The New York Times.

TITANIC SINKS FOUR HOURS AF[TER HITTING ICEBERG;]
866 RESCUED BY CARPATHIA, P[ROBABLY 1250 PERISH;]
ISMAY SAFE, MRS. ASTOR MAYBE, NOTED NAMES MISSING

The Lost Titanic Being Towed Out of Belfast Harbor.

PARTIAL LIST OF THE SAVED.

CAPT. E. J. SMITH.

12 A.M., VOTES FOR WAR, 373 TO 50; 500 ASKED FOR ARMY OF 1,000,000; GIGANTIC RESOURCES MOBILIZED

BRITISH WIPE OUT AN ENTIRE TURKISH ARMY; CAPTURE 18,000 IN 60-MILE DRIVE IN PALESTINE; HAIG STRIKES GERMAN LINE AT FOUR POINTS

THEODORE ROOSEVELT DIES SUDDENLY AT OYSTER BAY HOME; NATION SHOCKED, PAYS TRIBUTE TO FORMER PRESIDENT; OUR FLAG ON ALL SEAS AND IN ALL LANDS AT HALF MAST

LEAGUE OF NATIONS PLAN IS ADOPTED; PEACE CONFERENCE ACTS ON WILSON PLEA, STRONGLY SUPPORTED BY LLOYD GEORGE

SENATE SESSION ENDS, TREATY... THREE VOTES TAKEN, 39 T... MAY BE REVIVED AT TH...

PRESIDENT AND BRYAN SPLIT... WILSON FOR 1920 ISSUE, BRYAN... LODGE SEES COMPROMISE N...

ROOSEVELT TO SEEK POWER TO OFFER DEBT PAYMENTS; 3.2 BEER PASSAGE ASSURED

ROOSEVELT PROMISES A 'PARTNERSHIP' WITH BUSINESS, FARMERS AND WORKERS TO PROVIDE PROFITS AND HIGHER WAGES

LINDBERGHS AT SEA ON BRAZIL FLIGHT; 'O.K.' SHE REPORTS

PROHIBITION REPEAL IS RATIFIED AT 3:32 P.M.; ROOSEVELT ASKS NATION TO BAR THE SALOON; NEW YORK CELEBRATES WITH QUIET RESTRAINT

EXCHANGE, LABOR BOARDS NAMED; FARM BILL SIGNED

HITLER CRUSHES REVOLT BY NAZI RADICALS; VON SCHLEICHER IS SLAIN, ROEHM A SUICIDE; LOYAL FORCES HOLD BERLIN IN AN IRON GRIP

DOCTOR SHOOTS HUEY LONG IN LOUISIANA STATE CAPITOL; BODYGUARDS KILL ASSAILANT

LOUIS STOPS BAER IN 4TH AT STADIUM AS 95,000 LOOK ON

LEAGUE COUNCIL TOMORROW TAKES UP MUSSOLINI REPLY, ROME HOPEFUL, LONDON FIRM

'BIG 3' CHARTS TRIPLE BLOWS TO HUMBLE REICH AND AGREES ON A PEACE TO ELIMINATE TYRANNY; CARRIERS ATTACK MARSHALLS; 5TH ARMY GAINS

"All the News That's Fit to Print."

The New York Times.

LATE CITY EDITION

AMERICANS DRIVE FOUR MILES BEYOND THE ROER; OUR CARRIER AIRCRAFT SLASH AT TOKYO AGAIN; MARINES WIN HALF OF IWO'S CENTRAL AIRFIELD

OLD GLORY GOES UP OVER IWO

EGYPTIAN PREMIER SLAIN IN CHAMBER

Eisenhower Points New Push At Knockout Blow in West

SOVIET FORCES GAIN IN POLISH CORRIDOR

War News Summarized

JOINT ARMS BOARD SHAPED IN MEXICO

More Men, 30 to 34, to Be Drafted Unless Necessary to Industry

Foe's Manila Garrison Wiped Out; 2,146 Civilians Freed in Camp Raid

PRESIDENT ROOSEVELT IS DEAD; TRUMAN TO CONTINUE POLICIES; 9TH CROSSES ELBE, NEARS BERLIN

HITLER DEAD IN CHANCELLERY, NAZIS SAY; DOENITZ, SUCCESSOR, ORDERS WAR TO GO ON; BERLIN ALMOST WON; U.S. ARMIES ADVANCE

THE WAR IN EUROPE IS ENDED! SURRENDER IS UNCONDITIONAL; V-E WILL BE PROCLAIMED TODAY; OUR TROOPS ON OKINAWA GAIN

JAPAN SURRENDERS, END OF WAR! EMPEROR ACCEPTS ALLIED RULE; M'ARTHUR SUPREME COMMANDER; OUR MANPOWER CURBS VOIDED

QUEEN GETS NEWS AS CORONATION GIFT; THRONGS LINE HER PROCESSION ROUTE

ROSENBERGS EXECUTED AS ATOM SPIES AFTER SUPREME COURT VACATES STAY; LAST-MINUTE PLEA TO PRESIDENT FAILS

H-BOMB CAN WIPE OUT ANY CITY, STRAUSS REPORTS AFTER TESTS; U.S. RESTUDIES PLANT DISPERSAL

KENNEDY IS KILLED BY SNIPER AS HE RIDES IN CAR IN DALLAS; JOHNSON SWORN IN ON PLANE

21 DEAD IN LOS ANGELES RIOTS; 600 HURT; 20,000 TROOPS CALLED; PRESIDENT CONDEMNS VIOLENCE

KENNEDY IS DEAD, VICTIM OF ASSASSIN; SUSPECT, ARAB IMMIGRANT, ARRAIGNED; JOHNSON APPOINTS PANEL ON VIOLENCE

MEN WALK ON MOON

ASTRONAUTS LAND ON PLAIN; COLLECT ROCKS, PLANT FLAG

CREW OF CRIPPLED APOLLO 13 STARTS BACK AFTER ROUNDING MOON AND FIRING ROCKET; MEN APPEAR CALM DESPITE LOW RESERVES

U.S. AND SOVIET SIGN TWO ARMS ACCORDS TO LIMIT GROWTH OF ATOMIC ARSENALS; TRADE PACT DELAYED, TALKS TO GO ON

NIXON... HE URGES... FORD WI...

Jury Clears Simpson in Double Murder; Spellbound Nation Divides on Verdict

Diana Killed in a Car Accident in Paris

U.S. ATTACKED

HIJACKED JETS DESTROY TWIN TOWERS AND HIT PENTAGON IN DAY OF TERROR

U.S. AND BRITAIN STRIKE AFGHANISTAN, AIMING AT BASES AND TERRORIST CAMPS; BUSH WARNS 'TALIBAN WILL PAY A PRICE'

U.S. FORCES TAKE CONTROL IN BAGHDAD; BUSH ELATED; SOME RESISTANCE REMAINS

SADDAM HUSSEIN HANGED IN BAGHDAD; SWIFT END TO DRAMA; TROOPS ON ALERT

Christmas - 2008
from Joel Lane

The New York Times
THE COMPLETE FRONT PAGES 1851–2008

The New York Times

THE COMPLETE FRONT PAGES 1851–2008

Introduction by Bill Keller

Essays by Richard Bernstein, Ethan Bronner, Roger Cohen, Gail Collins, Helene Cooper, Thomas L. Friedman, William Grimes, Caryn James, Gina Kolata, David Leonhardt, Steve Lohr, Frank Rich, Carla Anne Robbins, Gene Roberts, William Safire, Serge Schmemann, Sam Tanenhaus and John Noble Wilford

Front Page News Summaries by James Barron

Black Dog
& Leventhal
Publishers
New York

Acknowledgments

The complexity of this multi-media book project, the first by The Times, called for the patient collaboration of two worlds: the electronic/digital universe, represented here by three DVDs containing every front page published by The New York Times since Day One, September 18, 1851; and the book you're holding, 456 pages with more than 300 selected front page images, original essays and other text that falls into the category of traditional "hard copy." Without the generous support and expertise of many colleagues, a few dedicated freelancers and a remarkably creative publishing partner, this unique endeavor would never have become a reality.

We are particularly grateful to Nancy Lee, J.P. Leventhal, Thomas K. Carley, Kenneth Richieri, Lee Riffaterre, Jim Mones, Marc Frons, Raymond Pearce, Alyse Myers, Harry Brindley, Gus Rylander, Jeff Tishman, Phyllis Collazo, Lioudmila Koudinova, Jeff Roth, Joan Netsky, Merrill Perlman, Rob Larson, Ranjit Prabhu, Mark O'Callaghan, Tomi Murata, Edith Berelson, Megan Considine, Ryan Murphy, Derek Gottfried, Rachel Camero, Keith Vachris, Theresa DeRosa and, on the publisher's staff, Janet Castiglione, Howard Musk, True Sims and Lisa Tenaglia.

—The Editors

Published by:
Black Dog & Leventhal Publishers, Inc.
151 West 19th Street
New York, NY 10011

Distributed by:
Workman Publishing Company
225 Varick Street
New York, NY 10014

Manufactured in Malaysia

Cover and interior design by Toshiya Masuda

ISBN-13: 978-1-57912-749-7

h g f e d c b a

Library of Congress Cataloging-in-Publication Data

The New York times : the complete front pages 1851-2008 / introduction by Bill Keller ; essays by Richard Bernstein ... [et al.].
p. cm.
1. History, Modern—19th century—Sources. 2. History, Modern—20th century—Sources. 3. United States—History—19th century—Sources. 4. United States—History—20th century—Sources. 5. American newspapers—Sections, columns, etc.—Front pages. I. Bernstein, Richard, 1944- II. New York times.

D351.N53 2008
909.8—dc22
2008020261

CONTENTS

HOW TO USE THE BOOK, DVD-ROMS, AND ONLINE ARCHIVE

THE BOOK

The more than 300 front pages in this book are divided into 16 eras. Each begins with a summary of the most important or interesting front page articles of the period, putting the front pages that follow into a historically contemporary context. The pages are in chronological order except for several full-page foldouts, which may be out of sequence (for production reasons) within the era. Summaries for these foldout front pages are indicated with a box if they are not in chronological order. For your convenience a magnifier is included to assist you in reading the articles as printed. If you would like to read the continuation of the article beyond page one, insert the appropriate DVD-ROM into your computer (see DVD-ROM and Online Access, below).

Each era also features at least one essay by a Times writer that relates to one or more front page news stories. The essays also include footnotes that refer to other Times articles, citing the headlines and dates of publication so they can be located on the DVD-ROM or in the Online Archives.

THE DVD-ROMS

There are three DVD-ROMs in this package and they include every front page ever published, from the very first issue of The New York Times (then known as The New-York Daily Times) on September 18, 1851, through April 1, 2008.

Insert DVD 1 to view pages printed between September 18, 1851, and December 31, 1899
Insert DVD 2 to view pages printed between January 1, 1900, and December 31, 1949
Insert DVD 3 to view pages printed between January 1, 1950, and April 1, 2008

Getting Started
To use the DVD-ROMs, you need a computer (either PC or Mac) with a DVD-ROM drive, Internet access and Adobe Reader 8.0 or later. Click on "Install Adobe Reader" on the main DVD-ROM page for a free installation of the latest version.

Please note: If you are using a Mac with OSX, the disks will not launch automatically.
Click on the Launch.pdf icon to begin using the disks.

NAVIGATING THE DVD-ROMS

The left navigation pane provides links to different decades, years and dates.

1. Click on a decade to show the years within that decade.
2. Click on a year to show the links for dates within that year.
3. Click on a date to view the full front page.
4. Click the minus sign (PC) or down arrow (Mac) next to a decade to hide links to the individual years and dates.

VIEWING A FRONT PAGE

1. Use the zoom-in button (+) and the zoom-out button (–) on the toolbar to navigate the text.
2. To continue reading past the front page, click on The New York Times masthead to access the Online Archives (further instructions below).

SEARCHING WITHIN A FRONT PAGE

This search will find a word or phrase within the page you are currently viewing.

1. In the search box on the toolbar, type in the word or phrase you want to find and press enter.
2. That word or phrase will then be highlighted in blue (if in a headline) or indicated with a box (if found within the text of an article).
3. Click on the highlighted box for a close-up view of that area.
4. The *Next* and *Previous* icons to the right of the search box will take you to each successive search result.

SEARCHING THE INDEX

This search will find all instances of a particular word or phrase from the DVD-ROM you are currently using. (To get your search results more quickly, use the Advanced Index Search.)

1. Click on the arrow to the right of the search box to access the Full Reader Search option.
2. On the initial search screen, type in the word or phrase you want to find and select DVD-ROM from the drop-down menu. Click Search.
3. A list of dates will appear in the results screen. Click on the plus sign (PC) or arrow (Mac) next to a date to show the search results from that front page.
4. Click on one search result and that front page will appear with the search text highlighed (See Steps 2 and 3 from Searching Within a Front Page).
5. (Optional) In the Sort By menu near the bottom of the Full Reader Search screen select sort by Date Modified to sort results chronologically.

ADVANCED INDEX SEARCH

This search will find all instances of a particular word or phrase from a select number of years or from the entire DVD-ROM you are currently using.

1. Click Advanced Search Options near the bottom of the Full Reader Search screen.
2. Click on the "Look in" drop-down menu and choose "Select Index." The Index Selection screen will appear.
3. Click "Add" on this screen and a finder window will open. Select the DVD-ROM from the drop-down menu and click on the Index folder.
4. A folder and .pdx file (for example, 1851-Index.pdx) for each decade and year on the DVD-ROM will appear as well as a folder and .pdx file for the entire DVD-ROM. If you'd like to search the entire DVD-ROM, move to Step 5. If you'd like to search a select number of years, move to Step 6.
5. Highlight the .pdx file for the entire DVD-ROM and click "Open." The index will appear on the Index Selection screen. Click OK. Move to Step 7.
6. Highlight the .pdx file for the year or decade within which you'd like to search and click "Open." The index will appear on the Index Selection screen. Repeat Steps 3-4 to add more indexes, and click OK.
7. The "Look in" menu on the Full Reader Search screen will now have selected "Current Selected Indexes" as its search. Type in the word or phrase you want to find and click Search.
8. Follow steps 3-5 from Searching the Index.

ONLINE ARCHIVES

To broaden your search to include articles and continuations throughout the paper, you will need to access the complete online archives of The New York Times.

1. To continue reading an article that begins on a front page within the DVD-ROMs, click The New York Times masthead on the top of the PDF. This will launch your Internet browser and lead you to the Times's Online Archives website. There, you will find a listing of articles from that front page and from the rest of the newspaper.
2. The front-page articles will be listed first. Click on an article title and the article preview page will open, listing the entire headline and a preview of the article.
3. For articles published between September 18, 1851, and December 31, 1980, click on the "Access Full Article" link on the bottom of the page and a PDF of the article will appear. Articles from January 1, 1981, to the present will be in a text-only format on the website.*

* If you are a home delivery subscriber, log in to The Times website for access to 100 full article views per month. If you are not a subscriber, you will have access to five full article views per session for the following years: 1851-1922 and 1987-the present. Articles published from 1923-1986 are subject to copyright law and are therefore not open to non-subscribers. Use the offer included in this book of 50 percent off six-months' home delivery of The Times to gain access to these articles—or purchase single and 10-pack articles through The Times website.

Please note:
The first Sunday edition of the paper was printed on April 21, 1861. There are no Sunday papers prior to this date.
The newspaper was not printed on the following dates:
January 2, 1852, 1853, 1862, 1863, 1864, 1865, 1866, 1867
July 5, 1861, 1862, 1863, 1864, 1865

There were three periods when The Times was on strike:

- December 9, 1962, to March 31, 1963. A western edition of the paper was printed during this time, and these papers are included on the DVD-ROM.
- September 17, 1965, to October 10, 1965. An international edition of the paper was printed during this time, and these papers are included on the DVD-ROM. There was only one edition of the paper on weekends during this time period.
- August 10, 1978, to November 5, 1978.

INTRODUCTION

BILL KELLER

"All the News That's Fit to Print"

The New York Times

Late Edition

VOL. CXXXIX . . . No. 48,144 — NEW YORK, MONDAY, FEBRUARY 12, 1990 — 40 CENTS

MANDELA, FREED, URGES STEP-UP IN PRESSURE TO END WHITE RULE

SPEECH IS RESOLUTE

He Asks Other Nations Not to Lift Sanctions Against Pretoria

By CHRISTOPHER S. WREN

Nelson Mandela leaving Victor Verster prison yesterday after spending 27 years in South African jails.

U.S. INVITES IDEAS FROM THE SOVIETS ON STRATEGIC CUTS

AN ADMINISTRATION SHIFT

Moscow's Earlier Suggestions on Reducing Nuclear Arms Have Been Spurned

By MICHAEL R. GORDON

Mike Tyson applying a cold towel to his swollen eye during a news conference after the fight.

Boxing Officials Could Overturn Defeat of Tyson

By PHIL BERGER

On Mandela's Walk, Hope and Violence

By JOHN F. BURNS

Bush Homeless Plan: 'Godsend' or False Hope?

Rural Doctor's Struggle to Care for the Poorest

The life of a newspaper revolves to a large, possibly ridiculous, degree around the making of a single page—the front page. For most of this paper's history, the news workday has been defined by the launching, refining, winnowing and arranging of those few articles that will represent the editors' best reckoning of what mattered most yesterday. That selection process was probably less consuming in 1851, when Page One of the new "New-York Daily Times" was crammed with so many items of news, in eyestrain type, that it's hard to imagine much was left out. Certainly the obsession with Page One is diminishing a little now, as we shift attention to our nonstop digital edition. But the climactic event of the newspaper day is still the afternoon Page One meeting, where editors from the various departments—Foreign, National, Metropolitan, Business, Culture, Sports and so on—nominate the articles they deem most important, most interesting, or right for "the mix."

And Page One is still what most stirs our ambition. Editors assure reporters that each page of the paper is precious, even those consisting of a narrow gutter alongside a department-store ad, but the front page is the showcase every reporter aspires to. Whether it comes shouted across a newsroom, telexed to a foreign bureau or in an e-mail message, there are few more satisfying phrases in our business than "You are fronted."

There are, of course, many articles on these pages that landed there due to the enterprise of a reporter who noticed something others missed, or who dug deep beneath the surface, or who, as we say in newsrooms, "wrote it onto the front." More often than not, though, making the front page is a matter of luck—of being in the right place when news is happening. The trick, such as it is, is making the most of an opportunity. As a correspondent, I had the astounding luck to be in the Soviet Union when it began to unravel, and then in South Africa when the black majority ended three centuries of white rule. I was fronted a lot, and I did not kid myself, at least I tried not to, that it was thanks mainly to the brilliance of my insights or the grace of my prose. How could you have such news handed to you—and such characters! Gorbachev! Yeltsin! Mandela! —and *not* be a regular presence on the front page? That I got lucky never diminished the kick of being fronted. It may have been Mandela's moment, but it was my rendering (and, pleasing me perhaps more than it should, my byline). When the front page was unfolded at the breakfast table, and when it is compiled in an album like this for the wonderment of future generations, Mandela is there—and so am I.

"All the News That's Fit to Print"

The New York Times

LATE CITY EDITION

Weather: Rain, warm today; clear tonight. Sunny, pleasant tomorrow.

VOL. CXVIII . No. 40,721 — NEW YORK, MONDAY, JULY 21, 1969 — 10 CENTS

MEN WALK ON MOON

ASTRONAUTS LAND ON PLAIN; COLLECT ROCKS, PLANT FLAG

Voice From Moon: 'Eagle Has Landed'

A Powdery Surface Is Closely Explored

By JOHN NOBLE WILFORD

HOUSTON, Monday, July 21—Men have landed and walked on the moon.

VOYAGE TO THE MOON

"All the News That's Fit to Print"

The New York Times.

THE WEATHER.

VOL. LXII...NO. 19,988. — NEW YORK, TUESDAY, OCTOBER 15, 1912.—TWENTY-FOUR PAGES. — ONE CENT

MANIAC IN MILWAUKEE SHOOTS COL. ROOSEVELT; HE IGNORES WOUND, SPEAKS AN HOUR, GOES TO HOSPITAL

Bullet In Right Breast, Doctors Say Wound Is Not Serious.

LUNG NOT PENETRATED

Roosevelt Walks from Hospital Unassisted, and Starts for Chicago.

MANUSCRIPT WAS A SHIELD

Assassin's Aim Good, but Papers in the Colonel's Pockets Save Him.

CALM ON OPERATING TABLE

Talks Politics with Physicians While Waiting for X-Ray Machine.

COLONEL CHECKS CROWD

"Don't Touch Him," He Says, as Rush is Made for His Assailant—Secretary Martin Fells Maniac.

Would-be Assassin Is John Schrank, Once Saloonkeeper Here.

A MANIAC ON THIRD TERM

Obsessed with Belief That He Was Commissioned to Remove Peril to Nation.

HAD DREAM OF McKINLEY

Martyred President, He Says, Told Him That Roosevelt Had Him Slain.

STARTED ON COLONEL'S TRAIL

Went South After Buying Revolver and Followed ex-President Closely.

WAS BAFFLED IN CHICAGO

Then He Went Early to Milwaukee and Planned Carefully to Make Sure of His Victim.

COL. THEODORE ROOSEVELT

The byline, you will notice, was a relatively late embellishment in The Times—nonexistent until the early 20th century, and relatively scarce until after midcentury, when newspapers found it advantageous to advertise (and appease) their stars, and when reporters were allowed to write with a more distinctive voice. Now we are promiscuous with bylines, not just to apportion credit or blame where it is due, not just to satisfy the needy egos of reporters, but also because we believe that over time the best reporters acquire an authority that resides not just in the reputation of the paper but in their own individual talent. Devoted readers of the front page have favorite bylines, the way opera lovers have favorite tenors and sopranos. This book, though, is, in large part, history written anonymously, its authors known by the mysterious "Special to The New York Times" or "From a Staff Correspondent of The New York Times."

Obviously the pages in this volume are selected for the events they recorded. They are organized, decade by decade, as a study guide to our development as a people—from civil war to civil unions, from suffrage to the Space Age, from the colonization of the East by the West to what has come to look a bit like the reverse. Some pages are so familiar as to be iconic ("MEN WALK ON MOON"), but one virtue of this generous compilation is that it makes so many stops along its 156-year trajectory, allowing for less obvious choices. It is a novel delight to turn a page and come across the beginning of the Pony Express, or General Custer's calamity at Little Big Horn, or the opening of the Brooklyn Bridge, or the verdict in the Scopes evolution trial. The attempted assassination of former President Theodore Roosevelt would not have made a more selective hit parade, but because it's here we can savor this extraordinary banner: MANIAC IN MILWAUKEE SHOOTS COL. ROOSEVELT; HE IGNORES WOUND, SPEAKS AN HOUR, GOES TO HOSPITAL.

The collection is capacious enough to offer many sideways glimpses of the American passage. The editors deemed frontable the phenomenal popularity of a book here ("Uncle Tom's Cabin," 1853) or a musical group there (The Beatles, 1964, who are treated with a kind of bemused condescension). One front page notes an ongoing debate about the religious convictions of Florence Nightingale. Attentive browsers will discover the day in 1961 when The Times reported that it had retained engineers and chemists to test major league baseballs; the paper had set out to resolve an argument that the sluggers Mickey Mantle and Roger Maris enjoyed a technical advantage over Babe Ruth, whose home-run record they were chasing. And the day in 1956 when reporter Allen Drury (later known for the novel "Advise and

The New York Times.

"All the News That's Fit to Print"

LATE CITY EDITION

NEW YORK, SATURDAY, OCTOBER 5, 1957.

SOVIET FIRES EARTH SATELLITE INTO SPACE; IT IS CIRCLING THE GLOBE AT 18,000 M. P. H.; SPHERE TRACKED IN 4 CROSSINGS OVER U. S.

HOFFA IS ELECTED TEAMSTERS' HEAD; WARNS OF BATTLE

COURSE RECORDED

Navy Picks Up Radio Signals—4 Report Sighting Device

560 MILES HIGH

Visible With Simple Binoculars, Moscow Statement Says

FAUBUS COMPARES HIS STAND TO LEE'S

ARGENTINA TAKES EMERGENCY STEPS

Device Is 8 Times Heavier Than One Planned by U.S.

SATELLITE SIGNAL BROADCAST HERE

Ex-Premier Mollet Accepts Bid To Form a New French Cabinet

City Sifts Charge That Schapler, Brooklyn Councilman, Sold a Job

Warsaw Crushes New Protest; Clubs, Tear Gas Rout Students

The New-York Times.

NEW-YORK, MONDAY, APRIL 10, 1865.

UNION

VICTORY!

PEACE!

Surrender of General Lee and His Whole Army.

THE VICTORY.

Consent") delivered this artful lead to an article that merged Hollywood and the Red Scare: "Arthur Miller, playwright, disclosed today a past filled with Communist-front associations and a future filled with Marilyn Monroe."

One thing I particularly like about absorbing history through this album of front pages is the several ways it puts history in its place.

For one thing, these front pages embed big events in a context. They show you what else was happening apart from the thing that made history. It is interesting to learn that on the date remembered for the orbiting of Sputnik, Jimmy Hoffa was elected head of the Teamsters. And you can appreciate how fraught the American situation was on March 21, 1933, from the juxtaposition of these two articles: the news that F.D.R. was seeking extraordinary executive powers to ease the pain of the Great Depression, and across the page a report that Hitler was assuming dictatorial control in Germany.

Another thing this collection does better than any history textbook is catch the news, not at its peaks and valleys but en route, as a running story. Between "THE WAR COMMENCED" in 1861 and "UNION / VICTORY!/ PEACE!" in 1865, you get the dailiness of civil war, the advances and retreats and political maneuvering. In this, and in subsequent wars, you follow the action not as seismic events but as the constant ache in a nation's life.

Another way these pages put history in perspective is by reminding us that it is not always clear, when you are living through events, what will really endure. More than a few pages here play up news that, in hindsight, mattered less than the editors believed. Other pages withhold excitement that now seems more than justified. Note, for instance, the wary second deck of headline on the first report of Edison's electric light: "CONFLICTING STATEMENTS AS TO ITS UTILITY." Or consider the report of Lincoln's Gettysburg address, which every student alive knows as a landmark of oratory. Readers of the Times on the morning of November 20, 1863, found the president's address modestly embedded in the second column of a long report on the dedication of the new national cemetery, under several decks of headline that scarcely note Lincoln's speech. (On the same day's page, a headline proclaims "A GREAT SPEECH," but it refers to a long-forgotten disquisition by the Rev. Henry Ward Beecher on Anglo-American relations.) You wonder whether readers coming upon Lincoln's remarks, unadorned and unappraised, recognized its magic without the intrusive voice of a correspondent or headline writer to tell them this was one for the ages.

The New-York Times.

VOL. XIV—NO. 4230. NEW-YORK, SATURDAY, APRIL 15, 1865. PRICE FOUR CENTS.

AWFUL EVENT.

President Lincoln Shot by an Assassin.

EUROPEAN NEWS.

"All the News That's Fit to Print"

The New York Times

Late Edition

U.S. ATTACKED

HIJACKED JETS DESTROY TWIN TOWERS AND HIT PENTAGON IN DAY OF TERROR

A CREEPING HORROR

Buildings Burn and Fall as Onlookers Search for Elusive Safety

President Vows to Exact Punishment for 'Evil'

A Somber Bush Says Terrorism Cannot Prevail

Awaiting the Aftershocks

Washington and Nation Plunge Into Fight With Enemy Hard to Identify and Punish

Newspaper editors—at least those of my generation and before—like to think of the newspaper as a gathering place, the village well, the office water cooler, where we pool our information and invigorate our sense of community. Even before we were polarized and atomized by the Web, that communal purpose of a newspaper was in decline. Still, I was struck by two headlines on pages 136 years apart. The first was a mournful line that began the coverage of Abraham Lincoln's assassination in the paper of April 15, 1865. It read simply: "AWFUL EVENT." The second was the banner in the paper of September 12, 2001: "U.S. ATTACKED." Quaint as the early version feels, it reflects the sense of the newspaper as a place where the nation assembles in moments of great stress, an affirmation that we are all in it together. The second headline reminds us that this relationship between the newspaper and its reader has not been altogether extinguished in our own century.

Earlier I described the front page as the editors' best reckoning of the news that mattered on a particular, remarkable yesterday. Like most things entrusted to human beings, the reckoning is sometimes wrong. (You will find no contemporaneous Page One treatment of the Holocaust, to pick one shameful misjudgment, although you will find chilling accounts of the forced deportation of Polish Jews and the horror of Kristallnacht.) The notion of "what mattered" is, necessarily, selective and subject to change over time depending on who is paying attention. (Surely women's rights "mattered" long before suffrage pushed the subject onto Page One in 1912.) As newspapers migrate to the never-ending and global cycle of the Internet, the very concept of "news"—not to mention "yesterday"—takes on new meaning. It is not unimaginable that in time the printed newspaper will disappear, or become, like vinyl records, a boutique item. Then there will be no more front page; just the home page.

So the front page is imperfect, evolving and quite possibly endangered. It is also absorbing, evocative and thought provoking. It is the face a newspaper presents to history, and this album of faces from the past century and a half is a treasury of ourselves.

Bill Keller is executive editor of The New York Times.

1851

A Nation Divided

1865

FRONT PAGE NEWS 1851-1865

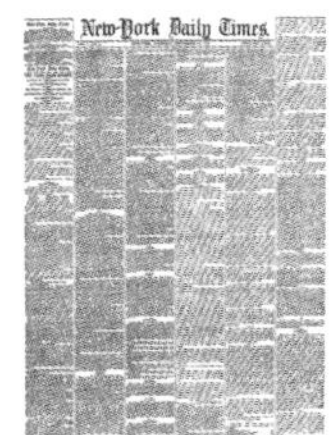

Volume I, Number One

SEPTEMBER 18, 1851

Into the rough-and-tumble competition of New York newspapers in the decade before the Civil War came a four-page broadsheet, apparently patterned after The Times of London. The New-York Daily Times was the brainchild of Horace Greeley's former right-hand man at The New York Tribune, and in less than two weeks, it would claim a circulation of 10,000, including "the most respectable families in town." But on its very first day, it blew a big local story. "Our item gatherer failed to discover the first spark of a fire" after fire alarms sounded, The Times acknowledged, "Failed" was the right word: Rival papers' item gatherers discovered an iron-foundry blaze on the Lower East Side that lit up the night skyline.

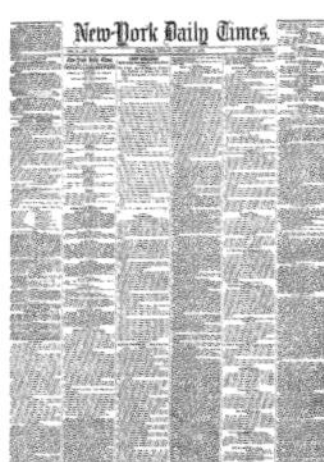

Uncle Tom's Cabin

JANUARY 14, 1853

"Uncle Tom's Cabin" was the antebellum era's top best-seller. It was in such demand that The Times, midway down the far-right column on a January morning, reprinted items about "Uncle Tom's Cabin" from newspapers in Paris and Honolulu. The novel began as Harriet Beecher Stowe's rebuttal to the Fugitive Slave Act, which made it a crime to "harbor or conceal" runaway slaves. "Uncle Tom's Cabin" had such an impact on the national consciousness, at least in the North, that years later, when Mrs. Stowe met President Abraham Lincoln, he said, "So you're the little woman who wrote the book that made this great war."

Perry Opens Trade With Japan

JUNE 13, 1854

Commodore Matthew C. Perry landed in Japan with an impressive flotilla and, The Times dryly observed, "rather a propensity for fighting." For Perry, this was a return trip. He was looking for answers to treaty proposals he had dropped off the year before. The isolationist Japanese had long shunned trade with the West, but the imperial government was intrigued by Perry's bravado and belligerence and agreed to negotiate a treaty. Success opened the way to trade with the U.S., and when the bargaining was over, Perry bragged that he accomplished his mission without firing a shot.

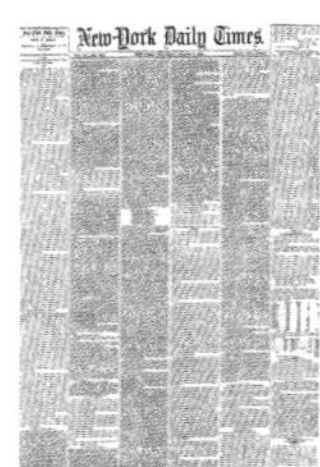

Nurse Nightingale's Good Works

AUGUST 2, 1855

Sometimes letters to the editor make the front page, as when a reader wrote to defend Florence Nightingale, the British nurse who had led nurses and nuns on missions to hospitals crowded with the wounded from the Crimean War. She had been concerned about poor sanitation and inadequate nursing. In New York there was concern in some Protestant quarters about her ties to Roman Catholics. "We know that in the East she ministered to the dying of every faith," the letter writer said in her defense, "and showed the most tender and delicate considerations for the religious feelings of all alike under her care."

The Fall of Sebastopol

SEPTEMBER 28, 1855

In The Times's early years, week-old foreign news was still fresh. The editors pieced together a series of short articles describing the end of the yearlong siege of Sebastopol, the decisive battle in the Crimean War. The fighting had gone on so long because the British and French were short on heavy artillery. When the French finally won a foothold on the edge of the city, the Russians sank their own ships to prevent their capture, and fled.

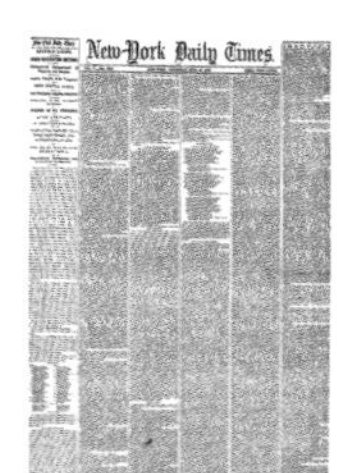

The First Republican Nominee

JUNE 26, 1856

John C. Fremont had name recognition from leading expeditions out west in the 1840's. He was also solidly against slavery, which made him appealing to the fledgling Republican Party, founded in 1854 by disaffected Midwesterners who had been Democrats, Whigs and Free Soilers. Theirs was an agrarian party that advocated free homesteads and free labor in the West and opposed the Kansas-Nebraska Act, which opened fast-growing territories to slaveholders. As the Republicans' first presidential candidate, Fremont won only 11 states to James Buchanan's 18. Millard Fillmore, attempting a comeback as the candidate of the Know-Nothing Party, carried one state—Maryland.

Dred Scott Decision

MARCH 7, 1857

President James Buchanan was counting on the Supreme Court to issue a decision in the Dred Scott case that would somehow calm abolitionists as well as slaveholders. The court dashed any chance of that—and of a second term for Buchanan—two days into his presidency, with an opinion that raised abolitionists' anger to the boiling point. The court said a slave had no legal rights in federal courts. It also dealt a broader blow to abolitionism by invalidating the Missouri Compromise and denying Congress the power to bar slavery in federal territories.

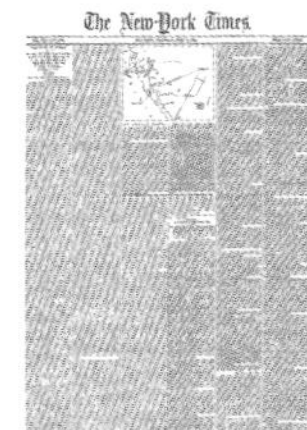

Garibaldi Unites Italy

JUNE 23, 1859

The Times's correspondent filed several thousand words about the "chit chat" in Europe concerning the Austro-Sardinian War, also known as the Second War of Italian Independence. Giuseppe Garibaldi, a hero of the Risorgimento in the 1840's, was maneuvering through Lombardy as the Battle of Magenta unfolded in Sardinia. That confrontation helped put the Austrian army on the run. Garibaldi would go on to capture Sicily and Naples, which he hoped would be united with the rest of Italy. They were, later that year.

'Insurgents' Raid Harper's Ferry

OCTOBER 18, 1859

Federal troops led by Colonel Robert E. Lee—who was 18 months away from resigning his Army commission to join the Confederates—were sent to crush what The Times called "insurgents" at the government arsenal at Harper's Ferry, West Virginia. The plan of attack had been dreamed up by the abolitionist John Brown, who had tried violence before: In 1856, he had murdered five proslavery Kansans. At Harper's Ferry, where he had planned to steal guns and ammunition, Brown's plan to incite Southern slaves to revolt never got off the ground. He barricaded himself in the arsenal until he was captured, and was tried for treason and hanged in less than two months.

Lincoln's Cooper Union Speech

FEBRUARY 28, 1860

Abraham Lincoln was stumping for the Republican presidential nomination when he appeared at Cooper Union in New York. No less a celebrity than William Cullen Bryant introduced him. Bryant said that Westerners like Lincoln formed a "bulwark" against slavery, and Lincoln told the crowd that he did not want slavery extended to western territories. He also brushed aside the idea that Republicans had fueled John Brown's failed raid at Harper's Ferry, and said Southerners wanted to "destroy the government" unless they could "construe or enforce" the Constitution as they wished. Their goal, he said, was to "rule or ruin in all events." The speech went over so well that later historians called it a turning point in Lincoln's drive for the nomination.

Pony Express Links the Nation

APRIL 3, 1860

Before East and West were linked by railroad, before cross-country telegraph and telephone cables, there was the Pony Express—several hundred horses, several dozen hell-bent relay riders, 2,000 dusty, sweaty miles and a mandate to get the mail through faster than ever before. On stagecoaches that made stop after stop, a letter could languish for a month before reaching an address in California. By ship, the mail took even longer. The Pony Express's promise to cut delivery time to about a week got the nation's attention, and The Times ran a short front-page item saying all the arrangements had been completed even before the first rider headed west from Missouri.

Civil War Begins at Fort Sumter

APRIL 13, 1861

Down to the last man who signed its secession ordinance, South Carolina was determined to fight. Its withdrawal from the Union in January 1861 was followed by the secession of six other Southern states in little more than six weeks. By spring, when the Southerners attacked Fort Sumter—which The Times spelled Fort Sumpter, with a p—the Union soldiers inside were running short on food and supplies. In northern cities like New York, eager volunteers rushed to sign up for duty in what they figured would be a speedy putdown of the Southern "insurrection."

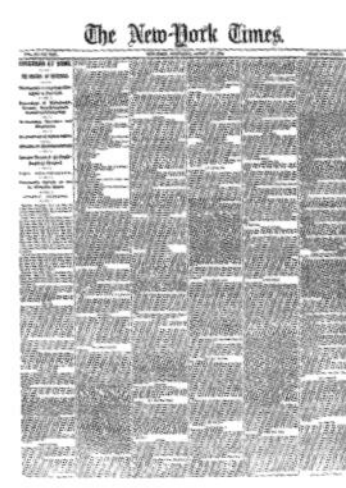

The Emancipation Proclamation

SEPTEMBER 23, 1862

Abraham Lincoln had opposed slavery but, in his first inaugural address, said he did not have the power "to interfere with the institution of slavery where it exists." Eighteen months into a war against states where it did exist, Lincoln announced a proclamation freeing slaves in Union-controlled territory. He had considered issuing it earlier but, on the advice of Secretary of State William H. Seward, had stalled—when Lincoln first toyed with the idea, General George B. McClellan had been unable to capture Richmond, and Seward did not want the Confederate leaders or the Northern rank and file dismissing the Emancipation Proclamation as a loser's cry for attention. Lincoln went ahead with it after Union forces scored a big victory at Antietam. The Times said the Emancipation Proclamation, "so long expected, so long delayed, bids fair to simplify at once the issues of the war."

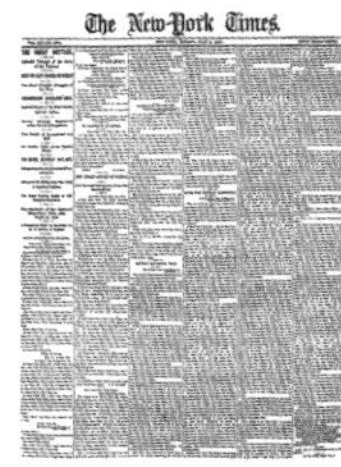

Confederate Rout at Gettysburg

JULY 6, 1863

Gettysburg proved to be a turning point in the Civil War, because it stopped a Southern advance that could have led to a Confederate occupation of Baltimore and Washington. Instead, after disastrous losses at Fredericksburg and Chancellorsville, Union troops routed the South in a three-day battle that The Times called a "tremendous artillery duel." Union General George G. Meade said his men were outnumbered, but still managed to fight off a fierce infantry assault known as Pickett's Charge on the second day. "Every charge [was] repulsed with great slaughter," The Times said, and when the smoke cleared, more than 50,000 soldiers were dead, including some 28,000 Confederates, about a third of the total Southern force.

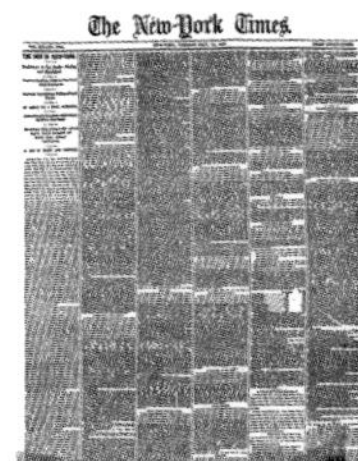

Draft Riots in New York

JULY 14, 1863

The mobs that rampaged through Manhattan were angry about a new federal law requiring local lotteries to fill out the ranks as recruitment lagged and desertions rose. The mobs included large numbers of Irish workingmen. (The Irish remained opposed to the war, in part because they feared being undercut in the job market by freed slaves.) A crowd of 50,000 overran a draft office on Third Avenue, destroying everything but what they wanted most—the names of the draftees, stored in a safe the rioters could not crack. Several thousand more attacked an armory downtown. The rioting continued for four days before 13 federal regiments arrived to restore order.

Lee Surrenders at Appomattox

APRIL 10, 1865

In the stillness of the Virginia countryside on a Sunday morning—the morning of Palm Sunday, no less—the South surrendered. Robert E. Lee, the statuesque Confederate general, was waiting for his Union counterpart, General Ulysses S. Grant, in Appomattox. Grant had not expected such a change of heart from Lee, who only two days before had written, "To be frank, I do not think the emergency has arisen to call for the surrender." Lee's turnabout had come so rapidly that Grant, mindful of appearances and respectful of a fellow West Pointer like Lee, apologized for being underdressed. Grant was not carrying his dress uniform, and wore "rough garb" to the meeting that ended four years of fighting. More than 600,000 soldiers had died, some 360,000 on Grant's side and nearly 260,000 on Lee's. Grant said that Lee's men could keep their horses and pistols; they soon stacked their rifles and headed for home. In Washington, President Abraham Lincoln was upbeat. "We are going to have good times now, and a united country," he said.

Booth Shoots Lincoln

APRIL 15, 1865

All Washington had heard the president was going to Ford's Theater. So had an actor named John Wilkes Booth, who remained a committed Confederate determined to exact revenge. He slipped into the president's box and leveled a single-shot pistol at Lincoln's head. He also stabbed an Army major who was a guest of the president. Then he leaped onto the stage, breaking his leg when he landed, but nothing could stop him. He picked himself up, shouted the state motto of Virginia—"Sic simper tyrannis" ("thus ever to tyrants")—and ran out the back door, where his horse was waiting.

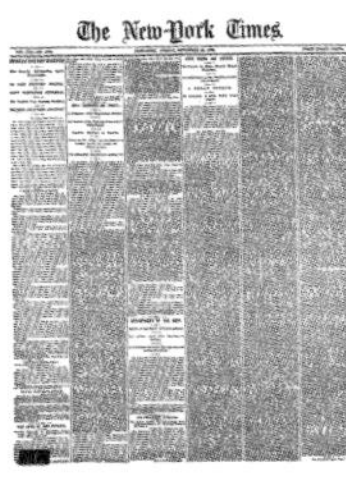

The Gettysburg Address

NOVEMBER 20, 1863

President Abraham Lincoln went to Gettysburg four months after the Union victory to dedicate the battlefield as a national cemetery. He was invited as an afterthought. The main speaker was Edward Everett, the 69-year-old former congressman, former secretary of state and former president of Harvard who gave a two-hour stemwinder. Lincoln's speech ran less than 280 words. It was so short that The Times printed it, in its entirety, on the front page (the 13,000-word text of Everett's speech appeared on page two), and The Times apparently garbled a key phrase. In the sentence that starts "It is for us, the living," The Times published the words "refinished work," while two of Lincoln's drafts say "unfinished work." Still, Lincoln had a famous beginning—"Four score and seven years ago"—and an ending that was a rallying cry for the North's ascendancy: "[W]e here highly resolve that these dead shall not have died in vain; that the nation shall, under God, have a new birth of freedom; and that government of the people, by the people, for the people, shall not perish from the earth."

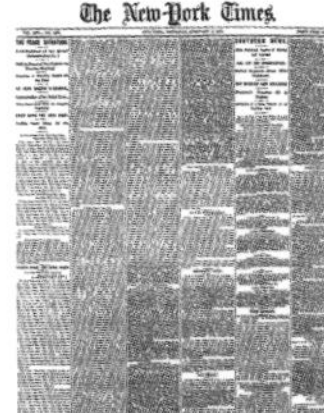

13th Amendment Bans Slavery

FEBRUARY 1, 1865

The 13th Amendment was the first amendment to the Constitution in 61 years, and at least the third official attempt to abolish slavery during the Civil War. The Senate had passed it in mid-1864, but it fell short in the House on the first try. When the House took it up again, the North was nine weeks away from winning the war, and the House chamber echoed with applause for each "yea" vote. The 13th Amendment went on to the states for ratification. Lincoln's home state of Illinois was the first, within 24 hours.

Grant Takes Richmond

APRIL 4, 1865

Union soldiers had mauled their way through the South's once-proud strongholds—Atlanta, Savannah, Charleston. Now General Ulysses S. Grant's men seized the Confederate capital itself, Richmond. The way was clear after Grant seized nearby Petersburg in a daylong firefight, and according to a telegram from a general in the first wave of troops storming Richmond, "The people receive us with enthusiastic expressions of joy." Not so those who fled on the single rail line that remained passable, among them Confederate President Jefferson Davis. Someone—fleeing rebels, arriving Union soldiers or itinerant vandals—set fire to the city.

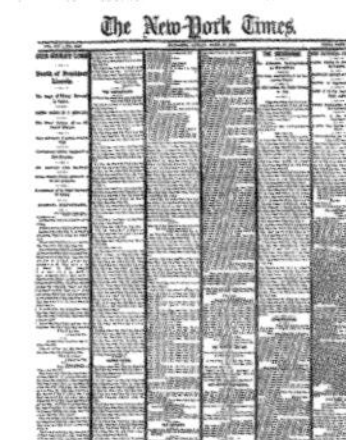

Stanton Breaks the News

APRIL 16, 1865

"Now he belongs to the ages," Secretary of War Edwin M. Stanton said. It was 22 minutes past seven o'clock on a Saturday morning in a borrowed rooming house in Washington. Abraham Lincoln, who had been carried there the night before from the theater across the street, was dead. Andrew Johnson would be sworn in as president three and a half hours later. The manhunt for John Wilkes Booth would go on for five more days. He had escaped into Union-occupied Virginia, where cavalry officers circled a barn where he was sleeping. They set it afire after he refused to come out with his hands up. Booth either committed suicide or was shot by a sergeant.

New-York Daily Times.

VOL. I....NO. 1. NEW-YORK, THURSDAY, SEPTEMBER 18, 1851. PRICE ONE CENT.

New-York Daily Times.

THE NEW-YORK DAILY TIMES IS PUBLISHED EVERY MORNING (*Sunday excepted,*) at the office, No. 113 NASSAU-STREET, between Beekman and Ann, just behind the Old Park Theater, and delivered to subscribers in the city, Brooklyn, Williamsburgh and Jersey City for six cents a week; or, when they prefer, they can pay in advance at the Desk for six months or a year at the same rate. Single copies, ONE CENT. Mail subscribers, FOUR DOLLARS a year.

THE NEW-YORK EVENING TIMES IS PUBLISHED EVERY EVENING, (*Sundays excepted,*) on the same terms as the Morning Edition.

THE NEW-YORK WEEKLY TIMES, A VERY LARGE NEWSPAPER FOR THE COUNTRY is published every *Saturday Morning*, at the low price of $2 per annum. Ten copies for $15, or twenty copies for $20, will be sent to one address, and the paper in no case continued beyond the time for which payment is made.

Payment in all cases must be paid in advance.

RAYMOND, JONES & CO. Publishers.

New-York Daily Times.

THE NEWS FROM EUROPE.

ARRIVAL OF THE EUROPA'S MAILS.

AFFAIRS IN ENGLAND.

The Election in France—Arrests, &c.

APPREHENDED DISTURBANCE IN AUSTRIA.

SOUTHERN EUROPE.

The Royal Mail Steamer *Europa* arrived at Boston yesterday morning, at about 6 o'clock. Her mails were sent on by the New Haven Railroad train, which left at 8 o'clock, and reached this city at an early hour last evening.

By this arrival we have received our regular English and French files, with correspondence, circulars, &c., to Saturday, September 6th—the *Europa's* day of sailing.

The news by this arrival has considerable interest, though it is not of startling importance.

In ENGLAND, political affairs are quiet. The *Humboldt* arrived at Southampton on Thursday, the 4th, with the news of the execution at Havana of the fifty men under Col. Crittenden's command. The details of the news are given at length in the London papers.

In FRANCE attention is chiefly absorbed with speculations on the approaching Presidential election. The Prince de Joinville is clearly to be a candidate, and will doubtless be a more formidable opponent of Louis Napoleon than any other that could be selected.

Another "Conspiracy" has been discovered in Paris ...

The Board of Assistant Aldermen closed their session for September, last evening. Our sketch of the proceedings is driven out by the Foreign News, but we are consoled by the reflection that our readers will find a full record of their doings in *The Evening Times*, which will be published at 1 o'clock this afternoon.

The Fountain in Washington Square goes on towards completion with considerable speed. It is to be a very large circular basin, with a central jet and several side jets. The excavation is made, the wall around the border of the basin is nearly done, and the workmen were yesterday laying a bottom of hard plaster. The fountain will be a very fine one, and will increase greatly the attraction of this beautiful park.

New-York Daily Times.

VOL. II....NO. 414. NEW-YORK, FRIDAY, JANUARY 14, 1853. PRICE TWO CENTS.

THE NEW-YORK DAILY TIMES.

A VERY LARGE DAILY NEWSPAPER—each number comprising Eight Pages, or Forty-Eight columns, and giving more reading matter than any other Daily Newspaper in the United States—is published EVERY MORNING, (*Sundays excepted,*) at No. 113 NASSAU-STREET, and is delivered to subscribers in New-York, Brooklyn, Williamsburg and Jersey City, for TWELVE AND A HALF CENTS a week, payable to the carrier. Single copies, TWO CENTS. Mail Subscribers, FIVE DOLLARS a year: six months, Two Dollars and a Half; three months, One Dollar and a Half. Three Dollars in advance required in all exchanges with Country Newspapers.

POSTAGE ON THE DAILY TIMES, sent to any part of the United States, paid in advance at the office where delivered—39 cents per quarter, or $1 56 per annum.

THE NEW-YORK EVENING TIMES.

IS PUBLISHED EVERY EVENING, (*Sundays excepted.*) One edition will be issued at 1. and the other at 3 o'clock, P.M. It will be sent by mail, or sold at the same rates as the *Daily Times.*

THE NEW-YORK WEEKLY TIMES,

A VERY LARGE NEWSPAPER FOR THE COUNTRY, is published every SATURDAY MORNING, at the low price of TWO DOLLARS per annum. Ten copies for FIFTEEN DOLLARS, Twenty copies for TWENTY DOLLARS, will be sent to one address; and the paper in no case continued beyond the time for which payment is made. Postage on the WEEKLY TIMES, sent by mail for one year, is as follows:

Within the County.............................Free.
Within the State...............................13 cents.
Within the United States......................26 cents.

THE TIMES FOR CALIFORNIA,

A LARGE NEWSPAPER OF EIGHT PAGES, or Forty-Eight columns, made up expressly for circulation in *California Oregon and the Sandwich Islands*, and containing only news of interest to readers in those sections of the country, is published on the departure of every Mail steamer. Price 3½ cents a copy.

Payments in all cases must be made in advance.

RAYMOND, JONES & CO., Publishers.

SPECIAL NOTICES.

NEW-YORK CRYSTAL PALACE.

☞ **Notice given by the Association for the** EXHIBITION OF THE INDUSTRY OF ALL NATIONS, to all parties in America desirous of contributing to the Industrial Exhibition to be opened in the City of New-York in May, 1853.

All persons desirous of obtaining a place in the Building, erected on Reservoir Square, in the City of New-York, by the Association for the Exhibition of the Industry of All Nations, are requested to send in their Applications for Space before the first day of February, 1853; immediately after which date the Association will proceed to decide on Applications and allot Space.

Each Application must furnish the Exhibitor's name and address in full, and state whether he is Manufacturer, Proprietor, or Agent. It must contain a concise description of the articles offered for Exhibition, and a statement of the precise dimensions of the Space required: if on Wall by Height and Length; if on Floor or Counter by Length and Breadth.

Applications must be signed by the persons proposing to exhibit, and be addressed to the Subscriber, at the office of the Association, No. 53 Broadway, New-York.

The Association hopes that attention will be given to the exact terms of this notice, and that its requirements will be carefully observed in making applications. By order,

W. WHETTEN, Secretary.

No charge made to exhibitors for space allotted.

January 5, 1853.

☞ **Mercantile Library Association.**—REGULAR NOMINATIONS FOR 1853:

For President—WILLARD L. FELT, with Willard Felt.
Vice-President—JOSEPH BLACK, with Benkard & Hutton.
Corresponding Secretary—JOHN F. HALSTED, with Wilson G. Hunt & Co.
Recording Secretary—S. U. F. ODELL, with Barclay & Livingston.
Treasurer—ABRAM HALSEY, Jr., with Bank of New-York.

DIRECTORS.

Douglas Leffingwell, with Ely Clapp & Bowen.
D. Reynolds Budd, " C. H. Leonard.
Wm. A. Marten, " T. G. & A. L. Rowe.
C. Y. Bradley, " Thos. Hunt & Co.
Geo. C. Wood, " Dibblee, Work & Moore.
Wm. H. Gilder, " Lewis B. Brown.
William M. Walton, " Macy Smith & Haslehurst.

By order Regular Nominating Committee.

WM. L. SEAMAN, Chairman,

M. L. B. MARTIN, Secretary.

☞ **Redemption from Spectacles**—Natural Sight Preserved and Restored, and near Sight Cured—Professor BROWNSON enables persons to preserve their natural sight to restore it after glasses have been used for years, and to cure near sight; all in a few weeks or months, without pain, risk or injury; at a reasonable expense. Weak, Sore and Diseased Eyes also treated. Several thousand references given. None but paid letters received. Students instructed. Medical advice given (Homœopathic and Hydropathic,) to invalids, &c., for Consumption, Dyspepsia, and other complaints of short or long standing. Explanatory pamphlets given to callers. Office Days in New-York, at No. 701 Broadway, from 9 to 3 every fourth Thursday during the Winter, viz: Jan. 13, Feb. 10, and March 10.

☞ **Spirit Rapping.**—Rev. Prof. MATTISON, A. M., delivers his second lecture on "Spirit Rapping," at the Tabernacle THIS EVENING, at 7½ o'clock. Subject: *Modern Necromancy; or Pretended Intercourse with the Dead.* The "Mediums" of the City are again invited to be present, to exhibit their marvelous phenomena; otherwise the public will judge whether the "Spirits" are not afraid of gas-light, and an intelligent audience. Doors open at 6½ o'clock. Tickets, 25 cents each.

☞ **Mechanics' Society**, Mechanics' Hall, No. 472 Broadway.—Lectures for 1853. Second Course. Commences at 7½ o'clock P. M.

Jan. 17—PARK BENJAMIN, Esq. Subject: *Fashion.*
Jan. 24—HENRY J. RAYMOND, Esq.
Jan. 31—Prof. BENJ. SILLIMAN, Sen. Subject: *The Influence of Science and the Arts on the Condition of Man, especially in our Country.*

☞ **Bleecker-street Sunday School Exhibition.**—In consequence of the storm on Wednesday evening, the Sunday School attached to the Third Universalist Church will repeat its Exhibition, in the Church, corner of Bleecker and Downing sts., on THIS (Friday) EVENING, commencing at 7 o'clock. Tickets, at 12½ cents each, may be obtained at the door.

☞ **Mercantile Library Association.**—The annual election for officers of this Association, will be held at the rooms, Clinton Hall, on TUESDAY, Jan. 18. Polls open from 9 A. M., until 6 o'clock P. M. By order.

JOSEPH BLACK, Recording Secretary.

☞ **Salamander Safes.**—WILDER'S PATENT with RICH'S IMPROVEMENT.—STEARNS & MARVIN, successors to Rich & Co., are the only manufacturers of Salamander Safes combining both patents. Depot No. 146 Water-st., New-York.

☞ **Miss Bacon's** EVENING COURSE OF INSTRUCTION at the Stuyvesant Institute.—The Second Lesson will be given THIS EVENING at 8 o'clock. Tickets for the term $5. Tickets for Single Lessons 50 cts.

☞ **Egyptian Antiquities.**—The opening of DR. ABBOTT'S Museum is postponed until further notice, to enable Dr. A. to complete the catalogue, rendered absolutely necessary by the great number of articles to be exhibited.

Amusements.

NIBLO'S.—Madame SONTAG has entirely recovered from her indisposition, and appears this evening in "The Child of the Regiment," the last time it will be performed by the NIBLO troupe.

BROADWAY.—Notwithstanding the storm last evening, Madame ALBONI had a large audience. "La Sonnambula" was again repeated, with Signor VIETTI as *Elvino*, the remainder of the cast being the same as that of Monday evening. The audience appeared to be better pleased with Signor VIETTI, than they were with his predecessor. Madame ALBONI was rapturously applauded throughout the Opera, and was forced to repeat the brilliant *finale*, after being three times "called out" amidst a shower of bouquets.

—There will be no Opera this evening, as the troupe will be engaged in rehearsing an Oratorio, which is to be performed on Sunday evening, at Metropolitan Hall, and in which the entire troupe, Orchestra, and Chorus, will appear. This evening's performances consist of "Petticoat Government," the ballet of "Giralda," the farce of "Married and Settled," and the pantomime of "Mons. Deschalumeaux."

WALLACK'S.—The drama of "Poor Cousin Walter," and the comedy of "Speed the Plough"—an excellent comedy, exceedingly well played.

BURTON'S.—Still the drama of "Paris and London," which attracts as large audiences as during the first week of its representation. The original comedy of "Laugh and Grow Fat," is also to be repeated.

BANVARD'S New Panorama of Jerusalem and the Holy Land, is still open at the Hall on Broadway, adjoining the Metropolitan Hotel.

☞ The number of deaths during the year 1851 was 18,934, which is 15 per cent. over the mortality of 1850; the latter, however, was a year of unusual health. The average of deaths was one to fifty-one and ninety-eight hundreths (51 98) of the population, or less than two per cent. Zymotic diseases (epidemic, endemic, and contagious) produce a greater mortality than any other class; the next to those, consumption and its kindred diseases. Consumption stands far above every other destroyer of human life in our climate. It has removed from the citizens of Massachusetts an average of *ten every day for the last three years.* It exhibits no partiality, unless it be to select its victims from the fairest and most promising. It is confined to no class of persons, or age, no season, no locality.

Typhus fever produced during the year 1851, about 4½ per cent. of the whole number of deaths; and diseases of the nervous system produced over 10½ per cent. Diseases of the circulative organs caused 2.46 per cent. of the deaths; and old age about 5 per cent., 3-5ths of which were females. Deaths from violent causes, including accidents and drowning, comprise about 4 per cent.

Agriculturists stand much the highest chance for long life, their average standing being *twelve years above the general average*, nearly nineteen above those returned as laborers, and eighteen per cent. above the average of mechanics.—*Boston Journal.*

What is birth to a man, if it shall be a stain to his dead ancestors to have left such an offspring?

New-York Daily Times.

THREE DAYS LATER FROM EUROPE

ARRIVAL OF THE ARABIA AT HALIFAX.

Cotton Declined—Breadstuffs Quiet.

HALIFAX TELEGRAPH OFFICE,
Thursday, Jan. 13—5 P. M.

The royal mail steamship *Arabia*, Capt. JUDKINS, from Liverpool, the 1st inst., for New-York, has just put in here short of coal, having experienced very heavy weather. She brings 48 passengers.

Owing to the occurrence of the Christmas Holidays she brings but little news.

ENGLAND.

Several appointments by the new ABERDEEN Ministry are published. Among them Villiers for Judge Advocate; Hayter, Secretary of the Treasury; Sir W. Page Wood, Vice Chancellor; Admiral Berkley, one of the Lords of the Admiralty; Lord Drumlanrig, Controller of the Household; Monsell, Clerk of the Ordinance.

Queen VICTORIA is stated to be in an interesting situation again.

KOSSUTH's mother died at Belgium on the 28th Dec. The Belgian Government refused KOSSUTH permission to visit her.

Mr. HEALD, the husband of LOLA MONTEZ, was drowned at Lisbon by the upsetting of a yacht.

A mutiny by the Chinese on board the ship *Gertrude*, bound from Amoy to Havana, had occurred; seventeen of them were shot, and the vessel put into Singapore.

FRANCE.

There is no news from the French Empire of any moment.

SPAIN.

It is reported that Mr. BARRINGER will shortly resign his appointment of American Minister at the Court of Madrid.

The Count VILLANUEVA, Conga Cuban intendantó, the richest man in Spain, is dead.

PORTUGAL.

An unexpected decree has been issued, converting all the Portuguese debts into 3 per cent.

TURKEY.

After a battle in Montenegro, an Armistice had been agreed upon until the Sultan's decision could be known.

INDIA.

The Calcutta mails of the 24th November, and Bombay to the 3d December, had reached England.

The news was quite unimportant.

The commercial accounts show but little change. Money was abundant.

COMMERCIAL INTELLIGENCE.

Liverpool Cotton Market.

The Cotton market had been dull all the week, and prices favored buyers, but quotations were only partially lowered to the extent of 1-16d. on American descriptions. The sales of Friday were 4 000 bales; and for the week they footed up 36 700, including 1,400 on speculation, and 450 bales for export. At the close of the year an error of 46,500 bales in excess upon the stock on hand had been discovered. The stock amounted to 577,820 bales. The following are the authorized quotations. Fair Orleans 6d.; fair Mobile 5⅞d; fair Uplands 5⅞d.

Liverpool Corn Market.

The Breadstuffs market has been quiet and the following are the ruling figures—WHEAT 7s. 9d. for White, and 7s. 3d. for red. FLOUR 28s. 6d. @29s for Phildelphia and Baltimore.

Produce Market.

RICE—Is rather dull. MOLASSES—No sales are reported. SUGAR—In fair demand for refining. COFFEE—Sales Domingo 44s; Bahia 41s. TEA—Rather slack till the holidays are over. 1 000 tons GUANO brought better prices. There had been no change in DYEWOODS, with fair sales. QUERCITRON BARK—Baltimore is quoted at 8s. SPIRITS TURPENTINE 50s. Sales 1,000 bbls. Rosin 5s. 6d. No sales of TURPENTINE or TAR. ASHES—Pots 26s. 6d.; Pearls 28s. PROVISIONS are unchanged. LARD nominally higher. TALLOW 46s. 6d.

London Markets.

COFFEE, 1s. dearer; BREADSTUFFS were barely maintained. COTTON has declined ⅛d. DISCOUNTS unchanged. MONEY in demand—Consols for Account, 100⅛, ex. dividend; BARING BROTHERS & Co. say the demand for American Federal Bonds and Inscriptions continues. There is no change in others; EAGLES are worth 76s. 5d. ℔ oz.

TRADE REPORTS—Are generally favorable. A fair business doing in Manchester.

Havre Cotton Market.

HAVRE, Dec. 29—*Tres ordinaire* Orleans, 85f.; *Bas* do., 78f. 50c.

FREIGHTS—Are unchanged.

Shipping Intelligence.

Arr. from Baltimore—27th, Alice, in the Clyde; Acadia, at Plymouth.
Arr. from Virginia—26th, Emma, at Texel.
Arr. from Charleston—19th, Maria, at Woolgast.
Arr. from Savannah—29th, Trenton, and Howard, at Liverpool.
Arr. from Mobile—27th, Carlo Mauran, in the Clyde.
Arr. from New-Orleans—28th, Navarre, at Teneriffe; 27th, Sea Nymph, in the Clyde; 28th, Heinrich at Bremerhaven; 30th, Charles Chaloner, Excelsior, Westmoreland, Liverpool; 31st, Azolus, do; 28th, Rebecca, off Ramsgate.

Passengers per Arabia.

Chevalier Sirben Ben, lady and servant, Sir Allan McNab and servant, Mr. Waller, lady and daughter, Mr. Henry, lady and three children; Miss Henry and servant; Mr. Hill and lady; Mrs. Artice; Messrs. Sayes, Smith, Davis, Weeks, Duncan, Girard, Roche, Parker, Kirkpatrick, Shipley, Van Blankenstein, Sharpstine, Hamilton, Mitchell, Farnes, Osborn, Bardnell, Samuel Johnson, Jay and friend, Halber, Hardhay, McGordon, P. B. Graham, Herbert, Griffin, Peteniard, Blanchard, Lucas, Williams.

Further News by the Illinois.

From a Private Correspondent at Panama.

The steamship *Columbus* arrived at Panama on the 19th, in 19 days from San Francisco. She reports the United States sloop-of-war *Portsmouth* at San Diego.

Spoke and was boarded by the whale-ship *Marengo*, of New-Bedford, off Cape St. Lucas—one year out, with 1,400 barrels of oil. Passed a clipper-ship, bound up, in latitude 12° 22', longitude 89° 52'.

The *Columbus* brought down 21 passengers.

By the arrival of the British Mail steamship *Bogota*, we learn from Valparaiso, 1st December, that business was improving there. Freights were high and vessels in great demand. One bark had been taken up at $25 per ton, for San Francisco—the current rate being $23. To Europe, the rate was £3 5s., and to the United States, $16 and upwards. Flour was at $8; Barley $3, and Beans $4 25. Coals were firm at last quotations.

The American bark *Trenton*, from Callao, was lost with a cargo of guano, about 300 miles west of Valparaiso. The captain and crew were saved.

The British steamer *Phosphorus*, of 45 tons, and drawing 2½ feet water, arrived at Valparaiso in 120 days from Liverpool.

On the 19th Nov. two shocks of an earthquake were felt at Valparaiso.

The British ship *Paragon* exchanged signals with the American clipper *Charles Ward*, in lat. 34° S., lon 73° E.

The following American vessels arrived at Valparaiso between 17th and 30th Nov.: 17th, *Huntress*, 112 days from Boston; 18th, *Zenobia*, 96 days from Rio; 23d, whaler *Edward Carey*, with 700 barrels oil; 30th, *Sumpter*, 126 days from New-York; 30th, *Sarah Snow*, 130 days from New-York; *Crusader*, not reported.

At Lima, an earthquake was felt on the 27th Nov.

☞ By comparing the Massachusetts Report of Births, &c., for 1851, with the United States Census for 1840, the increase of population during the last decade is ascertained to be 256,814, equal to 34.81 per cent. The County of Middlesex shows the largest increase, which is near 51½ per cent. Next follows Suffolk, with an increase of near 51 per cent. Next in order follows Norfolk, Essex and Worcester, whose population exhibits an increase in ten years of over 33 per cent. This increase is principally confined to the cities and manufacturing towns. The County of Nantucket has *decreased* during the same period over 6 per cent. The cities and villages of Boston, Lowell, Roxbury, Springfield, Chicopee, Lawrence, Worcester, Charlestown, Cambridge, the Chelsea, &c., have increased over 66 per cent.

The great increase of foreigners in the State is worthy of notice. In 1830 these were 1½ per cent. of the population. In 1840 they had increased to near 5 per cent., and in 1850 they amounted to 16½ per cent., or more than one-sixth of the entire population. According to the last centennial census, there were in this City 12,143 children of native, and 12,132 of foreign parentage. Of the births and marriages in Boston during the past three years, the foreign is nearly two to one over the native; and in regard to births, the same is true of Lowell, Fall River, and some other towns. The whole number of births in the Commonwealth during the year 1851, is 28,861, which is a larger number than that of any former year. The ratio of foreign to the whole number of births in the Commonwealth during the last three years, is nearly thirty per cent.

In all countries, the ratio of male to female births is stated to be 106 to 100; whereas during the past three years the ratio in the Commonwealth has been 108 to 100.—*Boston Courier.*

LATEST INTELLIGENCE

By Telegraph to the New-York Daily Times.

Mr. Gwin's Speech—Badger's Nomination Disliked at Mobile—The India Rubber Monopolists at Work in Congress.

Special Dispatch to the New-York Daily Times.

WASHINGTON, Thursday, Jan. 13.

Mr. GWIN's speech to-day on the Pacific Railroad was forcible and interesting. The bill will not pass in its present shape, but there is every indication that *some* measure to build the road will.

Private dispatches from Mobile state that the papers express the strongest disapprobation of the nomination of Mr. BADGER to the Supreme Court, as disparaging to the Bar and Bench of the Circuit—because the President falsified the principle on which he excluded Mr. CRITTENDEN, HOPKINS and MARSHALL,—because he does not live in the Circuit—because they want a young man, and because it is regarded as an effort to seduce the Senate from its independence, through its kind sentiments towards one of its members. The Bar of Mobile without distinction of party, will send remonstrances against his confirmation. Notwithstanding these attempts, Mr. BADGER will probably be confirmed to-morrow.

Ex-Governor CABELL died at Richmond, yesterday. He is father to the Representative from Florida.

There is much excited conversation among members, relative to investigations that concern the recent interference of an Attorney for the India-rubber monopolists, who is at the same time a Clerk of the U. S. District Court, to procure special legislation for the benefit of the monopoly, under color of a statute to punish contempt of Court. The proposition was pushed through the House and the Judiciary Committee, by concealing the fact that it was gotten up retroactively to affect a case already adjudicated.

Negotiations for the sale of the *Republic* are not yet concluded, because of a difference of $3,000.

Mr. UPHAM is better. His disease is Erysipelas.

S.

Washington Items.

WASHINGTON, Thursday, Jan. 13.

It is understood that the nomination of Mr. BADGER will be called up in Executive Session to-morrow. Whig Senators, to-day, express the hope of confirming the appointment. Meanwhile the following dispatches have been received by a member of Congress from reliable parties in Mobile.

"MOBILE, Jan. 11.—The papers express the strongest disapprobation of the nomination for Judge of the Supreme Court, as disparaging to the Bar and Bench of the Circuit, because the President falsified the principle on which he excluded CRITTENDEN, HOPKINS and MARSHALL; and because it is regarded as a corrupt effort to seduce the independence of the Senate by the kindly sentiments that exist in that body for one of its members."

"MOBILE, Jan. 12.—The bar of Mobile, without distinction of party, will send a remonstrance against the confirmation of BADGER's appointment."

And from another source,

"MOBILE, Jan. 12.—The nomination of Mr. BADGER meets with opposition at Mobile because he lives out of the Circuit—he is a Federalist in politics—his nomination is contrary to the principles on which the President rejected HOPKINS and MARSHALL—to his age, residence and qualifications, and because it is believed that it is a practice in the partiality of the Senate towards its own members to secure a seat in the Supreme Court to the Whig party."

SIDNEY WEBSTER, who will probably be Gen. PIERCE's Private Secretary, is still here, making arrangements preparatory to the General's removal to Washington.

Mr. KING seems better to day. The courteous treatment of the Senate has revived him.

It is rumored that fourteen Democratic Senators are opposed to JOHN A. DIX for a seat in the Cabinet.

Much feeling exists among members, relative to efforts made by the India Rubber monopolists to smuggle through Congress special legislation for their benefit. A son of a U. S. District Judge of New-York, a clerk of his fathers court being involved in it, the Houston Senate Committee, are about to make investigation concerning his connection with the cases, before his father.

XXXIId CONGRESS...Second Session.

SENATE....WASHINGTON, Thursday, Jan. 13.

The CHAIR laid before the Senate a communication from the War Department, with a statement of the expenditure of that department for 1852.

Mr. SMITH presented a memorial of 1,000 citizens of Connecticut, setting forth the claims of Doctor WELLS, as the discoverer of the anæsthetic agent.

Mr. MALLORY presented a memorial of officers of the Revenue service, asking for an increase of pay.

Mr. SEWARD offered a resolution, directing inquiry whether any action of Congress be necessary to the protection of New-Mexico from incursions of hostile Indians. Adopted.

Mr. BRIGHT submitted a resolution, which was adopted, directing the payment to the executors of Senator WHITCOMB of $175, to defray the expenses of the removal of his remains from New-York to Indiana.

Mr. CASS' resolution calling for the correspondence relative to SQUIERS' treaty with Nicaragua, and other matters, was taken up and adopted.

Mr. SHIELDS moved to take up the bill amending the charter of the City of Washington, by conferring upon the Corporation additional Police powers. Agreed to.

The resolution relating to Commodore MORGAN's conduct, while in the Mediterranean, was taken up.

Mr. SHIELDS presented a letter which he asked might be read, from Lieut. NELSON, vindicating the character and conduct of Commodore MORGAN.

Mr. HALE objected to the reading of the paper, and pending the question whether it be read or not, the subject was postponed till Monday.

The Senate then took up Mr. GWIN's bill, proposing the construction of a Railroad from the Mississippi to the Pacific with various branches.

Mr. GWIN addressed the Senate, in a written speech, for more than a hour, in support of the bill and in pointing out its feasibility and benefits.

Messrs. BELL, HAMLIN, MILLER, DAVIS, all followed, expressing themselves strongly in favor of the bill, but suggesting that time should be given to consider and determine the details.

Mr. SEWARD urged action on the measure. He was for it in any shape it might assume, now and at all times. No subject of equal importance could occupy the Senate. He was glad to see a return to the practiced business of Congress. After the debate on foreign affairs, he thought Congress should be called to the consideration of the internal improvements of the nation. He hoped the bill would be pressed and not suffered to remain unacted on any longer.

Mr. CASS was in favor of a road, but thought the vexed questions of the termini should be left to be settled by the Executive, after proper surveys and explanations.

Mr. BUTLER was opposed to the bill. He thought there ought to be proper explanations and surveys.

Mr. RUSK followed in support of the bill.

After further debate, Messrs. HAMLIN and RUSK submitted counter projects for the road, and all of them were ordered to be printed.

The subject was postponed till Monday, and the Senate adjourned.

HOUSE OF REPRESENTATIVES.

WASHINGTON, Thursday, Jan. 13.

The House resumed the discussion of the bill to prevent Frauds on the Treasury.

Mr. DARBY presented a memorial praying for a grant of land on the Western bank of the Mississippi River to aid in the construction of a railroad from New Orleans to Minnesota.

Referred to the Committee on Public Lands.

Mr. WILCOX rose to what he believed to be a question of privilege, and asked to be discharged from service as a member of the Committee on Military Affairs. The reason for this request was that he had been summoned by the Chairman to attend the sittings of the committee on Tuesday and Friday of each week. In pursuance of that summons, he had presented himself regularly at every meeting. Up to the present time there had not assembled a quorum for the transaction of business. He felt unwilling the public should hold him responsible for the business, the duty connected with which it was impossible for him to discharge without the coöperation of members of the committee. Important matters in the President's Annual Message, and the Report of the Secretary of War concerning the territories of Utah, New-Mexico and Oregon, and many other important matters from the Senate had been referred to that Committee. In fact the table of the Committee was groaning with the weight of business. The result of this neglect will be that the business will not be attended to, and will virtually be repudiated. The next Committee will look over the journal, and finding the matters not acted upon will take it for granted that the preceding Committee have repudiated the business. He did not wish the opprobrium attached to him for the neglect.

Mr. STANLY—I object for the reason the gentleman has shown himself to be a very attentive member, and we cannot do better by substituting another member.

A Voice—Exactly.

Mr. HAVEN—I hope the request of my colleague on the Committee will not be granted, for without his aid, and that of two or three others, we will not be able to get even a minority of the Committee, together. (Laughter.)

Mr. GORMAN—It is due to say, it is known to the country, that Mr. BISSELL, the Chairman, is confined to his bed by a grievous affliction, and Mr. GENTRY, by severe indisposition, cannot be there, nor has he been at any time during the session. I have been there almost every day since the session commenced. As there are some gentlemen who never go to the Committee, if I had time I should move to cut them off, and keep my friend on the Committee.

Mr. FREEMAN—I suggest to my colleague it would be very wrong to drive off an active member of the Committee, and it strikes me if this should be done there would be no work performed.

Mr. STEVENS, of Pennsylvania—I hope the gentleman from Mississippi will withdraw the application. I have the honor to be on the Committee on account of my great military services. (Laughter.) For four mornings I have been at the Committee Room three-fourths of an hour before the time, and I have always found the gentleman there alone.

Mr. WILCOX—I insist on my request to be discharged.

Mr. FLORENCE—I desire my colleague to answer me a question. He says the Speaker appointed him on the Committee because he desired to vindicate the truth of history. Now in what war was my colleague engaged?

Mr. STEPHENS—He placed me on the Committee on account of my examination of fortifications, circumvallations, gradations, and other things, the terms of which the gentleman knows, at Christiana. (Laughter.)

[It may be stated that FLORENCE was the foreman of the Grand Jury who examined into the Christiana riots.]

The question was taken, and Mr. WILCOX was not excused.

The House resumed the consideration of the bill to prevent frauds on the Treasury of the United States.

Mr. STEPHENS, of Ga., was free to state he thought the investigation by the Select Committee into the Gardiner claim fully and completely exonerated the Secretary of the Treasury from an improper connection with it. He then replied to the remarks of Mr. JOHNSON, of Tenn., and controverted the remarks of the last named gentleman, that it is *malum in se*, wrong in itself, for Members of Congress to appear before any tribunal in the prosecution of claims. They had always done so, and he had never heard of any imputation cast upon their characters for doing so. He had been informed that Col. BENTON appeared before the Mexican Board, also DANIEL WEBSTER, and Senators SOULE and BRIGHT, and members of the House, HOWARD, PHELPS and EWING—the last not now a member. He did not make this assertion to cast any imputation, for there is no law against any such thing.

Mr. PHELPS said he merely handed in papers to the Board for a constituent, got no compensation for it, and did not appear as counsel.

Mr. HOWARD made a similar explanation.

Mr. STANTON, of Tenn., said he appeared before the board now for a constituent who employed him as counsel and paid him for it. He had attended to thousands of cases for his constituents, and never received compensation, although he had been offered it.

Mr. STEPHENS replied, the explanations amount to this. The gentleman did not charge their constituents, but if money had been offerred, it would not have been considered improper to take it, any more than for prosecuting cases before the Supreme Court. His point was this, up to this time in our history such connection has never been deemed improper. There is no law against it. In the course of his remarks he alluded to the Galphin Claim, giving its history, and insisting it was an honest case, and in conclusion he would vote for the bill as an original proposition, and not with reference to past transactions.

Mr. STANTON, Tenn., did not see anything improper in appearing before a tribunal, established by Congress, for the adjudication of claims, but if Congress chose to establish this rule, and say a member of Congress shall not thus engage, he would be content.

Mr. JOHNSON, Tenn., asked his colleague whether he would justify CORWIN in retaining the money, if it was established beyond controversy that the GARDINER claim was allowed on forged papers, supported by perjury.

Mr. STANTON thought if such was the case, the money ought to be refunded. He had been told that CORWIN pledged himself to refund the money, if the fact of fraud is proved.

Mr. JOHNSON, Tenn.—I had no doubt that such an answer would be made by my colleague, for such was the opinion of every honest man.

Mr. ORR briefly defended the connection of WADDY THOMPSON, and the GARDINER claim, as counsel.

Mr. HOWARD, in his remarks, said there was no evidence before the Committee that CORWIN or THOMPSON knew the claim was a fraud.

PRESTON KING briefly explained the provisions of the bill, and the circumstances under which it was framed, when the House agreed to the several amendments pending, and the bill now presents the following features: First, all transfers and assignments hereafter made of any claim upon the United States, or any part or share thereof, or interest therein, whether absolute or conditional, and all powers of attorney, orders or other authorities for receiving payment of any such claim, or any part or share thereof, shall be absolutely null and void, unless the same shall be freely made and executed in the presence of at least two attesting witnesses, after the allowance of such claim, the ascertainment of the amount, and the issuing of a warrant for the payment thereof. Second, any officer of the United States or person holding any place of trust or profit, or discharging any official function under, or in connection with any Executive Department of the Government of the United States, or under the Senate or House of Representatives, who, after the passage of this act, shall receive any claim against the United States, shall in any manner, or by any means, otherwise than in the discharge of his proper official duties, aid or assist in the prosecution or support of any such claim or claims, shall be liable to indictment as for a misdemeanor, in any Court of the United States having jurisdiction for the trial of crimes and misdemeanors, and on conviction, shall pay a fine not exceeding twice the amount of gratuity, fee, or compensation, received by the person so convicted, or suffer imprisonment in the penitentiary not exceeding one year, or both, as the Court in its discretion shall adjudge. Third—Any Senator or Representative, who shall receive any gratuity from any claimant, certain or contingent, as prosecuting agent, or in any way assisting, shall be liable to indictment for misdemeanor, and on conviction pay a fine not exceeding twice the amount of the gratuity or compensation received by him, or suffer imprisonment in the penitentiary not exceeding one year, or both, at the discretion of the court. Persons having claims by inheritance, bequest, or marriage, are exempt from the above penalties. Fourth—Any person taking away, with intent to steal, records of a court of justice, shall be indicted for larceny, and on conviction shall be subject to a fine of $2,000, or suffer imprisonment in the penitentiary three years, or both. Fifth—Any officer having custody of official papers who shall destroy them, shall receive the same punishment as the above, and shall forfeit his office, and be forever disqualified from holding office under the Government of the United States. Sixth—For the prevention of bribes, any of the above-named offenders, on conviction, is to be fined not exceeding three times the amount so offered, promised, or given, and imprisonment in a penitentiary not exceeding three years, and the member, officer, or person convicted of so accepting or receiving the same, or any part thereof, shall forfeit his office and place; and any person so convicted under this section shall forever be disqualified to hold any office of honor, trust or profit under the Government of the United States. Seventh—The bill applies to all claims against the United States.

The question was stated on the bill.

Mr. SWEETSER moved it lay on the table, which was negatived.—Yeas, 11; Nays, 148. The affirmative votes were Holliday, Johnson of Arkansas, Meade, Millson, Polk, Stanton of Kentucky, Strother, Sweetser, Toombs, Welch, and White of Kentucky.

The bill was then read a third time, and, pending its passage, the House adjourned.

NEW-YORK LEGISLATURE.

SENATE....ALBANY, Thursday, Jan. 12.

Mr. BARTLETT from the majority of the Railway Committee, reported a bill to authorize the consolidation of Railway Companies.

Mr. BARTLETT dissents from the report.

Mr. CONGER introduced a bill repealing the act establishing a Teachers' Institute.

Mr. CONGER reported a bill to incorporate the American Geographical and Statistical Society.

Mr. MORGAN gave notice of a bill to amend the act of 1852, relative to the Harlem Railroad Company.

The Senate went into Committee on the bill relative to Savings' Banks and Savings' Institutions—rose and reported progress.

ASSEMBLY.

The general orders were taken up, and the following bills reported by the Committee of the Whole to the House:

To extend the time to collect taxes in Suffolk, Yates, Richmond, Dutchess and Niagara Counties.

To amend the charter of Buffalo City.

Mr. COOLEY's concurrent resolutions in regard to the Canals were received from the Senate, and laid over.

Mr. O'KEEFE gave notice of a bill relative to the Seaman's Fund, New-York.

BILLS INTRODUCED.

To repeal the Marriage Registry Act.

To incorporate Societies for Mental Improvement.

To amend the Act relative to Harbor Masters in New-York.

To authorize the Sackett's Harbor and Ellisburg Railway Company to issue preferred stock.

Further from Mexico—Loss of the Bark Sophia.

BALTIMORE, Thursday, Jan. 13.

The mail is through from New-Orleans. The papers contain the details of the news received from Tampico to the 27th ultimo. Among the leading officers of the regular Army who had pronounced in favor of the revolution, were COLS. CASANOVA, CRUZ and TENORIO.

The papers are filled with accounts of pronunciamentos—and the *El Tamaulipas* confidentially pronounces the Government of ARISTA doomed.

JUAN JOSE DE LA GARZA, provisional Governor of Tamaulipas publishes an address in which he justifies the revolution.

Cols. MEJIA and VEGA, had joined the revolutionists and within a few days a force of 1,500 men would be organized under the command of these Chiefs, which would march to occupy San Luis and other States of the Interior.

The Boston bark *Sophia*, from Liverpool, with a cargo of salt, went ashore near Charleston on Monday last, and after getting off, sunk in 7 fathoms of water. The vessel and cargo proved a total loss, but the passengers and crew were saved.

The Snow Storm.

NARROWSBURG, Thursday, Jan. 13.

Snow fell here for twenty-four hours, and is now about twenty inches deep. The train on the Erie Railroad have been greatly delayed, and the freight trains are scattered along the road wherever the storm overtook them. The Express trains of last night, and the day Express of to-day, going East, have passed this station. The weather is now mild.

OTISVILLE, Thursday, Jan. 13.

The Express train which left Jersey City at 5 P. M. yesterday, was detained at this place about twelve hours, being unable to force a passage through the snow in the cut, a few rods west of the station.

The Pennsylvania Kidnapping Case, &c.

BALTIMORE, Thursday, Jan. 13.

The case of RACHEL PARKER, the petitioner for her freedom, she having been kidnapped in Pennsylvania, was decided in her favor yesterday, the respondent abandoning the case. The citizens of Chester County, Penn., offered a reward of $1,000 for the apprehension of the murderers of JOSEPH C. MILLER, who assisted in the capture of RACHEL, and was shortly afterwards found dead in the woods near Stemmer's Run. The occurrence took place nearly a year ago, and it was supposed at the time that MILLER committed suicide through remorse.

No mail south of Richmond this morning.

The Murder of Mr. Rink in Philadelphia.

PHILADELPHIA, Thursday, Jan. 13.

The Coroner is engaged this morning investigating the murder of JOSEPH RINK. A number of persons were examined who saw the man running from the store; and a man answering the description given was arrested last evening, but discharged, not being identified. The murderer is described as about five feet ten inches high, stout with black hair, wearing a goatee and small moustache. And old pocketbook belonging to the deceased, in which he usually kept his notes, is missing, and the present supposition is that robbery was committed.

Massachusetts Legislature—Election of Public Officers, &c.

BOSTON, Wednesday, Jan. 12.

In the Legislature to-day, EPHRAIM WRIGHT, (Whig) was chosen Secretary of State, JACOB LOUD, Treasurer, also 9 Whig Councilmen; CHARLES THURBER, Whig, was chosen Senator, from Worcester, in place of Mr. KNOWLTON, Coalitionist, resigned.

Governor CLIFFORD will be inaugurated to-morrow, and will deliver his annual message.

Louisiana Election—The Steamship Cherokee.

NEW-ORLEANS, Wednesday, Jan. 12.

The majority for HEBERT, (Dem.,) for Governor in the whole State, is over 2,000—and the Legislature on joint ballot will give a Democratic majority, of probably 26.

The steamship *Cherokee* from New-York *viâ* Havana, arrived here on the 10th inst.—and sailed again at 8 o'clock this morning on her return.

Railroad Accident.

FREMONT, (Ohio,) Thursday, Jan. 13.

A passenger train from Toledo, this morning, ran off the track 8 miles west of this place. The engine, baggage express, and two passenger cars were badly smashed. Two men were seriously, and several others slightly injured—but no lives were lost. It is thought, however, that one man will not recover.

The Storm at Boston.

BOSTON, Thursday, Jan. 13.

The tow-boat *R. B. Forbes*, which was sent down to Minot's Ledge, yesterday, to take the place of the light boat *Brandywine*, was obliged to return to the City, it not being safe for her to remain. She reports bark *Turk*, from Malaga, for Boston, in Nantucket Roads, with both anchors down; the only vessel seen by her.

The Storm in the East.

BOSTON, Thursday, Jan. 13.

The storm still continues with unabated violence. Six to eight inches of snow have already fallen and badly drifted by a strong North-east gale. Neither the Fall River or Stonington trains have arrived, and are not expected to-night. The train via Norwich came through in good time this morning.

Hon. J. Butler King at New Orleans.

NEW ORLEANS, Wednesday, Jan. 12.

The Hon. J. BUTLER KING—late Collector of Customs at San Francisco, arrived here from California, in the steamship *Philadelphia*. He is going on to Washington.

The Weather and the Mails.

ALBANY, Thursday, Jan. 13.

The Southern mail due here at 11 o'clock last night, arrived here at 10 o'clock this morning.

The Western mails due here at 7 o'clock this morning, are not yet in. A heavy snow storm prevails.

The Snow Storm.

PHILADELPHIA, Thursday, Jan. 13.

The first New-York train to-day arrived here at 6 P. M. The Western train from Pittsburg reached here at 5 o'clock this morning. The Baltimore train arrived at the usual hour.

Railroad Accident.

CINCINNATI, Thursday, Jan. 13.

The train from Cleveland to Columbus, last night, ran over a tree at Lagrange—precipitating the locomotive and two passenger-cars into a ditch, and doing them much damage. No person was injured. The train was delayed twelve hours.

The Weather in New-Hampshire.

CONCORD, Thursday, Jan. 13.

Winter has returned again. The thermometer is now at 22°. This morning it was at 16°. The wind is northeast, and a snow-storm is commencing, with signs of a heavy gale.

Snow Storm at Boston.

BOSTON, Wednesday, Jan. 12—12 M.

A very severe snow storm commenced here early this morning, and still continues with every prospect of a heavy fall.

The Baltimore and Ohio Railroad.

WHEELING, Thursday, Jan. 13.

The excursionists return to-morrow. About eighty of them have gone on to Cincinnati.

It has stopped snowing, and the weather is cold.

Secretary Everett and the Colonization Society.

WASHINGTON, Thursday, Jan. 13.

Secretary EVERETT will deliver the address at the annual meeting of the American Colonization Society, in Washington, on Tuesday next.

Marine Disaster.

LEWES, Del., Thursday, Jan. 13.

The schooner *J. W. Conckin*, from New-York for Virginia came in collision with a Philadelphia schooner, and sustained some damage. She subsequently went ashore.

Death of Ex-Governor Cabell.

RICHMOND, Thursday, Jan. 13.

Ex-Governor CABELL, of Virginia, father of Hon. E. C. CABELL, of Florida, died here this morning.

THE NEW STEAMBOAT LAW.—The St. Louis *Intelligencer* says that the new law appears to meet with but little favor anywhere, and its usefulness or practicability, as we have heretofore stated, is very much doubted.

The St. Louis *Evening News* of Monday last, after announcing its postponement, denounces it as a "humbug, a bundle of absurdities—complicated, contradictory and impracticable," and adds that, "it is upheld by general ignorance, and by the salaried officials appointed to execute it, but who discharge their onerous duties by the palpable, gross, and unjustifiable nullification of the law itself."

Many features of the law, if properly carried out and made practically effective, would be of great benefit on our Western rivers, while others are a perfect nullity. Life boats in very many instances would be of incalculable benefit, but in others of no earthly use, especially in a narrow, shoal stream like the upper Ohio in Summer. Their Pittsburg *Gazette* has the following:

"Imagine one of our little 'dinkies,' drawing 18 inches water, "wrecked" on a "bar" in the Ohio. The raging surf roars around her, (over the left,) and imminent danger threatens the terrified passengers. The stout-throated captain cries, "Man the Life Boat!" the buoys are thrown out for the passengers who have fallen overboard, and then all who can get in are stowed safely away in its capacious hull. The oarsman "give way with a will," and in a short time the affrighted passengers are landed on the shore, blessing Congress for having thus interposed to save them from the horrors of shipwreck. After the "life boat" has thoroughly performed its mission, the captain probably wades ashore without taking off his boots.

Life boats, however, are very necessary, and hardly a week passes without recording a disaster by sea or lake, in which the life boat was found to be the principle saver of life. Early in December last, as we have published in our telegraphic reports, the crew of the bark *Isaac Stevens*, sixteen in number, were rescued by the steamship *Pacific*, in the Atlantic Ocean, by means of a life boat, sent out by the steamer, and manned by three of her crew. This life boat was built by Mr. FRANCIS, the inventor, who is now in this city.

UNCLE TOM'S CABIN.—The sale of "*Uncle Tom's Cabin,*" is prodigious. Five of the journals are now publishing it as a *feuilleton*. The future French opinions on American Slavery will be based on Mrs. STOWE's book.—*Paris Cor. of the Picayune.*

"Have you seen it?" asked a neighbor the next morning after a late arrival from California.

"No," was our reply, "but have you?"

"Yes, I sat up last night and read the first volume."

"Where did you get it?"

"I must not say, twenty-five names are now on the list."

We concluded there was no chance for us until the next arrival, if this copy must be thumbed by twenty-five readers.

P. S.—The *Messenger Bird* has since arrived and brought a supply of "*Uncle Tom's Cabin,*" and it has been our privilege to read the book. Most sincerely we hope every American at home and abroad may enjoy the same privilege. Especially we hope, those Senators and Representatives may read it, who voted for the Fugitive Slave Law.—those time-serving ministers of the Gospel who endeavor to justify American slavery by the Bible—those multitudes of christian professors who are so indifferent to the accursed evils of Slavery—and finally, we hope all ultra men both in the Colonization and Abolition ranks, will read the book.—*Honolulu* (Sandwich Islands) *Friend.*

☞ The Sacramento *Union* says, "The floodgates of the clouds seem to have been flung wide open on Monday, for such a fall of rain as came down, has seldom been experienced in this city—certainly not at any time during the present season. And the streets—what shall we say of the streets? Can that be called a street which is two-thirds water, and the other mud? Canals were almost as appropriate a term. One thing is certain, some tall specimens of wading are given, and boot-blacks find it convenient to abandon their fair weather position at the street corners. The class of worthies have become a kind of barometer, by which the weather is gauged. They will resume their places in a few days, and then look out for sunshine.

The Editor of the Chicago *Tribune* discourseth pleasantly of a New Year present he has received: We found in our Sanctum on New Year's day, standing on our new carpet, (that generous gift,) near a shelf of new books, (holiday presents,) a New Arm-Chair, evidently designed for the Editor of a Newspaper. So we sat down in it, and after trying it in various ways, and seeing specially whether it would balance itself on its two hind legs, as trained dogs do, (for this is the principal requisite of a chair,) we made up our irrevocable decision that it not only was a new Arm-Chair, but a very excellent Arm Chair, well-built, well balanced, well-painted, and well to do in the world every way, and that if we could only keep it where it was, one less of our friends would have to be kept standing, who might chance to call upon us. Well, that chair stands there yet. How it came there, we cannot say. There have been times when we have not kept our eye on it, and yet nobody has come to take it away, and it stands just where it did New Year's morning, and precisely where we are seated now. We are slowly but surely coming to the conclusion that it is ours—that it was a New Year's present, and that it will stand by us, like a tried friend, (or rather under us,) year after year. So far we are relieved, but the mystery of its origin still haunts us. Who made it? Who paid for it? Who brought it up the long flight of stairs? Who obtained entrance to our room? In fine, who was the kind, generous and mindful friend, that on the first day of 1853 remembered the Editor in his chairless estate and relieved him from being longer a *standing* joke? Who was it? Who? Who?

A little girl, scarcely two years of age, was killed one evening of last week in Suffield, by the explosion of one of the "camphene" or burning-fluid lamps which are now so generally in use. The mother of the child had temporarily left it in charge of a sister some five years old. The lamp had but one wick, the other having fallen through the tube and thus left a place for the fluid to run out if the lamp was handled carelessly. The elder child in endeavoring to light it, brought the lamp in proximity with flame, and the vapor or gas arising from the fluid at once took fire, blowing the lamp to pieces and shockingly burning the face of the little girl. She lived three or four days after the accident, her sufferings being prevented and her life prolonged by the plentiful application of *flour*.

A lady in Cincinnati having taken off the top of a camphene lamp to pour in more spirit, was holding it some five inches from the neck or tube of the lamp, where it was yet blazing, and the lower end of the wick extending into the lamp. While pouring in the fluid from a can, the blaze caught to the falling stream, when she instantly jerked out the wick, and some of the camphene falling upon her dress as she stood, carrying the blaze with it, set her dress on fire. Thos. G. Rees, being present, sprung instantly and caught her dress in his hands and smothered it out, the proof of his dexterity and fearless encounter of the flame may yet be seen on his fingers, they being crisped by the fire.

Michael Scott Gibson, an inmate of the State Lunatic Hospital at Worcester, escaped from that institution on the evening of the 1st inst., and has not since been heard from. At the March term of the Municipal Court in 1851, Gibson was tried and convicted on an indictment charging him with assaulting a female with felonious intent, and on the 12th day of that month was sentenced to ten years hard labor in State Prison. He remained in the prison until Nov. 20, 1852, when he was transferred to the Hospital at Worcester as an insane person, where he was properly treated until his escape.

The Portland *Advertiser* learns by a letter received by a gentleman of that city, that Miss Matilda Ann Planché, the authoress of "A Trap to Catch a Sunbeam," "Old Joliffe," and several other delightful little stories, was married on the 21st of Dec. last, to a young clergyman by the name of Mackarness. She intended publishing about Christmas time another of her little tales, to be entitled "The Evil Genius, or Influence."

The capitol of Florida is proposed to be removed, in accordance with a provision of the Constitution which requires that the seat of Government shall be permanently located within ten years after the admission of Florida as a State.

Mrs. Chisholm says the best time to select a wife is in the morning. If a young lady is at all inclined to sulks and slatternness, it is just before breakfast. As a general thing a woman don't get "on her temper" until after 10 A. M.

George Ticknor, the accomplished author of the "History of Spanish Literature," is preparing a memoir of Webster, which will be published expressly for the Massachusetts Historical Society.

THE NEW-YORK DAILY TIMES,

A VERY LARGE DAILY NEWSPAPER—each number comprising Eight Pages, or Forty-Eight columns, and giving more reading matter than any other Daily Newspaper in the United States—is published EVERY MORNING—(*Sundays excepted.*) at No. 138 NASSAU-STREET, corner of Beekman, and is delivered to subscribers in New-York, Brooklyn, Williamsburg and Jersey City, for TWELVE AND A HALF CENTS a week, payable to the Carrier; Single Copies, TWO CENTS. Mail Subscribers, FIVE DOLLARS a year; six months Two Dollars and a Half; three months One Dollar and a Half; Three Dollars in advance required in all exchanges with Country Newspapers.

POSTAGE ON THE DAILY TIMES sent to any part of the United States, paid in advance at the office where delivered—39 cents per quarter, or $1 56 per annum.

THE NEW-YORK EVENING TIMES

PUBLISHED EVERY EVENING, (*Sundays excepted.*) One edition will be issued at 1 and the other at 3 o'clock, P. M. It will be sent by mail; or sold at the same rates as the DAILY TIMES.

THE NEW-YORK WEEKLY TIMES,

A VERY LARGE NEWSPAPER FOR THE COUNTRY, is published every SATURDAY MORNING, at the low price of Two DOLLARS per annum. Two copies for THREE DOLLARS Five copies for FIVE DOLLARS, will be sent to one address; and the paper in no case continued beyond the time for which payment is made. Postage on the WEEKLY TIMES sent by mail one year, is as follows:

Within the County..........Free.
Within the State..........13 cents.
Within the United States..........26 cents.
Payments in all cases must be made in advance.

THE TIMES FOR CALIFORNIA.

A LARGE NEWSPAPER OF EIGHT PAGES, or Forty-eight Columns, made up expressly for circulation in *California, Oregon and the Sandwich Islands*, and containing only news of interest to readers in those sections of the country, is published on the departure of every Mail steamer. Price, 6 cents per copy.

RAYMOND, HARPER & CO., Publishers.

New-York Daily Times.

VOL. III....NO. 854. NEW-YORK, TUESDAY, JUNE 13, 1854. PRICE TWO CENTS.

New-York Daily Times.

JAPAN OPENED.

Satisfactory Result of Commodore Perry's Visit.

Three Ports Opened to American Trade.

Agreement to Furnish Coal to American Steamers.

INTERESTING NARRATIVE.

Detailed Account of Commodore Perry's Second Visit.

The *Susquehanna* arrived at Hong Kong from Japan on the 2d (April), bringing the gratifying intelligence that Commodore PERRY had succeeded in the objects of his mission in a manner that will confer honor on his country and enduring fame on himself. The precise terms of a Commercial Treaty had not been definitively arranged when the *Susquehanna* left the Yedó on the 24th of March; but enough had been done to establish a friendly feeling between the two countries. *The opening of Three or more ports to the Commerce of America, and the furnishing of Coals for its Steamers, may be considered as matters settled,* and Captain ADAMS held himself in readiness to proceed in the *Saratoga* to bear the intelligence to the Government at Washington.

We are enabled to furnish our readers with a detailed narrative of the proceedings in Japan, from which it will be seen that nothing could have been better or more fortunate than the course pursued by Commodore PERRY. Indeed we feel pretty certain that the most skillful diplomatist in Europe could not have brought matters to so speedy, pacific, and successful an issue. Commodore PERRY was known as a brave as well as accomplished seaman, but it was thought he had rather a propensity for fighting, which indeed, with such means at his disposal, and such people to deal with as the Japanese were ignorantly presumed to be, was deemed inevitable by most people, though, as our pages show, not by every one. Here however he has disappointed the world; and perhaps not a few in his squadron; but he has done what we did not do in China, and it was not expected any one could accomplish in Japan,—he *has peacefully and amicably opened it to the intercourse of his countrymen, without firing a shot or using an angry word.*

Commodore PERRY, in the *Susquehanna*, left the harbor of Hongkong on the 14th of January, accompanied by the *Powhatan* and the *Mississippi*, the sailing vessels, *Vandalia, Southampton, Supply* and *Lexington*, having some time before proceeded to the rendezvous at Napakiang in Loo Choo, where the squadron met on the 21st of January. Nothing of importance occurred at Loo Choo beyond visiting the capital, Shuidi, with the temples and forts, and admiring, as others have done, the picturesque and surpassingly beautiful scenery of the island.

The sailing vessels were dispatched for Japan on the last day of January, under command of Captain ABBOT, the steamships following on 7th February, and, along with the sloop *Saratoga* from Shanghae, joining the sailing vessels in the waters of Japan on the 12th, without accident beyond the temporary grounding of the *Macedonian*, which was lightened and speedily got off. The whole squadron then proceeded and anchored in the bay of Yedó, passing Uraga, where last year the interview and the delivery of the President's Letter took place. A few small forts, mounting ten or twelve guns each, were observed, but made no hostile demonstrations. Boats were not allowed to come alongside until the vessels had taken their stations, and then Government officers were directed to the *Powhatan*, (to which the Commodore's flag had been removed,) where they had an interview on the 13th with the fleet Captain ADAMS, to whom, after the exchange of compliments, the Japanese stated that in a few days a special high officer would be sent to Yedó to meet the Commodore and arrange everything in a courteous, frank, and friendly manner; but they objected that the vessels had come too far up, and recommended their return to Uraga, where the Emperor desired the meeting should be held as before; and that point they considered as of more importance than talking about the weather, which subject would seem to be the *pis-aller* of conversation in Japan as in all the rest of the world. We believe this was nearly all that passed during the first interview, and the duputation took leave in good humor, which grew to merriment, upon Captain ADAMS suggesting, that instead of returning to Uraga, perhaps a more favorable anchorage might be found higher up, and nearer the capital, which would also be more convenient for the high officers to be sent from Yedó, as well as in accordance with the customs of other nations.

The following day (14th) another interview was held on board the *Powhatan*, when the Japenese renewed their urgency about the meeting being held at Uraga, where on the previous occasion everything had passed in so amicable and pleasant a manner, and to which the Commodore had said he would return. Finding that Uraga was still objected to, they then proposed Kamakura, where the *Macedonian* had got ashore, and which they held to be a much more convenient place than Kanagawa, between the present anchorage and Yedó, as suggested by Dr. S. W. WILLIAMS. But after much talk on the subject, the Japanese at length left it to the Commodore to select a place for the interview. Before taking leave, the deputation said if the ships needed water or provisions, boats would be sent with supplies; but they were told that, except water, nothing else was likely to be required.

After mature consideration, Commodore PERRY decided to send Captain ADAMS in the *Vandalia* to meet the Governor of the Province at Uraga. Captain ADAMS was there informed by the Governor that everything was ready for considering the terms of a treaty between Japan and the United States, and if the Commodore (or, as he was termed, the Admiral) *would come to Uraga, it would be concluded before the going down of the sun.* It is supposed, however, that what was here meant by a treaty, was a favorable reply from the Emperor to the President's Letter on the subject. But Captain ADAMS reiterated, that the Commodore would not come to Uraga, where he had found the anchorage to be indifferent, but would meet the Japanese Commissioners at Yokohama, off the present anchorage of the flag-ship, ten to twenty* miles from Uraga. Captain ADAMS rejoined the squadron on the 24th February, and the following day the Japanese officers visited the flag-ship to settle the place of meeting, when the Commodore, among other things, told them that, having been entrusted with so many ships, which were seventeen thousand miles from home, he was reasonably anxious about their safety, and experience had proved to him that Uraga did not offer so secure an anchorage as where they now lay. Some discussion ensued, but finally it was arranged that the meeting should be he held at Yokohama.

* Our present information does not enable us to be more precise about the distance.

Eleven days afterwards the meeting took place; and in the interval, entertainments were interchanged by the American and Japanese officers. At one of two given by Capt. BUCHANAN, the Governor of Uraga, as we have seen in KEYING and other high Chinese officials, at once fell in with foreign observances in toasting and speechifying. Captain BUCHANAN proposed the health of the Emperor of Japan, which was drunk standing "with all the honors," and was acknowledged by the Governors of Uraga, who in return similarly proposed the health of the President of the United States. The Japanese took their liquor freely, especially champagne and liqueurs, greatly admiring the glassware that contained them; and expressed a hope that the time was at hand when they would be at liberty to visit foreign countries in steamers and ships of three masts.

It was during this interval that an officer of the squadron approached Yedó, and if he did not actually enter it, at least was near enough to judge of its appearance, and to ascertain, what, however, we believe a surveying party had done before, that close to the shore there is five fathoms water, so that it can be approached by large ships. The city is in the form of a crescent, and stands on an extensive plain with a magnificent back-ground of the mountains and wooded country; but it seems to possess no striking public buildings, while the dwelling-houses are generally of one story, and, therefore, present nothing imposing in their appearance, except their vast numbers, and space they occupy. The population of the capital has, however, been greatly exaggerated, for though it is certainly great, the Japanese officers themselves placed Yedó third among the cities in the world, London, they said, being the first, and Paris the second.

On the 8th, the preparations were completed for the reception of the Commodore, who, by the bye, insisted upon the removal of the screen-work which extended from the shore to the hall, and which shut out the public gaze. Between 11 and 12 o'clock, the marines having been mustered by Major ZEILIN, and the sailors by Lieut. PEGRAM, the whole in twenty-nine boats under command of Captain BUCHANAN, who conveyed the cortège to the shore, and waited the arrival of the Commodore and suite, consisting of Captain ADAMS, the Secretary, Mr. O. H. PERRY, and the interpreters, Dr. S. W. WILLIAMS and Mr. J. L. C. PORTMAN, who landed about noon, under a salute of seventeen guns from the *Macedonian*, the men in the boats standing up, and the officers on shore being uncovered. The procession then moved forward, the band playing "Hail Columbia" and the "President's March."

On entering the hall, the Commodore was received by four Commissioners, appointed for the purpose. They were:

First, HAYASHI, with the title of *Daigaku no kama*, or Prince Councillor.

Second, IDO, Prince of Tsus-sima, (the group of islands lying between Corea and Japan.)

Third, IDZUMA, Prince of Mimasaki, (a Principality lying west of Miaco.)

Fourth, UDONO, second assistant of the Board of Revenue.

The party being seated, the flag of Japan was run up on board the *Powhatan*, and saluted with twenty-one guns from the launches, after which another salute of seventeen guns was given to the Japanese High Commissioner, who through the interpreter presented his compliments and welcome to the Commodore and his officers, and particularly inquired about the health of the former. At a sign given the servants in attendance brought in laquered stands with tea and saki, sweetmeats and other conserves, and placed one beside each officer. The regalement seems to have been much the same as that which in China generally precedes the transaction of business with foreign officials; and while it was going on there was time to take a note of the place of meeting. The hall, which had been run up with great celerity, was about fifty feet long, forty wide, and twelve high, and surrounded with magnificent japonicas, some of them thirty feet in height, and in full bloom. Seats and tables about two feet high, covered with red cloth, extended the whole length of the apartment. The floor was covered with white mats, about three feet long by two wide; and the place was heated by highly ornamented braziers placed on beautiful Japan stands. The pillars supporting the erection were ornamented with purple crape, and the walls were richly adorned with paintings of birds and flowers. The hall was situated about five hundred yards from the landing-place, and was commanedd by the ships, which lay with their broadsides to it. Several native artists were present taking sketches of the strangers.

The refreshments being over, the Commodore and his personal staff were conducted by the Japanese Commissioners into another room in the rear, the entrance to which was covered with purple crape. The conference lasted three hours, and was carried on through the Dutch language, which the Japanese interpreters, MATS-MA-KI, and MICH-I-TASO, and Mr. PORTMAN, the Commodore's clerk, spoke fluently. *A very favorable answer was given to the President's letter*, which we presume was in terms a repetition of President FILLMORE'S; and it is stated that Commodore PERRY was fully satisfied on all points suggested by him, which, we again presume, were in accordance with Mr. Secretary WEBSTER'S letter of Instructions to Commodore AULICK accompanying the first letter to the Emperor. A draft Treaty, in English, Dutch, Chinese, and Japanese, was put into the hands of the Japanese Commissioners, who said that it would receive due consideration; but the old Emperor had died since Commodore PERRY was there last year, and his successor was a young man, who would require to consult his Council before coming to a determination; and the Commodore was reminded that Japanese did not act with the same rapidity as Americans did; which was thus illustrated: Should several Japanese meet together, desiring to visit the American ships, one would say: "It is a beautiful morning!" to which another would add, "How pleasant it is!" Then a third would remark, "There is not then a wave to be seen upon the water;" at length a fourth would suggest, "Come let us go and see the ships."

That the preliminaries of a treaty would be settled during the present visit was, however, more than probable. Its leading provisions, it is said, will be the opening of three or more of the ports of Japan to the commerce of the United States, and securing supplies of coals for the steamers of that country. In other respects the treaty, concluded or proposed, is understood to be nearly a counterpart of that with China, except, it is said, that the *Japanese objected to a clause admitting all other countries to the same privileges as America*; not like the Chinese, by whom, and not by Sir HENRY POTTINGER, as is generally supposed, the privileges of the English Treaty, were extended to all foreign countries. The Japanese would manifest more sagacity, and save themselves from incalculable vexation, were they to determine on allowing other nations to enjoy the same immunities as America, and no other, modeling all future treaties on precisely the same terms. But nothing can be as yet certainly known on the subject, for the *Susquehanna*, having been placed at the disposal of Mr. MCLANE, the Minister to China, and being under orders to be in Hong Kong in the beginning of April, was dispatched on the morning of the 24th March, the very day a Conference was to have been held for the purpose of considering the treaty.

As most of our readers may have forgotten the precise tenor of President FILLMORE'S letter to the Emperor of Japan, and as it is not long, we here insert it, appending an outline of Mr. Secretary WEBSTER'S instructions to Commodore AULICK, to whom the mission was originally entrusted:

"I send you, by this letter, an envoy of my own appointment, an officer of high rank in his country, who is no missionary of religion. He goes by my command to bear to you my greeting and good wishes, and to promote friendship and commerce between the two countries.

"You know that the United States of America now extend from sea to sea; that the great countries of Oregon and California are parts of the United States; and that from these countries, which are rich in gold and silver and precious stones, our steamers can reach the shores of your happy land in less than twenty days.

"Many of our ships will now pass in every year, and some perhaps in every week, between California and China. These ships must pass along the coast of your empire; storms and winds may cause them to be wrecked on your shores, and we ask and expect from your friendship and your greatness, kindness for our men and protection for our property. We wish that our people may be permitted to trade with your people; but we shall not authorize them to break any law of your empire.

"Our object is friendly commercial intercourse, and nothing more. You may have productions which we should be glad to buy, and we have productions which might suit your people.

"Your Empire contains a great abundance of coal; this is an article which our steamers, in going from California to China, must use. They would be glad that a harbor in your Empire should be appointed to which coal might be brought, and where they might always be able to purchase it.

"In many other respects commerce between your Empire and our country would be useful to both. Let us consider well what new interests may arise from these recent events which have brought our two countries so near together, and what purposes of friendly amity and intercourse this ought to inspire in the hearts of those who govern both countries."

The first half of Mr. Secretary WEBSTER'S instructions is devoted to the subject of coals, that being apparently the leading object of the mission; but Commodore AULICK was to avail himself of any and every opportunity when brought in contact with Japanese officials—either in treating about coals, or in delivering over certain shipwrecked Japanese—to impress upon them "that the Government of the United States does not possess power over the religion of its own citizens, and there is therefore no cause to apprehend it will interfere with the religion of other countries." This point, not without reason, as afterwards appeared, was held to be of the first importance, for even the question of commercial intercourse was made subsidiary, its success being regarded as unpromising; but in order to provide for any "favorable contingency," the Commodore was invested with power to negotiate a treaty, and was furnished with copies of those of China, Muscat, and Siam, as models, "the two latter containing guarantees for the protection of American sailors and property which may be cast ashore," which WEBSTER held to be more important than opening "one or more of the ports of Japan." If however the Commodore should succeed in effecting a treaty, Mr. WEBSTER concludes by saying, "it would be prudent to fix the period for exchanging the ratifications at three years."

During the conference on the 8th, Commodore PERRY mentioned that one of the marines had died, and he was desirous to have a piece of ground pointed out where this man and any others of the squadron that might die in Japan could be buried. The Commissioners first suggested Nanasáki, and next Uraga, but on both being objected to, a spot near the place of meeting was fixed upon. An account of the funeral by Captain SLACK, the officer commanding the marines, is given in another column, and cannot fail to be read with interest. We have only to add, that before the funeral took place, the Japanese officials came on board to view the body, for which purpose the coffin was opened; and after the burial one of them remarked that, according to the inscription on the lid, the man was a native of Ireland; not of America; but the explanation that followed proved quite satisfactory. In the course of the arrangements for the funeral, the prudence of President FILLMORE'S and Secretary WEBSTER'S assurance on the subject of religion was shown. The Japanese said they had observed it with pleasure, and quite understood the distinction between Protestants and Roman Catholics.

Before the interview broke up, the Commodore mentioned that he proposed to give his officers leave to go on shore for recreation. To this no great objection was made, and we believe that within a few days afterwards several the officers were taking exercise on shore. Rev. E. C. BITTINGER, the Chaplain, made several excursions among the villages and cornfields, which last he found in high cultivation. The houses were generally thatched, but those of the better sort were covered with tiles, having yards and small gardens within enclosures.

The following day, the same gentleman, finding the people neither unfriendly nor indisposed to receive him, and having obtained leave to go on shore, determined to visit two large cities some miles off, called Kanagawa and Kasacca, and with that view crossed an arm of the bay, which shortened the distance by several miles. He then proceeded through Kanagawa, supposed to contain from one to two hundred thousand inhabitants; and from the immense crowds that poured out everywhere to see the stranger, there can be no doubt of the population being very great. The crowds however, caused no inconvenience or impediment, for on a wave of the hand from the Japanese officials who accompanied Mr. BITTINGER, the people cleared a passage; and afterwards, a messenger having been sent forward for the purpose, the people packed themselves at the sides of the houses, and left the centre of the streets clear for the stranger. He entered some of the houses, which he found primitive in their furniture and arrangements; but, compared with other Oriental dwellings of the same class, neat, clean and comfortable. In some of them he observed clocks of Japanese manufacture. He also visited several temples, which though smaller than in China, have more gilding on their walls, and ornaments on their idols, and generally are in better order. The priests as well as the people were distinguished for their courtesy. The cities thus visited were not only very extensive, (estimated to be six miles long,) but with wide, well-formed streets. Kasacca is from fifteen to twenty miles distant, by land, from the ships; and Mr. BITTINGER being thus necessarily long absent, some anxiety was felt about him. As he was returning, a Japanese officer put into his hands an order from the Commodore for all officers to return on board, and shortly afterwards, a courier mounted on a splendid black horse, delivered a similar dispatch, and finding it was understood and acted on, turned round, and galloped back again to report the approach of the American officer, who concluded his journey by torch-light, and found on his arrival that everything that had occurred had been noted, even the number of buttons on his coat being recorded.

Four days after the interview, the presents were interchanged, time having been required to erect places for their reception. Those for the Emperor consisted of, among other things—

A Railway with Steam Engine—An Electric Telegraph—A Surf Boat—A Life Boat—A Printing Press—A fine Lorgnette—A set of Audubon's American Ornithology, splendidly bound—Plates of American Indians—Maps of different States of America—Agricultural implements, with all the modern improvements—A piece of Cloth—A bale of Cotton—A Stove—Rifles, Pistols, and Swords—Champagne, Cordials, and American Whisky.

And for the Empress, (presuming there is one,)—A Telescope—A Lorgnette in a gilded case—A Lady's Toilet-box, gilded—A Scarlet Velvet Dress—A changeable Silk Dress, flowered—A splendid Robe—Audubon's Illustrated Works—A handsome set of China—A Mantelpiece Clock—A Parlor Stove—A box of fine Wines—A box of Perfumery—A box of fancy Soaps.

Of the other presents, perhaps the one most valued was a copy of WEBSTER'S complete Dictionary to one of the Imperial interpreters. To the high officers were given books, rifles, pistols, swords, wines, cloths, maps, stoves, clocks, and cordials, the last of which they fully appreciated, and, as regards clocks, when it was proposed to bring an engineer from shipboard to set them agoing, the Japanese said there was no occasion for that, for they had clock-makers in Yedó who understood them perfectly. They were curious to know however about ERICSSON'S caloric engine, of which they had heard, but, from the Commodore at any rate, we suspect they would not receive a very favorable opinion of its practical utility.

Whatever may be thought of some of the other presents, the Railway and Telegraph, at which the world at the time was disposed to laugh, were happy hits. The Rail is only about three hundred yards in all, but being formed in a circle, the carriage can be driven at the rate of forty miles or more. Just at first the Japanese were chary of venturing into the car, but after a single trial there was much good humored competition for places. The Telegraph still more astonished them, but they will speedily understand it, and may possibly by this time be laying down the wires for themselves.

Christian Burial in Japan.

One of the standing opinions about the Japanese, destined to be thrown down by Commodore PERRY, has been, that they were invincibly intolerant of Christianity in any form. Indeed this has generally been assigned as the main reason for their exclusiveness. To the emblem of the Cross they still object, but the story of the expelled Portugese, that every Christian landing in Japan was required to trample on it, or on a representation of the Virgin and Saviour, must, if true, have been almost entirely confined to themselves and their coreligionists. More recent writers, who have been able to deny that such is now the custom, tell us, that "the practice of religious rights is prohibited by irrevocable Japanese laws;" but the following narrative of the funeral of a marine of the United States squadron shows that there is as little foundation for the one statement as the other:

On the 9th of March, the day following the first meeting be ween Commodore PERRY and the Imperial Commissioner from Yedó, to negotiate the terms of a commercial treaty, a soldier's and a Christian burial was given to a Marine, ROBERT WILLIAMS, who had died a few days before on board the steamer *Mississippi*. The party detailed for this purpose, consisted of several officers, one of them the Chaplain in his gown, an escort of eight marines in charge of a corporal, and four marines as bearers of the corpse. Two boats left the ship; one containing the officers, and the other the body and escort. Upon reaching the shore the party was met by several Japanese Officials, ready to conduct them to the grave. The escort landed first, and received the body with the usual honors. The little procession was then formed; first the escort, followed by the music (drum and fife); next the body borne on the shoulders of four messmates; and then the Chaplain with the other officers, and a few sailors from the boats bringing up the rear. In this order, with the music playing a Dead March, the party moved to the grave, winding through the streets of a village, a distance of nearly half a mile. On either side of the road, and on the surrounding hills, at the foot of one of which the grave had been made, thousands of people, men, women, and children, could be seen, all manifesting eager curiosity to witness a sight so entirely novel in *their* land.

I could not but think as we passed along, how strange, not only the procession, but each of us individually, must appear to that eager throng, not one of whom probably had ever before looked upon the face of a stranger from a foreign country; and yet their was no undue noise made, or apparent alarm on the part of any of them,—only intense interest in observing what was passing before them. As we neared the grave (which occupied a very pretty spot) the voice of the Chaplain could be heard,—"I am the resurrection and the life, saith the Lord; he that believeth in me, though he were dead, yet shall he live; and whosoever liveth and believeth in me, shall never die." As we gathered round the grave, and the reading of the beautiful and touching burial service proceeded, the scene was one of unusual interest; for the time, and place, and circumstances, all conspired to make it, as an incident, honorable to our short sojourn in a land, where for centuries, it is said the symbol of our religion has been trodden under foot. The Church burial service ended, the escort fired three volleys over the grave. I had expected that on this there would have been some commotion among the crowd, but I noticed only, at the first discharge, that for a moment there was a slight movement as of surprise, and then all were again quiet and attentive observers.

Having now committed to the earth, with all due honor, the remains of our deceased shipmate, the procession was re-formed, and with music to the front, again passed through the village and the thousands of spectators, to our boats on the beach. Here we took leave of the officials, who throughout the entire ceremony had conducted themselves with great propriety, and extended to us every civility; and returned to the ship, pleased with the consciousness of not only having witnessed, but assisted in giving such honors, in such a place, to a deceased brother. W. B. S.

The Resources of Japan.

Foremost among the resources of Japan are its fisheries. The sea and its productions, we believe, contribute fully as much to the sustenance of the natives, as do the fruits of the earth—rice, perhaps, excepted. One of their productions has a value which is not confined to the spot, but extends to us—to our enterprise, and our trade,—we mean the whale, or, as they call it, *kudsuri*. There is nothing of which such extensive use is made by the Japanese, both for rich and poor. It is found all around Japan, but particularly in the sea Keumano, which washes the Southern coast of the island Niphon, the most important territory of the Empire; and it also prevails in the islands of Tsussima and Goto, and upon the coasts of Omura and Nomo. These whales not only afford oil in great abundance, but their flesh, which is considered very wholesome and nutritious, is largely consumed. No part of them, indeed, is thrown away—all is made available to some useful purpose or another, excepting only the large shoulder bone. The skin, which is generally black; the flesh, which is red and looks like beef; the intestines, and all the inward parts; besides the fat or blubber, which is boiled into oil, and the bone which is converted to innumerable uses—all is made available to purposes of profit. We have gone into these few particulars respecting the whale, because it is that which has brought our countrymen into contact with Japan. Many of our ships have for some considerable time past frequented those seas for capturing the whale, an occupation which, it is found, might be pursued with great advantage, under a commercial treaty with the Government of Japan, whose inhuman laws at present not only prevent any assistance being rendered to shipwrecked mariners, but expose them to positive maltreatment, and even to violent death. To obtain redress in this respect was the primary object of Commodore PERRY'S expedition.

Japan abounds in natural and artificial productions of great value. Its mineral riches are enormous, and include metals of various kinds, especially gold, silver, and copper. Sulphur and nitre are also found in large quantities;—there is no want of coal, and there are precious stones of almost every variety; agates, sapphires, jaspers, cornelians, and even diamonds; while pearls are found in great plenty among the shells upon the coast. Then the fertility of the soil is very great. The mulberry tree grows extensively and affords food for countless myriads of silk worms. The *Kadsi*, or paper-tree, serves innumerable useful purposes, including the manufacture of cloth, stuffs and cordage. The *cerusi*, or varnish-tree, is another valuable production of the country, yielding large quantities of a milky juice which the natives employ to varnish, or *japan* as we call it, various articles. Then there are the bay-tree, the camphor-tree, the fig-tree, the cypress-tree, with very many more, all more or less valuable, and from which a great variety of useful things are made; and last, though not least, there is the tea-shrub, from the leaves of which the common drink of the people is brewed, and which is capable of yielding a valuable article of commerce. Trees growing nuts of various kinds are abundant; the maple is extensive and excellent; bamboos are very plentiful, and of great use, as they are everywhere in the Indies; they cultivate as much hemp and cotton as they can find room for in their fields; and as to rice, which is the main food of the natives, that grown in Japan is considered the best in all Asia, and it can be produced in almost any quantity. Their corns are of several sorts; besides the *komi* or rice, there are the *oomuggi*, a kind of barley; the *koomuggi*, their native wheat; and the *daidson*, a species of bean,—all of which abound with superior farina.

The manufactures of Japan have hitherto been confined almost exclusively to their own domestic wants; but many of them are, nevertheless valuable as articles of export. Our adoption here and throughout Europe of the term *japan* as applied to certain kinds of varnished ware, indicates how well known has been their peculiar excellence in, if not their invention of that useful art. They make various articles from the paper tree, resembling our *papier-mache*, which they paint, and varnish, on paper, very highly—and these might form objects of considerable trade. Their silks, muslins, and cotton goods are most of them very superior, and some of them are calculated to become highly *recherche*; and their carvings in wood, ivory, pearl, and fish-bone, are most ingenious and elegant. These are but a few of the products of their handicraft; but they are sufficient to show, taken in connection with their natural productions, how varied and how valuable are the resources of the Japanese.

Progress of the Chinese Revolution.

From the Commercial.

HONG KONG, Saturday, April 8, 1854.

For many months we have known nothing of the movements of the Northern Army of the insurgents. After penetrating to within a hundred miles of Pekin, they went into Winter quarters, and no actions of any importance have since taken place. TAE-PING-WANG maintains his position: and when certain reinforcements reach him, which have been seen moving northward, he will probably march for the capital. There great distress prevails, and the poverty of the treasury leads to increased oppression.

The issue of paper money and the debasing of the copper currency have been resorted to by the Government, but these measures can afford it but little effectual aid. Pekin must fall; and then the army of the North will spread itself over the neighboring country, and take possession of Soo-Chow and Hong-Chow, and other rich cities, which it has only to attack. The districts for a considerable distance around Nankin have peacefully submitted to the insurgents, and the taxes for some months past have been collected by insurgent officers.

To the South and West more activity has prevailed. Nearly all the cities of Ngunhwai and many of Hupeh are occupied by the rebels, who do not merely capture and pass through, as formerly; and lately we have heard of the capture of Wuchong and Hangkaw. Two days since, the powerful city of Changsha was reported lost. Although some part of this information may be erroneous, the tenor of it plainly indicates the total destruction of governmental power in the interior. Within a few days goods intended for the tea districts have been brought back, the owners finding it impossible to pass them through the country.

Warm weather is now rapidly approaching, and the camp at the North will soon be broken up. If Pekin falls, the power in those cities which have hitherto adhered to the Emperor must pass into the hands of the new party, and Canton can scacely be exempt from such change. Looking at the history of the past year, and the rapid progress of the insurgents, it seems probable that the coming Summer will decide the fate of China, and it is very desirable that some result be reached. The exigencies of commerce demand it.

The Streets—Genin again in the Field.

To the Honorable the Common Council of the City of New-York:

The undersigned, a resident of the Sixteenth Ward, would respectfully inform your honorable body that the said Ward is, at present, in a filthy and disgraceful condition. Such is the state of the streets in certain localities, that, unless they are speedily purified, nothing short of Providential interference can save the inhabitants from pestilential disease.

The stench arising from the abominations which have been suffered to fester and rot in the thoroughfares and byways, is, in some places, almost overpowering; and as the heat increases, and additions are made to the pestiferous mass, fever and cholera may be looked for as the unavoidable results.

Under these circumstances, and they are notorious throughout the ward, prompt sanitary action is required. Experience has taught the undersigned the futility of looking for it from the Street Department. He therefore asks of you, as guardians of the public health, such an appropriation as will suffice for the periodical removal of the elements of danger in this quarter of the City; probably $400 per week would effect the desired object and save the ward from the visitation of disease. For the sake of his own family and the families of his neighbors, the undersigned would be willing to assume the task of cleansing the ward and keeping it clean during the Summer months, if sufficient funds should be appropriated for that purpose—he of course giving bonds for the faithful application thereof, and receipts and vouchers for all moneys expended. JOHN N. GENIN.

☞ We learn by a note from Mr. F. COOMBS, that he has commenced a suit against Messrs. GROVER, BAKER & Co., for having accused him of fraudulently disposing of Sewing Machines of their make. He pronounces the assertion false and malicious.

LATEST INTELLIGENCE

By Telegraph to the New-York Daily Times.

CONGRESSIONAL PROCEEDINGS.

Interesting Debate in the House on Fixing a Day for Adjournment.

Resolution Naming August 14 Passed.

Negotiations for the Purchase of Cuba—Our Relations with New-Granada.

Correspondence of the New-York Daily Times.

WASHINGTON, Sunday, June 11, 1854.

The statement is traveling over the country that WARREN WINSLOW, who went to Madrid with dispatches to Mr. SOULE, in relation to the *Black Warrior* affair, is about to return to that Court with a specific offer for the purchase of Cuba. As much credence is given to the rumor, I may as well say it is unfounded. It is not even probable that Mr. WINSLOW will go to Spain again at all at present, so far as I can learn.

Our Government continues to press its demand for some arrangement by which we shall be enabled to settle at Havana, and without reference to Madrid, disputes arising in the ports of Cuba between the Spanish authorities and American citizens. Spain has manifested, as yet, no disposition to yield this point; and thus a serious disturbing element in our relations with that country continues to exist. The President will send a Special Commission to Madrid to aid in settling this point by the purchase of Cuba, if the present manipulations of the public pulse shall show that such a Commission will be popular, but he has not determined on that point yet. The Mesilla difficulty was settled by swallowing the question up in the greater one of purchase; and so all our Spanish difficulties will be arranged, by buying up the Island Colony whence all of them flow.

Each successive arrival from Europe brings additional evidence that the Spanish Court is coming down to the plain matter-of-fact proposition for the sale of Cuba to the United States. The members of the Government now talk freely of that measure, as of any other;—at the same time that they avoid coming frankly to the point of saying that they *will* sell, and of making a definite statement of terms. In short, they see that to this complexion they must come at last; but they prefer a little coyness, in hope of enhancing the price. The wisest Statesmen of Spain fully appreciate the fact that they would derive great advantages from a sale of the island to us. One hundred millions of dollars would firmly establish the Government, and leave an ample sum for the construction of railroads and other works of internal improvement, calculated to develop the natural resources of the kingdom and convert its rich waste into a productive self-sustaining country. Notwithstanding her great agricultural resources, but a very small portion of Spain does or can live thereby, for want of means to get the crops to market. While famine rages at one point, frequently two or three years' crops of wheat are rotting at thirty miles distance, because there is no method of bringing them to the point where needed. With railroads intersecting the country and reaching the seaboard, Spain might soon recover much of her former power and greatness. She has within her the surest element of prosperity,—unsurpassed agricultural resources. Make these available, and she will not need an overtaxed and distant colony to support her Government. Her statesmen see this of late; and many of them are anxious to finger our millions, that they may exchange the gold for railroad iron. Such arguments as these will be far more effectual in securing us the possession of Cuba than all the bullets and cannon balls we can muster.

I understand that the President and Secretary of State have had under consideration the subject of the passenger tax levied by the New-Granadian Government on American citizens passing through Panama to or from the Pacific. Mr. GREEN, our Minister to Bogota, has earnestly remonstrated against this tax, as unjust and violative of express treaty stipulation; and steps are about to be taken by our Government to resist its collection at all hazards. For this purpose a vessel of war will probably be sent to Aspinwall, and another to Panama.

The absent members of Congress come in very slowly; but the general expectation is that to-morrow the business of both houses will be recommenced in good earnest. There is much to be done, if Congress will only take hold with a view of accomplishing it. S.

THIRTY-THIRD CONGRESS......First Session.

SENATE—WASHINGTON, Monday, June 12.

A message was received from the House communicating the proceedings of that body on the occasion of the death of Hon. J. F. SNODGRASS of Virginia.

Mr. MASON delivered a eulogy upon the virtues of the deceased, and offered the customary resolutions—when the Senate adjourned.

HOUSE OF REPRESENTATIVES.

WASHINGTON, Monday, June 12.

PROPOSITION FOR ADJOURNMENT.

The SPEAKER announced the first business in order to be Mr. WALBRIDGE'S resolution providing for the adjournment of Congress on the 3d of July.

The rules were suspended by 104 against 38.

Mr. WALBRIDGE proposed to amend his resolution to adjourn July 17.

Mr. ORR offered a substitute—to adjourn the 14th of August. That would afford ample time for the transaction of other business.

Mr. HAVEN submitted the Senate's resolution for an adjournment from the 4th of July to the third Monday in October. He said, fix that time and all the necessary work will be done in the meantime. Congress had got into that kind of demoralization, so to speak, that they can do no valuable service till the members, after separating, shall come together at some future day.

Mr. ORR said his principle reason for voting for a suspension of the rules, was to defeat the Senate's resolution. He was opposed to taking a recess. It was unprecedented in the history of the Government. Congress should pursue the usual course.

Mr. HILYER proposed that Congress adjourn on the first Monday in August, and meet hereafter on the third Monday in October, in each year, instead of the first Monday in December.

Mr. MCMULLEN was opposed to fixing any day at present. Let Congress go to work, and transact the business before it, and then it would be time to provide for the adjournment.

Mr. HAVEN urged considerations why the Senate's resolutions should be adopted. He was satisfied if members stay here, they will keep the country in turmoil, without doing the public business. The private calendar has been taken up only twice. Disease is approaching us—the cholera is abroad. A quorum could only be maintained by the Sergeant-at-Arms scouring the city.

Mr. TAYLOR, of Ohio, said, if the 1st of August should be named, he would support the resolution. The business of Congress can be transacted in six weeks; the country demands it—we ought not to take recess.

Mr. HENN inquired whether if the Senate resolution should be adopted, members could not draw pay in recess; he understood that was the construction of the Comptroller.

Mr. HAVEN replied, the resolution was for adjournment, not recess; therefore members could not draw pay meantime.

Mr. CAMPBELL offered an amendment, which Mr. HAVEN accepted, providing no compensation shall be allowed members during recess.

Mr. DISNEY thought the whole matter premature, ill considered, and out of place. The Committees have their hands full of reports, and no one could say when Congress should adjourn.

Mr. JONES of Tenn. said the last ten days have been spent in idleness when there was not a working quorum in the House. He was opposed to recess, and thought all public business could be transacted by the 14th of August.

Mr. EWING could see no prospect of doing business if Congress remained here, and therefore was in favor of the earliest day of adjournment.

Mr. HILYER moved the whole subject be laid on the table. Negatived—56 against 97.

Mr. KEITT would prefer the 14th of September for adjournment. He understood the Democratic party came in power on a platform of principles many of which have not been carried out. [Laughter.] He wanted to give that party an opportunity to carry out their principles, one of which he understood to be a modification of tariff and free trade.

Mr. WALBRIDGE and Mr. HAVEN'S amendments were severally rejected.

Mr. ORR'S was adopted, by 71 against 69.

The question recurring on the adoption of the resolutions thus amended, fixing the 14th of August for adjournment—motion made to lay it on the table negatived. The resolution was then adopted—82 against 68.

Mr. HOUSTON made an ineffectual effort to introduce a resolution, that the daily hour of meeting shall be 11 o'clock.

Mr. HILYER asked leave to introduce a bill fixing the annual meeting of Congress the first Monday in Nov.

Pending the motion to suspend the rules, the House adjourned.

Messrs. Riddle, Goode, Gerrit Smith, Elliot, Trout and Sollers, were appointed a Select Committee on the Memorial of 2,000 Citizens of Delaware, praying the Government to effect some arrangement with Peru, by which, for a just and proper equivalent, the Peruvian Government will either cede to the United States Government one of the Guano Islands, or by removing the existing restriction on American vessels engaged in the guano trade, place the trade in the article on a more just and liberal commercial basis.

From Washington.

WASHINGTON, Monday, June 12.

The new City Government was inaugurated to-day, and the occasion was one of general rejoicing.

Mr. and Mrs. WM. F. RITCHIE arrived here this morning.

The New-York Light Guard in Boston.

BOSTON, Monday, June 12.

The New-York Light Guard, with Dodworth's Band, command much attention from our military and citizens generally. They are the special guests of the Boston Light Infantry. Capt. ROGERS, and this afternoon both companies were reviewed on the Common by Major General EDMANDS and staff.

In the evening the two companies, with numerous invited guests, partook of a sumptuous banquet in Faneuil Hall. Speeches were made by Governor WASHBURN, Mayor SMITH, Captains VINCENT and ROGERS, Lieut. CLAPP and others. It was a magnificently conducted affair throughout.

From Rio de Janeiro.

BALTIMORE, Monday, June 12.

The bark *Antelope* arrived here to-day with advices from Rio de Janeiro to the 1st of May. BREADSTUFFS were exceedingly dull with large receipts. No sales were reported, holders' views being above the market rates. The COFFEE market opened at an advance upon previous rates, with sales during the week of 35,000 bags at 4‖200@4‖300 for lots, and 4‖350@4‖400 for good firsts and superiors. At the close of the market good firsts could not be had at less than 4‖400. The stock in the market was small, and composed almost entirely of low qualities, the new crop being held back. STERLING EXCHANGE, 27¾d@28d. FREIGHTS dull.

Arrived at Rio 28th April—Ship Amelia, New-York; 29th, bark Stamboul, Boston. Sailed—25th, ship Tartar, for Philadelphia; 27th, bark Nautilus, and 28th, ship Susquehanna, both for New-York.

Fugitive Slave Excitement in Manchester, N. H.—Fatal Affray.

MANCHESTER, (N. H.,) Monday, June 12.

Much excitement was caused here yesterday and to-day, by a report that two persons from Virginia had arrived in Lowell in search of EDWIN MOORE, a colored barber, formerly resident in Lowell and now keeping shop here. MOORE is alleged to have escaped from Virginia, where he was a slave, twelve years since. A purse was made up for him to-day, and at noon he took the cars for Canada, accompanied by his wife and three children.

JOHN MARSHALL, a stable-keeper of this city, killed MICHAEL COLLAMORE, one of his employés, last evening, during a quarrel about wages. MARSHALL has been arrested.

Philadelphia New City Councils.

PHILADELPHIA, Monday, June 12.

The New City Councils were organized this morning. JOHN P VERREE was elected President of the Select Council, and JOHN H. DIEHL President of the Common Council. The vote in the latter body stood, DIEHL, Whig, 58; CRISPIN, Democrat, 10. A number of the seats of Democrats are contested, but they were sworn in by virtue of the certificates given by the Judges of Election.

New-Hampshire Legislature.

CONCORD, Monday June 12.

Wednesday next has been assigned for the choice, in Convention of the two Houses, of Secretary of State, Treasurer and Public Printer.

A large number of bills for banks, five cent Savings Institutions, and for the increase of bank capital have been introduced, indicating that bank matters will be a prominent feature of the session.

Fatal Railroad Accident.

PATERSON, N. J., Monday, June 12.

A lamentable accident happened in this city this morning. A gravel train had stopped until some cattle were driven off the track, and two laborers on the cars were throwing stones to assist in driving them away, when the train suddenly started, and both the men were precipitated on the track. The head of one of them was completely cut off, seven cars passing over him; and the other had the flesh torn from his legs, and is not expected to recover.

Fire at the White Mountains.

BOSTON, Monday, June 12.

The "Notch House" on the White Mountains was totally destroyed by fire on Friday last.

The Southern Mail.

BALTIMORE, Monday, June 12.

The Southern Mail as late as due is to hand but the papers contain no news worth telegraphing.

THE TURF OF 1854.

Trotting Match at the Centreville Course—The Judges' Decision Disputed—Union Course Races.

The Centreville Course was attended yesterday by a large number of persons from the City, to witness a trotting match announced to come off as follows:

"Mile heats, best three in five, top wagons. I. Woodruff names b. g. Wedge; Wm. Wheelan names br. g. Frank.

The Judges were selected by the parties interested in the race, and took their seats on the stand. The horses scored several times, and on the second turn they received the word *go*, and the gelding of Mr. WOODRUFF was full one length ahead at the time the word was given, and having the pole, *Wedge* had advantage over his competitor. As the steeds glided around the lower turn of the track, the brown horse of Mr. WHEELAN'S made a very bad break, and before he could be managed by his skillful driver, and compelled to settle down on a square trotting gait, he had made quite a run, but was checked as speedily as possible, and never made a skip or break after the first flare up. The horse under the management of Mr. WHEELAN exhibited most excellent speed under the existing circumstances, and with perfect ease he passed *Wedge* at the quarter pole, and left him in the rear for a long distance. ISAAC WOODRUFF urged *Wedge* to his utmost, but it was of no use, as he came very near being distanced at the first distance box, and only saved himself by making a desperate run on the back stretch, and thence homeward. Meanwhile, Mr. WHEELAN'S steed made no break up, and at one period he trotted a 2.40 gait, and finally came to the Judges' stand nearly an eighth of a mile in advance of Mr. WOODRUFF. As the contestants returned to the stand, the decision of the Judges was announced, as here annexed: "We decide that Mr. WHEELAN is distanced, in consequence of making a run on the lower turn of the course." This decision appeared to astonish the spectators, and was disputed. They finally pronounced it to be entirely wrong, and a direct violation of the "rules of the track." The result caused quite a sensation among the spectators. The feeling was against the Judges' decision, and the majority were in favor of Mr. WHEELAN, who could have won the race without a struggle, provided he had been permitted to trot the balance of the heats. It was, however, a fixed fact that the brown horse was "shut out," and the only excuse given was "foul driving" by Mr. WHEELAN, which yet needs confirmation, to induce many of the audience to believe the Judges were right in their decision as above given. Appeal being out of the question, the owners and driver of *Frank* left the course, and the money was given over by the stakeholder to the owner of *Wedge*. The people on the track, were somewhat disappointed at the singular termination of this match, and they left quite equally divided on the subject. In this instance the Judges assured the turfmen they had went in strict accordance with the *rules* and could not do otherwise. Only a few days ago a fine trotting match, of two mile heats, came off on Long Island between *Fanny D* and *Whalebone*, when the Judges paid no attention to the "rules" and decided against the mare on the second heat, when she really won the heat if the run of *Whalebone* had been deducted when they came to the stand.

The entire ground on the inside enclosure of the Union Course is now plowed up, and yesterday the celebrated Southern horses of Mr. GIBBONS arrived at the course, and during the day they galloped around on the rough turf, and were exercised in various ways by the men in charge of them. The great races on the Union Course, Long Island, will commence on Tuesday, 20th inst., and subjoined we give a list of the liberal purses offered by the proprietors:

First day Tuesday—Proprietor's purse $500, two mile heats. Same day—Purse $200, mile heats, best in five.

Second day, Wednesday—Proprietor's purse $700, three mile heats. Same day—Purse $100, mile heats; entrance $20 added.

Third day, Thursday—Proprietor's purse $1,500, four mile heats. Same day—Sweepstakes, mile heats; subscription $50 half forfeit, and $300 added by the proprietor, closed with the following entries: J. N. WHITTEN names ch. f. by imp. *Glencoe*, dam *Mary D*, by *Medoc*; R. TEN BROECK names gr. m. by *Glencoe*, out of *Sally Ward*, 4 years old; W. H. GIBBONS names b. f. by *Mariner*, dam *Cassandra*, 3 years old.

All the above mentioned purses and stakes are to be governed by the rules of the late New-York Jockey Club. N. B.—Entrances, for the purses, five per cent. to be added, and two or more to start to make a race.

The track will be in fine running order, and no trotting will be allowed on the track until the races are over.

The challenge offered by Mr. RICHARD TENBROECK, N. O., to run his horse against the best time ever made on the track, for a wager of $20,000, has been accepted by Col. GREEN and Capt. GREEN, of Baltimore. The forfeit money of $5,000, has been forwarded to Mr. MOREHEAD, Cashier of the Astor House, and the great race will probably take place on the Metairie Course, N. O., during the fall campaign. The acceptance of this challenge creates quite an excitement among the turfmen.

New-York Daily Times.

VOL. IV.....NO. 1208. NEW-YORK, THURSDAY, AUGUST 2, 1855. PRICE TWO CENTS.

New-York Daily Times.

FIRST OF AUGUST.

Anniversary of Emancipation in the West Indies.

PIC-NICS AT MORRIS' GROVE AND CLIFTON PARK.

Speeches of Judge Culver, Wm. L. Garrison and Others.

Yesterday was a great gala day with the people of color. They turned out in full force to celebrate another return of the day that brought the Emancipation Act into force in the West India Islands; and in picnics, parades, public meetings, and abundant speeches, made memorable the occasion. This is sensible—it is the true policy. The children ask, "Why this sacrifice?" and this thanksgiving? and their parents answering, must tell the story which it is well to tell—marking its return as a luminous day in the year—keeping the Emancipation Act fresh in its memory forever.

Of all the celebrations that took place yesterday, the most rational and imposing was that one projected by the City Anti-Slavery Society, though it was by no means the largest. Tickets were issued at (50 cents each) to all persons who desired to join in the celebration—each ticket entitling the holder to a ride on the Long Island Railroad from Brooklyn to Morris Grove and back. The cars left at 10 o'clock— our of them loaded with a motley colored company, the Railroad Company indulging them with four of their most aged and venerable cars—cars which probably ran behind the old engine *Ariel*, when it, first of all engines, penetrated the Island to its eastern end. We cannot say too much for the liberality of the Company. They gave us relics for our use that they must very tenderly cherish.

The weather proved to be the very finest of the season, though there was so thick a canopy of clouds in the morning, that many who had arranged to go stayed at home, and very many took their umbrellas along, who meant to have taken their wives and children also. One expressed a fear, as we were landing, that it would rain. "If it does," replied Mr. GARRISON, "we must say, 'the Lord reigneth, let the earth rejoice.'" "The earth may rejoice if it wants to, I shant," answered a farmer; "though so much of it as I own would rejoice much more in a good hot sunshine to-day."

Morris' Grove is some mile and a half west of Jamaica,—an oak wood, with noble chestnuts interspersed,—altogether a fine grove, and admirably adapted to the purposes of an out door meeting; only if it should rain, there is not a shed, shanty nor barn for a shelter for many a forty-acre lot's breath about.

The meeting opened with not more than two hundred and fifty people on the ground, but as the day wore on they were constantly gathering. At 4 o'clock there were not less than one thousand people on the ground. Of these, perhaps one fourth were white folks, the balance of all colors, handsomely assorted. There were as black men on the ground as ever fried in the sun of Guinea. One Venus especially struck us, with bare shoulders and arms, and a Bloomer hat upon her woolly head; she had a color that no residence in frozen climes could ever bleach out,—indeed, one would think that it would take many generations of amalgamation to render that skin translucent in the slightest degree. There were some of the rich mahogany color; others of all lighter shades up to that finest color in the world, a light tan color with the blood shining through. There were several very fine specimens of this sort of beauty—specimens of fine forms, elegant figures, and—what we white folks are wont to forget in making up our estimates of handsome women—with the colors nicely laid on by the artist Nature.

Of the ladies, too, in whose veins circle no drop of blood that owes origin to Africa, there was a brilliant selection,—for many of the slave's friends are very fair. Two or three blondes we noticed, either of whom would have turned poor NORTH's head, had he let the prussic alone and lived on to see this day. Of a different style was Miss G—— J——, who, dressed in white, with a belt of oak and maple leaves about the waist, and an oak leaf wreath about her head, received the highest admiration. Miss ANNIE W——E, tastily dressed in some thin light stuff that we know not the name of, with a wreath of wild flowers in her hair, particularly pleased our reporter. Miss J——A S——N, in a skirt of purple striped delaine with a black silk waist and an oak leaf crown, had a pure Grecian face, and a form and gait to match,—all these sylphs and graces, it is fair to presume, were either Abolitionists themselves or the daughters of Abolitionists, and as such they excited our strongest curiosity. "Fanatics" are apt to have homely wives but pretty daughters, evidently.

No band attended the Picnic-ers, contrary to the advertised intention WALLACE's Band had been engaged, but when its members saw how very black some of the picnic-ing faces were, they backed out of their engagement and went home with dumb bugles and reversed bassoons. Play their sweet music in the ears of niggers? Not they! WALLACE's is a high-toned band. Their instruments of brass and their stringed instruments create sympathies that are fit to delight the ears only of white folks. So WALLACE's high-toned band backed down, and the music was done *viva voce*, as the fine old Irish gentleman remarked—by word of mouth, as it were. This was a great disappointment, but we trust it will lead the colored people to depend more upon themselves for music than heretofore. They should get up a brass band of their own, and the very first thing they should do, would be to serenade WALLACE's high-toned band, to show them that a terrible rival is around. If they take our hint and get up a brass band, let them by all means keep all their engagements, even with white folks.

At 10½ o'clock, the reporters, (we like to give a matter in its chronological order,) Mr. GARRISON, and Judge CULVER, four colored clergymen, and the officers of the American Anti-Slavery Society, mounted the platform, and order spontaneously possessed the assembly. SIDNEY H. GAY, Esq., of the *Standard*, acted as President, and called upon Rev. JAMES M. WILLIAMS, pastor of a new colored church in Brooklyn, to make the opening prayer, which proved an appropriate and most suggestive one. The stately hymn "From all that dwell below the skies," was then lined by Rev. Mr. BROMLEY, of the Baptist Tabernacle Mission Church, and sung to the tune of "Old Hundred," a clean, yellow man, Mr. HAMILTON, with a noble voice, leading off.

Then President GAY introduced one as a man who carried a stiff backbone to Congress years ago, when backbones were scarce, and brought it back sound, and without a joint in it—Hon. Judge CULVER, of Brooklyn.

JUDGE CULVER'S SPEECH.

The Judge said that on such an occasion he felt a double train of emotions hurrying through his mind,—of joy with those who had lately gained their liberty; of sorrow with the millions that yet lack it. The text was always present to him then—"Rejoice with those that do rejoice, and weep with them that weep." Twenty-one years ago to-day the precious boon of Freedom was conferred by act of Parliament upon the Slave population of the West Indies. The speaker detailed the history of the Emancipation act, detailed the fears it gave rise to, and the bugbears its anticipation begot in the minds of the fearful. He eloquently pictured the well-remembered night of July 31, 1834, as the people gathered in watch-meeting to await the approach of the first hour of Freedom. The pregnant hour traveled easily up to its consummation—it was hailed with fervent prayer, with eloquent silence, and then with loud praises to God; but the insurrection, bloodshed, and throat-cutting, did not come off. The four American vessels in the harbor of St. Johns need not to have sailed, there was no demand for the British regiments, nor any call for the soldier's bayonet. As the case of the West Indies and our own are entirely parallel, in this peaceful history, we see unanswerable rejoinders to the arguments of the timid ones who now fear the consequences of immediate abolition in the United States.

The Speaker then turned to the political aspects of Slavery in the United States. Referred to the pretext of the Slave party for introducing Slavery into Kansas and Nebraska, on the ground of their alleged right to bring their local laws with them into the territories. It was remarked, he said, by a man who was once affected with a spinal complaint, that he had got over it because it was now settled in the law of physics that the man who had no backbone was not incident to the ailments that affected that member in those who had. It was remarked by that man that it was a great wrong to break the Missouri Compromise, but no harm could come of it, for Slavery could not get an entrance into the territories. He, (the speaker,) wondered if that old fogy had opened his eyes yet? He wondered if he had seen not long since six slaves advertised for sale in Nebraska? He wondered if EDWARD EVERETT preached this doctrine now which he did with the daring fact before him, that one-fourth of the colored people held as slaves at the time he made it, were held north of 36° 30'. Why, Slavery would come into New-York in ten days if there was no law against it. As a matter of political economy, Slavery should never for a moment be tolerated where it was practicable to drive it away. And no more striking illustration of the social effects of Slavery could be found, than in the comparison presented by those States in which it did and did not exist.

The Speaker gave, in elaborate detail, an account of the growth and prosperity of the State of New-York, as contrasted with that of Virginia—one circumstance of which, he stated, was the fact that the New-York *Tribune* circulated as much as all the newspapers in the whole State of Virginia, and had 90,000 left to give away. Virginia had 87,000 adult white persons not able to read or write—one in every five, whilst in New-York, notwithstanding her foreign population, the proportion was one in eighty-three. There was not one, he said, of the great party issues that had engaged the attention of the country for the last 70 years that had not been influenced by Slavery. The United States Bank, the Tariff, the Cheap Postage, the Free-Soil Policy, the Abolishing of Flogging in the Navy, Miss DIX's bill, the River and Harbor improvement, and every great enterprise, either in the cause of humanity or social amelioration and public improvement, met with opposition from the South. He referred, in conclusion, to the repeated breaches of faith with the North, which the Slave party had been guilty of, and expressed his determination never to abandon the cause of Anti-Slavery, and the rights of humanity, with which it was identical.

Judge CULVER made a good—a capital speech, and it was loudly cheered at the end, though it was only eighteen minutes short of two hours long. This would have been intolerable in a church, but in the cool wood, where one could move off the moment he felt weary, it was not tedious. When he concluded it was announced that the next order was lunching.

Now let no one imagine that there was an African Sängerfest repeated in the Grove. Instead, it was one of the quietest, snuggest, neatest times possible. There was not a drop of rum on the ground, from first to last—not a drop of beer except root beer, not a drop of cider, nothing stronger than soda water and black tea. Each family gathered around a bench, and emptying out the contents of their baskets, fell to, standing. It was essentially a cold cut. Nobody overate himself, if we may judge from our own experience. Indeed, "the press" generally was shy for a while that it would go hungry back to the meeting again, for the press is not over provident, and the chances for restoration for a consideration were not extraordinary. However, a good Quaker lady took pity on them, and furnished a handful of sandwiches and a beautiful loaf of cake to which they sat down, in thankfulness. A barrel full of ice water, with a dipper hanging on its edge, was close by, and a boy appearing opportunely with a basket of blackberries, "the press" was rescued from its danger of starvation. One straggling member afterwards fell in while foraging with a family of friends, and was treated to its most hospitable fare. For which, public thanks.

We should do injustice to the colored folks of Long Island if we omitted to say, however, that money would buy something eatable. An enterprising "gemman" from Brooklyn had candy, apple-fritters that looked like fried oysters, soda-water and cigars to sell. Another had ice cream and a rival in its sale. Uncle JOHN and Aunt PHEBE, of the town of Jamaica, drove up with their long, low "topped wagon," and when they had rigged out their table they spread it with a "ripping big" ham, fried eels and a loaf of bread. Then Uncle JOHN fed out to the multitude according to their demands—"a shillin's wuth," "a sixpenny wuth," or even "a three-pence wuth"—consisting of a slice of ham and a slice of bread. Now, Uncle JOHN was born a slave in Jersey, and there he married Aunt PHEBE and they jointly left, one morning, without a "Good bye," and all the Police, with old HAYS at their head, tried in vain to catch them while they rode down Broadway as large as life—"for the Lord protected them." Uncle JOHN loved to tell his story, and we noticed that when he got warm over it, he cut as thick slices for the three-penny customers as for the shilling, whereat his friends who had finished their lunch would punch him, and insist that he was losing money. Then the next three-cent customer would growl because his slice was not so large as his predecessor's. But Aunt PHEBE had seen Yorkers, and she could tell how much ham they give for a shilling in the gre't houses to York, and it wan't no use a talkin'. At one time Uncle JOHN got too busy to attend to his customers, and at least a dozen of the unwashed colored persons, with their work-clothes on, from the fields about, who wanted to get a bite, had to go off without feed, for he was in the midst of a theologico-political discussion of the colored question with a Rev. Mr. HODGES, of Brooklyn, a mulatto preacher, who has a church of his own and preaches on his own hook,—wears a knocked-in white hat, and is constantly disgusted with colored men who look up to GARRISON as a god, and don't appreciate work—hard, personal work—and the necessity of self-respect. Uncle JOHN thought Mr. HODGES was too confident of what negroes could do *in their own strength*. Mr. HODGES thought Uncle JOHN a very ignorant darkie, though he didn't call him "darkie." As we left the ground, we asked Aunt PHEBE if she had done well and had a good time.

"Oh, a blessed time," said she, "and done pretty well on the ham, but more 'specially on the fried eels—praise the Lord!" We congratulated her and praised her ham. "Yes," said she, "it was pretty good. Give Him the glory."

"But the change, Aunt PHEBE?"

"I'll keep that myself. He! he! he!" and the old lady laughed till the danger of suffocation was imminent.

There were no clams to be had on the premises, which greatly surprised us and disgusted one company, at least, of colored people from Bushwick.

The behavior of all parties on the ground was unexceptionable. Of course there was a little roughness on the part of the boys on the outskirts. There were no loose women about—a single colored couple, perhaps, excepted who came out in an omnibus. They arrived, glittering in gold and rustling in silks, while Mr. CULVER was speaking, and the first word that fell on their ears was a sacred one. They ejaculated an oath. "I didn't come here to hear about ——" said one, "and they ain't got no music." "Yes, they sing," answered a pretty Quakeress. "I want polka music and a dance," said she. The driver said we were going to Staten Island—he's a cheat. This is too great a shame!" and after one contemptuous exploration of the field, and a volley of oaths let off, they started back for the City, determined to get to the "Staten Island" place, if possible, "when there was some fun going on."

NOTABLE MEN IN THE AUDIENCE.

At 12½ o'clock the meeting was reopened. We then noticed on the ground, beside the smaller fry, such good Anti-Slavery men as ROLAND JOHNSON, Esq., and OLIVER JOHNSON, of course, Mr. LAUREN WETMORE, Hon. HENRY W. WOLCOTT, of New-Jersey, Mr. THOS. TRUESDALE, a cotton merchant of New-York, with his family, and JOSEPH POST, of Westbury, L. I.

AGAIN IN MEETING.

Mr. D. P. JOHNSON spoke to the audience of a colored woman who was present from Keokuk, Iowa, who had recently, he said, been emancipated by her mistress, an aged unmarried lady, who gave her and a large family their freedom, previous to her (the lady's) death.

CHARLOTTE PHILES, the colored person referred to, exhibited her credentials, and stated that she had raised $500 in Keokuk, which she had banked there, and that she had already collected $300 here towards purchasing her son and two sons in-law, who were still in Slavery.

The President appointed a Committee to make a collection towards defraying the expenses of the celebration, which otherwise would fall heavy on a few.

He then introduced, amid loud applause, Mr. W. LLOYD GARRISON, who said:

MR. GARRISON'S SPEECH.

MR. PRESIDENT, LADIES AND GENTLEMEN: If I had consulted the dictates of prudence, I should not be with you on this occasion; for in my own native State for some days past, I have been laboring under extreme debility, so as to make all effort laborious, and entire repose greatly to be coveted. Still, I gave my pledge, impossibilities out of the question, that I would come here and bear my testimony on this occasion in behalf of the glorious cause of liberty; and to-day I want to forget all about sickness. An Abolitionist has no right to talk about being unwell on the 1st of August. The event which we are here to celebrate, is a balsam to the body; it is a cordial to the mind; and the spirit which enters into sympathy and deep rejoicing with the emancipated in the isles of the sea, is a spirit that must and will forget that it has a body with it, but will try to do what may be done to say the right word on this occasion. After the very able, and elaborate, and eloquent speech made to us this forenoon, I can only come before you as the fifth wheel to the coach—altogether superfluous. And so I follow, rather as a matter of form than on the ground of necessity, but I can hardly hope to add anything to the interest which was given to our meeting this forenoon by the brave, and heroic, and intrepid man who stood before us to give us his word of testimony and approval. Mr. President, I am slightly beyond the meridian of life, and more than half of my life has been devoted to the Anti-Slavery enterprise. Whatever remains of that life will, by the help of God, be consecrated to the same glorious cause. Never, never, never, shall I relax one jot or tittle; never shall I cease to testify against Slavery so long as there remains in this guilty land one single slave to curse the soil, or to stain our national escutcheon. I was asked, not a great while since, by an Anti-Slavery woman, whether I did not grow weary in this cause? Whether I was not tired out, and desired repose? My answer was, and is, and will be to the end, I am tired of rascality and villainy, and corruption; I am tired of doughfaces, time-servers, and trimmers; I am weary of blood: I grow sick at heart in view of the oppression which is perpetrated upon millions of our countrymen at the South; but I never grow weary in denouncing all this,—on the contrary, at every fresh encounter with the Slave Power, as ANTÆUS when he touched his mother earth, I only derive therefrom the more strength and the more determination never to give up until *our* jubilee shall come. [Applause.] Alas, Sir, we are not here to celebrate an American Jubilee. Oh, no; there is nothing of this to talk about of an American character here, except that which is enough to suffuse every cheek with shame, and to make all the blood that is within our veins chill within us. There is nothing American about this celebration to-day. It is all foreign, to the eternal shame of this Republic. It relates to old England, the mother country, from whom our forefathers seceded in the times that tried men's souls. And she has taken the lead in the great and Godlike work of human enfranchisement, while we as a nation are trafficing in human blood, forging fetters for the enslaved, everywhere compromising the truth of Freedom, and everywhere lengthening the cords and strengthening the stakes of the Slave Power. West India Emancipation brings us here to-day. Thank God for that. Though we may not rejoice at an anniversary of the liberation of our own slaves, yet we may rejoice that the slaves of the olden time in the isles of the sea have been transformed by the magic touch of liberty into human beings, clothed with their God-given human rights, and now reposing in peace and safety under the flag of old England.

It was easy enough for them to be here, he continued, to celebrate the event which had called them together. It cost little for them to be here; but what a long and laborious struggle was it that had resulted in that grand event!—a struggle in which the only weapons employed by those who fought it—by CLARKSON, WILBERFORCE, MACAULAY, SHARPE, BUXTON, and the army of noble men and women whose names the world knew, and who nobly sustained them—were the word of God himself, and their determination to maintain it. In the endeavor to uproot Slavery they had to contend against the established Church, the aristocracy, and the mercantile influence of England. But where, he asked, were the West India Planters now? Like other men, they are without slaves in their hands. And where were the slaves? Enjoying, as men, the blessings of freedom.

> "God moves in a mysterious way
> His wonders to perform,
> He plants his footsteps on the sea
> And rides upon the storm.
> Blind unbelief is sure to err,
> And scan His works in vain;
> God is His own interpreter,
> And he will make it plain."

will make it plain! He had made it plain to-day. There was no darkness—it was all sunlight; and the same sunlight shown down on the emancipated sons of the isles of the sea, rejoicing over the wonderful event which God had brought to pass.

The opposition to Slavery in England at that day was not so strong, so terrible, and so difficult to encounter as that which we had still to encounter in our own land. It was strong enough, however, to try the temper of the strongest and the boldest. It required much faith in truth and justice and right, because at the outset, and till the end of the struggle, all the powers of the English Government, as well as the combined powers of the West India interest, were against the Anti Slavery movement. The mass of the people knew nothing of the horrors of Slavery—they were ignorant and indifferent; they were under the influence of men of high station and of great influence; they were under the influence of the established Church, and all these opposing powers had to be met. The pleas and defences put forth to justify West India Slavery then were precisely the the same pleas and the same defences which are made now against the abolition of Slavery in our own country. The cry of "Mind your own business" was the cry then as now. But it was every man's business to denounce tyranny wherever it existed, and abolish it wherever practicable. So the English West Indian Slaveholders asserted their right to our slaves. But the man who undertook to say that one man ought to own another was an idiot. Let no one argue with him. He did not need argument; he needed brains. There was not a man on God's earth who did not know that slaveholding was a damnable villainy. The men who opposed the Anti-Slavery movement were bereft of reason, for the instinct of reason was to recognize in man a brother man, and not a beast—not a thing in the shape of property. Another argument was that slaves were unfit for Freedom; that immediate liberation was the wildest thing in the world; that they must be prepared for it by a careful process—as if God had made a human being that was not fitted for Freedom. God never yet made a human being fit for Slavery, and no human being could be fitted for it until they had first broken his heart, and bowed down his spirit, and crushed his manhood, and brought him as near as possible to the condition of the irrational beast. Then they said again that the slaves were the inferior race, and that it was the will of God that the superior should govern and control the inferior. Inferior! Inferior in what, where all had had a fair chance and the same opportunities of improvement? Where had the experiment ever been fairly made, under equal circumstances, in which the result had not always been exceedingly honorable to the colored man, in competition with the white man? If there was an exception among men as to equality, tyrants, of all men, constituted that exception, and of all men were inferior to all other men, on account of their exceeding wickedness and villainy. The speaker then referred to the argument for Slavery based on Scripture, and proceeded to say that the slaves, on getting their freedom, would kill their former masters and torturers. Blood, blood, blood, was the argument and the objection. The reply, of course, was: it is a hallucination of your minds; you are deceived. The slaves do not cut your throats now, though you cut and lash and starve them—though you violate their wives or sell their children before their faces. But to the last stage of this struggle, the cut-throat argument was in unfailing requisition.

It was urged, also, that the slaves, when emancipated, would not work. But it was replied that the slaves themselves were to determine that. If men who would not work ought to be no other than slaves, then the slaveowners, as being the laziest of men, were the most deserving of slavery.

Fanaticism was also urged against those who took up the Anti Slavery movement. If emancipation took place, they said, then amalgamation would follow. That was the climax. Every white man would be sure to marry a black woman—a compliment, by the way, to the superior attractions of the colored ladies. But a slaveholder would sooner give up his hopes of heaven than amalgamation. There is no feature of Slavery they adhere to more firmly.

All the shades of complexion told a story of Slaveholding perfidy and villainy and violence in that one word—the Slaveholding amalgamation. See the audacity of the Slaveholders. Why did they abolish marriage in Slavery? For the sole purpose of gratifying the hellish lust of the masters, so as to give the slaves entirely over to their power. The result was that we dare not draw aside the curtain and reveal the horrors of the secret chamber. Oh, the results of that amalgamation! Sodom and Gomorrah realized and concentrated in that single word Slavery—a volcano of lust and impurity that was always in operation—always throwing out its lava tide of desolation and death, and rolling over the land blasting and blighting every green thing therein! The slaveholders pleaded that the true way of abolishing a thing was to do it gradually. But no amount of pressing could induce them to name a time. Like CHARLES JAMES FOX, the eminent British statesman, who was so notorious for getting involved in debts, and quite as notorious for never paying them, when dunned by SOLOMON, a Jewish money-lender, to name the time when he could discharge a heavy bill, answered, after much uneasy cogitation: "Well, SOLOMON, as you must have me fix a day, I believe I can name one. Suppose we say the Day of Judgment—or, as that will probably be a busy day for both of us, what if we should say the day after?" [Laughter.] So it would be with the slaveholders here—their day would be the day after the Day of Judgment. But they forget that there would be no day after the Day of Judgment for slaveholders in any part of the world. Again, the slaveholders asked: "Do you mean to deprive us of our property and of our vested rights? Give us full and entire compensation." But man never yet was the property of man; man never had any vested right in his fellow man. Finally they said if Slavery were abolished less sugar would be grown. Then chaos would come again. Every other argument was forgotten in that. But the argument should have been, not that less sugar would be grown, but that there would be no white mouths to consume it. They began by arguing that if the slaves were emancipated they would murder their former masters. And that being the case, what interest could slaveholders have in the amount of the sugar crop, since they could not enjoy it? That fact was forgotten. And if it were so, better have less sugar, but on more coerced pollution, no more degradation and brand ing irons, and slave extermination and maroon wars, and no more slave insurrections, and no longer any dread of them. [Applause.]

The speaker then referred to the cruelly exacting enactments of the West India slave code, which, he said, was a code that could be framed by none but devils, and which, though at the sacrifice of some sugar, had now gone to the bottomless pit.

They were to-day to rejoice over the downfall of a system like this. Emancipation produced the most marvelous transformation that had ever occurred in human history. He would go for less sugar, and take the blessings of liberty as an equivalent.

But with regard to this decrease in the production of sugar, he asserted that it was a Pro-Slavery lie. The sugar is raised and enjoyed by those who raise it, though the exportation is not so great. If it was argued that slaves would do no labor when emancipated, the reply was that God had instituted a law which allowed of no such event. "If man labors not, neither shall he eat." This the liberated slaves would soon learn for themselves; they would soon find out that Jordan is a hard road to travel. The colored people, by the manner in which they received their emancipation in the West Indies, showed their appreciation of liberty as no other people could have shown it, and offered an illustrious proof of the falsity of the charge of inferiority so frequently made against them. The results of emancipation have always been glorious. The emancipated have behaved not only well, but wonderfully well.

Mr. GARRISON went on in characteristic style to declaim against the Union, inveighing with great severity against the upholders of Slavery in the South, and those who abetted it in the North. This Union, he said, was a lie; the American Union was a sham and an imposture; it was a covenant with death and an agreement with hell, and their first business was to call for its utter dissolution and overthrow. If they had been deprived of their strength, like Samson, and betrayed like him to the Philistines of the South, they would rise and hurl down this accursed Government, and all go down together. He was sorry CHARLES SUMNER went for the Union; he was an infatuated man. He said it with all love and respect and veneration for him—for he loved, respected and venerated him highly. HENRY WILSON went for the Union; he belonged to the fusion party, whose identity was seldom preserved for a long time as the same. Whatever stood in the way of the slave's freedom he was for its overthrow. If it was the Church, he was for its overthrow. If it were clergymen, he pronounced them wolves in sheep's clothing—branding them as the basest of men Slaveholders, he had nothing to do with His appeal was not to them. They were insane. But he appealed to those who uphold the cause—those who were the props and pillars of the system—to the people of the North, intelligent, educated, cultivated, refined, powerful—to the people who constituted this American Republic. His appeal was to them in the name of God and common Liberty,—let us cease shaking hands with slaveholders, and give to the winds the cry, "No Union with slaveholders, socially, religiously, or politically!" Oh, for a jubilee, he cried, in our own country! The way to get it was to make no compromise with slaveholders or their abettors, and to regard nothing in the world so dear as Liberty. Taking this position, they should have resting upon their heads the blessing of those who were now ready to perish, and the blessing of Almighty God! [Loud and reiterated applause, amid which the speaker resumed his seat.]

Mr. MCKIMM, of Philadelphia, was next introduced, and stated some facts in reference to the rescue of Mr. WHEELER's slaves—the gist of which we have already published.

Three cheers were given heartily for PASSMORE WILLIAMSON, three more for the day we celebrate, and then all hands separated, in good spirits, and entirely satisfied with the 1st of August Pic-nic.

The Exclusively Colored Pic-Nic on Staten Island.

There was a split among the colored people. The lighter-hearted and more jovial didn't want to go with "the priests," but went in for a procession, and a parade, and a pic nic, with hot things to eat, &c., a dance and a good time with no white folks around.

By 9 o'clock in the morning, various military companies were duly equipped in uniform, and ready to start on the day's excursion—Staten Island being the locality fixed upon for the celebration. The sky was lowering; the prospect was discouraging; but the colored ladies, whose hams had been boiled on the previous day, whose sandwiches (with fresh mustard) had been newly prepared over night, could not be deterred from packing them into baskets, and bade defiance to the weather, in the lightest Summer dresses—mostly white or yellow—that we have seen around. Propitious were the fates. The clouds dispersed; the evil omens dissipated; not a drop of rain fell to mar the pleasure or spoil the speeches of the day.

Before 10 o'clock, the streets of the city were alive with drums. Even earlier, by an hour or two, the sidewalks gave evidence of a gathering of our colored brethren. Friend meeting friend, on the way to store or office, asked what it meant, and the reply he received was, "It is the first of August, the Anniversary of the Emancipation of the British West Indian Slaves."

The Twenty-first Anniversary certainly of a memorable day. The understanding which prevailed among the colored people, that the great gathering would be in St. John's Park, proved to be a mistake. The MacFarlan Guard met at the North Star House, in Church-street, and marched through several streets, among others down Hudson, and by St John's Park, afterward taking Mercer and Church streets, just looking into Broadway, and by way of Wall, Broad and Beaver streets, reaching the Battery. This Guard, a very respectable body of men, had picked a quarrel with the Hall Guard, commanded by Capt WILLIAMS, and the two companies refused to march together. Jealousy and bitterness were the unfortunate consequences. A third company that marched through our streets, also at variance with the rest, was the Independent Village Guards. Also we saw the Independent Attic Guard, of Brooklyn, and the Independent Cadets of New-York. Whether they fraternized or had their bickerings and animosities we did not find out. But they all arrived at Staten Island by different boats, which had not, it must be confessed, altogether a harmonious look.

Stapleton was the first place of resort, and the little village poured all its inhabitants into the streets to see the processions. We noticed that the German drinking houses were those principally, almost exclusively, patronized by our negro friends. GEISLER's hotel, corner of Patten and Gore streets, was the head-quarters of the McFarlan Guard. The others were distributed at various places, but chiefly at lager-bier saloons, of which a large number are to be found in the neighborhood of Vanderbilt's landing—most of them very low places. From what we observed yesterday, we concluded that everything but the Maine law flourished on Staten Island.

In the afternoon the Companies repaired to Clifton Park. A vast number of women and children, with numerous men not belonging to the military, had preceded them, and by 2 o'clock, there could not have been less than 5,000 colored people on the ground. The scene was novel, and considering the day and its associations, quite pleasing and picturesque. Colored ladies are so fond of gaudy hues, that we fancied a great many rainbows had been cut into small pieces to adorn the persons of these "images of God, cut in ebony." Colored venders of the fruits and other attractions of the season, were not sparsely distributed. Watermelons sold at nine cents each. Ice cream went rapidly at six cents a glass. Cold ham and vinegar had their attractions. Pork and beans were not despised; while eggs and green corn could not be supplied fast enough. These condiments were supplementary to the contents of large baskets which men and women bore on their arms, and seemed to labor under, as they ascended the hill, around which they sat in pretty family parties, benefit the shade of trees, talking loudly, laughing louder, and generally having the best possible time of it.

Then there were amusements. Did not the ladies swing, and scream aloud as the seup descended—for all the world as natural as any white lady! In the aerial cars, not only ladies and children adventured, but grown men sat therein, half in dignity, half in delight. There were also sports upon the grass,—rollings and tumblings to and fro. Really, as we have said, a very good time.

A little bickering we overheard. One yellow girl indignantly repudiated the charge of a black skin. She had never been so insulted before. Black she was not and black she would not be called. A colored lady got into a quarrel with an Irish laborer, who had laughed—as Irish laborers will—in a sneering, insulting fashion, at the procession. "They lifted the American Flag," she said, "and that's what you and your people can't dare to do without a lie." Her speech was not very lucid, but we caught her meaning.

In the course of the afternoon some speaking came off in the Park, from the stoop of a large building. About 700 persons listened, in semi-circle. The proceedings commenced with the hymn, "Before Jehovah's Awful Throne." Then followed a prayer by Rev. Mr. BARRIGER. Mr. JOSEPH TILLMAN was chosen President. He introduced Mr. STEPHEN MYERS, of Albany, formerly editor of the *Freeman's Advocate*, who said that he was very glad to meet them to-day in the Empire State.

MR. MYERS' SPEECH.

It was truly a glorious day for the colored people, since they had met to celebrate the anniversary—the twenty-first of the emancipation of the British West Indian slaves. Eight hundred thousand of those slaves, twenty one years ago, on this day, at the rising of the sun, became freemen. We hail it here, across the ocean, as an omen of a bright day of emancipation for ourselves also. We are met here to celebrate it in our hearts, and with the warm impulses of our thrilling bosoms;—to return thanks to the British people and to the British Government, for giving such an example to our legislators. It was a work not accomplished in a day. WILBERFORCE spent his life in the advocacy of the cause of the West Indian slave, in showing his countrymen the evils of Slavery, morally and politically. He has left a noble name on record,—a name that will grow forever, glowing brighter as it grows. CLARKSON also engaged in that struggle,—the noblest in which man was ever engaged, and proved to the satisfaction of the English people that Slavery, beside the sin of it, was actually a commercial injury and loss to the English nation. Now, continued Mr. MYERS, we do not come here, with flags, and drums and trumpets, for the mere purpose of enjoying ourselves, but to celebrate one of the greatest events recorded in the history of the world—the liberation at one stroke of the clock of 800,000 of our fellow-beings. Midnight passed and they were free. When the sun rose, they were found singing Hallelujah to the Lord. There was no revelry, no dissipation,—not a master was injured. All was peaceable, calm, great, sublime. The sun set the night before on 800,000 slaves; he rose upon 800,000 freemen. Were ever his rays as they tinged with radiance the summits of the hills, and the bare peaks of glistening rocks, so welcome to so many souls? There was no sleep that night for those 800,000. They watched and prayed—watched for the day, and prayed to the God who had made it the day of their deliverance. Oh, as the first red flashes went up from the East, and the shades of night began to loosen and dissolve, what sensations filled their breasts, as of prison doors to be opened, fetters to be unloosed, chains to be stricken off!

Why did he (the speaker) come here to talk of this? Because he anticipated another day of emancipation, when three millions and a half of his own race in this country should be set free. He thought, old as he was,—and they could see he was not a young man,—he should live to see it. Let the public instructors of the land do their duty. Let every pulpit, let every press take the right path, and the moral sentiment should be so irresistibly poured down upon the multitude, that opposition would die away out of sheer weakness.

He had been in the war of 1812,—at Chippewa, and all the great battle-fields of that eventful time. He had fought then for America, and he would fight again. The colored people would defend this land,—would defend American homes,—would protect the wives and children of Americans. Let another war break out, and the whole colored race would fight like brave soldiers, and never show their flying backs to the enemy. But if they were to be counted on in the time of danger, let the whites give them their rights now. We dug their trenches in the conflict before. Give us our legal rights, and we will dig their trenches, and carry their cannons on our backs, as we did before.

Mr MYERS spoke for about an hour, and spoke well. He was attentively listened to by a large audience, composed principally, but not exclusively, of colored people. He thought FREDERIC DOUGLASS equal in ability to any man in Congress. He said that a mammoth Convention of colored people would be held at Troy on the first Tuesday in September, and urgently recommended that fitting delegates should be sent.

The President then introduced Mr. JOSEPH W. SMITH, of New-York, who made a good speech. He, too, had been in the war of 1812. He had beaten the drum and had been beaten himself. He fought for this country's cause, not for his own, for he was told he was hired to beat music, that white men might march. But when the British ships began to pour in their shot, it was necessary to throw up trenches, and he went among the other colored men to do it. "Take care, or you will be killed," said the officers. They did not want us to be killed—they knew our value then. He was not in the habit of making Anti-Slavery speeches, but that flag before him, brought to his recollection the other day in the Park at New-York, when the Know Nothings held a meeting. He heard Col BALDWIN, of Virginia, speak there, and really, he seemed as if he meant to try and persuade the New-Yorkers to turn their State into a Slave State again. He said that God had sent the black men here to civilize them. Now, that was a lie, and he (the speaker) said so at the time, and would say so forever. The white man brought the black man here, and brought him, not to civilize him, but to demoralize him. He proceeded to recapitulate what the colored race had done for Americans in the last war, how they had bored holes in the bottoms of British ships, had borne great pieces of artillery on their shoulders up prodigious heights, how they had toiled and moiled, given their best sweat and blood, the zeal of their spirits and the strength of their sinews to the work. What for? Not to be spurned, reviled, despised, in recompense, but to be treated as men who had human feelings, all the year round, and not merely votes on the day of election. White men had tauntingly told him to go to his fatherland, if he needed rights. Then he would have to stay where he was, for his father was a white man. He thought they did well to celebrate the day of emancipation of British slaves, but there was another day of emancipation which they had forgot to celebrate, but which they ought, as natives of this country, not to overlook. He meant the day when the slaves of the State of New-York were set free. He would propose three cheers for that day. [The cheers were heartily given.] He thought the colored race depended too much upon the white man. They should not wait for the white man to lead their footsteps, but should march for themselves.

At this point of the Speaker's remarks, there occurred a disturbance in another part of the Grove, which drew off the male portion of the audience.

"Don't let the females go," cried the President. "No respectable female—no *respectable* female" will go—emphasizing the word respectable into very large capitals—"So now we shall see by a female's movement, whether she is respectable or not." The ladies did not move, fearful that if they yielded to their curiosity, they would be considered of no account. But the Speaker had lost his marrow, and with a benediction from Rev. Mr. BARRIGER, the meeting came to an end.

A procession was then formed, which marched to the house, occupied by the son of DANIEL MINTURN TOMPKINS. Afterwards they paraded the village, their two bands, (composed of Germans,) heading their respective divisions. It was rather bad for the cause, that owing to jealousy, respecting the marshalship of the day, and the arrangement of affairs in general, a good deal of discord, and some of the companies refused to march with the others, or even to associate with them. One of these companies had a ball in the evening on the Island, but a moonlight excursion which was talked of, was given up. The majority of the visitors returned to the City at 7 o'clock in the evening. A few of the more ardent amused themselves with firing pistols and crackers in the streets, until a late hour, as on the Fourth of July.

Evening Celebration in Brooklyn.

At 7½ o'clock in the evening a meeting was held at the Bridge-street African M. E. W. Church, when EDWARD CROVEY presided, assisted by JOHN J. WASHINGTON and Chaplain FREEMAN, as Vice-Presidents. JOHN F. THOMPSON acted as Secretary.

The exercises here were commenced with a prayer by the Chaplain, Rev. A. N. FREEMAN, which was followed by singing by the choir of the church, conducted by Prof. HAMILTON.

LEWIS TAPPAN, Revs A. N. FREEMAN, J. M. WILLIAMS, WM. H. HODGES, J. GIBBONS and JEREMIAH POWERS delivered addresses. At the close a collection was taken up, and at a late hour the meeting adjourned.

Much credit is due to Dr. RAY, Master of Ceremonies, and to the Committee of Arrangements for their management of the whole proceedings during the day—not an accident occurred or anything to mar its pleasure.

Quarantine Arrest.

To the Editor of the New-York Daily Times:

My attention has been called to an article in your paper of the 31st July, entitled as above, in which it is stated that "the Health Officer immediately went to a Justice and procured a warrant, which brought the offender, (meaning SILVIA,) within the Quarantine grounds, where he is safely locked up for the future hands of law and justice."

Being the Justice alluded to in the said article, and before whom Dr. THOMPSON made his complaint, I wish, in justice to the party accused, to state that SILVIA was not taken within the Quarantine grounds; that *he was not locked up*, but on the contrary, being informed that there was a complaint made before me against him, he *voluntarily* appeared at my office and entered into a recognizance for his appearance to answer the charge a the next Court of Sessions.

By inserting the above, you will confer a favor on yours, &c., THEODORE FREAN, Justice of the Peace.

QUARANTINE, Wednesday, Aug. 1, 1855.

Florence Nightingale Again—Christian Charity and Sectarian Bigotry.

To the Editor of the New-York Daily Times:

SIR: In a letter signed "Another Subscriber," in your journal of this morning, the writer while expressing belief in the truth of the information, which at your personal request I gave you relative to the religious faith of Miss NIGHTINGALE, corrects two errors in your printed statement of that information. Those errors are yours, as you are aware, and not mine, and you should have said so, instead of unjustly permitting me to be considered guilty of errors, which would naturally weaken reliance upon the other portion of my statement.

Every syllable stated in the letter of "Another Subscriber" I know to be correct. In the year 1842, I became first acquainted with the family, and was for some few years on terms of intimate acquaintance with them. Latterly I had not seen much of the NIGHTINGALE branch, but continued my relations with her uncle, W. S. SMITH, and W. CARTER, her cousin, now M. P. for Winchester, who is son of Mr. CARTER, so long the distinguished member for Portsmouth, and who is married to his cousin Miss NICHOLSON. I know Miss NIGHTINGALE to be a Unitarian, as far as it is possible to know any one's religion. She is so by birth, by profession, by practice and by expressed conviction. I see no more wrong in mentioning this truth, than in mentioning that Dr. POTTER is a Protestant or Dr. HUGHES a Roman Catholic. The deep wrong is done by those, who without any knowledge whatever of Miss NIGHTINGALE or her religious faith, rush in to contradict the truth and make the truth a reproach to her. There can be no object in this, beyond a desire to convert into a small sectarian triumph, that which is a triumph to humanity, and in which all men, without distinction of creed, who love and honor the good and beautiful, should rejoice. I know Miss NIGHTINGALE united with the rector of her parish, in Hampshire, in every work of love and charity, and in the absence of a Church of her own persuasion, attended the Parish Church. I know also that she and her family subscribed largely towards Roman Catholic schools established by some Belgian clergymen in the vicinity of London, for giving education and food to poor Irish children. I know that she served for several years in the hospitals of Germany, which I believe were chiefly under Roman Catholic direction. I believe that she has, since her return, before going to the East, united in many works for the benefit of her suffering kind, under the direction of the Bishop of London. We know that in the East she ministered to the dying of every faith, and showed the most tender and delicate considerations for the religious feelings of all alike under her care. As she thus ministered to, and sacrificed for all, without distinction of creed, so all should honor and love her without consideration of what may be her religious faith. It is painful then to see such controversies, but still more painful is it, and let me add, degrading and ungrateful to those who are guilty of it, to find Dr. HUGHES, through his organ in this City, trying to underrate one who has made such gentle sacrifice for so many of his creed, and representing her mission as a failure, because it was not directed by a Roman Catholic.

Yours truly, VERITAS.

Canandaigua not Decreasing.

To the Editor of the New-York Daily Times:

In your paper of yesterday, 30th inst., you published an article headed "Deserted Villages," in which you say:

"Even the beautiful and wealthy town of Canandaigua, so celebrated for its refined society and wealthy inhabitants, exhibits a *decrease* of population."

This is *not so*. By referring to *your own* paper of Friday, July 27, in which you copied from the *Evening Journal*, the results of the present Census in several cities and villages enumerated, you will find that the population of the *village* of Canandaigua in 1855 is 4,148, and do. do. do. in 1850 was 2,700—showing an *increase* in five years of 1,448, which is over 50 per cent., and greater in proportion than the increase of *New-York City*.

Please do us justice in *retired* Canandaigua.

Yours, respectfully, JOHN A. GRANGER.

CANANDAIGUA, Tuesday, July 31, 1855.

GENESEE COUNTY.—The following shows accurately the population of the different towns in Genesee County, as appears from the returns of the present census, and also the population of 1650. The increase of population in the County since 1850 is 2,458.

Towns.	Population 1855.	Population 1850.	Inc.	Dec.
Alexander	1798	1927	—	129
Alabama	2194	2054	140	—
Batavia	5302	4461	841	—
Byron	1641	1586	75	—
Bergen	1800	1897	—	97
Bethany	1879	1904	—	25
Darien	2172	2084	88	—
Elba	1901	1772	129	—
Le Roy	4553	3473	1080	—
Oakfield	1529	1457	72	—
Pavilion	1758	1640	118	—
Pembroke	2564	2279	285	—
Stafford	2035	1974	61	—
Total	30,946	28,488	2,889	391

We have now the population of Troy complete. We present below the population of each Ward in 1850 and 1855:

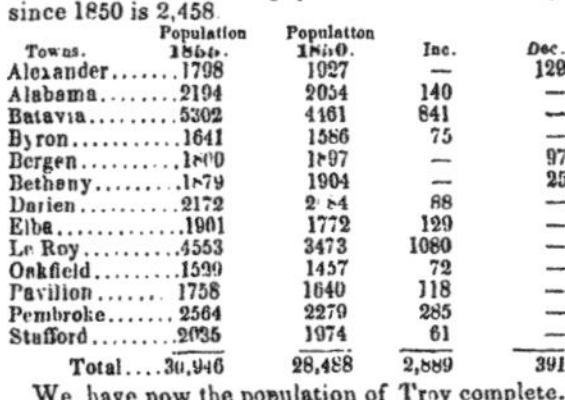

Wards.	1850.	1855.	Wards.	1850.	1855.
1	4,032	4,225	9	—	3,338
2	4,264	4,277	7	4,923	3,692
3	2,794	2,396	10	—	2,375
4	4,054	4,122	8	2,741	3,875
5	1,818	2,375	Green Island	150	8,500
6	4,139	2,599			
Total				28,935	36,771
					28,935
Total increase in five years					7,836

The Snake Humbug Exploded.

The following letter from Dr. PRESCOTT, of Concord, N. H., one of the most respectable physicians in the place, adds another to the many proofs that the snake story is one of the most barefaced and disgusting humbugs of the day. We trust the actors in it will be punished by public contempt and indignation, if in no other way:

CONCORD, N. H., Friday, July 27, 1855.

MY DEAR SIR: I had concluded to write you, after I understood that the man HILL had taken his child and snake to Boston for exhibition. I was called off in another direction, and I was prevented at the time.

My object in writing was to ask you to institute a close examination and satisfy yourself and the public whether the whole matter was a gross imposition, as I believed it to be, or otherwise.

But to-day I am gratified to learn, through the public press, that he has been detected, and I hope arrested in his mad and villainous career in this matter. While on exhibition here I saw the child and the snake, and considered it at the time, and so publicly declared it to be, an imposition, a gross humbug, but many thought otherwise. The little girl handled the serpent very carefully, and seized it suddenly by the nape of the neck, appeared agitated as through fear, or that the disgusting reptile was repugnant to her. She was asked if the snake ever bit her. She replied that it had bit her once. She was asked in my hearing, *when she first saw the snake?* She replied, "*father brought it in for me.*" I am highly gratified to learn that this unnatural and revolting spectacle has ceased to deceive a credulous public.

Most respectfully yours, &c.

Accident.

On Wednesday morning, as some men were endeavoring to lift a horse, that was supposed to be dead, on a cart in Greenwich-street, seeing the horse move, stopped the derrick, which in its fall struck the child of Mr. WITSCHIEF on the head, which injured it very severely. The horse had fallen last night under a load of marble, and was allowed to remain in agony all night in the street.

New-York Daily Times.

VOL. V....NO. 1258. NEW-YORK, FRIDAY, SEPTEMBER 28, 1855. PRICE TWO CENTS.

New-York Daily Times

AUTHORS AMONG FRUITS.

THE BANQUET OF THE PUBLISHERS.

GENIUS IN THE CRYSTAL PALACE

SEVEN HUNDRED GUESTS AT TABLE.

Letters--Toasts--Speeches--A Teetotal Entertainment.

The long promised Banquet tendered by the Book Publishers' Association of this City to the Authors, came off at the Crystal Palace last evening. In the arrangements for the event, the Publishers spared no pains. Everything was ordered upon a scale of great variety and elegance. The viands consisted almost wholly of fruits. The beverages were altogether destitute of alcoholic stimulant. The ladies were admitted among the guests—the gentlemen refrained from indulgence in cigars and wine—the place was kept a temperate and unusually comfortable for such an occasion—the tables were graced with the presence of wit and wisdom, and the evening passed off in a very successful manner.

APPEARANCE OF THE HALL.

The entire north nave of the Crystal Palace was given up to the Association. It was enclosed in the form of a pavilion, with longitudinal strips of red, white and blue, alternating. Six long tables, stretching from north to south, were flanked at the southern extremity by a dais, upon which rested the table for the officers of the evening and the speakers. Covers were laid for six hundred and fifty persons, but the number who actually took part in the destruction of the viands, and afterward were within ear-shot of the speakers, was about seven hundred. Upon each plate was placed a card bearing the name of a guest. The caterers of the occasion were COLEMAN & STETSON, whose entire force of waiters—one hundred and fifty—was transferred from the Astor House.

In front of the President's chair, resting upon a small platform, was placed a Cornucopia, from the mouth of which poured a luscious flood of the gifts of Pomona. From the other extremity hung a card, inscribed with the words: "May Plenty crown the humblest board." This appropriate emblem was a gift from the New-York Horticultural Society.

Above, elevated in the gallery, so that it cast a glow upon NOLL's Band that discoursed the finest of instrumental music till the evening ended, hung an illuminated motto in gas-work. It read as follows:

COMPLIMENTARY FRUIT AND FLORAL FESTIVAL

TO AUTHORS:

BY THE ASSOCIATION OF NEW-YORK PUBLISHERS.

September 27, 1855.

Below this was suspended another illumination, also in gas-work:

HONOR TO GENIUS:

Still further below, hung at the edge of the northern gallery, was a statue representing the Muse of History, enclosed in an illuminated Temple, in gas-work: the brow of the statue encircled by a brilliant crown, formed of minute points of light. The effect of this work was exceedingly elegant. Beneath it was a silken canopy, overshadowing the lower end of the room.

Back of the dais, the tricolor partition shut out the main body of the building, and above it was a gallery to which the ladies had access.

At each lady's place at table lay a small bouquet, wrapped in filigree. The number of ladies who occupied seats in the main Hall was very small—probably there were not above fifty in all. In the galleries there were many spectators, and nine-tenths of them ladies. All the points in the Palace from which a view of the Banqueting Hall could be obtained were occupied.

A strong force of Police was present, in uniform, and excellent order was preserved upon the floor by a detailed force under command of Sergeant JONES.

THE BANQUET.

Punctually at 6½ o'clock, the guests entered the Hall and took their places. WILLIAM APPLETON, Esq., President of the Association, presided. At his right sat Right Reverend Dr. POTTER, Provisional Bishop of this Diocese, who invoked the Divine blessing. A fierce and simultaneous onslaught upon the contents of the dishes was presently in order. Gentlemen with ladies and gentlemen without that privilege, alike endeavored to be polite, and displayed excellent capabilities of enjoyment. The beverages were coffee, tea and the simplest and earliest of liquids.

The President's table was honored by the presence of many familiar faces. WASHINGTON IRVING was there—fresh and genial, and the object of universal remarks. Dr. VALENTINE MOTT sat on the left of Mr. APPLETON, and near him Rev. GARDINER SPRING, Professor WEBSTER, Principal of the Free Academy; President WOOLSEY, of Yale College; Hon. CHARLES KING, President of Columbia College; Judge DUER, HENRY C. CAREY, Rev. Dr. ROBINSON and his lady, ("Talvi,") Professor DENISON OLMSTED, Judge JAY. Towards the eastern end of the table were Mayor WOOD and Hon. J. V. C. SMITH, Mayor of Boston, Rev. Dr. TYNG, Rev. H. WARD BEECHER, Rev. E. H. CHAPIN, Rev. Dr. OSGOOD, WM. C. BRYANT, Hon. ROBERT T. CONRAD, and Prof. S. F. B. MORSE. Among the persons at table we noticed, in the list of ladies, Mrs. BOTTA, (late Miss ANNE C. LYNCH,) Mrs. SIGOURNEY, "MINNIE MYRTLE," ALICE CAREY, Mrs. SCHOOLCRAFT of Washington, and the Misses WARNER. Ex-Mayor HARPER, Rev. Mr. MILBURN, N. P. WILLIS and a host of well-known faces—publishers, authors, and paper-men—were among the party. It was altogether a brilliant assemblage of the literary people of the City and its vicinity. On no former occasion has there been an opportunity to enjoy the sight of so many very great lions at once.

LETTERS FROM INVITED GUESTS.

Letters in response to invitations were received from the historian Prescott, Hon. Horace Mann, Grace Greenwood, Hon. Edward Everett, Ralph Waldo Emerson, Dr. John W. Francis, Dr. Francis Lieber, Rev. Henry Giles, Erastus W. Ellsworth, John Grigg, Hon. Robert C. Winthrop, Mrs. Sarah J. Hale, and others. Limited space forbids their publication.

Mr. EMERSON writes:

"The friendliest meeting of the authors and publishers of good books, I must think one of the fairest omens for mankind."

HORACE MANN says:

Your Crystal Palace is as famous a place as Mount Olympus; and the men and women whom you will assemble there will constitute a much more respectable company, and, I doubt not, will have a longer dynasty, than those who convened at the court of Jupiter. If there is any Mythological atheism in this, I hope my classical friends will pardon me. In such a company it would be an honor to be one of the *Dii Minores*. But I am one of the *Lares* only, stationed at a distant hearth-stone, and must remain and take care of the interests of my small family.

Mr. PRESCOTT sent a toast:

If toasts should be in fashion, will you allow me to send you one?

The Complimentary Festival to Authors and Publishers—By their fruits ye shall know them.

GRACE GREENWOOD has always something pleasant to say:

May you all find "it good to be *there*," and among the luscious fruits spread before you, may no "apple of discord" have place.

Hon. ROBERT C. WINTHROP writes of the influence of Publishers:

I know not a body of men within the limits of our wide-spread Republic, who, associated upon just principles, might wield a mightier power for good, than the Publishers and Booksellers of America. The Press, in one of its greatest departments, is in their keeping. Upon them, in no small degree, it depends what shall be the character of the reading, by which the American mind is to be trained up to the discharge of its unmeasured responsibilities. Theirs is the only *imprimatur* to which a Free People can ever submit. If, associating themselves together in a spirit of patriotism, they would put the ban of their rejection upon everything which panders to a depraved appetite or palters with a vital truth; they would effect an amount of good which no words could exaggerate, and would avert one huge half of all the danger which is threatening us, that our liberty may run into licentiousness.

Mrs. HALE sent with her letter a volume of poems—*Three Hours, or the Vigil of Love*—and referred to pages 19 and 20.

A. HART, of Philadelphia, wrote a brief declination, urging as his excuse the advent of a Hebrew Fast-day, (the Tabernacles,) and added a sentiment:

Authors, Printers, Publishers and Booksellers—The united efforts illumine the intellect of millions of inhabitants of this great Republic.

Hon. EDWARD EVERETT begged to be excused on account of ill-health.

Rev. HENRY GILES discoursed pleasantly of Literature:

Literature is the great common field where all creeds and nationalities can assemble in harmony, and in which the humanities and charities of our race are seen to be immortal and universal. The glory of literature to me is, that it allows nothing which is noble in man to die, and that amidst the clashings of opinions and the changes of ages, this gathers in what is chiefest in affection, grandest in sentiment, and truest in thought—from old HOMER to old CHAUCER—from old CHAUCER to young SHAKSPEARE, BRYANT, &c., and from PLATO to EMERSON.

STATISTICS.

Mr. G. P. PUTNAM, Secretary of the Book Publishers' Association, read an introductory statistical sketch of the Progress of American Literature. An association of Publisher's was formed eighteen years ago, at the old City Hotel. That, like this one, was intended to establish friendly social intercourse.

Mr. PUTNAM gave the following statistics of Books:

The records of American Publications, for the twelve years ending in 1842, show an aggregate of 1,115 different works. Of these, 623 were original, and 492 were reprints from foreign books. The full list of reprints would show very nearly the same number as the originals, viz.: an average of 52 of each, per annum. In the year 1853, there were 733 new works published in the United States; of which 278 were reprints of English works, 35 were translations of foreign authors, and 420 (a large preponderance) were original American works—thus showing an increase of about 800 per cent. in less than twenty years. As the average increase of the population of the United States in the same time,—great as it was—scarcely reached 80 per cent., it appears that literature and the book trade advanced ten times as fast as the population.

Mr. PUTNAM was exceedingly complimentary to the great names in American literature,—glanced at the progress made in mechanical execution,—and finally showed, by figures carefully cyphered out, that we no longer rely for intellectual nutriment upon the yield of British minds.

The statements were very elaborate.

REGULAR TOASTS—THE SPEECHES.

There were seventeen regular toasts, but to all of them responses were not made.

Mr. SUMNER was assigned to respond to "The Republic of Letters," but he did not appear.

To the second toast—

American Literature. Its youth gives brilliant promise of an honorable future: may its riper years show that it has been trained in the right schools.

WM. C. BRYANT responded happily. He was received with a hurricane of plaudits, and, when he could be heard, claimed that he was not the man the company should have called for. His superior modesty led him to say that there were worthier representatives of American Literature around him. He spoke of the time when he first appeared before the public as an Author—traced the changes in the popular feeling in regard to writers—and called up the memory of honest old COTTON MATHER, whose works counted up to as many days as there are in the year; and since whose time Literature has had much to learn. For more than a century after his time, the procession of American authors was a straggling one; now it is improving and increasing—it has brilliant essayists, learned metaphysicians, erudite philosophers. Every bush has its poet, starting up like the armed soldiers of RODERICK DHU from behind the rock and beneath the heather. What an immense Literature is that of our school-books! Will anybody undertake to enumerate the works that relate to questions of geography? Is there any end to the grammars? Can there be any complete catalogue of the authors who have toiled to make science easy by induction, by illustration, by the essay? Equal to that is the Literature that provides for the entertainment of the young. Not many years ago, Mr. B. said, he was in the Capital of the little Island of Malta, and was not displeased to find in its great Library a copious assortment of American books, selected by a lettered Scotchman, and comprising the writings of Miss SEDGWICK, Mrs. SIGOURNEY, and others of our female authors. Booksellers next claimed Mr. BRYANT's attention. Booksellers, it has been said, are the natural enemies of Authors. This he denied. It has been said, too, that the bookseller grows rich upon the works of the author. What else has he to grow rich upon? If there were no popular authors with fertile brains, there would be no wealthy publishers. The two classes grow and strengthen by each other's aid. Whenever I see a rich bookseller, said Mr. BRYANT, I know that there have been successful authors, and I have often wondered that among the subjects which have attracted the pens of authors, no one has ever thought of writing the Lives of Eminent Booksellers. What a study it would be, to portray the rise, the progress, the characters of the Publishers—to describe the generous bearing of that Bookseller who takes the author's manuscript, and, with scarcely a glance, consigns it to the Press, pays the author a handsome compensation, and only retains a trifling fee, scarcely worth mentioning, for himself. [Laughter.] Or, on the other hand, exhibit to the world the niggardly circumspection that inquires first, if the work of an author is likely to "pay," if it is published. Mr. BRYANT suggested the topic for the benefit of parties interested. In conclusion, he proposed the memory of ELAM BLISS.

Hon. EDWARD EVERETT was put down to respond to the third toast, but did not come. The toast was:

Literature and Statesmanship—When we are governed at home or represented abroad by a WHEATON, a BANCROFT, an EVERETT, a MARSH, a HAWTHORNE, a KENNEDY, here is hope for the dignity of the country and the interests of letters.

The fourth toast was in honor of "English Literature"—to which WILLIAM YOUNG, Esq., of the *Albion*, responded in a two minutes' speech, alluding to the news from Sebastopol. The fall of the fortress caused a perceptible elevation of the gentleman's patriotism. He was facetious upon himself in consequence of it.

"*The Clergy*" was responded to by Rev. W. H. MILBURN—the blind preacher. Mr. MILBURN made a very elegant little speech, in the course of which he referred in touching terms to his affliction. He said that in the economy of the Church to which he was attached it is incumbent upon the ministers, not only to preach the word, but to circulate good books. Mr. M. is in the twelfth year of his ministry: in this space of time he has traveled more than two hundred thousand miles in the performance of ministerial duties. The training of the Western preacher commences in the saddle. Mounted upon a noble steed the best he can procure—with limbs encased in leggings, and head surmounted by a straw hat, the young itinerant rides on from place to place, as duty calls. Dismounting at the door of the first convenient log cabin,—nicely adjusting upon his arm his saddle-bags crammed with books,—a rush-bottomed chair for a pulpit—he labors with the few who are drawn together by his ministry. Then his books are distributed. The Methodists, from the very first, therefore, have been the book publishers of the West. [Applause.] Hence their relation to "the trade" is more intimate than might be supposed. They are a kind of two-edged sword that cuts both ways. But their pay is small. They rejoice with exceeding great joy, if they succeed in obtaining one-half of their average allowance of $100. After humorous allusions to his own experience, Mr. MILBURN rebuked himself for the attempt to say anything at a literary festival—a man who could not read! Time was, when he was able to read; now he could not. Not that he had ever possessed the power of transferring ideas by the line, by the word, by the sentence, from the page to the mind. That privilege had been denied him. His reading had been but the child's perpetual spelling. He was only spelling—never reading. With shaded brow, with hand on cheek, with finger on eye, with velvet sweat rolling down the face, with scorching tears starting from tortured eyes—these had been his infirmities. But in the midst of all he had found Learning its own exceeding great reward. He had struggled thus for twenty years. In that space of time he had learned the riches of his mother tongue from the pages of SHAKSPEARE's dictionary—had studied eloquence from the pages of MILTON—had reaped knowledge from the light-giving mind of HOMER—and like solitary BARTIMEAS, had delighted to hear the words, if he could not see the face of the Son of Man. He magnified the position and office of the seller of a book. It was said of WOLFE, as he floated upon the St. Lawrence the evening before he met his death upon the plains of Abraham, that he said of GRAY's "Elegy," "I would rather have the reputation of being the author of that work than to be the conqueror of Quebec;" and so, to paraphrase the sentiment, Mr. MILBURN would rather have been the author of the *Sketch Book* (turning to Mr. IRVING, amidst great applause) than to have achieved any other work, or to have been known as the author of that noble Ode, commencing:

"The groves were God's first Temple;"

(turning to Mr. BRYANT,) than to have had the highest earthly honor. Had these been his, gladly would he have worn this badge of pain, (drawing a shade over his eyes,) and have worn it as a crown of triumph.

Mr. MILBURN's remarks were listened to with the profoundest attention. When he finished, he was conducted back to his seat.

The Fifth Regular Toast was—

The Fine Arts—The offspring of Free Institutions, and the ornament of a Practical People; their Use lies in their Beauty, and their Beauty lies in their Truth.

Rev. Dr. OSGOOD responded. He insisted that we were not indifferent to the Fine Arts. We have done, said he, a pretty little job of landscape gardening, with a Continent for a garden plot. We have placed the sculptor on a gigantic scale, hewing out of the most unpromising materials a homogeneous and glorious nation. But in the Departments that are deemed Fine Arts we have no need to be ashamed. We have a noble scroll of poets, from FRENEAU to BRYANT; a proud list of writers of fiction from BROCKDEN BROWN to IRVING; of painters, from WEST to POWERS. You, the most practical of our great men, have been patrons and lovers of the Fine Arts. FRANKLIN induced the first sculptor of note to visit us; FULTON contributed $5,000 toward printing an edition of an American poem! "Lightning MORSE" took a prize in his youth for an "Infant Hercules." The reverend orator insisted upon our need of amusement. The days of our festivities as yet have hardly commenced. We need to put aside the liquor and introduce the actor. Jonathan has initiated a reform. He becomes more and more a man of sentiment. Let him keep his prow bright—his threshing machine always geared—his long habit of threshing should teach him that—and he'd fast also to his wife's piano. He closed with a fine allusion to Bishop BERKELEY's never realized dream of founding a University in Bermuda.

The seventh regular toast was—

The Bench and the Bar—Illustrated by a MARSHALL, a STORY, a KENT and a WEBSTER, they prove that Literature and Law may mutually adorn each other.

To which Judge DUER responded at considerable length.

The eighth toast was—

The Publishers of Boston—A fraternity that has been illustrated by the patriotism of KNOX and the intelligence of an ARMSTRONG, a LINCOLN and a BALDWIN, may still be proud of the produce of their cultivated FIELDS.

Mr. LITTLE and Mr. FIELDS, of Boston, responded. The latter spun a few lines that held a delighted audience for about five minutes, and were rapturously applauded. The following are but bricks—our figure has changed—in the house:—telling of the "old time," he said:

> Tough days were those to launch a book—
> It makes us youngsters smile—
> For when they got a volume off
> Folks heard it creak a mile.
> But soon the times began to change,
> And change began to flow,
> And pockets tickled loud with cash
> That once were very low.
>
> How slow and sure they set their types!
> How small editions ran!
> Then fifty thousand never sold—
> Before the sale began.
> For how could they, poor plodding souls,
> Be either swift or wise,
> Who never learned the mighty art
> Of how to advertise.

Books of the modern times he thus hits off:

> The stranger begs him to re,
> To name the titles o'er,
> Of just a few, of all that's new,
> In his abundant store.
> So he begins—"The Sea of Blood!"
> "A work of wondrous power,
> Of which we've sold ten thousand sets
> Within the last half hour!
>
> This is the new Sensation book,
> A work of so much force,
> The first edition all blew up
> And smashed a cart and horse!
> A friend, who read the manuscript
> Without sufficient care,
> Was torn to rags, altho' he had
> Six cables round his hair!
>
> 'The Eggs of Thought' I'll recommend
> As very thrilling lays.—
> Some Poets poach, but here is one
> That all the papers praise.
> The School Commissioners out West
> Have ordered seventy tons,
> That widely they may be dispersed
> Among their setting suns.
>
> And here's a most astounding tale,
> A volume full of fire,
> The author's name is known to fame—
> *Stupendous Stubbs, Esquire!*
> And here 'The Howling Dites of Crime,'
> By A. Sapphira Stress,
> Two hundred men fell dead last night
> A working at the press!
>
> Our printers beat Briareus,
> As now the story stands,
> For that same worthy only had
> 'About a hundred hands!'"
> The old man groans in sad dismay,
> Then cries in trembling tones
> 'No more! give me a modest work
> We used to call 'Tom Jones!'"

The ninth regular toast was:

Our Lady Guests and their Writings—The New England Tone is re-echoed from the New Home of the Far West; and from a room on the banks of the Ohio, a touch of nature vibrates along *The Lofty and the Lowly* through the *Wide, Wide World*.

The tenth:

Institutions of Learning—The best operators for an active demand in the book market—they will never permit our judicious investments to fall below par.

President ALLEN, of Girard College, responded.

The eleventh toast was

The Printing press of the age of steam and electricity.

Rev. Mr. CHAPIN responded in his happiest style. He dwelt upon the beauty and the power of the press that with long, slim fingers picks up its messages of thought, scatters them quietly as snow flakes, though they fall like thunder-bolts on the ears of the people—that carries a sentiment by storm and again permeates the world unseen and unobserved, as the elements filter through the ribs of the earth. With a few bold strokes he pictured the rude first GUTTENBERG awkward press that tore the Bible away from the chained desk of the monastery, scattered its precious and holy truths abroad, and kindled a light to read them by. And then he pictured the press that brings us the last speech in the Fusion Convention and Confusion Caucus, reproduces the last groan of poor stricken Norfolk, and lays a daguerreotype of the world as it was at last sunset upon our breakfast table. It is wonderful to reflect, said he, that they will be reading what we are doing to-night, half-way to Albany in the morning before we are half out of bed. He described in a sort of charcoal sketch, the great publishers' establishment, such as HARPER's or APPLETON's, from the dark cellars where the old fire-eater puffs and works night and day, and the catacombs of types and vaults of plates, up through the many airy rooms where happy girls and men, with sleeves up-rolled, are performing the scores of processes that intervene betwixt the first handling of the much-loved MSS. and the well-bound book.

He spoke of the Press as the symbol of the general advancement of the age in science.

The rattle of the steam-press, he said, was more powerful than the rumbling of artillery. Each type as it clicks into place has a mark, though it be a thousand years ahead. Every new advance of the Press makes the Malakoff and Redan of Error tremble.

Not that the Press is always wholesome in its influence, or always right. But for the most part it must be. God never allows so great an engine to be used mostly for evil. Providence levies on telegraph and railroad, and hangs signal lanterns far out at sea on the prow of your steamship. In long grooves of the steam-press run the everlasting plans of Providence. The speaker enlarged on the *moral power* of the Press, and the alliance betwixt it and every other great invention, improvement or reform that marks the age. The audience applauded, bravoed and cheered when he sat down.

The next toast was—

The Sister Cities of Boston, New-York and Philadelphia, whose Chief Magistrates honor us to-night. While each aims to produce the best books of the best authors, and best reg...inted homes for them, the more rivalry the better.

Mayor SMITH replied in a jolly, off-hand style, creating much merriment, and a capital impression.

The next toast was—

The Newspaper.

Rev. H. W. BEECHER responded happily enough, but very heavily for him. His topic was the readers of books.

The next regular toast was:

The Publishers of Philadelphia—Who by honorable enterprise have so magnified the business that numbers BENJAMIN FRANKLIN among its founders, and which has since been adorned by the CAREYS, the THOMASSES, the GRIGGS and the HARTS of the city of Brotherly Love.

HENRY C. CAREY, Esq., of Philadelphia, was called upon to respond, but did not make his appearance, having left the hall.

The following was the last regular toast:

The Booksellers of the Union—So long as they are the medium for diffusing sound intelligence and the pure products of true genius, they deserve an honorable position in the community; for, in the ordinary business of their lives, they become benefactors to their country.

Volunteer toasts having been invited, the following were presented:

By JOHN KEESE, Esq.:

Woman. The rarest and most exquisite work of the great Author. Illustrated by the Graces, and published in Paradise.

By Dr. GARDNER:

Woman—the type of loveliness, a lettered angel,—she is an acknowledged standard work.

By Mr. MASON:

Our Guests—The Authors of America, whom we are proud to call friends, united we stand—divided we fall.

Mr. M. also proposed the health of the Mayor of the City of New-York.

His Honor Mayor WOOD responded briefly, and called up Professor MORSE, who, without speech, called in turn "Peter Parley" GOODRICH. Neither of these gentlemen, however, favored the audience with any remarks, as near as the reporter could ascertain, in the confusion occasioned by the movement of persons who, at this time, were crowding towards the stand; and then the exercises were closed with a musical medley by the Band. Take it together, the whole affair was a perfect success.

☞ A discovery has been made of a Gum similar to the Gum Arabic, which exudes from a tree in the northern part of Texas. It is said that a large extent of country is covered with these trees, which resemble the Musquito. The discovery is pronounced, in the Washington City *Star*, to be second only to the discovery of Gold in California.

ONE WEEK LATER FROM EUROPE.

Arrival of the America and Washington.

HIGHLY IMPORTANT WAR NEWS.

FALL OF SEBASTOPOL.

The City Destroyed by the Russians.

SUPPOSED DEATH OF GEN. BOSQUET.

FEARFUL SLAUGHTER ON ALL SIDES.

Reported Retreat of Gortschakoff towards Perekop.

Great Excitement throughout Europe

ATTEMPT TO ASSASSINATE NAPOLEON.

Austrian Proposal to Mediate In the Danish Difficulty.

CONSOLS 90 5-16 a 90 1-2.

COTTON EASIER—BREADSTUFFS UNCHANGED.

By the House Printing Telegraph—Office 21 Wall-st.

HALIFAX, N. S. Thursday, Sept. 27.

The Royal Mail steamship *America*, Capt. LANG, from Liverpool at 12½ o'clock on Saturday, the 15th inst., arrived here at about 6 o'clock this morning, bringing 116 passengers, and sailed again for Boston at 9 o'clock, where she will be due at a late hour tomorrow (Friday) afternoon. The *America* has experienced heavy gales during the passage to this port.

At 1 o'clock P. M., on the 15th inst., the *America* passed the Collins steamer *Pacific*, Capt. NYE, from New-York on the 5th inst., going into Liverpool.

The steamship *Union* arrived at Havre on the 5th and the *North Star* on the 12th inst.

THE WAR.

Fall of Sebastopol.

The news by the America confirms the accounts of the fall of the south side of Sebastopol, brought out by the steamer Washington, copious extracts from which will be found below, and to which we have, as yet, but very few details to add.

Vice Admiral BRUAT telegraphed:

CRIMEA, September 10—11 P. M.—I inspected to-day Sebastopol and its lines of defence. The mind cannot form an exact picture of our victory—the full extent of it can only be understood by an examination of the place itself. The multiplicity of works of defence, and the material means applied thereto, exceed by far anything seen in the history of the war.

The capture of the Malakoff has placed in the hands of the Allies a large amount of material and immense establishments—the importance of which it is not possible to state exactly. To-morrow, the Allied troops will occupy the Karabelnaia and the town, and under their protection an Anglo-French Commission will be occupied with making out a return of the material abandoned to us by the enemy. The exultation of our soldiers is very great.

SEPT. 12.—The enemy has destroyed the remainder of his fleet. Nothing now remains afloat.

The Allies are hastening preparations in case of GORTSCHAKOFF attempting to reach Perekop or to unite with LIPRANDI.

LOSSES OF THE ALLIES.

The London *Post* says the English loss in the assault on the Redan was five to six hundred killed and fourteen hundred wounded, including one hundred and forty one officers.

The *Moniteur* says that up to the morning of the 11th, 1,500 wounded, including 240 officers, had gone to the Ambulances. The number of the dead was not ascertained, but it is probably short of 2,000.

The Paris correspondent of the London *Times* writes that five French Generals were killed, besides ten superior officers.

It is also affirmed that Generals McMAHON and PONTEVES have died from the effect of wounds, and that General BOSQUET is either killed or wounded.

PELISSIER has been created a Marshal of France, and Paris completely illuminated on account of the victory.

A grand national *Te Deum* was celebrated at the Church of Notre Dame, the Emperor attending in person.

Queen VICTORIA has sent an address of thanks to her army, and directs General SIMPSON to congratulate Marshal PELISSIER on his brilliant victory.

Throughout France and England the rejoicing is immense.

Paris correspondence says PELISSIER has telegraphed for instructions in case GORTSCHAKOFF should ask to capitulate. The reply, as reported, is, in substance, that the Russians must surrender at discretion, lay down their arms, and give up all the fortified places in the Crimea including Odessa, and all their munitions of war, without doing any previous damage thereto. But GORTSCHAKOFF has not yet asked for terms.

Russian Report.

The Russian paper the *Brussels Nord*, says the resolution of Prince GORTSCHAKOFF exhibits the energy of a great commander. It saves Russia from an inextricable position into which a false interpretation of a point of honor would have forced her. The Russian army concentrated north of Sebastopol, will henceforth have that unity of movement and action which, until now, it has wanted. The Sebastopol of the South is replaced by Sebastopol of the North, a formidable position, bristling with innumerable guns, which a compact army henceforward will defend. Imperial history will do justice to Prince GORTSCHAKOFF, who, by making a momentary sacrifice, and avoiding a useless effusion of blood, has preserved for Russia an army trained to war by a struggle of a year's duration, and placed that army in a position which enables him to command the situation.

DENMARK.

A letter, dated Berlin, Aug. 4, says: Austria is said to have offered her mediation to Denmark, in her difference with the United States. Doubts are entertained as to whether the United States will consent to the compromise which Denmark intends proposing, of lowering the Sound dues generally, but Prussia would be quite ready to accept it.

RUSSIA.

A telegraphic dispatch from St. Petersburg states, that the Czar intends leaving there on the 13th for Moscow. At Warsaw he will be attended by Count NESSELRODE, who will, it is thought, arrange an interview for him with the King of Prussia.

HIGHLY IMPORTANT.

BY TELEGRAPH FROM LONDON TO LIVERPOOL.

LONDON, Saturday, Sept. 15—11 A. M.

The Paris Correspondent of the *Times* says, it is reported that 25,000 men have embarked at Balaklava for the North of Sebastopol; also, that the Russians are in full retreat toward Perekop.

The Paris *Debats* contains an editorial article, discussing the question whether Sebastopol is tenable by the Allies, while the Russians are masters of the forts on the north side, fronting the sea, and asserts that the town is quite tenable, the possession of Fort Chersone and Balaklava superceding the necessity of entering the harbor. The Russian armies will probably continue in observation within their strong positions until the Allies make some movement—hence all speculation as to the plan of the campaign must be purely imaginary.

The Baltic.

A dispatch from Dantzic, under date of the 14th inst., says that the block-ships are expected to be ordered home on Monday next.

Prince FREDERICK, of Prussia, is at present on a visit to Queen VICTORIA.

The *Times* suggests the celebration of a day of National Thanksgiving on account of the fall of Sebastopol.

It is rumored in the Clubs to-day that the Allies found 1,200 guns within the lines of Sebastopol, and also that the Russians are falling back upon Baktchiserai; but rumors from Paris are to the effect that Prince GORTSCHAKOFF will certainly hold the north side of Sebastopol to the last extremity. From the same source we learn that the allied Admirals have sent a dispatch stating that it is not expedient to enter the harbor of Sebastopol until Fort Constantine shall have been silenced. It is conjectured that the Allies will attack Fort Constantine from Fort Alexander and Artillery Bay.

FOREIGN COMMERCIAL INTELLIGENCE.

Liverpool Cotton Market.

Messrs. BROWN, SHIPLEY & Co. report the market easier, in consequence of the increased stringency in the Money Market, and the advanced rate of discount by the Bank. Prices, however, were not quotably lower. Messrs. DENNISTOUN & Co. say that the market opened at an advance of ⅛d., but afterwards receded and became dull, at last week's prices.

The sales of the week amounted to 46,000 bales, of which speculators took 6,000, and exporters about the same quantity. The sales of Friday were 6,000 bales. The following were the authorized quotations: New-Orleans Fair, 7½d.; Middling, 6⅞d.; Uplands Fair, 6¾d.; Middling, 6⅜d.; Mobile Fair, 6⅞d.; Middling, 6 3-16d.; Ordinary to Good Ordinary, 5½d.@5¾d.; Inferior, 4d.@5½d.

Messrs. DENNISTOUN & Co. quote Uplands Fair 6¾d. The stock on hand amounted to 514,000 bales, of which 329,000 were American.

State of Trade in Manchester.

The market was dull, but prices had undergone no change of moment.

Liverpool Breadstuffs Market.

The quotations vary materially, but most firms report the market stiffer and in some instances slightly higher, with a buoyant tone at the close, especially for Wheat, which is generally quoted at an advance of 1d.@2d.

BROWN, SHIPLEY & Co. call the market dull, and other Circulars say that it is quiet and unchanged. Western Canal FLOUR is quoted by BROWN, SHIPLEY & Co. at 40s.@41s.; Philadelphia and Baltimore, 41s.@42s.; Ohio, 42s.@42s. 6d.; White CORN, 43s.; Yellow, 39s. 6d.@40s.; Mixed, 39s.@39s. 6d.; White WHEAT, 12s. 3d.@12s. 7d.; Red, 11s. 6d.@11s. 9d. The weather had been very favorable, and the crop accounts were of a satisfactory character.

Liverpool Produce Markets.

From the Brokers' Circular.

ASHES dull, but prices unchanged. Old Pots sold at 30s.; New, 35s. Rough TURPENTINE nothing doing; Spirits in retail demand only. Common ROSIN steady, at 4s. 2d.@4s. 5d., and 9s. for fine. SUGARS advanced 1s.@1s. 6d. RICE active at former rates. Market bare of QUERCITRON BARK. LINSEED CAKE scarce.

OILS—Steady, with a moderate business; Linseed 43s. 6d.@44s.; Cod, £47; Sperm dull at £125; Pale Rape, 62s.; Palm in active demand at £44@£44 15s. Olive Oil in good request at 10s. advance. COFFEE—Active and buoyant. The prices of CURRANTS had considerably advanced. TEA—Steady. TOBACCO—Without change. Sales of Honduras LOGWOOD, £6; Domingo £5 7s. 6d.@£5 15s. No transactions in SEEDS. JUTE—Steady. Manilla HEMP, £40.

Liverpool Provision Market.

Messrs. RICHARDSON, SPENCE & Co. quote Provisions unchanged. A moderate business doing in BEEF and PORK. BACON selling at extreme prices, stock reduced very low, but arrivals daily looked for. LARD in speculative demand at 58s.@60s. TALLOW active at former rates.

London Markets.

Messrs. BARING BROS. quote an advance in SUGARS to the extent of 2s., the market closing with an active demand. COFFEE at auction has advanced 1s. TEA sold at 8½@9d. for Congou. TALLOW—Large deliveries at 57s. 6d. LARD—Buyers demand a reduction. WHITE WHEAT, 82s.@85s.; RED 76s.@80s. FLOUR, 42s.@46s. The Iron makers continued full of orders, but there was no change in quotations.

London Money Market.

The Bank of England had advanced its minimum rate of interest to 4½ per cent., and a further advance to 5 per cent. is looked for during the ensuing week. The Money Market exhibited increased stringency. CONSOLS for money closed at 90⅜@90½. The Bullion in the Bank of England had decreased during the week to the extent of £721,000. EAGLES quoted at 76s. 4½d. BAR SILVER, 5s. 1½d.

American Securities.

Very little had been done in AMERICAN STOCKS, and prices for the most part were nominal, and would probably remain so during the existing value of money.

Freights.

The Liverpool FREIGHT market was steady and prices unchanged.

The Latest Commercial News.

Messrs. BIGLAND ATHYA & Co., report: Liverpool, Saturday, 11 A. M.—COTTON unchanged. The market closed strong for everything in the shape of BREADSTUFFS. PROVISIONS very firm, stocks daily being reduced. BACON is dearer. BEEF and PORK meet with a moderate demand. CHEESE quiet. LARD rather easier, sellers at 59s.@59s. 6d. TALLOW active at 59s.@60s. for prime North American.

Passengers.

In Steamship America at Halifax from Liverpool.

Gen Paley, Bearer of Dispatches; Mr Molineux and lady, Miss Molineux, (two) Mr Pilkington and lady, Sez. Mr Chittenden and lady, Mr. Longman and lady, Miss Longman, Mrs. Read, Miss Gamble, Mrs Brodie, Mrs Allen, Misses Allen, Messrs. Quillan, Fleming, Gordon, Thompson, Wilson, Hewdson, Lloyd, Gass, Mathews, Letch, Jessie, Hammond, Davies, McDonald, Fraser, Master Leek, Hon. Jno. Howe, Messrs. Ferguson, Gamble, Kenny, Carr, Weir, Allen, Wilson, Allen, McCall, Law, Witte, Mason, Hewetson, Hewitt, Law, Emsor, Renalt, Castillon, Davis, Whiting, Chitson, Stewart, Castillon, Dyer, Lessan, Convers, Lawson, Jones, Brand, Neele, Betz, Rogers, Matthews, McCauley, Hart, walcker, Hobson, Maclegan, Pease, Kingston, Shaw, Mr. Scott and lady, Mr. Alberly and lady, Mr. Davis and lady, Mr. Gravelerans lady, Mr. Powell and lady, Mr. Walker and lady, Mr. Colgate and lady, Mr. Baring and lady, Mr. McAndrew and lady, Mrs. Downer, Mrs. Patterson, Mrs. Powell, Mrs. Lindley, Mrs. Edmunds, Mrs. Taylor, Mr. Colacho, Rev. Mr. Anguerro, Rev. Mr. Lench, Rev. Mr. Allen, Rev. Mr. Riley, Mathews, Collins, Wesley, Williams, Roberts, Carr, Griffiths, Wilson, Caruthers, Lloyd, Smith, Warren, Jr., Robinson, Read, Such, Hershaber, Hanmer, Nowell, Yates, Wilson, Aguira, Lato, Bringa, Highley, Hart, Bonsan, Stuart, Batchelder, Morton, Short, Parker, Cunningham, Marsden, Scott, Bundy, Wagner, Read, McMillan, Drinkwater, Simpson, Morley, Merrill, Gartz, Thompson, Longster, Bogle, Macnut, Kinder, Fleming, Hunter, Agent Associated Press at Liverpool.

Shipping Intelligence.

Arrived from New-York—4th, Blackfish, at Malaga; Archimede, at Trieste; Franklin, Bell, at Lisbon; 6th, steamer Union, Havre; 11th, Helen Mar, at Queenstown; 12th, steamer North Star, at Cowes; Isaac Webb, at Liverpool; William and Jane, off Dover; 13th, Grace, at Swansea.

Arrived from Boston—6th, Eagle, at Genoa.

Arrived from Philadelphia—31st, Star of Breeze, off Gibraltar.

Arrived from Charleston—8th, Superior, at Marseilles.

Arrived from Baltimore—10th, Howland, at Queenstown; 12th, Hudson, Daring, off Dungeness.

Arrived from New-Orleans—7th, Troy, at Genoa; Zephyr, at Marseilles; 12th, Weymouth, at Liverpool; 13th, George Green, at Liverpool; Lunar, at Deal; 3d, Mount Vernon, at Naples.

Sailed for New-York—8th, Carlo Mauran, from Stockholm; Cherokee, from Bordeaux; 10th, Empire State; 11th, S. Lindsey; 12th, American Union, from Liverpool; Elizabeth Hamilton, from Shields; Danube, from Cardiff; Excelsior, E. P. Saul, from Liverpool; 13th, Carolus Magnus, from Liverpool; 11th, Isabella, Mary Aldridge, from Helvoet.

Sailed for Boston—7th, Defiance, from Lisbon; 14th, Reporter, from Lisbon.

Sailed for Philadelphia—14th, James Brown, from Liverpool; 15th, Wyoming, from do.

Sailed for Baltimore—14th, Emily St. Pierre, from Liverpool.

Sailed for Savannah—12th, Florida, from Liverpool.

Sailed for New-Orleans—10th, Pelican State; 11th, Eudocia; 12th, Mary Glover; 13th, Bremen, from Liverpool; 7th, Sleman, from Antwerp.

NEWS BY THE WASHINGTON.

By the United States mail steamship *Washington*, Capt. CAVENDY, from Bremen and Southampton, we receive our files of European journals to the 12th instant.

The *Washington* has brought the important intelligence of the *fall of Sebastopol*. On the 8th inst., the Allied forces attacked the defences of Sebastopol, and the French, after several desperate assaults, carried the Malakoff.

The plan of the battle appears to have been as follows:—The place was attacked in four divisions. The British troops attempted the storming of the Redan, the French attacked the Malakoff, the extreme right of the French made a diversion on the Little Redan, and a united attack of the English, French and Sardinians was made on the Central Battery. All the attacks were made simultaneously with great spirit and energy, but the one which was eminently successful was led by Gen. BOSQUET and Gen. McMAHON on the Malakoff. Both the Redan and the Central Bastion were at times in the hands of the storming parties, but so accurately did the guns of the Russians cover these, that as soon as the English had gained possession of them it was found impossible to hold them.

The intelligence of the fall of Sebastopol was received in London with demonstrations of great joy. At the various theatres and places of public amusement the fact was officially announced, and the bands at each place immediately played the national anthems of England and France. Throughout England the demonstrations were general.

The following are the latest telegraphic dispatches brought by the *Washington* of the important event:

ALLIED ACCOUNTS.

Vice-Admiral BRUAT telegraphed on the 9th of September:

The assault upon the Malakoff Tower was made yesterday at noon, and later on the Great Redan and on the Central Bastion.

A gale from the North kept the ships at anchor.

The mortar-boats, to be enabled to fire, were obliged to enter Streletzka Bay.

They fired 500 shells against the Quarantine Bastion and Fort Alexander.

The six English mortar-boats, also at anchor in Streletzka Bay, fired about the same number of shells.

Last night violent explosions and vast conflagrations made us suppose that the Russians were evacuating the town.

To-day we ascertained that the Russian vessels had been sunk.

The bridge was covered with troops retreating to the north side.

After 8 o'clock the bridge was destroyed.

Only a few steamers remain in the port, anchored near Fort Catherine.

I approached this morning the Quarantine batteries on board the *Brandon* and ascertained myself that they are now evacuated.

They have just blown up.

Our soldiers have left their trenches and spread themselves in isolated groups on the ramparts of the town, which appears to be completely abandoned.

General SIMPSON telegraphed on the same day:

Sebastopol is in the possession of the allies.

The enemy, during the night and this morning, have evacuated the south side, after exploding their magazines and setting fire to the whole of the town.

All the men-of-war were burnt during the night, with the exception of three steamers, which are plying about the harbor.

The bridge communicating with the north side is broken.

General SIMPSON telegraphed on the 10th:

The casualties, I regret to say, are somewhat heavy. No General officer killed.

Names shall be sent as soon as possible.

General PELISSIER telegraphed on the 9th September:

Karabelnaia and the south part of Sebastopol no longer exist.

The enemy, perceiving our solid occupation of the Malakoff, decided upon evacuating the place, after having destroyed and blown up by mines nearly all the defences.

Having passed the night in the midst of my troops, I can assure you that everything in the Karabelnaia is blown up, and, from what I could see, the same must be the case in front of our left line of attack.

This immense success does the greatest honor to our troops.

I will send you a detailed account of our losses during the day, which, after so many obstinate combats, must be considerable.

To-morrow I shall be able to form an estimate of the results of this great day's work, a great portion of the honors are due to Generals BOSQUET and McMAHON.

Everything is quiet on the Tchernaya, and we are vigilant there.

The French Minister of War also received the following news:

CRIMEA, Sept. 9—8 P. M.

This morning I ascertained that the enemy has sunk his steamers.

Their work of destruction continued under the fire of our shells.

The explosion of mines successively, and on different points, made it our duty to defer our entrance into the place, which presents the spectacle of an immense conflagration.

Closely pressed by our fire, Prince GORTSCHAKOFF has demanded an armistice to carry away the remainder of the wounded near Fort St. Paul.

The bridge, as a precautionary measure, has been broken down by his orders.

I am collecting the returns of our losses, and you shall have them as soon as ready.

All goes on well.

We are vigilant on the Tchernaya.

PARIS, MONDAY—10 P. M.

A dispatch from General DELLA MARMORA announces that in the night which followed the capture of the Malakoff, the Russians retired, burning the town, destroying the buildings, and sinking their last ships.

It was General BOSQUET's *corps d'armée* which captured the Malakoff.

RUSSIAN ACCOUNTS.

Prince GORTSCHAKOFF telegraphed:

SEBASTOPOL, Sept. 9—8 P. M.

The enemy receives constantly reinforcements of fresh troops. The bombardment is fiercely violent.

TEN AT NIGHT—The garrison of Sebastopol, after sustaining an infernal fire, (*feu d'enfer*,) repulsed six assaults, but could not drive the enemy from the Korniloff Bastion (the Malakoff Tower.)

Our brave troops, who resisted to the last extremity, are now crossing over to the northern part of Sebastopol.

The enemy found nothing in the southern part but blood-stained ruins.

On the 9th of September the passage of the garrison from the southern to the northern part was accomplished with extraordinary success, our loss on that occasion being but 100 men.

We left, I regret to say, nearly 500 men grievously wounded on the southern side.

THE FALL OF SEBASTOPOL.

From the London Times, Sept. 11.

On Saturday, the 8th of September, within a few days of the anniversary of the landing of the Allied forces in the Crimea, and 316 days after the opening of the besieging batteries against Sebastopol, on the 17th of October, 1854, a final and victorious assault was made upon the southern part of the town. Before night the French flag waved in triumph on the Malakhoff Tower, which had fallen before the indomitable courage and perseverance of the assailants, and within a few hours more the Russian garrison had evacuated the Karabelnaia suburb and the southern portion of the fortress, *after blowing up the magazines and principal works, setting fire to the town in many places*, and then endeavoring to withdraw across the bar or from this terrific scene of devastation and defeat. So fell Sebastopol. The catastrophe surpasses in horrible interest all the preceding scenes of this gigantic contest. The columns of the Allied armies, combined in a fourfold attack, struggled all day with equal valor, though with unequal success, against the principal points marked out for assault. The extreme right of the French attack was directed against the work called the Little Redan, which was at first carried by the impetuosity of our Allies, though they were subsequently driven back by the fierce resistance of the Russians. The second and principal assault of the French army was against the Malakoff, which was carried by storm, and determined by its fall the fate not only of the day, but of the siege. A third attack was made by the British forces on the Great Redan, and, although we learn that the salient angle of this formidable work was at one moment carried and occupied by our troops, it must be added that they were subsequently driven out of it by the fire of the Russian batteries which commanded it, and this check in some degree diminishes the exultation which will be felt in this country at the triumphant termination of the siege. The French columns on the left also assailed, in the fourth place, the Central Battery, but failed to establish themselves in the work. We have no doubt that every man who attacked the defences of Sebastopol on that eventful day fought with the same undaunted gallantry and the same determination to carry the place or to perish in the attempt; and, although the results of these several attacks were unequal, all were animated by the same spirit and contributed to the great result. The first prize of this glorious victory belongs of right to our gallant allies the French, since the Malakoff Tower, the key of the main position, fell before the vigor of their assault; but, with that chivalrous feeling which is the noblest bond of men who have fought and conquered together, the names of all those who carried the rugged defences of Sebastopol deserve to stand side by side on one page, and no invidious distinctions shall sully or lessen their common renown.

The Russians on their side unquestionably defended the place with the utmost determination, and on more than one point they had the advantage over the besiegers. But it was the courage of desperation, for this effort was their last. No sooner were the outer works taken, which laid the town and the port at the mercy of the allied forces, than *the men-of-war and steamers in the harbor were all set on fire, blown up, sunk, or destroyed*, either by the fire of the allied batteries or by the orders of the Russian authorities. Such was the fate of the Russian Black Sea fleet, on

New-York Daily Times.

VOL. V.....NO. 1489. NEW-YORK, THURSDAY, JUNE 26, 1856. PRICE TWO CENTS.

REPUBLICANISM.

GRAND RATIFICATION MEETING.

Enthusiastic Indorsement of Fremont and Dayton.

Immense Concourse at the Tabernacle.

THREE MEETINGS AT ONCE.

TEN THOUSAND PERSONS PRESENT.

Procession to Col. Fremont's Residence.

SPEECH OF COL. FREMONT.

EXPANSION OF THE PLATFORM.

MRS. FREMONT CHEERED BY THE PEOPLE.

Speeches of Judge Emmett, Hon. Wm. A. Howard, Senator Trumbull, Attorney-General Kimball, and others.

Letters from Gov. Seward, Hon. Preston King, Hon. B. F. Butler, &c.

Unparalleled Enthusiasm—And no need for Tar-Barrels.

The REPUBLICANS OF NEW-YORK gathered in overwhelming numbers in and around the Broadway Tabernacle last evening, for the purpose of ratifying the nominations of JOHN C. FREMONT and WILLIAM L. DAYTON. At an early hour, crowds began to gather at the Tabernacle, and increased rapidly, until that spacious building was completely crammed. Full five thousand men were packed into the house when the hour arrived for the commencement of the proceedings. They blocked up the aisles; were wedged in among the seats; overflowed the platform; clung to the pillars; looked over one another's shoulders away up in the darkest corners of the galleries; peered over the heads of their fellows from the sills of the windows; preserved their good humor unimpaired amidst all the crowd and crush and jostle; and testified by the heartiest of all hearty plaudits their unqualified approval of the Candidates and the Platform. When the Tabernacle would hold no more people, the coming throng surged back and constituted itself into outside meetings. Two of these meetings were in progress at the same instant. One took post upon the steps of the Tabernacle, and the long covered-way, which leads to the door of the building, was densely packed with eager listeners. A second meeting was organized in front of the entrance on Broadway, and that thoroughfare underwent an hour's blockade. Speakers were abundant at all these meetings, and the enthusiasm was unbounded. Counting together the number of persons in attendance outside and inside of the Tabernacle, it is a moderate estimate to say that Ten Thousand Freemen of New-York assembled yesterday to do honor to their ticket.

The call for the meeting was circulated only two days beforehand, yet the response was as large as we have ever seen on occasions where there were weeks of preparation. There was no need o banners, or fireworks, or transparencies, or any other of the appeals that savor of clap-trap and humbug. A single band of music was present in the Tabernacle, but it was not found necessary to draw a crowd by burning a speck of tar, by firing a big gun, nor by flashing out a ray from a Drummond light. The people came, and heard, and listened courteously, and went away pleased that they had been enabled to take part in a demonstration that was as full of spirit and purpose as an egg of meat.

The proceedings were opened in the Tabernacle at 8 o'clock P. M. HIRAM KETCHUM, Esq., called the meeting to order, and proposed

For President—THOMAS B. STILLMAN.

The nomination was ratified with great unanimity.

Mr. STILLMAN, on taking the Chair, said: I thank you, fellow-citizens, for the compliment you have paid me by elevating me to the position of Chairman of this meeting. I have only to claim your indulgent consideration for any imperfections of which I may be guilty while I occupy this Chair and preside over your deliberations.

Mr. ISAAC DAYTON then came forward, and read the following list of Vice-Presidents and Secretaries, who were elected by acclamation:

VICE-PRESIDENTS.

Ward.		Ward.	
1.	Joseph Jameson, Joseph A. Gardiner.	12.	Thomas Carnley, Geo. J. S. Thompson.
2.	Edward Pepper, Joseph Manning.	13.	Gilbert D. Smith, Sandy Higgins.
3.	Robert B. Coleman, Andrew Jordan.	14.	Sanford L. Macomber, Henry Senden.
4.	Benjamin Sherwood, Henry H. Hewlet.	15.	John J. Tyler, John H. Powers.
5.	John Morton, Noah Worral.	16.	Henry Ivison, Ashael A. Denman.
6.	Noah L. Farnham, Pierre C. Van Wyck.	17.	Benj. F. Pinckney, Hermann Raser.
7.	Joseph B. Close, Robert Murray.	18.	Henry Brewster, T. G. Churchill.
8.	Henry Daved, Jonathan W. Allen.	19.	John C. Hull, Enos Montrose.
9.	Daniel French, R. L. Jaques.	20.	Johnson S. Fountain. Henry Camp.
10.	Robert T. Halleck, Pine Hopsins.	21.	Richard Mott, John D. Sherwood
11.	William Gray, Daniel D. Wright.	22.	Lebbeus B. Ward, John Ives.

SECRETARIES.

Robert J. Reid,	David R. Jaques
Hooper C. Van Vorst,	Henry B. Kent,
Thomas Doyle,	Wm. H. Anthon,
John Griffin,	Orgie Marian,
John Silcocks.	

The Chair announced that Judge EMMETT (temporary Chairman of the National Republican Convention at Philadelphia) would report to the meeting the proceedings of the National Convention. [Loud cheers.]

JUDGE EMMETT'S SPEECH.

Judge EMMETT said that, as he was not in the programme, he should have to crave indulgence for any imperfections he might make in his report of the proceedings at Philadelphia. He had no materials for making any report, but he believed all had read and approved of the platform which was there adopted. [Great applause.] He had always had an opinion that political Conventions in this country were bad things, nor had his opinion changed with regard to Conventions got up by men in power for the purpose of perpetuating their rule. Such Conventions were generally so many frauds upon the popular will. But the Convention at Philadelphia was of entirely a different character. [Applause.] Every man who went there went for the purpose of uniting with his fellow-citizens in support of the same great, noble, glorious cause as that which has assembled us together on this occasion. [Applause.] He had never before seen a political gathering so respectable in point of character or numbers as that which had assembled at Philadelphia. That Convention had opened his eyes. It had convinced him that no man could hope to arrive at any correct conclusions with regard to the history of parties as they now exist in this country, without studying with great care the principles upon which the Republican movement is based. In the Convention at Philadelphia were assembled men of all political parties. There were Old-Line Democrats there, and old fashioned Jeffersonian Democrats they were, too—[applause,]—and there were Old-Line Whigs there, and men who had belonged to all the respectable parties of the country. He could give no idea of the concert of action which prevailed among the delegates to that Convention. Every man went prepossessed for his favorite candidate; but every man also went convinced that the only road to success was in concession and harmony. So strong was this spirit of concession, so complete the harmony which prevailed, that instead of spending a week in deliberation and discussion, as it was supposed would be necessary, the work was accomplished in two days, and the nominations which were made were ratified with the greatest unanimity and enthusiasm. [Applause.] The delegates from the different States vied with each other in preserving the harmony of the Convention. There was (continued Judge EMMETT) one name mentioned in connection with the Presidency which elicited shouts of enthusiasm. It was the name of a favorite son of New-York. [Great applause.] Allow me to name him. It was WILLIAM H. SEWARD. [Tremendous cheers.] And, fellow-citizens, it is safe to assert that, had not his name been withdrawn at an early stage of the proceedings of the Convention, he would have been nominated by acclamation as our candidate for President. [Renewed cheers.] Mr. SEWARD has been charged with being a demagogue. He has been charged with ambition. His public acts are a sufficient refutation of the calumny. In all that he has done, he has given evidence of the purest patriotism and a profound love of his country. He is ambitious, but it is the ambition which should actuate the conduct of every lover of Freedom. [Great applause.] That matter, then, being settled, fellow-citizens, how shall I describe to you the manner in which the name of JOHN C. FREMONT was received. [Reiterated cheers and immense enthusiasm—the shouts for FREMONT entirely drowning the speaker's voice and preventing him from proceeding for several minutes.]

A VOICE—Three cheers for FREMONT.

The cheers were given with a will, and three more.

Judge EMMETT (resuming)—The rush that was made for FREMONT the moment his name was mentioned was, and still is, a mystery to me. That a body of men, who were versed in all the intricacies of politics, should have taken up a man who had no political antecedents, was a strange circumstance. But it was for that very reason that JOHN C. FREMONT [cheers] was taken up. It was because he had no political antecedents whatever. [Cheers.] It was because he was the representative of Young America. [Tremendous cheers.] It was because it was believed that he was better qualified than any of the old politicians, by those very reasons to lead us on to victory. [Applause.] Any attempt to say one word against his nomination would have been useless. Any one who had uttered a word against him, might as well have attempted to stop the torrent of Niagara with a pitchfork. [Laughter.] But there was no disposition on the part of any one to oppose his nomination. [Applause.] He seemed to be the choice of the Convention by common acclaim, by common consent. It seemed to be the general feeling that FREMONT was the man for the hour.

A VOICE—He's wide awake! [Cheers and laughter.]

Judge EMMETT—(continuing)—I have, since I came back to New York, met one man who was very curious to know what JOHN C. FREMONT had ever done. [Laughter.] I didn't tell him what he *had* done—but there are some things he has *not* done. [Applause.] He had no hand in the repeal of the Missouri Compromise. [Great applause.] He had no hand in the passage of the Kansas-Nebraska bill. [Renewed applause.] I think that's enough, fellow-citizens, [laughter,] for his negative qualities.

A VOICE—He had no hand, either, in the Ostend Manifesto. [Laughter.]

Judge EMMETT—He had not. I thank my friend for that suggestion. I will tell you what he has done. He conquered California with sixty-two men. [Great applause.] He has starved himself to feed his poor fellows. [Applause.] He not only went through his share of fatigues, and privations and hardships which his party endured, but he took a double share. [Applause.] That is the kind of man JOHN C. FREMONT is. [Uproarious cheering.] Many of you, my fellow-citizens, have read FREMONT'S book. Did you find anything in his writings which would disqualify him for the office of President? [Cries of "No! No!"] There is another thing he did. He won the heart and hand of THOMAS H. BENTON'S daughter. [Great laughter and three cheers for Mrs. FREMONT.] I tell you that is no small feather in his cap, and that it is by no means a small item in the qualifications he possesses for being the President of the United States. [Cheers and laughter.] For I hold, in the first place, that no man who has not had the courage to marry a wife [laughter, and cries of "Three groans for BUCHANAN,"] has courage to fill a responsible office. Do you believe that the son-in-law of THOMAS H. BENTON is deficient in a knowledge of the political history of the country. ["No, No."] JOHN C. FREMONT has taken his degree already by his marriage. I venture to say that his family connection with THOMAS H. BENTON has given him an opportunity, which he has improved, to render himself one of the best-informed politicians in this country. And he is as fresh as a rose this moment before you. [Laughter and applause.] He is not a hackneyed politician. He is unshackled by party obligations. He is unbound to any clique, and he is qualified to administer the affairs of Government as they were administered in better times, and as we hope they will be administered in the future. [Great applause.] So much for FREMONT. As soon, however, as we had got over the difficulty about the President, the same difficulty,—perhaps a greater,—was experienced in making our choice for Vice-President. There were in the minds of the members of the Convention many men of shining mark and great ability, whom they would have gladly seen elevated to the office. Foremost among these was Mr. BANKS. [Tremendous cheering.] I confess, fellow citizens, that I was at first in favor of taking up Mr. BANKS as the most available man—I believed he would be available because he was the man who led us on in our first triumph over our foe. [Applause.] But we were informed that he preferred to remain where he was, and we considered that he had received already the reward of his exertions, and we concluded that we might as well turn elsewhere—and that was the feeling of a great many in the Convention. The next man who rose before my mind, and before the minds of many others, was CHARLES SUMNER——

[The announcement of Mr. SUMNER'S name was the signal for a burst of enthusiasm which could not have been one tittle heartier than it was; cheers were given again and again for SUMNER, with repeated groans for BROOKS.]

Judge EMMETT—And I may say in regard to Mr. SUMNER, that it was the wish of many persons that he should have been the candidate for Vice President. We believed that as "the blood of the martyrs is the seed of the church," so every drop of blood that was extracted from Mr. SUMNER by the ruffianly assault of BROOKS, [groans for BROOKS,] would have been the seal of our success. But Massachusetts wouldn't part with SUMNER. Her Delegates said "No, we mean to send him back to the Senate again." [Cheers.] We said "We will elect him to preside over the Senate." "No," they said, "He shall go back to the Senate by our instrumentality alone, and not in any other way." I recollect, fellow-citizens, that it is narrated in the history of the Jews, that upon a certain occasion, they cut in pieces the body of a maiden, of their nation, who had been violated and afterwards murdered, and sent these pieces through all the tribes of their race to incite them to revenge. So would we have done had CHARLES SUMNER been nominated at our Convention. The blood which flowed from the wounds inflicted by the blows of BROOKS we would have scattered over the whole land and have roused every freeman to action from the mere exhibition of the outrage. [Applause.] But it is better as it is. His blood has already gone broadcast over the land. BROOKS [renewed groans] has received his reward in the voice of public execration, and SUMNER has received his, not alone in the expressions of sympathy which the assault upon him has excited, but in the guaranty it gives us that his career will not be eclipsed in splendor by that of any other man in the country. [Applause.] One word in regard to BROOKS——

A VOICE—Don't let us hear anything about him.

Judge EMMETT—Let us look at the case dispassionately. I hold that it is perhaps right in some cases for a man to take the law into his own hands—at least I thought so in the early part of my life, however wiser I may be now—[laughter]—and that a man may, under certain circumstances and in a good cause, be excused for not awaiting the tardy action of the law. But I say that any man who may be placed in such a situation is bound in the first place to consider whether he can do what he intends to do like a gentleman, and not in a cowardly manner. [Applause.] I do not say that Mr. BROOKS is a coward——

SEVERAL VOICES—"I do!" "He is!"

Judge EMMETT—I by no means feel disposed to style him a coward. I believe that a brave man sometimes commits blunders, and falls into errors. But this I may say—that Mr. BROOKS has not been brought up in the school of true courage.

VOICES—"That's it!"

Judge EMMETT—I believe that if he had taken time to think before he committed the assault, he would never have committed the deed, without, at least, giving his victim notice beforehand, and would not have struck a blow which incapacitated his opponent at once. I know nothing of the code of honor as practiced at the South, but I believe that none of those gentlemen who have approved of the conduct of Mr. BROOKS would have been willing to take his place. They declare that he did right, and applaud him for this deed as they would probably have applauded had an assassin killed LOUIS NAPOLEON but they wouldn't have done it themselves. [Laughter.]

Judge EMMETT here gave way for a moment, while Judge EDMONDS came forward and announced the arrival of Hon. WM. A. HOWARD, Chairman of the Kansas Investigating Committee. The announcement was received with loud applause, and

Judge EMMETT resumed—Now, fellow-citizens, let me say that we closed our labors at Philadelphia by putting in nomination Mr. DAYTON, of New-Jersey, for Vice-President. [Applause.] Mr. DAYTON was comparatively unknown to the Convention. Nobody mentioned his name till SUMNER and BANKS had been withdrawn. But the moment his name was mentioned, it ran through the Convention like wildfire. It is needless for me to detain you longer. You know what we have done as well as I can tell you. You know our principles. You have read our platform. Do you approve of it?

[Loud shouts of "Yes, Yes," and three cheers.]

Judge EMMETT—In one respect our opponents will have the better of us. We are not as yet a political party. We are the great heart of the nation, if you please, rising up in our strength; but we lack the tactics that our enemies possess. There are some old soldiers in their ranks. [Laughter.] They go in for the spoils. That is all they think of. For them they strive and struggle. They say that we shall quarrel over the spoils, and that we cannot satisfy all. But we are easy in our minds on that score. [Laughter.] We are not like those old, hackneyed politicians who, while they keep one eye on the patronage of office, keep the other upon the spoils of office. They say one to another, as Sir John Falstaff said:

"Choose me the best office, good Justice Shallow."

And then:

"Rob me the Exchequer first,
And do it with unwashed hands."

I have no doubt that SHAKSPEARE had an eye to Democratic office-holders when he penned that passage. [Laughter.] Our opponents say we are sectional, that we are Abolitionists, that we seek to create disunion and dissension. We know that this is not true. We know that we are not seeking to create dissensions. We know that we are conservative. We know that we are the best friends of the South at this moment. [Cries of "That's it."] Gentlemen, it is charged that Abolitionism is a crime. It is a word of reproach which is used in this country against any man who is supposed to be at all affected by a feeling of opposition to Slavery. It does no man any harm to examine himself on this subject of the abolition of Slavery. [Applause.] It is one of those things in which, if we are too careful not to inoculate ourselves, it will, as a distinguished delegate remarked at the Convention in Philadelphia, break out all over in the natural way [laughter,] and it is one of those things which we should never be afraid to look in the face, or to express our opinion upon. Applause.] I am not in favor of meddling with the institutions of the South where they now exist, where they are protected by the laws of the State, and where they form a portion of the social customs; [Cries of "That's the talk,] but, I think that the time will come when Slavery will cease to exist in this country; and I fervently and sincerely hope that that time is not far distant. [Cries of "So do we."] I believe that that time will come. I believe that there is an active principle now in operation which will carry that purpose into effect. A great duty is laid upon our shoulders; we owe the fulfilment of it to ourselves; we owe it to our country; we owe it to our posterity;—and if we are faithful to the trust reposed in us, our posterity will bless us yet, for the efforts we are making for its accomplishment. [Great applause.]

SPEECH OF THE CHAIRMAN OF THE KANSAS INVESTIGATING COMMITTEE.

WM. A. HOWARD was introduced amid vehement cheers. He said: When the Committee that I had the honor to be a member of, undertook the difficult and arduous duties assigned to them, of investigating the affairs, as far as they could, of Kansas, we decided that it was proper for us to pursue those investigations with as little prejudice as possible, and with all possible thoroughness and fairness, ["Hear, Hear," cheers, and cries of "Good"]—without favor or fear of any man or any men, and we found it necessary sometimes to act without reference to fear for ourselves. [Laughter and applause.] In order to discharge these most delicate, most important, and most difficult duties, we laid it down as a fundamental rule of conduct, that we would take no part in any public demonstration, that we would in no public manner express any views or any opinions with reference to any of these subjects, until we had closed our labors and put our seal to the record, as by it we were willing to live and die, and stand by it in despite of everything. [Loud cheers and cries of "Good."] We have steadily adhered to this purpose. Every one of us—at least, myself and my colleague, Mr. SHERWOOD, who constitute the majority of the Committee, [laughter and applause.] have steadily adhered to this rule, and acted upon this purpose; and I propose to do so to-night. We have some three or four days more labor to perform to close up this business, and until that is done you must hear no voice from me with regard to any of these matters about which there can be any difference of opinion among our fellow-citizens. [Cheers and cries of "Good."] But I confess that when I came in here and saw this "sea of upturned faces," although I never was an orator—never a man that could speak with much vehemence—[laughter]—yet, being a Western man, I have a soul in me—A VOICE—["And a backbone, too."]—and I confess I felt it was as much as I could do to hold back, for I found myself pulling off my overcoat before I really knew where I was. [Laughter and cheers.] But I am all right now. I cannot talk to you about Kansas affairs. I would like to address you on other subjects, but I have no strength. [Cries of "Go on."] No. I cannot go on. I lay on my back eight days at Detroit under the care of the doctor, in order to get to Washington, and the health thus restored I will not waste on you, I assure you. [Laughter and cheers.] I am here simply to make my apology, and to tender you my thanks for this cordial greeting. If we deserve anything it is well. If we don't deserve anything, we don't ask anything. We simply aimed to do our duty under all possible circumstances. If we succeed, we shall be glad of it. If not, it is too late to alter it now. But I may say this with regard to Kansas without entering on any discussion, or any question in discussion. I had read those accounts of outrages, of frauds, of invasions and violence. Many of them seemed to me like romance—like dreams. I thought, perchance, that the newspapers sometimes might have made glowing articles out of very common events. Previous to going there we took especial pains to provide ourselves with all the accounts of the sort that had ever been published. We got papers of different political views; we got files of them, cut them up, and made scrap-books of of them in order that we might get every yarn that had ever been told about anything in Kansas. [Cheers.] We proceeded with our investigation, and with these lights and in this way, we pursued our course. All I have to say about it now is, that instead of a dreamy romance that might be partly true and partly false, those things away in the distance, that may have been thought to concern me but little, and perhaps accounted nothing to anybody else, became to me a most fearful, living reality—[loud cheers]—terrible in its far-reaching consequences, and cutting the heart and so warming the blood that I can hardly contemplate it. But enough. This is no longer a romance to me. It is, as I have said, a reality—a reality very near and very present. But I have no more to say about it. I thank you again, fellow-citizens, for your cordial greeting, and I trust you will see the propriety of my excusing myself from entering into further details. Mr. HOWARD retired amid loud cheers.

THE RESOLUTIONS.

Judge EDMONDS then presented, amid enthusiastic cheering, again and again renewed, the following resolutions.

Resolved, That we accept the platform and the candidates of the Republican National Convention recently convened at Philadelphia, and will give them our cordial and earnest support, in the confident expectation that, through their instrumentality, peace and harmony will be restored to our people; the true principles of Freedom will be diffused abroad over the whole land, and the spirit of Proscription and Intolerance in every form will be effectually expelled from among us.

Resolved, That in common with the lovers of Liberty throughout the world, we have for years looked forward with anxious hope for the time when the avowal that "all men are by nature endowed with the inalienable right to life, liberty and the pursuit of happiness," should become a living reality to all the people; and supported by this hope—once strong, but daily growing weaker—we have submitted, at different periods of our national existence, to various measures, which were revolting alike to our love of Freedom and our sense of justice, but which promised a final and a happy end. At length, submission to such measures has ceased to be a duty, for that submission has but tended to the spread of Slavery, with all its swelling evils to the white man, and to the creation of a spirit of intolerance which has disturbed the public peace, been the cause of bloodshed, and invaded that freedom of thought and action which we have been fain to regard as the dearest birthright of every man among us.

Resolved, That the principle which lies at the foundation of the Pro-Slavery interest is, and must of necessity be, aggressive. We have therefore beheld it increasing largely the number whom it holds in bondage—violating and overthrowing the most solemn compromises—leading our public men to an unhappy but easy disregard of the most sacred pledges—threatening civil war—and converting even the seat of our Government into a scene of ruthless and violent invasion of the freedom of the press and of debate.

Resolved, That the manner in which a line of conduct so offensive has been welcomed and sustained throughout the whole slaveholding portion of the country, admonishes us that we have little more to hope from their forbearance; and that in ourselves alone are we to find any protection against the continued aggressions of a spirit which marks its progress with violence, and must attain its end in an intolerable bondage.

Resolved, Therefore, that we accept the issue between thraldom and Freedom thus forced upon us, and in accepting it we will not be unmindful of the spirit which once before prompted our people to pledge in the cause of Freedom life, fortune and sacred honor; nor that they who are thus warring upon us are our brothers still, heirs of the self-same heritage of Freedom with us, and members with us of the same national family. And while we pledge to the cause now first presented in distinct and palpable form before the country, our most earnest efforts, we do so with an abiding hope that we shall thus secure, in the end, harmony and happiness to all.

The Chairman then announced that the rallying song, copies of which had been distributed through the assemblage, would be sung to the music of the band, the audience joining in the chorus.

Several voices interrupted the presiding officer by demanding that the question be taken on the resolutions.

ANOTHER VOICE—Certainly, we will sing better after it. [Laughter.]

The question on the resolutions was then put and carried by an overwhelming "Aye!"

A gentleman then rose and led the meeting in singing the following verses:

RALLYING SONG.

TUNE—*The Marseilles Hymn.*

Behold! the furious storm is rolling,
Which Border-Fiends, confederates, raise.
The Dogs of War, let loose, are howling,
And lo! our infant cities blaze.
And shall we calmly view the ruin,
While lawless force with giant stride
Spreads desolation far and wide,
In guiltless blood his hands imbruing?
Arise, Arise, ye brave!
And let our war-cry be
Free Speech, Free Press, Free Soil, Free Men,
FRE-MONT and VICTORY!

Oh, Liberty! can he resign thee
Who once has felt thy generous flame?
Can threats subdue, or bolts confine thee—
Or whips thy noble spirit tame?
No! by the heavens bright bending o'er us!
We've called our Captain to the van—
Behold the hour—Behold the man!
Oh, wise and valiant, go before us!
Then let the shout again
Ring out from sea to sea,
Free Speech, Free Press, Free Soil, Free Men,
FRE-MONT and VICTORY!

Hurrah, Hurrah! from hill and valley,
Hurrah from prairie wide and free!
Around our glorious Chieftain rally.
For KANSAS, and for LIBERTY!
Let him who first her wilds exploring,
Her virgin beauty gave to fame,
Now save her from the curse and shame
Which Slavery o'er her soil is pouring.
Our Standard Bearer then
The brave Path-finder be!
Free Speech, Free Press, Free Soil, Free Men,
FRE-MONT and VICTORY!

The effect with which the vast mass of persons present joined in the chorus was indescribable. The audience wrought itself up into a perfect furore, and as the last sounds of the concluding stanza died away in a volume of sound the echoes of which made the very building shake, the whole assemblage rose to their feet *en masse*, and joined in a burst of cheering again and again renewed, amid waving of hats, handkerchiefs, and frantic demonstrations of delight.

SPEECH OF SENATOR TRUMBULL.

Senator TRUMBULL, of Illinois, was introduced by Judge EDMONDS as the colleague of Mr. DOUGLAS. He was received with vociferous cheers, followed by three groans for DOUGLAS. He said:

FELLOW CITIZENS: Coming as I do from what, a few years ago was the far distant West, where a great portion of my life has been passed, I should feel some hesitation in appearing before an audience in this the Commercial Metropolis of the Union and of the Western Continent, did I not know that you were all lovers of the same Constitution, and friends of the same Union, that we love and cherish in the distant prairies of Illinois. [Loud cheers.] It does my heart good to look round and over this vast assembly. I feel not unlike the inhabitants of Judea, when its shepherds of old went forth proclaiming glad tidings of great joy as they saw the star in the East. [Cries of "Good," and cheers.] It was a token to them of liberty—eternal liberty beyond the grave. [Loud applause.] This meeting is a token—a harbinger of that liberty which I trust will be perpetual in America. The questions at issue, at this time, before the people of the United States, are questions involving your liberty and mine. There is no use in disguising the real question at issue in this contest. And it is only necessary that that question should be understood, and we shall have a unanimous vote almost throughout the country, in the South as well as in the North. [Loud cheers.] For I tell you that it is by a misrepresentation of the sentiment of the North, by falsifying the principles of those who oppose the spread of Slavery, that the South has been roused and united together, and banded in a sectional party as one man against the North. It is because this body which has falsely arrogated to itself the name of Democracy—[hisses]—by assuming a name to which they have no title, by pretending to advocate principles which they daily trample in the dust, that the great masses of the people of this Union are sought to be misled. [Cheers.] I have no appeal, gentlemen, to make to your passions or your prejudices. I am one of those who believe that the heart of the great mass of people of this country, North and South, is sound when they properly understand the questions at issue. [Cheers.] I believe they are loyal to the Union and to the Constitution under which we live. [Renewed cheers.] But I believe there is a vast deal of misapprehension abroad. I believe that a party is now banded together in the country, inscribing on its banners principles, which, if not suppressed, will be destructive to the liberties of the country; and I wish, in the remarks which I shall make this evening, to appeal to the judgment and the candor of every impartial man who listens to me while I endeavor to unmask the hypocrisy of this party, which I say has thus falsely assumed the name of Democracy and ought never to be called by that name. [Cries of "Good" and cheers.] I, fellow-citizens, belong to that good old Democratic Party which believed in liberty of speech in protecting the rights of the people, in carrying on the Government under the Constitution as our fathers made and understood it. That Democracy I loved and cherished, and I was proud to be a member of it. [Cheers.] But not of that present party which has assumed the name—and to which I object—and for one I shall never call it by that name. I know there is something in a name. There is a poetry about it, and many persons have been misled by it, and I am sorry to see in our papers that the men now banded together to extend Slavery, to trample in the dust the most sacred guarantees of Freedom in our Constitution—I say I am amazed that any one understanding the question should ever apply to such a party, who are now showing themselves to be, instead of Democrats, tyrants and oppressors, the name of Democrats! [Loud cheers.] Now, I wish to treat them fairly, and let us inquire, first, what their views are. Have they put forward in their platform—do their leading men put forward in their speeches—Democratic principles? [Cheers and cries of "No."] Now, was it a part of the old Democratic creed that the Government should be economically or extravagantly administered? Which? [A voice—economically.] Well, this pretended Democratic Administration is expending more money every year, than any administration ever expended before, even in time of war. [Cries of "Good."] You are now in a time of profound peace, taxed more than seventy millions of dollars for these office-holders to fatten upon and carry the elections. Yes, to carry the elections; and that is the way that this poison is scattered over the land. It is by means of the money taken from your pocket and mine. For, you need not believe that these fat office-holders are not required to contribute from their earnings for the propagation of the falsehoods which are spread over the land. [Cheers and cries of that's a fact.] Well, again, what is the great principle that binds that party together? [A VOICE—Public plunder.] Public plunder some one says. I think so too. For we saw a few days ago a distinguished Whig gentleman, who had been a Whig all his life, and one of the most eloquent men in this land or any other, come out in the United States Senate and avow his adhesion to what he called the Democratic party, and he said that in doing so it required no change in principle or doctrine. And when he made the announcement, no sooner had he taken his seat, than the grand high priests of this party, arrogating that name, General CASS and Judge DOUGLAS, walked up and congratulated him, [cheers, laughter and hisses] and the next time we hear from the distinguished Senator from Louisiana (Mr. BENJAMIN) is (and this occurred only a few weeks ago) in the Cincinnati Convention making a President for the Democracy. Now, I'll tell you what I think of this party. I wanted for a long time some name to apply to it, and to get rid of further explanation, and by your permission, I intend christening it to-night. [Shouts of "Good," and "Go ahead."] You all know that there is an animal remarkable for the burdens it can bear—an animal that submits to draw heavy loads and grievous burdens, but that is little cared for by its master; for, when they have no longer any use for it, they turn it aside on a poor pasture to starve and to die—I believe they call it the ass. [Laughter, and a VOICE—"The jackass."] Don't mistake me. I am not going to call this party jackasses at all; but, by a slight transposition of the word Kansas, (for that is the origin of the party,) for any man who swears fealty to the Kansas bill, no matter whether he may have been a Whig or an Abolitionist, or what not, all his life, so as he goes for the Kansas bill, or the principles of the Kansas bill, he is a good enough Democrat at once. Well, then, by a slight transposition of the letters that spell the word Kansas, you can make Nak-ass. I therefore shall, during my remarks this evening—so as to save explanation every time I have to speak of the party—use the terms Nak-ass and Nak-asses. [Laughter.] What, let me ask, are the principles of this Kansas bill? Let me treat the author of that bill fairly. And I ask you, as I state now what he states to be the principles of it in the Northern States, if I do not state it fairly? He says it involves the principle of self-government, and he appeals to the people of the North in its favor. I know he does it in the State of Illinois, and I presume he does it here. He tells them that the Kansas bill simply leaves to the people of the Territory the right to regulate their own affairs in their own way; and isn't that right? He says that that is what the Kansas bill does. And he asks the question: "Now, if Slavery is an evil, and the people of Kansas want Slavery, ought they not to have it; and if they don't want it ought they not to exclude it? And are not they the proper judges, and what do you want to interfere with it for? Why can't you let the people manage that themselves in Kansas?" Now, haven't I stated it fairly? That is a powerful argument, gentlemen. The only difficulty with that position is, that there is not a word of truth in it. [Laughter.] Let me tell you what is in that bill. Why, it says in so many words, it being the true intent and meaning of this bill not to legislate Slavery into any State or Territory—(they stick in State so as to confuse a little)—if they exclude it therefrom, but to leave the people thereof perfectly free to regulate their own domestic affairs in their own way, subject to the Constitution of the United States. That is what is in the bill. Now, is that true? ["No."] Leave the people perfectly free to regulate their own domestic affairs in their own way! Now isn't it a part of the domestic affairs of the people in Kansas to choose their own Governor? Do n't you think it a part of your domestic affairs in New-York to choose your own Governor? [Cries of "Yes."] Well, you cannot do it if you go to Kansas, for the President of the United States appoints him. Why, fellow-citizens, when that bill was pending, this little stump speech, as Col. BENTON called it, which was thrust into the belly of the bill, was put in for no such purpose as Mr. DOUGLAS says; it was put in to be used at the four corners for electioneering purposes. There were men in Congress who saw that; and they thought they would test the sincerity of the framers of the bill. They accordingly proposed, as an amendment, that the people of Kansas,—you, when you go there, or your brothers, or your fathers, or your friends,—should have the right to elect their own governors. Who do you suppose voted for it? I'll tell you who did not vote for it. Every man who voted for the Kansas-Nebraska bill voted against it, and voted it down, except General SHIELDS, from my own State. And yet these men had the face to get up before the people of the North, and tell them, "Why, let the people of Kansas manage their own affairs as they please; what do you want to interfere with them for?" at the same time they would not let them elect their own Governor. Why, gentlemen, it is not only their Governor. It is just so with their judges. Even the clerk of a court cannot be appointed by the people of Kansas: for the President of the United States appoints the Judge and the Judge appoints the Clerk. The people cannot elect a Sheriff to perform any duties except to wait upon the Probate Courts and Justices of the Peace. I know they have got some bogus sheriffs there; but the Marshals, by act of Congress, perform all those duties. You see that is not what they intended by the bill. "Ah! but we did intend this," they say, "we intended to let the people of Kansas regulate the subject of Slavery for themselves." Did they? Was that your intention? Was that your intention when, in order to get at it, you trampled under foot a Compromise which was made nearly 40 years ago? Do you violate that? Yes. And the very author of the Kansas-Nebraska bill, but a few years ago, in speaking of the Missouri Compromise, said it had an origin akin to the Constitution, and that no hand had ever yet been found ruthless enough to attempt to destroy it. [Cheers.] His was the ruthless hand that was stretched forward to drag it under foot. [Terrific groans.] And he says now, to the people of the North, that the people of the Territory shall have the right to regulate the subject of Slavery for themselves. Well, I tell you he dare not say that in presence of the Southern Senators, on the floor of the Senate. I say he dare not say it there. Why, I tried him the other day. I asked him the question, and put it to him time and again. "Sir, do you mean to say, that under the Kansas-Nebraska bill, the people of Kansas have the right, through their Territorial Legislature, to exclude Slavery while it is a Territory?" What do you think he answered? Why, he went to bobbing around, and bobbing around. [Laughter.] And where do you suppose he brought up? Why, he brought up in the Supreme Court room, and said it was a judicial question. [Laughter and applause.] A judicial question? I then put it to him, for I did not mean to let him shrink—What did you put this in your bill for? Why did you say that the people of the Territory have the right to regulate their domestic institutions in their own way, if your bill did not mean it? Why did you not come out and state what it meant? Why was that put in? To that I got no answer. And yet, but a short time before, he had been proclaiming it aloud that he belonged to a National party, a party that advocated the same principles North that they did in the South, the same East that they did in the West—that knew no North or South, no East or West. But when you came to test him in the presence of the North and the South, the East and the West, he was as dumb as the man that never spoke. [Loud cheers.] Now, what *is* meant by that? I'll tell you how I understand it. In that same speech, which was made about four months ago, (and, no doubt, you have all read it,) he said the reason that I could not understand the Nebraska bill was that I was not a Democrat; all Democrats understood it alike. [Laughter.] Well, I brought some witnesses up, as I was not a very good Democrat in his opinion. I called up old Gen. CASS, who had said in his speech, a few days before, that the people in the Territory had a right, through their Territorial Legislature, to exclude Slavery at any time. He believes, you know, in popular sovereignty. That was a pretty good witness, I thought, at that time. Then I called to the witness stand Senator BROWNE, of Mississippi, and he said that the Kansas or Nebraska bill meant to confer upon the people of the Territory the right, when they formed a State Constitution, to have Slavery or not, as they liked. [Loud laughter.] Why, it is absurd, he says. How can that be? How did they get the power? We all contend, and that now is the doctrine of my colleagues, we all contend that Congress has no right to legislate on the subject of Slavery, and how, in the name of God, can Congress give to the Territory what it has not got? He looked upon it as an absurdity, and he stood between the two Democrats crosswise. [Laughter.] Now, he says, both of us have agreed to submit it to the court for decision. Did you ever hear of the case of a jury who, being sent to their rooms to decide on their verdict, and on being called back and asked if they had agreed, said "Yes," whereupon the clerk read the verdict: "We, the Jury, agree to disagree," while the Court reprimanded them and sent them back. I think it would be well to reprimand these gentlemen and send them home to reconsider the matter. [Cheers.] That is the great principle of the Nebraska bill. Why, he no more dare to make that Northern Speech in a Southern State, at any rate not before the Cincinnati Convention, than he would cut off his fingers. But again, how is that bill understood? What is the other principle in it? Why the South contends, and they are unanimous in that, that upon the idea of an equality in the rights of the States, a slaveholder has a right to migrate to any of the Territories, take his slaves with him and hold them as slaves so long as the Territory lasts. And they put it in this form: The Territories are the common property of the people of the Union. All have a right to go there alike, and it is unjust to the people of the Southern States not to allow them to take their property there, and hold it there as they hold it at home. I think that is fairly stating the position. I tried also to shake my colleague out of that hole, [laughter] but he took refuge again in the Supreme Court room; he did not want to prejudice the question when it came before the Supreme Court, and therefore he wouldn't give his opinion. [Applause.] Now that is the doctrine contended for. Look at its consequences. It takes Slavery not only into Kansas and Nebraska, but if the doctrine be true, it takes Slavery into every Territory—into Oregon and Minnesota as well as Kansas and Nebraska, because it argues upon that on the ground of equality of rights in the States. Then if you have a right to go into the Territories with your slaves, if you can go into one you can go into another; and this allows not only the right to take slaves into the Territories but also into the States, and the Southern citizen has just as much right to come to the City of New-York with his company of slaves, and hold them as slaves in your midst in spite of you, as he has to take them into Kansas. Now, I defy any man to find in the Constitution of the country any clause relating to equality of rights that does not apply as much to emigration from State to State as from State to Territory. But the truth is, he can take them into neither, and a moment's reflection will satisfy any of you of that fact. When an individual emigrates to another country or to a Territory, what does he take with him? Does he take the laws that he lived under at home with him? If he does, you will have as many laws in the Territory of the United States as there were tongues spoken in Babel. If every man were to do that, any person going to the Territories from New-York might bring your local ordinances with him; but you would think it rather strange to be punished out in Kansas for driving a dray without a license. [Laughter.] They have just as much right to enforce the license laws of the City of New-York in the Territory of Kansas, as they have to enforce the laws of the State of South Carolina there. [Cheers.] When you go into a Territory you go there to submit to the municipal laws there in force. If there was a law there in force establishing Slavery, of course you could take a slave there and hold him. But if there is no law on the subject of Slavery, why, it is a matter of course that the slave is free the moment he passes the boundary. [Applause.] It must be so, unless Slavery is the normal condition of man. [Laughter and cheers.] And they have just as much right to hold a white man a slave in Kansas as they have to hold a black man in the same condition. There is nothing in the nature of the skin. It is only because of the municipal regulation—because the men that hold slaves in the Sethern States—

[A VOICE—"There are white slaves there." Another Voice—"Plenty of them."]

Well, they will have a great many white slaves in the North if they are permitted to go on. [Cheers and cries of "that is true"] And that is the attempt now. It is not so much in reference to the welfare of the negro that we are here, but it is for the protection of the rights of the laboring whites, [cheers,] for the protection of ourselves and our liberties. And I protest against this Slavery propagandism, which, if it can take Slavery into the Territories, will then take it in to all the States of the Union.

[Here a person in the gallery got into a brawl with some of the audience in his vicinity, and kicked up a row, which for a short time interrupted the speaker's remarks. When quiet was at length restored, he resumed:]

And you need not tell me, fellow-citizens, that Slavery won't come into the North. I know it is a popular argument that Slavery can only exist where cotton and rice grow. That is a fallacy. It is not so at all. The products of Missouri do not differ from those of Illinois. The products of Maryland do not differ from those of Indiana. Slavery can just as well exist in Iowa or in Illinois to-day as it can in Kentucky or Maryland. I will tell you how Slavery came to be abolished in the Northern States. It was not because of its unprofitableness, but because of the principle of liberty which pervaded the North.—[loud cheers.] that principle of liberty which pervaded your fathers and mine, when they marched to the battles of the Revolution. They freed their slaves in the North, and emancipation was then popular. JEFFERSON was for it. All the early fathers of the Republic were for it. [A VOICE—"And WASHINGTON was for it."] And WASHINGTON, certainly. But a change has come over the spirit of the South. Slavery, which was then receding and being wiped out, because of the spirit of Liberty which was breaking brightly all over the land, has now become aggressive, and at this day an attempt is made to spread its black flag all over the Free Territories of the West. Next it will be over the Free States of the North. [Cheers and cries of "Never!"] Now, are you prepared for this? [Cries of "No, no."] How do they meet us? Why, they say you men who are opposed to the spread of Slavery are opposed to Free Government. I have already answered that. I have shown it is a humbug in the Kansas bill. What next? Why, they say we are Abolitionists. Well, that is just as false as their assertion that they are the friends of the Constitution and the true Democracy—just as false! When you look over the platform of the party which has just nominated Col FREMONT [loud cheers] you will find no such thing there. They emphatically pronounce against disunion. They declare that the union of these States must and shall be preserved—Oh! but I've heard it said, why you Republicans would repeal the Fugitive Slave law! You would abolish Slavery in the District of Columbia! You would incite the Slaves to insurrection, and set them to murder their masters. All this is in the imagination of the South—or it is not in their imagination, it is their invention. They know it is untrue. It is not found in the doctrines of the Philadelphia Convention. The principles of the Pphiladelphia Conaention are the principles of our fathers. And that those great forthers of ours, the framers of our Constitution, the authors of the Declaration of Independence, who proclaimed that their object was thorough union, perfect harmony, and the extension and preservation of the blessings of liberty to all this land; suppose that they were assembled here to-night, suppose that they were called upon as you were called upon, in 1854, to extend the territorial limits of this country, do you think they would have consented that Slavery should go into the new Territory? They would have done no such thing. It would belie their own history. Now let me put a question to you, as honest, temperate and candid men. If there was not a slave to-day in the United States, would you allow a slave to be introduced into the country? Would you allow Slavery to be planted here for the first time? [Loud cries of "No," from the entire meeting.] Then, for this is nearly the same thing, will you allow slaves to be freshly introduced into new territoty? Into a Territory almost as large as the thirteen original States? Into a Territory in which you are now laying the foundations of government? Will you allow Slavery to be introduced there? [Loud, redoubled shouts of "No, no."] Then, if that be your sentiment, you are for the platform enunciated at Philadelphia—for that is just what we said at that Convention.

The speaker said, he thought *Nakass* was a fitting name for the Democratic Party, for they do place heavy burdens on the people. Look, for instance, at the White House. There is an old ass there, who, now that they have no further use for him, they are about to turn into a meagre pasture, there to starve and die. But, meagre as is that pasture, there's food and space there for FILLMORE. [Laughter, cheers, and cries of "Yes, that's so.] There is one old ass in my own State, whom we will soon contrive to let down into that pasture. You all know who that is.

The speaker proceeded for some time in this strain, and presently said he would put to the meeting one definite question. Are you for the extension of Slavery? [Shouts of "No, no, no"—half the meeting rising to vociferate.] Because if you are, I tell you to vote for JAMES BUCHANAN—for he is pledged to extend Slavery, not only into the new Territories, but as a natural consequence into all the Free States.

The speaker again reverted to the present deplorable condition of affairs in Kansas; to the perpetual violation of all law and order there—and said that Slavery would be fastened on Kansas, unless the entire Free North aroused in their might and put it down. He did not wish to wrong the South—he did not object to the Fugitive Slave Law. He thought the South was entitled to it. [Shouts of "No, no;" hisses, cries of "Chair, chair—question, question."] But he would not take his oath to assist when called upon to catch a runaway negro. [Loud cheers.] Which was the only way to escape from that alternative? [Cries of "Elect FREMONT."] Yes, you have pointed out the way—you must, you will elect FREMONT. He then alluded to Mr. BUCHANAN, and to the position he occupied as a statesman. One great peculiarity of that gentleman was dullness of apprehension. Why, he could not understand the British Minister when he was Ambassador to England, and they proposed three times to arbitrate the Central American question. Lord CLARENDON spoke as plainly as a man could speak when in conversation with Mr. B. he submitted the question of arbitration. Mr. BUCHANAN did not understand that. And when afterwards they spoke to him about it at Washingeon, he replied, "Yes, he did recollect they said something about arbitration—but why didn't Lord CLARENDON propose to arbitrate in writing?" [Laughter.] Now, if any two private citizens have a dispute, and one says to the other, we will refer our difficulty to a mutual friend, is not that as intelligible a proposition to arbitrate as if he had written it, sealed it, and given it to the party he disputed with? After some further remarks, Judge TRUMBULL referred to the fillibustering designs of the present Administration on Cuba. The United States must have Cuba; it was only fair to buy it; so they proposed to buy it. But what if Spain were not willing to sell it? Well, then, they must have it any how. Oh! this is just another thing, that we can elucidate by the private life of each of us. Suppose I am to-night short of funds, and I walk home with any of you, and I propose to buy the contents of your pocket-book for ten dollars, and you reply: I have a great deal more in my pocket-book; I cannot afford to sell it you at that price. Well, I say, I must have it any how, I must take it from you. That is just the language our filibustering Government is using towards Spain. Are these the principles that ought to actuate a great people? Let us rather act on that fine saying of JACKSON'S, "Ask nothing but what is right, and submit to nothing that is wrong. [Loud applause.]

Whenever, continued the speaker, the doctrine of injustice shall prevail, the days of this Republic are drawing to an end, for the great God will not allow imposture and aggression long to prevail. In a just war we are invincible against the combined powers of the world; but in an unjust cause, he trusted in God that we were weak, indeed!

The speaker then proceeded to eulogize FREMONT, who was only in the vigor of his life. It had been tauntingly said of him, that he was but an engineer. But fifty years ago, that was also sneeringly said of a certain little corporal who, a few years afterwards, carried the banners of France triumphantly through nearly every country of Europe. So do I trust that our "engineer" will carry and wave aloft the banner of Liberty through every State of this Union. [Loud and continued cheering as the speaker retired to his seat.]

Cries for WILSON followed, and it was sometime before the Chairman was able to announce that he was not in the house.

The next speaker introduced to the meeting was FRANCIS B. KIMBALL, (Attorney-General from Ohio.) He said that he would not have appeared before the meeting at that late hour, if his design had been merely to make a speech. But he deemed that Ohio should mingle her voice in this great assembly. He was there to speak for Ohio, who had proved her devotion to the cause of liberty in the election of SALMON P. CHASE. There was no fear that Ohio would fall back in the great contest now im-

[*Continued on Eighth Page.*]

New-York Daily Times.

VOL. VI......NO. 1705. NEW-YORK, SATURDAY, MARCH 7, 1857. PRICE TWO CENTS.

LATEST INTELLIGENCE.

By Telegraph to the New-York Daily Times.

Magnetic Telegraph Co.'s Offices—4 Hanover-st., and 181 Broadway.

IMPORTANT FROM WASHINGTON.

Decision of the Supreme Court in the Dred Scott Case.

The Ordinance of 1787 and the Missouri Compromise Declared Unconstitutional.

MR. BUCHANAN'S CABINET.

WASHINGTON, Friday, March 6.

The opinion of the Supreme Court in the DRED SCOTT case was delivered by Chief Justice TANEY. It was a full and elaborate statement of the views of the Court. They have decided the following important points:

First—Negroes, whether slaves or free, that is, men of the African race, are not citizens of the United States by the Constitution.

Second—The Ordinance of 1787 had no independent constitutional force or legal effect subsequently to the adoption of the Constitution, and could not operate of itself to confer freedom or citizenship within the Northwest Territory on negroes not citizens by the Constitution.

Third—The provisions of the Act of 1820, commonly called the Missouri Compromise, in so far as it undertook to exclude negro slavery from, and communicate freedom and citizenship to, negroes in the northern part of the Louisiana cession, was a Legislative act exceeding the powers of Congress, and void, and of no legal effect to that end.

In deciding these main points, the Supreme Court determined the following incidental points:

First—The expression "territory and other property" of the Union, in the Constitution, applies "in terms" only to such territory as the Union possessed at the time of the adoption of the Constitution.

Second—The rights of citizens of the United States emigrating into any Federal territory, and the power of the Federal Government there depend on the general provisions of the Constitution, which defines in this, as in all other respects, the powers of Congress.

Third—As Congress does not possess power itself to make enactments relative to the persons or property of citizens of the United States, in a Federal Territory, other than such as the Constitution confers, so it cannot constitutionally delegate any such powers to a Territorial Government, organized by it under the Constitution.

Fourth—The legal condition of a slave in the State of Missouri is not affected by the temporary sojourn of such slave in any other State, but on his return his condition still depends on the laws of Missouri.

As the plaintiff was not a citizen of Missouri, he, therefore, could not sue in the Courts of the United States. The suit must be dismissed for want of jurisdiction.

The delivery of this opinion occupied about three hours, and was listened to with profound attention by a crowded Court-room. Among the auditors were gentlemen of eminent legal ability, and a due proportion of ladies.

Judge NELSON stated the merits of the case. The question was whether or not the removal of SCOTT from Missouri with his master to Illinois, with a view to temporary residence there, worked his emancipation. He maintained that the question depended wholly on the law of Missouri, and for that reason the judgment of the Court below should be affirmed.

Judge CATRON believed the Supreme Court has jurisdiction to decide the merits of the case. He argued that Congress could not do directly what it could not do indirectly. If it could exclude one species of property, it could exclude another. With regard to the Territories ceded, Congress could govern them only with the restrictions of the States which ceded them; and the Missouri act of 1820 violated the leading features of the Constitution, and was therefore void. He concurred with his brother Judges, that SCOTT is a slave, and was so when this suit was brought.

Several other Judges are to deliver their views to-morrow.

The following is Mr. BUCHANAN'S Cabinet, as confirmed by the Senate to-day:

Secretary of State—General CASS.
Secretary of the Treasury—Hon. HOWELL COBB.
Secretary of War—Hon. JOHN B. FLOYD.
Secretary of the Navy—Hon. ISAAC TOUCEY.
Secretary of the Interior—Hon. JACOB THOMPSON.
Attorney-General—Judge BLACK, of Pennsylvania.
Postmaster-General—Hon. A. V. BROWN.

Captain PETTIGREW, of the U. S. Army, is dead.

Extra Session of the United States Senate.

WASHINGTON, Friday, March 6.

Mr. SEWARD presented the petition of certain British subjects, setting forth that as Lord PALMERSTON'S act in surrendering the maritime rights of that Government is an act of high treason, those rights will revert to the British crown and nation as soon as the guilty party shall be impeached for that crime: that the petitioners have heard that the President of the United States is about proposing the terms on which the declaration of Paris will be agreed to by the United States; that such an act would be a connivance with Lord PALMERSTON in his attempt to possess himself of an arbitrary power foreign to the British Constitution and to the Constitution of the United States; and pray Congress to refuse their sanction to any convention with Great Britain founded on the illegal, treasonable and invalid declaration at Paris.

On motion of Mr. SEWARD the petition was laid on the table.

Mr. BIGLER presented the protest of forty-four members of the House of Representatives, and the protest of fifteen members of the Senate of Pennsylvania, against the proceedings under which Mr. SIMON CAMERON claims to represent that State in the Senate.

Mr. YULEE presented the credentials of Mr. MALLORY, elected Senator from Florida for six years from the 4th of March.

Mr. MASON was appointed to fill the vacancy in the Board of Regents of the Smithsonian Institution.

The Senate then went into Executive session, and afterwards adjourned till Monday.

The Inauguration Pageant—The Inaugural Address—Mr. Buchanan's Policy, &c.

Correspondence of the New-York Daily Times.

WASHINGTON, Thursday, March 5, 1857.

The event to which so many anxious thoughts were directed, and which, since November last, has engrossed so much attention, belongs now to history. At noon yesterday the Executive Administration of the Government passed quietly from the hands of FRANKLIN PIERCE into those of JAMES BUCHANAN, and the latter is now established as President at the White House. The inauguration pageant was the most imposing in numbers, and the most brilliant in display, ever witnessed here. Facility of transportation from all the principal cities, North, South, East, and West, offered inducements which did not exist on any former occasion, and were gladly appropriated for a sort of national holiday at the Capital. The day itself was genial and bright, inviting everybody to participate in the spectacle, and a cheerful sun lighted up the scene with unusual splendor, until about the hour when the inaugural was delivered, when clouds portentously lowered over the head of the new President and the assembled thousands. Various military companies from distant points enlivened the turn-out, and relieved the heaviness of the black-coated throng.

In the evening, the inauguration ball attracted several thousands of both sexes, and is admitted to have been, in arrangement, style, and appointment, the most successful affair of the kind ever attempted. Some idea of the scale upon which it was conducted, may be imagined from the fact that the cost reached about $15,000. Mr. BUCHANAN was present for a couple of hours, but it was observed that his usual gracious manner was evidently forced, rather than natural, owing to the debilitating effects of an epidemic which has prostrated most of the guests of the National Hotel. This trouble has been aggravated too by mental perplexities and much physical exertion all which have conspired to shake the remaining energies of a frame already tried by age and its insidious infirmities.

Little if any impression has been made by the Inaugural. No paper of the sort has ever been less discussed in political circles. As an intellectual production, it has no claim to superiority, and is below the standard of many of the papers prepared by Mr. BUCHANAN when Secretary of State, and even more recently as Minister to England. In point of policy, its chief effort seems to be the conciliation of every shade of opinion; and the careful reader cannot fail to observe that while Squatter sovereignty is condemned in one breath, it is approved in another, and that the same rule of expediency is applied to every other embarrassing or controverted question. Mr. BUCHANAN wisely relieves himself from a serious cause of embarrassment by adopting the one-term principle at the start, by which he will be enabled to act with more independence of party shackles, and to feel more personal ease in administering the Government. The temptation of a second term, and the power which that inclination gave to flatterers and time-servers, were the active causes which led to the humiliating downfall of the late incumbent. The Union-saving sentiments uttered by Mr. BUCHANAN will, doubtless, be echoed by that class of patriots who rely more upon the shouts over empty phrases than they do on the principles implanted in the Constitution, and by which alone the Union can be maintained in its integrity and strength.

It is very well known that the Message as originally prepared, did not meet the concurrence of Gen. CASS, or the new editor of the *Union*, when submitted to their inspection on Tuesday night; and but for alterations which were here required and made at the last hour, both would probably have retired from the positions assigned to them. With all his love of office, Gen. CASS was tenacious of his Squatter Sovereign bantling, and even went so far as to threaten to throw up the seals which glittered so invitingly before his eyes. This little episode may serve to explain the "individual" opinion which Mr. BUCHANAN expresses, as to the point of time when the people of a Territory may undertake to decide upon the subject of Slavery.

Until Gen. CASS gets fully established as Secretary of State, there will be no positive indication as to his Assistant Secretary. Gen. THOMAS, the present incumbent, whom Mr. MARCY advanced from personal partiality, is no favorite with Mr. BUCHANAN. The public will be greatly accommodated by any change that may be made in the Assistant Secretaryship of the Treasury Department, as it has been Mr. WASHINGTON'S misfortune to acquire a general unpopularity with all parties, and with the people of the District, to whom he is peculiarly obnoxious, for some reason or other.

A great deal is said in reference to Mr. BUCHANAN'S policy, as to the distribution of the patronage, but his mind is quite as liable to change in this respect as it did in regard to the principle of forming the Cabinet; and even more so, from the vast personal influences that will be brought to bear upon him in behalf of those who are in possession. OBSERVER.

The Inauguration Ball—Who were There and What was Done.

SPECIAL REPORT FOR THE NEW-YORK DAILY TIMES.

WASHINGTON, Thursday, March 5, 1857.

THE PREPARATIONS.

To the ladies who attend the quadrennial festival which marks the inauguration of a President, the Inauguration Ball is the great feature of the occasion, and it is certainly a most appropriate *finale*. Economical papas and departmental beaux thought that an X for a ticket, an X for a boquet, and an X for a carriage, was X-cessively X-travagant, and X-pensive, yet no X-cuse would be received, and they were forced to make the X-traordinary X-penditure. The ladies' tickets were huge enameled cards, bearing an engraved portrait of President BUCHANAN, surmounted by an arch, which rests upon emblematical pillars and a pedestal, completing the framework. These tickets were distributed with lavish profusion, and will probably be cherished by many a fair possessor as a *souvenir* of an occasion to be marked with a white stone.

Provoking was it to several who had expected to be present, that "Old Winter lingering in the lap of Spring," so deranged the express and baggage-arrangements between your City and this metropolis, that their wardrobes remained in transit, somewhere on the road. Like the lady of whom we read in a recent HARPER'S *Journal of Civilization*, they had, of course, "nothing to wear" in the trunks which had possession of a good share of their rooms, and so remained at home. Among the brilliant luminaries of fashion who were thus embargoed was Mrs. W*****l, of New-York—she arrived in good season, but her baggage, including a *ravissante costume de bal* made for the occasion was detained on the way. Is there no torture that can be inflicted upon those baggage-masters?

THE PAVILION.

As there is no hall in the "city of magnificent distances" large enough to contain more than 600 people, the managers were forced to erect a building expressly for the ball. It was, accordingly, put up on Judiciary-square, extending nearly 300 feet from the City Hall, with which it was connected at one end. Without, it resembled a huge railroad-contractor's shanty, as it was to be used, only for this occasion and then demolished—so architectural beauty was not deemed requisite. But within, it presented a fine appearance. The walls were lined with alternate stripes of "red, white and blue" glazed cambric, with national emblems at intervals on the walls. A seat ran around the sides, on a raised platform, and at the end next the City Hall, the entrance door opened on a wide gallery, from which a broad flight of stairs led down into the hall. The ceiling was of white cloth, studded with golden stairs, which twinkled as they were moved in unison with the measure of the dancers below, and reflected the blaze of light from large gas chandeliers. These chandeliers were an improvement on the wax-dropping candle sconces of the "Rough and Ready" Inauguration Ball in 1849.

The mayor's office, in the City Hall was fitted up for the reception of the President, and some half-a-dozen other rooms were used by the committees. The spacious hall of the Common Council was used as the ladies' dressing-room, excellent accommodations for hats and coats were provided in the basement, and up in the second story was a room where large punch-bowls and a long array of decanters showed that "total abstinence" was not the order of the night.

THE ARRIVALS.

Before ten o'clock the guests began to arrive, and so delightful was the clear, moon-light evening, that many who resided near the City Hall preferred to walk there. On they came, and soon a gay and brilliant throng emerged from the dressing rooms, and entered the hall. The proportion of ladies was marked, for although in New England it does not appear strange to see the fair sex predominate, it is a novelty here. Moralists naughtily commented on the fact that while every gentleman present, (even "the press,") had to pay ten dollars for a ticket, the ladies came without charge!

THE MUSIC.

Hopes had been entertained by the lovers of sweet sounds that the managers would be able to secure the fine band of DODWORTH or GILMORE, but they filled their orchestra with an *impromptu* conglomeration of musicians from the Navy-Yard, Baltimore and elsewhere, under the leadership of Mr. WEBER. Considering the material, and the little time for rehearsals, he did well with them. Here is the

PROGRAMME.

1. Inauguration March.....Nutzer.
2. Quadrille, Charivari.....Strauss.
3. Quadrille, Stradella.....Strauss.
4. Waltz, Epionen Tanze.....Strauss.
5. Quadrille, My Mary Ann.....Weber.
6. Quadrille, Schafer.....Labitzky.
7. Polka, Redowa, Minna Haha.....Wagner.
8. Quadrille, Wiena Carnivals.....Strauss.
9. Quadrille, Constitution.....Blsc.
10. Waltz and Polka, Venus Riegen.....Gung'l.
11. Quadrille, Postillion.....Strauss.
12. Quadrille, Medley.....Weber.
13. Polka, Redowa and Scottische.....Bergman.
14. Quadrille, (from opera Teufels Antheil)..Strauss.
15. Quadrille, Amoretten.....Strauss.
16. Waltz, Dreams on the Ocean.....Gung'l.
17. Quadrille, Concert Souvenir.....Strauss.
18. Quadrille, Almacks.....Strauss.
19. Polka, Redowa, Little Blossom.....Weber.
20. Quadrille, Sarah.....Strauss.
21. Quadrille, Louisen.....Strauss.
22. Waltz and Polka.....
23. Quadrille, Medley.....Weber.
24. Quadrille, Volsgarten.....Strauss.
25. Virginia Reel.

THE PRESIDENT'S ARRIVAL.

About eleven o'clock Mr. BUCHANAN arrived, accompanied by his niece, Miss LANE, who is to preside at the White House. He was received by Mayor MAGRUDER, who very discreetly spared him the infliction of a speech, and as he descended the stairway from the gallery, the band announced his arrival by striking up "Hail to the Chief." The President looked well, although a shade of anxious thought appeared at times to cross his fine countenance. He wore, of course, the Lancaster-made suit, of which, with its hidden stitching, we have all heard. Miss LANE is rather below the medium height, but has a fine figure, and is of that blonde Saxon type of beauty so familiar to Christendom since the multiplication of portraits of Queen VICTORIA. She wore a white dress trimmed with artificial flowers similar to those which ornamented her hair, and clasping her throat was a necklace of many strands of seed pearls. She was escorted by Senator JONES, and behind her, in full uniform, walked the veteran General JESSUP.

THE SCENE.

The pageant presented to the view of those in the gallery, as the President moved along the hall, was equal in magnificence to that witnessed at any European Court. The mass of humanity, "fair women and brave men," diplomatists, naval and military officers, opened to the right and left like the waves of the Red Sea, and reunited again as the President and his suite passed on, having saluted him with bow or curtesy. It was a rare scene to witness, and when, after having traversed the hall, the President received introductions to almost all present, there was no pushing or crowding. His presentations and conversations were of that unconstrained character which distinguishes refined society, Mr. BUCHANAN enlisting the good feeling of the ladies by his courteous demeanor and by his varied conversational powers.

THE NOTABLE GUESTS.

Mr. BRECKINRIDGE, the Vice-President, has many warm friends in Washington, who pressed around him to offer their congratulations. Ex-President PIERCE was detained at home (he is at Mr. MARCY'S) by the indisposition of his estimable lady, and the only representative of his Administration was his Private Secretary, SIDNEY WEBSTER, Esq., who escorted the beautiful Miss F**H, whose father's term of Senatorial office also expired yesterday. Elegantly dressed in white, trimmed with flowers, and with a cluster of flowers trailing from her classically formed head, she was decidedly the most showy among the fair demoiselles present.

La Reine du Bal was Mrs. D*****s, who was dressed in bridal white, and commanded admiration. Senator DOUGLAS escorted his niece, Miss G*****R, who is as fascinating as she is graceful. Senators CAMERON and DIXON, with their ladies, were the only politically Northern members of the upper-house present, but there was no lack of those from sunnier climes, with their ladies, among whom Mrs. S*****l, who is somewhat an oracle in political circles, was conspicuous. Mrs. Senator T******D, of New-Jersey, in white with silver trimmings, is always admired.

Fain would we chronicle the New-York belles who were escorted by Mr. CRUGER, the elegant costumes of the ladies of the diplomatic corps, among whom Madame DE SARTIGES is so prominent, and the other fair ones, many of whom mocked one's liveliest conceptions of Juno's regal beauty, and excited a regret that Phidias could not have immortalized them in marble. But as this report is to be sent by the early mails, we must pass them by—those who would have basked in the sunlight of their smiles and admired their toilettes, should have attended in person.

THE SUPPER.

A supper-room had been erected parallel with the large saloon, with which it communicated by several doors. Along one side of this room, opposite the entrances, was a buffet-table, nearly two hundred and fifty feet in length, behind which was an active body of waiters. The caterer was Monsieur GAUTIER, (the Delmonico of Washington,) who added to his high reputation by the gastronomic delicacies liberally provided. Prominent in the centre of the table, and visible from all parts of the room, towered a daintily decorated tower of confectionery, surmounted by a miniature American flag, bearing the National arms, and flanked by two banners, one inscribed with the name of the President, the other with that of the Vice-President. Lower down waved thirty-one flags, each one bearing the arms of a State. The designs for this exquisite and appropriate ornament were furnished by one of the first artists in the city—M. BESSAU.

BILL OF FARE.

Paté Truffle.
Saddles of Venison and of Mutton.
Boar's Head, stuffed and decorated.
Boned and roasted Turkeys.
Spiced Rounds of Beef.
Filets de Bœuf en Belle Vue.
Boned and Roasted Pheasants.
Tongues and Hams, decorated.
Aspic de Volaille.
Lobster, Chicken and Russian Salad.
Terrapins and Oysters.
Cream and Water Ices, in fancy moulds.
Marrons Glacés.
Charlotte Russe.
Meringues, Plombières, Bavaroises.
Jellies and Puddings.
Fancy Cakes, Preserved Fruits, Confectionery.
Roman Punch, Apple Toddy.
Wines, Liquors and Cordials.

An idea of the *quantity* provided of these delicacies may be formed from the fact that Monsieur GAUTIER used five hundred gallons of oysters, eight hundred chickens, one hundred gallons of ice-cream, one hundred pounds of bon-bons, &c.

Mr. BUCHANAN and suite were first admitted, with the Committee, to the table. They did not remain long, and then came that Balaklava charge which characterizes the onslaught at every festive scene, when the doors of the supper room are opened. "Onward they rushed," yet any one who used to attend the balls of LOUIS PHILIPPE can bear me witness that the Tuileries itself has witnessed some terrible scrambling. The action commenced by a running *feu de joie* from the champagne corks—forks were frantically demanded, and stupid youths would carelessly spill terrapin on ladies' dresses. Happy is your reporter to state that he saw no signs of intoxication nor rowdyism, and every one was good-natured, even the fair ones whose skirts were sadly stained by the negligence aforesaid.

Dancing was going on with unflagging spirit when your reporter was forced to leave, that he might transcribe his notes in season for the mail.

News from Kansas.

ST. LOUIS, Thursday, March 5.

A letter to the *Republican*, dated Westport, March 26, says that at a meeting of citizens at that place resolutions were passed to resist every effort and every movement intended or calculated to produce troubles similar to those of last year; extending hospitality and welcome to emigrants from all sections of the country; and pledging themselves to let the laws of Kansas and Missouri punish all violators of the law.

The Santa Fé mail arrived at Westport on the 26th ult. The party met no difficulty on the route, excepting from high streams and deep mud. The general news is unimportant. It is considered certain that Indian Agent DODGE was killed by the Apaches. All was quiet at Fort Bent.

ST. LOUIS, Friday, March 6.

The *Republican* contains a long communication signed by A. W. JONES, a resident of Lecompton, relative to recent affairs in Kansas; also, Governor GEARY'S letter and SHERRARD'S reply, together with the action of the Committee of the Judiciary in the Legislature on the matter, and the testimony taken before Judge CATO on the examination of JONES for shooting SHERRARD. The version now presented differs somewhat from previous reports. The communication casts much blame on Governor GEARY, and the Committee on Judiciary likewise censure his action JONES, who was held to bail in $5,000, has absconded.

Canal and Lake Navigation.

OSWEGO, Friday, March 6.

The schooner *Athenian*, which left Chicago last Fall with a cargo of 17,000 bushels of wheat for Oswego, and which was frozen in in the Welland Canal is now about two miles off this harbor. The Welland Canal is nearly free of ice.

The Missouri Legislature.

ST. LOUIS, Thursday, March 5.

Previous to the adjournment of the Missouri Legislature yesterday, a constitutional amendment limiting the State debt to $20,000,000 was passed.

Appointment of Commissioners to Remove Quarantine.

Special Dispatch to the New-York Daily Times.

ALBANY, Friday, March 6.

The Governor sent to the Senate this evening the names of Hon. GEORGE HALL, of Brooklyn, Hon. EGBERT BENSON, of New-York, and Hon. OBADIAH BOWNE, of Richmond, as Commissioners to remove Quarantine. The nominations were confirmed unanimously in open Senate. LEO.

NEW-YORK LEGISLATURE.

SENATE....ALBANY, Friday, March 6.

Mr. RICHARDSON reported a bill appropriating $15,000 to the Commissioners of Emigration, to pay the debts due Counties for the support of emigrant paupers.

Mr. NOXON reported favorably on the bill to make certain the record of marriages.

Mr. UPHAM reported favorably on the concurrent resolutions forbiding contractors to let out the waters of the Canals, under a penalty of the forfeiture of the contract and all the money due them.

Mr. C. P. SMITH reported favorably on the Bill amending the pilot law.

The Governor sent to the Senate, in special executive session, the nomination of EGBERT BENSON, GEO. HALL and OBADIAH BOWNE as Commissioners under the act for the removal of Quarantine.

The bill for the relief of the wives and minor children of drunkards was passed. Also, the bill changing the name of the Broadway Baptist Church; the bill for the relief of destitute children of seamen; and the bill to amend the charter of the Manhattan Savings Institution.

ASSEMBLY....ALBANY, Friday, March 6.

The Assembly was occupied all the morning in debating a resolution against printing the Excise report.

BILLS REPORTED FAVORABLY.

Providing an appropriation for two State Lunatic Asylums, and making an appropriation for the support of the pauper insane.

To authorize the formation of a new Railroad Company in place of the present Northern Railroad Company.

The twice reported bill taxing dogs.

NOTICES OF BILLS.

By Mr. JOHN J. RIELLY, to amend the law for the recovery of debts against vessels.

By Mr. MULLIGAN, to amend the Brooklyn Police bills.

By Mr. J. J. OWEN, to establish a State Printing office.

By Mr. SLUYTER, for the advancement of agricultural science in the State.

The Assembly agreed to hold evening sessions hereafter, every evening in the week except Saturday.

The concurrent resolutions, amending the Constitution so as to confer the right of suffrage to colored persons, were debated, but no question was taken.

From Louisville.

ARRIVAL OF DR. KANE'S REMAINS—DESTRUCTIVE FIRE, ETC.

LOUISVILLE, Friday, March 6.

An imposing procession of Masons in regalia, firemen and citizens, received the remains of Dr. KANE on their arrival here, this morning, and, marching through the principal streets, attended them to the steamer *Telegraph*, which will leave with them for Cincinnati at noon to-day. JOHN SCOTT, Agent of the Baltimore and Ohio Railroad, and WILLIAM R. PATTERSON, of Adams' Express Company, will attend to the transportation of the remains between here and Philadelphia.

The river is falling slowly. The water in the Channel is 7¾ feet deep. The thermometer is at the freezing point.

BREEDEN'S planing mill, three new stores, and two dwelling houses contiguous, on Main-street, were destroyed by fire last night. Mr. BREEDEN was the principal loser. Loss $30,000. Fully insured in Eastern offices.

New Jersey Legislature.

TRENTON, Friday, March 6.

The bill for the extension of the Morris and Essex Railroad to Jersey City passed the Senate to-day by 11 to 6. It now only requires the Governor's signature to become a law.

The bill to incorporate the Essex County Bank failed in the House by a vote of 26 to 28.

An attempt was made to reconsider the resolutions to meet the Committee of the New York Legislature on the Quarantine question, but in consequence of a dispatch stating that Mr. LEAVENWORTH'S bill had passed the New-York Legislature, the matter was laid over till Tuesday.

The Governor sent in the name of WILLIAM L. DAYTON, for Attorney-General, and that of Senator CHARLES P. SMITH, of Salem, for Clerk of the Supreme Court.

Markets by Telegraph.

NEW-ORLEANS, Friday, March 6.

COTTON—Sales to-day 7,000 bales. Prices stiffer but not quotably higher. Middling, 12¾c.@13¼c. *Receipts to-day*. 5,250 bales. SUGAR selling at 10c.; MOLASSES, 60c.; MESS PORK, (Eastern,) $22 50; LARD in kegs, $15c. Cotton freights to Liverpool, 15-32d. Sterling Exchange, 7¾ ⅌ cent. premium.

The Crowd in Broadway.

The Committee of the Board of Councilmen, to whom were deputed inquiry as to the practicability of some scheme to lessen the crowd in Broadway, met again yesterday in the City Hall Library, Councilman HASWELL in the Chair. In the way of evidence little was reached.

Captain HOPKINS, of the Third Ward, deposed to the fact that Broadway *is* obstructed, and that some of the causes of obstruction are susceptible of removal.

Mr. A. T. STEWART attended the meeting and offered some suggestions. He thought that the "snarl," or "jam," or "dead stand still," was inevitably produced so often as the omnibus drivers are compelled to neglect their proper duty in giving change to passengers. He would advise the employment of a "cad" at the door of each omnibus. He thought better regulations would most materially abate the evil. He censured the Mayor for neglecting to employ his own servants in getting up informations against infractors of the street regulations, and for inviting the public to become informers. Mr. STEWART adverted to a proposed railroad in Broadway; he believed the scheme was not dead; another bill was in readiness, but of course it would have his opposition—parties at each end of such lines being the only people benefited—the property along such lines being always deteriorated in value. The Committee appeared to be of the same opinion. Mr. STEWART praised the low omnibuses drawn by 4 horses, common in many English cities, as peculiarly accessible, very convenient, and not so liable to block the streets.

The Chairman expressed to Mr. STEWART his anxiety to adopt a plan which would at once widen both the sidewalk and the roadway. The other members of the Committee thought any such widening would be nugatory and inefficacious; there would be a corresponding addition to the throng. Others thought that the formation of the proposed side avenue, and compelling all licensed vehicles to pass down that avenue, returning by Broadway, would remedy the evil.

ROAD OPEN ACROSS THE ISTHMUS OF TEHUANTEPEC.—The New-Orleans *Picayune* has later advices from Tehuantepec, bringing the important information that the preliminary carriage road across the Isthmus had been completed after the almost incessant labor of 200 to 300 men for a period of several months. The two first carriages passed over the road to the Pacific terminus, on the 4th of January; among their occupants were the American Consul at Vera Cruz, Señor GUTIERES, formerly Secretary of the Treasury of Mexico, and others. The carriages returned next day, when there was great rejoicing in consequence of the glorious achievement, all along the Isthmus. The contract with the Mexican Government is now fulfilled, and the privileges guaranteed by it are secured. The perfect completion of the road will be pushed forward as rapidly as possible, and it will probably be opened on the 1st of June to the traveling public.

A DISTRESSING ACCIDENT.—We regret to learn that yesterday, in Baltimore, Mr. SAML. BUTTERWORTH, the Superintendent of the Branch Mint in New-York, while on his way to attend the inauguration was severely wounded by the accidental discharge of a pistol in the overcoat pocket of his friend and traveling companion, ISAAC V. FOWLER, Esq., Postmaster of New-York City. The weapon went off as Mr. F. was taking off his coat, and the ball entering Mr. BUTTERWORTH'S thigh ranged upwards. Though but a flesh wound, it is said to be severe.—*Washington Star.*

CALIFORNIA STEAMSHIP RUNNERS.

The Ticket-Swindlers' Own Story—Some of their Dodges—No Arrests made, and why it is hard to Punish them.

WARNINGS TO STRANGERS.

The ticket-swindlers are excited. They were very much stirred by our simple statement of a few of their villainous tricks upon unsophisticated countrymen who left in the *Illinois*. One who formerly was in the business and knows its workings volunteers a statement in extenuation of the abuses. He says the California steamship companies are more culpable than the runners, and he should like to see them bear a portion of the blame.

When the lines were first started, the steamship companies deemed it necessary to employ runners, at a regular salary, to go to the railway dépôts and hotels to solicit passengers. At that time there were no bogus offices. But the Companies soon found that the agent of one line would bribe the runners of the other. Then they adopted the plan of paying the runners a commission for each passenger they brought in. For a while it worked admirably. While the opposition ran strong between the Companies, both of them, weeks previous to the sailing of a boat, would extensively advertise and scatter handbills broad cast throughout the country, to the effect that the passage money was only $30 $40, or $50, as the case might be. Passengers for California flocked to the City, seduced by the prospect of so cheap a passage. Just previous, however, to the time of sailing, "as so many wanted to go," the price would be advanced to $100 or thereabouts. One boat started on the first of the month, the other on the 4th. It was of no use for the passengers to protest, and show the agent the advertisement, which stated that the fare was but $50, for the Company had the game all in their own hands. If, indignantly, the people refused to take passage in the first boat, it was their misfortune, as a still larger sum was asked on the next, the agent telling them that they should have gone in the first boat.

This method of the agents of the companies induced the runners to try a little speculation on their own risk. They reasoned thus: "If our employers advertise one price and charge afterwards what they please, let us by the same game turn a penny, too." At first they would buy four or five tickets at the low rate, and sell them at the advance. Respectable hotel-keepers furnished the necessary funds for the speculation, in return for which the runners sent countrymen to their hotels. This abuse has grown gradually into the outrageous system of ticket-swindling which is now practiced.

Most of the clerks in the regular offices, says our informant—a retired speculator in this line, remember—are aiders and abettors of the runners. They receive a large amount of the proceeds of the swindle. If they did not sell the runners the tickets by the quantity at $10 less per ticket than the regular price, the business would be stopped. But as things are managed now, the clerks in the genuine offices get the lion's share of the plunder, and the men who have to shoulder the infamy don't make such a large pile after all.

The clerks and runners are well acquainted. They drink together, and all that sort of thing. After the sailing of each steamer they adjourn to DELMONICO'S to dinner, and a division of the money.

This is the other side of the story; possibly there may be truth in it. At any rate it is all the ticket-swindlers have said to vindicate themselves.

It is positively denied, however, at the office of the United States Mail Steamship Company, that tickets are sold in large quantities to the runners, and none are sold below the regular price. It is impossible, they say, to keep the tickets out of the hands of these rascals, for if they refuse to sell them, the runners employ a stranger, who represents himself as about to emigrate with his family to California, and thus the tickets fall into their hands.

An instance was related us of the sharpness of these fellows in conducting their business. One of them who keeps a bogus concern in the vicinity of the Company's office, which is at No. 177 West-street, heard, just after the *George Law* sailed, that the price of passage by the *Illinois*, (the next steamer,) would be increased $25, as she was to carry out a company of United States Troops. His first thought was to obtain a large number of tickets at the low rate. But how could he procure them? He slipped off to Philadelphia, and bought them there, paying the money for 25 passages, at $100 each. But when he presented the agent's receipt at the New-York office, and asked for the tickets, Mr. RAYMOND refused to furnish them, on the ground that the Philadelphia agent had no authority to negotiate for passages, until he had been notified of any change in the price. The sharp ticket-swindler had the trouble and expense of his trip for nothing.

But unfortunately, the biters are not often bit—sorry statement as it is to make in this Christian age.

Upon the sailing of a steamer for California not long since, a party of five were met on the cars, as usual, while on their way to this City, by the man *going to California*. He knew exactly where Mr. RAYMOND'S office was in the City, the strangers having been posted as to the existence of bogus establishments: he knew the best hotel to stop at. The addition of so accommodating a person to their crowd was regarded as auspicious, and everything went on smoothly. As the steamer was to sail on the following day, no time was to be lost, and *the* office was soon reached by the valuable aid of the guide. Entering it the strangers inquire if Mr. RAYMOND is in? The clerk behind a high mahogany desk answers, "No, gentlemen, but he will be soon." This is Mr. RAYMOND'S office? they ask. "Yes, be seated gentlemen," is the courteous reply, "and make yourselves comfortable." A young man slips out of a side door, and in less than two minutes a dignified person enters at the front one. He has a business air, and scans the whole group with one eye as thoroughly as if his head were Argus', and every hair-pore were an eye. "There comes Mr. RAYMOND," says the clerk, as the portly gentleman makes a low bow and inquires—"What can I do for you, gentlemen?"

"W-a-ll, we're bound to the diggins, and want to know about the price of tickets. This is the true Californy ticket office of Mr. RAYMOND, isn't it?"

"Certainly, but there is a great crowd going, and I don't know as I can give you tickets by this steamer. How many are there of you?"

"Five, and—getting anxious—we must go if possible. There is no mistake neow, 'bout this office?" (looking round.)

"None whatever. Why, what makes you ask that?"

"Oh, we have been told that there is only one place in New-York where they sell the ginowine tickets, but that there are offices where strangers are sometimes taken in."

The guide reassures the company and points at the genuine poster on the wall. At this stage a young man enters quite out of breath, tips his hat, and addressing the bogus dignitary, hurriedly says:

"Mr. RAYMOND, there are so many passengers we shall want more blankets."

"How many do you want, Purser?"

"A hundred and fifty pairs."

"Very well—go down to the house of HARDHEAD, SNODGRASS, & BULWINKLE, and get them,—and, mind you, get the very best they have. We don't want any more of those coarse things we had before."

[Exit Purser.]

This stroke is a settler; Mr. RAYMOND finally promises to squeeze out five first-class cabin tickets at $200 each. No sooner said than done. The five travelers give their names. A young man reaches out the side door, and by the time some brief conversation is disposed of the said young man returns and hands something to the Clerk. The tickets are now all ready. And the Californians depart tickled at their success. In the morning as they go down to board the steamer to inspect their quarters they are surprised to observe another California ticket office, into which curiosity leads them. The scales now fall from their eyes—they have now found the office of the genuine RAYMOND—discover they have steerage tickets, and have paid $75 more for each one than there was any occasion for; the company is minus $375. This case occurred on the sailing of the *George Law*, and is likely to recur when the next steamer sails.

Is there no remedy for such rascalities? The law is no sort of bar to these vagabonds. The police they ask out to take a drink if they present themselves. The press has some terrors for them. It will be a disgrace to our times if a journal of civilization is not privileged to report, at an early date, their wholesale apprehension and punishment.

THREE DAYS LATER FROM EUROPE

ARRIVAL OF THE PERSIA.

Attacks on the Palmerston Administration.

Contradictory Rumors About the Persian War.

Reported Destruction of Canton.

Aid from Russia to China and Persia.

DEATH OF THE EARL OF ELLESMERE.

COTTON QUIET—GRAIN DULL.

Consols 93 5-8@3-4.

The British Mail steamer *Persia*, from Liverpool about 3½ o'clock A. M. of Saturday, the 21st, arrived yesterday afternoon.

The *Arago* arrived at Southampton on morning of the 20th, and the *New York* (S. S.) at Greenock, at 9½ o'clock A. M. of the same day

The news by this arrival has several features of interest. On the 20th, the night preceding the sailing of the *Persia*, DISRAELI, as the leader of the opposition in the House of Commons, made an attack on the Government financial scheme. The scope of DISRAELI'S proposal was to adjust the estimates for a period of three years, instead of for one year, so as to permit the complete repeal of the income tax at the expiration of three years from the present date. The debate was postponed.

The Persian difficulty, which a few days since appeared in a fair way of settlement, has taken a new turn for the worse—it being reported that FEROUK KHAN had, in consequence of the unexpected receipt of bellicose dispatches from his Government, broken off all negotiation with the British Minister at Paris, and would not now visit England. A statement opposed to this appears in a Paris Government journal.

The French Government has instructed its representatives at London, Vienna, St. Petersburg and Berlin to invite the Governments to which they are accredited to join in a Conference at Paris for the settlement of the Neufchatel affair. The Ministers of the above Powers resident at Paris will act as plenipotentiaries. The Conference will meet about the beginning of March, and it is believed will be protracted ere a satisfactory adjustment can be arrived at.

There is nothing nearer towards a settlement of the Danubian Principalities.

The London *Morning Advertiser* asserts that the Government has received a dispatch announcing the total destruction of Canton by the British.

After a long and painful illness the Earl of ELLESMERE died, on the 18th, at Bridgewater House, London, in the 57th year of his age. Lord ELLESMERE was distinguished as a munificent patron of art, as well as for his liberality of sentiment and his freedom from party fetters and rancor. As a poet he showed considerable talent, his works being a translation of GOETHE'S "Faust," and numerous translations of German lyrics, as also an original poem entitled "The Pilgrimage," descriptive of his travels in the East. He was the second son of the first Duke of SUTHERLAND, was educated at Oxford, and afterwards took the name of EGERTON, in place of his patronymic of Leveson-Gower. From 1820 to 1846 he was, for various terms, in the House of Commons; in 1827 was a Lord of the Treasury; from 1828 to 1830 was Chief Secretary for Ireland, and in 1830 was Secretary-at-War. He is succeeded in his titles and estates by his eldest son, Lord BRACKLEY, who is in a precarious state of health.

An explosion took place on the 19th, at the Land Hill Colliery, near Wombwell, on the South Yorkshire Railway. One hundred and sixty-six persons were in the pit at the time. Sixteen were drawn up alive, and the others remained for certain death, the interior of the pit having taken fire. Engines had arrived and the mouths of the shafts were being stopped up to extinguish the flames. Thirteen dead bodies had been found in the main tramways, but it would be some days before the pit could be safely entered to search for the rest. The pit had been worked but two years.

A report from the Russian Minister of War declares that the truce concluded with SCHAMYL, during the Turkish war, expired in May of last year, and that operations against the Circassians have been resumed along the whole line of the Caucasus.

Letters from St. Petersburg mention that it will be the beginning of April before the Emperor ALEXANDER sets out on his journey to Nice, and either on his way or his return, he will visit NAPOLEON at Paris.

The ratifications of the treaty signed between Russia and Persia, on the 5th of January last, were exchanged at Teheran on the 18th of the same month. This treaty cedes to Russia a track of land on the frontiers of Turkey, and situate between Bayazid and Nakhshivan, giving to Russia a complete command of the strategic road from Trebizonde on the Black Sea to the Persian frontier by Erzeroum. Russia has been endeavoring since 1828 to obtain the concession which Persia now grants. It is added that orders were immediately sent from St. Petersburg to construct a line of fortresses on the ceded territory.

The Brussels *Nord* publishes the details of the concession granted by the Russian Government for the great network of Railways to be constructed within ten years at an outlay of £45,000,000 sterling. The conditions are substantially the same as those already announced. Among the contracting parties are BARING BROTHERS, of London, and HOPE & Co., of Amsterdam.

We read in the Paris Correspondence of the London *Times:*

The last accounts received by the French Government from Persia announce that FIZLALI KHAN, who commands the advanced guard of the Persian army in Farsistan, had sent forward, on the 25th of December, a strong reconnoitering party of cavalry as far as 50 miles in advance of Shiraz. This demonstration, though so far from the British camp, had given rise to a report of an approaching attack on the English lines by the entire Persian army, but this is impossible, for the Persians, who have been joined by the Turcomans, have none but irregular cavalry in the province of Fars, with which it would be impossible to make an impression on the well-fortified position of the English army at Bushire.

Advices from the Principalities state that the Russian authorities had quitted Bolgrad, and surrendered the town to the commissioners sent from Jassy by the Moldavian Government. Col. BESSON, the French Commissioner for fixing the boundary of the Principalities, charged with tracing the Upper Yalpuk, has written that his labors are so far advanced that Komrat may be handed over to the Russian authorities on the 15th February.

In the House of Lords, Lord POLWARTH gave notice that he would move for any papers or correspondence relative to the cession of the islands of Haski, Gibleu, and Ghuragoul by the Imaum of Muscat to Her Majesty, and their erection into a colony; and also to call the attention of the House to a license granted on the 20th of February, 1856, by the Commissioners of Emigration to JOHN ORD and others, giving them the sole and exclusive right to raise and take away guano from these islands during five years.

It is announced that a commission is about to be appointed to choose a position to which to transfer the prisoners at Cayenne. Several places have been mentioned. One is New-Caledonia, and the other Algeria. Another idea suggested is to take possession of the Zephyrine Islands, opposite the coast of Africa, and which have the advantage of being detached from the continent or coast of Algeria.

W. H. RUSSELL, the London *Times'* correspondent, has entered into an engagement with Mr. BEALE, of London, to deliver three lectures a week, on the Crimea, till April, 1858, for a sum which rumor calls £10,000.

LONDON NEWS AND GOSSIP.

Mr. Disraeli's Attack on the Government—Lord Palmerston's Chances—Lord Derby's Motion Against the War in China—The Persian War Not Terminated—Lord Napier—Relations with the United States—Non-Appointment of Consuls—The Railroad Hoax—Death of the Earl of Ellesmere—Miscellaneous, &c.

Correspondence of the New-York Daily Times.

LONDON, Friday Evening, Feb. 20, 1857.

This night week we were in the midst of financial ministerial uncertainty. To-night we are in the crisis of ministerial existence. A grand *coup* is in the act of being made on the Palmerston budget by Mr. DISRAELI, the success of whose motion, if success it have, will be the knell of the present Administration. Whom that knell may summon to new official vitality

The New-York Times.

VOL. VIII.—NO. 2421. | NEW-YORK, THURSDAY, JUNE 23, 1859. | PRICE TWO CENTS.

THE WAR IN ITALY.

Movements of the Republicans and of Garibaldi's Corps—Plans of Kossuth—Napoleon III. and the Czar Alexander—Agitation of the English Middle Classes—The Battles of Magenta and Malesagno—Miscellaneous Facts and Incidents.

Special Correspondence of the N. Y. Times.

LONDON, Tuesday, June 7, 1859.

As some days must elapse before I can send you letters from Italy, I write on the eve of starting to give you a little of the chit chat received in private letters or from friends behind the scenes. The official bulletins telegraphed to Liverpool at the moment of the steamer's starting deprive "Own Correspondents" of the satisfaction of supplying latest news, so they are obliged to content themselves with securing from their friends at head-quarters the largest amount of non-official information, and in this department your correspondent flatters himself he will not be found wanting. The mystery in which all the movements of the combatants—especially of the allied armies—are shrouded, renders it extremely difficult for any one suspected of relationship with the Jenkinses to approach either camp. Even the London *Times* has had to overcome not a few obstacles before RUSSELL, (their famous correspondent from the Crimea and India,) furnished as he is with credentials from Lord ABERDEEN, could get permission to follow the allied army. He has finally succeeded, and his first letter from Vercelli appeared in the *Times* of yesterday. Colonel BLAKESLEY, that most un-English Englishman, sent by the *Times* to the Austrian camp, only succeeds in maintaining his footing there by becoming a very satellite of Austria; but, unfortunately for his friends, the *trop de zèle* manifested in their service has rendered his services *nil*, for when Englishmen are told that so far from pillaging the towns and country invaded on the Piedmontese Territory, the Austrian Army scarcely demanded sufficient for bare sustenance, they are inclined to ask, Is this a piece of satire, or is it meant as an insult to our understanding? His statement that the peasants are alike indifferent to Austrians, French, and Sardinians—that they incline to a Socialistic revolution, from their hatred to the wealthy classes—proves either his falsehood or his ignorance. But who can ignore Austria's hateful system of arousing the peasants against the upper classes, which succeeded so fearfully in Gallicia, and as signally failed in Italy, where rich and poor, beggars and nobles, recognize but one tyrant—Austria! and but one name for their enemies—*Tedeschi?* We are just now smiling at the admiration expressed by this gentleman for the behavior of the Milanese, among whom he believes that a powerful party, *opposed to Austrian rule, has determined to put down any disorders, and to leave their fate to be decided by the armies in the field:* I say we smile, for the Italians in London are on the *qui vive* for the telegram that at any moment may announce a revolution in Milan, which they have reasons for knowing must occur before twenty-four hours have passed. The news of the victory of the Piedmontese at Palestro, (on the left bank of the Sesia,) and of the French and Piedmontese at Magenta, needs no comment, though it is well not to put too implicit faith in the list of the enemy's killed and wounded, as the numbers vary with each fresh telegram; but, in order that your readers may be enabled to understand the contradictory acccounts that come from Tuscany, and the various surmises as to the reasons of GARIBALDI's movements in Lombardy, I will just briefly allude to the tacit arrangements made between the Governments and the people before the commencement of the war. In 1856, as you already know, a society was set on foot, secretly patronized by CAVOUR—with the Marquis PALLAVICINO for President, GARIBALDI for Vice-President, LA PARINA for Secretary—whose avowed object was the *unification* and *independence* of Italy. Overtures were made by this party to all the prominent men in Italy and their respective parties; and a large number, sinking their republican aspirations in the more important necessity of independence, accepted. MAZZINI and the staunchest republicans refused their adhesion, distrusting the intentions of the Piedmonmontese Government, and also because the programme excluded the idea of liberty, and the substitution of the word unification for unity admitted the division of Italy under different rulers But after the failure of the expedition to Naples in 1857, and the execution of ORSINI in 1858, this party immensely augmented its numbers, which have continued to increase up to the prepresent time. Threats of a French alliance having been thrown out in 1858, some of the chief partisans took the alarm, but reassured by the repeated assertions that no thought of French aggrandizement in Italy was entertained, they bent all their efforts to accustom the Italians, by means of the clandestine Press, to look upon VICTOR EMANUEL as future King of Italy; and there is every reason to believe that the King himself shares in this very natural ambition of exchanging a Piedmontese for an Italian crown. This propaganda, if not encouraged, was not disapproved of by CAVOUR, who, however, whether from necessity or from choice it matters not, came to a very different understanding with the Emperor at Plombières. For the precise terms of the agreement I will not vouch, but the following arrangement was to be effected, if possible: A brilliant victory by the allied armies over Austria being counted on, it was agreed that if after the first victory Austria should wish to come to terms, the *line of the Adige*, the river that separates Lombardy from Venice, should be named as the frontier line, Lombardy being annexed to Piedmont, Venice remaining to Austria until a fitting pretext should offer to deprive her of that also. If, however, she should remain obstinate, she must be fought clean out of Italy. This done, the division of the Peninsula was to be as follows: Savoy and Nice to be annexed to France, (in face if the map of Europe should be drawn afresh, according to nature's plan, Savoy goes to France of right;) the Kingdom of Northern Italy united under the sceptor of VICTOR EMANUEL, Tuscany and a portion of the States of the Church given to Prince NAPOLEON, and Naples and Sicily to MURAT. Of this arrangement not a word was breathed to the Italians; and as you know the extreme desire of the Tuscans to form part of a united Italy, no matter under what form of government, expressed in their clever device, V. I. V. A. VERDI, found vent at the out break of the war in the instant dethronement o the Grand Duke, and the proclamation of VICTOR EMANUEL as King Dictator. Great was the disappointment of the Tuscans when the King declined the offer of the dictatorship, and they were left to carry on their own Government, their enthusiastic soldiers prevented from fighting, while Parma and Modena, &c., were received as Piedmontese Provinces. True, the popular General ULLOA was sent to command them; but, then, his movements were so hampered by private orders that he could take no energetic steps, nor carry out any regular organization. What could it all mean? The arrival of Prince NAPOLEON was at first hailed as a signal for action, but his authoritative airs, his overbearing conduct to even the royal commissioners, explained the mystery to the Tuscans but too clearly. "Imagine our chagrin," wrote an ardent patriot the other day to a friend; "long since we resigned the hope of seeing the pure Italian tricolor wave from the towers of Florence; but when, in the place of the white cross of Savoy—the promise, at least, of Italian unity and independence—the Imperial arms appeared engrafted on our national colors, we felt that we were but exchanging the double-headed eagle for the scarcely less rapacious one-headed French bird of prey. Still we do not despair; we believe that VICTOR EMANUEL will not refuse us for his subjects when he understands that we dethroned the Duke, not for an exchange of masters, but solely with the desire of possessing an Italian Government." Now, you will observe that the *Times* correspondent in Tuscany noting the ill-humored dissatisfaction and disorganization that has taken the place of the enthusiastic unity with which the Tuscan crown was offered to the King of Piedmont, says: "*The point to which I wish to call your serious attention is that the Emperor and Count Cavour are no longer of one mind, for what at least concerns Tuscany.*" This is a mistake. NAPOLEON and CAVOUR are quite agreed to get Tuscany for Prince NAPOLEON if possible; but the Tuscans are determined to be ruled by VICTOR EMANUEL, and rumor says, but I will not vouch for its truth, that the King himself was not at all pleased at being compelled to refuse the dictatorship of Tuscany. A mere man of pleasure in time of peace, and a brave, reckless soldier in war, he has left and leaves the intrigues of diplomacy to CAVOUR, who, in common with the Piedmontese aristocracy, would prefer an enlarged Kingdom of Northern Italy, with Turin for the capital, to a United Italy, with the seat of Government at Rome; but it is very likely that the King, unaware up to the present time of the extraordinary enthusiasm prevailing for him throughout the Peninsula may not so readily consent to forego this so-coveted prize as his Imperial relation may have been led to expect! All will depend on the conduct of Naples. Should the two Sicilies declare for the King, it will be somewhat difficult for the Emperor, after his proclamation—which explicitly declares that he is desirous of giving Italy to herself—to force MURAT on the unwilling Italians; so we are anxiously expecting news from that quarter. In case the King should show symptoms of a wish to second the desires of the nation and become their King, rest assured that every Italian, even those who still refrain from fighting on account of the participation of NAPOLEON, will rally round his standard, and aid him to fulfill the national aspiration after unity and independence. All this will make clear to you the repugnance shown by the French and Piedmontese Governments to the admission of volunteers. Even now all those suspected of intercourse with MAZZINI are carefully prevented from setting foot in Italy, where PIETRI, the famous head of the French Police, with thirty of his chosen followers, is organizing a system of espionage on the Parisian model. PATERAS, a Neapolitan officer, implicated in PISACANE's expedition, went to Turin to offer his services, and was at once expelled. The newspaper entitled *La Nazione*, conducted by republicans, although entirely devoted to the King's interest, has been suppressed. Signors MAURICI, PANELLI, GUASTALLA, and a number of Italian gentlemen, wishing to join the volunteer corps, have been denied passports by the Sardinian Consul in London. COLOQUESE, MAGORI and others, furnished with passports by the Sardinian Consul, were arrested at Boulogne and imprisoned, and MAGORI sent back to England. Nevertheless, the whole corps of GARIBALDI is composed of ardent republicans, and, as the newspapers will have already informed you, they have conducted themselves in a manner worthy of their cause and of their gallant chief. It would seem to you exaggeration were I to detail, map in hand, all the *impossible* miracles, as the Italians would say, accomplished by this handful of volunteers, whose numbers have never yet reached a third of those of the Austrians. When first sent from the Lago Maggiore into Lombardy, GARIBALDI was promised that General NIEL should follow him immediately, but at the time of GARIBALDI's brilliant success from Varcse to Como, General NIEL had not stirred a step. The Italians are irritated at this, and hint that he has been sent on this perilous expedition in order that the Republican ranks may be thinned, if not annihilated, and at one time it was feared that the plan had succeeded, but GARIBALDI's smartness, his fertility in resources, and the desperate valor of his followers, supplied the place of numbers and assistance. I suppose you know that when called to the camp to receive the necessary instructions, he refused the plans drawn out for him, alleging that he must be left to his devices, or must resign his commission, as it was impossible to carry out any plan not suggested by the circumstances of the moment. This refusal gave great umbrage to the French, and to the staff-officers of the Sardinian army, but to accept GARIBALDI's resignation was to set him loose with his followers, to create revolution where he pleased. Besides he is a great pet of the King's, who inherits nothing of the timid, cautious, temperament of his father, which caused the guerilla chief to be a subject of hourly terror to CHARLES ALBERT during the campaign of '48. So GARIBALDI had his own way, and it was well he did, for under the peculiar circumstances, alone in an enemy's country, it was impossible to foresee the exigencies of the case. As it was, no sooner had the Austrians driven him out of Como—even while many were croaking over his failure, prophesying that he would be compelled to lay down his arms and retreat to Switzerland, he was just quietly recruiting his forces in the mountains, between the Lago Maggiore and Como—issued his proclamations to Lombardy to rise in insurrection—which order was instantly obeyed by the inhabitants of the Valtelline—then he pounced upon the Austrians as they were plundering Varese—engaged in another desperate combat at St. Fermo, (near Como,) and pursued his victorious march as far as Lecco.

Doubtless the next thing that we shall hear of him is that he has taken Bergamo and has effected a junction with the insurgents of the Valtelline, while the Milanese, driving out the Austrians, facilitate the march of the allied armies after their brilliant victory at Magenta. The young volunteers from GARIBALDI's camp write overjoyed at having been left alone to win the first laurels. Indeed, such is the enthusiasm that pervades the combatants, that Austria stands but a poor chance. In addition to the special objects of the war, the French feel that the honor of France is at stake. The Piedmontese regulars would not for worlds be thought inferior to their allies, and as for the volunteers, who have been considerably decried and sneered down, they have resolved to place not only their courage, but their obedience and constancy, above suspicion. Certainly they have succeeded to their hearts content, for at this moment GARIBALDI and his corps are the idols of the Italians and the admiration of Europe. GARIBALDI sends his dispatches direct to the King, whom alone you will remember he condescended to mention in his proclamation, and as VICTOR EMANUEL knows that he can count on the daring chief in any hour of need, it is not probable that he will allow him to be sacrificed to the exigencies of diplomacy. Of course the havoc made among these young patriots is frightful to contemplate.

The name at the head of the first list of the losses sustained by GARIBALDI is that of Captain IGNAZIO FRIGERIO, a Milanese nobleman, 44 years of age. One of the few partisans of the house of Austria, his father secured his entrance into the *guardia nobile* of the Emperor FERDINAND I., and soon after he was made Secretary of the Milanese Government, but hardly had the idea of national independence dawned on the Lombards in 1846 than the young IGNAZIO threw up his lucrative position, became an earnest apostle of the revolutionary ideas, and, as soon as the war broke out, one of the bravest soldiers in the Lombard division, where he attained the grade of captain. At the conclusion of the war of 1849, he retired with his noble wife and little sons to a voluntary exile in Genoa, where up to the commencement of the war he toiled for their support and education. In 1850 he published a work on military science which has been much praised by competent judges, and, openly avowing his republican principles, wrote constantly for *La Libertà*, a newspaper edited in Genoa. At the formation of GARIBALDI'S corps, his repugnance to share a war initiated by BONAPARTE was exceeded by his desire to fight the Austrians. The first to join the ranks, the post of his division was ever where danger was the greatest, and among the many slain FRIGERIO was the first to fall. Borne mortally wounded from the engagement at Como, he sank at once, leaving a widow whose ardent patriotism can alone sustain her under her irreparable loss, and three young sons, two of whom are in the Sardinian Navy. Captain D. CRISTOFORIS, a young engineer, 30 years age, who left London but a few weeks since, also fell in the same engagement. Of course we must hold ourselves prepared to read the names of our bravest and our best among the dead and wounded, but Philosophy is a poor comforter when the awful lists are actually before one's eyes!

KOSSUTH, with as many Hungarians as he can collect, starts to-day for Genoa, where General KLAPKA, Colonel KISS, General PERCZEL, General VETTER, Colonel YACZ, Colonel TELEKI, and others await him. Various are the surmises among English journalists as to the conditions existing between the Allies and the Ex-Governor of Hungary. The facts are these: Before the outbreak of the war, KOSSUTH and KLAPKA, making up their old differences, agreed to act in concert for the benefit of their common country, and the latter, on his return from Turkey, proceeded to Paris, where he held frequent interviews with Prince NAPOLEON, and thence to Turin, where he was received with open arms by Count CAVOUR, and also presented to the King. After sundry propositions and refusals on one side or the other, KOSSUTH at last offered to proceed to Genoa, and there issue a proclamation to the Hungarians calling on them to desert the Austrian army *en masse*, he to organize the deserters into a corps and become its military chief. When the number should reach 15,000 or 20,000, he demanded that with a small division of French troops, under a French flag, he should be authorized to cross the Adriatic and the Austrian provinces into Hungary, and there promote insurrection. The only objection made to this proposition was the displeasure of England at the double attack on Austria without rhyme or reason, and KOSSUTH was urged to make a tour through the Provinces, bending all his influence with the English people in the direction of non-intervention whatever turn the war may take. This course he has been pursuing with great energy for some weeks, commencing in London with the Lord Mayor in the chair, (a sign of the popularity of his theme, as years have passed since the powers that be have favored the illustrious exile with the light of their countenances,) and concluding with Glasgow, where the M. P.'s, and that warm friend of nationalities, Professor NICHOL, gave him every support. Meanwhile he issued an anonymous proclamation to the Hungarian troops, and now he has gone to Genoa to complete his share of the bargain. Whatever the English Government may think of this arrangement, depend upon it that the English people will hail with joy any event that may give brave Hungary a chance. The only thing to be feared is, that the desertion of the Hungarians once accomplished, (a most important point for the Allies,) the promises made to KOSSUTH, through KLAPKA, who it must be remembered has conferred with CAVOUR and Prince NAPOLEON, and not with the Emperor, will be set aside, and the expedition to Hungary abandoned, under the pretext that England protests against French intervention. As yet we have no means of judging how the public will view the scheme, as these facts are entirely unknown here, though the future will prove their accuracy. The current report is that the Grand Duke CONSTANTINE is spoken of as the future King of Hungary. This is not improbable, as, despite the promises made at Stutgardt, NAPOLEON has had immense difficulty in reconciling the Czar to his actual plans. This accounts for the procrastination and irresolution which marked the Imperial policy at the commencement of the year. However, all negotiations have been successfully concluded by LA BOUCIERE during his mission to St. Petersburgh. NAPOLEON has given his formal promise that Poland shall be prevented from rising, and shall be crushed if she attempts it. News of insurrectionary movements throughout the Turkish Empire will soon reach you, as these movements are already organized in Servia, Bosnia and Montenegro. Movements in Greece will follow. The Czar will be allowed to take what he can get in actual territory, and the remainder of the provinces to be organized under the protectorate of Russia. Such are the plans of the two Cæsars; how far they will be able to realize them remains to be proved.

4 P. M.—A telegram from Milan confirms the report of insurrection.

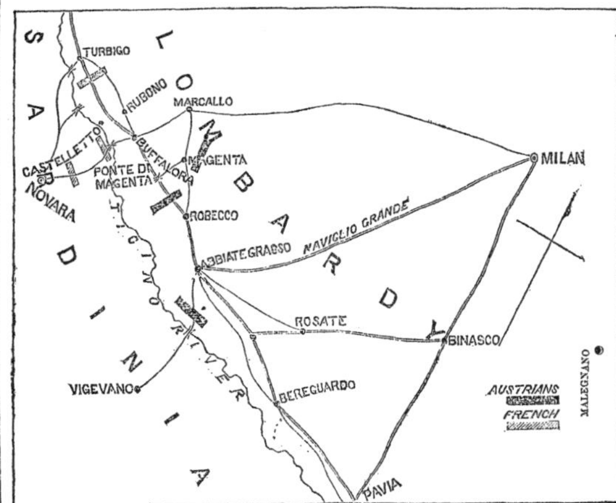

THE BATTLE OF MAGENTA

In the sketch which we publish above, of the points covered by the contending forces in the great battle of the 4th and 5th of June, our readers will, perhaps, find the means of understanding the nature of that battle more distinctly than any written account, or any map embracing more particulars, would enable them to.

The parallels on our plan represent the great canal, formed first in the twelfth century for purposes of navigation and irrigation, and subsequently improved and enlarged, especially under a skillful engineer of the sixteenth century, GIUSEPPE MEDA, who, like LEONARDO DA VINCI, and many other great artists of that wonderful age, was a painter as well as a hydraulist. The canal passes by Turbigo, Castelletto, and Rubono to Buffalora. Thence it widens, and taking in other branches, runs by the village of Ponte-di-Magenta and Robecco to Abbiate-Grasso, following in all this course a southeasterly direction, parallel with the river, and at an average distance of about two miles from its bank. At Abbiate-Grasso it connects with another great canal, which runs eastward by the "Vigevano road" to Milan. This latter canal is called the Naviglio Grande, and the name, for convenience sake, is often applied to the whole line from Milan by Abbiate-Grasso, up to Tornavento and the river. The whole length of the main course is about forty-six miles; and the size of the cut may be inferred from the fact that it is regularly navigated by fleets of boats fastened together by ropes, and called in the country language, *cobbie*.

On the 2d of June the Austrians, at Vigevano having learned to their amazement the passage of the Ticino, near Turbigo, on the morning of that day by the Imperial French Guard, threw three army corps, numbering more than 120,000 men, across the river, to Abbiate-Grasso, and marched northwards to arrest the French advance, following the line of the canal. The French, under MACMAHON, followed the Guard on the 3d. On the 4th the allied main body, under CANROBERT, was to cross near Buffalora, the Imperial Guard, with the Emperor, holding the bridge-head at that point, and MACMAHON, with the Sardinian King, reaching the town of Buffalora and Magenta. The arrival of CANROBERT was delayed by the state of the roads between Novara and the Ticino, and the battle was first severe at the bridge-head of Buffalora, from which it extended to the bridge over the Canal at Pontè-di-Magenta and to Magenta. The village of Pontè-di-Magenta was taken and retaken seven times. At 8 P. M. the Austrians gave way finally and fell back towards Robecco. On the next day, Sunday, the conflict was renewed, apparently on the road between Robecco and Magenta, but the Austrians fell back again, the French following them by Abbiate-Grasso along the line of the Canal, and also in the direction of Rosate. On the 8th the Allied Sovereigns entered Milan; and on the 9th the Austrians entrenched at Malegnano, beyond Binasco, ten miles to the southeast of Milan, were again attacked and defeated by the French *corps d'armée* of BARAGUAY D'HILLIERS. As the French Emperor, whose activity and ubiquity seem little less marvelous than the like qualities of his great namesake, left Milan but a few hours after he entered it, in the direction of Pavia, we may expect to hear soon of a fresh allied advance upon the line of the Adda, accompanied by demonstrations from the force under Prince NAPOLEON from the south of the Po.

OUR PARIS CORRESPONDENCE.

Interesting Details of the Battles of Palestro—Illuminations in Honor of the Victory of Magenta—Conspicuous Gallantry of Victor Emanuel—The Emperor's Brilliant Success as a General—The Zouaves and Turcos—Incidents of the War.

PARIS, Tuesday, June 7, 1859.

A great battle has been fought and the capital of Lombardy is in the hands of the allied army! The glorious news arrived in Paris at noon on Sunday, in the form of a dispatch from the Emperor to the Empress; and this dispatch hastily stuck up over town on large posters, contained only the following words: "Bridge of Magenta, 11½ o'clock A. M. A Great Victory! 5,000 prisoners; 15,000 of the enemy killed and wounded. Details hereafter." As you may well conceive, this news threw Paris into a high state of excitement, and the town has been a *fête* ever since. Flags were hoisted on all the public buildings, the guns of the Invalides were fired, and in the evening a general illumination took place, which was repeated in a more brilliant manner last evening. The Boulevards were crowded with people, and everybody appeared happy; but there was none of that uproarious, boisterous exhibition of pleasure we see at home: the fact is, the French have ceased to be a demonstrative people. You will perceive that the newspapers do not issue extras; the Governmen charges itself with the duty of first informing the public by means of handbills of these important events.

A subsequent dispatch from the Emperor to the Empress carries the loss of the Austrians at the battle of Magenta to 27,000 men—20,000 killed and wounded, and 7,000 prisoners. The same dispatch fixes the French loss in killed and wounded at 3,000. The immense disparity in these estimates, even as approximative figures, which in fact they can only be, proves that the Austrians must have fought with a great disregard for life, either against superior skill or superior numbers. Up to the present time we have no knowledge of the numbers engaged on the opposing sides; but a dispatch from Vienna anterior to the battle says that the entire Austrian force was recrossing the Ticino, and concentrating in a mass at Abbiate Grasso and Rosate, three and six miles south of the village of Magenta. It is probable that the Austrians had not all crossed the river at the time of the battle, and it is certain that the French had not all arrived at the scene of action in time to take part in the struggle. It is therefore estimated here that from 160,000 to 180,000 men were engaged in the battle; but on which side the preponderance lay we have yet no means of judging Three cannons and two flags were taken by the French, and one cannon was lost. The King, Marshal CANROBERT, and Generals MCMAHON and ST. JEAN D'ANGELY, (Commander of the Imperial Guard,) were all four wounded. General ESPINASSE, lately Minister of Interior, and General of Division in the corps of MCMAHON, was killed, as was also General CLERC, of the Imperial Guard. Gen. MELLINET was dangerously wounded.

If we now go back to the events which preceded the battle of Magenta, we shall find ample material for admiring the maiden generalship of LOUIS NAPOLEON. His long delay at Alessandria was to collect and organize perfectly his army, so that, notwithstanding its great bulk, it could be moved rapidly in any required direction; moreover, by collecting his army there, and sending in the direction of Montebello and Casteggio strong advanced posts, he constantly maintained the idea in the Austrian camp that he was going to attempt to cross the river into Lombardy below Pavia. The sequel proves that the Austrians regarded this as the probable point at which NAPOLEON would attempt to cross.

On the 30th of May, the Emperor NAPOLEON with his whole army commenced moving to the north, stopping first at Casale. Thus far the Austrians had no reason to believe that the plan of campaign had been changed, for they could not tell whether this movement was a *ruse* or not, and so they waited. General NIEL, however, as well as BARAGUAY D'HILLIERS, had disappeared suddenly, and as far as the first was concerned, no trace of him could be found by the Austrians, until he suddenly fell on Novara and took the place, much to their surprise; for they retreated precipitately, scarcely firing a gun.

On the 1st of June, the Emperor had formed his junction with the King still further north, at Vercelli. The 2d of June, their Majesties were at Novara, still further north, with the bulk of the combined armies. It was now evident to the Austrians, that the French were aiming for the bridge of Buffalora, on the direct road from Novara to Milan, and they commenced, too late, as usual, to recross the Ticino, and rush up on the Lombard side of the river to intercept the crossing at Buffalora. NAPOLEON, in order once more to deceive them as to his real designs, made a feint to cross the bridge of Magenta, and then ordered the corps of General NIEL to cross the bridge of Turbigo, which he did on the 3d of June, Friday. A smart conflict ensued on the soil of Lombardy, in which the French loss was 40 killed and wounded. The French remained masters of the field. During this time the Emperor and King were preparing to mar the Imperial Guard and the great body of the combined army over the bridge of Magenta, an operation which was commenced during Friday night and Saturday morning, but which was not entirely terminated at the time the great battle of Magenta was fought, on Saturday afternoon.

Here, then, we see that the Austrians have not only been out-generaled, but they have been beaten on their own soil, and in all probability by inferior numbers. While they were preparing to defend the river at Pavia and Piacenza, the Emperor was arranging his plans for crossing far away to the north at Novara. The moving of this immense army from Alessandria and Montebello to Novara in four days, with all its stores, artillery and material of war, in such perfect order as to be prepared at any part of its march for a grand pitched battle, was a feat which does the highest honor to the military skill of LOUIS NAPOLEON and his generals. For, while it was passing north, it must be recollected, it was moving along in sight almost of that part of the Austrian army still posted in the Piedmontese territory, on the line from Garlasco north to Novara.

The King's crossing of the Sesia at Palestro, with the occupation of that place, seconded very materially the movement of the French army on Novara, and the general plan for the crossing at Buffalora. It was a part of the *ruse*, and contributed very materially to its success.

Thus the three first days of June give us the scene of two immense armies, one on each side of a river, rushing up that river to a certain point where one wishes to pass and the other wishes to prevent the passage. The invading army arrives first, effects its passage, and is caught only at a distance of two miles from the river, when all the advantages of an attack during the crossing have been lost. Much bloodshed was thus saved to the invading army, for at any point lower down on the river a crossing could only have been effected with a great loss of men.

The road to Milan was thus rendered free, and at this moment this city is in the hands of the Allies, and Lombardy has been declared free from the dominion of Austria. The end of the occupation of Sardinia by the Austrian army has been as inglorious and ignominious as its commencement was high-handed and boasting. The Austrian army entered Piedmont with a great noise and with high-sounding pretensions. It attempted to cut off the junction between the French and Piedmontese armies as well in the direction of Novi as in that of Susa. When the allied army had collected its strength and taken the offensive, the Austrian army attempted first at Varese, then at Como, then at Palestro, and finally at the bridge of Magenta, to arrest its victorious march, but in each case with an inglorious defeat. The dilatory General GYULAI came very near having his retreat from Piedmont cut off by the French on the Lombardy side of the Ticino! While the manœuvering of the Austrian General has been bungling and slow, the movement of the French army along the whole face of the Austrian line, from the extreme south to the extreme north, is one of the most brilliant feats in the history of strategy and tactics.

What is to be the first result of the battle of Magenta, and the occupation of Milan by the allied sovereigns? The troops that still stand wondering at Stradella and Pavia at the sudden disappearance of BARAGUAY D'HILLIERS from their neighborhood, will be obliged to fall back rapidly on Cremona, for fear of finding an army marching in the direction of Lodi, to cut off their retreat. The same on the north: the troops that have been engaged against GARIBALDI will fall back upon Brescia, to prevent isolation from the main body of the Austrian army. Milan, which was in a state of revolt as soon as the news of the battle of Magenta arrived, and the whole Province of Lombardy, will declare the independence of the State, and will offer their assistance in cutting off the retreat of the Austrians, and in driving them from their strongholds of the Mincio. It would not be surprising, indeed, if the Emperor should be able to return to Paris in September, as he promised.

During the day we have had but two items of news from the seat of war, one of which announces that a deputation of the Municipal Council of Milan had proceeded to the camp of the two sovereigns to tender to King VICTOR EMANUEL, in presence of the Emperor NAPOLEON, the annexation of Lombardy to Piedmont. The other item is to the effect that the victorious army is pursuing the Austrians towards the river Adda, and that the latter have left behind in their flight an immense amount of provisions, guns, and material of war.

The two sovereigns were to have attended a *Te Deum* to-day, in honor of the success of their arms, in the ancient cathedral of Milan.

Generals MCMAHON and REGNAUD DE ST. JEAN D'ANGELY, have been named Marshals of France, on the field of Magenta. These two officers and Marshal CANROBERT, in the words of the Emperor's dispatch to the Empress, "covered themselves with glory."

General ESPINASSE, who was killed at the battle of Magenta, was the first high officer who passed into Lombardy. His body has been embalmed, and will be brought to Paris for interment. The King, VICTOR EMANUEL, was wounded in the arm.

The bravery of the King has gained for him the title, by election, of "Corporal" in the Third Zouaves. This magnificent regiment has been given by NAPOLEON to VICTOR EMANUEL as a body guard, since the battle of Palestro, in which, under the King's personal direction, they performed such wonders. The title of Corporal thus conferred is a high honor, and was in like manner conferred by the Old Guard on the first Emperor, after an unusual exhibition of personal courage on his part. VICTOR EMANUEL already wears the French military medal presented to him when he was in Paris four years ago. He is the only monarch upon whom this honor has been conferred, as the medal is only given for great deeds of personal courage on the field of battle.

A *Te Deum* was chaunted to-day at Notre Dame in honor of the battle of Magenta and the liberation of Milan, with great pomp. It was a *fac simile* of that which took place for the taking of Sebastopol. The metropolitan cathedral was decorated interiorly and exteriorly with great richness; the Empress and the Court attended in the state carriages; all the dignitaries of State, legislators and high military officers were required to attend in uniform; the National Guard and detachments of the Imperial Guard formed the lines and the escort of honor. As soon as the Empress issued from the Tuileries at the head of the Court procession on the way to the Cathedral, the cannon of the Invalides began to fire a salute. At the same moment there broke over Paris a dark and terrible thunder-storm, which persisted till the end of the ceremonies. The explosions of the earthly artillery alternated with those of the heavens, and with the torrents of rain that poured down the noise and the terrors of the battle were reproduced in the imagination in the streets of Paris. As her Majesty issued from the cathedral at the end of the *Te Deum*, the sky cleared off, the sun came out mild and clear, and at this moment we are enjoying a delicious moonlight evening, with individuals here and there lighting up for the third time their illuminations in honor of the victory.

We shall no doubt be able to send you the details of the battle of Magenta by the *Persia*, which sails three days later than the *Ocean Queen*. MALAKOFF.

PARIS, Thursday, June 9, 1859.

It would be difficult for you to picture to yourself the animation that reigns at Paris since the battle of Magenta and the liberation of the capital of Lombardy. To see the Boulevards in the evening is worth a trip across the Atlantic. There is none of that yelling, shouting, drunkenness and extravagance of joy, which would be manifested in Broadway if the American arms on some part of the frontier were to gain a great battle; there is the same animation here, but it is manifested differently. The streets are illuminated, all countenances are animated, everybody talks of war, but it is done quietly and with decorum. When Paris is excited there is *no rushing from place to place*, there are none of those always-out-of-breath people who alarm and inflame the rest, but instead, they repair in a mass to the favorite public promenades, and there, by looking in their neighbors' faces and seeing that they are no more excited than themselves, they promenade out their excitement.

In conversation every word pronounced has some connexion with the war; every mind and nearly every heart, unfortunately, is fixed on the plains of Lombardy. In the family circle the conversation rolls but upon one subject—the battle fought or the battle to be fought. At the *café* the only words that strike the ear are, the Austrians, the Piedmontese, GARIBALDI, the quadrilateral fortresses, the Ticino, the Po, the Zouaves, the Turcos. In the street it is still the same song; the air and the words are changed, but it is the same theme. There the Austrians, from *Autrichiens*, become "*Autrichemards*"; GARIBALDI, "*Garibalduche*," (*Anglice*, a "rough customer"); the Zouaves, "*Zouzous*," and VICTOR EMANUEL "the Corporal."

The theatres are preparing military spectacles, in hich, you will hardly need to be assured, the poor Austrians will be kicked, dog-baited, jilted in love, laughed at, and otherwise ill-treated, in mass and in detail. But in mounting these pieces the managers meet with a serious difficulty; none of their actors, even to the most insignificant of the supernumeraries, are willing to take the part of the Austrians, unless with double pay, and only then reluctantly. The result is unfortunate for those who accept, because the number being limited on account of the cost, their kicks, cuffs and misfortunes generally, are increased in proportion. It is a fact that actors sometimes by consenting to assume these ungrateful parts, fix upon themselves a public dislike which clings to them for years. The most supreme of insults just now among the *gamins* in the street, is "*Vous êtes un Autrichien!*" ("You are an Austrian!")

While the war does harm to one class, it brings happiness to another. We are having a perfect avalanche of bellicose literature, which gives bread to a crowd of enterprising minds otherwise without evident means of subsistence. Among the new sheets that have been started are, *The Army Bulletin*, *The Zouave*, *Italy*, *The Austrians in Italy*, *The Chasseur d'Afrique*, *The Voltigeur*, *The Grenadier*, *The Soldat du Train*, etc. But these small journals are like great passions, they light up quickly and are as quickly extinguished.

The Zouaves, especially since the affair of Palestro, have become the lions of the day in Italy. Their feats in the field, and even their words, are the constant subject of conversation and of repetition. During the fight at Palestro, a certain detached body of Zouaves which had to pass through several deep and muddy canals in their impetuous charge on the enemy's artillery, found their fleetness more impeded by the weight of their immense baggy trousers, soaked with water and mud, than by the balls of the enemy's guns. To disembarrass themselves of this impediment was but the work of a moment, and thus the Zouaves appeared on the field with a flag at half-mast, which might have been taken by the Austrians as a demand for quarters; but their actions in no manner corresponded to the color of their flag, and the grape and cannister continued to mow down their ranks until they reached and bayoneted the artillerymen on their guns. It was not till then that their Sergeant bethought himself of the fact that his men were in the undress uniform not recognized by the code, and that he suggested to them the propriety—to use a French phrase—of entering into order again.

The Tyrolese sharp-shooters in the Austrian army wear on their bonnets a tuft of plumes which resemble very much that of the Piedmontese sharp-shooters. At the battle of Palestro a regiment of these Tyrolese were hidden in the wheat, and the Zouaves deceived by the plumes, and approaching with confidence, received at thirty steps a most murderous discharge of balls along the whole line. The surprise lasted but a moment. "*Sac à terre!*" cried the Zouaves in one voice: "*A la baïonnette!*" Their Colonel did not try to oppose the torrent; the smoke of the discharge was not yet dissipated when the Tyroleans received the human avalanche, preceded by its thousand steel points, and were thus precipitated into the canal, where many hundreds were drowned or bayoneted. Not a single Tyrolean would have escaped, perhaps, if the Zouaves had had their linen instead of the woolen pantaloons, for they could not swim with these, and the enemy had thrown away their guns.

The *Patrie* relates the manner in which the King, VICTOR EMANUEL, was named Corporal (an honorary title the reader will understand) in the Third Zouaves, after the battle of Palestro. The Zouaves had been interring their comrades who had been killed. A deep trench was dug on an eminence, and when the bodies had been deposited and the trench filled up, all present went on their knees, and after a short prayer retired, bidding adieu to their dead brethren in arms. "Comrades!" exclaimed a Sergeant, as a funeral oration, "May God receive you! It was your turn to-day—to-morrow it may be ours!"

After this short and touching ceremony, the Zouaves about 400 in number, collected at a farm-house and were enjoying themselves with the abundant provisions they always know how to procure for themselves independent of their ordinary rations. The King's great bravery during the battle naturally came up for discussion, and various modes were proposed for properly informing his Majesty of their high appreciation of his valor. At last the proposition was made that he should be made Corporal of the Third Regiment of Zouaves. This was unanimously agreed to, and then the nomination was made with great formality. The oldest Sergeant standing up, solemnly proclaimed in a loud voice: "In the name of the 31 Zouaves, VICTOR EMANUEL, King of Sardinia, is named to the rank of Corporal in the said regiment!" The next day a memorandum of these proceedings was drawn up, signed by all the Zouaves, and sent to the King, who accepted the title as a high compliment.

The courage displayed by VICTOR EMANUEL was indeed well calculated to excite the enthusiasm of such soldiers as the Zouaves; seeing that they could not restrain him at Palestro, they adopted the plan of running before him. Thus his person was in some measure protected from harm.

The Zouaves are as kind and magnanimous to their prisoners as they are unequaled and admirable in their fighting qualities. An enemy who no longer resists is for the Zouave an object for protection and commiseration, and one can conceive of no nobler quality in a soldier than this. He takes pride in binding up and relieving the wounds he has just made. An Austrian officer at Palestro was seriously wounded; his horse carried him close to the French, where with difficulty he was clinging to his saddle. A Zouave stopped his horse and righted him in the saddle, when the Austrian repaid this act of kindness by placing his pistol against the Zouave's head and blowing his brains out. The officer was carried a prisoner to the French hospital, where great care will be taken to cure him, in order that he may be passed before a Court-martial and in his turn shot.

One of the circumstances to which the Zouave is indebted for his remarkable fighting qualities is the severe education through which he passes in the barracks. The gymnastics imposed upon him are something formidable. He is made to run by the hour at the top of his speed; he jumps, climbs, runs on his hands and feet, and is taught to do all this day after day, with musket and fixed bayonet in the hand. He is taught also to fence with his bayonet, and while he is thus fencing he actually leaps upon his enemy and stamps him to the ground. They do not care much about firing, preferring the bayonet and their rapid charges. A story is told in the papers which illustrates this fact. Just before one of the last combats they were distributing the cartridges to the different companies. When it came the turn of the Zouaves, they showed all the prudery of a young girl to whom one offers a present. They shrugged their shoulders, sidled away, said they didn't care about them, and they had to force them to accept. Then they took a cartouche delicately between the end of their fingers, and said, carelessly: "Pardon, Sergeant, I'll only take one!" What need, in effect, have they of cartouches? They go almost as rapidly as their balls, and they have their bayonets beside.

The Turcos have excited as much curiosity as the Zouaves. Their commander says that with the bayonet or in face of a battery of artillery they are splendid soldiers; their only fear is of mounted men; they do not stand well when threatened with cavalry. It is the habit of these savages in their native country to cut off the heads of their prisoners and the wounded on the field of battle. They have been taught by their French commanders that this will not be permitted under the French flag. At Magenta they were among the first in the action, and their mode of attack is represented as something peculiarly wild and savage. They attacked with loud cries, uttering all the oaths in the Mohammedan language. When they took prisoners they danced and yelled around them, putting them down on the ground—blasphemed outrageously over their heads, pronouncing in Arab all sorts of curses against their army and country—all of which must have astonished not a little the stoical Germans. The French commanders seem to be well satisfied, however, with this first trial of their half-tamed Kabyles. Their costume is the same as that of the Zouaves, only it is entirely green, and very picturesque. Like the Zouaves, they wear beards with shaved foreheads.

When the people in certain districts saw the regiment of Turcos arrive they barricaded themselves in their houses, uttering fearful cries. They avowed subsequently, when interrogated on the subject, tha the Austrians had told them that there were soldiers n the French army (referring to the Turcos) who lived only upon the meat of Christians! *Dei soldat che mangiano des Christiani*, they said. While one may find it astonishing that the Austrians should resort to such means of intimidation, it is not at all astonishing that the Turcos should have been recognized at first sight by these alarmed people, as the promised cannibals.

It is true that Captain JEROME BONAPARTE was at the

The New-York Times.

VOL. IX.—NO. 2520. NEW-YORK, TUESDAY, OCTOBER 18, 1859. PRICE TWO CENTS.

SERVILE INSURRECTION.

The Federal Arsenal at Harper's Ferry in Possession of the Insurgents.

GENERAL STAMPEDE OF SLAVES.

United States Troops on their March to the Scene.

Dispatches from our Special Correspondent.

WASHINGTON, Monday, Oct. 17.

The report that negroes have taken possession of Harper's Ferry, and now hold the Government Armory, has created great excitement here. It is said that troops from Fort McHenry, Baltimore, will be dispatched forthwith to the scene of disorder.

Dispatches to the President and Secretary of War confirm the report from Harper's Ferry. The President has telegraphed to Postmasters at Frederick and Baltimore for particulars. The train was fired into on the Bridge, and one man was killed. The insurgents have possession of the Bridge. A special train at Baltimore has been ordered to carry on troops. Frederick Volunteers have offered services.

WASHINGTON, Monday, Oct. 17.

The latest account says the insurgents are Government employes, headed by one ANDERSON, lately arrived there. It is believed to be an Abolition movement to protect runaways. A large number of negroes stampeded last evening from several localities. It is supposed that they are making for Harper's Ferry.

RELAY HOUSE BALTIMORE AND OHIO RAILROAD, Monday, Oct. 17.

Gov. FLOYD announced in the Cabinet meeting this morning that two months ago he received an anonymous letter stating that an Abolitionist movement was on foot, which would exhibit itself first at Harper's Ferry, about the middle of October, but he treated it with levity, and had not thought of it since. This seems to give the key to the insurrection.

A train has just arrived here with three companies, but without ammunition.

The eighty-five marines in company are fully equipped and supplied, and may divide. The marines were ready at Washington dépôt in one hour and twenty minutes from the first notice of the order.

BALTIMORE AND OHIO RAILROAD, PLANE NUMBER 4—9 P. M.

Our train of seventeen cars, with two hundred and ten Baltimore troops, eighty from Marines, and one hundred and twenty from Frederick, is just going on. Besides the above, there are one hundred and eighty Artillerymen from Fort Monroe. These constitute the whole force. Major REYNOLDS has command, until Major LEE, who is behind on a special train, with ammunition, comes up.

The insurgents have pillaged the pay-office. Gov. WISE has ordered out the Jefferson Regiment, and a horseman has been dispatched by the Baltimore and Ohio Railroad, with the Governor's orders. This messenger will endeavor to pass through the country, and deliver his message by three o'clock to-day. It is yet doubtful whether the troops will make an attack to-night or wait for daylight.

MONOCACY BRIDGE, Monday, Oct. 17.

A train has just returned from Harper's Ferry having been refused permission to pass. The insurgents are increasing. The baggage-master of the train was permitted to pass into the town, when he was marched into the Armory, where he found about six hundred runaway negroes. Mr. WASHINGTON, of Jefferson, also came down with his wife and servant. The latter was taken prisoner, and Mr. WASHINGTON and his wife were tied in their carriage. The place appeared to be deserted by the inhabitants. A few only remained. The baggage-master was permitted to return.

The same party reports about two hundred white men engaged in the insurrection. Everything had been plundered, and all appeared determined to fight. Mr. DIFFEY, master of trains, has telegraphed from Martinsburg, *viâ* Wheeling, that a body of armed men have taken possession of the Armory at Harper's Ferry and have planted guns in one bridge; they have stopped all our tonnage, and mail trains bound East are at the west end of the bridge. The telegraph wires are cut and there is no communication East. A body of armed men are getting ready to leave here at once to clear the bridge, that our trains can pass.

There is great excitement all through the neighborhood. It is now evident that the insurgents have fortified themselves and will make a desperate resistance. The Directors and families of the Pennsylvania Central Railroad are on an excursion, and have also been stopped at Harper's Ferry.

The following are the first dispatches received from the scene of disturbance, that were communicated to the Government:

"The express train east has been detained at Harper's Ferry in consequence of the railroad bridge and Armory being in the possession of an armed organized band of Abolitionists. They are 100, and perhaps more, in number. I took my baggage master and proceeded through the bridge, when I was stopped by three men having arms, who ordered me to halt or be shot down. I retired from the bridge and made my escape. I have been frequently shot at, and so have many others. All the watchmen of the bridge and Armory are under arrest. Moreover, every bridge around is guarded. HAYWOOD, the colored man, has been shot through the left side, greatly endangering his life. Inform the United States officials at once. There are some eight or ten men in the neighborhood of the Ferry in the greatest anxiety to know the issue of this dreadful affair. The captain of the band told me to notify you that no other trains should pass the bridge. Had you not better notify the Secretary of War of the circumstance?"

Our train is ordered to let Major LEE overtake us. The Frederick companies went at 3 o'clock, P. M., but have not since been heard from. We take on at this place two additional pieces of artillery, and an additional supply of ammunition from Frederick.

HARPER'S FERRY, Monday, Oct. 17.

Train arrived and halted below town, where runners communicated the state of affairs. Jefferson County Regiment had entered town, from Virginia side, and Frederick troops crossed the bridge; there had been a deal of firing. Some nine persons killed.

Mr. BECKHAM, Agent of the Railroad Company, was shot through, and his murderer fell almost at the same instant, pinned by a rifle ball from a friend of Mr. BECKHAM.

The troops have landed, and are in the town. The insurgents are willing to surrender, but on terms of safe conduct out of difficulty, otherwise they threaten to sacrifice the lives of LEWIS WASHINGTON and Col. DANGERFIELD, who they now hold as prisoners. Capt. AARON STEPHENS, of Norwich, Conn., is now dying of wounds, and makes the following statement:

"The plan has been concocting for a year or more. The parties rendezvoused at a farm a few miles from here, rented for the purpose by Capt. BROWN, of Kansas notoriety, under the name of Smith. Among the insurgents are KAGG, of Ohio; TODD, of Maine; WM. SEAMAN and Mr. BROWN, of Ohio." Q.

From the Associated Press.

BALTIMORE, Monday, Oct. 17.

A dispatch just received here from Frederick, and dated this morning, states that an insurrection has broken out at Harper's Ferry, where an armed band of Abolitionists have full possession of the Government Arsenal. The express train going east was twice fired into, and one of the railroad hands and a negro was killed, while they were endeavoring to get the train through the town. The insurrectionists stopped and arrested two men, who had come to town with a load of wheat, and, seizing their wagon, loaded it with rifles, and sent them into Maryland. The insurrectionists number about two hundred and fifty whites, and are aided by a gang of negroes. At last accounts fighting was going on.

The above is given just as it was received here. It seems very improbable, and should be received with great caution, until confirmed by further advices.

BALTIMORE, Monday, Oct. 17.

A later dispatch received at the Railroad Office, says the affair has been greatly exaggerated. The reports had their foundation in a difficulty at the Armory, with which negroes had nothing to do.

BALTIMORE, Monday, Sept. 17—1 P. M.

It is apprehended that the affair at Harper's Ferry is more serious than our citizens seem willing to believe. The wires from Harper's Ferry are cut, and consequently we have no telegraphic communication beyond Moncacy Station. The Southern train, which was due here at an early hour this morning, has not yet arrived. It is rumored there is a stampede of negroes from this State. There are many other wild rumors, but nothing authentic as yet.

The Secretary of War has telegraphed to Fort Monroe for three companies of artillery, who are expected to be in Baltimore to-morrow morning. A company of marines will leave the Washington Navy-yard at 3:20 o'clock to-day for Harper's Ferry

BALTIMORE, Monday, Oct. 17—2 P. M.

Another account received by train says the bridge across the Potomac was filled with insurgents, all armed. Every light in the town was extinguished, and the hotels, closed in all the streets, were in possession of the mob, and every road and lane leading thereto barricaded and guarded. Men were seen in every quarter, with muskets and bayonets, who arrested the citizens, and pressed them into the service, including many negroes. This done, the United States arsenal and government pay-house, in which was said to be a large amount of money, and all the other public works were seized by the mob. Some were of the opinion that the object was entirely plunder, and to rob the government of the funds deposited on Saturday at the pay-house. During the night the mob made a demand on the Wager Hotel for provisions, and a body of armed men enforced the claim. The citizens were in a terrible state of alarm, the insurgents having threatened to burn the town.

The following has just been received from Monocacy, this side of Harper's Ferry: "The mail agent on the Western-bound train has returned to Monocacy, and reports that the train was unable to get through. The town is in possession of the negroes, who arrest every one they can catch, and imprison. The train due here at 3 P. M., could not get through, and the agent came down on an empty engine."

BALTIMORE, Monday, Oct. 17—2½ P. M.

The Western train on the Baltimore and Ohio Railroad has just arrived here. Its officers confirm the statements first received touching the disturbance at Harper's Ferry. Their statement is to the effect that the bridge-keeper at Harper's Ferry, perceiving that his lights had been extinguished, went to ascertain the cause, when he was pursued and fired upon by a gang of blacks and whites. Subsequently the train came along, when a colored man, who acted as assistant to the baggage-master, was shot, receiving a mortal wound, and the conductor, Mr. PHELPS, was threatened with violence if he attempted to proceed with the train. Feeling uncertain as to the condition of affairs, the conductor waited until after daylight before he ventured to proceed, having delayed the train six hours. Mr. PHELPS says the insurrectionists number two hundred blacks and whites, and that they have full possession of the United States armory. The party is commanded or led by a man named ANDERSON, who had lately arrived at Harper's Ferry. Mr. PHELPS also confirms the statement in a previous dispatch, that the insurrectionists had seized a wagon, and loading it with muskets had dispatched it into Maryland. The military of Frederick had been ordered out.

Dispatches have been received from President BUCHANAN, ordering out the United States troops at this point, and a special train is now getting ready to convey them to the scene of disturbance. He has also accepted the volunteered services of Capt. SENICK's Company of Frederick, and has likewise ordered the Government troops from Old Point Comfort to proceed immediately to Harper's Ferry. This intelligence is authentic.

BALTIMORE, Monday, Oct. 17—3½ P.M.

The mail train going West got as far as Sandy, when Mr. HOOD, the baggage master, and another party, started on foot to the bridge. They went through the bridge, and were taken and imprisoned, but subsequently went before the captain of the insurrectionists, who refused to let anything pass. All of the eastward bound trains laying west of Harper's Ferry, have been taken; persons from this side the river, tying them together, and taking off the slaves. The mail train bound West has returned to Monocacy. There are from five hundred to seven hundred whites and blacks concerned in the insurrection.

The United States marines at Washington are under orders for Harper's Ferry. There is great excitement in Baltimore, and the military are moving. Several companies are in readiness to take the train, which will leave soon.

BALTIMORE, Monday, Oct. 17—4 P. M.

An account from Frederick says a letter has been received there from a merchant at Harper's Ferry, sent by a boy who had to cross the mountain and swim the river, which says that all the principal citizens are imprisoned, and many have been killed; also, that the railroad agent had been shot twice, and that the watchman at the dépôt had been shot dead.

BALTIMORE, Monday, Oct. 17—5 P. M.

A train filled with military, including the Law Greys, City Guards, Shields' Guards, and other companies, left here at 4 o'clock for Harper's Ferry. Representatives of the press accompanied the military.

BALTIMORE, Monday, Oct. 17—7 P. M.

A dispatch from Martinsburgh, west of Harper's Ferry, received *via* Wheeling and Pittsburgh, confirms the report of the insurrectionists having possession of the arsenal at Harper's Ferry, and says they have planted cannon at the bridge. All the trains have been stopped. A body of armed men was getting ready to proceed thither to clear the road. There was great excitement at Martinsburgh, Va.

RICHMOND, Monday, Oct. 17.

It is reported and believed that the Governor of Virginia has ordered volunteer troops to Harper's Ferry.

WASHINGTON, Monday, Oct 17—4 P. M.

On the receipt of the intelligence from Harper's Ferry, orders were issued for three companies of artillery at Old Point and the corps of marines at Washington Barracks to proceed thither without delay. The marines, ninety-three in number, left in the 3:15 P. M. train, with two twelve-pound howitzers and a full supply of ammunition. It is reported that they are under orders to force the bridge to-night at all hazards. Col. FAULKNER accompanies them.

It is reported, on good authority, that some weeks ago Secretary FLOYD received anonymous epistles stating that about the 15th of October the Abolitionists and negroes, and other disaffected persons, would make an attempt to seize the arsenal and hold the place, but the statement was so indefinite and improbable as to cause no fears of such an outbreak.

WASHINGTON, Monday, Oct. 17.—9 P. M.

In view of the possibility of the disturbances at Harper's Ferry extending to this vicinity, the Mayors of Washington and Alexandria have taken precautionary steps for its suppression. The President, through the Mayor of Washington, ordered a strong detachment of volunteer Militia to be posted at the National and Company armories, which was promptly done. Two hundred stand of muskets and a supply of ammunition will also be placed in the City Hall, for emergency. It is suggested by well-informed persons that the cause of the insurrection is the reported fact that not long since the contractor for the construction of a Government dam, at the Ferry, absconded, largely indebted to several hundred employes, who have taken this step to indemnify themselves, by the seizure of the Government Funds, which it was supposed were transported thither on Saturday. A gentleman just in from Harper's Ferry, thinks the blacks participated in the outbreak only on compulsion.

RICHMOND, Monday, Oct. 17—9 P. M.

There is great excitement here. Company F, with full ranks, has just left the Armory, expecting to take a special train to-night. There is a new company, with a similar uniform to the Greys.

The Greys leave for Harper's Ferry early in the morning. The Governor left to-night for Washington.

BALTIMORE, Monday, Oct. 17—9 P. M.

The *American's* special reporter telegraphs from Plane No. 4, 45 miles from Baltimore, and 31 from Harper's Ferry, at 8 o'clock, that the train consists of seventeen cars, with four hundred troops, under Maj. REYNOLDS, with a roadmaster and laborers to repair the track, and telegraphers to mend the lines. Three companies from Frederick were in an advance train. Col. HARRIS, of the United States Marines, commanding the expedition, follows in a special train. They will not reach Harper's Ferry before 10 o'clock.

MONOCACY BRIDGE, Monday, Oct. 17—10 P. M.

The train arrived here at 9 o'clock. LUTHER SIMPSON, baggage master of the mail train, gives the following particulars: I walked up the bridge; was stopped, but was afterwards permitted to go up and see the captain of the insurrectionists; I was taken to the armony, and saw the captain, whose name is BILL SMITH; I was kept prisoner for more than an hour, and saw from five hundred to six hundred negroes, all having arms; there were two or three hundred white men with them; all the houses were closed. I went into a tavern kept by Mr. CHAMBERS; thirty of the inhabitants were collected there with arms. They said most of the inhabitants had left, but they declined, preferring to protect themselves; it was reported that five or six persons had been shot.

Mr. SIMPSON was escorted back over the bridge by six negroes.

The train with the Frederick military is laying at Point of Rocks. A train with the directors of the Pennsylvania Railroad on board, is on the other side of Harper's Ferry. It was believed that the insurrectionists would leave as soon as it became dark. Orders have been received here that the train shall stop at Sandy Hook until Col. LEE, who is following in a special train, arrives. There are any amount of rumors, but nothing certain.

MONOCACY, Tuesday, Oct. 18—1 A. M.

The special train, with Col. LEE'S command, passed this station at 11:30 P. M. It is supposed that there is difficulty in adjusting the breaks in the road this side of Harper's Ferry, as nothing has since been heard of the expedition.

Episcopal General Convention.

RICHMOND, Monday, Oct. 17.

Both houses have agreed to hold their next Convention in New-York.

The report of the Committee on typographical errors in the standard Bible has been adopted, and Dr. MASON, of Maryland, appointed typographical corrector.

The order of the day was the consideration of resolutions by the Committe on domestic and foreign missions. A long debate took place. It chiefly related to the extension of missionary operations in Japan, China, &c. All the Committee's resolutions were adopted except the last, which was to memorialize the President, asking him to address the Court of Spain respecting religious toleration in Cuba.

Pending the debate the house adjourned.

The Sunday Law in Pittsburgh.

PITTSBURGH, Monday, Oct. 17.

Chief-Justice LOWRIE, whose driver was fined twenty-five dollars for violating the Sunday laws in driving his family to church, has published a card, in which he says he was quite ignorant that he had been allowing a trangression of the law, though he had studied it carefully, and officially declines carrying the case further, because there may be suitors before the Supreme Court in other cases, and they ought not to be embarrassed by having one of its Judges pecuniarily interested.

J. F. Shepard of the People's Five Cent Savings Bank of Boston.

BOSTON, Monday, Oct. 17.

J. F. SHEPARD of the People's Five Cent Savings Bank of this city, was brought before the Police Court this morning on a charge of defalcation, and on waiving an examination was bound over in the sum of $12,000 to stand his trial at the Superior Court

Death of John Calhoun.

ST. LOUIS, Monday, Oct. 17.

JOHN CALHOUN, Ex-Surveyor-General of Kansas and Nebraska, and President of the Lecompton Constitutional Convention, died at St. Josephs on the 13th inst.

The Attempted Insurrection at Constantinople

From the correspondence of the Paris papers are derived the following particulars of the recent attempt to overthrow the reigning dynasty of Turkey:

It is not yet three months since a secret society was founded which had for its daring object to seize the Sultan and his Ministers, and to modify the form of Government. The principal personage, Sheik AHMED, a Kurd, born at Suleymanieh, inhabited the médréeé (school) of the Mosque of Sultan BAJAZID. He is an enlightened man, free from fanaticism, much esteemed as a theologian and philosopher, and of incontestable honesty. Like most of the Turks, Sheik AHMED deplored the manner in which public affairs were conducted, the growing feebleness of the Empire, the administrative abuses, the financial disorders, the incessant and immoderate expenses of the palace; he severely criticised the acts of Ministers and the weakness of the Sovereign. He was listened to with deference, and his words derived great importance from the moral authority he enjoyed. Added to this, facts of daily occurrence confirmed those words, and increased the popular discontent. Around the Sheik were grouped men who shared his ideas, and frequently met. They comprised magistrates, clergy, military men, persons of the middle classes, and employes.

Among the Sheik's admirers and friends was the Circassian, HUSSEIN PASHA, a hot-headed, resolute man, distinguished, in 1855, in the Kars campaign. He was then Colonel of the First Regiment of Arabistan, and is said to have greatly distinguished himself in the repulse of the Russian attack. His conduct on that occasion won him a General's rank. Less fortunate last year in Montenegro, where his *corps d'armée* was roughly handled, and he himself had two horses killed under him, and escaped most narrowly, he was removed from his command. He went to Constantinople to demand a court-martial, which was refused. Left without employment, and considering himself unjustly treated, he became a malcontent. He deemed himself dishonored and his character became soured. He fell in with Sheik AHMED, and readily joined in his plans. According to the version before me, he was the arm of the plot, as the Sheik was its head. About two months ago, however, HUSSEIN was appointed to the staff of the army of Roumelia. At first he refused to go, but at last yielded and departed. It is said to have been then agreed that, in his absence, the direction of the movement should be intrusted to HASSAN PASHA, General of Artillery and member of the Secret Society, who commanded the Bosphorous, with all his batteries and military posts. DJAFER PASHA was another conspirator. He is an Albanian of high family, who in former days was more than once in arms against the Porte, but who, during the campaign on the Danube, joined the Sultan's army with 200 of his countrymen armed and equipped at his own charge. After the war they promised him much, but performed nothing; they would not even let him return to his own country, but compelled him to live in Constantinople on his pay of about £7 sterling a month. The conspiracy made many other recruits, some of them men of much importance. They include a great number of officers, and even non-commissioned officers of Artillery, Engineers, and the Guard. The number of officers comprised is estimated at not less than 850. There was a regular organization. The society was divided into two classes, chiefs and associates. Only the chiefs knew each other; the associates knew only their chiefs, each of whom grouped around him 100 to 150 men. I believe I may affirm that this society reckoned scarcely less than 15,000 to 18,000 men. The following was the plan of the conspirators: When the Sultan should be returning from the mosque, or when at night he should leave his kiosk at Topkaneh, to return to the palace with his habitual escort of palace officials and domestics, he was to be allowed to reach the narrowest part of the street which runs parallel with the Bosphorus from Topkaneh to Dolma Bagtchi. In that part is the post of Cabutach. The officers and the soldiers were to carry off the Sultan. All had been gained over, or nearly so, and the officer answered for his men. The Sultan taken, rockets were to be thrown from the stairs of Cabutach, to serve as a signal for the regiment quartered at Kulalee, some distance up the Bosphorus, on the opposite side. This regiment was to go by detachments to arrest the Minister of War, RIZA PASHA, in his yali at Beglerbeg, and the Grand Vizier, AALI PASHA, and the Minister of Foreign Affairs, FUAD PASHA, at their yalis at Canlidja.

Other Ministers and Presidents and Members of Councils were to be arrested, and, with the Sultan, were to be kept prisoners. According to one statement, the man who betrayed the plot, HASSAN PASHA, did so on account of a resolution taken to put them all to death, ABDUL MEDJID included. The general opinion in Constantinople, however, is said to be that there was no intention of proceeding to such extremities, and that HASSAN invented the story to extenuate his first fault. The conspirators had fixed (without consulting them) on a number of persons of distinction to replace the deposed dignitaries. The Sultan was to be declared deposed, and his brother or his eldest son (accounts vary) was to be put upon the throne. Everything was arranged. On Saturday, the 17th of September, the plot was to be carried out; but on the Wednesday night preceding HASSAN went to RIZA PASHA and told him all. Prompt measures were taken. In the night of Thursday, and on the Friday and Saturday, many arrests were made. The prisoners were sent to Kulalee, to Scutari, and to Daoud Pasha,

NEWS FROM EUROPE.

LONDON PAPERS BY THE HAMMONIA.

THE SAN JUAN DIFFICULTY.

Kossuth on the Late War.

The screw-steamship *Hammonia*, of the Hamburg line, from Southampton on the 4th inst., arrived here last evening.

The advices thus received are not so late as those supplied by the *North Briton*; but we are placed in possession of London journals to the day of sailing, and from them derive additional news of interest.

According to the *Daily News*, it is said to have been decided that the *Great Eastern* is to leave Portland on the 8th and proceed to Holyhead. Under the provisions of the mercantile marine acts the *Great Eastern* would not be permitted to carry passengers, and the Directors would be liable to heavy penalties if they did so before receiving the certificate of the Marine Department of the Board of Trade. No passengers will, therefore, be conveyed on her trial trip.

The *Times* says: "During the past week no fewer than forty total wrecks have been posted on the books at Lloyd's. Among the more calamitous was the destruction by fire of the ship *Schah Jehan*, from Calcutta to the West Indies, with 300 coolie emigrants. Another heavy loss is the total wreck of the *Sovereign of the Seas*. There are, in addition, several missing vessels, respecting which the most painful forebodings are entertained.

The London papers announce the death of that eminent non-conformist divine and theological writer, JOHN ANGELL JAMES. The event occurred at Birmingham on the 1st inst.

The convict bankers, Sir JOHN DEAN PAUL and STRAHAN, now in prison under sentence, will be released from confinement on the 23d inst.

The British ship *Providence*, arrived at Falmouth, reports that she was fired into while passing Tarifa, on the 9th ult. One man was wounded, some stanchions and chain-plates carried away, and eight planks of the deck ripped up.

According to a Spanish Ministerial organ, the Government of Madrid intends to fortify Tarifa very strongly.

THE SAN JUAN BOUNDARY DISPUTE.

THE LONDON TIMES ON THE MISSION OF GENERAL SCOTT.

We are glad to learn by the last steamer from America that Gen. SCOTT has been sent to take the place of the bellicose Gen. HARNEY in the command of the Pacific coast. Such a step on the part of President BUCHANAN is only what we had a right to expect from a politician who is old, experienced, and has a knowledge not only of his own country, but of our own. We may say, without fearing the charge of timidity, that we trust this difficulty will be settled peaceably, and according to the just rights of either party. It is so usual for men in command of American detachments or ships of war to indulge in vagaries like those of Gen. HARNEY that we are not disposed to dwell on the discourtesy of this officer; but the notion of disputing our right to an island which has been in the possession of the Hudson's Bay Company for an indefinite time, and which has remained in their hands since the treaty of 1846, and of doing this simply because it was pretended that an American had been arrested for an outrage on the Company's property, is something new in the annals of military achievements. Gen. HARNEY has been beyond doubt merely the representative of a class sufficiently abundant in the unsettled regions of America. The choice spirits who flock to California and Oregon from the more civilized parts of the Union are too much accustomed to administer justice on one another with the rifle and bowie-knife to take much thought about legal tribunals and established jurisdictions. They flocked into British territory, refused to pay taxes levied by competent authority, gave Gen. DOUGLASS plenty of trouble, and at last were only brought to order by the determination of the Government, supported by the mass of British-born subjects. Having been foiled in attempting to subject British Columbia to the reign of rowdyism, they have since endeavored to nibble at the possessions of her Britannic Majesty. The Island of San Juan is the spot which, by a forced interpretation of a very simple treaty, it is attempted to make American ground. It is only within the last few days that anything has been heard of this island—that its very name has been known generally—in the British metropolis. But for some time the idea of contesting our rights has been cherished by the local patriots, and some two months or more since it was determined to try what boldness and affected contempt of British remonstrances would do. In Gen. HARNEY the promotors of this enterprise had a fitting leader. Under pretence that an American had been illegally arrested by the Hudson's Bay Company, he declared that the time was come to assert by force the rights of the United States. Oregon is not now at six months' distance from Washington, nor are the Atlantic States divided by any lengthened term of voyage from the shores of England. Three months might be sufficient to settle the question of the Gulf of Georgia by the two Governments, and in that time it could not be pretended that the citizens of the United States were likely to suffer any great injuries or indignities. But to send a dispatch home requesting the settlement of the dispute, and then to offer arrangements with the British authorities during the necessary interval, would be a tame way of proceeding. It suits neither the temper nor the interests of a republican commander. Such a man may be swayed by two desires—the first to show his resolution to foreigners, war with whom forms almost the whole history of his country; the second to gain popularity in his native State for the Union in general, and open the way for future professional or political success. It is, no doubt, a great thing for a General to have the admiration of such a race as peoples California, to be their leader in an aggression which they will all support, and to be able to count on the suffrages of them, or those like them in other States of the Union. We cannot tell what may have already happened in those distant regions, but it is quite certain that if blood has been spilt, it must rest on the head of the officer who bethought himself of settling by a *coup de main* the difference in the construction of a treaty between his own country and such an empire as England. The naval force which Governor DOUGLAS can call to his aid is far from small, and the resources of the two countries in this respect are so different that we need have no fear of the result, should the intemperance of Gen. HARNEY and his supporters carry matters further than the patience of the British authorities can bear.

The circumstances of the landing are already pretty well known. There had been petty disputes for a month or two, the island having always been treated as British, and the Americans guilty of any encroachment having been resisted by the Hudson's Bay Company, when in July the claim of the United States to the island was first put in force by the landing of a body of troops. This took place on the 27th, the United States' Boundary Commissioner accompanying the troops. Having thus put an end, as far as in them lay, to any discussion of the rights of England, the Americans then bethought themselves of a conference with the British Admiral. Not a single British ship of war had been at the place for weeks previously; but, the fact of the American aggression having become known to the Admiral, he repaired to San Juan, and on the 11th of August, a fortnight after the invasion, a Mr. CAMPBELL, the United States' Boundary Commissioner, and Col. CASEY, of the American army, arrived in a packet-ship, and requested that Admiral BAYNES would come on board their vessel, and confer with them. This request, it is needless to say, was at once declined.

So stood matters at the last dispatch of mails from California. We trust that nothing has since happened to complicate the dispute. Should things remain as they were, the arrival of Gen. SCOTT with instructions from Washington will, no doubt, tend to bring matters to an amicable conclusion. The principal work, however, is to be done in the two capitals, and we would counsel the American Government, in all friendship and sincerity, not to minister to the ambitious passions of any man or class, by contesting rights which seem to us too strong for sophistry to overturn. There can be no doubt that the treaty of 1846 gave, and was intended to give, to Great Britain and the United States the free navigation of the Gulf of Georgia, and that this could be alone effected by making the channel which divides the two empires what it was always considered to be—the broad estuary which flows to the eastward of San Juan. This was the channel in those days when California had not yet been colonized, when British Columbia was yet unknown and unnamed, and when Oregon itself was a wilderness, wandered over only by the hunter and the trapper. Nothing was thought of other channels between San Juan and Vancouver, passable indeed to the steamers of the present day, but never navigated in those times, and surely never present to the minds of the statesmen who, map in hand, negotiated the Treaty of 1846. This is the view of the matter according to the spirit of the treaty, but if we take the letter it bears out no less our claims. The express words are, that "the line shall be continued westward along the 49th parallel of latitude to *the middle of the channel which separates the Continent from Vancouver's Island*, and then southerly, through the middle of said channel and Fuca Straits, to the Pacific Ocean." On these words the British Government is content to rest its claim, and it is mere surveyor's work to determine whether the line southward from the middle point of the channel, in 49° north, and through the middle of Fuca Straits, does or does not give the Island of San Juan to the British Crown.

THE FATE OF HUNGARY.

INTERESTING LETTER FROM M. KOSSUTH.

The following letter, addressed to JOHN MCADAM, Esq., of Glasgow, is published in the *Bulletin* of that city:

LONDON, Sept. 26, 1859.

MY DEAR SIR: The fatal day of Villafranca prostrated my hopes at a moment when we had the deliverance of my country within sight; nay, almost within the reach of our hand, like a ripe fruit ready to be plucked; and here I am again, a poor exile, as I was four months ago, only older by ten years from the bitter pangs of disappointment.

I say designedly "disappointment," and not "deceit." Of deceit I cannot complain, for I took good care to guard myself and my country against even the possibility of deceit; but I feel my heart nearly broken by disappointment, unwarranted by circumstances, unaccounted and unaccountable.

Without that thunderbolt from a clear sky—the Villafranca arrangement—this moment at which I write, Hungary would have already filled a page in the annals of history than which *none equal stands yet on* record; because the whole nation was united, ready, and resolved as scarcely ever before. All the feelings which sometimes bring division into a national household—difference of religion, language, race, and distinction of classes—had melted into one great common resolution—to get rid of the banditti rule of the House of Austria as soon as the war would take its logical expansion.

And the positive knowledge of this fact only adds to the bitter pangs of my disappointment. To be thus stopped at the moment when we were stretching out our hand to pluck the ripe fruit of liberty is distressing beyond description.

Well, it is as it is, and must be borne. It shall be borne undespondingly, though not without grief. If feel tranquil in my conscience that I have done the duty of an honest man and of a good citizen, by not neglecting to try whether or not events might be *turned, on a solid basis, to the profit of my native* land.

And some consolation I have besides. I had occasion to get reassured on the point that no diplomatic tricks—in fact, nothing that the lying craft of despots may devise—will ever for a moment divert my nation from its unalterable determination to take advantage of every reasonable opportunity for reasserting its independence.

I have learned that this resolution can as little be broken by terrorism as it can be shaken by any concessions which the HAPSBURGS may devise in the hour of their need. I have learned that Hungary knows how to endure, how to wait, but never will change. I know that the nation is as well disciplined as it is determined.

I have been confirmed, together with my nation, in the conviction that no great European question can ever receive its definitive solution without us; nor can Europe be brought to a settled condition without the rights and legitimate claims of Hungary being taken into due account.

From this conviction we desire the certainty of our future. We believe in our future freedom, therefore we shall be free. The corresponding resolution has with the whole nation become a religious creed.

To have learnt all this is some consolation; and one more I have—I have the satisfaction to know that by insisting on the guarantee of irretractible facts preliminary to my giving the signal for rising, I have preserved my country from great misfortunes for aims which were not our own, and have preserved its future uncompromised—intact. This, at least, is a bright speck on the dreary horizon of my deep grief.

I was particularly careful to warn my fellow-countrymen in exile not to be led away by impatience, to throw up their positions which they may have gained by industry, before events take a turn which will warrant my calling on them. I even warned, in public papers, my countrymen in America to wait, and not to stir. Thanks to this precaution, no harm has accrued to any one on my account. But *the prisoners of war from the Hungarian regiments* flocked spontaneously to our banner.

We had already five battalions (upwards of 4,000 men) organized—alas! in three weeks more we should have had 25,000 of them. When the war was brought to an untimely end, I considered it a duty to guarantee the condition of the gallant band. I wished them to return home, rather than be scattered in misery over the face of the earth, provided I could *secure to them a safe return.*

I therefore insisted on a double stipulation for them—that of amnesty, and that of exemption (*congé definitif*) from further Austrian military service. I succeeded in both regards. France insisted peremptorily, and Austria felt obliged to yield—both points are guaranteed as far as stipulations can guarantee; it remains to be seen how Austria (false Austria) will execute them.

On this point I want to be kept in knowledge, accordingly I ordered * * * * * * *

He reports that some of our home-going braves may possibly write to me under your address.

Excuse this liberty, and should any such letters come to your hands, do me the favor to forward them to me. There will be nothing in them of a compromising character. We are no conspirators, nor do we want to be conspirators. Our national cause has long ago outgrown such poor swaddling clothes—where the whole nation is one conspiracies are useless, as they are unwise.

I am like the birds of the air; I had given up my house, and have yet none—in fact, have no spot on earth to rest my weary head upon; therefore, till further notice, please (occasion arising) to send letters to the care of FRANCIS PULSKY, Esq., No. 13 St. Alban's Villas, Highgate-rise. London, N. W.

Allow me to trust that your friendly feelings towards me and mine have undergone no change by late events; and believe me to be, with particular consideration, yours ever truly, KOSSUTH.

JOHN MCADAM, Esq., No. 45 Hyde Park-street, Glasgow.

THE HUNGARIAN QUESTION AS EXPOUNDED BY KOSSUTH.

From the London Times.

M. KOSSUTH divides his attentions about equally between both sides, and after his chuckle over one monarch he proceeds immediately to make another as uncomfortable as possible. Hungary is represented as a simple volcano, only—and all the worse for that monarch—a most convenient and manageable volcano, ready to blow up whenever M. KOSSUTH tells it to do so. The concessions of the Austrian Court to the Protestants are dismissed with one contemptuous half-sentence, and Hungarian independence is described as biding its time, certain of the issue. He tells Austria that nothing but independence will satisfy Hungary, and that anything short of that will be accepted without thanks, as the forced gift of fear. We do not profess ourselves ready to take every word of M. KOSSUTH for gospel when he declaims and prophesies about Hungary. As a professed liberator he is, of course, bound to represent his country as aiming at a total rejection of the Austrian yoke, and never to be satisfied with anything else. At the same time, the facts which we all of us have before us are enough to show that Austria has but a weak and slippery hold of Hungary. She is somehow incapable of incorporating Hungary in her system, and making it feel at home in and a part of her Empire. How is this? Are we to take the pure unqualified "nationality" ground, and conclude that no people ever can be happy except under rulers of its own blood? Is it Austria's sole crime that Austria is not Hungary, and Hungary is not Austria? Nobody will, of course, deny the force of the nationality ground, and the liberation of Lombardy after five centuries of the German yoke will not weaken it; but the "nationality" ground is not everything or nearly everything. Nations have time after time been conquered by other nations, and have united afterwards with the conquerors, and the two have made one nation, and all the stronger and more powerful a one for the mixture. Look at the case of Ireland, so often quoted against us. Here there has not been that complete blending of races; but no one would for a moment say that Ireland was not incorporated into the English empire, and was not as substantial a part of us as Yorkshire, possessed of equal rights and privileges. The difference is, that liberty is a principle that incorporates, despotism is not. The process which incorporates a conquered nation with the conqueror is that of gradual concession, where disabilities are step by step removed, till after first yielding one point, and then another, there is at last produced a complete civil equality. But here lies the great difference between a free country and a despotism; the concessions of a free country are *trusted*, they are depended upon perfectly, because everybody knows that a free country *cannot* retrace a step of this kind; she is constitutionally incapable of it; it is not a matter of honor and keeping a promise, but of political nature; every concession is an advance in an order of things, and can no more be undone again than the course of the sun or the revolution of the seasons. But the concessions of a despotism cannot be trusted; they are not the gifts of an order of things, but of an individual will; they are given and taken away again as events dictate. This very case is one in point. The rights just conceded to the Protestants of Austria are only the same rights they enjoyed before the Revolution of 1848; they were then withdrawn; they are now granted again, but who can trust such a system of concession as this? Can the ruled nation feel any security in its position when it has only the will of an individual to depend upon? No, "Trust not in Princes nor in any child of man;" the individual's is a weak pledge indeed; an order of events is alone a sure security. Monarchs are censured for breaking their pledges, and they deserve the reproach, but the truth is they are men; they are individuals. Events take a turn, a prosperous crisis arrives, and they are immediately in the hands of the old party again. They can hardly, if they would, stand against the tide, and they forget their promises with their altered position. But the word of political nature is sure; the concessions of a free country advance and never can go back again, and they end in the complete incorporation of the conquered nation.

THE FRENCH ARMY—AN ORDER-OF-THE-DAY OF MARSHAL NEIL.

Marshal NEIL, on lately assuming his command at Toulouse, published the following order-of-the-day:

"SOLDIERS: The Emperor has deigned to confer on me the command of the sixth military arrondissement. In placing me at your head His Majesty accords me a proof his high confidence, of which I may well be proud. A recent and glorious war has shown once more what may be expected from the courage and devotion of the French soldier. At present, you are about to take advantage of the leisures of peace to improve your training and discipline, which are the first bases of the power of armies. The experience of the past will be turned to the advantage of the future, so that if war should again break out it may not be attended with less glory to our arms than in these later years, and that, under all circumstances, the Emperor may rely on your bravery and devoted loyalty. Unceasingly occupied in superintending and encouraging your labors, I shall always be happy to reward your services."

THE STATE OF ITALY.

CIRCULAR OF THE SARDINIAN GOVERNMENT.

Correspondence of the London Times.

PARIS, Sunday, Oct. 2—6 P. M.

A circular note has been sent by the Sardinian Minister of Foreian Affairs to the diplomatic agents of that country at the Courts of London, Paris, Berlin and St. Petersburgh, for the purpose of communicating it to those Governments. The document in question is couched, I understand, in lucid and earnest terms; and forcibly sets forth arguments in favor of the formation of a strong and independent Kingdom of Upper Italy, sufficiently powerful to counterbalance the influence of Austria, and keep in check her domineering tendencies. The constitution of such a State would, it is urged, dispel the apprehensions and tranquilize the mind of Europe, at the *same time that it fulfilled* the just wishes, so loudly and unanimously expressed, of those Italian countries which have lately shaken off tyranical governments. The note points out the impossibility of Piedmont's resisting Austria, should that Power, at any future time think fit to attack her, unless she be put in a more favorable position for so doing than has hitherto been secured to her. Intrenched in Venice and the quadrilateral, Austria will always press upon Italy, if there be not in that country a Power capable of inspiring her with respect. With Austria's fortresses overlooking her Lombard provinces, and with Austrian Dukes established by Austrian influence in the other countries adjacent, Sardinia would find herself hemmed in by hostile Governments, and her resistance to an attack might be desperate, but must be ineffectual. Signor DABORMIDA points out that peace, made on such bases, would be in reality only a truce, to be broken by Austria whenever she saw what she held to be a favorable opportunity. The people of Central Italy, with a true instinct of the necessities of the case, have shown—it is with great justice argued in the note—by their recent conduct how indispensable they deem the formation of the Kingdom of Upper Italy. Forgetting their long-standing feelings of rivalry, and discarding old jealousies, the different States voted, one after the other, with the utmost order and unanimity, their own annexation to Piedmont. Their wish, the note proceeds to say, has the strongest claim to respect; its realization would not be the sanction or introduction of a new and subversive principle, or of one opposed to European law and precedent, since the principle that would be recognized has already been acted upon in various European countries, in Greece, in Belgium, and in the Danubian Principalities, and since it is to its application that the present Emperor of the French owes his crown, and the present dynasty in England their first introduction as sovereigns of Great Britain.

PRESENT DIPLOMATIC ASPECTS OF THE QUESTION.

The *Journal des Débats* writes as follows on the difficulties of finding a solution for the Italian question:

"We do not pretend to give any solution of the difficulties which exist, and we should be greatly embarrassed to find one. Indeed, the annexation of the Duchies appears hardly possible without the coöperation of France, and hitherto France has declined to *deviate from the engagements entered into at Villafranca.* On the other hand, the restoration of the fallen Princes is impossible without the intervention of foreign aid, and both France and Austria have equally renounced that means of action. Even supposing the restoration accomplished, the question would not be settled. It must not be forgotten that the state of Central Italy before the war depended chiefly on Austrian domination in Lombardy and Austrian supremacy throughout Italy. The right of intervention attributed to Austria, and the possibility—or, to speak more correctly, the perpetual menace of that intervention, were the real bases of the thrones of the Archdukes and the indispensable condition of their maintenance. Now, that right of intervention, stipulated in private treaties between Austria and these Princes, it will be remembered, was one of the causes which led to the war; it has been destroyed by the French victories, and cannot be revived. And yet, not only the restoration, but also the maintenance of these Princes without the possibility of Austrian intervention, is hardly conceivable. Any one must be totally ignorant of Italy not to see that the Dukes would be at the mercy of every popular movement, and that as soon as it became known that no foreign Power would come to their aid they would not be able to stand. However, if we set aside these three solutions, the annexation to Sardinia, the restoration of the fallen Princes, and the erection of a new throne, what are we to look for in Central Italy? It is hardly too much to say, then, that the present state of affairs is a dead lock, extrication from which appears by no means easy. It is true, however, that everything has an end, that there is no drama or comedy without a conclusion, and that events, when human ingenuity is at fault, never leave embarrassing situations any great length of time without a solution."

DISTURBED CONDITION OF NORTHERN ITALY.

Correspondence of the London Times.

VIENNA, Friday, Sept. 30.

On the 22d inst., the anniversary of the day on which MANIN died, there were popular demonstrations at Venice and Verona. At Venice a kind of funeral procession went round the Place of St. Mark, and at Verona there was a promenade of the same description outside the walls of the fortress. Notwithstanding the introduction of drum-head law into the districts of Vicenza and Belluno, very many highway robberies are committed, and, as is said, by deserters from GARIBALDI's corps. On the 23d inst. twelve men in the uniform of the Sardinian volunteers attacked some travelers in the neighborhood of Verona, and several of the latter were severely wounded. Very many Austrian subjects cross the Po from the district of Rovigo, and join the Central Italian Corps, which has its outposts on the opposite *side of the river.* There is a brigade of Piedmontese Carabineers stationed at Vallegio, a small town near Villafranca, which gives great annoyance to the Austrians. The Piedmontese soldiers drill the fugitives from the province of Venetia, and when the latter have learned to handle their arms they join the above-mentioned Central Italian Corps. There is also a dépôt of firearms at Valleggio, at which any Italian who is inclined to fight for the liberty of his country may purchase a very fine rifle for the sum of five francs (4s.6d.) There are still about 4,000 Modenese soldiers in the Austrian territory, as not more than a score of the ducal troops have gone over to the National Party. The report that Austrian soldiers have recently been clothed in Modenese uniforms is so very absurd that it is not worth contradiction. The Lombards keep up the political agitation in Venice, and are to the inhabitants of that city what the Sardinians formerly were to the Milanese.

THE PAPAL STATES—SPEECH OF GARIBALDI.

On his arrival at Ravenna, Gen. GARIBALDI addressed the following words to the people who had assembled under the windows of the Governor's palace:

"We must arm while we are able to wield a weapon; independence is more difficult to preserve than to conquer. Armed as we are, our concord frightens our enemies; we shall always be united for the liberty and independence which Italy demands. When a whole people calls for it, it is God himself who inspires it with the thought, and in God's name we will defend it. To-morrow, at 6 o'clock, an enlistment-roll will be opened. Whoever writes his name in it shall be beloved by his country. *I shall myself undertake the duty of conducting this chosen detachment of my fellow-townsmen*—we shall be the stronger the more united we are. Ravenna is my native town, and its name shall remain *engraven in my* heart as long as I breathe."

The *Monitore* of Bologna publishes a letter from the Superieure of the Convent of Verrucchio, who declares that she has never seen a single soldier enter that building. This letter *is signed* "Fortunata Rinaldini," and legalized by "Pepoli." This declaration refers to a statement made by the clerical party, that the soldiers of the *insurgents* had entered the Convent and ill-treated the nuns.

MISCELLANEOUS.

The valedictory message of Gov. Hall, of Vermont, recommends economy in the State administration, and the abolition of State Attorney's fees, and the substitution of fixed salaries. The public institutions are in a prosperous condition, and the State Geological Survey is rapidly approaching completion. The Governor denounces the attempt to reopen the African Slave trade.

The recent failure of Henry Falls, carpet-dealer, in Cincinnati, is noticed by the Cincinnati *Times*. His liabilities are estimated at $50,000. It is stated that Mr. F. made collections of over $10,000 previous to his departure for parts unknown. The Sheriff levied on the establishment in satisfaction of a judgment in favor of Higgins & Co., of New-York, for $12,000.

The *Berliner Nachrichten* declares the story of the sale of Humboldt's library to Lord Bloomfield, to be altogether void of foundation; the more so as they have only just commenced to catalogue the collection—a task which is likely to consume a very considerable time, as it turns out to be far more extensive and valuable than was supposed.

A fire which occurred at Warsaw, N. Y., Oct. 14, destroyed property to the value of $13,000. It broke out in the planing mill of Gates & Hurd, and extended to Buxton's carriage factory. Loss on the former, $10,000; on the latter, $3,000. Insurance partial.

The *Critic* says: Mr. Robert Chambers is engaged upon a work that will excite much commotion in the literary world. He has a volume in the press refuting the antiquity of the Scottish Historical Ballads. We hear that he considers them to have been written in the early part of the eighteenth century.

A short time ago a cooper at Kierling, a village near Vienna, was sentenced to three months' imprisonment for having publicly found fault with the way in which the war was carried on in Italy.

The New-York Times.

VOL. IX—NO. 2633. NEW-YORK, TUESDAY, FEBRUARY 28, 1860. PRICE TWO CENTS.

REPUBLICANS AT COOPER INSTITUTE.

Address by Hon. Abraham Lincoln, of Illinois.

Remarks of Messrs. Wm. Cullen Bryant, Horace Greeley, Gen. Nye and J. A. Briggs.

The announcement that Hon. ABRAHAM LINCOLN, of Illinois, would deliver an address in Cooper Institute, last evening, drew thither a large and enthusiastic assemblage. Soon after the appointed hour for commencing the proceedings, DAVID DUDLEY FIELD, Esq., arose and nominated as Chairman of the meeting Mr. WILLIAM CULLEN BRYANT. The nomination was received with prolonged applause, and was unanimously approved.

SPEECH OF WM. CULLEN BRYANT.

MR. BRYANT, after the applause had subsided, said: It is a grateful office that I perform in introducing to you at this time an eminent citizen of the West, whom you know—whom you have known hitherto—only by fame, and who has consented to address a New-York assemblage this evening. The great West, my friends, is a potent auxiliary in the battle we are fighting, for Freedom against Slavery; in behalf of civilization against barbarism; for the occupation of some of the fairest region of our Continent on which the settlers are now building their cabins. I see a higher and wiser agency than that of man in the causes that have filled with hardy people the vast and fertile regions which form the northern part of the valley of the Mississippi—a race of men who are not ashamed to till their acres with their own hands, and who would be ashamed to subsist on the labor of the slave. [Applause.] These children of the West, my friends, form a living bulwark against the advance of Slavery, and from them is recruited the vanguard of the armies of liberty. [Applause.] One of them will appear before you this evening in person—a gallant soldier of the political campaign of 1856—[applause]—who then rendered good service to the Republican cause, and who has been since the great champion of that cause in the struggle which took place two years later for the supremacy of the Republicans in the Legislature of Illinois; who took the field against Senator DOUGLAS, and would have won in the conflict but for the unjust provisions of the law of the State, which allowed a minority of the people to elect a majority of the Legislature [Applause.] I have only, my friends, to pronounce the name of ABRAHAM LINCOLN of Illinois—[cheers]—I have only to pronounce his name to secure your profoundest attention. [Prolonged applause, and cheers for LINCOLN.]

Mr. LINCOLN advanced to the desk, and smiling graciously upon his audience, complacently awaited the termination of the cheering and then proceeded with his address as follows:

SPEECH OF MR. LINCOLN.

MR. PRESIDENT AND FELLOW-CITIZENS OF NEW-YORK: The facts with which I shall deal this evening are mainly old and familiar; nor is there anything new in the general use I shall make of them. If there shall be any novelty, it will be in the mode of presenting the facts, and the inferences and observations following that presentation.

In his speech last Autumn, at Columbus, Ohio, as reported in the NEW-YORK TIMES, Senator DOUGLAS said:

"Our fathers, when they framed the Government under which we live, understood this question just as well, and even better, than we do now."

I fully indorse this, and I adopt it as a text for this discourse. I so adopt it because it furnishes a precise and an agreed starting-point for a discussion between Republicans and that wing of the Democracy headed by Senator DOUGLAS. It simply leaves the inquiry: "What was the understanding those fathers had of the question mentioned?"

What is the frame of Government under which we live?

The answer must be: "The Constitution of the United States." The Constitution consists of the original, framed in 1787 (and under which the present Government first went into operation,) and twelve subsequently framed amendments, the first ten of which were framed in 1789.

Who were our fathers that framed the Constitution? I suppose the "thirty-nine" who signed the original instrument may be fairly called our fathers who framed that part of the present Government. It is almost exactly true to say they framed it, and it is altogether true to say they fairly represented the opinion and sentiment of the whole nation at that time. Their names, being familiar to nearly all, and accessible to quite all, need not now be repeated.

I take these "thirty-nine," for the present, as being "our fathers who framed the Government under which we live."

What is the question which, according to the text, those fathers understood just as well, and even better than we do now?

It is this: Does the proper division of local from Federal authority, or anything in the Constitution, forbid our Federal Government to control as to Slavery in our Federal Territories?

Upon this, DOUGLAS holds the affirmative, and Republicans the negative. This affirmative and denial form an issue; and this issue—this question—is precisely what the text declares our fathers understood better than we.

Let us now inquire whether the "thirty-nine" or any of them, ever acted upon this question; and if they did, how they acted upon it—how they expressed that better understanding.

In 1784—three years before the Constitution—the United States then owning the Northwestern Territory, and no other—the Congress of the Confederation had before them the question of prohibiting Slavery in that Territory; and four of the "thirty-nine" who afterward framed the Constitution were in that Congress, and voted on that question. Of these, ROGER SHERMAN, THOMAS MIFFLIN and HUGH WILLIAMSON voted for the prohibition—thus showing that, in their understanding, no line dividing local from Federal authority, nor anything else, properly forbade the Federal Government to control as to Slavery in Federal territory. The other of the four—JAMES MCHENRY—voted against the prohibition, showing that, for some cause, he thought it improper to vote for it.

In 1787, still before the Constitution, but while the Convention was in session framing it, and while the Northwestern Territory still was the only Territory owned by the United States—the same question of prohibiting Slavery in the Territory again came before the Congress of the Confederation; and three more of the "thirty-nine" who afterward signed the Constitution were in that Congress, and voted on the question. They were WILLIAM BLOUNT, WILLIAM FEW and ABRAHAM BALDWIN; and they all voted for the prohibition—thus showing that, in their understanding, no line dividing local from Federal authority, nor anything else, properly forbade the Federal Government to control as to Slavery in Federal territory. This time the prohibition became a law, being a part of what is now well known as the Ordinance of '87.

The question of Federal control of Slavery in the Territories seems not to have been directly before the Convention which framed the original Constitution; and hence it is not recorded that the "thirty-nine," or any of them, while engaged on that instrument, expressed any opinion on that precise question.

In 1789, by the first Congress which sat under the Constitution, an act was passed to enforce the Ordinance of '87, including the prohibition of Slavery in the Northwestern Territory. The bill for this act was reported by one of the "thirty-nine," THOMAS FITZSIMMONS, then a member of the House of Representatives from Pennsylvania. It went through all its stages without a word of opposition, and finally passed both branches without Yeas and Nays, which is equivalent to a unanimous passage. In this Congress there were sixteen of the "thirty-nine" fathers who framed the original Constitution. They were:

John Langdon,	Thos. Fitzsimmons,	Richard Bassett,
Nicholas Gilman,	William Few,	George Read,
Wm. S. Johnson,	Abraham Baldwin,	Pierce Butler,
Roger Sherman,	Rufus King,	Daniel Carroll,
Robert Morris,	William Patterson,	James Madison,
	George Clymer.	

This shows that, in their understanding, no line dividing local from Federal authority, nor anything in the Constitution, properly forbade Congress to prohibit Slavery in the Federal territory; else both their fidelity to correct principle, and their oath to support the Constitution, would have constrained them to oppose the prohibition.

Again, GEORGE WASHINGTON, another of the "thirty-nine," was then President of the United States, and as such approved and signed the bill, thus completing its validity as a law, and thus showing that, in his understanding, no line dividing local from Federal authority, nor anything in the Constitution, forbade the Federal Government to control as to Slavery in Federal territory.

No great while after the adoption of the original Constitution, North Carolina ceded to the Federal Government the country now constituting the State of Tennessee; and a few years later Georgia ceded that which now constitutes the States of Mississippi and Alabama. In both deeds of cession it was made a condition by the ceding States that the Federal Government should not prohibit Slavery in the ceded country. Beside this, Slavery was then actually in the ceded country. Under these circumstances, Congress, on taking charge of these countries, did not absolutely prohibit Slavery within them. But they did interfere with it—take control of it—even there, to a certain extent. In 1798, Congress organized the Territory of Mississippi. In the act of organization they prohibited the bringing of slaves into the Territory, from any place without the United States, by fine, and giving freedom to slaves so brought. This act passed both branches of Congress without Yeas and Nays. In that Congress were three of the "thirty-nine" who framed the original Constitution. They were, JOHN LANGDON, GEORGE READ and ABRAHAM BALDWIN. They all, probably, voted for it. Certainly they would have placed their opposition to it upon record, if, in their understanding, any line dividing local from Federal authority, or anything in the Constitution, properly forbade the Federal Government to control as to Slavery in Federal authority.

In 1803, the Federal Government purchased the Louisiana country. Our former territorial acquisitions came from certain of our own States; but this Louisiana country was acquired from a foreign nation. In 1804, Congress gave a Territorial organization to that part of it which now constitutes the State of Louisiana. New-Orleans, lying within that part, was an old and comparatively large city. There were other considerable towns and settlements, and Slavery was extensively and thoroughly intermingled with the people. Congress did not, in the Territorial act, prohibit Slavery; but they did interfere with it—in a more marked and extensive way than they did in the case of Mississippi. The substance of the provision therein made, in relation to slaves, was:

First—That no slave should be imported into the Territory from foreign parts.

Second—That no slave should be carried into it who had been imported into the United States since the first day of May, 1798.

Third: That no slave should be carried into it, except by the owner, and for his own use as a settler; the penalty in all the cases being a fine upon the violator of the law, and freedom to the slave.

This act also was passed without yeas and nays. In the Congress which passed it, there were two of the "thirty-nine." They were ABRAHAM BALDWIN and JONATHAN DAYTON. As stated in the case of Mississippi, it is probable they both voted for it. They would not have allowed it to pass without recording their opposition to it, if, in their understanding, it violated either the line properly dividing local from Federal authority, or any provision of the Constitution.

In 1819–20, came, and passed, the Missouri question. Many votes were taken, by Yeas and Nays, in both branches of Congress, upon the various phases of the general question. Two of the "thirty-nine"—RUFUS KING and CHARLES PINCKNEY—were members of that Congress. Mr. KING steadily voted for Slavery prohibition and against all compromises, while Mr. PINCKNEY as steadily voted against Slavery prohibition, and against all compromises. By this Mr. KING showed that, in his understanding, no line dividing local from Federal authority, nor anything in the Constitution, was violated by Congress prohibiting Slavery in Federal territory; while Mr. PINCKNEY, by his votes, showed that in his understanding there was some sufficient reason for opposing such prohibition in that case.

The cases I have mentioned are the only acts of the "thirty-nine," or of any of them, upon the direct issue, which I have been able to discover.

To enumerate the persons who thus acted, as being four in 1784, three in 1787, seventeen in 1789, three in 1798, two in 1804, and two in 1819–20; there would be thirty-one of them. But this would be counting JOHN LANGDON, ROGER SHERMAN, WM. FEW, RUFUS KING, and GEORGE READ, each twice, and ABRAHAM BALDWIN four times. The true number of those of the "thirty-nine" whom I have shown to have acted upon the question, which, by the text, they understood better than we, is twenty-three, leaving sixteen not shown to have acted upon it in any way.

Here, then, we have twenty-three of our "thirty-nine" fathers who framed the Government under which we live, who have, upon their official responsibility and their corporal oaths, acted upon the very question which the text affirms they "understood just as well and even better than we do now;" and twenty-one of them—a clear majority of the whole "thirty-nine"—so acting upon it as to make them guilty of gross political impropriety, and willful perjury, if, in their understanding, any proper division between local and Federal authority, or anything in the Constitution they had made themselves, and sworn to support, forbade the Federal Government to control as to Slavery in the Federal Territories. Thus the twenty-one acted; and, as actions speak louder than words, so actions under such responsibility speak still louder.

Two of the twenty-three voted against Congressional prohibition of Slavery in the Federal Territories, in the instances in which they acted upon the question. But for what reasons they so voted is not known. They may have done so because they thought a proper division of local from Federal authority, or some provision or principle of the Constitution, stood in the way; or they may, without any such question, have voted against the prohibition on what appeared to them to be sufficient grounds of expediency. No one who has sworn to support the Constitution, can conscientiously vote for what he understands to be an unconstitutional measure, however expedient he may think it; but one may and ought to vote against a measure which he deems constitutional, if, at the same time, he deems it inexpedient. It, therefore, would be unsafe to set down even the two who voted against the prohibition, as having done so because, in their understanding, any proper division of local from Federal authority, or anything in the Constitution, forbade the Federal Government to control as to Slavery in Federal Territory.

The remaining sixteen of the "thirty-nine," so far as I have discovered, have left no record of their understanding upon the direct question of Federal control of Slavery in the Federal Territories. But there is much reason to believe that their understanding upon that question would not have appeared different from that of their twenty-three compeers, had it been manifested at all.

For the purpose of adhering rigidly to the text, I have purposely omitted whatever understanding may have been manifested, by any person, however distinguished, other than the thirty-nine fathers who framed the original Constitution; and, for the same reason, I have also omitted whatever understanding may have been manifested by any of the "thirty-nine" even, on any other phase of the general question of Slavery. If we should look into their acts and declarations on those other phases, as the foreign Slave-trade, and the morality and policy of Slavery generally, it would appear to us that on the direct question of Federal control of Slavery in Federal Territories, the sixteen, if they had acted at all, would probably have acted just as the twenty-three did. Among that sixteen were several of the most noted Anti-Slavery men of those times—Dr. FRANKLIN, ALEXANDER HAMILTON and GOUVERNEUR MORRIS—while there was not one now known to have been otherwise, unless it may be JOHN RUTLEDGE, of South Carolina.

The sum of the whole is, that of our "thirty-nine" fathers who framed the original Constitution, twenty-one—a clear majority of the whole—certainly understood that no proper division of local from Federal authority, nor any part of the Constitution, forbade the Federal Government to control Slavery in the Federal Territories; while all the rest probably had the same understanding. Such, unquestionably, was the understanding of our fathers who framed the original Constitution; and the text affirms that they understood the question better than we.

But, so far, I have been considering the understanding of the question manifested by the framers of the original Constitution. In, and by, the original instrument, a mode was provided for amending it; and, as I have already stated, the present frame of Government under which we live consists of that original, and twelve amendatory articles framed and adopted since. Those who now insist that Federal control of Slavery in Federal Territories violates the Constitution, point us to the provisions which they suppose it thus violates; and, as I understand, they all fix upon provisions in these amendatory articles, and not in the original instrument. The Supreme Court, in the Dred Scott case, plant themselves upon the fifth amendment, which provides that "no person shall be deprived of property without due process of law;" while Senator DOUGLAS and his peculiar adherents plant themselves upon the tenth amendment, providing that "the powers not granted by the Constitution, are reserved to the States respectively, and to the people."

Now, it so happens that these amendments were framed by the first Congress which sat under the Constitution—the identical Congress which passed the act already mentioned, enforcing the prohibition of Slavery in the Northwestern Territory. Not only was it the same Congress, but they were the identical, same individual men who, at the same session, and at the same time within the session, had under consideration, and in progress toward maturity, these Constitutional amendments and this act prohibiting Slavery in all the territory the nation then owned. The Constitutional amendments were introduced before and passed after the act enforcing the Ordinance of '87; so that during the whole pendency of the act to enforce the Ordinance, the Constitutional amendments were also pending.

That Congress, consisting in all of seventy-six members, including sixteen of the framers of the original Constitution, as before stated, were preeminently our fathers who framed that part of the Government under which we live which is now claimed as forbidding the Federal Government to control Slavery in the Federal Territories.

Is it not a little presumptuous in any one at this day to affirm that the two things which that Congress deliberately framed, and carried to maturity at the same time, are absolutely inconsistent with each other? And does not such affirmation become impudently absurd when coupled with the other affirmation, from the same mouth, that those who did the two things alleged to be inconsistent, understood whether they really were inconsistent better than we—better than he who affirms that they are inconsistent?

It is surely safe to assume that the "thirty-nine" framers of the original Constitution, and the seventy-six members of the Congress which framed the amendments thereto, taken together, do certainly include those who may be fairly called "our fathers who framed the Government under which we live." And so assuming, I defy any man to show that any one of them ever in his whole life declared that, in his understanding, any proper division of local from Federal authority, or any part of the Constitution, forbade the Federal Government to control as to Slavery in the Federal Territories. I go a step further. I defy any one to show that any living man in the whole world ever did, prior to the beginning of the present century, (and I might almost say, prior to the beginning of the last half of the present century,) declare that, in his understanding any proper division of local from Federal authority, or any part of the Constitution, forbade the Federal Government to control as to Slavery in the Federal Territories. To those who now so declare, I give, not only "our fathers who framed the Government under which we live," but with them all other living men within the century in which it was framed, among whom to search, and they shall not be able to find the evidence of a single man agreeing with them.

Now, and here, let me guard a little against being misunderstood. I do not mean to say we are bound to follow implicitly in whatever our fathers did. To do so would be to discard all the lights of current experience—to reject all progress—all improvement. What I do say is, that if we would supplant the opinions and policy of our fathers in any case, we should do so upon evidence so conclusive, and argument so clear, that even their great authority, fairly considered and weighed, cannot stand; and most surely not in a case whereof we ourselves declare they understood the question better than we.

If any man, at this day, sincerely believes that a proper division of local from Federal authority, or any part of the Constitution, forbids the Federal Government to control as to Slavery in the Federal Territories, he is right to say so, but to enforce his position by all truthful evidence and fair argument which he can. But he has no right to mislead others, who have less access to history and less leisure to study it, into the false belief that "our fathers, who framed the Government under which we live," were of the same opinion—thus substituting falsehood and deception for truthful evidence and fair argument. If any man at this day sincerely believes "our fathers, who framed the Government under which we live," used and applied principles, in other cases, which ought to have led them to understand that a proper division of local from Federal authority, or some part of the Constitution, forbids the Federal Government to control as to Slavery in the Federal Territories, he is right to say so. But he should, at the same time, brave the responsibility of declaring that, in his opinion, he understands their principles better than they did themselves, and especially should he not shirk that responsibility by asserting that they "understood the question just as well, and even better, than we do now."

But enough. Let all who believe that "our fathers, who framed the Government under which we live, understood this question just as well, and even better than we do now," speak as they spoke, and act as they acted upon it. This is all Republicans ask—all Republicans desire—in relation to Slavery. As those fathers marked it, so let it be again marked, as an evil not to be extended, but to be tolerated and protected only because of and so far as its actual presence among us makes that toleration and protection a necessity. Let all the guarantees those fathers gave it be, not grudgingly, but fully and fairly, maintained. For this Republicans contend, and with this, so far as I know or believe, they will be content.

And now, if they would listen—as I suppose they will not—I would address a few words to the Southern people.

I would say to them: You consider yourselves a reasonable and a just people; and I consider that in the general qualities of reason and justice you are not inferior to any other people. Still, when you speak of us Republicans, you do so only to denounce us as reptiles, or, at the best, as no better than outlaws. You will grant a hearing to pirates or murderers, but nothing like it to "Black Republicans." In all your contentions with one another, each of you deems an unconditional condemnation of "Black Republicanism" as the first thing to be attended to. Indeed, such condemnation of us seems to be an indispensable prerequisite—license, so to speak—among you to be admitted or permitted to speak at all.

Now, can you, or not, be prevailed upon to pause, and to consider whether this is quite just to us, or even to yourselves?

Bring forward your charges and specifications, and then be patient long enough to hear us deny or justify.

You say we are sectional. We deny it. That makes an issue, and the burden of proof is upon you. You produce your proof, and what is it? Why, that our party has no existence in your section—gets no votes in your section. The fact is substantially true; but does it prove the issue? If it does, then, in case we should, without change of principle, begin to get votes in your section, we should thereby cease to be sectional. You cannot escape this conclusion; and yet, are you willing to abide by it? If you are, you will probably soon find that we have ceased to be sectional, for we shall get votes in your section this very year. You will then begin to discover, as the truth plainly is, that your proof does not touch the issue. The fact that we get no votes in your section is a fact of your making, and not of ours. And if there be fault in that fact, that fault is primarily yours, and remains so until you show that we repel you by some wrong principle or practice. If we do repel you by any wrong principle or practice, the fault is ours; but this brings you to where you ought to have started—to a discussion of the right or wrong of our principle. If our principle, put in practice, would wrong your section for the benefit of ours, or for any other object, then our principle, and we with it, are sectional, and are justly opposed and denounced as such. Meet us, then, on the question of whether our principle, put in practice, would wrong your section; and so meet it as if it were possible that something may be said on our side. Do you accept the challenge? No? Then you really believe that the principles which our fathers who framed the Government under which we live, thought so clearly right as to adopt it, and indorse it again and again, upon their official oaths, is, in fact, so clearly wrong as to demand your condemnation without a moment's consideration.

Some of you delight to flaunt in our faces the warning against sectional parties given by WASHINGTON in his Farewell Address. Less than eight years before WASHINGTON gave that warning, he had, as President of the United States, approved and signed an act of Congress, inforcing the prohibition of Slavery in the Northwestern Territory, which act embodied the policy of the Government upon that subject, up to and at the very moment he penned that warning; and about one year after he penned it he wrote LA FAYETTE that he considered that prohibition a wise measure, expressing in the same connection his hope that we should some time have a confederacy of Free States.

Bearing this in mind, and seeing that sectionalism has since arisen from this same subject, is that warning a weapon in your hands against us, or in our hands against you? Could WASHINGTON himself speak, would he cast the blame of that sectionalism upon us, who sustain his policy, or upon you who repudiate it? We respect that warning of WASHINGTON, and we commend it to you, together with his example pointing to the right application of it.

But you say you are conservative—eminently conservative—while we are revolutionary, destructive, or something of the sort. What is conservatism? Is it not adherence to the old and tried, against the new and untried? We stick to, contend for the identical old policy on the point in controversy which was adopted by our fathers who framed the Government under which we live; while you with one accord reject, and scout, and spit upon that old policy, and insist upon substituting something new. True, you disagree among yourselves as to what that substitute shall be. You have considerable variety of new propositions and plans, but you are unanimous in rejecting and denouncing the old policy of the fathers. Some of you are for reviving the foreign Slave-trade; some for a Congressional Slave Code for the Territories; some for Congress forbidding the Territories to prohibit Slavery within their limits; some for maintaining Slavery in the Territories through the Judiciary; some for the "gur-reat pur-rinciple" that "if one man would enslave another, no third man should object," fantastically called "Popular Sovereignty;" but never a man among you in favor of Federal prohibition of Slavery in Federal Territories, according to the practice of our fathers who framed the Government under which we live. Not one of all your various plans can show a precedent or an advocate in the century within which our Government originated. Consider, then, whether your claim of conservatism for yourselves, and your charge of destructiveness against us, are based on the most clear and stable foundations.

Again, you say we have made the Slavery question more prominent than it formerly was. We deny it. We admit that it is more prominent, but we deny that we made it so. It was not we, but you, who discarded the old policy of the fathers. We resisted, and still resist, your innovation; and thence comes the greater prominence of the question. Would you have that question reduced to its former proportions? Go back to that old policy. What has been will be again, under the same conditions. If you would have the peace of the old times, readopt the precepts and policy of the old times.

You charge that we stir up insurrections among your slaves. We deny it; and what is your proof? Harper's Ferry! JOHN BROWN! JOHN BROWN was no Republican; and you have failed to implicate a single Republican in the Harper's Ferry enterprise. If any member of our party is guilty in that matter, you know it or you do not know it. If you do know it, you are inexcusable to not designate the man and prove the fact. If you do not know it, you are inexcusable to assert it, and especially to persist in the assertion after you have tried and failed to make the proof. You need not be told that persisting in a charge which one does not know to be true, is simply malicious slander.

Some of you admit that no Republican designedly aided or encouraged the Harper's Ferry affair; but still insist that our doctrines and declarations necessarily lead to such results. We do not believe it. We know we hold to no doctrines, and make no declarations, which were not held to and made by our fathers who framed the Government under which we live. You never dealt fairly by us in relation to this affair. When it occurred, some important State elections were near at hand, and you were in evident glee with the belief that, by charging the blame upon us, you could get an advantage of us in those elections. The elections came, and your expectations were not quite fulfilled. Every Republican man knew that, as to himself at least, your charge was a slander, and he was not much inclined by it to cast his vote in your favor. Republican doctrines and declarations are accompanied with a continual protest against any interference whatever with your slaves, or with you about your slaves. Surely, this does not encourage them to revolt. True, we do, in common with our fathers, who framed the Government under which we live, declare our belief that Slavery is wrong; but the slaves do not hear us declare even this. For anything we say or do, the slaves would scarcely know there is a Republican Party. I believe they would not, in fact, generally know it but for your misrepresentations of us in their hearing. In your political contests among yourselves, each faction charges the other with sympathy with Black Republicanism; and then, to give point to the charge, defines Black Republicanism to simply be insurrection, blood and thunder among the slaves.

Slave insurrections are no more common now than they were before the Republican Party was organized. What induced the Southampton insurrection, twenty-eight years ago, in which at least three times as many lives were lost as at Harper's Ferry. You can scarcely stretch your very elastic fancy to the conclusion that Southampton was got up by Black Republicanism. In the present state of things in the United States, I do not think a general, or even a very extensive slave insurrection, is possible. The indispensable concert of action cannot be attained. The slaves have no means of rapid communication; nor can incendiary free men, black or white, supply it. The explosive materials are everywhere in parcels; but there neither are, nor can be supplied, the indispensable connecting trains.

Much is said by Southern people about the affection of slaves for their masters and mistresses; and a part of it, at least, is true. A plot for an uprising could scarcely be devised and communicated to twenty individuals before some one of them, to save the life of a favorite master or mistress, would divulge it. This is the rule; and the slave-revolution in Hayti was not an exception to it, but a case occurring under peculiar circumstances. The gunpowder plot of British history, though not connected with slaves, was more in point. In that case, only about twenty were admitted to the secret; and yet one of them, in his anxiety to save a friend, betrayed the plot to that friend, and, by consequence, averted the calamity. Occasional poisonings from the kitchen, and open or stealthy assassinations in the field, and local revolts extending to a score or so, will continue to occur as the natural results of Slavery; but no general insurrection of slaves, as I think, can happen in this country for a long time. Whoever much fears, or much hopes, for such an event, will be alike disappointed.

In the language of Mr. JEFFERSON, uttered many years ago, "It is still in our power to direct the process of emancipation, and deportation, peaceably, and in such slow degrees, as that the evil will wear off insensibly; and their places be, *pari passu*, filled up by free white laborers. If, on the contrary, it is left to force itself on, human nature must shudder at the prospect held up."

MR. JEFFERSON did not mean to say, nor do I, that the power of emancipation is in the Federal Government. He spoke of Virginia; and, as to the power of emancipation, I speak of the Slaveholding States only.

The Federal Government, however, as we insist, has the power of restraining the extension of the institution—the power to insure that a slave insurrection shall never occur on any American soil which is now free from Slavery.

JOHN BROWN'S effort was peculiar. It was not a slave insurrection. It was an attempt by white men to get up a revolt among slaves, in which the slaves refused to participate. In fact, it was so absurd that the slaves, with all their ignorance, saw plainly enough it could succeed. That affair, in its philosophy, corresponds with the many attempts, related in history, at the assassination of kings and emperors. An enthusiast broods over the oppression of a people, till he fancies himself commissioned by Heaven to liberate them. He ventures the attempt, which ends in little else than his own execution. ORSINI'S attempt on LOUIS NAPOLEON, and JOHN BROWN'S attempt at Harper's Ferry were, in their philosophy, precisely the same. The eagerness to cast blame on old England in the one case, and on New-England in the other, does not disprove the sameness of the two things.

And how much would it avail you, if you could, by the use of JOHN BROWN, HELPER'S book, and the like, break up the Republican organization? Human action can be modified to some extent, but human nature cannot be changed. There is a judgment and a feeling against Slavery in this nation, which cast at least a million and a half of votes. You cannot destroy that judgment and feeling—that sentiment—by breaking up the political organization which rallies around it. You can scarcely scatter and disperse an army which has been formed into order in the face of your heaviest fire, but if you could, how much would you gain by forcing the sentiment which created it out of the peaceful channel of the ballot-box into some other channel? What would that other channel probably be? Would the number of John Browns be lessened or enlarged by the operation?

But you will break up the Union, rather than submit to a denial of your Constitutional rights.

That has a somewhat reckless sound; but it would be palliated, if not fully justified, were we proposing, by the mere force of numbers, to deprive you of some right, plainly written down in the Constitution. But we are proposing no such thing.

When you make these declarations, you have a specific and well-understood allusion to an assumed Constitutional right of yours, to take slaves into the Federal Territories, and to hold them there as property. But no such right is specifically written in the Constitution. That instrument is literally silent about any such right. We, on the contrary, deny that such a right has any existence in the Constitution, even by implication.

Your purpose, then, plainly stated, is, that you will destroy the Government, unless you be allowed to construe the Constitution as you please, on all points in dispute between you and us. You will rule or ruin in all events.

This, plainly stated, is your language to us. Perhaps you will say the Supreme Court has decided the disputed Constitutional question in your favor. Not quite so. But, waiving the lawyer's distinction between dictum and decision, the Court have decided the question for you in a sort of way. The Court have substantially said, it is your Constitutional right to take Slaves into the Federal Territories, and to hold them there as property.

When I say the decision was made in a sort of way, I mean it was made in a divided Court by a bare majority of the Judges, and they not quite agreeing with one another in the reasons for making it; that it is so made as that its avowed supporters disagree with one another about its meaning; and that it was mainly based upon a mistaken statement of fact—the statement in the opinion that "the right of property in a slave is distinctly and expressly affirmed in the Constitution."

An inspection of the Constitution will show that the right of property in a slave is not distinctly and expressly affirmed in it. Bear in mind the Judges do not pledge their judicial opinion that such right is impliedly affirmed in the Constitution; but they pledge their veracity that it is distinctly and expressly affirmed there—"distinctly"—that is, not mingled with anything else—"expressly"—that is, in words meaning just that, without the aid of any inference, and susceptible of no other meaning.

If they had only pledged their judicial opinion that such right is affirmed in the instrument by implication, it would be open to others to show that neither the word "slave" nor "slavery" is to be found in the Constitution, nor the word "property," even, in any connection with language alluding to the things slave, or slavery, and that wherever in that instrument the slave is alluded to, he is called a "person;" and wherever his master's legal right in relation to him is alluded to, it is spoken of as "service or labor due," as a "debt" payable in service or labor. Also, it would be open to show, by cotemporaneous history, that this mode of alluding to slaves and Slavery, instead of speaking of them, was employed on purpose to exclude from the Constitution the idea that there could be property in man.

To show all this is easy and certain.

When this obvious mistake of the Judges shall be brought to their notice, is it not reasonable to expect that they will withdraw the mistaken statement, and reconsider the conclusion based upon it?

And then it is to be remembered that "our fathers, who framed the Government under which we live"—the men who made the Constitution—decided this same constitutional question in our favor, long ago—decided it without a division among themselves, when making the decision; without division among themselves about the meaning of it after it was made, and so far as any evidence is left without basing it upon any mistaken statement of facts.

Under all these circumstances, do you really feel yourselves justified to break up this Government, unless such a Court decision as yours is shall be at once submitted to as a conclusive and final rule of political action?

But you will not abide the election of a Republican President. In that supposed event, you say, you will destroy the Union; and then, you say, the great crime of having destroyed it will be upon us!

That is cool. A highwayman holds a pistol to my ear, and mutters through his teeth, "Stand and deliver, or I shall kill you, and then you will be a murderer!"

To be sure, what the robber demanded of me—my money—was my own; and I had a clear right to keep it; but it was no more my own than my vote is my own; and the threat of death to me, to extort my money, and the threat of destruction to the Union, to extort my vote, can scarcely be distinguished in principle.

A few words now to Republicans. It is exceedingly desirable that all parts of this great Confederacy shall be at peace, and in harmony, one with another. Let us Republicans do our part to have it so. Even though much provoked, let us do nothing through passion and ill temper. Even though the Southern people will not so much as listen to us, let us calmly consider their demands, and yield to them if, in our deliberate view of our duty, we possibly can. Judging by all they say and do, and by the subject and nature of their controversy with us, let us determine, if we can, what will satisfy them.

Will they be satisfied if the Territories be unconditionally surrendered to them? We know they will not. In all their present complaints against us, the Territories are scarcely mentioned. Invasions and insurrections are the rage now. Will it satisfy them if, in the future, we have nothing to do with invasions and insurrections? We know it will not. We so know because we know we never had anything to do with invasions and insurrections; and yet this total abstaining does not exempt us from the charge and the denunciation.

The question recurs, what will satisfy them? Simply this: We must not only let them alone, but we must, somehow, convince them that we do let them alone. This, we know by experience, is no easy task. We have been so trying to convince them from the very beginning of our organization, but with no success. In all our platforms and speeches, we have constantly protested our purpose to let them alone; but this has had no tendency to convince them. Alike unavailing to convince them is the fact that they have never detected a man of us in any attempt to disturb them.

These natural and apparently adequate means all failing, what will convince them? This, and this only: cease to call Slavery *wrong*, and join them in calling it *right*. All this must be done thoroughly—done in *acts* as well as in *words*. Silence will not be tolerated—we must place ourselves avowedly with them DOUGLAS' new sedition law must be enacted and enforced, suppressing all declarations that Slavery is wrong, whether made in politics, in presses, in pulpits, or in private. We must arrest and return their fugitive slaves with greedy pleasure. We must pull down our Free-State Constitutions. The whole atmosphere must be disinfected from the taint of opposition to Slavery, before they will cease to believe that all their troubles proceed from us.

I am quite aware they do not state their case precisely in this way. Most of them would probably say to us, "Let us alone, do nothing with us, and say what you please about Slavery." But we do let them alone—have never disturbed them—so that, after all, it is what we say which dissatisfies them. They will continue to accuse us of doing until we cease saying.

I am also aware they have not, as yet, in terms, demanded the overthrow of our Free-State Constitutions. Yet those Constitutions declare the wrong of Slavery, with more solemn emphasis than do all other sayings against it: and when all these other sayings shall have been silenced, the overthrow of these Constitutions will be demanded, and nothing be left to resist the demand. It is nothing to the contrary that they do not demand the whole of this just now. Demanding what they do, and for the reason they do, they can voluntarily stop nowhere short of this consummation. Holding, as they do, that Slavery is morally right, and socially elevating, they cannot cease to demand a full national recognition of it, as a legal right, and a social blessing.

Nor can we justifiably withold this on any ground save our conviction that Slavery is wrong. If Slavery is right, all words, acts, laws, and Constitutions against it, are themselves wrong, and should be silenced, and swept away. If it is right, we cannot justly object to its nationality—its universality; if it is wrong, they cannot justly insist upon its extension—its enlargement. All they ask, we could readily grant, if we thought Slavery right; all we ask, they could as readily grant, if they thought it wrong. Their thinking it right, and our thinking it wrong, is the precise fact upon which depends the whole controversy. Thinking it right, as they do, they are not to blame for desiring its full recognition, as being right; but thinking it wrong, as we do, can we yield to them? Can we cast our votes with their view, and against our own? In view of our moral, social, and political responsibilities, can we do this?

Wrong as we think Slavery is, we can yet afford to let it alone where it is, because that much is due to the necessity arising from its actual presence in the nation; but can we, while our votes will prevent it, allow it to spread in the National Territories, and to overrun us here in these Free States?

If our sense of duty forbids this, then let us stand by our duty, fearlessly and effectively. Let us be diverted by none of those sophistical contrivances wherewith we are so industriously plied and belabored—contrivances such as groping for some middle ground between the right and the wrong, vain as the search for a man who should be neither a living man nor a dead man—such as a policy of "don't care" on a question about which all true men do care—such as Union appeals beseeching true Union men to yield to Disunionists, reversing the Divine rule, and calling, not the sinners, but the righteous to repentance—such as invocations of WASHINGTON, imploring men to unsay what WASHINGTON said, and undo what WASHINGTON did.

Neither let us be slandered from our duty by false accusations against us, nor frightened from it by menaces of destruction to the Government, nor of dungeons to ourselves. Let us have faith that right makes might; and in that faith, let us, to the end, dare to do our duty, as we understand it.

When Mr. LINCOLN had concluded his address, during the delivery of which he was frequently applauded, three rousing cheers were given for the orator and the sentiments to which he had given utterance. There were then loud calls for Mr. GREELEY, who came forward and assured the audience that the orator of the occasion was a specimen of what free labor and free expression of ideas could produce. He was followed by Gen. NYE, who was called for a long time before he appeared; and when he did appear it was only to say that he could not allow himself to disturb the effect of the address to which they had listened, by any remarks of his. By and by there would be a more appropriate occasion, and when it came he promised to express his sentiment freely.

After a few words from Hon. JAS. A. BRIGGS and Judge CULVER, the audience separated.

NEWS BY TELEGRAPH.

THE LOSS OF THE HUNGARIAN.

Tardy Preparations for Visiting the Wreck.

FACTS ABOUT SUPPOSED PASSENGERS.

HALIFAX, Monday, Feb. 27—8 P. M.

Not another word, as yet, has been heard from the steamship *Hungarian*.

The revenue cutter *Daring* has not yet arrived at the scene of the wreck.

A party of divers has left here in the schooner *Ospray* to render assistance.

A hat-box marked "WM. BOULLENHOUSE, Sackville," has been washed ashore.

TORONTO, C. W., Monday, Feb. 27.

Letters received by the *Europa* by the friends of Mr. McKELLAR, M. P. P., state that he did not sail by the *Hungarian*, as was supposed.

ST. CATHERINES, C. W., Monday, Feb. 27.

Letters per the steamship *Europa* state that Hon. Mr. MERRITT, M. P. P., was not a passenger by the *Hungarian*, he being prevented by business from coming in her.

THE CATASTROPHE AT PORTLAND.

From the Portland Advertiser, Feb. 27.

We have no recollection of any catastrophe that has thrown such a gloom over our city as this. Many of those on board had connections or intimate frends here, and the anxiety of these connections and friends, and those who sympathize with them, has been heightened by the delay in the reception of news, and the mystery in which everything in regard to the disaster seems enveloped. Rev. Mr. GOSNER, of Montreal, who occupied the pulpit of the Park-street Church, and Rev. Dr. SHAILER, of the Federal-street Baptist Church, preached sermons yesterday specially upon the subject; and it was alluded to with much feeling in the sermons or devotional exercises in most of the other pulpits in the city.

The steamer *Bohemian*, which sailed from this port on Saturday for Liverpool, took in tow a large schooner, the *Sarah*, Capt. UPTON, and with a strong crew on board, accompanied by Capt. CRAWFORD, the efficient agent of the steamship line at this port; and from this source, if from no other, we hope eventually to get all the particulars that can be gleaned of the shocking catastrophe.

South Carolina Items.

MOVEMENTS OF ARCHBISHOP HUGHES—OBITUARY—BURNING OF A RICE MILL.

CHARLESTON, Monday, Feb. 27.

Archbishop HUGHES and Rev. Father MATHEWS have arrived here from New-York.

Capt. DESPERJOLS, of the French bark *Palmier*, just arrived from Pointpetre, Guadaloupe, died suddenly in a fit yesterday. He was a native of Bordeaux.

The *South Carolinian*, of yesterday, announces the death, by apoplexy, of Col. J. H. IRBY, formerly a Congressman.

The Canonsboro' Rice Mill, with 5,000 bushels of rice, was destroyed by fire yesterday. The mill was the oldest in the city. The residence of EDWARD LUCAS was also much damaged. The property was generally insured.

Excitement at Louisville, Ky.

ATTEMPT TO LYNCH A PRISONER.

LOUISVILLE, Ky., Monday, Feb. 27.

A man calling himself JOHN HASKELL, hailing from Massachusetts, (but others say an Englishman, a sailor recently from New-Orleans,) 42 years old, was arrested on Saturday last for an unnatural crime. His examination, to-day, was postponed on account of the illness of one of the witnesses. This forenoon a crowd gathered about the Court-house, increasing till 2 o'clock, when the Mayor ordered the steam fire-engine to the spot to drive away the crowd. This was temporarily successful, but towards dark the crowd swelled to several thousands, and an attack on the jail and the hanging of the prisoner were apprehended. The military were ordered to hold themselves in readiness. Two cannons were placed inside the jail, and the police marshaled, keeping the square in front of it clear, and arresting several intoxicated and turbulent persons. At 5 o'clock this afternoon Judge BULLOCK addressed the crowd, urging moderation, and saying that the persons interested in the prosecution desired no riotous conduct, but were willing that the prisoner should be dealt with by the law.

The crowd is now (9:30 P. M.) gradually dispersing, and although great indignation exists against the prisoner, the fears of an attack upon the jail to-night are subsiding.

Stand of Colors for the Seventh Regiment.

WASHINGTON, Monday, Feb. 27.

Both branches of the Common Council to-nigh passed, unanimously, resolutions of thanks to the military who visited the City on the occasion of the recent inauguration of the statue of WASHINGTON, and specially to the Seventh Regiment, National Guard, of New-York. They also voted to present to the latter in the name of the city a handsome stand of colors. Mr. WARD introduced the resolution.

From Texas.

REPORT OF THE RIO GRANDE COMMISSIONERS—ADJOURNMENT OF THE TEXAS LEGISLATURE.

WASHINGTON, Monday, Feb. 27.

The New-Orleans *Picayune*, of Wednesday, is received by Adams' Express.

The Galveston *Civilian*, of the 17th, says that Gov. HOUSTON has transmitted to the President the result of the labors of the Texas Commissioners on the Rio Grande. He says that unless immediate steps are taken for the efficient protection of the frontier of Texas, he will himself move to repel the present invasion and prevent a recurrence of the measures progressing in and out of Texas, looking to a protectorate in Northern Mexico. The Commissioners report that there is no certainty of quiet without a partial occupation of Mexico.

The Texas Legislature adjourned on the 13th inst., without action on the South Carolina resolutions.

The Marietta and Cincinnati Railroad.

SALE OF THE ROAD AND RECONSTRUCTION OF THE COMPANY.

BUFFALO, Monday, Feb. 27.

The Marietta and Cincinnati Railroad, with the property and effects belonging to it, was sold at Chillicothe yesterday by ORLANDO SMITH, in accordance with a decree of the Court. The property was purchased in the name of NOAH L. WILSON, DAVID GIBSON and others, Trustees, under a compromise-agreement for capitalization. The effect of the sale will be the reorganization of the Company free of debt, as the value of the property is to be represented entirely by the capital stock, all the mortgages being wiped out. The property was sold for the minimum fixed by the Court, two hundred thousand dollars.

Important Patent Decision.

PATERSON, N. J., Monday, Feb. 27.

Judge DICKERSON, of the United States Circuit Court, New-Jersey, this day granted an injunction at the suit of CHARLES GOODYEAR and the New-York Belting and Packing Company, restraining DUNBAR & JOSLIN, of Trenton, from making billiard strips, car springs, and other articles of India-rubber, in violation of the patent of CHARLES GOODYEAR. The defence was, that the defendants had patents for using sulphurates and shale; but it was proved, and not denied, that rubber cannot be vulcanized without the use of free sulphur.

Accident to the Steamer Jura.

BOSTON, Monday, Feb. 27.

The Cunard steamer *Jura*, from Liverpool on the 11th inst., put into New-Bedford this afternoon, having on Thursday, the 23d, broke her engine off Georges' Shoal. She will await the arrival of a steam-tug to tow her to New-York.

[It is needless to say that the dispatch in the morning papers of yesterday announcing the arrival of the *Jura* at this port was incorrect.—ED. TIMES.]

Fire in Philadelphia.

PHILADELPHIA, Monday, Feb. 27.

A fire broke out this evening in the drug warehouse of CHARLES ELLIS & Co., originating in the explosion of a can of ether in the packing-room, and seriously burning a female employe. The fire was extinguished with little damage to the building, but the extensive stock received much injury from the water.

Loss of the Steamboat Portsmouth.

ST. JOSEPH, Monday, Feb. 27.

The steamboat *Portsmouth*, of the Hannibal and St. Joseph Railroad Line, which left here on Saturday, bound for Kansas City, with a cargo of lumber and other stuff, struck a snag and sunk near Leavenworth on Sunday. She went down in twelve feet of water, and is a total loss. She is insured. Most of the cargo will be recovered.

Later from Minatitlan.

NEW-ORLEANS, Monday, Feb. 27.

Minatitlan dates of the 12th inst. are received. They state that the Mexican war-steamer *Fire* arrived there on the 7th, dismantled the fort and took the guns to Vera Cruz, by order of JUAREZ.

The United States Marines at Tehuantepec had interfered to prevent Americans from being driven out.

Adjournment of the Alabama Legislature.

MONTGOMERY, Ala., Monday, Feb. 27.

The State Legislature adjourned this morning. The Governor failed to approve the Convention bill.

Mr. JACKSON, ex-Speaker of the House of Representatives, died at Autauga on Sunday.

Arrest of an Alleged Counterfeit Money Dealer.

BOSTON, Monday, Feb. 27.

ALONZO P. BURRILL, a broker at No. 16 State-street, was arrested to-day upon the charge of dealing in counterfeit and broken bank-bills. Several hundollars of the stuff were found in his possession.

Murder in Georgia.

AUGUSTA, Ga., Monday, Feb. 27.

The Rome (Ga.) *Courier* of Saturday reports the brutal murder of ROBERT THOMPSON and his wife on the previous Tuesday. Mr. THOMPSON was a merchant and Postmaster of Sugar Valley, Ga.

Death of Dr. John Barker.

MEADVILLE, Pa., Monday, Feb. 27.

Dr. JOHN BARKER, President of the Alleghany College in this place, died suddenly at 2 o'clock on Sunday afternoon.

North River Opening.

RONDOUT, N. Y., Monday, Feb. 27.

The ferry between this place and Rhinebeck station is now running regularly, connecting with all trains on the Hudson River Railroad.

Markets by Telegraph.

PHILADELPHIA, Monday, Feb. 27.

FLOUR firm, at $5 75@$6 25 for superfine. WHEAT 2c.@3c. higher; sales of 4,500 bushels, at $1 55@$1 57 for white and $1 40 for red. CORN dull; sales of 3,000 bushels yellow at 75c.@76c. OATS 43c. @44½c. PORK—Mess, $18 75; Prime, $13@$15. WHISKY dull, at 23½c.@25c.

BALTIMORE, Monday, Feb. 27.

FLOUR quiet and firm; Howard-street, $5 50; Ohio City Mills held at $5 37½. WHEAT active; Red, $1 30@$1 33; White, $1 40@$1 50. CORN active and firmer, at 69c.@71c. by measure, and 73c.@74c. for White and Yellow, by weight. PORK steady; Mess at $18@$18 25; Prime advanced 50c., sales at $14@$14 50. WHISKY dull, at 24½c.

CHARLESTON, Monday, Feb. 27.

COTTON unchanged; sales to-day 1,700 bales.

SAVANNAH, Monday, Feb. 27.

COTTON—Sales to-day 650 bales, with more sellers than buyers, and holders pressing on the market.

AUGUSTA, Monday, Feb. 27.

COTTON—Sales unimportant, with little inquiry, and prices weak.

CINCINNATI, Monday, Feb. 27.

FLOUR dull and unchanged. WHISKY steady at $5 37½. PROVISIONS generally unchanged. LARD a shade easier. BACON and bulk meats—a small business doing, but held firmly. MESS PORK—no sales; offered at $17@$17 50.

NEW-ORLEANS, Monday, Feb. 27.

COTTON firm; sales to-day 10,500 bales. SUGAR steady, at 7⅛c.@7½c. MOLASSES, 38c.@39c. CORN firm; yellow, 75c.@78c.; white, 80c.@85½c. PROVISIONS firm; Mess Pork, $18 50@$18 75. Freights and Exchange unchanged.

Exchanges.

CINCINNATI, Monday, Feb. 27.

Money market firm, and the demand fully up to the supply. Sight Exchange on New-York unchanged.

Outrages on the Indians on the Mendocino Reservation.

If accounts that reach us from the Mendocino Reservation, says the Petaluma *Argus* of Feb. 4, are reliable, the villanies that are there perpetrated are exceeded only by the exploits of the valorous heroes of the North, and the whole affair is an outrage upon the Indians, and a swindle against the Government. Our information is direct, and comes to us under such circumstances as compel us to believe that it is reliable. Parties who have contracts for furnishing the Indians with beef and blankets are continually receiving money from the Government for articles the Indians never obtain. While the Indians are dispersed over the country, earning their own living and getting nothing from these contractors, the Government is daily charged for supplies that would be adequate to support every Indian on the Reservation. The blankets furnished the Indians, and for which the Government is charged at a high rate, are absolutely worthless—so rotten and damaged that they are of no value whatever. Nor is this all. The women are not protected against the abuses of unprincipled white men, but are subjected to indignities too revolting to describe, while the children are often sold to those who think they can make them serviceable. If these things are true, it is time this infamous system was abolished, and something else instituted in its place. For the sake of humanity we hope these things are not true; yet, in the face of so many acts of perfidy and cruelty on the part of those who are attempting to make money out of the Indians, nothing need surprise us.

The New-York Times.

VOL. IX—NO. 2663. NEW-YORK, TUESDAY, APRIL 3, 1860. PRICE TWO CENTS.

CONNECTICUT ELECTION.

The Opening Skirmish of the Presidential Fight.

Probable Success of the Republican Gubernatorial and Legislative Tickets.

GENERAL RESULTS.

FROM THE PALLADIUM OFFICE, (REP.)

NEW-HAVEN, Monday, April 2.

In 85 towns, or more than half the State heard from, Buckingham, Republican, leads over 1,000. This includes heavy majorities in Middletown, Waterbury, and most of the Democratic Districts. The House is Republican by an increased majority, and the Senate probably the same.

FROM THE HARTFORD COURANT OFFICE, (REP.)

HARTFORD, Monday, April 2.

It is impossible at the present time to give any correct opinion as to the result on Governor. It is believed, however, that BUCKINGHAM is elected.

FROM THE TIMES OFFICE, (DEM.)

HARTFORD, Monday, April 2.

Our returns show a net gain for SEYMOUR of 1,641, in thirty-seven towns and cities.

MAJORITIES FOR GOVERNOR.

MIDDLESEX COUNTY.

	Seymour, (Dem.)	Buckingham, (Opp.)
Middletown	290	—
Durham	—	19
Cromwell	69	—
Portland	379	—
Chatham	9	—

Democratic Representatives elected: Chatham, 2; Middletown, 2.

FAIRFIELD COUNTY.

	Seymour, (Dem.)	Buckingham, (Opp.)
Stamford	—	14
Darien	—	4
Greenwich	85	—
Norwalk	—	160
Wilton	—	51
New-Canaan	—	34
Ridgefield	—	87
Bridgeport	97	—
Danbury	—	35
Bethel	—	32
New-Fairfield	1	—

BRIDGEPORT, Monday, April 2.

The vote in this town to-day is the largest ever polled here. For Governor the vote stands as follows: Seymour, 1,200; Buckingham, 1,103; Seymour's majority, 97. James C. Loomis, Democratic Representative, has 56 majority. R. H. Winslow, Democratic Senator, from the Tenth District, has 83 majority.

BRIDGEPORT, Monday, April 2—11 P. M.

Representatives—Two Republicans are elected in Fairfield. There is a tie in Stratford. One Democrat is elected in Bridgeport, one in Westport, one in Weston, one in Easton, one in Monroe, one in Huntington, and one in Trumbull.

The Democrats are now marching in procession and cheering loudly. Bonfires are burning in the streets, and the greatest enthusiasm is manifested.

Norwalk elects two Republican Representatives, and the Republican legislative ticket was also successful in Ridgefield.

DANBURY—Wildman, Republican Senator, 34 majority. *Sheriff*—Seely, Republican, 10 majority. This is a reduction in the Republican vote of nearly three-quarters, as compared with the last election.

BETHEL—For Senator, 37 Republican majority.

ELEVENTH SENATORIAL DISTRICT—Republican majority, 26—a decrease of 100.

HARTFORD COUNTY.

	Seymour, (Dem.)	Buckingham, (Op.)
Hartford	349	—

COURANT OFFICE, HARTFORD, Monday, April 2—10 P. M.

Seymour in this city has 349 majority. Hartford County, with four towns to hear from, gives Buckingham 7,956, Seymour 8,268—making a Republican loss of 361 in the County, if the four towns to be heard from vote as they did last year.

Senators.—Two Democrats are elected and one Republican—the same as last year. The Republicans gain two Representatives in the County.

NEW-HAVEN COUNTY.

	Seymour, (Dem)	Buckingham, (Op.)
New-Haven	685	—
Waterbury	135	—

WATERBURY.—The election in this town has resulted in the triumph of the Democrats. The total vote polled is 1,600, of which Seymour has 867; Buckingham, 732—Seymour's majority, 135. The Democrats carry the entire State ticket by large majorities. For Representatives, Brown (Dem.) leads Welton (Rep.) 172; Coe (Dem.) leads Chase (Rep) 134. Of the adjoining towns, as far as heard from, five towns give a Republican majority, and nine a Democratic majority. Of these fourteen towns, the majority for Buckingham is 53. The Democrats appear to take their victory quietly, making no unusual demonstration.

OUR LATEST DISPATCHES.

HARTFORD, Monday, April 3—2 A. M.

Hartford, New-Haven, Tolland, New-London and Windham Counties give Buckingham 1,100 majority. The returns of Middlesex, Fairfield and Litchfield Counties will not vary the result a great deal.

Buckingham is elected, without doubt, and both branches of the Legislature are Republican by decided majorities, the House by a handsome increase over last year. This result insures a Republican United States Senator. It has been one of the hardest fought battles ever witnessed in this State.

NEW-HAVEN, Tuesday, April 3—2 A. M.

Eighteen towns in Hartford County give 398 Democratic majority. The other towns gave last year 192 Republican majority. The majority for Seymour in that County is 300.

New-Haven County, complete, gives Seymour 978 majority.

New-London County, complete, gives 600 Republican majority.

Windham County, complete, 1,116 Republican majority.

Fairfield County, eight towns, 126 Republican majority; it will probably be 200.

Litchfield and Tolland Counties gave 462 majority last year. The few returns now received show Republican gains.

Middlesex County gave 228 Democratic majority last year, and now in seven towns the Democrats gain 108, mostly in Middletown. The remaining seven towns, it is estimated, will make Seymour's majority in the county 350.

The House is Republican by nearly two-thirds.

The Senate, by returns and estimates, stands 13 Republicans to 8 Democrats.

If the towns to be heard from come in the same as last year, BUCKINGHAM, Republican, will be elected by about 1,000 majority.

FROM THE PACIFIC SIDE.

The Overland Mail of March 11—Still More Glowing Accounts from Washoe and Napa—Mining in Oregon—General and Commercial News.

MELOY'S STATION, Sunday, April 1.

The Overland Mail coach, with San Francisco dates to March 11, arrived at this station at about 12 o'clock last night.

SAN FRANCISCO, Sunday, March 11—12 M.

No arrivals. Sailed on the 10th, Ship *Emily*, FARNAM, for Callao.

There is not much for this mail.

During five days of last week the San Francisco Branch Mint coined $595,000 in double eagles.

MINING INTELLIGENCE.

Thirty tons of Washoe silver-ore, from the Ophir mine, has been smelted at the chemical laboratory of JOSEPH MOSHEIMER & Co., San Francisco, yielding an average of over $3,000 per ton, or about $100,000 in all. The company received a little more than $400 per ton for extracting the silver. Mr. MOSHEIMER is making preparations to establish a large smelting laboratory at Carson Valley.

Mr. W. S. TAYLOR, a reliable merchant, has just returned from the Washoe Mines. He informs the *Alta California* that he found 2,000 people at Virginia City, eating what they could get, sleeping on floors and in tents, and living generally in 1849-style. He went down 100 feet into the Mexican claim, in the Comstock Lead. Three men were engaged in digging the ore, two in carrying it up to the surface, and three in separating the rich ore from the poor. The vein is about ten feet wide. The ore pays $5,000 to the ton, and grows richer as they go deeper. Tunnels are being dug to reach other points of this lead. A tunnel is to be run 800 feet between the present mining places, and will go under Virginia City. His account is considered by the *Alta California* as entirely reliable.

Mr. ALPHEUS BULL, a banker, is now at the Washoe mines. He writes to a friend as follows:

"The country is unknown, and much that is said must be taken with a great deal of allowance. I saw but two claims that were paying an ounce of the mineral; the balance are undeveloped: hence their value is all conjecture. To me it appears to be a mineral country, and the relative success of the adventurers will, I apprehend, correspond with our early gold seekers in California."

A correspondent of the Sacramento *Union* writes from the Dalles, Oregon, under date of Feb. 10, concerning the new Similkameen gold mines, that the reports of rich gold fields are confirmed, but that the extent of them is not yet determined. Parties that have come into our valley the past week for supplies report that for 70 miles good prospects are found, and that the richest of all, some 40 miles from here, is the bar that was first discovered. Fifty-three men left this place for the mines yesterday. The tide has fairly set in, and nothing can prevent a rush to the mines. The snow has left us, and farmers have commenced putting in their Spring crops.

The last Yreka *Union* says that quartz mines in Jackson County, Oregon, continue yielding immense profits. From the accounts given, they excel anything yet known in California. A responsible merchant of San Francisco has paid a visit to these mines and returned. He called at the *Bulletin* office, and exhibited specimens of quartz taken from the Ish mine, seven feet below the surface. The ore in these specimens is evenly distributed through the rock, as if it had been broken and rounded into small pebble shapes and stirred in while the mass was hot. The owners of the mine claim that the quartz taken from it is worth $20,000 to the ton. They have already taken $200,000 worth out and can see as much more of equal richness in the small opening made in the ledge.

Valuable quartz discoveries are also reported at Yreka, a lead having been opened in the mountain at the head of Miner-street, from which $2,500 was taken the first day after its discovery.

MISCELLANEOUS.

The bill authorizing Butte County to subscribe $200,000 towards extending the Sacramento Valley Railroad northward to Oroville, has become a law.

The California Stage Company has expressed a willingness to carry a daily mail between California and Portland, Oregon, for the same pay the steamship company receives for carrying a tri-monthly mail between San Francisco and Portland.

At last accounts there was much activity in the organization of companies at the Napa quicksilver mines, and the work of opening them had commenced in six different places, creating a considerable demand for labor.

BY TELEGRAPH TO FRESNO CITY.

SAN FRANCISCO, Tuesday, March 13—5 P. M.

Arrived yesterday, ship *Reynard*, from Boston: to-day, ships *Harry Hastings*, *Great Republic*, *Ocean Telegraph*, *Expounder* and *Good Hope*, all from New-York; Danish ship *Carolina*, from Australia; steamer *Sonora*, from Panama.

Sailed, ship *Sparkling Wave*, for Realejo.

Sugar market buoyant; No. 1 China brisk, at 8½c.; jobbing sales of crushed, at 16½c.@17c.; 1,800 firkins of old butter, at auction, brought 8c.@10c. per pound. Provisions very dull. No sales from the fleet that arrived to-day. The market is generally weaker. The country trade is without improvement, and the city trade buy nothing until they are compelled to do so.

Eight buildings were destroyed by fire at Shasta, on the 10th. Loss, $15,000.

A telegraphic dispatch from Yreka last night says that GEORGE ISH and three others concerned in the Ish claim at Jacksonville, Oregon, have arrived at Yreka *en route* for the Atlantic States. A ledge of almost solid gold has been found on their claim twenty feet below the surface. THOMAS COROUGH was offered $80,000 for his fifth interest, but refused it, saying that the wealth of the ROTHSCHILDS would not tempt him to sell it.

The Pony Express.

THE ARRANGEMENTS COMPLETED—THE TIME TABLE.

ST. JOSEPH, Monday, April 2.

The arrangements are all completed whereby the first pony of the California express will leave here to-morrow, at 5 o'clock, P. M. In order to avoid the delay of letters from New-York and other Eastern cities, one day, viz.: over Sabbath, the day and hour of starting from here will be changed to Friday of each week, at 9 A. M. The next express will not leave here till Friday, the 13th day of April, after which it will start regularly every week. Time to Fort Kearney, 34 hours; Great Salt Lake, 124 hours; Carson City, 188 hours; Placerville, 226 hours; Sacramento City, 234 hours; and San Francisco, 240 hours. Dispatches will be telegraphed from the nearest telegraph station, which will be reached in about 200 hours. Dispatches will go from any point east to any place in California in about 205 hours. Dispatches are already coming in for this route.

Pennsylvania Legislature.

AN ADJOURNMENT PROBABLE TO-DAY—THE SUNBURY AND ERIE RAILROAD.

HARRISBURG, PA., Monday, April 2.

The Legislature will adjourn *sine die* to-morrow. Both Houses are still in session hurrying through the consideration of the calendar. The Committee of Conference on the Sunbury and Erie Railroad bill reported it in an amended form, postponing all foreclosure claims, the sale of the road, and other embarrassments under which the Company labor, until the 1st of May, 1861, and appropriating $600,000 to satisfy creditors, claimants for labor, materials, &c. The report met the concurrence of both Houses. The Committee of Conference reported that the General Appropriation bill passed by the Senate was rejected by the House. The Governor will call an extra session if the bill is not passed before the adjournment. The principal difference is in the matter of the salaries of the Judges of the Supreme Court, the House demanding that they shall be increased. The salaries of the Judges in Philadelphia and Alleghany County are increased by the Committee's report. The House is still in session.

Municipal Elections in Michigan.

DETROIT, Monday, April 2.

At the municipal election to-day in Ann Arbor the Republicans elected their Mayor and most of the City officers by increased majorities.

At Adrian the Republicans elected their Mayor by 90 majority.

At Grand Rapids M. L. SWEET, Republican, for Mayor, is elected by 15 majority.

At Jackson the Republican candidate for Mayor is elected by about 30 majority.

At Owasso, AMOS GOULD, Democrat, for Mayor, has over 200 majority.

At Ypsilanti, FALLETT, Democrat, for Mayor, has 100 majority.

At Niles, the Democrats elect their entire ticket by 50 majority.

At Pontiac, the entire Democratic ticket is elected by from 10 to 80 majority.

At Flint, Cold Water and Hillsdale, the Republicans elect their entire tickets by about the usual majority.

The Illinois Delegates to Charleston.

ST. LOUIS, Monday, April 2.

The *Republican* says that it is asserted that Hon. Mr. HUNTER, of Virginia, has addressed a letter to Mr. HERNDON, of Springfield, Ill., urging the delegates appointed by the Administration Democrats of that State, by all means to attend the Charleston Convention. The letter assures the delegates that they will be admitted to the Convention, and counsels them to pay no attention to what newspapers may say; and advises them to come by the Southern routes, intimating that funds will be provided for their expenses.

Messages for Europe.

A NEW LINE OF COMMUNICATION VIA ST. JOHNS, N.F.

ST. JOHNS, N. F., Monday, April 2.

Messages for Europe to go forward per steamship *Circassien* to Galway can be filed at No. 21 Wall-street to-day, and up to noon to-morrow. This is undoubtedly the speediest means of communication with Europe, as was shown by the last eastward trip of the *Prince Albert*, when dispatches from New-Orleans were delivered in London, Havre and Liverpool inside of seven days from date. The tolls on any message left at the above named office before to-morrow noon will be refunded in case the dispatch fails to be put on board the *Circassian*.

Election in St. Louis.

REPUBLICAN VICTORY.

ST. LOUIS, Monday, April 2.

Incomplete returns of one Councilman in each election district indicate that the Republicans have carried five Wards, and the Democrats three. There were no party nominations in two Wards, from which Independents were elected.

From New-Orleans.

ARRIVAL FROM HAVANA—AMMUNITION FOR MIRAMON—A FOOT-RACE.

NEW-ORLEANS, Monday, April 2.

The steamer *Habana*, from Havana 30th ult., has arrived. The markets are unchanged. The excitement about the captured steamers continued. It is reported that an agent of MIRAMON is in this city now after ammunition, etc.

"Unknown" won the foot-race yesterday for $5,000 by ten feet. SCHULTZ was ahead in the first hundred yards. Time, 18½ seconds. Another $10,000 race is proposed at Louisville.

Fires.

KEROSENE OIL WORKS AT HAMILTON, C. W.

HAMILTON, C. W., Monday, April 2.

WILLIAMS' Kerosene oil works were destroyed by fire on Saturday night last, together with 7,000 gallons of oil.

HOTEL AND STORES AT DANVILLE, PENN.

DANVILLE, Penn., Monday, April 2.

The Mansion House, SCROTH'S restaurant, BROWN'S saloon, SAVAGE'S jewelry establishment, and DORAN'S tailor shop, were destroyed by fire on Sunday morning. Loss, $15,000; partially insured. Fire supposed to have been the work of an incendiary.

BUSINESS PORTION OF JACKSONPORT, ARK.

MEMPHIS, TENN., Monday, April 2.

Almost the entire business portion of Jacksonport, Ark., was destroyed by fire on Wednesday last. Loss $150,000, insured for $81,000.

The Carstang-Shaw Case.

VERDICT FOR SHAW, THE DEFENDANT.

ST. LOUIS, Sunday, April 1.

Major WRIGHT closed his argument in the Carstang-Shaw case last evening. His speech occupied nearly eight hours in delivery, after which the jury retired, and in twenty minutes rendered a verdict for the defendant. A motion for a new trial was immediately filed by the plaintiff's counsel. In case the motion is refused, the case will be appealed to the Supreme Court.

The Great Western Railroad.

HAMILTON, C. W., Monday, April 2.

The traffic on the Great Western Railroad is rapidly increasing. The returns for the last fortnight show an increase of $12,000 over the corresponding period of last year.

The Slaver Orion.

THE OFFICERS HELD FOR TRIAL.

BOSTON, Monday, April 2.

MORGAN, CHAMBERLAIN and DUNNING, late officers of the bark *Orion*, an alleged slaver, are held in $5,000 each for trial. The examination will probably take place to-morrow.

FROM WASHINGTON.

Debate on the Davis Resolutions in the Senate.

Interesting Remarks of Messrs. Saulsbury, Ten Eyck, Brown and Wigfall.

The House upon the Utah Saints and their Sins.

Special Dispatch to the New-York Times.

WASHINGTON, Monday, April 2.

INDIAN AFFAIRS.

The annuity goods for the Indians in the Eastern District of Washington Territory will be dispatched over Lieut. MULLAN'S new wagon road, and distributed at Hellgate. The Expedition will be thirty-five days in reaching Fort Benton, but the good condition of the route in question leaves no doubt that it will be open in season to permit the movement of the troops, and the transportation of Indian supplies. One hundred thousand dollars more will be required to make this route good during heavy rains.

The Indian Bureau is now vigorously occupied in drafting the necessary instructions, and making arrangements to remit funds, and carry out the Indian treaties in Oregon, the appropriation for that purpose having passed Congress.

Pursuant to instructions from the War Department, the commanding officer at Fort Ridgely, will detail one of the foot companies of artillery under his command, for detached service, to be stationed temporarily at Yellow Medicine, for the protection of the Indians on the reserve at that place. The officer in command is to communicate directly with the Department Head-quarters.

Secretary COBB has appointed MURRAY WHALON, of Pennsylvania, secret agent of the Government on the Pacific coast, *vice* J. ROSS BROWNE resigned.

REVOLUTIONARY CLAIMS.

The bill which Hon. R. E. FENTON, of New-York, introduced at the commencement of the present session, having received the action of the Committee to which it had been referred, has been reported in the House of Representatives without amendment, and is in a position to be taken up at any time for consideration. It proposes to allow the officers of the Revolutionary army and their heirs the life half pay which was promised them by the Continental Congress, deducting therefrom all sums which the Government ever paid by way of commutation certificates, or as pay under the act of May 15, 1828. Whatever balance may be due on this basis, is to be paid without interest. The bill also provides 160 acres of land to the surviving children of each Revolutionary soldier who served fourteen days, or was engaged in battle, &c. There is a strong feeling in Congress in favor of the bill, and it will doubtless be taken up in the House and passed at an early day.

MISCELLANEOUS.

Gen. JEFFERSON DAVIS is again suffering from inflammation of the eyes. The surgical operation performed on one, last Saturday, it is apprehended will result in the loss of both.

Washington is likely to be favored with a street railroad war equal to that lately waged in Baltimore. The Senate is about to pass a bill granting the franchise to a squad of speculators over the heads of citizens claiming the grant. The House will arrest such legislation.

ARMY NEWS.

The two Superintendents of the General Recruiting Service are ordered to organize at Fort Columbus and Newport Barracks, four companies of recruits; two at each dépôt, of seventy-five men, or as near that number as possible, for the troops serving in the Department of Oregon, each company to have four lance sergeants, four lance corporals and two musicians. Non-commissioned officers are to be selected from the permanent party. Should there be a deficiency of recruits at either place to organize two companies, the Superintendents are to notify each other of the fact, that the deficiency may be supplied from the dépôt having a surplus, and such recruits will join the deficient company at Jefferson Barracks.

Recruits will be detached to Jefferson Barracks the 20th inst., and will move on the 1st of May following from St. Louis, by the Missouri River to Fort Benton, thence to Fort Dallas, by the route passed over by Lieut. MULLAN, of the Second Artillery. Brevet-Col. ROBERT C. BUCHANAN, of the Fourth Infantry, is assigned to the command, and will proceed to St. Louis in advance of the recruits, to superintend the arrangements of troops for the march. The other officers assigned to duty with the recruits are Capt. LENDRUM, of the Third Artillery; Capt JONES, of the Fourth Infantry; Lieuts. LIVINGSTON, of the Third Artillery, KANTZ, of the Fourth Infantry, and KELTON, of the Sixth Infantry, and Second-Lieut. STOUGHTON, of the Sixth Infantry, to report at Fort Columbus on the 15th inst. Capt. HENDRICKSON, of the Sixth Infantry, and Lieuts. MERCER, of the First Dragoons, SMITH, of the Sixth Infantry, and CARR, of the Ninth Infantry, are to report to Newport Barracks.

Brevet Col. JOHNSON, Acting Inspector-General, will inspect the recruits at Jefferson Barracks prior to their march from that post. On the arrival of the detachment at Fort Dallas, its distribution will be made under the orders of the commander of the Department of Oregon.

All officers of the Second Dragoons, of the Fourth Artillery, and of the Tenth Infantry, absent from Forts Kearney and Laramie, and the Department of Utah, except those on special duty, will report in person at Fort Leavenworth on the 25th inst., for duty, with a detachment of recruits to leave that post about the 1st of May following for Camp Floyd.

All officers absent from the First Dragoons, and the Eighth Infantry, stationed in the Department; from the Regiment of Mounted Riflemen, the Fifth and Seventh Regiments of Infantry, except those on other special duty than the recruiting service, will report in person at Fort Leavenworth on 25th of July next, for duty, with a detachment of recruits, to leave that post about the 1st of August following for the Department of New-Mexico. All officers absent from the Third Regiment of Infantry, except those on special duty, will report in person on the 1st of July next at San Antonio, Texas, to the commanding officer of the Department of Texas.

Officers who may report according to the above instructions, will join their respective posts and companies after executing these special orders. Should any officer be prevented by ill health from obeying these orders, before he can be excused he must present the certificate of the officer of the Medical Staff of the Army, which certificate must distinctly set forth the inability of the officer to perform the journey. In all cases the officer will be informed whether such certificate has been accepted.

From the Associated Press.

WASHINGTON, Monday, April 2.

The case of the United States against BOLTON, on an appeal from the Northern District Court of California, involving the title to three square leagues of San Francisco lands, was taken up in the Supreme Court to-day, WILLIAM B. REED making the opening argument for the United States. The Court, in view of the magnitude of the case, granted the request of BOLTON'S counsel, that three hours be allowed each for argument.

Col. BROWN writes to the War Department, from Brownsville, that reports the most false and exaggerated are put in circulation by persons interested in fomenting trouble on the Rio Grande border, immediately before the leaving of the New-Orleans steamer, for the evident purpose of exercising an influence on public opinion in the States. Hence such reports should be received with the greatest caution. He adds that the Cortinas movement was a mere raid, and the accounts largely magnified.

The State Department has written a letter to our Consul, Mr. HELM, at Havana, commendatory of his partial success in behalf of LIANO, a native Spaniard, but a naturalized citizen of the United States, who was summoned to military duty. In addition to other friendly offices, the Captain-General will submit the question to his Government, with a recommendation that LIANO be exempted from military duty. Secretary CASS has sent to Mr. HELM, for the information of the Captain-General, a copy of the instructions to our Minister to Berlin, Mr. WRIGHT, on the subject of interference with the rights of American naturalized citizens.

The majority of the House Committee on the Post-office are in favor of the Senate bill for a telegraph to the Pacific, but with amendments, reducing the price of messages 25 per cent. The Committee are divided as to the amount of subsidy the Government shall pay.

Mr. BURCH has been appointed a member of that Committee in place of Mr. ENGLISH, excused from service. This supplies a Representative from the Pacific, which was much desired.

It appears by a statement of the *Picayune's* Vera Cruz correspondent, of March 21, that Capt. ALDHAM wrote to MIRAMON protesting very strongly against wanton and inhuman destruction of English property and of non-combatants.

The Constitutional Union Committee to-night decided that the Chairman should convene the entire National Committee of Three Hundred simultaneously with the Convention to be held at Baltimore, May 9, to ratify nominations and take steps to further the organization for prosecuting the canvas.

SENATE.

WASHINGTON, Monday, April 2.

Mr. HUNTER, of Virginia, (Dem.,) from the Finance Committee, reported back the Indian Appropriation bill amendment, and gave notice that he would call it up to-morrow.

On motion of Mr. BENJAMIN, of Louisiana, (Dem.,) the bill for the final adjustment of private land claims in Florida, Louisiana, Arkansas and Missouri, was taken up.

Mr. BENJAMIN stated that the object of the bill was to prevent the presentation to Congress one at a time of these private land claims.

The bill was passed.

The bill to authorize the the location of certain warrants for bounty lands heretofore issued, on motion of Mr. HAMLIN was called up and passed.

The territorial resolutions of Mr. DAVIS, of Mississippi, (Dem.,) were called up.

Mr. SAULSBURY, of Delaware, (Dem.,) said the resolutions were the occasion of his speaking on the state of the Union and discussing its integrity; whether it is imperiled, and if so, who is responsible? and what remedies were there? He regarded the Federal Union as the palladium of our liberty, and would therefore oppose the political parties which threatened it. Some GIBBON would yet write the fall of the Union unless we timely pause and wisely act. It was scarce eighty years ago since the Revolutionary war was fought by those from the North, the South and the then West, who achieved a common liberty for them selves and their posterity. After that came the formation of the Federal Union, and there were conflicts then which were not irrepressible. Our fathers differed widely, but did not assume a moral government over the world. They knew no *capital* and *labor* States—now so called by political aspirants,—nor did they discuss the Slavery question; but they placed a clause in the Constitution relative to the escape of fugitives from labor from one State into another, which was a distinct and positive recognition of rights of property in slaves. It recognized the constitutional right of one man to have property in another man against the interference of States. He proceeded to discuss the Slavery questions presented from the earliest times to the present, and cited the first Fugitive Slave law of 1793, as recognizing property in slaves, and said he believed if ever there was a blot and blur on the history of the country, it was the Missouri Compromise. He charged the agitation of the Slavery question on the enemies of the Democratic Party heretofore and now. After condemning the hellish deed of Old BROWN, he referred to the political events of the day by an inquiry if the Union was imperilled. He believed that one man more than all others had brought the Union to the very verge of destruction by his teachings and advice. That man was an aspirant to the highest office of the land, was a teacher of the views of the Republican Party, and the same who recently delivered a speech in the Senate. The same man was once Governor of New-York, and refused to return to Virginia three men who escaped, charged with the crime of stealing slaves. If JOHN BROWN had carried all the slaves of Virginia to New-York, Mr. SEWARD would be a fortunate Governor for him in such an event. He quotes Mr. SEWARD'S Cleveland speech, showing that he was in favor of abolishing Slavery in the States and violating the Fugitive Slave Law. He there said "Slavery must be abolished, and you and I must do it." He also quoted from his letter to the colored citizens of Albany, that they had a right to complain of the Union, as it did not give them equal rights with others. When the Republicans assemble around the Council Board at Chicago, and call the roll of States, and there are no answers from the States where rest the remains of WASHINGTON, SUMTER and MARION, and nominate a candidate to rule over these subjected provinces, who had told the colored people that they had a right to impugn the memories of these Fathers of the Country, perhaps the patient sons of these Fathers will submit to the yoke. The motto of the banner of the Republican Party was lawlessness, and the party was bound to nothing, and its actions were duly determined by exigencies. In conclusion, he said Delaware was the first to adopt the Constitution, and will be the last to abandon it, and advocated the harmony of the Democratic Party as tending to destroy the evils which threatened the Union.

Mr. TEN EYCK, of New-Jersey, (Rep.,) said New-Jersey always had been true to the Union and Constitution, as understood by their framers and the statesmen of that day. The question was not now, Slavery in the States, but its extension into territory now free. None, except a few enemies of the Constitution, pretended that Congress had any right to abolish Slavery in the States in any way, but the question was as to whether in the broad domain, the common property of the Union, it should supplant free labor, enterprise and industry in the marts of commerce, colleges, schools and the golden harvest. The different systems of labor, slave and free, could exist in different sections of the country, but could not in the same field and workshop. The question was the introduction of Slavery into Territory where men are now free as the wild deer bounding over the prairie. He regarded Slavery as an evil. New-Jersey abolished it early, and then hoped others would, but because they did not it was no reason he should come here and villify and traduce members of the latter States. Slavery would have been abolished in many places if there had not been unwarrantable interferences with it. He proceeded to speak of the Fugitive Slave law, and said New-Jersey had had one of her own in force since 1793, and they had regarded it as obligatory on them. They had no doubt of its constitutionality. In one unreported case, Chief-Justice HORNBLOWER had discharged a slave because of a defect in the evidence, and had expressed an opinion as to the effect of its unconstitutionality, but it had not obtained with them. His people were in favor of executing the Fugitive Slave law, and he cited a case where a Representative of his State (Mr. STRATTON) advocated it, and sent three slaves back to bondage in a case before the Court, yet he was sent to Congress by a very large Republican vote. He contended that the principles of the Republican party were identical with those of JEFFERSON and the ordinance of 1787, and said that New-Jersey would stand with the Middle States in repelling ultraism and extravagance, and beg the other sister States, by the memories of Monmouth, Trenton, Saratoga, Bunker Hill, New-Orleans and Guilford, to maintain the Union.

Mr. BROWN, of Mississippi, (Dem.,) said it was well known that he contended that a territorial legislature could abolish Slavery by non-action, and that he favored Congressional protection of property in the Territories. For this the charges had been brought against him that he had departed from the usages of the party, and was interpolating new rules. He proposed briefly to deny these charges, for he had not attempted to interpolate in party usages anything not advocated by our fathers. He would show that in 1822, Congress, by an express law, overthrew and set aside certain laws of Florida Territory, and went further than that, by refunding certain monies paid under the repealed law, and substituted an independent law in its stead. It was thus asserted that Congress had the right to protect property in the Territories. He cited the case of a law passed in 1834, where Congress by direct law protected Slavery in Florida, which was voted for by WEBSTER, CLAY, FORSYTH and GRUNDY, and many other illustrious men of that Congress, and passed through both Houses of Congress without a dissenting voice, and was approved by President JACKSON. Yet he (BROWN) was denominated a heretic for advocating now what those illustrious men approved. He stood where they stood; he advocated their acts, and asked nothing new. Oh, Senators! he exclaimed, how have we fallen! He asked for no new theory, yet he had been condemned by Republicans and some Democrats for it. What depth of infamy was the South sinking to to allow these things to go on? He then referred to Mr. ATHERTON'S resolutions of the Thirty-fifth Congress, declaring that Congress had no right to make a distinction in the property of States going into the Territories, and, concluding, contended that this question of protection was never denied until the doctrine of "squatter sovereignty" came into Congress. He would maintain his position and allow no petty neighborhood politician to whistle him down.

Mr. WIGFALL, of Texas, (Dem.,) spoke at some length, saying, in the course of his remarks, that the people of a Territory could not admit or reject Slavery. The South asked that slave property might be placed on a footing with all other property. The first property man ever had was in men. He was opposed to starting new questions at this time, and would therefore vote for Mr. DAVIS' instead of Mr. BROWN'S resolution, although he regretted that any had been introduced. It was better to let the Charleston Convention nominate its candidate without a platform, fight the battle, starve out the Republicans, and discuss these things afterwards.

Adjourned.

HOUSE OF REPRESENTATIVES.

WASHINGTON, Monday, April 2.

Mr. HICKMAN, of Pennsylvania, (Rep.,) from the Committee on Judiciary, reported a bill to extend the right of appeal from decisions of Circuit Courts to the Supreme Court of the United States.

Mr. ELIOT, of Massachusetts, (Rep.,) introduced a bill for the removal of the obstructions at Hurlgate, and a bill for the improvement of Harlem River, which were referred to the Committee on Commerce.

Mr. MORSE, of Maine, (Rep.,) ineffectually endeavored to introduce a bill prohibiting the Chinese Coolie-trade in American vessels.

Mr. BURNETT, of Kentucky, (Dem.,) objected.

The bill for the suppression of polygamy in Utah was considered.

Mr. MILLSON, of Virginia, (Dem.,) said this bill should pass with as much unanimity as possible, for the crime of polygamy was not only extensively practiced, but attempted to be legalized by statute. He argued, in reply to Mr. TAYLOR, of Louisiana, (Dem.,) that Congress has power over this low and degrading imposture, and that the very first year after the adoption of the Federal Constitution, a law was passed for the punishment of certain crimes wherever the jurisdiction of the United States extended.

Mr. MCCLERNAND, of Illinois, (Dem.,) interrupting, said there was no instance in which Congress attempted to operate directly for the punishment of the crime in organized Territories.

Mr. MILLSON took issue, referring to the legislative history in support of the argument.

Mr. TAYLOR also controverted his position, but

Mr. MILLSON adverted to the gentleman's own State, Louisiana, to show when it was in a Territorial condition the penal laws were extended thither for the punishment of murder, arson, forgery, and every other crime.

Mr. PRYOR, of Virginia, (Dem.,) argued that the question of constitutional power is sustained by the uniform policy of the Government. Congress may supervise and annul the organic law of any incipient State. The Republican Party may associate polygamy and Slavery as the twin relics of barbarism, but he disputed the philosophy of the classification. He denied that they stand on the same ground and would fall together when driven from the shelter of a common security. In the interest of Slavery he repudiated the suggestion that the power which Congress possesses over the Territories for the punishment of crime and the suppression of polygamy may be perverted for the destruction of the rights and interests of persons holding slaves. The Territories are the common property of the people of the United States, and the power Congress possesses over them cannot be perverted for the benefit of any section repulsive to the justice and subversive of the equality of the States.

Mr. HOOPER, of Utah, (Dem.,) said polygamy was a part of the Mormon religious faith.

Mr. PRYOR replied, he had examined the disgusting and blasphemous farrago called the Mormon Bible, and he could not find therein a solitary word recognizing polygamy as a matter of religion. He did not, however, pretend to be acquainted with all the polemics of the Salt Lake Saints. The results of polygamy were seen in the bitter fruits of sedition and crime. This scandalous crime should be extirpated. It was offensive in the eyes of nations, and a reproach to civil liberty.

Mr. ETHERIDGE, of Tennessee, (Amer.,) said two colored persons were conversing about the millenium, when the lion and the lamb shall lie down together. One contented himself by remarking that the time had not yet come, while the other said, when it did come, the lamb would be found inside the lion. [Laughter.] We have here, however, the lion and the lamb lying down together, and it remains for the historian to find out which is the lamb, and which is the lion. The Democrats and Republicans harmonize on the vexed question of the power of Congress over the Territories. That his morality might not be questioned, he said he would vote for this bill or any other, and this disposition should be attributed to to his early teaching of piety. [Laughter.] He repeated that this question brings up the whole power of Congress to govern the Territories, by which the Democrats will be required to stand when the question of Slavery is involved. The Democratic catechism has been often revised, and so rapidly that people were not able to keep up with the changes, and now he was required to say that Congress has plenary power all on one side, provided it is in favor of the negro. This was not as yet published as the last authoritative exposition of the Democratic creed, but it would have endorsers more respectable than the Helper book. Incest, adultery and polygamy are kindred offences. If punishment may be extended to married persons they may to single ones. If the law may be applied to whites, it may be applied to blacks. The Constitution recognizes Slavery no more than it does husband and wife.

Mr. LAMAR, of Mississippi, (Dem.,) inquired whether the gentleman maintained and asserted the power of Congress to punish Slavery as a crime in the Territories.

Mr. ETHERIDGE replied—He was showing the difficulties gentlemen may have, for fear they will not see them. Whoever votes for the bill does so with a distinct understanding that Congress has power to punish adultery, and may extend the power to the interdiction of Slavery by unfriendly legislation. But he would vote for the bill because he believed Congress would always have too much good sense to do it. [Laughter.]

Mr. SINGLETON, of Mississippi, (Dem.,) asked whether the gentleman, in voting for this bill, voted for the principle that Congress has the right to abolish Slavery in the Territories?

Mr. ETHERIDGE repeated that he would vote for the bill in order to scour this nauseating offence, and because he thought Congress could prohibit it in Utah. It extends its provisions as well to blacks as to the whites. As to the operation on Slavery, the only guarantee he had was the good sense, liberality and fair dealing of Congress.

Mr. PRYOR remarked that the gentleman from Tennessee said he regarded every one voting for this bill as voting for the right of Congress to abolish Slavery in the Territories. That might be and was true as to the gentleman, but he (PRYOR) repudiated that view of the question. He observed a distinction between Slavery and polygamy under the Constitution.

Mr. ETHERIDGE—I know you do. You have said so. I was only speaking for myself.

Mr. LAMAR—My question is whether Congress has power to declare and punish Slavery as a felony in the Territories.

Mr. ETHERIDGE—I admit the power of Congress to legislate over black as well as white persons, and while this bill does not embrace black persons, Congress may do so. The gentleman from North Carolina, by offering an amendment, sought to dodge the question.

Mr. BRANCH, of North Carolina, (Dem.,) assured the gentleman he did not want to dodge. Polygamy might continue to exist before he would vote for the first section of the bill.

Mr. ETHERIDGE replied that the gentleman was not willing to face the responsibility by voting against the bill, but at the same time, afforded by his amendment a narrow plank by which his friends might escape from the burning wreck.

Mr. TAYLOR opposed the bill. It would be a dead letter on the statute book. He advocated Mr. BRANCH'S amendment, which would apply a remedy for the evil which all seem desirous should be extirpated. He argued that the Constitution is one of limited powers, and gave no authority to pass a measure like that under consideration.

A motion having been made to adjourn, Mr. SHERMAN, of Ohio, (Rep.,) said they should remain and continue the debate.

Mr. LAMAR was prepared to meet the question in a spirit of patriotism and not of party. The bill in effect declared that an entire community is guilty of felony. Owing to the great importance of the subject, it should receive a calm and not a hurried consideration.

Mr. NELSON, of Tennessee, (Amer.,) agreed that the bill was of great magnitude and should be carefully considered. After a liberal amount of discussion he would move the previous question, say late to-morrow afternoon.

The House refused to adjourn.

Mr. TAYLOR resumed and concluded his remarks.

The House then adjourned.

TURMOIL IN KENTUCKY.

Alleged Outbreak of Civil War—Letter from Cassius M. Clay—Doubts Thrown Over the Whole Story.

The neighborhood of Louisville, Ky., has been greatly disturbed by reports of serious outbreaks in Madison County, directed against the opponents of Slavery in that vicinity. The Louisville *Courier* of the 29th publishes the following note, brought by a "messenger in hot haste," who reported that as a committee of citizens attempted to drive away one HANSON, a member of the Fee Party expelled some weeks since, they were fired upon by a party of twenty-five men armed with rifles, and headed by a man named HALEY, who retired and fortified them in an old log-house. The Committee then dispatched the following letter:

RICHMOND, March 30, 1860.

Capt. John Morgan, Messrs. Allen & Goodloe, Bruce & Hunter:

GENTS: We send the bearer of this note requesting you to send us a *cannon*. We are in a serious difficulty with the Fee party in our county, *and we need a cannon to whip them out*. Your attention to this will much oblige a great many good citizens of this county—citizens who will remember the kindness. Send us cannon ball and cartridges, and everything necessary to load it. All expenses and damages, if any, will be promptly paid. Your friends,

ED. W. TURNER,
R. R. STONE,
MAJ. WM. HARRIS,
DR. WM. JENNINGS,
And others.

P. S.—If you can, send us some two or three of your boys who know how to load and shoot, and are competent to direct the piece, &c. E. W. T.

We have no one who has ever been accustomed to loading or shooting a cannon, and would like for some one to come who is competent. E. W. T.

The *Courier* adds that the cannon was forwarded and that the Lexington Rifles were ready to march but concluded to await further intelligence.

In addition, the *Evening Post*, of yesterday, publishes the following "private letter" from C. M. CLAY, dated March 29. Whether it was addressed to some one in this City, or elsewhere, is not stated:

"Yours of the 19th is received. I have only time to say that we are in a state of war. The oligarchy were aiming at *me*, in the expulsion of the Bereans from their homes, being in hopes that I would forcibly defend them, 'the Radicals.' Defeated by my Frankfort speech, rallying all the Conservative men to my standard, they churlishly gave in, yet fanning the discontent by garbling my speeches North, and circulating false rumors. HANSON'S return to his saw-mill at Berea (where he employed many Republicans) gave new fuel to the old fire. I went there on Saturday, and tried to induce him to leave, telling him he would bring on a fight, and advising the Republicans to keep apart from the movement. The mob at once cried out that I was then plotting an attack. On Monday they met at Berea, insulted the people by searching the houses, and not finding HANSON, they provoked a conflict; several were wounded, and the lynchers were *defeated*. On Tuesday they returned in force; but finding no one, they broke up the saw-mill and swore vengeance against me and the whole party. In the meantime, (on Tuesday,) I spoke at Richmond, stating that I was and had been *for peace*; that I stood upon the ground of my Frankfort speech, and should defend myself and friends. The mob increases in violence; I lie upon my arms awaiting an attack; my family absolutely refuse to retire, saying they will run bullets, and aid as in 1776. If driven into the woods, I shall attempt to hold my position as long as possible; standing on the Constitution, the laws and my right. I will defend them or die. The cannon at Lexington is sent for, and the Governor aids.

Is this my cause only, or that of the American people? Is it to be vindicated in this way, and now? Shall I stand or fall alone? 'May God defend the right!' Your friend, C. M. CLAY.

P. S.—My *daughters* are as firm as I and Mrs. C. C."

On the other hand, we have the following letter from our own correspondent at Louisville, dated the 29th, which denounces the whole story as a hoax:

THE IRREPRESSIBLE WAR—MADISON AND HOPKINS COUNTIES IN ARMS AGAINST THE "ABOLITIONISTS" AND "HELPERITES"—BUT ALL A HOAX.

Correspondence of the New-York Times.

LOUISVILLE, Ky., Thursday, March 29, 1860.

Some of the raciest jokes of the season occur in these parts. The Democrats of Lexington, Frankfort and Louisville, with Gov. MAGOFFIN, seem for a day or two past to have been roused to the highest pitch by great stories from the interior, warlike telegrams, wrought up with all possible pomp and circumstance. But they have already subsided, and are to day lying on their arms waiting for another "scare."

Yesterday we heard that two dozen or more of the expelled Abolitionists of Berea, headed by JNO. G. HANSON, had returned, and being ordered again to leave by the Madison County Vigilance Committee had shown fight, fired upon the Committee, killed two and wounded others, and then retreated to a block-house bristling with 200 guns, hoisted a flag, and swore they would not surrender! The citizens of Richmond, the county-seat of Madison, were marching to the seat of war *en masse*, armed to the teeth. The cannon, ammunition and militia boys of Lexington were sent for "to whip out the free party in Madison County." The Lexington Rifles, "in full dress," were about to start thither. Gov. MAGOFFIN had telegraphed to Louisville for percussion caps to fit the Miniés in the State Arsenal, and for a United States officer to accompany him and his numberless aids and the Frankfort militia to the Kentucky Solferino!

To-day, however, the whole thing turns out an arrant hoax from beginning to end! The Governor did indeed set out for the awful scene yesterday forenoon, but he got no further than Lexington before he concluded nothing would suffer for want of his august presence at the seat of war; and so he "turned tail," and found himself before his supper time back again at the seat of Government! I wonder any sensible body could have swallowed so bare-faced, self-evident a *canard*. Everything was so soon reported quiet in Madison—no "excitement" at Berea or Richmond. A small, insignificant, common-place row had occurred—nothing more—no bloodshed—nobody hurt or in danger! Those Madisonians, who, in the name of a "great many good citizens," sent that blood-and thunder dispatch to Lexington for help against the mighty "Fee party," appear to have done so more for deviltry than anything else. If not, they showed a marvelous distrust of their own strength, to invoke the chivalry of all Kentuck to their rescue from a petty Abolition handful! Be this as it may, our Democratic organ, this morning, announces that the troubles there have been "vastly exaggerated." "The Powers," to-day, assure us that "order reigns at Warsaw!"

One other joke, if you please. Some "scamp" in Madisonville, Hopkins County, the other day humbugged right well the distinguished editor of the Louisville *Courier*. The editor published with alacrity and prominence, a cock-and-bull-story addressed him from that quarter by one "E. W. M." But the Madisonville *Register* pronounces the entire tale a well-varnished hoax. He wrote that the intensest excitement pervaded Hopkins, owing to the presence, conduct, arrest and escape of a "Helferite," one "SANDERS, from New-Albany, Indiana," who traversed the country on horseback, with saddle-bags choke full of the "*Impending Crisis*" and "*Irrepressible Conflict*," and was conspiring with certain free negroes and slaves to murder at night certain planters, and then to run them off to the Ohio, opposite Evansville, where a "band of Helferites" would meet them and escort them over to free soil! The "Helferite" was seen by Mr. EDWARD SLOAN, reading some paper to his slaves by the roadside, who had left their work to listen to him. As SLOAN approached to question the stranger, the stranger rode away. SLOAN'S "old Sam" told him all SANDERS had said. Thereupon SLOAN gave the alarm in Madisonville; all the bells in town were rung, and the town put off in pursuit. They at last caught him, and were about to "string him up," when in the confusion and darkness he escaped! In the *melee* even the editor of the Madisonville *Register*, (who now turns up, to our *Courier's* chagrin, alive and kicking,) was mistaken for SANDERS, knocked down, and "very badly hurt!" "E. W. M." immediately sat down and wrote to the *Courier* a "catch-thief" letter, an epistolary advertisement, minutely describing the terrible fellow's appearance, age, &c., depicting the rage of the people of Hopkins, and indicating their willingness to give any amount for his capture. And yet this was all a baited bug-a-boo of "E. W. M's" invention!—a catch for the Louisville *Courier*! The *Courier* yesterday owns up, quotes the *Register's* extinguisher, and pronounces "E. W. M's" epistle of March 15, "the pure fiction of a scamp, whom 't were base to term a villain"—for he had "hoaxed the public," *alias* Hon. W. N. HALDEMAN.

PONTIAC.

The New-York Times.

VOL. X....NO. 2983. NEW-YORK, SATURDAY, APRIL 13, 1861. PRICE TWO CENTS.

THE WAR COMMENCED.

The First Gun Fired by Fort Moultrie Against Fort Sumpter.

THE BOMBARDMENT CONTINUED ALL DAY.

Spirited Return from Major Anderson's Guns.

The Firing from Fort Sumpter Ceased for the Night.

Hostilities to Commence Again at Daylight.

The Correspondence which Preceded the Bombardment.

The Demand for a Surrender and Major Anderson's Refusal.

THE RELIEF FLEET OFF THE HARBOR.

How the News is Received in Washington.

OUR CHARLESTON DISPATCHES.

CHARLESTON, Friday, April 12.

The ball has opened. War is inaugurated.

The batteries of Sullivan's Island, Morris Island, and other points, were opened on Fort Sumpter at 4 o'clock this morning.

Fort Sumpter has returned the fire, and a brisk cannonading has been kept up. No information has been received from the seaboard yet.

The military are under arms, and the whole of our population are on the streets. Every available space facing the harbor is filled with anxious spectators.

CHARLESTON, Friday, April 12.

The firing has continued all day without intermission.

Two of Fort Sumpter's guns have been silenced, and it is reported that a breach has been made in the southeast wall.

The answer to Gen. BEAUREGARD'S demand by Major [illegible] was that he would surrender when his supplies were exhausted, that is, if he was not reinforced.

Not a casualty has yet happened to any of the forces.

Of the nineteen batteries in position only seven have opened fire on Fort Sumpter, the remainder are held in reserve for the expected fleet.

Two thousand men reached this city this morning and embarked for Morris Island and the neighborhood.

CHARLESTON, Friday, April 12.

The bombardment of Fort Sumpter continues.

The Floating Battery and Stephens Battery are operating freely, and Fort Sumpter is returning the fire.

It is reported that three war vessels are outside the bar.

CHARLESTON, Friday, April 12.

The firing has ceased for the night, but will be renewed at daylight in the morning, unless an attempt is made to reinforce, which ample arrangements have been made to repel.

The *Pawnee, Harriet Lane*, and a third steamer are reported off the bar.

Troops are arriving by every train.

LATER DISPATCHES—HOSTILITIES STILL PRODEEDING.

CHARLESTON, Friday, April 12.

The bombardment is still going on every twenty minutes from our morters. It is supposed that Major ANDERSON is resting his ment for the night.

Three vessels-of-war are reported outside. They cannot get in. The sea is rough.

Nobody is hurt. The floating battery works well. Troops arrive hourly. Every inlet is guarded. There are lively times here.

CHARLESTON, Friday, April 12.

The firing on Fort Sumpter continues.

There are reviving times on the "Palmetto coast."

CHARLESTON, Friday, April 12—3 A. M.

It is utterly impossible to reinfofce Fort Shmpter, to-night, as a storm is now raging.

The morter batteries will be playing on Fort Sumpter all night.

FROM ANOTHER CORRESPONDENT.

CHARLESTON, Friday, April 12.

Civil war has at last begun. A terrible fight is at this moment going on between Fort Sumpter and the fortifications by which it is surrounded.

The issue was submitted to Major ANDERSON of surrendering as soon as his supplies were exhausted, or of having a fire opened on him within a certain time.

This he refused to do, and accordingly, at twenty-seven minutes past four o'clock this morning Fort Moultrie began the bombardment by firing two guns. To these Major ANDERSON replied with three of his barbette guns, after which the batteries on Mount Pleasant, Cummings' Point, and the Floating Battery opened a brisk fire of shot and shell.

Major ANDERSON did not reply except at long intervals, until between 7 and 8 o'clock, when he brought into action the two tier of guns looking towards Fort Moultrie and Stevens iron battery.

Up to this hour—3 o'clock—they have failed to produce any serious effect.

Major ANDERSON has the greater part of the day been directing his fire principally against Fort Moultrie, the Stevens and Floating Battery, these and Fort Johnson being the only five operating against him. The remainder of the batteries are held in reserve.

Major ANDERSON is at present using his lower tier of casemate ordnance.

The fight is going on with intense earnestness, and will continue all night.

The excitement in the community is indescribable. With the very first boom of the guns thousands rushed from their beds to the harbor front, and all day every available place has been thronged by ladies and gentlemen, viewing the spectacle through their glasses.

The brilliant and patriotic conduct of Major ANDERSON speaks for itself.

Business is entirely suspended. Only those stores open necessary to supply articles required by the Army.

Gov. PICKENS has all day been in the residence of a gentleman which commands a view of the whole scene—a most interested observer. Gen. BEAUREGARD commands in person the entire operations.

It is reported that the *Harriet Lane* has received a shot through her wheelhouse. She is in the offing. No other Government ships in sight up to the present moment, but should they appear the entire range of batteries will open upon them.

Troops are pouring into the town by hundreds, but are held in reserve for the present, the force already on the island being ample. People are also arriving every moment on horseback, and by every other conveyance.

CHARLESTON, Friday, April 12—6 P. M.

Capt. R. S. PARKER brings dispatches from the floating battery, stating that up to this time only two have been wounded on Sullivan's Island. He had to row through Major ANDERSON'S warmest fire in a small boat.

Senator WIGFALL in same manner bore dispatches to Morris Island, through the fire from Fort Sumpter.

Senator CHESNUT, another member of the staff of Gen. BEAUREGARD, fired a gun, by way of amusement, from Mount Pleasant, which made a large hole in the parapet.

Quite a number have been struck by spent pieces of shell and knocked down, but none hurt seriously. Many fragments of these missiles are already circulating in the city.

The range is more perfect than [illegible] the morning and every shot from the land tells.

Three ships are visible in the offing, and it is believed an attempt will be made to-night, to throw reinforcements into Fort Sumpter in small boats.

It is also thought, from the regular and frequent firing of Major ANDERSON, that he has a much larger force of men than was supposed. At any rate, he is fighting bravely.

There have been two rain storms during the day, but without effect upon the battle.

Everybody is in a ferment. Some of those fighting are stripped to the waist.

IMPORTANT CORRESPONDENCE PRECEDING THE BOMBARDMENT.

CHARLESTON, Friday, April 12.

The following is the telegraphic correspondence between the War Department at Montgomery and Gen. BEAUREGARD immediately preceding the hostilities.

The correspondence grew out of the formal notification by the Washington Government, which is disclosed in Gen. BEAUREGARD'S first dispatches.

[No. 1.]

CHARLESTON, April 8.

L. P. WALKER, Secretary of War:

An authorized messenger from President LINCOLN, just informed Gov. PICKENS and myself that provisions will be sent to Fort Sumpter peaceably, or otherwise by force.

(Signed,) G. F. BEAUREGARD.

[No. 2.]

MONTGOMERY, 10th.

Gen. G. T. BEAUREGARD, Charleston:

If you have no doubt of the authorized character of the agent who communicated to you the intention of the Washington Government to supply Fort Sumpter by force, you will at once demand its evacuation, and if this is refused, proceed in such manner as you may determine, to reduce it. Answer.

Signed, L. P. WALKER, Sec. of War.

[No. 3.]

CHARLESTON, April 10.

L. P. WALKER, Secretary of War:

The demand will be made to-morrow at 12 o'clock.

Signed, G. F. BEAUREGARD.

[No. 4]

MONTGOMERY, April 10.

Gen. BEAUREGARD, Charleston:

Unless there are especial reasons connected with your own condition, it is considered proper that you should make the demand at an early hour.

(Signed) L. P. WALKER, Secretary of War.

[No. 5.]

CHARLESTON, April 10.

L. P. WALKER, Secretary of War, Montgomery:

The reasons are special for 12 o'clock.

(Signed) G. F. BEAUREGARD.

[No. 6.]

CHARLESTON, April 11.

L. P. WALKER, Secretary of War:

Demand sent at 12 o'clock. Allowed till 6 o'clock to answer.

(Signed) G. F. BEAUREGARD.

[No. 7.]

MONTGOMERY, April 11.

Gen. BEURREGARD—Charleston:

Telegraph the reply of Maj. ANDERSON.

(Signed,) L. P. WALKER, Secretary of War.

[No. 8.]

CHARLESTON, April 11.

To L. P. WALKER, Secretary of War:

Maj. ANDERSON replies:

"I HAVE THE HONOR TO ACKNOWLEDGE THE RECEIPT OF YOUR COMMUNICATION DEMANDING THE EVACUATION OF THIS FORT, AND TO SAY IN REPLY THERETO, THAT IT IS A DEMAND WITH WHICH I REGRET THAT MY SENSE OF HONOR AND MY OBLIGATIONS TO MY GOVERNMENT WILL PREVENT MY COMPLIANCE." He adds: "Probably I will await the first shot, and if you do not batter us to pieces, we will be starved out in a few days."

Answer. G. F. BEAUREGARD.

[No. 9.]

MONTGOMERY, April 11.

Gen. BEAUREGARD—Charleston:

We do not desire needlessly to bombard Fort Sumpter, if Major ANDERSON will state the time at which, as indicated by him, he will evacuate, and agree that, in the meantime, he will not use his guns against us unless ours should be employed against Fort Sumpter. You are thus to avoid the effusion of blood. If this or its equivalent be refused, reduce the fort as your judgment decides to be the most practicable.

(Signed) L. P. WALKER, Secretary of War.

[No. 10.]

CHARLESTON, April 12.

L. P. WALKER, Secretary of War:

HE WOULD NOT CONSENT. I write to-day.

G. F. BEAUREGARD.

MR. FOX'S VISIT TO FORT SUMPTER.

CHARLESTON, Friday, April 11.

Intercepted dispatches disclose the fact that Mr. Fox, who had been allowed to visit Major ANDERSON on the pledge that his purpose was pacific, employed his opportunity to devise a plan for supplying the fort by force, and that this plan had been adopted by the Washington Government, and was in progress of execution.

THE KENTUCKY VOLUNTEER REGIMENT.

LOUISVILLE, Friday, April 12.

Dispatches have come here to hold the Kentucky Volunteer Regiment in readiness to move at a moment's notice from the War Department at Montgomery.

EXCITEMENT IN MOBILE.

MOBILE, Friday, April 12.

There is intense excitement and rejoicing here. Fifteen guns have been fired in honor of the attack on Fort Sumpter

THE CONFEDERATE STATES CONGRESS.

MONTGOMERY, Friday, April 12.

An extra session of the Confederate States Congress has been called for April 29.

THE NEWS IN WASHINGTON.

WASHINGTON, Friday, April 12.

The town was thrown into intense excitement to-night by the report of the commencement of hostilities at Charleston this morning at 4 o'clock. The more so because of the previous news of peace and landing of provisions at Fort Sumpter. The news came to-night from the Associated Press agent at Charleston, giving all the particulars of the correspondence between BEAUREGARD and Major ANDERSON, the commencement of the attack by the Secessionists, and ANDERSON'S response from his batteries.

The news was posted at once in all the hotels, and the wildest scene of excitement ensued. Among the Union men here there was general rejoicing that an issue was made at last, while no advocates of Southern rights were to be found.

Major ANDERSON'S fame is on every one's tongue about the hotels and streets. The news was at once taken to the White House. All visitors will be excluded, and the Cabinet summoned to await further information and act upon it. One thing I am certain of, from positive knowledge—that if this last information proves true, the Administration will support ANDERSON and his course with the whole power and means of the Government, at all hazards.

A crowd assembled at the telegraph office to await further news.

Everyone had been waiting anxiously all day for the report of an attack upon the Government supply vessels, which it was ascertained last evening would probably approach Charleston harbor some time during the night or this morning. The surprise occasioned by the report from repeated dispatches that they had entered the harbor without molestation, and were landing the supplies without any difficulty, present or apprehensive, created nearly as great an excitement as the later reports of battle. The President was informed by dispatches to three different parties, announcing the safe landing, until he finally concluded that they must be correct, and that better counsels were prevailing among the Southern men.

CABINET COUNCILS.

Mr. LINCOLN summoned the Cabinet together the second time to consult. They had met once at 10 A. M., and now convened again at 1 o'clock P. M. There was general rejoicing at the prospects of peace and final adjustment of our national difficulties, dampened somewhat, however, by fear that it would prove false. LINCOLN said to a friend that if these advices were correct, the crisis had been passed, and the whole question settled without firing a gun. He added that he did not consider the Government at war with the South, and did not intend it should by his act. It was in this view that the provisioning of the fort was ordered to be attempted, unaccompanied by armed demonstration. The President further said, while assuming that the supplies had been landed, that he did not consider maintaining supremacy of the Federal Government any victory over the South, but simply a vindication of the faith he had always reposed in the ultimate good sense, and sense of justice among the American people. The War Department did not place any reliance to-day on the peace dispatches. Secretary CAMERON declared that he saw no escape from conflict at both Forts Sumpter and Pickens.

LATER.—Notwithstanding a violent rain-storm, people are still thronging the streets, anxious to get the details of the fight at Charleston, but very little has leaked out except the leading statement that the fight has begun. The last rumor on the streets is that a breach has been effected in the walls of Fort Sumpter. Military men here say if this statement is part of the Associated Press news, it throws discredit on the whole story, as Fort Sumpter is too strong to be thus speedily reduced by any battery in the possession of the enemy. The motive of the statement that a breach has been effected, is supposed to be to discourage the President from sending additional forces there on the idea that the whole affair would be ended before reinforcements could arrive. This surmise is strengthened by the failure to get news of the arrival of the transports at Charleston, as there can be no doubt that some of them reached there before this. The President is anxious but calm at this trying hour of responsibility, confident in the rectitude of his course, and its approval by the people.

FOREIGN ASPECT OF SECESSION.

Mr. SEWARD and the President have consulted frequently with the foreign diplomats here concerning the present condition of our national affairs and the course of their respective Governments. On the part of the representatives of England and France, it is well understood that there is no spmpathy whatever for the South. Lord LYONS says that he sees no benefit to be derived by the English Government, or any foreign Power, from the subremacy of its people; that there is, of course no prospect of foreign supremacy on this continent in any event; while England and the United States have become so strongly united in mutual interests, that misfortune to one is disaster to the other in all points of material interests. The Southern Commissioners had reason to discover these facts while in Washington, and have probably given DAVIS and his compatriots some new ideas not at all flattering to their vanity and visions of ultimate success.

VIRGINIA TRAITORS.

The report that R. A. PRYOR, of Virginia, has joined the staff of BEAUREGARD, gives color to the rumor that several companies had left Richmond for Charleston, to join the rebel forces. Under the circumstances, the Virginia Committee who arrived to day, will get only cold comfort from Mr. LINCOLN, although they will be treated courteously, as the Administration cannot disclose its purposes while a rebellious army is opposing its power.

THE TRAITORS' MAILS TO BE STOPPED.

Should the news of to-night be confirmed, the Postmaster-General will suspend at once all mail communications with the rebel States.

THE DEFENCE OF WASHINGTON.

Two companies of the Second Cavalry are ordered to this city, to be selected by the officer in charge of the corps. Although Washington is not under martial law, all possible precautions are taken to guard against surprise. Mounted videttes are stationed [illegible] the approaches to the city, at a distance of several miles, to give notice of any coming hostile force.

FROM ANOTHER CORRESPONDENT.

ANOTHER ACCOUNT OF THE NEWS AT WASHINGTON.

The first dispatches from the seat of war were received in this city about 7 o'clock this evening. The excitement caused by the meagre intelligence was most intense. Bulletins were posted at the principal hotels, where immense crowds gathered to discuss the probable results. It is almost needless to say that while there was but one opinion as to the end, there was an infinite variety of conjectures as to the *modus operandi*. The public sentiment is very decided that in the war inaugurated to-day the Government will prove to be the victor.

NEVER THOUGHT OF EVACUATION.

There is no foundation for the long stories told of the original purpose of the Government to evacuate Fort Sumpter. Mr. LINCOLN has not entertained any such purpose. He has entertained no purpose but to maintain possession of the Government property and enforce the laws. All statements that negotiations were entered upon for the departure of Major ANDERSON'S command were mere *canards* got up for the purpose of covering political defeats. The policy of the Administration never depended upon the contingency of evacuation. It was fixed within ten days after Mr. LINCOLN'S inauguration. If evidence were wanting of this, it would be found in the fact that the Government was prepared to dispatch such quantities of men and material as left the port of New-York within four days.

FORETHOUGHT OF THE ADMINISTRATION—ITS EFFECT.

The rapid shipment of supplies, men and munitions was the result of forethought and previous preparation—the end of means long before matured. The Government continues to receive assurances of the popularity of the measures it has inaugurated. These come from all quarters, and from men of all parties. I was talking with a gentleman from Maryland this evening, who assured me that the steps taken to maintain the supremacy of the General Government had done more to stifle secession in his State than all the compromise propositions. He was at home yesterday when a dispatch was received that a conflict had taken place in the harbor of Charleston. About forty persons were present, including Republicans and "very few" Douglas Democrats and Bell-Everett men. There was a universal expression of hope that the Government would succeed. This feeling pervades the Border States to an extent that surprises all. The stern realities of an actual conflict appear to have sobered the people and brought them to realize the duties of the Government and their own responsibility as citizens.

DEMOCRATIC INDORSEMENT OF MR. LINCOLN'S POLICY.

I met a Democrat to-day, whom I have known all through the excitement of the last election as an out-and-out friend of the Southern Secessionists. He is a New-Yorker, and widely connected with its business, he himself being one of the heaviest dealers in sugars in your City. I was astonished to hear him proclaim unguardedly his approval of the policy of the Administration, his hope that the vigor displayed in the beginning would continue to the end, and his willingness to make all the sacrifices which war imposes upon commercial enterprise. He says that the prominent Democrat of the State of New-York who shall venture to give his aid and comfort to the Southern Confederacy is doomed to political oblivion. I could multiply a dozen such instances in my experience of to-day.

NO EXTRA SESSION OF CONGRESS.

There is little probability of an extra session of Congress. As was telegraphed you yesterday, there is no necessity for such a session. The Government has all the power which Congress could confer, except the money.

MONEY PLENTY.

Until the limit of Treasury Notes is reached, the Government has as much means at its disposal as its wants are likely to exhaust before the regular period for the assembling of the National Legislature. Were it to be called together now, it could do nothing more to maintain the national honor than Mr. LINCOLN is now doing, while it might seriously jeopardize the early success of the Government forces by needless but exciting debates. In the hands of a prudent, just and decided President, and an intelligent and harmonious Cabinet, the national honor and the national integrity is much safer than experience has proved it would be in the keeping of Congress.

LEO.

GENERAL WASHINGTON NEWS.

THE MORRILL TARIFF NOT SO BAD.

The alleged imperfections and imprudences of the Morrill Tariff, upon which an extra session has been defended, are found to be largely exaggerated, if not entirely unfounded. Mr. BARNEY assures me that he will find no difficulty in executing the law with his present force, and that its provisions are quite as explicit as such laws are usually made, and that the changes from the previous system are not so violent and general as is supposed. A gentleman from Maryland told me today that the new tariff was doing much to keep that State loyal. He represents the iron and coal interests of the State, and he thinks the same beneficial influences will be felt in Virginia and North Carolina, in both of which States the mining interests are fast becoming paramount.

FINANCES OF THE CONFEDERATE STATES.

The financial embarrassments of the "Confederate States" are betraying themselves at every turn. Yesterday's TIMES exposed some of the evidences of the pecuniary troubles of secession by calling public attention to the fact that the $5,000,000 of the $15,000,000 loan of the Confederate States are being "apportioned among" (that is, *forced* upon) the Banks of New-Orleans, Mobile, &c. Have you noticed, also, that the very first of the $1,000,000 Treasury Notes, issued by the Provisional Government of the seceded States, were taken "by the Secretaries of War and the Treasury in payment of their quarter's salaries." The significance of this fact is apparent when it is remembered that the test of financial soundness in any Government consists of its ability to pay all Government dues in gold.

An old Clerk of the Treasury Department, who was South last week on private business, met there Ex-Secretary HOWELL COBB, with whom he had some conversation relative to the financial condition of the Government of the United States. Mr. COBB'S experience in the Southern Confederacy does not seem to have improved his judgment at all in the matter of financial estimates, for he continues to come as wide of the mark as ever. In the conversation referred to, he expressed the opinion that the revenues of the Treasury would be only about $1,000,000 per month; that, under this state of facts, the funds would be speedily exhausted, and that, as there is authority to borrow only $27,000,000, which, with the $1,000,000 per month for the ensuing year, would foot up only $39,000,000, while the expenses of the Government must be about $65,000,000. the Treasury must be bankrupted inevitably.

The figures in the Department show, in fact, an increase of revenue over last year, and the revenue is coming in at the rate of $3,000,000 per month, instead of $1,000,000, which Mr. COBB graciously allows. During the two weeks ending April 9, 1860, the receipts in the Treasury were $1,471,241 48. The receipts during the corresponding fortnight of 1861 were $1,500,667 34; increase in 1861 $29,425 81.

It should be remembered, too, that these results are attained at a time when the new Tariff is operating unfavorably towards the Treasury, because goods are withdrawing from bond for consumption in cases where the duty is less under the old Tariff than under the new, while merchandise which can be taken out of bond at *reduced* duties under the new Tariff are allowed to remain. Unless a war shall occur, Government is likely to have abundant means during the coming year.

SUMPTER AND PICKENS CANNOT STAND BOMBARDMENT.

Gentlemen skilled as engineers, and whose judgment is usually sound, express the opinion that neither Pickens nor Sumpter can withstand bombardment, if their assailants are not operated against by land forces. The forts in question were not constructed to sustain a siege, but to defend harbors against hostile fleets. For the latter purpose they are admirably adapted; no "wooden walls" could withstand the fire from their batteries, or do themselves harm; but a well-sustained fire from different points on the adjacent shores, it is maintained, will reduce them both in time,—unless they have men enough and guns enough to promptly demolish the assailing forts.

SWAGGERING NAVAL OFFICERS.

An agent of the Navy Department might be profitably employed in an occasional stroll through the hotel lobbies at Washington, to notice the language and deportment of some who wear the naval buttons, and yet constantly and publicly swagger about the folly of the Government undertaking to bring the "Southern Confederacy" to terms. It is not often that a naval officer thus dishonors the button,—but when he does, if he has not the manliness to resign, it would be advisable to ship him to sea somewhere where he could do no harm if he should take the notion to turn traitor.

A. B. DICKINSON, on Thursday, formally accepted the mission to Nicaragua.

GUARD DUTY BY THE CLERKS.

It is suggested that the Secretaries of the various departments call upon the clerks to perform guard duty at each Department where they are stationed. In this way all the loyal employes will be very easily discovered, and the shakey ones detected. I have the assurance that the experiment is to be tried in connection with the present military movements in the city.

AFFAIRS IN NEW-GRANADA.

The Government of New-Granada has no force with which to render effective its recent decree of blockade of the forts of Rio Hacha, Santa Marta, Carthagena and Zapote, in the Atlantic, these forts being in the complete possession of the revolutionists. So far as the Pacific is concerned, the forts of Buenaventura, Tumaco, etc., have been partially blockaded for the past six months or more, by small vessels fitted out at Panama—but I believe this does not directly much concern American interests, although it does so indirectly, as the business of the Panama Railroad is somewhat lessened by any disturbances affecting the trade of the Pacific.

UNABATED RUSH FOR OFFICE.

There was a great rush at the White House again to-day of office-seekers. Most of them failed to gain admittance on account of the exciting news. The entire remainder of the Boston appointments were made, to-day, as follows:

Surveyor, CHARLES A. PHELPS.

Navy Agent, EUGENE L. NORTON.

United States District-Attorney, RICHARD H. DANA.

Marshal, JOHN S. KEYES.

A strong, but unsuccessful effort to defeat this slate was made.

The crowd of New-York office-seekers is increasing. CHARLES A. STETSON denies that he is a candidate for Marshal, or any other office.

CALIFORNIA APPOINTMENTS.

The following additional appointments have been made for California:

Appraiser, JOHN P. ZANE.

Collector at Monterey, JOHN T. PORTER.

Collector at Stockton, S. W. SPERRY.

Collector st Benicia, S. M. SWAIN.

Collector at San Diego, JOSHUA SLOANE.

Collector at San Pedro, OSCAR MACY.

WM. BELL has been appointed Postmaster at Great Salt Lake City, Utah Territory.

DISPATCH TO THE ASSOCIATED PRESS.

WASHINGTON, Friday, April 12.

The Virginia Commissioners arrived in this City, this morning, and during the afternoon they visited the President, not in their official capacity, and were received by him directly after the Cabinet meeting adjourned.

The President has made the following Massachusetts appointments:

CHAS. A. PHELPS, Surveyor of the Port of Boston in place of FLETCHER WEBSTER, who was removed at the earnest request of the Massachusetts Congressional delegation; EUGENE L. NORTON, Navy-Agent at Boston: RICHARD H. DANA, District-Attorney; JOHN S. KEYS, Marshal; JOHN A. GOODWIN, Postmaster at Lowell.

C. C. P. BALDWIN, Marshal, and GEORGE HOWE, Attorney for Vermont.

JAMES C. AIKEN, Marshal, and ED. G. BRADFORD, Attorney for Delaware.

LANSING G. VANCE, Postmaster at Morristown, Pennsylvania.

HARMON BENNETT, Postmaster at Norwich, New-York.

THE NEWS IN NEW-YORK.

Yesterday was a day of excitements. Rumors apparently well grounded concerning the progress of affairs at Charleston flitted through Wall-street, pervaded the thoroughfares and produced sensations of surprise, indignation and rejoicings, according to the nature of the mind to which they were brought. Dispatches were received stating that President DAVIS had, after consultation with his Cabinet, directed Gen. BEAUREGARD to allow unmolested passage of the Federal transports with their loads of supplies for Fort Sumpter, thereby obviating immediate hostilities; others that Maj. ANDERSON and Gen. BEAUREGARD were consulting together, and the probabilities were that the Fort would be surrendered so soon as its supplies were exhausted; and still others announcing that the war had actually begun. The first-mentioned dispatch was generally credited, and the feeling was almost universal that a great moral victory had been achieved by the United States Government.

At 5 o'clock in the afternoon, however, all uncertainty was set at rest. The telegraphic wire brought the long looked-for intelligence that WAR HAS BEGUN, and that the forces of the Confederated Traitors have struck the first blow. Expected as was the news, it produced a most remarkable and wide-spread sensation. Many had hoped the contest might yet be avoided; others thought the Federal Government would back down rather than shed blood; and others were certain that a Divine Providence would interfere to prevent so fratricidal a strife. The bulletin boards were surrounded; the streets near them were blockaded, and the fast-gathering multitude were only satisfied when the self-appointed reader had read himself hoarse in the frequent repetition of the brief announcement of the facts. Hundreds af anxious inquirers besieged the telegraph and publication offices, confident that there might yet be some item of information which was withheld from the masses, and they were only appeased when told that they were in possession of all, and that until this morning's papers were out they could have no more.

"Good, good," exclaimed many a one, as he read the statement, or as it was repeated to him by a friend, "at last we have reached a crisis; something *must* be done." The feeling of rejoicing was everywhere to be met, that Major ANDERSON had not lowered his flag, and that President LINCOLN had determined to sustain, even at so fearful a cost, the honor of the country. Of the very many with whom we conversed, and from whom we heard the freeset expression of opinions, we did not find a single individual who did not respond heartily to the sentiment, "Thank Heaven we have a Government." Speculations and wagers of all kinds were the order of the night, as to the probable effect of this or that battery, of the arrival and probable action of the fleet, and of the result of this first contest; and very long odds were offered and taken that Sumpter would silence Moultrie, and that the fleet, on arrival, would find but little to do. However that may be, the war has begun—the aggressors were the Confederated forces, the Federal post has returned vigorously the fire, and the entire moral support of the North stands about the President in this trying moment, as will the entire physical force stand at his side if a more trying hour should come.

THE PENNSYLVANIA WAR BILL.

HARRISBURGH, Friday, April 12.

The War bill passed both Houses to night, without amendment. Gov. CURTIN waited at the Executive office to sign it. It is signed.

The Charleston dispatches about hostilities were announced in both Houses, and produced a profound sensation.

Mr. SMITH, a Democratic member of the House, after the Charleston dispatches were received, changed his vote to aye on the War bill. All the Democrats of both Houses voted against it. The bill appropriates $500,000 for the purpose of arming and equipping the militia; authorizes a temporary loan; provides for the appointment of an Adjutant-General, Commissary-General, and Quartermaster-General, who, with the Governor, are to have power to carry the act into effect.

EFFECTS OF THE WAR IN BALTIMORE.

BALTIMORE, Friday, April 12.

The Charleston news was not generally promulgated here until after midnight. It produced a profound sensation, and general expressions of regret at

[*Continued on Eighth Page.*]

The New-York Times.

VOL. XI—NO. 3432. NEW-YORK, TUESDAY, SEPTEMBER 23, 1862. PRICE TWO CENTS.

HIGHLY IMPORTANT.

A Proclamation by the President of the United States.

The War Still to be Prosecuted for the Restoration of the Union.

A DECREE OF EMANCIPATION

All Slaves in States in Rebellion on the First of January Next to be Free.

The Gradual Abolition and Colonization Schemes Adhered to.

Loyal Citizens to be Remunerated for Losses' Including Slaves.

WASHINGTON, Monday, Sept. 22.

By the President of the United States of America:

A PROCLAMATION.

I, ABRAHAM LINCOLN, President of the United States of America, and Commander-in-Chief of the Army and Navy thereof, do hereby proclaim and declare, that hereafter, as heretofore, the war will be prosecuted for the object of practically restoring the constitutional relation between the United States and the people thereof in which States that relation is, or may be suspended or disturbed; that it is my purpose, upon the next meeting of Congress, to again recommend the adoption of a practical measure tendering pecuniary aid to the free acceptance or rejection of all the Slave States so called, the people whereof may not then be in rebellion against the United States, and which States may then have voluntarily adopted, or thereafter may voluntarily adopt, the immediate or gradual abolishment of Slavery within their respective limits; and that the efforts to colonize persons of African descent with their consent, upon the Continent or elsewhere, with the previously obtained consent of the governments existing there, will be continued.

That on the first day of January, in the year of our Lord one thousand eight hundred and sixty-three, all perons held as slaves within any State, or any designated part of a State, the people whereof shall then be in rebellion against the United States shall be then, thenceforward, and forever, free; and the Executive Government of the United States, including the military and naval authority thereof, will recognize and maintain the freedom of such persons, and will do no act or acts to repress such persons, or any of them, in any efforts they may make for their actual freedom.

That the Executive will, on the first day of January aforesaid, by proclamation, designate the States and parts of States, if any, in which the people thereof, respectively, shall then be in rebellion against the United States; and the fact that any State, or the people thereof, shall on that day be in good faith represented in the Congress of the United States by members chosen thereto at elections wherein a majority of the qualified voters of such State shall have participated, shall, in the absence of strong countervailing testimony, be deemed conclusive evidence that such State and the people thereof have not been in rebellion against the United States.

That attention is hereby called to an act of Congress entitled "An act to make an additional article of war," approved March 13, 1862, and which act is in the words and figure following:

"Be it enacted by the Senate and House of Representatives of the United States of America in Congress assembled, That hereafter the following shall be promulgated as an additional article of war for the government of the army of the United States, and shall be obeyed and observed as such.

ARTICLE—All officers or persons in the military or naval service of the United States are prohibited from employing any of the forces under their respective commands for the purpose of returning fugitives from service or labor who may have escaped from any person to whom such service or labor is claimed to be due, and any officer who shall be found guilty by a Court-martial of violating this article shall be dismissed from the service.

SECTION 2. And be it further enacted, that this act shall take effect from and after its passage."

Also to the ninth and tenth sections of an act entitled "An act to suppress insurrection, to punish treason and rebellion, to seize and confiscate property of rebels, and for other purposes," approved July 17, 1862, and which sections are in the words and figures following:

SEC. 9. And be it further enacted, that all slaves of persons who shall hereafter be engaged in rebellion against the Government of the United States, or who shall, in any way give aid or comfort thereto, escaping from such [illegible] and taking refuge within the lines of the [illegible] and all slaves captured from such persons or [illegible] them and coming under the control of the Government of the United States, and all slaves of [illegible] (or being within) any place [illegible] shall be [illegible] of [illegible]

SEC. 10. And be it further enacted, that no slave escaping into any State, Territory or the District of Columbia, from any of the States, shall be delivered up, or in any way impeded or hindered of his liberty, except for crime or some offence against the laws, unless the person claiming said fugitive shall first make oath that the person to whom the labor or service of such fugitive is alleged to be due, is his lawful owner, and has not been in arms against the United States in the present rebellion, nor in any way given aid and comfort thereto, and no person engaged in the military or naval service of the United States shall, under any pretence whatever, assume to decide on the validity of the claim of any person to the service or labor of any other person, or surrender up any such person to the claimant, on pain of being dismissed from the service.

And I do hereby enjoin upon and order all persons engaged in the military and naval service of the United States, to observe, obey and enforce, within their respective spheres of service, the act and sections above recited.

And the Executive will in due time recommend that all citizens of the United States who shall have remained loyal thereto throughout the rebellion, shall (upon the restoration of the constitutional relation between the United States and their respective States and people, if the relation shall have been suspended or disturbed,) be compensated for all losses by acts of the United States, *including the loss of slaves.*

In witness whereof, I have hereunto set my hand, and caused the seal of the United States to be affixed.

Done at the City of Washington, this Twenty-second day of September, in the year of our Lord one thousand eight hundred and sixty-two, and of the Independence of the United States the eighty-seventh.

ABRAHAM LINCOLN.

By the President.

WILLIAM H. SEWARD, Secretary of State.

GENERAL NEWS FROM WASHINGTON.

OUR SPECIAL WASHINGTON DISPATCHES.

WASHINGTON, Monday, Sept. 22.

THE PRESIDENT'S PROCLAMATION.

The great event of the day here is the proclamation of the President ordering the execution of the war measures of the last Congress, and promising freedom to the slaves in all States that persist in the rebellion against the Government. This act, so long expected, so long delayed, bids fair to simplify at once the issues of the war, and immediately to array against each other the unconditionally loyal and the rebellious of all shades and grades. If the cause of the Union and free institutions is strongest, this test will show it, and the only question of its triumph will then be the power in the Government to execute its policy with courage and vigor.

THE NEWS FROM KENTUCKY.

A special private dispatch, just received from Cincinnati, announces that BRAGG is marching on Louisville, Ky., and that Gen. NELSON has ordered the women and children to leave the city. BUELL is believed to have been outgeneraled, and to be several hours behind. The dispatch closes—"A General wanted for the West."

THE OLD ISSUE OF TREASURY NOTES.

I have the following statistics in regard to the old issue of United States Treasury Notes, receivable for duties, of the $60,000,0000 issue: $28,420,000 have been returned to the Department and burned; $43,000 have been returned, and are not yet burned; $4,000,000 have been redeemed, but not yet returned to the Department, leaving $27,537,000 yet outstanding As only about half the whole issue has yet been redeemed, and as the Government will be able to get no gold in payment of duties, so long as any of these notes remain in possession of the public, it is plain that the specie required to pay the interest falling due on Oct. 1—$4,000,000—as well as that falling due Jan. 1—$5,000,000—must be procured by the Government by purchase or loan.

Thirty thousand dollars of small currency notes were to-day paid out at the Treasury Department, and were all taken within an hour.

CONDITION OF GEN. HOOKER.

Gen. HOOKER is now with his friend, Dr. NICHOLS, at the United States Insane Asylum Hospital, near Washington. His wound is a rifle ball through the left foot. Although the wound is painful, it is not considered dangerous; yet it is sufficient to disable him for active service.

THE CONVALESCENT CAMP.

The Convalescent Camp, under the regulations of Gen. BANKS, is becoming an institution of very great utility. All stragglers and convalescents are immediately sent there, as are officers who have been absent without leave, or have overstayed their leave under circumstances that entitle them to lenity. Soldiers are classified according to the corps to which they belong, and are placed in charge of officers belonging to the same corps, who subject them to the daily drill of camp instruction. When the accumulation becomes sufficient to justify their removal, they are sent to their regiments and commands.

PENSIONS.

The Commissioner of Pensions has commenced making appointments of surgeons to make examinations and give certificates in cases of applications for pensions. The fees will make the offices desirable. The following are the appointments already made: Cincinnati, James H. Oliver; Indianapolis, Geo. W. Mears; Leavenworth, Kansas, Selden W. Jones; New-Philadelphia, Ohio, Wm. G. Smith; Terre Haute, Ind., Geo. W. Clippinger; Lafayette, Ind., O. L. Clark; Boston, Geo. S. Jones; Bangor, Me. Ralph J. K. Jones; Rochester, N. Y., Harvey F. Montgomery; Oswego, N. Y., Chas. C. P. Clark; Lyons, N. Y., Nelson Peck; Norridgewack, Me., Uno Robbins, Jr.

ACTING REAR-ADMIRALS.

The following naval officers have been made Acting Rear-Admirals and assigned to the command of the following squadrons, respectively: C. H. BELL, Pacific Squadron; CHAS. WILKES, "Flying Squadron," T. L. LARDNER, Eastern Gulf Squadron; C. H. DAVIS, Mississippi Flotilla.

From Salt Lake.

SALT LAKE, Monday, Sept. 22.

CHARLES MCBRIDE, from Virginia City, arrived here yesterday, one of a party of fifteen bound for the States. He says:

"The party were attacked by the Snake Indians at the City of Rocks, on the Humboldt route, 150 miles north. They fought the Indians for 20 miles, losing six killed and [illegible] all of their [illegible] JOHN CONNER, [illegible] SHAW, [illegible] had [illegible]

Reports of [illegible] daily, and [illegible]

THE LATEST WAR NEWS.

A Raid of Stuart's Cavalry Across the Potomac at Williamsport.

NO DAMAGE DONE.

The Reoccupation of Maryland Heights by Our Forces.

THE REBELS CONTINUIMG THEIR RETREAT

No Further Collisions at Last Accounts.

LATEST REPORTS FROM HEADQUARTERS.

HEADQUARTERS OF THE ARMY OF THE POTOMAC, Saturday Evening, Sept. 20, 1862.

The firing heard last evening in the direction of Williamsport, turns out to have been a raid of STUART's rebel cavalry. He crossed the Potomac on Friday night into Maryland, at that point, with his cavalry, one regiment of infantry, and seventeen pieces of artillery. The force sent up to drive him back, arrived near the town late in the afternoon. The firing heard was principally from the rebel guns. During the night they recrossed into Virginia and this morning they had disappeared from the opposite shore. No one was hurt.

The work of burying the dead is still continuing. They average about one thousand per day. To-morrow will probably finish it.

The Maryland Heights were yesterday occupied by a National force.

The indications are that the rebels are continuing their retreat into Virginia, leaving the line of the Potomac.

Divine worship was held at headquarters this evening, Bishop WHIPPLE, of Minnesota, officiating.

HEADQUARTERS, ARMY OF THE POTOMAC, Monday Evening, Sept. 22.

The following is the official report of loss in SUMNER's corps at the battle of the Antietam:

GEN. RICHARDSON'S DIVISION.

Killed	212
Wounded	899
Missing	24

GEN. SEDGWICK'S DIVISION.

Killed	335
Wounded	1,577
Missing	321

GEN. FRENCH'S DIVISION.

Killed	293
Wounded	1,321
Missing	203
Total loss in Gen. SUMNER's Corps	5,208

The loss in missing may be somewhat reduced by stragglers returning.

A train of cars crossed the Monocacy this morning. The road is now open to Harper's Ferry, where there is a sufficient Federal force for all purposes.

The rebels, in their hasty retreat from Maryland, left between 1,100 and 1,200 wounded between Sharpsburgh and the river. They are being paroled.

Twenty-six stands of colors were taken during the battle of the Antietam, and have been received at headquarters. Seven more are known to have been captured, and are in the hands of the different regiments which captured them.

OUR LATEST WASHINGTON DISPATCHES.

WASHINGTON, Monday, Sept. 22.

A special dispatch from Frederick states that some surgeons, just arrived from the army, report rebels still falling back from the Potomac. Not even their pickets are now to be seen.

Another dispatch states that our losses in the last fight are not nearly as great as at first reported, especially in SUMNER's Corps. In the California Regiment only one commissioned officer was killed (Lieut. WILSE) and one hundred and fifty privates killed and wounded.

The last reports from headquarters represented "All quiet along the lines."

THE WAR IN MARYLAND.

Another Account of the Great Battle of Antietam.

LETTERS FROM THE BATTLE-FIELD.

The Strong Position Chosen by the Enemy—How the National Forces were Arranged—Desperate Character of the Fighting—The Results, &c.

ON THE FIELD NEAR SHARPSBURGH, MD., Wednesday Evening, Sept. 17, 1862.

This day will be memorable for one of the bloodiest fought battles on the American Continent. The combined forces of the enemy, under JACKSON, LEE, LONGSTREET, and the whole rebel set, have made a stand near Sharpsburgh, and all day long, from 5 o'clock in the morning until now, (8 o'clock P. M.,) have been contesting with the Union Army under MCCLELLAN, led by BURNSIDE, HOOKER, SUMNER, KEYES, and the other heroes of the war. Nothing, I am sure, since the battle of Pittsburgh Landing, can compare with this day's fight, either in its collossal proportions, or in the bloody character of the struggle. Our advance overtook the rebel forces, apparently in full retreat toward the Shepherdstown ford of the Potomac, yesterday morning, and a temporary halt was ordered near Kedysville, a little village three miles north from Sharpsburgh. The enemy had taken possession of the Antietam Hills, on the right of the creek by that name, with Sharpsburgh in their rear. They were attacked yesterday by our batteries across this creek, for the purpose of occupying them until our whole force should come up, but no general engagement ensued. The rebels were evidently preparing for a last desperate stand, before the final attempt to cross the Potomac. Their failure to check our advance here they knew would be fatal to their whole army, for they could not escape safely into Virginia with our artillery and infantry assailing their rear.

The day closed without any decisive results, except that in every encounter our artillery practice was found to be too accurate and terrible for them, and [illegible] every position which they took [illegible]

[illegible] JACKSON [illegible] Maryland Heights [illegible] except the cavalry, which cut their way through and escaped,) abandoned the position, and was hurrying forward to reinforce the rebel troops at this point.

Thus the two armies, wearied by a harassing march over mountain ranges, and of four days' running fight from beyond Frederick, came together on this memorable field.

The enemy having chosen a strong position on the hills just beyond Kedysville, began a sharp cannonade at 5 o'clock in the morning. He found our boys wide awake, who replied firmly and steadily to the attack.

Gen. FITZ-JOHN PORTER had thoroughly examined the field on the previous day, and a council of the Generals had made a disposition of the various army corps for the grand contest. It will be sufficient, for the present purpose, to state that Gen. BURNSIDE took command of the extreme left, while the other Generals occupied the enemy's front and right. BURNSIDE, with Gens. RODMAN, WILCOX, COX and STURGIS Brigades, extended his lines as far as to the southeast of Sharpsburgh, with the stone bridge across the Antietam Creek in his front. Between their position and that of the enemy, who lay toward the village at the northwest, is a succession of hills running nearly north and south, the highest and most abrupt of which is that rising from the bed of the creek. Gens. HOOKER's and SUMNER's corps have been conspicuous throughout the bloody day, the early part of the fight being over their par of the field, while a fierce and protracted struggle was going on at the Stone Bridge, where Gen. BURNSIDE commanded in person. In the latter place we lost, in the forenoon, several brave officers and men. Gen. HOOKER is reported wounded; Lieut. Col. THOMAS BELL, of the Fifty-first, Pennsylvania Volunteers, was mortally wounded while leading his men to the attack at this place, and died soon after. Lieut. BEAVER, of the same regiment; Capt. MALCOLM WILSON and Sergeant HARRY H. STEWART, of the Second Maryland Regiment, Co. A, were also killed. Col. KINGSBURY, of the Eleventh Connecticut, was mortally wounded; and Adjutant ANDREW FOWLER, of the Fifty-first New York, is dead. Sergeant DAVIS, acting Lieutenant in the Twenty-first Massachusetts, had a leg badly shattered; Capt. MARTIN, Co. E, Second Maryland, lost a leg; and Color Sergeants OSBORN and HOOVER, of the Second Maryland, are both severely wounded; also Capt. NEILL, Thirty-fifth Massachusetts. I saw all these lying at a barn near the Stone Bridge, while the battle was progressing, having visited the spot for the purpose of obtaining a list (which is only partial,) of the killed and wounded.

I also saw lying dead on the field the following privates: James Kirby, Co. A, Second Maryland; Peter Daily, Co. I; Wm. Kelly, Co. H; Sergt. Jas. Clark, Co. H; John Q. Adams, Co. C; Daniel Fisk, Co. F, Sixth N. H.; Corp. Chas. M. Noyes, Co. K, Ninth N. H.; S. H. Case, Co. B, Seventeenth Mich.; Sergt. Howard Rand, Co. K, Sixth N. H.; Michael Boland, Co. G, Second Md.; —— Connerty, Co. G, Fifty-first N. Y.; Corp. Keefe, Co. I, Fifty-first N. Y.; Thomas N. Stockwell, Co. I, Fifty-first N. Y.; Robert C. Dale, Co. G, Fifty-first N. Y.; Geo. Summerlock, Co. A, Fifty-first Penn., and Thos. Davis, Co. I, Fifty-first Penn. I saw some half-dozen others on the east side of the bridge, whose names I could not learn, lying on the field. It was not safe to cross the bridge, but I was told several others lay on that side. It is impossible, in the present state of affairs, to obtain anything like an estimate of the numbers killed and wounded, but our losses have been very heavy.

The Irish Brigade, Gen. MEAGHER, in SUMNER's corps, occupied a very prominent position, and the brave General, I am told, had a horse shot under him. Some report him killed, but I cannot now learn that it is true. He rode in front of his brigade, and waving his flashing blade in the air, beckoned on his men to the attack. Wherever they made a charge the rebel lines were seen to waver and fall back.

The rebels kept as much as possible under cover of the ravines, and seldom advanced to the attack, but there has never been a battle, probably, where there was so little of woods for the rebels to conceal themselves in. The fighting has been mostly in the open field, with the exception of the sharp contest at the stone bridge, where woods (not dense) line both sides of the stream—and a considerable block of trees occupying nearly the centre of the right, where HOOKER was engaged.

The rebels have been driven back at least two miles since the fight began, so that Sharpsburgh has been, during the afternoon, about the centre of the rebel lines.

Three times the rebel caissons have been blown up by our shells. Five different conflagrations have occurred on the field of barns and houses which were set on fire by exploding shells, or purposely fired by the enemy. While I write the whole heavens are lighted up by burning barns and wheat stacks. It is an immense conflagration.

I made the following memoranda of events while overlooking the field:

Capt. COOK's Parrot Battery, Eighth Massachusetts, occupies the east hill opposite Sharpsburgh and the bridge, and does excellent practice on the enemy's position. Lieut. BENJAMIN, in charge of CARLISLE's Battery, also doing splendid execution. Twice the enemy's battery of six guns had been silenced or compelled to withdraw from the opposite hill.

The musketry firing down at the stone bridge, where WILCOX and STURGIS are engaged, is sharp and continuous. At 11 o'clock squads of rebels are seen "getting up" the hill. Our batteries are playing on them, which hurries their time. Shells burst, and solid shot plow up the ground all around them. Cheers from the ravine. The Seventeenth Michigan (new regiment and all brave boys) are charging down to the help of WILCOX. Our infantry are seen charging up the hill, and our batteries are ordered to cease firing to avoid hitting them. They are turned on the rebel batteries, which now open on the hill to the right of Sharpsburgh. Our infantry advance, and are shelled by the rebel batteries, and compelled to lie down and finally retire under cover of the next ravine. Our 20-pounder Parrots upset the rebel guns. Splendid shots by BENJAMIN. The Forty-fifth New-York come to the rescue, and are pressing by us toward the bridge. Gen. BURNSIDE has just sent orders for Gens. WILCOX and COX to cross the bridge with their brigades and occupy the hills south of the town. Our troops again advance, and as soon as they show themselves a new rebel battery of four guns, on the hill at the left opens upon us. At 12 o'clock a rebel caisson is blown up, the third one since morning.

Sharpsburgh is now the centre of the action in our front, while HOOKER is actively at work on the right. The firing in that part of the field is terrific and unceasing. The rebel lines are seen drawn up along the ravines at the northwest, and occasionally attempting to advance. In each instance they are met and driven back.

At 1 o'clock the fighting at the Stone Bridge has ceased, and WILCOX and COX have all passed over. We now have a large force on the hills confronting the rebel lines. They keep up a constant cannonade upon the Union troops. At 1½ P. M. a squad of seventeen rebels are brought to Gen. BURNSIDE as prisoners, who orders them sent to the rear. The spokesman of the party says: "I don't think there is a man of us who doesn't want to get out of the fight." Gen. COX is ordered to move up and occupy the hills south of Sharpsburgh. At 2½ P. M. there is a temporary lull of the firing, but it is very short. At 4½ P. M. our troops push up the hill (the rebels always continue to have us on the down-hill side of the fight) and a large force appears at their extreme left, advancing toward them over the hill. A perfect storm of shot and shell now greet the advance of our boys from a half dozen different batteries at once. On the right of our advance our troops push up toward the rebel lines and are met half way, at a ravine, where a fierce musketry fight continues for half an hour. The balls [illegible] up the dust in the plowed fields in all directions. The fight [illegible] and so many [illegible] from [illegible] quarters, it is difficult to distinguish friend from foe. Dust [illegible]

On the left of the town the Union forces have now gained the crest of the hill, the rebels giving back under their steady fire, and cheers and shouts ring along the line. The rebel flag waves sulkily in the heavy air, in close proximity to the cheerful Red, White and Blue, borne into the thickest of the fight by our brave boys. The Union troops hold their position at the Sharpsburgh road for half an hour, while a deadly contest is going on. Our artillery, which has crossed the bridge, now takes up a position at the left, to check the advance of the rebels, who are trying to flank us, and open a brisk fire. On come the rebel hosts in overpowering numbers, to flank the force on the hill, and WILCOX's Brigade, which has stood their ground for over an hour, now retire part way down the hill. A tremendous onset was now made from the south, the enemy apparently having received reinforcements, and our left is pressed back. The sun has set, but the contest only thickens with the close of the day. The enemy's shell begin to burst over our hospital near the bridge, and the horses at BENJAMIN's Battery are shot at the guns. He is ordered by Gen. BURNSIDE to withdraw them. Stragglers come in from the field, some wounded, some *tenderly* escorting comrades who are wounded—it generally takes two or three to perform this service for one man, and all hands wear a gloomy countenance and limp. Gen. BURNSIDE orders them back to their regiments, with a sharp reprimand. Among these delinquents is a Lieutenant of the Sixteenth Connecticut Regiment, whom the General reprimands, and orders his name to be taken. He goes limping, and says a ball hit him in the leg. "But you walked all the way from the field—why did you come here to exhibit your cowardice? You had better remained at home," said the General sharply. At the same instant a youth, not over fifteen, who had his arm torn by a shell or ball, came up, holding the bleeding member in his other hand. Look at that boy, Lieutenant, he has some excuse for leaving the field," but you have none. Shells now began to hum and burst all over the ground where we stood, and your correspondent began to think there might be danger in remaining longer in *that* place, so he *quietly* mounted his horse and *slowly* moved to the rear.

The rebels received a check soon after dark, and the contest ended for the night. It has been a most sanguinary fight. Our dead lie mingled with the rebel corpses on every part of this wide field—over a space of three or four miles. Many a poor fellow will lie on the cold, damp earth to-night, and pray for death to relieve him of his sufferings.

I shall endeavor to send fuller particulars of the fight than I am now enabled to do, as soon as they can be procured.

Both armies encamped on the field. To-morrow the dead must be buried, and possibly a renewal of the contest be had.

We shall have reinforcements of COUCH's Division this evening, from Harper's Ferry. E. S.

Events Succeeding the Great Battle—The Rebel Retreat Foreseen—Heavy Losses—Some of the Killed and Wounded—Incidents, &c.

ON THE FIELD, NEAR SHARPSBURGH, MD., Thursday, Sept. 18, 1862.

There has been no engagement to-day—only occasional firing between the pickets, who continue to confront each other on substantially the same field where the contest closed at sundown yesterday. The body of the enemy—if there be any body remaining—are at least three miles further toward the river than they were at the beginning of the battle yesterday morning. Competent judges, with whom I have conversed, among whom is Gen. GRIFFIN—a careful observer, and well versed in the ways of the rebels—believe that they are merely amusing us by these exhibitions of force, while the army proper is really on the retreat to the river, and should this hypothesis prove correct, we shall have a most mortifying result for all the labor, loss and bloodshed of this Maryland campaign. The rebel leaders have drawn after them from Washington an immense army, with its enormous train, which has marched, toiled, fought, and been dragged for fifty miles, over three mountain ranges, at an untold outlay of strength, expense and suffering; they will have supplied their starving army with all it needed; slaughtered and wounded thousands of our brave Union soldiers, and then have escaped back to Virginia to laugh in their sleeve at our laggard way of following up our successes. The old-fashioned way of waiting for the rebel army to make the first move to attack: to choose their own field of operations to fight us; lie still or retreat as suits *their convenience*, seems to be the humor of the hour.

What motives of "strategy" or mysterious plans requiring *time* for development, explains this failure to attack the rebels to-day, a mere novice in warfare has no right to draw in question. But one thing seems apparent to me, the Union army are eager to be "up and at them," and make an end of this rebel *canaille*, and of the rebellion, while we have them and it in our power. The humblest Union soldier will feel the mortification of permitting this ragged and wolfish lazaroni to escape our clutches, by crossing again into Virginia.

In order to ascertain the number of the killed and wounded, as near as might be, so soon after the battle, and to obtain such names of prominent persons who have suffered, I passed over the field to-day, and went to nearly all the hospitals where the wounded are being gathered in.

While the wounded are still on the field, and no official returns are made, it is, of course, impossible to obtain anything like a correct list of the killed and wounded. Lists will soon be prepared, however, and full accounts be sent forward. Every house and large barn contiguous to the field, is occupied by the wounded, where, I am happy to say, provision has very promptly been made for dressing wounds and rendering them comfortable.

The troops in HOOKER's, SUMNER's and RICHARDSON's corps have suffered greatly. Some officers of the General Staff estimate the number of wounded at 13,000, and say there are 5,000 on the field. My own judgment, after going pretty well over the ground is, that this estimate is greatly exaggerated, and that they do not amount to half that number, while the killed is very small in proportion to the wounded. I think six to eight hundred will cover the *killed*, and twenty-five hundred to three thousand the wounded, making a total of not to exceed *four thousand of killed and wounded.*

Gen. Rodman was shot through the body, the ball passing through the lung. Gen. Mansfield was instantly killed. Gen. Hooker was wounded in the foot. Gen. Hartsuff, of Ricketts's Division, wounded in the right iliac region; a serious wound. Col. Beal, 10th Maine, in the thigh. Col. Richard Oakford, of Scranton, Penn., (132d Penn. Vols.) was killed. Robert A. Abbott was seriously wounded in the lower jaw. Lieut. Jno. C. Dolan, injured in the hip by a shell. First Lieut. Sawyer, 7th Maine, killed, and about 100 privates of the same regiment wounded. Lieut.-Col. Fillebrown was thrown from his horse and injured, but not seriously. Gen. Max Weber was wounded seriously in the arm, and amputation may be rendered necessary. The Lieutenant-Colonel of the 49th New-York Volunteers, was dangerously wounded. Col. Kingsbury, of the Eleventh Connecticut, who was shot through the body twice and wounded in both feet, died this morning. Col. Childs, of the 4th Pennsylvania Cavalry, was killed while leading a charge on the right of the field. Gen. Richardson was wounded, and Gen. Hancock takes his command. Capt. Kelley, of the 8th Illinois Cavalry, was badly wounded on Monday in the mountain [illegible] Gen. Pleasanton's command, this cavalry did [illegible] artillery lost several other officers and men, whose names I cannot now obtain.

In Gen. King's Division the loss has been heavy. Col. H. A. V. Post, of the Second United States Sharpshooters, was wounded; also, Lieut. Chas. E. Cushing, Co. E, 22d New-York; Lieut. Whitman, Co. B, had his leg shot off—dead; Capt. Myers, Co. I, 14th Brooklyn—dead; Capt. O'Brien, Co. I, 24th Brooklyn—dead; Adgt. Parmele, 2d U. S. Sharpshooters—dead; Lieut. Seabury, 2d U. S. Sharpshooters—wounded; Lieut. Guest, 2d U. S. Sharpshooters—wounded; Capt. Chase, Co. A, 2d U. S. Sharpshooters—wounded; Sergeant-Major Shoot, 2d U. S. Sharpshooters—wounded.

In Caldwell's Brigade the loss was severe. The Fifth New-Hampshire Regiment have 119 killed and wounded, among which are fourteen officers. Some of these wounded are the following: Col. Cross, wounded in the head, slightly; Capt. Long, Co. G, wounded in the arm; Capt. Ranlet, Co. E, wounded in the thigh; Lieut. Graves, Co. H, forearm, slight; Lieut. Bean, Co. H, severely; Lieut. Gay, Co. H, mortally; Lieut. Parks.

KILLED IN MICHIGAN SEVENTEENTH REGIMENT.

Phelix Randall, Co. B.	Israel Colf, Co. C.
Andrew Salier, Co. C.	John A. Troy, Co. C.
Samuel Hunt, Co. D.	S. H. Hooley, Co. D.
Martin V. Moore, Co. D.	Daniel McMartin, Co. D.
Benjamin Ward, Co. D.	Almeron Palmeter, Co. D.
H. A. Smith, Co. D.	Henry Tomlinson, Co. D.
Wm. Woodward, Co. E.	Alex. McKinnon, Co. D.
Robert C. Irvin, Co. E.	Corp. Miron Hawley, Co. D.
Ephriam Micks, Co. F.	Silas Gardner, Co. D.
Delos Vandeberg, Co. H.	Mason Kearney, Co. I.
Frank Belknap, Co. I.	Wm. Clay, Co. K.
Oliver Cheeney, Co. K.	Leonard Ives, Co. K.
David D. Tompkins, Co. K.	Total, 25.

Mr. IVES, of Providence, an Aid of Gen. RODMAN, received a severe flesh wound in the thigh by a piece of shell. Probably not mortal. Mr. IVES is a brother of Capt. J. POYNTON IVES, who commanded the *Picket* in North Carolina, under Gen. BURNSIDE.

The Seventh Maine regiment (Third Brigade, SMITH's Division,) commanded by Major HYDE, went into the fight with 175 men and 14 officers, and came out with only 65 men and four officers unhurt.

Lieut. Butler, Co. A, was wounded and is missing; Capt. Jones, Co. B, wounded slightly; Adjt. Haskell was shot through both legs and his horse was killed; Lieut. Beason, Co. C, wounded in leg; Lieut. Goodman, Co. D, killed; Lieut. Emery, Co. E, wounded slightly; Lieut. Shorey, Co. F, wounded in the leg; Lieut. Warren, Co. H, wounded and missing; Capt. Cook, Co. I, wounded in leg; Lieut. Brown, Co. I. supposed killed; Capt. Cochran wounded in foot; Major Hyde wounded in hand and horse shot under him; not serious.

This regiment is now the body-guard of Gens. FRANKLIN and SMITH. The loss in this regiment is said to have been heavier than any regiment engaged, in proportion to numbers, since the beginning of the war. Their colors with "Williamsburgh" inscribed on them, were riddled with bullets. Capt. J. W. CHANNING has three bullet-holes through his clothes, and both he and Major HYDE came off the field with their clothing all bespattered with the blood of their comrades.

THE TURNER RIFLES.

Officers Killed.

Capt. Gustav A. Loreng, Co. C.
First Lieut. Jacob Pabst, Co. D.
Second Lieut. —— Krano, Co. G.

Some of the Wounded.

Capt. Robert Meikle, Pauls (?) Frick, —— Lohman, Capt. Weber, Lieut. Voelker.

Of enlisted men, there were twenty-six killed and eighty wounded.

THE FIRST DELAWARE—*Complete.*

Killed.

Capt. Watson, Co. A.	Corp. John Brierly, Co. A.
Capt. Leonard, Co. B.	Benjamin Lee, Co. A.
Capt. Richards, Co. C.	Mims J. Nelson, Co. E.
Ed. Moseley, Co. A.	Thomas Oskins, Co A.

Wm. McCoy, Co. D—shot in both hands.
Emanuel Deiasse, Co. F—left elbow.
Thos. G. Chance, Co. F—right knee.
Sergt. Chas. F. Holland, Co. E—right side.
Sergt. J. Spearsley, Co. H—left foot.
James E. Clark, Co. K—right thigh.
John Marshall, Co. A—left leg.
H. L. Savage, Co. G—little finger and right hand.
Geo. R. Ellis, Co. E—left leg.
Thos. Y. McCullen, Co. B—right shoulder.
Clarkson Cloud, Co. K—right shoulder.
Jos. Windser, Co. A—left leg.
Robt. Brierly, Co. A—abdomen.
James P. Dickerson, Co. F—abdomen.
Perry Wright, Co. D—right hand.
Wesley Freeman, Co. G—ball through right shoulder.
Wm. Porter, Co. H—bayonet thrust in hip.
Jesse Hurd, Co. K—struck by shell in the breast.
James Forgsum, Co. I—ball through right leg.
James Hilleyard, Co. F—right hand.
James Ross, Co. F—hand.
Ed. Ingham, Co. A—spent ball in breast.
Albert Nelson, Co. A—ball in back.
Corp. Geo. Camperson, Co. D—left knee.
Thos. Thornton, Co. I—flesh wound in left arm.
Corp. Patrick McClusky, Co. C—arm.
Jesse D. Furis, Co. A—wrist.
Sergt. J. Martin, Co. A—hand.
J. J. Kerbaugh, Co. A—right hand and one thumb amputated.
David M. Johnson, Co. E—left shoulder.
Henry Morris, Co. F—leg.
Patrick McGarraty, Co. C—right eye.
Corp. Henry Vinning—spent ball.
Jos. Fitzsimmons, Co. F—hip and back.
John Barton, Co. F—flesh wound in leg.
Thomas Workman, Co. F—neck.
Wm. Veach, Co. A—flesh wound in hand.
H. S. Chaffer, Co. I—flesh wound in left ear.
Sergt. M. Hill, Co. C—right foot.
Lieut. C. Tanner, Co. H—breast.
Jno. Walker, Co. H—left leg.
Jno. Curry, Co. H—left hand and right thigh.
Corp. Jos. Booth, Co. H—groin and leg.
Anthony Cheevers, Co. H—shoulder and leg.
Color Corp. Lewis Corell, Co. H—flesh wd. finger.
Daniel Reed, Co. H—flesh, left shoulder.
Jno. Shepherd, Co. A—left shoulder.
Wm. Wahl, Co. G—flesh wound in finger.
Patrick O'Brien, Co. E—flesh wound in left breast.
C. Platt, Co. A—hit by butt of a musket in breast.
Corp. Duley, Co. H—head and breast.
John Sweeney, Co. A—left side.
Jasper Calhoun, Co. A—left wrist.

In Gen. BURNSIDE's Corps there has been severe losses in officers and men. The great conflict culminated on the left, where he commanded, and a desperate effort was made to outflank WILCOX and COX's Divisions, which had gained the summit of the hills, and were fast turning the tide of battle. The contest here was desperate and bloody. To-day I can see our dead scattered over the hill side up which our gallant boys fearlessly charged the enemy. Nothing in modern warfare could exceed the steadiness and courage of the troops, who fought on this part of the field. To-day they occupy the hill, only a quarter of a mile in rear of the position which they took yesterday. The enemy's batteries of seven guns on the left of Sharpsburgh and about the same number on the right of the town continue to threaten our front lines. No material change has occurred since last evening in the position of the forces, but *we occupy the field of battle.*

Gen. BURNSIDE and Staff have remained constantly on or near the field, watching intently every movement of the rebels, who keep themselves habitually out of sight. We ought to learn a lesson from them in this respect. This afternoon the General and his Staff and his Aids might all have been seen lying on the ground, under the shelter of a large wheat stack during a heavy rain. Let those who covet the glory, and labors of the battle-field follow the march, and share the toils of our *working Generals*, and they will soon have enough of war.

On the right, in the extreme front, I found General COCHRANE, this morning, with his entire brigade engaged in picket service. Two hundred yards in advance of where he and Adjutant ROOME were, our lines of sharpshooters were lying along the ground, within short rifle range of the enemy's pickets. Every two or three minutes the sharp crack of rifles, and the "bim-m-m" of the bullet was heard, in some cases, passing directly overhead or on either side. Behind them, in a large plowed field, the rebel dead lay very thickly scattered about, in every conceivable position; while muskets, bayonets and the *debris* of the previous day's battle covered the ground. Beside the fence of a small square burying-ground I counted

[*Continued on Eighth Page.*]

THE EMANCIPATION PROCLAMATION

WILLIAM SAFIRE

Seen only as a matter of economic fact, the decade of the 1860's was marked by the largest liquidation of private property by any government in world history: the forced servitude of four million people, with "field hands" valued at over $1,000 each. Seen as a great milestone in the march to human freedom, the Emancipation Proclamation was the major moral turning point in American history.

For his first 18 months in office, Abraham Lincoln—a plurality president before secession, with 36 percent of the vote in a four-man race—believed that he had to insist that abolition was not his primary purpose.[1] The Republican platform he had run on in 1860 pledged no interference with slavery in the states where it existed. "My paramount object in this struggle is to save the Union," he wrote to New York Tribune editor Horace Greeley, who was demanding that he free the slaves, "and is not either to save or to destroy slavery."[2] But even as he wrote those words in August of 1862, his draft of the Emancipation Proclamation was a secret Lincoln held in his pocket. He was anxiously awaiting a military victory so that abolition would not seem to be an act of desperation in a war that was not going well against the superior generalship of the Confederacy's Robert E. Lee.

After the Union's victory at the Battle of Antietam,[3] Lincoln could declare, "the Father of Waters again goes unvexed to the sea"[4] and announce emancipation on September 22,[5] effective January 1, 1863. Northern reaction was not unanimously favorable; it included charges of hypocrisy because the proclamation exempted those slave states that did not secede, and meant that Lincoln "freed" only slaves where he could not free them and did not free those in states where he could.

Lincoln credited this portrait, taken before his Cooper Union address, with playing a key role in his election to the presidency.

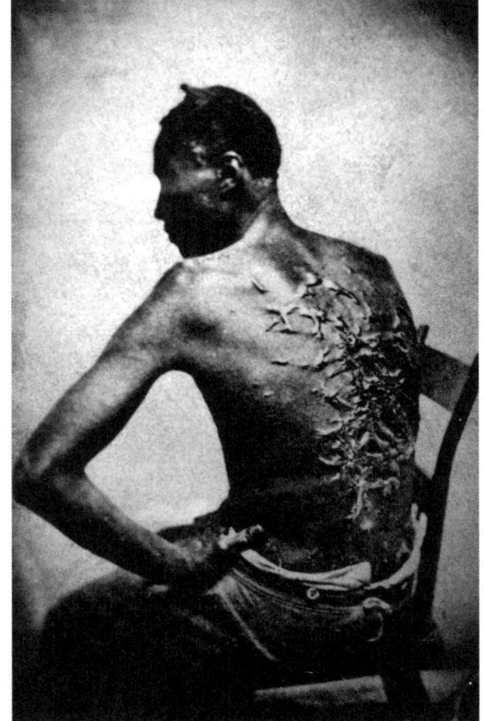

This 1863 photograph is a startling and graphic example of the beating and cruelty wrought upon slaves.

General Lee, commander of the Confederate forces in the U.S. Civil War, poses in uniform in 1863.

General Grant, commander of Federal troops during the Civil War, at Cold Harbor, Virginia, 1864.

FURTHER READING

1 "The Coming Administration," see November 8, 1860, front page.
2 "A Letter from President Lincoln," see August 24, 1862, front page.
3 "The Battle of Antietam.; The Great Victory," see September 20, 1862, front page.
4 "The President's Letter," see September 3, 1863, article.
5 "A Proclamation by the President of the United States," see September 23, 1862, front page.

The Battle of Gettysburg lasted three days, from July 1–3, 1863, and had the highest casualties of any battle in the Civil War.

Northerners who opposed abolition wished the Union would say "erring sisters, depart in peace" to the states that left, and complained that emancipation was not worth the horrendous casualty rate: in all, 600,000 Americans, north and south, died of wounds and war-related disease in the Civil War, in a population of 30 million, the equivalent today of six million deaths.

Lincoln had been cautioned by his political adviser, Montgomery Blair,[6] that emancipation could cost the new Republican party at the polls. There were fears that the proclamation would trigger bloody slave uprisings in the South, which would not only ensure a fight to the finish but also surely undermine prospects for ultimate reconciliation of North and South. Indeed, Union General George B. McClellan, who preferred a negotiated peace with the Confederacy to an unconditional victory that preserved the Union, ran against Lincoln in 1864; though he lost, he amassed 44 percent of the popular vote in the North.[7]

But strategically, emancipation meant that the Confederacy could no longer count on commercial support from abolition-minded England; more important to the conduct of the war, the fact of Lincoln's proclamation—which he couched in non-alarming, legalistic terms "with all the moral grandeur of a bill of lading," as one historian later put it—inspirited the majority of the North, to whom theories of "Union" and "majority rule" had been losing their appeal. Transforming what he called "this fiery trial" into a fight for human freedom reminded the majority of the nobility of the cause as the tide of the war was slowly turning.

The headquarters of the slave trading firm Price, Birch & Co. were immediately shut down after the Union troops seized Alexandria, Virginia, in 1861.

President Lincoln meets with General McClellan soon after the battle of Antietam, which was the single bloodiest day of combat in the war.

New York stations such as this one in City Hall recruited over 100,000 troops for the war.

At the moment he was to the sign the proclamation, he said to a small group of witnesses that "my right arm is stiff and numb" because all the handshaking he had to do that morning might make his signature seem shaky. But Lincoln added: "If my name ever goes into history it will be for this act, and my whole soul is in it." The signature on the document enshrined in the National Archives today does appear to reflect a slight quaver, but a smile is reported to have lighted Lincoln's face as he said, "That will do."

The Civil War was a terrible time for civil liberty. State legislators were arrested; some newspapers were shut down. Antiwar dissidents were reviled as "copperheads" (after the poisonous snake) and their leaders were arrested and denied access to civilian courts. Not until 1866, after the nation's most severe crisis had passed, did the Supreme Court, in Ex parte Milligan, rule against martial law where civil courts could operate.[8] America's wartime leaders have been embroiled in that security-versus-liberty controversy for the century and a half since.

The decade of the 1860's, in the war and its aftermath, was Lincoln's. His brief address at Gettysburg was a hymn to national birth ("conceived in Liberty"), death ("that these dead shall not have died in vain"), and resurrection ("a new birth of freedom"), a speech comparable in eloquence to the Sermon on the Mount.[9]

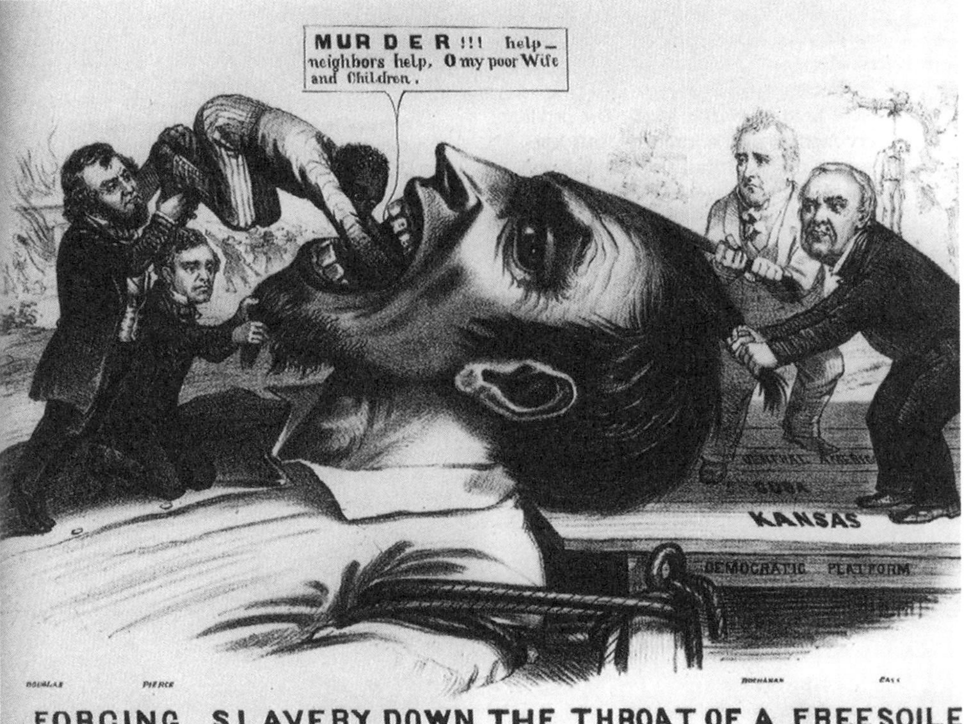

This cartoon depicts leading Democratic politicians forcing slavery down the throat of settlers of the western lands.

Abraham Lincoln and members of his cabinet at the signing of the Emancipation Proclamation.

6 "Montgomery Blair Dead," see July 28, 1883, article.
7 "Rebel Politics," see November 30, 1864, article.
8 "Washington, Special Dispatches to the New-York Times," see December 18, 1866, front page.
9 "The Heroes of July," see November 20, 1863, front page.

TO BE SOLD on board the Ship *Bance-Yland*, on tuesday the 6th of *May* next, at *Ashley-Ferry*; a choice cargo of about 250 fine healthy

NEGROES,

just arrived from the Windward & Rice Coast. —The utmost care has already been taken, and shall be continued, to keep them free from the least danger of being infected with the SMALL-POX, no boat having been on board, and all other communication with people from *Charles-Town* prevented.

Austin, Laurens, & Appleby.

N. B. Full one Half of the above Negroes have had the SMALL-POX in their own Country.

Newspaper advertisements often announced the arrival of African slaves to the American colonies.

Nor was he above accepting and reworking the words of others. William Seward, the political rival he appointed secretary of state, suggested that he add to his first inaugural address "a note of fraternal affection" to the departing Southerners. Seward's draft read, "I close…The mystic chords which…pass through all the hearts and all hearths in this broad continent of ours, will yet again harmonize in their ancient music when breathed upon by the guardian angel of the nation."

Lincoln, an unrecognized literary genius, took that draft peroration and unforgettably turned its metaphor into gold: "I am loth to close…The mystic chords of memory, stretching from every battlefield and patriot grave to every living heart and hearthstone all over this broad land, will yet swell the chorus of the Union, when again touched, as they surely will be, by the better angels of our nature."[10]

WILLIAM SAFIRE *is chairman of the Dana Foundation, which supports research in brain science, immunology and arts education. He was an Op-Ed columnist for The New York Times from 1972 to 2005 and currently writes the "On Language" column for the Times Sunday Magazine. The column, on grammar, usage and etymology, has led to the publication of 10 books. He is also the author of "Freedom," a novel about Lincoln and the Civil War. In 1978 Safire won the Pulitzer Prize for distinguished commentary, and in 2006 he was awarded the Presidential Medal of Freedom by George W. Bush.*

[10] "The Inauguration Ceremonies," see March 5, 1861, front page.

This painting depicts the Confederate attack on Federal troops during the Battle of Gettysburg, which is often cited as a turning point in the war.

The New-York Times.

VOL. XII—NO. 3676. NEW-YORK, MONDAY, JULY 6, 1863. PRICE THREE CENTS.

THE GREAT BATTLES.

Splendid Triumph of the Army of the Potomac.

ROUT OF LEE'S FORCES ON FRIDAY

The Most Terrible Struggle of the War.

TREMENDOUS ARTILLERY DUEL.

Repeated Charges of the Rebel Columns Upon Our Position.

Every Charge Repulsed with Great Slaughter.

The Death of Longstreet and Hill.

Our Cavalry Active on the Enemy's Flank.

THE REBEL RETREAT CUT OFF.

Chambersburgh in Our Possession.

Advance of the Militia under Gen. Smith to Important Positions.

The Rebel Pontoon Bridge at Williamsport Destroyed.

The Contents of the Captured Dispatches from Jeff. Davis to Lee.

A Peremptory Order for the Rebel Army to Return to Virginia.

OFFICIAL DISPATCHES FROM GEN. MEADE.

WASHINGTON, Saturday, July 4—10:10 A. M.

The following has just been received:

HEADQUARTERS ARMY OF POTOMAC, NEAR GETTYSBURGH, Friday, July 3—8½ P. M.

Major-Gen. Halleck, Genneral-in-Chief:

The enemy opened at 1 P. M., from about one hundred and fifty guns, concentrated upon my left centre, continuin without intermission for about three hours, at the expiration of which time, he assaulted my left centre twice, being, upon both occasions, handsomely repulsed, with severe loss to him, leaving in our hands nearly three thousand prisoners.

Among the prisoners is Brig.-Gen. ARMSTEAD and many Colonels and officers of lesser rank.

The enemy left many dead upon the field, and a large number of wounded in our hands.

The loss upon our side has been considerable. Maj.-Gen. HANCOCK and Brig.-Gen. GIBBON were wounded.

After the repelling of the assaults, indications leading to the beilef that the enemy might be withdrawing, a reconnoissance was pushed forward from the left and the enemy found to be in force.

At the present hour all is quiet.

My cavalry have been engaged all day on both flanks of the enemy, harassing and vigorously attacking him with great success, notwithstanding they encountered superior numbers both of cavalry and infantry.

The army is in fine spirits.

GEORGE G. MEADE,
Maj.-Gen. Commanding.

WASHINGTON, Sunday, July 5—4 P. M.

The latest official dispatch received here, up to this hour, from Gen. MEADE, is dated at Headquarters Army of Potomac, 7 A. M., July 4, which merely states that the enemy had withdrawn from his position, occupied for attack, on Friday. The information in the possession of Gen. MEADE, at that hour, did not develop the character of the enemy's movement, whether it was a retreat or a manœuvre for other purposes.

Reliable information received here to-day asserts that Gen. LEE's Headquarters were at Cashtown yesterday afternoon, and further represents that the rebels were fortifying at Newman's Cut, in the South Mountains, apparently to cover a retreat.

Later official dispatches are expected this evening.

SECOND DISPATCH.

HEADQUARTERS ARMY OF POTOMAC, July 4—Noon.

Maj.-Gen. Halleck:

The position of affairs is not materially changed since my last dispatch of 7 A. M.

We now hold Gettysburgh.

The enemy has abandoned large numbers of his killed and wounded on the field.

I shall probably be able to give you a return of our captures and losses before night, and a return of the enemy's killed and wounded in our hands.

GEORGE G. MEADE, Major-General.

THIRD DISPATCH.

HEADQUARTERS ARMY POTOMAC, July 4—10 P. M.

To Maj.-Gen. Halleck:

No change of affairs since my dispatch of noon.

GEO. G. MEADE, Major-General.

FOURTH DISPATCH.

WASHINGTON, Monday, July 6—12.30 A. M.

The following is the latest official dispatch:

HEADQUARTERS ARMY OF THE POTOMAC, Sunday, July 5—8:30 A. M.

MAJOR-GEN. HALLECK: The enemy retired under cover of the night and the heavy rain, in the direction of Fairfield and Cashtown.

Our cavalry are in pursuit.

I cannot give you the details of our captures in prisoners, colors and arms.

Upward of twenty battle-flags will be turned in from one corps.

My wounded and those of the enemy are in our hands. GEO. G. MEADE, Major-General.

THE PRESIDENT TO THE COUNTRY.

WASHINGTON, D. C., July 4—10:30 A. M.

The President announces to the country that news from the Army of the Potomac, up to 10 P. M. of the 3d, is such as to cover that army with the highest honor; to promise a great success to the cause of the Union, and to claim the condolence of all for the many gallant fallen; and that for this, he especially desires that on this day He, whose will, not ours, should ever be done, be everywhere remembered and reverenced with profoundest gratitude.

(Signed) A. LINCOLN.

THE GREAT BATTLE OF FRIDAY.

Our Special Telegrams from the Battle-Field.

NEAR GETTYSBURGH, Saturday, July 4.

Another great battle was fought yesterday afternoon, resulting in a magnificent success to the National arms.

At 2 o'clock P. M., LONGSTREET's whole corps advanced from the rebel centre against our centre. The enemy's forces were hurled upon our position by columns in mass, and also in lines of battle. Our centre was held by Gen. HANCOCK, with the noble old Second army corps, aided by Gen. DOUBLEDAY's division of the First corps.

The rebels first opened a terrific artillery bombardment to demoralize our men, and then moved their forces with great impetuosity upon our position. HANCOCK received the attack with great firmness, and after a furious battle, lasting until 5 o'clock, the enemy were driven from the field, LONGSTREET's corps being almost annihilated.

The battle was a most magnificent spectacle. It was fought on an open plain, just south of Gettysburgh, with not a tree to interrupt the view. The courage of our men was perfectly sublime.

At 5 P. M. what was left of the enemy *retreated in utter confusion*, leaving dozens of flags, and Gen. HANCOCK estimated *at least five thousand killed and wounded on the field.*

The battle was fought by Gen. HANCOCK with splendid valor. He won imperishable honor, and Gen. MEADE thanked him in the name of the army and the country. He was wounded in the thigh, but remained on the field.

The number of prisoners taken is estimated at 3,000, including at least two Brigadier-Generals—OLMSTEAD, of Georgia, and another—both wounded.

The conduct of our veterans was perfectly magnificent. More than twenty battle flags were taken by our troops. Nearly every regiment has one. The Nineteenth Massachusetts captured four. The repulse was so disastrous to the enemy, that LONGSTREET's corps is perfectly used up. Gen. GIBBON was wounded in the shoulder. Gen. WEBB was wounded and remained on the field. Col. HAMMELL, of the Sixty-sixth New-York, was wounded in the arm.

At 7 o'clock last evening, Gen. MEADE ordered the Third corps, supported by the Sixth, to attack the enemy's right, which was done, and the battle lasted until dark, when a good deal of ground had been gained.

During the day EWELL's corps kept up a desultory attack upon SLOCUM on the right, but was repulsed.

Our cavalry is to-day playing savagely upon the enemy's flank and rear. L. L. CROUNSE.

FROM ANOTHER CORRESPONDENT.

GETTYSBURGH, Friday, July 3.

The experience of all the tried and veteran officers of the Army of the Potomac tells of no such desperate conflict as has been in progress during this day. The cannonading of Chancellorsville, Malvern and Manassas were pastimes compared with this. At the headquarters, where I write, sixteen of the horses of Gen. MEADE's staff officers were killed by shell. The house was completely riddled. The Chief of Staff, Gen. BUTTERFIELD, was knocked down by a fragment of case-shot. Col. DICKINSON, Assistant Adjutant-General, had the bone of his wrist pierced through by a piece of shell. Lieut. OLIVER, of Gen. BUTTERFIELD's Staff, was struck in the head; and Capt. CARPENTER, of Gen. MEADE's escort, was wounded in the eye.

While I write the ground about me is covered thick with rebel dead, mingled with our own. Thousands of prisoners have been sent to the rear, and yet the conflict still continues.

The losses on both sides are heavy. Among our wounded officers are HANCOCK, GIBBON and a great many others whose names I feel restrained from publishing without being assured that they are positively in the list of casualties.

It is near sunset. Our troops hold the field, with many rebel prisoners in their hands. The enemy has been magnificently repulsed for three days—repulsed on all sides—most magnificently to-day. Every effort made by him since Wednesday morning to penetrate MEADE's lines has been foiled. The final results of the action, I hope to be able to give you at a later hour this evening.

S. WILKESON.

DISPATCH TO THE ASSOCIATED PRESS.

HEADQUARTERS ARMY OF THE POTOMAC, Friday, July 3—6 A. M.

The enemy's guns opened on our left wing at daylight, apparently to feel our position. They found us "at home," and soon suspended operations. They also endeavored to push forward their front on our right, but were driven back with loss.

9:40 *A. M.*—An hour ago, the enemy made a strong infantry attack on our right, and endeavored to break our line. The Twelfth corps, which formed our right, steadily drove them back for half an hour, when the enemy were reinforced, and a portion of the Sixth corps was sent to its support.

Failing in this, the enemy opened a heavy cannonade all along the line. The attack on the right is believed to have been a feint to cover a more formidable flank movement on the left. The cannonading is now heavy in that direction, and appears to be extending.

The Third Corps suffered greatly yesterday. The number of wounded is heavy, with a large number of officers. No estimate can be formed of the killed at this writing.

Heavy musketry has opened now on our right again and cannonading on our left is slackening. The enemy are fighting with the greatest desperation. Nothing can surpass the vigor and precision of our artillery.

Yesterday, the rebels took two of our guns, for want of horses and infantry support, but the division (HUMPHREY's, I think,) rallied and recaptured them. We took one from the enemy.

Comparatively few prisoners have been taken on either side up to this hour.

Ten o'clock A. M.—The cannonading has slackened.

Rebel prisoners say when their infantry charged our left-wing batteries yesterday, the massacre was beyond parallel. Some of the guns were masked, and did not open until the enemy were within canister range.

IMPORTANT SEMI-OFFICIAL DETAILS.

HEADQUARTERS ARMY OF THE POTOMAC, July 3, 1863.

The decisive battle has been fought to-day, and the enemy have been repulsed with terrific loss.

At daylight LEE's right wing batteries opened upon our left, and shortly after those of his centre followed. After half an hour's cannonading, doing but little damage to us, the fire slackened, and only occasional shots were exchanged.

Shortly afterward the enemy's left, composed entirely of infantry and sharpshooters, made an attack on our right wing. So sudden and impetuous was it accomplished that our skirmishers and front line were driven back from their intrenchments; but, by the aid of the batteries in the rear, and the indomitable bravery of the Twelfth corps, we regained the first position, capturing a considerable number of prisoners.

Several hours of ominous silence followed this repulse. At 1 o'clock the enemy fired two shots, apparently as signals for the grandest artillery fight ever witnessed on this continent. Before a moment had elapsed it is estimated that at least eighty guns opened upon us. Our batteries returned the compliment with interest. *The air seemed literally thick with iron*, and for more than an hour it seemed impossible that man or beast could live through it. Strange to say the enemy's accuracy of range, as exhibited on the two previous days, was wanting on this occasion. Most of their shells exploded far in the rear of our front, and generally missing our batteries.

Under cover of this *feu d'enfer*, LEE advanced his columns of infantry from the covers, and made several desperate attempts to carry the lines by assault; but each successive attempt was repulsed with terrible havoc to their ranks.

After an hour's incessant cannonading the fire grew less intense for a short time, but was again renewed for a little while, with great spirit. During this period, some of our batteries whose ammunition was expended and the men exhausted, ceased to fire, and on the approach of the reserve batteries, withdrew to the rear. The enemy only seeing the batteries withdrawing, and mistaking this for a retreat, made a massed infantry charge up the hill, and obtained a position in our lines, cutting to pieces and almost annihilating the small infantry supports; but before they had time to rejoice at their imaginary success, the fresh batteries poured in a deadly fire of canister and case-shot. The infantry reserves joined on either flank of the gap, charged them, and added greatly to their destruction. They were completely surprised; and *hundreds of them threw down their arms and asked for quarter*. Nearly the entire brigade of Gen. DICK GARNETT surrendered, and GARNETT himself, wounded, barely made his escape.

Longstreet was mortally wounded and captured. He is reported to have died in an hour afterward.

About 4:30 P. M. the artillery of the enemy slackened and had entirely ceased at 5, the last shots which they fired being far beyond their original position, and the infantry columns had withdrawn to their covers.

We took upward of three thousand prisoners. The enemy captured but few if any of our men.

The rebel prisoners report that *Gen. A. P. Hill was killed outright upon the field*, and that their officers suffered far greater casualties than in any previous engagement.

So terrific was the enemy's fire that the small house where Gen. MEADE and Staff were quartered, was perforated by several shots. Many of the Staff horses were killed around the house.

Gen. BUTTERFIELD was struck in the breast, and it is feared internally injured, by a piece of shell which exploded in the building. Lieut.-Col. JOSEPH DICKINSON, of the Staff, had his left arm perforated by a flying fragment of shell, and it seemed a miracle that no greater damage was done to life or limb.

Several of our general officers were wounded in the engagement. Gen. HANCOCK was wounded in the leg. Gens. GIBBON, WARREN and HUNT were wounded. In consequence of the excitement and difficulty in ascertaining their locations, the names of many prominent officers reported as killed or wounded cannot be ascertained to-night.

Too much credit cannot be given to our artillerists, who for hours stood to their guns under a broiling sun, and surrounded by the missiles of death, retiring only to give their positions to others, when their caissons and limbers were exhausted of ammunition. The infantry engaged also nobly did their duty, and the enemy to-day at their hands *has received the greatest disaster ever administered by the Union forces.*

All officers award the highest honors to Gen. MEADE for the able generalship he has displayed since he assumed command, and particularly for his coolness, decision and energy on this memorable 3d of July.

Last night, believing it to be his duty to the cause, and to learn how far he would be supported in the approaching conflict, he summoned his corps and division commanders for consultation.

DETAILS FROM OUR SPECIAL CORRESPONDENT.

HEADQUARTERS ARMY OF POTOMAC, Saturday Night, July 4.

Who can write the history of a battle whose eyes are immovably fastened upon a central figure of transcendingly absorbing interest—the dead body of an oldest born, crushed by a shell in a position where a battery should never have been sent, and abandoned to death in a building where surgeons dared not to stay?

The battle of Gettysburgh! I am told that it commenced on the 1st of July, a mile north of the town, between two weak brigades of infantry and some doomed artillery and the whole force of the rebel army. Among other costs of this error was the death of REYNOLDS. Its value was priceless, however, though priceless was the young and the old blood with which it was bought. The error put us on the defensive, and gave us the choice of position. From the moment that our artillery and infantry rolled back through the main street of Gettysburgh and rolled out of the town to the circle of eminences south of it. We were not to attack but to be attacked. The risks, the difficulties and the disadvantages of the coming battle were the enemy's. Our were the heights for artillery; ours the short, inside lines for manœuvreing and reinforcing; ours the cover of stonewalls, fences and the crests of hills. The ground upon which we were driven to accept battle was wonderfully favorable to us. A popular description of it would be to say that it was in form an elongated and somewhat sharpened horseshoe, with the toe to Gettysburgh and the heel to the south.

LEE's plan of battle was simple. He massed his troops upon the east side of this shoe of position, and thundered on it obstinately to break it. The shelling of our batteries from the nearest overlooking hill, and the unflinching courage and complete discipline of the army of the Potomac repelled the attack. It was renewed at the point of of the shoe—renewed desperately at the southwest heel—renewed on the western side with an effort consecrated to success by EWELL's earnest oaths, and on which the fate of the invasion of Pennsylvania was fully put at stake. Only a perfect infantry and an artillery educated in the midst of charges of hostile brigades could possibly have sustained this assault. HANCOCK's corps did sustain it, and has covered itself with immortal honors by its constancy and courage. The total wreck of CUSHING's battery—the list of its killed and wounded—the losses of officers, men and horses COWEN sustained—and the marvellous outspread upon the board of death of dead soldiers and dead animals—of dead soldiers in blue, and dead soldiers in gray—more marvellous to me than anything I have ever seen in war—are a ghastly and shocking testimony to the terrible fight of the Second corps that none will gainsay. That corps will ever have the distinction of breaking the pride and power of the rebel invasion.

For such details as I have the heart for. The battle commenced at daylight, on the side of the horse-shoe position, exactly opposite to that which EWELL had sworn to crush through. Musketry preceded the rising of the sun. A thick wood veiled this fight, but out of its leafy darkness arose the smoke and the surging and swelling of the fire, from intermittent to continuous, and crushing, told of the wise tactics of the rebels of attacking in force and changing their troops. Seemingly the attack of the day was to be made through that wood. The demonstration was protracted—it was absolutely preparative; but there was no artillery fire accompanying the musketry, and shrewd officers in our western front mentioned, with the gravity due to the fact, that the rebels had felled trees at intervals upon the edge of the wood they occupied in face of our position. These were breastworks for the protection of artillerymen.

Suddenly, and about 10 in the forenoon, the firing on the east side, and everywhere about our lines, ceased. A silence as of deep sleep fell upon the field of battle. Our army cooked, ate and slumbered. The rebel army moved 120 guns to the west, and massed there LONGSTREET's corps and HILL's corps, to hurl them upon the really weakest point of our entire position.

Eleven o'clock—twelve o'clock—one o'clock. In the shadow cast by the tiny farm house 16 by 20, which Gen. MEADE had made his Headquarters, lay wearied Staff officers and tired reporters. There was not wanting to the peacefulness of the scene the singing of a bird, which had a nest in a peach tree within the tiny yard of the whitewashed cottage. In the midst of its warbling, a shell screamed over the house, instantly followed by another, and another, and in a moment the air was full of the most complete artillery prelude to an infantry battle that was ever exhibited. Every size and form of shell known to British and to American gunnery shrieked, whirled, moaned, whistled and wrathfully fluttered over our ground. As many as six in a second, constantly two in a second, bursting and screaming over and around the headquarters, made a very hell of fire that amazed the oldest officers. They burst in the yard—burst next to the fence on both sides, garnished as usual with the hitched horses of aids and orderlies. The fastened animals reared and plunged with terror. Then one fell, then another—sixteen laid dead and mangled before the fire ceased, still fastened by their halters, which gave the expression of being wickedly tied up to die painfully. These brute victims of a cruel war touched all hearts. Through the midst of the storm of screaming and exploding shells, an ambulance, driven by its frenzied conductor at full speed, presented to all of us the marvelous spectacle of a horse going rapidly on three legs. A hinder one had been shot off at the hock. A shell tore up the little step of the Headquarters Cottage, and ripped bags of oats as with a knife. Another soon carried off one of its two pillars. Soon a spherical case burst opposite the open door—another ripped through the low garret. The remaining pillar went almost immediately to the howl of a fixed shot that WHITWORTH must have made. During this fire the houses at twenty and thirty feet distant, were receiving their death, and soldiers in Federal blue were torn to pieces in the road and died with the peculiar yells that blend the extorted cry of pain with horror and despair. Not an orderly—not an ambulance—not a straggler was to be seen upon the plain swept by this tempest of orchestral death thirty minutes after it commenced. Were not one hundred and twenty pieces of artillery, trying to cut from the field every battery we had in postion to resist their purposed infantry attack, and to sweep away the slight defences behind which our Infantry were waiting? Forty minutes—fifty minutes—counted on watches that ran! Oh so languidly. Shells through the two lower rooms. A shell into the chimney that daringly did not explode. Shells in the yard. The air thicker and fuller and more deafening with the howling and whirring of these infernal missiles. The chief of staff struck—SETH WILLIAMS—loved and respected through the army, separated from instant death by two inches of space vertically measured. An Aide bored with a fragment of iron through the bone of the arm. Another, cut with an exploded piece. And the time measured on the sluggish watches was one hour and forty minutes.

Then there was a lull, and we knew that the rebel infantry was charging. And splendidly they did this work—the highest and severest test of the stuff that soldiers are made of. HILL's division, in line of battle, came first on the double-quick. Their muskets at the "right-shoulder-shift." LONGSTREET's came as the support, at the usual distance, with war cries and a savage insolence as yet untutored by defeat. They rushed in perfect order across the open field up to the very muzzles of the guns, which tore lanes through them as they came. But they met men who were their equals in spirit, and their superiors in tenacity. There never was better fighting since Thermopylæ than was done yesterday by our infantry and artillery. The rebels were over our defences. They had cleaned cannoniers and horses from one of the guns, and were whirling it around to use upon us. The bayonet drove them back. But so hard pressed was this brave infantry that at one time, from the exhaustion of their ammunition, every battery upon the principal crest of attack was silent, except CROWEN's. His service of grape and cannister was awful. It enabled our line, outnumbered two to one, first to beat back LONGSTREET, and then to charge upon him, and take a great number of his men and himself prisoners. Strange sight! So terrible was our musketry and artillery fire, that when ARMSTEAD's brigade was checked in its charge, and stood reeling, all of its men dropped their muskets and crawled on their hands and knees underneath the stream of shot till close to our troops, where they made signs of surrendering. They passed through our ranks scarcely noticed, and slowly went down the slope to the road in the rear.

Before they got there the grand charge of EWELL, solemnly sworn to and carefully prepared, had failed.

The rebels had retreated to their lines, and opened anew the storm of shell and shot from their 120 guns. Those who remained at the riddled headquarters will never the crouching, and dodging, and running, of the Butternut-colored captives when they got under this, their friends, fire. It was appalling to as good soldiers even as they were.

What remains to say of the fight? It staggled surlily on the middle of the horse shoe on the west, grew big and angry on the heel at the southwest, lasted there till 8 o'clock in the evening, when the fighting Sixth corps went joyously by as a reinforcement through the wood, bright with coffee pots on the fire.

I leave details to my excellent friend and associate Mr. HENRY. My pen is heavy. Oh, you dead, who at Gettysburgh have baptised with your blood the second birth of Freedom in America, how you are to be envied! I rise from a grave whose wet clay I have passionately kissed, and I look up and see Christ spanning this battle-field with his feet and reaching fraternal and lovingly up to heaven. His right hand opens the gates of Paradise—with his left he beckons to these mutilated, bloody, swollen forms to ascend.

INCIDENTS OF THE BATTLE.

Capt. CUSHING, Company A, Fourth Regular artillery, was killed, and his battery suffered severely. The gallantry of this officer is beyond praise. Severely wounded early in the afternoon, he refused to leave his post beside his guns, but continued to pour grape and canister into the advancing columns of the rebels until they had reached the very muzzles of his pieces, and sure of their capture, were attempting to turn them upon our forces, when they were driven off by our infantry. At this moment Capt. CUSHING received his death wound, and fell lifeless to the earth. Heaps of corpses and wounded in front of his battery this morning, told a terrible tale of the effectiveness of its fire.

None of the company were taken prisoners by the rebels. After the battle but one gun of this battery remained uninjured—the rest having been dismounted or destroyed by the terrible fire of the enemy, which for the time was concentrated upon the batteries on this part of the field. In front of this position fell dead the rebel Gen. DICK GARNETT, who was courageously leading his men in this charge upon our batteries on Crow Hill. The rebel Gen. ARMSTEAD was also wounded here while advancing at the head of his brigade.

About fifty yards in front of our batteries was a stone wall, running from our centre in a southwesterly direction, behind which laid several of our regiments, picking off the enemy as they advanced up the slope of the hill. Notwithstanding the terrible fire poured into their ranks from our guns, so impetuous was the charge of the rebels that they drove our men from their position, and were advancing upon our batteries, several of which they captured, but the capture was only temporary. Gen. GIBBON's division, composed of Gens. WEBB's, HARRELL's and HALL's brigades, at the point of the bayonet, drove them back over the stone wall into the plain below.

Gen. GIBBON's division captured fourteen stand of colors and a large number of prisoners. Twenty-eight stands of colors in all were captured by the Second corps.

Gen. ARMISTEAD, when taken prisoner, asked immediately for Gen. MEADE, who was his classmate at West Point.

Col. WARD, of the Fifteenth Massachusetts, was killed.

Corp. HAYDEN, of the First Minnesota, was captured—escaped, seized a musket and seized a rare opportunity, and actually made ten rebels surrender. While marching them to Gen. GIBBON's quarters, a rebel behind a tree on the way drew a bead on him with his rifle. HAYDEN saw him in time to bring his piece to a level, and cry out, "Surrender." The fellow actually threw down his gun and joined the cavalcade, and HAYDEN came in with eleven captives.

Wounded prisoners taken in Gettysburgh this morning report that Gen. BRADLEY L. JOHNSON, of Maryland, was killed in Thursday's attack on our right. He was struck by a shell while charging our lines at the head of his division. Gen. HOOD is also repoited to have had his let shot off, and from the effects of which he has since died.

Rebel officers with whom I have conversed frankly admit that the result of the last two days has been most disastrous to their cause, which depended, they say, upon the success of LEE's attempt to transfer the seat of war from Virginia to the Northern Border States. A wounded rebel Colonel told me that, in the first and second days' fight, the rebel losses were between ten and eleven thousand. Yesterday they were greater still. In one part of the field, in a space not more than twenty feet in circumference, in front of Gen. GIBBONS' division, I counted seven dead rebels, three of whom were piled on top of each other. And close by in a spot not more than fifteen feet square lay fifteen "graybacks," stretched in death. These were the adventurous spirits, who in the face of the horrible stream of canister, shell and musketry, scaled the fence wall in their attempt upon our batteries. Very large numbers of wounded were also strewn around, not to mention more who had crawled away or been taken away. The field in front of the stonewall was literally covered with dead and wounded, a large proportion of whom were rebels. Where our musketry and artillery took effect they lay in swaths, as if mown down by a scythe. This field presented a horrible sight—such as has never yet been witnessed during the war. Not less than one thousand dead and wounded laid in a *space of less than four acres* in extent, and that, too, after numbers had crawled away to places of shelter.

The enemy's infantry, saving a small force of sharpshooters, was wholly out of sight at daylight on Saturday morning. There was talk on Friday night, after the battle, of organizing a column of pursuit.

Before the fighting was over—before sunset, considerably—the Signal Officers reported that an immense train of army wagons was going out of Gettysburgh northwest, on the road to Cashtown. Oh! that they could have run against the stonewall of the Harrisburgh army.

PARTIAL LIST OF KILLED AND WOUNDED.

Lieut. Dayton L. Card, commanding Co. E, 108th New York, was killed instantly by a shell. His body presented a ghastly sight. He was struck in the middle of the breast by a missle which exploded and tore him literally in two. Half of his face was also torn away by a fragment of shell.

Charles P. Leclear, Co. E, 108th N. Y.—killed.
J. Wickham, Co. E, 108th N. Y.—wounded.
Sergeant A. B. Hadley, do. do.—wounded.
Sergt. M. C. Bryant, Co. E, 108th N. Y.—wounded.
J. D. Anstak, Co. E, 108th New-York—wounded.

Cowan's New-York Battery—Killed.

Privates James Gray, Otis C. Billings, Jacob Y. McIlroy, Edmund Pete.

Wounded.

Lieut. Wm. P. Wright—right breast, probably mortally.

[Continued on Eighth Page.]

The New-York Times.

VOL. XII—NO. 3683. | NEW-YORK, TUESDAY JULY, 14, 1863. | PRICE THREE CENTS.

THE MOB IN NEW-YORK.

Resistance to the Draft---Rioting and Bloodshed.

Conscription Offices Sacked and Burned.

Private Dwellings Pillaged and Fired.

AN ARMORY AND A HOTEL DESTROYED.

Colored People Assaulted---An Unoffending Black Man Hung.

The Tribune Office Attacked---The Colored Orphan Asylum Ransacked and Burned---Other Outrages and Incidents.

A DAY OF INFAMY AND DISGRACE.

The initiation of the draft on Saturday in the Ninth Congressional District was characterized by so much order and good feeling as to well-nigh dispel the forebodings of tumult and violence which many entertained in connection with the enforcement of the conscription in this City. Very few, then, were prepared for the riotous demonstrations which yesterday, from 10 in the morning until late at night, prevailed almost unchecked in our streets. The authorities had counted upon more or less resistance to this measure of the Government after the draft was completed, and the conscripts were required to take their place in the ranks, and at that time they would have been fully prepared to meet it; but no one anticipated resistance at so early a stage in the execution of the law, and, consequently, both the City and National authorities were totally unprepared to meet it. The abettors of the riot knew this, and in it they saw their opportunity. We say abettors of the riot, for it is abundantly manifest that the whole affair was concocted on Sunday last by a few wire-pullers, who, after they saw the ball fairly in motion yesterday morning prudently kept in the back ground. Proof of this is found in the fact that as early as 9 o'clock, some laborers employed by two or three railroad companies, and in the iron foundries on the eastern side of the City, formed in procession in the Twenty-second Ward, and visited the different workshops in the upper wards, where large numbers were employed, and compelled them, by threats in some instances, to cease their work. As the crowd augmented, their shouts and disorderly demonstrations became more formidable. The number of men who thus started out in their career of violence and blood, did not probably at first exceed three-score. Scarcely had two dozen names been called, when a crowd, numbering perhaps 500, suddenly made an irruption in front of the building, (corner of Third-avenue and Forty-sixth-street,) attacking it with clubs, stones, brickbats and other missiles. The upper part of the building was occupied by families, who were terrified beyond measure at the smashing of the windows, doors and furniture. Following these missiles, the mob rushed furiously into the office on the first floor, where the draft was going on, seizing the books, papers, records, lists, &c., all of which they destroyed, except those contained in a large iron safe. The drafting officers were set upon with stones and clubs, and, with the reporters for the Press and others, had to make a hasty exit through the rear. They did not escape scatheless, however, as one of the enrolling officers was struck a savage blow with a stone, which will probably result fatally, and several others were injured.

From the above it will be seen that the drawing by Provost-Marshal JENKINS did not commence punctually at 9 o'clock, as was intended. Intimations had been received that a riot was probable, and Acting Assistant Provost-Marshal-General NUGENT was applied to for a force which would be sufficient to preserve the peace. At 10 o'clock, however, no other response had been made to this application than the arrival of a dozen policemen, and Provost-Marshal JENKINS decided to resume the drawing. The wheel was placed prominently upon the table, the blindfolded man stood beside it, the man whose duty it was turn the wheel was ready, and Mr. JENKINS announced that the draft, which was begun on Saturday, would be concluded. At this time there were about two hundred persons present, and, during the twenty minutes before the riot was inaugurated, they freely made use of excited and threatening language. These ruffians did not hesitate at all about joining the main body of the rioters as soon as they arranged themselves before the building, and their exit was the signal for the attack, which commenced with a volley of stones. When the office had been cleared of the officers and other persons, many of the more excited of the rioters rushed in and played instant havoc with the machinery, and demolishing the furniture and papers. The books, lists, records, and blanks were dragged into the street, torn into fragments, and scattered everywhere with loud imprecations and savage yells. The men seemed to be excited beyond expression, and in their futile efforts to wrench open the iron safe, which contained the names of the drafted, gave themselves wholly to devilish rage and fury.

The destruction of the material in the office was hardly accomplished when smoke was discovered to be issuing from the rear of the room, and this evidence of the building being on fire was received with vociferous shouts, and other indications of delight. As the flames gradually increased, the passions of the mob grew deeper, and their yelling and brandishing of clubs, and threatening of everybody connected with the enforcement of the draft was more emphatic. Some of the crowd supposed that the Enrolling officers had secreted themselves in the upper part of the building, and notwithstanding the fact that women and children were known to occupy the upper floors, the cowardly wretches threw stones and other missiles into the windows.

Fearing that these poor people would either be burned to death or maimed by these projectiles, Deputy Provost-Marshal EDWARD S. VANDERPOEL bravely stepped to the front, and assuring the rioters that they had utterly destroyed all the drafting paraphenalia, requested them to withdraw, or to do something to prevent the destruction of the helpless women and children. Suspecting from his uniform that he was one of the drafting officers, one of the rioters seized him and struck him. Mr. VANDERPOEL [illegible] and in a pacific man- [illegible] him with their hands [illegible] could not resist them, he withdrew to the place where the police were posted. The rioters followed him with great clubs, and the men, who were desperate, beat him upon the body and head. His head was so badly bruised that blood flowed profusely, when he was thrown down and kicked. He afterward escaped by the aid of the police and one or two of his friends; but the rioters followed him, striking him with clubs. He is so badly injured that there is but little probability of his recovery.

Meantime the fire spread from the enrolling office to the adjoining buildings, and the entire block was consumed.

ATTACK UPON SUPERINTENDENT KENNEDY.

Soon after the rioting began Superintendent KENNEDY hurried to the scene in a carriage, and as he alighted a portion of the crowd recognized him, greeting him at first with uncomplimentary epithets and afterwards with blows. A score or more of the ruffians fell upon him, and dealt heavy blows upon his head, face and body, injuring him severely. They doubtless would have killed him outright had not a strapping fellow in the crowd felt some compunction at the brutality of the rest and dashed in to the rescue. By vigorous blows he kept a clear space about Mr. KENNEDY's prostrate body until two policemen gathered up their Chief and removed him to a place of safety. In addition to his painful cuts and bruises, Mr. KENNEDY was also a sufferer in the loss of his watch, spectacles and gold-headed cane. The ruffians in this as in many other instances made plunder a part of their programme.

The rioters soon betook themselves to other places, apparently with no concerted plan but bent on fresh depredations.

THE ATTACK ON THE ARMORY IN SECOND-AVENUE.

At about 4 o'clock the crowd proceeded from the scene of their exploits in Lexington-avenue and Forty-fourth-street, to the armory situated on the corner of Second-avenue and Twenty-first-street. The building was a large four-story one, and was occupied for the manufacture of rifles and carbines for the Government. In the early part of the day the Police authorities had placed in the building a large number of Policemen, consisting principally of the Broadway Squad. Their instructions were to protect the building and the property therein, and to resist with force any attempt of the invaders to enter the premises. The mob on Second avenue, Twenty-first and Twenty-second streets rapidly increased, and at the time the first attempt was made to force the doors of the building, it amounted to from three to four thousand, the greater part of whom were boys. At this time some 18 or 20 men, followed by scores of youngsters, made an attempt to force the doors of the armory on Twenty-first-street. The doors were burst open by means of heavy sledges, and the crowd made a rush to enter the building. Those in charge of the building, acting under instructions, fired upon those who were entering, and four or five were wounded. One man, named MICHAEL VANEY, was shot through the heart, and died immediately. VANEY was a mechanic, and worked in the Morgan Iron Works. He was about 40 years of age, and resided in Twenty-third-street, between Avenues A and B. The other persons who were shot are not regarded as being seriously injured.

The shooting of VANEY, who was one of the ringleaders of the party making the attack, was the signal for a general onslaught upon the armory. Loud and deep were the curses uttered against the officers who had shot their leader, and for the next hour the paving-stones flew thick and fast, and not until the last pane of glass in the windows of the building had been broken, did they desist. It is proper to remark that nearly all those who threw the paving-stones were boys under twelve years of age. During all this time efforts of a desperate character were being made to fire the building. The doors on Second-avenue were finally forced open, and an excited multitude tried to effect an entrance. They were promptly repelled by those inside. Very soon they received reinforcements and again they made the attempt to enter, some of them with lighted torches in their hands. Meantime a dispatch was received by the officers of the Broadway Squad in charge of the building, from Police Headquarters, to the effect that inasmuch as it was impossible to reinforce them, and the attacking party so greatly outnumbered them, they must retire in the best manner they could. In a short time, they were all safely outside the building, with the exception of two of their number who were pelted on the head with brickbats; one of them was very seriously injured. The excitement against all policemen, at this time, ran so high that it was regarded a most hazardous undertaking for one to show himself to the excited populace. The fact that there was a private entrance in the rear was a most fortunate circumstance for them.

The police having vacated the premises, the mob found it comparatively an easy task to enter and fire the building. In fifteen minutes from the time the crowd had undisputed possession of it, the entire structure was a mass of flame. About half a dozen men remained inside as a sort of forlorn hope, and when all escape for them by the ordinary ways had been cut off by the flames, the poor fellows let themselves down from the windows of the third story in the best manner they could. One took hold of the window sill, and another slid down to his feet and then dropped to the pavement. In this way they all managed to escape; but two of them had each a leg broken, one had his skull so much fractured that he is not expected to recover, and another was so bruised and injured that when he was taken into a neighboring drug store life seemed extinct. Amid the excitement and confusion our reporter was unable to obtain the names of any of those who were thus injured.

SCENES BY AN EYE-WITNESS.

At 11 A. M. word reached the Park Barracks of the disturbance, and Lieut. REED and a detachment of the Invalid corps immediately repaired to the scene of the riot. They went by the Third avenue route, the party occupying one car. On the way up, crowds of men, women and children gathered at the street corners, hissed and jeered them, and some even went so far as to pick up stones, which they defiantly threatened to throw at the car. When near the scene of disturbance, Lieut. REED and command alighted, and formed in company line, in which order they marched up to the mob. Facing the rioters the men were ordered to fire, which many of them did, the shots being blank cartridges, but the smoke had scarce cleared away when the company (which did not number more than fifty men, if as many,) were attacked and completely demoralized by the mob, who were armed with clubs, sticks, swords and other implements. The soldiers had their bayonets taken away, and they themselves were compelled seek refuge in the side streets, but in attempting to flee thither several, it is said, were killed, while those that escaped, did so only to be hunted like dogs, but in a more inhuman and brutal manner. They were chased by the mob, who divided themselves into squads, and frequently a single soldier would be caught in a side street, with each end blocked up by the rioters. The houses and stores were all closed (excepting a few liquor shops, which had their shutters up, but kept the back door open,) no retreat was, therefore, open for him, and the poor fellow would be beaten almost to death, when the mob becoming satiated and disgusted with their foul work, he would be left sweltering in blood, unable to help himself.

Elated with success, the mob, which by this time had been largely reinforced, next formed themselves into marauding parties, and paraded through the neighboring streets, looking more like so many infuriated demons, the men being more or less intoxicated, dirty and half clothed. Some shouted, "Now for the Fifth-avenue Hotel—there's where the Union Leaguers meet!" Others clamored among themselves for the muskets which they had taken from the soldiers. The streets were thronged with women and children, many of whom instigated the men to further work of blood, while the injured men left the crowd, and found seats up the street corners, at one of which the reporter heard the following conversation between an intoxicated youth, who was badly wounded in the head, and an elderly excited woman, probably his mother:

Youth—"An' bedad, if it hadn't been for this lick, which the son of a —— guv me, I'd a belabored him 'afor this. And bedad I wud."

Woman—"Musshanuiusha, ye betters mind yer own bisernis."

Youth—"No, if SAM. GARRIGAN [or Galligan—REP.] had a' dun the business browner, it wud be all right."

From this it may be inferred that the Sam. Garrigan, or Galligan, mentioned in the conversation above, is the ringleader, of which there can be little doubt, as the reporter frequently heard Garrigan's or Galligan's name cheered and called the "Bully boy." Garrigan or Galligan, we believe, is a well-known wire-puller of the Ward, and from conversations between the men, we gleaned the following, which may be taken for what it is worth: 1. That Garrigan or Galligan is the ringleader. 2. That the mob, numbering about 500 men, assembled this morning at Central Park, armed and equipped, *i. e.*, with [illegible] sticks, and from there proceeded to the [illegible] office, where they commenced [illegible] considerably augmented, for, as yet, the workmen had not all gone to their day's work. As soon as the Provost-Marshal's Office had been gutted of its contents, and the adjoining building—a wheelwright's shop, in which there was much combustible material—had been fired, the telegraph wires were cut. Parties and bands of men and boys then visited the various workshops in the vicinity, and compelled the men to leave their work and join, threatening them with death unless they complied with their demands. It is said word was now sent by the rioters to Brooklyn, Jersey City and Albany of the outbreak, and a message, it is rumored, was received from the 'longshoremen of this City, stating that they would be up in the evening, armed to the teeth, to assist them.

By this time the Fire Department of the District arrived on the ground, and were preparing to work on the fire; but were prevented from doing so by the mob, who threatened them with instant death if their orders were disobeyed. The cars were stopped from running either way; the horses in several instances were killed, and the cars broken to pieces; the drivers were threatened with violence if they attempted to move on, as by this means the City authorities would hear of the outbreak.

The fire, which had now consumed the wheelwright's shop, had extended to the Provost-Marshal's office, which was soon enveloped in flames, from which issued a large and dark volume of smoke.

The rioters meantime danced with fiendish delight before the burning building, while the small boys and "Rocks" and "Softs" sent showers of stones against the office, smashing in the doors and windows, the fire seeming to do the work too tardily to suit them. The murky atmosphere and the heavy black clouds which lined the horizon, formed a strange, weird spectacle, which was made the more complete by the demoniac yells of the mob.

It now became evident to the firemen that if the flames were not subdued the whole block would be consumed; and, accordingly, several attempts to operate on the fire were made, but without success, as their apparatus was seized by the mob, and the firemen themselves were severely beaten. At this stage of the proceedings, Chief-Engineer DECKER, or some other high official of the Fire Department, appeared amongst the crowd, and, after much persuasion and talking, finally succeeded in quieting the rioters. The military, however, soon appeared on the ground, which aroused the ire of the mob, who renewed their violence with increased numbers.

To resume the thread of our report, the military being immediately routed, they fled to the side streets, where, as we have shown, they were shamefully maltreated. After this the mob concentrated and returned to the fire, where they found their friends awaiting them, with nourishment in the shape of liquors, which, as may be supposed, only added fuel to the fire already kindled: whisky soon accomplished its mission; the men became quarrelsome and squabbled amongst themselves. Some boasted of what they had done, one man boasting that he had nearly killed two soldiers, and wounded many more. Another, an obese, small, villainous-looking Irishman, who carried the butt of a bayonet, boasted that he had "done for" a nigger. Others, suffering from the wounds they had received, consoled themselves by exclaiming: "Never mind, SEYMOUR and WOOD are around, and will help us!" and "Old ABE will pay $300 to keep quiet," and the like. All vehemently protested against the "$300 clause," and were willing to be drafted, if the rich man would be made to shoulder the musket the same as they. Those who had done the most in routing the military, such as chasing a soldier until he fell from sheer exhaustion, and then beating him till he was near dead, were cheered and petted by their friends, who, both men and women, gathered around them by dozens.

During the row a man, said to be an officer or a policeman in undress uniform, shot a horse purposely, it is stated, because had the animal moved, it would be at the risk of the life of those standing around him; the owner (the horse was attached to a dray) endeavored to clutch the man, who dodged him and run up a flight of stairs in a house near by, with the probable intention of getting on to the roof to escape the mob, who were so infuriated at the deed, which they, of course, interpreted to be a retaliatory act on his part; he was pursued and dragged down stairs with his skull broken, when he was pitched to the mob, who, it is said, literally tore him to pieces. At this point a policeman who had become separated from his companions, who were stationed on a corner near by, in attempting to rescue the wounded man, found himself surrounded by the rioters, who commenced to pound and beat him shamefully; he drew his revolver and shot one man. The influence of this was electric; they rushed upon the unfortunate policeman, whom they deprived of his arms, struck him with their clubs and pelted him with stones. His companions, observing this, quickly formed in a line, but their attempts to make a stand were abortive; overpowered by superior numbers, they were utterly routed, several of their number being badly injured. The rest fled through the side streets, where they were chased by the infuriated mob; some jumped fences and hid in the corners of uncultivated lots, where they were found and maltreated shamefully. Two cases of the most painful description came under the reporter's observation: A policeman, having eluded their vigilance for several blocks, unable to run away further, threw himself down and begged for mercy. But his entreaties were unheeded; he was pelted with stones and beaten with clubs until his features could not be distinguished for the blood; even then their persecutions were continued, until, abandoning himself to his fate, the policeman feigned death; then, through the exertions of a few of the more humane of the rioters, he was left alone: friends soon rushed to his aid, and conveyed him to the Station-house. Another was beaten until his eyes were so clotted with blood that he could not see.

BURNING OF THE ORPHAN ASYLUM FOR COLORED CHILDREN.

The Orphan Asylum for Colored Children was visited by the mob about 4 o'clock. This Institution is situated on Fifth-avenue, and the building, with the grounds and gardens adjoining, extended from Forty-third to Forty-fourth-street. Hundreds, and perhaps thousands of the rioters, the majority of whom were women and children, entered the premises, and in the most excited and violent manner they ransacked and plundered the building from cellar to garret. The building was located in the most pleasant and healthy portion of the City. It was purely a charitable institution. In it there are on an average 600 or 800 homeless colored orphans. The building was a large four-story one, with two wings of three stories each.

When it became evident that the crowd designed to destroy it, a flag of truce appeared on the walk opposite, and the principals of the establishment made an appeal to the excited populace, but in vain.

Here it was that Chief-Engineer DECKER showed himself one of the bravest among the brave. After the entire building had been ransacked, and every article deemed worth carrying away had been taken—and this included even the little garments for the orphans, which were contributed by the benevolent ladies of this City—the premises were fired on the first floor. Mr. DECKER did all he could to prevent the flames from being kindled, but when he was overpowered by superior numbers, with his own hands he scattered the brands, and effectually extinguished the flames. A second attempt was made, and this time in three different parts of the house. Again he succeeded, with the aid of half a dozen of his men, in defeating the incendiaries. The mob became highly exasperated at his conduct, and threatened to take his life if he repeated the act. On the front steps of the building he stood up amid an infuriated and half-drunken mob of two thousand, and begged of them to do nothing so disgraceful to humanity as to burn a benevolent institution, which had for its object nothing but good. He said it would be a lasting disgrace to them and to the City of New-York.

These remarks seemed to have no good effect upon them, and meantime, the premises were again fired—this time in all parts of the house. Mr. DECKER, with his few brave men again extinguished the flames. This last act brought down upon him the vengeance of all who were bent on the destruction of the asylum, and but for the fact, that some firemen surrounded him, and boldly said that Mr. DECKER could not be taken except over their bodies, he would have been dispatched on the spot. The institution was destined to be burned, and after an hour and a half of labor on the part of the mob, it was in flames in all parts. Three or four persons were horribly bruised by the falling walls, but the names we could not ascertain. There is now scarcely one brick left upon another of the Orphan Asylum.

ATTACK ON THE TRIBUNE OFFICE.

During the greater part of the day, a crowd, composed principally of overgrown boys, amused themselves by going around to the various newspaper offices down town, cheering the bulletins which announced the progress of the riot in the upper part of the City, groaning the editors of such journals as were deemed obnoxious by the mob, and chasing and beating every person of color who chanced to make his appearance. The *Tribune*, as a matter of course, came in for the principal share of the groans, and it is but fair to add, that the *Daily News* monopolized the cheers. Various hints were given out by the rioters that the *Tribune* would be attacked in the evening, but they were not credited, or if they were, no preparations appear to have been made to repel it. About 7 o'clock, however, the crowd of boys began to be swelled by a different class of roughs, who appeared on the ground with clubs in their hands, and from their appearance, had evidently been engaged in the more bloody work up town. They immediately gathered around the *Tribune* office and commenced a series of the most unearthly groans and demoniac yells. In a few moments one of the more forward among them commenced an attack upon the door of the publication office, which was locked, but which soon gave way to the pressure of the mob, who, amid the crashing of broken doors and windows, rushed in [illegible]. In a moment more files of the *Tribune* were thrown out to the crowd and torn and scattered to the winds. In less than five minutes the office was completely gutted, and the desks and counters upset and broken. At length a platoon of the First Ward Police came rushing up Nassau-street, and on seeing them the mob, which numbered not less than four hundred men and boys, ran like so many sheep, leaving Printing-house-square, in less than three minutes, almost as clear of people as it is of a Sunday morning. It was a striking illustration of the cowardice of a mob when confronted by a handful of determined officers of the law. Several shots were fired by the policemen at ringleaders of the mob—but, so far as is known, none of them took effect. One of the policemen was also shot at by a rioter, the ball taking effect in the back. The wound is serious, but it is thought not dangerous. Before leaving the office, the rioters set fire to the building, but it was extinguished by a policeman before much damage was done.

OUTRAGES UPON COLORED PERSONS.

Among the most cowardly features of the riot, and one which indicated its political *animus* and the cunningly-devised cue that had been given to the rioters by the instigators of the outbreak, was the causeless and inhuman treatment of the negroes of the City. It seemed to be an understood thing throughout the City that the negroes should be attacked wherever found, whether they offered any provocation or not. As soon as one of these unfortunate people was spied, whether on a cart, a railroad car, or in the street, he was immediately set upon by a crowd of men and boys, and unless some man of pluck came to his rescue, or he was fortunate enough to escape into a building he was inhumanly beaten and perhaps killed. There were probably not less than a dozen negroes beaten to death in different parts of the City during the day. Among the most diabolical of these outrages that have come to our knowledge is that of a negro cartman living in Carmine-street. About 8 o'clock in the evening as he was coming out of the stable, after having put up his horses, he was attacked by a crowd of about 400 men and boys, who beat him with clubs and paving-stones till he was lifeless, and then hung him to a tree opposite the burying-ground. Not being yet satisfied with their devilish work, they set fire to his clothes and danced and yelled and swore their horrid oaths around his burning corpse. The charred body of the poor victim was still still hanging upon the tree at a late hour last evening.

Early in the afternoon the proprietors of such saloons and other places of business as had negroes in their employ, were obliged to close up for fear that the rioters would destroy their premises. In most of them the negroes were compelled to remain over night, not daring to go home lest they be mobbed on the way.

COURAGEOUS ACTION OF THE POLICE.

At about five o'clock a large body of rioters, differently estimated from one hundred to three hundred,—the latter much the nearer figure—marched down Broadway with a banner, inscribed "No draft" with the American flag, and with every conceivable diabolical weapon. They amused themselves *en route* by cheering and groaning at will, and occasionally killing or maiming every "nigger" they met. When below Fourteenth-street they avowed their determination of entering the La Farge House and seizing every colored servant there. Fortunately they were met at Amity-street—unexpectedly to them—by a body of Police some two hundred strong, under Inspector CARPENTER and Sergeant COPELAND. The Police instantly formed company front, and, with Inspector CARPENTER far in advance, at once charged on the "double quick." The fight for a few moments was savage and terrific. Men fell by the dozen under the sturdy blows of the Police, who had orders to "make no prisoners," and in five minutes naught was left of the lawless horde but the bodies of those ruffians who were knocked senseless lying on the ground. Too much credit cannot be awarded to the Police for their behavior on this occasion. They did not know whether one hundred or five thousand of the lawless were their adversaries, nor did they wait to ascertain. On they charged, and in five minutes were masters of the situation. Capt. CARPENTER was far ahead of his men, with reckless courage, rushing into the midst of the mob, and handling his club against fearful odds. It is a wonder he was not killed. This charge, and its success, must have had a salutary effect, being the first regular fight with the organized mob, and showing them that the Police are their superiors.

The Police, at the time they met the mob, were on their way to Mayor OPDYKE's house, in Fifth-avenue, which it was rumored was to be attacked. None of the Police were seriously injured in the encounter, while at least two of the rioters were killed, and ten or fifteen more were so badly used up that they will not be likely to take a hand in another riot at present.

THE ATTACK ON THE MAYOR'S RESIDENCE.

A short time previous to the fight above described, the mob had paid a visit to the residence of Mayor OPDYKE, No. 79 Fifth-avenue. Their number was estimated at about 500. As the police had not yet arrived upon the ground, it seemed a foregone conclusion that the Mayor's house would share the fate of others, and be pillaged and burned by the mob. While the rioters were about preparing for the attack, Judge BARNARD made his appearance, and by a well-timed speech persuaded them to desist from their purpose. While the Judge was addressing them, the ardor of the more violent roughs had time to cool, and on the conclusion of his remarks, they took up their line of march in another direction.

MEETING OF EX-OFFICERS AT THE ARMORY OF THE SEVENTH REGIMENT.

In accordance with the call of Gen. SANDFORD, the ex-officers now in the City, to the number of some two hundred or more, met at the armory of the Seventh regiment last evening, for the purpose of taking some action with reference to make their services of avail in the present emergency. In the absence of Gen. SANDFORD the meeting was organized by appointing Col. JULIUS W. ADAMS, late of the First Long Island volunteers, Chairman, and Capt. W. C. CHURCH, late of Major-General CASEY's staff, Secretary. On motion of Col. BAIRD, the officers present, willing to render service, were requested to record their names with the Secretary. It was also voted that the field officers present be appointed a Committee to devise a plan of operations. Gen. SANDFORD arriving in the meantime, the meeting resolved itself into a crowd, who gathered about him while he explained what action had been already taken to suppress disturbance, and what further measures were proposed to that end. He advised the officers representing different regiments to form a *nuclei* for as complete a reorganization of their several regiments as the exigency would permit. Officers of volunteer regiments were requested to enroll themselves under Col. J. M. DAVIES, late of the Harris Light cavalry, who would proceed immediately to perfect a regimental organization. All ex-officers of volunteer regiments now in the City are accordingly requested to report to Col. DAVIES, at the Armory of the Seventh regiment, at 8 o'clock this morning. They will come prepared to report the number of men they can procure to assist in quelling the riot. Discharged soldiers, citizens or others, organized or unorganized, willing to render service, are requested to report at the same time and place. They will be furnished with arms and equipments, and at once set to work.

CHARACTER OF THE MOB.

In the early part of the day yesterday, there were a number of respectable workmen and persons engaged in different occupations in the City, who were momentarily seduced from their labors and their work-shops, and went with the crowds in the street. But they at once saw the horrible character of the mob and the atrocious work they had on hand; they heard their threats and saw their shocking brutalities, and were only too glad to get out from among them. At last the mob or mobs were composed of only the vilest men in the City, and there was not a crime conceivable, from firing houses to hanging negroes, of which they were not capable. The reign of ruffianism was short, but it at last became a reign of the true article.

ROVING RIOTERS.

Some of the scenes in the side streets of the City, during the day were painful in the extreme, and humiliating to human nature. In the streets running north from Canal-street, where many colored people reside, mobs of foul-looking boys and men scoured up and down in the afternoon and evening, in pursuit of negroes, who were assailed wherever found; and our reporter observed in one gang, several women armed with sticks, rushing to and fro with the vile and cowardly crowd; but it is only justice to say that the voluble tongues of these women gave vent to their thoughts with an accentuation which was never acquired on this side of the Atlantic ocean. It was almost impossible to look down any street in that part of the City, or any other, without seeing a crowd roving hither and thither, or standing still in heated conversation. They seemed to have no special object in view. They appeared to have had no evil-defined atrocity to perpetrate. They were rather on the look out for something upon which to wreak their bad passions.

APPREHENDED ATTACK ON THE POLICE HEADQUARTERS.

At 1½ o'clock this morning, Inspector CARPENTER, at the head of 300 Policemen, marched from the Police headquarters to take down the body of the negro who was hung to a tree in Clarkson-street. They had gone but a short distance before they were recalled to repel an apprehended attack on the headquarters. No attack had been made when our paper went to press. The headquarters were guarded by 600 Policemen and 58 soldiers from the regular army, brought from Forts Hamilton and Lafayette.

THE HOUSES BURNED IN LEXINGTON-AVENUE.

Two fine brown-stone private residences in Lexington-avenue, between Forty-third and Forty-fourth streets, were entirely destroyed. One of them was occupied by a mechanic named WM. TURNER; the other one was believed to be the dwelling of a Deputy Provost-Marshal, who was connected with the enrolling and drafting office in Broadway, between Twenty-eighth and Twenty-ninth streets.

DESTRUCTION OF A BLOCK ON BROADWAY.

The drafting office for the Eighth Congressional District is located in Broadway, near Twenty-eighth-street. Here, under the direction of Provost-Marshal MANIERRE, the drafting was opened at 9 o'clock, and conducted without interruption until 12, when the announcement was made that further proceedings would be suspended until to-day. The mob soon afterward paid a visit to this place, sacked it, and then set it on fire. It was totally consumed, as well as the remainder of the block.

BULL'S HEAD HOTEL.

This famous hotel, for many years past kept by Mr. ALLERTON, and situated on Forty-fourth-street, between Lexington and Fifth avenues, shared the fate of so many other fine buildings in that part of the City. It was entirely destroyed, together with several barns, sheds and other out-houses on the premises. We do not understand that the cause of its destruction was owing to the fact that Mr. ALLERTON, or any one other person immediately interested in the establishment, was specially odious to the incendiaries. The mob entered the hotel in large numbers and demanded liquor. They took all there was in the house, and many of them drank to excess; they also took all the cigars they could find. Many of them then ransacked the house and took everything they could lay their hands upon. In a short time flames were discovered bursting from the second story windows, and before a single fireman was on hand the building was past all hope of being saved.

A STATION-HOUSE AND THE RESIDENCE OF THE CITY POSTMASTER BURNED.

About 9 o'clock, the rioters in strong force assembled at the Twenty-third Precinct Station-house, near Yorkville, and set fire to the building before their intentions could be frustrated. The books and records of the Precinct were saved by one of the Sergeants. The house of Mr. ABRAM WAKEMAN, Postmaster of the City, was also visited by the mob, and totally destroyed by fire.

THIEVES AND PICKPOCKETS.

This industrious class of our population availed themselves of the confusion to ply their arts, and in every instance with great success. Indeed the chief notice of a large portion of the rioters in joining the mob seemed to be the opportunity that would be offered them for promiscuous pillage and plunder. Many instances were reported of men being robbed of watches, pocket-books, breast-pins, &c., and all the houses that were burned were first plundered of their valuables by the mob.

THE POLICE.

The events of the day resulted in a great many casualties—a few fatal and many severe—among the Police. We have been able only to obtain a few names.

Officer SWAINSER, Twenty-ninth Precinct, struck in the head and badly cut; HOLMES, Twenty-ninth, cut in the head severely; MORRISON, Twenty-ninth, dangerously wounded; CHARLES B. LAW, Eighth, seriously; NOLAN McCARTY, Twenty-ninth, not expected to live; NOLEN WALSH, Eighth, badly cut; SUTHERLAND, Fifteenth, seriously cut and bruised.

PREPARATIONS FOR TO-DAY.

At 2 o'clock this morning the City was apparently quiet. A heavy rain fell about midnight which helped greatly to disperse the rioters. The preparations to meet the outbreak to-day, if it is renewed, we are assured are such as will prevent the recurrence of such scenes as were enacted yesterday. The rioters had it pretty much their own way yesterday, but if they resume their demonstrations to-day a good share of them will come to a bloody and well-deserved end of their career.

WHAT WAS DONE IN BROOKLYN—THE POLICE—THE NAVY-YARD—THE FIRE DEPARTMENT—THE PROVOST-MARSHAL'S OFFICE IN THE THIRD DISTRICT, ETC., ETC.

The riot in New-York has created an intense excitement in this city, and large numbers of persons crossed the river to see what was going on.

Capt. S. B. GREGORY, Provost-Marshal of the Third Congressional District, on hearing of the proceedings in New-York, packed up all his papers and transported them to a place of safety. There is nothing now in the building of the least importance to any one.

The draft, which was fixed for Wednesday morning, has been suspended for the present. Further notice will be given when the drawing will take place.

The number of persons enrolled in the different Wards comprising the District, and the number to be drafted, is as follows, all of the first class:

	No. Enrolled.	No. to be Drafted.
First Ward	707	180
Second Ward	944	257
Third Ward	1,057	340
Fourth Ward	1,367	369
Fifth Ward	1,960	551
Seventh Ward	1,374	373
Eleventh Ward	3,378	1,050
Thirteenth Ward	1,869	528
Fifteenth Ward	866	235
Nineteenth Ward	686	169

Of the second class about 11,000 persons are enrolled, making in all of both classes nearly 30,000.

Chief Engineer CUNNINGHAM, in view of the present exigency, ordered last night that in case of fire, the bells shall ring three rounds, designating the district, and then the general alarm. This is for the purpose of assembling all the firemen, so as to extinguish any fire that may occur. These orders will be in force until further directions.

The colored people are having a hard time of it. They are attacked everywhere and beaten. They crowded about the police stations last night, asking for protection, being prevented from going to their homes, or even walking the streets.

The police to the number of 100 went to New-York, in charge of Inspector FOULKE.

There was great commotion in the Navy-yard. The walls were manned and mounted with guns. Thirteen 18-pounders are mounted on the Flushing-avenue side, so as to sweep everything. Two 32-pounders command the main entrance, and all the vessels have been hauled into the stream, the guns shotted, and everything ready for any emergency.

Several companies of Marines, with 60 rounds of cartridges, and 12 boat-howitzers, rifled cannon, with ammunition-boxes, loaded with percussion shells, shrapnell, canister, and grapeshot, were sent to New-York toward evening. The Marines were accompanied by 300 sailors, armed with cutlasses and revolvers.

Some guns were taken from the State arsenal in Portland-avenue on Sunday night, which gave rise to the rumor that it had been attacked. The facts are that two companies of artillery, belonging to the Seventieth regiment militia have been ordered to Fort Hamilton, and the guns were taken for their use. They were placed on vessels at the foot of Little-street and transported to the fort. There are no arms in the building at present.

A Call to the Veteran Volunteers!

The veterans who have recently returned from the field of battle have again an opportunity of serving, not only their country, but the great emporium of New-York, from the threatened dangers of a ruthless mob.

The Commanding-General of the Eastern Department trusts that those who have exhibited so much bravery in the field of battle, will not hesitate to come forward at this time, to tender their services to the Mayor, to stay the ravages of the City by men who have lost all sense of obligations to their country, as well as to the City of New-York.

JOHN E. WOOL, Major-General.

P. S.—These men are requested to report to Maj.-Gen. SANFORD, corner Elm and White streets, on Tuesday, July 14, at 10 A. M.

CALLS FOR MILITIA TO MEET THIS MORNING.

The following calls were issued last evening:

NATIONAL ZOUAVES—ATTENTION!!—The officers and members of the Tenth regiment New-York volunteers, who are willing to assist in the enforcement of the laws, are requested to meet at No. 596 Broadway, Armory of Thirty-seventh New-York State Guards, as early this day as possible, in full uniform.

JOHN E. BENDIX, Colonel.

HEADQUARTERS EIGHTH REGIMENT N. Y. S. M.—The members, ex-officers and members [illegible] ment in the City, including troops are requested to meet at the Armory to-morrow, July 14, at 8 o'clock A. M. By order of Maj. LEANDER BUCK.

D. B. KEELER, Jr., Adjutant.

NINTH REGIMENT N. Y. N. G.—A meeting of the members and ex-members of this regiment will be held at the Mercer House, corner of Broome and Mercer streets, at 9 o'clock this morning, for the purpose of assisting in maintaining the State and City authorities in suppressing the riot. The call is signed by Lieut.-Col. RUTHERFORD, Maj. DIGGS, Capt. PICKETT, Capt. LANSING and Lieut. STRONG.

The following order was issued last evening by Gen. BROWN, commanding United States troops in this City:

HEADQUARTERS NEW-YORK, July 13, 1863.

ORDERS No. 1.—In obedience to the orders of the Major-General Commanding the Eastern Department, the undersigned assumes command of the United States troops in this City.

Lieut.-Col. FROTHINGHAM and Capt. REWELLE are of the Staff of the undersigned, and will be obeyed accordingly.

HARVEY BROWN, Brig.-Gen. Commanding.

TWENTY-SECOND REGIMENT N. G. S. N. Y.—All members of the Twenty-second regiment are requested to meet at the Segiment Armory, this morning, at 8 o'clock.

BOARD OF ALDERMEN.

The Conscription Act and the Riot—Alderman Farley's Opinion of both—Alderman Hall's Plan to Relieve Poor Conscripts.

The Board of Aldermen met by special call at 1½ o'clock yesterday afternoon, "to take action in such business as might come before them." The call was signed at about 9 o'clock in the morning, before the riot up town had begun, and the real object of the meeting was to authorize the Corporation Counsel to associate such eminent counsel with him as he might choose, and take steps to test the constitutionality of the National Enrollment Act, under which the draft is being made. Alderman FARLEY was the prime mover in the matter. The whole plan failed, however, for want of a quorum. A quorum failed to appear because of the excited state of feeling in the community, consequent upon the riot up town. It was at first designed to carry out Alderman FARLEY's idea, but the excitement that soon became alarming in the streets, led several of the Democratic members to the conclusion that it would be impolitic to take any action on the subject of the draft till quiet should be restored. Hence, when the Board met, only five members answered to their names—Messrs. HENRY, REED, JEREMIAH, HARDY and FARLEY.

Alderman JEREMIAH was called to the Chair, to fill the place of President WALSH. The roll being called and a quorum not appearing, the Chair asked the pleasure of the Board. Alderman FARLEY arose and said:

ALDERMAN FARLEY'S SPEECH.

Alderman FARLEY—Mr. President, I much regret that there is not a quorum present. I had hoped that the Board would be able to take some action to-day in regard to the General Government act for making a draft. In my district, I understand, the officers engaged in making the draft have been driven from their duty, and a serious riot is in progress. I regret that a disturbance of the kind should be initiated in the City in my district, because the people there will be wrongly charged with the responsibility of it. But the fault is not theirs, for they are as orderly and law-abiding as any community in the whole country. The persons creating the riot, and who are responsible for its consequences, came from New-Jersey. They crossed the river this morning from Weehawken and Guttenberg in crowds and proceeded to the place in the Ninth Congressional District, where the draft was in progress. They marched along the streets in a body, and on their way they forced workmen wherever they could from their labors to join them in resistance to the draft. You can, therefore, understand, Mr. President, that the fault of opposition to the draft, originating in my district, was wholly owing to the fact that the enforcement of the Conscription act was begun there. To this fact alone may be attributed the unfortunate circumstance of the first open opposition to the law being shown in my district. The persons who incited the trouble no doubt had been organized for the occasion, and a riot would have been set on foot by them in any other locality in the city, had the enforcement of the draft been first attempted elsewhere than in the district I have the honor to represent in this Board. I must repeat my regret at the absence of a quorum of this Board, for I had hoped that every member would rise in his seat and talk peace. The people are excited, and it is necessary that their excitement should be calmed down to a degree of respect for enacted laws. Then let them resort to the Courts to decide their grievances. The impression is strong that the Drafting act is unconstitutional, and until the question of its legality is decided by the proper judicial tribunals, they will regard any attempted enforcement of it as harsh and arbitrary. We should, therefore, talk and counsel peace, and quiet and aid the people to ascertain whether the law, which is so generally regarded as offensive and undemocratic, is in legal harmony with the fundamental law of our organization as a nation and Government. I suppose the question could be reached by any conscript getting out a writ of *habeas corpus*. I have a paper in my hand proposing a method whereby we should speedily test the question of the legality of the law. I had designed to offer it at this meeting, but it is of no use now. I hope, however, that every member of this Board will preach up peace. Let it be understood that the citizens of New-York are for law and order, and in favor of a just test of every measure that is obnoxious to them. The event of the riot to-day is unfortunate, because it will affect the reputation of the city, and possibly be a pretext for a declaration of martial law here. It affords the excuse probably desired by the Administration, for supplanting the civil by the military law in this Democratic City. The enactments of Congress and the acts of the Administration are already sufficiently burdensome to us, without recourse to such a sweeping assumption of authority as that. But we cannot say to what extent our rights [illegible] may be interfered with. Perhaps those in a position [illegible] to seize upon such an authority would be only too glad to have some sort of pretended excuse for prohibiting us from meeting here.

Adjourned.

No other remarks were made, and the President *pro tem.* declared the Board adjourned for want of a quorum, till the first Monday in August.

The paper to which Alderman FARLEY referred contained the following preamble and resolutions.

Whereas, It is apparent to all who are in any way conversant with the feelings and opinions of the population of this City, that a deep-seated and irradicable opposition pervades all classes against the provisions of the act of the late Congress of the United States, known as the "Conscription act;" and

Whereas, It is equally apparent that such opposition is taking form and shape, and will manifest itself at an early day in open armed resistance to the attempt of the authorities of the General Government to force citizens of this State, against their convictions and against their will, out of the limits or jurisdiction of their State; and

Whereas, The mutterings of the coming storm imperatively demand that the authorities of this City should take some steps to allay the excitement now daily and hourly increasing, and by mild and salutary measures to assist in abating the popular indignation against the manifest injustice about to be inflicted upon our citizens, consequent upon an enforcement of the provisions of the aforesaid act of Congress: be it therefore

Resolved, That the Counsel to the Corporation be and he is hereby authorized and directed immediately to take the necessary legal measures to test the legality of the act of the late Congress of the United States, known as the "Conscription Act," with reference to its application to this State.

Had it not been understood beforehand that there would in all probability be no quorum, Alderman HALL would have been on hand to offer the following as a substitute for Alderman FARLEY's paper:

Whereas, It is apparent that the three hundred-dollar clause in the National Enrollment act of the late Congress is calculated to inflict great privations upon the poorer classes of our citizens; therefore, be it

Resolved, That the Committee on National Affairs be and they are hereby instructed to report to this Board a plan whereby an appropriation can be made to pay the commutation of such of our poorest citizens as are likely to be most sorely affected by the enforcement of a conscription.

This plan was submitted by Alderman HALL to several of the Democratic members, and all who were consulted about it unhesitatingly declared themselves favorable to it.

It is not improbable that the Board will hold a meeting at an early day to consider it.

The Draft in the Eighth Congressional District, New-York City.

In the Eighth Congressional District, comprising the Eighteenth, Twentieth and Twenty-first Wards, the draft was yesterday morning commenced under the direction of Hon. R. F. MANIERRE, Assistant Provost-Marshal, at the headquarters, No. 1,190 Broadway. This is about the largest Congressional District in the City, and the number of names to be drawn will exceed 3,600.

The building was filled to its utmost capacity, except the space occupied by the Commissioners, and [illegible] the reporters [illegible] police force. [illegible] the outside [illegible] of the building [illegible] off with the [illegible]

[Continued on Eighth Page.]

The New-York Times.

VOL. XIV.....NO. 4230. NEW-YORK, SATURDAY, APRIL 15, 1865. PRICE FOUR CENTS

AWFUL EVENT.

President Lincoln Shot by an Assassin.

The Deed Done at Ford's Theatre Last Night.

THE ACT OF A DESPERATE REBEL

The President Still Alive at Last Accounts.

No Hopes Entertained of His Recovery.

Attempted Assassination of Secretary Seward.

DETAILS OF THE DREADFUL TRAGEDY.

[OFFICIAL.]

WAR DEPARTMENT, WASHINGTON, April 15—1:30 A. M.

Maj.-Gen. Dix:

This evening at about 9:30 P. M., at Ford's Theatre, the President, while sitting in his private box with Mrs. LINCOLN, Mrs. HARRIS, and Major RATHBURN, was shot by an assassin, who suddenly entered the box and approached behind the President.

The assassin then leaped upon the stage, brandishing a large dagger or knife, and made his escape in the rear of the theatre.

The pistol ball entered the back of the President's head and penetrated nearly through the head. The wound is mortal. The President has been insensible ever since it was inflicted, and is now dying.

About the same hour an assassin, whether the same or not, entered Mr. SEWARD's apartments, and under pretence of having a prescription, was shown to the Secretary's sick chamber. The assassin immediately rushed to the bed, and inflicted two or three stabs on the throat and two on the face. It is hoped the wounds may not be mortal. My apprehension is that they will prove fatal.

The nurse alarmed Mr. FREDERICK SEWARD, who was in an adjoining room, and hastened to the door of his father's room, when he met the assassin, who inflicted upon him one or more dangerous wounds. The recovery of FREDERICK SEWARD is doubtful.

It is not probable that the President will live through the night.

Gen. GRANT and wife were advertised to be at the theatre this evening, but he started to Burlington at 6 o'clock this evening.

At a Cabinet meeting at which Gen. GRANT was present, the subject of the state of the country and the prospect of a speedy peace was discussed. The President was very cheerful and hopeful, and spoke very kindly of Gen. LEE and others of the Confederacy, and of the establishment of government in Virginia.

All the members of the Cabinet except Mr. SEWARD, are now in attendance upon the President.

I have seen Mr. SEWARD, but he and FREDERICK were both unconscious.

EDWIN M. STANTON, Secretary of War.

DETAILS OF THE OCCURRENCE.

WASHINGTON, Friday, April 14—12:30 P. M.

President LINCOLN and wife, with other friends, this evening visited Ford's Theatre for the purpose of witnessing the performance of the "American Cousin."

It was announced in the papers that Gen. GRANT would also be present, but that gentleman took the late train of cars for New Jersey.

The theatre was densely crowded, and everybody seemed delighted with the scene before them. During the third act, and while there was a temporary pause for one of the actors to enter, a sharp report of a pistol was heard, which merely attracted attention, but suggested nothing serious until a man rushed to the front of the President's box, waving a long dagger in his right hand, and exclaiming "*Sic semper tyrannis,*" and immediately leaped from the box, which was in the second tier, to the stage beneath, and ran across to the opposite side, making his escape amid the bewilderment of the audience from the rear of the theatre, and, mounting a horse, fled.

The screams of Mrs. LINCOLN first disclosed the fact to the audience that the President had been shot, when all present rose to their feet, rushing toward the stage, many exclaiming "Hang him! hang him!"

The excitement was of the wildest possible description, and of course there was an abrupt termination of the theatrical performance.

There was a rush toward the President's box, when cries were heard: "Stand back and give him air." "Has any one stimulants." On a hasty examination, it was found that the President had been shot through the head, above and back of the temporal bone, and that some of the brain was oozing out. He was removed to a private house opposite to the theatre, and the Surgeon-General of the army, and other surgeons sent for to attend to his condition.

On an examination of the private box blood was discovered on the back of the cushioned rocking chair on which the President had been sitting, also on the partition and on the floor. A common single-barreled pocket pistol was found on the carpet.

A military guard was placed in front of the private residence to which the President had been conveyed. An immense crowd was in front of it, all deeply anxious to learn the condition of the President. It had been previously announced that the wound was mortal; but all hoped otherwise. The shock to the community was terrible.

The President was in a state of syncope, totally insensible, and breathing slowly. The blood oozed from the wound at the back of his head. The surgeons exhausted every effort of medical skill, but all hope was gone. The parting of his family with the dying President is too sad for description.

At midnight, the Cabinet, with Messrs. SUMNER, COLFAX and FARNSWORTH, Judge CURTIS, Gov. OGLESBY, Gen. MEIGS, Col. HAY, and a few personal friends, with Surgeon-General BARNES and his immediate assistants, were around his bedside.

The President and Mrs. LINCOLN did not start for the theatre until fifteen minutes after eight o'clock. Speaker COLFAX was at the White House at the time, and the President stated to him that he was going, although Mrs. LINCOLN had not been well, because the papers had announced that Gen. GRANT and they were to be present, and, as Gen. GRANT had gone North, he did not wish the audience to be disappointed.

He went with apparent reluctance and urged Mr. COLFAX to go with him; but that gentleman had made other engagements, and with Mr. ASHMUN, of Massachusetts, bid him good bye.

When the excitement at the theatre was at its wildest height, reports were circulated that Secretary SEWARD had also been assassinated.

On reaching this gentleman's residence a crowd and a military guard were found at the door, and on entering it was ascertained that the reports were based on truth.

Everybody there was so excited that scarcely an intelligible word could be gathered, but the facts are substantially as follows:

About 10 o'clock a man rang the bell, and the call having been answered by a colored servant, he said he had come from Dr. VERDI, Secretary SEWARD's family physician, with a prescription, at the same time holding in his hand a small piece of folded paper, and saying in answer to a refusal that he must see the Secretary, as he was entrusted with particular directions concerning the medicine.

He still insisted on going up, although repeatedly informed that no one could enter the chamber. The man pushed the servant aside, and walked heavily toward the Secretary's room, and was then met by Mr. FREDERICK SEWARD, of whom he demanded to see the Secretary, making the same representation which he did to the servant. What further passed in the way of colloquy is not known, but the man struck him on the head with a "billy," severely injuring the skull and felling him almost senseless. The assassin then rushed into the chamber and attacked Major SEWARD, Paymaster United States army and Mr. HANSELL, a messenger of the State Department and two male nurses, disabling them all, he then rushed upon the Secretary, who was lying in bed in the same room, and inflicted three stabs in the neck, but severing, it is thought and hoped, no arteries, though he bled profusely.

The assassin then rushed down stairs, mounted his horse at the door, and rode off before an alarm could be sounded, and in the same manner as the assassin of the President.

It is believed that the injuries of the Secretary are not fatal, nor those of either of the others, although both the Secretary and the Assistant Secretary are very seriously injured.

Secretaries STANTON and WELLES, and other prominent officers of the government, called at Secretary SEWARD's house to inquire into his condition, and there heard of the assassination of the President.

They then proceeded to the house where he was lying, exhibiting of course intense anxiety and solicitude. An immense crowd was gathered in front of the President's house, and a strong guard was also stationed there, many persons evidently supposing he would be brought to his home.

The entire city to-night presents a scene of wild excitement, accompanied by violent expressions of indignation, and the profoundest sorrow—many shed tears. The military authorities have dispatched mounted patrols in every direction, in order, if possible, to arrest the assassins. The whole metropolitan police are likewise vigilant for the same purpose.

The attacks. both at the theatre and at Secretary SEWARD's house, took place at about the same hour—10 o'clock—thus showing a preconcerted plan to assassinate those gentlemen. Some evidence of the guilt of the party who attacked the President are in the possession of the police.

Vice-President JOHNSON is in the city, and his headquarters are guarded by troops.

ANOTHER ACCOUNT.

though every body supposes them to have been rebels.

SATURDAY MORNING—1 O'CLOCK.

The person who shot the President is represented as about 30 years of age, five feet nine inches in height, sparely built, of light complexion, dressed in dark clothing, and having a genteel appearance. He entered the box, which is known as the State box, being the upper box on the right hand side from the dress-circle in the regular manner, and shot the President from behind, the ball entering the skull about in the middle, behind, and going in the direction of the left eye; it did not pass through, but apparently broke the frontal bone and forced out the brain to some extent. The President is not yet dead, but is wholly insensible, and the Surgeon-General says he cannot live till day-break. The assassin was followed across the stage by a gentleman, who sprang out from an orchestra chair. He rushed through the side door into an alley, thence to the avenue and mounted a dark bay horse, which he apparently received from the hand of an accomplice, dashed up F, toward the back part of the city. The escape was so sudden that he effectually eluded pursuit. The assassin cried "*sic sempre*" in a sharp, clear voice, as he jumped to the stage, and dropped his hat and a glove.

Two or three officers were in the box with the President and Mrs. LINCOLN, who made efforts to stop the assassin, but were unsuccessful, and received some bruises. The whole affair, from his entrance into the box to his escape from the theatre, occupied scarcely a minute, and the strongest of the action found everybody wholly unprepared. The assault upon Mr. SEWARD appeares to have been made almost at the same moment as that upon the President. Mr. SEWARDS wound is not dangerous in itself, but may prove so in connection with his recent injuries. The two assassins have both endeavored to leave the city to the northwest, apparently not expecting to strike the river. Even so low down as Chain Bridge, cavalry have been sent in

EUROPEAN NEWS.

TWO DAYS LATER BY THE EUROPA.

The Insult to Our Cruisers by Portugal.

The American Minister at Lisbon Demands Satisfaction.

Dismissal of the Commander of Fort Belan Requested.

Further Advance in Five-Twenties.

FINANCIAL AND COMMERCIAL.

HALIFAX, Friday, April 14.

The steamship *Europa*, from Liverpool on the 1st, via Queenstown on the 2d inst., arrived here at 2 o'clock this morning. She has 43 passengers for this port, and 30 for Boston. Her dates are two days later than those already received.

The steamship *Cuba*, from New-York, arrived at Liverpool at noon on the 1st inst.

THE STONEWALL AFFAIR.

A Lisbon dispatch, of the 31st of March, says that the American Minister at Lisbon has demanded satisfaction of the Portuguese Government for the firing upon the *Niagara* and *Sacramento* by the Portuguese forts. He also requests the dismissal of the Commander of Fort Belan, and a salute of twenty-one guns to the American flag.

Nothing as yet has been decided in regard to the matter.

A PROPHECY FROM RICHMOND.

The correspondent of the London *Times*, writing from Richmond on the 4th of March, says:

"I am daily more convinced that if Richmond falls and LEE and JOHNSTON are driven from the field, it is but the first stage of this colossal revolution which will then be completed. There will ensue a time when every important town of the South will require to be held by a Yankee garrison, when exultation in New-York will be exchanged for soberness and right reason, and when it will be realized that the closing scenes of this mightiest revolutionary drama will not be played out, save in the times of our children's children."

GREAT BRITAIN.

Parliamentary proceedings on the 30th ult. were unimportant.

In the House of Commons, on the 31st, Lord C. PAGET said that the Admiralty had received no proposal for sanctioning or supporting any fresh attempt to reach the North Pole. He was, therefore, unable to say what course the government would take if such a proposal were made.

Mr. NEWDEGATE put some questions as to the idea of the Pope taking up his residence in England, as

omize, but must maintain the position of Austria as a great Power.

INDIA.

A private Calcutta telegram of March 27 reports commercial affairs in much the same state as on the 25th, when slight improvement had taken place.

BRAZIL.

LONDON, Sunday, April 2.

The Brazilian mail has reached Lisbon, bringing the following dates:

RIO DE JANEIRO, Saturday, March 11.

Exchange 25⅝@26¼.

COFFEE.—Sales of good firsts at 65@66. Shipments 100,000 bags. Stock, 100,000 bags. Freights 50@62½.

BAHIA, Saturday, March 11.

Exchange 26¼.

Cotton nominal.

PERNAMBUCO, Saturday, March 11.

Exchange 26⅝@27.

Montivedeo has surrendered to Gen. FLORES. The Brazilians now occupy the city.

LATEST VIA LIVERPOOL.

LIVERPOOL, Saturday Evening, April 1, 1865.

The *Times* to-day has an editorial on the amended tariff law of the United States. It says:

"It is impossible to find an excuse for it. Tried by the light of reason or by the results of experience it is alike condemned."

It ironically credits the framers of the scheme with peculiar wisdom in selecting the 1st of April for its inauguration.

The *Army & Navy Gazette* says: "The work of the United States Navy has now been accomplished, and it must be confessed that in the hands of FARRAGUT and PORTER the high reputation which the officers and seamen of that Power established soon after the national existence of itself, has been greatly enhanced."

LATEST VIA QUEENSTOWN.

LONDON, Saturday, April 1.

There is no news of importance this morning.

PARIS, Friday, March 31—P. M.

The Bourse is steady. The Rentes closed at 67f. 30c.

COMMERCIAL.

LIVERPOOL MARKET.

LIVERPOOL, April 31.—Evening.

The Market report was received per *Moravian*.

COTTON—The stock of Cotton in port is 580,000 bales by actual count, being 13,000 bales below the estimates, of which amount 48,000 bales are American.

TRADE REPORT.

The Manchester market was firmer with an upward tendency.

BREADSTUFFS—The market is easier. Messrs. RICHARDSON, SPENCE & Co., and others, report: Flour dull and easier. Wheat quiet and quotations are barely maintained; red Western 8s.@8s. 8d. Corn inactive; mixed 27s. 6d.

PROVISIONS—The market is downward. WAKEFIELD, NASH & Co., and others, report: Beef has a downward tendency. Pork heavy and declined 2s. 6d. Bacon firmer and holders demand an advance. Lard dull and easier at 58s.@61s. Butter flat and declining. Tallow downward.

PRODUCE.—Ashes easier at 28s. 6d. for Pots, and 30s. for Pearls. Sugar, flat. Coffee, quiet and steady. Rice, quiet and steady. Clover Seed, firmer. Jute, 10s.@30s. lower. Cod Oil, quiet at 57s. Sperm Oil, no sales. Linseed Oil, steady. Resin, very dull. Spirits Turpentine, quiet at 65s.@66s.

PETROLEUM—BOULT, ENGLISH & BRANDON report: Petroleum firm, at 1s. 11d.@2s. for refined; no crude in market.

LONDON MARKETS.

FLOUR firm; WHEAT steady. IRON advancing; bars and rails, £6 10s.@£6 15s.; Scotch pig, 52s. 3d. SUGAR inactive. COFFEE active at a decline of 1s.@2s. TEA steady at 10½d. for common Congou. RICE steady. SPIRITS TURPENTINE firm at 67s. PETROLEUM steady at £18 for crude, 2s. for refined. SPERM OIL nominal at £82. TALLOW downward, at 40s @43s. LINSEED OIL flat.

LATEST COMMERCIAL

The New-York Times.

VOL. XIV......NO. 4225. NEW-YORK, MONDAY, APRIL 10, 1865. PRICE FOUR CENTS

HANG OUT YOUR BANNERS

UNION

VICTORY!

PEACE!

Surrender of General Lee and His Whole Army.

THE WORK OF PALM SUNDAY.

Final Triumph of the Army of the Potomac.

The Strategy and Diplomacy of Lieut.-Gen. Grant.

Terms and Conditions of the

the Richmond and Lynchburgh road to the Farmville and Lynchburgh road, I am at this writing about four miles West of Walter's church, and will push forward to the front for the purpose of meeting you.

Notice sent to me, on this road, where you wish the interview to take place, will meet me.

Very respectfully, your ob'd't servant,
U. S. GRANT,
Lieutenant-General.

APPOMATTOX COURT-HOUSE, April 9, 1865.

General R. E. Lee, Commanding C. S. A.:

In accordance with the substance of my letters to you of the 8th inst., I propose to receive the surrender of the Army of Northern Virginia on the following terms, to wit:

Rolls of all the officers and men to be made in duplicate, one copy to be given to an officer designated by me, the other to be retained by such officers as you may designate.

The officers to give their individual paroles not to take arms against the Government of the United States until properly exchanged, and each company or regimental commander sign a like parole for the men of their commands.

The arms, artillery and public property to be packed and stacked and turned over to the officers appointed by me to receive them.

This will not embrace the side-arms of the officers, nor their private horses or baggage.

This done, EACH OFFICER AND MAN WILL BE ALLOWED TO RETURN TO THEIR HOMES, not to be disturbed by United States authority so long as they observe their parole and the laws in force where they reside.

Very respectfully,
U. S. GRANT, Lieutenant-General.

HEADQUARTERS ARMY OF NORTHERN VIRGINIA, April 9, 1865.

Lieut.-Gen. U. S. Grant, Commanding U. S. A.:

GENERAL: I have received your letter of this date, CONTAINING THE TERMS OF SURRENDER OF THE ARMY OF NORTHERN VIRGINIA, as proposed by you. As they are substantially the same as those expressed in your letter of the 8th inst., THEY ARE ACCEPTED. I will proceed to designate the proper officers to carry the stipulations into effect. [sic: continues] pose of arranging definitely the terms upon which the surrender of the Army of Northern Virginia will be received.

Very respectfully, your obedient servant,
U. S. GRANT, Lieut.-General,
Commanding armies of the United States.

April 8, 1865.

GENERAL: I received, at a late hour, your note of to-day, in answer to mine of yesterday.

I did not intend to propose the surrender of the Army of Northern Virginia, but *to ask the terms* of your proposition. To be frank, I do not think the emergency has arisen to call for the surrender.

But as *the restoration of peace should be the sole object of all*, I desire to know whether your proposals would tend to that end.

I cannot, therefore, meet you with a view to surrender the Army of Northern Virginia, but *as far as your proposition may affect the Confederate States forces under my command, and tend to the restoration of peace*, I should be pleased to meet you at 10 A. M., to-morrow, on the old stage road to Richmond, between the picket lines of the two armies.

Very respectfully, your obedient servant,
R. E. LEE,
General, C. S. A.

To Lieut.-Gen. GRANT, Commanding Armies of the United States.

APRIL 9, 1865.

General R. E. Lee, commanding C. S. A.:

GENERAL: Your note of yesterday is received. As I have no authority to treat on the subject of peace, the meeting proposed for 10 A. M. to-day could lead to no good. I will state, however, General, that *I am equally anxious for peace with yourself*; and the whole North entertain the same feeling. *The terms upon which peace can be had are well understood. By the South laying down their arms, they will hasten that most desirable event, save thousands of human lives, and hundreds of millions of property not yet destroyed.*

Sincerely hoping that all our difficulties may be settled *without the loss of another life*, I subscribe myself,

Very respectfully,
Your obedient servant,
U. S. GRANT,
Lieutenant-General United States Army.

REJOICINGS.

WILMINGTON, Del., Sunday, April 9.

Wilmington is in an uproar and blaze of glory, rejoicing over the greatest of victories yet achieved

THE VICTORY.

Thanks to God, the Giver of Victory.

Honors to Gen. Grant and His Gallant Army.

A NATIONAL SALUTE ORDERED.

Two Hundred Guns to be Fired at the Headquarters of Every Army, Department, Post and Arsenal.

[OFFICIAL.]

WAR DEPARTMENT, WASHINGTON, D. C., April 9, 1865—9:30 P. M.

Lieut.-Gen. Grant:

Thanks be to Almighty God for the great victory with which he has this day crowned you and the gallant armies under your command.

The thanks of this Department and of the Government, and of the People of the United States—their reverence and honor have been deserved—will be rendered to you and the brave and gallant officers and soldiers of your army for all time.

EDWIN M. STANTON, Secretary of War.

WAR DEPARTMENT, WASHINGTON, D. C., April 9, 1865—10 o'clock P. M.

Ordered: That a salute of two hundred guns be fired at the headquarters of every army and department, and at every post and arsenal in the United States, and at the Military Academy at West Point on the day of the receipt of this order, in commemoration of the surrender of Gen. ROBERT E. LEE and the Army of Northern Virginia to Lieut.-Gen. GRANT and the army under his command. Report of the receipt and execution of this order to be made to the Adjutant-General at Washington.

EDWIN M. STANTON,
Secretary of War.

FROM RICHMOND.

Perils and Excitements of a Voyage Up the James—Scenes and Incidents Along the River.

From Our Own Correspondent.

RICHMOND, Va., Wednesday, April 5.

The inspiration of the scene and the scope of the which greets the vision is a gaily dressed tug, with a guard of marines, having in tow Admiral PORTER's barge with the President, on his return from Richmond, complacently seated in the stern sheets. It looks very much like a pic-nic. Following a short distance after is the President's handsome flag-ship, the *River Queen*. Not far behind is the beautiful steel gunboat *Bat*, ex-blockade runner, now general convoy to distinguished guests, and one of the fastest vessels in the navy. The *River Queen*, which took the President up the river, proceeded no farther than the obstructions at Drewry's Bluff. We are soon abreast of this historic fortification, and eager eyes scan closely its formidable walls and positions.

Here is the chief line of obstructions sunk by the rebels early in the war, and located as they are, directly under the guns of Fort Darling, subjecting every approaching thing to a terrible plunging fire, it is readily admitted that this was the impassable barrier to the naval advance on Richmond. The river here is very narrow, and the movement of large vessels attended with much danger. The obstructions were placed directly across the river, and filled it completely with the exception of a gap of fifty or sixty feet, left for the passage of the rebel fleet and flag-of-truce boats. They consist of the hulls of two or three old steamships, that formerly plyed between Richmond and New York. The wheel-houses, fast crumbling to decay, still rise above the water, and present the appearance of a melancholy ruin.

We pass so hurriedly under the guns of Fort Darling, that we have no good opportunity to observe its construction. We know it looks very strong, and on the north side it has one or two small outlying works on its flank. Our naval companions tell us that it is a casemated fortification, and with its surrounding field works, all parts of the fort itself, mounts not less than forty guns. All these, like hundreds more, are our trophies without blemish or injury.

Not far above Fort Darling lies the wreck of one of the famous rebel fleet in the James, the iron-clad *Virginia*. Whether she has been blown up or simply scuttled and sunk, cannot be ascertained from looking at her as she lies. She sank in deep water, and is careened over on her side, leaving a portion of her overhang visible above the water-line. Of the other iron-clad, the *Richmond*, we find no trace.

In the immediate vicinity of Fort Darling we pass through a very substantial bridge with a draw, used by LEE for the speedy transfer of troops from the north to the south side of the James. Ere reaching Richmond we pass two more of the same kind, though hardly so well built as the first; but all demonstrating that LEE had no pontoon bridges across the James anywhere—probably, because the rapid current rendered them unsafe, and probably, too, because he had not any pontoons to spare, when something else would answer just as well.

We have now steamed safely by all obstructions and chances of torpedoes, and the very pardonable trepidation which we felt in view of our possible danger, gives way to a feeling that just now is a moment in our lives, the significance, importance and sublimity of which cannot be justly appreciated. The City of Richmond is in view. The spires pointing heavenward; the smoke still rising from the conflagration's awful ruin, and the Stars and Stripes floating from a hundred house-tops and mastheads, all form a picture so sublimely grand and inspiring, that the human mind is simply lost in mute contemplation.

In a few moments we land at the Rockets, and a brisk walk of a mile and a half brings us to the

ances, while the Union guard outside seemed to richly enjoy the transition that the famous building had undergone, evidently having been there himself. The whirligig of time makes all things even, and the thousands of loyal officers and soldiers who have suffered the tortures and horrors of these dungeons may now contemplate their present uses with serene satisfaction, and yet without resentment.

A close inspection of Castle Thunder reveals one of the most hideous dungeons that can be conceived. We failed to see it, however, in all its filth and nastyness, for a strong force of men had been engaged two days in carrying out the accumulation of the past three years. The corporal of the guard who conducted us through, pointed out a spot on the floor on one of the main halls, not yet cleaned, where the dirt was three inches thick, and alive with vermin, *and yet on this floor, in this condition, prisoners were obliged to sleep either upon the dirt itself or upon palets of decaying straw.*

But I will not descant further upon this vile relic of the rebellion. Its career is too well known. The prisoners confined here, it will be recollected, were those against whom special vengeance was directed, prisoners of State, persons charged with harboring Union prisoners, Union officers charged with being spies, blockade-runners, &c. Well has it been said that a confinement in Castle Thunder is a foretaste of the tortures of the damned.

This building, together with the Libby belongs to the estate of JOHN ENDERS, and was leased by the rebel Government. They were originally built for stores, but subsequently turned into tabacco manufactories. But their base uses are now at an end.

This is the fourth day of the Union occupation, and the confusion in the city necessarily attendant upon such an evacuation, and such an occupation, is gradually subsiding. Could the ruins of the fire be removed from sight, Richmond would present an attractive appearance, for it is really a handsome city; but, after all, the saddest scenes are at the headquarters of the Provost-Martial, the Commissioners of Subsistence, and the office of Sanitary Commission, the latter being already established here. Gen. WEITZEL had no sooner established his headquarters here than thousands of citizens besieged him for rations. And as the city is now shut out from all supplies from the country, the crowd of applicants for subsistence is rapidly increasing. This morning there was nothing in the markets but a few small fish caught by negroes. The Capitol, the City Hall and the Capitol-square are filled with a great throng of all classes, condition, sexes and ages, with basket in hand and an appealing expression of face. What the regulations yet are in regard to the issue of rations to the citizens, I do not know, but a limited quantity is being supplied them at present.

In order to study this peculiar social feature of the rebellion, I mingled with these crowds this morning for a short time, to observe their temper, desires and condition. They were, of course, largely made up of what appeared to be the poorer classes, and many negroes were among them, some for subsistence for themselves and some as servants of families. I found many whose intelligent expression of countenance, fair features and attempted gentility of dress, indicated that they were of the higher classes, on whom the demands of want and hunger were as insatiable as upon those of less position. I noticed several ladies approach the officer in charge at the City Hall, genteelly attired, and with their faces so closely veiled as to defy the gaze of the keenest eye. They spoke in such tremulous

and is now dying.

About the same hour an assassin, whether the same or not, entered Mr. SEWARD's apartments, and under the pretence of having a prescription, was shown to the Secretary's sick chamber. The assassin immediately rushed to the bed, and inflicted two or three stabs on the throat and two on the face. It is hoped the wounds may not be mortal. My apprehension is that they will prove fatal.

The nurse alarmed Mr. FREDERICK SEWARD, who was in an adjoining room, and hastened to the door of his father's room, when he met the assassin, who inflicted upon him one or more dangerous wounds. The recovery of FREDERICK SEWARD is doubtful.

It is not probable that the President will live throughout the night.

Gen. GRANT and wife were advertised to be at the theatre this evening, but he started to Burlington at 6 o'clock this evening.

At a Cabinet meeting at which Gen. GRANT was present, the subject of the state of the country and the prospect of a speedy peace was discussed. The President was very cheerful and hopeful, and spoke very kindly of Gen. LEE and others of the Confederacy, and of the establishment of government in Virginia.

All the members of the Cabinet except Mr. SEWARD, are now in attendance upon the President.

I have seen Mr. SEWARD, but he and FREDERICK were both unconscious.

EDWIN M. STANTON,
Secretary of War.

DETAIL OF THE OCCURRENCE.

WASHINGTON, Friday, April 14—12:30 A. M.

The President was shot in a theatre to-night, and is, perhaps, mortally wounded.

Secretary SEWARD was also assassinated.

SECOND DISPATCH.

WASHINGTON, Friday, April 14.

President LINCOLN and wife, with other friends, this evening visited Ford's Theatre for the purpose of witnessing the performance of the "American Cousin."

It was announced in the papers that Gen. GRANT would also be present, but he took the late train of cars for New-Jersey.

The theatre was densely crowded, and everybody seemed delighted with the scene before them. During the third act, and while there was a temporary pause for one of the actors to enter, a sharp report of a pistol was heard, which merely attracted attention, but suggesting nothing serious, until a man rushed to the front of the President's box, waving a long dagger in his right hand, and exclaiming "Sic semper tyrannis," ...

SUMNER, COLFAX and FARNSWORTH, Judge CURTIS, Gov. OGLESBY, Gen. MEIGS, Col. HAY, and a few personal friends, with Surgeon-General BARNES and his immediate assistants, were around his bedside.

The President and Mrs. LINCOLN did not start for the theatre until fifteen minutes after eight o'clock. Speaker COLFAX was at the White House at the time, and the President stated to him that he was going, although Mrs. LINCOLN had not been well, because the papers had announced that Gen. GRANT and they were to be present, and, as Gen. GRANT had gone North, he did not wish the audience to be disappointed.

He went with apparent reluctance and urged Mr. COLFAX to go with him; but that gentleman had made other engagements, and with Mr. ASHMAN, of Massachusetts, bid him good bye.

When the excitement at the theatre was at its wildest height, reports were circulated that Secretary SEWARD had also been assassinated.

On reaching this gentleman's residence a crowd and a military guard were found at the door, and on entering it was ascertained that the reports were based on truth.

Everybody there was so excited that scarcely an intelligible word could be gathered, but the facts are substantially as follows

About 10 o'clock a man rang the bell, and the call having been answered by a colored servant, he said he had come from Dr. VERDI, Secretary SEWARD's family physician, with a prescription, at the same time holding in his hand a small piece of folded paper, and saying in answer to a refusal that he must see the Secretary, as he was entrusted with particular directions concerning the medicine.

He still insisted on going up, although repeatedly informed that no one could enter the chamber. The man pushed the servant aside, and walked heavily toward the Secretary's room, and was then met by Mr. FREDERICK SEWARD, of whom he demanded to see the Secretary, making the same representation which he did to the servant. What further passed in the way of colloquy is not known, but the man struck him on the head with a "billy," severely injuring the skull and felling him almost senseless. The assassin then rushed into the chamber and attacked Major SEWARD, Paymaster of the United States army and Mr. HANSELL, a messenger of the State

WASHINGTON, Friday, April 14, 11:15 P. M.

A stroke from Heaven laying the whole of the city in instant ruins could not have startled us as did the word that broke from Ford's Theatre a half hour ago that the President had been shot. It flew everywhere in five minutes, and set five thousand people in swift and excited motion on the instant.

It is impossible to get at the full facts of the case, but it appears that a young man entered the President's box from the theatre, during the last act of the play of "Our American Cousin," with pistol in hand. He shot the President in the head and instantly jumped from the box upon the stage, and immediately disappeared through the side scenes and rear of the theatre, brandishing a dirk knife and dropping a kid glove on the stage.

The audience heard the shot, but supposing it fired in the regular course of the play, did not heed it till Mrs. LINCOLN's screams drew their attention. The whole affair occupied scarcely half a minute, and then the assassin was gone. As yet he has not been found.

The President's wound is reported mortal. He was at once taken into the house opposite the theatre.

As if this horror was not enough, almost the same moment the story ran through the city that Mr. SEWARD had been murdered in his bed.

Inquiry showed this to be so far true also. It appears a man wearing a light coat, dark pants, slouch hat, called and asked to see Mr. SEWARD, and was shown to his room. He delivered to Major SEWARD, who sat near his father, what purported to be a physician's prescription, turned, and with one stroke cut Mr. SEWARD's throat as he lay on his bed, inflicting a horrible wound, but not severing the jugular vein, and not producing a mortal wound.

In the struggle that followed, Major SEWARD was also badly, but not seriously, wounded in several places. The assassin rushed down stairs, mounted the fleet horse on which he came, drove his spurs into him, and dashed away before any one could stop him.

Reports have prevailed that an attempt was also made on the life of Mr. STANTON.

MIDNIGHT.

The President is reported dead. Cavalry and infantry are scouring the city in every direction for the murderous assassins, and the city is overwhelmed with excitement. Who the assassins were no one knows,

SATURDAY, 1:30 o'clock A. M.

The President still lies insensible. Messrs. STANTON, WELLS, McCULLOCH, SPEED and USHER are with him, as also the Vice-President, the Surgeon-General, and other Surgeons.

There is a great throng about the house, even at this hour.

2 o clock A. M.

The President still lives, but lies insensible, as he has since the first moment, and no hopes are entertained that he can survive.

The most extravagant stories prevail, among which one is to effect, that Gen. GRANT was shot while on his was to Philaphia, of course this is not true.

Another is, that every member of Mr. SEWARD's family was wounded in the struggle with the assassin there. This also is untrue. Mr. FRED. SEWARD, the Assistant Secretary, and Major CLARENCE SEWARD, of the army, were wounded, neither of them dangerously.

THE CONDITION OF THE PRESIDENT.

WASHINGTON, April 15—2:12 A. M.

The President is still alive; but he is growing weaker. The ball is lodged in his brain, three inches from where it entered the skull. He remains insensible, and his condition is utterly hopeless.

The Vice-President has been to see him; but all company, except the members of the Cabinet and of the family, is rigidly excluded.

Large crowds still continue in the street, as near to the house as the line of guards allows.

THE SIEGE OF MOBILE.

Fierce Bombardment of the Spanish Fort—Mobile Papers Announce the Capture of Selma.

NEW-ORLEANS, Saturday, April 8, via CAIRO, Friday, April 14.

A special dispatch to the New-Orleans *Times*, from the Spanish Fort, dated April 5, says:

"A furious fire was opened on the rebel forts last night from our entire line. During the bombardment a small magazine in the Spanish Fort exploded. The damage is unknown. Quiet prevailed on the 5th. Deserters report from 18,000 to 20,000 troops in and about Mobile, including all the State Reserves, and about 2,000 in the Spanish Fort. The loss outside the Spanish Fort up to the 4th instant amounted to about 500 killed and wounded. The rebel loss exceeds ours."

Adjt.-Gen. THOMAS arrived at New-Orleans on the morning of the 7th.

Mobile papers of the 4th inst. announce the capture of Selma, Alabama, with 23 pieces of artillery, and a large amount of Government property.

Fort Sumter Celebration in Bangor.

BANGOR, Me., Friday, April 14.

The restoration of the Old Flag to Fort Sumter was celebrated here to-day by a national salute at noon, by a display of all the flags on public and private buildings, and by the raising of the Stars and Strips one thousand feet above the city by means of a monster kite bearing the name of U. S. GRANT.

The Madrid *Bolsa* says if the Pope should leave Rome, Spain would confer upon him the Balearic Isles.

The *Politica* says the Pope would rather inhabit the Montpensier Palace at Seville.

Lord PALMERSTON replied that the government respected the Pope personally very much, but for him to come to England would be both an anachronism and a solecism.

The revenue returns for the financial year, ending March 31, show a net increase of over £104,000 on the year. *Notwithstanding the great reductions in taxation, the revenue exceeds by nearly half a million sterling the estimates of Mr. GLADSTONE.*

Messrs. BARING's circular says that large business has been done in 5-20 bonds, and that prices advanced early in the week to 57⅛@58, but have since relapsed to 56⅜@57—the demand being chiefly from the continent.

On Friday, the telegrams per the steamship *Cuba* were received, and 5 20s again advanced to 57¾@58¼. Erie and Illinois Central Shares have also attracted attention, and have again advanced.

The Bank of England on the 30th ult. reduced its rate of discount to 4 per cent., at which there is a fair demand for money. This movement strengthened the English funds, and Consols are buoyant and advancing.

KELSON, TRITTON & Co., East India and general merchants, have suspended payment. Their liabilities are estimated at £900,000 sterling.

Another provincial bank has suspended, the Portsmouth and South Hants Banking Company. Their liabilities are about £170,000 sterling.

The Birmingham and Joint Stock Banking Company had agreed to take up the business of Atwood & Spooner's Bank, which lately suspended at Birmingham, and to pay the creditors 11s. 3d. on the pound.

The West India Mail steamer had arrived, with over two and a quarter millions of dollars in specie. She also brought several Captains of blockade-runners, whose occupations were gone.

THE ATLANTIC TELEGRAPH.

The French Government will probably send one or two steamers to accompany the two that are sent by the English Government with the *Great Eastern* across the Atlantic, at the time of laying the Atlantic cable, and it is hoped that the United States Government will do the same.

FRANCE.

Weekly returns from the Bank of France show an increase of cash on hand of over ten and a half millions francs.

In the French Chambers of the 30th. M. JULES FAVRE spoke upon the necessity for political liberty, but was interrupted by the President and declined to finish his speech. The amendment was rejected.

The amendment in favor of the liberty of the press was debated, but rejected by a large majority.

It is stated that NAPOLEON will leave Paris early in May, not returning until November. His physicians have recommended seven months' absence in the country air.

The Bourse is firm, 67.45.

SPAIN.

The *Epoca* states that the Minister of War tendered his resignation, and that Gen. LEOBSUNDI refused to place him.

A later dispatch says the Minister of War resigned from ill health.

Gen. RIVERA succeeded to the office.

DENMARK.

The King relieved M. HELLEEN, Minister of Justice, of his functions. HELLEEN represented the alliance between the Reactionary and extreme Democratic parties. It is supposed that all members of the late Cabinet will return to their posts.

ITALY.

In the allocutions delivered at the last consistory the Pope expressed surprise and sorrow at the sad events which have recently taken place in Mexico. His Holiness hoped MAXIMILIAN would abandon the course upon which he had entered, and satisfy the just desires of the Holy See. The Pope further thanked the Bishops of the Catholic world, especially those of Italy, for defending the religion and liberties of the Church, despite the decrees of the secular authorities.

PRUSSIA.

In the Military Committee of Chambers, the Deputies amendment was introduced with the object of effecting a reconciliation between the government and chamber, and proposing a maximum strength of the army at 180,000 men, which was rejected by 11 to 8. The committee also rejected the general military estimates and navy estimates and amendments, thus refusing the whole military and naval proposals of the government.

AUSTRIA.

Count MENSDORFF had made some ministerial explanation in the Lower House Reichsrath. He said the views of the government on the question of the Duchies would be communicated in the Federal Diet on the 6th of April.

As regards relations with Italy, he said the government desired to promote the material interests of the two countries, but that Italy maintained a hostile attitude to the government. He desired to econ-

COTTON—Sales to-day 6,000 bales, including 2,000 bales to speculators and exporters. The market is less firm but quiet and unchanged.

BREADSTUFFS—The market is quiet and steady.

PROVISIONS—The market is dull.

PRODUCE—The market is quiet and steady. Petroleum firm at 2s.@2s. 0½d. for refined.

LONDON, Saturday, April 1—Evening.

CONSOLS closed at 89¾@90. for money.

AMERICAN STOCKS—Illinois Central Railroad 61¾@62¼; Erie Railroad 36⅛@36¾; United States Five-twenties 57⅜@58¼.

Gen. Lee in Richmond—The Oath of Allegiance.

BALTIMORE, Friday, April 14.

The Richmond *Whig* of yesterday contains little of importance. It announces the arrival of Gen. LEE on the night previous.

The *Whig* publishes the oath of allegiance, which it says citizens will be required to swear and subscribe to. The Provost-Marshal's office is crowded with people anxious to take it, and the only question among citizens seems to be who shall be first to renew their citizenship.

Rejoicings at Cincinnati.

CINCINNATI, Friday, April 14.

Business was entirely suspended to-day. The city was universally decorated with flags, and great enthusiasm prevailed. The procession was an immense affair, comprising the entire police force, Gens. HOOKER and WALLICH, with their staffs, four regiments of National Guards, discharged veterans, ward organizations, the Fenian Brotherhood, the Fire Department, and a large number of colored citizens. All the bells in the city were rung, and salutes were fired at 6 o,clock this evening. To-night the city is brilliantly illuminated, and there is generally a display of fireworks.

Fire.

ROCHESTER, N. Y., Friday, April 14.

The cabinet warehouse of JAMES E. HAYDON, of this city, was partially destroyed by fire this morning. The stocks of HUMPHREY REEDY & Co., stove dealers, HASTINGS & McVEAN, paper dealers, S. B. ROBY, saddlery and hardware dealers, and the agency of the American Tract Society, were damaged. Total loss, $30,000; insurance, $20,000. The origin of the fire is unknown.

The Funeral of Gen. T. A. Smyth.

WILMINGTON, Del., Friday, April 14.

The remains of Brig.-Gen. T. A. SMYTH arrived here to-day at 1 o'clock, and will be interred on Monday afternoon with appropriate ceremonies.

An Unseaworthy War Steamer.

To the Editor of the New-York Times:

UNITED STATES STEAMER MUSCOOTA, HAMPTON ROADS, Va., Wednesday, April 12, 1865.

This vessel has returned to this port, having made her fourth attempt to make a cruise to the Pacific. On each occasion she has proved herself to be an unsafe sea boat. On her last trial she narrowly escaped being lost in the Gulf Stream. Inclosed you will find a list of her officers; please publish. Respectfully, &c.,

ARTHUR BURTIS, Jr., Paymaster.

List of officers attached to the U. S. steamer *Muscoota*, one thousand tons, 10 guns:

Commander GEO. M. RANSOM, Lieut. Thos. S. Spencer, Ass't Paymaster Arthur Burtis, Jr., Ass't Surgeon Danl. McMurtrie, Act'g Master Geo. R. Durand, Act'g Ensigns Robt. M. Clark, Jas. Courtney, John D. Thomas, Chas. A. Stewart, Second Ass't Engineers Robert H. Gunnell, Jas. H. Grasmer, Henry Snyder. Act'g Third Ass't Engineers Robt. L. Case, Geo. Taylor, Geo. Westinghouse, Jr., Masters Fred'k. A. Beatie, A. L. Spinney, Wm. Merrill, Captain's Clerk Geo. S. Dana, Paymasters Clerk P. B. Hathaway.

Arrivals in the City.

Gov. Jos. A. Gilmore, Concord, N. H., is stopping at the Fifth-avenue Hotel.

Hon. O. N. Shannon, Cincinnati; Gen. B. F. Stringfellow, Atchison; Dr. N. Greene, Louisville, and Wm. D. Griswold, Terre Haute, are stopping at the Metropolitan Hotel.

COLLISION.—The steamship *La Favorete*, while returning from a trial trip and passing up the East River, collided with the Catharine Ferry-boat *Manhassett*, as she was entering her slip on the Brooklyn side, doing considerable damage to the *Manhassett*, by tearing away a portion of the gentlemen's cabin, and somewhat injuring the hull. Fortunately nobody was hurt.

The Rebel Arms, Artillery, and Public Property Surrendered.

Rebel Officers Retain Their Side Arms, and Private Property.

Officers and Men Paroled and Allowed to Return to Their Homes.

The Correspondence Between Grant and Lee.

OFFICIAL.

WAR DEPARTMENT, WASHINGTON, April 9, 1865—9 o'clock P. M.

To Maj.-Gen. Dix:

This department has received the official report of the SURRENDER, THIS DAY, OF GEN. LEE AND HIS ARMY TO LIEUT.-GEN. GRANT, on the terms proposed by Gen. GRANT.

Details will be given as speedily as possible.

EDWIN M. STANTON,
Secretary of War.

HEADQUARTERS ARMIES OF THE UNITED STATES, 4:30 P. M., April 9.

Hon. Edwin M. Stanton, Secretary of War:

GEN. LEE SURRENDERED THE ARMY OF NORTHERN VIRGINIA THIS AFTERNOON, upon the terms proposed by myself. The accompanying additional correspondence will show the conditions fully.

(Signed) U. S. GRANT, Lieut.-Gen'l.

SUNDAY, April 9, 1865.

GENERAL—I received your note of this morning, on the picket line, whither I had come to meet you and ascertain definitely what terms were embraced in your proposition of yesterday with reference to the surrender of this army.

I now request an interview in accordance with the offer contained in your letter of yesterday for that purpose.

Very respectfully, your obedient servant,
R. E. LEE, General.

To Lieut.-Gen. GRANT, Commanding United States Armies.

Sunday, April 9, 1865.

Gen. R. E. Lee, Commanding Confederate States Armies.

Your note of this date is but this moment, 11:50 A. M., received.

In consequence of my having passed from

lations into effect.

Very respectfully,
Your obedient servant,
R. E. LEE, General.

THE PRELIMINARY CORRESPONDENCE.

The following is the previous correspondence between Lieut.-Gen. GRANT and Gen. LEE, referred to in the foregoing telegram to the Secretary of War:

CLIFTON HOUSE, VA., April 9, 1865.

Hon. Edwin M. Stanton, Secretary of War:

The following correspondence has taken place between Gen. LEE and myself. *There has been no relaxation in the pursuit during its pendency.*

U. S. GRANT, Lieutenant-General.

APRIL 7, 1865.

Gen. R. E. Lee, Commanding C. S. A.:

GENERAL: The result of the last week must convince you of the hopelessness of further resistance on the part of the Army of Northern Virginia in this struggle. I feel that it is so and regard it as my duty to shift from myself the responsibility of any further effusion of blood, by asking of you the surrender of that portion of the Confederate States Army, known as the Army of Northern Virginia.

Very Respectfully,
Your obedient servant,
U. S. GRANT,
Lieutenant-General,
Commanding Armies of the United States.

APRIL 7, 1865.

General: I have received your note of this date.

Though not entirely of the opinion you express of the hopelessness of further resistence on the part of the army of Northern Virginia, I reciprocate your desire to avoid useless effusion of blood, and therefore, before considering your proposition, *ask the terms you will offer, on condition of its surrender.*

R. E. LEE, General.

To Lieut.-Gen. U. S. GRANT, Commanding Armies of the United States.

APRIL 8, 1865.

To Gen. R. E. Lee, Commanding C. S. A.:

GENERAL: Your note of last evening in reply to mine of same date, asking the conditions on which I will accept the surrender of the Army of Northern Virginia, is just received.

In reply, I would say that *peace being my first desire, there is but one condition that I insist upon,* viz.:

That the men surrendered shall be disqualified for taking up arms again against the Government of the United States until properly exchanged.

I will meet you, or designate officers to meet any officers you may name, for the same purpose, at any point agreeable to you, for the pur-

a large procession is proceeding through the streets. Such an excitement was never before witnessed in this city,

ALBANY, Monday, April 10—1 A. M.

There is great rejoicing here over the news of the surrender of Gen. LEE and his army.

The news was received at about 10 P. M., and about midnight State and Pearl streets were filled with people anxiously awaiting the particulars.

The bells are ringing, cannon firing, while the multitude are indulging in fireworks.

The Governor was called up and briefly addressed the throng around his residence.

The State House and many private residences are illuminated.

PHILADELPHIA, April 9.

The glorious announcement of LEE's surrender was received here about nine o'clock. It was telegraphed to all sections of the city, and was announced in the several churches. The *Ledger* office was illuminated in five minutes. The bell of Independence Hall was rung by the order of the Mayor. The firemen immediately assembled and blocked up the streets. Salutes were fired, and the whistles of the steam-engines and the cheers of the assembled multitudes made the whole city ring.

WORCESTER, Mass., Monday, April 9.

The news of the surrender of LEE and his army created an intense excitement here to-night. The bells were rung, guns were fired, bonfires kindled, the fire companies turned out, and many stores and buildings were illuminated.

PITTSBURGH, Pa., Sunday, April 9.

The news to-night brought nearly the entire population into the streets. The recruiting booths were turned into bonfires, salutes were fired, speeches were made, and bands played.

TRENTON, N. J., Sunday, April 9.

The glorious news was received here with cheering and ringing of bells. The people are turning out *en masse* to receive and rejoice over the glad tidings.

PROVIDENCE, R. I., Sunday, April 9—Midnight.

Bells are ringing, cannon are firing, and the citizens are out rejoicing over the news of LEE's surrender. A large bonefire is burning on Weybosset bridge.

FROM THE PACIFIC COAST.

Juarez said to be Coming to Washington by way of San Francisco—French Forces in Sinaloa—French War Steamers in California Ports—The Overland Mails.

SAN FRANCISCO, Friday, April 7.

The steamer *John L. Stephens*, from Mazatlan, brings $93,000 in treasure and a thousand bags of silver ore.

The Mazatlan *Times*, the Imperialist organ, give the report that JUAREZ was en route for Cape St. Lucas, whence he would sail for San Francisco on his way to Washington.

A French naval expedition had sailed, it was supposed, for Guaymas.

An Imperial force has moved to Sinaloa.

A correspondent of the San Francisco *Bulletin*, writing from Mazatlan, March 4, says that JUAREZ is still at Chihuahua with his ministers raising troops, though money, arms, and ammunition are scarce.

The French war steamer *Victoria* and transport *Du Rhine* was at Santa Barbara, on the coast of California. They hope to obtain supplies of coal at San Francisco.

The daily Overland Mail, hence to Salt Lake, resumed its trips yesterday. The first mail this way since the interruption arrived last night.

The recent meeting in behalf of the Christian Sanitary Commission, resulted in remittances, by telegraph, within the past few days, of $20,000 in gold.

The scarcity of flour and wheat continues. Extreme prices are obtained, and consequently trade does not improve much.

The Union Convention of Washington Territory have nominated A. A. DEWY as Congressional Delegate.

Military celebrations for the national victories were held throughout the State to-day.

A mass meeting in aid of the Soldiers' Relief Association was held here to-night.

theme before us are far beyond the feeble descriptive powers of of the pen of your correspondent. No brilliant rhetoric, no vivid word-painting, no oratorical eloquence can portray the sublimity and immensity of the great victory. It is almost beyond the power of the human mind to comprehend its extent, and when you begin to descend to detail, the task is simply appalling in its magnitude. Think of a line of operations, held defensively and operated from offensively with such success, *thirty-nine miles long from flank to flank, thoroughly fortified throughout its entire length!* Think of the cities captured, of the fortificationss stormed and taken, with their hundreds of guns, great and small, of the material of war now in our hands, yet beyond the possibility of computation of the terrible battles, and the overwhelming defeat, and rout of the chief army of the reb ellion of the prisoners captured. Counted by the tens of thousands; of the terrified flight of the arch-traitor and his few desperate minions; of the triumphant entry of ABRAHAM LINCOLN into treason's fallen capital. Let every lover of his country depict the vast scene in his own imagination for words to fitly discribe it falls altogether.

Through the courtesy of Provost-Marshal Gen. PATRICK, I enjoyed an exceedingly pleasant sail from City Point to the Richmond wharves this morning, on his fleet flag ship, the *Mattino*. Accompanying the General were Hon. C. H. DANA, Assistant Secretary of War, his wife and son, and Hon. ROSCOE CONKLING, member of Congress from New-York. The snake-like bends of the James between City Point and Varina Landing, were quickly passed, and at the latter place assurance was given that the river was clear for our vessel to the very docks of Richmond; but I can assure you that the navigation of the tortuous channel of the James thence to Richmond, thickly sown with obstructions and supposed torpedoes, was an exceedingly delicate task, and full of excitement. Our pilot knew the channel of old, but he knew not the warlike devices of the enemy.

We were, however, very fortunate, and the approach to the city, especially during the last eight miles from Drewry's Bluff, was full of the intensest interest, for over these waters the Union flag had never before floated during the war. When we leave Dutch Gap and that famous canal, which looks as though it might have been washed out by a billow, we at once enter upon the lines held by the enemy. Howlett House Battery, famous for its determined resistance to our engeneering operations on the north side of the river, stands abandoned and gloomy, with its twelve large guns still in the embrasures, but all silent as we steamed rapidly by. Another long and large earthwork appears on the left bank, mounting eight or ten guns, and bearing directly upon the mouth of the canal. This, too, like the rest, is abandoned, with its armament unimpaired. We next pass the wreck of the rebel gunboat, blown up by our batteries during the effort made to run through our fleet some months ago.

The next point of interest is Fort Brady, on the north bank of the river, and the left of the position of our Army of the James. What strikes one as very remarkable here is the fact that owing to the intricate windings of the James there are two rebel batteries, Howlett House and another, absolutely in the rear of this former position of our army. Fort Brady is the point where Gen. GIBSON opened on the retreating rebel rams. Had there been larger guns at his disposal, the range is so good that they would have stood a poor chance of escape.

We are now fairly in that part of the river held solely by the rebels, and a knowledge of the channel and obstructions is absolutely necessary to a safe voyage. The gunboat *Monticello* is therefore hailed, and on asking for information, a pilot who has been up and down is tendered with much politeness. The obstructions sunk by our own fleet are soon passed, likewise the fleet of monitors, and the next object

comfortable room, amid hundreds of loyal guests.

L. L. CROUNSE.

First Impressions of Richmond—The Great Conflagration in the City—Who Was Responsible for it?—The Libby and Castle Thunder—Suffering for Food—Distribution of Supplies—Lee's Family.

From Our Own Correspondent.

RICHMOND, Thursday, April 6, 1865.

So many thousand facts are presented to the mind of the visitor here in such a very short space of time, that to record them systematically is almost impossible. The great features of the evacuation, the entrance of our troops, the conflagration, the President's visit and reception, have already been forwarded to you in detail by your correspondents who came in with the troops, and I will, therefore, allude to them only in a general way.

Let me say, though, at the outset, that the best part of the city is a ruin. That the awful fire kindled by the enemy, and which at first promised to consume but a few buildigns, was so fanned by the rising wind, that before it could be got under subjection, *thirty squares, comprising not less than eight hundred buildings in the very best and most valuable business part of Richmond were in ashes.* What the pecuniary loss is no one can estimate. Nearly all the principal mills, factories, warehouses, stores, banks and insurance offices were destroyed, and the losses being so heavy, the insurance companies, perhaps insolvent already from their countenance of the rebel currency, are now more than bankrupted, and thousands of property owners, computed wealthy in their actual possessions three days ago, are now reduced to beggary. It is among the things easily discernable, that this ruin, wrought by their own friends, to whom they have given all, and to whose tyranny they have submitted, with even cheerfulness, is the cause of far deeper gloom among many than that produced by the loss of the city or the defeat of their army. It is apparent indeed that the transfer of the city to the Union flag was not only *not distasteful to a very large portion of the people, many of them among the best classes, but even highly gratifying.* No captured city, not even Savannah nor Columbia, can present the ruin apparent here in Richmond. It will carry its painful evidences for half a score of years, and the only thing which will speedily alleviate the dire distress that must prevail, and give the city a chance for a speedy recovery from its present stagnation, is immediate peace. It is Richmond's only salvation. The origin of the fire and the incendiaries are so well and positively known that no extended investigation on these points is required. It seems that *Gen. Lee was not responsible for it, but that Jeff. Davis and his Secretary of War, Breckenridge, were.* The destruction of the supplies and the arsenal involved the destruction of the city, and it was so decided by the leading citizens. Gen. EWELL and Maj. CARRINGTON both protested against it in the most earnest manner, as did also a committee of citizens, but BRECKINRIDGE, in reply, exclaimed *that he didn't care a d—n if every house in Richmond was consumed, the warehouse must be burned.* Thus this wretched rebel, foisted into a powerful position with no constituents, is responsible for the dreadful ruin, and his master DAVIS is likewise responsible, because he silently countenanced it.

The fire was started in two places, among the supply warehouses near the wharves, and at the Danville Depot, where there were 1,500 hogsheads of tobacco belonging to the Confederate Government. This consumed the Danville Depot, also the Petersburgh Depot, and the bridge over the James to Manchester. The famous Libby Prison, and Castle Thunder, as I have already informed you, were not burned. They were reserved for a far more appropriate fate. I visited them yesterday, and found Castle Thunder used as a guard-house for factious and thieving negroes, caught in acts of plunder, while the Libby contained 700 rebel prisoners, officers and privates, temporarily shut up together. They looked through the iron gratings with gloomy counten-

pect their names were as foreign to them as the hunger they now sought to appease had been in days gone by. Many of the wealthiest families, however, who had the means, have far larger supplies of provisions on hand than was consistent with the repeated appeals of Confederate officials for such to spare from their bounty to feed the army.

The exodus of prominent citizens was confined mainly to those connected with the rebel government, and a few who had made themselves very conspicuous in rebel politics—all the rebel Cabinet and their chief assistants, though not much of their clerical force, got away. The preparations for the evacuation began very quietly among the officials. At noon of Sunday the important records of the departments were boxed up and carted to the depot; but very little suspicion was excited among the citizens as to the real state of the case. A strong guard was stationed at the Danville depot, and four trains were got ready, the first of which left, with DAVIS on board, at seven o'clock in the evening, and the last at midnight. DAVIS' family had gone into the country on the Friday preceeding, but not because of any apprehension that the city was to be given up. Very few families left the city, and there are very few vacant houses, the mansions of JEFF. DAVIS and GOV. BILLY SMITH being among those now in want of tenants. The family of Gen. LEE, consisting of his wife, who is an invalid, and three daughters, are among those who remain. They occupy a stylish house on Franklin-street, and for their protection a well disciplined guard is placed at the dwelling, and the family are scrupulously protected from annoyance of any character, the staring gaze of the passer-by hardly being allowed. This is the second time that Mrs. Gen. LEE has been in our hands. She was once captured by our cavalry near White House, in 1862, and sent through our lines to Richmond under flag of truce, by order of Gen. MCCLELLAN.

L. L. CROUNSE.

Union Sentiment in Richmond—Projects of Reconstruction—Distinguished Visitors—Recruiting Negro Troops—The Truth about Rebel Enlistment of Negroes.

From Our Own Correspondent.

RICHMOND, Friday, April 7, 1865.

I can give you news, to-day, which will gratify the heart of every loyal American. Virginia will return to the Union, and that right speedily. Desiring to ascertain the exact truth with reference to the alleged existence of a strong Union sentiment in the city, I availed myself of an opportunity to call upon certain gentlemen here whom I had heard alluded to by Secessionists as Union men, and I must say, that I spent two of the happiest hours of my life in full and free conversation with some of the most thorough and radical Union men in the country; men of wealth and position, whose faith has never wavered for an instant, and who, slaveholders, as they are, *demand that Virginia shall be taken back into the Union "under the Emancipation Proclamation;" that no vestige of the rebellion shall be tolerated; that the usurpation State, and Confederate, which has wrecked Virginia, shall not be recognized in a single respect;* that the State Government must be organized anew, by a convention of the people, as soon as that can be properly effected, and the State and its inhabitants thoroughly purged of treason in every shape.

Union sentiments, in this strong form exist here to a far greater extent than has yet been conceived; not alone among the poorer classes,—mechanics and laborers,—*but in wealthy and influential circles, where may be found men who have never lost faith in the Union;* who have confidently anticipated its triumph, and who greeted the old flag with tears of joy. They are men of the John Minor Botts school, and they are the leaven which shall leaven the whole lump here in this venerable old commonwealth of Virginia. They will delight to see the mass of the people treated with magnanimity, but they have felt too deeply the

Continued on Eighth Page.

The New-York Times.

VOL. XIII—NO. 3794. NEW-YORK, FRIDAY, NOVEMBER 20, 1863. PRICE THREE CENTS.

IMPORTANT FROM EAST TENNESSEE

The Rebels Advancing upon Knoxville.

THE PLACE COMPLETELY INVESTED.

HEAVY SKIRMISHING YESTERDAY.

The Position Very Strongly Fortified.

THE REBEL FORCES UNDER LONGSTREET.

KNOXVILLE, Thursday, Nov. 17.

The enemy began skirmishing from their position on Kingston Road, at 10 this morning. Our advance alone, composed wholly of mounted infantry and cavalry, occupied the position, under command of Gen. SANDERS, and each man fought like a veteran. At noon the enemy opened with artillery at short range, their battery protected by a large house. BENJAMIN's battery was the only one which replied, occupying the chief fortification, half a mile in front of and to the right of the town. A desperate charge was made by the enemy about 3 P. M. Our men were protected by rail barricades on the crest of the hill. Gen. SANDERS was severely wounded, and was borne from the field.

We yielded the position, and fell back about a third of a mile to a stronger one. We have lost about one hundred, one quarter of whom were killed. The enemy had completely invested the place, but Gen. BURNSIDE will defend it to the last man, and it is believed successfully. The troops are in the best spirits. Every important point is fortified, and confidence prevails that we shall whip the enemy out.

A MORE DETAILED ACCOUNT.

KNOXVILLE, Tenn., Tuesday, Nov. 17.

Gen. LONGSTREET, after crossing the Tennessee on Saturday morning, 14th inst., was attacked in the afternoon by Gen. BURNSIDE, who drove the advance guard back to within a mile of the river's edge by nightfall.

LONGSTREET crossed the remainder of his troops during the night, and on Sunday morning advanced in force.

Gen. BURNSIDE, finding it impossible to cope with him with the small force at his disposal, fell back to Lenoir, the rear guard skirmishing heavily with the enemy through the day.

Three desperate charges were made upon our positions during Sunday night, but they were handsomely repulsed.

On Monday morning Gen. BURNSIDE evacuated Lenoir, but owing to the energy with which the rebel pursuit was kept up, determined to give them a decided check, and accordingly came into line of battle at Campbell's Station, when a fight ensued, lasting from late in the forenoon until dark. Our first position commanding the road from both sides, the infantry deployed in front of this, and were soon attacked by the enemy, who made several gallant charges, and finally succeeded, by outflanking our men, in driving them to the cover of the batteries, which now opened a terrific and destructive fire. The rebels retired before it, gave way, and eventually fell back to the river.

It was now three o'clock in the afternoon. The rebels showing a desire to renew the attack, and having brought three batteries to their assistance, Gen. BURNSIDE fell back to a more desirable position and again gave them battle. The contest continued, closing at nightfall, with our troops in possession of their own ground.

The object of the fight having been attained, and as the detention of the rebels had enabled our trains to get all in advance, our troops fell back during the night and early Tuesday morning reached Knoxville, where a great battle is expected to be fought to-morrow.

Yesterday the rebel advance guard attacked our outposts upon the Loudon and Clinton roads and heavy skirmishing continued all day.

This morning the attack was resumed when the fog which set in during the night had lifted. The rebels finding it impossible to drive our men with infantry, brought several guns into position, and poured in a flanking fire.

In the afternoon they brought forward a heavy force of infantry once more, and, after a brief skirmish, charged our position. A terrific hand to hand conflict occurred—both sabres and revolvers being used on both sides. Our men fought with the greatest gallantry; but at last were compelled to fall back about a third of a mile, to a strong line, which they hold to-night.

We have to regret the wounding of Gen. SANDERS and Capt. SIKES, of the cavalry, who commanded the outpost. His condition is critical. Lieut.-Col. SMITH, of the Twentieth Michigan, was killed at Campbell's Station. Our loss in that fight was between two and three hundred. Our loss to-day will not exceed one hundred and fifty.

Our men are in the best of spirits and perfectly confident of success to-morrow.

LATE FROM CHATTANOOGA.

Correspondence of the New-York Times.

CHATTANOOGA, Monday, Nov. 16, 1863.

The stream of deserters from the enemy continues to increase. Among them are some of the Vicksburgh paroled prisoners, who are much exercised regarding their *status*. From information which they bring it is now rendered certain that LONGSTREET is operating against BURNSIDE in East Tennessee.

The weather for the past few days has been very fine, and the roads are in excellent condition.

REPORTS FROM REBEL SOURCES.

ATLANTA, Friday, Nov. 13.

Nothing from the front this morning. A party of Georgia State troops and Indians killed the notorious BRYSON and thirty-four of his men, a short time since, on the line between Georgia and North Carolina.

A special to the *Register*, dated Sweet Water, Nov. 12, says: "*The Federals have removed all their supplies to Knoxville for safety*, and are living on half rations. Several deserters, recaptured, were executed here yesterday."

A special to the *Intelligencer* says: "Two Yankee officers who deserted and came into our lines, report that GRANT expects soon to assault Lookout. His army is on half rations.

THE ARMY OF THE POTOMAC.

Cavalry Skirmish at Germanna Ford—Great Scarcity of Contrabands—The Army Being Paid Off.

WASHINGTON, Thursday, Nov. 19.

The intelligence received to-night from the Army of the Potomac is to the effect that a cavalry skirmish between 200 rebels and part of the Eighteenth Pennsylvania cavalry took place yesterday [illegible] on the Rapidan. The [illegible] our men fell back upon [illegible] loss was small. Som[illegible] [illegible] division drills, the country and weather being favorable for such purposes.

Hundreds of contrabands could be profitably employed in the army as drivers, teamsters, &c. In one artillery brigade alone, a sufficient number of soldiers are employed as wagoners and teamsters, to man a six-gun battery, for want of negroes.

Yesterday evening some cannonading was heard in the direction of the Rapidan south of Culpepper, but no particulars had been received when the messenger this afternoon left the army.

No sutlers have yet been granted right of transportation for their stores to the army. A few occasionally succeed in passing goods, but they are liable to arrest and confiscation.

Paymasters are busily at work in the discharge of their duties in almost all, if not all, the army corps.

THE HEROES OF JULY..

A Solemn and Imposing Event.

Dedication of the National Cemetery at Gettysburgh.

IMMENSE NUMBERS OF VISITORS.

Oration by Hon. Edward Everett—Speeches of President Lincoln, Mr. Seward and Governor Seymour.

THE PROGRAMME SUCCESSFULLY CARRIED OUT.

The ceremonies attending the dedication of the National Cemetery commenced this morning by a grand military and civic display, under command of Maj.-Gen. COUCH. The line of march was taken up at 10 o'clock, and the procession marched through the principal streets to the Cemetery, where the military formed in line and saluted the President. At 11¼ the head of the procession arrived at the main stand. The President and members of the Cabinet, together with the chief military and civic dignitaries, took position on the stand. The President seated himself between Mr. SEWARD and Mr. EVERETT after a reception marked with the respect and perfect silence due to the solemnity of the occasion, every man in the immense gathering uncovering on his appearance.

The military were formed in line extending around the stand, the area between the stand and military being occupied by civilians, comprising about 15,000 people and including men, women and children. The attendance of ladies was quite large. The military escort comprised one squadron of cavalry, two batteries of artillery and a regiment of infantry, which constitutes the regular funeral escort of honor for the highest officer in the service.

After the performance of a funeral dirge, by BIRGFIELD, by the band, an eloquent prayer was delivered by Rev. Mr. STOCKTON, as follows:

O God, our Father, for the sake of the Son, our Saviour, inspire us with thy spirit, and sanctify us to the right fulfillment of the duties of this occasion. We come to dedicate this new historic centre as a National Cemetery. If all the Departments of the one Government thou hast ordained over our Union, and of the many Governments which Thou has subordinated to the Union be there represented; if all classes, relations and interests of our blended brotherhood of people stand severally and thoroughly apparent in Thy presence, we trust it is because Thou hast called us, that Thy blessing awaits us, and that Thy designs may be embodied in practical results of incalculable, imperishable good. And so with thy holy Apostle and with the Church in all lands and ages, we unite in the ascription: Blessed be God, even the Father of Our Lord Jesus Christ, the Father of Moses, and the God of all comfort, who comforteth us in all our tribulation, that we may be able to comfort them which are in any trouble by the comfort wherewith we ourselves are comforted of God. In emulation of all angels, in fellowship with all saints, and in sympathy with all sufferers, in remembrance of Thy works, in reverence of Thy ways, and in accordance with Thy word, we love and magnify Thy infinite perfections, Thy creative glory, Thy redeeming grace, Thy providential goodness, and the progressive, richer and fairer development of thy supreme, universal and everlasting administration. In behalf of all humanity, whose ideal is divine, whose first memory is thy image lost, whose last hope is thy image restored; especially in behalf of our own nation, whose position is so peerless, whose mission is so sublime, and whose future is so attractive; we thank Thee for the unspeakable patience of thy compassion and for the exceeding greatness of thy loving kindness. In contemplation of Eden, Calvary and Heaven, of Christ in the God on the cross, and on the throne—nay, more—of Christ as coming again in all-subduing power and glory; we gratefully prolong our homage by this altar of sacrifice, on this field of deliverance, on this mount of salvation, within the fiery and bloody line of these mountains and rocks, looking back to the dark days of fear and of trembling, and the rapture of relief that came after, we multiply our thanksgivings and confess our obligations to renew and perfect our personal and social consecration to thy service and glory. O, had it not been for God! for our enemies, they came unresisted, multitudinous, mighty, flushed with victory and sure of success; they exalted on our mountains; they reveled in our valleys; they feasted, they rested, they slept, they awakened, they grew stronger, prouder and bolder every day; they spread abroad, they concentrated here; they looked beyond this horizon to the stores of wealth, to the haunts of pleasure and the seats of power in our Capital and chief cities; they prepared to cast the chain of Slavery around the form of freedom, and to bind life and death together forever. Their premature triumph was the mockery of God and man. One more victory, and all was theirs. But behind these hills was heard the feebler march of a smaller but still a pursuing host; onward they hurried, day and night, for their country and their God; footsore, wayworn, hungry, thirsty, faint, but not in heart; they came to dare all, to bear all, and to do all that is possible to heroes. At first they met the blast on the plain, and bent before it like trees; but then led by Thy hand to the hills, they took their stand on the these rocks, and remained as firm and immovable as they. In vain were they assaulted; all art, all violence, all desperation failed to dislodge them. Baffled, bruised, broken, their enemies retired and disappeared. Glory to God for this rescue! But, Oh! the slain, in the freshness and fullness of their young and manly life! with such sweet memories of father and mother, brother and sister, wife and children, maiden and friend. From the coasts beneath the Eastern star; from the shores of Northern lakes and rivers; from the flowers of the Western prairies; from the homes of the midway and the border, they came here to die for us and for mankind! Alas How little we can do for them! We come with the humility of prayer, with the pathetic eloquence of venerable wisdom, with the tender beauty of poetry, with the plaintive harmony of music, with the honest tribute of our Chief Magistrate, and with all this honorable attendances; but our best hope is in Thy blessings. O Lord, Our God, bless us. O, Our Father, bless the bereaved, whether absent or present. Bless our sick and wounded soldiers and sailors. Bless all our rulers and people. Bless our army and navy. Bless the efforts to suppress this rebellion, and bless all the associations of this day, and place, and scene, forever. As the trees are not dead, though their foliage is gone, so our heroes are not dead though their forms have fallen. In their proper personality they are all with thee, and the spirit of their example is here. It fills the air, it fills our hearts, and as long as time shall last it will hover in these skies and rest on these landscapes, and pilgrims of our own land and of all lands, will thrill with its inspiration, and increase and confirm their devotion to liberty, religion and God.

Mr. EVERETT then commenced the delivery of his oration, which was listened to with marked attention throughout. [The oration of Mr. EVERETT will be found on our second page.]

Although a heavy fog clouded the heavens in the morning during the procession, the sun broke out in all its brilliancy during the Rev. Mr. STOCKTON's prayer and shone upon the magnificent spectacle. The assemblage was of great magnitude, and was gathered within a circle of great extent around the stand, which was located on the highest point of ground on which the battle was fought. A long line of military surrounded the position taken by the immense multitude of people.

The Marshal took up a position on the left of the stand. Numerous flags and banners, suitably draped, were exhibited on the stand among the audience. The entire scene was one of grandeur due to the importance of the occasion. So quiet were the people that every word uttered by the orator of the day must have been heard by them all, notwithstanding the immensity of the concours.

Among the distinguished persons on the platform were the following: Governors Bradford, of Maryland; Curtin, of Pennsylvania; Morton, of Indiana; Seymour, of New-York; Parker, of New-Jersey, and Tod, of Ohio; Ex-Gov. Dennison, of Ohio; John Brough, Governor Elect, of Ohio; Charles Anderson, Lieutenant-Governor of Ohio; Major-Generals Schenck, Stahel, Doubleday, and Couch; Brigadier-General Gibbon; and Provost-Marshal-General Fry.

PRESIDENT LINCOLN'S ADDRESS.

The President then delivered the following dedicatory speech:

Fourscore and seven years ago our Fathers brought forth upon this Continent a new nation, conceived in liberty and dedicated to the proposition that all men are created equal. [Applause.] Now we are engaged in a great civil war, testing whether that nation, or any nation so conceived and so dedicated, can long endure. We are met on a great battle-field of that war. We are met to dedicate a portion of it as the final resting-place of those who here gave their lives that that nation might live. It is altogether fitting and proper that we should do this. But in a larger sense we cannot dedicate. We cannot consecrate, we cannot hallow this ground. The brave men, living and dead, who struggled here have consecrated it far above our power to add or detract. [Applause.] The world will little note nor long remember, what we say here, but it can never forget what they did here. [Applause.] It is for us, the living, rather to be dedicated here to the refinished work that they have thus so far nobly carried on. [Applause.] It is rather for us to be here dedicated to the great task remaining before us, that from these honored dead we take increased devotion to that cause for which they here gave the last full measure of devotion; that we here highly resolve that the dead shall not have died in vain; [applause] that the Nation shall under God have a new birth of freedom, and that Governments of the people, by the people and for the people, shall not perish from the earth. [Long continued applause.]

Three cheers were then given for the President and the Governors of the States.

After the delivery of the addresses, the dirge and the benediction closed the exercises, and the immense assemblage separated at about 4 o'clock.

About 3 o'clock in the afternoon, the Fifth New York regiment of heavy artillery, Col. MURRAY, was marched to the temporary residence of Gov. SEYMOUR, where they passed in review before the Governor, presenting a handsome spectacle. Upon the conclusion of this ceremony, which attracted quite a crowd of sight-seers. Gov. SEYMOUR presented a handsome silk regimental standard to the regiment, accompanying the gift with the following speech:

GOV. SEYMOUR'S SPEECH.

SOLDIERS OF NEW-YORK: We love our whole country, without reservation. But while we do so, it is not inconsistent with that perfect and generous loyalty to love and to be proud of our own State This day, when I took part in the celebration that was to consecrate yonder battle-field, while I felt as an American citizen, proud of my own country, and proud of the gallant services of her citizens, in every State, nevertheless my eye did involuntarily wander to that field where lie the glorious dead of our good and great State, and when I returned, to see marching before me your manly and sturdy columns, not knowing you belonged to New-York, my heart did quicken and my pulse tingle, to learn that you were acting commissions issued by myself; I am most proud and most happy that I have have this opportunity, on behalf of the merchants of the great commercial City of New-York; to present to you this glorious banner, which has been sent as a token of their confidence in your loyalty and your courage, and your fidelity in the hour of danger. Sergeant, I place these colors in your hands in the firm confidence that they will be borne through every field of triumph, of toil and of danger, in a way that will do honor to yourselves, to the great State which you represent, and the still greater country, to which we all belong. My God bless you as you serve your country in the distant field of danger We find in those glorious fields you left behind you are not indifferent to this conflict; are not indifferent to the welfare of the whole Union. I do not doubt, therefore, that when you shall return from your dangerous fields of duty, you shall bring back this standard to place among the archieves of our State with honorable mention of the services her sons have performed. I do not doubt that though it may perhaps be returned torn and stained, yet it will be still more glorious, and with glorious recollections clustering around it. In concluding these remarks, I ask in return of the men of New-York, to give three cheers for the Union of our country, and three cheers for the flag of our land.

Gen. SCHENCK followed in a short speech.

A subscription of $280 was made by the Marshals attending these ceremonies, to be devoted to the relief of the Richmond prisoners.

In the afternoon, the Lieutenant-Governor elect of Ohio, Col. ANDERSON, delivered an oration at the Presbyterian Church.

The President and party returned to Washingto at 6 o'clock this evening, followed by the Governors' trains. Thousands of persons were gathered at the depot, anxiously awaiting transportation to their homes; but they will probably be confined to the meagre accommodations of Gettysburgh till to-morrow.

DEPARTMENT OF THE GULF.

ARRIVAL OF THE CREOLE FROM NEW-ORLEANS.

The Attack upon Gen. Washburn's Column.

Our Entire Loss Six Hundred and Seventy-seven.

The steamship *Creole*, Capt. THOMPSON, arrived yesterday morning from New-Orleans, bringing dates to the 10th inst. Further accounts from the Teche country concerning the attack on WASHBURN's column represents our whole loss in killed and wounded and taken prisoners at 677. The Indiana Sixty-seventh was captured almost entire; the Sixtieth Indiana and Ohio Ninety-sixth lost largely. The rebel force was as five to one. We only excelled them in artillery, by means of which, at short range, it is thought, we killed a large number of the enemy. It is reported that the Thirteenth army corps, now in the Teche country, is ordered back to Memphis.

The attack was made by the enemy in force of 5,000 upon our rear guard, only 1,800 strong. The enemy captured two pieces of artillery, but one of them was subsequently retaken. The fight took place at Buzzard Prairie, on the east side of Bayou Teche.

Gen. PRICE was reported at Alexandria with 15,000 men, and for this reason, as well as the impossibility of getting supplies, it was deemed best to fall back.

Gens. THOMAS and WADSWORTH arrived in New-Orleans on the 10th inst.

THE DELAWARE ELECTION.

The Union Ticket Overwhelmingly Successful—Smithers, for Congress, Walked the Course.

WILMINGTON, Thursday, Nov. 19.

The election in this State passed off quietly. The Copperheads, seeing defeat staring them in the face, abandoned the contest. BROWN did not withdraw, but the leaders, knowing they would be compelled to proclaim themselves loyal men in order to vote, gave the key-note for the whole party to stay at home. SMITHERS walked the course. Newcastle County gives SMITHERS 4,014 votes, and BROWN 6 votes. In six Districts of Kent County, SMITHERS has 1,275 votes, BROWN none. In five Districts of Sussex County, SMITHERS has 844 votes, and BROWN 7 votes, showing a gain for SMITHERS over FISHER's vote of last year in this county.

J. T. HEALD,
Chairman State Committee.

GREAT BRITAIN AND AMERICA.

Welcome to Rev. Henry Ward Beecher.

Demonstration at the Brooklyn Academy of Music.

A GREAT SPEECH:

His Impressions of British Feeling Toward America.

An immense audience assembled at the Academy of Music, Brooklyn, last evening, to welcome and hear the Rev. HENRY WARD BEECHER. The meeting was under the auspices of the War Fund Committee, the entire proceeds to be devoted to the Sanitary Commission. Rev. Dr. STORRS made an eloquent address of welcome to Mr. BEECHER, who, on his appearance, was most enthusiastically greeted. When quiet was restored Mr. BEECHER spoke as follows:

MR. BEECHER'S ADDRESS.

I will not attempt to disguise the deep feeling with which your generous kindness, expressed in the words of my brother, affect me. I am more touched and more stirred by this sympathy than by all that I have seen and by all that I have experienced in the whole of my travel abroad; and I speak the simple truth, which has the witness in your hearts, that it is here in this city more than anywhere else that I desire to be so greeted. For as, when in England, it was my pride to be an American, so when I am in America, it is my pride to be a citizen of Brooklyn; and I accept your generous confidence, and this affecting testimony of it, in so far as it relates to me personally, with profound sensibility and with deep gratitude. I thank you; and yet I should be vain if I supposed that this was meant for me in my simple individuality. I am myself the effect of American institutions; I am made by them and if I have done any service to the public worthy of your regard, I owe it to this very public and the institutions which enrich it the power to do it any service. And I am glad that it is so—so deep are my feelings of patriotism, so profoundly am I impressed with the grandeur of this latest and ripest development of civil life, that I am more than willing to be sunk myself if my decadence and disappearance could add anything to the glory of my country. I would fain be as the oil in the lamp that gives its life, that the light may be bright which consumes it. And that which is my feeling is your feeling, and I know I bear your sympathy with me in this simple and artless expression of my feelings to-night. I am glad that you asked me to be present; and I am proud that it shall go abroad that when I came back to America, having witnessed as I could in Europe for the truth of our cause, the first place to greet me was my own home, where I am best known. It is, indeed, a wreath which I shall wear none the less because it is invisible. I went abroad, as you know, simply as a private citizen. It was tauntingly asked me, on my arrival in England, why, in the very height and paroxysm of our national agony, I abandoned the field to go abroad. I did not answer, but I now do answer. I foresaw that the Autumn and the Winter would require labors even greater than any period previous, and the excitement and the excessive labors of the two and a half years, or three years preceding, had not destroyed my health nor destroyed my constitution; but certainly I was jaded, and I feared to go into the labor of the Autumn and Winter, which required the best powers of every man, without my full strength; and since I could do nothing in the Summer, I took that opportunity, upon the generous invitation of my own people, to go abroad and rest, that I might come back to labor more assiduously. Allow me to say that this generosity of my own dear people was a comfort to me everywhere, and that in Great Britain—not because I disesteemed their kindness or undervalued their hospitality, but because it was something that I cherished with a secret pride—I refused to received their hospitality or, in the remotest degree, compensation in any form. I said to them, my own people sent me abroad, and it is their pleasure that I shall stand upon them for support, and I will not take one penny from the hand of an Englishman. [Applause.] You will not misunderstand me; it was not because I disdained their kindness, but because I valued yours. It was also said that I had come abroad sent by our Government. That would have spoiled it all. I had no official character, and would not have had one. I went simply as a private citizen, and I was there merely and only as an American citizen. And when, unsought and, indeed, against my feelings, if not against my judgment, I entered upon the labor of the past few weeks of my sojourn in England, I assumed the responsibility, I cannot say with trembling, for I am not accustomed much to tremble; but I assumed the responsibility with the gravest sense of what it was. I have felt the inspiration of nationality often, but I never before was placed between two such great people, where I saw them both in prospective, both in their present relations and in their future. I never before felt so much as I felt all the time, waking or dreaming, night or day, what it was to stand and plead for the unity of these two great nations, for the sake of struggling mankind; and it was at once an excitement to me and a support. But, after all, I did not know how my countrymen would regard my efforts. If you had disapproved, I should have been sorry that you disapproved, but not sorry for what I had done. I did the best I knew how to do, every time, everywhere disinterestedly, for the love I bear to the cause and to the principles which underlie it, and I had no word, could not have, from home whether my representations of policy, and of fact, and of history, and of the tendencies of things, would accord with yours, or whether I should not be caught up in the whirl of conflicting parties, my reasonings traversed, my arguments denied—not till I landed in Boston did I hear one whisper—and then I learned for the first time that my services had been accepted by my countrymen. [Applause.] But to-night I meet you, a citizen returned among his friends, profoundly thankful that the labor and the service which I attempted for the public good have the seal of their approbation. It is my purpose not to trespass any further upon your time in matters that are personal to myself. I know that you will not think me vain for what I have said, and I desire now this evening to speak upon that which you all have come to hear—namely, my impressions and experiences in respect to the condition of things in Great Britain, as they relate to this struggle and this country. Among the wise things said by that wisest of modern political writers, DE TOCQUEVILLE, is this: "That it is impossible to judge of the affairs of one country by applying to them the experiences and the rules of another one." There are many reasons why one would have presumed beforehand that it was easy to understand British feeling and British policy. There was a similarity of institutions and a sameness of radical principles; but that very similarity, since it begets, by different institutions and different vehicles, different policies in the end, is liable to deceive us, and we are liable to come to many conclusions, because, upon the face, things look like those to which we are accustomed at home. I myself have experienced that, for I had judged of the condition of England from the impressions produced upon me by my first four weeks' tarry there in the Summer. I should have judged very wrongly, as judged by my present convictions. Nor do I feel myself now adequate to analyze or state either the causes or the results of my feeling; I am quite aware that I am imperfect in my views in many directions. Nor can I presume to say that I present you opinions. My nature gives intensity to my expressions, and yet I wish beforehand to ask you to consider that the statements that I make are impressions liable to mistake, subject to corrections that may afterward be made in them. And with these preliminary remarks I will tell you what I saw and found. You are aware that the original expression of our people was almost universal that in Great Britain we should find a sympathizer, ready and prepared. One thing we counted sure, and that was, that if all the other nations stood aloof, there was one that would stand by us in the hour of our peril, and that was Great Britain. And the sharpness of our retaliatory complaints was acuminated by that very disappointment of a very confident conviction. When I was asked in Great Britain why the American Press so severely inveighed against England, and was almost silent in respect to France, I said: "Because we in our deepest hearts care for England, and not much for France." [Applause.] "Because under anger, and lower down than prejudice, when you strike the deeper feelings, the Americans know that they have an English origin, and they are proud of their history; when it gets back further than the present generation, [laughter;] and it was this growing affection and sympathy in the best natures and in the best parts of the best natures—it was this that made the disappointment of public expectation so sharp and so hard to be borne when Great Britain foiled our expectations and gave us no sympathy. We never asked for help. We never asked that she should lend us anything or stretch out so much as the little finger of her right hand. We did ask simply the generous confidence and generous moral sympathy and that was all, and that we did not get, and we felt sharply, the conduct of England. The expression of public feeling had an effect of throwing her moral weight against the North and for the South. So I told them. I carefully discriminated between the intention and the result. What men intend has much to do with judging of their moral character; but what men do does not depend always on their intention. And when, therefore, the British people disclaimed sympathy with the South, or a disposition to go against their own principles as represented by the North, I said to them, "What your intentions are you can best judge, but what the effect of your attitude is we on the other side can best judge," and we know that the moral influence of Great Britain has substantially gone for more than two years to help the rebellion of the slavocracy of the South, and to hinder the progress of free institutions in the North. And if there is rescue or relief—if there is redemption finally, Great Britain must stand aside, and it must be said: "The nation that boasted of her free institutions and her sovereign sympathy with the welfare of the common peoples has had no part nor lot in the great work." [Applause.] The denial of moral sympathy in Great Britain was only interpreted by the active exertions of certain parts of the British people on behalf of the South, so much so that it, I think, will scarcely be denied by any man that if the shipyards, and foundries, and looms, and shops of Great Britain had refused their succor to rebellion, the rebellion would have died out in the nation long ago. I said in private what it did not seem altogeter judicious ti say in public, that in some sense I might bring this war and lay it at the feet of the British people, and say, not that you intended it, but that the course of conduct pursued, legal or illegal, was such that, but for you, the rebellion would have perished almost in the beginning of it. [Applause.] And no man but knows that there was also in England an extraordinary spectacle of men who, from sheer hatred of war, by misjudgment and mistake were left to foment it. There never was a misposition more signal than that of the British public, as represented in their leading intelligent classes, in this conflict. There never was a case where a nation, by its upper classes, went so unquestionably in favor of slavery at the same time that they occupied themselves in the intensest denunciations of slavery—that went against free society at the very time they were particularly praising free society and arrogating to themselves its highest claims and honors. Under such circumstances we were, you recollect, drifting right toward war. I told the British people that war was not our choice, and yet terrible and cruel as it was, there was something in this struggle so near to us, and so indispensable to national life, that rather than that there should be interference, rather than there should be disruption and dismemberment, rather than that this republican free Government should fall, we would stand war with Great Britain, with France, with Europe. [Applause.] It would have been difficult to say this without the appearance of threat; but that difficulty was itself dissolved by the iterated and reiterated charges brought against me of having been bellicose in my own country, and of having threatened all manner of desolation to Great Britain; and my reply was this, that I felt a part, and full part in proportion, of the deep indignation which my own people felt against Great Britain, and that I had never desired war, and abhorred it, but that I held the great principles of free Republican Government to be so precious that we would not give them up, not even at the threat nor infliction of war, no matter who brought it upon us. This being the cruel disappointment that we experienced in our expectation of sympathy from Great Britain, you will ask me, "What did you find to the facts and condition of things?" I found, in the first place, on going there, that every man I met was a Southern man, not literally born in the South, but this is the division they have themselves made. These are the terms applied. They are Southerners and Northerners even more than we are here. I found that on the railways, on the boats, in the hotels, wherever there was a traveling public, there was a public that sympathized with the South, and adverse to the North. It was not an uncommon thing to hear a gentleman who had talked freely and kindly with me on other matters say as the news was discussed, "Bad news we have got by the last steamer." "Ah, what is the news?" being a little troubled. "I understand," he would reply, "that MEADE has driven LEE entirely out of Pennsylvania." [Laughter.] "God send us much more bad news, then," said I. But coming from communities enthusiastic and almost homogeneous on this subject, it was strange to my ears to hear well-dressed and well-read men congratulate themselves on disasters to the North, and rejoicing in the success of the South; and suah is the case. Nor will there return to your side one young man has been traveling that will not bring back to you this substantial account; that wherever he went almost every man whom he met, without exception, was against the North and in favor of the South; and you can well imagine the impression that would be made on the mind of such. They would say "There is no question about this matter—the whole British nation is against us." Go where you will, up or down, you will find it all the same, and that was the effect impressed upon my mind. On still further inquiry, I was disappointed to find that that boy to which I myself belonged—the Congregationalists, known as Independents in England. I had supposed, since they are set for a testimony for freedom and have been arrayed almost invariably on the side of struggling peoples and struggling liberties, I supposed I should find them right, I did not. I do not mean that there is not a very large part of that power whose principles are right. They will be included under the head which I shall mention by and by, but I am sorry to say that I did not find the influential and leading clergymen of that denomination, nor the influential and leading laymen on our side. They said that they sympathized with liberty. Yes, they sympathized with liberty just exactly as the icicles sympathize with sunlight and Summer. [Laughter.] It chills you to come near them; and I said to them, I want no such sympathy, and I want nothing if it cannot come from enthusiastic hearts, it does no good and we do not want it. I found also the most profound ignorance of our affairs and of the operation of our institutions, and that, too, in quarters where I had a right to expect more intelligence. I found the most active and unscrupulous efforts made by Southern men to stir up animosity toward our country. And let me say that the bad cause was better served than a good one there, as to some extent it has been in our own land, for I am sure that the South, for a bad cause, has more nearly put forth every particle of strength that it has to put forth than we have for a good cause. And as it is at home, it was abroad. Where we sent one man to England to influence public opinion, they sent a score; where we print one book of information, they a library; where we touched one spring, they touched a hundred. They seemed to pervade England, and they seemed, with the unerring instinct of selfishness and despotism, to know just where to undermine the generous and better feelings—just where to invoke the influence of ignorance—just where to touch men so that principle should fall and profit take its place. [Applause.] You may then imagine the surprise and skepticism with which, under these circumstances, I received the assurance of friends on every side that the great heart of the British nation was on our side. I had found nobody except unconditional friends of emancipation in whose society I was thrown—I had found almost nobody that spoke kindly of us on that seemed to be in sympathy with us, and yet my ears were filled with these assurances day and night. "You are mistaken, you are mistaken, this great English people are sound at heart." I said where under heavens do the English people keep their hearts, then? [Laughter and applause.] And if I had spoken in my early visit to England in June, I could not have spoken as I now do and shall. Neither on my first return from the Continent in September could I have understood and felt what I understand now, in some measure, and entirely believe that they were right, and that, after all, the great heart of the British nation is with us of the North. [Great applause.]

Let me take up, then, one part of society after another, and state, as I understand them to be, the facts. First, there is the great commercial class of England, those that are making money and those that have made it; if you please, call them the plutocracy. They are against us. In the first place there is a large class of men that are actively employed in supplying the South with all its necessaries—except principle, [laughter,] and they are making on suppose that they are making large fortunes. We cannot doubt which side they take. The next is a very large class of men who, for precisely an opposite reason, somehow are opposed to the North and in favor of the South; namely, those who have been accustomed to make money, but found this interrupting war has stopped their profits; and men that want to make money, but do not; they are opposed to us. And between these two classes lies an intermediate one of men, who are bewildered and perplexed, and see that business is more or less affected, as it is over the whole continent, by its sympathetic relations with this continent. They say when will this war end? and as the offensive is on the northern side, they feel as though whenever the North will stop *aggressing* the Sout the war will stop. So in the main they are against us. It may be lowered down to this: that while there are very noble exceptions here and there all through England—men that stand out of their class above and against it, not speaking comprehensibly, the commercial class of England are against the North, and in favor of the South. I have spoken of the religious people. It is very difficult for me to analyze the causes that have turned both the established churchmen and the dissenters in respect to their most influential men against us. I do not think so in respect to the laymen; but the influential layman and the influential clergymen, I think, are adverse to us as a body. The ground usually taken is this: that the North is not sincere; and secondly, that the war is a great sin. And nowhere else in this world is there so tender a conscience on the subject of the war as Great Britain—when she is not waging it herself. [Great applause.] She has, I believe, only three wars on hand now—in China, Japan, and, I believe, in Australia—no matter where it is, it is somewhere; and the rest of her leisure she occupies with a profoud regret and horror for this American war. If it was for but a ship on the sea, she was ready to go to war with us; if it was for the territory of a remote island in the Antartic Ocean, she was ready to go to war with the savages; if it was but to beat down the cities of Japan, she had no objection to burn the seat of 160,000 inhabitants in it; but when a people are making war for their own life, for everything that dignifies humanity, they stand throwing out their hands that men will make war. [Laughter.] But I am sorry to say that, while from the Friends, who have always maintained as against their own countrymen a consistent testimony against war, it should have been expected, from those men, that had no particular objection to the Crimean war, none to the opium war in China, and none to the war that they now have, if not on their hands, on the tips of their fingers. I told them to their faces, in Exeiter Hall, there was not a land on the face of the globe against which they had not dashed their bloody prows and that their flag was a symbol of their history—a cross inscribed on a field of blood. [Great applause.] The English nobility, as a class are also against us. I shall read some very noble exceptions by-and-by. But these exceptions do not alter the general statement that the nobility as a class are against us. For the most obvious reason we are not accustomed to estimate the effect of our example upon European institutions. When he takes his walk abroad, it is not the elephant that weighs and measures its own gravity as he treads on the field-mouse's tail. It is the mouse that meditates. [Laughter.] A gigantic nation as this, on such a continent as this, while we are treading on the steps of accomplishing history, we are not feeling the jar that we ourselves are making; but they that have thrones and aristocratic privileges do; and they are the best interpreters of the reactionary influence of Ameridan ideas and American institutions. And it was the *Saturday Review*, that scholarly, keen, brilliant, unprincipled paper of England; it was that paper that had the frankness to say that Americans must not think that their remarks were because they disliked us, but it was because they found our ideas and our example working in Great Britain, and they were obliged in order to defeat these ideas in England to attack us in America. They are there, fighting home battles; for there is an unerring instinct—there is this feeling—that if a Government con be so efficient, covering such a continent, and so ludicrously cheap, how can we maintain our expensive and complicated Government in our sphere? Lest they should not think of it themselves, millions of common people, who are being taxed perpetually, suggest it to their attention. Do you suppose they do not know it? Do you not know that the effect of our Revolution was to send revolution all through Europe? The causes of it were all prepared. It was the torch of our Revolutionary war that set fire to the trains that burned all over Europe. They don't forget it. They dread the reactionary influence of American ideas. Such prosperity—such power and at so little expense—with so few monopolies and prerogatives to the favored classes! Therefore, when they oppose us, it is not to be construed as malignant opposition to us—it is nothing more than another form of self-love, for it is self defending itself. If you had been born with a coronet on your head, you would have done just so. [Laughter.] In Parliament, if a vote were taken to-day according to the private thoughts, sympathies and wishes among members, I suppose they would vote five to one against the North and in favor of the South. It is believed, too, by those well informed, that at least a portion of the Government have been entirely willing to go into a rupture with the North, and that but for the unflinching restraints they would have done so long ago. It is the impression throughout the realm that the Sovereign of Great Britain has been from the first our judicious but our steadfast friend. [Prolonged applause.] It is believed and so represented to me that her never rightly estimated and lamented consort was our fast friend, and that among the last acts of his life were those which erased from documents presented to him sentences that would have inflamed the growing anger. [Renewed applause.] He died with the blessing upon his head, "Blessed are the peacemakers." [Applause.] All through in the British Government, as at present constituted, (and I shall read you their names bye-and-bye,) there are several that are known to be warm and disinterested in their regard for the North, as there are others in that Government who, it is known in England—at least it was so represented to me by those who ought to know—who would not hesitate to plunge the Continent in a war for the sake of disrupting this nation. And if you ask me what is the great underlying influence that has been at work upon the upper class of England, I answer thus:

1. Commercial interest and rivalry therein.
2. Class power and the fear of contagion and American ideas.
3. (I know not how I shall say it so that it shall be the least offensive to our friends on the other side, but they have not come and you have not come to the bottom of the conduct of Great Britain until you have touched that delicate and real foundation cause,) we are too large and strong a nation. [Laughter.]

This is, in my judgment, the right of the whole matter. A distinguished clergyman of London, personally kind and friendly to me, said to me in these very words: "Mr. BEECHER, you may just as well have it said to you; you have been growing so strong that we have felt for a good many years that we had got to take you down, and we were very glad when the job was taken from our hands by your own people." [Laughter.] When Mr. ROEBUCK—whose speech it was my great privilege to hear—[laughter]—declared that same fact in Parliament, it was cheered immensely, but reprobated in the *Times* and in the other presses that sympathized with the South, not because he had not spoken the truth, but because it was a truth not best to be spoken. [Laughter.] It is said (and I intended to have brought here to-night to have read) in one of their recent publications—and it was the immediate cause of one of my speeches there—that we were a lawless and arrogant set of men; were proud of our sudden growth; and it is said that even Mr. BEECHER himself was regarded as a specimen of what they should have to deal with in the nation supposed to be composed of men breathing that sort of threats. [Laughter.] Now when men make such lamentable mistakes as to suppose that such a peaceful man as I am is so dangerous, [laughter] is it to be supposed that they would not make a mistake in estimating the whole nation? [Renewed laughter.] It is the sun that makes the seeds grow. It is the light that stimulates the seeds into growth; but under all this is the dunghill that makes the heat that causes the seeds to spring up under the genial influences of the sun. And it is just exactly that hot bed at the bottom, underneath, that works up and turns aside what would be otherwise insufficient to do so, the natural sympathies from the North. It is just that which has prepared them for this, that and the other prejudice and misinformation. With this state of facts you will ask how is it then that the English people have been restrained? How is it that they have not gone into overt belligerency? That is the very question that I propose to answer and in the statement that the English heart is on our side. [Applause.] The nobility is against us; the Government is divided and a part is against us. I think I may say that while the brains that represent progress in Great Britain are in our favor, yet the conservative intelligence of Great Britain is against us, and that all there is on the surface of society representing its dignities, its power and intelligence is Anti-American. And the question I propose to you is how with the papers, magazines and universities—how with their titled estates opposed to us, that they have been restrained from manifesting this in open hostility? It is because there is a great underlying influence that restrains them—it is the influence of that underlife, and to a very great extent of the non-voting English who have produced this effect. It is a thing I could not understand at first, and which it is very difficult for us to understand—for whenever in our country there is a majority of the votes there is sure to be a direction of affairs. But it is not so in England. I learned that the men who could not vote where they were united and determined had the power to control the men who do vote. This is not an anomaly, then. It would be in our institution, but it is not in English institutions—among other reasons, because in a nation where one class have a preëminence and privilege and the underlying class have none, all the instinct of self-preservation teaches this favored class never to goad that great underlying class into madness. There is always that dragon of of revolution coiled up that they are afraid to arouse. Therefore it is, that when the great under class of England is determined in one direction, they always carry their point; first or last, the upper classes have to give way. Men whose fortunes are made—men whose only thought of the future is to carry the rich freights of the present along into their future—that class are generally against us. Men who have no fortune—men having very little in the present to care for, who are struggling for better fortunes for themselves and children—that class are on our side. They are in our favor, but they are a class who have not much voice—have very little expression, and they are therefore little heard. Their report is not wafted across, but their influence is felt on the other side of the sea. It seems to me that it is peculiarly fitting that we, who believe in the common people, should find ourselves opposed by the titled and strong, but should find our allies and fast friends in the emergency have been

[*Continued on Eighth Page.*]

The New-York Times.

VOL. XIV......NO. 4167. | NEW-YORK, WEDNESDAY, FEBRUARY 1, 1865. | PRICE FOUR CENTS.

THE PEACE QUESTION.

ITS LATEST ASPECT.

Three Commissioners Coming from Richmond.

They Apply for Admission to General Grant's Lines.

A. H. Stephens of Georgia, R. M. T. Hunter of Virginia, and A. J. Campbell of Alabama.

A FLAG OF TRUCE AND A PARLEY.

General Grant in Communication with the Government.

Expected Arrival of the Commissioners at Annapolis.

Special Dispatch to the New-York Times.

WASHINGTON, Tuesday, Jan. 31.

In regard to the rebel Peace Commissioners, the following facts are known:

ALEXANDER H. STEPHENS of Georgia, R. M. T. HUNTER of Virginia, and A. J. CAMPBELL of Alabama, the latter formerly of the United States Supreme Court, arrived at Gen. GRANT's lines last Sunday afternoon and desired permission to come to Gen. GRANT's headquarters.

After considerable delay and parley they were allowed to come to Gen. GRANT's headquarters at City Point. It appears that Gen. GRANT immediately notified the Government of the fact, but up to this time we are not aware of the decision arrived at, though they are expected to reach Washington presently, via Annapolis.

FROM GEN. GRANT'S LINES.

The Commissioners Appear in Front of Petersburgh—Application for a Permit to Come Through—Scenes under the Flag-of-Truce—Excitement among the Soldiers.

From Our Special Correspondent.

HEADQUARTERS FIFTH ARMY CORPS.
Sunday, Jan. 29, 1864—10 A. M.

For many days the weather has been intensely cold, and many cases of frost-bitten feet, ears, cheeks, &c., on our picket lines are reported. To-day the intense cold had moderated, and though the sun shone brightly and the air was calm, the roads were solid and travelers many.

In front of Col. HARRIMAN's brigade, of WILCOX's division, Ninth Corps, about noon to-day, a flag of truce was displayed on the parapet of the enemy's works, a few rods to the right of the crater. The bearer of the flag stated, that "Hon. ALEXANDER H. STEPHENS, Vice-President of the Southern Confederacy, and Hon. R. M. T. HUNTER, of Virginia, were desirous of proceeding to Gen. GRANT's headquarters; that they were expected, and would have approached our lines via the James River, but were unable to do so, owing to the ice in the stream."

The message sent by the bearer of the Confederate flag of truce was sent at once to the headquarters of the Ninth Corps.

The news that Messrs. STEPHENS and HUNTER were awaiting permission to enter our lines flew like wild-fire through the camps. They were distinguished men; they had made names for themselves before the war began, before acquiescing in the severance of the Republic, and the Union soldiers, who are reading men, knew it. Curiosity is one of the failings of the Union soldier, and, as the news of the flag passed from camp to camp, tents were evacuated, from bomb-proofs temporarily-buried soldiers emerged, pickets brought their rifled-muskets to an "order," and all, not otherwise engaged, covered the parapets of the works of the main and picket lines. As you know, for many days there has been a tacit understanding along this part of the line that there should be no firing; but, until to-day, the members of the corps did not think it conducive to their health to exhibit themselves prominently.

The white flag, however, brought both Unionists and Confederates within plain, point-blank shooting range of each other, and waiting for a reply to the rebel request, they showed themselves in clouds on the works of the contending armies. "How are you Fort Fisher!" says the Yanks; "Good-bye, European importations;" "Have you heard from HOOD?" "Did you know that your Virginian, THOMAS, had presented to Old ABE a 'worsted Hood'!" and many other remarks of a like nature.

The "Confeds" seemed to take it all in good part, and made, in some instances, quite happy replies, such as, "Fort Fisher may be gone up, but why don't you take Fort Crater?" "GWIN's a fool, and we don't care a d—n for anything more from Europe;" and "HOOD's hoodwinked old THOMAS, and you'll hear from him directly, I reckon."

So they passed the time intervening before the reply came. Men who, a few moments later, might be engaged in mortal combat, whiled away the closing hours of the beautiful Sabbath in seemingly friendly intercourse. But does any one dream that, if in the midst of this sort of national gathering, the order had been given, "Prepare for action," any of the soldiers, so jocose and free from care, would have disobeyed the command? No! But, shoulder to shoulder, they would have repeated the lesson they have been endeavoring to teach the foes of their country for these long years. In the soldier's life there is sunshine and shadow, but, alas! the shadow predominates. The Union soldier lives on in the hope that through the shadow will finally break the sun of peace, reflecting [illegible] city's clouds a rainbow of victory, telling in unmistakable colors of a "Union" conquered and thereafter indivisible.

As the bright orb of day neared the western horizon, and glanced upon the lofty spires of the yet unconquered "Cockade City," an officer from the headquarters of the Ninth Corps neared our foremost line. All were on the tiptoe of excitement; but, soldierlike, the gallant Colonel kept his own counsel; and, improvising a flag of truce from a white handkerchief, proceeded to scale the works; and, with one companion, advanced to the neutral ground.

After some minutes' waiting, he was met by four officers of the Confederacy, and a conference was held within a stone's throw of the scene of the terrible tragedy of the 30th of July last. What the result of this interview was, was not made public; but, it is believed that no word had been received from Gen. GRANT, and as a consequence, the "distinguished gentlemen" from Georgia and Virginia would have to bide their time, perhaps until to-morrow.

As the flags receded from each other, the thousands who covered the works suddenly disappeared, walking into their tents, crawling into their holes and descending into their bombproofs, to speculate upon the meaning of such a seemingly urgent desire on the part of the Vice-President and Ex United States Senator to enter the Union lines. Speculation upon this subject is not only rife among the soldiers, but among other thinking men, and the most extravagant propositions are put forth. Of course it is useless to speculate. It may be that the visit of these noted Southern gentlemen will be productive of good; but time alone will tell.

G. F. WILLIAMS.

REPORTS FROM BALTIMORE.

BALTIMORE, Tuesday, Jan. 31.

The *American*, this afternoon, publishes the following dispatch:

"The report has been current on the street since last evening to the effect that the Richmond *Sentinel* has announced the departure of three Peace Commissioners for Washington.

Up to noon to-day, we have no official confirmation of the rumor, though the assertion has been varied this morning by an equally positive announcement that Peace Commissioners, consisting of the rebel Vice-President ALEXANDER H. STEPHENS, and Ex-Senator R. M. T. HUNTER and Judge CAMPBELL had arrived at City Point and were expected to reach Annapolis to-day.

They are not spoken of as commissioners representing the rebel Government, but as citizens representing the people, on their way to Washington to confer with President LINCOLN on the subject of peace, precisely in the same capacity that Mr. BLAIR visited Richmond.

SECOND DISPATCH.

BALTIMORE, Tuesday, Jan. 31.

The *American* has the following special dispatch from Annapolis this morning:

ANNAPOLIS, Tuesday, Jan. 31.

Col. TYLER, of the Second Maryland Regiment, who arrived here this morning, says that on Sunday, ALEX. H. STEPHENS, R. M. T. HUNTER and two others reached our lines, and requested to come within our lines at Fort Hell, but were refused, and were awaiting permission from Gen. GRANT, who was then absent.

N. B.—I think the Commissioners were admitted nevertheless, and are now on their way to Washington. Hope to have something definite soon.

REPORTS VIA PHILADELPHIA.

PHILADELPHIA, Tuesday, Jan. 31.

A special dispatch to the *Evening Telegraph* says:

WASHINGTON, Tuesday, Jan. 31.

It is known in the best informed circles here that a commission from JEFF. DAVIS, consisting of Vice-President STEPHENS, R. M. T. HUNTER, and Gen. G. W. SMITH, have arrived at Annapolis with full power to arrange a settlement of our national difficulties.

It is believed from the understanding between Mr. BLAIR and Mr. DAVIS that the terms will be entirely satisfactory to the Administration and to Congress, and will chiefly consist of an amnesty to all offenders, and a withdrawal of the confiscation proclamation.

The Departure of the Commissioners from Richmond.

BALTIMORE, Tuesday, Jan. 31.

There is reason to believe that the Richmond papers of Monday contain an explicit statement of departure of commissioners for Washington.

From the Richmond Sentinel, Jan. 28.

It was a matter of pleasurable remark on yesterday that the President and Vice-President *had been engaged in a long consultation on public affairs.*

No Arrival yet from the James at Annapolis.

BALTIMORE, Tuesday, Jan. 31.

A dispatch from Annapolis to-night, says there has been no arrival from the James River, and there is no prospect of one to-night.

The Rebel Peace Commissioners.

The history and personal character of the rebel Vice-President, ALEXANDER H. STEPHENS, as well as his strenuous exertions to preserve the South from the folly and crime of secession, are well known to our readers. A. J. CAMPBELL, of Alabama, formerly occupied a seat on the Bench of the Supreme Court of the United States. It will be remembered that just previous to the capture of Fort Sumter, Mr. CAMPBELL appeared in Washington with Mr. FORSYTHE, of Mobile, CRAWFORD, ex-member of Congress from Georgia, and Mr. STEPHENS, on a mission to obtain the peaceful separation of the South from the Union. Since the commencement of hostilities his name has not been prominently before the public. Mr. R. M. T. HUNTER was formerly United States Senator from Virginia. He served a short time as rebel *Secretary of State.*

Return of Mr. Singleton.

Special Dispatch to the New-York News.

WASHINGTON, Monday, Jan. 30, 1865.

Gen. SINGLETON arrived in this city this evening, and immediately waited on the President. During his stay at Richmond he had frequent interviews with Mr. DAVIS and other prominent Confederate leaders, including Gen. LEE. Gen. SINGLETON represents those with whom he had intercourse as well disposed toward any movement calculated to restore peace on an honorable basis.

The Southern people remain firm in their determination to resist subjugation. The leaders are not averse to negotiation, provided it is not based on degrading conditions. They will meet us on equal terms, but not otherwise. They will not lay down their arms and accept whatever we choose to give them. There is no despondency in Richmond, but all, from Mr. DAVIS to the least important citizen, are desirous to have the war brought to a close.

FROM WASHINGTON.

ABOLITION OF SLAVERY.

Passage of the Constitutional Amendment.

One Hundred and Nineteen Yeas against Fifty-six Nays.

Exciting Scene in the House.

ENTHUSIASM OVER THE RESULT.

THE PEACE MISSION IN THE SENATE

A Resolution Calling for Information.

Passage of Retaliation Resolutions in the Senate.

Special Dispatches to the New-York Times.

WASHINGTON, Tuesday, Jan. 31.

THE PASSAGE OF THE CONSTITUTIONAL AMENDMENT.

The great feature of the existing rebellion was the passage to-day by the House of Representatives of the resolutions submitting to the Legislatures of the several States an amendment to the Constitution abolishing slavery. It was an epoch in the history of the country, and will be remembered by the members of the House and spectators present as an event in their lives. At 3 o'clock, by general consent, all discussion having ceased, the preliminary votes to reconsider and second the demand for the previous question were agreed to by a vote of 113 yeas, to 58 nays; and amid profound silence the Speaker announced that the yeas and nays would be taken directly upon the pending proposition. During the call, when prominent Democrats voted aye, there was suppressed evidence of applause and gratification exhibited in the galleries, but it was evident that the great interest centered entirely upon the final result, and when the presiding officer announced that the resolution was agreed to by yeas 119, nays 56, the enthusiasm of all present, save a few disappointed politicians, knew no bounds, and for several moments the scene was grand and impressive beyond description. No attempt was made to suppress the applause which came from all sides, every one feeling that the occasion justified the fullest expression of approbation and joy.

PETITIONS OF THE NAVAL CONTRACTORS.

The House Naval Committee having received a reply from the Secretary of the Navy to-day, unanimously instructed their Chairman to report a joint resolution, referring to the Navy Department the petitions of contractors asking for relief for losses in building double-enders, marine engines, &c., to be settled upon the principle of equity and justice. This is all the petitioners for relief ask, and without some such legislation the department cannot act in the matter.

THE TAX BILL.

The Ways and Means Committee to-day nearly finished the amendments to the tax bill. They expect to get through with the bill this week, and will report it at once.

THE NAVAL DEPOT AT CLEVELAND.

The Senate Naval Committee heard the arguments to-day in favor of a naval depot at Cleveland. The committee will not act definitely in regard to the matter until other parties have been heard.

THE TRADE IN COTTON.

The House Committee on Commerce to-day examined a large number of witnesses who are understood to have permits to trade in cotton with rebel States. These gentlemen, however, were very reticent, and the committee failed to elicit the required information as to how and where they got their permits.

Dispatches to the Associated Press.

WASHINGTON, Tuesday, Jan. 31.

THE VOTE ON THE AMENDMENT.

Soon after the passage of the Anti-Slavery Constitutional Amendment this afternoon, a salute was fired in honor of that event. The vote last June, when it was defeated for the want of the requisite two-thirds majority, was yeas, 96; nays, 65; absent, 21. Those who at that time voted against the amendment, but who changed their votes and cast them in the affirmative to-day, are Messrs. Baldwin of Michigan, Coffroth, McAllister, Ganson, Herrick, Radford, Steele, King, Rollins of Missouri, and Hutchins. Those who were absent on the former occasion, and who now voted aye, are as follows: Messrs. Brown of West Virginia, Davis of Maryland, Davis of New-York, Grinnell, McBride, Nelson, Pomeroy, Randall, Worthington and Yeaman. The following who were absent or not voting when the June vote was taken, voted nay: Messrs. Hall, Harris of Maryland, Harris of Illinois, Winfield, Ben. Wood and Townsend. Those who voted against the resolution last year, and were to-day absent or not voting, are Messrs. Lazear, Le Blond, McKinney, Marcy, McDowell and Rogers.

MR. WADE ON THE PEACE MISSION.

During the debate on the retaliation resolution, while Mr. WADE was speaking about Mr. BLAIR's mission to Richmond, Mr. JOHNSON asked how he came to go there. Mr. WADE replied: "I would like to know. Yes, Sir. I intend to know if there is power in the United States Senate to be informed on that subject. I intend to know why it was that any man was permitted to go with impunity through our lines, and confer with the arch traitor of the Confederacy, and come back here and go again." Mr. JOHNSON said he went in a Government vessel the last time. Mr. WADE responded: "Yes, I understand he went on a Government vessel. He had no more right to be on that vessel on a mission to hold communication with this arch traitor and devil, than he had to be on his road to the lower regions in a vehicle furnished by the Government."

THE CIVIL GOVERNMENT OF VIRGINIA.

The Alexandria (Va.) *Journal* says the civil government has been restored on the eastern shore of Virginia, and that in a few days civil government will be restored in every county where it was suppressed by the action of Gen. BUTLER.

THE SUBSCRIPTIONS TO THE SEVEN-THIRTY LOAN.

The financial arrangements just concluded between the Treasury Department and JAY COOKE contemplate the continuance of subscriptions to the seven-thirties through the national banks in New-York, Philadelphia, Boston and elsewhere, as heretofore.

THIRTY-EIGHTH CONGRESS.

SECOND SESSION.

SENATE.

WASHINGTON, Tuesday, Jan. 31.

PROTEST AGAINST THE BANKRUPT BILL.

Mr. WADE, of Ohio, (Union,) presented a joint resolution of the Ohio Legislature protesting against the passage of the bankrupt law, which was ordered to be printed and laid on the table.

THE DUTY ON IMPORTED PAPER.

Mr. WADE also presented a resolution of the Ohio Legislature in favor of the repeal of the duty on printing paper, which was ordered to be printed and laid upon the table.

EMPLOYMENT OF GENERALS.

Mr. WADE—I notice that the Secretary of War, in replying to a communication of the Senate about the employment of Generals, has made a mistake which I wish to correct. He says, among other things, that Gens. BANKS and LEE are before the Committee on the Conduct of the War. This is a mistake, and one which I wish to rectify, because it seems to be a standing one. I think it interferes with the disposition which the Executive wishes to make of these officers. Mr. WADE further stated that on the 14th of December, Gen. BANKS was before the committee for about two hours, to give testimony concerning the Red River expedition. One day in January the committee found him in the city, and called on him for a few minutes to explain some matters. Gen. LEE had not been before the committee since the 13th of January, when he gave testimony for about two hours. He (WADE) wished it to be understood that neither Gen. BANKS nor Gen. LEE were detained here by the Committee on the Conduct of the War.

CLERGYMEN AND THE DRAFT.

Mr. HARRIS, of New-York, (Union,) offered the memorial of certain ministers of the Gospel, asking that they be exempted from the draft. Which was referred to the Committee on Military Affairs.

THE SCHELDT DUES.

Mr. SUMNER, of Massachusetts, (Union,) from the Committee on Foreign Relations, reported a bill for the extinction of the Scheldt Dues. Which was ordered to be printed.

CONGRESSIONAL DIRECTORY.

Mr. ANTHONY, of Rhode Island, (Union,) introduced a resolution that a Congressional Directory be published hereafter, under the superintendence of the Joint Committee on Printing. Mr. ANTHONY explained that this would be more economical than the present arrangement, by which it was published under the auspices of the Postmaster of the House; but its chief benefit would be the appearance of the Directory at an earlier day in the Session than it now appears.

The resolution was adopted.

CALL FOR INFORMATION ON MR. BLAIR'S MISSION.

Mr. SUMNER offered the following resolution:

Resolved, That the President of the United States be requested, if not incompatible with the public interests, to furnish to the Senate any information in his possession, concerning any recent personal communications with the rebel JEFFERSON DAVIS, said to have been under Executive sanction, and also copies of any correspondence relating thereto.

Mr. CONNESS, of California, (Union)—I suggest to the Senator if it would not be better to leave out the verbiage, and make the resolution refer to the message of Mr. BLAIR.

Mr. SUMNER—I beg the Senator's pardon, but I prefer it as it is.

Mr. JOHNSON, of Maryland, (Union,) offered the following as an amendment by way of a substitute for Mr. SUMNER's proposition:

Resolved, That the President of the United States be requested, if not incompatible with the public interests, to inform the Senate if any person, and if any, who has, with his authority and assent, been in Richmond negotiating with the President of the so-called Confederate States, or with any other person or persons in that place, in relation to the termination of the present war, or with a view to ascertain, from such person or persons, upon what terms, if any, they would be willing to have said war terminated; and if so, to inform the Senate, also, what information he has obtained from such agent or person; also, if such person was in Richmond as aforesaid, whether he was authorized or permitted by the President of the United States to represent to the Confederate authorities upon what terms or conditions the President would negotiate in relation to peace, and, if so, what such terms and conditions were.

Mr. SUMNER said that the resolution he offered was much briefer and simpler than that of the Senator from Maryland. There were some words in Mr. JOHNSON's resolution which he did not like. He did not like to see the Senate adopt such a phrase as the Confederate authorities.

SEVERAL SENATORS—The resolution says "so called Confederate authorities."

Mr. SUMNER said he preferred to speak of them as rebel authorities.

Mr. DOOLITTLE, of Wisconsin, (Union,) suggested that both resolutions be printed and called up to-morrow.

This was agreed to and it was so ordered.

SECRETARY WELLES INTERROGATED.

Mr. HALE offered a resolution calling upon the Secretary of the Navy for information as to whether the arguments of the Judge-Advocate in the trial of Mr. SMITH, of Boston, had been printed by order of the Navy Department? What edition of the same had been published? What use has been made of the copies thus published? Also, whether any detectives have been employed by the Navy Department since January, 1864, and if so, how many, and how much they have been paid? what instructions they got, either written or verbal, from the Secretary or Assistant Secretary of the Navy? And especially whether any instructions were given to inquire into the conduct and business transactions of any member of either House of Congress? How much expense was incurred in this way? From what sources the funds were drawn, and by what authority?

Mr. CONNESS—I suggest that the resolution of the Senator from New-Hampshire lie over until the return of the chairman of the Committee on Naval Affairs, who is now absent.

Mr. HALE consented to the proposition, and the resolution was ordered to be printed.

NEW-YORK AND PACIFIC MAIL.

Mr. ANTHONY introduced a bill relative to mail service between New-York and the Pacific coast, which authorizes the Postmaster-General to contract for the transportation of the mails upon such lines by steamers on the Atlantic and Pacific coast, and by land transit across the Isthmus, semi-monthly, tri-monthly, or weekly, as in his judgment the public interest may from time to time require; the compensation not to exceed $400,000 for a semi-monthly, $600,000 for a tri-monthly, or $800,000 for a weekly line.

The bill was referred to the Committee on the Post-office and Post Roads.

THE BILL TO BRIDGE THE OHIO.

Mr. POWELL, of Kentucky, (Dem.,) asked that the Senate take up the bill to build a bridge across the River at Louisville.

The motion was disagreed to.

THE PROPOSED COMMITTEE ON CORRUPTIONS.

Mr. HALE then moved that the Senate proceed to the consideration of the resolution of Mr. DAVIS for the appointment of a Standing Committee on Corruptions of the Government.

Mr. DOOLITTLE suggested that as the animadversions of the Senator from New-Hampshire on the conduct of the Navy Department were likely to lead to protracted discussion, it would be well to make this the special order for some day, as there was very little time of the morning hour remaining.

Mr. HALE insisted on his motion.

Mr. HENDERSON desired to take up the bill to reimburse the State of Missouri for the expenses incurred in calling out the militia of that State.

The Senate refused to take up this bill and proceeded to the consideration of the resolution of Mr. DAVIS, upon which Mr. HALE was entitled to the floor.

Mr. HALE said he was opposed to appointing any more committees to investigate corruptions until some action was taken on frauds already discovered. He read at length from a report made by Hon. JOHN SHERMAN, when a member of the House, on the subject of naval contracts, to show that, while Congress had heretofore gone to great trouble and expense to discover frauds, yet none of the guilty parties had ever been punished.

THE QUESTION OF RETALIATION.

The morning hour expired, and the Chair decided that the retaliation resolution was in order on the proposition to recommit the papers on the subject to the Military Committee.

The subject was discussed by Messrs. HENDRICKS, WADE, SUMNER, SPRAGUE and HOWE.

Mr. SAULSBURY, of Delaware, (Dem.,) said that if all the allegations against the rebels as to their treatment of our soldiers be true, it was but another argument for peace. He was not ashamed to stand up in the Senate and advocate peace. He was not in the habit of endorsing what the President did. But if, as he heard, commissioners were on their way here to treat for peace, and this was the result of promises held out to the Confederates by the President, he was willing to endorse him so far.

The question was then taken on the motion to recommit the subject, and the Senate refused so to do. Yeas 10, nays 26.

YEAS—Messrs. Carlile, Davis, Hendricks, Powell, Richardson, Riddle, Saulsbury, Sumner, Van Winkle, Wright.

NAYS—Messrs. Anthony, Chandler, Clark, Collamer, Conness, Cowan, Dixon, Foster, Hale, Harlan, Harris, Henderson, Howard, Howe, Johnson, Lane of Indiana, Morgan, Merrill, Nesmith, Pomeroy, Ramsay, Sherman, Ten Eyck, Wade, Wilkinson, Willey.

The question then recurred on the amendment making retaliation comformable to the law of nations.

Mr. SUMNER moved further to amend by making it conform also to the usages of war as practiced among civilized nations. Mr. SUMNER called for the yeas and nays on the amendment, and it was adopted by a vote of 26 yeas against 13 nays.

YEAS—Messrs. Carlile, Cowan, Davis, Doolittle, Foote, Foster, Harlan, Harris, Henderson, Hendricks, Lane of Indiana, McDougall, Morgan, Nesmith, Pomeroy, Powell, Richardson, Riddle, Saulsbury, Sherman, Sumner, Ten Eyck, Van Winkle, Willey, Wilson, Wright.

NAYS—Messrs. Chandler, Clark, Collamer, Conness, Dixon, Farwell, Hale, Howard, Howe, Ramsay, Trumbull, Wade, Wilkinson.

Mr. SUMNER moved to amend by striking out the following; "Congress does not, however, intend by this to limit or restrict the power of the President to the modes or principles of retaliation herein mentioned; but only advises or requires a resort to them as demanded by the occasion."

Mr. SHERMAN, of Ohio, (Union,) suggested that the amendment be modified so as to strike out the words "to the modes or principles of retaliation herein mentioned."

This was adopted.

Mr. HENDRICKS, of Indiana, (Dem.,) offered as an amendment an additional resolution, declaring the sense of the Senate to be in favor of an exchange of prisoners.

Mr. HOWARD, of Michigan, (Union,) thought the subjects were so different that they should not be incorporated in the same resolution.

The amendment was adopted.

Mr. HENDERSON, of Missouri, (Union,) offered an amendment, advising the appointment of Commissioners of Prisoners, to look after the condition of our prisoners in the future.

The yeas and nays were called for, and the amendment was adopted.

YEAS—Messrs. Carlile, Collamer, Cowan, Davis, Doolittle, Foot, Foster, Harris, Henderson, Hendricks, Johnson, Lane of Kansas, McDougall, Morgan, Nesmith, Pomeroy, Powell, Riddle, Sumner, Ten Eyck, Van Winkle, Willey, Wilson, Wright—24.

NAYS—Messrs. Chandler, Clark, Conness, Dixon, Farwell, Hale, Harlan, Howard, Howe, Lane of Indiana, Morrill, Ramsay, Sherman, Trumbull, Wade, Wilkinson—16.

The resolution as amended was then passed and the Senate adjourned.

HOUSE OF REPRESENTATIVES.

WASHINGTON, Tuesday, Jan. 31.

MR. WOOD OFFERS A RESOLUTION.

Mr. FERNANDO WOOD asked leave to offer the following resolution:

Resolved, That it is the duty of the President to maintain, in every constitutional and legal manner, the integrity of the American Union, as formed by the Fathers of the Republic, and in no event, and under no circumstances, to proffer or accept negotiations which shall admit, by the remotest implication, the existence of any other Federal or Confederate Government within the territory of the United States.

Mr. FARNSWORTH, of Illinois, (Union,) objected to the reception of the resolution.

Mr. FERNANDO WOOD gave notice that he would next Monday move a suspension of the rules to introduce the resolution.

THE PRESIDENTIAL VOTE.

The Speaker appointed Mr. Stevens of Pennsylvania, Mr. Washburne of Illinois, Mr. Mallory of Kentucky, Mr. Davis of Maryland, and Mr. Cox of Ohio, as a committee on the part of the House to examine and count the votes for President and Vice-President of the United States, on the second Wednesday of February.

THE ANTI-SLAVERY AMENDMENT.

The House resumed consideration of the Senate joint resolution, proposing amendments to the Constitution of the United States.

Mr. MCALLISTER of Pennsylvania (Dem.) said when this subject was before the House on a former occasion, I voted against the measure. I have been in favor of exhausting all the means of conciliation to restore the Union as our fathers made it. I am for the Union and utterly opposed to secession or dissolution in any way or shape. The result of all the peace missions, and especially that of Mr. BLAIR has satisfied me that nothing short of recognition of their independence will satisfy the Southern Confederacy. It must therefore be destroyed, and in voting for the present measure, I cast my vote against the cornerstone of the Southern Confederacy, and declare eternal war against the enemies of my country.

Mr. COFFROTH, of Pennsylvania, (Dem.,) addressed the House in favor of the amendment, not, however, speaking for or against slavery. He argued the power of Congress to submit the amendment to the Legislatures of the States; that the South could defeat the amendment; that it must be submitted to the seceded States, or it would be recognizing their independence; that if this was done, it would apply only to those which adopted it. He also argued that the South would not remain in the Union under the Constitution as it now is, and that they would not come back after four years' fighting. All relating to slavery should be stricken from our statute books, and then, when the people of the South were tired and sick of this barbarous and inhuman war, and demand a cessation of hostilities, until it be ascertained if peace cannot be obtained, there will be no obstacles in the way of giving new guarantees to every person who shelters himself under the American Constitution. He also argued that slavery was the fruitful theme for the opponents of Democracy. It breathed life and existence into fanaticism, and unless that which sustained and fed fanaticism be removed from the political arena, the country would remain stationary, when all the rest of the world is moving. Change is the universal law of nature. What he had heretofore regarded as impolitic had ceased to operate. Having at the last session voted against the proposed Constitutional amendment, he would now vote for it. He had no doubt of the power to make the amendment in the manner proposed. In amending it three-fourths of the States represent the whole. The time has arrived to exercise the power. He believed that if Democratic policy and measures had been adopted, we should not now be engaged in war; but in the late Presidential election the people had endorsed the anti-slavery issue. He was prepared to follow it. The question had been settled by the verdict of the people, and so far as the National Government was concerned, it was not now a political issue. The adoption of the amendment would tend to restore all that is desirable to the prosperity of the country. He believed the best good of the Democratic party would be enhanced by the passage of the proposition, and it will open up a way to its triumph in the future.

Mr. BROWN, of Wisconsin, (Dem.,) spoke of the dangerous abuse of the power of the amendment. He had never been the apologist for slavery. He never thought it could be entirely destroyed. He was in favor of removing it, and then the people would place in power the Democracy. He gave this vote after much consideration, and as a Democrat, and would consistently stand by the organization of his party. No power on earth should prevent him from voting for the candidates of his party. His desire was the triumph of the party which has made this country great.

Mr. MILLER, of Pennsylvania, (Dem.,) said he owed it to himself and his constituents to reply to the sentiments of his colleagues just uttered on this floor. He wished to so act that when he returned home he would not be found derelict to the duty with which he had been entrusted, having taken an oath to protect, defend and preserve the Constitution of the United States. Long as the matter had been discussed here, it was very strange that no man had answered the question, what was to be done with the freed people, should such an amendment to the Constitution prove effective? Gentlemen on the other side had failed to make out a case. During this Administration the Constitution had been violated in all its important features.

Mr. HERRICK, of New-York, (Dem.,) in the course of his speech, said it was inconsistent that it would be a permanent institution. If he lived in Missouri or Kentucky, he should vote for the abolition of slavery therein; but as to Congressional action on that subject, it might be different. The question of slavery under the Constitution was reserved to the States respectively wherein it exists. In conclusion, he caused to be read a substitute which he desired to submit, providing that hereafter every sale and transfer of slaves shall be void and the slaves shall become free and from and after 1880 slavery shall cease, and Congress shall give compensation for the actual damage and loss suffered by loyal citizens of the United States.

Mr. HARDING, of Kentucky, (Dem.,) said truth and principle never change, but men change, and from time to time adopt opinions just as readily as they change their garments. But he would rather hold on to the Constitution, which was the only ark of safety. He denied that there was any constitutional power to deprive any State in the Union of its local self-government. Kentucky had been treated in bad faith. Not one of the pledges made to her had been fulfilled. She had been betrayed, and now it was sought suddenly to emancipate all her slaves. The policy would result in the destruction of the slaves, and the men who proposed to carry it out had no more love for the slave than Satan has for sinners.

Mr. KALBFLEISCH, of New-York, (Dem.,) opposed the proposition. He maintained that all our political misfortunes are attributable to a disregard of the Constitution. He had not learned his democracy from his inveterate enemies, and he would not be instructed by them now. This amendment, he contended, if adopted, would stand in the way of peace negotiations and a restoration of the Union. He said he should strive to uphold and carry out the pledges which he had made to protect and defend the Constitution. Apart from the question of power, this was not the time to attempt an amendment of the Constitution in the manner proposed. He denied that the result of the Presidential election was a favor of abolishing slavery everywhere. No such issue was made up in New-York.

The debate having closed, Mr. ASHLEY, of Ohio, (Union,) who had charge of the subject throughout, demanded the previous question, which was on the motion heretofore made by the gentleman, to reconsider the vote of last session, by which the constitutional amendment was lost for the want of the requisite two-thirds majority.

Mr. STILES, of Pennsylvania, (Dem.,) moved that the motion to reconsider be laid on the table.

This was decided in the negative. Yeas 57; nays, 111.

The question was then taken on the motion to reconsider, and it was decided in the affirmative. Yeas, 112; nays, 57.

Mr. MALLORY, of Kentucky, (Dem.,) raised the question that a vote of two-thirds was requisite to reconsider; but the Speaker overruled the point, saying all motions of this kind were governed by the rules.

Mr. MALLORY suggested a postponement of the vote until to-morrow, saying that several gentlemen who wished to record their names were absent. Let the time for taking the question be fixed so that all could have a fair warning.

Mr. ASHLEY replied that it had been universally understood that the question was to be taken to-day. He had consented to the extension of the debate even against the protest of his friends. It came with a very bad grace to ask for a postponement of the vote, considering the courtesy he had extended to the other side and the fair notice given.

Mr. BROWN, of Wisconsin, (Union,) asked the gentleman to give way in order that he might offer a substitute.

Mr. ASHLEY said he had one himself, which he preferred to the Senate's proposition now before the House.

Mr. ELDRIDGE, of Wisconsin, (Dem.,)—Why do you not offer it?

Mr. ASHLEY—Because I will not protract the proceedings.

The question was then taken on the adoption of the following Senate joint resolution, submitting to the Legislatures of the several States, a proposition to amend the Constitution of the United States:

Be it resolved by the Senate and House of Representatives of the United States of America in Congress assembled, two-thirds of both Houses concurring, that the following articles be proposed to the Legislatures of the several States as an amendment to the Constitution of the United States; when ratified by three-fourths of said Legislatures, shall be valid to all intents and purposes as a part of the said Constitution, namely:

ART. 13.—SECTION 1. Neither slavery nor involuntary servitude, except as a punishment for crime, whereof the party shall have been duly convicted, shall exist within the United States, or any place subject to their jurisdiction.

SEC 2. Congress shall have power to enforce this article by appropriate legislation.

There was much confusion throughout the proceedings, amid which the clerk proceeded to call the roll on the passage of the joint resolution.

The Speaker said, "Call my name as a member of this House."

The name was accordingly called.

When the Speaker answered to the name of SCHUYLER COLFAX, applause followed his response, and also burst out at other parts of the proceedings; which, however, the Speaker checked, and calling the House to order, said he hoped a better example would be set to preserve the decorum of the House.

Several members on the Democratic side of the House said those on the other side were as noisy as the persons in the galleries.

Mr. GANSON, of New-York, (Dem.,) had voted "no" on the question of reconsidering the vote by which the joint resolution was heretofore lost, now voted "aye," and Messrs. RADFORD and STEELE, (Dems.) of New-York, changed their votes in the same manner. These changes gave rise to applause, which was promptly checked.

The utmost interest was manifested throughout the calling of the roll, and there was strict attention on the part of the members to their responses; for, on the previous vote to reconsider, two-thirds of the members present had not voted in the affirmative, but a large majority of the members present had carried that question. It was therefore somewhat doubtful whether the pending joint resolution would be passed.

The votes of Mr. BALDWIN of Michigan (Dem.) and the gentlemen above mentioned however gave additional hopes to the friends of the measure.

When the calling of the roll was completed the Clerk proceeded to read the names, first of those who voted in the affirmative, and next of those who had voted in the negative. The House was now comparatively silent. The result of the vote was noted on a piece of paper and handed by the Clerk to the Speaker, who then announced the passage of the joint resolution by a vote of 119 yeas against 56 nays.

Thereupon rose a general shout of applause. The members on the floor huzzaed in chorus with deafening and equally emphatic cheers of the throng in the galleries. The ladies in the dense assemblage waved their handkerchiefs, and again and again the applause was repeated, intermingled with clapping of hands and exclamations of "Hurrah for freedom!" "Glory enough for one day," &c. The audience were wildly excited, and the friends of the measure jubilant. Never was a scene of such a joyous character before witnessed in the House of Representatives, certainly not within the last quarter of a century.

There was extensive hand-shaking and congratulation in every direction. The proceedings had attracted thousands of persons of both sexes, and having been brought to a close, those on the floor who had been admitted by the favor of the members, and the occupants of the galleries, hastily departed.

The vote on the passage of the joint resolution is as follows:

YEAS (DEMOCRATS IN ITALICS.)

Messrs. Alison, Iowa,
Ames, Massachusetts,
Anderson, Kentucky,
Arnold, Illinois,
Ashley, Ohio,
Bailey, Pennsylvania,
Baldwin, Michigan,
Baldwin, Massachusetts,
Baxter, Vermont,
Beaman, Michigan,
Blaine, Maine,
Blair, West Virginia,
Blow, Missouri,
Boutwell, Massachusetts,
Boyd, Missouri,
Brandagee, Connecticut,
Broomall, Pennsylvania,
Brown, West Virginia,
Ambrose W. Clark, New-York,
Freeman Clark, New-York,
Cobb, Wisconsin,
Coffroth, Pennsylvania,
Colfax, Indiana,
Cole, California,
Creswell, Maryland,
Davis, Indiana,
Davis, New-York,
Dawes, Massachusetts,
Deming, Connecticut,
Dixon, Rhode Island,
Donnelly, Minnesota,
Driggs, Michigan,
Dumont, Indiana,
Eckley, Ohio,
Eliot, Massachusetts,
English, Connecticut,
Farnsworth, Illinois,
Frank, New-York,
Ganson, New-York,
Garfield, Ohio,
Gooch, Massachusetts,
Grinnell, Iowa,
Griswold, New-York,
Hale, Pennsylvania,
Herrick, New-York,
Higby, California,
Hooper, Massachusetts,
Hotchkiss, New-York,
Hubbard, Iowa,
Hubbard, Connecticut,
Hubbard, New-York,
Hutchins, Ohio,
Ingersoll, Illinois,
Jenckes, Rhode Island,
Julian, Indiana,
Kasson, Iowa,
Kelley, Pennsylvania,
Kellogg, Michigan,
Kellogg, New-York,
King, Missouri,
Knox, Missouri,
Littlejohn, New-York,
Loan, Missouri,
Longyear, Michigan,
Marvin, New-York,
McAllister, Pennsylvania,
McBride, Oregon,
McClurg, Missouri,
McIndoe, Wisconsin,
Miller, New-York,
Morehead, Pennsylvania,
Morrill, Vermont,
Morris, New-York,
A. Myers, Pennsylvania,
L. Myers, Pennsylvania,
Nelson, New-York,
Norton, Illinois,
Odell, New-York,
O'Neill, Pennsylvania,
Orth, Indiana,
Patterson, New-York,
Perham, Maine,
Pike, Maine,
Pomeroy, New-York,
Price, Iowa,
Radford, New-York,
Randall, Kentucky,
Rice, Massachusetts,
Rice, Maine,
Rollins, New-Hampshire,
Rollins, Missouri,
Schenck, Ohio,
Scofield, Pennsylvania,
Shannon, California,
Sloan, Wisconsin,
Smith, Kentucky,
Smithers, Delaware,
Spalding, Ohio,
Starr, New-Jersey,
Steele, New-York,
Stearns, Pennsylvania,
Thayer, Pennsylvania,
Thomas, Maryland,
Tracy, Pennsylvania,
Upson, Michigan,
Van Valkenburgh, New-York,
Washburne, Illinois,
Washburne, Massachusetts,
Webster, Maryland,
Whaley, West Virginia,
Wheeler, Wisconsin,
Williams, Pennsylvania,
Wilder, Kansas,
Wilson, Iowa,
Windham, Minnesota,
Woodbridge, Vermont,
Worthington, Nevada,
Yeaman, Kentucky—119.

NAYS (ALL DEMOCRATS EXCEPT CLAY.)

Messrs. J. C. Allen, Illinois,
W. J. Allen, Illinois,
Ancona, Pennsylvania,
Bliss, Ohio,
Brooks, New-York,
Brown, Wisconsin,
Chanler, New-York,
Clay, Kentucky,
Cox, Ohio,
Cravens, Indiana,
Dawson, Pennsylvania,
Denison, Pennsylvania,
Eden, Illinois,
Edgerton, Indiana,
Eldridge, Wisconsin,
Finck, Ohio,
Grider, Kentucky,
Hale, Missouri,
Harding, Kentucky,
Harrington, Indiana,
Harris, Maryland,
Harris, Illinois,
Holman, Indiana,
Johnson, Pennsylvania,
Johnson, Ohio,
Kalbfleisch, New-York,
Kernan, New-York,
Knapp, Illinois,
Law, Indiana,
Long, Ohio,
Mallory, Kentucky,
Miller, Pennsylvania,
Morris, Ohio,
Morrison, Illinois,
Noble, Ohio,
O'Neil, Ohio,
Pendleton, Ohio,
Perry, New-Jersey,
Pruyn, New-York,
Randall, Pennsylvania,
Robinson, Illinois,
Ross, Illinois,
Scott, Missouri,
Steele, New-Jersey,
Stiles, Pennsylvania,
Strouse, Pennsylvania,
Stuart, Illinois,
Sweat, Maine,
Townsend, New-York,
Wadsworth, Kentucky,
Ward, New-York,
White, J. W. Ohio,
White, C. A. Ohio,
Winfield, New-York,
Ben. Wood, New-York,
F. Wood, New-York—56.

ABSENT, OR NOT VOTING.

The absentees, or those not voting, were:

Messrs. Lazear, Penn.,
Leblonde, Ohio,
Marcy, New-Hampshire,
McDowell, Indiana,
McKinney, Ohio,
Middleton, New-Jersey,
Rogers, New-Jersey,
Voorhees, Indiana—8.

All Democrats.

A motion to adjourn was carried amid the greatest confusion, yeas 121, nays 24.

The New-York Times.

VOL. XIV......NO. 4220. NEW-YORK, TUESDAY, APRIL 4, 1865. PRICE FOUR CENTS

GRANT.

RICHMOND

AND

VICTORY!

The Union Army in the Rebel Capital.

Rout and Flight of the Great Rebel Army from Richmond.

Jeff. Davis and His Crew Driven Out.

Grant in Close Pursuit of Lee's Routed Forces.

Richmond and Petersburgh in Full Possession of Our Forces.

ENTHUSIASM IN THE REBEL CAPITAL.

The Citizens Welcome Our Army with Demonstrations of Joy.

RICHMOND FIRED BY THE ENEMY

Our Troops Save the City from Destruction.

THE EVACUATION OF PETERSBURGH.

FIRST DISPATCH.

[OFFICIAL.]

WAR DEPARTMENT,
WASHINGTON, April 3—10 A. M.

To Major-Gen. Dix:

The following telegram from the President, announcing the EVACUATION OF PETERSBURGH and probably of Richmond, has just been received by this department:

EDWIN M. STANTON, Secretary of War.

CITY POINT, Va., April 3—8:30 A. M.

To Hon. Edwin M. Stanton, Secretary of War:

This morning Lieut.-Gen. GRANT reports Petersburgh evacuated, and he is confident that Richmond also is.

He is pushing forward to cut off, if possible, the retreating rebel army.

A. LINCOLN.

THE CAPTURE OF RICHMOND.

SECOND DISPATCH.

WAR DEPARTMENT, WASHINGTON, D. C.,
April 3—10 A. M.

To Maj.-Gen. Dix:

It appears from a dispatch of Gen. WEITZEL just received by this Department, that our forces under his command ARE IN RICHMOND, having taken it at 8:15 this morning.

EDWIN M. STANTON, Secretary of War.

THIRD DISPATCH.

WAR DEPARTMENT, WASHINGTON,
Monday, April 3—12 o'clock noon.

Maj.-Gen. Dix:

The following official confirmation of the capture of Richmond, and the announcement that the city is on fire has been received.

E. M. STANTON, Secretary of War.

CITY POINT, Monday, April 3—11 A. M.

To Edwin M. Stanton, Secretary of War:

Gen. WEITZEL telegraphs as follows:

"We took Richmond at 8:15 this morning. I captured many guns. The enemy left in great haste. The city is on fire in one place. Am making every effort to put it out. The people receive us with enthusiastic expressions of joy."

Gen. GRANT started early this morning with the army toward the Danville road, to cut off LEE's retreating army, if possible.

President LINCOLN has gone to the front.

T. S. BOWERS, A. A. G.

E. M. STANTON.

OUR SPECIAL ACCOUNTS.

Movements by Gen. Sheridan—His Call for Reinforcements—Four Thousand Prisoners Captured—Operations on the Petersburgh Front—The Gunboat Fleet Doing its Part.

From Our Own Correspondent.

HEADQUARTERS ARMY OF THE POTOMAC,
Sunday, April 2—6 A. M.

After we quitted the field on Friday evening the left of the Fifth Corps swung about half a mile further round, and drove the enemy before them. But intelligence being received from Gen. SHERIDAN that the condition of the ground on his front was such that he could not operate with cavalry, and his advance had, therefore, been compelled to fall back. The Fifth Corps was ordered to go to his assistance, in order to relieve it and prevent its withdrawal. Being perceived and taken advantage of by the enemy, Gen. MILES' division of the Second Corps was advanced by the left flank in its front, and it was then withdrawn to the Boydtown road.

Gen. MILES' division of the Second then fell back to a position on the plankroad behind a temporary embankment that had been thrown up on Wednesday, leaving in the line he recently occupied nothing more than skirmishers, who were directed to fall back if attacked. The Second Division of the Fifth Corps, Gen. AYERS, set out early this morning to support Gen. SHERIDAN, and the divisions of Gen. GRIFFIN and Gen. CRAWFORD followed it about noon. They all formed a junction with Gen. SHERIDAN's Corps at a distance of some five miles from the Mrs. Butler house, and a general engagement commenced there about 3 o'clock.

I was not able to go out, as the distance is too great for me to accomplish anything in time for the mail. I understand, however, that the combined forces of Gens. SHERIDAN and WARREN succeeded, after a hotly contested fight, in putting the enemy to flight. They captured four thousand prisoners, four batteries of artillery, a large train of loaded wagons and a number of cattle. The rebel loss in killed and wounded, as well as our own was very heavy, but I am unable to give any estimate of the number.

On our lines during the day there was no fighting except on the Twenty-fourth Corps front. The rebels assaulted the pickets of that corps, and attempted to retake the picket line, from which they were driven yesterday. They were speedily repulsed with a loss of about twenty-five killed and wounded and sixty-four prisoners. Our loss was fifteen in the aggregate.

In the afternoon our troops were massed at three places in the Ninth Corps front, at two in the Sixth, and one in the Twenty-fourth, one in the Twenty-fifth, and two in the Second, with a view of making several demonstrations on the enemy's works and going through them, if necessary, for the complete development of the plan of attack. In pursuance with this design our artillery opened a furious cannonading along the entire front at about 11 P. M., which was continued with little intermission until 6 o'clock this morning. At 3 this morning, such of our troops as it was deemed proper to send in were got into position in front of our works and held ready to make the assault.

I have not yet had time to ascertain which troops were led to the assault, nor the results at different points, and am only able to speak of the Second Division, Gen. POTTER's, of the Ninth Corps. This division was posted on that part of the line between forts Sedgwick and Davis, and some time before the hour of attack arrived the Brigade Commanders Gens. GRIFFIN and CURTIN, perceiving the opportunity to do so without endangering their own men made a sortie and captured one hundred and thirty-three men and four officers of the rebel pickets.

His picket-line was completely surprised, and only knew of the attack when called upon to surrender. At this hour, 6 A. M., there is exceedingly heavy firing along the entire line from Deep Bottom to the Boydtown plank-road, and the fleet of gunboats on the James River are participating in it.

The assault on the enemy's works commenced at 4 o'clock in several places, and is still progressing, but with what success is not yet known. In the front of the Second Division of the Ninth Corps there seems to be more artillery engaged than elsewhere on the line, except at the point where the gunboats are engaged. But Gen. POTTER and his two able Brigade Generals, GRIFFIN and CURTIN, are holding their men well up the work, and the determination is universal throughout the division to go through if required. Gen. POTTER and his staff are in the hottest part of the field, overseeing the assault in person. The General feels, no doubt, that his front is one of the most important positions on the whole line, and from its proximity to the rebel works, most liable to be broken through, except that opposite Fort Steadman, and he is consequently extremely solicitous respecting it. The front at Fort Steadman is ably defended by Gen. WILCOX.

LATER.

Part of the line on the left is said to have made a successful demonstration and captured a number of prisoners. If possible to get it through in time, I will send you particulars, dispatching it to City Point by express before the boat leaves.

Among the prisoners captured by the Ninth Corps are eight officers, one of them a Major. Col. GOWAN, of the Forty-eighth Pennsylvania, was badly wounded, as also Col. WINSLOW and Major STEINBERGE, of the One Hundred and Sixth New-York; Col. GREGG, One Hundred and Seventy-ninth New-York, badly wounded and reported dead. The fighting was so severe that the loss on both sides must necessarily be very heavy. The rebels fought our men hand to hand when we were about climbing the parapet of the fort, although lying down at the time to avoid the fire of our advancing line. Gen. GRIFFIN, of the Second Brigade of the Division, led the way into their works, and when Gen. POTTER sent to ask if he could hold the works, and if not to fall back, his reply was, "Tell Gen. POTTER I can hold the works. Send me more men if you can; but I will hold the works." He took command of the division on Gen. POTTER being wounded. Gen. CURTIN, of the First Brigade, also behaved with great gallantry, holding his men up to the works till an entrance was effected, and then dashing forward at their head driving the enemy before him. This fight, even if not ultimately successful, proves the old Ninth Corps to be equal to any emergency. The task set for it is the worst this army ever had to do, and so far it has accomplished the object unaided. Everybody here thinks those who are left of us will quarter in Petersburgh to-night, and that the old stars and stripes will wave over the cockade city ere the setting of the sun. In taking Petersburgh we draw the cord that will soon strangle the rebellion in Richmond.

Gen. WILCOX is also in the field with his staff. The lines here are also very close together, and if our forces should be repulsed and disordered, the enemy would have an excellent opportunity to inflict serious damage, and make us pay dearly for the temerity we have evinced in attempting to assault such almost impregnable works as those he occupies along this line.

Gen. HARTRANFT'S Division is engaged in the assault, but I am not able to say at what particular point or with what success. It is composed wholly of new troops who have never been in any engagement but that of the 25th ult., but they behaved so nobly on that occasion that great things are expected of them. And they have such regard for their brave and noble Division Commander that they will no doubt strive hard for the sake of his reputation and their own. Gen. PARKE, the Corps Commander, is also near the scene of action with his staff and within range of the enemy's guns directing the operations. From the present aspect of affairs he will have cause to be proud of his corps ere the day closes as we are no doubt already partially within the enemy's lines, strong as they are, whether we can hold them will soon be known. It is thought here that we can both take and hold them.

1 o'clock. A. M.—The demonstration in front of the Second division of the Ninth Corps promises to be a success. We have captured two of their forts, guns and all, and the line of works between and on either flank, and have taken two hundred more prisoners. The fight is still raging furiously. Our loss must be heavy, but at this hour it is impossible to give any estimate. We have succeeded in compelling them to bring their forces from the left and thus opened the way there for SHERIDAN and WARREN to operate successfully. Their force in this front, and which we are now fighting, is Gen. GORDON's corps, principally Southern troops from Alabama, Ga., and South Carolina. They have fought hard since the attack commenced, and still continue to dispute the ground inch by inch.

I regret to say that Gen. POTTER is severely wounded, being shot through the stomach. It is not classed as a mortal wound, but is highly dangerous.

I have not yet been able to learn how matters stand elsewhere, but we have now a strong force within their line of works and will hold them. By to-night, I hope to write you from Petersburgh,

H. H. YOUNG.

Skirmishing on March 30 Near Supporty Cross-Roads.

From Our Own Correspondent.

DINWIDDIE COURT-HOUSE, Va., Thursday, March 30.
Via WASHINGTON, Monday, April 3—8:45 P. M.

The advance of Gen. SHERIDAN'S command crossed Hatcher's Run yesterday, meeting only slight opposition and annoyance at that place from the enemy's cavalry.

W. H. F. LEE's cavalry, three brigades, was in front, but did not see fit to make a stand.

To-day, in an attempt to reach Supporty cross-roads, some of PICKETT's command and LEE's cavalry formed a line of battle and held the ground. In the skirmish that took place the following named persons were wounded:

KILLED AND WOUNDED.

John Leonard, Company F, Sixth United States Cavalry, left thigh, flesh; James N. Glosswax, Company A, Sixth United States Cavalry, hip; John Thompson, Company M, Sixth United States Cavalry; Henry M. Feelan, First United States Cavalry; Patrick Germon, Company F, Sixth United States Cavalry; John Mooney, Company M, Seventh Michigan; Sergt. Marsh, First Michigan, killed; Sergt. J. L. Culiek, Seventh Michigan, foot; Sergt. R. Harris, Fifth United States Cavalry; J. B. Morril, Company M, Fifth United States Cavalry; Sergt. Thomas M. Welles, Company F, Sixth United States Cavalry; Sergt. James Homer; Corp. E. Leabe, Fifth United States Cavalry, arm, severe; Sergt. J. Miller, Sixth United States; J. Davidson, First Michigan; Maj. Duggin, First Michigan; William Sherburne, Twentieth Pennsylvania; D. Duggin, First Michigan; George Nash; Corp. George Derrick; Sergt. Robert Rordan, Sixth New-York; Corp. George B. Lott, Twentieth Pennsylvania.

E. A. PAUL.

Details of the Victory.

Dispatches to the Associated Press.

HEADQUARTERS ARMY OF THE POTOMAC,
Saturday, April 1.

The greater portion of the army has not been engaged with the enemy to-day. The time has been occupied in erecting works on the new line, and repairing the roads connecting the different corps. The late rains had rendered it impossible to move the wagon trains as fast as the troops advanced. One train took forty-eight hours to move five miles with the assistance of one thousand men. But through the untiring industry and perseverance of the officers in charge of the Quartermaster's and Commissary Departments, the army has been almost as well supplied as while in their old quarters.

When the news of SHERIDAN's repulse reached here last night, a part of the Fifth Corps was at once despatched to his aid, and it is expected that to-night or in the morning we shall receive good news from that quarter.

It appears that SHERIDAN was moving on the road leading to a place called the Three Forks, about three miles from the Southside Railroad, when two cavalry brigades of PICKETT's division, which had been moved out in a great hurry, came down on a road running from Sutherland Station. As SHERIDAN's cavalry had most of them passed the junction, this movement of the enemy threatened to cut him off. He, however, discovered his danger in time to get his command back with only a slight loss, at the same time taking about 100 prisoners. Both the LEES were present, but one of them was at a respectful distance.

On being reinforced this morning by the Fifth Corps, the enemy fell back so rapidly that their dead and many of their wounded fell into our hands, as well as those of our own that were unavoidably left behind yesterday afternoon.

The attack made on the enemy's line in front of the Twenty-fourth Corps was led by FOSTER's division, and about two hundred prisoners were brought in, the One Hundred and Forty-eighth New-York taking most of them. Some three hundred or four hundred yards of ground was taken from them, and our picket line so much further advanced.

At 4 o'clock this morning this position was assaulted, and a few of our men captured; but in a very short time it was retaken, with about sixty prisoners and a stand of colors.

Our losses up to the present time will not exceed twenty-five hundred; while those of the enemy, on some parts of the line, at least, were greater than our own; but, of course, the total cannot be given.

Major DYKEMAN, of the Fifteenth New-York Heavy Artillery, is reported wounded and a prisoner.

Three sharpshooters were brought into the Fifth Corps headquarters this morning, sixteen cavalrymen belonging to WM. HENRY LEE's command.

They had been on picket duty and were cut off by the force which went to the assistance of SHERIDAN.

SECOND DISPATCH.

HEADQUARTERS OF THE ARMY OF THE POTOMAC,
April 1—Midnight.

A courier from Major-Gen. SHERIDAN has just arrived with the most cheering news.

The combined forces of cavalry and Major-Gen. WARREN's infantry advanced against the enemy this afternoon, driving them several miles, and capturing about 4,000 prisoners and a number of pieces of artillery.

They retreated to Five Forks, where they were flanked by a part of the Fifth Corps, which had moved down the White Oak road. It was here the large number of prisoners were taken.

The rebels then retreated south along the White Oak road, and were vigorously pursued by Gen. SHERIDAN, while MCKENZIE's cavalry from the Army of the James, advanced west on the Ford road toward the Southside road, and when the messenger left was only about three miles from it, and would undoubtedly reach it before morning.

Thus the last great line of railroad the rebels have to supply their capital and LEE's army by is about to be severed, and it is firmly believed that they will immediately leave their present position in Petersburgh and Richmond.

Sharp cannonading is now going on near the centre of the line, held by the left of the Sixth Corps.

REPORTS VIA BALTIMORE.

Capture of Forts Hell and Damnation—Heavy Losses.

Special Dispatch to the Evening Telegraph.

BALTIMORE, Monday, April 3.

The latest news here this morning is, that our forces had captured Fort Damnation last night, with all its armament and many prisoners. This fort is near Fort Hell, and one of the strongest and most important rebel forts.

It is also reported that Petersburgh has been captured.

The fighting has been terrible, and the losses heavy on both sides; but the rebel loss thus far is three times more than ours.

It is believed that SHERIDAN by this time has cut the Danville Railroad.

The Flood in the St. Lawrence—Submersion at Montreal—The Victoria Bridge in Danger.

MONTREAL, Monday, April 3.

The river rose several feet on Saturday and was piled with ice to a great heighth. One of the shoves came near striking a tube of the Victoria Bridge.

Yesterday morning, the river rose much higher, flooding William, Wellington and other streets. Between 5 and 6 o'clock in the evening, the ice shoved again and the water rushed over the revetment wall, flooding Commission-street. At about 11 o'clock, it again rose as high as St. Paul and St. Gill streets.

The Grand Trunk Railway track between Bonaventure and the tanneries is inundated.

The river rose a foot higher this morning.

The inundated parts of the city are covered with rafts formed with scows and boats.

At present, by far the greater part of the western end of the city is inaccessible except by boats.

The flood is causing the greatest suffering and distress.

Later—4 O'clock P. M.—The water is now slowly falling.

Fire at Louisville, Ky.

LOUISVILLE, Ky., Monday, April 3.

NUMONT's dry goods store, on Market-street, was burned this morning. EVERMAN's bakery and HELBURNE & Co.'s dry goods store, adjoining, were also injured by falling walls and water. The aggregate loss is $80,000, upon which there is very little insurance.

THE GLORIOUS NEWS.

Rejoicings in City and Country

Enthusiasm, Solemnity and Thanksgiving.

Business Suspended and Flags Displayed.

The Praise of the Army on Every Tongue.

Great Mass Meetings in Wall Street and at Union Square.

Patriotic Speeches and Patriotic Songs.

The Whole City Aglow with Excitement.

ILLUMINATIONS AND FIREWORKS.

At no time since the Fall of Sumter has the City of New-York been so thoroughly excited as it was yesterday upon the announcement of the occupation of Richmond. The news in the morning journals was sufficient to arouse the most latent patriotism, and cause the hardest heart to beat with gratitude. Scarcely, however, had the people settled themselves at their various avocations when a strange whisper filled the air, penetrating to the counting-room, the workshop and the school, as if by magic, and long before the newspaper extras stamped the joyful news upon the public mind, it was everywhere known that great news had come to hand, and that victory was ours. An interested crowd gathered about the TIMES Bulletin, and as the cheering words were read again and again, great hearty cheers went up from the multitude, and joy beamed from every eye. Soon the nimble feet of the newsboys had sped with the official dispatch throughout the town, and what had been but an intuitive surmise became a patent truth. The manifestations of exhilaration were boundless; flags were flung to the breeze from innumerable stores and dwellings, making Broadway to shine with the Stars and Stripes, and casting a stream of glory upon the harbor. At the ferries, as soon as the announcement was formally made, an order was issued to deck the boats with bunting, and at once the several fleets of double-enders steamed across the river gay with the flutter of our flag. The down-town shipping houses, most of which are provided with staffs, ran up their colors, so that South-street and West-street, Broad-street and Beaver-street, with the neighboring marts of traffic, vied in patriotic display with the hotels of Broadway and the mansions of the upper end. The magnetism of delight was upon every man. Not a dismal face, not an averted eye, not a pursed-up mouth was seen, nor a croaking tongue heard. No one suggested an "if" or a "but," but every one accepted the glad tidings as truth from the pen of an "honest man." Hand grasped hand in places where "how much" and "how low," are the ordinary salutation; "glorious news" and "thank God" sprang from lips more accustomed to "buyer sixty" and "seller ten;" hard pebbled spectacles that have weathered the beatings of the world and the buffetings of care for sixty years without a moisture, were wet with tears of gratitude, and men estranged for months grasped each others willing palm, while their hearts beat in harmonious thanksgiving. In the public and private schools as much and as genuine enthusiasm was displayed as in the harsher schools of Wall and William streets. Appropriate addresses were made in several of them by the Principals, and the national hymns were sung with a gusto which only school boys and girls can give. One theme was upon every lip—the boats, the cars, the restaurants, the stages, the streets were full of cheerful, happy, exulting, forgiving people, who waived all ceremony, all points of etiquette, and chatted busily each with his neighbor upon the one great occurrence of the day.

It would be idle to disguise the fact that our people rejoiced particularly over the fact that Richmond, the rebel capital, the home of the Confederate President, the seat of their government, the hub and centre of the contest, was at length occupied by our troops. Atlanta, Savannah, Wilmington and Charleston especially were each in turn the object of public attention and anxiety, but after all Richmond was the point after which the popular heart yearned. There it was that JEFF. and his satellites had reared their temple, there the skill of rebel engineers and the energies of their Gen. LEE had been spent in lines of defence and fortifications of strength. It has been the boast of any Southern man that come what might Richmond was forever theirs; that no power this side of Heaven could take it. For years this kind of talk has been made by the Southern people, and for years the sympathizing newspapers of this city and elsewhere have indorsed it, so that our people have felt within them an irrepressible longing for its possession. They wanted its lines of defence broken and its fortifications captured—they wanted JEFF. DAVIS driven out or hanged at his door post, and Gen. LEE swept from his intrenchments by besom of the Union. At length it came, and came, too, so suddenly, that the people were quite unprepared for it. It took the city several hours to accept the startling fact, to recognize its magnitude; and it is very doubtful if even yet the vast extent of the victory is duly appreciated. As each successive dispatch was placed upon the bulletins of the newspapers, the crowds increased in numbers, but the cup of enthusiasm was too full for further addition. Hardly would the paper be placed upon its board, before its contents would be thundered out to the people by some quick-sighted person, and after cheers were given for the news, he would be called upon for a repetition, and no let up was vouchsafed him until, hoarse with shouting and perspiring with exertion, he gave way to a successor, who, in turn, read and reread the stirring dispatches.

Many were the jokes made at the expense of JEFF. and his gray coats; many were the queer suggestions and odd ideas thrown out as to Mr. LINCOLN's probable course. One man, who kept the crowd near our bulletin in a constant uproar, suggested that it would be a good idea if Old ABE would take rooms at the Spottswood House, and issue from thence a proclamation of amnesty to every mother's son in rebeldom, always excepting old JEFF., MASON, and SLI-

[Continued on Eighth Page.]

The New-York Times.

VOL. XIV......NO. 4230. NEW-YORK, SUNDAY, APRIL 16, 1865. PRICE FOUR CENTS

OUR GREAT LOSS

Death of President Lincoln.

The Songs of Victory Drowned in Sorrow.

CLOSING SCENES OF A NOBLE LIFE.

The Great Sorrow of an Afflicted Nation.

Party Differences Forgotten in Public Grief.

Vice-President Johnson Inaugurated as Chief Executive.

MR. SEWARD WILL RECOVER.

John Wilkes Booth Believed to be the Assassin.

Manifestations of the People Throughout the Country.

OFFICIAL DISPATCHES.

WAR DEPARTMENT, WASHINGTON, April 15—4:10 A. M.

To Major-Gen. Dix:

The President continues insensible and is sinking.

Secretary SEWARD remains without change FREDERICK SEWARD'S skull is fractured in two places, besides a severe cut upon the head.

The attendant is still alive, but hopeless. Maj. SEWARD'S wound is not dangerous.

It is now ascertained with reasonable certainty that two assassins were engaged in the horrible crime, WILKES BOOTH being the one that shot the President, and the other companion of his whose name is not known, but whose description is so clear that he can hardly escape. It appears from a letter found in BOOTH'S trunk that the murder was planned before the 4th of March, but fell through then because the accomplice backed out until "Richmond could be heard from." BOOTH and his accomplice were at the livery stable at six o'clock last evening, and left there with their horses about ten o'clock, or shortly before that hour.

It would seem that they had for several days been seeking their chance, but for some unknown reason it was not carried into effect until last night.

One of them has evidently made his way to Baltimore—the other has not yet been traced.

EDWIN M. STANTON, Secretary of War.

WAR DEPARTMENT, WASHINGTON, April 15.

Major-Gen. Dix:

ABRAHAM LINCOLN died this morning at twenty-two minutes after seven o'clock.

EDWIN M. STANTON, Secretary of War.

WAR DEPARTMENT, WASHINGTON, April 15—3 P. M.

Maj.-Gen. Dix, New-York:

Official notice of the death of the late President, ABRAHAM LINCOLN, was given by the heads of departments this morning to ANDREW JOHNSON, Vice-President, upon whom the constitution devolved the office of President. MR. JOHNSON, upon receiving this notice, appeared before the Hon. SALMON P. CHASE, Chief Justice of the United States, and took the oath of office, as President of the United States, assumed its duties and functions. At 12 o'clock the President met the heads of departments in cabinet meeting, at the Treasury Building, and among other business the following was transacted:

First—The arrangements for the funeral of the late President were referred to the several Secretaries, as far as relates to their respective departments.

Second—WILLIAM HUNTER, Esq., was appointed Acting Secretary of State during the disability of Mr. SEWARD, and his son, FREDERICK SEWARD, the Assistant Secretary.

Third—The President formally announced that he desired to retain the present Secretaries of departments of his Cabinet, and they would go on and discharge their respective duties in the same manner as before the deplorable event that had changed the head of the government.

All business in the departments was suspended during the day.

The surgeons report that the condition of Mr SEWARD remains unchanged. He is doing well. No improvement in Mr. FREDERICK SEWARD.

The murderers have not yet been apprehended.

EDWIN M. STANTON, Secretary of War.

THE ASSASSINATION.

Additional Details of the Lamentable Event.

WASHINGTON, Saturday, April 15.

The assassin of President LINCOLN left behind him his hat and a spur.

The hat was picked up in the President's box and has been identified by parties to whom it has been shown as the one belonging to the suspected man, and accurately described as the one belonging to the suspected man by other parties, not allowed to see it before describing it.

The spur was dropped upon the stage, and that also has been identified as the one procured at a stable where the same man hired a horse in the evening.

Two gentlemen who went to the Secretary of War to apprize him of the attack on Mr. LINCOLN met at the residence of the former a man muffled in a cloak, who, when accosted by them, hastened away.

It had been Mr. STANTON'S intention to accompany Mr. LINCOLN to the theatre, and occupy the same box, but the press of business prevented.

It therefore seems evident that the aim of the plotters was to paralyze the country by at once striking down the head, the heart and the arm of the country.

As soon as the dreadful events were announced in the streets, Superintendent RICHARDS, and his assistants, were at work to discover the assassin.

In a few moments the telegraph had aroused the whole police force of the city.

Maj WALLACH and several members of the City Government were soon on the spot and every precaution was taken to preserve order and quiet in the city.

Every street in Washington was patrolled at the request of Mr. RICHARDS.

Gen. AUGUR sent horses to mount the police.

Every road leading out of Washington was strongly picketed, and every possible avenue of escape was thoroughly guarded.

Steamboats about to depart down the Potomac were stopped.

The Daily *Chronicle* says:

"As it is suspected that this conspiracy originated in Maryland, the telegraph flashed the mournful news to Baltimore and all the cavalry was immediately put upon active duty. Every road was picketed and every precaution taken to prevent the escape of the assassin. A preliminary examination was made by Messrs. RICHARDS and his assistants. Several persons were called to testify and the evidence as elicited before an informal tribunal, and not under oath, was conclusive to this point. The murderer of President LINCOLN was JOHN WILKES BOOTH. His hat was found in the private box, and identified by several persons who had seen him within the last two days, and the spur which he dropped by accident, after he jumped to the stage, was identified as one of those which he had obtained from the stable where he hired his horse.

This man BOOTH has played more than once at Ford's Theatre, and is, of course, acquainted with its exits and entrances, and the facility with which he escaped behind the scenes is well understood.

The person who assassinated Secretary SEWARD left behind him a slouched hat and an old rusty navy revolver. The chambers were broken loose from the barrel, as if done by striking. The loads were drawn from the chambers, one being but a rough piece of lead, and the other balls smaller than the chambers, wrapped in paper, as if to keep them from falling out.

CLOSING SCENES.

Particulars of His Last Moments—Record of His Condition Before Death—His Death.

WASHINGTON, Saturday, April 15—11 o'clock A. M.

The *Star* extra says:

"At 7:20 o'clock the President breathed his last, closing his eyes as if falling to sleep, and his countenance assuming an expression of perfect serenity. There were no indications of pain, and it was not known that he was dead until the gradually decreasing respiration ceased altogether.

Rev. Dr. GURLEY, of the New-York-avenue Presbyterian Church, immediately on its being ascertained that life was extinct, knelt at the bedside and offered an impressive prayer, which was responded to by all present.

Dr. GURLEY then proceeded to the front parlor, where Mrs. LINCOLN, Capt. ROBERT LINCOLN, Mrs. JOHN HAY, the Private Secretary, and others, were waiting, where he again offered a prayer for the consolation of the family.

The following minutes, taken by Dr. ABBOTT, show the condition of the late President through-out the night:

11 o'clock—Pulse 44.
11:05 o'clock—Pulse 45, and growing weaker.
11:10 o'clock—Pulse 45.
11:15 o'clock—Pulse 42.
11:20 o'clock—Pulse 45; respiration 27 to 29.
11:25 o'clock—Pulse 42.
11:32 o'clock—Pulse 48, and full.
11:40 o'clock—Pulse 45.
11:45 o'clock—Pulse 45; respiration 22.
12 o'clock—Pulse 48; respiration 22.
12:15 o'clock—Pulse 48; respiration 21—echmos both eyes.
12:30 o'clock—Pulse 45.
12:32 o'clock—Pulse 60.
12:35 o'clock—Pulse 66.]
12:40 o'clock—Pulse 69; right eye much swollen, and echmoses.
12:45 o'clock—Pulse 70.
12:55 o'clock—Pulse 80; struggling motion of arms.
1 o'clock—Pulse 86; respiration 30.
1:30 o'clock—Pulse 95; appearing easier.
1:45 o'clock—Pulse 86—very quiet, respiration irregular.
Mrs. LINCOLN present.
2:10 o'clock—Mrs. LINCOLN retired with ROBERT LINCOLN to an adjoining room.
2:30 o'clock—President very quiet—pulse 54—respiration 28.
2:52 o'clock—Pulse 48—respiration 30.
3 o'clock—Visited again by Mrs. LINCOLN.
3:25 o'clock—Respiration 24 and regular.
3:35 o'clock—Prayer by Rev. Dr. GURLEY.
4 o'clock—Respiration 26 and regular.
4:15 o'clock—Pulse 60—respiration 25.
5:50 o'clock—Respiration 28—regular—sleeping.
6 o'clock—Pulse failing—respiration 28.
6:30 o'clock—Still failing and labored breathing.
7 o'clock—Symptoms of immediate dissolution.
7:22 o'clock—Death.

Surrounding the death-bed of the President were Secretaries Stanton, Welles, Usher, Attorney-General Speed, Postmaster-General Dennison, M. B. Field, Assistant Secretary of the Treasury; Judge Otto, Assistant Secretary of the Interior; Gen. Halleck, Gen. Meigs, Senator Sumner, R. F. Andrews, of New-York; Gen. Todd, of Dacotah; John Hay, Private Secretary; Gov. Oglesby, of Illinois; Gen. Farnsworth, Mrs. and Miss Kenney, Miss Harris, Capt. Robert Lincoln, son of the President, and Doctors E. W. Abbott, R. K. Stone, C. D. Gatch, Neal Hall, and Mr. Lieberman. Secretary McCulloch remained with the President until about 5 o'clock, and Chief-Justice Chase, after several hours' attendance during the night, returned early this morning.

Immediately after the President's death a Cabinet meeting was called by Secretary STANTON, and held in the room in which the corpse lay. Secretaries STANTON, WELLES and USHER, Postmaster-General DENNISON, and Attorney-General SPEED, were present. The results of the conference are as yet unknown.

Removal of the Remains to the Executive Mansion—Feeling in the City.

WASHINGTON, Saturday, April 15.

The President's body was removed from the private residence opposite Ford's Theatre to the executive mansion this morning at 9:30 o'clock, in a hearse, and wrapped in the American flag. It was escorted by a small guard of cavalry, Gen. AUGUR and other military officers following on foot.

A dense crowd accompanied the remains to the White House, where a military guard excluded the crowd, allowing none but persons of the household and personal friends of the deceased to enter the premises, Senator YATES and Representative FARNSWORTH being among the number admitted.

The body is being embalmed, with a view to its removal to Illinois.

Flags over the department and throughout the city are at half-mast. Scarcely any business is being transacted anywhere either on private or public account.

Our citizens, without any preconcert whatever, are draping their premises with festoons of mourning.

The bells are tolling mournfully. All is the deepest gloom and sadness. Strong men weep in the streets. The grief is wide-spread and deep and in strange contrast to the joy so lately manifested over our recent military victories.

This is indeed a day of gloom.

Reports prevail that Mr. FREDERICK W. SEWARD, who was kindly assisting the nursing of Secretary SEWARD, received a stab in the back. His shoulder blade prevented the knife or dagger from penetrating into his body. The prospects are that he will recover.

A report is circulated, repeated by almost everybody, that BOOTH was captured fifteen miles this side of Baltimore. If it be true, as asserted, that the War Department has received such information, it will doubtless be officially promulgated.

The government departments are closed by order, and will be draped with the usual emblems of mourning.

The roads leading to and from the city are guarded by the military, and the utmost circumspection is observed as to all attempting to enter or leave the city.

AUTOPSY UPON THE BODY OF ABRAHAM LINCOLN.

WASHINGTON, Saturday, April 15.

An autopsy was held this afternoon over the body of President LINCOLN by Surgeon-General BARNES and Dr. STONE, assisted by other eminent medical men.

The coffin is of mahogany, is covered with black cloth, and lined with lead, the latter also being covered white satin.

A silver plate upon the coffin over the breast bears the following inscription:

ABRAHAM LINCOLN,
SIXTEENTH PRESIDENT OF THE UNITED STATES,
Born July 12, 1809,
Died April 15, 1865.

The remains have been embalmed.

A few locks of hair were removed from the President's head for the family previous to the remains being placed in the coffin.

THE ASSASSINS.

Circumstances Tending to Inculpate G. H. Booth—Description of his Confederate in the Crime.

WASHINGTON, Saturday, April 15.

There is no confirmation of the report that the murderer of the President has been arrested.

Among the circumstances tending to fix a participation in the crime on BOOTH, were letters found in his trunk, one of which, apparently from a lady, supplicated him to desist from the perilous undertaking in which he was about to embark, as the time was inauspicious, the mine not yet being ready to be sprung.

The *Extra Intelligencer* says: "From the evidence obtained it is rendered highly probable that the man who stabbed Mr. SEWARD and his sons, is JOHN SURRATT, of Prince George County, Maryland. The horse he rode was hired at NAYLOR'S stable, on Fourteenth-street. SURRATT is a young man, with light hair and goatee. His father is said to have been postmaster of Prince George County."

About 11 o'clock last night two men crossed the Anacostia Bridge, one of whom gave his name as BOOTH, and the other as SMITH. The latter is believed to be JOHN SURRATT.

Last night a riderless horse was found, which has been identified by the proprietor of one of the stables previously mentioned as having been hired from his establishment.

Accounts are conflicting as to whether BOOTH crossed the bridge on horseback or on foot; but as it is believed that he rode across it, it is presumed that he had exchanged his horse.

From information in the possession of the authorities it is evident that the scope of the plot was intended to be much more comprehensive.

The Vice-President and other prominent members of the Administration were particularly inquired for by suspected parties, and their precise localities accurately obtained; but providentially, in their cases, the scheme miscarried.

A boat was at once sent down the Potomac to notify the gunboats on the river of the awful crime, in order that all possible means should be taken for the arrest of the perpetrators.

The most ample precautions have been taken, and it is not believed the culprits will long succeed in evading the overtaking aim of justice.

The second extra of the *Evening Star* says:

"Col. INGRAHAM, Provost-Marshal of the defences north of the Potomac, is engaged in taking testimony to-day, all of which fixes the assassination upon J. WILKES BOOTH.

Judge OLIN, of the Supreme Court of the District of Columbia, and Justice MILLER, are also engaged today, at the Police Headquarters, on Tenth-street, in taking the testimony of a large number of witnesses.

Lieut. TYRELL, of Col. INGRAHAM'S staff, last night proceeded to the National Hotel, where BOOTH had been stopping, and took possession of his trunk, in which was found a Colonel's military dress-coat, two pairs of handcuffs, two boxes of cartridges and a package of letters, all of which are now in the possession of the military authorities.

One of these letters, bearing the date of Hookstown, Md., seems to implicate BOOTH. The writer speaks of "the mysterious affair in which you are engaged," and urges BOOTH to proceed to Richmond, and ascertain the views of the authorities there upon the subject. The writer of the letter endeavors to persuade BOOTH from carrying his designs into execution at that time, for the reason, as the writer alleges, that the government had its suspicions aroused. The writer of the letter seems to have been implicated with BOOTH in "the mysterious affair" referred to, as he informs BOOTH in the letter that he would prefer to express his views verbally and then goes on to say that he was out of money, had no clothes, and would be compelled to leave home, as his family were desirous that he should dissolve his connection with BOOTH. This letter is written on note paper, in a small, neat hand, and simply bears the signature of "Sam."

At the Cabinet meeting yesterday, which lasted over two hours, the future policy of the government toward Virginia was discussed, the best feeling prevailed. It is stated that it was determined to adopt a very liberal policy, as was recommended by the President. It is said that this meeting was the most harmonious held for over two years, the President exhibiting throughout that magnanimity and kindness of heart which has ever characterized his treatment of the rebellious States, and which has been so illy requited on their part.

One of the members of the Cabinet remarked to a friend he met at the door, that "The government was to-day stronger than it had been for three years past."

WASHINGTON, Saturday, April 15—3:30 P. M.

To-day no one is allowed to leave the city by rail conveyance, or on foot, and the issuing of passes from the Headquarters of the Department of Washington has been suspended by Gen. AUGUR.

Probable Attempt of the Assassins to Escape into Canada—Order from the War Department.

[CIRCULAR.]

WAR DEPARTMENT, PROVOST MARSHAL GENERAL'S BUREAU, WASHINGTON, D. C.—9:40 A. M. April 15.

It is believed that the assassins of the President and Secretary SEWARD are attempting to escape to Canada. You will make a careful and thorough examination of all persons attempting to cross from the United States into Canada, and will arrest all suspicious persons. The most vigilant scrutiny on your part, and the force at your disposal, is demanded. A description of the parties supposed to be implicated in the murder will be telegraphed you to-day. But in the meantime be active in preventing the crossing of any suspicious persons.

By order of the Secretary of War.

N. L. JEFFERS, Brevet Brig. Gen., Acting Provost-Marshal General.

MR. SEWARD AND SON.

Secretary Seward will Recover—Frederick Seward Still Very Low.

Special Dispatch to the New-York Times.

WASHINGTON, Saturday, April 15.

Mr. SEWARD will recover.

FREDERICK SEWARD is still unconscious. He breathes calmly and has an easy pulse. His head is dreadfully contused and lacerated.

An invalid soldier nurse saved Mr. SEWARD'S life.

GEN. GRANT'S MOVEMENTS.

PHILADELPHIA, Saturday, April 15.

Gen. GRANT arrived in this city late last night on his way to Jersey, but was intercepted on his way to Walnut-street wharf, by a dispatch from the office of the Associated Press, and it is supposed he returned to Washington immediately.

His Return to Washington—Dispatch from Mrs. Grant.

BURLINGTON, N. J., Saturday, April 15.

Lieut.-Gen. GRANT left Burlington for Washington, at 6 o'clock this morning.

MRS. U. S. GRANT.

WASHINGTON, Saturday, April 15.

Gen. GRANT, who left yesterday for New-Jersey, and who was informed of the assassination as he was leaving Philadelphia this morning, arrived here in a special train about noon, and immediately proceeded to the President's house.

The Theatres.

Dispatches from Boston announce that all the theatres in that city will be closed until further notice.

In this city a movement of the same kind has been inaugurated. Fox's Old Bowery Theatre will be closed this evening.

THE SUCCESSION.

Mr. Johnson Inaugurated as President.

The Oath Administered by Secretary Chase.

He Will Perform His Duties Trusting in God.

WASHINGTON, Saturday, April 15—12 A. M.

ANDREW JOHNSON was sworn into office as President of the United States by Chief-Justice CHASE, to-day, at eleven o'clock.

Secretary MCCULLOUGH and Attorney-General SPEED, and others were present.

He remarked:

"The duties are mine. I will perform them, trusting in God.

SECOND DISPATCH.

WASHINGTON, Saturday, April 15.

At an early hour this morning, Hon. EDWIN M. STANTON, Secretary of War, sent an official communication to Hon. ANDREW JOHNSON, Vice-President of the United States, that in consequence of the sudden and unexpected death of the Chief Magistrate, his inauguration should take place as soon as possible, and requesting him to state the place and hour at which the ceremony should be performed.

Mr. JOHNSON immediately replied that it would be agreeable to him to have the proceedings take place at his rooms in the Kirkwood House as soon as the arrangements could be perfected.

Chief Justice CHASE was informed of the fact and repaired to the appointed place in company with Secretary MCCULLOUGH, of the Treasury Department, Attorney-General SPEED, J. P. BLAIR, Sr., Hon. MONTGOMERY BLAIR, Senators FOOT, of Vermont, RAMSAY, of Minnesota, YATES, of Illinois, STEWART, of Nevada, HALE, of New Hampshire, and Gen. FARNSWORTH, of Illinois.

At eleven o'clock the oath of office was administered by the Chief Justice of the United States, in his usual solemn and impressive manner.

Mr. JOHNSON received the kind expressions of the gentlemen by whom he was surrounded in a manner which showed his earnest sense of the great responsibilities so suddenly devolved upon him, and made a brief speech, in which he said:

"The duties of the office are mine. I will perform them. The consequences are with God. Gentlemen, I shall lean upon you. I feel that I shall need your support. I am deeply impressed with the solemnity of the occasion and the responsibility of the duties of the office I am assuming.

Mr. JOHNSON appeared to be in remarkably good health, and has a high and realizing sense of the hopes that are centred upon him. His manner was solemn and dignified, and his whole bearing produced a most gratifying impression upon those who participated in the ceremonies.

It is probable that during the day President JOHNSON will issue his first proclamation to the American People.

It is expected, though nothing has been definitely determined upon, that the funeral of the late President LINCOLN will take place on or about Thursday next. It is supposed that his remains will be temporarily deposited in the Congressional Cemetery.

FROM RICHMOND.

WASHINGTON, Saturday, April 15.

The Richmond *Whig* of yesterday, contains the following:

HEADQUARTERS DEPARTMENT OF VIRGINIA, RICHMOND, Va., April 13, 1865.

Owing to recent events, the permission for the reassembling of the gentlemen recently acting as the Legislature of Virginia, is rescinded. Should any of the gentlemen come to the city under the notice of reassembling already published, they will be furnished passports to return to their homes. Any of the persons named in the call signed by J. A. CAMPBELL and others, who are found in the city, twelve hours after the publication of this notice, will be subject to arrest, unless they are residents of this city.

E. O. C. ORD, Maj.-Gen., Commanding the Department.

HEADQUARTERS DEPARTMENT OF VIRGINIA, ARMY OF THE JAMES, RICHMOND, Va., April 13, 1865.

GENERAL ORDERS No. 37.—Provost-Marshals will grant no passes to citizens from the North or to officers to come to this city, except on orders from the President, the Secretary of War, Lieut.-Gen. GRANT or the Department Commander.

Officers and soldiers now in the city will return to their respective commands at once, or be subject to arrest and confinement.

The Provost-Marshal-General is charged with the execution of this order.

By command of Maj.-Gen. ORD.

E. W. SMITH, Assistant Adjutant-General.

The *Whig* says: Maj.-Gen. GODFREY WEITZEL, commanding the Twenty-fourth Army Corps and Commander of the forces occupying Richmond, has been relieved from his command, and assigned to Petersburgh and vicinity. Maj.-Gen. E. O. C. ORD, commanding the Army of the James, assumes command of this department.

The report that Gen. R. E. LEE arrived in this city on Wednesday evening, was incorrect. The statement originated in the fact that Gen. CURTIS LEE had reached the city on a visit to his mother, Mrs. R. E. LEE. CURTIS LEE is a prisoner in the hands of the Union army, and, being at City Point, was kindly permitted to come to this city to see his mother, who was reported to be in ill-health.

The whereabouts of Gen. ROBERT E. LEE is not known here—at least, not outside of official circles. He is daily expected at Richmond.

Personal.

ST. LOUIS, Friday, April 14.

Maj.-Gen. BANKS and family left this morning for New-Orleans.

THE NATIONAL CALAMITY.

Popular Feeling in New-York and the Country.

REMARKABLE MEETING IN WALL-STREET.

Speeches of Representative Men.

Doings of the City Council and Other Public Bodies

Public Expression Throughout the Country.

Sympathy of the Nova Scotia Parliament.

A Rebel Flag Ordered to be Hauled Down.

PROCLAMATION BY GOV. FENTON.

EXECUTIVE CHAMBER, ALBANY, April 15.

The fearful tragedy at Washington has converted an occasion of rejoicing over national victory into one of national mourning. It is fitting, therefore, that the 20th of April, heretofore set apart as a day of thanksgiving, should now be dedicated to services appropriate to a season of national bereavement. Bowing reverently to the Providence of God, let us assemble in our places of worship on that day to acknowledge our dependence on Him who has brought sudden darkness on the land in the very hour of its restoration to Union, Peace and Liberty.

In witness whereof, I have hereunto set my hand and affixed the privy seal of the State, at the City of Albany, this 15th day of April, in the year of our Lord one thousand eight hundred and sixty-five.

(Signed,) R. E. FENTON.

By the Governor,
GEORGE S. HASTINGS, Private Secretary.

The State Legislature.

SENATE.

ALBANY, Saturday, April 15.

After an impressive prayer by Rev. Mr. SELKIRK, Mr. HUMPHREY said:

Mr. President—I understand that His Excellency the Governor is about to send a communication to this body, announcing the terrible calamity that has befallen our country. I move, therefore that no business be transacted until the reception of the communication from the Governor.

Subsequently Col. HASTINGS, the Governor's Private Secretary, appeared within the bar of the Senate and delivered the following message:

STATE OF NEW-YORK, EXECUTIVE CHAMBER, ALBANY, April 15, 1865.

To the Legislature:

It becomes my painful duty to announce to the Legislature the death of ABRAHAM LINCOLN, President of the United States. It is with emotions of profoundest sorrow that I make this announcement to your honorable body. Such an event is a national calamity, and under the circumstances now attending the bereavement, the nation weeps with heightened anguish. To be deprived of his wisdom, experience and counsel at a time when most important to return to the United States peace, fraternity and prosperity—at a time when the gigantic war which confronted him at the threshold of his Administration is about drawing to a close, and a final deliverance from our civil disturbances for which we have sacrificed so much, is a calamity that will cause the deepest sorrow and gloom to the millions of our land, and to the friends of freedom throughout the world.

This is the third time in our history that the Republic has been subjected to this trial, but it is hoped that our good cause and country, watered by a nation's tears and sanctified by its prayers, will pass in safety through the ordeal to a higher life and destiny. I have also to communicate to you the sad intelligence that our noble Secretary of State, and honored, favored son of New-York, WILLIAM H. SEWARD, was likewise a victim of the tragic plot of the assassins, and now lies in an unconscious condition. May God spare his life to this nation.

R. E. FENTON, Governor.

Mr. FOLGER moved the following resolution, which was adopted by consent, in silence:

Resolved, If the Assembly concur, that the message of his Excellency, the Governor, be referred to a joint committee of five from the Senate and seven from the Assembly, which was adopted and transmitted to the Assembly, when a recess was taken until 11:30 o'clock.

The President announced the committee on the part of the Senate: Messrs. Folger, Murphy, Andrews, Cook and Suffer.

Subsequently the committee reported the following through Mr. FOLGER:

The Joint Committee of the two Houses on the message of His Excellency the Governor, this day transmitted to the Legislature, makes the following report:

The Committee having in mind that the funeral ceremonies of the late President of the United States will probably take place on some early day in the next week, and that such day will be observed throughout the country as a day of solemn recognition of the tragic and awful event which now fills all thoughts, and the the Legislature will join in that observance, do unanimously recommend that on the day which shall be appointed for such obsequies, the two Houses of the Legislature do meet in their respective chambers, at the hour appointed for such funeral ceremonies, and that then, the two Houses being opened with prayer by clergymen especially selected for that service, resolutions appropriate to the occasion be offered. That the Joint Committee of the two Houses be now empowered to sit again to draft such resolutions, and report them on that day to the respective Houses, and do report the following resolution:

Resolved by the Senate, if the Assembly concur, That, viewing this unexampled and solemn event as demanding a cessation of legislative business, do now adjourn until Tuesday of next week, at 11 o'clock A. M.

CHARLES J. FOLGER,
Chairman of the Senate Committee.
THOMAS B. VAN BUREN,
Chairman of the Assembly Committee.

The report of the Committee was adopted, and the Senate adjourned until Tuesday morning, at 11 o'clock.

NEW YORK CITY.

Proclamation by the Mayor.

MAYOR'S OFFICE, NEW-YORK, April 15, 1865.

Citizens of New-York:

The death of the President of the United States may well excite your profound grief and amazement. I respectfully recommend that business be suspended, and that a public mourning for the departed Chief Magistrate be observed throughout the city.

C. GODFREY GUNTHER, Mayor.

Expressions of Sorrow.

But few words are needed to express the condition of our city since the reception of the news of President LINCOLN'S assassination. All men sorrow; all hearts are grieved and sickened at the great calamity which oppresses the nation, and universal gloom attests the sincerity of those who

[*Continued on Eighth Page.*]

1865

Colonialism

1877

FRONT PAGE NEWS 1865-1877

Austro-Prussian War

MAY 26, 1866

Europe was watching and waiting—dreading, The Times said, the first shot in Prussia's campaign to unify Germany under the Hohenzollerns and Prime Minister Otto von Bismarck. The Prussian force, which outnumbered the Austro-German enemy by some 100,000 men, made short work of the fighting: the war was over in seven weeks. The Prussians, having distracted the Austrians by striking an alliance with Italy that opened a new front in the war, delivered a knockout blow at the Battle of Königgrätz, bringing Germany under Prussian domination.

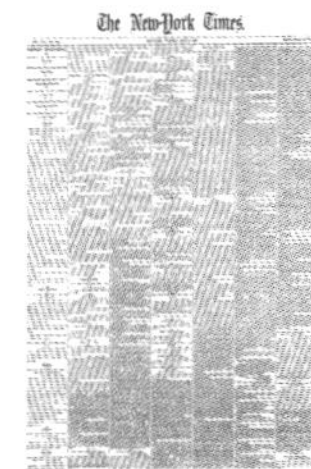

A United Neighbor

JULY 2, 1867

Under the British North America Act, Canada was to be a "dominion." (London decided not to call it a "kingdom" for fear of offending Washington.) The British divided what had been a single province into two—Ontario and Quebec—and joined them with the colonies of Nova Scotia and Brunswick. The Times reported that the new order promised more autonomy, but it also threatened unrest in the maritimes, where local newspapers bordered their front pages in black and some flags flew at half-mast.

The Alaska Purchase

NOVEMBER 13, 1867

The Times called the Alaska purchase "the formal transfer and delivery of Russian America." Angry taxpayers called the new territory "Icebergia," "Walrussia," "Seward's folly" or "Seward's icebox." The last two referred to Secretary of State William H. Seward, who arranged the $7.2 million deal to buy what many Americans figured was an endless, frozen wasteland at an inaccessibly remote corner of the continent. Russia's reason for unloading Alaska at two cents an acre was strategic: having lost the Crimean War, it did not want to risk a British incursion from Canada.

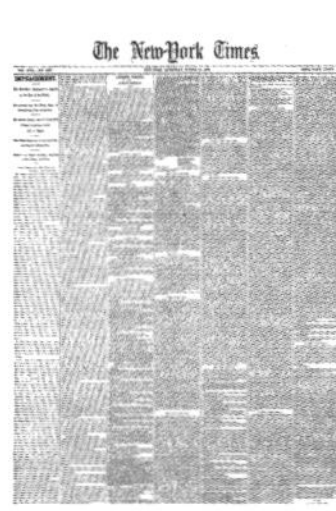

Johnson Escapes Impeachment

MARCH 14, 1868

For the first time in the nation's history, Congress moved to impeach a president. The reasons were political—not what the framers had had in mind when they spelled out the process. The Radical Republicans who took control of Congress in 1867 wanted to get rid of President Andrew Johnson, who was no pushover (he was a Democrat and a Southerner, though he had sided with the Union during the Civil War). The bickering turned ominous when they barred Johnson from replacing cabinet officials. Johnson ordered Secretary of War Edwin M. Stanton to resign, and they wasted no time approving impeachment charges. But he won his Senate trial by one vote. Historians say the proceeding ushered in a run of weak chief executives that lasted until an unelected one took over: Theodore Roosevelt, who was vice president when President William McKinley was assassinated in 1901.

14th Amendment Ratified

JULY 22, 1868

The Radical Republicans envisioned the 14th Amendment as yet another punishment for the South. But its promise of full voting rights backfired when they realized that it strengthened the South, at least in the popular vote—states in which blacks had had only three-fifths of a vote before the Civil War now counted blacks' votes the same as whites'. So Congress simply looked the other way when those states imposed poll taxes and other measures that effectively excluded blacks. The Supreme Court did not. In the 1950s, it made the 14th Amendment's "equal protection" clause a centerpiece of the decision that declared segregated schools unconstitutional—the legal foundation for later civil-rights laws and affirmative action.

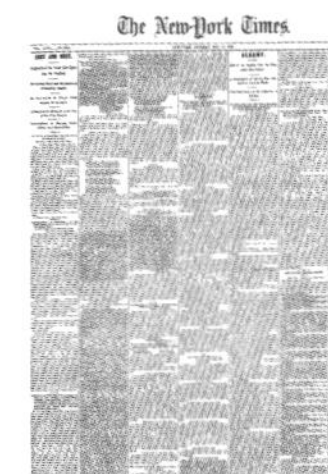

A Railroad Joins the Nation

MAY 11, 1869

"One, two, three...done." The telegrapher tapped the message from a ceremony in Utah, a ceremony that signaled nothing less than the uniting of the country. The new cross-country railroad line trimmed the time needed for passengers and freight to go from one coast to the other to a few days, not a few weeks or months. The Times said the railroad builders hammered a golden spike at the point where the line from the west met the one from the east. Muckrakers later exposed the huge financial fraud known as the Credit Mobilier scandal that had made investors rich, and historians later pointed out that the builders had swung at an ordinary iron spike (one made of too-soft real gold would not have taken the pounding).

Germans Occupy Paris

MARCH 3, 1871

It had been eight months since Napoleon III declared war on Prussia, convinced that his army, with its new and more accurate chassepot rifles, was invincible. The Prussian Prime Minister Otto von Bismarck had seen a fight with France as a way to bring unity to Bavaria, Wurttemberg and Baden—three German states Prussia did not already control. Bismarck proved right, and his generals proved better than the French at moving troops and supplies into position along the front. After a disastrous summer and fall in 1870, Napoleon was deposed and the Third Republic took over. France's fortunes did not improve, and by the spring of 1871, the Germans occupied Paris.

The Great Chicago Fire

OCTOBER 10, 1871

On a Sunday night in Chicago, a blaze started on Patrick O'Leary's property—legend has it that Mrs. O'Leary's cow knocked over a lantern. Unusually strong winds drove the flames, and soon all Chicago was on the run, even prisoners in the courthouse jail, who were released as the building burned. In time, the death toll was put at 300. Some 100,000 people lost their homes in the 29-hour inferno, which devastated four acres, 120 miles of wooden sidewalks and $200 million worth of property.

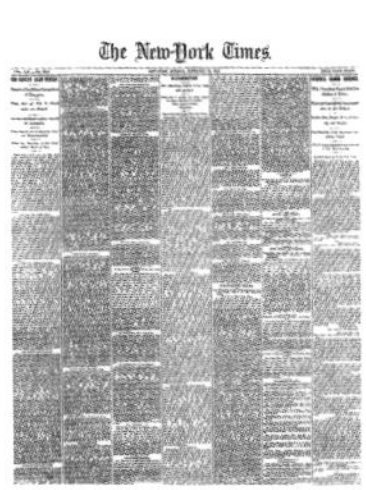

Congress Investigates the Klan

FEBRUARY 19, 1872

The Ku Klux Klan and other secret white supremacist groups sprang up after the Civil War, seeking by violence and intimidation to deprive former slaves of the rights and freedoms promised by Reconstruction. The Times said the Klan's tactics were nothing short of terror. The Klan maintained that it promoted "chivalry, humanity, mercy and patriotism." The Times reported, for example, that a congressional investigation found the Klan had used violence "as a means of intimidating and murdering negro voters during the presidential election of 1868." The investigation came months after Congress outlawed the Klan, though its principles (and some local chapters) lived on, and a revival before World War I renewed the murders, beatings and cross burnings across the South.

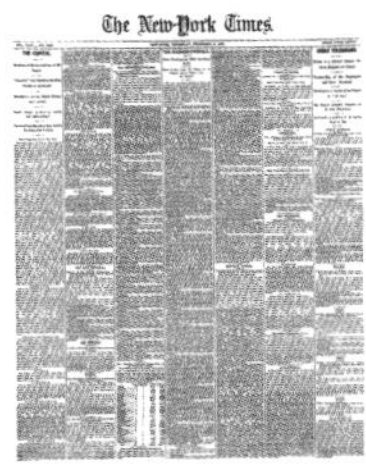

How Stanley Found Livingstone

DECEMBER 5, 1872

Times readers knew about the intrepid reporter Henry Stanley, his expedition to find David Livingstone in Africa and his famous catchphrase—"Doctor Livingstone, I presume." But Stanley's expedition had been paid for (and heavily ballyhooed) by the rival Herald, whose publisher, James Gordon Bennett, declared "I make news." Never mind that it was Stanley who had endured famine, drought and dysentery while protecting Bennett's investment. The Times's take was that having read all about it in The Herald, New York was not interested in hearing all about it. When Stanley gave a lecture in New York, The Times dryly noted in a medium-size article that "the hall was not one-third full."

Disraeli Deals For the Suez Canal

DECEMBER 16, 1875

The Suez Canal, the dream of a farsighted French engineer, had ruined the older, British-controlled overland route. But British Prime Minister Benjamin Disraeli saw an opening. He negotiated to buy the Egyptian khedive's share of the strategically important waterway. In the wake of the deal, The Times reported on the swirl of rumors in London—Russia was said to be jockeying for control of the canal, and Egypt was believed to be considering building a parallel railway. Neither happened; Disraeli's purchase paid for British authority to operate the canal for generations.

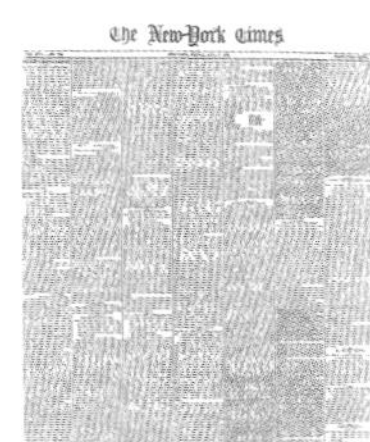

Custer's Last Stand

JULY 7, 1876

When word trickled in some two weeks later, it became clear that General George Armstrong Custer's ill-fated march to his own death and the massacre of more than 200 soldiers in the Black Hills of Montana—sacred territory to the Sioux and Cheyenne Indians camped there—had ended in disaster. Custer was a Civil War hero who had been dispatched to roust Indians from territory where white prospectors had struck gold, even though an 1868 treaty had promised the Black Hills to the Sioux "forever." Custer was overconfident and decided not to wait for reinforcements, ignoring the possibility that the Indians had him outnumbered—which they did, by roughly twenty to one.

Striking Rail Workers' Rampage

JULY 20, 1877

"Desperate Men on Strike," The Times declared in its headline on a story about the railroad workers' walkout, which had spread from the Baltimore & Ohio to the Pennsylvania Railroad. The B. & O., still reeling from the hard times that had followed the Panic of 1873, had cut wages twice in a matter of months. The strikers had imposed what The Times called a "blockade" that kept freight from reaching Washington —only one canal boat slipped past the "rioters" in West Virginia after being pelted with stones by strikers. For its part, the Pennsy angered workers by scheduling longer freight runs. Eventually President Rutherford B. Hayes sent soldiers to strike-torn West Virginia to guarantee that trains carrying mail would go through—a bloody prelude to later railroad violence.

The New-York Times.

VOL. XV......NO. 4576. NEW-YORK, SATURDAY, MAY 26, 1866. PRICE FOUR CENTS.

WASHINGTON NEWS.

Passage by the House of a Bill for the Equalization of Bounties.

Only 2 Votes in the Negative to 139 Affirmative.

Conference of Republican Senators on the Reconstruction Amendment.

The Disfranchising Section to be Rejected.

Raphael Semmes in Washington in Anxious Quest for Pardon.

Interview Between President Johnson and Mrs. Jefferson Davis.

Mr. Davis to be Allowed the Freedom of the Fortress Within Its Wall.

Rumored Postponement of His Trial Until Fall.

Special Dispatches to the New-York Times.

WASHINGTON, Friday, May 25.

MEETING OF THE REPUBLICAN SENATORS—RECONSTRUCTION.

The Republican members of the Senate held a caucus meeting for the purpose of trying to reconcile the various and conflicting opinions in regard to the plan of reconstruction and to settle upon the course to be pursued with reference to the confirmation or rejection of appointments by the President. Before anything definite had been accomplished the hour for meeting of the Senate arrived, and the caucus was adjourned, with an understanding that there should

EUROPEAN NEWS.

Listening for the First Gun of the Impending War.

Mobilization of the German and Italian Armies.

Relative Military Strength of Prussia, Austria, and Italy.

The Gayeties of the French Capital--Dancing Over a Valcano.

Timidity of Modern European Diplomacy.

Napoleon's Project for a Congress Favored Only by Austria and England.

OUR LONDON CORRESPONDENCE.

Europe Listening for the First Gun of the War—No Congress Possible—The Emperor's Speech—Mobilization of Armies—Who Shall Begin It?—The Attempted Assassination of Count Bismarck—The Treaties of 1815—Unities and Nationalities—Position of France—England Neutral—The Cause and the Result—War a Necessity—Princely Speeches.

LONDON, Saturday, May 12, 1866.

Europe has been waiting the past week, in anxious expectation, to hear the sound of the first cannon fired in a war which threatens to surpass all wars of modern times in the numbers of men and of nations engaged in it. But the gun has not been fired, and the question still is, who will fire it? There are scarcely two opinions about the probability of war. It seemed a week ago as if there were but one man in Europe who could command peace, and Europe waited for his word. That word has been spoken and Europe understands it to mean not peace but war.

The Emperor and Empress went to a *fête* at Auxerre, and in answer to a congratulatory speech of the

The New-York Times.

VOL. XVI.....NO. 4919. NEW-YORK, TUESDAY, JULY 2, 1867. PRICE FOUR CENTS.

EUROPEAN INTELLIGENCE.

Advices to Last Evening by Ocean Telegraph.

Distribution of Prizes at the Paris Exhibition.

Speech of the Emperor on the Peaceful Destiny of France.

Lord Stanley on the Alabama Negotiations.

Large Number of Claims Filed by Englishmen Against the United States.

Baron Von Beust Appointed Chancellor of the Austrian Empire.

FRANCE.

Distribution of Prizes at the Paris Exhibition—A Magnificent Spectacle—The Emperor's Speech.

PARIS, Monday, July 1—Evening.

The distribution of the prizes took place at the International Exposition to-day in the presence of a vast multitude of spectators, who filled all the aisles and circles of the great building and overflowed into the gardens of the Champ de Mars.

Their Majesties the Emperor NAPOLEON, and the Empress EUGENIE, together with the Prince Imperial, and His Imperial Highness, the Prince NAPOLEON, with their suites, proceeded to the Exposition in eight carriages, each drawn by six horses. They were accompanied by His Sublime Majesty, ABDUL AZIZ, the Sultan of Turkey and suite, in six splendid carriages, each drawn by six horses richly caparisoned.

When the initiatory ceremonies were concluded the Emperor rose from the throne and made a speech, in the course of which he said:

"Peoples and Kings have come here to crown the idea of peace and conciliation. France is proud to be great, prosperous and free; yet she is not unnerved by her material joys. The thoughtful can see the national fibres vibrate for the honor of France. But this noble susceptibility should not create fear for the world's repose, as we here prove our anxiety for peace."

The Emperor closed his speech by saying:

"This Exposition marks an era of harmony and progress, and the triumph of grand moral principles, which, with justice, can alone establish thrones and ennoble humanity."

Great enthusiasm followed the Emperor's speech. The cries of "*Vive Napoleon*," "*Vive l'Empereur*" continued for some minutes.

When the excitement had subsided, the Imperial Commission proceeded to announce the distribution of prizes.

At the conclusion of this ceremony, the Emperor and his distinguished visitor, the Sultan, accompanied by their suites, returned to the Tuileries.

A speech from Minister ROUHER preceded that of the Emperor.

The American Commissioner, Mr. BECKWITH, has been made an officer of the Legion of Honor.

GREAT BRITAIN.

The Alabama Negotiations Making Slow Progress.

LONDON, Monday, July 1—Evening.

In the House of Commons, this evening, Lord STANLEY, the Secretary of State for Foreign Affairs, stated that his Government was making slow progress in its negotiations with the Government of the United States in regard to the *Alabama* case, but he said he did not despair of achieving a happy result.

The Foreign Office would soon lay before the House all the documents and correspondence in the case.

A large number of English claims against the United States had been filed.

The Redistribution of Parliamentary Seats.

LONDON, Monday, July 1—Midnight.

In the redistribution of Parliamentay seats the Government concedes one additional member each to Liverpool, Birmingham, Manchester and Leeds.

RUSSIA.

Return of the Emperor to St. Petersburgh—General Rejoicing.

ST. PETERSBURGH, Monday, July 1.

The Emperor of Russia entered the capital at noon, and met with a warm reception by his subjects. There was an immense popular demonstration, and the streets were crowded, but there was no military display. At 1 o'clock the Czar attended a *Te Deum* at the Kazan Church, which was filled with the highest dignitaries of the Empire, the members of the diplomatic corps, the officers of the army and navy and the city functionaries.

He afterwards received the congratulations of the Diplomatic Corps at the Winter Palace.

Senator DOOLITTLE was presented.

The Commissioners of the Russian and American Telegraph are here. Their prospects of success are good.

AUSTRIA.

Baron Von Beust Appointed Chancellor of the Austrian Empire.

VIENNA, Monday, July 1.

Baron VON BEUST has received the appointment of Chancellor of the Austrian Empire, an office formerly held by Prince METTERNICH.

GERMANY.

Treaty Between Prussia and France in Regard to North Schleswig.

BERLIN, Monday, July 1.

The *Borse Gazette* of this evening says that a distinct understanding has been arrived at in Paris between the Prussian and French Governments in regard to North Schleswig, and that Flewsburg, Duppel and Alsen are to continue Prussian territory.

The same paper says that negotiations are still pending for the restitution of the property of King GEORGE of Hanover. Prussia makes it a *sine qua non* that he shall publicly abdicate.

FINANCIAL AND COMMERCIAL.

Financial.

LONDON, Monday, July 1—Noon.

Consols for money, 94⅛.

American Securities—Erie Railway shares.......43

Illinois Central Railway Shares.......79¾

United States Five-Twenties.......72¾

Atlantic and Great Western Railway shares.......24¾

LONDON, Monday, July 1—2 P. M.

Consols for money have advanced ⅛d., and are now quoted at 94¼.

American Securities are unchanged.

Atlantic and Great Western Railway shares 24¾.

LONDON, Monday, July 1—Evening.

Consols closed at 94⅛ for money.

American securities closed at the following rates:

United States Five-twenties.......72¾

Illinois Central Railway Shares.......79¼

Erie Railway Shares.......43¼

Atlantic and Great Western Consolidated Shares..25

FRANKFORT, Monday, July 1—Evening.

United States Bonds closed at 77⅜.

LIVERPOOL, Monday, July 1—Noon.

The Cotton market opens quiet and dull. The sales to-day will reach 8,000 bales. Middling Uplands, 11d.; Middling Orleans, 11¼d.

BREADSTUFFS.—The market is firm. Corn, 38s. for new California. Wheat, 13s. 9d. Barley, 4s. 10d. Oats, 3s. 8d. Peas, 38s.

PROVISIONS.—The market is generally without alteration. Pork, 74s. Beef, 135s. Lard, 48s. Bacon, 42s.@42s. 6d. Cheese, 63s.

PRODUCE—The market for articles of American Produce is generally unchanged. Linseed Cakes have declined to £9 15s. ℔ ton for thin oblong for feeding. Ashes—31s. for Pots. Resin—6s. 9d. for Common, and 12s. for fine. Spirits Turpentine—30s. Petroleum—1s. 2d. ℔ gallon for standard white, and 8d. for Spirits. Tallow, 44s. Clover Seed—American Red, 42s.

LONDON, Monday, July 1—Noon.

Sugar quiet at 25s. Iron—53s. 3d. Calcutta Linseed—64s. Oils unchanged, at £41 10s. for Linseed; £35 for Whale, and £130 for Sperm.

ANTWERP, Monday, July 1.

Petroleum—39 francs 50 centimes ℔ bbl. for refined.

LIVERPOOL, Monday, July 1—2 P. M.

The Cotton and Breadstuffs markets are without alteration.

In the Provision market Pork has advanced 1s. and is now quoted at 75s. Cheese has declined 1s. and is now selling at 62s. Other articles are unchanged.

In the Provision market Pot Ashes has advanced, and the price now is 31s. 6d. There are no changes to report in other articles.

LONDON, Monday, July 1—2 P. M.

The prices of all articles are the same as at noon.

LIVERPOOL, Monday, July 1—Evening.

COTTON—The Cotton market closed easier, but without change in prices. The following are the authorized quotations:

Middling Uplands.......11d.

Middling Orleans.......11¼d.

The sales of the day foot up 10,000 bales.

BREADSTUFFS—The market for Breadstuffs has been firm throughout the day. Corn closed at 38s. ℔ quarter for new mixed Western. California Wheat, 13s. 9d. ℔ cental. Barley, Oats and Peas unchanged.

PROVISIONS—The Provision market has been irregular. Pork has advanced 1s. for prime Eastern Mess, which closed at 75s. ℔ bbl. Beef steady at 135s. ℔ bbl. Bacon—The closing price for Cumberland Cut Middles was 42s. ℔ cwt. American Lard and Cheese unchanged.

PRODUCE—Petroleum advanced to 9d. ℔ gallon for Spirits; Standard White unchanged at 1s. 2d. Resin steady at 6s. 9d for common, and 12s. for fine American. Spirits Turpentine 30s. ℔ cwt. Tallow 44s. for American.

LONDON, Monday, July 1—Evening.

IRON lower; sales at 53s. ℔ ton for Scotch Pigs.

SUGAR steady at 25s. for No. 12 D. S.

LINSEEDS of all descriptions unchanged.

OILS steady at previous quotations.

MARINE NEWS.

The United States Steam-frigate Colorado.

LISBON, Monday, July 1—P. M.

The United States steam-frigate *Colorado* is at this port.

Arrivals Out.

QUEENSTOWN, Monday, July 1—2 P. M.

The steamship *City of Washington*, Capt. ROSKELL, from New-York on the 19th of June, arrived here to-day *en route* to Liverpool.

The steamship *Malta*, Capt. MCMICKAN, from New-York on the 18th ult., arrived at this port to-day on the way to Liverpool.

GLASGOW, Monday, July 1.

The Anchor line steamship *United Kingdom*, Capt. SMITH, which sailed from New-York on the 15th ult., has arrived in the Clyde.

Arrival of the Java at Halifax.

HALIFAX, Monday, July 1.

The steamship *Java*, which left Liverpool on June 23, arrived at this port at 2 o'clock this afternoon, and sailed at 4 o'clock for Boston, where she is due Wednesday morning.

AFFAIRS IN CRETE.

The Reported Turkish Victories Over the Cretans—Greek Blockade Runners—Turkish Violation of International Law.

WASHINGTON, Monday, July 1.

The latest official accounts received from Crete are dated the 4th of June. They contain no confirmation of the reported victories of OMAR PASHA, though these were said to have taken place on the 3d of June. According to advices from Heraclion, in Crete, OMAR PASHA attacked the Greeks with his whole army on the 1st of June, but from the fact that the Turks maintained an obstinate silence in regard to the issue of the battle, it is inferred that they were badly beaten.

Athens journals publish the official report of the commander of the Greek blockade-runner *Arcadi*, who has ventured for the twelfth time through the fire of Turkish cruisers to supply the Cretans with provisions, and to afford shelter to fugitive Christian families. Once when pursued by four Turkish frigates, the *Arcadi* succeeded in getting ahead of three of them, but was overtaken by the fourth, which opened fire. The Greek commander did not return the fire, in order not to violate international law, the ships being then in Turkish waters. The Turks continued to bombard the *Arcadi*, and killed one sailor and wounded two others. The *Arcadi* being then in sight of a Greek island, returned the fire, and inflicted far more severe damage upon the ship of the enemy, which was obliged to retire, while the *Arcadi* entered the Greek harbor and returned unmolested to Syria. The Turks, it is said, have become guilty of a breach of international law, without succeeding in stopping the Greek man-of-war.

The foreign Powers seemed to have relinquished their intention of advocating the right of suffrage for the Cretans, and with a view to induce unanimity of action, they confine their efforts to the proposal of a commission to examine the complaints and claims of the Cretans. But the Cretans state that they will not be satisfied with anything short of complete independence.

The Greek Budget for the current year has been published. The receipts amount to thirty-two millions drachms, and promise to reach forty millions. The highest receipts before the annexation of Ionian Islands to Greece never exceeded twenty-four millions. The expenditure for 1867 is estimated at twenty millions, so that there will be a considerable surplus.

Arrest of Counterfeiters at Boston.

BOSTON, Monday, July 1.

Two Italians, giving the names of ROSA MARIA and SALVADOR GRAZIA, were arrested this morning charged with making and circulating spurious coin of the denomination of five-franc pieces. They resisted the arrest, and one of them fired several shots from a revolver at the officers, but fortunately hit no one.

THE CONSTITUTIONAL CONVENTION.

Eighteenth Day's Proceedings.

ALBANY, N. Y., Monday, July 1.

The Constitutional Convention reassembled at 11 o'clock this morning.

Mr. ALVORD said that on Saturday last he gave notice that immediately after the reading of the journal this morning he would move a call of the Convention. He now made that motion, but being satisfied that it would not be sustained by the Convention he would withdraw the motion.

MEMORIALS.

By Mr. E. A. BROWN—Of the citizens of Lewis County for incorporating a liquor prohibition in the Constitution.

By Mr. FOWLER—Of the citizens of Chenango County, for a provision prohibiting towns and counties from donating any moneys to religious societies or corporations.

Also from the citizens of Madison for the extension of the suffrage to men and women alike.

By Mr. SCHELL—Of a member of the New-York Bar asking that the Constitution of the State provide that the code of laws known as the "Revised Statutes," shall be known hereafter as the "several statutes," and shall prescribe the manner in which the amendment shall be made by the Legislature.

RESOLUTIONS.

By Mr. WAKEMAN—To so amend the Constitution that the counsel for the accused may have the last appeal to the jury. Referred.

By Mr. FULLER—Relative to the Judiciary. Referred.

Mr. T. W. DWIGHT presented the following dispatch:

I approve the proposed clause relating to prisons, striking out compensation. Provision should also be made for removal, as in cases of other officers, for cause.

(Signed,) JOHN T. HOFFMAN.

At Mr. DWIGHT's request the dispatch was ordered printed with the memorial heretofore presented by the Prison Association.

Mr. WAKEMAN offered a resolution relative to the jury system. Referred.

Mr. BAKER offered a resolution prohibiting the Legislature from granting appropriations to any religious or sectarian institution. Referred.

GENERAL ORDERS.

The report of the Committee on Suffrage was called up. No other business being before the Convention M. J. TOWNSEND moved to postpone the consideration of the report until Tuesday, the 9th inst. Carried.

Mr. FULLER moved that the Convention now adjourn until Monday evening at 7:30 o'clock.

The motion was carried and the Convention adjourned.

THE DOMINION OF CANADA.

Inauguration of the Confederation—A General Holiday—Lord Monck Sworn in—Review of Troops.

OTTAWA, C. W., Monday, July 1.

This day has given birth to the political infant, the Dominion of Canada.

At 12:5 o'clock last night its advent was hailed by a salute of 101 guns and a bonfire, also by the ringing of bells. The day dawned clearly and brightly on its nativity, and the capital was dressed with bunting to testify the public pleasure. The flags hung out were of course the British, with a few, very few, French flags. It was evident that the celebration of the birth of the new State was to fall upon the shoulders of the authorities, the people generally taking a passive interest in it.

There is a feeling of anxiety as to how the union will work, rather than of confidence in it.

About the hour of 11 o'clock the streets became crowded, and the Russel House was the centre of news.

The groups of people wended their way toward the Parliament buildings to witness the arrival of His Excellency the Governor-General. A few minutes before 11 o'clock a guard of honor of 100 men of the Rifle Brigade, with the band, drew up, lining the approach to the entrance of the eastern block of the Parliament building.

At 11 o'clock precisely Lord MONCK, the Viceroy, drew up amid salutes of artillery. The guard presented arms and the band played "God Save the Queen."

The people looked on in silence at the pageant.

His Excellency entered the building and was then shut out from the public, where I am enabled to say that he took the oath of office as Governor-General of the Dominion of Canada before Chief-Justices DRAPER and RICHARDS, and Mr. Justice WILSON, HAGERTY and MONDALET.

His Excellency then proceeded to name the members of the Privy Council.

At this early hour it is impossible to give a positively correct list of the Council, but it is believed that the following members will form it: Hon. Messrs. J. A. McDonald, Alexander Campbell, Wm. McDougall, Wm. Howland, Alexander T. Galt, Geo. E. Cartier, J. Chapais and H. L. Langevin for Canada West and East, while Hon. Messrs. Tilley, Mitchell, Archibald and Kenney are the members of the lower Provinces.

This would form a council of twelve.

MACDONALD was then knighted and CARTIER made a Companion of the Bath, from which it will be seen that CARTIER is not so indifferent to the senseless titles in the gift of the crown as the Montreal *Minerva* and his friends would have Canadians believe.

The omission of BLAIR's and MCGEE's names will cause some dissatisfaction. This may be ascribed to Mr. CARTIER, who has got the Government formed to suit the views of the French Canadians.

Lord MONCK will remain at the head of Government for twelve months only it is reported, and will be succeeded by the Duke of Buckingham, with the title of Viceroy. This would be the next step toward monarchy, which could not be suddenly imposed upon the Canadians.

The only Lieutenant-Governor appointed, I am told, is Sir N. F. BELLEAU, who is the Executive for the Province of Quebec. The respective commanders of the forces of the other Provinces will for a time be acting Lieutenant-Governors—that is, administration of the Government.

This is all that is as yet known of the organization of the new Government.

After the affair was over Lord MONCK returned, after a salute of artillery, to Rideau Hall, the gubernatorial residence, and there was a petty review in front of the Parliament Building, the chief features of which were the firing of a *feu de joie* and the giving of three cheers.

I will wind up by saying that the celebration of the Union has not here at least been impressive, although it will be said by the Canadian Press, Ministerial side, to have gone off with *éclat*.

This day, July 1, will be henceforth known as Union Day.

Mr. MCGEE delivered an address of the new Dominion at Cornwall, on the 28th, and I give you the most important passages in it. Of the act of union he said, "It is not a question of men, nor even a question of policy, so much as meeting the new state of affairs upon which the country has entered, and as plainly as if it had been written. To the very letter does the union act convey to us the language of Great Britain regarding our new position and the new responsibilities which the country must assume. She says to us, "I have interfered in your legal affairs for the last time. You have come to me for an act of union, whereby your separate Provinces may be bound together, and I give it to you for your own good, that you may work it out in your own way; that henceforth you may go on according to your own desires and without interference from me. The people of the new Dominion number nearly four millions, and they are strong enough and should be wise enough to meet the new duties which this last gift from the imperial authority imposes. Added to these new relations with the empire, the observance of which should constitute a part of the new politics for the whole Dominion, there is a new duty which specially belongs to Canada. The Provinces of Ontario and Quebec, which from the weight of its population, has the lead in the shape of affairs of British America, and the responsibilities attached to this head ship, we are to work out the whole problem of British America, to show to the whole world, and especially to the other population in America, what representative government is. If our system should fail; if the new Constitution does not assure us in the enjoyment of representative government, we shall have no choice but to fall under democratic rule. Democratic rule, to speak from eleven years' personal experience, may be the worst system of tyranny, because the mere brute force of the majority bears down and tramples the rights of the minority. I don't deny that Democratic rule may be good in some respects; but our representative system, founded upon the recognition of the right of all classes, acknowledging the claims of minorities to protection from the tyranny of majorities, giving to every man, as far as the Constitution can give it, the rights of the largest measure of individual liberty, both of thought, action and a much higher system of government, is the highest system of free government yet instituted among men. In established representative institutions here we are doing true service to the people of the United States, we are teaching them the advantage of our form of government over theirs. If there are among our neighbors minorities, religious, political or social, borne down by the weight of the mere majority, they have only to look across the St. Lawrence to find a place of asylum where they can obtain that security denied them at home."

The Celebration at Toronto.

TORONTO, Monday, July 1.

To-day was observed as a general holiday; all business was suspended, and the city was gaily decorated with flags. The prominent feature in the day's celebration was the review of the troops, regulars and volunteers, which was witnessed by an immense concourse of citizens. To-night a monster concert was held at the Horticultural Gardens, at which the military bands were present. The principal buildings were illuminated, and a grand display of fireworks took place.

The Day at Halifax.

HALIFAX, N. S., Monday, July 1.

The inauguration of the Confederation of the Canadian, New Brunswick, and Nova Scotia Provinces was observed here to-day by a civic and military procession, a grand dinner and a public meeting. The celebration was a complete success.

ANOTHER STATEMENT.

HALIFAX, N. S., Monday, July 1.

The holiday for the new Dominion is a poor affair. The *Chronicle* and *Recorder* are out this morning in black.

Half the shops only are open.

The Scotch, English and Irish societies have refused to go in the procession.

Several flags are at half-mast.

The Anti-Unionists treat the whole affair with contempt.

Great excitement prevails.

Spring Flood in the Missouri River—Gen. Custer not Killed.

ST. LOUIS, Monday, July 1.

An Omaha dispatch says that the water from the mountains is coming down the Missouri river, overflowing the bottoms on the Iowa side, and also some places on the Nebraska side. Large quantities of Government freight are exposed on the bank of the river, which, it is feared, will be swept away. The foundation of the Northwestern Railroad depot on the Iowa side is under water for the third time this season. Part of the depot has been removed to Omaha.

Fifty Mormon missionaries have arrived in this city from Salt Lake, on their way to Europe.

The Government Commissioners have accepted the last completed section of the Union Pacific Railroad. Working parties on the road are fully protected against the Indians.

Gen. CUSTER at the last accounts was at the forks of the Republican River, ready to pursue the Indians if they should move southward.

A Conflict of Authority in Tennessee—Circular from Gov. Brownlow.

NASHVILLE, Monday, July 1.

Judge GANTT, Chairman of the Conservative Central Committee, recently addressed a circular to the County Courts, requesting them to appoint officers to hold the State elections, assuming that the law giving them the power had not been repealed. Gov. BROWNLOW issues a proclamation this morning, declaring that the County Courts have no authority to act as requested; that the power to appoint officers to hold elections has been taken from them, and conferred upon the Commissioners of Registration. He denounces the circular as seditious, wicked and revolutionary, and warns the County Courts against acting on its advice, as they will lay themselves liable to punishment. He concludes by ordering Gen. COWPER to dispose of the militia under his command so as to enforce the Franchise Law in its letter and spirit.

The political canvass in Tennessee is becoming animated and exciting.

A merchant named RICE was killed at Johnsonville yesterday. Politics was the cause.

Extensive Fire in Toledo.

TOLEDO, Monday, July 1.

A fire broke out this afternoon in the curtain factory of HALL & EVANS, No. 212 Summit-street, which, together with the confectionery establishment of S. C. FOX, and the hardware-store of C. BALLARD, were totally destroyed.

B. MELINK & Co.'s, wholesale furniture building and stock were badly damaged by water. The flames spread to the block on the opposite side of the street, occupied by RIGBY & Co., furniture; SCHAFER & Co., grocers; J. VAN BOOLEW, clothing; J. JANSON, auction and commission. The buildings and contents were considerably damaged. Total loss will probably reach $28,000; insured for $20,000.

Affairs in New-Orleans—Death from Yellow Fever.

NEW-ORLEANS, Monday, July 1.

The *Times* says the receipts of the city Treasury have averaged $60,000 per day since the Mayor's repudiation message was published. On Saturday there was such a demand for the city notes of the class denounced as illegal and fraudulent by the Mayor, that a premium was offered for them. The proclamation has had the effect of unusually stimulating the tax-payers.

Lieut. DEWEY, Twenty-eighth Cavalry, arrived yesterday from Indianola, Ill., with the yellow fever, and died at the St. Charles last night. This is the only new case reported.

An Oil Train on Fire—Destruction of Cars and Buildings at Cleveland.

CLEVELAND, Ohio, Monday, July 1.

A train of tank-cars, while unloading crude oil on the Atlantic and Great Western Road, at this place, to-day, took fire, probably from a passing engine, and destroyed three cars with a small quantity of oil. The fire communicated to BACKUS, WILLIAMS & Co.'s refinery, which was supposed to be fireproof, by the burning oil running in the doors. The refinery was totally destroyed. Loss, $56,000, on which there is but little insurance. ALEXANDER SCHOFIELD & Co., refiners, lose $5,000 on oil.

Mass Meeting at Richmond—Burial of Gen. Hill.

RICHMOND, Monday, July 1.

A large meeting was held to-night, and addressed by many prominent citizens, who urged all to register, and assured them that their rights were not affected by the Alexandria Constitution.

The remains of Gen. A. P. HILL were brought to the city to-day and interred in Hollywood Cemetery.

The first lot of new wheat was received here to-day.

Kentucky Tobacco Fair.

LOUISVILLE, Monday, July 1.

The Kentucky Tobacco Fair will be held here to-morrow.

Registration in Georgia.

SAVANNAH, Monday, July 1.

Fifty-nine whites and two hundred and eleven colored persons were registered to-day.

Appointment of Colored Policemen in Mobile.

MOBILE, Ala., Monday, July 1.

Five freedmen were to-day appointed on the police, and were sworn in by Mayor HORTON.

The Break in the Erie Canal.

ROCHESTER, N. Y., Monday, July 1.

The break in the Erie Canal, six miles west of this city, will probably be repaired to-day.

The Charleston Savings Bank Closed by Gen. Sickles.

From the Charleston Courier, June 28.

The Charleston Savings Bank was on yesterday closed by order of Gen. SICKLES, under the following circumstances:

It is stated that there are now in this command four United States soldiers who, at the beginning of the late war, were in Major ANDERSON's command, and stationed at one of the forts in the harbor. These men, some weeks ago made affidavit to Gen. SICKLES that they had, while in Major ANDERSON's command, made deposits of money in the Charleston Savings Institution, and that they could not subsequently obtain the return of their deposits, although they had made regular application for them. This affidavit was forwarded to the Treasurer of the Charleston Savings Institution, and the counsel of that institution made a written reply. In this it was stated that at the time that the commencement of hostilities was imminent, all deposits had been returned to all depositors who made application for them, and that some returns of deposits to United States soldiers, were made as late as October, 1861, but that there were upon the books the names of seven United States soldiers, including those of the men who made affidavit, whose deposits had not been returned.

The matter remained in abeyance until yesterday morning, when Gen. CLITZ, the Post Commandant, sent to the Treasurer of the institution an order to turn over to the military authorities the amount of deposits due the seven men referred to, with interest at seven per cent. per annum from the time of deposit to date, or that the assets of the institution should be turned over in satisfaction of the claim, or failing then, that the institution should be closed and taken possession of by the military authorities. The Treasurer locked the doors, turned the key over to the Provost-Marshal, and a policeman has now the building in charge, with orders to allow no person to enter.

There seems to have been some confusion in this matter. The Charleston Savings Institution, in which the soldiers' deposits were made, is in liquidation, and has no working existence. The Charleston Savings Bank is a new concern, and was only chartered after the close of the war. Both institutions have the same officers, it is true, but neither has any right to the assets, or is responsible for the liabilities of the other. The two institutions are altogether separate and distinct, but it seems that both have been summarily closed. As regards the rate of interest ordered by Gen. CLITZ to be paid, it may be mentioned that each depositor in the Charles own Savings Institution signed a contract in which he agreed to receive and require but 5 per cent yearly on whatever money he might deposit.

THE SURRATT TRIAL.

Cross-Examination of Lewis J. Weichman Resumed—Further Developments Regarding the Surratt Family—the Prisoner's Flight to Europe—His Confessions on the Voyage.

Special Dispatch to the New-York Times.

WASHINGTON, Monday, July 1.

The Surratt trial was the scene of a decided sensation to-day. After the cross-examination of WEICHMAN was concluded, about one o'clock. Dr. MCMILLAN, the Surgeon of the steamship *Peruvian*, on which SURRATT fled from Quebec to Liverpool, was called. The prisoner was visibly affected as the Doctor promptly identified him as the person to whom he was presented in a state-room on the steamer between Montreal and Quebec, and who was his fellow-passenger during the trip. He then began to narrate in a clear, connected, candid manner the various conversations the prisoner had with him. An account of one of SURRATT's trips to Richmond was being related, when the counsel for the prisoner pretended to misunderstand a portion of the narrative, and sought to confuse the witness by repeating his statements in an entirely different form. This the witness corrected several times, when at last he resented it as an insult, and in an impulsive and very forcible manner accused the prisoner's counsel of insulting the Government witnesses, and warmly denounced such conduct as only worthy of cowards and sneaks. This, of course, took the counsel by surprise, and produced a decided sensation in the Court-room. The defence immediately appealed to the Court, who rebuked the witness for his language, and at the same time rebuked the counsel for badgering the witnesses. Dr. MCMILLAN politely apologized to the Court, and then remarked that the counsel for the defence had a few days ago insulted the witnesses for the prosecution by saying that they ought to be in the penitentiary, and he believed himself as much a gentleman as either of them. The testimony was intensely interesting and very damaging to the prisoner. His examination was not concluded.

Since the commencement of the Surratt trial a fact has come to light regarding the Court which tried and sentenced Mrs. SURRATT, that deserves to be made public. It seems that after the trial and sentence the Court joined in earnestly recommending her to mercy, and that all the members thereof, except, perhaps, the Judge-Advocate-General, signed the recommendation. The paper is said to be in the handwriting of Hon. JOHN A. BINGHAM.

To the Associated Press.

WASHINGTON, Monday, July 1.

The Criminal Court-room was again crowded this morning with spectators, this being the day to which the Grand Jury of the June term had been adjourned. Chief-Justice Carter appeared upon the bench and ordered the roll of Grand Jurors to be called. Nineteen answered to their names; after which Judge Carter said there would be no further use for them this term, the irregular manner in which they had been summoned convincing him that no indictment they should find would be sustained by the Court; he, therefore, discharged them without day.

By agreement of counsel the cross-examination of Lewis J. Weichman was temporarily suspended in order to admit of the examination of Mr. Charles C. Dunn, who was then called and sworn and examined by Mr. Pierrepont.

Witness testified that in 1864 he employed John H. Surratt in the Adams Express office, witness being at the time agent of the Company; he was employed in the military freight depot, and entered upon his duties on Dec. 30; on Jan. 13, Surratt asked leave of absence, and witness expressed surprise that such an application should be made so short a time after he had been employed; Surratt said he had business in the country, and wanted to go there with his mother, and witness still refused; the next day Mrs. Surratt came and witness refused her also, and Surratt then left, and never came back to the office to resume his duties, nor did he ever return for his pay.

No cross-examination.

Lewis J. Weichman was then recalled, and was cross-examined by Mr. Bradley.

On April 2, 1865, witness went with Atzerodt to St. Aloysius Church, and there introduced him to Mr. Brophy, but does not recollect introducing him as his particular friend; recollects the date, because it was after the 1st and before the 3d of April.

Mr. Bradley—It is generally the case that the 2d comes between the dates named.

Witness said that he recollected it from another circumstance; it was on the night of April 1 that Gen. Augur's offices were burned, and witness was there with Mr. Jenkins; met Atzerodt again at Howard's stable, and Atzerodt was trying to get a horse to, he said, send off Payne; Atzerodt was at my room several times, and on one occasion he was there, and there was a bottle of whisky, and we took drinks all round; I went out that night to buy a bottle of whisky, and put it under my cloak, but do not remember that Howell or any one else gave me the money; it was on the 20th of March that Surratt got the letter addressed to James Sturdy; I recollect testifying to that fact at the conspiracy trial, and fixing it some time after the 4th of March; I fix the time because it was before the 25th that I saw the letter; saw Surratt and Payne fencing with bowie-knives on March 15. (Copious extracts were read from the testimony as given at the conspiracy trial, and witness was asked concerning discrepancies.) Atzerodt was at the house when Howell was there; Howell was there only once; Howell was a blockade-runner; I was not intimate with him, but treated him kindly; knew he was a blockade-runner, because Surratt said so; Howell taught me a cypher, but I do not recollect that the cypher was used in the secret service of the Confederacy; he taught me the cypher and I have used it, but I can't say that I was very familiar with it; I knew a gentleman here named Mr. Rockford; I never had a conversation with Mr. Rockford except in confession, except on one occasion, when I asked him if he would receive my confession; that was the only conversation I had with him outside of the confessional; I never considered myself under arrest the morning after the assassination; I don't recollect having been put in charge of an officer of the Metropolitan Police.

Witness' testimony was read as given on the assassination trial, wherein witness said he gave himself up to Major Richards.

Witness said he desired to correct that; he did not give himself up to Mr. Richards, but to one of his officers; when in Canada I did not consider myself under arrest; I was as much a detective then as McDevitt was, and was named as special officer in an order from the War Department; I was out of sight of the detective several times in Canada; in Quebec I went to a clergyman of my faith, and told him the situation I was in, and avowed my determination of coming back and testifying for the Government; I never told anyone that I would not have returned from Canada if I had not been compelled to do so; Mr. Stanton requested me to come back, and I came back as voluntarily as I could; on the occasion I drove Mrs. Surratt to the country I saw Mrs. Surratt and Booth in conversation as I went to Howard's stable for a buggy; at the conspiracy trial I did not detail the incidents in the order of succession they are now stated, because now my memory is clearer than it then was; I was then excited; my memory is clearer now than it was then; I know the succession was different then from what I have given it on this trial, because I have read the book within the last two years and the last month.

Q.—Have you not read it within the last two days? A.—Yes, Sir; I read it yesterday, but I cannot state what succession I gave the circumstances there because I did not pay special attention to that particular point; in testifying to the Commission relative to Mrs. Surratt's conversation with Mr. Lloyd on the way to the country, I said Mrs. Surratt leaned forward and whispered in Lloyd's ear; I said on this trial that I could hear the tones of the voice, but could not hear the words, but I think the statement is the same; I did not surrender myself to the Government when Mr. Carroll said they would have to put me in Carroll Hall Prison; I said I was at the disposal of the Government, and they could do with me as they pleased; I was in custody after that for thirty days; I did not consider myself in custody when I gave myself up to Major Richards' officer; from the time I gave myself up until I went to Canada I was always with an officer; on the afternoon of April 14 I got a buggy to take Mrs. Surratt to the country; Mrs. Surratt brought down an article wrapped up, and I fixed it in the buggy; in 1865 I testified that the package felt like two or three saucers; on Friday I drove up and down the road at Surrattsville several times, but I got out of the buggy and wrote a letter for Mrs. Surratt; I do not recollect that I was with Mrs. Surratt all the time after writing the letter until we started off; I don't remember seeing Mr. Lloyd come in in a buggy, but I do know I saw Mr. Lloyd and that he called attention to the fact that my buggy-spring was broken; at the conspiracy trial Mr. Lloyd expressed surprise that I should not have remembered the conversation between himself and Mrs. Surratt; I do not recollect Mr. Lloyd telling me that if I swore to a whisper I swore to a lie, and I don't remember what answer I made, or whether I made any answer; I did not tell John T. Ford that I told Secretary Stanton that I knew where Surratt was at the time of the assassination; don't remember to have conversed with John T. Ford about Surratt; I told Ford I had an interview with the Secretary of War, but I did not say that I knew where Surratt was, because I did not know where Surratt was; I might have told Ford that I had not seen John Surratt for two weeks before the assassination, and that I had seen a letter from Surratt dated Montreal, April 12; I did not tell Mr. Ford, Maddox and Gifford that I was told by Mr. Bingham if I did not tell more fully than I had done about these circumstances, that I would be treated as one of the conspirators; I never told any one that Mr. Bingham used threats about my testimony; I might have said here that my character was at stake, and that I would do all to aid the prosecution.

Question—Did you not state in substance that the office you received in Philadelphia was given in pursuance of a promise that you should be remunerated for your testimony, and should have the protection of the Government?

Mr. Pierrepont objected, and the objection was sustained, and the defence noted an exception.

Question—You stated on Saturday that you were removed from office because you voted the Radical Republican ticket; and now I ask if you have not stated that you were a Johnson man, and therefore entitled to hold your office?

Mr. Pierrepont objected.

Judge Fisher said it looked too much like bringing politics into a jury trial, and he would sustain the objection.

Witness was here interrogated as to the remarks made by Mrs. Surratt and Miss Annie Surratt on the night of the assassination, as testified to the other day, and he acknowledged that he did not testify to these facts before the Military Commission. I have since recollected the facts more clearly, and have written them down in my statement; I did not say that Mrs. Surratt asked me to pray for her intentions after the detectives had gone; she asked me to do so before the assassination; she made her request the evenidg of the 14th, before the assassination; I noticed Mrs. Surratt was nervous, and she asked me about the torchlight procession, and then asked me to pray for her intentions; the words were uttered in a tone loud enough for all in the parlor to hear them; I was at supper when I heard the footsteps on the steps as I have described them; when I went up stairs I found Mrs. Surratt in the parlor, and don't remember whether she left the room or not; I went to bed a few minutes before ten o'clock that night; Mrs. Surratt did not go down stairs that I remember; I did not see her leave the room on that night; no one, that I know of, came in the basement door; don't remember if Mrs. Surratt was absent on April 3; saw John Surratt in the evening of that day; I was not in the dining room on the evening of April 3 with John Surratt; Surratt was in the parlor; I don't remember whether Surratt went down to get his supper or not; have not said he did so, because I am not positive; I do not know that Mrs. Surratt remained at the table, and that Anna Surratt answered the door on the night of April 14; on the morning after the assassination I met Holohan in the street, and we then went home to breakfast, and I said I believed that Atzerodt had assassinated the President; at the breakfast table I said I would disclose all I knew; I remember a remark that was made at the table, that the death of Abraham Lincoln was nothing more than the death of a nigger in the army.

Q.—Who said that? A.—Anna Surratt.

Q.—Did you tell it at the assassination trial? A.—I did not.

Q.—Why did you not? A.—Because I had too much sympathy for the poor girl.

Q.—Why did you tell it now, then? A.—Because you drew it out of me, and because I have been hunted down and persecuted for the last two years on account of these people.

Mr. Bradley.—I did not ask you anything to induce you to make a voluntary statement.

Witness resumed, and in answer to a question said he had a *slight acquaintance* with Mr. Carlin; saw Carlin and Mr. Brophy together; I don't remember telling Brophy that I would never have testified if Capt. Gleason had not betrayed me; I don't remember telling either Carlin or Brophy that I did not wish to return from Canada, and would not have done so it the detective had not compelled me; that is simply an absurdity, and you will be satisfied that it is so before you are done with this trial.

Mr. Bradley—Well, suppose you let the counsel attend to that and give us the facts.

Witness resumed—I did tell Mrs. Brophy that Mrs. Surratt had said that she was going to find out what Booth and the other men were doing there, and she took John in the parlor, and when I asked Mrs. Surratt afterward, she said John was engaged in a *cotton speculation*; *I did tell Howell, the blockade-runner*, that my sympathies were with the South, because I often talked secesh with such fellows for buncombe; before the war any one would have been pleased to associate with Wilkes Booth, because he went in such good society; I have seen him in company with members of Congress and others; I was in Carroll prison with Mr. Hallohan and others; I was there thirty days, but I think Hallohan was released before I was.

At 12 o'clock the Court took a recess for half an hour.

Upon reassembling Louis J. Weichman was recalled and his cross-examination was continued by Mr. Bradley.

After the assassination trial I had a conversation with Mr. Lewis Carlin relative to the testimony I had given at that trial; I dont remember any particular evening; since the Court took a recess I saw Mr. Carlin and said "hallo, old fellow, I see you are going to be a witness against me;" he replied he could not help it; that it was his duty; never took a walk with Brophy and Carlin together; never went to Dunbaut's restaurant with him; don't remember telling Mr. Carlin that my conscience troubled me for the testimony given, and that I was going to confession to unburden my conscience; do not remember Carlin's telling me I had better go to a magistrate and make a statement, nor do I remember telling him that I would do so; I did not fear a prosecution for perjury; do not remember telling Mr. Carlin that the testimony was written out for me, and that I was compelled to swear to it; do not remember telling Carlin that I could have given an explanation of Mrs. Surratt's visit had I been allowed to do so; I say upon my solemn oath that I never said any of these things, and will put my word against the whole world on that point; the questions are perfectly surprising to me; do not remember telling Mr. Carlin about a child falling overboard and some man rescuing him; do not remember telling Mr. Carlin that I contemplated suicide; don't remember taking a revolver and threatening suicide; don't remember telling Mr. Carlin I was going to confession to ease my conscience; I deny telling Mr. Carlin my testimony would have been different if it had not been written out for me; I deny saying anything of what I have been questioned about alone; I did not state to Mr. Carlin that on April 14, 1865, before Mrs. Surratt and I went to Surrattsville and she spoke of getting a buggy, that I told her to send Booth, and she said Booth was not in town; I told Carlin nothing about breaking the spring of the wagon; I deny I ever told him.

Redirect by Mr. Pierrepont—I was confined in Carroll Prison as a Government witness; I was not confined there for any crime. (Paper exhibited.) I recognize it as a copy of the order appointing me a special officer; the original is in Mr. McDevitt's possession.

Mr. Pierrepont proposed to read the paper, and Mr. Bradley objected. The objection was overruled, and Mr. Bradley noted an exception. The paper is as follows:

HEADQUARTERS DEPARTMENT OF WASHINGTON, OFFICE OF THE PROVOST-MARSHAL-GENERAL, WASHINGTON, D. C., April 16, 1865.

SPECIAL ORDER NO. 68.—Extract—Special officers James A. McDevitt, Geo. Hollohan and Lewis J. Weichman, are hereby ordered to proceed to New-York City on important Government business, and after executing their private orders, return to this city and report at these headquarters. The Quartermaster's Department will furnish the necessary transportation.

By command of Major-Gen. AUGUR.

(Signed) F. INGRAHAM, Colonel and Provost-Marshal-General, Department North Potomac.

Official: J. P. RUSSELL, Captain and Assistant Provost-Marshal-General, Department North Potomac.

Witness resumed: It was on the morning of April 15, 1865, at breakfast, that Miss Anna Surratt said the death of Lincoln was no more than the death of a nigger, &c.

Mr. Pierrepont asked witness to state something more about his confession to Carlin and about his going before a magistrate, &c.

Mr. Bradley objected and said it was opening new matter.

Mr. Pierrepont contended that the witness could be asked to state all he said to Mr. Carlin.

Mr. Bradley said the witness had denied that he ever spoke to Carlin about the confession.

Judge Fisher admitted the question.

Witness said he never spoke to Carlin or Brophy about confession; never said anything to them about confession.

Mr. Pierrepont—That is all, then.

Witness—Are you done with me, Mr. Bradley?

Mr. Bradley—I do not know that I am. For the present I am, but I may have something further to say to you.

The witness then retired from the stand, and Dr. McMillan was called.

Mr. Bradley said he asked the prosecution to postpone the examination of Dr. McMillan, as the defence had not got a *subpœnæ duces tecum* to the Secretary of State, asking him to send to Court evidence in possession of the Department of State, which the defence must have in order to a proper cross-examination.

Judge Fisher said the cross-examination would not be reached to-day.

Mrs. Benson, late Mrs. Hudspeth, was recalled. (Photograph exhibited.) Witness recognized it as a resemblance to the individual who had dropped the letter in the New-York street-car.

Mr. Carrington explained that it was a picture of Booth.

By Mr. Bradley—The hand of the person who dropped the letter was remarkably small and delicate; I was attracted toward him particularly because I noticed he was disguised.

Dr. Lewis Joseph Archibald McMillan was called, and sworn: I am a surgeon, and am out of service now; two years ago I was in the service of the Montreal Ocean Steamship Company, and from April to October, 1865, I was Surgeon of the steamer *Peruvian*; left Quebec for Liverpool on September 16 1865, which was Saturday, and Sunday week, after we arrived at Londonderry, Ireland, and arrived at Liverpool the next day; I know the prisoner at the bar; he crossed the ocean with me to Londonderry on that voyage; I first saw the prisoner on the mail steamer *Montreal*, running between Montreal and Quebec, on the 15th of September, 1865; about a week or ten days previous a man named La Pierre, a priest, who, at the time lived in Montreal, came to me and said somebody was coming; and on the 15th of September I was going to Quebec on the steamer Montreal and there met this Mr. La Pierre again, and he said he would introduce me to his friend; he took me to a state-room of which La Pierre had the key; the state-room was locked and he unlocked it, and in the room I found the prisoner at the bar; Mr. La Pierre introduced the prisoner under the name of McCarty; I never suspected who the person was, and I passed the evening and night with him; the prisoner's hair was then short and of a dark brown color; I did not perceive that it was dyed, but I afterward found it out; the conversation that evening was general; La Pierre went to Quebec with us; when we got to Quebec we had breakfast on the steamer at seven or eight o'clock, and between nine and ten the passengers were transferred to the steamer *Peruvian*; upon reaching the *Peruvian* La Pierre said to me in Surratt's presence that he wished me to let Surratt occupy my room till the steamer left; I did so, and he occupied my room until the steamer left; the steamer left in half an hour, and La Pierre went ashore; that day, I remember, that either after lunch or dinner, the prisoner came to me and pointing to one of the passengers asked me if I knew who the gentleman was, and I said I did not know; Surratt said he thought the man was an American detective, and was after him; I told him I thought nothing of the kind, and asked him what he had done that he should be afraid of an American detective; he said he had done a good deed, and if I knew all he had done it would make my eyes stare; I said he need not be afraid of an American detective, because he was on a British ship and in British waters; he said he did not care if he was, for if he attempted to arrest him, this would settle him, and he exhibited a pistol; on the tug going from the steamer *Montreal* to the *Peruvian* I was introduced to ——

Mr. Bradley objected, unless it was shown what connection that had with Surratt.

Mr. Pierrepont said he proposed to show it was Beverly Tucker, Gen. Ripley, and others, who were in Montreal, and who were with Surrat in his flight.

Mr. Bradley asked if it was proposed to connect the men named with the conspiracy.

Mr. Pierrepont said it was proper to show who was on the tug, and were engaged in conversation with Surratt.

Judge Fisher said it could be shown what men spoke with Surratt.

Witness resumed and said he saw one speak to Surratt on the tug; on the voyage to Liverpool saw Gen. Ripley talk with Surratt; of my own knowledge I don't know who Gen. Ripley was, but the prisoner said he was Gen. Ripley, of South Carolina; there was among the passengers Mr. Cornell Jewett, the one they called Colorado Jewett; there was also a colored man, who said he had been in Jeff. Davis' employ; I know Beverly Tucker, and was introduced to him that morning on the tug going from the steamer *Montreal* to the steamer *Peruvian*; he went on board the *Peruvian*; the prisoner was called McCarty; we sailed about ten o'clock A. M.; after we got on board the steamer I perceived that Surratt's hair and mustache were dyed; he wore a pair of spectacles; he said he did not wear the spectacles because he was short-sighted, but because it aided in disguising him; I had conversation with the prisoner every day until we arrived at Londonderry; our conversation took place generally on the quarter-deck, and sometimes behind the wheel-house; I remember Surratt telling me he had been in the habit of going to Richmond with dispatches during the war, and bringing dispatches back to Washington and Montreal; he stated he was one time told in Montreal that he would meet a lady in New-York; that he met a woman in New-York and came to Washington and started for Richmond with four or five others; that after much trouble they crossed the Potomac, and, getting south of Fredericksburgh, they were driven on a platform car, and as they were drawn along they saw some men approaching, and found out they were escaped soldiers and were most starved to death, and that the woman said, "Let us shoot the d—d Yankee soldiers," and they shot them and then went on; he told me the name of the woman, but I cannot recollect it; I cannot remember the woman and would not like to say it; it sounded like Slater; the woman was conspicuous in Montreal during the trial of the St. Albans raiders, carrying messages; the soldiers referred to were unarmed.

Mr. Bradley said he could not see where this evidence was tending.

Judge Fisher said he could not see to what it tended now.

Mr. Pierrepont said they would connect it with the conspiracy.

Witness resumed and said Surratt told him he had received money from Benjamin, the Confederate Secretary of State; the amounts he named were $70,000 and $30,000; he said he was in Richmond a few days previous to its fall; he said one day that several of them were crossing the Potomac in a boat, when they were pursued by a gunboat and were ordered to surrender or they would be fired upon; a small boat was sent to them and they fired into the small boat as soon as it came alongside.

Witness was asked to repeat this sentence, and retorted by telling Mr. Merrick that he (Merrick) could understand it if he kept his ear open. He (McMillan) was not to be insulted, as all the witnesses had already been insulted, and he thought the insult to the witnesses was the act of a coward and a sneak.

Mr. Merrick asked if that was proper language for the witness to use.

The Court said it was not, but counsel must not worry and annoy the witness.

Witness said that Mr. Merrick had said the other day that all the witnesses ought to be in the Penitentiary, and he wanted it understood that he was as good as Mr. Merrick.

Witness then resumed and said—Surratt stated that he had frequently traveled to Richmond under the assumed names of Harrison and Sherman; upon reaching the coast of Ireland Surratt called me behind the wheelhouse and remarked that he saw foreign land at last and, putting his hand upon the pistol in his pocket, said he hoped to live to see the day when he could serve Andrew Johnson as Abraham Lincoln had been served; he said also that if an English officer attempted to arrest him he would shoot him; I told him if he did that he would meet with very little mercy in England; he replied that he knew that, but he would do it, nevertheless, for he would sooner be hanged by an English jury than a Yankee one, and if he went to the United States again he knew he would swing.

Mr. Bradley asked that the latter statement be repeated by the reporter. The witness was about to reply, when it was stated that he was not asked. The witness said he could tell all that was necessary, and, continuing his remarks, said that Mr. Merrick was not at all dangerous; he was not afraid of him.

At 2:20 the Court took a recess until 10 o'clock to-morrow morning.

Distressing Casualty at Norwalk, Conn.

Correspondence of the New-York Times.

NORWALK, Monday, July 1, 1867.

This quiet town was thrown into much excitement on Saturday night by the announcement that two sons of Mr. WILSON, a lawyer, aged 5 and 8 years, had been missing from their homes since the afternoon. All night parties of friends and neighbors were searching the roadways and woods, but without success. The search, with increased numbers, was continued until 3 o'clock yesterday afternoon, when the little fellows were found buried in a sand-bank, directly opposite their home. A slight excavation for building purposes had been made under the side of the road, and it is supposed that the children were playing there when the earth gave way, and the sand covered them to the depth of four inches. As no one was passing at the time, and the change in the bank was unnoticed until the afternoon, the place was not searched until then. The event has cast a shadow over the whole town.

Accident on the Wilmington and Manchester Railroad.

From the Charleston (S. C.) News, June 25.

The passengers by the Northwestern Railroad yesterday confirm the report of the accident on the Wilmington and Manchester Railroad, and bring further particulars. We learn that the accident occurred at Soldier's Creek, about thirty miles from Wilmington, at 5 A. M. Sunday morning. The heavy rains had caused the creek to rise, and the trestle was undermined, the embankment being washed away. This was not known to the engineer, and as the down train struck the trestle it gave way, and the engine and baggage and mail cars were precipitated into the creek. The engineer leaped from the engine and saved himself, but Mr. JACKSON HARRAL, a trestle builder, and Mr. O. J. BIRD, a section master, were caught in the wreck, and instantly killed. The engine went headforemost into the creek, but gained the opposite side, and stopped in a perpendicular position, with the smoke-stack and cow-catcher out of the water. The fall of the engine carried with it the baggage and mail cars; these were broken into fragments, and the mail agent was saved only by a miracle. Most of the mail matter was lost, and that saved from the wreck was too wet for distribution, and was carried back to Wilmington. Fortunately, the passenger cars were stopped when they were almost on the verge of the chasm, and the passengers escaped with a rough jolting and a few petty bruises. In consequence of this accident, we have been without a Northern mail since Saturday, but understand that repairs have been already commenced, and it is anticipated that the travel will soon be resumed along the road.

California Mining Stocks.

SAN FRANCISCO, Saturday, June 29.

Savage, $4,500; Crown Point, $2,200; Yellow Jacket, $1,640; Chollar Potosi, $450; Kentucky, $445; Ophir, $320; Belcher, $460; Imperial, $225; Overmann, $236.

The New-York Times.

VOL. XVII.....NO. 5034. | NEW-YORK, WEDNESDAY, NOVEMBER 13, 1867. | PRICE FOUR CENTS.

TELEGRAMS.

Withdrawal of the French Troops from Papal Territory.

The Suppression of the Temporal Power Declared Indispensable.

Italy Seeks to Dissuade the Powers from Joining the Conference.

Completion of Minister Menabrea's Cabinet.

FRANCE AND ITALY.

The Withdrawal of the French Troops to Civita Vecchia—The Proposed Congress Conference Objected to by the Italian Government.

PARIS, Tuesday, Nov. 12.

The *Moniteur* in its official column to-day, announce that the Emperor, seeing that Italy is resolved to do her duty and fulfill all her obligations under the September Convention, has withdrawn the French troops from the City of Rome and other parts of the Papal territory to Civita Vecchia.

The *Gazette* published the text of a diplomatic note from Prime Minister MANABREA, which declares that the suppression of the temporal power of the Pope is indispensable to the maintenance of good relations between Italy and France.

The French Government has issued a second note in regard to the proposed conference on the Roman question. In this document, even the third-rate Powers of Europe are called to participate. It is thought that none of them will decline.

The Government of Italy, which is hostile to the projected conference, has meantime sent a note to the European Powers in order to enable them to decide against the necessity of any conference whatever. In this note the Roman question is discussed from an Italian stand-point. The details, however, have not transpired.

Rear Admiral PROVANA DEL SABBIONE has been appointed Minister of the Marine, and his acceptance of the post completes the Cabinet of Gen. MENABREA.

FRANCE.

Resignation of Minister de la Valette.

PARIS, Tuesday, Nov. 12—Midnight.

The report of the resignation of the Marquis DE LA VALETTE, Minister of State for the Interior, is confirmed. The Emperor has appointed M. PINAREL his successor.

M. PIERRE MAGNE has also been appointed Minister of Finance.

Don MACEDO, Minister of Brazil to France, died to-day.

GREAT BRITAIN.

Serious Riot in Oxford.

LONDON, Monday, Nov. 11—2 P. M.

A serious riot is reported in Oxford, and troops have been ordered there to put it down.

LONDON, Tuesday, Nov. 12—Evening.

The measures taken to suppress the disturbance in Oxford to-day were effective, and the town is now quiet.

The Fenian Trials in Dublin and in Manchester.

DUBLIN, Tuesday, Nov. 12—Evening.

The trial of HALPIN before the Special Commission was concluded to-day. The jury brought in a verdict of "Guilty of treason and felony." The prisoner throughout his trial has maintained his claim of American citizenship. The Court has not yet pronounced his sentence.

MANCHESTER, Tuesday, Nov. 12—Evening.

The prisoners, ROBERTS, FEATHERSTONE and GOULD, were brought up before the Commission to-day, and were each sentenced to five years imprisonment.

All the indictments having been disposed of, the Special Commission for the trial of the Manchester rioters was dissolved.

SWITZERLAND.

Approval of the Postal Treaty with the United States.

BERNE, Monday, Nov. 11.

The Swiss Council has approved the new postal treaty negotiated with the United States of America.

PORTUGAL.

Prolongation of Admiral Farragut's Visit to Lisbon.

LISBON, Monday, Nov. 11.

It is understood that the United States fleet, under the command of Admiral FARRAGUT, now lying in this harbor, will not sail for some time to come, the Admiral having determined to prolong his stay in this port.

PRUSSIA.

A Delegate to the Diet Sentenced to be Imprisoned.

BERLIN, Monday, Nov. 11.

Herr TWESTEN, a Prussian deputy, has been tried and sentenced to two years' imprisonment for remarks on the Judiciary made by him in the Diet.

EUROPEAN MARKETS.

Financial.

LONDON, Monday, Nov. 11—Noon.

Consols for money........94¾
United States Five-Twenty Bonds........70 15-16
Illinois Central Railway Shares........83¼
Erie Railway Shares........46¾

No advices have yet been received of the prices of American securities in the New-York market.

FRANKFORT, Monday, Nov. 11—Noon.

United States Five Twenties for the issue of 1862, 76¾.

LONDON, Monday, Nov. 11—2 P. M.

Consols for money........94 7-16
United States Five-Twenty Bonds........70 15-16
Illinois Central Railway Shares........83½
Erie Railway Shares........46¾

LONDON, Monday, Nov. 11—3 P. M.

If REUTER's telegrams of the prices of American securities, and the quotation of gold in the New-York market, have come to hand he has not yet furnished them to the public.

In the absence of such advices the prices of American securities remain as already reported.

Consols for money are quoted at this hour at 94¾.

Whale oil has advanced to £39 ℔ 252 gallons.

FRANKFORT, Monday, Nov. 11—2 P. M.

United States Five-twenty Bonds, for the issue of 1862, 76¼.

FRANKFORT, Monday, Nov. 11—Evening.

United States Five-Twenties, for the issue of 1862, 76¾.

LONDON, Tuesday, Nov. 12—Noon.

The public are without advices from Reuter's Agency of the prices of American securities and the quotations of gold in the New-York market.

Consols, for money........94¾
United States Five-Twenty Bonds........71
Illinois Central Railway Shares........83¾
Erie Railway Shares........46¾

FRANKFORT, Tuesday, Nov. 12—Noon.

United States Five-Twenties for the issue of 1862, 76¾.

LONDON, Tuesday, Nov. 12—2 P. M.

Consols steady, at 94¾ for money.

Five-Twenties are dull, and have declined ¼, being quoted at 70¾. Illinois and Erie Shares unchanged.

LONDON, Tuesday, Nov. 12—Evening.

Consols closed at 94 9-16 for money.

No advices have yet been received by Atlantic Cable, and in their absence the following quotations are given without knowledge of the condition of the New-York market:

United States Five-Twenty Bonds........70 15-16
Illinois Central Railway Shares........84¾
Erie Railway Shares........47

FRANKFORT, Tuesday, Nov. 12—Evening.

United States Bonds are quoted at 76¾ for the issue of 1862.

Commercial.

LIVERPOOL, Monday, Nov. 11—Noon.

Cotton opened quiet, but at steady prices. The estimated sales to-day are 19,000 bales.

Middling Uplands........8 11-16d.
Middling Orleans........9 1-16d.

BREADSTUFFS—Corn, 48s. 9d. ℔ quarter for Mixed Western. Wheat, 17s. ℔ cental for White California, and 13s. 9d. for No. 1 Milwaukee Red. Barley, 5s. 4d. ℔ 60 lbs. for American. Oats, 3s. 11d. ℔ 45 lbs. for American. Peas, 50s. ℔ 504 lbs. for Canadian.

PROVISIONS—Beef, 105s. ℔ 304 lbs. for Extra Prime Mess. Pork, 72s. ℔ 200 lbs. for Eastern Prime Mess. Lard, 52s. 6d. ℔ cwt. for fine American. Cheese, 53s. 6d. ℔ cwt. for the highest range of fine. Bacon, 52s. ℔ cwt. for Cumberland Cut.

PRODUCE—No. 12 Dutch Standard Sugar, 26s. 6d. Resin—8s. 3d. for Common Wilmington, and 12s. for fine Pale. Turpentine, 27s. ℔ cwt. Petroleum—Spirits, nominal at 2s. ℔ gallon, and Refined, 1s. 5d. Tallow, 44s. 6d. ℔ cwt. for American.

LONDON, Monday, Nov. 11—Noon.

Calcutta Linseed, 68s. 6d. ℔ imperial quarter. Linseed Cakes—£11 ℔ ton for thin Oblong. Linseed Oil, £41 ℔ ton. Whale Oil, £37 ℔ 252 gallons. Sperm Oil, £114 ℔ ton.

LIVERPOOL, Monday, Nov. 11—2 P. M.

Cotton dull and unchanged.

No. 1 Milwaukee Red Wheat advanced to 13s. 10d. ℔ cental.

Cheese advanced to 54s. ℔ cwt. for the highest range of fine.

No changes in other articles since the noon dispatch.

LIVERPOOL, Monday, Nov. 11—3 P. M.

Cotton is dull, and Middling Orleans has declined to 9d. ℔ lb.

The other markets are without change.

LONDON, Monday, Nov. 11—2 P. M.

Linseed Cakes advanced to £11 5s. ℔ ton for thin Oblong, and Linseed Oil has declined to £40 10s. ℔ ton.

Cloverseed is quoted at 39s. for No. 1 American Red.

All other articles are as quoted in the noon dispatch.

ANTWERP, Monday, Nov. 11.

Petroleum 47½ francs for Standard White.

LIVERPOOL, Tuesday, Nov. 12—Noon.

Cotton dull. The estimated sales to-day are 8,000 bales. Middling Uplands, 8 11-16d.; Middling Orleans, 9d.

BREADSTUFFS—Corn, 48s. 9d. Wheat—17s. for White California, and 13s. 10d. for No. 1 Milwaukee Red. Barley, 5s. 4d. Oats, 3s. 11d. Peas, 50s.

PRODUCE—No. 12 Dutch Standard Sugar, 26s. 6d. Resin—8s. 3d. for Common Wilmington, and 12s. for Fine Pale. Tallow, 44s. 6d. Spirits Turpentine, 27s. Petroleum—Spirits, nominal at 2s.; Refined, 1s. 5d. Cloverseed, 39s.

PROVISIONS—Beef, 105s. Pork, 72s. Lard, 52s. 6d. Cheese, 54s. Bacon, 52s.

LONDON, Tuesday, Nov. 12—Noon.

Linseed Cakes, £11 5s. Calcutta Linseed, 68s. 6d. Linseed Oil, £40 10s. Whale Oil, £39. Sperm Oil, £114.

ANTWERP, Tuesday, Nov. 12—Noon.

PETROLEUM—47½ francs for Standard White.

LIVERPOOL, Tuesday, Nov. 12—2 P. M.

The Cotton market continues dull, but quotations are unchanged at this hour.

TRADE REPORT—The advices from Manchester to-day continue to be unfavorable. The market for goods and yarns was heavy, with a declining tendency.

BREADSTUFFS—Wheat is firm at 17s. for California White, and 13s. 10d. for Red Western. Corn—New Mixed Western steady at 48s. 9d. ℔ quarter.

PROVISIONS AND PRODUCE—There is no change to report in these markets.

LIVERPOOL, Tuesday, Nov. 12—Evening.

COTTON—The market closed heavy and declining under the influence of the unfavorable reports from Manchester. The following are the authorized closing quotations:

Middling Uplands........8⅝d.
Middling Orleans........8⅞d.

The sales of the day foot up 8,000 bales.

Breadstuffs, Provisions and Produce markets entirely unchanged. Sugars firm at 26s. 6d. for No. 12 Dutch Standard.

ANTWERP, Tuesday, Nov. 12—Evening.

PETROLEUM—The market is dull; Standard White is quoted at 47 francs 50 centimes.

EUROPEAN MARINE NEWS.

Arrivals Out.

LONDONDERRY, Monday, Nov. 11.

The Anchor Line steamship *United Kingdom*, Capt. SMITH, which left New-York Oct. 26, arrived at Moville to-day and sailed for the Clyde.

BREST, Tuesday, Nov. 12—Noon.

The steamship *Ville de Paris*, Capt. SURMON, from New-York on the 2d inst., arrived here this morning *en route* to Havre.

QUEENSTOWN, Tuesday, Nov. 12—Noon.

The steamship *City of Paris*, Capt. KENNEDY, from New-York on the 2d inst., arrived here this forenoon.

Marine Disaster.

QUEENSTOWN, Monday, Nov. 11—Noon.

The ship *Melbourne*, from Archangel for Boston, is at Cork in a leaking condition.

CENTRAL AMERICA.

Proposed Construction of a Railroad Through Honduras, from the Atlantic to the Pacific.

LONDON, Monday, Nov. 11—Noon.

A loan of one million pounds sterling to the Honduras Railway has been introduced in the market here.

This loan looks to the construction of a railway through Honduras, Central America, from Porto Cabello, on the Atlantic, to the Gulf of Fanseca, on the Pacific, the surveys of which were made under the old Squiers grant about eight years ago by a party of English engineers.

The proposed route is about 260 miles long, and the cost of construction will be about £6,000 per mile.

THE WEST INDIES.

Havana Markets and Marine Intelligence.

HAVANA, Tuesday, Nov. 12.

No. 12 Dutch Standard Sugar, 8¼@8½ reals.

Exchange on London, 14¾@15 per cent. premium.

Exchange on Paris, 2 per cent. premium.

Exchange on the United States at long sight for currency, 24@25 per cent. discount; for gold at long sight, 2¾ per cent. premium, and at short sight, 4¼ per cent. premium.

Arrived, brig *Cecilia* from Mobile and schooner *Anna Hatton* from New-York.

The schooner *Presto*, from Newport for Havana, was lost in a storm on the 5th inst., off New-Nassau.

The brig *Nasade*, from Lima for New-York, has put into Santiago de Cuba.

Sailed, steamer *Juniata* for Philadelphia, and steamer *Star of the Union* for New-Orleans.

The sanitary condition of the city is favorable.

THE DOMINION OF CANADA.

The Speaker of the Senate—The Militia Question.

OTTAWA, Canada, Tuesday, Nov. 12.

A movement is on foot in the Senate to petition the Imperial Parliament to make a change in the Constitution so as to provide for the election of the Speaker of the Senate by that body instead of by the Crown.

It is understood that the Government policy on the militia question is drill 100,000 men annually, twenty-five days. This makes the militia expenditure about $3,000,000 per year.

Escape of Counterfeiters from the Toronto Jail.

TORONTO, Canada, Tuesday, Nov. 12.

ULRICH and HARCQ, the two American counterfeiters confined in jail here awaiting extradition, escaped this morning by breaking their cells. They have not yet been recaptured.

HENRY WARD BEECHER and party arrived here to-day.

VIRGINIA.

Prize Fights at Fort Albany—Two Hundred Persons Arrested by the Military.

Special Dispatch to the New-York Times.

WASHINGTON, Monday, Nov. 11.

Gen. SCHOFIELD deserves credit for having rid the soil of Virginia of the detestable vice of prize fighting which has been carried on with impunity for the past two years on the south side of the Potomac. The pugilists and their crowds of thieves and rowdies from New-York, Philadelphia and Baltimore, would come here to arrange preliminaries and then charter boats to go down the river and fight in Virginia. This morning two fights had been arranged just over Long Bridge, within the walls of old fort Albany. Just as they got well started the Sheriff of Alexandria, with a posse of fifty soldiers from the Fourth Artillery, made a descent, and captured nearly everybody present and marched them through the wind five miles to Alexandria. No more such affairs will be permitted in Virginia while it is under military jurisdiction.

Associated Press Dispatch.

WASHINGTON, Tuesday, Nov. 12.

A large number of sporting men, black and white, belonging to this city and to other cities, left here between 3 and 6 o'clock this morning, in conveyances publicly advertised, to witness two separate prize fights at Fort Albany, Va., which is about two miles from Washington. The white pugilists were BOLSTER and MCLAUGHLIN, and the black fighters were SORRELL and BOVIE. The fight arranged between the latter parties excited the most interest, as it was to be the first of the kind between colored men. The crowd at Fort Albany were first disappointed at not witnessing a contest between the two white men, as the fight was declared "off," in consequence of the illness of MCLAUGHLIN, and the stakes were accordingly awarded to BOLSTER, who was on the ground. SORRELL, one of the black pugilists, then went into the ring, but BOVIE was not forthcoming. It was then reported that the latter would not appear, having been badly trained and fearing foul play. At this point the interesting concourse of black and white sports were startled by cries of "Police!" "Police!" "The military are coming!" "We've got to put for it!" A stampede at once commenced, but too late for all the spectators to escape from the military, who formed a cordon around the fort, and with fixed bayonets and pistols threatened death to every one who attempted to escape or break through the line. The number of persons captured was about two hundred. The troops were Company F, of the Fourth Artillery, who had been lying in the woods since daylight waiting for the "roughs" to appear. The Sheriff of Alexandria County was also present with a Police force from Alexandria County. The Sheriff of Alexandria County paroled a number of the prisoners, to appear at his office during the day, and the military escorted the remaining one hundred and fifty to Alexandria. SORRELL, one of the black pugilists, was among the few who made good their escape from the military. It is said that the seizure was made by direction of Gen. SCHOFIELD, who has declared that no more prize fights will be permitted to take place within his jurisdiction. On reaching Alexandria the prisoners, among whom were about twenty blacks, were marched into the jail. The reading of the law was called for by one of the prisoners, by which it appeared that the Riot Act is required to be read before arrests can be made, which was not done in this case. Therefore, the military and civil officers released the entire party after a course of lectures. SORRELL and BOLSTER, the two prize fighters, had previously made their escape—one by swimming the canal, and the other by a flank movement overland.

Arrest of a Delegate to the Virginia Convention.

RICHMOND, Va., Tuesday, Nov. 12.

The military authorities to-day arrested LEWIS LINDSEY, the colored delegate to the Virginia Convention, for using language calculated to array the whites and blacks against each other. He is to be tried by a military commission.

Arrest of Judge Parker at Winchester.

RICHMOND, Va., Tuesday, Nov. 12.

Judge PARKER, of Winchester, was arrested yesterday morning by the officer of the Freedmen's Bureau; charge not positively known. No order for such arrest was issued from headquarters here.

United States Circuit Court.

RICHMOND, Va., Tuesday, Nov. 12.

Chief-Justice CHASE will arrive here to-morrow to preside with Judge UNDERWOOD at the adjourned Spring Term of the United States Circuit Court, which commences to-morrow.

The Fall Term, at which JEFFERSON DAVIS will be tried, commences on the 25th inst. From the venire it appears that the jury will be largely composed of blacks.

MISSOURI.

Prairie Fires in the West.

ST. LOUIS, Tuesday, Nov. 12.

Accounts from different sections of Missouri and Kansas mention very serious losses to farmers from prairie fires. In some instances whole farms have been devastated, fences, barns, sheds, grain and hay stacks, orchards, and occasionally houses, being consumed. Many thousands of dollars worth property has been destroyed.

New Water Works for St. Louis.

ST. LOUIS, Tuesday, Nov. 12.

A contract was awarded to-day by the Board of Water Commissioners, to R. D. WOOD & Co., of Philadelphia, to supply water pipes and other castings for the new water works here. The contract amounts to over $1,250,000. Pittsburgh, Cincinnati, Philadelphia, Philipsburgh, N. J., and St. Louis, competed for the contract.

ARKANSAS.

The Convention Election—Probable Republican Majority.

MEMPHIS, Tenn., Tuesday, Nov. 12.

A special to the *Post* (Radical) from Little Rock, to-day, says that Arkansas will go largely for the Convention, with a working majority for the Republicans. About four-fifths of the registered votes were cast in the State. Montgomery, Perry, St. Francis, Dallas and Hotsprings Counties, complete, gives 200 for the Convention; the delegates are all Radical. Pulaski, Crawford, Conway and Sebastian Counties elect Radicals with the coöperation of the whites.

TENNESSEE.

Racing in Memphis.

MEMPHIS, Tenn., Tuesday, Nov. 12.

The attendance at the Memphis course to-day was again very large. The first race was for the Gayoso House stake of $400, heats free for all, and it was won by *Malcolm* in two straight heats; time, 1:50¾, 1:50¾. The second race was for the Association purse of $300, a two mile dash, free for all. Seven horses started, and the first heat was dead between *Duke of Orleans* and *Victorine*; time, 3:46. In a second trial *Duke of Orleans* won in 3:48¾.

NEW-YORK.

The New-York State Election.

ROCHESTER, Tuesday, Nov. 12.

The Monroe County Canvassers are in session to-day, and from their table we make the following majorities: McKean, 788; Hillhouse, 767; Gates, 772; Hammond, 581; Van Cott, 781; Powell, 760; De La Matyr, 618; Morgan, Republican Senator, 35; Powers, Democrat, for County Clerk, 206; Moore, Republican, for Sheriff, 943; Davis, Republican, for Assembly, 99; Wood, Republican, for Assembly, 132; Bradstreet, Democrat, for Assembly, 79.

ALBANY, Tuesday, Nov. 12.

The official Democratic majority on the State ticket in this county is 1,806.

Arrest of Supposed Burglars at Albany.

ALBANY, Tuesday, Nov. 12.

Detective KELLY to-day arrested two young Frenchmen, who gave their names as EMIL BONEL and ALFRED ROLAND, on suspicion of robbery. He found in their possession five sets of Priest's vestments, a communion cloth, &c., all valued at $1,500. They are supposed to be professional burglars.

Weston, the Pedestrian.

ROCHESTER, N. Y., Tuesday, Nov. 12.

WESTON arrived here at 12:20 o'clock to-night in good condition. He was met by a large crowd of citizens and went to Congress Hall, where he will remain the rest of the night. He made sixty-three miles to-day, six of them in a snow storm. The last thirty miles were made against a heavy head wind. He will leave this city at nine o'clock to-morrow morning.

PENNSYLVANIA.

Sinking of the Steamer Gen. Putnam.

PHILADELPHIA, Tuesday, Nov. 12.

Yesterday, about a mile above Newcastle, the steamboat *Major Reybold*, from Delaware City for Philadelphia, collided with the steamer *Gen. Putnam*, of the Light-house Department. The accident occurred about 10 o'clock in the morning, during a dense fog. The *Putnam* was from Wilmington, Del., bound to New-York. She immediately sank in about four fathoms of water. The Captain of the *Reybold* states that he gave the signals at regular intervals, but heard no response from the *Putnam*, whose Captain and crew were brought to this port by the *Reybold*. The damage to the *Reybold* was very trifling.

Execution of Neal Devaney.

SCRANTON, Penn., Tuesday, Nov. 12.

The execution of NEAL DEVANEY, aged 21 years, for the murder of his wife, CATHARINE DEVANEY, near Hazelton, Luzerne County, Penn., in July last, took place at 1 o'clock P. M., in the Jail-yard at Wilkesbarre. Two or three hundred people were present in the yard, and at least 5,000 people surrounded the Jail, covering the house-tops, trees, and every available resting-place.

He confessed his guilt on the scaffold, saying: "Gentlemen, I am guilty. DOMINICK TOOMEY swore falsely; he swore my life away. I forgive everybody; I forgive TOOMEY, too."

MASSACHUSETTS.

Gen. Banks Not in Mexico.

BOSTON, Tuesday, Nov. 12.

The advices purporting to come from the City of Mexico, announcing the arrival of Gen. N. P. BANKS in that city, have no foundation in fact. Gen. BANKS is at his home in Waltham.

Marine Disaster.

BOSTON, Tuesday, Nov. 12.

The schooner *Globe*, Capt. STRONG, owned by C. & E. J. PETERS, of New-York, loaded with coal, from Elizabethport for Haverhill, went ashore in entering Newburyport Harbor, on Hump Sands, on Sunday night. She is breaking up and will be a total loss. There is no insurance on the vessel.

KANSAS.

Murders at Leavenworth.

LEAVENWORTH, Kansas, Tuesday, Nov. 12.

The proprietor of the Planter's House, at Platte City, Mo., named JENKINS, was shot and instantly killed by a negro man this morning, who had been discharged for some misconduct. $500 reward has been offered for the arrest of the murderer.

In South Leavenworth, this morning, a mulatto woman shot and instantly killed another woman, the ball entering her ear. Jealousy is supposed to have been the cause.

OHIO.

Democratic National Convention.

CLEVELAND, Tuesday, Nov. 12.

The Cleveland *Plaindealer* to-day urges the selection of Cleveland as the place to hold the next Democratic National Convention, and says that prominent gentlemen agree to erect a grand temple to be used by the Convention in its session.

MARYLAND.

Baltimore Races—Second Day.

BALTIMORE, Tuesday, Nov. 12.

The second day's races of the Fall season on the Herring Run Course came off to-day. The track was again in very bad condition, owing to the storm of the previous evening, so much so that the first race—a five-mile dash between *Belle of Baltimore*, *Lucy* and *Lizzie* was postponed until to-morrow. The second race was mile heats, best three in five, to harness, for $250. There were three entries, *Kinadore*, *Lizzie* and *Frank*, and the race was won by the first named in three straight heats; time, 2:42, 2:46, 2:53.

GEORGIA.

Fire in Savannah.

SAVANNAH, Ga., Tuesday, Nov. 12.

A cotton factory with six adjoining houses was destroyed by fire to-day. The loss is estimated at $25,000, on which there is $11,500 insurance.

ALABAMA.

The Alabama Reconstruction Convention.

MONTGOMERY, Ala., Tuesday, Nov. 12.

In the Reconstruction Convention the whole day was consumed in considering the franchise question. The majority report, which embraces strong proscriptive features, will be adopted.

LOUISIANA.

Appointment of a Judge in New-Orleans.

NEW-ORLEANS, Tuesday, Nov. 12.

Gen. MOWER to-day appointed R. KING CUTLER Judge of the Second District Court of Louisiana, in place of Judge A. CAZABATE, resigned.

INCENDIARY FIRE IN FIRST-AVENUE.—A still alarm was given at midnight for a fire in the cellar of the tenement-house No. 215 First-avenue, and on the members of Engine Company No. 5 entering, they found a mass of straw and other inflammable materials on fire under the stairway, and also discovered PHINEAS JACOBS, who occupies the first floor as a dry-goods store, therein. As he acted in a suspicious manner, BENJ. J. GIRGUEL, Foreman of No. 5 Engine, ordered his arrest by the Police, and he is now held at the Seventeenth Ward Station-house to await further examination by the Fire Marshal.

RUSSIAN AMERICA.

Official Transfer of the Country to the United States Government.

NEW-ARCHANGEL, October, VIA VICTORIA, Sunday, Nov. 10, and SWINOMISH, W. I., Monday, Nov. 11.

The formal transfer and delivery of Russian-America to the United States Government took place to-day, by Capt. FESTREHOUFF, Acting Commissioner on behalf of the Russian Government, and Major-Gen. ROUSSEAU, on behalf of the United States.

At 3 o'clock P. M., a battalion of United States troops, under command of Major CHARLES O. WOOD, of the Ninth Infantry, was drawn up in line in front of the Governor's residence, where the transfer took place. By 3:30 a large concourse of people had assembled, comprising Americans, Russians of all classes, Creoles and Indians, all eager witnesses of the ceremonies.

Precisely at the last named hour the Russian forts and fleet fired salutes in honor of the lowering of the Russian flag; but the flag would not come down. In lowering it tore its entire width close by the halliards, and floated from the cross-trees, some forty feet from the ground. Three Russian sailors then attempted to ascend the inch-and-a-half guy ropes supporting the flag-staff, but each failed to reach his national emblem. A fourth ascended in a boatswain's chair, seized the flag and threw it in a direction directly beneath him; but the motion of the wind carried it off and caused sensation in every heart.

Five minutes after the lowering of the Russian flag the Stars and Stripes went gracefully up, floating handsomely and free, Mr. GEORGE LOVELL ROUSSEAU having the honor of flinging the flag to the breeze, the United States steamers *Ossipee* and *Resaca* at the same time honoring the event by firing salutes.

As the Russian flag was lowered Capt. PESTRECHOFF stepped forward and addressed Gen. ROUSSEAU as follows:

GENERAL: As Commissioner of his Imperial Majesty, the Emperor of Russia, I now transfer and deliver the Territory of Russian America, ceded by his Majesty to the United States.

Gen. ROUSSEAU, in response, as the American flag ascended, said:

CAPTAIN: As Commissioner on behalf of the United States Government, I receive and accept the same accordingly.

The Commissioners spoke in a tone of common conversation, and were only heard by Gov. MAKSATOFF, Gen. JEFF. C. DAVIS, Capt. KUSKOL and a few others who formed the troupe.

Several ladies witnessed the ceremonies, among them Princess MAKESATOFF, Mrs. Gen. DAVIS and Mrs. Major WOOD. The Princess wept audibly as the Russian flag went down.

The transfer was concluded in a purely diplomatic and business-like manner, neither bouquets nor speech-making followed. The entire transaction was concluded in a few hours, the *Ossipee*, with the Commissioner on board, steaming into the harbor at 11 o'clock this forenoon, and at 4 o'clock in the afternoon a dozen American flags floated over the newly-born American city of Sitka.

Terrific Hurricane—Narrow Escape of the United States Steamer Ossipee—Damage to Other Vessels.

NEW-ARCHANGEL, Nov. 2, VIA VICTORIA, V. I., Nov. 10, AND SWINOMISH, W. T., Nov. 11.

The United States steamer *Ossipee* was nearly wrecked on the night of the 27th ult, when 40 miles southeast of Archangel, in the most terrific hurricane witnessed on this coast during the past seventy years. She lost all her boats, and considerable of her sails and rigging was carried away, her chronometer was destroyed, and all the fires but four were put out; those remaining were kept alive by burning oil, tallow, grease, lard, candles and like substances. She shipped an immense sea, doing great injury to the powder in the magazine. Forty-six sailors were wounded while on duty, but providentially none were killed. Gen. ROUSSEAU and his son GEORGE and also the General's staff were on board. The hurricane lasted eighteen hours, and the entire storm between thirty-six and forty hours. Lieutenant Commander CROSSMAN and a boatswain named WILLIAM GREEN saved the ship by their heroic exertions in battening the hatchways when the storm raged with the greatest fury. The engineers and firemen all behaved nobly,

The *Ossipee* put into Sitka harbor on the evening of the 28th ult., having left here on the evening of the 26th.

The yellow fever has been thoroughly killed out.

The Revenue cutter *Lincoln* has gone to Staken River, with the United States surveying party in tow.

The chartered vessels *Milan* and *Buena Vista*, with Government stores for garrison, have arrived safely.

The hurricane swept over the harbor with terrific force. Fifteen vessels were at anchor in the harbor at the time. Three Russian vessels were driven ashore, and Sandwich Islands brig *Mameluke* was badly damaged. Several vessels dragged their anchors and bore down upon each other mercilessly, yet no serious damage was done. The steamship *John L. Stephens* was in their midst, but received no damage, though the midnight scene was entirely appalling.

A number of houses were blown down throughout the city, yet no lives were lost.

The Russian Commissioners have protested against the occupancy of the Fur Company's buildings by United States troops. By courtesy the troops are now sheltered and the supplies stored. The matter will be referred to Mr. SEWARD.

Much ill feeling has been exhibited since our occupation of the city. Several duels on paper have occurred, but they were settled without bloodshed. The parties are of high rank.

BOILER EXPLOSION.

The Terrific Explosion in Chicago on Sunday Morning—The Engineer Killed and Several Buildings Destroyed.

The Chicago *Tribune* of Monday gives a long account of the explosion of a boiler at a flouring mill in that city on Sunday morning last, by which four brick buildings were torn in pieces, a number of neighboring frame structures shattered, and the engineer and perhaps others killed. It says:

"Two o'clock arrived. CONNELL, the engineer, began to feel drowsy. He had been up every night during the week, and Saturday night had brought him no repose. He found it difficult to keep awake. Besides, what difference did it make? His engine was in beautiful trim, and every part had borne the test through a year's constant trial. So he went out into the engine-room, and, filling the furnace with coal, tried the gauges to see that everything was all right, and then, returning to the engine-room, lay down beside the engine, where the fly-wheel's whir lulled him first into a doze and then into a sound sleep. Coal makes a hot fire, and steam began to generate with greater rapidity. The engine's piston flew faster to and fro, and the fly-wheel began to revolve faster and faster. CAHILL, the miller, who was on the second floor, observed that the machinery was moving at a too rapid rate, and descended the stairs to regulate the gearing. He went below the frame-work of timbers that supported the mill-stones, and his hand was already upon the gear-wheel. But he did not turn it. That instant the most hideous, deafening sound that ever smote upon the ear, a noise like a peal of thunder, bursting close to the ground was heard. The air was filled with the rush of scalding steam—showers of bricks and iron flew in every direction. The earth trembled as at the shock of an earthquake, and huge buildings, on the opposite side of the river, shook to their foundations. The walls of the mill, and of half the block, had been rent asunder, and the entire mass had fallen to the ground, crushing everything that lay below like paper. The explosion had thrown the hot coals of the furnace in every direction, and in a moment flames broke out in scores of places throughout the block. The confusion that ensued exceeded a panic. People rushed forth from the lodging houses and from the tenements, in every stage of nakedness, and dashed through the streets and alleys, stopping not until they were blocks away, and when they paused even then, out of breath, believed that they were yet in the midst of danger.

The fact that the boiler was defective seems to be conceded. Indeed it had been a topic of discussion in the surrounding shops for six months; and the opinion had been often expressed that it would one day blow up the neighborhood. Mr. MARPLE states that the boiler was put in thirteen months since, and that about two months ago it was subjected to the proper test and declared to be safe. He had purchased two new boilers, and they were to have replaced that which exploded to-day. He had determined to dispense with that one, however, not because it was unfit or unsafe, but because it was not adapted to the requirements of the machinery in the mill.

FOREIGN NEWS BY MAIL.

ARRIVAL OF THE STEAMSHIP SCOTIA.

The Royal mail steamship *Scotia*, from Liverpool Nov. 2 and Queenstown Nov. 3, arrived at this port yesterday. Her advices are three days later than those received by the *City of New-York*.

Mr. DISRAELI was in Edinburgh Oct. 30. In the afternoon he was presented with the freedom of the city. The Lord Provost was careful to say that the honor was conferred upon Mr. DISRAELI as an eminent statesman and a man of letters, and that it had in no respect a political signification. Mr. DISRAELI accepted the situation, and scarcely touched upon politics. He, however, promised that the Government would take in hand the question of Education in Scotland. Leaving the music hall the Chancellor of the Exchequer went to the hall of the library of the University of Edinburg, where the degree of LL.D. was conferred upon him and Mr. LOWE, M. P., at the same time. In the evening Mr. DISRAELI was presented with a complimentary address by so-called workingmen of Edinburg.

At a meeting of the Council of the Reform League, on Oct. 30, a letter was read from the O'DONOGHUE, expressing approval of the recent discussion by the League of Irish affairs. He did not regard those proceedings as an incitement to physical force or to isolated deeds of violence, which everybody must reprobate, but as an expression of opinion that the appeal to physical force by ardent Irishmen cannot in reason be pronounced unwarrantable, and does not merit the brand of infamy which the faint-hearted and abettors of misrule would stamp upon it.

A great Protestant demonstration had taken place at Hillsborough, Ulster, and passed off quietly. The Marquis of Downshire presided.

At a meeting of the shareholders of the English and American Bank, in London, the resolution previously passed in favor of the concern being voluntarily wound up was confirmed.

At the meeting of the Grand Trunk, of Canada, Railway Company, it was stated that the total loss sustained by the Company from 1862 to June last, in American currency, amounted to no less than £311,000 sterling.

A dispatch from Athens, dated Oct. 26, says that according to the Greek journals the mission of ALI PACHA to Crete had proved a total failure, the insurgents demanding union with Greece. Fresh Turkish troops were said to have been sent to Crete, all the Egyptian troops having left, and frequent encounters were taking place between the Turks and Cretans, despite the armistice. French, Russian, Italian and Prussian vessels continued to transport Cretan fugitives to Greece.

FENIANISM IN ENGLAND.

The Murder Trials at Manchester—Scenes In and About the Court-house—The Witnesses and Their Testimony—Demeanor and Speeches of the Prisoners—The Death Sentence.

From Our Own Correspondent.

MANCHESTER, Saturday, Nov. 2, 1867.

Every hour the interest of this tragedy of the murder trials at Manchester has deepened. The law of England says that every man of those engaged in the release of KELLY and DEASEY were as guilty of the murder of the Policeman BRETT as the one who actually shot him. It is constructive murder. This was the charge of Chief-Justice BLACKBURN, and on this charge the Grand Jury has indicted the whole twenty-six for murder. Now this rule must work both ways, and it follows that the man who actually shot BRETT is no more guilty and no more deserving of death than any and all of the 26 indicted, or the forty or fifty said by the witnesses to have been engaged in the affray. But in no case can it be right to say that these men were engaged in a conspiracy for assassination and plunder. No one was robbed, no one, except by accident, was hurt, unless it was BRETT, and his death may have been by what is called "chance medley." It was sworn on the part of the prosecution that ALLEN and the rest who had revolvers fired at the ground or into the air, to frighten, and not to kill, the police and people, men and women who gathered around the prison van, from which they were seeking to release their imprisoned chiefs. No doubt it was a serious crime, unless justified by the imprisonment of KELLY and DEASEY, but it was not intended to be murder.

The Court-room, on Wednesday, was simply full. There were many ladies in privileged places—a few, even, on the platform which holds the Judge's bench. Some of the nobility of Lancashire—ladies as well as lords—occupied the grand jury box. The proceedings were more orderly and more dull than is usual in an American trial. In three days I have not heard one question objected to by the opposite counsel, nor has there been the least interruption. Leading questions are the rule, and some of the witnesses do little more than to say "yes," "yes," to questions which tell the story. The cross-examinations are searching, but there is little of which the most sensitive witnesses could complain. Only on Wednesday night, when a witness swore to the most direct and important circumstances in regard to ALLEN—swore that he saw him put his pistol through the ventilator, stoop down, take aim and shoot BRETT, not a word of which had he said when he was before the magistrates, and which he had apparently invented since, with an eye to the reward of two hundred pounds, did Mr. SEYMOUR startle the Court with a burst of most eloquent indignation.

THE WITNESSES.

Among the witnesses were four of the prisoners in the van, two interesting young women going to jail—one for the third time—for felony, and two little boys of ten and twelve, for larceny. The boys were in cells in the van, but declared that they saw ALLEN through a hole in the door release KELLY and DACEY, the Fenian prisoners. The jury went out to see the van, and found, I believe, that the narrow openings slant down to the floor, so as to make such recognition impossible. The felonious young women were among the clearest, promptest and most consistent witnesses. Each told her story like a book, and stuck to it bravely; only their stories point blank contradicted each other. The first swore that she was next to BRETT; that she cried out "O, CHARLEY, you'll be shot!" and that she got hold of his coat tails with both hands and pulled him down toward the floor, which brought his head even with the ventilator, when ALLEN shot him. The other swore just as positively that it was she who tried to take care of "CHARLEY"—that she was next him—that no one pulled him down, but that he stood bolt upright, and she had her hand on his shoulder, when a bullet came through the slats of the Venetian blind in the top of the door and killed him. Many of the witnesses contradict themselves; they contradict more or less each other, as usual; but the offer of a large reward has evidently affected the imaginations of many, and they swear to what they have heard or invented.

Some of the testimony is in the broadest Lancashire dialect, such as you hear sometimes on the stage. Mrs. BOUCICAULT, who should be Lancashire born, speaks it sweetly. They say "tew" for two, and "keow" for cow, as in Yankeeland; but they also say "douzen." On Wednesday morning a man kissed the book with a resounding smack, and said: "I saw a many roonin' daown the railway sloap, an' I thoat it was a pitch in"—which he explained to be a railway collision. ALLEN, he said, when caught by the crowd, was beaten over the head with his pistol and a brick, and he protected him.

On Wednesday night the streets through which the five prisoners are conveyed from the Assize Courts to the Jail were almost impassable from the crowd. I was wrong in saying that the van is guarded only by mounted Police. There is also a strong military escort; though a policeman in Court assured me that the feeling in the crowd is so strong against the prisoners, that if they are not hanged "Manchester will rise."

On Thursday morning the Crown called witnesses to prove the capture and remands of KELLY and DEASEY, the Fenians. We had upon the stand a Manchester Inspector, a giant of six feet three inches; a Dublin Police official, and a London detective Inspector from Scotland Yard. But it appeared that there had been an irregularity in the arrest and remands of the rescued Fenians. A Police Inspector had taken the responsibility of tearing up one warrant, and of writing the word "felony" into another, and the prisoner's counsel moved to quash the indictments for murder on the ground that the men rescued not having been in lawful custody, they had a right to get away, and their friends to help them. This was argued at some length, and the Court reserved the decision until after lunch, and then decided against the prisoners.

OPENING THE CASE.

There was no regular opening of the case for the defence, Mr. SEYMOUR preferring to reserve his forces for the summing up. Then the first witness, Miss MARY FLANAGAN, was called. A prettier Irish girl I have seldom seen, and that is saying a good deal. She was modest, lady-like, and, in her language and deportment, showed that she had received a careful education. Her parents keep a tavern some twelve miles from Manchester, and she has been a governess in a gentleman's family. She happened to know GOULD, one of the prisoners, and swore positively to having seen him at a time and place which made his participation in the riot impossible—nor could I see that the cross-examination of the Attorney-General shook or discredited her testimony. Mrs. LEARY, a very decent seeming woman, testified to having seen him at the same place and time. An old lady, her two sons, and another young man swore a clear *alibi* as to SHORE.

A sister of MAGUIRE swore that he never left her house until 7 o'clock on the night of the rescue. MARY INGHAM, a pale, pretty girl then came upon the stand, and pale and rigid as a statue—a more perfect *Jeannie Deans* than was ever seen upon the stage—told the whole story of her acquaintance with the soldier MAGUIRE, when and where she saw him that day, how he asked if he might go with her to a party, how he had often asked her to go with him to the theatre, and once she went, and how sure she was that on that fatal 18th of September he was at home; and her unshaken testimony was fully confirmed by four neighbors, whose houses almost touched that of the prisoner's sister. Here then were three as clear *alibis* as I ever heard, and the last a very strong one, out of the five prisoners on trial. No witness was called as to ALLEN, except a policeman to show that he was bruised and beaten, and his head bound up when the witnesses came to identify him; and none at all for LARKIN. On neither side was there any attempt to impeach a witness.

Unfortunately, as the crowd gathered again in the streets near the Assize Courts on Thursday night, the newspapers had the account of the shooting the night before of two policemen in Dublin. One dispatch said both were shot through the heart at midnight—another that both were shot in the stomach but mortally wounded. The jury ought not to hear of this occurrence—the provocation ought not to allude to it, but it can scarcely fail of having some influence upon the result of the trials going on in both Dublin and Manchester. These outrages are to be deplored and condemned, but that they have a cause is as evident as that they occur. In fact they could not happen if there were not the feeling which produces them, and that feeling is the deep hatred produced by centuries of wrong.

CLOSING ARGUMENTS AND VERDICT.

On Friday morning at 8:30 o'clock, in a cold rain-storm, I found the barricaded doors of the Assize Courts blocked up by a crowd struggling, as an English crowd always does, to gain admission. A few minutes after the doors were opened every foot of space was occupied; the jury was called over, the Judges took their seats, and Mr. DIGBY SEYMOUR, Queen's Counsel, commenced his plea on behalf of three of the prisoners, the two others being defended by Mr. Sergeant O'BRIEN. Mr. SEYMOUR is able and eloquent, but I think he weakened his case by denouncing Fenianism—which was really the crime for which all three men are on trial. He had raised the legal point that KELLY and DEASEY were not lawfully in custody, and therefore their rescue was justifiable, and the death of BRETT reduced to a case of manslaughter. The Court ruled that although the warrant was irregular, the magistrate acted rightfully in his discretion, and that the men were in the legal charge of BRETT. The speeches of both the counsel for the defence were professional and no more. There was no sympathy, and both earnestly condemned the cause in which the prisoners were engaged. This was well meant, but it would have come more naturally from the Attorney-General, who, on his part, refrained from any political allusions, and in no way pressed hardly upon the prisoners. He fairly and barely stated the case, without betraying the least earnestness. The summing up of the Judge, though no doubt intended to be strictly impartial, was harder upon the prisoners than the colorless speech of the handsome, *insouciant* Attorney-General.

The extraordinary circumstances of the trial were also commented upon, with an opposite effect, I suspect, from that intended. Never before in Manchester—seldom of late years in England—had a court of justice been so barricaded, so surrounded with Police, so filled with soldiers, who jostled civilians in the corridors, and the ring of whose muskets could be heard as they grounded arms in the great hall. Never were five manacled prisoners so guarded, and so escorted to and from the Court-house by regiments of horse and foot. All this preparation—this trial in a camp as if by a drumhead court-martial—must have effected the minds of the jury. They were to "save the country" by their verdict. The policeman at my side, between me and the prisoners, had a cartridge-box and Colt's revolver at his belt, and pointed out the Fenians he could spot among the audience.

At a few minutes past 6 o'clock the Judge finished his charge to the jury. He did not tell them they were judges of the law and the facts, as is done in America; he gave them the law, and left them the duty of deciding upon the facts. The jury retired, and for an anxious hour and twenty minutes the audience, which had been seated since before 9 o'clock in the morning, excepting an interval of half an hour, stood up and discussed the verdict. I felt sure that ALLEN would be found guilty; equally sure that they must acquit MAGUIRE. The *alibi* in his case was strong and consistent, and the Judge charged visibly in his favor. I was doubtful about the other cases, but two acquittals seemed probable. The jury came in after an absence of an hour and twenty minutes. The prisoners came up from below and took their places. The names of the five prisoners were called over, and the usual question put to the foreman, and five times he pronounced the terrible word, "*Guilty!*" All guilty of constructive murder. A man was killed by somebody, and they, with some scores of others, ruled by the Court to be equally guilty, were present aiding and abetting.

THE PRISONERS' SPEECHES.

And now commenced the most extraordinary scene I ever witnessed in a Court of Justice. When asked what they had to say why sentence of death should not now be passed upon them—a miserable and useless formality, since whatever they had to say should have been said to the jury before the verdict—each of the five prisoners addressed the Court, and each in his way was eloquent, and four were bold and defiant. The fifth, poor MAGUIRE, a soldier thirteen years in the Queen's service, declared, what I truly believe, that he never was a Fenian, had never been in any way concerned in the rescue, and was quietly at home in his sister's house, as was sworn by five unimpeached witnesses, added to a policeman who testified to his quiet habits. That a jury could condemn a man to death, on such a charge, with such a probability of mistaken identity, can only be accounted for by the fact that they were acting under a strong excitement.

The speeches of the four Fenian prisoners I can give *verbatim*, so far as their words are concerned; but no words can convey an idea of the courage, the heroism, the devotion with which these men met their fate. ALLEN's looks deceived me. For a boy of 19—and he does not look older—and one of ordinary opportunities, he showed an extraordinary spirit. There was not a tremor in his voice, which rang full and clear through the Court-room. I need not give all that was said, but in condensing the speeches I will give only the words and phrases of the speakers.

Continued on Eighth Page.

The New-York Times.

VOL. XVII.....NO. 5139. NEW-YORK, SATURDAY, MARCH 14, 1868. PRICE FOUR CENTS.

IMPEACHMENT.

The President Summoned to Appear at the Bar of the Senate.

His Counsel Ask for Forty Days to Prepare and File an Answer.

The Motion Denied and the Respondent Ordered to Answer on the 23d of March.

The Trial Ordered to Proceed Immediately Thereafter.

Speeches by Messrs. Stanbery, Bingham, Butler, Nelson and Others.

Special Dispatch to the New-York Times.

WASHINGTON, Friday, March 13.

The supreme majesty of the law and the power of this republican Government was illustrated anew to-day by the fresh scenes and proceedings in the great trial of impeachment. The business-like, almost matter-of-fact manner in which the Congress of the United States proceeds with this grave work is the most striking illustration of the innate love and reverence for law and order that characterize the American people. The numerous intelligent representatives of foreign nations who looked upon the proceedings of to-day must have been again impressed with the feeling that a nation that can without the ruffling of a single temper, or the trembling of a single interest, calmly address itself to so great an event as the trial of its Chief Executive, must be well-entitled to the proudest position upon the face of the earth.

The proceedings to-day were characterized by deeper interest, increased importance and greater solemnity than usual. The preparations for the formal opening largely balanced the general effect of the scene, and it is well at the outset to say that the arrangements for admission were all successfully carried out by the Sergeant-at-Arms, and a very disagreeable matter made as agreeable as possible. The audience began to gather in the Senate galleries as soon as the cordon of Police received word to let ticket-holders pass, and by 12 o'clock the seats were comfortably filled. A glance around the Chamber revealed a highly select and intelligent assemblage, two-thirds ladies, among whom were many faces remembered as having graced the same scene on the 4th of March three years ago. The morning had broken with threatening clouds, and was not conducive, therefore, to a brilliant display of toilets, though there was no lack of richness in the quality of the milder-toned fabrics. The thousand tickets were probably represented by nine hundred persons, as there was ample room, and no occupation of aisles, blocking up of doorways, or jostling or crowding anywhere except in the warmly-contested reporters' gallery, where those who say least about their privileges are pretty certain to get the least. Nearly all the spectators were the families of those persons to whom the tickets were distributed, the Diplomatic Corps being as largely represented in proportion as any other class. The floor of the Senate presented a scene as nearly the counterpart of that of the last inauguration as it well could be, without precisely the same material. Chairs had been placed for the House of Representatives. In the rear of the Senators and on the right of the Chief Justice was a table for the counsel for the defence, and on the left another for the Managers of the prosecution.

At 1 o'clock Vice-President Wade vacated the chair and asked the Chief Justice to assume the position of presiding officer. The Sergeant-at-Arms then made proclamation in the usual form, and Secretary Forney read the journal of the last Court-day's proceedings.

At 1:10 o'clock the Managers on the part of the House appeared and were duly announced. The Senators who had not yet been sworn, viz.: Edmunds of Vermont, Patterson of New-Hampshire, and Vickers, of Maryland, then advanced to the bar and were sworn by the Chief Justice. The return of the Sergeant-at-Arms to the summons, as sworn to by that officer, was then read, and the Chief Justice then ordered him to call upon the accused to appear and answer. In a loud voice, and amid the stillness of the whole Chamber, he called three times, "Andrew Johnson, Andrew Johnson, Andrew Johnson!" There were hundreds among that intelligent audience, who bent forward and eagerly strained their eyes, expecting the President to appear in response to that stentorian behest. But instead of the President, who should come in at the precise moment of the last call, like his very evil genius, but Benjamin F. Butler, all alone, stopping in a half-startled way at the first tier of seats, and looking up at the presiding officer as if to say "Here I am." There was a singularity about this coincidence, which was marked by a titter around the whole hall. The President's room, in the rear of the Senate Chamber, had been assigned for the use of his counsel, and the door in the rear corridor of the Senate lobby soon opened, and Ex-Attorney-General Stanbery, Judge B. R. Curtis, of Boston, and Hon. Thomas A. R. Nelson, of Tennessee, then appeared and took their seats. The members of the House of Representatives, which had resolved itself into a Committee of the Whole, having been notified that the Senate was in session as a court, then appeared headed by Mr. E. B. Washburne, Chairman of the Committee, escorted by the Clerk, McPherson, and Mr. Doorkeeper Lippincott, and followed by the Speaker, arm in arm with Mr. Schenck of the Ways and Means Committee, and then by the other members more or less in order of seniority, position or service in the House.

As soon as the presence of the House was officially announced, the Chief Justice declared it to be in order for the counsel for the defence to put in their answer to the articles of Impeachment. Mr. Stanbery at once rose, and in that characteristic bland, gentle, dignified manner of his, said he and his brothers, Nelson and Curtis, appeared in behalf of the President, and then read an authorization to that effect from the latter, which named also Messrs. Wm. Evarts and J. L. Black as counsel for the President. It is understood that Mr. Evarts signified his willingness to act at a late hour, and was unable to be present to-day. Judge Black also was not present.

Mr. Stanbery closed the reading of the authorization by submitting a motion that the President be allowed forty days time in which to file his answer to the articles of impeachment, and made a brief statement in support of the motion. Judge Bingham replied to this application that under the eighth rule of the Court no prayer of the kind could be granted, and continued at some length and with the vigor and force which always marks his arguments, to sustain this position. Judge Curtis, who is a man of good presence and pleasant address, said in response, that if the position assumed by Mr. Bingham was correct the rule had strangely misled the defence, and that it was contrary to custom in all other cases to compel an accused person to open his case when he pleads to the indictments. Mr. Wilson, in behalf of the Managers, supported Mr. Bingham, and then Mr. Stanberry closed the argument, which lasted less than an hour, by an earnest appeal against haste in so grave a trial; and begged that the impartially and dignity of the proceeding might not be impaired. The President stated the limitation of debate under the 20th rule, but there being no desire to extend it, Mr. Edmunds submitted an order fixing the trial for the 6th of April, whereupon Mr. Morton, of Indiana, moved that the Senate retire for deliberation, to which Mr. Sumner asserted, in his deep-voiced oracular manner, "That's the proper order," whereupon it was carried, and the Senators left their seats to consult in the reception-room. This was just 2 o'clock.

The Senate Chamber at once assumed the appearance of a recess. Just before the gavel fell members of the House gathered in knots, and discussed the question just argued; the galleries began their buzz of chatter and gossip; the reporters bulletined the situation, and put fresh points on their pencils; and some of the spectators, fatigued by the hours of waiting and one hour of listening, promenaded the corridors arm in arm, as though it were a fashionable reception. Some of the Senators, well knowing that the stifled propensities for debate would have free sway for ten minutes each, took the precaution to visit the restaurant before entering upon their deliberations.

What occurred in two hours or more of consultation is of course a secret, but I guarantee some will tell you more of that than they will of what was seen and heard with veritable eyes and ears. Report says of the "caucus," for that is what it was called by some inconsiderate person, was rather warm; that Mr. Sumner attempted to "dragoon" his brothers into denying the application *in toto;* that several of the Senators wouldn't be dragooned by him nor bullied by what he was pleased to term public sentiment;" that they exercised deliberate judgments, and that various propositions, varying from a grant of forty days down to a grant of no time at all, were discussed. The tendency, however, was largely in favor of about ten to fifteen days, and before the Senate was ready to appear, the keen instincts of vigilant reporters had flashed it over the wires that ten days had been settled upon.

At 4:10 o'clock the disorder of the floor and galleries was hushed; the Senators took their seats, and the Chief Justice, in his calm and polished manner, and in his blandest Supreme Court tones, announced that the motion was overruled, and that the respondent be ordered to file his answer on or before the 23d inst. "Jake Howard has carried his point," says some one. However, it is not too certain that it is more than half a point, for here Bingham made a request that the Court order the trial to begin immediately upon the filing of the replication of the Managers to the answer of the respondent. "The question shall the order be made" was put by the chair, the yeas and nays were called, and to the consternation of the advocates of impeachment it was lost by one vote, yeas 25, nays 26. Fifteen Republicans voting with eleven Democrats against it.

Mr. Sherman then moved the adoption of an order to fix April 6 for the day of trial. Mr. Wilson moved to amend by making it the 30th of March. Mr. Conkling came in with a lawyer-like, and practical substitute, that the trial shall begin on the filing of the replication, unless for cause shown the Senate shall otherwise order. Mr. Wilson withdraws his amendment, and permits Mr. Conkling's to come down pat on Mr. Sherman's original motion.

Thus far, Mr. Butler has not had anything to say. He now speaks. He makes a strong appeal against any delay; sets forth, as only he can, in that sharp, malicious, ugly way of his, chewing his under lip into mince-meat as he utters it, the fact that the country needs a speedy settlement of the question, and makes a forcible and vindictive argument, the bad taste of which is heightened by the calm, polished, but not very brilliant or argumentative reply of Mr. Nelson for the defence. Mr. Bingham then simply said that the order asked for by Mr. Conkling was entirely satisfactory to the Managers. Reverdy Johnson arose and naturally gravitated toward a speech, when Conkling, with admirable spirit, and in a manner which drew the heartiest commendation from every spectator, called him to order, and said that reluctant as he was, he must insist on the observance of the rule. Mr. Johnson drops into his seat like a bolt of iron, and he and Conkling exchanged explanations *sotto voce*, while the Chief Justice ordered the Clerk to call the roll on the amendment. The list was now scanned with intense interest; many expected to see a repetition of the former vote, for the question was substantially the same; but the shrewd observer saw that Conkling had relieved the Senate from embarrassment by giving them a business-like impartial and practical proposition which they adopted by a party division, 40 yeas to 10 nays. It did not change the aspect of the case at all.

The Court has now ordered the trial to proceed on the 23d, or as soon as the replication of the Managers is filed, unless the respondent can then show sufficient cause to warrant a further postponement, which will then be considered by the Court and decided according to the exigencies. All the progress was made to-day that was expected by any one—more than the prosecution hoped for; and the action of the Senate can be taken as settling one important fact, namely: That while there is every disposition to grant the President every privilege and all the time consistent with a full and impartial trial, there is a determination to permit no delays not absolutely necessary to the ends of justice.

At 5:15 P. M. the Court adjourned to the 23d inst., and the House retired to its own Chamber. The Chairman of the Committee of the Whole made his report; a session for debate was ordered for to-morrow; an adjournment was carried, and the crowd streamed out of the Capitol into the sunlight and wended its way dinnerward.

PRESIDENT JOHNSON AND HIS ADVISERS.

Affairs were very quiet at the White House to-day. There was no admission of visitors on account of the usual Cabinet meeting, which was attended by all the members excepting the Secretary of State, who was represented by Mr. Frederick Seward.

Mr. Stanbery and others of the President's counsel visited him during the forenoon, and were some time in conversation relative to the approaching trial. It has not yet been determined by the President as to who will form the addition to his present counsel; that will be decided upon probably during the coming week.

Adjutant-Gen. Thomas, who has attended several of the Cabinet consultations recently, was not present this morning.

Secretary Browning, after attending the meeting, repaired to the office of the Attorney-General for the purpose of engaging in any business there which might require his attention as the Acting Chief of that Department.

Judge Curtis and Hon. Henry Stanbery held long consultations this morning at the Attorney-General's office with reference to the proceedings which are now engaging their professional attention.

The President will give the sixth State dinner of the season this evening, to which some fifteen or twenty members of the House of Representatives have been invited with their families.

FORTIETH CONGRESS.

SECOND SESSION.

SENATE....WASHINGTON, Friday, March 13.

PREPARATIONS FOR THE IMPEACHMENT TRIAL.

The favored ticket holders to seats in the galleries commenced pouring into the Capitol by 10 o'clock, and by 11 o'clock the ladies' gallery was packed by as brilliant an audience as upon a full-dress opera night. None were permitted to pass the Supreme Court door without tickets, and guards were placed at half a dozen points, then on to the entrance of the galleries. A heavy police force was on hand. The rules were rigidly enforced, and hundreds of strangers, ignorant of the necessity of obtaining tickets, were turned back disappointed. The Senators' seats are arranged as before.

In the open space in front of the President's chair are two long tables, each furnished with seven chairs. One of the tables is intended for the Managers and the other for the counsel. Back of the Senators' seats, and filling the entire lobby, are about 200 chairs, intended for the accommodation of members of the House, Judiciary and others entitled to be present on the floor. Senators Howard and Anthony were in their seats early.

By 11:30 o'clock half the Senators had appeared and ranged themselves in little knots, discussing the momentous business of the day. It is noticeable that not a single negro is in the galleries. The section usually occupied by them is filled by ladies. There is no rush, and no crowding of doors and aisles; everything is conducted with perfect order and decorum.

A PRAYER FOR JUSTICE.

The chaplain invoked a blessing upon those now entering upon this high and important duty, and upon whom rest the eyes of the country and of the world; that they may be guided by Divine wisdom; that all their acts may be characterized by justice, and that this high Court may be led to such a verdict as God will approve in the high Court of Heaven, and to which all the people shall respond, heartily, Amen!

MAILS FOR LIBERIA.

Mr. Johnson presented a petition of the Colonization Society, praying that the Postmaster-General be authorized to enter into a contract to carry the mails to Liberia. Referred to the Committee on Post Offices and Post Roads.

PETITIONS.

Mr. Sumner presented the petition of drafted men of New-York, asking to be placed on an equal footing with volunteers with regard to pensions. Mr. Sumner also presented a number of petitions from shoe and leather manufacturers of various parts of Massachusetts, praying for a reduction of the tax. Referred to the Committee on Finance.

Mr. Cameron presented the remonstrance of the journeymen printers of Pennsylvania against the passage of a copyright law. Also, the petition of Lucretia Mott, President of the Anti-Slavery Society, praying for the establishment of a republican form of government in every State. Referred to the Judiciary Committee.

Mr. Frelinghuysen presented the petition of citizens of New-York and New-Jersey for a reduction of the army and navy, and of the general expenses of the Government. Referred to the Committee on Finance.

Mr. Morton presented the petition of the workingmen of Ohio for the passage of an eight-hour law. Referred to the Committee on Commerce.

THE JUDICIARY BILL.

The bill to amend the Judiciary act of Sept. 24, 1789, passed last evening, came over from the House signed, and received the signature of the President, *pro tem.*

PRIVATE BILLS.

Mr. Trumbull called up the bill for the relief of the heirs of Asbury Dickens, making an appropriation on account of his having acted as Secretary of State.

Mr. Trumbull offered an amendment, providing that none of the heirs who had taken part in the late rebellion, nor their assignees, shall participate in the benefit of this act, which was agreed to. The bill, after some discussion, was passed.

DIPLOMATIC APPROPRIATIONS.

On motion of Mr. Morrill, the Senate insisted on its amendment to the Consular and Diplomatic Appropriation bill, non-concurred in by the House, and Messrs. Morrill, of Maine, Howe and Buckalew, were appointed as a Committee of Conference on the part of the Senate.

Mr. Morgan introduced a joint resolution to carry into effect the resolution of March 2, 1867, providing for an exchange of documents. Referred to the Committee on the Library.

THE IMPEACHMENT TRIAL.

At the expiration of the morning hour, the President *pro tem.* announced that the chair was vacated for the Chief Justice of the United States. The Chief Justice entered by the side door after a short pause, and the Sergeant-at-Arms made a proclamation in the usual form. The Secretary of the Senate (Mr. J. W. Forney) read the journal of the last meeting of the Court. During the reading a long file of the members of the House could be seen through the half-open door.

On motion of Mr. Conkling the reading of the articles *in extenso* in the minutes was dispensed with.

At the conclusion of the reading, Mr. Howard, Chairman of the Committee of Seven, submitted the following order, which was adopted:

Ordered, That the Secretary inform the House of Representatives that the Senate is in its Chamber, and ready to proceed in the trial of ANDREW JOHNSON, President of the United States, and that seats are provided for the accommodation of its members.

The Chief Justice directed the Sergeant-at-Arms to attend to the execution of the order, and the Sergeant-at-Arms then opened the doors and announced: "The Managers of the Impeachment on the part of the House of Representatives!"

The Managers appeared, and by direction of the Chief Justice, took seats at the table on the left of the Chair.

Messrs. Stevens and Butler were absent.

Mr. Grimes suggested that the Senators who had not taken the oath be now sworn.

The Secretary called Messrs. Doolittle, Edmunds, Patterson, of New-Hampshire, and Vickers.

Mr. Doolittle was not present. Messrs. Edmunds, Patterson and Vickers came forward and the oath was administered to them by the Chief Justice.

The Sergeant-at-Arms then subscribed to the following affidavit, which was read by the Clerk:

The foregoing writ of summons addressed to ANDREW JOHNSON, President of the United States, and the foregoing precept addressed to me, were this day served upon ANDREW JOHNSON by delivering to and leaving with him copies of the same, at the Executive Mansion, the usual place of abode of the said ANDREW JOHNSON, on Saturday the 7th day of March instant, at 7 o'clock.

(Signed) GEO. G. BROWN,
Sergeant-at-Arms of the United States Senate.

The Chief Justice—The Sergeant-at-Arms will call the accused.

The Sergeant-at-Arms (in a loud voice) ANDREW JOHNSON, President of the United States—ANDREW JOHNSON, President of the United States, appear and answer to the article of impeachment exhibited against you by the House of Representatives of the United States.

The doors were thrown open at this point and every eye was turned that way for a moment. Mr. Butler entered and took his seat with the other Managers.

Senator Johnson rose and said something in a voice inaudible in the gallery; whereupon the Chief Justice said: The Sergeant-at-Arms will inform the Counsel of the President.

Messrs. Stanbery, Curtis and Nelson were ushered in at the side door and took seats at the table to the right of the Chair—Mr. Stanbery on the right, the others in the order named.

Mr. Conkling offered the following by direction of the Committee, in order, he said, to correct a clerical error.

Ordered, That the twenty-third rule of the Senate, for proceedings on the trial of impeachment, be amended by inserting after the word "debate," in the second line, the following words: Subject, however, to the operation of rule seven, so that, if amended, it will read as follows:

Twenty-third—All the orders and decisions shall be made and had by yeas and nays, which shall be entered on the record, and without debate, subject, however, to the rule seven, &c.

Rule seven provides that the presiding officer may in the first instance submit to the Senate, without a division, all questions of evidence and incidental questions.

Mr. Conkling explained that such was the original intention, but that the qualifying words were accidentally omitted. The order was adopted.

At 1:20 o'clock the Sergeant-at-Arms announced the members of the House of Representatives. The members entered and distributed themselves as far as possible among the chairs and sofas not already occupied by those having the *entree* to the Chamber under the rules. Many, however, did not find seats at once.

Mr. Stanbery then rose and said:

Mr. Chief Justice: My brothers Curtis, Nelson and myself are here this morning as counsel for the President. I have his authority to enter his plea. By your leave I will proceed to read.

Mr. Stanbery read as follows:

In the Matter of the Impeachment of ANDREW JOHNSON, President of the United States:

Mr. Chief Justice, I, ANDREW JOHNSON, President of the United States, having been served with a summons to appear before this honorable Court, sitting as a Court of Impeachment, to answer certain articles of impeachment, found and presented against me by the honorable the House of Representatives of the United States, do hereby enter my appearance by my counsel, Henry Stanbery, Benjamin R. Curtis, Jeremiah L. Black, William M. Evarts and Thomas A. R. Nelson, who have my warrant and authority therefor, and who are instructed by me to ask of this honorable Court for a reasonable time for the preparation of my answer to said articles. After a careful examination of the articles of impeachment and consultation with my counsel, I am satisfied that at least forty days will be necessary for the preparation of my answer, and I respectfully ask that it be allowed.

(Signed) ANDREW JOHNSON.

Mr. Stanbery—I have also a professional statement in support of the application; whether it is in order to offer it now the Chair will decide.

The Chief Justice—The appearance will be considered as entered. You can proceed.

Mr. Stanbery again read as follows:

In the matter of the impeachment of Andrew Johnson, President of the United States, Henry Stanberry, Benjamin R. Curtis, Jeremiah L. Black, William M. Evarts and Thomas A. R. Nelson, of counsel for the respondent, move the Court for the allowance of forty days for the preparation of the answer to the articles of impeachment, and in support of the motion make the following statement:

The articles are eleven in number, involving many questions of law and fact. We have, during the limited time and opportunity afforded us, considered as far as possible the field of investigation which must be explored in the preparation of the answer; and the conclusion at which we have arrived is, that with the utmost diligence the time we have asked is reasonable and necessary. The precedents as to time for answer upon impeachment before the Senate, to which we have had opportunity to refer, are those of Judge Chase and Judge Peck. In the case of Judge Chase time was allowed from the 3d of January until the 4th of February, next succeeding, to put in his answer, a period of thirty-two days, but in the case of Judge Peck there was but a single article. Judge Peck asked for time from the 10th to the 25th of May to put in his answer, and it was granted. It appears that Judge Peck had been long cognizant of the ground laid for his impeachment, and had been presented before the Committee of the House upon the examination of the witnesses, and has been permitted by the House of Representatives to present to that body an elaborate answer to the charges. It is apparent that the President is fairly entitled to more time than was allowed in either of the foregoing cases, and it is proper to add that the respondents in these cases were lawyers, fully capable of preparing their own answers, and that no pressing official duties interfered with their attention to that business; whereas, the President not being a lawyer, must rely on his counsel. The charges involve his acts, declarations and intentions; as to all of which his counsel must be fully advised, upon consultation with him, step by step, in the preparation of his defence. It is seldom that a case requires such constant communication between client and counsel as this; and yet such communication can only be had at such intervals as are allowed to the President from the usual hours that must be devoted to his high official duties. We further beg leave to suggest for the consideration of this honorable Court that, as counsel, careful as well of their own reputation as of the interests of their client, in a case of such magnitude as this, so out of the ordinary range of professional experience, where so much responsibility is felt, they submit to the candid consideration of the Court, that they have a right to ask for themselves such opportunity to discharge their duty as seems to them to be absolutely necessary.

(Signed) HENRY STANBERY,
BENJ. R. CURTIS,
J. L. BLACK,
WM. M. EVARTS,
THOS. A. R. NELSON,
Counsel for Respondent.

MARCH 13, 1868.

Mr. Bingham, Chairman of the Managers on the part of the House, said:

SPEECH OF MR. BINGHAM.

Mr. President: I am instructed by the Managers on the part of the House to suggest that under the 8th rule adopted by the Senate for the government of these proceedings, after the appearance of the accused, a motion for continuance is not allowed, the language of the rule being that if he appear and file an answer the case shall proceed as on the general issue. If he does not appear the case shall proceed as on the general issue. The Managers appeared at the bar of the Senate impressed with the belief that the rule meant precisely what it says, and that in default of an appearance the trial would proceed as on a plea of not guilty. If on appearance no answer be filed the trial shall still, according to the language of the rule, proceed as on a plea of not guilty.

Mr. Curtis, of counsel for the President, said:

Mr. Chief Justice: If the construction which the Managers have put upon the rule be correct, the counsel for the President have been entirely misled by the phraseology of the rule. They (meaning counsel for the President) have construed the rule in the light of similar rules existing in courts of justice; for instance, in a court of equity. The order in the subpœna is to appear on a certain day and answer the plea. But certainly it was never understood that they were to answer the plea on the day of their appearance. So it is in a variety of other legal proceedings; parties are summoned to appear on a certain day, but the day when they are to answer is either fixed by some general rule of the Tribunal, or there is to be a special order in this particular case. Now, here we find a rule by which the President is required to appear on this day to answer and abide; certainly that part of the rule which says, "to abide," has reference to future proceedings and the final result of the case, and so as we have construed the rule, or that part of it which relates to answering, it has reference to a future proceeding. We submit, therefore, as counsel for the President, that the interpretation which is put upon the rule by the Honorable Managers is not the correct one.

SPEECH OF MR. WILSON.

Mr. Wilson, one of the Managers, said: Mr. President, I desire to say, in behalf of the Managers, that we do not see how it would be possible for the eighth rule, adopted by the Senate to mislead the respondent or his counsel. That rule provides that upon the presentation of articles of impeachment and the organization of the Senate as hereinbefore provided, a writ of summons shall issue to the accused, reciting said articles and notifying him to appear before the Senate upon a day and at a place to be fixed by the Senate, and named in such writ, and file his answer to said articles of impeachment, and to stand to and abide such orders and judgments of the Senate thereon. The rule further provides that if the accused, after service, shall fail to appear either in person or by attorney on the day so fixed therefor as aforesaid, or appearing shall fail to file his answer to such articles of impeachment, the trial shall proceed, nevertheless, as upon a plea of not guilty.

Mr. Sherman moved that the day for answer be fixed as April 6.

SPEECH OF MR. BUTLER.

Mr. Butler asked to be heard on behalf of the managers, and asked why railroad speed should not be used on this trial. He said railroads and telegraphs could be used for bringing witnesses, &c., and affected all the business of life. He contended that the rules and precedents of ordinary courts were not applicable to this trial. In ordinary trials no dangers resulted from delay. In this case the necessity for prompt action was pressing. The respondent at the bar controlled the power of the nation, and might, in any moment of passion, prejudice or wrong, use it for the injury and ruin of the country. The business of the War Department would stop until the result of this trial was reached. The pulse of the nation beats in perturbation while the trial goes on. He claimed that an earlier day should be fixed for the defendant's appearance, and if then he can show that he has not had time to prepare, grant him the indulgence of further time. He said the defendant knew on the 22d of February what he would have to do, and he had fourteen days longer time for preparation than the Managers. He remarked that it could not be said hereafter that the charges brought were frivolous, because the accused says they are so grave that he will need forty days to prepare an answer to them. The learned counsel, in the professional statement submitted to the Senate, refer to the cases of Judge Chase and Judge Peck; and I presume that in the examination of the records of these cases, the attention of counsel was directed to the rules adopted by the Senate for the government of its action on the argument of these cases. By reference to the rules adopted by the Senate for the trial of Judge Peck, we find that a very material change has been made by the Senate in the adoption of the present rule—the rule in the case of Judge Peck being the third rule prescribing the summons, and required that, on a day to be fixed, the respondent should then and there appear and answer. The same rule was adopted in the Chase case; but the present rule in these cases, the words to which I have called the attention of the Senator, that he shall appear and file his answer to said articles of impeachment, and that appearing in person if he shall fail to file his answer to such articles the trial shall proceed nevertheless, as on a plea of not guilty. I submit, therefore, Mr. President, that the change which has been made in the rules for the government of this case must have been made for some good reason; what the reason may have been may be made a subject of discussion in this case hereafter. But the change meets us on the presentation of this motion, and we therefore on the part of the House of Representatives, which we are here representing, ask that the rule adopted by the Senate for the government of this case may be enforced. It is for the Senate to say whether the rule shall be sustained as a rule to govern the case or whether it shall be changed; but standing as a rule at this time, we ask for its enforcement.

SPEECH OF MR. STANBERY.

Mr. Stanbery said: The action taken by the Managers is so singular that in the whole course of my practice I have not met an example of it. The President of the United States, the Chief Justice, is arraigned on impeachment by the House of Representatives; a case of the greatest magnitude that we have ever had, and it is too grave to be treated as if it were a case before a Police Court to be put through with railroad speed on the first day of the trial. Where do my learned friends find a precedent for calling on the trial on this day? They say: "We have notified you to appear here to answer on a given day." We are here; we enter our appearance. As my learned brother, Mr. Curtis, has said, you have used precisely the same language that is used in a subpœna in chancery; but whoever heard that when a defendant in Chancery made his appearance he must appear with his answer, ready to go on with his case, and must enter on the trial. Of course we came here to enter our appearance; we state that we are ready to answer; we do not wish the case to go by default; we want time—reasonable time—nothing more. Consider that it is but a few days since the President was served with the summons; that, as yet, all his counsel are not present. Your Honor will observe that of five counsel who signed this professional statement two are not present, and could not be present, and one of them, I am sure, is not in the city. Not one of them, on looking at these articles, suspected that it was the intention to bring on the trial at this day. Yet, we understand the gentleman of the other side to say, "Read these rules according to their letter, and you must go on." If the gentlemen are right, if we are here to answer to-day, and to go on with the trial to-day, then this is the day for the trial. But article 9 says, "at 12:30 o'clock P. M. of the day appointed for the return of the summons against the person impeached," showing that this is the return day, and not the trial day. The managers say, that according to the letter of the eighth rule, this is the trial day, and that we must go on, and file our answer, or that without answer, the Court shall enter the plea of "not guilty" on the general issue, and proceed at once. But we say that this is the return day, and not the day of trial. The tenth rule says: "The person impeached shall be then called to appear and answer." The defendant appears to answer; states his willingness to answer, and only asks time. The eleventh rule says: "At 12:30 P. M. of the day appointed for the trial." That is not this day. This day, which the Managers would make the first day of the trial, is in the Senate's own rules put down for the return day, and there must be some day fixed for the trial to suit the convenience of the parties, so that the letter of one rule answers the letter of another rule. But pray, Mr. Chief Justice, is it possible that under the circumstances we are to be caught in this trap of the letter? As yet there has not been time to prepare an answer to a single one of these articles. As yet the President has been engaged in procuring his counsel and all the time occupied with so much consultation as was necessary to fix the shortest time, when, in our judgment, we will be ready to proceed with the trial. Look back through the whole line of impeachment cases, even in the worst times; go back to the Star Chamber, and every where you will find that even there English fair play prevailed. This is the first instance to be found on record anywhere, where, on appearance day, the defendant was required to answer immediately and proceed with the trial. We have not a witness summoned; we hardly know what witness to summon; we are entirely at sea. Mr. Chief Justice: I submit to this honorable body whether we are to be caught in this way? "Strike, but hear." Give us the opportunity that men have in common civil cases, where they are allowed hardly less than thirty days to answer, and most frequently sixty days. Give us time; give us reasonable time, and then we shall be prepared for the trial and for the sentence of the Court, whatever it may be.

SPEECH OF CHIEF JUSTICE CHASE.

The Chief Justice, rising, said: The Chief Justice would state, at the start, that he is embarrassed in the construction of the rules. The twenty-first rule provides that the case, on each side, may be opened by one person. He understands that as referring to the case when the evidence and the case are ready for argument. The twentieth rule provides that all preliminary or interlocutory questions and all motions shall be argued for not exceeding one hour on each side, unless the Senate shall, by order, extend the time. Whether that is intended to apply to the whole argument on each side, or to the arguments of each counsel who may address the Court, is a question which the Chief Justice is at a loss to solve. In the present case he has allowed the argument to proceed without attempting to restrict it, and, unless the Senate order otherwise, he will proceed in that course.

SECOND SPEECH OF MR. BINGHAM.

Mr. Bingham said—It was not my purpose, when I raised the question under the rule prescribed by the Senate, to touch in any way on the merits of any application which might be made for the extension of the time for the preparation of the trial. The only object I had in view, Mr. President, was to see whether the Senate were disposed to abide by its own rules, and by raising the question to remind the Senators of what they do know—that in this proceeding they are a rule and a law to themselves. Neither the common law nor the civil law furnishing any rule whatever for the conduct of this trial, save it may be the rule which governs in matters of evidence. There is nothing more clearly settled in this country and in that country whence we derive our laws generally, than the proposition which we have just stated; and hence it follows that the Senate shall prescribe rules for the conduct of the trial; and, having prescribed rules, my associate Managers and myself deem it important to inquire whether these rules, on the very threshold of these proceedings, were to be disregarded and set aside. I may be pardoned for saying that I am greatly surprised at the hasty words which dropped from the lips of my learned and accomplished friend, Mr. Stanbery, who has just taken his seat; that he failed to discriminate between the objection made here and the objection which might hereafter be made for the motion for the continuance of the trial. But, Mr. President, there is nothing clearer, nothing better known to my learned and accomplished friend than that the making of the issue before any tribunal of justice and the trial are very distinct transactions. That is perfectly well understood. A very remarkable case in the state trials lies before me, where Lord Holt presided at the trial of Sir Richard Brown Preston and others for high treason, and when counsel appeared, as the gentleman appears this morning, in the Court to ask for a continuance, the answer which fell from the lips of the Lord Chief Justice perpetually was, "We are not to consider the question of the trial, or the time of the trial, until a plea be pleaded, because," as His Lordship very well remarked, "it may happen that no trial will be required." Perchance you may plead guilty to the indictment, and so the rule lying before us contemplated. The last clause of it provides that if the defendant appear and shall plead guilty, there may be no further proceedings in the case, no trial about it. Nothing would remain to be done but to pronounce judgment under the Constitution. It is time for us to talk about the trial when we have an issue. The rule is a plain one, a simple one, and I may be pardoned for saying that I fail to perceive anything in rules ten and eleven to which the learned counsel have referred, which in any kind of construction can be applied to limit the effect of the words in rule eight, to wit: "That if the party fail to appear, either in person or by counsel, on the day named in the summons, the trial shall proceed as on the plea of 'not guilty;' and further, that, if failing on the day named in the summons, either in person or by attorney, to answer the articles, the trial shall nevertheless proceed as on a plea of 'not guilty.'" When words are plain in written law, there is an end of construction; they shall be followed. The Managers so thought when they appeared at this bar. All that they ask is that the rule be enforced, not postponed for forty days, to be met at the end of that time, perhaps, with a dilatory plea and a motion "If you please to quash the articles," or with a question raising the inquiry whether this is the Senate of the United States. It seems to me, if I may be pardoned in making one other remark, that in prescribing both these rules, that the summons shall issue to be returned on a day certain, given as in this case six days in advance. It was intended thereby to enable the party on the day fixed for his appearance to come to this bar and make his answer to these articles. I may be pardoned for saying further, what is doubtless known to every one within the hearing of my voice, that technical rules do, in no way control, or limit, or temper the action of this body; that under the plea of not guilty every conceivable defence which this party can make to these articles, if they be articles at all, if they be preferred by a competent tribunal at all, can be attempted. Why then this delay of forty days to draw up an answer? What we desire to know on behalf of the House of Representatives, by whose order we appear here, is, whether an answer is to be filed in accordance with the rule, and if it be not filed, whether the rule itself is to be enforced by the Senate and a plea of not guilty entered upon the accused—that is our inquiry. It is not my purpose to enter on the discussion at all as to the postponing of the day for the progress of the trial. My desire is for the present to see whether, under this rule and by force of this rule, we can obtain an issue.

DESULTORY DISCUSSION.

The Chief Justice—Senators, the counsel for the President submit that forty days be allowed for the preparation of his answer. The rule requires that, as every question shall be taken without debate, you who are in favor of agreeing to that motion say aye.

Senator Edmunds, rising, said: Mr. President, on this subject I submit the following order:

Ordered, That the respondent file his answer to the articles and impeachment on or before the 1st day of April next, and that the Managers of Impeachment file their replication thereto within three days thereafter; and that the matter stand for trial on Monday, April 6, 1868.

Senator Morton—I move that the Senate retire for the purpose of consultation.

Mr. Bingham—I am instructed by the Managers to request that the Senate shall pass on the motion under the eighth rule, and reject the application to defer the day of answer.

The Chief Justice—The Chief Justice will recognize the motion of the Senator from Vermont (Mr. Edmunds) as an amendment to the motion submitted by the counsel for the President.

Senator Conkling—What is to become of the motion of the Senator from Indiana, (Mr. Morton?)

Senator Sumner—What was the motion of the Senator from Indiana?

Senator Conkling—That the Senate retire for the purpose of consultation.

Senator Sumner—That is the true motion.

The Chief Justice put the question and declared it carried, and the Senate then retired from the Chamber at 2 o'clock P. M.

The galleries thinned considerably, while the Court held a long consultation, and the floor presented very much the appearance of a County Court-room when the jury had retired and the Court was in recess, not half the House and the other occupants of the floor remaining, and they scattered in knots among the Senators' seats and elsewhere; the Managers meanwhile, occasionally, consulted or pored over books bound in law calf. Mr. Stevens discussed with apparent relish some raw oysters brought him from the refectory. Mr. Wade was on the floor during most of the time occupied by the consultation. At 4:07 o'clock the Senators reëntered and took their seats.

When order was restored the Chief Justice said: The motion made by counsel is overruled, and the Senate adopts the order which will be read by the Secretary.

The Secretary read the order, as follows:

Ordered, That the respondent answer to the articles of impeachment on or before Monday, the 23d day of March, instant.

Mr. Bingham—Mr. President, I am instructed by the Managers to submit to the consideration of the Senate the following motion, and ask that it may be reported by the Secretary.

The Secretary read as follows:

Ordered, That before the filing of replication by the Managers on the part of the House of Representatives, the trial of ANDREW JOHNSON, President of the United States, upon the articles of impeachment exhibited by the House of Representatives, shall proceed forthwith.

The Chair put the question and said the yeas and nays appeared to have it, but the yeas and nays were demanded, and called with the following result:

YEAS—Messrs. Cameron, Cattell, Chandler, Cole, Conkling, Conness, Corbett, Drake, Ferry, Harlan, Howard, Morgan, Morton, Nye, Patterson of New-Hampshire, Pomeroy, Ramsey, Ross, Stewart, Sumner, Thayer, Tipton, Williams, Wilson, Yates—25.

NAYS—Messrs. Anthony, Bayard, Buckalew, Davis, Dixon, Edmunds, Fessendon, Fowler, Frelinghuysen, Grimes, Henderson, Hendricks, Howe, Johnson, McCreery, Morrill of Maine, Morrill of Vermont, Norton, Patterson of Tennessee, Saulsbury, Sherman, Sprague, Trumbull, Van Winkle, Vickers, Willey—26.

So the order was not agreed to. Mr. Wade did not vote.

Senator Sherman offered the following order, which was read:

Ordered, That the trial on the articles of impeachment shall proceed on the 6th day of April next.

Senator Howard—I hope not, Mr. President.

Senator Wilson moved to amend by making it the 1st, instead of the 6th of April next.

Mr. Butler—I would like to inquire of the President of the Senate if the Managers on the part of the House have a right to be heard upon this matter.

The Chief Justice—The Chair is of opinion that the Managers have a right to be heard.

SECOND SPEECH OF MR. BUTLER.

Mr. Butler—Mr. President and Gentlemen of the Senate: However ungracious it may seem on the part of the Managers representing the House of Representatives, and thereby representing the people of the United States, in pressing an early trial of the accused, yet our duty to those who send us here, representing their wishes, speaking in their behalf, and by their command, the peace of the country, the interests of the people—all seem to require that we should urge the speediest possible trial. Among the reasons why the trial is sought to be delayed, the learned counsel, who appear for the accused, have brought to the attention of the Senate precedents in early days. We are told that railroad speed was not to be used on this trial. Sir, why not? Railroads have effected everything else in this world; telegraphs have brought places together that were thousands of miles apart; it takes infinitely less time, if I may use so strong an expression, to bring a witness from California now than it took to send to Philadelphia for one in the case of the trial of Judge Chase; and therefore we must not shut our eyes to the fact that there are railroads, and there are telegraphs to give the accused the privilege of calling his counsel together, and of getting answers from any witnesses that he may have summoned and to bring them here. It should have an important bearing on the course we are to take that, I submit, is not to be overlooked. Railroads and telegraphs have changed the order of things. In every other business of life we recognize that fact. Why should we not in this? Passing from that which is but an incident—a detail, perhaps—will you allow me to suggest that the ordinary court of justice, the ordinary delays of courts, the ordinary time given in ordinary cases for men to answer when called before courts of justice, have no application to this case; not even, Sir, when cases are heard and determined before the Supreme Court of the United States, are the rules applicable to this particular case; for this reason, if no other,—that when ordinary trials are had, when ordinary questions are examined at the bar of any court of justice, there is no danger to the commonwealth in delay. The Republic may take no detriment if the trial is delayed. To give the accused time, interferes with nobody. To give him indulgence, hurts no one and may help him. But here the House of Representatives have presented at the bar of the Senate, in the most solemn form, the Chief Ruler of the nation, and they say, and they desire your judgment upon the accusation, that he has usurped power that does not belong to him. That he is at the same time breaking the laws solemnly enacted by you and those that have sent you here, by the Congress of the United States, and that he still proposes so to do. Sir, who is the criminal? I beg pardon of the counsel for the respondent. He is the Chief Executive of the nation. When I have said that I have taken out from all rule this trial. Because, I submit with deference, Sir, that for the first time in the history of the world has a nation brought its ruler to the bar of its highest court under the rules and forms provided by the Constitution, above all rule and all analogy, all likeness to an ordinary trial ceases there. I say that the Chief Executive, who is the commander of your armies, who claims that command, who controls, through his subordinates, your Treasury, who controls your navy, who controls all elements of power, who controls your foreign relations, may complicate, in any hour of passion, or of prejudice, the whole nation by whom he is the respondent at your bar. And, mark me, Sir, I respectfully submit that the very question here at issue this day, this hour, is whether he shall control beyond the reach of your laws, and outside of your laws, the army of the United States. That is the one great question here at issue: Whether he shall set aside your laws, set aside the decrees of the Senate and the laws enacted by Congress, setting aside every law, claiming the executive power only that he shall control the great military arm of this Government, and control it, if he please, to your ruin and the ruin of the country. Again, Sir, do we not know—may we not upon this motion assume the fact, that the whole business of the War Department of this country pauses until this trial goes on? He will not recognize, as we all know, the Secretary of War whom this body has declared the legal Secretary of War, and whom Congress, under a power legitimately exercised, have recognized as the legal Secretary of War. And do we not know, also, that while he has appointed a Secretary of War *ad interim*, he dare not recognize him, and this day and this hour the whole business of the War Department stops? Mr. Butler reminded the Senate that a gallant officer of the army, if confirmed by them to-day, who by right ought to have his commission and his pay commenced immediately when his appointment reached him, would have to wait, if this motion prevailed, for forty days—as long as it took God to destroy this world by a flood. [Laughter.] And for what I wonder?—that the intelligent and able counsel might delay the trial still longer, when one Department of the Government was already thrown into confusion, while they were blamed. But, he continued, that is not all. The great pulse of the nation beats in perturbation, while this strictly constitutional, but wholly anomalous proceeding goes on, and it pauses fitfully when we pause, and goes forward when we go forward. And the very question to-day in this country is arising out of the desire of men to have business interests settled, to have prosperity return, to have the Spring open as auspiciously under our laws as it will under the laws of nature. I say the very pulse of the nation beats here, and beating fitfully, requires us to still it by bringing this respondent to justice, from which God give him deliverance if he so deserve, at the earliest possible hour consistent with his right. Mr. Butler then urged that while all the time shown to be necessary when the case came to trial should be granted, no time should be fixed in advance. They should not presume in advance that the respondent could not get ready. Let him put in his answer, and then, if he showed the absence of necessary witnesses, the Managers would either acquiesce in a proper delay or admit all he sought to prove by the testimony. He would not deny the respondent a single indulgence consistent with public safety. They asked no more privileges than they were willing to grant to him. The great act for which he had been brought to the bar was committed on the 21st of February. He knew its consequences as well as they did. The House of Representatives had dealt with it on the 23d. On the 4th of March they had brought it before the Senate, with what they called its legal consequences, and now they were here ready for trial—instant trial. Some Judges had sat twenty-two hours in the day on the trial of great crimes, and they, God giving them strength, would sit here every day and every hour to bring this trial to a conclusion. He knew exactly what he had done. They had granted him more time, and now they asked that he should be prepared then to meet them. He hoped that hereafter no man, anywhere, would say that the charges upon which ANDREW JOHNSON was arraigned, were frivolous, unsubstantial, or of non-effect when counsel of the highest respectability, who would not for their lives say what they did not believe, told the Senate that, with all their legal ability, they could not put in an answer to the charges, so grave were they, in less than forty days—yea, fifty days. Mr. Butler concluded, after recapitulating the considerations which he thought ought to influence them in deciding this question, by reminding them that a speedy termination of the trial either way would bring quiet to the country, and praying them not to decide this question upon which the life of the nation depends, the greatest question that ever came before any body, on any of the ordinary analogies of law.

SPEECH OF JUDGE NELSON.

Judge Nelson, of counsel for the President, said—I have endeavored, in coming here, to divest my mind of the idea that we are engaged in a political discussion, and have tried to be impressed only with the thought that we appear before a tribunal sworn to try the great question which has been submitted for its consideration, and to dispense justice and equity between two of the greatest powers, if I may so express myself, of the land. I have come here under the impression that there is much force in the observation which the honorable Manager (Mr. Butler) made, "That this tribunal is not to be governed by the rigid rules of law, but is disposed to allow the largest liberty, both to the honorable Managers on the part of the House of Representatives, and the counsel on behalf of the President." I have supposed, therefore, that there was nothing improper in our making an appeal to this tribunal for time to answer the charges preferred, and that instead of that appeal being denied, much more liberality would be extended by the Senate of the nation, sitting as a Court of Impeachment, than we could even expect on a trial in a court of common law. It is not my purpose, Mr. Chief Justice, to enter at this stage into a discussion of the charges, although it would seem to be invited by one or two of the observations made by the honorable Manager, (Mr. Butler.) He has told you that it is right in a case of this kind to proceed with railroad speed, and in consequence of the great improvements of the age the investigation of this case can be proceeded with much more speedily than it could have been a few years ago. The charges made here are charges of the gravest importance. The questions which will have to be considered by this honorable body, are questions in which not only the representatives of the people are concerned, but in which the people themselves have the deepest and most lasting interest. Questions are raised here in reference to differences of opinion between the Executive of the nation and the honorable Congress, as to the constitutional powers and as to the rights which they respectively claim. These are questions of the utmost gravity, and are questions which, in the view that we entertain of them, should receive a most deliberate consideration on the part of the Senate. I trust that I may be pardoned by the Chief Justice and Senators for making an allusion to a statute which has long been in force in the State from which I come. I only do it for the purpose of making a brief argument by analogy. We have a statute in Tennessee which has long been in force, and which provides that when a bill of indictment is found against an individual, and he knows that, owing to excitement or other cause, he may not have a fair trial at the first term of the Court, his case shall be continued to the next term of the Court. The mode of proceeding, at law is not a mode of railroad speed. If there is anything under heaven, Mr. Chief Justice, which gives to judicial proceedings a claim to the consideration and approbation of mankind, it is the fact that justice and courts hasten slowly in the investigation of cases presented to them. Nothing is done or presumed to be done in a state of excitement; every moment is allowed for calm and mutual deliberation. Courts are in the habit of investigating causes slowly, carefully, cautiously; and when they form their judgment and pronounce their opinions, and when those opinions are published to the world, they meet the sanction of judicial and legal minds everywhere, and meet the approbation and confidence of the people before whom they are promulgated. If this is so—and this is one of the proudest characteristics in the form of judicial proceedings in courts—how much more ought it to apply in an exalted and honorable body like this, composed of the greatest of the United States, of Senators revered and honored by their countrymen, and who, from their position, are presumed to be free from reproach and to be calm in their deliberations. I need not tell you, Sir, nor need I tell many of these honorable Senators whom I address on this occasion, many of whom are lawyers, and many of whom have been clothed in times past with the judicial ermine, that in the courts of law the vilest criminal who ever was arraigned in the United States has been granted time to prepare for trial, and the right not only to be heard himself, but to be heard by counsel. No matter how great his crime; no matter how deep may be the malignity of the offence with which he has been charged, still he is tried according to the forms of law and is allowed to have counsel. Continuances are granted to him, and, if he is unable to obtain justice, time is given him and all manner of preparation is allowed him. If this is so in courts of common law, when they are fettered and bound by the iron rules to which I have adverted, how much more so ought it to be in a great tribunal like this, which does not follow the precedents of law, and which is seeking alone to obtain justice? Is it necessary for me to remind you and the honorable Senators that upon a page of foolscap there may be a bill of indictment prepared against an individual which might require weeks in the investigation? Is it necessary for me to remind this honorable body that it is an easy thing to make changes, but that it is often a laborious and difficult thing to make a defence against those accusations, reasoning from the analogy found by such proceedings at law. I earnestly maintain before this honorable body that suitable time should be given us to answer the charges preferred here. A large number of these charges involve an inquiry running back to the very foundation of the Government; they involve an examination of the precedents that have been sanctioned by different Administrations; they involve, in short, the most extensive range of inquiry, and the two last charges presented by the House of Representatives, if I may be pardoned for using an expression of the view I entertain of them, open up Pandora's Box, and will cause the investigation as to the great differences in opinion which have existed between the President and Congress, an inquiry which, so far as I can perceive, will be at most interminable in its character. Now, what do we ask here for the President of the United States, the highest officer in the land? We ask simply that he may be allowed time for his defence. On whose judgment is he to rely in relation to that? He must in a great part rely on the judgment of his counsel, to whom he has intrusted his defence. We, who are professionally responsible, have asserted in the presence of the Senate, in the face of the nation and of the whole world, that we believe it will require the number of days to prepare the President's answer which was stated in the proposition submitted to the Senate. Such is still our opinion. Are those grave charges to be rushed through the Senate, sitting as a judicial tribunal, in hot haste and with railroad speed, without giving the President an opportunity to answer them—that same opportunity which you would give to the meanest criminal? I do not believe, Mr. Chief Justice and honorable Senators, that you will hesitate one moment in giving us all the time that we deem necessary for preparing our defence, and that may be necessary to enable this body judiciously, carefully, deliberately and cautiously and with a view of its accountability, not only to its constituents but to posterity to decide this case. I have no doubt that the honorable Senators, in justice to themselves and in justice to the great land which they represent, will endeavor to conduct this investigation in a manner that will stamp the impress of honor and justice upon them and upon their proceeding, not only now but in all time to come after all of us shall have passed away from the stage of human action. Mr. Chief Justice, this is an exalted tribunal. I say it in no spirit of compliment, but because I feel it. I feel that there is no more exalted tribunal that could be convened under the sun, and I may say in answer to an observation of one of the honorable Managers, that I, for one, as an American citizen, feel proud that we have assembled here to-day, and assembled under the circumstances which have brought us together. It is one of the first instances in the history of the world in which the ruler of a people has been presented by a portion of the representatives of the people for trial before a Senate sitting as a judicial tribunal. While that is so, it is equally true on the other hand that the President, through his counsel, comes here and submits himself to the jurisdiction of this court, submits himself calmly, peaceably and with a confident reliance on the justice of the honorable Senate which is to hear his case. Mr. Chief Justice, I sincerely hope that the resolution offered by the Senator from Ohio will meet the approbation of this honorable body. I hope that time will be given, and that these proceedings, which in all time to come will be quoted as a precedent, will be conducted with that gravity, that dignity and that decorum which are fit and becoming in the representatives of a free and great people.

Senator Conkling submitted, as an amendment, the following:

"Ordered that unless otherwise ordered by the Senate for cause shown, the trial of the pending impeachment shall be proceeded with immediately after replication shall be filed."

The Chief Justice decided the amendment out of order as an amendment to the amendment offered by Senator Wilson.

Senator Wilson withdrew his amendment so that Senator Conkling's amendment to the motion of Senator Sherman might be in order.

REMARKS OF MR. BINGHAM.

Mr. Bingham said, I was instructed by the Managers to say that the proposition just suggested by the honorable Senator from New-York is entirely satisfactory to the Managers, on the part of the House; and to say further, that we believe it in perfect accord with the proceedings in this country. The Senate will doubtless remember that, in the trial of the Chase case, when a day was fixed for the trial, the Senate adopted an order which was substantially the same as the order suggested by the Senator from New-York.

It was as follows:

"*Ordered*, That the 4th day of February next shall be the day for receiving the answer and proceeding in the trial of impeachment against SAMUEL CHASE."

If nothing further had been said touching the original proposition, we would have been content and satisfied to leave the question, without further remark, to the decision of the Senate; but in view of what has been said, we beg leave to respond that we are chargable with no indecent haste when we ask that no unnecessary delay shall interpose in the trial between the people and a man who is charged with having violated the greatest trusts ever committed to a single person—trusts, which involve the highest interests of the whole people—trusts, which involve the peace of the whole country—trusts, which involve, in some sense, the success of this last great experiment of republican government on earth. We may be further pardoned for saying that it strikes us with somewhat of surprise, without intending the slightest possible disrespect to any member of the honorable body, that any proposition should be entertained for a continuance in a trial like this when no formal application has been made by the accused himself. To be sure a motion was interposed here to-day, in the face of the rules and of the laws of this body, for leave to file an answer at the end of forty days. The Senate has disposed of that motion, and in a manner, we venture to say, satisfactory to the whole country, as it is certainly satisfactory to the Representatives of the people at this bar; and, Sir, that being disposed of, and the Senate having determined the day on which answer shall be filed, we submit, with all due respect to the Senate, that it is but just to the people of the country that we shall await the incoming of that answer and the replication by the Representatatives of the people, and then see and know what colorable excuse will be offered, either by the President accused in his own person or by his representatives, why this trial should be delayed a single hour. If he be innocent of those grave accusations the truth will soon be ascertained by this enlightened body, and he has the right, in the event of the facts so appearing, to a speedy deliverance, while the country has a right to a speedy determination of this most important question. If, on the other hand, he be guilty of those grave and serious charges, what man is then within this body, or outside of it, ready to say that he should for a day or an hour longer disgrace the high position which has been held hitherto only by the noblest and most enlightened and most trustworthy of the land. We think that the Executive power of the nation should only be reposed in the hands of the men who are faithful to these great trusts of the people. This issue has been made with the President of the United States; and, while we admit that there should be no indecent haste, we do demand, in the name of the people, most respectfully, that there shall be no unnecessary delay, and no delay at all, unless good cause be shown for delay, in the mode and manner hitherto observed in proceedings of this kind.

Senator Johnson inquired whether there was any period fixed in which replication was to be filed.

Mr. Bingham replied that replication could only be filed with the consent and after consultation with the House; but he had no doubt it would be done within one or two days after answer was filed.

Senator Conkling called for the enforcement of

Continued on Eighth Page.

The New-York Times.

VOL. XVII......NO. 5250. NEW-YORK, WEDNESDAY, JULY 22, 1868. PRICE FOUR CENTS.

WASHINGTON.

Congress Declares the Fourteenth Amendment Adopted.

The Funding Bill Passed by the House.

Further Debate on the Bill to Reduce the Army.

Special Dispatches to the New-York Times.

WASHINGTON, Tuesday, July 21.

RATIFICATION OF THE FOURTEENTH AMENDMENT.

The concurrent resolution declaring the fourteenth article a part of the Constitution of the United States, passed both Houses to-day. In the House the Speaker presented a dispatch announcing the ratification of the amendment by the Georgia Legislature, thus making thirty States in all, or, twenty-eight exclusive of Ohio and New-Jersey, the requisite three-fourths, and placing the question beyond all doubt whatever. The President's approval of the resolution is not required.

PROSPECTS FOR AN ADJOURNMENT.

The question of adjournment was actively canvassed in both Houses to-day in private conversation by members, and in the Senate, Mr. SHERMAN, late in the afternoon, introduced a resolution providing for an adjournment on Thursday, stating that the state of business fully warranted the designation of that early day. After some talk, in which Friday, Saturday and Monday were all suggested, Mr. HENDRICKS stated that the President would, in case of such early adjournment, put sundry objectionable bills in his pocket, particularly that passed by the Senate last night, which reduces the army to 30,000 men, and distributes 1,000 muskets to the militia in each Congressional district. This brought Mr. SHERMAN to his feet in a very spirited speech, in which he said, in substance, that he offered the resolution because he believed the President would behave himself, and approve or disapprove the legislation of Congress in the ordinary manner, and not resort to the practice of pocketing important public measures. He still so believed; but if the threat of the Senator from Indiana was an indication of the President's action, then he was for staying here and compelling him to act on public measures as required by the law and the Constitution. He therefore asked that no action be had on his resolution for the present, and it went over. In the House a paper in favor of taking a recess until the middle of September was circulated and obtained eighty signatures, while a proposition for a positive adjournment received but forty. A resolution will be offered to-morrow to adjourn to meet at a certain day, when, if a quorum of the two Houses do not appear, their respective presiding officers shall adjourn them either *sine die* or until some day late in November, in terms and in fact coincident with the action last year. It is proper to state in this connection that the recent messages and proclamations of the President have done much to unsettle the faith that was beginning to develop in some minds, that he would at last yield his factious and useless opposition to the reconstruction work of Congress when those States were actually admitted to representation. But the belief of Republicans now is that he will scruple at no means in his power to overturn those Governments, or at least to promote dissension, strife and a feeling against the legality of the work of Congress. Hence, the possible necessity of such an adjournment as will leave it within the power of Congress to reassemble if the emergency requires. There was a more intense feeling against Mr. JOHNSON manifested in the private manner and conversation of members of both Houses to-day than has been apparent for several months, the result of the recent language used by the President in the performance of a duty imposed by law.

THE FUNDING BILL.

The Funding bill came up in the House to-day as the pending unfinished business, and argument was resumed on the substitute of Mr. BOUTWELL. The discussion developed the fact that the latter proposition was unexpectedly strong, and Mr. BOUTWELL pressed it with all his accustomed force and vigor. Privileged business intervening a vote was deferred until the evening session, when after further debate and various further amendments, Mr. BOUTWELL's substitute was rejected—yeas 67, nays 72. The bill, as matured in Committee of the Whole, was then passed—yeas 79, nays 68. It simply provides one class of bonds, running forty years, at 3 65 interest. It will probably go at once to a conference committee in the Senate. But Senator SHERMAN has not much hope that an agreement can be reached, the two propositions being so far apart in their most important details.

APPROPRIATION BILLS.

The Indian Appropriation and Deficiency Appropriation bills were agreed to to-day in both Houses, both having been reported from conference committees. The only other Appropriation bills not yet agreed upon are the District of Columbia, Charities and Alaska bills.

AD INTERIM APPOINTMENTS.

The bill regulating *ad interim* appointments is at length through both Houses. Mr. POMEROY to-day beat the Patent-Office ring in a handsome manner, and this point being carried, nothing else remained. The matter came up the first thing after the Alabama members, and the motion to lay the conference report on the table was lost by a large majority, as it would have killed the whole bill. The report was then agreed to, by yeas 80, nays 77, much to the surprise and chagrin of the defeated party, who supposed they had a large majority. This corrects a serious defect heretofore existing in the law. The Patent-office fund having been covered into the Treasury by an amendment to the Sundry Civil Appropriation bill, and Judge FOOTE having been favorably reported in the Senate for confirmation as Commissioner, the struggle over the office ends with this reorganization. The following is the bill in full:

An act to authorize the temporary supply of vacancies in the Executive Departments.

Be it enacted, &c., That, in case of the death, resignation, absence or sickness of the head of any Executive Department of the Government, the first or sole assistant thereof shall, unless otherwise directed, by the President of the United States, as is hereinafter provided, perform the duties of such head until a successor be appointed, or such absence or sickness shall cease.

SEC. 2. *And be it further enacted*, That, in case of the death, resignation, absence or sickness of the chief of any bureau, or of any officer thereof, except Commissioner of Patents, whose appointment is not in the head of an executive department, the deputy of such chief, or of such officer, or if there be no deputy, then the chief clerk of such bureau shall, unless otherwise directed by the President of the United States as hereinafter provided, perform the duties of such chief or of such officer until a successor be appointed or such absence or sickness shall cease, and no appointment, designation or assignment otherwise than as heretofore provided in the cases mentioned in the first, second and third sections of this act, shall be made except to fill a vacancy, happening during the recess of the Senate.

SEC. 3. *And be it further enacted*, That in any of the cases hereinbefore mentioned it shall be lawful for the President of the United States, in his discretion, to authorize and direct the head of any other Executive Department or other officer in either of those departments whose appointment is, by and with the advice and consent of the Senate, vested in the President, to perform the duties of the office vacant as aforesaid, until a successor be appointed, or the sickness or absence of the incumbent shall cease; provided that nothing in this act shall authorize the supplying, as aforesaid, a vacancy for a longer period than ten days when such vacancy shall be occasioned by death or resignation, and the officer so performing the duties of the office temporarily vacant shall not be entitled to extra compensation therefor; and provided, also, that in the case of the death, resignation, absence or sickness of the Commissioner of Patents, the duties of said Commissioner, until a successor shall be appointed, or such absence or sickness shall cease, shall devolve upon the Examiner-in-Chief, in said office, oldest in length of commission.

SEC. 4. *And be it further enacted*, That all acts heretofore passed on the subject of temporarily supplying vacancies in the executive departments, or which empower the President to authorize any person or persons to perform the duties of the head of any executive departments, or of any officer in either of the Departments, in case of a vacancy therein or inability of such head of a Department or officer to discharge the duties of his office, and all laws inconsistent with the provisions of this act be, and the same are hereby repealed.

MISSISSIPPI ELECTION RETURNS.

The following are the official returns of the recent election in Mississippi, as transmitted by Gen. GILLEM to Gen. GRANT, and sent to Congress to-day:

Counties.	No. of Registered Voters.	Constitution. For.	Against.
Adams	4,624	2,936	834
Amite	1,703	228	1,093
Attala	2,477	989	976
Bolivar	1,880	1,072	157
Calhoun	1,542	103	997
Carroll	4,037	276	2,727
Chickasaw	3,725	971	1,799
Coahoma	1,354	864	114
Choctaw	2,639	277	1,381
Claiborne	2,866	1,696	665
Clarke	2,188	998	835
Covington	688	93	440
Copiah	3,688	556	2,524
Davis	475	132	235
Desoto	4,706	413	2,107
Franklin	1,329	197	756
Greene	330	59	129
Hancock	857	143	404
Harrison	940	231	433
Hinds	5,974	2,869	2,044
Holmes	3,711	1,793	1,207
Issaquena	1,509	1,057	104
Itawamba	1,390	2?7	683
Jackson	828	123	383
Jasper	1,862	453	1,003
Jefferson	2,731	1,672	653
Kemper	2,313	1,021	953
Lafayette	2,839	298	1,895
Lauderdale	1,282	1,323	1,361
Lawrence	2,085	503	965
Leake	1,451	478	722
Lee	3,015	114	1,933
Lowndes	6,135	3,229	2,004
Madison	3,930	2,055	1,190
Marion	755	273	319
Marshall	4,707	1,587	2,279
Monroe	4,754	2,067	1,759
Neshoba	949	172	540
Newton	1,789	115	1,182
Noxubee	4,968	2,978	1,301
Oktibbeha	2,642	1,255	999
Panola	3,805	1,503	1,568
Perry	416	58	248
Pontotoc	2,043	698	929
Pike	2,191	511	1,196
Rankin	2,455	161	1,864
Scott	1,545	291	911
Simpson	972	49	682
Smith	1,078	8	827
Sunflower	1,064	374	301
Tallahatchie	1,675	196	1,031
Tippah	2,797	190	1,621
Tishemingo	3,504	479	1,860
Tunica	1,130	499	109
Wayne	941	391	219
Warren	7,630	4,851	1,316
Washington	3,885	2,733	251
Wilkinson	3,282	2,186	627
Winston	1,512	440	729
Yallobusha	3,640	932	1,963
Yazoo	4,219	1,816	1,490
Total	155,351	56,231	63,860
Majority against			7,629

VOTE FOR GOVERNOR.

Humphries, Dem. 63,321
Eggleston, Rep. 55,250
Majority for Humphries 8,071

On Members of Congress the vote was as follows:

First District.

C. H. Townsend, Democrat 11,029
Jefferson L. Wofford, Republican 5,823
Majority for Townsend 5,206

Second District.

T. N. Martin, Democrat 11,504
Jeuiel Railsback, Republican 6,068
Majority for Martin 5,436

Third District.

V. P. N. Turner, Democrat 11,681
C. A. Sullivan, Republican 10,181
Majority for Turner 1,500

Fourth District.

George C. McKee, Republican 20,444
George L. Potter, Democrat .... 15,?10
Majority for McKee 4,934

Fifth District.

W. T. Martin, Democrat 12 686
L. W. Pierce, Republican 11,886
Majority for Martin 800

With regard to the manner in which the election was conducted, Gen. GILLEM says:

"The troops in the State, amounting to 27 companies, were distributed at 63 posts and stations; and I may add that in every instance in which it was reported that fears of disturbance or interference with the elections was apprehended, regardless of the source from which the report emanated, troops were directed to be present and maintain order, and that no instance of intimidation or violence at the polls was reported by the commanders of posts or detachments; but on the contrary the elections are reported to have been conducted in an orderly manner. During the election commanding officers of the troops were directed to afford all necessary assistance to the civil authorities in the preservation of peace and good order. At the same time they were held responsible that force was only used when it was absolutely necessary."

In conclusion, Gen. GILLEM says:

"As is generally the case in elections, fraud is charged by both parties. All reports and complaints bearing on this subject are herewith transmitted for the consideration of the proper authority, merely remarking that I am satisfied that the election was as fair and 'free from intimidation or the influence of fraud' as it would be possible to secure under existing circumstances, and that no undue influence was exercised at the polls. If intimidation was used at all, it was beyond the power of the military to reach it. As the defeat of the Constitution renders it possible that the State may for a time remain under military control, I consider it my duty to call attention to the almost impossibility of finding persons to fill vacancies in civil offices who possess the necessary attainments, and who can qualify under existing laws. I would, therefore, recommend that section 9 of the act passed July 19, 1867, be so modified as to render eligible to office persons on the list of registered voters, to fill vacancies which exist or may occur in civil offices, State or municipal."

MEMBERS FROM ALABAMA.

Five of the six members from Alabama were sworn in to-day, viz.: Messrs. BUCKLEY, PIERCE, HAUGHEY, NORRIS and CALLIS. The remaining member is F. W. KELLOGG, of Mobile, who formerly represented the Grand Haven District, of Michigan. COLLIS' seat is contested by BURKE, also a Radical, on the ground of non-residence. COLLIS was an officer of the Veteran Reserve Corps, detailed for duty in the Freedmen's Bureau at Huntsville, where his regiment was subsequently. He was ordered to Nashville, and has never resided in the State. His family reside where they have for many years, in Grant County, Wisconsin.

PAY OF MEMBERS FROM THE SOUTH.

The House to-day agreed to pay the new members from the South from the date of their election. In the Senate, Mr. TRUMBULL, from the Judiciary Committee, reported in favor of paying the new Senators from the commencement of the Fortieth Congress, but the consideration of the report was postponed.

NOMINATIONS CONFIRMED.

The batch of nominations sent to the Senate yesterday were all reported on to-day, except Gov. COX, to be Commissioner of Pensions. The Foreign Relations Committee reported against ROSECRANS for Spain and MCCLERNAND for Mexico, but in favor of WATTS for Austria. No objection was urged against ROSECRANS, except the desire to retain the Hon. JOHN P. HALE, the present incumbent, in that position. The Finance Committee also reported against WELLS for Assistant Secretary of the Treasury, and COOPER for Commissioner of Internal Revenue. After the report in the latter case had been made, a message was received from the President withdrawing COOPER's name, and it is now understood that Mr. JOHNSON will appoint him Commissioner *ad interim* as soon as Congress adjourns. It is probable that these nominations will be acted on to-morrow.

OHIO RIVER BRIDGES.

The Senate to-night passed the General Railroad Bridge bill, which has been under discussion several days. They did not adopt the proposition to require the spans over the Ohio and Mississippi to be 500 feet, but accepted Mr. DOOLITTLE's substitute, authorizing a board of Government engineers to investigate the subject, and report whether the interests and safety of navigation require the spans to be of such length.

ARMY INTELLIGENCE.

Brevet Major-Gen. D. H. Rucker, Assistant Quartermaster-General, is relieved from duty as Chief Quartermaster of the Department of the East, and assigned to duty as Chief Quartermaster of the Department of Philadelphia. Brevet Major-Gen. Rufus Ingalls has been ordered to report to Brevet Major-Gen. McDowell, commanding the Department of the East, as Chief Quartermaster of that Department, in addition to his present duties in charge of the Department of New-York City. Brevet Col. F. J. Crilly, Captain and Assistant Quartermaster, is assigned to duty as Quartermaster of the District of and Post of Philadelphia. Brevet Major Joseph L. Crane, Chief Commissary of the Fourth Military District, has been ordered to take station at Cincinnati from Aug. 1 to Oct. 31, for the purchase and distribution of subsistence stores for the Fourth District.

By direction of the President, Brevet Brig.-Gen. CHARLES F. RUFF has been relieved and detailed as Professor of Military Science and Tactics at the University of Pennsylvania at Philadelphia.

FORTIETH CONGRESS.

SECOND SESSION.

SENATE....WASHINGTON, Tuesday, July 21.

On motion of Mr. MORGAN, the Joint Committee on the Library was discharged from the further consideration of the numerous petitions on the subject of an International Copyright Law.

POST ROADS.

Mr. RAMSEY called up the bill to establish certain post roads, which was passed.

THE FOURTEENTH AMENDMENT.

Mr. SHERMAN called up his concurrent resolution declaring the ratification of the fourteenth amendment, which was adopted.

It declares that three-fourths of the States—enumerating them—including Ohio and New-Jersey, having adopted the amendment, it has become a part of the Constitution of the United States.

PAY OF NEW SENATORS.

Mr. TRUMBULL offered the following:

Resolved, That the Secretary of the Senate be directed to pay to the Senators from Arkansas, Florida, North Carolina and Louisiana the compensation allowed by law, to be computed from the commencement of the Fortieth Congress.

Mr. SHERMAN suggested that the resolution ought to go to a Committee.

Mr. TRUMBULL quoted the precedents established on the case of the Senators from Tennessee. At the beginning of the Thirty-ninth Congress, Mr. DAVIES offered the resolution as dating back to a time—4th of March, 1867—when there were no Senators from those States. He denied that the Senators in question are constitutionally elected, in his opinion, and the Senators that came here a year ago are still the constitutional Senators from these States.

Mr. MORTON, at this point, objected to the further consideration of the resolution, and it was laid over.

STEAM PLOWS.

Mr. SHERMAN called up the joint resolution admitting steam plows free of duty for one year from June 30, 1868, which was passed.

BRIDGES OVER THE OHIO RIVER.

Mr. MORTON again called up the bill to authorize the construction of bridges across the Ohio River.

Mr. POMEROY repeated his objections to the requirement of 500 feet spans as impracticable with any but a suspension bridge.

Mr. CAMERON told a story of one ADAM HARNLEY, of Pennsylvania, with whom he had been present many years ago at a public meeting in Harrisburg, Penn., to discuss the feasibility of building a railroad thence to Lancaster, he (CAMERON) having expressed a favorable opinion. HARNLEY after the meeting was over said to him, placing his finger to his nose, that "It was all very well to talk about going from Hirrisburg to Lancaster in a day, but you and I knows better as dat." [Laughter.]

Mr. CAMERON expressed the opinion that bridge building is yet in its infancy, and generally favored the bill.

At 1 o'clock the Chairman announced the special order, the bill for the protection of American citizens in foreign countries.

Mr. NEWTON appealed to the Senator from California (Mr. CONNESS) to allow a vote to be taken on the pending bill.

Mr. CONNESS suggested an evening session for that purpose, and made a motion to that end.

Messrs. FESSENDEN and SUMNER urged the importance of holding an Executive session, there being much business on hand, in order to avoid being called together again for that purpose after the adjournment.

The motion for an evening session prevailed.

A PENSION BILL.

By consent of Mr. CONNESS, Mr. THAYER called up the bill granting a pension to the widow of Gen. FRANCIS T. RICHARDSON, killed at the battle of Antietam.

Mr. HARLAN moved to amend, that the pension be paid from the date of the passage of the bill instead of from the time of Gen. RICHARDSON's death in 1862. Rejected by 8 to 34.

Mr. YATES called up the bill granting a pension to the widow of the late Brig.-Gen. WALLACE.

After some opposition from Mr. CAMERON the bill was passed.

THE DEAF AND DUMB INSTITUTE.

Mr. CONNESS then consented, by request of Mr. MORRILL, of Maine, to allow the special order to go over, and Mr. MORRILL called up the bill making appropriations for the support of the Columbia Institution for the Deaf and Dumb and for other purposes, which was amended and passed.

THE INDIAN APPROPRIATION BILL.

Mr. HOWE, presented a report from the Committee of Conference on the Indian Appropriation bill.

Mr. COLE suggested that the bill as amended, with the report be printed, so that the Senators could examine the effect of the amendments. He said the bill does injustice to his section. Some discussion on the report ensued between Messrs. HENDERSON, CORBETT and HOWE. It was then adopted.

Mr. FESSENDEN moved to go into Executive Session.

Mr. CONNESS called for the yeas and nays, saying that the bill relative to the rights of citizens abroad could be passed in a few minutes.

The motion was agreed to by a vote of 25 to 24, and shortly after 3 o'clock the Senate went into Executive Session.

PROPOSED ADJOURNMENT.

When the doors were reopened, Mr. SHERMAN offered a concurrent resolution providing for an adjournment of the two Houses of Congress' *sine die*, on Friday next.

THE MILITARY BILL.

Mr. HOWARD and several other Senators expressed the hope that no day would be designated until after the bill for the reduction of the military peace establishment shall have become a law. They would not consent to place it in the power of the President to retain it in his possession and not return it to Congress. The constitutional limit of ten days could not apply in case there should be so early an adjournment.

Mr. HENDRICKS, in reply to the remarks which had been made, said he considered this a most dangerous bill, because it proposed to arm one political party against the other. It placed the control of the arms to be distributed with the Governors of the States designated, and this, too, immediately before the Presidential election. In regard to the ratio of distribution he asked what Maine wanted with seven thousand muskets, Massachusetts with twelve thousand and Indiana with thirteen thousand; and, in order to illustrate his argument, he referred to the fact that the Governor of Indiana being a candidate for reëlection, these arms placed at his disposal could be used according to his design and pleasure. And so with the other States. He commented upon the action of the Senate last night in rejecting Mr. VICKER's amendment providing that the distribution of arms, &c., shall not take place prior to the 1st of January, unless the President shall deem it necessary for the prevention of disturbance in the Southern States. This fact, he remarked, was significant of the design of the bill. Arms were to be distributed to all the States with the exception of Virginia, Mississippi and Texas, and these States were omitted because there was to be no election there. Therefore he argued that the only purpose of this distribution of arms before the election was to make a military force out of one party to overawe the other, and thus control the election. All he asked was a fair election, and that the people may vote without hindrance governed by their own judgment. Gen. GRANT had said in the last sentence of his letter accepting the nomination for the Presidency: "We want peace. Let us have peace." All parties should desire this, and quiet in the country. After this expression of the desire for peace on the part of the candidate of the Republican Party, we find here a firebrand—a measure calculated to excite passion and produce strife, and perhaps bloodshed. With a measure so threatening and dangerous in its character, the people would be slow to believe that that party desired peace. He hoped the President would exercise the power he possessed to prevent the bill from becoming a law. The President owed this not only to his constitutional duty, but to the peace and quiet of the country. He should defeat a measure so full of peril to the country, and which invited a conflict between the whites and blacks.

Mr. WILSON, in reply, said that not a single gun would be used unless there should be such a powerful combination to violate the law that it would be beyond the power of the civil authorities to disperse it, and then only in the hands of the militia as a *posse comitatus*. But of this the Senate had had to-day a passionate appeal from the Senator from Indiana, who talked about what the people would or would not do.

Mr. WILSON had no doubt that at the next election there would be a majority of a hundred Radicals in the House; not more than four States of the Union would be carried for SEYMOUR and BLAIR, and yet the Senator talked about overawing. Those who recently met in Convention in the City of New-York, assured their friends what they would do in the event of their success. WADE HAMPTON remarked in a speech that they would swear men to override the Constitution and laws. If we, said Mr. WILSON, have in the seven reconstructed States an honest election, I expect every one of them to vote the Republican ticket; and Gov. WISE had said he would vote for the Democratic candidate, not because he liked the platform, but because BLAIR promised, if placed in power, to overthrow the reconstructed States. Now, the way to preserve the public peace is to uphold law and order, and this is all that is itended by the bill. He was amazed that any man should rise up in opposition to it.

Mr. WILSON then referred to the New-Orleans and other riots, and asked who it was that had striven to provoke collision between the white and black races. There was not a repentant traitor in that Convention, not a man who was not as much a traitor as when he was warring in behalf of the rebellion in the Southern States. The Senator from Indiana had said Republicans had pardoned traitors. This was true; but those whom they had pardoned showed their repentance by their daily lives and conversation. The Democratic Party was the author of the rebellion. Every drop of blood shed in the war was owing to that organization. Every soldier who was wounded owes misfortune to the opposition of the Democratic Party to liberty. The members of that party fought against every law that tended to strike the fetters from the black man's limbs, and to defend and guard human rights. But, he said, we are stronger than muskets. God Almighty and Truth are on our side. We have justice and humanity, and a record brighter and purer and holier than any party in God's universe. History and the world attest it. We never fired on the flag of our country or raised the banner of revolt.

Mr. SHERMAN said he submitted the resolution providing for an adjournment in good faith, believing the Senators on both sides of the Chamber, the House and the President would enable them to close the business of the session. He had thought that the President would accord to the established custom, and sign, or without unnecessary delay disapprove of bills which might be submitted to him, in order that Congress might afterward act upon them. There was nothing in the condition of the public business which prevented an adjournment next Friday. All the ordinary bills are out of the way, and only a few remain to have the approval or dissent of the President. He, however, would never press a resolution of this kind in the face of what the Senator from Indiana says, viz: That the President intended to avail himself of his constitutional prerogative to defeat the will of Congress by withholding the bill which has been alluded to for ten days. He was willing to sit here through Summer's heat or Winter's cold, until the President either approved or disapproved of every act. The words of the Senator were not the kind of language to be used in this House. If the President would resort to the extraordinary expedient of withholding his signature to a bill which Congress deem proper for the public safety, he would not consent to adjourn until it was passed over his objections. He thought the Senator went out of his way when he stated what the President would or would not do. He repeated that in the face of what the Senator uttered, he was not willing to press the resolution until he knew what the President would do. This bill was debated last night at length. It enacted nothing but what was now the law of the land as to the distribution of arms. It was the duty of Congress to arm the loyal people in order that they might protect themselves. There was no danger of any of these reconstructed Governments violating the law and disturbing the public peace. The arms distributed to them would not be equal in number to the half million of arms now scattered among the rebels in the Southern States. He did not think, when he offered the resolution, that the Senator would make a partisan speech to excite the contempt and hatred of the country against Congress. In conclusion, he moved that the Senate now proceed to the consideration of the Executive business.

This motion was not acted on.

The Senate then agreed to the report of the Committee of Conference on the Deficiency Bill.

Mr. CONNESS took it for granted that the speech of the Senator from Indiana was deliberately made for political reasons. He expressed his thanks to the Senator from Ohio (Mr. SHERMAN) for the remarks made on the question of adjournment. It was plain to him that the message which had been received from the President during the last two weeks, and the proclamations he had issued, were of such a character as to justify the conclusion that they are incendiary and violative of his public duties, and, in his judgment, a scandal before the civilized world, and, in place of discussing the question of adjournment at this time, they would justify another impeachment by the House, trial by the Senate and expulsion from the place the President fills. It was not long since he escaped conviction by the merest chance in the world. The conduct of the first Minister of his Cabinet, the character of the political Convention to which he has joined his interest, the utterances of the men which composed it, and the letter of their candidate for the Vice-Presidency threatening rebellion—all justified what he (Mr. CONNESS) said; and in all probability we never shall be able until we take such action to guarantee peace to the nation. Let them renew the rebellion, and it will be fought out in a different way from the last. The Senator from Indiana quoted Gen. GRANT as saying: "Let us have peace." We ask and plead for peace; but we can have peace only on condition of obedience to law. The President by his communications and utterances, sets the example of disorder in the country. If we adjourn now, it will not be long before disorder is reëstablished.

Mr. HENDRICKS said it wanted but a few minutes to 5 o'clock, the time for taking the recess. He should like to have the time extended, in order that he might reply to the Senators who had assailed his position.

Mr. CONKLING objected.

The question of extending the time ten minutes was put to a vote. A majority, but not a quorum, voted in the affirmative. It was now 5 o'clock, and the Senate took a recess until 7:30 o'clock.

EVENING SESSION.

The Senate reassembled at 7:30 o'clock.

PACIFIC MAIL SERVICE.

Mr. RAMSEY called up the joint resolution authorizing the full amount of the subsidy of $500,000 to be paid to the Pacific Mail Steamship Company, for services between San Francisco, California, and China and Japan, which was passed.

SYMPATHY WITH THE CRETANS.

Mr. SUMNER reported from the Committee on Foreign Relations the following joint resolution, appealing to the Turkish Government in behalf of the people of Crete. He said it had been unanimously recommended by the Committee.

The following is the resolution:

Be it resolved by the Senate and House of Representatives in Congress assembled, That the people of the United States renew the expression of their sympathy with the suffering people of Crete, to whom they are bound by ties of a common religion and by gratitude due the Greek race of which the Cretans are a part: that they rejoice to believe that the suffering of this interesting people may be happily terminated by a policy of forbearance on the part of the Turkish Government, and they hereby declare their hope that the Turkish Government will listen kindly to this representation, and will speedily adopt such generous steps as will secure to Crete the much desired blessings of peace and the advantages of autonomic Government.

Resolved, That religion, civilization and humanity require that the existing contest in Crete should be brought to a close, and to accomplish this result the civilized Powers of the world should unite in friendly influence with the Government of Turkey.

Resolved, That it shall be the duty of the President to instruct the Minister of the United States at Constantinople to coöperate with Ministers of other Powers in all good offices to terminate the sufferings of the people of Crete, and that it shall be the further duty of the President to communicate a copy of this resolution to the Government of Turkey. The resolution was adopted.

GEORGIA AND THE FOURTEENTH AMENDMENT.

The Chair laid before the Senate a telegram from Gov. BULLOCK, of Georgia, announcing the ratification by the Legislature of that State of the fourteenth amendment.

BRIDGES OVER THE OHIO RIVER.

The special order, the bill to authorize the erection of bridges across the Ohio River, was taken up and Mr. VAN WINKLE addressed the Senate in opposition to the provision requiring 500 feet span over the channels, denying that Gen. WARREN had pronounced it necessary in the interest of navigation, as asserted by Mr. NEWTON on a former occasion. Truss bridges of such a span were impossible, in his opinion, and suspension bridges unsafe for railroad bridges.

Mr. MORTON replied at some length. He taxed Messrs. VAN WINKLE and RAMSEY with having used every endeavor to have the bill delayed, and intimated that the opposition of the former arose from his being a President of a railroad company that desires to build a bridge with short spans. He read a letter from the architect of the suspension bridge at Niagara, (Mr. LOGAN,) showing that that bridge, at 856 feet span, is crossed daily by trains, asserting that it would allow of their crossing at a speed of 30 miles an hour; that that gentleman is now building a new bridge over the Hudson of 1,600 feet span, capable of sustaining 35,000 tons. The latter gave a list of bridges of over 300 feet span here and in Europe. He contended that newspapers and business men everywhere favor requiring 50 feet span.

Mr. POMEROY made some further remarks, holding that the requirement of the 500 feet span amounts to a virtual prohibition of bridges, and that there should be a compromise between the railroad and river interests.

Mr. TIPTON spoke also in opposition to the bill.

Mr. DAVIS advocated it at length.

Mr. DOOLITTLE gave notice that at the proper time he would offer a substitute, authorizing the Secretary of War to appoint a board of no less than seven engineers to investigate in regard to the proper width and report at the next session, suspending in the meantime all building of bridges.

Mr. YATES pronounced in favor of the establishment of some minimum width of span.

After further discussion by Messrs. NYE and FRELINGHUYSEN,

Mr. NORTON professed his willingness to accept the amendment suggested by Mr. DOOLITTLE, to which Mr. POMEROY acceded.

Mr. VAN WINKLE said it would be acceptable with the following proviso, which he moved to read:

Provided, That this shall not apply to bridges already in process of construction.

Mr. SHERMAN opposed the proviso. He thought whatever rule is adopted should be applied to all bridges.

Mr. HENDERSON spoke briefly in favor of the amendment.

Mr. VICKERS produced a letter from Mr. GARRETT, President of the Baltimore and Ohio Railroad Company, stating that that Company has already expended $400,000 in building bridges across the Ohio River, under the present laws; that many prominent engineers concur in the opinion that a three hundred feet span is the limit that can safely be built, and that if this bill should be passed, the construction of the two bridges across the Ohio will be suspended, and it may be years before they can be recommenced.

Mr. VICKERS spoke in opposition to the bill.

Mr. VAN WINKLE's amendment was rejected.

Mr. WILLEY offered an amendment requiring the proposed Board of Engineers to examine the Steubenville bridge, and report whether it is an obstruction, and, if so, what should be done to remedy it.

The amendment was agreed to.

Mr. HENDRICKS offered another amendment providing that the bill shall not apply to the bridge in process of construction at Louisville, the same to be not less than four hundred feet span.

The bill then passed, and at 10:20 o'clock the Senate adjourned.

HOUSE OF REPRESENTATIVES.

Mr. WILSON, of Iowa, Chairman of the Judiciary Committee to which was referred the claims of the Representatives from the late rebel States to be allowed full pay from the commencement of Congress, reported a resolution that their pay shall commence from the date of their respective elections. Adopted.

COMMANDER HUGHES.

On motion of Mr. PIKE, the Senate amendment to the House bill, for the restoration of Commander A. K. HUGHES from the retired list to the active list of the navy, was concurred in, after striking out the name of Commander CELLEY for restoration.

PORTS OF ENTRY.

Mr. O'NEIL, from the Committee on Commerce, reported a bill changing the ports of entry from Plymouth to Edenton, N. C., and from Beaufort to Port Royal, S. C. Passed.

INTERNATIONAL METRICAL SYSTEM.

Mr. KELLEY introduced a bill to promote the establishment of an international metrical system of coinage. Referred to the Committee on Coinage.

REPRESENTATIVES FROM ALABAMA.

Mr. DAWES, from the Committee on Elections, reported that the credentials of the various Representatives elect from the State of Alabama had been examined and found in due form, and he moved that the test oath be administered to them.

Mr. BROOKS appealed to the House to say whether it was fair or just, when the people of Alabama were informed, under the act of March 23, 1867, that by abstaining from voting they could defeat the State Constitution and the election of members under it, to admit a set of representatives chosen by negroes, and by negroes alone. It was an outrage on the white people of Alabama, and on the whole white race of the country. The members were elected only by the negroes of Alabama, while the white people of Alabama by fraud, and by fraud alone, were kept from voting at that election.

Mr. DAWES replied to the remarks of Mr. BROOKS, which he spoke of as his accustomed speech. He would leave it to the gentleman from New-York to reconcile the inconsistency of his always preaching in favor of the representation of the late rebel States and his practical denial of it. He spoke of Mr. BROOKS' constant anxiety about the negro; an anxiety which troubled him by day and disturbed his sleep by night, lest by some chance the poor negro should get some advantage of him in the race of life. After further remarks in that satirical vein Mr. DAWES moved the previous question.

Mr. ELDRIDGE desired an opportunity to make some remarks.

Mr. DAWES declined to withdraw the call for the previous question.

The previous question was ordered and the report was adopted by a vote of 126 to 34.

The members elect from the State of Alabama were invited by the Speaker to approach and take the oath. Five gentlemen responded to the invitation and were about to be sworn, when Mr. BROOKS notified the Speaker that he desired the oath to be administered separately.

The Speaker said that was a subject for the decision of the House.

Mr. DAWES moved they be sworn in at once.

Mr. BROOKS said there were three cases to which he wished to call attention. He objected to the oath being administered to the person claiming to represent the Mobile District.

Mr. DAWES remarked that that gentleman was not present.

Mr. BROOKS—Who is the Representative from Mobile?

Mr. DAWES—F. W. KELLOGG.

Mr. BROOKS—KELLOGG, of Michigan. [Laughter.]

Mr. DAWES—No, Sir; KELLOGG, of Alabama.

Mr. ELDRIDGE said he hoped the gentleman from Massachusetts would not retire under the demagogical speech just made by him.

The Speaker stated that remark was not in order.

Mr. ELDRIDGE—Why not? It was certainly not meant for an insult to him. It was a compliment to his speech.

Mr. BROOKS demanded the yeas and nays on agreeing to the report. [Laughter.]

Mr. DAWES—The gentleman from New-York is laboring under a mistake, as usual.

Mr. BROOKS—There is also a person from the State of Maine to whom I object as being a resident of the State of Alabama.

The SPEAKER—The order of the House is that the gentleman shall be sworn in.

Mr. BROOKS—I do not suppose that the Speaker wants to violate the Constitution of the United States, and I ask him to read article one, section two of that instrument.

Mr. DAWES—The gentleman complains of one of those members because he was born in Maine. I should like to know where the gentleman himself was born.

Mr. BROOKS—I was born in Maine and went to New-York—not with a carpet-bag, but with a trunk—thirty years ago, and have resided there since.

The Speaker said he was required, by order of the House, to administer the oath of office. If the House directed the oath to be administered separately, he would of course obey that order; otherwise, he would swear these members collectively.

Mr. ROSS—One of those gentlemen is a friend of mine. He is a very good man, and I don't know that I will raise any objection to him.

Mr. ———Is he a neighbor of yours?

Mr. ROSS—He is. [Laughter.]

The oath was then administered to CHARLES W. BECKLEY, BENJAMIN W. NORRIS, CHARLES W. PIERCE, J. B. CALLIS and THOMAS HAUGHEY, and they took their seats as members from the State of Alabama.

VACANCIES IN EXECUTIVE DEPARTMENTS.

The Conference report on the bill to supply vacancies in the Executive Departments came up, when Mr. SPALDING withdrew the motion made by him yesterday to lay the report on the table.

Mr. HOLMAN renewed the motion. It was negatived.

The Conference report was then agreed to.

THE FOURTEENTH AMENDMENT.

A concurrent resolution was received from the Senate declaring the ratification by three-fourths of the States of the Union of the fourteenth article of amendment to the Constitution, and declaring that article a part of the Constitution.

Mr. BOUTWELL moved to refer it to the Committee on Reconstruction.

Mr. ELDRIDGE suggested that it be referred to the Judiciary Committee, as it involved some very important questions of constitutional law.

Mr. WASHBURNE, of Illinois, expressed the desire to have it passed at once by the House.

Mr. BOUTWELL thereupon withdrew his motion to refer, and moved the previous question.

Mr. WASHBURNE suggested that a dispatch had been received announcing that Georgia had ratified the amendment.

Mr. BOUTWELL sent to the Clerk's desk, and had read, the following dispatch:

ATLANTA, Ga., July 21, 1868.

To Schuyler Colfax, Speaker of the House of Representatives:

The fourteenth article and fundamental conditions adopted by a majority of thirty-four on joint ballot.

(Signed,) RUFUS D. BULLOCK, Governor elect.

Mr. BOUTWELL moved to amend the concurrent resolution by inserting Georgia.

Mr. BROOKS—On the proof of a telegram, how do you know that that came over the wires at all?

A Republican MEMBER—We will take it on faith.

The Speaker suggested a doubt whether that was the official notice required.

Mr. BOUTWELL withdrew the amendment.

The resolution was then agreed to, yeas 126, nays 32.

The States of New-Jersey and Ohio are included among those. Both have ratified the amendment.

THE FUNDING BILL.

The House then, at 2:15, resumed the consideration of the Funding bill.

Mr. BOUTWELL addressed the House in advocacy of the substitute proposed by him, providing for the issue of $400,000,000 fifteen years' five per cent. bonds, of $400,000,000, twenty years. 4½ per cent. bonds, and of $400,000,000, 25 years — per cent. bonds, principal and interest payable in coin, the latter class to be payable in the United States, or at London, Paris or Frankfotr—all such bonds to be exchangeable for five-twenty bonds.

In the course of his remarks he stated that with the adoption of his substitute there would still remain $$1,000,000,000 for which no provision would be made; but the $1,000,000,000 would be for something which is to come and go for the next fifteen years. That sum was composed as follows: Of five-twenty bonds, which may be paid in five years, but which the Government cannot be compelled to pay for twenty years, $300,000,000; of ten-forties, which may be paid in six or seven years, $263,000,000; of 1881 six per cent. bonds, $284,000,000; matured debt, $11,000,000, Total, $1,018,000,000—a sum which the Government could pay if it chose. He thought it politic to keep it in that condition.

He desired to show how the national debt was not disproportioned to the resources of the country, and instanced the fact that in the two years and nine months, between April 1, 1865, and Jan. 1, 1868, there had been paid out of the Treasury the enormous sum of $1,552,000,000, of which sum $485,000,000 went to the general expenses of the Government, and $1,067,000,000 to the reduction of the public debt. His opposition to the bill, as reported by the Committee on Ways and Means, was of the most serious character, inasmuch as it proposed to put it out of the power of the Government to pay its debt unless it went into the market to buy up its bonds. Referring to the advance on gold, he alluded to the fact that in 1866, with a circulating medium of $900,000,000, gold was at 128, whereas now, with a circulating medium of only $710,000,000, gold was at 143.

He could not explain the reasons for this in full, but he did not doubt that one cause of the increased price of gold was the accumulation of gold in the Treasury. If the theory of those who advocated a reduction of the circulating medium had been correct, gold should be to-day at 103 instead of 143.

He was opposed to the sale of gold, but thought that the gold in the Treasury might be utilized by the certainty of anticipating the payment of interest on all the debt on an abatement to be made, which would be so much gold thrown on the markets of the country.

Mr. SCHENCK opposed the substitute, and pointed out the difference between it and the bill reported by the Committee of Ways and Means. The bill provided for consolidating the public debt of the country, whereas the substitute did not present a scheme of consolidation. The question was, shall we commence a system of consolidation, using bonds of such a character and for such a time as that they will command credit at a low rate of interest, or shall we go on multiplying varieties of our public debt, pursuing temporary expedients, and issuing bonds to run for different lengths of time and at different rates?

Mr. PIKE remarked that he preferred some of the provisions of the Senate bill to those of either the bill of the Committee of Ways and Means or of the substitute. The most important was that allowing contracts to be made in gold. To him that was the most attractive feature in the bill. As to the provision for exchanging 6 per cent. bonds into 3 65-100 per cent. bonds, he deemed it an absurdity to make such a proposition. Was that a trade which anyone would desire to make?

Mr. ELDRIDGE asked Mr. PIKE whether he was in favor of paying the five-twenty bonds now due in greenbacks?

Mr. PIKE—If we had the greenbacks I would, but we have not the greenbacks.

Mr. ELDRIDGE—Then you are in favor of paying in greenbacks?

Mr. PIKE—Certainly I am, if we had the greenbacks to pay, but I am not in favor of issuing a batch of greenbacks for that purpose. Is the gentleman from Wisconsin in favor of that?

Mr. ELDRIDGE—I am in favor of paying the Five-twenties now due in greenbacks. I am in favor of withdrawing the National Bank currency, supplying its place with greenbacks, and paying the debt with them.

The colloquy between Messrs. ELDRIDGE and PIKE was pursued for some time, each charging the other with not answering questions directly; but it developed nothing more than expressed in the paragraphs quoted.

Mr. BOUTWELL resumed the floor, and in the course of his remarks, declared his belief that the foreign bondholders would exchange their six per cents into the bonds proposed in the third clause of his substitute.

Mr. RANDALL asked him what reason he had for thinking so?

Mr. BOUTWELL replied that there was a doubt existing as to the nature of the obligations assumed by this country. He was of opinion that three-fourths of all the bonds held abroad would be exchanged into the bonds contemplated by the third clause of his substitute. He was of that opinion from information received from German bankers, and from his own reflection as to what their interest was.

Mr. RANDALL—Do you believe that the principal of the five-twenties is payable in gold?

Mr. BOUTWELL—I will state exactly what my idea is. When by the act of 1862, we issued five hundred millions of five-twenties we stipulated that greenbacks should never be issued in excess of four hundred millions, but there was a stipulation over and above all law, inherent in the very nature of society, in the experience and traditions of all mankind. Every nation in its senses, actuated by honest purposes, when it resorts to forced loans or illegitimate means of raising money, by which its credit is impaired and its securities reduced below the value of gold, stipulates that every honest effort of that nature shall be directed to the resumption of specie payment, and the restoration of the public credit. That obligation rests upon us. According to the terms of the act of 1862, it does not appear beyond all cavil that we may not pay those bonds in greenbacks; but the same act also provides that we shall never issue more than $400,000,000 of greenbacks.

Mr. PIKE—The act of 1862 does not provide that.

Mr. BOUTWELL admitted that he was mistaken. It was the act of 1864 that provided it.

Mr. RANDALL expressed himself in favor of redeeming the five-twenties in greenbacks.

Mr. PIKE asked him where he would get the greenbacks to do it with.

Mr. RANDALL said he would issue them by authority of an act of Congress.

Mr. PIKE—A new issue.

Mr. RANDALL—Yes sir, as a substitute for the national bank currency. He went on to express his opinion that the question of funding the national debt was inopportune at this time. He was in favor of postponing the subject till the next session of Congress. The money market was not in a condition to warrant the United States in making any attempt now to fund the public debt, but if driven to the experiment he much preferred the bill of the Committee of Ways and Means to that of the Senate.

Mr. GARFIELD preferred the Senate bill to the bill of the Committee on Ways and Means and to the substitute. He had made a calculation recently, and had found that if the taxation in this country were held for twenty-one years as it was in 1866, without any change whatever, the last dollar of the public debt would be paid within that time. He hoped the House would disagree with the bill reported from the Committee of the Whole, and leave it as it came from the Senate with three terms of bonds. As to the question of paying the bonds in gold or greenbacks he had no concealment to make. He was ready to be questioned about it, and to answer all questions directly. He believed that when the law was passed Congress meant and thought and intended that every dollar of the bonds should be paid in gold. He did not believe that any member of Congress thought or intended so. He remembered that when the venerable gentleman from Pennsylvania (Mr. STEVENS) intimated that they were payable in greenbacks, the intimation struck the House with overwhelming surprise. It seemed to him that the question had reached an importance entirely beyond what it deserved.

Mr. PIKE—I was a member of Congress at the time, and I differed entirely from the gentleman.

Mr. WASHBURNE, of Illinois—I was a member also, and I agree entirely with the gentleman.

Mr. ELIOT—I was here too, and did not hear a word different from the idea of their being paid in gold.

Mr. BUTLER, of Massachusetts—I wish to say that I was not, but it is very plain what the law meant.

Mr. PIKE—I want nothing more than what the law said.

Mr. GARFIELD—Nothing but my respect for the age and venerableness of the gentleman from Pennsylvania, restrained me from reading what I had in my hand at the very moment when he made his remarkable speech the other day. Two sentences, plain and clear, in his own words, were uttered when the Five-twenty Bonds bill passed the House, in which he declared that the interest and principal were payable in gold. It is in the record, and if time be allowed I will read it now. Every one admits, however, that the interest of the five-twenties is payable in gold. As to whether the principal is payable in gold or greenbacks, there are two opinions. No one doubts that the greenbacks are payable in gold; so that it comes to that, at last, if the bonds are payable in greenbacks the greenbacks are payable in gold. That is the whole story.

REPORTS OF CONFERENCE COMMITTEES.

The consideration of the Funding bill was interrupted by reports from the Conference Committees.

Mr. DONNELLY made a report from the Committee of Conference on the bill of granting lands to the State of Minnesota, to aid in improving navigation of the Mississippi, that the Senate had receded from its amendment. The report was agreed to.

Mr. BUTLER, of Massachusetts, made a report from the Committee of Conference on the Indian Appropriation bill.

After considerable discussion the report was agreed to, and the House at 5 o'clock took a recess till 7:30 o'clock.

EVENING SESSION.

The House resumed its session at 7:30 o'clock.

Mr. BROOKS presented the memorial of C. HANSON, of New-York, and the Grand Holstein Ship Canal Company, setting out that the concession made to that Company by the Spanish Government has been ignored by the Prussian Government, which, he stated, has taken possession of the Holstein Territory, notwithstanding a clause in the treaty of peace that all the concessions made by Denmark shall be observed and carried out by Prussia. The petitioners ask indemnification for their outlay and loss, and that the President be authorized to exact it.

The memorial was referred to the Committee on Foreign Affairs.

THE DEFICIENCY BILL.

Mr. WASHBURNE, of Illinois, made a report from the Committee of Conference on the Deficiency bill.

Mr. BROOKS inquired of Mr. WASHBURNE what had been done about the river and harbor appropriation.

Mr. WASHBURNE said that a $1,500,000 had been inserted for rivers and harbors instead of the $7,000,000 in the House bill.

Mr. BROOKS—What is the amount in the Deficiency bill now?

Mr. WASHBURNE—About $3,500,000.

Mr. RANDALL—Has the River and Harbor bill been placed beyond resurrection in the Senate?

Mr. WASHBURNE—Yes, Sir; beyond resurrection for this session, and I hope for every session.

Mr. RANDALL—I join you in that hope.

Mr. EGGLESTON—I understand that the amendment in reference to the expenditure for rivers and harbors means this, that the Secretary of War is not authorized to appropriate any portion of the $1,500,000 for any works other than those named in the River and Harbor bill passed by the House.

Mr. WASHBURNE—That is the proviso to the amendment.

Mr. EGGLESTON—That is right.

Mr. WASHBURNE, of Illinois, said that he was glad to say to the House that the Deficiency bill just passed was the last of the appropriation bills, and the public could now figure up the entire amount of the money appropriated by Congress for the next fiscal year. He said the bills had been considered with the greatest care by the Appropriation Committee of both Houses, and he thought there were less objectionable items in the bills than there had been for many years. The expenditures had been largely cut down, and a great deal of vicious legislation that had crept in during the war had been purged from the statute books; and he could say, too, that the bills were all through in good season, and at a period anterior to the time of fixing the day of final adjournment. That was a matter which he believed was unprecedented in the history of the legislation of the House. Formerly, the most of the large appropriation bills were rushed through at the very last hours of the session, and in the most hurried and confused manner, but few of the members having any idea of what they contained. As to the amount of the appropriation for the present year, Mr. WASHBURNE said that there was the fixed sum for interest on the public debt, for pensions and for bounties, in the aggregate amounting to $190,000,000. That amount could not be lessened. It was the ordinary expenses for carrying on all the operations of the Government for the present fiscal year that this Congress was responsible for, and the people would demand to know what they were. Mr. WASHBURNE said that they would not reach more than one hundred and two millions, and that would be against seventy millions in gold coin in the administration of Mr. BUCHANAN. Considering all things—the increase of population, the natural increase of expenditures, and the increased prices of everything the Government had to buy, he considered the comparison a more favorable one, and the fact will forever stand out to the credit of this Congress. The estimates of expenditure for this year sent in by the present Democratic administration—

Mr. RANDALL, (with an air of astonishment)—The present what? [Laughter.]

Mr. WASHBURNE, (without noticing the interruption)—Were $372,000,000, including all interest on the public debt, pensions and bounties, but the entire amount appropriated by this Republican Congress, including such interest, bounties and pensions, will not amount to more than $292,000,000, a difference of $80,000,000 in favor of Congress. With these appropriation bills through, and without thrusting upon the country the schemes of robbery and plunder with which we are threatened, and which are now lying in wait, if we should now promptly adjourn and go home we would be welcomed by our constituents as faithful public servants.

The report of the Conference Committee was agreed to.

THE FUNDING BILL.

The consideration of the Funding bill was resumed, and the discussion was continued by Messrs. LAWRENCE, of Ohio, and BENTON in favor of the proposed measure.

Mr. SCHENCK closed the discussion, and advocated the passage of the bill as one that would put an end to all doubts and questions that perplexed and disturbed the public mind, fixing definitely the principle of exemption of bonds from all taxation, and fixing their mode of payment.

The debate being closed, Mr. HOLMAN moved to lay the bill on the table, which was negatived, yeas 35, nays 100.

The House then proceeded to vote on the amendments reported from the Committee of the Whole.

The first amendment, fixing the lowest denomination of bonds at $50, was agreed to without division.

The second amendment strikes out the provision for twenty, thirty and forty year bonds at various rates of interest, and substitutes for it one issue of forty-year bonds at 3.65 per cent. interest.

Mr. BROOKS demanded the yeas and nays.

The amendment was agreed to—yeas 74, nays 61.

The third amendment changes the language in regard to taxation of bonds, so that the income from them shall not ever be liable to income tax.

This amendment was agreed to—yeas 85, nays 63.

Amendments from four to nine being merely verbal, were agreed to.

The tenth amendment is to strike out the section of the Senate bill which legalizes coin contracts. The amendment was agreed to, yeas 87, nays 48.

The eleventh and twelfth amendments being merely verbal, were agreed to.

The thirteenth amendment being a new section offered in Committee by Mr. RANDALL, requiring sales, &c., of public bonds to be made by advertising for proposals, was agreed to without a division.

The fourteenth amendment being a new section, offered in Committee by Mr. LOGAN, requiring the tax on income of bonds to be assessed and collected by the Treasurer, was agreed to on a vote by tellers—yeas 90, nays 20.

The fifteenth amendment being a new section, was also offered in Committee by Mr. LOGAN, terminating the authority of the Secretary to issue bonds, &c., under existing laws, was agreed to without a division.

The question was then taken on Mr. BOUTWELL's substitute for the bill providing for three classes of bonds at 5 per cent., 4½ per cent., and 3.65 per cent., the latter payable in London, Paris, or Frankfort.

The substitute was rejected—yeas 66, nays 72.

Mr. WARD moved that the bill be laid on the table, which was rejected, only 34 voting in the affirmative.

The question then being on the passage of the bill, Mr. BOUTWELL rose and said that, inasmuch as this bill, if it passed, would postpone all possibility of paying off any portion of the public debt for forty years, which, to his mind, was equivalent to an indefinite postponement of all effort to pay the public debt of the country, he would be constrained to vote against it. It provided for a sinking fund by which there would be a residuum applicable to the public debt of more than $50,000,000 a year, and he asked how the people were to hold that accumulation of $50,000,000 a year for forty years. He considered the whole proposition so entirely unwise that he would be constrained to vote against it.

Mr. SCHENCK replied briefly to Mr. BOUTWELL's remarks, and reiterated the strong points of the bill.

The vote was taken, and the bill was passed—yeas 79, nays 68.

A motion to reconsider was laid on the table. The bill is in the same shape as it appeared at the close of Saturday's proceedings.

The House then, at 10:15 o'clock, adjourned.

MR. CHARLES FRANCIS ADAMS.

Public Reception in Boston Tendered Him and Accepted.

In compliance with the invitation and acceptance in the following letters, there will be a reception of Mr. ADAMS, in Horticultural Hall, Boston, to-morrow, at 12 M., to which all the citizens are invited:

BOSTON, July 6, 1868.

Hon. Charles Francis Adams.

DEAR SIR: You have returned to the United States after a long absence, during which you have represented the Government at the Court of St. James. Your term of foreign service has covered the most important period in the history of the United States since the establishment of their independence as a separate nation. And though you have not been personally present at home during the years of civil war, now happily at an end, you have been in active service on another field, engaged in the same great work with us of maintaining our integrity and rights as a nation.

The coincidence of eminent services abroad in three generations of lineal descendants in one family has no parallel in our history. And though our institutions and sentiments recognize no honorary titles of rank for individuals or families, it is peculiarly gratifying to us to witness the same traits and accomplishments which distinguished the ancestors, exhibited by their descendant.

As friends and fellow-citizens who, without distinction of party, and in common with all the people of the United States, have watched with intense interest the course of the American Legation at London while you have been at its head, and who feel a deep appreciation of the manliness, independence, courtesy and firmness with which you have represented us abroad, we ask leave to offer to you a cordial welcome on your return to Massachusetts. And it is our earnest wish that you will appoint some day agreeable to yourself, that we may offer to you in person the respect and gratitude which we feel for the great public services which you have rendered to our common country. We are very respectfully yours,

J. Wiley Edmands, William Ropes, J. M. Forbes, Edward Austin, Geo. Baty Blake, Jacob Bigelow, Richard H. Dana, Jr., James L. Little, Harvey Jewell, William Perkins, Peter Butler, J. Iasigi, N. H. Emmons, F. H. Bradlee, Samuel Batchelder, Geo. M. Barnard, Wm. Thomas, O. W. Peabody, Geo. C. Shattuck, F. E. Parker, F. W. Lincoln, Jr., Wm. Parsons, Ignatius Sargent, Edward S. Tobey, Edward S. Rand, Thos. C. Smith, Wm. Hilton, Samuel W. Swett, Patrick Grant, James H. Beal, H. P. Kidder, Albert Fearing, Israel Whitney, James Davis, Benj. S. Rotch, John Gardner, Josiah Quincy, Gardner Colby, Francis W. Palfrey, Charles E. Guild, Geo. H. Kuhn, John C. Lee, Charles H. Parker, Isaac Livermore, Henry A. Peirce, R. C. Mackay, Alpheus Hardy, James Sturgis, John Bertram, John M. S. Williams, J. A. Glidden, James S. Amory, Geo. B. Upton, Thornton K. Lothrop, E. R. Mudge, Sidney Bartlett, G. T. Bigelow, John H. Clifford, Nathaniel Thayer, Samuel Frothingham, Jr., George W. Lyman, John Amory Lowell, W. Amory, F. B. Crowninshield, J. Thos. Stevenson, Francis Bacon, Geo. Bemis, Wm. Gray, John G. Palfrey, Waldo Higginson, G. M. Dexter, Wm. B. Rogers, G. S. Hillard, J. J. Dixwell, George B. Emerson, Thomas Russell, John L. Gardner, Nathaniel Silsbee, Francis C. Lowell, Franklin Haven, T. Jefferson Coolidge, H. P. Sturgis, Charles G. Nazro, William T. Eustis, Geo. P. Denny, George C. Richardson, W. B. Spooner, Geo. Linder, Wm. Dwight, Thomas Gray, Peter Harvey.

MR. ADAMS' REPLY.

QUINCY, July 11, 1868.

Hon. J. Wiley Edmands and others, Boston.

MY FRIENDS AND NEIGHBORS: Your most kind and flattering letter of welcome to me on my return to private life among you, after a long absence abroad, was yesterday handed to me by a committee of your number.

I am not conscious of having done anything more than to try to do my duty. If it has happened that my service as a diplomatic agent clothed by his Government with grave responsibilities has met with some favor in the eyes of both the nations liable to be affected by it, I can only attribute it under Providence to a degree of good fortune that has seldom fallen to the lot of one similarly situated.

You are pleased to invite me to meet you in a manner which command from my sensibilities but one response. Not that I am eager to listen to or still less to take a part in my own praise, in recounting the history of the past. But I count among your number many of my oldest and best friends, in the midst of whom I have passed the best days of my life. It will delight me to seize this opportunity to renew my personal relations with all of those who have thought me worthy of such a manifestation of their regard, by a cordial exchange of greetings and mutual congratulations on our happy issue from past dangers. To that end it was the lot of all to work, each in his respective vocation. If my particular share of contribution to the common result has proved satisfactory to you, it is simply rewarding me to receive from those whom I highly esteem so generous an expression of their sense of it.

I remain your obedient servant,

CHARLES FRANCIS ADAMS.

The New-York Times.

VOL. XVIII.......NO. 5501. NEW-YORK, TUESDAY, MAY 11, 1869. PRICE FOUR CENTS.

EAST AND WEST.

Completion of the Great Line Spanning the Continent.

The Closing Work and Ceremonies at Promontory Summit.

The News Flashed by Telegraph Simultaneously Over the Country.

Rejoicings of the Metropolis at the Completion of the Enterprise.

Celebrations in Chicago, Philadelphia and Other Cities.

The Work Accomplished—Ceremonies at Promontory Summit.

Special Dispatch to the New-York Times.

PROMONTORY, Utah, Monday, May 10.

The long-looked-for moment has arrived. The construction of the Pacific Railroad is *un fait accompli*. The inhabitants of the Atlantic seaboard and the dwellers on the Pacific slopes are henceforth emphatically one people. Your correspondent is writing on Promontory Summit amid the deafening shouts of the multitude, with the tick, tick, of the telegraph close to his ear. The proceedings of the day are:

1. Prayer by Rev. Dr. TODD, of Pittsfield, asking the favor of heaven upon the enterprise.
2. Laying of two rails, one opposite the other—one for the Union Pacific Railroad, and one for the Central Pacific Railroad.
3. Presentation of spikes to the two Companies—on the part of California by Dr. HARKNESS, on the part of Nevada by Hon. F. A. FRITLE, and on the part of Arizona by Governor SAFFORD.
4. Response by Governor STANFORD on the part of the Central Pacific Railroad.
5. Response by General G. M. DODGE on the part of the Union Pacific Railroad.
6. Driving of the last spikes by the two Companies; telegraph to be attached to the spike of the Central Pacific Company, and the last blow to announce to the world by telegraph the completion of the Pacific Railroad.
7. Telegram to the President of the United States.
8. Telegram to the Associated Press.

Announcement in Washington of the Completion of the Road—Scene in the Telegraph Office.

Special Dispatch to the New-York Times.

WASHINGTON, Monday, May 10.

The completion of the Pacific Railroad has monopolized public attention here to-day to the exclusion of everything else. The feeling is one of hearty rejoicing at the completion of this great work. There were no public observances, but the arrangements made by the telegraph company to announce the completion of the road simultaneously with the driving of the last spike were perfect. At 2:20 this afternoon, Washington time, all the telegraph offices in the country were notified by the Omaha telegraph office to be ready to receive the signals corresponding to the blows of the hammer that drove the last spike in the last rail that united New-York and San Francisco with a band of iron. Accordingly Mr. TINKER, Manager of the Western Union Telegraph Office in this city, placed a magnetic bell-sounder in the public office of thta Company, corner Fourteenth-street and the avenue, connected the same with the main lines, and notified the various offices that he was ready. New-Orleans instantly responded, the answer being read from the bell-taps. New-York did the same. At 2:27 o'clock offices over the country began to make all sorts of inquiries of Omaha, to which that office replied:

"*To Everybody:* Keep quiet. When the last spike is driven at Promontory Point they will say 'Done. Don't break the circuit, but watch for the signals of the blows of the hammer."

At 2:27 P. M., Promontory Point, 2,400 miles west of Washington, said to the people congregated in the various telegraph offices:

"Almost ready. Hats off; prayer is being offered."

A silence for the prayer ensued. At 2:40 the bell tapped again, and the office at the Point said:

"We have got done praying. The spike is about to be presented."

Chicago replied:

"We understand; all are ready in the East."

Promonotory Point: "All ready now; the spike will be driven. The signal will be three dots for the commencement of the blows."

For a moment the instrument was silent; then the hammer of the magnet tapped the bell, "One, two, three," the signal; another pause of a few seconds, and the lightning came flashing eastward, vibrating over 2,400 miles between the junction of the two roads and Washington, and the blows of the hammer upon the spike were measured instantly in telegraphic accents on the bell here. At 2:47 P. M., Promontory Point gave the signal, "Done," and the Continent was spanned with iron. The same ceremony was observed at the military telegraph office in the War Department, where were present Secretary RAWLINS, Generals SHERMAN, TOWNSEND, and others. The President was unavoidably kept away by an engagement. The bell-taps here, too, repeated the blows of the hammer, and the completion of the great enterprise was known here before the echoes of the last stroke had died out of the ears of those present at the ceremonies on Promontory Point.

Rejoicing in This City—The Booming of Cannon and Chiming of Bells—Magnificent Thanksgiving Services at Old Trinity—Address by Rev. Dr. Vinton—Congratulatory Dispatches to San Francisco by Mayor Hall and the Chamber of Commerce.

It was apparent everywhere throughout the City yesterday that an event of more than usual importance was taking place, and that there was an evident disposition among the people to be jubilant. Especially was this the case in Wall-street, and in Printing-house-square and its vicinity. Flags were displayed on the City Hall, on all the newspaper offices, and on the prominent hotels. Every countenance seemed to bear a look of supreme satisfaction, and all were apparently awaiting with anticipations of delight the receipt of most welcome news. At length, soon after the sun had left the zenith, it came—the last rail of the road connecting our opposite ocean-bound shores was laid; the last spike (a gold one, by the bye) was driven; and thereupon there was booming of cannon, peals from Trinity chimes, and general rejoicing over the completion of the great enterprise, in the success of which not only this country, but the whole civilized world, is directly interested. According to the announcement made in yesterday's TIMES, there were special services in Old Trinity, and particular notice of the event was taken by the Chamber of Commerce. At 10 o'clock A. M., the Special Committee appointed by the Chamber at its last meeting proceeded to the office of the Western Union Telegraph Company, where Mr. S. B. RUGGLES, its Chairman, on behalf of the organization, handed to the operator, to be sent to San Francisco, the following

CONGRATULATORY DISPATCH.

From the Chamber of Commerce of New-York to the Chamber of Commerce of San Francisco, on the Completion of the Pacific Railway:

NEW-YORK, May 10, 1869—10 A. M.

The Chamber of Commerce of the State of New-York desires to unite at noon to-day with the Chamber of Commerce of San Francisco, in grateful thanksgiving to Almighty God, the Supreme Ruler of the Universe, on the completion of the continental line of railway, spanning the territory of the American Union and commercially uniting two great oceans of the globe; and in solemn recognition of the manifold benefits and blessings, industrial and commercial, moral and political, national and international, of this great avenue of intercommunication.

The new highway thus opened to man will not only develop the resources, extend the commerce, increase the power, exalt the dignity and perpetuate the unity of our Republic, but in its broader relations, as the segment of a world-embracing circle, directly connecting the nations of Europe with those of Asia, will materially facilitate the enlightened and advancing civilization of our age. By order of the Chamber.

SAMUEL B. RUGGLES,
WILLIAM E. DODGE,
GEORGE OPDYKE,
A. A. LOW,
Special Committee.

In a few minutes' time the lightning carried the congratulations of the Chamber across the Continent.

Up to the hour of going to press, no response had been received to the telegram sent to San Francisco by the Chamber of Commerce of th's City.

SERVICES AT TRINITY CHURCH.

Long before 12 M., the hour at which the special religious services in honor of the great event were to begin, Old Trinity was crowded with a congregation representing all conditions of our municipal society, anxiously awaiting the commencement of the exercises. At noon, after a voluntary on the organ had been performed, a long line of white-robed choristers and attendant clergymen emerged from the vestry and entered the chancel, all singing the following processional hymn:

"O come, loud anthems let us sing,
Loud thanks to our Almighty King,
For we our voices high should raise
When our salvation's rock we praise.

The depths of earth are in His hand;
Her secret wealth at His command;
The strength of hills that reach the skies
Subjected to His empire lies.

The rolling ocean's vast abyss
By the same sovereign right is His;
'Twas made by His Almighty hand,
That formed and fixed the solid land.

O let us to His courts repair,
And bow with adoration there;
Down on our knees devoutly all
Before the Lord our Maker fall."

Among the ecclesiastics in attendance were Rev. Drs. DIX, OGILVIE and VINTON, of Trinity; Bishop LITTLEJOHN, of Brooklyn; Rev. Drs. BURGESS and STUBBS, Rev. Mr. OBERLY, Rev. J. P. WHYTE, of Newport, R. I.; Rev. Professor JOHNSON, of the Episcopal Seminary, and many other clergymen of this City and Brooklyn.

When all had taken their places in the chancel, the Lord's Prayer was recited with great fervor by the clergymen and congregation in unison, Rev. Dr. OGILVIE leading. The collects for the fourth, seventh and eighth Sundays after Trinity were then read, and the following special prayer, set forth by authority of the Bishop of the Diocese, was recited by Rev. Dr. DIX:

"O God, the Creator of the ends of the earth, Who upholdest all things by the Word of Thy power, without Whom nothing is strong, nothing is holy; we bless and magnify Thy glorious name that by Thy goodness the great work which we commemorate this day has been accomplished, so that the extreme borders of our land have been joined and brought nigh together, and a pathway opened between remote parts of the earth, both for the commerce of the nations and for a highway and a way whereby Thy Gospel may have free course, and Thy holy name may be glorified. We thank Thee that the wilderness and the solitary place are made glad, and that the desert may rejoice and blossom as the rose. We come before Thee this day, in deep humility and thankfulness of heart, acknowledging that Thine, O Lord, is the greatness and power, and the glory and the victory and the majesty: for all that is in the heaven and in the earth is Thine. Thine is the kingdom, O Lord, and Thou art exalted as Head over all. Both riches and honor come of Thee, and Thou reignest over all; and in Thine hand is power and might; and in Thine hand it is to make great and to give strength unto all. Now therefore, our God, we thank Thee, and praise Thy glorious name, through Jesus Christ our Lord. Amen.

The *Te Deum Laudamus* was then sung, after which Rev. Mr. OBERLY read the lesson from the 7th chapter of Deuteronomy. The epistle was read by Rev. J. P. WHYTE, of Newport, R. I., and the ante-communion service by Rev. Dr. DIX, when the Nicene Creed was recited, and the anthem, "Great is the Lord, and greatly to be praised," was sung as an offertory selection.

ADDRESS BY REV. DR. VINTON.

Rev. Dr. VINTON then ascended the pulpit and delivered the following address:

FELLOW-CITIZENS AND BRETHREN: You have just listened to the anthem of praise and thanksgiving sent up from two separate and distinct organs, one in the chancel and the other in the loft; and yet so uniform were their strains that you could not distinguish the harmonies of one instrument from those emitted by the other. This intimate connection between those instruments is grandly typical of the great event we are here assembled to commemorate—the harmony of music and concord of one tune are practically illustrative of the joining of two oceans by railroad connection. In order to give impressiveness to the completion of a work so fraught with blessings to us as a people, the Chamber of Commerce of New-York have sent, by their Committee, a congratulatory dispatch to the Chamber of Commerce of San Francisco. [The reverend gentleman here read the dispatch, which may be found above.] This communication has probably reached its destination long since, even earlier than it is dated, owing to the difference in time between the two points; and about the time when we shall have closed these exercises, our strains of praise and thanksgiving will be taken up and reiterated on the shores of the mighty Pacific. This is indeed a great event of the world; it is one of the victories of peace—a victory grander than those of war, which leave in their track desolation, devastation, misery and woe. It is a triumph of commerce—a triumph indicating free trade as a future law of the nation. It is practically, in view of the results that will flow to the cause of Christianity in consequence of it, a fulfillment of the prophecy recorded in Holy Writ: "And the Lord shall be king over all the earth; in that day there shall be one Lord, and his name one."—Zachariah xiv., 9. We are told again that the Lord shall be king, and all the nations shall hear the voice of Zion. When we contemplate this achievement we can hardly realize its magnitude. Three thousand two hundred and eighty-five miles of continuous railway within four degrees of latitude and fifty degrees of longitude in the temperate zone. It begun when the nation was agitated by war, and is finished now when we enjoy a reign of peace. When the ocean route was discovered around the Cape of Good Hope, it was very properly regarded as a blessing to mankind—hence the designation by which it is known; but the completion of this mighty work, which connects the two oceans, is a still greater blessing. In the olden times, when camels—those ships of the desert—were the means used for transportation, for the furtherance of commercial traffic, it was found that wherever the caravans stopped there would spring up cities, and there would be evidences of civilization. So with this great work. It will populate our vast territory and be the great highway of the nations; their merchants will cross it to trade with us. But there is another aspect in which we view it as a blessing, and in connection with which we esteem it of still greater importance. It will preserve the Union of these States. Philosophers tell us, and we know it to be true, that where there are rivers which diverge in their courses, and have separate and distinct outlets, (as in Europe,) there the nations become diffused, and the peoples are separated and disunited. But where, on the contrary, the topography is such that the rivers all flow into one common central basin, there is necessarily a concentration of interests and of peoples, and that territory is marked out by God to be under one Government. By the operation of this natural law we must regard it as decreed that there shall ever be a unity of people and government in all that territory which lies between the Alleghanies and the Rocky Mountains. Beyond these lofty heights, however, we find the rivers diverging, as in Europe, and, following the rule that obtains in the Old World, there might be a diffusion of interests and a separation of governments in that section of the country divided from us by the Sierra Nevada and the Rocky Mountains. But this railway counteracts such natural tendency to disunion, has prevented a separation, and binds the States of the Atlantic and Pacific into one nation. Roman roads unified and consolidated the Roman Empire. They were made by the ambition of Emperors for the necessities of war and commerce; but, under Divine Providence, they were the highways along which the Apostles and the missionaries of Christ carried the good tidings of salvation to the tribes of the peoples. So this Pacific Railway is a means, under Divine Providence, for propogating the Church and the Gospel from this, the youngest Christian nation, to the oldest land in the Orient, now sunk in Paganism and idolatry, and so will revive the worship of the Triune God—the God of our salvation—in the farther East, the birthplace of Christianity. For this we celebrate this great event. Join with me, therefore, in singing an anthem of praise to God, "Glory to God in the highest; on earth peace, good will to men."

The choir then pealed forth the *Gloria* in MOZART'S immortal Twelfth Mass, the rendering throughout being superbly grand. Dr. DIX then offered up the prayer for the whole state of Christ's Church militant here on earth, and pronounced the benediction, after which the clergymen and choristers returned to the vestry, singing the recessional hymn, commencing:

"Bless'd be thou, the God of Israel,
Thou our Father and our Lord;
Bless'd thy Majesty forever,
Ever be thy name adored.

Thine, O Lord, are power and greatness,
Glory, victory, are thine own;
All is thine in earth and heaven,
Over all thy boundless throne."

The musical exercises throughout were of a superior order, and chained the attention of the immense congregation.

THE CHIMES.

When the religious services were ended, Mr. AYLIFFE struck up the chimes, beginning by ringing the changes on eight bells, and following with national and operatic airs. The ringing of the chimes attracted a large crowd to Broadway at the head of Wall-street, and it was not until the booming of cannon in the City Hall Park told of the receipt of an official dispatch by His Honor Mayor HALL, announcing the driving of the last spike in the last rail, that this crowd separated.

In Wall-street, and at the rooms of the Chamber of Commerce, the great event of the day was the subject of conversation and congratulation, and many announcements were made by the merchants of a determination to visit San Francisco, *via* the new route, during the coming Summer.

At the City Hall.

The flags on the City Hall were hoisted at an early hour, and preparations were made to fire one hundred guns as soon as the announcement was received that the last rail had been laid and the great work completed. At 3:16 P. M. the following dispatch was handed to the Mayor:

MAYOR BROWN, OF SAN FRANCISCO, TO MAYOR HALL.

PROMONTORY POINT, May 10, 1869.

To Hon. A. Oakey Hall, Mayor of New-York:

The last spike in the rail connecting the Atlantic and Pacific by rail has been driven at 3:10 P. M., (New-York time.)

A. S. BROWN, Mayor.

In a few minutes after the receipt of Mayor BROWN'S dispatch Mayor HALL sent the following:

MAYOR HALL'S REPLY.

EXECUTIVE DEPARTMENT, CITY HALL,
NEW-YORK, May 10, 1869.

To the Mayor of San Francisco:

New-York rejoiced when, almost half a century ago, by the completion of the Erie Canal, the silver chain of Western inland seas was riveted upon the Atlantic Ocean. The metropolis of America exults to-day, because by the completion of the Pacific Railway two extremities and coasts of an immense continent are commercially welded together. Apart from the relations of this grand event to Christianity, political economy, civilization and patriotism, it justifies the metropolis in the pardonably selfish expectation to soon become the commercial exchange of the world. Her newspapers, which have so largely contributed to this day's result, must soon accustom our citizens to phrases like this one: "The Asiatic freight train has arrived on time." So our flags are now flying, our cannon now booming, and in Old Trinity, at the head of Wall-street, a *Te Deum* imparts thankful harmonies to the busy hum about her church walls. Can it, then, be necessary, by mere words, to tender you fuller magnetic sympathy? As for congratulations to you, phrases seem inadequate to foretell the full fruition to your golden-gated city of enterprise of this beginning of railway intercommunication. Therefore let this 10th of May pass into the annals of San Francisco, New-York, and of every hamlet, village, town and city along the new highway, as an anniversary day.

A. OAKEY HALL,
Mayor of New-York.

The Mayor also gave orders to fire 100 guns in the City Hall Park in honor of the event, and Mr. ROOME having kept guns and ammunition in readiness, the first discharge was fired within five minutes after the receipt of the dispatch. A large number of persons congregated in the Park to listen to the booming of the cannon, which told of another great enterprise completed, and to congratulate each other on the event. Flags were hoisted on the Astor House and most of the private buildings so soon as the news was made public.

Celebrations in Chicago, Philadelphia, Buffalo and Other Places.

CHICAGO, Monday, May 10.

The celebration of the completion of the great interoceanic railway connection to-day was the most successful affair of the kind that ever took place in Chicago, and probably in the West. It was entirely impromptu, and therefore almost every man and woman and child in the city did their part toward making it a success. The procession was unique in appearance, and immense in length, which at the lowest estimate was seven miles. During the moving of the procession Vice-President COLFAX received the following dispatch:

PROMONTORY SUMMIT, Utah,
Monday, May 10.

To Hon. Schuyler Colfax, Vice-President:

The rails were connected to-day. The prophecy of BENTON to-day is a fact. This is the way to India. Signed

G. M. DODGE, JOHN DUFF,
SIDNEY DILLON, T. C. DURANT.

This evening Vice-President COLFAX, Lieutenant-Governor BROSS and others addressed a large audience at Library Hall, in which they spoke eloquently of the great era which this day marks in the history of our country.

During the evening there was also a general indulgence in fireworks, bonfires, illuminations, &c.

PHILADELPHIA, Monday, May 10.

At 2:30 o'clock precisely, Philadelphia time, the news was received of the driving of the last spike of the Pacific Railroad. Word was sent to the Mayor, and, in a few minutes, the bells on Independence Hall and various fire stations were rung, drawing a crowd into the streets, thinking a general alarm of fire was being rung. The people soon ascertained the reason of the ringing of the bells, and flags were immediately hoisted everywhere. A large number of steam fire-engines were ranged in front of Independence Hall, with screeching whistles, hose carriages, bells ringing, &c. Joy was expressed in every face at the completion of the great work of the century. The sudden flocking of the people to the State-house reminded one of the reception of the news of the surrender of LEE'S army, when a similar scene was enacted.

BUFFALO, N. Y., Monday, May 10.

A large crowd of citizens assembled at the Board of Trade rooms this afternoon, to hear the announcement by telegraph of the driving of the last spike in the rail connecting the Atlantic coast with the Pacific. The telegraph wire was attached to a large gong bell, and at 2:41 o'clock, city time, repeating strokes were simultaneously made. At the completion cheers were given, the "Star Spangle Banner" sung by the crowd, prayer offered and appropriate speeches made by Hon. D. S. BENNETT, HENRY A. RICHMOND and others.

SCRANTON, Penn., Monday, May 8.

Scranton celebrated the completion of the Pacific Railroad by the firing of cannons, ringing of bells, whistling of locomotives, and a general expression of joy by its citizens.

The Southern Pacific—Meeting of Directors at St. Louis.

ST. LOUIS, Monday, May 10.

Judge LEVI PARSONS, of New-York, President of the southern branch of the Union Pacific Railroad, running from Fort Riley, Kansas, down the Neosho Valley to Fort Smith, Ark., arrived here last night, accompanied by the following New-York directors: FRANCIS SKIDDY, ROBERT S. STEVENS, GEORGE DENNISON, THEODORE JOHNSON and H. H. JOHNSON. The party leave this afternoon for Junction City, for the purpose of making an inspection of the road. The road is a feeder to the Kansas Pacific Railroad. The survey was commenced in December last. Sixty miles will be built by next September, and the whole road is under contract. The Company have a grant of 1,350,000 acres of land, and $810,000 in county bonds have been subscribed toward the road by the counties through which it passes. Five thousand emigrants from Copenhagen have paid their passage, and 30,000 Swedes are expected during the season to settle on the lands belonging to the road.

WASHINGTON.

Minister Motley's Instructions—The Alabama Claims—The Belgian Mission—Case of the Mary Lowell.

Special Dispatches to the New-York Times.

WASHINGTON, Monday, May 10.

Mr. MOTLEY, the new Minister to England, is, it appears, to receive some written instructions of a general character in reference to the resumption of negotiations for the settlement of the pending questions between this country and Great Britain. It is stated that they will be very brief, and cover not so much what the present Administration would be willing to consider a satisfactory solution of the Alabama difficulty, as what it would be sure to reject. Mr. MOTLEY, whose return to Washington before he leaves is not looked for, will sail from New-York on the 19th inst.

THE ALABAMA CLAIMS.

A gentleman who arrived here to-day direct from London, and who is well acquainted with the leading statesmen there, says that Sir HENRY LYTTON BULWER had given notice that he would, on the evening of May 11, call up the *Alabama* Claims Treaty in the House of Commons. It was Sir HENRY'S intention to speak at same length, criticising the action of the British Ministry, and also taking exceptions to the course of Mr. SEWARD in precipitating action on this subject after the American people had condemned the Johnson Administration at the ballot-box. This speech from a man so strong in this nation as Mr. BULWER, will be looked for with much interest, and it is hoped here that the reception of Mr. SUMNER'S speech in England will not defer its delivery.

THE BELGIAN MISSION.

A large number of consular commissions were signed at the State Department during Saturday and to-day, and will be transmitted during the present week. The President visited the Department to-day, and rumor has it that it was in reference to the Belgian mission, and the making of some provision for J. RUSSELL JONES. It can be stated authoritatively, however, that there will be no immediate change in the representation of the United States at that Court.

THE MARY LOWELL.

The facts in the case of the *Mary Lowell*, that she was an American ship, seized while in British waters, under charge of a British officer, and condemned as a prize by the Spanish authorities, were officially communicated to the Foreign Office of Great Britain by the State Department some time ago. The claim has been presented by the English Government for settlement at Madrid, and here it is that another complication arises. It appears that the Spanish authorities insist that the vessel was not in British waters at the time, being more than three leagues from shore, which in the very nature of things will take some time to decide. The Spanish Government professes its ability to produce witnesses who will testify to this fact of locality at the time of seizure.

THE TAX QUESTION.

Two representatives of the New-York brokers' interest were here to-day, endeavoring to induce the reopening of the recent decision in the tax question, for the purpose of reviewing some of its points. In the absence of the Commissioner, Mr. DOUGLASS, Acting Commissioner, and Mr. SMITH, Solicitor, decided not to reopen the question. A communication was also presented from C. S. SLOANE, Esq., Chairman of the Executive Committee of the Stock Exchange, requesting that the time for making monthly returns for April should be extended, and that meanwhile a reconsideration of the original question should be had. Mr. DOUGLASS, for the Commissioner, assured the parties that the Department would not exercise any arbitrary power, but would exercise all the discretionary authority that seemed necessary to facilitate parties in accommodating themselves to the requirements of the recent decision.

THE NEW-YORK CUSTOM-HOUSE.

Considerable important information was, to-day, laid before the President with reference to irregular and fraudulent practices hitherto prevalent in the New-York Custom-house. The matters were referred to Special Agent HOWE for his investigation, and he will probably bring them to the attention of Collector GRINNELL.

PERSONAL.

JOHN CLEM, of Ohio, the famous drummer boy, who dropped his drum for a musket at Chicamauga, and shot a rebel Colonel who demanded his surrender, and was subsequently wounded in another engagement, has been appointed a cadet at large to West Point by the President. He was but 12 years of age when he beat his drum, and is scarce 17 now. He was cordially greeted by the President, General LOGAN and the Secretary of War, all of whom knew him well in the army.

Dispatches to the Associated Press.

WASHINGTON, Monday, May 10.

APPOINTMENTS.

THOMAS J. KINNEY has been appointed Assessor of Internal Revenue for the Ninth Illinois District, *vice* AMOS C. BABCOCK, who declined. JOHN P. TAGGART, of Galena, has been appointed Assessor of Utah, *vice* CAREY declined. No further appointment of Supervisors will be made until the return of Commissioner DELANO.

THE "JAR CASE."

The celebrated jar case of ROWLEY *vs.* MASON has assumed a new phase. Judge FISHER had decided in favor of ROWLEY, but on Saturday the same Judge granted a preliminary injunction staying the issue of a patent to ROWLEY, it being claimed that J. L. MASON was the original inventor, and reduced the article to practice.

DUTIES ON IRON TUBES AND FLUES.

The Secretary of the Treasury has decided that the tariff, as well as commercial usage, recognizes a distinction between wrought-iron tubes and wrought-iron flues, and that the former are liable to a duty of 3½ cents per pound, and the latter of 2½ cents per pound, under the existing laws.

ANNEXATION OF ST. DOMINGO.

Mr. FABENS, the confidential agent of the St. Domingo Government, recently had an interview with Secretary FISH. The subject or annexation will receive official consideration at an early day. The parties interested in the annexation movement furnish an extract of a letter from Professor GABB, who says he has prospected 200 miles of gold-bearing territory, surpassing in richness any known portion of California and Arizona.

REVENUE SUPERVISORS.

On the return of Commissioner DELANO several additional Supervisors of Internal Revenue will be appointed.

ARMY AND NAVY INTELLIGENCE.

Lieutenant-Commander A. P. Cooke has been ordered to the Naval Academy on the 1st of October next. Chief Engineer Henry Mason has been ordered to special duty in charge of the machinery at Providence. First-Lieutenant Moses Wiley, of the Sixth United States Cavalry, has resigned. Brevet Lieutenant-Colonel J. N. Benet, Major of the Ordnance Department, who has been assisting General Dyer while before the Court of Inquiry, has been ordered to return to his station and resume his duties as commanding officer of the Frankford Arsenal, Pennsylvania. Captain Edward Ball, of the Second Cavalry, has been ordered to join his company in the Department of the Platte.

ALBANY.

End of the Contest Over the Tammany Tax Levies.

A Reduction of About Two Millions at Length Made.

Final Adjournment of the Legislature at Midnight.

The Row About the New-York Tax Levies—The Republicans Stand Firm—So do the Democrats—A Dead Lock.

From Our Own Correspondent.

ALBANY, Monday, May 10, 1869.

The row about the Tammany tax levies still continues, with no better prospect of an adjustment than existed when the two Houses adjourned on Sunday morning. Tammany labored hard all day yesterday to buy over another Republican Senator, but without success. The new bribery bill (which, by the way, the Governor has not signed yet) looms up as a dark shadow in the future, and begins to strike terror to the hearts of men who have been trading their votes during this and previous sessions. It is important for the future moral effect of the law that an example should be made under it immediately, and the public will be glad to know that evidence is being collected for that purpose. In order that the imputation of partisanship may not attach to the movement, the law should be enforced against a Democrat and a Republican at the same time, and an example should also be made of one or more of the prominent lobbyists who have got rich by hanging around the Legislature during this and past years, disbursing the bribery funds. The influence of these scoundrels on the legislation of the State is even more than that of the members who sell their votes, for each one of them has corrupted scores of members, who, but for them, would never have thought of selling themselves.

At the opening of the Senate this morning Mr. FOLGER moved to take from the table several vetoes of the Governor, which was carried, and all were sustained. The Senate then resumed the consideration of the tax levies where they left off Sunday morning. Mr. TWEED moved that the Senate concur in the levies passed by the Assembly, whereupon Mr. FOLGER raised the point of order that both Houses having refused to agree through their respective Conference Committees in the levies as passed by the Assembly, the same were dead, and could receive no further action from the Senate. The President decided the point of order not well taken, and Mr. FOLGER appealed. After considerable discussion, in which Mr. CROWLEY sustained Mr. FOLGER, and Mr. MURPHY the President, a vote was taken on the appeal, which resulted yeas 16, nays 16—MATTOON voting, as usual, with the Democrats. The President gave the casting vote in the affirmative to sustain his own decision, whereupon Mr. FOLGER raised another point of order, that on an appeal from the decision of the President that functionary had no right to give the casting vote.

Lieutenant-Governor BEACH—The chair decides otherwise.

Mr. FOLGER—"Otherwise," (with emphasis;) that is nothing but a reiteration of the chair's decision.

A discussion then ensued as to the rights of the President in the case, Mr. MURPHY claiming that he had the right to give the casting vote, and citing a similar case on the part of the Speaker of the Assembly several years ago.

Mr. FOLGER said that was not a parallel case. The Speaker of the Assembly was a member-elect of that body, whereas the President of the Senate was not a member of the Senate, but merely the constitutional presiding officer. As a question of delicacy on the part of the President, he declined to say anything.

Mr. MATTOON here raised the point that no question was pending, and the discussion dropped.

Mr. TWEED'S motion to concur in the tax levies passed by the Assembly being again in order, Mr. MORGAN moved to strike out the clause in the City levy making an appropriation of twenty per cent. of the Excise fund (equal to about $300,000) for the support of private schools in New-York. He said these private schools were simply parochial schools, and as such were sectarian. The larger share of them were Catholic, but he was opposed to appropriating money for the support of any sectarian schools of any denomination. It was a stepping-stone to the destruction of the entire public school system of the State. Instead of encouraging these schools by giving them a share of the public money, the State ought to discourage them, and compel the children educated therein to come out and attend the public schools.

Mr. VAN PATTEN opposed the appropriation and every other scheme for perpetuating religious prejudice, by encouraging schools founded in opposition to the public schools of the State. If there were not accommodations sufficient for all the children in New-York, let them be increased; but if any religious denomination insisted upon educating its children in sectarian schools, let it support such schools by private aid, and not with the public fund.

Mr. MATTOON advocated the appropriation, because it would reach a class of children who would not otherwise be educated.

Mr. CREAMER also advocated it, and said that he had talked with leading men in other denominations besides the Catholic, and they were equally earnest with the Catholics in desiring an appropriation of this kind. He did not state who the "leading men" were, or to what denomination they belonged.

Mr. HUMPHREY protested against any further discussion of the School question at this time, as it would not make a particle of difference or change a single vote on this or any other item of the tax levies now under consideration.

Mr. MORGAN then withdrew his motion to strike out this clause, and Mr. TWEED withdrew his motion to concur; whereupon Mr. CREAMER moved that another Conference Committee be appointed, which was carried. Mr. O'DONNELL moved to instruct the Committee to adhere to the tax levies that passed the Senate—lost by the same party vote, Mr. MATTOON voting with the Democrats. During the discussion on this motion Mr. MORGAN informed the Democratic side of the Senate that the Republicans would not move a hair's breadth from the position they had taken, and that they could never pass the tax levies that were put through the Assembly by the Tammany Ring.

Mr. MATTOON took the occasion to deny the insinuations that had been thrown out about his deserting his party and going over to the Democrats. There was not a drop of Democratic blood in his veins and never would be. But he denied that this was, or ought to be regarded as a party measure. It was entirely a local measure that ought to be left to New-York. He had always been opposed to special legislation for the City of New-York, and was ready at any time to vote for the repeal of all the commissions that had been created for that City except the Police Commission, which he said he believed was satisfactory to both parties. On party questions he always voted with his party, and always should. He claimed to represent his constituents satisfactorily, and was perfectly willing to take their judgment on his course as a Senator.

The President announced the new Conference Committee on the part of the Senate to be Messrs. CREAMER and GENET, Democrats, and VAN PATTEN, Republican. Mr. VAN PATTEN declined to serve, as did also Mr. STANFORD and Mr. FOLGER. Mr. WILLIAMS was then appointed and accepted, but afterward changed his mind and withdrew from the Committee. On the part of the Assembly the Speaker appointed Messrs. CAMPBELL, GLEASON and LA BAR, Republicans, and Messrs. HITCHMAN and IRVING, Democrats. The only change in the two Committees, from those that were unable to agree before, is in the name of GLEASON on the Assembly Committee in place of TUTTLE.

The Committee went into session at noon, and the Senate adjourned to 3 P. M.

IN THE ASSEMBLY

the proceedings to-day were of little public interest. A few Senate bills of a local character were concurred in, and an attempt was made to concur in Swain's Two-tier Railroad bill, as it passed the Senate, but failed. Another mock session was held while waiting for the Senate's Conference Committee, and after that was agreed upon the House adjourned to 4 P. M. S.

The Tax Levies—Agreement of the Conference Committees—The Levies Reduced—Their Passage.

Special Dispatch to the New-York Times.

ALBANY, Monday, May 10.

The new Conference Committees on the tax levies, after being in session all day, came in at 9 o'clock this evening with a report that they had agreed unanimously on both the City and County levies. Senator WILLIAMS, who at first withdrew from the Committee, again changed his mind, and went back and took part in the deliberations, and signed his name to the report. The levies, as agreed upon, are in the aggregate $2,200,000 larger than those that originally passed the Senate—the increase on the City levy being $1,600,000, and on the County levy $600,000; but the items of the ring levies that passed the Assembly have been cut down in the aggregate about $2,000,000. The item appropriating 20 per cent. of the Excise income to private schools is retained, but the money is to be distributed under the direction of the Board of Education. On the whole, the Republican members of the Assembly Committee think they have got a pretty moderate levy.

It was ratified by the Assembly nearly unanimously, but in the Senate it met with a strong opposition. It had been agreed among the Republican members of the Senate, with the exception of MATTOON, who had gone over to the enemy, that they would adhere to the levies which passed their body; and when they saw WILLIAMS' name signed to the report of the Conference Committee they were satisfied that another of their members had gone over to the enemy, and the result proved that there were two more traitors in the camp; for, when the vote on concurring with the report of the Committee was taken, it was found that VAN PATTEN had also become a sudden convert to the Tammany levies. Both of these Senators tried to excuse themselves for the vote they gave, but it was done in such a stammering way and with such evidence of guilt as to become not only a mortifying but a sickening spectacle. MATTOON, who does his business boldly, was disgusted with his associates in treason, and did not hesitate to say he was ashamed of them. The vote stood 18 in favor of concurring with the Committee and 13 against. Mr. STANFORD was absent; but was prepared to vote with his party if his vote had been necessary. Had the report of the Committee been substantially in favor of the ring levies as they passed the Assembly, it was the design of the Republicans to leave the Senate, so that three-fifths would not remain to do business, and thus prevent a confirmation of the levies in case it could not otherwise be done. After finishing the two levies, both Houses passed concurrent resolutions to adjourn *sine die* at 12 o'clock midnight, which they did, and many of the members left in the early morning trains.

THE STATE LEGISLATURE.

SENATE....ALBANY, Monday, May 10.

The Senate met at 9 o'clock.

On motion of Mr. FOLGER, the veto messages of the Governor were taken from the table. The veto of the bill relative to filling the vacancy in the office of Justice of the Peace at Lowville was first considered. The veto was sustained, 23 to 1—Mr. MATTOON.

The veto of the bill to authorize the appointment of a President *pro tem.* of the Metropolitan Board of Police was sustained, 17 to 8.

The veto of the One Hundred and Twenty-fifth-street Railroad bill was sustained, 28 to 3—Messrs. CAULDWELL, GENET and MATTOON.

The veto of the Avenue C Railroad bill was sustained, 23 to 3—Messrs. CAULDWELL, GENET and MATTOON.

The veto of the bill in relation to filling the vacancies of Justices of the Peace in the several towns of the State was brought up. Mr. FOLGER thought the Governor partly right and partly wrong, and favored passing over the veto. The veto was sustained, 15 to 15—Messrs. Crowley, Folger, Hale, Kennedy, Mattoon, Morgan, Nicks, O'Donnell, Pulver, Parker, Stanford, Thayer, Van Petten, Chapman and Humphrey voting no. The veto of the bill to incorporate the Oswego Pier and Dock Company was sustained by 24 to 2, Messrs. MATTOON and VAN PETTEN voting no.

Under the order of messages from the Assembly, Mr. TWEED called up the question of concurring in the amendments to the Tax Levy bill. Mr. FOLGER raised the point of order that the Senate having agreed with the report of the Conference Committee, that they had failed to agree, and having discharged the Committee, no further action could be taken, and that the bill is dead.

The President overruled the point of order. Mr. FOLGER appealed from the decision. The Chair was sustained by 16 to 16—all the Democrats and Mr. MATTOON voting yea and the Republicans voting nay, the Chair giving the casting vote.

Mr. FOLGER raised the point of order that on a question of sustaining a decision of the Chair the President cannot give the casting vote. Mr. MURPHY took issue thereon. The Chair overruled the point of order. The question being on concurring with the Assembly amendment, Mr. MORGAN asked for a division of the question so as to vote separately on the proposition to appropriate twenty per cent. of the Excise fund for what he termed sectarian schools in New-York.

The proposition was discussed at some length by Messrs. MORGAN and MURPHY.

Mr. MORGAN withdrew his request for a division.

Mr. TWEED withdrew his motion to concur in Assembly amendments.

Mr. CREAMER moved that a new Conference Committee be appointed; which was carried, 17 to 15—Messrs. MATTOON and VAN PETTEN voting yea with the Democrats.

Mr. VAN PETTEN said he voted under a misapprehension, and moved to reconsider the last vote.

Mr. CROWLEY thought this idle, and said that it was evident the question must be compromised.

Mr. MORGAN said compromise was impossible. The Republican Senators have only to stand by the original Senate bill.

Mr. TWEED said there was no remedy for the dilemma except compromise.

Mr. FOLGER said the compromise must be in the Senate, and not with the Citizens' Association.

The motion to reconsider was lost, 16 to 16—the President voting no, and Mr. MATTOON voting no with the Democrats.

The President appointed the following as such Committee of Conference: Messrs. CREAMER, GENET, FOLGER.

The latter declined and Mr. STANFORD was appointed. Mr. STANFORD declined and Mr. VAN PETTEN was appointed. Mr. VAN PETTEN declined and Mr. WILLIAMS was appointed.

Mr. O'DONNELL moved to instruct the Committee to insist on the original Senate bill, or on the Assembly bill, as reported by its Committee. Lost, 16 to 16—Mr. MATTOON voting no, with the Democrats; the Chair also voting no.

The Senate took a recess until this afternoon, awaiting the Conference Committee's action.

AFTERNOON SESSION.

Mr. O'DONNELL introduced a bill, which immediately passed, protecting the fishing interests in Lake Ontario, bays, estuaries and River St. Lawrence.

Concurred in: The Assembly amendments to the bill for the construction of a new work and extraordinary repair on canals. The bill imposing a tax of three-quarters of a mill involves an expenditure of about one million and a half dollars.

The report of the Conference Committee on amending the General Excise law so as to retain the Senate amendments authorizing licenses to be granted for the sale of ale or beer for $10 was agreed to. Mr. MATTOON dissented.

The bill to incorporate the Brevoort Savings Bank, New-York, was passed.

On motion of Mr. VAN PETTEN, the Judiciary Committee, upon investigating the gun contract, was excused from reporting this session, and have leave to sit during the recess without expense to the State.

The report of the Conference Committee on the Tax Levies was received. The report of the City levy was concurred in—18 to 13—yeas all Democrats, and Messrs. VAN PETTEN, WILLIAMS and MATTOON; nays, all Republicans.

YEAS—Messrs. Banks, Beach, Bradley, Cauldwell, Creamer, Edwards, Genet, Graham, Hubbard, Mattoon, Morris, Murphy, Nichols, Norton, Pierce, Tweed, Van Petten, Williams—18.

NAYS—Messrs. Campbell, Chapman, Crowley, Folger, Hale, Humphrey, Kennedy, Morgan, Nicks, O'Donnell, Palmer, Parker, Thayer—13.

The report of the Committee of Conference on the County Levy was read, and concurred in by the same vote as the City Levy.

At 10:45, the levies being disposed of, a concurrent resolution was adopted to adjourn at 12 midnight.

On motion of Mr. THAYER, a new Committee of Conference on the Canal Appropriation bill was appointed, as follows: Messrs. THAYER, MORRIS and HUBBARD.

Recess for three-quarters of an hour.

EVENING SESSION.

Messrs. BRADLEY and CREAMER were appointed a committee to wait on the Assembly and inform them that the Senate was ready to adjourn. A committee was also appointed to wait on the Governor.

At 12 midnight, Lieutenant-Governor BEACH, after a few words of farewell, declared the Senate adjourned *sine die*.

ASSEMBLY.

On motion of Mr. HARTMAN, it was resolved that, if the Senate concur, the Assembly will adjourn *sine die* at 12 o'clock to-day.

The Speaker appointed the following as the Committee of Conference on the Tax Levies: Messrs. LA BAU, W. W. CAMPBELL, HITCHMAN, GLEASON and IRVING.

The Assembly took a recess for half an hour.

Upon reassembling, the Assembly concurred in the report of the Committee of Conference on the Canal Appropriation bill; also, the State Excise law.

Recess till 4 o'clock.

EVENING SESSION.

BILL ORDERED TO A THIRD READING.

For the construction of a railroad on Twenty-third-street, the charter to be sold at auction.

Mr. FREAR asked and obtained unanimous consent that said bill have now its third reading, and the bill passed—Mr. SELKREG alone voting nay.

Mr. W. W. CAMPBELL, of the Committee of Conference on the Tax Levies, made a unanimous report cutting down the City Levy $1,800,000, and the County Levy about $600,000. The report of the City Levy was concurred in, 94 to 11. The report on the County Levy was concurred in, 88 to 15.

The Senate bill to protect the fishing interests on Lake Ontario, its bays and entrances, and the River St. Lawrence, was passed.

At 11:15 o'clock a message was received from the Governor, vetoeing the bill relative to the assessment rolls in the town of Oswegatchie, St. Lawrence County. The Governor says the bill is a needless interference with the duties of the Town Assessors and Town Supervisors, which are regulated by the general laws. The City of Ogdensburg is a part of the town of Oswegatchie, and its citizens have their share in electing Supervisors of the town, whose jurisdiction extends over the city as well as the town for all town purposes. So long as the city continues a part of the town it is not right that any of the duties and powers should be devolved upon the Ward Supervisors, whose jurisdictions are much more limited. If the proposed change is necessary, there should be a general law passed.

The veto was sustained by a vote of 71 to 1.

Messrs. RICH, HUSTED and FERRIS were appointed a Committee to inform the Senate that the House was ready to adjourn; and Messrs. HIXON and MILLER were also appointed a Committee to inform the Governor of the same.

Mr. JACOBS called up his resolution instructing the Canal Board to inquire into the expediency of the building for the State a grain elevator in Buffalo.

The resolution was adopted, 43 to 24.

The Committee of Conference on the Canal Ordinary Repair Appropriation bill reported their failure to agree. Laid on the table and the bill killed.

Farewell speeches were made by Mr. SELKREG, Judge CAMPBELL and Mr. JACOBS. The Speaker, Mr. YOUNGLOVE, made the closing speech, and at 12:20 declared the Assembly adjourned *sine die*.

THE BILLIARD TOURNAMENT.

Close of the Tie Games—Foster Wins Against Snyder—The Winner of the Match Game in the Evening.

The closing game of the tie series of the tournament was played yesterday afternoon between FOSTER and SNYDER. It was to decide the choice for third and fourth prizes. There was not a game in the tournament proper that at all compares with this. It was played out in the shortest time, was marked by the largest run, and foots up the highest average. Both parties played strongly, the loser making an average of twenty-nine, going four times above triple figures, and one of these reaching above 200. FOSTER, on the other hand, ran up the tremendous number of 492 in the thirteenth inning. It was regretted that such a game as was that of yesterday afternoon had not occurred in the tournament proper, as it would undoubtedly have nerved up all the players, and as a result would have run up the grand averages many points from the lowest to the highest on the list. Below is presented a very full and concise table of the play, which gives the result in better form than any words can depict:

FOSTER—0, 0, 3, 21, 48, 6, 1, 90, 0, 63, 21, 3, 492, 69, 54, 6, 27, 3, 36, 6, 6, 0, 15, 12, 30, 21, 3, 3, 12, 57, 92.

SNYDER—0, 3, 3, 24, 0, 15, 13, 12, 42, 3, 249, 13, 27, 117, 3, 0, 0, 3, 123, 9, 6, 1, 10, 27, 0, 9, 30, 120, 9, 0.

Referee—R. SCOFIELD.

CYRILLE DION and JOHN MCDEVITT last evening played a game of three ball caroms for $250 a side, which, for closeness of score, was never excelled. MCDEVITT at one time was 60 points ahead, and toward the close of the game stood 35 ahead of his opponent, and had only 8 points to make to win. DION struggled manfully, and, although he was all over a loser apparently, ultimately won the game, amid deafening applause, by one run. Below is given the full score:

DION—0, 0, 0, 1, 0, 3, 2, 3, 0, 2, 2, 0, 1, 0, 0, 3, 0, 0, 4, 5, 2, 0, 0, 0, 2, 4, 1, 4, 0, 0, 0, 1, 0, 1, 4, 0, 2, 0, 0, 6, 2, 8, 1, 6, 1, 0, 0, 0, 0, 0, 0, 0, 0, 4, 0, 4, 10, 2, 5, 1, 2, 0, 1, 2, 0, 0, 0, 0, 0, 6, 0, 18, 0, 2, 0, 1, 0, 0, 2, 4, 0, 2, 0, 6, 0, 1, 5, 11, 9, 7, 1, 11, 0, 1, 5, 0, 0, 0, 0, 0, 0, 0, 1, 1, 0, 0, 0, 0, 1, 1, 6, 1, 19, 0, 2, 0, 0, 3, 0, 0, 15, 2, 0, 0, 0, 0, 6, 2, 0, 3, 5, 0, 3, 0, 16, 3, 2, 2, 1, 2, 3, 0, 1, 0, 1, 1, 14, 2. Total 300.

MCDEVITT—3, 1, 0, 1, 3, 6, 1, 0, 2, 0, 9, 0, 0, 0, 1, 1, 13, 0, 4, 1, 1, 0, 0, 0, 0, 13, 1, 3, 2, 5, 0, 7, 9, 1, 0, 0, 2, 2, 7, 5, 2, 5, 0, 0, 5, 0, 0, 0, 2, 0, 1, 0, 0, 1, 0, 1, 9, 0, 3, 2, 0, 1, 0, 0, 6, 3, 0, 7, 2, 1, 1, 0, 0, 0, 3, 0, 29, 0, 1, 2, 5, 4, 2, 0, 0, 2, 0, 1, 0, 0, 2, 0, 0, 0, 0, 1, 3, 0, 0, 0, 0, 0, 0, 6, 2, 0, 0, 0, 7, 0, 5, 6, 3, 0, 0, 0, 0, 0, 2, 1, 6, 27, 0, 0, 0, 0, 1, 0, 1, 0, 0, 4, 0. Total, 299.

The Massachusetts State Billiard Tournament at Boston.

BOSTON, Mass., Monday, May 10.

The Massachusetts Billiard Tournament, for the championship of the State, commenced this afternoon at the Olympic Theatre. The games to be played are 500 points each, push shot barred; the counting to be the same as in the New-York Tournament games. The first game was between R. E. WILMARTH and WILLIAM A. TOBIN, and was won by the former, 500 to 484. The winner's average was 12, and his highest runs 39, 42, 75, 27. TOBIN'S highest runs were 30, 72, 45, 40.

The second game was between J. H. FLACK and J. F. MURPHY, and was won by the former, 500 to 406. The winner's average was 13½, and his highest runs 30, 90, 24, 84. MURPHY'S highest runs, 138, 30.

In the evening the first game was between FLACK and TOBIN, and was won by the former, 500 to 395. The winner's average was 11 1-9, and his highest runs 51, 27, 33. TOBIN'S highest runs, 60, 27, 33, 36.

The next game was between WILLIAMS and DAVIS, and was won by the former, 500 to 471. The winner's average was 9, and his highest runs 48, 69, 42. DAVIS' highest runs were 39, 45, 39.

The Chess Tournament.

The tilt of Knights, Bishops, Kings and Queens commenced yesterday, at LIEDER'S Café Europa, Nos. 12 and 14 Division-street, about twenty-five members having signed their names as contestants for the prizes. The books will remain open during the week for fresh accessions, at which time they will be closed peremptorily, and no new entries will be allowed. Among the prominent signatures on the books are the names of Captain MACKENZIE, Major WERNICK, Messrs. MASON, DELMAR, KOPP, and others. There are also some new names, never before entered for a tournament. Up to last night at midnight, but few games had been played. During the week, the billiard tables will be removed to the floor above, and the chess-room capacity will be more than doubled. The present tournament promises to be extremely interesting.

The New-York Times.

VOL. XX.......NO. 6068. NEW-YORK, FRIDAY, MARCH 3, 1871. PRICE FOUR CENTS.

OCCUPIED PARIS.

Reception of the Invaders by the Inhabitants.

Gloomy Crowds and Closed Public and Private Buildings.

The Guards Prevent Violence With Difficulty.

The German Emperor Not to Enter the Humiliated Capital.

Return of the French Government as Early as Practicable.

OCCUPATION OF PARIS.

Agitation in the City on the Previous Night—Barricades Erected and Maintained—The Crowds Sad and Silent as the Hosts March In—Shops Closed and Newspapers Suspended—The National Guard Restrained with Difficulty.

LONDON, March 1.—There was much agitation in several quarters of Paris last night, and barricades were erected in the northern and eastern faubourgs. It is stated that they are only guarantees lest the Germans should overstep the assigned limits of occupation. The Governor of Paris is represented to have said he could only rely upon a certain number of the National Guard and troops of the line for interposition between the Germans and the populace.

LONDON, March 2.—Reports from Paris to yesterday evening state that the barricades between the Germans and the French were maintained. Immense crowds were in the streets, but they were sad and silent. No newspapers were published and the shops were closed. The National Guard at one time threatened to disobey orders and throw themselves on the Germans; but they were dissuaded from the rash attempt.

The German force in occupation of the north-western part of the city numbered 30,000 men, and was taken from the Sixteenth Prussian and the First Bavarian Corps.

The dividing lines were guarded by French and German soldiers.

Course of the Army of Occupation—A Commission Appointed to Hear Complaints—The Emperor Not to Enter the City—The Crown Prince to Conduct the Review—No Disturbances of Any Kind.

LONDON, March 2.—Paris dispatches state that several battalions of Germans entered the city at 7 o'clock yesterday morning, to prepare quarters. At 8½ o'clock the Palais d'Industrie was occupied. Some battalions soon afterward paraded in the Place de la Concorde. But a small number of the inhabitants were present, and no demonstrations were made.

There was soon a line of German troops along the Seine from the Pont du Jour to the Palais Bourbon, while on the right bank the French National Guards stopped the passage of all persons in uniform. Horse patrols circulated and occupied their quarters. No acts of depredation were committed.

The main body of occupation formed at Longchamps and in the Bois de Boulogne, where a review was held, and entered Paris at noon. The Emperor's staff are quartered at the Palace of the Elysée. Gen. KAMECKE commands the army of occupation.

A Prussian military commission has been established to receive the complaints of the inhabitants who have deserted the occupied quarters of the city. The public buildings have also been deserted and are closed. The Emperor declares he will not enter the city. The Crown Prince will therefore review the German Army.

The Emperor and Empress on a Tour of Inspection—Announcement of the Entry by Minister Washburne.

VERSAILLES, March 1.—The Emperor and Empress have just returned from Longchamps, where they inspected the Sixth and Eleventh Prussian and the First Bavarian Corps, 30,000 strong. The troops looked in excellent condition. The advanced guard entered Paris at 8 o'clock in the morning, without any disturbance.

WASHINGTON, March 2.—The following was received at the Department of State this morning:

PARIS, March 2, 1871—12:10 A. M.

Secretary Fish, Washington:

German entry into Paris peaceful and quiet. All quiet in the city.

(Signed) WASHBURNE.

RETURN OF PEACE.

Ratification of the Terms to be Exchanged Without Delay—The French Government to Return to Paris as Soon as Possible—Gens. Sheridan and Forsyth.

BORDEAUX, March 2.—An envoy, bearing the vote of the Assembly accepting the preliminary conditions of peace, will reach Paris at noon today. Ratifications will be exchanged without delay, so that the German forces may withdraw from the city this evening.

The employes of the Department of the Interior will return to Paris on Saturday, and it is believed the entire Government will be transferred to Paris again as speedily as the execution of the Peace Convention will permit.

Gens. SHERIDAN and FORSYTH, of the United States Army, have gone to Paris.

MISCELLANEOUS WAR NEWS.

Celebration of the Return of Peace at San Francisco—Ricciotti Garibaldi Claims the Prize for the First Prussian Flag Captured.

SAN FRANCISCO, March 2.—The celebration by the Germans in honor of the restoration of peace is to be on a grand scale. The day has not yet been fixed. The city and State officers have been invited to participate, but they have not yet accepted.

The prize of $500, offered by the Frenchmen in California for the first Prussian battle-flag captured in the war, has been claimed for RICCIOTTI GARIBALDI, who captured the flag of the Sixty-first Prussian Regiment, at Dijon, Jan. 23....The Irish societies have determined to make a united effort on St. Patrick's Day to raise funds for the relief of the suffering people of France.

GENERAL EUROPEAN NEWS.

Health of the King of Sweden—Opening of the German Parliament Again Postponed.

STOCKHOLM, March 2.—The Health of the King of Sweden is improving.

LONDON, March 2.—The *Opinion Nationale* says the meeting of the German Parliament has been postponed until the 20th of March.

WASHINGTON.

Rumors and Speculations About the New Congress—The Southern Pacific Railroad—No Hope for a Repeal of the Income Tax—Movements of the English Commissioners—The Senate and Revenue Bills—Statue of Roger Williams—Appropriation Bills, and Progress Thereon.

Special Dispatch to the New-York Times.

WASHINGTON, March 2.—There has been a breeze about the Capitol, today, concerning matters in the next Congress rather than in this. Numerous new and yet well-known faces have appeared on the scene, and the atmosphere has been thick with speculation and rumors touching upon the formation of the Committees of the next House, and particularly the Committee of Ways and Means. The interest centres in this Committee, and in its prospective chairman, most decidedly. Now the gossip goes to the effect that it was weeks ago decided by Speaker BLAINE that Gen. GARFIELD should be Chairman of that Committee. Today it is said that this arrangement has all been kicked over, and that Mr. BLAINE has been frightened out of his determination by the protectionists, who charge that GARFIELD's selection is in the interest of revenue reform. At all events there is something in the wind. Here, all of a sudden, are WHITE, NORDHOFF and GROSVENOR, three free-trade editors, in close consultation, as though each had a large sized flea in his ear. They hope yet to get GARFIELD, so it is said, but also comes down, coincidently Mr. SAM BOWLES, of the Springfield *Republican*, who takes a hand in, and to-night it is reported that Mr. DAWES is to have the Ways and Means Chairmanship, if he will take it. This report is also colored by the fact that the Southern members are said to have made a demand upon Speaker BLAINE to reconstitute the Committees on Claims and Appropriations more liberally, which means take WASHBURN and DAWES off, and put easy, pliable men in their places, so that the South may get its share of the people's money. Speaker BLAINE is not likely to lose his head in this direction, for he has nothing to lose, and everything to gain by resisting such demands. He never was in a position, and probably never will be again, where he had such complete opportunity to subserve the public interests only, to the exclusion of all personal considerations, and there is no doubt but that he will do his duty fearlessly. The success of the Administration depends largely upon the constitution of the Committees of the House, and such a Committee as that of Appropriations cannot be put in jeopardy by exchanging Mr. DAWES for any man less firm or less vigilant. The Ways and Means can be well filled with such a moderate protectionist as either Gen. GARFIELD or Hon. WM. A. WHEELER, present Chairman of Pacific Railroads, both of whom are able debaters, good parliamentarians, and men of unsullied integrity.

SOUTHERN PACIFIC RAILROAD.

The Conference Committee on the Southern Pacific Railroad bill, this morning, agreed on a report, the substance of which is as follows: The House bill is modified so as to authorize the construction of a branch from New-Orleans by way of Alexandria and Shreveport, to connect with the main line. This will require about 920,000 additional acres of land. The Southern Pacific Railroad of California, which by a charter heretofore granted, is authorized to build a line 700 miles long, from San Francisco to the thirty-fifth parallel, is now authorized to build to the thirty-second parallel, about 250 miles further, by the route surveyed to connect with the main line of the Texas Pacific, and its grant is extended accordingly. The report will be presented to-morrow, and its fate in the House, in view of these additions, is somewhat doubtful, as Mr. WHEELER, Chairman of the House Committee, is opposed to it in this shape.

INCOME TAX REPEAL.

Mr. HOOPER made a final effort in the House today to suspend the rules and pass the bill repealing the income tax, but failed worse than before, the vote standing yeas 91, nays 116, not only not two-thirds, but not even a majority. This, of course, is the end of the matter for this session. It will be tried again in the next Congress, but with what prospect, it is impossible to tell.

GEN. HOWARD VINDICATED.

The report of the Committee on Education and Labor, honorably acquitting Major Gen. HOWARD of all the charges brought against him under FERNANDO WOOD's resolution, was adopted in the House today by yeas 134, nays 52.

THE ENGLISH COMMISSIONERS.

The British members of the Joint High Commission and their attachés dined together tonight, at the head-quarters of the Commission, in the Philp mansion, on K-street. Their number was enlarged by the arrival of Sir STAFFORD NORTHCOTE. After dinner they attended a reception for the Diplomatic Corps given by Sir EDWARD THORNTON. On Saturday they will dine a number of invited guests, and on Thursday of next week they will dine with the President. The English members of the Commission were at the Capitol today, with Minister THORNTON and Gen. SCHENCK. They first visited the Senate, where they were received upon the floor, and were introduced to a number of Senators. They next visited the House of Representatives, where they occupied the front seat in the Diplomatic gallery. After witnessing the proceedings from the gallery for some time, Gen. SCHENCK escorted the Commissioners to the floor of the House, where he presented them to a number of leading members.

OREGON AND CALIFORNIA RAILROAD.

The Commissioners appointed to examine and report on the second, third and fourth twenty-mile sections of the road and telegraph line of the Oregon and California Railroad Company have made a statement that both the road and telegraph for those sections are of the first class and fully equipped. This makes eighty miles completed, the initial point being East Portland, Oregon. The President has ordered the issue of patents for the land granted to the Company by the law.

POWER OF THE SENATE OVER REVENUE BILLS.

Mr. SCOTT, in the Senate today, submitted the report of the Senate members of the Conference Committee on the income tax. The Senate is advised to hold to its right under the Constitution, to originate the resolution of repeal. The Committee takes the occasion of submitting its report to file a document giving the reasons which guided them. This opinion covers twenty-seven pages of legal cap paper, closely written, and reviews the precedents furnished by the practice of the British Parliament, the history of the adoption of the article of the Constitution whose meaning is in question, and an argument drawn from that history; the practice of Congress heretofore, and notes of commentators on the subject. The point involved is of more moment than may be thought at a first glance, and its correct settlement should be earnestly sought.

STATUES FOR THE CAPITOL.

Another new statue has come to the Capitol today, and will shortly be unboxed and set up in the old Hall of Representatives. It is a gift to the National Gallery by Rhode Island, which State has been the first to respond to the invitation of Congress for each State to place two statues in the Capitol. The first, placed in position a year ago, was a statue of Gen. GREENE, by H. K. BROWN, the best statue in the Capitol, and undoubtedly the best portrait-statue in this country. The statue now presented is of ROGER WILLIAMS, and is thoroughly ideal, there being no portrait, nor even so much as a description of ROGER WILLIAMS' personal appearance, in existence. It is not so much as known whether he was tall or short, corpulent or spare; and the unvailing will be accompanied with much interest from the desire to see the embodiment of the sculptor's conceptions.

VISITORS.

The city continues full of visitors, and the hotels are crowded to overflowing. Among the arrivals today at the Arlington are Gen. H. A. Barnum, of New-York, with Mrs. Barnum, a charming bride; W. S. Grosvenor, of St. Louis; Gen. Kilburn Knox, of New-York; C. S. Bunnell and W. W. Clark, of New-Haven; B. T. Morgan and M. L. Sykes, Jr., of New-York; Hon. Thos. Kinsella, of Brooklyn, and Hon. Alex. Mitchell, of Milwaukee: Hon. T. F. Randolph and Gen. Perrine, of New-Jersey; Police Commissioner Henry Smith; Commissioner of Charities, O. W. Brennan, and Mr. H. P. Farrington, of New-York.

RULERS OF THE DISTRICT.

The President today sent in a number of further appointments for the District of Columbia. They are marked by the same degree of excellence and fitness which characterized the selection of Governor. Gen. CHIPMAN, the new Secretary, won honorable fame in the war, and has since resided here in the successful practice of his profession. On the Board of Public Works are men of integrity, energy, nerve and taste. Mr. MULLETT fills the requirement that one member shall be a civil engineer admirably, and his energy and skill, combined with the enterprise of men like SHEPHERD and BROWN, will soon have a telling effect in the improvement of the city. One member of the Board of Health is a prominent colored man, Prof. JNO. M. LANGSTON, who is at the head of the Law Department of Howard University. The others are well-known physicians and private citizens. The high character of these appointments causes a feeling of regret that the President has not always felt equally untrameled in his selections.

APPROPRIATION BILLS IN DANGER.

There is great danger that one, if not two, of the principal Appropriation bills may be lost for want of time. But thirty-six hours remain for the entire consideration by the Senate of the Sundry Civil bill, which contains twenty-five millions, and today Mr. DAWES reported that the first Committee of Conference on the Legislative, Executive, and Judicial bill was unable to agree, and then proceeded to state the grounds of disagreement. These were the increased salaries for Judges of the United States Courts, the new State Department building, the proposed new park, the extension of the Capitol grounds, and the increased salaries of the Assistant Secretaries, Auditors, &c. Considerable discussion followed, particularly upon the necessity of a new building for the State Department, in which Gen. LOGAN indulged in his usual silly froth and foam about what he was pleased to term these outrageous expenditures. He seemed to be altogether oblivious of the part he played the other day in helping to log-roll through a million and a half for simply the beginning of various public buildings outside of Washington, and other schemes for Illinois and Missouri, to the extent of nearly a million more. In a few days Gen. LOGAN will be buried in the Senate, where his frothy declamation will be mainly of service in repelling the assaults of FRANK BLAIR. Subsequently a new Conference Committee was appointed—Messrs. DAWES, HOLMAN, and BURDETT. It is possible that some concession may be made on the subject of a new State Department, but the bill will fail, if the conference goes beyond that.

APPROPRIATION BILLS IN THE SENATE.

The Senate took up the Deficiency Appropriation bill today, and passed it about 3 o'clock. The Fortification bill was taken up and concurred in without any amendments. The River and Harbor bill was promptly taken up. This bill, in the Senate, is, by custom, referred to the Commerce Committee, and is the only appropriation bill which is not given to the charge of the Appropriation Committee. The consideration of the bill was continued till the hour of recess, and taken up again in the evening session, and has passed at 10 o'clock. Mr. COLE has called up the Sundry Civil bill, and hopes to make considerable progress with it, before the end of the sitting. The Senate has confined itself today pretty closely to the work of making appropriations, and the prospect is now that the last Appropriation bill will be enacted into law before the expiration of the session day after tomorrow.

STOPPAGE FOR AN OVERPAYMENT.

The New-Orleans, Opelousas and Great Western Railroad Company, at the close of the war, were indebted to the United States for railway material. By a general order of the Quartermaster-General, the disbursing officer of the War Department was authorized to deduct thirty-three and one-third per cent. from the credits of the Railway Company against the Quartermaster's Department for the transportation of troops and supplies of the United States. In a settlement made with the Company, the disbursing officer failed to make the deduction, and allowed the over credit upon the Company's indebtedness. Afterward, by a decree of the United States Circuit Court, the Marshal for the District of Louisiana sold the railroad with all its franchises. The purchaser paid to the United States the balance due from the Railroad Company for material, but the over credit was not considered in the settlement. The Railroad Company having wound up its affairs, and ceased its corporate existence, the Second Controller decides that the only party, excepting the disbursing officer, to whom in any event, the Government could look for indemnification is, the grantee of the United States Marshal; but that, as the terms of sale were in conformity with the decrees of the Court, the purchaser has a valid title as against the United States, and no trustee process, garnishment or attachment would lie for an indebtedness of the defunct Railroad Company to the United States. The stoppage was, therefore, properly made against the disbursing officer.

THE NEXT CONGRESS.

Caucuses of the Members Elect—Nomination of Officers of the House by Both Parties—The Old Incumbents Renominated by the Republicans.

WASHINGTON, March 2.—The Republican members elect to the ensuing Congress held a caucus, to-night, in the hall of the House of Representatives for the nomination of officers, Gov. BLAIR, of Michigan, in the chair, and Representatives AMBLER and MAYNARD acting as Secretaries. Speaker BLAINE, Clerk of the House MCPHERSON, and Doorkeeper BUXTON, were severally nominated by acclamation. Sergeant-at-Arms ORDWAY was nominated on the first ballot, the vote being for ORDWAY, 76; Gen. HERRON, 22, and Col. STOKES, member of the present Congress, 20. There were two ballots for Postmaster; W. S. KING, the present incumbent, was selected on the second, the vote being—KING, 67; H. SHERWOOD, of Michigan, 27; CYRIL HAWKINS, 12, and A. H. JONES, now a member from North Carolina, 11.

The Democrats and Conservatives held their caucus in the old hall of Representatives tonight. Hon. FERNANDO WOOD was chosen Chairman, and Representatives ADAMS, GETZ and SHOBER, Secretaries. Seventy-six members elect were present. There were twenty absent. Mr. KERR, on the part of the Committee heretofore appointed to inquire as to the credentials of certain members, made a report of the facts with reference to the members from Mississippi, and to the case of Mr. TIFT, of Georgia. On motion of Mr. KERR the subject was, after a considerable debate, recommitted to the Committee with instructions to take such action upon the organization of the next House as they may deem expedient. On motion of Mr. RANDALL, the case of the Tennessee delegation was referred to the same Committee with similar instructions.

Representatives MORGAN, of Ohio, and COX, of New-York, having been respectively placed in nomination for Speaker, Mr. RANDALL, on behalf of the Pennsylvania delegation, nominated GETZ, who, however, declined the nomination, expressing his thanks for the compliment. The caucus having balloted, Mr. MORGAN received the higher number of ballots, when the nomination was declared unanimous. The following-named gentlemen were then nominated by acclamation: for Clerk, JAMES G. BERRETT; Sergeant-at-Arms, NICHOLAS ISENBURY; Doorkeeper, OWEN THORNE; Postmaster, SEATON GALES; Chaplain, IGNATIUS T. COOPER.

On motion of Mr. RANDALL it was unanimously resolved that the Forty-second Congress ought to adjourn the first session at the earliest practicable time, and that those now present would continually vote to that end. The caucus then adjourned.

FORTY-FIRST CONGRESS.

THIRD SESSION.

SENATE....WASHINGTON, Thursday, March 2.

CREDENTIALS.

The credentials of Senators elect HENRY COOPER of Tennessee, and J. R. WEST of Louisiana, were presented, read and filed.

A REMONSTRANCE AND MEMORIALS.

Mr. HILL, of Georgia, presented a communication from the present and former members of the Legislature of Georgia, remonstrating against the character of the election of FOSTER BLODGETT as United States Senator from that State. It was ordered to be filed.

The Vice-President laid before the Senate the resolutions of the Common Council of Philadelphia in favor of a repeal of the income tax, and a memorial of WM. J. JESSUP, President of the Working Men's Assembly, New-York, praying for relief from the alleged combination of large operators and transportation companies to enhance the price of coal. Referred to the Committee on Education and Labor.

AN EASTERN QUESTION.

Mr. MORTON, of Indiana, offered a resolution calling on the President for any information communicated by the Legation at Constantinople, relating to the restrictions on the passage of the Straits of Dardanelles and the Bosphorus by ships of other nations. Adopted.

PACIFIC RAILROAD INVESTIGATION.

Upon conclusion of the morning orders, Mr. DAVIS, of Kentucky, moved to take up his resolution for an investigation into the condition of the Union Pacific Railroad. Negatived—yeas 13, nays 29.

FAILURE OF CONFERENCE COMMITTEES.

Mr. SCOTT, of Pennsylvania, from the Committee on Conference to which was referred the question at issue between the two Houses as to the right of the Senate to originate a measure repealing the income tax, made a report that the Committee had failed to agree; advising the Senate to adhere to its position, and stating that no further conference is necessary. The report was ordered to be printed.

Mr. SAWYER, of South Carolina, from the Committee of Conference on the Legislative, Executive and Judicial Appropriation bill, reported that the Committee of the two Houses were unable to agree, and asked to be discharged. It was so ordered.

NEW CONFERENCE COMMITTEES.

On motion of Mr. COLE, the Senate insisted on its amendments to the bill, and asked for the appointment of a new committee on the part of the House.

Messrs. Sawyer of South Carolina, Morrill of Vermont, and Thurman of Ohio, were appointed as the new Committee of the Senate.

The Senate insisted on its amendments to the Army and Naval Appropriation bills, and appointed the following Committees of Conference: On the Army bill—Messrs. Cole of California, Thayer of Nebraska, and Blair of Missouri. On the Naval bill—Messrs. Sprague of Rhode Island, Cragin of New-Hampshire, and Stockton of New-Jersey.

Mr. JOHNSON, of Virginia, was appointed on the Conference Committee on the Legislative Appropriation bill, vice THURMAN, excused.

DEFICIENCY APPROPRIATION BILL.

The Deficiency Appropriation bill was then considered as in Committee of the Whole, and the various amendments reported from the Committee on Appropriations, reducing the items were adopted, including an amendment limiting the total cost of the new Post-office and sub-Treasury building in Boston to $1,500,000; and, also, an amendment limiting the advertisement of mail contract-lettings to one newspaper in each State in which contracts are to be let.

Mr. COLE, of California, reported a new amendment making appropriations to supply deficiences in the items of compensation of clerks and messengers in the offices of the Assistant Treasurer in Baltimore and New-Orleans. Agreed to.

Mr. HOWE, of Wisconsin, moved an appropriation to provide for collecting, translating and publishing all the documents relating to the early history of the West, commencing with the discovery of the Great Lakes in 1669, and including the exploration of the Rocky Mountains in 1872. Agreed to.

Mr. CASSERLY, of California, commenting upon the large deficits in the bill for the Post-office Department, to which last year twenty-four million dollars were appropriated, receiving now an additional five millions, intimated that the regular Department expenditures were purposely underestimated last session, for political effect at elections. He understood the aggregate deficit under the bill amounted to nineteen millions.

Mr. COLE, of California, said it was impossible to state exactly the total amount, but that as reported from the Senate Committee, the estimate did not exceed ten millions.

Mr. EDMUNDS, of Vermont, said these deficiencies, though much larger under Democratic Administrations, were not then perceptible, inasmuch as under the loose practice of retaining balances in the Treasury, money intended for the use of one Department was diverted to the support of another without any settlement of accounts. A Republican Administration had reformed this gross abuse by substituting for it the present system of deficiency bills, whereby the actual expenditures of the Government were readily seen.

The bill then passed.

MORE APPROPRIATION BILLS.

The Fortification Appropriation bill was taken up and passed without amendment.

The River and Harbor Appropriation bill was then taken up. Pending its consideration the Senate went into Executive Session, and at 5 o'clock took a recess until the evening.

EVENING SESSION.

BILLS PASSED.

Bills were called up and passed as follows:

By Mr. WILSON, of Massachusetts—To authorize the promulgation of regulations for the government of the army.

By Mr. ANTHONY, of Rhode Island—For the recovery of damages for the loss of the sloop-of-war *Oneida.*

By Mr. CASSERLY, of California—To create ports of delivery at Eureka and Wilmington, in California.

By Mr. FOWLER, of Tennessee—Appropriating $18,500 for the damages to the building and grounds of the East Tennessee University, caused by Federal troops during the war.

SUNDRY CIVIL SERVICE APPROPRIATIONS.

Mr. COLE, of California, from the Committee on Appropriations, reported, with amendments, the Sundry Civil Appropriation bill.

DISAGREEMENT OF A CONFERENCE COMMITTEE.

Mr. SAWYER, of South Carolina, from the Conference Committee on the Legislative, Executive and Judicial Appropriation bill, reported that the Committee of the two Houses had failed to agree, and, on his motion, a new Committee was appointed on the part of the Senate. The new Committee are Messrs. EDMUNDS, HARLAN and DAVIS.

Mr. SAWYER stated that the subjects of disagreement were the increase of the salaries of the Judges of the District and Circuit Courts, the District Supreme Court and the Court of Claims, the establishment of the new Washington Park, involving the purchase of two squares of the Capital, and the increase of salaries of the heads of Bureaus, all of which were Senate amendments.

Mr. SHERMAN was in favor of the Senate receding from all these amendments, but would await the result of the appointment of a new committee.

RIVER AND HARBOR APPROPRIATIONS.

The River and Harbor Appropriation bill was then proceeded with as in Committee of the Whole.

The Committee on Commerce reported amendments making the following reductions, which were agreed to:

In the improvement of St. Mary's Falls Canal and St. Mary's River, Michigan, from $250,000 to $200,000.

For the improvement of Desmoines Rapids, from $275,000 to $200,000.

For the Falls of the Ohio River and the Louisville Canal, from $250,000 to $200,000.

For the East River, New-York, including Hell Gate, from $250,000 to $200,000.

The Committee also reported an amendment that the unexpended balance of appropriations of the River and Harbor Appropriation act of July 11, 1870, be reappropriated for the purposes therein specified. Adopted—yeas 29, nays 27.

The fourth section of the bill, directing the Secretary of War to prevent or remove obstructions in the navigable waters of the United States at the expense of the parties making such obstructions, was stricken out.

Mr. CHANDLER, of Michigan, offered an amendment providing for surveys of the Horse-shoe Shoals, in Delaware River, below Philadelphia, and of the harbor of Norwalk, Conn. Agreed to.

Mr. BLAIR, of Missouri, moved appropriations for improvements, as follows; harbor of Alton, Ill., $15,000; mouth of the Missouri River, $25,000; and for a general survey of the Mississippi River, from Alton, Ill., to the mouth of the Merrimac, including the harbor of St. Louis, $25,000. Adopted.

On motion of Mr. STOCKTON, $20,000 was appropriated for improving the Illinois River below Bordentown.

Mr. PATERSON moved an appropriation of $18,000 for the Fifteen-Mile Falls of the Connecticut River. Agreed to.

The bill was then passed.

DUTY ON COAL.

The House joint resolution repealing the duty on coal was referred to the Committee on Finance.

SUNDRY CIVIL EXPENSES.

The Sundry Civil Expenses bill was taken up. The bill was variously amended by the addition and reduction of items of appropriation; and without perfecting the bill, the Senate, at 12½, adjourned.

HOUSE OF REPRESENTATIVES.

EXPENSES OF DEFENDING A SEAT.

Mr. INGERSOLL, of Illinois, offered a resolution to pay to Mr. CONNOR, Representative from Texas, $2,000 for the expenses in defending the right to his seat. Adopted.

At a subsequent stage of the proceedings, Mr. PAINE, of Wisconsin, Chairman of the Committee of Elections, rising to a personal explanation, referred to the resolution for the payment of $2,000 to Mr. CONNOR for expenses in defending his right to a seat, and said that the subcommittee, consisting of Mr. POTTER, Mr. BARRY and himself, had agreed to report such a resolution, but at the same time he had proposed to call the attention of the House to the fact that it was introducing a new precedent, at least new since his connection with the House, although he found that in 1861 an allowance had been made to several sitting members for the expenses incurred by them in defending the right to their seats. Neither he nor any of the other two members of the subcommittee was in his seat this morning when the resolution was offered.

Mr. INGERSOLL explained how he came to offer the resolution. He had known nothing of the case until Mr. CONNOR politely requested him, this morning, to offer the resolution, as neither of the three members of the subcommittee was present, and as he was afraid, on account of the approaching close of the session, that there might not be another opportunity presented. He was not aware that there was any new principle involved, or he would not have presented it. He hoped that the question might be reopened, and considered fully and fairly by the House.

On motion of Mr. PAINE, the resolution adopted in the morning was rescinded, and the resolution came again before the House for action.

Messrs. POTTER, of New-York, and BARRY, of Mississippi, members of the subcommittee, stated the facts, which, in their opinion, entitled Mr. CONNOR to be allowed for his expenses.

Mr. DAWES, of Massachusetts, stated the circumstances under which he, as Chairman of the Committee on Elections in the Thirty-sixth Congress, had reported the resolution which was referred to as the precedent in this case. Although those circumstances justified that resolution, he regretted now that he had reported it, or that the House had adopted it, as the precedent was one which ought not to be followed. The whole system of contested elections was a great evil, and he questioned the propriety of paying either the contestant or the sitting member.

Mr. WASHBURN, of Wisconsin, suggested, as a jocular commentary on the resolution, that a million of dollars be appropriated to pay the expenses of all the sitting members who had incurred expenses in retaining their seats.

Mr. HALE, of Maine, a member of the Election Committee, protested against the resolution, and declared that not a single dollar should be paid to a member for defending his right.

Mr. CONNOR explained the circumstances under which he claimed that his case was a peculiar one, and that he should be allowed the expenses incurred by him in defending his right to a seat.

The question was then taken, and the resolution was rejected.

BILLS PASSED.

Mr. WASHBURN, of Wisconsin, moved to suspend the rules and pass the bill to authorize the restoration of JAMES BELGER to the rank of Major and Quartermaster in the army. Agreed to.

Mr. BINGHAM, of Ohio, from the Judiciary Committee, reported a bill to divide the State of Illinois into three Judicial Districts, and it was passed under a suspension of the rules.

Mr. STRICKLAND, of Michigan, moved to suspend the rules and pass the Senate bill to extend the time for the reversions to the United States of the lands granted by Congress to the State of Michigan for a railroad from Pere Marquette to Flint. Agreed to—86 to 41.

MANAGEMENT OF THE SOLDIERS' ASYLUM.

Mr. NEGLEY, from the Committee on Military Affairs, made a report in the matter of the charges as to the management of the National Asylum for disabled volunteer soldiers, that the charges made were without foundation. Ordered to be printed and recommitted.

INCOME TAX REPEAL.

Mr. HOOPER, of Massachusetts, moved to suspend the rules and pass a bill repealing the income tax. Negatived—yeas 91, nays 116. The result was received with laughter.

Mr. HOOPER remarked that as there was evidently a majority against the repeal of the income tax, he would not move to go into Committee of the Whole to take up the bill for its repeal, which is on the calendar of that Committee.

REMOVAL OF DISABILITIES.

On motion of Mr. BECK, of Kentucky, a Senate bill to remove political disabilities from several citizens of Kentucky was passed.

Mr. KELSEY, of New-York, noticing that it applied to several members of the Breckinridge family, asked Mr. BECK whether they had petitioned for the removal of their political disabilities.

Mr. BECK pledged his word that every person named in the bill had done so.

Mr. BECK also moved to suspend the rules and pass another Senate bill removing political disabilities from 3,264 persons in various States. Without reading the bill, it was negatived by 103 to 70, less than two-thirds in the affirmative.

Mr. TILLMAN, of Tennessee, moved to suspend the rules and pass a bill to remove political disabilities from several persons in his district, in Tennessee. Agreed to.

DISAGREEMENT ON APPROPRIATIONS.

Mr. DAWES, from the Conference Committee on the Legislative Appropriation bill, reported that the Committee had not been able to agree. He stated the difficulties which the Committee had encountered. The Senate had adopted 103 amendments to the bill. Most of them there was no difficulty in coming to an agreement upon. The amendments which the Committee had been unable to agree upon were few in number, but important in character. The first of them was as to the Judges' salaries. In addition to the increase of salaries of the Judges of the Supreme Court to which the House had agreed, the Senate proposed to raise the salaries of all the Judges of the United States Courts and of the Supreme Court of the District of Columbia and of the Court of Claims. The next was a proposition to erect a State Department which would ultimately cost four or five million dollars on the site now occupied by the War and Navy Departments. He thought that the Conference Committee might have agreed on that subject, because the State Department was now in a lamentable condition, with its records and archives exposed to fire, if the Committee had not in its deliberations punctured the whole thing by requiring the building to be of granite and to correspond with the Treasury Department. That provision seemed to have a wonderful effect in cooling the ardor that existed about it. But that was not all. Along with it was a proposition to make a splendid park, taking in all the public grounds from the Capitol to the White House, and defraying the expenses by the sale of other public grounds in other parts of the city. Another proposition was to extend the Capitol grounds north and south, at a cost estimated at $500,000, but which would not fall short of $1,000,000. The next proposition was to raise the salaries of all the Assistant Secretaries, the Second Controller, the Register, all the Auditors, the Commissioner of Customs, the Supervising Architect of the Treasury Department, all the Assistant Postmaster-Generals, and the Commissioners of the General Land Office, of Pensions, of Indian Affairs, and of Agriculture to $4,000. The House Conferees regarded themselves as instructed by the common sentiment of the House to oppose this elevation of salaries. For himself he was unwilling to enter upon the plan of enlarging the Capitol grounds at this time. He was unwilling to go further in raising judicial salaries than the House had gone, Raising the salaries of the Judges of the Supreme Court to $8,000). He was willing, under all the necessities of the Government, to agree to the commencement of our wing of the State Department to correspond with the Treasury Department, but he was not willing to have any fancy building erected on one side of the President's house and that magnificent pile of granite (the Treasury building) on the other. As to the increase of the salaries of officials, while he was willing to increase the salaries of some of these officials, he was not willing to increase the salaries of all of them.

NEW CONFERENCE COMMITTEES.

The Conference report was adopted and a new Conference Committee ordered. The Speaker appointed Messrs. DAWES of Massachusetts, HOLMAN of Indiana, and CULLOM of Illinois, as the new Conference Committee on the Legislative bill; Messrs. WASHBURNE of Wisconsin, STEVENS of New-Hampshire, and HALE of Maine, as the Conference Committee on the Naval Appropriation bill, and Messrs. DICKEY, BECK, and LOGAN, as the Conference Committee on the Army Appropriation bill.

The Senate amendments to the Army and Navy Appropriation bills were non-concurred in and a Committee of Conference ordered.

The House then, at 4:20 o'clock, P. M., adjourned.

JAPANESE EMBASSY.

The Members Presented to the President—Congratulatory Speeches—Friendly Relations of the Two Nations.

WASHINGTON, March 2.—The Japanese Embassy, which arrived here to-day, were presented to the President to-night, at 8 o'clock, in the Blue Parlour of the White House, by Secretary FISH. There were present, besides the President and Secretary FISH, Mrs. GRANT, Miss NELLIE GRANT, Mrs. FISH, HAMILTON FISH, Jr., BANCROFT DAVIS and Mrs. DAVIS, and others. The embassy, individually were introduced to Secretary FISH by Mr. BROOKS, the Japanese Consul at San Francisco, and by the Secretary to the President. They were subsequently introduced to the assembled company, when the introduction to the President had taken place, Prince MITS FUSIMI said:

MR. PRESIDENT: This audience has been sought that I might personally express to you my admiration of and interest in the many wonderful works of American enterprise, and I assure you that these expressions are not empty words but the hearty sentiments of our people. Intercourse between our respective countries has been regularly established through a monthly line of American steam-ships of surpassing excellence, whose trips, in connection with the great Pacific Railway, affords us a rapid and agreeable route to Europe, with every modern luxury of speed and convenience across your continent. Our travelers and students, like myself, on their way abroad will hereafter become better acquainted with your country and people. We shall constantly encourage intercourse and aim to annually increase more intimate and important relations. We sincerely hope for your kind co-operation and assistance, and shall welcome any augmentation of present mail and traveling facilities, to more closely unite our interests. The Government of Japan is well aware that education is the basis of all progress, and threfore sends her young men to receive a scientific education in America and Europe, hoping thereby to fitly prepare them to take a wise and discriminating part hereafter in the affairs of our own Government. With this view my brother, QUACHE NOMIA, was last year sent to this country under the traveling name of Adzumah Takahiss, and I am now on my way to Prussia for a like purpose. In leaving my brother in America I feel confident of a kind treatment and certain of your friendly assistance should our Chargé d'Affaires, INGOI AUNONI MARI, request it. Our Government has commissioned a diplomatic resident to this country to assure you that it is earnestly seeking for permanent progress in all that is great and good, as rapidly as it can acquire these cherished ends, and it desires, particularly, to cement more closely the already friendly relations and interests existing between our respective peoples.

The President replied:

PRINCE: It gives me much pleasure to receive you in this friendly and unofficial way, and to learn from your lips the amicable feelings of the people of Japan toward the United States. The people of this country reciprocate your wish that the present means of intercourse between the two nations, great and comfortable as you describe them to be, may be increased. The United States have seen with pride the young men of Japan, coming here to receive scientific educations. I shall take great pleasure in contributing to make their residence in this country agreeable and profitable to them. Sharing with you the opinion that education is the basis of progress, and the hope and belief that by acquiring it in the United States they will help to cement and extend the friendly relations which now happily exist between the two countries."

The Japanese Charge d'Affaires Presents His Credentials—Address to the Secretary of State, and Mr. Fish's Response.

WASHINGTON, March 2.—The Chargé d'Affaires of Japan, Mr. MORI, presented his credentials to the Secretary of State at about noon today. The following speeches were delivered on the occasion:

MR. SECRETARY: His Imperial Majesty, the Tenno of Japan, desiring to bring his people into more intimate connection with those of the United States of America, and thereby cement and increase a warmer friendship and more active intercourse, has appointed me as his Chargé d'Affaires to reside permanently in this City. In accordance with His Majesty's command I hand you a letter accrediting me as his first diplomatic resident to the United States of America, and in requesting permission to exercise my duties in this country, I assure you of my desire, while obeying my Sovereign, to promote at all times, as far as in my power, the warmest friendship between our respective Governments and peoples. Kindly permit me to look for your kind assistance in all our mutual affairs, and to assure you that your advice will ever be esteemed one of the greatest favors you can bestow.

The Secretary of State replied:

MR. MORI: The Government of the United States shares with His Imperial Majesty, the Tenno of Japan, the desire that the people of the two countries should be brought into a more intimate connection. It has learned with great satisfaction of your appointment as Chargé d'Affaires to reside permanently in Washington. In receiving you in that capacity, I take pleasure in assuring you that your friendly wishes will meet with a cordial response from the President and from the Government of the United States. I also beg to assure you that if I can at any time render you assistance in the discharge of your duties in relation to this Government, I shall esteem it a privilege to be permitted to do so.

Meteorological Record.

The following is the Signal Service report of the state of the weather and wind last night, Thursday, March 2, at 11:47 o'clock:

Place of Observation.	Height of Barometer.	Thermometer, Degrees.	Direction of the Wind.	Force of the Wind.	State of the Weather.
Augusta, Ga.	30.17	63	S. E.	Gentle.	Fair.
Baltimore, Md.	30.07	51	S. E.	[illegible]	Clear.
Boston, Mass.	30.00	40	S. W.	Gentle.	Fair.
Buffalo, N. Y.	29.62	54	S. W.	Brisk.	Cloudy.
Charleston, S. C.	30.17	61	S. E.	Gentle.	Fair.
Cheyenne, W. T.	29.84	19	S. W.	Gentle.	Clear.
Chicago, Ill.	29.81	32	N.	Brisk.	Cloudy.
Cincinnati, O.	29.72	62	S.	Brisk.	H. Rain.
Cleveland	29.63	61	S.	Brisk.	Cloudy.
Corinne	29.73	31	S. E.	Gentle.	Fair.
Detroit	29.53	53	S.	Brisk.	H. Rain.
Duluth, Minn.	29.95	27	S. W.	Brisk.	Cloudy.
Indianapolis	29.62	52	S. W.	Brisk.	H. Rain.
Key West	30.12	74	S. E.	Gentle.	Fair.
Knoxville, Tenn	29.93	60	W.	Gentle.	Rain.
Lake City, Fla.	30.09	68	S.	....	Cloudy.
Memphis	29.77	61	W.	Brisk.	L. Rain.
Milwaukee	29.88	27	S. W.	Gentle.	Cloudy.
Mobile	30.00	65	S. W.	Brisk.	Cloudy.
Nashville	29.81	63	S.	Brisk.	H. Rain.
New-Orleans	29.99	72	S. W.	Brisk.	Cloudy.
New-York	29.96	48	..	Calm.	Clear.
Omaha	30.10	31	N.	Gentle.	Clear.
Oswego	29.87	50	S. W.	Brisk.	Cloudy.
Philadelphia	30.01	56	W.	....	Clear.
Pittsburg	29.82	68	S.	Gentle.	Cloudy.
Portland, Me.	30.01	35	S. W.	Gentle.	Cloudy.
Rochester, N. Y.	29.69	51	S.	Gentle.	Clear.
San Francisco	30.38	55	W.	Brisk.	Clear.
Savannah	30.14	64	..	Calm.	Fair.
St. Louis, Mo.	29.88	37	W.	Brisk.	Cloudy.
St. Paul, Minn.	30.02	24	N. W.	Gentle.	Clear.
Toledo, O.	29.59	55	S.	Brisk.	H. Rain.
Washington	29.96	54	S.	Brisk.	Fair.
Wilmingt'n N. C.	30.20	62	S. E.	Gentle.	Cloudy.
Norfolk	31.14	58	S.	Brisk.	Cloudy.
New-London	30.01	35	S.	Gentle.	Fair.
Mt. Washingt'n	28.80	25	S.	Gale.	Cloudy.

Barometer corrected for temperature and elevation.

Arrival of Sir Stafford Northcote.

The Cunard mail steamer *Russia*, Capt. COOK, from Liverpool the 18th and Queenstown the 19th of February, arrived at this port yesterday morning. Among the passengers by the *Russia* were Sir STAFFORD NORTHCOTE, M. P., a member of the Joint High Commission; Mrs. STAFFORD NORTHCOTE, and Mrs. NORTHCOTE'S brother.

EUROPEAN CORRESPONDENCE

Interesting Summary of Events in England.

Britain's Attitude Toward France.

Momentous Reforms in the Army System.

Proceedings in Parliament—Condition of the Navy—The Approaching Royal Marriage—Small-Pox and the Methods of Prevention—The Case of Mr. Voysey—Sala's Suit.

The Cunard steam-ship *Russia*, which left Liverpool Feb. 18, and Queenstown Feb. 19, reached this port at a late hour Wednesday night. The dates are later by one day than those of the *Cimbria's* mail.

ENGLISH AFFAIRS.

Sentiment Respecting the Commission—Recognition of France's Government—The Nation's Attitude—Impression of the Blue Book—The Black Sea Question—Army Reorganization—The Royal Marriage—Effects of Small-pox—Sala's Suit.

From Our Own Correspondent.

LONDON, Saturday, Feb. 18, 1871.

The favorable impression caused by the announcement of the American Commission has been deepened rather than diminished by reflection. We are all naturally anxious to see the *Alabama* question honorably settled, but above all we are anxious to have it settled in our own mind. If we could only feel assured as to our duty in the matter, whether to yield or to resist, we should be quite ready for the worst in either sense. It has now been authoritatively explained both by Lord GRANVILLE and Mr. GLADSTONE that the Commissioners will not be authorized to commit their respective Governments to any agreement; that their task is simply to inquire, consult and recommend, and that it will then remain for the two Governments to consider how far their report or reports should be acted upon. As regards ourselves, any Ministry which may happen to be in office on the close of the investigation will, of course, be perfectly free to repudiate the advice alike of the English and American Commissioners; but practically, I feel confident that the verdict of our representatives, whatever it may be, will be adopted by this country—that is, of course, if it is substantially unanimous. The substitution of Sir STAFFORD NORTHCOTE for Sir JOHN ROSE will undoubtedly add to the weight of the Commission on this side. Sir JOHN is highly respected and esteemed, but he is not known to the whole country as the Ex-Minister for India is; and the presence of Sir STAFFORD by the side of Lord DE GREY will also serve to maintain the political equilibrium of the Commission, and secure for its report the favorable consideration of the Conservatives. Sir STAFFORD is a very able and enlightened man—by no means bigoted either in domestic or foreign politics. He was once private secretary to Mr. GLADSTONE, and it is a mere accident that he sits on one side of the House and his former chief on the other. He was in the Cabinet both with Lord DERBY and Mr. DISRAELI, his last office being that of Secretary for India.

RECOGNITION OF FRANCE'S GOVERNMENT.

Our Government has agreed, as the best thing, indeed almost the only thing, they can do for France, to recognize the new Government about to be formed in that country with all possible haste, as soon as it is legally constituted. The Blue Book, which has just been published, shows how persistently and desperately the French clung to the hope that somehow or other we should come to their rescue. Their disappointment at our refusal to interfere was very bitter, and we may expect to feel the effects of the resentment thus produced for a long time to come. Count BISMARCK is bound to do justice to the rigid impartiality of our Government, but we shall certainly be very foolish if we expect a fair, still less a generous appreciation of our policy from either side. Most assuredly we shall not get it. Our kind words and ready charity have only made the French more furious against us. They are quite satisfied that this is only a cheap way of purchasing their aid in the Russian difficulty. On the other hand, the Germans flatter themselves that they are quite shrewd enough to detect the reason of our neutrality in our impotence. Yet we have no cause to repent a line of policy, the steadiness and consistency of which have done a good deal to revive the drooping credit of the Foreign Office. Whatever may be said against a non-intervention policy, it requires, at least, a considerable degree of moral courage to sustain it, and as regards this courage, the Government have been superior to the bulk of the people. If we had drifted into the war, it would have been only through a kind of cowardice—through a terror of being thought afraid. And at one moment many of us were in a very dangerous mood of this kind. Happily the Government was steadfast, and the fit passed off. The debate of last night brought out very clearly both the difficulties with which the Government have had to contend and the peculiar perils which beset our action in regard to foreign affairs. In Lord PALMERSTON's account of his visits to France in 1814 and 1815, just published, there is a good story of the Emperor of Russia, who was so much struck with "the active swinging step" of the British troops that he gave orders to his own army immediately to adopt the same step. The Russians, however, were so confused and puzzled between the two steps, the old one to which they had been accustomed, and the new one they had not had time to learn, that they could not march at all. The whole thing was a failure. Now that is very much the position of this country in regard to foreign affairs. We have resolved to give up the old intervention policy, and have to a great extent done so, but the nation has not yet got into the way of non-intervention. We are in a transition state, but I suppose by and by we shall settle down into something like a consistent and intelligible policy. Mr. AUBERON HERBERT who started the debate, a perfervid Radical

The New-York Times.

VOL. XXI......NO. 6257. NEW-YORK, TUESDAY, OCTOBER 10, 1871. PRICE FOUR CENTS.

A CITY IN RUINS.

The Terrible Devastation of Chicago.

Three Square Miles in the Heart of the City Burned.

Twelve Thousand Buildings Destroyed---Loss $50,000,000.

Every Public Building, Hotel, Bank and Newspaper Swept.

Appeals to Other Cities and a Noble Response.

Frightful Details of the Disaster from Our Own Reporters.

Special Dispatch to the New-York Times.

ENGLEWOOD, (seven miles south of Chicago,) 5 P. M. MONDAY EVENING.

It is impossible to give in any approach to detail the devastation of Chicago. The fire of Sunday, previously reported, began in the lumber and coal tract, along the west bank of the river, laying in waste several squares, as previously reported, but the total of preliminary destruction among the cheap tenement structures and frame planing-mills of Canal and Clinton streets is lost and inconsiderable in the frightful sequel. The fire, early this morning, crossed the river into the large lumber and coal yards of the South Branch in the South Division, and the work of destruction of the city began in earnest. A violent south-west prairie wind prevailed and filled the air with fiery messengers of destruction before which the cheaper frame tenements of Market, Wells and Franklin streets melted away like wax. The most important city works first to be attacked were the extensive premises of the Chicago Gas Company, on the corner of Market and Adams, and opposite these on Adams-street the large City Armory and Police building, just undergoing repairs. The flames leaped like a prairie fire over the adjacent squares of cheap frame buildings on Wells and Lasalle streets and along the river, and its work, to be calculated only by millions, commenced in earnest after crossing Lasalle-street, where improvements of the best class existed. An area of desolation, of crumbling ruins, of ruined merchandise, the commercial and industrial wealth of Chicago, now extends throughout an extent, to give a sketch of the losses in which would be to reproduce the Business Directory of the city. Throughout the entire day the appalling visitation maintained its unstayed course. At present writing, among the unutterable confusion that reigns, individual loss and suffering is lost in a sea of misery that has overwhelmned more than one-half the population of the city either in their homes or their business.

Writing this at 5 P. M., from Englewood, seven miles south of the city, the junction of the Michigan Southern and Rock Island Railroads, the awful work of destruction still goes on with relentless fury. From Harrison-street, in the south, to Division-street, in the north, and from the river to the lake, an area of four miles long by one mile wide, the flames have swept everything before them. It is estimated that at least 100,000 people are homeless and in a suffering condition. The streets in the district still unburned are lined for miles with such household goods as have been saved from destruction. Most generous offers of assistance in money, food, or anything wanted, are coming in from almost every city and from throughout the country by telegraph. The Mayor has responded to several offers asking that cooked food be provided as soon as possible. Firemen are on their way here from Cincinnati, St. Louis and other cities. The water-works are entirely destroyed. Buildings are now being blown up on the line of the fire to attempt to arrest its progress.

It is now believed that the spread of the fire southward has been stayed at Harrison-street, but on the north side there is no diminution of its fury, and the entire division of the city is evidently doomed to utter destruction. There are grave fears that the flames may spread to the west side of the north branch of the river, and the inhabitants of the streets nearest the river are already moving to places, it is supposed, of greater safety. The Western Union Telegraph Company have now six wires working, east and south, running into a temporary office at the corner of State and Sixteenth streets. The North-western Railroad Company are running trains on both its branches, which are crowded with fleeing citizens. It is now positively asserted by some that the water-works are still intact, but the water has been shut off from the South and West Divisions on account of the quantity being used on the north side. A reliable gentleman just arrived from the North Division brings the joyful intelligence that the water-works are uninjured. God grant that it may prove true.

It is impossible now to give even an approximately correct statement of the losses, but a faint idea may be formed when it is stated that every bank in the city, except the small Savings institutions, one on Twenty-second-street, in South Division, and one on Randolph-street, in West Division, are destroyed. All wholesale stores, retail establishments, Post-office, the Court-house, Chamber of Commerce, every hotel in South Division, except Michigan-avenue Hotel, which, standing on the extreme southern limit, escaped, though it is badly scorched; every newspaper office, (the *Tribune*, which was supposed to be fire-proof, having finally succumbed,) every theatre, the six largest elevators, the immense depots of the Michigan Southern and of the Illinois Central Railroad, (both the passenger and freight depots of the latter,) more than a score of churches, and much of the shipping in the river all are destroyed.

Men who were millionaires yesterday morning are nearly penniless today; but more terrible than all is the awful certainty that many human beings have perished in the flames—how many no one can tell. Perhaps no one will ever be able to tell, but it is known that some have perished, and there is only a heart-sickening fear that the victims of the fiery monster may be counted by scores.

Hundreds of horses and cows have been burned in stables, and on the north side numbers of animals, though released from confinement, were so bewildered and confused by the sea of fire which surrounded them that they rushed wildly to and fro, uttering cries of fright and pain until scorched and killed.

Any attempt at a description of the scenes of this appalling calamity would be idle. The simple facts that the once great City of Chicago is destroyed, that hundreds of millions of active capital here have vanished, and that nearly one-third of Chicago's inhabitants are houseless dependents, are enough. Any attempt to embellish would be a mockery. As this awful day draws to a close, thousands of anxious eyes watch the clouds of smoke which still roll over the burnt district, with evident dread that a sudden change of wind may turn the flames upon that portion of the city yet spared.

There seems, however, little cause for apprehensions, and reinforcements of firemen from other cities are constantly arriving. Col. Z. G. WILSON, Superintendent of the Telegraph, is in receipt of dispatches from leading cities, announcing that aid is being provided for the sufferers. Col. CLOWRY, of St. Louis, telegraphs, that $70,000 have been subscribed by the merchants there. Cincinnati promises $200,000, and Cleveland is proportionately generous. All this and a great deal more will be needed to relieve the immediate pressing wants. Everything is being done by Gen. STAGER and his assistants to keep up communications for the citizens and Press with the world outside. Col. GEO. T. WILLIAMS, Superintendent at Cincinnati, reported promptly for duty this morning. About three-fourths of the United States mail was saved, and taken possession of by Col. WOOD, of the Post-office service.

The Chamber of Commerce occupied the south-east corner of Lasalle and Washington streets, and, with the building attached in the rear, had a frontage of 180 on Lasalle and 100 on Washington-street, owned by Chamber of Commerce Association, and leased to Board of Trade for ninety-nine years. Offices of leading produce-houses on first floor and basement. Exchange Hall above cost, about six years ago, $275,000. North-western National Bank, of STURGES BROTHERS, occupied the corner office. Insurance offices of GEO. C. CLARKE & CO., and Life Association in basement.

The Union National Bank building, a fine marble structure, opposite the Chamber of Commerce, was owned by W. F. COOLBAUGH and others, occupied by the Union Bank and the Merchants' National Bank, Yonkers Insurance and other insurance and real estate offices above, 100 by 100; cost of building, $150,000 on leasehold property.

Adjoining and south of the Union building, on Lasalle-street, was the Mercantile building, a fine marble structure; also, the very costly Oriental building and Dr. BASSETT's building. In the rear of these JAMES WADSWORTH was just completing a large area office building. The Merchants' Insurance Building, opposite the Union Building, owned and occupied by Merchants' Insurance Company on leased ground, cost $175,000 in 1868. The general office of the Western Telegraph Company and Gen. SHERIDAN's Head-quarters, Bank of SMITH BROS.

The west side of Lasalle-street, north from the Merchants' building to Randolph-street, was a line of costly structures, among them the Phœnix building of Messrs. BAIRD & BRADLEY, THOMAS HAYNES' marble building, the State Savings Institution and Savings Bank, and H. H. MAGEE's Milwaukee brick building occupied by the Home Insurance Company, and filled with offices above. These eight or nine buildings cost from $60,000 to $150,000 each.

The north side of Randolph-street was a continuous front of costly marble buildings from Lasalle to Clark-street. On the corner of the latter, the Sherman House, 180 by 160 feet, five stories high, owned by the heirs of the late F. C. SHERMAN, built in 1860 and extended in 1868, was occupied by Messrs. GEO. W. & D. A. GAGE and JOHN A. RICE, under a lease of five years from 1870, at $55,000 per year. The rentals of the building were nearly $150,000. Total loss in structure and contents, $550,000.

Adjoining the Chamber of Commerce on the east were NIXON's great building and W. S. JOHNSON's building, the two making a continuous structure 250 feet on Washington, and 180 on Clark, on leased ground, cost $250,000, occupied in offices above, and office of Pacific and Atlantic Telegraph Company in corner office on Ex-change place.

The block opposite the Court-house, on Clark-street, from Washington to Randolph, was occupied by Larmon Block, a five-story marble building, the Fifth National Bank, retail hat and drug-stores, and Bryant & Stratton's Business College above. Next north was Hooley's Theatre, formerly Bryan Hall, recently rebuilt, cost, $100,000. The remaining buildings northward were old and of light value, except the costly block of A. H. MILLER, jeweler, on the corner of Randolph, built six years ago, five stories high, cost $90,000; occupied as a first-class jewelry establishment. Riverside Improve-ment Company on third floor, and BAKER's engraving establishment. The Washington-street front of this square was brick and marble buildings, the finest being PARKER's new block, occupied by the new Bank of Illinois, of GEORGE SCHNEIDER, and others. Adjoining, on the east, was the *Daily Republican* office, and Judge OTIS' building, and King's block on the corner of Washington. The Manufacturers' National Bank of IRA HOLMES and others, occupied the corner of Dearborn-street. The Dearborn-street front of this block was a line of retail stores to the alley. Manniere's block, a fine structure, and the McElroy iron building, extended to the corner of Randolph. On the front on the latter street were the beautiful Updike building and a new stone block. Among the principal occupants were J. M. W. JONES' great stationery establishment, HORTON & LEONARD, printing house, SHOBER's lithographic establishment, BELDEN, clothier, and several leading wholesale liquor and clothing houses.

The residue of the square south of the Chamber of Commerce and NIXON & JOHNSTON's building was occupied by a long marble front block on Clark-street, by POPE's block and POPE's new and costly marble front "Open Board," Seeley's building and the costly Boone block of the Union Mutual Insurance Company made up the Lasalle-street front.

The block bounded by Clark, Washington, Dearborn and Madison, contained the costly Methodist Church building on the corner of Clark and Washington, Follansbe's Bank. The entire Washington-street front comprised retail establishments of the best class. The *Daily Times* building was in the middle of the Dearborn-street front of this square, also the marble Manniere block and S. B. COBB's buildings, extending to the corner of Madison-street, the south frontage of the square along the street containing CAMERON, AMBERG & HOFFMAN's stationery and bindery premises and a line of small stores. The Clark-street front of this square, south of the Methodist block, was occupied by CALHOUN's building and MORRISON's block, a very large and costly five-story structure, filled with stores and offices.

The square bounded by Madison, Clark, Dearborn and Monroe was probably one of the best built, and most compactly occupied, of any in Chicago. On Madison-street, commencing with the great marble Morrison block, at its north-west angle, and the continuous similar front of ROSENFELD & ROSENBERG, among occupants were G. E. STANTON's extensive fine grocery and liquor premises, *Kellogg's Railway Gazette* and *Inside Track* premises, SPALDING & LA MONTE's printing-house, the office of the *Evening Post*, the *Post* job offices, the *Evening Mail* premises, the *Bright Side*, the German *Staats Zeitung* office, in a costly marble building owned by the *Zeitung* Company. The Reynolds' block fronted 180 feet on Dearborn and 80 on Madison, filled with stores and offices. At the south-west angle of the square, on the corner of Dearborn and Monroe streets, stood the solid, detached and now destroyed building, the Post-office and Custom-house. Westward on Monroe was the great Lombard block, fronting 100 on Monroe and 180 on Custom-house-place, one of the most numerously occupied structures in the city. Here was the *Advance* office, the *Little Corporal*, the banking-house of BENJAMIN LOMBARD. West of this, on Monroe, were a line of handsome structures variously occupied, among others by the *Interior*. The square south from Madison-street on the west side of Lasalle contained Judge OTIS' block, and his new and splendid block, five stories high. Next this, south on Lasalle, was F. A. BRYAN's superb Bryan block, called the best office-building in Chicago, just completed, cost $200,000. West and south of this on Lasalle, and south-westerly and westward on Madison-street, the structures were of a cheaper and humbler class, with no notable values except to the suffering tenants.

Opposite on Lasalle from the Otis building was MAJOR's block, ANDREWS' block and Farwell Hall, representing a total value of nearly three-quarters of a million dollars, and filling the Madison-street front of this square to the alley. The fire-proof building of the Republic Life and W. K. NIXON's fire-proof office building, on the corner of Lasalle and Madison streets, completed the improvements of this square on the west. Next east of the latter, on Monroe, were the Kent Marble office building and the costly half-completed structures of J. P. SMITH and W. A. LANCASTER, eighty feet front five stories high. Next east was the extensive typefoundry of MARDER, LUSE & CO., and the marble Witkowsky Hall, later Olympic Theatre, occupied the corner of Clark. The principal buildings on the Clark-street front of this square were the Henderson block, the costly Arcade building, occupied by ADAMS, BLACKMER & LYON, Sunday-school publishers; TITSWORTH, clothing; LYON & HEALY, music; SMITH & NIXON, Steinway's pianos. The fine new marble building of MALCOM, McNEIL & CAMPBELL, and others occupied by wholesale paper stores, shoe and jewelry.

The improvements on South Clark-street, south of Madison, had recently commenced on a magnificent scale, the principal improvement being the great Pacific Hotel, to be completed in May, and to have been leased in this city the present week. The building, receiving its interior finish, covered the entire square bounded by Jackson, Clark, Quincy and Jackson streets; $800,000 already expended. Just north on Clark, at the corner of Adams, the Lake-side Printing Company were completing their costly edifice, 100 by 100.

Improvements of the best class had been pushed along Dearborn-street to Jackson-street. Among the notable structures below Monroe-street were H. H. HONORE's splendid buildings, one of them a sumptuously beautiful stone front, just being roofed. The Cook County National Bank was on the corner of Monroe and Dearborn. Next was the beautiful new Bigelow Hotel, 100 by 160 feet, just being furnished, having been leased to W. A. HUGHES; hotel owned by G. A. BIGELOW, cost, with furniture, $450,000, to have been opened in November. H. M. SHEPARD's building, marble front, 190 feet on Dearborn, cost last year, $100,000. Among its occupants the *Land Owner*.

On Adams-street, east of Dearborn, the beautiful building of the Academy of Design, the new marble blocks just occupied by the American Tract Society and the American Sunday School Union. These abutted on the Palmer House, an eight story structure on the corner of State and Quincy streets, finished by POTTER PALMER last year, W. P. F. MESERVE, lessee. Below Quincy, on State, the buildings were of a smaller class.

The block south of Washington-street, between Dearborn and State streets, presented at its north-west angle the large and costly Portland block, with the bank of Messrs. TAYLOR and others, and the German Savings Bank at the corner of Dearborn and Madison streets. Portland block was 180 feet square, five stories high, of Athens marble, and cost $300,000 before the war. Next on Madison, on the south, Dearborn Varieties, SMALL's stationery premises, Speed's block, and the Bank of the Merchants Loan and Trust Company and Savings Bank. On the State-street front of this square were Raymond block and POTTER PALMER's range of splendid five-story palaces, occupied by HOLLISTER & PHELPS, carpets; DOWNS, dry goods; CARSON & PERIE, ditto, and the great wholesale dry goods premises of ROSS & GOSSAGE.

The buildings on Clark-street, between Randolph and Lake, opposite the Sherman House, were small retail stores, occupying the Kingsbury lease, among the largest occupants, RAND McNALLY & CO., printers and publishers. Next north was SNOW's building, the banking-house of LUNT, PRESTON & KEAN, the bank of J. M. ADSIT, the North-western Railroad ticket-office, &c. Opposite, on the west side of Clark-street, were the banking-houses of the Traders' Bank, and the bank of GREENEBAUM & FOREMAN. The fine marble building of WM. B. OGDEN, built in 1851, the pioneer of its class of structures in Chicago, occupied the corner of Clark and Lake street. Among its tenants were the National Watch Company of Elgin. On the Lake-street side of the square between Clark and Dearborn streets, were MATSON & HOE's jewelry-store, and a line of elegant retail establishments in four-story brick buildings extending to DICKEY's building. On the south-west corner of Lake and Dearborn, opposite the Tremont House, occupied by the Merchants' Loan and Trust Company's Bank of S. A. SMITH and others. The basement was the banking office of WRENN, ULLMANN & CO. In the same building on Dearborn-street were the Gas Company's office and J. W. SMITH Merchants' Dispatch office. The next building was the *Evening Journal* office and COLBY & WIRT's furniture establishment. Next south the marble block of M. O. WALKER, adjoining the Matteson House, kept by HILL & CO., built in 1850. Value, with furniture, about $200,000. West of the Matteson, on Randolph-street, was a line of retail stores. B. F. CHASE's paper and painting establishment and the Chicago Museum of Col. WOOD, recently refitted. Loss, with contents, about $350,000.

The Tremont House was built by IRA COUCH in 1850, a model of its class; raised and rebuilt ten years ago; kept by JOHN B. DRAKE as a first-class hotel; 180 by 180, on Dearborn and Lake streets; five stories high; DRAKE's lease to expire in 1873; loss, with contents, $500,000. Stores underneath, Michigan Central and Great Western ticket offices; BEERS, clothing; EMERSON, hatter; COBB & PRITCHARD's extensive bookstore. The line of stores east on Lake-street were first-class retail premises—TOWNE, shoes; DALTON, house-furnishing, and others. On the south-west corner of State and Lake the European Hotel, four stories; loss about $100,000. On the State-street front of this square were HERRING's safes SCANLAN confectionery. LAFLIN's paper warehouse and ROUND's extensive printing establishment. Between this and E. H. SARGENT's drug store, on the corner of State and Randolph, were stove, hardware and produce houses. These latter also filling the Randolph-street front to the extensive livery premises, late RICE's, and EGGLESTON's furniture. MANN's drug-store occupied the south-west corner of Dearborn and Randolph streets. On the Dearborn-street front of this square were the Commercial Exchange Building, owned by GEORGE R. CHITTENDEN; a double marble structure, occupied by the banks of A. C. & O. F. BADGER, and Eames' Commercial National Bank.

The square bounded by Randolph, Dearborn, Washington and State streets contained the Crosby Opera-house on its central front on Washington, with the music stores of ROOT & CADY, W. W. KIMBALL, J. BAUER & CO., and WRIGHT's restaurant under it. The rear building contained ROOT & CADY's publishing rooms. The cost of the Opera-house, just being refitted at a cost of $50,000, was nearly $600,000, with its extension to State-street, occupied by SPEAR & CROFUT, carpets. The St. James Hotel, owned by Gen. W. L. STEWART, occupied the corner of State and Washington. The Third National Bank of J. IRVING PEARCE and others was in the costly marble McCormick Building on the north-west angle of the square, fronting on Dearborn and Randolph streets. Next south on Dearborn was the Rice Block, filled with offices and stores. South of this, on the same front, the Masonic Temple, built in 1856, a marble building containing HARDIN, CUSHMAN & CO.'s banking office and other banking offices.

To particularize further principal blocks is difficult. The iron-front stores on both sides of Lake-street, the great stores of Keith, millinery; Williams & Fitch, hats and caps; Burley & Tyrrell, crockery, Johnson, Spencer, & Co., cutlery; Hurlbut & Edsall, drugs; Doggett, Bassett & Hills, shoes; Durand, grocer, are a few of these names. South Water-street, east of State, was filled with heavy grocery firms. In this quarter of the city was the Adams House. The block on the east side of Michigan-avenue, from Wabash to Randolph-street, was lined with the great iron houses of HALE & AYERS, HALL, KIMBARK & CO., G. C. COOKE & CO., grocers; HIBBARD & SPENCER, hardware; and the magnificent marble armor building was occupied above by PULLMAN Palace offices and warehouse. In the rear of these the great depot grounds of the Illinois Central, Michigan Central, Chicago, Burlington and Quincy Railroad Companies. These buildings were the great Union Passenger House, the freight houses of vast capacity, and beyond these the great elevators.

On State-street, from Washington north to Randolph, stood a line of merchant palaces. On the corner of Washington POTTER PALMER's superb white marble building, 180 by 150, was filled through its six stories with the dry goods store of FIELD, LEITER & CO. The loss in building and contents will largely exceed one million. Next POTTER PALMER's store, occupied by ALLEN & MACKEY, carpets, the great Thayer & Tobey Furniture Warehouse, and GILES BROS.' costly jewelry-store and stock. Northward, on the corner, Garrett Block, occupied by the Chicago Omnibus Company. On State-street, south of Washington, the magnificent pile of buildings owned by HALE & BRO., Dr. WILLIAMS, PETER PAGE, STURGES BROTHERS, was known as Book-seller's Row, and contained the great book-houses of GRIGGS & CO., KEEN, COOKE & CO., and Western News Company. Boyce's building (in Marquette stone) was in process of construction on the Madison-street corner. On the Wabash-avenue front of this square were a line of costly buildings, owned by PETER PAGE and others, and occupied by PARDRIDGE, leading dry-goods, and APPLEBY, picture-frames.

On Wabash-avenue, between Washington and Madison, were the recently rebuilt block of JOHN B. DRAKE, JOHN V. FARWELL and THATCHER BROTHERS; occupants, HAMLIN, dry-goods; J. V. FARWELL & CO., dry-goods; F. C. & M. D. WELLS, stoves.

On the south-east corner of Wabash-avenue and Madison stood the Clifton House, Mr. JENKINS lessee; value of building and contents, about $150,000.

Below Madison, on Wabash-avenue and Michigan-avenue, the elegant residence section extended, only recently begun, to be invaded by business. On Wabash, north of Madison to the river, on Randolph and Lake streets to the lake shore, was the solidly-built wholesale quarter, a large portion of which was rebuilt in costly style a season or two since.

The Chicago Court-house was a structure extending from Lasalle-street to Clark, 180 feet front on each street, and 325 feet in length, contained the Court rooms, Recorder's and municipal offices, the valable law library, and the jail in the basement. It had been recently rebuilt and enlarged. The structure cost not far from $1,000,000.

The Devastation of Chicago---Map of the Burned District as Far as Heard From.

REFERENCES.

1. Court-house.
2. Chamber of Commerce.
3. Sherman House.
4. Tremont House.
5. Pacific Hotel.
6. Lake Shore and Michigan Southern, and Rock Island and Pacific passenger and freight houses.
7. Illinois Central, Michigan Central, and Chicago, Burlington and Quincy freight houses.
8. Chicago Water-works.
9. Chicago City Gas-works.
10. Pittsburg, Fort Wayne and Chicago, and St. Louis, Alton and Chicago Railroad passenger and freight houses.
12. Chicago and North-western Depot grounds.
13. Chicago *Tribune* office.
14. Chicago Shot-tower.
B. B. B. B. Elevators.

THE VERY LATEST.

Increased Spread of the Fire—The Southern Portion of Chicago Probably Destroyed—Telegraphic Communication with the City Cut Off.

Special Dispatch to the New-York Times.

CHICAGO, Oct. 10—1 A. M.—My associate in the city has been compelled to abandon his post, owing to the utter impossibility to keep up telegraphic communication. When he left the doomed City of Chicago the southern portion was threatened, in fact so great a hold had the flames obtained on the wooden buildings in that vicinity that the entire populace, men, women and children, were flying from their homes panic-stricken, and recklessly abandoning their household goods, it being apparently impossible to save even the veriest trifle. He comes to me prostrated by the excitement through which he has passed, and appears wholly unable to properly describe the scenes. As I have already telegraphed you, one-third of the citizens of Chicago are positively homeless, and ruined. As I write these lines the entire surrounding country is vividly lighted up by the glare of the burning city, and the scene even at this distance is appalling. The roads are thronged with fugitives who are vainly seeking shelter for the night. Vehicles of every description are constantly arriving, and I learn that all the roads leading from the city are in a similar condition. The agony and terror at present prevailing in the immediate neighborhood of Chicago must be simply awful and heartrending, and the spectacle is one that will probably never be witnessed on this Continent in a century.

Dispatches from the Associated Press.

CHICAGO, Oct. 9, 6 P. M., via CINCINNATI 11 P. M.—The progressing flames in the South Division were finally arrested about 1 o'clock P. M. This was accomplished by the blowing up and demolishing of several buildings on Wabash-avenue and Congress-street by Lieut.-Gen. SHERIDAN. The district burned over in the South Division embraces everything from the main branch of the Chicago River to the lake, and covering about 100 blocks. This district contained all the leading business houses, the banks, insurance offices, hotels, &c.; also, a large number of churches, including St. Mary's, Trinity, First Presbyterian, Second Presbyterian, St. Paul, Swedenborgian, &c. The Methodist Church, on the corner of Wabash-avenue and Congress-street, is saved. The Michigan-avenue Hotel, on the corner of Michigan-avenue and Congress-street, and the Congress Hall, directly adjoining, on Congress-street, are saved. Michigan-terrace, on Michigan-avenue, embracing the residences of Gov. Bross, Hon. John Young Scammon, S. C. Griggs, Peter L. Ross, and other leading citizens, is completely destroyed. All the newspaper establishments are totally wiped out. The *Tribune* building resisted the fire for several hours, but finally yielded when McVicker's Theatre, immediately adjoining, which also withstood the raging element, finally succumbed. In fact, all the buildings in the district which claimed to be fire-proof, shared the fate of those which could make no such claims. The Great Central Depot, at the foot of Lake-street, was a heap of ruins. About 9 A. M. most of the passenger cars of the Michigan Central, Burlington and Quincy, and Illinois Central Railroad were moved on the break-water and saved. West of Clark-street, in the Southern District, the fire extended south as far as Polk-street, sweeping everything before it. The distance burned over here is some three blocks wide and over half a mile in length, numbering about twenty blocks. The buildings were generally of the cheapest character, embracing saloons, small shops, poor residences, &c. The district burned over on the west side, commences at Taylor-street, running from De Koren to Jefferson. The fire ran thence four or five blocks north, and then moved diagonally toward the river, and finally the west limit was established on Clinton-street, and reaching thence to the river. It moved in this line northward until it reached the North-western and West-side Depots, where it stopped, a distance of nearly two miles from where it started. The Pittsburg, Fort Wayne and Chicago, and the Chicago and St. Louis Railroad Depots were in this district, and are destroyed.

Almost the entire Northern Division, from the main branch of the Chicago River to Lincoln Park, nearly two miles in length and one mile in width, is completely destroyed, including the Water-works, a large number of elegant churches, &c. This district embraces almost the entire business portion of the city.

The territory south of Harrison-street, in the South Division, reaching out many miles, and covered with dwellings, mostly of the better class, is untouched, and may now be regarded as safe from injury.

For miles and miles in every direction the sidewalks, lawns, vacant lots and front yards of dwellings are filled with people who have escaped from burning houses, taking with them only a scanty amount of furniture and clothing. The sight is truly a harrowing one. These people must receive immediate relief, or many will perish from exposure and starvation. As stated in my previous dispatch, it is utterly impossible to make an approximate estimate of the entire loss, but it can scarcely fall below $150,000,000. Of course, but a fraction of this amount can be recovered from insurance.

Gen. SHERIDAN has today telegraphed to St. Louis, to the Missouri depot there, to send at once 100,000 rations. He has also telegraphed to Omaha for two companies of soldiers and 100 tents. He will also order another 100,000 rations.

Mayor MASON has issued a proclamation calling a meeting to-night in the West Division, to see what the citizens can do for the relief of the sufferers.

There are at least 150,000 people who know not where they can get enough provisions to satisfy their hunger.

A late rumor from the North Division says the devastation is less wide-spread than heretofore reported.

I hear of no deaths reported by the disaster as yet, but undoubtedly many have perished.

THE FEELING IN THE CITY.

The Effect Upon Wall-Street—Rapid and Extensive Decline in Western Stocks—A Panic in the Market, Followed by Failures.

The news of the extensive conflagration in Chicago did not reach Wall-street until after the commencement of the regular business yesterday, for the reason that the morning papers had very brief accounts of the fire and the occurrence was not regarded as of great importance. As the day wore on, however, the full details of the terrible catastrophe begin to be received, and the news was posted on the telegraph and newspaper bulletins and made known by extras of the evening papers. The intelligence spread like wildfire, and reaching the stock market created the utmost consternation. Operators in stocks saw at once that such a terrible calamity must affect the values of the securities of all roads centering in or depending upon Chicago for business, and they immediately began throwing them over and selling short to a prodigious extent. The effect was electric. Stocks which had been considered among the best on the list, fell from one to two per cent. during the early transactions in the Long Room, and to a similar extent subsequently, so that at the close of the market in the afternoon they stood as much as nine or ten per cent. below the price in the morning, and bade fair to go still lower this morning. The excitement was intense during the entire day, and had not abated when the shades of evening closed upon the scene in front of the Exchange. Hundreds of speculators were ruined yesterday, and when the news of the decline in stocks reaches the country, where these securities are held, it is not at all improbable that the panic will extend thither and still further increase that which now overwhelms the great financial centre of the country. Thus the ruin attendant upon the fire in Chicago will not be confined to that city alone. Hundreds of homes all over the country will mourn losses consequent upon the fire, and the season which was believed to be the most prosperous for all classes known since 1865 may be made, by a single day's devastation, the most disastrous.

The panic in stocks was almost unparalleled. There was a universal depreciation of all values, and the extent of the decline will be seen by the following table:

	Highest.	Lowest.
N. Y. Central and Hudson consol....	92⅝	86
N. Y. Central and Hud. Certificates..	87½	84½
Erie....................	30¾	26
Reading....................	113⅝	108½
Lake Shore....................	106⅛	95½
Wabash....................	62	57¾
North-western....................	69½	63
North-western Preferred..........	90½	86
Rock Island....................	109½	99¾
Ohio and Mississippi..............	43¾	36½
Union Pacific....................	27¼	22¾
Hannibal and St. Joseph..........	63¾	55½
Western Union Telegraph..........	66¾	56¾
Pacific Mail....................	51¾	47
Pittsburg....................	120	117½

The above table gives but a faint idea of the panic which prevailed in the market. The room was crowded all day, and throngs were hurrying to-and-fro, some with faces blanched with fear, and others flushed with excitement. Rumors of failures were circulated far and near, and as the day closed at least half a dozen firms were reported as having failed to meet their engagements. Some of the cooler operators made fortunes by going short of the market in the first flurry, and scarcely any would have failed in this respect who had sold short at any time during the day. But in times of panic like these those who go short may find themselves long of the stock by reason of the inability of the parties to whom they have sold to receive it. It is thus that speculations cut both ways sometimes. It is not at all improbable that the failures of yesterday may be multiplied ten-fold today, particularly if the market continues to decline, as under the panic, it probably will.

THE GOLD MARKET.

Singular to relate, gold declined yesterday while it should have advanced. The market opened at 114⅞ bid, and closed at 113¾ bid. The market seemed paralyzed, and no one knew what to do. Against all the arguments that the losses by the Chicago fire must tend to enhance the price of gold, the price declined. At last the mystery was solved. A house which is intimately connected with Erie sold during the day about five millions gold against Erie Railway stock, which, it was said, they intended to ship to Europe. The sale had a depressing effect all around, and caused the carrying rate to close at sharp seven per cent. The effect of the Chicago fire upon the gold market cannot but be marked and immediate. The destruction of this immense property tends to derange the plans of shippers, as was observed yesterday in the produce markets of this City. The enormous stores of grain which have been destroyed were ready for shipment and were being hurried forward as fast as possible, and in some cases, doubtless, bills of exchange were drawn against grain which is now smouldering ashes. Besides this, the loss to the entire Western country is immense, and from it recovery must be slow. The Internal revenue receipts from this section will be small for months hereafter. Nor is this all. The general want of confidence in the security of the country and the railroads interested will extend to Europe, simultaneous with the cable despatches announcing the disaster, and in response we shall have demands for the liquidation of claims which might otherwise have awaited weeks or months in collection. This feeling of distrust will be increased by the panic of yesterday in the stock market and no one can tell where the trouble will end, nor what will be the nature of the demands made upon us. It is quite probable that the gold operators were panic-stricken as well as were the stock operators and that when a sober second thought is taken the reaction in gold will be as great as was the decline. The destruction of breadstuffs in Chicago is unfortunate at this time when the markets of Europe are far from being plethoric and the tendency will doubtless be to advance the price of these necessaries.

MONEY.

The rate of interest for money was suddenly increased yesterday from seven per cent. on call to one-quarter of one per cent. per day, and it is by no means improbable that even higher rates will be paid during today. The money which was sent to the West some weeks ago for the purpose of moving the crops will now have to remain there to relieve the suffering and aid in repairing damages. This prolonged withdrawal of currency will be doubly embarrassing at the present time when the commercial community has rather to expect extended and extensive accommodation. Indeed there is scarcely a merchant in this City but will feel the effect of this Chicago disaster. The great majority of our commercial men deal with that city extensively, and at this season especially are dependent upon it for returns with which to meet current and accruing obligations. If their creditors are ruined by the fire—as doubtless they are—the New-York merchant will not have the heart to press for payment, no matter how sorely he himself may be cramped by extending the accommodation. We may, therefore, see, as a not remote result of this disaster, failures of houses in this City, and, indeed, an avalanche of of trouble as great as that which followed the failure of the Ohio Life and Trust Company, some few years ago. In this emergency the importers who can will look to some tangible security, and discarding investments in anything else, will put their money in gold—which is the last refuge of the panic-stricken.

Aid for the Chicago Sufferers—Meetings to be Held Today.

At the request of a number of members, a meeting of the Chamber of Commerce will be held today, at noon, to take action for the relief of the suffering in Chicago. The Erie Railway and Hudson and Central Companies notified merchants yesterday that they would receive and forward, free of charge, on fast trains through to Chicago, all contributions which the citizens of New-York might make in aid of the sufferers.

Postmaster JONES has dispatched Mr. S. H. KNAPP, Superintendent of Mails, for Chicago, to

[Continued on Eighth Page.]

THE THIEVES CONVICTED

Complete Exposition of the Ring Accounts.

Official Report of the Joint Committee of Investigation.

Nearly $75,000,000 Spent from the Appropriations in Three Years.

The Tax-Payers in Debt One Hundred and Twenty Millions.

Some of the Robbers Pointed Out by Name.

The Schuyler Fraud Traced Home to Tweed.

The Joint Board of Supervisors and the Committee of Citizens met at 3 o'clock yesterday, in the Supervisors' room, in the new Court-house, Alderman J. G. DIMOND presiding.

WM. A. BOOTH rose and said: This meeting, I believe, has been called, Sir, at the instance of the Committee of Sixteen, of which I have the honor to be Chairman. That Committee, at last meeting, submitted their report in relation to the debt of the City, and also asked to be impowered to send for persons and papers. Since the meeting of that Committee the various Subcommittees, the various members of the Citizens' Committee, have been constantly at work at the investigation which had been assigned them. They had found every facility given them on the part of the new Deputy Controller as they had before on the part of the Controller. They have also had very pleasant intercourse in all their relations with the gentlemen associated with them on the Committee of the Board of Supervisors and the Board of Aldermen. The Committee found themselves at first embarrassed in their operation because the way was not clear for them without a conference with the Board of Supervisors. At the time that we asked for the conferring of power upon us we had no specific case, but we were aware from the course of the investigations that one or more cases must soon come up. We immediately after—the very next day—had occasion to suspend the action of one of our subcommittees, and on the following evening some persons called on me and informed me of several cases which showed absolute necessity for the possession of that power. There was one special case came before us in which it was stated that a certain party had erased the figures by a forgery from about $9,000 to about $49,000 by taking out the ink, replacing the paper and inserting the higher thousands and drawing a warrant for the higher paper, and received that pay from the Treasurer. Subsequently there came to my knowledge the names of the parties who had previously interviewed me at my house, and who implicated by name one of the highest City officials. For the want of the necessary power the Committee have not in that case, and in a great number of other cases where persons have been implicated, been able to pursue their investigation, and to satisfy themselves as to the correctness of these reports, and hence the imputation must rest, as it does, upon these parties who are said thus to be implicated. The Committee in pursuing their labors have purposed to give what they consider a full account of the City and County transactions for 1869, 1870 and 1871, up to the time that they entered on their labors, the 14th of September. They have taken off accounts to a considerable extent, appropriated for that purpose, but toward the middle of last week they learned that the new Deputy Controller was about to have all these accounts copied and published, and we were on Thursday shown a copy of the accounts of 1871, which were in proof sheet. Under those circumstances, the Committee came together on Thursday last, and, after a full conference, decided that they would change their course, unless they should receive further directions; and that was to suspend this week on these general accounts and confine themselves to the work given to sub-committees. We have invited this meeting in order to submit the report as far as prepared. The report on the Court-house, the report of printing, stationery, &c., cannot be prepared in time for this meeting. The Committee are now ready to submit the report of the sub-committee, whom we requested to confer with Mr. SCHUYLER in regard to the large payments made to him. We have also to submit the report on Armories and Drill Rooms pay-rolls, &c. In conclusion Mr. BOOTH submitted the following report:

REPORT OF HON. WILLIAM A. BOOTH, CHAIRMAN.

To the Chairman of the Joint Committee of Supervisors and Aldermen appointed to investigate the public accounts of the City and County of New-York:

The Committee of Tax-paying Citizens, who were appointed to make a thorough and exhaustive examination of the public accounts with the aid of experts, under their immediate supervision, and give the result of their investigations to the people of the City and State, respectfully report That, concurring in the appeal addressed to them, "that the good name of our City, its prosperity, and every interest dear to its people, must suffer from libels so gross, and attacks so false and exaggerated," they at once addressed themselves earnestly to the work which was assigned them, and have heretofore prepared a statement of the debt of the City and County, and the condition of the Sinking Fund, taken from the books in the Controller's office, which they believe to be perfectly accurate, which statement has already been published. Pursuing their investigations into the details of the accounts and of the bills which have been paid by the Controller during the past

The New-York Times.

VOL. XXI......NO. 6370. NEW-YORK, MONDAY, FEBRUARY 19, 1872. PRICE FOUR CENTS.

THE KUKLUX KLAN HYENAS.

Report of the Select Committee of Congress.

When, How and Why the Secret Order was Formed.

The Most Intelligent Negroes Selected for Immolation.

Extension of the President's Powers Recommended.

What the Minority of the Committee Have to Say.

WASHINGTON, D. C., Feb. 18.—The Joint Select Committee will, to-morrow, make their report on the condition of affairs in the late insurrectionary States. The Committee was organized April 20, and again met in Washington on the 7th of May last. On the 10th, a subcommittee of eight was appointed to proceed at once with the investigation, with authority to take testimony wherever they deemed it advisable, by a subcommittee of their own number, to be reported to a meeting of the full committee. Subcommittees were appointed to visit and take testimony in North and South Carolina, Georgia, Florida, Tennessee, Alabama, and Mississippi. The evidence taken in Washington and by a Subcommittee in South Carolina, having been reported to the Joint Committee, is now submitted and as an appendix to and part of the report is also submitted the report of the Subcommittee appointed to digest the record of the Executive officers of the States. The testimony taken in Georgia, Florida, Alabama and Mississippi by the Subcommittees visiting these States is not yet prepared and will be submitted with a supplement or supplementary report.

SCOPE OF THE INVESTIGATION.

IMMUNITY OF DISGUISED CRIMINALS.

THE HITHERTO SECRET ORDER.

OBJECT OF THE ORGANIZATION.

ORIGIN OF THE CORRUPTION IN THE SOUTH.

DEBTS AND ELECTION LAWS.

PATIENCE WITH THE SOUTH.

HOW TO CHANGE THE NEGRO VOTE.

BENEFICENT EFFECT OF THE ACT OF 1871.

RECOMMENDATIONS.

AS TO POLITICAL DISABILITIES.

HOW THE PEOPLE WERE FED.

The Report of the Minority of the Committee.

CARPET-BAGGERS AND SCALLAWAGS.

NO COMBINATION; NO CONSPIRACY.

The Latest Murder in Chelsea, Mass.

BOSTON, Mass., Feb. 18.—BARTHOLOMEW, who murdered STOKER in Chelsea last night, was arrested; also, Dr. SYDNEY B. WEST and MR. GILBERT, the two latter as witnesses of the homicide.

The Fishing Bounties.

Gen. BUTLER has written a letter to Gloucester, Mass., in which he expresses the conviction that the hopes of the passage of a bill granting bounties to fishing vessels are illusory, and says that it seems very clear to him that if laws should be passed repealing our duties upon fish and opening our ports to the Canadian fishermen before any bounty or any relief to the fishermen shall be enacted, then we are, indeed, without remedy.

WASHINGTON.

The Ridiculous Failure of the Arms Sale Question.

Mortification of Sumner and Schurz—Bonded Warehouse Reform—Civil Service—Indian Matters—Pensions—Miscellaneous.

Special Dispatch to the New-York Times.

WASHINGTON, Feb. 18.—When the debate in the Senate on the French arms resolution closed on Friday both SUMNER and SCHURZ were sick of their work, and the former was reported as confessing himself deceived as to the merits of the case.

POST-OFFICE COMPETITIVE EXAMINATION.

THE CHEROKEE LANDS.

THE TARIFF QUESTION.

THE BONDED WAREHOUSE REFORM.

THE APACHE RESERVATIONS.

GEN. ABBOTT'S CASE.

ARMY AND NAVY PENSIONS.

CIVIL SERVICE REFORM.

THE INDIAN BOARD SECRETARYSHIP.

THE LAND-OFFICE.

THE ALABAMA CLAIMS.

The Promise of the Parliamentary Session—Fresh Views of the English Press.

From the London Times, Feb. 6.

The Parliamentary Session of 1872 opens under circumstances which strangely illustrate the fallibility of political foresight.

FRANCE.

Orleanists Accused of Intrigue—Paying the Indemnity—The Old Nobility and "Henry V."

PARIS, Feb. 18.—The Monarchists in the Assembly are canvassing with great activity to obtain signatures to their forthcoming manifesto and to organize a strong and compact party.

SPAIN AND ITALY.

A Spanish Crisis—Gen. Sherman to be Feted at Pompeii.

MADRID, Feb. 18.—The Ministerial crisis continues.

ROME, Feb. 18.—Major-Gen. SHERMAN leaves this city Tuesday, for Naples. The Americans there are preparing a fête at Pompeii in his honor.

THE SNOW BLOCKADE.

Thrilling Adventures of the Detained Passengers—The Railroad Badly Equipped.

SALT LAKE, Feb. 18.—Thrilling narratives are given by passengers just through the snow-blockade of the Union Pacific Railroad.

Kansas Senatorial Bribery Investigation.

ST. LOUIS, Feb. 18.—A special dispatch from Topeka to the *Democrat* says: It is understood that the Senatorial Bribery Investigation Committee will report early this week the evidence taken.

Arrest of Liquor Dealers in Dakota Territory.

CHICAGO, Feb. 18.—A special from Fargo, Dakota Territory, says that Deputy United States Marshal LUTHER, assisted by a detachment of troops from Fort Abercrombie, yesterday arrested some twenty liquor-dealers charged with selling liquor on the Indian Reservation.

Telegraphic Brevities.

Preparations for the reception of the Grand Duke ALEXIS are actively going on at Havana.

The steamer *City of Mexico* arrived at Havana, yesterday, from New-York.

The residence of DAVID R. GOULD, at Quaker Hill, Dutchess County, with the furniture, was burned on Saturday. Loss, $6,000.

The Kuklux trials at Jackson, Miss., commenced on Saturday. Two hundred cases are to be tried.

The London Rowing Club accepts the challenge of the Atalanta Club, of New-York, to row a race with four-oared boats on the Thames in June.

Several buildings in Memphis were damaged by fire Saturday night. Loss, $10,000. HENRIETTA CONLEY, colored, was burned to death.

United States Deputy Marshal JOHN PEEKE, having in charge a man implicated in robbing the express at Muskogee, Indian Territory, was shot and mortally wounded by some teamsters, on the 15th.

Political Notes.

The Missouri regular Republican State Convention meets in Jefferson City on Thursday.

The Indiana Republican State Convention is to be held in Indianapolis on Thursday.

The Kansas Republican State Convention, to select delegates to the National Convention, meets in Lawrence, on Wednesday.

A delegate Convention of the National Labor Reform Party, to nominate candidates for President and Vice President, meets in Columbus, Ohio, on Wednesday next.

GENERAL ORDER BUSINESS.

Why President Grant Did Not Abolish it Before.

Extracts from Official Correspondence on the Subject.

Letters from Messrs. Boutwell, Grinnell and Murphy.

Consideration of the Steam-ship Discharge System.

The Treasury Department in Favor of Pier Warehouses.

Special Dispatch to the New-York Times.

WASHINGTON, Feb. 18.—The question has been repeatedly asked during the Custom-house investigation, Why did not the President pay some attention to the representations of the merchants who wanted the General Order business suppressed? The following correspondence between Messrs. GRINNELL, MURPHY and BOUTWELL, covers the whole subject, and answers the inquiry.

Very respectfully,
GEO. S. BOUTWELL, Secretary.

Respectfully, your obedient servant,
CHAS. G. FRANCKLYN.

I am, very respectfully,
GEO. S. BOUTWELL, Secretary.

The New-York Times.

VOL. XXII.......NO. 6619. NEW-YORK, THURSDAY, DECEMBER 5, 1872. PRICE FOUR CENTS.

THE CAPITAL.

Revision of the Committees of the Senate.

"Liberals" to be Placed on the Same Footing as Democrats.

Investigation Into the District Government Ordered.

Senator Sumner's Resolution on "Battles With Fellow-Citizens."

Power of Post Officials to Open Letters Not Addressed to Them.

Special Dispatch to the New-York Times.

WASHINGTON, D. C., Dec. 4.—The Committee appointed by the Senate Republican Caucus to rearrange the standing committees of that body will be able to report to-morrow, and it is probable that their report will be moved for adoption in the Senate, either to-morrow afternoon or on Friday morning. It is understood that they have substantially agreed upon a report. The policy pursued in regard to the "Liberals" is to leave them in the same attitude in which the Democracy have heretofore been placed when the committees have been revised, to wit: To leave them entirely unassigned, with a number of vacancies proportionate to the number of committees, and then to leave the members of the opposition to agree among themselves as to their respective assignments. In this manner Mr. Trumbull is dropped from the Judiciary and Public Grounds, Mr. Fenton from the Contingent Expenses, Finance, and Pacific Railroads, Mr. Schurz from Foreign Relations, Mr. Sprague from the Appropriations and Manufactures, Mr. Tipton from the Public Lands and Pensions, Mr. Rice from the Mines and Mining, and so on. Although the designations are not yet officially known, it is safe to predict that Mr. Edmunds will succeed to the Chairmanship of the Judiciary, and that Mr. Pratt will succeed him as Chairman of Pensions. New-York will lose her representation on the Finance Committee unless the Democracy should withdraw Mr. Bayard, which is not likely. Mr. Fenton will probably be supplanted on that Committee by Mr. Ferry, of Michigan, and on the Committee on Contingent Expenses, of which he has been Chairman, he will be succeeded by Mr. Windom, of Minnesota. Mr. Rice will be succeeded on the Committee on Mines and Mining probably by Mr. Hamlin, and he, in turn, on the Committee on Manufactures, by either Mr. Boreman, of West Virginia, or Mr. Robertson, of South Carolina. The vacancy on the Judiciary Committee, caused by the retirement of Mr. Trumbull, will be filled by a Western Senator, probably Mr. Wright, of Iowa, unless the Democrats consent to withdraw Mr. Thurman from the Judiciary. Mr. Trumbull will have no place on that Committee. Gen. Logan will doubtless be promoted to the second place on the Committee on Military Affairs, so that, with the retirement of Senator Wilson, he will become Chairman. The old Chairmen who will remain where they are now are Messrs. Sherman on Finance, Morton on Privileges and Elections, Cameron on Foreign Relations, Cole on Appropriations, Chandler on Commerce, Conkling on Revision of the Laws, Stewart on the Pacific Railroads, Frelinghuysen on Agriculture, Pomeroy on Public Lands, Ramsey on Post-offices and Post-roads, and a few others.

SCOLDING A WARD.

The poor, badgered, and tormented Government of the District of Columbia was overhauled again today by its ancient enemy, Mr. Roosevelt, of New-York. There is no other ward of Congress that passes through such ordeals as this local Government, into whose affairs every splenetic Congressman feels an inalienable right to meddle. Mr. Roosevelt therefore wants another investigation; and though a majority of the House agreed to his resolution, calling for information, there is no stomach for any such scenes as dragged through the weary months of last session. The Governor, Board of Public Works, and the House Committee on the District of Columbia will appear before the Committee on Appropriations for the purpose of explaining the items in the bill calling for an appropriation of a million and a quarter to reimburse the District for work done in front of the Government property.

REDUCTION IN THE REVENUE FORCE.

Secretary Boutwell, Commissioner Douglass, Ex-Commissioner Rollins, and Supervisors Simmons, of New-England, Tutton, of Pennsylvania, and Falton, of Maryland, were all before the Ways and Means Committee this morning in explanation and support of the proposed bill for the reduction of the force of internal revenue officials by the abolition of the office of Assessor and Assistant Assessor. Mr. Rollins made an especially clear and forcible argument in favor of the proposed measure, commending it in the heartiest manner. Ex-Commissioner Orton is expected to appear on the same side to-morrow.

THE MESSAGE.

The House went through the usual form of reference of the several portions of the President's Message, today, by a formal resolution offered by Mr. Dawes.

THE STEAM-SLOOPS.

The discussion in the House on the Naval Sloop bill developed nothing new today. It took a wider range, and under the lead of Messrs. Hale and Lynch, of Maine, took in the subject of fostering our ship-building interests generally. The Navy Department is thoroughly aroused on this measure, and is watching its progress very closely.

SENATOR SUMNER'S RESOLUTION.

Senator Sumner, in a conversation this morning, in which reference was made to his resolution concerning the perpetuation of the memories of the civil war, stated that he had not introduced the resolution with a view to initiate an irritating debate which should keep alive the bickerings of last session, but because he considered the measure proposed both just and logical, and the only means whereby the Government can be re-established upon a permanent basis. He declared it to be his intention and desire to make a brief historical speech, to show what civilized nations have done before us to prevent the perpetuation of memories of fraternal strife. His health, moreover, is such as to preclude him from participating in parliamentary conflicts, were he disposed to invite them. He spoke with considerable apprehension concerning his health, and remarked that on last evening he had experienced a renewed attack of his disease.

THE ST. CROIX LAND GRANT.

The representatives of the Bayfield and St. Croix land grant, in which Cornell University has so large an interest, state that they do not intend to ask further legislation from Congress, except the Secretary of the Interior should refuse to sign patents as fast as the road may be completed, in which event some mandatory legislation will be sought. The friends of the road will endeavor to induce the Wisconsin Legislature to confer the privileges of the old charter upon some new corporation which will complete the work. In addition to the recent decision in the Wisconsin Courts in favor of the grant, it is claimed that the decision of the United States Supreme Court last month in the Joy Cherokee land case settles the legal principle upon which the claim to the continuance of the Bayfield and St. Croix grant is based.

THE NORTH CAROLINA SENATORSHIP.

The election of Judge Merrimon to the Senate from North Carolina is claimed by North Carolina Republicans as a Republican triumph. He is reported to have announced, some little time ago, his intention, if elected to the Senate, to act with the supporters of the Administration. It was for this reason that the Republicans gave him their votes, when it had become plain that Senator Pool had no chance of re-election. Judge Merrimon and Judge Phillips, who has just been appointed Solicitor-General, were associated in the law business, and Judge Merrimon has the reputation of being an able and upright man.

INDIANS AS COTTON-GROWERS.

The Department of Agriculture has today received from Major T. D. Griffith, United States Agent for Choctaws and Chickasaws, several samples of cotton grown this year by members of those tribes in the southern part of the Indian Territory. Through the efforts of the present Agent, the Cotton Association of the Missouri State Fair at St. Louis extended its premium list to the Indian Territory, and the Indians were induced to exhibit a number of bales there, which, as well as the exhibitors themselves, attracted much attention. Among the samples are three which secured premiums of $500, $250, and $100 respectively; also one exhibited by Allen Wright, former Governor of the Choctaw nation, but too late to compete. A greatly-increased interest has thus been created among these people in the production of cotton, and it is believed that much larger crops will result from this well-directed labor.

GENERAL NOTES.

There is, so far as can be ascertained, very little favorable feeling toward renewing the law for a session of Congress on the 4th of March. It is doubtful if the proposition would now receive fifty votes in both houses. The usual holiday recess will be taken, beginning, probably, the Friday before Christmas, and ending Monday after New-Years. There will be the usual effort to have this recess dispensed with, but it will be even less earnest than usual. The Senate adjourned without transacting any business today. Vice-President Colfax being absent, Senator Anthony was chosen President of the Senate *pro tem.*, and the usual formal resolutions were passed. Certain North Carolina politicians suggest that the name of Senator Pool is entitled to some consideration in connection with a position in the Cabinet after March 4th. They maintain that the South deserves such a position, and that no one is better fitted for such station than a loyal Southern Republican. The House Committee on the Judiciary will soon report upon the case of United States Judge Delahay, of Kansas, against whom a memorial of impeachment has been presented.

Mr. Mullett, supervising architect of the Treasury, who has just returned from Boston, reports that the Government will proceed with the rebuilding of its buildings in the burned district without delay.

Dispatch to the Associated Press.

IMPORTANT DECISION.

Attorney-General Williams has decided, in answer to a communication from the Postmaster-General, that Post-office officials have no right to open or detain letters or other matter transmitted through the Post-office, though they may know that they contain obscene matter. The Attorney-General adds that Postmasters have no more authority to open letters, other than those addressed to themselves, than any other citizens of the United States.

SUDDEN ILLNESS OF MR. SUMNER.

Senator Sumner was seized with a rather sharp attack of his complaint, heart disease, while in the street last night. His friends have warmly urged his cessation from all his Senatorial labors, but he was in his seat today at the opening of the session.

A NEW LIGHT.

Notice has been received at the Light-house Board from the Government of the Dominion of Canada that a bright white light is exhibited on the light vessel, stationed off Sandy Beach Point, at the entrance of Gaspe Harbor, Province of Quebec, in addition to the red light formerly exhibited. The white light will show six feet above the red one from the mast of the ship, and at an elevation of thirty-five feet from the deck. The red light is likewise made more powerful. This change took place on the 10th of October last.

RAID ON SWINDLERS.

The police last evening closed up all the gift photograph swindling establishments in this city, and arrested the proprietors and clerks, and seized all the stock and cash on hand. The clerks were discharged on their own recognizance to appear at the Police Court to-morrow, and the proprietors were held to give bail.

THE LOST MISSOURI.

Report of the British Authorities at Nassau—Seventy-three out of Eighty-nine Persons Perished.

WASHINGTON, Dec. 4.—The Treasury Department has received the official report of the Court of Inquiry held at Nassau, N. P., under the act of 28 Victoria, upon the loss of the American steamer Missouri, which was burnt off Abaco, Oct. 28. The evidence is very voluminous, consisting of the testimony of most of the crew and officers saved. The Court finds:

First—That the vessel was hurriedly put to sea, and, although fitted with new boilers and newly-repaired machinery, no trial trip took place for the purpose of testing them.

Second—That the felting for the boilers was found to be either wanting or defective on the day appointed for sailing, and as there can be little doubt that the fire originated from the heating of the boilers, it can scarcely be questioned that the work of felting was imperfectly executed.

Third—That the Missouri was not provided with a sufficient number of boats, and such boats as she had were so secured as to be found difficult to be lowered.

Fourth—That on the alarm of fire all was confusion; that there was no discipline, no organization, or combined effort to save life; that each man acted independently to save his own life, and that no attempt was made to save the lives of the female passengers.

There were on board eighty-nine persons, of whom sixteen were saved and seventy-three perished.

THE INDIANS.

A Bill to Banish Whites from the Indian Territory.

ST. LOUIS, Dec. 4.—The *Democrat* has a special from Fort Gibson, Indian Territory, which says that a bill has passed the Cherokee National Council, now in session at Pahlequah, which banishes all white men from the nation. It has created much excitement, and there is great dissatisfaction among many of the most prominent citizens, who deem it a political crime. The question now agitated is whether or not the Chief will sanction or veto the bill.

BOSTON.

The Old South Church—The Republican Municipal Candidates.

BOSTON, Mass., Dec. 4.—The bill before the Massachusetts Legislature to lease the Old South Church to the Government for a Post-office, passed the House today on the third reading, by a vote of 144 to 47.

Henry L. Pierce, the Republican nominee for Mayor of Boston, dissents from the action of the Republican Convention in resolving to keep their nominations within the party, and declines the candidacy, saying in his letter: "As every citizen has a deep interest in the welfare of the city, all are entitled, irrespective of their political opinions, to a fair representation in its municipal government. I have long entertained this opinion. I should be untrue to myself did I now abandon it."

Dr. Haight, of New-York, Elected Bishop of Massachusetts.

BOSTON, Dec. 4.—The Protestant Episcopal Churches of Massachusetts held a special Convention at St. Paul's Church, today, for the election of a Bishop, to fill the vacancy caused by the death of Bishop Eastburn. About 100 churches were represented by 125 clerical and 200 lay delegates. Rev. A. H. Vinton was chosen Chairman.

Rev. Dr. Haight, of New-York, was chosen Bishop by both clerical and lay branches. In the former, on the fourth ballot, the vote stood: Benjamin J. Haight, 43; Alexander H. Vinton, 36; others, 4. The whole number of votes was 83; necessary for a choice, 42. Dr. Haight was then declared elected by the clergy, and a message from the laity was read announcing the same result to that body. In the Lay Delegate Convention, when the position of Dr. Haight was fully explained as a Liberal Churchman, he was elected on the second ballot. The following was the vote: Whole number cast, 66; necessary to a choice, 34; Benjamin J. Haight, 35; Alex. H. Vinton, 25; Alexander Burgess, 2. Rev. Messrs. Brooks, Paddock, and Potter had one each, and one was divided.

THE ELECTORAL COLLEGE.

Vote for President and Vice-President—Resolutions of Respect for the Memory of Horace Greeley.

ALBANY, N. Y., Dec. 4.—The Electoral College reassembled at 9 A. M., and proceded to vote for President by ballot, and it was found Ulysses S. Grant received all of the thirty-five votes. A vote for Vice-President was then had, and Henry Wilson was found to have also received all the thirty-five votes.

Hon. Andrew D. White, after alluding to the death of Horace Greeley, and speaking of his services, his high character, and the loss the country experiences in his demise, proposed the following:

"The Electoral College of the State of New-York, remembering that on this day the mortal remains of Horace Greeley are to be committed to the grave, desires to place upon the minutes of its proceedings an expression of the feeling of its members. The Electors have heard of the death of Mr. Greeley with deep sorrow; they remember him as one of those who labored at the foundation of the Republican Party most devotedly, and who fought its battles most fearlessly; they recall with reverence his faith in right, his hatred of wrong, his sympathy with the oppressed, his efforts to give courage to the struggling, his anxiety to better the condition of the poor, his unceasing labors to promote the moral and material advancement of his country. With the great body of their fellow-citizens of all varieties of opinions, they lament him not only as one from whom the country has received great good in the past, but also one from whom much thought fruitful of good was to be expected in the future. While the members of this Electoral College remain entirely firm in the conviction that in this their final expression this day, of the will of the people of this commonwealth, as to the choice of a Chief Magistrate of the United States, they are acting for the highest good of the nation, and for the continuance of a just, progressive, and pacific policy, they feel that the memory of the late opposing candidate is to be cherished tenderly. The College orders that its Secretaries make a record of this memorandum, and that they forward a copy of it to the family of the deceased patriot and philanthropist."

Wm. E. Dodge, of New-York, and Barney R. Johnson, of Binghamton, seconded the resolutions in brief but feeling terms, when they were adopted.

The following messengers to convey the vote of the College were then appointed: To Washington, Frederick Douglass, of Monroe; to the District Judge at Buffalo, S. H. Palmer, of St. Lawrence. The members were then called upon to sign the result of the vote in duplicate, which occupied considerable time.

The College then adjourned *sine die.*

NEW-ORLEANS, Dec. 4.—Today the Returning Board—not Warmoth's—declared the Electors on the Republican ticket elected by about 15,000 majority, and delivered to those Electors certificates of such election. At 4 o'clock the Electors, eight in number, proceeded to the State-house, (Mechanics' Institute,) and there, in due form of law, cast the vote of the State of Louisiana for Ulysses S. Grant for President, and Henry Wilson for Vice-President of the United States. Dr. L. Roudans was appointed as the messenger to carry the result of the election to Washington.

ANNAPOLIS, Md., Dec. 4.—The Electoral College met at noon today at the Capitol. Hon. Frederick Raine was chosed President, and made an appropriate address. Ex-Governor Bradford, one of the Electors at large, nominated Thomas A. Hendricks, of Indiana, President, and he received the unanimous vote of the College.

Ex-Governor Bradford, William Walsh, and James A. Buchanan, were appointed a Committee to prepare suitable resolutions to the memory of Horace Greeley.

COLUMBUS, Ohio, Dec. 4.—The Presidential Electors assembled today, and all cast their vote for U. S. Grant for President, and Henry Wilson for Vice-President.

BOSTON, Mass., Dec. 4.—The Electoral College of Massachusetts met today, and, after the customary formalities, cast their unanimous vote for Grant and Wilson.

CONCORD, N. H., Dec. 4.—The Board of Electors met at the State-house today, and immediately proceeded to vote for President and Vice-President by separate ballots. The result was a unanimous vote for Grant and Wilson. After preparing the certificates required by law, Capt. George W. Estabrook, of Concord, was elected messenger to carry to Washington the result of the ballots.

INDIANAPOLIS, Ind., Dec. 4.—The Presidential Electors today cast the votes of the State for Grant and Wilson. An appropriate resolution on the death of Horace Greeley was adopted.

NASHVILLE, Tenn., Dec. 4.—The Electoral College met today, and cast the votes of Tennessee for Hendricks, of Indiana, for President, and B. Gratz Brown for Vice-President. Resolutions of regret and sympathy for the death of Horace Greeley were adopted.

LITTLE ROCK, Ark., Dec. 4.—The Secretary of State today declared the Grant electors chosen in Arkansas by majorities ranging from 3,000 to 4,000. The electors met in the State House and cast their votes for Grant and Wilson.

ATLANTA, Ga., Dec. 4.—The electoral vote of Georgia was cast today with the following result: For President, B. Gratz Brown, 6; Horace Greeley, 3; Charles Jenkins, of Georgia, 2. For Vice-President, B. Gratz Brown, 5; Gen. A. H. Colquitt, of Georgia, 5; Gen. N. P. Banks, of Massachusetts, 1.

HARTFORD, Conn., Dec. 4.—The Connecticut Presidential Electors met here today, and cast their six votes for Grant and Wilson. Mr. E. A. Tucker, of New-Haven, was appointed messenger to convey a certified copy of the votes to Washington.

PROVIDENCE, R. I., Dec. 4.—The Presidential Electors met at Bristol, this afternoon, and cast the vote of the State for Grant and Wilson. Hon. Pardon W. Stevens was chosen messenger.

PHILADELPHIA, Penn., Dec. 4.—The Electoral College of Pennsylvania, met at Harrisburg today, and cast the twenty-nine votes of the State for Grant and Wilson.

TRENTON, N. J., Dec. 4.—The Presidential Electors met today, and cast nine votes for U. S. Grant for President, and nine votes for Henry Wilson for Vice-President of the United States, and appointed William Cloke as special messenger to carry the result to Washington.

SPRINGFIELD, Ill., Dec. 4.—The Electors of President and Vice-President met today in Representatives Hall and cast their votes for Grant and Wilson. Hon. W. D. Henderson was chosen messenger to carry the vote to Washington.

RICHMOND, Va., Dec. 4.—The Presidential Electors met in the State Library today, and, all being present, the full electoral vote of the State was cast for Grant and Wilson. Dr. W. W. Douglass was elected messenger to convey the vote to Washington.

ST. LOUIS, Dec. 4.—The Electoral College of Missouri met at Jefferson City this afternoon. After filling vacancies, and adopting resolutions of respect to the memory of Horace Greeley, adjourned until evening. There is said to be difference of opinion among the Electors as to who the vote shall be cast for, and a decision is not expected until a late hour.

ST. LOUIS, Mo., Dec. 4—Midnight.—The Electoral College, at its night session, reached no decision as to how the vote should be cast, and adjourned until to-morrow.

The Popular Vote, and Composition of the Electoral College.

The following table contains the popular vote for President, so far as it has been declared, and the electoral vote as decided by the popular vote. The death of Mr. Greeley has caused the votes in the Electoral College to be divided, as shown by our telegrams. Grant's majority in the twenty-seven States from which we have complete returns, is 668,169.

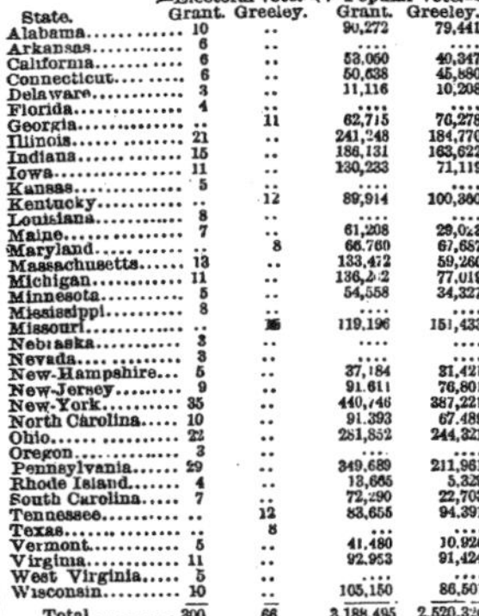

State.	Electoral vote. Grant.	Electoral vote. Greeley.	Popular vote. Grant.	Popular vote. Greeley.
Alabama	10	..	90,272	79,441
Arkansas	6	..	....	....
California	6	..	53,060	40,347
Connecticut	6	..	50,638	45,880
Delaware	3	..	11,116	10,208
Florida	4	..	....	....
Georgia	..	11	62,715	76,278
Illinois	21	..	241,248	184,770
Indiana	15	..	186,131	163,622
Iowa	11	..	130,233	71,119
Kansas	5	..	....	....
Kentucky	..	12	89,914	100,360
Louisiana	8	..	....	....
Maine	7	..	61,208	29,023
Maryland	..	8	66,760	67,687
Massachusetts	13	..	133,472	59,260
Michigan	11	..	136,2[illegible]2	77,019
Minnesota	5	..	54,558	34,327
Mississippi	8	..	....	....
Missouri	..	15	119,196	151,433
Nebraska	3	..	....	....
Nevada	3	..	....	....
New-Hampshire	5	..	37,184	31,421
New-Jersey	9	..	91,611	76,801
New-York	35	..	440,746	387,221
North Carolina	10	..	91,393	67,489
Ohio	22	..	281,852	244,321
Oregon	3	..	....	....
Pennsylvania	29	..	349,689	211,961
Rhode Island	4	..	13,665	5,329
South Carolina	7	..	72,290	22,703
Tennessee	..	12	83,655	94,391
Texas	..	8	....	....
Vermont	5	..	41,480	10,926
Virginia	11	..	92,953	91,424
West Virginia	5	..	....	....
Wisconsin	10	..	105,150	86,501
Total	300	66	3,188,495	2,520,326

Escape of Convicts from Sing Sing.

POUGHKEEPSIE, N. Y., Dec. 4.—Two convicts, named John Rieley and Robert H. pgood, escaped from Sing Sing Prison today, and up to the latest accounts had not been captured.

THE DIAMOND SWINDLE.

More Developments About the Great Hoax.

Report of Gen. Colton, the Manager of the Company, and of Clarence King, the Geologist.

The San Francisco papers received by yesterday's mails, are full of details respecting the exposure of the great diamond swindle. We give below the report of Gen. Colton, general manager of the Company. That body, after its receipt and the accompanying papers, unhesitatingly pronounced the whole scheme a fraud on a grand scale, which has cost those who were interested upward of $500,000. The following is Gen. Colton's report:

To the Board of Directors of the San Francisco and New-York Mining and Commercial Company.

GENTLEMEN: On the first of the present month I was tendered by your body the position of General Manager of your Company, under circumstances so liberal and flattering that I accepted the appointment, and proceeded at once to acquaint myself with the affairs and property of the Company.

On the 11th instant information having been received from Mr. Clarence King, United States Geologist, in charge of the survey of the fortieth parallel, from which it became probable that a great fraud had been perpetrated upon your stockholders, I immediately proceeded, under the earnest solicitation of your Executive Committee, to the purported diamond fields. My party was made up of Mr. Clarence King, who most generously consented to accompany the expedition, and Mr. Henry Janin, who had previously visited the ground and reported on its value; Mr. John W. Bost, ex-Surveyor-General of this State, and Mr. E. M. Fry, the last two gentlemen having been on the ground with what is known as the Roberts party.

We proceeded by rail to Black Butte Station, on the Union Pacific Railroad, in Wyoming Territory; there taking riding animals, we reached the ground on the 18th, it being in the Territory of Colorado, in a due south direction from Black Butte Station, and not to exceed fifty miles therefrom. The locality is perfectly easy of access in good weather, being situated on high table land, on the north side of a pine-clad mountain, plain to be seen in three hours' ride from our starting point. As all the gentlemen with me were familiar with the ground, we lost no time, and at once proceeded to prospect the property. At the head of what was designated on Mr. Janin's map and report as Ruby Gulch, I found a bare, solid table of sandstone about 320 feet long by 150 feet wide, cut up more or less by crevices, most of them emptying into Ruby Gulch, which runs parallel with the west face of the rock. On this table, as I am informed by Messrs. Bost and Fry, the Roberts party found the diamonds they brought to your Company. At the head of Ruby Gulch, and close by the edge of the rock, Mr. Janin pointed to the places where most of the dirt was taken, from which were washed the large number of diamonds and rubies taken by Gen. Dodge, Janin, Harpending, and Arnold to New-York, and afterward brought to San Francisco.

We proceeded at once to test the dirt in Ruby Gulch, and after making fifty-six different tests of the most thorough and careful nature, from surface to bedrock, the day closed on us without our having found a diamond or ruby outside the limits of the bare rock first described; whereas, on the Table Rock, visible to the naked eye, were many small rubies, and a few small, worthless diamonds which had been overlooked by previous parties.

The second day Gen. Bost and Mr. Fry devoted their time to various tests of the property, particularly in opening on this rock two crevices which showed unmistakable evidences of not having been tampered with. The result was they found no diamonds or rubies there or elsewhere during the whole day outside the previously described points where the first stones were found.

In the mean time Mr. Janin and myself proceeded first to the point on Diamond Creek where Arnold and others did their diamond washing. We found the gravel they had thrown away, and in testing it, discovered some small rubies, and found some of the same stones on several ant-hills near the trail they had traveled while there. We then proceeded on the eastern line of Mr. Janin's and Slack's survey of the original location, going north. Found all the stakes, and Mr. Janin, as we reached these, identified all the prospect holes on the line, from which he took the dirt with Mr. Arnold, and found diamonds and rubies, as set forth in his first report. We made five separate, distinct, and careful tests of the dirt, in and about each hole, making over thirty tests, and never in one instance found a diamond or ruby. We also dug new holes near his old ones and found nothing. In fact, after making numerous tests, ninety-three in all, in different places on the 160 acres of the original location, we never in a single instance found a diamond or ruby.

And to show you the correctness of our tests, I placed, several times, a very small ruby in the dirt each gentleman worked, and in every instance they found the stone, believing it to be a genuine find until I informed them otherwise. It further demonstrated how easy it was for one person even, who had the entire confidence of his associates, to commit numerous frauds on the various members of his party without their suspecting it.

Among other places I examined was a point of rocks near by and overlooking the place where Mr. Janin and others did the washing of the dirt that produced the precious stones brought to California in August last. On this point I found some rubies scattered on the bare rock, where, in my opinion, it would have been as impossible for nature to have deposited them as for a person standing in San Francisco to toss a marble in the air and have it fall on Bunker Hill Monument.

All these investigations forced upon my mind the irresistible conclusion that the general assortment of precious stones found on the ground were not placed there by bounteous nature, but were strewn by the designing hand of one whose supply was only sufficient to place a limited number in the most conspicuous places, where the eye of a coming expert would most readily discover them.

The previous party, after returning from the ground, related that in one hour's work ten men picked up 285 diamonds. It is understood these were all found in the locality before described. If so, it is to be regretted that they did not, in the eight days that they were on the ground, spend one hour more in prospecting other portions of the 3,000 acres they surveyed. In which event I feel certain that the second hour's labor would not have produced a single precious stone, leading, necessarily, to such further investigation as would have demonstrated that the diamonds that party found were all confined to the narrow limits of this small, barren, yet prolific spot, which fact would have prevented, in this city at least, many unfortunate complications.

Believe me, gentlemen, I was not unmindful of the great responsibility of carrying out the expedition, and of making this report, which pronounces today a property absolutely valueless having, when I left home, a cash value of many millions of dollars. The honor of this Board, and the interest of the community, demanded an immediate examination of the property, without a moment's delay and before any intimation could be given of our movements. It was not a journey to be coveted, for no mere pecuniary consideration, I am satisfied, would have induced any member of our party to undergo all the hardships and perils of such a trip in the mountains at this season of the year, camping and sleeping in the open air, surrounded much of the time by snow, with the thermometer 15° to 20° below zero.

In behalf of myself and the gentlemen who accompanied me, whose names are already given, the only remuneration we ask at your hands for undergoing the hardships of this journey, is that you will spare neither time, money nor skill in finding out the guilty parties to this unparalleled fraud, and bring them to speedy justice. The good name of the State and the credit of our mining interests demand it.

I have taken the liberty in this report of announcing the location of the so-called diamond fields of Arizona, from the fact that I consider it high time the alluring fascination of secrecy and mystery be stripped from this diamond excitement, and the world brought to understand that if there be any such immense deposits of precious stones as this present excitement has led them to believe, the deposit is yet to be found, as it is my honest belief, to this time, no new or rich discovery has been made in the section of country this mysterious whisper has pointed to.

In the few days I have been connected with the management of your company it is impossible for me to give you the least information as to who are the guilty parties in putting this fraud upon the world; but the unimpeachable integrity of every member of your board is a sufficient guarantee that this investigation will be so thoroughly conducted by you as to do justice to all parties concerned.

Trusting my course in this matter may meet the approval of your body, I remain, very respectfully. (Signed,) DAVID D. COLTON.

SAN FRANCISCO, Nov. 25, 1872.

CLARENCE KING'S STATEMENT.

At the same time was submitted a statement by Mr. Clarence King, United States Geologist, in which he says:

"Our first day was devoted to the sandstone table-rock, at the head of Ruby Gulch, where about all the stones collected by your parties have been gathered, and, had our critical work ended with the close of this one day, we should have left the ground confident believers in the genuineness and value of the fields. My suspicions were, however, aroused early in the second day's work, and I at once determined to made an exhaustive series of 'prospects,' of which the following are the results:

First—A nearly uniform numerical ratio exists between the rubies and diamonds.

Second—The gems, in nine cases out of ten, lie directly upon the hard surface of rock, or an indurated crust of soil. In the exceptional case, where I found them in crevices, there was always ample evidence that the sand or soil had been disturbed and broken up within a year.

Third—With the diamonds and rubies occur quartz pebbles of various sizes, and concretions of iron oxyd containing crystalline particles of quartz, which are found freely mingled with the soil from surface and bed rock: hence, if the gems were a natural deposit, being of a specific gravity intermediate between the quartz and iron concretions, they must have also settled through the earth to bed-rock. I therefore selected ground on and immediately about Table Rock, where the top was more or less strewn with the so-called rubies, carefully shoveled off the surface—inch of ground and gravel—and examined by means of sieves and pan-washing, all the material down to bed-rock. About thirty of these tests were made encircling Table Rock, and in no instance was a ruby or a diamond found.

Fourth—Ruby Gulch, leading directly from Table Rock to Arnold Creek, and by necessity receiving the wash of the gem-bearing surface of sandstone, was found to be extremely rich in rubies at the head; but this richness, instead of continuing down the bed, as if genuine it inevitably must be, proved to exist only in ground directly at the foot of Table Rock, where the soil was clearly disturbed, mixed, and smoothed over. I sank a series of four pits to bed-rock down the gulch at intervals, excavating probably a couple of tons of material, and although, as in every other instance, quartz, and even concretions were distributed throughout all the gulch soil, not a ruby or diamond was found.

Fifth—In the top of Table Rock, and in the midst of thickly-sown rubies are certain crevices not opened by your parties. They are filled with soil and pebbles, and more or less overgrown with grass, sage-brush and small cactus plants. We carefully removed the top inch, dug out the whole crack, finding no trace of diamonds or even rubies. In the crevices which bore unmistakable evidence of having been tampered with, we never failed to find rubies, and often small diamonds.

Sixth—Upon raised dome-like portions of Table Rock, rubies and diamonds lay upon the summits and inclined sides in positions where the storms of one or two Winters must inevitably have dislodged them, and where, moreover, they were unaccompanied by quartz or concretions.

Seventh—An exhaustive examination of the rock-material itself with a field microscope, revealed no grain, however minute, of either gem.

Eighth—In the ravines and upon the mesa near by, are numerous ant-hills built of small pebbles, mixed by the ants, and which we found to bear rubies on their surface. A still closer examination showed artificial holes, broken horizontally with some stick or small implement, through the natural crust of the mound; holes easily distinguished from the natural avenues made by the insects themselves. When traced to their end, each artificial hole held one or two rubies. Moreover, about these 'salted' hills were the old storm-worn footprints of a man. Many outside ant-hills were studied, but there were neither artificial holes piercing them, rubies within nor without, nor human tracks.

Ninth—I discovered in the Table three small emeralds. Summing up the minerals, this rock has produced four distinct types of diamonds, Oriental rubies, garnets, spinels, sapphires, emeralds and amethysts—an association of minerals I believe of impossible occurrence in nature.

Tenth—When altogether satisfied that the gems had been 'salted' on or about the Table, our party set out upon a series of outside prospects, which were carried on over all the mesa and its flanking cañons until the absolute valuelessness of the property was finally ascertained.

The results of these ten links of proof are: That the gems exist in positions where nature alone could never have placed them; that they do not exist where, had the occurrence been genuine, the inevitable laws of nature must have carried them. Finally that some designing hand has 'salted' them with deliberate fraudulent intent.

Furthermore, this is the work of no common swindler, but of one who has known enough to select a spot where every geological parallelism added a fresh probability of honesty. The selection of the geological locality is so astonishingly considered, the 'salting' itself so cunning and artful, the filling of all the conditions so fatally well done, I can feel no surprise that even so trustworthy and cautious an engineer as Mr. Janin should have brought home the belief he did, especially when, as his report states, he was not allowed to prospect exhaustively; nor do I wonder that your second party of ten men brought back a confirmation of Mr. Janin's opinion, since they, too, were hurried from the ground without actually testing it."

CENTRAL AFRICA.

Livingstone's Early Travels—Last Expedition—Origin of Stanley's Mission—His Journey Into the Interior.

Mr. Henry M. Stanley delivered the second lecture of his course last evening, at Steinway Hall, the subject being "The March of the *Herald* Expedition into the Land of the Moon." The flags and weapons of the fight and chase, which decorated the stage on the evening of the first lecture, occupied the same position as on that occasion. The hall was not one-third filled. Mr. Stanley appeared in a fancy white flannel suit, with Summer helmet and top boots. He was received with marks of applause, and commenced the lecture by an account of the early labors of Dr. Livingstone in Africa. From Kurumann, the station of his father-in-law, Rev. Robert Moffatt, he removed to Kolobeng, 200 miles north. From here he made his first journey north across the Kalahari Desert, and succeeded in discovering Lake Ngami. Mr. Stanley recounted the travels of Livingstone after his discovery of Ngami, westward across the continent to St. Paul de Loando, a Portuguese settlement, where, stricken by sickness, Livingstone lay prostrate for a long time, succored and tended by the Portuguese Consul. After his recovery he proceeded to the Cape, and from thence to England, where he remained two years. He then, for the first time, undertook a mission of discovery, under the auspices of the British Government, but was not very successful in the undertaking. He, however, settled beyond dispute the proper course of the Zambese. He again visited England, and at the urgent request of his friend, Sir Roderick Murchison, President of the Geographical Society, undertook the mission in which he is now engaged. He left England in 1865, for Zanzibar, via Bombay. Immediately after his arrival he struck into the interior. Letters were received from time to time by his friends, and all seemed going on well, when, in December of the same year, one of his escort, Musa, returned to Zanzibar, and stated that Livingstone and all his people had been massacred, and that he alone was the survivor. They were slain, he said, by the Zooloos, near Lake Shirwa.

Mr. Stanley then read the story of the murder as told by Al Musa to the English Consul at Zanzibar, and by him communicated to Lord John Russell. In October, 1867, Mr. Young, in the course of his expedition in the interior, heard that Livingstone had started for Ujiji. Nothing, however, was positively known of him save through rumors which reached the outer world from Arab sources. To resolve the doubts and ascertain the fate of Livingstone, Mr. James G. Bennett undertook to send an expedition in search of the Doctor, and sent the celebrated telegram to Mr. Stanley, then at Madrid, "Come to Paris;" and there took place the interview which led to Mr. Stanley's expedition. Mr. Stanley, in accordance with his instructions, proceeded to Zanzibar, where he found himself surrounded by innumerable difficulties. He was totally ignorant of the country and its inhabitants, and of all data on which to organize the expedition. He, however, hired some Arab traders, who had been in the interior, and acting under their advice purchased clothes, party-colored beads—each tribe using a certain color as currency—and a quantity of brass wire; beads passed for copper value, cloth for silver, and brass wire for gold. After accumulating the necessary stores, the expedition, among which were two white men, Shaw and Parker, left Zanzibar, the American flag flying from the Consulate, and a hearty farewell from the Consul's family ringing in its ears. From Bagonioyo, on the main land, the party journeyed on for sixteen days without much of interest occurring. They had cleared the jungle and arrived in a region like the Central Park stripped of its gravel walks and architectural ornaments. Symbamwhoubi, the city of the lions, was next reached, where the white strangers attracted no small curiosity, the Queen and many of her subjects turning out to gaze on them. The season of forty days rain had now set in, and the country in front was inundated. Ten days were occupied by the expedition in crossing this swamp, the Macata, and the mortality became so great that Stanley thought he should return to the coast. They, however, waded through and reached terra firma. At Umpawpaw, near which one of Benton's attendants was killed, Mr. Stanley experienced the plague of earwigs mentioned by Speke. The expedition next reached Ugogo, a nation of savages, who howled and jibbered at the white strangers, but let them pass uninjured. On June 23, the great plains of Unyanyembe—the lands of the moon—were reached, and messengers were dispatched to announce to the Arab Chiefs the arrival of the expedition. The Governor of Unyanyembe had a basin of good tea and a plate of "slapjacks" ready for Mr. Stanley. Here the Arab merchants endeavored to dissuade him from going to Ujiji, alleging that Livingstone was dead; but Stanley was not to be deterred, and he proceeded on his journey. Mr. Stanley retired amid much applause.

OCEAN DANGERS.

Arrival of a Disabled Boston Schooner at Newport.

Special Dispatch to the New-York Times.

NEWPORT, R. I., Dec. 4.—The schooner Game Cock, Capt. Andrew Patrick, arrived at this port this evening. During the recent gale which has been unusually severe along our coast, she lost her deck load, sails, and rudder. She is from San Domingo, and bound to Boston with a cargo of logwood.

A Steamer Short of Coal—A Brig Struck by a Squall.

HALIFAX, N. S., Dec. 4.—The steam-ship North American, overdue from Liverpool, put into Sydney, C. B., short of coal.

The brig Friend, of Harbor Grace, Newfoundland, was struck by a heavy squall on the 17th of November, off Cape Race. Lost her sails and spars and became leaky. The crew abandoned the vessel fifty miles south of Cape Race; were picked up and taken into North Sydney. There was a heavy gale, with lightning and rain, here yesterday.

LOUISIANA.

The Election Litigation—Continuation of Kellogg vs. Warmoth.

Special Dispatch to the New-York Times.

NEW-ORLEANS, Dec. 4.—The arguments of counsel in the case of Kellogg against Warmoth and others, before Judge Durell, was finished today. W. H. Hunt, Esq., closed for the complainant. It is expected that Judge Durell will deliver his decision on Friday next.

At the close of Mr. Hunt's argument the Court adjourned as a tribute to the memory of Mr. Greeley, in regard to whom Judge Durell made a handsome and complimentary allusion.

THE VIRGINIA LEGISLATURE.

Meeting of the General Assembly—Gov. Walker on the Kanawha—Greeley.

RICHMOND, Va., Dec. 4.—The General Assembly of Virginia met today, a quorum in each house being present. The Governor's message was read. The Governor speaks of the importance of the enlargement and completion of the James River and Kanawha Canal, but is satisfied that the United States Government will not, and really ought not to, undertake its completion, although its merits as a work of national importance are great. He hoped, however, that the Federal Government will lend the aid of its credit to the enterprise on safe and satisfactory conditions.

After the reading of the message, both Houses unanimously adopted resolutions of respect to the memory of the late Horace Greeley and adjourned.

THE WEATHER.

Synopsis and Probabilities.

WASHINGTON, Dec. 5—1 A. M.—The chief signal officer announces that the display of cautionary storm signals at the different lake ports will, on the 15th inst., be discontinued until the opening of navigation in the Spring.

SYNOPSIS.

The thermometer has remained high in the Gulf and South Atlantic States, with gentle variable winds, mostly northerly and easterly on the Gulf, with partly cloudy weather. On the lower lakes, and at the Canadian stations, south-westerly winds, cold and cloudy weather, with increased pressure prevail. In the Middle and Eastern States, northerly to westerly winds, unchanged temperatures, and pressures and clear weather. In the North-west, and thence over the upper lakes and to the Ohio Valley, southerly to westerly winds, cloudy and warm weather, and diminishing pressure.

PROBABILITIES.

On the lower lakes, and north-westward through the St Lawrence Valley, southerly to westerly winds, cloudy and milder weather, and failing barometer will prevail; in the Middle and Eastern States increasing temperatures, diminishing pressures, north-westerly to south-westerly winds, and partly cloudy weather; in the Gulf and South Atlantic States, southerly winds, increasing cloudiness, and warmer weather; in the North-west and over the upper lakes, and thence to Missouri and the lower Ohio Valley, south-westerly to north-westerly winds, rising barometers, colder and partly cloudy weather, with occasional snow. Warning signals continue at Duluth, Milwaukee, Chicago, and Grand Haven.

Sandy Hook Channel Obstructed.

The sea-going pilots by way of Sandy Hook report the channel-way obstructed by a sunken vessel, so as greatly to endanger the safe navigation of vessels entering and leaving the port. This wreck should be removed at the earliest possible time, for if not the masts of the wreck, now showing above water, will be broken off, leaving nothing visible to warn passing vessels of the danger. As many emigrant passenger vessels are now bound to this port, the authorities whose duty it is to attend to such matters, whether of the local or general Government, should see to the immediate removal of the obstruction, or we may be called upon to record some terrible wreck and loss of life.

The Thirty-Fourth-Street Cars.

To the Editor of the New-York Times:

Are not horse-cars run for the convenience and accommodation of the public, as well as the profit of the companies? This the Thirty-fourth-street Ferry line fails to do. The cars are few, slow and irregular, and those who rely upon them to catch a train often regret it bitterly. They have been entirely discarded by some Long Islanders, who find uncertain assistance worse than none. Far better were it did they not run at all, in which case the many sanguine would patronize the other lines, and not lose so constantly time, patience, and trains. Is there no hope for the better? OXENIA.

LONG ISLAND, Tuesday, Dec. 3, 1872.

Ice-Bound Crews.

A Christiania correspondent writes to the London *Times*: "About the beginning of November, the Norwegian Central Government at Christiania was informed by telegrams from its officials on the north-west coast that a number of those small craft which annually sail from the neighborhood of Tromsö, Hammerfest, &c., had not returned, and that there existed good grounds for believing that the crews, numbering about 100 men, were on Spitzbergen, which they were prevented leaving by ice. As there is, perhaps, no country which contains so many men acquainted with those inhospitable northern regions as Norway, it was at once presumed, it is to be feared but too correctly, that there existed no chance, except outward help, by which these poor castaway mariners could get away from such dreary Winter quarters, and that if no help could reach them there would be but a poor chance for any of the crews to outlive the Winter, unprovided as they were with suitable clothing, food, and other necessaries. To the great praise of the Norwegian Government, be it therefore said, the most energetic steps were at once taken, a naval officer was immediately sent out to the harbor of Tonsberg, where there is laid up in the usual Winter quarters the fleet of merchant sealers, and the seal steamer Albert was selected as being the most suitable ship with which to make the attempt to reach Spitzbergen. The Government consequently chartered the Albert, and by great exertions succeeded in properly manning and fitting her out in the shortest possible time. The Albert is a very strong steamer, built about five years ago in Bremen. She measures 700 tons, is sheathed with hardwood, and steams about nine knots. She is fitted out with the necessary clothing and food, carries heavy signal guns and rockets, and has two wooden houses with her, which it is intended to erect on shore at Spitzbergen at the most likely place for any stragglers to find them. The ship is commanded by Capt. L. Hansen, but the expedition is under the leadership of Capt. G. Otto—the former of the merchant navy, the latter a royal officer, but both men of great experience in the Arctic Seas."

CABLE TELEGRAMS.

Wreck of a Channel Steamer Between England and Ireland.

Twenty-One of the Passengers and Crew Drowned.

Consternation in London at the Prospect of "No Gas."

The French Assembly Debating on its Own Dissolution.

Blood-Hounds as Auxilaries of the Spanish Troops in Cuba.

GREAT BRITAIN.

Wreck of a Channel Steamer and Twenty-one Lives Lost.

LONDON, Dec. 4.—The steam-ship Cresswell, from Falmouth, for Cork, was lost during the voyage, and twenty-one of the passengers and crew perished.

Reported Wreck of the Dalmatian Unfounded—The Vessel at Liverpool—Breach of Promise Case—Emigration.

LONDON, Dec. 4.—The report received here on Sunday of the wreck of the steam-ship Dalmatian, and the loss of thirty-five of the persons on board, was untrue. The Dalmatian has reached Liverpool in safety.

Elizabeth Dredge brought suit today, in the Court of Queen's Bench, against Clinton Winans, a citizen of the United States, to recover $50,000 damages for breach of promise of marriage, but the case was compromised by Winans paying the plaintiff $7,500.

Mr. Robert Bowles was brought before the Lord Mayor at the Mansion House today, and again remanded for further examination.

The Crystal Palace will soon be lighted by gas manufactured from petroleum.

The number of emigrants that left Liverpool during November exceeded that of the previous month by 2,000.

The weather today throughout England is fair.

The Gas-Stokers' Strike in London—The City Partially in Darkness.

LONDON, Dec. 4.—Five hundred of the stokers employed by the London gas companies, who are now on a strike, have been summoned to appear before a Police Court under the "Masters' and Servants' act." The summonses of several of the strikers charge them with conspiracy. The companies have no dispositon to concede the demands of the stokers, and the latter announce that they are determined not to resume work until their companions, whose discharge gave rise to the strike, are taken back. Meanwhile the absence of gas is severely felt throughout London. Last night the city was in a state of partial darkness, and several of the theatres were compelled to omit their performances. There are no lights whatever in the underground railways. The price of candles has advanced.

Two thousand of the striking stokers assembled today in Trafalgar-square, and after listening to addresses from several of their leaders, formed in marching order and paraded through several streets of the city.

LONDON, Dec. 4—6 P. M.—Large portions of the city are in darkness to-night, the gas having been extinguished in many sections. The inhabitants are filled with consternation and dread, and the irritation against the striking stokers is very great.

FRANCE.

The Committee on Public Powers—Debate on the Dissolution of the Assembly.

PARIS, Dec. 4—Evening.—It is expected that the Committee of Thirty, to be elected by the Assembly to-morrow, and whose duty it will be to draw up a law regulating public powers, and prescribing the conditions of Ministerial responsibility, will consist of sixteen Monarchists and fourteen Republicans.

The party of the Right has rejected a proposition for even a partial renewal of the Assembly by appeal to the people.

A meeting of the party of the Left was held today, at which, after a powerful speech by M. Gambetta in advocacy of the dissolution of the Assembly, measures to that end were absolutely insisted upon.

SPAIN.

Carlist Operations and Rumors—Time Fixed for Issuing the New Loan.

PARIS, Dec. 4.—A dispatch from Bayonne, in the Department of Bas-Pyrenees, says 250 Carlists entered Spain from France yesterday.

There is much excitement in Malaga over apprehensions of a Carlist demonstration in that city. Many families are leaving, and troops are being quartered in the Custom-house and cathedral.

President Thiers has sent a dispatch to King Amadeus of Spain, congratulating him upon his convalescence.

LONDON, Dec. 4.—A dispatch from Madrid says a royal decree fixes the time for issuing a new loan to the amount of 250,000,000 pesetas for the 12th inst.

The announcement was made in this city today that the subscription books for a Spanish loan of £10,000,000 will be opened in the London market on the 12th.

CUBA.

Ferrol Insurgents Arrived—A Coolie Ship—The Spanish Army Reinforced by Blood-Hounds.

HAVANA, Dec. 4.—The steamer which arrived here yesterday from Spain, brought 200 sailors, who were implicated in the Ferrol revolt.

The steamer Fatchoy has arrived, with 1,000 coolies, who were sold previous to the arrival of the steamer.

The *Echo* (newspaper,) published in Sancti Espiritus, announces the arrival there of ten bloodhounds, to be used in capturing negroes still remaining in the mountains near that city. The hounds were purchased by order of the commanding General.

ITALY.

Heavy Rains in the North—Another Inundation Feared.

ROME, Dec. 4.—Dispatches from the north of Italy state that heavy rains have again swollen the waters of the River Po, and another inundation is apprehended.

Canal Navigation.

KINGSTON, N. Y., Dec. 4.—Canal navigation has about closed. Very few boats reached tide-water today; but it is expected that all loaded boats below Port Hixon, twenty-three miles from tide-water, will reach this place before the final close. Over a hundred loaded boats are reported on the canal. Very little ice has yet formed in the river above this point. Albany boats have reported a little floating ice, but navigation still unimpeded. One very cold night, however, would about close the river above here. Boats from this city to New-York are carrying immense freights. Buyers are securing their Winter stock, and sellers are rushing off their produce. No inconvenience has yet been experienced from the ice by them, though irregularity and delay have been caused by the heavy freights.

The New-York Times.

VOL. XXV.......NO. 7567. | NEW-YORK, THURSDAY, DECEMBER 16, 1875. | PRICE FOUR CENTS.

WASHINGTON.

THE DOINGS OF CONGRESS.

THE RESOLUTION ASKING FOR DOCUMENTS IN THE WHISKY SUITS WITHDRAWN—MR. MORTON'S RESOLUTIONS ON STATE RIGHTS LAID OVER—HOLMAN'S ANTI-SUBSIDY RESOLUTION PASSED.

Special Dispatch to the New-York Times.

WASHINGTON, Dec. 15.—Senator Stevenson to-day introduced in the Senate resolutions calling for copies of all letters, telegrams, orders, and instructions relating to the prosecutions of the Whisky Ring. He was not attempting to injure the proceedings, and reasonably withdrew his resolutions after a brief debate. Mr. Sherman said he thought the Secretary of the Treasury ought not to be embarrassed by the adoption of such resolutions. He said that this Whisky Ring was to be prosecuted to the last, no matter whom it hit, and he happened only this morning to have learned that it would embarrass the prosecution if the Secretary was obliged to give this information. Messrs. Edmunds and Conkling took the same view, but Senator Morton had no objections to the resolutions, and believed the publication asked for would be a complete vindication of the Administration and of the President. Senator Stevenson, in withdrawing the resolution, paid a high tribute to the Secretary of the Treasury. Mr. Randall's resolutions, offered yesterday, were not pressed to-day.

The resolution, prepared by Senator Morton defining State rights, printed in the TIMES of Monday, were introduced by him to-day. They were laid over, and soon after recess he will call them up for action. There is sure to be an interesting debate, and when they reach the House the majority of that body will be embarrassed with the disposition of them. The resolution to investigate the election in Mississippi will meet with opposition. The investigation which Mr. Morton proposes would lead to an examination of the composition of the Legislature, and it has been usually, if not universally, held that in deciding the right of a Senator to a seat the Senate could not go further back than the action of the Legislature which elected him. Even in the case of Louisiana, Congress was careful to leave to the Legislature the determination of its own membership. That the facts alleged in the resolution are not exaggerated is the prevailing opinion among Republicans.

Mr. Holman's anti-subsidy resolution was taken up to-day in the House, and passed by a vote of 218 to 35. Of the thirty-five negative votes, all except five came from Southern States, and three of those five, Kelley, O'Neill, and John Reilly, were from Pennsylvania; the other two were Dunnell, of Minnesota, and Page, of California. Taking the record made last session on this subject, it does not follow that all those voting for the resolution to-day will vote against Tom Scott's Texas Pacific scheme when presented to the House. When the Texas Pacific bill was before the House last February, thirty-seven members voted for that bill who recorded themselves earlier in the session in favor of Holman's resolution. Mr. Lamar, of Mississippi, has the distinction of being among the thirty-seven. His name is to-day recorded in favor of Holman's resolution, being the only member of the last House in the present Congress who voted against granting subsidies in December of last year, and for the Texas Pacific subsidy in the following February. Eight of the thirty-five voting nay to-day were members of the last House, and voted last year as they voted to-day. The absent and not voting members were thirty-four, namely: Atkins, Banks, Barnum, Bass, Bright, Buckner, Cochrane, Denham, Farwell, Hathorne, Hays, Hendee, Hoze, Hurlburt, Kehr, Lane, Mackey, of South Carolina, Meade, Phelps, Piatt, Powell, Pratt, Purnam, Ross of Pennsylvania, Schlecher, Stephens, Swann, Walker of Virginia, Walls, Walsh, Whitehouse, Williams, of New-York, Wilshire, and Woodburn. Of these, Bright, Buckner, Denham, and Swann voted last year for the Holman resolution, and also for the Texas Pacific subsidy. Hathorne, Hendee, Hurlburt, and Ross were also absent when the vote was taken last year.

Whatever changes may occur this Winter, when some specific subsidy scheme is presented to the House, the very decided vote of to-day strongly indicates that no subsidy can pass the House during the present session. It is equally clear that some of those voting aye to-day do not regard the resolution as conclusive, notably Mr. Lamar, the leading member from the South.

Mr. Springer, of Illinois, to-day offered a resolution in the House declaring that a third term in the Presidential office would be unpatriotic and fraught with peril to our institutions, and moved the previous question, which was seconded by a very large vote. Only two members, Page, of California, and Walls, colored, of Florida, stood up against seconding the motion for the previous question, and these were laughed down by the House. The vote on the passage of the resolution was yeas 218 and nays 18. Among those present and not voting was ex-Speaker Blaine. Of the eighteen negative votes, ten were from the South, five from the West, and one each from the States of Maine, Vermont, and New-York. Six colored members voted nay, and one (Rainey, of South Carolina,) dodged. McDougall, from the Auburn District, is the solitary third-term member from New-York.

THE HOLIDAY RECESS.

THE HOUSE DECIDES TO ADJOURN FROM DEC. 20 TILL JAN. 4—THE SENATE LIKELY TO CONCUR—SPEAKER KERR TO ANNOUNCE THE COMMITTEES NEXT MONDAY.

Special Dispatch to the New-York Times.

WASHINGTON, Dec. 15.—The adoption of the resolution by the House to-day to adjourn from Monday next to Jan. 4 was rather unexpected. It had been generally understood that the House would either adjourn from Thursday over the holidays, or adjourn until Tuesday next, and from some date next week until early in January. After conference at the session of to-day it was decided to adjourn to Friday, and then to Monday, it being given out by the Speaker that on that day he would be ready to announce the committees. The Senate will undoubtedly concur in the House resolution to-morrow, so that the recess will undoubtedly extend from Monday next to Jan. 4. The final work upon the committees will be pushed with vigor now, and as the skeletons have been made up the work of perfecting them will not be great. The effort to make Fernando Wood Chairman of the Committee on Ways and Means signally failed, as only a small number of his own delegation could be found to indorse him for the place. It may be regarded as definitely settled that he will not have that committee, and that, in consequence, there may be expected no little excitement when the announcement is officially made. Mr. Wood is not likely to submit tamely to such a slight. The best information places S. S. Cox at its head. There is no material change in the Chairmanships of the important committees since they were last given in these dispatches, and it is safe to say that there will be very few, if any.

EXECUTIVE BUSINESS.

NOMINATIONS BY THE PRESIDENT AND CONFIRMATIONS BY THE SENATE.

WASHINGTON, Dec. 15.—The President sent the following nominations to the Senate this afternoon: A. L. Johnson, of New-York, to be United States Circuit Judge for the Second Judicial Circuit; A. White, of Alabama, to be Chief Justice of Utah Territory; H. N. Blake, of Montana, Associate Justice of Montana Territory; D. P. Thompson, of Oregon, Governor of Idaho Territory; E. B. Smith, of Maine, Thomas Simons, of New-York, and A. S. Gaylord, of Michigan, to be Assistant Attorneys General; H. G. Sickel and Albert D. Wood, to be Pension Agents at Philadelphia; Robert M. Kelly, Pension Agent at Louisville, Ky.; Joseph M. Livermore, Surveyor of Eastport and the District of Passamaquoddy, Maine.

Registers of Land Offices.—W. R. Bates, East Saginaw, Mich.; W. B. Franklin, Chillicothe, Ohio; Thomas L. Bond, Salina, Kan.

Receivers of Public Moneys.—Thomas H. Pressnell, at Duluth, Minn., and Michael H. Fitch, at Pueblo, Colorado.

Postmasters.—Frederick E. Leiter, at Charlotte, Mich.; John T. Ogden, at Wellington, Ohio, and Samuel P. Baldridge, at Jackson, Ohio.

United States Attorneys.—E. B. Pomeroy, for Arizona Territory; D. P. Dyer, for the Eastern District of Missouri; C. O. Bradley, for Colorado Territory; G. W. Hazleton, for the Eastern District of Wisconsin; H. H. Wells, for the District of Columbia; C. S. Varian, for Nevada; J. B. Stickney, for the Northern District of Florida; J. K. Valentine, for the Eastern District of Pennsylvania; D. T. Corbon, for the District of South Carolina, and H. B. Whitfield, for the Southern District of Mississippi.

United States Marshals.—R. A. Clapp, for Nevada; Charles Hopkins for Washington Territory; H. W. Leffingwell, for the Eastern District of Missouri; R. W. Healey, for the Southern District of Alabama; W. F. Prosser, for Middle Tennessee, and William S. Swezey, for Wyoming Territory.

The Senate, in executive session, this afternoon, confirmed the following nominations:

Alexander L. Johnson, of New-York, to be Circuit Judge for the Second Judicial Circuit; C. N. Ringgold, Appraiser of Merchandise at New-Orleans; Albert D. Wood, Pension Agent at the Philadelphia (Penn.) Widows' Agency; Ferdinand Meyer, Supervisor of Internal Revenue, vice John McDonal, resigned; I. M. Bean, Collector of Internal Revenue for the First District of Wisconsin.

Registers of Land Offices.—James H. Moe, at Helena, Montana; H. L. Taylor, Wichita, Kan.; Alexander D. Fuckworth, North Platte, Nebraska; Charles M. Patterson, Marysville, Cal.; J. D. Hyde, Visalia, Cal.; John J. Henry, Fair Play, Colorado; Edward Stevenson, Ionia, Mich.; David W. Letchenthaler, Le Grand, Oregon; George R. Thomas, Cheyenne, Wyoming; Loren Listoe, Alexandria, Minn.

Receivers of Public Moneys.—Frederick J. Barton, East Saginaw, Mich.; J. C. Whipple, Cheyenne, Wyoming; E. B. Harrington, Beatrice, Neb.; W. F. Wright, North Platte, Neb.; P. J. Kaufman, Huntsville, Ala.; George B. Folsom, Taylor's Falls, Minn.; P. C. Stetten, Detroit, Minn.; J. M. Peck, Dardenelles, Ark.; H. M. Keyser, Helena, Montana; David D. Cone, Secretary to the President to sign land patents.

Postmasters.—Charles C. Ewell, at Kent, Ohio; Josiah Robbins, Niles, Ohio; Joseph M. Patterson, Piqua, Ohio; D. D. Taylor, Cambridge, Ohio; J. M. Todd, Bridgeport, Ohio; W. H. McCoy, Cadiz, Ohio; H. L. Robinson, Washington Court-house, Ohio; E. Y. Smith, Galion, Ohio; W. P. Wolf, Wilmington, Ohio; J. S. Crain, London, Ohio; O. T. Letcher, Bryan, Ohio; F. C. Wickham, Norwalk, Ohio; William Richardson, Chippewa Falls, Wis.; William P. Forsythe, Jefferson, Wis.; J. A. Wilcox, Berlin, Wis.; E. D. Henry, Omro, Wis.; James Gray, Romeo, Mich.; L. A. Hamilton, Owosso, Mich.; William Sayler, East Saginaw, Mich.; James W. Hine, Lowell, Mich.; John B. Handy, Three Rivers, Mich.; George R. Stone, Allegan, Mich.; Charles P. Crandall, Owatonna, Minn.; Clinton Spencer, Ypsilanti, Mich.; William P. Harding, Cambridge City, Ind.; Micham C. Garber, Madison, Ind.; B. W. Davis, Richmond, Ind.; A. F. Phillips, Kokomo, Ind.; Mrs. Sarah Sackleman, Busnville, Ind.; Elias Wilson, Millville, N. J.; Rachel McKibben, Middletown, Penn.; D. S. Gilger, Shamokin, Penn.; P. G. Clarke, Eutala, Ala.; Austin C. Chase, Syracuse, N. Y.; J. H. Taylor, Bozeman, Montana; Mrs. S. G. Ware, Salem, N. J.; Thomas B. Honks, Tribune, Penn.; J. K. Bowis, Bedford, Penn.; J. J. Smith, Sunbury, Penn.; James K. Dawes, Easton, Penn.; C. H. Brook, Conshohocken, Penn.; Luke Marvin, Duluth, Minn.; H. S. Haskell, Portage, Wis.; William Wallace, Battle Creek, Mich.; A. P. Hone, Shelbyville, Ind.; William N. Hughes, Columbia, Tenn.

The Senate also confirmed all the naval promotions made during the recess of Congress and sent to the Senate on the 9th inst., with the exception of the three following: Frank Plunkett, to be an Assistant Paymaster, and Passed Assistants Charles D. Mansfield and Charles S. Bartlett, to be Paymasters of the Navy, which three were not reported from the committee to whom they were referred.

NOTES FROM THE CAPITAL.

THE DOORKEEPER'S LIST OF APPOINTMENTS COMPLETED—CUBAN INTERVENTION—THE CENTENNIAL SUBSIDY—POSTAL CHANGES.

WASHINGTON, Dec. 15.—L. H. Fitzhugh, Doorkeeper of the House of Representatives, has completed his appointments. J. W. Jennings, of Texas, is his assistant; A. W. Fletcher, of Pennsylvania, Superintendent of the Folding Room; A. R. Rese, of Georgia, Superintendent of the Document Room; C. C. Aleshire, of Ohio, Assistant Superintendent of the Document Room; Lafayette Fitzhugh, of Texas, Document File Clerk. The Assistant Doorkeepers are divided among the States as follows: New-York, three; Arkansas, two, and one each for Ohio, Missouri, Virginia, West Virginia, Illinois, Indiana, Texas, North Carolina, Kentucky, Georgia, Alabama, and Mississippi, and one from the National Soldiers' Home. The clerks in the folding-room are divided as follows: Tennessee, two; Texas, two; Georgia, two; Pennsylvania, two, and one each to Ohio, Alabama, Louisiana, Indiana, Missouri, Wisconsin, California, Connecticut, West Virginia, and Illinois. The twenty-six pages and nine other persons in subordinate positions are divided among the States.

The resignation of Surveyor General Stratton has been placed in Senator Sargent's hands, to take effect Jan. 11. Mr. Sargent will recommend as his successor H. G. Rollins, who has so satisfactorily served as Register of the San Francisco Land Office during the past six years.

The published report that the United States have submitted proposals to Great Britain, France, and Germany, looking to an intervention in the Cuban question, is contradicted by the language of the President in his recent annual Message. In addition, it may positively be asserted that even if this Government should in future be inclined to such intervention, it would do so without asking or desiring the co-operation of foreign powers.

Representative Holman's resolution, agreed to in the House of Representatives to-day, against the granting of subsidies, was distinctly stated by him as not applying to the Centennial Exhibition.

The Postmaster General to-day issued an order changing name of Post Office at Greenburg, N. Y., back to its former name of Dobb's Ferry, thus continuing the Revolutionary name and favoring the inhabitants of the locality, who desired the change, and also for the additional reason that letters addressed to Greenburg often find their way to Greenbush.

Postal service was to-day ordered from Port Henry to Plattsburg, N. Y., and from New-Grinnell to Montezuma, Iowa.

The new District Jail, situated on the eastern branch of the Potomac, having been finished, the old structure which has so long disfigured Judiciary Square will be demolished. It has been presented for the last twenty years, by Grand Juries, as a nuisance, and was so insecure that prisoners had but little difficulty in effecting their escape. In this jail Dr. Charles John Gardiner, convicted of Mexico grant frauds, committed suicide, and Gen. Sickles during his trial for the killing of Philip Barton Key was a prisoner. It was frequently a place of political excitement during the days of slavery, when captured slaves were visited by their abolition friends, and the circumstances connected with their custody formed the subject of Congressional inquiry and exciting discussion.

The Commissioner of Patents yesterday heard the interference case declared between L. H. McCollough, of Indiana, and W. B. Watkins, of New-York, over the title and priority of the invention known to the public as the Police and Burglar Alarm Telegraph. The invention is of great value, and the case is being contested with much vigor.

A very large crowd of visitors was at the Executive Mansion to-day, including an unusual number of ladies. Among the callers who had audience with the President were Senators Hamlin, Ferry, Bruce, and Sargent, Col. S. S. Smoot, of this city, and a few others. The Attorney General and Secretary of War were in consultation with the President for some time during the day.

The balances in the Treasury at the close of business to-day were as follows: Currency, $9,736,718; special deposit of legal tenders for the redemption of certificates of deposit, $44,930,000; coin, $70,213,255, including $21,836,800 in coin certificates; outstanding legal tenders, $372,471,772.

The President has recognized Alfred Channing Bagshawe as Vice Consul of her Britannic Majesty at St. Louis, Mo.

Second Assistant Postmaster General Tyner is absent from his duties on account of illness at home.

There was a rumor in circulation to-day that Gen. Cowen, Assistant Secretary of the Interior, had been requested to resign, but Secretary Candler, who was interrogated on the subject, said that the rumor was entirely devoid of truth; that Gen. Cowen was entirely in accord with him and fully enjoyed the confidence of the President, and there was no desire whatever that he should retire from his present office.

THE ARMY AND NAVY.

WASHINGTON, Dec. 15.—The Army Register for 1876, just issued, shows that during the present year there were eighteen resignations, namely: One Paymaster, four Captains, seven First Lieutenants, five Second Lieutenants, and one Chaplain, and thirty-eight deaths, including two Brigadier Generals—Lorenzo Thomas and Alexander Shiras—two Colonels, two Lieutenant Colonels, six Majors, six Captains, twelve First Lieutenants, six Second Lieutenants, and two Chaplains. Nine officers were dismissed, three cashiered, and one honorably discharged.

The Chief of Engineers, the Chief of Ordnance, the Surgeon General, and the Chief Signal Officer of the Army are authorized to detail for duty at the International Exhibition of 1876 at Philadelphia as many enlisted men of their respective organizations as may be required by Major S. C. Lyford, Ordnance Department, Chairman of the board, on behalf of the United States executive departments, for purposes directly connected with the display to be made by the above bureaus of the War Department. The leave of absence granted Second Lieut. Thomas T. Knox, First Cavalry, Benecia Barracks, California, has been extended ten months.

Ensign Frank S. Holcum, ordered to the Hartford; Chief Engineer Elijah Laws, to duty in charge of the engineering stores at the navy-Yard, New-York; Passed Assistant Engineer James W. Holihan, to special duty at Philadelphia connected with the Centennial; Chief Engineer Robert Danby, detached from duty in charge of engineering stores at the navy-Yard, New-York, and placed on waiting orders; Master B. H. Buckingham has been commissioned a Lieutenant in the Navy to rank from July 3, last, and Master S. S. Primo to rank from June 5, last. Commander George W. Hayward has been ordered to New York to take command of the Supply, which goes into commission on the 21st inst. The Supply will take out supplies to our European Station and bring home works of art from the Mediterranean ports for the Centennial Exhibition.

WESTERN FREIGHT RATES.

Special Dispatch to the New-York Times.

CHICAGO, Dec. 15.—The managers of the eastern railroad lines in this city held another meeting to-day, and decided to advance rates on boxed meats five cents per hundred pounds. The rates take effect on the 24th inst. An attempt was also made to advance rates on grain, but after much discussion the subject was dropped for the present.

THE CANADIAN LUMBER MARKET.

OTTAWA, Dec. 15.—There is nothing doing in the lumber market as far as sales are concerned. It is estimated that a hundred million feet of sawn lumber is being wintered in Ottawa and vicinity—about the same quantity as last year. The prospect of a shortage in the British markets and Eastern States prompted the increased operations in the woods. The labor market is overstocked and wages very low.

THE OFFICIAL VOTE OF BOSTON.

BOSTON, Dec. 15.—Mayor Cobb's majority is 2,666 in a total vote of 27,200; the latter, with one exception, is the largest vote ever polled in this city. Of the Aldermen elect eight are Republicans and four Democrats. In the Common Council there are forty-nine Republicans and twenty-three Democrats. G. L. Ruffin, a colored lawyer, was elected a member of the Council, and is the first colored man ever chosen.

ROBBERIES BY MEXICAN BANDITS.

SAN FRANCISCO, Dec. 15.—A dispatch from San Diego says that a letter has been received by a merchant of that city from S. E. Gaskell, whose store at Campo was recently plundered by Mexican bandits, stating that the robbers assert their intention of attacking again with sufficient force to overcome all opposition. The letter urges a movement for their defense by citizens, little being hoped for from the military authorities.

THE BOSTON BASE-BALL CLUB.

BOSTON, Dec. 15.—The annual meeting of the Boston Base-ball Club was held here to-day, and the officers re-elected. The Treasurer's report shows the total income of the club for the year to be $37,767 06, and the total expenses $34,509 99, leaving a balance of $3,257 07. The Directors report the engagement of Murnan, Borden, McGinley, and Whitney, in place of four players gone to Chicago.

ALABAMA CLAIMS.

WASHINGTON, Dec. 15.—In the Court of Commissioners of the Alabama Claims to-day the arguments were concluded on cases No. 736, Eliza A. Pope; No. 737, Sarah Stevens, and No. 775, Samuel Stevens, for loss by the destruction of the Martaban by the Alabama; case No. 42, Alfred P. Pikes, and No. 43, T. H. Ellingwood, were finally submitted. The court then adjourned until to-morrow.

POLICEMAN SENT TO PRISON.

BOSTON, Dec. 15.—In the Superior Court at Dedham to-day, Police Officer E. F. Hunting, who shot and killed Charles F. Robbins at Graniteville Depot some weeks since, taking him for a burglar, was sentenced for manslaughter to three years at hard labor in the House of Correction.

TAXATION IN NEW-HAMPSHIRE.

CONCORD, Dec. 15.—A meeting of the Selectmen and Assessors of the different towns in the State was held here to-day to consider means for equalizing taxation throughout the State. A committee was appointed, consisting of two delegates from each county, to consider the matter and report to the next Legislature.

HOG PACKING.

ST. LOUIS, Dec. 15.—The *Live Stock and Commercial Record* reports the number of hogs packed here for the week ending to-day to be 39,364, and the average weight 272⅓ pounds; the total packing since Nov. 1, 137,418; taken by butchers, 14,360, and by shippers, 38,108.

A SHIP BURNED AT SEA.

BOSTON, Dec. 15.—A dispatch received here states that the ship Helen Morris, of Boston, Capt. Bursley, from Shields, for San Francisco, with coal, has been burned at sea. The Captain and twelve men landed at Valparaiso Nov. 28. The vessel was 1,225 tons register, built at Boston in 1868, and was owned by Baker & Morrill, of Boston.

DEATH SENTENCE COMMUTED.

ST. LOUIS, Dec. 15.—Mrs. Anna Hollinscheed, who was to be hanged at Herman, Mo., on the 17th inst., for the murder of her son-in-law, Christopher Albend, has had her sentence commuted to imprisonment for life by Gov. Hardin. Her husband, convicted and sentenced with her, will be executed at the appointed time.

ENGLAND AND THE EAST.

THE PURCHASE OF THE SUEZ CANAL SHARES.

VARYING VIEWS ON ITS EXPEDIENCY—GENERAL SENTIMENT FAVORABLE TO THE MEASURE—THE GOVERNMENT EMBARRASSED—MR. DISRAELI'S POSITION—ARMY MOBILIZATION.

From Our Own Correspondent.

LONDON, Saturday, Dec. 4, 1875.

The purchase of the Suez Canal shares is of course still uppermost in the public mind, and the first flush of excitement at the thought of England again playing a bold and decisive part in European affairs is gradually giving place to some uncomfortable doubts as to whether the *coup*, as it is called, is, after all, really so bold and decisive as was supposed, and whether it is likely to be altogether satisfactory in its results. A good deal of surprise has been occasioned by the discovery that the transaction gives to England the command of only ten votes at the meetings of the company, and it has also begun to dawn on people that the acquisition of shares in a joint stock company, of which England has just set an example, may establish a precedent which may be dangerously convenient to other powers, as it will enable them to carry on unscrupulous projects under cover of what they will be able to call legitimate trade. The growth of suspicion is further indicated in the rumor that the Russian Government intends to buy up a majority of shares in the canal, and the other equally significant report that the Khédive, having worked off his Suez stock at a good figure, is going in for a competing system in the shape of an overland line of railway through Egypt, which will dispense with the burning ordeal of the Red Sea passage. It is now known that the idea of this country acquiring a hold on the Suez Canal, though suddenly presented the other day in a new form, is not exactly an original idea. The question of bringing the enterprise under the control of England, in conjunction with other marine powers, was brought before Mr. Gladstone's Government, and declined for prudential reasons. During the reign of the present Ministry, there has been also communication with France on the subject, so that the French cannot justly complain of having been taken by surprise, since proposals were made to them which they set aside. The reports which have just arrived that the Khédive, having strengthened himself by an alliance with the English Government, has thrown himself vigorously into an aggressive movement not only against Abyssinia, but against Zanzibar, with a view to annex territory, are no doubt somewhat exaggerated, but they have been sufficient to suggest further doubts as to the expediency of the Government too closely identifying itself with that of Egypt.

THE PREVAILING SENTIMENT.

On the whole, however, the general feeling here still continues to be in favor of the step which has been taken. The reason of this is that it pleases two very opposite classes of people, who look at the question from different sides. On the one hand, are those who think that all the troubles of the Eastern question have been once for all set at rest by a financial investment which, even if it do not prove directly profitable, will keep the peace and help trade. On the other hand, there is another class who are delighted with this transaction, not as a final one, but as the beginning of a systematic and vigorous policy of intervention in European affairs in so far as our interests are concerned, and who imagine that, now the Government has taken the plunge, they will be committed to swim the whole passage. For the moment these two sets of people are at one; each is dazzled by its own side of the shield, and without thinking of the other side, sings the praises of Mr. Disraeli, whose magic wand has brought all this about. Some day, however, it will be discovered that the Government policy has two aspects, and that if the present investment is regarded as final, it will prove a delusion, while, if it requires to be supported and completed by ulterior measures, it is but the first step in a long and arduous journey which perhaps the country may not be altogether ready to undertake, or at least to pursue energetically.

THE GOVERNMENT'S EMBARRASSMENT.

It is this double view of the subject which embarrasses the Government, and makes it anxious to put off explanations as long as possible. Mr. Disraeli is evidently in doubt which theory of the situation to espouse. Should he go in for a big roar of the British lion and a lashing of the tail, and boldly avow that Russia is to be bearded in its den, or is he to adopt a mild, pacific tone, and congratulate the peace-at-any-price party on having averted war by the more holy influence of the breeches pocket? Some of the papers say that Parliament is to be called together immediately; others that it will not meet till the usual time in February or just before, and the latter will no doubt be found to be in the right. It would be extremely inconvenient for members of Parliament, especially country members, to come to town just now, when their houses here are all shut up, for a ten days' session, with Christmas immediately intervening; and Mr. Disraeli knows better than any man how to ingratiate himself into the weaknesses of humanity. Not for worlds would he interfere with the sacred rites of the domestic hearth, or disturb the family life of the country. At the same time, of course, he does not want his hand to be forced too soon, and to have to declare precipitately in what light he desires his policy to be viewed; and, indeed, not much good would come just now from any discussion. The country requires time to know its own mind, and to realize how far it is prepared to go. The Government may fairly plead that it knows what, in its own opinion, is for the best, but that the avowed adoption of a bold policy must depend on the support which it is likely to receive from the nation, and this must be ascertained before, in such a delicate game as foreign politics, it reveals its play.

THE OPINION OF COMMERCE.

The *Economist*, the chief organ of the commercial classes, has an article to-day on this question, which perhaps means a good deal more than is actually said. It is significantly headed "The Suez Canal Purchase, as far as We yet Understand it." At first, the writer says, the energy and novelty of the act charmed the many; but on consideration, the advantages seem to decrease and the price to increase; and it is very important that the world should know the reasons of the Government, supposing them to be satisfactory ones. Then he goes on to show that what has been bought is the dividends of the company at the end of nineteen years, (this income having been surrendered by the Khédive for that time,) and in the meantime five per cent. a year from Egypt. The Khédive is in a chronic state of embarrassment on account of his extravagance, and it is very difficult to say whether he will be able to meet the obligations which he has undertaken; and a new loan for Egypt is, for the present, out of the question. Consequently, the English Government will be kept in constant anxiety about Egypt. This will lead to missions and intervention, and will be perilous as regards our relations both with Egypt and with other powers, especially France. "The Khédive," the writer adds—and this is painfully true—"has long been known as one of the most confirmed speculators in Europe, and it is much to be feared that he now has the blank indorsement of the English Government, and that the money-lenders of Europe will again begin to lend to him at usurious rates, which they had just ceased to do." As to the Canal shares as a new commercial investment, the *Economist* holds that, if that were all, England would be much better without them, even apart from dividends, and looking only to the use of the Canal to commerce. There will, it is pointed out, be a constant and vital difference of opinion in the management of the canal between the English Government and other shareholders. The former will be satisfied if it pays in the long run, and will be anxious to keep it in good repair; the others will set themselves against expenditure, and be hungry for dividends. And in this contest the Government will be in a helpless minority, with everything it proposes suspected and distrusted. And, finally, how is "the road to India" to be secured? The purchase gives no additional rights against an enemy to England; and as to showing what we mean—if we mean war, is it wise to say so? If we do not mean war, is it wise to suggest the suspicion? The whole question is thus summed up: Are the shares worth four millions sterling, together with the jealousy of France and the necessity of interfering in Egypt? It will be seen that there are here some very pretty nuts to crack.

THE BRITISH ARMY.

The scheme for the mobilization of the British Army is another stroke of policy which is no doubt intended to have effect abroad. Certain bodies of troops are to be distributed through the kingdom in well-considered strategical relations to each other, and ready at short notice for any emergency. The regulars will, of course, be liable to go abroad, and the reserve forces and volunteers will then at once take their place, according to settled regulations. I need not trouble you with details; that is the general principle of the system. At each station full information will be provided as to roads in the district and all matters relating to tactics and strategy for the guidance of commanding officers, who will be bound to study the subject at each station where they happen to be posted. On the whole, the arrangements seem very practical and judicious, and it is said that they will be at once carried out. The serious question is, however, how far the Government has an active and efficient army qualified to do justice to such a plan. At present this may be doubted, for the regular battalions are seriously weak, and the reserves have practically no existence except on paper. Here, again, we must wait to know whether the Government is bold enough to carry out its schemes to the full extent, and there are many people who believe that this cannot be done without something in the nature of a conscription or universal service.

THE SEASON AND THE WEATHER.

In London the weather has become intensely severe, and to-day we are quite snowed up, besides being wrapped in a black, impenetrable fog. Locomotion is suspended, and even the few cabs which were in the forenoon seen staggering along the stiffening roads have disappeared.

FINANCE IN THE CITY.

The Stock Exchange has been rather holding its breath this week in fear of a great smash, or series of smashes, at the settlement. It is known that various speculators, including, it is said, Mr. Albert Grant, have suffered badly from being on the losing side of the market with Egyptians, and it was feared that some of them would collapse. But somehow they have tided over the evil day. J. H. F.

MALACCA.

ATTACK ON AND CAPTURE OF THE MALAY STOCKADE BY THE BRITISH.

LONDON, Dec. 15.—Sir William Jervois, Governor of the Straits settlements, telegraphs from Penang, dated the 14th inst., that on the 7th eighty men of the Tenth Regiment and 120 auxiliaries, consisting of irregular troops and Police, attacked from four to eight hundred Malays who were fortified behind a stockade within five miles of the Perak residency. After a sharp fight, the attacking party charged the Malays and routed them. From sixty to eighty of the enemy were killed or wounded, while only two of the British and six of the auxiliaries were killed and twenty-five altogether wounded. The troops are now meeting with no resistance and reinforcements are not required at present.

GERMANY.

DEPARTURE OF THE ARCHBISHOP OF COLOGNE FROM THAT CITY, NOT TO RETURN.

COLOGNE, Dec. 15.—The Archbishop of Cologne left this city yesterday, and is not expected to return. It is understood that he delegated his powers to subordinate Catholic ecclesiastics.

AFRICA.

CAPT. CAMERON'S EXPLORING EXPEDITION ARRIVES AT ST. PAUL DE LOANDA.

LONDON, Dec. 16—6 A. M.—The *Morning Standard* publishes a special dispatch from St. Paul de Loanda, stating that Capt. Cameron's exploring expedition arrived there Nov. 19, having traversed the continent from Ujiji. The expedition had been a complete success. All the men were well.

AN INTOLERANT PRIEST.

NEWPORT, Dec. 14.—Quite a number of residents of this quiet city are somewhat indignant because the Catholic Priest, Rev. Philip Grace, of St. Mary's Church, refused to permit the remains of a daughter of Manuel De Fray, who died here a few days ago, to be brought to the church for the purpose of having the usual burial service performed. He also refused to officiate at the house of the deceased, the reason being that the child was permitted to attend the Protestant school. In consequence of this decision the body of the child has been placed in the vault of the Protestant Cemetery to await further developments. No services have been held as yet, although the girl died on Friday. It is rumored that a Protestant clergyman will be called in to conduct the funeral services. It is a positive fact that the friends of the family have recommended such a step to be taken.

RAILROAD OPENING.

NEW-BEDFORD, Dec. 15.—The new railroad from this city to Fall River was formally opened to-day with appropriate ceremonies. An excursion train of five cars with the stockholders and officers of the railroad and City Government of this city went over the line this morning, and on their return brought twenty or thirty members of the Fall River City Government. Dinner was served at the Parker House, during which speeches were made by Mayors Howland, of New-Bedford, and Davenport, of Fall River; Presidents Howe, of the New-Bedford Railroad; Beauvais, of the Fall River Road, and others. The new road runs between the two cities in a nearly straight line, a distance of eleven and a half miles. Four way stations will be established, and the trains will run each way daily.

THE WHISKY TRIALS.

DISTRICT ATTORNEY DYER, OF ST. LOUIS, RENOMINATED BY THE PRESIDENT—HILL CONVICTED AT INDIANAPOLIS—RECTIFIERS PLEAD GUILTY AT COVINGTON, KY.

Special Dispatch to the New-York Times.

WASHINGTON, Dec. 15.—The name of D. P. Dyer was sent to the Senate to-day as District Attorney for the Eastern District of Missouri. This sets at rest the hostile reports that he was to be removed from the prosecutions of the St. Louis Whisky Ring, or that he would be left to drop out of office at the expiration of the time within which a nomination must be made. That the most efficient prosecuting officer employed by the Government at St. Louis should be retained is discouraging to the people who have been predicting so confidently the break down of the attack upon the Ring. The long and interesting dispatch from Chicago in this morning's TIMES, relative to the Chicago Ring, has created a good deal of excitement here to-day, though its revelations have been by no means unexpected. The dispatch has been eagerly read, and is the common theme of conversation to-night.

INDIANAPOLIS, Dec. 15.—Judge Gresham delivered his charge to the jury in James K. Hill's case this morning, and the jury retired at a few minutes after 10 o'clock, and at 4 o'clock returned a verdict of guilty on the first, second, and third counts, and not guilty on all the others. A motion for a new trial will be heard by the court to-morrow.

CINCINNATI, Dec. 15.—In the United States Circuit Court at Covington, Ky., to-day, J. M. Schnitker, F. R. Krueskamp, F. Macke, and Steinriede, engaged in the rectifying business, pleaded guilty of violations of the Revenue laws. Their sentences have not yet been announced.

THE BABCOCK COURT OF INQUIRY DISSOLVED AT THE REQUEST OF GEN. BABCOCK.

WASHINGTON, Dec. 15.—The President has received the following:

CHICAGO, Dec. 12, 1875.

To the President:

SIR: Since my request for a court of inquiry as the only apparent means open to me at the time of refuting charges made against me at St. Louis, a bill of indictment has been found in the United States Court, and I shall consequently be afforded a means of vindication before that tribunal. I therefore respectfully suggest the order convening such court of inquiry be revoked, as I trust that my case may be reached at an early day in the United States Court. Very respectfully your obedient servant,

(Signed,) O. E. BABCOCK.
Colonel of Engineers, United States Army.

In accordance with the above the following order has been issued:

WAR DEPARTMENT, ADJUTANT GENERAL'S OFFICE,
WASHINGTON, Dec. 15.

SPECIAL ORDERS No. 255.—The court of inquiry appointed in Special Orders No. 246, of Dec. 4, 1875, from this office, to assemble at Chicago, is hereby dissolved. The members and Judge Advocate will return to their stations.

By order of the President of the United States.
E. D. TOWNSEND, Adjutant General.

A telegram was received at the Department of Justice to-day from United States Attorney Dyer, at St. Louis, announcing that no more important trials would occur before January.

WRECK OF FISHING CRAFT.

SEVERAL VESSELS CAST AWAY ON THE NEWFOUNDLAND COAST—NINETEEN LIVES LOST.

BOSTON, Dec. 15.—Late Newfoundland papers received in this city this evening give particulars of ten distressing shipwrecks, involving the loss of nineteen lives. The first was that of the sloop Hopewell, with eight persons on board, which left St. Johns on the morning of Monday, Nov. 29, for Harbor Maine. The early part of the day was fine, but toward nightfall a heavy storm arose, accompanied by snow. The Hopewell proceeded on her voyage as far as the vicinity of Cape St. Francis, when she ran upon Biscan Rock about 8 o'clock in the evening. The storm being at its height, all hands, with one exception, were lost. The survivor, named Waugh, got on a rock and there remained until next day toward evening, when he was rescued after much trouble by Capt. Blandföde, of the steamer Hercules, who discovered the poor fellow waving a handkerchief. He had been on the rock about twenty hours at the mercy of every sea, and was almost exhausted.

The same day the schooner Water Witch left St. John's for a port in Conception Bay, and went to pieces near Pouch Cove, in the vicinity of Capt. St. Francis, at night, in the height of the storm. The shore line is almost perpendicular to the height of nearly six hundred feet. As the vessel was driven against the cliff those on board got on a ledge, where they clung all night, those whose footing was the least secure being swept off by the sea. Thirteen out of the twenty-four persons on board were saved, each one being made fast to about one hundred fathoms of line and hauled up the face of the cliff by the settlers in the neighborhood, who discovered the shipwrecked crew by their cries. There were four females among the lost.

Other marine disasters are mentioned, viz., a schooner, proceeding up Green Bay, with supplies from St. John's, was lost, and the Captain, his son, and two others perished. Three men belonging to Redhead Cove, in Trinity Bay, were lost by the capsizing of their boat. Two bodies were taken from a schooner ashore near Little Placentia. The schooner Phœbe Jane was lost near Filt Cove, when a female passenger and one of the crew were lost. The weather in Newfoundland has been extremely severe, the cold snap experienced here the last of November being felt there with increased severity.

THE WEATHER.

SYNOPSIS AND PROBABILITIES.

WASHINGTON, Dec. 16—1 A. M.—The area of lowest pressure is now central north of Lake Ontario, and falling barometer, southerly winds, and cloudy weather prevail in New-England and New-York; northerly winds, rising barometer, and clear weather in the Ohio Valley and Tennessee; southwest winds and higher temperature in the South Atlantic and Gulf States. The Ohio River has fallen.

PROBABILITIES.

For Thursday, in the South Atlantic and Gulf States, falling barometer, warmer, clear, or hazy weather, and southerly winds.

For Tennessee and the Ohio Valley, rising barometer, north-west winds, cooler, clear weather.

For the Upper Mississippi and Lower Missouri Valleys, rising barometer, lower temperature, north-west winds, and cloudy weather.

For the lake region, rising barometer, north-west and westerly winds, partly cloudy, warmer weather.

For the Middle States and New-England, rising followed by falling barometer, warmer weather, cloud and snow, except clear weather in the southern portions.

The Tennessee and Ohio Rivers will continue falling.

For the canal regions of New-Jersey and Virginia, the temperature will rise to freezing and above.

SAVINGS BANKS REDUCING INTEREST.

BOSTON, Dec. 15.—The Mechanics' Savings Bank to-day reduced the rate of interest to five per cent., to take effect after Jan. 1. This action is substantially the same as has been previously adopted by nearly all the savings banks in this city.

THE HUDSON CLOSED AGAIN.

POUGHKEEPSIE, Dec. 15.—The upper Hudson is closed again. The steamer Walter Brett, for Catskill from New-York, is frozen in at Rhinebeck. Its freight was forwarded by rail. No more boats can get north this season.

TWEED THOUGHT TO BE IN MONTREAL.

MONTREAL, Dec. 15.—It is reported that Tweed is here and hiding in a house on Union avenue. Mr. Tellier, of the New-York Merchants' Detective Agency, is in the city.

CONGRESSIONAL ELECTION.

NASHVILLE, Dec. 15.—Specials to the *American* say that the returns from the Fourth District of Tennessee render it certain that H. Y. Riddle (Dem.) is elected to Congress.

LATEST NEWS BY CABLE.

THE BREMERHAVEN EXPLOSION.

THE EXPLOSIVE CASE PREPARED WITH THE DESIGN OF DESTROYING THE MOSEL.

BREMEN, Dec. 15.—It is now ascertained that the passenger who owned the case of dynamite which exploded at Bremerhaven is named Thomassen, and not Thomas, as has been given heretofore. He has confessed to the authorities that he constructed the chest which exploded, and arranged a clock-work attachment to cause the explosion after a certain time had elapsed. He was occupied for a fortnight in filling the chest, and worked in a coach-house in one of the most frequented parts of Bremen.

The Police have examined the house alluded to, and found some of the packing material, but no explosives of any kind.

THOMAS STILL TRYING TO DESTROY HIMSELF—THE DIABOLICAL PLOT A CONSPIRACY INVOLVING ACCOMPLICES IN NEW-YORK.

LONDON, Dec. 16—5 A. M.—A special dispatch to the *Times* from Berlin says: Thomas has repeatedly torn the bandage from the wound he inflicted in his attempted suicide, and is now securely bound. He seems to be a Swabian by birth, but has been naturalized in the United States. He passed a week last October in Liverpool apparently trying to ascertain whether it would be best for him to put his infernal machine on board a steamer there or in Bremerhaven.

The number of the killed by the explosion already reaches eighty, and others of the injured are not expected to recover. Forty corpses were buried on Tuesday, together with some chests filled with unidentified fragments of bodies. The total number of killed and wounded is now estimated at 180.

BREMEN, Dec. 15.—Thomas, the passenger on the Mosel, and the owner of the cask of dynamite which caused the terrible disaster at Bremerhaven, has confessed his guilt, saying that he has accomplices at New-York. It is hoped that he will recover, so that the full particulars of his crime can be obtained.

The *Weser Zeitung* says authoritatively that it is now proved that the author of the catastrophe was a passenger named Thomas, who has acknowledged himself not only the possessor of the barrel which exploded, but that he intended bringing it on board the Mosel for the purpose of sinking that vessel. The motive for this diabolical scheme appears to have been to procure exaggerated and fictitious insurance, and to share afterward with others. Thomas is quite conscious, and answers all questions, but the bullets have not yet been extracted from his head.

From what is known, the barrel prepared for this shameful work was made strongly by a Bremen cooper and partitioned, one part containing the dynamite and the other the apparatus for exploding it. The plan probably was that the apparatus should be ignited by clock-work after Thomas had landed at Southampton, whither he took passage, and where probably the goods would be shipped. He intended to place his hellish machine on the Deutschland, but it was not in time." The *Weser Zeitung* adds: "In sober words we communicate this with certainty that the number of victims killed and wounded amounts to 170."

DRESDEN, Dec. 15.—William K. Thomas, since his attempt at suicide, has made a full confession at Bremen. He was born in New-York, married a New-Orleans lady, and has four children, the youngest a baby. He lived in Virginia during the war, and engaged in the business of blockade-running, whereby he grew rich. Since 1866 he has resided here and at Leipsic, and last at Strethlen, near Dresden. He appears to have lost his money and become embarrassed. He was twice in America during the past Summer. The last time he went without the knowledge of his family, and when he returned he wrote his banker here that he had made arrangements enabling him to pay his debts in December. He was highly esteemed by the people about here. His house has been searched, but nothing found connected with the disaster.

THE STEAMER L'AMERIQUE.

A VESSEL SUPPOSED TO BE THE MISSING STEAMER SEEN OFF CAPE ST. VINCENT.

LONDON, Dec. 15.—The steamer Indus, from Alexandria, Egypt, reports that on the 3d of this month, off Cape St. Vincent, (Portugal,) she passed a bark-rigged steamer in tow of a schooner-rigged steamer, both of the same company. The funnels were painted red with a black top. It is probable that the steamers in question were the disabled L'Amerique and the Ville de Brest, the latter having the former in tow.

THE DEUTSCHLAND DISASTER.

AN INVESTIGATION TO BE MADE BY THE BOARD OF TRADE—BURIAL OF VICTIMS.

LONDON, Dec. 16.—The *Times* announces that the Board of Trade have ordered an official inquiry into the loss of the Deutschland, to begin on Monday next at Poplar. Fourteen bodies of the victims were buried at Dover Court yesterday. The shops in that place and in Harwich were closed during the funeral, and deep sympathy was shown by all the inhabitants.

FRANCE.

LIFE SENATORS ELECTED YESTERDAY—REPORTED RESIGNATION OF M. LEON SAY, MINISTER OF FINANCE.

PARIS, Dec. 15.—The following were elected Senators to-day: Viscount de Lorgeril, Deputy in the Assembly for Côtes du Nord, and the Count de Douhet, Deputy for Puy de Dôme, both Legitimists; Hervé de Saisy, Deputy for Côtes du Nord, Bonapartist; M. Gouin, Deputy for Indre et Loire; M. Lepetit, Deputy for Vienne; M. Paul Morin, Deputy for Seine; M. Scherer, Deputy for Seine et Oise; M. De Tocqueville, Deputy for Manche; Gen. Chabron Le Tellier and Gen. Valaze, Deputy for Seine Inférieure, of the Left Centre; M. Carnot; M. Lanfray, Deputy for Bouches du Rhone; M. Rainpont, Deputy for Yonne, and M. Testelin, Deputy for Nord, of the Left: M. Corbon, Deputy for Seine; M. Crémieux, Deputy for Algiers; M. Littré, Deputy for Seine, and M. Scheurer Kestner, Deputy for Seine, Radicals.

The Right Centre proposed to annul the elections of the foregoing because of an infraction of the rule requiring secrecy, but after a heated encounter between M. Buffet and M. Gambetta the proposal was rejected by a majority of thirteen.

It is currently reported this evening that M. Léon Say, the Minister of Finance, has resigned.

EMPIRES EXPAND

ETHAN BRONNER

In March of 1866, a lugubrious Scottish missionary named David Livingstone landed on the lush coast of East Africa with a self-proclaimed mission: "to blaze a trail for the gospel." It did not go well. He converted precisely one man (who later lapsed). Livingstone disappeared into the bush, however, and thereby did blaze a rather different trail, an unintended one with global consequences. Henry Morton Stanley, a Welsh-born journalist, persuaded the owner of The New York Herald to send him to find Livingstone as a kind of attention-grabbing journalistic stunt. When Stanley did come upon him on November 10, 1871, he apparently did not utter the words, "Dr. Livingstone, I presume?"[1] But his dispatches set loose a Western frenzy toward Africa that carved the benighted continent among half a dozen imperial powers.

Like the Spanish and Portuguese who dug into the New World three centuries earlier, gold, glory and God motivated the men who followed Stanley. There was much talk of the need to "Christianize and civilize"—Thomas Carlyle, father of British imperialism, said it was the mission of the Anglo-Saxon race to take control of the world's backward regions—but the imperial endeavor was largely about money and adventure.

Britain took the biggest share of Africa, ultimately winning Egypt, Sudan, South Africa, Nigeria, Sierra Leone, Uganda and Kenya. At its height, the British Empire, upon which it was said the sun never set nor rose, covered 13 million square miles, one fourth of the planet and one fourth of the people on it as well.

France was not left behind. It had taken Algeria in 1830 and later extended its control to all of North Africa—Morocco and Tunisia. This was a time of enormous change for France.

FURTHER READING

1 "New Publications. How I Found Livingstone," see December 9, 1872, article.

Scottish missionary David Livingstone, while exploring and mapping Africa, lost contact with the outside world for six years before he was found by journalist Henry Morton Stanley.

The meeting of Stanley and Livingstone in 1871 near Lake Tanganyika with the famous supposed greeting, "Dr. Livingstone, I presume."

This late-19th-century cartoon depicts England at the height of its imperial power.

These Algerian recruits who served in the French army were known as Turcos.

A cigarette card depicting "manifest destiny" carries the image of pioneers and others moving west during the last half of the 19th century.

In a few decades it had gone from a land of artisans and peasants to an industrial power—not quite where Britain was, nor where Germany was about to be, but still important. Its imperial adventures in Africa were central to its prosperity.

Germany's birth as a nation and growth as an empire took place partly on the backs of the French. While the Paris of 1870 was an expanse of graceful avenues designed by Baron Haussmann, and a marked contrast with the labyrinth of narrow alleys of a few decades earlier, it was soon to suffer the shame of occupation. On January 18, 1871, France had the distinct humiliation of seeing the King of Prussia proclaimed German Emperor in the Hall of Mirrors at Versailles.[2] Peace was eventually signed and Paris returned to its rightful owners but at great cost—France lost the rich provinces of Alsace and Lorraine, recovered only in World War I.[3]

Other powers—Italy, Spain and Portugal—also participated in the great African land grab of the last decades of the 19th century. Ultimately, all the powers met in Berlin in 1884 to set up rules of the game.[4] They issued a proclamation a year later promising "to protect the natives in their moral and material well-being, to cooperate in the suppression of slavery and the slave-trade, to further the education and civilization of the natives, to protect missionaries and explorers." Profits were protected even more.

From the vantage of the United States, Europe's imperial habits were a matter of some disdain. The Americans considered themselves the bearers of a God-given mission to spread their way of life, which they defined through democracy and liberty but which included fierce continental expansion of their own.

As the Reverend Henry Ward Beecher of Brooklyn's Plymouth Church declared on Thanksgiving 1866 (in a sermon printed in the next day's Times): "I fervently believe that God has set apart this northern Continent as the place where first shall be shown what is the safety in Government, the power in war, the incalculable wealth of the industries of peace—of a free people."[5]

It had been less than a century since 13 coastal British colonies threw off their own imperial yoke and extended their boundaries to take in 3.7 million square miles, turning themselves into the world's biggest country after Russia and Canada.

Railroad officials and employees celebrate the completion of the first transcontinental rail line in America on May 10, 1869.

This cartoon called "The Two Young Giants" depicts the United States and Russia looking to expand commerce in Asia.

Their move west, spreading railway and telegraph lines, slaying tribal natives and bison along the way, had been bolstered by a collective sense of destiny. An American journalist named John L. O'Sullivan coined the phrase "manifest destiny" in discussing the annexation of Texas from Mexico in 1845. He used it again to justify barring England from taking Oregon, arguing it should be American. He said, "And that claim is by the right of our manifest destiny to overspread and to possess the whole of the continent which Providence has given us for the development of the great experiment of liberty and federated self-government entrusted to us."

By the 1860's and 70's, the United States was becoming a world power. And at that point the editors of The New York Times seemed to think the nation should focus far less on conquest and far more on decency and human development, especially for the less fortunate here and abroad. When they used the phrase "manifest destiny" it was with ironic distance, even anger.

This painting by John Gast, called "American Progress," depicts the allegorical female figure of America leading pioneers and railroads westward.

2 "Europe. William Proclaimed Emperor of Germany," see January 21, 1871, front page.
3 "Europe.; The Terms of Peace Read in the French Assembly," see March 1, 1871, front page.
4 "The Congo Conference.; Points of Dispute Shown in the Opening Speeches," see November 18, 1884, front page.
5 "Thanksgiving Day.; Observance of the Day as a National Festival," see December 8, 1865, front page.

The explosion of the U.S.S. Maine, which killed 266 crew members, instantaneous caused outrage that led to the Spanish-American War.

Cartoon depicting Theodore Roosevelt digging dirt on the Panama Canal and throwing it on Bogota, Columbia.

For example, in an editorial that ran on April 1, 1870, the paper called on Canada to follow the American example and throw off its British masters. The paper saw no point in trying to annex Canada to the United States, saying: "We are believers in 'manifest destiny' but our faith does not necessarily carry us to that extent."[6] It used similar language to dismiss calls for the annexation of Cuba.

On November 18, 1873, on its front page, the paper asserted that the United States stood ready to intervene in Cuba, which was suffering from Spanish atrocities, including slavery. There was a need to "take away the powers of the tyrannical masters of Cuba."[7] And two years later, The Times lamented the moves by Britain and France into the South Pacific, "dispossessing the weak natives of the South Seas." It said such moves would doubtless "be hailed by our manifest destiny friends."

It would be another generation before the Americans themselves went to war in Cuba and the Philippines. A few years later, President Theodore Roosevelt added his "corollary" to the Monroe Doctrine of the 1820's that told the Europeans to stay out of Latin America. The Roosevelt corollary stated that in case of flagrant or chronic wrongdoing by a Latin American nation, the United States could intervene in that country's affairs.[8] It would do so many times although whether it was to amend wrongdoing remains a matter of debate.

ETHAN BRONNER, *the former deputy foreign editor of The New York Times, is currently its Jerusalem bureau chief. A series of articles on Al Qaeda that he helped edit won the 2001 Pulitzer Prize for explanatory journalism. He also was education editor from 1999 to 2001 and national education correspondent from 1997 to 1999. Previously, Bronner wrote for Reuters and was the Boston Globe's Supreme Court and legal affairs reporter before becoming its Middle East correspondent, based in Jerusalem.*

6 "A Canadian Nationality," see April 1, 1870, article.
7 "Rebel Politics," see November 30, 1864, article.
8 "Washington, Special Dispatches to the New-York Times," see December 18, 1866, front page.

The New-York Times.

VOL. XXV.......NO. 7742. NEW-YORK, FRIDAY, JULY 7, 1876. PRICE FOUR CENTS.

THE LITTLE HORN MASSACRE

LATEST ACCOUNTS OF THE CHARGE.

A FORCE OF FOUR THOUSAND INDIANS IN POSITION ATTACKED BY LESS THAN FOUR HUNDRED TROOPS—OPINIONS OF LEADING ARMY OFFICERS OF THE DEED AND ITS CONSEQUENCES—FEELING IN THE COMMUNITY OVER THE DISASTER.

Special Dispatch to the New-York Times.

The dispatches giving an account of the slaughter of Gen. Custer's command, published in THE TIMES of yesterday, are confirmed and supplemented by official reports from Gen. A. H. Terry, commanding the expedition. On June 25 Gen. Custer's command came upon the main camp of Sitting Bull, and at once attacked it, charging the thickest part of it with five companies, Major Reno, with seven companies attacking on the other side. The soldiers were repulsed and a wholesale slaughter ensued. Gen. Custer, his brother, his nephew, and his brother-in-law were killed, and not one of his detachment escaped. The Indians surrounded Major Reno's command and held them in the hills during a whole day, but Gibbon's command came up and the Indians left. The number of killed is stated at 300 and the wounded at 31. Two hundred and seven men are said to have been buried in one place. The list of killed includes seventeen commissioned officers.

It is the opinion of Army officers in Chicago, Washington, and Philadelphia, including Gens. Sherman and Sheridan, that Gen. Custer was rashly imprudent to attack such a large number of Indians, Sitting Bull's force being 4,000 strong. Gen. Sherman thinks that the accounts of the disaster are exaggerated. The wounded soldiers are being conveyed to Fort Lincoln. Additional details are anxiously awaited throughout the country.

CONFIRMATION OF THE DISASTER.

DISPATCHES FROM GEN. TERRY RECEIVED AT SHERIDAN'S HEAD-QUARTERS—THEORIES OF THE BATTLE—PROBABLY TEN THOUSAND SIOUX IN POSITION—THE ATTACK CONDEMNED AS RASH BY OFFICERS OF EXPERIENCE—DISPOSITION OF THE WOUNDED.

CHICAGO, July 6.—At the head-quarters of Lieut. Gen. Sheridan this morning, all was bustle and confusion over the reported massacre of Custer's command. Telegrams were being constantly received, but most of them were of a confidential nature and withheld from publication. It is known that the unfortunate command broke camp on the North Rosebud on June 22 for the purpose of proceeding in a direction which would bring it to the point named about the 25th, at which place a bloody fight is reported to have taken time. The following dispatch, the last received at head-quarters in this city previous to the news of the massacre, confirms the accounts given to the extent of showing that Custer intended to go to that place.

CAMP ON THE NORTH ROSEBUD, June 21, 1876.
Lieut. Gen. P. H. Sheridan, Commanding Military Division of the Missouri, Chicago:

No Indians have been met with as yet, but traces of large and recent camp have been discovered twenty or thirty miles up the Rosebud. Gibbon's column will move this morning, on the north side of the Yellowstone, for the mouth of the Big Horn, where it will be ferried across by the supply steamer, and whence it will proceed to the mouth of the Little Horn, and so on. Custer will go up the Rosebud to-morrow with his whole regiment, and thence to the head-waters of the Little Horn, thence down the Little Horn. A. H. TERRY,
Brigadier General Commanding.

A dispatch received at the quarters of Gen. Sheridan this morning at 11 o'clock confirms the first reports received. The dispatch states that the forces were falling back, and that the wounded had been sent to Fort Lincoln. No details were given, but the officers at head-quarters regard it as a full confirmation of the engagement reported. In reply to an inquiry as to whether the attack was made by Gen. Custer of his own accord, or under orders from the department, an answer was given that Custer made the charge of his own volition. A still later dispatch from Lieut. Kinzie, of the Seventh Cavalry, was received, asking that he be transferred from the department where he is now on duty to the scene of action. This is also regarded as another confirmation of the bloody massacre reported. Gen. Custer's family are at Fort Lincoln, to which point the wounded are being conveyed.

So far as an expression in regard to the wisdom of Gen. Custer's attack could be obtained at head-quarters, it was to the effect that Custer had been imprudent, to say the least. It is the opinion at head-quarters among those who are most familiar with the situation, that Custer struck Sitting Bull's main camp. Gen. Drum, of Sheridan's staff, is of opinion that Sitting Bull began concentrating his forces after the fight with Crook, and that no doubt, Custer dropped squarely into the midst of no less than ten thousand red devils and was literally torn to pieces. The movement made by Custer is censured to some extent at military head-quarters in this city. The older officers say that it was brought about by that foolish pride which so often results in the defeat of men. It seems that a few days before Gen. Terry had offered four additional companies to Custer, but that officer refused them.

The information at head-quarters further is to the effect that Gen. Gibbon with his force was known to be moving up to Custer for the purpose of reinforcing him, and that he [Custer] knew of this, and knew that Gibbon would arrive by the following day after the engagement. I have it on as good authority as one of the leading officers at head-quarters, that Custer had been ordered by Terry to make a march toward the Little Big Horn and to form a junction with a column of infantry that was moving diagonally across the country to the same point. The two columns were then to co-operate and make an attack. Instead of marching from twenty to thirty miles per day, as ordered, Custer made a forced march and reached the point of destination two or three days in advance of the infantry; then finding himself in front of the foe he foolishly attempted to cut his way through and punish the red devils.

DISPATHES FROM GEN. TERRY.

PARTICULARS OF THE PLAN OF THE MOVEMENT UNDER CUSTER AS AGREED ON BEFORE THE MARCH.

Special Dispatch to the New-York Times.

PHILADELPHIA, July 6.—This afternoon Gen. Sheridan received two dispatches from Gen. Terry relative to the Indian battle in which Gen. Custer was killed, and this evening the telegrams were handed to your correspondent. Gen. Sherman says that he thinks the first dispatch giving the details of the battle was mislaid, or else some enterprising newspaper correspondent bought up the messenger and sent the account East, thus keeping the War Department in ignorance of the occurrence. From what he knows of the occurrence he believes that Gen. Custer attempted a battle without reconnoitering the position, and that he was too bold. He does not think the slaughter so great as at first reported. The first dispatch received by Gen. Sheridan was as follows:

CAMP ON YELLOWSTONE, NEAR MOUTH OF BIG HORN, July 2.

On the evening of the 28th we commenced moving down with the wounded, but were able to get along but four miles, as the hard litters did not answer the purpose. The mule litters did excellently well, but they were insufficient in number; therefore, the 29th was spent in making a full supply of them. On the evening of the 29th we started again, and at 2 A. M. the wounded were placed on the steamer at the mouth of the Little Big Horn. The afternoon of the 30th they were brought down to the depot on the Yellowstone. I send them to-morrow by steam to Fort Lincoln, and with them one of my aids, Capt. E. W. Smith, who will be able to answer any questions which you may desire to ask. Col. Sheridan's dispatch informing me of the reputed gathering of Indians on the Rosebud reached me after I came down here. I hear nothing of Gen. Crook's movements. At least a hundred horses are needed to remount the cavalrymen now here.

(Signed,) ALFRED H. TERLY,
Brigadier General.

The second dispatch was as follows:

CAMP BIG HORN, July 2.

I think I owe it to myself to put you more fully in possession of the facts of the late operations. While at the mouth of the Rosebud I submitted my plan to Gen. Gibbon and Gen. Custer. It was that Custer, with his whole regiment, should move up the Rosebud till he should meet a trail Reno had discovered a few days before, but that he should not follow it directly to the Little Big Horn; that he should send scouts over it and keep his main force further toward the south, so as to prevent the Indians from slipping in between himself and the mountains. He was also to examine the head waters of the Tollaska Creek, as he passed it, and send me word of what he found there. A scout was furnished him for the purpose of crossing the country to me. We calculated it would take Gibbons' column until the 26th to reach the mouth of the Little Big Horn, and that the wide sweep I had proposed Custer should make would require so much time that Gibbon would be able to co-operate with him in attacking any Indians that might be found on the stream. I asked Custer how long his marches would be. He said they would be at the rate of about thirty miles a day. Measurements were made and calculations based on that rate of progress. I talked with him about his strength and at one time suggested that perhaps it would be well for me to take Gibbon's cavalry and go with him. To the latter suggestion he replied: "That, without reference to the command, he would prefer his own regiment alone. As a homogenous body, as much could be done with it as with the two combined. He expressed the utmost confidence that he had all the force that he could need, and I shared his confidence. The plan adopted was the only one which promised to bring the infantry into action, and I desired to make sure of things by getting up every available man. I offered Custer the battery of Gatling guns, but he declined it, saying that it might embarrass him, and that he was strong enough without it.

The movements proposed by Gen. Gibbon's column were carried out to the letter, and had the attack been deferred until it was up, I cannot doubt that we should have been successful. The Indians had evidently prepared themselves for a stand, but as I learned from Capt. Benton that on the 22d the cavalry marched twelve miles; on the 23d, twenty-five miles; from 5 A. M. till 8 P. M., of the 24th, forty-five miles, and then after night ten miles further, resting, but without unsaddling, twenty-three miles, to the battle-field. The proposed route was not taken, but as soon as the trail was struck it was followed. I cannot learn that any examination of Tallaska Creek was made. I do not tell you this to cast any reflections upon Custer, for whatever errors he may have committed Custer's action is unexplainable in the case.

A. H. TERRY, Brigadier General.

These dispatches were all that either Gens. Sherman or Sheridan received up to midnight, and were sent to the Secretary of War.

DETAILS OF THE BATTLE.

GRAPHIC DESCRIPTION OF THE FIGHTING—MAJOR RENO'S COMMAND UNDER FIRE FOR TWO DAYS—EVERY MAN OF CUSTER'S DETACHMENT KILLED EXCEPT ONE SCOUT—AFFECTING SCENES WHEN RELIEF ARRIVED.

Special Dispatch to the New-York Times.

CHICAGO, July 6.—A special to the *Times* to-night from Bismarck, recounts most graphically the late encounter with the Indians on the Little Big Horn. Gen. Custer left the Rosebud on June 22, with twelve companies of the Seventh Cavalry, striking a trail where Reno left it, leading in the direction of the Little Horn. On the evening of the 24th fresh trails were reported, and on the morning of the 25th an Indian village, twenty miles above the mouth of the Little Horn was reported about three miles long and half a mile wide and fifteen miles away. Custer pushed his command rapidly through. They had made a march of seventy-eight miles in twenty-four hours preceding the battle. When near the village it was discovered that the Indians were moving in hot haste as if retreating. Reno, with seven companies of the Seventh Cavalry, was ordered to the left to attack the village at its head, while Custer, with five companies, went to the right and commenced a vigorous attack. Reno felt of them with three companies of cavalry, and was almost instantly surrounded, and after one hour or more of vigorous fighting, during which he lost Lieuts. Hodgson and McIntosh and Dr. Dewolf and twelve men, with several Indian scouts killed and many wounded, he cut his way through to the river and gained a bluff 300 feet in height, where he intrenched and was soon joined by Col. Benton with four companies. In the meantime the Indians resumed the attack, making repeated and desperate charges, which were repulsed with great slaughter to the Indians. They gained higher ground than Reno occupied, and as their arms were longer range and better than the cavalry's, they kept up a galling fire until nightfall. During the night Reno strengthened his position, and was prepared for another attack, which was made at daylight.

The day wore on. Reno had lost in killed and wounded a large portion of his command, forty odd having been killed before the bluff was reached, many of them in hand to hand conflict with the Indians, who outnumbered them ten to one, and his men had been without water for thirty-six hours. The suffering was heartrending. In this state of affairs they determined to reach the water at all hazards, and Col. Benton made a sally with his company, and routed the main body of the Indians who were guarding the approach to the river. The Indian sharpshooters were nearly opposite the mouth of the ravine through which the brave boys approached the river, but the attempt was made, and though one man was killed and seven wounded the water was gained and the command relieved. When the fighting ceased for the night Reno further prepared for attacks.

There had been forty-eight hours' fighting, with no word from Custer. Twenty-four hours more of fighting and the suspense ended, when the Indians abandoned their village in great haste and confusion. Reno knew then that succor was near at hand. Gen. Terry, with Gibbon commanding his own infantry, had arrived, and as the comrades met men wept on each other's necks. Inquiries were then made for Custer, but none could tell where he was. Soon an officer came rushing into camp and related that he had found Custer, dead, stripped naked, but not mutilated, and near him his two brothers, Col. Tom and Boston Custer. His brother-in-law, Col. Calhoun, and his nephew Col. Yates, Col. Keogh, Capt. Smith, Lieut. Crittenden, Lieut. Sturgis, Col. Cooke, Lieut. Porter, Lieut. Harrington, Dr. Lord, Mack Kellogg, the Bismarck *Tribune* correspondent, and 190 men and scouts. Custer went into battle with Companies C, L, I, F, and E, of the Seventh Cavalry, and the staff and non-commissioned staff of his regiment and a number of scouts, and only one Crow scout remained to tell the tale. All are dead. Custer was surrounded on every side by Indians, and horses fell as they fought on skirmish line or in line of battle. Custer was among the last who fell, but when his cheering voice was no longer heard, the Indians made easy work of the remainder. The bodies of all save the newspaper correspondent were stripped, and most of them were horribly mutilated. Custer's was not mutilated. He was shot through the body and through the head. The troops cared for the wounded and buried the dead, and returned to their base for supplies and instructions from the General of the Army.

Col. Smith arrived at Bismarck last night with thirty-five of the wounded. The Indians lost heavily in the battle. The Crow Scout survived by hiding in a ravine. He believes the Indians lost more than the whites. The village numbered 1,800 lodges, and it is thought there were 4,000 warriors. Gen. Custer was directed by Gen. Terry to find and feel of the Indians, but not to fight unless Terry arrived with infantry and with Gibbon's column. The casualties foot up 261 killed and fifty-two wounded.

THE SCENE OF THE MASSACRE.

DESCRIPTION OF THE REGION BY MAJOR GRIMES, WHO REMOVED THE FORTS IN 1868, UNDER THE TREATY.

Special Dispatch to the New-York Times.

ST. LOUIS, July 6.—The news of the massacre of Gen. Custer with seventeen commissioned officers and 315 men, near the Little Big Horn River, has created an extraordinary sensation here. Subsequent advices received at military head-quarters in this city substantially confirm the terrible news. Your correspondent this evening had a conversation with Major J. W. Grimes, one of the military officers stationed here, and who is very familiar with Indian affairs in the West. He is well acquainted with the country where the fight took place. He was detailed by the Government in 1868 to remove all the forts on the Powder River route, in accordance with the provisions of the Fort Laramie treaty of 1868. The battle occurred about twenty miles from the mouth of the Little Big Horn River, which empties into the Big Horn, and the latter into the Yellow Stone. The fight took place on the Crow reservation, about forty miles east of Fort C. L. Smith, the most northern of the Powder River Road forts, removed by Major Grimes in 1868. The country is diversified by mountain ranges and deep cañons, with intervening plateaus of sage brush prairies.

Ex-Gov. Fletcher, who was a member of the Peace Commission that went out last Summer, stated to-night that the present desperate condition of affairs is only a legitimate result of the present peace policy pursued by the Government toward the Indians.

THE CAUSES AND CONSEQUENCES.

FRUITS OF THE ILL-ADVISED BLACK HILLS EXPEDITION OF TWO YEARS AGO—ABILITY OF THE ARMY TO RENEW OPERATIONS EFFECTIVELY DISCUSSED—THE PERSONNEL OF THE CHARGING PARTY STILL UNDEFINED.

Special Dispatch to the New-York Times.

WASHINGTON, July 6.—The news of the fatal charge of Gen. Custer and his command against the Sioux Indians has caused great excitement in Washington, particularly among Army people and about the Capitol. The first impulse was to doubt the report, or set it down as some heartless hoax or at least a greatly exaggerated story by some frightened fugitive. At the second thought the report was generally accepted as true in its chief and appalling incidents. The campaign against the wild Sioux was undertaken under disadvantageous circumstances owing to the refusal of Congress to appropriate money for the establishment of military posts on the upper Yellowstone River. Gen. Sherman and Gen. Sheridan both asked for these posts, which, in case of anticipated troubles would give the troops a base of supplies about four hundred miles nearer the hostile country than they could otherwise have. The posts desired would have been accessible by steam-boats on the Yellowstone, which would have conveyed men and supplies. The House Committee on Military Affairs unanimously recommended their establishment, but the Committee on Appropriations refused to provide in their bills the necessary means. This is regarded as the immediate cause of the disaster. The remote cause was undoubtedly the expedition into the Black Hills two years ago in violation of laws and treaties, authorized by Secretary Belknap and led by Gen. Custer. If there had been a post at the head of navigation on the Yellowstone the expedition would doubtless have proceeded thence against the Indians in one invincible column. The policy of sending three converging columns so many hundred miles against such brave and skillful soldiers as the Sioux has been the cause of some uneasiness here among the few who have taken the trouble to think about the facts and prospects. The Sioux seem to have understood clearly the plan of attack, and threw themselves with their whole force first against Gen. Crook's column and now against Custer's, and both times inflicted serious disaster. The feeling was common to-day that the campaign is a failure, and that there must follow a general Indian war, promising to be costly in men and money. The Sioux are a distinct race of men from the so-called Indians of the South-west, among whom the army found such easy work two and three years ago. The Sioux live by the chase and feed chiefly upon flesh. The Southern Indians are farmers and eat fruits and vegetables, the latter are at their worst cruel, cowardly robber. The former are as much like the brave and war-like red men represented by the *Last of the Mohicans* as ever existed outside the covers of fiction and romance. This difference between the foes in the North and South-west seems not to have been well counted upon, nor provided for, and formed, as it might, prudently, no restraint upon the reckless fatal charge of the 300. If the tale told by the courier Taylor is true, the charge has scarce a parallel in the history of civilized or savage warfare. The massacre of Major Dade and his command in the Florida war is alone comparable with it in American history. The reason for an expedition against the Indians this Summer is not well understood, nor has any satisfactory explanation been published. The wild Sioux had never been willing to live upon the reservations marked out for them, and the understanding has been that they were to be whipped into submission, and compelled to live like Red Cloud and Spotted Tail, with their bands, about the Government agencies. The question of the policy and right of the war will now be renewed and discussed, and, indeed, is discussed to-day. Those who believe in the policy of the extermination of the Indians, and think the speedier the better its accomplishment, look upon the condition of war as inevitable, and are for pouring thousands of troops into the Indian country and giving them a terrible punishment. This class is small, even in the Army, where the policy of extermination is not popular save with a few high and restless officers. The invasion of the Black Hills has been condemned over and over again by the peace party, and there are very many who can truthfully say, "I told you so." From that unwarranted invasion the present difficulties have gradually sprung up, so that an expedition that originally cost a hundred thousand dollars perhaps, must lead to an expenditure of millions, which will advance civilization in no way, except by the destruction of the uncivilized. The Army, if the present campaign wholly fails, is in no condition to renew hostilities with sufficient force, and there is little reason to expect Congress will this session provide for an Indian war. Thus by force of circumstances a continuation of the war would probably be with the Government forces upon the defensive, protecting as far as possible agencies and settlements. There is another result that some hope for. It is the union of the three columns of troops and the delivery of a blow against the Indians that will place them at the mercy of the Army and compel them to sue for peace. The chances are, however, so far as the information now at hand may be relied on, that the Government forces are much too small in number, reduced as they are by two battles, to meet the powerful and exultant Sioux.

Until advised of the particular five companies of the Seventh Cavalry with which Custer charged the Sioux, with results so disastrous to his command, the War Department will not be able to furnish the list of casualties. From the dispatches printed to-day, based on the information furnished by Muggins Taylor, the scout, it is inferred that Capts. Thomas W. Custer and Myles Moylan, and Lieut. James Calhoun, of the Seventh Cavalry, and Lieut. A. B. Crittenden, of the Fourth Infantry, were among those killed. Capt. Custer was a brother of Gen. Custer, Calhoun was his brother-in-law, and Moylan was brother-in-law to Calhoun. Gen. Custer had but one brother in the Seventh Cavalry. The report that the General and his two brothers were killed doubtless arose from the relationship described between Custer, Calhoun, and Moylan. Crittenden was the son of Col. Crittenden, of the Seventeenth Infantry, and grandson of the late John J. Crittenden, of Kentucky. At his own request he was detailed for active service against the Indians and assigned to the Seventh Cavalry. The only dispatch received to-day at the War Department was one from Adjutant Gen. Crum, of Sheridan's staff, stating that Gen. Terry telegraphed from camp on Lone Horn River, under date of July 2, confirming the report of the fight on June 25 and the death of Gen. Custer. Terry's dispatches were sent to Sheridan at Chicago, and forwarded from there to Philadelphia, where Gens. Sherman and Sheridan now are.

VIEWS AT THE WAR DEPARTMENT.

THE CONFIRMATORY DISPATCHES FROM SHERIDAN'S HEAD-QUARTERS IN CHICAGO—FEELING AMONG CUSTER'S FRIENDS.

WASHINGTON, July 6.—Not until late this afternoon did the War Department receive confirmatory reports of the news published this morning of the terrible disaster in the Indian country. The absence of official advices in advance of the press reports, seemed to several Army officers, and to friends of those who are with Custer's command, fair grounds for arguing against the absolute correctness of the reports in the morning papers, but at the same time their was a profound anxiety to hear from Gen. Sheridan's Head-quarters, where it was considered certain that the earliest reports of any engagement that might hrve taken place would be forwarded. For this purpose Adjt. Gen. Townsend telegraphed early in the day for news from the Indian department, as also did Mr. Crosby, Chief Clerk of the War Department. In response to the latter the following came this afternoon from Chicago, signed by Assistant Adjt. Gen. Drum:

"Dispatches from Gen. Terry, dated from his camp, mouth of the Big Horn, July 2, confirm the newspaper reports of a fight on the 25th of June, on the Little Horn, and of Gen. Custer's death. Gen. Terry has fallen back to his present camp. I have sent full dispatches to the Lieutenant General, who will probably communicate them. I have not yet received Gen. Terry's report of the action, nor a list of the casualties."

In addition to the above a dispatch was received here to-day from Col. Ruggles, of Gen. Terry's staff, dated St. Paul, and addressed to Gen. Crittenden, announcing the death of his son, Lieut. Crittenden, in an Indian fight. There is the utmost anxiety in all quarters for additional news of the action, and the opinion is freely expressed among the officers of the Army that a war of considerable duration with the Indians seems inevitable, and these successes, it is feared, will have a very bad effect upon the Indians at certain agencies, particularly those at Red Cloud agency, who have been exhibiting a very uneasy spirit for some time past. Just at this time the Secretary of War and Gen. Sherman are both absent from Washington attending the celebration of the Army of the Cumberland in Philadelphia. The presumption is there will be an immediate conference upon the subject of the Indian war now fully inaugurated ted. It will be remembered that upon the ordering of the expedition into the Indian country, Gen. Custer was in this city and made an earnest application to join his command which had started while he was detained as a witness before a Congressional Investigating Committee.

Gen. Custer's old comrades in this city will hold a meeting on Saturday evening for the purpose of taking some action expressive of their esteem for him as a citizen and soldier, and adopting suitable resolutions regarding his death.

MISCELLANEOUS DISPATCHES.

A LIST OF OFFICERS KILLED—FEELING OVER THE DISASTER—A REGIMENT OF FRONTIERSMEN OFFERED FROM UTAH.

ST. LOUIS, July 6.—A telegram from Gen. Ruggles at St. Paul to Capt. Green Hale, commanding the cavalry at the arsenal here, gives the following as the names of the officers killed in the fight between the Sioux and Gen. Custer's command.

Gen. Custer,	Lieut. Smith,
Col. Custer,	Lieut. Porter,
Col. Yates,	Lieut. Harrington,
Col. Keogh,	Lieut. Calhoun,
Col. Cook,	Lieut. Reilly,
Lieut. McIntosh,	Lieut. Sturgis.
Lieut. Hodgson,	

Lieut. Harrington is missing.

Gen. S. D. Sturgis, in command of this post, received a telegram this afternoon from Assistant Adjt. Gen. Ruggles, at St. Paul, Minn., notifying him that his son was killed in the fight between the Sioux and Gen. Custer's command.

SALT LAKE, July 6.—The citizens here are very much excited over the Custer massacre, and several offers have been made to the Secretary of War to raise a regiment of frontiersmen in ten days for Indian service.

SAN FRANCISCO, July 6.—A dispatch from Virginia City reports great excitement at Custer's death. A meeting has been called to organize a company.

TOLEDO, July 6.—A special to the *Blade* from Monroe, Mich., the home of Gen. Custer, says the startling news of the massacre of the General and his party by Indians created the most intense feeling of sorrow among all classes. Gen. Custer passed several years of his youth at school in Monroe, and his parents have resided there many years. The town is draped in mourning, and a meeting of the Common Council and citizens was held this evening to take measures for an appropriate tribute to the gallant dead.

SKETCH OF GEN. CUSTER.

Major Gen. George A. Custer, who was killed with his whole command while attacking an encampment of Sioux Indians, under command of Sitting Bull, was one of the bravest and most widely known officers in the United States Army. He has for the past fifteen years been known to the country and to his comrades as a man who feared no danger, as a soldier in the truest sense of the word. He was daring to a fault, generous beyond most men. His memory will long be kept green in many friendly hearts. Born at New-Rumley, Harrison County, Ohio, on the 5th of December, 1839, he obtained a good common education, and after graduating engaged for a time in teaching school. In June, 1857, through the influence of Hon. John A. Bingham, then member of Congress from Ohio, he obtained an appointment to the United States Military Academy at West Point, and entered that institution on the 1st of July of the year named. He graduated on the 24th of June, 1861, with what was considered the fair standing of No. 34 in one of the brightest classes that ever left the academy. Immediately upon leaving West Point he was appointed Second Lieutenant in Company G of the Second United States Cavalry, a regiment which had formerly been commanded by Robert E. Lee. He reported to Lieut. Gen. Scott on the 20th of July, the day preceding the battle of Bull Run, and the Commander in Chief gave him the choice of accepting a position on his staff or of joining his regiment, then under command of Gen. McDowell, in the field. Longing for an opportunity to see active service, and determined to win distinction Lieut. Custer chose the latter course, and after riding all night through a country filled with people who were, to say the least, not friendly, he reached McDowell's head-quarters at daybreak on the morning of the 21st. Preparations for the battle had already begun, and after delivering his dispatches from Gen. Scott and hastily partaking of a mouthful of coffee and a piece of hard bread he joined his company. It is not necessary now to recount the disasters of the fight that followed. Suffice it to say that Lieut. Custer's company was among the last to leave the field. It did so in good order, bringing off Gen. Heintzelman, who had been wounded in the engagement. The young officer continued to serve with his company, and was engaged in the drilling of volunteer recruits in and about the defences of Washington, when upon the appointment of Phil Kearny to the position of Brigadier General, that lamented officer gave him a position on his staff. Custer continued in this position until an order was issued from the War Department prohibiting Generals of Volunteers from appointing officers of the regular Army to staff duty. Then he returned to his company, not, however, until he had been warmly complimented by Gen. Kearny upon the prompt and efficient manner in which he had performed the duties assigned to him. At the same time the General predicted that Custer would be one of the most successful officers in the Army. Nor were these predictions without a speedy realization. With his company Lieut. Custer marched forward with that part of the Army of the Potomac which moved upon Manassas after its evacuation by the rebels. Our cavalry was in advance, under Gen. Stoneman and encountered the rebel horsemen for the first time near Catlett's Station. The commanding officer made a call for volunteers to charge the enemy's advance post. Lieut. Custer was among the first to step to the front, and in command of his company he shortly afterward made his first charge. He drove the rebels across Muddy Creek, wounded a number of them, and had one of his own men injured. This was the first blood drawn in the campaign under McClellan. After this Custer went with the Army of the Potomac to the Peninsula and remained with his company until the Army settled down before Yorktown, when he was detailed as an Assistant Engineer of the left wing, under Sumner. Acting in this capacity he planned and erected the earthworks nearest the enemy's lines. He also accompanied the advance under Gen. Hancock in pursuit of the enemy from Yorktown. Shortly afterward, he captured the first battle-flag ever secured by the Army of the Potomac. From this time on he was nearly always the first in every work of daring. When the Army reached the Chickahominy he was the first man to cross the river; he did so in the face of the fire of the enemy's pickets, and at times was obliged to wade up to his armpits. For this brave act Gen. McClellan promoted him to a Captaincy and made him one of his personal aids. In this capacity he served during most of the Peninsula campaign, and participated in all its battles, including the bloody seven days' fight. He performed the duty of marking out the position which was occupied by the Union Army at the battle of Gaines' Mills. He also participated in the campaign which ended in the battles of South Mountain and Antietam. Upon the retirement of Gen. McClellan from the command of the Army of the Potomac, Custer accompanied him, and for a time was out of active service.

He was next engaged in the battle of Chancellorsville, and immediately after that fight he was made a personal aid by Gen. Pleasonton, who was then commanding a division of cavalry. Serving in this capacity he took an active part in a number of hotly-contested engagements, and marked himself as one of the most dashing, some said the most reckless, officers in the service. When Pleasonton was made a Major General his first pleasure was to remember the valuable services of his Aid de Camp. He requested the appointment of four Brigadiers to command under him, and upon his recommendation, indorsed by Gens. Meade and Hooker, young Custer was made a Brigadier General and assigned to the command of the First, Fifth, Sixth, and Seventh Michigan Cavalry. He did noble service at the battle of Gettysburg. He held the right of line, and was obliged to face Hampton's division of cavalry, and after a hotly-contested fight, utterly routed the rebels and prevented them from reaching the trains of the Union Army, which they hoped to capture. Custer had two horses shot under him in this fight. Hardly had the battle concluded when he was sent to attack the enemy's train, which was trying to force its way to the Potomac. He destroyed more than four hundred wagons. At Hagerstown, Md., during a severe engagement, he again had his horse shot under him. At Falling Waters, shortly after, he attacked with his small brigade the entire rebel rear guard. The Confederate commander Gen. Pettigrew was killed and his command routed, with a loss of 1,300 prisoners two pieces of cannon and four battle flags. For some time after this fight he was constantly engaged in skirmishing with the enemy, and during the Winter which followed in picketing the Rapidan between the two armies. He participated in the battle of the Wilderness in 1864, and on the 9th of May of the same year, under Gen. Sheridan, he set out on the famous raid toward Richmond. His brigade led the column, captured Beaver Dam, burned the station and a train of cars loaded with supplies, and released 400 Union prisoners. Rejoining Grant's Army on the Pamunkey, he took an active part in several engagements. After the battle of Fisher's Hill, in which he did most important service, he was placed in command of a division, and remained in that position until after Lee's surrender. At the ever-memorable battle of Cedar Creek his division was on the right, and not engaged in the rout of the morning, so that when Sheridan arrived on the field, after the twenty-mile ride, he found at least one command ready for service. His immediate order was "Go in, Custer!" The brave young General only waited for the word, he went in and never came out until the enemy was driven several miles beyond the battle-field. Nearly one thousand prisoners were captured, among them a Major General. Forty-five pieces of artillery were also taken. For this service Custer was made a Brevet Major General of Volunteers. Sheridan, as a further mark of approbation, detailed him to carry the news of the victory and the captured battle-flag to Washington. From this time on his fortune was made, and he continued steadily to advance in the esteem of his superiors and of the American people. When the rebels fell back to Appomattox, Custer had the advance of Sheridan's command, and his share in the action is well described in the entertaining volume entitled, *With Sheridan in His Last Campaign.* The book in question says: "When the sun was an hour high in the west, energetic Custer in advance spied the depot and four heavy trains of freight cars; he quickly ordered his leading regiments to circle out to the left through the woods, and as they gained the railroad beyond the station he led the rest of his division pell-mell down the road and enveloped the train as quick as winking. Custer might not well conduct a siege of regular approaches; but for a sudden dash, Custer against the world." After many another dash of the same kind as that described, Custer was mustered out of the volunteer service on the 1st of February, 1866, and on July 28 of the same year he was appointed Lieutenant Colonel of the Seventh United States Cavalry, and since that time has been almost constantly engaged in duty upon the frontier. Recently he has contributed several interesting articles to the magazines. Of his personal appearance, Col. Newhall, in *With Sheridan in His Last Campaign*, speaks as follows: "At the head of the horsemen rode Custer of the golden locks, his broad sombrero turned up from his hard, bronzed face, the ends of his crimson cravat floating over his shoulder, gold galore spangling his jacket sleeves, a pistol in his boots, jangling spurs on his heels, and a ponderous claymore swinging at his side. A wild, dare-devil of a General and a prince of advance guards." This description will be recognized by those who knew Gen. Custer as exceedingly true to nature. He was not a great General. He was a great fighter. His place in the Army will not easily be filled.

RECORD OF THE REGIMENT.

THE OFFICERS, AND WHAT THEY HAVE DONE—THE DATES OF THEIR PROMOTIONS.

The Seventh Regiment of United States Cavalry was organized by act of Congress July 28, 1866, and since then has been stationed at different posts until Nov. 27, 1868, when it was assigned to the Indian Territory. The following is a list of the regiment's officers: Colonel, Samuel D. Sturgis, of Pennsylvania, who entered the service on July 1, 1846, being then brevetted a Second Lieutenant in the Second Dragoons. He was promoted Second Lieutenant in the First Dragoons Feb. 16, 1847; First Lieutenant, July 15, 1853; Captain in the First Cavalry, March 3, 1855; Major, May 3, 1861; Lieutenant Colonel of the Sixth Cavalry, Oct. 27, 1863, and finally, to his present rank, May 6, 1869. Lieut. Col. George A. Custer, of Ohio, entered the Army June 24, 1861, as Second Lieutenant in the Second Cavalry; was promoted First Lieutenant in the Fifth Cavalry July 17, 1862; Captain, May 8, 1864, and Lieutenant Colonel of the Seventh Regiment, July 28, 1866. Major Joseph G. Tilford, of Kentucky, entered the service as Brevet Second Lieutenant July 1, 1851, and was elevated to the rank of Major Nov. 14, 1867.

Lewis Merrill, of Pennsylvania, entered the Army as Brevet Second Lieutenant in the First Dragoons July 1, 1855, and during the war served as Colonel of the Second Missouri Cavalry. He was brevetted Brigadier General of Volunteers and promoted Major of the Seventh Cavalry Nov. 27, 1868.

Marcus A. Reno, of Illinois, entered the service as Brevet Second Lieutenant in the First Dragoons July 1, 1857. During the war he was Colonel of the Twelfth Pennsylvania Cavalry, and was brevetted Brigadier General of Volunteers. He was made Major in the Seventh Cavalry Dec. 26, 1868.

Captains—Frederick W. Benteen, of Virginia, who entered the Army as Captain July 28, 1866, and served during the war as Captain, Major, and Lieutenant Colonel of the Tenth Missouri Cavalry; he obtained his present commission July 28, 1866. Myles W. Keogh, of the District of Columbia, was commissioned Second Lieutenant in the Fourth Cavalry May 4, 1866, and promoted Captain July 28, 1866. J. E. Tourtellotte, of Connecticut, was appointed Captain in the Twenty-eighth Infantry July 28, 1866; during the war he served as Captain, Lieutenant Colonel, and Colonel of the Fourth Minnesota Volunteers. Michael V. Sheridan, of Ohio, appointed Second Lieutenant in the Fifth Cavalry Feb. 23, 1866, and Captain in the Seventh July 28, 1866.

George W. Yates, of New-York, appointed Second Lieutenant in the Second Cavalry March 26, 1866, and Captain in the Seventh June 12, 1867. Thomas B. Weir, of Ohio, commissioned First Lieutenant July 28, 1866, and Captain July 31, 1867. Thomas H. French, of Maryland, commissioned Second Lieutenant in the Tenth Infantry May 13, 1864, and assigned to the Seventh Cavalry as Captain Jan. 1, 1871.

Owen Hale, of New-York, commissioned First Lieutenant July 28, 1866, and Captain March 1, 1869. Charles S. Ilsley, of Maine, appointed Second Lieutenant in the Sixteenth Infantry Feb. 23, 1866, and Captain in the Seventh Cavalry July 11, 1871. Miles Moylan, of Massachusetts, appointed Second Lieutenant in the Fifth Cavalry Feb. 19, 1863, and Captain in the Seventh Cavalry March 1, 1872. Thomas W. Custer, of Ohio, appointed Second Lieutenant in the First Infantry Feb. 23, 1866, and Captain in the Seventh Cavalry Dec. 2, 1875.

First Lieutenant—Thomas M. McDougall, of Wisconsin, appointed Second Lieutenant in the Fourteenth Infantry May 10, 1866, and First Lieutenant to the Seventh Cavalry Nov. 5, 1866. Henry J. Nowlan, of Corfu, appointed Second Lieutenant July 28, 1866, and promoted Dec. 3, 1866. James M. Bell, of Pennsylvania, appointed Second Lieutenant July 28, 1866, and promoted April 2, 1867. William W. Cooke, of New-York, appointed Second Lieutenant July 28, 1866, and First Lieutenant July 31, 1867. Henry Jackson, of Illinois, appointed Second Lieutenant July 28, 1866, and First Lieutenant July 31, 1867. Edward S. Godfrey, of Ohio, appointed Second Lieutenant June 17, 1867, and First Lieutenant Feb. 1, 1868. John F. Weston, of Kentucky, appointed Second Lieutenant Aug. 9, 1867, and promoted Nov. 27, 1868. Algernon E. Smith, of New-York, appointed Second Lieutenant Aug. 9, 1867, and promoted Dec. 5, 1868. Ed. G. Mathey, of Indiana, appointed Second Lieutenant Sept. 24, 1867, and promoted May 10, 1870. Donald McIntosh, of Oregon, appointed Second Lieutenant Aug. 17, 1867, and promoted March 22, 1870. James Calhoun, of Ohio, appointed Second Lieutenant in the Thirty-second Infantry July 31, 1867, and promoted Second Lieutenant in the Seventh Cavalry Jan. 9, 1871. Frank M. Gibson, of Pennsylvania, appointed Second Lieutenant Oct. 5, 1867, and promoted July 11, 1871. James E. Porter, of Maine, appointed Second Lieutenant June 15, 1869, and promoted March 1, 1872. William T. Craycroft, of Kentucky, appointed Second Lieutenant June 15, 1869, and promoted Dec. 2, 1875.

Second Lieutenants—Charles C. De Rudio, of New-York, appointed July 31, 1867. Charles Broroden, of Michigan, June 15, 1869. Benjamin H. Hodgson, of Pennsylvania, June 15, 1870. Winfield S. Edgerly, of New-Hampshire, June 15, 1870. Charles W. Larned, of New-York, June 15, 1870. Andrew H. Nave, of Tennessee, June 12, 1871. George D. Wallace, of South Carolina, June 14, 1872. Charles A. Varnum, of New-York, June 14, 1872. H. M. Harrington, of New-York, June 14, 1872. Luther R. Hare, of Indiana, June 17, 1874. James G. Sturgis, of New-Hampshire, June 16, 1875.

AN INTERVIEW WITH COL. CROFTON, COMMANDING GOVERNOR'S ISLAND—HIS RECOLLECTIONS OF GEN. CUSTER AND THE OFFICERS OF THE SEVENTH.

The massacre was of absorbing interest to the officers of Governor's Island, several of whom have served in the North-west and have been personally acquainted with Gen. Custer and all of the officers of the Seventh Cavalry. Col. Crofton, the commanding officer of the island, was connected with the service in the same detachment with Gen Custer, leaving it in 1874. "Yes," he said in answer to an inquiry from a TIMES reporter, "I have seen a little Indian fighting, and I tell you that it is the worst business a man can engage in. Here is Gen. Custer, one of the bravest of men and one of the best Indian fighters that ever lived, after years of successful experience beaten and cut down and all of his command with him. He who had so often baffled the wiles of the Indian and overmatched them in cunning, at length falls a victim to Indian strategy. I can look at it in no other manner, and I am pretty sure that when we get official reports we shall learn that the unfortunate General fell into a trap. I knew Gen. Custer well. He was a daring man. I remember an instance of his courage: We were on the Yellowstone River, Gen. Custer in command, and we were preparing to go up the stream. We were of course accompanied by a train, and it was necessary that the train should go along the bluff instead of along the bed of the river. So the General dispatched the train upon the hills and the two companies of cavalry jogged along below. After a while the General ordered a halt so that the train might not get too far behind. The men unsaddled their horses and gave themselves up to rest. Suddenly they were attacked by Indians. There were at least three hundred of them to eighty soldiers. Gen. Custer was not dismayed, however. He ordered his men to return fire, and they fought till their ammunition was exhausted. Then the men were just giving themselves up for lost when Gen. Custer ordered a remount, the horses having already been saddled. The men obeyed. 'Now charge for them,' shouted Gen. Custer. The command charged, and, without a single bullet, they put the Indians to rout, and escaped what a moment before seemed certain death.

It may be that Gen. Custer was too brave, too daring. Possibly he has been too rash, but I almost think not. Indians never fight, except, first, when they are cornered, and, second, when they have the advantage. The most natural theory is that Gen. Custer's command reached its point of attack too soon and was forced to attempt alone what was originally intended for the two divisions acting in concert. I hope the reports of the massacre are exaggerated, but from what I know of Indian warfare I cannot indulge the hope that they are. I have no doubt that if the Indians were successful they murdered every man in the command. I do not know all of the officers of the regiment, but some of them I know, and I know them to be as fine officers as there are in the service."

A TILDEN ELECTIONEERING TRICK.

STATE ENGINEER VAN BUREN'S REPORT TO THE CANAL BOARD—WHAT IT REALLY IS AND WHAT IT PURPORTS TO BE.

Special Dispatch to the New-York Times.

ALBANY, July 6.—State Engineer Van Buren's report to the Canal Board on pending contracts for extraordinary repairs on the canals was taken up at the meeting to-day and practically shelved. But Mr. Van Buren was careful to have an abstract of the document sent beforehand to the newspapers. The whole purpose of this report is for political effect, and nothing else. The ambiguous language, and the numerous exceptions and conditions, are in themselves sufficient to show that there is nothing serious in this latest proclamation of "reform." Van Buren gives a list of some thirty-eight pending contracts on which he pretends he has reduced the prices, and will save to the State on each contract sums ranging from $1,000 to $30,000, and that by these reductions only a small portion of the $499,000 which the last Legislature appropriated to pay for this work will be needed. This is his statement, the object, of course, being to show how much is saved to the State under Mr. Tilden's canal reform, and at the same time to have a loop-hole of escape from what he knew to be nothing but an electioneering falsehood. Mr. Van Buren qualifies his statement with suggestions that owing to legal difficulties it may be advisable to effect compromises with contractors where fraud and collusion cannot be charged. Now, the simple truth in regard to these contracts, as Mr. Van Buren and Gov. Tilden very well know, is that many of them have passed beyond the purview of the courts, the work being done and officially certified to in some cases by Gov. Tilden's own appointees. The only effect of resisting payment of these certificates would be such litigation as there was in the Schaub case, and a like result. In fact, Mr. Van Buren will not deny that he had Schaub's case down on his list, and the $9,000 due there would have gone to swell the bogus list of savings had it not happened that the man fought his case so vigorously in the courts as to get judgment just before Mr. Van Buren was ready to publish his report. Mr. Van Buren is one of the Canal Investigating Commission, put into State office by Gov. Tilden, and naturally is anxious to assist the election of his patron.

An analysis of the report in detail will be given at another time. It is sufficient to say here that those who really have any knowledge of the matter say that this latest contribution to campaign literature carries in it nothing but the promise of expensive and disastrous litigation to the State, with no return except the assistance it may render Mr. Tilden in his electioneering.

MR. BLAINE'S ILLNESS.

NO CHANGE IN HIS CONDITION—A EUROPEAN TRIP RECOMMENDED.

AUGUSTA, Me., July 6.—Mr. Blaine has now been home eight days. So far there has been no special change in his case. The nervous prostration is still the marked characteristic of his illness. He is not able to leave his room, and is almost constantly confined to his bed. His physician thinks that it will be many weeks before he will resume active work. A European trip is strongly recommended as soon as his strength is sufficient.

THE DEMOCRATS IN WASHINGTON.

A WEAK RATIFICATION OF TILDEN—A FOUR-MINUTE TORCH-LIGHT PROCESSION.

Special Dispatch to the New-York Times.

WASHINGTON, July 6.—The Democracy held their ratification meeting to-night, their speakers occupying the same stand erected for the Republicans after Cincinnati. There was a great torch-light procession, numbering probably two hundred, which was exactly four minutes marching slowly past THE TIMES office in double file. A good proportion of the torch-bearers were boys about the size of the pages at the Capitol. The Democratic processions in Washington will be larger if Tilden should be elected.

FRENCH POLITICS.

DIFFERENCES AMONG THE REPUBLICAN DEPUTIES ON MUNICIPAL MATTERS—REPORTED ATTEMPT TO SHOOT THE DUC DE CHARTRES.

Paris, July 6.—Differences have arisen among the Republican Deputies over the Municipal bill. The members of the Left, who yesterday agreed to a compromise on the bill, form the group known as the "Republican Left." Another section of the Left called the "Republican Union," which is under the direct leadership of M. Gambetta, held a meeting to-day and passed a resolution rejecting the compromise.

The journals hostile to Republicanism are jubilant over these dissensions. They declare that confusion has taken possession of the Republican Party, for now both the Republican Left and the Irreconcilable Radicals are opposed to M. Gambetta.

VERSAILLES, July 6.—In the Chamber of Deputies to-day M. Montjau, in view of the recent prosecution of *Les Droits de l'Homme* for publishing articles from the pen of Henri Rochefort, moved the abolition of the decree of 1852, prohibiting convicts from writing newspaper articles.

The New-York Times.

VOL. XXVI.......NO. 8066. NEW-YORK, FRIDAY, JULY 20, 1877. PRICE FOUR CENTS.

MARCHING ON ADRIANOPLE.

THE CAMPAIGN ACROSS THE BALKANS

SLIVNO AND KASANLIK THE POINTS SOUGHT TO CONTROL THE SOUTHERN OPENINGS OF THE BALKAN PASSES—THE TURKS MOVING ALL THE TROOPS SOUTH OF THE BALKANS TO OPPOSE THEM—KASANLIK OCCUPIED BY RUSSIANS—THE GRAND DUKE NICHOLAS TO OPPOSE AT TIRNOVA ANY FORCE DESIGNED TO MOVE AGAINST GEN. GOURKHO.

LONDON, July 19.—Dispatches to this morning's papers show that the Russians are endeavoring, with every prospect of success, to obtain possession of Kasanlik and Slivno, which would give them control of the southern debouchment of the two most important passes of the central Balkans. The statement of the *Times'* Adrianople correspondent, that the Russians were between Kasanlik and Schipka, is manifestly erroneous. For Schipka the dispatch should probably read Slivno. Turkish advices place the principal Russian force at Hainkoi, which is the southern debouchment of the chain Boghaz and Tchivarditzkor passes. The Turks seem to base their hope of repelling the invasion wholly on the arrival of Suleiman Pasha and his army. It is improbable that the Russians will give time for that before throwing forward a sufficient force to seize and hold the passes.

A Reuter telegram from Constantinople dated yesterday says: "Abdul Kerim telegraphs that he will cut off the retreat of the Russians who crossed the Balkans, and only waits the arrival of Suleiman Pasha to commence an attack.

"The Turkish fleet, with Suleiman Pasha's troops on board, passed Zante at 10 o'clock this morning.

"Twenty thousand regulars and 20,000 volunteers have left Constantinople for Adrianople. The Mussulman inhabitants of Adrianople are arriving here *en masse*, and are provided by the Government with lodgings in the schools."

A Ragusa dispatch of July 19 says: "Six Turkish battalions are marching from Scutari to Nisch."

A dispatch from Adrianople to-day says the Russians are advancing to destroy the workshops of the railway at Yeni Saghra. Mehemet Ali Pasha with a considerable force has left Adrianople to meet the Russians.

LONDON, July 20.—The *Standard's* correspondent at Constantinople telegraphs as follows: "I know, on very high authority, that the Porte does not expect to be able to prevent the Russians reaching Adrianople."

Various dispatches represent that the movement on Yeni Saghra was a feint. The real movement was directed toward a station further south, where the Russians have concentrated an Army corps under orders to proceed at once to Adrianople. It is calculated that the Turkish forces not already locked in the Danubian fortresses do not exceed 100,000, and that the Grand Duke Nicholas has a sufficient force at Tirnova to prevent their interfering with the movement on Adrianople.

The latest news from Constantinople is that the Russians, having taken Kazanlik, are marching on Philippopolis.

A *News* special from Elena says: "On Wednesday Gen. Gourko, who came through Tivarditzka Pass, immediately after passing through turned westward and marched on Kazanlik, sending at the same time a detachment to Yene-Saghra to cut the railway, and another to Esti-Saghra to occupy it and collect transport material. Reports were received to-day that his advanced detachments are already in Kazanlik. He may be there by this time; but if so I do not believe there has been time for intelligence to reach Elena. He intended as soon as Kazanlik was occupied to strike the defenders of Schipka Pass; and before marching he sent instructions that a column should march into the same pass from the northward and attack its defenses in front. It is reported to be very strongly fortified and held. Numbers of prisoners are engaged widening the Tivaritizka Pass, which will be practicable for the transport of vehicles in two days. Already batteries of field artillery have gone through. Gen. Gourkho keeps his communications quite open with the base at Tirnova.

The above is compiled from Gen. Gourkho's official dispatch and the narratives of officers who brought the reports from him.

RUSSIAN PROGRESS IN BULGARIA.

CONFLICTING REPORTS—THE ARMY AT RUSTCHUK SAID TO BE PREPARING TO ADVANCE—OCCUPATION OF LOFTCHA BY THE RUSSIANS—59,000 RUSSIANS ADVANCING ON WIDDIN.

LONDON, July 19.—A special dispatch from Paris to the *Pall Mall Gazette* has the following: "A telegram received here from Orsova states that the Russian advance in Bulgaria has slackened in consequence of dispatches received by Prince Gortschakoff from certain powers. The Russians will only resume the march after securing their rear, which is now only protected by the Fourth Corps, which is camped near Bucharest."

The *Daily News'* correspondent at Pavlo telegraphs under date of July 16, as follows: "The Army of Rustchuk has been permitted to commence an advance. Although the advance will be slow, yet I believe the masking policy is abandoned, and that Rustchuk and Shumla will be besieged by infantry. The advance will enable the cavalry to move forward and throw a circle of observation close around the rayon of the fortress and isolate it."

Reuter's telegram from Shumla says the Russians have occupied Loftcha, South of Plevna.

LONDON, July 20.—The correspondent of the *Times* at Bucharest sends the following: "Rustchuck appears to be completely surrounded, but we have no news as yet of the commencement of siege operations. When the blockade of Rustchuk is complete, so that its garrison cannot interfere with the Dobrudscha column, it is expected here that this Russian force will leave the line of the Tchernavoda Railway and envelop Silistria."

It is officially announced that the Russians have possession of the whole line of the Tchernavoda and Kustendje Railway, the Turks having evacuated and partly burned Tchernavoda on Tuesday night.

The *Post's* special from Nikopolis says 59,000 Russians are advancing from Nikopolis toward Widdin to besiege the fortress and prevent the advance of Turkish troops between Misch and Sophia. The Roumanians at Kalafat are resuming the bombardment of Widdin and will join in the siege.

The *Daily News* has received the following from Pavlo: "The news of Gen. Gourkho having crossed the passage of the Balkans has been received with extreme satisfaction at head-quarters, and immediately produced a determination in favor of prompt action on the part of the Rustchuk army. Rustchuk is to be at once invested, and if there is a Turkish army on the River Lom it will have to fight or retreat.

The Russian losses at Nikopolis are estimated at 1,200."

ABDUL-KERIM DISMISSED.

THE GENERALISSIMO SUPERSEDED BY MEHEMET ALI—OTHER DISMISSALS OF HIGH TURKISH OFFICIALS.

LONDON, July 19.—Reuter's Telegram Company has the following dispatch from Constantinople: "It is officially announced that Abdul Kerim had been dismissed, and Mehemet Ali appointed to succeed him. The dismissal of Redif Pasha is reported as probable, but has not yet been confirmed officially. Mehemet Ali is a Prussian, whose real name is Schultz. He has shown himself capable as division commander at Montenegro and elsewhere."

A later dispatch says that the Imperial steamer Sureja has left here to bring Abdul Kerim, Raouf and Redif Pashas back to Constantinople. Suleiman Pasha has been appointed commander of the army in Roumelia. Assim Pasha, now Minister of Justice, has been appointed Governor of Adrianople.

Dispatches to both the *Post* and *News*, from Constantinople, announce that Redif Pasha has been dismissed. The *News* special adds that Mahmoud Damad will probably succeed Redif Pasha. Perfect tranquillity prevails in the city.

TROUBLE IN THE GREEK PROVINCES.

EXCITEMENT IN THRACE AND MACEDONIA—GREEK VOLUNTEERS CROSSING THE FRONTIER.

LONDON, July 20.—The *Times'* Athens correspondent telegraphs as follows: "Official telegrams speak of great excitement in Thrace and Macedonia, especially Philippopolis, and of measures concerted by the Consuls and local authorities for securing the public safety. Many people here expect a rising of Greek Rayahs in a few days. There is no enthusiasm in Athens.

An Athens special to the Paris *Temps* reports that detachments of Greek volunteers have passed the Turkish frontier. The insurrectionary movement is expected to spread in Thessaly. The Minister of War is mobilizing the Greek troops and the Minister of the Interior is calling out volunteers.

A *Daily News* dispatch dated Athens, Thursday night, says the public mind is much agitated. The students have sent an address to the King, urging him to declare war against the Turks. The situation is critical. Volunteers are taking up arms. Massacres by Turkish irregulars are reported from various districts in Macedonia.

ENGLAND'S POSITION ON THE WAR.

STATEMENT OF EARL DERBY IN THE HOUSE OF LORDS—ENGLAND'S INFLUENCE IN THE CONTROVERSY—THE FLEET AT BESIKA BAY.

LONDON, July 19.—In the House of Lords this evening Lord Stratheden moved for the papers on the Eastern question. He criticised the neutrality policy of the Government as tending to diminish the influence of England both now and at the conclusion of the war.

The Earl of Derby replied that the British Embassy at Constantinople exercised the influence which fairly belonged to a neutral friendly power. As regarded the influence which England could exercise at the conclusion of the war, he could not conceive a position in which we could interfere with more influence or effect than at the close of the war, when both combatants were more or less exhausted, and we still uncommitted to any course and our forces fresh and unbroken. The Government had previously stated what they considered to be British interests. The Russian Ambassador had thanked him for giving so accurate a warning of the torpedoes which the Russian Government would have to avoid. He repeated the statements made in the House of Commons as to the reasons for the movement of the fleet to Besika Bay, that no explanation had been forwarded to the foreign powers concerning this movement, as none was called for or required. He promised that any authentic reports received concerning Russian cruelties should be presented to Parliament. But the statements now current were probably greatly exaggerated.

LONDON, July 20.—The English naval officers on leave in Constantinople from Besika Bay, have been recalled.

There is a rumor of a movement of the British fleet from Besika Bay.

WAR NOTES.

Prices advanced on the Paris Bourse yesterday in consequence of rumors of an armistice between Turkey and Russia.

The *Djeridic Havadis* states that Hobart Pasha has been ordered to bombard all places of importance on the Russian coast of the Black Sea.

The *Daily News'* dispatch from Constantinople announces that an Egyptian vessel has arrived in the Bosphorus with a regiment of cavalry.

Mukhtar Pasha telegraphs from Kars to Constantinople, under date of the 17th inst., that the revictualing and reorganization of Kars' garrison is now complete.

A Vienna dispatch to the *Standard* states that 40 citizens have been arrested in Belgrade as accomplices in the socialistic agitation. The rebellious spirit is spreading most alarmingly.

The *Times'* Paris correspondent states that Count Schouvaloff, in consequence of the bad impression produced by recent accounts of Russian atrocities, has sent an urgent telegram to Prince Gortschakoff, begging him to give the principal foreign correspondents every facility for visiting the places named as the scenes of these excesses.

A steamer, stated to be English, has arrived at the mouth of the Bojana with ammunition for the Turks. The Consuls at Scutari are endeavoring to ascertain the name of and the port the steamer came from, in order to inform their respective Governments. An Austrian Lloyd's steamer has embarked 800 Turkish wounded at Antivari for Constantinople.

RIFLE SHOOTING AT WIMBLEDON.

THE KOLAPORE CUP WON BY THE ENGLISH TEAM—THE ELCHO SHIELD WON BY IRELAND—LORDS AGAINST COMMONS—LORDS THE WINNERS.

LONDON, July 19.—At Wimbledon today, in the shooting for the Kolapore Cup, at 200, 500, and 600 yards, the score of the English team aggregated 608, and that of the Canadian team 586.

In the first stage of the shooting for the Elcho Shield, 800 yards, 15 shots each, Ireland scored 543, Scotland 530, and England 513. At the end of the shooting at the 900-yard range the score was: Ireland, 1,060; Scotland, 1,000; England, 991. The shooting for the shield terminated with the Irish team winning by a large number of points. The highest possible score was 1,800. Ireland scored 1,568; England, 1,464, and Scotland, 1,439.

The match between members of the Houses of Lords and Commons was won by the Lords by the following score: Lords, 404; Commons, 375. The highest possible score was 500.

THE CUBAN INSURRECTION.

AN ADDITIONAL REINFORCEMENT OF 25,000 SPANISH SOLDIERS TO BE SENT OUT IN OCTOBER—THE EXPENSES TO BE DRAWN FROM SPANISH MERCHANTS IN CUBA.

LONDON, July 19.—A letter to the *Daily News* from Madrid says: "The Spanish authorities are preparing to send 25,000 men to Cuba in October to fill the gaps caused by disease and death. The Ministers propose to raise the necessary funds to forward these reinforcements by another appeal to the Association of planters and financiers who furnished the advance for reinforcements sent out a year ago. Their privilege over the Cuban Customs revenue will be increased and prolonged to insure the payment of interest and the annual sinking fund. The Ministers have allowed the Cortes to understand that, if necessary, the Government will make even greater sacrifices. It is singular to observe that the improvement of Cuban affairs and the visible decrease of the rebellion does not convince most people of the ultimate pacification of the island."

COLONIZATION IN THE SOUTH.

WASHINGTON, July 19.—A private telegram from Spartanburg, S. C., says the pioneers of the Catholic Colony of St. Brendau arrived there yesterday in good spirits. Thirty thousand acres of land have been purchased in Transylvania and Henderson Counties, N. C., for colonization purposes. Arrangements have been made for the removal thither of 65 families from eight different States of the Union. They will turn their attention to farming and stock raising.

THE CROPS IN NEBRASKA AND IOWA.

OMAHA, Neb., July 19.—The *Herald* to-morrow morning will publish crop reports from 30 or 40 principal points in Nebraska and Western Iowa. They are without exception of the most favorable character, indicating the largest yield of all kinds of grain known for years. Barley and rye are nearly all harvested, and wheat will be begun next week. The quality and quantity are exceptionally good, and the acreage largely in excess of previous years.

CURRENT TOPICS ABROAD.

EARL BEACONSFIELD AND THE PIGOTT APPOINTMENT—PROBABLE ADJOURNMENT OF THE BRITISH PARLIAMENT AUG. 12—THE GENERAL ELECTIONS IN FRANCE TO BE HELD OCT. 14—THE SPANISH EXILES—LETTER OF ZORILLA.

LONDON, July 19.—In the House of Lords this afternoon Earl Beaconsfield explained that the appointment of Mr. T. Pigott as Controller of the Stationery Office was made on grounds of efficiency. He said that Mr. Pigott's resignation had been placed in his hands, but for reasons of high public duty he was bound not to accept it. In the House of Commons, Sir Stafford Northcote, Chancellor of the Exchequer, in reply to a question by the Marquis of Hartington, said that he hoped to close the session of Parliament about the 12th of August.

PARIS, July 19.—The *Figaro* announces that the date of the general elections has been fixed for Oct. 14.

Señor Zorilla writes to the *Echo Universel* denying that he and his friends were engaged in a conspiracy against the French Government, or that any arms had been found in their possession.

THE CHARTER OAK FAILURE.

A MEETING OF INDIGNANT CHICAGO POLICY-HOLDERS—A COMMITTEE APPOINTED TO GO TO HARTFORD.

Special Dispatch to the New-York Times.

CHICAGO, Ill., July 19.—A large number of policy-holders in the Charter Oak Life Insurance Company met here to-day, Rev. W. H. Ryder presiding. W. H. Wells, the Chicago agent of the company, gave an exposition of its status, after which several genetlmen expressed their views of the condition of affairs. If the charges made are true, said one speaker, Tweed was nothing compared to the wreckers of the Charter Oak. They had robbed the widows and orphans. Opposition was made to the proposition for the company to appoint a Receiver. One policy-holder believes that unless some change can be made and new stock brought into the company, so that Furber can not come in and acquire control of the whole thing, they might as well get right out of it now as in 10 or 15 years. Another gentleman, who had formerly been an agent of the company, denounced the arrangement with Furber, whereby he was to receive over $500,000, with 7 per cent. interest, as a fraud. Hon. William Bross moved the appointment of a committee of three to go to Hartford without delay, and to represent the interests of the Chicago policy-holders. He considered the old officers of the company either consummate scoundrels or grossly incompetent. Mr. Bross, W. J. Davis, and George Sherwood were named as the committee. The committee has no power to bind the policy-holders.

THREE HEAVY ROBBERIES.

ROCHESTER, N. Y., July 19.—A package containing about $17,000 in individual securities, including bonds of Bloomington and Empire, Illinois, Leavenworth City, St. John's Church, Canandaigua, and Erie and Pittsburg Railroad was stolen to-day from the First National Bank of Canandaigua.

WILMINGTON, Del., July 19.—The house of David Graves, at Brandywine Springs, near this city, was entered by burglars last night and robbed of $11,000 in United States bonds, about $100 in cash, some valuable jewelry, and numerous other articles.

NEWPORT, Perry County, Penn., July 19.—This morning, when the Cashier of the People's Bank of this place opened the bank safe, it was discovered that the cash drawer had been robbed of about $5,000 in money and $1,500 worth of bonds. The bank presented the same appearance as when closed last night. The bonds were of the following numbers and amounts: Issue of July 1, 1867, Nos. 124,413, 124,419, 58,644, 8,715, 30,539, each for $100; issue of July 1, 1865, Nos. 87,215, 91,318, 19,742, 119,789, 119,788, for $100 each, and No. 74,976 for $500.

THE SAN FRANCISCO MINT INQUIRY.

SAN FRANCISCO, Cal., July 19.—In the mint investigation this evening the commission resumed the examination of employes of the mint concerning the details of its management. Frank Pixley made some general charges to the effect that the mint was run as a political machine—that the employes had been used to locate desert lands, &c.—but was checked by President Low, who insisted upon the necessity of making specific charges in writing. The commission adjourned until Saturday at 2 P. M., when the Pinney charges will be taken up, to be followed by those preferred by Pixley.

MARINE DISASTERS.

BOSTON, Mass., July 19.—The schooner Dom Pedro, of 140 tons, Capt. David Speight, from Boston, bound to St. John, was run down and sunk last night off Boon Island by the United States revenue cutter Grant. At the time of the collision there was a thick fog, and the schooner had no port light set, which, with the absence of a torch-light and fog-horn, made the accident possible. The cutter was under steam, running for New-York. The schooner's Captain, crew, and five passengers, including three women, were saved. The Dom Pedro was about 10 years old, English built, and was valued at about $6,000. She had a general cargo valued at about $5,000.

BRUTAL MURDER OF A WOMAN.

WORCESTER, Mass., July 19.—At Auburn, this morning, Ellen Campbell, wife of Frank Campbell, a crippled pauper, was murdered by James Mulcahy, alias Wilkins. He broke each of the four limbs of his victim across his knee and pounded her head, destroying an eye and fracturing the skull. She lived four hours to tell the terrible story of her murder, and name the murderer. Mulcahy is under arrest. He admitted the commission of the act boastfully, and is evidently insane. He served two years in jail at St. John, New-Brunswick, and was released about three years ago.

STAGE-COACH ROBBERIES.

CHEYENNE, Wyoming Territory, July 19.—A coach from Deadwood was stopped last night near the Cheyenne River by three road agents, who robbed the passengers of about $50. Twelve miles further on they were again stopped by four robbers, who took the passengers' arms and part of their blankets. The treasure box was opened, but it contained no valuables. The up coach was also stopped last night near the Cheyenne River, the robbers securing only $13 from the passengers. There was no treasure in the coach.

MEXICAN MILITARY OPERATIONS.

GALVESTON, Texas, July 19.—A special dispatch from San Antonio last night says: "Gen. Pedra Valdez arrived by the Eagle Pass stage this morning, and will return on Friday. He has 290 men. Gen. Naranjo, on the other side, has 160 men, 100 of whom will join Gen. Pedra Valdez as soon as he crosses, which will be in six days."

NEW-ORLEANS, La., July 19.—Gen. Valdez, a leader in the Lerdo interest, is preparing for a movement into Mexico against Diaz. He is recruiting, &c., on this side, and will act in conjunction with Naranjo.

THE NEW STATE INSANE ASYLUM.

BUFFALO, N. Y. July 19.—On the invitation of the Board of Managers of the new State Insane Asylum, Dr. John Ordronaux, State Commissioner of Lunacy, Dr. M. B. Anderson and William P. Letchworth, all of the State Board of Charities, inspected the nearly completed work yesterday. They say the asylum, when completed, will be the finest in the country, and regret that progress is interrupted owing to the exhaustion of the appropriation.

DESPERATE MEN ON STRIKE.

TWO GREAT RAILROADS CRIPPLED.

THE RIOTERS ON THE BALTIMORE AND OHIO RAILROAD HELD IN CHECK BY UNITED STATES TROOPS—TWO TRAINS SENT OUT OF MARTINSBURG, ONE EAST AND ONE WEST—THE RAILROAD OFFICIALS HOPEFUL—ONE OF THE LEADERS IN THE STRIKE ARRESTED—PRESIDENT GARRETT'S APPEAL TO PRESIDENT HAYES.

Special Dispatch to the New-York Times.

BALTIMORE, Md., July 19.—The situation with regard to the strike on the Baltimore and Ohio Railroad is changed for the better, but the possibilities of trouble are not yet entirely averted. The United States troops, under command of Gen. W. H. French, arrived at Martinsburg early this morning, and at once went into bivouac. The strikers looked quietly upon them, but made no attempt to resist their movements.

Shortly after 10 o'clock hands were put on board of a train, and it was moved westward, but when it reached the head-quarters of the rioters, a mile west of Martinsburg, the men abandoned it, and the engineer ran it back to the town. New men were put on board with a detachment of 10 United States soldiers, and the train once more pulled out. A fireman named George Zepp, whose brother is ringleader of the mob, volunteered to do duty, and was followed up the track by his mother and sisters, who implored him to turn back. He resisted their entreaties, when a gang of strikers set upon him. He drew his revolver and drove them back, after which he mounted his engine, and the train went on. At latest advices it had reached Cumberland, and is expected to push on to-night as far as Keyser.

The first attempt to start a train east from Martinsburg was made at 3 o'clock this afternoon. It was placed in charge of William N. Clements, General Agent of the Baltimore and Ohio Railroad at Locust Point, and as the engine moved out of the siding at Martinsburg, the strikers gathered around it and made threatening demonstrations. They were well armed, and called to the engineer to stop or they would fire upon him. He paid no attention to them, and they charged down toward the locomotive as it moved slowly along the track. At this juncture the United States troops appeared with fixed bayonets, confronted the mob, and presented cold steel at them. At first the strikers appeared to be willing to make a fight, but as they advanced nearer to the serried line of bayonets, they wavered, and finally broke and ran for cover. Some of the leaders attempted to rally them, but they had no stomach for meeting the troops, and retired back into the town. The train went on, and to-night is well on its way toward Baltimore.

The movements of these two trains, one eastward and one westward, was undertaken by the railroad company with a view of demonstrating to the strikers that the company is abundantly able to carry on its operations under Federal protection, but as a matter of safety it was considered wise not to attempt any further movement of trains before to-morrow.

Advices from Martinsburg to-night say that the town is as quiet as the grave. The strikers have retired to their rendezvous, and are discussing what course of action they will pursue in view of the altered condition of affairs. The leaders are reported to be as desperate as ever, but they are not in favor of provoking a conflict with the Federal troops. They are rather disposed toward breaking up the camp and dispersing along the road in small bodies, with a view of inflicting damage wherever they may find it possible to do so.

The feeling among the railroad officials at Camden Station to-night is that they have won an important victory in the war, but that the future is still uncertain. Vice-President King, who has been managing affairs, has retired from duty to-night for the first time since Sunday night, but the events of to-morrow morning are looked forward to with a great deal of anxiety. The company will then undertake a general movement of trains east and west from Martinsburg, and it remains to be seen whether or not the strikers will continue hostile demonstrations.

Inspirited by the protection of the troops, the Sheriff of Berkley County this afternoon arrested at Martinsburg Dick Zepp, ringleader of the rioters, whose courage and desperation have placed him at their front. He was followed to jail by an angry mob of his friends, who were kept off by the bayonets of the troops. He had a hearing before a Justice of the Peace, and was released on bail to answer the charge of rioting.

The railroad authorities are solicitious that the blockade should be broken up by to-morrow on account of the commercial interests of Baltimore. The grain trade is calling for the delivery of shipments on their way from the West, but embargoed at Martinsburg, and the same thing is true of the live stock, coal, and petroleum interests. There are five or six vessels now waiting at the wharves here for petroleum that is held back on account of the strike, and the contracts of some live stock dealers have already been unavoidably broken because of the detention of the consignments to them. There are only about 200,000 bushels of grain in the elevators here, and there are charters for foreign ports to be filled within the next two days that will exhaust all this, and demand a heavy additional supply. The petroleum shipping companies are particularly frightened lest the strikers should undertake to set fire to their trains in the blockade. The stock of coal at Locust Point is also running low, and there is no relief from this trouble, because the Chesapeake and Ohio Canal hands are also on a strike and there is no coal coming eastward on that route. In order to fill the steamer and ship engagements maturing early next week for transportation to Europe, it is imperatively necessary that the blockade be immediately broken, and the emergency will force action of the most positive sort to-morrow.

There are fears of trouble on the Central Ohio Division of the Baltimore and Ohio Road. Advices late to-night say that the firemen are leaving their trains and threatening war. The extent of the difficulty is not entirely known, but notification has been sent to the Governor of Ohio that the company expects him to take whatever action is requisite. Matters up the main stem are in *statu quo*. No freight trains have been started from Wheeling to-day, the firemen and engineers refusing to go because of their fear of the strikers. No trains have arrived at or left Grafton, and the position there is in the hands of the strikers. A few trains have been run up the Parkersburg branch to Clarksburg, with the view of accumulating rolling stock on the main stem. At Keyser the strikers are very determined, and it is said that if they are driven out of Martinsburg they will make that their next rallying point. They refused to-day to allow a shifting-engine to move, and are more violent there than at any other point on the line except Martinsburg.

At Cumberland this morning a gang of rough-looking men attempted to board a passenger train, with the view of reinforcing the Martinsburg strikers, but were repulsed. The freight train westward from Martinsburg was also attacked at Cumberland to-night, but the mob contented themselves with throwing stones, and nothing serious occurred. The train eastward reached Baltimore about midnight without any further interruption. This finishes the programme for to-day, and to-morrow the railroad company will commence its movement of trains generally.

The west-bound freight train ran out of Cumberland about midnight without further interruption. The committees of strikers from the first, second, and third divisions of the road to-night met the strikers of the fourth division at Grafton. Resolutions were adopted declaring a determination that they will stand by each other and proposing plans for a compromise to be offered to the railroad company. Committees were appointed to act in conjunction with those from other divisions to meet the railroad official for the consideration of a basis of agreement. This effort will be fruitless. The company has resolved to hold to its ultimatum, and will not receive back in its employ any of the strikers. President Garrett has issued an order to-night that those who have been faithful shall be rewarded with medals and placed first on the list for promotion.

Dispatch to the Associated Press.

WASHINGTON, July 19.—The following dispatches were received at the War Department this morning from Col. French, commanding the United States troops at Martinsburg, West Va.:

MARTINSBURG, West Va., July 19.

To Adjutant-General, War Department:

Remained on the road till 6:30 A. M. President's proclamation not yet published; will be in an hour, when arrests will be made. Am in consultation with Col. Delaplaine.

FRENCH, Colonel Commanding.

MARTINSBURG, West Va., July 19.

Col. Vincent, Adjutant-General:

Proclamation printed. Now being circulated. After 12 o'clock, if the insurgents have not dispersed, the troops under my command will proceed to enforce the order of the President. At present everything seems quiet, and I doubt whether anything more than a demonstration will be required. Whatever action I may determine upon will be after consultation with and full concurrence of Col. Delaplaine, aid to the Governor.

FRENCH, Colonel Commanding.

Also the following from Gov. Matthews, of West Virginia:

WHEELING, West Va., July 18.

To Hon. George W. McCrary, Secretary of War:

The Legislature of 1875 prohibited the enrollment of the Militia of this State. There is now but one volunteer company which is valuable in this emergency. I have no doubt that within 10 days I could organize within the State a force sufficient to suppress any riot, but in the meantime much property will be destroyed, and, what is more important, valuable lives lost. I regret the necesity, but have not hesitated to assume the responsibility of applying to the President for assistance.

HENRY M. MATTHEWS, Governor.

The following telegram from John W. Garrett, President of the Baltimore and Ohio Railroad, was received by the President this morning:

CAMDEN STATION, BALTIMORE, July 18.

To his Excellency R. B. Hayes, President of the United States, Washington, D. C.:

I am informed that Gov. Matthews, of West Virginia, has telegraphed your Excellency that, owing to unlawful combinations and domestic violence now existing at Martinsburg and at other points along the line of the Baltimore and Ohio Railroad, it is impossible for any force at his command to execute the laws of the State, and has therefore called upon the Government for assistance of the United States military in this great and serious emergency. I have the honor to urge that the application of Gov. Matthews be immediately granted. It is impossible for the company to move any freight train because of the open intimidation of the strikers and the attacks that they have made upon men in the service of the company who are willing to work. Unless this difficulty is immediately stopped I apprehend most serious consequences, not only upon our line, but upon all the lines in the country, which, like ourselves, have been obliged to introduce measures of economy in these trying times for the preservation of the effectiveness of railroad property. May I ask your Excellency, if the application of Gov. Matthews be granted, to have me immediately advised through the Secretary of War, of the points from which the troops will be sent in order that no delay may occur in their transportation. If I may be permitted to suggest, Fort McHenry and Washington are points nearest to the scenes of disturbance, and from which the movement can be made with the greatest promptness and rapidity. It is proper to add that from full information on the subject, I am aware that the Governor of West Virginia has exerted all the means at his command to suppress the insurrection, and that this great national highway can only be restored for public use by the interposition of the United States forces. From an imperative sense of duty I am impelled to join in asking immediate action in order to prevent the rapid increase of the difficulties in the use of the lines between Washington City and Baltimore and the Ohio River.

JOHN W. GARRETT,
President Baltimore and Ohio Railroad.

WHEELING, West Va., July 19.—The Baltimore and Ohio strike has now become general, extending from Martinsburg to Parkersburg, Benwood, Columbus, Newark, and Chicago, and strengthens as it extends. The telegraph wires were cut west of Martinsburg by the strikers this afternoon.

CINCINNATI, Ohio, July 19.—The strike on the Baltimore and Ohio Railroad has extended to the Central Ohio Division, and all freight trains were detained at Newark to-day. It is stated that the strikers have threatened to use fire in case of the removal of trains. No demonstrations of violence have yet occurred, but are anticipated in case trains are taken out. The men, during the day, gathered about the depot in large numbers, but good humor prevailed. The engineers have not yet openly joined the firemen in the strike.

M. L. Doherty, Master of Traffic on the Baltimore and Ohio Road, called at the Governor's office to-day to consult in reference to military assistance to the authorities at Newark. Gov. Young was absent in Cincinnati. He is expected to return at midnight. There is no military company in Licking County, and the call on the Governor for aid is made on the supposition that the authorities at Newark are unable to control the strikers. The opinion prevails that the Governor cannot legally furnish military aid until the local authorities themselves declare their inability to control the strikers and protect property, and call for military assistance.

W. C. Quincy, General Manager of the Baltimore and Ohio Division west of the Ohio River, this afternoon held a conference with the old men at Newark, and offered to pay the old wages to such as would volunteer to take out trains; but the men, though willing to work, declined the offer for fear of their lives. It is stated on authority that the Baltimore and Ohio Road will employ on their Ohio Division experienced and skillful men to supply the places of strikers who have refused to go out on their trains. All is quiet here, the trains arriving and departing as usual.

BALTIMORE, Md., July 19—*Midnight.*—Officials at Camden Station furnish the following: "The eastward-bound freight train which left Martinsburg this afternoon arrived at Baltimore at 11:45 without accident or obstruction. The west-bound freight train which left Martinsburg at the same time arrived at Cumberland at 9:30. A mob of strangers assaulted the train on its arrival, but there being a squad of troops on board, no serious damage occurred."

THE PENNSYLVANIA RAILROAD.

REFUSAL OF THE TRAINMEN TO TAKE OUT DOUBLE TRAINS WITH ONE CREW—A BLOCKADE OF FREIGHT TRAINS AT PITTSBURG—WILLING CREWS DRIVEN OFF THE TRAINS BY VOLLEYS OF STONES.

PITTSBURG, Penn., July 19.—At noon to-day the freight train men on the Western Division of the Pennsylvania Railroad refused to go out with their trains. The strike is caused by the company's course in increasing the number of cars in the freight trains. Heretofore a conductor and his crew ran 17 cars. An order lately issued doubles this number, without increasing the strength of the crews. The strikers and their friends, in all nearly 500 persons, assembled at the outer depot, and by intimidation have prevented the crews from going out that otherwise would have remained at work. A man while attempting to couple cars was attacked and severely beaten. The ringleaders in this attack were arrested. The strikers then moved out on the line of the road toward East Liberty.

A placard was posted about the depot, signed by the President of the Trainmen's Union, calling a meeting of the train men at Phœnix Hall this evening.

At 3:30 P. M. to-day 18 trains were in the railroad company's yards ready to go out, but without crews to run them. The engineers were in readiness, but the company were not able to get men to take the strikers' places. The new order requiring double trains of two engines and 36 cars to be taken out by one crew went into effect this morning. The strikers claim that by this order two ordinary trains are taken out to Altoona, a distance of 116 miles, instead of to Derry, which is 48 miles. Formerly, a trip to Derry was considered a day's work, while now the trip to Altoona is considered a day's work. This, they say, would require one crew to do the work of two, and would enable the company to discharge one-half their number. It is said the strike was not prearranged, but was inaugurated by Conductor Ryan's crew, who sent word to the dispatcher that they would not take out their train. The dispatcher then asked two yard crews to take it out, and they, it is said, refused and were discharged. Subsequently Conductor Gordon ordered two men to take out an engine, but the strikers cut it loose from the train. Gordon then made another attempt, but the men on the train were stoned away and compelled to desert the engine.

When the trouble commenced at the outer depot this morning, a party of strikers lost no time in getting out to the East Liberty Stock Yards, and had a conference with the train and yard men there, which resulted in the latter joining the strikers. Trains were run upon side tracks and left there. The strikers then took possession of the main track and stopped all freight trains east or west. Those coming in from the east were allowed to proceed, after the situation had been explained, in order not to blockade the main track. It was necessary that some of the stock trains should be pulled up to the sidings to be unloaded, and this work was done by Pan Handle engines. None of those belonging to the Pennsylvania Railroad were allowed to be used. The main track at this point is wholly in the hands of the strikers. A west-bound freight train was stopped at Brinton's this afternoon by a party of strikers who had gone there for that purpose. The train was allowed to proceed, the men intimating that they would join the strikers as soon as they reached the city. The excitement along the road is intense, and it is feared the Fort Wayne and Pan Handle men will join the movement. The strikers threaten by force to release McCall, who was arrested for striking Superintendent Watt. No detention is offered to passenger trains, and no serious collisions have yet taken place.

PITTSBURG, Penn., July 19.—A large and very enthusiastic meeting of the Train Men's Union was held at Phœnix Hall, on Eleventh-street, to-night. Nearly all of the strikers were present, and the meeting was addressed by many speakers. But one sentiment was expressed—a determination to continue the strike. The meeting was very orderly. The strikers were joined at the meeting by the engineers and firemen of the Western Division and it was determined to have the fight on the reduction of wages which went into effect on June 1, and against the doubling of trains. The following resolutions were unanimously adopted as their ultimatum:

First—We, the undersigned committee appointed by the Western Division of the Pennsylvania Railroad Company, do hereby demand from said company, through its proper officers, the wages as per departments of engineers, firemen, conductors, and brakemen received prior to June 1, 1877.

Second—That each and every employe who has been dismissed for taking part or parts in the present strike or meetings held prior to or during said strike be restored to their positions as held prior to the strike.

Third—That the classification of each of said departments be abolished now and forever, and that hereafter engineers and conductors receive the same wages as received by engineers and conductors of the highest class prior to June 1, 1877.

Fourth—That the running of double trains be abolished, excepting coal trains.

Fifth—That each and every engine, whether road or shifting, shall have its own fireman.

The officers of the road claim that the double train arrangement is simply a pretext for the strike. They state that for three months past the frieght business has been very low, and that many crews have been kept in the employ of the company in anticipation of better business. During the last two weeks the decrease of freight has been so heavy that the company only had work for 15 or 18 of the 26 crews in their employ. They further state that the strike was gotten up because a large number of men expected to be thrown out of work by the new order.

THE CHESAPEAKE AND OHIO CANAL.

GEORGETOWN, D. C., July 19.—The canal-boat Ludlow Patton, the only boat that has been able to pass the blockade on the Chesapeake and Ohio Canal, arrived here to-day with 100 tons of coal for District merchants. She reports having met with considerable opposition from the strikers, who stoned and attempted to intimidate her crew.

CANADIAN RAILROAD HANDS DISSATISFIED.

LONDON, Ontario, July 19.—A deputation representing all classes of employes of the Great Western Railroad in this city, had an interview with Mr. Broughton, General Manager, at Hamilton, to protest against a reduction of wages. Mr. Broughton promised to consider the matter.

RUNS ON SAVINGS BANKS.

CHICAGO DEPOSITORS UNEASY—HEAVY DEMANDS MADE—SIXTY DAYS' NOTICE REQUIRED.

Special Dispatch to the New-York Times.

CHICAGO, July 19.—The uneasiness here yesterday among depositors of savings banks regarding the security of their deposits was by no means allayed to-day. Yesterday the State Savings Bank was the only one on which extra demands were made; to-day the Fidelity and others experienced somewhat of a run. Matters had a panicky outlook early in the day. At the State Savings Bank the crowd was very great and clamorous for their deposits. The bank officials finally took advantage of the 30 and 60 days' rule of limitation governing demands for deposits, and posted notice to this effect. Small accounts were settled on demand. There was a similar policy pursued, and with good effect, at other savings banks.

THE UNITED STATES INSURANCE COMPANY.

ST. LOUIS, Mo., July 19.—The United States Insurance Company, which a few days ago reinsurred its policies and retired from business, has declared a dividend of 80 per cent., payable in cash on or before the 23d of July. The whole amount this company received in cash subscriptions to its stock was $11 per share, or $22,000. The balance of the stock was paid up in dividends on stock notes amounting to $178,000. Besides these there have been dividends to stockholders amounting to $257,000, making a total of $435,000. The losses paid by the company in its 22 years of existence amounted to $1,700,000, and the company now returns to its stockholders the full amount of its stock.

THE REMONETIZATION OF SILVER.

Special Dispatch to the New-York Times.

CHICAGO, July 19.—At a meeting of the Textile Manufacturers' Association, of the West and South, held here to-day, and at which there was a large representation present, it was resolved that the remonetization of silver is considered an important means toward the re-establishment of industrial prosperity, and Congress is urged to restore the old silver dollar to its vacant place in the country's ancient coinage system.

SALE OF AN IOWA RAILROAD.

Special Dispatch to the New-York Times.

CHICAGO, Ill., July 19.—A special from Marshalltown, Iowa, states that the Central Railroad of Iowa was sold at auction in that city this afternoon. There was only one bid—that of the Farmers' Loan and Trust Company, of New-York, Trustee for the first mortgage bondholders—and on this the road was sold for $5,192,390.

SPRINGFIELD, Mass., July 19.—In the Northampton Bank burglary trial to-day, Edson concluded his testimony, bringing out no new facts. The trial will extend into next week.

NEW-HAVEN, Conn., July 19.—John H. Shields, the ringleader of the gang who violated Mrs. Ellen Warner on May 23, was to-day convicted, and sentenced to the State Prison for life.

CONCORD, N. H., July 19.—At a meeting of the Governor and Council to-day John S. H. Fink, of Portsmouth, and Isaac W. Smith, of Manchester, were nominated Justices of the Supreme Court.

NORHAMPTON, Mass., July 19.—The Selectmen have awarded the contract for building a bridge, in the place of the one destroyed by the tornado, to the Canton Bridge Company, of Canton, Ohio. The bridge will be of iron, about 1,225 feet long, and will cost about $27,000.

MOUNT WASHINGTON, N. H., July 19.—The first number of the daily newspaper *Among the Clouds*, projected by Henry M. Burt, editor of the *New-England Homestead*, to be printed on the summit of Mount Washington, has been issued. It is an eight-page paper, and will be published during the season.

THE NATIONAL FINANCES.

PROGRESS OF THE CONSOLIDATION.

CHANGE OF MANAGEMENT OF THE SYNDICATE OFFICE IN LONDON PROBABLE—THE PUBLIC SUBSCRIPTIONS TO THE FOUR PER CENT. LOAN—THE FIFTY-SECOND CALL FOR THE REDEMPTION OF $10,000,000 OF FIVE-TWENTIES—CONDITION OF THE UNITED STATES TREASURY YESTERDAY—REVENUE AND CUSTOMS.

Special Dispatch to the New-York Times.

WASHINGTON, July 19.—Mr. Bigelow, who has been connected with the syndicate operations at London for several years, has not been recalled, as has been stated in dispatches from this city, but it is probable he will be at an early day. All the expenses of the loan office at London are borne by the syndicate, but the Government designates the agents to transact the business, and these agents are qualified officers of the United States representing the Treasury Department. Recently the syndicate notified the Secretary of the Treasury that they believe the expenses of the London office could be reduced without impairing its efficiency, and Mr. Bigelow and one or two others were designated as officers whose services could be dispensed with. The recommendations of the syndicate have not yet been acted upon, but no doubt is entertained that they will be approved. Mr. Conant, late Assistant Secretary of the Treasury, was recently placed in charge of the London office, and in sending him there the purpose of the syndicate was doubtless to remove Mr. Bigelow. At the Treasury Department the charges recently published against Mr. Bigelow are positively denied.

The complete subscriptions to the 4 per cent. Consols of 1907, as reported to the Treasury Department, are as follows:

Washington...	$659,500	St. Louis......	137,350
New-York.......	2,591,500	Chicago......	391,050
Philadelphia..	145,650	New-Orleans..	265,650
Baltimore....	120,950	Cincinnati....	529,800
Boston........	756,000	San Francisco.	63,200
Total			$5,982,500
Syndicate			60,000,000
Grand total			$65,982,500

A San Francisco dispatch of to-day says: "The *Bulletin* this afternoon publishes an editorial on the manner of working off the 4 per cent. Government loan through the syndicate, embodying some facts showing the effect that course of action has produced on this coast, and what might have been accomplished had the loan been offered for popular subscription. The statements contained in the article are corroborated by the President of the Nevada Bank. They are in substance that that bank, representing the bank proper and several wealthy gentlemen of this city, offered a subscription of $20,000,000 to the syndicate, which was defeated by the refusal of the syndicate to concede out of the commission paid them by the Government the usual one-eighth of one per cent. allowed between bankers on this class of transactions, and, furthermore, that the Nevada Bank and its friends, had the loan been offered for popular subscription, stood ready to set its name at the head of the list for $100,000,000. It may be added that the $20,000,000 subscription proposed to the syndicate was intended as a permanent investment, and the Nevada Bank offered to agree not to resell the bonds within the term covered by the syndicate's contract."

The Treasury Department to-day issued the fifty-second call for the redemption of 5-20 bonds of 1865, being for $10,000,000, Consols of 1865, of which $7,000,000 are coupon, and $3,000,000 registered bonds. The principal and interest will be paid at the Treasury on and after the 19th day of October next, and the interest will cease on that day. Following are descriptions of bonds:

Coupon bonds dated July 1, 1865—$50, Nos. 24,001 to 30,000, both inclusive; $100, Nos. 40,001 to 52,000, both inclusive; $500, Nos. 34,001 to 42,000, both inclusive; $1,000, Nos. 64,001 to 75,000, both inclusive.

Registered bonds, redeemable at the pleasure of the United States after the 1st day of July, 1870—$50, Nos. 901 to 1,150, both inclusive; $100, Nos. 8,551 to 10,500, both inclusive; $500, Nos. 6,151 to 7,200, both inclusive; $1,000, Nos. 19,851 to 23,000 both inclusive; $5,000, Nos. 5,901 to 6,700, both inclusive; $10,000, Nos. 5,355 to 7,880, both inclusive.

The balances in the United States Treasury to-day were: Currency, $7,280,095; special fund for the redemption of fractional currency, $7,963,213; special deposit of legal tenders for the redemption of certificates of deposit, $59,355,000; coin, including $40,228,600 in coin certificates, $108,582,578; outstanding legal tenders, $359,764,332.

The receipts from internal revenue to-day were $380,681 17, and from Customs, $276,046 31.

THE DEMOCRATIC STATE OFFICERS.

NEARLY ALL OF THEM WILLING TO DEVOTE THEMSELVES TO THE SERVICE OF THEIR COUNTRY DURING ANOTHER TERM, IF THE PEOPLE SUBMIT TO IT.

ALBANY, N. Y., July 19.—In reply to inquiries relative to renomination, the present State officials have at various times made frank statements substantially to this effect: Treasurer Ross announced positively several days ago that he was a candidate for renomination, and would remain until the convention decided against him. He declared that he had not the slightest fear of being thrown over by the convention, unless he proved himself unworthy and incompetent within the intervening time till the convention. State Engineer Van Buren said that he would like a renomination, and expected to get it. The convention, however, would settle that, and he certainly would make no very direct appeal to it for a renomination beyond keeping up a good record. Attorney-General Fairchild stated very positively that he expected a renomination. Controller Olcott said that he would like a renomination, and hoped to get it. He had taken the place originally at Gov. Robinson's urgent solicitation, chiefly in order that he could superintend the final payment of the bounty debt, which the Governor was very anxious should be settled without any disturbance of State securities or the money markets and when that was accomplished he had informed the Governor of his willingness to withdraw and let some other party man come in. The Governor had not, however, expressed any consent to his withdrawal, and he had consequently remained. During the interval he had become interested in various financial and reformatory operations of the State and was averse to giving them up until they were finished. At the same time he was, he thought, quite young as a public officer, and could not feel like pressing his claims before a convention on any record which he had made, and would not press them. Secretary of State Bigelow has been absent for several days and his wishes and intentions were not obtained.

NAVAL INTELLIGENCE.

PORTSMOUTH, N. H., July 19.—The United States steamer Speedwell, Lieut.-Commander A. G. Kellogg, has been thoroughly overhauled at this navy-yard, and is ready for sea, with steam up, expecting orders to sail for New-London by to-night. She will take on board the Fish Commissioners, proceeding direct to Salem, Mass., which will be her head quarters the remainder of the season.

The United States steamer Enterprise has been floated out of the dry-dock, and it is now believed she can be got ready to sail for European waters about Aug. 30.

WASHINGTON, July 19.—Capt. William E. Fitzhugh has been ordered to command the Monongahela, in place of Commander S. D. Greene, detached from the command of that vessel and placed on waiting orders.

1877

America Comes of Age

1898

FRONT PAGE NEWS 1877-1898

Edison Flips the Switch

December 28, 1879

In 1878, Thomas A. Edison had promised to replace gas lamps, a staple of late-19th-century street corners and parlors, with electric ones. Little more than a year later, 84 incandescent electric lights were burning night and day in Edison's New Jersey laboratory. Soon he opened the world's first electrical substation, on Pearl Street in Manhattan. There, with generators, underground cables and fuses, he built the beginnings of the modern power grid—and arguably the beginnings of modern urban civilization, for better and worse.

When Oil Was $1.15 a Barrel

January 31, 1880

The Times's headline told, in three words, how oil was remaking post-Reconstruction America: "Fortunes in Petroleum." The biggest fortune was built on what The Times called "the great monopoly of oildom," John D. Rockefeller's Standard Oil. Rockfeller, the penny-pinching son of a snake-oil salesman, controlled 90 percent of the oil industry and a fortune that, by some estimates, would now be worth $200 billion. He later became a target of muckraking exposes by Ida Tarbell, investigations by government trust busters and a Supreme Court decision that broke up Standard Oil into more than 30 smaller companies. But Rockefeller remained synonymous with money—and later, philanthropy.

Chinese Exclusion Acts

March 10, 1882

Since the Civil War, thousands of Chinese immigrants had flooded the western United States, where working-class whites accused them of undercutting wages. Congress attacked the issue not by regulating pay but by suspending Chinese immigration for 10 years. Supporters complained, The Times said, that the Chinese "do not speak our language, do not care about our Constitution and laws, do not bear their share of taxation [and] do not perform military duty." Congress renewed the provision in 1892, and it remained on the books until 1943, when the U.S. and China were wartime allies against Japan and President Franklin D. Roosevelt demanded its repeal.

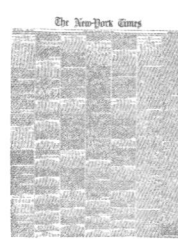

Brooklyn Bridge Opens

May 25, 1883

The Brooklyn Bridge was one of those they-said-it-couldn't-be-done creations that bound together two municipalities that had been as separate and distinct as the Left and Right Bank of Paris. Eventually Manhattan overshadowed Brooklyn, but nothing overshadowed the bridge. It was dreamed up by John A. Roebling, a German-born civil engineer who had written his college thesis on suspension bridges and had built spans supported by tightly wound ropes in Pennsylvania. For the Brooklyn Bridge, he used tightly wound cables of steel. He died while the bridge was being built, and it was finished by his son Washington, who got the bends after coming up from the caissons too quickly. After that, Washington Roebling would not go near the bridge. But he supervised the work by watching through a telescope in his office.

Geronimo Captured

August 22, 1886

Geronimo, a smart, aggressive commander who had eluded the U.S. Army across the Southwest, was captured after years of trying to defend his Apache Indians' right to what they considered their homeland. Geronimo surrendered, only to escape and surrender one last time in September. His American captors then double-crossed him, promising that he could go to the Apaches' Arizona reservation after an initial exile in Florida. They never let him get any farther west than Fort Sill, Oklahoma, although his fame was such that he rode in Theodore Roosevelt's inaugural parade.

Carrying the Torch

October 28, 1886

There she was in the distance, so new, so elegant, so symbolic: the skeleton that kept the Statue of Liberty's torch and crown aloft was designed by a young Parisian whose greater fame back home was yet to come, Gustave Eiffel. Engineers in the horizontal, low-lying city that was then New York realized that he put the future under her gown—the steel structure for what amounted to a 22-story skyscraper.

Gompers Leads Labor Federation

December 12, 1886

After organizing a nationwide general strike for an eight-hour workday, the newly formed American Federation of Labor elected its first president, Samuel Gompers. As a leader of the cigarmakers' union in New York, he had pioneered strikes and boycotts for higher wages. He also favored "political nonpartisanship," which meant avoiding alliances with such Marxist-leaning groups as the International Workers of the World. Gompers grew the A.F.L. into the nation's largest union confederation, with two million members by World War I.

Oklahoma Land Rush

APRIL 22, 1889

Everyone expected President Benjamin Harrison's order opening the Oklahoma Territory to settlers would mean one thing: a "mad rush to reach this far-famed land of plenty," as The Times put it. The federal government had driven five tribes of Indians onto reservations west of the Mississippi, opening a territory the size of Rhode Island and Delaware combined. Making good on the prediction of a mad rush, some 50,000 land-hungry whites swarmed in and staked their claims.

'The Great French Show'

MAY 19, 1889

Like later world's fairs, 19th-century expositions were a showcase for everything new, a see-and-be-seen circus of inventors, hucksters and crowds. The exhibits were temporary, housed in giant halls that were torn down after the last fair goer had finally gone home. The exhibition that opened in Paris in 1889 added something permanent to the cityscape and to the world's imagination: the Eiffel Tower, which reigned as the tallest structure in the world until the Chrysler Building and the Empire State Building came along in the 1930's.

How the West Was Won

NOVEMBER 22, 1890

Indians in the Dakotas had taken up a ritual called "ghost dancing," which they believed would hasten the return of dead relatives—and the demise of whites. Whites considered it a war dance because the dancers strapped on their rifles before the drums began, and Army brass feared another rout like the one that had killed General George Armstrong Custer at Little Big Horn. By year's end, impatient cavalrymen would kill Chief Sitting Bull and top off the conquest of the West by massacring some 200 Sioux Indians at Wounded Knee, South Dakota.

Homestead Steel Strike

JULY 7, 1892

The Homestead strike turned into a pitched battle—and a demoralizing setback for unions. It centered on a huge open-hearth mill where Andrew Carnegie's major domo, Henry Clay Frick, announced that he was lowering wages. Frick wanted humiliation for the largest union in the country, the Amalgamated Association of Iron and Steel Workers, about 15 percent of whose members had jobs there. The union rejected the pay cut and the workers took to the streets, where they faced off against Frick's Pinkerton detectives. At least 10 people on both sides were killed. The Pinkertons gave up, but not Frick. He got the Pennsylvania National Guard to move in five days later, clearing the way for strikebreakers to reopen the mill. By year's end, it was the union that gave up.

Parading to the World's Fair

OCTOBER 21, 1892

All Chicago turned out for a parade for the opening of the Chicago World's Fair, officially called the Columbian Exposition in celebration of Christopher Columbus and the 400th anniversary of his voyage to the New World. In the 19th century, he ranked as a hero, up there with George Washington and Abraham Lincoln and worthy of a fair that featured the famous "White City," the first large-scale installation of electric street lights.

Hawaiian Queen Loses Throne

JUNE 18, 1897

Queen Liliuokalani of Hawaii had taken issue with the treaty that gave Americans control of Pearl Harbor. The Americans' response was to depose her, with help from marines and a delegation led by Sanford B. Dole, the Hawaiian-born son of missionaries who was related to the American pineapple dynasty. Later they fended off an order from President Grover Cleveland to reinstate the queen, as well as a local "revolution" that tried to do the same thing. Now she challenged the Americans' seizure of more than 900,000 acres of Hawaiian land, a move that led to Hawaii's annexation in year 1898, which, in turn, led to statehood 61 years later.

The New-York Times.

VOL. XXIX.......NO. 8829. NEW-YORK, SUNDAY, DECEMBER 28, 1879.---TRIPLE SHEET. PRICE FIVE CENTS.

THE DEMOCRATIC INFAMY

POPULAR INDIGNATION IN MAINE INCREASING.

LITTLE SATISFACTION WITH THE GOVERNOR'S REPLY TO MR. MORRILL—FEARS THAT A PEACEFUL SETTLEMENT MAY NOT BE EFFECTED—THE REMOVAL OF ARMS BY THE GOVERNOR'S ORDERS.

The reports from Maine show that the indignation of the people is increasing, though moderate counsels prevail, and from all sides, from Democrats and Greenbackers as well as Republicans, come petitions urging Gov. Garcelon to seek the Supreme Court's decision. Public excitement is enhanced by the attempts of the Fusionists to seize the arms of the Militia. Many thinking men fear that a peaceful settlement cannot be secured. The Fusionists are calling meetings to sustain the Governor, who, at Lewiston last evening, said that his action in this matter was a deed of which he felt proud.

CONSIDERING THE END.

MR. MORRILL PREPARING AN ANSWER TO THE GOVERNOR—THE POSITION YESTERDAY.

BOSTON, Mass., Dec. 27.—A special dispatch from Augusta, Me., to the *Herald* says: "The bitter feeling and chance of trouble seem to increase rather than diminish. The Governor's letter to ex-Senator Morrill does not mean so much as at first sight it may appear to. He expresses a willingness to refer the points that have not already been adjudicated upon; but it is understood that he believes those points are extremely few, and that he has a decision of the court to back nearly every case. This leaves the hope for a peaceful settlement through the Morrill plan decidedly a faint one. Though the attempt was creditable, it looks now as if nothing can prevent trouble on the assembling of the Legislature but a square backdown on the part of the Fusionists, and how much chance there is of this one man can judge as well as another. Men who do not encourage violence openly do not hesitate to say that they fear and expect it. Congressman Frey's speech last night was not reassuring, and Congressman Reed thinks blood will be shed before the trouble is over. The excitement in country towns and villages grows more rapidly than in the cities even. In one of them it is understood that there is an excellent prospect of mob violence to-night, but it may be prevented. The meetings of both parties to-night will be numerous, and few of the speeches conducive to peace. To-morrow's sermons will be more warlike yet. Things are decidedly hot, considering that the mercury is below zero in the middle of the forenoon.

A correspondent of the Boston *Herald* telegraphs that paper from Augusta as follows: "Your correspondent met, last evening, one of the Republican Congressmen from this State, and had some conversation with him on the affairs in the State, and what the future was to bring with it. He declared himself unable to foretell, but said he should be gratified, not to say surprised, if a settlement was reached without bloodshed, which he evidently very much feared. He did not think any radical or violent talk would have much to do in increasing the popular excitement. All that was needed to enrage any honest citizen was to read the account of what the Governor and Council have done, and that would make any man's blood boil. He approved the statement of another Congressman, that he did not believe that eight such scoundrels could be found, out of the State Prison, as those who had perpetrated this outrage. This is pretty plain talk, and shows how deep the prevailing resentment is against the authorities. The gentleman declared that no excuse could be made for the crime. The most callow young lawyer who ever practiced before a justice court would be ashamed to have been guilty of trying to justify such infamy as the counting out of Skowhegan or Cherryfield, or the Sullivan and Gouldsboro case, or the Burnham-Cushman case in Aroostook. For such cases there never was a parallel. To read of them was all that was needed to excite an honest man's indignation. Speeches and editorials could only confirm and deepen the feeling which the contemplation of the facts inevitably created. Being told that a certain member of the Council was expected to speak to-night in a certain town, the Congressman asked, as if innocently desiring information, what would the people do with the fellow. 'Hang him, do you think?'"

AUGUSTA, Me., Dec. 27.—The Hon. Lot M. Morrill came to Augusta this morning by an early train and returned by special train at 5:30 o'clock this evening. It is understood that the object of his visit was to have a conference touching the points to be presented to Gov. Garcelon for submission to the Supreme Court. About 15 brief questions, it is said, have been agreed upon, but the letter has not yet been obtained. Mr. Morrill expresses great confidence that Gov. Garcelon will agree to submit the questions. Petitions are coming in rapidly from all parts of the State, urging the Governor to submit the questions to the Supreme Court.

BANGOR, Dec. 27.—Although the feeling is very intense, ordinary quiet prevailed on Friday, and all business proceeded as regularly as usual. The best citizens express great indignation at the moving of the arms through the streets on Christmas Day, but not the slightest tendency to disorder of any kind was manifested. The news of the clandestine removal of rifles of the Old Town Company from the armory by the Fusionists last night caused much comment and comparison with the lack of any disposition by the Republicans here to disturb the munitions at the arsenal or armory. Lieut.-Col. Daniel White, of this city, who succeeds to the command of the State Militia by the resignation of Col. Matlock, has issued a circular to the different companies, expressing the hope that all the present troubles will be peacefully settled, and asking reports of membership, arms, &c.

At a meeting of the Citizens' Executive Committee last evening, the following was adopted:

To the Public:

In view of the spontaneous uprising of our citizens at the sight of arms and ammunition transported through our streets on Christmas Day, stealthily and without written authority for the purpose, on behalf of the Governor of the State, of consummating by force the threatened crime against the decision of the majority as expressed at the polls, the undersigned, an Executive Committee of citizens, at a meeting held this evening, were unanimously of opinion that, while this uprising was but a natural expression of the indignation of our citizens, yet, if our Governor shall see fit to persist in this remarkable and alarming purpose of gathering munitions of war for use against the people, the responsibility therefor may well be left upon him, and the law-abiding citizens of Bangor will do nothing that would incur any degree of responsibility for the deplorable consequences which may ensue from turning the capital of the State into an armed camp. We, therefore, feel assured that there is no disposition on the part of the people to resist the execution of any order lawfully given by the Governor for the removal from our city of any property belonging to the State.

J. S. WHEELWRIGHT,	WHITING S. CLARK,
CHARLES G. STEARNS,	CHARLES S. LORD,
C. A. BARTELLE,	LYSANDER STRICKLAND,
G. R. LANCASTER,	HENRY LORD,
SILAS C. HATCH,	H. N. FAIRBANKS,
E. R. NEALLY,	C. U. CROSSMAN,
JOHN L. CUTTER,	B. B. THATCHER.
L. J. MORSE,	

Petitions signed by several leading citizens, including a number of the most prominent Democrats of the city, will be sent to the Governor, urging the propriety of complying with the proposition of Mr. Morrill for reference of the questions involved in the controversy of the returns to the Supreme Court.

The city is quiet and orderly. The report that the Republicans were forming a secret military association, with threats to seize the arms in the State Arsenal, is contradicted on the authority of the best-informed citizens of Bangor. There has been no purpose to trouble the Arsenal or any other property of the State.

Lieut. C. E. Miles, of Old Town, commanding the Hersey Light Infantry, has requested that the statement be made that he removed the arms of the company from the armory to his residence for safe-keeping on Thursday night, by order from Major M. M. Folsom and the State-house Clerk, Mr. French. Major Folsom is a townsman and an intimate political friend of Mr. Smith, Fusion candidate for Governor, and is next in rank below Lieut.-Col. Daniel White commanding the Militia. Although the removal of arms was decided upon in the city on Thursday afternoon, in view of the excitement here, as Lieut. Miles states, no consultation was had with Col. White, who was easily accessible, but action was taken on the orders of the clerk, who is not believed to have any authority to direct the movements of Militia. All military men here admit that the serious responsibilities of directing warlike operations in time of peace have been most carelessly and irregularly exercised in all the transactions in this vicinity.

PORTLAND, Me., Dec. 27.—The principal Protestant clergymen of Portland have united in a petition to the Governor to ask the advice of the Supreme Court in the present position of affairs. Episcopal Bishop Neely and the Rev. Dr. Hill are among the signers.

GARDINER, Me., Dec. 27.—Much dissatisfaction is reported among several prominent Democrats and Greenbackers on account of the clergymen addressing the indignation meeting on Monday night. There is much excitement here over the Bangor affair. A petition has been sent the Governor and Council, signed by 253 citizens of both parties, urging the propriety, expediency, and justice of asking the opinion of the Judicial Supreme Court, in accordance with the request contained in the communication from the Hon. Lot M. Morrill.

BELFAST, Me., Dec. 27.—Agreeably to a call, signed by a large number of Republicans, a citizens' meeting was held this evening. The meeting was called to order by Dr. J. G. Brooks, Representative-elect. Col. William A. Foger was chosen Chairman and A. C. Sibley Secretary. Speeches were made by several prominent citizens of this county, and many letters were read. The general tone of the speeches, letters, and resolutions were unqualifiedly condemnatory of the "counting-out" action of the Governor and Council, and while deprecating and disavowing all intention of resort to arms, yet advise that every constitutional right should be maintained, and where set aside or overridden must be contested step by step, and final resort must be at the bar of public opinion, as expressed at the polls in future elections.

WATERVILLE, Me., Dec. 27.—An indignation meeting of Republicans was held here to-night. Several brief speeches were made and appropriate resolutions were passed.

GOV. GARCELON FEELS PROUD.

CONSCIOUS OF DUTY DONE AND NOT AFRAID TO DIE IF NECESSARY.

LEWISTON, Me., Dec. 27.—The Fusionists had a large meeting in the City Hall to-night to ratify the action of the Governor and Council, 3,000 people being present and the crowd very enthusiastic. The meeting was called to order by D. T. Noyes, and the Hon. Nathan Morrill was nominated as Chairman, who made a brief speech of acceptance. A committee of seven, with Calvin Record as Chairman, was appointed to wait on the Governor at his residence and request him to address the meeting. The next speakers were T. B. Swan, of Mechanics' Falls, and T. B. Torrey, of Bath. While Mr. Torrey was speaking, Gov. Garcelon came into the hall, and was received with cheers, the audience rising.

Gov. Garcelon said: "I most heartily thank you for this expression of your confidence. A long life of 70 years has been spent in this community, and if there has been any act of mine in any way treasonable, or in violation of law and order, I am unconscious of it. I do not come to apologize for what has been done in the way of counting the returns made by the municipal officers; the records speak for themselves. Almost immediately after the election it was hinted that there would be unfair means used in counting the votes, and that an attempt would be made to steal the State. The election returns were placed in the hands of the Committee on Elections in October last. Until Nov. 17 no person save the committee had access to them. Prior to Nov. 17, I had hardly seen a newspaper for a fortnight, as I was busy removing my residence and office. That day I went to Augusta and went directly to my chamber in the Capitol. In five minutes I was called upon by a committee of Republicans, who demanded to see the election returns. The conference that followed has been reported, and has been reported correctly. The very fact of these Republicans presenting themselves served to make me more cautious in counting the returns in a lawful and constitutional manner. If there has been any act of my life of which I am proud, it is of the performance of my duty in tabulating and counting those returns. We have simply followed the Constitution and the laws, as interpreted by the Supreme Court time and time again.

"The Constitution prescribes certain things for cities and towns to do at election. If the requirements of the Constitution are not complied with, there is no legal election. These provisions were made for the purpose of securing an honest election. It turns out sometimes that there are informalities in the returns. The Legislature undertook to provide by law for correcting this. That correction must be made by the record. If there is no record, what can the returns be corrected by? If the record is like the returns, where can the correction come in? Now, when this avalanche of Republican statesmen came in on me at Augusta it popped into my head that their very object was to see the returns, and then go home and see that their records were made all right. In the case of Portland the returns were illegal, and the records were sent for. Lo! the record was found to be just like the returns. The Republicans say that the intention of the voter must be regarded, and not the Constitution and law. The Selectmen of the Town of Danforth had the presumption to go to the Clerk and demand that he change and correct the record. I have a letter from Mr. Berry, the Town Clerk, saying that he was threatened with a fine and imprisonment unless he complied. That is what comes of this amending records. Amend your records three months after the election, and where is the result of any election. The tabulations were made upon the basis of the Constitution, as explained by the court as far as possible, and if there is any one act of my life in which I am conscious of having performer my duty without fear or favor, it is in the performance of this duty thus imposed upon me. The circumstances that have surrounded me have been unfavorable. I have, in reality, had to face a frowning world on account of the foul lies of the Associated Press, and the vituperation and slander heaped upon me for over a quarter of a century."

Gov. Garcelon alluded to the unfavorable comments upon the action of William Pitt Fessenden from a Lewiston pulpit at the time of the impeachment trial of President Johnson, and said that the very clergyman who hurled anathemas upon him was obliged, publicly, to confess, three years after, that Mr. Fessenden was one of the most honest men ever known. "Every method that could be devised, the Governor continued, has been brought to bear on me to induce me to change my line of conduct; not only by usual forms of sour faces and vilification, but also by threats of assassination. I received a letter last night, warning me to be careful on my trip to Augusta, to watch the very food that I put into my mouth. This is only one of many similar letters from various parts of the State. I have faced more terrible guns than these paper bullets. I have slept where the bullets whistled through the trees, and I am not to be frightened by these despicable threats. If I am to be assassinated for obeying the laws of the State, my life could be offered on no better altar; it would cause more respect for the Constitution than ever before." The Governor's remarks were loudly cheered.

Mr. Neal, of Portland, made a brief speech, in which he named Gov. Garcelon for the Democratic Presidential nomination, amid loud applause. Solon Chase said he heard that the Governor was to speak here to-night, so he harnessed up the black colt and came down. It had popped into his head that the Governor had obeyed the law as he understood it. The only trouble with the Republicans was that they did not like to have the Governor administer their own medicine to them. The trouble was not with the man who enforced the law, but with the law.

Resolutions were read and adopted, praising Gov. Garcelon as a citizen and an officer, and denouncing the attacks upon his character. After the meeting, a procession was formed which marched to the Governor's residence with a brass band. The Governor was serenaded, and he made another brief speech.

APPROVING THE OUTRAGE.

MEETINGS CALLED BY GREENBACKERS AND OTHERS TO SUPPORT THE GOVERNOR.

ROCKLAND, Me., Dec. 27.—The Greenbackers have issued a call for a meeting of the citizens at Farwell Hall, Monday evening, to give expression to their determination to vindicate the integrity of the Constitution and laws, and to uphold the Executive of the State in the faithful discharge of his duty, and to rebuke violent and incendiary utterances.

BELFAST, Me., Dec. 27.—A call headed "Law and Order" invites the citizens of Belfast and its vicinity, who are in favor of sustaining the State authorities in the faithful discharge of their constitutional duty, and feeling that the treasonable utterances of the Republican meetings should not be permitted to go forth as the sentiments of the people of Maine, to meet on Monday evening to give expression to their views in regard to the threatening aspect of State affairs. Gov. Garcelon is invited to attend.

FAIRFIELD, Me., Dec. 27.—In accordance with a call, a meeting was held here this evening to ratify the action of Gov. Garcelon and his Council in the recent "count out," but more especially to give Councilor Brown a chance to defend himself before his townsmen, as at an indignation meeting held this week a resolution was passed personally condemning him for his action as Councilor in disfranchising his own town, and requesting society to ostracize him. Andrews Hall was well filled, many being obliged to stand. The meeting was called to order at 7:15. A. M. Gerald was chosen President, with four Vice-Presidents. Mr. Brown was then called on, and responded with a short speech, and by reading and explaining an abstract from the report of the Committee on Election Returns made by the Governor and Council, (which have been already published.) Mr. Brown, by way of introduction, said that the circumstances which called them together were peculiar. This meeting, like the preceding ones held in the same hall Monday evening, and in other parts of the State, was something which was never seen before in this loyal State, and was gotten up by men whose only desire was to elevate their own party. "We do not come here," he said, "to act on the defensive, but because we have been misrepresented." Mr. Brown argued that the Governor and Council had followed the Constitution to the letter; that they did not understand how to approach the case, and therefore approached it with the determination to do what was right, and that they had done that, and that their records would stand the investigation of honest men. Councilor Fogg then made a speech.

The following resolutions were adopted:

Resolved, That we, as citizens of the Town of Fairfield, believe the Governor and Council have canvassed the election returns in strict accordance with the Constitution and laws of the State, and that they are entitled to our respect and esteem for so faithfully performing their duties, and they shall have our support and services in whatever capacity they may be needed so long as they pursue a course in harmony with the laws and Constitution.

Resolved, That we believe the late treasonable meetings held by the Republican Party throughout the State are a part of the programme of a few unscrupulous partisans to create anger, hatred, and strife to cover up their own wrong-doing, making enemies where friendship should exist; that the expressions of many of their speakers and resolutions have come far short of the truth, honor, and decency.

Resolved, That we believe in honest and fair elections without intimidation, bribery, or fraud, and we consider either a crime as odious as treason.

Resolved, That the Associated Press is the tool of the Republican Party, in sending broadcast untruthfulness and inflammatory appeals in the interest of Senators Blaine and Hamlin, to the end that mob rule and violence shall take the place of the Constitution and the laws, and it should be abated, and we declare said association a nuisance.

Resolved, That those persons who at a former meeting in this hall induced boys and old men in their dotage to display their bigotry and ignorance, in heaping abuse on their fellow-townsmen, are deserving of our contempt and denunciation; and we hereby denounce those persons as unworthy of belief for those untruthful statements, and they should be shunned as enemies of society for their lack of common sense, decency, or self-respect.

Resolved, That the honorable Councilor of this district, the Hon. S. H. Brown, by an honest career in his profession among us for many years, by his earnest endeavors to promote the prosperity of this town in times of adversity, and many other ways, has endeared himself to his fellow-citizens, and has established his character as an honest, patriotic man, and disappointed partisans of any age or grade will do him no harm.

Resolved, That Alonzo Garcelon, for the unflinching discharge of his duty as chief Executive of this State, is deserving of the admiration and hearty support of every honest and patriotic citizen of the whole country.

Three cheers were given for Gov. Garcelon and Councilors Fogg and Brown, and the meeting adjourned.

EITHER BLACK-MAIL OR CRIME.

A MARYLAND EX-SENATOR CHARGED WITH OUTRAGEOUS CONDUCT.

SNOWHILL, Md., Dec. 27.—This portion of the Eastern Shore of Maryland has been more excited during the past few days than at any time since the Hearn-Duer homicide or the trial of that case. On Wednesday, Mrs. S. C. Polk, wife of a Pokomoke City shoe-maker, a comely-looking matron of 40, preferred charges of outrageous conduct against Col. W. I. Aydelotte, ex-State Senator, ex-member of the Maryland Boundary Commission, and a very prominent and wealthy Eastern Shore man. He is an Elder in the Presbyterian Church, and has borne an irreproachable character. Everybody believed, therefore, that it was a case of black-mail. Intense interest was taken in the hearing, which was not concluded until long after midnight last night. Mrs. Polk charges that, taking advantage of her husband's absence in Philadelphia, Col. Aydelotte, on four separate occasions last week and this, came to her house and made improper proposals to her, using force. On cross-examination she became very confused, and contradicted herself in many minor particulars. She gave her testimony in a manner which strengthened the black-mail theory, showing no delicacy or shame. Col. Aydelotte denied the charges point blank, but failed to explain satisfactorily the cause of his visits to Mrs. Polk's house. Justice Quinn gave his decision this afternoon, binding Col. Aydelotte over for the May term of the Circuit Court in $2,000.

APPOINTMENTS AT ALBANY.

ALBANY, N. Y., Dec. 27.—Gen. Carr, Secretary of State, has made the following appointments for his office: Deputy Secretary of State, Anson G. Wood, of Wayne; Chief Clerk, Lee Chamberlain, of Rensselaer; Land Clerk, Pirus H. Ferris, of St. Lawrence; Certificate and Alien Deposition Clerk, A. De Wagner Strickland, of New-York; Examiner, Frederick J. R. Chitty, of Warren; Clerk of Incorporations, William G. Carr, of Rensselaer; Book and Pardon Clerk, David J. Blauvelt, of Rockland; Stenographer and Clerk of the Board of Audit, W. H. Stevens, of Livingston; Statistics of Crime, W. E. Kisselburgh, Jr., of Rensselaer; Clerk in Charge of Historical and Ancient Records, Berthold Fernaw, of Hamilton; General Clerk, H. H. Cozzens, of Oswego; General Clerk, David Caswell, of Albany; Messenger, George H. Overacker, of Washington.

Gov. Robinson has appointed J. Roosevelt, of Hyde Park, Commissioner of the State Board of Charities, in place of James Roosevelt, resigned.

VALUABLE CHRISTMAS PRESENTS.

CINCINNATI, Dec. 27.—On Christmas Day, Robert Mitchell, of the wealthy furniture firm of Mitchell & Ramelsburg, of this city, had a family reunion at his residence, consisting of his wife, two sons and their wives, two daughters and their husbands, and a third daughter, 10 in all, among whom he divided equally $500,000 in stocks and other evidences of pecuniary value as Christmas presents.

EDISON'S ELECTRIC LIGHT

CONFLICTING STATEMENTS AS TO ITS UTILITY.

THE INVENTOR SAYS HE HAS SUCCEEDED IN GETTING A CHEAP SUBSTITUTE FOR GAS-LIGHT—A PUBLIC EXHIBITION PROMISED—PROF. MORTON'S CRITICISMS.

There was no lack of enthusiasm or of confidence about Mr. Edison as he greeted the TIMES reporter who entered his laboratory at Menlo Park, N. J., yesterday. The inventor, a short, thick-set man, with grimy hands, led the way through his workshop, and willingly explained the distinctive features of what he and many others look upon as an apparatus which will soon cause gas-light to be a thing of the past. The lamp which Mr. Edison regards as a crowning triumph is a model of simplicity and economy. In the lamp the light is emitted by a horseshoe of carbonized paper about two and a half inches long and the width of a thread. This horseshoe is in a glass globe, from which the air has been as thoroughly exhausted as science is able to do. So good a vacuum is produced that it is estimated that at the utmost no more than a one-millionth part of the air remains. The operation of pumping lasts one hour and a quarter. At the ends of the carbon horseshoe are two platinum clamps, from which platinum wires run outwardly through a small glass tube contained within a larger one leading out of the glass globe. The small tube contains air. Within it the platinum wires are met by two copper wires connecting with the conductors of the electricity. The air is left in the small tube, because otherwise the copper wires would be fused by the electric current. The carbonized paper is capable of being made incandescent by a current of electricity, and while it allows the current to pass over it, its resistance to the heat is strong enough to prevent it from fusing.

The first place visited was the room in which the furnace for carbonizing the paper is situated. The furnace is of the ordinary pattern, and on the coals rested a horseshoe mold, in which the bristol board to be charred was placed. Over each horseshoe a piece of tissue paper was placed, and the whole was washed until all the material of the card-board, except the carbon, was taken away. When the filaments were taken from the mold they resembled pieces of black thread. The particles hung tenaciously together, however, and the black horse-shoe was easily placed in the platinum clamps of the globe of the lamp. The exhausting of the air takes place after the carbon is put in position, and when this is done the lamp is complete. "As there is no oxygen to burn," said Mr. Edison, "you can readily see that this piece of carbon will last an ordinary life-time. It has the property of resisting the heat of the current of electricity, while at the same time it becomes incandescent, and gives out one of the most brilliant lights which the world has ever seen. The cost of preparing one of these little horse-shoes of carbon is about 1 cent, and the entire lamp will cost not more than 25 cents." Here the inventor gave a practical illustration of his invention. He was standing just under an ordinary gas chandelier in which two of his lamps were burning. He took one of the lamps out, and it appeared simply as a glass globe. He placed it back in the burner, and immediately a brilliant horse-shoe of golden light illuminated the globe. Mr. Edison then, by turning a screw in the lamp, brought the light down to a spark, turned it off completely, as gas can be turned off, and turned it on again to a brilliant incandescence by a twist of his fingers. He certainly demonstrated that in his own laboratory at Menlo Park, the electric light is as obedient to his will as the gas light is to the general public. The light from each lamp is of about the power of an ordinary gas-jet, but Mr. Edison claims that by increasing the electricity, he can raise the power to 15 gas-jets.

Eighty-four lights are burning night and day in the laboratory, and they are all supplied with electricity by an 80-horse-power engine, which is stationed in the basement of one of the buildings. This engine, in addition to feeding these lamps, furnishes the motive power for all the machines in the laboratory, and at night feeds the electric lights which have already been erected in Menlo Park in anticipation of the proposed grand illumination. The wires which are to convey the electricity to the lamps for the grand display are to be above ground, so that all spectators can see and investigate them. They will lead directly from the lamps to the generator in the laboratory, and any person can trace them from point to point.

From the furnace-room Mr. Edison conducted the reporter to the room in which his lamps are made, and where the air is exhausted from them. In this room, also, is Mr. Edison's machine for regulating the pressure of the electricity as it passes to the different lamps throughout his laboratory. This machine consists of a series of coils of copper, over which the electric current is continually passing, and each coil is connected with a series of lamps. If the pressure is too great on any series of lamps it is at once shown by the coil representing that series, and can be regulated in an instant. In this room, also, the carbonized paper is placed in the globes, and the lamp is completed. It is Edison's pet room, and here he spends most of his time when not engaged in studying out new inventions.

It has been asserted by some persons who are supposed to be conversant with the subject of electricity that in order to furnish lights for houses in this City a copper coil as large as an ordinary barrel would be required as a conductor from the central station to the different houses in two or three blocks. Regarding this, Mr. Edison said: "The size and amount of conductors for carrying electricity for lighting purposes depends, of course, upon the distance to which the electricity is to be carried. If I have to carry it 10 miles my conductor must be larger than it must be if I have to carry it 10 feet. My idea is to have central stations to cover, say a square of three or four blocks. The pipes containing the wires on a street, if this idea is carried out, will not exceed in size the circumference of your arm. They will be laid under the flag-stones just at the edge of the sidewalk, as gas-pipes are now laid."

"What will be the cost of these conductors," asked the reporter.

"The cost, compared to gas-pipes, will be very small, and there is very little chance of their getting out of order. The wire itself, which will convey the electricity, will be an ordinary No. 9 telegraph wire, the same wire that you see in use every day by the Western Union Company. That is as near the size of a barrel as I intend to get."

"How will the light be distributed?"

"Precisely as gas is now distributed. You see that I can turn that burner off entirely if I wish to; I can lower it or I can raise it, just as you can lower or raise a gas jet. Our electricity will go from our central stations just as gas flows from the meter. Whether the company will charge for the light according to the amount of electricity which each consumer uses, or whether so much a month will be charged to each consumer I cannot say. That is a question which the company will determine when the electric light is introduced."

"Do you intend to illuminate Menlo Park on New Year's Eve?"

"Not for the public as soon as that. Menlo Park is now illuminated every night to a certain extent. All the lamps that we have on hand are lighted nightly, but we cannot give the grand display that I intend to give until we have more lamps. You can say this, however, that the electric light is perfected, and that all the problems which have been puzzling me for the last 18 months have been solved. I expect to have every house here lighted, and a number of street-lamps going within 10 days. When I once get the light started, I shall keep them burning night and day for at least two weeks, in order to make a time test of my carbon. I believe that it is practically infusible, and I have confirmed my belief by experiments here in my laboratory for several weeks, but I want the public to believe it from their own knowledge, and the only way to make the public believe it is to show it to them. I think that my carbonized paper is the only substance which is capable of becoming thoroughly incandescent, and at the same time of offering to the current of electricity sufficient resistance to prevent it from melting away. The vacuum in the globe, of course, offers no oxygen of any consequence to burn; but the intense heat generated by the electricity would destroy any other substance than this carbonized paper. There is absolutely nothing there to fuse. It is carbon, pure and simple, and no machine known to this age can generate enough electricity to destroy it."

"Have any electricians responded to your invitation to see you and investigate your method of lighting by electricity?"

"No electricians have been here yet, nor are there likely to be any here. Electricians are a very scarce article in this country, although there are many persons here who call themselves electricians. They don't come here, because they know that if they do they will be convinced that my light is at last a perfect one. I am glad they don't come. Practical men, with experience, and what I call 'horse sense,' are the best judges of this light, and they are the men whom I like to welcome to my laboratory."

BUSINESS ASPECT OF THE MATTER.

CONFIDENCE OF THE COMPANY WHICH FURNISHES MR. EDISON WITH MEANS.

Mr. Edison's inventions and discoveries, in the way of electric illumination, whatever they may be, are the property of the Edison Electric Light Company, a corporation which supplies him with the money for conducting his experiments. Mr. Calvin Goddard, the Secretary of the company, told a TIMES reporter yesterday that the company had no doubt of Mr. Edison's having perfected his light to such an extent that it can be supplied equal to gas, be as easily managed as gas, and be furnished at a cost not greater than that of gas. The company, he said, was not yet quite ready, mechanically, to show the public the full and complete machinery and the manner of preparing the light, and the statement that a day had already been set apart to exhibit the completed light was incorrect. The first perfect demonstration of the success of the invention will be made at Menlo Park, but just when this will be done cannot yet be told. Time is needed to complete certain necessary fixtures. Among others a large number of lamps are still to be made. The company does not wish to invite the public to inspect the light until everything can be shown, and it is intended to exhibit the full capacity of the 80-horse-power engine to supply electricity to about 700 lamps. The objection which has been raised to the effect that one great difficulty in the way of the success of the light was in the large amount of copper necessary to carry the electricity, had been entirely avoided by Edison, according to Mr. Goddard. The objection was raised in Berlin, he said, in the experiments with the Jablochkoff candle, where the cost of the copper was very great. But this difficulty had been overcome, and the company had no fears on that score. When the light is introduced it is intended to generate the electricity by engines of comparatively small horse-power distributed over the City. Each engine will supply the lights for an area of a quarter to a half mile around it, the distance of the engines from each other depending upon the number of lights each has to supply. This arrangement will be made both for the sake of convenience and economy. To be ready for any emergency, as an accident to the generator, duplicate engines will be placed at each of the stations. It is understood that the Electric Light Company does not intend to take charge of the placing of the light, but will simply license others to do so.

A SCIENTIFIC VIEW OF IT.

PROF. HENRY MORTON NOT SANGUINE ABOUT EDISON'S SUCCESS.

Prof. Henry Morton, the President of the Stevens Institute of Technology, who is well known for his researches in physics, and whose experiments were a source of unfeigned pleasure and astonishment to Prof. Tyndall, recently sent a communication to the *Sanitary Engineer* protesting against the trumpeting of the result of Edison's experiments in electric lighting as "a wonderful success," when "every one acquainted with the subject" will recognize it as a "conspicuous failure." To this was added the statement that Edison "has done and is doing too much really good work to have his record defaced and his name discredited in the interests of any stock company or individual financiers." Edison, to whose attention this letter was called, was reported in a newspaper yesterday morning as inviting Prof. Morton or any other electrician to visit the Menlo Park laboratory and see the light in practical operation. In conversation with a TIMES reporter yesterday, Prof. Morton said that, for several reasons, he did not think he would accept Mr. Edison's kind invitation. "What is needed to be learned," said the Professor, "is the durability of these new lamps of Mr. Edison's, and the actual economy in the conversion of power into light by his arrangement. For example, according to the statement in the *Sun*, Mr. Edison places his present lamps and machines as yielding him what is equivalent to 10 gas-burners for every horse-power. Now, my own experiments with the best dynamo-electric machines—such as those of Siemens, Weston, Brush, and Maxim—using the ordinary carbon poles, show that we may obtain a light of from 1,200 to 1,600 candles per horse-power. Assuming a gas-burner to be equal to from 12 to 16 candles, this would be about 100 burners per horse-power. As compared, therefore, with the electric light obtained between carbon poles, Mr. Edison gets only 10 per cent., showing, therefore, precisely that enormous loss in the division of the light which has been alluded to before as one of the standing difficulties in the way of the practical application of such a system as Mr. Edison is working upon. This is taking simply his apparently rough estimate. For any definite and certain conclusions, prolonged and careful experiments, entirely under the control of the investigator, are absolutely necessary."

As regards the durability of Prof. Edison's new lamps, Prof. Morton was not at all sanguine. "Lamps," said he, "in all essential respects identical with these described by Mr. Edison have been in constant experimental use for several years past, with one invariable result, namely, that, while the carbon would operate successfully for periods varying from a few hours to several days, it has been found utterly impossible to render them reliably permanent. It is, therefore, in my estimation, here also necessary that experiments of some length, likewise under the entire control of the investigator, should be made in order that a decisive conclusion may be reached. With reference to the confident assertions of success which reach me from various quarters, I must fall back upon my experience of a little over a year ago. Every one remembers how, at that time, Mr. Edison read some remarks of mine by the light of his then brilliantly-glowing electric light, and pointed to it as a shining refutation. In turning over some old letters a few days since, I came across one from a friend of mine, who is a scientific man of high standing, and was at that time on very intimate terms with Mr. Edison. This letter is dated October, 1878, and in it I am assured that Mr. Edison's lamp is a perfect success, capable of replacing a gas-burner with perfect ease, and that when I see it I shall, no doubt, be charmed with its simplicity and efficiency. When I reflect that this previous complete success has been since abandoned by Mr. Edison, I feel that a little caution is needed in accepting the enthusiastic conclusions of his friends, even when they are illuminated by the shining electric lamps which occasion them."

"Can you tell me, Professor," asked the reporter, "what are some of the chief difficulties in the way of the success of Mr. Edison's light?"

"Well," Prof. Morton replied, "the first difficulty of all is the production of a lamp which shall be thoroughly reliable, and neither complicated nor expensive. All attempts up to the present lamp in this direction are acknowledged to be failures, and, as I have pointed out, there does not seem to be any novelty such as would authorize us to hope for a better success in the present one. The next difficulty is in the economical production of small lights by electricity. This is what is commonly meant by the phrase, 'dividing the electric light.' Up to the present time, and including Mr. Edison's latest experiments, it appears that this involves an immense loss of efficiency. Next comes the difficulty of distributing on any large scale the immense electric currents which would be needed, and to provide for their equal action at different points under varying conditions of the number of lights used. In reference to this, as far as I judge from the reports, Mr. Edison has been running not over 50 lights in all, while his 80 horse-power engine ought to supply 800 lights. The small number actually in use does not, therefore, develop this problem in any practical way."

"The question of measuring the current," added the Professor, as the reporter turned to leave, "the loss involved from the necessity of running the machinery without a moment's intermission during the entire time that any light is needed—in other words, the absence of any storing capacity in electricity—and various other matters of detail, while less important than the three principal difficulties which I have given you, are, nevertheless, very serious difficulties in the direction of a successful practical application of electricity for general illumination."

GEN. GRANT LEAVES PHILADELPHIA.

A QUIET RECEPTION IN WASHINGTON—NO PUBLIC DEMONSTRATION TO BE MADE.

PHILADELPHIA, Dec. 27.—Gen. Grant, accompanied by Mrs. Grant, his sons Jesse and Frederick, and the latter's wife, and by Gen. and Mrs. Sheridan, left the Continental Hotel a short time before noon to-day, and proceeded to the West Philadelphia Depot, where they took the 12:40 P. M. limited express train south for Washington.

WASHINGTON, Dec. 27.—Gen. Grant arrived here at 4 o'clock this afternoon, accompanied by Mrs. Grant, Col. Frederick Grant and wife, and Jesse Grant. About 300 persons assembled at the depot to meet the General, many of whom were ladies. The crowd gathered in the main room of the depot building, forming two lines across the room from the north entrance to the door leading to the track of arriving trains, a space between the lines being preserved by the Police for the passage of Gen. Grant and party to the street. On the platform in the depot yard there were assembled about 75 persons, among whom were Gen. Beale and family, Senator Cameron and wife, ex-Senator Pomeroy, Gen. Babcock, and Assistant Postmaster-General Tyner. Upon the arrival of the train, Gen. Beale and the persons with him entered Gen. Grant's car, and, after an exchange of salutations, the visitor and his traveling companions were escorted through the depot to B-street, where carriages were waiting to receive them. The General and Mrs. Grant were heartily cheered as they passed through the crowd from the depot. The party was rapidly driven to Gen. Beale's residence, in West Lafayette-square, passing the White House on the way. Gen. Grant will remain here until Tuesday, when he will depart for Havana by way of Cedar Keys, Fla. This evening he dined with Gen. Beale and family, and subsequently received a few personal friends who called to pay their respects. To-morrow he will dine with Senator Cameron, and on Monday will be entertained by Representative L. P. Morton, of New-York.

There will be no public demonstration whatever during Gen. Grant's visit to Washington. The house occupied by Gen. Beale is on the west side of Lafayette-square, at the corner of H-street and Connecticut-avenue and in full view of the White House. It is one of the historical residences of Washington, and was owned and occupied by Commodore Stephen Decatur when he fought the duel with Commodore Barrow, which resulted in the death of the former. Senator Cameron resides in the palatial residence built by ex-Gov. Shepherd, and occupied by that gentleman until overtaken by financial reverses. It is in Farragut-square, two blocks north of Gen. Beale's residence. Mr. Morton recently purchased the elegant residence owned and occupied by the late Samuel M. Hooper, a Representative from Massachusetts for many years, and, since the purchase, has expended $15,000 in improvements. Mr. Morton's house is one block from Lafayette-square, two blocks from the White House, and the same distance from the residence of Gen. Beale. Many of the residents of Washington did not know that Gen. Grant was to arrive to-day, and so little was said about it in the local newspapers that a large demonstration at the depot was avoided. As Gen. Grant was being driven off, followed by the cheers of the crowd, one of the old residents of the city who chanced to be passing, approached THE TIMES's correspondent. "What's the matter here?" he asked. "Gen. Grant has arrived," was the answer. "Is that so?" said the old resident; "where has he been?" The crowd, which was singing and cheering behind Gen. Grant's carriage, swept the old resident away before an answer could be made to his question, and it is probable that there is one man in Washington to-night who has not yet learned where Gen. Grant has been during the past three years, and who will doubtless continue in the belief that the ex-President has been a constant resident of Washington since President Hayes succeeded him in office. This old man is not singular in Washington, but is a representative of a large class of persons who resided here when slaves were publicly sold to the highest bidders, and who have neither the animation nor ambition to keep abreast with the progress of the times.

AUGUSTA, Ga., Dec. 27.—At a meeting of the City Council to-night, a resolution was unanimously adopted inviting Gen. Grant and party to stop here on their way to Florida, and extending to them the hospitalities of the city.

GENERAL RAILWAY NOTES.

ROCHESTER, N. Y., Dec. 27.—Mr. Vanderbilt having rejected the modification of his plans which the city adopted for the elevated tracks, it is reported to-day here that he has adopted a plan for the construction of the road south of the city, and that the work will be begun at once.

ST. LOUIS, Mo., Dec. 27.—Thomas Allen, President of the St. Louis, Iron Mountain and Southern Railway, is considering plans for an elevated track, to connect with the Union Depot, and it is probable that, if the city interposes no serious obstacles, such structure will be erected within a year. The project of bridging the Mississippi River at Carondelet, six miles south of the centre of the city, is being revived. The Missouri Pacific and St. Louis, Iron Mountain and Southern Roads now transfer, by ferry, about 300 cars daily at that point, and the revival of iron manufacture at the immense furnaces and rail-mills there make the bridge almost absolutely necessary to meet the demands of commerce, and contracts for the construction of the bridge, which is to cost between $2,000,000 and $3,000,000, will, no doubt, soon be let and the work pushed to speedy completion.

THE MARYLAND SENATORSHIP.

BALTIMORE, Md., Dec. 27. — Senator Whyte has given official announcement today that he is a candidate for re-election to the United States Senate. On the surface, chances are against his re-election. He counts on almost solid support from the Baltimore anti-Canal Ring Democrats. But many of the Democrats he counts on are said to be pledged to his opponent, A. P. Gorman. Whyte's supporters criticise Gorman's management of the Chesapeake and Ohio Canal, and of the Democratic Conservative Party in this State, and urge Whyte to enter the race to defeat Gorman by getting elected himself if he can; if not, by securing the election of some man who would be a truer representative of the Maryland Democracy than Gorman.

A JOKE ENDING IN DEATH.

CHICAGO, Dec. 27.—John M. Waite and M. B. Gould, both prominent and respected business men, thinking to play a practical joke upon a colored janitor, this afternoon disarranged the contents of Mr. Waite's room, and then, concealing themselves in a closet, waited until the janitor appeared. The latter becoming excited at the condition of the room, procured a revolver, and hearing a noise in the closet tried to pull the door open, and failing in that fired through the door. The shot passed through Mr. Gould's head, and he died soon after.

The Coroner's jury to-night rendered a verdict justifying the janitor and discharging him from custody.

ALMOST A DISASTROUS PANIC.

BALTIMORE, Md., Dec. 27.—A fellow in the front row of seats, at the performance at the Halliday-Street Theatre to-night, was creating a disturbance, and an officer took him out. Just as he reached the door he struck the officer and some person in the gallery cried "fight." The large audience took it for a cry of "fire," and a general rush for the street ensued. For a few minutes the excitement was great. Ladies and children screamed and cried, and three ladies fainted. After the manager had assured himself that all was right he secured the attention of the retreating audience, assured them that there was no fire, and quieted them. After the excitement had ceased, the play was continued.

THIRTY YEARS A MANAGER

ITALIAN OPERA FROM SONTAG TO MARIMON AND GERSTER.

WHAT AN INQUISITIVE VISITOR LEARNED WHILE TALKING TO COL. MAPLESON IN THE ACADEMY OF MUSIC—EIGHTEEN YEARS OF HER MAJESTY'S OPERA IN LONDON—A MANAGER'S TRIBULATIONS—REMINISCENCES OF SINGERS, COMPOSERS, DANCERS, CONDUCTORS, AND MANAGERS.

If music be the food of love, the lot of the caterer who furnishes such refreshment to the public is not the less full of anxiety and annoyance, and managerial enterprise in musical matters is not a whit less liable to end in disaster. Such, evidently, is the opinion of Col. James Henry Mapleson, for nearly 20 years the director of Her Majesty's Opera in London, and at present the manager of the Italian opera at the Academy of Music in New-York. The Academy of Music, which is not the handsomest or the most cheerful opera-house in the world, even when it is lighted up at night, and beauty in the boxes smiles radiantly at beauty on the stage, is a dark and dismal place on a Winter afternoon. A visitor to the manager of the opera, if the outer guard at the Fourteenth-street entrance decide that his business is important enough to need the Colonel's attention, is led through a little labyrinth out into the gloomy foyer, through the glass doors of which he looks bewilderedly across the vacant stalls of the vast auditorium, upon the full depth of the dimly-lighted stage, occupied, in the absence of *Amina* and *Astraflamante* and *Rhadames*, by scrub-women and carpenters. The manager's office opens into an obscure corner of this foyer. It is a cozy and cheerful room, and the visitor who has finally found it is pleasantly greeted by its occupant. If the prospects of Italian opera in America form the subject of the conversation, perhaps the Colonel will be in a rather gloomy frame of mind, as he was the other day. It was not the public he was disposed to find fault with. The newspaper critics, he thought, were unnecessarily severe—perhaps not intelligently so—and too scant with praise where praise was due. "Singers," said the Colonel, "are not made of metal. A manager can't do with them as he pleases. The extreme sensitiveness of a singer's organ is not taken into consideration in this country. The slightest change in the weather is apt to change a programme. Levy will tell you that even his cornet is affected by certain changes in the weather. And the newspaper men come here, some of them, at any rate, evidently determined to find fault. Campanini, for instance, sings *Elvino* as he has sung it here grandly and in perfect voice throughout, but perhaps in one little bit of recitative his voice is a trifle husky or his throat dry. Then it is announced the next morning that the tenor was in bad voice. The other night, when 'Sonnambula' was given, there were four vacant seats in the parquet; they had been reserved by a gentleman who exchanged his tickets for tickets to another performance at the last moment because of illness in his family. Every other seat in the house was occupied, and the receipts between $800 and $900 more than the previous night. Yet one of the newspapers announced that there was a poor house, and that announcement has gone Eastward ahead of us, together with the inference that Marimon does not draw in New-York. I think," continued the Colonel, "that I know when singers acquit themselves creditably; I am a musician myself, and have been a manager for 30 years."

I.

WITH SONTAG IN SCOTLAND.

"My first experience as a manager," said the Colonel; "let me see, that was in the Winter of 1848-9, when I was intrusted with the management of a concert company." The Colonel paused for a moment to audit a bill for colored fire at a dollar a pound, and while the visitor was trying to guess how many pounds were consumed during a performance of "Il Flauto Magico," he went on: "Yes, and a glorious company it was, too; I wish I had it now. It included Henrietta Sontag, who had just returned to the stage after an absence from it of about 18 years; Calzolari, a fine tenor; Belletti, the baritone who visited the United States with Jenny Lind; the great Lablache, the basso—yes, he was the father-in-law of the present Mme. Lablache—and Thalberg, the pianist, completed the party. We traveled through the English provinces and Scotland and Ireland. Yes, we did meet with adventure, for in the early part of February we got stuck in a snow-drift near Laurencekirk, in Scotland. In those early days no provision was made for such emergencies on the railroads, and there was no telegraph. We had been hurrying to give a concert at Aberdeen, but that made no difference. The snow was there and the road was blocked. For two days and a half the whole party lived in a peasant's cottage. Lablache, Thalberg, and the rest of us slept in an out-house; Sontag and her husband, Count Rossi, occupied the room of the daughter of the house. We lived on oatmeal porridge and vegetables; and Sontag, determined to keep up her practice, executed her scales and trills, greatly to the delight of many shock-headed, barefooted lads and lasses who gathered around the cottage to get a sight of the strange visitors. Finally we got away, and by giving two concerts a day for a time, and missing Aberdeen, got the tour dates right again, and thus filled out the season. The late Mr. Lumley, then manager of Her Majesty's, was delighted with the success of the tour, and presented me with £100 when we returned to London. Mme. Sontag gave me a beautiful clock. She appeared two seasons in London at that time, and then came to the United States. Afterward she went to Mexico, where she died. Sontag was induced to return to the stage, not only on account of her husband's losses in 1848, but because of Jenny Lind's refusal to sing longer in opera. Lind determined to give her attention exclusively to religious music, but she did not draw in sacred concert on the stage of Her Majesty's as she did in 'La Figlia del Reggimento.' Sontag was a light soprano, with a voice of very much the same quality as Lind's. She was paid a larger salary at Her Majesty's than Lind."

II.

VIARDOT AND ROGER.

Mr. Mapleson was placed in charge of another concert company the next season, of which the chief singers were Mme. Viardot and Roger, the great French tenor. They traveled over the same circuit as the Sontag troupe. At that time Meyerbeer was putting the finishing touches on the score of "The Prophet," which he had written for the Paris Grand Opera. Roger and Viardot had been engaged to create the parts of *Jean of Leyden* and *Fides*. The manager received by mail, during the tour, the voice parts of those two rôles for the singers to study. They were written upon the thinnest sort of paper, for the composer of "The Huguenots" was a very practical man, as well as a master of melody and harmony, and postage was very high in those days—10d. a quarter-ounce, or thereabouts. Viardot and Roger were both petulant enough about the manuscript, which they had to place over white paper in order to distinguish the characters; but, nevertheless, they set to work with energy to study the new music. Later, however, they were made still more petulant by the receipt of duplicate scores.

TECHNOLOGY AND PROSPERITY

DAVID LEONHARDT

On December 27, 1879, a reporter for The New York Times traveled to Menlo Park, New Jersey, to interview Thomas Edison in his workshop. There, Mr. Edison—"a short, thick-set man, with grimy hands"—showed off his latest invention, the electric lamp. It emitted light through a small horseshoe-sized piece of carbonized paper that was enclosed in a glass globe. Mr. Edison said he did not yet have enough lamps to give a grand New Year's Eve display in Menlo Park, but he believed that the general public would shortly be able to take advantage of his invention. It was, the reporter wrote, "an apparatus which will soon cause gas-light to be a thing of the past." (The Times's editors were a bit more skeptical. Under the main headline, "Edison's Electric Light," they wrote this sub-headline: "Conflicting Statements as to Its Utility.")[1]

Thomas Edison holding an electric light bulb, one of his numerous inventions that resulted in more than 2,000 patents during his lifetime.

The invention of the electric lamp—which remains a main source of artificial light more than 125 years later—put a capstone on the most prosperous decade Americans had yet known. The Civil War, for all its destruction, had also created an industrial infrastructure that could be put to more productive uses once the fighting ended. By 1869, the transcontinental railroad was completed, helping American farmers to send their crops to the nation's growing cities and from there to the rest of the world. The nation's steel industry was also becoming a global presence. Edison and Alexander Graham Bell were harnessing the power of electricity to change daily life. The oilmen of western Pennsylvania were making "fortunes in petroleum," as The Times reported in January 1880. It was no accident that Horatio Alger's stories found a mass audience during these years.

Edison's incandescent lamp soon established itself as the primary source of artificial light.

FURTHER READING

1 "Edison's Electric Light," see December 28, 1879, front page.

Oil derricks, like this cluster in Texas, created vast fortunes in the late 1800's and early 1900's for oil prospectors.

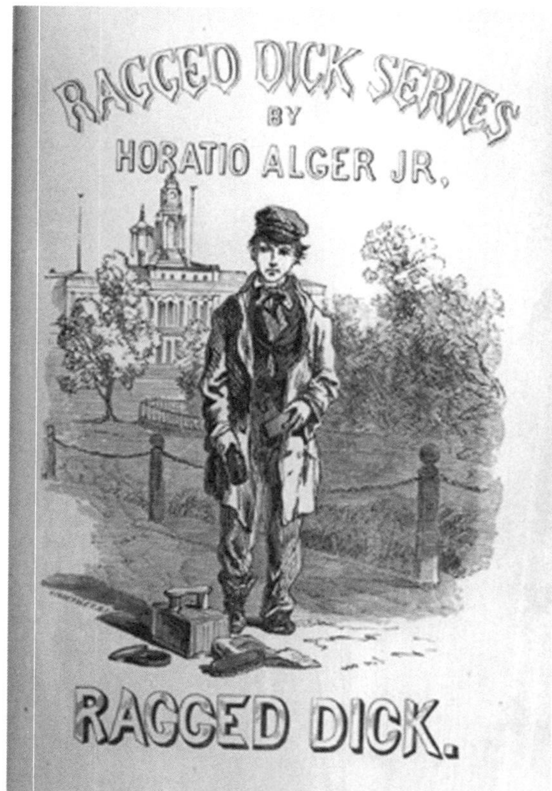

Horatio Alger's "Ragged Dick" is one of the author's many rags-to-riches novels that captured the imagination of Americans after the Civil War.

Animosity and violence against Chinese labor was on the rise in the late 1880's, particularly in the West.

If there is a modern equivalent to the 1870's, it would probably be the 1990's. As was the case during the early dot-com years, the technological advances following the Civil War made the country more wealthy—and more unequal. A legal climate that was becoming far more favorable to corporations played a role as well. Nearly every group of Americans benefited in the 1870's but the well-off benefited more than anyone else. They built mansions on New York's Fifth Avenue, in Philadelphia's Rittenhouse Square and at other fashionable city addresses. And like the 1990's, the prosperity of the 1870's didn't last much longer than the decade itself.

The post–Civil War boom eventually led to excesses such as land grabs, stock fraud and political corruption among railroads, banks and scores of other businesses that took decades to overcome. (There was an early sign of these excesses during the Panic of 1873, but the economy largely withstood the blow.)[2] In the 1880's, economic growth slowed, and in 1893 a panic more severe than the 1873 version sent the economy into a true slump.[3] The phrase is rarely used to refer to this period anymore, but the downturn of the 1890's was known then as the Great Depression.

Inequality continued to grow, but now the size of the nation's economic pie was not getting much bigger. So the affluent weren't merely reaping the largest income gains; they were making some of the only income gains. In most families, wages barely grew between 1880 and the end of the century—a widening income gap decades before the phrase became commonplace. "Suddenly Horatio Alger's vision of ample opportunity for anyone with 'luck and pluck' seemed no longer to describe the reality, much less the mood, of the time," Benjamin M. Friedman, an economist at Harvard, wrote in his recent history, "The Moral Consequences of Economic Growth." Many Americans, he added, had come "to believe that the country's best years were already in the past."

The frustrations led some Americans to look for scapegoats, which helped cause a backlash against both immigrants and blacks that was often vicious. Lynchings became more common; an average fo two black Southerners were lynched every week, on average, for an entire decade at the end of the 19th century. In 1882, meanwhile, Congress passed the Chinese Exclusion act,[4] an early step to tighten the nation's borders (even, ironically, as the Statue of Liberty was about to be hoisted on its pedestal on Ellis Island).

Organized labor also started to find its voice during these years; the American Federation of Labor was formed in 1886. Six years later, the workers of Carnegie Steel battled hand-to-hand with management-hired Pinkerton guards in Homestead, Pennsylvania.[5] In the 1880's thousands of white Americans also migrated south and west, to look for better times in the new state of Oklahoma.

Amid the strife, there were still signs of progress. The Brooklyn Bridge opened in 1883,[6] with much of the construction done by Andrew Carnegie's Keystone Bridge Company. The new suspension bridge not only allowed New Yorkers to "have their curiosity for sight-seeing abundantly satisfied," as The Times reported, but also added to a vastly improved national transportation network.

On May 1, 1893, the World's Columbian Exposition

2 "The Panic of 1873. Views of the Controller of the Currency," see November 30, 1873, front page.
3 "The Crisis and Its Causes," see July 31, 1893, article.
4 "No Chinese for Ten Years," see April 29, 1882, front page.
5 "Mob Law at Homestead," see July 7, 1892, front page.
6 "The Opening of the Bridge," see May 25, 1883, article.

HARPER'S WEEKLY
A JOURNAL OF CIVILIZATION

NEW YORK, SATURDAY, JULY 16, 1892.

TEN CENTS A COPY.
FOUR DOLLARS A YEAR.

THE HOMESTEAD RIOT.—Drawn by W. P. Snyder after a Photograph by Dabbs, Pittsburg.—[See Page 678.]
THE PINKERTON MEN LEAVING THE BARGES AFTER THE SURRENDER.

This cover of Harper's Weekly illustrates the conflict between workers and hired security police at the Carnegie Steel Company in the 1890's.

Strollers enjoy an outing on the Brooklyn Bridge during its construction in 1891.

The Statue of Liberty torch was on display in Philadelphia in 1884 prior to the statue's dedication in New York Harbor in 1886.

Crowds walk through the Columbian Exposition in Chicago, which celebrated advances in American technology in the late 1900's.

opened in Chicago when President Grover Cleveland threw a lever, celebrating American technological coming of age.[7] The fair had been scheduled to begin in 1892, for the 40th anniversary of Columbus's voyage, but it became such a sprawling spectacle that it had to be delayed until the next year. Still, it was a major success even before it opened, as thousands of people every week happily paid 25 cents ($6, in today's terms) to walk the grounds and watch, amazed, as construction workers built the exhibits. On display in the enormous buildings when the exposition finally opened were Eli Whitney's cotton gin, the world's largest conveyer belt, a 140,000-pound telescope and a map of the United States made entirely of pickles, according to the author Julie K. Rose. The exposition also included the famous "White City," a model of urban planning, with buildings by Louis Sullivan and Charles McKim. "Sell the cookstove if necessary and come," Hamlin Garland, who would later become a Pulitzer Prize–winning biographer, wrote in a letter to his parents. "You must see the fair."

The innovations on display in Chicago helped lay the groundwork for the prosperity that would follow. By the start of the 20th century, the economy was once again growing at a healthy rate, and a series of Progressive Era reforms ensured that the gains were more widely shared than previously. This combination of growth and reform—the Model T and the Sears catalog on one hand; the income tax, worker-safety rules, new public high schools and Theodore Roosevelt's trust-busting on the other—would again allow the typical family to enjoy rising living standards. The American century had begun.

DAVID LEONHARDT *writes the weekly Economic Scene column for The New York Times and is also a staff writer for The Times Magazine. He was one of the reporters who wrote the paper's 2005 series on social class in the United States. He previously worked for Business Week and for the metro desk of The Washington Post. Leonhardt came to The Times in 1999.*

7 "Opened by the President; Mr. Cleveland Presses the Magic Button at Chicago," see May 2, 1893, front page.

The New-York Times.

VOL. XXIX.......NO. 8859. NEW-YORK, SATURDAY, JANUARY 31, 1880. PRICE FOUR CENTS.

NATIONAL CAPITAL NEWS

SENATORIAL JEALOUSIES.

MESSRS. GROOME AND GORDON CONTENDING FOR THE CHAIRMANSHIP OF THE INTER-OCEANIC CANAL COMMITTEE.

WASHINGTON, Jan. 30.—It is said that Senator Gordon's bid for the Chairmanship of a special committee on the Interoceanic Canal has produced an unpleasant sensation in the mind of Senator Groome, of Maryland, who supposed that he had secured the place if such a committee should be appointed. On the 17th of December, Mr. Groome offered in the Senate a carefully-worded and comprehensive resolution providing for the appointment of a special select committee of nine Senators, whose duty it should be to take charge of all matters relating to an interoceanic canal, and asked for its immediate consideration. Mr. Pendleton offered an objection, and Mr. Ransom asked that the resolution lie over. It therefore went over under the rule. A day or two before Mr. Gordon offered his resolution, the publication of certain statements, of a nature to attract public attention to the importance of the canal question, was secured in several newspapers. The Monroe Doctrine was brought into prominence, and the views of Mr. Gordon were declared in connection with a reference to a mysterious interview said to have been held with the Secretary of the Navy. The way having thus been prepared, Mr. Gordon offered his resolution, which is almost the exact counterpart of Mr. Groome's, and it was passed before the friends of Mr. Groome saw its import. Immediately after its passage Mr. Hereford and Mr. Davis, of West Virginia, objected to the appointment of such a committee mainly on the ground of economy, and Mr. Hereford, a member of the Committee on Commerce, asserted that that committee, of which Mr. Gordon is Chairman, could easily attend to all the canal business. Mr. Davis's motion to reconsider is now pending.

It is said that several members of the Senate Committee on Commerce will insist that that committee shall take charge of this subject, and that it is not probable that a special committee will be appointed. By some Senators the action of Mr. Gordon in so unceremoniously endeavoring to appropriate the place which Mr. Groome had marked out for himself is regarded as peculiar, to say the least. Mr. Groome took his desk in the Senate less than a year ago, and his action may have seemed presumptuous to the Senator from Georgia, who has been a Senator since 1873. It may be that Mr. Gordon believes that he laid claim to the Chairmanship by his resolution offered on Dec. 2, the second day after the present session began. That resolution, however, did not provide for the raising of a committee, but only pledged the Government to protect any company to which Nicaragua might grant the right to build such a canal.

THE SWEETNESS OF SUGAR.

THE WAYS AND MEANS COMMITTEE GAINING MUCH INFORMATION—MR. M'KAY PRODUCES HIS CREDENTIALS.

WASHINGTON, Jan. 30.—The hearing on the sugar question was continued this morning by the Committee on Ways and Means. Mr. Henry A. Brown, the ex-Treasury Agent, who was before the committee yesterday, completed his statement, accompanying it with further experiments and demonstrations showing how a high grade of sugar can be artificially colored so as to make it represent a low grade under the Dutch standard. On being asked by Mr. Garfield what course he would recommend the committee to adopt, he said he would recommend the committee to allow the present tariff on sugar to remain as it is—Dutch standard and all—and to add to the power of the Secretary of the Treasury authority to employ polarization, which discovers immediately the crystallizable strength and consequent market value of sugar, and also to employ, when he saw fit, analyses, in order to detect other ingredients, in the export of fine sugars, lest the Secretary, in paying drawbacks, should be paying a drawback on sand and other articles. In addition to that, he suggested that all sugars be ground and brought to the consistency of the Dutch standard before being appraised.

Mr. French, Assistant Secretary of the Treasury, then made a statement as to the reasons which impelled the Secretary of the Treasury to issue orders in regard to the appraisement of sugar which have been so much complained of by the importers. He gave the history of two sugar cases, one in San Francisco and one in Boston, in which the question of artificial discoloration of sugar was tried before the courts, and from the decisions in which cases he deduced the principle that the Treasury Department was not only justified, but required to go behind the apparent coloring of sugar, and to ascertain its real value. "Formerly," said Mr. French, "color indicated the degree of sweetness—that is a convenient phrase to use—and when the Dutch standard was adopted, in 1861 and 1864, it was probably a just standard. The sugar as manufactured at that time was valuable according to its color. The whiter it was the purer and the more valuable. Since that time the methods then in use of manufacturing sugar have somewhat changed, and now, by the use of vacuum pans, instead of open kettles, and by the use of centrifugals for purifying, the process is changed, so that these crystallized sugars which come here in large crystals made in vacuum pans, (and which, I think, cannot be made in open pans,) do not by their color represent their true quality, even if fairly made. Even if made in the ordinary course of the manufacture of that kind of sugar, the sugar is sweeter than its color by the Dutch standard indicates, so that the Dutch standard is not the true standard, even if the sugar is honestly made."

Mr. French read to the committee a letter written by Mr. Nathaniel McKay to Sir Michael Hicks-Beach, the English Colonial Secretary, on the subject of his [Mr. McKay's] visit to British Guiana, in which letter he stated that he had been invested by the Committee on Ways and Means with semi-official authority to make a thorough investigation into the machinery and processes of making sugar in Demerara with the single purpose of establishing the fact whether artificial coloring was practiced there; that his examination had proved a complete vindication of the planters of Demerara.

Mr. Garfield asked the Chairman whether Mr. McKay had gone to Demerara as an agent of the Ways and Means Committee.

The Chairman stated that Mr. McKay had never been, either directly or indirectly, officially or unofficially, authorized by the committee to go to Demerara or anywhere else.

Mr. Garfield inquired whether any member of the committee knew of Mr. McKay having been deputed for such a purpose. Mr. Kelley said he did not know it, but he knew this, that when Mr. McKay was going to Demerara, he received a note from him [Mr. Kelley] and from another member of the committee, asking him [Mr. McKay] to bestow, while in Demerara, such attention as he could to the sugar question, and to investigate it. He thought it probable the Chairman had given Mr. McKay such a letter.

The Chairman stated that at the last session of Congress Mr. McKay called upon him with a letter from Mr. Kelley, which purported to be an indorsement of him [Mr. McKay] as to his intelligence and integrity, and fitness for some such duty; that he had asked his concurrence in the matter, which he [the Chairman] had refused. Subsequently, however, at the instance of Mr. Kelley, he had stated in writing that any information that could be procured relating to the sugar question would be of service to the committee.

Mr. McKay produced copies of the letters, the first being from Mr. Kelley, dated April 29, 1879, directed to Mr. McKay, invoking his [McKay's] aid in procuring information on which he [Mr. Kelley] might rely, in regard to the process of making sugar in Demerara; and the second being in the following words, from Mr. Wood: "I concur with Mr. Kelley, that a fair and honest inquiry into the manufacture of sugar at Demerara will be of much service to the Committee on Ways and Means in further investigations into the alleged coloring of sugar from these colonies." Mr. McKay replied that that was all the authority he had had, but he thought that that was sufficient authority for him, as a citizen of the United States visiting Demerara, to make the inquiry which he had made. He said he should like to state what he knew as to what Mr. French had done in regard to the Demerara people. He wanted to say that Mr. French had in the Custom-house of New-York two men from Demerara, who had stolen money from a sugar estate, and that he had put them there six days after the decision of Mr. Perot's case in Baltimore. Further discussion of this matter, which threatened to become rather personal, was forbidden by the committee, and Mr. McKay was subjected to an examination by Mr. Garfield as to what had taken him to Demerara.

Mr. McKay stated that he had gone there, not for the sole purpose of investigating the sugar question, but on business of his own. He was never concerned in the importation of sugar, but had a desire to take supplies from the United States to Demerara.

Further questions asked Mr. French elicited the fact that the report of a commission appointed by the colonial authorities of Demerara established conclusively the practice of fraudulent coloration of sugars there, and was in direct contradiction of Mr. McKay's report. Mr. French also stated in response to questions by Mr. Garfield that the effect of the recent Treasury orders as to the appraisement of sugar had been very favorable to the revenue.

The committee adjourned until to-morrow, when the hearing on the sugar question will close.

THE LAWLESSNESS OF THE UTES.

GOV. PITKIN'S STATEMENT OF THEIR DEPREDATIONS IN COLORADO.

WASHINGTON, Jan. 30.—Gov. Pitkin, of Colorado, resumed his testimony before the House Committee on Indian Affairs this morning. He stated that a band of Utes, under Antelope, entered the North Park, over 50 miles from the reservation, last May, drove the miners from their mines, burned immense forests, and destroyed large quantities of game, which the State is endeavoring to preserve by stringent Game laws. Colorow, in June last, drove miners and stockmen out of the North Park. He said the Indians did not remain on their reservation, but wandered as they pleased over the State. Warrants were issued from the District Court last July for the arrest of Indians who had bunred houses 40 miles away from the reservation, and Chief Douglass told the Sheriff, who followed the criminals on to the reservation, that he had no authority to go on the reservation, and refused to surrender the criminals. The Governor referred the matter to Gen. Pope. He presented the correspondence of Agent Meeker up to the time of his death, showing how he had been turned out of his house by Chief Johnson three weeks before the massacre, and his danger of being killed at that time, and of the employes being shot at while they were plowing. Gov. Pitkin described the interview of Captain Jack and three other chiefs with him in Denver shortly before the outbreak, when they came to secure the removal of Agent Meeker. He said their complaints against Meeker were that he was educating their children, endeavoring to induce them to work, and was plowing the land. They did not complain of want of food, encroachments by the miners, or dishonesty of the agent. He described the panic-stricken condition of the settlers along the border of the reservation after the Thornburgh massacre, and gave a long list of places that had called on him for troops and arms. He said that even now, after the panic had subsided, great apprehensions were felt by the settlers, and the opinion was general that an Indian war in the Spring was inevitable if the Indians were not removed.

TERRE HAUTE, Ind., Jan. 30.—Four Ute Indians, Ignatio, Salvero, Buckskin Charlie, and Ojo Bancho, to-day passed through here, in charge of Col. Page, on their way to Washington. None of the Indians can speak English, but Col. Page, who professed ignorance of the object of their visit, said they were going to Washington in obedience to the commands of the Secretary of the Interior. The tribes represented by these Indians were not concerned in the late insurrection, although they are generally hostile to Ouray, who, they say, owes his elevation to chicanery and fraud, in which Gen. Adams and others played an important part. They are from the Ute reservation in South-western Colorado, and are chiefs of tribes numbering 1,300 souls, including 350 warriors. Col. Page thinks the object of their visit to Washington is to discuss the expediency of removing the Utes to Oregon or elsewhere.

The people of Colorado look upon the return of Gen. Adams to secure the perpetrators of the recent outrages as a huge joke, since no one for an instant believes that he will be able to obtain possession of them.

THE DEMOCRATS AND THE EXODUS.

MORE PARTISAN TESTIMONY GIVEN BEFORE SENATOR VOORHEES'S COMMITTEE.

WASHINGTON, Jan. 30.—The Senate special committee to-day resumed the investigation of the causes of the colored exodus. Mr. Charles H. Otuy, who gave his direct testimony last Monday, was subjected to a rigid cross-examination by Senators Windom and Blair, in the course of which he acknowledged that he had not heard any member of the Washington Emigrant Aid Society advise the diversion of the exodus from Kansas to Indiana for political purposes, except Mr. Mendenhall, and could not name any other Republican in Washington outside of the Emigrant Aid Society who had advised or promoted the exodus for political purposes. He also stated that he had never heard of any colored men, other than Perry, Williams, and Evans, who were engaged in stirring up the colored people to emigrate from North Carolina. T. A. Boritz, a resident of Goldsboro, and the editor of a Democratic paper, said it was difficult to assign a reason for the exodus of colored people from North Carolina. It certainly was not on account of oppression; and he took occasion to indorse the evidence of O'Hara and Otuy so far as it related to the condition of the colored people in that State. On cross-examination, he admitted that there existed a belief among some of the blacks in North Carolina that penal laws were less severe in Indiana than in North Carolina, and he thought this had some effect in influencing emigration. M. T. Lenman, Sheriff of Putnam County, Ind., produced a printed circular which he had obtained from one of the North Carolina emigrants after he had reached Indiana. J. H. Clay, a colored man, was the author of it. It urges the colored men of North Carolina to go to Indiana, setting forth the attractions of that State, stating that its climate is healthful, that free schools for both races are maintained, that there are numerous colored churches, and that the blacks and whites stand equal before the law, and also stating that thousands of good farm hands and house servants can readily find employment at remunerative wages. Without concluding the examination of Mr. Lenman the committee adjourned.

NOTES FROM WASHINGTON.

WASHINGTON, Jan. 30, 1880.

The Secretary of the Treasury has increased the bullion fund of the Denver Mint $120,000, and authorized the purchase of silver by the Assayer in charge in lots of less than 10,000 ounces. This will enable the producers of Colorado to find a home market for their fine silver.

Although no official confirmation can be obtained of the story that the court which has been investigating the charges against Major Reno has recommended his dismissal, the accuracy of the report is generally conceded; and it is further stated, unofficially, however, that Gen. Sherman favors a milder course, and will recommend that Major Reno be suspended for one year.

The House Committee on Invalid Pensions unanimously agreed to-day to a resolution that all pension claims of an invalid character shall be reported to date from discharge where the disability was incurred previous to discharge; and where the disability was incurred subsequent to discharge, from the date of the disability; and all gratuitous pensions shall date from the passage of the act. All widows' pensions, where the husband was a pensioner, shall date from the death of the husband; and where the husband was not a pensioner, from the date of the disability.

INDIAN BUREAU SCANDALS

MR. HAYT'S DISMISSAL.

THE FACTS IN REGARD TO GEN. HAMMOND'S ALLEGED CONFESSION—WHY HAYT WAS REMOVED—AN EXPLANATION BY MR. A. C. BARSTOW

WASHINGTON, Jan. 30.—The sensational story published in some newspapers to-day in relation to the removal of Mr. Hayt from the office of Commissioner of Indian Affairs is positively denied by the persons whose names appear in the publication. Mr. Hayt's removal was directed by Secretary Schurz because Hayt admitted that he had withheld from the Secretary certain facts in relation to the San Carlos Agency and the silver mine in which Hammond and Hayt are alleged to have had a property interest, and not because of any testimony which Gen. Hammond gave before the commission now investigating the charges made against Hr. Hayt. The story to the effect that Gen. Hammond was secreted here in an obscure hotel, and that when taken suddenly sick yesterday he expressed a desire to make a "confession" to Secretary Schurz, is emphatically denied by Gen. Hammond. In conversation with the TIMES correspondent this evening, Gen. Hammond made in substance the following statement: He came here on Monday for the purpose of testifying before the commission, and was examined upon that day, but his testimony was not completed. The letter which it was alleged Hammond wrote Hart, agent at San Carlos, and in which he informed Hart that his resignation had been accepted, and that certain affidavits against him would not be filed, was presented to Gen. Hammond for identification, and he testified that he remembered having written to Hart on the general subject, but he did not believe that was the letter he wrote. He pronounced it a clever forgery, but admitted that if he did not know the subject matter, he would take it to be his own writing. The belief that the letter produced was not his instrument was induced by the date, which he thought was considerably removed from the period of his intercourse with Hart, and by the fact that the letter in question did not bear evidence of having been copied by means of a letter press. About this last point, however, there was a difference of opinion between Hammond and a member of the commission. Without completing his testimony, the commission adjourned until Thursday.

On the morning of that day Hammond met Gen. Fisk accidentally at the Riggs House, and a conversation ensued on the pending investigation. Nothing was said by Gen. Hammond about a confession "for the reason," said he, "that I had nothing to confess." While talking with Fisk, Gen. Hammond was suddenly seized with an acute pain, which proceeded from heart disease, to which he is subject and by which he has been frequently prostrated. He was taken to a room, and the two members of the commission, hearing of his sickness, called upon him. It was then arranged that the commission would call in the afternoon, and if Hammond felt strong enough, his testimony would be completed. In accordance with this arrangement, his testimony of Monday was read to him, and he proceeded to give further testimony. Upon this occasion he admitted that the letter, about the genuineness of which he was in doubt on Monday, must be the original letter sent to Hart, and this conclusion was reached after refreshing his memory by the examination of dates, and finding, upon a closer inspection of the document, evidence that it had passed through a copying-press. Gen. Hammond denies that there is anything in his testimony which connects Mr. Hayt or himself with having any interest in the mine at San Carlos, or that it in any way impeaches the integrity of Mr. Hayt. Secretary Schurz has not seen Gen. Hammond since he has been in Washington, and the entire story about the so-called confession is purely imaginary. Secretary Schurz will not say anything in addition to what he has already said, the substance of which was published in THE TIMES of to-day, about the removal of Mr. Hayt.

MR. BARSTOW'S EXPLANATION.

PROVIDENCE, Jan. 30.—The Hon. A. C. Barstow, Chairman of the Indian Commission, having been questioned concerning certain dispatches from Washington declaring that he had obtained Government contracts for supplies under an assumed name, in an irregular manner, &c., explains, in a letter to the *Journal*, the invariable mode of making contracts through sealed bids, publicly opened, the awards being made by a board of ten men, or a purchasing committee of five men, acting with the Secretary of the Interior and the Commissioner of Indian Affairs, or representatives of those officers. Mr. Barstow says:

"I am a stockholder in at least seven corporations, most of which sell their wares in every part of the land. I saw the wares of at least four of these corporations offered by their customers in competition last April, but only one of the offerings was accepted, and that one because, in the judgment of the professional inspector of this class of wares, whom I do not know and never saw, as well as of the Purchasing Committee of the Board of Indian Commissioners and of the department, the wares were best and cheapest. I never sat as Judge in any case in which I had the most remote personal interest, nor had I any real pecuniary interest in this small contract by the selling agent of the corporation, not under an assumed name. When the selling agent in New-York, and others of this corporation, desired to put in a bid for stores, I objected on the ground that I wanted nothing to do with Government contracts. When the matter was further pressed, I finally consented, providing the wares were offered at cost by the last inventory, the object being to furnish employment to men during a period of labor depression."

Mr. Barstow desires the reader to understand: First, that this thing was not done in a corner, "it was open, and was square and manly; all the interest I had in the matter was known to the committee—the slightest interest possible. Second, that the wares stood upon their own merit, that the award was made on the recommendation of an expert inspector, whom I never knew, saw, or conferred with, directly or indirectly, and by the Purchasing Committee, of which Gen. Fiske was one, and with which I did not act in this award or this class of awards. Third, that the Government got wares nice enough for the White House at less prices than very much inferior goods were ever bought by it or offered to it. Fourth, that, while the Government has been well served, I have not received any pecuniary advantage from any contract with it, Fifth, that if I erred in consenting to a bid being made by the selling agent of a corporation in which I am a stockholder, it was from a patriotic feeling, rather than from a desire for, or expectation of, pecuniary gain."

Concerning Mr. Hayt, Mr. Barstow says: "I have shared with the Secretary of the Interior, and with other men who have known him longer than the Secretary has, full confidence in Mr. Hayt's honesty. Whatever faults he had, I have seen nothing to lead me to doubt his integrity. I was not willing to hang him on suspicion, but I am willing to judge and condemn any man on proof of his guilt. If there has been any proof of that kind before the committee it has been since I left Washington. Of this I have no information except what I see in the newspapers."

CREAMERIES IN ROCKLAND COUNTY.

NYACK, N. Y., Jan. 30.—A new enterprise has been developed in Rockland County. This is the establishing of creameries in different parts of the county. Several of the leading and most influential property owners are engaged in this movement, and many farmers who until recently have not known the extent of the resources in their possession, have united with them in their efforts to carry the project to a successful consummation. For a long period of time, the farmers of Rockland County have been content, in a majority of instances, to gather from their land and stock enough to merely support them, and in some cases not enough for that. They are now awakening, however, to a knowledge of the fact that their land and stock form a capital from which a greater profit might be derived, and that their labors are necessary for the more rapid growth of the county and for the increased interest in its important industries. It is probable that the first creamery will be located at Spring Valley, and a meeting was held there yesterday to determine upon building sites, water facilities, &c.

EVILS OF RECEIVERSHIPS.

THE ATTORNEY-GENERAL SEEKING A REMEDY—EXORBITANT ATTORNEYS' FEES DEMANDED.

ALBANY, Jan. 30. — Attorney-General Ward has been giving his attention to the deep and well-grounded complaints against Receivers and Referees who have been bleeding broken or disabled corportions, and will to-morrow endeavor to check one or two attempts to deprive stockholders and policy-holders of large amounts of money which there seems to be great danger will be frittered away. A few days ago he was served with notice that Sewell & Pierce, of New-York, would petition Judge Westbrook to-morrow, in the Supreme Court, at Kingston, for an allowance of $11,000, which they demanded for legal services said to have been rendered to the Globe Mutual Life Insurance Company. These services, they allege, they rendered during the year 1878, before the company's troubles became known to the public. They say they have been partly compensated for their services. A second claim to be made by the same firm is for $10,000 for services alleged to have been rendered in 1879. The company transacted business only five months of the year 1879, so that the claim seems to the Attorney-General to be excessively high. Another petition, that deputy Attorney-General Everett will oppose, is that of Frederick T. Fairbanks. This petitioner is a stenographer in the office of Wingate & Cullen, and he demands that he shall be paid $993 18 stenographer's fees. The claim is made for taking 941 folios of testimony. This would make the charge more than $1 a folio, and 25 cents is considered as an extravagant charge by the Legislature. The work for which the charge is made is alleged to have been done in the accounting of the Continental Life Insurance Company, in which concern Wingate & Cullen are attorneys for the Receiver.

The Attorney-General has been receiving many letters from persons interested in the winding up of corporations in the hands of Receivers, complaining that inexcusable and irritating delay is common among the Receivers. He has, therefore, addressed a circular to about 40 of the institutions in charge of Receivers, calling upon them to furnish important information as to the manner in which they have managed their trusts, requiring an account of expenses and receipts, and some information as to when they will be able to wind up the concerns over which they were appointed. In carrying out his determination to remedy promptly some of the abuses practiced by Receivers, he will send to the Legislature a bill conferring upon the Attorney-General additional power to call Receivers to account, and to remove them in case they refuse to regard his demands for information.

SAD RESULT OF A MURDER.

DEATH OF MRS. HARRY W. BALDWIN, CRUSHED BY THE MYSTERIOUS TRAGEDY.

CINCINNATI, Jan. 30.—Mrs. Harry W. Baldwin died this morning at her father's residence in this city. Her death is the second act in the strangely mysterious Baldwin tragedy, which for nearly a year has baffled all attempts at unraveling. Mr. Baldwin, the son of a prominent banker, and a young man of fine promise and appearance, was found one night last March, opposite an Elm-street brothel, with a bullet-hole in his head. He was staggering, and the Police, supposing him to be drunk, took him to a station-house, where he died soon after in a cell. He had been away on a short business trip in Indiana, and was returning to his home and his young bride, when shot. The murder made a profound sensation at the time, and as the mystery of the crime grew with the investigations of the Police, public interest increased. For weeks the papers gave columns daily to speculations and theories of the murder, most of them connecting the affair with the house of ill-repute near which Mr. Baldwin was found.

These attempts to smirch the character of the murdered man added to the heavy weight of sorrow borne by his family. His wife of three months and his mother were nearly crushed. Late in the fall a son was born to the widow. She recovered from her illness at that time, but never regained her former health and spirits. Of late her illness assumed serious form and this morning she died, it is alleged, of a broken heart, though more natural causes are assigned by physicians. It is stated, also, that the strange circumstances of the crime and the constant attempts to prove that Baldwin had relations with women in the house of ill-fame, and was killed by one of them, have preyed upon the mind of his mother to a serious extent. A day or two ago there was a fresh revival of the case. One Peter Schwab gave testimony before the Grand Jury that he met Baldwin, on Saturday afternoon, before the murder, in a low variety show. There is most conclusive evidence, however, against this statement, and up to the present time not a particle of proof has been produced connecting the young man in any way with disreputable persons. The mystery of his death, it is thought, will never be solved.

DISCUSSING THE PRICE OF COAL.

PHILADELPHIA, Penn., Jan. 30.—The Lehigh Coal Exchange met here this afternoon. There was a large representation of operators and several members of the Schuylkill Coal Exchange present by invitation. After a long discussion, it was decided to make no change in line and city prices for February, except an advance of 25 cents per ton in furnace. It was contended that the iron trade was in the best condition to bear any increase in price which the market should warrant. The question of restricting production during the coming month was considered, and it was finally agreed to appoint a committee of three to confer with the Schuylkill trade upon that subject.

The committee subsequently met the members of the Schuylkill Exchange, and agreed upon the following prices for February: Lump and steam-boat, $2 65; for furnace, $2 50; for other grades, $2 50, with the exception of stove coal, $2 60, and pea coal, $1 55. The committee then had a consultation with Mr. Gowen, of the Philadelphia and Reading Company, who decided to let the tolls remain unchanged. For the present, also, the same rate of production at the mines will be maintained.

ARMY AND NAVY INTELLIGENCE.

WASHINGTON, Jan. 30.—Capt. A. N. Damrell is relieved from duty as Engineer of the Eighth Light-house District; Capt W. H. Heuer will report, by letter, to the Secretary of the Treasury for duty as Engineer of the Eighth Light-house District, in addition to his present duties under the Treasury Department, taking station at New-Orleans, La. Leave of absence until April 28 has been granted Capt. Evan Miles, Twenty-first Infantry.

Passed Assistant Paymaster John W. Jordon has been ordered to duty at Boston; Acting Sail-maker M. W. Watkins to the Vandalia.

CHESTER, Penn., Jan. 30.—Major-Gen. R. B. Marcy, Inspector-General of the United States Army, officially inspected the Pennsylvania Military Academy of this city to-day.

NEARLY BURIED ALIVE.

OTTAWA, Ontario, Jan. 30.—A small-pox patient had a narrow escape from being buried alive here on Wednesday last. He was laid in the coffin and placed in the grave before it was discovered that he was not dead. The grave-digger had thrown three or four shovelfuls of sand on the coffin, when he fancied he heard a noise. The coffin was immediately raised, and on the cover being removed it was found that the man still lived. He was taken back to the hospital.

AFFAIRS IN FOREIGN LANDS

EUROPEAN AND ASIATIC COMPLICATIONS.

THE PROPOSED INCREASE OF THE GERMAN ARMY—TURKEY'S OBLIGATIONS—RUSSIA'S WAR AGAINST THE TURCOMANS—THE AFGHAN TROUBLES.

LONDON, Jan. 30.—The strength of the German Army on a peace footing, as shown by the military budget of 1880–81, is 17,227 officers and 401,659 men. This does not include the projected increase, which the Cologne *Gazette* says is chiefly destined to reinforce the Alsace-Lorraine garrisons. The new field artillery regiment is to be stationed at Metz, and the heavy artillery will be divided among the fortresses of Alsace-Lorraine.

A Vienna dispatch denies the statement telegraphed from St. Petersburg on the 26th inst., that Austro-Hungary, England, and France had agreed to make a joint representation to the Porte for the speedy execution of the provisions of the treaty of Berlin respecting Montenegro and Greece and the question of reforms in Turkey.

In connection with the announcement that Gen. Turgukasoff has gone to Tiflis to participate in a council of war to decide whether the Turcoman campaign shall be defensive or offensive, the Moscow *Courier* says: "It is believed that a majority of the officers composing the military council at Tiflis think it impossible to take the offensive, in consequence of the scarcity of beasts of burden. It is also believed that Gen. Vonsach, who has gone to Tiflis, will assume the command of the Trans-Caspian forces, the health of Gen. Turgukasoff being seriously impaired."

CALCUTTA, Jan. 30.—Intelligence has been received here from Herat announcing that Ayoub Khan's Kabulese troops refuse to accompany him, and threaten to return to their homes unless their pay is forthcoming.

ATHENS, Jan. 30.—The Ministerial crisis has terminated. It has been decided that the Coumoundouros Ministry will continue in office without modification, and that their policy will remain unchanged.

LONDON, Jan. 31.—A Berlin correspondent reports that at the Government cannon foundry such large orders have been received that a number of fresh hands have been engaged, and all are working extra time.

A Vienna dispatch says: "It is reported that the Czarewitch recently remarked to some Polish magnates: 'I snall be proud to wear your glorious crown. Communicate this to your countrymen, and assure them of the favor of their future King.'"

POLITICS IN THE FRENCH SENATE.

A CONTEST FOR A VACANT LIFE SENATORSHIP—THE DUFAURE GROUP GAINING POWER.

LONDON, Jan. 30.—A dispatch from Paris says: "A coalition of the Moderate Republicans with the Conservatives yesterday elected M. Leon Say to the Presidency of the Senate Finance Committee over M. Calmon, a Vice-President of the Senate, who was the regular Republican candidate. On the Senate proceeding to elect a life Senator, vice Count Camille Bacchasson de Montalivet, recently deceased, the Extreme Left, whose turn it was to make a nomination, selected Dr. Paul Broca, the eminent anthropologist. M. Dufaure, Republican life Senator, with 12 or 14 followers who have practically ceased to belong to the Left Centre, and must henceforth rank as a distinct group midway between the Left and Right Centres, declined to be bound by the rotation system of the Left, and opposed the nomination of Dr. Broca on the ground of his Darwinian tendencies. They nominated M. Bertoland, a well-known advocate and Republican, but opposed to the anti-Jesuit clause of M. Jules Ferry's Education bill. The vote being taken, Dr. Broca received 126 votes, and M. Bertoland 118; scattering, 12, Dr. Broca thus receiving 3 less than an absolute majority. The election was then postponed. More than 100 Senators of the Right Centre supported the nomination of M. Bertoland. Manifestly, if the Dufaure group gains a few accessions through alarm at the radicalism of the Chamber of Deputies, it will be able to hold the balance of power. The rejection of clause 7 of the Education bill is now considered as certain."

LONDON, Jan. 31.—A Paris dispatch announces that the Senate has rejected two reactionary amendments to the Educational bill, but the votes were close, being 143 to 135 and 147 to 129.

In the division of the Chamber of Deputies on the question favoring political clubs, the minority consisted of 74 Conservatives and 106 members of the Advanced and Extreme Left. This is an additional proof that the Cabinet cannot rely upon the support of more than half of the Advanced Left. Eight Conservatives and 248 Republicans formed the majority.

BISMARCK AND THE ROMAN CHURCH.

THE POPE TO BE ASKED TO MAKE A STATEMENT OF GRIEVANCES.

LONDON, Jan. 30.—In connection with the announcement of the intention of Prince Bismarck to give explanations regarding the Church question, when the budget of the Ministry of Public Worship comes up for discussion next week in the Prussian Diet, a Berlin dispatch says: "As neither the Ultramontane press nor the Centre Party, nor the Prussian Bishops, can be regarded as impartial sources of information touching the plans of the Vatican, Prince Bismarck has determined to demand directly from the Pope what really are the grievances of the Church which prevent the establishment of a solid peace. When an answer is received Herr von Putt-Kammer, Minister of Ecclesiastical Affairs, will draft a bill abolishing the severest clauses of the May laws."

A dispatch from Rome to Reuter's Telegram Company says: "Telegrams received here state that Prince Bismarck and the German Crown Prince have agreed that it is advisable to re-establish harmony between the Romish Church and Germany. It is not yet known whether Prince Frederick William will visit the Pope."

CURRENT FOREIGN TOPICS.

LONDON, Jan. 30.—Lord Beaconsfield is suffering from an attack of gout.

Three deaths from starvation have occurred this week in the neighborhood of Parsonstown, County of Louth, Ireland. The Pope has sent 10,000 francs for the relief of the distress.

A dispatch from Rome says the condition of the Pope's health is causing anxiety. He suffers from fits of shivering and great prostration, but persists in his usual occupations.

A Reuter telegram from Rome says the Vatican has sent dispatches to St. Petersburg, through the Papal Nuncio at Vienna, authorizing the Bishops in Russia to adopt certain provisional rules, embodying concessions which, it is hoped, will facilitate the settlement of more important questions.

By the fire-damp explosion in the colliery at Meissen, Saxony, yesterday, 10 miners were killed, and 9 injured. Nine persons who were in the pit at the time of the explosion are unaccounted for.

CHEMNITZ, Saxony, Jan. 30.—A large spinning manufactory here has been totally destroyed by fire, throwing out of employment 500 persons.

MADRID, Jan. 30.—The Senate to-day, by a vote of 156 to 28, approved the articles of the Cuban Slavery Abolition bill as modified by the mixed committee of Senators and Deputies.

PARIS, Jan. 30.—The *Monde*, the organ of the Papal Nuncio here, referring to the mission of Mr. Parnell to the United States, says: "By the mouth of a Protestant, Catholic Ireland calls Protestant England to account. Whoever outrages justice paves the way for terrible expiations."

ST. PETERSBURG, Jan. 30.—The increase of infectious diseases in St. Petersburg is exciting some apprehension, the mortality from that cause for the week ending Jan. 17 being 19 per cent. of the whole mortality, or twice as great as usual.

In the case of Adjt. Baronoff, who was sentenced to be dismissed the naval service for insulting language in reference to the Minister of Marine, the Czar has ordered that he be placed on half pay instead of being dismissed. It is probable that he will be given command of one of the cruisers in the Pacific.

MAINE'S RESTORED HARMONY.

MORE FUSIONISTS TAKING THEIR SEATS—GOV. DAVIS'S MESSAGE.

AUGUSTA, Me., Jan. 30.—In the House to-day resolutions we introduced extending the grateful acknowledgments of the Legislature of Maine to the Senate and House of Representatives of Wisconsin for their appreciation of "the gravity and importance of the events, not only to ourselves but to the whole country, through which the people of this State have just passed, as expressed in the resolutions transmitted by their Governor, and for their generous sympathy and encouragement."

Several more Fusionists took their seats in the House to-day, and there are only four empty chairs in the Senate.

The Auburn Light Infantry left here this morning. There is no military or extraordinary Police force at the State-house now.

Gov. Davis started for his home in East Corinth this afternoon, and will return on Monday. In the meantime, he will finish his Message, which will be delivered the first of the week. Mr. Holbrook will be qualified as Treasurer the first of next week.

Immediately on taking his seat to-day, W. W. Perry, of Camden, a prominent Greenbacker, offered an order repealing that clause in the Constitution which requires certificates to be issued to members of the Legislature.

GEN. GRANT'S CANDIDACY.

CINCINNATI, Jan. 30.—In view of the newspaper charges that Mr. Halstead, of the *Commercial*, had started the story that Gen. Grant's friends had arranged to withdraw his name as a candidate for the Presidency, Mr. Halstead, in to-morrow's *Commercial*, will say: "There is a wide difference between that statement and the statement that Grant will not be a contestant for the candidacy." Mr. Halstead says he is called upon to confirm a report, said to have been traced to him, that he said George W. Childs had told him that he had a letter from Gen. Grant declining to be a candidate for the Presidency. There is no question of veracity between Mr. Halstead and Mr. Childs, for Mr. Childs never said anything of this sort, and Mr. Halstead never said that he did say so. Mr. Halstead further says that he was informed in Philadelphia that there would be authority for the statement that Gen. Grant was not a candidate, and must not be pressed into the contest as such; that the authorization would be distinct; and that the declaration would be decisive and made in good time. He has not understood that this statement has been denied, while a great deal of trouble has been taken within a few days to deny some things that have not been charged.

S. DANA HAYES'S DISAPPEARANCE.

BOSTON, Jan. 30.—Nothing has been heard from the missing State Assayer, S. Dana Hayes, and his friends are settling down to the conviction that he has left with the intention of remaining away for some time at least. The impression that he is temporarily insane is not so strong as at first. Those who saw him last are stout in their opinion that he was sound of mind. It is thought that he has gone to the western part of the country, or abroad, and that the occasion of his disappearance is domestic trouble. His attorney is settling up his affairs for the benefit of his wife, in accordance with his note of instructions. He was not in the least embarrassed financially, but was, as stated at first, in good circumstances, and enjoying a flourishing business. His absence is sincerely regretted by his many friends in this city.

A PRIZE MUSICAL COMPOSITION.

CINCINNATI, Jan. 30.—The prize of $1,000 offered for the best original composition by a native-born American composer, to be sung at the coming May musical festival, has been awarded to Dudley Buck, over 20 composers who entered into the competition. The title of the work is "Scenes from Longfellow's Golden Legend." The composition requires an hour for its performance. It is understood that Dr. Damrosch, of New-York, and Mr. Hamerick, of Baltimore, two of the five judges, favored a composition, also based upon Longfellow's poems, by George E. Whiting, formerly of Boston, and Theodore Thomas's vote decided the contest in Buck's favor.

ATTORNEYS IN TROUBLE.

LANCASTER, Penn., Jan. 30.—Messrs. Steinman and Hensel, attorneys and editors of the *Intelligencer*, appeared in court to-day to answer for contempt, and to show cause why they should not be disbarred, for an alleged libelous publication on the court. The respondents presented their answer, and an exhaustive argument was made for them by their counsel. The court reserved its decision.

AN UNHAPPY WIFE'S SUICIDE.

SCRANTON, Penn., Jan. 30.—Mrs. Phillips, wife of the Hon. Harry J. Phillips, an ex-member of the Pennsylvania Legislature, committed suicide to-night by taking poison. Her married life has been unhappy. Her husband deserted her several months ago, and they have not lived together since that time. Phillips is now on a visit in the Old Country.

A CHAMPION GAME OF BILLIARDS.

ST. LOUIS, Jan. 30.—The game of billiards played to-night between Sexton and Daly on one side, and Schaefer and Gallagher on the other, 400 points, championship game, was won by Sexton and Daly, with a score of 400 to 342. The winners' average was 18 4-22, and the losers' 16 5-21.

THE RECORD OF ACCIDENTS.

MILFORD, Penn., Jan. 30.—The body of a man was seen floating down the Delaware River, past this place, yesterday. It is thought to have been the body of Emmit Shamcon, a carpenter, who fell from the Delaware and Hudson Aqueduct, at Lackawaxen, Penn., New Year's Day.

A boy 9 years of age, son of L. W. Morss, of Sedgedale, Wayne County, Penn., ran into the house, a few days ago, to get a pistol to shoot a dog that had bitten a playmate. He put the pistol in his pocket, and when he attempted to draw it therefrom it was discharged, the ball passing through the abdomen and lodging in the back. It is thought he cannot recover.

AMBOY, N. J., Jan. 30.—Alfred Woolley, while riding out on horseback with his sister, at Centreville, this morning, attempted to adjust some loose fastenings upon the horse which his sister was riding, when the animal kicked him in the abdomen and face, causing fatal injuries.

BALTIMORE, Jan. 30.—John F. Hoffman, a brake-man on the Northern Central Railroad, was killed to-night near Eager-street, within the city. He was engaged in shifting cars, when the brake-chain broke and he fell between the cars, one of which passed over him.

FORT SCOTT, Kan., Jan. 30.—The boiler of Moloy's saw-mill, six miles north-east of this city, in Vernon County, Mo., exploded to-day, instantly killing Thomas Freeman, a laborer, and seriously injuring and scalding Henry Moloy, the owner. Plint Tinner, another laborer, was badly scalded, and two other men were slightly injured.

CRIME AND ITS RESULTS.

SAN FRANCISCO, Jan. 3.—Charley Taing, a Chinaman, was hanged at Colusa to-day for the murder of a Chinawoman, in Colusa County, in December, 1878.

PROVIDENCE, R. I., Jan. 30.—In Bristol, Simon J. Gray has been held for trial on a charge of rape on his daughter, whose husband demanded $2,000 in settlement of the charge.

ST. ALBANS, Vt., Jan. 30.—Isadore Marechal was arrested here to-day charged with having stolen silk valued at $4,000, from Block & Co., of Montreal, in October last. He is now in jail awaiting extradition, for which the Canadian Government will apply at once. Marechal has been arrested several times and has escaped from various prisons, including Sing Sing.

BOSTON, Jan. 30.—A dispatch from Ayer mentions the arrival of Abbott, in custody, on the charge of murdering Mrs. Crue at Groton. Several persons in the vicinity have recognized him. He declines to make a statement without the advice of counsel.

FORTUNES IN PETROLEUM

GREAT INTERESTS CENTRING IN THE OIL-FIELDS.

SIGNS OF EXCITING TIMES AHEAD—NEW FACTORS IN THE TRADE—THE ANTAGONISTIC COMBINATIONS—HOW MONOPOLY GREW AND PROSPERED—PROBABILITIES OF THE FUTURE.

OIL CITY, Penn., Jan. 29.—The oil market is as inflammable as the product whose fluctuations it records, and those who produce, refine, or speculate are always on the edge of an explosion that may blow their calculations all to the winds, or send the price of the product they are handling up or down to points that mean always ruin or disaster to some one. There is always an uneasy feeling in the oil regions, but of late it seems to have grown and increased. Possible sharp movements are just ahead, and there are new elements entering into the trade that defy all calculations and ignore all questions of supply and demand. The next 30 days promise to be full of exceeding interest and sharp business for the region bounded by Bradford, Pittsburg, and Cleveland; and to measure the causes of the present commotion, and to show what agencies are at work, these facts and supplemental speculative guesses have been put together. The real inside history of the oil movements and oil combinations can never be written, but enough is daily made apparent to show that nowhere outside of Wall-street and the grain centre at Chicago is there more fire, fever, and life of speculation than here in the oil district of Western Pennsylvania.

PRODUCERS AND REFINERS.

"I'll take it." "Sell you five more?" "Yes." "Five more! 10, 15, 20!"

The clock strikes 4 and the confusion ceases. Two hundred men drift away to their offices and homes, and the Oil Exchange closes for the day. Three hundred and fifty thousand barrels of crude oil have changed hands at an average price of $1.15 per barrel. Day after day, week in and out, this financial and business centre of oildom is thus boiling and bubbling away, for this is the crude oil market of the world.

Just now a new excitement is added to the score of excitements that forever keep the quotations running up and down the scale in obedience to no fixed rule, and yet answering so readily to the deft touch of the heavy operators and speculators. A new and important factor has been introduced into the trade by the election of James R. Keene, of New-York, to the Directorship of the Tide-water Pipe Line. Already his name on 'Change produces a halt in prices, keeping them within narrow limits of fluctuations. The speculators are waiting to see what the next move on the board will be. When the trade was in its infancy, calculations were easily made, and contingencies easily provided against by dealers, but to-day the oil market, like the stock and grain markets, is feeling the hand of the Californian and his followers, setting at naught all rules of supply and demand. Statistics are no more of use. Suppose, in illustration, that a prominent broker commences buying. "That's for Jim Keene," goes the whisper from mouth to mouth, and all hands join in with a rush. Those who are "short" rush to cover; the "longs" to get a heavier load before it goes higher; the waiting ones now think their opportunity has dawned, and they join the swarm of buyers. Everybody is buying, and none are anxious to sell. Prices jump. The "longs" become crazy—they cannot get oil enough. Higher and higher go their bids, until all at once some one seems to be selling. Somebody *has* been selling, quietly, but surely, and around goes another whisper. This time it is rapidly circulated among the bears that "Keene has begun to spill his oil." Then occurs a grand rush. All want to get from under. The result is, a few make money. Those who bought at the top and sold at the bottom, and *vice versa*, understand perfectly the meaning of the word "whipsaw."

There are four strings to the petroleum bow at present:

1. The producer, who holds territory in fee simple or by lease, puts down wells, and produces crude oil.
2. The refiners, who refine the crude product for illuminating and lubricating purposes.
3. The transportation companies, consisting of railroads and pipe lines.
4. The speculators.

The first string is a strong and powerful one, and has millions of capital and any amount of pluck and energy invested. The producer is well satisfied with his labor when his product brings $1 25 and upward per barrel. With any less price ruling he is inclined to be uneasy, and when less than a dollar is reached, he is very much dissatisfied. He lays all his trouble upon the three other strings. He sees his fellow-producers, and they get their heads together to devise ways and means whereby they can command a fair price for their product. Generally, before any feasible plan is perfected a rise in the market takes place, they become absorbed in selling their oil, looking up new territory, and banking their money. These diversions leave them no time to organize mutual protection leagues or unions, and so the movement goes to pieces for the time.

SPECULATORS AND TRANSPORTERS.

Until recently the speculators were local men of means—bankers, merchants, and capitalists. Lately, however, the low price of oil, with an easy money market, has attracted outsiders to the speculative pastures, and last October, when oil was ruling at 80 cents, a prominent Oil City banker, a heavy producer, and some Eastern capitalists, combined and bought largely, and forced the price to 90 cents. Here the market rested, seemingly having no more strength. At this price many of the Bradford producers sold their oil on hand, and contracted to sell all they could produce during the remainder of 1879; and, knowing the immense stocks on hand of both crude and refined, knowing the shipping season was over, they "went short" at 90, expecting to cover in at 75 or 70 before the end of the year. Then the combination pulled their string again and bought more oil, and prices went to $1. This seemed to be the top figure, and many joined the producers and went short at this figure.

November opened with the market at $89\frac{3}{8}$, and closed with it at $122\frac{1}{2}$. December opened at $126\frac{1}{4}$, and ruled about that figure until the 15th, when the price went off, and the year closed at $110\frac{5}{8}$. It is, therefore, easy to figure that the "shorts" were obliged to cover at the top, while the combination made a large amount of money. The prominent banker referred to, for instance, is credited with $500,000 as his share of the profits.

The refiners and transporters, though separate parties, have been accused of being practically one. The United Line, with its pipes and tanks for storing, touches every point in the producing field. This company stores and pipes oil. It makes connections with the wells and runs the producer's oil through its pipes to its immense tanks, giving the producer credit for the same, and issuing to him a United certificate, which he is at liberty to sell to any one who will purchase. This oil is to be delivered on demand, and at any point where the line runs. The Standard Oil Company, the great monopoly of oildom, is represented in the Board of Directors of the United Lines by its President and Secretary, although neither has ever attended any of the meetings. Mr. J. A. Bostwick, of New-York, is one of the Directors, and Mr. E. D. Worcester, Treasurer of the Lake Shore and Michigan Southern Railroad, is another. Reasoning from the facts already known, the situation seems to be about this: On one side there is the Standard Oil Company, the United Pipe Lines, and Mr. J. A. Bostwick, of New-York; while on the other side is the Tide-water Pipe Line, running from Titusville to Williamsport, connecting at the latter place with the Reading Railroad; the President of which road, Mr. Frank B. Gowen, and Mr. James R. Keene, and Mr. H. L. Taylor, of Fredonia, N. Y., have been elected Directors of the Tide-water Line. It is easy to see that this line can get to the sea-board with its crude oil through its own properties, while the Standard-Bostwick people are dependent on rail and water transportation over which they have no control.

But here other important indications must be noted. The City Council of Cleveland, Ohio, where the Standard works are located, two

The New-York Times.

VOL. XXXI.......NO. 9518. NEW-YORK, FRIDAY, MARCH 10, 1882. PRICE FOUR CENTS.

THE CHINESE BILL PASSED

A VOTE OF NEARLY TWO TO ONE IN THE AFFIRMATIVE.

MR. HAWLEY SPEAKS AGAINST THE BILL AND MR. JONES, OF NEVADA, FOR IT—AN INTERESTING ARGUMENT BY THE LATTER—VARIOUS AMENDMENTS ADOPTED—MR. EDMUNDS FINALLY VOTES IN THE NEGATIVE.

WASHINGTON, March 9.—The anti-Chinese bill passed the Senate to-day after another prolonged debate by a vote of nearly two to one. Two long speeches were made, one by Mr. Hawley against the measure, and one by Mr. Jones, of Nevada, in favor of its passage, and Mr. Edmunds, who had made the strongest argument affirming the right and power of the Government of the United States to exclude the Chinese, surprised many who had heard his remarks by making a speech against the bill when it came out of the Committee of the Whole and by voting in the negative on its passage.

The debate was resumed upon Mr. Farley's amendment prohibiting the courts from naturalizing Chinese, Mr. Hawley having the floor. Mr. Hawley, like his colleague, Mr. Platt, was opposed to the bill as making invidious discrimination between races, but he admitted the truth of Mr. Edmunds's proposition that the Nation could, and did, exercise the power to reject pauper, criminal, and idiotic immigrants. To legislate against a race would be to abandon principles that had challenged the admiration of the world. The passage of the bill might effect a change in the minds of the Nation's admirers. A few words in the bill might be quoted for centuries, in the same way that the Edict of Nantes was spoken of, or as the laws of China and Japan were frequently referred to. It would be ranked with such legislation as the alien laws, the Missouri Compromise, or the Fugitive Slave law. To make the law at all plausible, he suggested that the preamble should be changed so as to recite that because the Chinese do not come here to swear allegiance, do not speak our language, do not care about our Constitution and laws, do not bear their share of taxation, do not perform military duty, do not bring their wives and children, because they bring peculiar traits of character and strange religious belief, and because they come to establish a self-wilded peasantry when we want no peasantry, they shall be excluded. To admit these things would be to say that if the native of China would do those things he could come, but it only says something against a laborer of a peculiar color and merely expresses the opinion that the coming of Chinese laborers endangers the good order of certain localities. The obvious conclusion was that if the Chinaman comes he shall be insulted and driven to the sea-coast. Men rise and say that their coming will make a part of the people so angry that they will rise in rebellion and trample on their own laws. Mr. Hawley criticised at some length the manner of securing the modified treaty. On the same day that the Chinese had been compelled by bombardment to grant the Burlingame treaty, the fourteenth amendment was adopted, and a year later, Congress had declared, in the fifteenth amendment, that no person should be deprived of the right of suffrage by reason of race, color, or previous condition of servitude. Our radicalism was fading, and the Senate was now asked to deny to the Chinese the rights they were bombarded into accepting. In the Senator's estimation, right and power were confounded. While Congress had the right in a shallow and technical sense to do many things, it had in that sense the right to do many things that were wrong to do. He objected to basing the exclusion of Chinamen on the accident of color, and trusted that the Senate would be patient and not be driven to action by the fear of the arrival of a hundred Chinamen or by an indignation meeting. He thought the bill not indispensable to the country's welfare, and for one should not be ashamed to vote against it.

When Senator Jones, of Nevada, rose in his place it was expected that an interesting speech would be heard. The expectation was not unfulfilled. While Mr. Jones does not speak often enough to acquire grace of expression, and in uttering his views makes no sort of pretense to eloquence or oratorical effect, the fact that he speaks only when he has something to say, and then speaks with earnestness, assures him the respectful attention of his associates and of the galleries. He had waited, he said, to hear some good reason why the bill should not pass. He had been bewildered by Mr. Hoar's proposition that this Government could not exclude nations or people whose presence was objectionable, and had ransacked many books in the vain effort to discover any authority for such an assumption. In his estimation, Mr. Hoar's interpretation of the Constitution was a wrong one, and he regarded his ethnology and his logic as being equally faulty. Benjamin Franklin's writings were quoted to prove that at least one of the signers of the declaration of independence did not contemplate the occupation of this land by black and tawny people, but rather looked to its reservation for the benefit of the white race. He did not believe, with the Senator from Massachusetts, that the Chinese, whose condition had been the same for centuries, could be converted into good citizens in a single generation, or that it was right to attempt, as he had done, to deal with a race by individual instances. As a race they were without spirituality, honor, or sensibility. All injuries to them could be compensated by money. Mr. Jones denied the claim set up for them by Mr. Hoar that they were inventive, and said that he had looked up the matter. He found that Draper attributes to the Arabs and not the Chinese the discovery of gunpowder, and that Prof. Meyer, an eminent Orientalist, who had attempted to trace the discovery, expressed his belief that gunpowder had been introduced into China from India in the fifth or sixth century. They had been deprived of the credit of inventing the compass in the same way. He supposed that Mr. Hoar had found his information in an encyclopedia, but he had looked in the British Encyclopedia, and observed that even in that work the Chinese were not credited with these inventions.

Taking up another point, Mr. Jones said he had noticed that those who favored Chinese immigration were also in favor of a tariff to protect American labor. In his opinion such cheap labor as that secured by the importation of Chinese was detrimental to the cause of American labor, as cheap labor was a fallacy. The inevitable result of the contact of "the little brown man" with white men would be, if the Chinese continued to come, to equalize the condition of things in China and America. China was populous, yet poor. If labor would make a country rich China should be rich, for she had 400,000,000 of people, and the nation was poor. She was without intelligence, and there could be no wealth without intelligence. To dilute the intellectual energy of the American people would be disastrous to the Nation.

The Senators on the Democratic side listened with evident interest when Mr. Jones came to allude to the effect of the presence of a great African population in the Southern States. "Does any one on this side believe," asked he, turning to his Republican neighbors, "that if the African people in the Southern States were not surrounded and upheld by the whites they could maintain free Government there. I do not believe it." That opinion, he suggested, might be heresy, but he regarded it as correct. He asked Senators to reflect upon what might have been the condition of this country if the North had been crowded with blacks as the South is. The blacks had been an evil in the South, and many of the Southern people had been compelled to admit that it would have been a blessing if they had been absolutely excluded. The Chinese were more dangerous, obnoxious, and difficult of assimilation. China herself was an example to other nations, in that she had outlived many others, because she was exclusive, her people homogeneous. Mr. Jones closed his speech with an appeal to the Senate to heed the dispassionate judgment of 154,000 citizens of California and pass the bill.

Mr. Morrill spoke against the bill as a sudden closing of the doors to a friendly race and a violation of treaty obligations, which he feared the courts would not uphold.

Mr. Ingalls considered Mr. Farley's amendment objectionable in not being germane, the question of naturalization not properly entering into such a bill. He did not see why, if Massachusetts chose to admit Chinamen to citizenship, she should not be permitted to do so. Mr. Farley promptly replied that it was obvious that if Chinamen became citizens of Massachusetts they were citizens of the United States and could not be denied their privileges anywhere.

Just before the vote on this amendment was taken Mr. Edmunds objected to it as not properly connected with the bill, which merely proposed to regulate the coming and going of the Chinese, and expressed the opinion that anybody in favor of the substance of the bill would vote against it. Mr. Sherman stated his position, favoring limitation but not prohibition, and objecting to some provisions of the bill as harsh.

The vote was taken on Mr. Farley's naturalization amendment, which was adopted. Mr. Slater's amendment defining several classes of labor as unskilled, was rejected, and on Mr. Edmunds's motion, the words requiring that passports should be produced whenever legally demanded, were stricken out.

In the Senate, when the bill was reported from the Committee of the Whole, Mr. Ingalls called for a vote on his amendment to limit the exclusion of Chinese to 10 instead of 20 years. The amendment failed by a vote of 20 to 21. Mr. Ingalls then directed attention to the fact that section 14 provides that Chinese entering the country in violation of law shall be fined $100 or imprisoned, or be both fined and imprisoned, while the same section provides that violators of the law shall be sent out of the country by Collectors of Customs. It seemed to him that this would leave the Chinaman in a peculiar position. He asked for light, but no one explained what appeared to Mr. Ingalls to be an incongruity. No motion was made to amend. The Farley amendment was adopted by a vote of 25 to 22. Mr. Edmunds made a speech, protesting that the bill was against right policy, and that it threatened to destroy our trade with China by provoking unfriendliness. He declared that he should vote against it. On the passage of the bill, Mr. Mitchell, of Pennsylvania, attempted to make a speech during the calling of the roll, and was called to order for transgressing the rules. The bill was passed by a vote of 29 to 15, as follows: [Republicans in roman, Democrats in *italics*, Independents in SMALL CAPITALS:]

YEAS—Messrs. *Bayard*, *Beck*, *Call*, Cameron of Wisconsin, *Cockrell*, *Coke*, *Fair*, *Farley*, *Garland*, *George*, *Gorman*, Hale, *Harris*, Hill of Colorado, *Jackson*, *Jonas*, Jones of Nevada, Miller of California, Miller of New-York, *Morgan*, *Pugh*, *Ransom*, Sawyer, *Slater*, Teller, *Vance*, *Vest*, *Voorhees*, *Walker*—29.

NAYS—Messrs. Aldrich, Allison, Blair, *Brown*, Conger, DAVIS of Illinois, Dawes, Edmunds, Frye, Hoar, Ingalls, Lapham, McDill, McMillan, Morrill—15.

The bill as passed provides that from and after the expiration of 90 days after the passage of the act and until the expiration of 20 years after its passage, the coming of Chinese laborers to the United States shall be suspended, and prescribes a penalty of imprisonment not exceeding one year and a fine of not more than $500 against the master of any vessel who brings any Chinese laborer to this country during that period. It further provides that the classes of Chinese excepted by the treaty from such prohibition, such as merchants, teachers, students, travelers, diplomatic agents, and Chinese laborers who were in the United States on the 17th of November, 1880, shall be required, as a condition for their admission, to produce passports from the Government of China personally identifying them and showing that they individually belong to one of the permitted classes, which passports must have been indorsed by the diplomatic representative of the United States in China or by the United States Consul at the port of departure. It also provides elaborate machinery for carrying out the purposes of the act, and additional sections prohibit the admission of Chinese to citizenship by any United States or State Court, and construes the words "Chinese laborers" to mean both skilled and unskilled laborers and Chinese employed in mining.

WASHINGTON SOCIAL EVENTS.

SECRETARY FRELINGHUYSEN'S WEEKLY RECEPTION—COMING ENTERTAINMENTS.

WASHINGTON, March 9.—The usual Thursday evening reception at Secretary Frelinghuysen's residence was one of great brilliancy in spite of discouraging weather. Mrs. Frelinghuysen was assisted in receiving by her two daughters, and the company was entertained during the evening by musical selections by Miss Balch, Mlle. Nogueiras, and Mrs. Camp. The attendance was unusually large. Among the guests were President Arthur, Secretary and Mrs. Hunt, Attorney-General Brewster, Justice Strong, Senator Sawyer, the Chinese Minister and two secretaries, the Italian, Swedish, Austrian, Danish, Turkish, Haytian, and Portuguese Ministers, Representatives Kasson, Farwell, Bingham, Wadsworth, and Washburn, Major and Miss Herschel, of England; Gen. Drum and wife, Justice and Mrs. MacArthur, Mrs. Chauncey I. Filley, and Miss Mary Waite. The dresses were rich and in many cases elaborate. Mrs. Frelinghuysen wore a reception dress of black vengaline, trimmed with jetted lace; Miss Frelinghuysen, white nun's veiling and surah; Miss Lucy Frelinghuysen, Jacqueminot red satin, with Oriental brocade trimming and corsage bouquet of golden red. Baroness Fava, wife of the Italian Minister, wore a white moire silk with Spanish lace draperies, diamond and emerald ornaments. Countess Lewenhaupt, of Sweden, was attired in heliotrope satin and brocade, with heliotrope bouquet at the waist. Mme. Preston, of Hayti, wore blue silk, with white embroideries; Miss Herschel, black Spanish lace, with Etruscan gold ornaments; Mrs. Chauncey I. Filley, cream-tinted satin and brocaded velvet; Miss Nogueiras, black satin and lace, and other ladies were attired with equal richness.

The Chinese Minister has issued cards inviting the members of the Cabinet and diplomatic corps to meet Secretary Frelinghuysen on Saturday evening. Mme. Cheng will not appear, and only gentlemen are invited to partake of the hospitalities of the imperial Chinese Legation.

The President will give a dinner to the Justices of the Supreme Court, their wives, and a few other guests on Wednesday, March 15. This dinner has been postponed for some time awaiting the full complement of Judges on the Supreme bench.

WASHINGTON IMPROVEMENTS.

WASHINGTON, March 9.—Two subjects of great importance to the District of Columbia demand the attention of Congress. One is the reclamation of the Potomac flats and the other is the water supply of the city. The plan for reclaiming the flats has been fixed and the bill has been reported. The Senate sub-committee to which the water supply question was intrusted has prepared a bill providing for extending and raising the dam at Great Falls, for extending the aqueduct to the high ground north of the city, and for building a large reservoir at that point. Water cannot be supplied now in the higher parts of the city except by the use of steam pumps. The daily supply is about 27,000,000 gallons. The cost of the works provided for in the bill will be about $1,500,000.

TWO TENNESSEE MURDERERS.

NASHVILLE, Tenn., March 9.—The Supreme Court to-day refused to grant the petition for a new trial of W. W. Rea, sentenced last Saturday to be hanged April 25, in Giles County, for the assassination of James Goodrum. Rea still asserted his innocence. It is likely a petition will be presented to the Governor for a commutation of the sentence, on account of the conviction being based entirely on circumstantial evidence.

The Supreme Court to-day sentenced Andrew Jackson, white, to be hanged on April 28, in Dickson County, for the murder of James P. Clardy, on Jan. 25, 1881. Clardy was a bachelor, who resided alone, and was killed for his money.

FIRST BOAT THROUGH TO TROY.

TROY, N. Y., March 9.—The first boat from New-York arrived this morning. Navigation of the Hudson River opens two weeks earlier than usual.

BAIL IN STAR ROUTES CASES

GEN. BRADY REQUIRED TO FURNISH A LARGE BOND.

THE COURT HOLDS HIM IN $20,000 AND REBUKES HIS COUNSEL FOR ATTEMPTING TO BELITTLE THE CHARGE—THE OTHER CONSPIRATORS HELD IN SMALLER SUMS.

WASHINGTON, March 9.—The persons recently indicted for conspiracy and perjury in connection with the star route mail service were required to appear in court to-day and give bail. The first case called was that of Thomas J. Brady, formerly Second Assistant Postmaster-General. His counsel attempted to discredit the indictment against him, and declared that $1,000 would be sufficient bail in a case depending upon such a paper. Col. Bliss spoke of the magnitude of Gen. Brady's offenses and asked that the bail should be $20,000. The counsel for Gen. Brady did not induce Judge Wylie to regard the charges as of a trifling character. The Judge declared that the defense greatly underrated the gravity of the accusation, and rebuked them for suggesting so small a sum as $1,000. Here was a person holding a position of trust, and he is charged with violating that trust. Whether the charge could be sustained was a question, but for the present he would regard it as true. It was trifling to suggest such a sum as $1,000. In his opinion, the amount asked by the Government was not too large, and he therefore fixed the bail in that case at $20,000.

The list of defendants was then called. When the name of Alvin O. Buck, charged with conspiracy, was reached, Mr. Pelham said that Mr. Buck would be content to give $1,000. Mr. Bliss reported that Buck was probably loose and unlikely to appear when called, and their examination of the case showed that Mr. Buck was aware of the utter want of value in the land offered. Mr. Pelham said that whenever Mr. Buck was wanted he would be on hand. He had come all the way from Florida on a telegram to be here to-day. The court said he would fix the amount of bail at $2,000 in this case. Kate M. Armstrong, charged with conspiracy, was called. Mr. Pelham said that she would give $500 bail.

Mr. Bliss—This woman is a cook employed by Mr. Boone, and she has been used as a principal in obtaining contracts while occupying a position in the kitchen.

Mr. Pelham said that she was in the original charge, but had never been arrested and had not left the city.

Mr. Bliss—And she has been hiding. Our officers could not find her.

The court said that the bail would be $1,000.

When S. G. Cabell's name was called, Mr. Hine stated that he (Mr. Cabell) had recently received an award of 29 contracts, and the Government need not fear that he would not appear. His bail was fixed at $5,000.

The amount of bail in the other cases was fixed as follows: W. N. Minnix, $1,500, J. E. Kendall, surety; James W. Donahue, $1,000, John F. Donohue, surety; C. H. Dickson, $1,000; W. S. Barringer, $1,000; W. W. Jackson, $1,000; James B. Henderson, $2,000; J. R. Miner, $5,000; W. H. Turner, $2,500; E. J. Sweet, $1,000. Action in the cases of S. W. Dorsey and others was by the request of their counsel deferred until to-morrow.

When the case of Harvey M. Vail was reached, his counsel called attention to the fact that his client had been indicted under the name of Henry M. Vail. He supposed that as this error invalidated the indictment bail would not be required. At the request of Mr. Bliss bail was fixed in Vail's case at $1,000. It was understood, however, that if the error existed in the indictment the demand for bail would be withdrawn.

Mr. Bliss said it was desirable that some understanding be arrived at as to the time for pleading. The Government wished at least to get the conspiracy cases on trial before Summer. Mr. Wilson, for the defense, replied that on the return of indictments they had begun preparations to meet the cases at trial—that was, if they ever came to trial. He thought that they would be prepared to plead one week from to-day. By that time whatever they had to present to the court by plea or motion would be ready. The court could then fix a day for argument. This arrangement met the approval of the counsel for the prosecution, and was accordingly agreed to.

DEFECTS IN THE POSTAL LAWS.

MEASURES BEFORE CONGRESS TO PREVENT A REPETITION OF THE STAR ROUTE FRAUDS.

WASHINGTON, March 9.—The members of the star route ring were assisted in many cases by the Postmasters on their routes, especially by those at the terminal points. After having been awarded enormous pay for making better time, they failed to make the time required, and in many cases hardly attempted to make it. The Postmasters keep a report of the time of departure and arrivals for the use of the department. On some routes the Postmasters received very little from the Government, and were employed by the contractors and favored by them in many ways. When a contractor fails to make the time which is required by his schedule he is subject to heavy deductions from his pay. The frauds practiced by the contractors were, on many routes, as has been shown in THE TIMES, concealed by Postmasters, who made false reports concerning arrivals and departures. In the case of the line from Sydney to Deadwood, the Postmaster at Deadwood, Sol. Star, made a confession to the officers of the Government. The Postmaster at Sydney, the other end of the line, had also aided the ring by false certificates, and he confessed, but when the case was on trial a few days ago he refused to testify in behalf of the Government. Mr. Bingham, Chairman of the Post Office Committee of the House, has introduced a bill which provides that any Postmaster who shall make and render to the department any false register, record, certificates, or other report of arrivals or departures of the mails, or who, having knowledge of delinquencies of mail contractors, their agents, or carriers, shall fail to report the same promptly to the Postmaster-General, shall be deemed guilty of a misdemeanor, and upon conviction be punished by a fine of not less than $100 and not more than $1,000, and shall be imprisoned not more than two years. He has also introduced a bill providing for the punishment of Postmasters, Post Office Inspectors, or other officers employed in the service who do, or aid others in doing, anything forbidden by the postal laws, or who refuse to perform duties imposed upon them by law.

The auditor of the accounts of the Post Office Department, known as the Sixth Auditor of the Treasury, and in fact a subordinate of the Secretary of the Treasury, is an officer of great power. He examines and adjusts all of the department's accounts, superintends the collection of debts and penalties imposed on Postmasters and contractors, directs suits and legal proceedings, civil and criminal, takes all such measures as may be authorized by law to enforce the payment of money due to the department. J. M. McGrew was Auditor while Thomas J. Brady was Second Assistant Postmaster-General, and the revelations made since the investigation began prove that the ring would have found it difficult to rob the Treasury if the Sixth Auditor had been an honest officer, determined to do his duty and execute the law, and bring to justice notorious offenders. The Sixth Auditor is practically a law unto himself. His decisions on all accounts are final, unless an appeal be taken within 12 months to the First Controller of the Treasury. The House Committee on Post Offices will report a bill providing that all the Post Office accounts shall be finally revised by the First Controller. In this way a check will be provided similar to the checks to which all other Auditors of the Treasury are subjected. These bills are in the right direction, and it is hoped that the committee will continue to search for abuses which ought to be corrected by legislation.

NOTES FROM WASHINGTON.

WASHINGTON, March 9, 1882.

The national bank notes received for redemption to-day amounted to $172,000.

The receipts from internal revenue to-day were $381,783 70, and from Customs $684,078 29.

At the close of business to-day United States bonds had been redeemed as follows: Under the one hundred and fifth call, $19,658,050; under the one hundred and sixth call, $17,883,150; under the one hundred and seventh call, $2,839,750.

The House Committee on Patents to-day decided to report with a favorable recommendation Mr. Orth's bill authorizing the Commissioner of Patents to extend the patent of Clark Mills for a "mode of taking casts from the face of living persons" for a term of seven years, beginning April 1.

The bill for a commission to investigate the alcoholic liquor traffic was taken up by the Senate in the morning hour to-day, but was not finally acted upon. Amendments were adopted that not more than three of the five Commissioners shall be of the same political party, and that not more than three shall be Prohibitionists.

The Treasury Department to-day purchased 366,000 ounces of silver for delivery at the Philadelphia, San Francisco, New-Orleans, and Carson City Mints. It is understood that the Secretary of the Treasury will soon direct the transportation of $17,000,000 in gold from the Philadelphia Mint to the Treasury as provision for the expense of such transportation is made in the immediate deficiency bill.

The Secretary of the Treasury sent the following telegram to the Collectors of Customs at New-York, Philadelphia, Boston, Baltimore, and New-Orleans to-day: "Supreme Court, in case of Welsh against Merritt, has decided that duties accrue on imported sugars only according to their color as compared with Dutch standard. Instructions contained in circulars of July 19 and Sept. 2, 1879, to the contrary, are hereby revoked. Collect duties on apparent color of sugar as imported."

District Attorney Corkhill finished to-day the examination of the bill of exceptions in the Guiteau case. He says a large portion of it refers to the medical testimony, and that he had gone over these exceptions very carefully with Dr. Gray. He also says that it is a remarkable fact that there is no exception to any part of Dr. Gray's testimony. Mr. Corkhill said further: "To-morrow Judge Porter, Mr. Davidge, and myself will go over them again finally to determine upon their character. If there is a difference of opinion between counsel for the Government and Mr. Scoville, it will be left for the court to settle. Probably the exceptions will be argued in the General Term some time in April. I expect to ask the court to set them specially for argument some time in April."

In a report from the Committee on Commerce, made to the House to-day upon Mr. Crapo's bill "to amend the statutes relative to danger signals," it is asserted that from $5,000,000 to $7,000,000 of property, and from 300 to 1,500 lives are lost annually in fogs, falling snow, mists, and thick and hazy weather in waters navigable by course, and that the greater part of all of this loss may be directly attributed to the present defective signals and rules in force. The committee assert that a simple and far more efficient system of signals and rules can be adopted. They further say that the rules at present in force are complex, conflicting, and insufficient, and that the statutes and rules of the United States are in conflict with the Code of international rules to which the United States are not a party; that as a result of this state of things American ships, even when acting in conformity with the rules of the United States, are held responsible in foreign courts for damages resulting from collisions when the American vessels diviated from the international rules. The committee recommend the appointment of three international Commissioners, and also the appointment of a Board of Experts to determine the best apparatus to be used by vessels to determine the course steered in the night as a further protection against collision.

ASPIRING TO CONGRESS.

THE POSSIBLE CANDIDACY OF MAYOR MEANS, (DEMOCRAT,) OF CINCINNATI.

CINCINNATI, March 9.—A Washington dispatch, published in the *Commercial* of this morning, states that Mayor Means is to be put forward in the First Cincinnati District in the belief that he can carry the district for the Democrats. This is Congressman Butterworth's district, and, though it has been carried twice for Bullerworth, is usually considered Democratic. Inquiry to-day went to show that the Mayor would be much pleased with the nomination were he certain of commanding the full support of his party. His friends are urging him to make the race, but they admit that he has made enemies since he became Mayor who might prove troublesome. They would expect, however, to see him receive enough Republican support to overbalance what he might lose in his own party. When running for Mayor he was supported by Richard Smith, of the *Gazette* and a large following of religious and temperance people. He is wealthy, which is an important desideratum. Republicans say they would like to see him nominated for the reason that there is no man whom Major Butterworth could beat more easily. They say that his Republican friends would not support him for Congress.

SWEET & CO.'S FAILURE.

ASSIGNING THE PROPERTY TO TRUSTEES—APPRECIATION OF THE ASSETS.

BOSTON, March 9.—It is reported in State-street that certain large sales of Massachusetts Central bonds have been effected by Charles A. Sweet & Co., who suspended on Monday. It was given out on authority that the firm in question had made a private sale of $60,000 worth of Massachusetts Central bonds at 75, and that there was a demand for several more large blocks at the same figures. In the published statement of the assets of Sweet & Co., about $800,000 of Massachusetts Central bonds held by them was reckoned at 50 cents on the dollar. The difference will materially increase the assets. A meeting of the creditors was held this afternoon, at which the members of the firm proposed to assign all their property and assets to three Trustees—Samuel Atherton, James Beal, and George Whitney—who are to take charge of the affairs and settle up as soon as possible. The proposition was accepted by those present and the remaining creditors were advised to co-operate. The committee stated that, in its opinion, all claims would be met, dollar for dollar, and that Mr. Sweet will besides have left an ample competency. Thirty days are allowed the other creditors to agree to this plan, and it is understood that all will accept.

It is stated that the suspension has had the effect to frighten many of the employes of the Massachusetts Central Railroad about their pay for work done during the past two months. It is reported that above Hudson some of the workmen have been turned out of doors because of their inability to pay their board bills, already overdue. Some of the employes left their work temporarily yesterday because they had not been paid, and it is thought that more will follow their example unless a speedy settlement is effected with them.

NEW-JERSEY LEGISLATORS.

TRENTON, March 9.—The Republicans of the Legislature carried out the designs of the joint caucus in joint meeting to-day. When the joint meeting reassembled, a motion that a Police Justice of Jersey City be elected was carried. Farrier and Durell still maintained their opposition to Lawrence. One vote was needed to elect Lawrence. Mr. Shinn, of Atlantic, went to his rescue, and, voting with the 40 Republicans, elected him. Mr. Hobart introduced into the Senate a bill restoring to the New-Jersey Central Railroad its franchises after it shall have passed out of the hands of the Receiver.

SINDRAM AGAIN RESPITED.

ALBANY, March 9.—The Governor has this day granted a further respite to William Sindram, whose day of hanging in New-York was extended until Friday, April 7, only a few days ago until Friday, April 21, as otherwise the day would have fallen upon Good Friday.

AN OLD BANK CLERK'S FALL

THE FOURTH NATIONAL ROBBED OF A LARGE SUM.

SECURITIES WORTH $70,000 PLEDGED TO COVER MARGINS ON STOCK SPECULATIONS—THE AGED LOAN CLERK FOUND TO BE THE THIEF—HIS CONFESSION TO AN OFFICER OF THE BANK.

Wall-street during the past few days has been filled with stories of impending disaster. Prominent men were named as upon the verge of bankruptcy, and long-established houses were said to be in sore straits. Upon rumors such as these, mysterious and indefinite, the bears in the stock market were able to send down prices and reap heavy profits. Various banks were placed in the list of institutions said to be involved. It was alleged in positive terms that there was trouble in the management of the Fourth National Bank, and that developments were likely to appear which would startle the Street. The story grew as it passed around, and more than one broker sold stocks short in anticipation of some extraordinary sensation. To the feeling created by the vague but insinuating rumors afloat in this connection was due to no small extent the market's downward tendency in the early hours yesterday. Later in the day there was a move upward, and the bull operators seemed to have obtained relief from a heavy burden. The difficulty at the Fourth National Bank was made known. Its officers made public a detailed statement covering not only the financial status of the institution, but setting forth in full the causes which had given grounds for the sensational stories. All the allegations and insinuations by which it was sought to convince the public that the bank was financially entangled and embarrassed were met and were proved to be false.

But while the officers of the Fourth National were able to conclusively disprove the stories reflecting upon the institution's solvency, they at the same time were obliged to confess that a trusted employe had been dishonest and had successfully stolen and appropriated to his own use many thousands of dollars. The accused officer is R. H. Cornwall, who occupied the position of Loan Clerk. He is over 65 years of age, and the head of a large family. Heretofore no suspicion has ever been directed against him, and it was only after a thorough investigation had developed overwhelming evidence of his guilt that the bank officers were willing to believe that the crime was chargeable to him. Suspicions were awakened a week ago that something was wrong in the bank's accounts. Investigation brought to light the fact that over $70,000 in bonds and stock held as collateral were missing. There was ample testimony that Cornwall was the thief. Confronted with the evidence against him he made a clean breast of everything, and admitted that the entire $70,000 had been stolen by himself. He said he had no confederates, that he had been tempted, had unluckily given way, and was very, very sorry.

Cornwall had been in the employ of the Fourth National Bank over 11 years. His duty was to take charge of call loans and to assist the Cashier. When a customer asked a loan from the bank collateral security was passed upon by the Cashier. That officer accepting such securities would transfer them to Cornwall, whose duty it was to carefully examine them, see that they were as represented, and then file them away. His work was purely mechanical. His salary was less than $2,000 a year. Having filed the security his duty was to produce it on demand, and on no occasion was he ever unable to do this when called upon. The collateral was always forthcoming. Everything pointed to the clerk's thorough honesty. Recently, however, he suffered much from a chronic ailment, and for the past few weeks was obliged to remain away from the bank on several occasions. His home is in Plainfield, N. J. Last Friday was one of the days of his absence, and a message from Plainfield notified the bank officers that he would probably be detained out of town for the remainder of the week on account of sickness. Mr. Anthony Lane, the Cashier, undertook to personally attend to the sick man's work. He was not satisfied with the condition of things as he found them. A customer who wanted to square accounts called for $16,000 in bonds on deposit as collateral. Another customer wanted $5,000 in stock, which had been similarly placed. Cashier Lane was unable to find the whereabouts of either package. Singularly enough President Calhoun and his colleagues in the management of the bank instituted on this day an examination into the accounts of the Loan Clerk. Investigations in the Fourth National are made irregularly, made when least expected. There can be no preparation for them by the employes. The examination into Cornwall's accounts went along rapidly, and before the bank's closing hour on Friday it was established beyond question that the aged clerk had embezzled large sums. Cashier Lane went to Plainfield. Cornwall made a full confession. He said his thefts amounted to $70,000, and explained that he had been speculating in Wall-street. He was unable to make any proposition of compromise. Every dollar's worth of his property had been lost in the stock market. He seemed to be overcome by grief, and lay upon his bed throughout the interview, apparently exhausted.

Careful comparison of the securities in the bank's safes with the list of collateral charged against the bank bore out Cornwall's statement that $70,000 was about the amount stolen. The excess, so far as it could be discovered, was very slight. Cornwall's speculations in Wall-street were all with one house. Abstracting the securities from the bank, he carried them to this firm and placed them against margins on heavy orders. He was an enthusiastic bull. His orders were based upon the belief in the predictions which the Gould following so industriously circulated to the effect that prices were at their lowest and a heavy rise was certain. Unfortunately, Cornwall was mistaken. He uniformly found himself on the wrong side of the market. His $70,000 margins were soon completely wiped out, and he found himself penniless, with the certain detection of his crime staring him in the face. It was under this load that he sent word to the bank last Friday that illness would keep him from duty. His thefts were all of recent date, and all his losses in Wall-street are believed to have occurred within the past few months, while the market was completely under the control of the bears. The bank officers visited the brokers through whom Cornwall speculated and secured the return of all the stolen bonds and stock which had been put up on margins. They paid $70,000 in cash for the recovery.

Before connecting himself with the Fourth National Bank, R. H. Cornwall was a broker, and the greater part of his life was spent in Wall-street. For a time he was a member of the firm of George S. Robins & Son, paper dealers. As a broker he was connected with several of the first houses of the Street, and probably no man had a wider acquaintance among the influential operators. In his best days he was very rich, and his name was among the strongest among the brokers who built up and maintained the old Open Board. But over-enthusiasm worked his ruin in the stock market. He risked his all and lost. His failure occurred in 1870, and the clerical position in the bank at a small salary he gladly accepted as giving him an opportunity to insure self-support. At the time of his failure he was in business alone. His office was on Pine-street, near Nassau. Cornwall's personal appearance is not impressive. He is low in stature, and of frail physique. Always of a retiring disposition, he had few confidants. He was prominent in Methodist circles, of which church he has been for many years a member. His habits are said to have been irreproachable. He was not extravagant.

The Directors of the bank held a formal meeting to consider the embezzlement, and notification of Cornwall's crime was sent to the Controller of the Currency. As yet that officer has taken no action looking to the offender's arrest, though the delay is supposed to be because of Cornwall's sickness. If the arrest is not made soon, however, the Fourth National will institute proceedings. Vice-President Baldwin, asserting that the bank could readily stand the loss which it has suffered, supplied the following official statement of its financial condition at the beginning of the present year.

ASSETS.

Demand loans		$7,610,675 31
Bills discounted		8,598,148 83
Bonds deposited with Controller of Currency to secure circulation:		
United States 4 per cent. bonds	$400,000 00	
United States new 5s, 1881, (extended)	500,000 00—	900,000 00
Other stocks and bonds		103,291 38
Real estate		657,392 50
Cash:		
Specie	$4,348,482 00	
Legal-tender notes	493,933 00	
National currency	16,293 03—	4,858,708 03
Premiums paid		21,125 00
Interest due and uncollected		8,000 00
Total		$22,757,841 05

LIABILITIES.

Capital stock	$3,200,000 00
Deposits, (net)	17,524,679 41
Circulation	810,000 00
Dividends unpaid	147,824 22
Suspense account	18,515 17
Surplus and profits	1,161,822 25
Total	$22,757,841 05

Mr. Cornwall's house, in Plainfield, is a handsome frame structure, and is comfortably but plainly furnished. When a TIMES reporter rang the bell last evening the door was opened by a young girl, who said that Mr. Cornwall was at home. The reporter was shown into a sitting-room where a young man sat at a table. He said his father was the Loan Clerk of the Fourth National Bank, and was ill. He had been confined to his home for several weeks, suffering from inflammation of the bladder, and could not receive his most intimate friends. The reporter then explained the object of his visit and showed a memorandum which set forth that R. H. Cornwall, the Loan Clerk of the Fourth National Bank of New-York, had been detected as the embezzler of $70,000 of securities belonging to the bank. The young man closely scrutinized the paper and said he knew nothing about the matter. "Is this the first intimation you have had of the affair?" asked the reporter, and the young man, without seeming at all disturbed, replied: "This is the first time I have heard of any such thing in connection with my father and the bank." Then, after a pause, he added: "You cannot, of course, see my father, as he is very ill, but perhaps my brother George can tell you something about it. In a few moments George Cornwall, the brother referred to, entered the room. He carefully read the memorandum, and without betraying any excitement whatever, said, "I know absolutely nothing about it. This is news to me. My father is so ill that you cannot see him. I am sure there must be some mistake." He did not desire to disturb his father by asking him anything about the embezzlement, and as the reporter was about to depart from the house said, "I guess you will find that that report is a false one. It must be false."

There were no evidences of lavish expenditure of money in or around Mr. Cornwall's residence, and inquiry among the neighbors and among the business people elicited the information that the Cornwalls were looked upon as quiet, well-to-do persons, who had few intimate acquaintances. In fact, in the public places, where gossip about citizens generally is usually to be obtained without much difficulty, the Cornwalls were scarcely known at all.

FEATURES OF CHICAGO MARKETS.

CHICAGO, March 9.—There was a great deal of activity and irregularity in the produce markets to-day. Wheat was stronger, with a further widening of the difference between prices for April and May. There was some reason to think that the screws were tightened for next month, possibly in retaliation for the close call down to 1½, which had been resorted to by some of the shorts, and they retorted to-day by asking to have a price named for a basis to which to margin the property. At the Directors' meeting in the afternoon this request called out strong remarks from persons interested. The Directors agreed on 1.22. That will not hurt anybody. Corn was firmer in sympathy, but corn and oats were helped by news of an extensive snow-storm in Iowa. Provisions were described as "mushy" in the first part of the day, but they stiffened later in sympathy with grain. About 12:30 o'clock it was rumored that finances were much disturbed in London by the report that Russia had declined to explain Skobeleff's speech, though requested by Germany to do so. This caused a shaking up here, chiefly in wheat and corn. Our receipts were small, and that, with wet weather, was favorable to higher prices, though Liverpool and London reported a decline in wheat. Some persons who sold short on April wheat and bought for May are heavily taxed for the margins, which have been called freely on both deals.

P. P. Oldershaw, of this city, has made a formal demand on the New-York *Herald* for the name of the man who vilified our Board of Trade in that paper of Feb. 25. Mr. Oldershaw's name was taken in vain in that article, and he, therefore, thinks he has the right to know who made the charges of wholesale corruption here. An exporter stated to-day that the talk about one firm in Liverpool controlling the importations of cheese is simply absurd. He says if there is any one branch of trade more openly and closely competitive than are others it is the cheese trade. Instead of one, there are some fifty houses in the business. It is worthy of note that recently the Eastern markets have been looking to Chicago for their supply of salt mackerel. Early last Fall, anticipating the sharp advance which took place a little further along, Chicago dealers stocked up heavily. Consequently they have been in a position to undersell the Eastern trade. Evidence of this is furnished by the fact that for several weeks Cincinnati, New-York, Boston, and Providence have been drawing supplies from this point. We have shipped cheese to "the Western reserve," teas to New-York, grain, provisions, live stock and dairy products to all parts of the universe, but this, it is believed, is the first instance in which we have sent salt water fish to the sea-board. Scotland has evidently opened wide its potato bins. It is reported that contracts have been made for 80,000 bushels of this commodity, grown on Scottish soil, to be sold in this market. The price of home grown and Canadian consequently perceptibly weakened.

VIRGINIA OYSTER WARS.

FORTRESS MONROE, Virginia, March 9.—Another oyster war seems imminent, and a call to arms from the Governor of Virginia is almost hourly expected. Persons who to-day arrived here from Richmond and Lancaster Counties report that large fleets of alien oyster vessels are depredating upon the oyster-beds of the Rappahannock and other streams in that part of the State in defiance of the laws and the announcements of Gov. Cameron. A few weeks ago the Governor, at the head of an improvised naval expedition, pounced down upon these freebooters, capturing seven vessels and 61 prisoners. The former are now lying at the wharf at Mathews Court-house and the latter are behind the bars of the jail at the same place. The fate of these men, however, has not prevented others from similar offenses. These last marauders are said to be even bolder and more determined than those who were forced to succumb to Virginia's navy. It is said that, if interfered with by the inhabitants of the counties along the rivers upon which they are depredating, they threaten to kill all who approach them. The Whitworth guns sent to Mathews County were mounted upon the bank of the Rappahannock River, and are manned by the citizens of the county. The marauders, however, carry on their depredations beyond the range of these guns.

An appeal will at once be made to the Governor for such a military force as will either capture or drive off the tresspassers. A fund has been raised, it is said, by the oystermen of several of the large cities to defend those now in custody. Some of the ablest members of the Virginia Bar have been employed, and every effort will be made to secure the acquittal of the oystermen. The Executive has been asked to employ additional counsel to assist the State's Attorney in prosecuting them. It has been rumored that an attempt was to be made by the oyster thieves to release their friends now in jail. A strong guard is on duty there armed with muskets and supplied with an abundance of ammunition, besides having three Whitworth guns mounted on the banks of the river. The Governor will no doubt fit out another expedition and pounce down upon the freebooters before they can get beyond his jurisdiction. He is fully determined that the laws shall be enforced, even if blood has to be freely spilt in the efforts. As soon as the Legislature reassembles after the recess, the question of organizing a State navy will be agitated, and a proposition will be made to keep one or two fully equipped and armed revenue cutters on Chesapeake Bay and its tributaries to protect the oyster interests.

CONNECTICUT INSURANCE LAWS.

HARTFORD, Conn., March 9.—The Insurance Committee has been considering for some time the application of the Mutual Benefit Insurance Company of this city to be permitted to do an accident insurance business. The company is the one recently excluded from New-York for not complying with the laws. The committee has reported a bill in favor of allowing any life insurance company of this State to do an accident business. Probably no action which the committee may take will surprise the Legislature.

STATE LEGISLATIVE WORK.

THE APPROPRIATION BILL IN THE ASSEMBLY.

A LONG DISCUSSION ON THE APPROPRIATION FOR THE NATIONAL GUARD—MR. BROOKS ANSWERING CRITICISMS—A BILL TAXING BROKERS' SALES—MEASURES AFFECTING THE CITY.

ALBANY, March 9.—The Appropriation bill came up in Committee of the Whole to-day, was finally reported without amendment, and by the House ordered to a third reading. Much debate occurred over the Militia appropriation and the reasons for an increase of certain other items, and the members were kept in good nature by the sharp thrusts and retorts in which Messrs. Brooks, Benedict, Browne, Parker, and Roosevelt participated. Mr. Brooks, Chairman of the Ways and Means Committee, championed the bill and successfully defended it against all criticisms.

Mr. Benedict, of Ulster, was one of the first of this captious class to take the floor. He moved that the appropriation of $300,000 for the National Guard be reduced to $225,000. The sum, he said, was the same that was appropriated when the National Guard numbered upward of 20,000. During the past year the number had been reduced by mustering out of service more than 8,000 men. He failed to see where the economy was in appropriating for 12,495 men a sum that had been amply sufficient for upward of 20,000. Mr. Benedict referred sarcastically to the annual encampment which the Adjutant-General favored, as a means of bringing the Guard to a greater state of efficiency. This system of camp duty, claimed Mr. Benedict, would drive out of the ranks of the National Guard the best men who make citizen soldiers. The farmer, the citizen, the merchant could not leave his business to participate in an encampment. Mr. Brooks replied that it was quite possible for 12,495 men who were well drilled, well disciplined, and well equipped to be of far greater value to the State than 20,000 men who could boast of no such conditions. What the present Adjutant-General urged was urged in conformity to the wishes of the Governor, the Commander-in-Chief of the National Guard. It was not a wise thing to cripple the efficiency of the National Guard. The City of New-York still retained a remembrance of the past when millions of property were saved through the instrumentality of the National Guard.

Major Parker, of Albany, regretted that Mr. Benedict should have shown so much animus on this question, and particularly upon that portion of it relating to the disbandment of members of the Militia. He regretted very much the disbandment of the particular troop which had its head-quarters at Ellenville, Ulster County, and of which Mr. Benedict had had the honor of being a First Orderly Sergeant. Major Parker favored the appropriation as it stood, and so did Mr. Roosevelt, of New-York. The latter gentleman said that it was very unfair to cripple a scheme for placing the National Guard on a better basis by reducing the amount of appropriation necessary to carry out that scheme. Mr. Benedict's motion was put to a vote, and was lost by a vote of nearly two to one.

Mr. Browne, the young thorn of Otsego, desired some light on certain items. Why was there an increase of $2,000 in the expenses of the Executive Department, and why were the items of furniture for a number of the other departments inserted? Why had $10,000 been added to the item of printing? Why had there been an increase in sundry other items, all of which, by the way, were of such trifling importance that the laughter of the members was excited when Mr. Browne referred to them? Mr. Brooks calmly explained to his young friend why all this had been done. For the Executive Department $1,000 of the $2,000 increase was to meet a deficiency caused by offering rewards for fugitives from justice, and $600 was for the library. The printing item was increased because members (and here he looked severely at Mr. Browne) of the Legislature had by their votes authorized the printing of extra matter not called for in the contracts and of books for gratuitous distribution among the friends of members. The increase of $2,500 in the Attorney-General's office was to provide for a clerk. The amount would be saved to the stockholders in insurance companies and to the people 20 times over. Of all the cants in the world, said Mr. Brooks, quoting an author, the cant of criticism was the most tormenting. [Laughter.]

Mr. Brown was pricked by the quotation, and some amusing remarks followed between the two gentlemen. "I'm extremely sorry," interrupted ex-Gov. Alvord, "to see the minority in the House slowly breaking to pieces." The allusion to this exhibition of feeling between the Richmond and Otsego Democrats provoked a laugh. "And I," replied Mr. Brooks, turning the laugh upon the ex-Governor, "was just as sorry a year ago when I saw the majority breaking to pieces. On the theory that misery loves company, the member from Onondaga should be only too pleased to find himself in this company." Mr. Brooks concluded his defense of the appropriation bill by calling attention to the reductions which had been made in a number of items. The expenses of the Capitol had been cut down from $50,000 to $40,000, the useless office of Examiner of Weights and Measures had been abolished, and $5,000 had been cut out of the appropriation for the State Board of Health, of which he was himself a member. This concluded the long discussion, and the bill was given to the House in its entirety.

Several bills were ordered by the Assembly to a third reading. Among them was Mr. Monk's, abolishing the office of Deputy Commissioner in the city of Brooklyn. If the bill ever becomes a law, Mr. Whiting, Deputy Commissioner of Public Works, and the only office-holder of his kind, will be legislated out of office. The bill of Mr. Morrison, of New-York, incorporating the veterans of the Seventh Regiment and authorizing them to hold real or personal estate, was another measure which was thus progressed. A third was the bill of Mr. Raines, of Ontario, affording more protection to insured persons by requiring every policy of life or accident insurance to be indorsed with the application of the insured in full.

A bill by Major Haggerty, of New-York, provides a revenue for the State by a special tax on sales by brokers. By its terms "all brokers dealing in securities, corporate stocks, crude and refined petroleum, cotton, pork, grain, and flour shall pay to the State a tax on all sales thereof made by them at the rate of 2 cents on each $100 of the selling value of the securities, stocks, merchandise, and commodities sold. Such sales, on and after the 1st day of July next, shall be reported, and such tax be paid by the brokers making such sales monthly after the said 1st day of July to the State Controller. The said brokers shall, before making any sales referred to herein, pay to the Controller an annual license fee of $25, and shall pay a fine of $100 for each year in which he shall fail to pay such license fee. The taxes, license fees, and penalties prescribed by this act may be sued for by the Attorney-General, at the request of the Controller, in any court of record in this State." Section 2 authorizes the Controller from time to time, by a notice for 30 days published in the State papers authorizing the said reports to be made and the tax and license fee to be paid to the Commissioner of State revenue in any collection district designated in the notice. The Commissioner shall receive a reasonable percentage for this labor. Every broker upon whose sales a tax is hereby imposed shall keep a broker's book, in which he shall enter all contracts of and for sales made by him on the day on which the same is made, with the names of the parties, the day of sale, the subject and the price and amount of such sales. The Controller and any agent he may designate in writing shall have access at all reasonable times to and shall be permitted to inspect the contents of such books to ascertain the sales on which such tax is imposed. A failure to comply with this particular provision subjects the delinquent broker to a fine of $1,000 for each month during which, or any part of which, the failure shall occur. Making false returns renders the offender liable to a fine of not more than $5,000 and to indictment and punishment for a misdemeanor. The information obtained from these brokers' books is to be regarded as confidential, and to be used only for the purposes of this act. The taxes thus paid into the State Treasury are to be held for the general fund, and the payment in every fiscal year of the expenses, claims, and demands which shall be a lawful charge upon that fund while such taxes shall continue to be laid.

A bill by Mr. Van Allen, of New-York, changes the title of Inspector of Buildings to Superintendent of Buildings, gives him a deputy, and the Bureau of Inspection of Buildings such additional inspectors, clerks, and messengers as the Fire Commissioners may deem necessary, their action, however, to be subject to revision by the Board of Estimate and Apportionment. The appropriation, however, shall not exceed the sum now applied to the expenses of the Inspection Bureau. The Board of Estimate and Apportionment is furthermore directed, upon requisition of the Fire Commissioners, to appropriate a sufficient amount for the bureau's expenses for the remainder of the year.

Two bills by Mr. Shanley, of Kings, increases the salaries of members of the rank and file of the Police and Fire Departments of the City of Brooklyn from 20 to 25 per cent., and of the officers from 12 to 15 per cent. The proposed salaries are as follows: In the Police Department—Superintendent, $4,000; Inspector, $2,500; Drill Captain, $1,800; Captains, $2,000; Sergeants, $1,500; roundsmen, $1,300; detectives of five years of service, $1,500; other detectives, $1,200; patrolmen, $1,200; surgeons, $1,250. In the Fire Department—Chief, $4,000; Assistant Chief, $2,500; district engineers, $1,800; foremen, $1,300; ordinary engineers, $1,200; privates and firemen, $1,200.

A bill by Mr. Welch, of Niagara, incorporates the Niagara Falls Double Track Iron Bridge Company with power to throw a bridge for foot passengers and teams across the Niagara River between the Falls and the village of Suspension Bridge. The capital of the company is fixed at $100,000, and the privilege of increasing it another $150,000 is given. Mr. Catlin, of Westchester, presented a bill by request which gives those pilots whose services are declined by vessels of upward of 100 tons passing

The New-York Times.

VOL. XXXII.......NO. 9896. NEW-YORK, FRIDAY, MAY 25, 1883. PRICE FOUR CENTS.

AFFAIRS IN FOREIGN LANDS

THE BRITISH GOVERNMENT AND THE POPE'S CIRCULAR.

NO REQUEST MADE FOR ACTION BY THE VATICAN — IRISH DENUNCIATIONS OF THE CIRCULAR.

LONDON, May 24.—In the House of Commons to-day Lord Edmund Fitzmaurice, Under Foreign Secretary, replying to a question, said he had already stated, on March 19, that the Government had never entertained a scheme to establish a British Resident at the Vatican, and Mr. Errington had not since been a channel of communication between the Foreign Office and the Vatican. Mr. Errington had received no appointment from the Government, and, therefore, no pay. The Pope's circular to the Irish clergy had not been issued at the request of the British Government. Mr. Gladstone, replying to Mr. Charles Newdegate, Conservative, said that Earl Granville's letter of last year recommending Mr. Errington as a gentleman of honor and intelligence would remain in force so long as Mr. Errington answered that description. Sir Henry Wolff, Conservative, commented on what he termed the unsatisfactory answers of the Government.

Mr. Trevelyan refused in the interests of justice to answer a question in regard to the seizure of the *Kerry Sentinel*. Mr. Trevelyan, replying to Mr. Joseph Cowen, Radical, declared that Messrs. Davitt, Healy, and Quinn could obtain their release at any moment by complying with the law. The Judge who sentenced them, however, would be consulted as to the desirability of shortening their term of imprisonment.

A meeting of the Parnellite members of Parliament was held last night. Mr. Justin McCarthy, member of Parliament for Longford, who acted as Chairman, said it was the duty of Irishmen to contribute to the testimonial for Mr. Parnell. Referring to the Papal circular he said the Irish people had only to repudiate the fraudulent statements which had been made to the College of Cardinals. He should regret to see the priest divorced from Irish politics, for in times past he had been the only friend of the people. Mr. Biggar, member of Parliament for Cavan, spoke in condemnation of the circular.

LIMERICK, May 34.—The inhabitants of this city and county are preparing to give a hearty welcome to Archbishop Croke, who arrived in Ireland yesterday after his visit to Rome. The hills and villages of the county will be illuminated to-night in his honor.

DUBLIN, May 24.—Archbishop Croke, replying to an address of welcome at the Wicklow station, said it was the Pope's love for the Irish people that caused him to be so solicitous for their welfare. He was confident that when the Pope understood the situation better the efforts of the priesthood for the Irish would be crowned with success. Time would prove the correctness of his representations to the Pope. Meanwhile he urged the people to submit to the Vatican.

CORK, May 24.—The police to-day seized two suspicious-looking boxes which had just arrived from America.

THURLES, May 24.—Archbishop Croke, preaching from his pulpit in the cathedral to-day, said that the Pope had expressed sorrow that Ireland was troubled owing to the lawless views of a certain class and to secret societies. Archbishop Croke exhorted the people not to allow a word of condemnation to escape their lips against the Pope, who, he said, was their best friend. When the Archbishop was in Rome the Pope in addressing him said: "I am as good an Irishman as you are." The Archbishop expressed his intention of obeying the Pope's commands.

PROCLAMATION BY THE CZAR.

HE ANNOUNCES THAT HIS CORONATION WILL TAKE PLACE ON SUNDAY.

MOSCOW, May 24.—An imperial proclamation has been issued formally announcing that the coronation of the Czar will take place on Sunday, the 27th inst. The proclamation was made this morning by heralds-at-arms attended by several dignitaries from the circular platform before the Kremlin, which was used in ancient times for the promulgation of ukases and also for executions. The foreign Ambassadors who had been formally apprised of the time the proclamation would be issued were present attended by a large escort. After bugle blasts from the heralds the Secretary of the Senate read the proclamation, which was as follows:

> Our most august, high, and puissant sovereign, the Emperor Alexander, having ascended the hereditary throne of the Empire of all the Russias, the Kingdom of Poland, and the Grand Duchy of Finland, which are inseparable from it, has deigned, following the example of his predecessors and their glorious ancestors, to command that the holy solemnity of the coronation and anointment, in which the Empress will participate, shall, with the help of Almighty God, be performed on the 27th day of May. The solemn act is announced to all his majesty's faithful subjects in order that on the joyful day their most fervent prayers may be offered to the King of Kings, and that they may beseech the Almighty to send grace and blessing upon his Majesty's reign for the maintenance of peace and tranquillity, to the greater glory of His holy name and the constant prosperity of the empire.

The Emperor and Empress will only break their seclusion until Sunday to receive visits of foreign Princes. It had been decided not to hold a great diplomatic reception, but as the Emperor and Empress intimated their willingness to attend one reception, Gen. Schweinitz, the German Ambassador, as doyer of the diplomatic corps, will give a grand banquet and ball in their honor.

The banquet on Sunday will be a magnificent affair. On the Emperor's signal a Minister will present the guests with medals commemorating the coronation. The following is a list of the toasts: "His Majesty the Emperor," to be followed by a salvo of 61 guns; "Her Majesty the Empress," followed by 51 guns; "The Imperial Family," followed by 31 guns, and "The Clergy and all Faithful Subjects," followed by 21 guns.

BERLIN, May 24.—The *Provincial Correspondence* says: "The Czar has initiated and upheld a policy which has made it possible to settle all pending questions amicably. Germany joins with other countries in wishing for the welfare of Russia. She is convinced that the schemes of the Nihilists were directed against the peace of Europe, and that in preventing their accomplishment Russia rendered good service to civilization. The coronation is a festivity of peace."

CURRENT FOREIGN TOPICS.

GOTHENBURG, May 24.—The arctic exploring vessel Sophia, with Prof. Nordenskjold and other scientists on board, has sailed for Greenland.

VIENNA, May 24.—Lieut. Schlayer and the editor of a military journal fought a duel to-day with pistols. Lieut. Schlayer was killed.

PARIS, May 24.—Intelligence from Senegal is to the effect that a French column under Col. Desbordes has succeeded in driving the hostile natives back 60 kilomètres and that tranquillity has been established on the left bank of the Niger.

The Senate has adopted the report of the Committee on the Tonquin Credit bill, which points out that all hope of arriving at an understanding with China is not lost.

CHESTER, May 24.—Mr. W. H. Vanderbilt, accompanied by his son, arrived here to-day, and visited Eaton Hall, the seat of the Duke of Westminster.

BERLIN, May 24.—It is announced that Prince Bismarck will visit the Emperor William during the latter's stay at Gastein, and that if the Emperor Francis Joseph goes to Gastein Count Kalnoky, the Austrian Minister of Foreign Affairs, will accompany him. It is rumored that King Humbert and Signor Mancini, the Italian Foreign Minister, may also visit Gastein. Prince Bismarck has decided that if his health does not improve he will go to Kissingen at the end of June for a month, and will afterward proceed to Gastein.

LONDON, May 24.—A second meeting of influential ship-owners in favor of the construction of another canal across the Isthmus of Suez was held to-day. The meeting raised £20,000 for preliminary expenses, and resolved to inform the Government of the project.

In the opening cruise of the Northern Yacht Club, which took place to-day, the new cutter Marjorie, which was built by the owner of the Madge to compete with American yachts, reached the home anchorage four minutes ahead of the other boats although she made a late start.

Advices have been received from Mozambique that Makalolo and other chiefs on the Schiree River have declared war against Portugal.

In the House of Commons to-day, in reply to a question from Sir Henry Wolff, Lord Edmund Fitzmaurice said that Earl Granville was in communication with the authorities at Washington concerning the closing of American schools in Bulgaria. The Under Foreign Secretary, replying to a question from Mr. Charles Monk, member for the city of Gloucester, said that negotiations looking to a renewal of diplomatic relations between the British Government and Mexico were in an advanced state. He hoped that he would soon be able to make a fuller statement.

LONDON, May 25.—Herr Banks, Vice-President of the Hamburg Progressists, has committed suicide.

HOSTILITIES IN MADAGASCAR.

THE FRENCH OCCUPY SEVERAL PLACES AFTER HARD FIGHTING.

PARIS, May 24.—Advices have been received from Madagascar that a French detachment landed and carried several military posts which had been erected by the Hovas on Sakalava territory in defiance of French rights. It is stated that Admiral Pierre has bombarded Majunga and occupied the Custom-house there, thus securing the road and water-way leading to Tananrino, the capital of the island. The engagement lasted six hours. The Hovas suffered great loss.

It is semi-officially stated that the object of the French expedition to Madagascar is to obtain the payment of the sums due the French Government from Madagascar by holding the Custom-houses there as security for the amount. If the Hovas continue to resist, France will impose a treaty, placing French subjects in Madagascar on the same footing with English subjects.

LONDON, May 25.—The landing of the French in Madagascar has surprised the Malagasy Embassy, who state that the natives will fight the French to the death. Some of the members of the embassy will hasten home to assist in the defense of their country. Many rifles newly purchased are on their way to Madagascar, and are now nearly due. The Queen of Madagascar will issue a war loan. It is hoped that Americans and English will assist with money and arms.

OBJECTIONS TO JUDGE HOADLY.

CINCINNATI, May 24.—Representative Kahto, a leading Toledo Democrat, is in this city. He declares that Geddes is the coming Democratic nominee for Governor, and adds: "I tell you, Hoadly won't do. People in the country don't like the idea of a candidate who is the friend and attorney of liquor-dealers. Nor do the old Democrats like a man who has been a Republican or has voted against Bill Allen. Besides, a Toledo Democratic Catholic priest told me that it would not do to nominate Hoadly, as he was the attorney against the church property in the famous Archbishop Purcell case. He said the Catholics would vote against him for that, but Geddes would carry everything."

THE KENTUCKY REPUBLICANS.

LEXINGTON, Ky., May 24.—In the Republican Convention last night on the sixth ballot Thomas J. Morrow received the nomination for Governor by the following vote: Morrow, 539; Goodloe, 350. The nomination was made unanimous. The convention concluded its session to-day after nominating Gen. S. S. Fry, of Danville, for Lieutenant-Governor; Lewis C. Garrigus, an ex-Confederate, of Russelville, for Attorney-General; Leroy R. Hawthorne, of Newport, for Auditor; Mr. Flourney, of Paducah, for Treasurer; J. B. Pinkerton, of Grayson, for Superintendent of Public Instruction, and J. W. Asbury, (colored,) of Cynthiana, for Register of the Land Office.

ELECTIONS IN VIRGINIA.

ALEXANDRIA, Va., May 24.—The municipal election here to-day resulted in a victory for the Democrats. The exact vote will not be officially ascertained until a late hour, but the election of a Democratic Mayor and Council is assured. The Readjuster vote was very small.

RICHMOND, Va., May 24.—County elections were held throughout the State to-day. In many of the counties the contest between the Readjusters and Democrats was quite spirited, but the returns to-night do not furnish sufficient data upon which to base calculations as to the losses or gains on either side.

LYNCHBURG, Va., May 24.—The Democrats carried this city to-day, electing two-thirds of the Council and Aldermen.

AMASA STONE'S FUNERAL.

CLEVELAND, May 24.—The funeral services proper of the late Amasa Stone were held this afternoon at 3 o'clock at Lake View Cemetery. Col. John Hay and wife and other relatives were present. The body of Mr. Stone's son, Adelbert, was removed from Woodland Cemetery and interred with those of his father. The Rev. Arthur Mitchel conducted the ceremonies, and the Adelbert College Glee Club furnished music. Twelve of Mr. Stone's business associates and friends acted as pall-bearers. It was expected that the late millionaire's will would be opened immediately after the funeral, but owing to the depressed condition of Mrs. Stone, the reading was postponed. It is understood that Col. John Hay and Samuel Mather are mentioned as Executors of the estate.

AN ARKANSAS JUDGE SHOT.

NEW-ORLEANS, May 24.—A special to the *Times-Democrat* from Helena, Ark., says: "Immediately after the Circuit Court had adjourned for dinner to-day, and while its Judge, M. F. Saunders, was in the court-room looking up some authorities in cases which were pending before him, Dr. E. D. Moore approached him in regard to some matter in which Phillips County was indebted to him [Dr. Moore] for services rendered while Saunders was County Judge. Judge Saunders refused to listen to Moore, who became incensed and struck at the Judge and then fired twice at him, the second shot taking effect in his left hand. Both gentlemen are highly respected and the occurrence is deeply deplored by every citizen. Moore was arrested."

CIVIL SERVICE REFORM WORK.

ALBANY, May 24.—Civil Service Commissioner J. M. Gregory and Joseph H. Blackfan, Superintendent of the Foreign Mail Department, to-day established a local board of examiners, Albany being one of the 23 Post Offices to which the new civil service reform regulations apply. After a thorough examination of the Post Office, the Commissioner appointed as examiners Charles H. Zeilman, Superintendent of the Stamp Department; Joseph D. Craig, chief clerk to the Postmaster, and A. O. Sanford, Superintendent of the Mails. The first examination will be held about July 1. Dr. Gregory went to Saratoga this evening to spend a few days, after which he will return to Washington.

BOAT, BICYCLE, AND RUNNING RACE.

NEW-HAVEN, May 24.—An extraordinary race took place to-day from Birmingham to Milford Harbor. It was witnessed by about 1,000 people. The course was the Housatonic River and the direct road overland. Shell-boats were used on the river and bicyclists and pedestrians contested on land. The distance by water was 14 miles and by land 12 miles. The race was won by Terrence S. Allis on a bicycle in 1:38:30. Robert Swift sailed by the river in 1:53:30, and Charles Nettleton ran the distance in 1:57:30.

RECENT LOSSES ON THE LAKES.

CHICAGO, May 24.—Estimates of the loss from the storm of last Sunday and Monday foot up a little over $200,000 of property in ships and cargoes. Eighteen lives were lost and 15 vessels destroyed or damaged.

GRANT IN CHICAGO.

CHICAGO, May 24.—Gen. U. S. Grant arrived in the city this morning and left to-night for Galena.

GENERAL TELEGRAPH NEWS

IRON-WORKERS' TROUBLES.

A GENERAL STRIKE THROUGHOUT THE COUNTRY ORDERED FOR JUNE 1.

MILWAUKEE, May 24.—At a secret meeting of the employes of the immense rolling mills at Bayview, held last night, it was announced that a general strike of the iron-workers of the country would take place June 1, owing to a determination on the part of manufacturers to enforce a reduction all around of 20 per cent in wages. Between 4,000 and 5,000 men are constantly employed at Bayview by the North Chicago Rolling Mill Company, and the strike will prove a serious blow to the village. Many families are already preparing to leave the place, as the mill men are determined to shut down as soon as the strike takes place, which means a season of idleness of least six months at the very least, even if an agreement is reached at any time in the near future.

After the close of the mills the idea prevails in Bayview that the strike will be general and will extend from one end of the country to the other. The news of the determination of the large body of laborers to go out on a strike created great excitement to-day. Many of the men express the opinion rather freely that they would rather work for the reduced wages than to strike, but that the orders from the Amalgamated Iron and Steel Works Association are that no reductions must be acceded to, and that all work must cease as soon as the orders making the reduction are promulgated.

PITTSBURG, May 24.—Secretary Weeks, of the Western Iron Association, this evening received a telegram from an iron manufacturer in Chicago whose name he declines to give, stating that an arrangement had been made with the workmen under the terms of which work will be continued after June 1 on a conditional scale. The manufacturers regard this as conclusive evidence that all the mills outside of Pittsburg, Wheeling, and the Chenango and Mahoning Valleys will continue to work on conditional scales or resume on those terms after a few weeks as they did last year, and thus confine the strike to what was the final battle-ground at that time. Every mill that is able to resume work conditionally, it is claimed, weakens the Amalgamated Association, for its rules provide that after June 1 no work shall be done unless a scale is signed. This was the only change in the situation reported to-day. Numerous reports of contemplated compromises and other movements were circulated, but all have been authoritatively denied.

FALL RIVER, Mass., May 24.—Not long ago notice was posted in the iron works here that a reduction of 25 cents a ton would be made in the pay of puddlers and helpers, to go into effect to-day. A meeting of the men was held and it was decided to oppose the reduction. This morning the men assembled at the works, but refused to work unless the notice was withdrawn. This was not done; consequently, the workmen are now on strike. They claim that the rate of wages is now low enough, and that to yield would show a too submissive spirit on their part and pave the way for a future reduction.

A CLEVER EXPRESS ROBBERY.

TWO BAGS CONTAINING MONEY PACKAGES STOLEN AT CLEVELAND.

CLEVELAND, May 24.—The coolest and most adroit express robbery that has occurred for a long time in this part of the country was perpetrated to-day at the Union Railway Station. Alexander Granger, who has for several years had the delivering of money packages here, in order to expedite his work, has been in the habit of driving to the station in his own wagon to meet the 6 o'clock Lake Shore train from the West instead of waiting to take packages up in the safe of the big express wagon. This morning he was on hand as usual, and was handed two bags by the train-master. One had been made up in Chicago and the other contained the collections along the route. Granger's wagon stood at the easterly entrance of the station, in its accustomed place, two other express wagons standing near by, their drivers being in the station. The messenger carried his sacks to the wagon, threw them in, and was about to follow, when a man standing behind the iron grate window of the ice-room, a few feet away, called to him. Granger moved nearer to the window to hear better, when the man said: "What time does Hodge [a clerk in the express office] get down to his work?" "About 7 o'clock," said the messenger. "Well, tell him I will be up about 8:30," said the man, and then moved away. Granger went back to his wagon, saw that both sacks were there, and drove to the office. When the sacks came into the hands of the proper clerk he saw that the seals were not stamped. On investigation he discovered that both sacks contained small parcels of brown paper done up in the form of money packages. The theory of the police and express officials is that while the messenger's attention was called to the window the confederate of the man who hailed him took the sacks from the wagon and replaced them, although it is possible that the transfer was made before the bags came into his possession. The amount cannot be learned at present, as returns must first be had from the various offices along the line. It will run anywhere from $10,000 to $50,000. The Chicago agent has telegraphed that there was no bank money in either sack, as little of such money is coming toward Cleveland just now. In one there were 20 packages sent to the Lake Shore Railroad Company by various local agents. People about the station say that a suspicious-looking man has been seen to follow Granger about for several mornings.

AN INSURANCE COMPANY FAILS.

THE NEW-YORK MUTUAL ACCIDENT COMPANY IN A BAD CONDITION.

UTICA, N. Y., May 24.—The New-York Mutual Accident Insurance Company, with headquarters in this city, was to-day condemned by Superintendent McCall, of the Insurance Department. Application will be made to-morrow for the appointment of Receivers. The company was organized in 1881, with James Miller, then Mayor of Utica, as President; Taliesen Evans, ex-County Clerk, as Secretary, and John Chaler, County Treasurer; City Judge P. F. Bulger, and other prominent Uticans, together with Ira D. Warren, of New-York, and Alvin P. Higgins, of Brooklyn, in the directory. The Directors charge Secretary Evans with loose or fraudulent management, and say it has been impossible to get any statement from him of the company's affairs. On this information Superintendent McCall came to Utica, and for two days has been examining the company's affairs. He reports to Attorney-General Russell that the accounts are in wretched shape, and that the company has been managed in a slovenly and incompetent, if not in a fraudulent, manner. Evans claims that his accounts are all right, and that the failure of the company to meet its liabilities is due entirely to the failure of members to pay their assessments. His statement to the department last December showed total expenses for the year $9,276, of which claims paid amounted to only $2,612. The Superintendent is very severe on Evans and charges him with persistently violating the regulations of the company and with incomprehensible incompetency. Evans claimed a salary of $3,000, and says the company owes him $1,500. Other claims against the company aggregate $4,540, to pay which the treasury holds $6. On the last assessment only $184 was paid. The whole number of policies issued is 1,900.

PHILIP HART STILL MISSING.

TRENTON, N. J., May 24.—A visit to the little house on South Warren-street to-night, where the missing man, Philip Hart, had his store and dwelling, found Mrs. Hart surrounded by sympathizing neighbors. She said she had received a letter by this morning's delivery from one of her husband's sisters in New-York. The parents and relatives of the missing man have viewed every unknown body which has been brought to the Morgue, both in New-York and Brooklyn, during the past five or six days. None have proved to be that of Hart. The missing man wore a dark plaid suit and a derby hat. His wife does not believe she will ever again see him alive. Should nothing be heard of him this week steps will be taken next week to settle up his estate.

A JURY SICK WITH CHOLERA MORBUS.

PHILADELPHIA, May 24.—After a number of witnesses for the defense had been examined to-day in the trial of Lyons for the killing of Chung Wah You, one of the jurors complained to the Judge that nine of them were ill and unable to sit longer in the jury box. A recess was taken until 1 o'clock and a physician sent for. Upon the reassembling of the court Dr. Neff stated that he had attended the distressed jurymen and found that they were suffering from cholera morbus, but would probably be able to go on with the case in the morning. It was said that the jury, who have been locked up since they were sworn in, overfed themselves on veal which was served with their dinner last evening. The court adjourned until to-morrow morning at 10 o'clock.

POPE LEO AND THE IRISH.

CHICAGO, May 24.—One of the ablest Catholic clergymen of this city, the Rev. Father Hayes, of St. Ignatius College, said to-day that no notice of the Pope's letter had been received by any of the Catholic churches here. Father Hayes added: "Not a single Catholic has spoken to me upon the subject. I have not observed the slightest ripple. If there is any disaffection here, it is solely among the dynamite element or those closely allied to it. If the Pope did issue any circular to the Irish clergy, it must have been only to counsel prudence on their part in regard to matters of politics. I doubt the authenticity of anything alleged to have come from the Pope. This is not the time of our annual collection of Peter's pence in this city, but if there was a falling off in the collection at Baltimore, it must have been attributable to local causes and not from any influence of Pope Leo's attitude toward Ireland."

DISPLAY OF RAILWAY APPLIANCES.

OPENING OF THE NATIONAL RAILWAY EXPOSITION—OLD ENGINEERS.

CHICAGO, May 24.—The opening of the National Exposition of Railway Appliances occurred this evening in the presence of 5,000 people. Among those on the platform of the main exposition building were the Hon. E. B. Washburne, Mayor Harrison, Jesse Spalding, O. W. Potter, Edward Bronwaert, the French Consul; J. McGregor Adams, A. G. Darwin, and C. W. Rogers, of New-York, and Horatio Seymour, Jr., of Marquette, Mich. Prof. Swing offered prayer. Mayor Harrison, after welcoming the exhibitors and visitors, said that Chicago owed much of what she is to railroads. This city trusted corporations, not fearing that they would become monopolies. Speaking of the railroads of the world, he said there were 265,000 miles of track, of which 117,000 were in the United States. After presenting further railroad statistics Mayor Harrison introduced Vice-President French, who claimed that Chicago is and for a long time would continue to be the centre of the operative departments of the railroads of the country. He added: "The first object of congregating here this vast area of railway appliances is that those in charge of different departments of railroads may become acquainted with the improved appliances in their own and co-ordinate departments which have been developed just beyond the horizon of their labors, and of which they are more or less ignorant on account of their own individual sphere of work."

The Hon. E. Washburne then delivered the address of the evening: "The purpose of the Exposition," said he, "looking to the improvement in railway appliances and the advancement in railway knowledge, coupled with its benevolent object, must commend itself to all devotees of progress and all lovers of science and invention. When we look around and about us and behold this marvelous and wonderful display we are lost in admiration of the strength of the human understanding and the inventive genius of man. There have been expositions in many countries, and nations have vied with each other in the display of all that ingenuity and taste could suggest or wealth procure, but it is safe to say that the world has never seen a more creditable exposition than this, organized solely by private enterprise, and pushed to what we see before us by private citizens, with a degree of unselfishness and devotion rarely witnessed, and without pecuniary compensation. But they will find their reward in the gratitude of that great public which will appreciate all their labors and responsibilities and all the great services they have rendered to science and to mankind."

The veteran engineers were introduced. Horatio Allen, aged 84, is the man who brought the "Strowbridge Lion" to this country. He spoke briefly, saying that while America had gotten some ideas from England, nearly all the advancement was due to America. Engineer Hollingsworth, of Paterson, N. J., made a short speech. Joseph Whitehead was then presented. He was fireman on the Stockton in 1827 and served on the first locomotive ever run in England. When the wind was strong ahead the Stockton had to halt until the wind went down. The exercises ended with "God Save the Queen" by the orchestra. The great audience was then distributed through the buildings viewing the features of the exhibition. The larger engines attract much attention.

The heaviest, made by Cook, of Paterson, N. J., for the Southern Pacific, weighs 65 tons, and is 60 feet long. It is an 8-wheel driver, and has two sets of everything—cylinders, steam-chests, &c. This is probably the largest engine ever built. The most curious looking one is owned by the Reading Railroad Company. The fire-box and boiler is placed on top of the wheels and the heating surface is almost twice that in the ordinary low motion. This method of construction was adopted in order to burn coal dust which cannot be sold. The Brooks Works, of Dunkirk, N. Y., have seven locomotives on exhibition; the Baldwin Works, of Philadelphia, four; the Pittsburg Locomotive Works, three; the Dickson Manufacturing Company, of Scranton, Penn., one, but two more are on their way; Cook, of Paterson, one; the Rogers Works, of Paterson, one.

In the south corner of the building is the "curiosity shop," where old-style engines, cars, &c., are. It contains the Sampson, built in 1828 by Timothy Hockworth, New-Sheldon, Durham, and which for the last 35 years has been in service in a Nova Scotia coal mine. It has six small dirving wheels, and the boiler is covered with wooden strips. Mr. Davidson, the engineer who took it to Nova Scotia in 1843 and ran it up to last year, has charge of it. Near by is Arabian No. 1, a locomotive designed by Phinos Davis, and put in service on the Baltimore and Ohio Road in 1845. It is a peculiar-looking thing, though it did good work in its day. The opening of the fire-box is in front of the boiler, and the fireman, from his position, could "shoo" the cows from the track or jump off and remove obstructions. Next to this relic is an ancient tender and an old English coach—one of the first built. A few feet distant is a specimen of the early American carriages which ran on the "Tioga Railroad." It is about half the size of the cars now in use. A feature is the exhibit of the National Tube-works Company, just north of the fountain, the central figure being an imitation of an Egyptian obelisk, and the inclosure being surrounded with heavy tubing, surmounted in front by Carter H. Harrison's eagle. The obelisk is 36 feet high and 10 feet in diameter at base, with four large griffins in bas-relief at the corners. It is covered with red turcoman, the front being hung with steam gauges in arabesque patterns, and the other three sides being hung with brass fittings representing various Egyptian figures and hieroglyphs. The electric road will be in operation to-morrow.

THE WEATHER AND THE CROPS.

CINCINNATI, May 24.—The replies to a large number of inquiries addressed to correspondents in Ohio, Indiana, and Kentucky as to the effect of Monday's snow-storm and the frost of the succeeding night upon fruit and growing crops indicates that the injury was only slight. The most serious damage seems to have been from the breaking down of fruit trees by the snow clinging to the branches until they were overloaded. The injury from the frost will not amount to more than 5 per cent. This estimate seems a little remarkable when it is remembered that in some localities fully a foot of snow fell. It is explained by the fact that the weather remained cloudy and the snow soon disappeared. It will have the effect to make a backward season still more backward, which may prove an injury to corn. The farmers, however, are in good spirits.

COLUMBUS, Ohio, May 24.—Dispatches received here to-night from various points on the line of the Baltimore and Ohio Railroad and all divisions west of the Ohio River are all of a similar purport and to the effect that the heavy storm and cold wave which passed over the State has caused no damage to crops or fruit. The same is true of points in Indiana traversed by the Baltimore and Ohio. Secretary Chamberlain expresses the opinion that the storm will prove a benefit to the growing wheat, which has much improved during the past 10 days. The outlook for an extraordinarily large hay crop is most favorable at the present time.

AUGUSTA, Ga., May 24.—Late and more complete news from the growing crops in this section of Georgia and South Carolina state that the young cotton is suffering from the cold weather blight. Grain and garden crops are generally uninjured, but watermelon vines, quite a specialty in this section, are seriously damaged.

MONTGOMERY, Ala., May 24.—Light frosts were reported yesterday, but without damage to crops.

BOMBARDMENT OF MIRAGOANE.

PORT AU PRINCE, May 15.—The bombardment of Miragoane has begun and is making havoc among the insurgents. The rest of the republic is reported quiet, but the Government keeps silent in regard to passing events. In consequence of this silence the public believe that the real state of affairs is unfavorable. Volunteers are swelling the ranks of the Government army. The French Chargé d'Affaires was recently conveyed to Miragoane aboard the Haytian war steamer Sentinelli, with the object, it is supposed, of making certain proposals to the insurgents. He returned with an unfavorable answer.

Affairs at Cape Haytien are quiet. Seventeen prisoners have been pardoned.

A POLITICIAN'S SINECURE.

PHILADELPHIA, May 24.—At a meeting of the committee of the Gas Trustees to-day it came out that the pay of a lighter named William Walk had been drawn up to date in spite of the fact that he died two years ago. The wages were $40 a month, and they had been regularly signed for on the pay-roll of the Sixth District, where Walk used to be employed. It was stated that a prominent Fourth Ward politician had forged Walk's name, drawn the money every month, and employed a man to care for the lamps for $3 a week. The matter was referred to a sub-committee for investigation.

STORMS IN MISSOURI.

ST. LOUIS, May 24.—Information has just been received that very heavy wind and rain storms swept through Howell County, in this State, last Friday and Saturday, doing very great damage to farms and other property. Part of Howell Valley was flooded, and bridges and embankments on the Kansas City, Springfield and Memphis Railway were swept away or badly damaged, delaying trains several days. The little town of Moody was destroyed, every house being blown down. J. W. McKelvy and several other persons were badly hurt. The farmers in that vicinity also suffered severely, the houses and outbuildings of B. Hall, M. A. Greenstreet, G. W. Frew, and others being blown down and fences scattered over the country. Information also comes from Maries County that a tornado swept entirely across it, making a path a hundred yards wide, leveling forests, and sweeping the ground of everything in its way. The largest farm in the county, that of James Crisnon, which is three miles long, lost all its buildings, and the family barely saved their lives by rushing into the cellar of the milk-house. A horse was picked up and carried a quarter of a mile.

THE ITALIANS' SUCCESSFUL SIEGE.

BLOCKADING PHILADELPHIA STREETS UNTIL THEY ARE PAID THEIR WAGES.

PHILADELPHIA, May 24.—Fourth-street, between Walnut and Chestnut streets, was blockaded again to-day for several hours by the hundreds of unpaid Italian laborers besieging the office of the Philadelphia and Chester County Railroad Company. They were as quiet as men of their race usually are, but were evidently firm in their resolution to have their rights. While they waited Messrs. McCue, Catterbury, and other sub-contractors held a conference with W. W. Vogdes, the Treasurer of the road, which resulted, it was said, in the handing over to the contractors of $80,000 worth of the bonds of the company by the officers of the construction company through George F. Work. Money was raised upon these, and before noon the hungry Italians started for the scene of their labors with a portion at least of their hard-earned wages in their pockets. George F. Work to-day explained the troubles of the company in these words:

"D. R. Kelly, of New-York, got the control of our road from the construction company, of which I am an officer, and C. P. Durgan President. Kelly was to finish the road as far as Newtown-square by Sept. 1 and up to West Chester by Jan. 1. We were not to pay him anything until he had finished the road to Newtown-square, when we were to give him $200,000 or thereabouts. Kelly formed a partnership with Faulker, a banker, and Mr. King, a dealer in railroad supplies, both of New-York, and these gentlemen agreed to furnish him with the capital necessary to carry on his work on our road. They were to put up $150,000. They paid the first month's money, some $15,000, I believe, but then, for a reason that I do not know, suspended payment and thus crippled Mr. Kelly. The officers of the road and the construction company are not in the least to blame. I understand that a part of the wages due the men was paid to-day; the total amount due is $27,000. The road is to run from Thirteenth and Chestnut streets over the old West Chester Railroad to Abbottsford, thence to Newtown-square, and thence through Sugartown and Goshenville to West Chester."

DRILLING FOR PRIZES.

BEGINNING OF THE CONTESTS AT NASHVILLE —GRAND DRESS PARADE.

NASHVILLE, Tenn., May 24.—To-day's programme of the national competitive drill consisted of prize drills by the Treadway Rifles, of St. Louis, and the Houston Light Guards, of Houston, Texas, in the morning, and the Crescent Rifles, of New-Orleans, and Busch Zouaves, of St. Louis, in the afternoon, the drill being followed by a grand dress parade. The attendance was large and much enthusiasm was exhibited by the friends of the competing companies. The Treadway Rifles began their drill at precisely 10 o'clock and finished it 6¼ minutes ahead of the allotted time. The drill was a very fair one. Several breaks were made in the platoon movements. Stacking arms was good, fixing and unfixing bayonets fair; inspection was good. The wheels, with one or two exceptions, were neatly executed. The Houston Light Guards began at 11:15 o'clock and finished with eight minutes to spare. The inspection was fine, the individual errors few, the wheeling deficient, and the firing by company and fixing and unfixing bayonets excellent. The Crescent Rifles began at 2 o'clock and finished with 10 minutes and 30 seconds to spare. The manual was executed with but few individual errors. Their marching in company and platoon movements was good. In the extra time allowed him the Captain executed several difficult movements, as stacking arms without bayonets and wheeling in common time. The Busch Zouaves began at 3:30 o'clock and gave an excellent drill, which, although not according to the tactics, was much admired by the judges. The dress parade was then had, Gen. Bentley, of Iowa, reviewing the troops. To-morrow there will be an artillery drill and a sham battle, and on Saturday individual contests. The prizes will be awarded Saturday evening.

TWO WOMEN COMMIT SUICIDE.

FALL RIVER, Mass., May 24.—Mary Harrington, 50 years of age, who was quite wealthy, and resided in Sixth-street, committed suicide by hanging in a room at her residence at 5 o'clock this evening. An excessive use of liquor was the cause of the act.

PROVIDENCE, R. I., May 24.—Early this morning Nina Bell Chase, aged 21, shot herself in her room here. She had been living for a year with a man named William Paine, a stable keeper. Paine and his hostler went to a variety theatre last evening. The hostler left early, and Paine, on going to the woman's room, found the hostler there. An altercation ensued. After the men left the woman attempted to drink from a bottle of laudanum but was prevented. Paine afterward returned to her room and they talked for some time about the occurrence of the evening. Paine went to the door of another room in the building, and was talking with another woman when he heard the report of a pistol. The Chase woman had shot herself with a small revolver, and died before a surgeon could reach her. The police were not informed for nearly an hour, but they will investigate the case. The woman was married to a man named Manfield, living in Connecticut. Her father lives in Fall River, and her mother is in an insane asylum.

THE REV. JOSEPH COOK IN TROUBLE.

MONMOUTH, Ill., May 24.—The Rev. Joseph Cook, of Boston, lectured here last night on the subject "England and America Compared." While at supper in the dining-room of the Commercial House, he got into an altercation with a traveling salesman named Gill, from Indianapolis, and a scene followed. Gill, who sat at the same table with Mr. Cook, ordered raw beefsteak. It is said that Mr. Cook remarked that no gentleman would eat raw steak. Gill took offense and immediately proposed to fight. The clerk of the hotel was summoned and prevented an encounter with fists. The commercial traveler became exceedingly angry, and invited the Boston lecturer outside. Mr. Cook refused to go, and made his escape. Gill sent him a note requesting a meeting on the steps of the hotel, but he refused to leave his room without an escort, and sent for the City Marshal, who, in company with a police officer, escorted Mr. Cook to the Opera-house, returning with him to the hotel after the lecture. All the guests at the hotel, who were present, blame Mr. Cook for the part he took in the affair.

A WOMAN DENIED BY HER FATHER.

CINCINNATI, May 24.—A suit for slander brought by Miss Belle English against Clement L. English was tried in the Superior Court to-day, before Judge Force and a jury. The complainant alleged that Mr. English said to a reporter of a newspaper that the plaintiff was a blackmailer and not his daughter. The question at issue was her paternity. She brought proof showing that she was born in a private hospital in Clinton County, and placed in the care of a woman near by; that Mr. English brought his wife to the hospital, and that he paid plaintiff's expenses. Mr. and Mrs. English denied all knowledge of her. The jury, after a short deliberation, brought in a verdict in favor of the plaintiff, awarding her $2,500 damages.

REFORMED EPISCOPAL CHURCH WORK.

BALTIMORE, May 24.—The General Council of the Reformed Episcopal Church continued its session to-day, Bishop James A. Latane presiding. Reports of work done in the past two years were made by Bishop Charles E. Cheney, of Chicago; Bishop Samuel Fallows, of the West and North-west; Bishop P. F. Stevens, of Charleston, and Bishop James A. Latane, of Baltimore. Reports were received and read from Bishop E. Cridge, of British Columbia; Bishop John Sugden, of Sussex, England, and Bishop Edward Wilson, of Ottawa, Canada.

A KANSAS LOVER'S CHEERFUL WAYS.

LARNED, Kan., May 24.—Near Livingston, Stafford County, yesterday, George Cramer made a proposition of marriage to Miss Tillie Wensell, who refused him. He then drew a revolver, shot her twice, knocked her down with the weapon, and then cut his own throat. Both are expected to die.

AN OLD STAGE PROPRIETOR DEAD.

LOCKPORT, May 24.—George W. Rector died in Lockport to-day, aged 73. Forty years ago, before the era of railroads, no man in Western New-York was better known to the traveling public. He was for many years a hotel-keeper and stage proprietor in Niagara County.

TWO GREAT CITIES UNITED

THE BRIDGE FORMALLY OPENED.

IMMENSE CROWDS ATTRACTED BY THE CEREMONIES.

PROCESSIONS AND DECORATIONS IN BOTH CITIES, THE FORMAL TRANSFER OF THE STRUCTURE, ADDRESSES BY ABRAM S. HEWITT AND THE REV. DR. STORRS, AND FIRE-WORKS AND ILLUMINATIONS.

The Brooklyn bridge was successfully opened yesterday. A fairer day for the ceremony could not have been chosen. The sky was cloudless, and the heat from the brightly shining sun was tempered by a cool breeze. The pleasant weather brought visitors by the thousands from all around. Special trains were run from Philadelphia and Easton, Penn., and from Long Island points. Extra cars were attached to regular trains, and then there was barely standing room. It is estimated that over 50,000 people came in by the railroads alone, and swarms by the Sound boats and by the ferry-boats helped to swell the crowds in both cities.

The opening of the bridge was decidedly Brooklyn's celebration. New-York's participation in it was meagre, save as to the crowd which thronged her streets. Some of the Exchanges and business houses down town were closed; others stopped business about noon, but as a rule the stores were open as usual, and as a rule, too, patrons were as numerous as on the other days of the year, when no Brooklyn bridges are opened. The crowd from outside, with curious New-Yorkers, combined to give to the vicinity of Madison-square, to Broadway, and to City Hall Park, the customary gala-day crowds. Thousands of people crowded each one of the places named. The windows, the balconies, and the roofs of Broadway buildings had their throngs. There was no general decoration beyond the display of the American flags. These were flown wherever there was a staff surmounting a building, and in themselves gave the City a holiday appearance. Aside from this display there were not more than a score of buildings that were decorated. Of these the most noticeable were in the vicinity of the New-York approach at the publication offices of the *Sun* and the *Staats-Zeitung*. Festoons of bunting graced a half-dozen Broadway fronts. While the crowd of strangers were gathering along the line of march Superintendent Walling was personally superintending the police arrangements up town and Inspector Murray doing a like service with the large force detailed from the various precincts down town. The arrangements were well executed, and as a result there was no delay caused by the blocking of the streets. At about 9 o'clock a gang of workmen removed the unsightly fence which has been in front of the New-York approach and an equally impassable fence of about 50 policemen took its place.

Promptly at 11:15 A. M. the assembly was sounded at the armory of the Seventh Regiment, the escort to the President, the Governor, the Mayor and the other more or less distinguished guests. A half-hour later the regiment had been equalized by Adjt. Rand into 14 platoons of 20 files, or 40 men, each. A guard was detailed, and at 11:45, the regiment, Col. Clark commanding, left its armory and, headed by Cappa's band of 70 pieces and a drum corps of 22, started on its march. The men were dressed in Summer uniform, gray coats, white trousers, and white helmets. From Sixty-seventh-street and Fourth-avenue, through Sixty-sixth-street and down Madison-avenue, the regiment moved to Fifty-seventh-street. Passing through that street to Fifth-avenue, the regiment marched down the avenue with the perfect fronts and the long, swinging steps which have always marked it, to the Fifth-Avenue Hotel. At Twenty-third-street and Fifth-avenue the regiment halted. Two companies marched into Twenty-third-street, presented arms, and received the guests of the day. These occupied 24 carriages. In the first of these were seated President Arthur and Mayor Edson. These gentlemen were cheered as they appeared, and the President lifted his hat in acknowledgment of the compliment. In the second carriage were Secretary of State Frelinghuysen, Secretary of the Treasury Folger, and Trustee John T. Agnew. Postmaster-General Gresham, Secretary of the Navy Chandler, and Trustee John G. Davis occupied carriage No. 3. In the fourth carriage were Attorney-General Brewster, Marshal McMichael, of the District of Columbia; Mr. Allan Arthur, and Trustee J. Adriance Bush. The fifth had F. J. Phillips, the President's private secretary; Surrogate Rollins, M. W. Cooper, and Charles E. Miller as occupants. The sixth carriage was occupied by Gov. Grover Cleveland and Trustee Gen. Slocum. Seated in the seventh carriage were the Hon. Abram S. Hewitt, Controller Campbell, and Trustee Charles McDonald. Gov. Ludlow, of New-Jersey; ex-Gov. Fairbanks, of Vermont; Gen. W. S. Stryker, and Trustee Jenkins Van Schaick rode in the eighth carriage. Gov. Littlefield, of Rhode Island, and a member of his staff accompanied Trustee Henry Clausen in the ninth carriage. The remaining carriages were occupied by Gov. Cleveland's staff, Gen. Carr and staff, Gen. Shaler and staff, Gen. Ward and staff, Gen. Christensen and staff, and Gen. Fitzgerald and staff, all in full uniform. Among the gentlemen in citizen's dress who rode as guests were Collector of the Port William H. Robertson, ex-Secretary of the Treasury Windom, ex-Speaker of the House of Representatives Keifer, of Ohio; ex-Mayors Cooper and Grace, the Hon. S. S. Cox, the Hon. Orlando B. Potter, Joseph Lydecker, William H. Guion, Gen. Lloyd Aspinwall, W. A. Palmer, C. J. Hill, of New-Jersey; Senators Titus, Browning, and Grady, and Assemblyman Spinola. When the guests were all seated in their carriages the procession, preceded by a squad of 40 mounted policemen, commanded by Sergt. Ressell, passed down Fifth-avenue and turned into Broadway. President Arthur, of course, was the centre of observation. He was cheered and applauded, and bowed acknowledgments to the crowds in the windows and on the walks. When the procession passed Eighteenth-street the horses attached to the carriage in which the President and the Mayor was seated became frightened from some unknown cause and became unmanageable. They turned from Fifth-avenue down Eighteenth-street toward Sixth-avenue. A police officer caught the horses by the bridle and soon had them under control. At one time it looked as if there would be a runaway, and Mayor Edson prepared to jump from the carriage in case such a proceeding was necessary. President Arthur was very calm during the whole incident, which lasted but a minute or two, and so for that matter was the Mayor. When the horses were quieted and the carriage took its place in the procession again its occupants were greeted with the most hearty applause they received during the day.

Meanwhile City Hall Park and Printing-house-square had filled up with people until the spectators were packed in masses through which it was almost impossible to pass, and those who had tickets to attend the ceremonies had hard work to reach the bridge. Every available house-top and window was filled, and an adventurous party occupied a tall telegraph pole. It required the utmost efforts of the police to keep clear the necessary space. At 1:30 o'clock the procession reached the City Hall and halted. The guests in the carriages dismounted. The President was cheered. The crowd looked and asked for Gov. Cleveland, and was ready to cheer him, but they failed to recognize his portly form as he left his carriage and, with Gen. Slocum, walked up to join the Presidential party. The Aldermen, with the exception of Fitzpatrick, each carrying his staff of office and led by Sergeant-at-Arms Chambers with a gilt eagle perched on a long staff, the heads of the various departments, and a horde of minor office-holders, joined the procession of foot-men. Alderman Fitzpatrick told a TIMES reporter that, having worked and spoken earnestly against opening the bridge on May 24, he did not think it would have been consistent to attend the ceremonies. Then, too, he said, at the hour the bridge was opened he attended the funeral of an old and intimate friend, so that even had he desired to be on the bridge he would not have gone. The band struck up a lively march, the regiment broke into columns of fours, and the procession, like a huge gray and black serpent, wound its way to the entrance to the bridge. The regiment, or the greater part of it, marched upon the bridge at 1:50 o'clock. Preceding the President and Mayor Edson, who walked arm-in-arm, was a colored man carrying a yellow water-pail in one hand and a rack of glasses in the other. The President had to step carefully to avoid the water-carrier's heels. The crowd cheered the President. The darky took it as a salute to him, and smiled, unaware of his proximity to greatness. The procession disappeared through the entrance, and then the undistinguished guests followed. That is, those who had tickets followed. Those who hadn't tickets, and who were very curious, paid $2 to ticket speculators for the pieces of pasteboard which permitted them to pass over the span. During the rush white business cards of the requisite shape admitted a number shrewd enough to take advantage of the trick, but it was soon discovered and each card was thereafter carefully scrutinized.

When the President and Governor had walked about half the distance to the New-York pier, there was a commotion down the line, and Orator Abram S. Hewitt came struggling through the ranks trying to get somewhere near the head of the procession. The house-tops and upper windows of buildings almost as far as the eye could reach were black with eager sightseers, many of whom made use of opera-glasses and small telescopes to aid in getting a good view of the parade. The view from the bridge as the procession passed across was fine. All of the vessels in the harbor were gayly decorated with flags and bunting. The ferry-boats, tugs, and small craft on the rivers displayed flags. The pier-heads from which a view of the bridge was to be had were crowded with spectators. The vessels at the docks were packed with people, who took possession of them hours before the first gun was fired. The war vessels were anchored in a line below the bridge in the following order: Tennessee, Kearsarge, Yantic, Vandalia, Minnesota, and Saratoga. The first named was just above the Wall-street ferry, while the Saratoga was close to Governor's Island. Each man-of-war had a string of flags and bunting which reached from stem to stern and above the tops of the masts.

West of the New-York pier the Seventh Regiment halted and the men quickly formed in two ranks at the right of the promenade, presented arms, and the civilians passed by. The band halted under the pier arches and played "Hail to the Chief." At 2 o'clock the head of the column reached the pier, where several of the bridge Trustees, headed by Acting President William C. Kingsley, welcomed the chief magistrate and the Governor. As the party started forward after a temporary halt, a Signal Corps officer dipped a signal flag, and in 10 seconds a puff of smoke shot upward from one of the port-holes of the man-of-war Tennessee, followed instantly by a loud report. This was the first gun of the salute of 21 guns, and a moment later the guns of the Vandalia, the Kearsarge, the Yantic, and the Minnesota, and those at the Navy-yard and at Castle William, on Governor's Island, joined in the salute. The members of the Fifth United States Artillery presented arms on the river side of the pier, and then the head of the column reached the centre of the great bridge. When the procession reached the pier on the Brooklyn side, Mayor Low and the Brooklyn authorities stepped forward, the two Mayors locked arms, and the President was joined by Mr. Kingsley. A detachment of marines from the navy-yard stood guard at the Brooklyn pier, and east of the pier the Twenty-third Regiment was drawn up. The men presented arms as the guests passed by, the band greeted the party with "Hail to the Chief," and the immense crowd gathered on the Brooklyn approach cheered. The President and those near him took their seats in the building at the Brooklyn approach, but the great mass of those who had crossed from New-York were unable to get within hearing or seeing distance of the interior of the building. The jam was terrible, and it extended back half-way to the pier.

BROOKLYN'S GREAT DISPLAY.

Never in the history of Brooklyn did that city of anniversary events wear such a garment of colors as she did yesterday. To Brooklyn, which conceived the idea of a bridge and which furnished the bulk of the enormous sum required to build it, must be rewarded the lead in the celebration. The city fathers set the example and the citizens vied with one another in following it. There are 500 miles of streets in the city. It would be no exaggeration to say that from every block of that vast distance fluttered a flag or floated a lantern. It was in the lower end of the city, in the vicinity of the City Hall and on Columbia Heights in particular, that the decorative display was so attractive and in some instances so novel in its character. At an early hour in the morning a man crawled up the sides of the City Hall cupola and seated himself astride the neck of the blindfolded figure of Justice. He was joined by others, and when they had concluded their labors a pair of glistening bronze scales swung in their accustomed position, the flagstaff had been righted, and the national colors were flying from its truck. Far below it, from the staff on the roof, fluttered in the breeze the colors of the city itself, displaying the old Dutch motto "Een draght macht mocht." Every window in the building had its shield with its draping of miniature flags. The Ionic columns of the portico were draped with bunting. A similar display of flags and shields was made at the windows of the Municipal Building in the rear of the City Hall, and the dome of the Court-house adjoining was gorgeous in its dress of flying colors. The buildings about the City Hall square were heavy with bunting. Fulton-street in both directions, Court-street, Joralemon-street, Remsen and Montague streets, and Washington-street and Myrtle-avenue, all entering the square from as many different directions, presented a magnificent view of flags of all nations and Chinese lanterns strung from basement to roof on the private dwellings. The storekeepers on both sides of Fulton-street, from City Hall to ferry, gave up their windows and doorways to decorations. A jeweler had removed his wares and in the corner window had outlined a miniature representation of the bridge, massive gold chains forming the cables. In the window of another store was a floral piece, an excellent imitation of the bridge, 8 feet in length. Over the main entrance to the store was a large banner on which were inscribed the words: "Roebling—One of the few immortal names that were not born to die." On a transparency was inscribed the quotation: "Babylon had her hanging gardens, Egypt her Pyramids, Athens her Acropolis, Rome her Coliseum—so Brooklyn has her bridge. Over its broad roadway the teeming millions of the two cities may pass; under its spacious arch the commerce of the world may pass." Some windows were occupied with portraits or busts of the late Henry C. Murphy, John A. Roebling, and the present chief engineer of the bridge, Col. Washington A. Roebling.

An innumerable throng poured through the streets all the morning curious to view the decorations. Then as the hour of noon approached, by common consent it surged toward the Sands-street entrance to the bridge, where the ceremonies were to take place. Fulton and Washington streets, above and below Sands, were choked with a mass of men, women, and children. Policemen, under command of Drill Captain McKelvey, struggled to open a line through which the procession, in formation at the City Hall, could pass to the bridge. Boys recklessly clambered to the solitary section of an elevated railroad structure. Chief Campbell and Inspector Jewett directed the movements of 100 policemen, who kept a free roadway for a single block in front of the bridge entrance. The roofs of the buildings were peopled, the yards and rigging of every vessel along the river-front were manned, the piers were black with a mass of beings that, from the bridge overhead, looked like ants swarming over one another.

By noon the marines, the regulars, the members of the National Guard, and those who were to

The New-York Times.

VOL. XXXV......NO. 10,911. NEW-YORK, SUNDAY, AUGUST 22, 1886.----TRIPLE SHEET. PRICE THREE CENTS.

OLD WORLD NEWS BY CABLE

THE MAIN TORY EFFORT TO STAY IN WHILE THEY CAN.

STEPS ALREADY TAKEN TO DELAY MATTERS—AFGHANISTAN PERHAPS TO HELP THEM WITH THE IRISH QUESTION—GLADSTONIANS WHO ARE REALLY INDIFFERENT TO IRELAND.

BY COMMERCIAL CABLE FROM OUR OWN CORRESPONDENT.

Copyright, 1886, by the New-York Times.

LONDON, Aug. 21.—If it would not be literally exact to paraphrase for the present situation an ancient couplet so as to read:

"As bees on flowers alighting cease to hum,
So the Tories, settling into place, are dumb,"

it would be pretty near the truth. The new Ministry has talked a great deal, but has said nothing. That the Tories have got in, and that they mean by hook or by crook to stay in as long as they possibly can, is the gist of the Ministerial announcements. To promote this great end of drawing their own salaries, it is the desire of her Majesty's Government to avoid all controversial points and to postpone decision on all troublesome things until the latest possible day. Nothing could be more frank. Meanwhile the choice of the old device of pretending to need information and of appointing royal commissions to find out about things afresh has been resorted to, with fine indifference to the fact that the recommendations of similar commissions of inquiry have been piling up in the Irish archives since King John's time all unheeded. Side by side with this obvious scheme to gain time run politic efforts to satisfy the Tory clamor for repression and to seduce the Irish tenant class away from Mr. Parnell by promising vaguely some kind of land purchase plan later on. For the one, Buller will be sent to Kerry to attempt what even the League failed to do. For the other, there is a mysterious hint of great industrial, agrarian, and municipal reforms in the remote air.

This would all be very clever and pleasant if it only would work, but, unhappily, there are difficulties in the way. The Irish members have no idea of waiting till next Spring for the sake of easing the Ministerial path, and still less will the Irish farmers and Irish laborers submit through the Winter to impossible burdens in order that Lord Randolph Churchill may continue to be the leader of a House in which he has not got a majority. Both here and in Ireland the new Cabinet will encounter from the start all the opposition and resistance possible under the forms of law. The bribe will find no takers. Yet even the offering of it has raised trouble among the Liberal Unionists. Lord Hartington is said to have expressed strong dissent from Lord Randolph Churchill's evident intention of taking up Mr. W. H. Smith's old land purchase scheme. The *Spectator*, too, earnestly protests to-day against the idea of extending English and Scotch municipal principles to Ireland. It says that Lord Randolph Churchill's proposition "fills us with dismay. It is an odd way of keeping Parnellism out of College Green to install it in every commune." This seems like a declaration that the Unionists will not have anything whatever done in Ireland of a remedial nature, and that they object to even a guarded suggestion of such a possibility. This is, of course, the logic of the Unionists' position. To consent to any change, to concede any grievance, is to break down the dam for a home rule flood.

It would be pleasant if one could truthfully represent as resolutely opposed to these dullards, tricksters, and malcontents the 200 Gladstonians, all of whom are supposed to be animated by devotion to liberty, devotion to principle, and zeal for their cause. But this would not be at all true. There are a score or two in the lot who really believe in home rule, and are ready to make all sacrifices in order to keep it in the forefront of the agitation until it is achieved, and Mr. Gladstone and Mr. Morley are the only two men on the front bench in whose entire and deep sincerity one is able to believe. Mr. Labouchère, Mr. Conybeare, Mr. Stanhope, Mr. Stuart, and some others are equally firm; but the great majority of the others do not conceal their regret that the issue was raised at all, and while they have no intention of deserting Mr. Gladstone for a lesser light, they are still looking anxiously for a chance to reunite the party on almost any basis. For two days I had seen on the Terrace in dining rooms and in the lobby followers of Mr. Gladstone, Lord Hartington, and Mr. Chamberlain, all fraternizing, jovially, and cordially as if all the recrimination, bitterness, and accusation of treason and falseness of the last month were forgotten and all cause for ill feeling were now removed. Last night I asked an Irish leader how he explained this strange oblivion to all the meannesses and acrimony of June and July on the part of men who, by all the rules, ought to despise each other. He laughed at me. "You might as well expect American republicans," he said, "not to speak to one another over the Chinese question as look for real feeling among English politicians upon a mere Irish issue. What do they care for us one way or the other, or for anything else but getting as close as they can to the Treasury bench, where the honors and salaries are? You in America, we in Ireland, have the fortune or misfortune of being able to believe in abstract things and getting excited and enthusiastic over them. These Englishmen believe only, and are interested only, in themselves." I do not altogether follow this pessimism, but there is a truth in its gloomy view. When we are tempted to get sanguine about the prospects for home rule and a millennium generally, it will do no harm to remember this expression of the historic Irish view of the English character.

English comment on the Chicago Convention served in a way to illustrate this view. The reports to the *Times*, *Standard*, and *Daily News* have been unprecedentedly extensive for them, and the idea conveyed, whether justly or not, has been that the gathering was a pretty turbulent affair. All the Tory papers insist that, although nominally conservative elements are in control, really the dynamiters swayed the convention but dissembled their purposes. This false statement is nowhere taken up and controverted by the Liberal journals, which are too indifferent or ill informed to explain what the convention really did. The chief Gladstone paper, the *Daily News*, devotes itself to a whimsical paragraph on Mr. Finerty, quoting his "thirty generations" remark, and saying, "With such progenitors of course Mr. Finerty is not as other men, and has to think of the family feelings on the other side of the grave. Disaffection with him is a kind of worship of the ancestors, and this may be the first of the long-predicted effects on American life and character of contact with the Chinese." I quote this flippant thing to show what the biggest Liberal paper in England deems best worth comment in a great convention representing more supporters of Mr. Gladstone than went to the polls for him this Summer in all the three kingdoms. It helps one to realize that, despite Mr. Gladstone's championship, despite the formal adhesion of a vast majority of the British Liberal Party, Irishmen are still fighting with their hands tied and with the big odds of English indifference and levity against them. The Parnellite leaders here have been greatly relieved by the rebuke administered to the mouthy Mr. Finerty, and by the tone in which Mr. Davitt assumed that the latter went out on his own hook, as some uncertainty prevailed as to what he would be likely to do and say.

Probably Lord Salisbury and Lord Randolph Churchill will not be sorry to have the Afghan frontier issue assume importance enough to drive Ireland into the background, just as Mr. Gladstone's Ministry, it is believed, fostered it sixteen months ago to divert attention from the Egyptian muddle. The trick has been a familiar one in English politics since the Plantagenets invented French invasions to palliate the wool tax at home. It is not improbable that they will have their hearts' desire. The recall of the British commission is only relatively significant. Even if resolved upon in itself it means only that the English are tired of the intolerable delay which the Russians have managed to bring about. Its importance lies in the reasons actuating the Russians in desiring this delay. These reasons are at hand in the fact that the Trans-Caspian Railway, which in March of last year had only reached Kizil Arvat, now stretches through Askabad to Tschardschni, on the Oxus, on the frontier of Bokhara. In other words, Russia has held the Afghan frontier matter open until she was able to utilize it to her advantage. Now she is in a position to put the screws on England whenever she likes to menace Afghanistan and India at her pleasure. A rumor of English action this week sufficed to dash every Bourse in Europe, even without professing to signify anything. While awaiting further developments there is an uneasy feeling everywhere that Russia will avenge her checkmate on the Balkans by picking a quarrel in Asia. People even profess to know that this was understood perfectly at Gastein, and that the German and Austrian Emperors agreed to give Russia a free hand in the East if she gave a guarantee to keep quiet in Europe.

There is an understanding in Berlin, based on a letter received at Göttingen University, that a German Professor in an Argentine college has secured for Germany the whole southwestern portion of Patagonia beyond the line of 74° and southward of 48° as an imperial possession. There is some doubt expressed of the authenticity of this report on account of the supposed claims of Chili to the territory in question, but possibly there is a connection between this and the announcement that Baron Gutschmid, who is one of the cleverest and most energetic Germans in the commercial diplomatic service, has been removed from Spain, where he has quadrupled the German trade in a few years, to be Minister to Chili. Americans ought to find the rumor interesting.

Wilhelmj is forming a string quartet for a concert tour of Europe. It is expected to be the finest ever heard.

The little mimic Marshall P. Wilder sails on the City of Rome on Sept. 1, after a remarkable financial and social success.

Charles Duval, the cosmopolitan showman of Prince's Hall, thinks some of going to America in October.

The Empire opened to-night with two ballets, a concert and an English version of Adam's "Le Postillon de Longjumeau."

Boucicault, who is part lessee with Robert Brough of the Opera House at Melbourne, sailed for Australia with a burlesque company on Thursday on the Orient.

Lucille Saunders, of Hartford, who has studied in Paris for four years, made a successful début at a Covent Garden concert on Wednesday.

I am told by a Southwark banker that during the past month many thousands of pounds have been paid for Kent hops, chiefly by Liverpool buyers, for shipment to America. This export of hops, it is believed, has very rarely if ever happened before.

H. F.

NEW-JERSEY SOLDIERS CAMPING.

CAMP ABBETT, Sea Girt, N. J., Aug. 21.—The preparations that have been in progress for months for the encampment of the Second Division, National Guard of New-Jersey, at Sea Girt, are about completed and the regular routine of camp life will begin to-morrow, Sunday, when Gatling Gun Company B, of Camden, under command of Capt. Eckendorff, will arrive and be quartered on the camp grounds. The Third Regiment, from Elizabeth, under Col. Ropes; the Sixth, from Camden, under Col. Cooper, and the Seventh, from Trenton, under Col. Donnelly, will arrive early Monday morning. Gen. Sewell, in command, arrived this evening with his staff.

The grounds are in excellent condition, the grass having been closely cropped and the sod repeatedly rolled, making a perfectly level and even surface. The old farmhouse that has stood for near a hundred years on the most pleasant portion of the grounds, surrounded by shade trees, has been fitted up and will be occupied by Gov. Abbett and his family during the encampment. Tents for Gen. Sewell and staff officers are grouped around the frame building, and complete the camp headquarters. Tents to the number of 700 have also been erected for the accommodation of the different regiments. The new rifle range is in perfect order, and will be used by qualified marksmen of the Seventh Regiment during the week. The total number of men to be in camp during the week is 1,400.

THE MIKADO CONFERS ORDERS.

SAN FRANCISCO, Cal., Aug. 21.—Advices from Yokohama, per steamship City of Sydney, state that the Mikado has expressed his intention to the British and German Ministers of presenting imperial orders to the Prince of Wales and the Crown Prince Frederick William. The German Minister has been decorated by the Mikado with the Order of the Rising Sun of the first class. The same honor was offered to the British Minister, but owing to the regulations of his country he could not accept it. The conferring of these honors is due to the efforts of the British and German Ministers in securing a revision of the treaties with their respective Governments.

THE TENNESSEE GREENBACKERS.

NASHVILLE, Tenn., Aug. 21.—The Greenbackers met in this city to-day and held a conference. After organization a platform was adopted, which is a compilation of the National Greenback and Knights of Labor platforms. It says further: "That the imposition of a tax upon the people to pay any part of the bonds loaned to railroads or turnpike corporations of the State of Tennessee is a fraud that should not be submitted to by the people." After the adoption of the platform the convention unanimously nominated Thomas Snodgrass, of Crossville, Cumberland County, for Governor.

A CHAIR AS A BLUDGEON.

PHILADELPHIA, Aug. 21.—At an early hour this morning Patrick Cahill, a crank, called at the Mayor's office and insisted on seeing the Mayor. His progress up stairs was interrupted by John Dunn, night superintendent of the Mayor's office. Cahill quickly seized a chair and beat Dunn into a state of insensibility. The wounded man is now in a precarious condition. Cahill has been held to await the result of the injuries inflicted. Dunn was for many years connected with the *Press* of this city and was at one time its managing editor, under John W. Forney.

AN EXECUTOR WILL NOT SERVE.

BOSTON, Aug. 21.—The will of William Gray, Jr., was filed in the Suffolk County Probate Court this afternoon, and is dated Oct. 17, 1864. It bequeaths all his estate to his family and appoints his widow guardian of the children and his father, William Gray, Sr., Executor of the will. Mr. Gray has declined to serve, and a petition has been filed asking for the appointment of Edward Cunningham in his place.

A PHYSICIAN SHOOTS HIMSELF.

BALTIMORE, Aug. 21.—Dr. L. S. Bitting, aged 25, a young physician of this city, shot himself through the head this afternoon, causing death in a few minutes. No reason can be assigned for his act. He was the son of the Rev. C. C. Bitting, a prominent Baptist clergyman, who is now connected with the Board of Baptist Missions.

A BOAT ON A REEF.

PORT CHESTER, N. Y., Aug. 21.—George Quintard, of this place, on Thursday took about 60 of his friends to the Wild West show on Staten Island. On their return about 10 o'clock the boat was run on a reef at Hawthorn Beach. Her passengers were safely landed, after which the steamer was beached at Indian Harbor.

THEMES OF TALK IN PARIS

RIDICULE THAT MAY HELP BOULANGER.

RUMORS THAT THE PRESIDENT WILL RESIGN—THE TROUBLE WITH THE VATICAN—YOUNG MENIER'S MARRIAGE—DALY'S COMPANY AND MAIDEN EARS.

By Commercial Cable from Our Own Correspondent.

PARIS, Aug. 21.—I am as ashamed of writing always about Gen. Boulanger as readers can possibly be wearied with studying the stuff; but Paris declines to give anything else precedence. The concerted effort to smother him under ridicule has grown to the dimensions of a great movement headed by the *République Française*, backed by the Ferryites and more than winked at by his own colleagues, which fills the streets with the clamor of hawking burlesque satires on him and floods the press with onslaughts grave and gay. All this is said to mask a serious effort on the part of M. de Freycinet to get rid of him, and there are rumors of a scene between them in which Gen. Boulanger was forbidden to take his advertised tour of inspection on the Italian frontier. Certainly this has again been postponed—this time till the 28th. The gossips even mix M. Grévy in the matter, and aver that he is willing to resign and secure the succession to M. de Freycinet. If by no less heroic means the dangerous demagogue can be headed off the old gentleman had better hurry up, for the storm of sarcasm and gibes seems to have been too fierce to accomplish its object. Gen. Boulanger not only survives; he thrives under it. There can be no doubt that many of his actions are fussy and trivial. But, theatrical as they may seem, he is extremely popular with the crowd. His latest provision that reserve detachments, conscripts, young and territorial troops shall hereafter be met and marched to and from their destinations with martial music to preserve the army's prestige is one of those simple things which please everybody. Parisians are so delighted that they would find it easy to forgive him even if he had written the biography of himself now sold on the streets, as all his enemies charge and as some of his friends suppose he really did.

It is a pleasant phase of the colonial disputes that the storm centres a long way off. Paris and London having been prodigiously excited about the New-Hebrides last week, have now forgotten all about them until the next slow mail comes in bringing fresh fuel for a disturbance. In the interim we may occupy ourselves with the threatening trouble with the Vatican over the appointment of the Chinese Nuncio. It is not easy to discover the way to a dignified compromise. The French Government has said explicitly that it will never tolerate an act which will interfere with its protectorate over Christians in the Chinese Empire. The Pope has quite as distinctly announced his intention of sending a Nuncio or delegate who, in the order of things, could have no other functions. There is plenty of stubbornness at Rome and plenty of radical fire here which may readily provoke a rupture if the cool heads on both sides do not interpose. Neither the Vatican nor the republic could gain by such a quarrel.

The death of two more of Pasteur's patients in the provinces has created a painful impression, and the skeptics are rising of course in swarms to say "I told you so." The Czar's contribution, which raises the institute fund to $320,000, comes at an opportune time, for great hesitation was beginning to be marked here about the reality of the discovery.

The gossips divide their rhapsodies between Gen. Boulanger and the announced marriage of the famous Menier *fils*, the notorious amateur with circus and horse-training proclivities, with the no less celebrated beauty Mlle. Marsy, of the Comédie Française. Menier is a son of the chocolate manufacturer, the man who had the wit and courage to turn to good profit and advertisement the defect of his produce which made its repute by the melancholy fact of its getting white. In his old age he left his fortune and business to his sons, of whom this one has squandered a large portion in his private circus establishment. Dame rumor has long connected him with Mlle. Marsy, but no one foresaw her retirement from the stage, where she made a brilliant début, followed by a rather negative success. Still less did any one predict her marriage with this gentleman more than with any other of her many admirers.

The best and most novel advertisement given by the French press to Mr. Daly's company is the statement that young ladies can listen to the plays with impunity. This sensation was started by M. Sarcey, and the astounding fact of a theatre or company being able to give three successive representations without possible offense to maiden ears strikes the French as the wonder of the century. This virtuous element, allied to a desire for study of the language, would probably insure a Daly run did the troupe come in the Winter season. As it is, our compatriots are sure to be a winning attraction.

THE FINERTY EPISODE.

CHICAGO, Aug. 21.—The Irish Parliamentary delegates left for the East to-night. One of the American delegates, speaking of the convention, said: "The Finerty episode is much to be regretted, and I hold that those who were so clamorous for a speech did not show very much loyalty to the cause. He had plainly defined his position immediately after the adoption of the platform, and every one in the convention knew, or ought to have known, his views. He would either repeat them, or change position. To precipitate the first was unwise, and the latter could not be thought of, in a man of Finerty's firmness."

About the effects of the convention's work Mr. John F. Finerty would not venture an opinion. "I am not an officer of the League," he said in explanation of his refusal. Speaking of his own action in the convention, especially with reference to Michael Davitt, Mr. Finerty, said: "I think that the sentiments I uttered are shared by a majority of the Irish-American people, and I felt bound in duty, when I was forced upon the platform by the call of the convention and the direct invitation of the Chair, to assert openly the policy of the Radical element of the Irish Nationalists. I didn't think it well to let it go by default. I refrained from opposing the resolutions, and refused even to be a member of the Committee on Resolutions, so as not to embarrass the gentlemen from Ireland. I went to the meeting not intending to speak at all, and I didn't seek to bind the convention to my words. I am not a serf of anybody, and I do not think that Mr. Davitt had any right to impugn my motives in making the speech, and insinuating that I was eager to make it."

TRYING TO KILL HIMSELF.

FLUSHING, Long Island, Aug. 21.—Herman Schoenberger, a German, aged 56 years, of Manhasset, while temporarily insane this afternoon cut his right wrist with a razor. He ran through the house, the blood gushing from the wound. His wife and daughter aroused the neighbors. Six men succeeded in tying him to a bed. He may recover. He owns considerable property, and is in comfortable circumstances. He had been despondent for some time. Three weeks ago he tried to commit suicide by hanging himself from a beam in his barn.

HIS BODY COMING HOME.

LOUISVILLE, Ky., Aug. 21.—The body of young Frederick Pappenheimer, who killed himself yesterday morning at Mrs. Jarvis's boarding house, was shipped to New-York this evening at 7 o'clock, in care of the American Express Company. Nothing has been heard from his family. Mr. C. A. Bridges received a telegram from Mr. Pappenheimer's partner telling him to ship the body home. This is all that has been heard. There are no new developments in the case as to the causes which led to the rash act.

BIG FIRE IN SAN FRANCISCO.

SEVERAL BLOCKS DESTROYED — LOSS ESTIMATED AT $2,000,000.

SAN FRANCISCO, Cal., Aug. 21.—One of the largest fires which has ever visited this city occurred to-night. It started shortly after 6 o'clock, in Small's machine shop, on Brannon-street, between Fourth and Fifth streets, and spread with such rapidity that second and third alarms quickly followed. The fire ran north for half a block and south two and a half blocks, crossing Bryant, Brannon, and Bluxome streets, and extended from midway between Fourth and Fifth streets to the latter street. It was gotten under control two hours after it started. The loss is estimated at about $2,000,000.

It is impossible to ascertain the insurance or individual losses at this hour. The principal losers are: M. C. Hawley & Co., agricultural implements; W. B. Bradbury, planing mill; Gilbert & Morse, school furniture; Scutter, wagon works; Baker & Hamilton, agricultural implements; H. W. Rice, agricultural machinery; Walker & Son, wool warehouse; Whittier, Fuller & Co., paints and oils; Fuchs & Uhler, furniture manufacturers; Krelling Brothers, furniture manufacturers.

WOMAN AGAINST WOMAN.

MRS. CARR'S PERSISTENT PURSUIT OF MRS. COLLINS.

BOSTON, Aug. 21.—A suit of the most novel description was begun in the United States Circuit Court for this district to-day. The suit is instituted by Mrs. Elizabeth A. Carr, of Jacksonville, against Mrs. Frances F. Collins, who is named in the writ as of Boston, but who has, it is said, a residence in various parts of the Western hemisphere and whose domicile may be found in Eastern and Western cities and as far south as Honduras.

The plaintiff in the suit claims $20,000 damages for the alleged acts of the defendant in enticing away the plaintiff's husband, William P. Carr. The facts, so far as they appear, are that Mr. and Mrs. Carr went in 1884 to Jacksonville, where they kept a hotel during the Winter. Thither went Mrs. Collins, who at that time was living with her second husband in Providence, R. I., where Mrs. Collins had and still has property amounting, it is said, to $40,000.

Soon after Mrs. Collins's arrival at the hotel kept by the plaintiff, the latter became aware of certain familiarities between Mr. Carr and Mrs. Collins. Her suspicions that her husband was becoming infatuated with the defendant were verified when one morning she found both her husband and Mrs. Collins among the missing. In the course of a few days Mrs. Carr learned that the couple were stopping at Lake George. She went to Lake George, and with the assistance of friends succeeded in inducing the recreant husband to return to Florida. Matters after this progressed favorably until last November, when Mrs. Collins again put in an appearance at Jacksonville. After a short stay she and Mr. Carr simultaneously disappeared. Mrs. Carr subsequently ascertaining that the two were living together in Hot Springs, Ark. Mrs. Carr, it appears, did not make any further attempt to regain the affections of her husband, but brought a suit for divorce, alleging adultery with Mrs. Collins, and in last April she was given a decree of divorce by the Florida Supreme Court. She then, through her counsel, instigated proceedings against Mrs. Collins, which resulted in the latter's arrest on civil process yesterday by the United States Marshal and her appearance to-day before Commissioner Hallett, where she gave a bond for her appearance in court to answer the suit.

Mrs. Collins is about 35 or 40 years of age and of striking appearance, and was completely broken down when she was compelled to appear before the Commissioner.

NOT EASILY DAMAGED.

WONDERFUL ENDURANCE OF SOME CONNECTICUT CHILDREN.

NEW-HAVEN, Conn., Aug. 21.—Connecticut children have been proving this Summer that they can go through a wonderful amount of rough experiences and come out alive and well. Clifford Howe, a youth of 4 years, is the latest to prove his endurance. He is the son of Landlord Howe, of the Wallace House, in Cheshire. A day or two ago Clifford arose cheerfully, and, during the morning, tried to ride a horse. He got along famously until he fell to the ground, cutting his head open and generally shaking himself up. However, by the time afternoon had come Clifford was himself again, and he managed to see a baseball game, which was absorbing the interest of most of Cheshire's residents. He watched the game in safety, but while he was riding home he was accidentally pushed out of the wagon. Two wheels passed over his head, nearly scalping him. He was picked up and carried home, and the next morning there was not a happier or more active child in all Cheshire.

Mrs. J. Howard Burr, of Danbury, started to go down a flight of stairs with her baby in her arms. She caught the heel of her shoe in a stair rod and fell with her child to the floor below. Mrs. Burr was badly shaken up and her right arm was broken, but the baby came out all right and was not in the least injured by its share in the tumble.

Mrs. James Wallace, of No. 352 East-street, in this city, sat in a big armchair with her baby in her arms. Right back of her chair was an open window, and as she rocked backward and forward the child gave a sudden leap, sprang out of her grasp, and, before she fairly realized what had taken place, had fallen to the street below. Mrs. Wallace's room was on the second floor, and she ran down stairs fully expecting to find her baby terribly hurt if not dead. But in this she was mistaken, for when she reached the little one's side he was apparently very little the worse for his adventure. Half an hour later the baby was playing about the floor. There was not even a bruise on the little body and limbs.

A WIND WORTH MONEY.

VOLUNTEER FIREMEN ROUTED BY A RED-HOT BLAZE.

GLENS FALLS, N. Y., Aug. 21.—A disastrous fire broke out here to-day at the works of Finch, Pruyn & Co., lime and lumber merchants. The flames spread to the cooper's shop, office, and limekilns, and thence to a lumber pile a quarter of a mile long. A high wind blew directly over the village and sparks set fire to the Transportation Company's dock and storehouse. Hose companies were powerless to check the fire. Finch, Pruyn & Co.'s works were situated on a strip of land between the Hudson River and the canal, and the hose companies had to run a quarter of a mile to get back to the village where the transportation company's sheds were burning. The fire spread to the houses and down the canal banks to the lumber piles. The area of the fire is about three acres. Four hundred tons of coal in one shed is a mass of flames. Fire companies from neighboring towns are fighting the flames. Thousands of feet of lumber burning on both sides of the canal made the water almost boil.

Houses 300 feet away were set on fire by the intense heat. Hundreds of tons of lime were also destroyed. Six kilns were burned up and a storehouse containing thousands of barrels was also destroyed. The Volunteer Fire Department was utterly incapable of fighting the fire. People in the immediate vicinity of the conflagration fled from their homes, as the flames caught roof after roof. Fortunately the wind finally veered about and carried the sparks over the river. The firemen then prevented the flames from spreading further. Lumber piles are still burning. The damage is estimated at $50,000. The origin of the fire is at present unknown.

A COAL MINE FOR A GRAVE.

WILKESBARRE, Penn., Aug. 21.—The Nanticoke mine disaster has again been recalled by a letter from Gov. Pattison to the officers of the Susquehanna Coal Company, in which he states that he is in daily receipt of appeals from the relatives of the victims urging him to request the company to renew their efforts to recover the bodies. The officers of the company say further work of rescue is impossible. They might spend $100,000 and then not be able to find the bones of the men. They are willing to leave the whole question as to whether they are not right in their diagnosis to a board composed of 12 experienced and uninterested miners.

HE'S NO LANDLUBBER.

NEW-ORLEANS, Aug. 21.—The steamship Louisiana, of the Cromwell Line, arrived at her wharf this morning. This made her one hundredth trip from New-York to New-Orleans. Capt. E. V. Gager, who brought her in, has had command of her ever since her initial trip. Capt. Gager brought the first vessel of the Cromwell Line, the George Washington, to this port in 1863 and has been continuously in the service as Captain of various vessels ever since that time. He has made 330 voyages from New-York to New-Orleans and return.

CUTTING TO BE RELEASED

THE COURT THINKS HE HAS BEEN PUNISHED ENOUGH.

MEXICO WILL ALSO REMIT THE FINE, BUT WILL NOT ADMIT THAT SHE HAS VIOLATED ANY RIGHT.

EL PASO, Texas, Aug. 21.—By a special dispatch to the El Paso *Times* it has just been learned that yesterday the Second Chamber of the Supreme Tribunal of this State took up the case of A. K. Cutting, and, after reviewing the entire evidence, the argument began. This did not last long. The attorneys had previously come to an agreement that "the two months' imprisonment already suffered by Cutting be considered a complete purgation of his crime." This makes it certain beyond a doubt that the sentence which follows shortly will conform to this agreement among the attorneys. The case was heard with closed doors. The court holds that both Judge Castenador and Judge Zubia were exactly right in trying and sentencing Cutting, but, under the circumstances, thinks he has now, by two months' confinement, suffered enough, and they will order his release, to take effect probably by Tuesday or Wednesday of next week. The $600 fine is also to be remitted.

The court expressly reaffirms all that has been said in favor of the right of Mexico to try an offense committed in the United States. Therefore the status of the case as an international question is not and will not be in the least altered by the release of Cutting. It will come up again directly on a question of indemnity. Consul Brigham says he did not see how the release of Cutting at this stage would change anything but the personal comfort of Mr. Cutting. It was not so much a question of the personal liberty of Mr. Cutting as the broad principle at stake between the Governments, and, as he understood, the court had expressly affirmed the validity of the law which Secretary Bayard has rightly said that the United States could never permit to be enforced. It was likely that the point would come up again on the question of indemnity, which, he thought, would have to be paid.

WASHINGTON, Aug. 21.—No intimation has been received at the State Department of the alleged purpose of the Mexicans to pardon Cutting as soon as he shall have entered upon his term of imprisonment, but there is a disposition to believe that some way will soon be found to release him and thus to get rid of the annoying complication. Should this be done merely as an act of clemency on the part of the Mexican authorities, and without any avowed renunciation of the claim of extra-territorial jurisdiction, this Government will then undertake the task of securing such a renunciation so far as American citizens are concerned, since the claim is held to be abhorrent to all the principles of modern international law, as recognized and practiced by Governments which make any pretense to civilization. With Cutting out of the way as a direct issue, the subsequent proceedings would, of course, be carried on entirely through the leisurely channels of diplomacy, and without a hint or suspicion of possible war on either side.

It is admitted that the obnoxious law was, at the time Mexico declared her independence, a part of the French code, and that certain other powers of Europe may have set up and practiced upon similar claims at that time; but it is asserted that it has long since been abrogated or passed into disuse, and that such a claim would not now be assented to for a moment by the American Government, whoever might set it up. There are crimes, such as conspiracies to overthrow foreign Governments and the fitting out of filibustering expeditions, which, if committed by Americans upon American soil would not only render the criminal liable to arrest and punishment here for a violation of our own laws, but also, if subsequently caught within the jurisdiction of the offended Government, liable to apprehension and trial according to the laws of that power, without calling for other action on the part of our Government than the effort to see that the accused had a fair trial. But offenses against the persons or the interests of foreigners committed upon American soil, either by Americans or foreigners, are, it is claimed, within the sole and exclusive jurisdiction of American courts, and to this doctrine, it is asserted, all civilized Governments except Mexico assent.

It can be stated by authority that no demand for Consul Brigham's resignation has been made and that he is held in high esteem by the Department of State. So far as the department is officially informed his actions in connection with the Cutting episode have been wise, energetic, and creditable. It seems to be accepted in some quarters as proved that the department has made a mistake in its assumption that Mexico holds Cutting for an act committed upon this side of the boundary line. No mistake is acknowledged at the department, and so far as its present information goes the position taken by this Government is fully justified.

CITY OF MEXICO, Aug. 21.—The talk of a war has died out here, as it is generally regarded that the two Governments will arrange matters by diplomacy, but among Americans it is felt that a new treaty adapted to modern times should be negotiated. A Californian syndicate has taken a large mining property in the State of Michoacan, after coming to the conclusion that there is no danger of an interruption of peace. The capital of the syndicate is stated to be $350,000. English investors are making many inquiries regarding Mexican properties. Wholesale dealers are advancing prices on account of the depreciation in the value of silver.

SEVEN HURT, NONE KILLED.

WASHINGTON, Aug. 21.—What might have been a serious railroad accident occurred on the Metropolitan Branch of the Baltimore and Ohio Railroad where it crosses M-street, in this city. The Chicago express came round the Y at its usual rapid rate, and, coming upon the track of the Metropolitan Branch, it ran down at full speed before stopping to back into the station. While running at high speed the engineer saw the Hagerstown accommodation standing on the track ahead of him waiting to follow his train up to the station. He at once endeavored to check the speed of the express by putting on the air brakes, but they would not work, and in a moment his engine went crashing into the accommodation, badly wrecking the locomotive of the Hagerstown train and driving the tender through the front of the baggage car. The passengers in both trains were much shaken and bruised and six or eight persons were injured, but there was no loss of life.

Alfred Ray, a large land owner near Forest Glen, jumped from the train, rolled down the steep embankment, and it may be has sustained serious injury, and a lady on one of the rear cars was badly cut.

George A. Jeffries, living at Knowles Station, on the Metropolitan Branch, was injured about the head and hips.

Thomas Reed had a rib broken.

Mrs. Crossen, of Clifton, Va., received cuts about the body and had her thumb sprained.

James Reed was thrown from his seat and had his side injured.

Mr. Ray, an old gentleman living in the First Ward, also received slight injuries about the side.

A MINISTER'S FUNERAL.

LANCASTER, Penn., Aug. 21.—The funeral of the Rev. W. T. Gerhard tood place this morning at 10 o'clock. The services were held in the First Reformed Church, which was crowded. The opening service was read by the Rev. Dr. J. M. Fitzel, Pastor of the church. The Rev. Dr. J. Stahr, of Franklin and Marshall, read the lesson. The Rev. Dr. F. A. Gast, of the Reformed Theological Seminary, offered prayer. The Rev. Dr. Tibel announced the hymn and preached the funeral sermon, his text being: "Blessed are the dead that die in the Lord." After the sermon a short address was made by the Rev. Dr. Thomas G. Apple, President of Franklin and Marshall. At the conclusion of the services the procession moved to Lancaster Cemetery, where the interment was made. The pall bearers were the Rev. A. C. Wilmer, the Rev. W. F. Lichliter, of St. Luke's Reformed Chapel; the Rev. J. Max Hark, of the Moravian Church; the Rev. F. P. Mayser, of Zion Lutheran Church; the Rev. Dr. Theodore Appel, Superintendent of Reformed Missions, and the Rev. C. Elvin Houpt, of Grace Lutheran Church.

THE FLORISTS ADJOURN.

PHILADELPHIA, Aug. 21.—At to-day's session of the American Florists' Society interesting papers were read by J. H. Taylor, Bayside, N. Y.; William Hamilton, Allegheny, Penn., and J. D. Carmody, Evansville, Ind. The convention then adjourned.

BEQUEST TO A COLLEGE.

CHAUTAUQUA, N. Y., Aug. 21.—Miss Lindley, of Meadville, Penn., who died a few days ago, left $10,000 to Allegheny College, at Meadville, for the benefit of needy students.

A TRIPLE DROWNING.

HILLSDALE, Ontario, Aug. 21.—Thomas and William Taylor, brothers, and John Hamilton, were drowned while fishing in Orr Lake.

GERONIMO CAPTURED.

SURROUNDED BY THE MEXICANS WHILE TREATING FOR PEACE.

NOGALES, Arizona, Aug. 21.—News has just reached here that while negotiations were pending between the Mexican authorities and Geronimo, near Arispe, the Mexicans quietly surrounded the Indians, and that they now have them where there is no possibility of escape. Geronimo has been notified that the only terms will be an unconditional surrender. Capt. Lawton has been notified and is now moving toward Arispe.

WASHINGTON, Aug. 21.—Gov. Zulick, of Arizona, arrived in the city last night from the West and to-day had a protracted consultation with Secretary Lamar at the Interior Department respecting Territorial matters. The chief subject of discussion was the Indian situation in the Southwest. The Governor's attention being called by a reporter to the published statement that Gov. Ross and other Federal officials of New-Mexico had forwarded to the President a petition urging the removal of the Warm Spring and Chiricahua band of Apaches from Arizona, he said:

"I am glad to know that; the removal of these bands, which have so long terrorized the Southwest is, to my mind, an absolute and pressing necessity. I see that Geronimo is negotiating for terms, and in all probability he is anxious to surrender and return once more to his reservation and be forgiven; but this should not be permitted. Some time about the 1st of December last, I wrote to the Secretary of the Interior upon this subject and urgently requested that the Government adopt measures for the prompt and permanent removal of these bands from our Territory, and I am gratified to learn that Gen. Miles and Gov. Ross are so strongly and ably seconding my efforts. It is estimated that in the raids made by these Indians since their first surrender in 1878 there have been 2,500 persons murdered in Mexico, Arizona, and the adjoining Territories, besides the destruction of a vast amount of property. The reservation of San Carlos stands as a door opening through mountain ranges, every foot of which has been known to these Indians and their ancestors for centuries to the Sierra Madre range, whose almost inaccessible fastnesses present for them a home of perfect security.

"They are strong, muscular, and of endurance almost incredible to us of peaceful habits, capable of climbing with ease the most rugged mountains, and by the celerity of their movements defying the military to overtake and punish them on their marches. This is evidenced by the fact that Geronimo and his band when they left the reservation last Spring traveled 90 miles before they kindled a fire. When Chatto four years ago made his raid through New-Mexico and Sonora he went over 400 miles in six days, killing and murdering as he went. He was gone by the time the artillery and citizens were aroused to his presence, leaving a path of ruin and desolation behind him. There are now upon the San Carlos Reservation, which is a body of land 150 miles long by 100 miles wide, of Tonto, Mohave, San Carlos, and Yuma-Naches about 2,939, and of White Mountain Apaches 1,600. These are all peaceable and nearly self-supporting.

"The Chiricahua and Warm Spring Indians alone have defied every attempt to civilize them. Their treatment upon the reservation in former years has been an advertisement to other tribes that the greater and more numerous the outrages they commit upon unoffending citizens the more immunities are granted them. When wearied with bloodshed they return with perfidious faith to San Carlos. When year before last for the third time they had surrendered they were placed upon that portion of the reservation which had been claimed and occupied by the White Mountain Indians for a hundred years; were given improved farming utensils, seed, and everything necessary to till the soil, while the White Mountains, who have remained peaceful and are nearly self-supporting, were left to plow with tin cans, old hatchets, and anything else they could utilize for the purpose. The humane policy of the Government in supplying the Chiricahuas with the richest lands within the Territory, clothing and feeding them, has been repaid by treachery and bloodshed.

"It is hard to believe, but not a single hostile Chiricahua has ever been punished for his crime. I think I but voice the universal sentiment of the people of Arizona when I declare that there can be no proper or permanent peace so long as these hostile Indians are permitted to remain within the Territory. They have failed to observe every treaty stipulation made with them and cannot be trusted, as the past fully demonstrates. They are to-day, as they have ever been, a menace to our civilization, an obstacle to the introduction of capital and the acquisition of population."

"But where would you place them?" was asked.

"This question the Government must answer. In that question I am not deeply interested. We have borne the burden of their presence for many years, and we are now only anxious that the burden be transferred."

DEMOCRATS MUCH ALARMED.

AN UNFORTUNATE CONTRACT WITH A BOYCOTTED FIRM.

WASHINGTON, Aug. 21.—Officers of the Democratic Congressional Committee, who are busily engaged in sending out documents for use in the Fall campaign, have made a discovery which is giving them some concern. The contract for doing the printing for the committee was recently awarded to a firm in this city. The committee has been told that the firm does not employ union printers, and has for that reason been denounced as a "rat" office by the local Typographical Union, and put under the ban of a boycott by the Knights of Labor. The committee is tied up to the contract, and to be released from it would probably cost more than would be pleasant, considering that the committee is having hard work to secure the funds it wants for regular expenses. Chairman Kenna and his colleagues are hoping that their contract with a boycotted firm will not become generally known among the Knights of Labor, and are wondering what effect it would have if the Knights did know about it.

Col. Robert L. Taylor, who staid away from the Democratic Convention which nominated him for Governor of Tennessee because he was United States Pension Agent at Knoxville and did not care to violate President Cleveland's instructions to officeholders, is now in Washington. It is understood that he is here to present his resignation of the office of Pension Agent, as he proposes to make a lively canvass for the Governorship against his brother, who is the Republican nominee for the same high position. The latter is not under the necessity of giving up a good Federal office in order to electioneer for a State office.

HOW WATKINS WAS LYNCHED.

LOUISVILLE, Ky., Aug. 21.—A steamboat man who was an eye witness to the lynching of William Watkins, of this city, at Aurora, Ind., Thursday morning, for the murder of his employer. Helbert, arrived in the city to-day and told the story of the affair. His story is that Watkins staid with his victim, plunging the knife into him until life was extinct. The murderer was caught by the Sheriff of the county, and was on his way to jail when attacked by the mob. The lynching was no preconcerted affair. The people were considerably excited over the murder, and a crowd had formed near the distillery, where the prisoner was held by the Sheriff, but with no intention of lynching. This idea did not take definite shape till a man shouted out from the crowd: "Hang him!"

The suggestion thus thrown out was quickly acted upon. The words had hardly been spoken when a man near the Sheriff shook the folds from a rubber coat he carried on his arm and threw it over the head of the Sheriff. While a few men smothered the resistance of the Sheriff thus hampered, the rest of the crowd seized the prisoner and dragged him to an old well near by, pulled up the platform, tied the rope around his neck, and hoisted him by means of the old-fashioned sweep.

DROWNED WHILE BATHING.

SEABRIGHT, N. J., Aug. 21.—George V. Shiner, of New-York, a guest of the Peninsula Hotel, was drowned while bathing this afternoon. He was an expert swimmer, but venturing out too far, it is supposed, he got a cramp. The body was recovered in front of the hotel. Mr. Shiner was formerly a member of the firm of Harbison, Shiner & Co., dry goods merchants in Broadway. He lived at the Murray Hill Hotel.

ONE FOR THE MAYFLOWER

THE WINNER IN THE FIRST OF THE TRIAL RACES.

SHE BEATS THE OTHERS ON WINDWARD WORK IN SPLENDID STYLE—THE ATLANTIC LEADS GOING DOWN THE BAY.

The biggest boat was the leader yesterday. The first of the trial races to decide which of the four crack sloops shall defend the America's Cup this year was sailed under favorable conditions, and the new Boston sloop Mayflower proved herself a veritable skimmer of the seas. She started last and finished first, defeating the three other sloops in one of the prettiest yacht races ever seen in these waters. There have been more exciting races and more uncertain ones, but yesterday's contest was satisfactory because there were no accidents, no "flukes," no streaks of luck. It was plain sailing from beginning to end, and so far as any spectator could judge the boat that won was the boat that ought to have won; and she did in spite of certain mistakes of judgment which, being imitated by the Puritan, unquestionably lost that gallant yacht the second place in the race. The Atlantic was magnificently handled by Capt. Joe Ellsworth and sailed an admirable race, showing that the recent alterations made in her were wise. The Priscilla was also exceedingly well managed by her owner, Commodore Cass Canfield, and J. Frederick Tams, but the other boats had lighter heels. The Mayflower was sailed by Capt. Stone and the Puritan by her old skipper, Capt. Aubrey Crocker.

The E. Luckenbach did not figure as the judges' boat yesterday. Another tug belonging to the same owner and called the Luther C. Ward, a comfortable boat, left Pier No. 3 East River at 8:30 A. M. with ex-Commodore James D. Smith, Chairman of the Regatta Committee, a number of members of the New-York Yacht Club, and a variegated collection of newspaper men and carrier pigeons on board. There was a pretty bit of a wrinkle on the greenish gray water as the big two-masted tug steamed down the Bay, with her bright striped awnings spread and her flags flying. The rich blue of the August sky was decked with long white mare's tails and snow ball clouds that hovered around and looked as if they were puffing their fat cheeks for a good-natured blow. Coasters were making sail and lumbering down toward the Narrows in a way that showed that the softly piping breeze from the east-southeast had some backbone in it. The tug steamed down toward the Atlantic Yacht Club's anchorage, and the eyes of all on board began to search among the tangle of masts and spreading canvas for the giant mainsails of the racers.

Off Bay Ridge there was a small village of yachts bobbing up and down. The Mayflower was just getting under way, hoisting her big yellow mainsail as she slid out into the open water under her jibs. The Puritan was gliding away a little further to the south and getting up her club topsail as she went. Between the two boats was the Atlantic, with her saucy stern cocked up in the air, while away over by Staten Island the Priscilla was standing up like a lighthouse. All the sails gleamed white in the bright morning sun except the Puritan's mainsail, which was a trifle touched with mildew.

The British cutter Galatea, which came all the way across the ocean to hunt for the America's Cup, was lying calmly at her anchorage. She was a beautiful picture—one to fill a sailor man with enthusiasm. The judges' boat ran down near her and Lieut. Henn, her owner, and J. Beavor-Webb appeared at the rail. Lieut. Henn had on a white Tam o' Shanter cap, a dark blue reefing jacket, and white flannel trousers. His bronzed and bearded face was as full of smiles as a bottle of cocktails as he greeted his friends on the tug. His dingy was hauled alongside and he shouted in a cheery voice: "I'm going with you." He jumped into his boat and in a few moments was on the upper deck of the tug laughing and chatting in that genial manner of his which has already made him extremely popular among yachting men on this side of the Atlantic. The Galatea, under the charge of Mr. Beavor-Webb, subsequently made sail and went down into the Lower Bay to see some of the fun.

The tug next ran over to Tompkinsville, where she took aboard William Krebs, Secretary of the committee, and one or two other New-York Yacht Club members. Then she ran over toward Owl's Head and took up her position to windward of the buoy whence the race was to start. The course was from an imaginary line off Owl's Head to and around the Southwest Spit Buoy, No. 8½, to and around the Sandy Hook Lightship, keeping it on the starboard hand, thence back over the same course, finishing off Buoy No. 15, south of Fort Wadsworth.

It was now approaching the hour for the beginning of the contest, and the fleet of boats bearing spectators began to arrive. It increased during the day until a great crowd of steam and sailing craft of all descriptions, from stately steam yachts and dignified schooners down to the most awkward and lubberly old lighters, were outside the Narrows. Among those that went down were the steam yachts Electra, the flagship of the New-York Yacht Club; Stranger, Hinda, Vision, Angler, Empress, Ocean Gem, Mignon, Loando, Marion, Ruby, Inanda, Nooya, and Ruth, the schooners Estelle, which had a large party of ladies on board; Miranda, Fortuna, Grayling, Dauntless, Edith, and Lotus; the big yawl Cythera, the steamboats Columbia, Sylvester, and the police boat Patrol; the tugs E. Burgess, Cyclops, Joseph Stickney, Fred E. Ives, R. H. Williams, Jr., F. W. Vosburg, and James D. Nichol, and a kaleidoscopic collection of all sorts of sloops, cutters, yawls, sharpies, open jib and mainsail boats, catboats, rowboats, catamarans, and if any kind of craft has not been mentioned it was there just the same. The shores of Long Island and the heights of Fort Tompkins were covered with early risers, and wherever there was a good point of observation some one seemed to have found it, and staked out a claim on it.

And now the four flyers were hunting for positions up to windward of the starting line. It was just 10 o'clock when Capt. Luckenbach pulled the string and opened up the Luther C. Ward's whistle, letting out a long blast of warning. At this moment the Puritan was the windward boat of the fleet—that is, the nearest to Staten Island—and the nearest to the judges' boat, which was at the windward end of the starting line. The Mayflower was abreast of the Puritan, but further up the Bay. The Atlantic was the furthest boat west, but was on a line astern of the Mayflower, and the Priscilla was to leeward of them all. All were carrying, of course, mainsails and club topsails. The Priscilla held up also, her forestaysail and jib and her intermediate jib topsail up in stops. The other three had their jibs set, and their forestaysails and jib topsails in stops. The Galatea was lying off and on below the line watching the work of the four contestants.

The Puritan, Mayflower, and Atlantic stood on over toward the Staten Island shore. The Priscilla wore ship and went toward the middle of the Bay. The Atlantic, handled with consummate cunning by Capt. Ellsworth, ran to windward of the Puritan, as that crack was easing off, broke her forstaysail out of the stops, and headed for the line on the weather side of the fleet. The Puritan was the leading boat, the Atlantic second and windward, the Priscilla third and furthest to leeward, and the Mayflower fourth when the starting whistle blew at 10:10.

Like bursts of white smoke the Priscilla, Puritan, and Atlantic broke out their jib topsails, and a moment later the Mayflower followed suit. At the same moment the wind freshened up with a sudden access of enthusiasm and hauled squarely into the southeast. Close hauled, with everything pulling like mustard plasters, down went the sloops with smothers of white foam under their keen bows. The Priscilla and Atlantic forereached on the Puritan and the three boats crossed the line almost at the same time, making a marine picture full of splendid life. The Atlantic went across the line first, the Puritan second, the Priscilla third, and the Mayflower last. The time was as follows:

	H. M. S.		H. M. S.
Atlantic	10:12:07	Priscilla	10:13:29
Puritan	10:12:50	Mayflower	10:14:26

The Mayflower was jammed up to windward till her head sails shook as if she had the ague

The New-York Times.

VOL. XXXVI.....NO. 10,969. NEW-YORK, THURSDAY, OCTOBER 28, 1886. PRICE TWO CENTS.

WORKING FOR ROOSEVELT

SUPPORTERS FLOCKING TO HIM BY HUNDREDS.

ADHERENTS COMING FROM THE OTHER CANDIDATES — PREPARATIONS FOR GREAT MEETINGS IN HIS FAVOR.

Rain did not damp the Roosevelt boom yesterday apparently, for from early morning until late at night the headquarters in the Fifth-Avenue Hotel were thronged with the friends and workers of the energetic Republican candidate, who met many hundreds during the day, and received scores of letters containing assurances of support for him.

Mr. Roosevelt is gaining daily among the business men at a rate which has set the Hewitt men at their wits' ends to find a way to stop such inroads into their strength. This is particularly noticeable in the Stock Exchange, where the Democratic members who will vote for Mr. Roosevelt are numbered by the score. He will also have without exception the vote of the independent Republicans on the Exchange who supported Cleveland. It was at first thought best to organize a Roosevelt club on the Exchange, but the active Roosevelt men advised against it, believing that more could be accomplished by quiet work, and so the project was abandoned.

The roll of membership of the Down-town Roosevelt Club has now over 1,200 names, among those added yesterday being C. H. Delamater & Co., of the great Delamater Iron Works; Henry Clews, the banker; E. H. Ludlow & Co., the real estate men; Wetmore & Jenner, lawyers; Randolph W. Townsend, Ralph N. Ellis, A. F. Brombacher & Co., hardware; William M. Prichard, John M. Knox, lawyer; Stewart & Boardman, attorneys; Theodore W. Bailey & Co., Lefferts Strebeigh, lawyer; Austin Abbott, lawyer; William Fellowes Morgan, W. Gayen Dominick, W. A. Duer, George K. Otis, Walter Lawrence, and William D. Murphy.

An informal meeting of the Down-town Club was held at its headquarters, No. 47 Broadway, yesterday afternoon to make further arrangements for the mass meeting to be held on the steps of the Sub-Treasury, in Wall-street, Saturday afternoon. A committee from the Dry Goods Men's Club announced that it would participate in the meeting, marching down, a thousand strong, from the corner of Worth-street and Broadway, headed by the Twenty-second Regiment Band. The Down-town Club, with the Twelfth Regiment Band, will march up Broadway and down Wall-street to the meeting place, and speaking will begin at 3:15. Members of the Stock, Produce, and Real Estate Exchanges will join the two clubs at the Sub-Treasury steps, and as lively a meeting as has ever been seen on Wall-street is a certainty. Jackson S. Schultz will probably preside, and Gen. Stewart L. Woodford has telegraphed from Boston that he will be back in time to make a speech.

Mr. Roosevelt met 200 or 300 of the young men who are doing such excellent work for him at the rooms of the club during the afternoon, and being persuaded to "say something to the boys," thanked them most heartily for the work they had done in his behalf, a work the value of which could not be overestimated. He pleased them by informing them that the practical men in the Campaign Committee had said of their work that it was as practical and effective as any they had ever seen performed. Their work, said the young candidate, was especially gratifying because it came from a class of men who, he knew, would hold up his hands in any work he attempted for the best interests of the city. "The prospect of my election," he said, "has grown brighter day by day since my nomination, and while the fight has been an up-hill one the grade is growing less and less steep, until now we are on a level and daily getting the best of our enemies. If I am elected I know that all you will ask of me is to conduct the affairs of the city practically, well, and honestly, and that I promise you I shall do."

Richard Watson Gilder, editor of the *Century*, is an active supporter of Mr. Roosevelt and the principles he represents in this campaign. He has never before taken an active part in politics, but is this year doing what he can to assist in the election of Mr. Roosevelt. His first political speech was made in favor of Mr. Roosevelt's candidacy at the meeting of the Third Assembly District organization at the Cooper Institute on Tuesday evening.

Rufus Hatch, whom every one knows, and whom every one on the Street likes, is another of the very, very many men who have come to the conclusion that the proper man to elect Mayor is Mr. Roosevelt. At first he was a Hewitt man and believed him to stand the best show of an election, but he yesterday decided that if he voted for Hewitt he would be throwing away his vote, and so he has decided to vote for and support Mr. Roosevelt.

Owing to the rain last evening the Young Men's Roosevelt Club of the Twenty-first District made no parade. Instead it will parade, headed by the Ninth Regiment Band, on Saturday night. Members of the club are requested to meet at their headquarters in Morton Hall at 7 o'clock on Saturday evening. The club will make a good showing by turning out with full ranks.

The First Ward Roosevelt Campaign Club will have a meeting to-morrow evening at the Long Branch Hotel, No. 59 West-street, at which a number of good speakers will be present, including Gen. O'Beirne.

The colored voters of the Eleventh District will have a ratification meeting this evening at No. 106 West Thirtieth-street, near Sixth-avenue, at which Mr. Roosevelt, John C. O'Connor, Robert Ray Hamilton, and J. T. Van Rensselaer will make addresses. The colored men of the district propose to make it one of the liveliest meetings ever held in that vicinity.

Mr. Roosevelt will have a busy time this and to-morrow evenings. He will speak to-night at meetings in the Thirteenth, Eleventh, and Nineteenth Districts. To-morrow night he will speak at meetings in the Tenth, Eighteenth, Twenty-fourth, and Twenty-second Districts, and at the colored voters' mass meeting at the Grand Opera House Hall.

The Republican Club met last night at No. 32 West Twenty-eighth-street, and arranged for the appointment of special inspectors to look after affairs for Mr. Roosevelt on election day.

NOTES FROM NEWPORT.

NEWPORT, R. I., Oct. 27.—Mr. B. Powel, son of John Hare Powel, Mayor of Newport, is to be married to Miss Whipple, eldest daughter of Mr. and Mrs. John Whipple, formerly of New-York. Miss Whipple is a granddaughter of the late Gov. Thomas Swann, of Maryland. Mr. Powel's family came from Powelton, Penn., and are large real estate owners in Philadelphia; Mr. Powel is 18 years of age and Miss Whipple is about the same age.

A cottage site has been purchased on Conanicut Island by Mrs. C. H. Davis, of Washington, D. C.

Mr. Hugh K. Norman, of this city, was married to-day to Miss Dora Prindall, only daughter of Mr. and Mrs. Charles Prindall, of Gloucester, where the wedding took place. There were no bridesmaids and no ushers. The bride was dressed in a rich traveling suit. A reception followed the ceremony at the residence of the bride's parents. The presents were many and very costly. A solid silver tea service was presented by George H. Norman, the millionaire waterworks contractor, who provided at his own expense Newport's system of public water. The newly married couple will leave in a few days on their wedding tour, which will be spent in Europe.

PRESIDENT BARILLAS'S ESCAPE.

NEW-ORLEANS, Oct. 27.—A private letter received here to-day gives the particulars of an attempt upon the life of President Barillas, of Guatemala, who succeeded to the control of the Government upon the death in battle of Rufino Barrios a few years ago. The story goes that two merchants, druggists of Guatemala city, employed a servant of the President to administer poison with his food, and paid him $2,000 for the job. The man's courage failed him, however, and he went to the President, confessed the conspiracy, and delivered to him the poison and the money he had received. This was on the 10th inst. The would-be poisoners were arrested and were undergoing trial when the letter was written. If found guilty, of which there was no doubt, their execution was only a matter of a few days.

THE GREAT STRIKE IN CUBA ENDED.

HAVANA, Oct. 23.—The cigarmakers' strike, which had been in progress for some time past, has been settled. The operatives held another meeting in the Albisus Theatre, which, although a spacious building, was inadequate to contain all those who desired to enter. Mr. Upman, the manufacturer, was selected as the arbitrator between the manufacturers and their employes, and he succeeded in effecting an agreement. Work was resumed on Monday, Oct. 18. Most of the demands of the operatives were acceded to.

A VERY BAD MARKSMAN.

BIRMINGHAM, Conn., Oct. 27.—Ashbury Laity, a youth of 20, made up his mind to die to-day. He wrote letters to two young ladies, and facing a mirror tried to shoot himself in the head. He fired three times and was not wounded. Then he tried to jump over the banisters to the floor below, but was prevented. He was taken to the station house, and afterward released on a promise to consent to live. He is now guarded in his room.

TO BUILD ANOTHER MILL.

A PROPOSAL TO INCREASE THE SPINDLES OF FALL RIVER.

FALL RIVER, Mass., Oct. 27.—Quite a sensation has been created in this city of forty-odd mills over the report that some new ones are to be erected. The mill owners have long been complaining of the dullness in the print cloth market, and this argument has been used with telling force when the operatives have asked for an increase of wages. A few of the mills have of late shown a surplus. The Wampanoag has just increased its capital stock by the addition of 25,000 shares, made possible by the earnings over and above the dividends paid. The Stafford mills also have a surplus on hand, and the Directors have advised that a new mill be constructed. A special meeting of the stockholders will be called to consider the proposition.

The Stafford mills were incorporated in 1871, with a capital of $550,000. The last public statement of this mill, on March 17, showed a surplus of $108,898. The project has created considerable comment, and among the stockholders opposite views are freely expressed. It is claimed by these who are not in favor of any more cotton mills that the policy of the Directors is suicidal. They agree that the capacity for producing print cloths here is already immense, as viewed by the experience of past years, when goods have been piled up and no market could be found for them. Profits on the cotton industry have figured very small for the last five years in this city, and the stock on hand at present and a fair demand do not insure future prosperity. It is reasoned, therefore, that there should be fewer mills before there are more.

On the other hand, a number of the Directors, backed by others who have capital invested in the mill, are of the opinion that the outlook warrants the building of another factory. The Stafford mill has made money, as shown by the surplus, and the addition of new machinery would increase the value of the present investment. The corporation owns land on which to build the new mill. It is estimated that the new mill could be built for about $13 per spindle, and not much less, which would require an outlay of about $500,000. One of the last mills built here, in the construction of which due economy was practiced, cost for building, land, equipment, &c., $13 per spindle, and conditions have not materially changed. It is rumored that several other mills are to be erected.

TEMPORARILY EMBARRASSED.

A CINCINNATI DRY GOODS HOUSE ASKS FOR TIME.

CINCINNATI, Oct. 27.—A rumor that the wholesale dry goods house of Shipley, Dorsey & Co. was cramped, and had been compelled to ask for an extension of time from their creditors was the talk of the afternoon in business circles. Inquiry confirmed the report. The information given out was that the firm, becoming temporarily embarrassed, had asked their New-York creditors to grant an extension of time for two, four, six, eight, and ten months, without security, and the creditors had agreed to such an arrangement. The firm is said to be doing a business of about $1,500,000 a year. Some months ago they moved into a new building on Fourth-street, where they pay $18,000 a year rent. Their business has largely increased since the removal, and, it is stated, has grown beyond their capital. The statement made to the New-York creditors was that the firm has assets in the shape of stock, bills receivable, and real estate to the amount of $1,000,000, and liabilities of about $860,000. It is stated that prices have advanced since the house purchased its present stock, and that there will be no difficulty in meeting the obligations if the time is given.

FAILURES IN BUSINESS.

YORK, Penn., Oct. 27.—An execution was issued to-day against Thompson & Brother, cigar manufacturers, of Wrightsville, this county, for $9,500. There is said to be about $13,000 assets. The liabilities are $18,000.

ST. LOUIS, Oct. 27.—A deed of assignment for the benefit of creditors was filed in the Recorder's office to-day by Augustus A. Mellier, K. Duncan Mellier, and Alvin Mellier, composing the firm of A. A. Mellier & Co., doing a wholesale drug business at Nos. 909 and 911 Washington-avenue. The firm places their assets at $30,000, with liabilities estimated at $100,000, distributed about equally between creditors in the East and West. The assets are well secured. K. Duncan Mellier says that the cause of the failure is due entirely to many heavy losses by a decreased business and a shrinking in value of their stock.

VICKSBURG, Miss., Oct. 27.—Marx & Weinstein, dealers in dry goods, made an assignment to-day to E. F. Beck for the benefit of their creditors, none being preferred. The assets are about $13,000; liabilities, $11,000. Attachments amounting to $3,500 were issued to-day against the stock.

THE CROW-SIOUX FIGHT.

FORT KEOGH, Montana, Oct. 27.—The following additional particulars regarding the late fight on the Crow Reservation between a party of Crow and Sioux Indians, in which five of the Indians were killed and scalped, have just been reported: The expedition left the Yankton Agency a short time ago with the avowed intention of raiding the Crow camp on the Little Rosebud. Concealing their horses in a ravine, they went into the timber to reconnoitre. Their horses were found by the Crows and identified. A search was made and resulted in the killing of two Sioux and three Crows and the wounding of three of the latter. The remaining Sioux escaped to Fort Custer and reported the fight. The Crows had a war dance over the dead bodies of the Sioux, shot their bodies full of holes, and cut off the head of one with an axe. The report says the Crows are putting on paint and are preparing for war. It is purely an Indian quarrel and not dangerous to whites.

YALE UNIVERSITY HEREAFTER.

NEW-HAVEN, Conn., Oct. 27.—The corporation of Yale College held a meeting in this city to-day. The editor of the annual catalogue was directed to use the name of Yale University hereafter in that and similar official publications. The resignation of O. T. Sherman, who has been for several years in charge of the Thermometric Bureau of the observatory, was accepted. Mr. Sherman leaves New-Haven to pursue studies elsewhere. The honorary degree of Master of Arts was conferred on Elbert B. Monroe, of Southport, Conn., and on the Hon. Sidney B. Beardsley, of Bridgeport. Mr. Monroe is the donor of Dwight Hall, the new Young Men's Christian Association College Building, and is a graduate from the University of the City of New-York in the Class of '55. Mr. Beardsley is a Judge of the Superior Court of Connecticut.

CLARA MORRIS'S MANAGER SUED.

CHICAGO, Oct. 27.—J. H. McVicker, the proprietor of McVicker's Theatre, has begun a suit against Wesley Sisson, Clara Morris's manager, for $70,000 damages. As nearly as can be learned the suit is brought for alleged violation of contract, Mr. Sisson having decided to take Miss Morris to the Chicago Opera House for her engagement, which begins next week, instead of to McVicker's Theatre.

COLLEGE HILL PROPERTY SOLD.

POUGHKEEPSIE, N. Y., Oct. 27.—John Guy Vassar has purchased all the well known College Hill property from the New-York Mutual Life Insurance Company for $26,000. It originally cost $100,000. It is not yet known what Mr. Vassar intends to do with the property, but he says that "whatever is done will be for the good of the public."

A NEW BANK FOR BROOKLYN.

ALBANY, Oct. 27.—Bank Superintendent Willis S. Paine has authorized the Bedford Bank, of Brooklyn, to conduct a deposit and discount banking business, under the provisions of the State banking laws, with paid-up capital stock of $100,000. The officers of the bank are: Eugene G. Blackford, President; Howard M. Smith, Vice-President, and Douglass R. Satterlee, Cashier.

PERISHED IN THE FLAMES.

LYNCHBURG, Va., Oct. 27.—A fire at Pocahontas this morning destroyed 16 houses, including two hotels and several business houses. George Baber, of Lynchburg, perished in the flames. Several other persons are missing. The fire was the work of an incendiary. Heavy rain saved the town. The loss is $50,000; insurance unknown.

WILL HUNT THE KANGAROO.

NEW-HAVEN, Conn., Oct. 27.—A kangaroo rented from the New-York Central Park Museum escaped from a kangaroo show here to-night and jumped over the heads of a lot of boys and men who tried to catch him. A reward has been offered for his capture, and a body of men will hunt for him to-morrow.

LIBERTY'S GREAT STATUE

A GRAND CELEBRATION PROMISED FOR TO-DAY.

PROGRAMME OF THE EXERCISES ON BEDLOW'S ISLAND — FINAL ORDERS ABOUT THE PARADES.

The statue of Liberty yesterday was seen through a mist darkly. Piercing winds blew around Bedlow's Island, and the numerous workmen, who were not in any way protected from the weather, worked uncomfortably. The speakers' stand, and that for the use of musicians above it, were in readiness yesterday. Planks were removed and a semblance of tidiness was given to the island. A big barge, which looked extremely dismal, with its legend in red characters, "Eat, drink, and be merry," stood at the Bedlow's Island dock to land visitors. It will be used for that purpose this afternoon.

The following is the order of exercises on Bedlow's Island this afternoon:

1. Music during the landing and seating of the assembly.
2. Signal gun.
3. Prayer by the Rev. Richard S. Storrs, D. D.
4. Count Ferdinand de Lesseps, on behalf of Franco-American Union.
5. Presentation address, the Hon. William M. Evarts.
6. Unveiling.
7. Salute. A salvo from all the guns in the harbor.
8. Music.
9. Acceptance of the statue by the President.
10. Representative on behalf of the republic of France, Le Ministre Plénipotentiaire et Délégué Extraordinaire, A. Lefaivre.
11. Music.
12. Commemorative address, the Hon. Chauncey M. Depew.
13. Music. Doxology—tune, "Old Hundred;" in which the assembly is invited to join.
14. Benediction. Right Rev. Henry C. Potter, D. D. The assembly upon the island will be dismissed with the benediction, and will re-embark upon the steamers, which will return to their piers in the city, joining with the batteries in the general salute.
15. National salute. To be fired simultaneously from all the batteries in the harbor, ashore and afloat.
16. Illumination of the statue, with fireworks on Bedlow's and Governor's Islands and the Battery.

The music by Gilmore's Twenty-second Regiment Band, P. S. Gilmore Musical Director.

Major-Gen. Schofield's staff during the ceremonies attending the inauguration will be headed by Brevet Major-Gen. W. D. Whipple. Among his aides will be David H. King, Jr., Brevet Brig.-Gen. Charles H. Tompkins, Brevet Brig.-Gen. William W. Burns, Col. Daniel McClure, Col. Charles Sutherland, Col. Roger Jones, Brevet Lieut.-Col. J. H. Janeway, Lieut. E. L. Zalinski, Lieut.-Col. Marcus P. Miller, Lieuts. Benjamin H. Randolph, William W. Galbraith, Warren P. Newcomb, Harvey C. Carbaugh, Avery D. Andrews, Constantine Chase, J. Estcourt Sawyer, John Willis, C. B. Satterlee, Anthony W. Vogdes, Capt. James Halloran, Capt. J. A. Fessenden, Capt. David J. Craigie, and Brevet Brig.-Gen. Richard H. Jackson.

The naval parade will form off West Forty-fifth-street in two divisions. The following named vessels have been assigned places in the line:

FIRST DIVISION.

United States Coast Survey steamer Gedney; Belle Horton—Brooklyn city officials; Fra Diavolo, Marion, Hinda; Fred De Bary—Cercle Français de l'Harmonie and Woman Suffrage Association; Morrisania and Laura M. Starin—Grand Army of the Republic; Grand Republic—Veterans of the Seventh Regiment and the Brotherhood of Locomotive Engineers; Kaaterskill, H. E. Bishop, Livy, New-Haven, Magnolia, Mynders Starin, Sam Sloan, Eliza Hancox, barge J. S. T. Stranahan, and steamer N. J. Nelson.

SECOND DIVISION.

A. C. Cheney's Towing Line—A. C. Cheney, Prometheus, Terror, Conqueror, Camelia, Christiana, Saxon, P. C. Schultz; New-York, Lake Erie and Western Railroad Company's Vessels—Elmira, Buffalo, Van Houghton, Whipple, Roanoke, Governor Morgan, Don Juan; Pool & Co.'s Line—Chauncey M. Depew, J. H. Rutter, Blanche Paige, L. B. Dayton, C. F. Starin, American Eagle, H. M. Spraker; Perth Amboy Towing Line—Fannie P. Skeer, Isabel E. Wilbur, Isaac L. Fisher, Sallie P. Linderman; Bell Line Transportation Company—Robert Lockhart, Governor H. M. Hoyt, R. A. Packer; Schuyler's Towing Line—Niagara, Syracuse, Vanderbilt, Connecticut, Belle, America, Ontario, G. C. Adams, Quaker City, J. T. Easton, R. T. Banks; Moran's Towing Line—F. W. Vosburgh, George Garlick, Robert J. Moran, General Rosecrans; Reeve's Towing Line—Sammie, James Nichol, William Nichol, William N. Beach; Tice's Towing Line—Walter Tice, Nettie Tice, R. H. Williams, Charles E. Soper; Cornell's Towing Line—Cortes, J. C. Hart, E. H. Crosby, Townsend, William Street, C. G. Young, Thomas Dickson, E. Perry, J. M. Hedges, Hercules, R. M. Meade, Pratt; S. F. Shortland & Co.'s Line—James Watt, Thomas Shortland, General F. Sigel, Admiral, Border City, A. Mills, Carnie; David Bingham, May Clinton, S. R. St. John, Clara, Climax, Amelia, Victoria, Henry T. Sisson, Glen Cove, James A. Crawford, Fred E. Ives, Resolute, Thomas Walsh, E. J. Weed, Zouave, E. L. Levy, Glen Island, W. H. Vanderbilt, A. C. Gray, Mary Lewis, Gratitude, General Newton, Ocean King, Luckenback, Scandinavia, L. Ward, R. Burnett, Commodore Duryea, Mary H. Packer, Georgianna, Day Spring, W. J. McAldin, G. H. Dentz, James A. Garfield.

The following is a list of aides to Grand Marshal Gen. C. P. Stone: Gen. Henry A. Barnum, chief of staff; Capt Hugh G. Brown, Twelfth Infantry, Assistant Adjutant-General and Aide-de-camp; First Lieut. E. T. Brown, Fifth Artillery; Capt. Edward Field, Fourth Artillery; Brevet Capt. R. P. Strong, Fourth Artillery; Lieut. M. F. Waltz, Twelfth Infantry; Col. J. W. Jacobus, U. S. Volunteers; Lieut.-Col. F. A. Schilling, N. G. S. N. Y.; Major Lloyd Aspinwall, N. G. S. N. Y.; Major Charles Appleby, U. S. Volunteers; Major Benjamin J. Levy, U. S. Volunteers; Lieut.-Col. Gouraud, U. S. Volunteers; Capt. Charles H. McKenzie, U. S. Volunteers; Lieut. William F. Maher, U. S. Volunteers; Capt. Ferdinand Levy, U. S. Volunteers; Col. Frank S. Collins, N. G. S. N. Y.; Lieut.-Col. A. De Orville; Col. William E. Van Wyck, U. S. Volunteers; Lieut.-Col. A. M. Clark, U. S. Volunteers; Major G. M. Bundy, U. S. Volunteers; Major C. F. Ulrich, U. S. Volunteers; Col. Wilbur F. Brown, N. G. S. N. Y.; Gen. Anson G. McCook, U. S. Volunteers; Major David Scott, U. S. Volunteers; Frederick E. Blodgett, U. S. Volunteers; Lieut.-Col. Thomas Rafferty, U. S. Volunteers; Major John Van Duerson, Veteran Zouaves; Frank A. Sutton, Major James B. Horner, U. S. Volunteers; Col. John P. Walker, Gen. Kilborne Knox, Gen. J. Madison Drake, Col. John J. Garnett, Major H. W. B. Howard, Col. Edward H. Kent, Capt. James M. Brady, Col. Thomas C. Miles, Col. Granville P. Hawes, Capt. Frank M. Wilder, Col. J. B. Fassett, Major-Gen. James Hayes, Major-Gen. Charles H. T. Collis, Capt. H. Ansot, Capt. Henry Sinardi, Col. A. G. Dickinson, Col. Henry A. Gildersleeve, Col. Alfred Wagstaff, Gen. H. A. Tremain, Col. L. M. Dayton.

Gen. Horatio C. King, who has been assigned to the command of the Eighth Division, composed of independent military organizations, requests that these organizations shall form on East and West Fortieth-street, right resting on Fifth-avenue, at 9:30 A. M. The companies will form in column of twos on both sides of the street. The cavalry will form on West Fortieth-street, right resting on Fifth-avenue, and will have the advance of this division and will be followed by the Peekskill Cadets and the visiting companies from New-Jersey. Lieut.-Col. H. H. Beadle will act as chief of staff. The remainder of the staff will report at the Windsor Hotel at 8 A. M.

All day yesterday people came to the city in droves to participate in to-day's celebration. Extra heavily loaded trains, much behind schedule time, were the rule on every railroad entering the city. Every hotel was crowded to its utmost capacity last night, and there was hardly one of the better known hotels which did not have to turn away hundreds of would-be guests. This may be taken as an indication of the great crowds which will come to town to-day, when the carrying capacity of all the roads will be taxed to their utmost if the weather promises to be at all pleasant. Frenchmen were probably the most numerous among yesterday's arrivals, coming from all parts of the country and in great masses from the northern and western portions of this State, from Canada, and from the mills in Eastern Massachusetts and Connecticut. Last night's late trains added many to these contingents, and thousands more will reach here early this morning. A large party of Frenchmen engaged on the Panama Railroad and Canal are among the visitors.

In to-day's parade the Bartholdi Club, of New-York, will carry a banner the top of which, representing a hand holding the torch, was presented to it by M. Bartholdi, whom the club has enrolled as its first honorary member.

The following paper houses have agreed to close to-day: Charles Hubbs, Reynolds & Merriam, J. F. Anderson & Co., Miller & Flinn, Curran Brothers, Milton Hard's Sons, Clement Stockwell, Molleson Brothers, T. M. Bell, Miller & Loechner, Henry Lindenmeyr, Butler & Johnson, A. T. Hand, H. C. Hulbert & Co., M. Plummer & Co., Hastings & Todd, A. E. Crevies & Co., C. B. Hewitt & Brother, G. N. Miller & Co., Harris Brothers & Co., Horace Taylor, and L. Dejonge & Co. The members of the Building Material Exchange yesterday voted to have the Exchange closed to-day.

It was a matter of remark among those interested in making a success of the Bartholdi exercises that no tickets for the reviewing stand in Madison-square were sent to the Mayor. The Aldermen were supplied with a bundle of tickets of admission to the stand and most of them found their way into the hands of gin mill keepers and ward "heelers" of the lowest type. When a messenger was sent down to Richard Butler and the Committee of Arrangements from the Mayor's office a reply was given that all the tickets for officials had been sent to Alderman "Jim" Mooney.

Fourteen hundred policemen will be on duty taking care of the parade and the people who will flock to see it. Inspector Steers will have 250 at Madison-square. Superintendent Murray will command in person 500 men at the Battery, and Capts. Clinchy and Killilea will take 200 men over to Bedlow's Island. The remainder will be scattered along the line of march. The full detective force will be out.

The south roadway of the East River Bridge will be thrown open to-day for the use of pedestrians going from this city to Brooklyn. Those from Brooklyn must use the promenade.

President Cleveland and the members of his Cabinet who are to take part in to-day's ceremonies reached Jersey City soon after 9 o'clock last night in the fast train from Washington. As the President stepped from his car he was met by Station Master William Black, with whom he walked down the platform. Following him were Secretaries Bayard, Whitney, and Lamar, and Postmaster-General Vilas, with Col. Lamont bringing up the rear. All were quickly seated in two carriages, which were driven onto a Desbrosses-street ferry-boat, and, arrived in New-York, to Secretary Whitney's residence. The Presidential party will leave for Washington at 6 P. M. to-day.

CORNELL UNIVERSITY.

HONORARY DEGREES NOT TO BE CONFERRED IN FUTURE.

ITHACA, N. Y., Oct. 27.—At the meeting of the Board of Trustees of Cornell University this morning there were present President Adams and the following Trustees: George W. Schuyler, William R. Humphrey, Amasa J. Parker, Hiram Sibley, Henry W. Sage, Henry B. Lord, Lieut.-Gov. Jones, State Superintendent Draper, the Rev. Charles M. Tyler, and Messrs. Mynderse Van Cleef, George R. Williams, and J. De Witt Warner. Several matters of importance were discussed, but the only definite action taken during the morning session was relative to the matter of conferring honorary degrees, of which the Alumni of the university, with but very few exceptions, have recently expressed their disapproval. The action taken by the board last June, which favored the granting of honorary degrees, was unanimously rescinded, notwithstanding the fact that ex-President White is said to favor the idea.

At the afternoon session the question of the new law school was discussed, and a two years' course was decided upon with a Faculty comprising a resident Dean, a Professor, and Assistant Professor, and special non-resident Professors. This Faculty is to be chosen at the next meeting of the board, in January, 1887, when the public announcement of the law department will be made. The matter of State scholarships was also discussed with a view of devising a plan for procuring a full representation from the several Assembly districts in this State. A bill is to be submitted to the next Legislature on this subject. Appropriations were voted for the year, including a liberal allowance for the classical department.

The report of President Adams showed the institution to be in a flourishing condition in regard to the number of students and the efficiency of the Faculty. The whole number of students is 794, of which 370 are new students. The total number of Freshmen in full standing is 304. There are 33 post graduates.

The board adjourned to Jan. 20, 1887.

AN INSTITUTE BURNED.

THE CASE SCHOOL OF APPLIED SCIENCE IN RUINS.

CLEVELAND, Ohio, Oct. 27.—The Case School of Applied Science, founded by the late Leonard Case and endowed by him with property estimated to be worth $2,250,000, has been destroyed by a mysterious fire which broke out after midnight last night. The loss by the burning of the stately four-story structure, 92 by 167 feet, and the costly apparatus is nominally $200,000, the insurance upon which is comparatively trifling, but the loss which cannot be expressed in money is far greater. President Staley, who lately came from Union College, Schenectady, loses his valuable scientific library, his lectures, all the records of 25 years of educational work and some household goods. Prof. Albert Michaelson loses a costly collection of physical appliances, lectures, and all his mathematical calculations made here and while in the Annapolis Naval Academy, including important astronomical figures and his famous computations of the velocity of light. Prof. Hudson A. Wood loses one of the rarest collections of minerals and shells in the country. The scientific apparatus of the institution was bought in Europe for $22,000. One of the greatest losses was the relief map of Ohio, which excited much attention at the New-Orleans Exposition.

Adelbert College, which stands on contiguous ground, escaped. Its Trustees and Faculty to-day took formal action to express sympathy and offer rooms for the use of Case School classes. The offer was accepted, and study will be resumed next Monday. Prof. H. F. Reid, lately of Johns Hopkins University, arrived to-day to take a place in the Faculty as Professor of Mathematics. When he found the building burned he expected that he would be released from his engagement, but the Trustees notified him that he would be needed more than ever, as the intention is to continue the work and rehabilitate the school as speedily as practicable.

HIS CLOTHES CAUGHT FIRE.

NEW-HAVEN, Conn., Oct. 27.—Rudolph Lauze, aged 24, a clerk employed at Paul Jente & Brothers grocery, on Broadway, went into the cellar of the store this afternoon carrying with him a kerosene lamp. As he was about to return to the upper floor the lamp exploded, covering Lauze's face, hands, and clothing with oil, which instantly caught fire. A companion threw him upon the ground and had nearly succeeded in extinguishing the flames, when Lauze broke away from him, jumped to his feet, and ran up the stairs and into the street shrieking with pain. The flames burst out again, and were burning fiercely when the Rev. A. P. Miller, who was passing, pulled off his overcoat and threw it around Lauze, again subduing the flames. Lauze is frightfully burned about the body and neck. He was taken to the hospital where it is reported to-night that he has a bare chance to recover. He was to have been married to-morrow night to a Miss McAlpine, of this city. The cause of the explosion is unknown.

PRINCETON FRESHMEN HAPPY.

PRINCETON, N. J., Oct. 27.—The Princeton College Freshmen defeated the Vineland Preparatory School in a game of football this afternoon by 110 points to 0. The Freshmen commenced their scoring two minutes after the kick-off, and made touch-downs at short intervals all through the game. At the end of the first half the score stood 64 to 0. The second half lasted only 30 minutes, but during that time the Freshmen managed to score 46 points. The Freshmen team played well together, and did some very pretty passing. Hirst, Zeigler, Schoonmaker, Dohm, and Channing did the best work on the Freshmen eleven. Porter, '87, refereed the game.

BOYCOTTING KNIGHTS INDICTED.

PLYMOUTH, Mass., Oct. 27.—In the Superior Court the Grand Jury this afternoon reported an indictment against Peter McGeogh, of Lynn, and William Bokefer, of Salem, for conspiracy against the firm of Charles Harrington & Co. This is a well known boycotting case, in which the defendants, representing the State organization of the Knights of Labor, came to Plymouth and ordered out the men from the boot and shoe factory of Francis F. Emery until he agreed not to use Harrington's leather. The case is the first one of the kind in the New-England States.

JUBILANT REPUBLICANS.

NEW-BRUNSWICK, N. J., Oct. 27.—Although the Democrats have a majority of 1,200 the Republicans expect to carry the Third Assembly District of this county. The Democratic nominee is John Mulvey, a saloon keeper, who can hardly write his own name, and some of the party have revolted and placed an independent candidate in the field in the person of Freeholder Hezekiah Warne. As every Assemblyman will count in the contest for a successor to Senator Sewell the Republicans are jubilant.

A COUNTY TREASURER ROBBED.

LITTLE ROCK, Ark., Oct. 27.—Private advice from Desare, Ark., states that the County Treasurer of Prairie County was robbed this morning between the hours of 12 and 2 of about $11,000. Active measures are being taken to capture the robbers.

CHURCHILL AND THE IRISH

THE TORY LEADER'S SPEECH AT BRADFORD.

FOUR HUNDRED ADDRESSES PRESENTED TO HIM—HIS UTTERANCES SHARPLY CRITICISED BY THE PRESS.

LONDON, Oct. 27.—At the Conservative conference at Bradford yesterday the Right Hon. Henry Chaplin, member of Parliament, moving a vote of thanks to Lord Randolph Churchill for his speech and to the association, said he believed the time coming would be the worst the United Kingdom had ever experienced in agricultural depression. After speaking at the conference Lord Randolph addressed a large overflow meeting. His remarks were confined mainly to local matters.

Lord Randolph Churchill was presented with 400 addresses at Bradford to-day in the hall in which the Conservative conference was held. The hall was crowded. When he, accompanied by his wife, entered, both were greeted with prolonged cheering. Lord Randolph said he looked forward to a Winter of hard and heavy work. The Government were resolved to submit to the country real, genuine measures in accord with the reforming and progressive spirit of the age. Referring to the addresses he had received, he said they embodied a real and living political spirit, which could not fail to guide the future of the country. The vastness of the deputations who were present at the conference realized Lord Beaconsfield's prediction for the future of the Tory Party and the hold it ought to have on the masses of the people. He thanked the Dublin deputation for attending the conference, and said: "The Irish for the moment are influenced by agitators. Unfortunately, men who formerly occupied high Government offices are now using their reputations to weaken the Crown's authority. For these reasons constitutional principles are for the moment at a discount in Ireland." He desired to popularize constitutional principles in Ireland, which would benefit that country the same as England by a just, strong, and orderly Government. The fortunes of the Irish people were no longer to be the subject for sport and play, but the battle ground of political parties.

The *Standard* says: "Lord Randolph Churchill's speech fails to come to the level of the one made by him at Dartford. It is too long and much of it lacks interest." The *Times* says: "Exultation over the nervous prostration of the Gladstonians is very well in moderation, but it rather weakens some of Lord Randolph Churchill's own arguments. It is less called for when the Gladstonians are giving evidence of their vitality by their preparations for a counterblast at Leeds. Lord Randolph failed to avail himself of the chances at his command for a useful departure from the lines laid down in his former oration at Dartford. It is unfair and unwise to assume that the bulk of the Liberals will adopt or abet the tactics of the Parnellites. Despite the vagueness of Lord Randolph's proposal for a remedy, we do not think that the application of closure by a bare majority will commend itself to the Government."

Lord Randolph Churchill will not attend the Lord Mayor's banquet at the Mansion House on Nov. 9. Lord Randolph has been invited to a birthday party to be given by the Prince and Princess of Wales at Sandringham.

It is rumored that the political friends of Lord Hartington are urging him to postpone his departure for India, as they fear a Winter session of Parliament will be called, when his presence would be necessary.

Advices from Rangoon say that the rebellion in Myingyan is increasing. The mail for Yemsthen has been looted and the native escort killed. The British have organized forces to attack the rebels in the Membbo and Myingyan districts next week.

Sir A. E. Havelock, Governor of Natal, has informed the Legislative Council of that colony that the English Government has declined to consent to the absorption of Zululand. The Council proposes to decline to vote supplies unless the Governor explains the home Government's relations with the new Zulu republic.

Portugal has authorized the landing at Mozambique of the French Madagascar cable. Mozambique will become a station of the new line.

Miss Alice Whitacre, of Chicago, a soprano, has made a highly successful début in concert at Covent Garden. Two vociferous encores were given her. Mr. Randegger conducted the concert.

The Pondos invading Xesibiland have been dispersed.

NEWS OF THE FATHERLAND.

OPENING OF THE MERIDIAN CONFERENCE—THE BRUNSWICK PLOTS.

BERLIN, Oct. 27.—Emperor William to-day received several military reports, worked three hours, received Count Herbert Bismarck at 4 o'clock, and gave a large dinner party at 5. The Emperor proposes to attend a hunt on Saturday at Hubertustock. The King of Saxony, the Duke of Saxe-Altenburg, and other Princes will accompany him. Crown Prince Frederick William will return to Berlin on the 7th of November. The Crown Princess and family will remain in Italy for the Winter.

The international Meridian Conference opened to-day. Minister von Gossler presided. Delegates were present from all the German States and from Austria-Hungary, Belgium, Denmark, France, Italy, Holland, Portugal, Roumania, Russia, Spain, Sweden, and Switzerland. Ministers von Boetticher, Lucius, von Scholtz, and Freiburg were in attendance. Minister von Gossler made an address in which he referred to the importance of the decision of the conference and eulogized the services to science of the late Gen. Bayer. Dr. Foerster, of Berlin, was elected President; Drs. Struve, of the Pulkova Observatory, and Faye, of the Paris Observatory, Vice-Presidents, and Dr. Hirsch, of Neufchatel, Secretary.

Under the edict of Minister von Boetticher, requiring emigrants for America coming from Austria-Hungary to undergo an examination at Ratibor with reference to their pecuniary resources, 7,000 persons were examined during the quarter ending Sept. 30, though emigration was limited owing to harvest work, and 452 were not allowed to proceed, being without means.

It is reported that cholera has broken out in the villages of Finthen and Gonsenheim, near Mainz. The official autopsy on the bodies of victims disclosed signs of choleraic disease, but not of Asiatic cholera.

Since the arrest of Dr. Dedekind, a leading Guelphite, his Wolfenbuttel residence has been searched. Papers were found which compromised the Duke of Cumberland in the providing of funds for conspirators in Brunswick and Hanover. There have been further arrests of Hanover accomplices of Dedekind. The plan of the conspirators was to blow up with dynamite the residence of Count Gortz-Wrisberg, the Prime Minister of Brunswick.

Herr Wachtel, the singer, is worse. He is suffering with severe congestion of the lungs.

THE BULGARIAN CRISIS.

RUSSIAN PLOTS TO OUST THE REGENCY —A THREAT FROM KAULBARS.

SOFIA, Oct. 27.—M. Karaveloff refuses to go to Tirnova because of a fear of being insulted or assaulted. He argues that it is useless to convoke the Sobranje in the face of the Russian opposition. The Sobranje, he says, has no right to depose him from the Regency, and declares that if it does he will retire under protest.

A pro-Russian meeting, which has been called to take place in this city, and which Gen. Kaulbars had promised to attend, has been prohibited.

Gen. Kaulbars has informed the Regency that if the conspirators against Prince Alexander be punished the Russian Government will have recourse to extreme measures. The Regents, suspecting that it is Kaulbars's intention during their absence at Tirnova to assist the Zankoffites in Sofia to form a new Ministry, have taken the precaution to cause the arrest of all suspected persons, and have ordered the troops to be in readiness to suppress a revolt. A state of siege will be proclaimed in the event of a coup d'état being attempted.

Another Russian war ship is going to Varna.

A protocol has been signed renewing diplomatic relations between Servia and Bulgaria. It provides for a treaty of commerce and for the reference of several disputes to a joint commission.

LONDON, Oct. 27.—A state of siege has been proclaimed at Sofia.

ST. PETERSBURG, Oct. 27.—The *Official Messenger* says: "The anarchy which prevails in Bulgaria prevents the Russian Consuls from protecting the lawful interests of Russian residents. After Gen. Kaulbars had left Varna several Russians were arrested on illegal pretexts. Two Russian cruisers were therefore dispatched to that place."

PESTH, Oct. 27.—The *Nemzet*, a semi-official organ, dwells upon the advantages that would accrue to Italy by a close alliance with Austria-Hungary on the Balkan question. Other papers comment upon the isolation of England, and suggest the advisability of an alliance between Austria-Hungary, Italy, and England.

CONSTANTINOPLE, Oct. 27.—It has been officially denied that any agreement has been entered into by Turkey and Russia with regard to Bulgaria. The Porte has asked the withdrawal of Russian men-of-war from Varna.

CURRENT FOREIGN TOPICS.

BERNE, Oct. 27.—The Federal Government proposes to purchase all the railways in Switzerland.

VIENNA, Oct. 27.—Emperor Francis Joseph has started for Pesth to attend the opening of the delegations. It is expected the Empress will follow him.

The Reichsrath has agreed to abolish the freedom of the ports of Trieste and Fiumé. The House rejected a motion of Herr Stingl, a member of the Austro-German Club, for the conclusion of a customs treaty with Germany.

BELFAST, Oct. 27.—At the unveiling of a statue of the poet Davis in this city to-day Mr. Sexton, in replying to an address on "Young Ireland," referred to the recent riots in Belfast and observed that if the writings of Davis were better understood the downfall of faction and sectarian bitterness would be accomplished.

CAIRO, Oct. 27.—Judgment in favor of the Egyptian Government has been rendered in the case against Lawson, Ismail Pasha's agent, for seizing the Ismaila Palace.

PARIS, Oct. 27.—The *République Française* says that Gen. Boulanger, Secretary for War, will ask a credit for the army of 392,000,000f.

Floods are causing much damage in the Department of Vaucluse. The city of Avignon is partly submerged. Floods in the Rhône Valley have suspended railway traffic, destroyed several bridges, and caused other serious damage.

The *Siècle*, in an article similar to that in yesterday's *Temps*, declares that there is no question of calling upon England to evacuate Egypt. The *Paris* and *France* severely criticise the views expressed by the *Temps*.

DUBLIN, Oct. 27.—Mr. Lewis, in a farewell address to the Londonderry Loyalists, says he regrets handing over his seat in Parliament to one who, whatever his personal qualities may be, has been received and enlisted in America by Fenian dynamiters and advocates of murder.

ROME, Oct. 27.—Cardinal Jacobini, Papal Secretary of State, has requested the Nuncio at Paris to represent to the French Government the serious consequences that might arise from the adoption of a clause in the Primary Education bill of an odious character to the Vatican, and directed against the Catholic clergy in France. The clause referred to provides that education in schools shall be intrusted exclusively to the laity.

A DICTATORSHIP URGED.

A SCHEME TO MAKE PRESIDENT DIAZ PERMANENT RULER OF MEXICO.

NOGALES, Arizona, Oct. 27.—The proposal of prominent Mexicans to establish a Dictatorship to replace the Presidency of Mexico is attracting a great deal of comment. The Mexican papers, with few exceptions, have lately espoused the scheme and urge its adoption. *El Moniter Fronterisco* says: "Gen. Diaz prepared the road to the Dictatorship; the *Voz de Mexico* has entered the arena and proclaims it. Congress is called on to sanction the will of the Cæsar of the continent. Señor Romero Rubio works silently to realize this new plan. Not being able to bring to success his project to prolong the Presidential term he took up the Dictatorship, and so it happens that this project is fathered by a pillar of the Conservative Party, and the people seem to be indifferent to these attempts. Meanwhile the Gubernatorial press clamors for a Dictatorship for Gen. Diaz for 20 years. Why not make it hereditary? When nations do not possess the necessary manhood to be free nothing is more evident than that despots will take advantage of their indolence and erect thrones and assume the sceptre. It is nine years now that the men of Gurtober (Diaz's party) have climbed step by step the ladder which leads to despotism, and once there they have defied the public ire. Already they ignore the fundamental laws, and all that is wanted is the reign of a sole will. The life of a slave is sorrowful and we need to redeem it as men of action, men whose hearts belong to the country, not to the horde of speculators. If such men have disappeared we bow respectfully to the ruins of the republic and exclaim, 'Long live Porfirio!'"

La Voz de Mexico strongly urges in its latest edition that Gen. Diaz be made Dictator, and the organ of Montealegre demands that the General's term be made 20 years, and that the office be made hereditary.

WOMAN'S WORK FOR THE HEATHEN.

CLEVELAND, Ohio, Oct. 27.—The Women's Board of Missions of the Interior began its eighteenth annual session in Plymouth Church to-day, Mrs. Moses Smith, of Detroit, presiding. This board is auxiliary to the American Board of Commissioners for Foreign Missions, its object being to provide women missionaries to work among heathen women, and its jurisdiction embracing Ohio and the States and Territories to the West. The report of the previous annual meeting was submitted by the Secretary, Miss M. D. Wingate, of Chicago. Mrs. J. G. W. Cowles, of Cleveland, delivered the address of welcome. The report of Mrs. J. B. Leake, Treasurer, shows nearly $44,000 received from 24 States and Territories, from China, Turkey, and Canada, the disbursements leaving $800 in the treasury. In addition to addresses and reports exhibiting details of the work at home and abroad, letters were read from members, suggesting methods of raising money, the most unique of which was to persuade society ladies that it is good form to give money for the heathen. At a children's afternoon meeting stories were read to interest the little ones in the cause of missions. In the evening addresses were made by the Rev. Dr. Judson, Secretary of the American board, and others.

THE AMERICAN ORIENTAL SOCIETY.

NEW-HAVEN, Conn., Oct. 27.—The semi-annual meeting of the American Oriental Society was held at the Yale Divinity School this afternoon, and was largely attended by members of the society. Papers were read by Profs. Jackson, of New-Jersey; Hall, of New-York; Lanman, of Harvard, and Gottweir, of Columbia, and Gen. Henry B. Carrington, of Boston. Among those who took part in the discussion were Profs. Lyon and Gay, of Harvard; Hewell, of Amherst, and Day, Haskell, Harper, Vanname, and Harris, of Yale. In the absence of Prof. Whitney the Rev. Dr. Ward, of New-York, presided. The society adjourned to hold its annual meeting in Boston on May 2, 1887. To-night the members and their friends were given a reception by President Dwight, of Yale.

LABOR NOTES.

READING, Penn., Oct. 27.—The 300 employes in the rolling mill of the Reading Iron Works had their wages increased 10 per cent., to take effect Nov. 1. Puddlers, who formerly received $3 50 per ton, will now get $3 85.

WILMINGTON, Del., Oct. 27.—As the result of a conference yesterday evening with their employers the weavers at the Dean Woolen Mills who struck yesterday because of the discharge of one of their number returned to work this morning.

LANCASTER, Penn., Oct. 27.—The Penn Iron Company, of this city, has notified its employes of an advance in wages from $3 60 to $3 75 per ton for puddling, beginning Nov. 1, and a corresponding advance to the heaters and rollers.

TO PROTECT THEMSELVES.

NEW-BRUNSWICK, N. J., Oct. 27.—The people of Englishtown, Monmouth County, have organized a Vigilance Committee, and will prosecute some roughs who have been making life miserable to the town people. The roughs have instituted a reign of terror. They have assaulted several ladies, beaten two prominent citizens, made night hideous, and knocked down and robbed an aged man in the open streets. The citizens propose to put a stop to the outrages.

MARRIED FIFTY YEARS.

KEYPORT, N. J., Oct. 27.—Mr. and Mrs. Garrett Stout, of this place, celebrated their golden wedding this evening. Over 200 relatives and friends were present, including many grandchildren and great-grandchildren. Mr. Stout is 76 years of age, and has never used glasses. His wife is 69, and hale and hearty. The presents received were numerous and handsome.

THE WELTON WILL CASE.

NEW-HAVEN, Conn., Oct. 27.—Dr. Allan Hamilton, of New-York, testified to-day as an expert on insanity for the defense in the Welton will case. He declared that while Miss Welton may have been eccentric she was not, in his belief, insane. The hearing will be continued to-morrow.

ROOSEVELT SURE TO WIN

THAT'S WHAT LAST NIGHT'S MEETING INDICATES.

UNBOUNDED ENTHUSIASM AT THE GREAT RALLY.

COOPER UNION HALL FILLED AND MANY UNABLE TO ENTER—A RINGING SPEECH BY MR. ROOSEVELT—ADDRESSES BY MR. CHOATE, JUDGE DAVIS, AND OTHERS.

Red fire filled the open space in front of Cooper Institute last night, while rockets and roman candles illuminated the cloudy sky with a brilliant glare. The pavement in front of the building was black with people, who poured in a steady stream through the doors and down the stairs into the hall of the Cooper Union. They were going to one of the biggest and most enthusiastic Republican mass meetings ever held in this city—a meeting with old-time Republican flavor—a meeting that meant business and was full of hope.

Inside the place looked inviting. Just under the big clock over the platform hung a large crayon picture of Theodore Roosevelt, the candidate for the Mayoralty for whom that whole meeting was just bubbling over with enthusiasm and votes. Above the picture were four small American flags and a glittering eagle. Banners hung on the walls around, and a brass band, stationed at the south side of the platform, played plenty of inspiring music while the crowds were gathering. At 7:30 o'clock the hall was full and people were beginning to pick out available standing places along the wall. Every one looked hopeful and good-natured. They applauded the band and shook hands with one another, and showed every evidence of being of one accord on the question of Theodore Roosevelt's candidacy.

It was unquestionably a representative meeting, made up of men in all ranks of life. There were business and professional men, intelligent artisans and mechanics, young men just entering upon the discharge of their duties as citizens, and old men who had grown up with the party. There was also a goodly number of ladies present. The appearance of each of the speakers of the evening and of other well known men on the platform was greeted with hearty and prolonged applause.

Contrary to the expectation of the audience, Mr. Roosevelt appeared on the platform in company with Joseph H. Choate. The entire assembly arose to its feet and cheered in the wildest manner for several minutes. When the cheers died away some one cried, "Three cheers for the next Mayor!" and the building fairly shook with the volume of the shouts. When silence finally was obtained Elihu Root stepped to the front of the stage and was warmly received. He said:

"It is my pleasant duty to call this meeting to order, a wholly unnecessary duty because it is a meeting of the friends of order and law. [Cheers.] It is a still more agreeable duty to present to you a gentleman who has been selected as your Chairman, a man known and dear to you all, who took part in the foundation of the Republican Party, who has been one of its steadfast defenders and chief ornaments during the whole period of its existence, the one man who above all others in this city has enforced law and adorned Republican institutions, as a fitting presiding officer for a mass meeting assembled to advocate the candidacy of the youngest and most brilliant of the reformers and of the restorers of law—of order and law—in our city and of the golden days of the supremacy of the Republican Party. I call to your chair to-night Mr. Thomas C. Acton."

Mr. Acton could not have been more heartily welcomed than he was after Mr. Root's presentation, the vast audience fairly rising to receive him. "Can't you let Root's speech do for mine?" he asked as he stepped forward and shook Mr. Root's hands with old-fashioned heartiness. But evidently he had no idea of letting anybody serve as his proxy on such an occasion, and presently he was all over the stage and was talking with every part of his being warmly at work.

"I thank you," he began, "from the bottom of my heart. Such a greeting I never expected. Now I am here to show my earnestness in the cause of the young reformer. I knew his father, and I wish to tell you that his father did a great deal for the Republican Party, and the son will do more if you will give him a chance. [Applause.] He is the candidate of law and order; make no mistake about that. If he doesn't keep law and order I'll knock him out; make no mistake either about that. [Great laughter and cheering.] He is young, he is vigorous, he is a natural reformer. He is full, not of the law, but of the spirit of the law. The Cowboy of Dakata! [Applause.] Make the Cowboy of Dakota the next Mayor. [Great applause.] Now, the platform is full of speakers and I am through. I thank you once more, and we will go on with the regular order of business."

THE ORGANIZATION.

Mr. Acton then called on Col. S. V. R. Cruger to read the names of the Vice-Presidents and Secretaries. Ex-President Arthur's name was cheered, and other well known names were loudly applauded. Most of the gentlemen named were present. Following is the list:

VICE-PRESIDENTS.

Chester A. Arthur,
Hamilton Fish,
John Jacob Astor,
Levi P. Morton,
John Claflin,
George Jones,
Chauncey M. Depew,
D. O. Mills,
Salem H. Wales,
Whitelaw Reid,
Cornelius Vanderbilt,
William Dowd,
James D. Smith,
S. V. R. Cruger,
J. Hobart Herrick,
William W. Astor,
Brayton Ives,
Le Grand B. Cannon,
Edward H. Ammidown,
Joseph W. Drexel,
Jesse Seligman,
Alfred R. Whitney,
Cornelius N. Bliss,
Clarence A. Seward,
John F. Plummer,
James A. Jones,
J. A. Bostwick,
Charles H. Webb,
A. W. Kingman,
Horace Russell,
James M. Varnum,
Frederick Kuehne,
Charles E. Coon,
R. M. Galloway,
Jacob Hess,
John H. Hall,
George W. Smith,
John H. Watson,
Cyrus Busey,
George Starr,
Joel B. Erhardt,
Jacob Wendell,
Augustus Kountze,
Horace Porter,
William L. Strong,
A. M. Underhill,
Daniel Robinson,
John B. Dutcher,
Edward E. Eames,
H. W. T. Mali,
Robert G. McCord,
Joseph T. Low,
Thomas L. James,
William H. Webb,
David L. Einstein,
Alfred Ray,
John D. Lawson,
Edward M. Townsend,
M. C. D. Borden,
John Roach,
Charles Watrous,
John J. O'Brien,
S. B. Lichtenstein,
Myer S. Isaacs,
Richard Arnold,
Daniel F. Appleton,
George F. Baker,
Charles C. Beaman, Jr.,
E. D. Newstatt,
Henry Bergh,
Joel Maldhof,
Isaac H. Bailey,
Bernard Biglin,
Robert L. Belknap,
George W. Balch,
Henry Brewster,
Henry Clews,
Samuel Jacoby,
Hugh N. Camp,
Solon B. Smith,
William H. Gedney,
Jacob M. Patterson,
Signor W. Fay,
Leonard Hazeltine,
A. J. Juilliard,
Woodbury Langdon,
Walter H. Lewis,
John Schuyler Crosby,
Anson G. McCook,
J. M. Bundy,
Charles R. Hickox,
Joseph W. Howe,
Walter Howe,
H. O. Armour,
Robert Sewell,
Henry M. Flagler,
John H. Starin,
J. B. Houston,
H. H. Rogers,
Charles G. Landon,
Stephen R. Leshea,

William Turnbull,
Vincenzo Botta,
Julius Catlin, Jr.,
Birdseye Blakeman,
Joseph H. Brown,
J. Adriance Bush,
John H. Watson,
Richard Butler,
George M. Van Nort,
Benjamin Brewster,
Charles F. Ulrich,
William C. Le Gendre,
Giraud Foster,
F. E. Webb,
Edmund Stephenson,
Thomas F. Wentworth,
Edward C. Ripley,
C. Volney King,
Benjamin F. Manierre,
Theodore W. Dwight,
John M. Amory,
Sheridan Shook,
George E. Best,
Bruno W. Bergen,
Jefferson Clark,
James P. Foster,
David Mitchell,
John L. N. Hunt,
Edward M. Scudder,
James Q. Howard,
John Reisenweber,
James S. Lohmaier,
Denis F. Burke,
Francis A. Thayer,
Richard Deeves,
Alexander Caldwell,
George W. Hamilton,
Charles G. Cronin,
John Beattie,
Leopold Leo,
Samuel G. Jelliffe,
James W. Pratt,
William H. Barker,
George Dillenbeck,
Thomas S. Ormiston,
J. Romaine Brown,
L. B. Hutchinson,
David H. Knapp,
Joseph C. Jackson,
Lispenard Stewart,
Frederick W. Whitridge,
Edward Carlton, M. D.,
Mahlo Richardson, M. D.,
Samuel H. Randall,
Charles Whitlock,
David L. Blout,
Edward A. Dillenbeck,
Harris Cohen,
Henry Gleason,
Alexander Caldwell,
William Balser, M. D.,
Clarence W. Meade,
Cornelius Van Cott,
Thomas Allison,
Mortimer C. Addoms,
Michael Cregan,
Henry A. Barnum,
William T. Black,
James W. Perry,
Stephen N. Simonson,
William B. Hanson,
Conrad Weber,
Fernando Baltes,
M. L. Goldman,
Joseph C. Biglin,
Joseph P. Jardine,
George W. Blunt,
Charles E. Mammack,
Denis Shea,
William J. Gleason,
William H. Townley,
John Collins,
Henry H. Haight,
Thomas Rafferty,
John R. Pope,
Theodore Cole,
Joseph Haight,
Archibald S. Van Orden,
John Mulhall, Jr.,
Ernest Hall,
William H. Ten Eyck,
Thomas J. Rush,
John W. Marshall,
Henry L. Sprague,
John J. Clancy,
William O. Meagher,
Hiram Merritt,
Jeremiah Pangborn,
Isaac Wallach,
George W. Collin,
David W. Kohn.

VOTE FOR ROOSEVELT; DON'T THROW YOUR VOTE AWAY ON HEWITT

The New-York Times.

VOL. XXXVI.....NO. 11,007. NEW-YORK, SUNDAY, DECEMBER 12, 1886.----QUADRUPLE SHEET. PRICE THREE CENTS.

OLD WORLD NEWS BY CABLE

UNIONISTS THE CAUSE OF COERCION IN IRELAND.

DRIVEN TO IT BY THE LOGIC OF THEIR SITUATION—THE FUTURE OF THE LEAGUE—TOPICS TO COME BEFORE PARLIAMENT—NOTES ON MINOR AFFAIRS.

BY COMMERCIAL CABLE FROM OUR OWN CORRESPONDENT.

Copyright, 1886, by the New-York Times.

LONDON, Dec. 11.—It is nonsense, says Lord Salisbury, to talk of the tenants in the West of Ireland being oppressed or badly used. Nobody seeks to compel them to pay rents beyond their ability. If they can't pay they can go. A volume couldn't state more succinctly or describe more graphically the broad and lofty view of the Tory Premier on the Irish question. Since Marie Antoinette asked why the foolish people who were starving for want of bread did not eat cake there has been no other parallel for the grasp of the subject which Lord Salisbury shows. If he could put himself in the place of one of Lord Clanricarde's mountain cotters on a farm which never produced food enough for a family half fed and half clothed, with nothing but the leaking roof of a mud hut between them and the Winter storm, perhaps his easy phrase of pay or go would not strike him as such a complete and satisfactory settlement of the Irish problem. But Lord Salisbury is not wholly to blame for the fact that he learned nothing in the years when he earned his own living and is unable now to see any rights in the world save those of landed property. Why should the owner of Hatfield House be expected to have a keener eye for the dim and unfamiliar outlines of human rights than John Bright, George Trevelyan, and Mr. Chamberlain possess? I say nothing of Lord Hartington, who was bred to the purple, or of Banker Goschen, whose hereditary genius for the part of Shylock goes unquestioned. But if the Radicals, like others sprung from the people and trusted heretofore by the people, cannot see the right of the matter, it is not strange that Salisbury is blind.

The truth is, it is the Liberal Unionists who are pushing their Tory allies down the fatal incline toward the chaos of coercion. If they had the power all in their hands, the Tories would not be specially harsh toward Ireland. Indeed they might easily try and seek a compromise with the Parnellites, for they belong to the party whose principles—since Disraeli's time at least—are wholly opportunist; but the Unionists are under a cruel obligation to be logical. The necessity of justifying their secession weighs heavily on them. Hence it is that they feel forced to demand the most stringent measures of repression in Ireland. Hence it is that the *Chronicle*, which only a year ago was the organ of the democracy of London, leads all the Tory papers in the fierceness of its shouts for swift coercion. I doubt if, in the whole course of Irish history, more mean, cold-blooded, merciless things have been said about the country than were spoken at Tuesday's meeting and banquet. The old adage of the ferocity and bigotry of converts does not altogether explain the virulence of their attitude, for the bulk of them are not converts at all. In private confidences they deplore the miseries of Ireland as deeply as anybody, but they are filled with the idea that their public importance demands a consistent policy and are driven by the logic of their position to favor coercion, since it has become plain to all that theirs is no half-way house between that and home rule. So, alas, we have John Bright crying out for dragoons to cut down the starving peasantry, and Trevelyan framing excuses for rapacity on the part of rackrenting absentee landlords.

It is now that the full measure and importance of the fight which put Walsh in the chair of Laurence O'Toole becomes evident. If one of the English sycophants had been put in instead the League would now be crushed, with its leaders in prison and the whole island lying under martial law. If Rome is disposed to catechise Dr. McGlynn's views on land I wonder what it thinks of this higher prelate, who openly espoused and defends the *United Ireland* plan of campaign and outcrokes Croke in the firmness and frankness of his expressions of sympathy with the tenants. "Hereafter," says the *Saturday Review*, "as cheating on the turf is called welching, so the embezzlement of rents will be called walshing." The characteristic flout shows how grave a wound the Archbishop's arrow made. It is an open secret that the Government, which weeks ago, as I told you, resolved on proclaiming the League, still holds its hand because Walsh's attitude puts the whole Catholic Church in Ireland back of the League, and in case of attempted suppression would make every chapel in Ireland a meeting place for branches of the interdicted organization. The Ministry quite intelligibly shrinks from undertaking the thankless task against such odds. To suppress the League now means practically to re-enact the anti-Catholic penal laws of William and Anne. Ashbourne and Goschen perhaps do not object to this, but nobody else in or out of Parliament is ready to follow them; so the chances remain against a proclamation of the League. It still may be resorted to, but only on the Ministerial theory that it is better to do a thing foredoomed to be abortive than nothing at all.

As for the Irish, as I said last week, they are defiantly confident that whatever might be the case with a genuinely strong Government it is no Hicks-Beach who will terrify them as a ruler, no little Hughie Holmes who will puzzle and trap them as a lawyer. They feel themselves to be both bolder and shrewder than the men opposed to them at the Castle, and have no fear as to the outcome of the game with them. There is less clearness of opinion regarding Irish legislation. At the commencement of the session here the Unionists, who have locked their minds on this subject and thrown the key away, can exert a malignant influence far beyond their proportionate numbers and weight, and there is no telling what this may not accomplish—that is to say, assuming that the prophets are right in believing Ireland to be the chief and sole topic of discussion during the coming session.

This is by no means certain. It is undoubtedly true, so far as domestic matters are concerned, but the foreign question is likely soon to claim a solitary place in Parliamentary attention. The Bulgarian delegation will probably time their leisurely tour of Europe so as to be here when the session begins. They are peculiarly qualified to enlist English sympathies, for the most of them speak English perfectly, being graduates of Roberts College. This ought also to interest Americans, for the assertion comes from both Alexander of Battenberg and the Turkish Minister here that the whole movement of Bulgarian independence is directly due to that distinctively American institution. There is scarcely a man identified with the present Regency Government who is not under 40, and an Alumnus of Roberts. They form a class by themselves and are practically the only educated class in Bulgaria, and from their American training have learned what the ignorant Bulgar peasantry do not realize, that Russian despotism is just as hateful as Moslem tyranny. When these resolute, brave, wise young patriots come to England and tell here in the English tongue of their trials and aspirations, there need be no fear that their words will fall on deaf ears.

I get a hint that Austria is quietly moving to have the Bulgarians elect Prince Ferdinand of Saxe-Coburg, who is a Lieutenant in the Eleventh Austrian Hussars. He was born in Vienna, his age is 25, he is unmarried, and is handsome, popular, and highly eligible. If this is done it is likely that Russia will veto it or get Turkey to do so, which would serve to put Russia still more in the wrong and give Austria further ground for quarrel. Kalnoky has formally recognized the legality of the Sobranje. Hence, for Russia to reject an Austrian subject elected to the throne on the pretext of the illegality of the Sobranje would be a clear affront.

I believe the plan to be, if Russia rejects Ferdinand, the Sobranje is to recall Alexander. Austria is reluctant to consent to this, but England greatly desires it, and it may be that Kalnoky will eventually yield rather than take the responsibility of the initiative of war for the sake of putting Ferdinand on the throne. Turkey continues to play the melancholy and despicable part of a courtesan striving to placate all parties to the fight. The Armenian Gadban is working hard at Sofia in the Russian interest, but I understand White's reports from Constantinople express confidence that the Sultan will be all right when the time comes.

When the time comes is the scare. This is the phrase which haunts all Europe. Moltke's grave words of warning have sent all the Bourses on the Continent down like quicksilver. Nothing has come to reassure them. From two private sources in the north of Germany I learn of general officers who have arranged to move their families to Holland and England this Winter, thus arranging affairs in the full conviction that there will be war in the Spring. More and more people, everywhere, are reluctantly coming to believe this. The Germans are especially nervous over the prospect, having everything at stake. The belief is that the next war will be one the brunt of which will be borne by the cavalry, mounted infantry, and light artillery. Both the French and Russians have been greatly developing these branches. The Russians are said to have 90,000 cavalry ready to burst into Gallicia and Silesia, while the French concentrations of horse at Chalons sur Marne, Besançon, Bourges, and Sedan, attract much attention. The Germans do not forget that 20 years after the death of the Great Fritz, the wonderful military machine he constructed was knocked all to pieces at Jena, largely because the French had a leader whom they liked. There is much anxiety lest Boulanger may exert the same magnetic power and contrive a dash in force which would break the German lines and carry the war into the Fatherland. Hence elaborate and earnest preparations are making on both sides of the Rhine for a combat which will be truly a battle of giants when it comes.

President Cleveland's and Secretary Manning's remarks on fiscal affairs have been read here with great attention, and are commended universally as above the average of official utterances. There is little or no feeling here discernible on the fisheries question. The English have no special regard for the Canadians at best, and just now are too busy with Ireland and Russia to take the smallest interest in the question of cod bait. If public feeling controlled Iddesleigh, instead of red-tape traditions, he would settle the matter promptly on any reasonable basis proposed from Washington.

The Campbell case wearies and disgusts everybody, but the stockholders of evening papers will reap a rich harvest. There is an understanding that next week, if Lady Colin's case seems likely to fail, her counsel will produce letters which will make it impossible for Lord Colin ever to live in Britain again, even if they do not send him to prison.

The Japanese Princes, one of whom is an uncle of the Emperor of Japan, visited "The Mikado" last evening, and gazed in rather mystified gravity at the burlesque for some time, but finally saw the section of a joke.

Mr. Gladstone's health is said to be perfect and his voice has been much strengthened. He intends personally to lead his party in the coming session, at least for the opening weeks, and is preparing a great speech, which later will be circulated as a pamphlet throughout the kingdoms.

Early in February "The Pickpocket" will be withdrawn from the Globe and succeeded by a new comedy by Brandon Thomas and M. Duveray.

Ellen Terry resumed the rôle of Margaret at the Lyceum last night.

It is now definitely settled that Mary Anderson will make a provincial tour, opening in the Autumn in London under the management of Michael Gunn.

H. M. Imans has been engaged by D'Oyly Carte to play Pooh-Bah in "The Mikado."

Camille Saint-Säens has been in London during the week. The celebrated French composer has taken great interest in the concert given exclusively of his works by Herr Peiniger.

The Carl Rosa season of English opera at Drury Lane will be begun on May 2. During the season Corder's new opera, "Nordisa," will be given.

Frank Thornton has arrived in London from Australia. His tour there with "The Private Secretary" has been one of the most successful ever played in the antipodes.

It is whispered in the highest theatrical circles that Wilson Barrett, on his return to London, will not resume his position as lessee and manager of the Princess's Theatre. No details are given, but the report is generally believed to be correct. H. F.

ON TRIAL FOR CONSPIRACY.

NEW-HAVEN, Conn., Dec. 11.—The City Court room was crowded again to-day when the trial of Superintendents Wallace and Opdyke, charged with conspiracy to injure Thomas T. Meaney by blacklisting him, was resumed. Peter E. Bowman, Freight Agent of the New-York, New-Haven and Hartford Railroad, was the first witness. He testified that both he and Wallace had the power to employ or discharge men. He declined to answer whether he discharged Meaney or not, but stated that Meaney was not exactly discharged, being simply sent away to get a letter from Superintendent Opdyke, of the Northampton Road, by whom he had been discharged the month before. The witness further testified that he had been told by Superintendent Opdyke that Meaney had acted in a mean way in leaving his work. He also said on cross-examination that Superintendent Wallace had never ordered him to discharge Meaney. Attorney Ely, for the defense, then asked for a discharge for his clients on the ground that no combination had been proved between Superintendents Wallace and Opdyke. Judge Pickett declined to discharge the prisoners. After setting Dec. 21 as the day for hearing argument, the court adjourned.

A POOR REPORTER.

LANCASTER, Penn., Dec. 11.—In the editorial room of the *New Era* office this afternoon Samuel M. Sener, the court reporter, was assaulted by Charles Macnay, a prominent young grocer of this city. Macnay claimed that Sener, in reporting the case of embezzlement against J. Slater Erb, in which he was prosecutor, did him an injustice by omitting important testimony and misrepresenting the case generally, and yesterday he demanded a correction, which was promised, but not given. This afternoon he visited the editorial room and asked Sener if he proposed to make the correction. Sener replied that he would not, and Macnay struck him twice in the face, knocking him from his chair. Sener made no attempt to defend himself, but crawled under the table and as he emerged on the other side Macnay struck him again. Then the news editor came to Sener's assistance and held Macnay until the compositors who were summoned by his calls for help entered the editorial room. After treating Macnay pretty roughly they allowed him to depart and he left without his hat, which had been lost in the mêlée. Neither of the men was much hurt, but Mr. Macnay will probably not attack a reporter in his own office soon again.

TALK OF THE DAY IN PARIS

GOBLET'S HARD TASK AND THE NEW PLAY BY SARDOU.

BOULANGER COMING TO THE TOP—THE POINT HE HAS CARRIED—SARDOU TALKS ABOUT HIS PIECE.

By Commercial Cable from Our Own Correspondent.

PARIS, Dec. 11.—The *Lanterne* seems to give expression to the general impression of M. Goblet and his Ministry when it says: "We give the little Minister from Amiens 60 days." This extreme Radical prophecy of short life is matched by the sullen opposition of the organs of the Right, which shows that Goblet will not be able to break the mischievous and unnatural union of these two factions. Of course epigrams on the situation abound. It has already occurred to almost every Parisian journalist to say the new Ministry is the play of "Hamlet" with the Prince (who is M. de Freycinet) omitted. One jibe runs that M. de Freycinet was always liable to be tipped out by fortuitous chance, but it is only by such a chance that Goblet can stay in. To-day, however, badinage is yielding to a more serious view, as the difficulty had in filling the Foreign Office begins to shed significance on the situation. M. Floquet would have accepted the Premiership—nay, he did accept on condition the step was approved at St. Petersburg—but M. Laboulaye wired back that the Czar had not forgotten that M. Floquet was the man who publicly insulted his martyred father by the famous cry of "Vive la Pologne, Monsieur," and that Russian friendship would be impossible with him at the head of affairs. Hence the final selection of Goblet, who has offended nobody but the priests, actors, and Anarchists. But when Goblet tried to get a Foreign Minister the fat was in the fire. M. de Freycinet laughed at his request that he take the place. M. Duclerc was much obliged to him, but had other engagements; besides his selection would create a rupture with Germany.

M. Courcel was invited, but he refused unless the Duc d'Aumale was invited to return to France. This Boulanger overruled on a threat of resignation, so Courcel was impossible. How the place will be filled is not yet known, but the hitch suffices to show the public how delicate and dangerous the country's foreign relations are.

It shows even more clearly how like a colossus Gen. Boulanger bestrides the situation. The only man in the past Cabinet who dwarfed him was M. de Freycinet. In the new Cabinet he will be head and shoulders over all the rest, including the Premier. It is everywhere known that he decreed the refusal of the Council's offer and himself entered the new Cabinet on the onerous condition that the Ministry should adopt as its own his demand for an immediate extra vote of $60,000,000 for arming the French soldiers with the new repeating rifle and strengthening the Savoyard defenses. Whoever else may suffer, his position seems sure as long as the Goblet Ministry survives. He is the biggest man in it, and when it falls, either he will dictate its succession, or, if there is a dissolution of the Chamber, his name will be the strongest in France to conjure with in the elections, and the new Chamber will contain a large party ready to rally round him as the savior of the country.

A new piece by Sardou is always a chief event of the Paris theatrical season. "Crocodile" is to be a tremendous affair in five acts and three times five tableaus, thirty-four characters (not supers, any of them) and a heap of money to be spent on scenic effects without precedent and wondrous costumes. Sardou is a stickler for scenery. He sets his face against dress rehearsals before even a select few and often makes a radical change at the last moment. He is the scene shifter, stage manager, and pantomimist of his own characters, and he has even been known to dance in the front row at a rehearsal one of his own incidental ballets. At home at Marly he sits in his study like an alchemist in a laboratory. It may be said, indeed, that his plots are often mere experiments flung aside mercilessly if the philosopher's stone of a Famille Benoîton, a Théodora, or a Rabagas is not seen at the bottom of the crucible or in the transparent balloon of the report.

I managed to have an interview with Sardou to-day on the coming presentation of "Crocodile," about which Paris that enjoys itself is now itching with curiosity, but I fancy that Paris will have to wait a few days still before knowing anything of the production, and I only owe my own knowledge to the fact that I made Sardou furious by hinting that "Crocodile," in the opinion of some people, was only a warmed-up edition of "Foul Play" and "The Overland Route."

"What!" cried the pallid dramatist, throwing off his black velvet smoking cap, "are these accusations of plagiarism never to cease? Because there is a steamer in 'The Overland Route,' and a desert island in 'Foul Play' am I to be accused of going to modern English authors for my pieces? The British stage has done me the honor to knock at my door, but I have never ventured to pay them a return visit."

"I should like to be able to lay low this ghost, *cher maître*, by having some notion of 'Crocodile.'"

"Well I will do enough to satisfy the English-speaking world on that score. You may find one or two characters dead and buried when the first night comes on, for I kill, marry, acquit, and condemn ruthlessly as I go on; but of this you must take your chance. The 'Crocodile' in question is a ship in the Dutch service trading to Batavia, having on board a goodly show of passengers. Let me say something of my passenger list, for all have their say in the first act. In the first place we have Richard Kolt, the leading part, played by Marais. Richard is in love with Liliane, (Mlle. Legault.) Mlle. Leriche is an Englishwoman of a very flaring pattern. The daughters of America are represented by Miss Olivia, (Mlle. Baretty,) who is equally overcharged with national qualities rarely seen off the stage and so cool that in every emergency she takes notes. M. Jimmy (M. Berton) is the doctor of the ship, in love with Olivia. We have besides Mme. Jordaens, (Mlle. Claudia,) a widow; Peter Becque, (M. Frances,) a voluble French lawyer; a grotesque clergyman, (M. Boudier;) and two married couples who have left France to make their fortunes somehow. The wife of one of these, Gabrielle Bertholin, is played by the handsome Jeanne Delorme. I pass over the sailors and one Strapoulos (M. Herbert) who will become prominent further on. The 'Crocodile' is steaming on gayly and the audience is enjoying the social satire with which the dialogue literally reeks when crack! the vessel catches fire and the passengers are rescued. The boats are seen taking them away. It is not quite certain yet whether the Captain is to die in the wreck or not. This may cast a shadow over the piece, but we must only wait and see. And now, so far, do you see anything like 'Foul Play,' or your 'Overland Route'?"

"Oh, dear, no. I retract not only in my own name, but in the name of your accusers."

"The second act," continued Sardou, getting animated, "is upon an island where we find our passengers reduced to expedients. The stylish Widow Jordaens does the cooking; the handsome Gabrielle turns to washing, and we see the elements of modern society brought back to their original roughness. Here we dip into politics. A President is elected. This is Richard Kolt. The glib lawyer Peter Becque has his say all round, and, with the exception of Gabrielle, who puts in a blank voting paper, all share in the hope of a form of government worthy of the name; but alas! the sailors, ship carpenters, and others take the same view that M. Jules Grévy did many years ago—that no President is wanted. In the third act the Executive is at work when the curtain rises. Gabrielle and the widow have a tremendous lawsuit. Peter Becque is of course to the front. He pleads as if he were at home in court. As far as I can judge from the rehearsals, M. Frances will be wonderful in this part. At the end of the act comes a resolution worked up by Strapoulos, who urges the sailors to overthrow the President, and indeed the whole Government.

"I need scarcely tell you," continues Sardou, "that my passengers are rescued by a passing vessel, and that the love element of the piece now becomes in the ascendant. There is a big love scene between Kolt and Liliane, admirably rendered by Marais and Legault. The dénouement is humorous. Apart from the serious interest attached to the obtaining of a fortune by Kolt and his marriage to Liliane, one marriage was solemnized by a clergyman on the island, who now turns out to be a fraud; he is really a drummer for Cologne water. So much for my 'Crocodile.'

"Oh, by the way," added Sardou, as he was shaking hands, "I forgot to tell you that M. Massenet is providing music to accompany the new work. French pieces have always lacked the support of music, and this, at least, we borrow from your own 'Macbeth' and 'Midsummer Night's Dream.' There the piracy begins and ends. Au revoir."

To-night's dinner gathering of English-speaking journalists in Paris is the first step toward organizing a club on the basis of the Savage, of London, and the Lotos, of New-York. The project is an old one. Hitherto it has failed through rivalries and jealousies. To obviate the vexed questions of precedence, to-night's dinner will have no Chairman.

More elaborate preparations than usual are made for the celebration of the holidays. The shops are sumptuous with displays, and have an encouraging amount of patronage. It seems as if the shows of Paris had turned a corner from the path of depression so long traveled.

HEMMED IN BY FIRE.

TERRIBLE EXPLOSION IN A STEAM SUPPLY STATION.

BOSTON, Dec. 11.—Shortly before 7 o'clock this morning a terrible explosion occurred in the steam supply station of Hazlett & Underwood, at East Cambridge, by which several men were seriously wounded and two were probably injured fatally. On First-street are several large furniture factories which receive their power from Hazlett & Underwood's station. The power station was a building about 40 feet square, three stories in height, and was scarcely more than a wooden shell. In the boiler room was an immense bin piled high with shavings, which were the fuel used under the boilers. There was a number of workmen in the engine room this morning when the explosion took place, men who were employed in the neighboring factories and who had stopped on their way to work. The explosion occurred without a moment's warning, and the unfortunate men present were shrouded in one great sheet of flame. There was no way of escape until outside assistance was rendered. The building was soon a mass of fire, and the cries and shrieks of the imprisoned men were heart-rending. The southerly wall soon fell outward, and as soon as possible the unfortunate men were dragged from the ruins.

Harry Newhall, the engineer, was standing near the shaving bin when the explosion occurred, and was fairly covered with burning shavings. He managed to rush out, a mass of flames, and threw himself into the snow, rolling over until the fire was extinguished. He was fearfully burned, the flesh hanging in bloody strings from his arms, while his hair was completely burned off. He may possibly recover, although at a late hour to-night his case was considered critical. Fireman Albert Murray was badly scorched on the head and body, but will recover. Joseph Sears was badly burned, but his injuries are not considered fatal. Joseph Livenzea, 19 years of age, was horribly burned about the face, hands, and neck, and the hospital surgeons say he cannot possibly recover. The cause of the explosion is a mystery. It may have been caused by a spark in the shaving bin, or, as the room had no ventilation, it may have been caused by the generation of inflammable gas from the great pile of sawdust. The loss to the building will be fully $2,000.

WOODBRIDGE'S POSTMASTER.

WOODBRIDGE, N. J., Dec. 11.—James Freeman received his commission as Postmaster of this place yesterday and thus ended one of the most exciting and bitter personal contests that ever stirred the hearts of the people of this normally quiet village. The fight has been entirely Democratic in name and nature, and it all arose over the removal of the office from its long established position in the Masonic Hall building by D. P. Carpenter, who was appointed only a short time ago to succeed a Republican, and who now has to step down and out for his action in removing the office. The friends of the Masonic Hall position, led by ex-Assemblyman Savage, a son of George W. Savage, Consul to Belfast, had been using every means to have the office brought back, but without avail. Finally the ex-Assemblyman laid out plans to have Carpenter removed, and how successful he has been was seen yesterday, when his man Freeman took charge of the office, which is now in Main-street, and many of the most interested business men think it by far the best situation. The office will undoubtedly be brought back to the hall.

THE INDIANA ELECTION CASES.

INDIANAPOLIS, Dec. 11.—Judge Ayers, of the Civil Circuit Court, was expected to give his decision in the Lieutenant-Governorship case to-day, but has postponed it until Monday. The case will go to the Supreme Court in any event.

The examination of Messrs. Coy, Bernhamer, Spaan, and Counselman, charged with complicity in the Marion County election frauds, was begun to-day, but the defense interposed a demurrer that the facts stated did not make a crime against the United States, upon which the day was consumed in argument, the proposition being that the fraud must affect a Federal candidate in order to give the Commissioner jurisdiction. The Commissioner announced that he would give his decision on Monday. In his charge to the Grand Jury Judge Woods interpreted the law to give the Federal court jurisdiction of the offense, following the law as adjudicated in the Mackin case in Chicago. The case for the disbarment of Bernhamer for his complicity in the crime comes up before Judge Woods on Monday.

SENECAL'S APPEAL DISMISSED.

MONTREAL, Dec. 11.—A special cable dispatch says the appeal of L. A. Senecal, in the case of Hatton against Senecal, has been dismissed by the Privy Council. Action was taken by Mr. Hatton for the restoration of 35 bonds of the Montreal, Portland and Boston Railway Company, of the nominal value of $1,000 each. In default of producing the bonds it was asked that the defendant be condemned to pay $35,000, together with the amount of the interest coupons, &c. In the Superior Court the pretensions of the plaintiff, Mr. Hatton, were fully maintained, and Mr. Senecal was ordered to return the bonds or pay the amount claimed. Mr. Senecal appealed from the decision to the Privy Council.

THE COMSTOCKS DOWN.

SAN FRANCISCO, Cal., Dec. 11.—Mining stocks were all better this morning, excepting Consolidated Virginia, Sierra Nevada, and Utah. The first named opened at $37, the same as it closed last night, but dropped to $34 50, recovering to $36, to finally close at $33. Sierra Nevada opened 25 cents lower, closing at $8, a loss of 75 cents. Utah was weak at $9, at which it closed. The other stocks were strong, the advance ranging from 75 cents to $2 25 a share.

A LARGE BUILDING FALLS.

THE RUINS TAKE FIRE AND THREE MEN SUPPOSED TO BE LOST.

ST. LOUIS, Dec. 11.—About 2:30 o'clock this afternoon the roof of Shapleigh & Cantwell's hardware store, No. 414 to No. 420 North Main-street, fell in, carrying the four floors beneath it to the basement. The fourth floor was loaded with agricultural implements, the third with shelf goods, and the second with sample goods. Immediately after the crash the ruins caught fire from the boiler in the basement, and a general alarm was sounded, summoning the entire Fire Department. The water thrown on the Shapleigh building seemed to have no effect, and the firemen directed their attention to saving the adjoining buildings. A report quickly spread that at least a dozen men had been buried in the ruins, and the enormous crowd which had gathered in the vicinity looked on with horror. Men stood within 20 feet of the burning mass with the huge lines of hose emptying their contents into the roaring furnace. Shortly after the fire started the north wall of the building fell in, which materially lessened the danger to the firemen and made easier the work of saving the adjoining buildings, and by 3:30 the fire was under control. During the fire there was a constant fusillade of cartridges which were stored in the burning building, but the walls prevented the bullets from injuring any one. Most of the inmates of the building escaped with slight bruises, and as far as can be learned to-night only three are missing. They are John Mahan, porter; Arthur W. Palmer, clerk; Charles E. Reid, clerk.

Fireman Russell says that when he arrived on the scene he saw a man in the third story with the flames all around him. When he looked up an instant afterward the man had disappeared, and he supposes he must have fallen back into the burning building and perished. There were several narrow escapes. Walter B. Kincaid was standing in the archway between Nos. 416 and 418 when the first crash came and was struck by some of the débris, but escaped into the street. Joseph Furlong, an employe, was on the fourth floor, and was carried with the débris to the second floor, from whence he escaped with a broken leg. A man named Carpenter was assisted out badly injured and taken to a doctor's office. Fireman Jack Sheehan, of Hose Carriage No. 33, was struck on the head by falling timbers, and was taken away in a carriage. Joseph Chambers, foreman of engine No. 6, was struck on the head by falling bricks, and was seriously injured. Many others received slight cuts or bruises.

The Shapleigh Cantwell Hardware Company was one of the largest houses in the West. Their stock was valued at about $500,000, and is a total loss. The loss on building and stock, including the damage to adjoining buildings, will amount to $600,000; insurance, $400,000.

HORSEMEN AT ODDS.

THE TROUBLE IN THE NATIONAL TROTTING ASSOCIATION.

CHICAGO, Dec. 11.—The re-election of T. J. Vail as Secretary of the National Trotting Association was a surprise to many Chicago turfmen. Whether there will be an immediate break in the National Association as the result of his re-election is a question involved in considerable doubt. There is every probability of the organization of a Western association, but it is an open question whether the clubs that will form it will withdraw from or retain their membership in the National Association. The old association contains a considerable amount of money, and any member that withdraws forfeits all claim to that money. A desire to cut loose from Mr. Vail and his friends is expressed by a majority of the persons identified with trotting tracks of the West, but they have no desire to give their interest in the National Association's funds to the Vail side. It is claimed that St. Louis and Detroit will at once join hands to organize a new association. If this is true a Western association will be in existence inside of 60 days.

The St. Louis and Detroit Associations are enterprising and independent, and will come pretty near making a success of any project they embark in. If the telegraphic reports from New-York are correct, Judge Grant in an interview last night denounced as an unmitigated lie a statement that he had misrepresented his position toward Vail to H. V. Bemis, proprietor of the *Horseman*. He also said he went to the meeting of the board intending to sustain Vail. Mr. Bemis's reference to Judge Grant's position was made on information imparted by Messrs. Abercrombie, Hall, and Davis. Speaking of the Judge's remarks, Mr. Abercrombie said to-day: "I have sacredly withheld his expressions to me from the public, but now that he has seen fit to make such a furious and abusive denial of Mr. Bemis's statement I have nothing further to withhold. Judge Grant must now abide the consequences of his declarations and his rash denial. His action is beyond comprehension."

WALKING ON WATER.

A MAN TAKES A SHORT STROLL ON THE NIAGARA RIVER.

BUFFALO, Dec. 11.—An attempt was made to-day to outrival the feats of Donovan, Graham, Haslitt, Potts, and Allen in braving the terrors of Niagara, which, though a failure in one way, was a success in another. Mr. Alphonse King, who is the inventor of a water shoe, gave exhibitions some years ago in this country and Mexico and not long ago in Europe. He gave one in the Crystal Palace in London, and while there attracted the attention of Harry Webb, an old-time manager, who made him an offer of a year's engagement to come to this country. While here some time ago Mr. King had looked over Niagara River below the Falls and believed that he could walk across the channel on his patent shoes. He came to this country four weeks ago and has since that time been in New-York City practicing for the trip. While there, Thomas Bowe, hearing of King's determination to attempt the trip, made a wager of $1,500 with Webb that King could not walk 100 feet in the current. The money was deposited with a New-York newspaper, and on Friday afternoon Messrs. King and Webb, accompanied by A. C. Poole, of Poole's Eighth-Street Theatre, reached the Falls.

The trip to-day gave King two cold water baths, and demonstrated that while he could walk with or against the current all right it was impossible to walk across the river because of the eddies, which twice upset him. He retired confident that what he set out to do could not be done. King's "shoes" are of tin, 32 inches long, 8 inches wide, sloping at the top, and 9 inches deep. Each weighs 30 pounds. They are air-tight and have in the middle an opening large enough to admit the feet of the wearer. At the bottom are a series of paddles, which operate automatically as fins.

A TEMPERANCE MUDDLE.

DES MOINES, Iowa, Dec. 11.—While Mr. Kidd was considering whether to establish his big distillery here the constitutional prohibition amendment was pending in the Legislature. In order to facilitate the new manufacturing enterprise leading Republicans and temperance men lobbied a resolution through the Legislature that the amendment would not apply to spirits made for export beyond the State borders. The amendment failed in the courts, and the prohibitory laws followed. Recently a suit was brought under the law of last Winter to enjoin the distillery as a nuisance. The case was elaborately argued last week before Judge Given, of this city, who to-day in a long opinion denied the writ. In the arguments the defense relied on commercial comity between the States as establishing their right to do business, but Judge Given passes this by. He holds that the distillery began business under the law of 1857, and thinks none of the latter statutes interfere with this right. The prohibition question becomes daily more muddled in view of this decision, that of Judge Shiras, the straddling opinion of the Pharmacy Board, and the injunction issued against the latter body yesterday restraining them from canceling Sunday permits.

THE MINNEAPOLIS MILLERS.

ST. PAUL, Minn., Dec. 11.—The story regarding a scheme to consolidate the milling interests of Minneapolis is an "antique chestnut." The rumor was started some time ago and created some talk for one day, but investigation proved it to be without any foundation in fact. It is true that some such arrangement has been talked of for a long time in certain milling circles as one of the possibilities of the future, but there is no reason to believe that the matter has ever passed beyond the bounds of mere conjecture. When the rumor was revived some time ago leading millers declared that such a consolidation would be impracticable and out of the question. All of the big mills could not be induced to come in, and so the scheme could not be made to work. [The story alluded to is printed on the fourth page of this paper, and was sent out in substance by a press association.]

THE FEDERATION OF LABOR

TRADES UNIONISTS FORM A NEW ORGANIZATION.

THE KNIGHTS OF LABOR IGNORED AND A CONSTITUTION FOR THE NEW BODY ADOPTED—OFFICERS ELECTED.

COLUMBUS, Ohio, Dec. 11.—It will doubtless prove a trifle galling to Terence Vincent Powderly and his old Executive Board to learn that the trades unionists, who have been in session here for the best part of a week, have elected as President of their new organization, the American Federation of Labor, Samuel Gompers, the man he so vilified in the "secret" circular that was printed in to-day's TIMES. The fact that Mr. Gompers was elected without opposition may give Mr. Powderly an idea of the estimation in which he is held by trades unionists. The latter are now prepared to go their own way. They did not invite interference or opposition, in the first place, and if Mr. Powderly's lieutenants with his knowledge had not abused their powers so grossly there would be peace to-day between organizations that are now rivals. The new organization has no fear of the Knights, for its membership was in existence long before they were thought of. It begins life with 25 trades unions as a nucleus. There is reason to suppose that as many more will join the fold before another convention is held. Its primary object is to secure as members every trade and labor union in the country, and some of the steps it has taken to attain this object show the shrewdness of the builders.

Heretofore the Knights have been enabled to enroll all the workers in small communities. A glance at the Federation's constitution will show that such a field will no longer be left exclusively to the "noble order." The Knights have been enabled to secure many members by a promise of general assistance in case of a strike or lockout. Such assistance has proved by experience but a broken reed. The Federation's constitution provides that, under certain circumstances, assistance of a general character will be given in case of strikes or lockouts, and unionists know that their treasuries are seldom empty, and that among them a promise has usually amounted to fulfillment. Then members of the Federation will be allowed self-government. As among the Knights, a cigarmaker will not, among trades unions, be allowed to march into a silk mill and order a strike. The leaders of the new movement are tried men. The work is not new to them. They are acquainted with the weak spots in the "noble order" as well as in trades unions, and they have labored hard to construct such an organization that will not need constant tinkering. They think they have succeeded, and they talk like men who have satisfactorily accomplished a difficult task, upon adjournment late this afternoon.

The salient points in the constitution of the new organization are as follows:

This association shall be known as the American Federation of Labor, and it shall consist of such trades unions as shall conform to the rules and regulations.

The objects of the Federation shall be the encouragement and formation of local trades and labor unions and the closer federation of such societies throughout the organization, of central trades and labor unions in every city, and the further combination of such bodies into State, Territorial, and provincial organizations, to secure State legislation in the interests of the workingmen.

The establishment of national and international trades unions based upon a strict recognition of the autonomy of each trade.

To secure national legislation in the interests of the working people and influence public opinion by peaceful and legal methods.

The basis of representation in the convention shall be from national and international unions of less than 4,000 members, one delegate; 4,000 or more, two delegates; 8,000 or more, three delegates; 16,000 or more, four delegates, and so on, and from each local trade district or union not connected with a national head, one delegate.

No organization which has seceded from any local, national, or international organization shall be allowed representation or recognition in the Federation.

The officers shall be an Executive Council, with power to watch legislative measures directly affecting the interests of working people and to initiate, whenever necessary, such legislative action as the convention may direct.

This council shall use all possible means to organize new national and international and local trades unions, and to connect them with the Federation.

While we recognize the right of each trade to manage its own affairs, it shall be the duty of the Executive Council to secure the unification of all labor organizations so far as to assist each other in any justifiable boycott, and with voluntary financial help in the event of a strike or boycott duly approved by the Executive Council. When a strike has been approved by the latter, the particulars of a difficulty, even if it be a lockout, shall be explained in a circular issued by the President of the Federation. It shall then be the duty of all affiliated societies to urge their local unions and members to make liberal financial donation in aid of the working people involved.

The revenue of the Federation shall be derived from a per capita tax of ½ cent. per month from each member in good standing.

The salary of the President shall be $1,000 per year, with mileage and expenses.

Whenever the revenues shall warrant it the Executive Council shall authorize the employment of speakers in the interest of the Federation.

The remuneration for loss of time by the Executive Council shall be $3 per day and traveling and incidental expenses.

Any seven wage-workers of good character and favorable to trades unions, and not members of any body affiliated with this Federation, who will subscribe to the constitution, shall have power to form a local body to be known as a Federal Labor Union, and they shall have power to form their own rules in conformity with the constitution, and shall be granted a charter by the President of the Federation, provided the request for a charter be indorsed by the nearest local or national trades union officers connected with this Federation.

This constitution shall go into effect March 1, 1887.

The committee that conferred with the Knights of Labor who had been sent here by Mr. Powderly made the following recommendation:

"That the Executive Council of the newly organized Federation shall issue an address to the public upon the subject of our differences with the Knights of Labor. We might have terminated the conference the first half hour of the meeting, for it was evident the Knights of Labor committee had no power to act. In the interests of harmony we deemed it wiser to spend three hours in a friendly discussion with the hope of coming to an understanding."

The Federation elected as its President Samuel Gompers, of New-York. He is Vice-President of the International Cigarmakers' Union, and is considered one of the cleverest leaders in the trades unions of the country. He was born in London of Dutch parents. He has been a resident of this country since his thirteenth year, and worked at his trade, cigarmaking, since he was 10 years old. He is now 37, and has been a member of his union since its organization in 1864.

George Harris, of Reynoldsville, Penn., was elected First Vice-President. He was born in England in 1853. In 1883 he was elected President of the Miners and Laborers' Amalgamated Association of Pennsylvania, and still holds the office. His association has, he said to-day, a membership of over 35,000. The Knights, he thought, should not organize with "unfair" material or in districts in which unions were able to take care of workingmen's interests.

J. W. Smith, the Second Vice-President, is a member of the National Tailors' Union, and a resident of Springfield, Ill.

Gabriel Edmonston was elected Treasurer. He is a member of the Brotherhood of Carpenters and Joiners, and resides at Washington, D. C.

The Secretary of the Federation is P. J. McGuire, who occupies a similar office in the Brotherhood of Carpenters and Joiners. He is a man of brains as well as of mark in the labor movement, and to him more than to any other single man is due the successful organization of the Federation. Secretary McGuire is a most successful organizer, and is at the head of a union that has few equals. He believes the Federation has a bright future. He will not invite a contest with the Knights, but if it comes he will be their principal opponent.

Adolph Strasser, President of the International Cigarmakers' Union, expressed himself as follows, after adjournment:

"Our work will result in amalgamating all national and international trades unions. The Knights of Labor are defunct; it's no use talking about a corpse. They have lost 75 per cent. of the order in Massachusetts since Oct. 1 through the collapse of the Peabody strike."

J. R. Winders, San Francisco, said:

"I think the difficulties existing between the Knights and trades unions could be satisfactorily settled if No. 49, of New-York, was thrown into the ocean. Some of our radicals might be disposed of in the same way without causing a national loss."

Henry Emerich, of the National Furniture Makers, said:

"We have laid the foundation of a great labor movement."

George Block, National Bakers' Union, said:

"We will soon have all the trade and labor unions of the country in the Federation."

Christopher Evans, President of the federation of Miners and Mine Laborers, said:

"The convention could not have accomplished more."

Among the unions which were represented at the convention and are now members of the Federation are the Brotherhood of Carpenters and Joiners, organized in 1881 with a membership of 2,342; its membership now is 26,742; it has obtained an advance in wages of from

The New-York Times.

VOL. XXXVIII.....NO. 11,746. NEW-YORK, MONDAY, APRIL 22, 1889. PRICE TWO CENTS.

OKLAHOMA OPENED TO-DAY

BOOMERS READY FOR THE GREAT INWARD RUSH.

THE TURBULENT CROWD WAITING ON THE SOUTHERN BORDER—INFLUENCE OF THE OKLAHOMA LEAGUE.

PURCELL, I. T., April 21.—Final preparations were made to-day for the exodus into Oklahoma, which will begin to-morrow. Wagons were overhauled, supplies purchased, and guns and tools given careful inspection. The day was lovely, but there was no suggestion of Sunday in the street scenes. From the hill overlooking the beautiful valley of the Canadian a soft-toned bell called those religiously inclined to worship in the Catholic Mission of St. Augustine. In the town itself there are two insignificant church structures, but they are not centres of attractions to-day. The supreme moment is so near at hand that the thousands who have spent weary months in waiting can hardly contain themselves.

At 8 o'clock this morning the public square contained a large assemblage, and by 10 o'clock the throng had swelled to such an extent that passage was exceedingly difficult. Several prominent men were induced to mount improvised platforms and harangue the crowd on the great issue of the day. Judge Green of Kentucky, the only man in town who wears "store clothes" and a silk hat, spoke for a half hour. The people wanted light on the town site, school land, and other questions connected with the opening of Oklahoma, and he dispensed it with apparent knowledge of the situation.

The Judge is charged by many with being mixed up in town site schemes, and is not, therefore, deemed above giving advice which, if followed, would result to his personal advantage. He and others were surprised to discover this morning placards pasted about town, bearing this inscription regarding the late order made at the regular meeting of the Oklahoma legion:

Resolved, That we again pledge ourselves to protect our brother members in their long-respected rights on selected claims, and that all town-site sharks and claim jumpers shall be dealt with in a summary manner.

OKLAHOMA LEGION.

As the town is full of the gentry named in the notice, much uneasiness has been caused. There have been any number of attempts to discredit the existence of the Oklahoma Legion, but that it does exist and will wield a tremendous power in the near future, is conceded by many. One needs only to gain the confidence of boomers who have been here since the days of Oklahoma Payne, to ascertain that the league has a large membership, and that its purpose is to make good the claims of its members to the lands they have long since selected for occupancy.

A man whose connection with the organization cannot be doubted said this morning: "These doubting Thomases will learn to their sorrow, one of these days, that the Oklahoma Legion is alive and all-powerful. It owes its origin to the necessities of the hour, and is composed of men who are law-abiding and who propose to see fair play in the new territory. Every one of its members will locate on the claims they have already selected, and if he finds himself in danger because of his action he will be protected by his fellows, who are sworn to defend the rights of each.

"When one looks at the question carefully he will readily see that the organization of the league was the most natural thing in the world. Hundreds of men came to the borders of Oklahoma when the idea of opening the territory was first discussed and have remained there throughout the trying times which have followed. Each has had opportunity to become familiar with the country, and each made many acquaintances. When it became evident that the Springer bill was doomed, and that only a small part of the coveted lands would be opened this year, the boomers readily anticipated the very situation which now exists. They said to themselves: 'We have endured much to get ourselves a home in Oklahoma, and now there is a prospect that, after all, we will see our hopes crushed and the lands occupied by people who have suffered none of the privations through which we have passed.' With this possibility staring them in the face, the suggestion of a protective league was eagerly accepted and the Oklahoma Legion is the result. You can now judge for yourself whether the old-timers will come out second best in the coming fight for homes in the promised land."

The morning trains to-day brought many more pilgrims from the South, and they mounted the steep mountains outside the town in a picturesque procession. A carload of spades came in from Fort Worth, and the owner caused them to be unloaded at the station, where a great crowd had congregated. Then he mounted a freight car and announced that the lot would be disposed of at cost. It is reasonable to suppose that he did not confine himself strictly to the truth in this remark, but, nevertheless, every spade was sold within thirty minutes and the dealer had the money in his pocket. Spades are spades in this country just at present.

Mounted on a pony which evidently appreciated the fact that he had a tenderfoot aboard and acted accordingly, THE TIMES's correspondent made a tour of the outlying camps this afternoon. These begin at a point a mile west of the town and extend in a semicircle to the river bank. There are probably 1,000 wagons, with an average of five persons to each.

To one who has traversed the northern border of Oklahoma the difference in the make-up of the boomers is quickly apparent. Here the Southern type is all-prevailing, long-haired Texans, yellow as to complexion, lank as to form, and drawling as to speech, being in the majority. The outfits, while for the most part good, are not equal to those which will invade Oklahoma from the north. The man from Iowa, Kansas, or Illinois unquestionably is more thrifty than the Lone Star representative. He eats better food, too. Bacon and hominy constituted the noonday meal of the majority of Texans to-day, while many looked as if they were unable to afford these articles.

Suffering there is already, and how some of these people will manage to exist when they get across the river, is a question not easily answered. The case of the family found yesterday by the Deputy Marshals subsisting on crackers and cheese has many parallels. Probably the most pitiful case is that of a family of four, discovered this afternoon in a little hollow near Walnut Creek. They inhabited a tent, wonderfully constructed of bits of canvas and oilcloth, which seemed destined to go to ruin with the first gale of wind. An ordinary wagon stood outside, and a mule, which had seen its best days, was tethered near. The head of the family, a hollow-eyed and emaciated man, lounged on a ragged quilt spread on the floor of the tent, and three ragged, unkempt children sat listlessly by him. The wife and mother, whose appearance was on a par with the surroundings, bent over a skillet in which was frying a mess of wild mustard greens. There was nothing else eatable in sight, not even the seasoning, without which mustard greens are considered by epicures to be unpalatable.

It was a scene which called to mind Daniel Webster's experience with the family which, during the two days he remained with them, subsisted on grass fried in lard. There was evidently speedy need of charity and it was bestowed to-day, but of course the provision was only temporary. To-morrow, Providence permitting, this family will cross into the promised land, and if they do not starve to death in a week it will be because there are plenty of good people there.

There is only one regular ford here, and by daybreak the scenes recently witnessed at Arkansas City will be repeated on the road leading to the stream. There is great rivalry among the boomers for the honor of crossing first, and, as the road is narrow, it is not unlikely that many of the more adventurous home-seekers will seek to cross at other places where the stream seems fordable. The South Canadian is full of quicksand, and in the mad rush there may be some disasters. The Santa Fé crosses the river some distance below Purcell, and many of the boomers have prepared to pull their wagons over the bridge by hand and let their horses swim across. As there are many stock trains now running, the element of danger enters largely into this plan. From the great bluffs just north of Purcell a complete view of the exodus can be had.

This evening the current of street talk turned toward the town site speculators, and they were denounced by self-appointed orators, who are easily recognized as old-time boomers. There is an unmistakable hatred of the town-site men, and, although the law, as construed by Secretary Noble, renders them practically harmless, the rank and file are not yet fully posted and are disposed to push them to the wall. This feeling is almost sure to result in serious trouble next week.

The question of priority between squatter and filer is a vital one, and no two persons seem to be agreed as to the proper method of procedure. The non-mineral affidavit will be exacted from every applicant at the land offices. He must swear that he has been on his proposed claim, is familiar with it from actual observation, and that there exists no mineral or coal to his knowledge. This is a blow at the proxy system, and opens a wide gate for perjury.

The Santa Fé is arranging to run a number of trains into Oklahoma from this point in the morning to reach Guthrie at noon.

An order was issued last night to bar all commercial messages from the single wire between Purcell and Kansas City until next week. Another wire is being rapidly strung. Press messages from this town now go by way of Texas.

A detachment of the Fifth Cavalry arrived this evening, and went into camp four miles below the town. It will move up in the morning and guard the ford until noon.

Just at nightfall four Deputy Marshals came in with two horse thieves, whom they had captured, after a long chase, eight miles from Purcell. The streets were crowded, and as soon as the tidings spread, the Marshals and their prisoners were surrounded, and one loud-voiced cowboy implored his companions to lynch the thieves. "Hang them!" he shouted, and the crowd surged obediently forward. The Marshals kept cool and drew their revolvers, and the chief announced that the first man who attempted to harm the prisoners would be filled full of holes. He is known to be a man of his word, and the proceedings came to a sudden stop. The thieves were subsequently taken to the jail and placed under a strong guard.

To-night 300 town lots in Oklahoma City were sold at auction at a price ranging from $2 to $10 each. There are seventeen Oklahoma City townsite companies doing business here, and each is illegally disposing of lots. There will be music in Oklahoma City next week.

KANSAS CITY, April 21.—To-night being the last chance for persons bound for Oklahoma to move in time to reach that country by noon to-morrow, the Union station was thronged with a motley crowd as ever assembled in it. The Santa Fé, in addition to its two regular trains, sent out a special of eleven coaches, which represented nearly every line entering the city. The Rock Island also sent out an immense train. Innumerable cases of pocket picking have occurred during the past week, both in the station and on the trains.

To-day it was ascertained that three or four sharpers have been working a very smooth game. They would board an Oklahoma train, gain the confidence of a carload of "boomers," and finally suggest the organization of a colony. The sharpers would produce their pocketbooks and suggest a common fund and the actual settlers would follow suit. The common-fund idea invariably failed of consummation, however, but the pickpockets improved the opportunity by noting the size of each man's purse and its place of concealment. The sharpers would ride out a hundred miles or more and by that time would have succeeded in reaping their harvest. No arrests have been made yet.

A *Times* Arkansas City special says that it is reported there that Gen. Merritt has issued orders to the troops to take possession of all guns and pistols carried by the "boomers." They are not to be confiscated, but the idea is to hold them until the excitement is over as a precautionary measure against bloodshed. It is also said that liquor will be rigidly excluded.

MR. SPRINGER PLEASED.

SPRINGFIELD, Ill., April 21.—The Hon. W. M. Springer, Chairman of the Committee on Territories and author of the original Oklahoma bill, has returned to his home in this city, much elated at the success of the party of which he was the leader in succeeding after so many years in having the Oklahoma lands opened up to the settler. Mr. Springer is gratified rather than embarrassed at the excess of immigration into the Oklahoma country, and does not share the apprehensions so generally indulged in regarding probable lawlessness and bloodshed over disputed lands. He thinks the excess of immigration will only demonstrate the necessity of speedy action in the opening of the surrounding lands.

"The vast majority of the people who are going there," he says, "are seeking homes and not controversies. They want land. While most of them are going armed, their evident purpose is to be prepared to enforce law and order. There will, no doubt, many lawless characters follow the crowd, as in the case of any new community, no matter how favorably situated, but the way of the transgressor will be as hard in Oklahoma as in any part of the country. The people seem determined to have peace if they have to fight for it. In ten years from this time Oklahoma will be as populous as Kansas is now, and the overflow will slop over into Texas and Colorado, New-Mexico, Arizona, and Southern California, and the rebound will send thousands to Kansas, Arkansas, and Missouri. It will settle the Indian problem in the near future, not by extermination, but by making the Indian an individual landholder, by teaching him to earn his own living upon his own farm, and by making him a citizen of the United States, a voter, and a member of the body politic.

"If the commission appointed by the President meets with anticipated success, the Cherokee outlet, containing over 6,000,000 acres of land, will, in a few weeks or months, and without additional legislation, be opened up to settlement under the same terms as the land now being occupied."

THE OKLAHOMA COUNTRY.

Gen. Grant once said to a friend that if the Indian Territory was cultivated as it should be by white men instead of Indians, its products would feed the Nation. That remark indicates more forcibly than any description of land, water courses, and meteorological conditions can, the richness of the Territory, in a portion of which white men are to be permitted to settle for the first time to-day. The mad rush to reach this far-famed land of plenty has been graphically described from day to day by the correspondents of THE TIMES on the ground. To-day Oklahoma is open and the thousands of boomers who have been waiting for years to take up their abodes within its borders have at last their desire gratified.

Oklahoma lies in the heart of the Indian Territory, and some portions of its lands are as rich as any others on the continent. In shape it is an oblong square, at the southeastern end tapering down to a narrow strip hedged in by the Canadian River and the Pottawatomie Reservation. At the northwest and northeast also the boundaries widen out in narrow strips. Take a map of the State of New-York and stand it up on its Buffalo end, and a very clear idea will be obtained of the shape of the territory.

At present the only railroad entering Oklahoma is the Atchison, Topeka and Santa Fé. Several other lines, however, run near its borders, and will eventually enter its domains. The Atchison Road, after leaving Arkansas City, in Kansas, runs almost due south across the strip of land known as the Cherokee Outlet. It crosses the Ponca Reservation and skirts that of the Otoes and Missourias. It enters Oklahoma near Alfreed, and, continuing in a southerly direction, crosses the Red Fork of the Arkansas River or Cimarron River, as it is more commonly called, at Guthrie. It then runs through the settlements of Seward, Edmond, Oklahoma, Moore, Newman, and Walker, and crosses the Canadian River, on the southern bank of which is Purcell. The entire line within the limits of Oklahoma is less than one hundred miles, and the distance from Arkansas City to Purcell is only 143 miles.

On the western side of the Territory, running almost parallel with the railroad which skirts the eastern border, is the Abilene cattle trail and stage route. Situated on this trail, a few miles south of the Cimarron, is the Kingfisher stage station, the only important settlement in that part of the Territory. From Guthrie, where the Federal Government has established one of its land offices, to Kingfisher, where there is another, is less than thirty miles as the crow flies. The entire width of the body of the Territory is only forty miles.

To the north of Oklahoma is the Cherokee strip or Outlet, which is about sixty miles wide and which contains the reservations of the Nez Perces, Poncas, Otos, and Missourias. With the exception of these reservations the entire strip, which is about a hundred and seventy miles long from east to west, has been ceded to the United States by the Cherokees and will probably be opened to settlers in the near future. To the west of Oklahoma is the great reservation of the Cheyennes and Arrapahoes, while to the south is the Chickasaw Nation. On the east are the Pawnees, Sacs, and Foxes, Iowas, Kickapoos, and Pottawatomies.

The entire territory opened to settlement to-day is about the size of the States of Rhode Island and Delaware combined and comprises about 87 townships or something like 3,000,000 acres of land. There are about 3,200 sections of 640 acres or 12,890 quarter sections. No settler can acquire more than one-quarter section by settlement, and, as the boomers are said to outnumber the quarter sections, it follows that many of them will not get any land.

The country consists of undulatory plains and elevated prairies, and is watered by innumerable streams, which are tributaries to the Cimarron and Red Rivers. The climate is mild and salubrious, but generally dry, and is said to be the most delightful on the continent. The average mean temperature is from 55° to 60°, and the mercury is said never to go below 20° in the coldest Winter. The vegetation is very much like that of Northern Texas and Southern Kansas. The country is well wooded, a belt of forest known as the "Cross Timbers" being from five to thirty miles in width. Three important rivers traverse the Territory from west to east, namely: The Red Fork of the Arkansas, or Cimarron, the North Fork of the Canadian, and the Canadian River proper, the latter forming the southern boundary.

It may seem to the average reader of THE TIMES to be a long distance from New-York to the Promised Land, so-called, but an inspection of the railroad maps and time tables will convince any one that Oklahoma is really close at hand. From New-York to Chicago 24 hours is required by the fastest trains. Thence to Guthrie is 827 miles, and this distance is traversed by the ordinary trains in about 40 hours. Purcell is 64 miles south of Guthrie, and from there to Galveston, Texas, is 516 miles. To the heart of Oklahoma is less than half way across the continent.

SOME TARIFF PROBLEMS

CLASH OF NORTHERN AND SOUTHERN INTERESTS.

HOW TO RECONCILE REPUBLICANS OF LOUISIANA AND PENNSYLVANIA—FEARS FOR ANOTHER SHIP'S SAFETY.

WASHINGTON, April 21.—There is an expectation among some of the Southern Republicans that the Tariff bill of the Senate will undergo important changes before it is pushed through the next Congress. Mr. H. C. Warmoth, one of the leading Republicans of Louisiana and a large producer of sugar, says that he has no idea that the bill of last session will be passed with the sugar bounty provision approved in the Senate. It is his belief that the country will find that it is in need of all the revenue it is now receiving, and that there will be no occasion for making a great reduction in the sugar duties. The sugar producers of Louisiana do not want a bounty, he says, but wish to be regarded as engaged in one of the industries entitled to protection by duties. The bounty system will not be popular, and it would not be so satisfactory to the sugar planters and producers as a schedule of duties imposed according to the protection principle.

When this proposition is presented to the Fifty-first Congress, it is likely to provoke some opposition and a good deal of discussion from Western members on the Republican side, who have been introducing bills year after year for a repeal of all the sugar duties. The Southern Republicans who are anxious to make large profits on iron by enjoying the benefits of heavy duties in connection with cheap labor and other elements of production are likely to arouse the attention of the Western men who have been complaining of the burdens imposed upon them to swell the purses of manufacturers in the East. But the highest rates of duty on iron will not satisfy the Pennsylvania producers as well as the Georgia and Alabama men, who find iron ore and fuel in the same neighborhood. Just how the protection plan is to be adjusted so as to benefit Pennsylvania and Louisiana equally does not yet appear, but consideration of this matter promises to be interesting.

A good deal of anxiety has found expression in Washington because neither Admiral Kimberly's report from Samoa, under date of March 21, nor Lieut. Wilson's telegram from Auckland, under date of April 16, made any mention of the United States steamship Monongahela, which sailed from San Francisco Feb. 18 with supplies for the Samoan fleet, and some fear has been felt that she may have been lost at sea in the same storm that wrecked the vessels in the harbor in Apia.

As the Monongahela is a sailing vessel and was heavily loaded, she could not, under the most favorable circumstances, have reached the Samoan Islands much before March 30, the date on which the Alameda started for San Francisco with the last news that has been received from the islands, and on the date of the storm she was probably a thousand miles from Apia, and she undoubtedly encountered some of the very severe weather, which probably did considerable damage to her, and which may have driven her far out of her course. There will be, however, no reason to believe that she has been lost until later advices are received from Apia. Lieut. Wilson's silence need cause no anxiety, for, although he would probably have mentioned the arrival of the Monongahela if he had known of it, there is no reason to believe that he heard from Apia for at least three weeks before the date of his telegram from Auckland.

The store ship Monongahela is one of the old sailing ships of the navy, a vessel of 2,100 tons, displacement and bark rigged. For several years she has been stationed down at Callao as store ship for the Pacific squadron, but last year she was sent up to the Mare Island Navy Yard for repair with the intention of again sending her south. When the Samoan trouble broke out and it was learned that the United States had no coal supply at Apia, orders were issued to send the Monongahela to the islands with supplies of coal and material for the Pacific squadron gathered there.

The following are her officers: Commander George C. Wingate, commanding, Lieut. Commander William C. Gibson, Lieut. T. Dix Bolles, Lieut. (junior grade) Abraham E. Culver, Passed Assistant Surgeon Willard H. Crawford, and Passed Assistant Paymaster Arthur Peterson. The Monongahela is the vessel that was carried inland on the coast of Chili by a tidal wave, but again floated and put in service. She is a staunch, sound vessel, and if well handled there is no reason why she could not lay "bow to" in the open sea in perfect safety.

It is not often that the President of the United States is an object of less curiosity to a congregation than somebody else in it, even in Washington. That was the case to-day, however. The Church of the Covenant, in which the President is a pewholder, was entirely filled, excepting one centre pew that was evidently reserved. After the President, Mrs. Harrison, and Mrs. McKee had taken their seats, a party entered the church from N-street and was shown to the only pew remaining unoccupied. The party consisted of Mr. Ye Ha Yung, Mr. Ye Sang Jay, and Mr. Kang Chin He of the Corean Legation, an interpreter, and the two ladies of the legation, whose names are not easily recalled for use.

The ladies had never before attended a church service, but they were perfectly self-possessed as they made their way to the pew reserved for the party. They are both very small and were costumed in many colors and in a fashion strictly Corean, with curious little notched silk caps and tassels, skirts a trifle long and very full, and waistbands that were passed about the body directly under the arms. Throughout the service they were admirably attentive, although they knew not a word of what was said, and they did not appear to be aware that they were the chief objects of notice in a congregation that included the Chief Magistrate. When the service was ended they passed composedly out by the door they had entered, the ladies daintily picking up their long skirts as they tripped down the steps to enter the carriage that was waiting for them. At home no Corean woman appears in public.

The representatives of the nation who are here are impressed with the idea that whatever the Americans do is all right. Since they have seen several funeral services they have manifested a great deal of concern about what should be done in case of the death of the Queen dowager, who is eighty years of age and likely to die soon. They think that her death should be followed by appropriate services, and they have expressed regret that there is no church in which something like the American funeral services can be held. So much interest was felt in the Corean party and their odd costumes to-day that the President must have felt obliged to them for saving him from the undivided attention of the large congregation.

Some of the circumstances in connection with the recent agitation in the Treasury of the proposition to impose a duty on every Canadian-built freight car brought into the United States suggests the possibility that thrift on the part of American car builders has had something to do with it. The protest against the admission of such cars without the imposition of duty comes, it is said, from the Collector at Detroit. The ground upon which it is made, it is understood, is that there is no regulation in force that permits the entry of Canadian freight cars, even for convenience of exchange, although all cars that have been admitted from Canada have been allowed to come in under the impression that there was a permissive regulation on the subject.

It is now understood that Senator McMillan of Michigan has been active of late in directing the attention of the Treasury officers to the fact that the Canadian cars have been brought in without regard to limit of numbers, and that once in this country they have been kept here in service. Senator McMillan is a builder of cars at Detroit, and employs something like three thousand people in his works. The use of the Canadian cars, it is reported, injures the car building business. The demand for the imposition of duty on each freight car each time it enters the United States would, it is assumed, compel the abandonment of Canadian-built cars and the substitution of those of American build in their places. If Canada should retaliate by putting a duty on all American-built cars sent into Canada, the result might prove embarrassing to international traffic. The imposition of duty by the United States and by Canada would at first compel the shifting of all shipments of freights at the border, and, by increasing the expense, lead perhaps to a great reduction of business.

All keepers of lighthouses in the Government service will have to suffer a reduction of their salaries amounting to 4 per cent., from now until July 1. Formal announcement of this unpleasant fact has been made by the Lighthouse Board, with the approval of Secretary Windom. The necessity for it is due to the insufficient appropriation made for the salaries of light keepers for the current year, on the basis now allowed, and it is absolutely forbidden by law to expend more than the sum appropriated. A careful account will be kept of each deduction, and Congress will be asked next Winter to make good the amount. July 1, when the appropriation for next year will become available, salaries will be restored to the regular rates. The present deficiency was anticipated by the Lighthouse Board, and reported to Congress last Winter, but that body failed to provide for it.

The Civil Service Commission have been making all the necessary preliminary arrangements for supplying candidates for appointments in the Railway Mail Service, when that bureau of the Post Office Department comes within the scope of the civil service law, May 1. There are 5,320 officials at present in the Railway Mail Service, and of these only two—the general superintendent and one assistant general superintendent—are exempt from the application of the rules. The age limitation is 35 years. There is but one grade of examination, all appointments being made to class 1, which includes all places of $800 or less per annum. Places above $800 are filled by promotion or transfer.

With the consummation of the proposed application of the civil service rules to the Railway Mail Service, there will be a total of 27,200 offices of the Government under these rules, the list including the departmental, Customs, Postal, and Railway Mail Service.

MRS. SHEFFIELD DEAD.

PROPERTY THAT WILL GO TO YALE'S SCIENTIFIC SCHOOL.

NEW-HAVEN, April 21.—Mrs. Maria St. John Sheffield, widow of Joseph Earl Sheffield, donor of the Sheffield Scientific School, died at 8 o'clock to-night. She had been ill two weeks with paralysis.

Mrs. Sheffield was born in New-York in 1801. She married Joseph Earl Sheffield in 1822, and since then had resided in the old homestead on Hillhouse-avenue. In 1860, Mr. Sheffield gave to the scientific department of Yale, which was struggling for existence, the building now called South Sheffield Hall. The building was formerly used as a tavern, but was altered by Mr. Sheffield to meet the wants of the school. The name "Sheffield Scientific School" was not given to the department until several years later. By Mr. Sheffield's will the "homestead" was to go to the college after the death of Mrs. Sheffield. This property is now valued at $250,000. It is in the rear of the scientific school. Property on Chapel-street, in which the school has an interest, will increase the amount to nearly $600,000.

The school is now in need of room and this will be of great aid. The desired four years' course may soon be established. Mrs. Sheffield's six children all survive her. They are Mrs. Thomas B. Van Buren of Ten Neck, N. J.; Mrs. John A. Porter of New-Haven, Mrs. William Walter Phelps of Englewood, N. J.; Mrs. William J. Boardman of Cleveland, Ohio; George St. John Sheffield, Yale, '63, of Attleborough, Mass., and Charles J. Sheffield of Cleveland, Ohio.

THE GRASSHOPPER MUST GO.

FERGUS FALLS, Minn., April 21.—The war on the festive grasshopper is going to be instituted at once and fought to a finish. Capt. Chase, Chairman of the County Commissioners, who was called to St. Paul to consult with the Governor in regard to the matter, has been placed in charge, and will conduct the campaign. He will go to Perham, where he will meet Prof. Otto Luger, the State Entomologist, and a plan of action will be decided upon. Probably the first thing done will be to plow the land wherever the eggs are found. It is estimated that there are about five thousand acres on Perham prairie which will require this treatment. The eggs are found only on pasture land and timothy fields, and it is hoped that by plowing they can be killed off. The people of Perham are not as despondent as would be expected over the outlook, as they hope by starting in time to save their crops. Last year nothing was done until the hoppers hatched, when a reward of $1 a bushel was paid for catching them, and in this way over seventeen thousand bushels were caught. Col. Davidson of Perham was in town yesterday with samples of the eggs and parasites. The latter are very numerous wherever the eggs are to be found, and it is hoped they will fulfill their mission, which entomologists say is to kill the hoppers and destroy their eggs. The Clotherall prairies, about thirty miles this side of Perham, were afflicted last year and will also be plowed and treated in the same way as the fields at Perham.

BOSTON TO HAVE A FAST MAIL.

BOSTON, April 21.—General Superintendent Bell of the Railway Mail Service arrived here yesterday and had a conference with Postmaster Corse and other Post Office officials. The result is that after April 29 there will be a fast mail train between Boston and New-York, a thing which Boston has sought for a long time.

This insures faster time for mails, and all the matter will be worked on the trains. It is believed that the trains will leave each city at midnight and will go over the New-York and New-England Road, bringing the mails to each city in time for early delivery.

Superintendent Bigelow of the Railway Mail Service of New-England has induced the department to put an extra crew on the Boston, Springfield and New-York line. This crew will be split into two sections and added to the day lines east and west, leaving New-York at 9:01 A. M. and Boston at 8:30 A. M.

The day line east is due in Boston at 3:30 P. M., and it has been a common occurrence, owing to the imperfect assortment of the matter on the postal car, that this mail could not be delivered on the last carriers' trip in this city. Mr. Bigelow has received an allowance of ten men for this additional service.

The service between the West and Boston is to be improved also. Through Eastern mail arriving in Buffalo in the morning from the West has often been allowed to remain there twelve hours before starting on to Boston. This in future will be stopped, and all mail reaching Buffalo in the morning will be delivered in Boston the same day.

AN ELECTION CASE DECIDED.

LITTLE ROCK, Ark., April 21.—William Palmer and William Hobbs were acquitted and Thomas Hervey was found guilty in the Federal court yesterday, the jury returning a verdict after several hours' deliberation. This is the celebrated Plummerville election case, to which public interest has been directed for months past. The defendants were charged with refusing to allow two regularly qualified judges to act at the Congressional election held at the town last November. The testimony was expected to develop something which would lead to the detection of the four masked men who stole the ballot box on the night following the election, and also throw light on the mystery surrounding the subsequent murder of John M. Clayton. On the ground that the case could be better handled by Republican than by Democratic officials, President Harrison was urged to forthwith remove United States District Attorney House and Marshal Fletcher and replace them with Republicans, which was done.

The case, however, developed nothing and closes leaving the identity of the ballot-box thieves and assassins as great a mystery as before. Hervey was fined $100. Judge Brewer, who charged the jury and pronounced sentence, impressed every one by his impartial ruling throughout the trial, and his expressed determination to try the case on the law and evidence.

SERIOUS RUNAWAY IN BROOKLYN.

Mr. Frederick C. Fleck, aged twenty-five years, of 208 Centre-street, this city; his wife Annie, the same age; Miss Annie Kroner, aged eighteen years, and Mr. Frederick Coleman of 22 East Houston-street were riding through Prospect Park, Brooklyn, yesterday afternoon. They were occupants of a four-seated wagon, attached to which were two spirited horses.

Something frightened the animals near the Flatbush-avenue entrance and they ran away. All attempts to stop them were unavailing. They dashed out of the park, scattering pedestrians in all directions and finally brought up against an electric-light pole at Sixth and Flatbush avenues. The wagon was smashed, and all the occupants were thrown out with great violence.

Mrs. Fleck had her babe in her arms. Neither was harmed. Miss Kroner sustained a compound fracture of the right leg, and was removed to the City Hospital. Mr. Coleman had his scalp slightly cut, and Mr. Fleck suffered from shock and concussion. One of the horses was so badly damaged that it was thought best to end its existence.

THEIR FUN NOT APPRECIATED.

PHILLIPSBURG, N. J., April 21.—Congressman James N. Pidcock was recently married in Washington, D. C., and after an extended trip in the South he arrived with his bride at his home in White House Station. A number of his constituents arranged an old-fashioned "callthumpian" for the Congressman, and late at night a small army surrounded his house and began their fun. The bride and groom refused to respond, and the crowd became very disorderly. Windows and doors were smashed, fences razed, and weather boards ripped from the house. The outrage has provoked much feeling, and it is probable that the ringleaders will be indicted for malicious mischief.

A GIRL'S FIGHT FOR LIFE

TERRIFIC STRUGGLE WITH A CRAZY MAN.

A PRETTY HARLEM GIRL REFUSED TO MARRY JAMES DEMPSEY AND HE TRIED TO KILL HER—HIS SUICIDE.

Helen E. Stebbins is a pretty, ladylike girl who has lived with her uncle, George R. Storms, at 214 West One Hundred and Thirty-fifth-street for the past two years. Last October Powell & Co. of 72 Beaver-street opened a drug store at Seventh-avenue and One Hundred and Thirty-fifth-street, just across the street from where the girl lived, and put in charge of it James B. Dempsey, a good-looking man who had just passed his thirtieth year. In a few weeks Miss Stebbins and Dempsey became acquainted and their acquaintance rapidly ripened into friendship. Miss Stebbins was bright and intelligent and fond of music, and Dempsey was educated, fond of pretty girls, and music was his hobby. The consequence was that few evenings went by that these two young people were not together.

Some time in December Dempsey, whose love for the girl had become apparent even to the neighbors, asked her to marry him. Exactly what answer she gave is not known, but that it was a favorable one is evidenced by the fact that they were thereafter more together even than before. After a few weeks, however, there began to be trouble between them. Dempsey was erratic and extremely peculiar in many ways, and his fondness for other pretty girls rather annoyed Miss Stebbins. Girls used to come to the drug store to see him, and this his pretty sweetheart regarded as an infringement upon her own rights. Quarrels ensued, and the whole matter was ended by the girl's flat refusal to have anything more to do with the handsome druggist. This was in the latter part of December, and one night while in the back part of his store Dempsey swallowed a quantity of morphine and came very near dying. Somebody heard his groans, however, and summoned a physician, who pumped the poison out of him in time to save his life. When he became conscious Dempsey begged piteously to have Miss Stebbins come to see him, and she did so, and practically took care of him until he got well. Then she absolutely refused to have him come to her house or to talk to him, but he managed to meet her frequently in the streets and beg her to reconsider her determination. To all these appeals she turned a deaf ear.

Still the other pretty girls kept on coming to the drug store and Dempsey began to drink a little. Some time in the first part of February last he went on an extended spree, and while he was gone his backers discovered something about the girls and the previous sprees, and when Dempsey got back to the store after a week's absence he found that he had been turned out bag and baggage and another man put in his place. This calamity affected him greatly, and for a time he acted like a crazy man. He had no money, and it was only through the kindness of the father of his assistant in the store that he was given a place to live and enough to live upon. He was a first-rate druggist, and had an extended knowledge of medicine, which enabled him to in part repay his benefactor by taking care of the latter's sick child. Mr. Rosenstock, his friend in need, lives at 243 West One Hundred and Thirty-fifth-street, which is still almost across the street from Miss Stebbins's home, and ever since his discharge from the drug store Dempsey has continued his efforts to get the girl to marry him.

On Saturday afternoon last Dempsey told Mr. Rosenstock that his sister had arrived at Boston that day from abroad with a very sick child, and that she wanted him to come to her at once. He had no money, he said, and asked for $5 to pay his expenses. Mr. Rosenstock, who is kind-hearted, promptly gave him $10 and wished him godspeed. Dempsey left the house, but instead of going to Boston, he went to a near-by gun store and bought a cheap pistol. Then he spent the remainder of the time, until 8:30 o'clock, at a liquor saloon on Seventh-avenue, and at that hour he started for his ex-sweetheart's home. At the corner of Seventh-avenue and One Hundred and Thirty-fifth-street he almost ran into the girl, who was out on an errand for her uncle. He caught her by the arm and asked her earnestly to walk up the street with him, as he had something very important to say to her. His manner so impressed the girl that she consented to do so. Dempsey was lame in one leg—his only physical defect—and he walked very slowly. All the way up to One Hundred and Thirty-seventh-street he kept telling her of the importance of what he was going to say to her.

When they arrived at One Hundred and Thirty-seventh-street Dempsey turned abruptly into the street and, still holding the girl by the arm, walked up toward Eighth-avenue. This block is a lonely one, without any houses on either side. When they had gone about a hundred feet from the corner, Dempsey suddenly stopped and, drawing his new revolver from his pocket, said, "You will not marry me; now I will kill you and end my own life."

The girl caught a glimpse of the shining weapon, and, gathering up her skirts, she fled for her life. Dempsey was taken so by surprise at this action that he failed to fire, and when he recovered Miss Stebbins had gotten too far away for him to shoot her. His lameness prevented him from overtaking her, and she escaped. She ran down Eighth-avenue and One Hundred and Thirty-fifth-street to her home, and went in and locked the door. She told her uncle, who is employed in Stern Brothers's dry goods store, of Dempsey's attempt to kill her, and he advised her to go to bed. In the morning he said he would have the fellow arrested.

Hardly had the frightened girl gotten over her scare when the door bell rang and a messenger handed in a note from Dempsey. It read:

"You have run away from me. For God's sake let me hear from you. Come to Eighth-avenue and One Hundred and Thirty-fifth-street. I swear I will not harm you."

No attention was paid to this note, and an hour later another one came. Mr. Storms, who received this note, refused to open it, and then he and his niece, who were the only occupants of the house, locked up for the night and retired.

At 10 o'clock yesterday morning another note came from Dempsey, and this was returned unopened. Half an hour later Miss Stebbins was down stairs, when there came a ring at the basement door. She went to open it and got it just far enough open to see Dempsey there, glaring like a madman at her and holding a revolver in his hand. She screamed and tried to close the door, but the infuriated man pressed against it and prevented her. Then she screamed with all her might for help and Mr. Storms came running down to where she stood. As he reached the floor and got close to her Dempsey shoved back the door and, catching sight of Storms not five feet away, he raised his weapon and fired twice at him point blank.

Rage must have blinded him, for his bullets went wide of the mark. But Mr. Storms had had enough, and he gallantly ran back up stairs, leaving the girl alone to battle with the madman. The door which separated them was a light wooden frame, filled in the centre with panes of glass. With her back to this frail barrier, Miss Stebbins pushed with all her strength, until Dempsey, finding he could not push open the door, lifted his revolver, and with a single blow shattered every bit of glass in the frame. The crash so startled the girl that she jumped forward, and in an instant Dempsey was at her side, with his revolver pressed against her temple. With one frantic blow she struck the weapon up just as he fired, and the bullet grazed her forehead, the powder blackening and burning her skin.

Hardly knowing what she did, but with one overwhelming desire to save her life, the plucky girl then turned about and grappled with the murderous intruder as if she had been a man. She threw both arms about Dempsey's waist, pinning his arms to his sides, and held him there, panting and straining every nerve for the space of fully a minute. They were just about matched as to height, and during this awful minute they glared right into each other's eyes.

Suddenly Dempsey gave a jerk backward, and almost loosened the girl's hold upon him. But she got her hands clasped behind his back, and locked them there with the strength born of deadly fear. The brute tried to throw her down, but he was not a very strong man, and his lame leg prevented him from exercising all of his strength. Back and forward and from side to side of the narrow hallway these two people struggled until, with a last, convulsive effort, the girl lifted the man from the floor and threw him squarely on his back. She fell on him, and in the sudden shock her hands became loosened, and Dempsey wriggled his right arm, the hand of which still grasped the pistol, free from the girl's encircling arm.

Quick as a flash he raised the weapon to her head again, and again she dashed it up as it exploded. The bullet again grazed her head, and again her face was blackened and burned. But this was more than even this courageous girl could stand, and she got up on her knees and then to her feet and staggered to the steps leading to the floor above. There remained one bullet in Dempsey's revolver, and Dempsey seemed to realize that he had to kill himself. Lying there at full length on his back he raised the pistol to his right eye and sent the last bullet crashing through his brain.

Then Miss Stebbins, who had reached the front door, ran out into the street, shrieking wildly for help. She was caught at the corner by an acquaintance and was led back to the house. Her hands were bleeding from the effects of the blows she had struck at Dempsey's pistol and her face was black and scorched, but otherwise she was uninjured. Last night she had fully recovered, and she told a TIMES reporter the story of her terrible struggle for life with as much equanimity as if she were talking of the experience of some other woman.

In the meantime many persons attracted by the shots had run into the basement and found Dempsey there, unconscious and dying. He was taken in an ambulance to the Manhattan Hospital, where he breathed his last half an hour after his admittance.

Dempsey had no relatives here except a brother, who lives at 121 West Sixty-fifth-street. He was notified of the tragedy and arranged for the burial of the body.

The dead man is believed to have been crazy. Little is known of his history, but Miss Stebbins said that at one time during their courtship he showed her a newspaper clipping printed three years ago, which told of his attempt at suicide and his subsequent incarceration in a lunatic asylum. Both of his parents are dead.

TWO BIG MINNESOTA FIRES.

A LUMBER TOWN AND HALF A CITY SWEPT AWAY.

ST. PAUL, April 21.—A *Pioneer Press* special from Neenah, Wis., says: The woods near Marion, a station on the Milwaukee, Lake Shore and Western Road, forty miles west of Appleton, caught fire last night, and the flames spread with great rapidity. The town of Buckbee was entirely wiped out. Buckbee was a small lumbering town, and a great deal of lumber was stored there, which was consumed. The loss is estimated at $100,000. A train consisting of fourteen cars of lumber and five of logs caught fire near Marion and burned, causing a loss of about $75,000. The full loss on the lumber and dwellings at Buckbee and near Marion will amount to nearly $300,000. There has been but little rain in that section this season, and it is presumed that the fire originated from a spark from a passing locomotive.

At 4 P. M. Saturday the Meisenwinkle Woodenware Company's factory caught fire at Depere, burning the sheds containing staves and stock, and, in fact, everything belonging to it. While it was burning a heavy wind set in and blew sparks and coals of fire on the neighboring houses, making the largest fire ever seen in that city. Twenty dwelling houses were burned. The total loss on the dwellings and contents will probably amount to $200,000 or more, and it is said that not one-quarter is covered with insurance. The Meisenwinkle works, where the fire originated, suffers a loss of about $150,000, with an insurance of $60,000. When the fire first started, the Green Bay fire engine was sent for. The Green Bay and the Depere steamers were set in the middle of the burnt district, and were doing good work when the wind changed suddenly, and hemmed the engines in, driving the fire all to that immediate vicinity. The firemen had to abandon their engines and they were burned up. The steamers from Oshkosh and Appleton arrived at 11 P. M., and succeeded in getting the fire under headway. Depere is a city composed of two parts, East and West Depere. West Depere is the part that caught fire, and to-day there is not enough left of it to be identified. The people who were burned out have nearly all been taken under shelter by the neighbors of the east side. The full loss is estimated at over half a million dollars.

TWO HORSE CARS WRECKED.

THE FIRST SERIOUS DISTURBANCE IN THE MINNEAPOLIS STRIKE.

MINNEAPOLIS, April 21.—The first serious disturbance which has occurred in Minneapolis since the general tie-up of the car lines, a week and a half ago, took place this morning at Twelfth-avenue, South, and Washington-avenue. Two cars were thrown off the tracks, stones, bricks, bottles, and other missiles were used, and twenty-eight men were arrested.

Cars were run out as usual this morning on all the lines which have been operated for the past two days. No attempt had been made to start the Riverside avenue cars. This line runs through a portion of the city largely peopled by workingmen and they were not working to-day. The tearing up of a portion of the tracks during the night presaged trouble. Riverside cars were started early, and the crowds soon began to gather. At about 11 as two cars, going in opposite directions, approached each other at Twelfth and Washington avenues, South, stones and bottles were thrown from a saloon. This started the attack, and soon a crowd of about five hundred people had gathered.

The two cars were thrown over and badly wrecked. The scab drivers were stoned. The police were summoned and they too were stoned. Some persons received severe injuries, but they were hustled out of the way by their friends. The police were called from all the other lines of the city and the mob was finally dispersed. Owing to the withdrawal of all the officers from the other lines all street cars in the city were stopped.

HIS HEAD CUT OFF.

PARIS, Texas, April 21.—Deputy Marshal Fleming came in from the Territory yesterday and reported a ghastly find in the Choctaw Nation, fifty miles northeast of this city. While traveling along a country road with a guide in search of a band of criminals, he came upon the body of a man by the side of the road with his head cut entirely off, which was found sitting upright on the other side of the road with the face toward the body. There were seven bullet holes in the breast, and bloody stains showed that the crime had been committed only a few hours before. The man was neatly dressed, but there were no papers or any memorandum by which he could be identified. It was in a lonely place, with only one house within miles, and this was not far away. It was occupied by Indians, who first denied any knowledge of the body, and then told that it had been lying there for two weeks. Fleming knew better than this, as he had passed the same spot the evening before. After burying the man he came here and reported, and warrants were issued for the arrest of the Indians. Two Deputies and a strong posse left last night to arrest them and bring them here.

THE OATMEAL TRUST SUCCUMBS.

DES MOINES, Iowa, April 21.—H. R. Heath of this city, proprietor of the Des Moines Oatmeal Mill, has received a dispatch from Chicago signed by the Consolidated Oatmeal Company saying: "Have concluded to let combination go to pieces."

This means that the Oatmeal Trust is broken. "The trouble," said Mr. Heath, "is that people thought the oatmeal business was a big thing. All wanted to rush into it. The capacity of the mills two years ago was double the consumption. That led to the combination, but a large number of small mills have been started for the purpose of sharing the supposed profits or forcing the pool to purchase their plants. That is all over now. The longest pole knocks the persimmons and it will be hard for little mills to live. In oatmeal, as in all other manufactures nowadays, the only concerns that can make money are those which do a large enough business to reduce the cost of production to the lowest point."

THE DATE FOR A DEDICATION.

TRENTON, N. J., April 21.—The Rev. Thaddeus Hogan, pastor of the Catholic Church of the Sacred Heart in this city, announced at all the services to-day that the new church edifice which he has been building for the past two years will be dedicated on Sunday, June 30, and that Archbishop Corrigan has consented to deliver the sermon. Bishop O'Farrell of this diocese will dedicate the church, and Archbishop Ryan of Philadelphia will be the celebrant of the Pontifical mass. Archbishop Corrigan will receive a great welcome when he comes here. Before his appointment to the Archdiocese of New-York he was Bishop of the Diocese of Newark, which at that time included the entire State.

YALE'S DIVINITY SCHOOL.

NEW-HAVEN, April 21.—The seventh general catalogue of the Divinity School of Yale University contains notes of many matters of interest which have transpired between 1822 and 1888. The last catalogue was issued in 1872. The new one shows that the whole number of students from the beginning of the school and including those now in the school is 1,607, of whom 1,129 are now living. After the name of each person the number of years which he spent in Yale Seminary is given. Next follows a record of the time and place of birth, graduation, and ordination. Where by the act of ordination he was constituted pastor of a church the name and place of the church follows.

KILLED IN A RAILROAD WRECK.

BERWICK, Ill., April 21.—Two men were killed and three injured in the wreck of a mixed train on the Central Iowa Railroad last night near here. The wreck was caused by the breaking of a wheel as the train was going over the bridge at Cedar Creek. Two cars were hurled into the creek and took fire, burning the bridge. Conductor Colvin was instantly killed by the fall, and the son of Section Foreman Savage, the only passenger, was drowned. Express Agent Rogers, Brakeman Reed, and a mail clerk were badly mangled, probably fatally.

THE LONG SUSPENSE ENDED

PASSENGERS AND CREW OF THE DANMARK SAFE.

RESCUED AND TAKEN TO AZORES—ARRIVAL OF THE MISSOURI WITH SOME OF THE PASSENGERS.

COPENHAGEN, April 21.—A telegram from Lisbon to the United Steamship Company announces the safety of the crew and passengers of the steamer Danmark. The good tidings reached Lisbon from the Azores. It is stated that every one who was on the Danmark is safe, and that only an engineer was injured. Some of the passengers arrived at Lisbon to-day, a number are on their way to New-York, and the remainder are still at the Azores.

LISBON, April 21.—Forty-two of the crew of the Danmark have arrived here. Mr. Raben, the first officer, who is among them, reports that on April 4 the Danmark's shaft was broken. On the next day the disabled steamer met the steamship Missouri, from London March 28 for Philadelphia and Baltimore. The Missouri towed the Danmark until the 6th, when the latter seemed to be about to sink.

At first the Missouri was only able to take aboard twenty of the Danmark's passengers, but, after having jettisoned a portion of her cargo she found accommodations for all the crew and passengers of the Danmark. The Missouri then proceeded to the Azores, and left there the first and second officers and 320 passengers. She then continued her journey to Philadelphia, with 340 passengers and the remainder of the crew.

The Captain and three engineers of the Danmark left the Azores on the 14th for London.

The Danmark was about eight hundred miles from Newfoundland when the accident happened. Some say that the engines broke down. Engineer Kaas was found dead in the engine room after the accident. The Captain and three engineers proceeded to London on board a steamer from Demerara.

Forty-two sailors and all of the passengers left at the Azores by the Missouri came to Lisbon on the steamship Açor.

The death of the Danmark's engineer was due to the bursting of an engine pipe. The engineer was killed on the spot and the ship was badly damaged. In consequence of this damage together with the breaking of the shaft, the vessel was helpless in the heavy seas that prevailed.

The significance of the day was particularly felt by Messrs. Funch, Edye & Co., agents for the abandoned steamship Danmark, yesterday. At about 3 o'clock in the afternoon they received a dispatch from their agents in Copenhagen, stating that the passengers and crew of the deserted vessel had been saved. The steamship Missouri, said the dispatch, which left London March 28 for Philadelphia, had picked up all hands, had carried them to the Azores, and was on her way to Philadelphia, after leaving all but 340 on land there. This news had been received at Copenhagen from Lisbon upon the arrival there of the mail steamer from Fayal. The Missouri is expected now daily at Philadelphia.

There was no time lost in spreading the good news. P. S. Gottheil of Funch, Edye & Co. at once sent a copy of the dispatch to J. Roth, Passenger Agent of the Thingvalla Line. He was not at his office, but some clerks who had come down in expectation of possible news received the dispatch and at once joyfully set off after their superior. There had been during the last few days so many false rumors telling of the safety of the long-lost passengers that everywhere the first impulse was to doubt the authenticity of the news. There could be no mistake, however, this time as to its correctness. Though meagre in details it announced authoritatively the all-important fact that the passengers and crew were safe.

Mr. Gottheil, when asked last evening if he thought the report that the Captain of the Missouri had jettisoned his cargo was a probable one, said: "It does not seem to me that there would be any necessity of throwing the entire cargo overboard. The run from the point where the Missouri must have picked up the Danmark's people to the Azores is only a matter of about two days. Just for that time I should think room enough between decks could be made by throwing over 1,000 tons of the cargo. It seems strange to me also that if, as the press dispatch states, the chief engineer is dead, the owners have not notified us of the fact. The only word that we have had at all is contained in this dispatch:

"COPENHAGEN, April 21, 1889.

"Message received from Lisbon. Passengers, crew all saved, brought to the Azores by steamer Missouri; 340 follow Missouri to Philadelphia; remainder all in the Azores. THINGVALLA."

Neither did it seem likely to Mr. Gottheil that the accident had happened by the breaking of the shaft of the Danmark. This was of course possible, he thought. "I recall a case of an ocean steamer's shaft breaking and flying out so that before the engine could ordinarily have been stopped it would have torn a hole and have beaten through the bottom of the vessel. In that case, however, the engineer jumped in and, at the imminent risk of his life, stopped the engine before it had done much harm. Such an accident may have caused the disabling of the Danmark. I do not think it is probable that the Captain has yet left the Azores. As the only representative of the owners present, he would naturally remain in charge of the passengers until suitable and final disposition of them had been made."

It is two weeks to-day since the Danmark, abandoned and in a sinking condition, was sighted by Capt. Bond of the City of Chester on his way to Queenstown. The report first reached New-York on the 12th and was published the following morning. Since that time the Captain of every incoming steamship and sailing vessel has been eagerly questioned for the slightest clue which might throw some light upon the deepening mystery—what had become of the 667 passengers and 54 officers and seamen of the deserted ship. As the days went by and no news came, it looked very dark to the friends of those on board. Of the many theories advanced by different persons as to the fate of the seven hundred or more souls, the one held from the first by Messrs. Funch, Edye & Co. seems to have proved the true one.

The steamship Missouri, which, as reported, is the rescuing vessel, is a new freight ship, flying the British flag and commanded by Capt. Murrill. She is of 1,800 tons measurement, and is represented in Philadelphia by the firm of Peter Wright & Sons. She left London March 28, bound for Philadelphia, and has now been expected there for several days. It was evident, from the time that she left and from the course she would naturally pursue, that she would come close to the Danmark. The Danmark left Christiansand, bound for New-York, March 26, and her position when sighted, April 8, was 46° north 37° west. After the transference of the crew and passengers to the Missouri it was evidently deemed unsafe by the Missouri's Captain to take so large a number of people further than was absolutely necessary. Both the small size of his vessel and the insufficiency of his stores probably induced him to make the Azores as soon as possible. The speed of his vessel is about ten to twelve knots per hour in good weather, and she may now be expected in Philadelphia at any time.

The Azores or Western Islands are situated in the Atlantic Ocean, and extend in an oblique line from northwest to southeast. They are 800 miles from the nearest coast, that of Portugal.

DELAWARE BREAKWATER, Del., April 22—1 A. M.—The steamship Missouri, from London, with 340 of the passengers of the steamship Danmark, has just arrived here.

WATCHING IRELAND.

DUBLIN, April 21.—Thirteen families at Falcarragh, who had been evicted, but who had returned to their homes, were again evicted at 5 o'clock yesterday morning. Barricades had been erected, but the police met with no violent resistance.

The proposed Nationalist demonstration at Piltown, which was proclaimed by the Government, was held at Shough. The police were completely outwitted. While the crowd, headed by a band of music, were returning from the meeting, they were charged upon by hussars, but no one was injured.

LONDON, April 21.—It is stated that Lord Brownlow will succeed Lord Londonderry as Viceroy of Ireland.

DEFEATING THE EGYPTIANS.

SUAKIN, April 21.—A force of Soudanese to-day attacked and defeated a party of Egyptians from Suakin who were building a fort at Port Halaib. The Egyptians lost ten killed and wounded. They were forced to take refuge on the steamer Agami and have returned to Suakin.

CURRENT FOREIGN TOPICS.

VIENNA, April 21.—There was serious rioting in this city to-day arising out of the strike of tramcar drivers. Workmen in sympathy with the strikers blocked the streets and overcame the police. A force of cavalry had to be called out to quell the disorder. Many persons were injured and a large number were arrested.

BERLIN, April 21.—Emperor William proposes to make a trip in the Autumn to the North Cape. He will be accompanied by Saltzmann, the painter.

ROME, April 21.—Signor Crispi has invited M. Floquet and the members of the French Embassy here to a banquet on Monday next.

The New-York Times.

VOL. XXXVIII......NO. 11,769. NEW-YORK, SUNDAY, MAY 19, 1889.----SIXTEEN PAGES. PRICE FIVE CENTS.

LABBY'S ANNUAL MOTION

PROGRESS MADE IN HIS HOUSE OF LORDS FIGHT.

THE EMPEROR'S INTEREST IN THE GREAT STRIKE—SERVIA'S INTERESTING CELEBRATION—HOME RULE FOR INDIA.

BY THE COMMERCIAL CABLE FROM OUR OWN CORRESPONDENT.

LONDON, May 18.—There was a time, not very long ago, when Mr. Labouchère's standing motion to abolish the hereditary principle of the House of Lords obtained countenance from no English politicians of importance on either side of the House. Last night, when it came up for the fourth time during seven years, it was backed by the whole official leadership of the Liberal Party and beaten by only 41 votes in a house of 361. As it was, no Minister would have said a word in opposition if at the close of the debate the Government had not been taunted with silence on the Treasury Bench, which led Mr. Balfour to say a few unimportant words.

Mr. Labouchère's speech was in his wittiest and most sparkling vein, and was received with shouts of laughter, in which the Tories joined heartily. His description of the way in which, when plebeians are elevated to the House of Lords, they immediately set to work like the Chinese to ennoble their ancestors was made funnier by being pointed with some very apt personal examples. Guinness was made a peer, he said, because he brewed excellent stout, and it was thought that an honor to him would please the middle classes, but instantly he was elevated to the peerage he discovered that his family name used to be McGuinness, and that this family used its own title of Viscount Ivreagh. Others of the pompous fabricated genealogies in the new edition of Burke's "Peerage" were used with much effect to illustrate the same curious retroactive result of creating lords.

The speeches on the other side were made by minor young Tories, and were interesting only on two points, the first being the universal tribute they paid to the American Senate as the only wholly admirable and successful Second Chamber in the world, and the other being the statement made by young Curzon as to a talk he had with John Bright last year on the subject. Mr. Bright then told him that he had come to the conclusion that the best House of Lords would be one composed solely of such hereditary noblemen as owned the largest estates, and who would be elected by the other land owners of the various counties to represent them. This revelation of the strange reactionary lengths to which Mr. Bright's senile backward drift had carried him, once he was separated from Mr. Gladstone and got to associating with what Mr. Chamberlain calls "the Dukes and gentlemen of England," made a painful impression.

It is curious that no Tory spoke of the House of Lords save with an apology and the expression of a hope that some way would soon be found to improve its composition and character, and quite a number of Tories openly voted in the lobby with Mr. Labouchère. In many ways the debate and division were most interesting and significant of the present Parliament.

Unless things take a striking turn for the better in Westphalia in the next day or two, you may expect that William himself will visit the disturbed district and give the obdurate masters severe personal attention. It is impossible to get at the real merits of the huge labor dispute, but now that the Emperor has satisfied himself that the strikers are not affiliated with the Social Democrats, he has plainly decided to take their side against their employers as a matter of dynastic and personal politics. He can better afford to do this, as the general public are beginning to be seriously affected by the advance in the price of coal, and the common popular notion is that the mine owners have been working in a sort of trust combination to rob both the workmen and the consuming public.

Although various Kings and potentates are planning elaborate ceremonials to decorate their visits to one another this Summer, and the French Republic intends making the centenary of the fall of the Bastile the most imposing show Paris has ever witnessed, the really important public function of the year will be held far away from all centres of civilized European activity and population and will be indebted to kingscraft for only a little accidental lustre. I allude to the grand national commemoration next September of the fifth centennial of the battle of Kossovo in 1389, when Amurath, though losing his own life, destroyed the whole fabric of the Servian monarchy.

Before that fatal victory of Islam Servia had been a powerful dominion, extending from the Black Sea to the Adriatic and from Hungary southward to Thessaly. Now, after five centuries of most grievous bondage and benighted poverty, the Danubian Slavs have achieved some sort of freedom and are beginning to aspire to a union and restoration of their ancient strength. So long as King Milan was at the head of Servian affairs he served as a wet blanket to all such aspirations, but his boy has Russian blood and backing and may turn out to be the hero and statesman an oppressed people have been dreaming of so long. At any rate, the notion of a solemn commemoration next September has been spreading like wildfire, not only in Servia, but in Montenegro, Dalmatia, Bosnia, Croatia, and even to an extent in Roumania and Bulgaria.

In very many places Mohammedans are active on committees forwarding the celebration, but still more interesting and important is the way the matter is being taken up in the Austrian provinces mentioned above. Practically all the territories which Servia lost at Kossovo and has not since regained are held by Austria, and it is against her that the demonstration is really aimed. There is something like consternation at Vienna over the dilemma, it being equally dangerous to permit the manifestation and to forbid it. Of course, Russia's hand is suspected in the affair, and very likely not without cause. The present arrangement is to have the young King consecrated and crowned after the ceremony at the ancient seat of the last Servian Czar, which will be a sort of formal inauguration of a new Pan-Slavic crusade.

The latest candidate for home rule honors is India. According to recent advices, public and private, from Mr. Bull's large farm in the south of Asia, the inhabitants are pretty well aroused and mean business. The semi-Anglicized Hindu is a peculiar person, delicate in stature and small of head, conveying the impression at every age that he is not quite grown up; but he is intensely serious and would rather be fanatic in some patriotic or religious cause than anything else in the world.

Two causes have been at work to produce a general state of discontent. The first is the injustice of English rule coupled with the natural tendency to throw off the dominion of a foreigner, and second the spread of education. Not only have many young Indians been given a liberal education, both here and in the Indian capitals, in the beauty of free institutions and the inherent right of every people to govern themselves, but radical books and pamphlets of every sort, political and religious, have been scattered all over the country, translated and eagerly read. Indian newspapers are scurrilous and daring, and lose no opportunity to help along the fomentation. Indian finances are in a bad way. A large number of the small potentates are in the hands of money lenders, and it has been repeatedly and generally charged that the courts are absolutely corrupt, and that justice is for sale to the highest bidder.

There is little doubt that the sub-officials are a very bad lot and that the maladministration of affairs by them is so general and the ring so powerful that their superiors, sent out honorably to bask for a time in a tropical sun, have wisely concluded not to stir them up. Added to these there is the usual whisper of Russian influence. Russia is such a bugbear in some circles here that if rice didn't ripen or the tigers all died Russia would be held directly responsible.

However that may be, a great movement has started all over India. Mohammedans and Hindus are equally interested with the aim of getting a portion of the governing power into the hands of their own representatives. Their Congress has increased from 70 delegates at Bombay, in 1885, to 1,500 at Allahabad, in 1888. This Congress includes all the leading intellects of the people, and they have put forth a sort of declaration of rights, and are at present waiting to see what England does with it. They demand, first, the reconstruction of the Legislative Council; second, the absolute separation of judicial from executive functions in individuals; third, that the judiciary of the whole country shall be recruited from trained and competent legal sources; fourth, that the natives of India shall be freely admitted to administrative and executive positions. A qualified scheme of election is proposed, by which half the members shall be popularly elected. They also demand that the budget shall be submitted to them for criticism and investigation, and that native representatives shall have the power of interpellating the Government. This modest little bill of rights, backed as it is by popular unanimity, does very well for a start. Behind it, however, are whispers of demands even greater, with an ultimate scheme of democratic government pure and simple.

They absolutely dismiss any social questions an attempt to adjust which would create a breach between the Mohammedans and Hindus. The movement is a serious and thoughtful one, and is made with an evident appreciation of the increasing weakness of the English foreign policy and a consciousness that domestic affairs give Parliament all the work it can accomplish at the present time. It is rather ungrateful that English education should make the Indians so ready to turn on their philanthropic school teacher, but the world at large is very likely to side with the Indians. The position was very cleverly stated by a Baboo student at the Bishops' College. He said: "The English came into our country as peddlers; they continued in it as robbers, and they will soon be kicked out as lunatics."

An indignation meeting of unemployed actors, of whom there is an exceedingly large number in London just now, was held on Tuesday at the Surrey Theatre. The burden of the complaints was the pushing out of "trained actors" by young, educated, and well-connected amateurs. No scheme for bettering affairs was suggested.

"Her Father," an adaptation from José Echegaray, done at the Vaudeville Theatre on Thursday afternoon, turned out to be a rather heavy drama, conventional in interest and treatment. It was well received, however, and may do very well in this country.

"The Inheritance," by Cecil Raleigh, done at the Comedy Theatre on the same day, is a very good piece of dramatic work, the construction, characterization, and dialogue being equally commendable. The only thing against the play is the selection of the story, which concerns the effort of a sporting parson to disentangle himself from gambling creditors, to appease whom he has forged his brother's name. He lays a cunning plot for his brother's death by diluting chloral and leading him up to large doses, and then letting him take the undiluted drug in the same quantity. The dose is administered by the heroine and, as the sick man dies, and she is his heiress, the brother hints, and finally charges, that she murdered him. All is made right in a strong last act, and the play is the best piece of its kind seen here since "Captain Swift." Royce Carlton did admirable work as the guilty brother.

"The Grandsire," from the French piece "Le Filibustier," by Richepin, done at Terry's Wednesday, is pretty but inadequate.

Mr. Irving's decision to begin his next season, probably in the latter part of September, with Watts Phillips's melodrama, "The Dead Heart," is interesting, for a novelty has been expected. Thomas Wenman will not remain in the company after "Macbeth," in which he is playing Banquo, is taken off at the end of June.

H. F.

CONGRESSMAN GAY DYING.

NEW-ORLEANS, May 18.—Congressman Edward J. Gay is still confined to his bed at his plantation in Iberville Parish, with no signs of improvement and no hopes of recovery. He is helpless to the fullest extent and growing weaker every day.

A VICTIM OF HIGH TARIFF.

FAILURE OF THE ALMY MANUFACTURING COMPANY OF PHILADELPHIA.

PHILADELPHIA, May 18.—The failure of the Almy Manufacturing Company, which has made an assignment for the benefit of its creditors to H. Gordon McCouch, has created more comment among business men than the importance of the failure in a financial way would justify. The Almy Company has never been considered very strong, and its capital has always been somewhat limited. Mr. Almy was in business for himself on a moderate capital for the manufacture of worsteds and other woolen goods, but was not very successful, and three years ago he took in Mr. John Groom, who put in $15,000 or $20,000.

The most interesting point connected with the failure is that Mr. Almy and his partners have been high-tariff Republicans and were very earnest in their declarations before election that if Harrison was elected everything would be lovely with the manufacturers of Pennsylvania. The failure of the company following similar failures, and very material reductions in the operations of woolen mills in this city since the inauguration of President Harrison, has had a very demoralizing effect upon the spirits of high-tariff Republicans.

A leading merchant speaking of the Almy failure to-day said that many other failures would follow in a few years unless the tariff was materially changed, and particularly as regards wool, and it is generally admitted in the trade to-day that if the tariff bill which was before the last Congress admitting wool free had passed the Almy Company would not have failed and other mills which are now running on half time without profit would be running full time.

Mr. Almy says the company's liabilities are about $340,000, which includes about $80,000 in bonds of the company. The estimated assets are placed at $400,000, but they consist almost entirely of the company's mill property, which, if put up at a forced sale, would not bring one-third of that amount.

The failure is generally spoken of as a bad one in the sense that there is small prospect that the company will ever resume. The failure was anticipated in the trade, and caused little surprise. So little, in fact, that some of the high-tariff afternoon papers hardly notice it in their news columns.

According to Mr. Almy the causes of the trouble were various. Business had for some time been slow, there was a great deal of competition, sales had to be made on long time, and the company had incurred losses. The company's New-York commission house was Frederick Almy & Co., who were also the commission men for some Eastern mills. They had made advances to the Almy Manufacturing Company and, as they are also embarrassed, they could make no more.

As President of its manufacturing company Mr. Almy had tried to make arrangement with a commission house with larger capital, but, failing in that, he thought the best thing to do was to make an assignment.

These are the reasons that are given to the newspapers. The reason chiefly talked of among business men is the high tariff on wool.

The report telegraphed yesterday from Philadelphia announcing the failure of the Almy Manufacturing Company of that city and giving the Treasurer's statement that they had received word that their New-York house was going to make an assignment caused much surprise in the dry goods trade in this city. The New-York house referred to is the firm of Fred Almy & Co., dry goods commission merchants at 53 Leonard-street. Mr. Almy, after reading the press dispatch yesterday, said he had nothing to say at present in regard to the matter. His firm had not made an assignment, had not failed, had not suspended, and no notes had gone to protest. When asked if his firm was in financial difficulties or contemplated making an assignment, he declined to answer.

To others he is quoted as saying that he could not say what effect the assignment of the Almy Manufacturing Company of Philadelphia will have on his firm. It had accepted the company's paper for upward of $150,000, and he did not know whether the firm would have to make an assignment or not.

Mr. Almy has been in business in this city for about twelve years, his partners being Otto Von Arnim and Theodore Lamson. His father is the President of the Almy Manufacturing Company, and he was a Director in the concern. The New-York firm has done a large business for its capital, which was about $125,000. On Jan. 1 its statement showed liabilities of $339,000, all for acceptances which they claimed to have goods and accounts more than sufficient to cover. Mr. Almy is President of the Damon Manufacturing Company.

FIGHT FOR A CHILD.

NEWBURG, N. Y., May 18.—Mrs. Mary C. Eager of Warwick, this county, to-day produced before Judge Cullen, at Special Term of the Supreme Court, her little granddaughter, Grace Paddock, as directed by the writ of habeas corpus issued by Judge Barrett in New-York yesterday. William L. Paddock, a salesman in New-York, residing in New-Jersey, was married to a daughter of Mrs. Eager, and to them, some seven or eight years ago, was born the daughter Grace. Marriage proved a failure in this case, and the couple finally parted, each returning to the home of their parents, Mrs. Paddock taking with her the child.

The woman died two weeks ago and the father now claims the right to care for the child, which privilege is contested by the grandparents. The child seems to have inherited the mother's likes and dislikes and clung to her grandparents in court, paying no attention to her father.

Judge Cullen appointed Special County Judge F. V. Sanford a referee to take testimony, and awarded the custody of the girl to Mrs. Eager pending the decision of the court. Paddock is permitted to visit the child twice a week if he so desires.

A NEW STEAMSHIP FOR THE SOUND.

WESTERLY, R. I., May 18.—The General Assembly has passed an act authorizing the Providence and Stonington Steamship Company to increase the number of its Directors from seven to nine. The corporation has voted to accept this amendment to its charter. President W. M. Miller presided at the meeting and 10,483 shares were voted upon.

President Miller enlightened the stockholders concerning the long-delayed new boat of the line, the Connecticut, which he expects will be delivered to the company this week. The Cramps are putting in her engines, which lead to hopes for a speedy boat. She will be ready to join the Providence Line on the first Monday in June. The total cost of the craft will be $625,000.

TO FORECLOSE A MORTGAGE.

KINGSTON, N. Y., May 18.—About three years ago the Union Cement Company, which was organized by J. F. De Navarro of New-York City, made a contract to purchase the cement property owned by the Hudson River Cement Company at East Kingston, and commenced experimenting upon an extensive scale, but without accomplishing the desired result.

It is charged that the property was not paid for by the Union Company according to agreement, and they have refused to vacate it. A receiver, ex-Congressman James G. Lindsley of Rondout, has been appointed, and the first mortgage will be foreclosed.

A SCHOONER'S NARROW ESCAPE.

NORWALK, Conn., May 18.—Capt. William Allen of the schooner Henry Remsen, from New-York for Providence with iron, during the fog Thursday morning off Stamford had a narrow escape from being run into by the steamer City of New-York. Both craft were in shore and throwing their leads. The steamer was bound east and under good headway when the position of the schooner moving in the same direction was discovered. Capt. Allen put his helm aport and the steamer changed her course, just grazing the schooner as she passed. There were about eight fathoms of water under her keel.

RELEASED ON BAIL.

NEW-BRUNSWICK, N. J., May 18.—Judge Scudder to-day fixed bail at $10,000 each in the cases of General Freight and Passenger Agent Hendrickson and Construction Superintendent Hussey of the Raritan River Railroad, who were arrested for the murder of George Kessinger, killed in the fight to prevent the railroad from laying its tracks over the Furman brickyard at Sayreville. Charles and John Whitehead, rival brickyard proprietors, went bail for the men.

OCEAN BEACH ONCE, BELMAR NOW.

OCEAN BEACH, N. J., May 18.—The second special election to decide on a new name for this Summer resort has been held. The name of Belmar was agreed upon, only three votes being cast against it. The first name decided on was Elko, but the Summer residents objected so forcibly to the name that another election was held. The new name was suggested by H. Allaire, the wealthy architect of Monmouth County.

THE GREAT FRENCH SHOW

WHAT THE PRESENT VISITORS CAN SEE.

THE EIFFEL TOWER AND EDISON'S EXHIBIT—AMERICAN PICTURES VERY ATTRACTIVE—OTHER MATTERS.

BY THE COMMERCIAL CABLE FROM OUR OWN CORRESPONDENT.

PARIS, May 18.—Among more agreeable preoccupation, the return of the Deputies has almost passed unnoticed. The abandoned statesmen have cut out their work in practical divisions absolutely devoid of interest to the general public. The budget of necessity cannot be made a groundwork for discussion, because, like the celebrated four-cent Paris cakes, it is always *la même chose.* What will be more conflicting is the prologue. There are so many irons to be placed on the fire for future use, and ways and means to an end, while skillfully concentrated, must be artfully concealed, and all this will use up the better part of the first five or six sessions. From June 1, then, to the middle of the month, the budget will be itemized, and the end of June will send the Deputies to the provinces, when a tooth-and-nail fight for the general elections will begin.

The Haute Cour has not yet finished its labors, and in spite of the extraordinary reserve unusual to this gossipping town, it creeps out that Boulanger will be banished. Whether this is a result natural to the discovery and writing up of a long history of crime, or a foregone conclusion to Governmental necessity, is not divulged, and, to write frankly, no one seems to care anything about it. "The Marseillaise," momentarily at least, outfeasts the Boulanger anthem. Rumors concerning the health of the General became so persistently alarming that finally great scientific names were called in to vouch for the statements. When Dr. Bronardel, one of the most eminent French physicians, found words of precise meaning, and even dates of probable life, put in his mouth, he came out with a short clear letter stating that not only had he never seen Gen. Boulanger, but he knew nothing about his constitution, and that, had he been consulted as a physician, he would know enough to hold his tongue. This frank precision has bodkined gossip for the present.

The fun at the exhibition continues, and the Champ de Mars's atmosphere is more quicksilvery than ever. Nothing is finished yet, but the Eiffel Tower is open to the second platform. The public can go up there on foot, for the elevators cannot work before a fortnight. To open the tower even thus partially the workmen have labored all night, changing off hands as midnight hours advanced. M. Salles, son-in-law of M. Eiffel, assures me that no soldier on the battle field deserved better mention than these humble toilers, who, will never go down to history.

Except in block, it costs 2f. to climb up stairs to the first story, and 1f. more to mount one above. The ascension begins at 11 o'clock, and it would take too much cable space to describe the scene of yesterday amid the happy, patient crowd below and the glorious harvest of Russian, Flemish, and English restaurants above. Telephone communication regulates the number admitted at one passing. M. Eiffel remained all day, ever active and full of contented zeal, wherever he was recognized. Cheers were given a Mme. Sommer, who was the first lady to touch terra firma above, and next came in placid solemnity an Arab chief. All the French press came, and one or two foreign journalists. Each and all inscribed their names on the *Figaro* Eiffel sheet. This hands them down to French posterity.

There is no use in trying to epitomize the exhibition in routine, for it partakes of all the kaleidoscopic delight of every Parisian fête. One should be able to fly like a bird to every enticing necessity, and even then half the fun and wit would be lost. The Cairo donkey drivers have been reduced to a more quiescent mood, but owing to the change of surroundings, to the atmosphere perhaps, they certainly look more devilish than under the uniformly blue Cairo sky, with pyramids as a background. It is hard for them to be very reserved, for their very appearance with their daring patrons—for it does take a good deal of audacity to ride a donkey through the exhibition grounds—is a constant signal for wild applause. Half of these Arabs have to be imprisoned every night, and three were sent back to the Khédive yesterday. Like the dancers ambitiously called Almees, they are one of the great attractions, and Cairo-street is a swell resort and the proper place to be from 5 to 7 o'clock. The Algerian tent on the esplanade is really more interesting, because there are five women there, two of them beautiful types, but the distance over there is great and it has not yet grown into fashion.

I have enjoyed fully two comfortable views of the American picture exhibition. This has been a sly peep, for varnishing day has not yet been appointed. Some of the work from home will certainly astonish the critics here. I presume that Dewing will find gratification in the fact that his portrait of a lady, in yellow, entirely absorbed the jury's interest and admiration, and the Allegany landscape of Bolton Jones and the landscape of Wyant defeated all criticism. The portraits of Eastman Johnson and all the black and whites were respected centres. In its ensemble the home exhibition is already a pronounced success. Dannat, Sargent, Knight, and Weeks come out very strong in their respective showing and in their new and special exhibition pictures. The water colorists and pastellists have formally opened their expositions this week, the first afternoon bringing only invited guests. These particular exhibits are to be changed constantly. The pastellists are now the best.

In the machine gallery Edison's division is a crowded resort, and the poor fellow who attends to the phonograph will have a thorough French education before the season is over. He still looks a trifle blasphemous, in Anglo-Saxon, as he wipes his brow and casts up an agonized glance at the hated glass roof, but his attention and returning smile are purely French. The machine gallery is said to have wonderful ventilation resources somewhere, and it is becoming urgent for them to appear.

The Russian incident is closed. All the imperial crowns have disappeared, and Moscow and St. Petersburg emblems have replaced St. George. This takes away the official recognition from the year 1889, while it still leaves plenty of enthusiastic room for the French alliance belief. Politics have given great immunity to the Russian section, just as the patronage of the Prince of Wales has worked freedom for the English division. His Royal Highness is expected here, and all hands are at work to make the Saxon showing taut and clear.

The furniture section is almost empty. People delay bringing in their exhibits in dread of imitation, but May 20 has been officially made the ultimatum, and all must come to time or withdraw. No one goes to visit the superb horticultural display at the Trocadero, and it is a pity, for it is well worth the journey.

Dagnan Bouveret's Salon success, "Bretonne's au Pardon," has been sold by a Mulhouse gentleman for $6,000.

Coquelin was treated like a spoiled child at his farewell benefit in the Théâtre Français. He did a vast amount of work, appearing in portions of five of his best rôles, including Tartuffe, which he had never before played here. Notwithstanding the opinions expressed in his famous pamphlet on this subject, and contrary to its conclusions, the actor played the part according to tradition, and his attempt has been sincerely praised. A group of his friends intrusted to Madeleine Lemaire the presentation to him in the foyer of a plaque of lapis and silver and gold, with palms and laurel crowns engraved thereon, by Fannière. On one side was engraved "Coquelin—Comédie Française—1860-1889," and on the other "Coquelin—His Friends." The house was crowded, a good many well-known New-Yorkers being conspicuous.

There was a great counter-attraction, however, at the Opéra Comique in the première of Jules Massenet's "Esclarmonde" and the début of Miss Sybil Sanderson. On the evening before about 2,000 people had crushed into the building to listen in supposed select privacy to a dress rehearsal. The new opera tends entirely to the modern school. Thanks to the courtesy of Editor Hartmann, THE TIMES received the first published score, and its reading shows only intermittent concessions to melody. It is sensuous music, with sonorous orchestral effects, giving accompaniment to continued love duets. The soprano rôle is written for the exceptional voice of our Californian débutante. It ranges constantly in high notes above the line, and once Miss Sanderson takes and holds high G with ease and sweetness. It was called facetiously on the first night an "Eiffel Tower note." Miss Sanderson makes a beautiful picture in her picturesque costumes, and the dramatic rôle suits her style as well as the vocal score. She was received favorably.

At Cluny Théâtre "Trop Ainé," by MM. Valady and Dancourt, has not been the promised success, and there is no use in going into the details of the plot. The remarkably excellent troupe of the distant Cluny gave all their brightness and go to the piece, but it was unavailing. There was superb dressing on the part of the leading lady.

The theatres with the exception of the Français, the Grand Opéra, and, of course, the Opéra Comique are absolutely empty. No one can give a reason for this unprecedented abandonment. In 1878 the theatres enjoyed a harvest. Prices went up and staid up. It is now moved to close, as usual, in June, for with the exhibition, the bull-fight attraction, and the great Buffalo Bill show the theatres will stand no earthly chance.

Quite thirty thousand persons were present at the Wild West opening to-day, headed by President Carnot. The band mingled the "Marseillaise" with "Yankee Doodle." Great enthusiasm was caused by the shooting of the cowboys. The Indian tents are already a *chic* attraction, however Indian morality may suffer. The braves are courted and fêted by the prettiest women in Paris. Yesterday Valtesse and Depaix carried them cigarettes. Wherever you go you hear of nothing but "Buffalo Beel."

ONCE A RUSSIAN ALWAYS A RUSSIAN.

ST. PAUL, May 18.—Louis Niemo of the Dairy Commissioners' Department received yesterday a letter from Charlton F. Way of the American Consulate at St. Petersburg, in which he warns Russian and Polish Hebrew residents of the dangers attending their return to Russia. Gentiles who have been natives of the same country are also liable to be interfered with, but the interpretation of the Russian laws on the subject depends largely on the individual opinions of the officials who administer them. Mr. Way cites the case of a Polish Jew who came to the United States many years ago and became a naturalized citizen. He fought in the war of the rebellion, in which he lost an arm and was given a pension. Recently he returned to Russia and was at once imprisoned. After remaining in prison for a long time he was tried, convicted, and escorted to the frontier, because he had left the country before arriving at the age when he would become liable to perform military duty. While the American Government does everything possible to guard and protect citizens, native or naturalized, while abroad, there is no treaty with Russia on this point, and it seems to be the case there that when a man is once a Russian he is always a Russian and amenable to Russian laws.

IT IS NOT A TRUST.

ST. PAUL, May 18.—A local photographer, when asked concerning the proposed trust mentioned in a dispatch from Buffalo, answered that he did not know much about a trust, but he had heard something about a mutual benefit and protection association to be formed. The main object of the association will be to protect members from cheap photographers, who do all of their work with street exhibitions and can work at less expense than those who have more expensive establishments. It is proposed to make life insurance a feature of the organization, which is to be supported by initiation fees and regular dues. When a member dies his gallery will be placed in charge of a competent man and the proceeds given to the family, or the gallery will be sold and the money turned over to the heirs of the deceased. These are the principal objects of the proposed association, and the organization will probably be effected within a short time.

LITTLE LEFT FOR MRS. GAINES'S HEIRS.

NEW-ORLEANS, May 18.—Mr. W. W. Christmas and Dr. C. M. Kennedy, both of Washington, D. C., arrived last evening and took rooms at the St. Charles Hotel. Mr. Christmas is a son of James Y. Christmas and a grandson of the late Myra Clark Gaines. The object of the gentleman's visit to this city is to look after his interest in the succession of his grandmother. It is understood here that the heirs have very little interest in the Supreme Court judgment in their behalf, since the little lady litigant in whose name the suit is won had made over to lawyers and money lenders a great deal more than the amount of the judgment. Besides, she had previous to her death made a compromise with purchasers of the Blanc property to the amount of several hundred thousand dollars.

DELAYED BY A DENSE FOG

THE SERVIA RUNS AGROUND IN GEDNEY'S CHANNEL.

A LARGE SHIP ASHORE AT LONG BRANCH—THE THICK FOG A SOURCE OF DANGER AND DIFFICULTY.

The Cunard steamship Servia went aground and was held fast in the mud of Gedney's Channel at 10:15 yesterday morning. The dense fog which prevailed outside the Hook was mainly responsible for the Servia's mishap. As the tide began to ebb immediately, the steamship was all the more firmly settled in position, and to the 230 saloon passengers who spent the day in the fog it looked rather serious as night came on. A tug was hailed and brought the third officer of the Servia up to the city to report the unpleasant situation to Agent Brown. As there seemed no danger, however, that anything more serious would happen, Mr. Brown decided not to take off the passengers, but simply to wait for the tide, which was high at 10:35 P. M.

Later on, however, reports came from Sandy Hook that not only had the Servia been caught on the mud banks, but that the French steamer La Normandie had also experienced difficulty in getting out and had come to an anchor near the Servia. La Normandie had first fouled with Buoy No. 6 and carried it away from its moorings, its mooring chain becoming entangled in the big steamer's propeller. Worried lest in the darkness and fog with so many vessels gathered together in such close proximity, Mr. Brown decided to go to the Servia's assistance. He, therefore, ordered three tugboats to go down the bay to assist in pulling the Servia off at high water. He himself, with other members of the Cunard Line staff, embarked on the mailboat Fletcher and left Castle Garden for the Hook at 7:15. The E. M. Maillard, H. S. Nichols, and J. W. Burke left an hour later. At a late hour last night it was not known whether they had been successful in finding the Servia.

The French steamer's agents chartered the tug Pulver to proceed to the assistance of the Normandie, but that steamer at last was reported as having successfully gotten rid of the buoy chain and gone on to sea.

Among the Servia's passengers are Mr. and Mrs. W. E. Dodge, Capt. and Mrs. John Donohugh, Mr. and Mrs. John Grazier, Mr. and Mrs. Charles I. Goodale, Dr. and Mrs. W. J. Hill, B. F. Metcalf, James R. Macpherson, the Rev. and Mrs. C. B. Mitchell, W. E. Smith, Mr. and Mrs. Victor M. Smith, Mr. and Mrs. Jesse Seligman, Miss Seligman, the Rev. W. G. G. Thompson, and Mr. and Mrs. J. G. Warwick.

Mrs. Levi P. Morton and Miss Edith Morton were passengers on the steamer La Normandie. There were also on board Mr. and Mrs. Robert W. De Forest, the Misses De Forest, Mr. and Mrs. E. C. Moore, Frederic O. North, Capt. de la Peyriere, Consul Revoil, French Consul General at Costa Rica; Mrs. Revoil, Mr. and Mrs. William A. Slater, Rudolph Aronson, W. J. Brett, Count de Bresson, Francis Barton, N. R. Cottman, the Rev. Pius Conrad, Dr. Mariano Gonzalez, Dr. P. A. Kearney, and Dr. Ludger.

The dense fog which could be seen all day yesterday lying along the eastern horizon was a source of the greatest danger and difficulty to the pilots. Both outgoing and incoming vessels were subjected to delay and inconvenience, and during the day no incoming vessels crossed the bar.

The Hamburg-American Packet Company's new ocean steamer Augusta Victoria was earnestly awaited yesterday by some people who thought it possible that she would break the record. But the fog would have detained her, even if she had been pushed for speed, a very unusual thing on a steamship's maiden trip. This and many other things that occurred to annoy the seafaring portion of the community were laid up against the thick fog.

At about 1 o'clock the life-saving crew at Station 5, Long Branch, saw a big ship's royal masts towering over the fog in such a way as to indicate that she had gone ashore broadside to the beach. The waves brought her nearer and nearer every instant, and soon the outlines of her hull became visible about opposite the Howland Hotel. The life-saving crew put off to her, as the surf was rather heavy and the people on board the ship were in danger of being washed overboard and drowned.

It was ascertained that the ship was the Algoma, from Rio Janeiro for New-York, in command of Capt. Vero. She lay in an exposed position and was anxiously watched by hundreds of spectators on the beach. Capt. Vero went ashore in one of the lifeboats. It was thought last night that if the wind changed it would be possible to pull the Algoma off.

The agent of the Algoma is J. A. Whitney of 15 State-street, this city, who had left his office for the day before the report of her going ashore reached there. The Algoma is a British wooden ship of 1,184 tons burden. She was built in Maitland, N. S., in 1872.

Some little delay was experienced by the different ferries on account of the fog. On the North River the boats had a delay of about five minutes, but ran regularly otherwise. The Staten Island boats had some slight delay, beginning to feel the fog about 8:30. The fog down the bay was heavy, with a light south wind, and was what ferryboat pilots call a dark sea fog. It was quite heavy along the shore of Staten Island, so much so that it was difficult to see the dock lights on entering the pier. Owing to the light south wind the fog drove in from the sea up the bay, coming in heavy gusts, and then rifting for a moment only to settle down again heavily. On the East River the ferryboats experienced some slight delay. The great bridge was completely obscured from land view by the fog.

On board the North German Lloyd Werra, for Bremen, were Robert Garrett, Horatio Garrett, John W. Garrett, Mrs. T. Harrison Garrett, Miss M. E. Garrett, Mr. and Mrs. H. F. Billings, Mr. and Mrs. Julius Catlin, the Misses Catlin, Miss C. C. Crosby, Mr. and Mrs. Charles D. Fisher, the Misses Fisher, Dr. and Mrs. Joseph Kurtz, the Misses Kurtz, Dr. Carl Kurtz, Major W. Kaufman, Dr. Adolph Richter, and Capt. and Mrs. A. C. Tompkins.

The steamship Celtic, from Liverpool and Queenstown, was reported last night as anchored off the Scotland Lightship, waiting for the fog to lift.

NOTES FROM CUBA.

HAVANA, Cuba, May 18.—The dry weather continues and the large sugar estates are still working, although rain is much needed, the cane becoming hard and yielding little juice. Most of the smaller plantations have finished their crops, with a difference of 25 to 40 per cent. less production as compared with the previous crop. Much new cane will be planted, and the area for next season's grinding will be greatly increased. It is conceded that the crop of 1888-9 will fall short of that of 1887-8 fully 150,000 tons.

The tobacco crop promises to be abundant and of a good quality, and the production of potatoes is increasing every year, our market being well supplied with fine, large tubers, which are selling at wholesale for 2 cents per pound. Frequent fires have occurred among the sugar-cane fields, causing the destruction of large tracts of standing cane and burning over lands recently cropped. This, no doubt, is owing to the long-continued dry weather. Rain is very much needed all over Cuba.

The Madrid Government is at work on the Cuban tariff, and it is promised that some of the enormous duties will be moderated. Receipts at the various Custom Houses of the island show a large increase over those of 1888.

Notwithstanding the determined efforts of Capt. Gen. Salamanca, it has been found difficult to capture the bandoleros which have so long held sway in the country. Two of these have recently been condemned, and a reward of $2,000 gold is offered for their arrest and delivery to the authorities.

Representatives of the Government of Hayti have been trying to purchase one of the Spanish coast steamers to be used as a cruiser, but up to the present time they have not succeeded in doing so.

The city is generally very healthy.

OF INTEREST TO MARRIED WOMEN.

BISMARCK, Dakota, May 18.—The General Land Office has found out that a married woman cannot prove upon her homestead claim. A decision to that effect has been forwarded to the Bismarck Land Office. The victim is a young woman who lived nearly five years on her land, got married, completed her residence alone, and made final proof. The local office, following scores of precedents and the universal rule, accepted her proof. Some wiseacre in that unfortunate bureau, the General Land Office, has discovered that the young lady's residence followed her husband's and was merged in his. Her property rights are independent of his, and she has a perfect claim to her homestead if she sees fit to comply with the law subsequent to her marriage. Marriage cuts no figure under the homestead law, and she can complete the entry she has initiated, but she may be obliged to incur the expense of an appeal to the Secretary.

BUFFALO'S HOTTEST MAY DAY.

BUFFALO, May 18.—This has been the hottest day Buffalo has ever known in May. Officially the thermometer registered 88°. Down on the streets, where people moved and had their perspiring existence, it was 9° higher.

The New-York Times.

VOL. XL....NO. 21,243. | NEW-YORK, SATURDAY, NOVEMBER 22, 1890. | PRICE TWO CENTS.

ERRORS OF GOVERNMENT

THE WORK DONE YESTERDAY BY THE LAW AND ORDER LEAGUE.

JUDGE BONNEY'S ABLE DISCUSSION OF THE EXECUTIVE POWER AND THE ENFORCEMENT OF LAWS.

PITTSBURG, Penn., Nov. 21.—The International Law and Order League Conference to-day listened to letters from Judge Noah Davis, Senators Sherman of Ohio and Evarts of New-York, Secretary Windom, and Assistant Secretary Nettleton of the Treasury Department, and the Rev. Lyman Abbott, commending the work of the leagues and expressing regret at their absence. Mrs. J. Ellen Foster addressed the conference and tendered the fraternal greetings of the Non-Partisan Women's Christian Temperance Union.

Later in the day telegrams of sympathy and co-operation were sent to the Women's Christian Temperance Union, in session in Atlanta, Ga., and to the non-partisan Women's Christian Temperance Union in session in Allegheny. Mr. F. S. Spence, Secretary of the Temperance Alliance of the Dominion of Canada, gave a valuable account of the success attained in Canada in restricting the liquor traffic and enforcing advanced temperance legislation.

The election of officers for the coming year resulted in the re-election of the Hon. C. C. Bonney of Chicago as President, Lew Wallace, Bishop Ireland, Senators Colquitt and Moody, the Revs. E. E. Hale and Washington Gladden as Vice Presidents, L. Edwin Dudley of Boston Secretary, and Major E. L. Pond of Montreal Treasurer.

Inspector Archibald, Chief of Police of Toronto, described the methods of administration of the Police Department in that city that have made it rank so high among the cities of the globe. First among these causes he places a non-partisan Police Board; then a judiciary with a tenure lasting during good behavior, and lastly on a roused public sentiment that will sustain a most vigorous enforcement of law. As a result of Chief Archibald's twenty-five years' labor the city to-day is practically free from unlicensed liquor saloons, houses of ill-repute, and gambling dens, even bucket shops being suppressed.

This evening at a mass meeting held in the City Hall, Judge C. C. Bonney of Chicago, Dr. Edward Everett Hale of Boston, the Hon. John M. Langston of Petersburg, Va., and Mr. L. Edwin Dudley of Boston addressed the citizens of Pittsburg. Judge Bonney discussed "The Executive Power and the Enforcement of Laws." He brought the following severe indictment against our legislators and executives:

"Legislative work is notoriously poor. In quantity it is excessive, burdening the statute books with worse than needless details of administration; in quality it is crude and uncertain, requiring years to determine its real meaning and effect; in motive it is too often partial and sectional, instigated by some merely local interest or grievance, and not properly limited.

"But it is in the executive department of power that we see the gravest errors. We see as we survey the country executive position, high as the thrones of Kings and richly endowed with regal powers, occupied by commanders in chief who do not command; Governors who do not govern; executives who do not execute. We see those exalted public offices largely occupied with the affairs of the political party to which they respectively belong, and, when not so engaged, appearing more like the Chairmen of important committees than as the custodians and administrators of the great powers of government.

"The consequences have been most deplorable, dangerous classes and interests boldly intrude into the fields of active life, and audaciously contend with legitimate business and with lawful authority for possession and control. Innocence and justice walk in dread of contact with disorder and vice even in the highways of the people. False ideas of government infest the public mind, and it seems to be a common notion that any person may at pleasure dispute public authority, and that the only recourse in such a case is a lawsuit, more or less protracted, in which the wrongdoer will have a chance of success through some technical defect.

"Excessive political partisanship is to-day the deadliest living foe of peace, good order, and prosperity of the country. It cripples executive administration, and for the sake of their votes permits the dangerous classes to prey upon the people. The evils of that partisanship cannot possibly be overrated; the necessity for reform cannot possibly be exaggerated; but those evils will continue till the people rise and break the chains of partisan bondage and insist as a condition precedent upon their support that devotion to the country and ability to promote the general welfare, and not mere devotion to party and mere ability to promote its success, shall determine the selection of the persons by whom the great powers of government shall be held and exercised."

Judge Bonney cited approvingly the utterance of George Washington, who said: "All obstructions to the execution of the laws, all combinations and associations under whatever plausible character, with the real design to direct, control, counteract, or awe the deliberation and action of the constituted authorities, are destructive of the fundamental principle of government. They serve to organize faction, to give it an artificial and extraordinary force, to put in the place of the delegated power of the nation the will of the party, often a small but artful and enterprising minority of the community, and according to the alternate triumphs of different parties to make the public administration the mirror of the ill-concerted and incongruous projects in faction rather than the organ of consistent and wholesome plans, digested by common councils and modified by mutual interests."

Edward Everett Hale indorsed all that Judge Bonney had said, enforced the statement that the greatest peril to American institutions is from the growth of "bossism," or that spirit in American life which makes people willing to allow others to do their thinking for them and makes them indifferent to their obligations and duties as sovereign citizens.

CANNON BACK IN WASHINGTON.

HE IS CONFIDENT THAT THE REPUBLICANS CAN KEEP A QUORUM.

WASHINGTON, Nov. 21.—Representative Cannon was at the capital to-day, one day later than he had invited himself, to attend the first meeting of the Appropriations Committee, and he was strangely confident that there would be no difficulty in keeping a quorum of Republicans in attendance during the session. If the Republican members of the House attend at the opening in the same proportion that the Republicans of the Appropriations Committee have appeared, there would be less than fifty members out of 175.

Mr. Cannon is also impressed with the belief that the Republicans are to go on attending to business just as if nothing had happened. He ought to have added that the President is trying to have it understood that he desires the Republicans to attend early and to stay faithfully, as upon the legislation of the remaining part of the session he must build all his hopes of popularity in the next National Convention. When the Republicans find out that the President wants every man to be here, it ought to settle the question as to whether there is to be a quorum of Republicans present all the time or only on great occasions.

Mr. Cannon does not care to talk about the causes of Republican defeat. In that respect he is not so free-tongued as Representative Buchanan of New-Jersey, who wants to convict the people of lack of honesty and common sense. He says that the verdict did not count, for the people did not understand what the bill would do, and then he pitches into the retail dealers, calls them swindlers, and accuses them of making the McKinley bill odious by increasing prices right and left on goods that were not to be touched by the tariff.

NEWSPAPER INFLUENCE FOR HARRISON.

INDIANAPOLIS, Nov. 21.—Negotiations are in progress by Harrison Republicans for control of several daily papers whose alliance to Harrison is doubtful and whose influence would be necessary in this State to prevent systematic opposition to his re-nomination.

The papers which it is sought to bring under the control of a syndicate of the President's friends include the Evansville *Journal*, Terre Haute *Express*, Logansport *Journal*, Lafayette *Courier*, South Bend *Tribune*, and Fort Wayne *Gazette*. Several of these are such pronounced friends of Judge Gresham that the Harrison men regard their control as absolutely necessary to a solid delegation of Administration Republicans in the next National Convention.

Whether the plants will be purchased outright or leased has not yet been definitely settled.

CHANDLER'S DIRTY POLITICS.

NO RESULT OF THE EXTRA-SESSION MATTER—UNSEATING DEMOCRATS.

CONCORD, N. H., Nov. 21.—The extra legislative session conspiracy which Chandler has been engineering for some time past still hangs fire. The Governor and Council have been in session all day, and met again at 7 o'clock this evening, but adjourned shortly after until 9 o'clock to-morrow morning.

They sat with closed doors, but it was authoritatively stated that the question of an extra session was not broached in the Council Chamber until the evening meeting, when Gov. Goodell opened the subject deploring the necessity for calling the same, but expressing the opinion that such necessity existed and giving some of his reasons therefor. Councilor Merrill took the ground in opposition to the scheme and the adjournment was had before any other Councilor had expressed himself. There is a very strong feeling in the popular mind to-night that the Council will fail to agree upon the measure when it meets again in the morning, although Chandler, Moore, and others of the radical Republican element have been working desperately to that end all day.

Failing to get any consolation from the Democratic leaders yesterday looking to his retirement, Chandler had a dispatch sent to-day to Clerk Dickey asking for his resignation, but got no favorable response. There is a very general belief now that if the old Legislature is recalled Clerk Dickey will not only be at his desk, but that it will be impossible to remove him. The Governor and Council have not been idle during the day, although the extra-session business remains undisposed of. They have canvassed the returns of the votes for Senators in the various districts, and have perpetrated a great outrage in the estimation of fair-minded men of all parties.

In the Peterborough district, where the fact of the returns received at the Secretary's office show Hall, the Republican candidate, elected by 5 majority, and in the Nashua district, where the returns show a bare majority of 1 for Collins, Republican, the canvass was proceeded with, the result decided, and the decision arrived at that certificates be issued to these men, notwithstanding the fact that recounts have been called for by the Democratic candidates in both districts and are soon to be had.

This decision gives the Republicans absolute control of the organization of the Senate. Again, in the Somersworth district, where the returns show Felker, Democrat, elected by a narrow maojrity, they declared no election on the strength of an addenda which the Clerk of the town of Rochester made to his certificate, alleging that a mistake had been made in the footing of certain votes cast for the Prohibition candidate. This haste to issue certificates to Republicans in contested districts and to declare no election in a district where the returns show a Democrat chosen is denounced as an outrageously partisan exhibition. Undoubtedly Mr. Felker will petition the court for a mandamus to compel the issuance of his certificate.

HILL WILL BE A SENATOR.

WHAT THE POLITICIANS WHO KNOW HIM BEST THINK OF HIS ATTITUDE.

SYRACUSE, Nov. 21.—It is the impression up this way that Gov. Hill will allow himself to be elected to the United States Senatorship.

A local politician who has been admitted to the Governor's confidence on more than one occasion informs your correspondent that the election of a Democratic Assembly was as much a surprise to Gov. Hill as it was to the Republicans. "I am pretty well convinced," he said, "from what the Governor informed me two weeks before election that he had no idea of obtaining a majority in the lower house. As a matter of fact the Governor did not relish the idea of having behind him a Democratic Legislature. He feared that many of his political chickens would come home to roost, and that he would be confronted by reforms which he has been steadily advocating for the past six years because he realized there was not the slightest danger of having them reach him so long as the Legislature remained Republican."

"Then you think Gov. Hill will succeed Mr. Evarts?"

"Certainly. He need not retire from the Executive Chamber till the 4th of March, leaving for his successor to act upon the reform bills that the Republicans may pass upon Hill's previous recommendations. As it is his last year as Governor, the opportunity to avoid disagreeable legislation cannot be avoided. He will save himself from public abuse and obloquy and escape the charge of insincerity by retiring from office six weeks or two months before the Legislature adjourns."

"Has Gov. Hill expressed any wish for the Senatorship?"

"Only in this way: He regards himself as the leader of the party in the State, and rather than have any bitterness or ill feeling engendered among half a dozen ambitious men in the party, he will take the nomination—a proceeding which cannot be criticised, and which will certainly prevent any schism in the party. Besides, the Governor is of the opinion that he must make a record on the tariff issue. He cannot make any speeches as Governor of New-York, but as United States Senator he can play this point well."

"Why does he not propose Mr. Flower as a compromise candidate?"

"For the reason that Mr. Flower is his choice for Governor next year, as Mr. William F. Sheehan is for Lieutenant Governor."

"What will become of Lieut. Gov. Jones?"

"He will pay the freight."

IN MR. SCHOONMAKER'S PLACE.

A GOOD MAN TO DROP OUT OF THE INTER-STATE COMMERCE COMMISSION.

WASHINGTON, Nov. 21.—About the last of December the term of office of Commissioner Augustus Schoonmaker of the Inter-State Commerce Commission will expire and the President will have to name his successor. The law by which the commission was established provides that not more than three of the five Commissioners shall be of the same political party. Mr. Schoonmaker is a Democrat, and so are Messrs. Bragg and Morrison. There is not the slightest likelihood that the President will reappoint Schoonmaker. He will live up to his privilege and name a Republican in order to convert the commission into a Republican body.

Strangely enough, there have been few persons from New-York looking for this position. Mr. Platt would no doubt be glad if he could get one of his best heelers into it. The place is worth $7,500 a year, and yet while all of the dead ducks of the campaign are looking for something in the way of consolation money, none of them is mentioned for it.

There are several members now on the retiring list who are to ask the President to take care of them. Mr. Baker, the Rochester member, who was beaten in the nominating convention by Van Voorhis, is being referred to as a seeker for Gen. Batcheller's place in the Treasury. Representative Farquhar is in a like fix. Either of them would be glad of a comfortable Government position, and so would Mr. J. S. Sherman, who lost the Oneida district. If places are to be found for these men and for Gen. Grosvenor, and for others who do not care to stay in Congress for the remainder of their terms, Mr. Reed will have to set his electing committee at work and turn out a few more Democrats, in order to maintain the Republican majority that was built up in the last session.

The President will have some difficulty in finding a better man for the Inter-State Commerce Commission than Judge Schoonmaker. That he will select a man for the place for anything but political reasons no one imagines, and that he will make political matters in the State worse by an independent selection there is not much doubt. There is some concern among men who have business with the commission lest the Commissionership has been turned over to "Prince Russ," to be farmed out to the best account.

THE AUDITORIUM IN DANGER.

CHICAGO, Nov. 21.—At 10:30 P. M. to-night flames broke out in the Studebaker Building. The structure has been regarded as one of the finest in the city and immediately adjoins the Auditorium. For a time the fire looked threatening and sent forth volumes of smoke that filled the corridors of the Auditorium Hotel, creating quite a panic among the guests, who were about retiring for the night. Many in haste gathered their worldly effects together and were rushing up and down the hallways until fears were allayed by systematic action on the part of the hotel, employés. In the big Auditorium Theatre, which is surrounded by the hotel but separate from it, an immense audience was gathered, enjoying the "Babes in the Wood" pantomime. Only the people on the stage were aware of the proximity of the fire, as no smoke entered the big hall and the performance was uninterrupted, the management being assured that there was no danger to the great granite building and that the exits were more than ample, even in case of a stampede. The flames were confined almost entirely to the basement of the Studebaker Building, and the loss will not exceed $10,000; insured.

WORLD'S FAIR MANAGERS

PERMANENT SITE SELECTED FOR THE THIRD TIME.

ALL FURTHER DISPUTES SAID TO BE IMPOSSIBLE—THE APPORTIONMENT OF THE BUILDINGS.

CHICAGO, Nov. 21.—The most important event in the way of progress made in the Exposition this week was a permanent selection of a site for the third time, together with such a specific apportionment of buildings that all further disputes on this vexed question are said to be rendered impossible.

The fair will be held on the lake front and Jackson Park, with Washington Park and the Midway Plaisance to be used as overflow grounds. This is the apportionment for the lake front: Art building, decorative art building, music hall, electrical display, water palace, (if any,) and steel tower, (if any.) There will be exhibited in the South Parks the display of agriculture, forest products, forestry, machinery and appliances, viticulture, horticulture, floriculture, live stock, domestic and wild animals, fish, fisheries, fish products and apparatus for fishing, mines, mining and metallurgy, machinery, transportation, railways, vessels and vehicles, manufactures, electricity, ethnology, archæology, progress of labor and invention, and all of Department L, except music and the drama; the Government building, the State buildings, foreign buildings, and all other exhibits germane thereto. In connection with the lake front exhibit the citizens of Chicago will provide a two-million-dollar art institute.

This result was not arrived at until after a most disgraceful exhibition of petty bickering between the rival factions in this city devoted to the interests of the lake front and Jackson Park. A much larger number of exhibits was demanded by the lake-front people for this locality, and they had influence enough to secure action by the local Directory placing nearly all the interesting exhibits of a general character there.

This was before the meeting of the national committee. As soon as that body met, in effect it asked the local board to rescind its action and reapportion the exhibits. The Jackson Park people were responsible for this action by the national body, which had sense enough to secure an equitable distribution of the buildings, so that neither party can justly complain. By its firm stand on this question the national body has proved that it is the governing power and that its authority is supreme. The local board will hereafter be obliged to take a back seat.

A special committee appointed by Congress was in the city during the week for the purpose of inquiring into the expenditures of the national organization. The committee remained in session five days. All of the officers of the National Commission, with those of the local directory and prominent citizens of Chicago, were called to testify before the committee. A report will be submitted to Congress soon after the opening of next session.

The lady managers of the World's Columbian Exposition met Wednesday noon, and the following day elected Mrs. Potter Palmer of Chicago President and Mrs. Phœbe W. Couzins of St. Louis Secretary. About one hundred of the one hundred and fifteen lady managers are attending the session. Before their adjournment, which will probably be next Wednesday, a joint conference with a committee from the National Commission will be held, to define more clearly the powers and duties of the lady managers.

Members of the Government Board of Exhibit were in the city this week to decide upon a location for one of the Government displays. They went over the ground before the site question had been definitely settled and decided that Jackson Park was best adapted to the purposes of their contemplated exhibit. As the report favoring Jackson Park had not been acted upon at that time, the display was not fixed.

An invitation has been tendered to Chauncey M. Depew to speak in Chicago again on the subject of the World's Columbian Exposition.

Secretary Windom has decided that the $20,000 appropriated for the use of the Committee on Foreign Affairs is available for the purposes contemplated by Congress at any time the committee decides to begin work.

The City Council Committee on Finance has decided to recommend the issue of $5,000,000 of bonds, voted at the recent election, as soon as the local corporation is able to show that $3,000,000 of the popular subscription has been collected.

The Building Committee of the National Commission has made a report showing that expenses to date aggregate $51,000. The average expense of meetings of the National Commission is $14,000.

The most serious disagreement that has arisen between the national and local authorities is over the appointments of chiefs of bureaus. Members of the National Commission claim that there is a disposition on the part of Directors to ignore the authority of Director General Davis. This matter has been discussed at nearly every session of the commission this week, and is now being considered by the local directory. E. E. Jaycox, Master of Transportation, appointed by Director General Davis, has tendered his resignation as the easiest way out of the difficulties that surrounded his further occupancy of the place.

The proposition to increase the Buildings and Grounds Committee of the National Commission from six to eight members has been defeated.

Members of the National Live Stock Association, now in session, have sent a petition to the commission asking it to make cash premiums instead of medal awards at the exposition.

Congressman R. P. Flower, who is a member of the World's Fair Investigating Committee appointed by Congress, returned from Chicago yesterday, where the committee spent a week looking into World's Fair matters. Mr. Flower said to a reporter for THE TIMES that the national commission was altogether too large and too costly a body to be of any use to the projectors of the fair. This commission now numbers 106 men and 115 women.

"I am opposed," Mr. Flower said, "to the idea of permitting such a body to hamper the Chicago Board of Fair Directors with recommendations and diverse views, and to draw big salaries from the Congressional appropriation of $1,500,000 which should be applied to the legitimate purposes of the fair. I believe that it would be better for Chicago if the national commission should appoint a sub-committee of five good men to supervise the erection of the buildings and the work generally of the local board. This would stop many salaries, and Chicago would be enabled to go on with the preparations for the fair in her own way and with her own money."

Mr. Flower expressed the opinion that the site finally selected was the best one Chicago could offer, and that the outlook for the fair was very good at present.

A MINISTER UNDER CHARGES

FOR ACCEPTING A NOMINATION FOR A STATE OFFICE.

EUREKA SPRINGS, Ark., Nov. 21.—The fifty-fifth annual Arkansas Conference of the Methodist Episcopal Church, South, is in session here. It is well known that, under the order of passing character, the name of the Rev. T. M. C. Birmingham, the late candidate for Superintendent of Public Instruction, will be reached to-morrow, and it is certain that charges will be preferred against him for accepting the nomination on the Labor-Republican State ticket. The Democratic press in different parts of the State and many prominent clergymen, particularly the ministers and laymen from the Morrilton region, are clamorous for proceedings against him.

Mr. Birmingham has been advised by many friends to throw himself on the mercy of the conference, acknowledging that he was wrong. It is thought, however, that he will stand firm on the grounds of personal and political liberty, and that it was not unministerial for him to accept a nomination for an educational office. He is an able and courageous minister, who has heretofore stood high in the Church. He has held the office of Presiding Elder, and is usually Chairman of some of the most important committees.

The case is watched with great interest, as the Rev. N. B. Fizer, late candidate for Governor on the Labor ticket, is a member of the White River Conference of the same Church, and this trial will likely foreshadow its action in the case of Mr. Fizer.

SENATOR-ELECT KEYES'S RECEPTION.

PLAINFIELD, N. J., Nov. 21.—W. J. Keyes, who will represent Somerset County in the next New-Jersey Senate, gave a banquet to a large number of personal and political friends at his home in South Branch last night.

Among those present were Gov. Abbett and staff, Senator-elect Fred C. Marsh of Union, Assemblyman-elect Bergen of Somerset, ex-Congressman Clark, ex-Congressman Pidcock, ex-Assemblyman Klotz, James E. Martine, the Hon. John Veghte, Judge Bartine, and a hundred others, including several Republican friends of the host.

A FAMOUS FEUD ENDED.

BLOODY BATTLES RECALLED BY THE RELEASE OF "TOM" SMITH.

WINCHESTER, Ky., Nov. 21.—The last and one of the worst participants in the Perry County feud has been released from prison on bail of $8,000, and it is believed now that the French-Eversole war is over. The man in question is Tom Smith.

Together with a number of others of both the French and Eversole factions, he was indicted for the murder of Ed Campbell and John McKnight at the famous battles of these factions at Hazard in November, 1889. McKnight was killed about daylight of the morning of the fight, being shot through the heart as he opened the door, by three men concealed in the adjacent graveyard. It is claimed that Smith and Jesse Fields were two of the men. Smith is also indicted for the murder of Joe Eversole, the original leader of that faction, who, with Dick Combs, a young man who had no connection with either faction, was killed from ambush early in 1888.

Smith was released from jail on the ground that the confinement would kill him. His mind and health are evidently failing fast, and he will hardly live to be tried. Smith was a member of the French faction, and the leaders of that faction say the killing of Eversole and Combs was not done by members of that side, but that it was done in retaliation for the murder of William Gambritt, a Baptist minister, in the Fall of 1887.

Gambritt was killed by Joe Eversole, John Eversole, and John Campbell. The two latter shot him in the back while he was running, and Joe Eversole shot out his brains after he fell. The French side claim that it was friends of Gambritt who killed Joe Eversole, and that Smith was not present and knew nothing of the three men who killed Gambritt. John Eversole is the only one now living.

The fate of John Campbell, the other one, was tragic. In July, 1888, he, with several of the partisans of Eversole, went to kill John W. Morgan, a French sympathizer, but failed to find him at home. They were expected. French, with a number of his partisans from Breathitt County, and Campbell had posted Jonah Jones, a negro, at the mouth of a lane where French was expected to pass, with orders to kill the leader of the band and make his escape. After their failure to find Morgan, Campbell and his band got drunk, and, forgetting the orders given to the negro sentinel, went by the lane where he was posted. He thought it was the expected French crowd and fired at the leader, striking Campbell in the groin, from which he died after forty days of intense agony. These are instances that illustrate the growth of the mountain feud and show how hard they are to suppress.

THE BARKER FAILURE.

A HITCH IN THE NEGOTIATIONS OF THE RELIEF POOL.

PHILADELPHIA, Nov. 21.—There were rumors on the Street this afternoon that a hitch had occurred in the arrangements for the formation of a pool by several financial houses and banks to assist the Finance Company of Pennsylvania, whose difficulties were caused by the Barker failure, and that the money would not be subscribed. One of the officers of the Finance Company said this afternoon that some difficulty about the loan had arisen, but that it was removed. He stated that the company had first offered as security the property purchased by it for the Reading terminal, but it has since been discovered that the property could not be legally used by the Finance Company as collateral.

This was what had caused the difficulty in the negotiation of the loan, but other collateral had been offered and accepted by the syndicate, and the money would be subscribed. Drexel & Co. withdrew their offer to subscribe $100,000 toward the amount necessary to assist the company. In conclusion, he said that as yet the company had stood in no need of the money. Mr. A. J. Drexel, when asked about the trouble in raising the money, said: "No money has been subscribed as yet, only the arrangements to do so have been in course of negotiation."

It was stated at the office of Barker Brothers & Co. that no statement in regard to the firm's position would be made public this afternoon.

PITTSBURG, Nov. 21.—Fayette County is excited over the fact that Barker Brothers & Co. of Philadelphia had over $150,000 of the county's money, that being the proceeds of a bond sale. President Ewing of the Fayette County Bank says that institution holds securities from Barker Brothers in excess of the money deposited.

AN OKLAHOMA BANK FAILS.

GUTHRIE, Oklahoma, Nov. 21.—The Commercial Bank of this city, which is the largest bank in the Territory, made an assignment late last night for the benefit of creditors to the Sheriff as assignee. The proprietors have all left town.

The failure involves all that many of the depositors had. A large crowd has stood about the building all day. Orders of attachment are tacked upon the door of the bank in great numbers. The failure was caused by the collapse of the Newton (Kan.) National Bank a few weeks ago. The liabilities and assets cannot be ascertained.

A run was made on the other banks this morning, but upon showing ample funds the depositors were satisfied and the panic stopped.

CHICAGO HAS A NEW BANK.

MRS. GREEN AND SON WILL DO BUSINESS ON A BIG SCALE.

CHICAGO, Nov. 21.—Chicago will soon have a private bank, or rather a trust company, backed by an immense amount of money. Mrs. Hetty Green, known widely as the richest woman in America, and her son, E. H. R. Green, will be at the head of the concern.

Mr. Green said in regard to the project: "Arrangements are practically completed for the new business, or rather the new form of our old business. We will open a Trust company in Chicago. It will differ from the Jennings Trust Company in that we will not act for estates, as the members of that company do. Ours will be a mortgage business. We will loan money on securities and nothing more. We will loan it at a reasonable rate of interest and borrowers may take up their paper at any time. Ours will be a sort of private bank. It will be conducted on the principle of the Chemical Bank of New-York.

"My mother and myself will have the controlling interest, for we never invest in anything unless we have control of it. Others interested will be the Chemical Bank of New-York and Baring Brothers of London. San Francisco capitalists will also be interested. The nominal capital will be but $300,000, but the reserve will reach to about $150,000,000. The Chemical Bank of New-York is conducted on a similar plan. Its capital is small, but its reserve reaches about $30,000,000. This bank will be made, I think it is safe to say, one of the foremost financial institutions of America. Final details will be settled soon. Then we will procure suitable office, and begin business.

"We have started many banks and other financial projects. They have all been successful. This will be made, as the others have been, successful from the start. We have decided to make the city of Chicago our home, and we will open an institution in keeping with the future high rank Chicago will hold as a financial centre."

FUTURE OF THE BARINGS.

A LIMITED COMPANY TO BE FORMED AT ONCE.

LONDON, Nov. 21.—It is officially announced that arrangements for continuing the business of Baring Brothers & Co. have been concluded. A limited company has been formed and will be registered immediately, with a capital exceeding £1,000,000. Mr. Thomas Baring, member of Parliament, becomes Chairman of the company and devotes the whole of his fortune to the firm's credit. Other Directors are Viscount Francis Baring, member of Parliament; Mr. John Baring, Mr. Kirkman, and Mr. Hodgson.

The liquidation of the business of the old firm will be conducted by the remaing partners, Baron Revelstoke, Mr. Hodgson, Mr. Mildmay, and Mr. Norman. It is intendd to reserve to the old firm the right to pay off shareholders in the company on the payment of a substantial bonus which is yet to be decided upon. The guarantee fund has now reached £16,500,000.

BRAZIL'S NEW GOVERNMENT.

RIO JANEIRO, Nov. 21.—The Constituent Assembly, by a vote of 185 to 47, has recognized the legality of the provisional Government and adopted a resolution requesting the Government to continue its functions until a vote has been taken upon the question of a Federal Constitution.

Señhor Moraes has been elected President of the Congress.

A GREAT GAME PROMISED

YALE AND HARVARD'S STRUGGLE AT SPRINGFIELD.

HOW THE TWO FOOTBALL TEAMS WILL BE MADE UP WHEN THEY FACE ONE ANOTHER THIS AFTERNOON.

SPRINGFIELD, Mass., Nov. 21.—To-morrow afternoon at 2:30 o'clock there will be played on the level and solid field of Hampden Park, in this city, what promises to be the greatest football match in which Harvard and Yale teams have ever faced one another. As has been published in THE TIMES, the coming struggle will also be the hardest, and from all indications the most brilliant in the history of the present game itself, which dates back to 1876, when Harvard first introduced the Rugby game. Yale has had an uninterrupted string of victories since the first game she played against Harvard, when the crimson kickers went down to New-Haven and defeated the wearers of the blue.

This prestige, which Yale has acquired by hard work and study, is the very thing which Harvard graduates to-day are afraid of, and it is perhaps not strange that they should refrain from being sanguine of success on the eve of the present match. Still, Harvard has a better chance to win the game to-morrow than she has ever had before, for she has never turned out such a strong football eleven as she sent to this place this afternoon. With big, powerful fellows in the rush line; strong, active, young men behind the line, and every one of them drilled for months in the science of the game, the team is indeed a fine one.

The Harvard men are quartered at a boarding house kept by Mrs. Gardner almost within punting distance from the football field. They are in good physical condition. They went to bed at an early hour to get a good night's rest.

The Yale players did not come to town to-night. Adopting a characteristic Yale course, they went from New-Haven to Northampton to-day, and they will remain nineteen miles away from the field of conflict, in the quiet of the Northampton hills, until to-morrow morning, when they will take a train for this place, arriving here at 12:30 P. M. The Yale men are in good condition, and promise to play as brilliant a game as was ever played by a Yale team. The men have developed a wonderfully aggressive game, steadied by good team work and characterized by brilliant individual play, and their life and snap, together with their knowledge of football, make Yale's supporters look for a victory. Hence every one agrees that no matter which wins, there is going to be a grand struggle.

It is always the case just before a college match of any importance that rumors go floating about concerning the men who are to take part in the contest. To-night there are stories current to the effect that several players on each team are in poor form, but no reliance can be placed in such tales. The men are ready to battle for their lives. They will in all probability line up as follows:

Yale.	*Positions.*	*Positions.*	*Harvard.*
Hartwell	Left end	Right end	Cumnock.
Wallis	Left tackle	Right tackle	Upton.
Heffelfinger	Left guard	Right guard	Finlay.
Holcomb	Centre	Centre	Cranston.
S. Morrison	Right guard	Left guard	P.Traf'rd.
Rhodes	Right tackle	Left tackle	Newell.
Crosby	Right end	Left end	Hall'well.
Barbour	Qu'rt'r back	Quarter back	Dean.
McClung	L. half back	R. half back	Lake.
Williams	R. half back	L. half back	Corbett.
B. Morrison	Full back	Full back	B.Traf'rd.

It will be seen by this that Holcomb, a comparatively new man for Yale, will have to face the mighty Cranston of Harvard at centre, while Heffelfinger and Stanley Morrison, the Yale guards, will try strength and blocking tactics with Finlay and Perry Trafford, respectively. These men will play a good part of the game, although their work will not be as conspicuous as that of the rest of the teams. A football expert has already predicted that the game will turn on the centres.

The make-up of the Yale team was given to THE TIMES'S correspondent by Manager Sears, who denied that Capt. Rhodes would play at right end as reported. Rhodes, he said, would fill his regular position of right tackle. Manager Sears also said that Ben Morrison would be started out as full back, inasmuch as Yale did not believe Harvey would be strong enough to fill the position through a hard game. Harvey was injured in the Yale-Crescent game played in Brooklyn, but declares that he is all right now.

If an opinion were ventured before the game regarding the individual weaknesses of the two teams, it might be said that Yale's weak spots are centre, quarter back, and full back, while Harvard's failing is at full back, in the slowness of Birney Trafford's kick. Yale hopes to stop Trafford's kicking, while Harvard desires to get past Holcomb and down young Barbour before he has the time he needs to pass the ball. Yale's rush line averages 177½ pounds, 10 pounds more than Harvard's average, while Yale's rushers average over 6 feet in height. Harvard's average 5 feet 9 inches.

The field on which the game will be played is level and hard, a little too hard for a heavy fall, but just right for strong centre work and swift runs. New stands have been erected on three sides of the field. They are open stands and will seat 8,500 persons. Seven thousand more tickets for the game have already been sold than there is seating capacity to meet. When it is considered that about 20,000 persons will rush for seats, the jam and confusion likely to occur may be imagined. The 200 policemen engaged to control the crowd will have hard work. Instead of a fence to protect the inner field—such as has been provided at Eastern Park, Brooklyn, for the Yale-Princeton game—only ropes are stretched to keep back the people, and the difficulty which occurred last year is likely to be repeated.

College men have been flocking into town to-day and all the hotels are filled, many having hard work to find places to sleep, but so far there are in reality few other visitors here. The crowd that will see the game will arrive to-morrow on special trains from New-York and Boston and intermediate stations. About thirty Harvard men arrived this evening, among them being Coach George Adams, '86, who declared his confidence in the Harvard team. All has been done in the way of coaching the two teams that can be done. Each man has rehearsed the signals for the last time, and is now awaiting developments.

The ball given to-night at Union Armory on State Street was well attended and highly enjoyable. It was an agreeable repetition of the ball a year ago, when several residents of this city conceived the idea of having a social event already planned occur the eve of the Yale-Harvard game. Students of both colleges were invited, and in all there were about six hundred persons present. The managers of the event were George D. Pratt and H. G. Chapin, both residents of this city. Union Armory was tastefully decorated, among the adornments being seven Yale trophies representing Yale's prowess on water and field. Harvard men did not send any decorations.

Men have been about the Massasoit House all the evening flourishing money and talking a great deal about making bets, but the only bet of any account was one of $500 to $400 on Yale.

WILLIAMS DEFEATS DARTMOUTH.

WILLIAMSTOWN, Mass., Nov. 21.—The championship of the smaller New-England colleges, including Williams, Boston Technology, Amherst, Dartmouth, and Bowdoin was decided on the campus here to-day by Williams's victory over Dartmouth. It has been a stubborn and close contest, and Williams rejoices over the victory the more as it was hard won.

Williams played a steady, sharp game, the result of her long and careful training under Capt. Brown. Dartmouth was strong and aggressive, and lost because she did not make critical points tell. Street, Williams's fine half back, made the only touch-down, from which Brown kicked a very difficult goal. There were about 800 spectators, whose enthusiasm was tremendous throughout the game.

At the close the whole college in a body rushed from the campus with the team on their shoulders to the Post Office, where they cheered each member. To-night the town is red with bonfires and deafened with the sound of horns, guns, and cheers. It is needless to say that this victory is prized by the college above all except the championship in baseball. The teams lined up thus:

Williams.	*Positions.*	*Positions.*	*Dartmouth.*
Lafayette	Left end	Right end	Price.
Nelson	Left tackle	Right tackle	Folsom.
Hotchkiss	Left guard	Right guard	Carson.
Allen	Centre	Centre	Jones.
Sawtelle	Right guard	Left guard	Little.
Cluett	Right tackle	Left tackle	Lakeman.
Bigelow	Right end	Left end	Hall.
Brown	Quarter	Quarter	Allen.
Rogerson & Street.	Half backs	Half backs	Weston & Scruton.
Hall	Full back	Full back	Norton.

CAPT. POE IN UNIFORM AGAIN.

PRINCETON, N. J., Nov. 21.—The university eleven held their last public practice to-day, playing a very strong and aggressive game. Duncan Edwards, '85; Tracy Harris, '86; Spier, '87; Bird, '85, and Sam Hodges, '88, acted as coachers. Capt. Poe appeared in his football suit to-day for the first time since his injury, but did not play. He captained his team. He says that he will begin playing Monday. Spier and Warren are entirely recovered, and are playing a very strong game. Thomas, left guard, was injured to-day and carried from the field. He is troubled with a weak knee.

The eleven will continue practice Monday and Tuesday, especially preparing tricks and team play for the Yale game. Capt. Poe announced this evening in the *Princetonian* that the grounds will be closed to all students and outsiders during football practice. Competent coaches have been engaged for these days to correct all existing defects.

WESLEYAN BEATS BROWN.

SPRINGFIELD, Mass., Nov. 21.—Wesleyan defeated Brown at football on Hampden Park this afternoon by a score of 34 to 6. In the first half Wesleyan made 16 points by three touch-downs and two goals. In the second half Brown scored a touch-down and goal, while Wesleyan made three goals from touch-downs.

VANDERBILT VERSUS ARMOUR.

THE UNION STOCK YARDS DECLARE WAR ON THE "BIG FOUR."

CHICAGO, Nov. 21.—Vanderbilt versus Armour promises to be the situation growing out of the clash of opposing interests clustered in and around the Union Stock Yards. It was rumored on the Board of Trade to-day that the Union Stock Yards and Transit Company had declared war on the "Big Four," Armour, Swift, Morris, and Libby, and proposed to enter into competition with them, backed by the Vanderbilts of New-York and the Thayers of Boston.

At first regarded as only a joke, it was quickly substantiated from reliable sources. The Union Stock Yards and Transit Company does not propose to remain quiet and see their business taken away by Mr. Armour or anybody else. They propose to meet every move the "Big Four" can make. They have prepared the plans for the largest dressed-beef establishment in the world.

The new house will be located on a 100-acre section of land northwest of the stock yards. This land was recently purchased from Matthew Laflin for the sum of $600,000. The plant will cost from $5,000,000 to $7,500,000. In addition to this there will be constructed a new line of refrigerator cars. The estimated cost of the improvement is in excess of $10,000,000.

Mr. Armour is not at all disturbed. He heard of the proposed move on the part of the stock yards people several days ago. He referred a reporter to Mr. Martyn, who acted as his official representative.

"Have you heard that the Union Stock Yards and Transit Company proposes to establish an immense dressed beef house and compete with you?" was asked.

"I heard so several days ago," said Mr. Martyn, "and have heard enough to-day to convince me that the report is well founded. I hope it is true. It would be a good thing for the dressed beef business. It would interest men who are now killing live cattle in dressed beef."

"It is hinted that Mr. Armour is simply making a bluff for the purpose of forcing the Union Stock Yards and Transit Company to reduce their charges."

"Wait and see if it is a bluff," said Mr. Martyn. "It is impossible for us to remain where we are now."

"What effect will the threatened competition have on your trade?"

"The world is large enough for another big dressed-beef house. There is an immense undeveloped field in the dressed-beef trade. I would not be surprised if you should find on investigation that the new house will be built, not for the purpose of competing with us, but for the reason that it is a good and perfectly safe investment. It will bring the Eastern slaughterers to Chicago and put the dressed-beef trade on a permanent basis. We are honestly glad to learn of the establishment of this new house. It will be a good thing for Chicago and a good thing for us."

"Will the other packers—such firms as Hately Brothers, the Anglo-American Packing Company, Moran and Healy, and others move to the Indiana yards?"

"They will," said Mr. Martyn. "It will be for their interest to do so. There is not a packer in the yards who does not know that it is only a question of time when they will be compelled to move. Mr. Armour will duplicate at the new yards any plant now located in Chicago, pay the expenses of moving, and take in exchange the old plant."

It was generally understood on 'Change that Michael Cudahy is to be at the head of the new concern. In this connection it is significant that Mr. Armour and Mr. Cudahy recently dissolved a partnership which has made both of them millionaires several times over. Mr. Cudahy is now in Omaha and will not return to Chicago for several days.

H. Botsford, President of the Chicago Packing and Provision Company, said in reply to the question, "What will be the result of the establishment of a new stock yard in Indiana?"

"There will be a big struggle for supremacy. If Mr. Armour reduces yardage charges, the Union Stockyard and Transit Company will probably meet the reduction. If Mr. Armour reduces the charges for trackage the old company will do the same."

WISCONSIN SENATORSHIP.

A DOZEN OR MORE ASPIRANTS, WITH VILAS IN THE LEAD.

MILWAUKEE, Wis., Nov. 21.—Political interest now centres chiefly on the question as to who shall succeed John C. Spooner in the United States Senate. Among the dozen or so of persons whose names have been mentioned, there are four possibilities, two probabilities, and a claimed certainty. According to this subdivision, the names of the men in reversed order are: Col. W. F. Vilas; Col. Vilas and Gen. E. S. Bragg; Col. Vilas, Gen. Bragg, John Winans, and Gilbert M. Woodward.

The mention of the names of Col. "Gabe" Bouck of Oshkosh and of James G. Jenkins, United States District Judge of this city, are apparently without the consent or wish of the gentlemen named. Mr. Jenkins would be seriously thought of only in the unlikely event of a dead-lock, and gruff "Gabe" Bouck would sooner see his old comrade Bragg elected than to get the honor for himself. Winans and Woodward are more honored by their local admirers than seriously thought of by their party friends throughout the State.

Consequently whatever of real conflict there is narrows down to Bragg and Vilas. That it will be one to result in a factional fight in the party is the evident hope of the Republican organs. That it will be nothing of the sort is the clean determination of the two leaders and their friends. The chances are that Gen. Bragg will be relegated to the rear. He is not in accord with the now predominating influence of the party, whose battles he has fought in Wisconsin the past thirty years.

Notwithstanding that, the party managers and an overwhelming majority of the party papers in the State are already practically unanimous for for the ex-Cabinet officer, there are evidences that the prize is not to be secured without a struggle. S. M. Smead, of Fond du Lac, the recognized counselor of Bragg and leader of his forces, who was in the city recently, admits that the chances are seemingly in favor of Vilas. But he declares that the fight is by no means won. Mr. Smead laughed at the idea of a combination with the Republican members of the Legislature, and unreservedly announced that whoever received the caucus nomination would secure the certificate of election.

COL. KENNON'S SUDDEN DEATH.

Col. Beverly Kennon of 1,219 M Street, N. E., Washington, D. C., who arrived yesterday morning in Brooklyn with his wife and child to pay a visit to his father-in-law, James A. Griswold of 113 Columbia Heights, Brooklyn, died last evening from cerebral hemorrhage in the Brooklyn City Hospital. He had visited Brooklyn to watch by the bed of his father-in-law, who is rapidly sinking from softening of the brain, and yesterday afternoon he went out for a walk in Fulton Street. While in the drug store of Adrian Paradis he fell unconscious to the floor and was removed in an ambulance to the City Hospital, where he died without regaining consciousness.

Col. Kennon acquired his military title in the service of the Khédive of Egypt, where a movable turret for field service, which he invented, was used with effect at Alexandria. A report favorable to the adoption of the Kennon turret for use in the United States Army was made to the last Congress. Col. Kennon served in the Confederate Army and Navy. He was a native of Virginia and was about sixty years of age. His father was a Commodore in the United States Navy, and met his death by an explosion of a cannon in 1860.

TO HUNT FOR SEALS.

OTTAWA, Nov. 21.—The Fisheries Department is advised that leading capitalists in Vancouver, B. C., have organized a sealing and trading company and propose to equip a fleet for the purpose of engaging in sealing operations in Behring Sea.

INDIANS READY TO FIGHT

THE PINE RIDGE AGENCY PLACED IN IMMINENT PERIL.

EIGHT THOUSAND ARMED SIOUX CONGREGATED NEAR THE SETTLEMENT—GEN. BROOKE MASSING HIS TROOPS.

CHICAGO, Nov. 21.—News from the scenes of Indian disturbances have been coming to Gen. Miles's headquarters all day.

From the Pine Ridge Agency in South Dakota word comes that the Indians have the agency and the surrounding country in a state of terror. The ghost dances, under the lead of Little Wound and other chiefs, are still going on at Wounded Knee Creek and Porcupine. The Indians dance with their guns strapped to their backs. A large band of Indians are approaching from Rosebud Agency. These may join forces with the band at Wounded Knee Creek. If so, a fight may be looked for at any moment. Gen. Brooke, who is in command of the troops which arrived yesterday, has had consultation with the Indian agents. All view the situation as very grave. Until troops arrive to reinforce Gen. Brooke's command the Indians will not be molested in their wild actions. The wives and children of all the whites about the agency have left for safer places along the railroad.

Later news from Pine Ridge says that the dancing Indians at Wounded Knee Creek are growing more boisterous and threatening. When told that the troops were coming they answered scornfully that their Great Spirit was advising and encouraging them, and that troops could not stop their dance. A herder came in to-day and reported that several hundred Indians had congregated nine miles from the agency, and are waiting for the Rosebud Sioux to join them.

The news from Pine Ridge Agency through Omaha fully confirms that which comes direct. Things there are intensely uncertain. The troops from Omaha have arrived and are in good condition after their twenty-six-mile march over a strange and rough country. The troops have camped in the very heart of the reservation. The camp includes four companies from Omaha, a company of the Eighth Infantry which is serving as artillery, and three companies of cavalry from Fort Robinson. The camp is in command of Major Butler of the Second Infantry. Additional troops are coming from Forts Meade, Nibrara, and McKinney. Gen. Brooke is anxiously awaiting instructions from the department at Washington, which were due before he left Omaha. He wants orders as to whether or not he shall interfere with the ghost dance, the stimulating factor of the Messiah craze that possesses the Indians.

The Indians have become so bold in their frenzy that they declare that if the soldiers attempt to take away their chiefs, as has been proposed, they will cut the soldiers' ears off and kill them. Every officer on the ground views the situation as very critical. They know that from 6,000 to 8,000 Indians are likely to swoop down upon them at any moment.

"If this happens," one officer said, "nothing but a miracle could save us from Custer's fate. I hope to God that reinforcements will come before the red devils make their break."

The Indians that remain around the agency appear to be very friendly, but they are being closely watched, for Indian blood runs very thick. Red Cloud, the son of the famous old Sioux chief of that name, is still around the agency. He sympathizes with the Messiah fanatics, but instead of going off to the ghost dances hangs sullenly around the troops. If he makes a false move he will be looked up.

From Eureka, by way of Aberdeen, S. D., comes a dispatch which says that the settlers of Emmons and Campbell Counties are flocking into that place on account of a well-defined rumor that the Sioux take the warpath to-morrow. Five hundred people from the country are now in Eureka. La Grace, on the Missouri, is completely depopulated.

It was reported early this morning that two men had been shot and scalped by Indians in Campbell County. The Sheriff of Campbell County writes that there is a large body of Sioux on the east side of the Missouri. The people are greatly excited and are appealing to Gov. Mellette and Mayor Moody of this city for arms and ammunition.

From Mandan, N. D., comes a dispatch which says that the chances are against an immediate uprising, unless Sitting Bull makes up his mind it would pay. Sitting Bull would be arrested and put in irons, but the agent is afraid this would precipitate trouble. Agent McLaughlin has lost control of Bull and the other leaders. At Bull's camp the dance of 200 braves keeps up day and night. Indians with Sitting Bull do not welcome even friendly whites, and will not shake hands with them. They say all white men will be turned into buffalo and catfish in the Spring.

Indians from Pine Ridge are now with Sitting Bull inspiring his followers with Messianic heresy. Insufficient troops are at Standing Rock to justify such measures for the suppression of Sitting Bull as prudence would demand. In regard to a former report that the Indian police had thrown down their uniforms, the facts are that Agent McLaughlin sent them to arrest refractory Indians, and instead of obeying orders they threw off their clothes and joined in the dance. They returned to the agency without prisoners and offered no excuse. McLaughlin was afraid to punish them and condoned their offense.

Sitting Bull is jealous of the increase of cattle on Cannon Ball River belonging to white settlers. He teaches his followers that if a raid is made on the settlers and they are killed the Indians can surrender on the appearance of the soldiers and be forgiven. Then, because of the fate of former settlers, no new ones will come there. Indians who have followed the advice of Major McLaughlin, and accumulated property, are opposed to the proposed uprising. Young bucks who have nothing and older ones who are lazy, led by Sitting Bull, are causing all the trouble. Gov. Miller is in Mandan this evening.

THE GHOST DANCE.

HOW THE INDIANS WORK THEMSELVES UP TO FIGHTING PITCH.

ON WOUNDED KNEE CREEK, VIA PINE RIDGE AGENCY, S. D., TO RUSHVILLE, Neb., Nov. 21.—Accompanied by Buckskin Jack Russell, the scout; Major Burke, and a half breed named Half Eyes, a TIMES reporter has witnessed one of the famous ghost dances of the Sioux. Mounted on Cayuse ponies, the party started early last evening for the Wounded Knee. The trail lay over a rough, rolling country, where the buffalo grass is now yellow and short, and where snow lies in the depressions in the earth. Half Eyes was in the lead. The traveling was hard and extremely painful, and it was nearly daybreak when the low moaning chant of the Sioux and the snarling of their dogs were heard in the distance. The camp of the fanatics could not be seen until the ridges of a low chain of buttes were reached. From this elevation one could see the fires burning. The trip was extremely hazardous, owing to the frenzy of the hostiles and their knowledge of the arrival of the troops.

Half Eyes tethered the ponies near the ridge, and the rest of the trip was made on foot. The sky was just being painted by the rising sun when the expedition reached a clump of young cottonwoods, which skirted the banks of the Wounded Knee. From this point an excellent view could be had of the dance, which was still at its most exciting state. As near as Half Eyes could estimate, 182 bucks and squaws were in the dance.

A big tree stood in the middle of the circle formed by the Indians. Squatted on the ground, within a radius of sixty yards, were 400 other Indians, who were chanting with the dancers. Many of the reds were in war paint. Some of them were naked to the hips, and across their big muscular breasts were streaks of red and yellow paint. Beads tinkled from their porcupine-fringed legs, and eagle feathers hung from the crown of their black glossy heads. Some of the dancers were robed in white cotton cloth, which was pinned at the breast and drawn over the head in the form of a hood. Five medicine men sat on the ground outside of the circle; they were old men with wrinkled, skinny faces, and as the chant rose and fell, according to the vigor of the drumming, they waved medicine sticks above their heads. These sticks were painted green, with handles fashioned after the shape of snakes.

The dancers held one another's hands and moved slowly around the tree. They did not raise their feet as high as they do in the sun dance, most of the time it looked as though their ragged moccasins did not leave the ground, and the only idea of dancing the spectators could gain from the motion of the fanatics was the weary bending of the knees. Round and round the dancers went, with their eyes closed and their heads bent toward the ground. The chant was incessant and monotonous. "I see my father, I see my mother, I see my brother, I see my

10 Pages

The New-York Times.

10 Pages

VOL. XLI...NO. 12,751. NEW-YORK, THURSDAY, JULY 7, 1892. PRICE THREE CENTS

MORE GAINS FOR LIBERALS

THE TIDE IN ENGLISH ELECTIONS TURNS IN THEIR FAVOR.

EIGHT SEATS GAINED AS THE RESULT OF YESTERDAY'S RETURNS OF THE POLLINGS—A PLEASANT ENDING OF A DAY WHICH OPENED GLOOMILY—SOME OF THE SURPRISES TO THE GLADSTONIANS—THE INFLUENCE OF CHAMBERLAIN'S POLITICAL WORK—EFFECTS OF THE LABOR MOVEMENT—POLLINGS TO BE HELD TO-DAY.

BY THE COMMERCIAL CABLE FROM OUR OWN CORRESPONDENT.

Copyrighted, 1892, by the New-York Times.

LONDON, July 6.—After yesterday's hitch the Gladstonian boom is again under way, with a likelihood of not being interrupted, but the Liberals had worn the anxious seat smooth and shiny before the movement began.

To-day the budget of news opened gloomily enough for the Liberals at noon, with an unpleasant remainder from yesterday's pollings in the shape of the news of the loss of the seat of West Edinburgh. There was no reason on earth why we should not have had all these Scotch figures last night, except that the Sheriff of Edinburgh is a Tory, and could make himself disagreeable to the largest number of his neighbors by deferring the count till to-day.

The result in this district had been an almost foregone conclusion. Young Lord Walmer, who won this victory for the Unionists, is the son of Lord Selborne and son-in-law of Lord Salisbury, and so quite in the Cecil family swim. His seat in Hampshire, which he carried over with him when he deserted Gladstone in 1886, being now very shaky, it was decided to make a strenuous effort for him in Edinburgh, and a regular system of colonizing voters in the west district has been carried on during the past eighteen months. This is a familiar trick in Auld Reekie, where, long decrepit now, the jerry-built tenements are still standing which the Duke of Buccleugh hastily built in 1880 and filled with imported voters in the vain effort to beat Gladstone's first Midlothian candidature. This peculiar Scotch finesse played a part in to-day's election over in West Belfast, as well as accounting for Sexton's heavy defeat.

Still, though Walmer's success had been rather discounted, it made a discouraging overture to to-day's events. This despondency weighed heavily upon everybody's spirits. At the National Liberal Club, until after 11 o'clock to-night, twenty out of seventy-seven results came in without a single change, and with majorities running about as they did in 1886.

Then came news of two seats where the Liberals would have won but for Labor candidates, and of another—Glasgow, Camlachie—which was lost by Cunningham Graham's vicious stump candidature. People began to say that the jig was up and to curse all Labor candidates.

Then suddenly came a change. John Burns's great victory in Battersea was the first signal for cheers. Then came news of a triumph over a specially-noxious Unionist in Glasgow, and then tidings of three huge gains in London, aggregating a change of over 4,000 votes.

This was supplemented after midnight by a fourth London gain in Central Finsbury, where the learned Baboo Naoroji was elected. This is he of whom Salisbury spoke sneeringly as a black man, and this taunt was mockingly taken up by the cheering crowds to-night outside. This election of a full-blooded Indian to Parliament by a London constituency is certainly one of the most remarkable features of the whole strange fight.

All these gains were wildly cheered, but there was more astonishment over the double-barreled gains in Devonport, Portsmouth, and Oldham. Some sanguine folk had talked of these, but the actual fact staggered the listeners.

With North Salford they made twelve Liberal gains for the evening. These were offset by Camlachie, West Belfast, and the twin boroughs of Walsall, Wednesbury, which had fallen under the violent local influence of Chamberlain's Birmingham revolt, leaving the Liberals a net gain of eight on the day.

This tremendous display of power, within a certain midland area, by Chamberlain is really a wonderful thing. Its momentum has even sufficed to treble the unpopular Tory Matthews's majority, and turn the once potential Liberalism of Warwickshire into a ridiculous minority scarce worth counting. What makes the metamorphosis more striking is the fact that, as Birmingham becomes the focus of the Conservative forces, London reaches out for radical leadership.

Some other things have already developed in this election which the Liberals find difficulty in mastering. They have been fretting their hearts out the past two days because they have not made sweeping gains among the provincial boroughs. They have not, even now, realized the fact that their party's strength is no longer in the boroughs. Up to a dozen years ago it was, but all that is changed now. The small country shopkeepers, once their mainstay, are now all Tories, and the real Liberal strength is either in the great industrial sections of London and the north or among the agricultural laborers.

For this reason, the deepest interest attaches to the opening county division elections to-morrow. If the rural districts of Devon, Somerset, and East Anglia begin showing Liberal gains, as they are expected to do, we shall very soon find Gladstone's majority leaping up toward the historic figures of 1885.

To-morrow's polls will put all the borough elections, with a handful of exceptions, out of the way, and make a considerable beginning in the polling of the country districts. In all, seventy-three seats will be fought for to-morrow, of which the Tories now hold forty-six, the Unionists two, the Liberals seventeen, and the Nationalists eight.

This Tory preponderance is chiefly in London, where, out of fifteen seats, they now hold thirteen, and in the county divisions, where they have twenty-two out of twenty-six. The Liberals are entitled to expect several gains in London—probably three, possibly five or six—but the Tory local magnates have been careful, in selecting the first day's rural poll list, to pick as many safe seats as possible. This device is specially obvious in Ireland, where the solitary county division where the Tories have a ghost of a chance of winning—that is, South Dublin—is the only one which votes to-morrow. They expect this gain, which will be due, if at all, to Parnellite alliance and wholesale colonization, to produce an anti-home-rule effect on the remaining English polls.

Among the losses up to date, perhaps the Liberals feel most that of O. V. Morgan, who has an exceptional number of friends in the United States and Canada, and who sat for Battersea ever since the creation of that borough. Temporarily failing health compelled him, a while ago, to say he would not stand again, so John Burns was chosen as a candidate instead. Then Morgan, recovering his health, had to look for a new constituency, and unfortunately was beaten at Ashton.

The loss of Sir Horace Davey is regarded with much more complacency, even though it involves the loss of the seat as well. He is the most unpopular of all the dry-as-dust old fossils who have been clinging so long to Gladstone's skirts, wearying the patience of the younger Radicals. He lost Christchurch in 1885, Stockport and Ipswich in 1886, and now has given Stockton away. The legend of his malign effect has been so strong during these latter years that Liberal candidates have begged that he be not sent to make speeches in their behalf. This last failure will probably decide Gladstone to make him a peer. Then it will be impossible for him to bungle any more Parliamentary contests, which shows the House of Lords to be of some use after all.

Buchanan, who has been chased out of the seat of West Edinburgh by young Lord Wolmer, is an opinionated man, who carried the borough as a Unionist in 1885, became a Gladstonian, resigned to appeal to his constituents, and carried it for home rule in 1888. He might have made some figure in the House if he had ever been able to agree with any one.

Philip Stanhope is the only other Liberal thus far whose loss makes any other difference than the loss of a vote.

RETURNS OF THE POLLINGS.

MEMBERS CHOSEN AT THE ELECTIONS HELD YESTERDAY.

LONDON, July 6.—Dr. Charles Tanner (anti-Parnellite) was elected to-day, without opposition, to represent the Middle Division of County Cork in the House of Commons. Dr. Tanner was a member of the last Parliament, to which he was also elected without opposition.

Mr. Isaac Holden (Liberal) was returned to-day from the Keighley Division of Yorkshire without opposition. In 1885 the Liberal majority in the district was 2,245. In 1886 Mr. Holden was elected without opposition.

In the Hollamshire division of Yorkshire, Sir Frederick T. Mappin (Liberal) was returned without opposition. In 1885 the Liberal majority was 2,003. In 1886 Sir Frederick was elected without opposition.

Mr. William Abraham (Liberal) was elected without opposition in the Rhondda Valley Division of Glamorganshire, Wales. In 1885 the Liberal majority was 867. In 1886 Mr. Abraham was returned without opposition.

A mistake was made in the returns from Dundee last night. The corrected figures of the district, which returns two members, are: J. Leng, (Liberal,) 8,484; E. Robertson, (Liberal,) 8,191; W. O. Dalyleish, (Conservative,) 5,659; W. C. Smith, (Liberal-Unionist,) 5,066; Macdonald, (Labor,) 354. Liberal majority in 1886, 4,671.

Further returns have been received as follows:

East Edinburgh.—R. Wallace, (Liberal,) 3,876; McLeod Fullarton, (Liberal-Union,) 2,760; Wallace's majority, 1,116. In 1885 the Liberal majority was 2,408; in 1886, 1,441.

West Edinburgh.—Lord Wolmer, (Liberal-Union,) 3,728; T. R. Buchanan, (Liberal,) 3,216; Lord Wolmer's majority, 512. In 1885 the Liberal majority was 1,175; in 1886 the Liberal-Unionist majority was 600. Mr. Buchanan, who formerly represented the division, was elected in 1886 as a Unionist. Having changed his views on the home-rule question, he resigned and offered himself for re-election in February, 1888. In this election he was returned by 46 majority.

Central Edinburgh.—W. McEwan, (Liberal,) 3,691; A. K. Connell, (Liberal-Unionist,) 1,736; E. Wilson, (Labor,) 435. McEwan's majority, 1,520. In 1885 the Liberal majority was 1,246; in 1886, 1,624.

South Edinburgh.—Herbert Paul, (Liberal,) 4,565; Lewis McIver, (Liberal-Unionist,) 4,345. Paul's majority, 220. In 1885 the Liberal majority was 1,399; in 1886, 1,582.

Andover Division of Hampshire—Mr. William W. B. Beach (Conservative) has been returned without opposition. In 1885 the Conservative majority was 1,451; in 1886 Mr. Beach was elected without opposition.

Waterford—West Division.—Mr. Alfred Webb (anti-Parnellite) was returned unopposed. He sat in the last Parliament, to which he was elected without opposition.

Armagh—Northern Division.—Col. James Saunderson, (Conservative,) the well-known Orangeman, was returned without opposition. In 1885 the Conservative majority was 1,819; in 1886, 2,895.

Shropshire — Oswestry Division. — Stanley Leighton, (Conservative.) No opposition. In 1885 the Conservative majority was 981. In 1886 Mr. Leighton was elected without opposition.

Antrim—South Division.—W. G. E. Macartney, (Conservative.) No opposition. In 1885 the Conservative majority was 1,362. In 1886 Mr. Macartney was returned unopposed.

County Cork—East Division.—Capt. Donnellan, (anti-Parnellite.) No opposition. In 1885 the Nationalist majority was 4,048. In 1886 there was no opposition.

Manchester—South Division.—Sir H. E. Roscoe, (Liberal,) 4,345; Viscount Emlyn, (Conservative,) 4,064. Liberal majority, 281. Liberal majority in 1885, 670; in 1886, 335.

Manchester—Southwest Division.—Jacob Bright, (Liberal,) 3,924; Prof. Hopkinson, (Unionist,) 3,776; Liberal majority, 148. In 1885, Conservative majority, 567; in 1886, Liberal majority, 111.

Manchester—Northeast Division.—Sir James Ferguson, (Postmaster General, Conservative,) 4,239; C. P. Scott, (Liberal,) 4,129; Conservative majority, 110. Conservative majority in 1885, 1,445; in 1886, 327; in bye-election in 1891, 150.

Manchester—East Division.—Arthur James Balfour, (First Lord of the Treasury, Conservative,) 5,147; Prof. Munroe, (Liberal,) 4,749; Conservative majority, 398. Conservative majority in 1885, 824; in 1886, 644.

Manchester—North Division.—C. E. Swann, (Liberal,) 4,255; J. M. Yates, (Conservative,) 3,593; Liberal majority, 302. In 1885, Conservative majority, 975; in 1886, Liberal majority, 96.

Glasgow—Central Division.—J. G. A. Baird, (Conservative,) 6,085; Walter Menzies, (Liberal,) 5,245; Conservative majority, 840. In 1885, Liberal majority, 1,067; in 1886, Conservative majority, 1,356.

Glasgow—Blackfriars and Hutchestown Division.—A. D. Provand, (Liberal,) 4,146; Alexander Stuart, (Conservative,) 3,065; Liberal majority, 1,081. Liberal majority in 1885, 622; in 1886, 864.

Metropolis—Battersea Division.—John Burns, (Labor,) 5,616; W. M. Chinnery, (Conservative,) 4,057; Labor majority, 1,559. Liberal majority in 1885, 712; in 1886, 186.

Glasgow—Bridgeton Division.—Sir George O. Trevelyan, (Liberal,) 3,729; W. C. Maughan, (Conservative,) 3,351; Liberal majority, 1,378. Liberal majority in 1885, 121; in 1886, 797; in bye-election in 1887, 1,401.

Birmingham—West Division.—Joseph Chamberlain, (Unionist,) 6,296; Corrie Grant, (Liberal,) 1,879; J. W. Mahoney, (Labor,) 31; Unionist plurality, 4,417. In 1885, Liberal majority, 2,764; in 1886, Unionist unopposed.

Salford—South Division.—Sir H. H. Howorth, (Conservative,) 3,406; Alderman A. Forest, (Liberal,) 3,369; W. K. Hall, (Labor,) 553; Conservative plurality, 37. In 1885, Liberal majority 46; in 1886, Conservative majority, 157.

Middlesborough.—J. H. Wilson, (Labor,) 4,691; W. S. Robson, (Liberal,) 4,062; Mr. Bell, (Unionist,) 3,333; Labor plurality, 629. In 1885, Liberal majority, 2,926; in 1886, Liberal unopposed.

Birmingham—East Division.—The Right Hon. Henry Matthews, (Home Secretary, Conservative,) 5,041; H. G. Fulford, (Liberal,) 2,832; D. S. Collin, (Temperance,) 296; Conservative plurality, 2,209.

Birmingham—Central Division.—J. A. Bright, (Unionist,) 5,535; Mr. Herbert, (Liberal,) 1,522; Unionist majority, 4,012. In 1885, Liberal majority, 773; in 1886, Unionist unopposed; in bye-election in 1889, Unionist majority, 3,060.

Birmingham—South Division.—J. P. Williams, (Unionist,) 5,194; W. J. Lancaster, (Liberal,) 2,267; Unionist majority, 2,927. In 1885, Liberal majority, 1,787; in 1886, Unionist unopposed.

Birmingham—North Division.—Alderman W. Kendrick, (Unionist,) 4,841; Eli Bloor, (Liberal and Labor,) 2,084; Unionist majority, 2,757. In 1885, Liberal majority, 618; in 1886, Unionist unopposed.

Metropolis—Hampstead Division.—E. B. Hoare, (Conservative,) 3,848; J. S. Hanham, (Liberal,) 2,239; Conservative majority, 1,609. Conservative majority in 1885, 875; in 1886, 1,762; in by-election in 1888, Conservative unopposed.

Metropolis—Walworth Division.—W. Saunders, (Liberal,) 2,514; L. H. Isaacs, (Conservative,) 2,218; Liberal majority, 296. Conservative majority in 1885, 69; in 1886, 235.

Metropolis—Bermondsey Division.—R. V. Barrow, (Liberal,) 4,390; A. Lafone, (Conservative,) 2,732. Liberal majority, 1,658. In 1885, Liberal majority, 83; in 1886, Conservative majority, 358.

Metropolis—Southwark, West Division.—R. K. Causton, (Liberal,) 3,534; E. Bond, (Conservative,) 2,295. Liberal majority, 1,239. Liberal majority in 1885, 240; in 1886, 113; in bye-election in 1888, 1,194.

Glasgow—Tradeston Division.—A. Cameron Corbett, (Unionist,) 3,366; J. Caldwell, (Liberal,) 3,197; J. B. Burleigh, (Labor,) 783. Unionist plurality, 169. In 1885 Liberal majority, 1,118; in 1886, Unionist majority, 704.

Glasgow—Camlachie Division.—A. Cross, (Unionist,) 3,455; J. McCulloch, (Independent,) 3,084; Cunningham Graham, (Liberal-Labor,) 906; Hugh Awtt, (Liberal,) 179. Unionist plurality, 371. Liberal majority in 1885, 1,164; in 1886, 159.

Glasgow—College Division.—Dr. C. Cameron, (Liberal,) 5,804; Sir J. Stirling Maxwell, (Conservative,) 4,758; R. Brodie, (Labor,) 225. Liberal plurality, 1,046. Liberal majority in 1885, 1,523; in 1886, 655.

Salford—West Division.—Lees Knowles, (Conservative,) 4,152; B. Armitage, (Liberal,) 4,112. Conservative majority, 40. In 1885, Liberal majority, 273; in 1886, Conservative majority, 116.

Metropolis—Finsbury, East Division.—J. Rowlands, (Liberal,) 2,372; W. L. Shadwell, (Conservative,) 2,089. Liberal majority, 283. In 1885, Conservative majority, 20; in 1886, Liberal majority, 61.

Metropolis—Finsbury, Holborn Division.—G. Bruce, (Conservative,) 4,429; George Bateman, (Liberal and Labor,) 2,427. Conservative majority, 2,002. Conservative majority in 1885, 1,574; in 1886, 1,701; in bye-election in 1888, 965.

Metropolis — Bethnal Green, Southwest Division.—E. H. Pickersgill, (Liberal,) 3,206; T. Benskin, (Conservative,) 2,171. Liberal majority, 1,035. Liberal majority in 1885, 888; in 1886, 549.

Metropolis—Newington, West Division.—Capt. C. Norton, (Liberal,) 3,421; G. W. Tallents, (Conservative,) 2,328. Liberal majority, 1,093. Conservative majority in 1885, 645; in 1886, 382.

Glasgow—St. Rollox Division.—Sir J. Carmichael, (Liberal,) 6,247; the Hon. H. F. H. Elliott, (Unionist,) 4,891. Liberal majority, 1,356. In 1885, Liberal majority, 126; in 1886, Unionist majority, 110.

Aston Manor.—Capt. Grice Hutchinson, (Conservative,) 5,300; Mr. Ward, (Liberal,) 1,313. Conservative majority, 3,987. In 1885, Liberal majority, 1,153; in 1886, Conservative majority, 782; in bye-election in 1891, Conservative majority, 2,978.

Birmingham—Bordesly Division.—Jesse Collings, (Unionist,) 6,380; W. J. Davis, (Liberal and Labor,) 2,658. Unionist majority, 3,722. In 1885, Liberal majority, 1,327; in 1886, Unionist majority, 3,435.

Devonport, (Two Members.)—Hudson Kearley, (Liberal,) 3,354; E. J. C. Morton, (Liberal,) 3,325; Captain Price, (Conservative,) 3,012; Robert Harvey, (Conservative,) 2,972. Liberal majority, 313. In 1885, Conservative majority, 291; in 1886, Conservative majority, 980.

Metropolis—Bethnal Green—Northeast Division.—G. Howell, (Liberal,) 2,895; H. H. Marks, (Conservative,) 2,321; H. R. Taylor, (Labor,) 106; R. Ballard, (Independent,) 23. Liberal plurality, 574; Liberal majority in 1885, 1,251; in 1886, 372.

Metropolis—Hackney—North Division.—W. R. Bousfield, (Conservative,) 4,799; John McCall, (Liberal,) 3,280. Conservative majority, 1,519; Conservative majority in 1885, 416; in 1886, 1,503; in bye-election in 1892, 969.

Salford—North Division.—W. H. Holland, (Liberal,) 3,686; A. A. Baumann, (Conservative,) 3,399; Liberal majority, 287. Conservative majority in 1885, 176; in 1886, 159.

Metropolis—Rotherhithe Division.—C. Macdona, (Conservative,) 3,995; H. J. Glanville, (Liberal,) 2,765; Conservative majority, 1,230. Conservative majority in 1885, 527; in 1886, 1,087.

Oldham, (two members.)—J. M. Cheetham, (Liberal,) 12,619; J. T. Hibbert, (Liberal,) 12,541; Elliott Lees, (Conservative,) 12,205; J. M. Maclean, (Conservative,) 11,952; Liberal majority, 336. In 1885, one Liberal and one Conservative returned; in 1886, Conservative majority, 563.

Belfast — West Division.—Arnold Forster, (Unionist,) 4,316; Thomas Sexton, (Nationalist,) 3,427; Unionist majority, 889. In 1885, Conservative majority, 35; in 1886, Nationalist majority, 103.

Metropolis — Hackney — South Division.—Sir Charles Russell, (Liberal,) 4,537; T. H. Robertson, (Conservative,) 3,293; Liberal majority, 1,244. Liberal majority in 1885, 942; in 1886, 100.

Metropolis—Hackney—Central Division.—Sir. A. Scoble, (Conservative,) 3,478; J. F. Stewart, (Liberal,) 3,193; Conservative majority, 285. Conservative majority in 1885, 193; in 1886, 1,086.

Metropolis—Clapham Division.—P. M. Thornton, (Conservative,) 5,170; R. McKenna, (Liberal,) 4,526; Conservative majority, 644. In 1885, Liberal majority, 326; in 1886, Conservative majority, 469.

Portsmouth, (two members.)—J. Baker, (Liberal,) 9,643; W. O. Clough, (Liberal,) 9,448; Gen. Sir G. Willis, (Conservative,) 9,135; the Hon. Evelyn Ashley, (Unionist,) 9,000; Liberal majority, 313. In 1885, Liberal majority, 564; in 1886, one Unionist and one Conservative returned.

Walsall.—F. James, (Conservative,) 5,226; E. T. Holden, (Liberal,) 4,909; Conservative majority, 317. Liberal majority in 1885, 1,677; in 1886, Liberal unopposed; in bye-election, in 1891, Liberal majority, 538.

Metropolis—Finsbury—Central Division.—D. Naoroji, (Liberal,) 2,959; Capt. Penton, (Conservative,) 2,056; Liberal majority, 3. In 1885, Liberal majority, 547; in 1886, Conservative majority, 5.

Wednesbury.—Alderman Wilson Lloyd, (Conservative,) 4,986; the Hon. P. Stanhope, (Liberal,) 4,926; Conservative majority, 60. In 1885, Conservative majority, 195; in 1886, Liberal, majority, 662.

Cork City, (two members.)—William O'Brien, (McCarthyite,) 5,273; Maurice Healy, (McCarthyite,) 4,759; W. H. K. Redmond, (Parnellite,) 3,186; D. Horgan, (Parnellite,) 3,007; McCarthyite majority, 1,573. In 1885, Nationalist majority, 5,072; in 1886, Nationalist, unopposed; in bye-election in 1891, McCarthyite, majority, 1,512.

The following is a list of division changes not previously mentioned in which the representation is unchanged:

Paisley, Southhampton, Bath, Brighton, Bury, Chester, Gravesend, Ipswich, Plymouth, Salisbury, Taunton, Wakefield, Wigan, and Norwich.

FEATURES OF THE CAMPAIGN.

FIGURES OF THE RETURNS—MR. GLADSTONE'S CANVASS.

LONDON, July 7.—The total returns received up to 1 o'clock this morning show the election of 123 Conservatives, 93 Liberals, 19 Liberal-Unionists, and 4 Anti-Parnellites. Up to this time the Government has still a majority of 45.

The total Liberal gains are 29, and Conservative 14.

The total number of votes cast by the Unionists is 644,179; by the Opposition, 617,147.

Throughout the night the crowds in Fleet Street watching the bulletin boards at the various newspaper offices grew larger and larger. The greatest excitement prevailed, and when the results were posted they were greeted with cheers or groans, according to the political affiliations of the watchers. So vast were the crowds that traffic was completely blocked.

The newspapers issued a series of special editions giving the results up to midnight.

At 2 o'clock in the morning large and lively groups were still assembled about the bulletin boards eagerly discussing the situation.

Among the electoral weapons used by the Unionists is a flysheet giving an extract from Washington's Presidential valedictory, made in 1796. These passages are underlined:

"It is of infinite moment that you properly estimate the immense value of your national union to your collective and individual happiness. You should cherish an immovable attachment for it and frown upon attempts to enfeeble the sacred ties linking the various parts."

After the result of the polling in the east division of Manchester had been announced, Mr. Balfour, the successful candidate, made an address to an enthusiastic assemblage of his constituents and others, at the Manchester Conservative Club. He congratulated his hearers that the attempts of their opponents during the past six years to discredit their policy and to vilify their political characters had failed absolutely to shake the phalanx of unionism in Manchester. The flowing tide had not overwhelmed the popular intelligence.

It must be remembered, Mr. Balfour said, that their fight had been harder than in 1886. Six years of misrepresentation had brought back to the Gladstonian fold the less intelligent portion of the waverers who had abstained from voting in 1886. The polls were now as great as at any crisis in English history. Against an enormous voting power the Unionists had shown that they stood unconquered, and, he ventured to say, unconquerable. Mr. Balfour concluded by declaring that this night's work augured well for the future of the country.

The *Daily News* has received the following from its Edinburgh correspondent:

"Mr. Gladstone spent a comparatively quiet day at Dalmeny. He felt that, after yesterday's exertions in the windy weather, it would be advisable for him to curtail his intended route to Corstorphine, in which town arrangements had been made for him to address a political meeting. The demonstrations to-day were therefore less numerous than those which attended his triumphant drive of twenty-eight miles to Dalkeith yesterday, but were equally as enthusiastic.

"Mrs. Gladstone caught cold yesterday, and was to-day unable to accompany the party, which consisted of Mr. Gladstone, his daughter Helen, his son Henry, and a few friends.

"The small hall, with a most tiny platform, in which the meeting was to take place, was almost filled by the time the party arrived in Corstorphine. The Earl of Aberdeen's children, in the care of the family butler, were among those who had gathered in the hall to see and hear the 'Grand Old Man,' who was delighted to welcome them. The hall and all the adjacent streets were crammed with an enthusiastic crowd when Mr. Gladstone arrived in the town, and he was given an ovation.

"At the opening of his speech heavy thunder clouds gathered overhead, darkening the hall to such an extent that Mr. Gladstone was compelled to call for lights, for which seemingly no provision had been made. He explained that he needed lights, as he intended to read some notes he had made, showing that the Unionist poll in Scotland was about 30,000 votes, while the Gladstonian poll, including the votes wasted on Independent and Labor candidates, was about 47,000 votes.

At other points in his speech he apologized for assuming that Field Marshal Sir John Linturn Simmons was a Catholic.

"In noting Mr. Balfour's statement that the Government had distributed dividends, and the Opposition only prospectuses, Mr. Gladstone cited a dozen measures proposed by the Opposition which had been trampled on by 'Balfour and his mechanical majority.' 'Our dividends,' he said, 'were ready in our pockets. We were prepared to distribute them, but they were always voted down.' 'The prospectuses of the Liberal Party,' he continued in a splendidly-declaimed passage, 'are to be found in the legislation of the past sixty years, the last being the endeavor to establish real unity of the empire by meeting the just demands of Ireland.'

"Mr. Gladstone then began to comment on the polling, quoting figures to show that, while up to the present time the Ministerial votes in London had been increased by 9,000 over those of 1886, the Liberal votes had been advanced by 20,000. That, he said, was very significant. Greenock had been won gloriously. Perth had been lost by the operation of an ingenious process of which the Liberal Party had a monopoly. He dealt in a similar manner with results elsewhere.

"Mr. Gladstone intended to make only a half-hour speech, but he discoursed with much vigor for forty minutes.

"Then a local brewer named Usher, who was greeted with derisive shouts of 'Usher's Entire,' appeared on the scene with a huge manuscript containing a series of heckling questions. The audience became impatient at the interference of Mr. Usher, but Mr. Gladstone good-naturedly tried to obtain a hearing for the man, who stood stolidly facing the angrily-roaring crowd with dogged patience. When quiet had at length been restored, Mr. Gladstone patiently repeated to the implacable brewer passages from his former speeches, explaining his attitude toward the plan of campaign.

"Mr. Usher then collapsed before the stormy enthusiasm of the audience.

"At the conclusion of the meeting Mr. Gladstone returned to Dalmeny. He received a continuous ovation en route, and responded to the popular demonstrations in his usual happy vein."

The *Daily News* commenting on yesterday's elections says:

"The more cheering progress made by the Liberals yesterday strengthens the inference in favor of the return of Mr. Gladstone by an adequate if not substantial majority."

The *Chronicle*, after again reminding the Liberal Party that their losses are due to disregard of the claims of labor, calls the Battersea victory the prize result of the London elections. "Nothing equals it," says the *Chronicle*, "in significance and social value. John Burns is the premier-elect of London."

DISORDER IN IRELAND.

MORE FIGHTS AT POLITICAL MEETINGS—THE IRISH-AMERICAN COMMITTEE.

DUBLIN, July 6.—A crowd of anti-Parnellites to-day stormed the platform from which the Liberal-Unionists were addressing a meeting at Stranother, County Donegal. Among those on the platform was Mr. Donaldson, a Justice of the Peace. He was hit on the head and his skull was fractured. E. T. Herdman, the Conservative candidate for East Donegal, and D. B. McCorkill, the Conservative candidate for North Donegal, were also present. Each of them was cut about the head and face.

At an anti-Parnellite meeting held at Ballina, County Mayo, to-day, speeches were made by John Dillon and Daniel Crilly, who is the candidate in the North Mayo district. During the meeting the Rev. Father Conway, who was on the platform, bared his head and showed severe scalp wounds that had been inflicted by Parnellites. When his injuries were seen, over 100 Parnellite voters declared that they would desert the Parnellites and cast their ballots for Mr. Crilly.

The *Independent* (Parnellite) appeals to the authorities to prevent clergymen from acting as candidates' agents and from occupying polling booths to coerce voters, especially the illiterate ones.

The Irish-American committee who came to this country for the purpose of trying to establish harmony between the two Irish factions have thus far not been very successful. Their present policy is to hold informal conferences with the leaders of both sides.

To-day O'Neill Ryan of St. Louis, one of the committee, had a consultation with Dr. Joseph F. Fox, member of Parliament for the Tullamore Division of Kings County, who is one of the leaders of the anti-Parnellite division. Mr. Ryan was introduced to many of the leading members of the anti-Parnellite Party, but did not discuss the question of a reunion with their opponents. Mr. Ryan says that he believes that neither party will consider proposals looking to the establishment of peace until the respective strength of each side is ascertained at the polls.

The other members of the Irish-American Committee held interviews with Timothy Harrington and John Redmond, who have thrown the blame for the present contests on the anti-Parnellites, who, they claim, declined the proposal that all the old Irish members of Parliament should be allowed to retain their seats.

The committeemen strongly deny reports that they came to Ireland as emissaries of the Parnellite section in the United States. They claim that their visit to this country is the outcome of the policy of neutrality and union adopted in America. Until unity is restored between the warring factions in Ireland, they say, they do not hope for a reawakening of the interest of Irishmen in America in the Irish struggle for self-government. In proof of this they point out the paucity of the subscriptions for furthering the fight for home rule which have been sent from America since the split occurred in the ranks of the Irish Party.

Little notice is taken of the doings of the committee by the Irish press. This is chiefly owing to the paramount interest taken in the elections, and to the fact, which has been generally recognized, that it is an utterly hopeless task to attempt to bring about a reunion at the present time,

CORK, July 6.—It is reported that the assault made upon William O'Brien day before yesterday, as he was returning from a political meeting, has resulted in the serious injury of his left eye.

THE EVE-RODGERS SUIT.

MRS. RODGERS WANTS ALLEGED FRAUDULENT CONVEYANCES SET ASIDE.

NEW-ALBANY, Ind., July 6.—The Eve-Rodgers breach-of-promise suit will again appear in the Floyd Circuit Court in this city. Yesterday Mrs. Myra A. Rodgers filed suit against Nicholas Eve and his wife to set aside alleged fraudulent conveyances of property. The plaintiff alleges that on Nov. 5 Eve conveyed to John H. Lemon, for $4,000, certain lots on Oak Street which were in turn reconveyed to Eve's wife.

At the time the conveyances were made Mrs. Rodgers alleges that Eve was indebted to her in the sum of $2,500, damages for breach of promise, she having been awarded a judgment for that amount.

Mrs. Rodgers was married to Eve while her first husband was living, but whom she thought was dead. Her marriage with Eve was annulled, but he promised to marry her if she secured a divorce from her first husband. She was granted the divorce, but, as she says, Eve refused to keep his promise and married Mrs. Hanger of Somersburg.

Mrs. Rodgers sued Eve for $5,000 breach of promise, and also for $5,000 for seduction. The breach-of-promise case was tried in Jeffersonville and was decided against Eve, but he appealed to the Supreme Court.

A STRAIGHT REPUBLICAN TICKET.

NO FUSION WITH THE PEOPLE'S PARTY IN ARKANSAS.

LITTLE ROCK, Ark., July 6.—The Republican State Convention, which assembled to-day, carried out a cut-and-dried programme.

Despite the entreaties of some of the leading People's Party men, fusion was rejected. Powell Clayton peremptorily decided for a straight ticket, and ordered that William G. Whipple be put at the head of it. His orders were executed, and a full ticket was nominated. Whipple, the candidate for Governor, served two terms as Mayor of Little Rock. He is an attorney of no special importance. It is said he believes he can carry the State, and will make a thorough canvass.

The People's Party leaders are nonplused at Clayton's decision, but have decided to make a strong fight against both Fishback, the Democratic Gubernatorial nominee, and Whipple.

Nearly two-thirds of the delegates to to-day's convention were negroes. Of the white delegates nearly every one was a Federal office holder. The platforms of the Republican State Convention held here April 7 and of the National Republican Convention were indorsed.

ROBBED THE BANK AND FLED.

THE DEFALCATION WILL REACH ABOUT ELEVEN THOUSAND DOLLARS.

NASHVILLE, Tenn., July 6.—A sensation was created to-day by the announcement that Lester H. Gale, teller, and W. Turner, bookkeeper, of the City Savings Bank had both fled the city with between $10,000 and $11,000 of the bank's funds. The feeling of uneasiness on the part of some of the depositors did not last long, as all the checks presented were promptly paid. The bank had plenty of available money to meet all demands.

The Guarantee Company of North America is surety for Gale and Turner for $5,000 each. The American Surety Company is also surety for Gale for $5,000.

At the bank, President W. Settle stated that Gale and Turner disappeared after taking what cash the bank had on hand Saturday night. He said there was a further shortage due from money lost in speculation previous to their flight. He thought the total amount would not be more than $11,000.

The men fled Saturday night. The shortage was discovered last night. The principal part of the money was abstracted from a box in the vault. It is supposed the two men have gone to Mexico.

THE DEMOCRATIC COMMITTEE.

OFFICIAL NOTIFICATION OF ITS MEETING IN THIS CITY JULY 20.

INDIANAPOLIS, Ind., July 6.—A special from Logansport, Ind., to the *Sentinel* says that S. P. Sheerin, Secretary of the National Democratic Committee, has issued the following to-day from his office in this city:

"A meeting of the National Democratic Committee will be held at the Fifth Avenue Hotel in the city of New-York, Wednesday, July 20, 1892, at 8:30 P. M.

"The purpose of the meeting is the election of officers and the organization of the committee for the campaign."

New-Jersey Temperance Unions Meet.

OCEAN GROVE, N. J., July 6.—The Summer School of Methods of the Woman's Christian Temperance Union of New-Jersey began a two days' session in the tabernacle here this morning. Delegates were present from the principal unions in the State. The morning devotional service was led by Mrs. R. A. Phelps, President of the Asbury Park Union.

The following papers were read: "How to Secure a Large Audience at a Temperance Lecture," by Mrs. R. A. Anderson of Trenton; "Physical Culture," by Miss Ada Sulger, State Superintendent of Public Instruction, of Trenton; "What is a Model Woman's Christian Temperance Union?" by Mrs. H. H. Forrest of Philadelphia; "The Effects of Alcohol," by Dr. C. A. Dorman of Washington; "Journalism," by Mrs. Lucy A. Leggett of Washington. Miss Sulger, in her paper, said that women would be better morally and physically if they discarded corsets.

At the evening session Dr. Stokes, President of the Ocean Grove Camp Meeting Association, welcomed the members of the union. John G. Woolley of Minneapolis read a paper on intemperance, and made an earnest appeal for a united effort to close the saloons. Mr. Woolley is a reformed drunkard.

The services to-morrow will be unusually interesting.

Confident Fales Will Not Be Hanged.

NEWARK, N. J., July 6.—Robert Alden Fales, the boy murderer, who was sentenced yesterday to be hanged on Aug. 11, shows no sign of disturbance on account of his approaching fate.

His lawyers say they are confident that young Fales will not be executed. They have already commenced to prepare the necessary papers for a pardon or a commutation of the death sentence.

Ex-Judge Henry said to-day that he was firmly of the belief that the outcome would be the commutation of Fales's sentence to twenty years in prison. This is the sentence imposed for murder in the second degree in the State of New-Jersey.

Educators in the South.

ATLANTA, Ga., July 6.—The morning session of the Georgia Teachers' Association completed its work and made way for the Southern Educational Associations to meet at 3 P. M. The latter association was welcomed in the great hall of the Capitol by Gov. Northen, State School Commissioner Bradwell, Mayor Hemphill, and Hoke Smith, President of the Atlanta Board of Education. United States Commissioner William T. Harris delivered an address to-night on "Ten Years' Growth in Education."

Three Men Killed by a Fall of Coal.

WILKESBARRE, Penn., July 6.—By a fall of coal in the South Wilkesbarre shaft of the Lehigh and Wilkesbarre Coal Company this evening, two civil engineers and a timber man were instantly killed. The dead are: John Williams, aged twenty-six, civil engineer, a recent graduate of Lehigh University; John McCafferty, aged twenty-one, of Philadelphia, a civil engineer, who is comparatively unknown here, and Thomas Jones, aged forty-five, a timberman.

Passengers Lose Their Baggage.

CITY OF MEXICO, July 6.—A number of passengers of the steamer City of Panama, from San Francisco for Panama, came near losing their lives. A launch which was acting as tender to the steamer ran ashore at Tapachula and subsequently foundered. The passengers aboard were in great danger, but finally all of them were saved. They lost all their baggage, however.

A Move Against the Gloucester Track.

CAMDEN, N. J., July 6.—William J. Thompson, President of the South Jersey Jockey Club, was held in $1,000 bail this morning by Justice Cassady on a charge of maintaining a public nuisance at the Gloucester race track.

The complaint was backed by two affidavits.

MOB LAW AT HOMESTEAD

PROVOKED BY AN ATTACK OF PINKERTON DETECTIVES.

TEN MEN KILLED AND AT LEAST FIFTY WOUNDED.

FIERCE BATTLES FOUGHT AT THE STEEL WORKS—THE DETECTIVES ATTEMPT TO LAND FROM BOATS AND ARE DRIVEN BACK AND HELD UNTIL THEY SURRENDER.

PITTSBURG, July 6.—Mob law has prevailed at Homestead to-day. The Carnegie Steel Works strikers, made desperate by the prospect of defeat, fought for twelve hours with an organized and disciplined force of 300 Pinkerton men, and at the end of that time gained a signal victory. The Pinkerton men surrendered, and before morning will be lodged in the Allegheny County Jail, where they will be held to answer the charge of murder. The events of the day will rank as one of the most remarkable chapters in the history of labor riots.

It was shortly after midnight last night when word reached Homestead that two barges filled with Pinkerton men had left a point on the Ohio River, a few miles below Pittsburg, for Homestead, and that they would attempt to force their way into the mill before morning. The word was carried to Homestead at once, and before 2 o'clock 6,000 men, women, and children lined the river banks on the lookout for the Pinkertons.

The detectives had been rendezvoused some five or six miles below the city on the Ohio River, where two model barges had been prepared for them. These barges were of the best build, and were used in shipping iron rails down the river from the Carnegie mills at Braddock.

The holds were filled up with bunks, cooking arrangements, and other accommodations, and as an extra precaution, as if in preparation for the siege to which they were subjected, were lined with heavy steel plates on the inside, while the whole back deck was protected in a similar manner.

The barges were towed by two small steamers, and it was after 4 o'clock when they were sighted below Homestead. They headed for the river gate of the Carnegie mill yard. A thousand strikers were there before the gang planks could be thrown ashore. The mill yard fence had been run out into the river to protect just such a landing as was contemplated, but it fell like a paper wall before the rage of the strikers.

Rifles were in the hands of the Pinkertons, but not a man of the strikers fell back. The broad gang plank was run ashore. Eight Pinkerton men, walking abreast, stepped on its end. Only one man, a mill worker named William Foy, moved out to oppose them. There was a puff from the barrel of a Winchester, a sharp report, and Foy fell dead in his tracks. Instantly the Pinkertons were made to pay for their work. Every man of the first rank was shot down. Two fell into the water and were heard of no more. One other died, but his body was recovered, and the others were seriously injured.

That was the opening of the battle. The firing from the barges at once became general. A number of the strikers fell, and a great majority of the others started to run. But they did not go far before they returned to the front, more desperate than before. That was the only backward move of the strikers. During the rest of the day the workmen moved steadily forward from one point of vantage to another until the Pinkerton men were compelled to surrender.

From the first attack until noon the battle was continuous. When the Pinkertons failed to get into the mill the first time they made the attempt, the day was lost for them, but they did not seem to realize it. Three times during the morning they tried to land, but each time were repulsed. The strikers had obtained complete possession of the mill, and from behind furnaces and piles of iron they could shoot at anything that appeared over the side of the barges without danger to themselves.

The steamer Little Bill, which had towed the Pinkerton men to Homestead, was compelled early in the day to leave the barges on the bank and under the fire of the strikers to convey the wounded Pinkerton men to a place where they could obtain treatment. When this was accomplished, the Captain of the steamer tried to return and tow the barges into the middle of the river again, but he was not permitted to come near the bank.

In the meantime the strikers had secured two small cannons. One was planted on each side of the river. They were loaded with pieces of iron and were trained on the barges. Because of the poor aim of the gunners they did little execution, but each shot added to the terror of the Pinkertons. After noon the latter made no attempt to fight, and devoted all their energies to saving their lives. Three times they hoisted a white handkerchief as an appeal for a truce, but each time it was shot off the staff. Capt. Hynd and Supt. Kline of their force were disabled.

When it was found that little impression could be made by the cannon on the boats an effort was made to fire the barges and thus compel the detectives to leave the vessel or suffer the terrible fate of being burned alive. Hose was procured and oil was spouted on the decks and sides of the barges.

While this was being done barrel after barrel of oil was emptied into the river above the mooring place, the object being to allow it to float against the boats and then ignite it. This was attempted several times, but the boats did not burn, and then the mob hurled dynamite bombs at them.

Finally it was evident to everybody that they would soon die if they were not relieved, and the leaders of the strikers pleaded with their followers to allow the Pinkertons to surrender.

The appeal was drowned with shouts of "No!" "No!" "We'll kill them like dogs!" "They shall have no mercy!" but when, a few minutes later, the white handkerchief appeared on the top of one of the barges, the firing ceased and the strikers consented to a parley.

The Pinkerton men as soon as they found it was safe to talk, offered to surrender if the leaders guaranteed them protection. The promise was given, and 266 men marched off the boat and gave up their arms.

Then the promise that they should not be harmed seemed to be forgotten. They were driven like sheep between lines of strikers to the Opera House. All the way they were beaten first with fists, and then with clubs, and every conceivable weapon. Every man was sore and covered with blood before he found shelter.

Having locked the Pinkertons up and surrounded the building with an armed guard the strikers telegraphed Sheriff McCleary to come to Homestead and take the prisoners to jail. The Sheriff left Pittsburg on the first train. At midnight he had not returned, and it was reported from Homestead that the mob was reforming, and that many of the Pinkertons would be killed.

The record of the day's casualties is ten killed, seven workmen and three Pinkerton men, and at least fifty wounded, of which number probably twenty are seriously hurt. There are grave fears for what to-morrow will bring

10 Pages

The New-York Times.

10 Pages

VOL. XLII...NO. 12,842. NEW-YORK, FRIDAY, OCTOBER 21, 1892. PRICE THREE CENTS.

JUSTICE OVERTAKES DAVIS

THE HUDSON COUNTY BOSS AT LAST BROUGHT TO ACCOUNT.

INDICTMENTS REPORTED FROM TRENTON AGAINST HIM FOR CONSPIRING TO DEFEAT THE PUNISHMENT OF BALLOT-BOX STUFFERS AND FOR SUBORNATION OF PERJURY.

Nothing that has occurred in New-Jersey since the uncovering of the great ballot-box frauds in Hudson County in 1889 has so excited and interested the people as the story from Trenton yesterday that Jersey justice had at last found an opportunity to lay her hand upon "Bob" Davis, who is believed to have planned and superintended the perpetration of those frauds.

At the time they were committed he was the Sheriff of Hudson County, foresworn, it is charged, to protect the ballot-box stuffers from the law by packing his Grand Juries in their interest.

He is now a Police Justice in Jersey City, under Gov. Abbett's commission, and, by the election of a Board of Freeholders whom his gang placed in charge of county affairs, the Jailer of Hudson County.

The Federal Grand Jury at Trenton has just handed up two indictments against him for the part he took in trying to aid four of the convicted ballot-box stuffers to escape the punishment they so richly deserved.

One of these indictments is said to charge him with conspiracy with the ballot-box stuffers, and their lawyer, Charles J. Peshal, to defeat the ends of justice, and the second is said to charge him with subornation of perjury in connection with the efforts made to imprison them. It is said that United States District Attorney Henry S. White will arraign him and the others impleaded with him on Tuesday next.

When the ballot-box conspiracy became known, there were reasons for believing that Davis had been implicated in it; but while he consorted with the election sharks, procured bail for them when arrested, appeared in court at their trials to encourage them, and gave them employment in the public places in the community that he had put under his heel, specific proof of his guilty participation with them was never forthcoming.

When the election sharks were arraigned for trial, convicted, and sentenced to prison, it was hoped that the failure of his presumed promise to save them harmless would prompt them to revelations, but they have all sullenly taken the dose justice has meeted out to them, and loyally kept the great secret as to the conception and direction of the great frauds to themselves.

The incident that is at last to enable the courts to take him into custody, if the story that comes from Trenton be true—and THE TIMES's representative has unimpeachable authority for asserting that his indictment has been finally accomplished—attended the efforts of Judge Lippincott to get the gang into the State prison after the Court of Errors and Appeals—the court of final jurisdiction in the State—had affirmed their conviction.

About the time that memorable decision was handed down, Lawyer Peshal had attracted some attention to the methods by which he had saved Murderer Hallinger from the gallows on three occasions, when the local courts had ordered him to be hanged, and the ballot-box-stuffing fraternity had employed him to begin the endless series of appeals to the United States courts, that he had invoked so successfully in Hallinger's behalf, to keep the convicted election sharks out of prison.

Judge Lippincott got an inkling of the new means that were to be used in behalf of the convicts, who, by successive appeals to the State courts, had impudently defied his authority. Before Peshal could make a move he had had most of the convicted men corralled and hurried into the State prison.

But there were four of them whom he was unable to reach. They were Thomas Fallon, the janitor of the Street and Water Board Building—a position to which the board appointed his wife when he was finally hastened off to Trenton—Jacob Moschell, Thomas Durancy, and James Hart, comprising the first convicted Election Board. Judge Lippincott commanded Sheriff McPhillips from hour to hour to bring them into court, but the Sheriff pretended to be unable to find them.

They were being kept at large while Peshal perfected the papers for an appeal from the State to the Federal courts.

Late one Thursday night Peshal presented himself before Judge Green and asked for writs of habeas corpus for the four. His application was based on affidavits signed by the four prisoners, whom Judge Lippincott's energetic search had been unable to find, alleging that they were being "unlawfully detained, confined, and restrained of their liberty by John J. McPhillips, the Sheriff of Hudson County." Ex-Judge R. B. Seymour, who happened to be in court, heard the affidavit read. He concluded that if the affidavits were true the prisoners must be in the jail. There was no other place where the Sheriff could properly keep them.

Judge Seymour knew that Judge Lippincott was hunting for them anxiously, and he telegraphed to the Judge to inquire at the jail about them.

When the Judge asked at the jail office whether they were there, he was told that nothing was known of them there.

But when he opened court the next morning, the ring Sheriff marched the four into court to hear their sentences. The whole crowd had been informed that Peshal had perfected his appeal in Trenton at the time, and when they went into Judge Lippincott's presence in the morning they presumed that it would be only to serve notice of another appeal, and to give new bail to await the action of the Federal courts.

They were somewhat hasty, however, in going into court. When they presented themselves, the writs staying their sentence had not reached Judge Lippincott, and before it had arrived he had bundled them all off to Trenton on the double-quick and bidden the men who took them there to pay no attention to any papers that might be served on them while on the way.

For a wonder his directions were obeyed, and the four men, whose guilty friends had worked so hard to keep beyond the reach of the law, became the guests before many hours of State Prison Keeper Patterson.

Their affidavits that they were in custody when Judge Lippincott had been informed that they were not in jail led to an inquiry. Then it was learned that at the very time when the Judge had been informed that nothing was known of them they were in the parlor of the jail—the guests of "Bob" Davis, the jailer; that they had been taken there so as to be able to make the affidavit that they were "unlawfully restrained of their liberty," to lay the foundation for habeas corpus proceedings; that a notary visited them late at night to take their oaths, and that they had been secluded from the search of the court, Davis even going to the extent of directing his assistants in the jail to deny that the men were there, so that they could not be hastened away to prison before the proceedings being taken for their release were in shape. If they were in State prison serving a term to which they had been sentenced the case was closed against them, and no subsequent efforts for their relief would avail.

Judge Green said that he had been imposed upon; that men who were in jail as guests of the jailer were not restrained of their liberties; that perjury had been committed when they swore that they were and that the jailer had been party with the criminals to the crime of attempting to cheat justice by falsehood and deception. And when the October term of the United States courts opened in Trenton a few days ago he called the attention of the Grand Jury to the matter and asked that body to investigate and act.

The result is the indictment of Davis, and, it is said, of Peshal, too.

Judge Green did not call the attention of the Grand Jurors to the matter without a full knowledge of the facts. He had had an investigation set on foot, and "Bob" Davis, who was one of the witnesses, tried to evade his responsibility by asserting that he had taken the prisoners to jail in pursuance of a request of their bondsmen that they be apprehended. "Bob" Davis's testimony, under the questioning of Prosecutor Charles H. Winfield, was as follows:

"You know Moschell, Fallon, and Hart?" Winfield asked of Davis.

"Yes," was the jailer's reply.

"You are keeper of the county jail?"

"Yes."

"Did you see those three men last Thursday?" Mr. Winfield asked.

"Yes."

"Did you see them during the night preceding Thursday?"

"Yes."

"Where did you first see them during Wednesday or Wednesday night?"

"At the corner of Grove and Morgan Streets, two of them, Moschell and Fallon."

"Did you remain from that time in their company?"

"No, Sir; I told them their bondsmen wanted them returned to jail, and they told me they would be up there that night."

"What time did they come to jail that night?"

"Fallon came about twenty-five minutes before twelve, I think; Moschell came about a quarter to twelve; Hart didn't come until after twelve. Durancy didn't come at all. Notary Fish was waiting for them."

"Who requested Mr. Fish to come there?" asked the Prosecutor.

"I did."

"On Wednesday?"

"Yes."

"Before or after you saw Moschell and Fallon?"

"After I had seen them. I told them I wanted them in the jail between 11 and 12 o'clock."

"Why did you fix the time so late?"

"To give them a chance to bid their friends good-bye."

"How long did you keep them?"

"Until I turned the men over to the Sheriff on Friday morning. I sent for the Sheriff three times and could not get him. If I could have got him on Thursday I would have handed them over to the Sheriff then. I have no receipt for the prisoners on my record book. Nothing goes on that book without I have a commitment from the court. They were turned over by the bondsmen, and I hold the bondsmen for whatever charge there is."

"Then you didn't hold them that night? They were your guests simply?"

"No; they were held for the bondsmen."

"If they were not guests they were prisoners?" insisted Mr. Winfield.

"They were held for the bondsmen."

"You don't answer my question."

"I am answering you the best I can," retorted Mr. Davis.

"If they were not guests were they prisoners?"

"They were there for their bondsmen by virtue of the notice from the Sheriff to the bondsmen to turn these people in."

"Then you had nothing by which you held them?"

"Only by request of the bondsmen, who held me responsible."

"Have you any papers whatever by virtue of which you held these three men, or any of them?"

"If I did I would have a commitment."

"Did you have? Answer yes or no."

"I could not have it."

"You didn't have any paper?"

"Certainly not; only whatever notice was given by the Sheriff to the bondsmen to have those people turned into court."

"Where did these people sleep?"

"In the witness rooms."

"Were you present when they made their affidavit as to their petition?"

"Yes."

"By whom was the petition read?"

"I can't tell."

"Was this part of the petition read: 'The petition of Jacob Moschell, the complainant, shows and states that he is a citizen of the United States; that he is now unlawfully detained, confined, and restrained of his liberty by John J. McPhillips, Sheriff of Hudson County, State of New-Jersey, in the jail at Jersey City, in said County of Hudson and State of New-Jersey.'"

"I did not hear that part of it read to them."

The maximum penalty for subornation of perjury is $10,000 fine and five years' imprisonment.

TRENTON, N. J., Oct. 20.—The officials of the Federal Court are reticent about the indictment of ex-Sheriff Davis of Hudson County for the part he took in preparing the affidavits used in the habeas corpus application of the Jersey City ballot-box stuffers.

It is the common talk in Trenton that Davis is indicted. There were a large number of prominent Republicans on the Federal Grand Jury. It is also stated that Lawyer Peshall has been indicted, but no summons had been served on him at 6 o'clock. He was seen to-day and said:

"If there was anything illegal in the preparation of those affidavits I am the person to punish, because I, as their counsel, advised their preparation and signing. There is nothing in it. Let them indict me. I will make it merry for them."

MRS. HARRISON MUCH WEAKER.

A CHANGE FOR THE WORSE AFTER A COMPARATIVELY QUIET DAY.

WASHINGTON, Oct. 20.—There has been a change for the worse in the condition of Mrs. Harrison, and to-night she is weaker than she has been at any time since her illness began. She is greatly exhausted and cannot turn her head upon the pillow.

Her cough, which had ceased to trouble her, is now said to have increased in volume. This, coming as it does in paroxysms, has a very depressing and exhausting effect on the patient and tends to reduce her vitality.

Mrs. Harrison passed a comparatively quiet day and did not suffer so much from nervousness. She experienced more difficulty than usual, however, in taking nourishment, which she has heretofore taken with systematic regularity.

Although she is in such a very weak state yet her physician said to-night he did not apprehend any immediate fatal result, and he thought it probable that by morning she might rally and regain some of her lost strength.

At 10 o'clock Mrs. Harrison had rallied somewhat from her severe attack of prostration, and Dr. Gardner said she was resting a little more quietly and feeling a little stronger. The doctor said he was about to retire at that hour, and would be called if he was needed at the White House.

Mrs. Harrison's condition is so precarious that she may pass away within a few hours should another sinking spell occur. This may happen at any time now, from the natural effects of the disease and in the absence of any new complications.

WASHINGTON, Oct. 20—1 A. M.—At this hour Mrs. Harrison is no better. She is still very weak.

Sixteen Business Men Hurt.

NEW-HAVEN, Conn., Oct. 20.—An accident occurred here this afternoon, as a result of which sixteen local business men are covered with bruises to-night. This has been "Donation" day in New-Haven, and the committee in charge of receiving the offerings for the Orphan Asylum was taking them to that institution when the tally-ho upon which they were riding was overturned on Chapel Street and all were thrown to the ground.

Three of the party are painfully hurt. Harvey Munson, a prominent manufacturer, received a fracture of his left wrist and a deep gash on the nose. Joseph Manville struck on his head, and has a severe scalp wound. Benjamin H. Cobb escaped with a compound fracture of the left elbow and a nose badly bruised by the fall against the stone pavement.

All Quiet in Venezuela.

WASHINGTON, Oct. 20.—A cablegram was received at the Navy Department to-day from Admiral Walker, stating that the steamer South Portland, which sailed from New-York some weeks ago with arms for the insurgents of Venezuela, had arrived at La Guayra. The South Portland has been lying at Trinidad awaiting news of the result of the rebellion in Venezuela.

As the party for which the arms were intended was victorious, and is now in control of the Government, she had no difficulty in landing the arms.

Admiral Walker reported that the Chicago and Kearsarge were still at La Guayra, and that all was quiet.

Married by Gov. Chase.

CINCINNATI, Oct. 20.—A somewhat singular proceeding was the application here yesterday by Gov. Chase of Indiana for a clergyman's license to enable him to solemnize a marriage in Cincinnati. Gov. Chase, after taking an oath to support the Constitution of the State of Ohio, received the required license, and afterward Miss Harriet E. Chase, daughter of D. W. Chase of this city, and niece of the Governor, was married by him last night to Mr. Schuyler C. Durgea of this city.

A Large Paper Machine.

NIAGARA FALLS, N. Y., Oct. 20.—The largest paper machine ever made in this country has been ordered of Horne & Son, Lawrence, Mass., by the Niagara Falls Paper Company. This will be a 136-inch Fourdrinier machine, and is to be completed and set up before Feb. 1 next. The largest machine in England is said to be 150 inches wide. The previous largest one in this country is a 135-inch machine.

A War Ship for St. John's.

HALIFAX, N. S., Oct. 20.—The Newfoundland Government has asked the Admiralty to station a war ship at St. John's this Winter, and one of the fleet which usually goes south to Bermuda will likely be sent. It is said the Tourmaline will be the ship to winter there.

The war ship Pelican sailed for Bermuda this morning, where the crew will be paid off.

NOMINATED FOR ASSEMBLY.

A. L. Childs (Dem.) of Rochester, renominated; First Monroe District.

W. S. Church (Dem.) of Riga, renominated; Third Monroe District.

HARTER'S FRIENDS CONFIDENT.

HE CHALLENGES M'KINLEY TO MEET HIM IN JOINT DEBATE.

CLEVELAND, Ohio, Oct. 20.—The hottest political fight in Ohio this Fall is that being waged in the Fourteenth District, where Congressman M. D. Harter is making a most spirited canvass for re-election against E. G. Johnson of Elyria. The district gave Harrison over 1,600 plurality four years ago and McKinley 1,700 last Fall, but well-informed Republicans concede that if the election were held this week or next Harter would almost certainly be re-elected.

The nomination of Johnson, who is an active Foraker man, in Senator Sherman's home district was a bitter dose for the old-time partisans. Charles Horr of Wellington, one of the most influential men politically in the county, has bolted Johnson. This, of itself, would endanger his chances, but, besides, he has aroused the active opposition of the Prohibitionists. Reliable men say that not a single clergyman in his home county will vote for Johnson on the liquor question alone.

The Republicans are greatly scared, and are sparing neither men nor money in Johnson's behalf. McKinley, Sherman, and Foraker have made speeches, and other distinguished speakers are to follow.

The Hon. C. F. Ackerman, who is managing Harter's campaign, confidently predicts his re-election by 500.

Harter has written a letter to M. White of North Amherst authorizing him to say to the Republican Committee of his town and county that they may arrange for a joint discussion between Gov. McKinley and himself. He takes this step, he says, because McKinley's friends have sought to create the impression that he is unwilling to debate the general issues of the campaign with the Governor. If McKinley will meet him at Elyria, Mansfield, Columbus, Cleveland, Cincinnati, or Canton, Harter will give $100 to Oberlin College. Harter is going to New-York next week to speak at the meeting of bankers and merchants at the Sub-Treasury. If McKinley will discuss with him there, he offers to increase the gift to Oberlin College to $500.

A YOUNG WOMAN MURDERED.

HER BODY FOUND IN A FIELD—THE SUPPOSED ASSASSIN ARRESTED.

WILMINGTON, Del., Oct. 20.—The dead body of a white girl, sixteen years old, was found in a field back of the residence of Lewis P. Bush in the Eleventh Ward shortly before noon to-day. An examination of the body revealed that a shocking double crime had been committed during the night. Not satisfied with having committed a brutal assault, the perpetrator of the infamous crime added murder to his work.

The throat was cut from ear to ear, while the young girl's eyes were black and blue from beating. She had made a desperate struggle for her honor, and was only overcome by the superior brute force of her assailant. A large razor lying near the body told how the murder was committed. The weapon was besmeared with blood and was half open. There was every evidence of a desperate struggle.

The body has been identified as that of Katie Dugan, aged sixteen years, who lived with her parents at 1,110 West Front Street.

The girl's father, James Dugan, stated that about 8 o'clock last night he was entering his house near the scene of the crime when a young man of medium stature emerged from the shadow of the house and disappeared down the avenue.

It was not long after that when Katie put on a light evening coat and stated she was going out, but would return in a few minutes. Her younger sister, Lizzie, asked permission to accompany her, but this request was refused. The girl left the house and that was the last seen of her alive.

WILMINGTON, Oct. 21.—Detectives at 1 o'clock this morning arrested Richard Riley, on suspicion of being the murderer, at his home, 831 Bennett Street. He kept company with the murdered girl.

THE DUCHY OF BRUNSWICK.

THE PROVISIONAL GOVERNMENT IS THOUGHT TO BE NEAR AN END.

BERLIN, Oct. 20.—The Brunswick *Landes Zeitung* believes that the German Government has resolved finally to put an end to the Provisional Government of the Duchy of Brunswick. This, it is understood, foreshadows a declaration against the succession of the Hanoverian dynasty.

The Duke of Cumberland is the heir to Brunswick, but, owing to his refusal to give up his claim to the throne of the Kingdom of Hanover, he was not allowed to assume power on the death of the last Duke of Brunswick, Oct. 18, 1884.

Since October, 1885, the Government of the duchy has been administered by Prince Albrecht, brother of Emperor William I., he having been unanimously elected Regent by the Diet of Brunswick.

Newport's Democratic Rally.

NEWPORT, R. I., Oct. 20.—The Democrats opened their campaign here to-night amid great enthusiasm. A big procession paraded the streets and a Cleveland and Stevenson banner was raised in every ward. Then followed a grand rally in Democratic headquarters, over which Alderman Daniel B. Fearing presided.

Congressman Oscar Lapham was the chief speaker, making a convincing address upon the tariff. The time had come, he said, to decide whether it was to be a Government by the people or one by a moneyed aristocracy. Protection was an outrageous doctrine, tending to make monopolies all powerful in the Government. Protection formed a partnership between the Government and the money power, the money power to sustain the Government and the Government to sustain the money power. The speaker then went into a detailed convincing argument on the effect of tariff on the prices of various articles and its effect upon certain industries.

A Letter from Mr. Cleveland.

ST. PAUL, Minn., Oct. 20.—M. J. Donnelly of St. Paul wrote a letter to Grover Cleveland, giving the Democratic situation in the State as it appeared to him. He has received the following reply from Mr. Cleveland:

VICTORIA HOTEL,
NEW-YORK, Oct. 10, 1892.

M. J. Donnelly, St. Paul:

MY DEAR SIR: I desire to thank you for your recent letter, giving a statement of the political outlook in Minnesota. It would, indeed, be a glorious thing to see your State firmly placed in the Democratic column, and the determination and zeal of the Minnesota Democracy certainly gives hope for such a result.

Trusting that your predictions as to the outcome may be fully verified, and that the result in November may furnish a cause for Democratic rejoicing, I am, very truly yours,

GROVER CLEVELAND.

Sudden Death of ex-Mayor Oakley.

RUTHERFORD, N. J., Oct. 20.—As ex-Mayor Oakley was returning from Grace Church last night he was attacked by heart disease, and, with a companion named Douglass, sat down on the curbstone. After a little while Douglass asked Mr. Oakley how he felt, and, receiving no reply, asked again. For the second time he received no reply, and he then called for help. A passer-by, who answered the call, went for a doctor, but before the physician arrived Mr. Oakley died. He was the first Mayor of Rutherford, assuming the office about ten years ago, and was one of the most prominent Republicans here. He leaves a wife and three children.

Montana Strong for Cleveland.

MISSOULA, Mon., Oct. 20.—The Democrats have made a poll of this State, which shows that Cleveland will carry Montana by over 7,000, which is more than twice as much as was expected. The vote of the miners will be thrown almost solidly for the Democratic ticket.

The contest for the capital has narrowed down to Anaconda and Helena, and Marcus Daly, the special champion of the former, is using his money and influence in favor of Cleveland. The Populists will poll about 4,500 votes in the State.

West Virginia Polled.

WHEELING, West Va., Oct. 20.—Both of the great parties have concluded their poll of the State. The Democratic poll shows a majority of 800 and the Republican poll a majority of 1,000, indicating a close vote. The registration under the new election law is phenomenally large, the list in some counties being 50 per cent. in excess of the last Presidential vote.

MR. HIGGINS ALSO LEAVES

HE CAN STAND THE REPUBLICAN POLICY NO LONGER.

A TYPICAL PROTECTIONIST, BUT NOT A SUPPORTER OF A TARIFF ENACTED SOLELY FOR POLITICAL PURPOSES—SHAMEFUL ARGUMENTS ADVANCED BY THE M'KINLEYITES.

Another widely-known business man and influential Republican has publicly announced his purpose to vote for Grover Cleveland for President. He is A. Foster Higgins, head of the old and famous firm of Johnson & Higgins, average adjusters, and head of the firm of Higgins, Cox & Barrett, attorneys for the United States Lloyds.

Mr. Higgins, like Spencer Trask, whose change of political faith was made public yesterday, is a man of sincere and earnest convictions. He is, moreover, a typical protectionist, but his strong sense of justice compels him to repudiate the policy of the Republican Party as dishonest and mischievous.

For many years Mr. Higgins has been one of the most active and influential members of the Chamber of Commerce. He is Chairman of its Committee on Harbor and Shipping, and has given a great deal of his time to the advancement of public interests. He is also a Pilot Commissioner. Besides being a Director in the Knickerbocker Trust Company, he has a variety of important interests in this city and in Greenwich, Conn., where he resides.

Mr. Higgins has up to the present time been an ardent working Republican. He was one of the most zealous supporters of James G. Blaine for the Presidency, and actively supported Mr. Harrison in 1888. He has taken a conspicuous part in the defense of the protective system, having been the author of many communications to the public press on that subject. When asked yesterday about the change in his political views, Mr. Higgins said:

"It is with no little mental struggle that I yield to your request to express publicly the reasons which I have given privately for my intended withholding of my support and vote from the Republican Party at this coming Presidential election. This struggle arises from a sincere shrinking from any act which brings me personally before the public, and a very great disinclination by my words to throw discredit on the many very warm, honorable friends who I know will, regardless of anything I may say, persist in efforts to elect a Republican Government.

"I am still of the opinion and belief that it is to the interest of the United States to have within its own borders all industries which produce articles essential to our enjoyment of life, and that it is the privilege of the Government to contribute to the establishment of such industries by tariffs on foreign products of the same kind, but I most sternly draw the line at any and all tariffs which are plainly to pour money into the pockets of capitalists of industries well established and not needing any such tariffs to establish them, and also at all tariffs which are not in any respect for the general good, but solely to benefit certain local interests.

"Beyond these, when a tariff is openly confessed to be a matter of politics and enacted expressly to gain or retain political power in certain localities, by the pecuniary benefit the tariff is to confer on that locality, then the question must forcibly arise, is this the normal and necessary result of a protective system? If so, the evil is greater than any possible benefit which can be derived from the system. It is plain bribery and corruption, and cannot be maintained or defended by any honest person.

"Such I assert and believe to be the effect and operation of the McKinley bill. Its now very distinguished author and father, when shown the utter inconsistency of one of its items, whereby a duty of 97 per cent. ad valorem was to be placed on an article in the crude or raw condition, while in its completed form the duty was only 45 per cent.—the former bringing in its train a large percentage of labor and transportation going directly into the pockets of American laborers and American railroads, while in the latter not one dollar benefit would accrue to the citizens of the United States—replied to me, 'You are right. The item is all wrong. But it is entirely a question of politics. If we do not pass that item, we shall lose certain States to the party!'

"And when this bill was before the Senate, certain Senators, themselves Republicans, tried to amend the bill and correct grievous errors. Senator Teller arose and declared plainly that the passage of the bill just as it came from the House was essential as a political measure and necessary to the success of the Republican Party. And not a single voice was raised in rebuke of such a contemptible statement as an argument for the passage of a bill so fraught with burdens to the people.

"How such motives may have influenced and governed every item of the bill we have a right to infer, if it could be so openly avowed as a whole. Its authors do not hesitate to offer them and its political power to all members of their party, but when before the people they attempt to defend its character by statements calculated to blind inquiring minds.

"I heard a distinguished Senator, who was very active in its creation, state to an audience 'that in every instance where they had raised a duty on any product it was carefully gauged by and adjusted solely to equalize the difference between the wages paid in this country and those paid to the operatives who produced the same goods abroad.'

"Now, I cannot believe that the Senator intended to make a false statement, but such a statement is untrue, and a moment's reflection would have convinced him of its untruth. It was simply an evidence to my mind of a floundering attempt to justify a palpable outrage on the entire country on the plea of aiding the laborer.

"These things convince me that no political party can remain long in office without losing all sense of honor or of real public good. Everything is prostituted to retaining the party in power, that each may in some way reap an advantage. Protection is now prostituted to 'exclusion.' Not satisfied with a reasonable advantage and healthy competition, they openly declare that they intend to keep the markets of the United States exclusively for American manufacturers. This is not protection as I understand it or am willing to follow it. The party, therefore, that raises this standard can go on its way without my following.

"The safety of an institution consists largely of rotation in power. Thus the evils on both sides are brought to light. The Republican Party needs to be 'brought up with a round turn' and rebuked for daring to introduce bills and great measures involving the welfare, not only of the country, but of each individual, with a plain declaration that the prevailing and overpowering reason therefor is political. This can best be done by a change of administration, which I really hope will take place."

DISTRESSED BY MR. TRASK'S ACTION.

BALLSTON, N. Y., Oct. 20.—The defection of Spencer Trask of New-York from the Republican Party to Cleveland is the occasion of especial distress to the Republican machine in Saratoga County. He is one of the wealthiest Summer residents at Saratoga, having probably the finest house there, and conducts a branch of his stock brokerage business there through the Summer. He has always been depended upon to give liberally in influence and money to the county machine.

Within two years he was especially prominent in the Law and Order League which tried to enforce the anti-gambling laws at the famous Spa. His defection, coming at a time when George West, another opulent Republican, shows what is called "active indifference," is very discouraging to the Republican leaders, for the influence and cash of both have served in previous campaigns to bolster up halting members of the Grand Old Party who will now vote independently.

Frank Jones, the Postmaster here, one of the shrewdest of Republicans, said recently that the party, under the new apportionment making the whole county one Assembly district, had "just a chance of electing their Assemblyman."

Senator Harkness Badly Injured.

TOPEKA, Kan., Oct. 20.—F. P. Harkness, State Senator, and President of the Senate, was probably fatally injured this afternoon by being run over by a Union Pacific passenger train. He was en route from Clay Centre to Kansas City to meet his wife, who was returning from Albany, N. Y., their old home. At McFarland he left his train and started for another train on the next track, when the train he had just left started up and ran him down, crushing his ankle, breaking his leg, and badly injuring his thigh.

A Justice of the Peace Shot and Killed.

HAZLETON, Penn., Oct. 20.—At Audenried this morning Squire O'Donnell, a prominent politician and Justice of the Peace, was shot and killed by his constable, Isaac Phillips. It is understood that the men engaged in a political discussion, when the constable drew his weapon and fired three times, each ball taking effect. The Justice died soon after.

HAZERS SEVERELY PUNISHED.

FOUR SOPHOMORES WERE SUSPENDED AND ONE EXPELLED.

SOUTH BETHLEHEM, Penn., Oct. 20.—Four members of the sophomore class were suspended from the university to-day and one was expelled for hazing a "prep." The hazing took place in the Post Office Building in South Bethlehem. It consisted in compelling A. J. Baker, son of J. W. Baker of Lititz, Penn., to climb to the top of a room by means of a steam pipe, stand on a heater and sing, then catch with his mouth a piece of paper which was suspended from the ceiling with a string, and do the "bucket act." He did all of these things, as requested, but there was no force used.

About a week later Baker appeared at the room of one of the men and demanded $35.50 for damages. He claimed that his bill for injuries amounted to that sum and threatened to report the matter to the Faculty if not paid. As a matter of fact, his damages amounted to $5.50, which was paid by the hazers.

During the course of the interview with one of the men, named W. S. Murray, of Annapolis, Md., he intimated that Mr. Murray was a liar. Mr. Murray threatened to do violence to Baker, whereupon the latter obtained a warrant and had Mr. Murray arrested.

The case came up this morning and young Baker received a severe rebuke from Justice F. O. Fradeneck.

Last Monday Baker drew up charges against the hazers and presented them to the Faculty of the university. A special committee was appointed to hear the case.

At a special meeting of the Faculty this afternoon the evidence was submitted, and they decided as follows: J. J. Gibson of York, Penn., suspended for one year; W. S. Murray of Annapolis, Md., suspended; H. H. Wright of Cambridge, Md., suspended for one year; A. K. Kappella of Philadelphia, expelled; W. J. Collier of Duncannon, Penn., suspended for one term; H. A. White of Philadelphia, allowed to remain on probation.

O'REILLY'S DEATH-BED JOKE.

HE DISPOSES OF A FICTITIOUS ESTATE BY A WORTHLESS WILL.

ST. LOUIS, Oct. 20.—Edward O'Reilly died early in the morning of April 1 last, and developments in the courts to-day indicate that nearly the last act of his life was to play a first of April joke in the making of his will. This joke is exposed in a contest over his will, and cleared of all the legal cobwebs, the story is about this:

Mr. O'Reilly was very sick with consumption and had no family to care for him. Mrs. Emery D. Plant and her sixteen-year-old daughter, while visiting a charity hospital, met him. He took a great interest in the young lady, and she and her mother became interested in him. The upshot of it all was that he made a will leaving an insurance policy for $3,000 and some personal property to Miss Plant. He told her mother of this, and she was very kind to him. He was moved to St. Mary's Infirmary and had the best of care. Just after this change he amended his will, giving the Sisters of Mercy half and Miss Plant half his little fortune. The sisters nursed him tenderly, and when he died buried the body in consecrated ground with proper rites and ceremonies.

Then there arose a dispute over the will. Mrs. Plant did not know of the change, and to protect her daughter's rights employed an attorney. Indications pointed to an ugly contest, though the amount was small, until Mrs. Plant's attorney discovered, as he explained to-day, that there was no insurance policy—in short, that Mr. O'Reilly had nothing to give anybody. It seems he had a horror of falling into the hands of some medical college or of being buried in Potter's field. To save his body from the dissecting table and secure a consecrated grave he practiced the little fraud of making a will, and the trick seems to have worked.

EUROPE'S WINTRY WEATHER.

TEN FISHERMAN DROWNED OFF THE COAST OF SPAIN.

SAN SEBASTIAN, Spain, Oct. 20.—Very cold and stormy weather prevails along the coast. Last night the wind blew a gale. Two small fishing vessels were capsized off this port, and ten of the persons aboard of them were drowned. Nothing was known of the disasters until some of the survivers were washed ashore.

Reports from various places on the seaboard state that many small vessels have been wrecked and a number of lives lost.

VIENNA, Oct. 20.—Snow is falling here to-day, and the city and surrounding country bear a wintry aspect. All the foliage has disappeared and the hills are capped with snow.

It is snowing heavily in the highlands of Bohemia.

BERLIN, Oct. 20.—There was a heavy frost here last night. In Central Germany the rivers and canals are covered with ice. A heavy snowstorm prevails in the Hartz Mountains.

To Manage the Democratic Clubs.

WASHINGTON, Oct. 20.—Chauncey F. Black, President of the National Association of Democratic Clubs, has appointed the following Executive Committee to have entire management of the Association of Clubs for the next four years: R. G. Monroe, New-York; George H. Lambert, New-Jersey; H. W. Rusk, Maryland; A. T. Ankeny, Minnesota; William T. Wilson, West Virginia; Benton McMillin, Tennessee; James Fenton, Washington; C. C. Richards, Utah; N. W. McIvor, Iowa; Patrick A. Collins, Massachusetts; John C. Black, Illinois; Henry Watterson, Kentucky; J. S. Carr, North Carolina; Michael B. Harter, Ohio; Don M. Dickinson, Michigan; W. A. Clarke, Montana; Jefferson M. Levy, Virginia; Chauncey F. Black, President, Pennsylvania; Lawrence Gardner, Secretary, District of Columbia, and Roswell P. Flower, Treasurer, New-York, ex officio member.

Monmouth Bible Society Anniversary.

FREEHOLD, N. J., Oct. 20.—The Monmouth County Bible Society will celebrate its seventy-fifth anniversary in the Brick Church, Marlborough, on Thursday, Oct. 27. The exercises will commence at 10:30 A. M., when the anniversary sermon will be preached by the Rev. Theodore W. Welles of Paterson, N. J. The morning address will be delivered by the Rev. W. W. Moffett, the New-Jersey Superintendent of the American Bible Society. A historical address will be given at 2 o'clock by the Rev. George Swain, D. D., of Allentown. Following this will be an address by the Rev. Alexander MacLean, D. D., Secretary of the American Bible Society, and a Bible reading by "Gypsy" Smith. The delegates will be entertained at lunch by the ladies of the church.

Kansas Ministers Heard From.

TOPEKA, Kan., Oct. 20.—Just as everybody had imagined that the prohibition question had been dropped out of the campaign the Ministers' Association in a circular sets forth that the leaders of all the parties have purposely ignored this question in order to mislead the people and thereby secure the ordering of a constitutional construction at the election next month.

All ministers in the State are urged to explain from their pulpits that the adoption of the convention proposition would open the liquor question again, and to ask all parties to vote against it. But not one of the three parties will touch this question, leaving it to the individual opinion of the voters.

Nat Goodwin Wins at Faro.

LOUISVILLE, Ky., Oct. 20.—The sporting fraternity of this city was greatly excited this afternoon over a report that Comedian Nat Goodwin had made a winning of $7,000 at the faro bank over the "Boston," on Market Street, above Fourth. He played all last night and until 10 o'clock to-day.

His final and star play was calling the turn for $250, on which he won $1,000, coppering the losing and playing the winning card open for $250 each, winning all three bets and clearing $1,500 on the final turn. Feeling that that was enough for one day, he cashed in and quit.

Freight Wreck on the Pennsylvania.

ELIZABETH, N. J., Oct. 20.—A bad freight wreck occurred to-night on the Pennsylvania Railroad near Marion which blocked all travel for a couple of hours. The freight engine was thrown across the tracks and was badly shattered and several cars were wrecked. The disaster was caused by a defective frog.

THOUSANDS ON PARADE

PEOPLE'S DAY IN THE OPENING FÊTE AT CHICAGO.

GOVERNORS OF STATES, UNIFORMED SOCIETIES, AND CITY OFFICIALS MARCH THROUGH CROWDED STREETS—REVIEWED BY VICE PRESIDENT MORTON AND OTHER DIGNITARIES.

CHICAGO, Oct. 20.—Society set the glittering seal of her approval last night upon the World's Fair. To-day it was the turn of the people to express their approbation. Of Chicago's population, one in twenty marched in the civic parade, and the other nineteen, reinforced by a half million visitors from outside points, stood on the sidewalk, packed the streets, perched on roofs and window sills, and jammed the various stands along the line of march to see him do it.

The crowd was something gigantic. Chicago has at different times handled many a throng of visitors, but this one was away beyond anything she ever dealt with before. It is estimated that at least 1,200,000 people viewed the parade, and after it was over and done, the majority of the down-town restaurants were compelled to close their doors until they could attend to those who had already gained admittance. In the main, however, Chicago was equal to the occasion.

That the parade was handled in an almost perfect manner, that it was permitted to finish its march without let or hindrance, was due to the efficient work of Chicago's police force. It managed the crowds with discretion, made few arrests, and of all the features of a great day for this city their excellent work stands high.

The parade was scheduled to start from Michigan Avenue and Van Buren Street at 10:45. This would bring it past the reviewing stand at the Federal Building thirty minutes later; but, despite the utmost efforts of Grand Marshal Miles and his aides, it was exactly 12:23 o'clock when Chief of Police McClaughry at the head of the parade brought his bâton up to salute Vice President Morton, who received the parade on a tastefully-decorated stand, where he was surrounded by the members of the different legations and a throng of brilliantly-dressed ladies.

As the different Governors of the States passed the reviewing stand, some on horseback and others in carriages, each was greeted with a succession of cheers which kept him bowing for many minutes. After them came the rank and file of the parade, and in a formation of ten-file wide in double rank they rolled like a huge human wave past the reviewing stand for almost three hours. As each successive body reached the east side of the Federal Building it was greeted by one thousand little girls arranged in the shape and draped in the colors of the American flag. It was an inspiring sight, and not once did the little ones fail to receive an acknowledgment of their kindly greeting.

The Indian boys from the industrial school at Carlisle, Penn., created enthusiastic cheers as they came by. They carried long yellow poles, upon the end of which were fastened models of various tools emblematic of the different trades.

The weather was admirable for the parade. The sun shone warmly during the early portion of the day, but later the sky was overcast, and to the many spectators who stood hour after hour watching the stream flow past the fresh northern breeze was a trifle uncomfortable, but for the men who bore the burden of the day the temperature could not have been better adjusted. It is estimated that there were 75,000 men in line.

At the head of the parade, following the mounted police, came Sousa's Marine Band, acting as escort for the Mexican National Band. The visitors from beyond the Rio Grande were given a royal welcome. As quickly as the last strains from one band died away, the other took it up, and from the beginning to the end of the march there was continuous martial music at the head of the procession.

At the heels of the Mexican band was Major Gen. Miles, the Grand Marshal of the parade, resplendent in full military attire. Behind him clattered a score of aides de camp, clothed in black coats, trousers, and hats of a uniform description. Many of them were officers of the regular army, but the majority were men in private life.

The Chicago Hussars, in black with white trimmings, and accompanied by their bugle corps, was the escort to the Mayor of Chicago, the City Council in carriages, and the Governors of the different States, each of whom was surrounded by a brilliant staff. On either side of Mayor Washburne's carriage rode six hussars, acting as his private escort. As Governor after Governor went by each was greeted with cheers.

The second grand division was led by the Independent Order of Foresters, 12,000 strong, who made a fine appearance as they swept down the street in the regular formation of twenty front. The dark green of Italy flowed behind the crimson regalia of the Foresters, and the numerous Italian societies were cheered to the echo as they went by. In their rear was a big float representing "Columbus discovering America," and showing the Santa Maria approaching a rock-bound coast upon which a number of Indians stood, eagerly scanning the approaching vessel. Behind the float tramped 300 Grecians, wearing the decorations of their nation's flag—blue and white.

Eight thousand men of the Patriotic Order Sons of America were over an hour in going past. Then in close, even ranks came the descendants of the men who had won the battle of the Boyne, their persons and banners bearing knots of their favorite orange ribbons.

Three thousand five hundred men of the Chicago Turners' Society, headed by the National Commission of their order, looked exceedingly well in their neat uniforms of gray shirts, trousers, and hats. They were followed by 700 men of the Bohemian Turner societies, and these by 500 German veterans, who marched beneath the red, white, and blue of their adoption and the red, white, and black under which they had marched in less peaceful times.

There was a strong reminder of the heather as 1,200 Scots hove in sight. The bagpipes, which were many throughout their column, shrieked shrilly, and the men in tartans were a feature of the parade. The 250 representatives of the Royal Scots Regiment clad in the royal Stuart plaid called forth loud cheers of approval. Fifty men wearing the uniform of the famous Black Watch Regiment, who were next in line, were followed by a seemingly endless string of plaids.

The black and gold of the Sons of St. George followed the Highlanders. Then came rank after rank of Croation and Polish societies, in all about 2,000 men. After them came ten times as many ranks, each with its proportionate number of men, and every man a Swede. In four carriages were sixteen pretty girls representing in their attire the various national female costumes of Sweden and Norway.

The next division was made up of 2,000 boys from the grammar and high schools of Chicago, who were clad in various styles of uniform and gave vent every now and then to their school yells. Then tramped eight representatives of every Grand Army post in Chicago and Cook County, reinforced by numerous delegations from neighboring cities. The veterans were about 800 strong and at their rear was a float representing the famous old Monitor as she appeared before fighting the Merrimac. The Sons of Veterans, Modern Woodmen of America, uniformed ranks of the Royal Arcanum and Knights of Pythias, 2,000 men in all, closed the division.

The next division, under the command of Chief Marshal Cahill, was led by the Marshal, surrounded by a large staff in whose wake came the mounted members of the uniformed Knights of St. Patrick.

The second subdivision of this portion of the parade was the uniformed rank of the Catholic Order of Foresters, 850 strong, and comprising ten separate commanderies. The third subdivision had 4,440 men in line and showed the banners of forty-five courts and contained ten bands. The fourth subdivision had 2,550 men and thirty-four courts. The fifth division contained 2,544 men and thirty-one courts. Seven hundred men of the Hibernian Rifles came after the Foresters, and behind these 2,000 men of the Ancient Order of Hibernians, and then 5,000 more men of the Catholic faith who belong to the Archdiocesan Union, thirty-eight societies being represented.

The Catholic Knights of America, 1,000 men; the Catholic Benevolent Union, with 800; the Polish Catholic societies, with 1,000 men, and St. John the Baptist Society, with 1,000 men, were next in line. Miscellaneous Catholic societies numbering 1,200 men in the aggregate closed the grand division and the parade. In the rear of the Catholic Order of Foresters was a magnificent float, "Columbus," drawn by eight dapple-gray horses.

The route of the parade was as follows: Michigan Avenue, north to Van Buren Street, west on Van Buren to Wabash Avenue, north on Wabash Avenue to Lake Street, west on Lake to State Street, south on State to Adams Street, west on Adams to Franklin Street, south on

"All the News That's Fit to Print."

The New York Times.

COPYRIGHTED, 1897, BY THE NEW YORK TIMES COMPANY.

VOL. XLVI...NO. 14.300. NEW YORK, FRIDAY, JUNE 18, 1897.—TWELVE PAGES. PRICE THREE CENTS.

THE WEATHER.

The indications for to-day in this city and neighborhood are light showers, probably clearing to-night, northerly winds.

THE NEWS CONDENSED.

Stock market strong.

Wheat, 76⅝; corn, 29¼; cotton, 7¾.

CONGRESS—The Senate yesterday disposed of the schedule of the Tariff bill relating to spirits, wines, and beverages, and that relating to manufactures of cotton. The next schedule to be taken up relates to flax, and after that will come the wool schedule. The House was in session an hour and a half without transacting any business of consequence. Mr. Sulzer of New York made a short speech in which he expressed indignation because he was unable to get before the House the question of granting belligerency to the Cubans.—Page 4.

FOREIGN.—The Queen's eyesight is said to be sufficient to enable her to read proofs and correct them. The reports that she is growing blind are contradicted at Windsor, where she has arrived from Balmoral for the jubilee exercises. Seventeen bodies have been recovered from the Thames in three weeks. Most of the suicides are believed to be foreigners in London for the jubilee. Two Frenchmen were killed by Italians, and a Frenchman stabbed an Italian during labor troubles in France. A Paris reporter says the German Ambassador was near the Strasburg statue in Paris just before the bomb exploded. Emperor William has left Berlin for Cologne. He will take a cruise in the North Sea, and visit the Czar at St. Petersburg in August. Admiral von Tirpitz has been appointed Chief of the German Navy Department. The Rev. Father Kneipp of cold-water cure fame is dead at Woerishofen, Bavaria.—Page 7.

Page 1.

Queen Liliuokalani has filed a protest with Secretary Sherman against the annexation of Hawaii to the United States.

The new Democratic General Committee of Kings County met in Brooklyn last night for organization. James Moffett was elected Chairman.

The Executive Committee of the Citizens' Union will begin to-day securing a popular expression in favor of Seth Low's nomination by placing blanks for signatures in every prominent place in the city.

President Quigg of the Republican County Committee offered a resolution at a meeting of the County Committee last night which was a defiance of the methods of the Citizens' Union. The resolution was unanimously adopted after a speech by Mr. Quigg on the subject.

Strong opposition has developed to the Hawaiian annexation treaty in the Senate at Washington. Senator Davis declined to advance an opinion as to whether it will be considered at the present session of Congress.

Page 2.

One of the features of "Bunker Hill Day" in Boston was the presentation by the State of a figure of Winged Victory to the battle ship Massachusetts.

Page 3.

A committee of contractors waited on the striking tailors yesterday, and made an offer of settlement. The offer was declined.

The National Civil Service Reform League has written to the members of Congress protesting against the proposed amendment to the law that will exclude laborers from the classified lists.

John Kelly made a determined effort to commit suicide by jumping into the river from the Battery sea wall. When rescued he said that he had become crazy from nursing insane patients in a private asylum.

An attempt to wreck the New York express on the Baltimore and Ohio Southwestern about sixty-five miles east of St. Louis was foiled by one of the robbers, who warned the Sheriff. The latter reached the spot twenty minutes before the train was due. One robber surrendered and another was fatally shot. They had piled ties on the tracks. The express car carried $100,000.

Page 4.

In the trial of John S. Shriver in Washington, Judge Dittenhoefer advanced another ground to sustain his motion for an acquittal. The motion will be acted upon by Judge Bradley this morning.

The Senate made public yesterday the text of the Hawaiian treaty, President McKinley's message of transmittal, and the report of Secretary Sherman to the President which accompanied the treaty.

Page 5.

Miss Frances Archbold won the handsome silver prize cup for the women's handicap at the golf tournament, played on the Ardsley links. Her total score for the three days was 166 strokes.

Seven of the horses entered for the Suburban ran in races at the Brooklyn track yesterday. Ben Brush defeated Belmar and Havoc was beaten by On Deck. Great Bend won the Roslyn Stakes, and Free Lance the Myrtle Stakes.

Owing to the failure of the wind the races at the annual regatta of the New York Yacht Club were unfinished. At 9 o'clock last night the Colonia, Vigilant, and Wasp were becalmed about two miles north of the Southwest Spit. The Emerald gave up the race.

Page 7.

The Hoboken Turtle Club had its first outing of the year at the King's Bridge Hotel.

The Queens County Grand Jury yesterday indicted Mayor Gleason on the charge of having assaulted ex-Alderman John P. Madden.

Prince Ki Ye, heir to the Corean throne, who was here a week, left yesterday for Washington, where he will stop some time with the Corean Minister.

British and Canadian societies of New York City and vicinity will on Saturday begin their week of jubilee celebration with National sports and music at Ambr'ose Park, Brooklyn. Society dinners have been arranged for the ensuing week.

Residents of the Twenty-sixth Ward, Brooklyn, last night celebrated the passage of the bill for the improvement of Atlantic Avenue. The Brooklyn Music Hall was rented for the occasion. Prominent men made speeches, fireworks were let off on the streets, and several hundred citizens attended the banquet which followed.

Page 10.

The results of the first shipment of butter ever made by this Government to England have been communicated to Secretary of Agriculture Wilson in an official report from the experts.

Page 11.

G. H. Daniels, General Passenger Agent of the New York Central Road, spoke in advocacy of the Anti-Scalper bill before the Inter-State Commerce Committee in Washington.

The annual meeting of the Ogdensburg and Lake Champlain Railroad Company was held at Ogdensburg, N. Y., on Wednesday. The Central Vermont Railroad Company's interests favored a postponement of the election of officers, but the Parsons party opposed this and carried their point.

Page 12.

The will of Adam D. Wheelock of Brooklyn was filed in that city yesterday. The estate is left to his children.

Magistrate Simms, in the Morrisania Court, decided that a bicycle is not a carriage, and refused to punish a woman arrested for riding on the sidewalk.

The police court proceedings in the case of "Dan" Noble, who escaped from Auburn Prison twenty-four years ago, were checked by a writ of habeas corpus.

A report that charges against Surrogate Arnold had been made to the Bar Association was denied yesterday. The Surrogate says he can defend himself against any charges.

The Dry Goods Club celebrated its formal opening yesterday with a reception, which was attended by nearly all of the members, at its handsome quarters in the new building 377 and 379 Broadway.

The Cuban Junta has received a letter from Gen. Gomez, in command of the insurgent forces, that victory has attended the Winter campaign. None of the provinces are pacified, and independence is in sight.

The hearing in the case of Herman Tappan against the firm of Theodore W. Myers & Co., over the purchase of Bay State Gas stock, was continued before Magistrate Kudlich. Edward H. Myers, one of the firm, testified for the defense.

Jacob L. Kahn, a retail tobacco dealer and one of the District Attorney's witnesses in the suit against the trust, was assaulted by two men early on Thursday morning. He was knocked senseless as he approached his home, at 38 East Fourht Street.

Many prominent business men met yesterday and organized the Merchants' Association. Its object is to increase the jobbing trade of New York by bringing out-of-town merchants here at reduced railroad fares and showing them the advantages of the metropolis as a business centre.

Representatives of the Metropolitan Traction Company discussed the proposed improvements on the Sixth and Eighth Avenue Roads yesterday with the Sinking Fund Commission. The company expressed itself as willing to make the improvements under certain conditions. The Social Reform Club's resolutions annoyed the Commissioners.

AGAINST NEGRO LABOR.

White Cotton Mill Operatives in Charleston Object to Working with Colored Persons.

COLUMBIA, S. C., June 17.—As an outgrowth of the action of the Charleston Cotton Mill in displacing 300 white operatives with blacks upon resuming operations a few days ago, there is much suppressed excitement in the City of Charleston, where the mill it situated.

The situation is regarded as very grave, one involving a social problem of the greatest magnitude, and serious trouble is apprehended. Policemen are guarding the negro operatives and mill property in consequence of threats having been made.

It has been the policy of the Charleston papers, which are interested in the experiment to suppress complaints from the other side, and an approximation of the destitution of displaced operatives, was denied publication. Yesterday, however, it was printed in hand-bill form and displayed everywhere about the city, causing the greatest excitement.

After denouncing the policy of the mill owners, the bill reads, or at least part of it reads: "Proximity is the parent of social intercourse, which is longingly courted by the colored race, notwithstanding all that has been said to the contrary, and where does it abound more than in cotton mills?

"Yet Mr. Witte proposes to put the blacks and whites, male and female, side by side under one roof."

The bill goes on to say that the laboring side by side of colored men and women, and white men and women can only produce the worst results. The manifesto ends with an attack upon Mr. Witte, whom it styles "this mongrel cotton mill advocate," who would condemn the giving of Federal offices in this city to the negroes.

More than 50 per cent. of the population of Charleston is black, and if the experiment succeeds, the white operatives must leave town or starve, as there is no other employment open to them there.

OBJECTS TO THE ROBE.

Bishop Cheney of Chicago Rebukes the Council of Reformed Episcopal Church.

CHICAGO, June 17.—"I will not allow any one to take away my Christian liberty. That is what the Council of the Church at the New York meeting attempted to do."

This is the way Bishop Cheney of the Reformed Episcopal Church to-night spoke of the rule passed by the Council requiring that a certain robe should be worn in the pulpit.

"Let it be understood that we who opposed the rule will not withdraw from the Reformed Episcopal Churches," he continued. "My action in refusing to consent to wearing any garment suggested by the Council will not result in any serious action on the part of the Council or my Church. It is such a childish thing, so small, so insignificant, that I am astonished that the meeting considered the rule for a moment. The Eastern Churches all supported it, while the Western Churches were against it.

"The Synod of Chicago has never asked the council for a favor, nor have we sought for assistance. Rather the Council has come to the Synod of Chicago seeking for help. I would not be surprised, when the Council meets again in three years, if the local Synod would not be represented at the gathering."

SHE WANTED HER CAT.

Magistrate Wentworth Refused to Give Her a Summons for the Animal.

Magistrate Wentworth felt very much amused at Yorkville Court yesterday morning when approached by a respectably dressed woman with a baby in her arms, who asked his aid in recovering her pet Maltese cat.

"My cat has either strayed or been stolen," she said, "and I want a summons to find her again."

"Summons for a cat—a cat," laughingly said the Judge. "Leave your door open and she'll come back again."

"But will you assure me that my cat will come back?" continued the woman.

"You had better take care of your baby and not bother about a cat," answered the Magistrate.

When the woman insisted that she wanted to have her cat, the Judge said: "If you come to my house, I'll give you a cat with five kittens, and if that won't do, I'll give you thirteen cats and throw in a puppy with it."

"Thank you Judge," replied the woman, "I'll come to see you."

CIVIL VS. MILITARY LAW.

Proceedings in Nebraska Courts to Determine the Rights of Soldiers Against a Court-Martial.

OMAHA, June 17.—The Hon. W. R. Patrick was called to Fort Crook this afternoon to obtain if possible by legal process the release of five enlisted men who had been sentenced to thirty days in the guardhouse for mutiny.

The soldiers were detailed to clean the company commander's house. They did it, but protested, and for this they were tried by the post court and sentenced to thirty days in the guardhouse and to forfeit $10 pay. It is the intention of the attorney to commence habeas corpus proceedings in the Federal court in order to obtain the release of his clients.

VETERAN CHICAGO FIREMAN.

Death of Leo Meyers, Who Has Fought Flames All His Life.

CHICAGO, June 17.—Ex-Fire Marshal Leo Meyers is dying of paralysis. He was born here in 1834, the first child born of German parents in Chicago. At the age of three he tried to put out the kitchen fire, and he has been putting out fires ever since. At thirteen he joined the volunteer department, and when it was disbanded he became a paid fireman. He became Assistant Marshal in 1877, and Marshal a few years later.

His reputation as a fireman and for bravery and judgment is more than local.

PROTEST OF LILIUOKALANI

Hawaii's ex-Queen Says the Treaty Ignores the Rights of 40,000 Natives and Herself.

ROBS HER OF 915,000 ACRES

The Right of the Party in Power to Cede the Islands Once Repudiated by the United States—She Appeals to the People.

WASHINGTON, June 17.—About 3 o'clock this afternoon ex-Queen Liliuokalani filed the following protest in the office of the Secretary of State. It was delivered into the hands of Secretary John Sherman by Mr. Joseph Heleluhe, representing the native Hawaiians, duly commissioned by two of their patriotic leagues. Mr. Heleluhe was accompanied by Capt. Julius A. Palmer, the American secretary of Liliuokalani. Mr. Sherman treated the bearers most courteously, but gave no indications of his action in the matter:

I, Liliuokalani of Hawaii, by the will of God named heir apparent on the 10th day of April, A. D. 1877, and by the grace of God Queen of the Hawaiian Islands on the 17th day of January, A. D. 1893, do hereby protest against the ratification of a certain treaty, which, so I am informed, has been signed at Washington by Messrs. Hatch, Thurston, and Kinney, purporting to cede the said islands to the territory and dominion of the United States. I declare such treaty to be an act of wrong toward the native and the part-native people of Hawaii, an invasion of the rights of the ruling chiefs, in violation of international rights, both toward my people and toward friendly nations with whom they have made treaties, the perpetuation of the fraud whereby the Constitutional Government was overthrown and, finally, an act of gross injustice to me.

Because the official protests made by me on the seventeenth day of January, 1893, to the so-called Provisional Government was signed by me and received by said Government with the assurance that the case was referred to the United States of America for arbitration.

Because that protest and my communications to the United States Government immediately thereafter expressly declares that I yielded my authority to the forces of the United States in order to avoid bloodshed and because I recognized the futility of a conflict with so formidable a power.

She Was Unlawfully Coerced.

Because the President of the United States, the Secretary of State, and an envoy commissioned by them, reported in official documents that my Government was unlawfully coerced by the forces, diplomatic and naval, of the United States, that I was at the date of their investigations the constitutional ruler of my people.

Because such decision of the recognized magistrates of the United States was officially communicated to me and to Sanford B. Dole, and said Dole's resignation requested by Albert S. Willis, the recognized agent and Minister of the Government of the United States.

Because neither the above-named commission nor the Government which sends it has ever received any such authority from the registered voters of Hawaii, but derived its assumed powers from the so-called Committee of Public Safety, organized on or about the 7th day of January, 1893, said committee being composed largely of persons claiming American citizenship, and not one single Hawaiian was a member thereof or in any way participated in the demonstration leading to its existence.

Because my people, about 40,000 in number, have in no way been consulted by those, 3,000 in number, who claim the right to destroy the independence of Hawaii. My people constitute four-fifths of the legally qualified voters of Hawaii, and, excluding those imported for the demands of labor, about the same proportion of the inhabitants.

Because said treaty ignores not only the civic rights of my people, but, further, the hereditary property of their chiefs. Of the 4,000,000 acres composing the territory said treaty offers to annex, 1,000,000, or 915,000 acres, has in no way been heretofore recognized as other than the private property of the constitutional monarch, subject to a control in no way differing from other items of a private estate.

Confiscates Her Crown Lands.

Because it is proposed by said treaty to confiscate said property, technically called the Crown lands, those legally entitled thereto, either now, or in succession, receiving no consideration whatever for estates, their title to which has been always undisputed and which is legitimately in my name at this date.

Because said treaty ignores not only all professions of perpetual amity and good faith made by the United States in the former treaties with the sovereigns representing the Hawaiian people, but all treaties made by those sovereigns with other and friendly powers, and it is thereby in violation of international law.

Because by treating with the parties claiming at this time the right to cede said territory of Hawaii the Government of the United States receives such territory from the hands of those whom its own Magistrates (legally elected by the people of the United States and in office in 1893) pronounced fraudulently in power and unconstitutionally ruling Hawaii; therefore, I, Liliuokalani of Hawaii, do hereby call upon the President of that Nation to whom alone I yielded my property and my authority to withdraw said treaty (ceding said lands) from further consideration, I ask the honorable Senate of the United States to decline to ratify said treaty, and I implore the people of this great and good Nation, from whom my ancestors learned the Christian religion, to sustain their representatives in such acts of justice and equity as may be in accord with the principles of their fathers, and to the Almighty Ruler of the Universe, to Him who judgeth righteously, I commit my cause.

Done at Washington, D. C., United States of America, this 17th day of June, in the year eighteen hundred and ninety-seven.

LILIUOKALANI.

Joseph Heleluhe, Wekeki Heleluhe, Julius A. Palmer, witnesses to signature.

VIEWS OF A SENATOR IN PARIS.

Talks to The London Times's Correspondent About Hawaii.

LONDON, June 18.—The Times's correspondent in Paris says:

"To-day (Thursday) in the garden of the British Embassy I met a member of the American Senate, in high standing, who said to me: 'In one way or another we were bound to take Hawaii. It has, first of all, the advantage that it can be annexed without serious difficulty arising with any European power. Therefore we can satisfy our desire for some sort of annexation without running the risk of serious complications. Moreover, Hawaii is so near America that it is quite out of the question that it should belong to any other power, and its Government is so weak that it could not seriously resist if any other power really tried to take it.

"'Although not worth much, Hawaii will make an excellent coaling station, and it might prove otherwise useful in our hands. Unless we annex it now, we should expose ourselves to complications with the Japanese, who would soon outnumber the Americans in the islands, while now we have to fight nobody.'"

A Paris dispatch, published elsewhere in THE NEW YORK TIMES to-day, says that Senator Wolcott of Colorado attended the garden party in question.

Cow Swallows a Golf Ball and Dies.

ORANGE, N. J., June 17.—A cow belonging to School Commissioner George Kenney, died the other day in the field where is was pastured, and its owner supposing it had been poisoned ordered a post mortem. It was then found that the animal had swallowed a golf ball which had been dropped by a caddy for the Essex County Country Club.

TREATY STRONGLY OPPOSED

Senators Object to Acquiring Colonies and Opening Our Markets to Cheap Labor.

HAWAII MAY HAVE TO WAIT

The Plan Is to Let the Treaty Lie Over Until the Next Session, When the Objections Have Been Heard.

WASHINGTON, June 17.—Opposition to the Hawaiian annexation project has broken out much more violently than was anticipated by the Administration, and the treaty will be roughly handled when it comes up in the Senate for ratification. Whether the opposition will be able to muster sufficient strength in that body to defeat ratification is a speculative problem. It looks now as though the annexation party might not be able to command the necessary two-thirds vote. In any event, it is now taken for granted that favorable action at this special session, either in the form of treaty ratification or legislation sustaining the Administration plans, will be impossible.

The strongest, most dangerous opposition will be from two sources—those who are against the acquisition of remote territory by the United States and opposed on principle to the embarkation by this Government upon colonization schemes, and second, those who will fight annexation on the plea that the cheap labor of the Hawaiian Islands will seriously affect our agriculture, particularly checking the development of the beet sugar industry of the middle West, which gives promise of being an important addition to the production of the soil throughout a large section of the country.

There are many other reasons which will be urged, including, of course, the argument that by the taking of these remote islands the United States will no longer find it possible to sustain its hitherto impregnable position along the lines of the Monroe doctrine. President McKinley's message, which went to the Senate with the treaty, covers this point, but it will never be brought in when the context is being discussed.

Senator Davis, Chairman of the Committee on Foreign Relations, said to-day that the committee would take up the Hawaiian treaty at its next regular meeting, which will be held on Wednesday of next week, but that no special meeting would be held for that purpose. He said that the treaty would in any event be held in committee a sufficient length of time to permit all sides to be heard, but that the time would be controlled somewhat by the indications as to whether the Senate would consider the treaty at the present session. On this latter point the Senator declined to advance an opinion.

The programme now is that the treaty will be reported from the committee, and that after the Tariff bill has passed it will be called up. The Senate will be asked if a time for a vote can be fixed, and upon the objections by the opponents of the treaty its friends will say they are content to allow it to lie over until the next session. One reason for not pressing the treaty in the face of opposition is that the sentiment which may be only partially opposed to the treaty will be crystallized, which is not desirable.

It is also believed that Senators who are now undecided may become influenced favorably after mature consideration and after finding out what the drift of sentiment is in their States. It is well known that Senators cannot be held here after the tariff bill is passed.

GERMAN ANXIETY FOR SAMOA.

Vossische Zeitung Thinks Germany and England Should Act.

BERLIN, June 17.—The Vossische Zeitung thinks that the action of the United States imposes upon Germany and England the necessity of devising measures to prevent the adoption of a similar policy as to Samoa.

The Post, however, expresses the authoritative view held here when it says: "Germany has long regarded Hawaii as within the sphere of American interests, and can scarcely find any pretext either to question the right of the United States to annex or to interfere by protest or obstruction."

LEGISLATIVE PRINTING.

Contract for Two Years Awarded to C. Tollner, Jr., of Brooklyn.

ALBANY, June 17.—The State Printing Board at its meeting to-day awarded the contract for legislative printing for the two years beginning Oct. 1, 1897, to Charles Tollner, Jr., of Brooklyn, his bid being the lowest, at $68,611.30. The price of the last contract, which was awarded two years ago to the Wynkoop-Hallenbeck-Crawford Company, was in the neighborhood of $111,000.

The bids received were as follows: Charles Tollner, Jr., of Brooklyn, $68,611.30; Wynkoop-Hallenbeck-Crawford Company, $73,653.64; J. B. Lyon, $87,050.13; The Argus Company, $110,162.90; Weed, Parsons Company, $104,743.08; The Journal Company, $108,498.57.

ADAMS HOUSES RESTORED.

QUINCY, Mass., June 17.—The birthplaces of Presidents John and John Quincy Adams were opened to the public to-day for the first time since the work of restoring them was begun, and they were visited by large crowds of people from this city and surrounding towns. The John Adams house is in charge of Adams Chapter, Daughters of the Revolution, and the Quincy Historical Society has undertaken the work of preserving the John Quincy Adams house. Both of the old houses have been refurnished to correspond to old Colonial times.

CHICAGO BOARD OF TRADE ROW.

CHICAGO, June 17.—Amid catcalls and hisses Vice President Lyon of the Board of Trade adjourned the meeting of the members interested in the proposed warehouse amendment in the call room this afternoon.

A vote had been called for on the indorsing of a resolution against the proposed amendment, which is aimed to take away from "regular" elevator proprietors the right to store their own grain in their own buildings.

The "yeas" and "nays" seemed to be about equally divided, and Vice President Lyon made another effort to estimate the vote. Each side did its best to fill the big hall, a mighty bellow going up at each signal from the chair.

"The 'nays' have it," declared Mr. Lyon.

A general tumult followed, and the decision of the Chairman was disputed from different quarters of the room. One of the members who had advocated the amendment shouted a motion for adjournment. Another sprang to the floor and seconded it.

"I demand a division," screamed "Al" Farnum of Baldwin & Farnum. "It is impossible to tell which side has carried the question without it."

"Lay down!" came from a hundred voices, and then Bedlam broke loose, each side trying to make more noise than the other.

Lyon put the question without further comment. Only those in the front seats could make out what had been said, and the crowd in the rear had a pellmell rush to the corridor through the doors.

In vain Mr. Lyon smashed the handle off his gavel, and then substituted a rung of a chair. A dozen elevator men had held hasty conference, and while the Chairman was trying to secure order called for an adjournment until to-morrow. This was done in the hope that a reconsideration of the resolution might be taken. Mr. Lyon allowed the temporary adjournment to stand.

CITIZENS' UNION'S PLANS

To Secure Request of Thirty Thousand Voters for Seth Low's Nomination.

CITY FLOODED WITH POSTERS

In Every Prominent Place Will Be Found Blanks for Signatures—Nomination May Be Made June 30—Encouraging Reports from Labor Men.

The Citizens' Union will begin to-day the work of securing such an expression of the popular desire as Seth Low said would determine him in accepting the nomination for Mayor by the union. In his letter of June 7, Mr. Low wrote:

"If I were convinced that there was such a popular desire and that my candidacy would prove a unifying force among the friends of good government in the city, I should not hesitate to accept your nomination."

The Executive Committee of the union, at its meeting Wednesday night, determined to get an expression of popular desire at once, so that it will be possible to place Mr. Low in formal nomination by the first of July. It is well understood by members of the Committee of Two Hundred and Fifty that its letter and conference with Mr. Low was a practical selection and nomination of him for the Mayoralty; and the formal nomination will be made at the earliest possible day. This will probably be June 30, when the Committee of Two Hundred and Fifty will hold its next meeting.

To-day, when the people of New York go into the stores, or climb the elevated railway stations, they will find a profusion of posters asking voters to sign their names to a request for the nomination of Seth Low. These posters will be scattered over the city. They will be at all the Assembly district headquarters, in all prominent stores, placed conspicuously everywhere, and blanks for signatures will also be sent to every business office.

The following is the form of poster that will be found in the elevated stations:

> CITIZENS' UNION.
> If You Want
> HON. SETH LOW
> for Mayor,
> Sign your name in favor of his nomination and election.
> Blanks for signatures at general headquarters, 25 East Twenty-third Street, or at the following district headquarters:

A list of district headquarters will be given on each of these posters.

In the stores will be placed the following form:

> CITIZENS' UNION.
> If You Want
> HON. SETH LOW
> for Mayor,
> Sign Your Name
> Here.........

At the various district headquarters the following form will be found:

> CITIZENS' UNION.
> If you want
> HON. SETH LOW
> for Mayor,
> Sign your name in favor of his nomination and election.
> SIGN HERE...............

It is expected that within two weeks more than 30,000 names can be secured in this way. In this matter the union is following the example set in the campaign of Henry George, who received a popular expression of this sort before he accepted the nomination.

The Assembly district organizations are sending in daily to the Executive Committee resolutions and requests for the nomination of Mr. Low, and the volume of these requests already amounts almost to a public demonstration.

The committee is receiving encouraging news from the labor element. It is reported that a number of labor leaders, who have heretofore supported Tammany, have sent word to the Wigwam that they would not support it this year unless certain concessions, in the substantial form of municipal offices, were promised them. Tammany, it is said, was asked to reply to this proposition by the 11th of this month. That date passing without a reply, an ultimatum, it is said, was sent to the Wigwam that a reply must be forthcoming by June 20.

In the meanwhile, these labor leaders are waiting, but without much hope. The condition of the labor vote has changed materially, members of the Citizens' Union who are labor men declare, and none of the so-called leaders can any longer deliver the vote of his organization. Thousands of former Tammany voters in the ranks of labor, they say, have already allied themselves with the Citizens' Union.

JAMES MOFFETT, CHAIRMAN.

Democratic General Committee of Kings County Elected Officers.

The new Democratic General Committee of Kings County met in Brooklyn last night and organized by electing the following prearranged ticket: James Moffett, Chairman; William A. Doyle and Edward L. Walter, Vice Presidents; Robert T. Brown, Secretary; Michael J. Cummings, Corresponding Secretary; Arthur C. Salmon, Treasurer.

A resolution was passed authorizing the Executive Committee to take "such measures as may be necessary to provide for a conference with representatives of Democratic organizations in the Boroughs of Manhattan, Queens and Richmond and in connection with those organizations to make such provisions as may be necessary to call a city convention for the nomination of candidates for the coming election." The various committees will be announced later.

ONE KILLED, ANOTHER DYING.

Samuel Stimson's Carriage Struck by a Train at Herkimer.

LITTLE FALLS, N. Y., June 17.—The Adirondack express, which reached Herkimer about 5:30 P. M., struck a carriage containing Samuel Stimson and Miss Schermerhorn at the Main Street crossing in Herkimer. Stimson was instantly killed and Miss Schermerhorn is dying.

Samuel Stimson was one of the prominent Republicans of Central New York. He was a former Postmaster and Public Works Commissioner of Herkimer. Miss Schermerhorn was a teacher in the public schools.

Fresh-Air Fund Fair in Jersey.

SUMMIT, N. J., June 17.—The big fair and fête for the benefit of the Fresh Air and Convalescent Home was opened this afternoon on the grounds of the Casino Club, and a large and fashionable crowd attended it both afternoon and evening. It will close to-morrow night with a big dance. Each of the many picturesque booths is arranged to represent some well-known Mother Goose rhyme, and the young women in attendance are appropriately costumed to represent the characters.

TERMS OF PEACE SETTLED.

A Report that Turkey Will Accept the Conditions of the Powers.

LONDON, June 18.—The Athens correspondent of the Daily Telegraph, says:

"It is reported here to-night (Thursday) that the peace conference and the Porte have accepted a settlement, giving the Turks either the town of Ligaria, southeast of Milouna, or Nezeros, north of Larissa."

The Athens correspondent of the Daily Chronicle says the Porte has abandoned the policy of delay and decided to accept the advice of the powers.

CYCLONES AND HAIL IN SPAIN.

Crops Ruined, Cattle Drowned, and Lives Lost.

LONDON, June 18.—The Madrid correspondent of The Daily Mail says:

"A succession of cyclones and fierce hailstorms have destroyed the crops and vineyards in the Provinces of Valladolid and Guadalajara. In the district of New Castle houses have been flooded, hundreds of cattle drowned, and a number of lives lost."

CAT JUMPED TEN STORIES.

Remarkable Episode in the Career of a Chicago Feline.

CHICAGO, June 17.—Boozer, the office cat of The Journal, jumped out of a window on the tenth story of the building to-day. She fell 150 feet, into the alley below, where she was found by those who ran down expecting she was dead. But she wasn't.

A physician who was called in said Boozer was only shaken up a little. She was taken back to the editorial rooms.

FRIGHTENED BY A HYENA.

Chicago Cemeteries Being Guarded Against Expected Raids.

CHICAGO, June 17.—The hyena which gnawed its way out of the cage in Lincoln Park is still uncaught, although scores of policemen have scoured Lakeview, Buena Park, and the cemeteries.

Evidences of it were found in Graceland Cemetery, where it had partly unearthed a coffin. To-night there are guards at Graceland, Rosehill, and Calvary Cemeteries, and the police of Evanston, Ravenswood, and the northern suburbs are on the outlook for the grave digger.

MARRYING PARSON STRIKES.

Apparent End of Cheap Weddings for Chicago Couples.

MILWAUKEE, June 17.—The Rev. W. A. Hunkberger, who is known all over the West as the "marrying parson," and who has married as many as twenty couples in one day, has decided that he will marry no more people on Sunday. This will be a death blow to Milwaukee as the Gretna Green of Chicago unless some one arises to succeed Mr. Hunkberger.

In Summer and Winter, but especially in the Summer, it has been the fashion for excursionists to visit him and be married by him, and it was no uncommon thing for five or more couples to be waiting in the parsonage.

SCARLET FEVER IN PLAINFIELD.

Twenty-eight Cases Said to be Due to the Milk Furnished.

PLAINFIELD, N. J., June 17.—There is an epidemic of scarlet fever in this city, and within the past few days twenty-eight cases have been reported to the Board of Health.

It has been rumored that the cause of the epidemic is due to the milk furnished the people of the city, and it is quite likely that some steps will be taken to have this commodity thoroughly inspected as well as all cattle in this locality.

A statement was issued by Mayor Fisk to-day in which he says that he does not apprehend any great danger from the disease, and that it will not be necessary to close the schools.

BAD FEELING IN CANADA.

Friends of the United States Made Foes by the Tariff.

OTTAWA, Ont., June 17.—The feeling in the Canadian Parliament against the action of the United States toward Canada in tariff matters was again illustrated to-night when Mr. John Charlton protested in the strongest way against placing corn on the free list.

He admitted that free corn would be a benefit to the Canadian farmer, but said the Canadian Government ought not to give this advantage to the United States without receiving something in return. Several other speakers spoke in the same strain. In the past Mr. Charlton has always been favorable to the United States.

SOLD HIS WIFE FOR $100.

Jacob Zellar of Switzerland Has a Unique Transaction Near Alliance, O.

ALLIANCE, Ohio, June 17.—Jacob Zellar and Brecht Yanne, natives of Switzerland, rented a farm just east of this city two years ago. Zellar had a wife and family, while Yanne was single. Zellar's wife is comely, and it was not very long before Yanne became her ardent admirer. Zellar often complained of his hard lot, and regretted leaving Switzerland.

Last Sunday Zellar said that if he had $100 he would go back to Switzerland. "Sell me your wife, and stay away forever, and the money is yours," Yanne is said to have replied.

"Take the children, Brecht, and it's a bargain," said Zellar.

"Done," replied Brecht. The papers were made out and the money paid over that evening in the presence of several of their countrymen. To-day Jacob left Alliance for Switzerland.

THE WEATHER.

The local forecast may be found at the top of this page to the right of the title.

The storm has remained nearly stationary to the north of Montana, diminishing in intensity. The pressure is high over the Gulf, over Lake Superior, and off the North Pacific coast. Showers have occurred in the Middle Atlantic States, the Ohio Valley, the lake regions, Florida, and on the Middle Gulf coast. The temperature has risen in the South Atlantic States and Middle Mississippi Valley, and has remained nearly stationary elsewhere.

The record of temperature for the twenty-four hours ended at midnight, taken from THE NEW YORK TIMES's thermometer and from the thermometer of the Weather Bureau, is as follows:

	—Weather Bureau.—		TIMES.
	1896.	1897.	1897.
3 A. M.	60	63	66
6 A. M.	62	62	65
9 A. M.	62	64	72
12 M.	64	67	76
4 P. M.	63	67	72
6 P. M.	63	67	71
9 P. M.	63	64	69
12 P. M.	63	64	68

THE TIMES's thermometer is 6 feet above the street level; that of the Weather Bureau is 285 feet above the street level.

Average temperatures yesterday were as follows:

Printing House Square	69⅝
Weather Bureau	66
Corresponding date 1896	62
Corresponding date for last 20 years	70

CITIZENS' UNION DEFIED

President Quigg of the Republican County Committee Offers a Resolution Against Their Methods.

IT IS UNANIMOUSLY ADOPTED

He Also Says That the Attempt of Any Organization to Humiliate Any Other Organization Is An Act of Folly and Crime.

President Quigg of the Republican County Committee exploded what many of his associates describe as a "bomb" at last night's meeting of the County Committee in the Murray Hill Lyceum on East Thirty-fourth Street, near Third Avenue. After the routine business of the meeting had been disposed of Mr. Quigg asked George R. Bidwell to take the chair, and going upon the floor, Mr. Quigg then offered the following resolution:

Resolved, That it is not in the interest of a united and harmonious campaign for the good government of the city of New York to attempt at this time by forced and unusual methods to manufacture public sentiment in the interest of any particular candidate, nor can any candidacy prove a unifying force among the friends of good government in this city which is formally presented prior to the meeting of the Republican City Convention, or without regard to its action.

The crowd regarded this as a "drive" against the candidacy of Seth Low, and there was cheering. Mr. Quigg walked up and down in the centre aisle of the hall until order had been restored, and then he made his speech, which was taken by all the politicians who were present to mean that a warning was being served upon the members of the Citizens' Union. Mr. Quigg said, when Acting President Bidwell had restored order:

Chairman Quigg's Speech.

"I am one of those who realize that a successful campaign for good government in New York this Fall is serious business, to be gone about in a rational and considerate way. We have no single vote to trifle with. There may be ways to win other than the one which seeks to obtain every possible support by every just means, but I distrust them. I have deemed it my duty to offer this resolution as a frank statement of the position of this organization, profoundly hoping that it will escape misrepresentation. It is not a defiance. It is not a challenge. It is intended to operate only as a check upon violent and unreasoning persons who are placing in peril the cause which, no doubt, they really desire to promote.

"Mr. President, there ought to be only one ticket in the field this Fall against the ticket of a valorous enemy. It must be a ticket which measures up in the character of its candidates, in their representative quality and in their popularity before the people to the great end in view and the great emergencies of the situation. But it is impossible to know that we are safe in committing ourselves to any candidacies at this time, and it is very clear that any organization, great or small, which attempts to overreach or humiliate any other organization, great or small, commits an act of folly which, in view of the possible consequences, is an act of crime.

Criticises the Citizens' Union.

"Some days ago, three citizens of New York invited a fourth citizen to become a candidate for the office of Mayor as a representative of the cause of honest government. The reply they received was the reply which any self-respecting American gentleman would have given in similar circumstances. The gentleman addressed said prudently, and, of course, sincerely, that if the fact could be established that the people who intended honest government in New York wanted him to be their candidate, and if it could be proved that his candidacy would be a unifying force among them all, he would not refuse the use of his name. But he did not say to them: 'Go out upon the street corners, beat the drums, blow the horns, make all the noise you can, create by hook or by crook the impression that I am the only possible man who can win, and if you make noise enough, I will be your candidate.' He did not say this, nor did he mean it, and he must be pained and humiliated to discover that those who profess to be his friends, and are undertaking to appropriate his personality, have placed so mean a construction upon his words.

"Mr. President, there ought to be no attempt by a process of hot-house culture at this time to develop any man's candidacy or to promote any man's personal interests. Still less should there be an attempt by any element of the anti-Tammany party to coerce the action of any other element. And, Sir, in behalf of the great Republican Party of this city, I deem it my duty to give frank and sincere warning that these attempts cannot succeed in their purpose. The man who will be nominated by the Republican City Convention will be the man whose candidacy develops naturally out of the situation as it exists when that convention meets. No other man ought to be nominated, for no other man can win. I ask for a vote upon the resolution."

The Resolutions Adopted.

Mr. Quigg's resolutions were then unanimously adopted. There was much cheering. The politicians declared that Mr. Quigg had defied the Citizens' Union. They wondered whether it meant that Mr. Low would not be the choice of the Republicans. They said that the voice of Senator Thomas C. Platt had spoken.

After Mr. Quigg's resolutions had been unanimously adopted he relieved Mr. Bidwell of the chair, and Charles Butler of the Twenty-seventh Assembly District offered a resolution to the effect that the colored people ought to be better treated by the Republican organization. Mr. Butler spoke about promises that had been made but never kept. He asked that a committee of five be appointed to "investigate the situation of the colored vote as to appointments and representation." John S. Wise asked that the resolution be amended so as to include the "whites." There was much laughter at this.

Christopher Stewart of the Twenty-fifth Assembly District, who, like Mr. Butler, is a colored man, said that he opposed Mr. Butler's resolution and that the Republican Party always treated the colored voters properly. He said that Caleb Simms was an able representative of the Republican colored men. He moved that Mr. Butler's resolution be laid upon the table. This motion was carried, but Mr. Butler demanded that there be a division. This brought Abraham Gruber to his feet with the remark:

"That's the trouble. You are always looking for a division.

Gen. Collis Appears.

While the meeting was in progress Gen. C. H. T. Collis, Commissioner of Public Works, who has been outside of the regular Republican machine for several years, entered and was cheered. Gen. Collis has been named as a delegate from the Thirty-first Assembly District to the County Committee in the place of Mr. Roth, who withdrew in his favor.

Gen. Collis has concluded a treaty of peace with Senator Platt's machine. His presence last night was indicative of this fact.

President Quigg's efforts to harmonize the Republicans in this county were ratified last night when the County Committee adopted the following:

"Resolved, That the Republican County Committee heartily approves the measures that have been taken by the President and by the Committee on Organization, looking to a thorough and proper revision of the rolls of the election district associations, and to the enrollment of all qualified voters who desire to identify themselves with the Republican organization; and, be it further

"Resolved, That the County Committee urges the officers of every election district association so to conduct the contemplated revision and enrollment on the night of June 29, 1897, as to establish the fact that every Republican in the County of New

1898

The Age of Reform

1914

FRONT PAGE NEWS 1898-1914

Battleship Maine Blown Up

FEBRUARY 16, 1898

The explosion of the U.S. battleship Maine led to what Theodore Roosevelt called "a splendid little war," the four-month Spanish-American conflict in which the United States handily defeated Spain, freed Cuba, took over the Philippines as a protectorate and won Puerto Rico as an American possession. President William McKinley had sent the Maine to protect Americans in Havana after Cubans rioted. What caused the explosion—a Spanish mine, a bomb planted by Cubans hoping to draw the Americans into their fight or an accident aboard the 6,682-ton ship itself—was a mystery (and still is). But the jingoistic publisher William Randolph Hearst did not care. "Remember the Maine!" he urged readers before telling a reluctant reporter who was not finding much news on the scene, "You furnish the pictures and I will furnish the war."

Dewey Sinks Spanish Flotilla

MAY 1, 1898

Admiral George Dewey's squadron steamed toward the Philippines on orders from Theodore Roosevelt, an ambitious assistant secretary of the Navy who would soon go to war himself, charging up San Juan Hill with the Rough Riders. Luckily for Dewey and his sailors, the Spanish opened fire before the Americans were close enough. Now everything was up to Dewey, and as he maneuvered into Manila Bay, he knew it. "You may fire when ready, Gridley," he told his executive officer. It did not take long to decimate the Spanish flotilla. The Americans killed or wounded nearly 400 Spanish sailors without a single battle casualty.

British Lose a Key Battle in Boer War

JANUARY 29, 1900

The British outnumbered their independence-minded Afrikaner opponents by more than five to one in the Boer War, but manpower alone was not enough. They suffered defeat after defeat as the 19th century gave way to the 20th and pundits in London complained that incompetent generals had repeatedly gotten themselves into an impossible situation. At Spion Hop, the Boers forced the British to retreat amid heavy casualties. The fighting continued for two more years before the Boers conceded the loss of their independence in 1902 in a treaty that no less a figure than Rudyard Kipling said set the stage for apartheid.

Boxers Rebel in China

JUNE 8, 1900

"Protect the country, kill the foreigner," the Boxers shouted as they rampaged against foreigners in China. The Boxers belonged to a secret society whose name in Chinese meant "harmonious fists," and the roving bands who beat up Western missionaries knew how to use them. They also attacked the missionaries' Chinese converts and spread suspicion that the missionaries' real mission was not to save souls but to wipe out Chinese society. More than 200 foreigners and, by some estimates, 30,000 Chinese were killed before an international expeditionary force arrived and captured Peking.

Sun Sets on Victoria's Reign

JANUARY 23, 1901

Queen Victoria was born in a horse-and-carriage world that was revolutionized by steam and electricity during her 64 years on the throne. Railroads reached deep into lands where ocean-going explorers had done little more than plant the royal flag on the beach. British soldiers colonizing Africa used newfangled machine guns to shoot down tribesmen carrying little more than spears. The British would boast that the sun never set on her empire. They would also look back on the Victorian age for its formal manners and morés, often mistaken for prudery.

Elizabeth Cady Stanton Dies

OCTOBER 27, 1902

Elizabeth Cady Stanton "forged the thunderbolts, and I fired them," Susan B. Anthony said after Mrs. Stanton's death, at age 87. Mrs. Stanton had drafted the "Declaration of Sentiments" for an 1848 conference that ignited the decades-long campaign for women's suffrage and, ultimately, 20th-century feminism. "All men and women are created equal," she declared, improving on the Constitution and enumerating 18 "injuries and usurpations" of women by men—the same number of grievances the American colonists had put to King George III.

$600,000 for Tuskegee Institute

APRIL 24, 1903

The largest payoff from Booker T. Washington's "mass meeting" at Madison Square Garden in mid-April 1903 was $600,000 from someone who had not bothered to attend—the steel mogul Andrew Carnegie. The money went to Washington's Tuskegee Institute, which he had built into America's best-known black college. Washington, who had been born a slave in the 1850's, eventually raised $2 million for Tuskegee's endowment, mostly from other white industrialists, among them John D. Rockefeller.

Russian Strikers' Bloody Sunday

JANUARY 23, 1905

Czar Nicholas II had blundered through the Russo-Japanese War, while in St. Petersburg, workers had gone on strike to protest soaring food prices and official corruption. They gathered outside the Winter Palace, 150,000 strong, demanding such reforms as lower taxes, parliamentary elections and amnesty for political prisoners. It was an orderly demonstration by loyal Russians until palace guards raised their rifles and opened fire in what The Times called a "wholesale massacre." The attack touched off the revolution of 1905, which brought V. I. Lenin home from exile. "The revolutionary education of the proletariat," he declared, "made more progress in one day than it could have made in months and years of drab, humdrum, wretched existence."

Dreyfus Vindicated

JUNE 22, 1906

Captain Alfred Dreyfus of the French Army was disgraced in the 1890's—court-martialed on bogus treason charges against a backdrop of anti-Semitism and sharp political divisions between the left and the right. Then he was championed in Emile Zola's "J'accuse," a cry against injustice that won Dreyfus's release from prison. That led to another court-martial and another guilty verdict, but this time it was followed by a presidential pardon, reinstatement in the army, and promotion to major and the Legion of Honor. The Dreyfus Affair flared again almost 100 years later, when the French defense minister fired an army historian in 1994 over a paper that questioned Dreyfus's innocence.

Earthquake Rocks San Francisco

APRIL 19, 1906

The San Francisco earthquake would have registered about 7.8 if the Richter scale had existed then—strong enough to destroy wooden buildings and the new brick-and-stone City Hall alike. It was felt 3,000 miles away in Albany, New York, where a seismograph fluctuated at the moment the rumbling started. Two tectonic plates had slipped past each other along the San Andreas Fault. Soon a city that had been reduced to rubble was on fire as broken gas pipes and fallen electrical lines set off a conflagration that burned for three days. Some 500 people died, and 200,000 were left homeless.

The Unsinkable Ship Sinks. But Why?

APRIL 16, 1912

Titanic was as renowned for its watertight compartments as it was for its opulent first-class cabins—"Not even God could sink this ship," an employee of the White Star line said. But on its maiden voyage, confidence gave way to the catastrophe that became a legend: an iceberg seen too late, a collision too slight to be felt, a flood too big to be contained in the watertight compartments (and, a marine historian concluded in 2008, a rush of seawater hastened by cheap iron rivets in the hull that popped apart sooner than costlier steel rivets would have). Suddenly, Titanic denoted not fame but infamy and fallibility.

Wireless Message Spans Atlantic

OCTOBER 18, 1907

In 1907, "wireless" meant something completely different than it means in an age of cellphones and personal computers that do not need cables to connect to the Internet. The big advance in wireless technology in 1907 was slow and primitive: radio operators listening for the sound of dots and dashes amid the short-wave static, and relaying each message to the next station in a carefully placed chain. Still, it was a step toward binding the world together with fast long-distance communication.

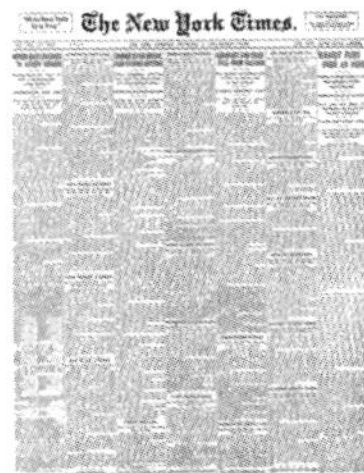

Wright's Record-Breaking Flight

SEPTEMBER 10, 1908

Five years after that first flight at Kitty Hawk, Orville Wright was trying for an Army contract—and setting aviation records again. He circled an Army parade ground near Washington for 62 minutes and 15 seconds, the first time he had flown that long. Eight days later, Wright's plane stalled and plunged to the ground. Wright's passenger died—the first airplane crash victim.

Peary Discovers the North Pole

SEPTEMBER 7, 1909

In six words, Commander Robert E. Peary wired the news that he had succeeded, and survived: "I have the pole, April sixth." It had taken Peary—whose expedition had been underwritten by The Times—five months amid treacherous avalanches and ice floes to return to a base station from which he could tell the world. He was not the only one making a claim on the pole. Dr. Frederick A. Cook announced that he had been there a year earlier. Cook's claim was eventually discredited (and he was jailed as a con artist in another scam). More recent scholars have questioned whether, because of honest mistakes in tracking the journey, Peary himself fell short.

Triangle Fire Kills 146

MARCH 26, 1911

On a Sunday, just another workday in the sweatshops of New York, a fire engulfed the top floors of a building where immigrant workers made ladies' shirtwaists. The managers escaped to safety, but not the workers, who were trapped by doors left locked to keep them at their sewing machines. The building's only fire escape broke away from the façade, useless. Some of the workers joined hands and jumped to their deaths on the pavement below. The official death toll, on the ground and in the burned-out factory, was 146. In the aftermath, garment workers' unions rallied, demanding safer working conditions, and the city adopted tougher fire and building codes.

Standard Oil in Pieces

MAY 16, 1911

In ordering the breakup of Standard Oil, the United States Supreme Court busted the nation's No. 1 trust. Standard Oil was John D. Rockefeller's creation. For 40 years, it had had a near-total monopoly on oil, from drilling and refining to pumping and selling. The Supreme Court said Standard Oil had to be dissolved because it exercised "unreasonable" restraint on trade. Standard Oil was so big that to comply, it had to be spun off into more than 30 separate companies that were, at least on paper, independent of each other. Some were huge in their own right, among them the corporate ancestor of Exxon, before it merged with Mobil.

Sun Yat-Sen's Blueprint for Revolution

OCTOBER 14, 1911

The Chinese Revolution propelled Sun Yat-sen to power, if only briefly, and The Times explained how he had plotted the revolt, making "secret journeys to England and America" to raise money. As the Qing dynasty fell, he planted the seeds of modern Chinese nationalism, describing the country's main ethnic groups—the Han, Manchu, Hui, Mongolian and Tibetan peoples—as its "five fingers."

Roosevelt Shot Before a Speech

OCTOBER 15, 1912

Former President Theodore Roosevelt—running again, this time as a third-party Bull Moose candidate—was leaving a hotel in Milwaukee to go give a speech. John Nepomuk Schrank, a deranged New York saloonkeeper who had shadowed Roosevelt across eight states, shot him in the chest. Roosevelt delivered his speech in his blood-soaked shirt. Only then, more than 80 minutes later, did he go to a hospital. The doctors decided not to operate, leaving Roosevelt with a bullet in his chest for the rest of his life.

Marching for Women's Suffrage

NOVEMBER 10, 1912

A nighttime march down Fifth Avenue in New York was another milestone in the push for women's suffrage. Some 20,000 marchers carried pumpkin-shaped lanterns, and the crowd of spectators along the sidelines numbered up to half a million. "It was a wonderful spectacle," The Times said, but it would take another eight years for the 19th Amendment to be ratified, giving women the vote.

Scott Dies at the South Pole

FEBRUARY 11, 1913

On the far frontier that was Antarctica, Captain Robert F. Scott reached the South Pole, only to discover that someone else had beaten him to it—the Norwegian explorer Roald Amundsen. Returning to his base, Scott died on the ice in temperatures of minus 40 degrees Centigrade. He was 10 miles from a depot where he would have found food and fuel. "We are weak," he wrote in his last message. "Writing is difficult. . . . These rough notes and our dead bodies must tell the tale."

Mrs. Pankhurst Deported

OCTOBER 19, 1913

The British suffragette Emmeline Pankhurst had been in and out of British jails often—her rap sheet included arson and vandalism tied to feminist protests. Edwardian Britain did not know what to make of her, and neither did Wilsonian America. When she arrived in New York in her sealskin coat, officials ordered her deported as an undesirable alien. As she left, she borrowed a line from, of all people, Patrick Henry: "Our motto is, 'Give us the vote or give us death.'"

Ford Raises Wages to $5 a Day

JANUARY 6, 1914

Henry Ford had a better idea for his workers: double their pay, to $5 a day. The business world was aghast, but he said they deserved it because Model T's were rolling off the assembly line in record numbers—one every 20 seconds or so. Soon thousands of job applicants were swarming at the factory gate—so many the police had to be called in when unrest flared. Ford stuck to his populism. "We believe in making 20,000 men prosperous and contented," he said, "rather than following the plan of making a few slave drivers in our establishment millionaires."

A Tougher Anti-Trust Law

APRIL 15, 1914

Teddy Roosevelt and the trust-busters had put the 1890 Sherman Anti-Trust Act to use. But President Woodrow Wilson wanted more regulatory power over monopolists. Congress answered Wilson with the Clayton Act, which took aim at interlocking boards of directors that gave a handful of moguls (and their friends) control over the companies that distributed and sold their goods. A second bill established what became the Federal Trade Commission.

"All the News That's Fit to Print."

The New York Times.

THE WEATHER.
Rain or snow, followed by fair; much colder, with a cold wave.

VOL. XLVII...NO. 15,008. NEW YORK, WEDNESDAY, FEBRUARY 16, 1898.—TWELVE PAGES. PRICE THREE CENTS.

THE NEWS CONDENSED.

Stock market strong.

Cash wheat, No. 2 red, $1.05⅝; cash corn, No. 2 mixed, 37⅝c.; cash cotton, 6⅛c.

CONGRESS.—The Senate yesterday adopted a resolution calling on the Attorney General for information as to the coming sale of the Kansas Pacific Railroad. The Attorney General promptly furnished the information called for. The House passed a bill regulating loans to officers of National banks.—Page 3.

FOREIGN—Lord William Nevill, fourth son of the Marquis of Abergavenny, was sentenced in London to five years' penal servitude for forgery. The Indian frontier war was discussed in the House of Commons. The Russian charge at Pekin discussed the question of the Southern Manchurian Railway with the Tsung-li-Yamen. The Ambassadors at Constantinople are trying to arrange for the autonomous Government of Crete without a provisional Governor. S. W. Rudolph of Philadelphia, an artist, expired at sea on the Aller, and was buried at Gibraltar. The British battleship Victorious is still aground at Port Said.—Page 7.

Page 1.

Fire of unknown origin destroyed the West End Hotel and seven cottages at Rockaway Beach.

The Classis of Kingston removed the Rev. Chandler A. Oakes as pastor of the Fair Street Reformed Church.

C. H. Rutherford of New York was arrested on the American Line steamer St. Louis at Newport News for passing a spurious check for $75 drawn on the Chemical National Bank of New York.

Handwriting experts at Zola's trial in Paris expressed the opinion that Count Esterhazy was the author of the bordereau, the writing which Dreyfus is serving a life sentence on Devil's Island.

It is reported that the Canadian Government has dispatched a note to Washington threatening to exclude Americans from the Klondike in case of hostile legislation by the United States.

A. J. Bowie, a mining engineer in the employ of James R. Keene, draws a dark picture of the outlook at the Klondike. Supplies, skilled miners, and machinery are wanting, he says, for successful work this year.

The proposed law taxing bachelors in New Jersey has brought to light a unique bachelors' club, which has hitherto been unknown to all but the initiated. Its objects are to promote gallantry toward the fair sex and discourage matrimony.

Señor Dupuy de Lome, the ex-Minister to the United States from Spain, with his family, reached the city last night en route for Spain. He declined to talk for publication, and was driven at once to the Hotel St. Marc. Two detectives from the Central Office met him as he landed from the Pennsylvania Railroad's ferryboat and remained on duty at the hotel all night. Señor de Lome and his party will sail to-day on the Britannic.

Page 2.

The Grand Trunk Railway is said to have purchased land near Toledo, which will give it an entrance into that city.

Contracts are said to have been made with the railroads to carry the greater part of Leiter's wheat holdings from Chicago to the seaboard. The Chicago market was strong yesterday.

It was said yesterday that the first of the four vessels being constructed for the American Mail Steamship Company will be ready in August, and that the new line will engage in the fruit trade between Jamaica and other West Indian points and the United States.

Page 3.

Arguments in favor of woman's suffrage were presented to the Senate and House committees in Washington by leading members of the National Woman Suffrage Association.

James B. Angell, United States Minister to Turkey, has announced his intention to resign in time to resume his duties as President of the University of Michigan next Fall.

Pay Director Luther G. Billings, United States Navy, has been convicted by a court-martial of falsehood and scandalous conduct, and sentenced to dismissal from the navy.

Addresses to the silver men of the country urging united action in coming elections have been issued by the Democratic and Populist and Silver Republican National Committees.

Proposals were opened in Washington for carrying the mails to Jamaica. The American Mail Steamship Company of New Jersey proposes to furnish four new American twin-screw vessels for 6⅔ cents per statute mile.

Commissioner Evans admitted the justice of THE NEW YORK TIMES's account of the abuses in the Pension Office. Reform in the selection and employment of clerks as well as a transfer of the bureau to the War Department have been proposed, but are not popular with Congress.

Page 4.

The old steamboat Narragansett, which has been fitted as a houseboat for detained immigrants, arrived at Ellis Island yesterday from Groton, Conn.

It is understood at Albany that the Democratic leaders propose next Fall to separate the State and Congressional campaigns, so that the fight for State officers and the Legislature shall be made on State issues and the fights in the Congressional districts on issues drawn to suit the conditions in each district. On the other hand, it is stated that the Republican leaders propose to make their fight chiefly on the financial issue.

The State Senate yesterday discussed the proposed Constitutional amendment providing for biennial sessions of the Legislature. There was a hearing before the Senate Cities Committee on the Brush bill relating to the Board of Health. Many bills of local interest were introduced in both houses, and others were reported favorably by committees. The Judiciary Committees of the Senate and Assembly will hold a joint meeting to-day to begin the preparation of a primary election bill.

Page 5.

A waiter's version of the story told by Beck of loaning $10 to Noonan, taking his cuff as security, tended to discredit the testimony given by Beck.

The twelfth annual convention of the American Newspaper Publishers' Association will begin its sessions at the Waldorf-Astoria this morning.

The Executive Committee of the Insurance Tariff Association will meet to-day and frame its recommendation in reference to the maintenance of rates.

Mrs. Clara Baldwin, daughter-in-law of William S. Baldwin, has had him committed for examination as to his sanity. He imagines, she says, that he is Napoleon's son.

George Richards, an old man, was killed at a Newark crossing by a fast train. He had warned the railroad previously that the place was inadequately guarded and dangerous.

Serious trouble was narrowly averted at a game of basket ball between a team of New Rochelle players and Connecticut Guardsmen. A rival local club annoyed the home team.

A girl from Rockland Lake died of rabies in Roosevelt Hospital. She is said last Summer to have fondled a dog afflicted with the disease, the saliva coming in contact with her chapped hands.

There was a large attendance yesterday at the auction sale of trotters and pacers in progress at Madison Square Garden, but the bidding lacked spirit, and a number of well-bred and speedy animals were knocked down at low prices.

The Board of Home Missions of the Presbytery held a special meeting yesterday, at which the Rev. Charles L. Thompson of the Madison Avenue Presbyterian Church was formally accepted as Secretary, to succeed the Rev. William C. Roberts.

John Moje, a Third Avenue saloon keeper, was fleeced of $200 in Philadelphia by three men. He says that he and his manager came up with one of the men and walked him about for six hours before he found a policeman, who arrested the man. Mr. Moje says a cigar he smoked dazed him.

Patrick Vaughan, the policeman who shot and wounded John Lawler, was discharged yesterday in Morrisania Police Court. Lawler pleaded for the officer. He said it was all his own fault, and vowed that he would live a better life in future, whereupon he was also discharged.

Nearly 700 covers, it is expected, will be laid at the banquet of the Merchants and Manufacturers' Board of Trade of New York, which will be held at the Waldorf-Astoria on Tuesday. The various industries and trades will be grouped at separate tables. Several United States Senators and Representatives will be present. A Reception Committee was appointed last night.

Page 7.

Charles L. Tiffany, who was eighty-six years old yesterday, received the congratulations of many old employes, some of whom have been with him for over forty years.

At a meeting of musical people at the home of Mr. and Mrs. A. W. Drake yesterday afternoon it was decided that the project to establish here a permanent orchestra should be energetically carried out. A committee will be appointed to raise the necessary amount, $1,000,000. There is already $115,000 in hand.

Page 9.

Opposition to the proposed combination of Western tin-plate manufacturers is developing in several quarters. New York dealers regard the scheme as impracticable.

A meeting of committees representing the Rapid Transit Commissioners and the Manhattan Railway Company was held, but a strict silence was maintained as to their proceedings.

Page 12.

Frank Moss denied yesterday the statement that the Society for the Prevention of Crime contemplates legal action against the promotion of William S. Devery to be Deputy Chief of Police.

The model tenement houses on Sixty-eighth and Sixty-ninth Streets, west of Amsterdam Avenue, were opened yesterday for inspection. One is ready for occupancy, and the first tenant will move in to-day.

Chairman Maxwell of the Brooklyn Committee of the Board of Education appeared before the Board of Estimate yesterday and asked for an allowance to pay the teachers for January. They will probably be paid Friday or Monday.

At the third monthly conference held under the auspices of the Charity Organization Society yesterday, the conditions of life of poor children in the city were discussed and the work done and in progress in their behalf was described. The necessity for more small parks in the congested districts was insisted upon, and examples were cited demonstrating the beneficial effects of rural surroundings upon health and morals.

Miss Dellaripha Richardson, daughter of the "Spite House" millionaire, appeared in Surrogate Fitzgerald's court yesterday during the hearing of the contest of her father's will brought by her brother and herself, made mysterious charges of murder and conspiracy, including the Surrogate in her accusations, and then went away. The evidence regarding Mr. Richardson's sanity when he made the will in dispute was concluded.

At yesterday's meeting of the City Council a resolution was introduced to compel department stores to pay a license of $500 a year for each department; another to investigate the price and quality of gas in various parts of the city, and a third contained a protest against the usurpation of municipal functions by the State Legislature. All were referred to committees. A protest from Queens against the centralization of all municipal power in Manhattan received scant courtesy from the Aldermen at their meeting.

Arrivals at Hotels and Out-of-Town Buyers.—Page 3.
Amusements.—Pages 6 and 7.
Marine Intelligence.—Page 2.
New Corporations.—Page 9.
Business Troubles.—Page 9.
Yesterday's Fires.—Page 2.
Insurance Notes.—Page 5.
Court Calendars.—Page 10.
Losses by Fire.—Page 2.
United Service.—Page 5.
Real Estate.—Page 10.
Legal Notices.—Page 5.
Railroads.—Page 2.

FIRE AT ROCKAWAY BEACH.

The West End Hotel and Seven Cottages Destroyed by Flames of Unknown Origin.

The West End Hotel and seven cottages at Rockaway Beach were destroyed by fire which started shortly after 11 o'clock last night in the hotel. The hotel was a four-story frame structure at the corner of Grove, Hammels, and Ocean Avenues. It contained 200 rooms and was owned by Paul Hauk, who lives in Seventy-fifth Street. He purchased it three years ago, paying $70,000 for it. He has since made extensive repairs and largely refurnished it.

The building was being repainted, and painters were at work in the building during the day. There was no one in the building when the fire started. The flames appeared to have spread through a large portion of the frame building when discovered. The fire was seen simultaneously by two policemen and a life saver.

When the volunteer firemen of Arverne, Hammels, and Rockaway Beach reached the building it was a mass of flame, and they turned their attention to the cottages, some of which were even then burning. Nothing was saved from the hotel. Four of the cottages were partially saved.

KINGSTON PREACHER REMOVED.

The Rev. C. A. Oakes No Longer Pastor of the Fair Street Reformed Church—He Will Appeal.

KINGSTON, Feb. 15.—The Classis of Kingston, after a special session which began yesterday morning and ended this afternoon, decided to dissolve the relations existing between the Rev. Chandler A. Oakes, Ph. D., and the Fair Street Reformed Church. Charges had been brought against Dr. Oakes by the consistory to the effect that the spiritual and financial condition of the church would be bettered by his dismissal. The case was summed up this afternoon for the consistory by the Rev. Dr. Oggel and by Dr. Oakes for himself. The Classis then retired, and after a deliberation of half an hour returned a verdict that the pastoral relations between Dr. Oakes and the church be dissolved on March 1. The vote of the Classis was 15 to 4.

Dr. Oakes is to be allowed to occupy the parsonage until April 1, and will be paid his salary up to June 1. The verdict was received in silence. Dr. Oakes announced his determination to appeal to the Synod, and said that he considered the offer of salary until June 1 as adding insult to injury.

"It is trying to bribe a man for a few hundred dollars, when life, honor, and justice are at stake," he said. This statement was received with applause. Moderator Davis stated that it would take twenty days for an appeal, and until that time the decision of Classis would stand as to the pastoral relations.

A committee, composed of Dr. Oggel, the Rev. Mr. McNair, Dr. Oakes's counsel, and the Rev. Herman Hageman, was appointed to revise the stenographer's minutes for the appeal. Dr. Oakes says he will preach in the church.

MISS DEANS'S CLAIM ON TRIAL.

Aged Witness Heard in the Suit for a Share of the Stewart Estate.

The actual trial of the suit brought by Miss Euphemia Deans against, ex-Judge Henry Hilton to recover a one-sixth interest in the old A. T. Stewart property at Thirty-fourth Street and Madison Avenue, was begun before Justice Scott.

Miss Deans, who is a school teacher, claims that through her mother she is one of the next of kin to the late A. T. Stewart. Her mother, Mary Bailey Deans, she contends, was an aunt of the dead millionaire. Judge Hilton denies the relationship.

The most important witness was James Bailey, eighty-six years old, who said he came to this country from Ireland on May 4, 1838. He said that when he came to this city in 1838 he met Mr. Stewart, to whom he had a letter of introduction from his mother, Mrs. Martin, and that Mr. Stewart spoke of him as the son of "his Aunt Mary." This testimony was intended to show the relationship between the plaintiff and her relatives in Europe. The case will go on.

The Southwestern Limited.

A fast limited train to St. Louis and Cincinnati without an excess fare, via New York Central-Lake Shore and Big Four route. Most comfortable train; leaves Grand Central Station—fourth of the Hudson River—every day at 1:00 P. M.—Adv.

ESTERHAZY IN THE TOILS

Handwriting Experts at Zola's Trial Affirm that He Was the Author of the Bordereau.

MME. DE BOULANCEY A FACTOR

She Received Letters from Esterhazy Animadverting on France and the Army—His Statements Startle the Court.

PARIS, Feb. 15.—The Zola trial will be concluded this week, according to programme, although it is expected that at least one night session will be necessary to get through on Saturday. So successful have been the efforts of M. Zola and his counsel, M. Laborie, to shatter the position taken by the Ministry on the Dreyfus case that already there are many who feel that Zola's acquittal is certain. When it is taken into consideration that the court was convened for the express purpose of securing a conviction, and that this seemed to be a foregone conclusion at the start, some idea may be obtained of the effect which the trial has had on public opinion in Paris. Even the Court itself, so bitterly hostile at the start, shows every day more and more evidence of being favorably disposed toward Zola. But this, of course, is no assurance that he will not be convicted by the Court.

It was rumored in the lobbies of the court to-day that MM. Laborie and Clemenceau are prolonging the examination of the witnesses in order to extend the trial, in the hope that the question of a revision of the Dreyfus trial will come before the Chamber of Deputies, now that it is generally admitted that Dreyfus was convicted on a secret document, and in the hope that something will happen in their favor.

While the examination of the experts proved rather tiresome, the fitnesses of their methods has turned favor toward Zola, and the mute sulkiness of the Advocate General is a strong indication of how matters are going.

To-day Col. Picquart seemed to come in for the hostility hitherto reserved for M. Zola. Mlle. Comminge's deposition tended to show that Lieut. Col. Paty du Clam wrote the telegrams, signed "Speranza," which were sent to Col. Picquart while he was in Tunis, with the intention to frighten him from following the Esterhazy trail. Col. Picquart's testimony created a deep impression.

It is said to-night that Commandant Ravary, who compiled the unsatisfactory report for the Esterhazy trial, has had a sudden attack of congestion of the brain. There were several quarrels outside the court to-day. In one case two barristers had a hand-to-hand fight.

High Prices Paid for Seats.

The visible excitement caused by the trial has greatly abated, but the real interest is absorbing and grows daily. The courtroom is packed, although the price of seats paid to those ready to wait all night to secure places has risen from 5f. to 25f.

Count Esterhazy will be examined to-morrow, so that this interest will be still higher, just as to-day's evidence exceeded yesterday's in exciting qualities.

When the trial is finished the discussion will be moved to the Chamber of Deputies and the Senate, where the Cabinet will be on its trial. There are still thirteen witnesses to be examined, and then will come the addresses of the Advocate General, M. Van Cassel; M. Laborie, and M. Clemenceau. M. Laborie is expected to speak four or five hours. M. Zola will speak very briefly.

The crowd present at the opening of the trial to-day was not so large as yesterday, and Zola's arrival at the court was not marked by any incident.

At the opening of the proceedings the Presiding Judge, M. Delegorgue, disallowed the request of counsel for M. Zola, M. Laborie, that the experts heard at the Esterhazy court-martial should be called to testify.

Gen. Gonse reappeared on the witness stand and protested against the assertion made by M. Jaures, the Socialist Deputy, on Saturday last, that the General Staff had refused to enlighten the Dreyfus affair.

M. Laborie, replying to Gen. Gonse, said that if he desired to throw light upon the case he could ask the War Minister's permission to do so.

To this Gen. Gonse answered that it was not within his province to transmit such a request to the Minister for War.

M. Crepieux Janin, a handwriting expert, was the next witness. He strenuously denied M. Teyssonnière's statement, made by the latter, who is also an expert in handwriting, to the effect that he had attempted to bribe M. Teyssonnière to modify his report of the Dreyfus bordereau.

M. Teyssonnière, M. Crepieux Janin added, had declared that it was on his (M. Teyssonnière's) report alone and not on M. Bertillon's that Dreyfus was convicted. This statement created a sensation.

M. Janin added that it was because M. Teyssonnière was angry with the witness for not sharing his opinion in regard to the Dreyfus case that he tried to compromise the matter. The witness further said he was a Frenchman and a Catholic, and exercised the profession of a dentist, and did not exercise the profession of an expert in handwriting.

M. Laborie Overruled by the Court.

Director Meyer of the French Record Office opened his testimony by affirming himself a Catholic. He declared that the published fac similes of the bordereau were as exact as possible, and he thought that Gen. Pellieux's contention that the fac similes looked like forgeries was an exaggeration. The witness added that he only desired an enlightenment of this sad affair, and if he was allowed to compare the fac similes with the original, if mistaken he would loyally say so. Continuing, the witness admitted that he had acted wrongly in refusing the examination of the bordereau to M. Bertillon, who, the witness asserted, had acted in a manner devoid of all sense.

M. Meyer concluded with saying that the handwriting of Major Esterhazy resembled that of the bordereau.

M. Laborie then asked permission to examine the experts Couard, Belhomme, and Varinard, but the Court refused the request, upon which M. Laborie drew up conclusions, asking the Court to take cognizance of the fact. But the Presiding Judge, before even hearing the question, refused to let it be put, after which the Court retired to deliberate and decided that the Presiding Judge was right in refusing to allow questions "the only effect of which would be uselessly to prolong the proceedings."

Prof. Ernest Molinier of the College of France testified that Major Esterhazy's handwriting absolutely resembled that of the bordereau.

M. Clémenceau, counsel for the Aurore, read letters from Mme. de Boulancey admitting the possession of letters which Major Esterhazy wrote her between 1881 and 1884, and containing serious animadversions on France and the French Army. Major Esterhazy, it appeared, asked that the letters be returned to him; but Mme. de Boulancey refused to do so, in order to be able to prove that she had not committed forgery.

M. Clémenceau urged the Court to appoint a magistrate to ask Mme. de Boulancey if, among the letters, there was not one containing the following expressions:

"First—Gen. Saussier [then the Commander in Chief of the French Army and Military Governor of Paris] is a clown. In our country the Germans would not show him in a circus." [Uproar in court.]

"Second—If the Prussians got as far as Lyons, they might throw away their guns and keep only their riding whips to drive the French in front of them.'" [Prolonged sensation.]

Blackboard for Demonstration.

Three amateur experts in handwriting testified that the fac simile was an exact reproduction of Major Esterhazy's handwriting, statements which caused further sensations in court.

M. Felix Frank, a lawyer of Brussels, testified that in order to demonstrate his evidence it would be necessary to have a blackboard, and that it would require an hour to demonstrate his theory.

Amid an uproar in court the session was suspended while a blackboard was procured and placed on an easel, after which M. Frank traced on the blackboard a fac simile of the bordereau and of Major Esterhazy's handwriting, and commenced his demonstration.

M. Frank made some long technical demonstrations and said:

"The majority of the experts started on the false idea that the writer of the bordereau had disguised his handwriting. The bordereau, however, was written naturally and in a running hand, which is identical with that of Major Esterhazy."

The latter, continued the witness, had recognized the bordereau as being his own handwriting, but had declared it had been traced by a forger. M. Frank proceeded technically to demonstrate the improbability of this explanation, showing how recurring words presented certain divergencies.

The lengthy demonstration of the witness caused impatience among the public in court, culminating in open murmurs, when M. Frank affirmed that the bordereau was written by one person alone, and added that this person was Major Esterhazy.

Annoyed at the murmurs, M. Frank turned and cried:

"I intended to end there, but since I am interrupted I will continue."

The Presiding Judge here remarked:

"I will ask you to use different language than that, which is discourteous."

M. Laborie thereupon intervened, asking the Presiding Judge to order silence in the court, pointing out that the lawyers were following the evidence with the closest attention.

"I am convinced," M. Frank resumed, "that the writer of the bordereau has a German mind."

The witness concluded with predicting that some day it would be recognized that the bordereau was not written by Dreyfus, which remark was greeted with murmurs.

The blackboard was then removed, and Prof. Grimaud of the Polytechnic School deposed that he signed the protests against the conduct of the Dreyfus affair because he was convinced that respect for the law, honor, and the fatherland was involved. The whole procedure struck this witness as being extraordinary. He added:

"In spite of the disguised threats and acts of intimidation of which I have been the victim, I here affirm that a revision of the case is a crying necessity, and I intend to do my utmost to obtain it."

The witness concluded with asserting his rights as a patriot and his love for the army, which brought forth hearty applause.

Prof. Havet of the College of France said he formerly was an expert, the bordereau and the letters of Major Esterhazy and Dreyfus, as well as a letter written by Dreyfus since his condemnation. The latter, the witness continued, was devoid of resemblance to the bordereau, of which he was convinced Major Esterhazy was the author.

Court was then adjourned. The crowd made no demonstration, and the officers, including Major Esterhazy and Gen. Pellieux, left amid silence.

At the Cabinet council to-day the trial of M. Zola and the publisher of Aurora was under discussion.

ARRESTED ON THE ST. LOUIS.

C. H. Rutherford in Custody at Newport News for Passing a Spurious Check on the Chemical Bank.

NEWPORT NEWS, Feb. 15.—A man representing himself to be C. H. Rutherford of New York, was arrested by Chief of Police Harwood on board the American Line steamship St. Louis this afternoon, charged with passing a spurious check for $75. Rutherford has been stopping at the Hygeia Hotel, at Old Point, for a week or two. He spent money freely, mingling among the guests of the hotel and the officers at Fort Monroe and soon became well acquainted. Saturday he requested Harry Phoebus, a druggist at Old Point, to cash a check for $75, drawn on the Chemical National Bank of New York. After placing the money to Rutherford Phoebus became suspicious, and telegraphed to the bank for information as to his responsibility.

He received a reply pronouncing the check worthless. Rutherford came to this city, and to-day he went to the shipyard where the St. Louis is tied up for repairs, and requested permission to inspect the vessel. While walking about the big liner he was confronted by the Chief of Police. He attempted to elude the officer, but was soon arrested. Rutherford is now in jail at Hampton. He will be tried as soon as the check is returned from New York. The incident has created a sensation at the hotel, where Rutherford made himself quite popular. It is understood that he swindled several military officers at the fort out of small sums of money.

A UNIQUE JERSEY CLUB.

Its Object Is to Promote Gallantry Toward the Fair Sex and Discourage Matrimony.

TRENTON, N. J., Feb. 15.—The bill introduced by Assemblyman Weller of this city to tax bachelors has brought to light the Bachelors' Club of Trenton. Although the club is one of the oldest in the State, it was not known that such an organization existed until it was forced to announce itself and to formally protest against the passage of the bill now pending. The object of the club as disclosed by its by-laws is rather unique. It is to widen the scope and increase the possibilities of gallantry, and at the same time discourage the seemingly inevitable result of the law of association between persons of opposite sex, namely, matrimony.

Article VII. of the constitution sets forth the principles upon which the club is founded, and is as follows:

"Section 1. No member of the Bachelors' Club shall call upon any one friend among the gentler sex, nor escort her to entertainments or social functions, except in case of formal invitation, oftener than once a month; and it is hereby made mandatory that each member shall call upon, escort to entertainments or social functions, or show some direct gallantry to friends of the gentler sex upon at least three separate and distinct occasions in each month.

"Sec. 2. Violation or disregard of the preceding section shall, after due hearing before the Executive Committee, be deemed sufficient cause for dismissal from membership."

The rigidity of this regulation has had the effect of depleting the membership from time to time, and has, to an extent, discouraged new acquisitions, but, despite this fact, the club has flourished and become popular. John Hartpence of the Supreme Court office has been President of the club since its organization, early in 1891, and J. Harry Woodruff has been Secretary and Treasurer. It is authoritatively stated that Senator Edward C. Stokes of Cumberland will be added shortly to the membership of the club.

MR. HOYT SUED FOR $10,000.

E. G. Bates Asks Damages in Boston as a Result of a Word War.

BOSTON, Feb. 15.—The trial of a suit for $10,000 damages against Charles H. Hoyt, playwright and ex-member of the New Hampshire Legislature, was begun before Judge Sherman and a jury in the Second Session of the Suffolk Superior Court this afternoon.

The suit is brought by Edwin G. Bates, a member of the firm of Bates & Rendis, music publishers, for alleged injuries to character and reputation. Mr. Bates is also musical director of the Castle Square Theatre. Mr. Bates alleges in his suit that in the Park Theatre one night Mr. Hoyt called him a liar and in an uncomfortable tone of voice added a boisterous, loud, and blasphemous tirade of words. He adds that this took place before a large concourse of people and in the presence of ladies, and that Mr. Hoyt after exhausting his vocabulary spit upon him.

It was alleged that Mr. Hoyt continued his talk at the bar of the Hotel Reynolds when Mr. Bates was not present. Mr. Bates says that he has been greatly injured in his feelings and put to great mental suffering, and asks $10,000 damages.

The trouble grew out of a controversy over the song "Sweet Daisy Stokes," which was sung by Otis Harlan in the play "The Black Sheep."

Mr. Hoyt says that any words spoken to the plaintiff were not publicly uttered or published, and were justified and proper, in that they were true.

Mr. Hoyt was in the court room accompanied by Fred Wright, his manager.

Mardi Gras—New Orleans, La.

35 hours New York to New Orleans via Southern Railway Limited, leaving New York 4:20 P. M., dining and sleeping cars. Fast Mail 12:05 midnight, through sleeping cars. Excursion tickets on sale Feby. 16th to 21st—Reduced rates. New York office, 271 Broadway.—Adv.

DARK TALE FROM KLONDIKE

A. J. Bowie, James R. Keene's Engineer, Says There Are Few Miners There.

EXORBITANT PRICES FOR FOOD

Many Men Drowned in the Ice Floe on the Way—Famine Sure to Kill Many Laborers—Corporations Needed for Good Work.

SAN FRANCISCO, Feb. 15.—A letter has been received from Augustus J. Bowie, a mining engineer sent to the Klondike by James R. Keene in the interests of a New York syndicate, dated at Dawson Jan. 3. After stating that the cold is 20 degrees below zero, with no wind, he says meat is sold at $1.50 per pound wholesale, and flour at $135 for a sack of fifty pounds. Men are paid $1.50 an hour who are not worth that much per diem. "Without exception," he says, "there are fewer mining men than in any other place I was ever in. They have not the slightest conception of mining. The only wonder to me is the fact that the place has been able to exist as long as it has under the terrible prices demanded for everything.

"People in San Francisco and elsewhere cannot conceive the condition of affairs here. Absolutely nothing is to be obtained, and it will be fully two years before the mines can be handled as they should be, on account of the want of ordinary essentials for work, let alone living. Wood sells at $50 per cord. There is plenty of it, but no means for quick or easy transportation. The mines are certainly extraordinarily rich, but the present system of work must be largely or entirely abandoned.

"Corporations must take hold and clean out the crowd of good-for-nothings." A new era will dawn. The Alaska Commercial Company and North American Transportation and Trading Company are the only two business concerns here, where there is ample room for more, if transportation lines were established. Situated as these companies are, they will throw every obstacle in the way of any and every body coming in to compete with them, and thus keep up their sales. They will slowly but surely absorb all the gold output by charging infamous prices for supplies. The Alaska Commercial Company during the present famine has never raised prices on any staple article and has been very just, but when the North American Transportation and Trading Company finds that the Alaska Commercial Company has sold out any article, it raises the price 300 per cent. or more. Coal oil is $40 per gallon, candles fetch $1 each, and are esteemed a luxury. The restaurants are closed up, as are the bakers, and choice bacon is a thing of the past. The poorest whisky, made on the spot, commands $5 a bottle, and you can buy but little at that figure.

"Light just now is the most important thing. One cannot buy candles or oil now for love or money. I have spent only one night in town, as the place is absolutely too disgusting for anything. Gin mills, women, dance houses, and gambling dens are everywhere.

"There is not the slightest doubt that many a poor fellow died en route here, and will yet move here. That is, a man who came in the other day by way of Dyea told me that on the way down he saw men's arms sticking out of the ice. Their bodies were out of sight. They were grasping oars, planks, and pieces of wood, which they had grabbed as they were drowning in the ice floe. The famine here cannot be pictured in too awful form. Soon the fuel will give out. Men cannot work without food, and there is no food for wood cutters. Some large strikes have been made on Eastern parties, $324,000 having been paid for three claims on Bonanza Creek, and $24,000 for two others. Twenty have been bought on Eldorado Creek for $100,000.

"Sulphur and Dominion Creeks now offer the best advantage for the money. The yield of all claims will, I think, be less than last year, as there are no supplies here, labor or materials to work with, and famine is sure to kill off many laborers. If I do not starve to death I shall be very lucky."

CANADA WILL RETALIATE.

Hostile Washington Legislation to be Met by Exclusion of Americans from the Klondike.

MONTREAL, Feb. 15.—A special dispatch from Ottawa says that the Dominion Government this afternoon dispatched a communication to Washington stating the determination of Canada, in the event of the passage by Congress of the bill introduced in the House by Mr. Payne and in the Senate by Senator Frye, to issue a proclamation barring all but British subjects from the right to mine in the Klondike or other Canadian territory in the Yukon region. The contents of the note, it is added, probably will be laid before the American Government by the British Ambassador, Sir Julian Pauncefote.

No official announcement has been made by the Government of the dispatch of such a note, but neither is it denied, and the general belief is that the step has been taken. There has been considerable agitation in favor of a move of this nature by the Canadian Government, and for some days the Government press has been hinting that it might have to come to that.

Sir Wilfrid Laurier and his Cabinet have been much annoyed at the threatened blocking of the "all Canadian Railroad" project by legislation at Washington, and the taunts of the opposition in Parliament probably have determined the Government to carry its plans through at any cost. It is known that the United States in its customs regulations at Port Wrangell, the Canadian Government may abandon the proposed Stickeen River route and build the railroad from Port Simpson, which will bring it all in Canadian territory.

KLONDIKE RELIEF DELAYED.

SEATTLE, Washington, Feb. 15.—The three-masted ship Lucille, chartered by the Government to convey to Alaska the army pack train of twenty-two officers and men and 110 animals, was libeled for $6,000 today by the Alaska Forwarding Company of San Francisco. Five officers of this company are also owners of the Lucille. A contract was entered into with Havner & Co., owners of the Lucille, to land the expedition at Skaguay, where the company intends to establish a pack train to be used over White Pass.

On the arrival of the Lucille at this port, Havner & Co. contracted to take the Government expedition, which is the advance detachment of the Klondike relief party. One thing after another delayed the departure of the Lucille, culminating to-day, when the San Francisco company libeled the ship because it was found that there was no room for both parties, and that the private expedition was to be left on the dock. A deputy marshal was put in charge of the ship. It is expected that the matter will be settled so that the Lucille can sail some time to-night or in the morning.

LOSS OF THE CLARA NEVADA.

SEATTLE, Washington, Feb. 15.—No further news has been received concerning the reported loss of the steamer Clara Nevada in Alaskan waters. Owing to the many conflicting rumors, hope for her safety has not yet been abandoned. Unless some unexpected report is received, no definite news is expected before next Thursday.

The latest report was brought down by the steamer Excelsior, which arrived today. Capt. Donnelson said that just before he left Juneau the steamer Coleman arrived and reported that wreckage and bedding marked "Hassler" had been washed ashore at Seward. He said: "The Clara Nevada was formerly a Government vessel, known as the Hassler, and I have no doubt that she is at the bottom of the sea, at least such part of her as was not burned, for the Seward citizens report having seen a blazing vessel on the water."

The Excelsior arrived at Juneau five hours after the steamer Rosalie, which reported passing the Clara Nevada.

The New Pennsylvania Limited.

With its new equipment, the Pennsylvania Limited is the most complete and the handsomest train in the world. Leaves New York every morning for Cincinnati, Chicago, and St. Louis.—Adv.

LAKE FISHERMEN LOST.

Carried Off on the Ice into Lake Erie—Between Twenty and Thirty in the Party.

BUFFALO, Feb. 15.—A number of men, estimated at between twenty and thirty, who were fishing through the ice on Lake Erie several miles up the lake, are believed to have lost their lives or to be adrift on the ice on the lake.

A heavy wind blowing from the east caused the ice to break away from the shore, and nothing can now be seen or heard of the men.

A large rescue party is on the way through a blinding snowstorm up the lake shore, but will not return before morning.

TALE OF MURDER MYSTERY.

A Jamaica (L. I.) Contractor Arrested as a Result of a Child's Strange Story.

Robert Brower, a contractor of Jamaica, L. I., was arrested last night by the police of Queens Borough on the strength of a story told by Mrs. Eliza Jackson of 102 Smith Street and her daughter Helen, aged seven years. The daughter says that on the morning of July 11 of last year she saw Brower and a young man employed by him place the body of a colored man in a box and bury it in his back yard.

Brower at first denied to the police that he had a colored man working for him at the time, but later admitted it, and said the man had gone away. Mrs. Jackson said that a son of Brower told her some time after the alleged interment that their colored man, named John, had been kicked by a horse, and had died and was buried in the yard.

RIOTERS KILLED IN HUNGARY.

Village Held Against Troops Sent to Restore Order—The Agrarian Socialist Movement.

VIENNA, Feb. 15.—The Agrarian Socialist movement in Hungary is becoming most serious. At Kistelek, in the Kaschau District, a thousand peasants are in open revolt. They have murdered the local magistrate, and are holding the village against the troops sent to restore order.

At Agrad, in the same district, in a desperate fight between the gendarmes and the peasants, four were killed and twenty wounded.

At Karasz the Socialists tried to liberate their imprisoned comrades, and the gendarmes were obliged to prevent an onset with leveled bayonets. A woman tried to wrest his rifle from a gendarme, and the latter stabbed her in the breast. She fell dead.

There have been many arrests and much disorder in other districts. At Szathmar a riot has been suppressed. The sale of gunpowder has been prohibited in the disturbed localities, and nobody is allowed out of doors after 7 in the evening without a special permit. There is talk of proclaiming a siege.

HANNA BRIBERY CHARGES.

C. C. Shayne Declines to Go to Ohio as a Witness.

C. C. Shayne, who was asked to appear as a witness before the committee of the Ohio Senate, which is investigating the bribery charges in connection with the election of Senator Hanna, has sent the following reply:

New York, Feb. 15, 1898.

Hon. Newman H. Burke, Chairman Senate Committee, Columbus, Ohio:

Engagements until after the London fur sales in March will prevent me from accepting your kind invitation. If, however, you desire a chapter for your Ohio political history, I refer you to my statements already published in the leading journals; or you can send a committee here, to whom every courtesy will be extended.

C. C. SHAYNE.

WEDDING OF MISS HANNA.

The Ohio Senator's Sister Married to a Young Man of Cleveland.

THOMASVILLE, Ga., Feb. 15.—Miss Lillian C. Hanna, the sister of Senator Hanna of Ohio, was married here this evening to S. Prentiss Baldwin of Cleveland.

The ceremony was performed at the country residence of Mrs. J. Wyman Jones, a sister of Miss Hanna, by the Rev. Mr. Whitney, rector of St. Thomas's Church of this city.

In addition to the family, those present were Gov. and Mrs. Merriam of Minnesota, Mr. and Mrs. Arthur Ely and M. A. C. Horse of Chicago, and Mr. and Mrs. Haskell of Cleveland.

Mr. Baldwin is twenty-eight years old; his bride is forty-five.

Glut of Money in Louisville.

LOUISVILLE, Ky., Feb. 15.—Owing to the money plethora the Louisville Clearing House Association has decided to reduce interest paid country correspondents from 2½ to 2 per cent. after March 1. The average balances of Louisville banks held for country correspondents is $10,000,000. Two years ago the banks paid 3 per cent. for country balances.

THE WEATHER.

The local forecast may be found at the top of this page to the right of the title.

The storm of Monday night in Illinois has moved very rapidly to New Jersey, increasing in intensity, a pressure of 29.34 inches being reported from Block Island and a northwest wind of sixty miles an hour from Norfolk. This storm has caused snow or rain from the Middle and Upper Mississippi Valley to the Atlantic Coast and violent gales in the lower lake region. A second storm of considerable intensity has appeared to the north of Montana. It has grown colder from the interior of the Middle and North Atlantic States to the Rocky Mountains.

The record of temperature for the twenty-four hours ended at midnight, taken from THE NEW YORK TIMES's thermometer and from the thermometer of the Weather Bureau, is as follows:

	—Weather Bureau.— 1897.	1898.	—TIMES. 1898.
3 A. M.	38	37	38
6 A. M.	37	33	36
9 A. M.	41	34	41
12 M.	45	37	42
3 P. M.	43	41	40
6 P. M.	39	40	38
9 P. M.	35	35	38
12 P. M.	32	39	39

THE TIMES's thermometer is 6 feet above the street level; that of the Weather Bureau is 285 feet above the street level.

Average temperatures yesterday were as follows:

Printing House Square....39¼
Weather Bureau....37¾
Corresponding date 1897....39¾
Corresponding date for last 20 years....32

The maximum temperature yesterday was 40 degrees at 1 P. M.; the minimum was 32 degrees at 4 A. M. The humidity at 8 A. M. was .73, and at 8 P. M., .93.

Poland! Poland! Poland!

The purest natural diuretic; positive cure. Physicians prescribe it. Circulars mailed (gratis). Poland Water Depot, 3 Park Place, near Broadway, New York.—Adv.

THE MAINE BLOWN UP.

Terrible Explosion on Board the United States Battleship in Havana Harbor.

MANY PERSONS KILLED AND WOUNDED.

All the Boats of the Spanish Cruiser Alfonso XII. Assisting in the Work of Relief.

None of the Wounded Men Able to Give Any Explanation of the Cause of the Disaster.

HAVANA, Feb. 15.—At 9:45 o'clock this evening a terrible explosion took place on board the United States battleship Maine in Havana Harbor.

Many persons were killed or wounded. All the boats of the Spanish cruiser Alfonso XII. are assisting.

As yet the cause of the explosion is not apparent. The wounded sailors of the Maine are unable to explain it. It is believed that the battleship is totally destroyed.

The explosion shook the whole city. The windows were broken in nearly all the houses.

The correspondent of the Associated Press says he has conversed with several of the wounded sailors and understands from them that the explosion took place while they were asleep, so that they can give no particulars as to the cause.

WHAT SENOR DE LOME SAYS.

He Declares That No Spaniard Would Be Guilty of Causing Such a Disaster.

Señor de Lome, the departing ex-Minister of Spain to this country, who arrived in this city last night, and went to the Hotel St. Marc, at Fifth Avenue and Thirty-ninth Street, was awakened on the receipt of the news from Havana.

He refused to believe the report at first. When he had been assured of the truth of the story he said that there was no possibility that the Spaniards had anything to do with the destruction of the Maine.

No Spaniard, he said, would be guilty of such an act. If the report was true, he said, the explosion must have been caused by some accident on board the warship.

THE MAINE'S VISIT TO HAVANA.

First American Warship to Visit Cuba Since the Struggle Began.

The Maine was ordered to Havana on Jan. 24 last, and was the first American warship to visit that port since the outbreak of the Cuban rebellion. In explanation of the visit of the American battleship to Cuba Secretary Long issued the following statement:

"So far from there being any foundation for the rumors yesterday of trouble at Havana, matters are now in such condition that our vessels are going to resume their friendly calls at Cuban ports and go in and out just as the vessels of other nations do. The Maine will go in a day or two on just such a visit. The department has issued orders for vessels to attend the public celebrations in Mobile and the Mardi Gras at New Orleans, and for the torpedo flotilla to visit Galveston, Texas."

The Maine was commanded by Capt. Charles D. Sigsbee. Her other officers were Lieut. Commander Richard Wainwright, Lieuts. G. F. Holman, John Hood, and C. W. Yungen, Lieuts. (junior grade) G. W. Blow, J. T. Blandin, F. W. Jenkins, Cadets J. H. Holden, W. T. Cluverius, Amon Bronson, and D. F. Boy'd, Jr.; Surgeon L. G. Heneberger, Paymaster C. W. Littlefield, Chief Engineer G. W. Howell, Passed Assistant Engineer F. C. Bowers, Assistant Engineers J. R. Morris and D. R. Merritt, Cadet Engineers Pope, Washington, and Arthur Crenshaw, Chaplain J. P. Chidwick, and Lieutenant of Marines A. W. Catlin.

The commander of the Maine, Capt. Sigsbee, is a favorite in the Navy Department. For four years he was Chief of the Hydrographic Office, and by his energy brought the office up to a high standard.

He justified the department's judgment in the selection by running his ship straight into a dock in New York harbor to avoid sinking a packed excursion boat. This was a display of quick judgment, nerve, and pluck that pleased the department so highly that the Captain was sent a complimentary letter.

ARMAMENT OF THE MAINE.

A Second-Class Battleship Built at the Brooklyn Navy Yard.

The Maine was placed in commission Aug. 17, 1895. She is a twin-screw, armored cruiser, with a belt of the belted type, and is known as a second-class battleship. Like the Texas, the Maine was built at a Government navy yard. The Texas was built at Norfolk; the Maine at the New York Navy Yard. Both ships were authorized when Secretary Whitney began the work of rehabilitating a then degenerate navy.

The Maine is of Navy Department designs throughout. The hull was built by navy yard workmen, and the engines were constructed by the Quintard Iron Works. That firm obtained the contract on its bid of $735,000. There were no other bidders.

The vitals of the ship are protected from gun-fire by an armor belt 180 feet in length. This belt has a maximum thickness of 11½ inches. Below the water line the armor tapers to a thickness of 6 inches. To deflect an end-on or a fore-and-aft fire, heavily armored and sharply inclined V-shaped bulkheads are placed forward and aft, the ends joining the armor belt. The bulkheads are 6 inches thick, and well backed.

In her main battery the ship mounts four 10-inch and six 6-inch rifles. A number of guns of smaller calibre are distributed in advantageous places. The 10-inch rifles are mounted in pairs in two steel turrets. One of these is situated aft, the other forward. The turret armor is 10½ inches thick. The protective power of these massive shields is increased by their circular shape, which tends to deflect a missile unless the impact is directly given.

The guns are breech-loading rifles, with bores 10 inches in diameter. The length of each gun is 320 inches. The weight is a little more than 24 tons. From them a full-service charge of 250 pounds of powder throws a 500-pound shell a distance of nine miles, with an initial velocity of 2,000 feet per second.

The 6-inch rifles are of the breech-loading pattern. These weapons measure 198 inches in length and weigh five tons each. The

"All the News That's Fit to Print."

The New York Times.

WITH ILLUSTRATED WEEKLY MAGAZINE

COPYRIGHTED, 1898, BY THE NEW YORK TIMES COMPANY.

WITH ILLUSTRATED WEEKLY MAGAZINE

VOL. XLVII...NO. 15,071. NEW YORK, SUNDAY, MAY 1, 1898.—TWENTY-FOUR PAGES. PRICE FIVE CENTS.

THE WEATHER.

Fair; variable north to west winds.

THE NEWS CONDENSED.

The Washington authorities expect news of victories over the Spaniards at Manila and in Cuba during the week.

Commodore Dewey may attack Manila at any time. Confidence is felt that the Spanish guns on shore are no match for the batteries of his fleet.

If he takes the city early news may be received over the cable, now controlled by Spain. News of a partial success would be sent to Hongkong by a gunboat and cabled from there.

China has not yet issued a neutrality decree. This is believed to be of great advantage to Commodore Dewey.

Preparations for the invasion of Cuba continue with the greatest activity. Trains filled with troops are arriving at Tampa, Fla., in rapid succession, and the fleet of transports is assembling.

It is not believed, however, that the departure of the advance guard can leave before Wednesday. Its destination is kept strictly secret, but the assertion that a landing will be effected at Matanzas is discredited in Washington.

Adjt. Gen. Corbin is still hampered in his efforts to organize the volunteer army by the objections of State authorities and officers of the National Guard to the places selected for camps.

The blockade of Cuban ports continues. The flagship New York was fired on with small arms by Spanish cavalry on the shore at Cabanas. Eleven shells were returned from the ship, and the enemy scattered.

Commodore Watson has been assigned to Rear Admiral Sampson's fleet. It is believed that the blockading fleet may be divided, part of it to be prepared to meet the Spanish fleet which left Cape Verde Islands on Friday.

The battleship Oregon, after a remarkably fast run from Punta Arenas, Chile, arrived yesterday at Rio de Janeiro.

The more important German journals have ceased to attack the United States, as the result of a hint from the Government. They now recognize that German interests lie with the fortunes of the Americans.

James Gordon Bennett's yacht Namouna is blockaded in the Mediterranean port of St. Tropez, in France, by Spanish warships.

Page 3.

All the arrangements were completed yesterday for the accommodation of the State troops at the camps. It was announced that the best of food and fresh meat and vegetables would be provided. The programme for the transferring of the men to the camps was also announced.

The regiment of recruits which William Astor Chanler has been forming was disbanded yesterday because Mr. Chanler had been informed by the President that his men were not needed. The Old Guard closed its tents, as enough men for two regiments have been enrolled. The Lafayette Post will furnish men for the regular army from its own recruits.

Page 5.

The Cuban Junta sent 150 Cubans to Tampa, where they will be equipped by the United States Government for immediate service in the field.

The American Line steamship Paris arrived at her dock yesterday, and she was enthusiastically greeted in the harbor. She will at once become an auxiliary cruiser and her crew will be mustered in to-morrow.

Page 8.

John Y. McKane, the ex-boss of Coney Island, was released from Sing Sing Prison. His homecoming was a signal for joyous demonstration by enthusiastic Coney Islanders, although McKane would allow no public reception. He broke down when he met his family.

Page 12.

Excise licenses this year will foot up about $5,100,000.

At the annual breakfast of the Wheaton Club of the Wheaton Seminary Alumnae Profs. Geddings and Backus, Dr. Lyman Abbott, Mrs. Kate Upson Clark, and others discussed education and dress reform.

Page 19.

Harold Frederic, in his cable letter to THE TIMES, reviews the war situation as seen through British spectacles, shows that the sympathy of Great Britain is with us, and that efforts to creat a pro-Spanish feeling have availed but little, even though there is a feeling of bitterness because of the proposed tonnage duties, and some disgust over the privateering methods of the blockading fleet at Havana. He shows how Great Britain was beaten in the diplomatic game in China by the shrewder Russians, notes the remarkable success of Stephen Crane's latest book, has a caustic review of the Burlington House exhibition of pictures, makes a few observations on Spanish and American gunnery, and relates some details of Whistler's latest scheme.

Page 24.

A New Jersey Justice of the Peace was cited to appear before himself as a witness in an assault case.

Many suits will follow the decision against the Mountain Water Company of New Jersey, brought by Harper, Hollingsworth & Co., for diverting the natural sources of Green Brook.

Yesterday was the last day allotted to Gov. Black for the disposal of the remainder of the bills left in his hands by the Legislature. He vetoed three items, aggregating $18,200 in the Supply bill.

"Buck" Davis, the desperado accused of murdering Mr. Blodgett, the general manager of the Edison Electric Light Company of Schenectady, N. Y., escaped from the jail at Salem, Vt., on Wednesday.

The Supreme Court at Bismarck, N. D., has reversed the decision of the lower court in a divorce appeal made on the ground that the plaintiff was not a bona-fide resident of the State, and warns all District Courts to look closely into the question of residence in all cases where divorce is sought by residents of other States.

Lewis Warner, the missing President of the Hampshire County National Bank and of the Hampshire County Savings Bank of Northampton, Mass., was seen at Westfield, Mass., on Friday afternoon, it is said. Attachments have been placed on the property of two Northampton firms as one result of his defalcations.

MILLIONAIRE KILLED BY CARS.

Theodore Wernwag Run Down by a Gravel Train Near Philadelphia.

PHILADELPHIA, April 30.—Theodore Wernwag, a wealthy banker of this city, was instantly killed to-day at Meadow Brook, a suburb of this city, by being struck by a gravel train.

Mr. Wernwag leaves a large estate, valued at upward of $1,000,000.

MAP OF THE PHILIPPINE ISLANDS TO WHICH DEWEY'S FLEET IS PROCEEDING.

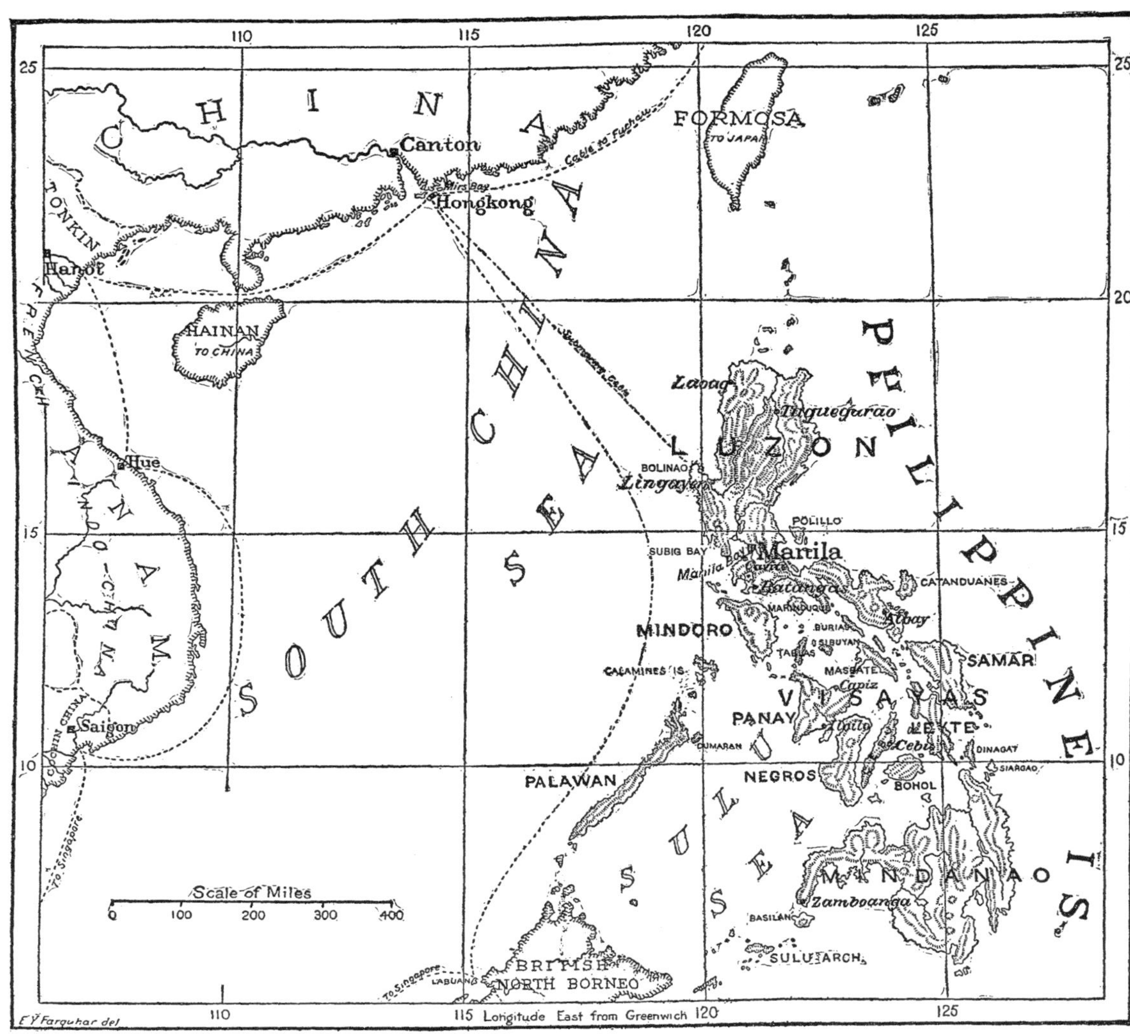

The Philippine Islands, a group of over 400 islands, extend across sixteen degrees of latitude between the Island of Formosa and the Molucca Islands. The largest of these islands are Luzon, Mindanao, Samar, Mindoro, Panay, Leyte, Negros, Masbate, and Zebu. The total area is estimated at 114,326 square miles, and the population about 7,000,000. They are all under Spanish rule, and are divided into forty-three provinces. Manila, on the Island of Luzon, is the capital, and the seat of the Governor General of the colony.

Manila is on the west coast of the island, and the Spanish fleet sailed from that port a few days ago, it was said, to meet the United States squadron, in command of Commodore George Dewey. These vessels have since gone into Subig Bay, a small inlet just north of the Bay of Manila. The United States squadron, which was at Mirs Bay, near Hongkong, has been sighted at Bolinao, a point about 100 miles north of Subig Bay. Bolinao is 550 miles from Mirs Bay, and in a straight line Mirs Bay is 700 miles from Manila. The dotted lines on the map show the cables, the only one from Manila going into the water at Bolinao, and running to Hongkong. In order to get authentic reports of the action taken by Commodore Dewey, it will be necessary for him to control this cable or to send a message from one of the mainland ports.

MANILA AWAITING ATTACK

Commodore Dewey Trying to Establish Communication With the Rebels, Says a Dispatch.

FLEET NOT YET HEARD FROM

A Report in Hongkong Says 50 or 60 Heavy Guns Command the Bay —A Blockade May Be Necessary in Consequence.

HONGKONG, April 30—2:30 P. M.—The British steamer Memnon, which has just arrived here from Manila, capital of the Philippine Islands, reports having seen the Spanish fleet outside Manila. She also met the British steamer Esmeralda, chartered by the banking companies of this place, which is on her way to Manila to take on board the specie there. She did not see any vessels of the United States fleet. The latter is supposed to be close in shore, trying to communicate with the insurgents, preparatory to continuing on to Manila.

If the reports which are current here are correct, the United States fleet has a difficult task to accomplish. It is said that the entrance of Manila Bay is commanded by from fifty to sixty heavy guns, well placed, and it is added that it will be impossible for the American warships to enter the bay without battleships, or without the co-operation of a strong land force. Therefore, it is believed Commodore Dewey will not attempt to force the entrance into the harbor, but will blockade the port until the insurgents move on Manila.

Agents of the insurgents here are trying to charter a steamer, in expectation of being able to transport a force of insurgents to the vicinity of Manila, and capture the strong fortress of Cavite, inside Manila Bay.

The cable to Manila is still intact, but the transmission of news regarding military or naval movements in the Philippine Islands is barred.

The British warships and torpedo boats at Hongkong have been forbidden to commence fresh repairs, which would seem to indicate the possibility of a movement in the near future upon the part of the British fleet.

THINKS MANILA EASY TO TAKE.

An Old Resident of the Philippines Arrives in San Francisco.

SAN FRANCISCO, April 30.—General interest is felt in the result of the impending fight off Manila, the cruiser Olympia having been built here. San Francisco is anxious that she should give a good account of herself.

Among the passengers on the steamer Gaelic, which arrived here to-day, is an old resident of the Philippines. He says that the forts at Manila are antiquated. There are three or four Krupp guns, but the remainder are of ancient model, and he does not believe the forts will be able to stand against our fleet for an hour. The Spanish troops, he says, are weak and disheartened after six months' hard fighting with the rebels, and are not likely to make much of a fight with well-armed foes. In fact, he does not think there will be any necessity for bombarding the City of Manila, for once the fleet has demolished the forts at the entrance to the bay, the city will probably capitulate.

As regards the Spanish warships, they are out of date, little or no discipline is maintained on board, and they will doubtless fall an easy prey to the United States fleet.

German business interests, it appears, are predominant there, and those of Great Britain come next in importance.

MADRID WITHOUT ADVICES.

No News Received There from Manila Up to 10 o'Clock Last Night.

MADRID, April 30—10 P. M.—Up to this hour no news has been received from Manila.

NEWS FROM DEWEY TUESDAY.

Washington Does Not Expect to Get Straight News Until a Gunboat Reaches Hongkong.

WASHINGTON, April 30.—The only cable connection between Manila and the outside world being controlled by the Spaniards, there is much speculation here as to where and how the first authentic news of the doings of Commodore Dewey's squadron off the Philippines will be received. It is accepted as certain that false and misleading reports of whatever is done will be sent out by the Spanish authorities, and as they have forbidden the transmission of code or cipher messages, there will be no opportunity for any story to come out of the place that is not made to read as the Spaniards want it.

The only way the people of this country can hope to get the truth about any engagement in Philippine waters, if there is one, will be from Commodore Dewey himself. The expectation at the Navy Department is that he will send either the Concord or the McCulloch with dispatches to Hongkong the moment anything decisive occurs. The McCulloch, which is a converted revenue cutter, will, it is thought likely, be chosen for this mission, as being better suited for dispatch work, though the cabled announcement from Hongkong that the Concord is expected back there "for orders" may mean that she will be the means of communication between the American fleet and the nearest available English cable station.

Two Days' Run from Manila.

Either the Concord or the McCulloch ought to make the run from Manila to Hongkong, under favorable conditions, in two days. As Commodore Dewey was not expected to reach Manila before this or to-morrow morning, naval officials here do not look for direct news from him before Tuesday or Wednesday of next week at the earliest. The possibility of the Asiatic Squadron bombarding any other town in the Philippines except Manila is said by officials of the Navy Department to be out of the question. It would be contrary to the recognied principles of international law, it is pointed out, for the fleet to bombard any unfortified place, and as Manila is the only town on the island that is fortified, it is the one liable to attack from the guns of the United States men-of-war.

While there is no doubt that one of the objects of Admiral Dewey is to crush the Spanish squadron in the Far East as the most effective method of protecting the important trade interests in that quarter, it is beyond doubt part of his purpose to seize and hold a port suitable for use as a coaling station. Notwithstanding the rumors that have come from Europe of interference to prevent the seizure of the Philippines or any part of them by Americans, it is not to be supposed for an instant that this Government will abandon in any degree this purpose. The coaling station is not only desirable, but is absolutely necessary from a naval point of view, unless the United States is prepared to surrender all commerce in American bottoms with Asia, and, fully realizing this, the naval officials will proceed with their campaign undeterred by European threats.

Our Retention of Manila.

Whether the station will be retained after the war by the United States will not now be determined. It is positively asserted that up to this moment these European menaces have taken no official form, and so far no protests have been lodged with the State Department. If any such should be made it would not be hard for this Government, by pointing to the wholesale seizures of almost the major part of the Chinese coast by the European powers, to justify itself in seeking to obtain at least so much of a foothold in that section of the globe as would suffice to give our warships a safe home port in time of stress and afford a moderate degree of protection to our commerce, which, in comparison with that of some of the European powers who have been most forward in their threats, is by no means insignificant.

It is semi-officially stated in the highest diplomatic quarters, representing France and Germany, that no protest or representation of any character respecting the operations of the American fleet at the Philippine Islands, have been made or are likely to be made. It can be stated also that neither the German nor the French Ambassador at Washington has received any instructions touching this subject, and the idea is scouted that such representation have been thought of in official quarters. The report that German warships have left Kiao-Chau Bay for the Philippines, in order to interpose armed resistance to a bombardment is denied. If a German warship had started from Nagasaki for Manila, as reported by cable, it is said this is for the purpose of protecting German residents, and not as a protest. These reports, it is pointed out, emanate from Madrid, and are designed to provoke irritation in this country against Germany and France.

So far as France is concerned, she is said to have no important interests in the Philippines. Her nearest interests are those at Tonquin. A leading diplomatic official, in discussing the report, said that if the United States designed territorial extension in the Philippines, then possibly the European powers might feel warranted in seeking an explanation. He said, however, that it was obvious the United States had no such territorial purposes, and that, lacking these, its effective conduct of the war was a subject solely for this country to determine.

Germany's interests in the Philippines are more extensive than those of France, but the German authorities have every confidence that these interests will be safeguarded and that no territorial questions will arise.

German Cruiser for Manila.

NAGASAKI, Japan, April 30.—The second-class German cruiser Irene, of 4,400 tons' displacement, 8,000 indicated horse power, and carrying a crew of over 350 men, has started for Manila to protect German interests. She is a steel vessel, built in 1887, and capable of steaming about nineteen knots. Her heaviest guns are four 5.9-inch rifles and eight 4.1-inch quick-firing guns.

The Saranac's Coal Liberated.

LONDON, April 30.—Advices from Iloilo say that the cargo of coal of the American bark Saranac, which was captured at that place by the Spanish gunboat El Cano, has been liberated.

Philippine Cable Service.

The Commercial Cable Company sends out the following notice:

"We are advised that private telegraphic service in code or cipher, to or from the Philippine Islands, has been suspended; also that direct communication between Hongkong and Manila has been established."

COMMODORE GEORGE DEWEY.

A Good Fighter and a Man to Inspire Confidence in Others.

Old naval officers who have known Commodore George Dewey, now in command of the Asiatic Squadron, during the greater part of his long service in the United States Navy say that he is a good fighter and a clear-headed and skillful commander. Moreover, he is regarded as "a fine fellow" by his brother officers. His dominant qualities, according to the testimony of old friends, are courage, manliness, frankness, shrewdness, and a keen sense of honor. As a naval officer he has always manifested the utmost confidence in himself, and thereby he has inspired confidence on the part of others. He is said to possess also the rare capacity of combining prudence with daring.

Of stanch Green Mountain stock, George Dewey was born in Vermont about 1838. He was appointed to the Naval Academy from that State Sept. 23, 1854, and immediately after his graduation, four years later, he was attached to the steam frigate Wabash of the Mediterranean Squadron. During the two or three years preceding the outbreak of the war of the rebellion young Dewey saw a variety of sea service and developed qualities which commended him to his superiors. He was at all times active and alert and fearless of danger. The opening of hostilities found him on board the steam frigate Mississippi of the West Gulf Squadron, and there, although serving in a subordinate capacity, he made a record which still shines in the annals of the navy.

In half a dozen engagements Lieut. Dewey distinguished himself for bravery. He figured in the capture of New Orleans in April, 1862, and did gallant service at Port Hudson in March, 1863. Later he was in various engagements with the Confederates below Fort Donelson, and he participated with personal credit in two attacks on Fort Fisher. Nearly all of the service in which Lieut. Dewey engaged during the rebellion was of a vigorous and dangerous character, and his bravery won repeated commendation from his commanding officers.

The frigate Mississippi was destroyed by the Confederates in the Mississippi River after a stubborn and gallant fight. The present Commodore was the last man to leave the sinking frigate, and Admiral Porter in commenting on this incident shortly afterward said: "It is in such trying moments that men show of what metal they are made, and in this instance the metal was the best."

It is the well-known "metal" of Commodore Dewey that gives his old associates in the navy the utmost confidence in the outcome of hte important manoeuvres in the neighborhood of the Philippine Islands. Rear Admiral Bunce, commandant of the Brooklyn Navy Yard, said last evening: "Dewey is a gallant officer and a good sea fighter. He will render a good account of himself. If there is any fighting to be done, he will be in it, and he will fight to the last."

Another old naval comrade of the commander of the Asiatic Squadron remarked that "Dewey will take good care of his fleet and will make the most effective use of it. He is sagacious and far-sighted as well as fearless and brave. The Spaniards are not likely to catch him napping. There is no officer of the United States Navy who could lead a fleet into battle with greater certainty of victory than Commodore Dewey. He enjoys one great advantage as a commander in having the implicit confidence of his subordinates. Every man who knows Dewey would follow confidently wherever he might lead."

Since his connection with the United States Navy Commodore Dewey has seen fifteen and a half years' sea service and twenty-three and a half years of service on shore. Almost at the close of the war of the rebellion he was commissioned Lieutenant Commander in recognition of gallant services. For the next few years he served on different ships of the European Squadron. In April, 1872, he was commissioned a Commander and placed in command of the Narragansett. Subsequently he served for awhile on the Government Lighthouse Board, of which he was Secretary part of the time. He was promoted Captain in September, 1884, and commanded the dispatch boat Dolphin. It was while in charge of the Dolphin that he paid several visits to this port and made a number of friends here. Returning to shore duty, Capt. Dewey served for three or four years as Chief of the Bureau of Equipment and Recruiting, with the rank of Commodore. He was promoted Commodore on Feb. 20, 1896, and on Jan. 3 last he was assigned to the command of the Asiatic Squadron.

A WEEK OF VICTORIES

Washington Authorities Think Decisive Successes at Manila and Cuba Are Near.

DEWEY IS RELIED ON TO TAKE THE PHILIPPINES.

No Spanish Guns on Shore Believed to Equal the Batteries on the American Warships.

Complaint that There Are Too Many Officers and Too Few Privates in the Army Now Assembling.

WASHINGTON, April 30.—Early news from Manila will be taken by the Administration as unquestionable proof of the complete success of Commodore Dewey in his expedition to the Philippines. Although much interest was manifested to-day in the movement of the army toward Cuba, there is much greater to hear from the Asiatic Squadron, separated as it is from any convenient point from which telegraphic tidings can be sent about its future movements, unless, as has been intimated, Manila or some other port is taken at which access to the cable line, now controlled by Spain, is made possible by capture.

Many inquiries were sent to the Navy Department to-day from the White House, and by persons interested in the personnel of the Asiatic Squadron, but at the department it was considered too early to expect news. If it comes to-morrow it will be good news. Postponement of it until the Concord or the McCulloch can bring dispatches to Hongkong, according to prior understanding, may not mean entire success, but it will afford the Navy Department some information about the strength of the Manila fortifiations and the character of the defense made by the Spanish commanders.

Only Manila May Be Bombarded.

Wild stories about the intended bombardment of the towns on the Philippine Islands have been published. There is no intention to violate international law by bombarding undefended or unfortified settlements.

If any firing is indulged in it will be in response to the guns of the Spanish ships or forts. Unless great improvements have been made in the works at Manila very recently the batteries there are unimportant, as compared with the powerful batteries on board the United States vessels. There will be no wanton shelling of houses and of people who are not prepared to defend themselves.

For some of the reasons that will constrain the vessels of Commodore Dewey's fleet to desist from attacking towns it is asserted at the Navy Department that there has been no bombardment along the coast of Cuba, either at Matanzas or Cardenas, or any other point, unless it was found by Admiral Sampson that batteries had been set up near houses, and subject to injury if the batteries chanced to be brought into use.

An examination of the charts leads naval officers to believe that the fort at Matanzas is inconvenient as a place of residence, and that the shots that would disturb the gunners and their commanders would probably be wide of the mass of inhabitants of the city.

War Department Very Busy.

No one who has not been in the neighborhood of the War Department can imagine the rush that is going on there and seems likely to be kept up until after the first expedition to Cuba is over. Every branch of the department is occupied, and in some of the bureaus the excitement is high.

It is evident that association with soldiers has not thoroughly steadied all the officers and clerks. The officers who served in the war of the rebellion are as frisky as the youngsters who have recently come from West Point and have yet to smell powder in action for the first time.

Very litle is known, outside of headquarters, about the movement upon Cuba, but as transportation has been supplied for 6,000 men, food for some time, an abundance of ammunition, all the equipage that can be imagined as necessaray for use in Cuba, the announcements in the newspapers are sufficiently corroborated in the department.

If all the arrangements work well, the coming week will record two reverses to Spain. Army and navy men agree that if the two undertakings are as successful as the Administration believes they will be, Spain will not be able to revive confidence anywhere in her ability to prevent the United States from ousting Blanco and his forces from Cuba. It is reported that the troops left behind at the different camps in the South are disappointed because they were not selected to accompany the advance to Cuba.

First Army May Be Enough.

Gen. Miles and Gen. Schofield are understood to have declared that the number to be sent over during the week will be enough, but if more are needed they can be easily added to the first body transported to the island.

Col. Hull of Iowa, Chairman of the House Committee on Military Affairs, regrets very much the differences in formation prescribed for the volunteer and regular forces.

"The army we are raising," said he to-day, "will be much more expensive than that with which we fought the rebellion. There will be a much larger number of officers to a given number of men that will call for higher pay, while it will cut down the force of privates. The only object has been to get in all officers as they were provided for in the militia. The companies should have had about twice as many privates and half as many officers as they will have."

The opportunity to secure prominent and honorable rank in the army has been sought to-day by a procession of men to the White House with or without their candidates for the positions of Major General or Brigadier General. It would not be difficult to form a regiment a day of Brigadier Generals from the number of applicants presenting themselves, principally on political grounds.

THE OREGON AT RIO DE JANEIRO.

Made Remarkably Good Time from Punta Arenas North—The Temerario 1,000 Miles South.

RIO DE JANEIRO, April 30.—The United States battleship Oregon arrived at this port at 6 o'clock this evening.

The arrival of the Oregon at Rio de Janeiro will ease the minds of all who have been anxious about the big battleship; she is now about 1,000 miles north of Buenos Ayres, where the Spanish torpedo gunboat Temerario has been waiting, it was supposed for the Oregon. The Oregon has made a remarkably good run. She left Callao, in Peru, on April 7, and was next reported at Punta Arenas, Chile, April 17. The distance from Callao to Punta Arenas is 2,800 miles, and she made that distance in ten days, which is at the rate of about 12 miles an hour. At Punta Arenas she had to wait to coal and for the Marietta, which had to take a longer course.

Big vessels go down as far as Pillar before entering the Straits of Magellan and pass through the rough waters that are always found in latitudes below 40, and are known among mariners as the "Rolling Forties." Vessels of small displacement enter Smyth Strait, which is considerably north of Pillar, and take a rather tortuous course through the archipelago and enter the Straits of Magellan proper at a point a little west of Punta Arenas.

The two vessels coaled at Punta Arenas, and left that port on the 22d inst. for the twenty-one-hundred-mile run to Rio de Janeiro. It took eight days to make this trip, and the same rate of speed, about twelve miles an hour, has been kept up. They will coal, and then start for the north. The next point at which they will probably touch will be Barbados, which is 3,200 miles from Rio de Janeiro.

WASHINGTON, April 30.—There was a feeling of relief among officials to-night over the safe arrival of the Oregon at Rio, well to the north and out of possible reach of the Spanish torpedo cruiser Temerario. The keenest interest is taken in her future movements, but on account of the extreme reticence of the naval authorities, the nature of the instructions which have awaited her at Rio are not known. The prevalent belief, however, is that her orders are to proceed to join Admiral Sampson's fleet without delay.

THE TOPEKA POSSIBLY SIGHTED.

May Arrive To-morrow—Believed to Have Been Seen Off the Banks.

ST. JOHN'S, N. F., April 30.—The British steamer Deddington, Capt. Trewin, fifteen days from Cadiz, arrived here to-day with a cargo of salt. She reports that yesterday morning, when off the Grand Banks, she sighted an unknown steamer, apparently a warship.

This vessel is thought to be the cruiser Topeka, which sailed from Falmouth, England April 19 The point at which the warship was sighted is about 900 miles from New York, and at the rate of speed shown so far the Topeka may be expected here late to-morrow.

CLIPPER GAP WORKS BLOW UP.

Supposed that Lightning Caused the Explosion—Extent of Damage to Property Not Ascertained.

AUBURN, Cal., April 30.—The Clipper Gap Powder Works, seven miles from here, were blown up this evening.

It is supposed lightning caused the explosion.

These works resumed operation a few days ago after several months' idleness. The extent of the damage has not been ascertained.

SUSPECTED SPIES ARRESTED.

Found Prowling About the Works of the Forcite Powder Company.

DOVER, N. J., April 30.—Two men, supposed to be Spaniards, were found prowling around the works of the Forcite Powder Company here this afternoon. They refused to tell their names and would not explain their presence. The watchmen of the company, who have been displaying unusual vigilance since the blowing up of the Atlantic Dynamite Works, at Kenvil, on Thursday, noticed the men, and on their refusal to tell their business, they decided to place them under arrest.

They fought desperately, but were overpowered and taken into custody. The men were placed in a cellar of a building and a strong guard placed over them. The authorities were notified and an investigation is being made. It is believed by many that the men were Spanish spies.

Carpenter Steel Works Guarded.

READING, Penn., April 30.—Beginning to-morrow, an armed guard of twelve men will protect the Carpenter Steel Works, in this city, where thousands of steel shells are being made for the big guns of the army and navy. This action has been taken by the management on account of the belief that the recent powder mill explosions were caused by enemies of the country.

THE WEATHER.

The local forecast may be found at the top of this page to the right of the title.

The pressure is low throughout the Southwest and the Missouri Valley. It is high in the lake regions and on the Middle and South Atlantic Coast. It has risen rapidly in the Northwest. The weather is nearly clear in the Atlantic Coast and Gulf districts. It is generally cloudy in the lake regions and Ohio Valley, and westward to the Rocky Mountains. Showers have fallen on the Middle and Northern Rocky Mountain plateau and slope, and in the Missouri and Upper Mississippi Valleys.

The temperature has fallen in the Northwest and risen in the lower lake region and North Atlantic States. For to-day fair weather is indicated in the Atlantic Coast districts and the Gulf States, cloudy weather and showers in the lake regions, the Ohio, Upper Mississippi, and lower Missouri Valleys. Showery conditions will continue in the Central Rocky Mountain districts. The temperature will be higher in eastern districts and will fall in the Central Missouri Valley.

The record of temperature for the twenty-four hours ended at midnight, taken from THE NEW YORK TIMES's thermometer and from the thermometer of the Weather Bureau, is as follows:

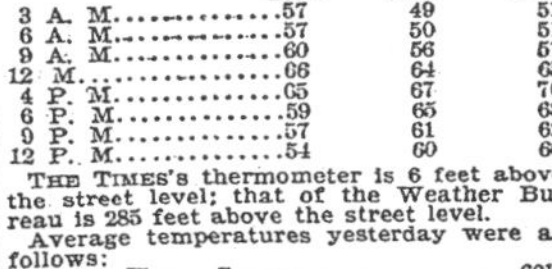

	—Weather Bureau.—		—TIMES.
	1897.	1898.	1898.
3 A. M.	57	49	51
6 A. M.	57	50	51
9 A. M.	60	56	57
12 M.	66	64	65
4 P. M.	65	67	70
6 P. M.	59	65	68
9 P. M.	57	61	62
12 P. M.	54	60	60

THE TIMES's thermometer is 6 feet above the street level; that of the Weather Bureau is 285 feet above the street level.

Average temperatures yesterday were as follows:

Printing House Square.......60½
Weather Bureau.......58
Corresponding date 1897.......59⅜
Corresponding date for last 20 years....53

The maximum temperature was 67 degrees, at 4 P. M., and the minimum 47 degrees, at 2 A. M. The humidity at 8 A. M. was 62 per cent., and at 8 P. M. 38 per cent.

DAILY, ONE CENT. SUNDAY, THREE CENTS.

"All the News That's Fit to Print."

The New York Times.

THE WEATHER.
Snow and colder, brisk north-easterly winds.

VOL. XLIX...NO: 15,618. NEW YORK, MONDAY, JANUARY 29, 1900.—Ten Pages and Supplement. ONE CENT In Greater New York and Jersey City. Elsewhere, TWO CENTS.

TO-DAY:

TEN PAGES,

WITH FINANCIAL REVIEW AND QUOTATION SUPPLEMENT.

THE NEWS CONDENSED.

FOREIGN.—Gen. Warren's entire force retreated to the south side of the Tugela River, under the personal direction of Gen. Buller, who reports that the place was "abandoned" because its perimeter was too large and there was little water. Circumstantial Boer accounts state that the republicans took Spion Kop by direct assault, driving the British step by step until they showed the white flag, and 150 of them surrendered. Other Boer reports place the British loss in dead left on the battlefield at 1,500 men. It is reported from London that Dr. Leyds, the Transvaal Agent in Europe, is trying to secure the mediation of Germany. He himself, in an interview, said that the Boers did not desire peace at this time on the basis of the status quo. Gen. Mercier was yesterday elected to the French Senate. The situation in China is receiving serious attention in Austria.—Pages 1 and 6.

Page 1.

The condition of P. D. Armour, the Chicago packer, is said to be very serious.

The Count and Countess de Castellane went to Lakewood yesterday.

A "blue law" 177 years old is being enforced in Baltimore.

A speech delivered by Brig. Gen. Hawkins Tuesday, before the officers of the Seventy-first Regiment, was made public yesterday. Gen. Hawkins contradicts the testimony of Gen. Kent regarding the regiment's movements at San Juan, and declares the whole trouble was due to the fact that the command was taken out of his brigade without his knowledge and contrary to his plans.

Page 2.

Quincy, Ill., police officers killed two safe blowers and wounded a third.

Charles Nord, a waiter employed in a café at 383 Bowery, was instantly killed last night in front of the place by an electric shock.

The Central Federated Union yesterday adopted a resolution that citizens only should be employed on the Rapid Transit tunnel work.

Page 3.

The Rev. Dr. W. S. Crowe lectured on "Christian Science" at the Church of the Eternal Hope.

David E. McClure, from papers found in his possession believed to have been a resident of Glasgow, Scotland, died in the Homeopathic Hospital, Brooklyn, yesterday from the effects of chloral, given to him by thieves, the police believe.

Page 4.

Mrs. Fannie Leslie of 1,090 Broadway, Brooklyn, committed suicide in a restaurant. Her mother, upon identifying her body at the Morgue, vowed to have vengeance upon the man with whom her daughter left home.

Mrs. Mary Gray Mexia, a New York woman, who claims to have been married by proxy in 1867 to Gen. Enrique A. Mexia of Mexico, will testify to-day at Dallas, Texas, in a contest of his will by a son of the General by another alleged marriage.

Page 5.

The Anti-Saloon League, an organization formed to work on political lines, began work here by holding services in many churches and halls in the northern part of the city.

The plans for the new buildings of Mount Sinai Hospital were on view at the annual meeting. It was announced that an additional $500,000 would be required to pay for them.

Page 7.

Bishop Satterlee, in Trinity Church yesterday, made a plea for the establishment of a National cathedral in Washington.

The Rev. Dr. Charles H. Eaton, in a sermon on "Brooklyn Mediaeval Theology," defended Unitarianism against the attacks of the Brooklyn revivalists.

Page 10.

The Post Office officials have decided to take action warning all citizens against the schemes of "green goods" swindlers.

The demands of Brooklyn High School delegates to the teachers' salary schedule conferences are reported to have dissolved an important meeting after a sharp war of words.

Amusements.—Page 6.
Arrivals at Hotels and Out-of-Town Buyers.—Page 2.
Court Calendars.—Page 9.
Marine Intelligence and Foreign Mails.—Page 5.
Real Estate.—Page 5.
Weather Report.—Page 2.
Yesterday's Fires.—Page 2.

PRESIDENT DIAZ'S SUCCESSOR.

It is Said Gen. Reyes Will be Mexico's Next Chief Executive.

Special to The New York Times.

MEXICO CITY, Jan. 28.—The gazetting of Gen. Bernardo Reyes to be Minister of War is but the carrying out of a plan long entertained by President Diaz of providing for the succession and retiring from active participation in public affairs. For years he has regarded Reyes as his right hand man. His political experience as Governor of Nuevo de Leon and his military career have endowed him with those qualities here considered necessary to the Chief Executive.

It was well known that four years ago President Diaz was sincere in his desire to retire. He feels that his mission has been fulfilled and that he merits a rest. The plan is to make Gen. Reyes the personal representative of the President, who will thus be relieved and enabled to make the tour which he has from time to time postponed, in deference to the pleadings of his advisers.

Four years hence it is expected that Reyes will succeed Diaz in proper person. The President will go abroad as soon as the preliminaries for carrying on the Government as indicated are fully completed.

GOT EVEN WITH INSURGENTS.

American Civil Prisoner Told Where Treasure Was Concealed.

Special to The New York Times.

SAN FRANCISCO, Jan. 28.—The transport City of Pekin brings a story from Manila to the effect that Harvey L. Jackson, a trader of Malolos, who succeeded in having $40,000 of insurgent coin turned over to the United States, is a beach comber in Manila, without funds to return to this country or start again in business.

Jackson did well as a trader at Malolos until the war came. Then the insurgents looted his store and took him prisoner, dragging him around from place to place.

When Lawton captured San Nicolas, Jackson escaped to the American lines, and in revenge promised to reveal the hiding place of the Spanish commander's treasure which Aguinaldo had taken. Under his guidance some soldiers recovered $40,000 in coin, but they found much more in coin and jewelry, which was divided among themselves. Several soldiers wore diamond rings and all had money to burn.

Jackson got nothing of the plunder, and his part in the recovery of the treasure was never reported to headquarters.

To Inspect the Semmes Statue.

NEWARK, N. J., Jan. 28.—The committee of citizens of Mobile, Ala., which has in charge the erection of a statue to the late Confederate Admiral Raphael Semmes, will arrive here on Tuesday to inspect the statue which has been cast by Ernest Vatier at his foundry in Market Street. The statue, which was begun last August, is not complete. It is of bronze, life size. The statue will be shipped next month.

VINDICATES 71ST REGIMENT

Gen. Hawkins Contradicts the Testimony of Gen. Kent.

NO NOTICE OF CHANGED PLANS

Says Trouble at San Juan Was Due to Men Being Taken Out of His Brigade Without His Knowledge.

When Brig. Gen. Hamilton S. Hawkins, United States Army, retired, reviewed the Seventy-first Regiment last Tuesday night at the armory, after the military ceremonies he met the officers of the regiment and a few special guests in the Colonel's room, and there made some remarks on the campaign against the Spanish in Cuba, and particularly as to the part played by the Seventy-first Regiment. While the General's remarks were not intended for publication, a number of the officers, after a conference, decided yesterday that they had such an important bearing in relation to the war history of the Seventy-first that they should be made public. Some of the officers go so far as to express the possibility of a new court of inquiry being appointed, in view of them.

Gen Hawkins was in command of the brigade of which the Seventy-first was a part. The importance of his speech lies in its contradiction of the testimony of Major Gen. Jacob Kent, who commanded the division in which the Seventy-first Regiment fought. This testimony appears in the proceedings of the court of inquiry. The officers of the Seventy-first have always claimed that the regiment, on account of its black-powder rifles and lack of experience, was intended for a reserve, and that it did not receive orders to cross the San Juan River. The testimony in question reads as follows:

Question by Col. Bacon—Then from the time you left Col. Downs at the forks (10 A. M.) until night, you sent no further orders to him?

Answer by Gen. Kent—No; I virtually abandoned him, as far as I was concerned. That belonged to his brigade commander.

In his speech, Gen. Hawkins took occasion to emphasize the fact that the Seventy-first was taken out of his brigade without his knowledge, and contrary to his plans and intentions, and that the whole trouble arose from that fact. After the regiment had been deflected into the trail, it was two miles away from Gen. Hawkins the distance between being an impenetrable jungle of cactus. Communication was practically impossible. Col. Downs has always claimed that he received no orders after 10 o'clock, and Gen. Hawkins's statement now that he did not know about Gen. Kent's plan to deflect the Seventy-first, the officers of the regiment take as a vindication of Col. Downs. Gen. Hawkins was not called before the court of inquiry, and the officers now claim that his testimony would have cleared every member of the regiment.

WHAT GEN. HAWKINS SAYS.

The remarks made by Gen. Hawkins were as follows. "When we were at Tampa the regular officers had an opportunity of watching the Seventy-first Regiment, and had all formed a good opinion of it. When the assignments were made, I felt myself especially honored to have the Seventy-first assigned to my brigade. Going down on the transports I saw little of it, but I saw that it was landed promptly.

"I remained on the transports after my brigade was landed, for the reason that I did not wish to have my personal horses swim out to sea, as most of you gentlemen remember was a common occurrence. I had determined that the navy should furnish small boats to act as sort of lane through which the horses could be taken ashore. It took so long that I turned the matter over to one of my trusted aides, and I left the transport.

"When I put my foot on land I was met by a civilian and told that a great battle had taken place at the front, and that we had met reverses. To substantiate this statement, he pointed up the hill at some Rough Riders who were returning wounded. I looked up the hill and did see some wounded men. I was then asked who was in command, and I said that I did not know, but that possibly I was.

"I then gave orders that my brigade and one or two other regiments should leave immediately for the front. I was struck by the prompt response of the Seventy-first. Going up the hill, you gentlemen will, no doubt, remember that we met some of the Rough Riders who were returning in a demoralized condition, and who reported that the Rough Riders had been annihilated, and that their Colonel had been killed. The first regiment I found coming up the hill was the Seventy-first, in good order. We found that the great battle had not taken place, so we returned to Siboney.

"We now come to the morning of the first day of July, when so many unfortunate occurrences took place. The orders were to start the night before, but we did not start until the morning. We had no orders to take the hill, and could receive none from Gen. Shafter. Gen. Kent seemed much troubled. Lieut. Miley of Gen. Shafter's staff, when the situation seemed critical, stated to Gen. Kent that if he had no objection, he would give orders to advance in the name of Gen. Shafter. To which Gen. Kent replied: 'Very well, Sir,' and started down the road to give the necessary orders.

SAYS KENT ACTED UNFORTUNATELY.

"My intention was that the Seventy-first should be in the second line, in rear of the Sixth and Sixteenth, to act as a sort of reserve, and when the final charge should come that my whole brigade should advance together. But Gen. Kent, without my knowledge, deflected the Seventy-first Regiment to the left when its head reached a trail discovered by the balloon.

"He evidently thought that my intention was to have the Seventy-first on the left of my brigade, and that this would be a shorter way to accomplish this object, but such was not my intention. It was a most unfortunate circumstance, for it removed the Seventy-first Regiment far from the rest of my brigade and placed it in the most trying position that troops could be thrown.

"When the Seventy-first came up the hill I placed them on the line, and as far as my observation went, it acted splendidly. The firing had ceased, but Gen. Shafter, who was in the rear had sent word to Lawton at El Caney, to leave and reinforce our right, as he was needed. It is certainly wonderful how fierce a battle seems when viewed from the rear. [Laughter.]

"I saw a shell burst over the left company of the Seventy-first Regiment. It did not become panic-stricken, but behaved in a soldierly manner, and quickly recovered itself and seemed to be kept well in hand by its officers.

"A battery seemed to be inactive, and I sent word to it to commence firing. My aide brought back a reply from its commanding officer that his men and horses were too much exposed and that he was going to move, which he did.

"I then placed two or three companies of the Seventy-first Regiment in the position vacated by the battery, and although just as much exposed, I heard no complaints from them or its officers of being in too much danger, and when I left on July 2, having been promoted, the Seventy-first was doing its duty.

"I have every reason to believe that if the Seventy-first Regiment was permitted to go where I intended that it should, and was not deflected to the left without my knowledge, it would have done equally well as the other two regiments of my brigade, and I am pleased to testify to the worth of the Seventy-first Regiment at any time.

COL. DOWNS PLEASED.

Col. Wallace Downs, formerly commander of the regiment, was asked what he thought of the remarks of Gen. Hawkins: "They are just what I should expect from a fair and impartial man," he said, "who was at the scene and knew how the Seventy-first was sacrificed by being thrown into the trail. I hear that Gen. Hawkins went even further, and said that the trail ought never to have been discovered.

"It is perfectly true that I was abandoned to my brigade commander by Gen. Kent, and as he had fixed it so that Gen. Hawkins was completely out of touch with me, I could get no orders from him. I am still waiting for them. Here is a fact that no military man has yet disputed:

"Gen. Kent gave me his last orders, he admits on the witness stand, at 10 A. M. The attack was not to begin on San Juan till after Lawton had taken El Caney. This capture was delayed, and finally, with every prospect of our position being made untenable, Col. Miley, at 12:20, ordered the regulars to attack the hill. I had been left to my brigade commander two hours before, and he could not communicate with me.

"If the blunder had not been made of pushing the Seventy-first into the trail that had been discovered only a few minutes before, and the outlet of which no one knew anything about, there would have been none of the bungling and confusion which interested persons tried to unload upon the Seventy-first. I am profoundly grateful to Gen. Hawkins for having let light in upon the situation at last."

Brig. Gen. George Moore Smith of the Fifth Brigade, who was among those present, also expressed his approval of the remarks of Gen. Hawkins.

BLUE LAWS IN BALTIMORE.

Every Store in the City Ordered Closed on Sunday—Police Take Names of All Offenders.

Special to The New York Times.

BALTIMORE, Jan. 28.—Not even a cigarette or a seidlitz powder could be bought in Baltimore to-day. For the first Sunday in many years every cigar store, corner grocery, bakery, and the like were closed up tight. Few drug stores kept open, and those that did displayed placards informing the public that the soda fountains were closed and that absolutely nothing would be sold without a prescription.

Five or six hundred policemen were kept busy all day taking the names of bootblacks, cabmen, and the keepers of little shops or fruit stands, for presentation to the Grand Jury. The Sunday newspapers were not stopped, but policemen took the names of the pressmen and other employes. The Police Department will hand in enough names to the Grand Jury to keep that body busy for nearly the rest of the term to the exclusion of the regular business for which it was chosen. Cases of petty offenders will receive attention while the gross violators lay low until the agitation blows over.

The down-town saloons which have a "pull" were given the tip that even side doors must be closed. Not a drink was obtainable for love or money.

The statute which the ministers' associations of various denominations insist upon being enforced is Article XXVII., Section 247, of the public general laws of Maryland. It is 177 years old, and reads as follows:

"No person shall work or do any bodily labor on the Lord's Day, commonly called Sunday, and no person having children or servants shall command or willingly suffer any of them to do any manner of work or labor on the Lord's Day, (works of necessity or charity always excepted,) nor shall any one suffer or permit any children or servants to profane the Lord's Day by gaming, fishing, fowling, hunting, or unlawful pastime or recreation."

This action of the authorities, it is asserted, will lead to a revision of the statute by the Legislature now in session.

ELOPERS COME TO NEW YORK.

Step-daughter of Thomas Nelson Page of Washington and Preston Gibson Are Married Here.

Special to The New York Times.

WASHINGTON, Jan. 28.—The magnificent home of Thomas Nelson Page, the author, was thrown into great excitement to-day by the announcement from New York of the elopement of his young step-daughter, Miss Mina Field, and Preston Gibson, son of the late Senator Gibson of Louisiana, and nephew of Justice White of the United States Supreme Court.

According to their usual custom, Mr. and Mrs. Page refuse to see representatives of the press, but a friend of the family has authorized a local paper to make a formal announcement of the marriage to-morrow morning, the date of the ceremony being given as Jan. 27. The place or name of the officiating clergyman is scrupulously withheld.

Miss Field is just seventeen, a petite brunette. She was until last Saturday a pupil at a fashionable finishing school at Dobb's Ferry, N. Y., and was to have been presented in society next Winter. She spent the Christmas holidays at her home in this city, one of the smartest junior dances of that season being given by Mrs. Page in honor of her two young daughters. These young women are among the heiresses of the capital, their father having been a brother and partner of Marshal Field of Chicago.

Young Gibson was a junior at Princeton, and like his bride spent the Christmas holidays in Washington, when an engagement of marriage is said to have come about.

The young people met in New York on Saturday, and are spending the early days of their honeymoon in that city. They are expected to return to Washington at the end of the month, when they will be received by the bride's family.

CASTELLANES AT LAKEWOOD.

The Count and Countess Guests of Mr. and Mrs. Dwight M. Harris—Outwit Crowd at the Station.

Special to The New York Times.

LAKEWOOD, N. J., Jan. 28.—Count and Countess de Castellane, Mr. and Mrs. George J. Gould, Mr. and Mrs. Snowden, Robert Collier, George Taylor, and S. L. Herbert arrived here on the 10:15 train from New York this morning. While the Count and Countess alighted from the front part of the parlor car and were received by Dwight Miller Harris, who escorted them to his private carriage in the rear of the station unnoticed, the rest of the party came from the rear end of the car and proceeded to the large coach of Mr. Gould, which was surrounded by four or five hundred people, all expecting to see the distinguished visitors enter the Gould coach.

During this commotion the Count and Countess were riding away with Mr. Harris to his beautiful colonial home on the lake just opposite the Gould mansion. During their stay here the Count and Countess are to be the guests of Mr. and Mrs. Dwight Miller Harris.

Luncheon was served on the arrival of the Castellanes at the Harris mansion, and later a visit was made to Georgian Court, where Mr. and Mrs. George J. Gould are entertaining some guests from New York and Philadelphia. Both families and their guests, with the Count and Countess, then drove to the Country Club, returning before dark.

It is expected that the Count will go to the Country Club to-morrow as the guest of Mr. Harris and engage in some shooting before the traps and take a turn at golf.

The grounds of Georgian Court were brilliantly illuminated to-night in honor of the Count and Countess. The Castellanes dined with Mr. and Mrs. Harris. Among those at the table were Mr. and Mrs. Edwin Gould, Miss May, Mr. and Mrs. E. Robbins Walker, Mr. Jones, Mr. and Mrs. James Converse, and Mr. and Mrs. Dwight Miller Harris.

NEW SCHOOL FOR WOMEN.

Sisters of St. Joseph Will Conduct One at Cliff Haven.

Special to The New York Times.

PORT HENRY, N. Y., Jan. 28.—The Order of the Sisters of St. Joseph, which conducts the Champlain Institute in this place, is about to erect on the Summer School property at Cliff Haven a collegiate institute for the higher education of women.

The building will be of the latest style with modern improvements. Each student will have her own separate apartment. The instructors will be selected from the most learned members of the order in various sections of this State. Sister M. Josephine, who has had great experience in this line as a public and parochial school teacher in New York City, has been selected as the head of the new institution.

BRITISH CAMPAIGN AN ENTIRE FAILURE

London Times Looks Forward to a Terrible Disaster.

FALL OF LADYSMITH CERTAIN

No Relief Could Reach Gen. White for a Month at Least.

HE CANNOT HOLD OUT.

Said to Have Expended His Rations Freely in His Confidence of Early Succor by Buller's Army.

LONDON, Jan. 29.—The week has opened with the utmost gloom for the British public, and the reaction is all the stronger because of the high hopes that were reposed in Gen. Buller's turning movement and of his announcement that there would be "no turning back."

The Times says: "The most carefully planned and executed movement of the whole campaign has entirely failed, and it can hardly be necessary to dwell upon the extreme probability that we shall learn, a little sooner or a little later, of a catastrophe almost without precedent in our military history, a catastrophe, indeed, without a parallel except in the surrender at Yorktown.

"We are checked at every point in the campaign. In fact, the campaign is still to begin. We wish we had clearer proofs that even now the Government has any adequate comprehension of the situation. The utterances of responsible Ministers have done nothing to reassure the country on this point.

MORE TROOPS NECESSARY.

"Heavy or light, the thing has to be done, and the Government ought to prepare for the immediate dispatch of 50,000 men and to take steps to send yet another 50,000, if those should be needed. The hopeless attempts to carry on the campaign with four widely separated columns, each unequal to its task, must be abandoned for a concentration of force and of purpose."

All the editorials this morning breathe the spirit of calm determination. Not one will allow that any reverse could deter the country from the object it has set itself to attain, whatever the sacrifices which may be involved.

CRITICISM OF THE GOVERNMENT.

Very frank criticism of the Government, however, is beginning to be heard even in quarters that have hitherto refrained. The Daily Mail boldly throws all the blame upon Sir Michael Hicks-Beach, Lord Lansdowne, and Lord Wolseley. It points to President Lincoln's dismissal of Simon Cameron from the post of Secretary of War as a precedent for "getting rid of incompetent Ministers."

The Morning Post dwells upon the danger of further rebellion at the cape, and of possible European complications. It urges that the navy be prepared for "any emergency."

The Standard and other papers reflect the anxiety of the public to learn how much truth there is in the Boer accounts of the fighting at Spion Kop. Gen. Buller's obscurity in his dispatches is bitterly criticised, as well as the evident fact that the censor is not only delaying but is removing all important matters from the newspaper dispatches. To judge with any accuracy of the extent of the disaster is virtually impossible.

THE FORCE ENGAGED.

It appears that Gen. Buller had altogether five brigades wholly or partly engaged, Gen. Coke's, Gen. Hildyard's, Gen. Hart's, Gen. Woodgate's, and Gen. Lyttleton's, and the 270 casualties already announced in Lyttleton's brigade are thus explained.

Much mystery still surrounds the retreat. It is possible that Gen. Buller has withdrawn his whole forces; but it is generally assumed that Lyttleton's brigade and Lord Dundonald's cavalry and other troops are still on the north side of the Tugela.

Gen. Buller's confidence that the Boers did not molest his retreat because they had been taught to respect the fighting powers of the British soldier, is not shared in London. It is thought rather that the Boers had some other plan in store, or did not wish to waste their men

CRITICISM OF BULLER.

At the service clubs the situation as revealed by Gen. Buller was considered very unpleasant. His excuses or explanations were characterized as very weak. The absence of water, which Sir Charles Warren was "led to believe" existed, and the facts that Spion Kop was "indeed a mountain," and that its "perimeter was too large," are all matters which even Gen. Buller's warmest admirers hold should have been ascertained before he attacked.

The comforting feature of the situation, however, is the fact that Gen. Buller's retirement across the Tugela was accomplished without loss, which puts an end to the unpleasant rumors that were in circulation here and on the Continent.

To Ladysmith the disappointment must be very bitter. A dispatch from the Boer laager near the town, dated Jan. 24, describes the garrison as "very evidently preparing a desperate coup in order to effect a junction with Gen. Buller's advancing army."

GEN. WHITE'S CONDITION.

It may be regarded as a certainty that, in the confident hope of early relief, Sir George White has lately been issuing extra rations, and this fact has given rise to an exaggerated idea as to the length of time the provisions would last.

Even should it be decided to send Gen. Buller reinforcements and to attempt to reach Ladysmith by a movement through the still more difficult country east of Colenso, it is extremely doubtful whether the garrison could hold out long enough, as such a movement would occupy at least a month.

MAY ABANDON LADYSMITH.

Open talk is heard of the absolute necessity of abandoning Ladysmith to its fate, while Lord Roberts reverts to the original plan of an advance over the Orange River upon Bloemfontein.

It is reported from Boer headquarters near Ladysmith that Gen. Buller had been down with fever, but had recovered.

Large arrivals of troops are due at Cape Town during the week.

There has been great activity in military quarters in all parts of England since Saturday morning.

The War Office, anticipating a great crush at the opening of Parliament, has placed new restrictions upon visitors during the session.

The situation at other points is unchanged, but indications that Lord Roberts is preparing plans for an advance across the Orange River come in a dispatch to The Daily Chronicle from Storkstroom, dated Jan. 25, which says that Thebits, an important position near Steynsburg, on the Stormberg-Rosmead line, is now occupied by the British, who are repairing the railway and bridges.

The correspondent observes that this will facilitate communication between Gen. Gatacre and Gen. Kelly-Kenny.

KILLED BY HIS OWN CROWD?

One of the Invaders of Frankfort, Ky., Reported Murdered on the Train Because He Yelled for Goebel.

Special to The New York Times.

LONDON, Ky., Jan. 28.—J. W. Bryant, who went to Frankfort a few days ago on the special train that carried more than 1,000 mountain men to the State Capitol, has hot returned, although it is certain he left Frankfort for his home Friday.

Two of the men who were on the special train and have returned here say that Bryant was shot and killed and pitched from the train window by the crowd as they were returning. Whether this be true or not, his family at East Bernsted, this county, are much worried about his whereabouts.

The two men who report that Bryant was killed are Messrs. Smith and Moore of this county and are reliable men. They say he was shot in the face and mouth and thrown from the car window because he yelled for Goebel.

ALL QUIET AT FRANKFORT.

Another Contest in the Legislature to Take Place To-day.

FRANKFORT, Ky., Jan. 28.—Politicians of both parties took a rest to-day, and the lobby of the Capitol Hotel was more quiet than it has been for several weeks. Last night the leaders of both parties were in caucus, that of the Republicans being prolonged until a late hour. No action of any kind was taken during the day, however. There were persistent rumors that another detachment of men from the mountains would arrive in Frankfort during the first half of the week.

E. G. Sebree, campaign manager for the Republicans, denied the story positively. "Nobody is coming that I know of," he said, "and if there was any organized movement among the Republicans to come to Frankfort I would know it. No such thing is contemplated by anybody."

To-morrow morning another contest will be heard in the House—that of Gill, Democrat, against Brister, Republican, from Logan County. This case was made a special order for Saturday morning at the same time as the Van Metter-Berry case. The majority of the Contest Committee is composed of Republicans, and will report in favor of Brister. A minority report will be presented in favor of Gill.

ANNA MAUD BOWEN DEAD.

Dean of Woman's Hall at Northwestern University.

Special to The New York Times.

CHICAGO, Jan. 28.—Miss Anna Maud Bowen, Dean of Woman's Hall, Northwestern University, dropped dead at noon today of heart disease. She was appointed Dean in June last year, and was the youngest woman ever appointed to the post.

She was born in Chicago in 1872, and entered the university in 1891 from the South-side High School. As freshman in the philosophical course she accomplished twice the amount of work that the ordinary student did, and finished the four-year course in three years, and was graduated in 1894 with the degree of Bachelor of Philosophy. In 1895 she was made a Fellow of Philosophy at Cornell, and after two years secured the degree of Doctor of Philosophy, being the youngest of 150 students. She then went to Leipsic.

Returning she was made Dean of the seminary at Martin's Ferry, Ohio, and then became an editorial writer on The Nation. She held the editorial position until her appointment as Dean last year.

FIRE IN HAWTHORNE MILLS.

Connecticut Factory Damaged on Account of Lack of Water.

Special to The New York Times.

GREENWICH, Conn., Jan. 28.—Fire in the Hawthorne Woolen Mills at Glenville, one of the mills in the American Felt Company's trust, did $5,000 damage to-day. Oily waste caused a spontaneous combustion in the stock room, and the flames burned through the ceiling to the weaving room above.

When the flames were discovered first it was found that the storage reservoir generally reserved for fire purposes was empty, and it became necessary to first start the water wheel to force the water into the tank, and then to start the engine to pump it into the building.

The floors were flooded to a depth of six inches before the fire was subdued.

P. D. ARMOUR SERIOUSLY ILL.

Special to The New York Times.

PASADENA, Cal., Jan. 28.—Mrs. Philip D. Armour, Jr., left Santa Barbara at 10 o'clock this morning with the body of her husband, and will arrive in Chicago some time Wednesday evening. The physicians have told Mr Armour, the father, that the trip to Chicago, with its attendant grief and excitement, would be almost certain to result in his death. His wife has decided to remain here with her husband, who is sadly in need of her care and encouragement. His condition is said to be very serious.

Mrs. Platt's Condition Improves.

WASHINGTON, Jan. 28.—The condition of Mrs. Platt, the wife of the Senator from New York, was reported to be better to-day.

BRITISH RETREAT OVER THE TUGELA

Warren's Force Crosses Under Buller's Personal Direction.

BRITISH DEAD MAY BE 1,500

Were Driven by the Boers from Spion Kop, Step by Step.

HOIST A WHITE FLAG

150 of Them Taken Prisoners in the Assault.

Spion Kop Lacked Water, Gen. Buller Reports, and Its Perimeter Was Too Large, So It Was "Abandoned."

LONDON, Jan. 29.—The War Office has received the following from Gen. Buller announcing that Gen. Warren has retreated to the south side of the Tugela River:

Spearman's Camp, Jan. 27, 6:10 P. M.

"On Jan. 20 Warren drove back the enemy and obtained possession of the southern crests of the high tableland extending from the line of Acton Homes and Hongers Poort to the western Ladysmith hills. From then to Jan. 25 he remained in close contact with the enemy.

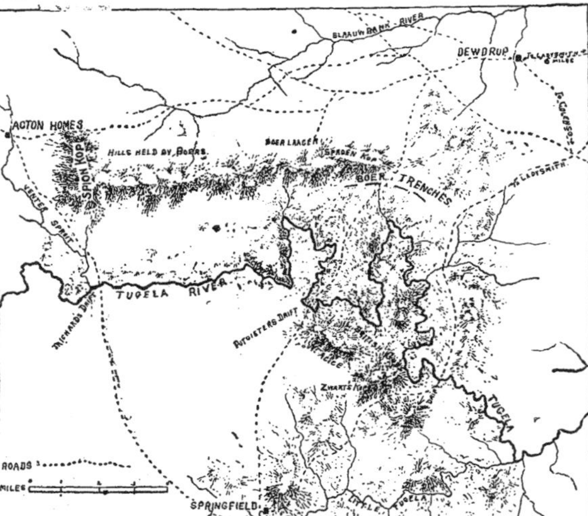

SCENE OF GEN. WARREN'S RETREAT FROM SPION KOP.

"The enemy held a strong position on a range of small kopjes stretching from northwest to southeast across the plateau from Acton Homes, through Spion Kop, to the left bank of the Tugela.

"The actual position held was perfectly tenable, but did not lend itself to an advance, as the southern slopes were so steep that Warren could not get an effective artillery position, and water supply was a difficulty.

"On Jan. 23 I assented to his attacking Spion Kop, a large hill, indeed a mountain, which was evidently the key of the position, but was far more accessible from the north than from the south.

"On the night of Jan. 23 he attacked Spion Kop, but found it very difficult to hold, as its perimiter was too large and water, which he had been led to believe existed in this extraordinarily dry season, was found very deficient.

"The crests were held all that day against severe attack and a heavy shell fire. Our men fought with great gallantry.

"I would especially mention the conduct of the Second Cameronians and the Third King's Rifles, who supported the attack on the mountain from the steepest side and, in each case, fought their way to the top, and the Second Lancashire Fusiliers and Second Middlesex, who magnificently maintained the best traditions of the British Army throughout the trying day of Jan. 24, and Thornycroft's Mounted Infantry, who fought throughout the day equally well alongside of them.

"Gen. Woodgate, who was in command at the summit, having been wounded, the officer who succeeded him decided on the night of Jan. 24 to abandon the position and did so before dawn Jan. 25.

"I reached Warren's camp at 5 A. M. on Jan. 25 and decided that a second attack upon Spion Kop was useless and that the enemy's right was too strong to allow me to force it.

"Accordingly, I decided to withdraw the force to the south of the Tugela.

"At 6 A. M. we commenced withdrawing the train and by 8 A. M. Jan. 27, (Saturday,) Warren's force was concentrated south of the Tugela without the loss of a man or a pound of stores.

"The fact that the force could withdraw from actual touch—in some cases the lines were less than 1,000 yards apart—with the enemy in the manner it did is, I think, sufficient evidence of the morale of the troops; and that we were permitted to withdraw our cumbrous ox and mule transport across the river, 85 yards broad, with 20-foot banks, and a very swift current, unmolested, is, I think, proof that the enemy has been taught to respect our soldiers' fighting powers."

WARREN WAS DRIVEN OUT

Boer Report of the Retaking of Spion Kop by Direct Assault in the Face of Heavy Fire.

BOER HEADQUARTERS, MODDER SPRUIT, Upper Tugela, Wednesday, Jan. 24, Midnight, (via Lorenzo Marques, Thursday, Jan. 25.)—Some Vryheid burghers from the outposts on the highest hills on the Spion Kop group rushed into the laager, saying that the kop was lost and that the English had taken it. Reinforcements were ordered up, but nothing could be done for some time, the hill being enveloped in thick mist.

At dawn the Heidelberg and Carolina contingents, supplemented from other commandoes, began the ascent of the hill. Three spurs, precipitous projections, faced the Boer positions. Up these the advance was made. The horses were left under the first terrace of rocks.

Scaling the steep, the Boers found that the English had improved the opportunity and intrenched heavily. Between the lines of trenches was an open veldt, which had to be rushed under a heavy fire not only from rifles, but of lyddite and shrapnel from field guns.

Three forces ascended the three spurs coordinately under cover of fire from the Free State Krupps, a Creusot, and a big Maxim. The English tried to rush the Boers with the bayonet, but their infantry went down before the Boer rifle fire as before a scythe.

The Boer investing party advanced step by step until 2 in the afternoon, when a white flag went up and 150 men in the front trenches surrendered, being sent as prisoners to the head laager.

The Boer advance continued on the two kopjes east of Spion Kop. Many Boers were shot, but so numerous were the burghers that the gaps filled automatically. Toward twilight they reached the summit of the second kopje, but did not get further.

The British Maxims belched flame, but a wall of fire from the Mausers held the English back. Their centre under this pressure gradually gave way and broke, abandoning the position.

The prisoners speak highly of the bravery of the burghers, who, despising cover, stood against the skyline edges of the summit to shoot the Dublin Fusiliers, sheltered in the trenches.

Firing continued for some time, and then the fusiliers and the Light Horse serving as infantry threw up their arms and rushed out of the trenches.

The effect of the abandonment of Spion Kop by the English can hardly be gauged as yet, but it must prove to be immense.

An unusually high proportion of lyddite shells did not explode.

LONDON, Jan. 28.—The following dispatch has been received in London from Pretoria, dated Jan. 25, via Lorenzo Marques, Jan. 28:

"The Government is advised that, after heavy fighting near Spion Kop, some British on the kop, being stormed, hoisted a white flag. One hundred and fifty prisoners. God be thanked! Although we also had to give brave and valuable lives."

1,500 BRITISH KILLED?

BOER HEAD LAAGER, Ladysmith, Jan 25—6 P. M.—The British dead left on the battlefield yesterday numbered 1,500.

BRITISH CAPTURE OF SPION KOP.

SPEARMAN'S CAMP, Friday, Jan. 26.—About 2 o'clock on the morning of Jan. 24, (Wednesday,) when heavy clouds rested upon the kopjes, the main point of the Boer position, Tabanyama, was stormed by the British infantry under Gen. Woodgate. Our

SUNDAY, THREE CENTS. DAILY, ONE CENT.

"All the News That's Fit to Print."

The New York Times.

THE WEATHER. Showers; southerly winds.

VOL. XLIX...NO. 15,730. NEW YORK, FRIDAY, JUNE 8, 1900.—FOURTEEN PAGES. ONE CENT In Greater New York and Jersey City. } Elsewhere, TWO CENTS.

THE NEWS CONDENSED.

Stocks dull.

Cash wheat, No. 2 red, 82¼c; corn, No. 2 mixed, 45¼c; oats, No. 2 mixed, 26¼c; cotton, middling, 8⅞c; iron, No. 1 foundry, $20; butter, creamery, extra, 19c.

FOREIGN.—A correspondent of The London Daily Express interviewed President Krüger near Machadorp, where his capital is situated, in a railway car fitted up for the emergency. The President and State Secretary Reitz said that the war was not over, and that guerrilla warfare would continue so long as 500 burghers were left to fight. He spoke hopefully of an early return to Pretoria, and said he would not leave the country. There are few telegrams from British sources. The list of casualties in the Thirteenth Yeomanry, captured on May 31, includes Sir John Elliott Cecil Power, Bart., killed, and the Earl of Longford wounded. The breach between Lord Lansdowne and Lord Wolseley has widened, and the latter has appealed to Premier Salisbury. Sir Alfred Milner, British Lord High Commissioner in South Africa, has sent a dispatch to the Colonial Office warning miners not to return to Cape Town from England. The situation in China grows worse. A big battle has been fought with the Boxers, in which 200 dead were left on the field. The British have landed 900 troops, a larger force than that of any other power. A detachment of 180 British marines is about to force a passage from Tien-Tsin to Peking. It is suggested in Berlin that there is a lack of harmony among the powers. The King of Sweden arrived at Paris to visit the exposition. The American Chamber of Commerce in Paris entertained the French Exposition officials. —Pages 1, 3, and 6.

CONGRESS.—The House yielded on the items in dispute on the Naval Appropriation bill and Congress adjourned. Mr. Cannon suffered a complete defeat; his proposed compromise being voted down. The closing scenes in the House were marked by great enthusiasm, roused by the singing of patriotic songs by the members, in which the galleries joined. Several Senators defended Commander Todd against the charges made in the House; after adjournment his suspension was revoked by Secretary Long.—Pages 1 and 2.

Page 1.

The Mayor of Newport threatened to arrest W. K. Vanderbilt, Jr., for fast locomobile driving. The Council will meet to-day to take action in regard to the speed rate.

Amendments to the Rules and Regulations of the Republican Party of the county, among other things providing for an executive committee, were adopted by the County Committee last night.

Page 2.

The American Ice Company has reduced the price of ice from 60 to 40 cents per hundred pounds.

Page 3.

Gov. Roosevelt addressed the boys of St. Paul's School at Concord, N. H.

One of the possibilities of the coming National campaign is a third Presidential ticket to be placed in the field by the National, or gold, Democracy.

The Democratic State Convention of Connecticut elected delegates to the National Convention and instructed them for Bryan and the Chicago platform.

Page 5.

Dr. Edward Everett Hale delivered an address yesterday at the annual commencement of Teachers College.

Page 6.

Capt. Frank F. Crenshaw and Capt. Flint are reported wounded in a dispatch from Manila.

The Secretary of War has directed the Military Governor of the Philippines to appoint a board to revise the tariff schedules.

Page 11.

President Wilson of the Consolidated Exchange replied to Moses Hirshfield's circular, defending his administration, and Gen. Watson and John Stanton joined with him in a statement of the Exchange's finances.

Page 14.

Capt. Frederick Bouchard of the barge Harvest Home late Wednesday night rescued a woman and child from drowning off Ellis Island.

Major Clinton H. Smith of the Seventy-first Regiment, who was dismissed from the National Guard of the State, has sent a letter of protest to Gov. Roosevelt. He declares that the officers of the Seventy-first will uphold him.

Arrivals at Hotels and Out-of-Town Buyers.—Page 3.
Business Troubles.—Page 12.
Court Calendars.—Page 12.
Insurance Notes.—Page 10.
Marine Intelligence and Foreign Mails.—Page 9.
Markets.—Page 9.
New Corporations.—Page 3.
Railroads.—Page 11.
Real Estate.—Page 12.
Society.—Page 7.
United Service.—Page 6.
Weather Report.—Page 3.
Yesterday's Fires.—Page 3.

BIG TORNADO IN THE WEST.

Much Damage in Indian Territory and Kansas—A Train Wrecked.

Special to The New York Times.

VINITA, Indian Territory, June 7.—The Town of Miami, Indian Territory, was struck by a tornado at 12:30 o'clock this morning. Several lives were reported lost, and great damage was done to property. Thomas Skinner, who had camped near the town, was sleeping in his wagon when the wagon was hurled into the Neosho River. Skinner was blown against a tree and instantly killed. Several persons were blown into the Neosho River, but were rescued easily on account of the river being low. The Christian church was completely wrecked, and the large livery barn of Manford Cooler was destroyed.

The loss in the town is estimated to exceed $10,000. Telegraph wires were blown down, heavy losses in hay barns and hay along the storm's path are reported. At Quawpaw, a few miles from Miami, nine large hay barns were destroyed, and all the barns at Oceuma were blown away.

The farmers began cutting their wheat a few days ago and the cyclone has destroyed nearly all the wheat along its path. Farmers were just laying by their corn and it is now blown down.

PARSONS, Kan., June 7.—A severe windstorm swept over this section, doing much damage to buildings, fences, trees, and growing crops. The clock tower of the Missouri, Kansas and Texas station was damaged and the elevator at St. Paul, Kan., twelve miles north of here, was destroyed.

At Emporia, Kan., the Crown Point Milling plant was badly damaged by wind and lightning. Many elevators and smokestacks of crushing mills were blown down.

The west-bound St. Louis and San Francisco passenger train was wrecked this morning two miles west of Oswego by a windstorm. The entire train was twisted loose from the engine and lifted from the track. Two express cars full of fruit were thrown about twenty feet and dropped on one side. Two tramps riding on the trucks were injured. The Pullman chair cars were thrown across the track.

CHETOPA, Kan., June 7.—A windstorm to-day almost destroyed the village of Faulkner, seven miles northeast of here. A schoolhouse, a church, and several dwellings were destroyed. The buildings were scattered over the adjacent country. Several farmhouses in the country were unroofed or blown from their foundations. Much damage was done to crops. No casualties are reported.

Twelve Injured in Wreck.

OMAHA, Neb., June 7.—The Milwaukee passenger train which leaves Council Bluffs at 11 A. M., was wrecked to-day at Persia, Iowa, by spreading rails. The dining car was overturned. Porter White and Conductor Kellogg were seriously injured. J. E. Boyer of Temona, Iowa, had his skull fractured, and will probably die. A Kansas City traveling man was seriously hurt, and eight other passengers were more or less injured.

"BOXERS" ENGAGED IN BIG BATTLE

Reported that 200 Dead Were Left on the Field.

UNITED STATES URGED TO ACT

Only Power Which Can Intervene Without Making Trouble.

British Land 900 Troops, and 180 Marines Start to Force a Passage from Tien-Tsin to Peking.

LONDON, June 8.—A dispatch from Shanghai, dated 7:30 P. M. to-day, says the Dowager Empress has ordered Gen. Neih-Si-Chong, with 3,000 men, to protect the railroad at Peking.

A severe fight, it is added, has occurred with the "Boxers," whose ranks include many soldiers from other Generals' commands. When the battle ended 200 dead were left on the field. The dispatch goes on to say:

"One hundred and eighty British marines, with a machine gun, are about to force a passage from Tien-Tsin to Peking. Altogether about 900 British have been landed from the fleet, a greater number than have landed from the combined vessels of the other powers. This evidence of Great Britain's intention to assert her position strongly gives great satisfaction here."

The Daily Express has the following dispatch from Shanghai, dated June 7:

"Attempts to repair the damage to the railway between Tien-Tsin and Peking have been frustrated by the Boxers, who, thousands strong, hold the line against the engineers, gangs attacking the trains arriving.

"The nearest undamaged point is forty-five miles from Tien-Tsin. All the children and ladies, except Lady Macdonald, have left the legations. There are the gravest fears for missionaries in outlying parts. They number hundreds, and the stations are isolated. Concerted action is impossible.

IMPERIAL EDICT IS EVASIVE.

The Peking correspondent of The Times, telegraphing yesterday, says:

"An imperial decree has been issued, but it is of the same evasive character as the preceding one. Throughout it is apologetic in tone and virtually gives justification to the 'Boxers' for their recent anti-foreign and anti-Christian outbreaks.

"The edict repeats the accusation against native Christians who 'joined the church for their own base ends,' and refers to the 'Boxers' as a 'brotherhood,' and not as rebels.

"It avoids all reference to the murders of missionaries or of native Christians, and implies that the destruction of the railway and mission property is due to lawless characters who have joined the Boxers to profit by the disturbances. It blames the officials, orders that the lawless shall be punished, and condemns the Chi-Li soldiers for assisting the disturbances. Nevertheless its character on the whole is quite unsatisfactory.

"The Tsung-li-Yamen undertakes that railway communication shall be restored by Saturday. They have protested against the arrival of more British guards."

WANT UNITED STATES TO ACT.

The morning papers, in long editorials dealing with the Chinese situation, refer to the possible course of the United States. The Daily Mail, which goes beyond any other in urging America to take the lead in intervention, under the caption "McKinley's Opportunity," says:

"The United States has secured definite pledges as to the maintenance of the open door, and their intervention would not produce friction, danger of which is to be anticipated should either England or Russia act alone. We have no desire to provoke a worldwide conflict. Yet our movements are regarded with so much suspicion by many Russians that serious complications might ensue did we land a strong force near Peking.

"The same applies to Russia, face to face with ourselves, but the United States has traditions of friendship with Russia and a community of interests with England. Their action would therefore assure the hostility of neither power. It need scarcely be said that they would have the moral support of the British people, and our material support also, if only the policy of our Government in the Far East were stronger than it is. They would certainly be assisted by Japan.

"In this way a world conflict, disastrous to the interests of all great States, could best be avoided and at the same time the pledges which the skillful negotiations of Mr. Hay have extracted from the various powers would be vindicated.

"The opportunity for America has come. Will she be equal to it, or will she let it slip from her hands and lose her vast potentialities of trade in Northern China?"

BRITISH INTERESTS IN CHINA.

Great Britain's financial interests in China, interests that can be named on the Stock Exchange, aggregate £40,000,000. These, on an average, have declined 1 per cent. There are also many trading companies and syndicates holding concessions which are capitalized for vast unknown sums. The English money in China is probably close to £500,000,000.

The report that Sir Claude Macdonald is too ill to attend to his duties is declared to be unfounded. He has been in constant communication with the Government.

COMMANDERS' INSTRUCTIONS.

The naval commanders in Chinese waters have received identical instructions as to procedure, the question of an emergency being left to their discretion. No fear is entertained for the safety of the legations at Peking. European residents, however, are escaping from the capital to the coast. Peking is still under control, according to a dispatch to the Morning Post dated yesterday, but in a very excited state. A thousand foreign guards were garrisoning the legation houses.

Six hundred international troops are at Tien-Tsin, with six guns. A dispatch to The Daily Mail from Shanghai, dated June 7, takes a gloomy view of things, which are pictured as going from bad to worse. The correspondent says:

"The authorities are displaying palpably guilty supineness in dealing with the Boxers; and the powers are more and more taking matters into their own hands. The Boxers' revolt is spreading and is rapidly changing its character. The Boxers are getting arms, preparing to meet force with force.

"There has been no communications between Peking and Tien-Tsin since Tuesday, although one miserable, half-hearted attempt has been made by Chinese soldiery to reach the capital. The troops were fired upon, and the train had to come back. Another station has been burned on the line."

BOXERS STILL RAIDING.

A news agency dispatch from Tien-Tsin, dated yesterday, says:

"The 'Boxers' are still raiding and pillaging over a wide area. They have wrecked and burned the stations at Long-Pong and Langoo. It has been definitely ascertained that Mme. Astier and Messrs. Ossent and Cades have been murdered. Gen. Nieh claims to have defeated the 'Boxers,' killing 500."

Telegraphing from Tien-Tsin, under date of June 6, a correspondent says:

"I left Tien-Tsin this morning en route for Peking, accompanied by Gen. Nieh, supposed to be one of the best of the Chinese Generals, with sixty troops. We proceeded to Lofa, a distance of thirty-one miles. We found the plate layers' cabins in flames and telegraph poles cut, and men engaged in destroying others in villages near the railway, where flags were seen bearing the inscription: 'Kill All Foreigners.'

"I saw smoke, evidently from burning houses, in the distance, but Gen. Nieh refused to proceed further, being in mortal fear of the Boxers, though the foreigners endeavored to persuade him to disentrain his troops, who are firmly convinced that it is useless to fight the Boxers, as other Chinese say they have seen Boxers hit with bullets rise and run away.

"There seems to be little prospect of a resumption of traffic to Peking unless the foreign powers assume control of the railway until the Chinese Government proves itself capable of managing communications with its capital."

GREAT BRITAIN'S ATTITUDE.

It is understood here that if the United States expects Great Britain to take independent or initiative action in China, as might be gathered from the special cable dispatches quoting Congressman Hitt, the Chairman of the House Committee on Foreign Affairs, it is depending on a contingency which appears very remote indeed.

A correspondent was informed officially to-day that the British Minister at Peking, Sir Claude M. Macdonald, and his assistants, are still in complete charge of the situation, and are relied upon to meet any circumstances which may arise, armed as they are with authority to requisition from the British-China squadron more troops if they are needed.

Replying to a private letter the other day, which suggested that Great Britain should show her teeth more, Lord Salisbury, it is learned, replied that "unfortunately England's teeth were now in South Africa."

SOUNDING THE POWERS.

In spite of the fact that it is officially stated that Great Britain has neither sounded other powers with the view of securing co-operation in a new and vigorous Chinese policy nor been sounded as to such action by any power, there are many rumors that such steps are under consideration. A member of a foreign Embassy in London says that it is certain the British Foreign Office is contemplating sending instructions to all its Ministers to secure the support of other governments, especially the United States Government, in a plan of action.

Although Russia might be included in this concert it would have for its ulterior object the frustration of any designs Russia may harbor for making capital out of the present troubled state of affairs in China. This statement the British Foreign Office categorically and emphatically denies.

ATTITUDE OF UNITED STATES.

WASHINGTON, June 7.—Perhaps a published rumor to the effect that the United States might join with other powers in prohibiting Russia from landing more troops than those of other powers in China led to the early appearance at the State Department to-day of Mr. De Wollant, the First Secretary of the Russian Embassy. The Ambassador, Count Cassini, is absent on leave from his post, and the First Secretary is acting as Chargé.

If that was the subject of his inquiries, the charge was speedily reassured, for the State Department has made no concealment of its policy respecting the Chinese situation, and has repeatedly intimated that it is concerned solely for the safety of the American Legation and Consulates in China, and for the direct interests of American citizens there.

An indication of the care exercised by the department in confining its officers strictly to these lines is afforded by the instruction to Minister Conger, sent yesterday, to draw upon Admiral Kempf for any force needed to protect his legation and such refugees as might claim the right of asylum there or in the consulates. The Minister was not even charged to send out the United States naval forces and marines to points where American missionaries are reported to be beset and in jeopardy, although much pressure has been brought to bear upon the State Department by the missionary interests to secure an order to this effect.

Mr. Conger's powers are regarded as ample, but he is not expected to take action in the matter of dispatching military expeditions to the interior of China that might be equivalent to a declaration of war. The department hopes to be able to adhere closely to the old-time policy of abstention from interference with internal matters in China, and especially to refrain from entangling movements in connection with the projects of other powers.

The Helena has not yet sailed from Manila to reinforce Admiral Kempf's force at Taku, and it is surmised that at the moment the order was received from the Navy Department, the vessel was either absent from Manila, or was not available for immediate service. The Navy Department was in communication to-day with Admiral Remey, presumably with reference to the speedy movement of the Helena, or some other ship, to Taku.

NO HARMONY AMONG POWERS.

BERLIN, June 7.—The Foreign Office regards the situation in China as no worse than it was last evening. No official reports indicating an unfavorable change have been received. The papers this evening, however, take a different view of the matter. The Vossische Zeitung says:

"Evidences are lacking of harmony among the powers interested in China, and the probability is that if the Boxer movement is allowed to spread and the dangers growing out of it become more serious this result will be owing to the want of harmony."

The National Zeitung, which expresses its views in similar terms, says it hopes that until the present troubles are over Russia, Great Britain, and Japan will bury their differences.

It is understood that Germany has officially declared her readiness to act in concert with the other powers. But, having no interests outside of Shan-Tung Province, she is not disposed to take the leading part in intervention in China.

The German newspapers claim to have discovered that the alleged secret agreement arrived at between Russia and Japan to act together against Great Britain in the Far East is purely fictitious. The National Zeitung avers that Great Britain stands hand in glove with Japan.

The officer commanding the German squadron at Che-Foo has been directed by cable to send a detachment of sailors and marines to Tien-Tsin and, after conferring with the German Minister at Peking, to arrange with the commanders of the other squadrons regarding further measures to be taken for the protection of Europeans.

Orders to Austrian Cruiser.

VIENNA, June 7.—The Austrian cruiser Zenta has been instructed to take part in the projected blockade, if finally decided upon.

ASKS MR. HAY'S AID.

Board of Foreign Missions Can Get No Reply from Peking.

The following letter was sent to the Secretary of State at Washington yesterday by the Secretary of the Presbyterian Board of Foreign Missions here:

Sir: Our board has fifty-eight American missionaries in the Shangtung Provinces, China, sixteen in Peking, and ten in Paotingfu, eighty-four altogether, besides, of course, large property interests.

We, as well as many relatives and friends, are intensely anxious about the personal safety of those missionaries, and particularly those at Paotingfu, where, according to the telegraphic dispatches in the daily press, some missionaries have recently been murdered.

A cabled inquiry of our own to Peking has brought no reply. I therefore venture to ask you to inquire by cable, through United States Minister Conger, whether the American missionaries are safe. We shall greatly appreciate your inquiry, and your prompt action will relieve a strain which is now very trying.

ARTHUR J. BROWN, Secretary.

A telegram was also sent to Secretary Hay by Darwin R. James, requesting that prompt attention be given to the above communication.

PLAN OF GOLD DEMOCRATS

May Place a Third National Ticket in the Field.

Executive Committee, After a Secret Meeting, Calls National Committee to Meet in July.

A third Presidential ticket to be placed in the field by the National, or gold, Democratic Party is one of the possibilities of the coming National campaign. This assertion was made yesterday afternoon by George Foster Peabody, Chairman of the National Committee. A meeting of the National Committee will be held in Indianapolis on July 25, at which time the course to be followed in the coming contest by the forces which battled for Palmer and Buckner four years ago will be mapped out.

The Executive Committee held a secret meeting in this city last Friday and after a full discussion of the National situation it was decided to authorize Secretary John P. Frenzel of Indiana to issue a call for a meeting of the National Committee.

Mr. Peabody yesterday explained to a reporter for THE NEW YORK TIMES the conditions which, in his opinion, might make it necessary for the gold Democrats to name their own ticket this year, as they did in 1896. He said:

"At our meeting last Friday we agreed that it would be wise for us to wait until after the Philadelphia and Kansas City Conventions have both been held before announcing what we intend to do this year. We will meet in Indianapolis three weeks after the holding of the Kansas City Convention. By that time the declarations of both conventions will have been made and we will have had time to form an opinion as to what to do. Of course, the question of candidates has been settled and we have some idea of what to expect in the way of platforms from the Philadelphia and Kansas City Conventions, but we will have to wait until we see the actual declarations made in those platforms.

"We want to see what the Republicans have to say on what is called imperialism, and then again the Republican currency plank may not be satisfactory. The same reasons apply to the convention to be held in Kansas City. It may be found that the delegates to that gathering will listen to reason, and that the conservative element is in control. Until we know the exact situation it would not be wise to commit ourselves to any policy.

"It had been hoped that it would not be necessary to reorganize our forces this year, but we decided that in our keeping reposed the old-fashioned Democratic principles, and that it was our duty to guard them well and to take in this coming campaign whatever action may be found necessary to keep those principles before the people."

Mr. Peabody has received many letters from Gold Democrats in all parts of the country asking him to have something definite done, and it was in response to these communications and visits from persons who took part in the fight of four years ago that Mr. Peabody summoned the Executive Committee to meet in this city last week. The committeemen who were here reported that there was much sentiment among those who cannot affiliate with the Republicans and who are opposed to William J. Bryan for the nomination of a third ticket. It is said that if at the meeting of the National Committee it is decided to hold a National convention it will probably be held in Indianapolis, as a compliment to the Indiana Gold Democrats, who were the first to take any action demanding that the anti-silver men in the party place a National ticket in the field. It was in Indianapolis that the Palmer and Buckner ticket was nominated in 1896.

The members of the National Committee are:

George Foster Peabody, New York, Chairman; John P. Frenzel, Indiana, Secretary and Treasurer; J. M. Faulkner, Alabama; P. J. Cole, Arizona; C. B. Moore, Arkansas; E. B. Pond, California; Louis R. Ehrich, Colorado; Joel A. Sperry, Connecticut; John S. Russell, Delaware; D. G. Ambler, Florida; Thomas F. Corrigan, Georgia; Benjamin T. Cable, Illinois; John R. Wilson, Indiana; Edwin Ludlow, Indian Territory; L. M. Martin, Iowa; Eugene Hagan, Kansas; Zack Phelps, Kentucky; M. R. Spellman, Louisiana; C. Vey Holman, Maine; William Pinckney Whyte, Maryland; N. Matthews, Jr., Massachusetts; Thomas A. Wilson, Michigan; F. W. M. Cutcheon, Minnesota; H. M. Street, Mississippi; L. C. Krauthoff, Missouri; A. H. Nelson, Montana; Euclid Martin, Nebraska; G. Woodbury, New Hampshire; William J. Curtis, New Jersey; William B. Childers, New Mexico; Charles Tracey, New York; H. E. Fries, North Carolina; H. L. Whitehed, North Dakota; Talfourd P. Lenn, Ohio; C. E. S. Wood, Oregon; S. T. McCormick, Pennsylvania; C. C. Mumford, Rhode Island; W. R. Davie, South Carolina; John B. Hanton, South Dakota; Michael Savage, Tennessee; M. L. Crawford, Texas; Parley Williams, Utah; W. H. Creamer, Vermont; Joseph Bryan, Virginia; Hugh C. Wallace, Washington; Randolph Stainaker, West Virginia; Ellis B. Usher, Wisconsin.

ELKINS FOR VICE PRESIDENT.

His Name Considered by New Jersey—Views of Senator Stokes.

Special to The New York Times.

TRENTON, N. J., June 7.—A number of the New Jersey delegates to the Republican National Convention have been here this week attending the Supreme Court. When asked as to the attitude of the New Jersey delegation on the Vice Presidency, each one said that the delegation was entirely at sea in the matter, but it was ascertained that the name of Senator Stephen B. Elkins of West Virginia is being considered with favor.

Senator Stokes of Cumberland County, one of the party leaders, when seen at his office in the Mechanics' Bank, of which he is President, was free to say that while he regarded the situation as perplexing and while he had no personal preferences, it seemed clear to him that Senator Elkins was the most desirable candidate from a party point of view.

"He combines," said Senator Stokes, "more elements of availability than any other prominent Republican. Born in Ohio, brought up in Missouri, where he taught school and was admitted to the bar, identified for fourteen years with the development and political life of New Mexico, and now a resident of West Virginia, he is representative of the West and South, and his large business connections make him acceptable to Pennsylvania, New Jersey, and Maryland, while New York would probably regard him with almost as much favor as Cornelius N. Bliss.

"No," said Senator Stokes, "don't ask me to say to what extent Mr. Elkins's name is being considered by our delegation. These are merely my personal views as to his availability territorially and to the business world. Whether the convention accepts the logic of the situation or not remains to be seen."

DARKNESS AT BATH BEACH.

Electric Lights Extinguished, Creating Confusion and Annoyance.

Every electric light at Bath Beach suddenly went out early last night while a big crowd of visitors was moving about among the various concert halls and other places of amusement there. Up to 1 o'clock this morning the defective circuit had not been repaired, and for several hours total darkness prevailed in almost every direction. A dozen or more kerosene lamps furnished all the illumination that existed during that time.

To judge from the noises that rose from the beach for a couple of hours after the dark season began, it was with no slight difficulty that the visitors found their way to the trolley cars. Exactly what happened is still a matter for conjecture, and it is expected that later discoveries will expose many incidents both comic and criminal, as there was abundant opportunity for either.

NEW REPUBLICAN RULES

Adoption of Amendment Providing for Executive Committee.

TEN EYCK MAY BE CHAIRMAN

Not to be Hampered by County Committee's President—Making Way for General Greene.

The Republican County Committee met in special session at the Murray Hill Lyceum last night. In the absence of President Lemuel E. Quigg, who is confined to his home by illness, McDougall Hawkes of the Twenty-fifth Assembly District presided.

Secretary George R. Manchester, in obedience to the action taken at the meeting of the Executive Committee in the afternoon, presented amendments to the rules and regulations of the Republican Party of the County of New York.

These amendments provided, first, that the County Committee elected at the official primary in August, 1900, shall meet for organization on the third Thursday in December, 1900.

This, it will be noticed, is subsequent to the Presidential election.

Next, it was decided to amend Article 4 by striking out the words "and also the Executive Committee," and "these bodies," and substituting therefor "that body," so that the paragraph shall read: "The President shall be the Chairman of the County Committee, and it shall be his duty to preside at all meetings of that body, and he shall be ex-officio a member of all standing and special committees."

Article 5 was amended to add after the "Treasurer" "and the Chairman of the Finance Committee," and, to add to the clause the following:

"The Executive Committee shall meet for the purpose of organization within ten days after its appointment upon the call of the President of the County Committee, and shall forthwith elect its Chairman, who shall be ex officio a member of the Finance Committee and the Committee on Election Officers.

"The Executive Committee shall meet on the call of its Chairman to consider such business as may be brought forward. Meetings of the committee must be called by the Chairman upon the written request of seven members of the committee, stating the object for which a meeting is desired."

This divorces the Chairman of the Executive Committee from the Presidency of the County Committee.

Another amendment provides that delegates to each convention shall be apportioned among the several units of representation according to the primary election law.

Either the County Committee or the Executive Committee may call future conventions, and all delegates must be elected on the official primary day in September of each year, except in Presidential years, when they shall be chosen in August.

All the amendments were adopted on motion of Postmaster Van Cott.

Leader Charles A. Hess of the Twenty-fifth District presented the resignation of Arthur T. Sturges. In his place Gen. Francis Vinton Greene was unanimously chosen.

This prepares the way for the election of Gen. Greene to the Presidency of the committee at the meeting to be held on June 21.

It is generally understood that Aqueduct Commissioner William H. Ten Eyck will be the Chairman of the proposed Executive Committee. Other members will be F. S. Gibbs, Collector of Customs George R. Bidwell, John Sabine Smith, Postmaster Cornelius Van Cott, Gen. Francis Vinton Greene, and Lemuel E. Quigg.

GEN. GREENE TO SEE MR. PLATT.

Conference of Republican Leaders Is Announced for To-day.

Senator Platt and Chairman Odell of the Republican State Committee are in town. The former was very much fatigued on his return from Washington, and retired early. Mr. Odell had no news.

It is admitted, however, that there will be a conference to-day, at which Messrs. Platt, Odell, and Gen. Francis V. Greene, the coming President of the Republican County Committee, will be present.

Chairman Odell had several callers yesterday, including Congressman James S. Sherman of Oneida, who is said to have Gubernatorial aspirations, and Lieut. Gov. T. L. Woodruff, who would like to be Vice President. Mr. Woodruff would not discuss the Vice Presidency.

ELEPHANT PUT TO DEATH.

Hanged on a Mammoth Freight Derrick.

Special to The New York Times.

BALTIMORE, Md., June 7.—Sport, the big elephant of Bostock's Zoo, was put to death by hanging at 6 o'clock this evening. The novel execution took place in the Bolton yards of the Pennsylvania Railroad here. The gallows was the powerful derrick used by the railroad for lifting stone and other heavy freight. The mammoth beast was given large quantities of ether before the execution. Chains were placed about his neck so as to draw upon his windpipe and choke him to death. As the derrick raised the beast, he trumpeted fiercely for a moment, and then was still. Life was extinct in nine minutes. A number of physicians witnessed the hanging and made an examination of the body afterward.

While Sport was being transported in a freight car from Scranton, Penn., in company with an elephant named Jolly, which died of heart disease yesterday, the big beasts became playful. Sport backed with some force against the door, which gave way beneath his weight. The elephant was precipitated from the moving train to the ground. He fell on his back and emitted a terrific scream. The train was stopped and a wrecking crew was telegraphed for. When they arrived Sport was lifted by a derrick into the train. When examined by Baltimore surgeons it was found that while Sport had broken no bones, he had suffered partial paralysis of the spinal column. It required a number of conferences to determine how to kill the big beast.

LAKE BORGNE CANAL BOUGHT.

Alabama Products Will Reach New Orleans by an All-Water Route.

Special to The New York Times.

NEW ORLEANS, June 7.—A company with ample financial backing has just purchased the Lake Borgne Canal property, on which a vast amount of money has been spent, and will push the work to completion. This waterway will connect Lake Borgne and the Mississippi Sound with the Mississippi River seven miles below New Orleans, and will furnish a connecting link between the extensive system of inland waterways made available by the costly work that is being done in improving and opening the Warrior River. The purpose is to establish an unbroken line of slackwater navigation from the Alabama coal and iron fields to New Orleans.

By this route the products of the far interior of Alabama, including coal, iron, turpentine and resin, pitch pine and other timber of value, will find their way down the Warrior and Alabama Rivers to Mississippi Sound, and thence by a sheltered route behind the chain of islands which inclose the sound to Lake Borgne. After crossing Lake Borgne they will reach the canal, and passing through it, be afloat in the Mississippi River, reaching New Orleans by an all-water route without once breaking bulk. This water way will enable the Alabama coal mines to undersell the Pittsburg coal combine in Southern markets, and will also open up a large export business in naval stores for New Orleans.

MAY ARREST MR. VANDERBILT.

He Runs Down a Child—Mayor of Newport Threatens Him for Fast Locomobile Driving.

Special to The New York Times.

NEWPORT, June 7.—Rumors of complaints regarding the speed which William K. Vanderbilt, Jr., has been driving his locomobile through this city have been heard for the past three days, but nothing official has been done by the local authorities until to-day, when Frederick Sheldon, one of the prominent cottagers, called upon Mayor Boyle and lodged a complaint against Mr. Vanderbilt, for the speed with which he passed through the city this morning. According to his complaint, he had a narrow escape from being badly injured. Mr. Sheldon demanded that something should be done to prevent Mr. Vanderbilt from driving his machine at the speed he has been going, and after fully explaining the circumstances, he drove home satisfied.

Later Mr. Vanderbilt chanced to meet the Mayor and his Honor threatened him with arrest if he persisted in racing his locomobile through the streets of Newport.

This afternoon Mr. Vanderbilt came from the Herreshoff works at Bristol, landing at Bristol ferry, where his locomobile was in waiting and, with a party of guests, drove into Newport with his usual speed.

Later as Mr. Vanderbilt was passing along the lower part of Thames Street in a runabout automobile a little girl, who attempted to run across the roadway, was struck by one wheel and was thrown to the ground. Mr. Vanderbilt immediately stopped the automobile and jumping to the roadway quickly picked the child up in his arms and held it until the mother arrived.

The child apparently was not injured, and after handing her over to her mother Mr. Vanderbilt informed the parent that any medical attention or care the child might need, as a result of the accident, would be furnished at his expense.

The farmers in Middletown are considerably worked up over the rapid speed with which W. K. Vanderbilt, Jr., passed through that town a few days ago with his "lightning machine," as it has been named in the rural districts, and the Council will hold a special meeting to regulate the speed of such carriages.

The Ordinance Committee of the City Council of Newport will hold a special meeting to-morrow afternoon to take action in regard to the speed rate and other matters pertaining to the regulation of automobiles in Newport.

BOSTON AND ALBANY LEASE.

Provisions of the Bill to be Reported in Massachusetts Senate.

Special to The New York Times.

BOSTON, June 7.—In the Massachusetts Senate to-morrow Senator Soule, Chairman of the Committee on Railroads, will present the Boston and Albany lease as recommended in the bill voted by the committee after a protracted session last evening. The vote was virtually 12 in favor to 3 against the measure in committee. Senators Joy and Ross and Representative Blood dissent, while Representative Weston reserves his right to dissent, although his name does not appear as against the bill.

By the terms of the bill the Commonwealth does not waive or release any rights or privileges that it may now have, but expressly reserves and retains such rights. These include the right to reduce rates and fares, to compel service, &c. It is stipulated that there shall be no higher rate for freight from any point to Boston than is charged to New York. Nor shall the New York Central diminish or allow to be diminished the facilities for travel and business over the Boston and Albany. It shall expend not less than $250,000 per year, beginning July 1, 1901, until the full sum of $2,500,000 shall have been expended in improving East Boston terminals and double-tracking the Grand Junction Railway.

No change in the lease shall be valid unless it is approved by the Massachusetts Legislature. Whenever the Railroad Commissioners shall deem that the provisions of the act are not complied with they shall transmit a statement to the Attorney General, who shall institute proceedings to obtain compliance. The Supreme Judicial Court of Massachusetts is given full jurisdiction to act on the petition of the Attorney General, and to enforce its decree against the lessee.

The term of the lease is for ninety-nine years, and the act takes effect July 1 1901. There is no referendum attached

WILLIAM T. PARKER DEAD.

Became Suddenly Insane at the Harvard Law School Examinations.

Special to The New York Times.

CAMBRIDGE, Mass., June 7.—William Thornton Parker, Jr., of the Harvard Law School died this afternoon at 3 o'clock at the Cambridge Hospital of an abscess on the brain caused by overstudy. Thornton was one of the hardest working students in the Law School, and as this was his last year he had been applying himself with unusual vigor.

A few days ago he was taking the examination in Constitutional law when suddenly in the midst of the examination he became insane, and waving his hands wildly, cried out a number of unintelligible sentences. His condition became rapidly worse, and he died this afternoon. He came from Springfield, Mass., and was about twenty-four years of age. He was also a graduate of the Massachusetts Institute of Technology, where he obtained the highest honors.

COLLEGE ATHLETE DROWNED.

S. L. Bahny Loses His Life While Swimming in Mohawk River.

Special to The New York Times.

SCHENECTADY, N. Y., June 7.—The commencement of Union College this year is again overshadowed by the drowning fatality. S. L. Bahny of Olean, a member of the Class of 1902, and a well-known athlete, lost his life this afternoon while swimming in the Mohawk River.

With four companions, Leroy Taylor, George Walrath, E. H. Rider, and W. J. Dickenson, Bahny essayed to swim across the stream. He lost his strength when about half the distance had been accomplished, and cried for help. Taylor, who was about twenty-five yards from Bahny, went to his assistance and tried to tow him ashore. Bahny, however, struggled, and finally succeeded in getting so firm a hold on the would-be rescuer that the two men sank to the bottom. On coming to the surface Taylor freed himself from the grasp of Bahny and made the rest of his way to shore. Walrath then tried to save Bahny, but after a struggle of several minutes he, too, was forced to seek his own safety. Bahny's body was recovered shortly afterward.

ACTOR'S BRAVE RESCUE.

Grasps Two Drowning Women by the Hair and Swims Ashore with Them.

Special to The New York Times.

PORT JERVIS, N. Y., June 7.—Richard Lyle of New York City, in company with Miss Niva Sutterly and Mrs. Beatrice Jensen, was enjoying a boat ride on Culvert Lake, near Branchville, N. J., to-day. The ladies decided to exchange seats during the trip, and as they were passing him, Lyle, who weighs 200 pounds, leaned toward the ladies and the boat capsized. When the three returned to the surface the boat had drifted away, but Lyle, who is an expert swimmer, grasped the ladies by the hair, and holding their heads above the water, swam to shore. The ladies fainted, but restoratives were administered, and they are now none the worse for their experience.

Lyle and the ladies are members of the Lyle theatrical company of New York, which is playing at Branchville, and when Mr. Lyle appeared on the stage last evening he was greeted with tremendous applause by the audience, who had heard of his brave deed.

THE HOUSE YIELDS; CONGRESS ADJOURNS

Senate Wins Fight Over Naval Appropriation Bill.

BAD DEFEAT FOR CANNON

His Proposed Compromise Voted Down—Cummings Tells Him He Is "Only a Toy Musket."

Special to The New York Times.

WASHINGTON, June 7.—The fifty-sixth Congress, first session, adjourned this afternoon at 5 o'clock. Joseph G. Cannon, Representative from Illinois, and hitherto the real leader in the House on the Republican side, at midnight the victor over the Senate in the long contest over the Naval Appropriation bill, may have held the opinion, before to-day's session was at an end, that it should have adjourned yesterday, for the sole purpose in holding it together seems to have been to administer to him a complete, conspicuous, and unexpected defeat.

When the two houses dispersed late last night the Senate was smarting under what it considered the insulting treatment accorded to the Naval bill conferrees and the Senate in overturning the conference report on the Appropriation bill and adjourning without attempting to bring about another meeting. Even the form of the new conference was offensive, for the House had taken the matter out of the hands of the Naval Committee and placed it in the care of the Committee on Appropriations. This meant that Mr. Hale and his associates of the Senate were to meet the men who had inspired the opposition that had made possible the prolongation of the session.

A REACTION IN THE HOUSE.

Before the House met to-day a reaction had set in, not altogether an uninspired reaction, for Senators who understood the situation were at work. Fifteen or twenty of them visited the House from time to time to warn their representatives not to join the crusade against the Hydrographic Office of the Navy Department merely to contribute to the political strength of the Coast and Geodetic Survey.

The reaction had been fully established before a vote was reached. Mr. Cannon, still aglow and confident after the rout last night of the Hydrographic office forces, marched up with abundant confidence. The deposed conferrees of the Naval Committee were buoyed up by the assurances and the promises of the visiting Senators. Upon a viva voce vote to recede and concur, which preceded in order the motion of Mr. Cannon to non-concur, Mr. Dayton (Rep., W. Va.,) of the Naval Committee won by a few votes.

Mr. Cannon believed that the rollcall would sustain him and preserve the fruits of the victory achieved last night. The roll-call showed 118 votes to accept the proposition of the Senate, and only 96 for Cannon. Cannon was a beaten leader. He surrendered without conditions, giving over the charge of the bill to Mr. Dayton, one of the men last night discredited and deposed. Everything remaining in dispute went the Senate's way.

For a time it was uncertain whether the President, after his experience of yesterday, would not decline to again wait upon Congress, adopting instead the practice of his predecessor, and ask committees of that body to wait upon him at the White House after the Naval bill had been completed. He was informed, however, when the agreement had been reached, and sent word that he would come to the President's room at the Capitol between 4 and 5. When he reached the Capitol he had little to do, and he was on his way back to the White House a few moments after 5.

HOUSE YIELDS TO SENATE.

WASHINGTON, June 7.—The story of to-day's contest over the Naval Appropriation bill is practically a story of the proceedings in the House with reference to the bill. The Senate simply waited on the House.

Early in the day the conferrees on the bill decided to report a disagreement. Their conference developed the fact that the representatives of both houses were willing to make mutual concessions, and in reality an agreement practically was reached, though it was decided to first report a disagreement to both houses in order to test the feeling.

The tentative agreement eliminated all inland and coast work, confined the survey to the ocean, eliminated all reference to the lakes and to "hydrographic surveys," and reduced the $100,000 appropriated by the Senate amendment to $50,000. The amendment as thus agreed upon was as follows:

Ocean Survey—Including the waters of Cuba and the Philippine archipelago, but not the coast thereof, and for the purchase of nautical books, charts, and sailing directions, and freight and express charges on the same, $50,000.

Mr. Cannon, on behalf of the House conferrees on the Naval Appropriation bill, formally reported the disagreement to the House. The former conferrees, who were superseded last night after a bitter fight, evidently were ready to resume the struggle. Mr. Cannon moved that the House recede and concur in the Senate amendment with an amendment which struck out the word "hydrographic" and provided for ocean, but not coast, surveys.

In his statement Mr. Cannon said the proposed amendment was in harmony with the instructions given by the House a week ago not to agree to any surveys for the coasts of the great lakes, the seaboard, or the islands of our new possessions. The amendment would confine the naval surveys to the deep water of the ocean.

DAYTON MOVES TO RECEDE.

Mr. Dayton, (Rep., West Va.,) one of the superseded conferrees, moved to recede and concur in the Senate amendment in order to bring the question squarely before the House. This motion took precedence over that of Mr. Cannon.

Mr. Moody, (Dem., Mass.,) who last night charged the conferrees with betraying their trust, apologized for his words amid applause.

Mr. Cummings, (Dem., N. Y.,) one of the conferrees, said the apology was "justly due and handsomely done."

He then explained the difficulties under which the old conferrees had labored. He contrasted the result of their work with that of the new conferrees, who, he said, had offered a new proposition which practically violated the House instructions while technically observing them. He somewhat startled the House by referring to a "junketing trip" which Mr. Cannon had taken as the guest of the Coast Survey, and then proceeded to pay his respects to the Chairman of the Appropriations Committee. Mr. Cummings wields a keen blade and the House enjoyed his dextrous thrusts.

CUMMINGS ON CANNON.

He pictured Mr. Cannon, the Chairman of the great Appropriations Committee, as a lion lashing his sides and roaring while the crowd of jackals followed as they smelt fresh meat. Then he described how the House, following blindly the lion's leadership, had done everything it could to degrade its conferrees, despite their appeals that they were powerless.

"I told you," said he, with great vehemence, "that we were up against a stone wall, but you turned us down and turned the controversy over to the Appropriations Committee to settle. And they went up against the same stone wall, with the result that they are back here crawling before this House with another proposition. Why, if you were so loyal, did you come crawling back into the House?" he asked, addressing Mr. Cannon. "Why did you not continue your opposition?" Then, with sarcasm and with a contemptuous wave of his hand, he said as took his seat:

"You have been misnamed; you are no Cannon, you are a toy musket." This shot

"All the News That's Fit to Print."

The New York Times.

THE WEATHER.
Fair; wind northeasterly, becoming southerly.

VOL. L...NO. 15,926. NEW YORK, WEDNESDAY, JANUARY 23, 1901.—SIXTEEN PAGES. ONE CENT In Greater New York, Jersey City, and Newark. } Elsewhere, TWO CENTS.

QUEEN VICTORIA DEAD AT OSBORNE

Passed Away Quietly at 6:30 o'Clock Last Evening.

SCENE AT THE BEDSIDE

Family, with Bowed Heads, Listened to Bishop's Prayers.

QUEEN BADE THEM FAREWELL

Said to Have Spoken Words of Great Moment to Prince of Wales.

ALBERT EDWARD NOW KING

Privy Council and Parliament Will Meet in London To-day, and the Proclamation of the New Monarch's Succession Will Follow—Grief Over the Queen's Death and Admiration for Her Character Universal in the United Kingdom, the British Colonies, Europe, and America—Arrangements for the Funeral Not Yet Announced.

COWES, Isle of Wight, Jan. 23.—Queen Victoria is dead. The greatest event in the memory of this generation, almost the most stupendous change in existing conditions in England that could be imagined, has taken place quietly, almost gently, upon the anniversary of the death of Queen Victoria's father, the Duke of Kent.

The end of this splendid career came in a simply furnished room in Osborne House. This most respected of all women, living or dead, lay in a great four-posted bed. Around her were gathered the majority of her descendants. Well within view of her dying eyes there hung a portrait of the Prince Consort. It was he who designed the room and every part of the Castle. In scarcely audible words the white-haired Bishop of Winchester prayed beside her, as he had often before prayed with his sovereign, for he was her Chaplain at Windsor.

With bowed heads the imperious ruler of the German Empire, the man who is now King of England, the woman who has succeeded to the title of Queen, the Princes and Princesses, and those of less than royal designation listened to the Bishop's ceaseless prayer.

Naturally, the family, while recognizing the claim for public information, insist that some details of the events around the deathbed shall be sacred for the present, and have imposed the strictest secrecy on the whole household. The Queen is, however, said to have bidden farewell, in a feeble voice, to her family. She first recognized the Prince of Wales, to whom she spoke a few words of great moment; then Emperor William and the others present filed past and heard a whispered good-bye. All those in the bedroom were in tears.

Six o'clock passed. The Bishop continued his intercession. One of the younger children asked a question in a shrill, childish treble, and was immediately silenced. The women of the royal family sobbed faintly and the men shuffled uneasily.

THE END QUITE PEACEFUL.

At exactly 6:30 Sir James Reid held up his hand, and the people in the room knew that England had lost her Queen. The Bishop pronounced the benediction.

The Queen passed away quite peacefully. She suffered no pain. Those who were now mourners went to their rooms. A few minutes later the inevitable element of materialism stepped into this pathetic chapter of international history, for the Court ladies went busily to work ordering their mourning from London.

The wheels of the world were jarred when the announcement came; but in this palace at Osborne everything pursued the usual course. Down in the kitchen they were cooking a huge dinner for an assemblage the like of which has seldom been known in England, and the dinner preparations proceeded just as if nothing had happened.

An incident characteristic of the Queen's solicitude for others occurred two days ago, when, in one of the intervals of consciousness, she summoned strength to suggest to her dressers, who had been acting as nurses, that they take the opportunity of getting some fresh air.

QUEEN ASKS FOR HER DOG.

On Monday afternoon the Queen asked that her little Pomeranian be brought to her bedside.

It was feared that the Queen was dying at about 9 o'clock yesterday morning, and carriages were sent to Osborne cottage and the rectory to bring all the Princes and Princesses and the Bishop of Winchester to her bedside. It seemed then very near the end; but, when things looked the worst, the Queen, in one of the rallies due to her wonderful constitution, opened her eyes and recognized the Prince of Wales, the Princess, and Emperor William. She asked to see one of her faithful servants, a member of the household. He hastened to the room, but before he got there the Queen had passed into a fitful sleep.

Four o'clock marked the beginning of the end. Again the family were summoned, and this time the relapse was not followed by recovery.

The Prince of Wales was very much affected when the doctors at length informed him that his mother had breathed her last. Emperor William, himself deeply affected, did his best to minister comfort to his sorrow-stricken uncle, whose new dignity he was the first to acknowledge.

OUTSIDE OSBORNE HOUSE GATES.

No member of the royal family left Osborne House yesterday for the customary drives. A changing group of correspondents and townspeople loitered about the gates all day long, but never reached the proportions of the crowd of Monday.

It was a melancholy day. Occasional drizzles obscured the emerald hills beyond the castle. Greater simplicity or a more entire lack of any of that pomp traditionally attached to royalty could not be found in any country house in the kingdom than here, where the best-beloved monarch of centuries was dying and the ruler of another great nation waited by her bedside as grandson rather than as Emperor.

Two stalwart policemen guarding the gates against intruders were the sole reminders of officialdom. They were compelled in the morning to refuse admission to three dusky visitors from India who drove up arrayed in such gorgeous robes that the bystanders instinctively lifted their hats, mistaking them for potentates. The trio announced themselves as lecturers touring England in behalf of a foreign mission, and insisted upon an audience with the Prince of Wales to tender the sympathies of India.

Many of the country gentry and a few titled personages appeared at the lodge and registered their names in the visitors' book, the thrifty flunky who officiated doing a profitable business by selling the original copies of official bulletins to souvenir enthusiasts. Artists and photographers obtained pictures of the gates and grounds and any prominent persons who appeared.

THE LORD CHAMBERLAIN ARRIVES

Everybody feared that the Queen would never waken from the sleep which the noontime bulletin spoke of, and everybody was watching the flag on the castle tower, expecting it to sink to half mast. Lord Clarendon, the new Lord Chamberlain, with Prince Christian of Schleswig-Holstein and the Duke of Argyll, arrived at Osborne in the afternoon. The arrival of the Lord Chamberlain was an ominous sign, as he announces to a new monarch his accession to the throne.

When the 4 o'clock bulletin announced that the Queen was sinking, all the watchers at the gates of Osborne House made up their minds to remain to the end. The cold was intense, and a few favored ones sought shelter in the royal lodge, just inside, where they waited in absolute silence.

NEWS OF THE EVENT ANNOUNCED.

The telephone bell rang at 7:04 P. M., but before a royal servant had time to take the message the Chief of the Queen's Police emerged from the darkness, and, with bared head, said:

"Gentlemen, the Queen passed away at 6:30."

All present reverently uncovered, and then shrill whistles outside and the ringing of the bells of the bicycles in waiting were the signals for messengers to race to Cowes with the news. In a few moments the place was deserted. Simultaneously, mounted messengers, on white horses, dashed from Osborne. What happened within the royal residence is purely surmise.

On their arrival at Cowes the correspondents found the news had been known both at East and West Cowes fifteen minutes before it had been announced to those in waiting at the gates of Osborne House. The streets were already filled with sorrowful crowds discussing her Majesty's death.

Prince and Princess Louis of Battenberg arrived at Osborne just too late to see her Majesty alive.

From all parts of the world there are still pouring into Cowes messages of condolence. They come from crowned heads, millionaires, tradesmen, and paupers, and are variously addressed to the Prince of Wales and the King of England.

RESULT OF ROBERTS'S NEWS?

The record of the last days of the reign of Victoria is not yet fully known. The correspondent of The Associated Press was the only correspondent admitted to Osborne House, and his interview with Sir Arthur John Bigge, private secretary to the late Queen, was the only official statement that was given out.

For several weeks the Queen had been failing. On Monday week she summoned Lord Roberts and asked him some very searching questions regarding the war in South Africa. On Tuesday she went for a drive, but was visibly affected. On Wednesday she suffered a paralytic stroke, accompanied by intense physical weakness. It was her first illness in all her eighty-one years, and she would not admit she was sick. Then her condition grew so serious that, against her wishes, the family were summoned. When they arrived her reason had practically succumbed to paralysis and weakness.

The events of the last few days, described in the bulletins, are too fresh to need repetition.

THE LAST BULLETINS.

OSBORNE HOUSE GATES, Isle of Wight, Jan. 22.—An official bulletin issued at 8 o'clock said:

The Queen this morning shows signs of diminishing strength, and her Majesty's condition again assumes a more serious aspect.
JAMES REID.
R. DOUGLAS POWELL.
THOMAS BARLOW.

The bulletin issued at noon said there had been no change for the worse in the Queen's condition since the morning bulletin.

At 4 P. M. another bulletin was posted. It said the Queen was slowly sinking.

At 6:45 P. M. the end was announced as follows:

Her Majesty the Queen breathed her last at 6:30 P. M., surrounded by her children and grandchildren.
JAMES REID.
R. DOUGLAS POWELL.
THOMAS BARLOW.

THE QUEEN'S FUNERAL.

Will Probably Be at Frogmore—Many Royalties Expected.

COWES, Isle of Wight, Jan. 23.—The body of Queen Victoria is being embalmed to-night, and will probably be taken to Windsor on Saturday.

The coffin arrived last evening from London.

Emperor William's arrangements are not settled, but it is believed that he will not depart until after the funeral, which will probably be a ceremony never before equaled in this country.

LONDON, Jan. 23.—There is little doubt that the funeral of Queen Victoria will take place at Frogmore, Hertfordshire, though nothing in regard to this matter has yet been announced.

Her Majesty was so closely related to the European Courts, big and little, that the gathering of royalties at the obsequies will be unprecedented.

ATHENS, Jan. 22.—King George will start for London to-night.

PARIS, Jan. 23.—The French Government will be represented at the funeral of Queen Victoria by an extraordinary embassy.

The members have not yet been chosen, but the embassy will be headed by Vice Admiral de Lajaille, who on several occasions welcomed Queen Victoria at Cherbourg in the name of France.

TO-DAY'S CEREMONIES.

Privy Council and Parliament to Meet—The Proclamation of the King.

LONDON, Jan. 23.—The Privy Council will meet in London to-day, and the proclamation of the King will take place thereafter at all places required by custom.

The King will come to London to preside over the Council. The Ministers will attend, give up their seals of office, be resworn, receive the proclamation of the King, pass votes of condolence and congratulation, and adjourn.

After giving up their seals the Ministers receive them back from the new ruler. The Privy Councilors will also be sworn afresh.

Shortly before midnight yesterday an official announcement was issued calling Parliament to assemble at 4 o'clock this afternoon to enable members of the House of Lords and House of Commons to take the oath of allegiance to the King. Precedent orders that Parliament shall meet within twenty-four hours of the death of the ruler.

At the offices of the Lord Chamberlain and of the City Remembrancer, at the Guildhall and at the College of Heralds, the officials were busy yesterday preparing for the formalities which for the first time in a generation, are to take place—the proclaiming of a new ruler of the United Kingdom. All the ancient gazettes, Court circulars, and other papers which describe the ceremonial of 1837 were taken from the libraries, that the officials might familiarize themselves with the ancient pageantry whereby a sovereign is proclaimed. The City Remembrancer said yesterday:

"It will depend on the pleasure of the new monarch to decide how far the ancient customs will be modified to suit modern methods; but, in a country where precedents are so firmly adhered to as England, it may be anticipated that we shall follow closely on the acts which prevailed when the Queen ascended the throne. The Privy Council, which is a very large body, will meet at once at St. James's Palace, where the form of proclamation declaring that 'we, etcetera, with one voice and consent of tongue and heart declare and proclaim the high mighty Prince Albert Edward, etcetera, who, by the death of the monarch, has become our only lawful and rightful liege, etcetera.'

"This proclamation will give the new title the King may assume, but this is not yet announced to us. The proclamation will then be sent to Heralds' College, and the following day the Earl Marshal, the Garter King at Arms, the Herald's Pursuivants, and other officials, with the college members and the Household troops, will proceed from the palace, clad in their splendid surcoats, and proceed to Trafalgar Square. There the King at Arms will halt, command silence, and read the proclamation. Proceeding down the Strand to Temple Bar, a halt will again be made, to demand an entrance into the City to proclaim the King. There the Lord Mayor and Sheriffs, in their state carriages, will form a great procession, and when the Earl Marshal's party comes just within the City boundary the proclamation will be read again, and the procession will pass down Ludgate Hill and Cheapside to the Royal Exchange, where similar ceremonies will close the spectacle."

DEEP GLOOM IN LONDON.

Places of Amusement All Closed—How the News Was Received.

LONDON, Jan. 23.—Silence, gloom, and darkness characterize London to-night. From Whitechapel to Mayfair streets usually gay with nightly festivity are dark, deserted, and desolate, and this depression of the public mind is likely to continue for many days to come.

Only a few hours ago the pleasure-seeking populace was hurrying to the theatres and music halls, only to find in every case the doors closed and big, black-bordered bills announcing that the performances had been suspended. The people, thus turned into the streets, gave for a short time an unusually thronged appearance to the West End. Many turned in the direction of Buckingham Palace and Marlborough House, where absolute silence reigned. Small bills, signed "Balfour," were posted outside, announcing the death of the monarch.

Everywhere, in vehicles and on the streets, the one topic of conversation was what would happen under the new reign, rather than the life and death of Victoria. Much interest was evinced in the way in which the enormous fortune of the dead Queen would be distributed, the general notion being that Osborne House would go to Princess Beatrice, and that she and Princess Christian would come into a considerable portion of Queen Victoria's wealth.

The probability that the King will take up a practically permanent residence in Buckingham Palace was much canvassed. This is a question that comes very much home to Londoners. Queen Victoria's preference for Balmoral Castle and Osborne House has been a complaint of long standing in the metropolis, and it is hoped that the new reign will see a change in this respect. The presence of the Court in London would give a brightness and gayety to the city which have long been absent.

Not until Queen Victoria has been laid to rest beside the Prince Consort at Frogmore will the theatres or music halls reopen. Moreover, business will come to a practical standstill. Music in all the hotels and public places ceased last evening. Fashionable resorts were empty, and very few of the nightly habitués were in evidence.

Americans who have passed through great National calamities may recall the crêpe-draped buildings and the National hush; but they can ill-conceive, since the death of Lincoln, any such expression of gloom as has already fallen on the United Kingdom. Marlborough House, so long the home of the new monarch; Buckingham Palace, where Queen Victoria made her last stay in London, and St. James's Palace, the residence of so many former monarchs, are to-night all black and deserted. Sentries in black overcoats keep silent vigil before the closed gates and bolted doors.

Early in the evening from St. Paul's, Westminster Abbey, and other churches bells were solemnly tolling or ringing muffled peals. In some cases the shops were already exhibiting signs of mourning. Beyond these things, however, and the boys crying extra editions in every direction, there was little that would outwardly indicate the passing of the country through an experience novel to almost the whole people.

SORROW IS UNIVERSAL.

Telegrams arriving from all parts of the country and the colonies re-echo the deep feeling of sorrow pervading all classes. These show that everywhere bells have been tolled and public performances and private functions suspended.

In Dublin the expressions of regret were universal. The bells of St. Patrick's Cathedral were tolled. Earl Cadogan, the Lord Lieutenant, was absent from Dublin yesterday, but it is expected that he will return immediately to preside at a meeting of the Irish Privy Council to proclaim the new King.

The news was received with the greatest sorrow at Balmoral, Windsor, and Eton, where Queen Victoria was regarded in an especially personal manner by the inhabitants.

Princess Beatrice telegraphed the tidings to ex-Empress Eugénie at Farnborough.

SCENES YESTERDAY AFTERNOON.

The gloomy faces of the crowds incessantly approaching the bulletin board at the Mansion House indicated yesterday how little the public hoped to receive better news of the condition of the Queen. Men of all ages and conditions, women and even children were content to spend a long time in awaiting their turn to get within reading distance of the board. As the throng moved slowly past the notice board, those who were unable to get there personally sent messenger boys with notebook and pencils to copy the text of everything posted. The grief of all was evident. Never were there so many black ties in the city before the actual arrival of a time of general mourning.

There was a remarkable scene outside the Mansion House early in the afternoon. On receipt of the alarming reports something resembling a groan was uttered by the hundreds of people assembled, and then some one started singing the national anthem. All heads were bared, and in a moment the crowds were singing "God Save the Queen" with a fervor proving how earnestly they wished for her Majesty's recovery. The passengers in passing carriages, cabs, and omnibuses joined in the singing, the drivers reverently doffing their hats.

At 4:35 P. M. the following was posted:

Osborne, 4 P. M.

My painful duty obliges me to inform you that the life of our beloved Queen is in the greatest danger. ALBERT EDWARD.

In reply the Lord Mayor, Frank Green, dispatched the following:

"I have received your Royal Highness's sad intimation with profound grief, which is shared by the citizens of London, who still pray that under Divine Providence the irreparable loss to her Majesty's devoted family and loyal subjects throughout the empire may still be averted. Will your Royal Highness be pleased to accept this heart-felt expression of my deep and sincere sympathy?"

THE FINAL ANNOUNCEMENT.

The latest bulletins previous to the announcement of the Queen's death, especially the message sent by the Prince of Wales, dispelled the last gleam of hope. The crowds silently dispersed from in front of the Mansion House, and only a few groups awaited the appearance of the inevitable announcement. This came at 7 o'clock in the form of a dispatch to the Lord Mayor from the new King as follows:

Osborne, 6:45 P. M.

My beloved mother has just passed away, surrounded by her children and grandchildren. ALBERT EDWARD.

The Lord Mayor immediately sent the following reply:

"Your Royal Highness's telegram announcing the nation's great loss I have received with profound distress and grief, and have communicated this most sad intimation to my fellow-citizens. Her Majesty's name and memory will forever live in the hearts of her people.

"May I respectfully convey to your Royal Highness and to all the members of the royal family the earnest sympathy and condolence of the City of London in your great sorrow?"

The scrap of paper a foot square, posted on the wall of the Mansion House, gave the first notice to London's homeward hurrying thousands of the death of the Queen. Excavations by which the street had been torn up made access to the bulletin difficult, but the bared heads of a silent group under a flickering gas jet told the crowds on the 'bus tops and sidewalks that the Queen was no more.

"BIG BEN" IS TOLLED.

A quarter of an hour later more than a thousand newsboys had invaded the streets with black-ruled newspapers, crying, "Death of the Queen," while through the dark streets boomed the deep-toned notes of "Big Ben," the big bell of St. Paul's Cathedral, the bells of the city re-echoing the news.

The shops closed as soon as the bells began to toll, and the blinds of the Mansion House were drawn down as soon as the message from the Prince of Wales was received by the Lord Mayor.

The bell tolled at St. Paul's Cathedral was the gift of William III., and is used only on occasions of the death of royal personages, Archbishops of Canterbury, Lord Mayors of London, and Bishops of London. The tolling continued for two hours at intervals of a minute and could be heard for miles in the direction of the wind.

Some hundreds of people stood in front of the cathedral around the spot where Queen Victoria prayed on the sixtieth anniversary of her accession to the throne.

LONDON PRESS COMMENTS.

Universal Grief Reflected in Editorials—Labouchere's Warm Eulogy.

LONDON, Jan. 23.—All the morning papers appear in heavy mourning borders, with editorials eulogistic of the dead Queen and recalling the leading events and characteristics of her reign. Very few political references as to the future are made. The Daily Mail says:

"We can but regret that the Queen was not permitted to see the end of the South African struggle. She has been taken from us in a dark hour which, we may hope, is a prelude to the dawn, and when we can ill spare her ripe experience and her vast knowledge of measures and men."

"Let us think of her this morning," says the Daily Chronicle, "by her highest title, not by her crown and sceptre, but by her own magnificent and splendid ideal of womanhood. This it is which touches the heart's core of a proud and imperial race. We have lost mother, wife, and Queen."

The Chronicle remarks that President McKinley was slightly premature in sending a communication to "His Majesty, the King," inasmuch as the Prince of Wales has not yet been proclaimed by the Privy Council.

The Daily Telegraph publishes two editorials under the captions "The Queen" and "The King." In the latter it says:

"Most happily for him, he has, with infinite credit to himself, passed through a period of probation in some ways more difficult and certainly more prolonged than that to which any successor to a throne in modern times has been subjected. He assumes the burden of his imperial task equipped with all the invaluable experience which the most painstaking discharge of great duties could secure him during the lifetime of his august mother. So accustomed have we become to his direct, personal patronage of every charity and every beneficial movement, many of which he initiated himself, that we are apt to forget the exhausting nature of the strain almost daily imposed upon his strength. He has won among the masses of the people a popularity that has been vouchsafed to few of his predecessors."

The Times says:

"The confidence inspired by her personal character enabled Queen Victoria on many occasions to use her intimate knowledge with effect in smoothing the rugged places of international relations or in modifying a policy which, through sheer inadequacy of information, would have led to undesirable friction. We have also to thank the Queen for influence of the most potent kind consistently and vigorously used to enforce high ideals of social and personal virtue, of religious faith and of Christian life."

Referring to the intellectual upheaval and the enormous social and economic progress which characterized the Victorian era, The Times expresses regret that the impetus has to some extent spent itself.

"At the close of Victoria's reign," continues The Times, "we find ourselves somewhat less secure of our position than we could desire, somewhat less abreast of the problems of the age than we ought to be, considering the initial advantages we secured."

"The great English-speaking Republic beyond the Atlantic has not failed to send us officially by the mouth of President McKinley, and unofficially by innumerable newspaper articles and other tokens of popular feeling, proof of how heartily and profoundly it shares in our grief. Need we say for ourselves and our colonies how dear to us in such an hour is the fellowship in woe which our American kinsmen so generously and warmly tender us?"

In another article The Times says:

"If anything can in some measure console the nation for the irreparable loss it has sustained, it is the well-founded conviction that the Queen has left behind her a worthy successor, who may be trusted to walk in her footsteps.

"In the whole range of English social and political life no position is more difficult to fill satisfactorily and without reproach than that of the heir apparent, and it may be justly said that the way this position has been filled has contributed to the remarkable increase in the devotion to the throne and the dynasty which has been one of the most striking characteristics of Victoria's reign.

"As Albert Edward has been a scrupulously constitutional Prince, we may confidently predict that he will be a scrupulously constitutional King. In the fulfillment of this onerous task he will have by his side a Queen who is already enthroned in the hearts of her loving subjects."

Henry Labouchère, M. P., in Truth has a remarkable tribute to Queen Victoria, a tribute all the more remarkable because of his democratic ideas and frank criticisms of royalty.

"Among all her millions of subjects," he says, "there are but few who will not mourn for her loss as for one of their own household. Nor will the mourners be found among her own subjects alone. It is not too much to say that never in the history of the world has a single death caused such universal grief. Alike in happiness and sorrow, she lived a life beyond reproach, without thought of self and unreservedly devoted to the duties of the hour. Although occupying perhaps the proudest position ever filled by a woman, and never wanting in a certain queenly dignity, her tastes, habits, demeanor, and even her dress were marked by the rarest simplicity.

"She has been indeed the mother of her people, and as a mother she will be mourned. In all the affairs of State she manifested the same wisdom that inspired her private life, nor did her own country alone enjoy the fruits of her experience and sagacity. Through her kindred and descendants abroad her influence for many years has been felt in Continental politics, always on the side of peace; and, in at least one crisis, she is known to have rendered service to the whole of Europe.

"Her sudden and lamentable breakdown was due entirely to worry and overwork. She had been greatly distressed by events in South Africa and by domestic griefs."

The Daily News says that Queen Victoria was always a peacemaker. It refers to the incident of her modifying in a pacific sense Lord Russell's dispatch in the Trent case.

The Standard, expressing regret that the Queen was not spared to see peace restored in South Africa, says: "The end for which she strove and prayed has yet to come, and the hope is perhaps visionary that the common grief of Britons and Afrikanders may abate those racial animosities which stand in the way of pacification."

Referring to the conspicuous success of Queen Victoria's reign, The Standard says:

"There was a time when republicanism was a serious phrase on English lips. To-day no whisper of discontent with the monarchical Constitution breaks the mourning of a loyal nation around the bier of the sovereign. It will be said of her in the annals of our land that she strengthened the Throne by loving the people, and that she was a great Queen and the mother of Kings because she was a good, noble, and true-hearted woman."

THE NATIONS' TRIBUTES.

Enmity for Great Britain Hushed and Only Sympathy Expressed.

PARIS, Jan. 23.—The news of the death of Queen Victoria was known in Paris at 8 o'clock last evening through special editions of the evening papers, which newsboys carried throughout the city. Great sympathy was expressed on all sides.

As soon as definite information reached Parliament the Presidents of the chambers announced that the next session would be adjourned as a sign of mourning.

When the news was known at the Ministry of Foreign Affairs, M. Delcassé, the Foreign Minister, went to the British Embassy to express to the Acting Ambassador the condolence of the French Government. President Loubet postponed his visit until the return of Sir Edmund Monson.

Not until then, moreover, will the arrangements relative to mourning be made. The British flag, draped with crape, will be placed over the entrance to the embassy to-day.

Last evening there was a steady stream of callers to inscribe their names in the register at the embassy.

Few and far between, indeed, are the Paris papers this morning which do not sound the note of regret at the passing of Victoria. In addition to long obituaries, special writers publish appreciations, reviewing the Queen's life work, noting in what respects it contributed to the greatness of the British nation, and speculating in some cases upon the reign about to open. Foremost of these special writers is M. Hanotaux, who, in Le Journal, refers to the extent of England's debt to Victoria.

"Her temperament and judgment, thanks to the precious lessons of Lord Melbourne," says M. Hanotaux, "were in complete accord with English Parliamentary institutions. Her success as a sovereign was due to her close attention to the affairs of State, her frequent journeys, her interviews with foreign statesmen, and above all, to the extraordinary position of being allied to several of the reigning sovereigns of Europe."

Le Gaulois says:

"Her action may be summed up in a brief phrase, little authority and much influence. The changes which are about to take place express better than blind and foolish flattery the place she occupied in Europe. That will be her true funeral oration, the final word of which will be that she, the possessor of most ordinary faculties, accomplished more than certain conquerors, and has left a greater gap than Catherine or Elizabeth."

Le Siecle says:

"Doubtless the Prince of Wales will follow the good example of his mother, whose death will mark no change of policy or opinion in Great Britain. He will peaceably enjoy the loyalty of the empire, accorded during the long reign of the Queen."

Le Temps, discussing the outlook, says:

"The sadness, alarm, anxieties, moral sufferings, and pecuniary cares arising out of the Transvaal war have created a new feeling in England. Queen Victoria has been like a mother of a family, a living link with the prosperity of the past, an anchor of security for the British people. With her disappearance will come the unknown, the groping into the dark future."

BERLIN, Jan. 22.—The news of the death of Queen Victoria had been hourly expected in Berlin, and on its arrival special editions of the newspapers sold like wildfire, the announcement being read with silent and respectful sympathy. The fact that Empress Augusta Victoria started to-day for Homburg to be near Dowager Empress Frederick added to the sad circumstances of the occasion.

Immediately after the receipt of the news Count von Eulenburg, the Chief Court Marshal, ordered the flags half masted on all public buildings. Although the hour of the evening was somewhat advanced, a number of the embassies and legations, including the United States Embassy, did the same.

Special mourning orders to the Schloss, the army, the Court, and the public departments were issued this evening. These will be published to-morrow and go immediately into effect.

The German nation fully shares in the feelings of the British people toward the venerable and illustrious sovereign who has just breathed her last.

Semi-official paragraphs in the press this evening rebut the idea, commonly held in Germany, that the new King will be inclined to be hostile toward Germany. On the contrary, they assert that he will act in the interests of Great Britain and the British people alone.

A sense of gratification is felt by all Germans that Emperor William was present at Osborne during the last hours of Queen Victoria's life and that the lofty feelings of filial piety which prompted his action have met with such full and unqualified recognition on the part of the British nation.

THE HAGUE, Jan. 22.—The Dutch press printed the news of the death of Queen Victoria with mourning borders.

The Court will go into mourning; but it is probable that there will be no change in the arrangements for the marriage of Queen Wilhelmina.

ROME, Jan. 22.—A most painful impression was produced by the receipt of the news of Queen Victoria's death.

King Victor Emmanuel, Queen Helena, the Pope, and members of the Government immediately telegraphed condolences.

GRIEF IN CANADA.

Flags at Half Mast Everywhere and Amusement Places Closed.

TORONTO, Ontario, Jan. 22.—To Torontonians no tidings fraught with greater sorrow ever flashed over the wires than those which recorded the death of the Queen. All classes of the community show their heartfelt grief. From early morning till the announcement of her Majesty's death, great crowds gathered and waited around the different newspaper offices, eagerly scanning each bulletin as it was posted up. When at last the dreaded news came, heads were reverently uncovered, and the crowds dispersed silently. For half an hour the bells kept tolling their mournful messages, while national flags, half-masted, swung from every pole.

The children in every school in the city this forenoon sang for the last time "God Save the Queen." The Mayor will proclaim a day of mourning.

MONTREAL, Jan. 22.—The bulletin officially announcing the death of her Majesty turned Montreal into a city of mourning. No sooner was the fact announced than the fire bells began to ring out at minute intervals, and mingled with them came the tolling of the big cathedral bells of both the English and Catholic churches. Flags appeared at half-mast everywhere, and the crowds in the streets and at the bulletin boards of the various papers, their heads in most cases bared, reverently read the announcement.

All entertainments of a social nature have been canceled, and even skating rinks, hockey rinks, and places of public amusement have been closed.

OTTAWA, Jan. 22.—The news of the Queen's death reached Ottawa at 2 P. M. The Secretary of State at once issued a proclamation continuing in office all who held positions under the Crown. This is merely formal.

All public buildings in the Dominion at once placed the union jack at half mast, and it will so remain until sundown on the day of the Queen's funeral.

ST. JOHN'S, N. F., Jan. 22.—The announcement of Queen Victoria's death has called forth expressions of the keenest regret in Newfoundland, the oldest colony of the British Empire. The Colonial Cabinet met this evening and adopted resolutions of condolence, which were cabled to London.

To-morrow will be observed as a day of mourning throughout the colony.

Arrangements are being made for the proclamation of the new sovereign upon receipt of an official intimation of his accession.

HALIFAX, N. S., Jan. 22.—Symbols of mourning for Queen Victoria are everywhere displayed. Flags fly half-mast on ships and from the frowning fortress, and the royal standard, for the first time in many years, is half-mast at the Citadel.

All performances have been canceled, and on the day of the Queen's funeral the tolling of half a hundred bells will mingle with the loud notes of minute guns for the departed sovereign.

A sketch of the life of Queen Victoria will be found on Pages 6 and 7 of this issue.

AMERICAN TRIBUTES TO QUEEN VICTORIA

President McKinley Cables Condolences to the New King.

WASHINGTON FLAGS LOWERED

Such a Mark of Respect Had Never Been Before Paid on the Death of a Monarch—Action by Congress.

WASHINGTON, Jan. 22.—Four days of anxiety, in a large measure, prepared official Washington for the news which was flashed across the cable this afternoon from England. So it happened that all things that could be decently done in anticipation of the death of Queen Victoria had been disposed of, and all was in readiness for the execution of the formalities which are indispensable to such occasions. The President and his advisers were in receipt from time to time of all news which came from Osborne House. When the end came it found appropriate measures of condolence framed, and even orders, ready for execution, looking to the half-masting of the flags over the executive departments and the carrying out of the usual formalities.

The half-masting of the National ensign was an unusual tribute. This has been done once or twice on the occasion of the funeral of some great ruler, but never before in the case of the death of a monarch. The adjournment of the House was also an unusual mark of respect.

THE PRESIDENT'S MESSAGE.

The news announcing the death of Queen Victoria was conveyed to President McKinley simultaneously with its receipt by the newspapers. Soon afterward the President sent the following message of condolence to the new King:

Washington, Jan. 22, 1901.

His Majesty the King, Osborne House, Isle of Wight:

I have received with profound sorrow the lamentable tidings of the death of her Majesty the Queen. Allow me, Sir, to offer my sincere sympathy and that of the American people in your personal bereavement and in the loss Great Britain has suffered in the death of its venerable and illustrious sovereign, whose noble life and beneficent influence have promoted the peace and won the affection of the world.
WILLIAM McKINLEY.

Secretary of State Hay cabled the following message to Ambassador Choate at London:

Department of State, Jan. 22, 1901.

Choate, Ambassador, London:

You will express to Lord Lansdowne the profound sorrow of the Government and people of the United States at the death of the Queen and the deep sympathy we feel with the people of the British Empire in their great affliction. JOHN HAY.

The actual dispatch of the message from the President to the new King of England and from Secretary Hay to Ambassador Choate was delayed only long enough to receive the physicians' statement announcing the demise of the Queen, and then they were sent forward at once and copies were furnished to the press.

The flag on the Executive Mansion was placed at half-mast at 3:30 o'clock.

THE SENATE'S RESOLUTION.

The Senate was in executive session when the news of Queen Victoria's death was announced, but the bulletin announcing her death was passed around by the doorkeepers. Expressions of regret and of admiration for the virtues of the dead sovereign were heard on all hands. Senators Allison and Morgan held a hurried consultation, as the result of which the latter drew up a resolution, which the former presented when the executive session closed. The resolution was as follows:

"That the death of her Royal and Imperial Majesty, Victoria, of noble virtues and great renown, is sincerely deplored by the Senate of the United States of America."

The resolution was adopted unanimously. Afterward Mr. Allison offered the following resolution:

"That the President pro tem. of the Senate cause to be conveyed to the Prime Minister of Great Britain a suitably engrossed copy of the foregoing resolution."

This was agreed to.

Senator Lodge, evidently voicing the sentiment of most of his colleagues, said later:

"The Queen's death is to the people of the United States a real sorrow. Her reign, the longest in English history, has been a great and memorable one, but it has perhaps nothing greater or more memorable than her own ability and purity of character; her fidelity to her high duties, and her devotion to those ideals of conduct and domestic life which appeal most profoundly to all English-speaking people. The Queen has always been a steadfast friend to the United States, and during her long life has made that friendship traditional in her family. Americans can never forget that England was withheld from active interference in our own civil war largely, if not wholly, by the influence of the Queen and the wise counsels of Prince Albert."

THE HOUSE ADJOURNS.

The House received the news at about 2 o'clock, and for the time being it was the theme of universal discussion among the members. Speaker Henderson had shown deep interest in the Queen's condition, and the first bulletin announcing her death was taken to him in his private office and to Chairman Hitt of the Committee on Foreign Affairs. Mr. Hitt conferred with his colleagues as to the precedents in such cases, and then framed a brief and expressive resolution of sympathy and respect to be introduced in the House later. For a time it was feared that this might give rise to some expressions from Boer sympathizers, but, on the contrary, it was developed that the sentiment of respect for the departed sovereign was shared by all alike.

At the conclusion of the general debate on the District of Columbia Appropriation bill Mr. Hitt offered the resolution, which was as follows:

"Resolved, That the House of Representatives of the United States of America has learned with profound sorrow of the death of her Majesty Queen Victoria and sympathizes with her people in the loss of their beloved sovereign; that the President be requested to communicate this expression of the sentiment of the House to the Government of Great Britain; that, as a further mark of respect to the memory of Queen Victoria, the House do now adjourn."

The reading of the resolution was listened to with impressive silence. Mr. Hitt stated very briefly that this resolution followed the precedents in similar cases. It was, he said, copied almost literally from the resolution adopted upon the occasion of the death of the President of the French Republic, and followed the expression adopted upon the death of the Czar of Russia. He did not, he said, think that the occasion called for any extended remarks, and asked for a vote.

The resolution was unanimously adopted, and the House at 5:05 P. M. stood adjourned until noon to-morrow.

After the adjournment members gathered in knots and discussed the event, the tributes being to the womanly virtues and purity of home life of the Queen, no less than to her national service.

PRAISE FROM CABINET MINISTERS.

Secretary of State Hay, on being informed of the Queen's death, declined to make a statement for publication on the ground that, being under obligation to send an official message to the British Government on the subject, he did not feel called upon to make a further supplementary private statement.

Attorney General Griggs said:

"Hers has been a noble life. Whether she was greater as a Queen or as a woman is hard to say. Her good influence upon

"All the News That's Fit to Print."

The New York Times.

THE WEATHER.
Rain and warmer; winds south, becoming west.

VOL. LII......NO. 16,476. NEW YORK, MONDAY, OCTOBER 27, 1902 —FOURTEEN PAGES. ONE CENT In Greater New York, Jersey City, and Newark. Elsewhere, TWO CENTS.

REPUBLICAN APATHY STIRS UP GOV. ODELL

By His Orders the State Will Be Flooded with Oratory.

Afternoon Meetings of His Tour Were Failures, Although Those at Night Were Well Attended—His Itinerary.

Special to The New York Times.

ALBANY, Oct. 26.—Upon the suggestion of Gov. Odell the State will be flooded with Republican oratory during the coming week for the purpose of dispelling the apathy which he has found on his trip to be generally prevalent. The State Committee will instruct the county leaders throughout the State to organize meetings in all of the principal cities and towns and will agree to furnish speakers. Job Hedges and Linn Bruce, who have been with the Governor's party, already have had engagements made for them for every night this week, and dozens of Republican spellbinders from New York, Buffalo, and other places will be sent into the country districts.

Gov. Odell and Chairman Dunn have no doubt about the result of the election if the Republican vote which has been registered is put into the ballot boxes. Their minimum estimate is 50,000 majority in the State. The reports which have been sent to Chairman Dunn and which have inspired his confidence in the outcome have been based largely on the registration. But Gov. Odell's experience on his tour has led him to the conclusion that the conditions existing in the State this year are peculiar and that it would be unwise to be overconfident.

Nearly every one of the afternoon meetings which Gov. Odell and Senator Depew addressed on their tour which ended at Jamestown last night was a failure. The explanation given by the Republican leaders who arranged the meetings, that the people were too busy to come out, was not satisfactory to the Governor, and their statement that he could count absolutely on the Republican vote being brought to the polls on the day of election was not relied on. The view of the Governor was that leaders who failed to make a good showing of attendance at meetings to be addressed by himself, Senator Depew, and such interesting campaign orators as Job Hedges and Linn Bruce were not to be fully trusted to get their people to the polls.

So he decided that things needed a stirring up and communicated with Chairman Dunn, with the result that it has been planned to make the present week notable in the history of the Republican organization of the State for the number of meetings arranged and the number of orators sent out by the State Committee to address them.

The night meetings of the Governor's tour were all well attended, with the exception of the one at Lockport, which Job Hedges was sent out from Buffalo to address. Mr. Hedges said on his return that the band composed about one-tenth of his auditors. The night meeting at Syracuse was entirely satisfactory in point of attendance, and so were the night meetings at Rochester and Buffalo. At each place the meeting was held in the largest hall in the city and the hall was crowded. At Rochester people were turned away. But the greatest outpouring of people and the greatest enthusiasm were encounterd at Jamestown. It was said by the local leaders that the attack which had been made on Gov. Odell by David B. Hill had aroused the Republicans of Chautauqua as nothing had done since the campaign had begun and that their coming out in such large numbers, not only from Jamestown, but from various points in Chautauqua and Cattaraugus Counties, was largely due to a desire on their part to show how they felt about Hill's attack on the Executive.

Tuesday the Governor will go to Binghamton, which is the home of Chairman Dunn, to address a meeting, and Thursday he will go to New York, where he will address two meetings that evening. His last meeting will be at Patchogue Friday evening.

WRECKED HIS AMBULANCE TO SAVE A WOMAN.

Man Whose Hand Had Been Cut Off by a Trolley Car Had to Wait.

While responding to a hurry call on Thirty-fourth Street, between Second and Third Avenues, last evening, a Bellevue ambulance was wrecked by coming in contact with a lamp post at Thirty-first Street and First Avenue. Neither the ambulance surgeon, Dr. Orr, nor Driver Duhy was injured, although both were thrown out. The ambulance had swung into First Avenue from Twenty-sixth Street and was going north at a rapid pace. Near the corner of Thirty-first Street a woman weighing over 200 pounds stood waiting for a Belt Line car. The driver clanged his bell, but the woman seemed paralyzed with fear and did not move. It was a question between running down the woman and wrecking the vehicle.

Driver Duhy swerved the horse up on the sidewalk and into a lamppost, wrecking the ambulance and the post. As soon as the accident occurred, Dr. Orr telephoned at once to the hospital and another vehicle was sent to Thirty-fourth Street in charge of Dr. Sahrenback.

The ambulance had been called to attend Luke Ronan, a laborer of 302 East Thirty-fourth Street, who had been rendered unconscious and had his right hand cut off at the wrist. He was crossing Thirty-fourth Street, when he was struck by east-bound Thirty-fourth Street cross-town car 3,289 and thrown about ten feet. The man landed on the fender of west-bound car 1,278 of the same line. He rolled off and fell under the car, the wheels of the forward truck passing over his right hand at the wrist and severing it.

When the second ambulance arrived Ronan was unconscious and the doctor said he had a probable fracture of the skull. He was taken to the Polyclinic Hospital at 214 East Thirty-fourth Street on account of his weak condition.

FLOOD IN BRUNSWICK, GA.

Business Interrupted and Lights Put Out—Railroads Suffer.

BRUNSWICK, Ga., Oct. 26.—As a result of heavy rains which have continued for forty-eight hours, five blocks in the centre of the city are under water to-night, and considerable damage has been done. On Newcastle Street, between Monk and Mansfield Streets, the water has rushed into the stores, and is from ten to fifteen inches deep. The city Fire Department Headquarters is under water, the jails are both flooded, and from Bay to Union Street, a distance of a quarter of a mile, traffic is impossible.

The Brunswick Electrical Supply Company's plant is crippled, and not a lamp furnished by that concern is burning to-night.

A heavy northeaster has been prevailing for two or three days. Railroad traffic has been interfered with badly, and several washouts have been reported on the Southern Railway, between Brunswick and Jesup, and on the Brunswick and Birmingham. All mails are belated, both arriving and departing.

INDEX TO DEPARTMENTS.

ALMERIC PAGET INJURED; ONE OF HIS EYES REMOVED.

W. C. Whitney's Son-in-Law Accidentally Shot by a Friend While Gunning in England.

LONDON, Oct. 26.—Almeric Hugh Paget, who married Miss Pauline Whitney of New York, has been accidentally shot by a friend while shooting in the country.

After the accident Mr. Paget was hurriedly brought to London, where it was found necessary to take out one of his eyes.

It is believed that the sight of the other eye will not be affected.

Mr. Paget is a grandson of the first Marquis of Anglesea, and a cousin of the present head of the house. He was born in 1861. His father was the late Gen. Lord A. H. Paget. On Nov. 12, 1895, he married Miss Pauline Whitney, daughter of William C. Whitney of this city.

Mr. Paget's eldest brother, Major Gen. Arthur Paget, married Miss Mary Stevens, daughter of the late Mrs. Paran Stevens.

The friends of Mr. Paget in this city received word of the accident to him yesterday, but had no details in regard to his injuries.

MR. CHAMBERLAIN TO VISIT SOUTH AFRICA.

The Colonial Secretary to Start at the End of November—Will Examine the Administrative Problems in the Colonies.

LONDON, Oct. 27.—It is officially announced that the Right Hon. Joseph Chamberlain, the Colonial Secretary, has decided personally to visit South Africa, and to examine on the spot the problems presented by the termination of the war and the settlement of affairs in the new colonies.

King Edward has given his approval of this plan, which, it is said, has also the full approval of Premier Balfour and the other members of the Cabinet.

Mr. Chamberlain proposes to start for South Africa toward the end of November and to return in the early part of March. His visit will embrace the Cape, Natal, the Orange River Colony, and the Transvaal.

The Colonial Secretary hopes to have an opportunity to confer while in South Africa with representatives of all the different interests concerned, and to consider their views in his future policy.

It is said that Lord Milner has been consulted with regard to Mr. Chamberlain's trip, and that he cordially welcomes the idea.

The Times says it understands that Mrs. Chamberlain (who was Miss Mary Endicott of Salem, Mass.,) will accompany her husband to South Africa, and that J. Austen Chamberlain (the Postmaster General) will answer Colonial Office questions in Parliament during his father's absence.

By The Associated Press.

LONDON, Oct. 27.—The striking precedent to be established by Mr. Chamberlain in visiting a colony in the course of his term of office is the subject of universal and approving comment this morning.

The Daily Telegraph thinks that this step will be the precursor of similar visits to Canada and Australia. Various references are made to the "new diplomacy" and the "new statesmanship," as well as to the political aspects of the absence of the strongest Minister at a time when the Government is passing through a critical phase of its existence.

There are also some hints that Mr. Chamberlain will be glad to be absent during the awkward discussions arising from the Government's Education bill. On the whole, is warmly welcomed as being timely and however, the Colonial Secretary's decision sensible.

HAS ADDICKS GIVEN UP?

He Causes a Report to be Spread That He Has Abandoned the Fight in Delaware.

Special to The New York Times.

WILMINGTON, Del., Oct. 26.—J. Edward Addicks, Republican National Committeeman, this evening sent word to this city from Claymont through one of his trusted lieutenants that he had abandoned practically the fight in Delaware. Mr. Addicks told his friend to have printed the statement, "that the election in Delaware, so far as Mr. Addicks is concerned, is in the hands of the friends of the President." Mr. Addicks's mouthpiece declared that this means that Mr. Addicks will quit the fight, which, being further interpreted, means that the contributions to the Union Republican campaign fund will not be forthcoming.

Mr. Addicks's position is said to have been due to a conference of the Addicks Republican leaders at Philadelphia last evening when the situation was carefully reviewed, and Mr Addicks finally stated that he was weary of electing members to the Legislature who afterward went back on him.

The discouraging feature to the Union Republicans was the situation in Sussex County, where in districts he has formerly carried a fusion has been made between the anti-Addicks Republicans and the Democrats, by which the latter support the regular Republican candidates for the Legislature.

Mr. Addicks's leaders did not see how they could overcome this as the opponents of Mr. Addicks were carrying the war into the Addicks stronghold. In Kent County there has been a heavy registration and the Democratic leaders are claiming the county, while the Addicks men stand to lose the county ticket in both lower counties.

When this statement became known late to-night among a small group of politicians it caused a sensation. The Regular Republican leaders, however, rather discredit the report of Addicks's withdrawal. Horace Greeley Knowles, one of the anti-Addicks leaders, declared that he put but little faith in anything said by Mr. Addicks of a political nature, and it was merely a scheme to throw the Democrats off the track.

Another prominent Regular Republican said:

"Addicks is trying to keep us from getting on to him. He probably knows that we will have a number of Pinkerton detectives to watch the operations of his lieutenants in the use of money and the statement is merely to make us relax our efforts. Addicks this time has got hold of a hot potato and he cannot drop it if he would. He will be routed on election day."

ELIZABETH CADY STANTON DIES AT HER HOME

Noted Advocate of Woman's Suffrage Nearly 87 Years Old.

Her Championship of Her Political Belief Almost Lifelong—Her Companionship with Miss Susan B. Anthony.

Mrs. Elizabeth Cady Stanton died at 3 o'clock yesterday afternoon at her home in the Stuart Apartment House, 250 West Ninety-fourth Street. Had she lived until the 12th of next month she would have completed her eighty-seventh year. Mrs. Stanton had been ailing for several months, but had not been seriously ill. Of recent years she became very stout, and this, combined with her naturally large frame, made the use of a cane necessary. Saturday she was confined to her bed. Though physically incapacitated, her mental powers were as much in evidence as ever, and only in the first part of the week she had written two articles for publication. Early on Saturday Mrs. Stanton dictated to her secretary a letter.

Toward nightfall she lapsed into semiconsciousness and so continued until the end. Her son, Robert L. Stanton, and her daughter, Mrs. Margaret Lawrence, resided with their mother. Six children survive—Henry, Theodore, Mrs. Margaret Lawrence, Mrs. Stanton Blatch, Robert L., and G. Smith Stanton. All reside in New York, except Theodore, who represents Harper's Weekly and several other American publications in Paris.

The funeral will be held Wednesday and the interment will be at Woodlawn Cemetery.

Mrs. Stanton was born Nov. 12, 1815, in Johnstown, N. Y. She was the daughter of Supreme Court Judge Daniel Cady and wife of the late Henry Brewster Stanton, noted abolitionist and journalist. She began her education at the Johnstown Academy, and later became a pupil at Emma Willard's Seminary, in Troy, a school noted then throughout the country. She was graduated with the class of '32. Eight years later, while attending a world's anti-slavery convention in London, she made the acquaintance of Lucretia Mott, which resulted in the joint issuance of a call for a woman's rights convention. Mrs. Stanton was on her wedding trip at this time. The convention was held at her home, Seneca Falls, July 19 and 20, 1848.

The first formal claim for suffrage for women was then made. In 1854 she appeared before the New York Legislature and addressed it on "The Rights of Married Women." Six years later she took the stand that drunkenness should constitute a cause for divorce. She was instrumental in having the question of woman suffrage submitted to Kansas in 1867 and Michigan in 1874. She was President of the National Committee of her party from 1855 to 1865. She was also identified with the Women's Loyal League and was President of the National Women's Suffrage Association until 1883. In 1868 she sought to become an actual political factor by entering the lists for Congress. For the past quarter of a century and over she had annually addressed a committee of Congress in favor of an amendment for women to the Constitution of the United States.

"At the time of her death she was honorary President of the National Women's Suffrage Association. Mrs. Stanton's mother was Margaret Livingston, a daughter of James Livingston, an officer in the American Army during the Revolution. Her father's ancestors came from Connecticut. Mrs. Stanton began to take a great interest in the laws as they applied to women by having access to her father's office, and in which she spent a great deal of time. She began to hold that the statutes were unfair toward women. Before she knew how great a project was confronting her, she had become the evangel of equal rights.

"After graduation from the Willard Seminary in Troy, Mrs. Stanton came to find herself in sympathy with the principles enunciated by her cousin, Gerritt Smith, the anti-slavery agitator. She became desirous of knowing just what the conditions were in the South, and it was at the house of an abolitionist that she met her future husband.

Through her efforts, practically unaided, she caused the passage of a "Woman's Property bill" by the New York Legislature, delivering a two-hour speech thereon. With her work as an anti-slavery advocate and claimant for women's rights, she also found time to devote to the cause of temperance.

She was wont to tell that as early as her sixteenth year she became a believer in woman's rights. Her vexation and mortification were great when her brothers went to college and she could not also go. About this time she was often in a tilt with the law students in her father's office over the rights of women. When they could not score any other way they would mention "The Taming of the Shrew," not at all to the liking of their opponent.

Mrs. Stanton met Daniel O'Connell in London. "He was," she said, "tall, well developed, and a magnificent-looking man, and probably one of the most effective speakers Ireland ever produced." She was in Paris in 1840 at the time the body of Napoleon Bonaparte was brought to France from St. Helena by the Prince de Joinville, and witnessed the wild excitement over the event.

While the Stanton family was living at Chelsea, Mass., Whittier became a regular visitor. During such time he unfolded to Mrs. Stanton one of the most deeply interesting pages of his life, a sad romance of love and disappointment. Mrs. Stanton first met Miss Susan B. Anthony when the latter was a demure young Quakeress. The two ever worked together in friendship and sympathy. Mrs. Stanton said of their joint labors:

"We never met without issuing a pronunciamento on some question. In thought and sympathy we are one, and in the division of labor we exactly complemented each other. In writing we did better work than either could alone. While she is slow and analytical in composition, I am rapid and synthetic. I am the better writer, she the better critic. She supplies the facts and statistics, I the philosophy and rhetoric, and, together, we have made arguments that have stood unshaken through the storms of long years—arguments that no one has answered. Our speeches may be considered the united product of our two brains."

The crowning work of Mrs. Stanton's life is held to be by many the "Woman's Bible." Lady Henry Somerset and Miss Frances E. Willard discussed the project of this Bible with Mrs. Stanton, but finally withdrew their names from the committee, fearing that the work would be too radical. Miss Anthony and Mrs. Stanton were the founders of the Loyal League, which had for its object the relief of the suffering families of Union soldiers, the heads of which were at the front. In 1886 Mrs. Stanton and Miss Anthony issued in collaboration three volumes entitled "History of Women's Suffrage."

It is a noteworthy fact that Miss Anthony finished the fourth volume only last week. In 1895 Mrs. Stanton published "Eighty Years and More," being a volume of reminiscences of her life. She was the author of scores of essays upon marriage, divorce, and allied subjects. From 1870 to 1880 she devoted the greater part of her time to lecturing. On Nov. 12, 1895, she was the central figure in a most memorable reception which took place in the Metropolitan Opera House, this city, and was attended by prominent suffragists from every part of the country. This reception marked the completion of her eightieth year.

TRIBUTE FROM MISS ANTHONY.

ROCHESTER, N. Y., Oct. 26.—The news of the death of Elizabeth Cady Stanton fell with almost crushing weight upon Miss Susan B. Anthony, who had planned to go to New York on Nov. 12 to assist the venerable advocate of woman's suffrage in the celebration of her eighty-seventh birthday. Miss Anthony said to-night:

"Through the early days, when the world was against us, we stood together. Mrs. Stanton was always a courageous woman, a leader of thought and new movements. I always called her the philosopher and statesman of our movement. She was a most finished writer, and every State paper presented to Congress or the State Legislatures in the early days was written by Mrs. Stanton.

"I cannot express myself at all as I feel. I am too crushed to say much, but, if she had outlived me, she would have found fine words with which to express our friendship."

"What period of your lives gave you the greatest pleasure?" was asked.

"When we were digging together. When she forged the thunderbolts and I fired them. The greatest campaign we ever had together was in 1869, at the constitutional convention held in Kansas for suffrage and the same year in New York State.

"In spite of her big family, to whom she was devoted, and the great amount of work she did outside her home, she was one of the finest housekeepers I ever saw."

PHILADELPHIA PASTOR HITS AT DR. PARKHURST.

Charges Him with Preaching Communistic Doctrines—Criticises His Defense of a Starving Man's Right to Steal.

Special to The New York Times.

PHILADELPHIA, Oct. 26.—"Higher Ideals of Honesty" was the subject of a sermon preached at the Walnut Street Presbyterian Church to-day by the Rev. Dr. S. W. Dana, who in the course of his remarks criticised recent utterances of the Rev. Dr. Parkhurst of New York. He said in part:

"'Thou shalt not steal,' has placed upon it many an interpretation according to one's personal wish or conduct. Some are honest in spots, but not at the very roots of their being. They will deal fairly with their brother man and rob the Government if they have a chance. As a member of a political party, or a Legislature, or a corporation, they will connive at that which they would blush to do as a private citizen.

"Then where, too, there is so much wild talk in these days about municipal, State, or National ownership of all land, with the rich products beneath the surface and abundant harvests of the surface, some imbibe the idea that, as a part of the Government, they have a right to their neighbor's possessions.

"The newspapers of last Monday gave some extracts from a sermon by the Rev. Dr. C. H. Parkhurst of New York. He is quoted as saying: 'Some may not think it quite prudent to preach this doctrine. If I were dying of starvation and had no means of buying a piece of bread, and were to go by a baker's shop, I should help myself to it. The way I should reason would be: "That bread belongs to the baker, but it is more God's bread. I am one of God's little boys, and, therefore, look upon this loaf as an answer to the prayer I offered my Father this morning, 'Give me this day my daily bread.'"'

"This sounds plausible, and we have often heard such decisions from communistic preachers and from the mouths of the poor, who in their distress have justified their conduct in taking that which belonged to their neighbor. But we hardly expected such statements from a Christian pulpit. If a man is justified in stealing bread when hungry, by the same process of reasoning he will steal clothing to protect his body, and coal and wood to cook his food. According to this theory, is there any right of personal property? The fallacy of all reasoning of this kind is the assumption that life is the first necessity, and that it must be preserved at all hazards, even if every law is violated.

"In a bread famine our municipal government might be justified in taking possession of the bakeries of the city and managing them in the interests of the whole, but 'God's little hungry boys' had better not take their law into their own hands and break into a baker's shop or they will not be counted honest in the sight of God or man."

NEGRO MOBBED BY WHITES.

Wheelman Who Ran a Woman Down Roughly Handled—Crowd Knocked Him Down and Kicked Him.

White persons in the neighborhood of Thirty-sixth Street and Eighth Avenue mobbed a negro, Moses Mimms, at that corner last night, when he ran down Mrs. Elizabeth Klicks of 306 West Thirty-first Street, as he was riding a bicycle. He was knocked down again and again, struck a number of times and kicked as he lay in the street. Men and women hit him, while many women shouted in glee or rage as they saw the man being maltreated. Two policemen saved him by charging through the mob and leading him to the station house. He was bruised and cut, but not dangerously hurt, and he was locked up without being sent to a hospital.

Mr. and Mrs. Klicks were walking up Eighth Avenue during the evening. Mimms was riding through Thirty-sixth Street. He lives at 444 West Thirty-fifth Street and is thirty years old. He wore the uniform of the Calumet Wheelmen.

As he was about to cross the avenue Mimms noticed he was in line with Klicks and would run him down if he kept on, turned his wheel and dodged as Mr. Klicks, seeing his danger, dodged also. Mrs. Klicks tried to dodge, and, as the negro kept his wheel going while looking for a chance to get by, he ran into her, knocking her off her feet. She rolled into the gutter. Mimms fell off his bicycle.

Klicks helped his wife to her feet. The surrounding crowd of white people who had seen the accident immediately seemed to conclude that the negro was a clumsy man and altogether to blame, and they went at him like madmen. As he arose to his feet, he was sent spinning again by a man who struck him in the neck.

"Now, do him up," shouted another man, rushing up, while the crowd which quickly gathered tried to hem in the negro. But he saw his desperate situation, and with a wild dive jammed himself through the crowd and ran like a frightened deer up the avenue. But the crowd had no intention of losing him.

The colored man only got a few rods away when he was knocked over again. He got up but went down, and then a man kicked him. The negro shouted in his terror, and had such a look of fear on his face that with the shouts he made many people fell back. But others pressed forward and hit the negro as he got up again, and then a number joined in the kicking. Women stood by and shouted to the men encouragingly while the mob surrounded the negro and the men beating him all the time increasing until nearly 1,000 persons were at that point.

It was all happening quickly, and as the human ring was being formed Policemen McManus and Flynn of the West Thirty-seventh Street Station had run up. They tried to push through the crowd, but failed until they drew their clubs and stepping back a few steps shouted to the crowd to make way, and then they ran at the mob and deliberately forced their way through by their own impetus, both being large men.

Some hard characters were close to Mimms and seemed to be beating him more for their own amusement and because the man was colored than through any indignation over the accident. McManus and Flynn no sooner appeared through the edge of the crowd than these men saw them, and at once dashed back, through the crowd and across the street. The policemen did not pursue, but seized Mimms and stood for a few seconds to show the crowd that they were going to protect him. No further molestation was offered the negro, who sat breathing hard with several cuts in his head, his body bruised, and his clothing in a ragged and dirty condition. He recovered rapidly when he found he was safe. The policemen gave him some time to get strength to walk to the station, and with a policeman on each side of him he went to the station house.

Mrs. Klicks was found to be badly hurt. She had a gash in her head, concussion of the brain, and what the physicians feared might be a fracture of the skull. She was unconscious, and a surgeon took her hastily to Roosevelt Hospital in an ambulance, from a drug store at Thirty-fifth Street, to which she had been carried by several men. Her condition was then very serious.

WILLIAM TELL FEAT HAS TRAGIC ENDING

Marksman Misses Apple, Hits Man's Head on Which It Rested.

Fatal Shooting Causes Panic Among Audience in a Hall at Cold Spring Harbor.

COLD SPRING HARBOR, N. Y., Oct. 26.—John Volkman, a barber who was employed by George Van Ausdall, was accidentally shot and killed last night on the stage of Thespian Hall by Charles Meinel of a company which has been giving a two weeks' show there in connection with the sale of a medicine. One of the star features of the show was Meinel's feat of shooting an apple from the head of any person who would volunteer to stand up and allow the apple to have his head for a resting place. When no one volunteered a member of the troupe performed this service.

Saturday afternoon while at work Volkman expressed his willingness to act as the support of the apple, and those who were in the shop at the time tried to dissuade him from taking the risk. One man went so far as to jokingly bid him good-bye, and ask where he wished to be buried. His employer, who knew he would probably try the daring act, made every effort to keep him from the hall, even delaying work in the shop in the hope that this feature of the performance would be over. Volkman reached the hall, however, in time to volunteer.

Meinel did not appear to be in good shooting trim last night, and had been jeered but a short time before because he had missed a card at which he had been shooting.

When Volkman had had the apple placed on his head Meinel began shooting at a distance of about twenty feet. The first two shots missed, but the third struck Volkman in the forehead and he dropped to the stage.

There was a wild scene in the body of the hall, which was crowded. Women screamed and fainted, and many rushed for the exits.

Dr. Soder, the manager of the show and medicine company, went to the aid of the injured man, and Dr. Baldwin of Main Street was summoned. They extracted a part of the bullet a couple of inches from where it entered, this portion having passed through the flesh between the bone and skin and lodged just inside the skin. The examination showed that the remainder had crushed through the frontal bone. Volkman died within an hour. Meinel was arrested by Constable James Wright, and held for a hearing on a charge of manslaughter.

Dr. Gibson of Huntington, the Coroner, reached here this morning and examined three witnesses, Thomas Keegan, Albert Waters, and Horace Allen, Jr. He then postponed the inquest until to-morrow morning, and notified District Attorney Livingston Smith, who will be here in the morning to take charge of the investigation.

Dr. Baldwin, in the presence of the Coroner, this morning performed the autopsy. This showed that the bullet had divided upon hitting the frontal bone two and a quarter inches above the eyebrow line. The smaller fragment had taken the course already described, and the other passed through the bone and into the brain, taking a backward and upward course, and lodging against the skull at the top and rear of the head.

Volkman was eighteen years of age. His father and mother reside in New York, but at present are in Germany.

FELL 250 FEET TO DEATH.

Two Men Instantly Killed, One Fatally Hurt—Rope Holding Swinging Scaffold on the Chimney Slipped.

By the slipping of a rope of a swinging scaffold on the tall chimney of the eleven-story refinery of the American Sugar Refining Company, on the northwest corner of Kent Avenue and South Second Street, Brooklyn, yesterday two men fell 250 feet, and were instantly killed, and another, who fell 70 feet to the roof of the building, was mortally injured.

The men killed were John Mulroy, twenty-five years old, and John Williams, twenty-seven years old, both living in Newark, N. J. Mulroy, it is said, was to have been married soon. The man fatally injured was Henry Cooper, also of Newark, who was removed to the Eastern District Hospital in a critical condition. He received a compound fracture of both legs and internal injuries.

The fourth man on the scaffold was John Murray, who saved his life by clinging to a rope until he was rescued. The refinery is known as the Brooklyn house of the American Sugar Refining Company. The chimney is about 275 feet from the ground, and was built in 1877. An iron ladder reaches to the top from the roof of the building.

About two weeks ago some of the bricks at the top dropped to the ground between the sugar refinery building and a building on the river front. At that time several men were injured, and one, William Naher, had his skull fractured and was removed to the Eastern District Hospital, where he is still.

Cooper obtained a contract to repair the chimney, and the work began yesterday. A stationary scaffold was built around the four sides of the chimney near the top, and when the brickwork was finished a swinging scaffold was suspended from the stationary structure. The rope holding the swinging scaffold was tied around one of the stout timbers of the stationary scaffold.

This swinging scaffold was on the north side of the tall chimney yesterday morning, and the four men got on it to do the "painting," as the mortar work was called. Cooper and Murray were on the land side of the scaffold, and the two men killed on the East River side. The scaffold was about thirty feet below the stationary structure when Cooper gave orders to lower it a little more. Williams lowered his end a few feet and fastened it, but a few minutes later, without any warning, the side nearest the river suddenly slipped down the rope, precipitating Mulroy and Williams to the ground. Almost every bone in their bodies was broken. Murray, who was nearest the rope on the other side, quickly seized a grip on it, while Cooper just missed getting a similar grip as he fell.

The first intimation people in the street had of the accident yesterday was when they heard the cries of the falling men. Murray's cries for help were also heard, as he hung in midair, and several men hurried up the iron ladder to the stationary scaffold, and hauled him up to it by a rope.

Spanish Leather Concern's Plant.

Special to The New York Times.

MOUNT HOLLY, N. J., Oct. 26.—A Spanish leather concern employing over 800 hands is negotiating for the purchase of suitable quarters for the removal of its plant to this place. The concern caters to the Cuban trade especially. Antonio Cabrisas, the President of the concern, is here looking over the contemplated site.

Mr. Cleveland's Gift to a College.

Special to The New York Times.

VILLA NOVA, Penn., Oct. 26.—Ex-President Grover Cleveland has given 200 volumes to the library of Villa Nova College. The college last Commencement Day conferred the degree of Doctor of Jurisprudence on Mr. Cleveland.

IRISH ARE PURCHASING QUANTITIES OF ARMS.

Manufacturers Must Not Send Arms to Proclaimed Districts Without a License.

LONDON TIMES—NEW YORK TIMES Special Cablegram.

LONDON, Oct. 27.—The Times says that, "in consequence of the consignment of unusual quantities of arms and ammunition to Ireland," the Chief Constable of Birmingham has issued a circular to the local manufacturers calling attention to the necessity they are under of observing the terms of the Peace Preservation act.

This measure forbids the consignment of arms or ammunition to any person in a proclaimed district without a license.

According to reports printed in the London papers some of the Irish members of Parliament have recently been advocating armed resistance to British rule, or at any rate expressing regret that such resistance cannot be organized.

The Nationalists have in other ways committed acts which are declared to be of a treasonable character. For instance, at a meeting of the Corporation of Limerick on Oct. 2, a resolution was agreed to, on the motion of Councillor Prendergast, to confer the freedom of the city on a Capt. O'Donnell, who was stated to be a Limerick man who had served on the Boer side during the late war in South Africa. The resolution, after some delay, was seconded by Councillor Slattery and passed without discussion, the Mayor immediately calling on the Council to proceed to the next business.

A recent number of The Irish People gives a list of thirty-one Nationalists who are now undergoing or awaiting sentences under the Crimes Act. It includes the following members of Parliament: William Redmond, (six months,) Michael Reddy, (seven months,) Haviland Burke, (five months,) William Duffy, (arrested,) John O'Donnell, (arrested,) J. P. Farrell, (awaiting sentence,) P. A. McHugh, (awaiting sentence,) and John Roche, (four months' hard labor.)

Many of the convicted Nationalists were charged with sedition.

BICYCLIST ELWELL KILLED.

His Neck Broken by a Fall from a Motor Cycle—He Had Toured Europe and Asia.

Frank A. Elwell of 5 Arlington Place, Brooklyn, who has traveled over a large part of the world upon a bicycle, was killed yesterday at Hicksville, L. I., by a fall from a motor cycle.

Elwell was a member of the Alpha Motor Cycle Club, and, with about seventy other members of the club, was upon a ride over Long Island. The party had reached Hicksville and sat down to dinner, but had not missed Elwell, who had fallen behind, when a stray bicyclist rushed into the room where they were assembled and cried out that he had just come upon a man, evidently a member of the party, lying dead beside his cycle.

Several members mounted in haste and rode back. They found Elwell quite dead. It was evident that the front fork of his machine had broken while he was riding at a high rate of speed. He was projected over the handlebars, landed upon his head, and his neck was broken, so that death came instantly. Coroner Remsen of Hicksville viewed the body and gave permission for its removal to Brooklyn.

Elwell had a wife but no children. His father was once the editor of a paper in Portland, Me., of which place the dead man was a native. His bicycle tours during the past twelve years have covered most of the countries of Europe and Asia.

TRAINMEN WANT MORE PAY.

80,000 Employes of Western Railroads Expected to Ask for a 20 Per Cent. Increase.

Special to The New York Times.

CHICAGO, Oct. 26.—Eighty thousand employes of Western railroads are expected to demand a 20 per cent. increase in wages, following similar action taken by 7,000 yardmen in the Chicago district Saturday. Chicago will be the centre of the fight, for this district has for years set the wage scale on the roads running west from a line through Duluth, Chicago, Cairo, and New Orleans. If successful here, the union officials believe they will win in the other centres, and on this account will bring all their power to aid the local men.

So important is the situation in Chicago, as affecting probable success in other sections, that Grand Master P. H. Morrissey of the Brotherhood of Railway Trainmen, who has been ill in Cleveland for several weeks, was brought to this city to-day.

Morrissey at once went into secret conference with Vice Grand Master W. G. Lee, also of Cleveland. It is believed they considered the question of the time for action in other parts of the West, but neither of them would discuss the purpose of the meeting.

Interest in the movement already has spread to the Switchmen's Union of North America, an independent body.

Roadmen want the same increase as do the yardmen. The freight conductors are paid 3 cents a mile, and the brakemen 2 cents. This scale was set in the old days when the trains were small and the engines light, and it was expected the conductors would earn from $3 to $4 a day and the brakemen from $2 to $3.

MYSTERIOUS EYE DISEASE.

Is Contracted from House Dust and Destroys Sight.

Special to The New York Times.

TRENTON, N. J., Oct. 26.—The physicians of McKinley Hospital here have noticed within the month a peculiar form of eye disease contracted from house dust, in one case destroying the sight of an eye.

About ten days ago Mrs. Isaac Cooper was in the cellar of her home directing her servants in clearing it out. She took a dust brush from a servant and used it herself on some dust. Immediately after she felt an itching of the left eye, rubbed it, and the eye became very much inflamed. It grew rapidly worse and her husband, Dr. Cooper, sent here to the hospital, where, despite all that could be done, the sight left the eye, and Dr. Vischer, a specialist from Philadelphia, was summoned. Apparently nothing touches the disease and the specialist says the sight is gone for ever.

The physicians are puzzled over the case, which is similar to that of other patients received this month, all of whom had been dusting their homes.

Supposed Stradivarius Violin Found.

Special to The New York Times.

ORANGE, N. J., Oct. 26.—A "find" of what is said to be an Antonius Stradivarius violin has been brought to light by A. A. Denis of this city, who bought the instrument in Morristown about two years ago. He paid $35 for it and purchased it for the use of his daughter. No particular value was placed on the "fiddle" at the time, although many noticed the richness of its tone. An expert found the Stradivarius label inside and the date 1719. Mr. Denis has been offered $1,500 for the violin, but he holds it at a higher figure.

SCORE HURT IN COLLISION

Trolley Car Hits an Automobile Near Yonkers and Turns Over.

Accident Occurs at Edge of a Steep Embankment on Warburton Avenue—Party in Auto Escape Injury.

YONKERS, Oct. 26.—In front of Greystone this afternoon a collision between a trolley car and an automobile was responsible for the more or less serious injury of more than twenty persons.

According to the story told by the motorman, the car was passing Samuel J. Tilden's old residence, in Warburton Avenue, and the automobile was going along in the same direction and ahead of the car. The wheels of the machine, which was a big one weighing three tons, seemed somehow to be caught in the car tracks. The unexpected stoppage caused the car to run into it, and the shock was so violent that the car was flung from the track and over upon its side.

On one side of the track was a steep embankment, at the foot of which are the tracks of the New York Central Railroad, but the car was thrown the other way. While, therefore, it did not roll any great distance, the passengers were tumbled over and jumbled together topsy-turvy, and most of them were more or less hurt before it was possible to get them out of the wreck.

The automobile shot forward some distance after being hit, but was able to make its way to town in spite of the accident and a very much damaged tire. The chauffeur, who was arrested, gave his name as W. B. Raymond of 850 Eighth Avenue, New York City. He declined to say who owned the automobile or who was in it. The occupants were two women and a man, but the owner, the chauffeur says, was not in the party.

Joseph Nagle, the motorman of the car, lays the blame upon the chauffeur. The man and the women in the automobile escaped so far as could be learned without injury. Most of the people in the car disappeared without giving their names and none was dangerously injured. Some of them went home at once and summoned doctors to attend them there; others went to the offices of doctors along Warburton Avenue and neighboring streets; still others were taken to St. John's Riverside Hospital.

Those who were taken to the hospital are as follows:

BAILEY, Miss WENONAH, of Amsterdam Avenue, New York, a guest of Miss MacClintock; face cut, shoulder cut and bruised, cuts from glass about body.

CALLAHAN, Miss KATIE, of this city; scalp wounds and bruises.

MacCLINTOCK, Miss MERLE, of Mount Vernon, torn and lacerated; one ear almost torn off; bruised and cut by glass.

Harry Genabach, Miss Mamie Mahoney, Miss Mamie O'Brien, S. L. Ascher, and Martin Ryan were treated for cuts and bruises and went to their homes.

At the office of Dr. Miles there were treated James Arthur of 118 New Main Street, this city, and his three nephews, George, James, and William Arthur. All four had scalp wounds and were cut by glass and bruised about the body. They went home.

The names of the others injured could not be learned, the doctors refusing to tell, simply contenting themselves with saying they had treated a certain number. Their numbers, combined with those whose names are given, bring the total up to twenty-two.

EXCITEMENT IN WISCONSIN.

La Follette's Attack on Senator Spooner May Cost the Governor Thousands of Votes.

Special to The New York Times.

MILWAUKEE, Oct. 26.—That Gov. La Follette, in his speech at Appleton Saturday, in which he declared that Senator Spooner must declare in favor of the State Republican platform to get the Administration support for re-election, meant to administer a telling blow to the Senator, is practically admitted by the State organ of the administration, when it says:

"The answer stamped the Governor as being absolutely consistent and honest in his advocacy of strict compliance with platform pledges. Had he been an opportunist, merely seeking for votes, here was an opportunity such as would not be again presented to him. If he desired to repudiate, or even modify, his attitude toward a single plank in the State platform he could have done so, but to have done so would have laid him open to the charge of inconsistency. It was a supreme moment, and Gov. La Follette rose to the occasion."

Protests against the Governor's attack are rising from all parts of the State. Senator Spooner is silent under the Governor's attack, refusing to make any statement except that he will continue this week on his schedule of speeches advocating the election of the entire State ticket.

That Gov. La Follette's attack will cost him thousands of votes seems to be foreordained and it is admitted even by his friends.

GREEN BAY, Wis., Oct. 26.—As a result, it is said, of Gov. Lafollette's latest attack on Senator Spooner the Governor will not be able to secure the hall for his speech here to-morrow. The hall is owned by Senator Hagemeister, one of the strongest Spooner Republicans in the State.

NEW POST FOR WU-TING-FANG.

PEKING, Oct. 26.—An edict has been issued appointing Wu-Ting-Fang to succeed Sheng as Commissioner for the new commercial treaties negotiations.

Sheng has resigned this office in order to bury his father, who died last Friday, and to perform other filial duties.

Sheng was formerly Director of Telegraphs and Railroads. He was also Taotai of Shanghai during the period of the Boxer rising. He is said to be greatly disliked by foreigners, and has been described as thoroughly unscrupulous and cunning.

It has been rumored that the powers were opposed to Sheng's holding the position which he has just resigned. It is a post of the greatest importance in connection with China's foreign trade.

TO TEACH GIRLS FARMING.

Special to The New York Times.

WELLESLEY, Mass., Oct. 26.—Wellesley College, ever progressive, is planning to take up farming. A new department of learning is to be installed, which will teach young women scientific gardening—how to treat diseased wheat and grain, and how to become expert grafters. The promoters of the new idea at Wellesley assert that no other female institution in America possesses equal advantages and facilities to conduct such a department, and as an argument point to the spacious, well-kept grounds of the college and the world-famed Hunnewell estate, with its magnificent greenhouses.

Besides the farming department, there will be an up-to-date dairy, in which the fair agriculturists will learn the science of perfect butter-making. In a poultry yard they will learn to rear and feed chickens.

In England there is a horticultural college at Swanley, which covers all departments except cattle raising. Hundreds of women graduates have been taught there.

"All the News That's Fit to Print."

The New York Times.

THE WEATHER.

Fair; wind variable.

VOL. LII.....NO. 16,630. NEW YORK, FRIDAY, APRIL 24, 1903.—SIXTEEN PAGES. ONE CENT In Greater New York, Jersey City and Newark. Elsewhere, TWO CENTS.

MANCHURIA CRISIS; JAPAN IS AROUSED

Russia Demands Sovereignty in the Country.

She Presents a New Agreement for China to Sign.

Refuses to Evacuate Manchuria Till This Is Done—One Clause of the Agreement a Slap at the United States—Orders to Japanese Warships.

LONDON TIMES—NEW YORK TIMES Special Cablegram.

LONDON, April 24.—The Peking correspondent of The Times says that Russia has presented seven new demands as conditions for carrying out the Manchurian convention and evacuating Niu-Chwang and the two southern provinces of Manchuria.

First, it is demanded that there shall be no new treaty ports and no new foreign Consulates in Manchuria. This, says the correspondent, is a slap in the face for the United States, which proposed the opening of treaty ports at Mukden and Taku-Shan.

Second, it is required that the customs revenues of Niu-Chwang be paid into the Russo-Chinese Bank, and not the Chinese customs bank.

Third, it is demanded that no portion of Manchuria be alienated to another power.

Fourth, none but Russians are to be employed in an administrative capacity in Manchuria, military or civil.

The fifth clause, which is described by the correspondent as somewhat obscure, demands that the Chinese administration continue in the same status as at present.

Sixth, it is provided that Russia is to have the right to own telegraph wires wherever there are Chinese telegraphs in Manchuria, using the same poles.

Seventh, it is required that Russia shall control the sanitary regulations of the treaty port of Niu-Chwang.

By The Associated Press.

PEKING, April 23.—Russia has demanded that China sign an agreement practically ceding to her the sovereignty of Manchuria and excluding other nations from that country. The Russian Chargé d'Affaires, M. Plancon, has informed Prince Ching, President of the Foreign Office, that no further steps in the evacuation of Manchuria will be taken until this agreement is signed.

Prince Ching has refused the Russian terms, but his refusal probably pleases Russia as well as his acceptance would have done, because either alternative means the relinquishment of Chinese sovereignty in Manchuria.

The Russian demands are as follows: First, no more Manchurian ports or towns are to be opened; second, no more foreign Consuls are to be admitted into Manchuria; third, no foreigners, except Russians, are to be employed in the public service of Manchuria; fourth, the present status of the administration of Manchuria is to remain unchanged; fifth, the customs receipts at the port of Niu-Chwang are to be given to the Russo-Chinese Bank; sixth, a sanitary commission is to be organized under Russian control; seventh, Russia is entitled to attach telegraph wires to the poles of all Chinese lines in Manchuria, and, eighth, no territory in Manchuria is to be alienated to any other power. No explanation has been given to the Chinese of the Russian interpretation of the fourth demand.

The Chinese officials are greatly disturbed, but they are powerless.

While the foregoing demands were before the Chinese for consideration M. Plancon assured his colleagues explicitly that the only reason for the delay in restoring the Government of Niu-Chwang to the Chinese was the organization of the sanitary commission.

There has been considerable feeling in British circles over the appointment of a Russian Customs Commissioner in Niu-Chwang, but this revelation of Russia's determination to maintain control of Manchuria and close the "open door" there robs the appointment of its importance.

JAPANESE WARSHIPS ORDERED TO NIU-CHWANG.

YOKOHAMA, April 23.—Three Japanese warships have been ordered to Niu-Chwang.

Marquis Ito has held a secret conference with the leading Japanese statesmen.

The Russian demands for privileges in Manchuria have excited the Japanese press, which insists on vigorous action, and is confident that the United States as well as Great Britain will support Japan.

An arrangement has been reached by which the political crisis has been averted. The Government's naval proposals remain unchanged.

FIGHTING IN MACEDONIA.

Greeks Said to Have Tortured Bulgarians—Battle Near Prilip.

LONDON TIMES—NEW YORK TIMES Special Cablegram.

LONDON, April 24.—The Sofia correspondent of The Times says there are several revolutionary bands in the North of Adrianople Vilayet.

It is stated that the village of Sarmashik, where a conflict recently occurred, has been plundered by Bashi-Bazouks and gendarmes.

A Doubnitza telegram says the remnant of Saieff's band has been captured.

Col. Yankoff publishes a letter in The Dnevnik saying that thirty Bulgarian insurgents recently captured in Thessaly were tortured by Greeks, and that one succumbed.

An official telegram from Constantinople, says the Vienna correspondent of The Times, confirms the rumor that the holy men sent by the Sultan are detained at Ipek by the Albanians as hostages for the Sultan's good conduct.

There has been a conflict north of Prilip between Turkish troops and a revolutionary band twenty-five strong. The Turks lost six killed and seven wounded, and the insurgents seven killed and wounded. The members of the band covered their retreat by throwing dynamite bombs.

INDEX TO DEPARTMENTS.

THE KING'S VISIT TO PARIS.

A "Slightly Querulous Note" in German Comments on It.

LONDON TIMES—NEW YORK TIMES Special Cablegram.

LONDON, April 24.—A slightly querulous note, says the Berlin correspondent of The Times, is perceptible in some of the German comments on King Edward's forthcoming visit to Paris. No one professes any objection, but the event is described as one which the Germans may regard with equanimity and at the same time any reference in this connection to Germany and her policy is resented.

The Neueste Nachrichten professes to be unable to understand why what it considers "a flavor of ill-will against German policy" should be imported into the compliments passing between England and France.

The correspondent says this refers apparently to The Times's editorial contrasting the dignity and calm of French policy with the restlessness of the German Foreign Office.

W. K. VANDERBILT 'RETURNS TO PARIS.

His Visit to London Was in Connection with His Approaching Marriage, but His Plans Are Still a Mystery.

LONDON, April 23.—William K. Vanderbilt has returned to Paris. His hurried visit to London was connected with the procuring of a special marriage license.

There is much discussion as to whether a license can be issued under the circumstances. It is said that the Ecclesiastical Court could not refuse a license, whatever its feelings in regard to divorced persons; but it is added that it could delay matters, probably a fortnight, by requiring the production of documents which would have to be sent from America. At the Archbishop of Canterbury's office it was said to-day that the Archbishop had the undoubted right to refuse to issue a license. No application, however, has yet been received from Mr. Vanderbilt.

For an ordinary license one of the parties must live in some parish here for three weeks and have the banns read out in church on three successive Sundays. The French formalities require a residence of six months.

PARIS, April 23.—There continues to be much mystery concerning the plans for the Vanderbilt-Rutherfurd wedding. All the parties who are in a position to speak authoritatively decline to disclose the plans, and close friends of the parties have not yet been informed as to the time or place for the ceremony. One of the intimate friends of Mr. Vanderbilt and Mrs. Rutherfurd said it was generally believed they intended to make the ceremony as private and quiet as possible.

It is said that the report that the marriage would take place on Saturday in London did not come from an authorized source, though Mr. Vanderbilt's trip to London is considered by his friends as indicating preparation for the ceremony to take place there.

The Duchess of Marlborough has been here for several days, coming from Vienna, presumably to attend the wedding. She drove in the Bois this afternoon, and it is thought, called at Mrs. Rutherfurd's residence. All inquiries at Mrs. Rutherfurd's house relative to her plans meet with evasive responses.

Mr. Vanderbilt and Mrs. Rutherfurd are indignant at the persistent inquiries made regarding their engagement. A photographer stood outside Mrs. Rutherfurd's residence most of the day, trying to get a snapshot of her for American papers.

CARPENTERS TO MAKE PEACE.

Orders Sent to Men in New York to Resume Work Pending a Conference.

INDIANAPOLIS, April 23.—It was announced from the National headquarters of the United Brotherhood of Carpenters and Joiners this evening that orders will be telegraphed to the striking members of the brotherhood in New York City to-morrow morning to suspend all hostilities and resume work.

The committees to be chosen by the brotherhood and the Amalgamated Society of Carpenters will hold a conference May 4 to devise means by which the society may become a part of the brotherhood.

BRIDGE WORKERS' SETTLEMENT

Wage and Hour Agreement in Pittsburg District to Last Until 1905.

Special to The New York Times.

PITTSBURG, April 23.—Official announcement was made to-day at the headquarters of Local Union No. 3 of the International Association of Bridge and Structural Iron Workers of the settlement of the wage scale for the entire Pittsburg district until Jan. 1, 1905. The agreement was entered into with the National Association of Manufacturers and Iron and Steel Erectors.

The early settlement was brought about through the ending of the trouble of the union with the American Bridge Company. The strike against that corporation was ended Tuesday night, after which the general agreement was made. Any differences that may arise from May 1 until the expiration of agreement, on Jan. 1, 1905, shall be settled by arbitration.

The wages of structural iron workers are advanced from 47½ to 50 cents an hour, with an eight-hour work day. The wage rate is not uniform over the country, but the working rules are the same.

MRS. HANNAH SOUTHWICK DEAD

She and Her Brother, Whose Father Served Under Washington, Held the Age Record for Twins.

PAWTUCKET, R. I., April 23.—Mrs. Hannah Southwick, eighty-eight years old, an original Daughter of the Revolution, died here to-day. She and her brother, Jeremiah, who died recently in Franklin, Mass., held the distinction of being the oldest twin brother and sister living in the United States.

They were born in Cumberland in 1815. Their father, John Haselton, crossed the Delaware with Washington and was the first man in the party to land.

$600,000 FOR TUSKEGEE AND B. T. WASHINGTON

Andrew Carnegie's Contribution to the Endowment Fund.

Also to Provide Life Income for Mr. and Mrs. Washington — Philanthropist Has Been Giving $10,000 a Year to the Institute.

As a result of the Tuskegee mass meeting held on April 14 at Madison Square Concert Hall, Andrew Carnegie has donated $600,000 toward the endowment of the Tuskegee Normal and Industrial Institute in Alabama, and for a life income for its President, Booker T. Washington, and his wife. Mr. Carnegie, it has also become known, has been giving $10,000 to the institute for four years past.

The following letter making known the six-hundred-thousand-dollar gift was sent to William H. Baldwin:

"New York, April 17, 1903.

"William H. Baldwin, Jr., Trustee:

"My Dear Friend: I have instructed Mr. Franks, my cashier, to deliver to you, as Trustee of Tuskegee Institute, $600,000 5 per cent. United States Steel Company first mortgage bonds toward the Endowment Fund.

"I give this without reservation except that I require that suitable provision be made from the gift for the wants of Booker Washington and his family during his own or his wife's life. I wish that great and good man to be entirely free from pecuniary cares that he may be free to devote himself to his great mission.

"To me he seems one of the greatest of living men, because his work is unique, the modern Moses, who leads his race and lifts it through education to even better and higher things than a land overflowing with milk and honey. History is to tell of two Washingtons, one white, the other black—both fathers of their people.

"I am satisfied that the serious race problem of the South is to be solved wisely only through Mr. Washington's policy of education—which he seems to have been specially born—a slave among slaves—to establish and in his own day greatly to advance.

"Glad am I to be able to assist this good work in which you and others so zealously labor. Truly yours,

"ANDREW CARNEGIE."

When seen last night at his room in the Manhattan Hotel, Mr. Washington was still in a state of great elation over the good news which he received last Saturday.

"It would be impossible to express adequately my thanks to Mr. Carnegie," he said. "Not only those directly interested in the welfare of Tuskegee Institute will be glad to hear of the generous gift, but I think all the people of the South, both white and black, will be filled with gratitude."

About the condition made by Mr. Carnegie relative to Mr. Washington himself, the latter refused to say anything except that he, of course, appreciated the kind thought.

The Endowment Fund Committee, the members of which are William H. Baldwin, Jr., Robert C. Ogden, J. G. Phelps Stokes, and George Foster Peabody, will take action on the gift, he said, when three of them, now at the Southern Educational Conference in Richmond, return to New York. It will be for them to accept the gift and approve the conditions.

Mr. Washington made known the fact that heretofore has been hidden from the public, that Mr. Carnegie has been giving $10,000 a year to Tuskegee. The attention of the millionaire was first forcibly called to the work being done by Booker T. Washington by the latter's book, "Up from Slavery." This volume is in the library at Skibo, Mr. Carnegie's estate in Scotland.

The first gift that Mr. Carnegie made to the Alabama institution was in the form of a twenty-thousand-dollar library, which was given as a result of a visit that the negro educator made to the philanthropist about four years ago. Since then the $10,000 has been received regularly every year.

"The income of the $600,000 is not to be used for the construction of any new buildings or for equipment," said Mr. Washington, "nor is the capital to be touched at all. The yearly interest on the bonds is to go toward the defrayal of the current expenses of the school, which amount to $152,000. As it is now, I have to raise the greater part of this sum by private contribution every year, and of course the $30,000 will be a great help. However, I don't want the impression to be given that the generous gift of Mr. Carnegie entirely relieves the needs of Tuskegee. With the present endowment of $110,000 and the new gift of $600,000 there is still $1,000,000 necessary before the income will meet the current expenses."

Mr. Washington made a personal visit to the residence of Mr. Carnegie yesterday morning and thanked him for the gift. He says that although Mr. Carnegie did not distinctly say so, it is probable that the mammoth meeting in Madison Square Garden last week and the speech of Mr. Cleveland may have had something to do with the large donation. It is Mr. Washington's hope that this liberality will open up the way to future gifts by Northern friends of the negro. Since the meeting last week he has succeeded in getting as much as $18,000 to be used in defraying the current expenses of Tuskegee.

Mr. Carnegie has never visited the institute, and his knowledge of it is, therefore, the result of reading and hearing speeches. Mr. Washington expressed the hope that no very long time would pass before the school had the pleasure of welcoming the man who has done so much for it.

"I want to express my gratitude to the people of the North," Mr. Washington added, "for the uniform courtesy and warmth with which they have received me. My stay here has been made as pleasant for me as possible. That it has been satisfactory is shown by this last gift, not to speak of the others."

Mr. Washington will leave to-morrow for Hampton, where on Tuesday he will deliver an address at the dedication of the building erected by Mrs. C. P. Huntington as a memorial to her husband.

ENTHUSIASM AT RICHMOND.

Tuskegee Trustees and Others Express Their Gratification at Mr. Carnegie's Big Gift.

Special to The New York Times.

RICHMOND, Va., April 23.—The announcement of Andrew Carnegie's gift to Tuskegee Institute was made known here to-night, and created unbounded enthusiasm.

William H. Baldwin, Jr., President of the General Education Board, when seen to-night at the conference at the Academy of Music made the following comment:

"Washington's work and self-denial are worthy of recognition by all people, and this generous gift will aid materially in helping him meet the expenses of the rapidly growing work of Tuskegee."

President Edwin A. Alderman of Tulane University and a Director in the Southern Education Board said:

"I consider Tuskegee Institute a great experiment station for the training of a backward race for useful and honorable life in this Republic. Booker T. Washington has infused this institute with his own sanity, sympathy, and patriotism. His work for it is one of the notable educational achievements of the generation. Mr. Carnegie has done a high patriotic service in relieving the institution from want and wasteful struggle. Nowhere will the news of this great beneficence be received with more genuine gladness and approval than in the South and by the Southern people."

Col. G. R. Glenn of Georgia, assistant agent of the Peabody Fund in the South, said:

"I believe Principal Washington is worthy of all the cordial sympathy and practical co-operation that have come to him from all parts of the country. Mr. Carnegie's great gift will tremendously increase the efficiency of the Tuskegee Institute. As a Southern man interested in the practical and useful education of all our children, I rejoice to learn of this additional gift for the industrial training of the children of the negro race."

President Robert C. Ogden expressed his satisfaction in the following terms:

"Mr. Carnegie's gift is a source of encouragement to Booker T. Washington and the cause for which his life stands. The great hope is that this gift may stimulate and inspire other generosity. The sums needed for education of our backward populations are vast, and when men of wealth realize that, the burden of Washington and others will be greatly lifted."

George Foster Peabody, Treasurer of the General Education Board, said:

"The gift of Mr. Carnegie is an indication of the appreciation by shrewd business men of two main features respecting Southern education. First, that the ideal of industrial education as set forth at Tuskegee is the most hopeful and worthy of substantial assistance by means of permanent endowment.

"Second—That Northern men who were factors in the abolition of slavery are redeeming an obligation to the country as well by helping negro education into which the South has put so many millions. His provision for Mr. Washington also indicates his appreciation of the value of true manhood, common sense, and social service.

"This gift also indicates that Mr. Carnegie appreciates that only a portion of the great sum needed should come from one man, for the annual need of the institution is more than four times the interest on the magnificent sum given by Mr. Carnegie for an endowment."

Said Edgar Gardner Murphy, Executive Secretary of the Southern Education Board:

"As I understand the terms of the gift, it will have two effects: First, it will help Tuskegee to make its work still more effective and practical; secondly, it will relieve the institution of the necessity of paying a salary to Booker T. Washington. It will partly save him from the necessity of constantly leaving his proper work to seek money in the North, and will thus enable him to give himself more strictly and completely to the administration of the school."

TUSKEGEE AND ITS PRINCIPAL.

Remarkable Career of Booker T. Washington — What He and His Wife Are Doing for Their Race.

Booker Taliaferro Washington, the admitted leader of his race, and who has been the head and life of the Tuskegee Normal and Industrial Institute since 1881, when he founded it, has been linked so inseparably with this institution that its life during the past twenty-two years has been his life. Born in slavery, he has by his faithful and unselfish devotion to the work of uplifting his people won the highest eulogies of public men and has the undivided confidence of the people of his own State of Alabama as well as that of the people of the North.

Prof. Washington was born a slave at Hale's Ford, Va., during either 1857 or 1858. The place of birth and his home during the first few years of his life was one of those one-room log cabins with uncouth chimneys and wood glued upon the end such as even yet may be seen in some parts of the South. The floor of the cabin was hard-trodden earth, and the walls had no windows, a circumstance which was of little account, as the door rarely was closed, and even when it was both air and light had perfectly free passage between the logs of the walls where the mud chinking had fallen out.

A few years later Washington's mother moved to Madison, West Va., along with the other chattels of the family that owned them. Here Washington was put to work in the salt furnaces during the greater part of each year, and was at this work when the war ended, bringing them somewhere about eight years of age. At this period the boy, between his working time, managed to go to school for a couple of months each year, and when unable to do so he would devote his nights to study.

This kept up until in 1871 he heard of the Hampton Institute, in Virginia, and made up his mind to go there. With just enough money to carry him to Richmond he started and got there shelterless and friendless. A hole under the sidewalk gave him his first night's lodging, and in the morning he got work unloading pig iron from a nearby vessel. With what he thus secured he got to Hampton with fifty cents in his pocket. Working his way through the institution and graduating with honors, he returned to West Virginia, where he taught school for a time and then was able to spend a year at Wayland Seminary in Washington. From there he was called back to Hampton as a teacher and remained for two years.

When application was made to Gen. S. C. Armstrong by the citizens of Tuskegee, Ala., in 1881 for some one to start an institution at that place on the plan of Hampton Institute, Prof. Washington was recommended. He went there and found no lands, no buildings, nothing in fact but the promise of the State to pay $2,000 annually toward the expenses of the school. His work began in a small shanty and church with one teacher and thirty students. From that time until now the growth of the Institute has been phenomenal, and full credit is given alone to the able management of President Washington. Now there are more than forty buildings, about 2,000 acres of land, and its property in the aggregate is valued at nearly $1,000,000.

There annually more than 1,000 young colored men and women are taught how to make their lives count for the most possible for themselves, for their race, and for the general public. It is an intensely practical school. The students who are studying farming do all the work of the land. Of the buildings, nearly all of which are of brick, all but the first three or four were built by the students of the mechanical arts department, beginning with the making of the bricks and the cutting of the timber. Tuskegee is the largest school in the world for negro pupils, conducted wholly by negro teachers. Its executive force and instructors, numbering nearly 100, are all of the negro race, and with the exception of the Board of Trustees, none of whom resides at the school, there is no one of any other race connected with the institution.

Prof. Washington first became a National character in 1894, when he spoke for the negro on the opening day of the Atlanta Exposition. Previously he had acquired more or less local fame as an orator, but on this occasion he was hailed as the successor of Frederick Douglass as the leader of the negroes. Since then he has been in demand as a public speaker upon the question of his race. As such he has appeared before the best known organizations and people of the country. He was called into consultation by President McKinley on matters affecting the negro, and has also been consulted by President Roosevelt. At no time, however, has there been the faintest suggestion of mingling in politics on his part. Harvard University conferred the degree of Master of Arts upon him in 1896.

In 1893 Washington married Miss Maggie Y. Murray, who has since been closely identified with the work of her husband, and is one of the leading spirits of Tuskegee. She, too, has been prominent in many National movements for the uplifting of the negro women, and is Chairman of the Executive Committee of the National Association of Colored Women. She is the President of the Mothers' Club at Tuskegee, the work of which is teaching the poor colored mother to be cleanly, to learn to economize time, and to recognize the necessity of sanitation. She also has been one of the leaders in the movement against the intemperance of the blacks in the South and has accomplished much for the benefit of her people.

CITY BONDS STILL INVALID.

Special to The New York Times.

MADISON, Wis., April 23.—Gov. La Follette to-day returned to the Senate without approval the Wipperman bill to legalize municipal bonds that were issued without having been authorized by a vote of the people, as required by law. Action on the veto was postponed until next Wednesday morning.

Many cities of the State are seriously affected by the veto. The cities of Janesville, Beloit, Superior, and other places issued bonds without having held a prior popular election on the proposition, which the Supreme Court has held to be necessary, and the bonds will be legally worthless unless the present measure is passed over the veto.

THE PRESIDENT'S VACATION ENDED

He Holds a Reception at a Yellowstone Park Hotel.

Resumes His Tour To-day—Has Been Much Benefited by His Stay in the Park—Amusing Incidents.

CINNABAR, Mont., April 23.—President Roosevelt's vacation it at an end. He greeted the members of his party and a large number of persons at the Mammoth Hot Springs Hotel in Yellowstone Park to-day, and will resume his tour to-morrow.

The President, who arrived at Fort Yellowstone yesterday, is the picture of health, and the time he has spent in the park has been of great benefit to him. He speaks in enthusiastic terms of the park. Word went out several days ago that he would meet the people living in the park and vicinity this morning, and when he arrived at the Mammoth Hot Springs Hotel he found 200 men and women waiting to greet him. The President addressed them briefly, speaking of the good time he had had during the past two weeks, and then shook hands with each one. He spent the rest of the day inspecting the post and horseback riding with Major Pitcher. Before starting to-morrow he will participate in the laying of the cornerstone of the new gate at the northern entrance to the park.

The President and those who accompanied him on his tour of the park are delighted with the trip. No accident occurred to mar the pleasure of the party, and, for the most part, they were favored with delightful weather. John Burroughs, who accompanied the President most of the time, was also greatly benefited by his out-door life, and his face is as bronzed as that of the President. The President spent most of his time studying the habits of the different species of game that abound in the park. He would lie for hours near a herd of elk or mountain goats, and would frequently walk eight or ten miles to observe them. He also studied bird life with Mr. Burroughs, and showed himself particularly well posted on this subject. Mr. Burroughs was able to show him but one bird with which he was not acquainted, namely, the soltaire.

Mr. Roosevelt's camp was composed of two Sibley tents and one wall tent without board floors, and while everything was very simple, it was quite comfortable. The party that accompanied him was a small one, consisting of Major Pitcher, Mr. Burroughs, two orderlies, and two cooks. There also was a small force to man the pack wagon.

While there were no accidents a number of amusing incidents occurred. One of them happened at the time of the President's visit to Geyserland a few days ago. The President and Mr. Burroughs were on skis and started to race down hill. The snow was soft, and Mr. Burroughs, who had never used a ski before, soon found himself with his head in the snow and his feet in the air. He had hardly struggled to his feet when the President repeated the performance. Neither was hurt, but Major Pitcher secured excellent photographs of the catastrophe, which he has promised to have developed.

On another occasion the President had just commenced to shave himself when Mr. Burroughs discovered a number of mountain goats jumping down a steel hill. He called the President's attention to the sight, and Mr. Roosevelt came running out without hat or coat, and with his face covered with lather.

The party was fortunate in running across game. Thousands of elk and deer and quite a number of mountain sheep and goats were encountered and their habits were closely studied. The President and Mr. Burroughs also saw many strange birds, and the latter is quite enthusiastic over some of the feathered tribes that inhabit the park. Mr. Burroughs tells a good story in connection with the birds. The party were sitting around the camp fire one night when Mr. Burroughs, whom, by the way, the President has nicknamed "Oom John," on account of his flowing white whiskers, heard a strange call. He did not recognize it and asked Bill Hoffer, the guide and trapper, what it was.

"That's an owl," said Bill.

"Oh, no," replied the President and Mr. Burroughs, "an owl does not sound that kind of a call." Thereupon the party started out to locate the bird. They finally discovered it perched on the topmost bough of a tall tree. It was too far away to be plainly discerned with the naked eye.

"You keep that bird treed, Oom John," said the President, "and I will go and get the glasses."

When the bird was brought into vision by the powerful glasses, it proved to be a dwarf owl. Bill Hoffer was vindicated.

The President had a number of narrow escapes. One day, in company with Major Pitcher, he fired a new revolver at a tree. The weapon was defective, and the empty shell flew back and struck the President on the cheek, drawing blood. If it had struck a little higher up it would have injured, if not blinded, one eye.

The President rode a big gray horse during the whole of his stay. The horse belongs to Troop B, Third Cavalry, and is one of the surest-footed animals in the Park. He showed what he could do on the first day out. To reach the first camp it was necessary to traverse for about two miles a narrow mountainous trail, which was covered with ice. Some of the party dismounted and led their horses down the trail, for a misstep meant death or serious injury, but the President stuck to the saddle and guided his mount safely down the trail.

The longest walk enjoyed by the President was taken on Easter Sunday. He started out alone in the morning, declining the offer of other members of the party to accompany him. He spent the day in climbing mountains and walking along the trail. He covered fully twenty miles, and did not return to camp until 7 o'clock in the evening. When Major Pitcher found that the President was determined to go by himself, he induced him to take a revolver so that he could signal, in case of accident.

PENNELL INSURANCE FIGHT.

BUFFALO, April 23.—The effort of the company which issued a policy for $15,000 on the life of Arthur R. Pennell to have J. Frederick Pennell interpleaded in Attorney Wallace Thayer's suit against the insurance company came to an abrupt ending at the Special Term of the Supreme Court this afternoon. Charles B. Sears, attorney for the administrator, in open court withdrew all claim for the payment of the policy to the estate, and thus put an end to the motion for interpleader.

The case having taken that turn, the sealed instructions which A. R. Pennell left with his attorney, Mr. Thayer, regarding the purpose of the $25,000 trust which he left with him, were not produced in court.

It was reported they were opened, and the attorneys, on finding they named Mrs. Burdick as a beneficiary, decided a contest would be useless. The attorneys refused to affirm or deny the report that the instructions had been opened. It is generally believed, however, that they were.

A POSTMASTER UNDER ARREST.

Special to The New York Times.

TOLEDO, Ohio, April 23.—Deputy United States Marshal B. J. Wagner arrived to-day from Middlebass with Postmaster Herman Wehrle of that famed resort, the latter under arrest on a charge of embezzlement of funds belonging to the United States Government. The warrant was signed by Post Office Inspector Moore, who charges embezzlement of $4,367.87. Col. Moore says the misapplication of Government funds extends as far back as Nov. 1, 1902, and he cannot say how much further. Col. Moore expresses the opinion that the actual sum embezzled is far in excess of the amount stated in the warrant. It is alleged that Wehrle has been issuing bogus money orders.

COL. JOSEPH K. RICKEY DEAD.

Coroner Says He Committed Suicide by Taking Carbolic Acid—Carried from Throng in Broadway.

Col. Joseph Karr Rickey, famous throughout the country as the originator of the concoction bearing his name, died suddenly yesterday in his home at 24 West Twenty-fifth Street.

Although the members of the family denied that the Colonel had taken poison, Coroner Scholer announced last night that Dr. Weston had performed an autopsy on the body and had found a small quantity of carbolic acid in the stomach.

"Col. Rickey committed suicide," the Coroner said. "The autopsy settles all doubt on the matter. The man had a fatty heart, and as I could find no traces of carbolic acid on his lips or his tongue, I concluded at the time that he must have died of heart disease. I think he must have taken the acid with whisky. On account of the condition of his heart, it would only require a small quantity of the acid to kill him."

His physician, Dr. A. S. Maddox, had counseled him to remain within doors, but Col. Rickey, who was a familiar figure on Broadway and in the leading hotels, insisted on going out daily. He appeared to be considerably improved yesterday, and he started for a walk. He visited the Hoffman House and then stood on the corner of Broadway and Twenty-fifth Street watching the passing throng. Suddenly he reeled and clasped one hand to his breast. Policeman Riordan ran to his assistance and escorted him to his home. He died soon afterward. It was said that he had been despondent lately.

Col. Rickey was born in a small town in Wisconsin in January, 1842. A few years later the family moved to Keokuk, and subsequently to Fulton, near St. Louis, Mo. At the outbreak of the war he ran away from home and enlisted in the Confederate Army, and while in St. Louis formed the acquaintance of Miss Sallie Howard, who was at a convent where the Colonel's sister was a pupil. Miss Howard became the Colonel's wife, and she and two children survive.

Col. Rickey was one of a quartet of famous Colonels who were known in nearly every city in the country—Col. William Hyde, Col. Broadhead, Col. "Gus" Prather, and Col. Rickey. Col. Rickey had a very wide acquaintance with members of Congress and he took an active part in promoting legislation. At one time he was the owner of the Shomaker Building, on Pennsylvania Avenue, in the capital city.

Col. Rickey had three children—Natalie Kyle Rickey, Alby Prather Rickey, and William Hyde Rickey. Natalie married Robert Spencer of St. Louis. She and her husband are dead. Alby Prather is the widow of Leslie Hanchett of St. Louis, and William Hyde is in business in the West. For several years Col. Rickey engaged in the stock brokerage business in St. Louis with his son-in-law under the firm name of Rickey & Spencer. For about ten years he resided in this city, where he was interested in a mineral water company.

The Colonel was prominent in the Missouri Society. He was a racegoer and was considered an expert poker player.

"Al" Smith said of Col. Rickey yesterday: "Joe and I were boys together. He was the soul of honor. He was as square as a die, and if he was your friend you could command his last dollar. He has given away a fortune to those he deemed in need." The Colonel was a very warm friend of William J. Bryan. The body was taken to Fulton, Mo., last night, where the funeral is to be to-morrow afternoon.

LEE RETURNS TO MISSOURI.

At the Solicitation of His Wife He Will Make a Full Confession Concerning "Boodle."

Special to The New York Times.

ST. LOUIS, April 23.—Lieut. Gov. John A. Lee returned from Chicago to-night, and to-morrow will appear before the local Grand Jury, which is investigating boodling in the State Legislature. He came back on the advice of his wife, who, after a conference with Circuit Attorney Folk, went to Chicago to see him.

Mr. Lee looks careworn and ill. He says he has been maligned, and not half the charges brought against him can be proved. He asserts that he is suffering from a malady which compels him to rest from all exertion, bodily and mental, and that when he fled the State to avoid appearing before the Grand Jury it was with no purpose of remaining away longer than necessary to fit himself for the ordeal.

He declares he was not "bluffed" into returning to St. Louis by Mr. Folk's threat to permit Daniel J. Kelley to turn State's witness and that he is unjustly accused of attempting to shield his friends while exposing his enemies in the "boodle" scandal.

After spending a few minutes at home Mr. Lee visited Circuit Attorney Folk in his office. Attorney General Crow was present. The Lieutenant Governor spent some time in conference with the two officials, who are prosecuting the "boodle" investigation, and it is said on good authority that he pledged himself to tell the Grand Jury to-morrow several important things which he did not tell in his previous examinations.

THE CRIM SALE OF ANTIQUES.

Special to The New York Times.

BALTIMORE, April 23.—Collectors from New York, Philadelphia, Washington, and other cities were included in the scores of bidders and buyers at the second day's sale of the famous collection of antiques of the late Dr. William H. Crim.

T. F. Manning of New York secured two bargains. One was an old Cononial sideboard with swell front, claw feet, and cut glass handles, for $375, and the other six fine Sheraton chairs, at $57.50 each.

A feature of the day was an exciting contest over an exquisite old china cabinet, elaborately inlaid, which was one of the best pieces in the collection. It was started at $200, and slowly advanced to $500. Then the bidding became spirited. The piece was desired by ex-Gov. Bulkeley of Connecticut and Mrs. John A. Cayle of Lancaster, Penn., and the price was quickly run up to $1,000. Mrs. Cayle finally obtained the cabinet for $1,525. She also bought a number of other articles.

The Lafayette bed—a mahogany bedstead of the Empire style, handsomely carved and painted, which was made for Lafayette in Baltimore prior to his first visit—went to Mr. Brinkhurst of Wilmington, Del., for $700. A portrait of Gilbert Stuart, which was started at $25, was secured by R. F. Phifer of New York for $200.

An old mahogany serpentine front Chippendale sideboard went to F. Kellar of Philadelphia for $97.50. A revolver was purchased for the Smithsonian Institution for $5.

C. H. Pond of New York bought six solid mahogany inlaid Chippendale arm dining chairs for $660, a mahogany Chippendale inlaid table for $200, two mahogany chairs for $60 each, an open grate, with massive brass columns and brass blower, for $65, and a mahogany bureau for $100. Mr. Goff paid $100 each for two mahogany knife boxes, with silver monograms, which belonged to Charles Carroll of Carrollton.

DECISION IN BANKRUPTCY.

Special to The New York Times.

CHICAGO, Ill., April 23.—"The filing of a petition in bankruptcy, followed by seizure and by adjudication in bankruptcy, is a seizure of the property by the law for the benefit of creditors and an appropriation of it to the payment of the debts of the bankrupt. It is a seizure of the property by legal process, equal in rank to any of the same force and effect as by execution and attachment."

In these words the United States Circuit Court of Appeals to-day gave the first decision of the kind in regard to title to property. The decision was given in the bankruptcy case of Alexander Rodgers, a seed merchant, who failed in May, 1901.

The lower court had denied that the Chicago Title and Trust Company, trustee, was in actual possession of the property of the bankrupt, title to which was really in the name of holders of certain warehouse receipts. Newton Wyeth, representing the trustee, appealed from this ruling, and the higher court has now set aside the other order.

WIFE SEIZES PAPERS FOR JAMES N. TYNER

Gains Access to Assistant Attorney General's Safe.

HIS DISMISSAL FOLLOWS.

Official and His Sister-in-Law's Son Under Cloud in Connection With the St. Louis Turf Fraud Scandal.

Special to The New York Times.

WASHINGTON, April 23.—The developments to-day in the Post Office scandal were the most startling and sensational that have come out of an executive department in a long time. The safe in the office of James N. Tyner, Assistant Attorney General for the Post Office Department, who was permitted to resign last March on condition that he stayed away from the department until his resignation took effect on May 1, was emptied of all its papers by Mrs. Tyner and by the mother of Harrison J. Barrett, a former Assistant Attorney General, whose conduct in connection with the St. Louis turf scandal is under investigation. The actual work was done by a safe expert, acting under the direction of the two women, who assert that they were obeying Mr. Tyner's orders. They decline to give up the papers, and the Assistant Attorney General has been summarily removed from office. The facts in the case have been sent to Attorney General Knox for action, and criminal proceedings are expected.

As long ago as the beginning of March the evidences of irregularities in Mr. Tyner's office were so complete, and the case was so flagrant, that Postmaster General Payne demanded the Assistant Attorney General's resignation. Mr. Tyner, it is said, pleaded for mercy, and his appeal was seconded by a tearful and pathetic one made by his wife. Mr. Payne was finally so affected that he consented to modify his demand, with the proviso that Mr. Tyner stay away from the department.

A leave of absence was given to him for the purpose. Meanwhile the investigation into the conduct of Barrett, who is Mr. Tyner's nephew, proceeded. George A. C. Christiancy, one of the Assistant Attorneys, who is a candidate for Mr. Tyner's place, acted as chief of the bureau.

The office, on the fifth floor of the Post Office Building, comprises three rooms, the doors of which open on the corridor. Two of these doors are always kept locked, and the third serves as the general entrance room. The safe is in the last of the rooms which is kept locked.

Just as the department was closing for the day, at about 4 o'clock Tuesday afternoon, Mrs. Tyner entered the office. Some subordinates were sitting in the outer room. She disregarded them and walked into the second room, where Mr. Christiancy was working. She walked past him into the third room, where the safe is. Mr. Christiancy walked in after her.

Mrs. Tyner is a little, gray-haired woman, with a positive manner and a strong dislike for Christiancy. She spoke to him peremptorily.

"Mr. Christiancy," she said, "when Andrew comes send him in to me. Now you will please leave the room."

LEFT MRS. TYNER ALONE.

She took off her jacket as she said this, and Mr. Christiancy thought she was going to wash her hands. He went out, and she closed the door after him. After that none of the persons in the office knew anything of what was taking place in the inner room until Mrs. Tyner opened the door and came out. To all appearance she had been alone all the time.

As was subsequently learned by Mr. Payne, as soon as Mrs. Tyner was alone in the room she opened the door leading into the corridor. There were waiting for her Mrs. Barrett, her sister, who is the mother of Harrison J. Barrett, and an expert in the employ of the Mosler Safe Company of Broadway and Duane Street, New York. This man's name is G. G. Hamner. The Mosler Safe Company built the safe in the office.

Hamner opened the safe and the two women took out everything in it. Not so much as a scrap of paper was left in the fire-proof box, which was kept for the storage of important documents. They made the papers up into a package, and about that time "Andrew" arrived, and was sent in by Mr. Christiancy. He is Andrew Hogan, a negro messenger attached to the office.

Mrs. Tyner handed the package to Hogan and directed him to take it up to Mr. Tyner's house. If he passed through the outer office the suspicions of the clerks would be excited by the package, so she let him out through the door opening into the corridor, and Hogan, suspecting nothing wrong, took it away.

Mrs. Tyner let Hamner and Mrs. Barrett out through the same door, but they were observed by a negro charwoman, who had also seen them come in, and whose curiosity was keenly excited by these peculiar proceedings. After giving them time enough to get away Mrs. Tyner opened the door leading into the outer office, and walking majestically past Mr. Christiancy and the clerks, went into the corridor, and vanished.

A moment later Mr. Christiancy went into the room and discovered the safe empty with the door standing open. It only took a minute to see what had taken place, and then he rushed to the Postmaster General's office to report the affair to Mr. Payne. The Postmaster General immediately sent to Chief Inspector Cochran for two of his men, and dispatched them post haste to Mr. Tyner's house with instructions to recapture the papers. The Tyner party beat the Inspectors to the house, and when they arrived a few minutes later Mrs. Tyner was ready for them. She told them she had acted under Mr. Tyner's orders, and that she would not let the Inspectors see her husband or look at the papers. She would not even let them look at the papers while she herself held them.

REMOVED HIM FROM OFFICE.

Mr. Payne then sent for Mr. Hamner, who made a full statement of the case, and furnished all that was lacking in the way of evidence. The next day the Postmaster General removed Mr. Tyner from office, and to-day the correspondence in the case was made public. Mr. Payne's letter was as follows:

Washington, April 22, 1903.

Hon. James N. Tyner, Assistant Attorney General for the Post Office Department:

Sir: You are hereby removed from the office of Assistant Attorney General for the Post Office Department.

I deem it proper to give you the reasons for this summary action on the part of this department. Early in the month of March I communicated to you through a mutual friend a request for your resignation. After a painful interview with you, and a more painful one with Mrs. Tyner, I consented to modify the demand for your resignation so that it might take effect on May 1, 1903, with the proviso, however, that you were given leave of absence from the time of the acceptance of the resignation to the date of its taking effect, with the understanding that you were not in any way to undertake to discharge the duties of the office.

Late yesterday afternoon Mrs. Tyner came to the office of the Assistant Attorney General for the Post Office Department, entering in the regular way, went through the main office to the private office, closing the door behind her. She then unlocked the door entering from the public hall into the private room and admitted her sister, Mrs. Barrett, whose son was formerly assistant in your office, and whose conduct is now under investigation by the department. She also

"All the News That's Fit to Print."

The New York Times.

THE WEATHER.
Fair; light to fresh north winds.

VOL. LIV....NO. 17,178. NEW YORK, MONDAY, JANUARY 23, 1905.—TWELVE PAGES. ONE CENT In Greater New York, Jersey City and Newark. | Elsewhere, TWO CENTS.

CZAR'S SUBJECTS ARM FOR REVOLT

St. Petersburg Strike Leaders Decide to Fight.

WORKMEN WANT REVENGE

Rumors of Outbreaks in Finland and Elsewhere.

DOWAGER CZARINA FLEES

Joins Czar at Tsarskoe-Selo—Number Shot in Capital Placed as High as 5,000.

ST. PETERSBURG, Monday, Jan. 23.—Leaders of the strikers who came into conflict with the troops yesterday assembled last night and decided to continue the struggle with arms.

The strikers, goaded to desperation by the events yesterday, a day of violence, fury, and bloodshed, are in a state of open insurrection against the Government. It is rumored that 30,000 or 40,000 armed strikers from Kolpino, sixteen miles distant, are marching on St. Petersburg.

The workmen are now arming with every available weapon for a renewal of the struggle. They have few firearms, but are turning the implements of trade into improvised weapons.

There are rumors of trouble in Finland and disaffection on the part of the troops. Strike leaders say they are awaiting news from Moscow and other large cities, where the troops are not believed to be so loyal as the Guards regiments.

The Moscow Regiment yesterday refused to fire on the working people.

No one knows how many men, women, and children were killed and wounded yesterday by the volleys of the troops. Some estimates are as high as 5,000, but 500 is probably nearer the true number.

The Emperor is at Tsarskoe-Selo, whither the Empress Dowager has fled.

PEACEABLE MEN SHOT DOWN.

Petitioners Met by the Troops of Grand Duke Vladimir.

Special Cable to THE NEW YORK TIMES.
Copyright, 1905, THE NEW YORK TIMES.

LONDON, Jan. 22.—St. Petersburg's streets were the theatre to-day of scenes unparalleled in the history of the world. A wholesale massacre of Russian strikers occurred, and the dead and wounded are numbered by thousands.

The strikers undertook to-day to present to the Czar a petition for the redress of their wrongs.

Instead of meeting the Czar they had to deal with Grand Duke Vladimir, and the morgues and hospitals are full of the victims of his cruelty. The correspondent of The Daily Mail, in telegraphing an account of the tragedy, says:

"This morning all was still and strangely quiet. It was bitterly cold, with a piercing wind and driving fine snow. People muffled in furs went to church as usual. A few strolled toward the Palace Square to see what was to be seen, and, finding nothing, started away again.

"There were no troops in front of the palace, and the bridges across the Neva were open to traffic.

"St. Petersburg under the freshly fallen snow was a white, fair city, from which the gilt minarets of the Admiralty, the cathedral, and the St. Peter and St. Paul fortress shot up tongues of flame in the growing sunshine.

"The church bells were calling. Swift sleighs with splendid horses were gliding by. It was impossible then to connect the scene with the pitiful tragedy that was so swiftly to follow.

"At 10 o'clock the troops began to move about, passing in different directions along the radiating suburban thoroughfares. Cavalry, infantry, and Cossacks in small detachments made no great military display, but infantry and some Guards marched away in regiments, their fixed bayonets glittering wickedly.

"The official programme was going to be literally carried out. Evidently no procession from any industrial suburb was to be allowed to approach the centre of the capital.

"An hour later a little tour in a fast sleigh showed that Central St. Petersburg was ringed with a triple cordon of defenses, terrible as those of Liao-Yang, as if to resist an invading army.

"Out on every main road, on the Ekaterinoffsky Prospect on the left bank of the river, at every strategic point where there were cross-roads, detachments of troops were placed on the further side. Every bridge crossing the Neva to Vassili Ostrov was strongly held, while from the inside of the great courtyards of the Winter Palace a mass of troops came out into the Palace Square.

"Most noticeable, as always, were the Preobrajensky Guards in their striking uniform, and the Pavlovsky Guards in high bronze helmets. There were also grenadier guards and the glittering cuirasses and eagle caps of the cuirassiers of guards, the Czarina's regiment, mounted all on black.

"The cavalcade was a magnificent sight as it wheeled round in the great square.

"It was plain thus early that there would be no demonstration in front of the Palace. It only remained to see with how much consideration any attempt to hold one would be repressed.

"It was not long to wait before all uncertainty was removed. What followed it is impossible to describe, because it is impossible to know what occurred in many places widely apart.

"The narratives of eye-witnesses are as yet uncollected, but from many different directions people set out upon the projected pilgrimage, only to be shot down in masses by their uniformed brothers almost before their procession had started from the suburbs.

"The Putiloff strikers left their barrack homes about the factory according to their programme, bringing with them their wives and children, even their babies, as had been arranged. Father Gopon marched at their head, bearing a crucifix aloft above the great roll containing the precious petition.

"They marched down the Peterhoff Chaussée, where the works stand, down hill to where, at the Neva gate, the triumphal arch erected after the Turkish war stands at the junction with the main Baltic thoroughfare.

"There the Ismailovsky Guards, a regiment of which the Czar is honorary Colonel, were drawn up in waiting.

"As the head of the procession approached the acting Colonel called upon them to stop. Father Gopon, still holding the crucifix, advanced and demanded that the Colonel receive and forward the petition.

"This request was declined. Then, after a minute's hesitation and discussion, the procession continued to advance. A sharp order was given. The soldiers raised their rifles, and a volley rang out, but they had only used blank cartridges.

"Another order. This time ball cartridge, and men, women, and children fell in heaps.

"Father Gopon, still clutching the crucifix, stood among the dead and dying with the petition.

"Still another volley, and then the crowd no longer. The procession turned and fled, all but 300, who were lying dead, and 500 writhing wounded.

"Some who had revolvers fired as they fled. Others carried icepicks, some had stones, but practically they were unarmed.

"It was all over with the Putiloff strike procession, and at 11:41 o'clock the strikers were still in sight of their works. As they retreated the soldiers followed, and before a quarter of an hour most of them had fled to their homes, and there only remained the dead and wounded, who were removed with the usual Russian skill to be taken to hospital or home.

"What happened to the Putiloff contingent happened at other places. A procession starting its advance found its progress barred almost before it was begun, and as it attempted to continue it was mowed down by volleys.

"Twenty thousand people started from Kolpino, a manufacturing village twenty-five miles away. At the Moscow arch, on the confines of the town, they met with six volleys. A thousand fell dead and 1,500 were wounded.

"From up the river a great crowd marched to the Nevsky gate, where 500 fell dead and 700 were founded.

"The Vassili Ostrov workers only lost 200 killed and 700 wounded."

TROOPS FIRE AT LODZ.

Many Demonstrators Shot Down—Rising in Finland Feared.

LONDON TIMES—NEW YORK TIMES Special Cablegram.
Copyright, 1905, THE NEW YORK TIMES.

PARIS, Jan. 22.—A dispatch from St. Petersburg gives an account of a public demonstration at Lodz, a manufacturing town in Russian Poland, in which the crowd carried flags and raised cries of "Long Live Poland!"

Troops stationed in houses along the route of the procession fired upon it through the windows. Some persons were killed and several wounded.

Great excitement prevails.

Another St. Petersburg dispatch says very serious news has been received from Finland, where all the factory hands are on strike and a general rising is feared.

CIVIL WAR THREATENED.

Workmen Have Lost Faith in Czar, and Now Mean to Fight.

ST. PETERSBURG, Monday, Jan. 23.—A condition almost bordering on civil war exists in the terror-stricken Russian capital.

The city is under martial law, with Prince Vassilchikoff as commander of over 50,000 of the Emperor's crack guards. Troops are bivouacked in the streets and at various places on the Nevsky Prospect, the main thoroughfare of the city.

It is rumored that M. Witte will be appointed dictator to-day, but the report is not confirmed.

A member of the Emperor's household is quoted as saying that the conflict of yesterday will end the war with Japan, and that Russia will have a Constitution or Emperor Nicholas will lose his head.

The authorities, while they seem to realize the magnitude of the crisis with which the dynasty and the autocracy are confronted on account of yesterday's events, are apparently paralyzed for the moment.

An official statement was promised at midnight, at which hour it was announced that it had been postponed till to-morrow.

Intense indignation is bound to be aroused all over Russia. The workmen and revolutionists expect news from Moscow and other big centres, where the troops are not of the same class as the Guard regiments of St. Petersburg.

The Warsaw and Baltic Railroad is reported to have been torn up for a mile and a half, but the damage is said to have been repaired.

The blood which crimsoned the snow has fired the brains and passions of the strikers and turned women as well as men into wild beasts, and the cry of the infuriated populace is for vengeance.

The sympathy of the middle classes is with the workmen. Comment on the action of the troops and authorities is very bitter, and sarcastic remarks are made that officers are braver against the defenseless public than against the Japanese, and that "ammunition may be scarce in the Far East, but is too plentiful here."

If Father Gopon, the master mind of the movement, aimed at open revolution, he managed the affair like a genius, for he has done a great deal to break the faith of the people in the "Little Father," who, they were convinced and who Father Gopon had taught them to believe, would right their wrongs and redress their grievances.

Maxim Gorky, the Russian novelist, expresses the opinion that yesterday's work will break the faith of the people in the Emperor. He said last evening:

"To-day inaugurated revolution in Russia. The Emperor's prestige will be irrevocably shattered by the shedding of innocent blood. He has alienated himself forever from this people.

"Gopon taught the workmen to believe that an appeal direct to the 'Little Father' would be heeded. They have been undeceived.

"Gopon is now convinced that peaceful means have failed and that the only remedy is force. It is now the people against the oppressors, and the battle will be fought to the bitter end."

At a big meeting last night the following message from M. Gorky was read:

"Beloved Associates: We have no Emperor. Innocent blood lies between him and the people. Now begins the people's struggle for freedom. May it prosper. My blessing upon you all. Would I might be with you to-night; but I have much to do."

A workman who was introduced to speak in Father Gopon's name made a fiery speech. He appealed to the Liberals to furnish arms. The meeting adopted a letter denouncing the officers and regiments that fired on the workmen and another letter extolling the Moscow regiment which refused to fire.

The following is the text of a letter addressed by Father Gopon to Emperor Nicholas on Saturday night:

"Sovereign: I fear your Ministers have not told you the full truth about the situation. The whole people, trusting in you, have resolved to appear at the Winter Palace at 2 P. M. in order to inform you of their needs. If, vacillating, you do not appear before the people, then the moral bonds between you and the people, who trust in you, will disappear, because innocent blood will flow between you and the people.

"Appear to-morrow before your people and receive our address of devotion in a courageous spirit. I and the representatives of labor and my brave workingmen and comrades guarantee the inviolability of your person."

With darkness it was feared that the mob might begin to loot and pillage, and even burn; but beyond the breaking of a few windows in the Nevsky Prospect and the pillaging of fruit shops, little disorder was reported. Some windows of the palace of Grand Duke Alexis were smashed.

Most of the theatres were closed, but at the People's Palace, which was open, two Liberals attempted to harangue the audience, proposing at the close of the performance that the audience testify to their sympathy with their fallen brothers. The orators were promptly arrested, but the audience walked out.

St. Petersburg is sleeping quietly at this hour, 4:45 A. M., worn out by the excitement of a long day. Laborers and spectators have long since left the streets, and the military and police have had little to do for hours beyond driving off occasional riotous bands of irresponsible rogues bent on window-breaking and marauding and dispersing groups of too demonstrative Socialists or Liberals returning from protracted meetings where their minds were filled with incendiary speeches.

Since midnight the Russian capital has been as peaceful as it was the preceding night; but in the Palace Square and in all the principal streets and open places throughout the town bivouac fires are gleaming and infantrymen sleeping near their stacked rifles or marching hither and thither.

Cavalrymen on wearied horses are patrolling the long thoroughfares. No further firing has been heard and no more reports of collisions have been received.

A renewal of rioting is not expected until late in the morning, if at all to-day, as the strikers, thoroughly wearied by yesterday's events, will be inclined to wait until the military precautions have somewhat relaxed.

Two hundred journalists and professional men met in this city on Saturday evening to discuss means to avoid bloodshed. A committee, consisting of the authors Kharsenieff, Gorky, Annensky, and Gesief, several professors, and the workmen's advocate Kedrim, was appointed to interview Minister of the Interior Sviatopolk-Mirsky.

They arrived at the Ministry of the Interior at 10 o'clock Saturday night, but were received coldly, the officials declaring that it was impossible for them to see the Minister that night. The committeemen announcing their intention to wait till the Minister would see them, they were persuaded to go away by Assistant Minister Rydzefsky, who, being told that their errand was to prevent bloodshed, resolutely refused to call Prince Sviatopolk-Mirsky and ironically told the committeemen they had better persuade the workmen to abandon their plan of a procession to the palace.

Thus rebuffed, the committeemen proceeded to M. Witte's residence. M. Witte received them affably and offered tea to them, which they declined. Having heard them, M. Witte expressed himself with great sympathy, but maintained that all measures had been decided without consulting him, adding: "I am nothing in the administration."

M. Witte then referred them to Minister Sviatopolk-Mirsky, regretting his inability to do anything, and advising them to get the demonstration abandoned. He said the workmen had taken a wrong course, which was incompatible with autocracy. The Emperor could only receive a deputation by application through proper channels.

He then telephoned to Minister Sviatopolk-Mirsky and tried to persuade him to receive the committee. The Minister, however, still declined, and the deputation departed.

Late last night at a conference of editors of St. Petersburg newspapers it was agreed to address to the censorship administration a protest against the censorship of the day's events, and it was also resolved to send a deputation to negotiate with the workmen's union regarding the resumption of work by the printers.

DAY OF TERROR IN CZAR'S CAPITAL

Troops Slay Women and Children with Men.

LED BY PRIEST TO DEATH

Workmen Force Guards to Fire to Stop Them.

BARRICADES IN STREETS

A General Killed and Other Officers Attacked—Crowds Shout "Down With the Czar."

ST. PETERSBURG, Jan. 22.—This has been a day of unspeakable horror in St. Petersburg.

Minister of the Interior Sviatopolk-Mirsky presented to his Majesty last night the invitation of the workmen to appear at the Winter Palace this afternoon and receive their petition, but the Emperor's advisers had already taken the decision to show a firm and resolute front, and the Emperor's answer to the 100,000 workmen trying to force their way to the Palace Square to-day was a solid array of troops who met them with rifle, bayonet, and sabre.

The priest Gopon, the leader and idol of the men, in his golden vestments, holding aloft the cross and marching at the head of thousands of workmen through the Narva Gate, miraculously escaped a volley which laid low half a hundred persons.

The figures of the total number killed or wounded at the Narva Gate, the Moscow Gate, at various bridges and islands, and at the Winter Palace vary. The best estimate is 500, although there are exaggerated figures placing the number as high as 5,000.

Many men were accompanied by their wives and children, and in the confusion, which left no time for discrimination, these shared the fate of the men.

One Regiment Mutinied.

The troops, with the exception of the Moscow Regiment, which is reported to have thrown down its arms, remained loyal and obeyed orders.

The military authorities had a firm grip on every artery in the city. At daybreak guard regiments, cavalry, and infantry held every bridge across the frozen Neva, the network of canals which interlace the city, and the gates leading from the industrial section, while in the Palace Square, as the storm centre, were massed Dragoon regiments, infantry, and Cossacks of the Guards.

Barred from the bridges and gates, men, women, and children crossed the frozen river and canals on the ice by twos and threes, hurrying to the Palace Square, where they were sure the Emperor would be present to hear them.

But the street approaches to the square were cleared by volleys and Cossack charges. Men and women, infuriated to frenzy by the loss of loved ones, cursed the soldiers while they retreated.

Strikers Built Barricades.

Men harangued the crowds, telling them that the Emperor had foiled them and that the time had come to act. Strikers began to build barricades in the Nevsky Prospect and at other points, using any material that came to hand, and even chopping down telegraph poles.

Fighting meantime continued at various places, soldiers firing volleys and charging the mob. The whole city was in a state of panic. Women were running through the streets seeking lost members of their families. Several barricades were carried by the troops.

Toward 8 o'clock in the evening the crowds, exhausted, began to disperse, leaving the military in possession. As they retreated up the Nevsky Prospect the workmen put out all the lights.

The little chapel at the Narva gate was wrecked.

On Kaminostov Island all the lights were extinguished.

Every officer wearing the uniform of the Emperor who was found alone was mobbed. A General was killed on the Nicholas Bridge, and a dozen officers were seized, stripped of their epaulets, and deprived of their swords.

Troops Spared Father Gopon.

There was a very dramatic scene at the Narva Gate when Father Gopon, in golden vestments and bearing aloft an ikon, and flanked by two clergymen carrying religious banners, approached at the head of a procession of 8,000 workmen.

Troops were drawn up across the entrance. Several times an officer called upon the procession to stop, but Father Gopon did not falter. Then an order was given to fire, first with blank cartridges. Two volleys rang out, but the line still did not waver.

Then, with seeming reluctance, an officer gave the command to load with ball, and the next volley was followed by shrieks of the wounded.

As the Cossacks followed up the volley with a charge the workmen fled before them, leaving about 100 dead or wounded.

It was evident that the soldiers deliberately spared Father Gopon. One of the clergymen by his side was wounded, but he escaped untouched and hid behind a wall until the Cossacks passed. He was then spirited away by workmen.

The Scenes in Palace Square.

The most harrowing scenes of the day were around the Palace Square.

This enormous place back of the Winter Palace is surrounded by gardens fronting the Admiralty and by a vast semi-circular building containing the offices of the General Staff, the Ministry of Finance, and the Foreign Office. In the centre of the block is cut an arched gateway surmounted by a bronze quadriga. The gateway serves as an entrance to the Grand Morskaia, one of the most fashionable streets of the city, which crosses the Nevsky Prospect.

Beyond the semi-circular building is a wide space leading to the Moikai Canal, and beyond this stands an enormous square building, the headquarters of the St. Petersburg Military District. From this building the Grand Duke Vladimir had issued orders for the whole military preparations, and from it he directed the day's operations.

In the centre of the square stands a great granite column supporting a statue of Victory, commemorating the defeat of the Napoleonic invasion, at which a veteran guard in the uniform of the period of Alexander I. stands sentinel.

Like a Military Camp.

When The Associated Press correspondent arrived at the Palace Square early this morning he found a considerable crowd of demonstrators already lining the railings of the Admiralty Gardens and the Boulevard. The square itself presented the appearance of a military encampment.

Several companies of the Pavlovsky and Preobrajensky Guards had piled their arms, while the men were sitting around campfires or stamping on the snow to keep warm. Beyond the infantry stood squadrons of the Chevalier Guards and the Horse Guards, without their lances, cuirasses, or the usual gay trappings.

The men carried carbines slung across their shoulders, and their stirrups were covered with felt or straw to keep off the cold. All the soldiers wore bashliks, or hoods, to protect their ears from the keen, searching wind. A field kitchen steamed merrily, disseminating the odor of viands.

Many of the men wrestled or boxed, cracking jokes as one or another rolled on the snow.

A whole row of ambulances drawn up near the palace served as a grim reminder of the stern business on hand.

Meanwhile pickets were stationed at all the entrances of the palace, and cavalry patrols kept promenaders moving along the sidewalk. Sleigh traffic continued uninterrupted till the time came for the cavalry to charge.

The crowd of strikers in and outside the Admiralty Gardens continued to grow hourly, swelled by arrivals from the Nevsky Prospect, which debouches upon the boulevard skirting the Gardens.

Constantly Reproached Troops.

The strikers manned and held a small edifice at the corner of the Gardens and poured out constant objurgations and reproaches at the troops. It was in vain that officers requested them to disperse.

"We have come to present our homage and grievances to the Emperor."

"Let the Emperor come out and hear us; we do not wish to do harm."

"Long live Nicholas II.! If he only listens to our grievances we are sure he will be just and merciful!"

"We cannot longer endure our sufferings. Better die at once and end all!"

Such were the cries repeatedly heard.

Many strikers brought their wives and children. "You soldiers are our brothers; you cannot shoot these little ones," they exclaimed. But as the pickets and patrols continued driving off the people the demonstrators began to give way, and the bitterest insults and oaths, in which the Russian vocabulary is particularly rich, became frequent.

"We are not Japanese; why brutalize us? Will you shame the mother who bore you, who was a Russian like ourselves?" were some of the cries that were heard. Later such expressions as "Scoundrels!" "Mercenaries!" "Dogs!" and worse were heard. A long-haired student among the crowd hurled an insulting epithet at an officer, who sent a couple of men to arrest him.

The crowd tried to rescue the student, but he was dragged and kicked across the sunlit square, his long hair tossing in the wind. The crowd broke out into a storm of hoots and hisses. Then a young workman jeered at a soldier, who applied his rifle butt, and, with the help of comrades, dragged the workman, despite his piteous pleadings, to the lockup.

Every time the troops moved the crowds hissed them. Strikers also gathered at the entrance of the Grand Morskaia and of the avenue leading to the Moika. The crowd at the latter place swelled to huge proportions, blocking the bridge across the canal.

Ordered to Disperse Crowd.

The order came at 1:30 P. M. to clear off the crowd. The Colonel commanding the Horse Guards uttered a short, sharp command; the troopers drew their swords and advanced at a quick trot, and then broke into a gallop, heading straight for the Moika, where they were lost in a cloud of snow.

Shrieks from the wounded resounded. Then came silence, broken only by the galloping of ambulance horses.

The next twenty minutes passed without incident. Nothing indicated the approach of the horrible butchery which was destined to stain the corner of the Admiralty Gardens with human blood.

The crowd there persisted in refusing to move on, clamoring for the Emperor and continually hurling abuse at the troops, but attempting no violence.

Two companies of the Preobrajensky Guards, of which Emperor Nicholas himself was formerly Colonel, which had been standing at ease in front of the Palace, formed up and marched at double quick toward the fatal corner.

Events followed with awful swiftness.

The commanding officer shouted "Disperse! Disperse! Disperse!"

Many in the crowd turned to flee, but it was too late. A bugle sounded and the men in the front ranks sank to their knees and both companies fired three volleys, the first two with blank cartridges and the last with ball.

A hundred corpses strewed the sidewalk. Many women were pierced through the back as they were trying to escape.

The Associated Press correspondent, standing behind the troops, saw mangled corpses of persons of all ages and both sexes strewing the ground. One boy of thirteen had his skull pierced and rent by bullets. Great splashes and streams of blood stained the snow.

Only a few of the victims remained alive, for the fatal volley was fired at a distance of not more than twenty paces, and so the ambulances had little to do.

Sleighs Carried Off the Dead.

The police recruited a large number of sleighs to carry off the dead.

Heartrending scenes were witnessed as wives, husbands, and mothers came up to claim their dear ones and were carried off with them in the sleighs.

Meanwhile the crowd had drifted up the Nevsky Prospect, yelling, "Murderers! Murderers!" and the square resumed its calm aspect, the troops returning to their stations.

It was now the turn for the crowd stationed at the Morskaia entrance to the square, where the Horse Guards repeated the exploit with which they had cleared the Moika, and drove the people pell mell down the thoroughfare.

From thenceforward the Palace Square ceased to be the centre of interest. The Associated Press correspondent went to the Grand Morskaia, and stood a whole hour near the corner of the Nevsky Prospect. The fashionable hotels on either side of the Grand Morskaia were crowded, but the doors were closed except to well-known visitors. Fashionable jewelers' and other stores were barred, but mostly unshuttered. Quite a number of prominent personages stood on the sidewalks watching the developments.

Secretary Spencer Eddy of the American Embassy chatted with Grand Duke Boris, who had driven up in a stylish sleigh, drawn by a magnificent trotter. M. Bompard, the French Ambassador, drove past with his wife. As a couple of squadrons of red-capped hussars trotted by the officers gave the command, "Use the flats of your swords."

Then the troopers moved off and disappeared down the street, the crowds shrieking "Murderous dogs!" but quickly vanishing before them. A few who were wounded were picked up and conveyed to a drug store on the opposite corner of the Grand Morskaia and the Nevsky Prospect.

An Impromptu Oration.

No troops were visible for as much as half an hour. A crowd quickly formed outside the drug store, and an orator was found for the occasion. Standing on the steps of the drug store, he addressed the impromptu meeting thus:

"Comrades: We came humbly and peacefully to meet the Emperor and lay our grievances before him; but the Emperor refuses to see us, and instead soldiers were sent to shoot us down. Then all I can say is he is no Emperor." "Down with the Emperor!" shouted the crowd.

The orator proceeded:

"We have suffered under the sway of the Chinovniks." ("Down with the Chinovniks!" exclaimed the crowd.) "We hoped for redress, but hope is no longer possible; we can win our rights only by fighting." ("Down with the autocracy!" yelled the crowd.)

"Our only chance of redress is from representatives of the people." ("Long live the Constitutional Assembly!") "Then all I have to say is, To arms, comrades, to arms!"

"To arms!" was the thunderous response.

The crowd, now aroused to a state of frenzy, at the sight of the wounded who were being brought out of the drug store and placed in ambulances, saluted them as martyrs. Every head was uncovered as the victims were conveyed away.

The wilder element in the crowd had now obtained the upper hand and pro-

INDEX TO DEPARTMENTS.

"All the News That's Fit to Print."

The New York Times.

THE WEATHER.

Partly cloudy and warmer to-day; fair to-morrow.

VOL. LV...NO. 17,711. • • NEW YORK, SUNDAY, JULY 22, 1906.—36 PAGES, In Three Parts, Including Pictorial Section. PRICE FIVE CENTS.

$5,819,580 BOND AWARD TO S. BYERLEY, CLERK

Central Park West Man Figures in Federal Canal Issue.

REFUSES TO TALK ABOUT IT

Fisk & Robinson Get $15,000,000 of the Issue—The Average Price Is Above $104.

In an apartment at 428 Central Park West lives Samuel Byerley, who, according to the City Directory, is a clerk. On the records of the Treasury Department in Washington Mr. Byerley stands as the successful bidder for $5,819,580 of the new issue of Panama Canal bonds. Whether he is representing some large financial interest in this transaction or has made a plunge on his own account, Mr. Byerley refused to say last night.

When the bids for the Panama bonds were opened in Washington on Friday, several bids of Mr. Byerley were found among them. Three were for $1,000,000 each at 104.125, 103.900, and 103.975. Each of these came within the figures under which awards could be made, although their average was not so high as that of the other two big bidders, Fisk & Robinson of New York and the Merchants' National Bank of Philadelphia.

Afterward, according to the Washington dispatches, another Byerley bid was found, this time for $5,000,000 at 103.867. This bid was the lowest on which awards were made, and on it the New Yorker got only $2,819,580 of bonds. It was announced, however, that in case of default of some of those to whom awards had been made Mr. Byerley would get more.

No business address is given opposite Mr. Byerley's name in the City Directory, and his name does not appear in any of the financial directories.

When a reporter called last night at the Byerley flat, on the first floor of 428 Central Park West, near 103d Street, Mr. Byerly talked through a young woman. He refused to say whether his bids had been made for his own or another's account. Neither would he say where he was employed as a "clerk."

Special to The New York Times.

WASHINGTON, July 21.—Awards under the $30,000,000 issue of Panama Canal bonds were made to-day, the average price realized by the Government being above $104.

Fisk & Robinson of New York get half the issue, Samuel Byerley of New York gets $5,819,580, and the Merchants' National Bank of Philadelphia $3,000,000. Should some of the bidders default, Mr. Byerley will get over $2,000,000 more under his lowest bid, which was for $5,000,000 at 103.867.

Secretary Shaw was asked to-night if he knew who Byerley was. He replied in the negative. Other Treasury Department officials were asked the same question, and all denied all knowledge of the man. Some of them were a great deal surprised and much interested when informed that Byerley was a "clerk." They wanted to know where he worked and who his employer was.

Mr. Shaw has not made any investigation of the standing of the bidders, nor has he made any formal allotment. He will make his allotments on Aug. 1, and before that date the bidders must put up the premiums. The Secretary has the right to reject any and all bids, and he will reject any for which the bidder has not put up his premium by Aug. 1. If a bidder pays his premium there will be no investigation into his antecedents, place of employment, or personal character; if he does not he will not get the bonds.

Byerley was at the bottom of the list, having just squeezed within the limit, and for some reason there is an idea here that some of those above him are likely to drop out by failing to produce the premium between now and Aug. 1. On just what that theory rests nobody seems to know, or at least nobody is willing to say.

The awards above $50,000 were:

Fisk & Robinson, New York City—$5,000,000 at 104.23; $5,000,000 at 104.10; $5,000,000 at 103.89. Total, $15,000,000.

Samuel Byerley, New York City—$1,000,000 at 104.125; $1,000,000 at 103.990; $1,000,000 at 103.975, and $2,819,580 at 103.867. Total, $5,819,580.

Merchants' National Bank, Philadelphia—$1,000,000 at 104.36; $1,000,000 at 104.16; $1,000,000 at 103.93. Total, $3,000,000.

Victor Spanner, East Orange, N. J.—$600,000 at 104.31.

John H. Waring, Washington—$600,000 at 103.875.

John W. Mitchell, Washington—$500,000 at 104.

Eva McLain Meding, Washington, $500,000 at 104.

Henry H. Deane, Jacksonville, Fla.—$400,000 at 104.07.

M. J. Dyke, Windber, Penn.—$200,000 at 104.56, and $200,000 at 104.06.

B. H. Warring Washington—$300,000 at 104.125.

Palmetto National Bank, Columbia, S. C.—$300,000 at 103.875.

Merchants' National Bank, Baltimore—$100,000 at 104.109 and $200,000 at 103.8755.

Columbia National Bank, Buffalo—$300,000 at 104.

H. G. Bonner, Windber, Penn., $200,000 at 104.30.

Keystone National Bank, Pittsburg, $200,000 at 104.

First National Bank, Cheyenne, Wyoming, $150,000 at 104.

Yankton National Bank, Yankton, S. D., $150,000 at 104.

Second National Bank, Jersey City, $150,000 at 104.

First National Bank, Grafton, W. Va., $150,000 at 104.

German-American National Bank, Fort Wayne, Ind., $130,000 at prices ranging from 104.51 to 103.91.

Frank L. Kuhn, Cleveland, $100,000 at 104.75.

Tiffin National Bank, Tiffin, Ohio, $100,000 at 104.

Windber National Bank, Windber, Penn., $75,000 at 104.

First National Bank, Pearlsburg, Va., $75,000 at 104.

First National Bank, Crete, Neb., $60,000 at 104.

National Bank of Barre, Vt., $50,000 at 104.0625.

First National Bank, Pendleton, Oregon, $50,000 at 104.25.

First National Bank, Portsmouth, N. H., $50,000 at 104.

First National Bank, Oswego, N. Y., $50,000 at 104.10.

First National Bank, Hopkinsville, Ky., $50,000 at 104.

Mr. Robinson of the firm of Fisk & Robinson of New York, the largest buyer, and Mr. Ayers of the Merchants' National Bank of Philadelphia, the third largest buyer, had a conference at the office of Secretary Shaw this afternoon in reference to the price they would ask for such bonds as they did not wish to retain for themselves, and 104 4 plus 3 per cent. interest after Aug. 1 was agreed upon. As the bonds pay 2 per cent., the buyer will have to pay 1 per cent. interest after Aug. 1.

Secretary Shaw to-day said that he was especially gratified at the patriotic spirit manifested by a great many of the bidders. They were willing, he said, to subscribe for the bonds even at a high rate, in order to show their appreciation of the Government's efforts to build the canal in the shortest possible time. He said that many private persons had put in bids for comparatively large amounts, and it might take several days to ascertain whether all of these parties would be able to pay for the bonds.

The Secretary will at once designate as Government depositories all National banks whose bids were $103.50 or better, irrespective of whether their bids were successful or not, and in this way he expects to put into circulation at least $20,000,000. This will leave the Treasury cash in splendid shape and enable the Secretary to meet any money stringency this Autumn with another distribution of $20,000,000 or less. For the present deposit of $20,000,000 the Secretary will require the deposit of Government bonds as security, and it is expected that in this way a large part of the present issue of twos will be absorbed.

WEDS W. R. TRAVERS'S WIDOW

F. C. Havemeyer, Jr., Married to the Former Miss Harriman.

Frederick C. Havemeyer, Jr., son of Henry O. Havemeyer, was married to Mrs. Lillie Harriman Travers, divorced wife of the late William R. Travers and daughter of Oliver Harriman, at noon yesterday by the Rev. Father Michael C. O'Farrell, pastor of Holy Innocents Church, at 126 West Thirty-seventh Street. The ceremony was performed at the parsonage, 139 West Thirty-sixth Street, the only witness being Henry Havemeyer, the bridegroom's brother.

Mr. Havemeyer is a Catholic and Mrs. Travers is a Presbyterian. The fact that she was divorced was not in question, because of the death of her husband. The wedding was a quiet one. Immediately after the ceremony Mr. and Mrs. Havemeyer drove away. Their honeymoon plans were not divulged.

The former Mrs. Travers is a younger sister of Mrs. William K. Vanderbilt, who was formerly Mrs. Samuel S. Sands and who upon the death of Mr. Sands married Louis M. Rutherford. Mr. Havemeyer's bride is also a sister of Mrs. S. H. Olin, whose first husband was the late William E. Dodge. Oliver H. Harriman is her brother.

Mrs. Havemeyer was divorced from Mr. Travers in Rhode Island. She sailed for Europe before the news of the divorce had been made public. In the following Autumn Mr. Travers committed suicide. He had been suffering from melancholia. He left a large fortune to his sisters and niece. Returning to America the following Winter, Mrs. Travers was active in Newport society. She lived at Newport for several weeks this Summer, having apartments with her brother, Robert M. Harriman, at the Dennison cottage, in Catherine Street. She left there for New York early last week, the understanding being that she would sail for Europe soon for an automobile tour.

Mr. Havemeyer has been to Newport frequently this Summer as a guest of his sister, Mrs. Cameron McR. Winslow.

TROLLEY WIRE AROUND A CAR

Brooklyn Passenger Burned in a Novel Accident.

The trolley pole of a Brooklyn Crosstown car of the Erie Basin line jumped the wire at Willoughby Avenue and Pearl Street last night. In some unknown way, when an attempt was made to replace the wheel the wire snapped and twined around the pole.

The accident was not noticed for a minute as the car forged ahead under power, but finally the pyrotechnic display from the pole and the roof of the car attracted the attention of the conductor. The car was brought to a standstill, but by this time the electric fire from above was so startling that the passengers became panic stricken.

The car was well filled with passengers and most of them jumped to the street. In the scramble several persons were hurt. Frank Donnelly of 242 Carlton Avenue came in contact with the live wire and sustained severe burns of the left arm.

When the car stopped it was found that the cable for nearly a block had been torn down and was emitting electric flame. So great was the excitement around the scene of the accident that a policeman called the reserves from the Adams Street Station.

The wire was still sputtering when the reserves arrived. After the crowd had been forced back a hurry call was sent to the Brooklyn Hospital for an ambulance. The surgeon who arrived found that none of the passengers, with the exception of Donnelly, had suffered serious injury. The trolley wire continued to sputter and emit fire for nearly an hour, when employes of the company arrived and repaired the damage.

GOURDAIN PLANS HIS JAIL.

Warden and Guards Engaged—Preparing to Give Back Money.

Special to The New York Times.

CHICAGO, July 21.—Louis A. Gourdain, who has been vainly trying to have himself put in the Illinois State Prison, came back to Chicago this afternoon with several new ideas. He said he would start at once building his "penitentiary annex" at Joliet and have it all ready in case the United States Supreme Court fails to grant his desires.

"Monday I will start to give away $4,000,000 to persons who have lost money investing in my enterprises, which the Government has held illegal. I figure that I have taken in from $800,000 to $1,500,000 a month in the last five years. I shall post notices to that effect in every Post Office in the United States. That's the only way I can get a list of the names.

"While in New York I engaged a warden and an assistant warden for my penitentiary annex. They will leave jobs in another prison. I'll pay them double the salaries of those officials in the Joliet Penitentiary. I have hired six Chicago men as guards. They will receive double the salary of guards at Joliet.

"I will have plans and specifications for my prison annex on Monday. Architect Campbell of Joliet is preparing them. The prison will be 40 by 40—a replica of the one owned by the State.

"I will make shoes, shirts, and coats, and shovel coal in my little penitentiary."

American Princess Chimay Not Dead.

PARIS, July 21.—The announcement published in London and New York that the Princess Chimay, formerly Clara Ward of Detroit, Mich., is dead, is erroneous. The report was founded on the death here of Princess Pierre Caraman Chimay, wife of the Belgian Minister to Luxemburg.

Latest Shipping News.

Arrived—SS Caledonia, Glasgow, July 14.

DREYFUS IS DECORATED WHERE HE WAS DEGRADED

Cross of the Legion of Honor Pinned on His Breast.

OFFICERS CONGRATULATE HIM

Ceremony in the Courtyard of the Military School—An Attack of Heart Weakness Afterward.

PARIS, July 21.—In the presence of a distinguished military assemblage Major Alfred Dreyfus, wearing the full uniform of his rank, this afternoon received the Cross of Chevalier of the Legion of Honor.

The ceremony, which took place in the courtyard of the Military School, was rendered doubly impressive by being held on the very spot where the buttons and gold lace were stripped off Dreyfus's uniform and his sword was broken twelve years ago.

The decoration of the Major assumed the aspect of a notable demonstration. His brother officers, who were prominent figures in various stages of the controversy, were among the spectators, and outside the circle of troops stood Mme. Dreyfus and the little son of Dreyfus, Brig. Gen. Picquart, who shared in the court's acquittal of the famous prisoner; Anatole France of the French Academy, and Alfred Capus, and other literary men, who aided in Zola's campaign for a revision of the first trial.

Previous to the ceremony Major Dreyfus was presented to Gen. Gillain, commander of the First Division of Cavalry; Gen. Percin, and other prominent officers, who warmly shook hands with him, testifying their satisfaction at his return to the army. The officers then repaired to the courtyard, where trumpeters sounded four calls announcing the ceremony.

The courtyard, from which the general public were excluded, as the ceremony was purely official, was encircled by two batteries of the Thirteenth Artillery, commanded by Col. Targe, who made the recent discoveries at the War Office leading to the rehearing of the case against Dreyfus and his acquittal.

Gen. Gillain, accompanied by a number of army officials, entered the circle with trumpets and drums sounding. Major Dreyfus took up a position by the side of Col. Targe, while Gen. Gillain, stepping into the centre of the circle, announced the decoration of Targe as a Commander and Dreyfus as a Chevalier of the Legion of Honor. Dreyfus and Targe, with their sabres drawn, then advanced to the centre of the troops, taking a position before Gen. Gillain. The latter first bestowed the decoration on Targe, and then, turning to Dreyfus, the General said:

"In the name of the President of the Republic and in virtue of the powers intrusted to me, Major Dreyfus, I hereby name you a Chevalier of the National Order of the Legion of Honor."

After pinning the cross on Dreyfus's breast and felicitating him on his well-earned honor, the General gave the Major the military accolade, the trumpets sounding and the spectators applauding. Dreyfus briefly expressed his acknowledgments.

The troops then defiled before Gen. Gillain, Dreyfus occupying the post of honor on Gen. Gillain's right, Col. Targe and the other Generals being stationed on his left.

When the march past was completed the trumpets again sounded four calls, announcing the close of the ceremony, which had lasted only about five minutes, and Dreyfus and Targe were immediately the centre of an eager crowd of officers and friends. One of the first to reach Dreyfus was his little son, who rushed forward and threw his arms around his father's neck, sobbing violently.

The officers who had not taken official part in the ceremony also came forward to greet their comrade. As Dreyfus received the well wishes of his relatives and the officers, his face, usually impassive, twitched with emotion, and it was with difficulty that he preserved his soldierly calm.

Turning to Anatole France, Dreyfus said:

"I thank you more than I can say, you who have always struggled for my cause."

M. France replied:

"We merit no thanks, for what has been done was in the interest of right and justice. We felicitate you all the more since so many others who have struggled for justice have died before it was attained."

Col. Targe terminated his felicitations by conducting Major Dreyfus to the officers' quarters, where Mme. Dreyfus was waiting for him. The meeting between the husband and wife was most affectionate, the spectators withdrawing to permit them to be alone.

Shortly after this Dreyfus, accompanied by his wife and son, emerged from the Military School and entered a carriage. As the Major appeared the crowd in front of the main entrance gave him a hearty ovation, waving handkerchiefs and shouting "Vive Dreyfus!" "Vive la République!" "Vive l'Armée!"

The carriage was then driven swiftly in the direction of Dreyfus's home. On reaching his residence the Major, who is affected with heart weakness, suffered a violent attack, but thanks to his strong will power the faintness soon passed away and he was able to receive Procurator General Baudouin and Brig. Gen. Picquart, to whom he expressed his sincerest thanks for their exertions on his behalf.

FERRYBOAT RAMS HER SLIP.

Three Hurt at the Gates by a Boost Given by the Tide.

While making her slip at the foot of Liberty Street early yesterday morning the Jersey Central ferryboat Bound Brook rammed the bridge with such force as to cause the injury of three persons just outside the entrance gate.

The tide, the cause of the trouble, carried the boat with great force into the slip, the shock of the impact throwing several of the passengers to their knees, while two persons outside the entrance were injured by flying timbers. The third person was hurt by having his left leg run over by a wagon. The horse attached to it became frightened at the noise of the collision.

The injured were Julius Modeska of 865 Greene Avenue, Brooklyn; John Jones of 144 Perry Street, Manhattan, and Joseph Kepstein of 386 Johnson Avenue, Jersey City. They were sent to their homes. None of the passengers on the boat was hurt, nor was the vessel injured in any way.

LINER FINLAND ASHORE.

Red Star Steamship Starting for New York Grounds in the Scheldt.

FLUSHING, Holland, July 21.—The Red Star Line steamship Finland, Capt. Apfeld, which sailed to-day from Antwerp for Dover and New York, is ashore in The Scheldt.

Assistance has been sent to her.

COOLER SUBWAY NEXT MONTH

Plant at the Bridge Will Reduce the Heat Eight or Ten Degrees.

The new plan for cooling the Subway station at the Brooklyn Bridge, involving a draught of air, the temperature of which will be lowered by water pumped from two driven wells at the north end of the station, will be put into operation early next month.

The cooled air will be forced by electric fans through ducts which will run along the ceiling of the Subway above the station platforms. In this way it is expected that the temperature will be reduced from eight to ten degrees.

The temperature of the water will be from 52 to 62 degrees and the combined water output of the wells will be 40 gallons a minute. The coils wihch will receive the water will have a surface sufficient to cool 75,000 cubic feet or more of air a minute. The four fans will be nine feet in diameter.

FOUR BATHERS DROWNED.

Father Lost While Trying to Save His Daughter at Atlantic City.

ATLANTIC CITY, N. J., July 21.—Four bathers were drowned in the surf within one hour late to-day. The dead are:

Thomae, Robert L., aged 49, Camden, N. J.

Thomae, Miss Helen D., 13 years, Camden, N. J.

Sharpless, C. W., 28 years, Jenkintown, Penn.

Whitlock, Walter N., 57 years, 205 East Grace Street, Richmond, Va.

Connected with the double tragedy in which the Thomaes were drowned are several peculiar circumstances.

The two entered the water shortly after 5 o'clock. Mrs. Thomae did not don a bathing suit, but sat on the shore watching the father give the little girl her first lesson in swimming. Finally, tired with the exercise, Thomae went upon shore and joined his wife. Helen remained behind, wading in the water that did not reach her waist. The first inkling Mr. Thomae had of her danger was when he heard a cry of "Papa! papa! Help me!"

Before he could reach his daughter a swirling current had carried her beyond his depth. Striking out, he managed to reach her side, and, seizing her bathing suit, attempted to swim ashore.

For fully ten minutes he struggled in the waves, but becoming exhausted, the father sank, still clutching the bathing suit of the now lifeless girl. The life guards used every effort to rescue the two, but were unable to do so because of the heavy undertow.

Sharpless and a friend were bathing, when the former got beyond his depth. He was carried out by the tide, and before the life guards could reach him life was extinct.

Whitlock was ill when he entered the surf, and he was not missed by friends until the body was washed upon the beach.

HAVE BURGESS ARRESTED.

Suterville's Constable Also Held on Engineer's Complaint.

Special to The New York Times.

McKEESPORT, Penn., July 21.—The trouble which began last week between the Baltimore & Ohio Railroad and the Borough of Suterville broke out in a fresh place to-day, when the Burgess of Suterville and his brother, the town constable, were placed under arrest charged with assault and battery by two engineers whom they had been instrumental in fining for alleged fast running of trains through the borough.

John Burton and Newton Hurley are the engineers appearing as prosecutors. A few days ago they were dragged from their engines, they assert, by Burgess William Oberdick and his brother, Edward Oberdick, the town constable, and haled before a Squire, who fined them each $19 and costs for fast running of their engines. The engineers affirm that the Burgess and his brother beat them in making the arrest. The hearing has been set for Monday.

The Council of Suterville had passed an ordinance regulating the speed of trains to fifteen miles an hour while passing through the borough, and Burgess Oberdick made an attempt to enforce its observance.

DAYLIGHT HURTS WIRELESS.

Continuous Arctic Day Interferes with Service in Alaska.

WASHINGTON, July 21.—It has long been known that wireless telegraphy is easier at night than in the day, but that fact was lost sight of in the establishment of that method of communication in Alaska, between Fort Michaels and Nome, where it had been found impossible to maintain a cable owing to the ice movements and currents.

Reports to the War Department now show that for the first time trouble has been experienced in working the system in Alaska, and as the trouble was coincident with the beginning of continuous day north of the Arctic Circle that fact is supposed to account for the difficulty. However, it is said that the interruption has never extended over the whole day at any time.

ZION SALARIES, $1 A YEAR.

Amount Allotted to All City Officials by the City Council.

Special to The New York Times.

CHICAGO, July 21.—After to-day the salaries of Mayor, Chief of Police, City Treasurer, Commissioner of Public Works, City Attorney, Fire Marshall, City Collector, Commissioner of Health, and Aldermen of Zion City will be $1 a year, the City Council having passed an ordinance to that effect.

Some time ago citizens presented a petition asking that several of the high-sounding offices be dispensed with as a matter of economy, but the Council took this means to accomplish the same end. The actual work of a number of the officials is done by deputies or assistants, to whom small salaries are paid.

HIS SUIT REJECTED, HOTEL MAN A SUICIDE

R. T. Sullivan of the Blossom Heath Inn Shoots Himself.

DIED IN GIRL'S APARTMENT

It Is Said That He Wanted Miss Jessica Buck to Break Her Engagement to Dr. B. H. Waters.

Robert T. Sullivan, manager of the Blossom Heath Inn, on the road between White Plains and Larchmont, N. Y., died from the effects of a pistol wound in the head, in the apartment of Miss Jessica Buck, at 211 West 101st Street, yesterday, under circumstances which are to be investigated by Coroner Shrady and the police of the West 100th Street Station.

According to what the police were told by Dr. B. H. Walters of 59 West Thirty-sixth Street, an employe of the Health Department, who was a friend of Sullivan, and Dick Walker, the dead man's negro valet, Sullivan shot himself at 4 o'clock yesterday afternoon. The police were not informed of the shooting until 9 o'clock last night. They are not satisfied with the story of the affair as it came to them, and Coroner Shrady, upon their advice, decided to hold up the funeral and make an investigation.

Sullivan had been missing from the Blossom Heath Inn for several days. He told Charles B. Fleming, the proprietor of the place, that he was going to New York. He didn't say why he wanted to go to the city. When Sullivan failed to return yesterday Fleming decided to send Walker to New York to hunt for him. He gave the valet the addresses of several places, including the Milford apartment house, where Miss Buck lived, and told the negro to bring the manager back to the inn.

Walker, according to what he told the police last night, found Sullivan about 3 o'clock yesterday afternoon in Miss Buck's apartments. He said that Sullivan had known Miss Buck for two years, and was in love with her. It was said, however, that Miss Buck was engaged to marry Dr. Waters.

When the valet found Sullivan he told him of Fleming's anxiety, and asked if he did not wish to return to the inn.

"All right, Dick," Sullivan is reported as having answered. "I'll get ready at once." Walker said that Sullivan then stood before a looking glass to adjust his collar.

"This collar isn't fit to go out in," he said. "Dick, go out and get me another." The valet was away about five minutes. When he came in, he said, Sullivan spoke to Miss Buck.

"Well, we'll have one more drink before we go," he said to her. "Go out and get some cracked ice and I'll mix it." Miss Buck, according to Walker, went into the kitchen of the apartment to get the ice. Then Sullivan told Walker to go to an adjoining room for his coat.

While Walker and Miss Buck were both out of the room they heard two shots. They ran in and found Sullivan upon the floor with blood flowing from a wound in his right temple. He had a revolver in his right hand.

Miss Buck, according to Walker's story, immediately ran out of the house. She is said to have gone to the home of a friend on Lexington Avenue. Walker said he locked the door and went to a telephoned and called up Dr. Waters. He said that Dr. Waters came to the house, and after examining the body decided to notify the police of the West 100th Street Station.

It was 9 o'clock when notification of the suicide was received at the station, however, and the police thought it a peculiar case.

Coroner Shrady was notified, and after hearing the story told by Walker and Dr. Waters,, decided to hold the case open Walker said he learned that Sullivan had had luncheon yesterday with Dr. Waters and a Mrs. Peters, Sullivan's sister.

Dr. Waters said late last night:

"My engagement to Miss Buck was announced to our personal friends a few days ago. Mr. Sullivan, who was an estimable young man, had long been attached to Miss Buck, and felt the matter very keenly."

Coroner Shrady, in searching Sullivan's clothes, found a bankbook showing deposits exceeding $500 in the First National Bank of Mamaroneck, N. Y. The amount of a racing slip, which showed that a bet had been lost by Sullivan, nearly counterbalanced the deposit account.

At 2 o'clock this morning the police had not found Miss Buck. Manager Fleming at the Blossom Heath Inn telephoned into the city that he did not believe that Sullivan had killed himself because of unrequited love. He said that Sullivan had been depressed for some time, but he could not assign any reason for the man's melancholy.

JEWELS AND VALET GONE.

Alexander R. Peacock Fears He Trusted His Man Too Far.

Special to The New York Times.

PITTSBURG, July 21.—Alexander R. Peacock, who was one of Andrew Carnegie's younger partners, has been robbed of diamonds and other jewelry valued at several thousand dollars. He accuses his valet of the theft.

Mr. Peacock has figured in several exciting episodes, one a dash across the continent in a special train. Last May he decided that he would have a valet, and so went to New York and engaged Fred Bennett, 24 years of age, then at the Waldorf-Astoria. Mr. Peacock found him all that had been represented. In fact, he was so pleased that he trusted the man with all of his valuables and gave him the freedom of his mansion. Bennett, in his spare moments, romped with the Peacock children.

By and by various articles disappeared. Several servants were suspected and were discharged. Several days ago Mr. Peacock left the city, and Bennett was practically in charge. Peacock's secretary visited Detective Headquarters this morning, after a record trip in Mr. Peacock's red automobile, and reported that the Peacock diamonds had been stolen and also that Bennett was missing.

Forty-nine Jersey City Saloons Quit.

The Jersey City Excise Board notified Chief of Police Murphy yesterday that they had put forty-nine saloons out of business by refusing licenses to the proprietors on the ground that the places they kept were disorderly. The patrolmen were furnished with a list of these places with instructions to close them. They agreed to sell only "soft" drinks.

FLEET THREATENS MUTINY.

Russian Sailors at Sevastopol Make Demands—Soldiers Arrested.

SEVASTOPOL, July 21.—A meeting of 2,500 sailors from the warships here today drew up economic demands for presentation to Admiral Skrydloff.

Unless these demands are fulfilled the men say the whole of the Black Sea fleet will revolt.

ST. PETERSBURG, July 21.—Two squadrons of dragoons and hussars have been sent to Kronstadt, where there is a recurrence of the ferment among soldiers and sailors.

Fourteen men of the Second Battalion of the Preobrajensky Regiment, including two non-commissioned officers, have been arrested for agitating and conveyed to the Fortress of St. Peter and St. Paul.

BRYAN'S DAY WITH CROKER.

Stud and Kennels of the Latter's Farm Near Dublin Inspected.

DUBLIN, July 21.—Mr. and Mrs. William J. Bryan have arrived here.

They spent yesterday with Richard Croker at Mr. Croker's farm, near Dublin. Mr. Croker had invited a number of his American and local friends to meet Mr. and Mrs. Bryan, and the day was spent in inspecting the stud and kennels.

Mr. and Mrs. Bryan expect to be back in London to-morrow evening.

MRS. McCLURG IS A PILOT.

Gets Papers Enabling Her to Navigate the Great Lakes.

CHICAGO, July 21.—Mrs. Ogden McClurg of this city, a daughter-in-law of the late Gen. A. C. McClurg, to-day received final papers as pilot and master on the Great Lakes. She is the first woman to receive such papers on the lakes.

Mrs. McClurg is now the Captain of the Sea Fox, the McClurg steam yacht, a boat of 74 tons.

PLAN TO GET ROCKEFELLER.

Prosecutor Says He Would Be Arrested on His Golf Links.

Special to The New York Times.

CLEVELAND, July 21.—Prosecutor David of Hancock County, where the State has taken action against John D. Rockefeller and the Standard Oil Company for alleged violation of the Valentine Anti-Trust law, to-night told how he would proceed. After a conference with Prosecutor Wachenheimer in Toledo he said:

"Unless John D. Rockefeller, through his attorneys, enters his appearance in Findlay and gives bond, the Sheriff of Hancock County will make an honest and vigorous effort to arrest him. If he comes to Ohio he must either submit to arrest or enter an appearance and make bond.

"There is no desire on the part of the Hancock County authorities to inconvenience Mr. Rockefeller, but if he comes to the State and refuses the alternative I have mentioned he will be arrested even on his own golf links if found there."

WIRELESS FROM WELLMAN.

He Hopes to Start on His Aerial Voyage in the Middle of August.

DANE'S ISLAND, Spitzbergen, by Wireless Telegraphy to Hammerfest, Norway, July 21.—Wireless communication has been opened from this place, 700 miles from the pole.

Everything is progressing favorably at Camp Wellman. The balloon house is under construction.

Walter Wellman hopes to start on his aerial voyage toward the pole by the middle of August.

WOULDN'T SPEND GOLD.

Mortality Among Canal Laborers Leads to Decision to Pay in Silver.

PANAMA, July 21.—Henceforth the Panama Canal Commission will pay all laborers in silver.

It seems that simultaneously with the previous decision to pay the men in gold the mortality among the West Indian laborers increased considerably, and rumor has it that in many instances the negroes have preferred practically to starve to spending the gold coin, little of which they had ever seen.

BIG GAS WELL NEAR ALBANY.

Men Boring for Water Cause a Terrific Explosion.

ALBANY, July 21.—For many hours a stream of natural gas has been spouting from a well on the farm of James Hilton near Voorheesville, about twelve miles southwest of Albany.

The gas was discovered while the well was being bored yesterday afternoon. With a terrific explosion it burst forth, throwing stones and sand 200 feet into the air. This morning the pressure was reduced somewhat, but the gas still continues to rush from the well. The boring of the well had advanced about 150 feet when the gas came.

AMERICA GOOD ENOUGH.

Conclusion of Old Mr. Chapman After Meeting a Chill in England.

Gideon Chapman of Washington, Penn., who is 87 years old, returned yesterday from his first visit in fifty-five years to Colchester, England, his birthplace. He is sorry he went.

The old man, who is reputed well-to-do, said his relatives, of whom there were only a few left in Colchester, looked with suspicion on him when he appeared there several weeks ago, and it was not until they learned that he was well off in a worldly sense that their welcome warmed.

Everything in the old country had changed since he was there last, Mr. Chapman said. As much as he loved England, he said, he loved America better now. Pennsylvania was good enough for him.

The Cunarder Etruria, the vessel in which Mr. Chapman returned home, was the first of the transatlantic liners to reach New York this year via the northerly, or shorter, course. She made a splendid run, her time from Queenstown to Sandy Hook being 6 days, 5 hours, and 55 minutes.

DUMA DISSOLVED; ARMY IN CAPITAL

Martial Law Declared—Dictatorship May Be the Next Step.

NO PARLIAMENT TILL MARCH

Czar's Decision Taken at a Conference Attended by the Grand Dukes and Trepoff.

ST. PETERSBURG, Sunday, July 22.—Russia's first experiment in parliamentary government came to an ignominious end to-day with the promulgation of two imperial ukases, the first dissolving the present Parliament and providing for the convocation of its successor on March 5, 1907, and the second proclaiming the capital of Russia and the surrounding province to be in a "state of extraordinary security," which is only infinitesimally different from full martial law. This measure of safety is to provide for the outbursts which undoubtedly will be provoked by the dissolution of the Duma. It is now but a step to a dictatorship.

The texts of the two ukases, both of which are addressed in the stereotyped form to the Ruling Senate, are as follows:

According to Paragraph 105 of the Fundamental Law we order the Imperial Parliament dissolved, and fix the time for the convocation of the newly elected Parliament as March 5, 1907.

Regarding the time for the new elections to the Imperial Parliament we will later issue special indications.

The Ruling Senate will not fail to take proper measures to place this into effect.

Peterhof, July 21. NICHOLAS.

In consideration of a report of the Council of Ministers presented to us regarding the necessity in the future for the preservation of order and public safety in the City and Province of St. Petersburg, we consider it necessary to declare in the above city and province, instead of the state of reinforced security which now prevails there, a state of extraordinary security. The Prefect of the City and the Governor of the Province are intrusted with the rights thereto appertaining.

The Ruling Senate will not fail to take proper measures to place this into effect.

Peterhof, July 21. NICHOLAS.

With these orders, which were promulgated at 3 o'clock this morning, Emperor Nicholas by a stroke of the pen set Russia back to where she stood two years ago—in the full grip of autocracy and irresponsible government—wiping out for six months at least the whole structure of Parliament, erected at such cost.

There is little doubt that the convocation of the new Assembly will be still further postponed unless the new Parliament promises to be more amenable than the present.

The delay in fixing the time for the elections seems to indicate a decision to change the present basis of suffrage to a basis of universal suffrage, by means of which the advisers of the Emperor hope to swamp the educated Liberals, the Socialists, and the workmen with the vast mass of the peasantry.

The only uncertainty is the coming storm—when and where will it break? The advocates of the "mailed fist" believe that by dissolving Parliament and provoking a collision now they will find the revolutionary leaders unprepared for an uprising, whereas further delay would give the Revolutionists the time needed to organize and to continue the corruption of the army.

There are no precedents in Russian history for the execution of an order of prorogation, but Monday probably will find the Tauride Palace in the possession of the military and the surrounding streets held by the Emperor's Guards.

The Constitutional Democratic caucus adjourned before the news of the dissolution of Parliament was received, but the information has already reached the leaders of the party. A meeting has been summoned for to-day to discuss procedure and whether they shall attempt, like the French Third Estate, to continue existence as a revolutionary body in defiance of the sovereign's will.

A large part of the Province of Kieff, where armed uprisings are anticipated in consequence of the dissolution of Parliament, has been placed under martial law.

It is positively asserted that on Thursday an imperial ukase authorizing the dissolution of Parliament was signed, and was to be enforced yesterday, but on Friday the execution of the ukase was postponed.

Last night a final conference on the subject was held at Peterhof. Exactly who was present cannot be learned, but it is understood that the Grand Dukes, Gen. Trepoff, and other Court officials, and one or two Ministers were at the palace.

Evidently the Government is not blind to the fact that the dissolution of Parliament will be accompanied by riots and bloodshed, if nothing worse. Troops are being massed at St. Petersburg, Moscow, and other centres, and, in addition to the Guard Regiments which were hurriedly marched into the capital on Thursday night, the entire Twenty-third Division of Infantry arrived here yesterday afternoon from Pskoff.

The arrival of the additional troops at the capital was followed by the strengthening of the patrols throughout the industrial quarters, where the workmen yesterday were greatly excited by the complete suppression of the Socialistic press. Orders were issued to all printing offices to notify the Chief of Police immediately of any attempt to set up the address of the lower house to the country. The temper of the masses can be judged by the fact that mobs resisted the closing of the offices of the Socialist papers on Friday night and that at meetings of the proletariat organizations of Moscow it was resolved to make the dissolution of Parliament the signal for a general strike.

The Socialists and the Group of Toil in Parliament prepared for the present emergency They drafted an address for issuance to the country the moment the dissolution was declared.

Bloodshed on a large scale, with a dictatorship in the background, is considered to be the inevitable sequel of the dissolution of Parliament, but the supporters of dissolution declared that the

"All the News That's Fit to Print."

The New York Times.

THE WEATHER.
Fair to-day and to-morrow; rising southerly winds.

VOL. LV...NO. 17,617. NEW YORK, THURSDAY, APRIL 19, 1906.—TWENTY TWO PAGES. ONE CENT In Greater New York, Jersey City and Newark. Elsewhere, TWO CENTS.

OVER 500 DEAD, $200,000,000 LOST IN SAN FRANCISCO EARTHQUAKE

Nearly Half the City Is in Ruins and 50,000 Are Homeless.

WATER SUPPLY FAILS AND DYNAMITE IS USED IN VAIN

Great Buildings Consumed Before Helpless Firemen—Federal Troops and Militia Guard the City, With Orders to Shoot Down Thieves—Citizens Roused in Early Morning by Great Convulsion and Hundreds Caught by Falling Walls.

SAN FRANCISCO, April 18.—Earthquake and fire to-day have put nearly half of San Francisco in ruins. About 500 persons have been killed, a thousand injured, and the property loss will exceed $200,000,000.

Fifty thousand people are homeless and destitute, and all day long streams of people have been fleeing from the stricken districts to places of safety.

It was 5:13 this morning when a terrific earthquake shock shook the whole city and surrounding country. One shock apparently lasted two minutes, and there was almost immediate collapse of flimsy structures all over the city.

The water supply was cut off, and when fires started in various sections there was nothing to do but let the buildings burn. Telegraph and telephone communication was cut off for a time.

The Western Union was put completely out of business and the Postal Company was the only one that managed the roof sliding into the courtyard, and the smaller towers tumbling down. The great dome was moved, but did not fall.

The new Post Office, one of the finest in the United States, was badly shattered.

The Valencia Hotel, a four-story wooden building, sank into the basement, a pile of splintered timbers, under which were pinned many dead and dying occupants of the house. The basement was full of water, and some of the helpless victims were drowned.

Fires Start in Many Places.

Scarcely had the earth ceased to shake when fires started simultaneously in many places. The Fire Department promptly responded to the first calls for aid, but it was found that the water mains had been rendered useless by the underground movement.

Fanned by a light breeze, the flames quickly spread, and soon many blocks were seen to be doomed. Then dynamite was resorted to, and the sound of frequent explosions added to the terror of the people. These efforts to stay the progress of the fire, however, proved futile.

The south side of Market Street, firemen and United States soldiers, who assisted them, blew down building after building. Their efforts, however, were useless, so far as checking the headway of the flames was concerned.

The shortage of water was due to the breaking of the mains of the Spring Valley Water Company at San Mateo. The water needed so badly in the city ran in a flood over San Mateo.

Burning of the Opera House.

The fire swept down the streets so rapidly that it was practically impossible to save anything in its way. It reached the Grand Opera House on Mission Street, and in a moment had burned through the roof. The Metropolitan Opera Company from New York had just opened its season there, and all the expensive scenery and costumes were soon reduced to ashes.

From the opera house the fire leaped from building to building, leveling them almost to the ground in quick succession.

The Call editorial and mechanical departments, in the handsome building at Third and Market Streets, were totally destroyed in a few minutes, and the flames leaped across Stevenson Street toward the fine fifteen-story stone and iron building of Claus Spreckels, which, with its lofty dome, was the most notable structure in San Francisco. Two small wooden buildings furnished fuel to ignite the splendid pile.

Thousands of people watched the hungry tongues of flames licking the stone walls. At first no impression was made, but suddenly there was a cracking of glass and an entrance was effected. The inner furnishings of the fourth floor were the first to go. Then, as if by magic, smoke issued from the top of the dome.

This was followed by a most spectacular illumination. The round windows of the dome shone like so many full moons; they burst and gave vent to long, waving streamers of flames. The crowd watched the spectacle with bated breath. One woman wrung her hands and burst into a torrent of tears.

"It is so terrible," she said.

The tall and slender structure which had withstood the forces of the earth appeared doomed to fall a prey to fire, was ruined, though its massive walls were not all destroyed.

A little further down Market Street, the Academy of Sciences and the Jennie Flood Building and the History Building kindled and burned like so much tinder. Sparks carried across the wide street, ignited the Phelan Building, and the army headquarters of California, Gen. Funston commanding, were burned.

Still nearing the bay, the waters of which did the firemen good service along the docks, the fire took the Rialto Building, a handsome skyscraper, and converted scores of solid business blocks into smoldering piles of bricks.

Thousands Watch the Flames.

Banks and commercial houses, supposed to be fireproof, though not of modern build, burned quickly, and the roar of the flames could be heard even on the hills, which were out of the danger zone. Here many thousands of people congregated and viewed the awful scene.

Great sheets of flame rose high in the heavens, or rushed down some narrow street, joining midway between the sidewalks, making a horizontal chimney of the former passageway.

The dense smoke that arose from the entire business district spread out like an immense funnel and could have been seen miles out at sea. Occasionally as some drug house or place stored with chemicals was reached, most fantastic effects were produced by the centred flames and smoke which rolled out against the darker background.

One of the first orders issued by Chief of Police Dinan this morning was for the closing of every saloon in the city. This step is taken to prevent drink-crazed men from rioting in the streets.

Mayor Schmitz sent out word to the bakeries and milk stations throughout the city that their food supplies must be harbored for the homeless. Provisions were made to place tents in every park in the city, and those who have lost all will be given food and shelter.

Early in the morning the prisoners confined in the city prison on the fifth floor of the Hall of Justice were transferred in irons to the basement of the structure. Later they were removed to Pacific Division of the United States Army, were asked to send troops.

A thousand men from the Presidio, sent by Gen. Funston, arrived downtown at 9 o'clock to patrol the streets. The Thirteenth Infantry, 1,000 strong, arrived from Angel Island a little later and went on patrol duty at once.

The soldiers were ordered to shoot down vandals caught robbing the dead and to guard with their lives the millions of dollars' worth of property placed in the streets to escape the flames.

The First California Artillery, 200 strong, two companies, was detailed to patrol duty on Ellis Street. Two more companies patrolled Broadway in the Italian section. The Ellis Street contingent of guardsmen were under the command of Capt. G. A. Grattan. Capt. William A. Miller commanded the forces on Broadway.

The city is under martial law, and all the downtown streets are patroled by cavalry and infantry. Details of troops are also guarding the banks.

Early this morning Mayor Schmitz, who established his office at Police Headquarters, named the following citizens as a Committee of Safety:

James D. Phelan,	Paul Cowles,
Herbert Law,	M. H. De Young,
Thomas Magee,	Claus Spreckles,
Charles Fee,	Rudolph Spreckles,
W. P. Herrin,	C. W. Fay,
Thornwell Mullalley,	John McNaught,
Garret W. Enerney,	Dent Robert,
W. H. Leahy,	Thomas Garrett,
J. Downey Harvey,	Frank Shea,
Jeremiah Dinan,	James Shea,
John J. Mahoney,	Robert Pisis,
Henry T. Scott,	T. P. Woodward,
I. W. Hellman,	Howard Holmes,
George A. Knight,	George Dillman,
I. Steinhart,	J. B. Rogers,
S. G. Murphy,	David Rich,
Homer King,	H. T. Cresswell,
Frank Anderson,	J. A. Howell,
W. J. Bartnett,	Frank Maestrettl,
John Martin,	Clem Tobin,
Allan Pollock,	George Toumey,
Mark Gerstle,	E. D. Pond,
H. V. Ramsdell,	George A. Newhall,
W. G. Harrison,	William Watson.
R. A. Crothers,	

THE BUILDINGS DESTROYED.

A Partial List of the Structures Torn Down or Injured.

SAN FRANCISCO, April 18.—The following is an incomplete list of the buildings destroyed or injured:

Call Building, entirely destroyed.
Claus Spreckels Building, burned out.
Hearst Building, collapsed.

ALL SAN FRANCISCO MAY BURN; CLIFF HOUSE RESORT IN SEA

Flames Carried From the Business Quarter to Residences

PALACE HOTEL AND MINT GO; BIG BUILDINGS BLOWN UP.

Other Shocks Felt During the Afternoon—Insane Asylum Is Wrecked and Hundreds of Former Inmates Are Roaming About the Country—Reports of Heavy Loss of Life at San Jose.

SAN FRANCISCO, Thursday, April 19.—12:15 A. M. (3:15 A. M. New York Time.)—At midnight the fire still roars. Fleeing inhabitants can see from miles around the pillars of fire towering skyward. The crash of falling ruins and the muffled reports of the exploding dynamite reach the ear at regular intervals.

A disaster that staggers comprehension and in point of terror and damage is unprecedented on the coast has not yet reached its culmination.

The Merchants' Exchange Building, one of the handsomest and most substantial edifices in the city, is in flames, as is also the Crocker-Woolwarth Building.

The former building is a fourteen-story structure, seven floors of which are occupied by the Southern Pacific Railway Company as offices. The Crocker-Woolworth Building is a twelve-story terra cotta and granite structure and stood directly opposite the Palace Hotel.

The immense D. O. Mills Building is surrounded by fire and probably will latter place was closed, and this dispatch is written on a doorstep near Chinatown, the illumination of the burning buildings furnishing light for the writer.

It appeared that the great Mills Building would block some of the southward sweep of the blaze, as it had already checked an advance northward earlier in the night. If this proves true the limits of the fire will be determined, but predictions on this point are as unreliable as the strong wind, which every five minutes is changing from one direction to another.

The city to-night in face of its appaling disaster, is fairly quiet and orderly. Liquor cannot be had anywhere and the formidable presence of Federal troops, militia and naval reserves has had its effect on the element that might be disposed to be disorderly.

The Mayor's proclamation authorizing the shooting of looters on sight has been scattered broadcast in circulars and few reports of thieving are received.

It is impossible to give anything like an accurate statement concerning the killed. Unquestionably many people were either killed outright, imprisoned or rendered unconscious in collapsed

"All the News That's Fit to Print."

The New York Times.

THE WEATHER.

Unsettled Tuesday; Wednesday, fair, cooler; moderate southerly winds, becoming variable.

For full weather report see Page 23.

VOL. LXI...NO. 19,806. NEW YORK, TUESDAY, APRIL 16, 1912.—TWENTY-FOUR PAGES, ONE CENT In Greater New York, Jersey City, and Newark. { Elsewhere, TWO CENTS.

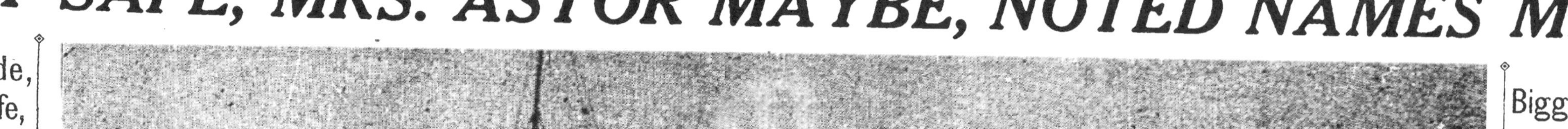

TITANIC SINKS FOUR HOURS AFTER HITTING ICEBERG; 866 RESCUED BY CARPATHIA, PROBABLY 1250 PERISH; ISMAY SAFE, MRS. ASTOR MAYBE, NOTED NAMES MISSING

Col. Astor and Bride, Isidor Straus and Wife, and Maj. Butt Aboard.

"RULE OF SEA" FOLLOWED

Women and Children Put Over in Lifeboats and Are Supposed to be Safe on Carpathia.

PICKED UP AFTER 8 HOURS

Vincent Astor Calls at White Star Office for News of His Father and Leaves Weeping.

FRANKLIN HOPEFUL ALL DAY

Manager of the Line Insisted Titanic Was Unsinkable Even After She Had Gone Down.

HEAD OF THE LINE ABOARD

J. Bruce Ismay Making First Trip on Gigantic Ship That Was to Surpass All Others.

The admission that the Titanic, the biggest steamship in the world, had been sunk by an iceberg and had gone to the bottom of the Atlantic, probably carrying more than 1,400 of her pas- ... nd crew with her, was made

Biggest Liner Plunges to the Bottom at 2:20 A. M.

RESCUERS THERE TOO LATE

Except to Pick Up the Few Hundreds Who Took to the Lifeboats.

WOMEN AND CHILDREN FIRST

Cunarder Carpathia Rushing to New York with the Survivors.

SEA SEARCH FOR OTHERS

The California Stands By on Chance of Picking Up Other Boats or Rafts.

OLYMPIC SENDS THE NEWS

Only Ship to Flash Wireless Messages to Shore After the Disaster

LATER REPORT SAVES 866.

BOSTON, April 15.—A wireless message picked up late to-night, relayed from the Olympic, says

"All the News That's Fit to Print."

The New York Times.

THE WEATHER.
Fair to-day and to-morrow; rising southerly winds.

VOL. LV...NO. 17,617. NEW YORK, THURSDAY, APRIL 19, 1906.—TWENTY TWO PAGES. ONE CENT In Greater New York, Jersey City and Newark. Elsewhere, TWO CENTS.

OVER 500 DEAD, $200,000,000 LOST IN SAN FRANCISCO EARTHQUAKE

Nearly Half the City Is in Ruins and 50,000 Are Homeless.

WATER SUPPLY FAILS AND DYNAMITE IS USED IN VAIN

Great Buildings Consumed Before Helpless Firemen—Federal Troops and Militia Guard the City, With Orders to Shoot Down Thieves—Citizens Roused in Early Morning by Great Convulsion and Hundreds Caught by Falling Walls.

SAN FRANCISCO, April 18.—Earthquake and fire to-day have put nearly half of San Francisco in ruins. About 500 persons have been killed, a thousand injured, and the property loss will exceed $200,000,000.

Fifty thousand people are homeless and destitute, and all day long streams of people have been fleeing from the stricken districts to places of safety.

It was 5:13 this morning when a terrific earthquake shock shook the whole city and surrounding country. One shock apparently lasted two minutes, and there was almost immediate collapse of flimsy structures all over the city.

The water supply was cut off, and when fires started in various sections there was nothing to do but let the buildings burn. Telegraph and telephone communication was cut off for a time.

The Western Union was put completely out of business and the Postal Company was the only one that managed to get a wire out of the city. About the roof sliding into the courtyard, and the smaller towers tumbling down. The great dome was moved, but did not fall.

The new Post Office, one of the finest in the United States, was badly shattered.

The Valencia Hotel, a four-story wooden building, sank into the basement, a pile of splintered timbers, under which were pinned many dead and dying occupants of the house. The basement was full of water, and some of the helpless victims were drowned.

Fires Start in Many Places.

Scarcely had the earth ceased to shake when fires started simultaneously in many places. The Fire Department promptly responded to the first calls for aid, but it was found that the water mains had been rendered useless by the underground movement.

Fanned by a light breeze, the flames quickly spread, and soon many blocks were seen to be doomed. Then dynamite was resorted to, and the sound of frequent explosions added to the terror of the people. These efforts to stay the progress of the fire, however, proved futile.

The south side of Market Street, from Ninth Street to the bay, was soon firemen and United States soldiers, who assisted them, blew down building after building. Their efforts, however, were useless, so far as checking the headway of the flames was concerned.

The shortage of water was due to the breaking of the mains of the Spring Valley Water Company at San Mateo. The water needed so badly in the city ran in a flood over San Mateo.

Burning of the Opera House.

The fire swept down the streets so rapidly that it was practically impossible to save anything in its way. It reached the Grand Opera House on Mission Street, and in a moment had burned through the roof. The Metropolitan Opera Company from New York had just opened its season there, and all the expensive scenery and costumes were soon reduced to ashes.

From the opera house the fire leaped from building to building, leveling them almost to the ground in quick succession.

The Call editorial and mechanical departments, in the handsome building at Third and Market Streets, were totally destroyed in a few minutes, and the flames leaped across Stevenson Street toward the fine fifteen-story stone and iron building of Claus Spreckels, which, with its lofty dome, was the most notable structure in San Francisco. Two small wooden buildings furnished fuel to ignite the splendid pile.

Thousands of people watched the hungry tongues of flames licking the stone walls. At first no impression was made, but suddenly there was a cracking of glass and an entrance was effected. The inner furnishings of the fourth floor were the first to go. Then, as if by magic, smoke issued from the top of the dome.

This was followed by a most spectacular illumination. The round windows of the dome shone like so many full moons; they burst and gave vent to long, waving streamers of flames. The crowd watched the spectacle with bated breath. One woman wrung her hands and burst into a torrent of tears.

"It is so terrible," she said.

The tall and slender structure which had withstood the forces of the earth appeared doomed to fall a prey to fire. After a while, however, the light grew was ruined, though its massive walls were not all destroyed.

A little further down Market Street, the Academy of Sciences and the Jennie Flood Building and the History Building kindled and burned like so much tinder. Sparks carried across the wide street, ignited the Phelan Building, and the army headquarters of California, Gen. Funston commanding, were burned.

Still nearing the bay, the waters of which did the firemen good service along the docks, the fire took the Rialto Building, a handsome skyscraper, and converted scores of solid business blocks into smoldering piles of bricks.

Thousands Watch the Flames.

Banks and commercial houses, supposed to be fireproof, though not of modern build, burned quickly, and the roar of the flames could be heard even on the hills, which were out of the danger zone. Here many thousands of people congregated and viewed the awful scene.

Great sheets of flame rose high in the heavens, or rushed down some narrow street, joining midway between the sidewalks, making a horizontal chimney of the former passageway.

The dense smoke that arose from the entire business district spread out like an immense funnel and could have been seen miles out at sea. Occasionally as some drug house or place stored with chemicals was reached, most fantastic effects were produced by the centred flames and smoke which rolled out against the darker background.

One of the first orders issued by Chief of Police Dinan this morning was for the closing of every saloon in the city. This step is taken to prevent drink-crazed men from rioting in the streets.

Mayor Schmitz sent out word to the bakeries and milk stations throughout the city that their food supplies must be harbored for the homeless. Provisions were made to place tents in every park in the city, and those who have lost all will be given food and shelter.

Early in the morning the prisoners confined in the city prison on the fifth floor of the Hall of Justice were transferred in irons to the basement of the structure. Later they were removed to Pacific Division of the United States Army, were asked to send troops.

A thousand men from the Presidio, sent by Gen. Funston, arrived downtown at 9 o'clock to patrol the streets. The Thirteenth Infantry, 1,000 strong, arrived from Angel Island a little later and went on patrol duty at once.

The soldiers were ordered to shoot down vandals caught robbing the dead and to guard with their lives the millions of dollars' worth of property placed in the streets to escape the flames.

The First California Artillery, 200 strong, two companies, was detailed to patrol duty on Ellis Street. Two more companies patrolled Broadway in the Italian section. The Ellis Street contingent of guardsmen were under the command of Capt. G. A. Grattan. Capt. William A. Miller commanded the forces on Broadway.

The city is under martial law, and all the downtown streets are patroled by cavalry and infantry. Details of troops are also guarding the banks.

Early this morning Mayor Schmitz, who established his office at Police Headquarters, named the following citizens as a Committee of Safety:

James D. Phelan,	Paul Cowles,
Herbert Law,	M. H. De Young,
Thomas Magee,	Claus Spreckles,
Charles Fee,	Rudolph Spreckles,
W. P. Herrin,	C. W. Fay,
Thornwell Mullalley,	John McNaught,
Garret W. Enerney,	Dent Robert,
W. H. Leahy,	Thomas Garrett,
J. Downey Harvey,	Frank Shea,
Jeremiah Dinan,	James Shea,
John J. Mahoney,	Robert Pisis,
Henry T. Scott,	T. P. Woodward,
I. W. Hellman,	Howard Holmes,
George A. Knight,	George Dillman,
I. Steinhart,	J. B. Rogers,
S. G. Murphy,	David Rich,
Homer King,	H. T. Cresswell,
Frank Anderson,	J. A. Howell,
W. J. Bartnett,	Frank Maestrettl,
John Martin,	Clem Tobin,
Allan Pollock,	George Toumey,
Mark Gerstle,	E. D. Fond,
H. V. Ramsdell,	George A. Newhall,
W. G. Harrison,	William Watson.
R. A. Crothers,	

THE BUILDINGS DESTROYED.

A Partial List of the Structures Torn Down or Injured.

SAN FRANCISCO, April 18.—The following is an incomplete list of the buildings destroyed or injured:

Call Building, entirely destroyed.
Claus Spreckels Building, burned out.
Hearst Building, collapsed.

ALL SAN FRANCISCO MAY BURN; CLIFF HOUSE RESORT IN SEA

Flames Carried From the Business Quarter to Residences

PALACE HOTEL AND MINT GO; BIG BUILDINGS BLOWN UP.

Other Shocks Felt During the Afternoon—Insane Asylum Is Wrecked and Hundreds of Former Inmates Are Roaming About the Country—Reports of Heavy Loss of Life at San Jose.

SAN FRANCISCO, Thursday, April 19.—12:15 A. M. (3:15 A. M. New York Time.)—At midnight the fire still roars. Fleeing inhabitants can see from miles around the pillars of fire towering skyward. The crash of falling ruins and the muffled reports of the exploding dynamite reach the ear at regular intervals.

A disaster that staggers comprehension and in point of terror and damage is unprecedented on the coast has not yet reached its culmination.

The Merchants' Exchange Building, one of the handsomest and most substantial edifices in the city, is in flames, as is also the Crocker-Woolworth Building.

The former building is a fourteen-story structure, seven floors of which are occupied by the Southern Pacific Railway Company as offices. The Crocker-Woolworth Building is a twelve-story terra cotta and granite structure and stood directly opposite the Palace Hotel.

The immense D. O. Mills Building is surrounded by fire and probably will latter place was closed, and this dispatch is written on a doorstep near Chinatown, the illumination of the burning buildings furnishing light for the writer.

It appeared that the great Mills Building would block some of the southward sweep of the blaze, as it had already checked an advance northward earlier in the night. If this proves true the limits of the fire will be determined, but predictions on this point are as unreliable as the strong wind, which every five minutes is changing from one direction to another.

The city to-night in face of its appaling disaster, is fairly quiet and orderly. Liquor cannot be had anywhere and the formidable presence of Federal troops, militia and naval reserves has had its effect on the element that might be disposed to be disorderly.

The Mayor's proclamation authorizing the shooting of looters on sight has been scattered broadcast in circulars and few reports of thieving are received.

It is impossible to give anything like an accurate statement concerning the killed. Unquestionably many people were either killed outright, imprisoned or rendered unconscious in collapsed

"All the News That's Fit to Print."

The New York Times.

THE WEATHER.

Unsettled Tuesday; Wednesday, fair, cooler; moderate southerly winds, becoming variable.

For full weather report see Page 23.

VOL. LXI...NO. 19,806. NEW YORK, TUESDAY, APRIL 16, 1912.—TWENTY-FOUR PAGES, ONE CENT In Greater New York, Jersey City, and Newark. { Elsewhere, TWO CENTS.

TITANIC SINKS FOUR HOURS AFTER HITTING ICEBERG; 866 RESCUED BY CARPATHIA, PROBABLY 1250 PERISH; ISMAY SAFE, MRS. ASTOR MAYBE, NOTED NAMES MISSING

Col. Astor and Bride, Isidor Straus and Wife, and Maj. Butt Aboard.

"RULE OF SEA" FOLLOWED

Women and Children Put Over in Lifeboats and Are Supposed to be Safe on Carpathia.

PICKED UP AFTER 8 HOURS

Vincent Astor Calls at White Star Office for News of His Father and Leaves Weeping.

FRANKLIN HOPEFUL ALL DAY

Manager of the Line Insisted Titanic Was Unsinkable Even After She Had Gone Down.

HEAD OF THE LINE ABOARD

J. Bruce Ismay Making First Trip on Gigantic Ship That Was to Surpass All Others.

The admission that the Titanic, the biggest steamship in the world, had been sunk by an iceberg and had gone to the bottom of the Atlantic, probably carrying more than 1,400 of her pas- ... nd crew with her, was made

Biggest Liner Plunges to the Bottom at 2:20 A. M.

RESCUERS THERE TOO LATE

Except to Pick Up the Few Hundreds Who Took to the Lifeboats.

WOMEN AND CHILDREN FIRST

Cunarder Carpathia Rushing to New York with the Survivors.

SEA SEARCH FOR OTHERS

The California Stands By on Chance of Picking Up Other Boats or Rafts.

OLYMPIC SENDS THE NEWS

Only Ship to Flash Wireless Messages to Shore After the Disaster

LATER REPORT SAVES 866.

BOSTON, April 15.—A wireless message picked up late to-night, relayed from the Olympic, says that the Carpathia is on her way

[illegible] even the Postal was forced to suspend.

Electric power was stopped and street cars did not run, railroads and ferry-boats also ceased operations. The various fires raged all day and the fire department has been powerless to do anything except dynamite buildings threatened. All day long explosions have shaken the city and added to the terror of the inhabitants.

Following the first shock there was another within five minutes, but not nearly so severe. Three hours later there was another slight quake.

First Warning at 5:13 A. M.

Most of the people of San Francisco were asleep at 5:13 o'clock this morning when the terrible earthquake came without warning.

The motion of the disturbance apparently was from east to west. At first the upheaval of the earth was gradual, but in a few seconds it increased in intensity. Chimneys began to fall and buildings to crack, tottering on their foundations.

The people became panic-stricken, and rushed into the streets, most of them in their night attire. They were met by showers of falling bricks, cornices, and walls of buildings.

Many were crushed to death, while others were badly mangled. Those who remained indoors generally escaped with their lives, though scores were hit by detached plaster, pictures, and articles thrown to the floor by the shock. It is believed that more or less loss was sustained by nearly every family in the city.

Steel Frame Buildings Stand.

The tall, steel-frame structures stood the strain better than brick buildings, few of them being badly damaged. The big eleven-story Monadnock office building, in course of construction, adjoining the Palace Hotel, was an exception, however, its rear wall collapsing and many cracks being made across its front.

Some of the docks and freight sheds along the water front slid into the bay. Deep fissures opened in the filled-in ground near the shore, and the Union Ferry Station was badly injured. Its high tower still stands, but will have to be torn down.

A portion of the new City Hall, which cost more than $7,000,000, collapsed, ablaze, the fire covering a belt two blocks wide. On this, the main thoroughfare, were many of the finest edifices in the city, including the Grant, Parrott, Flood, Call, Examiner, and Monadnock Buildings, and the Palace and Grand Hotels.

At the same time commercial establishments and banks north of Market Street were burning. The burning district in this section of the city extended from Sansome Street to the water front, and from Market Street to Broadway.

Fires also started in the Mission, and the entire city seemed to be in flames.

Long Detours Around Fires.

The flames, fanned by the rising breeze, swept down the main streets until within a few hundred feet of the ferry station, the high tower of which stood at a dangerous angle.

The big wholesale grocery establishment of Weelman, Peck & Co. was on fire from cellar to roof, and the heat was so oppressive that passengers from the ferry boats were obliged to keep close to the water's edge, in order to get past the burning structure.

It was impossible to reach the centre of the city from the bay without skirting the shore for a long distance so as to get entirely around the burning district.

About 8 o'clock the Southern Pacific officials refused to allow any more passengers from trans-bay points to land, and sent back those already on the boats. The ferry and train service of the Key Route was entirely abandoned owing to damage done to the power house by the earthquake at Emeryville.

Lack of Dynamite Felt.

There was little dynamite available in the city. The Southern Pacific soon brought some in. At 9 o'clock Mayor Schmitz sent a tug to Pinola for several cases of explosives. He sent also a telegram to Mayor Mott of Oakland. At 10:30 he received this reply to his Oakland message:

"Three engines and hose companies leave here immediately. Will forward dynamite as soon as obtainable."

The town of San Rafael, despite its own needs, sent fire fighting apparatus here.

Mayor Schmitz gave orders to use dynamite wherever necessary, and the

less intense, and the flames, finding nothing to consume, gradually went out, leaving the building standing, but completely gutted.

At California and Sansome Streets stood the Mutual Life Building, a modern structure of architectural beauty, to which the flames were soon communicated. An attempt was made to save it, but the fire was irrepressible. The flames gained, and in a few moments the big building was beyond hope. The Anglo California Bank was swept by the flames and came down in a rush.

Time and again attempts were made with dynamite to clear a space which should prevent the flames from spreading to other buildings, but freely as the explosive was used the fire crept and climbed from one structure to another.

An unusually loud report showed that a gas house at Eighteenth and Market Streets had blown up. The fire caused by the explosion quickly communicated in various directions. As the gas house exploded a feeling of despair overcame the men who were performing the rescue work.

Scare at Palace Hotel.

The Palace Hotel, the rear of which was constantly threatened, was the scene of much excitement, the guests leaving in haste, many with only the clothing they wore. Finding that the hotel was surrounded on all sides by streets, and was likely to remain immune, many returned and made arrangements for the removal of their belongings, though little could be taken away owing to the utter absence of transportation facilities.

The Parrott Building, in which was located the chambers of the State Supreme Court, the lower floors being devoted to an immense department store, arises they will be taken to a branch county jail on the Mission Road.

The Mayor also established a base of rescue, and soon had forces out where they could accomplish most. Many men were sent down to the lodging house district near Market Street. There it was found that many frame buildings, packed with people, had collapsed, burying their occupants in the ruins.

The rescuers jumped into the wrecks and pulled out the dead, the dying, and the injured. Practically every physician in the city immediately volunteered his assistance, and soon there was a well-equipped medical corps organized which began ministering to the injured.

For hours bodies were taken out in the lodging house district, and hundreds of men volunteered to go into the ruins to get more.

The pretentious City Hall, bounded by Larkin and McAllister Streets and City Hall Avenue, was badly shattered by the earthquake, and the ruins later were burned. It took twenty years to build the City Hall, the pride of the coast. When the first shock was felt the building rocked and swayed until it cracked. Part of the interior fell and the ruins caught fire. An alarm was turned in and the firemen responded. Chief Sullivan, awakened by the shock at his quarters in a firehouse, hastened to put on his clothes. As he reached for them the tower of the California Hotel dropped upon his building and crushing through the roof killed him.

The firemen arrived at the City Hall, but were helpless. They hitched their hose to the fire plugs, but there was no water supply.

Every possible precaution has been taken to guard property. Immediately after the destructive shocks the police turned out on guard, and the Governor and Gen. Funston, commanding the

aged.

The White House, walls badly cracked; all plate glass windows gone; every piece of stock in building removed before 9:30 A. M.

Winchester Hotel, Third Street, totally destroyed by earthquake shock.

Grand Opera House, entirely destroyed.

Claus Spreckels house and stables, Van Ness Avenue, badly damaged and will have to be largely rebuilt.

St. Luke's Episcopal Church, Van Ness Avenue, will have to be pulled down.

Mechanics' Library Building, Post Street, cornices fell to street; building slightly injured.

Crocker Building, Market and Post Streets, slightly damaged, principally around light shaft.

Lick House, walls and roof largely caved in.

Upham Building, Pine and Battery Streets, totally destroyed; loss, $550,000.

Fire house adjoining California Hotel in Bush Street; Chief Sullivan and wife, sleeping in engine house, severely bruised by bricks crashing through roof from hotel.

California Hotel, Bush Street, upper walls collapsed and upper floors wrecked.

The building in course of construction to be occupied by the Hamman baths will have to be rebuilt. It is in Post Street near the Olympic Club. The walls are badly warped and twisted and the roof has fallen in.

San Francisco Gas and Electric Company's Post Street plant, only slightly injured.

St. Francis Hotel, exterior slightly cracked and seamed, but not seriously injured.

Pacific Union Club, Post and Stockton Streets, front injured and fissures in rear wall.

St. Dominic's Church in Pierce Street, total loss. The interior of the church is wrecked and there are fissures in the walls. The structure will have to be pulled down. The parochial house in the same block is nearly a wreck. It is estimated that the loss to the parish is $300,000.

The ornamental top on St. Dunstan's, the apartment house at Sutter Street and Van Ness Avenue, fell into the street.

The Concordia Club building in Van Ness Avenue has several fissures in the side, and rebuilding will be necessary.

The Hotel Grinado, badly damaged; stone coping about roof fell.

EARTHQUAKE'S AUTOGRAPH AS IT WROTE IT 3,000 MILES AWAY.

Tracing Made by the Seismograph Needle in the Office of State Geologist John M. Clarke, State Museum, Albany, Showing How the Earthquake Traveled Across Continent in 19 Minutes.

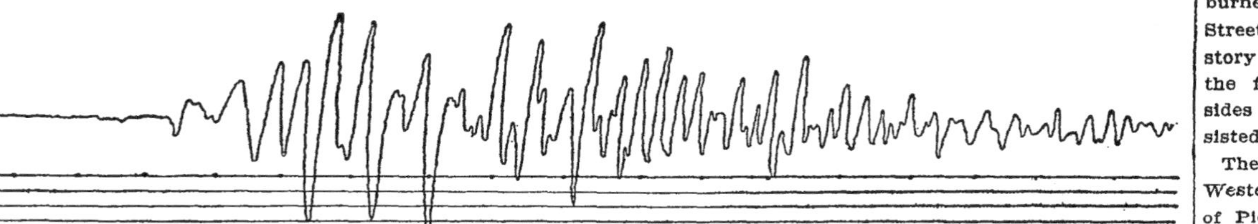

The drawing represents the vibration of the north and south pendulum of the seismograph during the time of the most intense activity, beginning in San Francisco at 5:13 A. M., in Albany at 8:32. In Albany the violent agitation ended at 8:43 A. M. The straight lines at the side of the wavy line indicate the normal condition of the record as the recording drum revolves, and this serves to show the contrast between the ordinary progress of the record and that during a disturbance. The spaces between the dots indicate lapses of one minute each.

The same violent disturbance was noticeable on the seismograph at Washington between 8:32 and 8:35 A. M., thus verifying the time of transit across the continent—19 minutes.

burn. The Lick House, the Occidental Hotel, and the Russ House in this immediate vicinity are in immediate danger.

The exact loss of life never will be known. Hundreds have been incinerated. To-night the city resembles one vast shambles with the red glare of the fire throwing shadows across the worn and panic-stricken faces of the homeless.

At the morgue in the Hall of Justice fifty bodies lie. Before the eyes of an Associated Press reporter three thieves were shot dead.

The Japanese quarter has been burned and the people fled in terror, packing on their backs what household effects they could tie together.

At 9 o'clock to-night an Associated Press man who went to a high hill overlooking the city noted that the sky on the east and south sides was illuminated for a distance of four or five miles. The illumination on the southern side was in a duller glow, showing that the flames were not consuming property of such great proportions as was the case on the east side.

In the business district toward the water front the flames were either checked or blocked at about Washington Street, and at the corner of Kearny Street the Hall of Justice could be noted standing, but it was impossible to determine what damage had been done to the interior. From the Hall of Justice to the south the fire cut its way through some of the choicest buildings in the city, the Pacific Mutual and the Italian-American Bank Building being reduced to ashes.

Down Kearny Street on both sides at 10 o'clock the conflagration was still raging with fury, but the direction of the wind prevented its advance up the hills to the west toward the residence quarter.

To the west of Kearny, up to Dupont, most of the buildings were burned as far south as California Street. All around the new fourteen-story Merchants' Exchange Building the fire burned fiercely, licking the sides of the steel giant, but it resisted the influence of the heat.

Then came the destruction of the Western Union Building, at the corner of Pick and Montgomery Streets. In this building were the offices of the Associated Press. Earlier in the day the occupants had been ordered out by the authorities on account of danger, and The Associated Press established a temporary station in The Bulletin editorial rooms. Then the

buildings which were afterward burned.

At 10 o'clock the Occidental Hotel began burning and the great Crocker Building containing the Crocker-Woolworth National Bank was ablaze.

On Geary Street the Albert Pike Memorial Temple of the California bodies of the Scottish Rites Masons, containing scenery that cost $20,000 and costumes valued at $15,000, collapsed. The new Jewish synagogue adjoining was cracked to its foundations.

While five dying men were taken from a collapsed building at Second and Jessie Streets Fathers Hogan, Rogers, and Huber of St. Patrick's Church granted them the last rites of the Catholic Church. This ceremony was performed while a mass of coping overhead threatened to crush the priests to death. Three of the men died.

A shoemaker, Joseph Lindsay, was four hours in a demolished building and when dug out it was found that he had not been hurt.

The entire Larkin Street frontage of the City Hall for a distance of several hundred feet was thrown out into the street, and that thoroughfare for two blocks is piled high with boulders of mortared brick and twisted iron.

Latest reports from Leland Stanford University at Palo Alto indicate that the magnificent stone buildings of that institution have suffered severe damage. Many of the buildings were ruined by cracks that split them from cornice to foundation.

The University of California at Berkeley, across the bay, escaped serious injury. The buildings are intact. Only a few structures collapsed in Berkeley, the shock being slight there.

Artillerymen from the Presidio with their supply wagons and the army commissary wagons are aiding in getting the fleeing inhabitants and their baggage out of the threatened quarters.

270 Dead in an Asylum.

The insane asylum at Agnews is a total wreck, 270 of the inmates being killed. It is reported that the attachés of the institution who were about at the time of the earthquake were saved. The ruins took fire shortly after the collapse. One hundred and twenty bodies have been removed.

There were about 700 persons in the building. Hundreds of the inmates who escaped death are roaming about the country in a state of panic.

Half San Francisco Gone.

OAKLAND, Cal., April 18, 10 P. M.—It looks now as if the entire City of San Francisco would be burned.

At 10 o'clock to-night the fire

...hite Star Line offices, 9 Broadway, at 8:20 o'clock last night. Then P. A. S. Franklin, Vice President and General Manager of the International Mercantile Marine, conceded that probably only those passengers who were picked up by the Cunarder Carpathia had been saved. Advices received early this morning tended to increase the number of survivors by 200.

The admission followed a day in which the White Star Line officials had been optimistic in the extreme. At no time was the admission made that every one aboard the huge steamer was not safe. The ship itself, it was confidently asserted, was unsinkable, and inquirers were informed that she would reach port, under her own steam probably, but surely with the help of the Allan liner Virginian, which was reported to be towing her.

As the day passed, however, with no new authentic reports from the Titanic or any of the ships which were known to have responded to her wireless call for help, it became apparent that authentic news of the disaster probably could come only from the Titanic's sister ship, the Olympic. The wireless range of the Olympic is 500 miles. That of the Carpathia, the Parisian, and the Virginian is much less, and as they neared the position of the Titanic they drew further and further out of shore range. From the Titanic's position at the time of the disaster it is doubtful if any of the ships except the Olympic could establish communication with shore.

Titanic Sank at 2:20 A. M. Monday.

In the White Star offices the hope was held out all day that the Parisian and the Virginian had taken off some of the Titanic's passengers, and efforts were made to get into communication with these liners. Until such communication was established the White Star officials refused to recognize the possibility that there were none of the Titanic's passengers aboard them.

But by nightfall came the message from Capt. Haddock of the Olympic to Cape Race, Newfoundland, telling of the foundering of the Titanic and of the rescue of 655 of her passengers by the Cunarder Carpathia, which, the wireless message said, reached the position of the Titanic at daybreak. All they found there, however, was lifeboats and wreckage. The biggest ship in the world had sunk at 2:20 o'clock yesterday morning.

Mr. Franklin admitted late last night that the Parisian and the Virginian, though they were among the first to answer the Titanic's calls for help, could not have reached the scene before 10 o'clock yesterday morning, seven and a half hours after the big Titanic buried her nose beneath the waves and pitched downward out of sight. The Carpathia, so the wireless dispatch from Capt. Haddock to Cape Race announced, reached the scene of the Titanic's foundering at daybreak, several hours before the expected arrival of the Virginian and the Parisian.

1,465 Lives Lost First Report.

It is unbelievable, so White Star Line officials were compelled to concede finally, that the Carpathia should have failed to pick up every lifeboat which still floated on the waves. If they failed to pick up more than 655 passengers, it was because the others of the ship's complement had gone with her to the bottom.

But it was not until nearly nightfall that the extent of the disaster was realized. Before that the reassuring nature of the bulletins issued by the White Star line was sufficient to quiet the fears of those who had relatives or friends aboard the unfortunate ship and to prevent widespread belief in a serious disaster.

Capt. Haddock's message from the Olympic, which is printed in another column of THE TIMES, strongly indicated that none but the 655 taken from life boats by the Carpathia had been saved. This message was delayed immediately to the White Star offices, but Mr. Franklin positively declined to make the text of the message public. He offered still the hope that passengers were aboard the Parisian and the Virginian, and even when the admission was wrung from him that there seemed little hope of the saving of any others than the 655 aboard the Carpathia, he clung to the hope that in some unexplained way there were other passengers abroad the two Allan liners.

First Reported Titanic in Tow.

Throughout the day there had been reassurances that the Titanic was being towed to port by the Virginian, and when Capt. Haddock's message proved this to be untrue only the admission was made at the White Star offices that the Titanic had sunk. Mr. Franklin said that Capt. Haddock's message was brief and "neglected to say that all the crew had been saved." But the inference was not that all the passengers had been saved. Rather it was that many of them had died, and presently Mr Franklin admitted the fear that there had been a terrible loss of life on the Titanic.

This version of Capt. Haddock's wireless had been given at the White Star offices:

Capt. Haddock of the Olympic sends a wireless message to the White Star offices here that the steamer Titanic sank at 2:20 A. M., after all the passengers and crew had been lowered to life boats and transferred to the Virginian. The steamship Carpathia, with sev...red passengers of the Titanic, ...en route to New York.

At 9 o'clock, however, he modified this statement, declaring:

As far as we know the situation, there have been rumors from Halifax that three steamers were at the scene of the Titanic's sinking, namely, the Virginian, the Parisian, and the Carpathia. We have heard from Capt. Haddock of the Olympic, who says that the Titanic sank at 2:20 o clock this morning. Haddock also informs us that the Carpathia has 675 survivors on board. It is very difficult to say whether the Virginian and the Parisian have any survivors on board until we can get a report from those vessels.

Fears Serious Loss of Life.

We have asked for that report from Capt. Haddock, and we are expecting a reply at any time. The Carpathia is proceeding to New York direct. We very much fear that there has been serious loss of life, but it is impossible for us to say definitely concerning this sad part of the situation until we are able to reassure ourselves whether or not any of the Titanic's passengers are aboard the Allan liners.

We are hopeful that the rumors which have reached us by telegraph from Halifax that there are passengers aboard the Virginian and the Parisian will prove to be true, and that these vessels will turn up with some of the passengers. It is the loss of life that makes this thing so awful. We can replace the money loss, but not the lives of those who went down.

Another version of the message from the Olympic was current last night and included the sentence: "Loss likely total 1,800 souls." This sentence was not in the message received by THE TIMES from Cape Race nor in that sent to the White Star line offices.

Continued on Page 2.

THE PROBABLE LOSS.	
Number Aboard.	
First cabin	325
Second cabin	285
Steerage	710
Crew, (estimated)	800
Total	2,120
Saved.	
By the Carpathia	866
Probably drowned	1,254

The Lost Titanic Being Towed Out of Belfast Harbor.

CAPT. E. J. SMITH,
Commander of the Titanic.

PARTIAL LIST OF THE SAVED.

Includes Bruce Ismay, Mrs. Widener, Mrs. H. B. Harris, and an Incomplete name, suggesting Mrs. Astor's.

Special to The New York Times.

CAPE RACE, N. F., Tuesday, April 16.—Following is a partial list of survivors among the first-class passengers of the Titanic, received by the Marconi wireless station this morning from the Carpathia, via the steamship Olympic:

Mrs. JACOB P. ——— and maid.
Mr. HARRY ANDERSON.
Mrs. ED. W. APPLETON.
Mrs. ROSE ABBOTT.
Miss G. M. BURNS.
Miss D. D. CASSEBERE.
Mrs. WM. M. CLARKE.
Mrs. B. CHIBINACE.
Miss E. G. CROSSBIE.
Miss H. ROSEBIE.
Miss JEAN HIPACK.
Mrs. HY. B. HARRIS.
Mrs. ALEX. HALVERSON.
Miss MARGARET BAYS.
Mr. BRUCE ISMAY.
Mr. and Mrs. ED. KIMBERLEY.
Mr. F. A. KENNYMAN.
Miss EMILE KENCHEN.
Miss G. F. LONGLEY.
Mrs. A. F. LEADER.
Miss BERTHA LAVORY.
Mrs. ERNEST LIVES.
Miss MARY CLINES.
Mrs. SINGRID LINDSTROM.
Mr. GUSTAVE J. LESNEUR.
Miss GIORGETTA A. MADILL.
Mme. MELICARD.
Mrs. TUCKER and maid.
Mrs. J. B. THAYER.
Mr. J. B. THAYER, Jr.
Mr. HENRY WOOLMER.
Miss ANNA WARD.
Mr. RICHARD M. WILLIAMS.
Mrs. F. M. WARNER.
Miss HELEN A. WILSON.
Miss WILLARD.
Miss MARY WICKS.
Mrs. GEO. D. WIDENER and maid.
Mrs. J. STEWART WHITE.
Miss MARIE YOUNG.
Mrs. THOMAS POTTER, Jr.
Mrs. EDNA S. ROBERTS.
Countess of ROTHES.
Mr. C. ROLMANE.
Mrs. SUSAN P. ROGERSON. (Probably Ryerson).
Miss EMILY B. ROGERSON.
Mrs. ARTHUR ROGERSON.
Master ALLISON and nurse.
Miss K. T. ANDREWS.
Miss NINETTE PANHART.
Miss E. W. ALLEN.
Mr. and Mrs. D. BISHOP.
Mr. H. BLANK.
Miss A. BASSINA.
Mrs. JAMES BAXTER.
Mr. GEORGE A. BAYT...
Miss C. BONNELL.
Mrs. J. M. BROWN.
Miss G. C. BOWEN.
Mr. and Mrs. R. L. BECKW...
Miss RUTH TAUSSIG.
Miss ELLA THOR.
Mr. and Mrs. E. Z. TAYLOR.
GILBERT M. TUCKER.
Mr. J. B. THAYER.
Mr. JOHN B. ROGERSON.
Mrs. M. ROTHSCHILD.
Miss MADELEINE NEWELL.
Mrs. MARJORIE NEWELL.
HELEN W. NEWSOM.
Mr. FIENNAD OMOND.
Mr. E. C. OSTBY.
Miss HELEN R. OSTBY.
Mrs. MAMAM J. RENAGO.
Mlle. OLIVIA.
Mrs. D. W. MERVIN.
Mr. PHILIP EMOCK.
Mr. JAMES GOOGHT.
Miss RUBERTA MAIMY.
Mr. PIERRE MARECHAL.
Mrs. W. E. MINEHAN.
Miss APPIE RANELT.
Major ARTUR PEUCHEN.
Mrs. KARL H. BEHR.
M... ...SSETTE.
Mrs. WILLIAM BUCKNELL.
Mrs. O. H. BARKWORTH.
Mrs. H. B. STEFFASON.
Mrs. ELSIE BOWERMAN.

The Marconi station reports that it missed the word after "Mrs. Jacob P." In a list received by the Associated Press this morning this name appeared well down, but in THE TIMES list it is first, suggesting that the name of Mrs. John Jacob Astor is intended. This supposition is strengthened by the fact that, except for Mrs. H. J. Allison, Mrs. Astor is the only lady in the "A" column of the ship's passenger list attended by a maid.

NAMES PICKED UP AT BOSTON.

BOSTON, April 15.—Among the names of survivors of the Titanic picked up by wireless from the steamer Carpathia here to-night were the following:

Mr. and Mrs. L. HENRY.
Mrs. W. A. HOOPER.
Mr. MILE.
Mr. J. FLYNN.
Miss ALICE FORTUNE.
Mrs. ROBERT DOUGLAS.
Miss HILDA SLAYTER.
Mrs. P. SMITH.
Mrs. BRAHAM.
Miss LUCILLE CARTER.
Mr. WILLIAM CARTER.
Miss CUMMINGS.
Mrs. FLORENCE MARE.
Miss ALICE PHILLIPS.
Mrs. PAULA MUNGE.
Mrs. JANE ———
Miss PHYLLIS O. ———
HOWARD B. CASE.
Miss MINEHAN.
Miss BERTHA ———

to New York with 800 passengers from the steamer Titanic aboard. They are mostly women and children, the message said, and it concluded: "Grave fears are felt for the safety of the balance of the passengers and crew."

Special to The New York Times.

CAPE RACE, N. F., April 15.—The White Star liner Olympic reports by wireless this evening that the Cunarder Carpathia reached, at daybreak this morning, the position from which wireless calls for help were sent out last night by the Titanic after her collision with an iceberg. The Carpathia found only the lifeboats and the wreckage of what had been the biggest steamship afloat.

The Titanic had foundered at about 2:20 A. M., in latitude 41:46 north and longitude 50:14 west. This is about 30 minutes of latitude, or about 34 miles, due south of the position at which she struck the iceberg. All her boats are accounted for and about 655 souls have been saved of the crew and passengers, most of the latter presumably women and children.

There were about 2,100 persons aboard the Titanic.

The Leyland liner California is remaining and searching the position of the disaster, while the Carpathia is returning to New York with the survivors.

It can be positively stated that up to 11 o'clock to-night nothing whatever had been received at or heard by the Marconi station here to the effect that the Parisian, Virginian or any other ships had picked up any survivors, other than those picked up by the Carpathia.

First News of the Disaster.

The first news of the disaster to the Titanic was received by the Marconi wireless station here at 10:25 o'clock last night [as told in yesterday's New York Times.] The Titanic was first heard giving the distress signal "C. Q. D.," which was answered by a number of ships, including the Carpathia,

"All the News That's Fit to Print."

The New York Times.

THE WEATHER. Fair to-day; fair, colder to-morrow; fresh westerly winds.

VOL. LVII...NO. 18,164. * * NEW YORK, FRIDAY, OCTOBER 18, 1907.—EIGHTEEN PAGES And Part I. of Autumn Review of Books. ONE CENT In Greater New York, Jersey City, and Newark. { Elsewhere, TWO CENTS.

ANK HERE IS SAFE IN HEINZE CRASH

learing House Committee Finds the Mercantile National in Sound Condition.

UTTE BANK CLOSES DOORS

tto Heinze & Co. Suspended from Stock Exchange—Ridgely Likely to Succeed Heinze in the Mercantile.

At the instance of the New York Clear- House Committee, which met late sterday afternoon, an examination of e Mercantile National Bank, from the esidency of which F. Augustus Heinze signed in the morning, was made last ght. For this work the committee se- cted James G. Cannon, Vice President the Fourth National Bank; Edward wnsend, President of the Importers and aders' Bank, and Walter E. Frew, Vice resident of the Corn Exchange Bank. arly this morning they made a report, ying that the bank5s capital was intact, d that it would open for business as ual this morning.

In addition to this move by the Clearing ouse, Mr. Heinze's resignation was fol- wed by announcements of the suspen- n of Otto Heinze & Co. on the Stock xchange and the closing of Heinze's itte Savings Bank.

At the meeting at the Clearing House the afternoon there were present J. dward Simmons, President of the Fourth ational Bank, and Alexander Gilbert, resident of the Clearing House and of e Market and Fulton National Bank, esides three members of the official earing House Committee—William A. ash, President of the Corn Exchange ank; Dumont Clarke, President of the merican Exchange National Bank, and dward Townsend. James T. Woodward, resident of the Hanover National Bank d Chairman of the Clearing House ommittee, was out of town, as was also . Barton Hepburn, President of the hase National Bank and another mem- er of the committee.

During the meeting the affairs of the ercantile National and the events of e last few days in Wall Street, partic- arly the sensational incidents connected ith the United Copper Company, were refully gone over, and the resolution ached to make an examination of the ercantile National at once, that insti- tion being a member of the Clearing ouse, and therefore subject to examina- on by it. It was virtually decided that the examination proved the bank to in sound condition the Clearing House, hich means all the great banks which e members of it, would stand by the ercantile National and see it through ny troubles which might follow the vents of the last few days.

The committee, therefore, selected the ankers named to make the examination, nd this committee went up to the West- rn Union Building, where the Mercan- le National Bank offices are, and be- an an examination of its books, which sted far into the night. Practically all he officers of the bank and the greater art of the clerical staff remained on and to help the committee in the work.

Upon leaving the bank the committee ent immediately to the home of J. Ed- ard Simmons, at 28 West Fifty-second treet. At midnight the following state- ent was given out by Mr. Simmons:

"Mr. Nash, the Acting Chairman of he Clearing House Committee, states hat the committee, with the full co-op- ration of the officers and Directors of he Mercantile National Bank, made an xamination of its condition after the ose of business to-day. The examina- on was very thorough, and was not ompleted until a late hour. Mr. Nash nd his associates were convinced from he result of the examination that the ank was perfectly solvent and able to eet all its indebtedness. The capital of 3,000,000 is intact and with a large sur- lus."

Mr. Simmons was asked if this meant that the Clearing House had decided to tand by the bank in case there was a un.

"There certainly can be no other mean- ng to the action the Clearing House has aken," he said.

Mr. Simmons said the bank would open ts doors this morning, as though nothing ad happened.

"Has it been decided yet who will be the President of the Mercantile National?" Mr. Simmons was asked.

"There is little doubt that Mr. Ridgely vill accept the Presidency," he replied. He has not yet signified his intention f accepting, but I am quite sure he will ake the position offered him."

Charles A. Hanna, the National bank xaminer in this city, made arrangements o receive a duplicate report from the Clearing House Examination Committee or the purpose of informing Controller of the Currency Ridgely of the status of he bank.

Heinze Out; Offer to Ridgely.

An offer of the Presidency was made o Mr. Ridgely in Washington in the norning by telegraph, following the res- gnation of F. Augustus Heinze, who withdrew from the office after a pro- racted meeting of the Board of Directors. The Directors met at 11 o'clock in the morning and were in constant session until after 1 o'clock. It was then an- nounced that Mr. Heinze had resigned the Presidency. In doing so he made the following explanation:

In view of the difficulties in which my brother's firm finds itself, I have determined that it is proper that I should give liberally of my time in assisting them to straighten out their affairs. In aid of this, I have, after consulting with my fellow-Directors of the bank and my personal friends, and consulting as well my own personal interests as a large stockholder of the bank, this day resigned as its President, remaining, however, as a Di- rector, and have joined with by fellow-Directors in a request that Mr. Ridgely accept the place made vacant by my resignation.

The condition of the Mercantile and the effects upon it of the developments of the last few days in the affairs of the copper company of its former Presi- dent were carefully gone into. The dis- cussion of the situation was vigorous, and there were plainly differences of opinion, but the final result of the meeting was

Continued on Page 4.

AMERICAN HOTEL FOR BERLIN.

It Hears of a Colossal Structure to be Run on Our Lines.

Special Cable to THE NEW YORK TIMES.

BERLIN, Oct. 17.—It is announced here that an American syndicate has acquired a block of choice property in Berlin at the corner of the Unter den Linden and Pariser-Platz, for the pur- pose of erecting a colossal building containing a palatial hotel, a grand opera house, and a roof garden, the whole establishment to be run upon American lines.

The opera house, it is stated, will have seating capacity for three thou- sand persons.

It is understood the plans for the colossal edifice will soon be laid before the Kaiser with a request for his ap- proval of them. His assent will have to be given before the building can be erected. It is said the structure will cover more ground than is covered by the Waldorf-Astoria, and that it will exceed in magnificence any building of its kind in Europe.

AGED WOMAN'S BACK BROKEN.

Struck by an Auto While Returning from Father Mayer's Funeral.

Mrs. Amelia Greenblatt of 115 East Eighth Street attended the funeral yester- day of her late pastor, the Rev. John B. Mayer, in the St. Nicholas Roman Catho- lic Church in Second Street. The service ended at noon and Mrs. Greenblatt started from the church to go to her home.

She crossed the sidewalk and stepped into Second Avenue almost in front of an automobile driven by Rudolph Plain of 379 Gates Avenue, Brooklyn. Plain, who was driving from the Williamsburg Bridge toward Bond Street, sounded his horn loudly as he came down the avenue into which throngs were flocking from the church.

The loud blast of the horn startled Mrs. Greenblatt, who is 54 years old, and she stood still, apparently stupefied by her danger. Plain put on his brakes and tried to swing his machine to one side. Before he could stop the car, however, it had struck the woman and flung her to one side against the curbstone.

Women in the crowd screamed in horror. Policeman Burke of the Fifth Street Station lifted the woman in his arms and put her in the tonneau of the auto which Plain had succeeded in stop- ping. Then he ordered the chauffeur to drive up Avenue A to Bellevue Hospital at top speed.

The trip to the hospital of more than a mile was made in less than three minutes. Physicians who examined Mrs. Green- blatt said that her spine was broken.

The Rev. Father Mayer, whose funeral Mrs. Greenblatt had attended, died on Monday at the age of 56. He was born in Germany, came here in 1870 and was ordained a priest and assigned to the St. Nicholas Church seven years later. His long pastorate there endeared him to the German population of the parish over which he presided and hundreds visited the church yesterday.

PUMP THEM IN—KIPLING.

Immigration of Whites to Canada Will Keep Out Yellow Men.

TORONTO, Oct. 17.—"Pump in the im- migrants from the old country; pump them in."

That is the solution Rudyard Kipling suggests for the Asiatic problem on the Pacific Coast. Mr. Kipling, accompanied by his wife, arrived here last night from a tour of the Canadian Northwest.

"Immigration is what Canada wants in the west," said Mr. Kipling. "You must have laborers there. You want immigra- tion, and the way to keep the yellow man out is to get the white man in. If you keep out the white then you will have the yellow man, for you must have labor. Work must be done and there is certain work a white man won't do so long as he can get a yellow man to do it. Pump in the immigrants from the old country. Pump them in. England has five millions of people to spare."

Mr. Kipling expressed the opinion that both in the mother country and in Can- ada the labor party is opposed to immi- gration. "In England," he said, "the party is opposed to immigration because it would remove its great grievance with regard to the unemployed. In Canada there is a feeling in opposition to immi- gration because labor feels that it will be swamped."

Mr. Kipling, on being asked if the state- ment which appeared in a local paper that he was in Canada on behalf of the British Government and to formulate a scheme for their consideration as to Asiatic im- migration was true, laughed and said: "I have still some sense of humor left." Pressed for an answer in the affirmative or negative, he said, laughing merrily: "Well, say that I am."

GOV. SMITH FREES SLAYER.

Atlanta People Think He Indorses the Unwritten Law.

Special to The New York Times.

ATLANTA, Oct. 17.—By granting a par- don to L. D. Strong of Macon to-day, Gov. Hoke Smith, in the opinion of many here, indorsed the "unwritten law."

Six months ago Strong, who is a promi- nent business man of Macon, killed Henry Smith, a Macon merchant, alleging, on the girl's confession, that Smith had mis- treated Strong's 16-year-old sister. Strong went to Smith's place of business and shot him five times in the presence of many people. Smith lived a few minutes, and as he died, swore that he was inno- cent. Public sympathy was with Strong, but the jury convicted him and he was sent to the penitentiary. At once a move- ment for pardon was begun, and it cul- minated to-day when Gov. Smith, on the recommendation of a prison commission, gave him freedom.

MAGILL ON THE STAND.

Says Nagging of His Mother and Sister Caused Wife's Despondency.

DECATUR, Ill., Oct. 17.—Taking the stand to-day in his own behalf, Fred H. Magill, accused of murdering his first wife in order that he might wed Faye Graham, told in a matter-of-fact way of the events that led up to Mrs. Magill's death and the finding of her body by him the next morning.

Just before he retired that night, the witness said, his wife requested him to get her a bottle of beer. He got a bottle from the ice chest and then retired. In the morning when he awoke he saw his wife was not around. He made search of the house and found her in the spare room, lying with a blanket wrapped tight- ly around her head. He spoke to her, but got no reply, and upon examination he found she was dead. Witness said he de- tected the odor of chloroform.

Asked what, in his opinion, caused his wife's despondency he replied:

"Her headaches and the nagging of my mother and sister."

Magill was on the stand four hours. His testimony concluded the case for the de- fense.

CONRIED AND BOYD AT ODDS IN STOCKS

Opera Director's Brother Han- dled the Dealings of the Opera House Superintendent.

PROFIT FIGURES WIDE APART

$40,000, Says Boyd, Perhaps $300, Says Conried, and He'll Pay in Due Time.

Feeling that he was not getting rich enough from his salary as Superintendent of the Metropolitan Opera House and having heard of the many opportunities for obtaining money following the antics of the bulls and bears in Wall Street, Andrew Boyd who, besides having been Superintendent of the Opera House for many years is a close personal friend of Heinrich Conried, decided last January that he would take a little flyer in stocks with his savings. To-day he is a sadder, but wiser man. He met the same fate as many other lambs, though, he says, in a different way from many of them.

In his career in the theatrical business Mr. Boyd has always made it a prac- tice to lay aside a little for a rainy day. This little he put in the bank from time to time until it grew to $1,000. Then he bought a bond. This nucleus made him all the more anxious to save, and another bond and yet others were added to the savings until the amount had reached about $10,000, all in interest bearing bonds.

Then, last January, when the stock market was active, Mr. Boyd grew inter- ested in it through Alexander Conried, a stock broker, brother of Heinrich Con- ried, Director of the Metropolitan Opera Company.

Alexander Conried has no office, and, so far as known, he has no direct con- nection with any brokerage firm in "the Street." He is what is known as a "wandering broker," taking business from whom he can get it and putting it where he thinks it will be to his best advantage. Mr. Boyd says he gave Mr. Conried $6,000 to be used as margin in stock specula- tions.

The stocks that Conried bought for Boyd, copper being among the number, began to drop rapidly. The $6,000 in margins soon became $5,000, then $4,000, $3,000, $2,000, and $1,000, and when the $500 mark had been reached, according to Boyd, Conried told him he would have to advance more money if he would save the $6,000 he had already put up.

Then it is said he gave Conried $4,000 in bonds as additional margins. This money Boyd thought had saved the day for him. He watched the quotations in the papers, and each day he noticed, so he says, that his stocks were get- ting better and better. Finally he fig- ured out for himself a large profit, and asked Mr. Conried for it. He says he didn't get it, and on this point Mr. Con- ried agrees with him, but adds that there were no such profits as Mr. Boyd had figured out.

Mr. Boyd took his side of the case to a lawyer yesterday. When Mr. Conried heard of this he consented to give his version of the affair, and it is a very dif- ferent version, to a TIMES reporter.

"My trades for Mr. Boyd were just the same as trades for all other clients," he said.

"Mr. Boyd did put up margins for me to buy stocks for him, but it is absurd to say that I made $40,000 in the market for him and failed to turn it over to him. I bought copper around 118 and it went off. I bought other stocks for him and they went up. I really think that the amount of his winnings in the market would reach only about $300.

"It is quite true that when I closed out his account I owed him several thousand dollars, and could not pay it to him at the time the account was closed because the money was locked up in several other ac- counts, and I had to wait until they were straightened out. I have paid him a part of the money, and expect to close out the balance within a few days. The whole thing is really very greatly exaggerated."

J. VIPOND DAVIES HURT.

Consulting Engineer Stops Runaway and Saves Children—His Hip Broken.

J. Vipond Davies, chief consulting en- gineer of the Hudson Tunnel Company, who lives in 24 Bowne Avenue, Flushing, Queens Borough, had one hip broken and received internal injuries yesterday morn- ing while preventing a team of runaway horses from running down a group of school children.

Mr. Davies was on his way through Amity Street, Flushing, to the Main Street railroad station to catch the 8:30 o'clock train for Long Island City, when two teams of horses hitched to moving vans, owned by G. Anderson & Son, which were backed against the sidewalk, took fright at an automobile driven by William Haak of Franklin Place. One of the teams became unmanagable and started off.

The horses were heading direct toward a group of school children when Mr. Davies sprang and caught the nearest horse by the bridle. He was swung from his feet, but managed to change the course of the team from the street to- ward the sidewalk.

Mr. Davies was clinging to the bridle when the team crashed into a tree. He was thrown against the tree and fell to the ground so that the front wheels of the van passed over his legs. The team was checked by the collision and the horses were quickly caught, while Mr. Davies was picked up and carried into the office of Dr. E. T. Lawrence at 147 Amity Street.

When Mr. Davies learned the extent of his injuries, at his own request he was taken to his home. His condition is said to be serious.

THIS ISSUE OF THE NEW YORK TIMES includes AUTUMN BOOK LIST NUMBER of The New York Times Saturday Review (FIRST SECTION)

Second Section To-morrow.

FIRST WIRELESS PRESS MESSAGE ACROSS THE ATLANTIC

Signalizing the Opening of the Marconi Service to the Public, and Conveying a Message of Congratulation from Privy Councillor Baron Avebury, Formerly Sir John Lubbock.

Form 13

THE WESTERN UNION TELEGRAPH COMPANY.

INCORPORATED

24,000 OFFICES IN AMERICA. CABLE SERVICE TO ALL THE WORLD.

This Company TRANSMITS and DELIVERS messages only on conditions limiting its liability, which have been assented to by the sender of the following message. Errors can be guarded against only by repeating a message back to the sending station for comparison, and the Company will not hold itself liable for errors or delays in transmission or delivery of Unrepeated Messages, beyond the amount of tolls paid thereon, nor in any case where the claim is not presented in writing within sixty days after the message is filed with the Company for transmission.

This is an UNREPEATED MESSAGE, and is delivered by request of the sender, under the conditions named above.

ROBERT C. CLOWRY, President and General Manager.

RECEIVED at 813 Sixth Ave. Corner 46th St.

TELEPHONE: 3907 BRYANT.

1B Lr Sn Dh & 53 Collect D, P R, Land lines,

London Via Marconi Wireless Glace Bay N S Oct 17th,

Times, New York.

This message marks opening transatlantic wireless handed Marconi company for transmission Ireland Breton limited 50 words only send one many messages received Times signalize event quote trust introduction wireless more closely unite people states Great Britian who seem form one Nation though under two Governments and whose interests are really identical.

Avebury Marshall ....1210 Am Oct17th

ALWAYS OPEN. MONEY TRANSFERRED BY TELEGRAPH. CABLE OFFICE.

The above message was immediately followed by others which appear in another column of The Times this morning.

MARCONI CONGRATULATES THE NEW YORK TIMES

GLACE BAY, NOVA SCOTIA, Oct. 17.—Mr. Marconi says: "Congratulate New York Times on having received first westward press message."

FROM THE PRIME MINISTER OF FRANCE.

WEST STRAND, London, Oct. 17, via Marconi Wireless Telegraph to Glace Bay, N. S.—THE NEW YORK TIMES's Paris correspondent forwards to me the following message for transmission across the Atlantic by Marconi wireless telegraph:

"Dans l'inauguration du prodigieux mode de communication mis désormais à leur disposition, les deux grandes républiques ne peuvent que trouver une heureuse occasion de se feliciter et de formuler les voeux les plus cordiaux pour le mantien de la paix dans le travail pour le bonheur des peuples dans la solidarité."

"CLEMENCEAU."

[Translation.]

In the inauguration of the marvelous means of communication put at their disposition from this time forward, the two great Republics could not but find it a happy occasion to congratulate themselves and to express the most cordial wishes for the maintenance of peace in the work for the happiness of the people in the joint responsibility.

CLEMENCEAU.

MISS VANDERBILT MUST TAKE CHANCES

By No Means Certain She Will Be Admitted to Austrian Court in Vienna.

A HIGH OFFICIAL SAYS SO

Unless Emperor Dispenses with Proof of Considerable Ancestral Nobil- ity She Will Be Shut Out.

Special Cable to THE NEW YORK TIMES.

VIENNA, Oct. 17.—A Court official of high rank, of whom I inquired what would be Miss Gladys Vanderbilt's status with respect to the Court in the event of her marriage to Count Sze- chenyi, said:

"The lady in question would be re- ceived at Court in Budapest, but not in Vienna, unless the Emperor should dispense with the proof of nobility with respect to sixteen of her ancestors, which otherwise she would be required by Austrian Court etiquette to furnish.

"Such a concession is sometimes made, and very likely it would be made in the case we are speaking of, out of consideration for the social standing of Count Szechenyi and the importance of the Vanderbilt family."

It seems, in view of this authoritative statement, that Miss Vanderbilt, if she marries the Count, may find herself in a rather unpleasant predicament when she comes to live in Vienna.

NEWPORT, Oct. 17.—Miss Gladys Van- derbilt is not spending all the time with her fiancé, Count Szechenyi, although he is a guest at her mother's house. This morning she was at the Casino with a number of young women friends, the Count remaining at The Breakers.

At noon she drove about town in her basket phaeton with her chum, Miss Jo- sephine Pearson. They had a "college ice" together in a Thames Street drug store. Miss Vanderbilt seemed to be thoroughly enjoying the absence of a crowd of curious sightseers, and to fully appreciate the fact that she was being left entirely unnoticed.

This evening Miss Vanderbilt and Count Szechenyi attended a dinner given in their honor by Mrs. Charles H. Baldwin at Snug Harbor, and later accompanied Mrs. Baldwin and her other guests to the Opera House to see William Collier in "Caught in the Rain." This was Miss Vanderbilt's first appearance at the New- port Opera House since her engagement, and she and the Count were naturally the centre of attraction between the acts.

H. P. WHITNEY ARRESTED?

Colorado Authorities Accues Visitors of Slaughtering Deer Wantonly.

Special to The New York Times.

DENVER, Col., Oct. 17.—Two men who say they are Frank Carnegie, nephew of Andrew Carnegie, and Harry Payne Whit- ney of New York, came to Colorado two weeks ago to hunt bear. They hired guides and started out with a pack of hounds. Reaching the game country, they began to slaughter deer promiscuously, both for the sport and for bait for traps.

Deputy Warden Bush finally arrested the hunters and their guides, took them before a Justice of the Peace, and prose- cuted them for wanton destruction of deer. Bush says he had an offer of $300 to drop the case before the trial. After the trial began, he says, the Justice was called out of court by his wife, and when he returned he dismissed the case. The State Game Warden is investigating the case.

ROCKEFELLER TOO SAVING.

Supt. Jones of Forest Hill Resigns Be- cause Expenses Are Cut.

Special to The New York Times.

CLEVELAND, Oct. 17.—Asserting that John D. Rockefeller wants to cut ex- penses too much, C. C. Jones, for some seven months superintendent of the Forest Hill estate, has resigned, and will leave for New York on Nov. 15. Jones says that Rockefeller insisted on curtail- ing expenses to such an extent that he could not keep up the place. He allowed some trimming of costs when he took the position, but recently, he says, Mr. Rockefeller wanted to reduce the pay of the men and he demurred. An argument followed and Mr. Jones resigned.

"When I came here I thought I was to run the estate," said Mr. Jones, "but soon found that such was not the case. Mr. Rockefeller insisted on changes and orders that I did not believe were for the best, and I found that I couldn't look after the place as it should be and follow the suggestion that he made, so I quit."

SAVED BY SENATOR SCOTT.

He Stops Runaway and Rescues Two Mexican Women.

Special to The New York Times.

CITY OF MEXICO, Oct. 17.—United States Senator Nathan B. Scott of West Virginia, here on a pleasure trip, made a daring rescue of two prominent Mexican women in a runaway accident in one of the principal streets here last evening.

Senator Scott, who is almost 65 years old, jumped from the sidewalk, seized the reins, and stopped the runaway horses after a desperate struggle.

Latest Shipping News.

Arrived—S. S. Emilia, Trieste, Sept. 4; S. S. Olinda, Nuevitas; S. S. Fagertun, Port Antonio.

DEUTSCHLAND STUCK CLOSE TO HER PIER

Capt. Kaempff Gives Up Attempt to Get Liner Off After Three Hours' Work.

PASSENGERS SENT TO BED

Hundreds of Friends Exchange Greet- ings with Them as Seven Tugs Strive in Vain.

The Hamburg-American liner Deutsch- land from Hamburg for this port, stuck in the mud last night in the Hudson River, with her big freeboard actually scraping against the end of her Hoboken pier. After waiting for nearly three hours in the hope that the big ship might be warped into her dock, her 500 cabin passengers and 300 steerage passengers reluctantly went to bed, convinced that it would be morning before they could set foot on American soil.

During the time that a flotilla of tugs struggled to pull the ship off the mud and up to her pier hundreds of persons wait- ing to welcome home-coming voyagers lined the pier, exchanging greetings with the marooned passengers, for though the boat touched her pier there was no way for the passengers to reach it except by sliding down a forty-foot rope ladder, and this Capt. Kaempff would not permit.

The accident came as a climax to a voyage replete with fog and rough weath- er. Soon after leaving Hamburg the liner ran into weather that compelled her to slacken speed, and soon after there fol- lowed forty-eight hours of dense fog. De- layed by these conditions, the Deutsch- land did not reach Quarantine until 9 o'clock last night, instead of early yes- terday morning, when she was due.

It was an hour later before the big boat slowed down near her pier to let the tugs make their lines fast to her. Usually there are at least fourteen tugs employed to swing the steamship into her dock, but last night only seven an- swered Capt. Kaempff's call.

Six of these made lines fast to one side to pull the stern around, while the other made fast to her bow, against which it shoved, apparently without effect. The tugs puffed and steamed, but the ship scarcely moved, and in the meantime the tide was rapidly running out.

For half an hour the struggle was kept up, and then the Deutschland's keel touched bottom. Amidships, one side of the boat grated against the pier, while the bow and stern swung far away from the structure.

WIRELESS JOINS TWO WORLDS

Marconi Transatlantic Service Opened with a Dispatch to The New York Times.

MESSAGES FROM EMINENT MEN

Prime Minister Clemenceau, the Duke of Argyll, Lord Avebury and Others Send Greetings.

10,000 WORDS THE FIRST DAY

Marconi in Personal Supervision at Glace Bay and Greatly Pleased with the Results.

SIR HIRAM MAXIM'S TRIBUTE

His Message to Peter Cooper Hewitt in New York, Who is Trying to Pick Up the Oversea Messages.

By Marconi Transatlantic Wire- less Telegraph to The New York Times.

LONDON, Oct. 17.—This mes- sage marks the opening of the transatlantic wireless service. It is handed to the Marconi Company here for transmission to Ireland, and thence to Cape Breton, Nova Scotia, and New York. As it is limited to fifty words, I can send at present only one of the many messages received for transmission to The New York Times to sig- nalize the event. This message, from Privy Councillor Lord Ave- bury, formerly Sir John Lubbock, follows:

"I trust that the introduction of the wireless will more closely unite the people of the United States and Great Britain, who seem to form one nation, though under two Gov- ernments, and whose interests are really identical. AVEBURY."

MARCONI'S CONGRATULATIONS.

The above message, received early yesterday morning, was quickly followed by one from The Times's correspondent at Glace Bay, as follows:

"Glace Bay, N. S., Oct. 17.

"Mr. Marconi says: 'Congrat- ulate New York Times on having received first westward press mes- sage.'"

Then came in full the original message filed by The Times's cor- respondent in London, from which the short dispatch above was con- densed, to meet the fifty-word limit imposed by the Marconi Company upon the first message transmit- ted. The full message follows:

MESSAGES FROM EMINENT MEN.

By Marconi Transatlantic Wire- less Telegraph to The New York Times.

LONDON, Oct. 17.—This mes- sage marks the opening of the transatlantic wireless service. It is now eleven years since William Marconi, in May, 1896, announced in New York that he had discov- ered the secret by which messages might be flashed through space without the assistance of wires or cables such as were used in the or- dinary methods of telegraphy at that time. Mr. Marconi's state- ments were received with skepti- cism, and his prediction of the won- ders which he felt confident could be worked by means of his applica- tion of the Hertzian waves was openly disputed even by electricians, who ought, from their knowledge of the feats achieved by the electric spark, to have recognized that the limits of its potentialities had not been reached.

Mr. Marconi, as this message tes- tifies, has now accomplished all that he expressed his confidence in being able to do. This message, which I have handed in at th Lon-

"All the News That's Fit to Print."

The New York Times.

THE WEATHER.

Fair to-day and probably Friday; wind light to fresh southwest.

VOL. LVII...NO. 18,492. * * * * NEW YORK, THURSDAY, SEPTEMBER 10, 1908.—SIXTEEN PAGES. ONE CENT In Greater New York, Jersey City, and Newark { Elsewhere, TWO CENTS.

BOSSES HAVE DECIDED TO ACCEPT HUGHES

Parsons, Whom the "Test" Results in Manhattan Surprised, Admits It.

RENOMINATION NOW SURE

The Governor Will Have 513 Delegates at Least, 8 More Than Are Needed—Woodruff Talks.

Developments in the Republican camp yesterday practically insure the renomination of Gov. Hughes at the Republican State Convention, which will meet in Saratoga next Monday.

While there was at first an effort among the Republican leaders who have opposed the Governor's renomination to magnify the opposition shown in the primary "tests" on Tuesday and to minimize the pro-Hughes sentiment, President Herbert Parsons of the Republican County Committee lost no time in climbing down from the fence and making a dash for the Hughes band wagon.

Republican State Chairman Timothy L. Woodruff gave out a long statement in which he sought to justify the objections of the anti-Hughes leaders to the Governor's renomination. Chairman Woodruff did not deviate yesterday from the position he has maintained for the last few weeks—that "the delegates must decide." It is asserted, though, that Mr. Parsons is not playing a lone game, but merely had the good sense to head a procession that may develop into a foot race of bosses and bosslets into the Governor's camp, and that Mr. Woodruff in all probability will be the second in line.

Test Made It Clear—Parsons.

President Parsons, who has been subjected to a great deal of pressure emanating from Oyster Bay and from the managers of the Taft campaign, made his first open statement on the question of the Governor's renomination yesterday. He said:

"The result of the test votes taken in this county shows that a considerable majority of the enrolled Republicans prefer that Gov. Hughes should be renominated. We took the test to put the question up to them, and, if their desires were explicit, to act accordingly. The test shows that there is some bitter opposition. But in view of the controlling sentiment in favor of the Governor's renomination, which the test has made clear, it is my opinion that a large majority of the delegates from New York County to the State Convention will favor Gov. Hughes's renomination."

Hughes Sure of 513 Delegates.

If President Parsons, who will control the delegation from New York County, makes good his statement, the renomination of Gov. Hughes is assured. New York County has 187 delegates in the State Convention. A simple majority of one from that number will give the Governor 94 of the New York delegates.

The number of delegates from up State either instructed for, committed to, or reliably classed for Gov. Hughes, number 362. Friends of State Chairman Timothy L. Woodruff, who is leader of the Republican organization in Kings County, admit that 57 of the delegates from Kings at least will go to the State Convention either pledged to or instructed for Gov. Hughes.

This will give the Governor a total of 513 delegates, according to the present line-up. Only 505 delegates are needed to nominate. And a dozen counties, with an approximate aggregate of 100 delegates, are in the doubtful column, with a probability that a majority will go to the convention to work for the renomination of Gov. Hughes when they learn that a large majority of the New York delegates will be for the Governor, and that nothing can be gained by opposing his renomination.

Those Pledged to Him Now.

Here is a list of up-State counties where the delegates have either been instructed for Gov. Hughes, stand committed to him, or can be depended upon to be for his renomination at the Saratoga Convention:

County	Delegates	County	Delegates
Broome	12	Monroe	56
Cattaraugus	11	Nassau	9
Cayuga	12	Oneida	22
Chautauqua (2 A.D.)	8	Oswego	12
Chenango	7	Rensselaer	19
Clinton	7	Rockland	5
Cortland	6	Saratoga	11
Delaware	9	Schuyler	4
Dutchess (1 A.D.)	7	Steuben	15
Erie	53	Suffolk (2 A.D.)	3
Franklin	8	Tompkins	6
Greene	6	Westchester	29
Herkimer	9	Wyoming	6
*Jefferson	13	Yates	4
Lewis	5		
Total			362

*All of 1st and part of 2d A. D.

In the Doubtful Column.

Here are the counties placed by the leaders in the doubtful column:

County	Delegates	County	Delegates
Essex	6	Seneca	5
Orange (1 A.D.)	9	Sullivan	5
Otsego	8	Ulster	14
Queens	18	Washington	9
St. Lawrence	18		
Total			93

The Anti-Hughes Force.

Here are the up-State counties which either have elected or will elect anti-Hughes delegates:

County	Delegates	County	Delegates
Albany	28	Orange (1 A.D.)	8
Chemung	8	Putnam	3
Columbia	7	Richmond	8
Dutchess (part 2 A. D.)	7	Schenectady	11
		Schoharie	5
Fulton and Hamilton	5	Suffolk (2 A.D.)	7
		Tioga	6
Jefferson (2 A.D.)	1	Warren	6
Montgomery	8	Wayne	9
Niagara	13		
Ontario	9		
Total			143

These delegates have been instructed for Senator Horace White of Syracuse or Speaker James W. Wadsworth, Jr.:

FOR WADSWORTH.

County	Delegates	County	Delegates
Allegheny	9	Livingston	7
Chautauqua (1 A.D.)	10	Orleans	6
Genesee	7		
Total			39

FOR WHITE.

County	Delegates	County	Delegates
Onondaga	30	Madison	8
Total			38

Both State Chairman Woodruff and County President Herbert Parsons of the Republican County Committee said yesterday that it would be futile to attempt at this time to figure out to a mathematical certainty how many delegates from their respective bailiwicks would be against the Governor at the convention. These delegates, it would seem, constitute about the only element of uncertainty in the situation, but in the aggregate they will not have any effect on the result.

Self-Justification by Woodruff.

The analysis by State Chairman Woodruff of the result of the primary test was strangely in contrast with the statement of President Parsons, based on the returns from the districts in which the primary test was made. While President Parsons insisted that the returns disclosed a decided Hughes sentiment, Mr. Woodruff in his statement asserted that these same returns justified the declaration of the leader that the Governor was unpopular with the Republican voters. Mr. Woodruff said:

"The magnitude of the opposition man-

Continued on Page 2.

NO WATER TO FIGHT A FIRE.

Low Pressure Gives Brooklyn Factory Blaze a Dangerous Start.

Inadequate water pressure permitted a fire which started shortly before midnight last night on the third floor of the six-story factory building at 552 to 556 State Street, Brooklyn, to spread so rapidly that twenty minutes after the fire had been discovered Deputy Fire Chief Lally sent in five alarms.

For ten or fifteen minutes after their arrival the firemen were unable to throw streams of water into the flames, and even after that time the pressure was not up to the standard. The water tower threw a spray of water which might almost have come from an atomizer, so small was it.

By midnight every one of the six floors, which were occupied by the Empire Cork Specialty Company, was in flames, and fire was leaping out of all the windows and threatening momentarily to communicate the blaze to the tenements on either side of the factory or to those in the rear of it in Atlantic Avenue. The tenants in these buildings were ordered out by the police.

It took the reserves from five precincts to handle the crowds, which were record ones, for Brooklyn. Deputy Commissioner Baker took charge of the police.

Chief Croker and Deputy Fire Commissioner Wise responded to the fifth alarm, and Chief Croker took command. By 12:30 o'clock he believed that it was under control. The tenements adjoining the burning building on both sides had been somewhat injured by flames.

The damage was estimated at $75,000 to the building and stock of the cork company. The factory is owned by Percy G. Williams, the theatrical manager:

The blaze tied up the trolley cars, which run through Atlantic Avenue or up Flatbush Avenue from Fulton and Livingston Streets. The lines affected included the Flatbush Avenue, Seventh Avenue, St. John's Place, Fifth Avenue, and Third Avenue.

TESTS CHURCH WELCOMES.

Minister, Disguised as Workingman, Cordially Greeted in All But One.

Special to The New York Times.

CHICAGO, Sept. 9.—To disprove the assertion of the Socialists that the churches only welcome the rich and scorn the workingman, the Rev. John Thompson, pastor of the McCabe M. E. Church, spent his August vacation disguised as a workingman and attending services at nine wealthy churches of the city.

In a threadbare and shiny blue serge coat, trousers that were worn at the edges, a cheap cotton shirt and tie, old shoes and a black felt hat, the minister was so well disguised that even his friends might have passed him by. In fact he sat in a street car beside one of the members of his own congregation and was not noticed.

"I made the experiment," he said today, "to find what, if any, truth there might be in the charge that the workingman and the poorly dressed visitor are not made welcome in our churches. I found, as I had hoped, that it was just the other way.

"In the nine churches that I visited I found the congregation always attentive, and in eight of the churches the ministers were cordial. In the ninth, I must say, I was surprised to see how crusty the minister was, and I was practically repulsed when I spoke to him at the end of the service."

THINK PRISONER IS MONROE.

Man in Trenton Jail Said to Answer the Desperado's Description.

Special to The New York Times.

TRENTON, Sept. 9.—"Samuel Worthington," who was arrested here for stealing a ride on a train and is now serving thirty days in jail, may prove to be "Bill" Monroe, the Orange County desperado, who is wanted for assault and arson at Middletown, N. Y.

Monroe has been chased in many directions by Sheriffs' posses. Only recently he attended the fair at Middletown, N. Y., disguised as a woman and tacked a notice on a tree stating that he had made such a visit.

"Worthington" gave his address as Middletown, and admitted that he had been arrested once for horse stealing and another time for assault. He said that he served time for these offenses in Pennsylvania.

Squire Manfred Naar, who committed Worthington to jail, communicated with the Sheriff of Orange County asking that some one who knows Monroe be sent to Trenton to see whether Worthington is the much-sought-for outlaw. A Deputy Sheriff of Orange County has started for this city for this purpose.

GLAD HE LED LYNCHERS.

Ex-Senator Sullivan Will Stand Consequences for Directing Shooting.

MEMPHIS, Sept. 9.—A special from Oxford, Miss., quotes former United States Senator W. V. Sullivan as follows with reference to the lynching last night:

"I led the mob which lynched Nelse Patton, and I'm proud of it. I directed every movement of the mob, and I did everything I could to see that he was lynched. Cut a white woman's throat! And a negro! Of course I wanted him lynched. I saw his body dangling from a tree this morning, and I'm glad of it.

"When I heard of the horrible crime I started to work immediately to get a mob. I did all I could to raise one. I was at the jail last night and heard Judge Roane advise against lynching. I got up immediately after and urged the mob to lynch Patton.

"I roused the mob and directed it to storm the jail. I had my revolver, but did not use it. I gave it to a Deputy Sheriff and told him to 'shoot Patton, and to shoot to kill.' He used the revolver and shot. I suppose the bullets from my gun were some of those that killed the negro.

"I don't care what investigation is made, or what are the consequences. I am willing to stand them. I wouldn't mind standing the consequences any time for lynching a man who cut a white woman's throat. I will lead a mob in such a case any time."

Claim of $1,000 Filed Against Thaw.

PITTSBURG, Penn., Sept. 9.—A claim of $1,000 was filed before Referee in Bankruptcy Blair against Harry K. Thaw today by Dr. Jackson R. Campbell of New York.

CROKER IS FOR BRYAN, ALSO FAVORS BETTING

Thinks Republican Anti-Trust Laws Have Not Helped Condition of the Individual Citizen.

GAMBLING IS HUMAN NATURE

America with Hughes Anti-Betting Laws Is a Free Country No Longer—King Edward the Finest Sportsman.

Special Cable to THE NEW YORK TIMES.

DUBLIN, Sept. 9.—"I am out of politics," said Richard Croker to the correspondent of THE NEW YORK TIMES, who saw him to-day in his beautiful Irish home some miles out from this city. "I know nothing of what is going on, and, anyhow, there is too much water between here and America for me to do anything. Moreover, anything I do say is so misrepresented. "Why," exclaimed Mr. Croker, indignantly, "only the other day it was said that I hoped Taft would win!"

"Your sympathies are with Bryan then?" he was asked.

"Certainly, I hope Bryan will win. He would make a fine President."

"What are his chances?"

"That I do not know, but there has been a great change in public feeling in recent years."

"How will the Republican anti-trust laws affect the issue?"

"They look very nice on paper, but how do they affect the individual? Have they lessened the cost of living or increased the wages of the individual? I say they have not. I judge things by their results, and I say the individual is no better off to-day. As a matter of fact, the cost of living has never been higher and wages are no better. That is the result which has been brought about under the Republican régime."

"What do you think the Democrats will do with regard to the New York Governorship?"

"That I don't know," replied Mr. Croker, and for a moment he contemplated the graveled walk upon which we were standing. Then, looking up with a gleam of scorn in his gray eye, he said:

"Look what they've been doing there! Why, they've broken up horse racing!"

Gov. Hughes's Anti-Betting law was, in Mr. Croker's opinion, enough to damn any party.

"They are ruining the country; ruining the race tracks, in which a great deal of money is invested; ruining the breeders of horses, many of whom are breaking up their studs, and that in a free country! It is a free country no longer. You have more freedom over here. I go to race meetings here and I see a fine crowd of people, ladies and gentlemen, enjoying themselves, and King Edward himself at their head.

"King Edward is the finest sportsman in the world. If there was anything wrong in it do you think he would be at the head of all kinds of sport in this country? In London you have a national sporting club. They encourage all kinds of sport and are allowed to make a certain amount of money; the rest goes to hospitals and charities."

Mr. Croker added that he was not against a certain supervision of betting and gambling and would favor the introduction of the Paris mutuel system of betting, but he certainly would not endeavor to stop betting altogether. It was in human nature to gamble and in the spirit of free people.

"That's why it is tolerated over here; because it is the will of the people, and that's why the King is at its head."

Continuing his argument as to the ethics of gambling, Mr. Croker said it was in the very essence of human nature to gamble.

"If I insure this house," he said, indicating the beautiful mansion in which he lives, "I merely bet with the insurance company that it will be burned down, and the company bets it won't; and if I insure my horse, I bet he will break his neck, and the company takes the risk that he won't. It is the same, to a large extent, in business of all kinds."

"But, Mr. Croker, a man may bet with what he cannot afford to lose; he may mortgage his coat."

"That," replied Mr. Croker, "is his own affair. If he didn't put his money on a horse he would probably get rid of it some other way."

Mr. Croker added that there was no reason why gambling laws should not apply equally to the Stock Exchange and the race track.

"Gov. Hughes's policy," he said, "would get us back to the Puritanical days of the Know Nothings."

Mr. Croker hopes to visit New York in the Fall, but his mission there will have nothing to do with politics.

PARKER UNWILLING.

Doesn't Desire to Hold Public Office Again, He Says.

Alton B. Parker, who returned here from Washington yesterday, made it plain that, as THE TIMES indicated, he does not intend to run for Governor.

"I am not willing to run for Governor of New York," said Judge Parker. "I did not feel that the situation and the question presented justified me in saying more yesterday than that it is my desire never again to hold public office. My friends, I felt, would understand that I said precisely what I meant, and my answer was intended to inform them and no one else."

Judge Parker will entertain Mr. Bryan at dinner next Sunday.

OGDEN M. REID A REPORTER.

Starts on the Staff of His Father's Newspaper and Seems to Like It.

Ogden Mills Reid, only son of Whitelaw Reid, Ambassador to St. James's, is now hunting down the elusive political item as a reporter on his father's newspaper, The Tribune. He began yesterday, and last night he was waiting in vain at the Hotel Knickerbocker to form the acquaintance of William James Conners of Buffalo and the Democratic State Committee. Later, at an hour when the seasoned reporter would have called it a day's work, he cheerfully volunteered to go on a still hunt for Republican State Chairman Timothy L. Woodruff, who is a mighty difficult man to find after Republican State Headquarters has closed for the day.

"He takes to the work as a fish takes to water," said one of the veteran workers on The Tribune, in discussing young Mr. Reid's first day as a newspaper reporter.

Young Mr. Reid's appearance as an active worker on The Tribune staff recalls the story printed recently in THE TIMES that Whitelaw Reid had refused several offers to purchase his newspaper on the ground that he desired to leave it as a legacy to his son.

The latter is a Yale graduate of the Class of 1904. Subsequently he took a course at the Yale Law School. At the university he was chiefly noted for his interest in aquatic sports. In appearance he does not greatly resemble his father, the Ambassador.

MRS. LAWSON RESCUED AT SEA

Hangs On to Railing of Steam Yacht Capsized in Collision.

Special to The New York Times.

BOSTON, Mass., Sept. 9.—Mrs. Arnold Lawson's ability to maintain a hold on the railing of the steam yacht My Gypsy saved her from drowning this afternoon.

When the yacht was struck by the outward bound fishing vessel Boyd and Leeds Mrs. Lawson caught the railing as she was going overboard, and held on until rescued by the tug Metropolitan. At times she was immersed in the sweeping seas, but when the yacht had been righted from the effects of the collision she pluckily returned to it and informed the party of friends aboard that her experience was "nothing."

The My Gypsy, which is the yacht that Thomas W. Lawson gave his deceased wife, in charge of Capt. Crockstad, had just cleared for a short sail, and Mrs. Lawson was sitting at the stern of the boat on deck. Capt. Crockstad tried to run the My Gypsy across the bow of the schooner.

The bowsprit of the Boyd and Leeds caught the signal mast of the steam yacht. The yacht was suddenly careened to port.

Mrs. Lawson, when the boat began to capsize, was swept down the deck on her yacht chair. When the chair hit the rail she was thrown overboard, but managed to get a hold on the rail.

The big ocean tug Metropolitan closed in, and the crew reached out and hauled Mrs. Lawson aboard their boat.

THREAT TO BURN WHITEFACE.

Man Arrested for Attempt to Blackmail Mountain Lumber Company.

Special to The New York Times.

LAKE PLACID, N. Y., Sept. 9.—Probably never before has a mountain been made a medium for blackmail, but that is the use to which John St. Clair of Bloomingdale is charged with putting Mount Whiteface in a letter to the T. J. & J. Rogers Company of Ausable Forks, demanding the immediate payment of $200 under penalty of a fire, which, in addition to burning the company's holdings of about 15,000 acres of timber land about the base, would probably have swept the entire mountain, destroying forever the wonderful scenic beauty of Whiteface.

The letter was sent to the company over the name of L. H. Murphy. The company officials decided to set a trap for the man. A check for $100 was mailed to L. H. Murphy, at Bloomingdale. St. Clair, it is charged, called for mail in the name of Murphy, and he was followed to this village by ex-Sheriff S. W. Barnard. After an unsuccessful attempt to cash a check for $100 at the American House, the man succeeded in getting it cashed by a tradesman and was arrested by Deputy Sheriff Allen.

WANAMAKER BUILDING PLANS.

$6,000,000 Raised for Construction of Last Section of Philadelphia Store.

PHILADELPHIA, Sept. 9.—A mortgage for $6,000,000 on the Philadelphia store of John Wanamaker, including the property bounded by Chestnut and Market, Thirteenth and Juniper Streets, and the properties 1224 and 1226 Market Street, was recorded to-day. The mortgage, or trust deed, was to secure $6,000,000 worth of 5 per cent. five-year gold bonds, of which the Land Title and Trust Company is made trustee.

The purpose of Mr. Wanamaker is to borrow $6,000,000 and to issue 6,000 bonds of $1,000 each, secured by these properties. This, it is understood, is to complete financial arrangements by which Mr. Wanamaker will begin at once the construction of the last section of his store on the Chestnut Street side.

By the terms of the mortgage or trust deed Mr. Wanamaker can sell the old plant to replace it with the new one, but he must keep up the insurance on the properties and pay taxes, &c.

Officers of the trust company say all the bonds have been subscribed for at par by financial men of this city and New York.

TO BUY FRANKLIN HOUSE.

Say American Syndicate Has Option on Building in Paris.

PARIS, Sept. 9.—Michael J. Doyle of Philadelphia announced to-day that he had secured an option for an American syndicate upon the house in this city built and occupied by Benjamin Franklin when he was cultivating friendly relations with France during the American Revolution. The receptions given by Mr. Franklin in this house made it famous.

Subsequently Napoleon I. lived there for a time, and after his divorce from Josephine he turned the property over to her. Mr. Doyle declines to give the names of those interested or the purposes for which it is planned to use the property.

Special to The New York Times.

PHILADELPHIA, Sept. 9.—The Michael J. Doyle mentioned in a dispatch from Paris is probably Michael Francis Doyle, a well-known lawyer, who has been abroad for some time and is prominent in civic associations.

Nothing was known here of his intention to purchase the Franklin house, and if he was acting for a syndicate, it is probable that they have kept their plans secret for fear of enhancing the price.

AERONAUT AND TIGER FALL FROM BALLOON

Men, Women, and Children Flee in Terror as Animal Lands in Fair Grounds.

ATHLETE SERIOUSLY HURT

The Tiger, Uninjured by 100-Foot Drop, Takes Refuge in the Balloon Tent.

Nearly 15,000 persons, many of them children, yesterday being Children's Day at the Richmond County Fair, stood in the fair grounds at Dongan Hills, S. I., late in the afternoon looking up into the air, where young William Coby, in spangles and tights, sat smiling and bowing on a trapeze attached to a balloon which slowly rose above the heads of the crowd. The young trapezist had one arm around a pet tiger cub, which he supported on the trapeze, and which with him was soon to drop in a thrilling dive with a parachute.

Children shouted in delight, and men and women waved hats or handkerchiefs at the athlete. Suddenly from somewhere in the crowd there arose a cry. Instantly it was taken up by others, and presently the multitude were shouting to the trapezist:

"Look out! Your balloon's on fire."

Coby, looking downward, had not seen a spiral of flame which caught the eye of some one in the crowd as it ate its way around one of the hempen supports which attached the trapeze to the balloon. He was nearly 100 feet in the air, but perhaps the voices of the crowd reached his ears. At any rate he turned his eyes upward.

Then he leaped into activity. He tried to free his parachute and prepare for the leap which would enable him to float easily to the ground. But he was an instant too late, however. Before he could free the parachute the bar on which he stood working at the ropes with nervous fingers dropped from the supporting balloon.

A cry of horror arose from the crowd as Coby's figure whirled downward, spinning over and over in the air. Beside him in the downward dive shot the tiger cub, its paws and tail thrashing around in the air.

It was only a few seconds before Coby and his tiger cub struck the turf on the inside of the race track course from which they had ascended. Instantly the crowd pressed forward. But suddenly men and women, dragging children by the hands or carrying infants in their arms, turned back in a wild panic, and fled toward the grandstand, opposite which the balloon ascension had been made.

"The tiger! Look out for the tiger!" was the cry that went up.

Apparently uninjured by its fall the tiger cub made for the crowd in long leaps. Although the crowd did not know it, the animal's only object apparently was to gain the shelter of the tent used to house the balloon. Once within the tent it lay whimpering in terror.

Coby was carried to his dressing tent, and there Dr. Mord from the Smith Infirmary looked him over. He found that the man had received internal injuries and a severe concussion of the spine, and advised his immediate removal to the infirmary. He was taken there in an ambulance.

Coby is only 18 years old, and lives at 903 Bremer Street, Milwaukee. He is a professional balloonist and parachute jumper, and had been exhibiting daily at the fair since its opening on Monday. The police arrested his manager, Frank Robinson, later, asserting that he had not used proper precaution in seeing to it that the balloon and its apparatus were in proper shape before permitting the ascent. Robinson was bailed out by the officials of the fair. The balloon dropped near by, and was found to be only slightly damaged. Robinson wanted to reinflate it and make an ascent himself, but this was not allowed.

Samuel Haber of 209 Spring Street, Manhattan, got a fractured kneecap in the excitement following the fall of Coby and the tiger cub. He was running from the animal when he fell. He, also, was taken to the infirmary.

Yesterday was Democratic day at the fair, and among the visitors were Charles F. Murphy, Col. Henry Watterson, J. Hamilton Lewis, and State Chairman Conners.

HUMAN DYNAMO IN TEXAS.

Electrically Charged Boy Furnishes Power for Fan or Lights.

Special to The New York Times.

GALVESTON, Texas, Sept. 9.—A living storage battery is the only thing to which E. G. Atloy, an American born child of Russian parents, living with his widowed mother in Houston, Texas, can be compared. The boy, who is 7 years old, is a human magnet, and possesses all the electric properties of a dynamo engine in addition.

A metal filling had been put in one tooth, and when the boy came home he picked up the knob used to connect an electric fan with an electric light wire in his mother's residence and thrust it into his mouth.

A threaded metal cap was on the end which screws into the cup for the electric bulb. As the metal cap touched the metal tooth filling the boy's head jerked slightly and the fan began to revolve and then to buzz frantically at full speed. This kept up as long as the circuit was completed in the boy's mouth.

The mother was frightened and feared witchcraft, but the boy seemed pleased at the sensation.

A piece of iron held in the boy's hand for a few moments becomes highly magnetized. A hammer with an iron handle held in his hands will attract tacks at a distance of four feet.

The boy says that he feels only an agreeable sensation. He has red hair of the reddest possible hue, large freckles, and blue eyes.

FIREMAN'S SON STARTS A FIRE

Eight-Year-Old Boy Wanted to See the Engines Turn Out.

Acting Capt. Rehahn of the 152d Street Police Station was at a small fire in the cellar of the tenement at 2,805 Eighth Avenue last night, when he heard a boy say to another that he knew who started the fire. Rehahn grabbed the youth, who led him to Colonial Park, where in some bushes the policeman found eight-year-old William Donnelly, Jr., son of a fireman, who lives at 2,811 Eighth Avenue.

According to Rehahn, the boy admitted that he started the blaze to see the engines turn out. Young Donnelly was paroled in the custody of his father, who will take him to the Children's Court today to answer a charge of malicious mischief.

MRS. SAGE 80 YEARS OLD.

She Receives Many Flowers and Telegrams at Long Island Home.

Special to The New York Times.

LAWRENCE, L. I., Sept. 9.—An unusual number of parcels and telegrams came here yesterday for Mrs. Russell Sage. Most of the parcels contained flowers, and the telegrams and letters were for the most part congratulations upon her eightieth birthday.

Mrs. Sage spent the day quietly at her home. It is the cottage in which Mr. Sage died, and is one of the favorite houses maintained by Mrs. Sage.

Several friends called to pay their respects to Mrs. Sage on her birthday, but many did not know she was in town. She was pleased at the receipt of congratulations sent by institutions she had helped. She expects to remain in her Lawrence cottage thoughout September.

HARRIMAN IN FAST RUN.

Line Clear for His Special Train Speeding to Omaha.

OGDEN, Utah, Sept. 9.—E. H. Harriman's special train reached Ogden at 5:15 o'clock this afternoon. The train consists of several private cars and a baggage car. Every district on the Salt Lake Division has been kept clear during the day to give the special right of way for a record run. One of the fastest trips on record was made between these points.

After a stop of twenty minutes at Ogden, the Harriman party pulled out for Omaha, and another record run is scheduled for the thousand-mile journey.

BOSTON PAWNSHOPS BUSY.

Loans Taken Out on $425,000 Worth of Property in Two Days.

BOSTON, Sept. 9.—Personal property valued at $425,000, including more than 700 watches, was pawned in the City of Boston yesterday and to-day. O. W. Farley of the loan division of the Bureau of Criminal Investigation spent the busiest day in the history of the department recording the loans.

No reason for the unusual amount of pawning is known except that yesterday followed a holiday.

WILL BUY CHEYENNE CANYON.

New York Syndicate to Add to Attraction of Famous Scenic Resort.

Special to The New York Times.

COLORADO SPRINGS, Col., Sept. 9.—A syndicate of New York capitalists has secured an option on the famous South Cheyenne Cañon including the seven falls at the head of which Helen Hunt Jackson, the poet, was buried, also the cave of winds and the Manitou cliff dwellers' ruins.

The purchase price is given by Attorney R. S. Ellis, who represents the owners, as $500,000. Although a payment has been made, the names of the purchasers are withheld at present. The buyers plan considerable outlay to add to the attraction of these famous scenic environs, which are visited by thousands of tourists annually.

RETALIATE ON ERIE ROAD.

$2 a Mile Charge for Observation Engine Forces Inquiry by State Board.

Special to The New York Times.

TRENTON, Sept. 9.—The State Railroad Commission is indignant at the proposition of the Erie Railroad to the effect that it will charge $2 a mile for an observation engine for a tour of inspection by the commission over the Erie lines in this State. This would make the trip cost the State $800. The Commissioners aver that there must be something radically wrong with the Erie lines that the officials should seek to put such a price on an observation engine for the use of the three Commissioners to get the best possible view of the tracks, &c.

In retaliation the commission has put all of its force of inspectors on the Erie lines, and will order a thorough report of the Erie system at once.

Under the law the commission is entitled to ride free of expense on all lines in the State, but the law is silent on observation engines.

GUN FIGHT TO CATCH WOMAN.

Alleged Black Hand Agent Opens Fire on Officers Who Try to Capture Her.

BESSEMER, Mich., Sept. 9.—Mrs. Frank Galler, who, it is alleged, as a "Black Hand" agent, has for several weeks been terrorizing business men, was captured here to-day after a gun fight with officers. She is the wife of a miner.

Five officers were lying in wait at Powder Mill Creek, near a box where money was to be deposited. About 4 o'clock the woman cautiously crept along the road, grabbed the box, and ran. Upon being pursued by officers she drew a pistol and began a fusillade. The fire was promptly returned, until officers who were stationed at a turn in the road grabbed the woman and placed her under arrest. The woman's husband, Frank Galler, has also been jailed. The couple, with four children, came from Venice, Italy, five years ago.

POLICEMAN ARRESTS 15 MEN.

Overawes Fighting Striking Lamplighters and Strikebreakers with His Gun.

Alone and unaided Policeman McGrath of the West 152d Street Station arrested fifteen Italians at 185th Street and Broadway last night, thirteen of whom were striking lamplighters and the other two strikebreakers. McGrath, who was on a bicycle and in plain clothes, saw the thirteen attack the two, and threatening to shoot them he managed to make them all stand.

He was pondering over what to do with his prisoners when he saw Sergt. Kennison on the steps of his home near by. He called him and the two men managed to make the fifteen walk to the horse shed of a near-by roadhouse, where they kept them until they summoned the patrol wagon from the station.

All fifteen were taken to the station, where Frank Masietto of 2,515 Amsterdam Avenue and Joseph Maglieri of 570 West 165th Street, the strikebreakers, were held for carrying concealed weapons. The other thirteen, among whom the police said was the leader of the strikers, Joseph Vende of 517 West 168th Street, were all charged with disorderly conduct.

WRIGHT FLIES OVER AN HOUR

Follows 57-Minute Flight at Fort Myer with One of 62 Minutes 15 Seconds.

AMERICA RULES IN AVIATION

Lieut. Lahm Also Makes Trip with Wright and Record for "Doubles" Is Smashed.

PLANES OBEY EVERY TOUCH

In Early Morning Flight Aviator Outdoes Delagrange — Achievements Watched by High Officials.

Special to The New York Times.

WASHINGTON, Sept. 9.—In three successive flights in his aeroplane to-day, Orville Wright broke three world's records and wrested from France for America the laurels of the air.

In his first flight at an early hour this morning he drove his machine in circles over the Fort Myer parade ground for 57 minutes and 31 seconds, beating the previous endurance record made by Delagrange by 25 minutes 46 1-5 seconds.

In his second flight, late in the afternoon, he remained in the air for 62 minutes and 15 seconds, surpassing his own previous record by 4 minutes and 44 seconds.

His last flight was made with Lieut. Lahm of the Signal Corps in the seat beside him. Together they sailed for 6 minutes and 16 seconds, surpassing the record for doubles formerly made in Virginia by Orville Wright and his mechanician by 2 minutes and 36 seconds.

As far as altitudes attained were concerned the most spectacular flight of the day was the first. Then with few people to watch him Wright determined to familiarize himself with the upper air. From his normal course of some forty feet above the parade ground Mr. Wright turned the nose of his skimming craft upward for little runs at a height of 150 feet from the ground.

But as a demonstration of perfect mastery of his planes, and consequent mastery of the air, the long flight in which he broke his own and all other records for endurance was unequaled. When Mr. Wright descended from his morning flight he said that if he had known how near the hour limit he had come he would have stayed up longer, and there is no doubt that he would have done it. But the experience he gained in his 57 minutes of constant attention to the tricks of aviation in his early flight told its own story in the inventor's assurance in the afternoon, and in the perfect response to the slightest touch he made on his three levers.

Leading Officials Watch Flight.

The most representative company that has yet watched the daily experiments gathered this afternoon, following the report of Mr. Wright's early success. Gen. Nelson A. Miles came to Washington for the express purpose of watching the flights, and studied the manoeuvres of the inventor. Secretary of War Wright and Secretary of the Navy Metcalf were on the grounds long before the flight took place, and the army was represented by Gens. Oliver and Murray, Col. Hatfield, and many others. The French Military Attaché, Major Fournier, who recently witnessed some of Wilbur Wright's attempts at Le Mans, was also present. The crowd numbered several thousands.

It was 5:17:45 o'clock when the heavy weights dropped from the derrick and gave the forward impetus to the airship, waiting balanced on its monorail. Wright had taken his seat a moment before without the least apparent uneasiness, and in a businesslike way took hold of the controlling levers.

As viewed from behind at close quarters the enormous planes with the large twin propellers whirring with an irregular rattle behind them seemed to flutter off down the parade ground like a wounded bird. As the distance increased, however, the impression of irregular motion conveyed by the propellers was lost, and the machine seemed to be sliding over the grass on its skids like an iceboat over a frozen lake. The aeroplane was fully 100 yards from the starting point before it could be seen that it had left the ground, and was skimming the highest weeds under its own power.

Then like a giant gull, snow white in the sunlight, the tips of the planes tilted to the left, and still on the rise the aeroplane passed over the aerodrome at the other end of the field, missing its gable roof by only a few feet. Mr. Wright held his planes and rudder rigid until a complete half circle had been described, and then brought the ship back to an even keel as he sped up the field along the side of Arlington National Cemetery.

Dips Machine to the Crowd.

The crowd, intent on watching the start had given only a straggling cheer as the falling weights jerked the machine along the starting rail, and the cheer was quite lost in the whir of the propellers and the backward rush of a powerful current of air. But as Wright soared over the spectators crowding around the starting point, a long yell told their spontaneous enthusiasm. The aviator did not move his hands from the levers to wave an acknowledgment, but instead he dipped the nose of the bird-like structure, swooped to within twenty feet of the ground, and returned as a

"All the News That's Fit to Print."

The New York Times.

THE WEATHER.
Fair, warmer to-day; clouding to-morrow; light, variable winds.

VOL. LVIII...NO. 18,854. * * * NEW YORK, TUESDAY, SEPTEMBER 7, 1909.—EIGHTEEN PAGES. ONE CENT In Greater New York, Jersey City, and Newark { Elsewhere, TWO CENTS.

PEARY DISCOVERS THE NORTH POLE AFTER EIGHT TRIALS IN 23 YEARS

GAYNOR, UNPLEDGED, CONSENTS TO RUN

Writes Business Men He Will Accept Support of Any Party, but Make No Promises.

SAYS TAMMANY IS FOR HIM

Assured by Leaders of the Nomination, He Declares—Is for War on Machine Control and "City Spoliation."

Supreme Court Justice William J. Gaynor of Brooklyn has announced his willingness to become a candidate for Mayor in a letter written to a committee of influential Brooklyn citizens, who urged him soon after his return from Europe to enter the fight. The long-awaited declaration of his position was made public last night together with the names of the committee of citizens and their letter to the Brooklyn jurist.

Justice Gaynor reviews the entire Mayoralty situation, assails "mere political control," which has resulted in "spoliation of the city treasury." He declares, however, that he has reason to believe that he will receive the Democratic nomination and Republican support, as well as that of the Independence League.

An interesting part of the letter is that in which Justice Gaynor refers to the printed statements that he would not receive the indorsement of the Republican organization unless he made some definite pledge of his position. While declaring that he does not believe that the majority of the organization demand any such condition of him, he emphatically states that he will pledge himself to no organization.

"I shall not take a nomination from any organization to which is annexed any pledge, promise or condition whatsoever other than to be Mayor in fact, and do my duty if elected," says he.

In referring to his expectation of welcoming all voters to his standard, Justice Gaynor says: "When an organization or party vouches for one and nominates him and wants him elected I have always understood that it welcomes help from any and all quarters to elect him."

Promises from Tammany.

He goes on to make the significant declaration that he has received assurance from influential Democrats that the Tammany City Convention will give him an "unconditional nomination" and that "no one can prevent the election of delegates who will nominate me." He states that he is aware that there is opposition to him in the organization, but that he does not believe "an undivided delegation can be brought into the convention opposed to my nomination."

"As to the Independence League," he continues, "inasmuch as it has always stood for the uplifting of city government, I think I may justly expect its support."

Justice Gaynor concludes with a solemn pledge to discharge his trust with fidelity and honesty, ending with the words, "No party or party machine can drag us down if we stand fast together: on the contrary, we may lift city politics up in all parties, and make the spoliation of the city's treasury, through mere machine political control, a thing impossible in the future."

Here is Justice Gaynor's answer:

Justice Gaynor's Letter.

Sept. 4, 1909.

"Messrs. Abraham Abraham, James McMahon, Archibald R. Watson, Judson G. Wall, Michael H. Drummond, James Creelman, Charles M. Higgins, M. M. Belding, Jr., and Frank J. Price

Dear Sirs—Your letter added to my very great anxiety, already caused by similar letters and requests and public discussion, but has finally helped to enable me to see my way through it. I put myself in your hands, and consent to be a candidate for nomination for Mayor. No doubt you have observed that several bodies of citizens have nominated me already. I specially note your statement, 'We do not care who, or what party convention, joins in nominating and voting for you if you will give us your consent to run,' etc. It requires me to say something of recent occurrences in order that there may be no misunderstanding, and I trust I may say it without a bit of unkindness to any one.

The Republican City Committee has met since your letter was written and apparently give out a statement that the Republican City Convention will not nominate any one who will not pledge himself in advance not to accept a nomination from the Democratic City Convention also. Although published in all of the newspapers, and in no way questioned, I have doubted whether it was in fact authorized. I know that many Republicans will not acquiesce in it. As is well enough known, I have long been of those who look upon such extreme partisanship in city or local elections as most unfortunate. Its main result is to play everything year after year into the hands of party machines.

In years gone by I have worked shoulder to shoulder with Republicans and Democrats alike and together in efforts to prevent official wrongdoing and lift the city Government up and make it intelligent and decent. I so worked successfully with those who prevented the fraudulent purchase of the water company, and other even worse things, still in general remembrance, and with those who moved upon and destroyed John Y. McKane and his corrupt control, results and benefits from which were accepted by leaders and the machines of both parties in turn through series of years.

We never paused then to inquire of one another's politics, or to put any ban or bar on one another because of politics, and we shall not do the like now. Must I now in order to run for Mayor first get up and unjustly offend men who so worked with us then, and thousands of others who gave us their good-will and sympathy in such work, by saying that I shall not suffer the city convention of their party to also nominate me? If I should do so I could not expect their votes.

The great bulk of the voters here who are Democrats in National politics are in favor of intelligent and good local government the same as the corresponding bulk of Republican voters are. How much better it would be for the city if they should work together instead of proscribing and ostracizing each other.

Base Men in the Minority.

Base men are in the minority in all parties and everywhere. There are 75,000 or more voters in this great city who now never allow National politics to influence their votes in city elections. What,

Continued on Page 7.

HARRIMAN SUFFERS RELAPSE.

Diagnosed as Acute Indigestion—His Physician Says, 'We Hope for the Best.'

Special to The New York Times.

TURNER'S, N. Y., Sept. 6.—That E. H. Harriman has had a relapse was admitted this afternoon by Dr. W. M. Gordon Lyle, his physician, at the Harriman home here. Acute indigestion is Dr. Lyle's diagnosis of his patient's trouble.

The attack came on yesterday after Mr. Harriman had appeared to be doing nicely for several days. A telephone message was sent from the Harriman home in the early hours of this morning to Miss Taylor, Superintendent of St. Luke's Hospital nurses' registry, at 214 West 108th Street, Manhattan, asking her to send her best nurse here with all speed. The nurse arrived within three hours.

According to Dr. Lyle, Mr. Harriman is resting easily to-night. He said that it was he who sent for the nurse. There is a report that there are four other nurses here, but this could not be confirmed. Certain it is that Mr. Harriman's state of health is such that both day and night nurses are required.

When Dr. Lyle was seen this afternoon he was much perturbed over the presence here again of newspaper men. It was pointed out to him, however, that they were withdrawn on the understanding that the press was to be apprised of any change in Mr. Harriman's condition through his office at 120 Broadway. He was told that nothing could be learned from that source to-day.

"It is true," said Dr. Lyle, "that Mr. Harriman has had a relapse. Yesterday he had a sharp attack of indigestion, but he is better to-day, and is now resting comfortably. We hope for the best."

Mr. Harriman's entire family is at Tower Hill, while Judge Robert S. Lovett, general counsel to most of the important Harriman interests, was summoned to Arden and arrived last night. It is said that two of the physicians who were called into consultation with Dr. George W. Crile, the Cleveland surgeon, shortly after Mr. Harriman's return from Europe, are again at Arden. They are Dr. Walter B. James of 17 West Fifty-fourth Street and Dr. George E. Brewer of 61 West Forty-eighth Street.

Dr. Lyle gave out this bulletin at 4 P. M.: "Mr. Harriman had an attack of acute indigestion at 11 P. M. last night, having partaken of a dinner a little heartier than his strength would allow. His condition is improved to-day, although there are still slight indications of a bad stomach."

At Dr. Brewer's home last night it was said that the doctor was at Cedar Camp in the Adirondacks, so far as any of his household here knew. He may have gone to Arden from there, however. There was no response to the telephone when a TIMES reporter tried to reach Dr. James's house over the wire.

DYNAMITE HOUSE AND PLANT.

Official Who Had Discharged Men Kicks Explosive to the Ground.

Special to The New York Times.

TYRONE, Penn., Sept. 6.—The handsome residence of Thomas Calderwood, an official of the American Lime and Stone Company, and all of the buildings of the company at the quarry near here, were completely wrecked and one unidentified fire engineer was killed by explosions of dynamite early to-day.

Calderwood some time ago discharged some foreign employes of his company, and it was the general belief here that the explosions were acts of revenge.

Mr. Calderwood arose at 5 o'clock and smelled something burning. Upon investigation he found a large bundle of dynamite securely bound with wire on his kitchen window. He immediately tore the window open and kicked it to the ground, and shouted for his wife and daughter to run for their lives. They had barely reached the street before the explosion occurred. Every window in the house was smashed to atoms. The doors and walls were badly damaged. Windows for blocks were broken.

At the quarries a ton of dynamite had been stored. The whole amount was exploded, completely destroying the buildings about the works, and blowing large steel car 100 feet from the tracks.

The home of Harry Houck, near the quarries, was completely destroyed. The scales used for weighing cars were wrecked, and windows were broken in the houses within a radius of five miles.

HUGHES'S DEPUTIES AT RACES

Make No Secret of Their Mission, but Find No Betting at Sheepshead Bay.

Four investigators of race-track conditions from Albany visited the Sheepshead Bay race course yesterday, as the representatives of Gov. Hughes, after presenting themselves, with credentials which were accepted, to Sheriff Hobley of Kings County.

The investigators made no secret of their mission, but made no claim to official standing of any kind, except to say that they came to observe what was going on and ascertain the conditions concerning betting at the race track for a report to the Governor.

The visitors watched the proceedings of the holiday crowd through the afternoon, and agreed that they saw nothing fitting the description of race-track betting published in an afternoon newspaper early last week, which report caused Gov. Hughes to request reports from the New York police officials and the officials of Kings County on the matter of race-track bookmaking.

MISS STEWART A PRINCESS.

Emperor Francis Joseph Confers the Rank in Her Own Right.

VIENNA, Sept. 6.—Emperor Francis Joseph has conferred upon Miss Anita Stewart, whose marriage to Prince Miguel of Braganza will take place Sept. 15, the rank of Princess in her own right.

Miss Anita Stewart is the daughter of Mrs. James Henry Smith by her first husband, William Rhinelander Stewart, whom she divorced in South Dakota to marry Mr. Smith. When Mr. Smith died in Kobe, Japan, he left his stepdaughter an income of $40,000 a year, to which her mother will add another $40,000 a year on her marriage to Prince Miguel next month in London.

In order to get the consent of his father, Dom Miguel, the Prince had to renounce all claim to the throne of Portugal in favor of his younger brother, Prince Francis Joseph.

LONDON APPLAUDS PEARY'S EXPLOIT

Instant Acceptance of His Report a Contrast to Skepticism Toward Dr. Cook.

HAD AWAITED HIS VERDICT

Admiral Nares Thinks It Peculiar That the Announcements Should Come So Close Together.

Special Cable to THE NEW YORK TIMES.

LONDON, Sept. 6.—The news that Commander Robert E. Peary had reached the north pole was made known throughout London by late editions of the evening papers, which displayed the brief announcement, under headlines which suggested none of the reservations with which the reports of the discovery by Dr. Cook have been received.

In marked contrast with the skepticism with which Dr. Cook's reports were printed is the immediate and whole-hearted acceptance of Peary's dispatch. Nothing could show this better than a comparison of headlines upon the two announcements.

A Difference in Headlines.

"North pole reached by Peary. Official news that the American flag was hoisted April 6, 1909." That is the way in which Commander Peary's dispatch is presented to its readers by a London paper which headed Dr. Cook's report as follows: "The north pole reported discovered. American explorer's statement."

With the general public a similar readiness to accept Commander Peary's statement is strikingly apparent and bears out the saying frequently heard here recently to the effect that had it been Commander Peary instead of Dr. Cook who had come forward with a bare announcement of the discovery of the pole not a single voice would have been raised in question. It is a testimony to Commander Peary's high reputation as a man and an explorer that the world accepts his word without a shadow of hesitation.

Had Awaited Peary's Testimony

Mr. Peary's announcement is hailed with peculiar satisfaction, because, throughout the controversy that has been raging in the last few days, it has been stated again and again that Mr. Peary's testimony would settle the question definitely. "Peary will know the truth," it was said. Thus, Peary is the witness for whom the whole world is waiting. There was a consensus of opinion among the people with whom I talked to-night that if Commander Peary contests the claims put forward by Dr. Cook, the latter will find it an extremely difficult task to establish his pretensions to be the discoverer of the pole, even should the "proofs" which he is now withholding prove to be as good as he says they are.

Cook Expects Confirmation.

Dr. Cook, on being informed in Copenhagen to-night of the news from Mr. Peary, said:

"*I hope it is true, for Peary's reports will confirm all my claims.*"

An arctic explorer to whom to-night I showed Mr. Peary's message to THE NEW YORK TIMES, saying, "I have the pole," made the comment that Mr. Peary, by implication, denied any other claim to the honor of discovering the pole, and that, consequently, it was to be inferred that the confirmation which Dr. Cook expects from Mr. Peary is hardly likely to be forthcoming.

Peculiar Coincidence, Says Nares.

Sir George Nares, who led the arctic expedition of 1875-6, when interviewed to-night with regard to Commander Peary's message announcing the discovery, said:

"It is difficult to avoid the conclusion that Commander Peary's Eskimos at Etah must have known that Dr. Cook had crossed Smith's Sound and passed Etah last Winter to reach Ellsmere Land. Dr. Cook, then," continued the Admiral, "gets down from his Eskimo headquarters at Annotook to Upernavik by a Greenland route never before traversed, passing all the sea glaciers in Baffin Bay just in time to catch a Danish Government vessel which leaves Upernavik early in the year before the whaling vessels are due.

"My first impression was that Dr. Cook had got hold of Commander Peary's Eskimos in some way or other and ought to have communicated either with Commander Peary or with the Eskimos at Etah.

"The question now arises how it comes about that Cook and Peary announce at practically the same time the discovery of the north pole. Is it not a peculiar fact that this coincidence takes place, in view of the possibility of news having reached Etah of the success of one or the other of the men?"

Capt. Scott of the exploring ship Discovery stated to-night that Commander Peary's message put it beyond doubt that the Stars and Stripes was the first flag to fly at the north pole.

The Proper Witness Arrives.

"Just at the very moment when men were saying that only the evidence of an independent witness who had himself visited the north pole could estab-

Continued on Page 2.

In order not to miss The New York Times of to-morrow, in which will be printed exclusively Lieut. Peary's own story of his discovery of the North Pole, order a copy from your newsdealer early to-day.

COOK GLAD PEARY REACHED THE POLE

Unmoved When, Wreathed with Flowers at Banquet, He Hears the News.

HOPE NOW FOR OTHERS

Believes More Expeditions Will Reach the Pole Within the Next Ten Years.

COPENHAGEN, Sept. 6.—Copenhagen was electrified to-night by the report of Commander Peary's announcement that he had reached the north pole. Dr. Cook was immensely interested and said:

"That is good news. I hope Peary did get to the pole. His observations, and reports on that region will confirm mine."

Asked if there was any probability of Peary's having found the tube containing his records, Dr. Cook replied:

"I hope so, but that is doubtful on account of the drift. Commander Peary would have reached the pole this year, probably, while I was there last year. His route was several hundred miles east of mine. We are rivals, of course, but the pole is good enough for two.

"The fact of two men having reached the pole along different paths," continued the explorer, "should furnish large additions to scientific knowledge. Probably other parties will reach it in the next ten years, since every explorer is helped by the experience of his predecessors, just as Sverdrup's observations and reports were of immeasurable help to me.

"I can say nothing more concerning Commander Peary's success without knowing further details, than that I am glad of it."

While Dr. Cook was conversing casually this morning with some friends, a possibility of the dénouement which electrified the world to-day was laughingly suggested. Dr. Cook remarked:

"It is quite possible that Peary will turn up now. He is about due to get back if he carries out his plans."

Those who have had the best opportunities to become acquainted with Dr. Cook here believe that he is not likely to enter into a controversy with Commander Peary.

It is doubtful if history furnishes a more dramatic episode than the breaking of the news to Dr. Cook that Peary had realized the goal of his life's ambition and repeated struggles. Dr. Cook was seated at a dinner, surrounded by explorers and correspondents, in the gilded ballroom of the Tivoli Casino. Around his neck was hung a garland of pink roses, according to the Scandinavian method of honoring heroes, which the explorer wore blushingly and with visible embarrassment. Several speeches, acclaiming him, had been given and repeated toasts to him drunk with clamorous cheers.

Amid this scene a whisper went around that Peary had planted the Stars and Stripes at the pole. Cook was perfectly cool and unmoved. He made a striking speech, in which he paid high tribute to the work of Sverdrup, who sat near, to whose discoveries he largely owed his success; to John R. Bradley, who had financed the expedition; to "the intelligence, endurance, and faithfulness" of the Eskimos who had assisted in the preparations, and those who had accompanied him. The whole story of the expedition, he said, has not come out, and will not come out for some time, nor will it come out in installments, but only when it is completed.

Dr. Cook did not permit the whispers which came to his ear of Peary's success to move him in the least, but when he had finished he was surrounded by correspondents who looked for some sign of emotion, but the explorer said smilingly: "I am glad."

Nothing but arctic exploration has been thought of here for the last few days. The people at first refused to believe that such a report as that telling of Peary's success had been received. They thought it must be a canard or a practical joke. The Danish news agency, which received the telegram from London, feared that it had been imposed upon and cabled to London for confirmation before it would circulate the report.

Minister Egan characterized it as one of the most dramatic events of history. The rumor spread that Peary was returning by way of Denmark, and this made an immense sensation. Some questioned the authority of the Peary telegram on the ground that it was improbable that a scientific man would use such dramatic language.

After the dinner to-night Dr. Cook stood about talking with Sverdrup and the other guests in a most unconcerned manner. Later, with the roses still decorating his shoulders, his hosts led him through the Casino grounds to an automobile. A crowd of several hundred, half of the number being women, surrounded and followed him, cheering, but the people were not able to get near enough to shake hands, because of a cordon of police.

Notifies The New York Times That He Reached It on April 6, 1909.

HE WIRES FROM LABRADOR

Returning on the Roosevelt, Which He Reports to Bridgman Is Safe.

IS NEARING NEWFOUNDLAND

Expects to Reach Chateau Bay To-day, When He Will Send Full Particulars.

McMILLAN SENDS WORD

Explorer's Companion Telegraphs Sister: "We Have the Pole on Board."

SEVEN VAIN EXPEDITIONS

Many Years Consumed in Learning the Feasible Route—Picked Men Were His Assistants.

Commander Robert E. Peary, U. S. N., has discovered the north pole. Following the report of Dr F. A. Cook that he had reached the top of the world comes the certain announcement from Mr. Peary, the hero of eight polar expeditions, covering a period of twenty-three years, that at last his ambition has been realized and from all over the world comes full acknowledgment of Peary's feat and congratulations on his success.

The first announcement of Peary's exploit was received in the following message to THE NEW YORK TIMES:

> Indian Harbor, Labrador, via Cape Ray, N. F., Sept. 6.
> THE NEW YORK TIMES, New York:
> I have the pole, April sixth. Expect arrive Chateau Bay, September seventh. Secure control wire for me there and arrange expedite transmission big story. PEARY.

Following the receipt of Commander Peary's message to THE NEW YORK TIMES several other messages were received in this city from the explorer to the same effect.

Soon afterward The Associated Press received the following:

> INDIAN HARBOR, Via Cape Ray, N. F. Sept. 6.—To Associated Press, New York:
> Stars and Stripes nailed to the pole. PEARY.

To Herbert L. Bridgman, Secretary of the Peary Arctic Club, he telegraphed as follows:

> Herbert L. Bridgman, Brooklyn, N. Y.:
> Pole reached. Roosevelt safe. PEARY.

This message was received at the New York Yacht Club in West Forty-fourth Street:

> INDIAN HARBOR, Via Cape Ray, N. F., Sept. 6.—George A. Carmack, Secretary New York Yacht Club:
> Steam yacht Roosevelt, flying club burgee, has enabled me to add north pole to club's other trophies. (Signed) PEARY.

Cipher Shows Authenticity.

The telegram to Mr. Bridgman was sent in cipher. The cipher used was a private one and indicated clearly that the dispatch was undoubtedly from Commander Peary.

Commander Peary also sent a message to his wife at South Harpswell, Me., where she has been spending the Summer.

"Have made good at last," said the explorer to his wife. "I have the old pole. Am well. Love. Will wire again from Chateau."

The message was signed simply "Bert," an abbreviation of Robert, Commander Peary's first name. Mrs. Peary sent a wife's characteristic reply, with love and a blessing and a request for him to "hurry home."

By a strange coincidence, Mrs. Frederick A. Cook, too, was in South Harpswell, Me., when she received the first news from her husband.

Peary's Companion Reports.

Two messages were received in this country also from Donald B. McMillan, who accompanied Peary. Mr. McMillan was an instructor in mathematics and physical training at the academy in Worcester, Mass., until the close of school last year, when he obtained a leave of absence of two years to go on the Peary expedition.

In addition to his message to Dr. D. L. Abercrombie, Principal of the academy, Mr. McMillan sent the following to Mrs. W. C. Fogg, his sister, who is Postmistress at Freeport, Me.:

> Indian Harbor, Sept. 6, 1909.
> Mrs. W. C. Fogg, Freeport, Me.:
> Arrived safe. Pole on board. Best year of my life. BEN.

Follows Cook's Report Quickly.

These messages, flashed from the coast of Labrador to New York and thence to the four corners of the globe while Dr. Frederick A. Cook is being acclaimed by the crowned heads of Europe and the world at large as the discoverer of the north pole, added a remarkable chapter to the story of an achievement that has held the civilized world up to the highest pitch of interest since Sept. 1, when Dr. Cook's claim to having reached the "top of the world" was first telegraphed from the Shetland Islands.

The two explorers, Dr. Frederick A. Cook and Commander Robert E. Peary, both Americans, had been in the arctic seeking the goal of centuries, the impossible north pole, whose attainment has at times seemed beyond the reach of man. Both were determined and courageous, and both had started expressing the belief that their efforts would be crowned with success.

Peary the Better Known.

Peary was well known to both scientists and the general public as a persistent striver for the honor of reaching the "farthest north." Dr. Cook, on the other hand, had held the public attention to a lesser degree. He made his departure quietly and his purpose was hardly known except to those keenly interested in polar research.

Then suddenly, and with no word of warning, a steamer touched at Lerwick, in the Shetland Islands, and Dr. Cook's claim to having succeeded where expedition after expedition of the hardiest explorers of the world had failed was made known. Dr. Cook's announcement was that he had reached the pole *on April 21, 1908.*

Three days later Dr. Cook arrived at Copenhagen and received a welcome such as no explorer had ever received before.

Peary Announces Success.

Five days after the receipt of the Lerwick message, almost to the hour, came the sensational statement from Indian Harbor, Labrador, that Commander Peary also had been successful on his third expedition to the coveted goal, the date being April 6, 1909.

He filed his brief messages and continued on his way to the south, leaving the world to marvel at a dramatic situation such as has seldom been recorded—the double achievement of a purpose that for almost ten centuries had baffled the endeavor of man and had taken many an explorer to his death in the frozen north.

It is almost certain that Commander Peary did not know of Dr. Cook's announcement when he sent his messages from Indian Harbor.

Under ordinary circumstances Commander Peary's announcement would have evoked world-wide interest, but the existing conditions conspired to add many times to the importance of his communication.

According to Dr. Cook's account of his expedition, he buried the American *flag at the pole in a metal tube;* Peary's words would indicate that the Stars and Stripes were raised by him and left standing.

How the News Came.

The message from Commander Peary to THE NEW YORK TIMES was received in New York at 12:39 yesterday through the Postal Telegraph Company. It was handed in at Indian Harbor, Labrador, and was sent from there by *wireless telegraph* to Cape Ray, Newfoundland, and from Cape Ray to Port aux Basques by the Newfoundland Government land lines; thence to Canso, Nova Scotia, by cable, and to New York from there over the lines of the Commercial Cable Company.

PEARY REPORTS TO THE TIMES

ANNOUNCES HIS DISCOVERY OF THE POLE AND WILL SEND A FULL AND EXCLUSIVE ACCOUNT TO-DAY.

Indian Harbor, Labrador, via Cape Ray, N. F., Sept. 6.

The New York Times, New York:

I have the pole, April sixth. Expect arrive Chateau Bay September seventh. Secure control wire for me there and arrange expedite transmission big story.

PEARY.

PEARY'S MESSAGE TO HIS WIFE.

SOUTH HARPSWELL, Me., Sept. 6.—Commander Robert E Peary announced his success in discovering the North Pole to his wife, who is summering at Eagle Island here, as follows:

INDIAN HARBOR, via Cape Ray, Sept. 6, 1909.

Mrs. R. E. Peary, South Harpswell, Me.:

Have made good at last. I have the old Pole. Am well. Love. Will wire again from Chateau.

(Signed) BERT.

In replying Mrs. Peary sent the following dispatch:

SOUTH HARPSWELL, Me., Sept. 6, 1909.

To Commander R. E. Peary, Steamer Roosevelt, Chateau Bay:

All well. Best love. God bless you. Hurry home.

(Signed) JO.

CONFIRMED BY FELLOW-VOYAGER.

INDIAN HARBOR, Labrador, Sept. 6, 1909.

Dr. D. W. Abercrombie, Worcester Academy, Worcester, Mass.:

Top of the earth reached at last. Greetings to Faculty and boys.

(Signed) D. B. McMILLAN.

DR. COOK CABLES THE TIMES.

To the Editor of The New York Times:

COPENHAGEN, Sept. 6.

Glad Peary did it. Two records are better than one, and the work over a more easterly route has added value.

COOK.

WASHINGTON CREDITS PEARY.

Believes Cook, Too, but Has Said That He Must Produce Records.

Special to The New York Times.

WASHINGTON, Sept. 6.—There was instant acceptance among the geographers in Washington of the assertion in Commander Peary's laconic cable message that he had discovered the north pole. And there was just as ready rejoicing for Peary is popular with the scientific men in the National capitol, and they are ready to take his word at its face value without examination or delay.

In the manner of their acceptance of this announcement of a second discovery of the point that has baffled discovery for so many years there is a sharp contrast to the attitude of the same men toward the announcement from Dr. Cook. Most of them, indeed, accept Cook's assertion, and announce their belief that the Brooklyn man actually did reach the north pole in April, 1908. But there

"All the News That's Fit to Print."

The New York Times.

THE WEATHER. Fair, warmer Sunday; rain probably Monday; moderate south winds. For full weather report see Page 10, Part 3.

VOL. LX...NO. 19,419. ** NEW YORK, SUNDAY, MARCH 26, 1911.—90 PAGES, In Eight Parts, Including Picture Section and Review of Books. PRICE FIVE CENTS.

141 MEN AND GIRLS DIE IN WAIST FACTORY FIRE; TRAPPED HIGH UP IN WASHINGTON PLACE BUILDING; STREET STREWN WITH BODIES; PILES OF DEAD INSIDE

LIMANTOUR, VICTOR, PROMISES REFORMS

He Remains in Mexican Cabinet and de la Barra Will Displace Creel.

FORCE WILL MEET FORCE

Minister, However, Appeals to Mexicans and Nations to Believe in the Government's Good Faith.

FROM VICE PRESIDENT CORRAL.

Mexico City, March 25.

To the Editor of The New York Times:

The resignation of Gen. Diaz's Cabinet has been well received, because its object is to make it easier for the President to introduce reforms in public administration which it is thought will contribute to reestablish peace.

RAMON CORRAL.

FROM MINISTER OF WAR COSIO.

Mexico City, March 25.

To the Editor of The New York Times:

I am not in a position to answer your question since it is for the public to discuss the effects of the resignation.

G. COSIO.

Señor Limantour seems to have gained full sway in the Mexican Government. He is to remain as Minister of Finance. Ambassador de la Barra, with whom he had long consultations in New York, has been summoned from Washington to be Minister of Foreign Affairs in place of Enrique Creel, Limantour's rival. Four other new names are on the Cabinet slate.

Señor Limantour in an interview appeals to all Mexicans to rally to the Government. He promises needed reforms, but declares force will be met with force.

The Maderos, who were in New York, have gone to Texas to be nearer to Francisco I. Madero, the rebel leader.

Insurrectos have appeared at new and widely scattered places. Successful operations are reported in Coahuila and Neuvo Leon in the North and Guerrero and Oaxaca in the South.

APPEAL BY LIMANTOUR.

Assures Mexicans of Reform and Appeals for Their Support.

Special to The New York Times.

MEXICO CITY, March 25.—Señor José Yves Limantour, whose return to this city has been followed by the upsetting of the Diaz cabinet, and who is expected to be a figure of great importance in the new Ministry, in an interview with the correspondent of THE NEW YORK TIMES this afternoon outlined the policy which he believes will be followed by the Government. Señor Limantour, whose resignation went in with those of his colleagues, spoke as an individual.

"I hope and earnestly trust," he said, "that the present difficulties will soon be solved in the best interests of the country and to the satisfaction of all reasonable and patriotic citizens; and I feel that I can say that the administration of Gen. Diaz is prepared to take such measures and implant such reforms as will satisfy the best public opinion of the country; and that, while meeting force with force, it will leave nothing undone in the present circumstances to unite all good Mexicans.

"A united Mexico is our watchword. I ask all patriotic and progressive Mexicans to be patient, and while the Government is working at the problem before it that they practically display the love of the fatherland, which has been and must be the basic principle of Mexico's proud position in the world. The putting aside of all personal resentments is imperatively demanded and a common cause to overcome a national difficulty is a necessity.

"If the citizens and friends of Mexico will continue to prove their devotion to the glorious past and the promising future of this nation in a brief time all complexities can readily be overcome. The Mexican people and the Governments friendly to us must believe—and I say this in all solemnity of verity—that the Government is determined to properly and progressively satisfy all legitimate demands for reformative measures, and that it is doing this in its line of duty as a representative Government, honestly, sincerely, and fearlessly."

The resignation of the Cabinet yesterday is taken as an indication that Señor Limantour's policies are prevailing with President Diaz. Señor Limantour's recognized value in his present office and his unfamiliarity with diplomatic duties is advanced as a strong argument against a change in his office, and he will remain as Finance Minister.

While high officials will not admit that Gen. Bernardo Reyes has been recalled from Europe, it can be stated with practical certainty that the summons has gone to him. To Gen. Reyes, who has long been called the "idol of the Mexican Army," may be intrusted the task of handling the rebellion, as Minister of War and Marine. He will succeed the aged Gen. Cosio, who has been severely criticised for the campaign so far conducted. Gen. Reyes, who has long been abroad on a mission to study the military methods of Europe, was last heard from in Rome, whence he had gone from Paris.

Six Chosen For Ministry.

MEXICO CITY, March 25.—Although no official announcement has been made, it is known that five of the new members of President Diaz's Cabinet have been chosen and it is almost certain that Jose Yves Limantour will remain as Minister of Finance. Other selections besides that of Señor de la Barra as Minister of Foreign Relations, are:

DEMETRO SODI, Judge of the Supreme Court, Minister of Justice, succeeding Justino Fernandez.

NORDBETT DOMINGUEZ, Postmaster General, Department of Communications, succeeding Leander Fernandez.

MANUEL MAROQUIN, well-known civil engineer, Department of Fomento, succeeding Olegario Molina.

JORGE VERA ESTANOL, attorney, Minister of Education, succeeding Justo Sierra.

So far as official announcement of the

Continued on Page 9.

TO-DAY'S SUNDAY TIMES

CONSISTS OF

Part I. Pictorial Section.

II. News Section.

III. and IV. Sporting News, Wireless and Cable Sections.

V. Magazine Section.

VI. Review of Books.

CONTENTS

VII. Theatres, Society, Fashions, Resorts, Music, Queries.

VIII. Business Section.

WIRELESS NEWS BY KITES.

Got Calls 4,000 and 6,000 Miles Away, Say San Francisco Men.

SAN FRANCISCO, March 25.—Notable achievements in wireless telegraphy are reported by a party that conducted experiments in receiving messages with the aid of high-flying kites on a beach near the Golden Gate last night.

The experimenters say they have distinctly heard calls from San Juan, Porto Rico, Washington, D. C.; Key West; Fla.; Brooklyn Navy Yard, Colon, Guantanamo, Cuba, and the station at Otichishi, Japan, which is 4,900 miles distant. They also detected an indistinct Marconi spark, which they believe was sent from Cornwall, England, a distance of 6,500 miles.

The receiving aerials were strung between two pairs of 16-foot kites, which rose to a height estimated at 1,500 feet.

To-day reports of the experiments are being prepared for transmission to the War Department, together with suggestions for the use of such an appliance for the detection of distant activities of enemies.

SENDS WIRELESS 2,500 MILES.

The White Star Liner Megantic Forwards a Message to England.

HALIFAX, N. S., March 25.—What is said to be an entirely new feat in direct wireless communication, the sending of a message over the Atlantic a distance of 2,500 miles from a ship at sea to England, was reported by the White Star Dominion liner Megantic, which arrived to-day from Liverpool.

While off the coast last night Purser Pomeroy of the Megantic sent a wireless dispatch to Liverpool via Poldhu, Cornwall. The message was received and to-day when the ship docked, a reply by cable was handed to the purser.

Hitherto messages from ships in this part of the Atlantic have gone by way of Cape Race or Glace Bay and a range of 600 miles has been considered as practically the limit.

RAILROAD STRIKE IS OFF.

kQueen & Crescent Firemen Return to Work, Both Sides Yielding Points.

Special to The New York Times.

CINCNNATI, Ohio, March 25.—The strik eof firemen on the Queen and Crescent road, which caused considerable loss of freight and passenger service, was called off late to-night following a conference of the road's officials and representatives of the Firemen's Union. Both parties found it necessary to concede points of difference.

The company retains the right to employ such firemen as are now in service between Oakdale and Chattanooga, and to give them one-half the passenger and preferred freight runs.

It is understood that the strike, which has lasted sixteen days, has cost the company at least $250,000, besides the cost of operating trains with new firemen.

It is significant that the agreement is not signed by Vice President Powell of the road, who took the matter out of the hands of General Manager Baker. It is signed by Baker for the road and Vice President H. O. Teat, Chairman J. L. Payne(Vice Chairman G. A. Odenwald, and Secretary-Treasurer J. L. Fetterman of the Firemen's Union.

TALK OF CHARGES AGAINST THE MAYOR

Civic Organizations Taking Up Magistrate Corrigan's Attack—Want Police Control Shifted.

MAY GO TO THE GOVERNOR

Former District Attorney Philbin Says the Force Is Demoralized and Gaynor Doesn't Understand It.

An attempt was made yesterday to start an official investigation of police conditions in this city. Various civic organizations communicated with Magistrate Joseph E. Corrigan, who in a letter to the newspapers described the situation as intolerable and put the blame directly upon Mayor Gaynor.

It is the intention of the organizations to find out if things are as bad as has been set forth by Magistrate Corrigan and to have the responsibility placed somewhere.

Magistrate Corrigan has been asked to submit all the information and data relating to the subject he has on hand or can get, and he will comply with the request. This is as far as the Magistrate will go, he said, as he considers that he has done his duty in drawing the attention of the public to the abuses.

"I have nothing to add to what I stated in my letter," said Magistrate Corrigan yesterday, "but I am ready to stand by everything I wrote. My deductions are more than borne out by the letters which I receive by every mail. Most of these are from responsible people and contain specific instances of how the police of New York City are demoralized. These letters I am willing, with the consent of the owners, to turn over to any investigating committee, with any other information which I possess. I hope a full investigation will be made, either by the Grand Jury or some civic body."

Magistrate Butts Takes Notice, Too.

It was reported that the civic organizations will endeavor to have police control taken entirely out of the hands of the Mayor. It was said that they will even go so far as to bring charges before the Governor against the Mayor if he does not remedy defects of his own accord.

City Magistrate Butts substantiated in a measure yesterday the charges of Magistrate Corrigan. On Thursday Magistrate Butts praised Magistrate Corrigan's sincerity and courage, and he was not invited to the meeting of Magistrates on Thursday evening at which thirteen Magistrates disclaimed sympathy with Magistrate Corrigan's attack.

Magistrate Butts's position was defined when two policemen from the West 126th Street Station offered newspaper clippings in the Harlem Court describing proceedings at the Polo Athletic Club as a basis for warrants for the boxers. They said they had been unable to get into the club

"It is a barefaced confession of the general inefficiency of the Police Department for you to offer me such evidence," said Magistrate Butts. "It reflects small credit on the police affairs of the city. How absurd it is for you men to come here and ask for a warrant or even a summons, when you make no straight charge based upon any real evidence that a crime has been committed.

"Now, understand me! I do not blame you two men or your Lieutenant or your Captain, but it certainly shows inexperience, if not stupidity, in the police administration of the City of New York. The court is powerless to put in motion its processes on such 'evidence' as this. The application for a warrant is denied."

Among those who openly backed up Magistrate Corrigan's charges yesterday were former District Attorney Eugene A. Philbin, who helped to break up the old police "system," convicting a number of Captains for neglect of duty and forcing others to retire from the department.

Force Demoralized, Says Philbin.

"I consider the police force of New York the finest body of men in the world for its size," said Mr. Philbin. "For the most part it is made up of splendid fellows, but they are now working purely under the stimulus of their own innate virtue. The force as a force is demoralized: never in my time has it been in such a state, and I believe that whether his statement was judicious and well timed or not, Magistrate Corrigan was entirely correct in his description of the conditions.

"Men are afraid of their commanding officers, not in the old sense of knowing that they must obey them, but in the sense of having no confidence in them. They are afraid to make an arrest, almost to call their souls their own. Of course, such a condition is intolerable.

"A Captain in the old days was held strictly accountable for what happened in his precinct, and although an honest patrolman, with a grievance or a wrong to report, did not have a chance in the world if he went to Headquarters with it, the discipline was splendid and New York was protected. I did my best to destroy that old system while I was in the District Attorney's office, thinking that thereby I could do a permanent good to the city. It seems, however, that I really did an injury, as so far nothing has been found as a substitute for what was called the police 'business.'

Criticisms of the Mayor.

"I do not believe that Mayor Gaynor is fully informed on police matters, or so thoroughly conversant with them as those who have studied them for years. In my opinion the only solution is to appoint a Police Commissioner for a long tenure of office, say fourteen years, so that he may be free from all influence.

"I am convinced that all the Magistrates who signed the statement condemning the action of Magistrate Corrigan, though they believed it impolitic and, perhaps, tending further to upset the discipline and efficiency of the force, really agreed with him."

James Forbes, Secretary and Director of the National Association for the Prevention of Mendicancy and Charitable Imposture, who is well acquainted with police conditions in New York, also supports Magistrate Corrigan.

"There is no question about it," he said, "the whole police force of the city is utterly demoralized. The police realize that the Mayor dislikes the police, mistrusts them, takes every opportunity to side against them.

"Now, the police force is a peculiar body, with a psychology all its own. They are very closely bound together, so that the slightest influence spreads at once through the entire force, and the Mayor's constraint, which has been carried to the extent of persecution, has simply wiped out their spirit."

Letters to Corrigan.

Letters from all kinds of people praising him for the stand he has taken in regard to the police continue to pour in on Magistrate Corrigan. The following is from a prominent lawyer:

"I congratulate you on having at last brought the public to a realization of present conditions. Whatever the other

Continued on Page 8.

The Flames Spread with Deadly Rapidity Through Flimsy Material Used in the Factory.

600 GIRLS ARE HEMMED IN

When Elevators Stop Many Jump to Certain Death and Others Perish in Fire-Filled Lofts.

STUDENTS RESCUE SOME

Help Them to Roof of New York University Building, Keeping the Panic-Stricken in Check.

ONE MAN TAKEN OUT ALIVE

Plunged to Bottom of Elevator Shaft and Lived There Amid Flames for Four Hours.

ONLY ONE FIRE ESCAPE

Coroner Declares Building Laws Were Not Enforced—Building Modern—Classed Fireproof.

JUST READY TO GO HOME

Victims Would Have Ended Day's Work in a Few Minutes—Pay Envelopes Identify Many.

MOB STORMS THE MORGUE

Seeking to Learn Fate of Relatives Employed by the Triangle Waist Company.

WINDOWS MARKED X FROM WHICH FIFTY GIRLS JUMPED—SOUTH SIDE OF BUILDING
COPYRIGHT BY AMERICAN PRESS ASSOCIATION

The Burning Building at 23 Washington Place.

Three stories of a ten-floor building at the corner of Greene Street and Washington Place were burned yesterday, and while the fire was going on 141 young men and women—at least 125 of them mere girls—were burned to death or killed by jumping to the pavement below.

The building was fireproof. It shows now hardly any signs of the disaster that overtook it. The walls are as good as ever; so are the floors; nothing is the worse for the fire except the furniture and 141 of the 600 men and girls that were employed in its upper three stories.

Most of the victims were suffocated or burned to death within the building, but some who fought their way to the windows and leaped met death as surely, but perhaps more quickly, on the pavements below.

All Over in Half an Hour.

Nothing like it has been seen in New York since the burning of the General Slocum. The fire was practically all over in half an hour. It was confined to three floors—the eighth, ninth, and tenth of the building. But it was the most murderous fire that New York has seen in many years.

The victims who are now lying at the Morgue waiting for some one to identify them by a tooth or the remains of a burned shoe were mostly girls of from 16 to 23 years of age. They were employed at making shirtwaists by the Triangle Waist Company, the principal owners of which are Isaac Harris and Max Blanck. Most of them could barely speak English. Many of them came from Brooklyn. Almost all were the main support of their hard-working families.

There is just one fire escape in the building. That one is an interior fire escape. In Greene Street, where the terrified unfortunates crowded before they began to make their mad leaps to death, the whole big front of the building is guiltless of one. Nor is there a fire escape in the back.

The building was fireproof and the owners had put their trust in that. In fact, after the flames had done their worst last night, the building hardly showed a sign. Only the stock within it and the girl employes were burned.

A heap of corpses lay on the sidewalk for more than an hour. The firemen were too busy dealing with the fire to pay any attention to people whom they supposed beyond their aid. When the excitement had subsided to such an extent that some of the firemen and policemen could pay attention to this mass of the supposedly dead they found, about half way down in the pack, a girl who was still breathing. She died two minutes after she was found.

The Triangle Waist Company was the only sufferer by the disaster. There are other concerns in the building, but it was Saturday and the other companies had let their people go home. Messrs. Harris and Blanck, however, were busy and their girls—and some men—stayed.

Leaped Out of the Flames.

At 4:40 o clock, nearly five hours after the employes in the rest of the building had gone home, the fire broke out. The one little fire escape in the interior was never resorted to by any of the doomed victims. Some of them escaped by running down the stairs, but in a moment or two this avenue was cut off by flame. The girls rushed to the windows and looked down at Greene Street, 100 feet below them. Then one poor, little creature jumped. There was a plate glass protection over part of the sidewalk, but she crashed through it, wrecking it and breaking her body into a thousand pieces.

Then they all began to drop. The crowd yelled "Don't jump!" but it was jump or be burned—the proof of which is found in the fact that fifty burned bodies were taken from the ninth floor alone.

They jumped, they crashed through broken glass, they crushed themselves to death on the sidewalk. Of those who stayed behind it is better to say nothing—except what a veteran policeman said as he gazed at a headless and charred trunk on the Greene Street sidewalk hours after the worst cases had been taken out:

"I saw the Slocum disaster, but it was nothing to this."

"Is it a man or a woman?" asked the reporter.

"It's human, that's all you can tell," answered the policeman.

It was just a mass of ashes, with blood congealed on what had probably been the neck.

Messrs. Harris and Blanck were in the building, but they escaped. They carried with them Mr. Blanck's children and a governess, and they fled over the roofs. Their employes did not know the way, because they had been in the habit of using the two freight elevators, and one of these elevators was not in service when the fire broke out.

Found Alive After the Fire.

The first living victim, Hyman Meshel of 332 East Fifteenth Street, was taken from the ruins four hours after the fire was discovered. He was found paralyzed with fear and whimpering like a wounded animal in the basement, immersed in water to his neck, crouched on the top of a cable drum, and with his head just below the floor of the elevator.

Meantime the remains of the dead—it is hardly possible to call them bodies, because that word suggests something human, and there was nothing human about most of these—were being taken in a steady stream to the Morgue for identification. First Avenue was lined with the usual curious east side crowd, Twenty-sixth Street was impassable. But in the Morgue they received the charred remnants with no more emotion than they ever display over anything.

Back in Greene Street there was another crowd. At midnight it had not decreased in the least. The police were holding it back to the fire lines, and discussing the tragedy in a tone which those seasoned witnesses of death seldom use.

"It's the worse thing I ever saw," said one old policeman.

Chief Croker said it was an outrage. He spoke bitterly of the way in which the Manufacturers' Association had called a meeting in Wall Street to take measures against his proposal for enforcing better methods of protection for employes in cases of fire.

No Chance to Save Victims.

Four alarms were rung in fifteen minutes. The first five girls who jumped did so before the first engine could respond. That fact may not convey much of a picture to the mind of an unimaginative man, but anybody who has ever seen a fire can get from it some idea of the terrific rapidity with which the flames spread.

It may convey some idea, too, to say that thirty bodies clogged the elevator shafts. These dead were all girls. They had made their rush their blindly when they discovered that there was no chance to get out by the fire escape. Then they found that the elevator was as hopeless as anything else, and they fell there in their tracks and died.

The Triangle Waist Company employed about 600 women and less than 100 men. One of the saddest features of the thing is the fact that they had almost finished for the day. In five minutes more, if the fire had started then, probably not a life would have been lost.

Last night District Attorney Whitman started an investigation—not of this disaster alone but of the whole condition which makes it possible for a firetrap of such a kind to exist. Mr. Whitman's intention is to find out if the present laws cover such cases, and if they do not to frame laws that will.

GIRLS JUMP TO SURE DEATH.

Fire Nets Prove Useless—Firemen Helpless to Save Life.

The fire, which was first discovered at 4:40 o'clock on the eighth floor of the ten-story building at the corner of Washington Place and Greene Street, leaped through the three upper stories occupied by the Triangle Waist Company with a sudden rush that left the Fire Department helpless.

How the fire started no one knows. On the three upper floors of the building were 600 employes of the waist company, 500 of whom were girls. The victims—mostly Italians, Russians, Hungarians, and Germans—were girls and men who had been employed by the firm of Harris & Blanck, owners of the Triangle Waist Company, after the strike in which the Jewish girls, formerly employed, had become unionized and had demanded better working conditions. The building had experienced four recent fires and had been reported by the Fire Department to the Building Department as unsafe, on account of the insufficiency of its exits.

The building itself was of the most modern construction and classed as fireproof. What burned so quickly and disastrously for the victims were shirtwaists, hanging on lines above tiers of workers, sewing machines placed so closely together that there was hardly aisle room for the girls between them, and shirtwaist trimmings and cuttings which littered the floors above the eighth and ninth stories.

Girls had begun leaping from the eighth story windows before the firemen arrived. The firemen had trouble bringing their apparatus into position because of the bodies which strewed the pavement and sidewalks. While more bodies crashed down among them, they worked with desperation to run their ladders into position and to spread firenets.

One fireman, running ahead of a hose wagon, which halted to avoid running over a body, spread a firenet, and two more seized hold of it. A girl's body, coming end over end, struck on the side of it, and there was hope for an instant that she would be the first one of the score who had already jumped to be saved.

Thousands of people, who had crushed in from Broadway and Washington Square and were screaming with horror at what they saw, watched closely the work with the firenet. Three other girls, who had leaped for it a moment after the first one, struck it on top of her, and all four rolled out and lay still upon the pavement.

Five girls who stood together at a window close to the Greene Street corner held their places while a fire ladder was worked toward them, but which stopped at its full length two stories lower down. They leaped together, clinging to each other, with fire streaming back from their hair and dresses. They struck a glass sidewalk cover and crashed through it to the basement. There was no time to aid them. With water pouring in upon them from a dozen hose nozzles the bodies lay for two hours where they struck, as did the many others who leaped to their deaths.

One girl, who waved a handkerchief at the crowd, leaped from a window adjoining the New York University Building on the westward. Her dress caught on a wire, and the crowd watched her hang there till her dress burned free and she came toppling down.

Many jumped whom the firemen believe they could have saved. A girl who saw the glass roof of a sidewalk cover at the first-story level of the New York University Building leaped for it, and her body crashed through to the sidewalk.

On Greene Street, running along the eastern face of the building, more people leaped to the pavement than on Washington Place to the south. Fire nets proved just as useless to catch them and the ladders to reach them. None waited for the firemen to attempt to reach them with the scaling ladders.

All Would Soon Have Been Out.

Strewn about as the firemen worked, the bodies indicated clearly the preponderance of women workers. Here and there was a man, but almost always they were women. One wore furs and a muff, and had a purse hanging from her arm. Nearly all were dressed for the street. The fire had flashed through their workroom just as they were expecting the signal to leave the building. In ten minutes more all would have been out, as many had stopped work in advance of the signal and had started to put on their wraps.

What happened inside there were few who could tell with any definiteness. All that those who escaped seemed to remember was that there was a flash of flames, leaping first among the girls in the southeast corner of the eighth floor, and then suddenly over the entire room, spreading through the linens and cottons with which the girls were working. The girls on the ninth floor caught sight of the flames through the windows, up the stairway, and up the elevator shaft.

On the tenth floor they got them a moment later, but most of those on that floor escaped by rushing to the roof and then on to the roof of the New York University Building, with the assistance of 100 university students who had been dismissed from a tenth story classroom.

There were in the building, according to the estimates of Fire Chief Croker, about 600 girls and 100 men. The bodies of those

"All the News That's Fit to Print."

The New York Times.

THE WEATHER.

Fair to-day; probably fair to-morrow; moderate west winds.

For full weather report see Page 11.

VOL. LX...NO. 19,470. * * * NEW YORK, TUESDAY, MAY 16, 1911.—TWENTY-TWO PAGES. ONE CENT In Greater New York, Jersey City, and Newark. { Elsewhere, TWO CENTS.

DIAZ NOW READY TO QUIT AT ONCE

Is Believed to Have Informed Madero That He and Corral Are Prepared to Resign.

WANTS TO NAME 4 MINISTERS

While Madero's New Demands Include Resignation of Diaz and the Entire Cabinet.

FEDERALS ABANDON SONORA

Troops Concentrating in Mexico City—Hermosillo Evacuated—Rebels Get Another Border Town.

BY STEPHEN BONSAL.

Special Correspondent of The New York Times.

Copyright, 1911, by The New York Times Co.

MEXICO CITY, May 15.—The statement from an insurgent leader to THE NEW YORK TIMES, republished here by The Diario del Hogar, a paper with a wide circulation and with an anti-Diaz policy, created a great sensation this afternoon.

It is apparent that the light seen by every one else has not escaped those at the Palace.

The principal demands of Gen. Madero were received this morning. The revolutionary leader states that they are greater than they were before the capture of Juarez, but only commensurate with the proportions of that victory. He demands the immediate resignation of Diaz; secondly, the issuance of orders for new elections; thirdly, the resignation of the whole Cabinet.

These demands are under consideration. While they have not been rejected and Madero's threat to march upon Mexico City if they are rejected is obviously exerting great weight, a counter-proposition has been made by the Federal Government here to Madero through Judge Carbajal.

If my information is correct, Gen. Diaz offers to resign immediately without any further delays, and promise the same for Vice President Corral, but he asks Madero to consent that four members of the present Cabinet, or rather four Ministers whom he may select, shall remain.

These are understood to include Señor de la Barra, Minister of Foreign Affairs, and Señor Vera Estanol, Minister of Education and the Interior. Further, Gen. Diaz sets great store upon Gen. Reyes being appointed Minister of War immediately upon his arrival in this country, possibly on May 21.

It is thought there in circles sympathetic with the revolution that, for the purpose of stopping bloodshed and reestablishing law and order at the earliest possible moment, Gen. Madero may accept the Diaz counter-proposition.

With the good news that the negotiations are progressing and bid fair to have success, the atmosphere of the capital has cleared wonderfully and the city wears a more cheerful aspect. Business, of course, is practically at a standstill, but the tension in the foreign colony, as well as among the Mexicans, is greatly relaxed.

An incipient riot in the Bolsa district last night was suppressed so quickly that we have no means of discovering its character, if it had any.

From outside the city, however, cumulative news continues to pour in of the peaceful advance of the revolution. Town after town has fallen, no resistance being offered, nor was law and order interrupted. Pachuca, only three hours away from the capital, was attacked this morning. Half the town seems to be in the possession of the revolutionists, and it is expected that the conquest will be completed to-night.

The railway from Puebla to Oaxaca, after many interruptions and robberies, committed apparently by unattached bandits to the detriment of passengers and freight patrons, has suspended operations, but the main railway communication with the southern part of the republic is uninterrupted.

The plight of Americans on the wing is deplorable. Many instances are heartrending. There are 600 at Vera Cruz awaiting transportation, and this does not include about forty distressed citizens who, I am informed, have applied at the consulate there for transportation, if possible, or relief in any event.

Fifty American families, members of the railroad colony, have left Aguas Calientes in the last forty-eight hours, leaving only four families there. The American Smelting and Refining Company there is advancing money to all its married American employes who are leaving for the United States by many routes, and thus the whole colony is deserted.

A similar exodus is taking place in other sections of the republic, of which, however, owing to the interrupted wires and difficulty of communication our information is very meagre. Americans on the Pacific side seem concentrating at Colima, from which place

Continued on Page 7.

THE FIRST AERO-TAXI.

Will Carry Passengers from Lucerne at a Fixed Rate a Kilometer.

Special Cable to THE NEW YORK TIMES.

PARIS, May 15.—According to the Temps, the first aero-taxi will be put into service in a few days at Lucerne.

The innovation is due to the enterprise of the Compagnie Trans-Aerienne, which has just sent to Lucerne a biplane fitted with a taximeter. The aeroplane will be piloted by the aviator Erbster, and will carry passengers on cross-country flights at so much per kilometer registered on the dail.

It is calculated that the aero-taxi will ultimately become a far cheaper conveyance than the streets taxicab, owing to the bee-line route it will be able to follow in the air, where, furthermore, trouble owing to congested traffic is non-existent.

SHACKLETON NOT A RIVAL.

Not Going to Crocker Land—Glad to Hear of American Expedition.

Special Cable to THE NEW YORK TIMES.

LONDON, May 15.—Sir Ernest Shackleton has no intention of leading an expedition to Crocker Land and cannot understand how his name came to be connected with such a report. When THE NEW YORK TIMES correspondent questioned him concerning it, he said:

"I cannot understand who originated the story. I expect some private conversation has been retailed for public consumption. I have discussed privately among people I know possible expeditions ranging from New Guinea and the Amazon to the Kara Sea.

"It is interesting to hear that the Museum of Natural History in New York is sending an expedition to Crocker Land, because it is certainly a tract that ought to be explored. I have no intention of butting in anywhere on any other expedition, and, anyhow, I am not going anywhere this year. I wish success to the Americans."

Sir Ernest thinks highly of the prospects of the American expedition.

FIREMEN OVERCOME RIOTERS.

Two Thousand Strikers, After Fierce Battle, Driven Back by Water.

Special to The New York Times.

GRAND RAPIDS, Mich., May 15.—A score of men and women were injured and many members of a mob of 2,000 striking furniture workers and sympathizers were hurt in a riot at the plant of the Widdicomb Furniture Company to-night. Several of the injured may die.

After a fierce battle with revolvers, clubs, stones, and missiles of almost every description, in which the police were badly beaten, a fire engine company attacked the mob with streams of water, and succeeded in quelling the disturbance to a certain extent. Many women were active among the rioters.

The trouble started when a mob of about 300 men, women, and boys attacked a closed automobile driven by Ralph Widdicomb of the furniture company, who was taking several strikebreakers from the factory. One of the policemen on guard at the plant attempted to make an arrest, and the mob closed in on him. Other policemen with drawn revolvers quickly arrived, but were overwhelmed.

A squad of reserves was rushed to the scene and soon began firing, and the fire was returned by the rioters. Several police officers were knocked senseless by missiles hurled by women.

Mayor Ellis made a fruitless attempt to quell the riot before the Fire Department was summoned. A terrific battle ensued as the firemen began to lay their lines. The mob was finally broken up and the strikebreakers were spirited away.

CORNER ERMINE MARKET.

St. Louis Firm Puts Up Prices for the Coronation.

Special to The New York Times.

ST. LOUIS, Mo., May 15.—Owing to the scarcity of ermine on the European market, St. Louis controls an important feature of the coronation festivities. A St. Louis concern, the F. C. Taylor Fur Company has been quietly cornering the catch of the trappers of Alaska and Canada and are now preparing to ship 100,000 of the little white skins to London. The value of this shipment is estimated at $175,000.

The Taylor Company has been working so quietly that even the agents for the Royal Furriers, who visited St. Louis several months ago, did not know that there was a supply here. The world was scoured by this agent and every one of the available furs bought up.

After the English agent left St. Louis the fur company began getting their skins out of storage, and when they counted up found that they had more than 200,000. Six weeks ago they shipped about 80,000 skins, and within the next week will have sent out about 100,000 more.

The furs are not being shipped directly to London, but they will eventually reach that place, probably by the first of June. The wholesale price of the skins has risen from about one dollar each to almost double that price.

MRS. DODGE SENTENCED.

Not Less Than Four Nor More Than Six Years in Vermont State Prison.

GUILDHALL, Vt., May 15.—A sentence of not less than four nor more than six years in the State prison at Windsor was imposed to-day upon Mrs. Florence L. Dodge, who was convicted on Saturday of manslaughter in shooting William Heath at her home at Lunenburg on Sept. 17.

Mrs. Dodge received the sentence without the slightest evidence of emotion. Her counsel stated that they would take no exceptions to the sentence. Mrs. Dodge will probably be taken to the State prison to-morrow.

When asked by the court if she had anything to say, Mrs. Dodge replied:

"I have nothing further to say than I have said all the time: 'I am innocent.'"

$250,000 FOR RIOT LOSS.

United States Express Company Sues Jersey City.

TRENTON, N. J., May 15.—In an effort to recover $250,000 damages as the result of rioting incident to the recent strike, Edward T. Platt, Treasurer of the United States Express Company, brought suit in the Supreme Court here to-day against the Mayor and Aldermen of Jersey City.

It is charged that the Mayor and police failed to suppress the mobs and rioting and the city is held to be responsible for the damage done to the company's property and for the interference with its business.

COUNTERFEIT PLANT TAKEN IN A RAID

Four Men and a Woman Captured on Charges of Making Bogus Indian-Head Bills.

ALL READY TO LEAVE TOWN

Band Said to Have Made Plans to Flood Alaska with the Bad Five-Dollar Bills.

Through the arrest yesterday of four men and a woman, the seizure of a lithographic stone, upon which had been engraved a fac simile of the Indian head five dollar bill, many engraving tools and printing apparatus, the Secret Service men believe they have ended a plot which had for its object the flooding of Alaska with counterfeit money.

For weeks the Government sleuths have been watching the band and they swooped down upon them yesterday when the experimental printing plant had been closed, the apparatus packed ready for shipment and those charged with being interested in the making of bad money had their tickets already purchased for Chicago.

The prisoners are James Glenard, his wife and Marko Pagonich of 216 East Sixteenth Street; Samuel Pekovich of 616 Eleventh Avenue, and Mlahailo Karahasvick, an engraver, of 433 East Sixth Street. With the exception of the Glenards, the prisoners are from Montenegro. Pagonich's card sets forth that he is President of the Alaska King River Mining Company of Douglas, Alaska. Glenard said he had been for fifteen years a member of the New Orleans police force. Three years ago, he said, he left there and went to San Francisco, where he and his wife ran a boarding house. The pair came to New York six months ago. Mrs. Glenard has two gold upper front teeth in each of which is set a diamond.

After weeks of shadowing, Richard H. Taylor, in charge of the local Secret Service, with John Henry and Frank Burke and others of the force, went to the Glenard house about noon yesterday. On the way they arrested Karakasvick. They told those in the Glenard flat that they were Government agents and demanded to know why the band had pawned so much jewelry lately. Nothing was said about counterfeiting and the three men and the woman readily consented to go to the Secret Service office in the Custom House. While this was going on other Secret Service agents went to 6 Paterson Street, Hoboken, and seized the plant. Those arrested were confronted with the evidence and each was questioned separately. After the examination they were locked up, some in the Old Slip and others in the Greenwich Street station.

The development of the plot has been carefully watched by the Secret Service men. Karakasvick, it is said, had been under suspicion before in connection with the counterfeiting of Austrian notes. In watching him the agents say they discovered the identity of the others.

The plot started six weeks ago, when some of those under arrest lived at 402 Eighth Avenue. Five weeks ago the Glenards moved to 216 East 16th Street and that became the headquarters. It took weeks of patient work to complete the lithograph stone. This was ready three weeks ago and those engaged in the plot rented and furnished a floor in the Hoboken house. They furnished it, bought a fine hand press, paper, ink and other necessaries. Two days ago the first proofs were run off on the press. Then everything was packed up preparatory to moving to Chicago. The proofs are now in the hands of Taylor and his men. The sleuths say the work is remarkably good. The stone was engraved to imitate the silk fibre as in a genuine bill.

While the preparatory work was in progress the funds of the band ran short, and it was then they had resorted to pawning their jewelry. Their returns would have been quick, for had they decided to print here, the agents say, they could have turned out at least sixteen bills an hour.

Glenard protests that he was forced into the plot by threats against himself and his wife. At first, he said, he believed that the other men were engaged in making stock certificates for the Alaska mine. He admits that toward the last he knew that bad money was to be made and when he wanted to back out threats were made against his life.

TO SELL "SPENDTHRIFT" FUND

There's a Chance That the Purchaser May Profit 1,000 Per Cent.

Special to The New York Times.

CAMBRIDGE, Mass., May 15.—Hammond Braman, college man, former banker and broker of this city, stands to lose the $50,000 "spendthrift trust fund" created for him by his father unless he bids it in or has it bid in to-morrow when it is put up at auction.

In the Boston papers to-day appeared an announcement that the auction would take place to-morrow by order of the Board of Trustees in Bankruptcy. Further particulars were to be obtained from Clarence W. Rowley, attorney at law. The advertisement was headed as follows:

> Win or lose a $50,000 fortune.
> Now tied up in a Spendthrift Trust.
> If the man dies without a child, you get the whole. If the man dies leaving a child, you get nothing. He hasn't any child now and we don't think he ever will have any.

Braman went into bankruptcy about three years ago. The Old Colony Trust Company is trustee of the Braman fund. If Hammond Braman dies without issue those who take a chance in the auction may realize 1,000 per cent. on their investment. Braman is the son of Grenville T. W. Braman, formerly a member of the firm of Braman & Dow.

PROF. WHEELER RESIGNS.

Instructor at Yale, Divorced for Cruelty, Leaves the College.

Special to The New York Times.

NEW HAVEN, Conn., May 15.—Prof. [illegible] Lord Wheeler of the Sheffield Scientific School, Yale, forwarded by telegram from Chicago. his resignation to [illegible] university corporation at its May meeting to-day, which was attended by [illegible] members except President Taft and [illegible] Baldwin.

[illegible] statement given out by Secretary [illegible] the corporation to-night says that the resignation was received, and was accepted, in accordance with a rule which requires a professor's resignation to lie upon the table for one meeting.

The statement adds that "it will be acted upon at the next meeting, and, in the meantime, he will not exercise his functions as a professor at the university. Prof. Wheeler's classes were to-day turned over to other instructors during the remainder of the school year.

MRS. TAFT BETTER; NO ALARM FELT NOW

President Returns to Washington, Gets Reassuring Telegram, and Goes to Theatre.

WIFE LEAVES THURSDAY

Daughter Will Act in Her Place at White House Social Events for a Time.

Mrs. Taft, whose illness caused the President to return to New York Sunday night to see her at his brother's house, 36 West Forty-eighth Street, was so much improved yesterday morning that the President took an early train for Washington. In the evening, when he received a reassuring telegram, he went to the theatre. The telegram said that Mrs. Taft would return to Washington on Thursday afternoon.

Announcement was made at the White House that the programme which Mrs. Taft has mapped out for the Spring will be adhered to. The dinner to the Fur Seal Commissioners on Thursday night and the garden party Friday evening will be given. Miss Helen Taft, who is now with her mother, will act as mistress of the White House on both occasions.

Dr. Evan W. Evans, Henry W. Taft's family physician, called at the house yesterday morning to see the wife of the President, and remained about half an hour. Mrs. Taft was getting along so nicely that it was not thought necessary to issue a formal bulletin. She is rapidly recovering from her nervous attack.

The President had two callers before he left his brother's house yesterday morning. Henry L. Stimson, who is to join the President's Cabinet as Secretary of War, came to talk over matters connected with his appointment. Mr. Stimson was to have been sworn in as Secretary of War this week, but it was announced yesterday that he would not take the oath until next Monday.

The other caller was Postmaster General Hitchcock, who had been spending the week-end in New York. When he read of Mrs. Taft's illness he drove to the house to inquire about her.

The President, accompanied by Major Butt and Henry W. Taft, came out of the house at 9:40, and entered a waiting automobile. The presence of a squad of police and secret service men outside the door served to attract a small crowd, who cheered when the President came down the steps, smiling broadly as he raised his grey Fedora hat.

The President's automobile was preceded down Fifth Avenue by two bicycle policemen and followed by two automobiles containing detectives and secret service men. The President sat with his brother. At the Pennsylvania station he boarded the private car Ideal, which was attached to the 10:08 train.

PRIEST ARRESTS A BOY.

Crap Player Tried to Strike Father Brann, the Latter Declares.

Father Henry A. Brann of St. Agnes's Church, at 143 East Forty-third Street, was seated at a front window of the rectory yesterday afternoon when he noticed a group of boys playing dice on the sidewalk opposite. He quietly left the building, but five of the lads saw him and ran. Isadore Berkowitz, 15 years old, a telegraph messenger living at 1,571 First Avenue, however, endeavored to seize 8 cents they abandoned on the sidewalk and was caught by the priest.

Near Lexington Avenue and Fifty-first Street the boy attempted to strike the priest, but Father Brann managed to hold the youngster until the arrival of Patrolman McMahon.

The priest accompanied the prisoner and the patrolman to the East Fifty-first Street Station, where the boy was charged with juvenile delinquency and sent to the Children's Society. He denied that he had tried to strike the priest, but said his coat was pulled half off and he was endeavoring to get it upon his shoulders.

MUCKRAKING TO CEASE.

President Cannon of Fourth National Bank Tells a Western Audience So.

Special to The New York Times.

OMAHA, May 15.—There is to be an end of muck-raking and the magazines which have heretofore devoted so much space to articles of this character are to take up religion and "play up" theology as it has never been done before, according to James G. Cannon, President of the Fourth National Bank of New York, who to-day addressed the Omaha Ministerial Union on the subject of the "Forward Movement." Mr. Cannon said:

"If there is not the greatest ingathering in the churches it will be the fault of the men in charge, for we are going to have the subject of religion so 'played up' in the papers and magazines that the man who wants to promulgate religion will not have a single excuse for failing to get busy among his friends and neighbors.

"The magazine editors who have been muckraking all their lives are seeing that the thing must end, and that the only step toward progress consists in building man up."

WEAPON BILL PASSES.

Only Seven in Assembly Vote Against It and It Goes to Governor.

Special to The New York Times.

ALBANY, May 15.—By a vote of 123 to 7, the Assembly to-night pased the Sullivan dangerous weapon bill. The bill makes the sale or carrying of dangerous weapons without a permit a felony, and provides that dealers in such weapons must keep a register, in which the name of a purchaser must be recorded.

The bill has already passed the Senate, and now goes to the Governor.

STANDARD OIL COMPANY MUST DISSOLVE IN 6 MONTHS; ONLY UNREASONABLE RESTRAINT OF TRADE FORBIDDEN

And of Such Unreasonable Restraint the Supreme Court Finds the Standard Guilty.

DECISION PLEASES TAFT

Decision Reads "Unreasonable" Into Law and Is What Trusts Wanted, Says La Follette.

LOWER DECISION MODIFIED

More Time Given and Injunction Against Doing Business Meanwhile Is Removed.

JUSTICE HARLAN DISSENTS

Objects to Limiting the Sherman Law by the Use of the Term "Unreasonable."

WHAT STANDARD WILL DO

Chicago Counsel Says It Will Go On as Usual After Changes Are Made.

Special to The New York Times.

WASHINGTON, May 15.—Final decision was returned late this afternoon by the Supreme Court of the United States in one of the two great trust cases which have been before it for so long—that of the Standard Oil Company. The decree of the Circuit Court for the Eighth Circuit directing the dissolution of the Oil Trust was affirmed, with minor modifications in two particulars. So far as the judgment of the court is concerned the action was unanimous, but Justice Harlan dissented from the argument on which the judgment was based.

The two modifications of the decree of the Circuit Court are that the period for execution of the decree is extended from thirty days to six months, and the injunction against engaging in inter-State commerce on petroleum and its products pending the execution of the decree is vacated. This latter modification is made distinctly in consideration of the serious injury to the public which might result from the absolute cessation of that business for such a time.

Broadly speaking, the court determines against the Standard Oil Company on the ground that it is a combination in unreasonable restraint of inter-State commerce. For the first time since it has been construing the Sherman Anti-Trust act the court takes that position, and thus definitely reads the word "unreasonable" into the law. It was on this ground that Justice Harlan dissented. This decision, therefore, is a practical reversal of the position taken by the court in the trans-Missouri case, one of the first cases under the Sherman law.

In that case Justice White joined with the late Justice Brewer in a dissenting opinion, while Justice Harlan was with the majority of the court. That decision held, as Justice Harlan now holds regarding the Standard Oil Company, that the combination complained of was in restraint of inter-State commerce and therefore under the inhibition of the statute. Justices White and Brewer then held that the combination complained of was an "unreasonable" restraint of commerce, and so brought itself under the ban of the law.

Justice Harlan sharply criticised the majority of the court for taking this position. He declared it to be a menace to the institutions of the country. He said it was amending the Constitution by judicial interpretation, and was unjustified. And he asserted that one of the greatest dangers to the country was the willingness of the courts to take such action.

How Decision Was Received.

The decision was received with varying emotion by the crowd in the little court room. Attorney General Wickersham hailed it as a victory for the Administration. Frank B. Kellogg, the Assistant "Trust Buster," who has had the chief management of the case from the Government from its inception, was of similar opinion. Progressive Senators like La Follette openly expressed distrust of the effect of the decision, and Senator Kenyon, who only a few weeks ago left the Department of Justice to enter the upper house of Congress, spoke of it as a "dangerous decision."

While in the Department of Justice, Mr. Kenyon was in charge of the prosecution of the Beef Trust, the members of which will be indicted individually on the criminal count. The department hopes to bring these cases to trial in the near future.

Trust lawyers who were in court did not display any willingness to comment on the decision. But among the lawyers who heard the Chief Justice deliver his epitome of the opinion, which he did without referring to the printed text of the decision, and who were not connected with this case, the opinion prevailed that the decision was distinctly favorable to "big business." For a long time there has been open expression of the hope on the part of "big business" that when the decision in the oil and tobacco cases did finally come down, they would at least point a way under which the big corporations could continue to do business, and that the present general method would not be utterly destroyed.

President Taft himself, in messages to Congress and in public speeches, has declared himself earnestly in favor of retaining the economy and efficiency of combinations and of destroying merely those practices which unduly restrained inter-State commerce and stifled competition. There was a time when the President was in favor of some amendment to the Sherman law in the effort to reach this situation. But he finally came to the conclusion that it was impracticable to write the word "unreasonable" into the law, and pointed out that more and more the Supreme Court was tending toward the point where its decisions in trust cases would be based on that construction of the statute.

Way Out for Corporations.

Now it seems to have been done, and the forceful personality of Chief Justice White has so impressed itself upon the court that he has carried seven of the other Justices with him. Representatives of "big business" who heard him this afternoon did not hesitate to declare emphatically that the decision was all that the big corporations could ask. They regarded with especial favor the establishment of the proposition that a combination must be in "unreasonable" restraint of commerce to be unlawful.

This they believe points out the way by which the big corporations in the country can continue to exist. They recalled with satisfaction the fact that President Taft has specifically declared that it is not mere size which puts a corporation or combination under the ban of the law; it is not the breadth or scope of its operations, or the amount of its capitalization, but whether or not it does two things; fixes prices and controls output.

The representatives of corporations here to-day find in Chief Justice White's decision a practical agreement with the position of President Taft. They have been satisfied with that position and have realized for a long time that business must conform to such standard. Now they find relief in the decision of the highest court in the country, and some of them expressed the opinion this evening that the effect on the general business situation would be good.

There is very little difference in the views of the progressives and those of big business men here as to the effect of the decision. But whereas the corporation representatives regard it with favor, the progressives find in it cause for distrust and dissatisfaction. This view was especialy emphasized by Senators La Follette and Kenyon.

La Follette Not Satisfied.

"In the light of what Justice Harlan in his dissenting opinion said of the Chief Justice's decision," said Senator La Follette, "I think that if it is true that the court holds that the law applies only to unreasonable restraint of trade it is a very dangerous decision. In that view of it I should say it is precisely what the trusts want, and they, more than any others, will be pleased with the decision. The court has amended the Sherman anti-trust law just as it was attempted over and over in the Senate to do it. What they did not get in the Senate they have now got from the court.

"If Justice Harlan interprets the decision correctly we shall have a plenty to do now with the law so amended. Every trust will now come into court and claim justification on a special set of facts going to support the claim that it is not restraining trade unreasonably, and it is to be expected that courts will make use of a sliding scale of reasonableness to apply to each case. I fear that the court has done just what the trusts have wanted it to do and what Congress has refused steadfastly to do."

Senator Kenyon of Iowa took a view similar to that of Senator La Follette. He said:

"I think the court has amended the anti-trust law, and it will lead to trouble. The courts will now be obliged to consider the reasonableness or unreasonableness of trust operations, and to-day's decision will prove to be only the beginning of a long and hard fight. It suggests that legislation will be demanded by the people to make good what has been taken from the law, but it is not easy to see just what legislation will fit the situation.

"I am inclined to feel that nothing short of jail sentences will accomplish any positive results. There has been discussion of the limitation of investments, with safeguards against stockholders being in more than one corporation, but all that is probably far in the future, and I do not care to talk about it. I do not hesitate to say, however, that there is danger in this decision."

On the other hand the decision was regarded by many as a great victory for the Government. Among these were Senator Cullom of Illinois, who sat through the greater part of the Chief Justice's delivery of the decision, and also through Justice Harlan's dissenting opinion. Senator Bailey o Texas manifested great pleasure in the decision. He went in and out of the court chamber several times in the afternoon, and after the adjournment of the court walked out through the Capitol and stood for several minutes talking with a group of Justices, including Chief Justice White, Justice Holmes, and Justice Van De Water.

"It is a correct interpretation of the law," said Senator Bailey, "and no corporation will be able under its operation to organize a trust or engage in business in violation of law. I think the Supreme Court has now made it impossible for a corporation to defy the law."

What Wickersham Says.

Attorney General Wickersham and Solicitor General Lehmann were surrounded as soon as the court adjourned by those who wanted to learn their views of the decision. Mr. Wickersham commented very briefly and then went to the Department of Justice, where he promptly withdrew into his private office and prepared a statement in which he formally expressed his view of the victory won by the Government. The statement says:

"The Attorney General stated, with respect to the decision in the Standard Oil case rendered by the Supreme Court today, that the court unanimously affirms the decree rendered by the Circuit Court in favor of the Government in every particular save that it gives the defendants six months instead of thirty days' time in which to comply with the decree.

"Substantially every position contended for by the Government in this case is affirmed by the Supreme Court. In the reasoning by which the Chief Justice reaches the conclusion in which the whole court concurs he expresses the view that only contracts, combinations, &c., which in any way unreasonably or unduly restrain inter-State trade and commerce or which are unreasonably restrictive of competitive conditions are within the prohibition of the first section of the Sherman act. Justice Harlan, on the other hand, dissents from this view and contends that every contract, &c., which does restrain trade and commerce is within the inhibition of the statute, but he concurs with the whole court in the decree of affirmance.

"The Chief Justice further holds that the second section of the act seeks, if possible, to make the prohibitions of the act all the more complete and perfect by embracing all attempts to reach the ends prohibited by the first section that is, restraint of trade by any attempt to monopolize or monopolization thereof, even although the acts by which such results are attempted to be brought about, or are brought about, be not embraced within the general enumeration of the first section. He further hold that the criterion by which it is to be determined in all cases, whether a contract, combination, &c., is a restraint of trade within the meaning of the law, is the direct or indirect effect of the acts involved."

OPINIONS ON THE DECISION.

Attorney General Wickersham: "Substantially every proposition contended for by the Government is affirmed."

Frank B. Kellogg, counsel for Government: "It is a complete victory for the Government."

Senator Kenyon, formerly Assistant Attorney General: "I think the court has amended the anti-trust law, and it will lead to trouble."

Senator La Follette: "I fear that the court has done what the trusts wanted it to do, and what Congress has steadily refused to do."

Alfred D. Eddy, Standard Oil counsel in Chicago: "The business of the Standard Oil Company will go on as usual, although changes will be made."

Courtroom Crowded.

It has been a long time since there was such a scene in the Supreme Court as that of this afternoon. With the House not in session at all, and the Senate engaged in interesting controversy for only a few minutes, the court was the chief attraction for the ordinary visitors to the Capitol. And of course there were many more persons interested in the two trust cases than could possibly find room in the restricted quarters of the great court.

Long before noon there was a long line of waiting men and women in the corridor before the door of the courtroom, a line that extended clear across the rotunda of the Capitol. And despite the oppressive atmosphere of the courtroom very few of those who managed to get in left and made room for others.

As the afternoon waned there were many significant nods about the room and gestures at the big clock over the head of the Chief Justice, showing how the audience took note of the fact that it had got beyond the hour of closing for the Stock Exchanges. Every Justice on the bench had at least one opinion to deliver, and they prosed along through them until it began to look as if there would be no trust case to-day.

At length it came the turn of the Chief Justice. The aged Justice Harlan had lingered a weary time over a number of railroad cases, and when Chief Justice White began to read, and it was seen that he was delivering not an opinion, but the orders of the court on certain motions, it began to look as if the trust cases would surely go over for another fortnight. Then the Chief Justice announced that he had the opinion and judgment of the court in a case, and there was a rustle of sudden expectancy. But instantly it appeared that it was not a trust case.

This decision dragged along to its close and the audience of Senators and Congressmen scattered about inside the rail, along with the Attorney General and the representatives of the Department of Justice, and the trust lawyers shuffled wearily, as if thinking that they had wasted a day for nothing. Then the Chief Justice plunged into the great decision. With an added note of solemnity in his manner he said:

"I have the opinion and judgment of the court in No. 358," and everbody in the room knew that the Standard Oil decision was coming.

Chief Justice Reads Decision.

The Chief Justice did not read the long opinion, but, speaking extemporaneously, delivered a synopsis of the decision. He spoke, as usual, rapidly and with great variation in volume of voice, so that at times his words were distinctly audible in every part of the room and at other times even the stenographers directly in front of him were unable to catch a syllable. Several times Justice McKenna, who sits at his left hand, leaned over and suggested that he raise his voice so that he could be heard. Once or twice on such suggestions the Chief Justice repeated what he had said, and then for a time would speak forcibly, so that all could hear.

Always with earnestness and conviction the Chief Justice spoke, often accompanying his words with a gesture. When he discussed the motive of the men who enacted the Sherman law his voice rang through the courtroom as he said:

"The writers of that law were legislating for freedom."

It was just one minute to 4 o'clock when the Chief Justice began speaking in the Standard Oil case. He was forty-nine minutes delivering his synopsis.

It was just twelve minutes of 5 o'clock when the Chief Justice concluded, and the audience gathered in the crowded courtroom breathed a sigh of relief at the final gratification of a nation-wide curiosity in regard to the fate of one of the most gigantic business organizations known in the world's history. The Chief Justice gathered up his papers, flung his silken

"All the News That's Fit to Print."

The New York Times.

THE WEATHER.

Fair and cool to-day; increasing cloudiness, probable local rains, slightly warmer to-morrow.

For full weather report see Page 20.

VOL. LXI...NO. 19,621. * * * NEW YORK, SATURDAY, OCTOBER 14, 1911.—TWENTY-TWO PAGES ONE CENT In Greater New York, Jersey City, and Newark. { Elsewhere, TWO CENTS.

WAIT ALL NIGHT AT POLO GROUNDS

Most of the Seats for To-day's Great Game Have Gone to Speculators.

FEW TICKETS FOR THE FANS

But Some 200 Faithful Souls Camp in the Dark at the Closed Gates.

CLUB OFFICIALS CENSURED

The Scalpers and Hotel Stands Have Seats A-plenty at $8 and $10 Apiece—$450 for a Box.

When Umpire William J. Klem, or one of the three other arbiters assigned to the opening of the world's champion series between the New York National League Baseball Club and the Philadelphia American League Club, cries. "Play ball," at 2 o'clock this afternoon, the new stands at the Polo Grounds undoubtedly will be packed as tightly as it is possible to pack human beings, with enthusiastic baseball fans, but whether the enthusiasm will be for the home team, the Giants, or for the Philadelphia Athletics is a question which occasioned considerable discussion yesterday wherever the fans congregated.

When the Giants won the game, some days ago, which made them pennant winners in the National League, New York's baseball enthusiasts expressed their pleasure in the wildest praises of the club and in the making of bets that the Giants would "clean up" the Athletics as they had done in 1905, when the same clubs met for the world's championship. It took only two days—Thursday and yesterday—to turn many of the eagerest rooters into Philadelphia partisans, and the manner in which the sale of tickets was conducted provided the reason.

William M. Gray, Secretary of the New York Baseball Club; issued a statement last night saying that the charge had been called to his attention that the club had permitted ticket speculators to obtain possession of about all the tickets for the world's series. He denied that such was the case and offered $5,000 for proof that the club was party to any such arrangement.

The Victims Not Convinced.

But it would take more than any official announcement by Mr. Gray or any proffer of reward if he be proved wrong to convince the thousands who had followed directions and written for tickets, with money orders and checks inclosed, that something hadn't been radically wrong with the ticket distribution arrangement which reseulted in their receiving no tickets. All day yesterday from dawn to dark thousands of excited fans stormed the offices of the New York Baseball Club.

They wanted tickets most of all, but failing these they couldn't see why they shouldn't have their money back at once instead of waiting until next week as requested.

Thousands of Forged Tickets.

On top of the indignation caused by the distribution of the tickets among scalpers came the disclosure that thousands of tickets have been forged and are being offered for sale. The counterfeit is a careless, crude bit of work, and the names of President John T. Brush and Treasurer John Whalen at the bottom of the ticket are printed instead of the autographs of these officials being reproduced.

The figures on the ticket are of a different style, but in spite of these differences, many people were so anxious to buy tickets that they bought the counterfeits last night. The management has given orders that all tickets be carefully scrutinized at the turnstiles to-day. The original tickets were plain, ordinary pasteboards, such as any printing shop could easily turn out, and much criticism is being directed at the management because they did not adopt a ticket which would be more difficult to reproduce.

The National Commission will meet this morning at 10 o'clock and will probably order an investigation of the ticket scandal.

Police Commissioner Waldo had ordered details of policemen to prevent speculation in tickets anywhere near the St. James Building, but there wasn't a speculator in the city rash enough to offer tickets in the very halls where the disappointed fans were waiting. Had he done so he would probably have been mobbed.

In many other places about town, however, tickets were for sale in any quantities desired. Only the price differed from that which the club had advertised. Three-dollar seats commanded $5 to $10 with the prospect that these prices would advance again to-day.

One man proudly exhibited a piece of pasteboard entitling him to a box for the series. He declared he had paid $450 for it. Several speculators offered boxes for $200. The scandal in which the ticket sale had resulted finally brought about an investigation by the Post Office authorities. Too many tickets and checks or money orders seemed to have gone astray in the mails. They decided, however, that there had been no fraud.

District Attorney Whitman expressed a willingness to undertake an investigation, declaring that one should be made if conditions governing the ticket sale were such as thousands of disgruntled fans charged. He declared, however, that he of course wouldn't take the initiative, and admitted that he had been expecting all days to receive from some source a complaint on which he could act. Should such a complaint be made to-day he said he would immediately begin an investigation.

Public clamor drove the National Baseball Commission, composed of August Herrman, Ban Johnson, and Thomas J. Lynch, to seek a conference with President Brush of the New York Baseball Club in the Hotel Imperial last night. It is known that they discussed the ticket situation, but no action was taken, and the commission will not meet until to-day.

Offer of a Reward.

Secretary Gray's retort followed his interview with a newspaper man who did not mince his words. In full it read:

A newspaper reporter told me to-day it had been stated to him that a ticket speculator named Marks had arranged with certain New York Club officials which enabled him to secure one thousand tickets to the world's series at 50 cents advance per ticket. This statement I brand unqualifiedly as a malicious, malignant lie, and I will give five thousand dollars ($5,000) to any one who can prove that any such arrangement with Marks or any other living individual existed whereby they could secure a single ticket for speculative purposes.

I would not have worked night and

COFFEE STILL GOING UP.

Rumor of an Arbuckle Corner Helps Advance Price Nearly a Cent.

Coffee, which has been climbing steadily in price for several years, but with more speed for the past few weeks, advanced nearly a cent a pound on the Coffee Exchange yesterday during a session of the heaviest trading that market has ever seen. The December option for the standard grade went to 14.95 cents per pound, which is nearly double the price at this time in 1910, and represents a rise of about 3½ cents per pounds since the first of the year.

The present levels are the highest in a generation, and are due to the Brazilian Government's action five years ago in discouraging further planting of coffee trees, and in taking out of the world's markets under its valorization scheme the surplus supplies of the staple.

These supplies are now held in warehouse, and are being marketed gradually. Actual coffee is selling still higher than the Exchange future contracts, and Arbuckle Brothers paid yesterday 16½ and 16¾ cents per pound for 150,000 bags of spot coffee. The news of the heavy buying by the Arbuckles gave rise to rumors that the firm had cornered coffee, and induced many of the shorts on the Coffee Exchange to cover.

William A. Jamison, one of the partners of Arbuckle Brothers, issued a statement last night denying that his firm had a corner in the staple or were fixing the price. The advance here, he explained, was due to the rise in coffee prices on the European Exchanges, and New York prices, he said, were still below those in the other markets of the world.

"We are buying coffee entirely for distribution, roasted or green," he said, "and are selling at a fractional advance over the prices at which we have bought. We are not piling up stocks for a corner. Prices to the consumer have not been much affected by the advance in raw coffee. Most of the coffee sold in this country is marketed under trade names at standard prices, and these prices have in most instances been maintained."

NO CHURCH DOOR FEES.

Apostolic Delegate Directs That Custom Prevalent Here Be Dropped.

Special to The New York Times.

ST. LOUIS, Mo., Oct. 13.—The practice in some Roman Catholic Churches of asking a contribution at the door, thus exacting a fee for a seat in church, is ordered discontinued in a circular letter addressed to all Archbishops and Bishops of the Church in the United States, and sent out by Mgr. D. Falconio, Apostolic Delegate at Washington, D. C.

Father D. S. Phelan, editor of The Western Watchman, has received the first copy in St. Louis. The letter is phrased in the most sweeping terms, and condemns the practice in the strongest language.

The order applies to all Catholic churches in America, and Mgr. Falconio's order becomes effective at once, the clergy being directed to rearrange for the collection of their revenues. Mgr. Falconio speaks of the practice as "bringing scandal to both Catholics and non-Catholics," and regrets that complaints, on investigation, have been shown to be "too true." The order is evidently the result of many years' careful investigation, for Mgr. Falconio refers to a complaint made to him by the Cardinal Prefect of the Propaganda in 1908. The circular warns that any clergyman who disobeys the order will be "condignly punished."

The Roman Catholic archdiocesan authorities stated last night at the headquarters of Archbishop Farley, St. Patrick's Cathedral, Fifth Avenue and Fiftieth Street, that no letter from Papal Delegate, His Right Reverence Mgr. Falconio, had been received by them.

"There is nothing new or revolutionary about the letter that Mgr. Falconio is reported to have written," said a spokesman of the Archbishop last night. "There is an old law of the Church against collecting fees from those about to attend mass. The Papal Delegate before Archbishop Falconio sent letters to heads of dioceses on this subject when it was reported that this law had been violated. The universal custom about the payment of pew rent is that pew holders are entitled to their pews only at the high mass on Sundays and holy days of obligation, and that at the earlier masses, usually low masses, at which there is no music, attendance is unrestricted to the faithful. As the communicants of Roman Catholic churches usually outnumber by three or four times their seating capacity, a sufficient number of masses at convenient hours are invariably provided, so that non-pewholders can attend the religious services which conscience and the laws of the Church require."

TO TRY NEW FLIER TO-DAY.

Wrights' Motorless Glider Arrives at Their Kill Devil Hill Camp.

Special to The New York Times.

MANTEO, N. C., Oct. 13.—Orville Wright promised this afternoon that his new "buzzard" biplane will have its first try-out to-morrow if the winds prove favorable.

The arrival of the machine, which the Wright brothers expect to soar like a bird, was the feature of the day in the aviators' camp, near Kill Devil Hill. Two crates, one six by eighteen feet, with a depth of eighteen inches, and the other considerably smaller, were unloaded from the little gasoline boat that landed at Kitty Hawk Bay yesterday afternoon, and the machine was carted to the beach a mile away. The cases were immediately stored in the hangar, and the parts will be assembled early to-morrow.

The Wrights have given up as hopeless their efforts to make the tests secretly. To-day Lorin and Wilbur Wright received several reporters and extended to their visitors an invitation to return to camp to-morrow for the initial trial of the machine they believe will demonstrate their ability to soar indefinitely in a motorless glider.

Alexander Ogilvie, the English aviator with the Wrights in their camp on the beach, will try out the new machine with Orville.

Orville Wright continues to refuse to describe the new glider. It looks much like the old machine, he says, and his advice to questioners is, "Wait until to-morrow and see." Crated as it was it was impossible to get an idea as to what shape the machine will assume when it is assembled.

DELAYS MISSISSIPPI FLIGHT.

Aviator Robinson Unable to Start, Owing to Cross-Currents.

MINNEAPOLIS, Minn., Oct. 13.—Having emerged safely from an automobile accident to-day, Aviator Hugh Robinson attempted to start on his hydro-aeroplane flight from Minneapolis to New Orleans. His frail craft was buffeted by the winds and careened dangerously. From the time that he struck the cross-currents and was forced to seek safety on the shores of Lake Calhoun, until dusk, the aviator stood prepared to try again.

Robinson had set great store by to-day—Oct. 13—because it was his birthday anniversary. He is 30 years old.

SAW J. B. M'NAMARA AT EXPLOSION SCENE

Los Angeles Times Employe, Long Missing, Identifies Prisoner as Alley Loiterer.

FIGHT OVER UNION PREJUDICE

Whole Day Occupied with the Examination of One Venireman Without Reaching a Decision.

Special to The New York Times.

LOS ANGELES, Cal., Oct. 13.—William Brown, a former employe of The Los Angeles Times, to-day positively identified James B. McNamara, on trial for murder in connection with that disaster, as the man who was seen hanging about in the alley that ran back of the main building of the destroyed plant on the night of the explosion, Oct. 1, 1910.

The morning session of the trial was about half over when Joseph Ford, Assistant District Attorney, entered the courtroom, bringing with him a man. Ford entered inconspicuously, and, taking his companion within the rail, seated him a dozen feet away from and facing McNamara.

The man fixed his gaze on the prisoner. Immediately the latter called Clarence Darrow, his chief counsel, over to him, and whispered:

"They've brought that fellow here to identify me."

The stranger kept his place for a few minutes, all the while scrutinizing the defendant. Then he went to Ford and both withdrew. Ford refused to say who he was, but acknowledged that he had brought him there to identify J. B. McNamara as "some one" the stranger knew. It developed later that the stranger was Brown. McNamara himself said that he had never seen him before.

Brown was employed in the paper stock room of The Times at the time of the explosion, and is now a teamster. He is known to have reported to the Grand Jury that he had seen a strange man loitering about in the vicinity of the alley in which the explosion is known to have occurred. Brown has been searched for by the prosecution for some time, and was lately found.

His identification of the prisoner is said to be positive and to put the matter of McNamara's presence on the corner of First and Broadway, the night of the explosion and within an hour of the time, beyond all doubt.

Trial to be a Long One.

Proof that the trial of McNamara will be a long-drawn and fiercely contested one was given to-day in the determination evinced by both sides in the struggle that has arisen over the selection of a jury. Neither State nor defense is going to expend a challenge unnecessarily.

To the watchers in the press seats and to the crowded court room, the lines on which the trial will be waged became plain as the contest proceeded. The defense will, in all probability, make much of the supposed prejudice against McNamara because of his affiliations with labor unions, and the prosecution will just as probably endeavor to belittle and avoid that issue.

Throughout the tedious proceedings the prisoner rarely moved and hardly ever glanced around. He is growing paler under the strain, and his eyes appear more deeply sunken. His beard is not heavy, but he showed the lack of a shave when he came into court this morning. This being commented upon, Sheriff Hammel announced that he had sworn in a barber as a Deputy Sheriff, whose sole duty will be to give the prisoner and the jurymen also a daily shave.

Every effort is being made to provide for the comfort of the twelve talesmen now under guard. The best of meals possible to provide are sent to their prison, and to-night, with a number of detectives guarding them, they were taken on an automobile ride in the city. Last night was chilly and several of the veniremen protested at the shortness of the blankets provided by the State. Their feet stuck out, they say. That will be remedied to-night by the addition of quilts from the county jail.

It was ascertained to-night that it is the intention of the State, provided the court will permit the introduction of the testimony, to get Ortie E. McManigal to tell the story of the attempted destruction of the Blackwell's Island bridge over the East River, New York, on the night of April 1, 1908, by loosening the guy ropes that held firm a ten-ton derrick of the Pennsylvania Steel Company. The derrick was on the top of a high temporary tower, and but for the fact that a watchman discovered the loosened guy rope in time the heavy derrick would have crushed the structure below it in falling.

McManigal's First Big Job.

This, it is said, was one of the first big jobs that McManigal attempted alone. He had, so he is said to have informed District Attorney Fredericks and the Burns Detective Agency, been ordered to dynamite the bridge, and would have done so, but lost his nerve at the critical moment. He will, if allowed by the Judge, tell that story immediately after relating how he and others dynamited the Boston Opera House.

It was 10:14 o'clock when court convened. H. S. Poppenbush was selected to fill the vacancy in the panel caused on Wednesday by the withdrawal of one talesman because of physical disability.

District Attorney Fredericks informed the court that he would like to withdraw his objection to the unanswered question directed to G. T. Nelson, one of the veniremen on Wednesday. The question was:

"With reference to the officers and men who direct the management of the affairs of labor unions, do you believe that the great majority of them are lawless men?"

Lecompte Davis, for the defense, at once asked the question of Mr. Nelson, who replied:

"I do not believe I can answer that question. I do not know anything about the officers."

"Well, what is your belief about them?"

"I don't know anything about them."

"You realize the defendant is on trial for a matter that concerns labor organizations, and you have no opinion about the majority of the officers being lawless men?"

"A great many are and a great many not."

"Don't you know, Mr. Nelson that you are prejudiced against officers of the labor unions?"

"No, I should say not so."

Argument of Counsel.

"This is the first juror," began District Attorney Fredericks, "and I doubt whether we will ever get a juror who has not formed some opinion on this case."

Court reconvened at 2:10 o'clock, and Judge Bordwell announced that the veniremen were excused until to-morrow morning, as the argument between opposing counsel concerning Nelson's competency as a juror would consume the remainder of the day, which it did without any decision respecting Mr. Nelson's fitness to serve being reached.

AUTHOR MIGHELS DIES OF GUNSHOT WOUND

Lingered a Week After Fatal Accident While Hunting on a Western Ranch.

JUST BACK FROM HONEYMOON

Well-Known Novelist and Short Story Writer Only Lately Returned from Europe.

Special to The New York Times.

RENO, Nev., Oct. 13.—Philip Verrill Mighels, author and playwright, succumbed last night to a wound inflicted by himself while hunting quail near Golconda a week ago. He was unconscious toward the last, and made no statement. His wife was present at the end. It was thought for a time that the author would survive his wound.

Mr. Mighels was visiting on the Bliss ranch. He went out to hunt quail one morning about a week ago. He fired and wounded a quail, and as the bird was fluttering on the ground he struck it with the butt of his gun. The weapon was exploded and the entire charge of shot entered Mighels's right side.

Philip Verrill Mighels was born in Carson City, Nev., forty-two years ago, the son of Henry Hust Mighels and Lucy Ellen Verrill. He attended private schools in Carson City and the Carson City High School. He studied law and was admitted to the bar at the age of 21. Two years later he went to San Francisco and engaged in newspaper work. His stories and sketches soon attracted favorable attention, and he came to New York in 1894. From that time he devoted himself solely to writing.

Mr. Mighels was married soon after he settled in New York to Mrs. Ella Stirling Cummings, who had been a Commissioner from San Francisco to the Chicago World's Fair, and was herself an author of short stories. The marriage took place near Atlantic Highlands, in a little country church. In July, 1909, they were divorced in San Francisco, Mrs. Mighels alleging desertion. His earliest collection of poems called "Out of a Silver Flute" contains a poem in which the poet describes his courtship.

Mr. Mighels was married a second time a little more than a year ago. He went abroad with his bride, and only returned to America a few weeks ago. He stopped a few days in New York and then went on West. Mr. Mighels had previously spent four years in Europe, from 1897 to 1901. His New York home was at 201 West 104th Street.

Mr. Mighels's publishers, Messrs. Harper & Brothers, said that the author's most popular book was undoubtedly "Bruvver Jim's Baby," which he published in 1904. This story Mr. Mighels later dramatized. His other stories are "Nella, the Heart of the Army," "When a Witch is Young," "The Crystal Sceptre," "The Inevitable," "The Ultimate Passion," "Chatwit, the Man-Talk Bird," and "The Pillars of Eden."

NOT ILL, SAYS WISTER.

Author Off on Hunting Trip—Leaves Ranch for Here To-morrow.

RIGBY, Idaho, Oct. 13.—Owen Wister, the author, left his ranch in Jackson's Hole, Wyo., this afternoon for a short hunting trip.

Before leaving he said that rumors of his ill-health were unfounded, and added that he expected to leave Jackson's Hole for New York on Oct. 15.

SUFFRAGIST FOR ALDERMAN.

Socialists Nominate Miss Elizabeth Dutcher of Brooklyn.

The Socialist Party organization in the Forty-second Aldermanic District, Brooklyn, nominated a suffragist for Alderman yesterday. She is Miss Elizabeth Dutcher of 80 Pierrepont Street, well known in society. She has long been regarded as an ardent suffragist.

Miss Dutcher has also done a great deal to better the conditions of the working girl. She is a settlement worker and has worked in the Little Italy section of South Brooklyn.

PASTOR'S WIFE BANKRUPT.

He Had Left the Pulpit to Engage in Real Estate Deals.

Mrs. Martha W. Norton, wife of the Rev. Robert F. Norton, formerly assistant pastor at St. aMrk's M. E. Church and Beverly Road and Ocean Avenue, Flatbush, Brooklyn, who left the pulpit recently to engage in real estate development in Far Rockaway, filed a petition in bankruptcy yesterday in the United States District Court in Brooklyn, admitting liabilities of $90,852.61, and naming no assets.

It is said that Mrs. Norton's trouble was occasioned by the fact that she indorsed many notes of her husband's to enable him to carry on his real estate speculation. He has been unable to handle this, it is said, owing to its failure to move rapidly as he had planned.

Among Mrs. Norton's creditors are the First National Bank of Port Jefferson, the First National Bank of Islip, the First National City of Brooklyn, and the Bank of Lawrence. Judge Veeder appointed Charles A. Tipling as referee to take testimony on the petition.

Dr. Norton's former home, which he left last Spring to go to Far Rockaway, was a handsome residence at 950 Ocean Avenue, Flatbush

REGISTRATION FAR BELOW LAST YEAR'S

Drop of 15 Per Cent. on First Day from 1910 in Manhattan and Bronx.

REPUBLICAN DISTRICTS HIT

An Actual Gain in Queens, Which Is Building Up Rapidly—A Challenge List of 42,209 Names.

The first day's registration in this city for the election this Fall showed a big drop from the figures of last year, when leaders of all parties bewailed the poor showing made. The total was 150,415, a decrease of 18,358.

In Manhattan and the Bronx the decrease was 13,541 or nearly 15 per cent. Nearly ever district showed a drop of from 200 to 400 and some a good deal more. The falling off was especially heavy on the west side, which is normally Republican. The Fifteenth, where Albert Ottinger is leader, showed a decline of 1,300, the Seventeenth, Abraham Gruber's bailiwick, nearly 700, and the Nineteenth about the same. The Twenty-first showed a similar drop. The only district to report a gain was the Eleventh, where there was an increase of 60.

In Brooklyn the drop was 4,568. There were increases in a few districts, which was attributed to the shifting of population.

In the Borough of Queens, where the population is increasing rapidly, there was an actual gain of 136. There was a falling off of 112 in the First District and of 39 in the Second. These were overcome by gains of 51 in the Third and 136 in the Fourth.

In Richmond the decrease was 395.

FIRST DAY'S REGISTRATION.

Boroughs.	1911.	1910.	1909.
Manhat. and Bronx.	82,469	96,010	101,954
Brooklyn	61,283	65,851	69,931
Queens	11,928	11,892	13,941
Richmond	3,625	4,020	4,221
Grand total	159,415	177,773	190,055

Manhattan and the Bronx.

A. D.	1911.	1910.	1909.
First	1,557	1,870	2,227
Second	1,986	2,170	2,309
Third	2,344	2,588	2,665
Fourth	1,531	1,753	1,841
Fifth	1,859	2,377	2,412
Sixth	1,972	2,032	2,119
Seventh	1,753	2,051	2,183
Eighth	1,642	1,908	1,871
Ninth	1,633	1,866	2,091
Tenth	1,625	1,855	1,979
Eleventh	2,317	2,247	2,526
Twelfth	2,059	2,391	2,716
Thirteenth	1,857	1,969	2,304
Fourteenth	2,180	2,211	2,685
Fifteenth	2,560	3,870	3,652
Sixteenth	1,824	2,070	2,134
Seventeenth	2,449	3,115	3,571
Eighteenth	1,855	2,007	2,194
Nineteenth	3,295	3,925	4,153
Twentieth	1,950	2,268	2,527
Twenty-first	2,831	3,647	3,924
Twenty-second	2,056	2,371	2,486
Twenty-third	5,273	6,479	5,963
Twenty-fourth	1,530	1,576	1,659
Twenty-fifth	2,180	2,758	2,930
Twenty-sixth	2,030	2,344	2,508
Twenty-seventh	1,634	2,290	2,398
Twenty-eight	1,420	1,497	1,797
Twenty-ninth	2,174	2,933	3,095
Thirtieth	3,234	3,639	3,991
Thirty-first	2,698	3,257	3,473
Thirty-second	5,013	5,081	5,399
Thirty-third	2,578	2,947	3,260
Thirty-fourth	3,985	4,367	4,663
Thirty-fifth	3,928	3,938	4,267
Total	82,469	96,010	101,954

Brooklyn.

A. D.	1911.	1910.	1909.
First	2,239	2,622	2,894
Second	1,804	1,979	2,350
Third	1,811	2,032	2,458
Fourth	2,279	2,517	2,507
Fifth	3,136	3,364	3,437
Sixth	2,345	2,552	2,706
Seventh	1,930	2,122	2,249
Eighth	1,860	2,046	2,295
Ninth	3,629	3,609	3,986
Tenth	2,675	3,062	3,498
Eleventh	2,562	3,031	3,157
Twelfth	3,387	3,918	4,133
Thirteenth	1,852	1,902	2,005
Fourteenth	1,954	2,043	2,030
Fifteenth	2,154	2,089	2,200
Sixteenth	3,764	4,127	3,993
Seventeenth	2,919	3,272	3,435
Eighteenth	4,334	4,586	4,636
Nineteenth	1,906	2,013	2,226
Twentieth	2,458	2,565	2,818
Twenty-first	1,419	1,598	1,699
Twenty-second	5,210	5,347	5,698
Twenty-third	3,562	3,455	3,521
Total	61,283	65,851	69,931

Queens.

A. D.	1911.	1910.	1909.
First	2,419	2,531	3,212
Second	2,249	2,288	2,806
Third	3,849	3,798	4,238
Fourth	3,411	3,275	3,693
Total	11,928	11,892	13,949

Richmond.

A. D.	1911.	1910.	1909.
First	3,625	4,020	4,221

The falling off was not unexpected and was indicated plainly by the small number of voters who appeared in the early hours. The present is decidedly an off-year in politics, as there will be no State ticket and no city ticket to elect. The only State officers to be chosen are members of the Assembly, and the only city officials, members of the Board of Aldermen. In New York County only two officers are to be elected on the county ticket, Sheriff and Surrogate. There are also four Justices of the Supreme Court to be elected in this county. Brooklyn is to vote for county officers and for Justices of the Supreme Court.

The importance of the election, therefore, does not compare favorably with any of the last three years. There was a Presidential election in 1908, and the first day's registration reflected the interest of the voters. In 1909 there was an election for Mayor and other city officers, and the sharp three-cornered contest between Gaynor, Hearst, and Bannard brought out a big registration, but less than the year before. Lst year the canvass was for Governor and other State officers. The registration again fell off, and it was the general expectation that there would be a further decline this year.

John R. Voorhis, State Superintendent of the Metropolitan Elections District, had provided the Inspectors of the various election districts with challenge lists in advance of the opening of the registration books. The aggregate of the names on these lists was 42,209. They were made up of deaths, obtained from the Board of Health, convictions of felonies from the court records, and removals. The removals were obtained by a house-to-house canvass. Formerly they were obtained from the Post Office, but this year any information from that source was refused. Armed with these lists, it was expected that the Inspectors would see that no floaters registered on the name of those no longer qualified to vote.

Voters who neglected to register yesterday will have another chance to-day, and the two final days for registration will come on Friday and Saturday of next week.

REGISTRATION IN THE STATE.

Confusion Over Recent Levy Law Decision—Strike at Ogdensburg.

SARATOGA, N. Y., Oct. 13.—The registration for the first day in Saratoga County is reported light in all the villages, showing a decrease from last year in practically every district. Consider-

Continued on Page 4.

JUSTICE HARLAN ILL.

Oldest Member of the Supreme Court Has Acute Bronchitis.

WASHINGTON, Oct. 13.—Associate Justice John Marshall Harlan of the Supreme Court of the United States is suffering from an attack of acute bronchitis at his home in this city.

Justice Harlan is 78 years old, and his condition is regarded as grave because of his advanced years. He is the oldest member of the Supreme Court.

150 SAILORS UPSET IN BAY.

Boats from Cruiser California Struck by Ferryboat from Oakland.

SAN FRANCISCO, Oct. 13.—A launch and its tow of three boats from the cruiser California, flagship of the Pacific Fleet, were struck by a ferryboat in San Francisco Bay to-night while returning from the Oakland Mole after the Oakland reception to President Taft.

About 150 officers and sailors were in the small craft, and many were thrown into the bay.

It is said all but one sailor were rescued.

SUES HUSBAND'S PARENTS.

Mrs. Stearns Asks $50,000 for Alleged Alienation of His Affections.

Special to The New York Times.

CHICAGO, Ill., Oct. 13.—Edgar G. Stearns, Western selling agent for the United States Rubber Company, and his wife, Mary Pyott Stearns, were made defendants in a suit for $50,000 damages filed in the Circuit Court to-day by their daughter-in-law, Irene Corbett Stearns. The suit is for the alleged alienation of the affections of David Stearns, son of the elder Stearns, and husband of the plaintiff.

The suit comes as a climax to the runaway match of the younger Stearns and his wife, whose maiden name was Irene Corbett, two years ago. Miss Corbett was employed as a stenographer in the office of the elder Stearns.

Following the marriage the elder Stearns, it is said, threatened to separate the couple on the ground of his daughter-in-law's religion.

Mrs. Stearns's attorney states that the younger Stearns has not contributed to the support of his wife since last February.

ROCKEFELLER SEEMS WELL.

Attended to Business Abroad, It is Stated—Sails To-day.

Special Cable to THE NEW YORK TIMES.

LONDON, Oct. 13.—William Rockefeller and Mrs. Rockefeller have booked passages by the Campania, which leaves Liverpool to-morrow.

Efforts to locate Mr. Rockefeller since his arrival in England by the Mauretania were unavailing. His presence on that vessel was known to very few passengers. Dr. Sydney Jones, the Mauretania's doctor, said that he never saw Mr. Rockefeller on the trip, and did not know he was aboard till Sunday.

Asked by THE NEW YORK TIMES correspondent if it was possible that a passenger could be seriously ill on the ship and be attended by a private doctor without his knowledge, he replied that it was possible, but highly improbable.

Standard Oil men here say they do not believe the reports of the serious illness of William Rockefeller, as they would be informed if he were really ill.

There were rumors in the financial district yesterday that Mr. Rockefeller was seriously ill abroad, and that his visit had been shortened on that account, but there was no definite information to that effect. These reports brought the following statement from a member of the family last night:

"The day before sailing for Europe on the Mauretania, William Rockefeller attended the regular Tuesday meeting of the Executive Committee of the Union Pacific. He attended to other routine business and did not appear to his business associates to be suffering. It is well known that Mr. Rockefeller occasionally had tonsil trouble. On the day of his father's departure for Europe, William G. Rockefeller stated to an inquirer that no special signifcance attached to the trip, and that he expected his father would return within about six weeks."

KILLS WOMAN HE'D ANNOYED.

Italian Shoots Her Down Near Her Home, Then Ends His Own Life.

As her son was running to greet her and her sister was waving to her from a window, Mrs. Annie Bowman was shot down and killed yesterday afternoon near her home at 1,113 Sixty-seventh Street, Brooklyn. Her slayer, James V. Sorrenti, who had been annoying her with his attentions for years, promptly killed himself.

Sorrenti was known among his friends as "the lady-killer" and he did his best to live up to his reputation. He first met Mrs. Bowman, who had a husband and three children, three years ago, and though Mrs. Bowman was eight years older than he, he began to make violent love to her. The Bowmans moved several times to be rid of him, but he always followed.

At last they came to Sixty-seventh Street, which had the advantage of being close to the home of Mrs. Bowman's sister, Mrs. Charles Leboe, at 1,113 Sixty-eighth Street.

In a little while Sorrenti came and this time took rooms next door. Bowman warned him that he had better clear out or he would have him arrested or would kill him, and the man did move just around the corner to the home of his brother, Peter, 6,511 Eleventh Avenue.

Mrs. Bowman told her husband at breakfast yesterday that she had a premonition of fear. Three days ago Sorrenti had met her and told her that he had drawn all his money and was going back to Italy. She must come with him, he declared. If she did not, he would surely kill her. Bowman, however, did not take the thing seriously, and went off to his work and his wife went downtown and bought a new hat.

After dinner she started to her sister's. The lots are not built up thickly in that district, and as she went she could see Mrs. Leboe in the window waving her hand, and she waved back. Paul, her son, 13 years old, was in his aunt's house and as soon as he saw his mother ran to meet her.

Then Mrs. Leboe saw a man creeping through some shrubs behind Mrs. Bowman and tried to warn her. Sorrenti sprang out behind Mrs. Bowman, and before she could turn fired at close range. The first shot pierced her heart. As she fell to the ground another shot struck her behind the left ear.

Children on the street saw the murder and fled in terror. Sorrenti cast one glance around, then put the revolver to his temple and pulled the trigger. As Paul reached his mother he fell on her and began to caress her. When he realized she was dead he turned on the Italian and kicked him. Bicycle Patrolman Roland Chataway came up quickly and summoned Dr. Cooke from the Norwegian Hospital. With great difficulty they dragged Paul away, and then they found that Mrs. Bowman was dead and Sorrenti dying. He was hurried to the hospital and died there at 6 o'clock.

PLAN BEHIND CHINA REVOLT IS REVEALED

Vast Scheme to Overthrow the Manchu Empire Silently Progressing for Years.

PEOPLE AND ARMY RIPE

Letters of Sun Yat Sen to British-American Bankers Tell Details in Seeking Funds.

MANIFESTO TO THE WORLD

Chinese Bankers Guarantee Offered—Five of Ten Army Divisions in Rebel Control.

REPUBLIC IS REVOLT'S AIM

Military Government First, to be Followed by Universal Suffrage and a President.

SUN YAT SEN FOR THE POST

May Have Got Funds Which Started Revolution in This Country—Rebel Success Grows.

Special Cable to THE NEW YORK TIMES.

LONDON, Oct. 13.—Evidence of a remarkable character came to-day into possession of the correspondent of THE NEW YORK TIMES showing that the Chinese rebellion is no mere sporadic outbreak, but the outcome of an organization secretly elaborated during the past three or four years by a body of most astute Chinese progressives under the leadership of Dr. Sun Yat Sen. This evidence is authoritative and conclusive.

Some of it I am at liberty to publish; the remainder I can only outline, owing to the delicate position in which its revelation would place the informants.

Documents amply prove that Dr. Sun Yat Sen and his associates have been making secret journeys to England and America, using every endeavor to raise a vast sum of money in the two countries to finance a Chinese rebellion. On more than one of these visits to London Dr. Sun Yat Sen has discussed his plans of campaign, and early this year he stated to a friend that he was going back to China, and that, if his disguise was not penetrated and he himself captured, the insurrection would begin in the early Summer. He still wanted further funds, however, and it was the fear that his mission might become known to the authorities, and that he himself might be done away with by means similar to those by which he was once kidnapped in London, that made it necessary for him to leave the country before he could convince the financiers whom he approached that the arms of the rebels would be crowned with success and a Chinese republic proclaimed.

Told Financiers in London.

For the best of reasons Dr. Sun Yat Sen did not disclose his full plans even to some of his most intimate friends. The latter were known to the Chinese authorities, and he felt that such knowledge would place them in a difficult position. But to a group of English and American bankers to whom he had applied for a loan he told the whole story of his projected campaign. In the early part of the negotiations Dr. Sun Yat Sen had stated that he had guarantees up to a large amount, and in reply to a request for information about these guarantees, the leader of the rebellion sent the following letter to the capitalists referred to. He wrote from New York, where he was working out the military part of his scheme.

New York.

Dear Mr. ——:

I am very sorry I have been too late to meet you in New York, as was arranged when we were at —— Club in London. In regard to the matter of getting a loan for a political object in China by the guarantee of Chinese merchants abroad, I have succeeded in bringing in a Chinese bank and three rice mills in Bangkok, Siam, and some merchants in Singapore and three mine owners in the Malay States who are willing to give such a guarantee. Their property, taken together, amounts to about $20,000,000, or about £4,000,000.

In order to make sure of our success we need a loan of £500,000 to perfect our organization, which will enable us to capture at least two rich provinces by the first surprise. After gaining this footing we will establish a provisional Government. Then we shall be able to give a substantial guarantee of a national character for a greater loan to further our movement to its completion.

We want you to find out for us positively whether there are any such capitalists who are willing to furnish us money; if so, under what condition.

"All the News That's Fit to Print."

The New York Times.

THE WEATHER. Fair Tuesday and Wednesday; moderate west winds. For full weather report see Page 22.

VOL. LXII...NO. 19,988. NEW YORK, TUESDAY, OCTOBER 15, 1912.—TWENTY-FOUR PAGES. ONE CENT In Greater New York, Jersey City, and Newark. Elsewhere, TWO CENTS.

MANIAC IN MILWAUKEE SHOOTS COL. ROOSEVELT; HE IGNORES WOUND, SPEAKS AN HOUR, GOES TO HOSPITAL

COL. THEODORE ROOSEVELT

Bullet In Right Breast, Doctors Say Wound Is Not Serious.

LUNG NOT PENETRATED

Roosevelt Walks from Hospital Unassisted, and Starts for Chicago.

MANUSCRIPT WAS A SHIELD

Assassin's Aim Good, but Papers in the Colonel's Pockets Save Him.

CALM ON OPERATING TABLE

Talks Politics with Physicians While Waiting for X-Ray Machine.

COLONEL CHECKS CROWD

"Don't Touch Him," He Says, as Rush Is Made for His Assailant—Secretary Martin Fells Maniac.

Special to The New York Times.

MILWAUKEE, October 14.—Col. Theodore Roosevelt was shot and wounded in the right breast in front of the Hotel Gilpatrick shortly before 8 o'clock to-night. Col. Roosevelt was about to enter his automobile to go to the Auditorium for his evening address, when a man rushed up and fired at close range.

The bullet entered the flesh under the right nipple, but its force was broken by the manuscript of the speech which Col. Roosevelt had prepared for this evening. He at first declared he had not been wounded, but on the way to the hall a hole was noticed in his overcoat and it was found that his shirt was covered with blood. Nevertheless he insisted on delivering his speech, and went on, for fifty minutes, even though his weakness became so apparent that physicians insisted that he should stop.

Talked Politics at Hospital.

After his speech he was taken to the Emergency Hospital to have his wound examined.

At 10:30 o'clock Col. Roosevelt was sitting on the operating table talking politics with the physicians while they were awaiting the arrival of an X-ray machine.

Col. Roosevelt left the hospital at 11:25 P. M. He was able to walk unassisted.

"I am feeling fine," he said.

Surgeons Say Wound Is Slight.

Col. Roosevelt left at 12:50 A. M. for Chicago. Before he left surgeons who had attended him gave out the following statement:

"Col. Roosevelt is suffering from a superficial flesh wound in the right breast. There is no evidence of injury to the lungs. The bullet is probably somewhere in the chest wall. There is only one wound and no sign of injury to the lung. The bleeding is insignificant. The wound has been sterilized externally with gauze by Dr. R. T. Fayle, the consulting surgeon of the Emergency Hospital. The bullet passed through Col. Roosevelt's army overcoat and other clothing and through a manuscript and spectacle case in his breast pocket, and its force was nearly spent before it penetrated the chest. The appearance of the wound also showed evidence of a much-spent bullet.

"Col. Roosevelt is not suffering from the shock and is in no pain. His condition is so good that surgeons did not object to his continuing his journey to Chicago in his private car. In Chicago he will be placed under surgical care.

"The X-ray photograph has been finished and the Colonel is feeling fine. He is seeing the newspaper men, and presently will go to his car to start for Chicago.

"Dr. F. L. TERRELL,
"Dr. R. G. FAYLE,
"Dr. JOSEPH COLT BLOODGOOD of Johns Hopkins.
"Dr. F. A. STRATTON."

The X-ray of Col. Roosevelt's wound shows that the bullet lodged in the abdominal wall and did not penetrate the lung.

Just as the Roosevelt special train was leaving here a sudden change in plans was made and the engineer was ordered to hold the train.

It was stated that the bullet penetrated three inches of the abdominal wall, and the wound is more serious that at first thought. This was shown by the X-ray photograph which has just been developed.

A special train was to bring from Chicago four surgeons. They are Drs. John B. Murphy, Arthur Bevan, A. R. Ochsner and L. L. McArthur.

It was finally decided at 12:45 that Col. Roosevelt should go on to Chicago, and the train started.

The positive statement that Col. Roosevelt was not injured seriously was made by Dr. Stratton, who said that there was no cause for alarm as to the Colonel's condition.

'The wound was a superficial one," said Dr. Stratton. "The bullet is imbedded in the muscular tissue. All that we did at the hospital was to put on an antiseptic dressing. You may say Col. Roosevelt is not in a dangerous condition. There is no truth in the report that the bullet penetrated the abdominal wall. If the bullet had reached his lungs it would have been evident and he would have had coughing spells."

How the Shooting Occurred.

The man who did the shooting said he was John Schrank of 370 East Tenth Street, New York City. Papers found on him showed he had been following Col. Roosevelt for some time, and that he was a crank on the subject of the third term.

As no secret had been made of the plans of Col. Roosevelt, a crowd was in front of the hotel to see him leave for the Auditorium. When he came out a cheer was set up and to it he responded smilingly, raising his hat and bowing. Several persons pushed to the front to see him better or to try to shake his hand, as is usual. There were cries of encouragement from all sides.

No special pains had been taken to protect the Colonel under the circumstances, and the members of his party — Philip Roosevelt, a cousin; Henry F. Cochems, the Bull Moose leader here; Albert H. Martin, one of his secretaries, and Capt. A. O. Girard of this city—were not on guard.

When the party had crossed the sidewalk to the automobile Col. Roosevelt's companions stood aside and let him step in. Mr. Martin entered immediately after him. There was another cheer and Col. Roosevelt faced the crowd and raised his hat, smiling.

A stocky man had been standing at the edge of the sidewalk only a few feet from the Colonel. When he pushed his way forward little attention was paid to him because many admirers of the Colonel have done such things. Col. Roosevelt, in fact, looked benevolently upon him and smiled. The man suddenly produced a pistol and fired pointblank.

Football Player Fells Man.

The fellow still had his pistol raised and seemed about to fire again, but here Mr. Martin saved his chief. He had seen the pistol and had leaped forward to shield the Colonel. Too late for that, he jumped just as the shot was fired and landed on the assailant.

Martin, who is six feet tall and a former football player struck squarely on the man's shouders and bore him to the ground. He threw his right arm about the man's neck with a deathlike grip and with his left arm seized the hand that held the pistol. In another second he had disarmed the fellow.

Col. Roosevelt had barely moved when the shot was fired, and stood calmly looking on, as though nothing had happened. Martin picked the man up as though he were a child and carried him the few feet which separated them from the car, almost to the side of the Colonel.

Roosevelt Averts Lynching.

"Here he is," said Martin, "look at him Colonel."

All this happened within a few seconds and Col. Roosevelt stood gazing rather curiously at the man who attempted his life before the stunned crowd realized what was going on. Then a howl of rage went up.

"Lynch him! Kill him!" cried a hundred men.

The crowd pressed in on the man and Mr. Martin and Capt. Girard, who had followed Mr. Martin over the side of the automobile, were caught with their prisoner in the midst of a struggling throng of maddened men. It seemed for the moment that he would be torn to pieces, and it was Col. Roosevelt himself who intervened. He raised his hand and motioned to the crowd to fall back.

"Stop, stop!" he cried. "Stand back! Don't hurt him!"

The crowd at first was not disposed to heed his words, but at length fell back and permitted Mr. Martin and Capt. Girard to carry the man into the hotel. After a short struggle he gave up and was taken without resistance out of the reach of the crowd.

"Are you hurt, Colonel?" a hundred voices called out.

"Oh, no!" he responded, with a smile. "Missed me that time; I'm not hurt a bit."

"I think we'd better be going on," he said to the other members of his party, "or we will be late."

Colonel Learns He Is Wounded.

No one in the party, including Col. Roosevelt himself, entertained the slightest notion that he had been shot. He felt no shock or pain at the time, and it was assumed that the bullet went wild. As soon as Col. Roosevelt had assured himself that the assassin was safe in the hands of the police he gave orders to drive on to the Auditorium.

The party had driven hardly one of the four blocks from the hotel to the Auditorium when John McGrath, another of Col. Roosevelt's secretaries, uttered a sharp exclamation and pointed to the Colonel's breast.

"Look, Colonel," he said. "There is a hole in your overcoat."

Col. Roosevelt looked down, saw the hole, then unbuttoned the big brown army coat which he was wearing and thrust his hand beneath it. When he withdrew it, his fingers were stained with blood.

He was not at all dismayed.

"It looks as though I had been hit," he said, "but I don't think it is anything serious."

Dr. Scurry Terrell of Dallas, Tex., Col. Roosevelt's physician, who had entered the automobile just before it started, insisted that the Colonel return to the hotel. He would not hear of it, however, and the car was driven on to the Auditorium.

Speaks Despite Doctors' Protest.

As soon as they reached the building, Col. Roosevelt was taken into a dressing room and his outer garments were removed. Dr. Terrell, with the help of Dr. John Stratton of Milwaukee and Dr. S. S. Sorenzon of Racine, Wis., who had been in the audience and came to the dressing room on a call from the platform, made a superficial examination of the wound. They agreed that it was impossible to hazard a guess as to the extent of the Colonel's injuries and that he should by all means go at once to a hospital.

"I will deliver this speech or die, one or the other," was Col. Roosevelt's reply.

Despite the protests of his physicians, he strode out of the dressing room and onto the stage.

Audience Shocked by the News.

A large crowd packed into the big building, cheered loudly as he entered, and without a word to indicate what had happened went to his seat. For several minutes the crowd, no man of whom suspected that the Colonel bore a bullet in his body, kept up its cheering.

Then Mr. Cochems stepped to the front of the platform and held up his hand. There was something in his manner which had its effect upon the crowd and the cheering died suddenly away.

"I have something to tell you," said Mr. Cochems, "and I hope you will receive the news with calmness."

His voice shook as he spoke and a deathlike stillness settled over the throng.

"Col. Roosevelt has been shot. He is wounded."

Shows His Blood-stained Shirt.

He spoke in a low tone, but such was the stillness that every one heard him. A cry of astonishment and horror went up from the crowd, which was thrown into confusion in an instant. Mr. Cochems turned and looked inquiringly at Col. Roosevelt.

"Tell us, are you hurt?"

Men and women shouted wildly. Some of them rose from their seats and rushed forward to look more closely at the Colonel.

Col. Roosevelt arose and walked to the edge of the platform to quiet the crowd. He raised his hand and instantly there was silence.

"It's true," he said. Then slowly he unbuttoned his coat and placed his hand on his breast. Those in the front of the crowd could catch a sight of the bloodstained garment. "I'm going to ask you to be very quiet," said Col. Roosevelt, "and please excuse me from making you a very long speech.

"I'll do the best I can, but you see there is a bullet in my body. But it's nothing. I'm not hurt badly," he went on.

A sigh of relief went up from the crowd, and then an outburst of tumultuous cheering. Thoroughly reassured by the Colonel's action that he was in no serious danger, the people settled back in their seats to hear his speech.

Col. Roosevelt began to speak in a firm voice, somewhat lower than its usual tone, and except that his gestures were less emphatic than usual there was nothing about the man to indicate his condition. After he had been speaking a few minutes, however, his voice sank somewhat and he seemed to stand rather unsteadily.

Dr. Terrell and Col. Cecil Lyon stepped up to him and the doctor insisted that he stop.

"I'm going to finish this speech," said the Colonel, ener-

Continued on Page 2.

Crank's Reasons for the Shooting in Two Documents.

MILWAUKEE, Oct. 14.—A written proclamation found in the clothing of the man who shot Col. Roosevelt to-night read:

September 15, 1912, 1:30 A. M.—In a dream I saw President McKinley set up in a Monk's attire in whom I recognized Theodore Roosevelt. The President said: "This is my murderer; avenge my death."

September 12, 1912, 1:30 A. M.—While writing a poem some one tapped me on the shoulder and said: "Let not a murderer take the Presidential chair. Avenge my death."

I could plainly see Mr. McKinley's features.

Before the Almighty God, I swear this above writing is nothing but the truth.

Another note found in the man's pocket reads:

So long as Japan could rise to the greatest power of the world despite her surviving a tradition more than 2,000 years old, as General Nogi so nobly demonstrated, it is the duty of the United States of America to uphold the third term tradition. Let every third termer be regarded as a traitor to the American cause. Let it be the right and duty of every citizen to forcibly remove a third termer. Never let a third term party emblem appear on the official ballot.

I am willing to die for my country. God has called me to be his instrument, so help me God.

INNOCENT GUILTY.

Written in German at the end of this note was: "A strong tower is our God."

Would-be Assassin Is John Schrank, Once Saloonkeeper Here.

A MANIAC ON THIRD TERM

Obsessed with Belief That He Was Commissioned to Remove Peril to Nation.

HAD DREAM OF McKINLEY

Martyred President, He Says, Told Him That Roosevelt Had Him Slain.

STARTED ON COLONEL'S TRAIL

Went South After Buying Revolver and Followed ex-President Closely.

WAS BAFFLED IN CHICAGO

Then He Went Early to Milwaukee and Planned Carefully to Make Sure of His Victim.

Special to The New York Times.

MILWAUKEE, Wis., Oct. 14.—For a time the man who shot ex-President Roosevelt refused to give h.. name, but he finally admitted that he was John Schrank of 370 East Tenth Street, New York.

In making a full confession he told of a carefully laid plot to shoot the Colonel, often frustrated, but finally successful. The man talked freely after his first refusal to give his name. He said:

"I formerly ran a saloon at 410 East Tenth Street, between Avenues D and C, New York City. I was born in Erding, Bavaria, two hours out of Munich, the capital. I am 36 years old and came to this country when 9 years old, with my parents. I have been engaged in the saloon business as proprietor and as an employe nearly all my life, until I decided that it was my duty to kill Col. Roosevelt.

"I have been personally acquainted with Roosevelt since the former President was Police Commissioner of New York in 1895. I was first attracted to him as a politician during the convention in Chicago. Then I began to think seriously of him as a menace to his country, when he cried 'Thief' at that convention. I looked upon his plan to start a third party as a danger to the country.

"My knowledge of history, gained through much reading, convinced me that Roosevelt was engaged in a dangerous undertaking. I was convinced that if he was defeated at the Fall election he would again cry 'Thief,' and that his action would plunge the country into a bloody civil war.

Dreamed McKinley Came to Him.

"I deemed it my duty, after much consideration of the situation, to put him out of the way. I was living at my home address at the time, but soon after I had a dream in which former President McKinley appeared to me. I was told by McKinley in this dream that it was not Czolgosz who murdered him, but Roosevelt. McKinley, in this dream, told me that his blood was on Roosevelt's hand, and that Roosevelt had killed him so that he might become President.

"I was more deeply impressed by what I read in the newspapers than others, and after having this dream was more convinced than ever that I should free the country from the menace of Roosevelt's ambition.

"On Sept. 21 I removed to the White Hotel at 156 Canal Street, near the Bowery. I did this as my first step in a plan to kill Roosevelt. I went soon afterward to a gun store on Broadway and purchased a revolver.

"I then purchased a ticket to Charleston, S. C., and went to that city by steamer. My first plan was to catch the Roosevelt party in New Orleans, but I found that to be impossible.

Starts on Colonel's Trail.

"I accordingly went to Charleston, and upon my arrival there had $300 left. I left a bag at the Hosley House in that city, which contained, besides the box in which the revolver I had purchased, had been packed, a deed to property on Eighty-first Street, in New York, worth $25,000, and my naturalization papers. That bag is there now.

"Not being able to carry out my plan in Charlestown I proceeded to Atlanta, Ga., thence to Chattanooga, Tenn., and from there to Evansville and Indianapolis, Ind., and to Chicago.

"In each one of these cities I tried

"All the News That's Fit to Print."

The New York Times.

THE WEATHER.
Fair Sunday, moderate northwesterly winds; Monday, fair, warmer; variable winds.
For full weather report see Page 19.

VOL. LXII...NO. 20,014. • • • • • NEW YORK, SUNDAY, NOVEMBER 10, 1912.—98 PAGES, In Eight Parts, Including Picture Section and Review of Books. PRICE FIVE CENTS.

400,000 CHEER SUFFRAGE MARCH

20,000 Women in Great Parade Fifth Avenue a River of Fire.

LITTLE JEERING FOR THE MEN

Good-Natured Chaff from the Sidelines and Applause from Women Paraders.

MISS LA FOLLETTE ON FLOAT

Suffrage States in Chariots Escort Four New Additions — Every Woman Carries a Lantern.

About 20,000 women, girls, some of them very little ones, by the hundreds, and several thousand men and boys marched last night for the glory of woman suffrage. It was a wonderful spectacle, and was witnessed by a crowd that jammed Fifth Avenue from Fifty-ninth to Fourteenth Street, where the paraders turned east to Union Square. The watching throngs, the police estimated, numbered 400,000 to 500,000 persons.

The demonstration was in striking contrast to the parade earlier in the year, when the women and girls passed through inadequately policed lines of spectators, many of whom jeered and ridiculed the cause the marchers represented. Last night there was none of that, and the crowd was as big as Fifth Avenue could hold.

There was of course plenty of noise, mostly cheering, but it was of the complimentary and admiring sort. It took nearly two hours for the women to pass a given point, and the only reason they were able to do so in that time was because they marched in columns of fifteens and twenties instead of by fours and twos as is sometimes the case with long-drawn-out demonstrations in New York.

Police Learned Their Lesson.

The police learned a lesson last Spring, and the orders that went out from Police Headquarters yesterday gave to Inspector Lahey a sufficient number of men to keep the crowds in check, and, to the credit of the bluecoats, it must be said that they carried out the orders faithfully. Here and there a break into the lines would occur, but the police were always able to force the crowds back to the sidewalk before any damage was done.

As for the parade itself, it was a line, miles long, of well-dressed, intelligent women, deeply concerned in the cause they are fighting for; of girls in their teens, overflowing with enthusiastic exuberance, and of men, some of them old and tottering, but the majority young, husky fellows, who marched as haughtily as their sisters and carried high the yellow pennants of the cause and the big yellow, pumpkin-shaped lanterns that more than anything else made last night's parade a thing beautiful to look upon. With the exception of a few of the men's organization, practically every person in that vast line of marchers held aloft one of those gleaming lanterns.

Long River of Fire.

The picture was that of a long river of fire that beginning somewhere north of St. Patrick's Cathedral ended in a blazing display no less brilliant in Union Square, where the orators of the movement assembled at the close of the parade to tell those who would listen why votes for women are just as good for New York as for California, Michigan, Oregon, and Wyoming and the other States that have voted the franchise to women.

The parade was timed to start at 8 o'clock, and that was the time it started. There was no delay and there was no halting once the columns got under way.

It was not necessary to flash the word down the line that the suffragists were coming. The glare of those big pumpkin-shaped lanterns was all that was needed. First, to those who banked the sidewalks from curb to walls south of Fifty-eighth Street, it appeared like a single big line of fire that was yards wide and only inches deep. But the width of the picture was short lived, and as the minutes passed the red river grew longer and longer until, when the head of the column reached a point abreast of St. Patrick's Cathedral, the spectacle as seen by those south of Forty-second Street was that of a rolling stream of fiery lava.

Mrs. Hale on White Horse.

At the head of the procession, riding a snow-white horse that was as well-behaved as he was lively stepping, was the Grand Marshal, Mrs. Beatrice Forbes-Robertson Hale. Beside her rode Col. Frederick Stewart Greene, who looked as though he was mighty proud of the honor of being the chief aid to the leader of the greatest parade women ever held in this section of the country. After Mrs. Hale came banner bearers of the National American Woman Suffrage Association, among them the venerable Dr. Anna Howard Shaw, the veteran suffragist of them all, who, despite her years, walked as briskly and as proudly as did any of her younger sisters. Everybody appeared to know who the white-haired lady wearing a great blue sash was, and for her there was a hearty cheer all along the line. Associated with Dr. Shaw as banner bearers were Miss Caroline I. Reilly, Mrs. Mary Ware Dennett, and Mrs. Frances Bjorkman.

After the banner-bearers came the chariots, each driven by a girl in Grecian costume and each representing one of the ten States that have voted for woman suffrage. First of the suffrage States to get the honor of a Grecian chariot was Wyoming.

Scorned the Chilly Air.

The torch-bearers who preceded the Wyoming chariot were Miss Keith Wakeman and Mrs. H. Simpson, while the woman who stood up in the chariot and tugged at the reins was Miss Inez Milholland, the militant young woman who has become a famous advocate of the rights of women in America. Miss Milholland made a fine picture, and when somebody asked her if she were not a bit chilly because of the flimsy looking costume she wore she replied, "I will never get cold in a cause such as this."

After Idaho came Colorado, where women have been voting for some years, and the young woman who saw to the proper navigation of this chariot was Miss Florence M. Cooley, while the torch-bearer, who marched gayly ahead, was

Continued on Page 8.

HOLD-UP MEN ESCAPE IN TAXI.

Felled Cashier in Brooklyn Factory and Fled with Payroll Cash.

Two men armed with revolvers made their way unnoticed late yesterday afternoon to the fourth floor of the factory of the Interstate Novelty Electric Company, 104-110 South Fourth Street, Williamsburg, held up the bookkeeper and took $954 which had been brought to the factory to pay off the hands. Though they were stopped on the way down by two employes they managed to reach the street in safety, and, jumping into a waiting taxicab, were whisked over the Williamsburg Bridge to Manhattan, where all trace of them was lost.

Because of advance orders the employes were working overtime, and were not to be paid off until 7 P. M. The bookkeeper, Barnard Goldstein, remembers having seen a taxi standing in front of the factory when he returned from the bank with money for the pay roll. The chauffeur seemed very busy reading a book. He walked into his office and rolled up the cover of his desk. As he sat down in the chair two men rushed into the room, pointed revolvers at him and cried "Hands up!" Goldstein says he attempted to grapple with the robbers, when one of them hit him on the head with the butt end of a revolver. He was then gagged and the money taken from his wallet.

When the police arrived they found Goldstein unconscious on the floor of his office. Ambulance Surgeon Eberle from the Williamsburg Hospital was called in and revived him. He could remember only vaguely the appearance of the two men. The $954 which they took was all in small bills, so that they will have no trouble in getting rid of it.

HE HAD NEVER TASTED BEER.

Patrolman on Excise Duty Therefore Loses Case Against Bartender.

Magistrate Harris, sitting in the Snyder Avenue Police Court, Brooklyn, was astonished yesterday when a policeman, assigned to excise duty, and testifying in the case of a bartender, said that he had never tasted lager beer in his life. The teetotaler who had been detailed to get evidence against law-violating saloonkeepers was Patrolman Walter D. Martin of the Excise Squad. He appeared as a witness against a bartender employed in a Rogers Avenue saloon, who was charged with selling beer on Sunday.

"Will you swear that the drink served to you was beer?" asked the court.

"No, I cannot do that," replied Martin. "I did not taste it."

"Why not?"

"Because I don't drink, not even when assigned to investigate excise cases," explained Martin, while the Magistrate, apparently amazed, stared at him. "I hate the stuff and never taste it."

"You mean to say that you never tasted beer; that you cannot swear that it is such when it is placed before you, and yet are assigned to excise duty?"

Martin admitted that this was the case. The complaint was dismissed.

COAL STILL GOING UP.

Prices to be Advanced Again with First Touch of Winter.

CHICAGO, Nov. 9.—Prices in all grades of coal will be advanced with the first touch of real Winter, according to men closely connected with the mining industry. The Northwest, they said, will face a desperate situation, as coal will have to be transported by rail instead of by lake shipments. It was also argued that because of the shortage in anthracite, due to labor difficulties and the lack of a reserve supply, the Eastern and Middle West producing districts could only supply their immediate territory.

Producers of anthracite, it was said, faced a shortage of twenty million tons at the close of the Summer. To overcome this the producers are confronted with the necessity of 2,500,000 tons a month more than the normal production.

INDIANAPOLIS, Nov. 9.—Coal prices here and throughout the State are higher this year over last by more than $1 a ton for anthracite, while all soft coals show an increase of from 25 to 50 cents. The increase in anthracite is said by the dealers to be due to the miners' strike, while the higher prices for soft coal is in consequence of an increased demand to replace hard coal.

In addition to this there is a car shortage which has prevented the shipment of coal.

RIVES DENIES RESIGNATION

But Vestryman Says Divorced Man Is No Longer on Church Register.

Special to The New York Times.

POUGHKEEPSIE, Nov. 9.—Reginald W. Rives, who, it was reported in yesterday's papers, was forced to resign as vestryman in the Zion Episcopal Church at Wappinger's Falls on account of domestic troubles which culminated in a recent Reno divorce, denied to-day that he had retired, and said that the report probably had its origin in a visit he had paid to the new rector, Dr. Cunningham.

An investigation into the records of the church by another vestryman disclosed the fact that Mr. Rives's name is no longer among those of the church officers.

In regard to the report that the finances of the church will be injured by the non-attendance of Mr. Rives's two sisters, Mrs. John Boreland and Mrs. Walter Smith, who have followed their brother out of the church, officials declared to-day that the institution was never in better condition.

WENT TO HIDE AND DIED.

Seekers Find Boy Playmate Strangled in His Own Coal Bin.

His head firmly lodged between slats at the top of a coal bin, Maurice Fulton, 7 years old, of 1,257 Lincoln Place, Brooklyn, met death yesterday by slow strangulation, while his playmates in a game of hide-and-go-seek were searching all over the neighborhood for him.

The boys were playing in front of Maurice's house, and when it was his turn to hide he slipped down into a cellar and attempted to get into the coal bin. The bin was boarded up to a height of five feet, and above that were vertical slats close together and running to the ceiling. The lad managed to squeeze his head through between two of these slats, and then evidently lost his foothold.

After several minutes' vain search, the other boys went down into the cellar and were horrified to find Maurice dead in this position.

Latest Shipping News.

Arrived—SS Cowrie, Rotterdam, Oct. 25; SS Bristol City, Madeira, Oct. 25; SS Maracaibo, Mayaguez, Nov. 2.

DYNAMITER MAKES AMAZING CONFESSION

McManigal, on Witness Stand, Tells of Many Explosions for Which Union Paid.

SENT SOUVENIRS TO FAMILY

Sent Spoon After Every "Job"—Names Frank C. Webb of New York as One Who Knew of Work.

INDIANAPOLIS, Nov. 9.—How he carried dynamite in suit cases on passenger trains and checked the explosive at railway stations without thinking of danger to others; how he waited to place bombs so night watchmen would not see him, and how from every city where he blew up a "job" he sent a souvenir spoon home to his wife in Chicago were related by Ortie E. McManigal on the witness stand in the trial of the forty-five accused dynamite plotters to-day.

"Ping," an alias of Herbert S. Hockin, McManigal said, was the password he gave to labor leaders in various cities so they would know he was the man sent to do a "job." He named Frank C. Webb, New York; Michael J. Young, Boston; Richard H. Houlihan, Chicago; James Cooney, Chicago, and Frank M. Ryan, all officials of the International Association of Bridge and Structural Ironworkers, as among the defendants, besides the McNamara brothers, who knew he was employed as a dynamiter.

Young and Webb, he said, pointed out non-union jobs for him to blow up. Hockin, now Secretary of the union, he described as the chief of the McNamara dynamiting crew, and said Ryan, President of the union, had spoken to him about an explosion.

"Did you send anything to your family after you blew up the job in Boston?" was one question asked McManigal.

"Yes," he answered, "I sent home a souvenir spoon. I always sent home souvenir spoons from the cities where I blew up jobs."

At the outset McManigal asserted he attempted to protect the lives of people whenever setting off a bomb. At his first job in Detroit, June 25, 1907, he told of pushing a garbage barrel against the rear door of a restaurant so the people would not run out and be injured or killed at an explosion across an alley.

"In June, 1907, Hockin came to me while I was working on the Ford Building in Detroit," said McManigal. "He said the Executive Board of the union had decided to clean out the open-shop concerns, and I was the man to do it. He said, 'You used to work in a stone quarry and you know how to use explosives. You'll be paid by the union.'

Explosion at Ford Building.

"I protested, but he told me if I didn't do as the Executive Board said he'd see that I was boycotted against getting a job. I finally consented.

"Where to get the dynamite was the next question. I decided to go to my uncle, William Behm, at Bloomville, Ohio, who had a stone quarry. I went to Bloomville June 22 and brought back to Detroit in a suitcase 35 pounds of dynamite, some fuse, and caps.

"I told Hockin I had the dynamite in my room. He said, 'All right. You've gone this far, and you had better pull off the job between 1 and 2 A. M.'

"I went to my room and prepared three bombs, each with fifty feet of fuse. I then went back to the Ford Building and waited in an alley to see if there were any police about. Seeing none, I put one bomb in the firebox of the boiler in the building under construction, another in an air compressor, and a third near the cylinder. Joining the ends of the fuse at one point, I lit all of them. They were fixed to go off at about 1 A. M. It was then about 10 o'clock.

"I again looked about the alley. I noticed a kitchen door at the rear of a restaurant opened on the alley opposite where the bombs were, and, thinking some people might run out at the first explosion and be injured by the second or third explosion, I shut the door and jammed a barrel of garbage against it. Then I went to my room and waited to hear the noise.

"It came about 1 o'clock. Later I heard the newsboys calling 'Extra.' It reminded me I still had some explosives in my room. What should I do with them? I didn't dare to go out with a package. That would excite suspicion. So I took what dynamite I had left to the bathroom, and, cutting it into small pieces, flushed it out."

"Did you see Rockin the next day?" asked District Attorney Miller.

Wanted to Be Let Alone.

"Yes; he had paid me $20 for expenses to Bloomville. He said I would be fully compensated for my work as the Executive Board had set aside a certain amount for each job, but he said I must keep at it. He said I would receive $125 for a job at first, and I was to send a newspaper account of each explosion so he could get the money from the International Union. The clipping was a kind of a certificate that the explosion had occurred.

"Thinking the police were watching me, as it was my first explosion, I decided to leave Detroit. I wanted to work and for them to let me alone. But Hockin kept after me, saying 'We've got the goods on you now and you have to keep at it, for we are going to clean out the National Erectors' Association.'

"I went to Chicago and worked there. The next February Hockin came to my house in South Sangamon Street and said he had a job for me at Clinton, Iowa. I went to Clinton. It was a double-track railroad bridge across the Mississippi River. I pulled off the job pretty much in the same way as the other one, placing thirty sticks of dynamite at various places. One lot failed to go off on account of being frozen.

"When I saw Hockin again he looked greatly worried, explaining they had found the frozen dynamite and had arrested a man. He thought it was me and was afraid I would tell. He paid me my expenses and said he would see I was paid for my work. Later I was told to go to a union headquarters in Chicago. When I got there Richard H. Houlihan, Financial Secretary of a local union, handed me an envelope containing $165, adding a friend had left it for me.

"Hockin said he was going to keep me pretty busy after that, and he was going to Buffalo, N. Y., to look over a job, and when I got a telegram signed 'Ping' or 'Clark' I was to come. A few days later I got a telegram, saying, 'Meet me in Buffalo and make it heavy, meaning

Continued on Page 3.

TO-DAY'S SUNDAY TIMES

CONSISTS OF

FAST EXPRESS KILLS SCHOOLBOYS IN AUTO

Hurled Down Steep Embankment by Pennsylvania Train Near Red Bank, N. J.

GUARD BAR RAISED TOO SOON

Freight Train Cuts Off View of Express from Crossing Tender and Two Boys Are Killed.

Special to The New York Times.

RED BANK, N. J., Nov. 9.—James H. Stevenson, a schoolboy living at Hazlet, near here, was instantly killed, and Alexander Hall of New York, his chum, was mortally injured this afternoon when an automobile in which they were going duck shooting was struck by a Pennsylvania Railroad express train on the New York & Long Branch Railroad near young Stevenson's home.

The two boys were hurled from the automobile down a steep embankment. A hundred people waiting for trains at the Hazlet station saw the boys hurled from their automobile and made a rush to their assistance. The first to arrive found one of the boys dead, his body terribly mangled, and the other so badly injured that he died an hour later.

The railroad flagman is blamed for the accident. As the boys drove up to the tracks they found the guard bars down and stopped their automobile. A freight train was then passing. As the freight train cleared the roadway the guard bars were raised, it is said, and the street opened to traffic.

Young Hall, who owned the automobile and was driving it, moved forward to cross the tracks. He had just reached the track when a train going at a rate of fifty miles an hour crashed into the automobile. It had been cut off from the view both of those in the automobile and of the flagman by the freight train, while the noise of the freight train had drowned the noise that otherwise would have warned of its approach.

The crossing, which is on the main road from Keyport to Holmdel, has long been known as one of the most dangerous along the Jersey Coast, as the railroad traffic and vehicular traffic are both very heavy. Peter O. Weighan, the railroad flagman, is 70 years old. When he learned the fatal result of his error in opening the gates too quickly he was stunned. He said the noise of the freight train completely drowned out the noise of the express and that he opened the gates fully believing the tracks to be clear.

Parker Stevenson, father of one of the boys, is a retired Brooklyn commission merchant with a Summer home at Hazlet. The son had been commuting to Brooklyn for several years in order to attend school with his companion on the fatal automobile ride. Alexander Hall was the son of Charles Mason Hall of 255 West Ninetieth Street, New York. Both boys were 15 years old. Young Hall came to Hazlet yesterday, in company with his sister, to visit the Stevensons over the week-end.

Mrs. Stevenson fainted when she was told of her son's death, and her condition to-night is said to be serious. Mr. Stevenson was away from home on an automobile trip to Red Bank, and did not learn of the tragedy until several hours after it happened.

ENGLAND WARNS TRIPLE ALLIANCE

Asquith Hints at Irreconcilable Divergence—Churchill Says Fleet Is Ready.

VICTORS NOT TO BE ROBBED

Premier Declares, However, the Great Powers Are Working for Peace Freely and Frankly.

SERVIA IS THE DANGER POINT

Triple Alliance Ready to Prevent by Force Its Annexation of Ports on the Adriatic.

By Marconi Transatlantic Wireless Telegraph to The New York Times.

LONDON, Sunday, Nov. 10.—For the present the actual war operations in the Balkans are completely overshadowed by the diplomatic situation.

Premier Asquith's speech at the Guild Hall last night had been as eagerly awaited as any of the many historic pronouncements ever delivered at the Lord Mayor's banquet. In it he expressed hope but did not relieve public anxiety, for he refrained at this stage from even indicating in the most general way the points, some of them full of difficulty, which must inevitably emerge for solution. Then Mr. Asquith added:

"For the moment and so long as a state of belligerency continues, his Majesty's Government, so far as their influence goes, would deprecate the raising and pressing of isolated questions, which, if handled separately and at once, may lead to irreconcilable divergence, but which may well assume a different and perhaps more tractable aspect if they are reserved to be dealt with from the wider point of view of a general settlement."

There is such a danger point as Mr. Asquith suggests. Austria has already in a measure taken that separate action which the British Government is deprecating.

The instruction to the Austrian Minister, Ugron, on returning to Belgrade are to point out to Servia that Austria is determined under no circumstances to permit Servian occupation of Durazzo.

Winston Churchill, First Lord of the Admiralty, who spoke before Mr. Asquith at the banquet, made an announcement which, like the Premier's speech, did nothing to relieve the anxiety. He said:

"At the present time a strong British fleet is cruising in the Eastern Mediterranean. More than twenty battleships and cruisers are to be found where they are wanted and when they are wanted in those classic waters, now the theatre of such tremendous events.

"The absence of these powerful forces at the time of this crisis in European afairs requires especial vigilance from the Admiralty, and certain precautions designed to increase our immediate preparedness, have been taken.

"We have no reason to apprehend trouble of any kind, but my advisers of the Admiralty are satisfied that our fleet and flotillas in home waters are by no means unequal to any task which might devolve upon them.

"It would be a poor thing to belittle or deprecate the undoubted resources of the British naval power in serious times like these, and there is no reason whatever to do so, for that power has not often stood upon a firmer basis than it does to-night."

"CAN'T ROB VICTORS"—ASQUITH

British Premier Says Powers Are Agreed—Deprecates Raising Special Questions.

LONDON, Nov. 9.—"Upon one thing I believe the general opinion of Europe to be unanimous—that the victors are not to be robbed of the fruits which cost them so dearly."

This was the statement made by Premier Asquith to-night during a speech at the Guild Hall banquet on the Near Eastern situation.

The Prime Minister referred to the unsuccessful efforts of the powers to prevent the conflict and to the great changes the war had made in the map of Europe. He said that the fall of Constantinople might occur at any moment, and added:

"In these anxious times it is satisfactory to be able to announce that the relations of England with the other powers, without a single exception, were never more friendly and cordial." Mr. Asquith continued:

"The great powers are working together with a closeness of touch and a frankness and freedom of communication and discussion which is remarkable and which may seem almost unintelligible to those who believe that, because for certain purposes the powers have been and are ranged in different groups they must therefore in a time of a European crisis be arrayed in opposite camps."

The map of Europe will have to be recast, the Premier declared, and nowhere was there a disposition to belittle the magnitude of the struggle or dispute the decisiveness of the result.

"England," he said, "has no direct

Continued on Page 3.

RANCHER LEFT $1,140,245.

Zimmerman Made Loans Worth $260,000 to Cattlemen, All Good.

KANSAS CITY, Mo., Nov. 9.—An administrator's report of the estate of J. K. Zimmerman, a cattleman of Waco, Texas, who died in Excelsior Springs, Mo., Oct. 6, filed in the Probate Court here to-day, values the estate at $1,140,245. Administrators found that $260,000 of this amount represented loans to Texas cattlemen in sums of $5,000 to $25,000, of which the only record kept was a penciled notation on a slip of paper. All were found to be gilt-edged.

Mr. Zimmerman died intestate. He was buried in his old home in Hanover, Penn. He was unmarried, and often had told friends he never would make a will because of a superstition that once a will was made death of the maker would follow soon. Several probable Zimmerman heirs have been located, among them Mrs. Emma Chance of Kewanee, Ill.

$6,000 FOR MISSING BOY.

Colored Woman Believed to Have Kidnapped Child from Summer Camp.

Special to The New York Times.

PHILADELPHIA, Nov. 9.—A circular offering a reward of $6,000 for the recovery of Robert Dunbar, Jr., 4 years old, who was supposed to have been kidnapped from a Summer camp at Swazie Lake, near Opelousas, La., was received to-day at the detective bureau from the Burns National Detective Agency.

The child disappeared from his parents' tent. He is presumed to have been taken away by a colored woman about 30 years old. She was seen at Baton Rouge accompanied by a child answering the description of the missing boy on Sept. 25, and was traced to Burnside, twenty-eight miles distant.

The circular stated that the boy might have been carried away for the purpose of securing a ransom for his return, although no demands had been received from any source.

BURN ROOSEVELT'S PICTURE.

Connecticut Social Club Takes It Out on Lawn and Makes Bonfire.

Special to The New York Times.

MERIDEN, Conn., Nov. 9.—An exclusive social and Republican organization in this city, known as the Home Club, is in chaotic condition as the result of the action of some of the dyed-in-the-wool Republican members who destroyed the photograph of ex-President Rosevelt, which was presented by him to the club, with his autograph, when he was President.

When the election of Wilson was indicated late Tuesday night the picture was taken from a prominent place on the wall o fthe clubroom by one member, and thrown to the floor. Another member thrust his foot through the canvas, and then it was taken to the lawn in front of the club building and burned.

AKED SEEKS CITIZENSHIP.

English Pastor Applies for Full Naturalization at San Francisco.

Special to The New York Times.

SAN FRANCISCO, Cal., Nov. 9.—The Rev. Dr. Charles F. Aked, who came here last year from the Fifth Avenue Baptist Church in New York to assume the pastorate of the First Congregational Church in San Francisco, applied to-day for full admission as a citizen of the United States.

According to his application he came to this country on April 17, 1909, and obtained his first papers on July 5 in that year. His five years of residence expired last July, but as he could not get papers in time to vote at the election this week he decided to wait until it was over. He must now obtain papers from New York to show that he had lived three and a half years there. To-day two residents of this city swore that he had lived here since April 11, 1911.

TAKES FIRST RAILROAD RIDE.

Mrs. Keith Is 113, and Her Youngest Son, 89, Was with Her.

JOPLIN, Mo., Nov. 9.—Mrs. H. Keith, 113 years old, and her youngest son, 89 years old, took their first ride on a railroad train yesterday. They came from their home, which is several miles from a railroad, in Southern Arkansas.

Charles McManamy was the first patrolman in uniform they ever saw.

"Are you a policeman?" asked Mrs. Keith. "Well, we want you to show us how to get uptown. This is the first time my son and I have ever been in Joplin. We came up to see the sights and are going back home to-morrow."

Mrs. Keith said that she has three sons older than the one who accompanied her here. The eldest is 95, she said. All live with their mother, or near her home. Her husband was killed in the civil war.

SCHRANK'S TRIAL PUT OFF.

District Attorney Takes Time to Notify Roosevelt of It.

Special to The New York Times.

MILWAUKEE, Nov. 9.—Col. Roosevelt was notified by the local District Attorney to-day that he could appear if he wished as a witness against John Schrank, who shot him recently. The trial, which had been slated for to-day, was postponed to next week. It is not thought here that Col. Roosevelt will care to make the trip, as his evidence is not necessary.

The State plans to keep the date of trial secret, rush the proceedings, and have Schrank on his way to prison before the general public knows the trial has been started.

Schrank is undecided about engaging a lawyer. "If Roosevelt comes to Milwaukee, then I will certainly get a lawyer," he is said to have remarked. "If he does not, then I think I will not get an attorney, but will take my medicine."

CANCELS OIL LAND LEASES.

Mr. Taft Voids Grants Made by Indians to Uncle Sam Oil Company.

WASHINGTON, Nov. 9.—At a hearing in the White House President Taft sustained to-day the action of the Department of the Interior in canceling leases entered into by the tribal council of the Five Civilized Tribes of Indians with the Uncle Sam Oil Company of Oklahoma for several hundred thousand acres of oil land. The oil company had appealed to the President.

Secretary of the Interior Fisher said after the hearing that bids for leases of the same land, in smaller quantities than those made out to the Uncle Sam Company, would be opened in Oklahoma next week.

ROBERT ROOSEVELT HURT.

12-Year-Old Cousin of the Colonel Knocked from Horse.

WASHINGTON, Nov. 9. — Robert Roosevelt, the 12-year-old son of R. B. Roosevelt, a cousin of Theodore Roosevelt, was slightly injured to-day when knocked by tree branches from a horse he was riding in Rock Creek Park.

The horse ran away. When a policeman returned with it the youth pluckily insisted upon riding the horse home, rather than go in a carriage and he had his way about it.

TURKS LOSE KEY TO ADRIANOPLE

Unconquerable Bulgars Take Two Dominating Forts by Assault.

EXPECT SURRENDER HOURLY

Artillery Rushed Up to Hold the Forts and City's Position Is Hopeless.

POUNDING TCHATALJA LINES

Savoff's Main Forces Crowding In on Nazim Pasha's Army, Which Is Steadily Weakening.

By LIEUT. WAGNER,
The Only Correspondent at the Front on the Bulgarian Side.
By Marconi Transatlantic Wireless Telegraph to THE NEW YORK TIMES.
By arrangement with The Vienna Reichspost.
Copyright, 1912, by THE NEW YORK TIMES Company.

HEADQUARTERS OF THE BULGARIAN ARMY, Nov. 9.—The capture by the Bulgarians of two important positions on the northwest and southeast of the girdle of forts around Adrianople, which I have already reported, took place during Thursday night.

After a fierce artillery fire a brigade, followed by reserves, was commanded to storm the outworks of Kartaltepe and Papaztepe.

In spite of Turkish searchlights and a hail of Turkish projectiles the Bulgarian infantry were at last successful in taking both forts by the assault.

The Bulgarians immediately brought up reinforcements, notably artillery, repelled all counter-attacks, and commenced to fortify the captured positions, which are on the near side opposite Adrianople.

Of the two captured forts Kartaltepe is, in particular, extremely strong. It is situated on a hill, 143 meters high, and dominates both the city and its outlying girdle of forts.

The capture of those forts with the simultaneous storming of the fortress of Karkostepe renders any further defense hopeless. The capitulation of the fortress is expected hourly.

Closing in on Tchatalja.

HEADQUARTERS OF THE BULGARIAN ARMY, Friday, Nov. 8.—Supported by the positions they have already won, the Bulgarians are employing their whole strength in the attack on the remaining lines of the Turkish position at Tchatalja.

The third army has already pushed forward in the forest land south of Lake Derkos, while the first army is in action about the Turkish main position, east of the town of Tchatalja.

The Bulgarians have not yet succeeded in entirely breaking through the Turkish position, which consists of several lines drawn up one behind another, but the beating down of the Turkish defense is now only a question of a very short time.

The Turkish troops fight very unequally. Some detachments, which have obviously not been in action before, resist stubbornly. The remains of Nazim Pasha's army are now showing those signs of generally weakened powers of resistance which are usually exhibited by beaten troops.

The capitulation of Adrianople is imminent. The negotiations for the surrender of the fortress, which have been started, have not yet led to any result, but as the Bulgarians have successfully driven in the last great Turkish sortie and won a dominating position on the northwest front of Adrianople all further defense of the place is hopeless.

Men Fought Hand to Hand.

The fighting on the Tchorlu River was of an appalling character. The river is still dammed in many places by corpses and material of war, while the water runs red with the blood of dead and wounded men.

In the forest to the north there was bitter fighting at close quarters, and the animosity on both sides was so great that men threw away weapons and sprang at one another's throats.

Frightful scenes were also enacted at the capture of Istranja and on the occasion of the unsuccessful advance northwestward from Kapaklibunar. Attacked in superior force from three sides, the Turkish troops rushed in headlong flight back on Kapaklibunar, but before they could reach it they were slaughtered by Bulgarian artillery and infantry fire.

Although they, too, were exhausted by many days' fighting and the forced marches, the Bulgarian troops by their ruthless pursuit drove asunder all the units of Nazim Pasha's army.

CONSTANTINOPLE, Nov. 9.—The Turkish garrison of Adrianople claims to have inflicted a severe defeat on the Bulgarians in a two days' battle on the west front of the fortress near Marash.

An official report, dated yesterday, has been received from the Civil Governor of Adrianople, in which he says the battle began at 8 o'clock Thursday morning and continued until 7 o'clock in the evening. After half an hour's pause fighting was resumed with renewed vigor and continued all night and the whole of the next day until nightfall last night.

The Turkish report says the Turkish troops attacked with fixed bayonets

"All the News That's Fit to Print."

The New York Times.

THE WEATHER.
Increasing cloudiness, warmer, probably snow; Wednesday, clearing; brisk southeasterly winds.
☞For full weather report see Page 22.

VOL. LXII...NO. 20,107. • • • NEW YORK, TUESDAY, FEBRUARY 11, 1913.—TWENTY-FOUR PAGES. ONE CENT In Greater New York, Jersey City, and Newark. | Elsewhere, TWO CENTS.

SCOTT FINDS SOUTH POLE; THEN PERISHES WITH FOUR MEN IN ANTARCTIC BLIZZARD; BODIES FOUND AFTER EIGHT MONTHS

ARMED TRUCE IN MEXICO CITY; MADERO RETURNS

Called Upon by Diaz for His Resignation, the President Cries, "I Will Die First!"

REBEL LEADER INSISTENT

Says He Held Off to Prevent Slaughter, but the Federals Have Not Done the Same.

BATTLE PREDICTED TO-DAY

Both Sides Have Been Strengthening Their Positions and Seeking Reinforcements.

FOREIGNERS NOT MOLESTED

Executions Take Place at the Palace—Son of Reyes Kills Himself.

NORTHERN GENERALS WAITING

Washington Hurries Warships to Convenient Ports to Watch Events in Republic.

General Diaz to The Times.

By Cable to the Editor of THE NEW YORK TIMES.

MEXICO CITY, Feb. 10.—The revolt is in progress and in a few hours will have to be decided. All the chances are in our favor. I will protect all your citizens and properties.

FELIX DIAZ.

Special Cable to THE NEW YORK TIMES.

MEXICO CITY, Feb. 10.—The city at 10 o'clock to-night was quiet.

The Federals and Revolutionists still held their positions. The Government was taking ammunition to the palace under a heavy guard.

Gen. Diaz says he delayed battle in order to avoid slaughter of non-combatants, but as the Government has not refrained from hostile movements he has about lost patience.

Fighting, it is expected, will begin at daybreak.

Special Cable to THE NEW YORK TIMES.

MEXICO CITY, Feb. 10.—An armed truce prevailed between the Federals and the revolutionists all day.

Gen. Diaz still held the arsenal and had practical control of all the heavy artillery. He is equipped with rifles and machine guns and has an unlimited supply of ammunition. According to reports, he is arming and drilling several hundred men in the arsenal.

A conference was held this morning between Gen. Diaz, two of his suporters, and Cabinet Ministers at a café in the centre of the city. What occurred at the conference was not made public, but after it was over a red flag was raised on the arsenal, and war without quarter was declared.

Several cannon were taken from the arsenal last night to the suburbs. They were placed where they would command the Chapultepec Castle. Officers in the castle say they will raze it if necessary to save it.

The movements of President Madero are kept secret. It is reported that he went to Cuernavaca last night and returned to the city at dawn this morning. Gen. Felipe Angeles, commander of Cuernavaca, it is said, is at Contreras, twelve miles south of the capital, with about a thousand Madero troops.

Gen. Angeles, it is said, has some heavy artillery.

The populace is maintaining neutrality.

A small riot in the Colonia del Carmen early this morning was stopped by mounted police.

The number of dead has not been reported, as it is impossible to pass the lines.

Genovevo de la O and Felipe Neri, rebel leaders from the State of Mexico, occupy a position within ten miles of the capital at Tlalpam and Xicpimilco, awaiting the orders of Gen. Diaz to enter the capital. Tlalpam is five miles beyond the Country Club. Foreigners are leaving that place.

Messengers were sent to Gen. Diaz this morning, protesting loyalty to him and asking permission to enter and join his forces. He sent an officer with instructions to take the positions and waih further orders.

Higinio Aguilar and Gaudencio de la

Continued on Page 8.

EDISON 66 YEARS OLD TO-DAY

Wife Will Make Him Quit Work Long Enough to Dine with Friends.

Special to The New York Times.

WEST ORANGE, N. J., Feb. 10.—Thomas A. Edison, who will be 66 years old to-morrow, will pass the day just as he does the other 364 in the year, with the exception of an occasional Sunday, when he yields to the insistence of Mrs. Edison and goes to church. He will work in the laboratory and offices, but has promised to "knock off" in the evening to be the guest at a family dinner party which Mrs. Edison is arranging.

The employes of the works will observe the day by wearing buttons or pins bearing the numerals "66." The workers at the Edison plant are grateful because since Edison took charge of the commercial branches in December many of the pay envelopes of the humbler employes have been fattened.

The production of the kinetophone, tha further perfection of the storage battery, and the development of the disk phonograph record are among the achievements of the inventor during the past year. For his storage battery Edison received the Rathenau medal, donated by Emile Rathenau of Berlin.

"I feel like twenty-five," said Edison this afternoon. "I'm sure I'm going to keep right at it, too, for a good many years more."

POPE DECORATES EDITORS.

Medals to Cardinal for Those Who Compiled Catholic Encyclopedia.

Cardinal Farley received from Pope Pius X. yesterday the "Pro Ecclesia et Pontifice," an important decoration, to be bestowed upon the Board of Editors of the Catholic Encyclopedia. The order was instituted by Pope Leo XIII., July 17, 1888, and the decoration was made a permanent distinction only in October, 1898. It is to reward those, who, in a general way, deserve well of the Pope. The medal is made of gold, silver, and bronze. It is cross shaped, made rectangular in form by fleurs de lis, fixed in the angles of the cross. In the centre of the cross is a small medal with an image of its founder, Pope Leo XIII. The ribbon is purple, with delicate lines of white and yellow on each border. The decoration is worn on the right side of the chest.

The Board of Editors of the Catholic Encyclopedia consists of Charles G. Herbman, Ph. D., L. L. D., Professor of Latin Language and Literature at the College of the City of New York; Edward A. Pace, Ph. D., D. D., Professor of Philosophy at the Catholic University in Washington; Conde B. Pallen, Ph. D., L. L. D., of New Rochelle; Mgr. Thomas J. Shahan, D. D., rector of the Catholic University, Washington, and the Rev. J. J. Wynnee, S. J.

Dr. Pallen has just returned from Rome, where he presented the Pope with a set of the Vatican edition of the encyclopedia.

LEFT CHANGE FOR $50 BILL.

Clerks Wonder if Their Customer Was Absent-Minded or Crazy.

All day yesterday the clerks at the Broadway and Thirtieth Street store of Hackett Carhart & Co. expected to see a wild-eyed man run in and demand if any one had seen on Saturday a perfectly good $50 bill. No such person turned up, and last night as the employes put out the lights they wondered if there really could be any one in this city who cared so little for money.

On Saturday afternoon a customer asked to be shown some neckties. He seemed perfectly rational and betrayed no more than the proper amount of interest in the adornment of his person. He selected ties worth $4.50 and handed the salesman a $50 bill. This was sent on its way to the cashier for change and the ties were wrapped up. The man took his parcel, put it in his pocket, and quit the store. When the salesman received the change he had gone. The man ran out into Broadway, but the customer had disappeared.

The salesman reported the incident and the cashier decided at once that the note must be a counterfeit. But examination proved that it was genuine.

SOON TO WED, DISAPPEARS.

Rockfellow's Friends Unable to Account for His Sudden Departure.

Special to The New York Times.

PLAINFIELD, N. J., Feb. 10.—Rowland C. Rockfellow, son of the late Mayor George W. Rockfellow, disappeared from his home on Saturday, leaving two notes for his mother, who was prostrated by his absence. His wedding to Miss Rae Warnock, daughter of Mr. and Mrs. W. W. Warnock, was set for Tuesday night, Feb. 18, and one of the letters addressed to his *mother said:*

"I wil lnot be responsible for any debts unless contracted by myself." The wedding invitations had been issued when the young man disappeared.

Mrs. Rockfellow said to-day that she could not account for her son's action. She exhibited the other note he had left, which read:

> Dear Mother: I have been a good boy. I am not dishonest, but I can't help going away. Don't blame me.

W. R. Causbrook, district manager of the Public Service Corporation's local office, where Rockfellow was employed as cashier, said this afternoon that his accounts were correct. His fiancée, Miss Warnock, said she had not had any quarrel with Rockfellow. The first intimation she had had of his absence, she asserted, was on Saturday night when he failed to appear at a dinner party given to them.

WILSON WON'T SEE CASTRO.

Declines Request of ex-President of Venezuela for an Interview.

TRENTON, N. J., Feb. 10.—Representatives of ex-President Castro of Venezuela came to Trenton to-day to obtain an interview for the General with President-elect Wilson. Castro wished to see the Governor, but Mr. Wilson declined to receive him on the ground that he would not mix in any affairs of the Taft Administration before his inauguration as President.

Castro has been building hopes on the possibility of friendly action by Mr. Wilson. He has said that if Mr. Wilson was President instead of Mr. Taft he would have no trouble in obtaining admission to this country. When Mr. Wilson visited Ellis Island some time ago the ex-President expressed much regret that he had been unable to see him. One of Mr. Wilson's companions on that trip, Mrs. J. Borden Harriman, did ask Commissioner Williams to let the Governor's party talk with Castro, but Mr. Williams refused the request curtly. Mr. Wilson seemingly did not know of Mrs. Harriman's request at the time it was made.

SCOTT'S LAST MESSAGE TO THE WORLD.

Not Faulty Organization, but Misfortune, Caused the Disaster Which He Foresaw—Asks Aid for Families of the Dead.

MESSAGE TO THE PUBLIC.

The causes of this disaster are not due to faulty organization, but to misfortune in all the risks which had to be undertaken. One, the loss of pony transport in March, 1911, obliged me to start later than I had intended, and obliged the limits of stuff transported to be narrowed. The weather throughout the outward journey, and especially the long gale in 83 degrees south, stopped us. The soft snow in the lower reaches of the glacier again reduced the pace.

We fought these untoward events with will and conquered, but it ate into our provisions reserve. Every detail of our food supplies, clothing and depots made on the interior ice-sheet and on that long stretch of 700 miles to the pole and back worked out to perfection. The advance party would have returned to the glacier in fine form and with a surplus of food but for the astonishing failure of the man whom we had least expected to fail. Seaman Edgar Evans was thought to be the strongest man of the party, and Beardmore glacier is not difficult in fine weather. But on our return we did not get a single completely fine day. This, with a sick companion, enormously increased our anxieties. I have said elsewhere that we got into frightfully rough ice, and Edgar Evans received a concussion of the brain. He died a natural death, but left us a shaken party, with the season unduly advanced.

But all the facts above enumerated were as nothing to the surprise which awaited us at the Barrier. I maintain that our arrangements for returning were quite adequate, and that no one in the world would have done better in the weather which we encountered at this time of the year. On the summit, in latitude 85 degrees to 86 degrees, we had minus twenty to minus thirty. On the Barrier, in latitude 82 degrees, 10,000 feet lower, we had minus thirty in the day and minus forty-seven at night pretty regularly, with a continuous headwind during our day marches.

These circumstances came on very suddenly, and our wreck is certainly due to this sudden advent of severe weather, which does not seem to have any satisfactory cause.

I do not think human beings ever came through such a month as we have come through, and we should have got through in spite of the weather but for the sickening of a second companion, Capt. Oates, and a shortage of fuel in our depots, for which I cannot account, and, finally, but for the storm which has fallen on us within eleven miles of the depot at which we hoped to secure the final supplies. Surely misfortune could scarcely have exceeded this last blow!

We arrived within eleven miles of our old One Ton camp with fuel for one hot meal and food for two days. For four days we have been unable to leave the tent, the gale blowing about us. We are weak.

Writing is difficult, but for my own sake I do not regret this journey, which has shown that Englishmen can endure hardships, help one another, and meet death with as great a fortitude as ever in the past. We took risks. We knew we took them. Things have come out against us, and therefore we have no cause for complaint, but bow to the will of Providence, determined still to do our best to the last.

But if we have been willing to give our lives to this enterprise, which is for the honor of our country, I appeal to our countrymen to see that those who depend on us are properly cared for. Had we lived, I should have had a tale to tell of the hardihood, endurance, and courage of my companions, which would have stirred the heart of every Englishman.

These rough notes and our dead bodies must tell the tale, but surely, surely, a great, rich country like ours will see that those who are dependent on us are properly provided for.

March 25, 1912. (Signed) R. SCOTT.

INDICT WALSH, NEWELL AND FOYE

True Bills Found Against Police Captain and Lawyer on Bribery Charge.

WHITMAN AFTER HOCHSTIM

Ready Now to Indict One of the Heads of Syndicate Running Disorderly Hotels.

WALDO HUNTING DOWN GRAFT

Big Police Official Reported Called for Examination To-day—Costigan Aids Curran Inquiry.

The Extraordinary Grand Jury returned indictments yesterday against Police Capt. Thomas W. Walsh, Patrolman Charles E. Foye, and Edward J. Newell, the lawyer. Walsh and Newell were charged with bribery and against the lawyer there was a second indictment charging him also with misdemeanor. The first bill found against Newell a fortnight ago was dismissed and the new ones returned. Foye was charged with perjury because of his sworn testimony before the Curran Committee that Chairman Curran had tried to persuade him not to press a charge against a saloonkeeper whom he had arrested.

The witnesses against Walsh and Newell were Thomas J. Dorian and Nathan J. Michaels, the managers of the Hotel Avenel; George A. Sipp, and Patrolman Eugene Fox. All of them were willing witnesses except Michaels. Sipp's story, covering five years of paying graft to Capt. Walsh for protection, was corroborated by Dorian before the Curran Committee, and then Dorian fled the city. District Attorney Whitman made a long and fruitless effort to find him. It was learned that he was receiving his weekly pay from the hotel syndicate that employed him, and a search began for evidence to show that these payments were really made to keep Dorian away.

Mr. Whitman threatened to proceed against the syndicate and to indict Dorian. Then Dorian returned and told a story to Mr. Whitman that not only confirmed the confession made by Fox, but gave information that showed that the disorderly hotel syndicate had paid graft to the police for many years in the many districts in which they owned hotels. It was discovered that there were several of these hotels in various sections of the city. Yesterday Mr. Whitman said that he was ready to submit enough evidence before the Grand Jury to indict at least one of the leading spirit of the syndicate.

Whitman After Hochstim.

The man that Mr. Whitman is after is Max Hochstim, who, with Philip Blau, Jacob Spielberg, and a man named Fromberg, composed the Baltic Hotel Company that owns the Hotel Avenel and other hotels of the same character. Mr. Whitman learned yesterday that Mrs. Hochstim owns thirty-nine shares of the Baltic Hotel Company, and that Hochstim owns one share. The sixty other shares are scattered. Some of the information against the syndicate was gathered yesterday in the course of the investigation in connection with police graft bearing upon the cases directly aimed against Walsh and Newell.

The moment the indictment against Newell was returned Justice Goff issued a bench warrant for his arrest. It was served by Detective Flood of Mr. Whitman's office, who found Newell in his office at 42 Broadway. He was brought before Justice Goff and his bail on the bribery charge was fixed at $2,000, while the $1,000 on which he was held on the misdemeanor charge was continued. A surety company furnished the bail, and Newell went about his business. Foye is away on a vacation. He will be taken into custody this morning as soon as he returns and bail will be set. If he fails to furnish it he will be locked up. No action was taken against Capt. Walsh because of his illness. As soon as he is physically able to go abroad he will be arraigned and released on bail.

W. M. K. Olcott, Newell's lawyer, had a talk with Mr. Whitman between the time of Newell's indictment and his arraignment in court. Before Mr. Whitman went home last night it was said that there were prospects that Newell would tell all he knew of his connection with Sipp and Capt. Walsh.

It was explained that if he told all he knew it would be to the effect that a well known lawyer handed him $1,000 to give to Sipp in return for Sipp's promise to remain out of this State until after Jan. 1, 1914; that he held out $300 to pay himself for the services he had rendered Sipp while the latter was a prisoner at Atlantic City on the charge made against him by the police and that the money came originally from Capt. Walsh. But if Newell's story goes beyond this transaction it might reach a point where the system of the police to get legal services from certain influential sources, directly or indirectly, would be uncovered.

Newell Proved Obdurate.

When Newell was indicted first for a misdemeanor, under Section 2,441 of the

Continued on Page 9.

Death Wipes Out Brave Party on Return Trip to Winter Quarters

LEAVES MESSAGE TO PUBLIC

Disaster Not Due to Faulty Organization, but to Misfortune, His Last Word.

THREE BODIES IN ONE TENT

There Scott, Wilson, and Bowers Succumbed to Starvation and Exhaustion.

OATES BRAVED DEATH ALONE

Knowing His Fate, He Marched Out Into the Blizzard—"Brave Soul," Wrote Scott.

EVANS KILLED BY A FALL

Storm Wrecked Last Hope of Saving Themselves When Only 11 Miles from a Food Depot.

REACHED POLE JAN. 18, 1912

Found Amundsen's Records There—Perished March 29, 1912, and Bodies Were Found in the Following November.

By Lieut. E.R.G.R. EVANS, R.N.
Second in Command of the Scott Expedition.

Special Cable to THE NEW YORK TIMES.

CHRISTCHURCH, New Zealand, Feb. 10.—Capt. Robert F. Scott's antarctic ship, the Terra Nova, on Jan. 18, this year, arrived at Cape Evans, the base on McMurdo Sound, where it was to meet the explorers on their return from the expedition in search of the south pole and bring them back, if they were ready. It was learned from the shore party found at this base that Capt. Scott and the four men with him had reached the pole on Jan. 18, 1912, but all had perished on the return journey, about the end of March. Their bodies were not found until a searching party discovered them on Nov. 12, nearly eight months after the disaster.

Capt. Scott, Dr. Edward A. Wilson, chief of the scientific staff, and Lieut. H. R. Bowers had made their way back to within 155 miles of Cape Evans, when they were caught in a blizzard and were overcome about March 29. They were then within eleven miles of One Ton Depot, where they would have found shelter and supplies.

Previously Petty Officer Edgar Evans and Capt. L. E. G. Oates of the Inniskillen Dragoons, who had been in charge of the ponies and dogs, had succumbed. Evans was the first to give way, dying from concussion of the brain due to a fall on Feb. 17. Oates died from exposure on March 17.

Found Amundsen's Records.

The records of Capt. Scott were recovered by a relief expedition. They showed that he and his party had reached the south pole on Jan. 18, 1912. There they found the tent and records left by Capt. Roald Amundsen when he quit the pole on Dec. 17, 1911.

Six other men of the Scott expedition who had been through a perilous experience were found to be safe and well. They composed Lieut. V. L. A. Campbell's expedition, which had been sent to make geological investigations to the east of Cape Evans. The Terra Nova has been unable to take the men off the year before on account of ice, and they were left to spend another Winter in the antarctic. In this party were Dr. Levick, Priestly, Abott, Browning, and Dickerson.

Relief Party Had to Return.

Before the Terra Nova sailed for New Zealand last March Surgeon Atkinson, who had been left in charge of the western party until Capt. Scott's return, dispatched Garrard and Demetri with two dog teams to assist the southern party, whose return to Hut Point was expected about March 10, 1912. Atkinson would have accompanied this party, but was kept back in medical charge of Lieut. Evans, the second in command, who, it will be remembered, nearly died from scurvy.

This relief party reached One Ton Depot on March 3, but was compelled to return on March 10, owing primarily to the dog food running short, also to persistent bad weather and the poor condition of the dogs after the strain of a hard season's work. The dog teams returned to Hut Point on March 16, the poor animals being mostly frostbitten and incapable of furthe work.

Garrard collapsed through an overstrained heart. His companion was also sick. It was impossible to communicate with Cape Evans, the ship having sailed on March 4, and the open sea lying between Atkinson and Keohane.

The only two men left sledged out to Corner Camp to render any help that might be wanted by the southern party. They fought their way out to Corner Camp against the unusually severe weather, and, realizing that they could be of no assistance, they were forced to return to Hut Point after depoting one week's provisions.

In April, when communication with Cape Evans was established, a gallant attempt to relieve Lieut. Campbell was made by Atkinson, Wright, Williamson, and Keohane. This party reached Butter Point, when they were stopped by open water. Their return was exciting and nearly ended in disaster, owing to the sea ice breaking up.

Search Party's Journey.

The search party left Cape Evans after the Winter on Oct. 30 last. The party, which was organized by Surgeon Atkinson, consisted of two divisions, Atkinson taking the dog teams with Garrard and Demetri, and Mr. Wright being in charge of a party including Nelson, Gran, Lashley, Crean, Williamson, Keohane, and Hooper, with seven Indian mules. They were provisioned for three months, as they expected an extended search.

One Ton camp was found in order, and all provisioned.

Proceeding along the old southern route, Wright's party sighted Capt. Scott's tent on Nov. 12. Within it were found the bodies of Capt. Scott, Dr. Wilson, and Lieut. Bowers. They had saved their records, hard pressed as they were.

From these papers the following information was gleaned:

The first death was that of Seaman Edgar Evans, petty officer

Capt. Robert Falcon Scott.

The continuation of the authentic narrative of Capt. Scott's expedition will appear exclusively in The New York Times to-morrow.

WOMEN'S SUFFRAGE

GAIL COLLINS

Elizabeth Cady Stanton, seated, often wrote speeches for her fellow suffragist, Susan B. Anthony.

As the United States rang in the 20th century, the nation was celebrating the New Woman, an independent, spirited creature who was literally freewheeling. Bicycling had become the new passion for middle-class Americans, and after generations of being trapped in corsets and weighed down by ankle-length skirts, women were suddenly permitted to go whizzing down the streets in clothing that would not wrap itself around the wheel spokes. "Not the least good thing the bicycle has done has been to demonstrate publicly that women have legs," said Life magazine.

Only one thing, it seemed, was missing: "We have got the new woman in everything except the counting of her vote at the ballot box," said Susan B. Anthony.[1]

Anthony and her great friend Elizabeth Cady Stanton would both live to see the new millennium, but they knew they would not live to see American women given the right to vote. It should have happened after the Civil War, Stanton said shortly before her death in 1902, "and like all things too long postponed, now gets on everybody's nerves."[2]

Southern senators had no intention of expanding the right to vote to black women when they were so busy disenfranchising black men. The powerful liquor lobby, well aware that women voters would support Prohibition, lent its hand in keeping the lid down tight. Despairing of ever getting a constitutional amendment through Congress, the suffrage leaders dedicated themselves to amending the state constitutions, one by one.

It was a long, depressing slog with occasional bright dots of success sprinkled through years and years of petition signing and testimony before state legislatures. "To get the word 'male' in effect out of the Constitution cost the women of the country fifty-two years of pauseless campaign," said Carrie Chapman Catt, who had led the drive during most of those uninspiring crusades. She counted up 56 referendum campaigns (all directed, of course, at the exclusively male

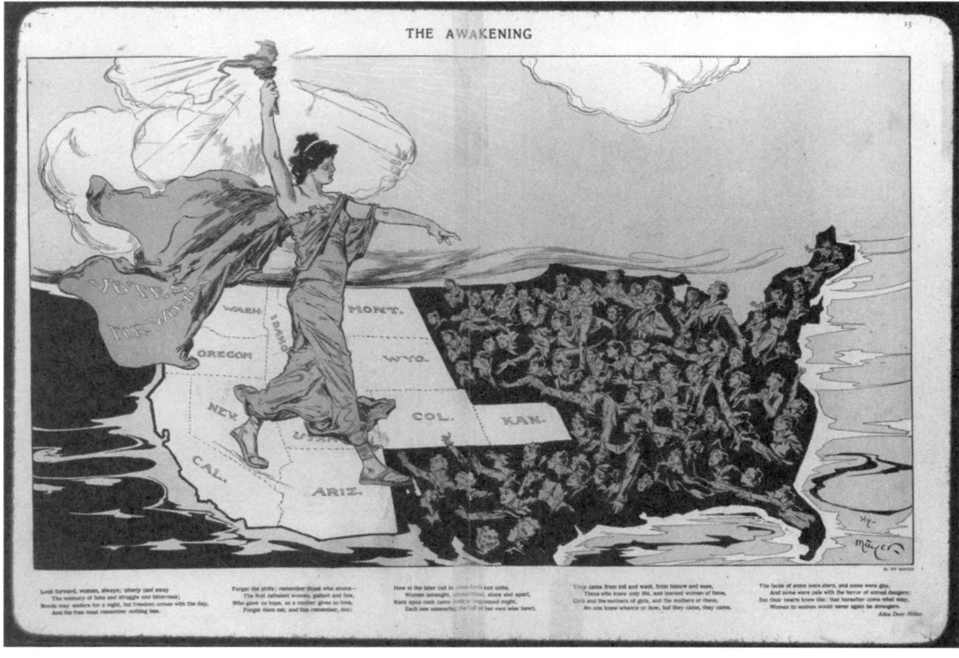

In 1915, women in the western United States had the right to vote while those in the East did not.

voters), 480 campaigns to get legislatures to consider suffrage amendments, 47 campaigns for constitutional conventions, 277 campaigns directed at state party conventions, 30 campaigns to get national parties to put suffrage in their platforms and "19 campaigns with 19 successive Congresses."

Obviously, none of that sounded like much fun. "The only method suggested for furthering the cause was the slow process of education," said Stanton's daughter Harriot Stanton Blatch. "We were told to organize, organize, organize to the end of educating, educating, educating." Blatch, who married an Englishman and lived in London for 20 years, had close contact with the British suffrage movement and knew that parades, sit-ins and the occasional mass arrest were far more interesting.

The younger generation—those new women who were turning up as college presidents, labor organizers, settlement house workers, journalists and consumer activists—started demonstrating what their idea of a suffrage movement would look like. In California, where a critical referendum on votes for women was underway in 1911, there were parades, pageants and billboards all over the state, with everyone draped in what was now the official suffrage color, yellow. Even advertising experts jumped into the fray, and readers were suddenly confronted by ads that announced Shredded Wheat was "a vote for health, happiness and domestic freedom," and showed a woman dropping a cereal biscuit into the ballot box. The referendum passed and California women were enfranchised—a huge victory for women all around the country.[3] "We all shouted for joy, some hugged and kissed one another, some cried and some jumped up and down for joy," wrote a housewife in Kansas.

In 1912, 10,000 women marched in New York, in a demonstration that was particularly notable for its egalitarian cast—the mixture of society women, the usual middle-class suffrage suspects and the working class.[4] Workers carried banners depicting their trades. (Dressmakers had a sewing machine and the writers bore aloft pictures of the novelist Harriet Beecher Stowe.) And in 1913, the greatest march of all would take place in Washington, organized by Alice Paul.

Of all the young American women who went to England and came back determined to use civil disobedience to break the Congressional stalemate on suffrage, Paul stood in a class

FURTHER READING

1 "Miss Susan B. Anthony Died This Morning," see March 13, 1906, front page.
2 "Elizabeth Cady Stanton Dies at Her Home," see October 27, 1902, front page.
3 "Suffrage Wins By 2,500," see October 14, 1911, article.
4 "Suffrage Army Out on Parade," see May 5, 1912, front page.

Some 20,000 women marched in a massive, pre-election parade in New York on October 23, 1915, in support of suffrage.

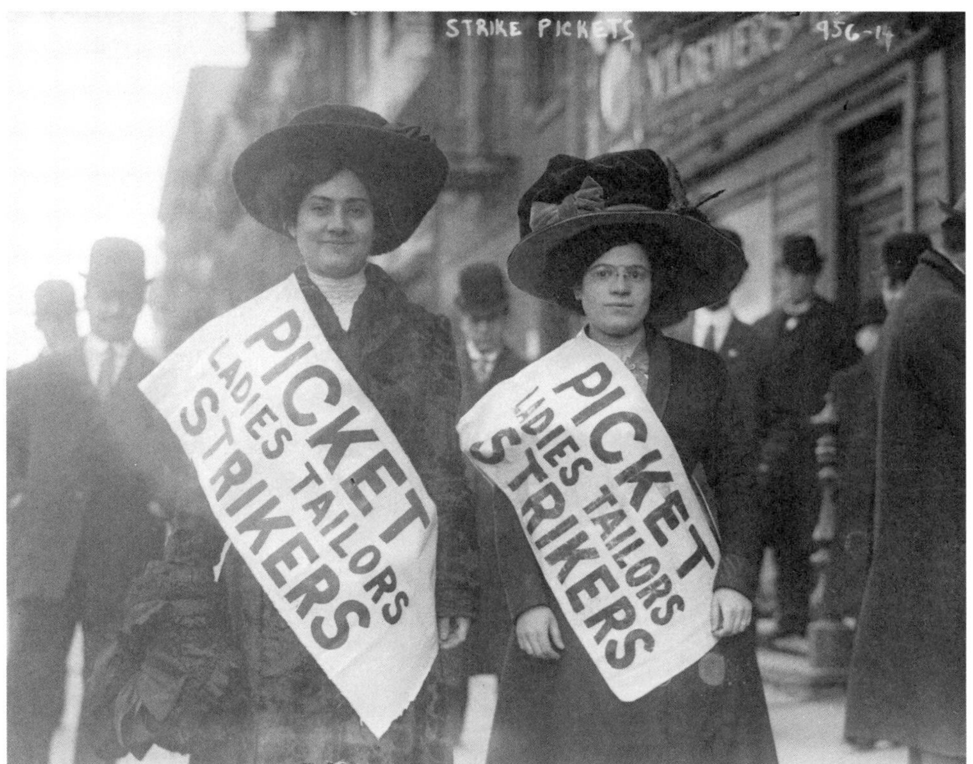

Women, like these tailor industry workers, were active in the labor union movement.

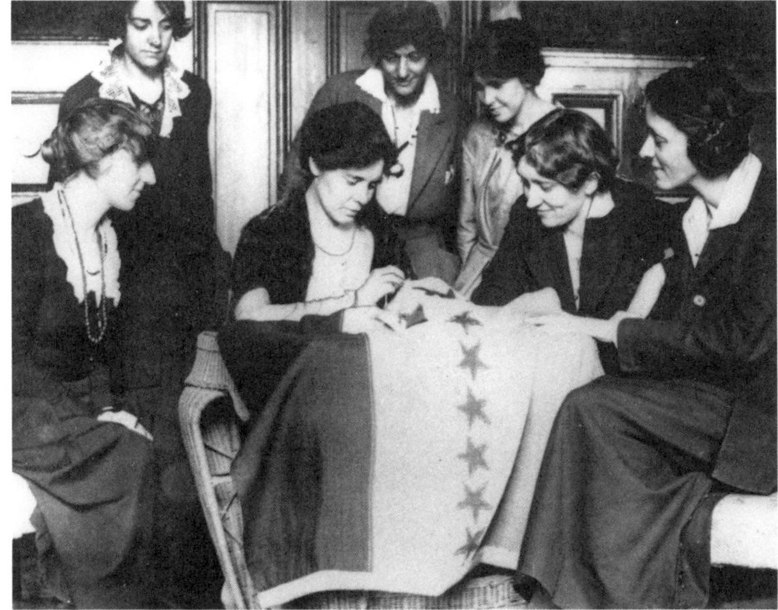

Suffragist Alice Paul sewed a star on the Suffrage Flag as each state ratified the constitutional amendment giving women the right to vote.

Universal suffrage for women collided with racist attempts to disenfranchise blacks, as this political cartoon depicts.

The cover of the official program of the Women's Suffrage Procession in Washington, D.C., in 1913.

by herself. Small, frail looking and so obsessed with the cause that she refused to waste more than 30 cents a day of the movement's money on food, her single-mindedness drove opponents crazy. Some claimed that the lack of nutrition had made her insane, and one referred to her as an "anemic fanatic."

But when it came to staging a really good parade, Paul took second place to no one. On the day before Woodrow Wilson's inauguration, she assembled 8,000 marchers, 26 floats, 10 bands and 6 chariots in a display led by Inez Milholland, a beautiful suffragist who, in a strategy far ahead of its time, tried to woo young women into the cause by assuring them that fighting for the right to vote was good exercise. Over half a million people gathered to watch the women march, and when Wilson arrived in town by train, he was greeted by an empty station.[5]

One of the downsides to Paul's single-mindedness was her willingness to ignore any political issue that got in the way of suffrage, including racial justice. Southern women had made an unholy pact with the male power structure, to support votes for white women and total political suppression for blacks. With her eyes on that constitutional amendment, Paul attempted to placate the racists by announcing that black women would have to march at the back. She had not reckoned with Ida B. Wells-Barnett, the Chicago civil rights activist and journalist, who disappeared into the crowd and then emerged to join Illinois delegation as it walked past.

For Wilson, a man who loved to bask in the admiration of intelligent women, it was painful to have them angrily picketing his White House and demanding to know how he could fight for democracy abroad while disenfranchising them at home. Over the first years of his administration, Paul would continually up the ante—pickets, then arrests, then hunger strikes. Her will was stronger than the president's, and Wilson eventually threw himself behind the suffrage drive. Thanks to his pressure, the amendment passed Congress in 1919.[6] One Congressman left a hospital bed to lend his support, and another refused to have a broken arm and shoulder set for fear of missing the vote. And when the final state, Tennessee, ratified the amendment in 1920, the deciding vote was cast by the youngest lawmaker,

Prominent suffragettes greet Rebecca L. Felton, the first woman to serve in the U.S. Senate, in November of 1922.

24-year-old Harry Burn, who changed from no to yes after his mother wrote a letter telling him to be a "good boy" and vote for suffrage.

GAIL COLLINS *was the editorial page editor of The New York Times from 2001 to January 2007 and currently is on a second tour as an op-ed columnist. Previously, Collins wrote for the New York Daily News and New York Newsday. Collins also founded the Connecticut State News Bureau, which reported on statehouse issues and local politics across the state from 1972 to 1977. She is the author of several books including "Scorpion Tongues: Gossip, Celebrity, and American Politics" and "America's Women: Four Hundred Years of Dolls, Drudges, Helpmates, and Heroines."*

Women join men at a polling place in New York City after winning the right to vote in 1920.

5 "5,000 Women March, Beset by Crowds," see March 4, 1913, article.
6 "Suffrage Wins in Senate," see June 5, 1919, front page.

"All the News That's Fit to Print."

The New York Times.

THE WEATHER

Cloudy, cooler to-day; probably fair to-morrow; light to moderate west winds.

☞For full weather report see Page 5, Sporting Section.

VOL. LXIII...NO. 20,357. NEW YORK, SUNDAY, OCTOBER 19, 1913.—90 PAGES, In Eight Parts, Including Picture Section and Review of Books. PRICE FIVE CENTS.

LOYAL FEW HEAR SULZER FAREWELL

Admirers Present Loving Cup and the Impeached Governor Again Denounces Murphy.

LETTER FROM ROOSEVELT

Regrets Governor Did Not Give Details of His Defense "So I Could Speak More Strongly."

BIG OFFERS FOR LECTURES

One as High as $100,000 for Season —Mr. and Mrs. Sulzer Go to Cooperstown To-day.

Special to The New York Times.

ALBANY, Oct. 18.—In a drizzling rain about one hundred men, headed by a band, marched to the Executive Mansion to-night and presented to William Sulzer a silver loving cup and to Mrs. Sulzer a huge bouquet of American Beauty roses. The procession was led by William Furlong, an undertaker, and at its head was carried a transparency, reading on one side, "Our Bill; He Dared to do Right," and on the other, "William Sulzer, Victim of Corrupt Bossism." Each of the paraders wore a lithograph of Sulzer in his hat. One of the onlookers was Patrick E. McCabe, Clerk to the Court of Impeachment, and the gathering led him to remark:

"That is a collection of the rarest political crackpots I have ever seen."

The paraders consisted of a mixture of all parties, most of them in the disappointed class. Mr. Sulzer's Secretary, Chester C. Platt, walked between Calvin Keesch and Jay W. Forrest.

The loving cup was engraved:

"To William Sulzer, Impeached Governor; a victim of corrupt bossism. Friday, October 17, 1913."

The cup was wrapped in manila paper, instead of reposing in a silk-lined box as is customary. The wrapper of the bouquet was similar to that of the cup.

Stood on Chairs and Davenports.

The line of march lay over streets which were being improved, and the paraders had to wade through a great deal of mud. When they arrived at the "People's House" the doors were thrown wide open, and most of the crowd rushed into the hall, at the end of which stood Mr. Sulzer and his wife. Soon the couple were hidden by the crowd, and there was a lively scramble for standing room on chairs and davenports.

Mr. Sulzer started in to shake hands with all of his callers, but he never completed his task. They crowded into one corner of the hall around him and refused to move. Some one said a few words of consolation to him, only to be interrupted by Mrs. Sulzer.

"The action of the court is the least of our troubles," she said. The crowd began to cheer and shout.

"We'll have you back here next year, Bill," one man yelled. Applause greeted this, and another enthusiast cried, "Hurrah for the next President of the United States," whereupon there was more cheering. Three cheers and a tiger for Mrs. Sulzer followed.

Attendants moved the crowd back from Mr. Sulzer, and the speechmaking began. Chester C. Platt read a speech assuring Mr. Sulzer that he had been removed because he would not obey the bosses. Mention of the name of Charles F. Murphy brought hisses. The crowd frequently interrupted Mr. Platt with remarks about Mr. Sulzer's enemies. "Lynch him!" shouted one man at the mention of the name of an Assemblyman. J. W. Forrest presented the loving cup to Mr. Sulzer.

Again Sulzer Defies Murphy.

The impeached Governor in a speech reiterated his assertion that his removal was due to his displeasing Tammany Hall.

"Had I obeyed the boss, instead of my oath of office, I would still be the Governor and the 'organization' would be patting me on the back and telling the people that I was a second Andrew Jackson," he said. "Tammany Hall, through the agency of Chief Murphy, has succeeded in taking away the office the people gave me by the largest plurality of votes any candidate for Governor ever received in the history of the State; but Tammany Hall cannot succeed in taking away my manhood, my self respect, and my determination to keep up the struggle, day in and day out, for honest government, which should be the hope and the aim of every decent citizen.

"My condemnation by the boss is intended to serve as a warning and a precedent to all who may follow me of what will happen to them if they do not 'obey orders,' but I believe my fate will have a good effect in the end and do more than any other single thing I could do to forever destroy the terrors of corrupt 'bossism' in the State of New York.

"Instead of my removal from office serving as a warning to public officials who may have the temerity to set themselves up between a band of plundering criminals and the taxpayers they despoil, it may be a blessing in disguise and bring about great reforms, better conditions and honest government, whereby the taxpayer will get a dollar's worth of results for every dollar of his money expended."

New Letter from Roosevelt.

A letter which Col. Roosevelt wrote to Mr. Sulzer on Oct. 3 last was given out by Mr. Platt. It was in response to a letter from Mr. Sulzer, telling Col. Roosevelt that on advice of counsel Mr. Sulzer could not permit a letter he wrote to the ex-President regarding the impeachment case to be made public. The letter from Col. Roosevelt follows:

My Dear Governor: I thank you for your letter, and I am sorry that I have to leave before your defense is made public. I wish it had been possible for you to write to me the letter of which you wrote, giving me the definite facts as to the effort by Mr. Murphy and his associates to bend you to their interests against the cause of honesty and decency in popular Government and their promise of immunity to you from impeachment if you would cease your attacks on the men who have been guilty of misconduct and theft in connection with public office, and if you would cease your demand for direct primaries. Such a letter, giving me in detail the facts, would of course have enabled me to speak much more strongly than I have spoken.

Again thanking you and begging that you will extend my heartiest regards to Mrs. Sulzer, I am, faithfully yours,

THEODORE ROOSEVELT.

Mr. Platt read several telegrams received by Mr. Sulzer. One from J. L. Woods Merrill of Kansas City offered "ten thousand dollars guaranteed to you to explain in Convention Hall here your impeachment by Murphy and Tammany as judges and jury and the verdict by them for continued graft and rubber-stamp government." Another, from Henry Neil of Chicago, guaranteed Mr. Sulzer $100,000 for one season to lecture "on your heroic sacrifices for honest

Continued on Page 2.

McCALL AND MITCHEL MEET.

"Hello, John," "Hello, Judge," Their Greeting at Irish Ball.

E. E. McCall, the Tammany candidate for Mayor, and John Purroy Mitchel, the Fusion candidate, met last night and greeted each other smilingly. Both were guests at the Irish Ball given in the Lexington Avenue Opera House by the United Irish Societies of New York.

Mr. McCall arrived at the ball at 11:35 o'clock and was escorted to a box in the gallery by Chairman Thomas Kelly of the Ancient Order of Hibernians and Thomas Rock, Chairman of the Reception Committee of the ball. The Tammany candidate shook hands with scores of his friends who visited him in the box in the fifteen minutes that he stayed to watch the dancing. As Mr. McCall was departing, Mr. Mitchel's auto drove up in front of the Lexington Avenue Opera House. When Mr. Mitchel stepped from his motor, some one said to him:

"You're just in time to see the Judge. He is upstairs."

"Is that so?" said Mr. Mitchel with a smile. "That's an opportunity."

Then Mr. McCall walked out of the entrance to the opera house surrounded by his friends. Someone called his attention to the fact that Mr. Mitchel's party had arrived. Mr. McCall stopped and, when he saw Mr. Mitchel, waved his hand and said with a smile:

"Hello, John."

Mr. Mitchel lifted his hat and returned the smile as he said:

"Hello, Judge."

Then Mr. McCall climbed into his auto as his opponent started upstairs. After being introduced, Mr. Mitchel said that he was going to dance. He selected for a partner Miss E. A. Kelly, daughter of J. C. Kelly of 208 East Eighty-fifth Street. When he walked onto the floor with his partner, the music was drowned in cheers and applause. When this ended they began to waltz as the orchestra played, "The Little Girl of My Dreams."

TIMES TARIFF DATA OFFICIAL

Paris Consul General Posts It to Inform Exporters of New Duties.

Special Cable to THE NEW YORK TIMES.

PARIS, Oct. 18.—Copies of THE NEW YORK TIMES for Sept. 30, containing tables of the new tariff duties, are at a premium here, as they are the only source of information in Paris concerning the revised schedule as completed.

THE NEW YORK TIMES correspondent to-day supplied the Consul General with a copy of this issue, and it has been posted at the consular offices in the Avenue de l'Opéra, with a notice to would-be exporters of goods to America that it may be regarded as being as near as possible official until a copy of the new law is received from Washington.

Consul General Mason said: "This is the greatest boon possible. I wish to thank THE NEW YORK TIMES for its aid and also to congratulate the newspaper on its enterprise in publishing such a useful number.

"The only official document we have is a copy of the bill as it passed the House without Senate changes. We have been besieged all the week by persons seeking definite information, as tremendous shipments have been held up. With the aid of THE TIMES we shall be able to give adequate information."

CLOSE STEAMSHIP OFFICES.

Austrian Police Seize Canadian Pacific Railway Branches.

Special Cable to THE NEW YORK TIMES.

VIENNA, Oct. 18.—All the Canadian Pacific Railway agencies in Austria were closed and sealed to-day by court representatives, bringing the company's business practically to a standstill.

Samuel Altmann, the company's agent, who was arrested Thursday on a charge of helping Austrians to evade military service by emigrating to Canada without passports, is not allowed out on bail, the alleged reason being that there has been collusion in the matter. It is rumored that high functionaries, implicated in the affair and alleged to have accepted bribes, were found on a list in Altmann's house.

Domiciliary visits were made here this afternoon to the offices of eight other steamship lines belonging to the pool, who are suspected of practices similar to those charged to the Canadian Pacific.

LUCKEY AMAZED CURTISS.

Inventor Tells How Winner of New York Times Race Learned Aviation.

Special to The New York Times.

PENN YAN, N. Y., Oct. 18.—When Glen Curtiss heard that William S. Luckey won THE NEW YORK TIMES race around Manhattan Island, he said that this was one of the surprises aviation is continually springing. About a year ago, he said, Luckey appeared at the Curtiss camp in Hammondsport for training as an aviator. He was nearing the half century mark in years and had spent a long stretch of his life in New York manufacturing trunks for travelers, but had decided to take his turn at roaming and purposed to travel through the upper air. It was almost funny, the inventor said, to think of this sedate looking gentleman starting out to do Beachey and other youngsters. But Luckey's business training stood him in good stead and by methodical plugging he soon learned the management of the machine. His name proved a misnomer however during his early exhibitions and hard luck followed him. He stuck to it, though, and his final mastery of the intricacies of aviation may be best testified to by those four hardy fliers who with him fought their way around Manhattan sky scrapers in the teeth of a gale.

J. J. HILL IN TRAIN CRASH.

Shaken Up When Express Hits Local in Wisconsin—Man Killed.

WINONA, Minn., Oct. 18.—A northbound express train with James J. Hill in his private car at the rear crashed into a local southbound passenger on the Burlington Road at Nelson, Wis., to-day, killing Fireman Elliott of De Sota on the local.

The express train was late and running about 50 miles an hour, and the engineer failed to note the block signal in the fog. The local train was about to take the siding when the engineer observed the express train rapidly aproaching. He reversed his engine and jumped.

The conductor on the local was standing on the car platform and was thrown some distance, his shoulder being dislocated. The express messengers on the fast train and a few of the passengers on the local were more or less injured but none seriously. Mr. Hill was shaken up but not much hurt. Travel on the main line was blocked for some hours.

CITY REGISTRATION TOTAL IS 669,639

Figures for All Five Boroughs Show 26,031 Increase Over 1909.

MUCH LESS THAN 1912

Manhattan the Only Borough to Fall Behind the Registration Figures of 1909.

Registration for this year with the four days' figures complete shows a gain throughout the entire city over the figures of 1909, the last Mayoralty year, of 26,031. Manhattan was the only borough that fell behind the figures of 1909. The loss was more than made up, however, by the big gains in Queens and the Bronx.

The former borough showed by far the largest gains, more than 12,000 voters registering there this year than in 1909. There was a gain in Queens over the figures of last year, when a President was elected, of nearly 2,000.

The total registration for the entire city this year was 669,639, as compared with 643,608 in 1909, and 705,286 in 1912, the figures for last year being more than 35,000 better than this year. Brooklyn did better than 1909 by about 7,000, although it fell behind last year by more than 17,000.

The Bronx went fully 18,000 better than in 1909, and a little over 200 better than last year. In Queens the registration was 12,000 better than in 1909 and about 2,000 better than last year.

The registration in Manhattan fell about 11,000 below those of 1909 and fully 20,000 behind 1912.

Richmond made a better showing by 1,000 than in 1909.

The falling off in the downtown districts in Manhattan continued and the up town Republican Districts showed a corresponding increase over 1909.

In Manhattan, 64,199 people registered yesterday; in Brooklyn, 62,894; in Queens, 14,207; in the Bronx, 20,494, and in Richmond, 4,641. The total for the day for all the boroughs was 166,435.

The following are the complete figures for the four days of registration this year as compared with the figures of 1909, 1910, and 1912.

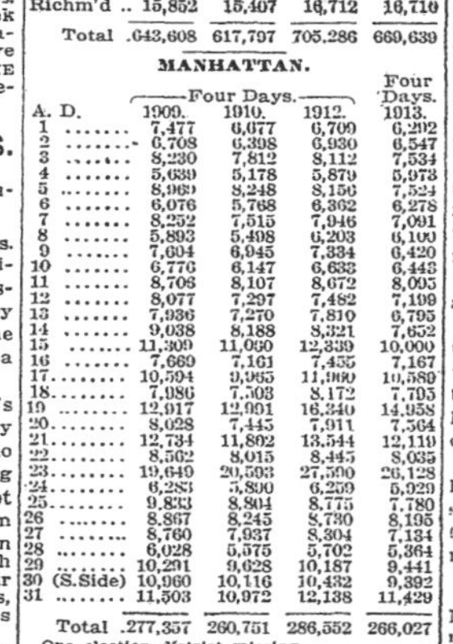

REGISTRATION FOR FOUR DAYS.

Boroughs.	Four Days. 1909.	1910.	1912.	Four Days. 1913.
Manhat ...	277,357	260,751	286,552	266,027
Bronx	65,966	65,412	83,580	83,714
B'kyln ...	235,401	229,195	259,655	242,788
Queens ..	48,972	47,032	58,787	60,400
Richm'd ..	15,852	15,407	16,712	16,710
Total	643,608	617,797	705,286	669,639

MANHATTAN.

A. D.	Four Days. 1909.	1910.	1912.	Four Days. 1913.
1	7,477	6,677	6,709	6,292
2	6,708	6,398	6,930	6,547
3	8,230	7,812	8,112	7,534
4	5,639	5,178	5,879	5,973
5	8,969	8,248	8,156	7,524
6	6,076	5,768	6,362	6,278
7	8,252	7,515	7,946	7,091
8	5,893	5,498	6,203	6,100
9	7,604	6,945	7,334	6,420
10	6,776	6,147	6,633	6,443
11	8,706	8,107	8,672	8,095
12	8,077	7,297	7,482	7,199
13	7,936	7,270	7,810	6,795
14	9,038	8,188	8,321	7,652
15	11,309	11,060	12,339	10,000
16	7,669	7,161	7,435	7,167
17	10,594	9,965	11,900	10,589
18	7,986	7,503	8,172	7,705
19	12,917	12,001	16,340	14,958
20	8,028	7,445	7,911	7,564
21	12,734	11,802	13,544	12,119
22	8,562	8,015	8,445	8,035
23	19,649	20,593	27,590	26,128
24	6,283	5,890	6,259	5,929
25	9,833	8,804	8,775	7,780
26	8,867	8,245	8,730	8,195
27	8,760	7,937	8,304	7,134
28	6,028	5,575	5,702	5,364
29	10,291	9,628	10,187	9,441
30 (S.Side)	10,960	10,116	10,432	9,392
31	11,503	10,972	12,138	11,429
Total	277,357	260,751	286,552	266,027

One election district missing.

THE BRONX.

A. D.	Four Days. 1909.	1910.	1912.	Four Days. 1913.
30 (N.Side)	3,494	3,225	3,353	3,187
32	20,233	19,980	24,838	24,824
33	11,251	10,513	12,511	11,922
34	16,407	16,649	23,735	23,784
35	14,581	15,045	19,143	19,997
Total..	65,966	65,412	83,580	83,714

BROOKLYN.

A. D.	Four Days. 1909.	1910.	1912.	Four Days. 1913.
1........	9,035	8,505	9,039	8,094
2........	7,353	7,082	7,054	6,375
3........	7,721	6,899	6,913	6,521
4........	8,934	8,877	9,375	8,607
5........	10,935	10,802	12,191	10,984
6........	8,833	8,518	9,098	8,673
7........	8,163	7,838	8,279	7,831
8........	7,888	7,247	7,691	6,988
9........	14,086	14,128	17,367	16,300
10........	10,449	9,962	10,932	9,683
11........	10,020	9,689	10,856	9,470
12	11,826	11,902	12,941	12,167
13	7,611	7,126	8,166	7,530
14	7,396	7,212	7,478	6,833
15	8,337	7,919	8,871	8,411
16	14,518	15,057	19,449	19,418
17	10,088	9,693	10,702	9,880
18	14,841	15,932	20,095	19,260
19	8,011	7,582	8,309	7,669
20	9,957	9,346	10,368	9,520
21	5,995	5,481	5,992	5,507
22	19,806	19,341	22,674	21,300
23	13,134	12,967	15,820	15,556
Total..	235,461	229,195	259,655	242,301

QUEENS.

A. D.	Four Days. 1909.	1910.	1912.	Four Days. 1913.
1	10,513	9,612	11,224	11,375
2	10,140	9,200	11,224	11,618
3	15,424	15,151	19,771	20,613
4	12,895	12,069	16,568	16,794
Total..	48,972	47,032	58,787	60,400

RICHMOND.

A. D.	Four Days. 1909.	1910.	1912.	Four Days. 1913.
1	15,852	15,407	16,712	16,710

GETS $100 PEARL IN OYSTER

And Point o' Woods Lifesaver Develops Inordinate Love for Them.

SAYVILLE, L. I., Oct. 18.—Charles Hildreth, a Point o' Woods life saver, bit on something yesterday as he was eating raw oysters. It was a big pearl, and he rushed with it to the nearest jewelry shop. There he was told it was worth $85.

"I'll try a bit further," he said.

He went to the store of H. L. Terry & Son, and received an offer of $100. He decided to keep it awhile. Meantime, he is developing an extraordinary taste for oysters.

"Lightning has been known to strike twice in the same spot," he says.

TO-DAY'S SUNDAY TIMES

CONSISTS OF

I. Pictorial Section.

II. News Section.

III. and IV. Cable, Wireless and Sport Sections.

V. Magazine Section.

VI. Book Review.

VII. Society, Fashions, Music, Drama.

VIII. Real Estate, Business, Financial.

INVITES GERMANY TO HALT NAVY PLANS

Winston Churchill Officially Proposes a Cessation of Battleship Building for a Year.

Special Cable to THE NEW YORK TIMES.

LONDON, Oct. 18.—Speaking at a great Liberal meeting in Manchester to-day, Winston Churchill, the First Lord of the Admiralty, in behalf of the Government made a specific offer to Germany of a year's "naval holiday," wherein both nations would agree to halt the construction of battleships.

Widespread interest was aroused by the proposal, and much significance is attached to the offer, which was made while he was discussing the naval expenditures of $375,000,000 a year and warning the nation of the inevitably heavy increase in armaments if the rivalry continued.

The pith of his speech was contained in this paragraph:

"Now, we say in all friendship and sincerity to our great neighbor, Germany: If you will put off beginning to build your two ships for twelve months, we will put off in absolute good faith the building of our four ships for exactly the same period."

If Great Britain and Germany took the lead, Mr. Churchill added, there was a good prospect of success in getting other powers to agree to a naval holiday, thus relieving the taxpayers of a burden of millions of dollars.

Mr. Churchill first advocated a naval holiday on March 26, when he was speaking in the House of Commons on the naval estimates, but Germany did not accept his offer.

LONDON, Oct. 18.—In his speech at Manchester Winston Churchill, in the middle of lamentations over the "serious misdirection of human energies" involved in the huge expenditure on armaments, remarked that the only way of effecting retrenchment was along the lines of an international agreement. Then he went on:

"The proposal I put forward in the name of the British Government for a naval holiday is quite simple. Next year apart from the Canadian ships, or their equivalent, and apart from anything that may be required by any development in the Mediterranean we shall lay down four great ships to Germany's two. Now, we say to Germany: 'If you will put off beginning to build your two ships for twelve months, we will put off in absolute good faith the building of our four ships for exactly the same period.'"

Mr. Churchill then expressed the opinion that if Great Britain and Germany took the lead, all the other great countries would follow suit, and they would all be just as great and as sound as if they had built the ships at present projected. If Austria and Italy did not build, the obligation, he said, would be removed from France and Great Britain, and the fact that the triple alliance (Germany, Austria-Hungary, and Italy,) was building no ships would make the proposal possible without the slightest danger or risk. The First Lord then added:

"Isn't it likely that so great and memorable an event would produce an effect on the naval construction of the United States and Japan? Scores of millions would be rescued for the progress of mankind."

Mr. Churchill added: "That is the proposal I make for the year 1914, or if that year is thought to be too near, for 1915."

The speaker said he was impervious to the objections which would be raised by armament firms here and in other countries, remarking:

"They must be our servants and not our masters."

The First Lord warned his hearers that apart from such an agreement "the naval expenditure of next year will be substantially greater than that of this year. Whatever may be necessary for the safety of our country and the maintenance of our influence all over the world will have to be done."

Mr. Churchill thought the fact that the situation in Europe was much clearer now than it had been for some time, the strong evidences of a desire for peace and the greatly improved relations between Great Britain and Germany rendered the moment favorable for the resumption of the consideration of the suggestion of a naval holiday to which friendly reference was made in a speech by the German Imperial Chancellor."

FOUR IN AUTO DROP 80 FEET; UNHURT

Driver Puts on Full Speed and Shoots Out Over Precipice at Jersey City Heights.

As Harry McCloskey of 53 Prospect Street, Jersey City, was driving his automobile along Palisade Avenue on the Heights shortly after 9 o'clock last night, he intended to cross the long bridge that spans the Ravine Road, but his wheels skidded sharply on the asphalt, wet from the evening's drizzle, and instead of taking the bridge the machine turned to the right and ripped its way through a flimsy wooden fence.

Mr. McCloskey felt the car take the grassy embankment beyond the fence and start rapidly down it. Then he did some swift thinking. He had to think not only for himself and his car but for his brother and sister, who were with him, and two women whom they had invited for an evening drive. Their alarm was great enough, but his was greater, for he knew the lay of the land just at that point and knew that within a few more seconds his machine would reach the brink of a sheer drop of eighty feet.

Mr. McCloskey knew that running under the bridge and almost at right angles to the avenue whose slippery pavement he had just left, was the Ravine Road, leading off into Hoboken. He knew that that road was sunk in a rocky chasm, its jagged wall practically as precipitous as the walls of a room. He knew, too, that the height of that wall was just about eighty feet.

It was very dark there just then and neither he nor any of the frightened members of his party could see clearly ahead of them. But Mr. McCloskey had seen it all a hundred times in broad daylight. The edge of the sharply slanting grassy bank was just ahead of him and protected by no wall or barrier of any sort. The only barrier was that wooden fence along Palisade Avenue and his car had torn its path through that without wasting a moment's time.

All this flashed into Mr. McCloskey's mind as swiftly as the thoughts of a dream. He wondered what he could do and in the press of the instant, he could think of only one course—to put on full speed and see what shooting out into space would do for them. His hands had not left the wheel and they were at the brink. Mr. McCloskey shut his eyes and put on full speed. Out over the precipice—the car seemed to plunge forward.

And then it dropped. Those who had witnessed the start of the accident and had rushed forward to the railing of the bridge heard the screams as those in the car, as, with lights on and seats full, it dropped 80 feet to the road below. They heard the thump of its landing.

They waited for a brief instant of silence and then exclamations of surprise, mingled with startled, nervous laughter, came up from the Ravine Road. The car had fallen the eighty feet, but it had landed right-side up.

The speeding car had shot so far forward that it landed beyond the sidewalk, and beyond even the middle of the road. It had bounded once, and on reaching the ground again had struck against the further curb. The impact smashed the right front wheel. And that was all that happened to the car.

Besides his brother Robert and his sister, Catherine McCloskey, Mr. McCloskey's other passenger was Miss Roslyn Kramer of 233 Ralph Avenue, Brooklyn. Mr. McCloskey himself is 20 years old, and the prediction in Jersey City last night was that an enterprising firm would soon be blazoning forth the make of the car that safely took the eighty-foot drop to the Ravine Road.

As to the occupants, one of them, Miss Grace Platt of 62 Booream Avenue, Jersey City, had jumped before the car fell—jumped and landed so that she fell on the grassy embankment. She was jarred and bruised, but not so seriously hurt but that she was able to go to her home with the rest of the quaking, thankful party. Harry McCloskey was still at the wheel of the car when it landed in the road below. He found afterward that a pain in his side came from the dislocated rib.

The accident was entered in the blotter in the Jersey City Police Headquarters in these words, with some of the names misspelled:

"At 8:40 an automobile with a New Jersey license No. 48080 owned and driven by Harry McCloskey, of 53 Prospect Street, Jersey City, in which were four other passengers, Robert McCloskey, Catherine McCloskey, of 53 Prospect Street; Rosalind Kraemer, of 233 Ralph Avenue, Brooklyn, and Grace Platt, 52 Booream Avenue, Jersey City, was going north on Palisade Avenue and when 80 feet south of the Ravine Bridge skidded and broke through the fence, ran down an incline, and dropped seventy-five feet to Ravine Road. Grace Platt injured in the right side, treated by Dr. Mereheimer, of 258 Palisade Avenue, and taken home in his automobile. The other passengers escaped injury. The front wheels of the automobile were broken."

HUERTA WILL STICK; SCOFFS AT FLIGHT

Means to Re-establish Peace in Mexico, He Says, and Within the Law if Possible.

DIAZ AT HAVANA, GOES ON

Confident of Election to the Presidency — Vera Cruz Nervous Over His Coming.

MEXICO CITY, Oct. 18.—Provisional President Huerta has not resigned, nor has he fled from the capital. When seen at the National Palace at 5 o'clock this afternoon he said he had no intention of doing either.

"When I resign," he added, "it will be to seek a resting place six feet in the soil. When I flee the capital, it will be to shoulder a rifle and take my place in the ranks to fight the rebels."

This was President Huerta's answer to questions whether there was any foundation for the reports, which have been freely circulated in the capital and have found their way to the United States.

Gen. Huerta looked the picture of health and energy. Attired in a new suit, he greeted the correspondent with cordiality, motioned him to a seat, asked for a cigarette, and listened to the explanation of the motive for the visit.

"So it is reported that I have fled," said the President. "You can see for yourself that I am here at my post. To say that I have resigned or intend to resign is an absolute falsehood. I have no intention of resigning.

"Within the Law if Possible."

"Should the elections, which will be held as I have promised, indicate another for the Presidency, I shall step aside. Until that time you will find me here complying with my promises to the nation, which are to re-establish peace—within the law if possible, but to re-establish peace."

President Huerta interspersed his remarks with anecdotes, illustrating his points.

"Another thing," said the President. "I have money for my requirements. Don't think that I haven't. Where did I get it?" Here he tapped his chest with a satisfied smile, adding: "But I have it."

On the question of pacification, he said that before the end of the month the Government would have retaken Torreon and made headway toward the pacification of the State of Durango.

"I have 8,000 men at Hipolito," said the President, "moving on Torreon, and 2,000 more are proceeding north from Zacatecas."

In reply to a suggestion that further rumors were afloat to the effect that a troop train proceeding to Torreon had been blown up, he exclaimed:

"More lies! Nothing of the kind has occurred."

To the statement that a report was current that all Americans had been ordered to leave the capital, Gen. Huerta answered with a gesture of disgust.

"What nonsense!" he replied. "As I have repeatedly said since I came to the Presidency, foreigners, from Hottentots to the most enlightened, have received and will continue to receive every guarantee. Mexicans likewise who obey the laws have nothing to fear from me. Transgressors must watch out. They shall be punished through every means the law affords."

Says Foes Started Rumors.

In the opinion of Gen. Huerta, the sensational rumors originated with the enemies of the administration in the capital and elsewhere for the effect they would have with the revolutionists.

Gen. Huerta is working fifteen to eighteen hours daily, sleeping at odd times when fatigue overtakes him. He adopts various ruses to escape from the scores striving to reach him with personal affairs. He slips out of unused entrances and takes roundabout routes to hide his whereabouts. Col. Carlos Aguila, his son-in-law, who is with him almost continuously, sought him to-day in half a dozen haunts before locating him in the palace.

There is no truth in the report that Americans have been ordered out of Mexico. Several American residents here have received cablegrams in the last few days from relatives in the United States begging them to leave.

One business man has been instructed by his firm in the United States to wind up his business and quit the country. This has given rise to various disquieting rumors.

Accuse 74 Deputies of Sedition.

Seventy-four of the 110 members of the Chamber of Deputies, arrested by order of President Huerta last week, were formally declared prisoners to-day by the second Judge of the Federal District, who has had charge of the investigation into the cases. The period in which charges had to be filed against the Deputies or their liberty given to them expired to-day.

The charges made against the Deputies to-day were for political offenses, designated by the law as rebellion, sedition, and insults to important public functionaries.

Ten Deputies, against whom there was said to be insufficient evidence,

Continued on Page 9.

BIG FIRE IN ONEIDA.

Other Cities Help Check Flames That Destroy Several Buildings.

ONEIDA, N. Y., Oct. 18.—Fire that was brought under control to-night after it had burned for several hours caused a property loss here of approximately $120,000. Engines from Rome and Canastota at a late hour were aiding the local department in fighting the flames.

Among the properties partly or wholly destroyed were the lumber yard of R. B. Ruby, the hardware store of George H. Ruby & Son, a three-story brick building taking up an entire block and containing a large stock of hides and pelts, a coal elevator of C. A. Frost & Son, two small dwellings, and a barn. The fire started in a paint store.

CYCLIST FALLS ON COFFIN.

Hurled from His Motor Cycle, He Dives Through Side of Hearse.

Special to The New York Times.

BLOOMINGDALE, N. J., Oct. 18.—Losing control to-day at Union Square of a high-powered motor cycle, John Roach of Butler was thrown from the machine and went head first through the glass doors in a hearse. He fell on the top of the coffin bearing the body of Oscar Vreeland.

The funeral procession had to halt, and several of the mourners were called to assist the undertaker in extricating Roach. He was badly cut by his passage through the thick glass.

MRS. GLIDDEN IN ACCIDENT.

Wife of Cup Tour Founder in Auto That Kills a Boy.

CAMBRIDGE, Mass., Oct. 18.—An automobile occupied by Mrs. Franklin J. Burnham of Colorado and Mrs. Charles J. Glidden, wife of the founder of the Glidden Cup automobile tours, knocked down and fatally injured seven-year-old William Boyle in Cambridgeport to-night. The boy was taken into the car and hurried to the Relief Hospital, where he died. The chauffeur, Charles J. Holmes, was arrested on a charge of manslaughter and released on bail furnished by Mrs. Burnham.

FINDS TRACES OF RADIUM.

But Prof. Shrader Fails to Reduce Gas in a Spring to Salts.

WILLIAMSTOWN, Mass., Oct. 18.—Prof. J. H. Shrader of the Department of Physics at Williams College announced to-day that he had found traces of radium in a spring near this town. According to the experiments made, the presence of the rare and valuable element seems to be manifested in the form of gas, and so far all efforts on the part of Prof. Shrader to reduce it to salts of radium have proved unsuccessful.

The small quantities of radium that scientists have so far obtained have come from deposits of pitchblende found in various parts of Europe.

WILSON'S GIANT POTATO.

President Gets 6¾ Pound "Sample of Democratic Prosperity."

WASHINGTON, Oct. 18.—A big sweet potato, weighing six and three-quarter pounds, was removed from the desk of President Wilson to-day to the White House kitchen and to-night it will grace his family dinner table.

The potato, on view to the President's callers all of yesterday, was the gift of Charles E. Robinson of Lincolnton, N. C. The donor sent it, he said, "as a sample of Democratic prosperity."

ANSWERS COAL TRUST SUIT.

Lehigh Company Denies It Operates Roads as Common Carrier.

PHILADELPHIA, Oct. 18.—The Lehigh Coal & Navigation Company, one of the defendants in the Government's Hard Coal Trust suit, filed its answer to-day denying any community of interest with the Philadelphia and Reading Coal & Iron Company, and the Reading Company, other corporations named in the litigation.

The company admits that it constructed, owns and formerly operated the Lehigh & Susquehanna Railroad, and that it owns and controls coal lands estimated to contain more than 500,000,000 tons of available anthracite in the Lehigh region, from which it produces 3,700,000 tons a year.

Although maintaining that under its charter it has the power to engage in the business of a common carrier, the company denies that it operates any line of railroad as a common carrier.

SERVES PAPERS ON WALDO.

Colored Deputy Catches Police Commissioner at Headquarters.

Deputy Sheriff Lee, a colored member of Sheriff Harburger's staff, was congratulated yesterday by the Sheriff for his success in serving papers on Police Commissioner Waldo. Lee said that, after trailing the Commissioner for half a day on Friday, he had darted past three uniformed men and served Mr. Waldo as he was about to enter an automobile at Police Headquarters.

The papers were in Amos Culleson's taxpayer suit against the purchase of 650 revolvers for the Police Department. The complaint alleges that the specifications were drawn so as to exclude all except Colt's revolvers. The law firm of Beardsley, Hemmons & Taylor of 50 Wall Street, said that several subpoena servers of their office had failed in the effort to serve the Police Commissioner.

VAN ALEN PEARLS HIDDEN?

Necklace Found in Mrs. Thompson's Corsage, Boston Reports.

Special to The New York Times.

BOSTON, Mass., Oct. 18.—The opinion prevails in custom house circles that developments in the case of Mrs. May Van Alen Thompson, the Newport society woman who arrived from Liverpool on Thursday, will prove sensational.

The charge is published here to-day that Miss Wilkins, one of the matrons in the customs service, searched Mrs. Thompson on the day of her arrival and found a valuable pearl necklace in her corsage.

The work of appraising the contents of the twenty-five trunks has begun, the officials having abandoned the idea of sending them in bond to New York. The trunks contain gowns, laces, and coats, as well as gems which Mrs. Thompson failed to declare. Her contention has been that she is a non-resident of the country, and, therefore, is not obliged to make any declaration. Officials at this port say her contention will not stand, as it has been found by Treasury officials that Mrs. Thompson's husband is listed as a qualified voter and citizen of New York City.

MRS. PANKHURST IS BARRED OU

Taken to Ellis Island fro Liner and Ordered Deported After Hearing.

MAY GO ON 'HUNGER STRIK

Inquiry Board Decides Again Suffrage Leader on Grounds of "Moral Turpitude."

APPEAL TO WASHINGTO

Counsel Hope to Get Her Free Suffragists in Many Cities Pro test—Postpone Garden Meeting

Mrs. Emmeline Pankhurst, leader the British militant suffragettes, arriv in this port yesterday morning on French liner Provence, but was allowed to land at the pier. She w taken to Ellis Island, and after a he ing before a board of special inqui was ordered deported as an undesira alien on the grounds of "moral tur tude." Last night she slept in the ro where not long since Prince Pignat was confined. The deportation ord has been appealed to Washington.

After the Provence cleared Quarant at 7 A. M. she was boarded by Imm gration Inspector George W. Moo from Ellis Island, who went imme ately to the music room, on the prom nade deck, and took his seat at a tab He then sent a steward to ask M Pankhurst to appear before him. A other Immigration Inspector, Jam MacGregor, sat at a table at the oth side of the music room and question the rest of the first-cabin passengers

Dressed in a long sealskin coat, co ering an olive broadcloth suit, with blue cloth hat surmounted by a bla plume, the militant leader entered t music room, followed by at least fi reporters and photographers. She d not appear to be at all uneasy at t prospect of being questioned, and h a good, healthy color in her cheek She smiled pleasantly when asked sit down, and said that she was p fectly willing to give the Inspector a information that the United State Go ernment might require.

Questioned by Inspector.

Inspector Moore conversed with Mr Pankhurst in subdued tones in ord that he might not be heard by t throng surrounding them. She inform him that her age was 51 years, and th she was born in Manchester, En land. The next question put to her w whether she had been convicted arson, to which Mrs. Pankhurst repli

"I have not. My last conviction w for conspiracy. There is a long list crimes in England for which they co vict women now that is a relic of th time when the men were fighting fo suffrage."

When she admitted the convictio with its three years' sentence, of whi she served only three months, the I spector said:

"Mrs. Pankhurst, I am sorry to i form you that it is my duty to deta you and escort you to Ellis Islan where you will appear before the Boa of Special Inquiry when your right t enter the United States will be decided

After learning that she was not t be allowed to land at the pier whe suffragists were waiting to greet he Mrs. Pankhurst, still smiling and pe fectly collected, went up on the prom enade deck and gave an interview t the reporters.

"I have come here to tell the Ame ican people the whole story of ou activities in England in the fight fo suffrage," she said. "My mission t this country is similar to that of me who have come to represent Ireland t this great republic of the West. I com to appeal for help. Redmond an O'Connor came here to appeal for he for Ireland.

Attack on "King" Asquith.

"I wish that it could be understoo that our movement in England is di rected against 'King' Asquith, and no against King George. There is jus one obstinate old gentleman now i England who bars the way fro women getting the vote. It is Asquit who is blocking suffrage there.

"Our cause there differs materiall from the cause here. I am not come t the United States to teach the wome of America how to get the vote. The are too intelligent for that, and ar making phenomenal strides in securin their end."

Mrs. Pankhurst was then asked b the reporters if she would have carrie out her hunger strike to the end and died for the cause. In answer she ros to her feet and exclaimed dramaticall

"Our motto is, 'Give us the vote o give us death.'"

At that moment the band of th Provence, standing on deck nearby struck up a ragtime melody, which wa translated into English as, "Oh, Those Pretty Blue Eyes," and rendered it dif ficult for Mrs. Pankhurst to make he self heard.

Just before the Provence arrived at her pier, shortly after 8 o'clock, In spector Moore requested the chief of ficer of the Provence to have some ex tra guards at the gangway.

"You never can tell what these women might be up to," he said.

There was no demonstration at landing time, however Miss Joan Wickham, the advance agent of Mrs. Pankhurst, was on hand with a bunch of white asters, and brought a message by cable from Beatrice Harraden. She went on board, accompanied by Miss Mary Keegan, Miss Elsie Mackenzie, Mrs. Lavinia Dock, and Mrs. Henry Butterworth, and all were indignant when they were informed that the English leader was to be detained. Their condolences were interrupted frequently by the siren of the

"All the News That's Fit to Print."

The New York Times.

THE WEATHER

Fair to-day and to-morrow; diminishing northwest winds.

☞For full weather report see Page 20.

VOL. LXIII...NO. 20,436. .... NEW YORK, TUESDAY, JANUARY 6, 1914.—TWENTY-TWO PAGES. ONE CENT In Greater New York, Jersey City and Newark, { Elsewhere TWO CENTS.

FIND CORPORATION CHECK TO N. E. MACK

State Contractor Freely Tells of Contributions at Whitman's Graft Inquiry.

TERM "HEELER" DEFINED

Otherwise a State Committeeman Useful in Getting Contracts—Doyle Paid to the G. O. P.

Testimony regarding a check given as a campaign contribution by a corporation and countersigned by a member of the corporation, by mere chance was brought out yesterday in the John Doe inquiry which District Attorney Whitman is prosecuting in the search for graft. The testimony was the result of Whitman's policy of questioning all State contractors who come his way. Mr. Whitman has the cancelled check in his possession.

The check for $50 is made out to Norman E. Mack, former Chairman of the Democratic National Committee and former Chairman of the Democratic State Committee. The check is dated Oct. 28, 1911, at which time Mack was the State Chairman, with offices at 1 West Thirty-fourth Street.

George Sherrill, Democrat, a middle-aged contractor of Hudson Falls, N. Y., was the man who told about the check. Sherrill incidentally is a State employe. Under cross-examination by Assistant District Attorney Clark the contractor spoke of his contribution with apparent pride. He said that the check which he sent to Mack was the first check which he drew on his bank account in the Hudson Falls National Bank. This bank account was opened shortly after C. Gordon Reel, then State Highway Commissioner, notified Sherrill that two repair contracts were awaiting him in the Highway Department. Sherrill had obtained the contracts without the formality of bidding.

After he made his contribution according to the testimony, Sherill obtained two road contracts amounting to $75,000.

Sherrill is an officer of the Sherrill Engineering & Contracting Company of Hudson Falls, incorporated in this State. The check bears the signature of this corporation and also the signature of "George Sherrill, Treasurer." It bears the indorsement of Norman E. Mack and the handwriting is similar to that on many checks of individuals which were made out to Mack in 1911, which are now in District Attorney Whitman's possession. The check was indorsed over to Arthur A. McLean, Treasurer of the State Committee, and was cashed at the Fourth National Bank of this city on Nov. 1, 1911, the depository of the Democratic State Committee.

Jury May Inspect Check.

Under Section 44 of the Corporation Law of this State it is illegal knowingly to accept a campaign contribution from a corporation. Arthur A. McLean already has been indicted on two counts under this section. Everett Fowler of Kingston and James K. McGuire, ex-Mayor of Syracuse, have been indicted under the same section for soliciting contributions from corporations. It could not be learned yesterday what action is expected in the present case. The special Supreme Court Grand Jury which indicted Fowler, McLean, and McGuire, will meet again to-day and it is likely that the new Mack check will be laid before it.

Mack's name has been brought out in the John Doe inquiry a number of times, but Sherrill's check is the first corporation check indorsed by Mack which has been found. A check for $250 made out by Seneca P. Hull, a contractor of Cortland, N. Y., to Mack furnished the basis of an extortion indictment against Everett Fowler, but this was the check of an individual and not of a corporation. When a report of the Hull matter appeared in the newspapers Mack explained that he never had paid any attention to financial matters when he was Chairman of the State Committee except to indorse and turn over to McLean all the checks that were sent to him.

Sherrill, the contractor, at present is one of the adjusters of claims in the Department of Public Works. He testified yesterday that he had entered upon his State duties in 1911, but it was not brought out whether he was a State employe at the time he made the $50 check payable to Norman E. Mack. Sherrill testified that he was responsible to John Mahr, claim agent under Duncan W. Peck, the Superintendent of Public Works.

When Assistant District Attorney Clark was questioning him about his relations with the Department of Public Works, Sherrill gave another bit of interesting information. He told about sending a campaign contribution to Peter Manweller, who, Sherrill asserted, was employed as a private secretary by the Superintendent of Public Works.

"What were your relations with Manweller?" asked Mr. Clark.

"Why, I sent him a campaign check, too, for $100," replied Sherrill.

"Did Manweller ask you for $100?" Mr. Clark asked.

"I never talked to him at all. I just understood that he was the man to send the money to. I think I have the check at home and I'll send it when I get home."

Cornelius J. Reardon, Republican, a contractor from Glens Falls, a schoolmate of ex-Gov. John A. Dix, confined almost all of his testimony to C. Gordon Reel, the former State Highway Commissioner. Reardon said that he had finished the construction of a road for the State nearly two years ago. Although this road had been approved by all the State authorities interested, he said, there was still $800 due him from the State.

Told He Must "Divvy."

"Did you ever talk with Reel about the delay?" asked Mr. Clark.

"Yes, but he referred me to some one else," replied the witness.

"Who was that man?"

"I don't know who he was, but it was a man in the Highway Department. That was when Reel was in office. This man said I had to 'divvy' if I expected to get my money. I got hot and told him to go to the deuce."

"Do you think that Reel tried to help you?"

"No, I got the idea that Reel was trying to put me in touch with some one who should hold me up."

Reardon said that he went to Reel a number of times, once to get a repair contract.

"I heard they were handing them out in Albany," he said, "so I went up to get a hand-out. Reel said: 'The contracts are here, but we'll have to take care of our friends first.'"

"Didn't you regard yourself as a friend?" asked Mr. Clark.

"No," replied the witness. "I was a Republican, and I said good day."

Reardon explained that he sought the aid of Charles R. Foley, who was Dep-

Continued on Page 2.

PATERSON THEATRE BURNS.

Firemen Hurt in Fighting Flames—Loss Put at $100,000.

Special to The New York Times.

PATERSON, N. J., Tuesday, Jan. 6.—The Paterson Opera House, the most important theatre in this city, was destroyed early this morning by a fire which was discovered burning briskly back of the stage soon after midnight last night.

All the available fire-fighting apparatus of Paterson was called out to fight the flames, which for a time threatened to wipe out an entire business block in Main Street.

At 2:30 o'clock, however, the fire was brought under control. In fighting the blaze several firemen were overcome, and two of them were injured seriously. An early estimate of the property damage was $100,000.

The opera house, at which a stock company was playing this week, was built first more than ten years ago, and in its time has been burned four times. The last time, which was some three years ago, it was destroyed completely.

There was a panic among the Italians living in neighboring tenements, and many were rescued scantily clothed.

FLATBUSH HOMES BURNED.

G. H. Orton's Family Didn't Know Roof Was Blazing Overhead.

Neighbors rang the front door bell of the residence of George H. Orton, one of the department managers of the Standard Oil Company, at 1,689 East Twenty-first Street, Flatbush, at 9 o'clock last night to notify the family, who were seated downstairs, that the third floor and roof were burning. As they ran upstairs to save their valuables on the second floor, the flames enveloped the entire upper part of the house and ate their way rapidly downward.

By the time the Fire Department had arrived the fire had jumped several feet to the home of William Brittigan, secretary for Joseph P. Day, the real estate dealer. The Orton house was almost totally destroyed and that of Mr. Brittingan was badly damaged. The entire loss will be nearly $20,000.

The fire is believed to have been caused accidentally by Miss Catherine Orton, the fifteen-year-old daughter of Mr. Orton, who, half an hour before the fire was discovered, had been rummaging through a clothes closet on the third floor and had thrown away a match which she thought was out.

CUTS ATLANTIC RATES.

North German Lloyd Announces Reductions in Eastward Fares.

Special Cable to THE NEW YORK TIMES.

LONDON, Tuesday, Jan. 6.—A telegram from Berlin to The Times says the dispute between the Hamburg-American and North German Lloyd Companies is now being reflected in fresh communications from both sides to the press, but as the date of the conference in Paris is still more than a fortnight distant there is time enough to see whether the war between the German lines will be maintained.

The North German Lloyd Line yesterday announced the following reduced steerage rates from America eastward:

For express steamers from New York, $32; for postal steamers from New York, $30.

From Galveston and New Orleans, $30.50; from other North American ports, $27.50.

It is now suggested in some quarters that the dispute between the German lines may be settled by the intervention of the Emperor.

REPORT ON BURKE CHARGES

Inquiry Abroad Into Panama Commissary Purchases Completed.

Special to The New York Times.

WASHINGTON, Jan. 5.—The War Department to-day received a bulky report from the principal agent of the department sent abroad a month ago to investigate the relations of John Burke, the assistant purchasing agent of the Panama Railroad, with various firms from which supplies have been bought for the railroad.

Secretary Garrison issued orders to Major Frank C. Hobbs of the United States Engineer Corps, who is in charge of the Washington office of the purchasing department of the Panama Canal, to seal up the report and forward it at once to Col. Goethals, with directions to act as his judgment prompted him.

"I told him," said the Secretary, "to prosecute Burke if there was law for it and the offense was shown. If there was no law for it and the offense charged had been committed to dismiss the man at once and put some one else in his place."

Secretary Garrison has had no response as yet from the Department of Justice in reply to his inquiry whether or not Burke could be prosecuted as an official of the Government for violation of the Federal statute against the acceptance of bribes or gratuities in connection with any public business. He is, however, assured on high legal authority that there is abundant law for a prosecution, and if the facts shown by the investigation, in Col. Goethals's judgment, justify a prosecution Burke may be brought to account for what has occurred in connection with his administration of his office.

Secretary Garrison did not read the report of the investigation abroad, and is not informed of its nature or contents. Preferring to have the judgment first of Col. Goethals upon it he had it sent at once to the Isthmus. The entire investigation has been under the direction of Col. Goethals, although the tracing of contracts in the United States and in Europe was done under the direction of Major Hobbs. Major Hobbs refused to discuss the report in any way.

Mr. Garrison said to-day that Mr. Burke had not at any time asked him for an interview, and, so far as he knew, had not come to Washington at any time to make any representations in regard to the charges made against him.

Latest Shipping News.

ARRIVED—SS Caroline, Havre, Dec. 23.

CARDEN REMOVED FROM MEXICAN POST

British Minister, Accused of Anti-American Tendencies, to Go to Brazil.

NOT OFFICIALLY CENSURED

But English Opinion Is That He Was Indiscreet—No Successor Yet Named.

Dispatch to The Associated Press.

LONDON, Jan. 5.—Sir Lionel Carden, British Minister to Mexico, is soon to be transferred to Rio de Janiero as Minister to Brazil. He was appointed to Mexico July 18, 1913, to succeed Francis William Stronge.

The successor to Sir Lionel Carden at Mexico City will probably be Charles Murray Marling, senior counselor in the British Diplomatic Service, now accredited to Turkey.

Sir Lionel Carden's transfer, which is a promotion as far as salary is concerned, although the two legations possess the same standing in the service, would have been made some time ago except for the fact that the British Foreign Office would not make the change while the Minister was under fire for the alleged interviews in which he was made to reflect upon the policy of the United States toward Mexico.

The diplomatic change in Mexico will be received with surprise when it becomes known on this side of the Atlantic, for, while Sir Lionel's actions and general demeanor since the outbreak of the Mexican troubles have been considered somewhat indiscreet by the general public, nobody here believed he had done anything to justify the attacks upon him which appeared in some of the American papers. In fact, it is expected that the official statement which will doubtless be issued when the changes are made will explain that Sir Lionel's transfer to Rio de Janeiro in no way casts discredit upon the Minister.

Sir Lionel Carden probably will come to England before going to his new post. It is said by his friends that when he went to Mexico he had the choice of going directly to Rio de Janeiro to succeed Sir William Henry Doveton Haggard, who had reached the retiring age, or of spending six months in Mexico as Minister there before proceeding to Brazil. Owing to the state of health of his wife, who is not strong, Sir Lionel decided to go to Mexico first.

Unfortunately, he went to Mexico with a reputation of being anti-American at a time when the best understanding between the United States and Great Britain was most desirable. Naturally the British Government defended Sir Lionel against the attacks made upon him, but the belief prevailed that it would be better to find another post for him.

The salary of the British Minister at Rio is $17,500, with a house allowance of $1,250, while that at Mexico City is $5,000 less, and no house allowance is made.

Charles Murray Marling, the probable successor of Sir Lionel, has had a long and varied career in the *Diplomatic* Service, which he joined in 1888. Most of the time he has occupied diplomatic posts in the East, at Constantinople, Athens, and Teheran; but he has also served at Paris, Sofia, Madrid, and Rio de Janeiro.

The officials of the Foreign Office were not prepared this evening to discuss Sir Lionel Carden's transfer, and were considerably surprised to discover that the intentions of the Government had leaked out. It is generally understood, however, that the Government takes much the same view as the public, that the Minister has not been entirely discreet in handling the situation in Mexico, although the Government does not believe that he has done anything to justify the very severe criticism leveled against him.

Nothing has become public here as to any differences between the American *naval authorities in Mexican waters* and Sir Christopher Cradock, the Admiral in command of the British warships there.

When it was suggested to-night to the American Ambassador, Walter H. Page, that the Ambassador might have had something to do with Sir Lionel Carden's transfer, he declined to admit responsibility, but suggested that Sir Lionel himself might have been the agency.

That the transfer was not a surprise to the Ambassador was indicated by the fact that he volunteered the name of the Minister's successor, saying that he understood that Mr. Marling was to take the post. Mr. Page denied that he had visited the British Foreign Office in connection with the rumors regarding Sir Christopher Cradock.

Special Cable to THE NEW YORK TIMES.

LONDON, Tuesday, Jan. 6.—Nothing is printed in the London newspapers this morning in relation to the reported transfer of Sir Lionel Carden from his post as Minister to Mexico to that of Minister to Brazil.

CARDEN WON'T ADMIT IT.

Says He Has Not Received Notice—Suggests Forced Loans to Huerta.

Special Cable to THE NEW YORK TIMES.

MEXICO CITY, Jan. 5.—Sir Lionel Carden says he has not received notice that he has been transferred from this capital to Rio de Janeiro, and says he does not believe the news would be given to the press before he had been notified.

The report has not become public here, but diplomats say that the reported action of the British Government does not surprise them, as it has been well known that Sir Lionel's activity here has not met the approval of Washington.

Mexican officials say that they have not been informed regarding the change, but would be sorry to see the Minister leave, as he has maintained excellent relations between Great Britain and Mexico.

It is generally believed here that his transfer would materially improve conditions in the Diplomatic Corps, removing much friction of which he is said to have been the occasion.

Dispatch to The Associated Press.

MEXICO CITY, Jan. 5.—Sir Lionel Carden had not been advised of his in-

Continued on Page 3.

KAISER STRIPS HEIR OF HIS AUTHORITY

Prince Reduced to Subordinate Rank Owing to Telegram to Zabern Commander.

Special Cable to THE NEW YORK TIMES.

BERLIN, Jan. 5.—The Berliner Zeitung am Mittag states that the Crown Prince has been practically stripped of all military authority in consequence of his telegram congratulating Col. von Reuter, the commander of the regiment that usurped the civil authority at Zabern, Alsace, on his "firm stand."

The journal states that as soon as the existence of the telegram was verified a conference of "competent authorities" was summoned, and it was determined to recall the Prince from Danzig, where he was in command of the "Death's Head" Hussars, within twenty-four hours. The position he now occupies on the General Staff in Berlin is stated to be a "wholly subordinate one."

In Court quarters it is pointed out that the feud between the Kaiser and his heir has apparently been aggravated, because the Crown Prince was not invited to attend the Emperor's New Year dinner to the commanding Generals, though he was "ordered" to appear after dinner and listen to a two-and-a-half-hours' disquisition by his parents on the 1913 "Kaiser manoeuvres."

The Crown Prince has had several differences with the Kaiser. In November, 1911, it may be recalled, much comment was caused by the Crown Prince's action in enthusiastically applauding in the Reichstag speakers who attacked the Imperial Chancellor, Dr. von Bethmann-Hollweg, on the occasion of a debate on the Moroccan settlement with France. The Prince ostentatiously showed his approval of references to the "German sword" and every word uttered against France and Great Britain. A day or so later the Kaiser voiced his displeasure with the Crown Prince through an inspired telegram published in The Cologne Gazette. This was regarded as a public and semi-official rebuke, and fully confirmed the reports that the Kaiser had reprimanded his son for having openly shown his approval of the attacks on the Government's Moroccan policy.

In October of last year the Crown Prince again rebelled against the Kaiser's Government. He intervened in characteristic fashion in the controversy regarding the thrones of the Duchy of Brunswick and the Kingdom of Hanover by writing a vigorous letter to the Imperial Chancellor, declaring that his brother-in-law, Prince Ernest Augustus, son of the Duke of Cumberland, should not be permitted to enter Brunswick as reigning Duke until he "clearly and categorically" renounced his and his offspring's claims to the throne of Hanover.

In June 1912, there was whispered gossip in naval circles that the Kaiser had made his parental and military authority felt by the Crown Prince by ordering his son to remain with his regiment in Danzig in order to prevent him from going to Kiel for the races. This discipline was meted out, it is said, because the Crown Prince planned to enter a boat against his father's.

It was announced last month that the Crown Prince was to join the General Staff of the army in Berlin after having been for more than two years at Danzig as Colonel of the "Death's Head" (First) Hussars. The newspapers intimated then that the Crown Prince did not like the transfer and was doing his utmost to have it revoked.

READY TO ORDER A VOLLEY.

Admissions by Col. von Reuter—Civilian Arrested for Laughing.

STRASBURG, Jan. 5.—Zabern, the now famous little garrison town of Alsace, narrowly escaped widespread carnage on Nov. 28, according to the testimony of Col. von Reuter, commander of the Ninety-ninth Infantry Regiment, when he was brought before a court-martial here to-day.

The Colonel was charged, together with Lieut. Schad of the same regiment, with various offenses against the law.

On the witness stand the Colonel swore that he had fully made up his mind to order the troops to open fire if necessary to "restore order," and he accompanied Lieut. Schad, when the troops were clearing a square, in order personally to give the command to fire if necessary, as he did not wish to leave the responsibility to so young an officer.

The Colonel said that on that date he replied to an official, who asked whether he (von Reuter) would allow it to come to bloodshed, as follows:

"Certainly! Blood may flow, and, under certain conditions, the story will be a *good one if it happens; for we are* protecting the prestige and the honor of the whole army and the greatly shaken authority of the Government."

Addressing the court, the witness added:

"I was convinced that our Government was allowing its reins to drag on the earth"

Col. von Reuter seems to have acted under the impression that he was the supreme arbiter at Zabern. He informed the civil authorities of his intention to proclaim martial law, although this was the Emperor's prerogative, and he told the Public Prosecutor that "jurisprudence ends here."

The conditions in Zabern were unsatisfactory before his arrival there, said the Colonel, many brawls between soldiers and civilians having preceded the incidents in which Lieut. von Forstner took such a prominent part. The soldiers preferred to pass their time in barracks when off duty rather than lay themselves open to insult in the streets.

Lieut. Schad, who is one of the youngest officers of the regiment, was the man who on Nov. 29 in the course of a riot ordered his men to clear one of the squares of Zabern and arrest everybody who stood still even for a moment. Among those taken into custody were several civilian Judges of the city. Lieut. Schad also led a squad of soldiers to a bedroom on the second floor of a private house and there arrested a man who had laughed scornfully at the soldiery. He also vied with Lieut. Baron von Forstner, now in prison undergoing a sentence for his illegal acts in Zabern, in displaying great anti-civilian activity, and is accused of illegal deprivation of liberty, of willful assault, and of disturbance of the peace.

FLYING MADE SAFE; WRIGHT EXPLAINS IT

Inventor Tells How His Stabilizer Balances Aeroplanes and Prevents "Overcontrol."

Special Cable to THE NEW YORK TIMES.

LONDON, Tuesday, Jan. 6.—The Daily Mail prints this morning a cable dispatch from Orville Wright in which he explains his stabilizer for aeroplanes. It is the first description of the device that Mr. Wright ever has given out for publication.

His dispatch to The Daily Mail follows:

"DAYTON, Ohio, Jan. 5.—The stabilizer with which experiments have been carried on the last several months consists of two parts. One is controlled by a pendulum, for maintaining the literal balance of a flying machine; the other controlled by a vane, for fore and aft balance. The power for warping the wings and turning the elevator is furnished by a small windmill, attached to the aeroplane so that the stopping of the motor does not affect the operation of the device.

"The general principles of this stabilizer are the same as disclosed in the patent taken out by the Wright brothers in Europe several years ago, but the mechanism has been changed and improved. One of the important improvements is a device for preventing overcontrol when the aeroplane has been thrown out of balance in one direction and the elevator is turned or the wings warped to bring it to level again. This device gradually brings the elevator and wings back to their normal positions as the machine is approaching the level, so that when the level is finally reached the controls do not turn the machine on over past level.

"To make a turn the operator simply sets the steering level to one side. The device automatically brings the aeroplane to the proper angle, so that it neither slips inward nor skids outward; it regulates the angle of banking more accurately than can the average aviator. Messrs. Griffiths Brewer and Alec Ogilvie of England had short rides on the machine during the first tests of the device last September. ORVILLE WRIGHT.

The Daily Mail says: "The news that Orville Wright has made a new contribution to the art of flying, only second in importance to his invention of the first practical aeroplane, will thrill the world. When Orville Wright makes the claim that his stabilizer renders flying 'as nearly foolproof as anything can be,' the world will believe him, for it knows he is no talker and boaster."

Griffiths Brewer, who has just returned from the United States after having made several flights at Dayton with Orville Wright, said last night that the Wright stabilizer could be brought into play within a minute while the machine was rising in the air. He says it also can be switched on or off at the will of the pilot, and that the balance it secures is much better than a pilot could maintain himself. The Wright device, he says, weighs no more than thirty pounds.

CARDINAL GIBBONS'S LEGACY

Will Use for Education Large Sum Inherited from Miss Andrews.

BALTIMORE, Md., Jan. 5.—As residuary legatee under Miss Eliza Andrews's will, which was probated today in the Orphans' Court here, Cardinal Gibbons may receive between $200,000 and $500,000. The Cardinal said the money would be used for Catholic educational work.

The estimated value of Miss Andrews's personal property is $600,000, and it was said her holdings of real estate would be found to be of equal value. Specific monetary legacies in the will for religious and charitable purposes aggregate $21,000.

Miss Andrews lived here for many years until her death last month. Her father was Dr. Thomas F. Andrews, a distinguished medical practitioner in Norfolk, Va., before the civil war.

MISS WILSON AT MARDI GRAS

President's Daughter to Attend Twelfth Night Ball in New Orleans.

Special to The New York Times.

NEW ORLEANS, Jan. 5.—Miss Eleanor Wilson, the President's daughter, and Miss Helen Woodrow Bone, his niece, arrived in New Orleans to-night to attend the ball of the Twelfth Night Revellers to-morrow night. They are the guests of the Misses Mary and Lucy Smith, relatives of the Wilson family. Mrs. Woodrow Wilson is expected to arrive to-morrow afternoon. An invitation was extended to the President and he may accept.

The Twelfth Night ball is the first of the big Mardi Gras entertainments, and the Revellers form one of the most exclusive of the carnival societies. Their annual ball usually is the chief event of the year in the débutante circles.

MOB THRASHES WIFE BEATER

Her Complaint Brings Chastisement to Father of Six.

ROCHESTER, N. Y., Jan. 5.—Twenty citizens of the town of Almond, Allegany County, went to the home of Edward Davidson last night and gave him a severe beating. The men wore bran sacks over their heads.

Davidson has a wife and six small children. Yesterday morning Mrs. Davidson tramped fourteen miles through the snow to Almond and reported that Davidson had beat her severely. A mob immediately formed.

GIVES $10,000,000 TO 26,000 EMPLOYES

Ford to Run Automobile Plant 24 Hours Daily on Profit-Sharing Plan.

MINIMUM WAGE $5 A DAY

No Employe to be Discharged Except for Unfaithfulness or Hopeless Inefficiency.

Special to The New York Times.

DETROIT, Mich., Jan. 5.—Henry Ford, head of the Ford Motor Company, announced to-day one of the most remarkable business moves of his entire remarkable career. In brief it is:

To give to the employes of the company $10,000,000 of the profits of the 1914 business, the payments to be made semi-monthly and added to the pay checks.

To run the factory continuously instead of only eighteen hours a day, giving employment to several thousand more men by employing three shifts of eight hours each, instead of only two nine-hour shifts, as at present.

To establish a minimum wage scale of $5 per day. Even the boy who sweeps up the floors will get that much.

Before any man in any department of the company who does not seem to be doing good work shall be discharged, an opportunity will be given to him to try to make good in every other department. No man shall be discharged except for proved unfaithfulness or irremediable inefficiency.

The Ford Company's financial statement of Sept. 20, 1912, showed assets of $20,815,785.63, and surplus of $14,745,095.57. One year later it showed assets of $35,033,919.86 and surplus of $28,124,173.68. Dividends paid out during the year, it is understood, aggregated $10,000,000. The indicated profits for the year, therefore, were about $37,597,312. The company's capital stock, authorized and outstanding, is $2,000,000. There is no bond issue.

About 10 per cent. of the employes, boys and women, will not be affected by the profit sharing, but all will have the benefit of the $5 minimum wage. Those among them who are supporting families, however, will have a share similar to the men of more than 22 years of age.

In all, about 26,000 employes will be affected. Fifteen thousand now are at work in the Detroit factories. Four thousand more will be added by the institution of the eight-hour shift. The other seven thousand employes are scattered all over the world, in the Ford branches. They will share the same as the Detroit employes.

Personal statements were made by Henry Ford and James Couzens, Treasurer of the company, regarding the move.

"It is our belief," said Mr. Couzens, "that social justice begins at home. We want those who have helped us to produce this great institution and are helping to maintain it to share our prosperity. We want them to have present profits and future prospects. Thrift and good service and sobriety, all will be enforced and recognized.

"Believing as we do, that a division of our earnings between capital and labor is unequal, we have sought a plan of relief suitable for our business. We do not feel sure that it is the best, but we have felt impelled to make a start, and make it now. We do not agree with *those employers* who declare, as did a recent writer in a magazine in excusing himself for not practicing what he preached, that 'movement toward the bettering of society must be universal.' We think that one concern can make a start and create an example for other employers. That is our chief object."

"If we are obliged," said Mr. Ford, "to lay men off for want of sufficient work at any season we purpose to so plan our year's work that the lay-off shall be in the harvest time, July, August, and September, not in the Winter. We hope in such case to induce our men to respond to the calls of the farmers for harvest hands, and not to lie idle and dissipate their savings. We shall make it our business to get in touch with the farmers and to induce our employes to answer calls for harvest help.

"No man will be discharged if we can help it, except for unfaithfulness or inefficiency. No foreman in the *Ford* Company has the power to discharge a man. He may send him out of his department if he does not make good. The man is then sent to our 'clearing house,' covering all the departments, and is tried repeatedly in other work, until we find the job he is suited for, provided he is honestly trying to render good service."

ARMY POLO PLAYER DYING.

Lieut. Armstrong Fractures His Skull in Cavalry Match.

EL PASO, Texas, Jan. 5.—Lieut. Eugene V. Armstrong, Thirteenth Cavalry, was probably fatally injured on Sunday afternoon in a polo game at Washington Park between teams from the Fifteenth and Thirteenth Cavalry. Lieut. Armstrong was thrown in a collision with a fellow-player and his skull was fractured. Five doctors have agreed that an operation cannot save him.

Lieut. Armstrong was one of the army's best polo players, and had participated in Eastern tournaments with the Meadow Brook and other crack teams. He is a native of Pennsylvania, but his parents now live at Cook's Bridge, Del., from which State he was appointed to West Point. He graduated in the class of 1904.

BRIDAL GOWNS GO IN FIRE.

Brooklyn Man's Wife-to-Be Loses Trousseau in Ansonia, Conn.

ANSONIA, Conn., Jan. 5.—One store was burned out, three others were damaged, and a dozen families made homeless when fire swept a three-story brick business and tenement block here to-day.

Miss Annie Aarons, who is to be married to-morrow evening to Philip Leift of Brooklyn, N. Y., lost all her wedding outfit and presents, and her bridesmaid, Miss Esther Cohen of Worcester, Mass., lost all her gowns.

A HOGARTH DIES IN POVERTY

Descendant of the Artist Lived for Many Years on Poor Relief.

Special Cable to THE NEW YORK TIMES.

LONDON, Jan. 5.—Miss Susannah Hogarth, aged 79, a descendant of the artist, has just died in Ilford in poverty.

For many years she lived on poor relief and then on an old-age pension, only her landlord knowing her descent.

ANOTHER HAITIAN REVOLT.

Gen. Zamor Takes Refuge in American Consulate at Cape Haitien.

CAPE HAITIEN, Jan. 5.—A column of regular troops has been ordered by the President of the republic to proceed immediately to the northeastern frontier districts to suppress an insurrection which has started there.

Gen. Zamor, the Governor of the Northern Department and ex-Minister of War, has taken refuge in the American Consulate.

DIVING POOL FOR RUTGERS.

Mrs. Robert Balentine Presents It at the Cost of $20,000.

Special to The New York Times.

NEW BRUNSWICK, N. J., Jan. 5.—Dr. William H. F. De Marest, President of Rutgers College, announced to the undergraduate body to-day the gift of a $20,000 swimming pool.

Mrs. Robert Balentine of Newark has presented it to the college.

NO CHICAGO SUBWAY BIDS.

Method of Payment for $131,000,000 Job Fails to Interest Contractors.

CHICAGO, Jan. 5.—Apparently nobody wants to build Chicago's *$131,000,000* subway. This was the day for opening bids, but none was received.

Mayor Harrison hoped that some contractor would take the contract, content to take his pay out of the earnings of the system in that part of twenty years—the longest franchise the city can grant—which remained after the work was completed.

BREAK DEADLOCK BY FORCE.

Asbury Park Council Organizes with Aid of the Police.

ASBURY PARK, Jan. 5.—With the aid of the police, the Fusion members of the Council this evening succeeded in breaking the deadlock which has existed since they assumed office on Jan. 1. One of the Democratic members, technically under arrest, was brought into the room where the three Fusion members were holding their meeting by Chief of Police W. H. Smith.

As soon as he had crossed the threshold the election of Dr. F. F. Coleman as President took place. It was not necessary to have the vote of the Democrat, but his presence in the room to make a quorum was necessary.

It is likely that the Democrat will take the case to court.

STOVE SETS CHILD AFLAME.

Badly Burned Despite Catholic Sisters' Valiant Efforts to Save.

Margaret Markowitz, a ten-year-old pupil of the Cliffside, N. J., parochial school, tumbled much in the wet snow at recess time yesterday morning, and her schoolmates took her into the schoolroom and placed her in front of the stove to dry her clothing. In some way her clothing caught fire, and the flames quickly enveloped her.

Sister Therese of St. Joseph's Order, standing near, wrapped her habit about the child and smothered the flames, but not before the girl had been badly burned. She was taken to the North Hudson Hospital, where, it was said last night, skin grafting would have to be resorted to to save her life. The child's home is on the River Road, Shadyside.

TEAR UP GRADE CROSSING.

City Officials of Memphis Take Drastic Action After Accident.

MEMPHIS, Tenn., Jan. 5.—Heading a large force of workmen, Mayor E. H. Crump and Thomas Dies, Commissioner of Public Utilities, to-day tore up the railroad tracks at the grade crossing where five persons were killed and several wounded last night when a freight train on the Nashville, Chattanooga & St. Louis Railroad crashed into a street car.

The freight train was operating on a track that city officials had ordered removed several days ago. The railroad authorities had made no move to comply with the order and the Mayor's action resulted. According to witnesses there were no lights on the rear of the freight train and no switchman at the crossing.

ARRESTS BRIGHT'S DISEASE.

California Physician Describes New Remedy and Its Effects.

Special to The New York Times.

LOS ANGELES, Cal., Jan. 5.—A newly discovered treatment of "washing" the kidneys with an alkaline solution is declared by Dr. A. T. Charlton of the County Hospital to be a positive "arrest" of Bright's disease in any stage, and Dr. Charlton to-day cited as proof twenty cases in which he applied the method.

"It is well known," he said, "that Bright's disease is caused by the kidneys being unable to purify the blood as it passes through those organs. With my new discovery I wash the kidney clean and, by using the alkaline solution, change the reaction of the blood from acid to alkaline. This overcomes the toxicity and cleanses the entire system of its poison."

Dr. Charlton's most severe test was that of John Frohman, a laborer, who was brought to the hospital in the dropsical, or last stages, of the disease. By using a "high irrigation" pressure, Dr. Charlton declared, he had not only enabled Frohman to leave the hospital, but that the man would live his natural span of days so far as his kidneys were concerned.

Dr. Charlton said he was engaged in making a minute report of his discovery, its application, and the cases treated by him, to the American Medical Association and to several other scientific bodies.

THIRTY-TWO LOST ON THE OKLAHOMA

Eight Saved from Oil Ship Which Buckled When Suspended Between Waves.

SOME ADRIFT IN LIFEBOAT

Crew from the Bavaria Rescued Exhausted Officers in a Gale Off Sandy Hook.

WIRELESS BROUGHT AID

Spanish Liner's Lifeboat Was Smashed in Going to Rescue Before Bavaria's Arrival.

A wireless message which was received in this city by the Hamburg-American Line at 9 o'clock yesterday morning from Capt. Graalfs of the Bavaria, brought word that the vessel which was wrecked on Sunday fifteen miles off Sandy Hook was the oil tank steamer Oklahoma, owned by the Gulf Refining Company of this city. The first meagre dispatches told of the rescue of eight officers and artificers of the liner by the Bavaria and of the loss of thirty-two men, including Capt. Cates, a passenger.

At 9 o'clock last night, in answer to urgent messages from the Hamburg-American Line asking for more details, this wireless dispatch was received from Capt. Graalfs telling of the disaster:

Hamburg-American Line, New York:

On Jan. 5, at 6 A. M., we sighted the signals of distress of a vessel; wind north northeast, velocity 8, high, rough sea. At dawn we saw the forward part of a steamer, floating on the water; tank steamer Oklahoma, New York. At 8 o'clock in the morning we were close to the wreck and lowered a boat with six men, who succeeded, after great effort, in seizing a rope that was thrown to them.

The men of the Oklahoma lowered themselves into the boat, quite exhausted from their experience of the last twenty-four hours. Capt. Gunther stated that last Sunday, at 7:30 A. M., during heavy weather, without any previous warning, the ship suddenly broke in two right behind the bridge. In about twenty-two minutes the after part of the ship, with the crew of thirty-two men, sank into the deep, the stern pointing upward with the propellers twirling. The fore part was kept afloat by the bulkhead, the stem up to the rear edge protruding from the water.

The lifeboats either went down with the ship or were smashed by he waves immediately after the catastrophe. On the evening of Jan. 4 a Spanish steamer appeared, but was unable, owing to the bad weather, to accomplish anything. *Immediately after the Bavaria,* the United Fruit steamer Tenadores arrived on the scene of the disaster, but there was nothing left to be done, the boat from the Bavaria having taken off all the men. The life-saving work took place 39.7 North. 73.45 West. GRAALFS.

Saw Lifeboat Launched.

Another wireless message from Capt. Graalfs was received, which said:

According to statements made by some of the men saved, a boat from the sunken part of the Oklahoma with from eight to ten men was seen. Whereabouts unknown.

From the account given by Capt. Graalfs shipping men in this city decided that the *Oklahoma* had been "hogged" by the sea, or caught on the crests of two gigantic waves fore and aft that left the vessel without any support amidships. It was not uncommon, they pointed out, for a ship to be thus caught and lifted up by two waves, especially in rough weather like that prevailing on Sunday, but some of the big transatlantic liners have safely withstood the strain of similar tests.

According to officials of the Hamburg American Line, the Bavaria sailed from Philadelphia on Sunday with a part cargo, bound for Boston to take on more freight. She will arrive in Boston some time this afternoon.

The first definite news received in this city as to the fate of the Oklahoma was contained in this wireless message from Capt. Graalfs of the Bavaria, sent to the agents of his line here yesterday morning:

By wireless via Cape May: Hamburg-American Line, New York City.

At 8 A. M. saved eight from American tank steamer Oklahoma from New York. They are Capt. Alfred Gunter, first mate; Bartil Ivarson, second mate; Knute Dahle, third mate; Karl Eklund, wireless operator; William Davis, boatman; Rassmusson, carpenter; Harman Ericksen, and Quartermaster Hamilton Powell. Rest of thirty-two hands seem to have gone down with after part of ship. Accident happened Sunday morning at 8. Rescue 8 A. M. to-day. GRAALFS.

Not until 9 o'clock yesterday morning, more than twelve hours after the "S. O. S." signal was flashed over the ocean to summon aid to the Oklahoma, was the name of the wrecked ship known. On Sunday the ship was reported to be the Wasca, and no such name was recorded in the maritime registers. Then it was said that the vessel in distriess was the Koenegin Luise, a North German Lloyd liner, that is safe in Australian waters. Then a wireless message suggested that the sinking ship might be the tank steamer Delaware. No one suspected that the wrecked vessel was the Oklahoma until Capt. Graalf's message was received.

Names of Those Lost.

Immediately after the receipt of this message the Hamburg-American Line asked Capt. Graalfs by wireless for fur-

"All the News That's Fit to Print"

The New York Times.

THE WEATHER
Rain to-day and Thursday; rising northeasterly winds, probably becoming gales late to-day.
For full weather report see Page 19.

VOL. LXIII...NO. 20,535. NEW YORK, WEDNESDAY, APRIL 15, 1914.—TWENTY-TWO PAGES. ONE CENT In Greater New York, Jersey City and Newark. | Elsewhere TWO CENTS.

ATLANTIC FLEET ORDERED TO TAMPICO; HUERTA REFUSES TO SALUTE OUR FLAG; SAYS HE WILL UPHOLD MEXICO'S HONOR AND PREPARES MESSAGE TO CONGRESS

HUERTA PREPARES A MESSAGE FOR SUBMISSION TO CONGRESS

Members of That Body Say They will Probably Approve His Patriotic Action.

MEXICO, April 14.—President Huerta has prepared for submission to Congress an important declaration.

Congressmen say it is probable that they will approve his highly patriotic action.

Special Cable to THE NEW YORK TIMES.

VERA CRUZ, April 14.—Foreign Minister Portillo y Rojas, in his last note to Nelson O'Shaughnessy, American Chargé, clearly sets forth the Mexican Government's declination to honor the American flag with a salute at Tampico. He says that President Huerta considers the sovereignty of Mexico would thus be degraded, and is not disposed to yield to the pressure of any nation over his army's actions. He considers that international law and usage were not tampered with by the Dolphin launch incident, and is disposed to uphold the honor and sovereignty of Mexico at any cost.

It is said here to-night that Secretary Daniels has advised the New York and Cuba Mail Company that its boats are now at the disposition of the American Government and may be called upon for service at any moment for removing refugees from Tampico.

Seven Battleships and Two Cruisers Get Orders for Service.

SOME GO SOUTH TO-DAY

President Wilson Determined to Employ Adequate Force to Compel Respect for Flag.

CABINET IN LONG SESSION

Blunt Refusal of Demand for Satisfaction Precipitates Speedy Action.

DANGER OF STEP REALIZED

Some Officials Fear Huerta Will Hand O'Shaughnessy His Passports, Making Crisis Acute.

15,000 MEN IN NAVAL FORCE

Including 2,500 Marines, Ready for Landing—The Louisiana Going from Here.

Special to The New York Times.

WASHINGTON, April 14.—As a result of the refusal of the Mexican Government to fire a salute to the American flag as reparation for the indignity offered to an officer and men from the gunboat Dolphin at Tampico, President Wilson to-day ordered the entire North Atlantic battleship fleet to that Mexican port. Late to-night the Navy Department received word from Admiral Badger that four battleships were ready to sail from Hampton Roads to-morrow morning.

On the face of it this action means that if the salute is not forthcoming, the United States will use force to back up its demand for reparation. But the Administration steadfastly refuses to give any detailed explanation of the matter.

Rumor of Three Day Limit.

Daniels' Formal Statement.

VILLA ROUTS 15,000, TAKES SAN PEDRO

Victorious Rebel Army Enters the Town Headed by Captured Military Band.

11 DAYS OF FIERCE FIGHTING

Both Sides Lose Heavily—One Report Says 5,000 Were Wounded, but This is Questioned.

Special to The New York Times.

The Chase After Velasco.

WAR TALKS BY TELEPHONE.

Rebel Version of Conversations with Federals Before Torreon.

MR. DOOLEY ON AGITATORS

A little philosophy about the I. W. W.'s and others who are much in evidence just now

IN NEXT SUNDAY'S TIMES.

Also a fine portrait of Shakespeare by a new process in commemoration of the 350th anniversary of his birth.

TRUST BILL IN; DEFINES UNIONS

They May Carry Out Legitimate Objects, but Can't Violate the Sherman Law.

CURBS COURT INJUNCTIONS

Interlocking Directorate Ban Excludes Small Banks—Holding Company Provision Easier.

JURY TRIALS FOR CONTEMPT

Measure Consolidates Administration's Programme and May Be Reported in Ten Days.

Special to The New York Times.

WASHINGTON, April 14.—A more definite idea of the Administration's programme for trust legislation was obtainable to-night when Representative Henry D. Clayton of Alabama, Chairman of the House Judiciary Committee, made public the revised Anti-Trust bill. It links the anti-trust question with that of union labor.

May Not Satisfy Labor.

Continued on Page 3.

BRYAN STILL HOPEFUL.

May Get Away to Florida in a Few Days, He Says.

Special to The New York Times.

GUARD COLOMBIA TREATY.

Sudden Shift at Washington—To be Published at Bogota.

Special to The New York Times.

MUSICIAN KILLED BY TRAIN.

Woman Tries to Save L. L. Glover on Third Avenue Elevated.

THREATENS GIRL TO WED HER

Handley, Defied at the Last, Takes Poison in City Hall, Atlantic City.

Special to The New York Times.

COMMISSION PLAN WINS.

Orange, by a Majority of 243, Changes Style of Government.

Special to The New York Times.

MAIL TRUCK OVERBOARD.

Why Some New Jersey Towns Missed the Morning Newspapers.

WHITMAN SCOUTS CIROFICI'S STORY

To Investigate Report That "Dago Frank" Was Drugged Before Confession.

CLANCY TO BE QUESTIONED

District Attorney Learns Italian Offered to Exonerate the Three Other Gunmen.

NO "DOLLAR JOHN" PLOT

Father Cashin and Miss Cirofici Tell How Confession Was Made—To Move for Becker Trial To-day.

Information from Sing Sing Prison reached the office of District Attorney Whitman yesterday which caused him to smile at the whole structure of the "Dago Frank" Rosenthal murder confession made just before the gunmen were to pay the death penalty Monday morning.

"Horrible Travesties," Says Cashin.

No "Dollar John" Murder Plot.

Three Ignorant of Confession.

Continued on Page 6.

CITY MUST INSURE 100,000 WORKERS

The State, Too, Put Within the Scope of the New Compensation Law.

A BROAD INTERPRETATION

Would Bring the Mayor and All Other Officials Within the Law's Provision.

VINCENT ASTOR ILL AT FIANCEE'S HOME

Has Acute Congestion of the Right Lung—Condition Is Serious.

WEDDING PLANS HALTED

Stricken on Monday Night, Following Previous Attack of Bronchitis—His Mother at Bedside.

Vincent Astor is seriously ill with acute congestion of the right lung at Hopeland House, Staatsburg, N. Y., the country home of Robert P. Huntington, the father of his bride-to-be.

STEEL WAGE CUT PLANNED.

No Escape If Railroad Rates Are Increased, Independents Announce.

Special to The New York Times.

1914

The Great War

1921

FRONT PAGE NEWS 1914-1921

Assassin Unleashes World War I

JUNE 29, 1914

Two bullets fired at royals in eastern Europe became the 20th century's shots heard around the world. The heir to the Austro-Hungarian throne, Archduke Ferdinand, was a target for a nationalist Serbian gunman because he favored soft-pedaling the nationalist factions that were agitating across the far-flung multinational Empire controlled by his uncle, Emperor Franz Joseph. (The assassin also killed Ferdinand's wife, Duchess Sophie.) Austria soon declared war against Serbia, and Austrian artillery pounded Belgrade. In Washington, President Woodrow Wilson preached noninvolvement, telling Americans to remain "neutral in fact as well as in name" and "impartial in thought as well as in action."

Conflict Spreads Across Europe

AUGUST 5, 1914

In August 1914, one declaration of war followed another across Europe. So did rapid mobilizations. Austria had been counting on the German Foreign Office to keep Russia from getting involved. But in August, Germany itself went on the offensive against Russia and, a few days later, so did France. Then Britain declared war on Germany after the Germans invaded neutral Belgium. Austro-Hungary was soon at war against Russia and, a few days later, France and Britain. By the end of the month, even Japan had joined the lineup—against Germany.

Protesting 'The Birth of a Nation'

APRIL 15, 1915

In Europe, German Zeppelins were attacking British towns from the air. In the United States, movie goers were reliving the Civil War through D.W. Griffith's silent film "The Birth of a Nation." Historians praise its cinematography and big-budget extravagance—and condemn its racist storyline. It drew almost daily demonstrations at the Liberty Theater in New York as the National Association for the Advancement of Colored People pressed to have the most offensive scenes edited out.

Lusitania's Last Voyage

MAY 8, 1915

The warnings were all over the papers about U-boats with torpedoes, but still a stylish crowd boarded the British liner Lusitania in New York on May 1. In the Atlantic six days later, a German attacked. One survivor reported: "The ship rose in the air, and she slipped down as if she was gliding down a greased surface." The Lusitania was gone in little more than 15 minutes, and so were nearly 1,200 people, among them the New York railroad heir Alfred Gwynne Vanderbilt, who had handed his life jacket to another passenger.

Lusitania's Aftermath

MAY 31, 1915

In the United States, where the Wilson administration clung to neutrality, the sinking of the Lusitania inflamed public opinion—all the more so when Germany called the attack "justified self-defense." Washington countered that the Lusitania had not been armed or carrying guns. But in its hold there had been more than a hundred tons of ammunition, and the Germans claimed the passengers had included Canadian troops whose mission was "the destruction of the brave German soldiers." Washington continued to resist going to war over Germany's submarine offensive.

Attack on Verdun

MARCH 3, 1916

All was quiet on the western front in 1915, but not for long. The focus on eastern fronts from Galicia to Gallipoli ended when the Germans tried to ring French fortifications around Verdun and shell them with artillery. That was exactly what the French claimed its infantry was doing to the Germans. The result was the longest, bloodiest battle in World War I, with more than a quarter-million soldiers killed. The French were outmanned and outmaneuvered but held the Germans to small, incremental advances through the spring and early summer. Then General Philippe Petain of France began organizing counterattacks. In Washington, President Woodrow Wilson stuck to his pledge of neutrality, even as protégés of prominent Democrats like William Jennings Bryan tried to goad Wilson into joining the conflict.

Easter Rebellion Collapses

APRIL 30, 1916

The six-day Easter Rebellion began when militant, independence-minded Irish Republicans seized locations in Dublin—not nationwide, as they had planned. Their newly proclaimed "Irish republic" collapsed as British troops arrived and arrested the organizers, who were tried for sedition and executed. But Britain failed to re-establish its authority, which eventually led to the Irish civil war.

Chasing Pancho Villa

MAY 10, 1916

The Mexican revolutionary Pancho Villa had made trouble on both sides of the border, executing U.S. citizens in Mexico and swooping down on an Army staging ground in New Mexico, so President Woodrow Wilson dispatched troops on a misadventure to catch him. Major General Frederick Funston—"Fearless Freddie," a pint-size hero of the Spanish-American War—plotted the maneuvers while General John J. Pershing headed into the field. But they never got their man. Villa finally "retired" in 1920, but only after Mexico officially pardoned him. By then Funston was dead, of a heart attack, and Pershing had gone on to command American troops "over there" in World War I.

Rasputin Murdered

JANUARY 3, 1917

The Russian nobles who plotted to murder Gregory Rasputin could not have imagined that it would involve so much work. First the scraggly-bearded "mad monk" of the last days of Imperial Russia survived cyanide-laced tea cakes and wine, followed by a gunshot in the back and, a few hours later, more bullets (after he came to and tried to flee). Finally they dumped him in the icy Neva River, where he drowned. The nobles believed that Rasputin, who had great influence with Tsar Nicholas II and the Empress Alexandra, was negotiating a secret peace treaty with Germany to undercut the Russians' offensive on the eastern front.

U-Boats on the Prowl

FEBRUARY 1, 1917

Germany countered the allied blockade—and intensified the pressure on President Woodrow Wilson to enter the war—by declaring unrestricted submarine warfare in British waters. Wilson's response would be to break off diplomatic relations as the Germans sank the American steamer Housatonic. There were no casualties; everyone aboard was rescued by a passing British ship.

U.S. Joins the War

April 6, 1917

President Woodrow Wilson had won a second term in 1916 with the slogan, "He kept us out of war." A month after inauguration, Wilson changed his tune. "The world must be made safe for democracy," he declared—and that meant appropriating $3 billion, mobilizing an army of a million soldiers and joining the conflict. Among the 50 "no" votes in the House was that of the only woman in Congress, Representative Jeanette Rankin of Montana (elected in 1916). "I want to stand by my country, but I cannot vote for war," she declared, tearfully, on the House floor.

Bolsheviks Seize Power

November 9, 1917

"This is only a preliminary step toward a similar revolution everywhere," the Bolshevik leader, V.I. Lenin, declared after the overthrow by armed sailors who stormed the Parliament in Petrograd and overthrew Premier Alexander Kerensky. Kerensky had lost the support of the military after he fired a top general, and the revolutionaries after he refused to push through their social and economic programs. With Russia in chaos and Lenin and Leon Trotsky in charge, the Soviet government soon negotiated a separate peace in World War I, giving Germany control of 300,000 square miles of territory, including Ukraine, Finland, Poland and the eventual Baltic states.

Theodore Roosevelt Dies

January 7, 1919

"Now look—that damned cowboy is President of the United States," Republican strategist Mark Hanna declared. But Theodore Roosevelt was a Harvard-educated, trust-busting, progressive, war-hero cowboy. He was sworn in after a remarkably rapid rise in politics: in five years he had gone from New York City police comissioner to governor of New York (elected on his Rough Rider fame in the Spanish-American War) to vice president to president on William McKinley's assassination. Attempting a comeback on the third-party Bull Moose ticket in 1912, he lost to Woodrow Wilson. Roosevelt died at age 60 at his home on Long Island.

Czar Abdicates in Russia

March 16, 1917

Russia and its royal Romanovs had teetered through World War I, absorbing two million casualties in 1915. Now the monarchy toppled as Bolshevik unrest swept St. Petersburg, and Czar Nicholas II abdicated after months of famine and chaos, allegations of corruption and suspicions of secret alliances with German enemies. Power passed to Grand Duke Mikhail, who renounced the throne after one day. The Romanovs, fleeing into exile in the Ural Mountains, were executed by a Red Army firing squad in 1918.

Armistice Ends World War I

November 11, 1918

When the fighting stopped, the cheering began in Times Square. Kaiser Wilhelm had abdicated, and leaders of the German and allied armies had signed the documents in a railroad car. The price had been high all around. America, which had joined the war only the year before, recorded 53,500 battle deaths and 63,000 deaths from disease and accidents. European casualties from four years of conflict ran into the millions. President Woodrow Wilson called World War I "the culminating and final war for human liberty," but it turned out to be the prelude to an even greater drama of suffering.

Britain Takes Control of Palestine

September 23, 1918

The fighting was over in Europe, but continued in the Mideast. British General Edmund Allenby's infantry corps had been battered by the Turks in 1917, when the Balfour Declaration had offered Jews a "national home" if the "civil and religious rights of existing non-Jewish communities in Palestine" were left alone. That point created huge headaches later. But Allenby's rout of three Turkish divisions was one for the record books. Military historians consider it the last great cavalry victory. It opened the way to Haifa and Nazareth, where the Turkish-allied German commander was forced to flee in his pajamas.

League Plan Approved in Paris

January 26, 1919

President Woodrow Wilson staked his prestige on establishing the League of Nations. At the Paris conference to negotiate a treaty officially ending World War I, Wilson saw enduring alliances and multilateral institutions as essential to guaranteeing "permanent arrangements that justice shall be rendered and peace maintained." But the U.S. was returning to isolationism. The Republicans had won control of the Senate in the midterm congressional elections, a twist that spelled trouble for Wilson's League.

Germans Sign Versailles Treaty

June 29, 1919

The official end of World War I, the Versailles Treaty, came five years to the day after the assassination of Archduke Ferdinand that drew Europe into war. President Woodrow Wilson hoped for peace with reconciliation, but that was not to be. Under the treaty, Germany faced heavy punitive reparations, which fed the economic turmoil in the 1920's that contributed to the rise of Nazism. Already, Germans were angry; in Berlin, The Times reported, "the air is charged with the spirit of rebellion."

Defeat in the Senate

November 20, 1919

The Treaty of Versailles went down to defeat in the Senate, dooming President Woodrow Wilson's dream of the League of Nations. The opposition was led by Henry Cabot Lodge, a Republican who had become chairman of the Senate Foreign Relations Committee after the Democrats lost control of the Senate in the 1918 elections. Wilson himself had had a stroke in October, and all communications with him went through the First Lady, Edith Bolling Galt Wilson. She kept the diagnosis secret, and for much of Wilson's final months in office was suspected of virtually running the country.

Red Scare

January 3, 1920

The U.S. roared into the twenties with a Red Scare—nationwide raids ordered by Attorney General A. Mitchell Palmer, who considered Communism the new No. 1 enemy. Contributing to the hysteria were a string of bombs sent through the mail. One exploded on Palmer's own doorstep. Under two wartime laws, large numbers of labor organizers and immigrants were hauled in from coast to coast, among them five members of the New York State Assembly expelled as "little Trotskys in our midst." Dozens were detained for long periods without being charged, and as public opinion shifted, the raids backfired on Palmer, dooming hopes of succeeding President Woodrow Wilson.

No Chance for Compromise

January 9, 1920

The White House and President Woodrow Wilson's opponents in Congress had bickered and squabbled and danced around the idea of a compromise on the League of Nations treaty—a compromise that would allow the U.S. to send a delegate to the League's first meeting, scheduled for January 10. Wilson remained opposed to Senator Henry Cabot Lodge's "reservations," and finally the Democratic patriarch William Jennings Bryan broke with Wilson. Lodge saw no hope, either.

"All the News That's Fit to Print."

The New York Times.

THE WEATHER

Local showers today; Tuesday, fair; fresh, shifting winds, becoming northwest.

For full weather report see Page 17.

VOL. LXIII...NO. 20,610. NEW YORK, MONDAY, JUNE 29, 1914.—EIGHTEEN PAGES. ONE CENT In Greater New York, Jersey City and Newark. { Elsewhere TWO CENTS.

CALIFORNIA GOES ON ROCKS IN FOG

Tory Island, Off Northwest Irish Coast, Scene of Mishap to Anchor Liner.

IN NO IMMEDIATE DANGER

Bows Badly Stove In and Ship Taking Water Through Two Holes in Hold.

PASSENGERS STILL ABOARD

Ship Carries 1,000 Persons—Rescue Vessels, Called by Wireless, Standing By Throughout Night.

Special Cable to THE NEW YORK TIMES.

LONDON, June 28.—The Anchor liner California, with more than 1,000 persons aboard, has gone ashore on Tory Island, off the northern coast of Ireland. The destroyer Swift, the fastest and largest vessel of her class in the world, and other vessels have gone to her assistance in response to wireless calls for aid.

The ship is said to be in no immediate danger.

The accident to the California occurred in a thick fog. The latest news received early this morning was that although the position of the liner was serious, no lives had been lost.

In reply to a wireless message, the Captain sent the following details:

California ran ashore Tory Island in fog, about half mile from lighthouse. Did not hear foghorn blowing. Quiet sea. No danger. Three men of war and steamer Cassandra standing by to transfer passengers.

The California went on the rocks with such force that the lower part of her bows were badly stove in, and the two front holds soon filled with water. She is in five fathoms of water forward and seven fathoms aft. There was no panic on board.

News has been received from Londonderry that the landing of the Irish passengers may be expected before noon today.

News of the stranding was caught by the Malin Head wireless station and the entire torpedo boat destroyer flotilla which was for duty off the Ulster voast looking for gun runners, was called up and wireless orders were given to all the destroyers from the cruiser Hecla in Lough Swilly to hurry with all speed to the scene of the accident.

Subsequently orders were received by all the telephone and telegraph stations on the coast from Bangor to Bunbeg, County Donegal, to keep their offices open all night.

By 11 o'clock six destroyers were making for Tory Island.

LONDONDERRY, June 28.—In a thick fog and rain which rendered Tory Island invisible from the mainland, the Anchor Line steamer California, bound from New York for Glasgow, went ashore tonight on the rocks off that island. Wireless calls for help brought speedy assistance from a number of small gunboats and torpedo boats which were patrolling the Northwest Irish Coast for gun runners in connection with the Ulster movement.

The latest news received here is that the California is stuck fast on the rocks, but is in no immediate danger. She struck with such force that the lower part of her bows was badly stove in, and she is making water through two holes in her forehold and second hold.

The steamer, which has on board 121 saloon and more than 300 second cabin passengers, lies in five fathoms of water forward and seven fathoms aft.

The passengers and crew are still on board. There was no panic when she struck the rocks.

Several steamers, including one liner, and the gunboats are standing by, and other vessels are expected to arrive at the scene during the night.

LONDON, June 28.—Capt. Coverley of the California late tonight sent out this wireless dispatch:

"Ran ashore in fog about half mile from the lighthouse. Did not hear foghorn. Sea quiet. Three men-of-war and steamer Cassandra standing by to transfer passengers."

CARRIED 841 PASSENGERS.

Place Where California Struck Ten Miles Out of Her Course.

The California sailed from New York at noon on Saturday, June 20, for Glasgow via Moville with 116 first-class, 850 second-class, and 375 third-class passengers. She signaled Malin Head yesterday afternoon, and should have been off Moville about 8 o'clock. Tory Island is more than ten miles out of her course.

The California carried a crew of 240 officers and men, and was commanded by J. A. Coverley, one of the most experienced Captains in the Anchor Line service. This was his second voyage on the California after having been twelve years on the Calabria in the New York-Mediterranean service, and more recently in command of the liner Elysia in the Indian service of the Anchor Line.

The California is the second largest vessel of the Anchor Line in the New York trade, and was built at Glasgow by D. & W. Henderson Bros. in 1907. She is 470 feet long, with a beam of 58 feet 2 inches and a depth of hold of 23 feet 6 inches. She is a twin-screw steamer, with an average speed of 15 knots.

The Captains and other officers of the Anchor Line are accustomed to fog around the coasts of Scotland and Ireland and always keep a man on the lookout on the foc'sle head, as well as

Continued on Page 3.

STAYS IN AIR 21 HOURS.

Berlin Aviator's Feat Held to be a World's Record.

BERLIN, June 28.—Herr Landmann, an aviator, today concluded a non-stop flight of 21 hours 49 minutes.

It is asserted that this flight constitutes a world record.

Twenty-one hours would be almost enough to carry the seaplane America either to the coast of Ireland, or to the Azores. Plans for the forthcoming trans-Atlantic flight are based on the America's reaching the Azores in twenty hours.

DEWEY IN CANAL PARADE.

Will Be Invited to Make Trip Aboard His Old Flagship Olympia.

Special to The New York Times.

WASHINGTON, June 28.—Admiral George Dewey may take his old flagship, the Olympia, through the Panama Canal next March in the naval parade. Rear Admiral Clark, retired, has been ordered to take command of his old ship, the Oregon, for the occasion, and Secretary Daniels said this afternoon that he had decided to invite Admiral Dewey to take part. If the Admiral does not feel like making the journey via the canal, he may go overland to San Francisco and go aboard the Olympia upon the arrival of the pageant fleet there.

The President and Secretary Daniels will make addresses upon the arrival of the fleet at the exposition city. It is likely that Admiral Dewey and Admiral Clark also will speak. The entire brigade of midshipmen will be taken to San Francisco for the occasion. This will probably take the place of their annual cruise.

The Oregon and the Olympia will be moored at a specially constructed wharf and will be on exhibition throughout the entire exposition. Behind them will be anchored seven typical modern naval ships—a dreadnought of the New York or Oklahoma type, a battleship of the Connecticut or Minnesota type, an armored cruiser of the Tennessee or Montana type, one of the three scout cruisers, a destroyer, a submarine, and a collier, each of the latest build. In addition, the entire Atlantic Fleet will remain throughout nearly the whole of the exposition.

Neither Admiral Dewey nor Rear Admiral Clark has been aboard his ship since relinquishing their commands shortly after the close of the Spanish-American war.

A NEW GAME FOR BROADWAY.

But Auto Owners Hope Trundling Stolen Tires Won't Become Popular.

Harry E. Sullivan with his brother and two women rode up to Shanley's Restaurant, in West Forty-third Street, last evening in a limousine auto with a new white tire strapped like a life preserver to the back. Two men who had the appearance of chauffeurs came down the street after the owners of the auto entered the restaurant. With businesslike briskness they unbuckled the new white tire and trundled it down the street. The taxicab starter at Shanley's scratched his head. Then he spoke to Patrolman Louis Fick.

"They did it so natural," he explained, "that I didn't think to bother them."

The patrolman jumped into an auto and started in pursuit of the tire. By its tread-prints on the damp pavement he followed it down to Ninth Avenue, up to Forty-fourth Street, around the corner, and there the artful dodgers foiled him by rolling it into the street where its trail was lost in a maze of tire tracks. The tire was worth $75.

"If it's as easy as that," said Mr. Sullivan when he heard of his loss, "rolling rubber hoops in Broadway is apt to become a popular pastime. The first rule of the game is: 'A rolling tire must gather no moss.'"

SCORES BRYAN AND TREATY.

Francis B. Loomis Calls Colombian Agreement "Stupendous Blunder."

Special to The New York Times.

SAN FRANCISCO, June 28.—Bryan's proposed treaty between the United States and Colombia is vicious as to motives and purpose, says Francis B. Loomis, former Assistant Secretary of State. In a statement here tonight Mr. Loomis said:

"Bryan's Colombian treaty is a covert attempt to loot the United States Treasury by lobbyists and political brigands, into whose hands the Secretary of State is playing.

"Bryan and the President are trying to besmirch and discredit the achievement of the previous Administration, which made the canal a reality.

"The treaty is one of the most stupendous blunders made by Bryan, who is running wild with his 'world peace' theories. The United States owes Colombia nothing, either by treaty or otherwise.

"Mr. Bryan's contention that the people of Latin America feel aggrieved because we refuse to permit the Colombian troops to cross the Isthmus for the purpose of engaging in bloody encounters, and closing the lines of transit is not supported by ascertainable facts. The truth is the important Governments of South America such as Argentina, Brazil, and Chile care nothing about Colombia, and they deplore her misdeeds as much as we do."

STATE'S TOLL OF ACCIDENTS

Automobiles Killed Nearly Half as Many as Railroads in April.

Special to The New York Times.

ALBANY, June 28.—There were nearly half as many deaths in New York State from automobile accidents during April as there were from railroad accidents. This is shown in the vital statistics issued by the State Department of Health for April. The deaths resulting from railroad accidents numbered 58, from automobiles 25, from street cars 15, and other vehicles 20. Landslides killed 12 individuals, and 3 others died from injuries inflicted by animals. There were 128 suicides during the month and 35 homicides.

The other external causes of death ran the total up to 735 for the month.

$120,000 FOR SHACKLETON.

Sir James Caird's Gift for His Antarctic Expedition.

Special Cable to THE NEW YORK TIMES.

LONDON, June 28.—Sir James Key Caird, the millionaire jute manufacturer of Dundee, has given $120,000 toward the expenses of the Shackleton antarctic expedition.

Sir James made the gift after Sir Ernest Shackleton had personally explained to him the programme which he hoped to carry out.

Sir Ernest says the gift puts the expedition on a sound basis, and there is now no fear that it will not start well equipped.

FEDERALS DESERT AGUASCALIENTES

Town South of Zacatecas Evacuated by Huerta's Forces, but Villa Turns Back.

IS CAMPAIGN ABANDONED?

Border Hears His Ammunition Is Exhausted — Row with Carranza Will Not Down.

ENVOYS WAIT ON CARRANZA

Rebel Chief Said He Must Consult Generals—Reply Called Favorable.

ZACETAS, June 27, via El Paso, June 28.—Aguascalientes, capital of the States of the same name, has been evacuated by the Federals, according to information reaching Gen. Villa's headquarters today.

Owing to this, his plan of campaign has been changed, and the troops of the division are returning to Torreon.

Part of the division left last night. The rest will leave for the north today. Gen. Villa will follow his troops during the day. Last Wednesday it was announced that the Villa troops would be taken toward Aguas Calientes overland.

Late reports show that the losses of the Federals here were much greater than at first supposed. The number of prisoners taken by Villa's troops exceed 4,300. The number of killed was close to that figure.

The latest casualty report of the Constitutionalists was over 700 dead and 1,100 wounded, but these figures are not complete.

EL PASO, June 28.—Gen Villa's campaigns are apparently postponed indefinitely.

Lack of ammunition is given as the principal cause, but recent developments, still concealed in the Carranza-Villa estrangement, are believe by partisans of trangement, are believed by partisans of the quiet situation below this point.

The victory of Zacatecas, won by Villa last week, occasioned the expenditure of nearly all his ammunition during the four days of almost continuous fighting.

Since then Villa has not been able to replenish his supply from the United States on account of the strict embargo by United States troops along the frontier. It is said that he has not been assisted in this regard by Gen. Carranza, who could draw on the arsenals at Monterey and Saltillo.

He has only the little ammunition left after the fighting at Zacatecas and an unstated quantity captured from the Federals there.

Gen. Villa returned today to Torreon, according to telegrams from him dated from that place. Some matters connected with his relations with Carranza, it is stated, will be taken up by Villa as well as the obtaining of ammunition for his army.

The statements of Alfredo Breceda, one of Carranza's agents at Washngton, fell here today as oil on the fire.

Carranza and Villa adherents are now outspoken in their views of the recent estrangement, and regard Breceda's statements as an additional indication that discussion of the matter will not subside for some time. Breceda's remarks closely followed in effect those made a few days previously by Roberto Pesqueira, Constitutionalist confidential agent. The Villa men have remained silent.

CARRANZA-HUERTA DEAL?

Report of Peace Negotiations Comes from Mexico City.

VERA CRUZ, June 28.—Secret peace negotiations between Gen. Carranza and President Huerta have been in progress in the capital, according to Antonio Magnon, an American who arrived from Mexico City today. Mr. Magnon said it was positively known that representatives from Carranza had been in the capital for several days in conference with President Huerta, but that the details of the discussions had been kept secret.

It was thought in the capital that a peace agreement between Huerta and Carranza based upon Huerta resignation, was certain to come soon, Carranza having been forced to make some concessions because of his disagreements with Gen. Villa and Gen. Angeles.

It is reported in Mexico City that supporters of Villa and Carranza have been fighting near Monterey.

Mr. Magnon said also that President Huerta's volunteer forces at San Luis Potosi, including all the noted chieftains, such as Gen. Pasquale Orozco and Gen. Antonio Rojas, had refused to cooperate further with the regular army or to withdraw toward the capital, but would fight the Constitutionalists in that region. The volunteer leaders, most of whom are veterans of the three years' border warfare, and all frontiersmen, and, according to Mr. Magnon, say that the Federal recruits are hopeless as soldiers and only hamper the actions of the veteran volunteers.

Gen. Joaquin Maass, Federal commander at San Lois Potosi, went to the capital last Friday to confer with President Huerta, Mr. Magnon said, and was still there when Magnon left Saturday. Mr. Magnon said Gen. Maass, whom he had known for years, confirmed the reported action of the volunteers.

The Federals are fortifying Aguascalientes against a Constitutionalist advance, but it is understood in the capital that Gen. Villa plans to direct his next blow against Queretaro, cutting both the National and Central Railways and compelling the abandonment by the Federal forces of much territory in order to prevent themselves from being cut off from the capital.

Mr. Magnon said that he learned at Soledad that the Federals were gathering railway equipment for the narrow

Continued on Page 5.

Propose Pan-American Memorial to Columbus

A splendid tomb topped by a great light is proposed to be erected in Santo Domingo, in the Caribbean Sea, by subscriptions from peoples of all lands. See NEXT SUNDAY'S TIMES.

OUR GUNS FIRE ON SANTO DOMINGO

Few Shots from the Machias Stop Bombardment of Puerto Plata by President Bordas.

WARNED BY CAPT. RUSSELL

Told Not to Endanger Foreigners in Attack on Rebels There—Refugees Taken Off by Our Boats.

Special to The New York Times.

WASHINGTON, June 28.—Following general instructions from the Navy Department to protect the lives and property of Americans and foreigners in Santo Domingo, the little American gunboat Machias on Friday afternoon entered the inner harbor of Puerto Plata, and with a few shots from her main battery silenced a battery of President Bordas's forces that was bombarding the town.

The bombardment was in violation of emphatic orders from Capt. Russell, commanding the American squadron, that the attack on the city, which is in the hands of rebels, be conducted in such a way as not to imperil the lives of foreigners.

Capt. Russell is in personal command of the first line battleship South Carolina, that was detached from service at Vera Cruz when conditions in Santo Domingo became threatening. His dispatch to the department, which, like all dispatches from Santo Domingo, took two days to come, makes no mention of casualties. His dispatch follows:

PUERTO PLATA, June 26, 1914.

This afternoon, about 5:30, when the Bordas artillery ashore fired shells into the city of Puerto Plata, the Machias anchored in the inner harbor and with some shots from her main battery stopped the artillery fire into the city, after which there was no further firing. We have the situation well in hand, and no additional vessels, either United States or foreign, will be needed to prevent the bombardment of Puerto Plata. The prompt stopping of the artillery fire into the city this afternoon will have a very reassuring effect upon the Americans and other foreigners in the city, who have recently displayed great anxiety about their protection and safety.

At 8:30 P. M. Friday the revenue cutter Algonquin took on board forty-two persons for passage to San Juan, thirty-three being Porto Ricans and nine Americans, ten men, thirteen women, and nineteen children, and then steamed for San Juan. The Clyde Line steamer Seminole, from Norfolk en route to Santo Domingo City, arrived at 3 P. M. Friday, and after delivering mail took away from Puerto Plata four persons—one French, two Spanish, and one Chinaman. The Clyde Line steamer Algonquin, en route to New York, arrived at 7 P. M. Friday and took away from Puerto Plata twenty-four persons—five Americans, thirteen British, three French, and three Cubans. These passengers were put on board the three vessels named by the South Carolina boats. RUSSELL.

The Navy Department today was emphatic that Capt. Russell's summary enforcement of his orders indicated no change in policy, and that the silencing of President Bordas's battery did not mean that American intervention on a wider scale would be undertaken. The orders had been emphatic, and the attacking forces seemed to think they could be disregarded with impunity. The United States has never indicated its sympathies as to the contending forces, though as under the treaty it was responsible for the Custom House at Puerto Plata, its obligation in this instance was clearly not to encourage attack by the Government's troops.

The Machias is a gunboat of 1,177 tons, 204 feet in length, and with 32 feet beam. Her main battery consists of eight guns of about 4-inch calibre and four smaller guns. She was formerly used by the Naval Militia of Connecticut.

Secretary of the Navy Daniels said the other day that there was no intention to send more ships to the island, and Friday's incident is not thought to have changed his mind on that score.

$500,000 FIRE AT DOVER, N. J.

Incendiaries Destroy Richardson & Boynton Stove Plant.

DOVER, N. J., June 28.—All of the plant of the Richardson & Boynton Company, except the shipping department building, was destroyed by fire today. The firm manufactured stoves and ranges, and its plant, which was Dover's largest industry, covered thirty acres of ground. The loss is $500,000, partly covered by insurance. The works, which ordinarily employ 1,100 men, were shut down three weeks ago for repairs.

Charles Helfer, a night watchman, says he made the rounds of the works at 6:30 A. M. and found everything all right. At 7:30 o'clock he saw smoke coming from the trimming shop. Men who were in the street say they saw flames in three or four different places at the same time.

Dover's two steamers and an auto chemical engine and truck manned by the Volunteer Fire Department responded to the general alarm. All the buildings were frame except the shipping building, which is built of concrete. The water pressure was inadequate, and the flames spread rapidly to the casting and cleaning shop, the mounting, boiler, patent filing, drill and patternmakers' shops, each in a separate building. Three Lackawanna Railroad box cars in the yard near the shipping building were burned. All the finished stock on hand was in the shipping building. The firemen concentrated their efforts to save that building.

For an hour or two there was fear the flames might spread to the town. The firemen successfully defended the nearest buildings.

Incendiarism is suspected. Secretary and Treasurer W. L. R. Lynd, who is also Mayor of Dover, said he couldn't account for the fire. There was no fire in any building of the plant, and the engines had been cold since the shutdown. It is recalled that a threatening letter was sent to Mayor Lynd demanding he should prevent the delivery of the Slattery anti-Catholic lectures. He declined to interfere, and the lectures were delivered on May 15 and 16 last.

The plant will be rebuilt at once. At noon a gang of laborers was put to removing the débris. The company has offices in New York.

HEIR TO AUSTRIA'S THRONE IS SLAIN WITH HIS WIFE BY A BOSNIAN YOUTH TO AVENGE SEIZURE OF HIS COUNTRY

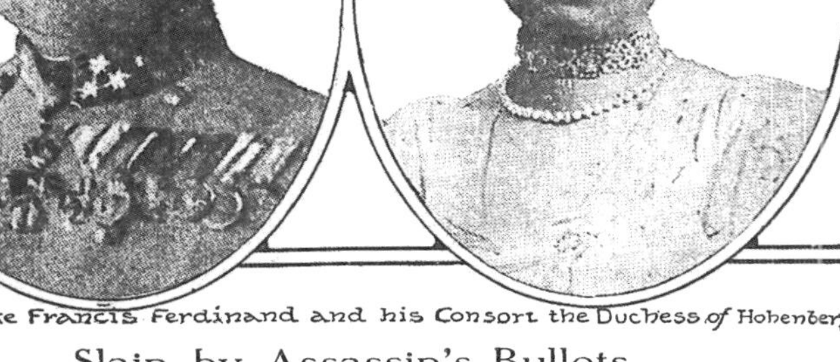

Archduke Francis Ferdinand and his Consort the Duchess of Hohenberg

Slain by Assassin's Bullets.

Francis Ferdinand Shot During State Visit to Sarajevo.

TWO ATTACKS IN A DAY

Archduke Saves His Life First Time by Knocking Aside a Bomb Hurled at Auto.

SLAIN IN SECOND ATTEMPT

Lad Dashes at Car as the Royal Couple Return from Town Hall and Kills Both of Them.

LAID TO A SERVIAN PLOT

Heir Warned Not to Go to Bosnia, Where Populace Met Him with Servian Flags.

AGED EMPEROR IS STRICKEN

Shock of Tragedy Prostrates Francis Joseph—Young Assassin Proud of His Crime.

Special Cable to THE NEW YORK TIMES.

SARAJEVO, Bosnia, June 28. (By courtesy of the Vienna Neue Freie Presse.)—Archduke Francis Ferdinand, heir to the throne of Austria-Hungary, and his wife, the Duchess of Hohenberg, were shot and killed by a Bosnian student here today. The fatal shooting was the second attempt upon the lives of the couple during the day, and is believed to have been the result of a political conspiracy.

This morning, as Archduke Francis Ferdinand and the Duchess were driving to a reception at the Town Hall a bomb was thrown at their motor car. The Archduke pushed it off with his arm.

The bomb did not explode until after the Archduke's car had passed on, and the occupants of the next car, Count von Boos-Waldeck and Col. Morizzi, the Archduke's aide de camp, were slightly injured. Among the spectators, six persons were more or less seriously hurt.

The author of the attempt at assassination was a compositor named Gabrinovics, who comes from Trebinje.

After the attempt upon his life the Archduke ordered his car to halt, and after he found out what had happened he drove to the Town Hall, where the Town Councillors, with the Mayor at their head, awaited him. The Mayor was about to begin his address of welcome, when the Archduke interrupted him angrily, saying:

"Herr Burgermeister, it is perfectly outrageous! We have come to Sarajevo on a visit and have had a bomb thrown at us."

The Archduke paused a moment, and then said: "Now you may go on."

Thereupon the Mayor delivered his address and the Archduke made a suitable reply.

The public by this time had heard of the bomb attempt, and burst into the hall with loud cries of "Zivio!" the Slav word for "hurrah."

After going around the Town Hall, which took half an hour, the Archduke started for the Garrison Hospital to visit Col. Morizzi, who had been taken there after the outrage.

As the Archduke reached the corner of Rudolf Street two pistol shots were fired in quick succession by an individual who called himself Gavrio Princip. The first shot struck the Duchess in the abdomen, while the second hit the Archduke in the neck and pierced the jugular vein. The Duchess became unconscious immediately and fell across the knees of her husband. The Archduke also lost consciousness in a few seconds.

The motor car in which they were seated drove straight to the Konak, where an army Surgeon rendered first aid, but in vain. Neither the Archduke nor the Duchess gave any sign of life, and the head of the hospital could only certify they were both dead.

The authors of both attacks upon the Archduke are born Bosnians. Gabrinovics is a compositor, and worked for a few weeks in the Government printing works at Belgrade. He returned to Sarajevo a Servian chauvinist, and made no concealment of his sympathies with the King of Servia. Both he and the actual murderer of the Archduke and the Duchess expressed themselves to the police in the most cynical fashion about their crimes.

ARCHDUKE IGNORED WARNING.

Servian Minister Feared Trouble if Heir Went to Bosnia.

Special Cable to THE NEW YORK TIMES.
[Dispatch to The London Daily Mail.]

VIENNA, June 28.—When the news of the assassination of the Archduke Francis Ferdinand and the Duchess was broken to the aged Emperor Francis Joseph he said: "Horrible, horrible! No sorrow is spared me."

The Emperor, who yesterday left here for Ischl, his favorite Summer resort, amid acclamations of the people, will return to Vienna at once, in spite of the hardships of the journey in the terrible heat.

The Archduke, who was created head of the army, went to Bosnia to represent the Emperor at the grand manoeuvres there. This was the first time the Archduke had paid an official visit to Bosnia. The Emperor visited the provinces immediately after their annexation, in 1908, and the manner in which he mixed freely with the people was much criticised at the time, as those in his party were always afraid lest some Slav or Mohammedan fanatic might attempt the monarch's life. The Emperor's popularity, however, saved him from all danger of this kind.

Before the Archduke went to Bosnia last Wednesday the Servian Minister here expressed doubt as to the wisdom of the journey, saying the country was in a very turbulent condition and the Servian part of the population, might organize a demonstration against the Archduke. The Minister said if the Archduke went himself he certainly ought to leave his wife at home, because Bosnia was no place for a woman in its present disturbed state.

The Minister's word proved correct. The people of Sarajevo welcomed the Archduke with a display of Servian flags, and the authorities had some difficulty in removing them before the Archduke made his state entry into the city yesterday, after the conclusion of the manoeuvres. In these manoeuvres were the famous Fifteenth and Sixteenth Army Corps, which were stationed on the frontier throughout the recent Balkan war, and they carried out the evolutions before the Archduke.

Greeted with Cheers.

The details of the tragedy, as received in Vienna, were as follows: The Archduke was driving in a motor car toward the Town Hall in Sarajevo, with the Duchess of Hohenberg by his side. A large crowd assembled to watch them go by. The Archduke, raising his hand to his military cap, acknowledged the cheers, while the Duchess was smiling and bowing, her pretty face framed by her blonde hair.

Suddenly the Archduke's sharp eye caught sight of a bomb hurling through the air. His first thought was for his wife, and he threw up his arm in time to catch the bomb, which thus was turned aside from its course and fell on the pavement and exploded. The Archduke's motor car hastened on its way, its occupants unharmed, but the two Adjutants who were seated in the next motor car were injured by splinters from the bomb. Several persons on the pavement were very seriously hurt by the explosion of the bomb, which was thrown by a young man named Tabrinovitch, (Gabrinovics,) who is a typist from Trebenje, in Herzegovina, and is of Servian nationality. He was arrested some twenty minutes later.

The Archduke and his wife left the Town Hall, intending to visit those who had been injured by the bomb, when a schoolboy 19 years old, named Prinzip, who came from Grahovo, fired a shot at the Archduke's head. The boy fired from the shelter of a projecting house.

Wore Bullet-Proof Coat.

The boy must have been carefully instructed in his part, for it was a well-guarded secret that the Archduke always wore a coat of silk strands which were woven obliquely, so that no weapon or bullet could pierce it. I once saw a strip of this fabric used for a motor-car tire, and it was puncture-proof. This new invention enabled the Archduke to brave attempts on his life, but his head naturally was uncovered.

The Duchess was shot in the body. The boy fired several times, but only two shots took effect. The Archduke and his wife were carried to the Konak, or palace, in a dying condition.

Later details show that the assassin darted forth from his hiding place behind a house and actually got on the motor car in which the Archduke and his wife were sitting. He took close aim first at the Archduke, and then at the Duchess. The fact that no one stopped him, and that he was allowed to perpetrate the dastardly act indicate that the conspiracy was carefully planned and that the Archduke fell a victim to a political plot. The aspiration of the Servian population in Bosnia to join with Servia and form a great Servian kingdom is well known. No doubt today's assassination was regarded as a means of forwarding this plan.

Break News to Children.

The Archduke's children are at Glumex, in Bohemia, and relatives already have left Vienna to break the news to them. The Duke of Cumberland motored to Ischl immediately upon receipt of the news and was received by the Emperor, who will arrive in Vienna at 6 o'clock tomorrow. The bodies of the Archduke and his wife will not be brought to Vienna until tomorrow a week.

The Archduke Charles Francis Joseph, the new heir to the throne, is at Reichenau, near Vienna, with his wife, Princess Zita of Parma, and their little son and daughter. He is expected in Vienna tonight.

When the first news of the assassination became known in Vienna, early this afternoon, crowds collected in solemn silence and discussed the report, which was not credited at first. Every one connected with the press was stormed by crowds asking whether confirmation had been received, and on hearing the truth they said, "How awful!" and then dispersed, to go about their ordinary business or pleasure. The newspapers are getting out extra editions, and the whole city talks of nothing else.

New Heir Popular.

The Archduke Charles Francis Joseph, who is now heir to the throne, always has enjoyed great popularity. He was trained for the throne from the first, although he was kept somewhat in the background, being sent to country garrisons. He was not allowed to undertake to act as the representative of the Duchy of Vienna to as great an extent as the Viennese would have wished. This, however, did not detract from his popularity, while the Princess Zita, his wife, won all hearts before she married the heir to the throne, and the birth of a son two years ago completed her popularity, if, indeed, anything was lacking.

General opinion here connects the assassins with the Servian faction, and it is feared that it will lead to serious complications with that unruly kingdom, and may have far-reaching results. The future of the empire is a subject of general discussion. It is felt that the Servians have been treated too leniently, and some hard words are being said about the present foreign policy.

All the public buildings are draped in long black streamers and the flags are all at half-mast.

BRAVERY OF ARCHDUKE.

Gave First Aid to Those Wounded by the Bomb.

SARAJEVO, Bosnia, June 28.—Archduke Francis Ferdinand, heir to the Austro-Hungarian throne, and the Duchess of Hohenberg, his morganatic wife, were shot dead in the main street of the Bosnian capital by a student today while they were making an apparently triumphant progress through the city on their annual visit to the annexed provinces of Bosnia and Herzegovina.

The Archduke was hit full in the face and the Duchess was shot through the abdomen and throat. Their wounds proved fatal within a few minutes after they reached the palace, whence they were hurried with all speed.

Those responsible for the assassination took care that it would prove effective, as there were two assailants, the first armed with a bomb and the other with a revolver. The bomb was thrown at the royal automobile as it was proceeding to the Town Hall, where a reception was to be held, but the Archduke saw the deadly missile coming and warded it off with his arm. It fell outside the car and exploded, slightly wounding two aids de camp in a second car, and half a dozen spectators. It was on the return of the procession that the tragedy was added to the long list of those that have darkened the pages of the recent history of the Hapsburgs.

As the royal automobile reached a prominent point in the route to the palace, an eighth grade student, Gavrio Prinzip, sprang out of the crowd and poured a fusillade of bullets from an automatic pistol at the Archduke and the Duchess. Both fell mortally wounded.

Prinzip and a fellow-conspirator, a compositor from Trebinje, Nedeljo Gabrinovics, barely escaped lynching by the infuriated spectators and were finally seized by the police, who afforded them protection. Both men are natives of the annexed province of Herzegovina.

Wards Off the Bomb.

The first attempt against the Archduke occurred just outside the Girls' High School. The Archduke's car had restarted after a brief pause for an inspection of the building, when Gabrinovics hurled the bomb. This was so successfully warded off by the Archduke that it fell directly beneath the following car, the occupants of which, Count von Boos-Waldeck and Col. Merizzo, were struck by splinters of iron.

Archduke Francis Ferdinand stopped his car, and after making inquiries as to the injuries of his aids and lending what aid he could, continued his journey to the Town Hall. There the Mayor began the customary address, but the Archduke sharply interrupted and snapped out, "Herr Burgomeister, we have come here to pay you a visit and bombs have been thrown at us. This is altogether an amazing indignity."

After a pause, the Archduke said: "Now you may speak."

On leaving the hall the Archduke and his wife announced their intention of visiting the wounded members of their suite at the hospital on their way back to the palace. They were actually bound on their mission of mercy when, at the corner of Rudolf Street and Franz Josef Street, Prinzip opened his deadly fusillade.

bullet struck the Archduke in the face. The Duchess was wounded in the abdomen and another bullet struck her in the throat, severing an artery. She fell unconscious across her husband's knees. At the same moment the Archduke sank to the floor of the car.

Plunges Into River.

After his unsuccessful attempt to blow up the imperial visitors Gabrinovics sprang into the River Miljachka in an effort to escape, but witnesses plunged after him and seized him.

A few yards from the scene of the shooting an unexploded bomb was found,

"All the News That's Fit to Print."

The New York Times.

THE WEATHER
Fair today; partly cloudy, warmer Thursday; moderate east to southeast winds.
☞For full weather report see Page 19.

VOL. LXIII...NO. 20,647. NEW YORK, WEDNESDAY, AUGUST 5, 1914.—TWENTY PAGES. ONE CENT In Greater New York, Jersey City and Newark. | Elsewhere TWO CENTS.

ENGLAND DECLARES WAR ON GERMANY; BRITISH SHIP SUNK; FRENCH SHIPS DEFEAT GERMAN, BELGIUM ATTACKED; 17,000,000 MEN ENGAGED IN GREAT WAR OF EIGHT NATIONS; GREAT ENGLISH AND GERMAN NAVIES ABOUT TO GRAPPLE; RIVAL WARSHIPS OFF THIS PORT AS LUSITANIA SAILS

Kaiser Hurls Two Armies Into Belgium After Declaring War.

LIEGE ATTACK REPULSED

German Guns Are Reported to be Bombarding Both That City and Namur.

BELGIANS RUSH TO ARMS

Parliament Acclaims King's Appeal and Votes $40,000,000 for National Defense.

FRENCH BORDER CLASHES

Stronger German Forces Crossing the Border Near Mars-la-Tour and Moineville.

RUSSIANS ATTACK MEMEL

Seacoast Town of Germany Defeats Attempt of Enemy to Capture It.

NEW YORK TIMES-London Chronicle Special Cable Dispatch.

BRUSSELS, Aug. 4.—The German Minister informed the Belgian Government at 6 o'clock this morning that its reply to Germany's request for leave to cross its territory was unsatisfactory and that a state of war existed between Germany and Belgium.

The news was given to the outside world by the Prime Minister at the opening of Parliament, and spread like wildfire through the streets, which were soon filled with crowds of excited people.

At the Ministry of War Count von Lichtenvalde said he had news that German forces were already on Belgian soil near Liege.

He also stated that in response to the telegram from the King of the Belgians King George had sent a eelegram saying that he would respect the independence, integrity, and neutrality of Belgium.

A scene of tremendous enthusiasm took place in the Chamber when the Premier invited the co-operation of all parties and announced that the King had appointed M. Vandervelde, the Labor leader, a member of the Ministry. The latter said that the workingmen of Belgium would defend their country when attacked with the same ardor with which they had defended their liberties in the past.

Le Peuple, the labor organ, says:

"Why do we, irreconcilable antimilitarists, applaud those who offer themselves in defense of their country? It is because it is necessary to protect our hearths, homes, and families, and our ancient freedom at the price of our blood.

"Go, sons and workers! Register as recruits. We prefer to die for progress and solidarity to living under a régime of brutal force and savage violence."

To night there is great excitement in the streets of the capital. All classes of the people are filled with grim determination to defend their country to the last.

The civil guard is protecting German citizens at the railway stations.

The speech made in the House of Commons by Sir Edward Grey has been received with enthusiasm by all classes of Belgians.

Liege Repulses German Attack.

By The Associated Press.

BRUSSELS, Wednesday, Aug. 5.—War has been begun by Germany upon Belgium. A formal declaration of hostilities against this country has been issued by the Kaiser's Government, and at least two columns of German troops have crossed the frontier.

Word reaches here that the cities of Liege and Namur are already being shelled by the invaders.

It is reported that following a demand by the Germans for the surrender of the City of Liege an engagement ensued, in which the Germans were repulsed. All Germans have been expelled from Liege and Namur.

This violation of Belgian neutrality followed the failure of a second German ultimatum to induce Belgium to permit the passage of the Kaiser's troops to the French border.

This ultimatum stated that Germany was prepared to carry through by force of arms, if necessary, any measures she considered essential. It was delivered by the German Minister in Brussels last Monday night, as the reply of Germany to the refusal of Belgium to accede to Germany's first ultimatum.

Germany further stated that if Belgium adopted a hostile attitude against the German troops and put difficulties in the way of their advance, Germany would be obliged to regard Belgium as her enemy. In that case, Germany would not enter into any undertaking with Belgium, but "would leave the final relations of the two States to the decision of arms."

Following this German troops crossed the frontier at Gemmenieh, near the junction of the Dutch, Belgian, and German frontiers.

Another report says that a German force invaded Belgium near Verviers, east of Liege.

King Albert presided yesterday over a joint session of the Senate and Chamber of Deputies, and in an address stated that never since 1830 had a graver situation confronted a neutral nation. He said it was imperative that every Belgian should do his duty and resign himself to every sacrifice that might be necessary to prevent the violation of Belgian soil.

The King went on:

"Our Fatherland is in danger. Let me make an appeal to you, my brothers. At this supreme hour the entire nation must be of one mind. I have called together the two houses of Parliament so that they may support the Government in declaring that we will maintain untarnished the sacred patriotism of our fathers. Long live independent Belgium!"

A scene of stirring enthusiasm followed. Deputies and Senators stood and shouted in chorus the closing words of King Albert's speech.

Premier de Broqueville then made a statement as to Germany's ultimatum to Belgium and the reply of Belgium, stating that the Government would not sacrifice the country's honor, and that the nation would resist by every means in its power all encroachments on its rights. He added:

"The word is, therefore, To arms! In this land of ours we shall not weaken, and even if we are conquered we never shall submit. Belgium, supported by the united energy of her sons, will not perish."

Another prolonged patriotic demonstration followed, the Queen and her children, who were present, being loudly cheered.

The Chamber afterward passed a bill appropriating $40,000,000 for purposes of defense.

M. Vandervelde, the Socialist leader, has joined the Belgian Cabinet, so that all political parties may be represented in the Government.

A special train, carrying all the securities of the National Bank of Belgium, left for Antwerp during Monday night.

Queen Elizabeth and Princess Marie also left Brussels yesterday for Antwerp.

The newspaper Chronique announces that the authorities have seized the wireless installation set up by the German School here.

Over 17,000,000 Fighting Men of Eight Nations Now Engaged in the Colossal European War

DUAL ALLIANCE.

	Regular Army.	Reserves.	Total War Strength.
Germany	870,000	4,430,000	5,300,000
Austria-Hungary	390,000	1,610,000	2,000,000
Total	1,260,000	6,040,000	7,300,000

TRIPLE ENTENTE AND ITS ALLIES.

	Regular Army.	Reserves.	Total War Strength.
Russia	1,290,000	3,300,000	4,590,000
France	720,000	3,280,000	4,000,000
England	254,500	476,500	731,000
Belgium	42,000	180,000	222,000
Servia	32,000	208,000	240,000
Montenegro	50,000	......	50,000
Total	2,388,500	7,444,500	9,833,000
Grand Total			17,133,000

The above figures do not include the naval forces of the nations.

MORE INVADERS IN FRANCE.

German Activity Increases, but Only Outposts Are Engaged.

PARIS, Aug. 4.—Increased aggressiveness is being shown by German forces on the eastern frontier.

One body of troops today crossed into French territory near Mars-la-Tour, where one of the most important battles of the Franco-Prussian war was fought on Aug. 16, 1870.

Another German detachment entered the village of Moineville, in the Department of Muerthe et Moselle. A parish priest was killed.

Other detachments visited outlying farms at Lepuix, near Belfort, and requisitioned cattle. Several Germans were taken prisoners and brought into Belfort.

German troops today cut the telephone and telegraph wires on French territory along the border.

No engagement in force was reported, but the French outposts have been harried since last night by numerous raids of the enemy. The French, however, refused to be drawn beyond the six-mile zone left unoccupied along the frontier.

A German army aeroplane last evening dropped three bombs on the French fortified town of Luneville, southeast of Nancy. Some damage was caused, but there were no casualties.

A squadron of the Eleventh Dragoons, stationed in Belfort, rendered funeral honors today at Joncherey to a German Lieutenant, the first victim of the actual conflict between France and Germany.

The Temps publishes a résumé of the incidents on the frontier. It says several German reconnoitring parties crossed the frontier to ascertain the strength of the French covering troops. It is assumed by the military authorities here that the Germans would have made a sudden attack in great force on Nancy if the French troops in the vicinity had been found in minor strength.

Several parties of Germans entered the zone to round up the cattle. These were not interfered with, but when a squadron of German cavalry crossed the line near Belfort, a squadron of French cavalry was sent out and the German troops retired.

The first town entered by the Germans was Longlaville, near Longwy. Later they invaded Cirey-sur-Vezouze.

RUSSIANS ATTACK MEMEL.

Garrison at German Seaport Town Beat Off Their Assailants.

BERLIN, Aug. 4.—A body of Russian frontier guards from Krottingen was driven back yesterday by a part of the garrison of the German seaport of Memel, the most northerly town in German territory.

SERBS WHIP 10,000 AUSTRIANS.

Heavy Loss by the Invaders at Semendria Reported.

PARIS, Aug. 4.—A dispatch from Nish, Servia, to the Matin says the Austrian troops were defeated with heavy loss in a battle with the Servians on Sunday near Semendria.

Three regiments of Austrian infantry, comprising nearly 10,000 men, supported by heavy artillery, advanced against the Servians, but were repulsed, leaving many of their number dead and wounded on the field.

A large force of Austrian troops, aided by a flotilla of monitors, composed of twenty vessels, has been trying for six days to cross the River Save into Servian territory, but has not succeeded in landing.

LONDON, Aug. 4.—Servian mobilization has been completed, according to a Nish dispatch to the Exchange Telegraph Company. Ninety-five per cent. of those liable for active service have responded to the call.

The Servian Government has prohibited the sending of press dispatches, which is taken as a prelude to an invasion of Bosnia.

Cunarder Slips Out; Will Pick Up British Cruisers as Escorts.

GERMAN WARSHIPS NEAR

Liner to Head for Newfoundland, Where Other English Ships Will Meet Her.

FRENCH CRUISERS OUTSIDE

Wireless Code Messages from Telefunken Station at Sayville Aid German Cruisers.

TO BE SENT TO WASHINGTON

The Dresden Reported Off Cape Cod in an Attempt to Cut French Cable.

OUR DESTROYERS PUT OUT

Liner Olympic Sails In Under Convoy of Cruiser Essex—German Warships Outclassed.

Cruisers Off the Coast

French.—Cruisers Conde and Descartes.
British.—Cruisers Berwick, Essex, and Lancaster.
German.—Cruisers Dresden, Strassburg, and Karlsruhe.

As the Cunard liner Lusitania left this port for Liverpool at 1 o'clock this morning, she was picked up outside Sandy Hook by the British cruiser Essex, which had just convoyed the White Star liner Olympic to the end of its transatlantic journey past three German cruisers off this coast and almost into New York Harbor.

The Lusitania was due to leave its pier at 12 o'clock. It was expected at that time that a wireless message would be received from either the Berwick, Lancaster, or Essex, the three British cruisers now off the Atlantic Coast, that one or all of them would escort the Lusitania on its trip across the Atlantic.

Word that the Lusitania could leave port safely had not come through the air at 12 o'clock. Capt. Dow had not yet received the word to cast off. It was believed by the crowd at the pier that at the last minute it had been decided that the danger was too great, and that the sailing was to be postponed.

A few minutes before 1 o'clock Chief Officer Johnson, who had been sent to the British Consulate, returned in an automobile to the pier and hurried on board the Lusitania.

Captain Orders Lights Out.

A few minutes later Capt. Dow gave the order, "All lights out." Those at the pier heard the order repeated again and again from one end of the boat to the other, and then, practically dark, the big ship glided out into the river.

It was not known to be a certainty that the Lusitania would have the convoy of the Essex until after the Olympic arrived.

The Lusitania has on board 100 passengers in the first cabin, 30 in the second, and 50 in the third, and carried 2,200 sacks of mail. All passengers were notified that lights in the staterooms must be blanketed when the vessel passed Ambrose Channel, and in the passageways of the ship oil lamps were to replace the customary electric lighting. The ship is to make the trip with no lights showing except the running lights at the masthead and on the sides. Passengers were allowed on deck, but warned that no lights must be shown.

Among the prominent passengers is William P. T. Hollingsworth, member of the American Chamber of Commerce in France. He is going abroad for his wife, five daughters, and one son, who are at a watering place on the northern coast of Normandy. G. Menier, the chocolate manufacturer, who owns the Island of Anticosti in the Gulf of St. Lawrence, is also returning for his family, who are at the same watering place.

Alice Gutterman, daughter of Mrs. Simon Stern, widow of the dry goods merchant, is going abroad to seek her mother, who is in the north of Italy. Lieut. C. E. Lockhart, R. N., is going back to England to join the navy, under orders. J. J. Cawthra of Toronto, Jaquin Bonilla, Consul General of

Continued on Page 5

GERMAN FLEET SINKS A BRITISH MINE LAYER

Scoutship Pathfinder Is Chased By the Kaiser's Warships But Makes Its Escape.

LONDON, Aug. 4.—A British mine-laying ship has been sunk by a German fleet.

The British scoutship Pathfinder was pursued by the fleet, but managed to make her escape.

There are seven mine-layers in the British Navy—the Intrepid, Andromache, Latona, Thetis, Iphigema, Apollo, and Naiad, all of 3,400 to 3,600 tons. Only the Intrepid and Naiad carry any guns.

BATTLE IN THE NORTH SEA?

London Paper Reports One Going On, Says Wounded Are Landed.

Special Dispatch to The Central News of America.

LONDON, Aug. 4.—A special of The Star, published at 11 P. M., asserts that a naval battle has been going on some hours off the north of Scotland and that several wounded marines and seamen have been landed at Cromarty.

TWO GERMAN WARSHIPS TAKEN, ANOTHER SUNK

French Fleet in the Mediterranean Reported to Have Won a Victory.

PARIS, Aug. 4.—An unofficial report from Algiers says that a French fleet has captured two German cruisers, the Goeben and the Breslau.

A Havas dispatch from Algiers says that it is reported there that French warships have sunk the German cruiser Panther.

A previous report from the Governor of Algeria, in a telegram to the French Government, said that the German cruiser Breslau fired eight broadsides (about sixty shells) into the French fortified town of Bona this morning.

One man was killed and some buildings were damaged.

The German gunboat Panther, which is reported to have been sunk by French cruisers, was one of the smallest vessels in the Kaiser's navy, but also one of the most renowned, for it happened that four times she was the storm centre of various incidents of international politics. It was the Panther that blew the Haitian gunboat Crete-à-Pierrot out of the water in Bnaives Bay in 1902.

In the fall of 1905, when she was still stationed in South American waters, her commander sent a detail of sailors ashore at Itajahy, Brazil, to seize a deserter. This action was disavowed by the German Government and the vessel's commander reprimanded.

Thought the Breslau Had Escaped.

LONDON, Aug. 4.—The Breslau bombarded Bona at 4 o'clock this morning, and afterward steamed off at full speed in a westerly direction, according to a dispatch received at the French Embassy.

BORDEAUX, Aug. 4.—Two German steamers in this port have been seized.

CONSPIRACY SCARE ON THE VATERLAND

Tale of Plot to Blow Her Up Brings Launches With Searchlights, and 50 Policemen.

Fifty policemen and detectives, eight scout launches with searchlights, and a great number of the dock employes were on guard last night at the piers of the Hamburg-American Line after Chief of Police Hayes of Hoboken was informed by Pier Supt. Bode that there was a plot to blow up the Vaterland.

Bode went to Chief Hayes at 7 o'clock and said that a man had told him of overhearing the plot being hatched in a resort in River Street. The man, whose name Bode refused to tell, gave the names and addresses of the men in the plot.

Chief Hayes rushed a detachment of men to the piers. The Burns Detective Agency, also notified by Bode, sent men who were stationed on the Vaterland and the piers. Swift motor launches with searchlights were sent for, and within an hour the river was being patroled for several hundred yards either way from the piers. The three great searchlights of the Vaterland were brought into play, and every craft that approached was watched closely. The men on guard were relieved at midnight by another force. Supt. Bode was alarmed and spent the night at the piers.

Chief Hayes sent detectives to find the alleged plotters, and said he expected to arrest them by noon today. He said that he was fearful of international complications if the Vaterland were damaged or destroyed while in dock at Hoboken.

The piers of the North German Lloyd were also under strict guard last night and no one could approach them unless he could give an account of himself that was satisfactory to the men on watch.

British Declaration of War With Germany, Following Rejection of Her Demand

LONDON, Aug. 4.—Great Britain declared war on Germany at 7 o'clock tonight.

An earlier announcement that Germany had declared war on Great Britain was due to an error in the Admiralty's statement.

The Foreign Office's Statement.

The British Foreign Office has issued the following statement:

"Owing to the summary rejection by the German Government of the request made by his Britannic Majesty's Government that the neutrality of Belgium should be respected, his Majesty's Ambassador at Berlin has received his passports and his Majesty's Government has declared to the German Government that a state of war exists between Great Britain and Germany from 11 o'clock P. M., Aug. 4."

Declaration Announced to Germany.

BERLIN, Aug. 4.—Shortly after 7 o'clock this evening William Edward Goschen, the British Ambassador, went to the Foreign Office and announced that Great Britain had declared war with Germany. He then demanded his passports.

England Calls All Unmarried Men From 18 to 30 To Serve King and Country in This Hour of Need

LONDON, Wednesday, Aug. 5.—A War Office advertisement appears in the morning papers headed: "Your King and Country Need You."

The advertisement says that the empire is on the brink of the greatest war in the history of the world, and appeals to all unmarried men between the ages of 18 and 30 years to join the army immediately.

State of War Exists, Says Britain, as Kaiser Rejects Ultimatum.

MUST DEFEND BELGIUM

King George Issues Call to Arms and Thanks the Colonies for Their Support.

ENVOY LEAVES BERLIN

British Foreign Office Makes Final Announcement One Hour Before Time Limit.

VOTE $525,000,000 FUND

England Takes All Foreign Warships Building in Her Ports—Two from Turkey.

JAPAN TO AID ENGLAND

To Smash the Kiel Canal Probably English Fleet's First Attempt Against Germany.

Special Cable to THE NEW YORK TIMES.

LONDON, Wednesday, Aug. 5.—War is on between England and Germany. An ultimatum to the German Government that the neutrality of Belgium must be respected was rejected by the Kaiser's Government and the British Foreign Office announced last night that a state of war existed.

The time limit for Germany's reply was set at midnight, but the Foreign Office announced that as Germany had given his passports to the British envoy at an earlier hour, the state of war existed from 11 o'clock.

King George has issued his proclamation mobilizing the army and has sent a message to the colonies thanking them for their hearty support in the hour of national emergency.

The Government has assumed control of all the railways and the Admiralty has taken over all the foreign warships now building in English ports.

The House of Commons has voted a fund of $525,000,000 for the emergency.

England Cool in Great Crisis.

England is facing this, the greatest crisis in her history, with calmness and courage. Sir Edward Grey's exposition has made it clear that the war is none of her seeking, and that she goes into it because her honor and her self-preservation alike compel her to do so. There is neither any sign of panic nor flame of war fever. All parties and all classes present a united front. The few exceptions are not worthy of mention. The protests that the Labor members of Parliament and a few Liberals have made in the House of Commons do not represent the prevalent feeling either in the ranks of labor or among the avowed pacificists. The peace-at-any-price advocates are submerged beneath the huge majority who would have welcomed peace with honor but prefer war to dishonor.

Liberal newspapers like The Westminster Gazette, The Daily Chronicle, and even The Daily News accept the situation as inevitable.

"'Here we stand, and we can do no other.' The Germans will recognize that famous phrase," says The Westminster Gazette, "and understand that it expresses the feelings of the vast majority of the British people."

The demeanor of the crowds last evening and this morning began to betray growing excitement. A procession of a thousand young men marched along by Whitehall and up the Strand, cheering. It was headed by a squad carrying the Union Jack of England and the tricolor of France. As it passed Trafalgar Square there was some booing, but the cheering outweighed it. Fleet Street last evening was jammed by crowds watching the bulletins. Occasionally they sang "The Marseillaise" and "God Save the King."

Soon after the announcement of Germany's declaration of war against Belgium was displayed on the bulletin boards the crowds, evidently believing no greater news was likely to come, quietly dispersed, and by 11 o'clock Fleet Street was as quiet as usual.

Would Smash Kiel Canal.

Premier Asquith's statement in the House of Commons yesterday that the German Government had been asked to give satisfactory assurances on the question of Belgium's neutrality by midnight was generally regarded as meaning that England was prepared to strike at once if the reply was unfavorable.

The German fleet is concentrated for the defense of the Kiel Canal. Its destruction will be the first object of the Briaish fleet.

Germany's compliance with the British ultimatum was not expected. Germany, according to a statement emanating from her London embassy, would have consented to refrain from using Belgian ports and would have confined her violation of neutrality to the inland districts if Great Britain would agree to hold aloof. It is obvious that a compact on such lines would have been useless to Great Britain. Belgian neutrality is strategically important in two ways—by sea to Great Britain and Germany and by land to Germany and France. If England abandoned it in its land aspect, nobody, not even the Belgians, would have been willing to defend it when it was threatened in its sea aspect.

It seemed unlikely from the start that Germany would desist, because it was a matter affecting the military plans of her General Staff. The whole German theory of war is to make plans years ahead and have everything, down to the last railway siding, ready for their execution and to carry them out without deviation. It is probable that the present plan was made as long ago as when Anglo-German hostility was an axiom, and there was no question in German minds of so shaping their strategy as to keep Great Britain neutral.

German Ships in Peril.

As was anticipated, Germany's first naval effort was to deal a heavy blow to the Russians in the Baltic, but as yet there is insufficient evidence that it succeeded or that the Russian fleet was rendered powerless. Germany's most urgent need, according to experts, is to assemble all her available naval forces on the west, principally in the North Sea, but, these experts say, the Germans are not likely to seek battle, hoping the strength of their adversaries may be reduced by the action of mines and torpedoes.

Two German cruisers seem to be in peril. The battle cruiser Goeben, on the way from the Mediterranean, is reported to have passed Gibraltar, steaming westward. She will not venture through the English Channel, and must travel homeward via the west coast of Ireland and north of Scotland. An attempt certainly will be made to intercept her, and the need of carrying assistance to her may bring about a fleet action. The German cruiser Breslau is reported to have shelled Bona before proceeding westward toward Gibraltar. Her position seems perilous in the extreme.

Control of Railway Lines.

The Government took over the railways to complete the co-ordination of the railway facilities, in view of the military and naval requirements and the needs of the civil communities. The staff of each railway remains as before. Supreme control is vested in a committee composed of the General Managers of the chief railways.

The Acting Chairman is H. A. Walker, manager of the London & Southwestern, who is well known among American railway men. The committee was formed some days ago. The Great Eastern is not represented, possibly because its General Manager, H. W. Thornton, is an American.

News Flashed to Navy.

When the announcement of the state of war was made by the Foreign Office, and the quietness of the Summer night was suddenly broken by the raucous cries of the news venders, the streets were practically empty. The ordinary troops of theatregoers were conspicuous for their absence.

Midnight was considered the fateful hour when orders would be flashed by wireless to the British Navy to begin operations.

Reports which had spread during the evening that German warships had sunk a British mine finder and chased the destroyer Pathfinder, were taken as another instance of Germany's method of taking an unfair advantage and acting before war actually was declared.

Sir John Jellicoe, who has been long regarded as predestined to head the fleet in case of war, has taken supreme command, with Rear Admiral Madden as Chief of Staff. Sir John Jellicoe, who is familiarly known as "J. J.," is a typical, keen-faced officer, distinguished for his personal courage as well as for scientific gunnery. He has the German decoration of the Red Eagle. Lord Kitchener is taking the Administrative part of the work of the War Office, where Lord Haldane is assisting Mr. Asquith.

The only panicky note which struck the English press hard came from The Evening News, which came out in a poster headed "Treachery" and stating that Lord Haldane's German sympathies made his apointment to the War Office a matter of suspicion to France. THE NEW YORK TIMES correspondent saw Lord Haldane at Whitehall yesterday afternoon walking toward Westminster. When accosted he said there was nothing he could say.

Lord Haldane did yeoman service when at the War Office, and a Liberal paper says the worst news Germany could receive is that he has returned to the department.

England's war with Germany is likely to be purely a naval conflict for the time being. Germany will keep her fleet sheltered at Wilhelmshaven and trust to her submarines and torpedo boats to reduce the strength of the British investing fleet. The reported sinking of a minelayer probably is due to this. The feature of the Anglo-German war will be the strewing of the North Sea with floating mines.

Asquith's Impressive Speech.

The first chapter of the critical events of the day was unfolded when Premier Asquith read his statement in the House of Commons. The Premier read in a firm and measured voice, and his hand shook as he held the typewritten copy. His words were

"All the News That's Fit to Print."

The New York Times.

THE WEATHER
Fair today and tomorrow; slowly rising temperature; light to moderate variable winds.
For full weather report see Page 14.

VOL. LXIV...NO. 20,900. .... NEW YORK, THURSDAY, APRIL 15, 1915.—TWENTY-TWO PAGES. ONE CENT In Greater New York, Jersey City and Newark. { Elsewher TWO CENT

PLOTZ DISCOVERS TYPHUS VACCINE

Physician Not Yet 25, Who Isolated the Bacillus, Achieves a New Triumph.

DR. ZINSSER IS INOCULATED

Member of Rockefeller Expedition Takes Prophylactic Before Going to Serbia.

ACCLAIMED BY COLLEAGUES

Young Bacteriologist Congratulated by Members of the New York Pathological Society.

Dr. Harry Plotz, the young bacteriologist of Mount Sinai Hospital, who discovered the bacillus of typhus fever last year, but was not permitted to announce his discovery before a body of physicians because the news had appeared in THE NEW YORK TIMES before it was communicated to them, was acclaimed last night as a distinguished scientific investigator by 250 members of the New York Pathological Society and visiting physicians who gathered at the Academy of Medicine to listen to Dr. Plotz and his co-workers relate the results of their experiments.

Not only was the discovery of the causative agent of the disease fully confirmed by proofs of the highest scientific character, and accepted as final by men who are considered among the foremost laboratory investigators in the world, but the announcement was made that Dr. Plotz had continued his experiments to such a length that he had discovered an antityphus vaccine, in other words, a protective agent against the disease.

Dr. Zinsser Inoculated.

As conclusive proof of the acceptance of the vaccine as a prophylactic agent, it was further stated, to the amazement of a large number of the physicians present, that Dr. Hans Zinsser, the eminent bacteriologist who holds the professorship of bacteriology of the College of Physicians and Surgeons of Columbia University, who is also President of the New York Pathological Society, and who is now on his way to Serbia as a member of the Rockefeller expedition to take up the fight against typhus, had been inoculated with the protective vaccine prior to his departure. Other members of the Rockefeller expedition were inoculated also at their request.

While the pathologists and bacteriologists of Mount Sinai recommend the use of the vaccine, they do not guarantee its efficacy, as the studies relating to it are still in progress and may not be completed for a long time.

Dr. Plotz, who is not yet 25 years old, was curious while a medical sudent as to the origin of a fever called Brill's disease, which was supposed to be related to typhus fever. He entered the Pathological Laboratory of Mount Sinai Hospital as an interne for the sole purpose of solving the mystery, and he found the germ of Brill's disease at the first attempt. There he isolated the germ of true epidemic typhus fever. He compared the two and found them to the same.

Brill's Disease and Typhus.

In other words, Brill's disease and typhus fever are the same ailment, differing only in their virulence and the resulting mortality.

Dr. Plotz's discovery is now conceded to be one of the most important contributions made to medical science in America. Among those who congratulated the young physician and acknowledged that he had confirmed the claim of his preliminary report were Dr. Hideyo Noguchi and Dr. Samuel J. Meltzer, the distinguished investigators of the Rockefeller Institute for Medical Research; Dr. Nathan E. Brill, the discoverer of Brill's disease; Dr. William Hallock Park, chief of the bacteriological department of the Board of Health of this city; Dr. F. S. Mandelbaum, and Dr. E. Libman of the pathological department of Mount Sinai Hospital.

Dr. Plotz himself had the satisfaction of announcing that a world-famous physician, Dr. William H. Welch, head of the Medical Department of Johns Hopkins University, had done himself the honor of christening the newly acknowledged germ; its name is bacillus typhii exanthematus, but it is far from being as big as its designation would seem to indicate, since it is only microscopic in size.

Three papers were read at the meeting, all relating to the typhus experiments at Mount Sinai. They were read by Dr. Plotz himself and two of his coworkers, Dr. Peter K. Olitzky and Dr. George Baehr. Dr. Plotz's paper dealt with the bacteriological studies, Dr. Olitzky's with the serological aspects of the investigation, and the third, which was read by Dr. Baehr, but which was prepared by the three physicians, was a description of the experiments themselves.

Controversy of Physicians.

Dr. Plotz, then a medical student at the College of Physicians and Surgeons, apparently began to inquire into the cause of Brill's disease about the time that Dr. Brill was engaged in rather a warm discussion (which was conducted in various medical publications) with two well-known members of the United States Public Health Service, Dr. Anderson and Dr. Goldberger, concerning the nature of the disease. The Federal doctors believed Brill's disease was typhus. Dr. Brill maintained that they hadn't proved it.

As soon as Dr. Plotz went to work in the Mount Sinai laboratories he set about his typhus work, and, in all, examined the blood of about forty patients suffering from Brill's disease. He isolated a bacillus. About this time, as a result of the wars in the Balkans, several cases of European epidemic typhus arrived at this port and were taken to the isolation hospitals in the lower bay. Dr Joseph O'Connell, Health Officer of the Port, permitted Dr. Plotz to get

Continued on Page 3.

15 DEAD; 20 INJURED IN DETROIT COLLISION

Freight Cars Run Into a Trolley Crowded with Laborers on Their Way Home.

DETROIT, April 14.—Fifteen persons were killed and about twenty were injured late today in a collision between a Detroit City street car and a string of freight cars pushed by a switch engine on the Detroit, Toledo & Ironton Railroad. Most of the dead are foreigners whose homes were beyond the western limits of the city Four of them are women. The street car was heavily loaded with passengers homeward bound from their day's work.

As the car approached the railroad crossing it stopped and the conductor ran ahead to see if the track was clear. He signaled the motorman to wait, but apparently the latter, who is said to have been inexperienced, misunderstood his meaning. He applied the power and the car ran rapidly down an incline and onto the railroad tracks.

The freight cars struck the trolley fairly in the middle, smashing it almost to bits. The wreckage was pushed along 100 feet, several of the dead and injured dropping along the street before the train was brought to a standstill. Others were crushed in the splintered mass of steel and wood and it was several hours before they could be extricated and their exact number known.

Many private automobiles rushed to the scene of the accident and these, together with the ambulances which responded to the call for help, carried the injured to the hospitals.

EGG NEGRO SCENES IN LIBERTY FILM PLAY

Police Quell Disturbers at "Birth of a Nation," and Arrest Indignant Southerner.

A mixed crowd of white men and negroes who had obtained seats in the front row of the gallery started a demonstration against the film play, "The Birth of a Nation," at the Liberty Theatre at 10:30 o clock last night.

Policemen, ushers and private detectives who had been stationed at convenient intervals in anticipation of a demonstration swarmed down upon the noise makers and seized two of the leaders. As they did so two eggs splattered over the screen, blotting out portions of a picture showing a white Southern girl in the act of leaping off a cliff to escape from a negro pursuer.

A white man, who gave the name of Howard Schaeffle, was hurried from the theatre after private detectives had asserted it was he who threw the eggs. He cried out, "Rotten, rotten" as the detectives pushed him down the stairs toward the street. He was taken to the West Thirty-seventh Street station on a charge of disorderly conduct.

A negro who walked with a slight limp followed the white man out with the help of detectives. He protested loudly that "that play's a libel on a race. It's got to be stopped."

A negro arose some minutes after the main party had left.

"On the anniversary of Lincoln's assassination," he shouted, "it is inappropriate to present a play that libels 10,000,000 loyal American negroes. I think President Lincoln wouldn't like this play. The negro, who said his name was Cleveland G Allen and that he was the head of a colored news agency, was ushered to the street.

At the West Thirty-seventh Street Station Schaeffle was searched and a paper bag containing three eggs was found in his overcoat pocket.

"I was taking the eggs home for breakfast," he said, "and I stopped in to see this play. I am a Southerner and a libertarian, and I believe in the education and the uplifting of the negro. It made my blood boil to see the play and I threw the eggs at the screen. The play will have to be removed from the boards."

Schaeffle said he was born in Maryland. A negro lawyer, escorted by a delegation of negroes who had not been in the theatre, appeared at the station to take charge of Schaeffle's case.

The management of the theatre pointed out this scene as a refutation of the charge that the play was meant to libel the negroes, or show them in an especially bad light. The management insisted that most of the applause during the progress of the play was for scenes showing negroes performing heroic acts.

10 MEN IN CENTRAL HOLD UP

Stop Freight Train Near Buffalo, Load Auto Trucks and Escape.

BUFFALO, Thursday, April 15.—Ten masked and armed men held up a New York Central freight train at Sanborn, about fifteen miles from Buffalo, at 2 o'clock this morning, uncoupled and looted the cars. Ten automobile trucks were filled with the stolen goods.

Engineer Goss of Syracuse escaped from the robbers and ran his engine eight miles to Suspension Bridge for help. The robbers had disappeared when a posse arrived on the scene.

MRS. ROOSEVELT IN HOSPITAL

Wife of ex-President to be Operated Upon Today.

Mrs. Theodore Roosevelt was brought to the Roosevelt Hospital by Colonel Roosevelt late last night where she became a patient.

While no information could be obtained at the hospital beyond the admission that the wife of the former President was there, it was understood that she would be operated upon today. She had been ill at her home in Oyster Bay, and was brought in when her physicians decided that an operation was necessary.

Colonel Roosevelt remained with her at the hospital for some hours and then left for home. The nature of her ailment could not be ascertained and it is not known what physicians are attending her.

$72,908 TO FIGHT CANCER.

Large Gifts Announced to Harvard Medical School.

BOSTON, April 14.—Gifts amounting to $72,908, to be devoted to cancer research at the Harvard Medical School, were announced at a meeting of the Harvard Overseers today.

Of this sum $50,000 was provided by the will of Philip C. Lockwood of this city.

VILLISTAS SURROUND BIG CARRANZA ARMY

State Department Advices Say That Obregon's Retreat Is Cut Off in Celaya Battle.

MORE SHOTS CROSS BORDER

American Aviators Ordered to Brownsville to Patrol River While Siege Goes On.

Special to The New York Times.

WASHINGTON, April 14.—In the clash of the large armies representing the Villa and Carranza factions, General Villa seems to have succeeded in surrounding the force of General Obregon near Celaya, in Central Mexico. The progress of this battle, which is of first importance in the present military contest, was thus summed up by the State Department:

"The department is in receipt of advices, dated April 13, from San Luis Potosi, stating that heavy fighting around Celaya favors the Villa forces, which have surrounded Obregon and two of his subordinate commanders. The lines extend from Celaya through Queretaro to La Griega. It is estimated that 45,000 troops are engaged. Obregon's retreat is said to be cut off at La Griega by Generals de Las and Argumedo.

"The San Luis Potosi district is quiet and in undisputed Villa control. Trains are in operation from San Luis Potosi to Aguascalientes, east of San Luis Potosi, to Las Palmas and south to San Felipe. Trains also arrived occasionally from Saltillo."

Success in this battle has been claimed by both factions, and officials have been puzzled by the conflicting reports. Carranza was first to claim "a great victory," but this action was characterized the next day by General Villa as a mere skirmish, and he announced that everything favored the final success of his army.

A victory for the Villa forces here would open the railway and telegraph lines from the American border to the City of Mexico by removing Obregon, who now holds Queretaro, where the two main lines of railway from the north meet. A victory for Obregon would divide Villa and the northern armies from the Zapata forces which hold the capital.

The battle line, according to the State Department account, extends east and west, from Celaya through Queretaro to La Griega, a distance of about thirty miles.

Danger at Tuxpam.

The situation around Tampico and Tuxpam is causing great concern to officials of this and other Governments. Admiral Caperton, who hurried to Tampico from Vera Cruz several days ago to protect American and foreign interests, today made a report by radio on the situation around Tuxpam and was instructed to afford full protection to American and foreign interests at that point.

There are a number of foreigners and Americans that wish to leave Tuxpam and Admiral Caperton will be looked to for their care and protection. The commander of the army transport Sumner, which has been ordered to Tampico to take care of refugees, has been instructed to co-operate with Rear Admiral Caperton in affording safety to Americans or foreigners at Tuxpam. Should Americans or foreigners find it necessary to flee from Tuxpam they will be taken on board the transport Sumner and on the naval vessels commanded by Admiral Caperton.

More Bullets Cross Border.

The Mexican border conditions became threatening again today. General Frederick Funston sent a report to the War Department saying some of the combatants in yesterday's attack on Matamoros had fired bullets across the border at Brownsville. General Funston, who has command of American forces on the border, with headquarters at San Antonio, notified Secretary Garrison that he was proceeding to Brownsville from his headquarters at Fort Sam Houston to take personal charge of the situation.

General Funston has specific instructions of a secret character as to how to handle any contingency on the border, but before taking any vigorous action in the direction of stopping the Mexican fire toward the American side he must report to Washington and ask for instructions. As understood here General Funston must not return the fire of the Mexicans without specific orders from Washington.

General Funston forwarded to the War Department a report from Colonel Blockson covering yesterday's hostilities, saying they extended from a point half a mile in front of the right flank of Carranza's trenches around Matamoros to about a mile from the Brownsville pumping station. It was near the latter point that the Mexican bullets fell on the American side. During the battle the Villistas used two field pieces and fired about twenty cannon shots into Matamoros.

AVIATORS TO PATROL BORDER.

Ten Men from Army School Ordered to Brownsville.

WASHINGTON, April 14. — First Lieuts. T. Dewmilling and Byron Q. Jones and eight enlisted men with an aeroplane from the army aviation school at San Diego, were ordered today to Brownsville, Tex., to aid in the enforcement of neutrality at that point during the fighting across the Rio Grande at Matamoros.

Because of the circuitous course of the river between Brownsville and Matamoros and the heavy growth of vegetation lining the river banks, an aeroplane, in the opinion of army officers, affords the best means of patrolling that section of the border.

The expedition is already on its way from San Diego.

VILLA LAND LAW READY.

Refers to the Confiscation of the Untilled Tracts.

EL PASO, April 14.—Manuel Bonilla, in charge of agrarian reforms in Chihuahua State, said here today that the Villa Government had no intention of confiscating mines or arable land which could not be worked on account of existing conditions.

He reported that Francisco Escudero, the Villa Secretary of Finance and Industry, had completed the law referring to the confiscation of untilled land, which would be presented soon to General Villa for his signature. Escudero had drawn up the amendments to the old Federal mining law regarding confiscation of unworked property, which has occasioned opposition on the part of American and other foreign mine owners.

MAY SEEK TO INDICT RIGGS BANK OFFICERS

Matter of Counter-Suit Left to Attorney Brandeis by Accused Treasury Heads.

CONGRESS TO TAKE A HAND

Abolition of Controller's Office Already Being Broached—Hearing on Injunction Comes Up Tomorrow.

Special to The New York Times.

WASHINGTON, April 14.—Counsel for both Controller of the Currency John Skelton Williams and the Riggs National Bank put in a busy day getting ready for the hearing in the District Supreme Court on Friday, when the Riggs Bank officials will ask for a continuance of the temporary injunction to prevent the conversion into the general fund of the Treasury of $5,000 alleged to be due the Riggs Bank as interest on Government bonds—the point on which the great fight legally hinges. Both Joseph W. Bailey, attorney for the bank, and Mr. Williams said they thought they would be prepared for the battle by Friday, but the Controller afterward qualified his statement by saying that he had not asked Louis D. Brandeis, special counsel for the Department of Justice, whether he would seek a postponement in order to complete preparation of his case.

It became known today that a determined effort would be made by a Republican Senator at the next session to induce Congress to abolish the office of Controller of the Currency, or at least to remove most of the powers at present attached to the office. It has been argued that the creation of the Federal Reserve Board, with its corps of examiners, made the Controller's office unnecessary. When Mr. Williams was asked about this report he laughed.

"I have been told by two persons who ought to know that they could get $1,000,000 from certain bankers in return for my resignation," he said.

The Controller was non-committal in regard to the statement that he was preparing to ask for criminal indictments against three officials of the Riggs Bank on the ground that they had violated the National Banking act. It was learned that this matter was being discussed with Mr. Brandeis, who had not yet had time to go through the great mass of papers turned over to him by the Controller's office, and that it would depend entirely upon his decision, to be reached after conferences with Attorney General Gregory and Jesse C. Adkins, an ex-Assistant Attorney General engaged for this case, whether the evidence would justify criminal charges.

Mr. Brandeis took up his quarters this morning at the Department of Justice, where a room was set apart for his use, and was closeted a long time with Mr. Gregory, Mr. Adkins, Assistant Attorney General Warren and District Attorney Laskey. Mr. Laskey's arrival at the Department of Justice created a stir, as he would be the official in charge should criminal proceedings grow out of the case.

Much interest is being taken in the efforts of the Riggs to align other national banks in the fight to curtail the powers of the Controller, which have been considerably broadened by the present incumbent. Copies of The News Leader, published in Controller Williams's home town, Richmond, Va., which reached Washington today, contained an interview with the Controller's brother, Langbourne M. Williams of the firm of John L. Williams & Sons, in which he said that in his opinion the Riggs National Bank officers were putting up the cry of persecution to anticipate any possible action the Government might take against them.

DOOMS OFFICE OF CORONER.

Gov. Whitman Signs Bills Abolishing It on Jan. 1, 1918.

ALBANY, April 14.—The office of Coroner in New York City will be abolished on Jan. 1, 1918, under the terms of the Stoddard bill, signed today by Gov. Whitman. The terms of office of the present Coroners will expire on that date.

Their duties would be transferred to a chief medical examiner to be appointed by the Mayor.

Additional charges were filed with Governor Whitman today by the City Club of New York against Coroner Patrick D. Riordan, whose removal is asked for on charges growing out of his conduct at the inquest following the fatal collision on the Manhattan Elevated Railroad on Dec. 9 last. The present charges recite that the Coroner, who was supposed to be on night duty, could not be reached until shortly before midnight, and even then did not reach the police station, where the bodies of the two victims lay until 2:15 A. M., when, the complaint alleges, "he was unfit and incapacitated for duty by reason of the fact that he had apparently imbibed too freely of some alcoholic beverage."

DIVER REACHES THE F-4.

Walks Along Lost Submarine 288 Feet Below the Surface.

HONOLULU, April 14.—Chief Gunner's Mate Frank Crilley went 288 feet under water here today and walked along the submarine F-4, which disappeared March 25. The depth is said by naval officers to be a world's diving record.

He found the F-4 lying on a smooth, sandy bottom with no coral growths to impede hoisting operations. She lay on her starboard side, her bow pointing shoreward. Two parted lines were found attached to the craft.

After Crilley reported, it was said that further observations probably would be made before an attempt is made to raise the F-4.

Crilley went down in an ordinary diving suit, and the recompression chamber designed to reduce pressure on the diver was not used.

Crilly was under the water two hours. It took him five minutes to make the descent and he was on the bottom twelve minutes. An hour and forty-five minutes was required to bring him to the surface in order to accustom him gradually to the change in air pressure.

SAY BENEDICT XV. WAS MISQUOTED

Papal Court Angered by Interview Crediting Him with Favoring Stoppage of Arms.

POPE MAY DISAVOW IT

Many Protests from the United States, Britain, and France Reach the Vatican.

Special Cable to THE NEW YORK TIMES.

MILAN, April 14 (Dispatch to The London Daily Chronicle).—The German-American interview with the Pope has aroused bitter indignation at the Papal court, where the statements attributed to Benedict XV. are openly characterized as fantastic and false.

The Vatican correspondent of the Corriere della Sera, who enjoys exceptional privileges in obtaining information direct from the Holy See, states that in consequence of the serious nature of the misrepresentations and the storm of telegraphic inquiries and protests showered upon the Vatican by Roman Catholic clergy and laity in the United States, Britain, and France, His Holiness probably will communicate a formal disavowal of the interview in the forthcoming issue of the Osservatore Romano.

The correspondent adds that the declarations alleged to have emanated from the Pope are plainly in contradiction with the marked change unfavorable to the Germanic cause which for some time past has been apparent in the political attitude of the Holy See.

Il Secolo has searched the Vatican registers in vain for any entry of a private audience accorded Karl von Wiegand. My own information is, however, that the German journalist was warmly recommended for such an audience in a note addressed to Cardinal Gasparri, the Papal Secretary, by Baron de Ritter, Bavarian Minister to the Pope. Very significant, indeed, is the fact that the clerical newspapers subsidized by the Vatican in reproducing the text of the alleged interview retransmitted from London and Cologne suppressed altogether the paragraph which urged President Wilson to hasten the dawn of peace by stopping the exportation of munitions of war to the Allies.

The leading organs of the Italian press find it easier to regard flagrantly unneutral advice of this sort as a Germanophile journalistic sop thrown to the greedy German appetite across the Atlantic than as an authentic utterance of so astute a diplomatist as Benedict XV.

Special Cable to THE NEW YORK TIMES.

PARIS, April 14.—A report that the von Wiegand interview with the Pope was obtained practically under false pretenses causes great satisfaction to the French press. Equal interest is roused by Dr. Eliot's pro-Ally speech, which is widely quoted as representing the real sentiments of Americans.

The Journal des Débats discusses Ambassador Bernstorff's Washington difficulties. It says:

"Count Bernstorff's action in publishing his note before handing it to Washing is probably a clumsy attempt to put pressure on President Wilson by an appeal to public opinion. It is another instance of the brutality of German methods, which are successful possibly against weak peoples, but are unlikely to prevail against mighty America."

That sums up French opinion of the subject. The affair is regarded as one more error of German diplomacy.

PUBLISHED IN BERLIN, TOO.

Alleged Interview with Pope Elicited Inspired Comment.

Special Cable to THE NEW YORK TIMES.

LONDON, Thursday, April 15.—The London Times says the "interview with the Pope" was published in Berlin Saturday evening by the Lokalanzeiger, which said that "at its request Mr. von Wiegand had placed a copy of his manuscript at its disposal."

On Sunday the Lokalanzeiger published a note, obviously dictated by the German Foreign Office, to the effect that the Pope's remarks evidently meant that the United States ought to cease to supply munitions of war to the Allies. The inspired writer remarked that the interview would take "a very important place among the various reports from von Wiegand's pen about his meetings with prominent personages of the present time," and proceeded:

"Cautious though the expressions of the Pope in general are, his urgent appeal to all Americans, both Government and people, to avoid everything which might prolong the war can scarcely be regarded as anything else than an admonition to abandon all deliveries of arms to the belligerents. The glowing love of peace and of mankind which is expressed in the Pope's every word will therefore not meet with unmitigated admiration in the countries of our enemies.

"It must, however, be beyond doubt, and for us a matter of importance that cannot be exaggerated, that the words of Benedict XV. will produce among the hundreds of thousands of North American Catholics a very valuable support for the elements in the United States—they are none too big—especially the German-Americans and Irish, which are laboring for the observance of the strictest neutrality."

COTTON TO REMAIN FREE.

British Government Decides Not to Make It Contraband.

LONDON, April 14.—The British Government has decided against placing cotton on the contraband list.

A question was asked in the House of Commons this afternoon on this subject, and Neil Primrose, Under-Secretary of State for Foreign Affairs, on behalf of the Foreign Office, replied that after careful consideration it had been found that the military advantages to be gained by declaring cotton contraband were insufficient to render such a step expedient.

NEUVE CHAPELLE BLUNDERS COSTLY

Sir John French Reports That the British Lost 12,811 There.

ORDERS BADLY EXECUTED

This Resulted, He Says, in Disorganization of Troops After the Victory Was Won.

GUNS ENDANGERED INFANTRY

Troops Had to be Recalled Because the British Artillery Fire Could Not Be Stopped.

LONDON, April 14.—Field Marshal Sir John French, commander of the British expeditionary forces on the continent, reports the British losses in the three days' fighting at Neuve Chapelle last month, as follows: Killed, 190 officers, 2,337 men; wounded, 359 officers, 8,174 other ranks; missing, 23 officers, 1,728 men; total casualties, 12,811.

The report continues:

"The enemy left several thousand dead on the field, and we have positive information that upward of 12,000 wounded were removed by trains. Thirty officers and 1,657 of other ranks were captured."

The British commander's dispatch concerning the battle is long, and says among other things:

"Considerable delay occurred after the capture of Neuve Chapelle, and the infantry was greatly disorganized. I am of the opinion that this delay would not have occurred had the clearly expressed order of the general officer commanding the First Army been more carefully observed."

Field Marshal Sir John French's report, which covers the battles of Neuve Chapell and St. Eloi under date of April 5, was published in the official Gazette today. The Commander in Chief writes:

"The event of chief interest and importance which has taken place is the victory achieved over the enemy in the battle of Neuve Chapelle, which was fought on March 10, 11, and 12.

"The main attack was delivered by the troops of the First Army under command of General Sir Douglas Haig, supported by a large force of heavy artillery, a division of cavalry, and some infantry of the General Reserve. Secondary and holding attacks and demonstrations were made along the front of the Second Army, under direction of its commander, Sir Horace Smith-Dorrien.

Praise for Sir Douglas Haig.

"While the success attained was due to the magnificent bearing and indomitable courage displayed by the troops of the Fourth and Indian Corps, I consider that the able and skillful dispositions which were made by the general officer commanding the First Army contributed largely to the defeat of the enemy and to the capture of his position. The energy and vigor with which General Sir Douglas Haig handled his command show him to be a leader of great ability and power.

"Another action of considerable importance was brought about by a surprise attack made by the Germans on March 14 against the Twenty-seventh Division holding the trenches east of St. Eloi. A large force of artillery was concentrated in this area under the cover of a mist and a heavy volume of fire was suddenly brought to bear on the trenches.

"At 5 o'clock in the afternoon this artillery attack was accompanied by two mine explosions, and in the confusion caused by these and by the suddenness of the attack the position of St. Eloi was captured and held for some hours by the enemy.

"Well-directed and vigorous counter-attacks, in which the troops of the Fifth Army Corps showed great bravery and determination, restored the situation by the evening of the 15th."

The dispatch describes further operations, saying:

"On Feb. 6 a brilliant action by the troops of the First Corps materially improved our position in the area south of La Bassée Canal. During the previous night parties of the Irish Guards and the Third Battalion of the Coldstream Guards had succeeded in gaining ground from which a converging fire could be directed on the flanks and rear of certain brick stacks occupied by the Germans, which had been for some time a source of considerable annoyance. At 2 P. M. the affair commenced with a severe bombardment of the brick stacks and the enemy's trenches.

"A brisk attack by the Third Battalion of the Coldstream Guards and Irish Guards from our trenches west of the brick stacks followed and was supported by the fire from the flanking position which had been seized the previous night by the same regiments.

"The attack succeeded, the brick stacks were occupied without difficulty, and a line was established north and south through a point about forty yards east of the brick stacks.

Fifth Corps Suffered Most.

"The casualties suffered by the Fifth Corps throughout the period under review, and particularly during the month of February, have been heavier than those on other parts of the line. I regret this, but do not think, taking all circumstances into consideration, that they were unduly numerous. The position then occupied by the Fifth Corps had always been a very vulnerable part of our line. The ground was marshy, and trenches were most difficult to construct and maintain. The Twenty-seventh and Twenty-eighth Divisions of the Fifth Corps had had no previous experience in European warfare, and a number of the units composing the corps had only recently returned from service in tropical climates. In consequence, the hardships of a rigorous Winter campaign fell with greater weight upon these divisions than upon any other in the command.

"Chiefly owing to these causes the Fifth Corps, up to the beginning of March, was constantly engaged in counter-attacks to retake trenches and ground which had been lost. In their difficult and arduous task, however, the troops displayed the utmost gallantry and devotion, and it is most creditable to the skill and energy of their leaders that I am able to report how well they have surmounted all their difficulties and that the ground first taken over by them is still intact and held with little greater loss than is incurred by the troops in all other parts of the line."

Describing an attack on the German trenches near St. Eloi on Feb. 28 by Princess Patricia's Regiment, of the Canadian contingent, under command of Lieut. C. E. Crabbe, the Commander-in-Chief says:

"The services performed by this distinguished corps have continued to be very valuable since I had occasion to refer to them in my last dispatch. They have been most ably organized and

Continued on Page 2.

TWO WARSHIPS HIT BY DARDANELLES FORTS

Allied Cruiser and Destroyer Shelled—Turks Massing on Gallipoli Peninsula.

CONSTANTINOPLE, April 13, via Wireless to Berlin and London, April 14.—An official statement issued by the Turkish War Office tonight says:

"Some enemy patrol ships today (Tuesday) bombarded unsuccessfully the batteries at the exit of the Dardanelles. A cruiser and a destroyer both were struck by shells."

Special Cable to THE NEW YORK TIMES.

ATHENS, April 14, Dispatch to The London Daily News.)—The Turks are daily massing troops on the Gallipoli peninsula, especially at Kiled Bahr, and all the heavy guns which were formerly around Constantinople, Principo, and Marmora seaports are being removed to the Dardanelles.

A great number of German aeroplanes have arrived. The day before yesterday a German aeroplane threw three bombs at an allied transport. The damage caused is unknown.

Warships bombard the Turkish position daily.

The Governor of Smyrna has refused to allow the male Turkish population in the neighborhood of Burla to leave. It is thought they will be pressed into service in case of the landing of an allied force. From Burla to Smyrna the Turks have made trenches to be used at the first opportunity. On the mountain above the village of St. Georges they placed thirty large guns.

UPHOLDS LANGUAGE OF BERNSTORFF NOTE

Hamburg Nachrichten Talks of "Enemies Who Pretend to be Neutral."

AMSTERDAM, (via London,) April 14.—The Hamburg Nachrichten, commenting on the German memorandum to the State Department at Washington recently given out for publication by Count von Bernstorff, the German Ambassador, declares that the United States allows England to act as she pleases and supplies her with all the war materials she requires, and continues:

"Many a one who has had to observe this procedure of the United States has struck the table with his fist. The anger created in Europe is greater than the people over there allow themselves to imagine.

"Our Foreign Office has now found the right language against France, against England, and, without any sort of consideration, against the United States, too. With consideration and forbearance we get no further forward. The German people will gradually finish with their declared enemies, although tremendous efforts will be required, but behind them stand other enemies who pretend to be neutral and claim from us the rights of neutrality, together with every consideration, but who, nevertheless, continuously and zealously support our enemies and assist them in their war against us.

"It is time that a strong word went to Washington. In expression it will be polite, but its meaning can only be: Are you neutral, or are you our enemy?"

MINISTERS DIVIDED ON SUBMARINE POLICY

German Chancellor Said to Be Opposed to It on Account of Neutral Opinion.

Special Cable to THE NEW YORK TIMES.

LONDON, April 14.—A correspondent of the London Daily News sends the following from Rotterdam:

"From a highly dependable informant who has been closely associated with German diplomatic circles I learn that the policy of submarine piracy against mercantile shipping has caused and is still causing serious trouble in the German Government, which is almost equally divided as to the value of the policy. When it was first proposed it produced a pronounced split in the Government. The whole idea originated with Admiral von Tirpitz, but was strongly opposed by the Imperial Chancellor, who adopted the view that any such policy would undoubtedly produce an extremely bad effect in neutral countries.

"For some time the proposition was keenly debated, the Chancellor adhering strongly to the point that whatever the advantages, they would be infinitesimally small compared with the effect produced among non-combatants. Von Tirpitz, however, realizing the high seas fleet was still at the mooring posts, argued that the only feelings to be consulted were those of Germans and that in view of the forced inactivity of the German high seas fleet and the fact that German mercantile marine interests had been annihilated, something must be done to justify Germany's claim to sea power. Ultimately the Kaiser's assent went to the high seas party and the piracy was begun.

"To this day the Chancellor is strongly opposed to the policy, a fact that accounts for the different methods adopted by submarine commanders in dealing with vessels. 'No discretion' said my informant, 'is allowed commanders of submarines. It is all due to the difference of opinion that exists in Government. Orders given those responsible for submarine policy differ from day to day.'"

A ONE-DAY STRIKE CALLED IN MILAN

Protest Against Killing of a Man by Police at War Meeting—Genoa Dockers to Go Out.

MILAN, (Via Paris,) April 14.—The workmen in all the manufactories and the employes of the street railway, gas, and automobile services agreed today to join a twenty-four-hour general strike.

The strike was called by the extremists in the Labor Party as a protest against the killing of a man by the police while they were charging a crowd last Sunday which had gathered for a mass meeting at which Italy's attitude in the war was to be discussed.

GENOA, (via Paris,) April 14.—Owing to differences between the dockers and the steamship companies a general strike in the harbor of Genoa has been called for tomorrow.

ZEPPELIN RAIDS ENGLISH TOWN

Aircraft Flies Over the Tyne District and Drops Incendiary Bombs in Several Places.

VERY LITTLE DAMAGE DON

Warnings Are Sent of the Airship's Approach and Pilot Is Baffled by Darkness.

AIMED AT BIG GUN WORK

Great Armstrong Plant at Elswi Supposed to Have Been Objective of the Raiders.

Special Cable to THE NEW YORK TIME

NEWCASTLE, Thursday, April (Dispatch to The London Da Chronicle.)—A Zeppelin raid was ma over the Tyne district last night so after 8 o'clock. The whole region, fr Newcastle to the coast was plunged i darkness.

The first news of the attack came fr Blyth, eleven miles northeast of Ne castle, and stated that the airship w heading in from the East at great spee As it passed over Blyth, it dropp eight bombs on the outskirts of t town.

After leaving Blyth the giant aircra changed its course and evidently tended to make for Newcastle, but pilots obviously were baffled by t darkness. Bombs were launched fr the giant aircraft from time to ti haphazardly, but very little dama was done.

The airship evidently reached the Ty at Wallsend, and then proceeded eas ward toward South Shields. As it dre near Wallsend bombs were dropped a one of them fell on the railway, narrow ly missing a crowded passenger tra which was on its way to Newcastle.

Between Blyth and Wallsend the Ze pelin passed over Cramlington a dropped several bombs in the neig borhood. One house was set on fire.

Altogether the raid is estimated have lasted twenty-five minutes, a so far as can be ascertained, no gre amount of damage was done. A m was injured by a shell splinter at Cho pingtot.

Most of the bombs discharged were an incendiary kind. Information h been received that while passing ov Wallsend the Zeppelin dropped a bo which struck a house in which was woman. She had a miraculous escap being only slightly injured by a pie of flying masonry.

Soon after midnight the lights in New castle and the surrounding district we switched on again, and the military a thorities announced that no further da ger was to be apprehended.

Only one Zeppelin seems to have bee engaged in the raid. The night w ill-suited to the raider, and in the dar ness it appears to have completely lo its bearings.

Five bombs were dropped at Wallsen Two of them fell in a field, and wh they struck the earth the missiles ga off a brilliant flame by which they we located by a farmer, who handed the over to the police.

The steel cases, or cylinders, were fi or six inches in diameter, about eighte inches long, were coated with some i flammable material, which had be burned off, and the steel tubes we fuzed by the intense heat. One of t witnesses, who examined them, state that they had contained petrol and su phur. They were embedded in the ear about two feet.

From Wallsend the raider cross the Tyne and five or six minutes lat was reported at Weston and then South Shields, passing eastward a homeward.

Newcastle was altogether misse probably because when the warni came, every light in the town was once extinguished and the trams stoppe running.

Though there was immense excit ment here, there was no panic. On th contrary, all the familiar warnings dangers of being out of doors were dis regarded by the townsfolk and th streets were crowded with people.

One bomb dropped at Beaton, withi three miles of Newcastle and Elswick This is the nearest point to Newcastl that was reached. Everywhere th coming of the raider was flashed, an the country villages, towns, and citie were all in darkness.

SHELLS FIRED AT RAIDER.

Guns at Cramlington Aimed at the Big Airship.

Special Cable to THE NEW YORK TIME

LONDON, Thursday, April 15.—A dis patch to The Daily Chronicle from New castle says that guns at Cramlingto opened fire on the enemy airship. Eigh shells were discharged and could be seen quite distinctly as they burst in the sky and within such a short distance o the German raider as to make matters uncomfortable for it.

The troops stationed at Blyth als fired at the Zeppelin as it passed ove the town, according to the dispatch which says the craft was last observed passing over Sunderland and travelin out to sea.

The district which was raided by the German airship is one of the most important industrial centres of the Kingdom. The chief town, Newcastle-on-Tyne, is not only a large seaport, but is one of Britain's biggest coal exporting and shipbuilding centres. The celebrated Armstrong Works, at Elswick, may almost be regarded as the English equivalent of the Krupps. Here the building of the largest warships, with all their armor, guns, machinery and fittings, is carried on and

"All the News That's Fit to Print."

The New York Times.

THE WEATHER
Fair today and Sunday; fresh to strong southwest to west winds.
For full weather report see Page 21.

VOL. LXIV...NO. 20,923. NEW YORK, SATURDAY, MAY 8, 1915.—TWENTY-FOUR PAGES. ONE CENT In Greater New York, Jersey City and Newark. | Elsewhere TWO CENTS.

LUSITANIA SUNK BY A SUBMARINE, PROBABLY 1,000 DEAD; TWICE TORPEDOED OFF IRISH COAST; SINKS IN 15 MINUTES; AMERICANS ABOARD INCLUDED VANDERBILT AND FROHMAN; WASHINGTON BELIEVES THAT A GRAVE CRISIS IS AT HAND

SHOCKS THE PRESIDENT

Washington Deeply Stirred by Disaster and Fears a Crisis.

BULLETINS AT WHITE HOUSE

Wilson Reads Them Closely, but Is Silent on the Nation's Course.

RUMOR OF CONGRESS CALL

Loss of Lusitania Recalls Firm Tone of Our First Warning to Germany.

CAPITAL FULL OF RUMORS

Reports That Liner Was to be Sunk Were Heard Before Actual News Came.

Special to The New York Times.

WASHINGTON, May 7.—Never since that April day, three years ago, when word came that the Titanic had gone down, has Washington been so stirred as it is tonight over the sinking of the Lusitania. The early reports told that there had been no loss of life, but the relief that these advices caused gave way to the greatest concern late this evening when it became known that there had been many deaths. Although they are profoundly reticent, officials realize that this tragedy, probably involving the loss of American citizens, is likely to bring about a crisis in the international relations of the United States.

It is pointed out that the sinking of the Lusitania is the outcome of a series of incidents that have been the cause of concern to this Government in its endeavor to maintain a strictly neutral position in the great European war.

It is impossible to say tonight what effect the loss of American lives on the Lusitania will have on the Government. Judged from the little that can be learned it is a safe prediction that President Wilson will endeavor to ascertain all the facts, including evidence as to whether a German submarine was responsible for the sinking of the vessel, before proceeding to determine the course to be pursued. The news that many lives had been sacrificed, probably as many as a thousand, was given to him at the White House about 1 o'clock this evening, but no word came from him as to what effect this intelligence had on him.

The State Department tonight sent instructions to the American Embassy in London to send the names of any Americans who might have been killed or injured in the disaster. A bulletin from THE TIMES, saying probably 1,000 lives had been lost, was sent to the White House as soon as received and laid before President Wilson. The news that two torpedoes had been fired into the Lusitania by a submarine and that the Lusitania sank fifteen minutes afterward was also sent to the White House, but reached there after the President had gone to bed. The President retired about 11 o'clock.

Rumors of Congress Session.

There were reports this evening that Congress would be called in extra session, but these were not justified and the most that can be said is that while the Government is greatly concerned over the situation, it has shown no inclination toward excitement or taking hasty action.

This afternoon and early this evening officials were relieved over the reports that no lives had been lost. But in spite of the calmness in the upper official circle during this period, there was little effort elsewhere to conceal the view that even if no Americans went dow with the liner this Government might find itself face to face with a grave situation.

The statement from London that the Lusitania was torpedoed without warning were regarded as showing the delicacy of the situation, for this Government, in the warning it delivered to Germany concerning the proposed submarine warfare on merchant ships, laid down the principle that the obligation to visit and search a merchant ship before sinking or taking her captive was imposed on the German Government.

But it is too soon to say or even to attempt to predict, wha course the United States Government will adopt. It is clear that the first move of the Government will be to ascertain all the facts obtainable and that the inquiry will be pursued, as far as possible, by officers of the United States. Until such an investigation has been completed and President Wilson and his advisers have determined what attitude the facts warrant the Government in adopting, no formal diplomatic action may be expected. For the present the higher officials content themselves with a refusal to answer questions as to the position likely to be taken and with expressions of the hope that the early reports that no lives were lost in the Lusitania are true. That was Secretary Bryan's way of treating the matter before the alarming bulletins began to arrive.

What impresses Washington most tonight is that the loss of American lives was apparently the result of the action taken in the face of the warning given to Germany that such an outcome of a German attack might bring about a rupture in the friendly relations between the two countries. The language employed in that warning note was regarded as too drastic by some public men here, but the defense of its use was that it would be better to be outspoken before any critical incident than to wait until it occurred, when public feeling in this country might be aroused to the highest pitch and demands made for redress against Germany.

While there was interest here in the last voyage of the Lusitania on account of the risk she ran, it was not an intense interest. The feeling among officials and others appeared to be that the Germans would not go to the extreme of sinking a passenger vessel with women and children and many American citizens aboard. Even the advertisement inserted in American newspapers last Saturday by the German Embassy, warning Americans not to take passage for Europe in the ships of Germany's enemies, did not cause any alarm here with particular reference to the Lusitania, although it produced a feeling of irritation.

President Wilson Shocked.

President Wilson had just finished luncheon and was preparing to go golfing when the first news of the Lusitania disaster reached the White House. It came in the form of a newspaper bulletin and was received by Rudolph Forster, the executive clerk to the President. Mr. Forster, who was in the executive offices, wrote a note to the President telling him of the report. It was said afterward that the President was greatly shocked and perturbed, but that he expressed thankfulness that no lives had been lost, as the bulletin had it.

The President canceled his golfing and decided to remain at the White House. A little later, when further bulletins were positive in stating that no lives had been lost, the President went motoring. Tonight he received press bulletins concerning the Lusitania in his study in the White House. These were sent to him from the telegraph room of the executive offices. It was said that he had no visitors during the evening. A bulletin saying that probably 1,000 lives were lost in the disaster was sent to him shortly before 10 o'clock.

Secretary Bryan was at luncheon at

Continued on Page 2.

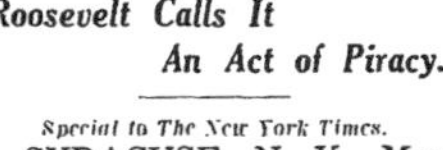

Roosevelt Calls It An Act of Piracy.

Special to The New York Times.

SYRACUSE, N. Y., May 7—Colonel Roosevelt tonight characterized the sinking of the Lusitania as "an act of piracy."

"I do not know enough of the facts," said the Colonel, "to make any further comment or to say what would be proper for this Government to do in the circumstances.

"I can only repeat what I said the other day when the Gulflight was attacked. I then called attention to the fact that months before the German war zone was established, and deeds such as the sinking of the Lusitania were threatened, that if such deeds were perpetrated they would represent nothing but mere piracy."

THE LOST CUNARD STEAMSHIP LUSITANIA

Cunard Office Here Beseiged for News; Fate of 1,918 on Lusitania Long in Doubt

Official news of the sinking of the Lusitania yesterday reached New York in fragmentary reports, and several hours elapsed between the first unverified rumor of the disaster and the cable messages that told at night of the saving of some of the passengers and gave meagre details of the most sensational incident of its kind in the war.

The early accounts that indicated all on board had been saved reassured hundreds of friends and relatives of passengers. Later it was made known that lives had been lost and probably many persons had been injured.

Among the prominent passengers rescued was George A. Kessler. The list of those of whom no word was received included A. G. Vanderbilt, Charles Frohman, Charles Klein, Justus Miles Forman, and Elbert Hubbard, besides persons widely known in society.

A cablegram sent to Farley Hopkins of The Yale News staff at New Haven, by his father, who was aboard the Lusitania, stated that the vessel was sunk not beached, that three hundred persons had been already landed, and that the rest in small boats were making for shore. The message reached New York at 8:15 o'clock and was signed "Lee Higginson & Co., London."

Message to Cunard Office.

The first word of the sinking of the Lusitania received here reached the local offices of the Cunard Line, 21 State Street, at 11:41 o'clock yesterday morning, but was not made public until late in the afternoon. The message, which was sent from the head office in Liverpool, read:

> The Lusitania we regret to advise, an unconfirmed report states to have been torpedoed by a submarine at 2 P. M., Friday, ten miles from Kinsale, and sunk at 2:30. There is no news as to the safety of passengers or crew.

Following this dispatch there was a message which had been picked up by the wireless station at Land's End, evidently a distress call from the liner, which said:

> Come at once. Big list. Position ten miles west Kinsale.

A third dispatch from Queenstown stated:

> All available craft in harbor dispatched to assist. Weather here beautifully fine. Wind southeast, light.

By 3 o'clock in the afternoon the news of the sinking of the Lusitania had been spread in the city and the Cunard offices were besieged by relatives and friends of the passengers on board. Owing to the alterations in and additions to the passenger list on sailing day, last Saturday, it took some time to get the correct figures, which were finally given out as 290 first, 601 second, and 362 third class passengers. Of the cabin passengers thirty-six had been transferred fro mthe Cameronia on Saturday morning. This delayed the Lusitania's departure from 10 o'clock to 12:28.

1,918 Persons on Board.

The officers and crew numbered 665 men instead of the usual complement of 950, on account of fewer men being carried in the engineers' and stewards' departments. Thus there were in all 1,918 persons on board.

The Cunard agentstold all inquirers that they would give out the messages as fast as they were received and had no intention of keeping back the news from the public. Several bulletins were received from the Liverpool office, but few of them contained any definite statements and they were cancelled, in some instances, within an hour. One received at 4 P. M. read:

> Motor fishing boats towing two boats filled with passengers, probably fifty. Tug Stormcock making Kinsale. Some passengers on board. Many rescue vessels are row apparently making Queenstown.

The first dispatch stating positively that the Lusitanit had sunk reached the Cunard office at 5 P. M. It read:

> Old Head Kinsale Station reports about twenty boats, all belonging to Lusitania, are in vicinity where sunk. About fifteen boats are making for the spot to resume.

An unconfirmed report was received late in the afternoon that all the passengers and crew had been saved in small boats and rafts. This information was given out to the people waiting in the Cunard office, and many of them went home. It was estimated that fully 500 inquiries were received by telephone and telegraph in the afternoon from relatives and friends of passengers on board. Long-distance calls were received from St. Louis, Atlanta, Montreal, and Toronto.

The next bulletin made public at the Cunard office was the following:

> Liverpool, May 7.
> 1:51 P. M., (New York Time.)
> Following received by Admiralty, Galley Head, 4:25 P. M.: Several boats, apparently survivors, southeast nine miles. Greek steamer proceeding to assist.

The next bulletin was:

> Liverpool, May 7.
> 2:33 P. M., (New York Time.)
> Queenstown wires Old Head: Large steamer just arrived in vicinity, apparently sending assistance. Tugs, patrols, &c., now n the spot, taking boats in tow. Motor fishing boat with two Lusitania boats bearing probably for Kinsale. We have wired Kinsale agents to render every assistance, to advise us if any boats are towed in there.

This was followed by:

> Liverpool, May 7.
> 4:04 P. M., (New York Time.)
> Cork newspaper reports that 300 passengers landed at Clonakilty. Old Head wire begins: Cancel last message. Stormcock taking passengers and boats from motor fishing boat, proceeding Queenstown.

First News of Loss of Life.

The Cunard office at 9:25 o'clock at night received the following cablegram from the Cunard offices at Liverpool:

> Liverpool, May 7.
> 8:29 P. M. (New York Time.)
> Admiralty have nad message from Queenstown saying between 500 and 600 landed at Queenstown, including many hospital cases, some of whom have died. Also number landed at Kinsale.
> CUNARD, Liverpool.

At the same time the Cunard Line gave out the following cablegram from its Liverpool office in reply to a private inquiry:

> Brethertons and family are safe.

The message evidently referred to Mrs. Cyril H. Bretherton of Los Angeles and two children, who were in the second cabin. Mr. Bretherton came here from Los Angeles with his wife and children for a visit to relatives in England. He remained in New York a long time before sailing.

A report that Cornelius Vanderbilt had received a cablegram from his brother, Alfred G. Vanderbilt, who was a passenger on the Lusitania, was denied by Mr. Vanderbilt when he called up himself to get news.

Robert S. Franks, Vice President of the Carnegie Corporation of New York, who lives at West Orange, N. J., waited all afternoon to get news of his niece, Miss P. Hutchinson.

Toward evening the crowd diminished in the office, as it was believed that no more news would be received until this morning.

The Cunard Company gave out the following statement late in the afternoon:

> The Cunard Company's whole concern is with regard to the possible loss of life of passengers and crew. The material loss is covered by insurance. According to meagre reports so far received the Lusitania was torpedoed without warning, and sank within a very short space of time. A large number of ships are known to be afloat, and the weather is reported to be fine and calm. Every effort is being made to obtain further details, and all information will be published without delay.

The Cunard office gave out the following bulletin shortly before 10 o'clock at night:

> LIVERPOOL, May 7, 9:25 P. M., (New York Time.)—Queenstown wires that First Officer Jones states about 500 to 600 lives saved. This includes passengers and crew, and is the only estimate we are able to make. In the meantime we are going through hotels, lodging houses, &c., tonight, and will wire tomorrow fullest possible list. In the meantime injured and dead are taking up our attention.
> CUNARD, Liverpool.

Reports 450 Rescued.

The following was given out at the Cunard office at 10:30 o'clock at night:

> Liverpool, May 7, 9:45 P. M..
> (New York time.)
> Queenstown wires the tug Stormcock landed 150, including passengers and crew. It is reported that the trawlers Dock and India Empire have about 200 on board. The tug Flying Fish has 100, and three torpedo boats brought in 45 living and 4 dead. We are putting the survivors in

Continued on Page 3.

Loss of the Lusitania Fills London With Horror and Utter Amazement

Special Cable to THE NEW YORK TIMES.

LONDON, Saturday, May 8.—Stupefaction is the word which best describes the first impression created by the news of the sinking of the Lusitania. People seemed unable to realize that at this stage of the world's progress such a deep could be committed as an act of war.

"I have no words for it," said Lord Rosebery, and everywhere one found the same sentiment repeated.

It was some hours between the time the first reports of the disaster were received at the Admiralty and the time the news was made public by a communiqué from the Press Bureau. During this interval the news spread quickly through official, Parliamentary, shipping, and newspaper circles.

At the Cunard offices in the later hours of the afternoon men rushed in asking, "Is it true?" When and how they heard the news was a mystery. Shipping offices could give little or no information until the official statement was issued that the Lusitania was sunk by a submarine at 2:33 P. M., eight miles south of West Kinsale.

Shortly after 7 P. M. a dispatch reached THE NEW YORK TIMES correspondent from Liverpool that it was stated that many passengers and crew were unofficially reported saved. But at that hour this information was without foundation. The chief reports here were to the effect that only 300 out of 1,900 souls on the mammoth liner had been saved. Seeing that the vessel had sunk so quickly, it was argued that the loss of life must have been great, that the torpedo must have created such havoc that an immediate heavy list would follow, and in that event the boats were already hanging out on their davits the difficulty of manning and filling even half of them in the time available would have been so great that the possibility of saving a majority of the people aboard was minimised.

When first moments of dull horror passed speculation began. One of the first theories advanced was that to have caught the Lusitania the German sub-marine could not have given the speedy liner any warning. Previously reported activities of German submarines in the waters to the southwest of Ireland encouraged the belief that several vessels of the underwater fleet must have been on the lookout for the Cunarder so as to demonstrate to the world that German warnings were not empty threats.

It was suggested that as the incoming transatlantic liners usually followed a certain distinct track, running close to the southern shore of Ireland it was an easy matter for two or more submarines, to lie in wait for the Lusitania, and once she was observed to let torpedoes go at her vast length presenting a huge target.

Early in the afternoon it was not known at the Cunard offices where the Lusitania had met destruction. It was suggested that the company was unaware whether she was steaming to Liverpool by the north or south of Ireland and that her choice of course was probably directed by Admiralty orders received by her captain. That she was being convoyed was generally assumed, and as an addendum to this assumption, it was believed that Germany would invoke the fact of convoy as a reason wherefor no warning could be given.

Scene in the Strand.

There was a remarkable scene in the Strand when the news first became known. A newsboy shouting out the contents of a bill of an evening paper "Lusitania torpedoed and sunk, official!" was stopped outside the Hotel Cecil by a police constable, who refused to believe the news. He intimated the lad would be arrested if it were shown he was crying out false news. The boy promptly showed the policeman the official news of the disaster in the "stop-press column" and he was allowed to proceed. The incident attracted a huge crowd and in a few minutes the boy had sold all his papers.

The official news was first published at 5:45 P. M. and created a profound impression on the public, and especially in the west end hotels where the guests gathered round the newspaper ma- [illegible] Many Americans, mostly business men are at present staying at the Hotel Cecil, Savoy, and other big hotels in Northumberland Avenue and those who had expected relatives and friends to arrive in London today hurried in taxicabs to make inquiries at the Cunard offices. Americans in evening dress rose hurriedly from the dinner table when they heard the news and drove off to the shipping office in Cockspur Street. Americans did not attempt to hide their anger. A group outside the Carlton Hotel hailed a newsboy and on glancing at the official statement became infuriated, shouted and shook their fists in disgust.

Vain Inquiry At Ship Office.

Describing the scene inside the London Cunard office, says The Chronicle:

"One or two middle-aged ladies sat about quietly reading newspapers splendidly hoping against hope. Early in the long vigil the overstrung nerves of one young girl gave way and she shrieked in hysterics. She had a brother and sister on the vessel, but all she could be told was that the boat had gone down and that it was hoped that the passengers were safe.

"A Canadian officer from the War Office asked for news of Lady Allan and a General whom he thought were on board the vessel. He went away as barren of news as the others waiting uatiently around.

"One man told me quietly he had four friends on board who had persisted in spite of all warnings in sailing on the ship. In a corner sat an old, white-headed clergyman and his wife, waiting with tear-filled, tragic eyes for news of their son, who was returning from America on the torpedoed liner.

"Inquiries as to the safety of this friend and that relation were continually arriving by telegraph and telephone. The American Ambassador sent a representative to discover all that was known, and requested that he be kept in telephone communication.

"To every one the company officials were courteous and considerate alike, speaking in quiet reassuring tones, moving silently about the anxious grief-stricken crowds. On a long office counter newspaper men, British and American, quietly scribbled their messages. At intervals of an hour or so (they really seemed like days or years) cables wereed across the counter, were hastily copied on huge sheets of paper, and pinned conspicuously on the walls. Their import was passed with miraculous rapidity from lip to lip, but mostly they left nobody much wiser or more hopeful.

"In the small hours of this morning the crowds were hardly less. Those who had left earlier in the night now returned and new watchers were constantly arriving. There could be no sleep for any of them this night."

BERESFORD BLAMES A LACK OF CRUISERS

Great Britain Needs More to Protect Her Trade Routes, Says Naval Critic.

Special Cable to THE NEW YORK TIMES.

LONDON, Saturday, May 8.—Lord Charles Beresford, ask for an expression of opinion on the sinking of the Lusitania, said he thought it was due to a shortage of cruisers to protect the trade routes.

This had been his opinion for years, he said.

Admiralty Puts Embargo On News Dispatches

LONDON, May 8.—It is stated that the British Admiralty is not withholding any verified facts regarding the Lusitania, but declines to pass dispatches based merely on rumor.

It is expected that the Admiralty will issue a statement as soon as authenticated facts are available.

DEATH OF FROHMAN IS FEARED IN LONDON

"What Is America Going to Do About It?" Asks British Colleague of Manager.

Special Cable to THE NEW YORK TIMES.

LONDON, May 7.—The theatrical world of London is stunned over the reported fate of Charles Frohman. Mr. Frohman is a familiar figure in the theatrical life of London, and theatre managers and players alike regarded him highly. Speaking tonight, Frederick Harrison, lessee of the Haymarket Theatre, after expressing his intense shock over the report of Mr. Frohman's drowning, asked abruptly:

"What is America going to do about the torpedoing of the Lusitania? What is Washington to say about the drowning of American citizens? Is America going to take it lying down?"

Mr. Harrison spoke of Mr. Frohman as one of his most intimate friends and a man whose loss the entire theatrical world, here and abroad, would feel keenly.

"Only three days ago I received a letter from Mr. Frohman, written in New York April 21," said Mr. Harrison. "In it Mr. Frohman, after speaking of his intention to make a trip to see me and other theatrical managers on business, wrote: 'I hope to see you soon.' From the letter I took it he was sailing within a few days.

"All I can say is that the theatrical profession loses a clever man and a very kind friend. Mr. Frohman had tremendous influence in the theatrical field and his energies were directed the right way. The sinking of the Lusitania is a terrible act and Germans ought to be held by America to the fullest accountability."

AMERICANS IN LONDON ARE DEEPLY STIRRED

A. J. Drexel Denounces Sinking of the Lusitania — Pinchot Refrains from Commenting.

Special Cable to THE NEW YORK TIMES.

LONDON, May 7.—Anthony J Drexel, at his home in Grosvenor Square, denounced the sinking of the Lusitania to THE NEW YORK TIMES correspondent as "the most infernal outrage that has happened during the war." Mr. Drexel sailed on the Lusitania for New York on March 13, when Captain Dow was in command. He came back on the American liner New York with Harry Lehr because of Mr. Lehr's fear of sailing on a steamer flying other than the American flag.

"I don't see how the American Government," said Mr. Drexel, "can do anything but go into the war itself. If the lives of its citizens are to be snuffed out this way by the Germans America must act sternly if Americans are to feel that the protection of their country means anything. Can it be that America will supinely allow the Germans to murder her citizens? For my part, I expect the Government at Washington to take drastic measures now with Germany. If it means war to protect our citizens, I'm for war. I feel helpless to express my feelings of dismay and horror over this damnable thing. How do we know the Germans will not torpedo a ship flying the American flag? Where is this terrible work of the Germans to end? What is to be done with the Kaiser, who has the blood of innocent American men and women on his hands! Is America to raise no voice in protest?

"Her protest must be in thunder tones, maybe of cannon, that strike to the depths of the Berlin iniquity."

Gifford Pinchot, who says he still holds an official commission from the American Government in the war relief work, expressed himself tonight at the home of his brother-in-law, Sir Alan Johnstone, where he has been staying since the Germans escorted him out of Belgium, would not speak of the Lusitania case because of his connection with the Government.

"I wish I were able to speak, but I must remain silent," he said as tears came to his eyes. Mr. Pinchot had arranged to return to New York on the Lusitania a week from tomorrow, having got word from Washington several days ago that it was inadvisable for him to try to carry out his work in the war zone. When he heard of the torpedoing of the Lusitania Mr. Pinchot got into touch with the American Line to make reservation on the St. Paul tomorrow for himself and his wife. When he talked with THE TIMES correspondent tonight he was not sure he would be able to get the accommodations he wanted, and said he might have to postpone going.

"But I'll go back to New York on a steamer flying the American flag," he said.

Lord Rosebery said regarding the torpedoing of the liner: "The thing is beyond all expression.

SOME DEAD TAKEN ASHORE

Several Hundred Survivors at Queenstown and Kinsale.

STEWARD TELLS OF DISASTER

One Torpedo Crashes Into the Doomed Liner's Bow, Another Into the Engine Room.

BOATS PROMPTLY LOWERED

But Ship Goes Down So Quickly Many Must Have Gone with Her —No Officers Reported Saved.

ATTACKED IN BROAD DAY

Passengers at Luncheon—Warning Had Been Given by Germans Before the Ship Left New York.

LONDON, Saturday, May 8.—The Cunard liner Lusitania, which sailed out of New York last Saturday with 1,918 souls aboard, lies at the bottom of the ocean off the Irish coast.

She was sunk by a German submarine, which sent two torpedoes crashing into her side, while the passengers, seemingly confident that the great, swift vessel could elude the German underwater craft, were having luncheon.

How many of the Lusitania's passengers and crew were rescued cannot be told at present. Official statements from the British Admiralty up to midnight accounted for not more than 500 or 600, and unofficial reports tell of several hundreds landed at Queenstown, Kinsale and other points.

Up to midnight 520 passengers from the Lusitania had been landed at Queenstown from boats. Ten or eleven boatloads have come ashore and others are expected.

A press dispatch says seven torpedoes were discharged from the German craft and one of them struck the Lusitania amidships.

Probably at least 1,000 persons, including many Americans, have lost their lives.

Sank in Fifteen Minutes.

The stricken vessel went down in less than half an hour, according to all reports. The most definite statement puts fifteen minutes as the time that passed between the fatal blow and the disappearance of the Lusitania beneath the waves.

There were 1,253 passengers from New York on board the steamship, including 200 who were transferred to her from the steamer Cameronia. The crew numbered 665.

No names of the rescued are yet available.

Story of the Attack.

The tug, Stormcock, has returned to Queenstown, bringing about 150 survivors of the Lusitania, principally passengers, among whim were many women, several of the crew and one steward. Describing the experience of the Lusitania, the steward said:

"The passengers were at lunch when a submarnie came up and fired two torpedoes, which struck the Lusitania on

"All the News That's Fit to Print."

The New York Times.

THE WEATHER
Fair today and Tuesday; gentle, moderate, shifting winds.
For full weather report see Page 13.

VOL. LXIV...NO. 20,946. NEW YORK, MONDAY, MAY 31, 1915.—FOURTEEN PAGES. ONE CENT In Greater New York, Jersey City and Newark. { Elsewhere TWO CENTS

GERMANY REPLIES THAT IT WAS 'JUSTIFIED SELF-DEFENSE' TO SINK LUSITANIA; CAN NO LONGER 'OBSERVE REGULATIONS' WOULD ARBITRATE HER ATTACKS ON OUR OWN VESSELS; WASHINGTON DISTURBED BY THE NOTE, WHICH IS NOT FINAL

VON JAGOW EXPLAINS NOTE

Believes it Essential to Establish First 'a Common Basis of Fact.'

NOT GERMANY'S FINAL WORD

Hopes We Will Let Her Know Wherein Our Understanding of the Case Differs from Hers.

GERMANY HAS SUPPLIES

And Is in No Danger of Being Starved Out by the Embargo on Foodstuffs.

BUT WOULD CHANGE POLICY

Should Great Britain Return to the Contraband Rules "Generally Accepted Before the War."

BERLIN, May 30, (via London, Monday, May 31, 3:30 A. M.)—Gottlieb von Jagow, the Imperial German Foreign Secretary, received the correspondent of The Associated Press today and outlined the reasons which impelled the German Government to send an ad interim note to the United States Government, instead of a final and definite reply to the American representations regarding the Lusitania and other ships that have been torpedoed and Germany's submarine policy.

"The issues involved," said Herr von Jagow, "are of such importance, and the view in regard to the Lusitania show such variance, that the German Government believed it essential to attempt to establish a common basis of fact before entering into a discussion of the issues involved.

"We hope and trust that the American Government will take the same view of the case and let us know in what points their understanding of the facts differs from the German viewpoint as set forth in the note, and in what points they agree, before looking for a direct answer to their communication.

Hopes for Common Basis.

"The American note, of course, leaves the way open for a preliminary discussion of the situation as suggested in the German note. I hope that such a common basis of fact, once established, may serve as the groundwork for further conversations."

The Minister was unwilling to give a more definite outline to or to comment on the suggestion that an arrangement might be reached on a basis of an inspection and certification by the American Government of passenger ships, not carrying war cargoes, pointing out that he did not feel entitled to anticipate, as the other departments of the Government must be heard before suggestions could be definitely taken up or discussed.

Dr. von Jagow expressed pleasure at the newspaper announcement that American Line steamers were not carrying contraband, but he suggested the advisability of supplementing such newspaper statements by more definite authoritative announcements.

Points to British Embargo.

Replying to a question, Dr. von Jagow said that Germany had been willing from the outset to abandon her submarine war against merchantmen in response to a return by Great Britain to the regulations of war regarding contraband generally accepted before the war, the specific condition being the lifting of the embargo on foodstuffs and raw material, now on the list of conditional contraband.

It was not Germany's fault, but Great Britain's, he said, that the well-meant proposals of the United States for a compromise failed.

"The question of foodstuffs and raw materials," Dr. von Jagow said, "is not a question of necessity for Germany but one of principle. Germany has shown, I think, that it cannot be starved out by Great Britain's em-

Continued on Page 2.

Full Text of Germany's Reply to the United States

Berlin, May 29, via London, May 31,—1:08 A. M.

The undersigned has the honor to submit to Ambassador Gerard the following answer to the communication of May 15 regarding the injury to American interests through German submarine warfare:

The Imperial Government has subjected the communication of the American Government to a thorough investigation. It entertains also a keen wish to co-operate in a frank and friendly way in clearing up a possible misunderstanding which may have arisen in the relations between the two Governments through the events mentioned by the American Government.

Regarding, firstly, the cases of the American steamers Cushing and Gulflight, the American Embassy has already been informed that the German Government has no intention of submitting neutral ships in the war zone, which are guilty of no hostile acts, to attacks by a submarine or submarines or aviators. On the contrary, the German forces have repeatedly been instructed most specifically to avoid attacks on such ships.

If neutral ships in recent months have suffered through the German submarine warfare, owing to mistakes in identification, it is a question only of quite isolated and exceptional cases, which can be attributed to the British Government's abuse of flags, together with the suspicious or culpable behavior of the masters of the ships.

The German Government, in all cases in which it has been shown by its investigations that a neutral ship, not itself at fault, was damaged by German submarines or aviators, has expressed regret over the unfortunate accident, and, if justified by conditions, has offered indemnification.

The cases of the Cushing and the Gulflight will be treated on the same principles.

An investigation of both cases is in progress, the result of which will presently be communicated to the Embassy. The investigation can, if necessary, be supplemented by an international call on the International Commission of Inquiry, as provided by Article III. of The Hague agreement of Oct. 18, 1907.

When sinking the British steamer Falaba, the commander of the German submarine had the intention of allowing the passengers and crew a full opportunity for a safe escape. Only when the master did not obey the order to heave to, but fled and summoned help by rocket signals, did the German commander order the crew and passengers by signals and megaphone to leave the ship within ten minutes. He actually allowed them twenty-three minutes' time, and fired the torpedo only when suspicious craft were hastening to the assistance of the Falaba.

Regarding the loss of life by the sinking of the British passenger steamer Lusitania, the German Government has already expressed to the neutral Governments concerned its keen regret that citizens of their States lost their lives.

On this occasion the Imperial Government, however, cannot escape the impression that certain important facts having a direct bearing on the sinking of the Lusitania may have escaped the attention of the American Government.

In the interest of a clear and complete understanding, which is the aim of both Governments, the Imperial Government considers it first necessary to convince itself that the information accessible to both Governments about the facts of the case is complete and in accord.

The Government of the United States proceeds on the assumption that the Lusitania could be regarded as an ordinary unarmed merchantman. The Imperial Government allows itself in this connection to point out that the Lusitania was one of the largest and fastest British merchant ships, built with Government funds as an auxiliary cruiser, and carried expressly as such in the "navy list" issued by the British Admiralty.

It is further known to the Imperial Government, from trustworthy reports from its agents and neutral passengers, that for a considerable time practically all the more valuable British merchantmen have been equipped with cannon and ammunition and other weapons and manned with persons who have been specially trained in serving guns. The Lusitania, too, according to information received here, had cannon aboard which were mounted and concealed below decks.

The Imperial Government, further, has the honor to direct the particular attention of the American Government to the fact that the British Admiralty, in a confidential instruction, issued in February, 1915, recommended its mercantile shipping not only to seek protection under neutral flags and distinguishing marks, but also, while thus disguised, to attack German submarines by ramming. As a special incitation to merchantmen to destroy submarines, the British Government also offered high prizes and has already paid such rewards.

The Imperial Government, in view of these facts, indubitably known to it, is unable to regard British merchantmen in the zone of naval operations specified by the Admiralty Staff of the German Navy as "undefended." German commanders consequently are no longer able to observe the customary regulations of the prize law, which they before always followed.

Finally, the Imperial Government must point out particularly that the Lusitania on its last trip, as on earlier occasions, carried Canadian troops and war material, including no less than 5,400 cases of ammunition intended for the destruction of the brave German soldiers who are fulfilling their duty with self-sacrifice and devotion in the fatherland's service.

The German Government believes that it was acting in justified self-defense in seeking with all the means of warfare at its disposition to protect the lives of its soldiers by destroying ammunition intended for the enemy.

The British shipping company must have been aware of the danger to which the passengers aboard the Lusitania were exposed under these conditions. The company in embarking them, notwithstanding this, attempted deliberately to use the lives of American citizens as protection for the ammunition aboard and acted against the clear provisions of the American law, which expressly prohibits the forwarding of passengers on ships carrying ammunition, and provides a penalty therefor. The company, therefore, is wantonly guilty of the death of so many passengers.

There can be no doubt, according to the definite report of the submarine's Commander, which is further confirmed by all other information, that the quick sinking of the Lusitania is primarily attributable to the explosion of the ammunition shipment caused by a torpedo. The Lusitania's passengers would otherwise, in all human probabilty, have been saved.

The Imperial Government considers the above-mentioned facts important enough to recommend them to the attentive examination of the American Government.

The Imperial Government, while withholding its final decision on the demands advanced in connection with the sinking of the Lusitania until receipt of an answer from the American Government, feels impelled, in conclusion, to recall here and now that it took cognizance with satisfaction of the mediatory proposals submitted by the United States Government to Berlin and London as a basis for a modus vivendi for conducting the maritime warfare between Germany and Great Britain.

The Imperial Government, by its readiness to enter upon a discussion of these proposals, then demonstrated its good intentions in ample fashion. The realization of these proposals was defeated, as is well known, by the declinatory attitude of the British Government.

The undersigned takes occasion, et cetera, JAGOW.

The President's Note of May 13, to Which the Above Is the Reply.

The Secretary of State to the American Ambassador at Berlin:

DEPARTMENT OF STATE
Washington, May 13, 1915

Please call on the Minister of Foreign Affairs and after reading to him this communication leave with him a copy.

In view of recent acts of the German authorities in violation of American rights on the high seas, which culminated in the torpedoing and sinking of the British steamship Lusitania on May 7, 1915, by which over 100 American citizens lost their lives, it is clearly wise and desirable that the Government of the United States and the Imperial German Government should come to a clear and full understanding as to the grave situation which has resulted.

The sinking of the British passenger steamer Falaba by a German submarine on March 28, through which Leon C. Thrasher, an American citizen, was drowned; the attack on April 28 on the American vessel Cushing by a German aeroplane; the torpedoing on May 1 of the American vessel Gulflight by a German submarine, as a result of which two or more American citizens met their death; and, finally, the torpedoing and sinking of the steamship Lusitania, constitute a series of events which the Government of the United States has observed with growing concern, distress, and amazement.

Recalling the humane and enlightened attitude hitherto assumed by the Imperial German Government in matters of international right, and particularly with regard to the freedom of the seas; having learned to recognize the German views and the German influence in the field of international obligation as always engaged upon the side of justice and humanity; and having understood the instructions of the Imperial German Government to its naval commanders to be upon the same plane of humane action prescribed by the naval codes of other nations, the Government of the United States was loath to believe—it can not now bring itself to believe—that these acts, so absolutely contrary to the rules, the practices, and the spirit of modern warfare, could have the countenance or sanction of that great Government. It feels it to be its duty, therefore, to address the Imperial German Government concerning them with the utmost frankness and in the earnest hope that it is not mistaken in expecting action on the part of the Imperial German Government which will correct the unfortunate impressions which have been created, and vindicate once more the position of that Government with regard to the sacred freedom of the seas.

The Government of the United States has been apprised that the Imperial German Government considered themselves to be obliged by the extraordinary circumstances of the present war and the measures adopted by their adversaries in seeking to cut Germany off from all commerce, to adopt methods of retaliation which go much beyond the ordinary methods of warfare at sea, in the proclamation of a war zone from which they have warned neutral ships to keep away. This Government has already taken occasion to inform the Imperial German Government that it cannot admit the adoption of such measures or such a warning of danger to operate as in any degree an abbreviation of the rights of American shipmasters or of American citizens bound on lawful errands as passengers on merchant ships of belligerent nationality, and that it must hold the Imperial German Government to a strict accountability for any infringement of those rights, intentional or incidental. It does not understand the Imperial German Government to question those rights. It assumes, on the contrary, that the Imperial Government accept, as of course, the rule that the lives of noncombatants, whether they be of neutral citizenship or citizens of one of the nations at war, cannot lawfully or rightfully be put in jeopardy by the capture or destruction of an unarmed merchantman, and recognize also, as all other nations do, the obligation to take the usual precaution of visit and search to ascertain whether a suspected merchantman is in fact of belligerent nationality or is in fact carrying contraband of war under a neutral flag.

The Government of the United States, therefore, desires to call the attention of the Imperial German Government with the utmost earnestness to the fact that the objection to their present method of attack against the trade of their enemies lies in the practical impossibility of employing submarines in the destruction of commerce without disregarding those rules of fairness, reason, justice, and humanity which all modern opinion regards as imperative. It is practically impossible for the officers of a submarine to visit a merchantman at sea and examine her papers and cargo. It is practically impossible for them to make a prize of her; and, if they cannot put a prize crew on board of her, they cannot sink her without leaving her crew and all on board of her to the mercy of the sea in her small boats. These facts it is understood the Imperial German Government frankly admit. We are informed that in the instances of which we have spoken time enough for even that poor measure of safety was not given, and in at least two of the cases cited not so much as a warning was received. Manifestly, submarines cannot be used against merchantmen, as the last few weeks have shown, without an inevitable violation of many sacred principles of justice and humanity.

American citizens act within their indisputable rights in taking their ships and in traveling wherever their legitimate business calls them upon the high seas, and exercise those rights in what should be the well-justified confidence that their lives will not be endangered by acts done in clear violation of universally acknowledged international obligations, and certainly in the confidence that their own Government will sustain them in the exercise of their rights.

There was recently published in the newspapers of the United States, I regret to inform the Imperial German Government, a formal warning, purporting to come from the Imperial German Embassy at Washington, addressed to the people of the United States, and stating, in effect, than any citizen of the United States who exercised his right of free travel upon the seas would do so at his peril if his journey should take him within the zone of waters within which the Imperial German Navy was using submarines against the commerce of Great Britain and France, notwithstanding the respectful but very earnest protest of his Government, the Government of the United States. I do not refer to this for the purpose of calling the attention of the Imperial German Government at this time to the surprising irregularity of a communication from the Imperial German Embassy at Washington addressed to the people of the United States through the newspapers, but only for the purpose of pointing out that no warning that an unlawful and inhumane act will be committed can possibly be accepted as an excuse or palliation for that act or as an abatement of the responsibility for its commission.

Long acquainted as this Government has been with the character of the Imperial Government, and with the high principles of equity by which they have in the past been actuated and guided, the Government of the United States cannot believe that the commanders of the vessels which committed these acts of lawlessness did so except under a misapprehension of the orders issued by the Imperial German naval authorities. It takes it for granted that, at least within the practical possibilities of every such case, the commanders even of submarines were expected to do nothing that would involve the lives of noncombatants or the safety of neutral ships, even at the cost of failing of their object of capture or destruction. It confidently expects, therefore, that the Imperial German Government will disavow the acts of which the Government of the United States complains; that they will make reparation, so far as reparation is possible, for injuries which are without measure, and that they will take immediate steps to prevent the recurrence of anything so obviously subversive of the principles of warfare for which the Imperial German Government have in the past so wisely and so firmly contended.

The Government and people of the United States look to the Imperial German Government for just, prompt, and enlightened action in this vital matter with the greater confidence, because the United States and Germany are bound together not only by special ties of friendship, but also by the explicit stipulations of the Treaty of 1828, between the United States and the Kingdom of Prussia.

Expressions of regret and offers of reparation in case of the destruction of neutral ships sunk by mistake, while they may satisfy international obligations, if no loss of life results, cannot justify or excuse a practice the natural and necessary effect of which is to subject neutral nations and neutral persons to new and immeasurable risks.

The Imperial German Government will not expect the Government of the United States to omit any word or any act necessary to the performance of its sacred duty of maintaining the rights of the United States and its citizens and of safeguarding their free exercise and enjoyment. BRYAN.

CONSIDERS IT DISAPPOINTIN

Dissatisfaction With th Reply Is Reflected in Government Circles.

PROMPT REJOINDER LIKEL

Answer Will Probably be Sent Berlin Within 24, or at Most 48, Hours

TO RESTATE OUR POSITIO

With an Intimation That a Early and Definite Reply Is Desired.

WILL REQUIRE REPARATIC

And Assurances of Future Respe for American Rights—Newspape Echo Capital's Disapproval.

WASHINGTON, May 30.—Ge many's reply to the American n concerning the sinking of the Lu tania, with a loss of more than American lives, produced a feeling profound disappointment here. D satisfaction at the failure of Germa to answer the demands of the Unit States was reflected in Governme circles generally.

President Wilson had retired early before the text arrived—but from reading of the summary published day and Ambassador Gerard's for casts, he had an accurate impressi of what it contained.

Secretary Bryan would make comment. Other Cabinet officers we reticent, but there was little concea ment anywhere that the answer fro Berlin had produced a grave situati in the relations between the Unit States and Germany. Just wh course of action the United Stat will pursue is undetermined.

Press dispatches giving the text the reply came during the evening a were sent to the White House. T official text from Ambassador Gera arrived just before midnight, and w be placed before the President ear tomorrow. There will be a Cabin meeting on Tuesday.

Prompt Answer Probable.

From a previous knowledge of Pres dent Wilson's position, it was genera ly predicted tonight that a prompt a swer would be sent to Berlin, perha in awenty-four or forty-eight hou This is expected to give the Americ Government's understanding of t facts—that the Lusitania was n armed and carried no concealed gun that she sailed from the United Stat a peaceful merchantman, and that u der all rules of international law a humanity the vessel should have bee visited and searched and her passe gers transferred to a place of safet whether she carried ammunition not. American law does not prohib the carrying of ammunition on pa senger ships, it will be asserted, b only self-exploding material, and th liners in the past have been pe mitted to carry arms and ammunitio by special ruling of the State Depar ment on the meanings of Feder statutes.

Germany's failure even to discus the reparation demanded by th American note, and her evasion of th request that guarantees be given th American vessels and lives be not e dangered in the future are the mai points, however, which the Unite States Government, it was generall believed tonight, would advert in th second note.

Doesn't Remove Risks.

The expressions of regret and of fers of reparation for unintentiona attacks on neutral ships are expecte to have little weight in determinin the nature of the response of th United States. When the note May 13 was sent it was pointed ou that such promises did not remov the risks to which American vesse and lives were subjected—and to sup port this contention the United State will add, it is said, that the Ameri can steamer Nebraskan was orpedoe

"All the News That's Fit to Print."

The New York Times.

THE WEATHER
Partly cloudy today; fair tomorrow; not much change in temperature; light northwest winds.
☞Fo full weather report see Page 19.

VOL. LXV...NO. 21,223. ... NEW YORK, FRIDAY, MARCH 3, 1916.—TWENTY PAGES. ONE CENT In Greater New York, Jersey City and Newark. { Elsewhere, TWO CENTS.

ATTACK ON VERDUN IS RESUMED; NEW ASSAULTS AT DOUAUMONT ARE BEATEN OFF, PARIS SAYS

EGIN WITH HEAVY GUNFIRE

ut the German Infantry Suffer Severe Checks as They Move Up.

HELLING NORTH FRONT

ill Across the Meuse and the River Crossings Subjected to Bombardment.

RENCH AIRMEN ARE BUSY

ssail Supply Stations Back of the German Lines, Dropping Scores of Bombs.

LONDON, March 2.—German attacks great violence have been resumed to e north of Verdun.

Following severe artillery fire along e entire front, from west of the Meuse beyond Douaumont to the eastward, veral very strong assaults were made the latter region, according to the ght bulletin of the French War Of-ce.

These attacks, which Paris characteres as pushed with "extreme violence," ere repulsed by French infantry, whose re, it is stated, "decimated the enemy nks." French artillery also was active in the engagement.

La Côte du Poivre, to the west of Douamont, and Le Mort Homme, lying cross the Meuse southeast of Forges, kewise were targets of the German ins. Bombardment of the latter point ad the principal crossings of the river gan last night with great vigor.

In the Woevre district, east of Verdun, tle activity has been shown by the ermans except in the vicinity of Fress, where, after a severe bombardment, attack was made on the French positions only to be repulsed, according to aris.

French airmen have been engaged in fensive operations to counteract the ork of the foe. One squadron of aeroanes assailed the station at Chamey, southwest of Metz, dropping fortyar bombs. Forty bombs were dropped the railway station at Bensdorf, to e eastward of Metz.

Paris Story of New Attack.

The night report of the French War ffice is as follows:

In Belgium destructive fires have een directed by our artillery against he German organizations to the east f Steenstraete.

Between the Somme and the Oise a erman work was destroyed by our atteries in the region of Beauraignes.

In Champagne a German aeroplane, helled by our batteries in the vicinity f Suippes, fell in flames within the nemy lines.

In the Argonne we executed concenrated fires to the north of Harazée nd on the Cheppy Wood.

In the region to the north of Verdun nd in the Woevre the activity of the nemy artillery, which had abated omewhat during the preceding days, ras considerably increased during the ourse of the day along the entire ront, and principally on Le Mort Homme, the Côte du Poivre, and in he region of Douaumont. At the lastamed point the bombardment was ollowed by several attacks of infantry f extreme violence. This series of ttacks was repulsed by our troops, hose fire decimated the enemy ranks. Our batteries replied energetically verywhere to the bombardment and helled the enemy's roads of communiation.

To the northeast of St. Mihiel our ong-range guns bombarded the railay station at Vigneulles. According o our observers, two fires were started, several trains were hit, and a locomotive was blown up.

In Upper Alsace there has been reat activity on the part of both arlleries in the sector of Seppois.

Last night one of our bombing quadrons dropped forty-four shells f all calibres on the station at hambley, which appeared to have uffered serious damage. Notwithtanding a lively cannonade, the aeroanes returned in safety to our lines. Today our aeroplanes likewise ropped forty shells on the railway tation at Bensdorf and nine projeciles on the enemy establishments at vricourt.

Heavy Assault on Fresnes.

The French War Office announcement the afternoon said that there were termittent bombardments of the Vern and Woevre fronts during the night. German attack on Fresnes was relsed, it is said. The report reads:

In the Artois district, to the east of he road running from Neuville to La olle, we had caused the explosion of mine, located under an old crater, hich was occupied by the enemy. We ook possession of the new crater.

In the region of Verdun the enemy ombarded violently last night Le Mort Homme (The Dead Man), at the Côte e l'Oie, between Malancourt and Forges, as well as the principal crossngs of the River Meuse. There was ttle activity on the part of the artilery to the east of the Meuse.

In the Woevre district, after an inense retaliatory fire from the artilery, the enemy yesterday evening delivered a spirited attack on our posiions at Fresnes. They were at once riven back by our counterattack from

Continued on Page 3.

British Recapture 800 Yards of Trenches; Heavy Gunfire May Portend Big Offensive

LONDON, March 2.—The recapture of 800 yards of trenches along the Ypres-Comines Canal in Flanders is announced in the official statement of the War Office tonight. A small salient in the German lines at that point has also been won by the British forces. The statement is as follows:

> We recaptured the trenches at the bluff of the Ypres-Comines Canal, which were lost Feb. 14, and also captured a small salient in the original German lines.
>
> A counterattack launched by the enemy some hours later was repulsed. German mine galleries in the captured trenches were destroyed. We have taken 180 prisoners, including four officers.
>
> There has been much artillery activity on both sides today from Vierstraat to Boesinghe.

Special Cable to THE NEW YORK TIMES.

ROTTERDAM, March 2, (Dispatch to The London Daily Telegraph.)—From many points on the Belgo-Dutch frontier comes news of tremendous artillery actions along the Yser front, also in the neighborhood of Ypres.

For three days and nights the guns have roared almost without cessation. Their thunder has reached the ears of people, and shaken windows in places more remote from the front than ever before.

According to definite reports reaching the frontier the German front trenches have been subjected to a fearful bombardment.

GERMAN ATTACK PICTURED BY FOE

Unrolling Like Gray Carpet, They Come On, Despite Big Guns and Rifle Fire.

MACHINE GUNS STOP THEM

And Then the Bayonet Ends It—2,000 Brandenburgers Still Held in Fort.

Special Cable to THE NEW YORK TIMES.

PARIS, March 2.—Accounts that reach Paris from Bar-le-Duc, Chalons, and other junction points to which most of the Verdun wounded have been taken, make it clear that the French soldiers have retained complete confidence; despite the extraordinary fury of the bombardment, which all agree far surpassed anything ever known before on this front.

An auxiliary surgeon, who has just returned from Bar-le-Duc, says:

"It is a pity that a neutral observer is not able to compare our wounded with the German prisoners, taken after the Champagne bombardment. Even when unhurt, the latter were utterly dazed. The majority could not speak coherently, but just managed to babble words of terror or relief at their escape.

"Ours naturally feel the shock, but show it rather in excitement or fever than in lowered morale. Their eyes show that each is eager to describe his part in what all declare a victory. Fully two-thirds express regret at having to leave before we finished off the Boches. All are perfectly confident about the final outcome.

"I spoke with one of a batch of German prisoners, all Prussians, young and well equipped. They had come from Serbia after six weeks' rest. They were very different from the confident group I saw after the Marne. They looked thoroughly beaten. One youth I interrogated talked French well. He said to me:

"'We were told that this was the last battle of the war, that the French were tired and had no cannon. So we were literally stupefied when your cannonade replied, fully as effective as ours. My regiment attacked south of Beaumont. We lost quite half of our men in the first discharge of the French guns. The rest retired speedily. We in the front were glad to crawl to your trenches. We have escaped from hell.'"

A Young Soldier's Story.

One youngster of the class of 1914, who has a broken arm, is quoted as giving this vivid account of the early fighting:

"They told us the Boches had 400,000 picked men and 2,000 guns. I can well believe it, but they have lost more than a third of the former at least.

"As for the cannonade, it was a regular deluge. Our trenches were demolished as if they had been deliberately turned upside down by a giant hand. After six hours of that there was nothing left to defend, so we retired to the support trenches near Anglomont. We had to crawl, and, what with shell holes, corpses, and barbed wire, it was no trip in a sleeping car.

"Then the enemy began to advance. They looked like a big gray carpet being unrolled over the country. Our guns had the range exactly, but the gaps filled up as by magic.

"We opened fire at 200 yards. I guess there were few misses at that close, but we might as well have been firing peas. They never even hesitated.

"Then our mitrailleuses got going. That was different. Whole rows of the enemy toppled over like corn under the scythe. They stopped; then we

Continued on Page 3.

MUD OF WOEVRE HINDERS ADVANCE

But German Howitzers Pound Away Busily at French Targets as Infantry Creep On.

BATTLEGROUND IS TITANIC

Attacking Troops Show Tireless Energy Amid Difficulties—Losses Declared Small.

By Baron KURT VON REDEN.

Special Cable to THE NEW YORK TIMES.
The Berlin Tageblatt Dispatches.

ORMONT FARM, via German Great Headquarters, Feb. 29, (via London, March 2.)—A monster circle of fire spreads before me, and the howitzer battery, which a while ago was firing near me, has driven off and is already going into action again far ahead of me. This is the only one of the many I can follow, so far as my field glasses can reach.

In time a little order comes out of this chaos. Slowly I find the connection between the continuous wailing and crashing all around. By individual batteries, I can already discover the targets at which they are firing—a flat, bare ridge, then a patch of woods, then a long-range fort with many batteries and fortification works.

The French line is plainly marked by the continuous heavy explosions on its crest. One also sees the delicate outlines of little mounds, which are the fortifications we are bombarding in order to hold them down to let the German infantry advance.

A new page of history has been turned here before my eyes—a tenfold magnification of the picture of the battle of Sedan. Only a part of the battle around Verdun can be seen here, and yet this section is titanic in extent.

Today there is deep mud everywhere. The snow does not last, and we hope for dry days.

I have spoken with troops that stormed the strongly fortified and far-dominating Hill 344 last Wednesday. When the splendid German artillery succeeded in completely silencing the heights, the infantry was turned loose and stormed through the shredded barbed-wire entanglements.

The bald, towering hill lies just before me. It formed a connecting link between the defenses on both sides of the Meuse.

As the infantry advanced, a frightful fire from some far-distant French flanking batteries laid a checkerboard pattern of bursting shells on the foreground, through which the brave troops stormed with indescribable defiance of death till at last they reached the top of the hill.

But the worst was still to come. The French now laid a fierce concentric fire upon this important hill, possession of which was decisive for the terrain on both sides. Thus the German troops were completely cut off for two days as on an island and forced to hold out. There was, of course, not a ghost of a chance to bring on the field kitchens.

But, despite everything, these heroes beat off violent counterattacks and held out until a whole strip of the front was in their possession.

Prisoners have just been passing by me—Europeans in faultless new uniforms and colored soldiers in picturesque rags, and without the new protective steel helmet. They, too, narrate how they were completely cut off by the German fire, and finally surrendered.

The troops that have enjoyed a little rest after the heavy days are just going forward again. The men are

Continued on Page 3.

Mine Field Is Set Adrift Off the Coast of Sweden

LONDON, Friday, March 3.—A Stockholm dispatch to The Morning Post says that, according to a message from Karlskrona, Sweden, a whole mine field of several hundred mines is drifting from the north, presumably having been set adrift by the ice and wind.

The message adds that explosions are occurring hourly, and that navigation in the neighborhood of the Swedish islands is perilous.

TAMMANY STARTS BOOM FOR GERARD

Ambassador to Germany Urged at Syracuse Convention as Gubernatorial Candidate.

SEABURY IS IN THE FIELD

Conway and Treman Also Receptive—Osborn to Run for the United States Senate.

Special to The New York Times.

SYRACUSE, March 2.—As the result of informal conferences between Tammany Leader Charles F. Murphy and Democratic leaders from up-State, while the unofficial State convention was in progress here, it has been determined that only a Democrat who can command the unqualified support of President Wilson will receive the support of the Democratic State organization in the Fall primaries as a candidate for the Gubernatorial nomination.

Mr. Murphy, it is said, told up-State men with whom he talked that he would be pleased if they could bring forward some strong Democrat from up-State who could be groomed for the race. Should they fail to do so, Mr. Murphy thought New York City could supply the man needed. If the Tammany chieftain had any particular man in mind when he made this statement he gave no intimation of the fact to the conferees from up-State.

Judging, however, from the talk among the score or more of influential Tammanyites who attended the convention, James W. Gerard, whom President Wilson appointed Ambassador to Germany, is looming large on the Democratic horizon as a possible prospective standard bearer in the Gubernatorial fight.

According to reports received from abroad, Ambassador Gerard's return to the country is expected before long. It has also been reported that he is to make speeches for President Wilson throughout the country in the national campaign.

It is not thought the views of either Mr. Gerard or the Democratic leaders at Washington have been obtained regarding the plan to have Mr. Gerard run, which as yet is said to be purely tentative and likely to remain in that stage until he arrives here and can give his assent to the program. The advantages of having Mr. Gerard lead the fight, as seen by the Democratic leaders who are anxious to have the plan carried out, are these:

There could be no question about the President's support of Gerard.

Mr. Gerard, besides being high in the favor of the Federal Administration and having proved himself thoroughly qualified for public office, is highly regarded in Tammany circles. Mr. Gerard was Treasurer of Tammany Hall in several of its most successful campaigns, and has always been a good organization man.

The selection of the present Ambassador to Germany, it is thought, would conciliate the German-American element and attract their support to the Democratic ticket in a year when it is realized that a special bid must be made for German-American votes.

Mr. Gerard, it is thought, would insure the support of Mr. Hearst and his newspapers for the Democratic State ticket at least.

One Democratic leader suggested that the wealth of Mr. Gerard might prove one of his chief attractions in the eyes of certain Democrats high in the party councils in this State, who expect that his nomination would bring a lot of "easy money" into the sadly depleted Democratic campaign treasury.

Seabury Is Receptive.

Among prospective candidacies in connection with the Gubernatorial campaign the one most widely discussed among the delegates and visitors at yesterday's convention was that of Judge Samuel Seabury of the Court of Appeals.

Judge Seabury, according to his friends, would like to exchange his seat on the bench for the Governor's chair. He received in round numbers 647,000 votes as a candidate for Judge of the Court of Appeals in 1914. This was only 40,000 votes less than Governor Whitman received. The big vote has commended him to a good many of the Democratic leaders, but there is opposition to him in many quarters because of his earlier connection with the Independence League and other radical movements.

Ex-Lieut. Gov. Thomas F. Conway, running mate of ex-Governor Dix, also will be a candidate in the Fall primaries for the Gubernatorial nomination. Mr. Conway has the support of the Democratic organiation in the Northern Tier counties.

Charles E. Treman, who was Superintendent of Public Works in the Dix administration, is another up-State Democrat who figured clearly in the convention gossip on Gubernatorial possibilities. Mr. Treman is a wealthy merchant whose home is in Ithaca. He is regarded as an independent Democrat.

It is fully expected that Chairman William Church Osborn of the Democratic State Committee before long will announce his candidacy for the United States Senate as successor to Senator James A. O'Gorman, whose term expires at the end of the present year. The general belief among Tammany men at the convention was that Senator O'Gorman would return to the practice of law. Samuel Untermyer, is also said to be anxious to go to the Senate.

There are many indications that the hope expressed well-nigh universally by Democrats who attended the convention that Governor Whitman would be nominated by the Republicans for a second term will not be fulfilled. If William Barnes has his way—and Mr. Barnes is thought to have sufficient influence in the Republican State organization to have his way—Mr. Whitman will be dropped at the end of his present term.

PRESIDENT DENIES HE FAVORS WAR AS GORE CHARGES IN SENATE DEBATE; BRITAIN'S ORDERS TO ARMED LINERS

STATEMENT FOR MR. WILSON

What He Told Congressmen on Crisis Given to The Times.

STRIVING HARD FOR PEACE

But Move in Congress to Limit His Power Was Drifting Toward Conflict.

BERLIN ATTITUDE STIFFENED

Gerard Says Germans Think Congress 5 to 1 Against Wilson—War Talk Laid to Bernstorff.

Special to The New York Times.

WASHINGTON, March 2.—Sensation followed sensation today in the delicate controversy over the armed ship issue. Besides the statements in the Senate indicating a critical condition in the relations between Germany and the United States, a story went the rounds—rapidly, gaining a bit as it went, as such stories usually gain—that Count von Bernstorff, the German Ambassador, had informed Secretary Lansing that if the United States severed diplomatic relations with the Berlin Government Germany would declare war. It was asserted that the President had so quoted the German Ambassador in talks with leaders in Congress who called at the White House to discuss the armed ship situation.

A careful inquiry this evening, while it brought refusal from the State Department and the German Embassy to discuss any matter of such a confidential character, produced from the Embassy an oral denial of that portion of the report that put Count von Bernstorff in the position of having asserted that Germany "would declare war" in the event of a breach of relations. Little, if any, doubt exists, however, that Count von Bernstorff has stated, although it is not asserted that he did so directly to Secretary Lansing, that a diplomatic break "would mean war."

Dissension Here Stiffens Germany.

Today James W. Gerard, the American Ambassador, cabled to the State Department that the statement was being circulated in official circles and through the newspapers that Congress stood five to one against President Wilson on the armed ship issue. The effect of this belief is reflected in press dispatches from the German capital. The impression here is that German officials have convinced themselves that the United States is afraid of war, and that Germany's back has been stiffened immoderately in dealing with this country in the Lusitania and armed ship questions.

There is general confidence that the warning resolutions will be tabled in the Senate tomorrow. Some of the President's supporters are hopeful that the House will be influenced by the example of the Senate and will decide to vote down the similar resolutions pending in that body. But it is only a hope, for practically every member of the House is willing to admit that the confusion there is so great that it would be mere surmise to say what the House would do if a warning resolution came before it for action.

Tonight Representative James R. Mann, the Republican floor leader, visited the President at the latter's invitation. He would not say afterward what their conference had developed. Secretary Lansing also had a conference with the President this evening.

Confusion existed tonight in every portion of the capital which touches the Government. Many men—most of them members of Congress—see a breach with Germany without taking into consideration that the President will go to extremes to prevent it. Some of them are saying privately that the President wants war and that his course in the armed ship controversy is directed toward that end. One may hear all sorts of ill-considered statements in this town tonight.

Gloom at the Capital.

It is undeniable that a feeling of gloom exists in many quarters here and that opinion is general that the situation of the relations between Germany and the United States is very delicate indeed. But among a considerable number who have some knowledge of the attitude of the Administration, the understanding prevails that there can be no severance of relations unless a Teutonic submarine sinks a merchant ship with the consequent loss of American lives. A refusal by Germany to modify her armed ship order is not regarded as making a break certain.

There were so many stories in circulation today as to what President Wilson had said to Congressional leaders with regard to his attitude toward the armed ship order and toward Germany as a nation, that a friend of the President consented to tell what he knew of the matter. He explained that he was not speaking in any official or authoritative way, but it was evident that he was fully acquainted with the scope and the character of the conversations that had taken place between the President and leading Senators and Representatives during the past week. This friend of the President said that what he would tell was not the President's position as explained to any particular group of legislators, but was what the President had told to all of those who had called on him at his invitation. Some of the conversations took a wider scope than others.

The President, according to this friend, told his Congressional callers that the way to avoid war was to have the people of the United States stand solidly behind the Executive in his handling of the armed ship negotiations. That course proposed in Congress—the resolution of warning—would lead toward war and not away from it. A yielding now on the part of the Government in dealing with the Central Powers would, the President thought, result in further curtailing of American rights on the seas, and the Government could not afford to yield. The United States must stand by international law itself, the President was indicated as saying. If it did otherwise, circumstances as they occurred would change the law of nations and the outcome would be confusion and no fixed rules for international observance. It would not be long under these conditions before international law would be wiped out. If this Government made a concession to Germany on the issue involved in the armed ship controversy we would be obliged to make concessions to England and other nations, and the whole fabric of international law would fall to pieces.

Might Cause a Break.

The President was asked by some of his congressional visitors what would happen if Congress adopted one of the pending resolutions warning Americans not to travel on armed ships. According to the President's friend, he said such action would encourage Germany to disregard American rights on the seas. What would happen, he was asked, if a German submarine sank an armed merchantman having Americans on board? The President was represented to have said in answer that possibly the only thing that could happen would be a break in relations between the United States and Germany. Congressmen who have visited the White House to discuss the armed ship issue have told their legislative associates that the President said that if a merchant ship was sunk without warning by a German submarine and American lives were lost, he would dismiss the German Ambassador and the Austrian Chargé d'Affaires, recall Ambassadors Gerard and Penfield and prepare for emergencies, but the President's friend did not mention this in his explanation of the President's position.

What would be the next step, the President was asked by some of the Congressional leaders—the step following a break in diplomatic relations? The President's response to this was that it had been represented to him that this might lead to war.

Another question put to the President, according to the version given today, was: What would be the effect of war upon the United States? To this the President is represented to have answered that if we were forced into hostilities, our position might have the effect of bringing the war to an end much sooner than appeared at present.

The President was told that some persons were saying that he wanted war with Germany. Apparently his response to this was made with some emphasis. Why should anybody think he wanted war? His whole course had shown that he was doing everything to preserve peace. His course was the course that would lead to peace, while the course of those who desired to adopt a resolution warning Americans not to travel on armed merchant ships would lead to war. Only the support of the Congress and the people for the Executive in conducting the present negotiations would preserve peace. The President is represented to have spoken of having been jeered, sneered at, and ridiculed for his efforts for peace. At this point the President is understood to have exclaimed in effect: "In God's name, could any one have done more than I to show a desire for peace?"

In the course of his conversations with Senators and Representatives President Wilson expressed the opinion that if a merchant ship carrying Americans was sunk by a Teutonic submarine and the lives of Americans were sacrificed, it would be impossible to hold the American people. They would decide the issue for themselves.

Full Text of British Instructions to Armed Liners; Approach of Submarine to be Deemed Hostile Act

LONDON, March 2.—The British Admiralty tonight officially made public the Admiralty orders to armed merchantmen, given Oct. 20, 1915.

The orders say that the armament of such vessels must be used solely for resisting an attack by an armed vessel and for no other purpose. As British submarines and aircraft are ordered not to approach merchantmen, the orders say, the approach to a British merchantman of a submarine is to be regarded as done with a hostile intention.

The official statement reads as follows:

> In view of the recent issue by the German Government of a memorandum on the treatment of armed merchant ships, the Admiralty has decided to make public the instructions actually governing the actions of British merchant vessels armed for self-defense:
>
> *Instruction, dated 20th of October, 1915, in re the status of armed merchant ships:*
>
> (1) The right of the crew of a merchant vessel to forcibly resist visit and search and fight in self-defense is well recognized in international law and expressly admitted by the German prize regulations in an addendum issued June, 1914, at a time when it was known that numerous merchant vessels were being armed for self-defense.
>
> (2) Armament is supplied solely for the purpose of resisting attack by an armed enemy vessel and must not be used for any other purpose whatsoever.
>
> (3) An armed merchant vessel, therefore, must not in any circumstances interfere with or obstruct the free passage of other merchant vessels or fishing craft, whether these are friendly, neutral, or hostile.
>
> (4) The status of a British armed merchant vessel cannot be changed upon the high seas.
>
> *Rules to be observed in the exercise of the right of self-defense:*
>
> (1) The master or officer in command is responsible for opening and ceasing fire.
>
> (2) Participation in armed resistance must be confined to persons acting under the orders of the master or the officer in command.
>
> (3) Before opening fire the British colors must be hoisted.
>
> (4) Fire must not be opened or continued from a vessel which has stopped, hauled down her flag, or otherwise indicated her intention to surrender.
>
> (5) The expression "armament" includes not only cannon, but also rifles and machine guns in cases where these have been supplied.
>
> (6) The ammunition used in rifles and machine guns must conform to Article XXIII., Hague Convention, 1907, that is, bullets must be cased in nickel or other hard substance and must not be split or cut in such a way as to cause them to expand or set up on striking a man. The use of explosive bullets is forbidden.
>
> *Circumstances under which armament should be employed:*
>
> (1) The armament is supplied for the purpose of defense only. The object of the master should be to avoid action whenever possible.
>
> (2) Experience has shown that hostile submarines and aircraft have frequently attacked merchant vessels without warning. It is important, therefore, that craft of this description should not be allowed to approach to short range, at which a torpedo or bomb launched without notice would almost certainly be effective. British and allied submarines and aircraft have orders not to approach merchant vessels. Consequently it may be presumed that any submarine or aircraft which deliberately approaches or pursues a merchant vessel does so with hostile intention. In such cases fire may be opened in self-defense in order to prevent the hostile craft from closing to a range at which resistance to a sudden attack with bomb or torpedo would be impossible.
>
> (3) An armed merchant vessel proceeding to render assistance to the crew of a vessel in distress must not seek action with any hostile craft, though if she herself is attacked while doing so fire may be opened in self-defense.
>
> (4) It should be remembered that the flag is no guide to nationality. German submarines and armed merchant vessels have frequently employed the British, Allied or neutral colors to approach undetected. Though, however, the use of disguise and false colors to escape capture is a legitimate ruse de guerre, its adoption by defensively armed merchant ships may easily lead to misconception. Such vessels, therefore, are forbidden to adopt any form of disguise which might cause them to be mistaken for neutral ships.
>
> *Admiralty comment:*
>
> These instructions, which are those at present in force, are the latest issued. Successive issues have been made, not by reason of a change in policy—the policy throughout has remained unaltered—but by improvement in wording and greater clearness of expression, to emphasize the purely defensive character of the armament of merchant vessels.
>
> It is because of the distorted interpretation given these instructions as a whole and the very forced character of the interpretation given by the German Government to portions which they quote from an earlier issue of the instructions that the Admiralty felt it desirable, with a view to allaying neutral anxiety, to publish these in extenso.

SENATE TO KILL WARNINGS

Leaders Plan Vote Today That Will Sustain the President.

POLL SHOWS BIG MAJORITY

Stone Differs from President on Armed Liners, but Fights to Leave Him Unhampered.

LODGE BACKS EXECUTIVE

Williams and Others Join Lively Debate—Gore's Statements Disclaimed by Leaders.

President Officially Denies Senator Gore's Statement

Special to The New York Times.

WASHINGTON, March 2.—The White House issued this statement tonight: "When the attention of the White House was called to certain statements in Senator Gore's speech this afternoon, the President authorized an unqualified denial of any utterance to which any such meaning could be attached."

Special to The New York Times.

WASHINGTON, March 2.—The Senate today was the centre of the international storm. It has been many years since the elder statesmen were so sharply stirred as they were today when Senator Gore of Oklahoma, a radical Democrat and close friend of William Jennings Bryan, declared that he had it on good authority that President Wilson had said he expected war and that war would not be altogether an evil, as American participation might end the European struggle by midsummer, and so do a great service to civilization.

Senator Stone of Missouri, Chairman of the Committee on Foreign Relations, who has seen the President several times lately, when challenged to deny the statement, said the President had never intimated that he thought war would be good for the United States or that he thought American participation in the European struggle would end it by midsummer.

Representative Flood, Chairman of the House Committee on Foreign Affairs, who has participated in several White House conferences during the past ten days, denied tonight that the President had made any statement in his presence justifying the expressed apprehension of Senator Gore.

"The President has said nothing in my presence that would justify such a report as Senator Gore informed the Senate he had received," said Mr. Flood. "I have heard the President say nothing to indicate that war with Germany might not be a bad thing for this country or that he desired war. On the contrary, the President told us that he was working night and day to keep this nation out of war. Several members of the House asked me recently if the President had made any statement justifying the circulated reports, and I told them flatly that he had not."

The White House announced that in regard to "certain statements in Senator Gore's speech, the President authorized an unqualified denial of any utterances to which any such meaning could be attached."

Even before Senator Gore spoke in favor of his resolution warning Americans from armed belligerent ships, Mr. Stone had made a profound impression by reading a prepared statement in which he formally announced his divergence from the President and summarized the President's view as being that if the "German Government should persist in their policy (of sinking armed merchantmen without warning) he would sever diplomatic relations and submit the matter to Congress, which under the Constitution is the war-making power."

Senate to Take the Lead.

In spite of his differences with the President, Mr. Stone is working diligently to obtain for the President the prompt defeat of the Gore and Jones resolutions of warning in the Senate. But today's debate in the upper house was precipitated by Mr. Stone's speech, which was regarded as the more important because it was read from prepared manuscript. Yesterday the Senate was ready to wait for action in the House on the resolutions offensive to the President. But last night Mr. Stone decided that the House was so at sea, with ideas so far from crystallization, that the Senate should take lead.

With a view to getting the prompt votes sought by the President, Mr. Stone made his statement today, indicating his intention to prepare a compromise resolution that might bring almost the unanimous support of Congress to the aid of the President. But in doing so he explained his fundamental differences from the President on the question of armed merchantmen. This evening he seemed to have almost despaired of

"All the News That's Fit to Print."

The New York Times.

THE WEATHER

Fair Sunday; Monday partly cloudy; light, variable winds.

For full weather report see Page 23.

VOL. LXV...NO. 21,281. NEW YORK, SUNDAY, APRIL 30, 1916.—96 PAGES, In Seven Parts, Including Picture and Rotogravure Section and Review of Books. PRICE FIVE CENTS.

CONFEREES OPEN MEXICAN PARLEY; VIEWS CONFLICT

Obregon Asks for Withdrawal of Our Troops and Scott for Co-operation.

BOTH QUESTIONS DEFERRED

Long Discussion Over the Conditions in Territory Where Pershing's Men Are.

CORDIALITY SHOWN AT END

Impressive Military Display Marks Reception of Obregon and Staff in El Paso.

From a Staff Correspondent.

Special to The New York Times.

EL PASO, Tex., April 29.—The first conference between the representatives of the United States and Mexico began at 5 o'clock this afternoon in the Mexican Customs House in Juarez, and at exactly 7 o'clock, when the four American Army officers and six Mexican representatives left the building, General Scott was seen to pat General Obregon on the shoulder as they went down the steps.

Both the American Chief of Staff and the Mexican Minister of War were smiling, and the conferees of both sides shook hands with one another. Beyond this manifestation of cordiality, they disclosed nothing that had occurred at the discussion of the operations of the American punitive expedition in Mexico, but THE NEW YORK TIMES correspondent is able to state with authority that this is what occurred at the first conference:

General Obregon communicated to General Scott what amounted to a demand that all American troops be withdrawn from Mexico. This was discussed for a few minutes, then it was practically tabled.

Scott's Counter-Proposal.

General Scott presented then the counter-proposal that the Carranza Government co-operate with the American force in Mexico in further pursuit of the Villista bandits. After brief discussion this counter-proposal was tabled to be taken up again at a later conference.

It was agreed between the representatives of the two Governments that these two proposals could not be passed on until there had been discussion regarding the actual conditions prevailing in Mexico in general, and particularly in the State of Chihuahua. Thereupon a prolonged discussion of conditions in the northern State in which the American troops are now situated began. This discussion lasted throughout the remainder of the conference.

General Scott said after the first conference:

"You may say for me that the meeting was very satisfactory. I will notify General Obregon as to the time of our next meeting."

The Mexican representatives have with them the Civil Governor of Chihuahua, Ignacio Enriquez, a clean-cut young Mexican who was educated at the University of Illinois. He is here practically as a "witness in the case."

In presenting their arguments in the discussion of conditions in the North of Mexico, the official representatives will call Enriquez to bear testimony that the State is now under the control of Carranza. And the reports of Mexican secret agents are already here, to be introduced as documentary evidence to the same end.

Mexicans Prepare a "Brief."

The Mexicans have prepared their case like a lawyer's brief. Another "witness" will be Luis Gutierrez, Military Governor of Chihuahua. From sources which THE TIMES correspondent is unable to disclose it was learned authoritatively tonight that General Obregon has complete authority to conduct the conferences without awaiting new instructions of any sort from General Carranza.

General Scott, however, will communicate each day while the conferences are in progress with the Washington Administration and receive new instructions with which to enter the next session.

General Scott is communicating the result of the first conference to Washington this evening, and expects further instructions by tomorrow morning.

The next conference was tentatively set for tomorrow to be held in the same room in the Mexican Custom House. The time is undecided. General Scott will set the hour after hearing from Washington. Those in a position to know estimated tonight that the conferences would last at least four or five days, and probably longer.

The officials who attended the conference this evening were:

Representing the United States, General Hugh L. Scott, Chief of Staff; General Frederick Funston, Lieut. Col. R. E. L. Michie of the General Staff, and Captain Fitzhugh Lee, General Funston's Aid.

Representing Mexico: General Obregon, the Minister of War; General Jackinto Trevino, commander of the Department of the Northeast; General Luis Gutierrez, General Plutarco, and General Elias Calles, Military Governor of Sonora.

The Mexicans also had present as an interpreter Andreas Garcia, their consul at El Paso, and there was an American interpreter with General Scott.

General Calles arrived here this morning. He had not been included in the list of conferees at first, but yesterday telegraphed a request that he be allowed to attend, and was invited by General Funston. The representatives of both countries agreed at this evening's conference that they would make no official statements for publication until all of the conferences were over.

Obregon and Suite Received.

The first official conference, which did not begin until 5 o'clock this afternoon, followed an exchange of formal visits on the part of the representatives of the two Governments. The American officials took the initiative and made the first call last night, motoring across the international bridge and visiting General Obregon and his associates in the Juarez custom house.

The Mexican officials paid a return visit this morning, General Obregon and his large retinue of Generals and minor officers calling on Generals Scott and Funston in their private car parked near the railroad station here. But before they reached the car the Mexicans had an opportunity to learn that despite the fact that about 12,000 American troops are now in Mexico there is still an impressive number of them at this particular point of the border.

When the Americans crossed the

Continued on Page 6.

VILLISTAS SMASHED, ARMY OFFICERS THINK

Americans' Hard and Frequent Blows Have Taken Fight Out of Scattered Bandits.

By FRANK B. ELSER.

Special Correspondent of The New York Times.

RANCHO PROVIDENCIA, Chihuahua, Mexico, April 28, (by Carrier to Headquarters of General Pershing, Namiquipa, thence by Wireless to Columbus, N. M., April 29.)—Officers of the Seventh Cavalry arriving at this camp this afternoon from Minaca, Santo Tomas, and other towns in the Guerrero district were of the opinion that Villa forces in the Sierra Madre, in broken up bands, had been hit so hard and so often since the Americans came into the country that all the fight had been taken out of them.

These officers said that to the Americans had been given valuable assistance by the Carranzistas during the thirty-day campaign, which closed with the defeat of the last band of Villistas of considerable size at Temachi on Saturday, April 22.

Carranzistas, with large reinforcements from Torreon and from Zacatecas, San Luis Potosi, and other States in the southern part of the Republic, began to arrive today. As they have nothing in common with the natives of this region, it is now believed that they are in a position to keep Villistas from reassembling in numbers sufficiently large to do damage or levy tribute.

The opinion prevails among men arriving from the west that Villa is dead. This opinion is said to be entertained by natives regardless of political leanings.

CONFEREES DEADLOCK ON ARMY BILL ITEM

Can't Agree on Number of Regulars, on Volunteer Reserve or on Nitrate Plant.

WASHINGTON, April 29.—Conferees of the House and Senate, after three days of deliberation on the Army Reorganization bill, the first of the big preparedness measures, have come to a complete deadlock over several important features. It was strongly intimated tonight that they would report a disagreement and ask their respective branches of Congress for further instructions.

"Hopelessly apart on the size of the regular army, on the proposals for a volunteer reserve army, and on a Government nitrate plant," was the report of one member of the conference tonight, and he declared Congress would be asked in the near future to pass again on these features of the measure.

The Senate conferees are insisting determinedly upon the provision in the Senate bill for a regular army of 250,000 men and Representative Kahn, the Republican House conferee, is standing with them. Representatives Hay and Dent, however, are insistent upon the House provision for 140,000 men.

Representative Kahn pointed out to the conferees today that his amendment for an army of 200,000 had been defeated by only a small majority when the House had the bill under consideration. Since that time, big army men contend, international developments have caused a change of feeling on the part of many representatives. Some Administration leaders think the House might now be brought to accept the 250,000 Senate proposal should the conferees fail to agree.

It was said tonight that should a disagreement be reported the Senate might agree to give up its volunteer army plan and accept instead the National Guard reserve provision of the House bill, and might also abandon the Government nitrate plant provision, which, it is conceded generally, never will be accepted by the House.

900 RECRUITS A WEEK ARMY'S AVERAGE NOW

5,417 Men Enlisted in Last 44 Days—18,413 Applicants Rejected.

WASHINGTON, April 29.—Figures compiled by the War Department based on reports from recruiting stations in all parts of the country show that 5,417 recruits have been obtained for the army in the last forty-four days. This is a fraction over one-fourth of the total of 20,000 men to be added to the regular army under the Hay emergency resolution, which was passed by Congress immediately after the Pershing expedition went into Mexico. At the present rate of enlistment it will take all Summer to obtain 20,000 recruits.

During the forty-four days in which the enlistment has been pushed under high pressure the recruiting officers have received applications from 23,830 young men. Of this number the applications of 18,413 were rejected on account of failure to measure up to the high standard required by the recruiting officers.

Every five days the War Department receives telegraphic reports showing the progress in recruiting, the last of these periods having ended at noon yesterday. These reports show that the recruits are being obtained at the rate of about 900 a week. To date the enlistment record has been as follows, for each of the periods:

Period Ending	Applications.	Acceptances.
March 20	2,453	550
March 25	2,653	840
March 31	3,863	551
April 5	2,880	629
April 14	4,968	1,048
April 21	3,575	772
April 28	3,436	718
Total	23,850	5,417

Chicago has been the banner recruiting centre for the country, reporting that during the last forty-four days there have been 2,440 applications and 521 recruits accepted. San Francisco ranks second with 2,762 applicants and 464 recruits accepted, while New York City is third, with 2,122 applicants and 392 recruits accepted. St. Louis stands fourth with 884 applicants and 242 recruits accepted, while Philadelphia has a records of 582 applicants, of whom 221 were accepted.

COMPULSION VOTE GROWS.

Scottish Trades Union Congress Now Stands 66 to 46 Against.

GLASGOW, April 29.—The Scottish Trades Union Congress, by a vote of 66 to 46, today declared its opposition to compulsory military service.

The vote is considered significant, as heretofore the Scottish trades unionists have been virtually unanimous against compulsory service.

8,970 BRITISH AT KUT SURRENDER TO TURKISH FOES

Tigris Force Which Gen. Townshend Led Almost to Bagdad Is Starved Out.

RELIEF FORCE 20 MILES OFF

Hordes of Turks, Strongly Intrenched, Twice Defeated Efforts to Reach Town.

FLOODS ALSO HALT ADVANCE

England Laments Surrender, but Praises Commander for His Brilliant Defense.

LONDON, Sunday, April 30.—The British Tigris army under the command of Major Gen. Charles Townshend, which has been besieged at Kut-el-Amara, has surrendered to the Turkish foes. Exhaustion of supplies compelled the force to yield.

This official announcement was made here yesterday:

> After a resistance protracted for 143 days and conducted with a gallantry and fortitude that will be forever memorable, General Townshend has been compelled by the final exhaustion of his supplies to surrender.
>
> Before doing so he destroyed his guns and munitions.
>
> The force under him consists of 2,970 British troops of all ranks and services, and some 6,000 Indian troops and their followers.

The eventual surrender of General Townshend had been expected since the recent failure of the forces under Lieut. Gen. Gorringe and General Keary to break through the Turkish position at Sannayyat, about twenty miles below Kut-el-Amara on the Tigris River, and an unsuccessful attempt to send to the blockaded army provisions by steamers. It had been touch and go with the small British force for many days.

The location of Kut-el-Amara, on a peninsula extending into the Tigris River, made it impossible to send supplies by air as there was no landing place for aeroplanes.

While a supply vessel a few days ago got beyond the main Turkish lines at Es-Sinn, it was a forlorn hope, as the Turks investing the city, advised of her coming, could have easily sunk her from shore, even if she had escaped the artificial barriers in the river.

As for the forces, which attempted to relieve General Townshend, they met with almost continual misfortunes. Several times when it was believed they were on the point of success, rising waters made further progress impossible. After penetrating Turkish positions they were compelled to fall back or remain stationary, owing to the impossibility of attacking the position at Sannayyat, which was surrounded by water. The British troops did actually attack the prepared position there, after wading through mud and water waist deep, but while meeting with some success, failure at other points made their sacrifices futile.

The British public never lost faith in General Townshend, and even now that he has been forced to capitulate after destroying everything at Kut-el-Amara that might be valuable to the Turks, they look back upon his campaign as a brilliant one.

END OF 10 MONTHS' CAMPAIGN.

Surrender Is a Climax of Disasters to British Forces.

The surrender of General Townshend's army to the Turks is one of the few instances of the war in which an entire fighting unit of important numbers has laid down its arms. It is one of the largest body of troops of the Entente Allies which has surrendered at one time and larger than any other captured French or British force.

Signs have not been wanting for a month that the Anglo-Indian force at Kut-el-Amara was in sore straits. Communication had been kept up by aeroplanes, but the official British statement of Friday that a vessel loaded with food had grounded four miles below the city was a strong indication that the force had lacked supplies to a dangerous degree.

A recent Turkish official bulletin said the position of the British at Kut-el-Amara was critical and that they were expecting to receive small supplies of food by aeroplane.

Up to a late day General Townshend had kept alive the hope that he would be relieved. King George sent a message of encouragement to him several weeks ago, and in a message sent out as late as April 7 the General said he expected to be relieved soon.

Less than a score of miles away down the Tigris is a relief army which for months had been attempting to reach the besieged forces. A few weeks ago several successes over the Turks were announced and hope then ran high in England that the mission would succeed.

The Kut-el-Amara disaster is an unfortunate ending of a campaign which for a short time promised to be crowned with remarkable success, by the capture of Bagdad.

It was early in June, 1915, that General Townshend, moving northward on his way to Bagdad, captured Kut-el-Amara with the Turkish force of 730 men and the Governor.

Led 40,000 Men Northward.

Townshend had with him two divisions of Anglo-Indian troops, or a few over 40,000 men. There are no towns deserving the name between Kut-el-Amara and Bagdad, and, receiving fresh supplies the following week, Townshend

Continued on Page 2.

Turks Report That the Kut Garrison Numbered 13,300 And That Surrender Was Made Without Conditions

LONDON, April 29.—A Constantinople dispatch, received by way of Berlin, says that the Vice Chief Commander of the Turkish Army announces that the British garrison at Kut-el-Amara, under General Townshend, which surrendered unconditionally, numbered 13,300 men.

Although the British report puts the size of the surrendered garrison at 8,970 men, it refers to the Indian troops "and their followers." This may account for the additional 4,300 reported from Constantinople and the seeming discrepancy between the British and the Turkish official reports of the surrender.

ROOSEVELT STIRS CHICAGO AUDIENCE

"I'm Proud of You!" He Cries as Diners Cheer His Plea for Preparedness.

WANTS UNIVERSAL SERVICE

Objects to Uncle Sam with a Chinese Pigtail, and Liberty as a Female Huckster.

Special to The New York Times.

CHICAGO, April 29.—Into the Middle West, territory classed by many political leaders as only lukewarm toward his doctrines of preparedness, Colonel Roosevelt today brought from New York his views, conceded to be preliminary to an avowed Presidential candidacy.

If his political chances are to be judged by the warmth of his welcome, his most ardent friends could not have been disappointed. For the reception he got from the time he stepped off the Twentieth Century Limited this morning until he had concluded his address before the Illinois Bar Association tonight was enthusiastic, and bore all the appearance of spontaneity.

He came to Chicago to address the jurists on "National Duty and International Ideals" in a 4,000-word speech, which was interpreted as a straight-out declaration of the issues on which the Roosevelt-for-President campaign shall be based.

A crowd of 1,000 or more greeted the Colonel when he arrived at the La Salle Street Station and thousands cheered him as he passed through the streets in his motor car. On every side the slogan: "We want Teddy! We want Teddy!" adopted by hundreds of delegates to the Republican National Convention of 1912, was chanted. In many ways the scenes enacted were not unlike those witnessed at the time of the 1912 convention upon the arrival of the Colonel, only the situation was more tense then and the crowds greater in size.

If the reception today was a manufactured one, it was well staged and the Roosevelt adherents, far from admitting that it was arranged in advance, assert that little publicity was given to the fact that the Colonel was to arrive here at a certain hour.

The cordiality of the earlier reception was repeated tonight at the Illinois Bar Association dinner at the Hotel La Salle, which was attended by Governor Dunne and hundreds of prominent jurists and attorneys of the State. In all more than 1,300 obtained seats, and the entire nineteenth floor was given over to the affair.

Hundreds of applicants were turned away. It was the biggest dinner ever held in Chicago, according to the management, and this gave an inkling of the interest which the Colonel has aroused in the campaign he has undertaken.

He Assails Wilson's Policies.

The jurists and their guests gave the Colonel a rousing reception and listened with the deepest attention to his carefully prepared address, much of which was in the form of an attack upon the Wilson Administration and the country's policies in handling international problems. If it has accomplished nothing else, the trip has served to place Colonel Roosevelt before the people of the Middle West as openly and uncompromisingly a candidate for the Republican nomination. Where there were a number, and among them several political leaders of prominence, who found it difficult to believe that Colonel Roosevelt actually hoped to capture the Republican Convention after sending the Republican ticket to defeat four years ago there are none now.

"Yes, Teddy's in it for sure," was a remark frequently heard from the lips of those who watched his strenuous entry and heard his address.

Colonel Roosevelt, by his appearance here, has unquestionably created a new atmosphere in connection with national preparedness. He has added, also, a new "punch" to the pre-convention campaign, and where it was lagging a bit has set it ahead at least two weeks in this section. Where many had given little heed before to the fact that the National Convention was only a few weeks off they have been brought to a full realization of the fact that the decision must soon be made, and that if Roosevelt is to be headed off the job must quickly be undertaken.

The greatest demonstration came tonight at the dinner when the jurists, attorneys, and their guests rose and shouted themselves hoarse when the Colonel placed himself on record for universal service founded on a modified form of the Swiss system.

From the moment that he began to speak the Colonel had the crowd with him, and his words were interrupted a score of times by applause. At the final outburst, spontaneous and sustained, with the diners on their feet, waving napkins and shouting, the Colonel gave way to the emotions he felt.

"My heart is thrilled," he exclaimed when his voice could be heard above the din. "I know you are sound. I knew the West meant business—that you would stand for the nation.

"By George, I'm Proud of You!"

The cheering was redoubled and drowned out the Colonel's voice for more than a minute, and he stood there, his face glowing.

"I can't do you the good you have done me," he continued, pounding with his clenched fist to emphasize his feelings. "But I'll go on with my head up and my heart strong to preach preparedness to the people.

"By George, I'm proud of you—it's great! And I can't tell you how glad I am that you showed your feelings in this manner when I spoke of universal service in which all of us would take our man's part in upholding the welfare of this nation.

"I did not know how you'd take it when I said that but I believe in it with all my heart, and I didn't care a darn what the effect would be, I was going to tell you what I thought and felt. I'm proud of you as American citizens. I can't tell you how proud I am."

And the demonstration did not end there. At the conclusion of the

Continued on Page 3.

GERARD APPRISED OF KAISER'S STAND

Berlin Believes the Ambassador Has Been Told What Germany's Reply Will Be.

WASHINGTON GETS NO WORD

Awaits Envoy's Report on Visit to the Emperor—President Will Allow No More Parleying.

BERLIN, April 29.—Ambassador Gerard was received in audience by Emperor William last night and conferred with other leaders of the Empire. No intimation has been given as to when the German reply to the American note will be ready, except a hint contained in a Berlin dispatch to the Cologne Gazette, which said:

"The consultations at Great Headquarters probably are near a conclusion. The visit of the American Ambassador was designed to permit him to consult with persons in authority there over the situation. It is assumed their final decision also will be communicated to him there."

The Tageblatt explains this morning that its statement that the basic features of the answer already have been settled was misunderstood. The paper asserts it meant only to say that a draft of the answer had been made, but that a decision had not yet been reached. The wording of this morning's statement indicates clearly, however, that there was no misunderstanding on the part of the readers, but that the Tageblatt made an error yesterday.

There is virtually no comment in the press upon the situation except that from the pen of Count Ernst von Reventlow, who still appears to believe a breach with the United States is inevitable.

The official organ of the Hansabund, the organization of commercial interests, refers to the gravity of the decision to be reached. It says the representatives of commerce, industry, and trade belonging to the Hansabund are certain the decision will be reached with the dispassionate care which it demands, but are equally certain that Germany's dignity as a nation and its freedom to use all weapons of defense will be fully regarded.

The Hansabund hopes, however, it is declared, that an honorable and peaceful understanding will be reached, but that if such a solution proves impossible all Germans will stand united behind the Emperor.

PRESIDENT WILL NOT PARLEY.

Germany Must Comply or Break Will Follow—Optimism Abating.

Special to The New York Times.

WASHINGTON, April 29.—The feeling of optimism that has prevailed here over the indications that Germany would meet the American demands for the abandonment of present methods of German submarine warfare began to wane today on account of the view that appeared to prevail in Berlin that the issue would be discussed between the two Governments before the German answer was transmitted. This Government wants no discussion. It holds that the time for discussion has passed. There is every reason to believe that President Wilson has determined to break relations with Germany if his demand is not complied with literally.

The supposition in some quarters that Emperor William asked Ambassador Gerard to convey a message to President Wilson which would suggest a modification of the American attitude or permit a discussion of the principle involved, has not tended to increase the hopefulness of those who understand the President's position. Even the Kaiser's personal request along such lines would not influence the President, it is gathered, to consent to further exchanges concerning the merits of the submarine controversy.

Much of the optimism that has prevailed here has been based on information to the German Embassy that the Berlin Government would endeavor to meet the desires of the United States. In German circles this optimism continues, and it is shared to a great extent by officials of the Washington Government. But those officials in a position to know the inside of the situation are not indulging in any high hopes. They know the determination of President Wilson to have a settlement of the submarine issue one way or the other, and realize that he has made up his mind that a severance of diplomatic relations must come if Germany attempts to evade the American demand by suggestions of parley or otherwise.

The President, there is good reason to believe, has decided irrevocably that he will take the course set forth in the note to Germany if a satisfactory answer is not forthcoming, and will not be influenced by opposition in Congress or elsewhere. The pro-German deluge of telegrams to Senators and Representatives has not had the slighest effect on the President. If anything, this phase of the German propaganda has made the President and his advisers even more determined to adhere to the course they have outlined.

Mr. Gerard was expected to have reached Berlin on his return from his visit to the Kaiser some time today. At the State Department just before the closing hour it was said that no message had come from the Ambassador as to his conference with the German Emperor and none was expected today on account of the unusual delays in telegraphic transmission of cipher dispatches. The department has not heard from the Ambassador since he cabled that he had been invited by the Kaiser to visit him, and was leaving Berlin for the front on Thursday.

It was reported today that the Administration was becoming anxious over the failure of the German Government to respond to its demand, which called for a declaration "immediately" that present methods of German submarine warfare had been abandoned and made effective, but nothing to bear out that impression was obtained in official quarters. The Administration has no inten-

Continued on Page 2.

DUBLIN REVOLT IS NEAR COLLAPSE; POST OFFICE REBELS SEIZED IS BURNED; WIMBORNE TELLS STORY OF RISINC

Redmond Tells Nationalists to Aid the Troops in Suppressing Revolt

LONDON, April 29.—John Redmond, leader of the Irish Nationalists, has placed himself absolutely at the disposal of the authorities and is in constant touch with them. He has instructed Nationalist supporters in all parts of Ireland to hold themselves at the disposal of the military authorities.

In many places besides Dublin the Nationalist voters have already, on their own initiative, mobilized in support of the troops. At Tipperary yesterday volunteers offered their services.

Irish Rebels Proclaimed Republic; Seven Headed It, Wimborne Says

Failure to Cut Wire to Curragh Camp a Fatal Error—Sailors Landed from Fleet to Aid Troops in County Galway.

DUBLIN, April 29.—Baron Wimborne, Lord Lieutenant of Ireland, expressed to The Associated Press at the Viceregal Lodge today the assurance that the seditious movement would be suppressed in the course of a few days.

The Viceroy was full of praise for the loyalty displayed by the great majority of the Irish people, and considered the momentary success gained and the damage done by the rebels as small when viewed in connection with the surprise of the outbreak and the evident preparations made for it.

The country outside of Dublin, except for a few isolated places, has, he declared, remained peaceful.

Requested to give an account of what had happened since the rebels had proclaimed an Irish republic last Monday afternoon, Baron Wimborne said:

"The outbreak began Monday morning about 11:30 o'clock. About that time information was received that Dublin Castle had been attacked, Stephens Green occupied, and the Post Office seized by the rebels. Telephonic communication with the Curragh Camp was immediately obtained by the authorities and the reserve troops there were brought to Dublin that night and the following morning.

"Meanwhile the situation at the Castle, which had never been captured by the rebels, was strengthened. The only casualty there was the shooting of a policeman at the gate. A very few hours after the outbreak large forces had been assembled in the Castle, which, however, was never in real danger.

Failed to Cut Wire to Curragh.

"The rebels had cut telegraphic communications with the country districts and England, but had not succeeded in discovering a telephone wire which connected the Curragh Camp with headquarters. This was one of their great mistakes. They did not cut communication with North Ireland, with which we have at all times been able to converse.

"At one time the rebels had possession of the Broadstone Railway Station, which was not protected.

"On Tuesday morning all the reinforcements we had called from Curragh had reached Dublin, and since that moment the rebels have not attempted anything except sniping from certain localities and houses. It is so easy for them to abandon houses by back doors and to get away to other advantageous positions.

"The military cannot distinguish the rebels from other citizens. Sometimes they leave their houses after hiding their rifles and cartridges and mingle with the ordinary inhabitants. After taking observations of the soldiers' positions they return to commence sniping again. Most of the houses they occupy they have entered by force, and not because the householders sympathize with their movement. As a matter of fact, the general run of people do not sympathize with them.

"Since the number of troops has increased, the position of the rebels has remained the same. When their activities at any point become too lively the troops throw a few shells into the houses they occupy and such explosions have caused fires, while other fires have been started by the rebels themselves.

"They have barricaded Sackville Street and are in possession of all the houses there, but they were shelled out of Liberty Hall by a gunboat on Tuesday, and we occupied their headquarters immediately. They burned Linen Hall barracks, and other small fires have occurred.

"In the early stages of the revolt the Sinn Feiners fired on the members of the fire brigade, but later we cleared the area around the fires, and the firemen were able to extinguish the flames.

"Wednesday the military arrangements were completed by the arrival of further reinforcements, and the rebels were hemmed in in Sackville Street. The work of disposing of the troops to deal with the snipers occupied a lot of time and much care, but eventually this district and other rebel quarters were surrounded. Everything done has been carried out according to plans.

"A big cordon has been drawn all around Dublin and shorter cordons around the inner districts.

Fighting in Galway.

"Regarding the situation in the provinces on the whole, it is very good. We were naturally apprehensive lest there might be some response there to the Dublin movement. Fighting occurred in Galway near Athenry, where the police are now in possession of the town, but the rebels are encamped in a ruined castle. There also has been fighting in a Galway town which the rebels attacked and compelled us to land men from the fleet to support the military.

"Encounters took place at Enniscorthy, County Wexford, and there were certain rebellious assemblages in Meath and Louth, but on the whole reports are quiet. This applies also to Cork, Limerick, Kerry, Clare, Kilkenny, Mayo, Sligo, Tipperary, Leitrim, Kildare, Roscommon, and all of Ulster."

When asked concerning the origin and connections of the rebel movement with the Germans, the Viceroy said there was an absolute certainty the rebellion was timed to take place with the knowledge of Germany, and was intended to bring about the withdrawal of troops from England to Ireland.

"As to the landing of Sir Roger Casement," said Baron Wimborne, "that was all arranged in Germany with the connivance of the Sinn Feiners. On the night of his arrest a motor car upset into a river and the occupants, who were drowned, both wore Sinn Fein badges. The Germans do not seem to have supplied the rebels with arms, which are of all descriptions, even including fowling pieces.

"A proclamation issued by the rebels announcing the foundation of the Irish Republic was signed by seven persons, including J. T. Clark, Connolly, Pearce, and MacDermott."

Augustine Birrell, the Chief Secretary for Ireland, who was present during the interview with the Viceroy, supplemented his remarks by saying the situation would be dealt with according to martial law, which now is in full operation in Ireland, and deprives the citizens of the right of a civil trial. Mr. Birrell was not overwilling to give information as to occurrences, but he said he was satisfied that the situation was well in hand and that the suppression of the movement was a matter of a short time.

The visit of The Associated Press Correspondent to the Viceregal Lodge followed a long drive in an open motor lorry through the disturbed sections of the city and past barricades, where soldiers knelt or lay down in replying to the rebel snipers. Occasional bullets whistled overhead and the rattle of a machine gun salvo was heard.

No soldier is permitted to walk about without a rifle, as such a proceeding would bring almost certain death. Citizens stood behind curtains and windows as the automobile of the correspondent dashed by. Only a few venture onto the porches, and they fear to go to the stores to obtai nprovisions.

Boys Shot in Bread Line.

This fear was fully justified, as The Associated Press Correspondent saw two small boys shot while waiting at a bakery for bread during the morning. In other parts of the city, also, many civilian casualties were caused, but the number either of the soldiers or civilians killed or wounded could not be obtained.

The rebels today have been confining their activities to sniping in various parts of the city. The scenes of their operations have been circumscribed to the districts about Sackville Street, the cattle market, and Stephen's Green, where they are surrounded by vigilant troops in complete cordons, while the city itself is cut off from approach by another cordon whose limits are around the circular road which surrounds the city.

Every civilian is regarded with suspicion, and passage through the lines can be obtained only with the best of credentials and passes.

Outside the three areas already mentioned as being in possession of the rebels, numbers of isolated snipers occasionally fire pot shots at passing soldiers. These snipers are difficult to locate. At a hotel on the north wall dozens of shots went through windows and struck walls, while spent bullets dropped everywhere in the streets.

BANK SAVED BY STUDENTS.

Trinity College Opened Heavy Fire on Rebels and Drove Them Off.

LIVERPOOL, April 30.—How Trinity College students saved the Bank of Ireland is told by a resident of Liverpool who has just arrived from Dublin.

"It was the intention of the Sinn Feiners," he said, "to take this institution and its valuable contents, and a body of rebels came along with the express purpose of putting this intention into execution. Opposite the bank stands famous Trinity College, where an officer's training corps of students is stationed, and the young officers had a warm reception in readiness.

"The rebels came along in great style, anticipating no trouble and shooting down the half-dozen soldiers always on guard at the bank. But as they advanced there was a rifle volley, and some of the attacking party dropped to the ground.

"The college had been transformed into a veritable fortress. In the windows were sandbags, loopholed, behind which the officers were waiting to give battle. The insurgents were stupified, and for a moment hesitated as to what they should do. Then several sprang forward, shouting to their comrades, and the rebels pressed on.

"Again came a volley from the windows of Trinity College. More men fell and the rebels broke in disorder and fled."

LEADER CONNOLLY KILLE

Artillery Used Agains Dublin Section in Which Rebels Are Corralled

CASUALTIES EXCEED 10

Sackville and Grafton Street Reported to Have Been Set on Fire.

MANY LADS IN THE REVOL

Old Men, Too, Joined the Rank —Little Disorder in Other Parts of Ireland.

LONDON, Sunday, April 30.—Fie Marshal Viscount French, commande of the home forces, reports that th General Post Office at Dublin, whic has been the principal stronghold of th Sinn Feiners, has been burned down.

James Connolly, one of the leaders the rebels, is reported to have bee killed.

It is said Connolly undertook to issu to persons desiring to leave Dublin pas ports bearing the words: "Pass beare James Connolly, Commandant Gener of the Irish Republican Army."

Many of the rebels have been mad prisoner, and the revolt in Dublin is o the verge of collapse.

In the rest of Ireland the situation generally satisfactory.

It is reported that the casualties the street fighting in Dublin excee 100, and that the troops have been con pelled to resort to cannon in one sectio A dispatch received yesterday afterno said that Sackville and Grafton Stree were in flames, and that artillery wa being used on the houses, the in habitants having been removed.

The recent news that the rebels ha been driven out of St. Stephen's Gree with bombs, suffering heavy losses killed, wounded, and prisoners, has no been confirmed officially.

From inquiries made among the mil tary authorities at Dublin, the corre spondent of The Evening Star conclude that there probably are not more tha 1,500 or 2,000 men and lads actually en gaged in the rebellion, so far as th central part of the city is concerned Among them are quite a number of ol men who were closely associated wit the Fenian troubles, and some youth of 16 or 17. This is shown, the corre spondent says, by the appearance of th prisoners already brought in.

Of the situation outside Dublin litt is known beyond the official admissio that the disaffection has spread to var ous localities in the west and south Ireland. Field Marshal French's state ment of Friday night described thes disturbances as local in character, an so far as has been revealed by informa tion which has passed the censorshi they have not been attended by heav fighting.

A dispatch from Tralee yesterda said that Austin Stack, commander the Tralee corps of Sinn Feiners, an Cornelius Collins, an accountant in th General Post Office at Dublin, who ar charged with abetting in the importa tion of arms from the enemy, wer taken from the Tralee jail under strong military and police escort an removed on a train to an unknown de tination. There was no demonstration

SCENES IN EMBATTLED CITY.

Newspaper Men Landed with Birrel in Midst of the Fighting.

DUBLIN, Thursday, April 27, (vi London, April 29.)—Fifteen hundred o so armed men of the Sinn Fein had hold on Ireland's capital today. Afte four days of fighting their rebel flag sti flew from a number of central points.

Since Monday some of the chief pos tions in the city have been in the hand of the rebels. In defending these strong holds against regular troops and Iris Nationalist volunteers the rebels ar fighting with desperation for their live which they know may be forfeited o the charge of treason.

Regulars now command all the rebe positions, the fall of which is merely question of time.

The streets of Dublin were deserted to day, except for sentries and militar guards. Business was at a standstill Civilians peeped anxiously from behin curtained windows. Field guns wer barking, machine guns rattling, and rifl fire was pattering, apparently fron every quarter at the same time.

Birrell Landed with Newspaper Men

When The Associated Press corre spondent landed early this morning a the quay near the Custom House th pinging of bullets from rifles of sniper in the vicinity was frequent. Augustin Birrell, the Secretary for Ireland, ha made the passage from England wit the newspaper men. As he steppe ashore he shouted cheerily: "I wis you luck, gentlemen! I don't know wha will happen to you, now that you ar here!"

Soldiers and rebels fired at each othe from street corners, wharves, roofs, an

"All the News That's Fit to Print."

The New York Times.

THE WEATHER
Fair today; Thursday unsettled, warmer, probable showers; variable to southeast winds.
For full weather report see Page 23.

VOL. LXV...NO. 21,291. ..... NEW YORK, WEDNESDAY, MAY 10, 1916.—TWENTY-FOUR PAGES. ONE CENT In Greater New York, Jersey City and Newark. | Elsewhere, TWO CENTS.

4,500 MILITIA CALLED FOR MEXICO; 4,000 MORE REGULARS ALSO TO GO; COAST ARTILLERY FORCE DEPLETED

CYMRIC IS LOST; HAD NO WARNING, HER OFFICERS SAY

White Star Steamship Sinks at Sea Many Hours After Being Torpedoed.

FIVE OF HER MEN KILLED

Others Are Landed on Irish Coast—No Americans in the Crew.

WASHINGTON SEEKING FACTS

State Department Will Ascertain if German Pledge Was Violated by Submarine.

Cymric Got No Warning, Say Officers Who Saw U-Boat

BANTRY, May 9, (via London, May 10.)—One hundred and seven members of the crew of the Cymric arrived at Bantry this evening. Several, suffering from broken limbs, were sent to the hospital.

The officers of the Cymric declare that the vessel was torpedoed without warning. A submarine was seen, but it disappeared immediately after firing the torpedo.

The Cymric, although badly damaged, made her way for some hours, but finally sank. Many of the crew, on their arrivel here, were barefooted and only partially clad.

Special Cable to THE NEW YORK TIMES.

LONDON, May 9.—The White Star steamship Cymric, which was torpedoed yesterday, sank this morning.

The American Embassy has been notified by the American Consul at Liverpool that he understood there were no Americans aboard the Cymric. The vessel carried no passengers, and the crew, the Consul said, was entirely British.

The Embassy has not been informed as to the incidents surrounding the torpedoing of the ship, and is waiting to ascertain if the Germans gave warning and otherwise conformed to the promises to America in the latest note.

THE NEW YORK TIMES correspondent is authorized officialy to say that the Cymric was unarmed.

By The Associated Press.

LONDON, May 9.—Lloyd's reports that the White Star liner Cymric sank at 3 o'clock this morning. All those who were on board at the time were saved.

American Consul Frost, at Queenstown, has telegraphed to Consul General Skinner here that he has gone to Bantry to meet the survivors.

Consul Frost's message announced that five members of the crew of the Cymric were killed by an explosion.

London dispatches yesterday said the 13,000-ton steamship Cymric had been torpedoed by a German submarine. A message from Queenstown last night said the vessel, torpedoed at 4 o'clock Monday afternoon, was still afloat and was proceeding to an Irish port. The Cymric left New York on April 29 with a large cargo of war munitions for Liverpool. She had been in service as a freighter for several weeks, and carried no passengers.

CYMRIC TORPEDOING MAY INVOLVE PLEDGE

Washington to Gather All Facts of Disaster—Status That of a Merchantman.

Special to The New York Times.

WASHINGTON, May 9.—The State Department is getting reports of the torpedoing of the White Star steamship Cymric and will consider them with a view to determining if any action shall be taken. Consul Frost, at Queenstown, reported in one dispatch that it appeared that the vessel was torpedoed without warning, and in a later message said:

"Absence of warning inferrable."

A statement by Consul Frost that the Cymric was on Admiralty service does not appear to impress officials, who have consistently held that the mere chartering of a merchant vessel by an Admiralty office to carry supplies does not give the vessel the character of a warship, but leaves her status the same as that of a merchant vessel engaged in ordinary trade.

While there was decided reticence at the State Department today with respect to the Cymric case, one of the highest officials in a position to speak with authority did not hesitate to explain that there was a clear distinction between a merchant vessel chartered by the British Admiralty to carry supplies and a merchant vessel under Government requisition. In the first instance, it was said, the status of the vessel as a private merchantman was not changed. But if she was requisitioned by the Admiralty and officers and crew were entirely under its orders, she became a national ship of the British Government, and as such was not entitled to the immunity from attack without warning or even without visit and search, upon which the Government of the United States has insisted in its long controversy with Germany.

Wants All the Facts.

Although a positive statement on the subject was refused, it was inferred that

Continued on Page 4.

American Note Is in Berlin; Lansing Expects No Reply

BERLIN, May 9, via London, May 10.—President Wilson's reply to Germany, accepting Germany's promise of a change in her methods of submarine warfare, has reached Berlin, but has not yet been handed to the German Government by Ambassador Gerard.

WASHINGTON, May 9.—Secretary Lansing let it be known late today that the United States did not consider that its response to the German note called for a reply from Germany.

Unless Berlin specifies to the contrary, it will be assumed that Germany accepts the American view as stated.

$250,000 FORTUNE HIDDEN IN RUBBISH

Woman Recluse in Broadway Hotel Had Wealth Concealed in Strange Nooks.

IMMURED FOR FIVE YEARS

Jewelry Worth Hundreds of Dollars Found in a Piano and Cast-off Clothing.

Not even a death notice marked the passing of Miss Caroline E. Marshall, who died on March 2, 1915, a lonely recluse shut in her three-room suite at the Hotel Wallick, from which she had not emerged for five years, although in going through her belongings it was found that she was possessed of a fortune of $258,072, according to the schedules filed yesterday by Anthony P. Luden, transfer tax appraiser.

In an affidavit by Joseph H. A. Symonds of Press & Symonds, attorneys for the executrices of the will strange facts in the life of Miss Marshall were revealed. This affidavit says that the rooms were so cluttered up with trunks, bundles, pasteboard boxes, and old newspapers and magazines as to necessitate a long search for the assets. Only a narrow passage for entry to and egress from the rooms was left by the accumulation of years.

In a dresser drawer were found two certificates for stock of the New York Central Railroad, one for twenty-eight shares and the other for one share. Another certificate for one share was turned out of a pasteboard box which was filled with old and worn kid gloves. Money in various amounts was found concealed in boxes and old clothing.

In the living room there was a grand piano. Hidden among its strings was some valuable jewelry. Still more was discovered in an old box containing cast-off clothing in the bottom of a closet. This lot was appraised at $1,200. Among the other items that were found were three checks dated in 1909, which had apparently not been presented for collection. They were found to be worthless, the maker of one of them having since died.

When the search for a will was made none could be found. Even the carpet was torn up, but no valuables were revealed beneath it. A will made in 1893, however, was found in a safe deposit box at the Second National Bank. When it was made certain that no later will was to be found about the rooms in the hotel search for the heirs was begun. This carried the correspondence of the attorneys as far as New Zealand, where one of the beneficiaries was found living. Miss Marshall had had little communication with any of the beneficiaries for several years, and, according to the affidavit, she had no intimate friends.

Only one of the witnesses to the will was found living, and it was upon the testimony of this survivor that the will was probated.

The total assets of the estate were valued at $258,072, and the net estate at $241,062. The taxable interests of the beneficiaries were: New York Homeopathic Medical College and Hospital, $10,030; Edmund C. Marshall, brother, $72,481; Mary L. Van Ness, sister, $42,031; Maud I. Marshall, niece, $9,066; Sarah Edith Marshall Parker, niece, $28,482; Thomas William Marshall, grand nephew, $28,521; Edward Landor Marshall, grandnephew, $28,521; P. Agnes Luttgen, niece, $692, and Mary Knapp Marshall, niece, $399.

The assets of the estate were: 416 Spring Street, $16,500; 248 Eighth Avenue, $29,500; 38 West Sixteenth Street, $35,000; 303 Canal Street, $28,500; 182 Spring Street, $21,000; 184 Spring Street, $12,500, and 122 Duffield Street, Brooklyn, $6,500. The realty was subject to tax liens amounting to $2,975. Bank deposits were $42,088; personalty, $43,851; notes, $159; bonds of the West Shore Railroad Company, $44,088, and 254 shares of the New York Central Railroad Company, $20,828.

BRITAIN CALLS MARRIED ELIGIBLES NOW ABROAD

All Who Are Ordinarily Residents of Great Britain Must Report for Military Duty.

LONDON, Wednesday, May 10.—All Englishmen, whether single or married, eligible for military service, who are living abroad, but who are ordinarily residents of Great Britain, must return to England forthwith and report for military duty.

This announcement was made in the House of Commons yesterday by Sir George Cave, the Solicitor General.

GREEK VILLAGE SHELLED.

Germans and Bulgars Destroy Houses and Inhabitants Protest.

PARIS, May 9.—A dispatch to The Havas Agency from Athens says:

"The village of Mayada was bombarded yesterday by the Germans and Bulgarians, who threw thirty heavy shells causing much damage, including the destruction of a number of houses. The reason for the bombardment is not known. The civil population is protesting."

IRISH HARMONY LIKELY TO RESULT FROM LATE REVOLT

Redmond and Carson to Issue a Manifesto to the People of Ireland.

MAY ADVANCE HOME RULE

Conscription for the Emerald Isle Finally Rejected by the House of Commons.

CASEMENT TRIAL PUBLIC

Strong Feeling Against Executions Shown in Parliament by Questions to the Premier.

LONDON, May 9.—Irish politics are again in the foreground as a result of the recent rising and the consequent convergence of sentiment between John Redmond, the Nationalist leader, and Sir Edward Carson, the Ulster leader.

The conference of these leaders yesterday on the disarmament question, and today's significant debate in the House of Commons on the possibility of bringing Ireland within the purview of the Conscription bill, have given this matter still greater importance, and it looks as though Ireland's unfortunate experience might become the indirect means of adjusting in a manner satisfactory to all parties the difficult home rule problem, which has been hung up during the war.

It is understood that a manifesto to the Irish people has been agreed upon, but the contents of the manifesto have been withheld until Thursday, so as to enable its simultaneous publication throughout Ireland. Various rumors were current in the lobbies of Parliament tonight concerning negotiations between the Government and the Irish parties, but nothing is likely to be decided upon by the latter until after Premier Asquith's pronouncement on the Irish situation, which is expected tomorrow.

During the committee stage of the Military Service bill in the House of Commons today, Sir John Brownlee Lonsdale, whip of the Irish Unionist Party, moved that Ireland should be included in the operation of compulsion.

Premier Asquith, replying, said the question of compulsion was not a matter of agreement with Ireland and that if the motion were persisted in there would be protracted discussion which would prevent the measure becoming a law at the earliest possible moment.

The Premier said that a very large number of the representatives of Ireland were not at the moment prepared to accept compulsion in Ireland, and that it was not desirable that the country should be plunged into a controversy on the subject at this time. Ireland had just undergone a terrible ordeal, but the result of it he believed would be to establish the foundation among loyal Irishmen of a larger measure of agreement than there ever had been in the past.

The Premier asked what could be worse than that the representatives of Ireland should be forced into a conflict at this moment. The Government, he added, was reviewing with the utmost care the military arrangements in Ireland and the matter of bearing arms, and he hoped a common agreement would be reached.

Sir Edward Carson deprecated the exclusion of Ireland from compulsion. He blamed the Government for failing to suppress the anti-recruiting campaign in Ireland, which he believed had largely led to the recent disastrous events.

John Redmond challenged Sir Edward's assertion that in the recent government of Ireland the Nationalists had the power but not the responsibility.

"Certainly, since the Coalition Government was instituted," said Mr. Redmond, "I have had no power in the government of Ireland. My opinions have been overborne and my suggestions rejected. It is my profound conviction that if we had had power and responsibility during the last few years the recent occurrences in Ireland would never have arisen."

Mr. Redmond proceeded to declare it unfair to leave the impression that Ireland had not done well in recruiting. She had more than 150,000 men now with the colors, men who had displayed bravery and covered themselves with glory, said the Nationalist leader. He opposed conscription for Ireland because he believed compulsion the worst possible way to get men in Ireland, and after recent events his deliberate opinion was that it would be not only wrong, but well-nigh insane, to attempt to enforce conscription, and it would be a fearful responsibility if, in the face of this deliberate opinion, Ulster men should persist in the attempt to force conscription upon Ireland.

Mr. Redmond besought the House, not only for the sake of Ireland, but for the sake of the empire, not to proceed with this course.

"Nobody is more anxious than I," he continued, "to respond to the Ulster appeal for co-operation. I have hoped against hope, and hope still, even in the dark, miserable circumstances of the moment, that we might come together. Aye, and before long, I hope with all my heart that out of these miseries we may be able, by taking a large, generous view, something like a statesmanlike and far-reaching view of the empire's highest interests, that out of this turmoil and tragedy we may evolve some means of putting an end to these difficulties, so that we may have a united Ireland, where the people and the Government have both power and responsibility."

Winston Spencer Churchill considered that Mr. Redmond had rendered immense services to the empire and that Great Britain owed a deep debt to the Nationalist Party for their exertions in the present struggle, "the first struggle," said Colonel Churchill, "in which Ireland has been a valiant friend on our side."

He would feel the same reluctance, he declared, in pressing an Irish question against Mr. Redmond's opinion as he would feel against pressing a South African question against the opinion of General Botha.

"The whole future of Ireland," he continued, "depends upon two men, Sir Edward Carson and Mr. Redmond, and there is no difficulty they cannot surmount if they act together."

The Lonsdale motion was voted down without division.

It is understood that Colonel Churchill has decided to resume politics. His

Continued on Page 3.

Plot to Assassinate Sweden's King Fails

STOCKHOLM, May 9, (via London.)—The Aftonbladet today prints a rumor of an unsuccessful plot by Socialists and Anarchists against the life of King Gustave.

"Sensational rumors are current," says the newspaper, "of a plot by the young Socialist-Anarchist Party against the life of the King of Sweden in revenge for the conviction of three Socialist leaders of the anti-Militaristic Congress recently held. The attempt on the King's life was planned to be made at the horse show, but the conspirators were foiled by the mobilization of the entire detective force and the placing of a cordon of detectives in plain clothes around the King."

FRENCH REPULSE 4 VERDUN ATTACKS

Heavy Masses of Germans Are Flung at Hill 304, but All in Vain, Paris Says.

ASSAILANTS' LOSSES HEAVY

A Renewed Counteroffensive by French East of the Meuse Wins Back More Lost Trenches.

PARIS, May 9.—Four attacks in force by the Germans, three of them of a very violent character, were made in the region of Hill 304 at Verdun last night and today, but all were beaten off by the French, according to the night bulletin of the French War Office.

In addition to this furious fighting on the west bank of the Meuse, the French troops have been continuing their counter-offensive on the east bank of the river, and, it is officially stated, have won back more of the trenches which were captured by the Germans northwest of Thiaumont on Sunday.

Three of the German attacks near Hill 304 were made during the night. One of these was started at 3 o'clock in the morning, great masses of men assailing Hill 287, west of Hill 304. The second aimed at the trenches northeast of Hill 304. In the third the Germans struck at the wood to the west of the hill. Heavy losses were suffered in the repulses, according to the War Office report.

Today the Crown Prince's forces, moving to attack a trench, west of Hill 304, were stopped by the French curtain of fire.

The War Office report of tonight is as follows:

> In Champagne our artillery shelled the trenches and batteries of the Germans north of Ville-sur-Tourbe and the enemy communications in the region of Somme-Py.
>
> On the left bank of the Meuse the bombardment was less intense. In the course of the day an enemy attack against a trench west of Hill 304 was stopped short by our curtain of fire and the enemy was not able to debouch.
>
> On the right bank and in the Woevre the artillery action was intermittent.
>
> Latest reports show that in the night of May 8-9 the Germans launched in the region of Hill 304 three very violent attacks, which were carried out by heavy effectives—one, reported in the communication of this morning, against our positions on Hill 287; another against our trenches northeast of Hill 304, and the last against the wood to the west. All these attacks, broken by our fire, cost the adversary very serious losses.
>
> Our batteries took under their fire revictualing convoys and enemy detachments on the road between Essey and Bayonville, northwest of Pont-à-Mousson.

The afternoon bulletin had this to say of operations in sectors outside of the west of the Meuse region:

> An intense bombardment was conducted by the Germans in the sectors of Eix and Chatillon and between Douaumont and Vaux.
>
> There was grenade fighting at Apremont and in the valley of the Fecht.
>
> South of Autreches, near Soissons, the Germans attempted an attack, but were repulsed.
>
> At Bolante, in the Argonne, the French captured two small German posts, killing all the occupants.
>
> Elsewhere on the front there were no important developments.

Berlin Reports Repulses of Foe.

BERLIN, May 9, (by Wireless to Sayville.)—The German Army Headquarters statement today says:

> In connection with our successes at Hill 304 we took, south of Termiten Hill, to the south of Haucourt, several trenches by storm. Attempts by the enemy to recapture with strong forces the terrain lost on Hill 304 failed. The enemy's losses were heavy.
>
> Other attacks by the French on the east bank of the Meuse, in the district of Thiaumont farm, were equally unsuccessful. The number of French taken prisoner there increased to 3 officers and 375 men, besides 16 wounded. Nine machine guns also were taken.
>
> On other parts of the western front there were only a few patrol enterprises which proved successful for the Germans.

LONDON, May 9.—The British official statement tonight reads:

> Last night there was mining activity on the front between Neuville-St. Vaast and Souchez, also northeast of Armentières and east of Ypres without effecting any change in the situation.
>
> There was quite unimportant artillery activity today.

The Belgian official communication reads:

> There was some slight artillery action at divers points on the front.

MACHINE GUNS SAVED FRENCH.

Old Style Weapons Strengthened by Use of New Automatic Rifles.

PARIS, May 9.—The latest assaults of the Germans at Verdun have served to demonstrate the efficiency to which the French have brought the use of the machine gun. The French front line

Continued on Page 3.

OBREGON HALTS PROTOCOL

His Request That Americans Quit Mexico at Set Date Refused.

SUGGESTS BORDER PATROLS

McQuatters, Mining Man, Leaves Conference After Mexicans Protest at Presence.

EXTRA TROOPS IN EL PASO

Infantry Battalion Sent There to Prevent Disorder—Funston Delays His Departure.

EL PASO, Texas, May 9.—Fear of a break between the United States and Mexico over American troop dispositions in Mexico was allayed tonight when, afer a three and a half hours' discussion, Generals Scott and Obregon, the American and Mexican conferees, agreed to hold another conference, probably tomorrow.

The conference today began shortly after 5 o'clock, with Generals Scott, Funston, and General Alvaro Obregon and Juan Amador, Mexican Sub-Secretary of Foreign Affairs, taking part. A. J. McQuatters, mining man, who has participated in three other conferences, was present at the beginning, but withdrew on complaint of the Mexican representatives that his business connections rendered his presence undesirable.

It is understood that General Obregon again brought up the subject of a definite date for American troop withdrawal from Mexico. He again was informed, it was said, that the American Government was firm in its refusal to make this concession. It was suggested to him that in view of the Big Bend raid, under the nose of Carranza troops, the United States scarcely could consider the de facto Government fully capable of coping with the bandits.

Obregon to Consult Chief.

In the face of this statement General Obregon is understood to have asked for more time to consult with General Carranza.

General Funston had planned to leave here tonight for San Antonio, where, at his headquarters in Fort Sam Houston, he was to take charge of the new troop dispositions that will come with the dispatch of 8,000 militia and regular army men to the border. After the conference it was announced that he had postponed his departure. This circumstance added to the optimism that prevailed following the announcement that negotiations would continue.

All day today there was a hint of war in the atmosphere of El Paso. Prior to the conference the word went out that only one thing could prevent a break between the United States and Mexico—complete reversal by General Obregon of the attitude he took at yesterday's meeting with Generals Scott and Funston, when he declined to sign the tentative agreement for Mexican and American troop co-operation unless it was modified to set a date for American withdrawal from Mexico.

There were few optimists to point out that in the end the Mexican Minister of War must concede the point of the United States. A great majority concluded that he was more likely to withdraw from the negotiations. Activities of the American military men here added to the apprehension. It was learned that messages had been sent to General Pershing at the front, warning him to prepare for any contingency. All along the border the word had gone out to the scattered detachments of the American Army patrol to be on guard. Hope still was entertained, it was said, that the situation could be adjusted.

New Proposal for Patrol.

General Obregon went into the conference this evening announcing that he had a new proposal to make to the American representatives. He intended to ask, he said, that a common border patrol should be stretched along the border, American troops guarding the Mexican side, and Mexican troops patrolling the American side.

On his return to his private car in Juarez, after the conference, General Obregon made the following statement to the press:

> On the instructions of the First Chief I have proposed a plan for the patrol of the frontier by troops of both countries. Each country, under this arrangement, would patrol its own side and co-operate with the other in running down and breaking up the outlaw bands who have committed a number of depredations lately. We are proceeding amicably in the conference. I should like to say for the benefit of the yellow press that I delivered no ultimatums tonight.

General Scott is understood to have said he would be glad to present the proposal to the Washington Government.

General Obregon after the conference called Consul Garcia of El Paso and Samuel Belden, Carranza lawyer in San Antonio, into a short conference. General Gavira, Commander of Juarez, called upon him to receive orders relating to troop movements in the State of Chihuahua. The War Minister's entire office force was engaged in coding messages to be sent to Mexico City, keeping General Carranza fully informed as to the progress of the conferences.

Amador Protests to Scott.

Juan Amador, Mexican Sub-Secretary of Foreign Affairs, called on General

Continued on Page 2.

Carranza Organ Sees a Serious Menace of War; Assails Our Attitude and Expedition as Unjust

MEXICO CITY, May 9.—Commenting editorially today on the gravity of the international situation, growing out of the border raid at Glenn Springs, Texas, El Pueblo, the official Government organ, says:

> We are confronted by the most serious, the most grave moment of our national life. We are facing the tremendous danger of war, which we have never desired and never desired provoked, and which surely is not desired by the United States.
>
> The nation ought to know the truth and ought to consider that all the sacrifices, all the anguish, which our struggles to purify our political organization and reconquer the liberties of the people have cost should not be rendered sterile by an absurd and unjust war.
>
> From the beginning the struggle to implant a constitutional form of government has been met with constant difficulties from Washington, which we have met with impartiality, good faith, and a legitimate defense of the general interests of the country. In the United States, refugee Mexicans, in union with capitalists, Catholics, and American adventurers, have plotted to undo the work of the revolution.
>
> The stupid aggression of Villa and his bandits is not an isolated factor, but is connected with the work of these divers elements along the frontier, who daily try to overthrow the Constitutionalist Government and disturb the tranquillity of the United States.
>
> Far from trying to reach an agreement that would be sensible and equitable, so that the roots of these conspiracies might be cut, once for all, the United States sends a so-called punitive expedition into Mexican territory and prolongs the conflict, instead of settling it through diplomatic channels. Historic precedents do not uphold these proceedings.
>
> We have yet the right to believe that President Wilson, who knew how to face the great crisis of the European war, who has proclaimed and sustained his pacific theories, who has seen through the schemes of filibusters, and who has opened his arms to the Latin-American republics in an appeal for continental solidarity under the Monroe Doctrine, will not retrace his steps, will not tear up the foundations of his prestige by unchaining a war which nothing can justify, and sacrifice a people already weakened and bled by their internal struggles.
>
> Against such a war are the collective interests of both countries, but if, unfortunately, we are dragged into such a war, President Wilson may rest assured that never again will the United States have the confidence of a single Latin-American nation. And as for Mexico, while one Mexican stands, the ground which he covers will be his home, his religion, his honor.

Dr. Atl, leader of the Mexican Labor Party, and intimate friend of General Carranza, sent a cablegram tonight to President Wilson, declaring that the Mexican people and all Latin America wanted "a catergorical declaration" from him as to his policy toward the Latin-American republics.

NEAR AGREEMENT ON ARMY INCREASE

Senate Conferees Reconciled to Surrender of Volunteer Reserve Provision.

TRAINING CAMPS INSTEAD

Regular Army of 180,000, Federalized Militia, and Government-Operated Nitrate Plant.

WASHINGTON, May 9.—Agreement on the army reorganization bill was in sight tonight. Conferees of the Senate and the House, who will renew their deliberations tomorrow, expect to be able to reach a compromise so that the first of the big defense measures may be on the President's desk next week. The Senate today again committed the bill to conference.

That the Senate conferees would have to surrender the volunteer army reserve of 261,000 men which the House so strongly repudiated yesterday was admitted tonight by Senate leaders, but they hope to strengthen the provision of the House bill authorizing citizen instruction camps so that military training for thousands of citizens may be afforded and a nucleus of a volunteer army thus be built up. The Senate conferees believe it would be useless to hold out longer for the volunteer army, in view of the House insistence that the National Guard should constitute the main reserve military defense force. Under the House bill as it stands thousands of civilian training camps might be instituted under direction of the Secretary of War.

It was predicted tonight that the conferees would agree on a regular standing army with a peace strength of 175,000 or 180,000 men, with the Senate expansive organization system, which would make possible recruiting to a strength of 220,000 in time of need. The House bill provides for a peace strength of 140,000 and the Senate bill for a peace strength of 250,000. The conferees also are expected to agree to the main features of the House bill regarding the reorganization and federalization of the National Guard, thus providing for a defense reserve of approximately 400,000 men.

The House amendment for a nitrate plant probably will be accepted. Under it $20,000,000 would be appropriated for a plant to be operated exclusively by the Government. Agreement on minor features of the bill, such as military training in schools and colleges and organization details, is expected without much delay.

COL. BROWN IN HOSPITAL.

Cavalry Leader Who Was with Pershing Arrives at Fort Bliss.

Special to The New York Times.

EL PASO, Texas, May 9.—Colonel W C. Brown of the Tenth Cavalry arrived at the base hospital at Fort Bliss today suffering from hernia. Before going to the fort he called on General Funston at the headquarters car in El Paso and begged for permission to be allowed to return to the front at once.

"I can outride and outfight any of those young men at the front," Colonel Brown told General Funston. "I can get fixed up tonight and leave in the morning for Namiquipa."

General Funston ordered him to the base hospital.

Colonel Brown, who is 61 years old, has been one of the foremost cavalry leaders in the dashing campaign of General Pershing's men against Villistas. On April 1 he led troopers of the Tenth against a band of the outlaws at Aguascalientes, and thirty of the bandits were killed, the survivors fleeing.

MEN MOBILIZING IN THREE STATES

Funston Orders Them to Fort Sam Houston, Douglas, and Columbus.

UNDER WAY IN TWO DAYS

Militia Will Be Mustered Into the Regular Service as Soon as They Reach Camps.

SAN ANTONIO, Texas, May 9.—It was announced at headquarters this afternoon that General Funston had designated Fort Sam Houston as the mobilization point for the organized militia of Texas. He named Douglas the mobilization point for the Arizona National Guard, and the New Mexico militia will be mobilized at Columbus, N. M.

Officers at headquarters estimated that the mobilization at all three points should be completed within a week. It was indicated that the troops might be held in camp for a brief period before being sent to their border stations.

Immediately on receipt of telegraphic advices from General Funston naming the mobilization points the Governors of the States affected were notified of his action. It is their duty to order the militia of their respective States to the designated points at once, subject to the orders of General Funston. The movements should be well under way, it was said, within the next day or two. The camp at San Antonio will be by far the largest, containing approximately 2,500 men when all organizations have been assembled.

Under instructions from the War Department, the militia troops will be mustered into the United States service as fast as they reach mobilization camps. Major Orrin R. Wolfe, in charge of militia affars for the Southern Department, will serve as general mustering officer for all three States. In Texas he will have as assistants Captains John D. Long and James R. Love, Jr., both of whom are now on duty with the State troops as inspectors and instructors. There will be two assistant mustering officers for the militia of each of the two other States, appointed on the recommendation of the commanders at Columbus and Douglas.

General Funston left El Paso tonight and will reach headquarters here tomorrow night. He will immediately give attention to the problem of disposing of the militia to the best advantage along the border. Tentative plans for disposition have been worked out by Major Malvern-Hill Barnum, Chief of Staff, and will be submitted to General Funston for approval.

Following is the preliminary disposition of regular troops ordered to the border:

Regimental headquarters and one battalion of the Twenty-first Infantry, Yuma, Ariz.

Two companies of the Twelfth Infantry, now at Yuma, to rejoin the regiment at Nogales.

One battalion of the Twenty-first Infantry to Nogales.

Regimental Headquarters and two battalions of the Fourteenth Infantry to Douglas.

Third Infantry from Plattsburg, N. Y., to Rio Grande City.

Eleven companies of coast artillery equipped as infantry to Fort Sam Houston for distribution along the Texas border.

Three batteries of the Third Field Artillery to Fort Sam Houston for distribution.

Half a company of the Nineteenth Infantry left here today to strengthen the

Continued on Page 2.

38,500 MEN FOR FUNSTON

Texas, Arizona, and New Mexico to Send Their National Guard.

CANADA BORDER DRAWN ON

Funston's Call for More Men Impels Washington to Take Vigorous Steps.

ARREDONDO ALLEGES PLOT

Carranza Ambassador Asserts Raids Last Week Were Planned in U. S.

Special to The New York Times.

WASHINGTON, May 9.—Vigorous steps for the protection of the American border against further raids from the Mexican side and to meet any contingency in the border situation were taken by President Wilson today. The President called the National Guard of Texas, Arizona, and New Mexico into the service of the United States. These troops, numbering about 4,500 men, will be used for border patrol duty and will release regulars that can be utilized for service in Mexico.

President Wilson at the same time directed Secretary Baker to send to the border about 4,000 more regulars, all infantry and coast artillery. The call for militia and more regulars—which will add about 8,500 men to the border patrol—was made by the Administration on the urgent recommendation of Major Gen. Frederick Funston, supported by strong appeals from the border States for better protection.

Regulars Ordered to Border.

The additional regulars ordered to the border today are:

> Thirtieth Regiment of Infantry, Colonel Edwin A. Root, from Plattsburg Barracks, New York.
>
> Third Regiment of Infantry, Colonel Robert L. Hirst, the First Battalion of which is at Fort Ontario, N. Y., and the Second and Third Battalions, and machine-gun company of which have been stationed at Madison Barracks, N. Y.
>
> Headquarters, Second Battalion, and machine gun company, Fourteenth Infantry, Colonel Richard H. Wilson, from Fort Lawton, Wash., and the Third Battalion of the same regiment, from Fort George Wright, Washington.
>
> Headquarters, machine gun company, and Second Battalion of the Twenty-first Infantry, Colonel Francis H. French, from Vancouver Barracks, Wash., and the First Battalion of the same regiment, from the Exposition at San Diego, Cal.
>
> In addition, ten companies of coast artillery stationed at Gulf and Atlantic Coast posts were ordered to San Antonio, Texas, to serve as infantry with the border patrol. The coast artillery companies ordered out were: One Hundred and Twenty-seventh, Galveston; One Hundred and Sixty-fourth, New Orleans; Twentieth and Seventy-seventh, Pensacola, Fla.; Seventy-fourth, Savannah, Ga.; Thirty-first, Fort Caswell, N. C.; Forty-first and Sixty-ninth, Fort Oglethorpe, Ga.; One Hundred and Twelfth, Delaware River, (Forts Du Pont, Delaware, and Mott;) One Hundred and Third, Fort Howard, Md.; 145th, Charleston, S. C.

Coast Artillery to Go.

In view of the pressing need for relief of troops now stationed on the border and required for expeditionary service, Secretary Baker, after a conference with the President, announced at 11 o'clock tonight that it had been decided to make use of the Coast Artillery, and a beginning was made by issuing the orders for the organization of a provisional regiment consisting of the eleven companies. This will make a regiment of 1,000 men.

The entire command will not be drawn from any of these forts and the regiment to be formed in this manner will be about one-third of the whole number of men at these various posts from Delaware to Texas. The provisional regiment will rendezvous at San Antonio under orders from General Erasmus M. Weaver, Chief of the Coast Artillery, who will tomorrow designate the Colonel and field officers who will have command of the regiment.

This is only a beginning of the use of the Coast Artillery under a regimental organization for patrol duty. There are now enrolled in the Coast Artillery corps through the United States between 19,000 and 20,000 men. Nearly all of them are available for field service. The War Department was not anxious to use the Coast Artillery, but in view of the recommendations of Generals Scott and Funston for more men for border patrol it was found necessary to do so. By detailing caretakers at many of the less important posts along the Atlantic and Pacific Coasts, it is contended, it will be entirely practicable to form ten or fifteen regiments for border patrol duty.

Trains for Troops.

Arrangements have been made for trains to carry these troops to San Antonio and it is expected that they will be able to detrain there in about three days.

Secretary Baker also announced at 11 o'clock that in addition to using the Coast Artillery orders had been issued moving five batteries of the Fifth Field Artillery from Fort Sill, Okla., to the border. The disposition of these five batteries will be left entirely to the discretion of General Funston. The sixth battery of the Fifth Artillery is already

"All the News That's Fit to Print."

The New York Times.

THE WEATHER
Cloudy, warmer, probably rain tonight and Thursday; wind variable.
For full weather report see Page 21.

VOL. LXVI...NO. 21,529. ... NEW YORK, WEDNESDAY, JANUARY 3, 1917.—TWENTY-TWO PAGES. ONE CENT In Greater New York, Jersey City and Newark. | Elsewhere, TWO CENTS.

GERMANS SAY SWORD WILL ANSWER ENTENTE'S REJECTION OF PEACE; WASHINGTON DOUBTS U-BOAT REVIVAL

WILSON MAY SOON RECALL PERSHING AS CARRANZA ASKS

Commission Expected to Send Troop Withdrawal Question to the White House.

FLETCHER TO GO TO MEXICO

Ambassador Sees President as Arredondo Leaves for Short Visit to His Chief.

TEXT OF PROTOCOL ISSUED

Pledges Americans to Hold Up All Other Questions Until Our Soldiers Come Back.

Special to The New York Times.

WASHINGTON, Jan. 2.—President Wilson is contemplating the early withdrawal of the American troops commanded by Major Gen. John J. Pershing, from the Mexican State of Chihuahua, to the American border. It could not be ascertained from what was gathered here today that the positive decision had been reached to withdraw the expedition, but there appeared to be ample ground for the statement that the President is seriously considering preparations for the voluntary withdrawal to the border independent of the Atlantic City protocol which General Carranza has declined to sign in its present form.

Franklin K. Lane, Chairman of the American section of the Joint International Commission, made public today the text of the protocol signed at Atlantic City on Nov. 24. This protocol was not to become effective until approved by both Governments. The action of General Carranza in withholding his approval is based on his desire for a modification of the agreement and his preference for the withdrawal of the troops without any agreement, and voluntarily on the part of the United States Government.

Secretary Lane's action in giving out the text of the protocol, as signed by the Commissioners, although not approved by the de facto Government, was explained in an authoritative quarter as meaning that the efforts of the Commission to obtain the consent of both Governments to a troop withdrawal agreement had failed, and that the endeavor to settle this matter by commission was to be abandoned.

Wilson Expected to Act.

The refusal of Carranza to approve the protocol and the disinclination of the American Commissioners to acquiesce in the de facto Government's desire for its modification are expected to be followed by early announcement, perhaps tomorrow, that the American Commissioners have decided to refer the question of withdrawing the troops to the President for independent action. The belief grew strong today that the President soon would authorize the announcement that it has been decided voluntarily to withdraw the troops without making an agreement for their recall.

The expedition is costing the United States Government about $14,000,000 a month. High army officials are in favor of early withdrawal as a military measure, pointing out that the American troops have been idle for many months, and that no good purpose is being served by their continued presence in Mexico. It is known that army officials do not regard the position which the Pershing forces occupy as a strong military line, and that for protection of the border against raids they, from a strict military viewpoint, would be in a stronger strategic position if withdrawn to the American side of the line.

Arredondo Leaves Capital.

Secretary of State Lansing announced that Eliseo Arredondo, the Mexican Ambassador-designate to the United States, had called at the State Department to say farewell, preparatory to his departure for Queretaro, for a conference with General Carranza. Mr. Arredondo left Washington at 6:15 o'clock tonight and is traveling via St. Louis. He told Secretary Lansing he expected to be gone about three weeks and was leaving his family in Washington because he expected to return to his post. Ramon P. de Negri, who has been placed temporarily in charge of the embassy, accompanied Mr. Arredondo to the State Department and was introduced to Secretary Lansing, but not as a permanent successor to the Ambassador-designate.

Mr. Arredondo denied that he had been recalled, and from an authoritative official source it was learned that the Washington Government possessed no information to indicate that the request for him to confer with General Carranza was intended as any offense to the United States Government.

Henry P. Fletcher, Ambassador of the United States to Mexico, who has not yet gone to his post, though his appointment was confirmed by the Senate some months ago, conferred with the President at the White House late this afternoon, under an appointment made by Mr. Wilson. At this conference there was an exchange of ideas on the Mexican situation. It is believed that Mr. Fletcher has been directed to prepare to go to his post in Mexico City in a short time.

Chairman Lane and his American associates on the International Commission, George Gray and John R. Mott, met in the office of the Secretary of the Interior for the consideration of the Mexican situation. Mr. Lane asserted that the American Commissioners were not yet ready to announce their atti-

Continued on Page 8.

Allies Captured 583,000 Men in 1916; 119,300 in the West

ON THE FRENCH FRONT IN FRANCE, Jan. 2.—During the course of last year, according to authoritative figures, 78,500 Germans were captured on the French front by the French and 40,800 by the British, while in Serbia and Macedonia the Entente allied armies took 11,173 Bulgarians and Turks prisoner.

During the same period the Italians made prisoners 52,250 Austrians, while the Russians captured more than 400,000 Germans and Austrians.

This gives the Allies a total of 583,000 prisoners for the year.

JUDGES PUT SWANN CASE UP TO WHITMAN

They Hear District Attorney's Answer to Delehanty, but Decide Not to Act.

HE ACCUSES BRECKENRIDGE

But Latter Denies He Served Employers While in Office—Union Men in Court Today.

The Court of General Sessions will not hear the charges of misconduct in office made against District Attorney Edward Swann. The Judges reached that decision, informally, yesterday, as was forecast. The next move in the case is therefore up to Governor Whitman, with whom ex-Judge James A. Delehanty filed the allegations that Mr. Swann had tried to dismiss indictments against labor leaders for their part in garment strike riots, in reciprocation for those leaders' services in the last election.

A dispatch to THE NEW YORK TIMES from Albany last night said that, while there was a general feeling that Mr. Whitman would entertain the charges against the District Attorney, it was not likely that any public announcement regarding the case would be forthcoming from the Governor for several days.

Mr. Whitman, it was added, had his first glimpse of the Delehanty letter embodying the charges, and spent the greater part of yesterday afternoon in conference with Franklin B. Lord, his legal assistant, considering them. It was assumed that if the Governor decided to entertain the complaint he would proceed under the Sherman-Moreland act, which would involve a resubmission in legal form of the charges and the appointment of a Commissioner to take testimony and report his findings to the Governor.

Under the Constitution the Governor has power to remove a District Attorney against whose official conduct complaint has been made after giving to him an opportunity to be heard. From such a decision there is no appeal, but it is known that Mr. Whitman is adverse to any such drastic action in the Swann matter.

Demands a Thorough Inquiry.

The decision of the Court of General Sessions not to take up the case was reached at a conference shortly after Mr. Swann had appeared before one of the Judges and presented his formal answer to Mr. Delehanty's charges. That answer already had appeared in the newspapers as a public statement antedating its formal presentation to the court.

After the Clerk of the Court had received Mr. Delehanty's memorandum of charges filed with him, Mr. Swann appeared before Judge Joseph F. Mulqueen in Part I. of the court and said:

"I appear before your Honor because of the fact that by virtue of your designation to sit in Part I. for this month you are the Presiding Judge of the Court of General Sessions.

"Without previous notice or intimation I was apprised by the newspapers on Sunday morning that after my office had closed Saturday evening and my staff and I had left for the holiday a communication had been addressed to this court by a gentleman who, by appointment, had sat as Judge for the year just passed, in which certain statements had been made attacking my official conduct as District Attorney and charging an attempted deceit upon this court.

"I beg to hand you herewith a statement upon the matter regarding which I earnestly request most careful and speedy attention upon the part of yourself and your associates upon this bench. Public welfare and my own reputation as a former Judge, as District Attorney, and as a citizen, require that a thorough examination of the facts be made by this court.

"All the papers in the cases are at your disposal, and I will await instructions and directions from the Judges of this court."

Calls Situation "Unprecedented."

In connection with Mr. Swann's submission of the cases to the Judges of General Sessions, all the defendants in the labor riot cases are to be produced in court this morning in proof of the prosecutor's assertion that they are available for trial, although their bail bonds have been discharged and they are at liberty.

Judge Mulqueen told Mr. Swann, in reply to his formal statement, that the situation was unprecedented in the Court of General Sessions. He advised the District Attorney that he might file his statement and it would be brought to the attention of all the Judges. Judges Otto A. Rosalsky, Charles C. Nott, Jr., T. C. T. Crain, William H. Wadhams, and Mulqueen lunched together later to discuss their action in the affair. Judge Malone was unable to attend because of illness. Judge John F. McIntyre, who was elected to succeed Mr. Delehanty, also was absent.

No member of the court would talk for quotation after the meeting, but two Judges said it was the sense of all that no action should be taken by the General Sessions bench, and that, while they had agreed that each member of the court should have a copy of the accusing memorandum and the reply to it in order that they might meet later to take them up if they wished to do so, it was practically certain that no such meeting ever would take place. The Judges felt, as explained yesterday, that since the matter was before the Governor, and his authority was higher than theirs, it would be useless as well as inappropriate for them to go into the case.

Fear of Fusion by Tammany Seen.

These were only the formal activities, however, of a day that fixed the Delehanty-Swann controversy firmly on a political basis. From the first Mr. Swann had asserted that the whole matter was a Republican plot, and last night he broadened this statement with the promise that he would involve prom-

Continued on Page 6.

HINT THAT NOBLES KILLED RASPUTIN STIRS PETROGRAD

Gossip Alleges a Plot Involving a Prince Allied to the Czar by Marriage.

MONK'S BODY RECOVERED

Divers Said to Have Found It in the Neva—Story of Shots in a Garden.

SUSPECTED AS PRO-GERMAN

Rasputin, Whose Life Was Twice Before Attempted, Viewed as Emperor's Evil Genius.

Special Cable to THE NEW YORK TIMES.

LONDON, Jan. 2.—The Daily Chronicle's Petrograd correspondent sends the following account of the assassination of the notorious Russian monk Rasputin:

"The story of an event that overshadows all others in interest at the present moment is told in veiled form. On Friday night two young men belonging to the highest Petrograd society drove up in a motor car to the house on Corokhavaya Street occupied by a man whose name is notorious throughout Russia. This man was taken in the car to a large house on the Moïka Canal owned by Prince Yusupoff Sumarokoff-Elston. The garden attached to the house extends from the canal to Offitszerskaya Street.

"At 3 o'clock Saturday morning a policeman on the Moïka and another policeman on Offitszerskaya Street heard the sound of shots and cries from the garden. The policeman on Offitszerskaya Street saw several persons coming out of a gate and asked them what had happened, but received no explanation. Shortly afterward a motor car drove up into the garden and another car arrived at the door of the house on the Moïka. The judicial authorities were called up and traces of blood were seen on the snow in the garden.

"According to one version, the body of the murdered man was put into a car, wrapped up in a fur coat. One of the young aristocrats took his seat beside the chauffeur, and the car was driven to an island at the mouth of the Neva.

"In the course of Saturday and Sunday an investigation was made by the judicial authorities, a number of persons were examined, and the main facts as to the assassination were established. In the ice on a branch of the Neva, near Petrovsky Island, a freshly made hole was discovered. Near the hole were traces of blood, and not far away lay a pair of goloshes with suspicious red marks. Divers were set to work, and it was rumored last evening that the body had been discovered.

"Extraordinary interest has been aroused by the event, due not only to the personality of the murdered man, but also to the high rank of the persons immediately concerned. One of them, a handsome young man of 30, received part of his education in England and some years ago was very popular in fashionable society in London. It is said that he and several of his friends and relatives cast lots to see who should accomplish the act. The name of a well known and formerly reactionary Deputy is also mentioned in connection with the event."

The Daily Chronicle adds that Felix, Prince Yusupoff, belongs to the Sumarokoff-Elston branch of one of the noblest houses of Russia. He is 29 years of age and was married three years ago to Princess Irene of Russia, second cousin of the Czar and eldest daughter of the Grand Duke Alexander.

Rasputin Suspected as Pro-German.

This is the third time that report has come out of Russia announcing the assassination of the notorious mystic and adventurer, Gregory Rasputin, who is supposed to have exercised such an influence for evil upon the mind of the Czar of Russia. The first time was in July, 1914, when, exiled from Petrograd, he was stabbed by Julia Guseva at Tyumen, Siberia; then on May 11, 1916, his death was reported from Bucharest.

It has been stated by those who have been in a position to penetrate the domestic surroundings of the Russian imperial family that the interest of the Czar in Rasputin was purely that of an investigator, who used the monk as a means to gather information from and at times to communicate with the mass of the people from whom his exalted birth and rank separated him. From Rasputin, it is said, Nicholas learned of the horrors of vodka, and immediately set about to eliminate them.

When Rasputin lay wounded in Tyumen in 1914 his Majesty sent to him the Court physician, Professor Sergius Petrovitch. It was than Rasputin made this startling accusation against Illiodor, "the mad monk," who is now in New York:

"It is all that cursed Illiodor. But, to the confusion of himself and my enemies, I will live, and they will have nooses put around their necks."

When interrogated, the Guseva woman declared that she had attempted to kill Rasputin because he had spread temptation among the innocent. No connection could be established between her and Illiodor.

The attempted assassination of last Spring is supposed to have been due to political causes. Rasputin had been well acquainted with General W. A. Soukhomlinoff, who was Russian Minister of War during the fatal campaign in East Prussia, when traitors were believed to have betrayed the Russian armies in the field and left them without reserves of munitions at home. In June, 1915, Soukhomlinoff resigned and was later arrested and lodged in the fortress of Peter and Paul.

Among the witnesses sought was Rasputin, who was known for his pro-German sympathies. It was said that he had been discovered by the secret political police and would create a sensa-

Continued on Page 4.

French Cabinet Outlines Plans for Reconstruction

WASHINGTON, Jan. 2.—Plans for the reconstruction of Northern France after the war, worked out by a French Cabinet Committee and outlined in official reports received here, embrace a carefully prepared program for restoration of normal conditions immediately after peace is declared.

Provisions are included for the return of refugees to the enemy occupied districts as expeditiously as possible, prefects of the departments already having reported the number to be repatriated, and a system having been worked out for the return first of those whose presence is an immediate necessity. A central labor bureau has been established in Paris to estimate the labor demand and supply. Prefects in the invaded district have been provided with funds to purchase agricultural machinery.

ACCUSES RAILROADS IN 8-HOUR FIGHT

Brotherhood Chief Charges That They Permit Train Delays to Pile Up Expenses.

FRETS UNDER THE DELAY

Predicts Additional Litigation by the Transportation Companies—Labor Leaders Call a Meeting.

CLEVELAND, Jan. 2.—W. G. Lee, chief of the Brotherhood of Railroad Trainmen, issued a statement here today charging that the railroads of the country are permitting delays to trains and overtime which would not ordinarily be permitted in order to prove the enormous expense that would follow obedience to the Adamson law. The statement asked whether if the Supreme Court declared the law either constitutional or invalid, the brotherhoods should continue to await the eight-hour day. The statement follows:

"The railways enjoined the Government from enforcing the Adamson law. Additional litigation will thereafter very likely be started by the railways on the plea of determining to whom does the law apply, or how does it apply?'

"Already the railroads are permitting delays to trains, overtime, &c., that would not be permitted under normal conditions.

"Recall, if you can, an instance where labor organizations have attempted to enjoin the Government from enforcing a Federal statute. Such organizations are law abiding instead of law breakers.

"Remember, the railways are not enjoining the brotherhoods, but are enjoining the Government.

"The question is, after the Supreme Court has said the law is or is not constitutional, shall the employes, who President Wilson and Congress declared should have the eight-hour basic work day, forget their request and continue to wait?"

Mr. Lee denied a report that a sealed statement putting the Adamson law situation up to the men had been sent out by the chiefs of the four brotherhoods.

It was learned from an authoritative source today that the General Chairmen of the four brotherhoods will hold a meeting in Chicago on Jan. 11 to consider the situation.

DISCUSS WILSON PROGRAM.

Newlands Shows Labor a Loophole in Arbitration Bill.

Special to The New York Times.

WASHINGTON, Jan. 2.—The Administration railway strike prevention program, for which President Wilson has asked urgent consideration in Congress, made little progress today at the first hearing before the Interstate Commerce Committee. Frank Morrison, Secretary of the American Federation of Labor, appeared before the committee to say that organized labor would oppose any measure that carried compulsion of any character, and Andrew Furuseth, representing the Seamen's Union, expressed the opposition of his organization to the plan to prohibit strikes and lockouts during Government investigation of industrial disputes.

None of the heads of the four big railway brotherhoods was present, but P. J. McNamara, Vice President of the Brotherhood of Locomotive Firemen and Engineers, said that they might present their views later in the week. Ex-Senator Faulkner of West Virginia, representing the railroads, told the committee that his clients did not disapprove the general principles involved in the strike-prevention program, but that they might wish to suggest alterations in the details of the bills before the committee.

Frank W. Whitcher, President of the Massachusetts State Employers' Association, and Everett P. Wheeler, representing the Reform Club of New York, addressed the committee in favor of the President's recommendations. Mr. Wheeler advocated industrial arbitration, recalling as an example of the success of the plan the arbitration board appointed by President Roosevelt in the Pennsylvania coal strike. He also mentioned the system employed by the Borough of Manhattan in giving all borough employes against whom charges were preferred a hearing before a board of three, in which they were represented by one of their own number.

At the close of Mr. Whitcher's address, after a discussion of the dangers of injunctions as a method of preventing strikes, Senator Newlands called the speaker's attention to the provision in the President's program which prevents the calling of strikes during a Government investigation.

"You realize, do you not," he asked, "that there is nothing in this provision which prevents an individual from giving up his employment?"

It is understood that this idea is to be urged by the supporters of the bill as a defense against the claims of organized labor that the measure interferes with the "right" to strike.

It was tentatively decided by the committee to limit the presentations of both the railroads' and the brotherhoods' side of the arguments to two days each in order to hasten the work on the bills. It was indicated at the White House today that the President does not believe an extra session will be necessary to obtain the adoption of his program, in spite of the evident great opposition to the Strike Prevention act in both houses of Congress.

THINKS PLEDGES SAFE

Belief at Capital That Germany Will Not Dare Break Promises.

WOULD DASH PEACE HOPES

President Expected to Continue His Efforts, with Safety of America in View.

ALLIED NOTE FORWARDED

Ambassador Sharp, at Paris, Directed to Send It to Berlin in Original Text.

Special to The New York Times.

WASHINGTON, Jan. 2.—The State Department today instructed Ambassador Sharp at Paris to communicate to Germany and the other members of the Central group of belligerents the joint answer of the Entente Governments rejecting the German peace offer.

In some quarters this is regarded as the final act in the Teutonic effort to bring about the negotiation of arrangements for ending the war. But from what is known of President Wilson's interest in the matter it is believed that he will not permit the attitude of Great Britain, France, Russia, and Italy to discourage him in furthering his own peace movement, and it is expected that he will not allow the exchanges he initiated to lapse with the receipt of the forthcoming answer of the Entente to his note of Dec. 18, to which the Central Powers have already made a sympathetic reply.

It was through Ambassador Sharp that the Entente nations forwarded their response to the German peace proffer. The Ambassador cabled the response to the State Department in English, and as he has the original communication in Paris, the State Department has instructed him to use the original text in communicating the document to Berlin and the other capitals of the Teutonic league. He was also instructed to send the Entente note in French, the language in which it presumably was written when it was handed to Mr. Sharp. Through this means the document will be laid before the Central Powers in its original form, and will not be subjected to the danger of error by sending it again by cable to Germany and her allies.

Viewed as Complete Rejection.

Berlin press dispatches indicate that the German Government regards the Entente answer as a complete rejection of the offer of the Central Powers, and this view agrees with the expressed opinion in high German circles here. Whether the idea is being disseminated that Germany looks upon her peace movement as a failure with the purpose of arousing President Wilson to greater activity in pressing his own particular peace endeavor is of course problematical, but that interpretation is given to the German expression by some observers in Washington.

Those who have followed the situation closely and have some knowledge of what is going on in the German mind are satisfied that the Berlin Government does not intend to take any action that would cast peace to the winds as long as the very faintest hope exists of inducing the Entente Powers to exchange views with their enemies. It is understood that Germany has no intention of showing resentment of the action of the Entente by resuming submarine warfare on a reckless scale or doing anything that will endanger the prospect of help from the United States Government. To that extent at least the peace movement has been of benefit to the United States. It seems to insure that the pledges given to this Government by Germany in connection with the Sussex case will be lived up to. In fact, it is broadly intimated that this is to be expected, and the intimation is coupled with the explanation that there is no occasion for Germany to change her present methods of submarine warfare because she is doing very well under them; that is, she is doing great damage to the commerce of her enemies, particularly Great Britain.

Germany, it is evident, realizes that if she should begin reprisals against Great Britain on account of the rejection of the peace offer, she would imperil the continuance of what she probably considers the friendly help of President Wilson. Besides, it is said, if she is honest in her desire for peace a this time, she knows that her only opportunity of bringing about a peace conference is through the President. In these circumstances it is believed here that until the President's efforts have reached finality, one way or the other, Germany will take no action in the way of reprisal or otherwise that might put her in the bad books of the Wilson Administration.

President's Real Purpose.

No word comes from the White House as to how the President views the situation. Those who know Mr. Wilson, however, and understand his methods and habits of thought are satisfied that he will cling tenaciously to his desire to bring the war to an end as quickly as possible. They realize that the policy of taking a hand in a peace movement has been in his mind for a long time, and that he is not disposed to drop it lightly in the face of the discouragement given by the Entente answer to Germany.

It is said in some quarters here that the President is playing a bigger game than is involved in bringing peace at this time. In making his suggestions to the belligerents he had in mind the material interests of the United States, and

Continued on Page 2.

Says Central Powers Face Starvation And Must Give Up Before Next Fall

Special Cable to THE NEW YORK TIMES.

LONDON, Wednesday, Jan. 3.—The Morning Post publishes the following, dated Dec. 26, from its Budapest correspondent:

"Taking for granted that the peace offer of the Central Powers and the efforts of neutrals will fail to bring about a speedy end of the war, the question arises how long the Central Empires will be able to hold out. Setting aside military considerations, and basing one's theory purely on economic grounds, it is evident we are within measurable distance of the limit of endurance of their much-suffering peoples.

"It is plainly apparent to any one who has made a study of the economic conditions in Germany and in the dual monarchy that the peace offer made in the middle of December was chiefly prompted by the knowledge that relief must come within six months from the present time at the outside if internal troubles of the most serious character are to be avoided. In Austria-Hungary the available stocks of food will not even last for six months.

"But supposing, by imposing severe privations on the people, the authorities should succeed in quieting them until the end of June, how is the population—increased, it must be borne in mind, by some 26,000,000 mouths in the occupied regions—to be fed during the months of July and August? For by that time, according to statisticians, not a grain of wheat or maize will be left. Even if the spoils in Rumania should afford some relief, which is a most questionable supposition, there will thus be two months to be bridged over before the earliest crops can be harvested, and in that period starvation on a scale hitherto unknown in the world, save perhaps in India, will present itself.

"When it comes to that, of course, peace will have to be made on any terms. The feeding of the army is the main concern of the Central Empires, not that of the population, as may be imagined; yet even this cannot be managed for more than another six months, even allowing for the fact that the Austro-Hungarian forces behind the front are on half rations and that very soon, in all probability, the men on the western front will fare no better. The fact is, the time has come when the question of feeding even the army gives rise to the gravest apprehension. Although the peasantry and land owners have been stripped of everything in the way of cereals, the army has not enough food to carry it through the Winter. Local authorities in different districts have petitioned the Government to supply food for distribution among the poor, but the Government can do nothing, for the military authorities are supreme.

"Even if a peace conference were called together tomorrow peace would probably still be some months off, and it is not at all probable that the blockade would be raised in the meantime, that is to say, while negotiations were in progress.

"Under these circumstances, the Central Powers have but a very limited time in which to bring about an understanding as regards the conference itself. The people are already desperate, and the troops may become desperate, too, as soon as they experience on their own persons the horrors of the present food shortage."

"It is rumored that after his coronation as King of Hungary the new Emperor-King will take the question of peace in hand and go to Berlin to discuss the position with Emperor William. The newspapers express great hopes of his energetic will to attain this end, and if those hopes are well founded, as is generally believed here, some most unexpected events may be in store for the peoples of the Central Powers."

SENATE DELAYS VOTE ON PEACE

Lodge and Gallinger Object to Summary Indorsement of Wilson's Note.

FORECASTS PARTY DEBATE

Stone Presses for Prompt Action — Believed to be Result of President's Call.

Special to The New York Times.

WASHINGTON, Jan. 2.—It became increasingly apparent today that the Administration was determined to have the approval of the Senate for its move toward getting a statement of terms from the belligerents, and that this was one of the objects which impelled President Wilson to pay his sudden visit to the Capitol yesterday to see Senator Stone, Chairman of the Committee on Foreign Relations. A determined move by Senator Hitchcock of Nebraska and Senator Stone to obtain immediate consideration for the Hitchcock resolution indorsing the President's note was again temporarily blocked today by Republican opposition.

The temper of the debate today foreshadows a probable general discussion of the relations of the United States with Europe when the Hitchcock resolution finally does come before the Senate for a vote. Both Senator Lodge, the ranking Republican member of the Committee on Foreign Relations, and Senator Gallinger, the Republican floor leader, in asking that the question be deferred made much of the point that the President's act involved the whole subject of future American foreign policy, and the latter mentioned specifically the Washingtonian theory of avoiding entangling alliances and the Monroe Doctrine. So vital a matter, they said, could not possibly be permitted to pass without discussion.

Senator Lodge contended that the resolution ought to go to committee for consideration before the Senate took action. "It involves a very large and very grave problem," he said, "and should not be passed as if it were a general matter, with no specific importance. It is certainly too important for us to allow it to pass without discussion. There must be opportunity to amend it.

"We ought to have all the official papers in the case before us in order to consider it properly. At present we have only the President's note in official form. For other documents we are compelled to rely on newspaper reports. We should have before us for the consideration of so grave a matter the German reply to the President's note, the Spanish note, and the reply of the Entente Allies to the German note.

"There was a very important statement of the Secretary of State, in which

Continued on Page 2.

ENTENTE'S REPLY TO WILSON READY

Final Draft, Approved by France and Britain, May Be Sent Today.

CITES PURPOSES OF PEACE

Note Explains How Allies Hope to Pave the Way for Ending All War.

LONDON, Jan. 2.—The final draft of the reply of the Entente to President Wilson's peace note, which already has been approved by France and Great Britain, has been forwarded to Italy and Russia. As no changes have been suggested thus far from those quarters it is not improbable the note will be delivered to the American Ambassador in Paris, William G. Sharp, within a short time. It is understood here that the note may possibly be handed to Mr. Sharp tomorrow. However, Belgium made her request at the last moment that the statement of her case be added to the reply to the Central Powers, and similar additions or delays may occur in the case of the note to President Wilson.

In its present form the reply is about the same length as the note to the Central Powers, and has the same characteristics of general and guarded language. One of the most important points is a differentiation between peace among the present belligerents and such future arrangements as may be made for permanent peace, the purpose being to show neutral upholders of a future permanent peace that this is attainable not alone by first concluding the present war, but also by concluding the kind of a peace which will pave the way for a permanent peace.

While the original draft, like the reply to the Central Powers, was written largely in France, Foreign Secretary Balfour also has had a considerable part in it, particularly in regard to phrases seeking to elucidate the situation for the benefit of public opinion in neutral countries.

CRITICISE ENTENTE REPLY.

English Papers Say Its Translation from French Was Crudely Done.

Special Cable to THE NEW YORK TIMES.

LONDON, Jan. 2.—Criticism of the literary aspects of the Entente's reply to the Central Powers continues. The Westminster Gazette thinks the note "about as sad a piece of English as could be" and cites the following inadequacies of translation.

"When we read that the allied nations have for thirty months been engaged in a war and turn to the original French we find the verb 'ont Subi,' which surely means have had to endure. Sham is a somewhat crude and harsh rendering of 'prétendue' and certainly sanctions conveys something different to the mind from the English penalties, and vide" is rather hollowness than the empty pretense of the enemy declaration."

The Manchester Guardian devotes an editorial to the use of the word penalties as equivalent for French "sanctions," declaring that the meaning which the English Foreign Office translation found for sanctions' has no existence in the French language, according to the Littré's monumental dictionary

BERLIN PRESS BELLIGERENT

Nation Summoned to Rally to von Hindenburg to Resent "Insult."

HOPE NO LONGER FOR PEACE

Papers Declare Germany Must Continue War with Weapons of Land, Sea, and Air.

WILL STRIKE AT BRITAIN

"We Know Where She Is Vulnerable"—Tone of Allies' Note No Surprise.

Heads of Teuton Parliaments to Hold Important Meeting

LONDON, Jan. 2.—A dispatch to the Exchange Telegraph from Copenhagen says:

"The Vienna Reichspost says it learns that an important meeting of the Presidents of the German, Austro-Hungarian, Bulgarian, and Turkish Parliaments will be held in Berlin on January 18."

LONDON, Jan. 2.—Comments of the German papers on the Entente reply to the German peace proposal are sent by Reuter's correspondent at Amsterdam as indicating the universal conviction that peace is now impossible and that the Central Powers must continue to prosecute the war with the utmost vigor.

The Berlin Lokal-Anzeiger considers that nobody will be shocked, because the Entente's refusal was anticipated.

"But," it adds, "every one will be surprised and shocked at the shallowness, levity, and mendacity of the reasons given for the refusal, and it is difficult to explain how ten serious men were able to affix their signatures to the document without blushing. Our answer can only be given on the battlefield."

The Vossische Zeitung says: "All possibility of further negotiations has disappeared under this scornful reply. There is only one rejoinder, namely, warfare until the cold steel of our arms has brought the fever temperature of our enemies down to something near normal."

Wanted Peace, Will Accept War.

The Berlin Tageblatt says: "We would gladly have written 'Peace be unto thee' over the gate of the new year, but it would be childish to seek in the Entente's reply any expressions but those of an absolute 'No.' Who in the world can now doubt that the Entente plans, which aim at the dismemberment of Germany, Austria-Hungary, and Turkey will be resolutely repelled by the German people?"

The Kreuz-Zeitung says: "The form of the Eentente's rejection makes it an insult. Our reply can only be given with the sword."

The Vorwärts says: "Since our enemies desire to continue the war, no choice remains to the German people. There will be no illusion; behind the refusal lies the hope of finally being able to lay Germany prostrate. It is to the interest of the whole German people to frustrate this design.

The Rhenische Westphalische Zeitung says: "The German people to one man will now gather around von Hindenberg. The last plea for indulgence falls to the ground. All our sharp weapons must come into use on land and sea and in the air. We know the points where Great Britain is vulnerable.

The Cologne Gazette's Berlin correspondent considers that no way is left open for further negotiations, and adds: "It is not yet decided what the Government will do, but it is not improbable that Germany will again precisely define the German view direct to the neutrals."

Says Peace Dream Is Over.

BERLIN, Jan. 2, (via Amsterdam and London.)—"The peace dream is over for the present," says the Täglische Rundschau. "Whoever abandoned himself thereto will be sobered by the Entente reply and will adapt himself to the hard reality.

"If the German offer is today rejected the thought of peace is not by this refusal suffocated. The British, French, and Russian people have been deluded into the belief that our offer of peace was a confession of our weakness and an attempt to save ourselves before the collapse. When the coming months of the war show that this lie, too, is shivered on the German arms revulsion must come, and then woe to those rulers who will have to answer for the useless bloodshed."

ENTENTE'S REFUSAL NO SHOCK TO BERLIN

Gist of Answer to Peace Proposal Discounted—Analysis Based on Early Summary.

From a Staff Correspondent.

By Wireless to THE NEW YORK TIMES.

BERLIN, Jan. 1, (via Tuckerton, N. J., Jan. 2.)—A Havas agency version

"All the News That's Fit to Print."

The New York Times.

THE WEATHER
Rain Thursday; fair, cold wave by night Friday.
For full weather report see Page 21.

VOL. LXVI...NO. 21,558. NEW YORK, THURSDAY, FEBRUARY 1, 1917.—TWENTY-TWO PAGES. ONE CENT In Greater New York, Jersey City and Newark. | Elsewhere, TWO CENTS

GERMANY BEGINS RUTHLESS SEA WARFARE; DRAWS 'BARRED ZONES' AROUND THE ALLIES; CRISIS CONFRONTS THE UNITED STATES

Text of Germany's Note to the United States

Washington, D. C., Jan. 31, 1917.

Mr. Secretary of State:

Your Excellency was good enough to transmit to the Imperial Government a copy of the message which the President of the United States of America addressed to the Senate on the 22d inst. The Imperial Government has given it the earnest consideration which the President's statements deserve, inspired, as they are, by a deep sentiment of responsibility.

It is highly gratifying to the Imperial Government to ascertain that the main tendencies of this important statement correspond largely to the desires and principles professed by Germany. These principles especially include self-government and equality of rights for all nations. Germany would be sincerely glad if in recognition of this principle countries like Ireland and India, which do not enjoy the benefits of political independence, should now obtain their freedom.

The German people also repudiate all alliances which serve to force the countries into a competition for might and to involve them in a net of selfish intrigues. On the other hand, Germany will gladly co-operate in all efforts to prevent future wars.

The freedom of the seas, being a preliminary condition of the free existence of nations and the peaceful intercourse between them, as well as the open-door for the commerce of all nations, has always formed part of the leading principles of Germany's political program. All the more the Imperial Government regrets that the attitude of her enemies, who are so entirely opposed to peace, makes it impossible for the world at present to bring about the realization of these lofty ideals.

Germany and her allies were ready to enter now into a discussion of peace, and had set down as basis the guarantee of existence, honor, and free development of their peoples. Their aims, as has been expressly stated in the note of Dec. 12, 1916, were not directed toward the destruction or annihilation of their enemies and were, according to their conviction, perfectly compatible with the rights of the other nations. As to Belgium, for which such warm and cordial sympathy is felt in the United States, the Chancellor had declared only a few weeks previously that its annexation had never formed part of Germany's intentions. The peace to be signed with Belgium was to provide for such conditions in that country, with which Germany desires to maintain friendly neighborly relations, that Belgium should not be used again by Germany's enemies for the purpose of instigating continuous hostile intrigues. Such precautionary measures are all the more necessary, as Germany's enemies have repeatedly stated, not only in speeches delivered by their leading men, but also in the statutes of the Economical Conference in Paris, that it is their intention not to treat Germany as an equal, even after peace has been restored, but to continue their hostile attitude, and especially to wage a systematical economic war against her.

The attempt of the four allied powers to bring about peace has failed, owing to the lust of conquest of their enemies, who desired to dictate the conditions of peace. Under the pretense of following the principle of nationality, our enemies have disclosed their real aims in this way, viz.: To dismember and dishonor Germany, Austria-Hungary, Turkey, and Bulgaria. To the wish of reconciliation they oppose the will of destruction. They desire a fight to the bitter end.

A new situation has thus been created which forces Germany to new decisions. Since two years and a half England is using her naval power for a criminal attempt to force Germany into submission by starvation. In brutal contempt of international law, the group of powers led by England does not only curtail the legitimate trade of their opponents, but they also, by ruthless pressure, compel neutral countries either to altogether forego every trade not agreeable to the Entente Powers or to limit it according to their arbitrary decrees.

The American Government knows the steps which have been taken to cause England and her Allies to return to the rules of international law and to respect the freedom of the seas. The English Government, however, insists upon continuing its war of starvation, which does not at all affect the military power of its opponents, but compels women and children, the sick and the aged, to suffer for their country pains and privations which endanger the vitality of the nation. Thus British tyranny mercilessly increases the sufferings of the world, indifferent to the laws of humanity, indifferent to the protests of the neutrals whom they severely harm, indifferent even to the silent longing for peace among England's own allies. Each day of the terrible struggle causes new destruction, new sufferings. Each day shortening the war will, on both sides, preserve the lives of thousands of brave soldiers and be a benefit to mankind.

The Imperial Government could not justify before its own conscience, before the German people and before history the neglect of any means destined to bring about the end of the war. Like the President of the United States, the Imperial Government had hoped to reach this goal by negotiations. After the attempts to come to an understanding with the Entente Powers have been answered by the latter with the announcement of an intensified continuation of the war, the Imperial Government—in order to serve the welfare of mankind in a higher sense and not to wrong its own people—is now compelled to continue the fight for existence, again forced upon it, with the full employment of all the weapons which are at its disposal.

Sincerely trusting that the people and the Government of the United States will understand the motives for this decision and its necessity, the Imperial Government hopes that the United States may view the new situation from the lofty heights of impartiality, and assist, on their part, to prevent further misery and unavoidable sacrifice of human life.

Enclosing two memoranda regarding the details of the contemplated military measures at sea, I remain, etc.,

J. BERNSTORFF.

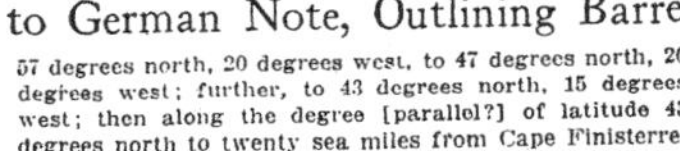

Text of the Annex to German Note, Outlining Barred Zones and Prescribing Conditions for American Vessels

WASHINGTON, Jan. 31.—Following is the text of the annex to the German note presented to the State Department by Count von Bernstorff:

MEMORANDUM.

"From Feb. 1, 1917, sea traffic will be stopped with every available weapon and without further notice in the following blockade zones [" barred zones," according to a version received via Sayville] around Great Britain, France, Italy and in the Eastern Mediterranean:

"In the north:

[The Sayville version says: "In the North Sea, the district around England and France, which is limited by a line twenty nautical miles."]

"The zone is confined by a line at a distance of twenty sea miles along the Dutch coast to Terschelling Fireship; the degree [meridian?] of longitude from Terschelling Fireship to Udsire; a line from there across the point 62 degrees north, 0 degrees longitude, to 62 degrees north, 5 degrees west; further to a point three sea miles south of the southern point of the Faroe Islands; from there across a point 62 degrees north, 10 degrees west, to 61 degrees north, 15 degrees west; then 57 degrees north, 20 degrees west, to 47 degrees north, 20 degrees west; further, to 43 degrees north, 15 degrees west; then along the degree [parallel?] of latitude 43 degrees north to twenty sea miles from Cape Finisterre, and at a distance of twenty sea miles along the north coast of Spain to the French boundary.

"In the South—The Mediterranean:

"For neutral ships, remains open the sea west of the line Pt. Des Espiquettes to 38 degrees 20 minutes north and 6 degrees east; also north and west of a zone sixty sea miles wide along the North African Coast, beginning at 2 degrees longitude west. For the connection of this sea-zone with Greece there is provided a zone of a width of twenty sea miles north and east of the following line: 38 degrees north and 6 degrees east to 38 degrees north and 10 degrees west, to 37 degrees north and 11 degrees 30 minutes east, to 34 degrees north and 22 degrees 30 minutes east.

"From there leads a zone twenty sea miles wide, west of 22 degrees 30 minutes eastern longitude, into Greek territorial waters.

"Neutral ships navigating these blockade zones do so at their own risk. Although care has been taken that neutral ships which are on their way toward ports of the blockade zones on Feb. 1, 1917, and have come in the vicinity of the latter, will be spared during a sufficiently long period, it is strongly advised to warn them with all available means in order to cause their return.

"Neutral ships which on Feb. 1 are in ports of the blockade zones can with the same safety leave them.

"The instructions given to the Commanders of German submarines provide for a sufficiently long period during which the safety of passengers on unarmed enemy passenger ships is guaranteed.

"Americans en route to the blockade zone on enemy freight steamers are not endangered, as the enemy shipping firms can prevent such ships in time from entering the zone.

"Sailing of regular American passenger steamers may continue undisturbed after Feb. 1, 1917, if

(A) The port of destination is Falmouth.

(B) Sailing to or coming from that port course is taken via the Scilly Islands and a point 50 degrees north, 20 degrees west.

[" Along this route," says the Sayville version, "no German mines will be laid."]

(C) The steamers are marked in the following way, which must not be allowed to other vessels in American ports: On ship's hull and superstructure three vertical stripes one meter wide, each to be painted alternately white and red. Each mast should show a large flag checkered white and red, and the stern the American national flag. Care should be taken that, during dark, national flag and painted marks are easily recognizable from a distance, and that the boats are well lighted throughout.

(D) One steamer a week sails in each direction with arrival at Falmouth on Sunday and departure from Falmouth on Wednesday.

(E) United States Government guarantees that no contraband (according to German contraband list) is carried by those steamers.

[" Two copies of maps on which the barred zones are outlined are added," says the version received via Sayville.]

THIS PORT CLOSED

Collector Malone Stops All Outgoing Ships at Narrows.

GERMAN SHIPS SEARCHED

No Evidence of Unusual Activity on Vessels at Hoboken.

GUARD SET ON THIS SIDE

Police Ordered Out at Midnight to Keep Watch Over Ships Off 130th Street.

ANXIOUS FOR SHIPS AT SEA

Shipping Men in This and Other Ports Fear for Them in Blockade.

Col. House Hurries Off to Washington

Colonel E. M. House left hurriedly for Washington on the Pennsylvania Railroad at 12:30 o'clock this morning. He entered the station through a private stairway and secluded himself in the car before the train was opened to the general traveling public.

The Port of New York was sealed tight last night by order of Dudley Field Malone, Collector of the Port. Vessels of every description, including tugboats, were turned back at Quarantine by the torpedo boat stationed there to maintain the neutrality of the United States.

The purpose of Mr. Malone's order remained a mystery upon which he declined to throw any light. He has full authority to act upon his own initiative in case of emergency, as he is held responsible for enforcing neutrality.

Even naval officers are under orders to take instructions from Mr. Malone in all matters affecting the neutrality of New York.

Rumors that the crews of the German ships interned at Hoboken would attempt to scuttle the vessels and destroy the machinery in the event of war, sprang up everywhere last evening as soon as the German note was made public. Collector Malone called up Chief of Police Patrick Hayes of Hoboken, who was attending the annual patrolmen's ball, and the Chief, with half a dozen plain-clothes men, left the dance and hurried down to the piers to reinforce the eleven men of the Neutrality Squad on guard there. Deputy Collector George F. Lamb was present.

A thorough search made by the neutrality guards under Roundsman Miles disclosed no evidence of any preparations to justify the rumors. The Hamburg-American and North German Lloyd liners have been tied up at the piers for two years and a half, during which time there has been no opportunity to dredge out the slips, so it was said that they were practically lying in the mud, and that scuttling them would be rather pointless.

As to the possibility of an attempt to escape from the harbor, it was said that none of the ships had enough coal to last for more than a single day's steaming, at the end of which period they must inevitably be captured, even if they could pass the destroyers on guard at the Narrows. The Vaterland has more coal than any of the others, but in her case it was said that most of the officers of the interned liners have been living on board of her and that the coal was needed to get up steam for heating and lighting.

Watch Put on German Ships Here.

At midnight Police Inspector Thomas Ryan of the Sixth Inspection District, including the district between 110th Street and Spuyten Duyvil and West of Fifth Avenue, received orders to keep in reserve all men who were about to go off duty at that hour. Twenty

Continued on Page 2.

BRITAIN TO MEET GERMAN MENACE

Fleet of 4,000 Vessels Ready to Chase U-Boats and Protect Merchant Ships.

PORTS WILL BE KEPT OPEN

Liverpool and Bordeaux to be Especially Protected — Fore and Aft Guns for All Vessels.

Great Britain and her allies are prepared to meet Germany's moves in her submarine campaign, it was authoritatively asserted in shipping circles last night. The Entente Powers were convinced weeks ago that ruthless warfare with undersea boats would be decreed sooner or later and have known for ten days that the decision had been reached, it was said.

The ports of Liverpool and Bordeaux will be kept open at all hazards, British steamship representatives asserted, even if it becomes necessary to convoy every merchant ship which crosses the Atlantic. The first step to be taken by the British Admiralty, which virtually controls the merchant fleets of the Allies, will be to arm every ship with guns fore and aft for defensive purposes, it was predicted.

To meet the emergency the British Government has been assembling for months, it was said, a large fleet of small, fast cruisers to be used as "submarine chasers." This type of war craft has proved very effective against undersea boats, well informed shipping men declared. Agents of British lines declared the Admiralty now has a fleet of 4,000 vessels available to keep the sea lanes clear of raiders and submarines and to act as convoys.

There are said to be hundreds of patrol boats and mine sweepers, independent of torpedo boat destroyers, which are on the lookout to convoy liners and freighters when they arrive in the danger zone bound for French or British

Continued on Page 3.

"Barred Zones" and "Safety Lanes" Outlined in Germany's Note.

Surrounding the British Isles and bordering the coasts of France, Belgium, and Holland is a "barred zone" (indicated by black areas on the map) twenty nautical miles wide. The boundaries of a secondary "barred zone," shutting off the British Isles and running as far south as Cape Finisterre, on the northwestern coast of Spain, are indicated by a heavy black line. This zone is pierced by the route to Falmouth, as laid down for one American ship a week in the annex to the German note.

In the Mediterranean the safety zone leading to Greek territorial waters is indicated by the white areas shown in the map of that sea. The territorial waters of France, Italy, and the British possessions in the Mediterranean are apparently included in the barred zones.

CHANCELLOR TELLS GERMAN DECISION

He Outlines to Reichstag Committee Measures for Defense by Land and Sea.

AGREED ON AT CONFERENCE

Results of Headquarters Discussion Quickly Told to German Leaders.

BERLIN, Jan. 31, (via London.)—The Imperial Chancellor, Dr. von Bethmann Hollweg, is to make a statement on foreign affairs and the military situation this afternoon to the Ways and Means Committee of the Reichstag. According to the newspapers, the Chancellor will make important declarations regarding "the decisions of the Government," and will explain the grounds upon which these decisions are based.

BERLIN, Jan. 31, (by Wireless to Sayville.)—In its announcement today reporting the result of the recent conference at German Great Headquarters, the Overseas News Agency says:

"Chancellor von Bethmann Hollweg and Foreign Secretary Zimmermann have returned from Great Headquarters, where the planned ofensive of the Entente was discussed at the meetings, and a unanimous agreement regarding all measures of defense was formulated. The Central Powers calmly await coming events, conscious of their own power."

LONDON, Jan. 31.—Chancellor von Bethmann Hollweg and Foreign Secretary Zimmermann have returned to Berlin from headquarters at the front, where a complete agreement on measures to be taken by Germany on land and water was reached, according to a Berlin telegram transmitted by Reuter's Amsterdam correspondent.

Kaiser Predicts "Hard Times."

AMSTERDAM, Jan. 31, (via London.)—The Reichsanzeiger publishes an Imperial rescript conveying the German Emperor's thanks for birthday congratulations extended to him. It says:

"From these numerous manifestations there ring out with the overwhelming force of unanimity indignation at the contemptuous rejection of our peace

Continued on Page 2.

A SHIP A WEEK FOR US

To and From Falmouth on a Prescribed Route.

BECOMES EFFECTIVE TODAY

Bernstorff Delivers a Note Which Ends Germany's Pledges to Us.

BECAUSE OF PEACE FAILURE

The Kaiser Now Proposes to Employ All Means of Sea Warfare at His Command.

CAPITAL TAKES GRAVE VIEW

President Studies Note Alone—Break Predicted in Some Quarters.

President Amazed by News; Spends Evening Studying Note

WASHINGTON, Jan. 31.—When The Associated Press dispatches telling of the German note began arriving at the White House today President Wilson was in his office talking with a friend. Secretary Tumulty hurried to him with the news. The President could not believe it until he was assured that the information was contained in a formal note already before the State Department.

The President went to bed at 11 o'clock after spending the evening alone in his study with a copy of the German note. This apparently disposed of suggestions that some action might be taken before morning.

The President saw no callers, but is understood to have used the telephone freely.

As far as could be learned, no plans have been laid for him to go before Congress, as he did to announce the sending of the Sussex note threatening to break off diplomatic relations.

Special to The New York Times.

WASHINGTON, Jan. 31.—The United States Government tonight faces its greatest international crisis since the Lusitania was sunk. With full knowledge that her action almost certainly means a break with America, Germany announced to this Government today that she intended to abandon the pledges she gave last year to observe the rules of international law in the conduct of her submarine warfare against merchant shipping. How a break can be avoided, observers here are unable to see. The gravity of the situation cannot be exaggerated.

Beginning at midnight tonight the German U-boats will sink without warning any merchant vessel, neutral as well as enemy, entering a prescribed zone that extends from north of the British Isles around into the Mediterranean to include even the waters of Greece.

That is the sum and substance of Germany's communication to this Government today, delivered to Secretary Lansing in Washington by Count von Bernstorff, the Kaiser's Ambassador, and to Ambassador Gerard, in Berlin, by the Imperial Foreign Office.

Recalls Final Warning.

The United States Government is on record as determined to break diplomatic relations with Germany if pledges concerning submarine warfare are not observed in letter and in spirit. Today's notification of the Imperial Government brings the United States to the point where it must decide whether it intends to make good the following warning to Germany, contained in a note of April 18, 1916:

"Unless the Imperial Government should now immediately declare and effect an abandonment of its present methods of submarine warfare against passenger and freight-carrying vessels the Government of the United States can have no choice but to sever diplomatic relations with the German Empire altogether. This action the Government of the United States contem-

"All the News That's Fit to Print."

The New York Times.

THE WEATHER
Clearing today; tomorrow probably fair; southwest gales.
For full weather report see Page 21.

VOL. LXVI...NO. 21,622. NEW YORK, FRIDAY, APRIL 6, 1917.—TWENTY-TWO PAGES. ONE CENT In New York City. | TWO CENTS New England and Middle States. | THREE CENTS Elsewhere.

HOUSE, AT 3:12 A.M., VOTES FOR WAR, 373 TO 50; $3,000,000,000 ASKED FOR ARMY OF 1,000,000; NATION'S GIGANTIC RESOURCES MOBILIZED

HUGE BUDGET FOR WAR

$3,401,000,000 Needed for the Army and Navy at Once.

ESTIMATES GO TO CAPITOL

Taxation and a $3,500,000,000 Bond Issue Considered as a Means of Getting Funds.

MAY RAISE INCOME LEVIES

Fixed Price of 3½ for Bonds Considered—Daniels Explains the Navy's Plans.

Special to The New York Times.

WASHINGTON, April 5.—Three billion four hundred and one million dollars is needed immediately to place the United States on a proper war footing and to meet the first expenses of actual operations in the war with the German Government. This fact was disclosed when William G. McAdoo, as Secretary of the Treasury, today sent to the Capitol the first of the estimates from the various executive departments of the Government based on "military necessity." These estimates call for the appropriation of $3,401,865,684.87, of which the sum of $3,400,932,484.87 is for the army and navy alone, while the rest is for use by other departments as collateral war expenditures.

This total of $3,400,932,484 will enable the Government to raise, organize, equip and officer an army of 1,000,000 men during the next year, but will not pay for the employment of that force beyond June 30, 1918; it will enable the navy to raise its enlisted strength of 150,000 men and the Marine Corps to increase its enlisted personnel to 30,000 men, in addition to certain active operations in the war.

The total of $3,400,932,484 is also in addition to the sum of $517,273,802 already provided for the navy's use during the next fiscal year by the Naval act of March 4, 1917, and the sum of $240,000,000 carried by the Army Appropriation bill which passed the House yesterday under a suspension of the rules.

Hastening War Measures.

Great strides toward getting the fighting forces of the United States ready for the war were taken by the various branches of the Government today. These included:

First—Secretary of War Baker conferred at the Capitol with Chairman Chamberlain of the Senate Military Committee regarding the wishes of the President for authority to raise not less than 1,000,000 men, including the expansion of the regulars and guard forces during the coming year, and the raising of a force of approximately an additional 1,000,000 men next year.

Second—The Administration bill providing for the creation of this new army was sent to the Capitol with its provisions for raising two separate forces of 500,000 men each, to be composed of men between the ages of 18 and 25, to be obtained by a selective draft system.

Third — Chairman Fitzgerald and members of the House Appropriations Committee began consideration of the stupendous war budget within ten minutes after it had been received by the House of Representatives.

Fourth—Senator Simmons of North Carolina, Chairman of the Senate Finance Committee, conferred with House leaders regarding plans to meet the financial demands for preparedness by a bond issue of $3,500,000,000, bearing interest at not exceeding 3½ per cent.

Fifth—Members of the House Naval and Military Affairs Committees conferred on proposals that a lump sum of $3,500,000,000 be placed in the hands of the President to spend on the army and navy as he deems necessary, thereby abandoning the ordinary policy of making specific appropriations in separate bills and making the details public.

Although the needs of the army and navy were not given in detail, the estimates submitted today by Secretary McAdoo, acting for the other departments of the Government, show that they cover all phases of the needs of the Government from doubling the number of men in the navy and marine corps and to quadrupling the number of men in the present regular army and National Guard force to providing extra watchmen for the State, War, and Navy Building.

McAdoo's Detailed Estimates.

These are the important recommendations made by Secretary McAdoo in his estimates to prepare the United States for entry into the war with the German Government:

First—To make an army of 1,000,000 men ready for war both in personnel and material within a year—$2,932,537,933.

Second — To increase the enlisted strength of the navy from its present authorized emergency strength of 87,000 men to full war strength of 150,000 men, and to increase the Marine Corps from present authorized emergency strength of 17,500 men to full war strength of 30,000 men—$175,855,761.87.

Third. Extraordinary expenditures on materials for the naval establishment, including guns, ships, and

Continued on Page [illegible]

American Men in Belgium May Be Interned in Germany

LONDON, April 5.—A dispatch to the Exchange Telegraph from The Hague says:

"A frontier correspondent asserts that he understands General von Bissing, the German Governor General in Belgium, intends to order the internment of all Americans between the ages of 17 and 45 living in Belgium.

"The correspondent adds that they will be sent to Western Germany, probably to Aix-la-Chapelle."

FIVE GERMAN SHIPS AT BOSTON SEIZED

Crews Dispossessed Early This Morning On Port Collector's Order.

600 GUARD. LINERS HERE

Malone's Neutrality Squad On Watch and He Waits Up All Night.

BOSTON, Friday, April 6. — Five German steamships, which have been in refuge at this port, were ordered seized, and their crews dispossessed, by Collector of the Port Edmund Billings early this morning. The vessels taken over are the Amerika and Cincinnati, passenger ships, and the Wittekind, Köln, and Ockenfels, freight steamers.

Malone Waits Up All Night.

Anticipating the passage by Congress of a declaration of war by this country against Germany, Dudley Field Malone, Collector of the Port of New York, prepared to remain in his office all night. He has upward of 600 special guards about the German ships now in this port, the bulk of them in Hoboken, where are the greatest of the German vessels, and on which are 1,200 men and 350 officers. At midnight Mr. Malone said, "I am waiting," and authorized the statement that the heavy guards had been sent out.

It was evident that the guards were vigilant to prevent possible destruction of the vessels.

German officers and sailors aboard the interned liners in Hoboken, including the great Vaterland, were calm and ready for whatever might be demanded of them. Some officers thought the ships would be seized, others that, as German property, they would be held inviolate by this Government. Over the fact that the machinery of all of the ships has been damaged so that none now are navigable, there was unconcealed satisfaction.

Government tugs aided yesterday in moving the Maia and the German sailing vessel Indra, which have been at anchor near Staten Island since the beginning of the war, across the bay to an anchorage near the City Dock at Brooklyn. The Portonia, which was moved from an anchorage in the bay to Brady's Dock, Staten Island, on Wednesday, was also moved yesterday across the bay to an anchorage near the Brooklyn shore. The idea of the movement was to concentrate separated ships in the event of action by the Government.

The Teuton ships at this port are:

German.

Name and Dock.	Tonnage.
President Grant, Hoboken	18,072
President Lincoln, Hoboken	18,100
Vaterland, Hoboken	54,284
Nassovia, Hoboken	3,902
Armenia, Hoboken	8,544
Bohemia, Hoboken	8,414
Pisa, Hoboken	4,967
Pennsylvania, Hoboken	13,333
Harburg, Hoboken	4,472
Magdeburg, Hoboken	4,497
Adamsturm, Hoboken	5,000
Matador, (sailing,) Hoboken	1,468
George Washington, Hoboken	25,570
Kaiser Wilhelm II., Hoboken	19,360
Friedrich der Grosse, Hoboken	10,771
Prinzess Irene, Hoboken	10,893
Grosser Kurfurst, Hoboken	13,102
Barbarossa, Hoboken	10,984
Hamburg, 135th Street	10,531
Koenig Wilhelm II., 135th Street	9,410
Allemania, 135th Street	4,680
Prinz Eitel Friedrich, 135th Street	4,650
Prinz Joachim, 135th Street	4,760
Portonia, Stapleton	2,778
Maia, Stapleton	2,555
Clara Mennig, Stapleton	1,085
Indra, (sailing,) Stapleton	1,748

Austrian.

Name and Dock.	Tonnage.
Dora, Brooklyn	7,037
Ida, Brooklyn	4,730
Martha Washington, Stapleton	8,312
Himalaia, Newark Bay	4,948

Malone Confers at Washington.

WASHINGTON, April 5. — Collector Dudley Field Malone, who has general supervision over the war-bound German merchant ships in New York harbor, conferred with Secretary McAdoo today, and it was understood that the question of taking possession of the vessels was under consideration. Secretary Wilson, who would have jurisdiction over the crews of the ships under the immigration law, conferred with Secretary McAdoo last night.

A final decision as to whether the ships shall be taken over had not been reached today, and depends upon the final interpretation by the Government upon the Prussian-American Treaty of 1828, which, the American Government contends, has already been violated in several respects by Germany. The formal abrogation of the treaty has been considered.

In case the ships are taken, it is believed that they will first be turned over to the Shipping Board for repairs to their machinery, which was damaged when diplomatic relations were broken off.

DETAILS OF THE ARMY BILL

Universal Service Embodied in Measure Presented to Congress.

SELECTIVE DRAFT AT ONCE

Regulars and Militia to be Put On a War Footing and 500,000 Others Called.

MEN 19 TO 25 MUST ENROLL

President Authorized to Enlist 500,000 More When Needed —Want Military Graduates.

Special to The New York Times.

WASHINGTON, April 5.—A bill embracing the War Department's recommendations for temporarily increasing the military establishment of the United States for use in the existing emergency was submitted to Senator Chamberlain, Chairman of the Senate Committee on Military Affairs, and to Chairman Dent of the House Military Committee today by Secretary Baker.

The bill provides for the raising of the regular army to full war strength, the drafting of the National Guard into the Federal service and raising it to war strength, and the enlistment of 1,000,000 additional men by selective drafting. Under the terms of the bill it is estimated that authority is granted to the President to raise and maintain an army of 1,727,846 men, including regulars, National Guardsmen, and those to be drafted under the principle of universal military service. This force would be made up about as follows:

Regular army, including five increments of increase, provided for by the National Defense act of June 3, 1916, when raised to full war strength—287,846 men.

National Guard, when raised to full war strength—440,000 men.

Additional force of men to be chosen by selective drafting—500,000.

Second additional force of men to be chosen by selective drafting—500,000.

Total—1,726,846.

Million Men This Year.

It is not the present intention of the Administration to raise and equip a force of more than 1,000,000 during the next twelve months. This is about all that could be brought together and properly trained with our present military facilities during the first year. If the bill is adopted the Government would begin raising the regular army to full war strength, would draft the National Guard ino Federal service and begin raising its units to maximum war strength, and then raise the balance by selective drafting.

The enlisted men to bring the regular army and the National Guard up to war strength are to be raised by voluntary enlistment, but if the President decides that they cannot beso raised he may resor to selective draft. All other forces provided for by the bill which the War Department sent to the Capitol today are to be "raised and maintained by selective draft exclusively."

The bill submitted today is intended to serve only the needs of the Government during the present emergency and is not a permanent plan for the increase of the army. In voicing his indorsement of the principle of universal military service the President has adopted that method of obtaining soldiers only for the purposes of the present war. What is to happen after the war is over is considered another matter from the immediate and practical needs of the Government at the present time.

The selective draft, under the terms of the bill, will take in men between the ages of 19 and 25, which means that all males between these ages will have to present themselves for registration under penalty of imprisonment for failure to do so. The drafting is to be determined in proportion to the population of the various States, or at the ratio of about 1,100 for each Congressional district. Credit is to be given to each State and Congressional district for its quota of men furnished to the regular army or National Guard forces.

The act is not to be construed to compel the service of those whose creeds forbid participation in war.

The President is also authorized by the bill to exclude or discharge from the draft the following: Custom House clerks, persons in the United States mail service, workmen in Government armories, arsenals, and navy yards; mariners actually employed in American sea service, pilots, persons engaged in munition and military industries, those with dependents, and those physically or morally unfit.

To Train an Army of Officers.

In drafting its program the General Staff recognized the fact that the United States must start at the beginning and train first an army of 100,000 officers and noncommissioned officers to undertake the training of the thousands of youths who will enter

Continued on Page 3.

German Warships Seize Ship That Helped Save U-Boat

COPENHAGEN, April 5, (via London.)—The Tidens Tegen's Trondhjem correspondent sends a story of the capture by the Germans and taking into port of the Norwegian steamer Nanna, after the Nanna had endeavored to tow a helpless submarine in the North Sea to a German port. The steamer was taken to Hamburg by German torpedo boats and is being held there.

According to the story, the Nanna agreed to tow the helpless submarine, but the towline broke off the west coast of Jutland. The submarine thereupon signaled for assistance and eight German torpedo boats appeared. The crew of the Nanna was ordered below and the torpedo boats took the steamer, together with the submarine, to Cuxhaven.

The Germans, so the story goes, refused the request of the Norwegians to be piloted back through the minefield. Instead the Nanna was taken to Hamburg, where she is still detained, despite persistent efforts by the Norwegian authorities to obtain her release.

AMERICAN SHIP SUNK; CREW SAVED

Unarmed Missourian, Returning in Ballast, Is Destroyed in the Mediterranean.

REPORT 5 OTHER SHIPS LOST

Two of Them Belgian Relief Vessels with Valuable Cargoes —Americans on Board Others.

WASHINGTON, April 5.—The sinking without warning of the unarmed American steamor Missourian, which left Genoa April 4, with thirty-two Americans among her crew of fifty-three, was reported to the State Department today by Consul Wilbur at Genoa. The crew was saved. The Consul's dispatch, which was undated, follows:

"Unarmed American steamer Missourian, 4,981 net tonnage, Master William Lyons, built at Sparrows Point, owner American Hawaiian Steamship Company, fifty three crew all told, including master and officers, thirty-two American citizens, balance various nationalities, according to records this office sailing from Genoa, April 4, in ballast, bound for the United States, sunk without warning, according telegram just received from master, as follows: 'Dated Porto Mauridio, 5th. Sunk without warning, crew saved, leave for Genoa, 7 o'clock P. M., April 5. (Signed) Lyons.' As soon as master and crew arrive will prepare and transmit full report."

The American steamship Missourian, owned by the American-Hawaiian Steamship Company and chartered by the France and Canada Steamship Company, left this port on March 5 for Genoa. The ship was unarmed and carried a general cargo. The Missourian was a vessel of 7,914 tons gross, and was built at Sparrows Point, Md., in 1904. She was first named the Missouri. For many years she was engaged in the New York-Panama trade, and was transferred to the Atlantic trade after the beginning of the European war. She was for a time in the service of the United States Government, having been taken over as a transport shortly after General Funston was sent to Vera Cruz in 1914.

AMERICANS ON 2 SHIPS SUNK.

Saved from British and Norwegian Freighters Destroyed by U-Boats.

WASHINGTON, April 5.—Destruction of two more vessels, one British and one Norwegian, with Americans on board, was reported to the State Department today by Consul Lathrop at Cardiff. The Norwegian steamer Sandvikgoole was sunk by a submarine believed to have been German, while the British steamer Lincolnshire was sunk without any submarine being seen. Crews of both vessels were in small boats for two hours, in dangerous positions, before being rescued. Consul Lathrop's reports follow.

"Frank Kragle, American fireman on the Norwegian unarmed steamer Sandvikgoole, England to Gothenburg, cargo iron and iron ore, reports vessel sunk by submarine, believed German, about noon, March 27, five miles off Aberdeen. Warned, sank fifteen minutes after crew left. Weather clear and cold, sea rough, wind high; no vessel in sight; no passengers, crew rescued after two hours by British mine sweeper; landed Aberdeen; no casualties.

"Felix Morris, colored American Seaman on British unarmed steamer Lincolnshire, New York to France, reports vessel torpedoed without warning afternoon March 29, fourteen miles off Irish coast. Vessel sank six minutes after crew left. Weather clear, very cold; sea moderate; wind fresh; no vessel in sight; no passengers, submarine unseen;

Continued on Page 2.

32,000 PLANTS OFFERED

No Nation Ever Had Such Enormous Resources for Waging War.

TWO YEARS OF PREPARATION

Summary of What Has Been Achieved in Naval, Military, and Industrial Fields.

OUR NAVY READY FOR ACTION

Army Waits on Congress—Extraordinary Work by the Council of Defense.

WASHINGTON, April 5.—Actual and potential resources which, all told, probably never have been equaled by those of any other nation in the history of the world, are brought into the great war under the American flag.

Into the balance against Germany are thrown a navy in strength and efficiency among the foremost afloat, an army comparatively small but highly efficient, backed by a citizenry of upward of 20,000,000 capable of military duty, industrial resources incomparably the greatest in the world, already mobilized for public service, and the moral force of more than 100,000,000 Americans awakened to their country's peril and united behind their President with a patriotic fervor reincarnating the spirit of '76.

Although much remains to be done, officials believe the nation's destinies are secure now, no matter how stubborn or prolonged the pressure of German militarism or how wide the scope of German intrigue. The slowly maturing preparedness sentiment has borne fruit in military, naval, and industrial measures which already have put the United States on a defense basis not even hoped for two years ago. What more it will do, the President believes, can be measured only by what the Administration finds will be necessary.

The navy, always the first line of defense, has cleared its decks of antiquated incumbrances, has added new units modernized to meet the German tactics, and through the patriotic cooperation of ship and material makers is hurrying to completion other mighty fighting craft that will be the last word in power and efficiency. Authorized but ten days ago to recruit to the full war strength of 87,000 men, the navy already has almost attained the total. To provide additional officers a class of midshipmen has been graduated three months ahead of its time. A newly organized coast patrol of submarine chasers is on duty, and hundreds of small craft to augment it are under construction.

Army Waits on Congress.

Army preparations are less complete because of the uncertainty over what Congress will authorize for that branch of the service. The regulars, numbering nearly 120,000 and trained and equipped in a way which their officers believe matches, unit for unit, the boasted efficiency of Germany's best, are ready to respond overnight to whatever call may come. The National Guard, 150,000 strong and hardened by months of service at the border, already has many units in active service for police duty throughout the country and can be fully mobilized on short notice. Without additional authorization by Congress the regulars and guardsmen could be recruited to a combined strength of 700,000, and detailed plans for whatever larger army may be authorized have been prepared, and great quantities of equipment for it purchased.

Industrial preparations, thanks to lessons of the war and the patriotic attitude of industry, have produced a great, compact scheme of national resources with almost unlimited possibilities. The Council of National Defense, in daily conferences with the nation's leading financial, commercial, scientific, and labor chiefs, not only has worked out a definite and detailed industrial mobolization plan, but has secured the indorsement and pledges of the men who can put it into effect at a moment's notice, bringing to the aid of the military arms of the service the full resources of the richest nation, organized with characteristic Yankee skill and business thoroughness.

For military reasons only a small part of the details of these preparations has been permitted to reach the public. It is known, however, that for many months the Government has considered war more than a possibility, and has strained every resource to make ready. In the tense waiting period since relations were broken, the President, while hoping fervently that hostilities could be avoided, has kept the whole machinery of the Government in motion day and night to prepare against eventualities. To any close observer at the capital it now is apparent that Germany again has misjudged if she thought to find the United States hopelessly impotent and unprepared.

Shipyards in Nation's Service.

The Navy Department, in order to complete in record time the enormous

Continued on Page 4.

List of Fifty Members of House of Representatives Who Voted Against the Adoption of War Resolution

WASHINGTON, Friday, April 6.—The fifty Representatives who voted against the war resolution were:

ALMON,	FULLER, (Ill.)	WOODS, (Iowa.)
BACON,	HAUGEN,	IGOE,
BRITTEN,	HAYES,	JOHNSON, (S. D.)
BROWNE,	HENSLEY,	KEATING,
BURNETT,	HILLIARD,	KING,
CARY,	HULL, (Iowa,)	KINKAID,
CHURCH,	MISS RANKIN,	KITCHIN,
CONNOLLY, (Kan.)	REAVIS,	KNUTSON,
COOPER, (Wis.)	ROBERTS,	LA FOLLETTE,
DAVIDSON,	RODENBURG,	LITTLE,
DAVIS,	SHACKLEFORD,	LONDON,
DECKER,	SHERWOOD,	LUNDSEN,
DILL,	SLOAN,	McLEMORE,
DILLON,	STAFFORD,	MASON,
DOMINICK,	VAN DYKE,	NELSON,
ESCH,	VOIGT,	RANDALL,
FREAR,	WHEELER,	

GERMANY GARBLES WILSON'S ADDRESS

Nothing About Mexican Intrigue or Spies Allowed to Reach the Public.

PRESS FURIOUS AT WILSON

His Distinction Between German Government and People Called False.

COPENHAGEN, April 5, (via London.)—The German public up to the present time has had no opportunity to hear the full story of the reasons leading up to the entry of the United States into the war, as only condensed and expurgated versions of President Wilson's message appeared in German newspapers yesterday under headings indicating that this was practically the complete text. This in part is apparently due to the fact that the first version of the speech telegraphed from England to neutral countries on the Continent on Tuesday were sharply condensed, whole sections having been eliminated, particularly from the latter part of the message.

President Wilson's reference to the attempt to embroil Mexico against the United States is deemed improper reading for Germans, nor are they allowed to hear President Wilson's reasons for the conviction that the autocratic German Government has not only no friendship for America, but is ready at any opportunity to plot against its security.

The reference to dynastic wars, too, is twisted into a shape which has aroused indignant comment from every German newspaper.

The full text of the message was received in Copenhagen only today. It reads almost like another document as compared with the earlier version. The first part of the two versions is substantially the same, except for condensations and omission of non-essential matter. The second part has been cut wholesale. The President's reasoning on the inadvisability of armed neutrality is given completely; no reference is made to the proposed financing of the Allies, and the paragraphs relating to Russia are dismissed in two sentences. Only the briefest summary is made in the German papers of the concluding paragraphs of the message.

But a comparison of this tabloid version as received in Denmark with that published in Berlin shows that the German censors' pencils had been vigorously employed to strike out references to the conduct of German agents, which constitutes one of the main items of President Wilson's indictment of the autocratic German Government.

Says Democracy Has Failed.

Special Cable to THE NEW YORK TIMES.

BERLIN, April 5, (via London.)—Regarding President Wilson's declaration that American hostility was not directed against the German people, but against the German Government, the Lokal-Anzeiger says it is the acme of hypocrisy to say that an autocratic Government provoked the war against the will of the German people.

"It is impossible," says the Lokal-Anzeiger, "that the ruler of a nation who has at his disposal the reports of his Ambassador and numerous other sources of information regarding the events of the early part of August, 1914, in Berlin, should really believe that this war was not begun with the assent of the German people. If he ever read the report of the Reichstag session of Aug. 4 he must know that his contention is untrue. If he upholds it, despite his better knowledge, he only does it to prove by an untruth his untenable theory of the only true and gratifying democracy, and his whole cardboard house of artificial evidence miserably collapses by which he seeks to prove to Congress the justification and honesty of his policy and the noble spirit of his attitude.

"The history of the war has proved the actual contrary to Wilson's contention. Those nations whose fate is determined by parliamentary representation have become tools without a will in the hands of small groups of vainglorious men and have been degraded to mere pawns on the chessboard of political intrigue. It is also true that the foreign policy of parliamentary government States remains the secret of a few men, just as it does in monarchical States. We cannot presume that this well-known fact, the truth of which is acknowledged by the radical press of all countries, should have remained

Continued on Page 3.

FRANCE AROUSED BY OUR DECISION

Members of Both Chambers Cheer for America—Many Cities Adopt Resolutions.

POINCARE CABLES WILSON

Deputies Suggest Offering Us the Port of Brest as a Naval Base.

PARIS, April 5.—This was America's day in France. Extraordinary scenes of enthusiasm over the United States's entry into the war were witnessed in both houses of Parliament, while municipal councils met in cities throughout the Republic and adopted resolutions acclaiming the United States.

In Paris the American flag was seen everywhere. The appearance of the Stars and Stripes in different parts of the city multiplied rapidly as the day advanced, and soon the available supply was exhausted. Such was the demand for newspapers that the evening editions giving the vote of the United States Senate on the war resolution were quickly exhausted. The crowded subway cars were more animated than at any time since the war began, while knots of soldiers and civilians in front of all cafes and at all street corners discussed the great event with manifest satisfaction.

The sentiment in Paris and throughout the country is epitomized by President Poincaré in the following cablegram he sent today to President Wilson:

At the moment when, under the generous inspiration of yourself, the great American Republic, faithful to its ideals and its traditions, is coming forward to defend with the force of arms the cause of justice and of liberty, the people of France are filled with the deepest feelings of brotherly appreciation.

Permit me again to convey to you, Mr. President, in this solemn and grave hour, an assurance of the same sentiments of which I recently gave you evidence, sentiments which, under the present circumstances, have grown in depth and warmth.

I am confident that I voice the thought of all France in expressing to you and to the American nation the joy and the pride which we feel today as our hearts once again beat in unison with yours.

This war would not have reached its final import had not the United States been led by the enemy himself to take part in it. To every impartial spirit it will be apparent, in the future more than ever in the past, that German imperialism, which desired, prepared, and declared this war, had conceived the mad dream of establishing its hegemony throughout the world. It has succeeded only in bringing about a revolt of the conscience of humanity.

In never-to-be-forgotten language you have made yourself, before the universe, the eloquent interpreter of outraged laws and a menaced civilization.

Honor to you, Mr. President, and to your noble country. I beg you to believe in my devoted friendship.

RAYMOND POINCARE.

Brest to Be American Port.

The first war measure to be taken in connection with the expected entrance of the United States into the war, which was introduced in the Chamber today, provides for an agreement with the United States, if necessary, for the use of the Port of Brest by American naval forces. The measure provides generally for the utilization of the port to the best interests of the national defense.

Not since the historic session of Aug. 4, 1914, has there been a parallel to the scenes in Parliament. Alexandre Ribot, the venerable Premier, arose immediately after the Chamber came to order and began an address in solemn and impressive tones to the silent assemblage which filled every part of the House. The Deputies listened with unbroken attention until the first mention of the United States. Then they broke out in applause. At first it was a decorous clapping of hands, and then the whole House spontaneously arose, cheering for the United States and President Wilson.

The American Ambassador, William G. Sharp, was in the diplomatic gallery. The Deputies turned toward him and the demonstration continued. The Am-

Continued on Page 6.

DEBATE LASTED 16½ HOURS

One Hundred Speeches Were Made—Miss Rankin, Sobbing, Votes No.

ALL AMENDMENTS BEATEN

Resolution Will Take Effect This Afternoon with the President's Signature.

KITCHIN WITH PACIFISTS

Accession of the Floor Leader Added Others to the Anti-War Faction.

Special to The New York Times.

WASHINGTON, Friday, April 6.—At 3:12 o'clock this morning the House of Representatives by the overwhelming vote of 373 to 50 adopted the resolution that meant war between the Government and the people of the United States and the Imperial German Government.

War will formally begin this afternoon when President Wilson will approve the resolution which was passed by the Senate Wednesday night and was approved by the House this morning without the crossing of a "t" or the dotting of an "i."

The House presented an impressive spectacle as the roll call proceeded on the adoption of the war resolution. Nearly every member was in his seat.

The galleries were crowded for the most part by men and women who had sat there all the evening, some of them since 10 o'clock yesterday morning when the House met. Some of the men and women were in evening dress. Men and women who were in the diplomatic box had come directly from dinner parties.

There were crowds also in the corridors outside the galleries, seeking a chance for a peep at the events inside.

Usually when the roll of the House is called there is much confusion, and it is often difficult to hear the responses of the Representatives as their names are droned by the reading clerk.

But there was a marked difference this morning. The House, which had been full of levity at times during the long debate, felt the solemnity of the moment. No sound disturbed the proceedings. Every member's answer came distinctly and was heard by the throng that listened almost breathlessly to the "Ayes" and "Noes" that followed the calling of the roll.

Miss Rankin Votes "No."

Miss Jeanette Rankin, the woman Representative from Montana, had been absent from the House most of the evening, but took her accustomed place while the roll call was in progress. When her name was called she sat silent. "Miss Rankin," repeated the clerk. Still no answer. The clerk went on with his droning, and floor and galleries buzzed.

On the second roll call Miss Rankin's name was again called. She sat silent as before. The eyes of the galleries were turned on her. For a moment there was breathless silence. Then Miss Rankin rose. In a voice that broke a bit but could be heard all over the still chamber she said:

"I want to stand by my country, but I cannot vote for war. I vote no." The "No" was scarcely audible.

And the maiden speech of the first woman Congressman ended in a sob. She was deeply moved and big tears were in her eyes.

It was a sympathetic House, however, and although most of the persons there were plainly in favor of the war resolution, a wave of applause swept through floor and gallery.

When the roll call had been completed and a slip containing the count handed to Speaker Clark the latter's gavel came down with a bang. The House became quiet instantly.

"On this motion," said the Speaker "the Ayes are 373 and the Noes are 50."

The cheers that followed drowned the Speaker's announcement that the resolution had been adopted. Then the floors and galleries cleared, Representatives and spectators knowing that war had again come to the United States.

The Senate adjourned Wednesday night, to meet again at noon today. As the resolution must be returned to the Senate, while that body is in session President Wilson will not receive the historical document for signature until this afternoon. From the moment of his approval war will be on.

The Early Morning Scenes.

At 1:20 o'clock this morning, when Representative Kelly of Pennsylvania began to express his views, the tally list showed that he was the eightieth member to address the House on the war resolution.

At that hour the galleries were crowded, women forming a majority of the spectators. All through the evening

"All the News That's Fit to Print."

The New York Times.

THE WEATHER
Fair today and tomorrow; moderate northwest to north winds.
For full weather report see Page 21.

VOL. LXVII...NO. 21,839. ... NEW YORK, FRIDAY, NOVEMBER 9, 1917.—TWENTY-TWO PAGES. ONE CENT In Greater New York. | TWO CENTS Within Commuting Distance. | THREE CENTS Elsewhere.

REVOLUTIONISTS SEIZE PETROGRAD; KERENSKY FLEES; PLEDGE IS GIVEN TO SEEK "AN IMMEDIATE PEACE"; ITALIANS AGAIN DRIVEN BACK; LOSE 17,000 MORE ME

WOODS MUST GO AS POLICE HEAD, HYLAN DECIDES

Mayor-Elect Will Ask Him to Retire if He Fails to Resign.

SUCCESSOR NOT YET FOUND

Murphy Will Refrain from Interference, Congressman Smith Declares.

HYLAN SHOCKS JOB HUNTERS

Announces Dela in Considering Appointments—Craig Against Pay-as-You-Go Plan.

Mayor-elect John F. Hylan, it was said yesterday, has no intention of retaining Arthur Woods at the head of the Police Department. Friends of the Mayor-elect said that he expected to find a man after his own liking, who measured up to the job, to succeed the Police Commissioner before Jan. 1, when the Mayor-elect assumes office. Unless Judge Hylan had received the resignation of Commissioner Woods by the time he was ready to appoint his successor, the Police Commissioner, it was said, would be asked to retire.

At the headquarters of Judge Hylan persons who enjoy the confidence of the Mayor-elect said last night that he regarded the administration of the Police Department under Commissioner Woods as having been one of the vital issues in the campaign, even though less attention was paid to it by Judge Hylan in his speeches than to some other branches of the Mitchel Administration. The wire-tapping episode, which aroused such a storm of protest in certain quarters at the time of the charities investigation, and in which the Police Department under Commissioner Woods was directly concerned, was condemned both by Tammany Hall and its organized allies, the Democratic Fusion Committee and the Business Men's Association, in their platforms. Judge Hylan, it was said, felt that he was bound by the terms of the platform on which he was elected.

Expect Woods to Resign.

It is the belief of Judge Hylan's friends that Commissioner Woods will follow the usual practice and submit his resignation when the change of administration occurs, even though a provision in the New York City Charter provides for a five-year term, which in the case of the present incumbent does not expire until April, 1919. But even should this belief not prove justified, the Charter provisions relating to the Police Commissionership are regarded by Judge Hylan's friends as sufficiently plastic to provide the Mayor-elect with the means of creating a vacancy at the head of the Police Department whenever he desires to do so.

It was said at Hylan headquarters last night that the Mayor-elect as yet had not given serious consideration to the task of finding a successor for Commissioner Woods. Reports indicating that the Police Commissionership would go to a "good Tammany man," of whom some have been named in the speculation over patronage, and that Charles F. Murphy, leader of Tammany Hall, was particularly anxious to have his wishes consulted in the filling of this office, it was said both at the headquarters of Judge Hylan and at Tammany Hall, might be discarded as without justification.

Judge Hylan, it was said last night by his friends, was keenly alive to the fact that Mayors stood or fell by the public verdict on the administration of the Police Department. Leader Murphy also, it was asserted, was not oblivious of the fact that, while Judge Hylan was Mayor, Tammany would be on trial, and that any attempt on the part of Tammany Hall to lay violent hands on the Police Department would arouse a storm of resentment at the very beginning of the new administration. Among the friends of Judge Hylan the prediction was made freely yesterday that the Mayor-elect would make clear to the political leaders that he did not need any help in picking a new Police Commissioner.

A statement made yesterday by County Clerk William F. Schneider, Chairman of the Democratic Fusion Committee, which body was largely instrumental in making Judge Hylan the nominee for Mayor, was regarded as not altogether void of significance.

Wants Hylan to be Foot Free.

"The appointment of a Police Commissioner should be left entirely to the Mayor," said Mr. Schneider. "The political organizations which were behind Judge Hylan's candidacy should scrupulously avoid any divided responsibility in the administration of the Police Department. Tammany's political foes have always made the Police Department an issue in city elections, and the course of Tammany in relation to police administration has been disastrous to that organization. The selection of a Police Commissioner should be undertaken by Judge Hylan solely on his own responsibility and without any interference or advice by politicians."

Leader Murphy did not appear at Tammany Hall yesterday. It was learned that the Tammany chief was preparing to go away for a rest, as is his practice after a hard-fought campaign. In his absence Congressman Thomas F. Smith, Secretary of Tammany Hall, did the talking.

"Mr. Murphy has been leader of Tammany Hall for sixteen years," said Congressman Smith. "In all that time he has neither recommended nor had anything to do with the selection of a Police Commissioner. There is every

Continued on Page 3.

Insists Emperor Charles Will Be Polish Ruler

Special Cable to THE NEW YORK TIMES.

THE HAGUE, Nov. 8.—In spite of recent denials, the Lokal-Anzeiger repeats that the Austrian Emperor is to be named King of Poland. It says this was decided on at a Crown Council on Monday.

Poland is to be joined to Austria, and Galicia is to belong to the future Kingdom of Poland. Lithuania and Courland will be separate States, such as Prussia, and be represented by Grand Dukes. The paper points out that in Austria even the Germanic parties appear to approve this, but that special emphasis is laid on and guarantees demanded for "the strengthening of Germanic-Austria."

The paper seems to question whether German interests have been sufficiently consdiered in this settlement.

THREAT OF DICTATOR IN GERMAN SNARL

Government Attempts to Force Dropping of Demand for Radical Vice Chancellor.

HERTLING DENIES PROMISES

Opposition to Attack Chancellor as Soon as Reichstag Meets Unless He Yields.

COPENHAGEN, Nov. 8.—The threat that a military dictatorship is inevitable unless insistence upon a radical Vice Chancellor is dropped and the Government of Count von Hertling as it now stands is accepted is held out over the progressive democratic elements in Germany.

Count von Hertling, through a semi-official note in the Norddeutsche Allgemeine Zeitung, announces that no promises whatever were made to give the radicals the two posts they desired. Representatives of the Reichstag majority have issued an equally authoritative announcement that they adhere to their old position.

The radical press indicates that the Chancellor's compromise proposal to appoint a radical Deputy to the newly created Ministry for occupied territories with a seat in the Prussian Cabinet is not acceptable because such a post would be merely temporary, and the occupant would be powerless in the face of the military authorities.

The situation is drifting rapidly toward the goal desired by the reactionaries, that is, a split in the present alignment in the Reichstag and the formation of a new coalition embracing the Conservatives and the National Lib... bloc, which would have a bare majority in the Reichstag, is by no means impossible, despite the apparent unity proclaimed by the majority caucus.

The Catholic Centrum is by no means adverse to following the Chancellor along a road marked with party advantages. The National Liberals, who for the most part are Conservatives and annexationists and whose hearts never were in the present majority bloc, intimate strongly in their formal announcement of Herr Friedberg's withdrawal of his acceptance of the Vice Presidency of the Prussian Cabinet their dissatisfaction with the attitude of the Radicals and the Socialists.

The Socialists apparently have abandoned the dictum expressed by Philipp Scheidemann on Sunday that the new von Hertling Government, which differs from that of Dr. Michaelis only in the person of its chief, provided all necessary guarantees of responsible popular Government as a pre-condition to peace.

The Tageblatt and other Radical newspapers say that if Chancellor von Hertling bows to the "hidden powers" and the influence of the Court clique, the opposition will introduce on Nov. 22, when the Reichstag reconvenes, a resolution of lack of confidence in the Government. Count von Hertling's position is much like that of Dr. Michaelis after his "as I interpret it" speech.

LONDON, Nov. 8.—The German political crisis is represented as being as acute as ever in special dispatches from Amsterdam. Some say that Count von Hertling's Chancellorship is in danger of immediate shipwreck.

The refusal of Herr Friedberg, leader of the National Liberty Party, to accept the Vice Presidency of the Prussian Ministry and the prospect that Dr. Helfferich is to be retained as Vice Chancellor are regarded as matters impossible of settlement. Count von Hertling is reported to have succumbed to military and junker influence.

The Cologne Gazette blames the Progressives and the Socialists for the reawakening of the crisis, and says that the prospect for a political truce has disappeared.

OTTO H. KAHN TALKS FINANCE WITH WILSON

New Yorker at the White House Discusses Economic Condition of the Country.

WASHINGTON, Nov. 8.—Otto H. Kahn, head of Kuhn, Loeb & Co., called today on President Wilson. He would not discuss his visit except to say that it was for the purpose of talking over the economic condition of the country.

Otto H. Kahn has given considerable attention to the question of war taxation, and has advocated methods that would lay as little strain as possible on business in general while taking heavy levies from profits or incomes which could afford it without danger of drying up the sources of revenue. In May, when the question of taxing profits was beginning to receive much consideration, he pointed out that a very heavy tax on excess profits would be more desirable than a moderate tax on general profits.

"It appears," he said at that time, "that a 40 per cent. tax on excess profits over and above the average earnings for the last three years would yield for the present year the amazing total of at least $800,000,000 in addition to the yield from the corporate income tax at the rate of 4 per cent."

In August he urged that undue burdens on incomes and business profits should be avoided, while the taxes should be laid as widely as possible in order not to lay so much burden on any one as to be crushing.

"All I am advocating," he said at that time, "is in effect that in the public interest not too much be exacted at once, but that by dividing the burden over a reasonable number of years, capital in no one year, and especially not during the first year of the war, should be so excessively taxed as to produce an unscientific and dangerous strain. If the great fund of capital is suddenly and too greatly reduced the effect upon commerce and industry is apt to be sudden and withering."

CADORNA IS OUTFLANKED

A General Among the Troops Cut Off on the Middle Tagliamento.

INVADERS CAPTURE 80 GUNS

Berlin Reckons Total at More Than 2,300; That of Prisoners Over 250,000.

ROME ADMITS WITHDRAWAL

Official Report Shows That Rearguard Actions Are Proceeding West of the Livenza.

BERLIN, Nov. 8, (via London.)—Austro-German forces in Northern Italy have crossed the Livenza River, and in outflanking operations on the middle Tagliamento have captured 17,000 Italian troops, among them a General. Eighty guns have been added to the booty, which now includes more than 2,300 guns. The total number of prisoners taken since the drive began now exceeds 250,000.

These developments of the campaign are announced in the afternoon report from Army Headquarters, the text of which follows:

Our detachments, advancing on the mountain roads, have broken the resistance of the enemy rear guard. By an outflanking movement our attacking columns cut off the retreat of the enemy troops still holding out on the middle Tagliamento between Tolmezzo and Gemona and on the permanent fortified works of Monte San Simeone.

Up to the present 17,000 Italians, among them a General, with 80 guns, have had to surrender.

In the plain, fighting has developed along the Livenza River. By a vigorous advance German and Austro-Hungarian divisions, in spite of destroyed bridges, have forced the crossing and have thrown the enemy back westward.

The total number of prisoners captured has now been increased to more than 250,000 and the booty in guns to more than 2,300.

Tonight's report says:

In Italy we are fighting our way forward in the mountains and on the plains.

Retreat Continues, Rome Reports.

ROME, Nov. 8.—The withdrawal of the Italian line was continued yesterday, the War Office announced today. The larger units retired unmolested.

Italian troops fought numerous rearguard actions, in the course of which they succeeded in holding up the Austro-German advance temporarily. Italian airplanes continued bombarding hostile forces along the Tagliamento and brought down five enemy machines.

The text of the statement follows:

During yesterday we continued the withdrawal of our line. The larger units have retired without being molested by the enemy.

Numerous engagements took place between the hills of Vittorio and the confluence of the Monticano and the Livenza, in the course of which our brave troops succeeded in detaining the enemy's advance.

In spite of strong resistance on the part of hostile machines, our aviators renewed their bombardments of enemy troops along the Tagliamento. Five enemy airplanes were brought down.

As the Vittorio hills and the Monticano River lie to the west of the Livenza, the statement of the Italian War Office is equivalent to an admission that the Austro-Germans have crossed the latter stream.

Final Stand Beyond the Livenza?

By The Associated Press.

ITALIAN ARMY HEADQUARTERS, Nov. 8.—The bulk of the Austro-German invading forces today presents a main frontage of about thirty-five miles along the Tagliamento River, with reconnoissance parties thrust forward eight or ten miles west of the river, for the purpose of feeling for the points of least resistance. This is producing detached engagements, but no battle in force has yet occurred.

The Livenza River, to which the Italian withdrawal is now in progress, is only one of a series of successive defense parallels. The Italian Army still has in reserve large bodies of troops, which, however, naturally feel the effects produced by the recent retirement of their main body. Heavy reinforcements at this moment, therefore, would render invaluable assistance, in the opinion of the military authorities.

The enemy territorial occupation in Eastern Friuli presents a sinister aspect far beyond its military purport. The Alps heretofore have been the traditional boundary between the Northern Teutonic and the Southern Latin races. The Austro-Germans recognize the Alpine boundary, except for Trent and Trieste.

Now for the first time the Teutonic forces are occupying territory in the Friuli plains, which are the easternmost part of Venetia and age-long possessions of the Latins. Such an invasion strikes at the very heart of the principle of nationality, and also thrusts a Teutonic wedge southward along the Adriatic. This brings up the grave question of whether Germany will finally secure territorial lodgment with ports and naval bases on the Adriatic, thus realizing her aim to

Continued on Page 4.

British Government Denies Lack of Concern for Italy

LONDON, Nov. 8.—The following official announcement was issued tonight:

"A statement from a correspondent of The Associated Press at Italian Headquarters appeared in the British press today. This statement set out to remind the Allies that something more than assurances were needed for getting reinforcements in men and munitions to the threatened Italian lines, and purported to reflect the feeling of Italians, who were represented as distrusting the allied efforts to help them. It was also stated that the enemy masses were so overwhelming that nothing but effective reinforcements would turn the tide.

"This alarmist statement is absolutely uncalled for and is calculated to do grave harm by suggesting that the seriousness of the military situation in Italy is not appreciated by her allies, and that the latter are not giving her the support she requires. There is no truth whatever in these assertions. The statement that the enemy masses are overwhelming is an absurd exaggeration."

The Associated Press issued this statement last night:

"The dispatch to which the foregoing British official statement refers was sent by The Associated Press correspondent at Italian Headquarters on Nov. 7. This correspondent is an American Staff man, who was present at the beginning of the Italian retreat and accompanied the Italian Army back to its present position.

"The dispatch in question was passed by the Italian military censors at General Cadorna's headquarters, and, as it was sent through France, also passed the French censorship."

LONDON HAILS OUR WAR MISSION

Comes at Critical Period of the War with New Assurance of Victory.

ENVOYS MAKE BRISK START

Begin Conferences on First Day —Benson Visits Jellicoe— Trip Was Uneventful.

Special Cable to THE NEW YORK TIMES.

LONDON, Nov. 8.—The American mission, headed by Colonel E. M. House, arrived in Europe at a crucial period of the world war. With Russia in the throes of a fresh revolution that may lead to anything, and with Italy engaged in a desperate struggle against both a foreign enemy and internal difficulties the landing of the American mission at a British port is an encouragement to the stalwart and a rebuke to the faint hearted.

To England in particular it possesses special significance. It is a concrete expression of the union of Anglo-Saxon races in the greatest war for liberty the world has ever seen, and also an augury of the victorious overthrow of despotic forces which make the world unsafe for democracy.

The statement which Colonel House gave to the British press tonight supplemented the announcement issued in America by the President. In all quarters it is hailed as a plain definition of the objects aimed at by America and a pledge of America's intention to fight on till those ends are attained.

Great Britain's confidence in the issue of the struggle has never been seriously undermined. There have been times of depression when the end seemed far distant but the country as a whole has set itself resolutely to travel the long and weary road. England never for one moment doubted its ability to win through itself.

There were those who questioned the possibility of a final decision being reached in this war. There still are a few of these, chiefly to be found among that clique which believes that a negotiated peace with an unregenerate and unrepentant Germany is an acceptable solution.

America's clear perception of the issue at stake and America's undivided purpose to fight, as Colonel House put it, until it becomes certain that no group of selfish men can again bring about disaster to the world, more than counterbalances all that history has written, or may yet write, on the wrong side of the allied ledger.

Colonel House explained today to the English newspaper representatives the circumstances under which the American mission had come to participate in the Allied War Council shortly to be held in Paris. He was asked if the United States was going to sign the pact of London and he quietly, but clearly, made it patent that the question did not arise.

Various phrases in President Wilson's announcement drew a query as to whether any criticism of the past conduct of the war by allied Governments was implied.

Colonel House decisively negatived any such suggestion. In this respect it may be stated emphatically that the American participation in the war council of the Allies is most heartily welcomed by those who most clearly see

Continued on Page 11.

AWAITS LIGHT FROM RUSSIA

Washington Reserves Judgment, Hoping Revolt Is Only Local.

EXPECTS A COUNTER-MOVE

Kerensky, with Conservatives and Perhaps the Army Behind Him, May Save the Country.

DARK DAYS SEEN AHEAD

And Allied War Conference Faces Another Huge Problem —Bigger Burden for Us.

Special to The New York Times.

WASHINGTON, Nov. 8.—Until accurate official reports are received, official and diplomatic Washington are reserving judgment on the new Russian crisis and all that it involves, including possibly civil war, and a still further weakening of Russia's position in the war against Germany.

Dark as the news dispatches make the situation in Petrograd appear, there is a strong hope among officials and diplomats that there may be a silver lining to the cloud. On every hand keen sympathy was expressed for Premier Kerensky and those who have been standing with him against terrific odds in opposing the extremist elements who, by their activities, have threatened to disorganize the Russian military machine, and have worked for separate peace, regardless of its effect on the future of Russia and her pledges to her allies.

The State Department has received no official confirmation of the Maximalist successes in Petrograd. In the last six days Secretary Lansing has received only two messages from Ambassador Francis, and neither dealt with the political situation. One bore date of Friday last and the other of Tuesday.

The Russian Embassy officials said they had no advices from Petrograd on the basis of which comment could be made. Jean Soukine, First Secretary, after a telephone conversation this afternoon with Ambassador Bakhmeteff, who is in Memphis, stated that in the absence of official intelligence the Embassy held that the action of the Maximalists in Petrograd, as told in the news dispatches, was local to the capital and by no means representative of the will or of the Russian nation.

This point was emphasized here today that the dispatches from Petrograd stated that the Maximalists had taken control of the telegraph offices and that this put them in a position to exaggerate reports of the situation in their own favor.

First Secretary Soukine stated that the Embassy was unable to present the views of the Government, being without instructions, but he pointed out that Petrograd was the centre of Bolsheviki activity. To this fact, he said, was due the present situation in Petrograd, which did not represent the conditions throughout Russia. Mr. Soukine stated that the local character of the disturbance was proved by the fact that the Central Executive Committee of the Petrograd Council of Soldiers' and Workmen's Delegates did not express the will of the Pan Russian Council's Executive Committee, which only a few days ago refused to approve the creation by the Petrograd Council's Executive Committee of a military revolutionary committee, and at the same time urged that measures be taken to prevent the consummation of the designs of the Bolsheviki.

The embassy officials suggested that "Petrograd is likely to be isolated." No interpretation of this statement was given, but it was believed to indicate a belief that the Bolsheviki would find themselves without national support and that the army might decline to accept orders from their Military Revolutionary Committee, which now, according to the announcement in Petrograd, is the sole Governmental authority.

Expect a New Government.

In many quarters it was thought that another Government will be formed for Russia, now that some members of the Provisional Government had been arrested. The new Government would probably be formed at Moscow, it was said, and be dominated by the conservative Socialist elements, although it might be a coalition, including members of the Constitutional Democratic Party as well as Socialists and Laborites, of which last-named party Premier Kerensky is a member.

No doubt was expressed in diplomatic circles that the Allied Powers would recognize any Government formed to oppose the Bolsheviki, even if the latter maintained their hold upon Petrograd. Moscow was regarded as the probable choice for the provisional capital, because all the elements there have been in sympathy with the Government as against the extremist Socialists. Moscow also is held to be a more purely Russian city, and, as compared with Petrograd, practically free from the elements that have made the life of the Government precarious.

It is believed that unless the army goes over en masse to the Bolsheviki, the temporary ascendency of the rad-

Continued on Page 2.

Reverses Cited as Showing Greater Need Than Ever For Unified Direction of Allied War Policy

By CHARLES H. GRASTY.

Special Cable to THE NEW YORK TIMES.

ROME, Nov. 8.—My observations here confirm previous insistence upon the urgent need of centralized methods of managing the war. At bottom this war is the biggest business enterprise ever undertaken, and, while the Kaiser handles his end of it as such, each of the Allies is more or less playing its own separate game. With an infinity of resources, they have discussed and postponed critical decisions until the advantage has been lost.

To mention one recent instance: If the Korniloff movement had been handled by the Allies as the Kaiser would have handled such an opportunity, the Russian situation might have been stabilized and the Italian drive rendered impossible.

There has not been a single allied action, with the exception of the battle of the Marne, ranking as a great aggressive stroke. The Allies are not organized to initiate and execute big policies. Instead of looking ahead and planning on a big scale, they yield where pressure is applied, with the result that usually they trail along a few days or weeks behind Germany. Purely local and political matters divide and divert attention in the allied Chancelleries.

Coming on top of many previous heartbreaking lost opportunities, the present menace in Italy is quite serious enough to rally the Entente Powers at last into substituting for the town meeting some plan under which they can see the war situation as a whole and concentrate with foresight, originality, and driving power, as we understand those things in America.

In a word, after three years, it is time to quit playing amateur against professional. If America gives the lead, all the rest will follow, as there are directed against us none of the petty jealousies peculiar to Europe, and all the allied countries have complete confidence in our disinterestedness and sound leadership.

Plans for the conduct of the war on the basis of a unified western front extending from the North Sea to the Adriatic are now under consideration by Premiers Lloyd George and Painlevé and other high civil and military officials in conference in Rome.

STOCKS TUMBLE ON RUSSIAN NEWS

Flood of Liquidation Hits Exchange, Heightened by Action of Short Sellers.

NEWS CHECKS BROAD RISE

No Action Considered Yet in Regard to Publishing Proportion of Short Sales.

The stock market suffered one of the most drastic declines of the year yesterday, following the receipt of dispatches which told of the Kerensky Government's downfall. Owners of securities considered the Russian news more disturbing than developments on the Italian front, although in banking circles the new republic's reversion to a condition of political chaos did not seem to increase pessimism over the war outlook greatly. In a wild hour of trading the active speculative stocks dropped 4 to 11 points from their previous levels, thereafter recovering part of the distance under active bidding from investors and traders who covered short contracts and what looked like banking support.

The decline was made all the more emphatic because it occurred suddenly in the midst of a rather broad rise of prices. Starting slightly higher than Wednesday's closing quotations, the prominent railroad and industrial shares advanced in many cases more than a point before 11 o'clock, and were moving along normally when the first reports came from London of the changed conditions in Russia. There was a quick drop of a couple of points in the next quarter hour, and then a short period of steadiness, a lull before the storm.

Big Sales of Steel Common.

When brokerage houses with wire connections began to get in their orders after flashing out the Russian news, a flood of selling struck the Exchange, which was heightened by the operations of short sellers in the Street and out. Steel common was poured forth in blocks running as high as 5,000 shares, and International Mercantile Marine preferred dropped under heavy selling from 98 to 91½, frequently by quarters and half points, and without a period of recovery. Reading, Southern Pacific, New York Central, and Union Pacific were pressed for sale, and numerous high-grade railroad bonds lost more ground than in any preceding day since Jan. 1.

The movements of some of the more active stocks from their best to their lowest prices, with their net declines, are in the following table:

	Decline From Top.	Net Decline.	Last Price.
American Can	5½	2¼	30¾
American Smelting	5¼	4	70⅝
American Sugar	6¼	5½	90
Atchison	8½	2⅛	82¾
Baldwin Locomotive	7½	3¾	51¼
Bethlehem Steel	9½	8⅛	73
Brooklyn Rapid Transit	5¼	2⅜	45¼
Canadian Pacific	4⅞	2⅞	133⅜
Crucible Steel	7	3½	52
General Motors	5¾	3	80
In. Mer. Marine pf	11	5	94
New York Central	3⅞	2⅝	65
Reading	6½	3¾	68¾
Republic Iron & Steel	6⅞	4½	68⅝
Union Pacific	5¼	3	109⅝
United States Steel	7⅛	4¾	90¾

Russian Bonds Decline.

The Russian situation had a naturally adverse effect on the Russian bonds dealt in on the Curb. From Wednesday's last price of 56 the 5½s declined to 48, with sales of $30,000, and the 6½s dropped from 64 to 58 with transactions involving $25,000. Russian exchange fell away from 13.35 cents per ruble to 11.75 cents for transfers by check, approaching the previous minimum record of 11½ cents. At times the market was report-

Continued on Page 2.

HOPE STRONG MAN WILL RULE RUSSIA

Zemstvos' Agent Here and Herman Bernstein Agree That Kerensky Must Go.

GREAT REACTION EXPECTED

Salchnovsky Thinks Revolt May Lead to Constitutional Monarchy.

The elimination of Kerensky from the affairs of the Russian Government was declared to be the most probable as well as the most desirable result of the present Maximalist revolt by persons familiar with Russian affairs and in sympathy with the moderate parties there.

Alexander Sakhnovsky, head of the American offices of the Union of Zemstvos, predicted that the reaction toward a stronger form of government might go as far as the setting up of a constitutional monarchy under the Grand Duke Michael, who was named as the successor of Nicholas in the first announcements of the revolution last March, but was immediately pushed out of the way by the tide of radical sentiment.

"Russians who have landed in New York within the last few days," said Mr. Sakhnovsky, "bring reports that the whole nation outside of the radicals of Petrograd is disgusted with the violence, disorder, and uncertainty which have prevailed for months past. There is a strong tide setting toward a more compact and powerful government, and Moscow would undoubtedly be the natural centre of such a movement.

"In Moscow the Bolsheviki are not 1 per cent. of the total population, and all Russia outside of Petrograd would stand together, I believe, against the extreme policy of the Maximalists. This will be particularly true if, as is possible, Lenine and Trotzsky call in the German fleet to their aid.

"In any event, it will take a stronger Government than that of Kerensky to bring about order. The excellence of Kerensky's motives and ideals is recognized, but he is too gentle a man for his position at the preesnt time. It has been shown that the policy of mildness with the Bolsheviki does not pay. Moreover, he lacks the executive experience which is necessary to the head of the Government. A man like Prince Lvoff would be considerably more useful, and I believe, from the reports I receive, that sentiment in Russia is setting in that direction.

"As for the Grand Duke Michael, he has always been very popular, and the fact that he has married a woman not of royal blood, the divorced wife of a Moscow lawyer, has increased his popularity. I am confident that Russia as a whole will not yield to a faction of Petrograd."

Herman Bernstein, who was in Petrograd during the Maximalist riots of last July, said that he was confident that Trotzsky was only the agent of Lenine, who from his hiding had been directing this revolt, as he had done the rising of that period.

"It can't win," he said, "for Lenine and Trotzky are both extremely unpopular. They had a better chance last July, when, if they had only had well-laid plans, they would have been able to dominate Petrograd. As it was, they failed at the time, and the popular execration directed against Lenine after the bloodshed of July was such as to convince me that he will never be able to dominate the Russian people.

"But undoubtedly Kerensky cannot

Continued on Page 2.

MINISTERS UNDER ARRES

Winter Palace Is Taken After Fierce Defense by Women Soldiers.

FORT'S GUNS TURNED ON IT

Cruiser and Armored Cars Also Brought Into Battle Waged by Searchlight.

TROTZSKY HEADS REVOLT

Giving Land to the Peasants and Calling of Constituent Assembly Promised.

PETROGRAD, Nov. 8.—With the aid of the capital's garrison complete control of Petrograd has been seized by the Maximalists, or Bolsheviki, headed by Nikolai Lenine, the Radical Socialist leader, and Leon Trotzsky, President of the Central Executive Committee of the Petrograd Council of Workmen's and Soldiers' Delegates. Their action has been indorsed by the All-Russia Congress of Workmen's Councils.

A proclamation has been issued declaring that the Revolutionary Government purposes to negotiate an "immediate democratic peace," to turn the land over to the peasantry, and to convoke the Constituent Assembly.

Premier Kerensky has fled. He is variously said to be headed for Moscow and the northern front of the army, and orders for his arrest have been issued. Last night he was reported to be at Luga, eighty-five miles southwest of Petrograd. Several members of his Cabinet have been taken into custody.

The Preliminary Parliament is declared dissolved.

Little serious fighting has attended the revolt so far. The Provisional Government troops holding the bridges over the Neva and various other points yesterday were quickly overpowered, save at the Winter Palace, the chief guardians of which were the Women's Battalion. Here last night a battle royal took place for four hours, during which the Bolsheviki brought up armored cars and the cruiser Aurora and turned the guns of the Fort of St. Peter and St. Paul upon the palace before its defenders would surrender.

Prior to the attack the Workmen's and Soldiers' leaders sent the Provisional Government an ultimatum demanding their surrender and allowing twenty minutes' grace. The Government replied indirectly, refusing to recognize the Military Committee.

Vice President Kameneff of the Workmen's and Soldiers' Delegates told The Associated Press today that the object of taking possession of the posts and telegraphs was to thwart any effort the Government might make to call troops to the capital. The Russkia Volia and the Bourse Gazette have been commandeered.

The city today presented a normal aspect. Even the noonday band accompanying the guard of relief under the previous administration continued its function. There were the customary lines in front of the provision stores and children played in the parks and gardens. There was even a notable lessening of the patrols, only a few armed soldiers and sailors moving about the streets

How the Revolt Developed.

The Maximalist movement toward seizing authority, rumors of which had been agitating the public mind ever since the formation of the last Coalition Cabinet, culminated Tuesday night, when, without disorder, Maximalist forces took possession of the Telegraph office and the Petrograd Telegraph Agency.

Orders issued by the Government for the opening of the spans of the bridges across the Neva later were overridden by the Military Committee of the Council of Workmen's and Soldiers' Delegates. Communication was restored after several hours of interruption. Nowhere did the Maximalists meet with serious opposition.

An effort by militiamen to disperse crowds gathered in the Nevski and Letainy Prospekts during the evening provoked a fight in which one man is reported to have been killed. Minor disturbances, some of them accompanied by shooting, occurred in various quarters of the city. A number of persons are reported to have been killed or wounded.

Yesterday morning found patrols of soldiers, sailors, and civilians in the streets maintaining order. Further than a continuation of suppressed excitement, the streets of the city presented no unusual aspects. The shops and banks which had opened for business began closing up about noon.

Shortly after noon a Soviet force occupied the telephone exchange, where a small guard had been stationed for weeks. An effort by Government forces to retake the exchange led to a brief fusillade, by which it is believed a number of casualties was caused. The Maximalists remained in possession of the building.

Toward 5 o'clock in the afternoon the Military Revolutionary Committee issued its proclamation stating that Petrograd was in its hands. It read:

> To the Army Committees of the Active Army and to all Councils of Workmen's and Soldiers' Delegates and to the Garrison and Proletariat of Petrograd:
>
> We have deposed the Government of Kerensky, which rose against the revolution and the people. The change which resulted in the deposition of the

"All the News That's Fit to Print."

The New York Times.

THE WEATHER
Overcast, rising temperature today; tomorrow unsettled; wind south.
For weather report see next to last page.

VOL. LXVIII...NO. 22,263. NEW YORK, TUESDAY, JANUARY 7, 1919 TWENTY-FOUR PAGES. TWO CENTS Metropolitan District 50 Mile Radius | THREE CENTS Within 200 Miles | FOUR CENTS Elsewhere

THEODORE ROOSEVELT DIES SUDDENLY AT OYSTER BAY HOME; NATION SHOCKED, PAYS TRIBUTE TO FORMER PRESIDENT; OUR FLAG ON ALL SEAS AND IN ALL LANDS AT HALF MAST

ITALIAN CITIES GIVE PRESIDENT AMAZING GREETING

He Regards Popular Demonstrations as Proof That the Masses Are with Him.

LEAVES TURIN FOR PARIS

Vast Throngs Turn Out Everywhere to Acclaim—He Responds to Their Spirit.

MAKES MANY SPEECHES

Three in Genoa and Five in Milan—Shows Weariness Under the Great Strain.

By RICHARD V. OULAHAN.

Copyright, 1919, by The New York Times Company.
Special Cable to THE NEW YORK TIMES.

TURIN, Jan. 6.—President Wilson's reception at Turin was a repetition of the demonstrations at Rome, Genoa, and Milan. There was continuous cheering by enormous crowds massed behind the soldiers as he passed this morning from the railroad station to the municipality, where he received the freedom of the city.

The President was acclaimed by a great throng when he appeared at a window of the Philharmonic Club.

The heavy rain and the early hour of his arrival did not affect the enthusiasm of the people, many of whom shouted, "Viva Wilson, god of peace!"

The President has been deeply moved by the character of the demonstrations, and has responded gleefully. He said that Sunday's demonstration in front of the palace at Milan was the most spontaneous and inspiring he ever saw. On that occasion he led the band as he stood on the balcony of the palace, and threw kisses with both hands to the delight of the people.

Another striking ovation occurred at a gala performance of "Aïda" at La Scala, in Milan, when the President and Mrs. Wilson appeared in the royal box. Mrs. Wilson drew admiring comment, and shared the popularity of her husband.

President Wilson departed for Paris this afternoon. He was fatigued after his strenuous Italian tour, and he probably will go to some quiet place near Paris to rest, perhaps for a week.

It is obvious that the President is popular here in Italy where he is regarded as the exponent of the prevention of future wars.

Confident of Italian Support.

Copyright, 1919, by The New York Times Company.
Special Cable to THE NEW YORK TIMES.

MILAN, Jan. 5.—President Wilson's visit to Italy, which ends with his departure from Turin tomorrow, already has had an important result in establishing a sympathetic point of contact between the President and the Italian Government. Those accompanying the President have been impressed with the sincerity and cordiality of Italy's greeting.

Even before he came to Europe, President Wilson had knowledge of the closeness to and personal relation toward America felt throughout Italy, but not until his arrival in Rome did he fully appreciate how the people were permeated with the desire to turn that relationship into a closer bond. Everywhere the President went the Italians showed an understanding of his principles for producing permanent peace. Their attitude toward Americans generally is so friendly as to leave no doubt as to the genuineness of the expressions that they looked to the President to establish a basis for freeing Europe from future wars.

It is difficult to convey to the American mind how these kindly people impressed upon President Wilson and those accompanying him the faith they placed in his regard for their interests and those of the entire world. Very generally they are sympathetic with the aspirations of their Government for the retention of Dalmatia and other nearby provinces, taking the position that the future safety of Italy demands this outcome, but they showed a heartfelt, even affectionate,

Continued on Page Six.

Secret Treaty Gave England Supervision of Mesopotamia

PARIS, Jan. 6.—Supervision of the affairs of Mesopotamia after the conclusion of peace was assigned to Great Britain by a treaty concluded between France and England concerning the future of Asia Minor early in the war. The existence of this treaty only recently has become known publicly, and no previous mention has been made of the important country of Mesopotamia.

Under the terms of this treaty France was to assume direction of the destinies of Syria, Lebanon, and Armenia Minor, (that part of Armenia to the west of the Euphrates.) Palestine was to be under international protection, while Mesopotamia and portions of the Arabian peninsula were to be under the supervision of Great Britain. It was settled that the largest possible autonomy would be assured to the races and peoples in these countries, and an economical administration and equality of rights were also agreed to.

What disposition the Peace Conference will make of this and other secret treaties is much discussed in Paris.

PEACE CONFERENCE TO BEGIN MONDAY

Wilson Back in Paris Today to Begin Series of Preliminary Discussions.

WILL SAIL ABOUT FEB. 12

Plans to Address Congress on Peace Problems and Return to Paris After March 4.

By CHARLES A. SELDEN.

Copyright, 1919, by The New York Times Company.
Special Cable to THE NEW YORK TIMES.

PARIS, Jaan. 6.—It seems to be definitely settled that the Peace Conference will begin a week from today, Monday, Jan. 13. President Wilson is expected back in Paris tomorrow, and Premier Clemenceau tomorrow or next day.

The selection of a Secretary General for the conference is the one big post yet in abeyance. The most likely man for this important place is M. Dutasta, the French Minister to Switzerland. The other powers have been asked by France if he would be acceptable to them. An affirmative reply is expected.

It is supposed the honor of presiding at the conference will be passed around more or less. No doubt the conference will begin under the Presidency of Clemenceau, but he will frequently leave the chair to talk, so in the course of the proceedings it is probable that British, Italians, and Americans all will have a chance to conduct the general meeting.

To Begin Series of Conferences.

PARIS, Jan. 6.—President Wilson is due back in Paris at 8 o clock tomorrow morning. There will be no formalities over his arrival. He will proceed to the Murat residence for a series of conferences which will begin to give concrete form to the work of the Peace Congress.

Lord Robert Cecil, the British authority on a League of Nations, will be one of the early arrivals in Paris after the President. Premier Lloyd George, if the British Cabinet situation permits, is expected toward the end of the week, and Foreign Secretary Balfour is ready to come from Cannes whenever needed.

Lord Robert Cecil, it is understood, is ready to present a quite definite plan giving the British viewpoint on a Society of Nations. Leon Bourgeois is prepared to outline the French plan, while the American delegates have been engagde actively in putting their views into definite shape.

Among those likely to see the President are Senator Owen of Oklahoma, Premier Venizelos of Greece, and a Zionist delegation for discussion of questions concerning Palestine, Syria, and Armenia. Parts of the Polish, Czechoslovak, and Serbian delegations have arrived and are seeking interviews with the President, who doubtless will confer with all of them. The outlook is for a busy week preparatory to the assembling of the interallied conference next week.

President Wilson will return to the United States to attend the closing sessions of the present Congress, according to present plans, and will come back to France for the later sittings of the Peace Congress. The President will make several addresses to Congress, and after March 4, it is expected, will return to France.

President Wilson, according to present plans, intends to leave Europe about Feb. 12 for the United States. The President not only intends to be in Washington for the closing sessions of the present Congress, but to deliver several addresses concerning the settlement of the war and the establishment of a peace which it is hoped will be durable.

WASHINGTON SORROW KEEN

News of Ex-President's Death Received There As Stunning Blow.

OFFICIALS PROMPT TO ACT

Baker and Daniels Order Army and Navy Tribute Throughout the World.

FLIERS GO TO OYSTER BAY

Ten Will Watch Over Sagamore Hill—Military Funeral if Family Wishes It.

Special to The New York Times.

WASHINGTON, Jan. 6.—News of the death of ex-President Roosevelt, who for seven years occupied the White House, not only created profound sorrow, but broke upon the nation's capital with a stunning blow.

Men of all sorts were eager for details of the death, and quickly bought the "extras" that soon appeared on the streets. At the Capitol, in the embassies, throughout the Government executive departments, and among the rank and file of the people anxious interest was manifested and keen sorrow was expressed.

As soon as news reached the White House Joseph P. Tumulty, the private secretary to the President, sent a cablegram to President Wilson in Italy officially notifying him. The flag over the White House was lowered to half mast and orders were issued to half-mast the flags on every Government building in Washington. Flags on business houses and private dwellings were likewise half-masted.

The United States Supreme Court, when notified of the death of Colonel Roosevelt by Attorney General Gregory, adjourned at once, and both the Senate and the House of Representatives adjourned after paying tribute to the former President. The bust of Colonel Roosevelt in the Senate corridor was shrouded in crape.

Secretaries Baker and Daniels issued orders under which the American flag will be half-masted all around the world wherever there are American soldiers, sailors, or marines. The flags at army camps and cantonments or forts in this country as well as those floating from the staffs of headquarters of the various army camps in France, Germany, Luxemburg, Siberia, and in Northern Russia will be half-masted.

Secretary Daniels has this message sent by telegraph, cable, or radio to all American naval ships and stations this morning:

"Ex-President Roosevelt died this morning. Colors are to be half-masted until sunset this evening."

Orders were issued by the heads of the various other executive departments for the half-masting of flags over offices under their jurisdiction throughout the world.

Secretaries Baker and Daniels stated tonight that a military funeral would be ordered for Colonel Roosevelt if it should accord with the wishes of Mrs. Roosevelt and other members of the family. Unofficially these officials had been informed that Mrs. Roosevelt desired to have a private funeral, but before hearing that report arrangements had been made to consult the family with regard to the funeral.

As a tribute to the memory of Colonel Roosevelt, whose youngest son, Quentin, an aviator, was shot down in France, General William L. Kenly, Director of Military Aeronautics, today ordered that two flights of army airplanes hover continuously over Sagamore Hill, Oyster Bay, day and night until the day of the funeral. There are five planes in each flight and the first of these fliers left Hazelhurst Field, at Mineola, L. I., this afternoon and dropped wreaths in front of the Roosevelt home. This was done as a tribute from the army air service to Colonel Roosevelt.

General Kenly said tonight that he would fly from Washington to Sagamore Hill in an army airplane to attend the funeral.

Poincare Says France's Heart Goes Out to Mrs. Roosevelt

PARIS, Jan. 6.—President Poincaré, when informed by The Associated Press of the death of Theodore Roosevelt, said:

"I am very much affected by the report of President Roosevelt's death. It was so unexpected. After the President had left the hospital some days ago we thought that all danger had passed.

"Well do I remember the dignified letter which I received from Mr. Roosevelt after the death of his son Quentin, in which he informed me that he was coming to France to visit the grave of his son. It is distressing to me to think that poor Roosevelt will not have an opportunity to lay flowers on the grave of his heroic son.

"The whole heart of France goes out to Mrs. Roosevelt in sympathy.

"Friend of liberty, friend of France, Roosevelt has given, without counting sons and daughters, his energy, that liberty may live. We are grateful to him. We wish to express to Mrs. Roosevelt our most sincere condolence."

CONGRESS MOURNS COLONEL'S DEATH

Both Houses Adopt Appropriate Resolutions and Then Adjourn for the Day.

TRIBUTES TO HIS MEMORY

Ex-President Eulogized by Members of Both Parties—Lodge Agitated While Speaking.

Special to The New York Times.

WASHINGTON, Jan. 6.—Profound regret over the death of ex-President Roosevelt was expressed in both Houses of Congress today. Senate and House both adjourned for the day out of respect for his memory. Flags on the Capitol were flown at half mast.

In the Senate a resolution of regret was offered by Senator Martin of Virginia, the Democratic floor leader, who spoke upon it, being followed by Senator Lodge of Massachusetts and Senator Calder of New York. In the House a similar resolution was offered by Representative Rainey of Illinois, who spoke upon it, and was followed by Representative Hicks of Oyster Bay.

Vice President Marshall, presiding over the Senate, appointed fifteen Senators as a committee to attend the funeral, while Speaker Clark appointed twenty-six Representatives. They will leave Washington tomorrow.

When the Senate met, the Chaplain, the Rev. Forest J. Prettyman, standing at the Vice President's desk, where ex-President Roosevelt sat while Vice President, offered the following prayer:

"Almighty God, as we meet today to represent this mighty nation, the shadow of a great loss falls upon us. One of the men of might, a leader of men, a patriot and a scholar, has passed from us. He was honored by his countrymen in being called to preside as Vice President over this body and then called to be our Chief Magistrate. His name has added luster to the history of our country, and his achievements have increased our influence in the life of the world.

"Throughout the nation there goes a sense of sorrow that this strong man, so brave and chivalrous and true, has come to the end of his great career. We pray Thy blessing upon his devoted wife and children as they mourn his loss. We pray Thy blessing upon the country he loved so well, that in this hour of great responsibility we may measure up

Continued on Page Two.

Extremists Start New Revolt in Berlin; Call On Masses to Destroy the Government

By LEONARD SPRAY.

Copyright, 1919, by The New York Times Company.
Special Cable to THE NEW YORK TIMES.

ROTTERDAM, Jan. 6.—I have just heard by telephone from Berlin that a revolutionary movement against the Government is in full swing.

The movement was organized by the Independent Socialists and the Spartacus League. An appeal has been issued by these elements to destroy the Government and "establish the power of the revolutionary proletariat."

An armed conflict began at 2 o'clock.

AMSTERDAM, Jan. 6.—The Spartacus group on Sunday evening made another attempt to seize the reins of power in Berlin and occupied the office of the Wolff Bureau, the semi-official news agency. The last telegram received here from the Wolff Bureau announced the seizure.

Private advices say that the Spartacides occupied the offices of half a dozen big newspapers, including the Socialist Vorwärts. Among the other offices occupied were those of the Tageblatt, Vossiche Zeitung Lokal-Anzeiger, and Morgen Post.

It is added that the newspapers were not expected to appear on Monday with the exception of Vorwärts, which was to be issued by a committee of revolutionary workingmen.

The office of the Wolff Bureau has been closed by the Spartacides and the news agency has ceased operations. This office and those of the leading Berlin newspapers are concentrated in a small area south of Unter den Linden which is accessible from Oranienburg, a workingmen's quarter.

Oranienburg is one of the strongholds of the Spartacides. They had previously seized newspaper offices, but were unable to gain control of the city.

Reports are in circulation here that a general coup d'etat has been attempted by the Spartacides.

Former President Theodore Roosevelt
Who Died in His Sleep at His Home in Oyster Bay Yesterday Morning.

ROOSEVELT'S END SHOCKS PARIS

Public, Unaware of His Illness, Had Looked Forward to His Proposed Visit.

PARIS, Jan. 6.—Theodore Roosevelt's death came as a shock to Paris, which was unaware of his illness. The public had been expecting the fulfillment of his proposed visit to France.

The news of Colonel Roosevelt's death was communicated by The Associated Press to the Peace Commission and other officials in diplomatic circles, eliciting general expressions of regret.

J. J. Jusserand, the French Ambassador to the United States, said: "The unexpected death of one who has upheld all his life the principles of virile manhood, straightforward honesty, and fearlessness, will be mourned all over the world, nowhere more sincerely than in France, whose cause he upheld in her worst crisis in a way that shall never be forgotten."

Henry White, one of the American Peace Commissioners, said: "I have heard of Mr. Roosevelt's death with deep sorrow, because of the loss to the nation of a great public servant and to myself of a lifelong friend."

Herbert C. Hoover said: "The news of Mr. Roosevelt's death comes to me as a distinct shock. America is poorer for the loss of a great citizen, the world for the loss of a great man. His virility and Americanism have been one of our national treasures."

Colonel E. M. House said: "I am greatly shocked to hear the news that comes from America. The entire world will share the grief which will be felt in the United States over the death of Theodore Roosevelt. He was the one virile and courageous leader of his generation, and will live in history as one of our greatest Presidents."

Colonel House sent to Mrs. Roosevelt a cablegram, saying

"Mrs. House shares with me the great sorrow which all Americans feel over the death of your distinguished husband."

Secretary Lansing said "The death of Colonel Roosevelt removes from our national life a great American. His vigor of mind and ceaseless energy made him a conspicuous figure in public affairs. Friends and enemies alike recognized the force of his personality, and the great influence he had in holding public thought and purpose. His patriotism and devotion to his country will long be remembered by all his fellow-citizens, while his sturdy Americanism will be an inspiration to future generations."

Loss to Whole Country, Says Cardinal Gibbons

BALTIMORE, Jan. 6.—Cardinal Gibbons said tonight:

"It was a terrible shock to me to learn of the death of former President Roosevelt. I had been intimately acquainted with him from the time he was elevated to the high office of President of the United States, and we were very dear and good friends. It is a terrible loss to me and to the whole country."

W. H. TAFT REGRETS DEATH OF COLONEL

Says Roosevelt's Patriotic Americanism Will Be Missed—"I Am Very, Very Sorry."

HARRISBURG, Penn., Jan. 6.—William H. Taft today said:

"I am deeply shocked by the death of Colonel Roosevelt. I saw him in the hospital six weeks ago, and he seemed to be very vigorous. He was suffering from rheumatism, but his voice was strong, his personality was as vigorous as ever, and his interest in the questions of the day as tense and acute as always. I mourn his loss personally, and I greatly regret it for the sake of his country."

Asked if he thought Colonel Roosevelt's death would affect the international future of the nation, Mr. Taft replied:

"That's a very difficult question to answer. His influence and advice were important. His patriotic Americanism will be missed, of course. I am very, very sorry."

Daughter Hears News in South.

AIKEN, S. C., Jan. 6.—Mrs. Richard Derby, who was Miss Ethel Roosevelt, left here today for Oyster Bay, N. Y. She was accompanied by Major Thomas Hitchcock, at whose home she and her two children had been guests for several weeks. Dr. Derby, her husband, is attached to a medical unit overseas.

CITY GRIEVES FOR COLONEL

Flags at Half Mast on Public Buildings and Courts and Aldermen Adjourn.

New York City was quick to pay tribute yesterday to Colonel Theodore Roosevelt, directly the news of his death became known. Flags on buildings were placed at half mast; the Board of Aldermen after adopting a resolution in Colonel Roosevelt's memory adjourned in tribute to him. Courts were adjourned after presiding Judges spoke in praise of the late ex-President, and many civic, educational and other organizations met and adopted resolutions. A number of organizations appointed memorial committees to represent them at the funeral services.

On his return from Albany late yesterday afternoon, Mayor Hylan sent the following telegram to Mrs. Roosevelt:

In this hour of your great bereavement permit me to extend to you in the name of the people of the City of New York the sincere sympathy that we all feel for you. Your loss is shared by the entire nation.

Alderman John S. Gaynor, Republican leader, offered the following resolution at yesterday's meeting of the board:

The sudden death of Colonel Theodore Roosevelt is a great blow to the people of this city.

Among us he was born, and here he commenced that remarkable public career which led him to the highest office in the gift of the people of the land.

As Police Commissioner of the City of New York, member of the State Legislature, United States Civil Service Commissioner, Assistant Secretary of the Navy, Governor of this State, Vice President, and then Chief Executive of this great nation, the services he rendered to his country and to humanity throughout the world will ever be enshrined in the memory of man.

A more forceful, vigorous, loyal

Continued on Page Five.

EMBOLISM CAUSED DEATH

Blood Clot, Physicians Announce, Killed Col. Roosevelt in His Sleep

WORKED UP TO THE LAST

Worn by Illness, Former President with Indomitable Will Kept Up Activities.

WAS IN PERIL IN HOSPITAL

Embolism Then Threatened His Life—Rheumatism Traced to Tooth Infected 20 Years Ago.

Special to The New York Times.

OYSTER BAY, L. I., Jan. 6.—Theodore Roosevelt, former President of the United States, died this morning between 4 and 4:15 o'clock while asleep in his bed at his home on Sagamore Hill, in this place.

His physicians said that the immediate cause of death was a clot of blood which detached itself from a vein and entered the lungs.

His sudden death took by surprise his physicians as well as all others who had been with him lately. It was announced that the blood clot was not directly due to the inflammatory rheumatism from which he had been suffering for two months, but must be traced to earlier conditions. One of the contributing causes was the fever which he contracted during his explorations in Brazil, when he discovered the River of Doubt early in 1914. This fever left a poison in the blood which had been a partial cause of several attacks of illness which he had suffered since that time.

Colonel Roosevelt was working hard as late as Saturday, dictating articles and letters. He spent Sunday quietly, but looked and felt well, until shortly before 11 o'clock, when he had difficulty in breathing. After treatment he felt better and returned to bed.

Mrs. Roosevelt looked in to see how he was sleeping at 2 o'clock this morning. He then appeared normal. Two hours later, James Amos, an old negro servant of the family, formerly with them at the White House, thought that there was something wrong with the manner in which Colonel Roosevelt was breathing. Amos had been placed in the next room to keep a close watch over Colonel Roosevelt, and went at once to the bedside. He was alarmed at the hollow sound of his breathing and summoned the trained nurse. When she arrived, the breathing had stopped. Dr. George W. Faller of Oyster Bay, the family physician, was summoned, and found that life had left the body a few minutes before.

Statement By Physicians.

Later, the following statement was given out by Dr. Faller and Drs. John H. Richard and John A. Hartwell of New York, who had Colonel Roosevelt under their care at Roosevelt Hospital:

Colonel Roosevelt had been suffering from an attack of inflammatory rheumatism for about two months. His progress had been entirely satisfactory and his condition had not given cause for special concern. On Sunday he was in good spirits and spent the evening with his family, dictating letters. He retired at 11 o'clock, and at 4 o'clock in the morning his manservant who occupied an adjoining room, noticed that, while sleeping quietly, Colonel Roosevelt's breathing was hollow. He died almost immediately, without awakening. The cause of death was an embolus.

GEORGE W. FALLER, M. D.
JOHN H. RICHARDS, M. D.
JOHN A. HARTWELL, M. D.

An embolus is a clot of blood. Dr. Faller said that it had probably occurred in the lungs, but might have been in the brain.

Colonel Roosevelt was taken from Roosevelt Hospital to Oyster Bay to spend Christmas with his family, but was expected to return for further treatment. The inflammatory rheumatism was due, in the opinion of his physicians, to an infected tooth, which had originally given trouble twenty years ago. Inflammatory rheumatism is not known to be a cause of embolism, and it is not believed that the rheumatism was responsible for his death, although it may have contributed to it.

Colonel Roosevelt suffered from pulmonary embolism at the Roosevelt Hospital three weeks ago, and was then in a critical condition for a time, but his recovery was thought to be thorough.

Mrs. Roosevelt was the only member of the family at home when the death occurred. Captain Archibald Roosevelt had left yesterday with his wife, formerly Miss Mary S. Lockwood, for Boston, on receiving word that her father was dying. Lieut. Col. Theodore Roosevelt, Jr., is in France with the Army of Occupation. Captain Kermit Roosevelt is also in France. His daughter-in-

"All the News That's Fit to Print."

The New York Times.

THE WEATHER
Fair today and Tuesday; diminishing northwest winds.
For weather report see next to last page.

VOL. LXVIII...NO. 22,206. .... NEW YORK, MONDAY, NOVEMBER 11, 1918. TWENTY-FOUR PAGES. TWO CENTS Metropolitan District 50 Mile Radius | THREE CENTS Within 200 Miles | FOUR CENTS Elsewhere

ARMISTICE SIGNED, END OF THE WAR! BERLIN SEIZED BY REVOLUTIONISTS; NEW CHANCELLOR BEGS FOR ORDER; OUSTED KAISER FLEES TO HOLLAND

SON FLEES WITH EX-KAISER

Hindenburg Also Believed to be Among Those in His Party.

ALL ARE HEAVILY ARMED

Automobiles Bristle with Rifles as Fugitives Arrive at Dutch Frontier.

ON THEIR WAY TO DE STEEG

Belgians Yell to Them, "Are You On Your Way to Paris?"

LONDON, Nov. 10.—Both the former German Emperor and his eldest son, Frederick William, crossed the Dutch frontier Sunday morning, ac-

Kaiser Fought Hindenburg's Call for Abdication; Failed to Get Army's Support in Keeping Throne

By GEORGE RENWICK.

Copyright, 1918, by THE NEW YORK TIMES.
Special Cable to THE NEW YORK TIMES.

AMSTERDAM, Nov. 10.—I learn on very good authority that the Kaiser made a determined effort to stave off abdication. He went to headquarters with the deliberate intention of bringing the army around to his side. In this he failed miserably.

His main support consisted of a number of officers, nearly all of Prussian regiments, who formed themselves into two regiments and placed themselves at his Majesty's disposal. To do anything with such support was seen, of course, to be Gilbertian.

During the night the Kaiser called the Crown Prince, Hindenburg, and General Gröner to him, and the consultation lasted a couple of hours. Both officers strongly pressed the Kaiser to bow to the inevitable, and Hindenburg informed him that any more delay in coming to a decision to abdicate would certainly have the most terrible consequences and lead to serious events in the army. For those consequences Hindenburg said he must refuse responsibility.

The Crown Prince, it is said, was the first to give way. General Gröner fully supported Hindenburg's view, but when the conference broke up the Kaiser remained unconvinced of the advisability of abdication. He is said to have come to his final decision an hour or so later, after several communications had reached him from Berlin and after another short and stormy talk with Hindenburg.

Meanwhile, his son-in-law, the Duke of Brunswick, for himself and his heir, had abdicated. "Brunswick's Fated Chieftain" was forced without fighting to abdicate. Reports have it that the republican movement in Brunswick, which long before the war was chafing under autocratic conditions, began to be noticed even before it was set in motion at Kiel.

Kaiser Shivered as He Signed Abdication

LONDON, Nov 10—Emperor William signed his letter of abdication on Saturday morning at the German Grand Headquarters in the presence of Crown Prince Frederick William and Field Marshal Hindenburg, according to a dispatch from Amsterdam to the Exchange Telegraph Company.

The Crown Prince signed his

BERLIN TROOPS JOIN REVOLT

Reds Shell Building in Which Officers Vainly Resist.

THRONGS DEMAND REPUBLIC

Revolutionary Flag on Royal Palace—Crown Prince's Palace Also Seized.

GENERAL STRIKE IS BEGUN

Burgomaster and Police Submit—War Office Now Under Socialist Control.

LONDON, Nov. 10. — The greater part of Berlin is in control of revolutionists, the former Kaiser has fled to Holland, and Friedrich Ebert, the new

Socialist Chancellor Appeals to All Germans To Help Him Save Fatherland from Anarchy

BERNE, Nov. 10, (Associated Press.)—In an address to the people, the new German Chancellor, Friedrich Ebert, says:

Citizens: The ex-Chancellor, Prince Max of Baden, in agreement with all the Secretaries of State, has handed over to me the task of liquidating his affairs as Chancellor. I am on the point of forming a new Government in accord with the various parties, and will keep public opinion freely informed of the course of events.

The new Government will be a Government of the people. It must make every effort to secure in the quickest possible time peace for the German people and consolidate the liberty which they have won.

The new Government has taken charge of the administration, to preserve the German people from civil war and famine and to accomplish their legitimate claim to autonomy. The Government can solve this problem only if all the officials in town and country will help.

I know it will be difficult for some to work with the new men who have taken charge of the empire, but I appeal to their love of the people. Lack of organization would in this heavy time mean anarchy in Germany and the surrender of the country to tremendous misery. Therefore, help your native country with fearless, indefatigable work for the future, every one at his post.

I demand every one's support in the hard task awaiting us. You know how seriously the war has menaced the provisioning of the people, which is the first condition of the people's existence. The political transformation should not trouble the people. The food supply is the first duty of all, whether in town or country, and they should not embarrass, but rather aid, the production of food supplies and their transport to the towns.

Food shortage signifies pillage and robbery, with great misery. The poorest will suffer the most, and the industrial worker will be affected hardest. All who illicitly lay hands on food supplies or other supplies of prime necessity or the means of transport necessary for their distribution will be guilty in the highest degree toward the community.

I ask you immediately to leave the streets and remain orderly and calm.

WAR ENDS AT 6 O'CLOCK THIS MORNING

The State Department in Washi gton Made the Announcement at 2:45 o'Clock.

ARMISTICE WAS SIGNED IN FRANCE AT MIDNIGHT

Terms Include Withdrawal from Alsace-Lorraine, Disarming and Demobilization of Army and Navy, and Occupation of Strategic Naval and Military Points.

By The Associated Press.

WASHINGTON, Monday, Nov. 11, 2:48 A.

"All the News That's Fit to Print."

The New York Times.

THE WEATHER
Fair today; tomorrow rain or snow; moderate northwesterly winds.
For full weather report see Page 19.

VOL. LXVI...NO. 21,601. NEW YORK, FRIDAY, MARCH 16, 1917.—TWENTY PAGES. ONE CENT In Greater New York. | TWO CENTS New England and Middle States. | THREE CENTS Elsewhere.

REVOLUTION IN RUSSIA; CZAR ABDICATES; MICHAEL MADE REGENT, EMPRESS IN HIDING; PRO-GERMAN MINISTERS REPORTED SLAIN

RAILWAY STRIKE ORDERED TO BEGIN TOMORROW NIGHT

Managers and Heads of Brotherhoods End Final Conference, Both Defiant.

WILSON NOW THE ONLY HOPE

President Seems to Have No Authority, but May Make Appeal to Patriotism.

FIVE DAYS' GRACE FOR MILK

Travelers to Have Time to Get Home—Appeals for the Public's Approval.

The eight-hour fight between the 250 railroads of the United States and the 400,000 trainmen has placed the country again face to face with a nation-wide railway strike.

The National Conference Committee of the Railways yesterday defied the ultimatum of the four brotherhoods that the eight-hour day should be put into effect at once, and the labor chiefs formally served notice that their strike order stood and that a progressive

Government Heads Hold a Mysterious Conference

Special to The New York Times.

WASHINGTON, March 15.—A conference surrounded with much mystery took place late this afternoon in the office of the Secretary of State. In addition to Secretary Lansing, it was attended by Mr. Baker, the Secretary of War; Mr. Gregory, the Attorney General; Mr. Daniels, the Secretary of the Navy; Mr. Polk, the Counsellor of the State Department, and Mr. Woolsey, personal legal adviser to the Secretary of State.

After the conference it was said by one of those who attended it that no particular subject had been discussed. It had been devoted, he indicated, to many questions that naturally came up for discussion at this critical period in the international relations of the United States. Elsewhere, however, the impression was given that the conference was called to consider matters of rather pressing importance.

FRYATT'S FATE FOR OUR GUNNERS

German Threat to Put to Death Crews of Any Armed American Ships They Capture.

WARNING IN MUNICH PAPER

Assumes That President "Realizes Fate to Which He Is Sub-

LONDON HAILS REVOLUTION

Expected Czar's Overthrow and Sees Brighter Prospects for the Allies.

THINK THE COUP DECISIVE

Well-Informed Observers Believe the Patriotic War Party Has Made Its Control Secure.

FEAR NO SEPARATE PEACE

With Weak Ruler Deposed and Pro-German Advisers Ousted, They Predict New Victories.

Special Cable to THE NEW YORK TIMES.

LONDON, Friday, March 16.—It is the belief in well-informed circles here that the Provisional Government which has been set up in Russia by the military party will be able to keep the upper hand in maintaining a policy that means the uninterruptedly vigorous prosecution of the war to a victorious end.

The overthrow of the Czar was expected, and observers here are confident that the Grand Duke as regent will have the solid support of the war party, while they are equally sure of the elimination of any element with a pro-Ger-

Duma Appeals to the Army for Unity Against Foe; Gives Pledge of No Weakening or Suspension of War

LONDON, March 15.—The Reuter correspondent at Petrograd telegraphs under date of yesterday:

"The Military Committee of the Duma has asked all the officers not yet employed by the committee to undertake the organization of the soldiers who joined the people, and help guard the capital. The committee issued a statement, pointing out that at the present moment, when facing an enemy who wished to take advantage of the temporary weakness of the country, it was absolutely necessary to make every effort to maintain the power of the army. It added that the blood of the Russians who had died during the two and a half years of war pledged the people to do this.

"The President of the Duma sent telegrams to the commanders of the Baltic and Black Sea fleets, to the chiefs of the armies on the northern, southwestern, western, Rumanian, and Caucasus fronts, and to the Chief of the General Staff, requesting that the army and navy preserve absolute calm, and to be sure that the struggle against the foreign enemy was not suspended or weakened even for a single moment. The telegram sent these commanders added:

> As hitherto, the army and navy must continue firmly and valiantly to defend the country, and while the Provisional Committee is aided by the military element in the capital and with the moral support of the people in restoring calm and regular activity, each officer, soldier, and sailor should fulfill his duty.

"The officers of the Petrograd garrison at a general meeting unanimously agreed to recognize the authority of the Executive Committee of the Duma until the formation of a permanent Government.

"An imperial bodyguard regiment rode into Petrograd today. It is estimated that there are now 60,000 troops in the capital."

People in Revolt Burn and Slay in Streets of Russia's Capital

Fashionable Hotel Riddled by Machine Guns When Pro-German Shoots at Crowd—Count Fredericks's Home Set on Fire and Family Ill-Treated—General de Knorring Shot.

Stuermer and Protopopoff Reported Assassinated

Special Cable to THE NEW YORK TIMES.

ons. On the whole, however, the bloodshed, compared with the magnitude of the achievement, has been infinitesimal. Regiment after regiment, brought in from outside the capital, promptly joined their comrades on the side of the people, and when a special body of

ARMY JOINS WITH THE DUMA

Three Days of Conflict Follow Food Riots in Capital.

POPULACE TAKE UP ARMS

But End Comes Suddenly When Troops Guarding Old Ministers Surrender.

CZAR FINDS CAPITAL GONE

Returns from Front After Receiving Warning from Duma and Gives Up His Throne.

Empress Reported Under Guard or Hiding From Angry People

Special Cable to THE NEW YORK TIMES.

PETROGRAD, March 14. (Dispatch to The London Daily Chronicle.)—The Empress of Russia has been placed under guard.

LONDON, March 15.—According to information received here the Russian people have been most distrustful during recent events of the personal influence of Empress Alexandra. She was supposed to exercise the greatest influence over Emperor Nicholas.

It is stated that her whereabouts

Leading Figures in Russian Revolution.

Czar Nicholas II Who has Abdicated.

Czarevitch Alexis 12 Yrs old who will succeed to the Throne.

As was the case last Fall, when the railroads and the unions broke off diplomatic relations, the only hope of averting a strike lies with President Wilson, and both the managers and the brotherhood leaders remained in New York overnight in the expectation that Mr. Wilson would take a hand in the situation. However, it is a moot question what steps the Government could take to prevent paralysis of transportation facilities and consequent weakening of the nation's resources in the international crisis. The general opinion among officials in Washington last night seemed to be that the President could do little beyond appealing to the patriotism of both sides. A provision to empower him to take over the roads in such an emergency was among the Administration recommendations for railway legislation which failed at the last session of Congress.

Daniel Willard, President of the Baltimore & Ohio, and a member of the National Defense Council, who has been watching the strike developments in New York for the last three days, left late yesterday afternoon for Washington.

Last August after the two sides broke, President Wilson sent the members of the United States Board of Mediation and Conciliation to New York to bring the two sides together. The board failed, and when a strike order was about to be issued, the President sent his Secretary, Joseph P. Tumulty, to New York, with a request that the managers and the labor leaders come to the White House. It was after he kept the two sides in Washington all during the month of August that the Adamson law was passed after a call for a national strike, effective Sept. 4, had been issued. Both sides as represented here now are in readiness to go to Washington.

Monday is decision day for the Supreme Court, and if it should hand down a decision on the Adamson law then it might lead to a renewal of conferences between the two sides regardless of the strike situation. The railroad managers have all along expressed the opinion that the law would be held invalid. The haste of the brotherhoods in forcing the issue has caused the managers to believe that the labor leaders also think the law will be thrown out. While the brotherhood heads say the action of the court one way or the other will not affect their demands, the railroad managers believe that the invalidating of the Adamson law would give them an advantage.

The word of the deadlock here yesterday was flashed to all parts of the country last night, and notices of embargoes and strike preparations were put out by nearly all of the railroads. Appeals to the patriotism of the men were made by many roads. President Wilson was among the first to get notice of the break.

Joseph Hartigan, City Commissioner of Weights and Measures, was quick to appeal to the brotherhoods to permit the movement of food trains into this city. In reply to his plea he received this letter, signed by the chiefs of the four organizations:

"Every indication now seems to warrant the statement that the freight train, engine, and yard employes on certain railways entering this city will peaceably withdraw from service at 7 P. M., Saturday, March 17, and that the employes on other lines will continue in service for several days thereafter, making it possible, in our opinion, to furnish this city food and fuel supplies for several days after the strike becomes effective.

"We regret exceedingly the necessity

Continued on Page 20.

BERNE, Switzerland, March 15, (via Paris.)—The crews of armed American merchantmen who venture to fire upon German submarines before a state of war exists between Germany and the United States, must expect to meet the fate of Captain Fryatt, warns the Munich Neueste Nachrichten, a copy of which has reached Berne, in commenting on the announcement of the State Department that American merchantmen will be armed.

"We assume," the newspaper says, "that President Wilson realizes the fate to which he is subjecting his artillerymen. According to the German prize laws it is unneutral support of the enemy if a neutral ship takes part in hostilities. If such a ship opposes the Prize Court then it must be treated as an enemy ship. The prize rules specify as to the crews of such ships. If, without being attached to the forces of the enemy, they take part in hostilities or make forcible resistance, they may be treated according to the usages of war.

"If President Wilson, knowing these provisions of International law, proceeds to arm American merchantmen, he must assume responsibility for the eventuality that American seamen will meet the fate of Captain Fryatt."

The Captain Fryatt referred to in the foregoing dispatch was Captain Charles Fryatt of the Great Eastern Railway steamer Brussels. He was tried before a German naval court-martial in July, 1916, and sentenced to death, on a charge that he had attempted to ram the German submarine T-33. The sentence of the court-martial was executed.

STONE ASKS FOR LIST OF AMERICAN SHIPS

Senate Adopts His Resolution, Which Causes Much Speculation in Washington.

Special to The New York Times.

WASHINGTON, March 15.—Senator Stone of Missouri caused some comment at the Capitol today by introducing a resolution directing the Secretary of Commerce to give the Senate a full list of sea-going vessels applying for American registry between Jan. 1, 1916, and March 15, 1917; the name and character of such vessels before and after registration, the names of the ships' owners, and the precise date of application for registry and date of receiving it. The resolution was read and adopted without discussion, and Secretary Redfield will forward the information tomorrow.

There was a good deal of speculation as to why Mr. Stone, Chairman of the Committee on Foreign Relations, should want this information made public. One suggestion was that he might think that some belligerent nation was permitting its ships to be registered in the United States, so that through the later torpedoing of these ships by German submarines the United States might be drawn into the war. It was suggested that if Mr. Stone wanted the information for his own use, he could have got it by telephoning the Department of Commerce.

Mr. Stone showed no desire to explain his resolution and seemed prepared to rebuff questioners. He said that his resolution spoke for itself. When asked if the changes in the ownership of the Algonquin had prompted his resolution, the Senator said that he would not be interviewed.

As the situation is explained to THE NEW YORK TIMES correspondent, the revolution simply means that German sympathizers within the Russian Government have been overthrown, and that no chance remains for a separate peace being secretly arranged with Germany. This, it is felt, is the real basis of the revolution that has worked such a sudden change in Russian politics.

This revolution, which has been on the verge of boiling over for months, reached its crisis three days ago, when the military leaders, with the Duma behind them, started outbreaks in Petrograd and Moscow. It is evident from the way in which the uprising was conducted, says THE NEW YORK TIMES correspondent's informant, that it had been carefully planned and skillfully executed.

"After it got under way," he says, "there was no hesitation of movement until the members of the military party were masters of the situation. The details of what occurred in Petrograd and Moscow are lacking, but enough is known to show that they have been in a fever of sanguinary revolution for the last three days.

"Dashes of troops against the headquarters of the pro-German leaders, with the capture of Protopopoff and Stürmer as prisoners of war, were conspicuous features of the revolution. The houses of German sympathizers were burned in both cities, and the occupants either taken captive or forced to flee.

"Now that the military party is in control the situation is said to be settling down, with every prospect that the aim of the Revolutionists will be accomplished."

In fact, the situation was described last night as being "entirely satisfactory."

For months, said the informant of THE NEW YORK TIMES correspondent, Great Britain had been expecting an outcome of the Russian political crisis that would mean the solid intrenchment of the war party and the downfall of those seeking a separate peace with Germany. Now it may be confidently expected that Russia will play her part in the war with even greater vigor than before.

German-Born Czarina Blamed.

The Daily Chronicle in its leading article says:

"From a very early period the German-born Czarina and the clique of pro-German reactionaries whom her influence made powerful with the Czar were bent on ending the war prematurely in the interests of reaction. The Ministers set up under these auspices have for over two years acted in defiance of public opinion. Their policy was not obscure; they hampered the army in respect of munitions, disorganized the country in respect of its distributive services, brought about artificial famine in a land which is one of the world's chief food producers, and themselves, through police agents, tried to stir up abortive revolts in order that they might plead military failure and internal revolution as a reason for withdrawing from the war.

"The people foiled them for long by magnificent and much enduring patriotism. When the Government left the army without munitions the local authorities—the zemstvos and unions of towns—stepped in and organized their

Continued on Page 2.

Exchange Telegraph's Copenhagen correspondent sends the following:

"A telegram to the Extrabladet reports that the Russian Consul in Haparanda states that the pro-German ex-Prime Minister, Boris Stürmer, and Minister of Home Affairs Protopopoff have been murdered."

Special Cable to THE NEW YORK TIMES.

LONDON, Friday, March 16.—Belated dispatches from Petrograd, giving details of the revolution in Russia, are arriving here. A dispatch to The Morning Post, dated Wednesday, says:

"Every weapon save only heavy artillery has been freely used in Petrograd streets for four days past, and today there is still considerable firing at various points at intervals. Rifles, revolvers, machine guns, and armored motors—all have been used and are still in use.

"The military hotel, formerly the Astoria Hotel, which lodged exclusively officers from the front, their wives and families, with the majority of officers present here as representatives of the Allies, was subjected to a heavy fusillade from machine guns on armored motors, entirely as the result of what was represented as provocation on the part of a pro-German resident, who fired upon the people from the windows.

General's Daughter Wounded.

"The daughter of the Russian General Prince Tumanoff, who is now commanding a cavalry division at the front, was severely wounded in the neck, and her rooms were ruined by the fusillade. A mob of armed men—soldiers, sailors, and civilians—thoroughly searched the Astoria, and disarmed all the Russian officers, but showed marked consideration for the allied officers.

"Similar scenes have been enacted throughout Petrograd, while in the transpontine regions occupied by the factory population, heavy fighting has been in progress for days, until the alleged excessive cruelty of the police caused the Cossacks and soldiery to espouse the side of the people.

"The ease with which the whole of the capital fell into the hands of the revolutionaries very greatly mitigated the bloodshed inevitable in civil tumults, but the butcher's bill is undoubtedly heavy enough."

Supplementing this by a telegram dated Thursday the same correspondent says:

"Precisely one week ago peaceful street demonstrations, at first largely composed of women and childen, were made in protest against the inadequate supply of black bread. The police, unable to cope with the movement, which they felt bound to crush by the usual police methods, called in the aid of the Cossacks.

"The workmen, who had held aloof from the overt demonstrations as organized bodies and who were at first represented only by the younger, irresponsible workingmen, were enraged at the rough treatment by the police of their women and children and were encouraged by the obvious reluctance of the Cossacks and soldiery generally to back up the police oppression. Finally the Cossacks turned on the police, who fled before them, and there was a pandemonium of irregular shooting.

"Matters were not improved by the setting at liberty of political prisoners and criminals and the burning of pris-

voy also came in it felt that the old régime had fallen indeed.

Rowdy Element Breaks Loose.

"In the meantime the red revolutionary parties were preaching anarchy in all its forms, and the rowdy elements of the population of the great city were busy indulging their professional instincts.

"Happily the worst incentive to violence—alcohol in all its forms—was almost unprocurable, and the disciplined sense of the soldiery, who now formed the majority, was against excesses which disgraced what was now felt to be the great cause of national freedom.

"M. Rodzianko, at the head of the Duma Committee, soon issued commonsense orders for the disarming of civilians and for the checking of red revolutionary manifestations. The soldiers and people themselves put a stop to the looting. Throughout the city a careful search was made for stores of foodstuffs, which were promptly put on sale. The results warrant the belief that unscrupulous profiteering on an incredible scale had long been prevalent.

"At the present moment a careful search is being made for higher military officers and other functionaries, who are being induced to accept the new conditions and carry on their public duties or undergo arrest. The secret police, that scourge of the Russian nation whose service is despised by all, and which has been for a generation past the refuge for defaulters and detected miscreants of all other public services receive no mercy, but the ordinary police are being merely put under arrest.

Police Stations Destroyed.

The Petrograd correspondent of The Daily Chronicle sent the following, bearing Wednesday's date:

"In Moscow, Kiev, and Kharkoff the troops have signified adherence to the new movement, and in Moscow the police have surrendered of their own accord. The Department of Police in Petrograd has been rifled and the building of the secret police, that hotbed of political intrigue, has been burned, and all police stations in town looted and their contents burned or scattered.

"The ordinary and political police, in some cases, were killed. In other cases, they were dragged from their hiding places and lodged in dark cells in the fortress of St. Peter and St. Paul, where so many have suffered martyrdom for Russian freedom. The political prisoners, victims of the old régime, have been freed from the jails, and many are now taking part in the reorganization of the Government."

Count Fredericks's Home Burned.

LONDON, Friday, March 16.—The Times Petrograd correspondent describes the sacking of the residence of Count Fredericks, Minister of the Imperial Court and Aide de Camp to the Emperor, as one of the most deplorable incidents of the revolt.

Count Fredericks's house was set on fire. His aged wife was carried out fainting. His daughter, who is frail, rushed out, carrying her favorite dog. The girl was ill-treated by the drunken mob, and the dog was killed. Both women eventually were taken to a place of safety.

Count Fredericks is now in attendance upon former Emperor Nicholas.

General de Knorring was ordered to report to the Duma, but refused to comply with the summons. On the contrary, he armed himself and the janitor

Continued on Page 2.

is in seclusion, fearing the populace.

The Empress Alexandra before her marriage to the Emperor of Russia in 1894 was the German Princess Alix of Hesse-Darmstadt.

PETROGRAD, March 15.—Emperor Nicholas of Russia has abdicated, and Grand Duke Michael Alexandrovitch, his younger brother, has been named as Regent.

The Russian Ministry, charged with corruption and incompetence, has been swept out of office. One Minister, Alexander Protopopoff, the head of the Interior Department, is reported to have been killed, and the other Ministers, as well as the President of the Imperial Council, are under arrest.

A new national Cabinet is announced, with Prince Lvoff as President of the Council and Premier, and the other offices held by the men who are close to the Russian people.

Petrograd has been the scene of one of the most remarkable risings in history, beginning with minor food riots and labor strikes last week Thursday. The people's cry for food reached the hearts of the soldiers, and one by one the regiments rebelled, until finally those troops which had for a time stood loyal to the Government gathered up their arms and marched into the ranks of the revolutionists.

Duma President Leading Figure.

Michael V. Rodzianko, President of the Duma, was the leading figure among the Deputies, who unanimously decided to oppose the imperial order, issued last week, for a dissolution of the House. They continued their sessions, and M. Rodzianko informed the Emperor, then at the front, that the hour had struck when the will of the people must prevail.

Even the Imperial Council realized the gravity of the situation, and added its appeal to that of the Duma that the Emperor should take steps to give the people a policy and government in accordance with their desires and in order that there should be no interference with carrying on the war to a victorious ending.

The Emperor hastened back to the capital, only to find that the revolution had been successful and that a new Government was in control.

The Empress, who, it is alleged, has been influential in the councils opposed to the wishes of the people, is reported to have fled or to be in hiding.

Although considerable fighting took place, it is not believed that the casualties are large. One report says that they do not exceed 500.

A few defenders of the old régime put up a last feeble defense last night from the roofs of the wrecked Astoria Military Hotel and St. Isaac's Cathedral, facing on two sides of the same square.

The city is now quiet and perfect order prevails. So far as is known, no foreigners were injured.

The Imperial Palace at Tsarskoe-Selo is said to have been in a state of siege, but thus far no firing has been reported between the guards defending the palace and the revolutionists and troops.

According to one report the Emperor expected trouble to follow from his decree dissolving the Duma, and so warned the residents of Tsarkoe-Selo to arrange to remain in the suburb for an indefinite period.

Began From Strikes a Week Ago.

The most phenomenal feature of the revolution was the swift and orderly transition whereby the control of the city passed from the régime of the old Government into the hands of its opponents.

The visible signs of revolution began on Thursday, March 8. Strikes were declared in several big munitions factories as a protest against the shortage of bread. Men and women gathered and marched through the streets, most of them in an orderly fashion. A few bread shops were broken into in that section of the city beyond the Neva, and several minor clashes between strikers and police occurred.

Squads of mounted troops appeared, but during Thursday and Friday the utmost friendliness seemed to exist between the troops and the people.

This early period of the uprising bore the character of a mock revolution, staged for an immense audience. Cossacks, charging down the street, did so in a half-hearted fashion, plainly without malice or intent to harm the crowds, which they playfully dispersed. The troops exchanged good-natured raillery with the working men and women, and as they rode were cheered by the populace.

Long lines of soldiers stationed in dramatic attitudes across Nevsky Prospect, with their guns pointed at an imaginary foe, appeared to be taking part in a realistic tableau. Machine guns, firing rounds of blank cartridges, seemed only to add another realistic touch to a tremendous theatric production which was using the whole city as a stage.

On Saturday, however, apparently without provocation, the troops were ordered to fire on people marching in Nevsky Prospect. The troops refused to fire, and the police, replacing them, fired rifles and machine guns.

Then came a clash between troops and police, which continued in desultory fashion throughout Saturday night and Sunday. The Nevsky Prospect was cleared of traffic by the police and notices were posted by the commander of the Petrograd military district warning the people that any attempt to congregate would be met by force.

Until Sunday evening, however, there was no intimation that the affair would grow to the proportions of a revolution. The first serious outbreak came at 6 o'clock, when the men of the Volynsky Regiment shot their officers and revolted when they received an order to fire upon striking workingmen in one of the factory districts.

Another regiment detailed against the mutineers also joined the revolt. The news spread rapidly to the other barracks and four more regiments went over. Some of the revolting troops marched to the St. Peter and St. Paul Fortress on the left bank of the Neva, and after a brief skirmish with the garrison took possession of it.

Dissension spread among the troops, who did not understand why they should be compelled to take violent measures against fellow-citizens whose chief offense was that they were hungry and were asking the Government to supply bread. Several regiments deserted. A pitched battle began between the troops who stood with the Government and those who, refusing to obey orders, had mutinied, and even slain their officers.

A long night fight took place between the mutinous regiments and the police at the end of St Catharine Canal, immediately in front of the historic church built over the spot where Alexander II. was killed by a bomb. The police finally fled to the rooftops all over the city and were seen no more in the streets during the entire term of the fighting.

Turning Point in Revolution.

Still, on Monday morning the Government troops appeared to control all the principal squares of the city. Then came a period when it was impossible to distinguish one side from the other. There was no definite line between the factions. The turning point appeared to come about 3 o'clock in the afternoon. For two hours the opposing regiments passively confronted each other along the wide Liteiny Prospect in almost complete silence.

From time to time emissaries from the revolutionary side rode to the opposing ranks and exhorted them to join the side of the people. For a while the result seemed to hang in the balance. The troops appeared irresolute, awaiting

Grand Duke Michael Alexandrovitch who has been named Regent

Michael Rodzianko, Head of the Revolution and the Temporary Government

Prince Lvoff Heads Cabinet; Milukoff Foreign Minister

PETROGRAD, via London, Friday, March 16.—The members of the new National Cabinet are announced as follows:

Premier, President of the Council, and Minister of the Interior—Prince Georges E. Lvoff.

Foreign Minister—Professor Paul N. Milukoff.

Minister of Public Instruction—Professor Manuiloff of Moscow University.

Minister of War and Navy, ad Interim—A. J. Guchkoff, formerly President of the Duma.

Minister of Agriculture—M. Ichingareff, Deputy from Petrograd.

Minister of Finance—M. Tereschtenko, Deputy from Kiev.

Minister of Justice — Deputy Kerenski of Saratoff.

Minister of Communications—N. V. Nekrasoff, Vice President of the Duma.

Controller of State—M. Godneff, Deputy from Kazan.

cording to advices from The Hague. His reported destination is De Steeg, near Utrecht.

The former German Emperor's party, which is believed to include Field Marshal von Hindenburg, arrived at Eysden, [midway between Liege and Maastricht,] on the Dutch frontier, at 7:30 o'clock Sunday morning, according to Daily Mail advices.

Practically the whole German General Staff accompanied the former Emperor, and ten automobiles carried the party. The automobiles were bristling with rifles, and all the fugitives were armed.

The ex-Kaiser was in uniform. He alighted at the Eysden station and paced the platform, smoking a cigarette.

Many photographs were taken by [of?] the members of the Imperial party. On the whole the people were very quiet, but Belgians among them yelled out "En voyage a Paris." (Are you on your way to Paris?)

Chatting with the members of the staff, the former Emperor, the correspondent says, did not look in the least distressed. A few minutes later an imperial train, including restaurant and sleeping cars, ran into the station. Only servants were aboard.

The engine returned to Visé, Belgium, and brought back a second train, in which were a large number of staff officers and others, and also stores of food.

The preparations began for the departure at 10 o'clock this morning, but at 10:40 o'clock the train was still at Eysden. The blinds of the train were all drawn.

The Daily Mail remarks that, if the party arrived in Holland armed, all of them must be interned.

While other dispatches con-

Continued on Page Three.

afterward.

Before placing his signature to the document, an urgent message from Philipp Scheidemann, who was a Socialist member without portfolio in the Imperial Cabinet, was handed to the Emperor. He read it with a shiver. Then he signed the paper, saying:

"It may be for the good of Germany."

The Emperor was deeply moved. He consented to sign the document only when he got the news of the latest events in the empire.

The ex-Kaiser and former Crown Prince were expected to take leave of their troops on Saturday, but nothing had then been settled regarding their future movements.

GERMAN DYNASTIES BEING WIPED OUT

King of Wuerttemberg Abdicates — Sovereign of Saxony to Follow Suit.

PRINCES MAY BE EXILED

Socialists Are Demanding That Every Sovereign in the Empire Shall be Dethroned.

LONDON, Nov. 10.—A Havas dispatch from Basle says:

"Wilhelm II., the reigning King of the monarchy of Württemberg, abdicated on Friday night."

A Wolff Bureau dispatch from Stuttgart, by way of Amsterdam, says that the King has issued a proclamation saying that his person would never serve to hinder the development of the wishes of the people.

According to a report received from Berne, the German Socialists are demanding that every dynasty in Germany be suppressed and all the Princes exiled. It is reported that the Kings of Bavaria and Saxony intend to abdicate soon.

Here is a list of the rules, until several days ago, of the various parts of the German Empire. Those who have abdicated and those reported to be on the point of abdication are marked by an asterisk:

ANHALT—Duke Edward, son of the late Duke Friedrich of Anhalt and of Princess Antoinette of Saxe-Altenberg. Succeeded his brother April 18, 1861.

BADEN—Friedrich II., succeeded to

Continued on Page Two.

MORE WARSHIPS JOIN THE REDS

Four Dreadnoughts in Kiel Harfor Espouse the Revolutionary Cause.

GUARDSHIPS ALSO GO OVER

Those Protecting Mines in the Great Belt and the Baltic Abandon Their Posts.

LONDON, Nov. 10.—The crews of the German dreadnoughts Posen, Ostfriesland, Nassau, and Oldenburg, in Kiel Harbor, have joined the revolution, says a Copenhagen dispatch. Marines occupied the lock gates at Ostmoor and fought down a coast artillery division which offered resistance.

According to the British Wireless Service three German destroyers have anchored outside of Stockholm. All the guardships in the Baltic, it is said, have joined the revolutionary movement.

Six more cruisers flying the red flag arrived at Hamburg last night, says a Wolff News Agency dispatch received in Copenhagen.

An Amsterdam dispatch states that the Berlin Vossische Zeitung and Vorwarts confirm the fact that the inception of the revolution at Kiel was mistaken for the idea that a cruise had been ordered and that it was intended to give battle to the British fleet.

Up to Friday night the number of persons killed at Kiel was twenty-eight, according to information re-

Continued on Page Three.

Socialist Chancellor, has taken command of the situation. The revolt is spreading throughout Germany with great rapidity.

Dispatches received in London today announce these startling developments. The Workmen's and Soldiers' Council is now administering the municipal government of the German capital.

The War Ministry has submitted, and its acts are valid only when countersigned by a Socialist representative. The official Wolff telegraphic agency has been taken over by the Reds.

The red flag has been hoisted over the royal palace and the Brandenburg Gate. The former Crown Prince's palace is also in possession of the revolutionists.

There was severe fighting in Berlin between 8 and 10 o'clock last night and a violent cannonade was heard from the heart of the city.

Burgomaster and Police Join.

A Copenhagen dispatch states that Dr. Liebknecht, the famous Socialist, who spent many months in prison for antagonizing the German Imperial Government and who was recently released, has issued the following announcement in Berlin in behalf of the Workmen's and Soldiers' Council:

"The Presidency of the police, as well as the Chief Command, is in our hands. Our comrades will be released."

A dispatch from Berne states that the Burgomaster of Berlin has placed himself and his staff at the disposal of the new Government.

Some German newspapers describe the movement as Bolshevism. The people are shouting "Long live the Republic!" and singing the "Marseillaise."

Officers Shelled by Reds.

When revolutionary soldiers attempted to enter a building in Berlin in which they supposed that a number of offi-

cording to a Wolff Bureau dispatch, has issued the following proclamation:

Fellow-Citizens: This day the people's deliverance has been fulfilled. The Social Democratic Party has undertaken to form a Government. It has invited the Independent Socialist Party to enter the Government with equal rights.

cers were concealed shots were fired from the windows. The Reds then began shelling the building. Many persons were killed and wounded before the officers surrendered.

When the cannonade began the people thought the Reichsbank was being bombarded, and thousands rushed to the square in front of the Crown Prince's palace. It was later determined that other buildings were under fire. Among those killed in the fighting at the "Cockchafer" Barracks was one of the workmen's leaders known as "Comrade" Habersroth.

The Reds, at last reports, were maintaining order.

Berlin was occupied by forces of the Soldiers' and Workmen's Councils on Saturday afternoon, according to a Wolff Bureau report received in Copenhagen. News of Emperor William's abdication was received in the city on that afternoon with general rejoicing, which was tempered by the fear that it had come too late.

Russians Aid in Outbreak.

How far the example of the Russian Bolsheviki influenced the German upheaval is an interesting question. Red flags figured frequently in the various risings and Chancellor Ebert's motor car floats the international emblem.

The shoulder straps were torn from the uniforms of officers in a number of German cities and even the soldiers' insignia were stripped from them. Russian prisoners played a part in the demonstrations in two or three towns.

Delegates of the revolutionary German navy arrived in Berlin on Friday, according to a dispatch from Copenhagen. They conferred for several hours with the Minister of Marine and with members of the Reichstag majority parties.

It is stated that Hugo Haase, a Socialist leader in the Reichstag, has the situation at Hamburg in hand.

It is officially announced from Berlin, according to a Copenhagen dispatch, that the War Ministry has placed itself at the disposal of Chancellor Ebert. This action was for the purpose of assuring the provisioning of the army and assisting in the solution of demobilization problems.

Serious food difficulties are expected in Germany, owing to the stoppage of trains. The Council of the Regency will take the most drastic steps to re-establish order.

In the new German Government there will be only three representatives of the majority parties, namely, Erzberger, Gothein, and Richthofen, says a dispatch from Copenhagen. The other posts will be occupied by Socialists and independents.

Reds Announce Success.

BERLIN, Nov. 9, (German Wireless to London, Nov. 10)—(Associated Press.)—The German People's Government has been instituted in the greater part of Berlin. The garrison has gone over to the Government.

The Workmen's and Soldiers' Council has declared a general strike. Troops and machine guns have been placed at the disposal of the Council. Guards which had been stationed at the public offices and other buildings have been withdrawn.

Friedrich Ebert (Vice President of the Social Democratic Party) is carrying on the Chancellorship.

The text of a statement issued by the People's Government reads:

In the course of the forenoon of Saturday the formation of a new German People's Government was initiated. The greater part of the Berlin garrison, and other troops stationed there temporarily, went over to the new Government.

The leaders of the deputations of the Social Democratic Party declared that they would not shoot against the people. They said they would, in accordance with the People's Government, intercede in favor of the maintenance of order. Thereupon in the offices and public buildings the guards which had been stationed there were withdrawn.

The business of the Imperial Chancellor is being carried on by the Social Democratic Deputy, Herr Ebert.

It is presumed that, apart from the representatives of the recent majority group, three independent Social Democrats will enter the future Government.

Scheidemann Exhorts Calm.

Deputy Scheidemann, (leader of the majority Socialists in the Reichstag,) in a speech today, said:

"The Kaiser and the Crown Prince have abdicated. The dynasty

Continued on Page Four.

hand, and the allied Governments and the United States, on the other, has been signed.

The State Department announced at 2:45 o'clock this morning that Germany had signed.

The department's announcement simply said: "The armistice has been signed."

The world war will end this morning at 6 o'clock, Washington time, 11 o'clock Paris time.

The armistice was signed by the German representatives at midnight.

This announcement was made by the State Department at 2:50 o'clock this morning.

The announcement was made verbally by an officila of the State Department in this form:

"The armistice has been signed. It was signed at 5 o clock A. M., Paris time, [midnight, New York time,] and hostilities will cease at 11 o'clock this morning, Paris time, [6 o'clock, New York time.]

The terms of the armistice, it was announced, will not be made public until later. Military men here, however, regard it as certain that they include:

Immediate retirement of the German military forces from France, Belgium, and Alsace-Lorraine.

Disarming and demobilization of the German armies.

Occupation by the allied and American forces of such strategic points in Germany as will make impossible a renewal of hostilities.

Delivery of part of the German High Seas Fleet and a certain number of submarines to the allied and American naval forces.

Disarmament of all other German warships

END OF AN ERA

WILLIAM GRIMES

When the guns of the First World War fell silent, Europe lay lifeless. Millions had died. Northern France and Belgium were in ruins. Russia was convulsed by revolution. Some of the most advanced economies in the world had sputtered to a dead halt. Mass starvation loomed.

In this dark hour, Woodrow Wilson lit a fire of hope. In January 1919, he set sail from New York for the great conference in Paris at which the allied powers—Great Britain, France, Italy and the United States—would remake the world.[1] He brought with him a vision of peace, justice and cooperation, expressed in a declaration of principles called the Fourteen Points.[2]

The instrument for realizing this vision, specified in Point 14, would be an international, or supranational, organization called the League of Nations, created "for the purpose of affording mutual guarantees of political independence and territorial integrity to great and small States alike."

Wilson looked into the future and saw an end to the petty machinations of kings and princes. Diplomacy would be based on "open covenants of peace, openly arrived at" rather than secret treaties. Blind territorial ambition would be checked, military competition curtailed, the rights of small nations secured, freedom of the seas and of trade guaranteed, the aspirations of oppressed peoples for nationhood honored. The war to end wars would usher in the millennium, a peaceful, prosperous future for mankind.

The League was American idealism at its best and worst—lofty in conception, even inspiring, but completely unrealistic. The European powers were far more interested in punishing Germany and grabbing as much territory as possible from Germany, Austria-Hungary and the Ottoman Empire. The newly liberated small countries of central Europe, already at each other's throats, shared the same lust

President Wilson was awarded the Nobel Peace Prize in 1919 for his efforts to form the League of Nations.

American troops of the First Infantry Division pause near St. Mihiel, France, in July of 1918.

Exuberant American troops embark for France in 1917, anxious to meet the enemy.

FURTHER READING

1 "Bugles Greet Delegates," see January 19, 1919, front page.

2 "Text of President Wilson's Speech," see January 9, 1918, front page.

The Big Four chat at Versailles. From left, David Lloyd George of Great Britain, Vittorio Orlando of Italy, Georges Clemenceau of France and Woodrow Wilson of the United States.

President Wilson waves his hat from the deck of the U.S.S. George Washington as it steams into New York Harbor July 9, 1919, bringing the president home from the Versailles Peace Conference in France.

for weapons and land as the great powers. Georges Clemenceau, the French premier, remarked dismissively, and tellingly, "I like the League, but I do not believe in it."

If Wilson's idealism irritated his fellow leaders at the conferences—Clemenceau, the British Prime Minister David Lloyd George and the Italian Premier Vittorio Orlando—it struck a chord with millions of Europeans, and with oppressed minorities across the globe. Wherever he went in France and Italy, Wilson was greeted by ecstatic throngs. (The innumerable Avenue Wilsons throughout France bear witness to this euphoria.) The League of Nations seemed to many people, not all of them dizzy utopians, Europe's last chance to rise above its own bloody history. "We were journeying to Paris, not merely to liquidate the war, but to found a new order in Europe," the British diplomat Harold Nicolson wrote. "We were preparing not peace only, but Eternal Peace."

Failure was built into the League's structure. Since it had no military forces, and no power to impose binding arbitration, its role would be, in essence, advisory. It would take a unanimous vote by all member states to pass most decisions—a fatal flaw, as it turned out. Severely compromised from its birth, the League came into being with the signing of the Versailles Treaty on June 28, 1919.[3] Forty-four nations signed its charter. The United States was not among them.

In the end, Wilson found his worst enemies at home. Having carried the day in Paris, he returned to confront a skeptical Congress, wary of any organization that might commit the United States to the military defense of League members. The battle lines were drawn for a political struggle over the Versailles Treaty that severely damaged Wilson's reputation and ultimately took his life.

Senator Henry Cabot Lodge, the Republican chairman of the Senate Committee on Foreign Relations and a confirmed Wilson hater, led opposition to the League, demanding changes to the treaty, known in the language of diplomacy as reservations.[4] A more adroit politician than Wilson might have worked out a compromise and learned to live with modest revisions that would ensure Congressional passage of the treaty.

Wilson, however, behaved like a man possessed. The concept of principled opposition was foreign to his nature. During the war, he had stifled dissent through two pieces of repressive legislation, the Espionage Act[5] and the Sedition

Act,[6] that declared open season on socialists, union organizers, German-Americans and critical newspapers.

Similarly, critics of the League of Nations were dismissed as venal ignoramuses or "bungalow minds." Ignoring his closest advisers, Wilson refused to consider Lodge's proposed amendments. He alienated Irish-Americans by refusing to put the issue of Irish self-determination on the table. From the outset, Wilson ruled out any changes whatsoever to the treaty. As the campaign for its passage gathered steam, he became increasingly vindictive, erratic and self-righteous. "Dare we reject it and break the heart of the world?" he asked the Senate.[7]

English King George V meets with President Wilson at Charing Cross in London.

The sticking point was Article X of the League Covenant,[8] which required members "to respect and preserve as against external aggression the territorial integrity and existing political independence of all Members of the League." George Washington had warned the American people against foreign entanglements. The events of the last four years had proved him prescient. The League, to many Senators, looked like a standing invitation to involve the United States in foreign adventures.

Hiram Johnson (left) and William E. Borah led Senate isolationists in their successful fight to kill the League of Nations.

Enraged at Congressional sniping, and undermined by the testimony of his own diplomats, Wilson took his case to the people. In September 1919 he embarked on a cross-country speaking tour designed to build support for the League and put pressure on Congress, whose members he urged to "put up or shut up."[9]

In failing health, he delivered speeches that often crossed the border between impassioned and hysterical. Despite his efforts, opposition to the League gained momentum. Debilitated by arteriosclerosis and congestive heart disease, Wilson began sinking alarmingly. On October 2, back in Washington, he suffered a major stroke that left him incapacitated, a condition concealed from the American people by his wife and doctor for the remainder of his term of office.

America never ratified the Versailles Treaty or joined the League of Nations, which became a byword for failure. Unable to keep the peace, slow the European arms race or resolve conflicts, it limped along until World War II put it

Senator Henry Cabot Lodge's main objection to the League of Nations was the Article X provision.

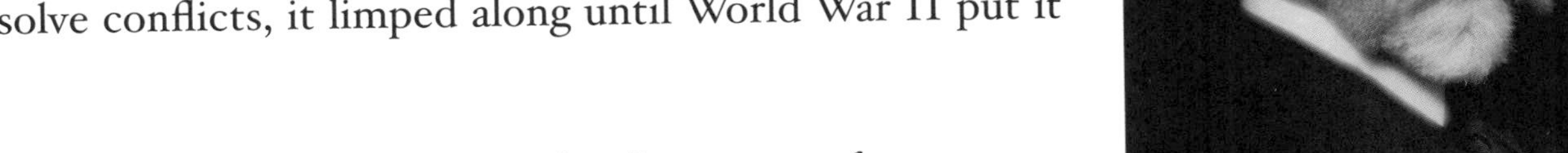

3 "Enemy Envoys in Truculent Spirit," see June 29, 1919, front page.
4 "Lodge Outlines Five Reservations to League Plan," see August 13, 1919, front page.
5 "President Calls Conferees, Urges Press Censorship," see May 24, 1917, front page.
6 "Sedition Bill Sent to Wilson by House," see May 8, 1918, article.
7 "Text of President Wilson's Speech to Congress, Explaining the Work of the Peace Conference," see July 11, 1919, article.

out of its misery. William L. Shirer, the great CBS correspondent, walked past the League's Geneva headquarters in 1938 with a colleague who called the building "a granite sepulchre." Turning to Shirer, he said, "There, my friend, are buried the dead hopes of peace for our generation."

WILLIAM GRIMES *writes abituary articles for The New York Times. From 2004 to 2008 he reviewed nonfiction books as a daily book critic and previously contributed articles for The Times's Style and cultural sections. He also was the chief restaurant reviewer for The Times from 1999 to 2003. Grimes is the author of "My Fine Feathered Friend," "Eating Your Words" and "Straight Up or On the Rocks: The Story of the American Cocktail."*

8 "Root for Modified League of Nations; Against Article X," see October 20, 1920, front page.

9 "Defends Article X.; Challenges Foes, President Tells Indianapolis Crowd He Fights as American. Not Party Man," see September 5, 1919, article.

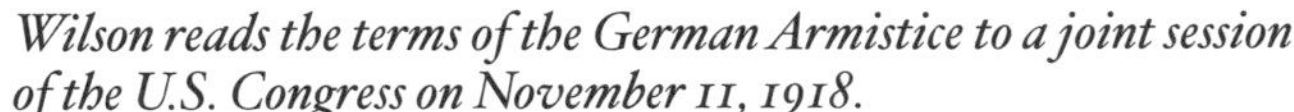

Wilson reads the terms of the German Armistice to a joint session of the U.S. Congress on November 11, 1918.

"All the News That's Fit to Print."

The New York Times.

THE WEATHER
Fair today; Tuesday, warmer; moderate southerly winds.
For full weather report see Page 17.

VOL. LXVIII...NO. 22,157. NEW YORK, MONDAY, SEPTEMBER 23, 1918.—EIGHTEEN PAGES. TWO CENTS Metropolitan District | THREE CENTS Within 200 Miles. | FOUR CENTS Elsewhere.

BRITISH WIPE OUT AN ENTIRE TURKISH ARMY; CAPTURE 18,000 IN 60-MILE DRIVE IN PALESTINE; HAIG STRIKES GERMAN LINE AT FOUR POINTS

PUTS RISE IN FOOD AT 3 1-2 PER CENT. SINCE LAST YEAR

Hoover Bureau Asserts That Increases Have Been Popularly Overestimated.

FARMERS' RECEIPTS SOARING

Prices Up 35 Per Cent., but Margin Narrowed Between Producer and Wholesaler.

BIG JUMP IN SOME FOODS

But General Cost Far Below That of Rent, Clothing, Transportation, and Other Items.

Special to The New York Times.

WASHINGTON, Sept. 22.—An analysis of the food situation and the increase in living costs was made today by the Food Administration, which holds that increases have been greatly overestimated by laying too much emphasis on special cases.

A table showing the relative increases and decreases in costs during 1917 and 1918 was made public to show that, according to wholesale quotations, the average increase in the national expenditure for foods grouped as breadstuffs, vegetables, meats, &c., for the second period of 1918, was only 3.5 per cent. over the same period in 1917. This is arrived at, however, by placing the decrease in the expenditure for vegetables at 63.1 per cent. Fruits jumped 80 per cent., oils and nuts 54 per cent., and poultry and eggs 16.5 per cent.

"The attached table," says the Food Administration, "is a computation of the national food bill for each three months, beginning with the second quarter of 1917, down to the second quarter of 1918. It is based on taking the total food consumed by the nation divided into the items of breadstuffs, vegetables, meat, dairy products, &c., at the average wholesale price for the quarter, and thus arriving at what the nation, as a whole, actually expended.

"The figures show that during the last twelve months there has been an increase in the national food bill per quarter from $2,563,600,904 to $2,693,731,871, or 3½ per cent. While this is the whole nation's expenditure at the wholesale prices and thus clearly indicates the national trend, it does not follow that there are no local variations.

"In those sections where there has been a great local increase in population there has been a disturbance of distribution and prices have increased to a larger per cent. On the other hand there are corresponding sections of the community where actual decreases or no increases have taken place.

"The cost of rent, clothing, transportation and other items of living has advanced several times as much as the aggregate increase in the cost of foodstuffs. There has been more than a 35 per cent. increase in prices paid to the farmer, but also a reduction of speculation and profiteering and narrowed margins between farmers and wholesale prices under food regulations."

Here is the Food Administration's analysis of the situation:

SECOND QUARTER 1917.	Total Cost.	Cost Per Capita.
Breadstuffs	$314,906,915	$3.0382
Vegetables	330,709,747	3.1905
Sugar	200,674,663	1.9363
Fruits	78,281,156	.7550
Oils and nuts	52,302,765	.5046
Fish	26,140,445	.2522
Meats	764,802,651	7.3804
Poultry and eggs	221,956,895	2.1417
Dairy products	573,665,667	5.5354
Total	$2,563,600,904	$24.7353
THIRD QUARTER 1917.		
Breadstuffs	$393,732,314	$3.7844
Vegetables	152,884,830	1.4694
Sugar	205,327,030	1.9734
Fruits	71,290,290	.6852
Oils and nuts	58,304,496	.5604
Fish	26,326,613	.2530
Meats	777,833,981	7.4705
Poultry and eggs	226,038,723	2.1726
Dairy products	584,068,678	5.6138
Total	$2,495,407,855	$23.9847
FOURTH QUARTER 1917.		
Breadstuffs	$348,554,753	$3.3372
Vegetables	136,890,969	1.3107
Sugar	210,439,897	2.0148
Fruits	70,506,614	.6750
Oils and nuts	68,485,873	.6558
Fish	33,133,947	.3172
Meats	878,708,620	8.4131
Poultry and eggs	266,500,892	2.5516
Dairy products	641,510,693	6.1421
Total	$2,654,751,258	$25.4175
FIRST QUARTER 1918.		
Breadstuffs	$351,952,618	$3.3567
Vegetables	143,179,060	1.3655
Sugar	190,016,407	1.8122
Fruits	75,057,007	.7158
Oils and nuts	72,652,456	.6929
Fish	40,621,802	.3875
Meats	838,387,663	7.9961
Poultry and eggs	304,216,881	2.9014
Dairy products	676,389,410	6.4510
Total	$2,692,483,304	$25.6791
SECOND QUARTER 1918.		
Breadstuffs	$340,626,283	$3.2216
Vegetables	[illegible]	1.1768
Sugar	[illegible]	1.7930
Fruits	103,881,429	.9868
Oils and nuts	81,964,541	.7786
Fish	24,702,491	.2349
Meats	938,780,260	8.8912
Poultry and eggs	262,577,561	2.4947
Dairy products	619,553,054	5.8863
Total	$2,693,731,871	$25.6919

Allies Have Taken 185,000 Prisoners in Two Months

PARIS, Sept. 22.—In a review of the battles in France during the last six months, the Havas Agency credits to the American troops the re-establishment of the balance on the western front, and points out the entire change that has taken place in the last two months. It goes on:

"In the last two months alone the Allies took 185,000 prisoners.

"The enemy losses in men who will never be able to return to the ranks are estimated at 600,000—a void which the 1920 class will not suffice to fill."

GERMANS RUSHING TO HELP BULGARS

Reinforcements Sent in Effort to Check the Allied Push.

ITALIANS JOIN IN THE DRIVE

Strike Enemy's Line East of Monastir—Serbs Advanced Twelve Miles on Friday.

WASHINGTON, Sept. 22.—Serbian troops pressing the Bulgarians and Germans in Central Macedonia advanced more than twenty kilometers Friday, and are now within four miles of the Uskub-Saloniki Railroad, the main artery for the supply of the Austro-German and Bulgarian forces opposing the British and French armies on the Serbian right.

The cutting of this railroad, it is said here officially, will force the retirement of the enemy left wing and cause a general readjustment of the enemy lines in this entire section.

Following is the text of the Serbian official statement:

We yesterday (Friday) advanced more than twenty kilometers toward the north. Our troops are several kilometers to the north of Kavarda. In addition to this town we have liberated another fifteen villages. Twelve guns have been taken by our cavalry.

Fresh Bulgarian and German troops are arriving continually to reinforce the enemy lines. During the retreat the Bulgarians set fire to the villages and plundered all that remained to the poverty stricken population, thus treating them as enemies, in spite of the claims of the Sofia Government that this population is not Serbian, but Bulgarian.

ROME, Sept. 22.—In conjunction with the general Entente allied offensive against the Teuton and Bulgarian forces in Macedonia, Italian troops yesterday began a vigorous advance in the bend of the River Cerna, to the east of Monastir. The official statement issued today by the Italian War Office says that the front enemy positions were captured.

PARIS, Sept. 22.—Concerning operations on the Macedonian front, Army Headquarters today made public the following:

Army of the East.—Bulgarian forces have been defeated and are being pursued between the Cerna and the Vardar, despite increasing rearguard resistance.

Serbian forces have advanced in the region of Cebren. On the right they captured high crests near Porta and Czena. Bulgarians burned villages which they had abandoned, and one complete battery of field pieces fell into our hands. Our aviators bombarded the retreating enemy with machine gun fire.

On both sides of the Vardar and north of Monastir there is great artillery activity.

VIENNA, Sept. 22, (via London.)—An official statement issued at the War Office today says:

"On the Albanian coast further Italian attacks were repulsed."

BUENA VENTURA SUNK; 64 OF CREW MISSING

American Steamer Returning from France Torpedoed—30 Survivors Land in Spain.

CORUNNA, Spain, Sept. 22.—Three officers and twenty-seven of the crew of the American steamer Buena Ventura have arrived here. The vessel was torpedoed last Monday. Three boats with sixty-four of the crew are missing.

The Buena Ventura was proceeding from Bordeaux, where she had unloaded a cargo of petroleum for Philadelphia.

The vessel was of 4,881 gross tons and belonged to the United States Steel Products Company.

AUSTRIANS IN MUTINY, HOIST THE RED FLAG

Regiment at Rovno Refuses to Go to France and Is Joined by Two Others.

BASLE, Sept. 22.—An Austrian regiment at Rovno, in the Russian province of Volhynia, is reported in a dispatch received here from Kiev to have refused to go to the battlefront in France.

The Austrians unfolded the red flag and are said to have been joined by two other regiments.

AMERICANS SLAIN BY RUSSIAN REDS, GERMAN REPORTS

Correspondent Says Vologda Leader Urged Murder of Allied Citizens.

FINLAND OFFERS REFUGE

But Asks Norway, Sweden, and Denmark to Help Share the Burden.

KAISER'S ORDER TO TEUTONS

Says All Germans and Austro-Hungarians in Russia Must Join Soviet Troops.

AMSTERDAM, Sept. 22.—The Russian People's Commissary at Vologda, according to the Petrograd correspondent of the Hamburg Nachrichten, has urged on the population of the entire Vologda Province south of Archangel Province the most ruthless persecution of British subjects and French and American citizens.

Rioting against Entente nationals has taken place in various towns, the correspondent says, and some Frenchmen and Americans are being murdered.

HELSINGFORS, Sept. 22, (via Copenhagen,) (Associated Press.)—"In view of the condition of anarchy and murder at Petrograd and the defenseless situation of a great part of the population," says an official statement issued here, "Finland's Government feels that on purely humanitarian grounds it cannot refuse to permit Russian, English, American, and Italian refugees to come to Finland."

The Finnish Government, however, the statement says, is compelled by the scarcity of provisions to beg the three Scandinavian countries—Norway, Sweden, and Denmark—to help in harboring a portion of the refugees.

LONDON, Sept. 22.—It is understood in official circles here that arrangements are progressing for the mutual repatriation of British subjects in Russia and Russians in Great Britain.

Information is said to have been received from M. Tchitcherin, the Russian Foreign Minister, which leads to the belief that British subjects will be got out of Russia safely.

PEKING, Sept. 22, (Associated Press.)—News has been received here that the German Emperor on Sept. 10 issued an order to all Austro-Hungarians and Germans in Russia, saying it was their first duty to join the Russian Soviet troops, and to oppose Japan and her allies, "who threaten to restore the Eastern front."

ARCHANGEL REVOLT WAS QUICKLY ENDED

Allied Diplomats and Military Chiefs Took Charge and Established a Protectorate.

ARCHANGEL, Sept. 11. (Associated Press.)—Colonel Tchaplin, leader of the recent attempt to overthrow the Provisional Government headed by M. Tschaikovsky, in Northwestern Russia, has resigned his post as Commander of the Russian Forces and has been succeeded by Colonel Ivanoff.

The labor disputes in Archangel are being rapidly settled. American soldiers who had been operating the street-car system have been transferred to other duties.

As a result of the attempt to overthrow the Government the Allied diplomatic and military chiefs assumed temporary direction and established a protectorate in the region in the rear of the Allied front pending the adjustment of political disputes. This decision followed the arrest of M. Tschaikovsky and all but two members of his Government early last Thursday by a party of conservative officers headed by Colonel Tchaplin, who sought to establish a new régime.

M. Tschaikovsky and his ministers were taken on a ship en route to the Solovetsk Monastery, whence they have been returned by order of the Allied Ambassadors with the approval of American Consul General Poole. Meanwhile the Allied forces, including the American troops, patrolled the city, assuring tranquility and a just settlement of all disputes. Following is the text of the proclamation, which was signed by the American, French, British and Italian Ambassadors and Consul General Poole:

"To the People of the Northern Region: The undersigned representatives of the Allied nations and the commanders in chief of their forces seeing the confusion created in the minds of the people by proclamations by leaders of the oppos-

Continued on Page Three.

"German People, Be Hard," Hindenburg Tells Well-wishers

AMSTERDAM, Sept. 22.—Field Marshal von Hindenburg, replying to greetings sent to him from a patriotic meeting in Juterbog, said:

"The first replies from the enemy camp to the Austrian note reveal our enemies' state of mind. In the face of this there can be only one watchword, 'German people, be hard.'"

COPENHAGEN, Sept. 22.—America's answer to Austria-Hungary's recent peace note and the speech of Premier Clemenceau of France on the same subject should, according to the Lokal-Anzeiger of Berlin, be posted on billboards and be communicated to the German people by the distribution of millions of pamphlets.

"No German man or woman who knows the contents and significance of these declarations," the newspaper declares, "can doubt that peace is attainable only either through our victory or at the price of our utter destruction."

OUR MEN VICTORS IN ST. MIHIEL RAIDS

They Take 34 Prisoners and Gain Information of German Activities.

AMERICAN BARRAGE DEADLY

Germans Slow in Returning Our Fire, Which Killed Sixty at Haumont and Charey.

WITH THE AMERICAN FORCES IN LORRAINE, Sept. 22, (Associated Press.)—American troops made two successful raids on the German lines northeast of St. Mihiel early this morning, taking twenty-nine prisoners in the region of Haumont and five southeast of Charey. Both raids were preceded by barrages.

Patrols from the region of Haumont reported that at least forty Germans were killed or injured. Other patrols from the Charey region estimated that the barrage killed at least a score of Germans.

The prisoners taken southeast of Charey were machine gunners, the Americans capturing two heavy machine guns. At Haumont the Germans were captured in dugouts, where they had taken refuge from the stiff American barrage.

The Germans answered with their artillery along the American line. The first American barrage began soon after midnight. The other started at 2 o'clock. Both continued for two hours.

A unit of the American raiders entered Haumont, where the Germans had been using a church tower as an observation post. Sharp fighting took place in the streets of the village, the Americans getting the better of the Germans and obtaining the information desired. They then returned to their own lines.

A patrol found several new dugouts east of Haumont and indications that the Germans were continuing to dig in. Another patrol reported enemy trenches and numerous machine gun emplacements south of Dommartin.

When the American barrages started the Germans apparently believed that another offensive had opened, and filled the sky with rockets and signal shells. The heavy shelling apparently caused confusion on the enemy front, because it was more than twenty minutes after the first barrage before the Germans replied.

Sept. 21—German airplanes were active last night in the region between the Moselle River and St. Bénoit, northeast of St. Mihiel. The forward areas were bombed practically all night.

German artillery kept up a harassing fire on the Bois-le-Prêtre, Rappes Woods, and the village of Fey-en-Haye. The road to Thiaucourt is being shelled intermittently.

The Germans are reported to be working on dugouts to the west of Pagny and to the east of Haumont. Similar activity has been observed north of Dampvitou and south of Dommartin.

Operating a German Railroad.

WITH THE AMERICAN ARMY ON THE LORRAINE FRONT, Sept. 22, (Associated Press.)—The American engineers detachment is now operating a complete German narrow-gauge railroad in the St. Mihiel salient, the Americans having captured thirty-eight one-man gasoline locomotives in the course of their offensive.

In Thiaucourt the Americans took

Continued on Page Two.

BRITISH IMPROVE POSITIONS

Take Prisoners in Night Attacks on Northern Hindenburg Outposts.

WIDE ADVANCE AT GAVRELLE

German Defenses All Carried on a Two-Mile Front North of the Scarpe.

NEW THRUST NEAR EPEHY

Germans Yield Several Points of Resistance—Artillery Is Active on French Front.

LONDON, Sept. 22.—British troops last night pushed their lines forward at four points on the front facing the northern part of the Hindenburg line.

The most extensive gain was made north of the Scarpe River, near Gavrelle, where they threw the Germans back on a two-mile front.

Further south, at Moeuvres, a German attack was repulsed yesterday afternoon, and Haig's men improved their positions.

To the right of this sector, south of Villers-Guislain, the Germans attacked last evening and were driven back after sharp fighting, the British following up their advantage and advancing their line.

East of Epehy the British attack of yesterday was renewed, and Little Priel Farm and other points of resistance were carried.

In each of these operations a number of Germans were captured.

Only local actions were fought today, but the British made slight gains south of Villers-Guislain and near Zillebeke, in the Ypres sector.

The French War Office reports some artillery activity north of the Aisne and in the St. Quentin region.

Haig's Important Gain Near Epehy.

WITH THE BRITISH ARMY IN FRANCE, Sept. 22, (Associated Press.)—A midnight advance of the London and English county troops resulted in the regaining of a large portion of the ground lost last Saturday after an attack along the fragments of the Hindenburg outpost line between Cambrai and St. Quentin.

During Saturday morning these battalions, with yeomanry and Australians on their right, stormed a series of redoubts and farms forming the backbone of the outpost system opposite Bellenglise and Vendhuille, a mile and a quarter west of the Scheldt Canal, between St. Quentin and Cambrai. They occupied the Guillemont, Quennemont, and Little Priel farms, the Tombois redoubts, and a chain of strong trenches, heavily banked with fire, connecting these positions.

Early Saturday afternoon counterattacks were delivered by Alpine Corps and the 38th Thuringian and 2d Guards Divisions, which were massed in the main Hindenburg system on the western bank of the canal. They drove in great strength down the trenches, but the British bombed them back slowly.

Four hundred prisoners had been taken by the British during Saturday morning, and half of those were released by the counterassault. The British retired about half way to their original positions west of Epehy and Ronssoy, maintaining a maximum advance of nearly a mile at some places, and stubbornly held their ground for the remainder of the day.

The result of the fighting of the last thirty-six hours has been the bringing of the British front within about three-quarters of a mile of the main Hindenburg system opposite Bellicourt on the canal and within a mile and a quarter of the Vendhuille bridgehead, eleven miles south of Cambrai.

Trench warfare, with constant bombing, is inevitable in the present phase of the British operations. The ground in front of the 3d and 4th Armies as far as the canal and for a half mile beyond is covered with ditches, redoubts, and fortified farms, making surprise attacks of great weight impossible.

The Germans are fighting stubbornly in the way they like best. While they are able to keep intrenched in the region of deep ravines and broad gullies they have less fear of the tanks or of being otherwise overwhelmed. Fresh German infantry has been put into the battleline.

The weather is inclement, which has hampered the fighting troops.

Swiss Hear Bavarian Prince Shot at Hindenburg In Rage Over Differences, but Missed the Marshal

Special Cable to THE NEW YORK TIMES.

ZURICH, Sept. 22.—Many Swiss Socialist journals have heard from indirect sources that serious differences have arisen between South German politicians and the Prussian dictators.

The Central Schweiz Demokrat reports that a Bavarian commander attempted in an access of rage to attack Hindenburg, and German deserters are quoted as saying that a Bavarian Prince tried to shoot Hindenburg, but that the Field Marshal was not wounded.

These reports may be sensational versions of recent stories coming through neutral countries that Crown Prince Rupprecht was at odds with Hindenburg and was trying to dodge responsibility for the check of the July offensive. He is known to have left the Somme front for a time in August on a "vacation."

HAIG'S MEN FIGHT IN RAIN AND MUD

Soldiers Suffer from the Lack of Shelter After Their Rapid Advance.

SLOW ADVANCE NEAR EPEHY

Germans' Reinforcements Held Them Up Saturday, but Lost Ground Yesterday.

By PHILIP GIBBS.

Copyright, 1918, by The New York Times Company.
Special Cable to THE NEW YORK TIMES.

WAR CORRESPONDENTS' HEADQUARTERS, Sept. 22.—We have been having some wild weather here, with heavy rain, and the men in the fighting fields have been wet and muddy.

It is not pleasant in these fields, where even behind the lines twenty miles deep along all the front there is little shelter for the troops, except tents in swamps, a few groups of huts, slimy dugouts and tarpaulin sheets stopping up monstrous shell holes in broken houses.

The British armies are fighting, working, and sleeping in wet clothes, because when it rains so heavily as during the last few days waterproof capes are of slight avail against the storm, tents are leaky, and oozy mud and water squelch into marching boots.

There is something grimly picturesque about these rain pictures of the war. The steel helmets of a battalion marching up to the line are washed by the downpour and gleam with a blue light. Their rifles are tied about with rags to keep them dry. The rain pours down their shiny capes and beats into their mud-splashed faces. Great guns go by on caterpillar wheels, which grind up the soft tracks; field batteries move forward with the gunners hunched forward on mules which are flaked with mud up to the ears, and gun wheels splash through the young ponds.

Gangs Busy Repairing Roads.

The long roads through the battlefields, the Albert-Bapaume Road, the Arras Road, the Amiens-Péronne Road, those highways down which so much history of this war has passed with fire and fury, are golden tracks where the sun breaking through clouds shines on their puddles and on their rain-washed surface, and where gangs from labor battalions are at work filling up recent shell holes, smoothing out the bumps and gullies made by the heavy traffic of moving armies.

Storms break over the dead woods on either side of these highways, etched black against the gray of the sky or its white cloud-mountains, and out of the wet earth where countless trenches and shell craters are waterlogged there rise the ruins of this world of ours—the high jagged walls of fallen houses, bits of churches, abbeys and monasteries with their stones washed white in the rain, masses of broken brick work from which the iron girders stick out, twisted fantastically, where once there were villages of France; and here and there a pile of rubbish which was a mill or sugar factory or wayside shrine.

The wind howls through these ruins and the rain beats down upon them, and British soldiers wander through them with steel helmets lowered to the storm or crouch in the scanty shelter they can give. Horses and mules are stabled there in roofless rooms, and gun limbers are stacked in gardens where flowers still grow in a wild chaos of sandbags and barbed wire, and away over the desolate fields of thistles which cover some of the litter of the infernal strife long trains are

Continued on Page Two.

TURKS OUTWITTED BY GEN. ALLENBY

Were Apparently Unprepared to Face Hostile Operations on So Large a Scale.

COUNTRY MOST DIFFICULT

British Fought Over Steep Hills and Masses of Boulders Till Foe Was Routed.

By W. T. MASSEY.

Special Cable to THE NEW YORK TIMES.

WITH THE BRITISH ARMY IN PALESTINE, Sept. 20.—It is impossible to estimate the vast quantity of captured machine guns, motors, ammunitions, stores, and rolling stock which the Turk will find it difficult to replace. On the low ground in the passes a great quantity of transport is immovable because the men had taken the horses to try to escape from the advancing troops, or they had been smashed by aircraft action.

Railway communications have been damaged everywhere, and Arab regulars and Bedouin levies have done invaluable service in cutting the Hedjas Railway north and south of Derat and the line running westward thereof.

Though some of the enemy are putting up vigorous rearguard fights in the hills they cannot stop our progress, but large parties are bewildered at meeting our forces in unexpected places. We continually hear of Turks retiring on positions we occupied several hours previously.

Yesterday Londoners and Indians made a swift march from Wadi Faliak across marshy ground to Tul Keram, where with the aid of a mounted brigade they rounded up much transport on the move. From Tul Keram the infantry moved to the north of the railway which the Australians destroyed yesterday, and deny this pass to Samaria to the Turks. Other infantry which carried the coastal defenses in one marvelous rush faced east.

The progress in the rough hilly country is rapid, considering the ease with which the mountain tracks could be defended by few machine guns. Some of the troops are approaching Samaria and Sudieh.

Though they first stubbornly resisted, the rearguards of the Turks are now retreating hastily toward El Afule and Beisan, where our cavalry is waiting for them.

The attack near Nablus road, which began the operations, was brilliantly conducted. Welsh, Indian, and Cape Colony battalions all shared in the success. The mixed brigade commenced a most difficult night march on Wednesday over a mountainous country east of the road, getting over the watershed, then clambering down the steep faces of hills where they commence to fall toward the Jordan Valley.

The leading battalion passing over the rocks of the Wadi Samieh took the enemy posts and allowed the second battalion to pass through to the second objectives. These taken, the third battalion went on, driving the enemy from other strong points, then gave way to the fourth battalion, which faced west and carried the important feature El Mugheir with a rush and another hill westward. A Cape company battalion captured a hill northeast and took one gun.

Another brigade operation westward was equally meritorious. It attacked Forfar and Bidston Hills, about a mile and half apart, the southernmost hill being taken from the north, the north-

Continued on Page Two.

TURKS TRAPPED BY CAVALRY

Anglo-Indian Horsemen in Swift Dash Northward Bar Line of Retreat.

OCCUPY TOWN OF NAZARETH

While Hedjaz Arabs East of the Jordan Destroy Railroads and Bridges.

AIRMEN SLAUGHTER FOE

120 Cannon, Besides Airplanes and Vast Transport, Taken by Allenby's Fighters.

LONDON, Sept. 22.—The Turkish Army operating in Palestine between the Jordan and the Mediterranean has been virtually wiped out by the British under General Allenby.

In the rapid sweep forward of the British Army, following the overwhelming of the Turkish defense system north of Jerusalem, 18,000 prisoners have been rounded up so far, large numbers of the enemy have been killed or wounded, and in addition to the capture of 120 guns, booty including four airplanes and a large quantity of uncounted transport has fallen into the hands of the pursuing forces.

Cavalry units have advanced sixty miles from their original positions and occupied Nazareth, El Afule, and Beisan.

The British losses were surprisingly slight considering the importance of the advance.

Turks Cut Off from Escape.

The text of this evening's announcement follows:

By 9 o'clock on Saturday night on our left wing the infantry about Birafur had reached the line Beitdajan-Samaria-Birafur, shepherding the enemy on the west of the Jerusalem-Nabulus road into the arms of our cavalry operating southward from Jenin and Beisan.

Other enemy columns vainly attempted to escape into the Jordan Valley in the direction of Jisr-ed-Dameer, which still is held by us. These columns suffered severely from our aircraft, which constantly harassed them with bombs and machine-gun fire from low altitudes.

In the vicinity of Lake Tiberius our cavalry detachments hold Nazareth and the rail and road passages over the Jordan at Jisr-ed-Dameer.

Already 18,000 prisoners have been captured and 120 guns collected.

The appended statement was issued earlier in the day:

Palestine—By 8 P. M. on Sept. 20 the enemy resistance had collapsed everywhere save on the Turkish left in the Jordan Valley.

Our left wing, having swung around to the east, had reached the line of Bidieh, Baka, and Messudieh Junction, and was astride the rail and roads converging at Nabulus.

Our right wing, advancing through difficult country against considerable resistance had reached the line of Khan-Jibeit, one and one-fourth miles northeast of El-Mugheir and Es-Sawieh, and was facing north astride the Jerusalem-Nabulus road.

On the north our cavalry, traversing the Field of Armageddon, had occupied Nazareth, Afule, and Beisan, and were collecting the disorganized masses of enemy troops and transport as they arrived from the south. All avenues of escape open to the enemy, except the fords across the Jordan between Beisan and Jisr-ed-Dameer, were thus closed.

East of the Jordan Arab forces of the King of the Hedjaz had effected numerous demolitions on the railways radiating from Derat, several important bridges, including one in the Yurmak Valley, having been destroyed.

Several days must elapse before accurate figures of captures can be given, but already more than 8,000 prisoners, 100 guns, large quantities of both horse and mechanical transports, four airplanes, many locomotives, and much rolling stock have been counted.

Very severe losses have been inflicted on the masses of Turkish troops retreating over the difficult roads by our air services.

A German airplane, later ascertained to have been carrying mails, landed in the midst of our troops at Afule. The pilot, who believed the place still to be in Turkish hands, de-

Section 1

"All the News That's Fit to Print."

The New York Times.

THE WEATHER
Cloudy, probably rain Sunday; Monday clearing; southeast winds.
For full weather report see Page 22.

Section 1

VOL. LXVIII...NO. 22,282. NEW YORK, SUNDAY, JANUARY 26, 1919—108 PAGES, in Nine Parts, Including Picture and Magazine Sections (Rotogravure) and Book Section. FIVE CENTS In Greater New York | Elsewhere SEVEN CENTS

LEAGUE OF NATIONS PLAN IS ADOPTED; PEACE CONFERENCE ACTS ON WILSON PLEA, STRONGLY SUPPORTED BY LLOYD GEORGE

MOVE TO CANCEL 15 BILLIONS IN WAR EXPENSES

House Bill Revokes $7,179,156,944 in Contracts and $8,221,029,294 in Authorizations.

AFFECTS ARMY AND NAVY

Committee Has Not Yet Found Time to Cut Allotments to Other Departments.

BIG SAVING IN THE ARMY

Reduction in Ordnance Department Alone $9,217,648,304, and Quartermaster $3,756,135,307.

Special to The New York Times.

WASHINGTON, Jan. 25.—The cessation of war saved the nation billions of dollars through the cancellation of contracts and authorizations. In the deficiency bill reported to the House by the Appropriations Committee, today, contracts for $7,179,156,944 are ordered canceled and authorizations amounting to $8,221,029,294 are withdrawn. If the war had continued another six months it is estimated that the expenditure of both these amounts, or more than $15,000,000,000 would have been necessary.

The bill carries recommendations for appropriations of $29[illegible],244,329.45 for the various services of the Government, divided as follows: War Department, $6,473,782.68; Navy Establishment, $280,762,225.36; Civil Service, $7,853,750.57; Navy Department, $154,570.84.

The largest items for which appropriations are recommended follow:

War Department—Temporary employes, $4,000,000; disposition of remains of officers and men, $2,473,782.68.

Navy Department: Bureau of Navigation, $1,531,178.64; Bureau of Yards and Docks, $6,100,000; Bureau of Construction, $15,000,000; Bureau of Steam Engineering, $4,330,882.

Representative Swagar Sherley, Chairman, in his report said:

"The repeal of appropriations and withdrawal of authorizations has been confined to the military and naval establishments, not because funds voted to other departments are all required, for such is not the fact, but because the magnitude of the task made impossible at this time a review of the other departments, and it is hoped that in connection with the Sundry Civil and other bills many of these surplus funds may be dealt with. The committee in recommending that various sums shall be covered into the Treasury does not mean to affirm in any sense that the total of the moneys left with the various bureaus is needed or should be expended, or to approve or disapprove various activities set forth in the hearings. There should, and doubless will be, large savings made from these balances.

"What the committee has endeavored to do is to cover into the Treasury such sums that plainly are not needed, but as it is necessarily uncertain just to what extent the Government may be able by cancellation of contracts and discontinuance of projects to reduce its obligations, the committee has deemed it wise to leave funds amply sufficient to meet such obligations. To have undertaken to pass judgment on remaining activities would have been to usurp the prerogatives of many of the committees and would have required a detailed examination that would have taken many additional months.

"The labors of the committee have been greatly added to because of the absence of any uniform system of keeping accounts by the various departments, and it desires to express the hope that Congress may provide soon for such a system of accounting. While the work of the committee by some may be thought unnecessary on the ground that the departments probably would not have expended the sums anyway it was the judgment of the committee that it was wise directly to provide against their expenditure, and it cannot be doubted that the examination of their balances and survey of their activities and needs by the various corps of the army and navy brought about by the action of the committee should enable these departments to make savings of many millions."

The following table shows the savings in cancellation of contracts and authorizations:

ARMY ESTABLISHMENT.

Purpose.	Appropriations.	Authorizations.
Sig. Serv....	$83,373,20[illegible].04	$45,000,000.00
Mil. Aeron..	85,000,00[illegible].00	....
Airc'ft prod.	402,000,000.00	....
Qm. Corps...	3,740,385,307.76	15,750,000.00
Med. Dept...	54,145,513.73	65,000,000.00
Eng. Corps..	792,580,435.76	200,000,000.00
Ord. Dept...	1,503,369,009.75	7,714,279,294.70
Chem. Warf.	183,932,610.66	150,000,000.00
Total army	$6,844,795,077.70	$8,190,029,274.70

NAVAL ESTABLISHMENT.

Purpose.	Appropriations.	Authorizations.
Aviation	$98,000,000.00	....
Navigation ..	4,500,000.00	....
Ordnance ...	164,833,843.69	$31,000,000.00
Public Works	2,173,627.00	....
Sup. and Ac.	23,096,000.00	....
Steam Eng..	1,420.33	....
Marine Corps	41,216,075.06	....
Total navy	$334,361,866.98	$31,000,000.00
Grand total army and navy	$7,179,156,944.68	$8,221,029,294.70

Combined appropriation and authorization, $15,400,186,239.38.

Text of the Resolution to Create a World League As Unanimously Adopted by Peace Conference

PARIS, Jan. 25.—Following is the text of the resolution relating to the creation of a League of Nations, which was adopted by the plenary session of the Peace Conference today:

The conference, having considered the proposals for the creation of a League of Nations, resolved that:

It is essential to the maintenance of the world settlement which the associated nations are now met to establish that a League of Nations be created to promote international obligations and to provide safeguards against war.

This league should be created as an integral part of the general treaty of peace and should be open to every civilized nation which can be relied on to promote its objects.

The members of the league should periodically meet in international conference and should have a permanent organization and secretaries to carry on the business of the league in the intervals between the conferences.

The conference therefore appoints a committee, representative of the associated Governments, to work out the details of the constitution and the functions of the league and the draft of resolutions in regard to breaches of the laws of war for presentation to the Peace Conference.

Responsibility.

That a commission, composed of two representatives apiece from the five great powers and five representatives to be elected by the other powers, be appointed to inquire and report upon the following:

First—The responsibility of the authors of the war.

Second—The facts as to breaches of the laws and customs of war committed by the forces of the German Empire and their allies on land, on sea, and in the air during the present war.

Third—The degree of responsibility for these offenses attaching to particular members of the enemy's forces, including members of the General Staffs and other individuals, however highly placed.

Fourth—The constitution and procedure of a tribunal appropriate to the trial of these offenses.

Fifth—Any other matters, cognate or ancillary to the above, which may arise in the course of the inquiry and which the commission finds it useful and relevant to take into consideration.

Reparation.

Following is the draft of a resolution in regard to reparation which the conference adopted:

That a commission be appointed, which shall comprise not more than three representatives apiece from each of the five great powers and not more than two representatives apiece from Belgium, Greece, Poland, Rumania, and Serbia, to examine and report

First—On the amount of reparation which the enemy countries ought to pay.

Second—On what they are capable of paying, and,

Third—On the method, the form, and time within which payment should be made.

International Legislation.

A resolution in regard to international legislation on industrial and labor questions was passed. It reads:

That a commission, composed of two representatives apiece from the five great powers and five representatives to be elected by the other powers represented at the Peace Conference, be appointed to inquire into the conditions of employment from the international aspect and to consider the international means necessary to secure common action on matters affecting conditions of employment and to recommend the form of a permanent agency to continue such inquiry and consideration, in co-operation with and under the direction of the League of Nations.

This resolution was adopted regarding international control of ports, waterways, and railways:

International Control.

That a commission composed of two representatives apiece from the five great powers and five representatives of the other powers be appointed, to inquire and report upon the international régime for ports, waterways, and railways.

CROMWELL DEATHS NOW CONFIRMED

Bordeaux Police Chief Reports That Young Women Committed Suicide.

PARIS, Jan. 25, (Associated Press)—The Commissioner of Police at Bordeaux confirms the report of the suicide of the Misses Gladys and Dorothea Cromwell.

The American Red Cross Headquarters here, in answer to inquiries, says it has been informed that the Misses Cromwell sailed on the French steamer La Lorraine. Friends of the twin sisters accompanied them to the pier.

The officer in charge of the Red Cross party on board the ship sent by wireless to the Red Cross a copy of the note found in the stateroom occupied by the sisters in which they said they intended to commit suicide.

The drowning of the Misses Dorothea and Gladys Cromwell from the French liner La Lorraine soon after the vessel sailed from France is still a mystery to members of their family in New York.

Seymour L. Cromwell, the only brother of the young women, discredits the reports and declared last night at his residence, 169 East Seventy-fourth Street, that he believed a mistake had been made, because of the conflicting dispatches and a cheerful letter he had received from his sisters less than a week ago.

Mr. Cromwell said late last night:

"Not only I, but the State Department and of course the Red Cross have sent cables to France endeavoring to find out some definite explanation. As yet I have received no satisfying word, but I was given to understand when the cables were sent that no answer would be forthcoming for thirty-six hours.

"The only thing that can convince me that such a thing could ever have happened would be to receive a wireless from the liner Espagne stating that my sisters were not aboard that vessel. Returning from France on La Lorraine is one of my most intimate friends and also two close friends of my partner in business. Wireless messages have been sent to these friends, but as yet no answer has come."

The Misses Cromwell were 32 years old and not 22 as first reported.

SEEK TO INSTALL STATE SOCIALISM

North Dakota Nonpartisan League, Controlling Legislature, Plans Legislation.

Special to The New York Times.

BISMARCK, N. D., Jan. 25.—Seven million dollars would be invested by North Dakota in the establishment of a State bank and a system of terminal elevators and flour mills under the industrial program introduced in the State Legislature by the Nonpartisan League, which controls both houses.

Complete revision of the State's scheme of taxation, by which the taxation burden would be transferred from personal property to corporations, incomes, and land, also has been proposed, and has the support of the league majorities, which are bound by a caucus pledge to pass all legislation indorsed by such caucus.

The abandonment of the old system of appointive State officials for fixed terms also is due, with the substitution of the Socialist plan, by which officers such as State Tax Commissioners, educational directors, charitable institution directors, &c., may be removed at will.

These, in a general way, are the big problems which confront the Legislature, now twenty days old, and which William Lemke, Vice President of the Nonpartisan League, says will be adjourned by Feb. 10.

This is the first State Legislature completely controlled by the nonpartisans. They have more than two-thirds of the members of the House and Senate, and by using emergency clauses in their administration measures they will come very near to beating referendum of their bills, as 30,000 signatures are required to refer bills to which emergency clauses are attached, and the State has only about 100,000 voters all told.

In carrying out their program for industrial enterprises, the nonpartisans

Continued on Page Five.

REDS WANT PARLEY NEARER

Tchitcherin, Foreign Minister, Says Princes' Islands Are Too Remote.

BUT WILL CONSIDER PLAN

Promises to Do So on Receipt of Confirmation of Council's Reported Decision.

TAKES A SUPERCILIOUS TONE

Invitation Comes, He Says, When Soviets Have Settled Internal Troubles of Russia.

PARIS, Jan. 25.—M. Tchitcherin, the Bolshevist Foreign Minister, has sent a wireless message to the Soviet representative in Sweden asking for confirmation of the decision of the Supreme Council of the Peace Conference to send a mission to confer with representatives of the different factions in Russia on Princes' Islands.

M. Tchitcherin's message says that the islands are too remote for such a meeting. He objects to the isolation of the islands as tending to surround the conference with secrecy, and also objects to leaving to the Entente the choice of participants.

This proposition of the Supreme Council, the message says, is made at a time when the Bolsheviki are victorious over their opponents and the internal situation of Russia has been settled, but the Soviet Government, on receipt of the confirmation requested, will carefully consider the proposal.

More Russians Enter Protests.

The Council of the national and democratic bloc of Russian political organizations abroad has sent a strongly worded protest to Premier Clemenceau against the decision of the Supreme Council to call a conference of the Russian factions.

"We would be men without honor and courage if we accepted for a single moment a truce such as proposed to us while all that are dear are in danger of death—violent death by execution or assassination or slow death through hunger," the protest says.

"The interest of humanity in general and democracy in particular requires the establishment in Russia of a régime based on the sovereignty of the people freely expressed. An improvised meeting at the Princes' Islands cannot be an expression of this sort. Russia has long clamored for the free election of a Constituent Assembly. The attempt was stifled by the Bolsheviki by force of arms, and they are today asked to make the voice of Russia heard!"

The Russian Bolshevist Government at Moscow, according to information received by the Socialist newspaper L'Humanité, is surprised that the suggestion made by the allied and associated Powers for a conference between the Russian factions comes at a time when the Bolsheviki are victorious in the field. The Bolsheviki, however, the advices add, do not reject the principle of a conference.

Vladimir Bourtzeff, a well-known Russian revolutionist, in an article in the Matin says that the Russian parties opposed to the Bolsheviki will positively refuse to attend the conference on Princes' Islands, because they look on the Bolsheviki as traitors to the fatherland and as murderers who have dishonored Russia.

Vasili Maklakoff, the latest Russian Ambassador accredited to France, according to the same article, says that all Russians in Paris feel deeply humiliated by the proposal of the allied and associated Powers. The Ambassador adds that a party truce and cessation of hostilities, as requested by the Allies, could have only one result—the hampering of the armies which are about to liberate Northern Russia—without putting an end to the reign of terror. The Ambassador is also quoted as declaring that only the Bolsheviki will profit by such a conference.

Alluding to the decision of the Supreme Council of the Peace Conference to send a delegation to meet representatives of the various Russian factions, which decision has been objected to in some Russian quarters as not in the real interest of the Russian people, M. Maklakoff said yesterday:

"The presence of France and America at the Peace Conference is a guarantee that any unfriendly intention toward Russia, even if there were such, would not be countenanced. It is most strange, however, that France, which on Dec. 29, in alluding to Bolshevism while stating her attitude toward Russia, declared that she would 'never have anything to do with crime,' should now have joined in the proposal to hold a discussion with Bolshevist delegates at the Princes' Islands."

It may be noted in connection with the attitude of Ambassador Maklakoff to-

Continued on Page Three.

Text of Wilson's Speech to Peace Conference Pointing Out Need of a League of Nations

PARIS, Jan. 25.—President Wilson's address before the Peace Conference today was as follows:

Mr. Chairman—I consider it a distinguished privilege to be permitted to open the discussion in this conference on the League of Nations. We have assembled for two purposes, to make the present settlements which have been rendered necessary by this war and also to secure the peace of the world, not only by the present settlements but by the arrangements we shall make at this conference for its maintenance.

The League of Nations seems to me to be necessary for both of these purposes. There are many complicated questions connected with the present settlements, which perhaps cannot be successfully worked out to an ultimate issue by the decisions we shall arrive at here. I can easily conceive that many of these settlements will need subsequent consideration; that many of the decisions we make shall need subsequent alteration in some degree, for if I may judge by my own study of some of these questions they are not susceptible for confident judgments at present.

It is therefore necessary that we should set up some machinery by which the work of this conference should be rendered complete.

We have assembled here for the purpose of doing very much more than making the present settlements that are necessary. We are assembled under very peculiar conditions of world opinion. I may say, without straining the point, that we are not the representatives of Governments, but representatives of the peoples.

It will not suffice to satisfy governmental circles anywhere. It is necessary that we should satisfy the opinion of mankind.

The burdens of this war have fallen in an unusual degree upon the whole population of the countries involved. I do not need to draw for you the picture of how the burden has been thrown back from the front upon the older men, upon the women, upon the children, upon the homes of the civilized world, and how the real strain of the war has come where the eyes of the Government could not reach, but where the heart of humanity beats.

We are bidden by these people to make a peace which will make them secure. We are bidden by these people to see to it that this strain does not come upon them again. And I venture to say that it has been possible for them to bear this strain because they hoped that those who represented them could get together after this war and make such another sacrifice unnecessary.

It is a solemn obligation on our part, therefore, to make permanent arrangements that justice shall be rendered and peace maintained.

This is the central object of our meeting. Settlements may be temporary, but the action of the nations in the interest of peace and justice must be permanent. We can set up permanent processes. We may not be able to set up a permanent decision.

Therefore, it seems to me that we must take as far as we can a picture of the world into our minds. Is it not a startling circumstance, for one thing, that the great discoveries of science, that the quiet studies of men in laboratories, that the thoughtful developments which have taken place in quiet lecture rooms have now been turned to the destruction of civilization? The powers of destruction have not so much multiplied as they have gained facilities.

The enemy, whom we have just overcome, had at his seats of learning some of the principal centres of scientific study and discovery, and he used them in order to make destruction sudden and complete. And only the watchful and continuous co-operation of men can see to it that science, as well as armed men, is kept within the harness of civilization.

In a sense the United States is less interested in this subject than the other nations here assembled. With her great territory and her extensive sea borders, it is less likely that the United States should suffer from the attack of enemies than that other nations should suffer. And the ardor of the United States—for it is a very deep and genuine ardor—for the society of nations is not an ardor springing out of fear or apprehension, but an ardor springing out of the ideals which have come in the consciousness of this war.

In coming into this war the United States never for a moment thought that she was intervening in the politics of Europe, or the politics of Asia, or the politics of any part of the world. Her thought was that all the world had now become conscious that there was a single cause of justice and of liberty for men of every kind and place.

Therefore, the United States should feel that its part in this war should be played in vain if there ensued upon it abortive European settlements. It would feel that it could not take part in guaranteeing those European settlements unless that guarantee involved the continuous superintendence of the peace of the world by the associated nations of the world.

Therefore, it seems to me that we must concern our best judgment in order to make this League of Nations a vital thing—a thin sometimes called into life to meet an exigency—but always functioning in watchful attendance upon the interests of the nations, and that its continuity should be a vital continuity; that its functions are continuing functions that do not permit an intermission of its watchfulness and of its labor; that it should be the eye of the nations, to keep watch upon the common interest—an eye that did not slumber, an eye that was everywhere watchful and attentive.

And if we do not make it vital, what shall we do? We shall disappoint the expectations of the peoples. This is what their thought centres upon.

I have had the very delightful experience of visiting several nations since I came to this side of the water, and every time the voice of the body of the people reached me, through any representative, at the front of the plea stood the hope of the League of Nations.

Gentlemen, the select classes of mankind are no longer the governors of mankind. The fortunes of mankind are now in the hands of the plain people of the whole world. Satisfy them, and you have justified their confidence not only, but have established peace. Fail to satisfy them, and no arrangement that you can make will either set up or steady the peace of the world.

You can imagine, I dare say, the sentiments and the purpose with which the representatives of the United States support this great project for a League of Nations. We regard it as the keynote of the whole, which expressed our purposes and ideals in this war and which the associated nations have accepted as the basis of a settlement.

If we return to the United States without having made every effort in our power to realize this program, we should return to meet the merited scorn of our fellow-citizens. For they are a body that constitute a great democracy. They expect their leaders to speak; their representatives to be their servants.

We have no choice but to obey their mandate. But it is with the greatest enthusiasm and pleasure that we accept that mandate. And because this is the keynote of the whole fabric, we have pledged our every purpose to it, as we have to every item of the fabric. We would not dare abate a single item of the program which constitutes our instructions; we would not dare to compromise upon any matter as the champion of this thing—this peace of the world, this attitude of justice, this principle that we are the masters of no peoples, but are here to see that every people in the world shall choose its own masters and govern its own destinies, not as we wish, but as they wish.

We are here to see, in short, that the very foundations of this war are swept away. Those foundations were the private choice of a small coterie of civil rulers and military staffs. Those foundations were the aggression of great powers upon the small. Those foundations were the holding together of empires of unwilling subjects by the duress of arms. Those foundations were the power of small bodies of men to wield their will and use mankind as pawns in a game. And nothing less than the emancipation of the world from these things will accomplish peace.

You can see that the representatives of the United States are, therefore, never put to the embarrassment of choosing a way of expediency, because they have had laid down before them the unalterable lines of principles. And, thank God, these lines have been accepted as the lines of settlements by all the high-minded men who have had to do with the beginning of this great business.

I hope, Mr. Chairman, when it is known, as I feel confident it will be known, that we have adopted the principle of the League of Nations and mean to work out that principle in effective action, we shall by that single thing have lifted a great part of the load of anxiety from the hearts of men everywhere.

We stand in a peculiar cause. As I go about the streets here I see everywhere the American uniform. Those men came into the war after we had uttered our purpose. They came as crusaders, not merely to win a war, but to win a cause. And I am responsible to them, for it falls to me to formulate the purpose for which I asked them to fight, and I, like them, must be a crusader for these things, whatever it costs and whatever it may be necessary to do in honor to accomplish the object for which they fought.

I have been glad to find from day to day that there is no question of our standing alone in this matter, for there are champions of this cause upon every hand. I am merely avowing this in order that you may understand why, perhaps, it fell to us, who are disengaged from the politics of this great continent and of the Orient, to suggest that this was the keystone of the arch, and why it occurred to the generous mind of your President to call upon me to open this debate. It is not because we alone represent this idea, but because it is our privilege to associate ourselves with you in representing it.

I have only tried in what I have said to give you the fountains of the enthusiasm which is within us for this thing, for those fountains spring, it seems to me, from all the ancient wrongs and sympathies of mankind, and the very pulse of the world seems to beat to the fullest in this enterprise.

CONFERENCE ACTS SWIFTLY

Hears Speeches in Favor of League and Gives Quick Approval

FIRST ADDRESS BY WILSON

Lloyd George Warmly Voices Great Britain's Support of the Proposal.

ORLANDO ALSO BACKS IT

Wilson and House Are American Members of Commission to Draft League Plan.

Delegates of Great Powers on Peace League Commission

PARIS, Jan. 25.—The delegates of the Great Powers on the League of Nations, it was learned tonight, will be:

For the United States—President Wilson and Colonel Edward M. House.

For Great Britain—Lord Robert Cecil and General Jan Christian Smuts.

For France—Leon Bourgeois and Ferdinand Larnaude, Dean of the Faculty of Law of the University of Paris.

For Italy—Premier Orlando and Viterio Scialoia.

For Japan—Viscount Chinda and K. Ochiai.

The delegates of the small nations will be announced later.

PARIS, Jan. 25, (Associated Press.)—The plenary session of the Peace Conference today unanimously adopted the project to establish a League of Nations and name a commission to draft the complete plan.

President Wilson and Colonel House are the two American members of the commission.

The session of the conference began at 3 o'clock in the afternoon in the Salle de la Paix of the Foreign Office with the same imposing setting as the first session, but with little ceremony and a manifest purpose of business.

M. Clemenceau was again in the chair, with President Wilson and the full American delegation at his right, and Premier Lloyd George and the British delegation at his left.

When the session opened it was addressed by President Wilson on the subject of the proposed world league.

The President declared that the conference had solemn obligations to make a permanent settlement.

With great earnestness he asserted that the conference could not complete its work until some further machinery of settlement should be set up.

"We are not here alone," he went on, "as representatives of Governments, but as representatives of peoples, and in the settlements we make we need to satisfy, not the opinions of Governments, but the opinion of mankind."

League Must Have Continuity.

The President contended that a League of Nations must be a vital thing and not casual or occasional. It must have continuity.

"It should be the eye of nations, an eye which never slumbers," he added.

On his travels, the President said, people everywhere had greeted the league as the first thing in their interest.

"Select classes of men no longer direct the affairs of the world," said the President, "but the fortunes of the world are now in the hands of the plain people."

The wish of the people, therefore, must be heard. The war had swept away those old foundations by which small coteries had "used mankind as pawns in a game." Nothing but emancipation from the old system, he contended, would accomplish real peace.

The President said he had seen American soldiers in the street—soldiers who had come, not alone for war, but as "crusaders in a great cause." He added, "And I, like them, must be a crusader, whatever it costs to accomplish that end."

After declaring that the conference was for the purpose of a settlement arising out of the war and to make

Section 1

"All the News That's Fit to Print."

The New York Times.

THE WEATHER
Fair and continued cool Sunday; fair Monday; moderate winds.
For full weather report see Page 23.

Section 1

VOL. LXVIII...NO. 22,436. NEW YORK, SUNDAY, JUNE 29, 1919. 122 PAGES, In Nine Parts, Including Picture and Magazine Sections (Rotogravure) and Book Section. FIVE CENTS In Greater New York | Elsewhere SEVEN CENTS

PEACE SIGNED, ENDS THE GREAT WAR; GERMANS DEPART STILL PROTESTING; PROHIBITION TILL TROOPS DISBAND

WILSON PROMISES TO ACT

Must Wait Until Complete Demobilization, His Word from Paris.

THIS WILL TAKE 7 WEEKS

President Calls Attention of Congress to His Request for Repeal.

LIQUOR MEN UNPREPARED

Had Hoped Until Announcement That Executive Would Intervene at the Eleventh Hour.

Special to The New York Times.

WASHINGTON, June 28.—President Wilson will not lift the ban which provides for war-time prohibition until the demobilization of the army has been terminated.

But when demobilization has been completed, the President will lift the ban. Formal announcement to this effect was made at the White House tonight. The President is in agreement with A. Mitchell Palmer, his Attorney General, that he cannot at this time lift the ban on wartime prohibition. He agrees with the Attorney General that the language of the law is such that he will be free to act on his own initiative, without Congressional action, not immediately after the signing of the treaty of peace, but when the army has been demobilized. As the army has not yet been demobilized, and there are yet a million men in the army, called into service under the emergency of war, the President, in the failure of Congress to vest him with power to call off wartime prohibition, takes the position that he cannot interfere with the putting of wartime prohibition into effect.

The responsibility for putting wartime prohibition into effect is put squarely up to Congress by the President. He takes the position that the law calling for wartime prohibition was an act of Congress, that its terms are clear, and that he had asked Congress to provide for the repeal of the legislation. Congress, having failed to act so far, has left the President's hands tied with legal strings so far as lifting the ban is concerned, and he makes this situation very plain in a cablegram sent to the White House just before he left Paris today.

President Wilson's cablegram was made public at the White House at 8 o'clock tonight by Joseph P. Tumulty, the Private Secretary to the President.

In his message the President said that he could not act until the army had been completely demobilized, and since there were still a million men in the service there was no chance of his taking immediate action. He called attention to the fact that the present difficulty could have been obviated if Congress had heeded his recommendation of several months ago.

The President in his message left no doubt as to what action he will take when demobilization is terminated.

"When demobilization is terminated," says the final sentence of his cablegram, "my power to act without Congressional action will be exercised."

When demobilization has been terminated will be determined by the President upon information to be supplied to him by Secretary Baker and by Attorney General Palmer. The prospects are that six, or perhaps seven, weeks will elapse before demobilization is terminated, which means that the President will probably not be in position, under his construction of the law, to act before the middle or latter part of August in lifting the ban.

It means that wartime prohibition will go into effect on July 1, even though there is no adequate provision legally made for its real enforcement, and that it will remain in effect until the termination of demobilization unless Congress meanwhile adopts the President's request for a repeal of the legislation which provided for the institution of wartime prohibition.

Congress is free at any time to enact the necessary legislation. So far all attempts to bring about repeal have failed on Capitol Hill and there is no present indication that Congress intends to change.

Not only has the President asked Congress to repeal the legislation standing in the way of lifting the ban, but in his cabled statement of today the President declares without equivocation that he will exercise his power to act when demobilization is terminated, and makes it clear he will then lift the ban unless Congress by repealing the act of Nov. 21, 1918, does away with wartime pro-

Continued on Page Eleven.

President Sends A Prohibition Message; Says He Will Act When Demobilization Ends

WASHINGTON, July 28.—The following message from President Wilson, stating his stand on the prohibition question, was made public at the White House tonight by Secretary Tumulty:

I am convinced that the Attorney General is right in advising me that I have no legal power at this time in the matter of the ban on liquor. Under the act of November, 1918, my power to take action is restricted. The act provides that after June 30, 1919, "until the conclusion of the present war and thereafter until the termination of demobilization, the date of which shall be determined and proclaimed by the President, it shall be unlawful, &c." This law does not specify that the ban shall be lifted with the signing of peace, but with the termination of the demobilization of the troops, and I cannot say that this has been accomplished. My information from the War Department is that there are still a million men in the army under the emergency call. It is clear, therefore, that the failure of Congress to act upon the suggestion contained in my message of the twentieth of May, 1919, asking for a repeal of the act of Nov. 21, 1918, so far as it applies to wines and beers, makes it impossible to act in this matter at this time. When demobilization is terminated, my power to act without Congressional action will be exercised. WOODROW WILSON.

VIOLENCE GROWS IN BERLIN FERMENT

Bomb Hurled at Building in Which Officials Were Conferring on Strike.

SHOTS FIRED AT MINISTERS

Railway Strikers Ignore Orders from Noske and Union Chiefs to Resume Work.

Copyright, 1919, by The New York Times Company.
Special Cable to THE NEW YORK TIMES.

BERLIN, June 28, (via Copenhagen.)—Vorwärts, even Die Freiheit and also Ledebour, in his first speech after his release from prison, earnestly warn the people against riots and political revolt which, in view of the enormous military strength gathered in Berlin, can only lead to awful bloodshed.

Doubtless the big leaders of the Independent Socialists do not wish any outbreaks at present. Nevertheless the air is charged with the spirit of rebellion, and nobody here would be surprised if tomorrow there were a repetition of the events of January and March on a much larger scale.

The minor leaders of the Independents, Communists and Sparticides desire to inflame this unrest, communicating it to ever-growing circles of the workers, and inciting the lawless elements to the most audacious and wholesale crimes. Unknown parties shortly after 2 o'clock this morning threw a bomb against the façade of the building of the Public Works Department. It exploded with a terrific noise, shattering about 200 windows. Nobody was hurt. Later, when the ministers and the railway employes' delegates left the building, after trying vainly all night to reach an agreement, unknown persons fired revolvers at the government members, without hitting any one.

Incite Lawlessness in Berlin.

Though ten or more members of the Executive Committee of the Berlin Soldiers and Workers' Councils, after being arrested yesterday on suspicion of conniving with the Hamburg revolutionists for the overthrow of the Federal Government, have been released for lack of evidence nobody doubts for one moment that telephone congratulations were exchanged between them and the Hamburg revolutionists, as overheard by officials, but the identity of the man who answered the Hamburg announcement of the successful revolt with "Bravo!" and promised the Executive Committee's aid in starting a revolt against the Government in Berlin could not be established.

Members of that Executive Committee have never made any secret of their intention to overthrow the Government at the first opportunity, and doubtless the weaker heads among them yesterday believed that the time had come. The lawless element believe this, and it cannot be denied that they are quite right, if the absence of any effective policing of the capital is any justification.

Insecurity has reached an incredible degree. Lately men disguised as officers have been ascending street cars and, with pointed revolvers, collecting pocketbooks and jewels from the passengers in true Wild West fashion. This

Continued on Page Three.

DUTCH UNWILLING TO GIVE UP KAISER

Majority of the People Firmly Opposed to Yielding to Allies' Demand.

HOPEFUL AT AMERONGEN

Troelstra Says Chamber Would Surrender Ex-Ruler to Germany Only.

Copyright, 1919, by The New York Times Company.
Special Cable to THE NEW YORK TIMES.

THE HAGUE, June 27.—The question of the delivery of the ex-Kaiser is again on the tapis here. There is no doubt that a majority of Netherlanders are already forgetting Germany's and the ex-monarch's record and violently oppose his surrender.

Appeals such as the recent one from the German Officers League and echoes from the German press only serve to strengthen these feelings. The officers' appeal stated that the German officers would be dishonored forever if Holland delivered the ex-Kaiser to the Allies, and ended with the statement: "It is even yet not certain whether a German can be *found* to sign the peace treaty."

The NEW YORK TIMES correspondent questioned Pieter Troelstra, the Socialist leader, the report emanating from Germany that the Dutch Social Democrats opposed the surrender of the ex-Kaiser. Troelstra replied:

"Our party has taken no official attitude. As we have not yet considered the question officially no resolution has been taken and no official correspondence carried on.

"It is true that we are against his surender on principle and would oppose it. I consider that we must wait until we receive the allied demand, so that the matter is not urgent.

"I can certainly say that as Socialists we believe in the right of asylum. English Socialists defend the right of asylum and London has always been a city for political refugees. Switzerland and the Netherlands have been free for centuries and it is a matter of tradition."

When asked if the question were put to a vote in the Dutch Chamber other parties would oppose the delivery of the ex-monarch, Troelstra replied in the affirmative.

"It is impossible," he said, "to deliver a refugee to an enemy. It is against all rights. If Germany should demand the Kaiser it would be another question. We should be in favor of that. I feel nothing but antipathy for his personality, but only his own Government has a right to demand him. I believe that all parties would vote in favor of a demand from the German Government."

Plead Ties with Dutch Queen.

Copyright, 1919, by The New York Times Company.
Special Cable to THE NEW YORK TIMES.

BERLIN, June 28.—The League of Officers of the Former Prussian Army and German Navy has addressed a message to the Dutch Queen pleading that she had refused to extradite the "*all highest war lord*, our beloved unforgettable King, his Majesty Kaiser Wilhelm, who because of high treason in his own country, and not forced by the enemy's arms,

Continued on Page Three.

LEAGUE OPPONENTS UNITING

Republican Senators Now Seem Agreed on Policy of Reservations.

McCUMBER IS WON OVER

But North Dakota Senator Opposes Any Action Nullifying the Covenant.

SHANTUNG ACTION ASSAILED

Borah Calls It Indefensible—Norris Demands a Reservation Regarding It.

Special to The New York Times.

WASHINGTON, June 28.—With unexpected swiftness the Republican opposition in the Senate to the League of Nations covenant, as embraced in the Treaty of Peace, began to crystallize today, after the cables had brought word that Germany had signed the treaty, and that the President, in his message to the American people, had expressed the hope that the treaty would be "ratified and acted upon in full and sincere execution of its terms."

The President's message, coupled with his statement in interviews at Paris that he hoped the Senate woud ratify the treaty with the League of Nations covenant in it, without amendment, had the effect, it appeared, of bringing closer the elements of opposition among the opponents of the League. Instead of influencing wavering Senators toward an attitude favoring the ratification of the League of Nations covenant, the President's appeal appeared to have exactly the opposite effect.

While the opponents of the covenants, before Germany signed, were admittedly divided as to a policy to pursue in fighting the covenant when the treaty should come before the Senate, they seemed, for the first time since the League fight started, to have come to some general agreement.

Every Republican Senator to whom THE NEW YORK TIMES correspondent talked said decisively that he believed that, if the League covenant was to be accepted by the Senate some character of qualifying resolution would have to be passed, along with the treaty ratification, to express dissent from features objected to.

Even Senator McCumber of North Dakota, the one Republican member of the Foreign Relations Committee who has all along advocated adoption of the covenant, after the President's message had been read in the Senate, said that he believed it would be necessary for that body to adopt "explanatory reservations" in the ratification of the treaty, respecting features involved in the covenant. Mr. McCumber spoke of such reservations being necessary as to the Monroe Doctrine and the right of the United States to determine its purely domestic questions, like immigration, racial equality, and the tariff.

The North Dakota Senator made it clear that he would not favor any resolution of reservation that would have the effect of nullifying the covenant. He wanted the treaty of peace ratified, with the League of Nations included. But he insisted that the Senate should not hesitate to express its dissent from features that affected purely American affairs. If this were not done, he said, there might come some development in the future that might impel the Senate to take action which, in effect, would take America out of the League.

McNary for Interpretation.

Senator McNary, Republican, Oregon, who only a few days ago announced himself as favoring the League of Nations, declared today that he would not oppose a resolution that would enable opponents of the covenant to make clear their dissent from matters to which they objected. This, he said, might be done through a resolution of "interpretation," which was another way of saying one of "qualification."

At the same time Senator McNary agreed with Senator McCumber that no resolution ought to be adopted that would have the effect of rejecting the League of Nations covenant.

Talk of direct amendment of the covenant was not so insistent today among the more radical Senators. They appeared to be willing now to stand behind qualifying resolutions that would amply set forth the features subject to objection. They maintained, however, that Article X., guaranteeing the territorial integrity of members of the League, should come out. On this point

Continued on Page Five.

Wilson Says Treaty Will Furnish the Charter for a New Order of Affairs in the World

WASHINGTON, June 28.—The following address by President Wilson to the American people on the occasion of the signing of the Peace Treaty was given out here today by Secretary Tumulty:

My Fellow Countrymen: The treaty of peace has been signed. If it is ratified and acted upon in full and sincere execution of its terms it will furnish the charter for a new order of affairs in the world. It is a severe treaty in the duties and penalties it imposes upon Germany; but it is severe only because great wrongs done by Germany are to be righted and repaired; it imposes nothing that Germany cannot do; and she can regain her rightful standing in the world by the prompt and honorable fulfillment of its terms.

And it is much more than a treaty of peace with Germany. It liberates great peoples who have never before been able to find the way to liberty. It ends, once for all, an old and intolerable order under which small groups of selfish men could use the peoples of great empires to serve their ambition for power and dominion. It associates the free Governments of the world in a permanent League in which they are pledged to use their united power to maintain peace by maintaining right and justice.

It makes international law a reality supported by imperative sanctions. It does away with the right of conquest and rejects the policy of annexation and substitutes a new order under which backward nations—populations which have not yet come to political consciousness and peoples who are ready for independence but not yet quite prepared to dispense with protection and guidance—shall no more be subjected to the domination and exploitation of a stronger nation, but shall be put under the friendly direction and afforded the helpful assistance of governments which undertake to be responsible to the opinion of mankind in the execution of their task by accepting the direction of the League of Nations.

It recognizes the inalienable rights of nationality, the rights of minorities and the sanctity of religious belief and practice. It lays the basis for conventions which shall free the commercial intercourse of the world from unjust and vexatious restrictions and for every sort of international co-operation that will serve to cleanse the life of the world and facilitate its common action in beneficent service of every kind. It furnishes guarantees such as were never given or even contemplated for the fair treatment of all who labor at the daily tasks of the world.

It is for this reason that I have spoken of it as a great charter for a new order of affairs. There is ground here for deep satisfaction, universal reassurance, and confident hope.

WOODROW WILSON.

DEPORT THIRTY 'RED' AGITATORS

Fifteen Have Been Shipped Away in a Week—18 More Waiting at Ellis Island.

MOST OF THEM ANARCHISTS

Number Includes Some Suspected of Having a Hand in Plot Against Officials.

The deportation of alien agitators and conspirators who have abused their sojourn in America by preaching the overthrow of the United States Government, some of them coming under suspicion of the Secret Service for plots against President Wilson and other high public officials, has begun. Within the last seven days, fifteen of these disturbers, among them the editors of two anarchist newspapers, have been deported from New York, and eighteen others are now on Ellis Island awaiting the sailing of ships that will return them to the lands of their nativity.

The Secret Service agencies of the Government have been quietly, but thoroughly, at work for weeks, and every day or two a new batch of aliens who have urged the destruction of American institutions are rounded up and their records submitted to the proper authorities with a view to immediate deportation.

In the last four weeks thirty anarchist, I. W. W., and Bolshevist agitators have been deported by way of Ellis Island. This number does not include the Seattle and Spokane I. W. W. disturbers and other radicals who were sent East for deportation as a result of Bolshevist strikes in the Pacific Northwest several months ago. Some of those agitators also have been deported, and the cases of several others, recommended for the "homeward voyage, are soon to be decided by the courts.

Most of the deportations have taken place since bombs were set off at the homes of Attorney General Palmer and

Continued on Page Nine.

AMERICA GREETED BY KING GEORGE

"Brothers in Arms Will Continue Forever to be Brothers in Peace."

SENDS MESSAGE TO WILSON

"We Lay Down Our Arms in Proud Consciousness of Valiant Deeds Nobly Done."

LONDON, June 28, (Associated Press.)—King George has sent the following message to President Wilson:

"In this glorious hour when the long struggle of nations for right, justice and freedom is at last crowned by a triumphant peace, I greet you, Mr. President, and the great American people in the name of the British nation.

"At a time when fortune seemed to frown, and the issues of the war trembled in the balance, the American people stretched out the hand of fellowship to those who on this side of the ocean were battling for a righteous cause. Light and hope at once shone brighter in our hearts, and a new day dawned.

Together we have fought to a happy end; together we lay down our arms in proud consciousness of valiant deeds nobly done.

Mr. President, it is on this day one of our happiest thoughts that the American and British people, brothers in arms, will continue forever to be brothers in peace. United before by language, traditions, kinship, and ideals, there has been set upon our fellowship the sacred seal of common sacrifice. GEORGE, R. I.

After news of the signing of peace had been received here the following was issued over King George's signature:

The signing of the treaty of peace will be received with deep thankfulness throughout the British Empire. This formal act brings to its concluding stages the terrible war which has

Continued on Page Three.

ENEMY ENVOYS IN TRUCULENT SPIRIT

Say Afterward They Would Not Have Signed Had They Known They Were to Leave First by Different Way.

CHINA REFUSES TO SIGN, SMUTS MAKES PROTEST

These Events Somewhat Cloud the Great Occasion at Versailles—Wilson, Clemenceau, and Lloyd George Receive a Tremendous Ovation.

President Wilson Starts for Home

PARIS, June 28, (Associated Press.)—President Wilson left Paris on his homeward journey tonight. His train started from the Gare des Invalides for Brest at 9:45 P. M.

Mr. Wilson's party was accompanied to Brest by General Leorat and Colonel Lobez, the President's French aids, and also by Stephen Pichon, French Foreign Minister; Georges Leygues, French Minister of Marine, and Captain André Tardieu, a member of the French peace delegation. Ambassador Wallace, General Pershing, Premier Clemenceau, and Colonel House were at the station to say good-bye.

The crowd in the station, numbering upward of a thousand, wildly cheered the departure of the President, who raised his hat to cries of "Vive Wilson." Mrs. Wilson threw kisses to the crowd as the train departed.

The superdreadnought Oklahoma will accompany the George Washington to the United States.

VERSAILLES, June 28, (Associated Press.)—Germany and the allied and associated powers signed the peace terms here today in the same imperial hall where the Germans humbled the French so ignominiously forty-eight years ago.

This formally ended the world war, which lasted just thirty-seven days less than five years. Today, the day of peace, was the fifth anniversary of the murder of Archduke Francis Ferdinand by a Serbian student at Serajevo.

The peace was signed under circumstances which somewhat dimmed the expectations of those who had worked and fought during long years of war and months of negotiations for its achievement.

Absence of the Chinese delegates, who at the last moment were unable to reconcile themselves to the Shantung settlement, struck the first discordant note. A written protest which General Smuts lodged with his signature was another disappointment.

But bulking larger than these was the attitude of Germany and the German plenipotentiaries, which left them, as evident from the expression of M. Clemenceau, still outside of formal reconciliation and made the actual restoration to regular relations and intercourse with the allied nations dependent, not upon the signature of the "preliminaries of peace" today, but upon ratification by the National Assembly.

To M. Clemenceau's warning in his opening remarks that they would be expected, and held, to observe the treaty provisions loyally and completely the German delegates, through Dr. Haniel von Haimhausen, replied after returning to the hotel that had they known that they would be treated on a different status after signing than the allied representatives, as shown by their separate exit before the general body of the conference, they never would have signed.

Under the circumstances the general tone of sentiment in the historic sitting was one rather of relief at the uncontrovertible end of hostilities than of complete satisfaction.

The ceremony had been planned deliberately to be austere, befitting the sufferings of almost five years, and the lack of impressiveness and picturesque color, of which many spectators, who had expected a magnificent State pageant, complained, was a matter of design, not merely omission.

The actual ceremony was far shorter than had been expected, in view of the number of signatures which were to be appended to the treaty and the two accompanying conventions, ending a bare forty-nine minutes after the hour set for the opening.

Premier Clemenceau called the session to order in the Hall of Mirrors at 3:10 P. M.

The signing began when Dr. Hermann Müller and Johannes Bell, the German signatories, affixed their names. Herr Müller signed at 3:12 o'clock and Herr Bell 3:13 o'clock.

President Wilson, the first of the allied delegates, signed a minute later. At 3:49 o'clock the momentous session was over.

The most dramatic moment connected with the signing came unexpectedly and spontaneously at the conclusion of the ceremony, when Premier Clemenceau, President Wilson and Premier Lloyd George descended from the Hall of Mirrors to the terrace at the rear of the palace, where thousands of spectators were massed.

GREAT DEMONSTRATION FOR ALLIED LEADERS.

With the appearance of the three who had dominated the councils of the Allies there began a most remarkable demonstration. With cries of "Vive Clemenceau!" "Vive Wilson!" "Vive Lloyd George!" dense crowds swept forward from all parts of the spacious terrace. In an instant the three were surrounded by struggling, cheering masses of people, fighting among themselves for a chance to get near the statesmen.

It had been planned that all the allied delegates would walk across the terrace after signing, to see the great fountains play, but none of the other plenipotentiaries got further than the door.

President Wilson, M. Clemenceau and Mr. Lloyd George were caught in the living stream which flowed across the great space, and became part of the crowd themselves. Soldiers and bodyguards struggled vainly to

"All the News That's Fit to Print."

The New York Times.

THE WEATHER
Fair today, with diminishing northwest winds; Friday fair, warmer.
For weather report see next to last page.

VOL. LXIX...No. 22,580. NEW YORK, THURSDAY, NOVEMBER 20, 1919. THIRTY-TWO PAGES. TWO CENTS Metropolitan District | THREE CENTS Within 200 Miles | FOUR CENTS Elsewhere

SENATE SESSION ENDS, TREATY IS DEFEATED; THREE VOTES TAKEN, 39 TO 55, 41 TO 50, 38 TO 53; MAY BE REVIVED AT THE DECEMBER SESSION

PRINCE SPENDS DAY SEEING NEW YORK; 'HAVING FINE TIME'

Mingles Democratically with People and Wins Their Hearts with His Smile.

ENJOYING EVERY MINUTE

Visits Movies, Wall Street, and Woolworth Tower, and Says He Will Come Again.

WALKS UNNOTED ON AVENUE

Tops Off His Busy Day Dining with Fellow-Britons and Dancing with Our Debutantes.

The second day of the visit of the Prince of Wales to New York, during which many thousands of Americans and hundreds of his own countrymen lavished attentions upon him, served to lift to new levels the high favor with which he was received when he arrived. Not only did he endear himself to countless new friends, but with his simple enjoyment, his quick response, he contrived to seem a very old friend indeed to those who had known him for all of two days.

New York, which was curious and interested when he arrived and frankly approving by the time he had made his first tour of the city and uttered his first little speech, had, in the words of one of the many speakers who paid him honor, "quite capitulated to him" by the time he reluctantly left the last of a series of brilliant functions last night.

Nor was the Prince reticent about letting the city know he reciprocated all its warmly expressed feeling. As on the day of his arrival, he talked on each occasion seriously for a few moments of the part he hoped to play in deepening the ties of friendship between the United States and Britain.

But each time he digressed long enough to assure his hearers that he was "having a fine time," and each time he became a little more emphatic in his assurances—which impressed his listeners as being meant as much as anything to convince himself—that he was coming back soon and would stay longer when he came.

Though he was never entirely out of the willing hands of his American hosts during the day, they did surrender him to a degree in the evening that he might enjoy the hospitality of those over whom he some day is destined to rule. The members of seven British societies, most of whom doubtless saw him for the first time, felt the appeal of his clean, bright youth just as quickly and as warmly as have Americans, and lost no opportunity to give noisy and hearty evidence that they liked his looks and his actions and the way he talked.

Enjoys Day Heartily.

With the more formal ceremonies of welcome out of the way, the Prince had a better time of it and found the long program laid out for him less exacting. He was treated to a variety of experiences, he met all sorts of people, he was not called upon to do a great deal of talking, and he gave himself up heartily to those opportunities to play which the wise elders who surrounded him had interspersed in his day.

At that, he was tired and, at times, a bit nervous. But that seemed to make no difference. The smile—one might almost call it a grin—which has earned for him the popular title of "the smiling prince," was seldom absent.

And when he reached the Madison Avenue home of Mrs. Whitelaw Reid, late last night, to be the guest of honor at a great ball she gave him, in which all of society's best participated, he was about the last man present to manifest any willingness to quit dancing and go home.

He danced with many of the débutantes of the season, and with a fair share of the matrons of earlier ones. The slim figure in evening clothes with the broad blue ribbon of the Order of the Garter slashing the white shirt front, topped by that unmistakable mop of smooth blond hair, was an active, a conspicuous, and a popular one.

Proves Himself Real Democrat.

Edward Albert found every opportunity during the day to exhibit that democracy for which he has expressed so much liking, both here and in Canada, and which many of those who have admired him have ascribed as one distinct source of his own appeal. He was called upon to meet and to mingle with many elements, to respond, as it were, to a great variety of stimuli, and he proved equal to each occasion, leaving every function he attended with a trail of good wishes behind him.

The city showed itself anything but

Continued on Page Three.

Panama Canal Toll Records Broken by October Traffic

PANAMA, Nov. 19.—The tolls collected from ships passing through the Panama Canal during October exceeded those of any previous month.

They amounted to $661,000 as compared with the next highest month, May, 1918, when $644,000 was collected.

Commercial vessels to the number of 196 passed through the canal in October.

HARDING BLAMES THE SPECULATORS

Break in Stocks, He Said, Followed 'Unbridled Speculation' in the Market.

WARNINGS WERE UNHEEDED

Reserve Board Refused to Withhold Credit from Commerce and Industry for Stock Trading.

WASHINGTON, Nov. 19.—The recent break in the New York stock market was due to "unbridled speculation," Governor Harding of the Federal Reserve Board said in a letter tonight to Senator Owen of Oklahoma, who had asked for a direct explanation of the price crash.

Speculators took no heed of warnings issued by the Board and by the Federal Reserve Bank at New York that reserves were declining and that a halt must be called, Mr. Harding said, and the speculative movement continued. These circumstances, he added, then forced the New York bank to call the attention of rediscounting banks to the situation, in order that demands of regular customers for call money in handling commercial transactions might be protected.

Text of the Letter.

The text of Governor Harding's letter follows:

"My Dear Senator: Receipt is acknowledged of your letter of the 14th instant.

"The Federal Reserve act is intended for the benefit of commerce and industry and not for the stimulation of the investment market or of speculative movements. The short title of the act reads, as follows: 'An act to provide for the establishment of Federal Reserve banks, furnish an elastic currency, to afford means of rediscounting commercial paper, to establish a more effective supervision of banking in the United States.'

"Section 13 of the act provides in part that Federal Reserve Banks may discount notes, drafts, and bills of exchange arising out of actual commercial transactions: That is, notes, drafts, and bills of exchange issued or drawn for agricultural, industrial, or commercial purposes, or the proceeds of which have been used, or are to be used, for such purposes. It provides further that nothing contained in the act shall be construed to prohibit such notes, drafts, and bills of exchange, secured by staple agricultural products, or other goods, wares or merchandise from being eligible for such discount 'but such definition shall not include notes, drafts, or bills covering merely invstments or issued or drawn for the purpose of carrying or trading in stocks, bonds, or other investment securities, except bonds and notes of the Government of the United States.'

"The Board has repeatedly called attention to the fact that resources obtained from the Federal Reserve banks should not be used for speculative purposes, and at various times when there has been unusual speculative activity it has issued public warnings as to the bad effect of such activities upon the banking situation. The first warning of this kind was issued as long ago as October, 1915, and the warning has been repeated on several occasions since that date when conditions made it necessary. On June 10, 1919, the Board made public a letter which it had addressed to all Federal agents, reading as follows:

"'The Federal Reserve Board is concerned over the existing tendency towards excessive speculation, and while ordinarily this could be corrected by an advance in discount rates at the Federal Reserve Banks, it is not practicable to apply this check at this time because of Government financing. By far the larger part of the invested assets of Federal Reserve Banks consists of paper secured by Government obligations, and the board is anxious to get some information on which it can form an estimate as to the extent of member bank borrowings on Government collateral made for purposes other than for carrying customers who have purchased Liberty Bonds on account, or other than for purely commercial purposes.

"This letter was sent out for the purpose of ascertaining to what extent Government obligations were being used to secure loans from Federal Reserve Banks

Continued on Page Two.

DEADLOCK ON COAL CONTINUES DESPITE GARFIELD'S APPEAL

New Joint Sub-Committee Meets but Operators Fail to Present Counter-Demands.

SAYS PUBLIC IS PARAMOUNT

Fuel Administrator Asserts People Will Not Stand Excessive Prices or Prolonged Tieup.

COAL SHORTAGE GROWING

Supplies to Cleveland Plants Cut Off—Kansas City Coal Scanty.

Special to the New York Times.

WASHINGTON, Nov. 19.—Conferences between the coal operators and miners of the Central Competitive field were again adjourned tonight without anything like a definite agreement having been reached, despite the fact that Fuel Administrator H. A. Garfield made an address before the joint session of the scale committees this morning, in which he said that the public, "the chief party in interest in the present controversy, was not in a mood to tolerate either excessive prices or prolonged stoppage of production."

The most hopeful note was sounded this evening by representatives of the operators after a session of a committee of sixteen, formed of eight representatives of the Scale Committee of the operators and eight acting for the miners. The operators said that some progress had been made and that there would be another joint session at 10 o'clock tomorrow morning.

John L. Lewis, Acting President of the United Mine Workers, upon leaving the conference said that the miners were still in a receptive mood, but that no proposal had been submitted by the operators as yet. He did not discourage those who expressed the hope that some result might be approached at tomorrow's renewal of the conference but said that nothing "concrete" had, as yet, been accomplished.

It had been hoped that the address by Dr. Garfield, which was delivered at an open meeting in the morning, would bring immediate results. In this, at least, the situation was disappointing. Once behind closed doors, the representatives of the operators and miners again locked horns and fenced for advantage. Dr. Garfield's address had carried the conviction that the Government did not intend to permit a heavy increase in the price of coal to the consumer and the operators felt that they wanted further time to consider their proposal in view of that situation.

Garfield May Speak Again.

As the situation stands now, it seems probable that the Fuel Administrator, as the representative of the public, will have something further to say within the next forty-eight hours unless the end of the disagreement is in sight.

Attorney General Palmer announced today that he had summoned the operators and miners of Alabama and of the New River District of West Virginia, to meet with him tomorrow to discuss charges made by the miners that union men who want to return to work in these districts are being discriminated against. The operators have made the charge that the order recalling the strike order was not issued in proper form, with the seal of the union attached.

In regard to the latter charge Mr. Palmer said today that the Department of Justice was satisfied with the manner in which Acting President Lewis and other officials of the United Mine Workers of America had complied with the instructions of the court. An investigation, he said, showed that the order recalling the strike order had been issued in proper form.

Garfield Explains His Purpose.

WASHINGTON, Nov. 19 (Associated Press)—Dr. Garfield, addressing the joint session of the Scale Committees in the morning, explained that his purpose was to furnish the conference with the data which he would use in determining what wage advances, if any, agreed to by the operators and miners could be borne properly by the public.

"I represent the people of the United States in a different sense from the Secretary of Labor," he said. "It is part of Mr. Wilson's function to effect conciliation. It is my sole function to exercise those powers conferred on the Fuel Administration; to see that an adequate supply of coal is furnished the people of the United States, and to

Continued on Page Five.

Public Opinion Is Trying Unions, Says Gov. Roberts

NASHVILLE, Tenn., Nov. 19.—Governor A. H. Roberts issued a statement here today declaring Tennessee labor unions were on trial at the bar of public opinion. When the toiler "becomes an anarchist or engages in lawlessness," he said, "he then forfeits his right to the sympathy of the law-abiding man.

"No man can fight under two opposing flags. The people should awake to a realization of the dangers confronting them.

"The coal miners have utterly disregarded the order revoking the strike because it is said to have been printed on plain paper, signed with a typewriter, and did not have the seal of the union. No one would be foolish enough to believe that this was not a mere accident."

PLOT TO PUT BOMBS IN CHRISTMAS MAIL

Philadelphia Police Report Discovery of Nation-Wide Red Conspiracy.

AIMED AT HIGH OFFICIALS

Explosives Were to be Concealed in Ribbons and Holly Marked as Gifts to Victims.

Special to The New York Times.

PHILADELPHIA, Nov. 19.—Discovery of a Red plot to slay officials with explosive Christmas mail packages was announced this afternoon by James Robinson, Superintendent of Police.

Information of the plot, which he considers reliable, indicates it is nation-wide, and directed against Federal, State and city authorities who took part in the national roundup of radicals planning the overthrow of the Government.

Immediate steps were taken to prepare Federal investigators, postal authorities, and the police of the large cities for action against the mail plot, which is scheduled to begin operation just before and during the Christmas holidays.

Evidence that bombs were to be sent through the mail concealed in ribbons and holly was reported to Superintendent Robinson by Andrew Emanuel, head of the bomb squad, who said he unearthed it during his investigation of radical activities here. The information was verified, according to Emanuel. The information is believed to have emanated from an anarchist "squealer."

A memorandum issued by the Bureau of Police is as follows:

"Superintendent of Police Robinson is in possession of reliable information that the members of a certain radical organization with headquarters in the principal cities of the United States, are preparing to sen out, prior to and during the Christmas holidays, packages of neat appearance, which would probably be considered as Christmas gifts by the persons who receive them, to the United States Government officials and officials of the States and cities whose duties have required them to take an active part in the suppression of Bolshevist and anarchist movements.

"The radicals say that when the officials receive and open the packages they will be greatly surprised, as an explosion will result.

"The superintendent has sent the information to the Government officials in this city, and to Chief of Police Quigley of Rochester, N. Y., who is chairman of the Board of Governors of the National Bureau of Criminal Identification, and President of the International Association of Chiefs of Police, with the request that the matter be given wide publicity."

Todd Daniel, District Superintendent of the Department of Justice, and George A. Leonard, Chief Postal Inspector, were apprised of the plot. The city's Bomb Squad has been doubled, and determined efforts are being made to arrest the organizers of the conspiracy before it begins operation.

WASHINGTON, Nov. 19.—Department of Justice officials said tonight they were without information as to the discovery by the Philadelphia police of a nation-wide plot to kill Federal, State, and municipal officials by means of bombs sent through the mails at Christmas time. The Bureau of Investigation of the department, however, immediately asked its Philadelphia agents for details of the Reds' conspiracy as gathered by the police there. Officials also began checking over the long list of radicals who are under surveillance by the department to ascertain their latest activities.

EXPECT TO REVIVE TREATY

Hitchcock Believes Wilson Will Send It to Senate Again.

PEACE RESOLUTION BACKED

Republicans Count on Putting Through Plan at the Session Next Month.

TO TEST PUBLIC SENTIMENT

Situation May Be Changed if the Opinion of the Country Asserts Itself.

Mr. Taft Still Hopes For a Compromise

When ex-President William Howard Taft, who is staying at the Hotel McAlpin, was told last night of the defeat of the Peace Treaty he made this comment:

"I'm longing for a compromise. That's all I have to say tonight. Why not agree on a preamble and not sacrifice so much?"

Mr. Taft indicated to his questioner that he had no further statement to make at the time.

Special to The New York Times.

WASHINGTON, Nov. 19.—After the Senate had adjourned late tonight Senator Hitchcock, who has led the fight for the Administration forces, declared that the treaty was not dead and that he believed the President would resubmit it at the next session of Congress in December.

"The President can send it back," he said. "I do not, however, know what course he will follow, as I have not discussed that with him, and have not been in communication with the President since the action taken by the Senate tonight."

Senator Lodge, Chairman of the Foreign Relations Committee, admitted that the President could resubmit the treaty if he saw fit, but added that the Republicans' attitude would be unchanged. He was asked if he considered the treaty dead.

"It is dead in this Senate," he said. "They killed it, just as I told them they would if they voted against it," he added, with an emphatic gesture.

Senator Lodge said that he did not care to discuss at length the action taken, which spoke for itself. He did, however, express the belief that, by refusing to accept the majority reservations, the Administration Senators must accept the responsibility for the treaty's defeat at this session.

In his opinion, Senator Lodge said, the President would have to wait until Congress reconvened in December to withdraw the treaty. The action of the President in withdrawing the treaty, Mr. Lodge held, would be an admission on the President's part that it had been rejected.

It is understood that Senator Lodge will press the adoption of his concurrent resolution declaring that a state of peace exists at the opening of the regular session of Congress in December. The Republicans express confidence in their ability to put the resolution through.

The text of the Lodge resolution is:

Whereas, by resolution of Congress, adopted April 6, 1917, and by reason of acts committed by the then German Government, a state of war was declared to exist between that Government and the United States; and,

Whereas, the said acts of the German Government have long since ceased; and

Whereas, by an armistice signed Nov. 11, 1918, hostilities between Germany and the Allied and Associated Powers were terminated; and

Whereas, by the terms of the Treaty of Versailles, Germany is to be at peace with all the nations engaged in war against her whenever three Governments, designated therein, have ratified said treaty; now, therefore,

Be it resolved by the Senate, (the House of Representatives concurring) that the said state of war between Germany and the United States is hereby declared to be at an end.

It is understood that Administration leaders will fight this plan for ending the war, and there is a constitutional question whether Congress can do so by a resolution not requiring the President's signature.

After the Senate adjourned it was admitted on all sides that the future treaty situation was decidedly mixed. Senator Hitchcock was asked whether President Wilson was likely to call the Senate immediately in special session for a reconsideration of the treaty. Mr. Hitchcock answered that he thought the President would not show quite so much

Continued on Page Two.

President Wilson's Final Appeal to Democrats That Helped to Defeat the Lodge Reservations

WASHINGTON, Nov. 19—Following is the text of the President's letter, addressed to Senator Hitchcock and read at the Democratic conference this morning:

My Dear Senator—You were good enough to bring me word that the Democratic Senators supporting the treaty expected to hold a conference between the final votes on the Lodge resolution of ratification and that they would be glad to receive a word of counsel from me.

I should hesitate to offer it in any detail, but I assume that the Senators only desire my judgment upon the all-important question of the final vote on the resolution containing the many reservations of Senator Lodge. On that I cannot hesitate, for, in my opinion, the resolution in that form does not provide for ratification but rather for nullification of the treaty. I sincerely hope that the friends and supporters of the treaty will vote against the Lodge resolution of ratification.

I understand that the door will then probably be open for a genuine resolution of ratification.

I trust that all true friends of the treaty will refuse to support the Lodge resolution.

Cordially and sincerely yours,

WOODROW WILSON.

URGED THE SENATE TO SAVE EUROPE

Gen. Smuts, in Belated Message, Pleaded That We Not Blast the World's Hopes.

SPOKE FOR HIS PEOPLE

South African Leader Said League Alone Could Prevent Dissolving Civilization.

JOHANNESBURG, Union of South Africa, Nov. 19 (Associated Press).—Lieut. Gen. Jan Christian Smuts, British member on the League of Nations Commission, in "a message from South Africa to America," appeals to America "not to blast the hopes of the world" through non-ratification of the treaty covenant by the Senate.

[This appeal was received in the offices of the New York newspapers just a few moments after word came from Washington that the Senate had adjourned without acting on the treaty.]

General Smuts says:

"I am told that the League is in danger in the American Senate. I can scarcely believe it. But if so, may I send a message from South Africa to America.

"My people are a small people, my voice in their behalf is weak. But the greatest leaders in America before now have listened to me.

"I trust my appeal will not be resented. I appeal to America not to blast the hopes of the world. America has established a great record in the war. She has shown herself capable of the highest altruism. When human freedom was endangered and appealing hands were stretched out, America rose to the height of her great opportunity, shamed the cynics who believed she was merely bent on money-making and rushed whole-heartedly to the rescue of those great human ideals for which the Allies were fighting. Her great act of unselfishness and moral idealism in the most critical stage of the war saved world democracy.

"Today the world is no less endangered, the machinery of the League is wanted to save civilization from dissolving into fragments, from falling into decay. It alone can save tottering Europe.

"No nation put more faith, more effort into the construction of the League than America. It now only remains to ratify and pass the covenant. Other nations have approved it. Even distant Asia is represented. Japan has given her approval, while America alone hesitates and falters.

"Will the great leaders now lag behind the racks? I cannot believe it. I cannot believe that America will, after all, block the way, that the purely American viewpoint will be allowed to override the wider interests and necessities of our own civilization in the greatest crisis in history.

"America has proved true to the best ideals of free and peaceful Government, and can only be true to herself by remaining true to these ideals as embodied in a League for the whole human race It is in the power of America to lift the heavy weight of despair which today is bearing down Christendom. We all pray to her to do so. We pray her to sign the great covenant and complete the work for humanity which she so unselfishly set out in the war to do."

EXECUTE MOROCCAN REBELS

Spaniards Put to Death 21 Tribesmen Who Slew Officers.

MADRID, Nov. 18—Twenty-one Moroccan tribesmen were executed at Tetuan, east of Tangier, this morning following their conviction by a courtmartial of killing their officers while the tribesmen were in the service of the Spanish Government, according to advices received here.

'NULLIFICATION,' SAID PRESIDENT

Asked Democrats Through Hitchcock to Defeat the Lodge Treaty Plan.

PARTY CONFERENCE AGREED

Lodge Retorted, Declaring the Senate Had Equal Responsibility for Treaties.

WASHINGTON, Nov. 19.—A letter from President Wilson advising Senators to vote against ratification of the treaty with the Foreign Relations Committee's reservations embraced in it was laid before a conference of the Administration forces in the Senate this morning by the Democratic leader, Senator Hitchcock, and had much to do with swaying the minority.

In his letter the President declared that the Lodge resolution really meant "nullification" of the treaty.

The decision of Democratic friends of the treaty to vote against a ratification resolution containing the Lodge reservations was affirmed at the conference of Democrats. Senator Hitchcock announced that enough Democrats to insure its defeat had agreed to vote against the Lodge resolution.

No compromise plan was drafted by the Democrats but it was suggested that after the prospective defeat of the Lodge reservations a committee of Democrats would be appointed to confer with the Republicians to that end.

Democrats who attended the conference were not bound by any conference agreement and said they were willing to accept many of the majority's reservations, but could not accept the preamble or those dealing with Article X, Shantung, equality of voting and one or two others. If the majority declined to compromise, it was said, responsibility for failure of the treaty would rest on that side of the chamber. Various compromise measures were considered at the conference.

Republican Leader Lodge in a formal statement predicted that the Senate would "not obey the orders" of President Wilson with regard to the treaty.

"The Senate has equal power and responsibility with the President in the making of treaties," said Senator Lodge. "They will not, in my opinion, obey the orders of the President, who undertakes to command the Senate to ratify the treaty without the reservations adopted by a large majority of the Senate, which Americanize it and make it safe for the United States. What he commands will not, in my judgment, be done."

It was learned that a proposal to modify the preamble reservation of the committee so that the reservations would not require affirmative acceptance by the other powers had been under serious consideration by the Republican leaders. They were said to have manifested a willingness to insert a proviso by which the reservations could be accepted by the other powers by merely "not objecting" to them.

Just before the Senate convened and while the Democratic Senators were meeting, Senator Lodge held a conference with Will H. Hays, Chairman of the Republican National Committee.

SWISS ACCEPT THE LEAGUE.

Decision of the National Council Subject to Referendum.

BERNE, Nov. 19.—Switzerland's adhesion to the League of Nations was voted by the Swiss National Council today. The vote came after eight days of debate, the count being 124 in favor of joining the League to forty-five against.

The decision of the council is subject to a referendum.

LODGE RESOLUTION BEATEN

Lost by 39 to 55 the First Time and 41 to 50 Afterward.

FULL RATIFICATION FAILS

Defeated by 38 to 53—All Attempts at Compromise Are Beaten.

PEACE DECLARATION MOVED

Lodge Proposal Goes Over to Next Session—11 Hours of Tense Struggle.

Special to the New York Times.

WASHINGTON, Nov. 19.—The treaty of peace with Germany, after a long and bitter parliamentary struggle, came to a vote in the Senate tonight and in each of three tests was defeated. The first vote was on the question of ratification with the Lodge reservations. Thirty-nine Senators voted for ratification on these terms and 55 voted against. The second vote was on the same question, revived by a motion to reconsider, and this time 41 Senators voted for, and 50 against. The third and final vote was on the question of ratification without reservations of any kind; 38 Senators voted "yes" and 53 "no." The Senate then adjourned sine die at 11:10 o'clock.

Immediately after the last vote, which spelt the doom of the treaty as far as this session of Congress is concerned, Senator Lodge, the majority leader, offered a concurrent resolution declaring peace to exist between Germany and the United States, this being done so as to pave the way for an independent treaty with Germany.

As the House had adjourned sine die, the Lodge resolution had to go over until the next session of this Congress, which meets December 1.

After the Democrats for the second time had voted down the Lodge resolution of ratification, Senator Underwood, Democrat, of Alabama, offered the substitute resolution of ratification without reservations. Although Senator Lodge and those working with him had blocked all previous efforts of the Democrats to obtain a vote on any resolution of their own through parliamentary points of order, Mr. Lodge allowed the Underwood resolution to come to a vote.

Seven Democratic Senators voted against it and one Republican Senator, Mr. McCumber of North Dakota, voted for it. The vote on the resolution ended the efforts of the minority to save the treaty.

Proposes Notice to Wilson.

After the Senate had voted, Senator Fletcher, Democrat, of Florida, suggested that the Senate communicate word of its action to President Wilson. Upon this Senator Penrose, Republican, of Pennsylvania, exclaimed:

"Oh, he'll know about it well enough."

Senator Lodge remarked that the President would undoubtedly take official cognizance of the action of the Senate. He referred to the procedure under other treaties where Presidents had done this.

The Democratic forces made repeated efforts to obtain a vote upon substitute resolutions of ratification with mild reservations. At every point in this struggle the Democrats were outvoted by the Republican majority. Throughout the last stages of the fight Senator Lodge held his forces solidly together, with the single exception of Senator McCumber, who voted for the Underwood substitute.

The middle-ground Senators who had been counted upon by Mr. Hitchcock to come to his relief at the last moment and bring about a parliamentary twist by which the Democrats could substitute their reservations, declined all overtures for compromise. Senators Lenroot, McCumber, Kellogg, Edge and others of the so-called mild reservationists told the Administration Senators during the last hour of the fight on the Senate floor that the Administration leaders had lost their opportunity for compromise, and that they intended to stand by the majority program.

Hitchcock's Efforts Fail.

Appeals were made by the Democratic leader for the Republicans to leave the way open for compromise, but these were abruptly thrust aside. Senator Hitchcock implored the middle-grounders not to shut the door to agreement.

During the final moments of the fight Senator Swanson, Democrat of Virginia, walked over to Senator Lodge while the minority moves for substitute resolutions were in progress, remarking

"For God's sake, can't something be done to save the treaty?"

"Senator, the door is closed," replied Senator Lodge. "You have done it yourselves."

The defeat of the treaty was witnessed by crowded galleries which followed the various manoeuvres with acute interest. Crowds stood in the corridors leading to

"All the News That's Fit to Print."

The New York Times.

THE WEATHER
Fair and colder today; Sunday fair with slowly rising temperature.
For full weather report see Page 16.

VOL. LXIX...No. 22,624. ••• NEW YORK, SATURDAY, JANUARY 3, 1920. TWO CENTS Metropolitan District 50 Mile Radius | THREE CENTS Within 200 Miles | FOUR CENTS Elsewhere

REDS RAIDED IN SCORES OF CITIES; 2,600 ARRESTS, 700 IN NEW YORK; DEPORTATION HEARINGS BEGIN TODAY

30 ENEMY SHIPS OFFERED FOR SALE BY SHIPPING BOARD

Chairman Payne Announces Intention to Get Government Out of Shipping Business.

LIMITS BIDS TO AMERICANS

Vessels Must Fly the American Flag and Ply on Routes Designated by the Government.

LEVIATHAN IN THE LIST

Also the Big Mount Vernon and George Washington—Safeguard Against Alien Purchase.

Special to The New York Times.

WASHINGTON, Jan. 2.—Thirty former enemy-owned passenger ships seized by the United States Government when this country entered the war were offered for sale today, with the condition that the purchasers shall be Americans, and the ships must be used on lines to be designated by the Shipping Board and must fly the American flag.

The group offered for sale today includes the Leviathan, largest ship afloat; the George Washington, used by President Wilson in his trips to the Peace Conference, and other well-known vessels.

In connection with the offer Chairman John Barton Payne of the Shipping Board announced that it was the intention of the board to get the Government out of the shipping business as rapidly as possible by selling to private interests all passenger and cargo ships, including former enemy-owned tonnage, unless Congress stepped in and blocked such a program.

Shipping experts have pointed out that passenger liners operated by the United States might find it difficult to compete with foreign owned liners as a result of a decision of this Government not to sell alcoholic drinks on its passenger ships. Officials of the Shipping Board would not discuss this question. They did not admit that it had anything to do with the decision to dispose of passenger liners to private interests. The decision, it is stated, is simply in line with the general policy to get the United States out of the commercial shipping business as soon as possible.

The Internal Revenue Bureau must determine as to the privileges which may be enjoyed by passenger shipping owned by private interests and flying the American flag, and the Shipping Board has no part in the settlement of this issue.

Chairman Payne said he was unalterably opposed to a policy of Government ownership of commercial shipping, and it also became known that the decision of the board to sell its liners was determined principally by the cost of refitting the former enemy ships from their present condition of transports to first-class passenger vessels, which would be nearly $50,000,000. It was found, for instance, that rewiring of the Leviathan would cost half a million dollars.

Details Terms of Sale.

Ships will not be sold at bargain prices, however, and Government control will continue until satisfactory bids are obtained.

The Shipping Board tonight issued a call for bids for the Leviathan and twenty-nine other former German and Austrian owned passenger liners and combination passenger and cargo ships. The Leviathan was formerly the Vaterland. The complete list of former enemy owned tonnage now offered for sale follows:

Vessels of First-Class Passenger Type—Leviathan, Agamemnon, Mount Vernon, Von Steuben, George Washington, Martha Washington, America, De Kalb, Aeolus, Huron, Princess Matoika, Pocahontas, Callao, Moccasin, Black Arrow and Otsego.

For Steerage and Cargo—Eton, Madawaska, Mercury, Powhatan, Orion, Antigone, Susquehanna, President Grant, Nansemond, Artemis, Philippines, Wyandotte and Freedom.

Steps looking toward the sale of other passenger and cargo vessels, now completed or in course of construction in American yards, will be taken shortly, the effort being made to stimulate the sale to private account. The call for bids issued tonight was restricted to former enemy-owned ships, in order to dispose of them at this time if possible. Conditions of the sale will be somewhat different from those governing the sale of new tonnage.

Proposals will be received by the Shipping Board up to and including Jan. 20, and these specifications are made:

"Proposals to be accompanied by a certified check for 2½ per cent. of the total amount bid. Bids to be on either lump sum per ship or per gross ton dead weight. The following information should accompany all bids:

"First—Trade or service in which ships will be placed if bid is accepted.

"Second—Such assurance as may be possible that service will be permanent.

"Third—The amount of United States tonnage now owned by bidder.

"Fourth—Percentage of foreign ownership or interest in partnership, company or corporation bidding.

"Fifth—Foreign interest in bid, if any.

"Sixth—Particular fitness of bidder for service.

"All bids to be based on taking title of ships, it being understood and agreed that any commitments of the Shipping Board involving operation, repairs, or

Continued on Page Six.

2,396 Ships Passed in 1919, Was Panama Canal Record

PANAMA, Jan. 2.—Traffic through the Panama Canal in 1919 exceeded that of any previous year. Two thousand three hundred and ninety-six ships of 7,128,000 net tons, in addition to naval ships displacing 1,000,000 tons, passed through the waterway. The cargoes of the merchant ships amounted to 7,711,000 tons.

Ships measuring 7,000 tons, carrying 10,000 tons of cargo, were 2 per cent. greater than in any previous year. December broke the monthly record, 283 ships of 957,000 net tons, carrying cargoes of 953,000 tons, traversed the canal. The tolls collected amounted to $891,378 for December and $6,972,004 for the year.

AMERICAN SHIPS GOING CARGOLESS

Prohibition and High Freights Sent 21 Away Empty from Marseilles.

RECORD OF THE LAST MONTH

Better Organized British Agencies Had Already Taken the Cream of Port's Business.

Copyright, 1920, by Chicago Tribune Company

MARSEILLES, Jan. 1.—Twenty-one American freighters have been forced to leave Marseilles during the last month without cargoes owing to prohibition in the United States, which makes wine, the principal export of France, contraband in America, and to the low exchange, which makes it impossible for boats paying American salaries to handle French cargoes to ports outside of the United States.

There are seven boats flying the American flag in port here waiting for cargoes, but indications are that they will have to depart light.

Captains of these boats state that unless the United States Government establishes transportation agencies in the leading ports throughout the world the United States merchant marine will be unable to compete with Great Britain and other countries, which, they declare, owing to influential local representatives, are able to pick off the cream of the shipping business and leave what is undesirable for the United States boats.

Among the American boats being held here for cargoes are the schooner Lucia, which brought a cargo of coal from Norfolk, Va.; the Melbourne, which brought to France a cargo of kernels from West Africa, and the Mantchain, which brought Lagos goods.

All along the Gold Coast of Africa an American boat does not get a show at any desirable cargo, Captain C. B. Foster, of the Melbourne, said. "This is not unexpected, because British shipping gets preference among British colonies; but I don't know a single place where the United States shipping has an edge. We consider ourselves lucky if we can get an even break."

Captains Charles Willard of the Lucia and C. Coater of the Mantchain, both old seamen, made the same comment.

"If the United States Government or Shipping Board would get able seamen, those who know this game from the galley up, to represent us in the various ports, we might get a chance at the desirable cargoes. As it is, a United States boat has to take what it gets," Captain Foster stated. "The British Government especially makes it a rule to have a man who knows what he is doing go after business for British ships. It is time the United States took a step in that direction unless it wants to sell out altogether."

The longshoremen were granted all their demands and have returned to work, after tying up shipping here for some time by a strike.

EBERT URGES GERMANS TO RESTORE THE NATION

Declares That This Year Will Show Whether They Are to Endure or Collapse.

BERLIN, Jan. 1.—President Ebert requested the Chancellor to publish the following New Year manifesto today:

"In the year just ended chaos was averted and the unity of the empire was maintained and consolidated. Under the pressure of a reckless force we were compelled to conclude a peace threatening the honor and welfare of our nation and placing the fruits of our work of past and future years at the mercy of foreigners.

"The year which begins must decide whether Germany, despite all difficulties, will maintain herself as a nation and State and develop her economic life on a sound basis or whether, through internal quarrels, she will definitely collapse and bury the hopes, even of her future generations.

"With these prospects of our fate before my eyes, I urge all those calling themselves Germans, in view of the common danger, to close their ranks in order that each according to his capacity may help to the utmost in the restoration of the Fatherland."

SENATE COALITION FORMING TO SEEK TREATY HARMONY

Democrats to Act Through Mild Reservationists, Who Are to Sponsor New Plan.

TO OFFER DRAFT TO LODGE

McNary Warns of Support of Conciliation Committee Unless Efforts Continue.

CONFERENCES ARE GROWING

Democrats Defer to Wilson by Refraining from Direct Com promise Proposal.

Special to The New York Times.

WASHINGTON, Jan. 2.—The Democratic program for a compromise on the peace treaty is now in the making.

While the Senate Democrats are opposed to offering direct proposals, a way around the difficulty has been found. The Democratic suggestions are to come ostensibly from the mild reservationist group of Republicans.

Democrats will claim no credit for helping frame the compromise. They will not even admit having a hand in it, but they will vote for it.

The Democratic program is to be handed to the mild reservationists within a short time, according to present plans. This may be within twenty-four hours, or within a week. It embodies four points, upon which Democratic leaders have already tentatively outlined their position to the mild reservationists. These points will relate to the preamble, Article X., Reservation 14, and Shantung.

The mild reservationists are to hand the Democratic proposals to Senator Lodge, after they have worked out an agreement with the Democrats on them. Upon Mr. Lodge's verdict, his friends say, will depend their acceptance or rejection by the additional Senators whose support is necessary to effect ratification. Senator Lodge's position is such that it appears certain he will withhold his assent from these or any other proposals until there is absolute certainty that they will command 64 votes.

With the situation in this state today, leaders on both sides agreed that the final settlement and ratification are probably many days off.

Leaders on Both Sides Confer.

Both Mr. Lodge and Mr. Hitchcock today held important treaty conferences. The Republican leader saw Senator Swanson, a Democratic member of the Foreign Relations Committee; Senator McNary, mild reservationist leader; Senator Lenroot, strong reservationist, and Senator Capper, a Lodge reservationist. Mr. Hitchcock called in Senators Swanson and King, the latter of whom has written a set of reservations.

The net result of the conferences, according to those who attended them, was to increase the hopefulness which nowadays pervades the Capitol, but no definite basis for which has yet been found by even the most optimistic Senator.

Senator Swanson, it was stated after his conference with Mr. Lodge, did not ask the Republican leader to consider any concrete program.

Mr. McNary discussed the forthcoming Democratic proposals and the possibility of getting enough votes for them. He also advised Mr. Lodge that unless evidences of activity were continued Senator Underwood's resolution for an official conciliation committee would be adopted after the recess with the aid of several Republican votes.

Senator Lodge has already expressed his hostility to this resolution and is understood to be somewhat disturbed at the prospect that Republicans will support it in sufficient numbers to pass it, with the aid of the Democrats. Mr. Lodge's opposition to it is founded, it is understood, upon his unwillingness that the Democrats should even appear to get credit for bringing about a settlement.

Senator Lenroot said that his talk with Senator Lodge added nothing to his information concerning the situation, but he hinted that the next day or two might bring interesting developments.

Mr. Capper found Mr. Lodge quite as partial to the Lodge reservations as he ever was, and said that he and the Republican leader agreed thoroughly that the Lodge program must stand without vital change.

Senator Lodge said after his conferences that the outlook was good. He was still waiting, he said, for something concrete from the other side. So far as he is concerned the program on which he stands is known, and his sponsorship of that program has not diminished.

Hitchcock Predicts Concession.

The Democratic conference in Senator Hitchcock's office did not produce all that was expected of it by some Senators in the way of tangible results. This, however, was due to the absence of certain Democrats, whose advice was desired. At its conclusion Mr. Hitchcock denied that the Democrats would submit definite proposals, on the ground that they were not in a position to do so. He said that the Hitchcock reservations which he presented at the last session represented the extent to which he was authorized to go.

"I am not in a position to offer a compromise and have not been asked to do so," said Senator Hitchcock. "If

Continued on Page Three.

Paris Opera Chorus Strikes and Prevents Performance

PARIS, Jan. 2.—A large audience which gathered to attend the opera tonight was disappointed when the manager announced that a sudden strike of the employes would prevent the performance. The members of the orchestra and of the chorus and the supers announced their intention to strike early tonight when their demands were not met by the management. The electricians and mechanics did not join the strikers.

A concert for the benefit of devastated regions, arranged for Sunday, has been postponed.

LONG ISLAND TRAIN HITS AUTO; KILLS 2

Crushes Car at Babylon Pike Crossing and Carries It, with Dead, Quarter of a Mile.

THREE OTHERS ARE INJURED

Driver with Four Fares Speeding Toward Crossing Failed to Heed Danger Whistle.

Special to The New York Times.

MERRICK, L. I., Jan. 2.—At an unprotected crossing where the tracks of the Long Island Railroad cross the Babylon Turnpike between Freeport and this village the Speonk express shortly after 6 o'clock tonight struck a touring car in which were five persons. Two of them were killed and the others so badly hurt that they were rushed to the Nassau County Hospital in the effort to save their lives. The dead were:

The Dead.

CARROW, ANDREW H., 26 years old, of Baldwin.
MANGLES, FLORENCE, 22, of Bellmore.

The Injured.

HOBARTH, ANNA, of Roosevelt.
KEENE, ROYAL B., the driver of the car.
KELSKY, MICHAEL, of Hempstead.

A remarkable feature of the accident was that the express train lifted the automobile and with its occupants carried it for a quarter of a mile. When the train came to a stop about 500 yards from the station here the car, a crumpled, shattered mass of wreckage, fell off the front of the engine and with it tumbled out the living and the dead. Nothing was left at the turnpike crossing to show that there had been a collision there.

Keene, the owner of the car, drove for hire and he was traveling from his starting point, believed to have been Mineola. Miss Mangles and Miss Hobarth worked at the Doubleday-Page plant at Garden City. With them was Kelsky. They were evidently going home. It is thought that Carrow was a "fare" picked up on the way. Just how the accident happened was not known this evening, but it is generally thought that Keene was speeding his car along the Babylon road and that he did not hear the whistle of the approaching locomotive above the noise of his engine. This is borne out by the fact that there was no attempt to turn the car aside.

Keene was a friend of two young men who were killed by a train at the same crossing about two months ago. Carrow came to Long Island from Florida about four years ago and was married to a Baldwin girl.

THREE HELD IN AUTO DEATH.

Killing of Man in Yonkers Under Investigation by Police.

Three men are under arrest at Yonkers on a charge of homicide in connection with the death of William J. Duvall of Warburton Avenue, Hastings, whose body, hidden among bushes, was found lying near the estate of Samuel Untermyer on Warburton Avenue, Yonkers, yesterday morning.

The men, William Rohbach, Michael Ritz, and Thomas Mallon, all of Hastings, are being held on order of Coroner George Engle, who believed Duvall met with foul play.

Five deep wounds, apparently knife wounds, which, the Coroner says, could not have been the result of an automobile wreck, were found on Duvall's head and neck. Duvall and the three men under arrest were acquaintances.

The three men admit that while they were on their way to Hastings from Yonkers in their automobile at 2 o'clock yesterday morning the car struck and killed the man. Finding he was dead and fearful of the consequences, they dragged his body fifty feet from the roadway and threw it down a slight embankment.

HINTS AT LENITY TO KAISER

Belgian Jurist Says Allies Do Not Wish to Make Him a Martyr.

THE HAGUE, Jan. 2, (Associated Press.)—H. Carton de Wiart, former Belgian Minister of Justice, whose opinion is considered reliable in Dutch circles, writes in the Libre Belgique of Brussels that the allied demand for the extradition of the former Emperor William, which is expected in the near future, will not be based on any existing international law or on stipulations in The Hague Convention of 1900, but on a "new moral right."

The former Minister hints that it is the probable intention of the Allies not to punish the former Emperor severely as, he says, this would make him a martyr in the eyes of the German people.

RAIDS ON 13 CENTRES HERE

Federal Officers Seize Hundreds of Reds at Their Meeting Places.

NOVY MIR PAPERS SEIZED

Eight Hundred Warrants Out in New York City and More in New Jersey.

HEARING AT ELLIS ISLAND

Aliens to Be Deported Promptly —Citizens Will Face Trial for Anarchy.

Without a hint of its intention, the full force of the Federal authorities fell on radicals from coast to coast last night and, as reports came into the Government headquarters where William J. Flynn, chief of the Department of Justice Bureau of Investigation, sat directing the drive, it was said that thousands of agitators aiming at the overthrow of the Government had been trapped in the nation's greatest series of raids.

The blow was aimed at one organization only—the Communist Party of America. This band of followers of the Lenin-Trotzky doctrine of violent government has been conducting a campaign against American institutions and, admittedly, has been in close co-operation with Petrograd. Early in the drive of last night it was ascertained, that some of the highest disciples of Sovietism in this country were sought for deportation.

Flynn Says 700 Were Caught.

"I believe that with these raids the backbone of the radical movement in this country has been broken," declared Chief Flynn at 12:30 this morning. Two hours later he said that more than 700 persons had been seized and examined as a result of the raids here.

Among the prisoners that came into headquarters late were twenty-five women, half of them apparently girls of high school age. They were taken in a descent on The Communist World's publication establishment, at 207 East Tenth Street. Four of the girls were later released.

Another person who was arrested was Julian Codkind of 133 East Ninety-seventh Street, who, the Federal authorities say, is employed in the City Department of Finance, and that he told them that he believed in the principles of the Communist Party, and that the entire nation would soon adopt them. The agents also asserted that Codkind told them he believed in the overthrow of the Government if it became necessary. His arrest took place a few minutes after he had been elected Secretary of the English-speaking branch of the organization in Harlem.

Harry Winitsky, secretary of the National Communist Party, who is now out on bail under charges of criminal anarchy in this State, also was arrested. He did not give his right name and seemed anxious to avoid attracting attention. Winitsky was recognized by an operative of the Department of Justice. When his identity became known he demanded that Dudley Field Malone be sent for. He told the officials that he was a lawyer and so did not have to answer questions.

Thirteen Headquarters Raided Here.

While the agents in thirty-three cities were out on their mission, operatives in New York City raided thirteen Communist Party and Communist Labor Party headquarters. They placed under arrest several hundred men, and, according to Chief Flynn, expected to have the remainder of those named in the deportation warrants in custody before morning. One of the first places to receive the attention of the New York raiders was the publication plant of the Novy Mir, a Russian newspaper printed at 77 St. Marks Place. A quantity of literature was seized at the newspaper offices and at the meeting places.

The raiders failed to meet with any resistance, and the "visits" were quiet affairs. Instructions had been issued to the raiding parties to act with as little force as possible.

It was announced while the raids were still in progress that a special board of inquiry would convene this morning on Ellis Island for the purpose of hearing the cases of the men arrested last night. It was stated that the men arrested in New York, New Jersey, and the western part of New England would certainly be tried by this court, but that it had not been definitely decided whether Western, Southern, and Far Western radicals would come before it.

Those proved to be aliens will be deported without delay, as 3,000 deportation warrants had been prepared for service in the raids. In all, 812 warrants were written and ready for local reds. Naturalized citizens caught by the Federal agents will be turned over to the State authorities for prosecution under State law. In New York, it was said, a direct request would be made to Governor Alfred E. Smith that

Continued on Page Two.

Raiders Ordered to Make Cleanup Thorough; Warned Against Violence or Taking Valuables

The following instructions as to the conduct of the raids were issued in identical form to all Department of Justice men engaged in the action throughout the country:

INSTRUCTIONS.

Our activities will be directed against the radical organizations known as the Communist Party of America and the Communist Labor Party of America, also known as Communists.

The strike will be made promptly and simultaneously at 8:30 P. M. in all districts. The meeting places of the Communists in your territory, and the names and addresses of the officers and heads that you are to arrest, are on the attached lists.

You will also arrest all active members where found.

Particular efforts should be made to apprehend all the officers, irrespective of where they may be, and, with respect to such officers, their residence should be searched and in every instance all literature, membership cards, records and correspondence are to be taken.

When a citizen is arrested as a Communist, he must be present with the officers searching his home at the time of the search.

Meeting rooms should be thoroughly searched.

Locate and obtain the charter. All records, if not found in the meeting rooms, will probably be found in the home of the Recording Secretary or Financial Secretary, but in every instance, if possible records should be found and taken.

All literature, books, papers, pictures on the walls of the meeting places, should be gathered together and tagged with tags which will be supplied you, with the name and address of the person by whom obtained and where obtained.

In searching meeting places, a thorough search should be made and the walls sounded.

It is an order of the Government that violence to those apprehended should be scrupulously avoided.

Immediately upon the apprehension of the alien, or citizen, search him thoroughly. If found in groups in a meeting room, they should be lined up against the wall and searched. Particular efforts should be made to obtain membership cards on the persons who are taken.

Make an absolute search of the individual. No valuables, such as jewelry and moneys, to be taken away from those arrested.

After a search has been made of the person arrested you will take all the evidence you have obtained from his person and place in an envelope, which will be furnished you, placing the name, address, contents of the envelope, by whom taken and where, on the outside of the envelope and deliver to me with the alien.

Everybody will remain on duty until relieved, without exception.

Flashlights, string, tags and envelopes should be carried, as per instructions.

In searching rooms of an alien pay particular attention to everything in the room and make a thorough search thereof.

You are also warned to take notice "that no violence is to be used."

You will communicate with me by telephone from your several districts, the number of the telephone herewith given.

Attached you will find a list of those to be apprehended in your district, and you will also apprehend all those found arrested with these names at the time of the arrest whom you find to be active members of the Communist Party.

You are also instructed to use reasonable care and good judgment.

SOVIET OFFERS PEACE TO ITALY

Foreign Minister Holds Out Trade Opportunities Through Black Sea Ports.

REDS NEARING THAT COAST

Armies Marching on Mariupol, on Sea of Azov—Agent at Dorpat Offers Great Concessions.

LONDON, Jan. 2.—Tchitcherin, Bolshevist Foreign Minister, has proposed to Italy a resumption of relations between that country and Soviet Russia, pointing out that the "imminent capture of the Black Sea coast by the Soviets will open the Black Sea route to Italy," says a Moscow wireless message received here.

The Bolsheviki, the message continues, have occupied the important stations of Yusovo and Dolia and are marching toward Mariupol (an important seaport on the Sea of Azov).

A quantity of guns and booty was captured in this section, as was also the entire Markhoff division, one of General Denikin's finest corps, the Moscow report adds.

An earlier Moscow wireless reported a rapid advance in the Donetz coal region in South Russia. It was claimed that all of the railway junctions between Bakhmut and Lugansk had been occupied and that the Red lines were less than 65 miles east of Lugansk. (Lugansk is about the same distance from the Sea of Azov.)

With the capture of Novocherkassky thousands of prisoners were taken, according to the Soviet report, which declares the occupation of Ilovavskoye deprives the enemy of the only railway leading up to the front.

On the eve of his return to Copenhagen to resume the prisoner exchange negotiations with Maxim Litvinoff, the Bolshevist representative, James O'Grady, told The Mirror correspondent that he believed the pourparlers would be successful and that the repatriation of British prisoners and British civilian residents in Soviet Russia would be effected by the end of January.

Mr. O'Grady said his consultations since his return from Copenhagen would aid materially in bringing about a settlement. He expressed it as his opinion that Russia would save herself if left alone.

DORPAT, Jan. 1.—Bolshevist Russia is willing to make great concessions to the big powers in the interests of peace, but will not hold out the olive branch to General Denikin, according to M. Klishke, Secretary of the Soviet delegation conferring with Esthonian delegates here.

"A year ago we would have considered peace with General Denikin," he said, "but now it is a fight to the finish."

M. Klishke added the Bolshevist army now numbered 3,000,000 men and declared it to be "invincible."

"Soviet Russia, however," he declared, "would be glad to disband the entire force if peace with the world could be achieved."

Bolshevist agents have reported that France is trying to organize a huge offensive against the Soviet government, he said.

RAILROAD DEFICIT BIG IN NOVEMBER

Excess of Expenditures Was About $64,500,000, the Largest of the Year.

COAL STRIKE CUT TRAFFIC

Eastern Roads Especially Were Hard Hit by the Difficulties with Miners.

WASHINGTON, Jan. 2.—The Government deficit from railroad operation during November will be approximately $64,500,000, a high record for the year, according to figures compiled and made public tonight by the Bureau of Railway Economics. Net operating income for the month was estimated to have fallen below $20,000,000, which the Bureau of Economics declared to be the lowest in thirty years when computed on a basis of percentage of investment.

Gross revenues for the month were estimated at close to $436,000,000. This figure is only slightly below the high mark of a year ago, but the heavy expenses, due in part to the coal strike, which also reduced the revenues, left as net little of the operating revenues.

The Government's net loss, the bureau estimated, on the basis of Interstate Commerce Commission figures, has reached $548,000,000 in the twenty-three months of railroad operation. The bureau placed the loss for the eleven months of 1919 at more than $331,000,000.

December return on the rail operation was forecast as bringing another decline to the estimate in the statement issued a few days ago by Director General Hines, who pointed to the inevitable loss in revenues incident to the coal strike.

The November earnings as computed by the bureau with comparative figures for the corresponding month in 1918 follow:

	1919.	1918.
Revenues	$436,000,000	$440,400,000
Expenses and taxes	417,000,000	383,900,000
Net income	19,000,000	56,500,000

While the November revenues were said by the bureau to show an increase of $149,200,000, as compared with the average for the month in the three-year test period before the war, expenses and taxes also have increased more than $213,000,000. The increase in operating revenues was traceable largely to the heavy passenger traffic, which was represented to have been about 10 per cent. higher than the November average of the test period. Freight traffic, however, was estimated to have dropped several per cent.

The Eastern roads, which in other months have offset losses accumulated by lines in other sections, were unable to meet their actual operating expenses and taxes for the month, the Bureau of Economics figures revealed. Expenses and taxes of the Eastern lines were shown to have been $4,200,000 in excess of operating revenues.

Lines in the West, however, did better in earnings than in most previous months, due to the heavy grain movement and also to the fact that they did not suffer from loss of revenue through the closing of mines. Their earnings were placed at about $20,000,000.

RAID FROM COAST TO COAST

Secret Service Men Make Simultaneous Swoop.

PREPARING FOR SIX MONTHS

Have Evidence Showing Campaign to Form Soviet Councils and Overthrow Government.

MORE RAIDS WILL FOLLOW

Deportation of Prisoners Accused of Advocating Revolution Will Be Asked.

Special to The New York Times.

WASHINGTON, Jan. 2.—A nation-wide raid on members of the Communist Party and the Communist Labor Party was conducted tonight by agents of the Department of Justice. In thirty-three cities of the country, extending from the Pacific to the Atlantic, and many neighboring towns, Secret Service operatives, armed with thousands of warrants, set out to make wholesale arrests. According to reports reaching here the total of arrests up to a late hour had reached nearly 2,600.

Excerpts made public from a manifesto of the Communist Party revealed that the organization contemplates the overthrow of the American system of government and its replacement by a "workers industrial republic," or Soviet system. It was said tonight at the Department of Justice that the Communist Party and the Communist Labor Party—between which there is little difference—supported the Third International,—which was formed under the auspices of Lenin and Trotzky at Moscow, March 6, 1919.

Totals of the Arrests.

Up to midnight these unofficial reports of total arrests from the centers of Red activities had been received:

Ansonia	12	Louisville	21
Baltimore	35	Manchester, N. H.	65
Berlin, N. H.	40	Meriden	3
Boston	37	Milwaukee	50
Buffalo and vicinity	135	Nashira, N. H.	161
Bridgeport	15	New York City	700
Cambridge	1	Oakland, Cal.	18
Cleveland	100	Portland, Ore.	20
Chelsea	24	Philadelphia	200
Chicopee	16	Pittsburgh	21
Detroit	400	St. Paul	9
Denver	6	St. Louis	25
Erie, Pa.	2	Springfield, Mass.	65
Grand Rapids	6	Toledo	8
Holyoke	20	Youngstown	16
Haverhill	21	Wellesley, Mass.	2
Hartford	2	Waterbury	7
Kansas City	12	Worcester	65
Lawrence	19	Wilkesbarre and vicinity	70
Lowell	46	Connecticut towns	11
Lynn	47	Rhode Island cities	30
Los Angeles	1		
Total			2,585

Simultaneously with the announcement of the country-wide raids, Attorney General Palmer gave out a copy of a letter he sent on Dec. 29 to Maclay Hoyn, State's Attorney of Illinois, who last night put 200 radicals in jail on his own authority and declared that he had been asked by the Department of Justice to hold off. Mr. Hoyn asserted that this was "pussyfoot politics" on the part of the Attorney General, and also said that the Reds had been warned of the forthcoming raids.

Mr. Palmer's letter shows that raids upon an extensive scale were contemplated at the time he wrote to Mr. Hoyn. For this reason the Attorney General requesed the State's Attorney to postpone independent action for ten days.

This formal statement on the raids was issued by the Department of Justice:

"Agents of the Department of Justice took into custody tonight several hundred members of the Communist Party and the Communist Labor Party of this country, located in thirty-three cities, on the charge that these organizations advocate and teach the overthrow of the United States Government by force and violence. The only difference between the Communist Party and the Communist Labor Party is one of leadership. Both of these parties, since their organization early last September, have been endeavoring to bring about the establishment of a Soviet form of Government in this country, similar to that which now obtains in Russia."

Quotes Communist Manifesto.

The extract from the manifesto of the Communist Party as made public was as follows:

"The Communist Party of America is the party of the working class. The Communist Party of America proposes to end capitalism and organize a workers' industrial republic. The workers must control industry and dispose of the products of industry. The Communist Party is a party realizing the limitations of all existing workers' organizations, and proposes to develop the revolutionary movement necessary to free the workers from the oppression of capitalism. The Communist Party insists that the problems of the American worker are identical with the problems of the workers of the world.

"The Communist Party is the conscious expression of the class struggle of the workers against capitalism. Its aim is to direct this struggle to the conquest of political power, the overthrow of capitalism and the destruction of the bourgeois State.

"The Communist Party prepares itself for the revolution in the measure that it

"All the News That's Fit to Print."

The New York Times.

THE WEATHER
Rain today; Saturday local snows, colder; moderate shifting winds.
For full weather report see Page 23.

VOL. LXIX...No. 22,630. NEW YORK, FRIDAY, JANUARY 9, 1920. TWO CENTS Metropolitan District 50 Mile Radius | THREE CENTS Within 200 Miles | FOUR CENTS Elsewhere

PRESIDENT AND BRYAN SPLIT ON TREATY; WILSON FOR 1920 ISSUE, BRYAN WOULD YIELD; LODGE SEES COMPROMISE NOW IMPOSSIBLE

SOCIALISTS ELATED; SEE PROPAGANDA IN ASSEMBLY'S ACT

Excluded Members Raised from a Harmless Minority to a Political Force, Says One.

PREPARE APPEAL TO LABOR

Issue Statement Declaring Lusk Committee Feared Possible Disclosures.

SUBMIT LIST OF QUESTIONS

Public Men Differ as to Assembly's Attitude—Craig Approves; Hylan Demurs.

Roused by the action of the State Assembly in excluding the five Socialist members at its opening session on Wednesday Socialist leaders in the city worked feverishly yesterday preparing the defense they will make before the Assembly Judiciary Committee on Monday. Besides denying the charge that the platform of their party is inimical to the best interests of the United States and to the State of New York the Socialists will contend that the action of the Assembly was entirely due to the Lusk Committee, which feared important disclosures which the Socialists intended to submit.

After a committee of eight members of the Socialist Party had held a long session at the People's House, 7 East Fifteenth Street, a statement was given out in which it was intimated that the British Secret Service was behind all the activities of the Government officials in this country who are seeking evidence against Russian Soviet representatives here.

It was further intimated that R. N. Nathan, said to be Chief of the British Secret Service here, had participated in the raids on the Rand School and the Soviet Bureau, and that the original papers which he had obtained, which were of "great commercial importance" to the United States, had enabled his own Government "to obtain commercial and diplomatic advantages in its relations with the Soviet Government of Russia." To head off these disclosures, the Socialists said, the Assembly took the drastic action it did.

Commended and Condemned.

The Assembly's action was both commended and condemned by officials here. It was made clear that the Board of Aldermen would not follow the example of the Albany legislators and seek to exclude the four Socialist members of the local board. F. H. LaGuardia, the Republican President of the Aldermanic Board, said he did not believe such measures should be applied here, and warned against steps which might create a real anti-American, anti-Government party in this country.

At the People's House, which contains the New York County headquarters of the Socialist Party, there was excitement all day, the Socialists condemning what they called the Albany outrage. The most important conference was that of the committee of eight, consisting of S. John Block, Jacob Hillquit, William Karlin, Algernon Lee, Julius Gerber, I. M. Chatcuff and Aldermen Beckerman and Vladeck. This committee had the task of preparing the defense, and prominent lawyers, it was said, will be called in. The fight to save their seats in the Assembly, it was said, would be carried to the Supreme Court of the United States if necessary.

No statement was available at the conclusion of their session, but Mr. Block, the Chairman, said the official reply of the Socialist Party to the State Assembly would be made today. "It will be an answer to and an exposure of the falsity of much that is contained in the resolution submitted by Majority Leader Simon L. Adler," he said. "The exact nature of what legal action will be taken has not yet been decided upon."

While the Special Committee and its counselors are conferring on the legal status of the Legislature's action, an effort to arouse the sympathy of working people in this city is to be made at a meeting at the People's House on Monday night. As it was explained by Assemblyman Louis Waldman of the Eighth District, the Socialists, who are particularly interested in the affair, expect to consolidate all the radical organizations "for the purpose of fighting to a finish the usurpation of power by the Assembly." To this conference have been invited representatives of the Labor Party, the Committee of Forty-eight, organizations affiliated with the Central Federated Union, the United Hebrew Trades, the International La-

Continued on Page Five.

"Soviet Ark" Reported Near Entrance to the Kiel Canal

LONDON, Jan. 8.—A wireless message received late today gave the position of the United States transport Buford, the "Soviet Ark," in the North Sea somewhat north of the entrance to the Kiel Canal, but not far enough north of the waterway to warrant the assumption that she is making for the straits rather than for the canal.

Wireless messages from the Buford have been picked up by the English stations since the vessel sailed from New York with the 429 undesirables aboard more frequently than is usual in the case of transports. As far as can be learned, however, the reports have referred to the latitude and longitude of the vessel. None of them, it is said, has mentioned untoward incidents as having occurred among the deported throng.

STEEL STRIKE ENDS, FOSTER RESIGNS

National Committee Blames Courts, Press, Troops and Officials for Collapse.

AND THE SECRETARY QUITS

Will Redouble Organization Efforts, He Says, Professing No Discouragement.

PITTSBURGH, Pa., Jan. 8.—The strike in the steel mills and furnaces, called Sept. 22, and which at its inception involved 367,000 men, officially was called off here tonight by the National Committee of the Steel Workers' Union after an all-day meeting.

Announcement that the National Committee had decided to proceed no further was contained in a telegram sent to the headquarters of the American Federation of Labor in Washington, heads of all international unions interested and organizers and field men in all strike districts. The committee at the same time accepted the resignation of William Z. Foster as Secretary-Treasurer, effective Feb. 1.

Foster was the storm centre of the strike, the alleged vehicle, it was asserted, by which radicals of labor, "boring from within," were aiming to wrest control of the American Federation of Labor from President Gompers and the conservative leaders. He will be succeeded as Secretary-Treasurer by James G. Brown, former President of the Timber Workers' International Union and Foster's chief aid in the conduct of the strike.

"The Steel Corporation, the telegram said, "with the active assistance of the press, the courts, the Federal troops, State police and many public officials, have denied the steel workers their rights of free speech, free assemblage and the right to organize and, by this arbitrary and ruthless misuse of power, have brought about a condition which has compelled the national committee for organizing iron and steel workers to vote today that the active strike phase of the steel campaign is now at an end.

"A vigorous campaign of education and re-organization will be immediately begun, and will not cease until industrial justice in the steel industry has been achieved. All steel workers now are at liberty to return to work, pending preparation for the next big organization movement."

The telegram was signed by John Fitzpatrick, Chairman; D. J. Davis, Vice President of the Amalgamated Association of Iron, Steel and Tin Workers; Edward J. Evans, International Union of Electrical Workers; William Hannon, International Union of Machinists, and William Z. Foster, Secretary of the committee.

Mr. Fitzpatrick declined to discuss the action of the committee, but Secretary Foster said:

"The strike has encouraged the steel trade unions to redouble their efforts. It has been proved that the men in the steel industry can be organized and they have secured the confidence of men in other unions."

Reviewing the strike, Mr. Foster said that it had its inception at St. Paul in 1918 and he was called in as secretary of the committee then formed to organize the steel trades. All preliminary work was completed and the strike called Sept. 22 last. Nine States were affected and 367,000 quit work.

Steel Corporation executives said they were not surprised that the strike had been called off, as the strikers have been drifting back to work for several months. Many mills, it was added, had long ago been able to operate full time with full forces, the principal trouble being the lack of common labor, which formed the backbone of the strike.

CONVENTION GOES TO COAST

To Meet in San Francisco June 28 to Name Party Ticket

COMMITTEE BACKS WILSON

Upholds His Course in Regard to Treaty and Reservations.

PARTY'S RECORD LAUDED

Democrats Cite Federal Reserve and Farm Loan Systems, as Well as War Record.

Special to The New York Times.

WASHINGTON, Jan. 8.—The Treaty of Versailles and the League of Nations and President Wilson's opposition to reservations, the policy of the Administration in respect to labor and its establishment of the Federal Reserve and farm loan systems were indorsed by the Democratic National Committee today. It was decided to hold the national convention in San Francisco on June 28.

The meeting, one of the most enthusiastic held in years, was attended by leading Democrats, including two aspirants for the Presidency, Attorney General Palmer and former Speaker Champ Clark, both of whom were rousingly welcomed. William Jennings Bryan did not attend the sessions but appeared at the Shoreham Hotel where the committee met and held an informal reception. The conservatives apparently avoided him, but he was surrounded by his old admirers.

In effect the resolutions adopted by the committee accepted the challenge of Senator Lodge to make the treaty a campaign issue. They indorsed unhesitatingly everything President Wilson did at Paris and his present opposition to Republican reservations. This action, taken in advance of the reading of the President's letter at the Jackson Day dinner, showed that the national leaders were in harmony with him on his stand on the treaty.

The resolutions, adopted unanimously by a rising vote, follow:

> The Democratic National Committee rejoices with the nation at the rapid return to health and vigor of Woodrow Wilson, the leader of democracy, after his physical breakdown, due largely to overexertion in his efforts in behalf of worldwide peace.
>
> We indorse his courageous and patriotic endeavor to bring the nations of the world to peace by such mutual understanding as will enable them to settle their differences by amicable methods rather than by war.
>
> We affirm our approval of the Treaty of Versailles and we condemn as unwise and unpatriotic the attitude of those Senators who would defeat its ratification, either directly or by overwhelming it with reservations that are intended to and will have the effect of nullifying it.
>
> The failure of the Senate Republican leaders to offer or to permit consideration of interpretative reservations that will preserve the general purpose of the treaty and to so permit its ratification condemns them to the criticism of the nation and to the contempt of the world.

Party's Record Praised.

When the Democratic Party came into power in 1913 under the leadership of Woodrow Wilson, it found the nation in a condition of comparative industrial and commercial depression, its financial system not functioning and the banking system of the country in the hands of a few men at whose will panic periodically occurred. Banks, both national and State, failed with ominous frequency, causing bankruptcy and ruin, stopping the wheels of industry and deterring enterprise. Farmers were denied reasonable credit for the prosecution of their business by their local banks. Special interests were clamoring for even more power than that long exercised by them. Those and other ills had existed for sixteen years under Republican rule, without any relief.

To remedy these conditions, the Democratic Administration, supported by a Democratic Congress called in special session, entered immediately upon a vigorous constructive program. It established a currency and banking system that distributed money as needed to the localities where it was created, freeing the currency of the country from the domination of a few men, and enabling the nation to finance itself through the greatest war the world has known, as well as to feed, clothe and finance the other countries associated with us in the de-

Continued on Page Three.

Text of President's Letter Defining His Treaty Stand

Special to The New York Times.

WASHINGTON, Jan. 8.—The letter of President Wilson read at the Jackson Day dinner tonight was as follows:

THE WHITE HOUSE, WASHINGTON, January 8, 1920.

My Dear Mr. Chairman:

It is with keenest regret that I find that I am to be deprived of the pleasure and privilege of joining you and the other loyal Democrats who are to assemble tonight to celebrate Jackson Day and renew their vows of fidelity to the great principles of our party, the principles which must now fulfill the hopes not only of our own people but of the world.

The United States enjoyed the spiritual leadership of the world until the Senate of the United States failed to ratify the treaty by which the belligerent nations sought to effect the settlements for which they had fought throughout the war. It is inconceivable that at this supreme crisis and final turning point in the international relations of the whole world, when the results of the great war are by no means determined and are still questionable and dependent upon events which no man can foresee or count upon, the United States should withdraw from the concert of progressive and enlightened nations by which Germany was defeated, and all similar Governments (if the world be so unhappy as to contain any) warned of the consequences of any attempt at a like iniquity, and yet that is the effect of the course which the United States has taken with regard to the Treaty of Versailles.

Germany is beaten, but we are still at war with her, and the old stag is reset for a repetition of the old plot. It is now ready for a resumption of the old offensive and defensive alliances which made settled peace impossible. It is no open again to every sort of intrigue.

The old spies are free to resume their former abominable activities. They are again at liberty to make it impossible for governments to be sure what mischief is being worked among their own people, what internal disorders are being fomented.

Without the covenant of the League of Nations there may be as many secret treaties as ever, to destroy the confidence of governments in each other, and their validity cannot be questioned.

None of the objects we professed to be fighting for has been secured, or can be made certain of, without this nation's ratification of the treaty and its entry into the covenant. This nation entered the great war to vindicate its own rights and to protect and preserve free government. It went into the war to see it through to the end, and the end has not yet come. It went into the war to make an end of militarism, to furnish guarantees to weak nations, and to make a just and lasting peace. It entered it with noble enthusiasm.

Five of the leading belligerents have accepted the treaty and formal ratifications will soon be exchanged. The question is whether this country will enter and enter whole-heartedly. If it does not do so, the United States and Germany will play a lone hand in the world.

The maintenance of the peace of the world and the effective execution of the treaty depend upon the whole-hearted participation of the United States. I am not stating it as a matter of power. The point is that the United States is the only nation which has sufficient moral force with the rest of the world to guarantee the substitution of discussion for war. If we keep out of this agreement, if we do not give our guarantees, then another attempt will be made to crush the new nations of Europe.

I do not believe that this is what the people of this country wish or will be satisfied with. Personally, I do not accept the action of the Senate of the United States as the decision of the nation.

I have asserted from the first that the overwhelming majority of the people of this country desire the ratification of the treaty, and my impression to that effect has recently been confirmed by the unmistakable evidences of public opinion given during my visit to seventeen of the States.

I have endeavored to make it plain that if the Senate wishes to say what the undoubted meaning of the League is I shall have no objection. There can be no reasonable objection to interpretations accompanying the act of ratification itself. But when the treaty is acted upon, I must know whether it means that we have ratified or rejected it.

We cannot rewrite this treaty. We must take it without changes which alter its meaning, or leave it, and then after the rest of the world has signed it, we must face the unthinkable task of making another and separate treaty with Germany.

But no mere assertions with regard to the wish and opinion of the country are credited. If there is any doubt as to what the people of the country think on this vital matter, the clear and single way out is to submit it for determination at the next election to the voters of the nation, to give the next election the form of a great and solemn referendum, a referendum as to the part the United States is to play in completing the settlements of the war and in the prevention in the future of such outrages as Germany attempted to perpetrate.

We have no more moral right to refuse now to take part in the execution and administration of these settlements than we had to refuse to take part in the fighting of the last few weeks of the war which brought victory and made it possible to dictate to Germany what the settlements should be. Our fidelity to our associates in the war is in question and the whole future of mankind. It will be heartening to the whole world to know the attitude and purpose of the people of the United States.

I spoke just now of the spiritual leadership of the United States, thinking of international affairs. But there is another spiritual leadership which is open to us and which we can assume.

The world has been made safe for democracy, but democracy has not been finally vindicated. All sorts of crimes are being committed in its name, all sorts of preposterous perversions of its doctrines and practices are being attempted.

This, in my judgment, is to be the great privilege of the democracy of the United States, to show that it can lead the way in the solution of the great social and industrial problems of our time, and lead the way to a happy, settled order of life as well as to political liberty. The program for this achievement we must attempt to formulate, and in carrying it out we shall do more than can be done in any other way to sweep out of existence the tyrannous and arbitrary forms of power which are now masquerading under the name of popular government.

Whenever we look back to Andrew Jackson we should draw fresh inspiration from his character and example. His mind grasped with such a splendid definiteness and firmness the principles of national authority and national action. He was so indomitable in his purpose to give reality to the principles of the Government, that this is a very fortunate time to recall his career and to renew our vows of faithfulness to the principles and the pure practices of Democracy.

I rejoice to join you in this renewal of faith and purpose. I hope that the whole evening may be of the happiest results as regards the fortunes of our party and the nation.

With cordial regards,
Sincerely yours,
WOODROW WILSON.

To Hon. Homer S. Cummings,
Chairman Democratic National Committee, Washington, D. C.

BOOM FOR HOOVER STARTS PROMPTLY

Selection of San Francisco for Democratic Convention Gives Impetus to His Candidacy.

POSITION REMAINS UNKNOWN

Friends Say He Represents Best Opinion in East and West and Would Get Women's Votes.

Special to The New York Times.

WASHINGTON, Jan. 8.—The selection of San Francisco as the city in which to hold the Democratic National Convention has given a decided impetus to the movement to bring about the nomination of Herbert Hoover for President on the Democratic ticket.

That was generally admitted today in political circles after the announcement of the decision had been made. Later, when it became known that President Wilson and William Jennings Bryan had taken almost directly opposite positions on the question of making the Treaty of Peace and the League covenant an issue of election, the belief was expressed that this situation would aid the Hoover candidacy.

Talk of Hoover for President was heard on every side as soon as it became known that the California city had been selected as the scene of the convention. Hoover is a Californian, although most of his career has been staged in other parts of the world, and his friends are urging that he is not only of the West but representative of the thought and desires of the Middle West and the East as well and an international figure at the same time.

It is likely that a "favorite son" boom for the nomination of Hoover will be started soon in California and will spread to other parts of the West. In his speech tonight James W. Gerard, who has announced himself a candidate for the Democratic nomination, quoted

Continued on Page Three.

Treaty Effective at 4 Tomorrow; Fourteen Nations at Ceremony

Supreme Council to Go Out of Existence—Armenian Mandate May Be Offered to Norway—Memorandum to Italy Pat Fiume Under League.

By EDWIN L. JAMES.

Copyright, 1920, by The New York Times Company.
Special Cable to THE NEW YORK TIMES.

PARIS, Jan. 8.—It was announced by the French Foreign Office tonight that the Versailles Treaty would be put into effect Saturday afternoon at 4 o'clock.

This announcement came after the new date of Jan. 15 had been tentatively set earlier in the day.

It is understood that Premier Clemenceau decided suddenly to let pending disputes with Germany go over until after the exchange of ratifications, thus restoring the policy the Council had been pursuing. The "Tiger" does not want the new conference tied up with the German situation.

The following nations will participate in the ceremony: France, Great Britain, Italy, Japan, Belgium, Bolivia, Brazil, Guatemala, Peru, Poland, Siam, Czechoslovakia, Uruguay, and Germany.

Resent Our Aloofness.

I speak conservatively when I say European diplomats regret America's absence from the conferences of the powers. In fact, they resent it. It is causing the sharpest comment which has thus far greeted America's rôle as peacemaker. One allied diplomat remarked:

"The Allies wish to act in accord with Washington on all of the portentous questions before us. America has largely determined the Adriatic issue up to this time, and she is responsible for our having to pass on it now. America has a vital interest in the Russian problem, and recognized her responsibility there by making an accord with Japan on Siberian action. America has had to do with the Turkish situation being in its present ugly state, and her co-operation is needed for its settlement. Let these facts sink in.

"Now the world needs that our labor be done quickly. Clemenceau will probably be President of France on Feb. 17, and we want to finish before that interruption comes.

"Now look at the Adriatic situation. This is the time for all concerned to make concessions and reach an agreement. America has played and still does play, a big rôle. How are we to know what concessions America will make, how are we to negotiate with America, if she has no representative at our conferences?

"It may be said that we can reach our conclusions and then submit them to America. But suppose they do not suit Washington? What then? Must we start all over?

"The same holds true for the Russian and Turkish questions. We have to have America's accord, and it looks as if America is making it hard to get it."

Ambassador Wallace thinks that he has no authority to sit in at these conferences of the Premiers and has asked Washington to instruct him. If the Premiers should send an invitation to Ambassador Wallace to attend some of their sessions, as they did send to Ambassador Davis at London, he would attend. However, it should be pointed out that the London Conference was different from the pending meetings, because at these definite and final conclusions are expected to be made.

The allied diplomats give every indication of being sincere in their complaint that America occupies the position of a world power without wishing to shoulder the responsibility of helping to shape policies to the success of which her assent is regarded as essential.

The Temps tonight expressed regret that the American Government will not participate in the coming conference, and says:

"Peace is not achieved. Neither in the Adriatic nor the Orient can the question in suspense be settled without the co-operation of the United States. The United States on its side cannot disinterest itself from European affairs. Whether one wishes it or not, from henceforth all affairs of the world are in a pool.

"It is today true of the nations of the modern world as it has been for a long time true of individuals within a na-

Continued on Page Twenty.

TO KEEP UP WORK FOR COMPROMISE

Underwood and McNary Hold the President's Statement Leaves Way Open.

PARTY LINES ARE TIGHTENED

Middle-Ground Republicans and Many Democratic Senators Doubtful of the Outcome.

Special to The New York Times.

WASHINGTON, Jan. 8.—Most Senators who discussed the President's statement and the Jackson Day dinner speeches agreed tonight that the result will unquestionably be the stiffening of the lines of the Lodge reservationists and a consequent handicap to any compromise movement.

Senator Underwood, after learning the President's position, said he still thought his resolution for a conciliation committee offered the solution of the difficulty. He pointed out that Mr. Wilson did not entirely close the door to Senate action, although he conceded the President left the opening very small. Mr. Underwood indicated that he intended to go ahead.

Senator McNary, leading Republican worker for a compromise, holds that the President's attitude need not prevent a compromise, and for that reason he would not abandon his efforts, he said. Most mild reservation Senators, however, took the view after hasty reading of the President's statement that he had made it all but impossible for treaty ratification, except through a Democratic revolt against his leadership and acceptance of the Lodge reservations. Such ratification, they pointed out, would be futile, for Mr. Wilson would not accept it.

Friends and supporters of Senator Lodge said they welcomed the issue. The difference between Mr. Bryan and the President, they said, greatly

Continued on Page Four.

CLASH AT JACKSON DINNER

Wilson Declares Senate Must Not Alter Treaty's Meaning

BRYAN FOR CONCESSIONS

Says the Party Cannot Afford Delay—Not a Candidate for President.

WILSON SILENT ON 3D TERM

Democratic Presidential Aspirants Claim Record of Achievement by Party.

Special to The New York Times.

WASHINGTON, Jan. 8.—A sharp clash of views over the Peace Treaty between President Wilson and William J. Bryan developed tonight at the Jackson Day dinner here, following a meeting of the Democratic National Committee at which it was decided to hold the party's national convention at San Francisco, beginning June 28.

The President, in a letter read at the dinner, came out squarely for the treaty "without changes which alter its meaning," although he said that "there can be no reasonable objection to interpretation accompanying the act of ratification." He declared unequivocally that if the meaning of the treaty were changed by the Senate he would favor an appeal to the country with the treaty and the league covenant as an issue.

As one of the guests of honor at the dinner Mr. Bryan made a speech which contained a plea for keeping the treaty out of politics. He argued that the treaty should be ratified without delay; that there should be compromise on the part of the Democratic Senators if necessary to bring this outcome.

To Mr. Bryan the main thing was to ratify the treaty and establish peace with Germany. With the Republicans controlling the Senate, he held, theirs should be the responsibility and the Democratic minority should not put obstacles in their way. Thus the issue between President Wilson and Mr. Bryan was definitely drawn.

The President has taken up the challenge of Senator Lodge to bring the treaty into the Presidential political campaign. It is evident also that his letter is intended as notice to the Senate that if the treaty's meaning is changed or it is so ratified as to require its resubmission ot the allied powers the President will refuse to resubmit it. We cannot "rewrite this treaty," he said.

Lodge Says Treaty Hopes Fade.

Senator Lodge accepted the challenge of the President. He issued a statement tonight after learning what was in the President's letter, in which he said that the issue was clearly drawn.

"The President has made his position very plain," said the Senator. "He rejects absolutely the reservations adopted by a decisive majority of the Senate. He says we must take the treaty without any change which alters its meaning, or leave it. He will permit interpretations, whatever that may mean, expressing its undoubted meaning, when there is hardly a line of it which has not been questioned and received many meanings.

"This permission is valueless. He stands as he has always stood, for the treaty just as it is.

"The issue is clearly drawn. The reservations intended solely to protect the United States in its sovereignty and independence are discarded by the President. The President places himself squarely in behalf of internationalism against Americanism.

"I have hoped that in the Senate we might have come together and ratified the treaty, protected by the principles set forth in the fourteen reservations. The President, I fear, has made this hope impossible. If it is impossible, then we must bear the delay inseparable from the President's attitude and appeal to the people, which I for one shall most cordially welcome."

Big Demonstration Over Letter.

The reading of the President's letter was punctuated by the wildest enthusiasm at both sections of the dinner, which was held at two hotels, the Willard and the Washington, with the same speakers at each. Homer S. Cummings, Chairman of the Democratic National Committee, who presided at the larger of the two dinners, which took place at the Willard, was obliged to pause time and again in his reading of the letter until the enthusiastic Democrats present had given vent to their enthusiasm.

Several times the diners rose en masse and cheered. The women present in that great gathering of men were quite as enthusiastic as those of the other sex.

What was perhaps the greatest burst of cheering came at the Willard dinner, when Chairman Cummings read the portion of the President's letter suggesting the submission of the treaty issue to a referendum of the American people if the Senate altered the covenant. We

1921

The Turbulent Twenties

1929

FRONT PAGE NEWS 1921-1929

Irish 'Free State' Established

DECEMBER 7, 1921

After the Easter Rising in 1916 and a paramilitary campaign by the newly organized Irish Republican Army in 1919, home rule in Ireland became a priority for Great Britain. London offered something less than full independence, proposing to make Ireland a "free state" dominion within the British Empire, like Canada and Australia. Ireland's nationalist president, Eamon de Valera, sent delegates to the negotiations, but the suggestion of a treaty for "free state" status apparently came as a surprise to Belfast. A civil war erupted even before the new dominion officially came into existence, along with Catholic-Protestant conflicts that lasted through the rest of the 20th century.

Gandhi Arrested

MARCH 11, 1922

British authorities charged Mohandas K. Gandhi with sedition, the price he paid for leading the independence movement against colonial rule in India. Gandhi had fashioned a nationwide agenda for nonviolent noncooperation, promoting a boycott of all things British, from British-made products to British-run institutions like courts and government offices. His arrest came a few weeks after he had called off the mass civil disobedience because violence had erupted in one village. In the meantime, London papers had been agitating for Gandhi's arrest, and the secretary of state for India was forced to resign for not apprehending him sooner.

Isadora Duncan Detained

OCTOBER 2, 1922

A brouhaha at the pier in New York was probably just what Isadora Duncan, the flamboyant pioneer of modern dance, wanted as she returned to the United States. Her European trip had netted her a Russian husband and a new identification with Communism. Immigration officials had them detained, purportedly on suspicion that they were Bolshevik agents. But they were soon released and went on to Boston, where a patriotic crowd at a dance performance booed her onstage. She responded theatrically, by angrily baring a breast and shouting, "This is red, and so am I."

King Tut's Tomb Discovered

FEBRUARY 17, 1923

Adventure-seeking Europeans made archaeology something of a sport in the early 20th century, underwriting extensive digs across the Middle East, from Cairo to Amman and Babylon. The goal was to uncover ruins and remains of long-buried biblical empires not yet plundered by grave robbers. One longtime British Egyptologist, Howard Carter, discovered King Tut's tomb in the nick of time—Carter's backer, the Earl of Carnarvon, had run out of patience and would not pay for another year of Carter's hunting. But his excavations led to the greatest find of all, a warren of secret chambers filled with hundreds and hundreds of funerary relics that had not been touched in 3,000 years, including the boy king's solid gold coffin.

Hitler's Beer Hall Putsch

NOVEMBER 10, 1923

"No one leaves the room alive without my permission," Adolf Hitler announced during his first attempt to seize power, in Bavaria. Hitler's machine-gun-toting storm troopers first surrounded a giant Munich beer hall during a political rally, then he led the state commander and two other officials into an anteroom where he harangued them until they went along with his insurrection plan. Hitler climbed on a table, fired his pistol in the air and declared, "The national revolution has begun." It quickly fizzled. A Nazi march to Berlin, inspired by Mussolini's march on Rome in 1922, dissolved when German troops opened fire, killing 16 Nazis. Hitler was jailed for the plot; in his cell he started writing "Mein Kampf."

Teapot Dome Scandal

JANUARY 27, 1924

Just as "Watergate" became synonymous with White House political scandal in the 1970's, "Teapot Dome" was synonymous with high-stakes political and financial corruption in the 1920s. A Senate investigation found that Albert B. Fall, the secretary of the interior under President Warren G. Harding, had pocketed several hundred thousand dollars from leasing federal petroleum reserves to two oil barons. ("Teapot Dome" was the name of one of the reserves, in Wyoming.) Fall was later convicted of taking bribes, and two other Harding protégés committed suicide, one a Republican bagman in the Justice Department (dubbed the Department of Easy Virtue because pardons and permits could be had for cash). President Calvin Coolidge, who had been Harding's vice president and who became president when Harding died in disgrace in August 1923, sidestepped the scandal and won election on his own in 1924.

Leopold and Loeb Confess

JUNE 1, 1924

Nathan F. Leopold and Richard A. Loeb were two college-age buddies from well-to-do Chicago families who believed that they were smart enough to pull off the perfect murder, just for thrills. They kidnapped 14-year-old Robert Franks, bludgeoned him to death and buried his body in a railroad conduit. There the killing became less than perfect: Leopold lost his glasses—a clue that pointed detectives to the pair. At their trial, Clarence Darrow's defense was a carefully reasoned condemnation of capital punishment, and it worked. The judge sentenced them to life terms for the murder and 99 years for the kidnapping. Loeb was killed in prison in 1936, slashed by another inmate. Leopold, paroled in 1958, died in 1971.

Democrats Split Over the Klan

JUNE 28, 1924

The first big fight at the 1924 Democratic National Convention was over whether to denounce the Ku Klux Klan, which was viciously anti-black, anti-Semitic and anti-Catholic—but popular with white Southern Democrats. No less a Democratic eminance than William Jennings Bryan argued against even referring to the Klan by name. He said that doing so would only give the Klan more publicity. Eventually that approach won out, by one vote. Agreeing on a nominee took another nine days and 103 ballots; he was John W. Davis, a Wall Street lawyer and former congressman, who lost to President Calvin Coolidge in November.

'Why We Go to Cabarets'

NOVEMBER 26, 1925

Ellin Mackay's scorching manifesto about café society was front-page news because of who she was, a debutante whose millionaire father had presided over the completion of the first trans-Atlantic cable. She shocked capital-S society with her put-downs of the boys she had grown up with: "If our elders want to know why we go to cabarets, let them go to the best of our present-day stag lines. There they will see extremely unalluring specimens." She had a different reaction to Irving Berlin. Short and Jewish, he was not exactly a poster boy for High Society. But Ellin married him, even though her father threatened to cut off her inheritance.

Sinclair Lewis Refuses a Pulitzer

MAY 6, 1926

Of the nine Pulitzer Prizes awarded in 1926, one was refused—something that had never happened before and has happened only once since (William Saroyan turned down a Pulitzer for drama in 1940). Sinclair Lewis said he could not accept a Pulitzer for his third novel, "Arrowsmith," because "all prizes, like all titles, are dangerous." He objected to the language used to explain what the prize was for—a work depicting the "wholesome atmosphere of American life." He said that meant that winners could be chosen "not according to their actual literary merit but in obedience to whatever code of good form may chance to be popular at the moment." He had no such qualms when he won the Nobel Prize for Literature in 1930.

Dempsey Beats Tunney

SEPTEMBER 24, 1926

Prize-fighting was to the Jazz Age what professional football is these days—the sport with a special hold on the national consciousness. And there was no more famous fighter in the Jazz Age than Jack Dempsey, the heavyweight champion since 1919. So when Gene Tunney defeated him in the rain in Philadelphia, the crowd of 135,000 was stunned and Dempsey was succinct: "I have no alibis to offer." Tunney also won the rematch, in 1927, despite a knockdown in the seventh round and the infamous "long count" controversy that followed.

The Big Broadcast

JANUARY 22, 1927

The year had begun with the first coast-to-coast radio broadcast, of the Rose Bowl. Three weeks later, broadcast engineers in Chicago hooked up their microphones and sent the third act of Gounod's "Faust" down the line, live. The singers sounded good. The Times said that static, "the foil of best laid radio plans," did not interfere until the final moments.

The Dawn of Television

APRIL 8, 1927

Before "Howdy Doody" and "The Honeymooners," before MTV and VH1, before high-definition and plasma screens and TiVo, there was Herbert Hoover giving a speech. He was anything but charismatic, but to bend Marshall McLuhan's famous phrase, the message was the medium. It was the first public demonstration of television, and while bugs remained to be worked out, The Times was awed: "It was as if a photograph had suddenly come to life and begun to talk, smile, nod its head and look this way and that."

Sacco and Vanzetti Executed

AUGUST 23, 1927

The execution went on as scheduled, even though someone else had confessed to the robbery-murder and even though intellectuals like Professor Felix Frankfurter of Harvard Law School had argued that the defendants were victims of a "Red scare"—the kind of post–World War I hysteria that had prompted Woodrow Wilson's attorney general, A. Mitchell Palmer, to round up "alien Bolsheviks." But Chief Justice William Howard Taft refused to leave his vacation home for a last-minute appeal, and Governor Alvan T. Fuller of Massachusetts refused to grant clemency to Nicola Sacco and Bartolomeo Vanzetti. They had been obscure anarchists before they were arrested for a 1920 factory-payroll robbery in which the paymaster and a guard were shot to death. Their defenders maintained that they were framed and that the trial was essentially a political prosecution.

Einstein Expands Relativity Theory

JANUARY 12, 1929

It had been years since Albert Einstein had posited a relationship between energy and mass with the equation that every science student learns as $E=mc^2$. For a decade he had been working on a theory to unify gravity and electromagnetism as different manifestations of a single fundamental field. He would continue his work on a unified field theory through the 1950s, trying to reconcile it with the other, contradictory centerpiece of modern physics, quantum theory.

Evolution on Trial

JULY 22, 1925

The Scopes case put Charles Darwin's theory of evolution on trial against the idea that the Bible's account of creation was literally true. Southern states where Protestant fundamentalism had taken hold had statutes to keep teachers from teaching evolution. In Tennessee, John Scopes was indicted for teaching "that man has descended from a lower order of animals." His trial brought two of the nation's best-known lawyers to a rural courtroom: Clarence Darrow, who defended Scopes, and William Jennings Bryan, who had volunteered to prosecute the case. Darrow called the proceeding the first of its kind "since we stopped trying people for witchcraft." He lost the case but succeeded in ridiculing the creationists—and Bryan, who died of a heart attack less than a week later. Scopes was fined a nominal amount ($100) but Tennessee's anti-evolution law remained on the books until 1967, when it was overturned by the Tennessee Supreme Court.

Lindbergh's Trans-Atlantic Flight

MAY 22, 1927

"Well, I made it," Charles A. Lindbergh said when he climbed out of the cockpit at Le Bourget airport outside Paris. What an understatement—Lindbergh's history-making flight had been followed, hour by hour, as his little single engine plane bounced and bumped over the Atlantic for 3,600 miles. No detail was too small for headlines—"Ate Only One and a Half of His Five Sandwiches"—and exclamation points. Another detail proved he had packed light, to save weight. At the U.S. Embassy in Paris, where he spent the night, he had to borrow the ambassador's pajamas.

"All the News That's Fit to Print."

The New York Times.

THE WEATHER
Fair today and Thursday; no change in temperature; north winds.
Temperature yesterday—Max., 40; min., 30.
For full weather report see Page 23.

VOL. LXXI....No. 23,328. NEW YORK, WEDNESDAY, DECEMBER 7, 1921. TWO CENTS In Greater New York | THREE CENTS Within 200 Miles | FOUR CENTS Elsewhere

IRELAND TO BE A FREE STATE WITHIN THE BRITISH EMPIRE; AGREEMENT SIGNED GIVING HER A STATUS LIKE CANADA'S; ULSTER CAN STAY OUT; PARLIAMENT CALLED TO RATIFY

HARDING PROPOSES FLEXIBLE TARIFF AND LABOR REGULATION

Asks Congress to Extend the Powers of the Present Tariff Commission.

WOULD FUND FOREIGN DEBT

Will Not Denounce Trade Treaties and Wants Merchant Marine Act Changed.

AGAINST TAX-EXEMPT BONDS

Many Arms Conference Delegates in Throng Which Listens to President's Address to Congress.

Special to The New York Times.

WASHINGTON, Dec. 6.—In an address which President Harding pointed out was not only a message to the Congress but to the people of the entire country he made an appeal today for the united support of his party in the accomplishment of legislation that he considers vital to the peace, prosperity and security not only of the United States but of the world. Senators and Representatives of both parties agreed that it was a very frank expression of the views and hopes of the Chief Executive. In much that he said the President won the outspoken approval of the Democrats as well as the Republicans.

[The full text of the message is published on Page 8.]

Not since the war days has a more representative audience listened to an address by a President on the opening of Congress. Occupying seats of honor directly in front of the rostrum from which the President spoke were statesmen of Europe and the Orient who are representing their respective countries at the Conference for Limitation of Armament. They were an intensely interested body of men who, observing the strictest decorum, did not join in the applause that continually interrupted the delivery of the address.

Behind the diplomats and foreign delegates were grouped the members of the Senate and House, Secretary Hughes and the other members of the Cabinet being in the first row of seats in the House reservation. There were just two uniformed personages on the floor. One was General Pershing and the other his aid, Major Quekenmeyer.

Refers Twice to Arms Conference.

Twice in the course of his address, once at the beginning and again as he concluded, the President referred to the Conference for Limitation of Armament now in session in Washington.

"It is gratifying to report," he said at the start, "that our country is not only free from every impending menace of war, but there are growing assurances of the permanency of the peace which we so deeply cherish."

"Agreeable to your expressed desire," he said, in concluding his address, "and in complete accord with the purposes of the executive branch of the Government, there is in Washington, as you happily know, an international conference now most earnestly at work on plans for the limitation of armament, a naval holiday, and the just settlement of problems which might develop into causes of international disagreement.

"It is easy to believe a world hope is centred on this capital city. A most gratifying world accomplishment is not improbable.

Procedure to Avoid Strikes.

Discussing at considerable length the problem of capital and labor, the President pointed out that the right of labor to organize is as necessary and as fundamental as is the right of capital to organize, and that the right of labor to negotiate through its chosen agents is as essential as is the right of capital to organize to maintain corporations and to limit the liabilities of stockholders. But, he added, just as it is undesirable that a corporation shall not be permitted to impose undue exactions upon the public, it is just as essential that labor shall not be permitted to exact unfair terms of its employers, or subject an innocent public to distress in order to gain its end.

In the same way that nations are seeking procedures to settle their difficulties without resort to war, the President suggested, some procedure should be found whereby labor and capital can reach agreements without resort to those forms of warfare" which are recognized as strikes, lockouts, boycotts and the like.

"Inescapable" World Relationship.

Other outstanding features of the address were the earnestness and the unqualified positiveness with which the President asserted the "inescapable relationship" of the United States to the affairs of the world in finance and in trade. The United States, he declared, would be unworthy of its best traditions, "if we were unmindful of social, moral and political conditions which are not of direct concern to us," but which,

Continued on Page Nine.

Text of Agreement to Establish the Irish Free State

LONDON, Dec. 6 (Associated Press.)—The text of the agreement signed this morning by the British Government and the Irish representatives follows:

Article I.—Ireland shall have the same constitutional status in the community of nations known as the British Empire as the Dominion of Canada, the Commonwealth of Australia, the Dominion of New Zealand and the Union of South Africa, with a Parliament having powers to make laws for peace and order and good government in Ireland, and an executive responsible to that Parliament, and shall be styled and known as the Irish Free State.

Article II.—Subject to provisions hereinafter set out, the position of the Irish Free State in relation to the Imperial Parliament, the Government and otherwise shall be that of the Dominion of Canada, and the law, practice and constitutional usage governing the relationship of the Crown or representative of the Crown and the Imperial Parliament to the Dominion of Canada shall govern their relationship to the Irish Free State.

Article III.—A representative of the Crown in Ireland shall be appointed in like manner as the Governor General of Canada and in accordance with the practice observed in making such appointments.

Article IV.—The oath to be taken by the members of the Parliament of the Irish Free State shall be in the following form:

"I do solemnly swear true faith and allegiance to the Constitution of the Irish Free State as by law established, and that I will be faithful to his Majesty King George V., and his heirs and successors by law, in virtue of the common citizenship of Ireland with Great Britain and her adherence to and membership of the group of nations forming the British Commonwealth of Nations."

Article V.—The Irish Free State shall assume liability for service of the public debt of the United Kingdom as existing at the date thereof and toward the payment of war pensions as existing on that date in such proportion as may be fair and equitable, having regard for any just claims on the part of Ireland by way of set-off or counter-claim, the amount of such sums being determined, in default of agreement, by the arbitration of one or more independent persons being citizens of the British Empire.

Article VI.—Until an arrangement has been made between the British and Irish Governments whereby the Irish Free State undertakes her own coastal defense, defense by sea of Great Britain and Ireland shall be undertaken by his Majesty's imperial forces, but this shall not prevent the construction or maintenance by the Government of the Irish Free State of such vessels as are necessary for the protection of the revenue or the fisheries. The foregoing provisions of this article shall be reviewed at a conference of representatives of the British and Irish Governments to be held at the expiration of five years from the date hereof with a view to the undertaking by Ireland of a share in her own coastal defense.

Article VII.—The Government of the Irish Free State shall afford to his Majesty's imperial force (a) in time of peace such harbor and other facilities as are indicated in the annex hereto, or such other facilities as may from time to time be agreed between the British Government and the Government of the Irish Free State, and (b) in time of war or of strained relations with a foreign power such harbor and other facilities as the British Government may require for the purposes of such defense, as aforesaid.

Article VIII.—With a view to securing observance of the principle of international limitation of armaments, if the Government of the Irish Free State establishes and maintains a military defense force, the establishment thereof shall not exceed in size such proportion of the military establishments maintained in Great Britain as that which the population of Ireland bears to the population of Great Britain.

Article IX.—The ports of Great Britain and the Irish Free State shall be freely open to the ships of the other country on the payment of the customary port and other dues.

Article X.—The Government of the Irish Free State agrees to pay fair compensation, on terms not less favorable than those accorded by the Act of 1920, to Judges, officials, members of the police forces and other public servants who are discharged by it or who retire in consequence of the change of government effected in pursuance of the hereof paragraph.

Provided that this agreement shall not apply to members of the auxiliary police force or persons recruited in Great Britain for the Royal Irish Constabulary during the two years next preceding the date hereof. The British Government will assume responsibility for such compensation or pensions as may be payable to any of these excepted persons.

Article XI.—Until the expiration of one month from the passing of the Act of Parliament for the ratification of this instrument, the powers of the Parliament and Government of the Irish Free State shall not be exercisable as respects Northern Ireland, and the provisions of the Government of Ireland Act of 1920 shall, so far as they relate to Northern Ireland, remain of full force and effect, and no election shall be held for the return of members to serve in the Parliament of the Irish Free State for the constituencies of Northern Ireland unless a resolution is passed by both houses of Parliament of Northern Ireland in favor of holding such elections before the end of said month.

Article XII.—If before the expiration of said month an address is presented to his Majesty by both houses of Parliament of Northern Ireland to that effect, the powers of the Parliament and Government of the Irish Free State shall no longer extend to Northern Ireland, and the provisions of the Government of Ireland Act of 1920 (including those relating to the Council of Ireland) shall, so far as they relate to Northern Ireland, continue to be of full force and effect, and this instrument shall have effect, subject to the necessary modifications;

Provided, that if such an address is so presented, a commission consisting of three persons, one to be appointed by the Government of the Irish Free State, one to be appointed by the Government of Northern Ireland, and one, who shall be Chairman, to be appointed by the British Government, shall determine in accordance with the wishes of the inhabitants, so far as may be compatible with economic and geographic conditions, the boundaries between Northern Ireland and the rest of Ireland, and for the purposes of the Government of Ireland act of 1920, and of this instrument the boundary of Northern Ireland shall be such as may be determined by such commission.

Article XIII.—For the purpose of the last foregoing article the powers of the Parliament of Southern Ireland under the Government of Ireland Act of 1920, to elect members of the Council of Ireland, shall, after the Parliament of the Irish Free State is constituted, be exercised by that Parliament.

Article XIV.—After the expiration of said month, if no such address as mentioned in Article XII. hereof is presented, the Parliament of the Government of Northern Ireland shall continue to exercise as respects Northern Ireland the powers conferred upon them by the Government of Ireland Act of 1920, but the Parliament of the Government of the Irish Free State shall in Northern Ireland have in relation to matters, in respect of which the Parliament of Northern Ireland has not the power to make laws under that act (including matters which, under said act, are within the jurisdiction of the Council of Ireland), the same powers as in the rest of Ireland, subject to such other provisions as may be agreed to in the manner hereinafter appearing.

Article XV.—At any time after the date hereof the Government of Northern Ireland and the Provisional Government of Southern Ireland, hereinafter constituted, may meet for the purpose of discussing provisions, subject to which the last of the foregoing article is to operate in the event of no such address as is therein mentioned being presented, and those provisions may include: (a) Safeguards with regard to patronage in Northern Ireland; (b) safeguards with regard to the collection of revenue in Northern Ireland; (c) safeguards with regard to import and export duties affecting the trade and industry of Northern Ireland; (d) safeguards for the minorities in Northern Ireland; (e) settlement of financial relations between Northern Ireland and the Irish Free State; (f) establishment and powers of a local militia in Northern Ireland and the relation of the defense forces of the Irish Free State and of Northern Ireland, respectively, and if at any such meeting provisions are agreed to, the same shall have effect as if they were included among the provisions subject to which the powers of Parliament and of the Government of the Irish Free State are to be exercisable in Northern Ireland under Article XIV. hereof.

Article XVI.—Neither the Parliament of the Irish Free State nor the Parliament of Northern Ireland shall make any law so as either directly or indirectly to endow any religion or prohibit or restrict the free exercise thereof or give any preference or impose any disability on the account of religious belief or religious status, or affect prejudicially the right of any child to attend school receiving public money without attending the religious instruction of the school, or make any discrimination as respects State aid between schools under the management of the different religious denominations, or divert from any religious denomination or any educational institution any of its property except for public utility purposes and on the payment of compensation.

Article XVII.—By way of provisional arrangement for the administration of Southern Ireland during the interval which must elapse between the date hereof and the constitution of a Parliament and a Government of the Irish Free State in accordance therewith, steps shall be taken forthwith for summoning a meeting of the Members of Parliament elected for the constituencies in Southern Ireland since the passing of the Government of Ireland act in 1920 and for constituting a Provisional Government. And the British Government shall take steps necessary to transfer to such Provisional Government the powers and machinery requisite for the discharge of its duties, provided that every member of such Provisional Government shall have signified in writing his or her acceptance of this instrument. But this arrangement shall not continue in force beyond the expiration of twelve months from the date hereof.

Article XVIII.—This instrument shall be submitted forthwith by his Majesty's Government for the approval of Parliament and by the Irish signatories to a meeting summoned for the purpose of members elected to sit in the House of Commons of Southern Ireland, and, if approved, it shall be ratified by the necessary legislation.

Signed on behalf of the British delegation:

LLOYD GEORGE.
AUSTEN CHAMBERLAIN.
BIRKENHEAD.
WINSTON CHURCHILL.
WORTHINGTON-EVANS.
GORDON HEWART.
HAMAR GREENWOOD.

On behalf of the Irish delegation:

ART OF GRIOBHTHA (ARTHUR GRIFFITH).
MICHAEL O. O. SILEAIN (MICHAEL COLLINS).
RIOBARD BARTUN (ROBERT C. BARTON).
E. S. DUGAN (EAMON J. DUGGAN).
SEORSA GHABGAIN UI DHUBHTHAIGH (GEORGE GAVAN DUFFY).

Dated the 6th of December, 1921.

ANNEX.

An annex is attached to the treaty. Clause 1 specifies that Admiralty property and rights at the dockyard port of Berehaven are to be retained as at present date and the harbor defenses and facilities for coastal defense by air at Queenstown, Belfast, Lough and Loughswilly to remain under British care, provision also being made for oil, fuel and storage.

Clause 2 provides that a convention shall be made between the two Governments, to give effect to the following conditions: That submarine cables shall not be landed or wireless stations for communication with places outside of Ireland established, except by agreement with the British Government, that existing cable rights and wireless concessions shall not be withdrawn except by agreement with the British Government, and that the British Government shall be entitled to land additional submarine cables or establish additional wireless stations for communication with places outside of Ireland, that lighthouses, buoys, beacons, &c., shall be maintained by the Irish Government and not be removed or added to except by agreement with the British Government, that war signal stations shall be closed down and left in charge of care and maintenance parties, the Government of the Irish Free State being offered the option of taking them over and working them for commercial purposes, subject to Admiralty inspection, and guaranteeing the upkeep of existing telegraphic communication therewith.

Clause 3 provides that a convention shall be made between the two Governments for the regulation of civil communication by air.

'IRISH FREE STATE' CREATED

All of Ireland Outside of Ulster to Have Dominion Rule.

ULSTER CANNOT STOP IT

Redrawing of Her Frontiers to Follow if She Finally Refuses to Join.

NAVAL RIGHTS RESERVED

Control of Finances, Land Forces and Powers of Council of Ireland Given to New State.

Special Cable to THE NEW YORK TIMES.

LONDON, Dec. 6.—"Ireland shall have the same constitutional status in the community of nations known as the British Empire as the Dominion of Canada, the Commonwealth of Australia, the Dominion of New Zealand and the Union of South Africa, with a Parliament having powers to make laws for the peace and order and good government of Ireland and an Executive responsible to that Parliament, and shall be styled and known as the Irish Free State."

Such is the first article of the "treaty between Great Britain and Ireland" which was signed some minutes after 2 o'clock this morning on behalf of Great Britain by Lloyd George, Austen Chamberlain, Lord Birkenhead, Winston Churchill, Sir L. Worthington-Evans, Sir Hamar Greenwood and Sir Gordon Hewart, and on behalf of Ireland by Arthur Griffith, Michael Collins, Robert Barton, E. J. Duggan and Gavan Duffy.

The signatures were affixed to the document in that historic room of 10 Downing Street on whose walls hang the portraits of the greatest British Premiers of the past and of one American, George Washington, the Father of His Country.

It was that same room, Lord Birkenhead pointed out today, which "witnessed the fateful and melancholy discussions that preceded the final recognition on the part of the statesmen of this country that the American colonies were lost. It was in that room," said the Chancellor of the Exchequer, "in which the anxieties, uncertainties and vicissitudes of the war met with daily reflection, that yesterday was entered upon, in my judgment, a new phase which promises, after all these bitter centuries and generations, that at last an era may dawn which will enable us, of our day and generation, to say that we have not achieved less in settlement here at our own doors of the issue which seems, but is not, domestic than we achieved in the fields of arms when we preserved the security and existence of these islands from the greatest menace that assailed them since the Napoleonic period."

The Cabinet met this morning and approved the agreement reached between the British and Sinn Fein delegates. The Premier was heartily congratulated.

Parliament to Meet Next Week.

Now that the treaty of settlement has been signed the next step will be to submit the terms to the British Parliament for approval. For this purpose both Houses have been summoned to meet on Wednesday next, Dec. 14, by which time it is hoped the agreement as signed by the Sinn Fein delegates will have been ratified by the Dail Eireann.

This meeting of Parliament will be the first of a new session, and this will give added importance to the opening ceremony.

The King will open the session in person and in full state. The greatest emphasis will thus be laid upon it as a great historic occasion, on which the King's speech will no doubt lay due stress. There will be no other business to place before the Houses at this stage, and a day or two would be enough to secure the object in view. Then Parliament would adjourn until the date of assembly previously fixed, Jan. 30, unless there should appear a reason for a meeting a week or two earlier. But the preparation of the necessary bill for giving effect to the Anglo-Irish agreement will require time and its completion before the end of January is unlikely.

The terms of the agreement were carried to Dublin by E. J. Duggan, one of the Sinn Fein plenipotentiaries, adn Desmond Fitzgerald, Dail Minister of Publicity.

Meanwhile at the house in Hans Place occupied by the delegates and at the Secretariat in Cadogan Gardens the process of packing up began. There was noticeable slackening in the care with which doors had been guarded ever since the Sinn Feiners came to London; and women secretaries were bustling about packing up big files of documents and getting their own baggage ready. Formal orders had not yet been issued to them, but they expect to leave by the mail train tomorrow night, arriving in Dublin on Thursday morning.

None of the delegates was ready to discuss the settlement, and equal reticence was shown by the rest of the party. They seemed, however, confident that the agreement would be accepted by the Sinn Fein generally, and when it was suggested that De Valera's speeches in the last day or two looked rather ominous, one of the secretaries declared he thought his utterances on Monday quite moderate.

A poster of The Freeman's Journal

B.R.T. DIVIDENDS PAID DAY OF RECEIVERSHIP

Checks for $236,250 Mailed by Operating Company Just Before Garrison Took Charge.

HECTIC HOLIDAY FOR HEDLEY

Got $1,000,000 on New Year's Eve to Stave Off the Failure of Interborough.

Stories of quick shifts of millions between holding companies and subsidiaries in both the Interborough and Brooklyn Rapid Transit systems on the eve of receiverships were told in the Transit Commission's hearing yesterday by James R. Sheffield, trustee in bankruptcy for the Interborough Consolidated Corporation, and Howard Abel, Controller for the B. R. T.

On Dec. 31, 1918, a few hours before Lindley M. Garrison was appointed receiver for the New York Consolidated Railroad Company, which operates the subway and elevated lines of the B. R. T. system, the companys officers rushed out checks for the last payment of a 1¼ per cent. dividend on $18,900,000 of stock, amounting to about $236,250. The dividends had been declared in the preceding September. As holder of approximately 96 per cent. of the stock of the New York Consolidated, the Brooklyn Rapid Transit Company received the larger part of this payment.

A year later President Frank Hedley and other officers of the Interborough were spending a "hectic New Year's Eve," and finally obtained a loan of $1,000,000 from its bankrupt holding company, the Interborough Consolidated, to aid in averting a receivership for the subway and elevated lines of Manhattan and the Bronx.

A few days before this New Year's Eve loan the Interborough Rapid Transit Company had finished paying back to the Interborough Consolidated $800,000 borrowed from the treasury of the holding company the day before it went into bankruptcy in March, 1919. Mr. Sheffield, trustee in bankruptcy for the Interborough Consolidated, had demanded the return of that $800,000 on the ground that the loan was "illegal."

He also had demanded from the Interborough payment of a note for $500,000, due on April 1, 1919, but which was

Continued on Page Five.

German Explosion Kills 100, Sets Dynamite Works Afire

BERLIN, Dec. 6 (Associated Press).—It is reported that 100 persons lost their lives today as the result of the explosion of an oil tank in the Nobel Dynamite Works at Saarlouis, Rhenish Prussia.

The works are burning.

SAYS UNION ABUSES RAISE BUILDING COST

Witness Tells Lockwood Committee of Expenses Piled Up by Labor Inefficiency.

The Lockwood committee opened a new phase of its housing inquiry late yesterday afternoon by examining witnesses in an endeavor to learn to what extent housing construction was loaded with high costs due to the inefficiency of labor. C. G. Norman, Chairman of the Board of Governors of the Building Trades Employers' Association, detailed a long list of abuses he alleged existed in building trade unions, resulting from severe membership and production restrictions demanded by the organizations.

Patrick J. Crowley, successor of Robert P. Brindell as Chairman of the Building Trades Council, having jurisdiction over 115,000 workers, explained the inefficiency of labor by the phrase "more pay, more pep," and declared he had heard no complaints lately regarding the inefficiency of labor.

Samuel Untermyer, senior counsel to the committee, and Henry Mayer, assistant counsel, again took up the affairs of Inside Electrical Workers' Union 3, which is said to have collected $250,000 a year on "permit" cards which enabled non-union journeymen to work on union jobs if they paid $2.50 a week for journeymen's cards and $1 a week for helpers' cards. Mr. Untermyer examined Joseph Lawlor, Treasurer of the union, concerning the $26,000 of the funds alleged to be missing, but Lawlor became involved in confused statements, saying he believed that William A. Hogan, the financial secretary, had turned the money over to the union, and then that he did not know whether Hogan turned the money over to him or not, finally returning to his original statement.

In introducing the examination of

Continued on Page Six.

America Will Enter No Alliance; Three More Chinese Advisers Out

No Treaty on Far East Likely, but a Less Formal Agreement—Project Shaping Slowly.

By EDWIN L. JAMES.

Special to The New York Times.

WASHINGTON, Dec. 6.—Whatever plans are being worked out for an international treaty, protocol, resolution, agreement, or understanding among three, four, five, six, seven, eight or nine powers to establish a Far Eastern policy do not now form a proper subject for public consideration, according to the official view of the American delegation to the armament conference.

It is stated by spokesman for the delegation that much progress has been made in the working out of a Far Eastern agreement. But just what that "progress" means and just what it is purposed to commit the nation to the Amerlacn representatives are not yet prepared to say.

While reports originating from other delegations are being published all over the world, emphasizing the idea of an alliance of the United States with other nations, the Amerlacn delegates think the time is not fit to present the American views on what might be a suitable arrangement.

Efforts made today to induce the American representatives to set correspondents on the right path amid the eddies of conflicting rumors as to what was being done brought only the instructive statement that what had been been published about treaties and alliances was not within gunshot of the truth. But just what the truth is—that is not forthcoming.

Observers, and many visiting diplomats, have commented frequently upon the secrecy of the conference since its first days. Not a few of the old-school diplomats who are here and at work feared that the Americans were going to stage the conference doings in the open. It is probable that there was a general expectation that some of the real negotiations would be done at public meetings. It even looked that way just after the first two open sessions.

But the fears of the old school diplomats have proved groundless. For two weeks there has not been a plenary session, and it has become evident that the plenary sessions will be full-dress occasions for announcing decisions previously reached.

While there is no official statement on the subject, there appears no reason to suppose that the American delegation is going to undertake to involve this country in an alliance to take the place of the Anglo-Japanese alliance or to serve any other purpose. Nor will there, in all probability, be any treaty, three-

Continued on Page Four.

Attaches of Delegation Resign in Protest Against 'Negative Results' of Conference.

Special to The New York Times.

WASHINGTON, Dec. 6.—As a protest against "negative results" of the conference concerning China's aspirations, three additional attachés of the Chinese delegation to the Washington conference, two of them superior advisers, today tendered their resignations. This action followed that of Dr. Philip K. C. Tyau, Secretary General of the delegation, yesterday.

Those who resigned today are Yuho M. T. Liang, ex-Minister of Foreign Affairs; Tzu-Chi Chow, ex-Minister of Finance, superior advisers, and Vice Admiral Ting-Kan Tsi, associate director of the revenue council and adviser to the delegation. He was an adviser to the office of the President of China during the incumbency of the late Yuan Shih-Kai. A report that Lieut. Gen. Fu Hwang, adviser to the delegation, also had resigned, was denied.

It was uncertain tonight whether the resignations would be accepted.

China's attitude was criticised by an American official, who said that China had nothing to gain by such a course. He pointed out that the conference was making great progress, and that China found herself in a very strong position, face to face with all the nations interested in the Far East, with their representatives disposed to do everything possible to aid in restoring China's integrity and rehabilitating her finances.

There is divided opinion in the Chinese delegation as to the situation that that country is facing in the conference. One Chinese adviser, deprecating the resignations, said that the action had been premature and would fail of the expected effect. Some of them resigned for the political effect at home, while others, it was said, were absolutely sincere in the course taken.

Another spokesman for China counseled a more determined attitude on the part of China and an insistence that the Shantung Railroad dispute be adjusted first, rather than the minor differences now under consideration in the parley. He said he was in a position to say that the leaders in the conference had decided just how far the Far Eastern matters should be settled and that China would be forced to take what was given her. In his opinion, the conference leaders have agreed not only upon a naval ratio but upon other matters. China, he said, would not be allowed to change her tariff treaties and most of the things in dispute would be left to a commission to study and report upon to another conference.

"We are not too sensitive about the

Continued on Page Four.

Carson Sees for Britain Day of 'Abject Humiliation'

Special Cable to THE NEW YORK TIMES.

LONDON, Dec. 7.—The Morning Post says that after reading the terms of the Irish agreement the comment of Lord Carson, former Ulster leader, was:

"I never thought I should live to see a day of such abject humiliation for Great Britain."

CANADIAN ELECTION LIBERAL LANDSLIDE

Premier Meighen Loses His Seat and His Protection Policy Is Repudiated.

OTTAWA, Dec. 6.—Premier Meighen was defeated in his home constituency, Portage La Prairie, Manitoba, in the Canadian general election today. His opponent was Harry Leader, Progressive.

Returns received tonight indicated the defeat of the Meighen Government and a landslide for the Liberals, led by W. L. Mackenzie King. Seven members of the Cabinet were defeated.

Mr. King, the Liberal leader, was elected in North York, Ontario, a division normally Conservative, by 1,000 majority. T. A. Crerar, leader of the Progressive Party, was elected in Marquette, Manitoba.

In the eastern part of the dominion the Liberals made a clean sweep. Quebec, with sixty-five members in Parliament, will be represented entirely by Liberals. Five of the seven defeated Cabinet members were candidates in Quebec constituencies.

Nova Scotia, with sixteen seats, gave them all to Liberals, two members of the Government going down to defeat in that province. Liberals were reported elected in three out of the four Prince Edward Island divisions, and in six of the eleven constituencies in New Brunswick.

The Cabinet members defeated were F. B. McCurdy, Minister of Public Works, Colchester, N. S.; E. K. Spinney, Minister without portfolio, Yarmouth, N. S.; L. P. Normand, President of the Privy Council, Three Rivers, Quebec; C. C. Ballantyne, Minister of Marine and Fisheries, Montreal, Quebec; A. Fauteux, Solicitor General, Terre Bonne, Quebec; L. G. Belley, Postmaster General, Charlevoix, Quebec; Rudolphe Monty, Secretary of State, Beauharnois, Quebec.

Premier Meighen issued the following

Continued on Page Twelve.

ULSTER RESERVED; DUBLIN REJOICES

Craig Cabinet Begins Sessions to Consider the Terms of the Agreement.

NORTH DISLIKES THE OATH

But Waits to See if Sinn Fein Is Really Friendly—Dail's Acceptance Predicted.

Special Cable to THE NEW YORK TIMES.

BELFAST, Dec. 6.—News that the settlement had been achieved between the British Government and the Sinn Fein delegates caused some surprise in Belfast, particularly in view of De Valera's declaration at Galway in regard to allegiance. The disposition of Ulster people is not to enter upon any hasty criticism or comment, but to wait until the terms are revealed. Should the position of Ulster be safeguarded and southern Ireland accept allegiance and a recognized position within the British Empire there will be a general feeling of satisfaction in the north that the strife in Ireland has been brought to an end.

A specially convened meeting of the Ulster Cabinet was held today. After considering the terms for two and a half hours the Cabinet adjourned further consideration until tomorrow.

Colonel Spender, Secretary to the Northern Cabinet, was asked for the Cabinet's first impression of the terms of settlement. He said they were somewhat puzzled and were anxious to have certain points cleared up. Colonel Spender added that if the proposed changes in area affected any great tract of territory or meant any great disturbance of population they would not be acceptable to Ulster. He understood, however, that they really meant small adjustments along the frontier.

Asked if the form of oath was acceptable, Colonel Spender said that the Ulster people did not like it, but if it were acceptable to the British people they could not object. He regarded with suspicion the fact that the Sinn Feiners were not prepared to take the ordinary form of oath.

Likes the Option for Ulster.

In one form, Colonel Spender remarked, the latest proposals meant an advance, because the former ones provided for forcing Ulster to go in under an all-Ireland Parliament while these gave an option. If the good-will of the Sinn Fein was forthcoming, he added, and there was an intention on their part

Continued on Page Two.

"All the News That's Fit to Print."

The New York Times.

THE WEATHER
Rain today; Sunday fair; strong northwest winds.
Temperature yesterday—Max., 45; min., 36.
For weather report see next to last page

VOL. LXXI....No. 23,422. *** NEW YORK, SATURDAY, MARCH 11, 1922. TWO CENTS In Greater New York | THREE CENTS Within 200 Miles | FOUR CENTS Elsewhere

WILL DROP ELEVATED OR ACCEPT RECEIVER, INTERBORO DECIDES

New Contract Freeing Subway of $7,600,000 Annual Rent the Alternative.

OWNERS PLAN COURT FIGHT

Interborough Also Wants $30,000,000 for Third Tracks and the New Power Houses.

TO OPPOSE BETTER SERVICE

Ready to Quit if Transit Board Compels Improvements Which Eat Up Present Savings.

The Interborough Rapid Transit Company has refused to make any further payments due on its lease of the elevated lines owned by the Manhattan Railway Company. It has asked the latter company to make a new agreement which would shift from the Interborough payments of $7,600,000 a year, save it from the responsibility of the deficits on the elevated system, and yield in return annual interest payments on betterments aggregating between $1,000,000 and $2,000,000 a year.

In this way the Interborough has answered the question, frequently asked, as to what adjustment could be made in the matter of the lease so far as it concerned the consolidation plan of the Transit Commission.

The Interborough is prepared to consent to the appointment of a receiver for its property if it fails to obtain relief from the payments to the Manhattan Company or if the Transit Commission insists upon enforcing expected orders directing the company to increase its service to the point of absorbing the savings derived from the present restriction of service.

This new development has been known to the commission for some time and it was suggested that this knowledge was responsible for the amendment to the Public Service Commission law introduced in the Legislature at the instance of the commission. The amendment directly bearing on the situation provides that the commission have power to order that the present service of the elevated lines shall not be disturbed in any way, even if separated from the Interborough system.

Rental a Heavy Burden.

Under the terms of the lease between the two companies the Interborough is pledged to pay the Manhattan Company 7 per cent. on a valuation of $60,000,000 for the use of the elevated, at the rate of $1,050,000 every quarter, and to pay in addition taxes and interest on bonds aggregating $3,400,000 a year. These payments, it has been asserted, are responsible for the financial condition of the Interborough and one of the principal reasons why the company has been compelled to pinch service on its subway system, pass interest payments on securities, and delay payments for necessary material.

The new agreement between the Interborough and Manhattan companies, suggested by the former, provides that the Manhattan Company shall pay the Interborough $30,000,000 for the third tracks and power houses built by the Interborough. The plan also requires the Manhattan Company to pay the interest due on this money, to be adjusted on the basis of interest fixed when it was obtained; to relieve the Interborough from all payments of any kind named in the present lease, and to operate the lines independently of any relationship between the two companies save that ordered by State authorities.

Such a plan would leave the Interborough in possession of the new extensions, valued by the company at approximately $17,000,000. These extensions are considered of small moment in the transit system of the city, for the reason that they run in territory where the traffic is not heavy. They were built with an eye to future growth and in the hope that some day they would yield substantial profits.

All of Extensions Short.

One of these extensions is from 155th Street, the original terminal of the Ninth Avenue line, which is owned by the Manhattan Company, to Jerome Avenue, a distance of about three-quarters of a mile. It joins the Jerome Avenue line, which is part of the subway system. Another extension runs from the station of the Third Avenue line at Fordham Road near 190th Street to Gun Hill Road and thence to White Plains Road, about one mile and three-quarters. The third extension is from the Second Avenue line at Fifty-seventh Street, across Queensboro Bridge to Queensboro Plaza, where it joins rapid transit lines to Astoria and Corona, about one mile and a quarter.

It is the opinion of the Interborough that these extensions can be operated without loss, because of the belief that the railroad law of the State would compel the Transit Commission to fix a fare to cover operating expenses. That the commission, under any amendment of the Public Service Commission law, could compel the company to operate these bits of road at a loss is considered unreasonable by the company's lawyers. Such a situation, it was said, would compel the company to carry passengers free because they had paid a fare to the Manhattan Company, or compel the Manhattan Company to carry free passengers who had paid fares to the Interborough. There would have to be a fare for a ride on the lines of the two companies, it was explained, which would reimburse both, under any plan of adjustment.

These extensions, it was said, would not be operated at a loss, and litigation

Continued on Page Three.

University Course to Make Bellhops and Head Waiters

BOSTON, March 10.—Bellhops and head waiters de luxe are to be turned out by Boston University. Seventy-five men have signed for a six weeks' course for college men who work in Summer hotels during their vacation.

The course, which is to start at the university next week, will show the young men how to become any sort of hotel official. It will be given by the vocational department of the College of Business Administration.

RUM RUNNER KILLS BOOTLEGGER IN BOAT

Man Aboard the Imatra Opens Fire on Motor Craft After Dispute.

WOMAN LEADS GUN FIGHT

Wounds Detective in Fusillade Preceding Capture of $10,000 in Whisky.

An alleged bootlegger was killed in a motor boat off a Brooklyn pier last night in a controversy over several cases of liquor which men of the crew of the tramp steamer Imatra had bargained to sell to five young men who came alongside the vessel in a small power craft. A man charged with the shooting was arrested and two men found in the motor boat were taken into custody. The other two are being searched for by the police.

The dead man was George Rauch, 26, of 154 South Fourth Street, Brooklyn, who was one of the five in the motor boat which was to transport the liquor, which had been smuggled into this country. Charged with shooting him, Albert Fosberg, 32, chief engineer of the steamer Imatra, was locked up at the Butler Street Police Station in Brooklyn.

The four men in the motor boat with Rauch, according to the police, were Samuel Kirnsky, 807 Manner Street, Woodhaven, L. I.; Benjamin Raphael, 482 Henry Street, Manhattan, and his two brothers, Lester and Moe Raphael, 155 Henry Street, Manhattan.

Party Comes for Liquor.

According to the story told to the police by Benjamin Raphael and Kirnsky, the party first visited the steamer in the afternoon, making arrangements to purchase several cases of whisky, which were to be taken off last night. In accordance with this arrangement, the party drew alongside the steamer at 7 o'clock in the 30-foot motor boat Harding. The men first said they didn't get the whisky, but later admitted that they got two cases, for which they said they paid $180.

Fosberg, who is charged with homicide in connection with the death of Rauch, tells a different story. He said the men came aboard the steamer and took off two cases, promising to return to the ship and get additional cases and then pay for the whole. Instead of climbing back aboard the vessel, Fosberg said, the men started the boat's motor and drew away.

At sight of the men getting away with the whisky, Fosberg said, he ran back into his room and got a revolver. He said, according to the police, he fired only one shot at the motor boat. That shot took effect in Rauch's chest, causing his death, the police said.

The motor boat continued on to the foot of Montague Street, half a mile away, and the Poplar Street Police Station was notified. Rauch was taken off the boat and was later pronounced dead by Dr. Thompson of the Long Island Hospital.

After leaving the dead man in charge of Benjamin Raphael and Kirnsky, the two other members of the party sped away in the boat. The police said the prisoners admitted later that the boat carried two cases of whisky, and was to land at East Houston Street. The police in Manhattan were notified to look out for the boat.

Benjamin Raphael and Kirnsky are said to have told the police, after admitting that they had actually got whisky, that they paid the third mate, Brynols Garge, $70, and the first mate, whose name they didn't know, $110.

Fifteen Shots Fired in Raid.

A pistol fight between alleged bootleggers and two detectives in which fifteen shots were fired and at least one person, a detective, was wounded, followed a raid yesterday afternoon on a house at 18 Charlton Street. The house is believed by the police to be the terminus in this city of a gang of rum smugglers operating by automobile between this

Continued on Page Fourteen.

FORD'S 'FREEZE-OUT' OF RAIL PARTNERS BLOCKED BY I. C. C.

Small Stockholders of D., T. & I. Defeat Alleged Scheme to Get Rid of Them.

PREVENT LEASE OF ROAD

Commission Sustains Their Contention That It Is Against Public Interest.

WILL KEEP THEIR SHARES

Proposed Lessee Was a Company Owned Entirely by Members of the Ford Family.

Henry Ford, who urged the railroads of the country to "get rid of the unproductive stockholders," has been blocked by the Interstate Commerce Commission in an alleged attempt to "get rid of" the minority stockholders in the Detroit, Toledo & Ironton Railroad Company, Mr. Ford's interesting railroad adventure.

Notice of the decision against Henry Ford was received yesterday in a registered letter from the Interstate Commerce Commission at Washington by Alexander L. Strouse, of Frank, Weil & Strouse, 187 Madison Avenue, counsel for some of the small stockholders.

Leon Tanenbaum and Benjamin M. Strauss of this city and several others, who charged that Mr. Ford was trying to "freeze them out," remain as active associates, though on a small scale, in the automobile manufacturer's railroad enterprise. These men have refused offers of several times the market value of the stock and have represented themselves as determined to remain business colleagues of Mr. Ford, in spite of the latter's well-known aversion to partners of any nationality and in spite of his newspaper campaign against Jews. The holdings of the minority stockholders are less than 2 per cent. of the total.

Stockholders' Contention.

The minority stockholders in their proceedings before the Interstate Commerce Commission alleged that Ford had tried to destroy their rights in the D., T. & I. by leasing the property to a company owned exclusively by the Ford family. They opposed the lease as being against public interest and being purely a device to deprive the small stockholders of any influence or share of profit in the enterprise. The decision of the Interstate Commerce Commission upholding the minority stockholders against Ford and denying permission to make the lease was rendered on Tuesday of last week.

The proceedings had created widespread interest, especially among small holders of stock in different railroads, because of Ford's denunciation of what he called "unproductive stockholders." He had asserted in interviews that the future of the railroads was imperilled by the necessity of paying large dividends to them. Dividends, according to the automobile man, should go only to the "productive stockholders," who were defined by him as employes of the road, persons active in the management and others who continued to contribute actively to its success.

The lease transferring everything of value from the old company to the new would have left the minority stockholders, according to their contention, holding a 2 per cent. interest in the hollow shell of the old company and no interest at all in the new. They alleged that they were victims of an attempt by Ford to translate his railroad theories into practice.

Mr. Ford's Statements.

During the course of the litigation, interviews and statements by Ford, telling what he would do if the Pennsylvania or New York Central were turned over to him, were held to have an interesting bearing on the legal merits of the case, as showing what was going on in Mr. Ford's mind at the time he sought to engineer the alleged "freeze-out" lease. Mr. Strouse made application for permission to cross-examine Ford.

One of the statements of Mr. Ford, ridiculing arguments as to the necessity of protecting the rights of widows and orphans by safeguarding stock from railroad manipulation, was printed by the United States Chamber of Commerce as an authorized interview. In it Mr. Ford urged the policy of "getting

Continued on Page Three.

Plan to Cut Europe's Armies in Half Submitted to League by Commission

By EDWIN L. JAMES.

By Wireless to THE NEW YORK TIMES.

PARIS, March 10.—A temporary mixed commission of the League of Nations Assembly has transmitted to the Governments which are members of the League a draft plan for European armament limitation modeled on the Washington naval reduction treaty. The members have been asked to notify the commission how the allotments of troops compare with their ideas of their needs for national defense. Of course, the plan, which was drafted in accord with instructions of the last League Assembly, held in September, is only in a formative state. The commission will meet again on July 15 and continue work on a scheme to be presented to the third Assembly of the League, which meets in Geneva in September.

The League commission's plan, which was presented at a recent meeting by Lord Esher, representing England, embraces all European countries except the Central Powers, whose armies are limited by the peace treaties, and Russia. The unit taken is 30,000 men. There would be the following allotment of units: Belgium, 2; Czechoslovakia, 3; Denmark, 2; France, 6; Great Britain, 3; Holland, 3; Norway, 2; Poland, 4; Portugal, 1; Rumania, 3; Sweden, 2; Spain, 3; Switzerland, 2.

This would mean forty-six units, or a total of 1,380,000 soldiers for Europe, which would be a reduction of about 50 per cent. under the present armies.

The League Commission also has under consideration another plan to apply the ratios of the Washington naval treaties to the navies of the league members not parties to the Washington agreement.

The weakest point of the League plan is the absence of Russia from the plan. Russia not being a member of the League, the commission naturally could not lay down the size of her army. It is the intention of the League leaders to try to get Russia into limitation negotiations and some statesmen hope to raise the matter at Genoa.

As the plan stands it will meet the opposition of France. France's probable reply to it will be a demand that the League be given some sort of Federal force to enable it to insure observance of the terms of any such limitation agreement.

The plan was tentatively adopted at a meeting of the commission two weeks ago but was kept secret at the time.

Germans to Clear Buildings Of All Monarchical Insignia

BERLIN, March 10 (Associated Press).—All insignia of monarchical Germany must be removed from public buildings, Minister of the Interior Adolf Koester today told the Reichstag. He added that the Government had decided to fix a definite period within which this decision would be carried out.

Exceptions will be made, he said, only where these emblems have been structurally incorporated in buildings where their removal would destroy the architectural value and effect.

All paintings, busts and statues in Government offices must also be removed if their retention is incompatible with the Republican régime. This order will chiefly apply to portraits of former Emperor William, although Herr Koester said exceptions might be made if their removal destroyed the "artistic and historical unity" of the interior decorations.

JURIES OF CITIZENS TO BAR BAD PLAYS

Conference of Actors, Dramatists, Managers and Vice Crusaders Fixes Details.

TO AVOID POLITICAL CENSOR

Theatrical Contracts to Stipulate That They Must Obey Jury's Findings.

The organization of a voluntary jury system, designed to eliminate indecent plays and thereby make unnecessary a political censorship of the stage, was launched late yesterday afternoon at a meeting of dramatists, managers and producers, actors and vice crusaders at the American Dramatists' Society, 148 West Forty-fifth Street.

An important feature of the proposed jury system is the insertion of a clause in all future contracts between dramatists and producers and between actors and producers that they will abide by the decisions of the jury.

Those attending the meeting were informed that Mayor Hylan's approval of the undertaking had been given in an informal manner. Early next week a committee will endeavor to see the Mayor and obtain his formal approval.

Many Interests Represented.

The details of the jury system were worked out at a meeting representing the Authors League of America, through Jesse Lynch Williams, President; Channing Pollock, Vice President, and Le Roy Scott, Chairman of the Executive Committee; its subsidiary, the American Dramatists, represented by Owen Davis, Eugene Buck and George Creel; the Actors' Equity Association, represented by John Emerson, President; Frank Gillmore, Executive Secretary, and John W. Cope of the Equity's council; the Producing Managers' Association, represented by William A. Brady, Charles Coburn and Winthrop Ames; the Better Public Shows Movement, represented by John S. Sumner, head of the Society for the Prevention of Commercialized Vice; Edward J. McGuire and A. G. Boyle of the Y. M. C. A., Mrs. Herbert J. Glover of the Welfare Board of the Protestant Episcopal Church, Mrs. Marian Tucker and Cranston Brenton and Mrs. Coffin of the Drama League.

"These people believe that a political censorship is impossible without destroying all that is finest in what affects," explained Channing Pollock, spokesman for a committee delegated to give out the facts concerning the meeting after its adjournment. "They believe that the theatre is not in a bad way. However, they agree that there are four or five bad plays and that there is a tendency to produce other plays without which the theatre would be better off."

To Draw a Panel of 300.

Their program contemplates the drawing of a panel of 300 citizens. Nominations are to be submitted by the organizations on the joint committee representing the theatrical organizations on the one side, and the Better Public Shows Movement and the City Administration on the other. Each group will be permitted to nominate 150 candidates for the panel, the qualifications for which will be chiefly "good citizenship and common sense," according to Mr. Pollock.

"If a complaint against a given theatrical production is received by the city officials," said Mr. Pollock, "they may call for a jury of twelve to be selected from the panel above described, as representing the theatre on the one side and the public on the other. Each side will have two peremptory challenges. First, they must decide whether any part of the production is objectionable from the point of view of public morals. Second, is the play as a whole objectionable? A vote of 9 to 3 constitutes a verdict. If the jury decides that a manager must readjust his play, he will have one week in which to make the changes. Then the jury will review the play. If the jury decides that the play as a whole is objectionable, all interests, including the dramatists, owners, producers, actors and the public, agree that the play shall be taken off and that there shall be no appeal to the courts. This agreement is to be included in every contract made by the managers with both dramatists and actors.

"We agree with the public," said Mr. Pollock. "The theatre must be a decent place."

AGUINALDO COMING HERE.

Filipino General Accepts Invitation of Spanish War Veterans.

MANILA, P. I., March 10.—General Emelio Aguinaldo has accepted an invitation to be the guest of the Spanish-American War veterans at their annual convention in Los Angeles next Summer. It will be his first visit to the United States.

General Aguinaldo will be the honorary chairman of the Filipino mission, which is expected to sail for the United States late in April to lay before President Harding claims of the islanders to independence.

SENATOR STANFIELD, THE 'WOOL KING,' ACCUSED OF FRAUD

Idaho National Bank Charges That He Formed a Company to Defraud His Creditors.

HURT BY DROP IN SHEEP

Had Just Bought 400,000—Attempt to Set Aside His Transfer of Real Estate.

THREATENS LIBEL ACTIONS

But Idaho Commissioner Defies Him and Asks Why He Doesn't Pay Farmers What He Owes.

Special to The New York Times.

PORTLAND, Ore., March 10.—Robert Nelson Stanfield, the "wool king" and United States Senator from Oregon, elected in 1920 over former Senator Chamberlain is in difficulties and is rushing home from Washington to save what he can out of property imperiled by the drop in the prices of wool and sheep.

Prayer that a deed of conveyance of real estate made by Stanfield through the R. N. Stanfield Company be set aside is made in an action filed in the Circuit Court today by the First National Bank of Weiser, Idaho, against Stanfield, the R. N. Stanfield Company and the Columbia Basin Wool Warehouse Company.

Claims for about $75,000 against Stanfield on notes for money loaned him during the last year or two are advanced.

The allegation is contained in the complaint that the R. N. Stanfield Company was formed "to hinder, delay and defraud his creditors." When the deed of conveyance was made out, the complaint sets forth, the Wool Warehouse Company assumed the obligation of payment for a mortgage of $200,000. The plaintiff asks that the value of the warehouse liens on real estate be adjudicated and that the plaintiff's rights be determined.

The complaint states that several large judgments against the defendant have been secured in various courts of Oregon and in Boise, Idaho.

Miles Cannon, Idaho Commissioner of Agriculture, announced today that he would welcome suit against him for criminal libel, threatened by Senator Stanfield. The Capitol News this week printed a special dispatch from Washington to the effect that Senator Stanfield had instructed several sheep companies in Idaho and Oregon to start libel suits against Commissioner Cannon because of a published statement by Cannon that these companies had failed to pay for hay and feed furnished in the Spring of 1921 and that many claims have been filed with his department.

Senator Stanfield also advised the managers of his companies to consult attorneys concerning possible action against Cannon on the ground of criminal libel, the dispatch said. When this dispatch was called to the attention of Commissioner Cannon he said:

"I am prepared to make sensational disclosures if this matter is pushed. I made the reports with regard to the Stanfield companies strictly in accordance with the statutes and the evidence submitted to my office. I have not published half the evidence in my possession and I am not particularly worried over this threatened action for alleged criminal libel."

Section 2,059 of the Revised Idaho Statutes, under which Mr. Cannon is acting, reads:

"The Department of Justice is directed to investigate all cases reported to it where a producer of agriculture or products or live stocks have suffered loss in the marketing of his products or has failed to receive a fair and just reasonable compensation by reason of fraud, injustice, extortion, manipulation or profiteering on the part of others."

On Feb. 11 Commissioner Cannon telegraphed to Senator Stanfield at Washington as follows:

"Please wire me immediately whether there are any legal or moral reasons why your sheep companies operating in the State of Idaho should not pay farmers for hay sold and delivered in the Spring of 1921. Quick answer required."

It is known that Mr. Stanfield's losses of wool and sheep have been enormous. In many cases sheep were bought at $16 and when the bottom dropped out of the market they went down to $6.

The Idaho action came to a head when it was published this week that Stanfield had just made a purchase of 400,000 to 500,000 head of sheep. The Idaho Commissioner believes that if Stanfield had money for such a purchase as this, he had money enough to pay the Idaho farmers for hay sold to the Stanfield Companies last year.

United States Senator Stanfield of Oregon is himself authority for the statement that he is America's largest producer of wool and mutton. Here is his autobiography as supplied to the Congressional Directory:

"Robert Nelson Stanfield, Republican, of Portland, Ore., was born at Umatilla, Umatilla County, Ore., July 9, 1877; educated in the public schools and State normal schools of Oregon; engaged in the live stock industry, being America's largest producer of wool and mutton; also engaged in banking, particularly in the financing of livestock producers; served three terms in the Oregon State Legislature; one term as Speaker of the House of Representatives; married to Inez E. Hill in 1897; one daughter, Miss Barbara Stanfield, who is now 17 years of age; nominated as Republican candidate for the United States Senate over one other opponent; elected United States Senator Nov. 2, 1920, defeating the incumbent opponent by 16,500 votes."

GANDHI ARRESTED ON CHARGE OF SEDITION; LONDON REPORTS INDIA QUIET THUS FAR; LORD DERBY TO TAKE MONTAGU'S PLACE

Martial Law After Day of Terror in the Rand; Strikers Kill a Manager and Ten of Police

JOHANNESBURG, Union of South Africa, March 10 (Associated Press).—Bold moves by the striking miners, accompanied by fierce fighting between strikers, commandos and police, made the day one of terror in the Rand. Martial law eventually was proclaimed.

Manager Brodigan of the Brakpan mine, the centre of much of the day's fighting, and two special constables were captured and taken out on the veldt and shot. Seven special constables protecting the mine were killed. The strikers also captured twenty-seven policemen at Newlands, west of Johannesburg, where spirited fighting occurred, threatening to shoot them all if other police came to the rescue.

At Fordsburg one man of a commando, or force of burghers, was killed and thirteen members of the commando and four policemen were wounded. The sound of artillery firing at Fordsburg was audible here.

With the proclamation of martial law and the seizure of the strikers' headquarters, where all documents were confiscated, the populace felt a sense of relief. The Ministers of Justice and Defense have issued a statement denying reports of a contemplated native rising in the Rand. They assert there is no disposition on the part of the natives to give trouble. Meanwhile military units are enrolling with remarkable speed and a citizens' protection league is being formed to run public services.

Firing started at Benoni early this morning. Street fighting followed, both sides suffering casualties. Many pedestrians were hit. For two hours the ground between the market square and the workers' hall was a battle area. Then the police formed with the object of surrounding the hall. There was continuous sniping and three persons fell dead, one of them a policeman.

LONDON, March 10.—Premier Smuts of the Union of South Africa today told the legislative Assembly, which is engaged in a discussion of the struggle in the Rand, that the people were face to face with one of the gravest situations that have yet arisen in the country. The Laborite members and Ministerialists are accusing each other of responsibility for the disturbance.

According to the Reuter correspondent at Johannesburg, Premer Smuts declared the behavior of the Rand natives had been beyond reproach, "but the whites had nothing to be proud of." He said the Government had given instructions that very strong measures must be used to suppress lawlessness.

BIG HOUSING BILL NOW SURE TO PASS

Machold Announces Support of Metropolitan $100,000,000 Building Fund Measure.

LOCKWOOD IS ACCUSED

Absence From Hearing Said to Have Endangered Other Bills—He Denies It.

Special to The New York Times

ALBANY, March 10.—As the result of developments at the Capitol today the passage in both branches of the Legislature of the Lockwood committee's bill which would enable the Metropolitan Life Insurance Company to devote $100,000,000 of its investable funds to housing relief in New York City seems assured. The prospect is also that both Senate and Assembly will act favorably on five other measures already on the calendar of the Senate which are directly concerned with rents and housing.

The financial part of the Lockwood committee's program, however, has been placed in jeopardy through the conduct of Senator Lockwood himself, which has greatly puzzled his colleagues in the Senate. After serving notice that he would move to discharge the Cities Committee from further consideration of those of his committee's bills not already reported, and after filing with Senator Gibbs, Chairman of the Cities Committee, a petition in which seven other members of that committee joined him, demanding that the bills be reported promptly, Senator Lockwood departed for New York City and was not in attendance when the committee met to take action on his bills.

Under the circumstances no action could be taken. At an earlier stage of the session the loss of time would not necessarily prove fatal. But final adjournment is only a week away and bills reported from committees automatically go on what is known as the general orders calendar in the Senate, where they remain until advanced to third reading. General orders is the last order of business in the Senate and is seldom reached during the closing week of a session. In fact, Senator Lusk announced today, while measures on the general orders calendar were under consideration, that the Senate probably would not return to that order of business again before the session ends next Friday. The general orders calendar in the Senate, during the final days, is the morgue to which undesirable measures are consigned if they have not already been left there.

It will probably be necessary when the bills finally are reported by the Senate Cities Committee for Senator Lockwood to ask that they be immediately advanced to final reading when they can be read and acted on. One solitary objection will prevent this, for bills can be advanced in this fashion only by unanimous consent.

The petition sent to Chairman Gibbs of the Cities Committee read as follows:

"We, the undersigned, members of the Cities Committee, respectfully request that you report promptly for the consideration of the Senate, the bills introduced by the Joint Legislative Committee on Housing.

"Very truly yours,
"CHARLES C. LOCKWOOD.
"SEYMOUR LOWMAN.
"HOMER E. DICK.
"WILLIAM W. CAMPBELL.
"PARTON SWIFT.
"C. ERNEST SMITH.
"JAMES J. WALKER.
"PETER J. McGARRY."

Senators Walker and McGarry were the only Democratic signers.

As a result of the petition, Senator Gibbs called a meeting of his committee, which was held immediately after the Senate had adjourned for the day. Only five members appeared, Senator Lockwood not being among them, and three, Campbell, Dick and Smith, had signed the petition. The others were Senator Gibbs and Senator Fearon.

"The five did not constitute a quorum, so we had no right to take action on

Continued on Page Three.

OUR RHINE CLAIM IS NOT ALLOWED

Finance Ministers Continue the Division of German Payments Among Allied Powers.

BOYDEN ASKS $241,000,000

Question Will Go to Governments Upon Whom Washington Is in a Position to Use Pressure.

By EDWIN L. JAMES.

Special Cable to THE NEW YORK TIMES.

PARIS, March 10.—The Washington Government today asked the Finance Ministers of the allied nations engaged in a conference here for dividing up German payments to the Reparation Commission for a settlement of the claim of $241,000,000 of the American Government for the cost of the American Army of Occupation. The allied Ministers did not comply, but by subsequent action presented a direct refusal to grant the American demand.

The American communication was in the form of a statement by Roland W. Boyden, American member of the Reparation Commission, who is sitting in the allied Finance Ministers' meeting. Although the official communiqué makes no mention of the matter, it is understood Mr. Boyden recalled that the Berlin treaty reserved for America the benefits she would enjoy under the Versailles Treaty; that the Versailles Treaty provided that costs of the armies of occupation was a lien on German payments of prior validity to general reparations; that the Allies having practically paid themselves for their occupation costs, the $241,000,000 due America should be paid before any allotment was made for general reparations.

To grant the American demand the allied Ministers, after having allotted sums to meet the French, English and Belgian army occupation costs, would have to assign funds to meet the American claim. What the Finance Ministers did was to complete the division of the 1921 payments and then provide for the allocation of the 1922 payments by Germany, which action included allocation of funds for other purposes than payment of the armies of occupation. No provision was made for meeting the American demand, nor will any be made before the end of the Ministers' conference tomorrow, it was stated tonight officially.

Say We Should Collect Our Own.

The attitude of the Finance Ministers is in accord with that of their Governments, which is that America, having a separate treaty with Germany, should collect direct from Germany. It is always possible the allied Governments may find delicate reasons for changing this attitude, but as the matter stands at present the Allies do not feel that they should collect for America.

The American action is important because for the first time it raises the issue of the validity of the Berlin treaty, that is, it raises the question whether it is a first mortgage, ranking with the Versailles treaty, or a second mortgage ranking after it. It is true the Berlin treaty, in its text, reserves for America the rights she would have had under the Versailles treaty. But that reserving is done by America and Germany, without the consent of the Allies, who under the Versailles treaty, according to the European interpretation, already held a first mortgage on all German resources.

It was the expectation of the allied nations that following the signing of the Berlin treaty Washington would negotiate with them to establish American rights under the Berlin treaty. This was pointed out in the Paris dispatches of THE NEW YORK TIMES last September, which dispatches brought a statement from Washington that no such negotiations were necessary. Because the allied nations owe America immense sums of money and America can bring pressure

Continued on Page Two.

ARREST IS MADE QUIETLY

Leader Taken Into Custody on Order of Government at Delhi.

NEW PLOTS WERE REVEALED

British Opinion Strongly Urged Seizure of Gandhi, First Ordered Last Month.

LORD DERBY TO TAKE OFFICE

Montagu Speaks Today at Cambridge—Resignation of Viceroy Regarded as Inevitable.

BOMBAY, March 10 (Associated Press). — India's non-co-operationist leader, Mohandas K. Gandhi, has been arrested at Ahmedabad, 310 miles north of Bombay. He is charged with sedition.

Special Cable to THE NEW YORK TIMES.

LONDON, March 10.—The announcement by the India Office late tonight that a telegram had been received stating that Gandhi had been arrested and adding there had been no trouble so far follows upon Delhi reports that the Indian Government had decided upon his arrest for today.

London newspapers have been urging that this step should be taken for weeks, and Montagu's statement in the Commons on Feb. 14 that the official order for Gandhi's arrest actually had been issued the week before and then canceled led to charges, as one paper puts it this morning, of "vacillation, hesitation and lack of consistent steadiness" against the Indian and Home Governments.

Montagu on Feb. 14 told the House of Commons that the Government of India had been informed that if in their judgment Gandhi's arrest became necessary they would receive the whole-hearted support of the Imperial Government.

"Last week the official order for his arrest was actually issued," he said, "but since then there has been a dramatic change in the situation, Gandhi and his colleagues having decided not to pursue the policy of civil disobedience, volunteer processions or other illegal activities."

In view of this development the Government of India was holding its hand.

Publication of the Indian Government's demands and the resignation of Montagu have been followed by further sensational disclosures of widespread activities of Indian seditionists and in view of insistent demads of English newspapers it was felt the Indian Government could not longer delay action against Gandhi.

Special Cable to THE NEW YORK TIMES.

LONDON, March 11.—Several political correspondents this morning mention the prediction made in some quarters yesterday that Lord Reading's resignation would shortly be announced.

In that case the Duke of Devonshire is said to be the likely successor.

LAHORE, India, March 10.—Lajpat Rai, a prominent Indian Nationalist, today was sentenced to two years' imprisonment, one year at hard labor was imposed for violation of the Seditious Meeting act, and the other year for violation of the Criminal Law Amendment act. The sentences are to run consecutively.

He was sentenced last December to six months' detention and a fine of 500 rupees, but about a month later he was released and re-arrested immediately on the charge of violating the Criminal Law Amendment act.

DERBY TO TAKE INDIAN OFFICE.

Announcement of His Appointment Is Expected on Tuesday.

Special Cable to THE NEW YORK TIMES.

LONDON, March 10.—It is understood that the Premier has invited Lord Derby to succeed Mr. Montagu as Secretary of State for India.

The opinion in authoritative circles is that Lord Derby will accept and that announcement of his appointment may be expected on next Tuesday.

Reading's Resignation Expected.

LONDON, March 10 (Associated Press).—It was stated authoritatively tonight that an announcement of the name of the successor of Mr. Montagu had been postponed until Monday or Tuesday. It was added that it was virtually certain the new Secretary would not be Andrew Bonar Law. The eventual resignation of the Earl of Reading as Viceroy of India is still regarded as inevitable.

The India incident has intensified the strong feeling between the Liberal and Conservative wings of the Coalition Ministry. The Liberal newspapers without exception lament that Mr. Montagu allowed himself to be drawn into a "false step." But some of them think the result would have been the same in any case, because had he consulted the Cabinet and the Cabinet had refused to permit publication of the India statement the Secretary still would have resigned as a protest.

While awaiting reports from India as to the effect of Mr. Montagu's resignation, the position of Viceroy Reading is the chief subject of the discussions of the press. Official circles which deal with Indian affairs do not concur in the prevailing opinion that the Viceroy necessarily will follow the Secretary of State for India in quitting the Government. It is stated that the Earl of Reading certainly was in his right as

"All the News That's Fit to Print."

The New York Times.

THE WEATHER
Fair and mild today and Tuesday; gentle to moderate variable winds.
Temperature yesterday—Max. 79, Min. 60.
For full weather report see Page 21.

VOL. LXXII....No. 23,627. NEW YORK, MONDAY, OCTOBER 2, 1922. TWO CENTS In Greater New York | THREE CENTS Within 200 Miles | FOUR CENTS Elsewhere

BIGGEST CONVENTION BANKERS EVER HELD OPENS HERE TODAY

Special and Regular Trains Bringing Delegates From All Parts of Country.

TEXANS ON CHARTERED SHIP

Hotels Swamped by Advance Guard of Financiers—10,000 Are Expected.

BRANCH BANKS FIGHT DUE

Independents Complete Plans to Attack System on Floor of Convention Today.

The forty-eighth annual convention of the American Bankers' Association, which will begin at the Hotel Commodore today, will bring together the largest assemblage of bankers ever gathered in one city. More than 6,000 bankers from all over the country had registered at the Commodore last night. Thousands more are due today. Guy Emerson, Executive Manager of the Local Committee of One Hundred, which has charge of registrations, announced that the committee would probably have to make arrangements to take care of 10,000 guests, instead of the 7,500 that had been expected. The record attendance at previous conventions of the Association was 4,600.

Delegates poured into New York yesterday on special trains as well as the regular trains arriving at Grand Central Terminal and Pennsylvania Station. More specials from the West and South are due this morning. Texas delegates and their guests chartered a special steamship for the trip north, and the ship was reported nearing port last night.

Father Knickerbocker's resources for lodging and entertaining guests are being strained by the enormous influx of bankers with their wives and daughters. The hotels are crowded. All reservations have been taken at the Commodore, which is the headquarters for the convention, and at other big hotels. The committee, however, has a central organization with a list of hotel rooms vacant in all the first-class hotels of the city.

Registering the Delegates.

More than 1,200 persons are busy registering the delegates, fifty at a time being assigned to meet the onrush of newcomers at the registration desks. The clerks are worn out so quickly that new shifts have to be put on duty every little while. A complete post office substation has been installed in the lobby of the convention hall on the ballroom floor of the Commodore. It is run by post office employes on general delivery lines and is already doing 200 per cent. more business than the general delivery department at City Hall Station.

New York is extending itself in every way to welcome and entertain the visitors. Mayor Hylan has welcomed them officially in the name of the city. Smokers, fashion shows, dinners, theatre parties and sight seeing excursions by motor and boat have been arranged. The New York bankers and their wives have made all sorts of social arrangements. Special attention is to be paid to the wives and daughters of the delegates. For one, Mrs. Otto H. Kahn has offered her private golf course at Cold Spring Harbor, L. I., to the women attending the convention.

As they approach New York, prominent bankers from all parts of the country are unanimous in advancing optimistic opinions on the general condition of affairs in their own cities. Interviews from representative bankers from various Federal Reserve cities, in widely separated parts of the country, which were obtained yesterday, emphasized the belief that the prospect is for good business, but no boom.

The convention will last from Monday to Friday. The business part of the program will begin this morning. General sessions will be held on Tuesday, Wednesday and Thursday mornings. On Friday will come the wind-up, and the delegates will be on their way home Saturday.

A fight by independent bankers against the branch bank system is expected to be the big issue at the convention. The agitation over this question is said to be a vital factor in the record-breaking attendance at this year's conventtion.

Independent bankers from all parts of the country plan a strenuous fight on the floor of the convention to compel the association to go on record by a formal vote against the branch bank system. The convention will be asked to favor legislation now before Congress, which is being besieged by the anti-branch faction with requests to enact laws against such institutions at the next session.

Strong Opposition Expected.

Strong opposition is expected by the anti-branch men. Although a vast majority of the out-of-town bankers, who make up most of the membership of the association, are against the branch system, the anti-branch faction says "a bitter minority, aligned with the great financial institutions of Wall Street," favor the branch system and are opposed to the convention taking any action against it.

According to the anti-branch adherents, representatives of several big banking institutions have made advances looking toward a compromise which would put the convention on record as merely opposed to further extension of the branch system, and recognizing the right of national banks to establish branches in States which have passed

Continued on Page Four.

Fire Prevention Week Opens; Read the Warnings and Help

Fire Prevention Week begins today and will last until Oct. 9. Placards and warnings to the public will be posted in conspicuous places all over the city, and the removal of waste materials and odds and ends which clutter up homes and factories and make good material for starting fires, will be urged.

Big placards will appear on both sides of the Fifth Avenue buses. The Woolworth stores in the metropolitan district will display placards in their windows, prepared by the company. The Hotels Imperial, Pennsylvania, Ambassador, McAlpin, Breslin and the Margaret in Brooklyn, will have fire prevention messages printed on their menus.

MILLER DECLINED 'DRY' NOMINATION

Governor Gives Out Letter Showing He Refused to Seek Votes Under "False Colors."

"NEVER A PROHIBITIONIST"

Was Unwilling to Indicate Approval of the Fundamental Principle of That Party.

Special to The New York Times.

ALBANY, Oct. 1.—Because it was reported that Governor Miller had been seeking the Prohibition nomination for Governor or an endorsement of that party, which nominated George K. Hinds of New York, the Governor made public tonight a letter from Coleridge A. Hart, Chairman of the Prohobition Party in Westchester County, offering the Governor the party's endorsement, and his reply declining on the ground that his acceptance would place him in the position of sailing "under false colors."

On Sept. 27 Mr. Hart wrote the Governor as follows:

My dear Governor Miller:

The Prohibition Party expects to hold its State Convention on the 30th day of September, at 3 o'clock P. M., at 206 Schermerhorn Street, Brooklyn, N. Y.

On conferring with various party leaders, I find a desire on the part of many members of our party to nominate or, rather, endorse you as our candidate for Governor, upon the ground, not that you are a prohibitionist, much less a third party prohibitionist, but that you have courageously stood for the enforcement of law, including the Prohibition law.

Will you accept such nomination if tendered you?

With kindest regards, I am,

Very truly yours,
COLERIDGE A. HART.
County Chairman.

The reply of Governor Miller, dated Sept. 29, read as follows:

My dear Mr. Hart:

After careful consideration of the suggestions contained in your letter of Sept. 27, I have reached the conclusion that I cannot accept a nomination by the Prohibition Party. I am not now and never have been a prohibitionist. I understand that the leaders who might tender me a nomination would understand that, but that might not be the case with those who have been voting the Prohibition ticket year after year from principle. My acceptance of the nomination might indicate to them an approval of the fundamental principle of their party, and I cannot afford to be put in the position of seeking votes under false colors.

I also feel that loyalty to my party associates would prevent me accepting the nomination if one were tendered.

Yours very truly,
NATHAN L. MILLER.

LENIN TO RESUME WORK.

Wil lPreside Over Cabinet Meeting Tomorrow, It Is Announced.

Special Cable to THE NEW YORK TIMES.

MOSCOW, Oct. 1.—Premier Lenin will preside over a Cabinet meeting Tuesday next, it is announced here today.

The reasons for this rather unexpected emergence from retirement which it was reported would last until the beginning of November, is not stated, but THE NEW YORK TIMES correspondent learns, firstly, that Lenin's health has shown even more rapid improvement than was hoped, and, secondly, that his return is not unconnected with the Near Eastern crisis and in a lesser degree with the Urquhart contract, whose ratification is understood to be related to the course of international affairs.

COPELAND TO ACCEPT; HYLAN, LIKE HEARST, WILL SUPPORT SMITH

Tammany Jubilant Over Publisher's Attitude After Ex-Governor's Opposition.

MAYOR MAY SPEAK TODAY

Health Commissioner, Nominated for Senate, to Consult Him Before Making Statement.

SMITH WILL TALK TONIGHT

Republican Leaders Say Miller's Up-State Plurality Will Overcome Democratic Vote Here.

The announcement of William Randolph Hearst that he would support the Democratic State ticket, including former Governor Alfred E. Smith, the nominee for Governor, was received yesterday with jubilation by Tammany leaders, important and petty. It was agreed by all of them that Mr. Hearst's statement of his position, in directing the editor of the New York American to support the ticket, had given to Mr. Smith what they regarded as an even chance of election where he had only a hope. Mr. Smith's stand at the Syracuse convention, in keeping Mr. Hearst off the ticket, was said to have strengthened him among up-State Democrats. As one Tammany leader phrased it, Mr. Smith's chance of election had doubled since last Friday.

One immediate effect of the Hearst declaration was to make it certain that Dr. Royal S. Copeland would accept the nomination for United States Senator. Dr. Copeland, who was at his Summer home at Suffern, had nothing further to say, but is expected to issue a formal statement today accepting the nomination, after he has conferred with Mayor Hylan, to whom he owes appointment as Health Commissioner. The reason for the delay in the acceptance was said to be the desire of Dr. Copeland, a member of the City Administration, to act with courtesy toward the Mayor.

"I have been in the country ever since the convention started," Dr. Copeland said, "and courtesy demands that I consult friends before I make known my position. There are a few I want to talk to, including the Mayor. It is much better for me to do that and then accept the nomination, if I decide to, than to accept and talk with them afterward."

Congratulated by McAdoo.

Dr. Copeland said that he had received hundreds of congratulatory messages, including telegrams from former Governor James M. Cox of Ohio and William G. McAdoo.

Mayor Hylan had nothing to say about the Democratic ticket yetserday, but he is expected to come out in support of it today. Although the Democratic leaders still credited Mr. Hearst's supposed Presidential aspirations and a desire on his part to be "regular" in preparation for his candidacy in 1924 as the principal motive for his support of the ticket, it was said that fear of the possibility of the removal of Mayor Hylan by Governor Miller, should he be re-elected, might have been a contributing factor.

So far as the Mayor is concerned, a member of his cabinet admitted that his support of Mr. Smith, whom he is known to dislike, might have in it something of the quality of self-preservation. Whether Governor Miller has anything of the kind in mind or not is not known, but there may be said to be no question in the mind of some of the Mayor's friends that Governor Miller, if re-elected, might be expected to remove Mayor Hylan if, as expected he should get into a deadlock with the Transit Commission over its proposed reorganization plan.

Denial was made by persons close to Charles F. Murphy, leader of Tammany, that there had been any agreement with Mr. Hearst to give him the support of the New York State delegates to the next Democratic National Convention in return for his support of the State ticket this year. It was said that word had been sent to friends of Mr. Hearst, if not to Mr. Hearst himself, that Tammany would not oppose any fight he might make for the Democratic nomination for President, but would keep an open mind concerning him with final decision postponed until the convention.

Mr. Murphy could not be reached last night at his Summer home at Good

Continued on Page Ten.

Woman Sends 42,000 Cents To Pay Greenwich Taxi Bill

Special to The New York Times.

GREENWICH, Conn., Oct. 1.—A wealthy woman residing in a fashionable section of Greenwich moved to her Winter home in New York City last week leaving a bill of $420 owing the Greenwich Cab Company for taxicab fares. A representative of the company had visited her estate here on two occasions in an effort to collect the bill before she left, but was unsuccessful.

Yesterday the woman sent a taxicab from New York to the cab company's office here with a large keg containing 42,000 one-cent pieces. With it she sent $1 to pay for the taxi that had made the two trips to her home here for the purpose of collecting the money, and her photograph, under which was written "O la la."

It took four men to carry the keg into the Putnam Trust Company office and place it in a private vault.

FOUR 1920 INCOMES EXCEEDED $5,000,000

Rockefeller's Estimated Above $8,000,000—Henry Ford and Probably Edsel in the Group.

CORPORATE INCOMES DROP

They Were $1,508,763,645 Less Than in 1919—This State Pays 23.69 Per Cent. of Tax.

Special to The New York Times.

WASHINGTON, Oct. 1.—Returns of the personal incomes of $5,000,000 or more were made by four persons in 1920, according to statistics of incomes made public tonight by the Internal Revenue Bureau. One of the returns was made by a "single man," undoubtedly John D. Rockefeller, who is a widower. The other three were joint returns of husbands and wives.

Of the four, two were made by residents of New York State and two by residents of Michigan. The identity of those making the returns is not given. It is recognized, however, that Mr. Rockefeller is one of the New Yorkers. Admittedly, also, one of the great incomes from Michigan was returned by Henry Ford.

There are those who believe that both returns of $5,000,000 or more from Michigan were made by the Ford family and that the second income of $5,000,000 from that State was returned by Edsel Ford and his wife. Those who should know about the large fortunes of residents of Michigan are at a loss to make a better guess.

The net income returned by Mr. Rockefeller is not established definitely. His return is grouped with those of two other persons who made returns on incomes of from $2,000,000 to $3,000,000, the grand total of the three incomes being $12,909,188. Mr. Rockefeller's net income in 1920, therefore, must have been not less than $6,909,188. It probably was slightly in excess of $8,000,000.

This, however, does not take into consideration deductions and income from tax-exempt securities, in which Mr. Rockefeller has very heavy holdings.

Two Net Incomes $16,463,642.

The two net incomes of New Yorkers of $5,000,000 or more totaled $16,463,642 and the total tax paid on them was $10,568,387.

The two incomes reported by residents of Michigan totaled $13,456,335 and the total tax paid was $8,617,007.

There were nineteen incomes reported of $1,000,000 to $1,500,000, three of $1,500,000 to $2,000,000, four of $2,000,000 to $3,000,000 and three of $3,000,000 to $4,000,000.

One woman reported an income of $1,000,000 to $1,500,000 and one an income of $3,000,000 to $4,000,000.

The other reported net incomes numbered:

Amounts.	Number of Incomes.
$1,000 to $2,000	1,909,965
2,000 to 3,000	1,638,657
3,000 to 4,000	856,095
4,000 to 5,000	431,141
5,000 to 6,000	177,147

Big Fall in Corporate Incomes.

The number of corporation income tax returns for the calendar year 1920 was 345,595. Of these, 203,233 reported net income amounting to $7,902,654,813; income tax, $636,508,292; war profits and excess profits tax, $988,726,351; total tax, $1,625,234,643.

For the calendar year 1919 the number of corporation returns was 320,198, of which 209,634 reported net income totaling $9,411,418,458, and taxes aggregating $2,175,341,578.

There were 160 corporations that filed returns for 1920 reporting net income of $5,000,000 and over, and 836 that filed returns of from $1,000,000 to $5,000,000.

The numbers of other corporation net income groups were:

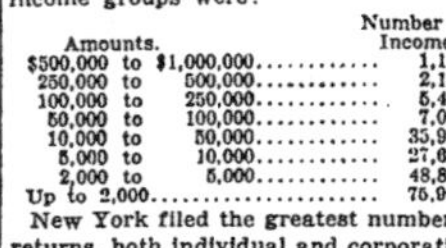

Amounts.	Number of Incomes.
$500,000 to $1,000,000	1,142
250,000 to 500,000	2,124
100,000 to 250,000	5,497
50,000 to 100,000	7,092
10,000 to 50,000	35,994
5,000 to 10,000	27,615
2,000 to 5,000	48,868
Up to 2,000	75,905

New York filed the greatest number of returns, both individual and corporation, and reported the greatest amount of net income, followed by Pennsylvania and Illinois. The total number of returns filed by New York was 1,103,129, of which 1,047,634 were personal and 55,495 were corporation.

Pennsylvania filed 691,575 returns, of which 672,746 were personal and 18,827 were corporation.

The total number of returns filed in Illinois was 563,594, of which 542,467 were personal and 21,127 were corporation.

New York Pays 23.69 Per Cent of Tax.

The aggregate net income reported by New Yorkers was $5,989,253,419, on which the tax amounted to $639,799,964. The net income reported by individuals was $4,030,632,696 and by corporations $1,958,620,723. The net income reported by New York was 18.93 per cent. of the

Continued on Page Twelve.

ISADORA DUNCAN AND POET HUSBAND DETAINED ON LINER

State Department Said to Frown on Dancer's Soviet Proclivities.

HELD ON BOARD THE PARIS

Will Be Called Today Before Special Board of Inquiry at Ellis Island.

YESSININ POWDERS HIS HAIR

Isadora Brushes Off Youthful Consort's Locks When Photographers Appear.

Isadora Duncan, originator of the modernized classic dance, born in California and, according to herself, the great-granddaughter of General William Duncan of the Revolutionary War, arrived here yesterday on the French liner Paris from Havre with the following entourage: her husband, Serge Yessinin, the young Russian poet; Woldemar Wetluguine, a Russian author, who acts as her secretary; her two children, maid and valet.

The titian-haired dancer, who expected to be welcomed at the pier by a committee from her native State, was astounded when the Immigration Inspector told her that he was going to order the officers of the Paris to detain her, her husband and her secretary on board for the night, to be sent to Ellis Island this morning for examination by a special board of inquiry.

There was no explanation as to why the dancer and her party had been ordered detained, but it was understood that the instructions came from Washington and that Soviet opinions expressed by the dancer were involved. She had some difficulty in getting into France recently, and for similar reasons, it was said, on her return from Russia. Her last visit to New York was in 1917, when she brought several war orphan girl dancers. She has twenty-five more of them on the way from Russia now, ten boys and fifteen girls, she said.

Has Suite de Luxe on Liner.

Miss Duncan was plainly vexed with the attitude of the Immigration Inspector and said so frankly to the reporters in her suite de luxe on the promenade deck of the Paris. She reclined on a couch with her left arm thrown gracefully round the neck of her blonde husband, who had powdered his hair, and the other hand clasped that of her sister-in-law, Mrs. Augustus Duncan. S. Hurok, her manager, who had come to meet her, stood on guard at the door of the suite. Later he sent a telegram to the State Department in Washington. The dancer seemed chiefly concerned over the young poet to whom she was married eight months ago, and at intervals in the interview she patted his round, boyish face and told him in French to be "tranquil."

That is about all the French the young husband understands. Officers of the Paris said that during the voyage the secretary had been kept busy acting as interpreter for the newlyweds. Miss Duncan wore a round white soft felt hat with a narrow black band, a crimson silk gown and red morocco leather Russian boots. She dusted the powder from the poet's hair before the photographers posed them together.

Working for Art, Not Politics.

In a statement which had been prepared by her husband and Secretary Wetluguine before the party had been ordered detained, Miss Duncan said:

"Here we are on American territory. Gratitude, that is our first thought. We are the representatives of young Russia. We are not mixing in political questions. It is only the field of art that we are working. We believe the soul of Russia and the soul of America are about to understand each other.

"We are come to America with only one idea—to tell of the Russian conscience and to work for the rapprochement of the two great countries. No politics, no propaganda!

"After eight years of war and revolutions a Chinese wall is surrounding Russia. Europe, itself torn by war, hasn't enough strength to tear down that Chinese wall. Russia is in the shadows, but it is misfortune that has helped us. It is during the Russian famine that America made a generous gesture. Hoover has destroyed the Chinese wall.

"The work of the American Relief Administration is unforgettable. Above everything else I wish to emphasize the fact that today there are only two countries in the world—Russia and America.

"In Russia there is an avid thirst to study America and her sweet people. May it be that art will be the medium

Continued on Page Three.

KEMAL ORDERS ALL CHANAK MOVES HALTED, BUT HIS TROOPS REMAIN CLOSE TO BRITISH, ARMISTICE MEETING SET FOR TOMORROW

Soviet in Note to Allies Seeks French Support For Admission to Near East Conference

By WALTER DURANTY.

Special Cable to THE NEW YORK TIMES.

MOSCOW, Oct. 1.—Russia at last has found the means she has been seeking of diplomatic intervention in the Near Eastern imbroglio.

She has addressed to the Foreign Ministers of England, France and Italy a note of protest against the allied blockade of the Black Sea, consequent on the occupation of the Dardanelles and Bosporus, couched in a form calculated to further present Russian diplomacy, which aims at participation in the conference that is to decide the status of Constantinople and the Straits.

Whereas previous notes failed to attain this result, the note published today contains passages directed right at France, whom Russia judges far more likely than England to oppose her admission to the conference. The said passages emphasize the fact that "freedom of the Straits," as interpreted by the Allies, means freedom only for Britain and her friends and that the British Fleet must be the supreme arbiter by reason of England's naval supremacy.

The Russians know well that this very point has been loudly raised by the less Anglophile elements in the French press and that, diplomatically speaking, it is quite an open question whether among "Britain's friends" today France herself can be included. In other words the note clearly intimates to France that she can count on Russian support for any interpretation of the phrase "freedom of the Straits" that will not leave them at the mercy of the dominant naval power.

NEW DEMAND FOR THRACE

Kemal's Reply to Allied Note Calls for Immediate Surrender.

BUT HE MAKES CONCESSIONS

Will Stop Operations Toward Chanak and Constantinople Pending the Parleys.

TURKISH TRICK AT ERENKEUI?

London Times Hears Pretended Evacuation Masked a Futile Attempt to Seize a New Position.

CONSTANTINOPLE, Oct. 1 (Associated Press).—Orders for the cessation of military movements in the Chanak region of Asiatic Turkey and for the suspension of the activities of the Turkish irregular forces in Thrace have been issued by Mustapha Kemal Pasha, the Turkish Nationalist leader.

The Turkish Nationalist authorities have agreed to an armistice conference in Mudania on Tuesday and have requested the Allied High Commissioners to appoint delegates. The Nationalists will be represented by Ismet Pasha and possibly by Hamid Bey.

Kemal's Reply Published in Paris.

PARIS, Oct. 1 (Associated Press)—The text of Mustapha Kemal's reply to the allied joint note of Sept. 23 was made public tonight by the Foreign Office.

The reply is dated Sept. 29 and promises immediately to stop the military operations which have been developing toward Constantinople and Chanak "in pursuit of the Greek armies." It accepts the proposal for an armistice conference at Mudania next Tuesday with representatives of the Entente.

Dealing with Thrace, the reply is worded by marked firmness. It credits the Entente with sentiments of justice toward Turkey, but demands that Thrace shall not be left one day longer under the Greek Army, saying that it is indispensable that Thrace shall be evacuated immediately and restored to the Angora Government up to the west of the Maritza River, including Adrianople.

The note, which is signed by Yusuf Kemal, Minister of Foreign Affairs, begins by saying that a formal reply to the Entente's note will be sent in a few days by his Government.

"Confident in the assurances which M. Franklin-Bouillon has given the Commander-in-Chief of the Turkish armies, in accord with the representatives of the Entente Powers meeting in Paris, and persuaded that negotiations will at once be proceeded with to establish a just peace," the note continues, "an order has been given to stop immediately our military movements, which have been unceasingly developing in the direction of Constantinople and Chanak-Kalen in pursuit of the Greek armies.

"The assurances given by M. Franklin-Bouillon have established the sentiments of justice with which the propositions of the Entente are truly inspired, with a view to assuring the rights of Turkey.

Insists on Getting Thrace Quickly.

"Nevertheless, as the maintenance of Thrace, if only for a day more, under the administration and occupation of the Greek Army is a cause of danger of every kind and grief to Turkey's peoples, it is indispensable that Thrace to the west of the Miritza River, with Adrianople, be evacuated immediately and restored urgently to the Government of the Great National Assembly of Turkey."

The reply, in conclusion, accepts Mudania for a conference on Oct. 3 and names Ismet Pasha, commander of the armies on the west front, as Turkish representative, and asks to be informed as to the names of the Generals representing the Entente Powers.

The Nationalists' note of acceptance of the allied proposals, according to a Havas dispatch from Constantinople, provides that the British and Turkish forces shall temporarily hold their present positions, without any further movement, until the armistice conference called at Mudania makes its decision.

The dispatch adds that the peace conference, if all goes well at Mudania, should be held about Oct. 15, according to the belief prevalent in Turkish quarters. In the meantime it is felt that the Mudania meeting, if it is finally approved of by Great Britain and Italy, will relieve the tension. In view of General Harington's efforts to preserve the peace, and in consequence of the approval of the conference by the French and the Turks, there is little doubt in Constantinople that the meeting will take place as planned.

The call for the Mudania conference already has been accepted by France, and it is believed here that Great Britain and Italy, if they have not already done so, will reply favorably to the invitation to attend. The acceptance of the two latter powers is considered so certain that it was said in official quarters here today that General Harington would be the British representative and General Mombelli would act for Italy. France has designated General Charpy.

Evacuation of Erenkeui Denied.

LONDON, Oct. 1.—A dispatch to The London Times from Chanak, dated Saturday, says that Friday's optimistic opinion on the situation, based on the apparent evacuation of Erenkeui, was scarcely justified. The Kemalist cavalry, instead of retiring, advanced around the British flank, with the in-

PROPOSE THAT ALLIES HOLD THRACE A MONTH

French Envoy and Kemal Would Then Have Control Transferred to Turks.

WHO WILL EXPEL GREEKS?

Not the British, Paris Fears, and So Sentiment There Is Not Very Optimistic.

By EDWIN L. JAMES.

Special Cable to THE NEW YORK TIMES.

PARIS, Oct. 1.—The Quai d'Orsay announced this afternoon that the special French envoy of Kemal Pasha, Henry Franklin-Bouillon, had arranged, subject to the approval of the Governments concerned, a conference at Mudania for Oct. 3, to arrange the military positions to be occupied by the various armies concerned pending the drafting of peace terms with the Turks.

According to the announcement, this conference is expected to consider "the conditions under which the evacuation of the neutral zone of Chanak and of Thrace can be assured." The French Government makes it known this evening that it has accepted the proposal. All depends on what the British Government decides. It is expected here that London will accept the conference.

However, it must be recalled that yesterday morning General Harington sent to Mustapha Kemal a demand that the Turks evacuate the territory they hold around Chanak, and stating that until that was done the British would attend no conference with them, at Mudania, Venice or anywhere else.

According to the Quai d'Orsay, acceptance by the Allies of the plan for the Mudania conference would mean "the immediate halting of the Turkish troops."

This justifies the remark that in the Chanak district the Turks could not advance any further without literally treading on the toes of the British. But this condition derives some importance if it is true, as reported, that 300 Turkish troops succeeded Wednesday evening in crossing the Bosporus, near Beikos, into Thrace, and if it is true that the Turks are organizing in Thrace.

According to the Havas Agency, Kemal and Franklin Bouillon agreed on the following provisions relating to Thrace:

"Thrace would be immediately occupied by the Allies, who would provisionally assure the administration by means of about 1,000 men stationed at Adrianople and little detachments placed at strategic points like Gallipoli, for

Continued on Page Two.

DEFENSE OF THRACE IS GREEKS' NEW AIM

Will Aid Entente and Resist Turks Says Gonatas, Leader of Successful Revolt.

NOT READY FOR REPUBLIC

Leader Told the New King That Reaction Would Be Crushed and Won His Collaboration.

ATHENS, Oct. 1 (Associated Press).—"I am not, as you have seen, a Robespierre, and I don't even want to be thought of as a military dictator," said Colonel Gonatas, leader of the revolutionary movement, today in discussing the Grecian revolt, which probably will go down in history as one of the most capably organized and one of the swiftest military upheavals ever affecting the nations of the world.

Colonel Gonatas modestly disclaimed that his brain was the creative force and his the genius which brought the movement to its amazingly quick conclusion.

"It was the officers about me," he said, "and they did me the honor to make me their leader."

A handsome man of about 45 years of age is Colonel Gonatas. His black hair, brushed back, crowns an intellectual face which often breaks into a pleasant smile as in French he talks of the revolution.

"We who made this revolution," continued Colonel Gonatas, "earnestly hope the people of the United States will understand why we made it and that they will give their sympathy to us, and generally speaking, espouse our cause. For this revolution had to come. It was the very logic of human events.

The King an Embarrassment.

"We were misgoverned at home, and because of that we met military disaster abroad. So we decided to come home and remove both the King and the Government—to put our house in order. We removed the King because he was an embarrassment in our relations with the countries of the Entente. He was an embarrassment, so we asked him to make way for his son.

"We brought with us to Athens an army of sufficient size to render all resistance ineffective, and we carried through the revolution without shedding a single drop of blood. We arrested five civilians who we consider were responsible for our defeat in Asia Minor and two officers for trying to foment resistance to us without governmental authority.

"It was a matter of honor with us to protect the King. Constantine left yesterday for Palermo on the Steamer Patrias, which sails sometimes for America, accompanied by an honorary escort of torpedo boat destroyers provided by the Revolutionary Committee.

"Until tried by special tribunals, the civilian prisoners will be transferred to and kept on an island in the Aegean Sea."

These civilians include such men as former Premiers Gounaris and Stratos.

Program of New Regime.

Colonel Gonatas explained his immediate program to the correspondent as follows: Collaboration with the Entente countries, the immediate reinforcement of the Thracian front and the active pushing of the war against the Turks, if necessary, and then securing the unity of all parties at home, "which have been separated up to now by hatred, one against the other." Thus, he added, it was hoped to save Greece.

Asked if the revolutionists had any idea of creating a republic, Colonel Gonatas replied:

"I personally think the time has not yet arrived for Greece to become a democracy. Some years must pass before the people can govern themselves in the form of a republic.

"We visited King George and explained to him our movement. We told

Continued on Page Two.

Kidnapper Abandons Voth Baby; Stolen Child Restored to Mother

As mysteriously as she was kidnapped on Wednesday afternoon, 3-month-old Mildred Voth was restored last night. The child was found abandoned in the hallway of an apartment house at 18 West 100th Street, near Central Park West, by George Burns, the janitor, who heard an infant faintly crying. Burns started for the West 100th Street Station and met a patrolman who accompanied him there. Detectives Dent and Boyle of the West 123d Street Station were notified that the infant was believed to be the one sought throughout the city for five days.

Julius Voth, an electrician of 307 West 133d Street, sped to the West 100th Street Station, identified the baby and sent for his wife. Mrs. Voth, a frail woman, sleepless and worn after the long hunt with its many disappointments, went to the station, looked at the wailing baby and cuddled it in her arms with the cry:

"Thank God, it's Mildred!"

Laughing and crying, Mrs. Voth assured detectives anxiously watching her that she could not be mistaken. The blue blanket in which the infant was wrapped was the one stolen from the baby carriage, which was found many hours after the kidnapping. The child still wore the white coat, trimmed with blue, in which it was clad when it disappeared, and its undergarments were ones in which the mother had dressed it on Wednesday before she went shopping. Mildred was well nourished and appeared to have been kindly treated. The scratch on her left cheek, which had been given as one means of identification, still was visible, though it was healing.

Mrs. Voth said she believed that the kidnapper, thought to have been a wealthy woman starving for a child, became frightened as the hunt proceeded, aided by every means of publicity, and decided to surrender the baby.

Detectives made inquiry in the neighborhood of the apartment house where Mildred was found, but could find no one who had seen anyone near the place with a baby.

Mildred was stolen about 4 o'clock on Wednesday afternoon in front of a Woolworth store at 208 West 125th Street by a woman who, Mrs. Voth believed was one who folloed her from another store after bending over the coach to admire the baby. The coach was abandoned in Madison Avenue near 109th Street.

Cosgrave's Uncle Is Shot Dead in Dublin By Four Armed Youths Holding Up Saloon

By Wireless to THE NEW YORK TIMES.

DUBLIN, Oct. 1.—The operations of an armed gang of young fellows representing themselves as members of the Irish republican army, but really out for loot, were responsible for a painful tragedy in Dublin last night. These fellows have been choosing the closing time for licensed houses Saturday nights as a favorable opportunity to carry on their nefarious traffic. Last night four of them entered the public house in James Street of Mrs. Bridget Burke, and one of them shot dead Patrick Cosgrave, uncle of President Cosgrave.

They burst into the shop, called "Hands up!" and, dividing, some made for the till. The customers were ordered to stand still. Mr. Cosgrave caught hold of the revolver of one of the raiders near the door. The latter shouted, "Let it go!" Cosgrave told him not to get excited and all would be right, but the raider wrested the weapon from his grasp, and immediately there was a shot. The man at the till got up, and all rushed for the door. Mr. Cosgrave fell, shot through the chest, death following a few moments later, life being extinct when he was brought to Stevens Hospital.

President Cosgrave and members of the police were on the scene shortly afterward.

The dead man was 65 years old. The Cosgrave family is connected with the Burkes by marriage. Mrs. Burke is the mother of Miss Joan Burke, Irish singer, known in Ireland and other lands for her beautiful voice. Her father died a short time ago, and her brother fell in the 1916 rebellion, fighting on the rebel side.

The house of last night's tragedy was frequently visited by the British during the Black and Tan régime, and Burke was seized as a suspect and imprisoned.

The affair emphasizes the extreme gravity of the situation created by the activities of irresponsible men armed with guns, whom it is difficult to track down at present.

"All the News That's Fit to Print."

The New York Times.

THE WEATHER
Fair and cold today and Sunday; northwest winds.
Temperature yesterday—Max., 25; min., 12.
☞ For weather report see next to last page.

VOL. LXXII....No. 23,765. *** NEW YORK, SATURDAY, FEBRUARY 17, 1923. TWO CENTS In Greater New York | THREE CENTS Within 200 Miles | FOUR CENTS Elsewhere

TUT-ANKH-AMEN'S INNER TOMB IS OPENED, REVEALING UNDREAMED OF SPLENDORS, STILL UNTOUCHED AFTER 3,400 YEARS

ESSEN IS COWED AFTER WOUNDING OF TWO SOLDIERS

Fight in Beer Hall Causes the French to Turn Out a Stronger Military Display.

CITY NOW WITHOUT POLICE

Chief Arrested, Men Disarmed and Records Seized—Frequent Clashes Elsewhere.

JAIL FOR 2 BURGOMASTERS

Electric Plant Director Is Fined 5,000,000 Marks—Berlin Supplies Funds for Strikers.

Special Cable to THE NEW YORK TIMES.

DUESSELDORF, Feb. 16.—Every day is adding more and more to the casualty list of the Ruhr occupation.

Last evening in a beer hall at Essen two French soldiers were slightly, and one German policeman gravely, wounded.

At Gunkenrath a French sentinel fired on and killed a German workman who was trespassing on the railroad track.

At several points last evening sentries and posts fired shots as warnings and with every rifle discharged the tension is growing.

The affair at Essen was the most important as affecting the situation in the town. It began, as trouble may at any time begin, trivially enough. Eight French soldiers and two Belgians went into the beer house and called for drinks about 9:30 in the evening. As usual the landlord refused to serve them and the soldiers, as has become their habit, began to draw beer themselves. In protest the landlord called in the German policeman on duty at the door, and, according to all accounts of both the Germans and the French, this policeman entered excitedly with his revolver in his hand crying "Hands up!"

At once the affair which had been a burlesque became serious. The French soldiers instead of obeying such a peremptory order began to draw their revolvers. Then the German fired. Before he could be overpowered he had wounded two men slightly and it was not till he fell with a bullet through his body that he stopped firing.

Attracted by the noise the German police patrol entered at that moment and prevented further fighting.

Police Headquarters Raided.

Today the affair had an aftermath. With armored cars and machine guns a detachment of French troops rode through the town and wheeled sharply into the police barracks before it was known what was intended. They arrested the chief of police, disarmed eighty men in the station and took possession of all records.

Everywhere throughout town patrols have been moving about all day, and as if in warning to the nationalist trouble makers, the French are displaying their strength.

Yesterday the town was silent, depressed and suspicious. Today it is cowed. The French have the whip hand and even the most ardent nationalist must admit it.

All through the province the measures of the French for repressing organized resistance and propaganda are increasing in severity. Over half the newspapers in the Ruhr have now been suspended for one cause or another, police who do not salute, being arrested in batches, and with every new batch the penalty is being increased.

To all this tightening up the Germans are making as yet no new reply. The telephones of Düsseldorf, Essen and several other places are still suspended.

At Bochum the municipal employes today struck for four hours as a protest against the arrests which have been made in the town and against the requisitioning of automobiles. The only return to work was at Duisburg, where the tramway employes have been granted a 110 per cent. increase in wages at a time when the mark is improving by leaps.

Yesterday for the first time the effect of the export prohibition order became evident. As fewer freight trains are leaving the district fewer are coming in, and from 200 the number out and in, has fallen to about 40. If that falling off continues a food shortage, which always threatened, may become a reality, and both the French and Germans are doing their utmost to deal with the situation when it arises, each with the hope that their efforts will rally the masses to their support. The Germans are organizing storage and distribution centres as if for a siege, and at the same time the French are accumulating all the food they can in the district. The number of military trains has been largely increased and food is being brought from France far in excess of what is needed by the troops.

To counter all this effort to obtain local support among the workers the Germans have now nearly completed their arrangements for payment of workers forced out of employment by the prohibition of exports. Big firms are prepared themselves to stand a loss, but to small firms the Government, through the Employers' Association and the Reichsbank, is prepared to give all the help that is needed. The total wages roll which it is estimated will have to be met is something like 50,000,000 gold marks a month, and the Government, which in November last asked for a moratorium in reparation payments, seems now prepared to pay this sum to workmen in order to support resistance to the French. So far there has, however, been little or no closing down, and except at the coalpits where little or nothing is being done except for repairs and local consumption work, the Ruhr seems almost normal.

Quick Retaliation by French.

ESSEN, Feb. 16 (Associated Press).—Following the wounding of two French soldiers by German security police in a café brawl last night, Essen was the

Continued on Page Three.

89 M. P.'s Ask Harding's Aid; 'One Hope of Saving Europe'

By Wireless to THE NEW YORK TIMES.

LONDON, Feb. 16.—Signed by eighty-nine Labor and Co-operative members of the British Parliament, the following cablegram was sent to President Harding today:

"America with Britain unwittingly made France's present destructive action possible. We appeal for American co-operation today as the one hope of saving Europe."

Among those who have signed the message are Arthur Henderson, George Lansbury, R. E. Buxton and John Hodge.

$500,000 GEM THEFT SUSPECT ARRESTED

"Marshall" Held as Leader of Gang That Robbed Mrs. Schoellkopf at Drinking Party.

CAUGHT ON MONTREAL TRAIN

Another Arrest Here Said to Have Furnished Clue—Companion Also in Custody.

Inspector John D. Coughlin at Police Headquarters last night announced that the debonair "Marshall," alleged leader of the gang that robbed Mrs. Irene Schoellkopf of $500,000 worth of jewelry in an apartment at 64 West Fifty-second street aerly on the morning of Jan. 1, had been arrested yesterday on a train between Schenectady and Troy. The arrest was made by Detectives Daly, Horan and Buckley of Inspector Coughlin's staff. They caught "Marshall" when he was attempting to return from Montreal and took him to a house at 75 Lancaster Street, Albany, which he said was his home, to look for the stolen jewels. The detectives reported to Inspector Coughlin by telephone from the Lancaster Street house that they had not found the booty.

The man alleged to be "Marshall" was traveling under the name of M. D. Biddulph. According to the police, his full name is Matthew Darian Biddulph. The police say that he is an ex-convict, and that he is known to the police all over the country under the aliases of R. H. Matthews, R. H. Harrison and John F. Derby. According to the police, his photograph is No. 17,555 in the Rogues' Gallery at San Francisco, and he has been arrested many times, and convicted several times.

Inspector Coughlin said the man was wanted in Los Angeles and San Francisco on the charge of passing worthless checks.

Search of the records at Police Headquarters last night showed that "Marshall" had been arrested for passing a worthless check at the Yale Club in New York City in 1917, but had got off with a suspended sentence.

"Marshall," when arrested, said he was 27 years old and gave his occupation as traveling salesman and actor. Under the name of Biddulph, Inspector Coughlin said, the man had had some success as a moving picture actor, appearing in Universal photoplays. By a coincidence, the last film in which he is known to have appeared was called "Wanted at Headquarters," in which he played a "heavy" part—in other words played a movie villain. This was in 1919.

Companion Also Arrested.

The detectives arrested with "Marshall," a man who identified himself as George F. Daley of 83 Clinton Street, Albany. As far as known, Daley had no connection with the Schoellkopf case, but the police are holding him to investigate why he was traveling with "Marshall." Daley is said to be a New York billposter, with an address in the vicinity of Broadway and 82d Street.

The arrest of "Marshall" and Daley followed a few hours after Horan, one of the detectives who made these arrests, had locked up a man named Charles Curtis in New York. Horan and his partner, Detective Owens, have been detached from all other duty to work exclusively on the Schoellkopf case for several weeks. In the line-up at Police Headquarters yesterday morning, Horan and Owens recognized Curtis, who had been arrested as a suspect in another case, as a man they had been looking for as a friend of one of "Marshall's alleged confederates in the Schoellkopf robbery.

Curtis was released from the charge on which he was first held, but Horan immediately rearrested him on the charge of suspicion of burglary in another jewel theft—the robbery of Mrs. Lillian Myers of $50,000 worth of jewels in her apartment at 300 West Forty-ninth Street on July 21 last. Curtis is believed to have given the information on which Horan and the other

Continued on Page Six.

ANDERSON ENRICHED BY REALTY TRADING, IS STORY TO PECORA

Prosecutor Quotes Him as Saying $24,700 Came, in Currency, From Deals.

CONTRADICTS HIS AFFIDAVIT

Report to Anti-Saloon Directors in 1919 That Money Came From Loans Is Recalled.

GRAND JURY MOVE HINTED

Inquiry Will Be Pressed "In Some Other Way," Brackett Is Warned in Letter.

In a letter to ex-Senator Edgar T. Brackett, counsel for William H. Anderson, State Superintendent of the Anti-Saloon League, Acting District Attorney Ferdinand Pecora yesterday indicated that unless Mr. Anderson answered questions relating to the source and expenditure of the publicity fund of $24,700, he would take Grand Jury action. Mr. Pecora's letter was in reply to a reiteration by Mr. Brackett that Mr. Anderson should not submit replies to questions pertaining to the fund, details of which Mr. Anderson professes to have withheld from the Board of Directors of the League.

Intimating that he questioned the accuracy of statements made by Mr. Anderson, Mr. Pecora disclosed that Mr. Anderson had asserted he had obtained the money through realty investments negotiated by a friend at a time when he was earning $4,000 a year as an official of the League in Maryland. Mr. Pecora quoted Mr. Anderson as saying that the profits were in excess of $24,700, the sum which he alleged he had loaned the League here for its work when the necessary expenditures exceeded the income. Mr. Pecora pointed out that Mr. Anderson was unable to give the location of any of the realty and declined to divulge the name of his investor friend. Mr. Anderson told the Acting District Attorney that he had received the profits in currency, which he placed in his safe rather than in a bank, acording to the letter to Senator Brackett.

Text of Pecora's Letter.

Mr. Pecora's letter follows:

Feb. 16, 1923.

Hon. Edgar T. Brackett, 120 Broadway, New York City.

Dear Senator Brackett:

Much as I regret your adherence to your advice to Mr. Anderson to refuse to answer certain questions which I have asked him as to the sources from which he obtained the sum of $24,700.00, which he claims to have expended on behalf of the Anti-Saloon League during the years 1913 and 1914, and details of such expenditure, I recognize fully your unquestioned right to advise him as his counsel in such manner as you may deem to be in accordance with his own interests.

You express the view that it would seem grotesque to base any prosecution of Mr. Anderson on the facts which have been shown. You also recognize that the ascertainment of the sources from which Mr. Anderson obtained the $24,700, and the methods by which he expended the same, properly comes within the scope of the inquiry which this office is making in so far as light may be shed on the question as to whether the representations which Mr. Anderson made to the Directors of the league in connection therewith are true or false.

In connection with his expenditure of $24,000, Mr. Anderson has declared to me, among other things, that the monies were paid out by him in currency from time to time to certain persons whose identities he will not disclose; that these payments were made for publicity work on behalf of the league; that he has no vouchers or written records of any kind which would show the respective dates and specific amounts of such payments, and that he cannot from memory give such data; that he cannot produce a single copy or piece of printed matter that was used in such publicity work; that all of said monies came from his personal means which he did not keep in any bank or other such depositary, but which he kept in a safe in the office of the respective headquarters of the league in the States of Maryland and New York; and that he made such expenditures upon his own initiative and judgment; and without his having consulted the Board of Directors of the league in New York with regard to them.

Tried to Trace Money.

In view of the unusual circumstances under which, according to his own statements, Mr. Anderson made

Continued on Page Four.

Idaho Assembly Bars Japanese From Leasing Any Lands There

BOISE, Idaho, Feb. 16.—The Assembly of the Legislature, by a vote of 54 to 6, today passed a measure to prohibit the leasing of lands in the State to Japanese. The measure, according to its author, Representative Gillis, while aimed primarily at the Japanese, is applicable to all aliens.

Speaking to the Assembly, Representative Gillis said he feared an influx of Japanese and other aliens to Idaho through refusal of the Federal Government to re-lease land now occupied in Washington, and because of other States passing anti-leasing laws.

ENGINEER AMBUSHED AND SLAIN AT DOOR

Earl Remington of Los Angeles, Who Made Planes in War, Is Found Dead in Driveway.

WIFE ASLEEP IN THE HOUSE

Victim, Shot as He Stepped From Automobile, Met Death He Had Feared.

LOS ANGELES, Feb. 16.—Earl Remington, wealthy electrical engineer, found dead from gunshot wounds in the yard of his home here early today, had lived in fear of death for the last week, according to his wife, who was so prostrated with grief that she could not be seen until late today.

Two persons took active parts in the slaying of Remington, according to police conclusions announced late tonight.

Mrs. Remington said her husband had been acting strangely and showed extreme nervousness. Noises outside the house, particularly at night, seemed to distress him, she said. Remington had offered their home, which is in an exclusive residential district, for sale, the widow stated, but had instsucted her never to permit any stranger to enter the house.

Although Remington telephoned to his wife yesterday that he was going to their ranch near Chino and would not return until late, it has been established, according to the police, that he did not go to the ranch.

Detectives are attempting to trace his movements yesterday in the hope of finding some clue to the slaying. They stated they had found two friends of the dead man who said they saw him at 5 o'clock yesterday afternoon.

That Remington was slain by some one having a grudge against him is the opinion expressed by the detectives.

Whether an attempted burglary of the office of the safe company of which Remington was the head, on Oct. 15, 1922, had anything to do with the engineer's death also is being investigated. Two of the company's safes were broken into, according to a report, but nothing of value was taken. The police are working on the theory that papers may have been taken at that time which were used later in a blackmailing plot against Remington.

Remington evidently was murdered at about last midnight.. A dozen neighbors heard the fatal shot, and his wife lay sleeping within a few feet of him; but the body was not found until 6 o'clock this morning, when Charity Dawson, a negro maid, started downstairs to light the gas heating plant of the house at 1,409 South St. Andrews Street, a fashionable neighborhood.

There was a trail of blood on the driveway and a riddled leather portfolio which Remington had carried. The maid called Mrs. Remington, and the whole neighborhood was soon aroused by their screams.

Remington left his offices early in the afternoon for a trip to his Chino ranch. He was not seen thereafter by either employes or family until his body was found. He rang up his wife at 3:30 P. M. and told her he was going to Chino, according to the maid.

Remington, the police believe, drew up in his Ford coupé at the side of his house, perhaps at the order of his assailant. He stepped around to the back of the car, shifting the leather portfolio now high, now low, in front of his body in an effort to shield himself.

There was a loud report, perhaps two. One charge from the shotgun tore its way to the engineer's heart.

As he staggered away from the machine he fell on his back, arms spread out.

Mrs. Remington, according to the maid, did not hear the report of the gun. As her husband lay dying she was asleep in a bedroom in the northeast corner of the house, directly above the driveway. From her window she could have looked down on the struggle.

Neighbors playing cards heard the shots but thought they were automobile engines backfiring, or tires exploding. If the Remington dog had not been chloroformed for rabies about two weeks ago, the engineer might still be alive, according to the maid. She believes the dog might have awakened the family. Remington had no children.

"The motive may have been robbery, it may have been revenge," said Detective Sergeant Cline after talking with Mrs. Remington.

Remington was Vice President of the International Electric Protective Association, and had a wide reputation as a safe and bank designer.

Aviation was his sporting diversion, and he was adept at stunt flying. During the war he organized and was general manager of an aviation company here.

Charge Hawaiian Coolie Labor Plot.

Special to The New York Times.

WASHINGTON, Feb. 16.—Charges were made today by the Executive Council of the American Federation of Labor that for two years there had been an intensive agitation for the importation of 50,000 Chinese coolies into the Hawaiian Islands, where they would be placed under bond making them "debt slaves" for five years or less if they became rebellious. The council instructed the Federation's legislative representatives to do all in their power to prevent any enactment of laws that would in any degree open the gates to this character of immigration.

SENATE APPROVES BRITISH-DEBT BILL; FINAL VOTE, 70-13

46 Republicans, 24 Democrats Favor It—Borah Among the Four Republicans Opposed.

BITTER DEBATE TO FINISH

Many Assail "British Victory," but Glass Wins Applause by Recalling Allies' Sacrifices.

ONLY ONE AMENDMENT

Settlements With Other Allies Must Have Congress Approval—Bill Now Goes to Conference.

Special to The New York Times.

WASHINGTON, Feb. 16.—The Senate passed the British Debt Refunding bill tonight by a vote of 70 to 13, forty-six Republicans and twenty-four Democrats voting to ratify the settlement as agreed to by the Debt Funding Commission, while nine Democrats and four Republicans were recorded in favor of repudiating the settlement.

The final roll-call was ordered at 7:20 o'clock tonight. The Administration victory was much more impressive than had been anticipated, it having been predicted that between fifteen and twenty Senators would oppose the bill when the vote on passage was reached.

The measure passed with only one amendment—that proposed by Senator Robinson of Arkansas, which gives to Congress the right to pass on settlements that may be arrived at in the future with other debtor nations. An amendment to equalize the interest rates and require Great Britain to pay the same interest as the United States itself pays on the loan was defeated, 61 to 21.

It is expected that the House will promptly accept the Robinson amendment and that the bill will be in the hands of the President early next week.

All efforts to amend the bill with regard to interest rates or in other important particulars were signally defeated. An amendment proposed by Senator Harris of Georgia, which authorizes the appointment of three Democrats on the Funding Commission, would undoubtedly have carried, but was withdrawn when the Republican leaders promised to give this matter early consideration when it is presented to the Senate in the form of an independent bill. The Republicans appear as anxious as some of the Democrats to have the minority share the responsibility of adjusting the more than $11,000,000,000 debt now due this country by its former associates in the European war.

Sharp Debate Continued All Day.

Eight lively hours preceded the passage of the bill. At times the debate was spirited to the point of bitterness, but the clean-cut Administration victory was never in doubt. The defeat of the Hitchcock amendment to maintain the British interest charges at a rate as high as rates paid by this Government and a speech by Senator Glass of Virginia broke the back of the opposition. The impassioned plea of the Virginia Senator for favorable action and his fervid defense of Great Britain came near the close of the long day. When Senator Glass concluded it appeared for a minute or two as if the session might have to suspend while Senators, Republicans as well as Democrats, pressed forward to shake his hand and congratulate him.

The leaders of the opposition were La Follette, Reed of Missouri, McKellar, Heflin, Trammell and Norris, while Smoot, Lenroot, Glass and Underwood commanded the defending forces. La Follette made the longest of all the speeches, a carefully prepared utterance in which he denounced Secretary Mellon, ridiculed the President and assailed the majority membership of the Finance Committee for what he charged was its undue and unwarranted haste in rushing the bill to a final vote.

The last day arguments of the opposition were based principally on the claim that the United States, in agreeing to fix the interest Great Britain will pay at 3 per cent. for the first ten and 3½ per cent. for the remaining fifty-two years, had, in fact, canceled what they claimed was approximately $1,666,000,000 of the interest charges.

La Follette Ridicules Harding.

Opening the debate, Senator La Follette recalled the White House dinner of a year ago, which was attended, among others, by J. Pierpont Morgan, Charles H. Sabin and Secretary Mellon, all of them, declared the Wisconsin Senator, of the international banking group.

Continued on Page Five.

KING IN NEST OF SHRINES

Series of Ornate Covers Enclose Pharaoh's Sarcophagus.

WHOLE FILLS LARGE ROOM

Mortuary Chamber Opens Into Another Room, Crowded With Great Treasure.

EXPLORERS ARE DAZZLED

Wealth of Objects of Historic and Artistic Interest Exceeds All Their Wildest Visions.

KING TUT-ANKH-AMEN,
wearing the crown and royal vestments, as he appeared to his contemporaries. From a multi-colored decoration on the walls of the tomb of Huy, his Viceroy, discovered some years ago near the tomb of the King.
Courtesy Metropolitan Museum of Art.

Special Cable to THE NEW YORK TIMES.

LUXOR, Egypt, Feb. 16.—This has been, perhaps, the most extraordinary day in the whole history of Egyptian excavation. Whatever any one may have guessed or imagined of the secret of Tut-ankh-Amen's tomb, they surely cannot have dreamed the truth as now revealed.

The entrance today was made into the sealed chamber of the tomb of Tut-ankh-Amen, and yet another door opened beyond that. No eyes have yet seen the King, but to practical certainty we know that he lies there close at hand in all his original state, undisturbed.

Moreover, in addition to the great store of treasures which the tomb has already yielded, today has brought to light a new wealth of objects of artistic, historical, and even intrinsic value which is bewildering.

It is such a hoard as the most sanguine excavator can hardly have pictured, even in visions in his sleep, and puts Lord Carnarvon's and Mr. Carter's discovery in a class by itself and above all previous finds.

Official Opening Sunday.

Though the official opening of the sealed mortuary chamber of the tomb has been fixed for Sunday, it was obviously impossible to postpone until then the actual work of breaking in the entrance. This was a job involving some hours of work, because it had to be done with the greatest care, so as to keep intact as many of the seals as possible, and also to avoid injury to any of the objects on the other side which might be caused by the falling of material dislodged.

All this could not be done on Sunday while the official guests were kept waiting in the singularly unpleasant atmosphere of the tomb, so an agreement was made with the Egyptian authorities by which the actual breaking through of the wall should be done in their presence today.

Consequently, Howard Carter was very busy inside the tomb all morning with Professor Breasted and Dr. Alan Gardiner, whose assistance has been invaluable from the beginning of the work of examining seals and deciphering and copying inscriptions of all kinds. They had finished by noon, and the tomb was closed till after luncheon, at which Lord Carnarvon, Mr. Carter and Lady Evelyn Herbert entertained all those invited to be present today.

Official Story of Inner Tomb.

It was after 1 o'clock when the official party entered the tomb, and the operation was begun which was to result in such astounding discoveries, of which I am able to give the following authoritative description:

Today between the hours of 1 and 3 in the afternoon the culminating moment in the discovery of Tut-ankh-Amen's tomb took place when Lord Carnarvon and Howard Carter opened the inner sealed doorway in the presence of Lady Evelyn Herbert, Abdel Hamid Suliman Pasha, Under Secretary of Public Works; Pierre Lacau, Director General of the Antiquities Department; Sir William Garstin, Sir Charles Cust, Mr. Lythgoe, the curator of the Metropolitan Museum of Art of New York; Mr. Winlock, Director of the

GOV. REILY RESIGNS PORTO RICO OFFICE

Tells President Ill Health Forbids Him to Resume Executive Duties.

HAD BEEN LONG UNDER FIRE

Offended by His Inaugural Address, Unionists Made Many Charges Against Him.

WASHINGTON, Feb. 16 (Associated Press).—The resignation of E. Mont Reily as Governor of Porto Rico was received at the White House early this evening, but no announcement was made concerning it, although there was every indication that it would be accepted.

The text of the cablegram of resignation, as made public at the White House, follows:

Hon. Warren G. Harding, President of the United States:

On account of very serious injury while in the States, my trip to Porto Rico prostrated me, and I have been confined to my bed since, not being able to resume my official duties. My physicians inform me it will be several months before I can recover and I must have complete change and rest, free from all care. This being the case, I feel that I should resign and look after my health first.

I would like for my resignation to become effective April 1, believing that by that time I will be able to travel, and if I am not can be taken to a hospital here until I am able to do so.

In offering my resignation, I cannot do so without expressing to you and Secretary Weeks my appreciation of the unfailing loyalty and support you have both continually given to me in my arduous and trying work here.

Your recent statement to me that you were for me 100 per cent. had its echo in the great demonstration tendered me on my return, and shows that the work of your Administration in Porto Rico has not been in vain, but has been appreciated. It was a complete vindication of our American policies instituted in the islands two years ago.

A delegation composed of men of all political parties called on my Secretary yesterday, requesting that I withhold my resignation until you could be communicated with. I have notified them my resignation was irrevocable. Ninety per cent. of the people of the Island are for you and the things you stand for, and are pleading that no backward step be taken in-

Continued on Page Five.

GOETHALS DEMANDS COAL FOR UP-STATE

"We Want Action, Not Conferences," He Says in Message to Federal Fuel Distributer.

SEIZURE IS THREATENED

Insists Shipments to Canada Be Diverted—People Will Get Coal, He Asserts.

General George W. Goethals, State Fuel Administrator, serving notice on the Federal Fuel Distributer that "we want action, not conferences" for the relief of suffering localities in Northern New York, suggested in two telegrams yesterday immediate authorization by the Federal officials of drastic relief measures.

Diversion to up-State towns of coal now moving to Canada, priority of New York shipments over shipments to Canada and seizure of cars en route to Canada were some of the measures suggested.

"The people in that part of the State are going to get coal," General Goethals asserted in making public the telegrams. "I am awaiting action from Washington on the telegrams. In case I don't get it, I am not saying what I am going to do."

The seizure of one car of coal consigned to Canada for use of the Saratoga Springs Hospital was authorized yesterday by the shipper, John F. Bermingham, President of the Lackawanna Coal Company. General Goethals called this to the attention of F. R. Wadleigh, Federal Fuel Distributer, in one of his telegrams and asked why the Government could not require the Delaware & Hudson Railroad "to supply our needs."

Reports from Mr. Kilmer to the State Fuel Administration offices yesterday were that people up-State were "on the point of taking coal off the tracks." The people were ready "to take the law in their own hands," he stated and added that "no juries in the afflicted communities would ever vote for conviction."

Predictions of epidemics from influenza and pneumonia unless coal arrived at some of the up-State points today were made by Mr. Kilmer.

General Goethals told reporters that priority must be given both to an emergency shipment of 20,000 tons, which is required immediately, and to future regular allotments.

Schools at many points in the Saratoga district have been closed for lack of fuel, reports to the State Fuel Administration said. Two schools in Corinth have been closed, and unless some coal arrives before Monday, or the school authorities can get some wood, the high school also will close. The school at Schuylerville was ordered closed yesterday for an indefinite period because of the lack of fuel.

Louis Cohen, a landlord of 514 West 152d Street, was sentenced to thirty days in the workhouse in the Court of Special Sessions yesterday for failing to supply sufficient heat and hot water for the house at 522 West 146th Street.

Probation officers reported that the building was badly in need of repairs. Window panes were out and doors were loose, they said, and the temperature recently had been several degrees below the legal minimum.

Mrs. Bertha Becker, who owns a building at 524 West 151st Street, was fined $250 on a similar charge in Special Sessions.

Won't Stop Coal to Canada.

WASHINGTON, Feb. 16.—The proposal for an embargo on anthracite exports, especially to Canada, has been carefully considered and definitely abandoned, it was said today at the White House.

In the view of high Government officials an embargo would have no material effect on the coal shortage which is being experienced in sections of New York and New England.

Doctor and Chauffeur Killed When Train Wrecks Ambulance at Jersey Grade Crossing

A fatal grade crossing accident occurred last evening at Hackensack, N. J., where a train running forty miles an hour, on the New Jersey and New York branch of the Erie Railroad, smashed into an ambulance, crushing a hospital interne and a chauffeur to death. James Reape, 38 years old, of 99 Nassau Street, Brooklyn, the chauffeur, was instantly killed. Dr. Louis Nishawitz, 25, of 830 Kelly Street, the Bronx, an interne at the Hackensack General Hospital, was mortally injured. His skull was fractured and his left leg and right arm were cut off. He died in the hospital half an hour after the accident. The ambulance was wrecked.

Dr. Nishawitz lost his life in the performance of his duty, as he was answering a call to take a sick woman to the hospital from her home on Hudson Street, Hackensack. After the accident a second ambulance was sent for the woman, but the delay had been fatal, and she was dead on its arrival.

The accident occurred about 5:50 P. M. at the Essex Street crossing. The train was a Haverstraw express, carrying commuters from New York.

Owing to a sharp curve south of Essex Street, the engineer could not see the crossing until he was close to it. The crossing gates should have been lowered, but were not. John Burke of Pearl River, N. Y., the gate tender, said the gates were frozen and out of commission. According to Burke, he stood in the middle of the road and swung a red lantern, but the ambulance driver did not heed. Burke was arrested on a technical charge of manslaughter.

Dr. Nishawitz was the son of Max Nishawitz, a shoe merchant in the Bronx. The physician was a graduate of De Witt Clinton High School and the Long Island College Hospital.

Harding Threatens to Cut Shipping Fleet Unless Congress Passes the Subsidy Bill

WASHINGTON, Feb. 16.—The Administration Shipping bill was restored tonight to its former place as the unfinished business of the Senate, after having been laid aside since early in the week to allow consideration of the British debt settlement legislation. This was done on motion of Senator Jones of Washington after advocates of the measure had demonstrated their superior strength by voting down, 38 to 30, a motion by Senator Robinson of Arkansas to adjourn.

The vote on adjournment was not regarded as an accurate test of the strength of the forces supporting and opposing the Shipping bill, as several Senators on both sides were absent.

Opposition of the shipping measure are expected, when the Senate meets tomorrow, to counter with a proposal to lay the bill aside again in favor of the Capper Truth-in-Fabrics bill, and it was considered possible that a test vote on the merchant marine legislation may result.

Although the future of the subsidy bill in the Senate has not been clearly indicated in the face of claims and counter-claims on the possibility of its passage, it was said at the White House today that President Harding would not call a special session of Congress to consider the merchant marine situation if the Shipping bill should fail.

Mr. Harding was said to feel that the necessity for action looking to a solution of the shipping problem had been clearly demonstrated, and to have reached the decision that if the Shipping bill is not enacted the Government will proceed at once to take such steps as will diminish in a very great degree the present losses of the Government's fleet.

Detailed reports on the operation of Shipping Board vessels, showing net losses on individual voyages running as high as $100,000, had been studied by the President and his advisers, it was said, and the consensus of opinion was that the losses would be wiped out under the necessary economics which would follow the return of the shipping to private ownership.

"All the News That's Fit to Print."

The New York Times.

THE WEATHER
Fair today and tomorrow; moderate west and southwest winds.
Temperature yesterday—Max. 44, min. 30.
For weather report see next to last page.

VOL. LXXIII....No. 24,031. * * * NEW YORK, SATURDAY, NOVEMBER 10, 1923. TWO CENTS In Greater New York | THREE CENTS Within 200 Miles | FOUR CENTS Elsewhere

REICHSWEHR TROOPS CRUSH BAVARIAN REVOLT; LUDENDORFF AND HITLER TAKEN, NOW MISSING; AMERICA REJECTS INQUIRY WITH FRENCH LIMIT

CUVILLIER IS HELD, CORRIGAN CLEARED OF LIBEL ON ENRIGHT

Crain Decides That Liquor Graft Charges Against Commissioner Are "Unsustained."

SCORES POLICE TESTIMONY

False Code of Loyalty Shields Dishonest Men on the Force, Judge Declares.

CIVIL SUITS TO BE PRESSED

Magistrate Cannot Escape, Say Enright and Counsel—Assemblyman Talks of New Fight.

Assemblyman Louis A. Cuvillier was held for the Grand Jury yesterday on a charge of criminally libeling Police Commissioner Enright by sending a telegram last April referring to "Enright and his graft collectors" in connection with charges of police corruption in prohibition enforcement. The charge against Magistrate Joseph E. Corrigan, co-defendant with Mr. Cuvillier, was dismissed.

The accusations of "grafting" against Commissioner Enright were "unsustained." This was the decision of Judge Thomas C. T. Crain, before whom, as committing Magistrate, the charges and countercharges were aired.

"After seeing and hearing seventy-one witnesses and reading their testimony as transcribed on 3,283 pages of typewriting and weighing the summations of counsel, I am glad to feel required to say that nothing brought to my attention gives ground to believe that Commissioner Enright is dishonest," Judge Crain said.

Judge Crain, at the same time, denounced vigorously the grafting, inefficiency and untruthfulness on the part of the police which the evidence was held to have disclosed. The force, as a whole, he declared, "has been inefficient in connection with the Mullan-Gage law," and "a considerable number" in it have made the law the occasion for "theft and extortion."

Immunity Plea Fails.

"Very probably," he said "he (the Commissioner) knew much more about it than has been disclosed upon this inquiry. But to 'know' in a popular sense of the existence of unworthiness, corruption, dishonesty and graft in the force is one thing, and to be able to prove it by legal evidence as to sustain dismissals against legal proceedings for reinstatement is quite another."

The plea of Assemblyman Cuvillier that as a legislator immunity was granted by the State Constitution from libel action by Commissioner Enright, was held by Judge Crain to be without merit. Neither was the contention that the crime, if any, was in Albany County, where the telegram was filed, a sound one, the Judge decided. Mr. Cuvillier was held in $500 bail, which he furnished. Assistant District Attorney Ferdinand Pecora said that the case would be taken to the Grand Jury as soon as possible.

The Assemblyman in a statement declared that the decision "will give all the more incentive to begin on Jan 1, when the new Legislature convenes, my fight to rip wide open politically the City of New York."

The dismissal of the charge against Magistrate Corrigan was on the ground that the evidence showed that so far as he was concerned the telegram was published "unintentionally" and "inadvertently." The Magistrate's testimony had been to the effect that when he realized the full import of the reference to Commissioner Enright he had taken steps to prevent its publication. While his defenses of justification and excuse tended to throw doubt upon the plea of inadvertence, Judge Crain said, the doubt had been dispelled by careful weighing of the evidence. He chided the Magistrate for his utterances on police conditions, which, he said, "were spoken on commendable impulse but without deliberation."

Refers to Police Testimony.

The chief points in Judge Crain's findings with regard to general conditions in the Police Department were these:

The testimony given by members of the force "is often regrettably inaccurate and unreliable," and sometimes "appears to be designedly false."

"The testimony of most officers examined in this proceeding was neither clear nor frank. They seemingly sought to thwart the purpose of the inquiry. The testimony of some of them appeared to be purposely untrue.

"It is deducible from the testimony that the force as a whole has been inefficient in connection with the enforcement of the Mullan-Gage law; that some in it were themselves violators of that law and that the existence of the law was made by a considerable number of the force the occasion for theft and extortion."

"Aware of the unpopularity with many of the Mullan-Gage law some laxity on the part of the police in enforcing it, repugnant to many, was perhaps to be looked for, but laxity with reluctance to enforce an unpopular law is one thing and open, unashamed connivance at its breach and participation in the profits accruing from its violation another.

"The bootlegger must not be the patrolman's intimate. He must not be the captain's entertainer. He must not be the inspector's backer and banker.

"Entrenched behind the false code of so-called loyalty and honor which seal the lips of many honest men on the force and deters such from disclosing what they know of graft, and protected by the timidity of their victims, who are themselves wrongdoers, the corruptionists of the force despise public opinion and defy

Continued on Page Eight.

Saves $25,000 From Bandits By Throwing Money on Engine

DETROIT, Mich., Nov. 9.—Quick thinking by the driver of a Ford Motor Company pay-car today saved a bag containing $25,000 when four armed bandits tried to hold him up. As the bandits intercepted the car the driver leaped from the machine and placed the bag on a passing locomotive of the Detroit, Toledo & Ironton Railroad, Ford's own railroad.

The pay-car was on the way from the River Rouge plant to a construction camp at Flat Rock when the bandits intercepted it. They disappeared after the bag was tossed onto the locomotive.

LLOYD GEORGE HOME, GETS GREAT OVATION

Crush of Thousands in London, Hailing Him as Victor, Follows Southampton Uproar.

HE CHAMPIONS FREE TRADE

Attacks Baldwin's Proposals Vigorously—Paints Vision of Anglo-American Co-operation.

Special Cable to THE NEW YORK TIMES.

LONDON, Nov. 9.—An extraordinary welcome was accorded to David Lloyd George tonight on his arrival, with Dame Margaret and Miss Megan, at Waterloo Station.

Southampton had done its best to greet him as he stepped off the White Star liner Majestic. It had given him its freedom and received in return a speech full of enthusiasm for all he had seen in his American and Canadian tour and of hopes of what the United States and Great Britain might accomplish working together for freedom, justice and, above all, fair play.

But the friendliness of the seaport borough was nothing compared to the wild enthusiasm for the ex-Premier shown by the London crowd. It was frankly political. In an interview Mr. Lloyd George had given at Southampton he had come out flat-footedly for free trade. He stood, he declared, by his April speech at Manchester, in which he had said: "If there is going to be a fight about free trade, let us clear the decks; let us get rid of the McKenna tariff, Paris resolutions and Safeguarding of Industries act."

He had also hinted at a reunion of the Liberal Party, and implied his willingness to serve under Mr. Asquith if necessary, and so he was received not only as one who, in the belief of his admirers, had achieved wonders by his American tour, but as one of the chief leaders in a great political fight which is just beginning.

A more or less formal welcome was to have been tendered to the ex-Premier at Waterloo. It was to come from both his political supporters and representatives of the free churches, and was to be enlivened by Welsh songs by Welsh choirs. The railway company had prepared for the demonstration by shutting off taxicabs from the station, putting up trophies and flags and arranging to run the train in at the most commodious platform.

Crowd Takes Full Charge.

The stage, in fact, was set, but the crowd took charge. The choir, indeed, sang and made its harmonious ring above the cheers and shouts, but that was all of the set program which was carried dout.

As soon as Mr. Lloyd George alighted the police summed up the situation and saw that they must get him away from his admirers as quickly as possible. They surrounded him and fought their way down the platform to an automobile awaiting him. It was adorned with flags, flowers and a bunch of Welsh leeks, and had a large laurel wreath in front with the words "Well done."

The police got the ex-Premier's party into the car and told the chauffeur to start. He tried, and gave up. The crowd was all around him. It was shouting and cheering, and singing "For He's a Jolly Good Fellow." It was yelling for a speech and pressing forward to shake Mr. Lloyd George's hand. The chauffeur simply dared not move.

At last Mr. Lloyd George rose, and removing his hat, said a few words.

"I only want to thank you from the bottom of my heart," he said, "for your kindness. I have had a very remarkable trip in Canada and America. I have experienced kindness beyond expression, but one is always glad to see one's own people again."

Then the police cleared the people back an the automobile started, very slowly.

Continued on Page Three.

MRS. STOKES WINS AGAINST HUSBAND'S 5-YEAR DIVORCE SUIT

Jury in 65 Minutes and on One Vote Absolves Her of Misconduct.

SHE WILL SUE IMMEDIATELY

Is Now Receiving $18,000 a Year From Stokes as Separation Allowance.

TEARFULLY THANKS JURORS

Stokes, Apparently Unmoved, Walks From Room While Wife Is Being Congratulated.

After deliberating an hour and five minutes, and taking a single ballot, a Supreme Court jury decided yesterday afternoon that the charges made by W. E. D. Stokes against his wife had not been sustained, and that he was not entitled to the divorce for which he has been fighting for five years.

The jury had filed out when Justice Mahoney, at the conclusion of Max D. Steuer's summing up for Stokes, finished his charge at 4 o'clock. The lights in the surrounding buildings and in the courtroom had been turned on when, at 5 o clock, an attendant announced the arrival of Justice Mahoney.

"A verdict," was the word that swept through the room. Mrs. Stanley Richter, daughter of Samuel Untermyer, Mrs. Stokes's counsel, stopped chatting with Mrs. Stokes, and Mr. Untermyer took a seat beside his client. The room was quite still as the jurors filed in. Court Clerk George F. Lyon called the roll. The points at issue were framed in sixteen questions involving Mrs. Stokes and several corespondents.

Jury Voted "No" on All.

"Gentlemen of the jury," asked Clerk Lyon, "have you agreed upon a verdict?"

"Yes," replied Foreman Harry U. Hitchcock, an engineer, about 60 years old. "We vote 'No' on all of them."

Fifteen of the sixteen questions in the framed issues charged Mrs. Stokes with misconduct with Hal Billig, a cousin; Roland Miller, her half-brother; George Schroeder, S. Montgomery Roosevelt and Will H. Myer. Since no testimony was adduced concerning any of these men, Justice Mahoney directed the jury to eliminate them from its consideration and answer "No" to the charges.

The only question left for the jury to declare a verdict upon, and on which they voted "No," was interrogatory No. 9 which was:

"Did the defendant, Helen Elwood Stokes, commit adultery with one Edgar T. Wallace in or about the months of April, May and December, 1914; April, 1916; November, 1917, and January, February and March, 1918, at the premises 13 East Thirty-fifth Street, in the Borough of Manhattan, City of New York, State of New York?"

Mrs. Stokes Tearfully Happy.

Mrs. Stokes, joyful to the point of tears, was congratulated by her mother, by Mr. Untermyer and his daughter, and then she walked over and thanked each juror with a handshake. Stokes displayed no visible emotion, and after his negro valet had helped him on with his coat he walked out of the courtroom.

Mr. Steuer completed his summing-up at 3:15, having spoken for six hours, the same length of time as occupied by Mr. Untermyer, who protested frequently that Mr. Steuer's argument was not based solely upon the evidence.

"Mrs. Stokes," said Mr. Steuer, "was a fine witness. She is more astute, more calculating than any witness I have ever seen. Minutes before I had formed a question she knew the answer. She was always stepping in front of me. I had no chance with her and freely admit it. She couldn't be cross-examined."

Regarding the denial of the corespondent, Edgar T. Wallace, of any intimacy with Mrs. Stokes, Mr. Steuer said

"If Wallace admitted it, you wouldn't believe him. Who would expect a skunk like that, a man who induced a married woman to come to his apartment, renewing an old flame, luring her away from her elderly husband—who would expect a skunk like that to go on the witness stand and admit it and expect to be believed, as he tells you he would have done?"

Says Munchausen Was Outclassed.

"And that story about the ring. Why, Munchausen was beaten by hundreds of miles by the one who made up that story. Would you believe such gibberish as that? Since when do men as childish pranks loan to women of that age dia-

Continued on Page Three.

Bank Books Found Ten Years After Death Add $15,588 to Fortune of Brooklyn Family

How the family of James Hughes, a Brooklyn merchant, who died on Feb. 5, 1913, came into an unexpected additional fortune of $15,588 from his estate, which had been distributed long ago to his heirs, was described in a report submitted yesterday to the Brooklyn Surrogate's Court. The money is represented by six bank books, which were put aside by Hughes several months before his death and had remained concealed and untouched for more than ten years.

Two of his daughters, Mrs. Mary A. Bryne and Sarah J. Hughes of 958 Bedford Avenue, had recalled that their father had mentioned a trust fund for his wife and children, but his will made no mention of it and a search for additional property had failed to reveal anything more when the estate was distributed.

A few days ago Mrs. Bryne and her sister Sarah were having Hughes's former store cleared and a man removing the stuff dropped a bundle of papers. He was about to throw it out when the sisters interposed. They opened it and within the core of other papers they found six bank books, showing deposits in the South Brooklyn Savings Bank, which had been accumulating interest all these years. The name of Mrs. Catherine Hughes, the widow, appeared on one of the books, and the names of five children on the others. The accounts had been opened by Hughes when his sons and daughters were children.

Alexander Campbell, attorney for the family, told the Court yesterday that Mrs. Bryne and Sarah Hughes had told him of finding the books and had informed him that their father had mentioned a trust some time in 1912, when he showed books to them bearing their names. The girls supposed the trust had been cancelled.

According to the trust books the money will be distributed as follows: To Mrs. Catherine Hughes, the widow, $1,119; Mrs. Bryne, $1,048; Sarah J. Hughes, $3,373; Annie E. Hughes, $3,132; George L. Hughes, $3,314; Catherine R. Hughes, $3,287, and $314 to James F. Hughes.

DEADLOCK ON PARIS TERMS

Coolidge Declares Inquiry Would Be Restricted to an Audit.

HUGHES CALLS PLAN FUTILE

President Sees Help on Reparations Blocked, but the Door Is Still Open.

POINCARE DEFENDS STAND

Declares That Only Parliament Can Cut Down French Claims on Germany.

Special to The New York Times.

WASHINGTON, Nov. 9.—The American Government has decided that it cannot favor or participate in any expert inquiry on the capacity of Germany to pay reparations if the scope of the investigation is to be limited as proposed by the French Government. The stumbling block in the diplomatic conversations between Secretary Hughes and Premier Poincaré is the rigid insistence of the latter that the scope of the inquiry be limited to an examination into Germany's "present" capacity to pay during the next six years.

M. Poincaré fixed 1930 as the deadline beyond which the experts should not go in determining what Germany can pay, and in the formulation of a financial plan for making such payments. In announcing the failure of the Franco-American negotiations, Secretary Hughes late this afternoon declared the official opinion of the American Government to be that it would be useless and futile to undertake the suggested inquiry along any such limited lines as are insisted upon by the French Government.

In the opinion of the American Government it was, and still is, imperative that some sound financial plan for German reparation payments be formulated and adopted by the powers to prevent financial and economic disaster in Europe. It was because of such a need that this Government considered it desirable there should be an expert inquiry for the purpose of ascertaining the capacity of Germany to pay and recommending to the Reparation Commission a practical plan of payment.

The whole idea of the American Government, it was officially said at the State Department today, was that the proposed expert inquiry should have latitude sufficient to enable the establishment of some sound basis for economic recuperation in Europe.

Hold That Aim Is Frustrated.

Any attempt to establish the year 1930 as the limit beyond which the experts should not inquire is believed by President Coolidge, Secretary Hughes and members of the Cabinet to be an absolute frustration of the kind of inquiry demanded by the situation. It was officially stated both at the White House and the State Department that the narrowed scope of the inquiry as favored by France could lead to no practical result, and therefore it would be useless to undertake it.

No written statement was issued by the State Department, but an informal oral announcement of the Government's decision was authorized by Secretary Hughes at 5 o'clock in the afternoon, after Ambassador Jusserand had delivered to him the final word of the French Government. M. Jusserand called after receiving a long cablegram from Premier Poincaré, in which it was made plain that France insisted upon its decision to have the inquiry limited to investigation of Germany's capacity to pay up to 1930.

President Coolidge an hour earlier had authorized the statement, through his official spokesman at the White House, that if the inquiry were to be limited to consideration of "present" German capacity to pay, or to German capacity up to 1930, it would be, in this Government's judgment, "wholly futile and useless" to hold the inquiry.

Coolidge Wants More Than Audit.

This was not the only limitation suggested by the French Premier that was unsatisfactory to the United States, but it alone was sufficient to defeat the project. Both at the White House and the State Department, it was pointed out that the greater part of the six-year period, in any event, would be absorbed in the moratorium which economic authorities admit must be granted to Germany. The White House spokesman stated that if the experts could not deal with the situation beyond 1930 their rôle would be reduced to that of mere auditors, instead of the kind of competent financial experts whom the United States Government has had in mind.

President Coolidge, it was added, did not perceive, after most careful conference and consideration of the whole subject, how the United States could be of real help through participating in so limited an inquiry. The work of mere auditors, it was stated, could not go far enough to enable them, under such restrictions, to propose an adequate financial plan.

Great disappointment is felt by the American Government over the refusal of France to favor an inquiry of broad latitude. As to the next step in the situa-

Continued on Page Two.

London Looks for Pressure On France to Pay Debts

LONDON, Nov. 9 (Associated Press).—Tonight's news from Washington of the failure of the negotiations for a reparation conference will hardly come as a surprise to British official quarters.

The general view is that the next step may be a formal request by the American and British Governments for the payment of the war debts owed them by France as a means of bringing economic pressure, and so inducing France to adopt a more moderate policy.

TITUS DE BOBULA JAILED IN BUDAPEST

Husband of Mrs. C. M. Schwab's Niece Arrested for Plot to Overthrow Government.

SAID TO BE FORD EMPLOYE

Arrest of Ulain Reveals Hitler's Plan for Coups in Germany, Hungary and Austria.

Special Cable to THE NEW YORK TIMES.

VIENNA, Nov. 9.—Titus de Bobula, an American, has been arrested in Budapest on the charge of complicity in the conspiracy headed by Deputy Ulain of the National Assembly to overthrow the Hungarian Government.

The Arbeiter Zeitung says de Bobula is the son-in-law of Charles M. Schwab and an employe of Henry Ford, and that he has been using Ford funds to finance the conspiracy. [De Bobula is not Mr. Schwab's son-in-law. He married a niece of Mrs. Schwab.]

The American Legation in Budapest is taking steps to obtain the release of de Bobula.

Besides Ulain and de Bobula sixteen Hungarians and five emissaries of Hitler have been arrested.

VIENNA, Nov. 9.—The attempted Ludendorff-Hitler coup in Bavaria has brought to light a vast Fascista plot for coups d'état in Austria and Hungary, and perhaps Turkey and Bulgaria.

Several weeks ago Chancellor Seipel of Austria sent troops to the Bavarian border to prevent Bavarian and Austrian National Socialist troops under Hitler from effecting a union to overthrow the Austrian Government. Hitler was formerly an Austrian officer.

Then a Fascista plot was discovered in Budapest. Police seized papers on one Ulain, a radical Nationalist Deputy, while he was on a train en route to Munich. These papers showed that he was working with Ludendorff and Hitler and that a treaty of alliance had been concluded between Bavarian and Hungarian reactionaries. With Bavarian aid a Hungarian military dictatorship was to have been set up.

Count Bethlen, Premier of Hungary, ordered the arrest of several Nationalist leaders and also of seventy Bavarians who had recently arrived in Hungary under the pretense of working for a brewer. The overthrow of the Hungarian Government was planned to take place at the end of November.

The detection of the plot by the Austrian and Hungarian officials prevented the spread of the conspiracy, but it is believed that Hajas and Pronax, the real chiefs of the Hungarian irregulars, are still at liberty because of their influence.

It is stated that several Italian Fascisti are implicated in the Bavarian-Hungarian move. Hitler is said to have obtained certain Italians because he agreed to the co-operation of demand that southern Tyrol remain Italian property.

BUDAPEST, Nov. 9 (Associated Press).—Among others arrested in connection with the Ulain conspiracy is Deputy Homonnay, an intimate of Ulain.

The putsch in Hungary was planned for the end of November, when, it was supposed by those in the conspiracy, Hitler would control all of Germany and be in a position to send 5,000 troops. Among the papers found on the prisoners, according to the police, is a list of political leaders to be executed in case of success. The first name on the list was that of Count Albert Apponyi.

VIENNA, Nov. 9 (Associated Press).—The Bavarian coup has profoundly disturbed all elements in Austria. While it is too early to obtain an expression of the official attitude, the newspapers unanimously term the movement "fool-

Continued on Page Two.

All American Vessels Must Remain 'Dry'; Coolidge Won't Lift Ban, Despite Treaties

Special to The New York Times.

WASHINGTON, Nov. 9.—President Coolidge authorized the statement today that there would be no change in relation to the prohibition against American ships carrying liquor within or outside of the three-mile limit, regardless of any treaty that might be made with Great Britain or other countries.

The Presidential spokesman stated that Mr. Coolidge did not intend to change the Harding order, which barred the carrying of liquor on American flag vessels outside of the three-mile limit. As to the carrying of liquor within the three-mile limit, that was prohibited under the Supreme Court decision.

It has been indicated that if Great Britain entered into a treaty with the United States which permits the search of vessels of British registry anywhere within a twelve-mile limit, concessions would be made whereby British lines would receive the privilege of carrying liquor in bond, including rations for the crews, into American ports.

Leaders of Revolt Disappear After Capture; Bavarian Premier Still a Prisoner of Hitlerites

MUNICH, Nov. 9 (Associated Press)—The whereabouts of General Ludendorff and Adolph Hitler was a mystery tonight. Neither Dr. von Kahr, the Military Dictator, nor General von Lossow, Commander of the Bavarian Reichswehr, has given any indication of his intentions toward the captured General and his Fascist prompter.

In official quarters here it is declared both men gave Dr. von Kahr and General von Lossow and other Bavarian officials unequivocal assurances of loyalty and promised that they would not attempt a coup or embark upon any political adventure without duly apprising official quarters.

LONDON, Nov. 9.—A dispatch to The Daily Mail from Berlin says martial law has been proclaimed throughout Bavaria and that any death sentences pronounced by court-martial are to be executed within three hours.

The dispatch adds that, according to a communication from Munich, Adolph Hitler escaped and is believed to be at Rosenheim, near the Austrian frontier, trying to rally his followers.

A dispatch to the Central News from Paris says a dispatch received in the French capital from Munich declares that Adolph Hitler was seriously wounded in the Reichswehr attack.

BERLIN, Nov. 9 (Associated Press).—The followers of Adolph Hitler are still holding Premier von Knilling of Bavaria, who was placed under arrest by them during Thursday night's coup.

FAILURE OF REVOLT HALTS PARIS PLANS

Report Got Abroad That Poincare Was About to Call Out More French Troops.

ARMS CONTROL IS PRESSED

German Nationalist Dangers Expected to Bring the British and French Closer Together.

By EDWIN L. JAMES.

Special Cable to THE NEW YORK TIMES.

PARIS, Nov. 9.—At 5 o'clock this morning Premier Poincaré was busy on the German situation. After having read all reports available he sent messengers to the Allied Ambassadors in Paris asking them to get instructions from their Governments preparatory to a meeting of the Conference of Ambassadors at 5 o'clock this afternoon to discuss measures to be taken. However, the afternoon brought so many conflicting reports as to just what had happened in Bavaria and then the official announcement from Germany that the Ludendorf-Hitler putsch had failed, that the meeting was adjourned until tomorrow.

M. Poincaré had prepared for the adoption by the Allied Governments of his note sent to Berlin yesterday saying France would not tolerate the establishment of a military dictatorship in Berlin, the program of whose authors was repudiation of the Treaty of Versailles.

Previous to the receipt of late news from Berlin M. Poincaré had summoned to the Quai d'Orsay the Minister of War and the Minister of the Interior, which gave rise to a report he was preparing to call up one or more French classes for military action in case Ludendorff, regarded here as the agent of the former Crown Prince, should gain control of Germany.

Regardless of the immediate fate of the Ludendorff attempt, it is probable that the recrudescence of the strength of the German Nationalists opposed to execution of the treaty will have an effect, especially since the dropping of the experts' inquiry.

The ultimatum period for German acceptance of the allied demand for resumption of military control expires tomorrow, and there is every evidence that England is deeply interested in this situation. For, although England has got out of the peace settlement most of the material advantages coming to her, after all, England has more at stake in the Treaty of Versailles than that. All Englishmen bear in mind the danger they saw before the war in the building of a great German war fleet, and at the Peace Conference the first and foremost British claim was annihilation of the German fleet and imposition of restrictions against her building another. Were the anti-treaty leaders to gain control in Germany, could England, by use of her fleet alone, prevent the prolific German shipyards from building fighting craft? Perhaps for the English as well as for the French the chief prospect for forcing Germany to fulfill the treaty, either in the clauses especially interesting to France or clauses especially interesting to England, lies

Continued on Page Two.

BERLIN ROYALISTS UPSET BY FIASCO

Bavarian Putsch Calls a Halt on Plans to Form a New Coalition Government.

FRENCH WARNING RESENTED

Poincare's Message Is Regarded as "Unwarranted Intervention" in German Affairs.

BERLIN, Nov. 7 (Associated Press).—The Nationalist leaders in the Reichstag make no concealment of their chagrin over the fiasco of the Hitler "putsch" in Bavaria, which they obviously view as having done irreparable damage to the swing to the Right among a large body of the voters. Incidentally the movement has seriously handicapped the negotiations proceeding between the members of the Nationalist Party and the German People's Party for the formation of a bourgeois Cabinet, a movement which had received fresh impetus today when Chancellor Stresemann's party adopted a resolution to suggest to the Chancellor the advisability of inviting the Nationalists into such a coalition.

With the Munich débâcle awaiting final political liquidation, the belief is expressed in political circles that the Nationalists in the present situation suggest a heavy liability to such a four-party constellation, which, were it formed, in all probability would demand the retirement of Dr. Stresemann. Neither the Chancellor, the Democrats nor the Clericals thus far have indicated their attitude toward the proposed bourgeois Cabinet.

Nationalists Blame Stresemann.

The leaders of the Nationalist Party have issued a communiqué throwing all responsibility for recent events in Germany upon the Reich Government. It declares that the immediate creation of a government inspiring national confidence is the most urgent duty at the present time.

The German People's Party brands the insurrection as a "criminal coup d'état" in that it is the gravest menace to national unity, co-ordination of economic conditions and efforts to salvage the complicated situation in the Ruhr and Rhineland.

Vorwärts reproaches the Government for its tolerance of Bavarian flouting of the Central Government. It asserts that if Chancellor Stresemann had diverted some of the energy he directed toward Saxony to Bavaria, the Munich putsch would have been impossible.

The Socialist organ charges that Nationalistic circles in Berlin possessed knowledge of the coming insurrection, "in that the conspicuous demand that Stresemann retire oddly enough synchronized with Munich events."

Reply to French Ambassador.

M. de Margerie, the French Ambassador, visited Chancellor Stresemann this afternoon and informed him that, while the French Government did not desire to intervene in Germany's internal affairs, it felt anxiety over the present events.

The Chancellor replied that he shared the views of the French Government with regard to the necessity of a democratic and constitutional Government, being himself a constitutional Chancellor.

Chancellor Stresemann's Government today informally apprised the diplomatic missions in Berlin that its authority had not been impaired by the putsch and that the Munich episode was considered as having been disposed of, in so far as it threatened to become a menace to the Berlin Government's stability.

French opposition to the establishment of a limited directorate, or even a dictatorship, which Premier Poincaré is said to have expressed informally through the French Ambassador, is viewed in semi-official circles here as unwarranted intervention in German internal affairs.

"Admonition from the French Government, or support from that source, is not required by Germany in connection with her efforts to adjust internal affairs, and it may even be suggested that support from this source would rather discredit the cause of democracy," says the National Zeitung.

BRIEF BATTLE ENDS REVOLT

Army Storms Building Held by Rebels, Who Quickly Give Up.

KAHR IS AGAIN IN CONTROL

Dictator and Lossow Pretend to Yield, Then Suppress 'Beer Hall Revolution.'

BERLIN GREATLY RELIEVED

Word Came at Dawn Bavarian Officials Would Put Down the Outbreak.

By CYRIL BROWN.

By Wireless to THE NEW YORK TIMES.

BERLIN, Nov. 9.—The loyal Reichswehr, commanded by the disloyal General von Lossow, today stormed the Bavarian War Ministry Building wherein Hitler, Ludendorff and their followers had entrenched and fortified themselves. There were small losses on both sides. Hitler and Ludendorff were captured. According to one report, Hitler made his escape, but another report says that the whereabouts of both Ludendorff and Hitler is unknown.

After no great defensive fight, the two leaders are down and out and thoroughly discredited, even if they should get light sentences in treason trials.

So far as Berlin is concerned, the Ludendorff-Hitler putsch was all over this morning with no shouting. The Bürgerbrau coup d'état was the craziest farce pulled off in memory, making the Kapp putsch look like a gilt-edged revolution.

As reported, the Berlin Government was taken completely by surprise and thoroughly alarmed, spent much paper money printing proclamations to the people. The important practical measure, however, was to make General von Seeckt Dictator with cart blanche order to clean up rebellious Bavaria, or rather the rebellious outsiders, Hitler, Ludendorff and their followers.

The Stresemann Government and President Ebert spent the early morning hours in anguish until at 5 this morning there arrived a radio message from the Chief Burgomaster of Nürnberg, who happens to be a Socialist, reading:

"Herr von Kahr, General Lossow and Colonel Seiffert have declared that their agreement with the action of Hitler and Ludendorff was extorted from them under duress and that they repudiate this movement in every form, shape and manner. These gentlemen hope in the course of today to master this putsch. If Reischwehr troops should enter Munich these facts will be communicated to them *for their information.*"

Von Kahr and Lossow Act Quickly.

At the same time General von Lossow sent a wireless to the North Bavarian troops to the same effect. Dr. von Kahr further sent out an order to all Bavarian officialdom, particularly to officials controlling the border, first, to arrest on sight all members of Hitler's national Socialist organization and all members of the Oberland League; secondly, to look for and arrest on sight both Hitler and Ludendorff "wherever met."

On receiving this wireless from Nürnberg the Stresemann Government not only breathed easier but sent out a circular message to all foreign embassies and ministries in Berlin that the Munich putsch was squelched. These messages were delivered about 6 o'clock when the American and other foreign Ambassadors, Ministers and minor diplomats were still sleeping. And whereas up to this magic hour, when Stresemann got the wireless flash of not only no danger but a victory, the heart of Berlin was cordoned by heavily armed Green police, ruthlessly throttling all motor traffic as being suspicious, immediately thereafter the police reserves went home and have not been seen all day. Berlin was quiet all night and all day. There was not even a vestige of demonstration, disorders or plunderings.

There are deeper political results of the amateurish and abortive putsch in Munich, however. It clears the air and definitely eliminates Hitler and his national Socialist followers as well as Ludendorff. At the same time this coup strengthens the real reactionaries of Bavaria, which is overwhelmingly Catholic and monarchistic, and loyal to Crown Prince Rupprecht, who shrewdly has kept himself in the background. By the bulk of Bavarians Ludendorff and Hitler were considered interlopers, outsiders and non-Bavarians, which they were. Now that Hitler and Ludendorff are removed, the real show has a chance of starting on clean lines. Munich is reported all quiet tonight.

Steps Taken to Suppress Putsch.

By Wireless to THE NEW YORK TIMES.

COBURG, Nov. 9.—According to official news received here from Munich, von Kahr, Lossow and Seiffert withdrew their consent to the putsch which had been exacted from them at a meeting at Munich immediately afterward and having established headquarters at the Reichswehr Barracks at once proceeded with the organization of the suppression of the Hitler putsch with, as seems now, complete success.

They immediately issued the following

Section 1

"All the News That's Fit to Print."

The New York Times.

THE WEATHER
Fair and cold today; tomorrow, fair and warmer; northwest winds.
Temperature yesterday—Max., 28; Min., 7.
For weather report see page 7, Part II.

Section 1

VOL. LXXIII....No. 24,109. **** NEW YORK, SUNDAY, JANUARY 27, 1924. Including Rotogravure Picture Section in two parts—Magazine and Book Sections in Rotogravure. FIVE CENTS In Manhattan, Bronx and Brooklyn | Elsewhere TEN CENTS

COOLIDGE, IN MIDNIGHT STATEMENT, TAKES UP OIL SCANDAL; PROMISES FACTS WILL BE REVEALED AND GUILT PUNISHED; SPECIAL COUNSEL FROM BOTH PARTIES TO BRING OUT TRUTH

JAPAN'S REGENT WED WITH SHINTO RITES; ALL TOKIO REJOICES

Hirohito and the Princess Nagako Announce Their Nuptials to Spirits of Ancestors.

NO FOREIGNERS ADMITTED

Millions Throng Streets, Cheering Bridal Pair—Public Celebrations Are Deferred.

BRIDE IN MARVELOUS GOWN

Kimonos of Silk Are Richly Embroidered—Prince Attired as a Japanese Gentleman.

TOKIO, Jan. 26 (Associated Press).—In the sacred precincts of the imperial palace, and in accordance with an ancient marriage ritual antedating the Christian era, Prince Regent Hirohito was married this morning to Princess Nagako, eldest daughter of Prince Kuni.

Residents of Tokio indulged in joyous celebration of the event, the first public expression of joy since the disaster of last September. Great crowds gathered in the streets, which were gayly decorated for the occasion, and thronged the open spaces in the vicinity of the palace for a glimpse of the royal couple.

The wedding was celebrated with Shinto rites, and comprised an announcement of the event to the imperial spirits which are enshrined in the Kashiki-Dokoro, or Holy of Holies, in front of which the pair took their vows. The spirits of 122 royal predecessors witnessed the union and gave their blessings, according to devout Japanese belief. The royal couple exchanged bowls of sacred rice wine to plight their troth, after the ancient custom.

Previously, as in the case of accession to the throne, the party, including members of the royal family and officials of the household, assembled and for two hours went through a slow movement toward the shrine, every step in which, including the sounding of the clappers, was according to the imperial wedding law.

No foreigners witnessed the ceremony, only the members of the royal family and the highest dignitaries of the empire being permitted to attend the rites.

The garb of the regent was the simple dress suit of a Japanese gentleman for such occasions, except that the upper cloak was red with a shade of yellow running through it, the patterns embroidered on it representing mandarin ducks. The Hakama, or loose trousers, were of white silk with patterns of butterflies, while the obi, or belt, was of black leather decorated with carved stones.

Bride's Costume Elaborate.

The bride's costume was far more elaborate. The chief garment, or Karaginu, was a dazzling kimono of scarlet and purple silk, with the chrysanthemum crest in white embroidered on it. The mo, or skirt, was another piece of artistic weaving, being of white silk handsomely embroidered. The uwagi, or outer dress, was of purple silk decorated with designs of pine trees and tortoises, symbols of long life. A long robe, known to Japan as the uchiginu, and the itsutsuginu, or fifth dress, were of rich silk handsomely embroidered.

In the case of the Prince the hakama, which formed a train, were of purple silk.

The bride carried a fan of gilded wood on which appeared paintings of flowers of all colors. The fan was so carried that the bride might give and receive with it, as it is not permitted to touch sacred things with one's own hands.

Accompanying the Regent were the sceptre and crown. The shrine itself was decorated with offerings of fruit and chrysanthemums.

The ceremony was comparatively simple, being comparable to a civil wedding in Christian countries, according to Japanese students. The official public celebration had been postponed until later in the year owing to the country's mourning. The public ceremonial will include a great banquet attended by court officials and diplomats.

The object of the banquet will be to make official announcement to the people and to foreign powers of the fact that the heir to the throne has been married.

Tremendous crowds greeted the Prince and his bride as they passed to and from the palace before and after the ceremony. Flags were flown from many buildings, even the refugee barracks in the public parks being gaily decorated. Many of the spectators climbed upon great piles of debris left by the earthquake and fire in September to catch sight of the wedding procession.

Elaborate precautions were taken to guard against any untoward incident. Ten thousand police and soldiers lined the routes taken by the bride and bridegroom, who approached the palace by separate thoroughfares. The crowds

Continued on Page Six.

Sofia Blames Neuilly Treaty For Ravages of Wolves

Copyright, 1924, by The New York Times Co. Special Cable to THE NEW YORK TIMES.

PARIS, Jan. 26.—Bulgaria is suffering more heavily this Winter than ever before from ravages of wolf packs and, according to Sofia dispatches, she is blaming her misfortune on the Treaty of Neuilly. The country always has been cursed with wolves, but heretofore at the beginning of Winter the population has made a short, quick war on the invaders, which were driven back to the mountains. The Treaty of Neuilly, however, has disarmed the Bulgarians and the people are unable to drive the wolves away. The result is that flocks in many places have been decimated and a number of peasants have been killed by packs, which now are bold enough to raid villages far from the mountains.

MINE BLAST TRAPS 45 IN PENNSYLVANIA

Rescue Work Starts Quickly but Is Hampered by Debris in Coal Workings.

FOURTEEN ESCAPE IN DAZE

Group Seeking Entombed Men Are Overcome—Hope of Saving Victims Small.

Special to The New York Times.

INDIANA, Pa., Jan. 26.—Rescue crews are working feverishly tonight to reach forty-five coal miners who were trapped in Mine 8 of the Barnes & Tucker Co. at Shanktown, fifteen miles northeast of this place, by a gas explosion this afternoon at 3:30 o'clock.

The day shift had just completed its labors for the week and was preparing to leave the workings when a terrific explosion occurred, bringing tons of débris crashing to the floor and blocking all but one of the headings.

Fourteen men made their escape, but the others were cut off. From present indications the rescue teams will not have worked their way through the débris until midnight or later, and the fear is that the forty-five are dead or will be suffocated by the deadly afterdamp or drowned by the rising water before they are reached.

Mine 8 is worked chiefly by aliens and there is a marked absence of the usual hysteria attending such tragedies. The situation is made all the more dramatic by the stoic calmness of the women and the occasional whimpering of children.

Efficient rescue teams, working in short relays, are proceeding to their work with the precision gained by their class instruction and are making steady headway into the headings where the missing workers are.

The explosion this afternoon is believed to have completely wrecked the operation. The detonation was audible over a wide area. The rumbling, which died away as suddenly as it came, left a stillness which was broken by screams from the women who instinctively knew the always feared tragedy had come.

The mine rescue teams were quickly on the job and word was sent to surrounding towns for assistance and to mine inspectors. Within ten minutes the first relief crew had entered the mine and began to attack the barrier of débris.

Soon afterward fourteen men, pallid beneath their grime and with wild eyes, emerged from the only heading that was open. They expressed the belief that their fellow-workers had been killed.

Risking their lives in an attempt to rescue some of their companions, three miners who were standing at the

Continued on Page Seventeen.

$81,000 IN STOLEN SCHOELLKOPF GEMS FOUND IN DENVER

Jeweler Who Bought $300,000 Loot for $10,000 Leads Way, Though Near Death.

HIS PARTNER A SUICIDE

Ends Life on Same Day That Two Men Are Captured and Accused of Hold-Up.

ROBBERY DETAILS KNOWN

Trio Rented Apartment Underneath Actor's and Waylaid Woman Leaving New Year Party.

District Attorney Banton announced last evening the recovery of $81,000 worth of the $300,000 in gems stolen New Year's Eve a year ago in the hold-up of Mrs. Hugo C. P. Schoellkopf following a card party in a house in West Fifty-second Street. He also disclosed confessions by two of the three robbers which showed that they had disposed of the entire loot for less than $10,000 to an itinerant jeweler in the theatrical district within twelve hours of the crime.

The prosecutor also revealed that Eugene Moran and Albert Hurwitch, the robbers, were the principal witnesses before the Grand Jury which returned an indictment against John W. Mahan, the alleged "fence," on Jan. 18, charging him with criminally receiving the $300,000 in gems. He added that Mahan after being nursed back to health in a hotel here, accompanied a detective and Mr. Schoellkopf's secretary to Denver, Col., where he recovered $81,000 of the gems in a sealed jar from a man with whom they had been secreted less than a week after the hold-up.

Mr. Banton told also of the suicide of Henry Hirsch, partner of Mahan, in his apartment at 1,356 Waldron Avenue, the Bronx, on Nov. 2 last, the day that Moran and Hurwitch were captured by Detective Sergeants Owens and Horan at Trenton, N. J., after a countrywide search for them. Hirsch shot himself through the head, Mr. Banton said, but it was not known whether his suicide was due to the arrest of the two robbers.

Mahan Was on Verge of Death.

Mahan, who had an office in the Loew Building at 1,550 Broadway, had gone to Miami Beach late last Summer. When the detectives surprised him in a hotel there they found that he was a victim of arterio-sclerosis and was on the verge of death with a blood pressure of 220. Mahan collapsed when the detectives revealed their identity, but after physicians and nurses had worked over him for more than twelve hours he consented to accompany the detectives back to New York.

He was not placed under arrest at the time, to avoid complications which might arise over extradition proceedings. On the train coming to New York he suffered another relapse, and on the arrival of the detectives with the man at Pennsylvania Station an ambulance was summoned and he was secretly taken to an apartment in the Biltmore Hotel.

The detectives, after conferring with District Attorney Banton and Inspector Coughlin, head of the Detective Division, called in specialists and nurses to attend Mahan, and four days later he consented to accompany the detectives to Denver. Moran and Hurwich, the robbers, were to be called to trial before Justice Tompkins in the Criminal Branch of the Supreme Court on the day following the announcement of Mahan's arrival here.

When they were taken into court for

Continued on Page Fifteen.

Must Pay Collision Damages Though She Was Not in Auto

The Appellate Division of the Supreme Court in Brooklyn yesterday confirmed verdicts aggregating $30,000 awarded in suits brought against Mrs. Cora Riggi of 421 East Twenty-first Street, Brooklyn, wife of a wealthy candy manufacturer, as a result of a collision April 19, 1922, in which her automobile was involved. The plaintiffs were Mr. and Mrs. Howard C. Smith and their two children and Frank H. Trecartin, all of 136 Seventh Avenue, Brooklyn. They alleged they were thrown from the automobile with which Mrs. Riggi's car collided at Garfield Place and Eighth Avenue, Brooklyn. Mrs. Riggi was not in her machine at the time.

REPUBLICAN CHIEFS AT SEA ON SURTAXES

Concession to Democrats in House Termed 'Suicidal' Course in the Steering Committee.

NO COMPROMISE IS URGED

Party Measure With the Lowest Rate Possible Is Advocated, Despite Probable Defeat.

Special to The New York Times.

WASHINGTON, Jan. 26.—Against their will, but through a combination of circumstances, Republican members of the Ways and Means committee may yet be forced into uniting behind a tax-reduction bill with surtax rates approaching as near the Mellon plan as possible, thus abandoning any idea of compromising with the Democrats on a measure that would be sure to gain the approval of a majority of the House.

The Republican steering committee met today. Some of those present declared that it would be suicidal to try to compromise with the Democrats for the reason that any bill which would obtain Republican support in the House would have to have a surtax maximum as high as Mr. Garner's Democratic bill, and thus the Mellon bill would be turned into a Democratic plan. It would be best, they argued, to bring out a bill with as low a surtax maximum as possible, and then if it were defeated in the House, the Ways and Means members could point out that they had done all they could, and that the Democrats and insurgent Republicans were to blame for the overthrow.

Stand By Mellon's Figures.

These men would like to see a maximum surtax of 25 per cent. reported to the House, but they realize that this is highly improbable because of the mixed views of the Republicans on the Ways and Means Committee, who can hardly agree on less than 32 per cent. So the suggestion was made to make the rate as near to Mr. Mellon's 25 per cent. as could be agreed upon. There were arguments from those of other views, however, counter claims being made that about half the Republican members of the Ways and Means Committee could not conscientiously support a low rate, and that, anyway, a low rate would be smothered on the floor.

So far as could be ascertained, the Steering committee reached no agreement on policy, and will meet again next week to consider the situation again. Observers declare that it is not surprising that the committee cannot unite, when it comprises such varying elements as Representatives Graham, of Illinois, Sanders, of Indiana, Anderson, of Minnesota, Tincher, of Kansas, Darrow, of Pennsylvania, Magee, of New York, Sinnott, of Oregon, and Speaker Gillett of Massachusetts, and Representative Longworth of Ohio, ex-officio members.

There is a decided trend in the Steering Committee, however, toward making the tax reduction bill purely a Republican plan and standing on that idea, whether it is defeated or not. This view is in consonance with that of the Administration, leaders stated today.

Democrats Refuse to Recede.

Democrats today reiterated their refusal to recede from the Garner rate of a 44 per cent. maximum surtax rate, their tactics being to try to get the bill through Congress with as high a maximum as possible, thus placing before President Coolidge the responsibility of vetoing the bill. The Democrats are anxious now that the Republicans alone shall frame the bill in the committee, as they are convinced that, if a low rate measure is sent to the floor, it can be torn to pieces in the House.

The one step taken on the bill by the Ways and Means Committee today was to defer until Monday a final settlement of the community property tax. Mr. Mellon recommended that husbands and wives should not be allowed to file divided returns on property owned jointly, for the reason that the dual returns bring in far less revenue than when combined. Eight Western States allow husbands and wives to divide their returns under State laws, and so their Representatives on the committee, especially Representative Hadley of Washington, fought the proposal vigorously.

Secretary Mellon's idea was rejected

Continued on Page Fifteen.

PRESIDENT TAKES HOLD

Will Not Prejudge, but Will Act on Facts When Revealed.

NO ONE MUST BE SHIELDED

Guilt Will Be Punished, Liability Enforced, Illegal Contracts Canceled.

END OF LONG PARTY COUNCIL

Executive's Post-Midnight Utterance Takes Up Call for Action and Pledges Results.

Special to The New York Times.

WASHINGTON, Jan. 27.—President Coolidge will name special counsel representing both the Republican and the Democratic Parties to prosecute those guilty of fraud in connection with the leasing of oil lands in the Naval Reserves of Wyoming and California.

Announcement of the President's purpose was made soon after midnight this morning, when a formal statement was issued from the White House.

Pointing out that it was not for the Executive to pre-judge a case which must be passed on by the courts, Mr. Coolidge went on to declare that he would take the proper action whenever facts were revealed to him that required it.

He went on to state that he felt action was warranted on the evidence already presented before the Senate Investigating Committee.

With his understanding that men of both political parties were involved in the scandal, he then said that he purposed to select counsel of high rank from both parties to prosecute cases where it seemed there was guilt.

He added as a climax to his statement: "If there is any guilt, it will be punished; if there is any civil liability, it will be enforced; if there is any fraud, it will be revealed; and if there are any contracts which are illegal, they will be canceled. Every law will be enforced, and every right of the people and the Government will be protected."

Had Started New Inquiry.

Previous to this announcement by the President he had taken action to bring the oil scandal to a head. He had ordered Secretary Work of the Department of the Interior to submit to him expert advice as to the wisdom of the leases made by ex-Secretary Fall with the Sinclair and Doheny interests, and their validity.

Ths action, it was announced, was preliminary to the President's decison to assume full leadership of the party in the scandal casting its shadow over public officals and the Republican Administration.

That President Coolidge meant to act long before any indictment was presented to the Grand Jury became known yesterday. He had been advised by lawyers that the law had not been complied with in several respects, and that the leases with Edward L. Doheny and Harry L. Sinclair are invalid and could be annulled, irrespective of whether fraud was committed in their making. It is expected they will be annulled early next week.

Republican leaders have been confer-

Continued on Page Three.

The President's Statement

Special to The New York Times.

WASHINGTON, Sunday, Jan. 27.—The following statement was issued by President Coolidge soon after midnight this morning:

It is not for the President to determine criminal guilt or render judgment in civil causes; that is the function of the courts. It is not for him to prejudge. I shall do neither. But when the facts are revealed to me that require action for the purpose of insuring the enforcement of either civil or criminal liability, such action will be taken. That is the province of the Executive.

Acting under my direction, the Department of Justice has been observing the course of the evidence which has been revealed at the hearings conducted by the Senatorial committee investigating certain oil leases made on naval reserves, which I believe warrants action for the purpose of enforcing the law and protecting the rights of the public. This is confirmed by reports made to me from the committee.

If there has been any crime, it must be prosecuted. If there has been any property of the United States illegally transferred or leased, it must be recovered.

I feel the public is entitled to know that in the conduct of such action no one is shielded for any party, political or other reasons. As I understand, men are involved who belong to both political parties, and having been advised by the Department of Justice that it is in accord with former precedents, I propose to employ special counsel of high rank drawn from both political parties to bring such actions for the enforcement of the law. Counsel will be instructed to prosecute these cases in the courts so that if there is any guilt it will be punished; if there is any civil liability it will be enforced; if there is any fraud it will be revealed; and if there are any contracts which are illegal they will be canceled.

Every law will be enforced. And every right of the people and the Government will be protected.

NEW CONGRESS MOVE TO VOID OIL LEASES

Garrett Introduces in House Joint Resolutions Which Will Get Wide Support.

SENATE TO ACT TOMORROW

Coolidge Is Asked to Bring Suit for Cancellation, Employing Outside Legal Talent.

Special to The New York Times.

WASHINGTON, Jan. 26.—Joint resolutions declaring the Sinclair and Doheny leases of the naval oil reserves void were introduced in the House this afternoon by Representative Garrett, the Democratic leader, who requested the President in the resolutions to bring suit for the cancellation of the leases and to stop any further extraction of oil from the reserves. Mr. Garrett suggested that the President should employ legal talent outside the Department of Justice.

The resolutions were identical, one relating to the Sinclair leases of Naval Reserve No. 3, or Teapot Dome, April 7, 1922, the other dealing with the Doheny lease of Naval Reserves Nos. 1 and 2, in California, April 25 of the same year. The Sinclair lease concerned the Mammoth Oil Company, the Doheny contract, the Pan-American Petroleum and Transport Company.

The resolutions, Mr. Garrett stated,

Continued on Page Three.

HULL SAYS SCANDALS ARE CAMPAIGN ISSUE

Democratic Chairman Declares People Must Vote For or Against Corrupt Government.

CALLS FOR HOUSE CLEANING

He Asserts That Coolidge Sat in the Cabinet That Approved the Oil Leases.

Special to The New York Times.

WASHINGTON, Jan. 26.—Cordell Hull, Chairman of the Democratic National Committee, declared tonight in a statement that the Teapot Dome scandal stood out "as the greatest political scandal of this or any other generation." There have been a multiplicity of scandals in the three years of the Republican Administration he said, and these have furnished an additional issue for the coming election

"Shall the United States have corrupt government or clean government?"

The statement also attacks the President for inactivity in dealing with the Teapot Dome scandal. It states that while Vice President he sat in the Harding Cabinet while the leases were discussed and not until yesterday did he say anything about the developments in the investigation into the naval oil leases.

Chairman Hull's Statement.

Chairman Hull's statement reads:

"The multiplication of scandals under the Republican National Administration which came into power on March 4, 1921, with the Teapot Dome naval oil scandal standing out as the greatest political scandal of this or any other generation, has created an additional political issue for the 1924 campaign, which, without lessening the importance of many other sharply drawn vital issues, is of paramount importance to every voter and to every citizen regardless of political affiliations."

The issue bluntly stated is:

"Shall the United States have corrupt government or clean government?

"When this Administration came into power on March 4, 1921, it was dominated by the most reactionary element ever known in the history of a political party, which was in league with the most selfish and predacious financial and industrial special interests ever grouped together for public plunder and national exploitation. The Republican reactionary leaders construed the huge majority of 1920 as a license to use the Government for their own selfish and party ends. The predatory special interests, which own and financially support the reactionary element in the Republican Party, levied tribute upon the masses of the people as did the bandit Tarif and his followers in Spain in the eighth century, and have looted the Government of property and resources. Administration officials have even

Continued on Page Three.

ROOSEVELT RETELLS STORY

'Worried' and 'Scared,' He Says, About Payments by Sinclair to Fall.

STICKS TO FIRST VERSION

Wahlberg Contradicts Him—Checks Made Out to Zev's Trainer, He Says.

DOHENY READY TO CANCEL

Makes a Conditional Offer to Committee to Give Up the Oil Leases.

Special to The New York Times.

WASHINGTON, Jan. 26.—Before Archie Roosevelt was recalled today by the Senate committee investigating the Naval Reserve oil leases, Edward L. Doheny, through Gavin McNab, his attorney, offered to reconvey his contracts under certain conditions without awaiting any action by a board of experts.

The committee also received from G. T. Stanford, attorney for Harry F. Sinclair, a note signed by ex-Secretary Fall for $25,000 which was said to have been given for the Liberty bonds which J. W. Zevely testified yesterday had been loaned to Mr. Fall by Mr Sinclair.

Mr. Roosevelt was cross-examined first by Senator Smoot, who said "it was the universal opinion that there was nothing definite arrived at last Monday, when Mr. Roosevelt outlined for the committee the nature of his conversation with Mr. Wahlberg, and when for the first time, the $25,000 Liberty bond transactions was referred to. Mr. Stanford, of counsel for Mr. Sinclair, also took part in the cross-examination of Mr. Roosevelt, his questions being much along the same line as those asked by the Senator from Utah.

Mr. Wahlberg was also recalled today. It was quickly apparent that his memory had been greatly refreshed since his appearance last Monday. He admitted this on the stand today. He insisted that when he was before the committee on Monday he was suffering from loss of sleep, and that fact, he declared, explained why he knew so much more today than he did then.

When Mr. McNab submitted Mr. Doheny's offer to reconvey the California oil land lease the committee listened in silence and no member commented on it. The attitude of the committee remains as it was—that is, it will make its own recommendation and in its own time.

As on yesterday, the Democratic caucus room in the Senate Office Building, in which the hearings are now being held, was jammed. Word had gone out that Archie Roosevelt was to be subjected to a cross-examination to show, if possible, that the testimony he gave on Monday could not be substantiated, and that Wahlberg, with his memory refreshed, would take the stand and repudiate the statement that he had told Roosevelt that $68,000 of Sinclair's money was paid to the foreman of the Fall ranch in New Mexico.

Archie Roosevelt came in with his brother, Colonel Roosevelt, Assistant Secretary of the Navy. He was smiling when he took the stand, and was not moved in his testimony wherein he admitted several times that he was greatly "worried" and "scared" over the affair.

Mr. Wahlberg today was at one time vehement to the point of belligerency. He even repudiated the "six or eight cows" story he told on Monday in telling the story about the alleged payment to the foreman of Fall's ranch.

When Mr. Stanford, counsel for Sinclair, stepped into the proceedings the question of checks was apparently cleared up, for, as subsequent questions indicated, the alibi of Mr. Sinclair is that the checks which Mr. Wahlberg referred to in his talk with Mr. Roosevelt were two checks—one for $25,000, another for $43,000—which, it was testified, Mr. Sinclair made out to the order of Sam Hildreth, his race-horse trainer, just before Mr. Sinclair left for Europe on Jan. 16.

Mr. Wahlberg swore these were the checks he had in mind. He said they were on his desk when he talked with Mr. Roosevelt on the day Mr. Sinclair sailed. Mr. Roosevelt, on the other hand, asserted that the conversation took place on Jan. 18, two days after Mr. Sinclair quit the country, and his sworn testimony was that Mr. Wahlberg referred to "canceled" checks, and the checks which he says were on his desk, Mr. Wahlberg admitted today, had not even started on their way to Mr. Hildreth when he said he talked with Mr. Rooosevelt.

Senator Walsh read to Wahlberg parts of his previous testimony which were in contradtion of what he said today. Senator Lenroot, backing up Walsh, demanded to know why Wahlberg had not thought of the Hildreth checks when he was on the stand Monday.

Then it was that Wahlberg offered a "loss of sleep" explanation, as well as the worried condition in which he said he found himself when he came to realize that Roosevelt was going to testify about $68,000 worth of checks which, he declared, as described by Roosevelt, never existed.

It was announced tonight by Senator Lenroot that ex-Secretary Fall would not take the stand before 10 o'clock Tuesday morning. Mr. Fall is said to

Enright Keeps Secret Squads to Check Up On His Flying Vice and Liquor Battalion

When Commissioner Enright on Friday night relieved the thirteen District Inspectors of the work of suppressing vice, gambling and violations of the Volstead act throughout the city he retained two secret squads of detectives to act as a check on the plain clothes men of the reorganized Special Service Division, assigned to vice and liquor work, under Deputy Chief Inspector Samuel G. Belton.

For the six years that Enright has been Commissioner he has maintained a force of twenty "confidential" detectives in his office, under Sergeant Fred Kruse. A squad of twenty-five plain clothes men also has operated under secret orders from the office of Chief Inspector Lahey. These two squads did espionage work for Enright and Lahey when reports were received that the Inspection District plain clothes men were not as viligant in the enforcement of the laws assigned to them as they might be.

The identity of these men was kept secret from the other members of the force, and it was understood that when they became dissatisfied with conditions in a district reports which they made to the Commissioner or the Chief Inspector always led to raids over the heads of the Inspectors by the Special Service Division and the Inspectors were called "on the carpet" before the Chief Inspector.

It was said at headquarters yesterday that the two secret squads would continue to act independently of the Special Service Division, and would even increase the scope of their work until Enright and Lahey become satisfied that Deputy Chief Belton has his new organization operating in an efficient manner.

Commissioner Enright "cleared" the reorganized Special Service Division out of Police Headquarters yesterday, assigning Belton and his men to the old Elizabeth Street Station as a base of operation.

The first raid made by members of the reorganized division resulted in sixty-four men, arrested on suspicion of gambling at 304 Bowery at 5 P. M. yesterday, being discharged by Magistrate Weil in the Night Court. Two plain clothes men told the Court they were sent to the place on an order direct from Police Headquarters. They alleged that they found indications that the place was being used for betting on horse races. They admitted they hadn't seen gambling.

72-Mile Gale and Cold Wave Sweeping City; Zero Weather Is Predicted for Today

The city was swept early yesterday by a gale which brought a cold wave that continued all day.

It was the coldest Jan. 26 since 1905, according to the Weather Bureau. The temperature was 6 above zero at midnight last night and still dropping. It was said at the Weather Bureau last night that the temperature might drop to zero this morning.

So strong was the northwest gale that it smashed a plate glass window in the Pacific Bank, Seventh Avenue at Forty-ninth Street. The mishap set off a burglar alarm, bringing policemen and private detectives, who remained on guard until the window was boarded up. Reaching a velocity of seventy-two miles an hour at times, the wind rattled windows and kept many awake.

The cold wave struck New York shortly before 1 A. M. At midnight the temperature had been 28 above zero. It dropped to 25 at 1 A. M., 23 at 2 o'clock, 19 at 3 o'clock, 17 at 4 o'clock, 16 at 5 o'clock, 14 at 6 o'clock, and 13 at 7 o'clock.

After 7 A. M. the wind dropped to forty miles an hour and the sun began to warm up the city. The temperature rose at 8 o'clock to 14 degrees, where it stayed until noon, when it shot up to 17 degrees. At 1 P. M. it reached 18, the top point.

During the afternoon as the sun moved toward the horizon, the temperature fell gradually to 13 at 6 o'clock. There was a brisk gale meanwhile.

At 8 P. M. the temperature was 10 degrees, or 18 below that at midnight yesterday. It fell to 7 degrees at 10 o'clock, and continued to decrease gradually late last night and early this morning.

The Weather Bureau forecast that the cold would continue until noon today, when there would be a slight rise in temperature. "Fair and cold" was the formula announced for today. The weekly forecast for Jan. 28 to Feb. 2 was as follows:

"Fair until Wednesday or Thursday, when unsettled weather will set in, attended by snow, and possibly rain. Cold at beginning of week, rising temperature middle of week, and considerably colder at end of week."

Several other cities in the East reported much colder weather than New York. At 8 o'clock last night it was 4 below zero in Portland, Me.; zero at Buffalo, 2 above zero at Albany, 6 above at Boston and 6 above at Pittsburgh.

The coldest place in the United States yesterday was Duluth, Minn., which had a temperature of 22 below zero at 8 A. M. It was 64 above in Key West, Fla., at the same time.

Section 1

"All the News That's Fit to Print."

The New York Times.

THE WEATHER
Fair today; tomorrow, unsettled; shifting westerly winds.
Temperature yesterday—Max., 67; Min., 47.
For weather report see Page 2, Part 2.

Section 1

VOL. LXXIII....No. 24,235. * * * * NEW YORK, SUNDAY, JUNE 1, 1924. Including Rotogravure Picture Section in two parts—Magazine and Book Sections in Rotogravure. FIVE CENTS In Manhattan, Bronx and Brooklyn | Elsewhere TEN CENTS

COOLIDGE CONFERS WITH ROOT ON COURT; DEMOCRATS BACK IT

President Believed to Be Preparing to Open Fight With Senators for His Plan.

LONG WHITE HOUSE PARLEY

Ex-Secretary Praises President's Stand, but Refuses to Reveal Results.

SWANSON ANSWERS PEPPER

Report Signed by Democratic Senators Upholds Harding Scheme for American Membership.

Special to The New York Times.

WASHINGTON, May 31.—Entrance of the United States into membership in the Permanent Court of International Justice, created by the League of Nations, as a leading issue in the coming campaign was brought forward prominently today by a conference which Elihu Root had with President Coolidge, following the latter's reiterated support of the Court plan as advocated by ex-Secretary Root, and urged upon the Senate by President Harding and Secretary Hughes.

That the Democrats intend to make court membership a feature of the Democratic platform was indicated by Democratic leaders today when the attitude of the Democratic Party, as represented in the Senate, was shown in the report made by Senator Swanson, ranking minority member of the Foreign Relations Committee. This report virtually supports the proposal as urged by President Coolidge and his predecessor, except that it refrained from suggesting some reservations which were recommended by President Harding. The entire Democratic membership of this committee accepted the League of Nations Court, and thereby offered to uphold the hands of the President, who has been deserted by his party in the Senate committee.

Something like the situation which developed in the Republican Party during the Wilson Administration, when the party divided on the League of Nations, is threatened today, according to Republican leaders of the irreconcilable group who are opposed to our adhering to the International Court, foreseeing, they declare, that this will be the opening wedge for entering the League of Nations at a later date.

Root Worries Republican Senators.

The group in the Senate which got behind the Pepper plan was greatly concerned over the conference Mr. Root had with the President. They said that they might meet with strenuous opposition from Mr. Root and a number of other leading men and publicists, and if the former should become aggressive in advocating the President's proposal undoubtedly a bitter fight would develop at the convention which would be carried into the campaign.

While Mr. Root would not say anything about his conference other than to express gratification with the President's strong position on the World Court, as expressed in his Memorial Day speech, it is known that the Court was the chief subject of discussion at the luncheon table at which William M. Stearns was the other guest. Mr. Root declined even to give any idea of the strength of the World Court proposal in the country and said that he would not take any active part in the convention or the deliberations of the Resolution Committee over the plank on the Court.

That President Coolidge intends to fight the element in his party which has ignored his recommendations on the Court as well as the bonus and the Bursum pension bill is becoming more apparent each day. The Republican leaders who once dropped in at the White House frequently are not seen there since the Senate rejected the bonus veto and there appears to be a feeling of estrangement between the same Senate Republicans and the White House.

It was said today that President Coolidge would stand more squarely on his own ideas of policies and Government efficiency following the convention. One of his advisers said recently that he was carrying out inherited policies and therefore did not feel that he could take a position different from that laid down by his predecessor. After the platform at Cleveland has been adopted, his advisers say, he will become more assertive and will carve out his own ideas. Those who know the President well say that he will show himself in a stronger way after the convention and that he intends to make his first big fight with the Senate faction over the World Court.

Democratic Report Upholds Court Plan.

Not twenty-four hours after President Coolidge had rebuked the irreconcilables for their insistence that the United States must not approve membership in the Permanent Court of International Justice except under reservations that the participating nations could not accept, the Democrats of the Senate Foreign Relations Committee submitted a minority report completely upholding the ideas of President Harding, President Coolidge and Secretary Hughes on entrance into the Court.

The report, submitted by Senator Swanson of Virginia, said that the injection of the Pepper program had prevented hope of congressional action at the present term of Congress unless Mr. Coolidge could within a week's time, swing his recalcitrant party leaders in the Senate into line.

As a matter of fact, with the time

Continued on Page Two.

Coolidge Sends Telegram To Zeta Beta Tau Services

Harold Riegelman, executive of the Zeta Beta Tau Fraternity, yesterday made public the following telegram he received from President Coolidge with reference to the memorial services held in Providence, R. I., on Friday, in honor of Roger Williams:

"Please be good enough to communicate my good wishes and felicitations to the Zeta Beta Tau Fraternity in connection with the memorial services you are holding May 30. There is something peculiarly appropriate in the fact that these Jewish young men should be holding such exercises in Rhode Island. That Commonwealth owed its establishment to the determination of founders to secure the right of complete freedom in religion. Our Americans of the Jewish faith were largely moved to cast their lot here by exactly the same consideration.

"It is occasion of congratulation to both them and our nation that they were able to find here the liberal institutions which they sought and under which they have helped to make our country what it is.

"CALVIN COOLIDGE."

FIND BISHOP BROWN GUILTY OF HERESY

Trial Bishops Unanimous in Declaring His Doctrine Contrary to That of the Church.

DEFENDANT WILL APPEAL

Asserts Case Has Made Fundamental Issues Plain and His the Last Heresy Trial.

Special to The New York Times.

CLEVELAND, May 31.—William Montgomery Brown, retired Protestant Episcopal Bishop of Arkansas, was found guilty of heresy today by the unanimous vote of seven of his peers in the House of Bishops. Sentence was postponed until Oct. 14, to give Bishop Brown time to prepare the basis for his appeal.

The Court of Trial Bishops ruled that the twenty-three counts in the presentment, consisting of extracts from his book, "Communism and Christism," proved that the defendant believed and taught, "publicly and advisedly, doctrine contrary to that held by the Protestant Episcopal Church in the United States of America."

In a statement following the verdict Bishop Brown declared that his trial, which was the first trial of a Bishop in the Protestant Episcopal Church in the United States on a heresy charge, was the last heresy trial in history. The trial, he said, meant "the subordination of every dogma to the progressive revelation of science."

The verdict was delivered at 3:30 this afternoon in the dimly lighted hall of Trinity Cathedral, which has been the scene of the trial since last Tuesday. As the seven Bishops filed into the hall the 400 men and women in the audience rose. Bishop Brown placed on the table the four-year-old daughter of a former parishioner. Presiding Bishop John G. Murray of Baltimore took his place under the stained-glass representation of the Christ with arms outstretched. Bishop Brown took the little girl in the white dress and placed her on his knee.

Announces Verdict of "Guilty."

Bishop Murray then read the following decision:

The Court, having fully heard the allegation and proof of the parties in the above entitled cause, and having deliberately considered the same after the parties have withdrawn, and every member of the Court, sitting in the cause at the conclusion of the same, having disclosed his opinion as to whether the accused is guilty or not guilty with respect to each particular charge and specification contained in the presentment, does hereby pronounce and record its decision and judgment as follows:

The accused is guilty of holding and teaching publicly and advisedly doctrine contrary to that held by the Protestant Episcopal Church of the United States of America in the manner and form as set forth in the presentment as to each of the charges and specifications of the presentment.

The Court announced it would be glad to permit Bishop Brown an opportunity to make a statement, if he wished, as to why sentence should not be passed on him, and that such a statement might be made at noon on Oct. 14, 1924.

Joseph W. Sharts, counsel to Bishop Brown, said he would take the time offered, and announced he would begin preparation to appeal the case.

Heresy in the Protestant Episcopal

Continued on Page Three.

JAPANESE PROTEST SAYS EXCLUSION VIOLATES TREATY

Asserts 1911 Compact Gives "Liberty of Entry, Travel and Residence" to Both Peoples.

CITES NOTICE TO RUSSIA

Our House Resolution on the Treatment There of "Particular Race" Is Recalled.

ASSERTS ASSIMILABILITY

Note, Which Also Blames Congress, Is Made Public by Hughes Without Comment.

Special to The New York Times.

WASHINGTON, May 31.—The Japanese note of protest against the exclusion clause of the new immigration bill, recently cabled from Tokio, was delivered to Secretary Hughes today by Ambassador Hanihara.

The discriminatory legislation recently enacted by Congress, the note asserts, is in entire disregard of the spirit and circumstances that underlie the conclusion of the Treaty of Commerce and Navigation concluded between the United States and Japan in 1911. Discussion of the question of legal technicality, as to "whether and how far" the provisions of the immigration act are inconsistent with the terms of the treaty, will be reserved for another occasion, the note says.

After reciting the circumstances which led up to the conclusion of the "gentlemen's agreement," and declaring that Japan has always striven to carry out its provisions, the note states that the sweeping provisions of the immigration act have "made it impossible for Japan to continue the undertakings assumed under the 'gentlemen's agreement.'" and that the "patient, loyal and scrupulous observance by Japan for more than sixteen years of these self-denying regulations, in the interest of good relations between the two countries, now seems to have been wasted."

Taking up the question of assimilability of the Japanese, the note declares that few immigrants of foreign stock may well be expected to assimilate themselves within a single generation; that the Japanese immigration to the United States dates from the last few years of the nineteenth century, and the period is, therefore, too short to judge of the adaptabilities of the race.

The note further declares that the "pressure of the invidious discriminations" to which the Japanese residents of some States in America have been subjected have not provided a general atmosphere in which to demonstrate their adaptability.

Text of the Japanese Protest.

The text of the protest of the Japanese Government is as follows:

Japanese Embassy,
Washington, May 31, 1924.
Honorable Charles E. Hughes, Secretary of State.

Sir: In pursuance of instructions from my Government, I have the honor to present to you herewith a memorandum enunciating the position of Japan on the subject of the discriminatory provisions against Japanese which are embodied in section 13 (C) of the Immigration act of 1924, approved May 26, 1924.

MEMORANDUM.

The Japanese Government are deeply concerned by the enactment in the United States of an act entitled the "Immigration Act of 1924." While the measure was under discussion in the Congress they took the earliest opportunity to invite the attention of the American Government to a discriminatory clause embodied in the act, namely, section 13 (C), which provided for the exclusion of aliens ineligible to citizenship, in contradistinction to other classes of aliens, and which is manifestly intended to apply to Japanese. Neither the representations of the Japanese Government nor the recommendations of the President or of the Secretary of State were heeded by the Congress, and the clause in question has now been written into the statutes of the United States.

It is, perhaps, needless to state that international discriminations in any form and on any subject, even if

Continued on Page Thirteen.

Japanese Kills Himself Near Tokio Embassy; Hara-kiri Victim Assails Us, Asks Vengeance

By WILFRID FLEISHER.

Copyright, 1924, by The New York Times Company.
By Wireless to THE NEW YORK TIMES.

TOKIO, May 31.—An unidentified Japanese, over 40 years old, committed hara-kiri, which is the traditional Japanese method of suicide, by disemboweling himself in front of the residence of Viscount Inouye early this morning on the edge of the compound where stand the ruins of the former American Embassy which was destroyed in the earthquake.

He left two letters. One was addressed to "The American Ambassador and American people." The other to "The people of the Japanese Empire."

The tragedy was discovered by a maid servant of Viscount Inouye, who found the body propped up against a tree stump in the garden.

Using a small dagger six inches long, the man had slit his abdomen crosswise and then upward in the classical way, and he also slashed his neck. The two letters lay beside the corpse.

The police were immediately informed, and a crowd soon athered around the corpse, including several American marines who are quartered in the embassy compound. The unknown was clad in a foreign style suit without shoes, but was otherwise well dressed. A mat was placed over the corpse, which was removed later in the morning.

The letter addressed to the American Ambassador was opened by the police and made public this evening. It reads:

"To ask the reflection of the American people I hereby entreat by my death his Excellency Cyrus E. Woods, American Ambassador, who well understands Japan and has great sympathy for the Japanese people, to convey my request as follows:

"That a law shall be enacted to remove the exclusion clause from the new Immigration bill. I request by my death the withdrawal of the Japanese exclusion clause because I greatly regret that your country, which has always advocated peace from a humanitarian viewpoint and has been known as a leader for peace throughout the world, enacted the Japanese exclusion clause in complete disregard of humanity.

"The indignation caused by this insult is impossible to overcome. If there is any ground for this affront we should repent it and overcome the indignation, but when there is not the slightest cause for the offense given us it is quite impossible to overcome our indignation even if we wished to.

"I am a Japanese. We are now humiliated by your country in the eyes of the world without any justification—if there is any justification it applies for your country only—I prefer death rather than to feel resentment.

"After my death I will ask the reconsideration by the people of your country through Jesus Christ and pray for the greater happiness of your people. At the same time I pray God for the removal of the injurious anti-Japanese clause from the immigration bill, which has subjected the Japanese to great insult and humiliation."

"A NAMELESS SUBJECT OF THE JAPANESE EMPIRE."

TOKIO, May 31 (Associated Press).—It is understood that the letter addressed to the Japanese by the man who committed hara-kiri urged the nation to rise to avenge the insult embodied in the action of America.

The incident has created a sensation in Tokio, despite efforts of the police to suppress the details.

Several minor incidents illustrate the growth of the anti-American spirit throughout Japan engendered by the passage of the Exclusion act by the American Congress. At Wakayama, a city forty miles from Osaka, the Young Men's Association passed a resolution demanding the withdrawal of the American missionaries from that district.

Three women's organizations of Tokio have passed resolutions urging women not to buy American toilet articles, and the press reports a movement among Buddhist and Shinto leaders to bar Christians from Japan.

Publicists, journalists and former officials have formed the "Taibei Doshikai" (Anti-American Association) to carry on the national agitation against exclusion

FRENCH VOTES HERE SOUGHT FOR SMITH

Leader of Move Says Governor Would Seek Repeal of Dry and Immigration Laws.

LETTERS ARE GIVEN OUT

Ask Every French Society to Pledge Its Support to Democratic Candidate.

A plan to deliver the "French vote" in the Presidential campaign to Governor Smith, in the expectation that if elected President he would work for the repeal of the prohibition and immigration laws, reopening America to French wines and liquors and to immigrants from Latin countries, was revealed yesterday.

The plan became known through a letter of protest written by Frank D. Pavey, President of the Federation of L'Alliance Française in the United States and Canada, to Gaston Liebert, former Consul General of France in New York and now Director of the French Bureau of Information here.

Mr. Pavey, who is a Republican, made public his letter yesterday. It was the third communication in a controversy between Mr. Pavey and M. Liebert as to whether L'Alliance Française of New York, of whose Administrative Council Mr. Pavey is a member, should affiliate with the Central Committee of French Societies of New York, which M. Liebert first projected.

Mr. Pavey has opposed vigorously the idea of affiliation, on the ground that L'Alliance Française was devoted exclusively to social and educational work, while the Central Committee of French Societies was nationalistic and political in its aims. M. Liebert has denied that there was any idea of political propaganda in the organization of the Central Committee.

Support of Governor Smith Urged.

Further inquiry, after a copy of Mr. Pavey's letter was received by THE NEW YORK TIMES, showed that Clement Rueff, an importer, as President of the French Democratic Club of New York, Inc., and President of the Smith-for-President Committee of that club, had sent a circular letter on May 19 to various French societies, urging them to support Governor Smith's candidacy.

It was learned also that the Courier des Etats Unis, the French newspaper published in New York, supported the Smith-for-President movement in an article which included the circular letter sent out by Mr. Rueff's committee, and ended with an editorial exhortation to all citizens and societies of the French language to elect a "Democrat of the integrity of Governor Smith" and "sweep out the Republicans from power."

Mr. Rueff in a reply to Mr. Pavey's letter yesterday said the French Democratic Club was supporting Governor Smith for President in the interests of both France and the United States and that it was fighting for the repeal of the prohibition law for the sake of personal liberty.

Mr. Liebert said he would answer Mr. Pavey later.

The circular letter sent out by the Smith-for-President Committee was signed by Mr. Rueff as President of the club and of the committee, and was typed on the letterhead of the Club Democratique Français (French Democratic Club of New York, Inc.) of 114 West Forty-eighth Street under date of May 19. Underneath the club title on the letterhead were the words: "Comité Smith pour Président."

Translation of the Letter.

A translation of the letter, made by an officer of one of the societies which received it, follows:

Mr. President: We have the honor

Continued on Page Six.

LA FOLLETTE MOVES QUICKLY IN CONGRESS

Goes to Capitol, Calls Followers, Gets Swift Report to Senate on Rail Labor Bill.

MAY BLOCK ADJOURNMENT

Followers Say He Is Determined to Get Barkley Bill Made Law at Any Cost.

Special to The New York Times.

WASHINGTON, May 31.—The fur began to fly in Congressional circles today when Senator La Follette, who hurried back to Washington yesterday, made his appearance at the Capitol, summoned several of the progressive and radical Democrats and Republicans and demanded action by Congress on proposals for rail and farm legislation.

The Wisconsin Senator was in his best fighting trim, and within three hours after he reached his offices the Senate Interstate Commerce Committee voted to report favorably the Howell-Barkley bill, which would do away with the Railroad Labor Board. This is one of La Follette's pet measures and has the backing of the railroad brotherhoods.

Senator La Follette was not content with stirring up the Senate, but called into conference Representative Nelson of Wisconsin, leader of the progressive-radical bloc of the house, in an effort to get some arrangement whereby the Howell-Barkley bill, in the shape agreed to by the Senate committee, would stand a chance of speedy adoption in the House if approved by the Senate.

While Senator La Follette would make no statement on his plans, it was stated on good authority that he expects to have a busy time of it next week. He will probably make a speech on Monday or Tuesday, demanding action on some of the measures asked by the radicals and progressives and attacking the tactics of the more conservative elements in both the big parties in opposing these bills.

Senator La Follette is expected to give warning that he certainly will enter the campaign as an independent candidate for the Presidency unless the leaders of the Republican and Democratic Parties agree to put through before taking an adjournment the program of legislation which he advocates. It is conceded that no such arrangement will be agreed to by the party leaders and the entrance of La Follette into the Presidential race is accepted here as virtually certain.

The coming of Senator La Follette to Washington two days before the date he had scheduled for his return has again raised the question as to the likelihood of Congress being able to reach an agreement to adjourn on June 7.

Those who have been following the course of the Howell-Barkley bill and other measures which Mr. La Follette favors had about reached the conclusion that there was little chance of such bills being passed before adjournment. Now the picture is somewhat altered. It was said in one quarter today that Mr. La Follette was prepared to organize the progressive and radical elements and try to prevent adjournment next Saturday unless the Howell-Barkley bill was adopted and signed by the President or adopted and passed over a presidential veto, as the case might be.

The possibility of an organized fight for the adoption of some farm relief bill also looms up with the reappearance of La Follette. It is evident that in any event, even if adjournment can be forced without regard to La Follette's dictum, the Wisconsin Senator intends to make all of the political capital he can out of the situation.

Senator La Follette as soon as he reached his office at the Capitol soon after 10 A. M., got to work on the telephone rallying the Progressive and radical forces. As a result there was a

Continued on Page Eight.

Coolidge Takes Mellon's Tax Bill Report Down the River on the Mayflower for Study

Special to The New York Times.

WASHINGTON, May 31.—President Coolidge received today a report on the tax bill from Secretary Mellon and General Lord, Director of the Budget. He took it with him on the Presidential yacht Mayflower this afternoon for study during a week-end cruise.

There was a report today that the President would delay action on the tax bill until the very latest period, to see what action Congress takes on four or five bills which were not recommended by the budget and which would greatly increase the deficit. Due to holidays and Sundays, the President has until midnight June 7 for final action on the revenue bill, and by that time, it is believed, the course of Congress on the other large appropriations pending will be known.

None of the bills outside the budget that would entail large expenditures has yet passed through Congress. The Veterans' Bureau reorganization bill, with an appropriation of $32,000,000, has gone through the Senate, and the German relief bill, costing $10,000,000, through the House, but neither the Postal Salaries bill nor the Reclassification bill has been approved by either House.

Secretary Mellon had a long conference with the President following the presentation of his report. He declined to make known whether he had recommended the veto of the tax bill or to indicate the nature of his report.

Besides making an analysis of the bill himself, Secretary Mellon had the benefit of surveys of the bill made by experts of the Treasury, and when he talked to the President he dealt principally with facts and figures. He is known to have eliminated practically everything bordering on guesswork. He told the President what, after these surveys, he thinks the tax bill will accomplish and what he thinks it will fail to accomplish in meeting the demands of the Treasury under reduced taxes and for the money necessary to meet the soldiers' bonus.

President Coolidge will receive copies of THE NEW YORK TIMES by airplane tomorrow morning on the Mayflower in Chesapeake Bay near the entrance of the Potomac River. He asked that papers be delivered to him and suggested the use of a speed boat, but the Naval Air Service decided to obtain the yacht's position tomorrow by radio and then to have Lieutenant E. H. Carlison fly a Martin monoplane about the vessel and drop the papers to her deck.

DR. M. L. BURTON PICKED BY COOLIDGE TO NOMINATE HIM

Head of Michigan University, Who Is Not a Delegate, Will Get In on a Proxy.

HE IS A LONG-TIME FRIEND

Herbert S. Hadley, President of University in St. Louis, Is Mentioned for Vice President.

SUPPORTERS PUSH BORAH

Assert He Could Lead the Ticket in 1928—He Is Cold to Their Appeals.

Special to The New York Times.

WASHINGTON, May 31.—Dr. Marion Leroy Burton, President of the University of Michigan, has been selected by President Coolidge to place him in nomination at the Republican convention. The announcement of his selection was made today by William M. Butler, Chairman of the Coolidge Campaign Committee, who will become Chairman of the Republican National Committee with the resignation of John T. Adams in June.

For the first time in two decades the honor of placing the name of a Presidential candidate before the Republican convention goes to a man who is not a delegate to the convention. He will be furnished a proxy, since under the rules of the Republican Party the nominating speech must be made by a delegate. Dr. Burton has been a personal friend of President Coolidge since the former was President of Smith College at Northampton, the home of the President.

Mr. Coolidge is expected to dominate the action of the convention not only as to who shall be Chairman of the Resolutions Committee, which will draft the platform, but he and his advisers, it is understood here, will pick out the candidate for Vice President. This elimination of candidates for both places is now going on quietly and is being conducted by Mr. Butler and William M. Sterns of Boston.

Republican leaders agree that the President should have the decision as to his running mate and the character of the platform in most respects, although the Senate leaders are expected to fight the World Court proposal sponsored by the President in his Memorial Day address. This will be about the only point of difference between the President and the Senate leaders.

The name of Herbert S. Hadley, who was prominent in the 1912 campaign, was mentioned today as one of the men engaging the attention of the Coolidge leaders for the Vice Presidential nomination. He was desired to make the nominating speech, but was unable to accept because it interfered with his duties as President of the Washington University of St. Louis, whose commencement day falls on the same day as the opening of the Cleveland Convention. Mr. Hadley is a former Governor of Missouri. Another Missouri man, the present Governor Hyde, has been discussed, but late developments indicate that he is not receiving serious consideration by the Administration, although he is an avowed candidate and one of the few in the field.

Senate leaders, even those of the conservative faction, are anxious to influence Senator Borah to accept the nomination for Vice President. They say that he would strengthen the ticket and would become the candidate for President in 1928. Senator Borah thus far has declined to give any attention to the appeals that have been made to him. He does not intend to go to the Cleveland convention, and for that reason he shied from the honor of placing the President in nomination.

Dr. Burton is a noted educator, who has not taken any active interest in politics. He was President of Smith College, Northampton, Mass., from 1910 to 1917, and later was head of the University of Minnesota. Since 1920 he has been President of the University of Michigan. He is a powerful speaker.

Dr. Burton Leaves for Capital.

ANN ARBOR, Mich., May 31.—Dr. Marion Leroy Burton, President of the University of Michigan, left today for Washington.

Will Ask Party Pledges for Filipinos

Special to The New York Times.

WASHINGTON, May 31.—Manuel Quezon, Speaker of the Philippines Assembly, will appear before the Resolutions Committee of the Republican National Convention in Cleveland to urge that a plank be incorporated in the platform definitely committing the party to a policy of independence for the Philippines. Mr. Quezon will asw the Resolutions Committee of the Democratic National Convention to insert a like plank in the platform at the New York convention.

Twenty Girls May Be Lost As California School Burns

LOS ANGELES, Cal., May 31.—Between fifteen and twenty girl inmates are believed to have perished in a fire tonight which destroyed the Hope Development School for Subnormal Girls at Playa del Rey, near here.

Nineteen of the school's thirty-nine girl inmates have been removed to a hospital at Venice, three and a half miles north, injured by the flames or from jumping from the second story of the three-story building.

MEN HE BEFRIENDED BEAT, BIND, ROB HIM

Pair Posing as Collegians Hold Up Phipps Moshier, a Wealthy Columbia Man.

ESCAPE IN HIS SPORTS CAR

Leave Him Hobbled and Gagged in a Field Off Country Road, After Debating Murder.

A hold-up, in which a wealthy manufacturer's son was bound, gagged and threatened with death Thursday night near Fishkill by two men he had befriended, came to light yesterday when the State troopers sent out a general alarm for the automobile they stole from him. The man's assailants had planned their attack all the way from Westfield, Mass., where they had struck up an acquaintance with him on the basis of their mutual friendship with certain college men.

The victim was Phipps G. Moshier, 25 years old, a Columbia graduate, son of a manufacturer living at 20 Hayden Row, Hopkinton, Mass. Corporal C. G. Gilbert of Troop K, stationed at Fishkill, confirmed the story yesterday and said that a general alarm had been sent out for the robbers and the stolen machine, a 1924 sport model Buick, painted gray, with a red line around the body and bearing on both sides Moshier's initials in red. At the rear were two spare balloon tires and a trunk rack.

Moshier told this story:

"I was driving to New York on business. I was in Westfield, Mass., near Springfield, Monday, when two men of about my age, very well dressed and of refined manner, came to the curb and admired my automobile. They drifted into other conversation, in which it developed they knew a number of Yale graduates with whom I had gone to school at Exeter. One of them gave me to understand that he was a Yale graduate and the son of a business man in Albany. He said he was not in good standing with his father, but was on his way to Albany to right himself and go into business with him. As I was going to Albany, by way of Pittsfield, I invited them to ride with me.

Invited Him to Dinner.

"We got to Pittsfield late on Monday. There they sent telegrams. They gave me their names and addresses which I placed in a notebook, but they later stole the notebook and all I recall about their names is that one was nicknamed 'Friday' and the other 'Sook.' They were good spenders, not sponging on me for anything. At Pittsfield they left for Albany, as I had to remain over. I told them that in Albany I would put up at the Hotel Wellington. The one who said he lived in that city said he would like me to have dinner at his home there and meet his father.

"I reached Albany Wednesday. At the hotel was waiting a note from one of them, expressing regret that I had not been in when he called. I tore up the note, unfortunately. They showed up later in the day and we went out to dinner. I declined the invitation to have dinner at the home of the man who said he lived in Albany.

"I remained at the Wellington Wednesday night. Apparently, they went to their homes in that city. On Thursday, as they had said they were going to New York, we set out together in the car. The man who had said he was in bad standing at home told me he had squared matters and had received permission and funds to go to New York for a few days to see some shows.

"We were about a mile from Fishkill at 9 o'clock Thursday night, I at the wheel, one of them beside me and the other in the rear seat of the open car, when one of them asked me to slow down so that he could light a cigarette. That had been done many times on the way and I thought nothing of it. As I

Continued on Page Fourteen.

New Maid Vanishes in Hour; $25,000 in Gems Also Disappear From West Side Apartment

A young woman, employed as a maid by Mrs. Herman Plaut of 150 West Seventy-ninth Street reported for work at 8 o'clock Thursday morning. An hour later she disappeared. Soon afterward it was discovered that a case of jewels valued at more than $25,000 was missing.

Mrs. Plaut was the only member of the family at home when the robbery occurred. Her husband, who is in the lighting fixture business, had gone to his office at 423 East Twenty-third Street. Their daughter had gone shopping.

The jewel case, containing several valuable diamond rings, a lavalliere, bar pins, watches and bracelets, was lying on Mrs. Plaut's dressing table. She had worn some of her jewelry at a dinner the night before and expected to use it again that night.

After the departure of her family Mrs. Plaut went to her bedroom. She missed the jewel case and called for her maid. There was no answer. She then called for the cook. But the cook had not seen the maid either. The elevator operator and the doorman were questioned; but neither had seen the girl leave the house.

The Plaut apartment was thoroughly searched and it was found that a door leading to a back stairway, which in turn led to the cellar, had been unbolted. A black hat, a coat, and a suit case filled with clothes were found in the new maid's room.

Detectives investigated the maid's references and found them to be genuine. The detectives believe that the jewels, within easy access, were too great a temptation for the young woman.

TWO RICH STUDENTS CONFESS TO KILLING FRANKS BOY IN CAR

Sons of Wealthy Chicagoans Hit Him With a Chisel and Then Gagged Him.

THEN DISPOSED OF BODY

Youth's Clothing, Which They Stripped From Him, Burned in Home of One Slayer.

LONG PLANNED SUCH CRIME

Once Thought to Kidnap Rosenwald's Grandson—Chauffeur Upset Their Alibi.

Special to The New York Times.

CHICAGO, May 31.—The kidnapping and murder of Robert Franks, 14-year-old son of the millionaire Jacob Franks, while he was returning home from school on May 21, was confessed at [illegible] o'clock this morning by Nathan F. Leopold Jr. and Richard Loeb, likewise sons of Chicago millionaires. This was the climax of a police inquisition that had lasted throughout the night and started with the arrest of the youths Friday.

The two youths are post-graduate students of the University of Chicago. Leopold is reputed to be the youngest graduate of that institution and Loeb the youngest of the University of Michigan. Leopold is 19 and Loeb within a month of the same age.

They admitted that they had seized the boy, placed him in a hired automobile and slain him five minutes afterward while the car was driving through a heavily traveled street. First hitting him on the head with a chisel, they insured his death by choking him with a gag. They put acid on his face in an effort to so disfigure it that identity would be destroyed. Leopold wrote the letter to Jacob Franks, demanding $10,000 ransom. Loeb was the one who telephoned to the Franks home from the drug store and gave directions for the delivery of the ransom.

Ransom and the "adventure" of crime were the motives for the deed, although both received liberal allowance from their parents. Long having had kidnaping in mind, they had discussed making a victim of the grandson of Julius Rosenwald, head of Sears Roebuck & Co., of which firm young Loeb's father, Albert H. Loeb, is Vice President.

Death Penalty for Both Crimes.

Kidnapping is a capital offense under the Illinois laws, so that should they be proved guilty of the kidnapping and murder the two youths could be sentenced to death on two counts.

"I have a hanging case," said Robert E. Crowe, State's Attorney, after he had reviewed all angles of the confessions. "The State is ready to go to trial immediately." Chief Justice Caverly of the Criminal Court, stating that he would urge an immediate trial, said "Justice should be served within thirty days."

Plans have been completed for quick action in the courts. The inquest, indefinitely postponed the day after the body was found, will be reopened Monday morning and it was announced that the case would be the first to be submitted to the June Grand Jury. State's Attorney Crowe said it was possible to try the slayers of the boy for two crimes in case indictments were returned.

Mr. Crowe declared the confessions had revealed that the students had no intention of returning the boy to his parents if the ransom had been paid. They expected to destroy all evidences of the crime.

The attitude of Leopold and Loeb when they were first arrested inclined the State's Attorney and the police to doubt their guilt. Both asserted their innocence and courted the fullest investigation, even to saying they did not desire freedom until they had been fully cleared, a position endorsed by their parents.

Leopold's arrest had been due to tracing to his ownership the pair of spectacles found near the body of Robert Franks when it was discovered nude at a railroad culvert near a swamp. He explained the presence of the glasses there by saying he visited the swamp frequently to study the habits of birds.

In offering an alibi, Leopold told of having spent the afternoon with Loeb in his automobile and the evening with Loeb and two girls in riding around and visiting cabarets.

The suspicions of the State's Attorney became strongly aroused when Loeb contradicted Leopold and declared he was not with his chum in the evening.

Chauffeur Blasts Leopold's Alibi.

Checking up on Leopold's story when doubt began to be cast on it, Mr. Crowe learned from the Leopold family chauffeur that the youth's car had not been out of the garage on the day of the kidnapping. Hunting for a red car similar to Leopold's, detectives found that one had been hired by Leopold from an automobile renting agency under the name of Morton D. Ballard on May 21.

When confronted by the chauffeur's information the prisoners showed signs of fear and the examiners, confident that they would break, pressed the examination vigorously. Soon they broke down and confessed, a court stenographer taking down their statements.

The confessions told how the chums planned their crime as far back as last November. They intended the ransom money should be given to them by Mr. Franks or any detectives he might have with him from a moving Illinois Central train going south and that then they would flee with the money in the opposite direction in an automobile.

Jacob Franks, the father, was told to go to the Vandebogart drug store

"All the News That's Fit to Print."

The New York Times.

THE WEATHER
Partly cloudy today; tomorrow, probably thunder showers.
Temperature yesterday—Max., 70; Min., 62.
☞For weather report see next to last page.

VOL. LXXIII....No. 24,262. * * * NEW YORK, SATURDAY, JUNE 28, 1924. TWO CENTS In Greater New York | THREE CENTS Within 200 Miles | FOUR CENTS Elsewhere

KLAN ISSUE OVERSHADOWS ALL ON EVE OF BALLOTING; PLANK SPLITS PLATFORM MAKERS, M'ADOO WINS ON LEAGUE; LAST NOMINEES ARE IN, UNDERWOOD AND DAVIS STRONGER

RUHR THROWN OPEN TO 210,000 EXILES BY FRENCH AMNESTY

Jail Sentences Also Are to Be Suspended or Reviewed by Herriot's Order.

BERLIN PROPOSAL REFUSED

Premier Won't Let Rail Tax Receipts Be Diverted From Bond Interest Payments.

MARX REPLIES TO ALLIES

Note on Resumption of Military Control Said in Berlin to Be Unconditional Acceptance.

By EDWIN L. JAMES.

Copyright, 1924, by The New York Times Company. Special Cable to THE NEW YORK TIMES.

PARIS, June 27.—Premier Herriot has instructed General Degoutte, commanding the Franco-Belgian forces occupying the Ruhr, to permit with few exceptions the return to the industrial region of all Germans expelled since the beginning of the occupation in January of last year.

While the exact number affected is not known because their families were sent out with all Germans against whom expulsion orders were issued, it is understood the new order will permit the return to their homes of about 210,000 persons. The only exceptions are those expelled for serious non-political crimes, whose number is small. M. Herriot had previously authorized the return of 60,000 Germans expelled from Rhineland territory exclusive of the Ruhr.

It is further announced that the sentences on all Germans condemned to prison for taking part in the passive resistance program without criminal violence will be suspended and that persons convicted for crimes of violence will have their cases reviewed for the purpose of exercising the largest measure of clemency.

This measure is quite in accord with M. Herriot's position that exploitation of the Ruhr should now be given up in favor of putting into operation the Dawes plan, and that regardless of the merits of the expulsion of those who interfered with this exploitation there is no use prolonging their deportation. There is some criticism of the Premier's measure before putting into operation the experts' plan, on the ground that he could have used permission to the expelled Germans to return as a card in the coming negotiations with the Germans.

Coincident with the announcement of this move, it has been made known that M. Herriot sent a note to Berlin rejecting the German proposals in regard to the Ruhr Micum accords. These proposals were made two days before M. Herriot became Premier, and stated that the Germans could not renew the agreements for deliveries by the Ruhr industrialists unless the French agreed that the 200,000,000 gold marks railroad tax planned by the Dawes report should be used to repay the industrialists. Inasmuch as the Dawes plan intended the railroad tax to meet the interest charges on an issue of bonds to be delivered to the Allies, it was perfectly apparent that the German demand amounted to an effort to reduce the amount Germany would have to pay under the experts' system.

In rejecting this proposal M. Herriot said France and Belgium wished the accords prolonged on the present basis until the Dawes plan went into effect.

The Micum accords expired April 15 and were renewed by M. Poincaré for two months. When they again expired on June 15 the Germans agreed to a fifteen-day extension, because of the French political crisis. Therefore on Monday the Ruhr agreements technically expire again. On June 30 also the German reply to the allied demand for the resumption of military control of the Reich is due.

While the issue of military supervision will probably go into the interallied conference which opens July 16 the French wish to have the Micum accords kept out of the conference for the reason that the British do not recognize the legality of the Ruhr occupation and it would be embarrassing to have the Ruhr situation considered in London under such conditions.

BERLIN SAID TO AGREE TO MILITARY INQUIRY

Reply to Ambassadors' Demands Being Sent to Premier Herriot by Courier.

By T. R. YBARRA.

Copyright, 1924, by The New York Times Company. Special Cable to THE NEW YORK TIMES.

BERLIN, June 27.—The German Government's answer agreeing to resumption of allied military investigation into the alleged warlike preparations in Germany will be dispatched from here tonight. The Government heads arrived at an agreement regarding the tenor of the note Wednesday, since when slight changes have been made in the original text outlined.

The note will not be telegraphed, but taken direct to Paris by courier, who will hand it personally to Premier Herriot, who is exofficio Chairman of the Conference of Ambassadors, which sent the allied demand for resumption of military control, to which Germany is now replying.

The reply covers five typewritten pages, taking up the question with con-

Continued on Page Seven.

Convention Disturbs Cabinet; Coolidge Shuts Off the Radio

Special to The New York Times.

WASHINGTON, June 27.—Democratic noise over the radio disturbed the Cabinet meeting at the White House so much today that the receiving set was shut down while President Coolidge and his lieutenants held their session.

In the afternoon, however, the machine was turned on again and yells of "'Ray for Al!" piercing cries of "Mac'll do!" and blasting music from the band in Madison Square Garden filled the corridors of the executive offices.

TO FLY BY NIGHT WITH PACIFIC MAIL

New Transcontinental Postal Airplane Service to Start Next Tuesday.

3,000 MILES IN 35 HOURS

Special Letter Boxes Here for the Air Mail—40 Pilots to Operate in Relays.

New red, white and blue mail boxes will be placed in the business sections of the city next Monday to serve New Yorkers who wish to have letters delivered in San Francisco within thirty-six hours. They are the new air mail letter boxes and serve to announce the inauguration of a new transcontinental postal airplane service.

The air carriers will begin their daily flights on Tuesday. This is an auspicious event, not circus or spectacular flying, but the beginning of the operation of a through air mail service 365 days in the year, through Summer heat and Winter storms, flying through the entire night as well as by day.

Tuesday at 11 A. M. the first winged pony express will hop off from Hazlehurst Field, Long Island, carrying mail for the Golden Gate, 3,000 miles away. According to schedule the mail should arrive in San Francisco at 5:45 on the afternoon of the following day. The mail planes will leave the Pacific Coast for the Atlantic daily at 6 A. M. with mail due to arrive here 32 hours later.

To Illuminate the Heavens.

By night the highways of the heavens will be illuminated to guide the pilots as they fly over twelve States, making thirteen regular stops. Arrangements have been made with the rail mails so that offices not located on the air mail route may dispatch mail matter to connect therewith. For example: Philadelphia may dispatch to Los Angeles, by rail to New York or Cleveland, thence by air to San Francisco; thence by rail to Los Angeles.

The regular stops on the air mail route from New York are Bellefonte, Cleveland, Bryan, Chicago, Iowa City, Omaha, North Platte, Cheyenne, Rawlins, Rock Springs, Salt Lake City, Elko, Reno and San Francisco.

Any mailable matter will be carried by airplane, including sealed parcels not exceeding fifty pounds in weight and not exceeding forty-eight inches in length and girth combined, if postage is paid at the rate of 8 cents an ounce for each zone or part zone in which mail is carried by plane. The rate of postage to San Francisco is 24 cents.

Attached to all of the air mail letter-boxes is a map showing the air-highway across the continent and giving information regarding rates of postage between the various stops. Mail should be placed in letter-boxes about three hours before 11 o'clock in the morning, when the plane leaves for the West.

Special airplane stamps are not required. Any stamps good for postage may be usel. Also, it is not necessary to post mailable material in the special air mail boxes. The new boxes are merely a convenience for those who wish to post letters at the last minute. All mail for airplane dispatch should be prominently marked "Via Air Mail."

Air Mail Boxes Here.

The new boxes here are located at Times Square, General Post Office lobby, Pennsylvania Station, Fifth Avenue and Thirty-fourth Street, City Hall, Grand Central Station, Broadway and Wall Street, Broadway and Twenty-third Street and Fifth Avenue and Forty-second Street.

John H. Bartlett, Acting Postmaster General; Superintendent Peter A. McGurty and a large number of Post Office officials will be present at Hazelhurst Air Mail Field to view the first flight and bear witness to the beginning of a new epoch in the history of the Postal

Continued on Page Eight.

LAST NOMINEES IN FIELD

Call of the States Ends With Sixteen Candidates Named.

MANY SECONDING SPEECHES

John W. Davis, Glass, Cox, Silzer, C. W. Bryan and Brown Added to the Long List.

WOMEN LEAD IN ORATORY

They Stir Up Weary Delegates and Start Real Demonstrations.

Today's Official Program.

FIFTH SESSION.

Following is the official program for today's session of the Democratic Convention:

Convention called to order by the Hon. Thomas J. Walsh, Permanent Chairman, at 9:30 A. M., Daylight Saving Time.

Invocation by the Rev. John Roach Straton, pastor of Calvary Baptist Church of New York.

Report of Committee on Resolutions.

Roll-call of States for vote on nominations for President.

Adjournment.

By ELMER DAVIS.

The Democrats are through at last with making nominations for the Presidential nomination. They devoted six hours and a quarter yesterday to that necessary but painful task, finishing up a work that had been begun on Wednesday afternoon and carried forward through most of Thursday's sessions.

According to the stenographic record, only about 40,000 or 50,000 words were spoken yesterday, but anybody who had to sit through it all would be willing to swear that there were at least 40,000,000.

The convention is supposed to resume its operations at 9:30 o'clock this morning, though it will probably start late, as usual. The adoption of the platform, probably after considerable argument, is the first thing in the order of business. Before the day is over the balloting for the Presidency may begin.

Six new Presidential candidates were placed before the convention yesterday. Ohio nominated James M. Cox; Nebraska, Governor Charles W. Bryan; New Hampshire, Governor Fred W. Brown; New Jersey, Governor George S. Silzer; Virginia, Senator Carter Glass, and West Virginia, John W. Davis.

This makes sixteen candidates presented altogether. Oscar W. Underwood, Joseph T. Robinson and William Gibbs McAdoo were nominated on Wednesday, and Alfred E. Smith, Willard Saulsbury, David Franklin Houston, Samuel M. Ralston, Jonathan M. Davis, Albert C. Ritchie and Woodbridge N. Ferris on Thursday.

If you don't see your favorite among the belauded sixteen, don't worry. A lot of other people will be voted for on the first ballot, and later. Quite possibly the eventual nominee of this convention will be somebody who has not been formally placed in nomination at all.

But the nominations were not half of it yesterday. There were also seconding speeches. Mr. McAdoo was seconded seven times, Governor Smith four times, and Senator Underwood once. This makes their total score: McAdoo 11, Smith 7 and Underwood 2, for all of them had been extensively seconded on Thursday. Messrs. Silzer, Ritchie, Davis, Glass and Brown also were seconded yesterday.

The big wind accompanying the thunderstorm of Wednesday evening had a higher velocity than the winds that blew in Madison Square Garden from 11:40 yesterday morning till nearly 6 o'clock last night, but the Democratic wind was considerably larger in volume. Under the influence of this fearful

Continued on Page Three.

© Campbell Studio.

THE FIRST WOMAN TO BE PLACED IN NOMINATION FOR THE VICE PRESIDENCY.

Mrs. Leroy Springs, National Committeewoman From South Carolina, Whose Name Will Be Put Forward by That Delegation.

TO PRESENT WOMAN FOR VICE PRESIDENT

Mrs. Leroy Springs of South Carolina to Be First of Her Sex Put in Nomination.

SENATOR WHEELER O. K.'S IT

Says Comely and Brilliant Southerner Would Improve Situation in the Senate.

Mrs. Leroy Springs of Lancaster, S. C., is to be the first woman in American history to be placed in nomination for the Vice Presidency.

Those behind the move do not expect Mrs. Springs to be nominated—that is not the end they have in mind. They simply believe that this woman—generally conceded to be one of the most brilliant as well as one of the handsomest in the convention—is entitled to a fine compliment.

Mrs. Springs caught the fancy of the convention from the start and when it was suggested that she preside over the Committee on Credentials there was a chorus of unanimous ayes.

And Mrs. Springs handled her committee like a veteran, winning the plaudits of her colleagues not only for the ability she showed but for the courtesy and fairness of her every act.

The decision of friends of Mrs. Springs to place her in nomination for Vice President was conveyed to the press section by a member of the South Carolina delegation.

"We have," he said, "the leading woman Democrat of the South in this delegation of ours and we have decided when our name is reached in the roll of States to offer her as a candidate for the Vice Presidential nomination. While she probably will not go over the line a winner she will at least, we are sure, receive a rousing compliment such as has been accorded to few women in our history."

Mrs. Springs was taken completely by surprise when told of the plan. Not a hint of what was going on had been permitted to reach her. She refused to believe the report was accurate.

"It simply cannot be true," she exclaimed, "but it certainly is nice for all these good friends of mine to consider me worthy of such a compliment. Of course, I know it is just a delightful tribute. There isn't a chance in the world of my being nominated. Just the same I appreciate it very, very much."

Under the Constitution a candidate for the Vice Presidency must be thirty-five years old. Mrs. Springs admits she meets this Constitutional provision. To the casual observer, she might seem to be below the age limit and therefore ineligible.

Senator Wheeler of Montana, when

Continued on Page Three.

'DARK HORSES' BUSY ON TRACK STRATEGY

All Decide to Canter Under Wraps in Early Balloting, Waiting for Break.

RALSTON TALK STRONGER

Supporters of All Candidates Find Encouragement in Acclaim Which Delegates Gave Names.

With fourteen "dark horses" entered in the race for the Democratic Presidential nomination and waiting to be off when the convention, possibly today, starts balloting on candidates, interest in "Tom" Taggart's entry, United States Senator Ralston of Indiana, continued strong last night.

According to those actively identified with the Ralston boom, he grew in strength throughout yesterday, a day most of the leaders, great and small, spent at the Garden sitting with their respective delegations, listening to nominating speeches and intent on gauging sentiment for the several candidates through the degree of enthusiasm with which their names were received. Scores of conferences, held while the speech-making was in progress, convinced the friends of the Hoosier candidate that with Governor Smith and William G. McAdoo out of the way, a drift toward him would set in very promptly.

Pending their expected elimination, it was stated last night, it is possible that Senator Ralston may be found drifting along with his thirty Hoosier votes and little or nothing more recorded in his favor. Those active in his support are anxious to avoid during the early balloting any unusual showing of strength which might arouse antagonism in the camps of other "dark horses." They are intent on shaping their strategy so that the potential strength of their candidate will be disclosed when the crucial stage of the struggle is reached and not before. They profess to be confident that from that time on he will continue to show gains on each successive ballot.

Unite on Early Strategy.

Mr. Taggart has been actively engaged in establishing among promoters of lesser booms a modus vivendi which he believes will endure throughout the early part of the battle.

The strategy to be pursued by the leaders behind the standards of the fourteen candidates is this:

Each, including favorite sons to whom delegations from their own States are more or less loosely committed, will bend every effort toward holding on to his own delegates during the early stage of the balloting, neither attempting to

Continued on Page Three.

Octogenarian Runaway Gets His Wish; Wanted All His Life to See a Convention

James John Brady, the 82-year-old Civil War veteran who ran away from Mrs. Florence Grey's boarding house in Vincennes, Ind., last Sunday and came to New York on money he had saved from his pension because he wanted to attend a Democratic National Convention and see the Brooklyn Bridge before he died, realized one of his ambitions yesterday. If it doesn't rain, he will realize the other today.

From 10:30 A. M. until nearly 4:30 in the afternoon Brady sat in the centre of the space reserved for spectators on the floor of Madison Square Garden. Charles A. Greathouse, member of the Democratic National Committee from Indiana, sent the runaway an alternate's ticket after reading in THE TIMES that Brady had appeared penniless and exhausted at the Travelers' Aid Society, 144 East Forty-fourth Street, after vainly attempting to get a convention ticket at the Indiana headquarters at the Hotel McAlpin.

Although Brady, who was born in Fourteenth Street, but hasn't been in New York since he left here as a lad of 14, protested that he couldn't possibly get lost, one of the Travelers' Aid Society workers went with him to the Garden.

Brady went to bed early to make ready for today's program. At 10:30 o'clock, unless the weather prevents, he will be taken across the Brooklyn Bridge in an automobile by William Crockett, architect of the Travelers' Aid Society building.

When Louise Closser Hale, who also comes from Indiana, heard of Brady's presence in New York, she sent him tickets to "Expressing Willie," in which she is appearing at the Forty-eighth Street Theatre. Brady attended the performance Thursday night. Yesterday Mrs. Grey, the runaway's landlady in Vincennes, sent him $40 to get him home. The railroad fare is $33, so he had $7 to spend.

KLAN HOLDS UP PLATFORM

Committtee in Session Early This Morning Over Question.

34 TO 20 FOR NAMING KLAN

McAdoo League Plan, Calling for a Referendum, Is Adopted by Vote of 34 to 16.

BAKER CONTINUES STRUGGLE

He May Take 1920 Plank to the Convention—Child Labor Plank Turned Down.

The McAdoo forces triumphed in the Resolutions Committee yesterday when by a vote of 32 to 16 the committee adopted the McAdoo policy on the League of Nations, with a plank declaring approval of the League but making adherence to it dependent upon a referendum of the people.

With the League plank adopted, the committee proceeded to take up the Ku Klux Klan plank. A poll indicated that 34 members of the committee favored a plank which did not mention the Klan by name, while 20 were for a plank which should denounce the organization specifically.

Three planks with respect to the Ku Klux Klan were presented. That which omitted the name of the Invisible Empire was prepared by William J. Bryan. That naming the Klan was the proposition of the anti-Klan forces in general.

There was, however, an additional plank presented from Alabama, the home State of Oscar W. Underwood.

The Composite Klan Plank.

The composite plank of the opponents of the Klan reads:

> We condemn political secret societies of all kinds as opposed to the exercise of free government and contrary to the spirit, if not the letter, of the Constitution. No member of such society can justly claim to be a disciple of Thomas Jefferson.
>
> We therefore pledge the Democratic Party to oppose the efforts of the Ku Klux Klan or any similar organization that inteerferes with political freedom or religious liberty, or which engenders racial prejudices.

It declares, further, that a religious test cannot be required for any office of trust in the Government, and that there shall be no effort to arouse religious dissension.

The Bryan plank, which leaves out any specific mention of the Klan, reaffirms the devotion of the Democratic Party to the fundamental principles contained in the Constitution, providing for the free exercise of religion, freedom of speech, freedom of the press and the right of the people to free assembly.

The third, or so-called Alabama plank, is long, reviewing the history of organizations of that character and making specific reference to the "Know-Nothing Party" of 1856.

It declares that the Democratic Party openly opposed the "Know-Nothings," and that there is no reason now why it should not specifically oppose the Ku Klux Klan.

Taking the floor under the same five-minute limitation rule on speakers that obtained when the League was under discussion, Mr. Bryan spoke in opposition to naming the Invisible Empire in the party declaration. He declared that four years hence the Klan organization would have been forgotten, and he pleaded with the committee to avoid any action that would divide the Democratic Party. He said he could support no movement which would array one set of men against another.

Sharp Battle Over the League.

Chairman Homer Cummings said at a late hour this morning that the committee expected to complete its deliberations in time to present a complete report to the convention when it meets at 9:30 o'clock this morning.

After five hours of spirited debate, in which William J. Bryan and most of the Senate members of the committee opposed a plank declaring for entrance into the League immediately and without reservations, as proposed by Newton D. Baker, the referendum section was adopted. Mr. Baker, although standing alone, vigorously upheld the position of Woodrow Wilson and told the committeemen that they would not dare to strangle this great Wilson policy if the War President were living.

At 12:30 this morning the Resolutions Committee by a decisive vote adopted the completed League of Nations plank with the referendum provision.

William J. Bryan, Senators Pittman, Walsh and Caraway and Representative Garrett, among others, favored this plank. Mr. Baker opposed it and demanded the incorporation in the platform of the 1920 plank, which declared for full entrance into the League.

Mr. Baker will present a minority report to the convention.

Text of the League Compromise.

The text of the League compromise plank as drafted reads:

The Democratic Party pledges all its energies to the outlawing of the

Continued on Page Two.

16 Candidates for President Now Before the Convention

When the roll-call of States was completed yesterday sixteen candidates for the Presidency had been nominated by the Democratic National Convention. Among the nominees are five United States Senators and the Governors of six States. Here is the list, in order of the candidates' respective States:

Senator O. W. Underwood.Alabama
Senator J. T. Robinson.....Arkansas
William Gibbs McAdoo....California
Ex-Senator W. Saulsbury..Delaware
Senator Samuel M. Ralston...Indiana
Governor Jonathan M. Davis..Kansas
Governor Albert C. Ritchie.Maryland
Senator W. N. Ferris......Michigan
Governor Chas. W. Bryan..Nebraska
Governor F. H. Brown.N. Hampshire
Governor G. S. Silzer....New Jersey
Governor Alfred E. Smith.New York
David Francis Houston....New York
Ex-Governor James M. Cox....Ohio
Senator Carter Glass.......Virginia
John W. Davis........West Virginia

RAIL LABOR CHIEFS STAND BY M'ADOO

Statement Signed by Forty Officials Declares Organized Workers Are For Him.

MAKE THIRD-PARTY THREAT

Gompers and Holland Repudiate Inclusion of Federation and State Workers.

Forty officials of railway labor unions who are working for the nomination of William G. McAdoo issued a statement through his headquarters yesterday saying that organized labor was overwhelmingly for him.

The statement was received with surprise among the 350 labor leaders in New York, and Samuel Gompers, who is Chairman of organized labor's Non-Partisan Committee, made the following comment:

"No one has the right to speak for the American Federation of Labor."

The railway unions' statement said:

"The political situation so far as the labor vote is concerned is without parallel. There is no precedent for it in our political history. There are here today more than forty representatives of leading labor organizations, including those of railroad labor, working day and night for the support of Mr. McAdoo's candidacy. These men are all here because of their own convictions, supported by the rank and file of their organizations.

"The sentiment among the great mass of organized wage earners is overwhelmingly for McAdoo, and, in the judgment of these same leaders, he must be the nominee if these leaders are to go to the Convention for Progressive Political Action on July 4 at Cleveland and vote against the placing of an independent candidate in the field.

"They have the necessary votes to prevent the successful launching of an independent movement. There is no other available Democratic candidate to whom the workingman will give the same unqualified support. Neither the Republican Party nominee nor the platform adopted by the Republican Convention is acceptable to the organized workers affiliated with the Conference for Progressive Political Action.

"If Wall Street, the Democratic bosses and the representatives of big business wish to divorce these workers from the Democratic Party in the present campaign they will continue their opposition to Mr. McAdoo. They do not realize the state of mind of labor and of the masses of the people for a truly progressive candidate.

"The present activities of some of the Democratic bosses can be likened to nothing more clearly than to the fiddling of Nero while Rome burned."

The statement was signed by Timothy Shea, Assistant President of the Brotherhood of Locomotive Engineers and Firemen; A. O. Wharton, member of the Federal Labor Wage Board; B. M. Jewell, President of the Railroad Employes Department of the A. F. of L.; J. A. Franklin, President of the Brotherhood of Boilermakers and Iron Shipbuilders; J. G. Luhrson, President of the Railway Telegraphers and E. Millimen, Vice President of the Maintenance of Way Employes.

At the Hotel Aberdeen headquarters of the Federation surprise was expressed that the railway men should have issued a statement on behalf of organized labor. It was pointed out that organized labor officially has no candidate, that its policy with respect to candidates is non-partisan, and that if the candidate is to its liking it will support him, whoever he may be. At the same time it was said that the railway unions would be expected to support whatever candidate was nominated if he were agreeable to the representatives of the mass of organized labor.

Federation representatives believe that the platform will strike a truly progressive note with regard to those planks in which labor is interested. These include an unqualified demand for State action on the Federal Child Labor amendment; abolition of the Railroad Labor Board section of the Esch-Cummins act and a clear-cut attack on the abuse of the injunction in industrial disputes.

It was reported yesterday that in re-

Continued on Page Five.

STORM OVER KLAN MENACING

Leaders Expect Lively Contest Today on the Convention Floor.

SERIOUS SCHISM IS FEARED

McAdoo Proposal for Klan Compromise Is Promptly Rejected by Smith.

CANDIDATES MORE ACTIVE

Delegates Appraise Dark Horses With a View to Second Choice in Case of Deadlock.

By RICHARD V. OULAHAN.

No more confused party situation could possibly exist than that which confronted the Democratic National Convention when it adjourned at 6 o'clock last evening until 9:30 o'clock this morning.

The Ku Klux Klan issue is the centre of the whirligig of uncertainty in which the Democratic Party finds itself involved after its convention has been in session for four days without having accomplished anything of a definite or forward character. The Klan question overshadows everything, even the important matter of choosing the party's candidate for President.

A cloud no bigger than a man's hand when leading Democrats and party workers began assembling in New York last week for the party's quadrennial gathering, the Ku Klux problem has blackened the entire Democratic sky and promises a storm that may play havoc with party interests during the political campaign of 1924.

Today the convention's Committee on Resolutions, its members overworked, drowsy from lack of sleep, overwrought, will bring into the convention the platform of principles which the committee was engaged in drafting last night. At least the expectation was that the platform would be presented.

Nothing known of the proceedings behind the closed doors of the room in the Madison Square Hotel, opposite the Garden, in which the Committee on Resolutions has been holding its sessions, justified the contention of optimistic leading Democrats that there was a prospect of a unanimous agreement on a Ku Klux Klan plank which would enable the convention to dispose of this awkward embarrassment without exposing to the country a serious schism ominous of the preservation of party solidarity in the months preceding the Presidential election.

Sessions to Go Into Next Week.

In the midst of the confusion one fact stands out clearly. That is that the Democratic Convention will go over into next week. How long its duration will be nobody knows. It threatens to be the longest national gathering in the party's history. With that meticulous regard for the sensibilities of voters who believe in keeping holy the Sabbath day, there will be an adjournment from this evening until Monday morning.

What today will bring forth in the historic interior of Madison Square Garden is as much a matter of uncertainty as everything else involving the convention other than an extension of the convention's sessions into next week. The whole day may be devoted to discussing the platform, with assurance of a battle royal between the McAdoo and the anti-McAdoo forces over the question of condemning the Ku Klux Klan by name. It is possible—barely possible—that before the convention takes its week-end adjournment on Saturday night balloting on a choice of a Presidential candidate will be in progress without any definite result.

Sunday promises to be a day of conferences among leaders with a view to determining upon a way to lead the party out of the maze in which it finds itself through the foremost position given the question of religious liberty.

Last night it was the understanding that such conferences will be held. They probably will comprise three groups, each meeting separately, but with one group seeking to serve in a mediatory and conciliatory capacity. A group composed of leading men—and perhaps including some women—will make an effort to bring into harmony the diverse views of the McAdooites and the anti-McAdooites over the Klan. These arbiters are certain to have a difficult task in the conditions that now prevail, in which old party chiefs, veterans of many political conventions, cool and collected in most circumstances, are showing a tendency to see red.

Candidates Are Still Active.

Meanwhile, the matter of choosing the Democratic candidate for President to oppose Calvin Coolidge has been shoved into what seems to be a secondary place. But proponents of the selection of this Presidential aspirant or that have not lost sight of it.

While there appears to be a rather general feeling that no light on the Presidential situation is possible while the Ku Klux issue remains unsettled, undercurrents are at work that affect the matter of a Presidential choice.

The situation with reference to candidates underwent no perceptible change yesterday other than that there was an increase in the tendency on the part of

"All the News That's Fit to Print."

The New York Times.

THE WEATHER
Cloudy and colder today; cloudy and rain tomorrow.
Temperature yesterday, max. 37, min. 28.
For weather report see next to last page.

VOL. LXXV....No. 24,778. *** NEW YORK, THURSDAY, NOVEMBER 26, 1925. TWO CENTS In Greater New York | THREE CENTS Within 200 Miles | FOUR CENTS Elsewhere in the U. S.

DEMOCRATS SPLIT OVER REDUCTIONS IN NEW TAX BILL

Rainey Declares He Will Lead Fight for Drastic Changes in the Measure.

TAKES ISSUE WITH GARNER

Illinois Ways and Means Member Assails Personal Exemptions and Surtax Cut.

SAYS RICH MEN FARE BEST

Coolidge Expresses Pleasure Over the Revision and Assurance of Early Passage.

Special to The New York Times.

WASHINGTON, Nov. 25.—President Coolidge expressed his pleasure over the shape taken by the new $336,236,000 tax reduction bill during a call made upon him today by Chairman Green of the Ways and Means Committee. It is understood that the President was particularly gratified by the non-partisan aspect of the bill and the assurance that it would be hurried through the House.

But at the same time the President was expressing his satisfaction a startling break developed among the Democrats of the Ways and Means Committee who have been helping draw the tax bill. Representative Rainey of Illinois came out with a statement bitterly assailing the bill in nearly every important particular, and announcing that he proposed to lead a fight in the House to make drastic changes in the measure.

Mr. Rainey's views are diametrically opposed to tax principles laid down by Representative Garner, the ranking Democrat of the committee, and are against the compromises made by Mr. Garner with the Republicans for the sake of harmony.

Mr. Rainey wants the personal exemptions to remain as they are, the estate taxes to stay at a 40 per cent. maximum, the surtax to be set at a 25 per cent. maximum, the earned income limit to be retained at $10,000, and the retroactive action in applying 1921 rates to estates falling under 1924 schedules to be stricken out of the bill. He says he will make a hard fight on the floor for each of these aims.

Points to "Bad Features."

"The bill is non-partisan in its commendable features, which are many, and in its bad features, which in my judgment are serious. There is, however, a chance to amend it on the floor. We have raised the exemptions and have relieved nearly 2,000,000 taxpayers of the payment of $5 or $6 each in income taxes per year—a relief which they did not ask and did not want—and we have relieved less than 4,000 men of the payment of $100,000,000 in taxes every year—a greater relief than they asked for or expected. Forty-two men in the United States have been relieved of $20,000,000 in taxes per year, and we call this result 'trading' and 'balancing.'

"If this was a 'trade' it is not difficult to see who got the better of it. To relieve 2,000,000 men of a conscious contribution which they were perfectly willing to make of $5 or $6 each per year is dangerous indeed from an economic standpoint. It leads in the direction of old-age pensions, widows' pensions, unemployment pensions, subsidies to industries in order to enable them to pay a better wage, &c.

"We have raised the earned income allowances so as to apply to incomes of $20,000 a year, an unexpected gratuity. We have made the reduced estate taxes retroactive in 1924, relieving the estates of persons now deceased of the payment of $20,000,000 within the next twelve months into the Treasury of the United States—an unexpected gratuity.

"If we had stopped the surtax rate at 25 per cent. and had permitted the very satisfactory exemptions to remain where they now are, and if we had not made the estate tax retroactive, and had permitted the earned income allowance to remain as it now is, we would have had sixty or seventy million dollars to apply to the relief of the taxpayers who are really burdened and who really carry on the industries of the country, to wit: Those who pay on incomes of between $25,000 a year and $70,000 a year. These taxpayers will never know there has been a reduction in the income tax rate, and they constitute that class which expected it most and which need it most.

Says the Rich Get the Most.

"The elimination of estate taxes points in the direction of the complete destruction of this kind of taxes. The war between the States led by Florida, anxious to furnish a refuge safe from taxation for the very rich, will go merrily on. The men of large incomes get more out of this bill than in their wildest dreams they ever expected. We are generous indeed in the bill to this class of our citizens. We gave them a maximum surtax rate of 20 per cent. when they were only asking for a maximum rate of 25 per cent.

"We have repealed the publicity provisions so that the public cannot tell how fast the number of men who receive incomes of $1,000,000 a year and over is increasing, and we have relieved their estates after they die from taxes. We have reduced the taxes on grain alcohol 50 per cent., losing revenue variously estimated at from $4,000,000 to $8,000,000 per year.

"This made it necessary to retain the stamp taxes on conveyances to the

Continued on Page Four.

Crime Wave in Washington As Police Tag Automobiles

WASHINGTON, Nov. 25 (AP).—Coincident with the efforts of the Washington police to unravel and enforce an ever-changing multitude of traffic regulations, a crime wave has swept over the Capital.

Daylight hold-ups, heretofore rare in Washington, have become almost daily occurrences. Residences as well as stores have been robbed and in one case a bandit spent an hour in a private residence trussing up the occupant, his wife and the maid, and then made away with jewelry and other valuables, using the owner's automobile to accelerate his departure.

Complaints have been made that while these crimes have been committed large numbers of the police force have been busy tagging automobiles for over-parking or chasing other machines for minor infractions of the regulations.

ELLIN MACKAY CALLS CABARETS A REFUGE

Society Girls Seek Escape From Promiscuity of Smart Functions, She Writes.

DODGE 'POISONOUS' TYPES

Prefer Rubbing Elbows in Cabaret to Meeting "Unalluring Stag Lines" in Homes.

Miss Ellin Mackay, daughter of Clarence Mackay, has written a magazine article in which she asserts that young people go to cabarets to "have privacy and to escape" from the "unalluring" and "poisonous" individuals with whom young people are obliged to dance at parties in smart homes and clubs.

Miss Mackay's article is printed in the forthcoming issue of The New Yorker and is entitled "Why We Go to Cabarets."

"We go," she says, "because we prefer rubbing elbows in a cabaret to dancing at an exclusive party with all sorts and kinds of people."

The taste of the young people for cabarets is greatly deplored by their elders, who miss the dowagers on gold chairs and other features of the old-time balls, according to Miss Mackay. Then, taking the defensive, she continues:

"Cabaret has its place in the elderly mind beside Bohemia and Bolshevik, and other vague words that have a sinister significance and no precise definition.

The "Unalluring Stag Line."

"But if we can't defend the cabaret at least we can tell why we go there. It is not, as our elders would have it, because we 'enjoy rubbing elbows with all sorts and kinds of people.' We do not particularly like dancing shoulder to shoulder with gaudy and fat drummers. We do not like unattractive people. But, at least in the cabaret, though we see them and are near them, we do not have to dance with them. If our elders want to know why we go to cabarets let them go to the best of our present-day exclusive parties and look at the stag lines. There they will see extremely unalluring specimens.

"There is the young man who is well read in the Social Register, who talks glibly of the Racquet Club while he prays that you won't suspect that he lives far up on the west side. There is the gentleman who says that he comes from the South who lives just south of New York, in Brooklyn. There is the partner who is inspired by alcohol to do a wholly original Charleston, a dance that necessarily becomes a solo, as you can't possibly join in, and can only hope for sufficient dexterity to prevent permanent injury to your feet. There are hundreds of specimens, each poisonous in his own individual way."

Besides those "poisonous specimens" the débutantes and post-débutantes have to face, according to Miss Mackay, are "hundreds of pale-faced youths, each exactly alike," and "numberless colorless young men."

"The stag line," she sums it up, "is not a collection of which any hostess can be proud."

After describing a memorable leap year party at the Colony Club, she con-

Continued on Page Two.

AIR PLANS IGNORED, SAYS PATRICK, URGING A SEPARATE CORPS

Army Aviation Chief Complains of Shelving of All His Proposals.

MAKES REPORT TO DAVIS

He Again Asks Equipment and Personnel Increase and a Distinct Flying Unit.

ANTI-AIRCRAFT FIRE UPHELD

General, However, Declares Planes Are Surest Air Defense—Deplores Appropriation Cuts.

Special to The New York Times.

WASHINGTON, Nov. 25.—Major Gen. Mason M. Patrick, Chief of the Army Air Service, in his annual report to Secretary of War Davis charges that "not one" of the recommendations which he made in his last annual report for an increased Air Service, the correction of "the unsatisfactory condition with reference to commissioned personnel," and legislation for "the development of civil aviation" has been followed by tangible affirmative action. He adds that after his observations of the past year he is "still convinced that every one of these recommendations should at once be approved and carried out."

In his latest report, General Patrick reiterates his statements made before the President's Air Board favoring the conversion of the Army Air Service into a corps which would bear the same relation to the War Department that the Marine Corps does to the navy. He told the members of the Air Board that he favored such an arrangement pending the ultimate establishment of a Ministry of Defense, which, he hoped, would combine under one head the army, the navy, the Marine Corps and the air services of the two departments.

Besides these major changes in the administration of the Army Air Service, General Patrick demands the creation of a separate budget for the air corps, a separate promotion list for the Air Service, the provision of "sufficient funds to supply safe flying equipment for at least existing units and personnel," and funds for an adequate housing program for personnel of the Air Service, also the adoption of a definite aircraft building program to cover a period of years.

Praises Loyalty of Personnel.

In concluding his report General Patrick says: "During the past year much has been done to better the Air Service, its training and equipment. The spirit which animates it is evidenced by the fact that more flying was done than in any previous peace year, with a resulting improvement in the effectiveness of this arm. In its readiness to do its part in any emergency I commend the greater part of my personnel for its loyalty and for the hard work done under trying conditions."

No mention is made by General Patrick of any of the controversies which have developed in the department over the administration of the air forces or of the charges made by Colonel Mitchell, which have led to court-martial proceedings against him.

Discussing the much debated question of the value of anti-aircraft apparatus as a means of defense against attack by aircraft, General Patrick declares in his report that "the surest defense against aircraft is other aircraft," although he says that "undoubtedly a small amount" of anti-aircraft apparatus is an important part of defensive measures.

"In my report last year," General Patrick says, "I recommended specifically the following:

"Provision for an increased air service, correction of the unsatisfactory condition with reference to commissioned personnel, legislation for the development of civil aviation.

"During the year just passed not one of these recommendations has been followed by tangible affirmative action. I have had an additional year in which to observe the operation of the Army Air Service and I am still convinced

Continued on Page Nine.

William T. Dixon Dies From Bullet Wound After Acting in Tragic Play for Charity

Special to The New York Times.

BALTIMORE, Md., Nov. 25.—William Thomas Dixon, gentleman farmer and horseman, was found by his wife with a bullet wound in his temple today at his home, Greenpoint Farm, ten miles from Chestertown. A pistol was lying near him and he died about an hour later without having been able to make any statement.

No note or explanation of his death was found, and it is said that Mrs. Dixon has declared her husband had no reason to want to end his life.

Mr. and Mrs. Dixon took part in a play for charity in the Baltimore Auditorium Sunday evening. It is said that Mr. Dixon had been greatly impressed by several tragic situations in the play, and members of the family believe these may have preyed on his mind. His health had been poor for some time.

Mr. Dixon was from an old Maryland family. He was the son of Isaac Dixon, for years previous to his death the head of the paper firm of Smith, Dixon & Co. of Baltimore. An uncle of the dead man, William T. Dixon, was President of the National Exchange Bank of Baltimore.

Mr. Dixon was the President of the Kent County Horse Show, which gave an exhibition on last Armistice Day.

During the eight years in which they lived at Greenpoint Farm Mr. and Mrs. Dixon entertained their friends frequently. Their house was a social centre for that part of the county. They went to the farm when they were married. Mr. Dixon studied at Johns Hopkins University and was inclined to take up business pursuits. The Greenpoint Farm had been in the family for a long time, and he became interested in it. He lived the life of a gentleman farmer there, raising horses and food products.

Mrs. Dixon was Miss Crisfield of Kent County. Three children are living.

Mr. Dixon's mother, Mrs. Elizabeth White Dixon, lives in Baltimore. A brother, Isaac Dixon, is a student at Princeton. His sisters are Mrs. H. Childs Frick, wife of the son of H. C. Frick of Pittsburgh; Mrs. H. Ridgely Simpson, Mrs. John L. Dorsey and the Misses Catherine and Deborah Dixon. Mr. Dixon was about 37 years old.

New Mineral Named 'Kempite' Found by Stanford Scientist

PALO ALTO, Cal., Nov. 25 (AP).—Professor A. F. Rogers of the Department of Mineralogy of Stanford University today announced the discovery of a mineral in alum rock, a famous deposit at San José, that has never before been entered in the mineralogical annals of the world. He has called this discovery "Kempite" in honor of Professor James F. Kemp of Columbia University, New York.

The new mineral is a manganese oxychloride and has no commercial value.

The alum rock formation was at first supposed to be a meteorite but was later found to be a plain boulder heavily charged with manganese. The formation was broken up for this manganese during the World War and many experiments of its remaining contents were undertaken.

CHAPMAN REJECTS COMMUTATION ORDER

Coolidge Acts on Federal Sentence to Allow Connecticut to Hang Convict.

NEW REPRIEVE TO MARCH 3

Supreme Court Will Decide if Slayer Has Legal Right to Refuse.

Special to The New York Times.

HARTFORD, Conn., Nov. 25.—The recipient of a commutation of his Federal sentence from President Coolidge, which he refuses to accept, Gerald Chapman will now carry directly to the United States Supreme Court his fight to prevent death on a Connecticut gallows. On Friday Governor Trumbull will grant a reprieve, which will prevent the hanging of Chapman on Dec. 3, and fix a new date for his execution, March 3.

At the hearing on the writ of habeas corpus issued by Judge Thomas, already set for next Monday at Wethersfield prison, the State will argue that his Federal sentence having been commuted Chapman is the State's prisoner. His counsel will contend that he has the right to refuse, and has refused the commutation and is still a Federal prisoner who must serve out his unexpired term at Atlanta before he is legally in the custody of the State of Connecticut.

First and foremost the Supreme Court will be called on to decide whether Chapman can legally refuse to accept commutation of the Federal sentence. If it decides he must accept the commutation the other point is untenable.

President's Order Read to Chapman.

The fact that the President had ordered commuted Chapman's sentence of twenty-five years for the robbery of a New York mail truck was first made known today when it was read to the prisoner by Warden H. K. W. Scott at Wethersfield. States Attorney Alcorn and George H. Cohen, acting United States Attorney, of New Haven, had spent Monday with Attorney General Sargent in Washington discussing the situation caused by Chapman's effort to be transferred to Atlanta, and rumors were rife in Washington Monday night that the President, acting with Attorney General Sargent's approval, would either pardon Chapman or commute his sentence. No official word was forthcoming. The commutation of sentence, however, was signed by the President on Monday night and delivered to Mr. Alcorn, who brought it back to Hartford with him and gave it to Warden Scott this morning.

With the Warden when he went to Chapman's cell were United States Attorney Cohen and Joseph M. Freedman of Chapman's counsel. After the President's order had been read to him Chapman declared that under no circumstances would he accept the commutation, thus carrying out instructions that had been previously given to him by his counsel.

"I refuse absolutely to accept it," said Chapman.

A copy of the order was offered to Mr. Freedman, but he declined to touch it until it was understood that receiving it was in no way to be considered an acceptance of the commutation, but rather as information for counsel in the preparation of Chapman's case in the Federal courts.

Text of the President's Order.

The text of the President's order follows:

To all to whom these presents shall come, greeting:

Whereas Gerald Chapman was convicted in the United States District Court for the Southern District of New York of robbery of mail matter and placing the life of the mail carrier in jeopardy, and was sentenced Aug. 23, 1922, to imprisonment for twenty-five years in the United States penitentiary at Atlanta, Ga.; and

Whereas the said Gerald Chapman began his sentence in the Atlanta penitentiary on Aug. 25, 1922, and escaped therefrom March 27, 1923, was recaptured March 28, 1923, and escaped from the Athens (Ga.) Hospital on April 4, 1923, and was recaptured and returned to the Atlanta penitentiary Jan. 22, 1925; and

Whereas the said Gerald Chapman was transferred to the Connecticut State Prison at Wethersfield, Conn., by an order dated Jan 24, 1925, duly signed by the Attorney General; and

Whereas it has been made to appear to me that the ends of justice will be served by a commutation of the sentence in this case;

Now therefore, be it known that I, Calvin Coolidge, President of the

Continued on Page Ten.

HERRIOT IS CALLED TO FORM CABINET; SUCCESS IN DOUBT

Radical Chief Is Appealed To by French President When Doumer Fails.

SOCIALIST LEADERS SPLIT

Majority of Executive Committee Vote Against Joining Government of Any Other Party.

DISREGARD HERRIOT'S PLEA

President Doumergue Reluctant to Entrust Power to Faction Forming Small Part of Chamber.

Special Cable to THE NEW YORK TIMES.

PARIS, Thursday, Nov. 26.—In the present situation of political parties in the Chamber France does not yet seem able to get rid of dictation by the Left and by the Socialist section of the Left.

Despite the defeat of M. Painlevé last Sunday, despite the wishes of the Senate, of the President of the Republic and of the greater part of the public to obtain a central government fairly representative in the present crisis of the whole opinion of the country, all efforts to make such a government have failed.

Where M. Briand could not succeed Senator Paul Doumer has failed and President Doumergue has had to make an appeal to Edouard Herriot, who last April was turned out of office by the Senate following the revelation that his Government had secretly caused the legal limit of circulation of the Bank of France to be exceeded in order to meet a Treasury emergency.

But the leader of the Radical faction of the Left bloc, who accepted the task yesterday and promised a reply today after he had consulted the various parties, appears to be meeting with no better success. With the hope that the Socialists would consent to join the Government M. Herriot tentatively decided upon the following combination in which liberal provision was made for his allies:

President of the Council and Minister of the Interior—EDOUARD HERRIOT.
Minister of Justice—M. CHAUTEMPS or LEON BLUM, the latter a Socialist.
Minister of War—PAUL BONCOUR, Socialist.
Minister of Foreign Affairs—ARISTIDE BRIAND.
Minister of Public Instruction—M. LOCQUIN, Socialist, or M. DALADIER.
Minister of Finance—LOUIS LOUCHEUR.
Minister of Public Works—M. MOUTET, Socialist, or FREDERIC BRUNET.
Minister of the Colonies—HENRY BERENGER.
Minister of Agriculture—COMPERE MOREL, Socialist.
Minister of Labor—M. LEBAS, or M. LOCQUIN, Socialist.
Minister of Commerce—M. PASQUET.

M. Herriot is said to have made a "moving appeal" to the Socialist leaders and obtained vague promises of support. But by a vote of 13 to 10 the Executive Committee of the party at a meeting held at midnight adopted a resolution against participation in any government constituted by another party, thereby making the strongest bid for an opportunity to form the next Government themselves.

After heated discussion resulting in a split the majority of the committee adopted the principle of refusing to join forces with any other group. Thereupon a resolution was adopted by the minority expressing faith that the parliamentary group in the Chamber would work out a plan in the present grave crisis in conjunction with the Socialists. Some of the militant Socialists after tonight's meeting said the vote was a definite step toward a split in the Socialist Party.

During the last two days the Socialists have been advertising the fact that they are now quite ready to take power themselves and they have been busy casting Cabinets with Paul Boncour as Premier, Vincent Auriol as Finance Minister and themselves in all the chief ministerial offices. But they have waited in vain for a call from the Elysée to form this government.

In the Chamber of 582 deputies their number is less than a sixth, and in face of public opposition to any such flagrant minority rule President Doumergue has refused to yield to their pretentions. In asking M. Herriot to form a Ministry he put the issue plainly before the Radical leader and party as to whether they are to conform to Socialist

Continued on Page Two.

REVEAL PLAN TO IMPEACH 'MA' FERGUSON, CHARGING NEGLECT OF DUTY AS GOVERNOR; SAY HER HUSBAND DICTATES OFFICIAL ACTS

Gov. Ferguson Issues 105 Thanksgiving Pardons, Bringing Total During Administration to 1,126

AUSTIN, Texas, Nov. 25 (A. P.)—Governor Miriam A. Ferguson late today issued 105 clemency proclamations to Texas prison inmates, effective Thanksgiving Day.

This is the largest number of such proclamations yet to be issued at one time by the Governor. Since her inauguration on Jan. 20, the Governor has granted clemency to 1,126 prisoners.

Today's 105 clemency proclamations reduced the Texas prison population to 3,462. Forty-eight full pardons, forty-nine conditional pardons, seven paroles and remission of one fine constituted the woman Governor's Thanksgiving bounty to Texas convicts. Two of the full pardons and seven of the conditional pardons were granted to women.

The proclamations show that twenty-seven were convicted of murder, manslaughter and assault to murder, and that most of the convicts have served the greater part of their sentences.

Governor Ferguson's exercise of the pardoning power has been brought up in the criticism of her administration. The conference of legislators on Monday night decided that her acts of clemency would be investigated at the proposed special session of the Legislature. Recently the Central Texas Methodist Conference assailed the pardon policy as liberating "criminals, a large percentage of whom are bootleggers."

HER FOES DISCLOSE AIMS

Declare Special Session Is to Oust Family From Texas Politics.

HUSBAND IS STORM CENTRE

Speaker of House Asked for Governor and Was Told "He" Was in Conference.

SHE IS CALLED A FAILURE

Legislators Declare That the Next Executive of Texas Will Be a Man.

From a Staff Correspondent of The New York Times.

AUSTIN, Texas, Nov. 25.—The meaning of developments here in the past few days is that a group of Texas legislators is seeking to impeach Governor Miriam A. Ferguson, the "Ma" Ferguson of the 1924 election headlines, whose husband, James E. Ferguson, was impeached as Governor eight years ago on the charge of improper use of State funds.

If the attempt to impeach Mrs. Ferguson is carried through, it will be on grounds of incompetence and waste of State funds. In other words, it is charged that the State's first woman Governor is a failure.

No evidence has been produced here to show whether the attempt to impeach the Governor will succeed. Nobody believes that she has been guilty of any criminal actions, but many Texans are convinced that she is Governor in name only, and that her husband, "Jim" Ferguson, is the real Governor.

He is not accused of any criminal actions either, but the anti-Ferguson element charges that he has dictated his wife's acts as Governor in such a way as to waste huge sums of the State's money.

The anti-Ferguson group at the State Capitol made it plain today that they intend to oust Mrs. Ferguson as Governor and Ferguson from Texas politics altogether, if they possibly can, and that they are convinced that Texas has had enough of women Governors.

"The next Governor of Texas will be a man," said a spokesman for the group.

Speaker Says Husband Is Aimed At.

Speaker Lee Satterwhite of the Texas House of Representatives, who announced yesterday that he would call a special session of the House looking toward the impeachment of any State official whose conduct warranted it, if Mrs. Ferguson refused to grant the petition asking her to convene the session, made the following statement tonight to a reporter for THE NEW YORK TIMES:

"If it comes to a question of impeachment, the Legislature will not hesitate to impeach the Governor because she is a woman. It takes this stand because she is not the Governor actually, but only technically. Her husband really sits on the throne, and if he has no regard for her honor, obviously he cannot expect the Legislature to have any sympathy for her.

"If Mrs. Ferguson had been elected Governor on her own initiative, and if she were now in fact Governor of Texas, and if her official family should lead her into the trouble which she now faces, you could not prevail upon any Texas Legislature, composed of gentlemen of the chivalrous traditions of the State of Texas, to attempt to impeach her.

"But the fact is that she is only an accident in the Governor's office and is under the domination of her husband, who dictates every official act of hers.

"Therefore, the Legislature will not hesitate to impeach her if the facts justify an impeachment. For her sake, I hope they will not. If they do, it will be an impeachment of her husband and not of her, for as I said before, she is not really the Governor.

Tells of "Jim's" Dominance.

"She functions as Governor as far as affixing her signature to official documents is concerned, but further than that I doubt whether she functions at all. She may possibly overrule Jim in some questions of pardoning prisoners. All her important official acts as Governor, however, are performed upon the dictation of her husband.

"During the legislative session no legislator ever thought of going to consult Mrs. Ferguson about any matter of legislation. If Jim wasn't there when a legislator went to the Executive Office, he waited until Jim was there.

"I had an experience about six weeks ago which is typical. I came down here to discuss some matter with the Governor. When I walked into the waiting room and asked for the Governor, his secretary said he was in conference. You will notice that we say 'he' down here when we mention the Governor.

"While I was waiting, Mrs. Ferguson appeared in the rotunda and I walked out and talked with her for five or six minutes. It was just a social visit. I did not even think of discussing the object of my call with her. Then I went back to wait my turn to see the Governor-

GLORIA GOULD TAKES RESIDENCE IN PARIS

It Is Believed There to Be Preliminary to Suit to Divorce H. A. Bishop Jr.

HUSBAND IS NOW IN MAINE

Relatives and Friends of Couple Here Say They Are Unaware of Any Court Action.

Special Cable to THE NEW YORK TIMES.

PARIS, Nov. 25.—Mrs. Henry A. Bishop Jr., who was Miss Gloria Gould, has taken a house in Paris on the Rue Spontini. It is understood that her intention is to establish a legal residence in France for the purpose of suing for a divorce.

The records of the Palace of Justice as yet contain no mention of her application.

The sudden departure of Mrs. Gloria Gould Bishop for France on Oct. 3 gave rise to rumors that she intended to obtain a divorce from her husband, Henry A. Bishop Jr. When Mrs. Bishop arrived in Paris with her young daughter on Oct. 11 she said:

"The report that I intend to divorce my husband is ridiculous and the first I heard of it was from ship reporters as I was leaving New York."

When she was asked why her departure had been so hasty, she replied that it had not been so hasty as had been made out. She declared that she had gone abroad for a long rest from her work as managing directress of the Embassy, a new moving picture theatre in the Times Square district.

George J. Gillespie, counsel for Mrs. Bishop in the litigation over the Gould estate, when asked last night if the Paris report that Mrs. Bishop was to sue for divorce was true, said:

"The only comment I can make is that I can shed no light on the subject at all."

Mrs. Henry A. Bishop, mother of the husband of the former Gloria Gould, said at her home in Bridgeport:

"I don't know anything at all about it."

She added that her son was spending a long vacation in the Maine woods far from a telephone.

At the home of Miss Katherine Jordan, who was Mrs. Bishop's maid of honor, Mrs. Frank Bertram Jordan, her mother, said that Miss Jordan's comment on the dispatch was the same as Mrs. Bishop's.

Mrs. Gloria Bishop is the youngest daughter of the late George J. Gould by his first wife. She is a sister of Mrs. Anthony J. Drexel, Lady Decies, Mrs. Carroll J. Wainwright, Jay Gould,

Continued on Page Two.

FIRE RAZES 3 BLOCKS IN ROCKAWAY GALE

Unexplained Blaze on Ocean Front Burns Largest Dance Pavilion in Whole City.

DAMAGE PUT AT $100,000

Jamaica Causeway Speeds Aid—New Water System Halts Spread of Flames.

Fire which started in an unexplained way in Louis A. Phillips's dance pavilion at Beach 102d Street and the Boardwalk at Seaside, Rockaway, last night burned that structure and, fanned by a high wind, spread through three blocks on the ocean front, destroying the Atlas Bathing Pavilion, the Auto Race Speedway and twelve concession stands. The loss was estimated at $100,000.

Five companies of firemen poured water on neighboring buildings, all, like those destroyed, of frame construction, to prevent a conflagration which it was at first believed might wipe out the whole section. The wind, however, was blowing toward the sea, and the speedy arrival of fire companies from Ozone Park and Woodhaven over the new Jamaica Bay Causeway, coupled with the high water pressure recently installed in the neighborhood, saved the other buildings. They included Morrison's Theatre at Ocean Avenue and 102d Street and Steeplechase and Thompson's parks at Ninety-eighth Street, on either side of the burned area.

Phillips's pavilion was one of the largest structures of its kind in Greater New York, a mammoth wooden building, 75 feet wide and 275 feet long, extending, until the filling in for the boardwalk was begun, 200 feet into the ocean. During the Summer it was the meeting place of many of the larger political clubs of the city, Long Island and New Jersey for rallies, picnics and dances attended by several thousand persons.

The pavilion and the other structures were closed for the Winter and no one was supposed to be in them, but, like other seaside places, it may have been the meeting place of tramps.

Blaze Fanned by Wind.

The fire, whipped by the wind, reduced it to ashes and the flames and sparks were blown eastward, setting fire almost immediately to adjoining concession stands between it and the Atlas Bathing Pavilion at 101st Street and the adjacent Auto Race Speedway at 100th Street.

Here a block of vacant land intervened between the Speedway and a row of concession stands, but the sparks were blown across it and the latter also caught fire, while other sparks, despite the direction of the wind toward the sea, were settling on buildings across Ocean Avenue toward the mainland.

Fire companies from Far Rockaway, Rockaway Park and Rockaway Beach were summoned in the first two alarms and two additional alarms summoned apparatus from Ozone Park and Woodhaven.

The latter used for the first time the Jamaica Bay Causeway from Woodhaven across Jamaica Bay to Beach Ninety-fifth Street, making the journey in fifteen minutes, whereas the old way overland would have required three-quarters of an hour.

It was the first time also for a test of the new water pressure system of the Rockaways in an actual fire. Hitherto the pressure there has been fifteen pounds, but the new system developed a maximum of ninety pounds and, with all the fire companies pouring streams on the burning buildings and on others to soak them thoroughly against the flames, the pressure was never lower than seventy-five pounds.

When the fire companies saw that the burning buildings could not be saved most of them concentrated on preventing the spread of the blaze to adjoining structures, and they confined the fire so well to the three blocks between 102d Street and Ninety-ninth Street that only one building in adjacent territory was damaged. It was Philip Jolly's Pavilion at 102d Street and the Boardwalk, where a few sparks, settling in a direction opposite to the wind, fell on the roof and burned part of the building.

Morrison's Park, at 102d Street and Ocean Avenue, and Steeplechase and Thompson's parks in the opposite direction, were not damaged.

Cold and Cloudy Promised Here Today; New England to Have White Thanksgiving

The New England States, where Thanksgiving Day had its inception 300 years ago, will be the only part of the East where typically cold and crisp Thanksgiving weather, with snow on the ground, will prevail today, according to the official forecast. In this city it will be partly cloudy and cold, with a temperature probably in the vicinity of freezing. Southward to the Gulf States unsettled, showery weather, with moderate temperature, will prevail until late in the day.

Yesterday's snow flurries, which began at noon and kept up intermittently until 6 o'clock in the evening, when they turned to rain, resulted in a fall of only fifteen one-hundredths of an inch. It was sufficient, however, to make the footing slippery and uncertain, and taxicabs and other automobiles skidded perilously as they turned corners.

Snow shovels were in use in Buffalo yesterday for the first time this Winter, according to an Associated Press dispatch. The snow flurries of the early part of the week developed into a heavy storm which continued all forenoon. The fall there was about one inch.

The highest temperature here yesterday was 37 degrees, registered shortly after noon. The lowest was 28 degrees at 5 in the morning.

San Antonio, Texas, managed to be quite comfortable with the thermometer at 78, while New Orleans was only two degrees lower.

Special to The New York Times.

WINSTED, Conn., Nov. 25.—Visiting Winsted when a light snowstorm was in progress today, George Stumpf of Hall Meadow issued a cheering statement. He declared Winter would not be as severe as many have predicted and based his prediction of mild weather on the short hair on his horse, which, he said, was "no longer than in Summertime," and on husks leaving the corn partially exposed.

"Charlie Chuck" lends support to Mr. Stumpf's prediction, as groundhogs continue to roam above ground.

ALL THAT JAZZ

CARYN JAMES

In 1922, F. Scott Fitzgerald suggested calling his new story collection "Tales of the Jazz Age," but his editor, Maxwell Perkins, came back with news that the sales force hated the title.[1] "They feel there is an intense reaction against all jazz," he wrote, and the word alone would "injure the book." Fitzgerald, 25 years old and already a best-selling novelist, wrote back: "It will be bought by my own personal public. . . . That is, by the countless flappers and college kids who think I am a sort of oracle." Fitzgerald was right, of course.[2] He kept the title and is credited with having invented the phrase "jazz age," a term that still evokes vivid images of dancing the Charleston at drunken, all-night parties.

To a country emerging from the darkness of World War I, the sunny 1920's quickly came to mean youth, sexual freedom and hedonism, an appealing departure that would reverberate though the rest of the century. In the 1960's, a similar cultural shift would be called the "generation gap"; by the end of the century the kind of fame Fitzgerald enjoyed would belong to the age of celebrity. Fitzgerald was the oracle of both.

He reflected and helped shape the period with his personal fame—Scott and Zelda Fitzgerald leaping in fountains made them legends in their own time—and because his work was both popular and enduring. "The Great Gatsby"[3] (1925), with its self-made hero and dreams of endless possibility, is central to the American identity, and its eloquent romanticism makes it a classic, but it didn't sell as well as works by Fitzgerald and others that spread a wilder image of jazz babies.

Edna St. Vincent Millay's[4] famous line, "My candle burns at both ends," which appeared in her 1922 poetry collection "A Few Figs from Thistles," set the tone and theme for the

American writer F. Scott Fitzgerald, a chronicler of the 1920's lifestyle, with his family aboard a ship in 1926.

Edna St. Vincent Millay, whose poetry set a tone for the decade of the 1920's, was known for the line, "My candle burns at both ends."

FURTHER READING

1 "The Man Who Made Great Novels Greater," see March 26, 1950, article.
2 "Scott Fitzgerald: Ten Years After," see December 24, 1950, article.
3 "Scott Fitzgerald Looks into Middle Age," see April 19, 1925, article.
4 "Edna St. V. Millay Found Dead at 58," see October 20, 1950, article.

This flapper on the cover of Life Magazine was an icon of the times, dancing the Charleston and wearing the distinctive flapper fashion.

Sinclair Lewis poses with his bride, the journalist Dorothy Thompson, as they return from Europe in 1928.

decade. And two of the period's most popular works of fiction sold the allure of the slightly disreputable. The Armenian-born, London-based writer Michael Arlen's 1924 novel "The Green Hat," in which a well-bred, sympathetic heroine has a string of casual lovers, was a huge best seller on both sides of the Atlantic. It was so scandalous that when it became a Greta Garbo movie four years later, with the more suggestive title "A Woman of Affairs," the movie credits skittishly dropped any mention of the book and the plot didn't mention that the heroine's husband had syphilis.

Anita Loos's 1926 best seller "Gentlemen Prefer Blondes" was presented as the diary of a gold-digging flapper, Lorelei Lee (before the movies recast her as Marilyn Monroe in the 50's). With their tantalizing portraits of this new freedom, such fictions allowed readers to live vicariously, to sit back and read about the world changing around them—often in that sinful New York City—even if they sat in cozy armchairs in Middle America.

The image of the jazz age could spread through fiction because the publishing world was so different in the days when movies were silent (before 1927) and broadcast television nonexistent. A flourishing tabloid press kept photographs of flappers in view, but mainstream magazines were immensely influential too. In 1920 alone Fitzgerald had five stories published in the Saturday Evening Post, including "Bernice Bobs Her Hair" (something proper young ladies didn't do), in which the Midwestern heroine is transformed from an innocent into a flirt.

The revolt against staid 19th-century morality was evident even in writers who weren't especially jazzy. Sinclair Lewis, one of the decade's best-selling novelists, undermined the deadness of bourgeois America in works like "Main Street" and "Babbitt."[5] And Fitzgerald's own fiction included a cautionary undercurrent often overlooked in his day, a realization that high-spirited hedonism would eventually have to deflate; Gatsby, after all, is killed. As the decade went on, ominously if unknowingly headed toward the great stock market crash of '29, the very titles of Fitzgerald's story collections signal the change, from the youth and brash confidence of "Flappers and Philosophers" in 1920 to "All the Sad Young Men" in '26.

The soundtrack to all this was real jazz, epitomized by the music of Duke Ellington,[6] which crossed over from Harlem to white America. And in literature the Harlem Renaissance, the flowering of black writers embracing their own experience and culture, ran parallel to and sometimes intersected the Fitzgerald line. The Great Migration from the rural south to the urban north set the groundwork for poets like Langston Hughes and Countee Cullen, and fiction writers like Nella Larsen and Jean Toomer, whose 1923 "Cane,"[7] a poetic fiction about Southern and Northern black characters, remains one of the most respected works of the decade.

As dynamic as the Harlem Renaissance was in its day, its long-term influence was even more striking. Zora Neale Hurston,[8] along with Hughes and others, founded the literary journal "Fire!" in 1926, but the works for which she is now known didn't arrive until the 30's: she collected folktales in the story collection "Mules and Men" (1935) and used Southern dialect in her novel "Their Eyes Were Watching God" (1937). Literature as a means of exploring black culture was the Harlem Renaissance's crucial legacy to younger writers like Richard Wright, whose "Native Son" (1940) was a galvanizing indictment of racist society, and Ralph Ellison, whose "Invisible Man" (1952) still stands as a masterpiece about a black man, or anyone, defining a self.

The movement's publishing landmarks were just as valuable. Claude McKay's 1928 novel "Home to Harlem"[9] became a best seller, but even as he made that breakthrough he faced a generation gap and philosophical differences within his own community. W.E.B. Du Bois criticized the novel for its blunt descriptions of street life and sexuality, setting off a debate about the kind of image black artists should create that continues even now.

By the end of the decade, the old guard and the new of both races were still engaged in that generational tug of war. In February 1928, a short article in The Times ran under the headline "Sees Derby as Foe of Jazz." It reported that the president of Smith College had told an alumnae dinner, "We have turned the corner and are now moving with our backs to the jazz age...We are reverting to Victorian formalism." The evidence: "Men are beginning to wear black derby hats."

5 "The Man From Main Street," see September 24, 1922, article.
6 "Duke Ellington, a Master of Music, Dies at 75," see May 25, 1974, front page.
7 "Cane," see January 19, 1969, article.
8 "Looking For Zora; Zora," see December 30, 1979, article.
9 "When Spring Comes to Harlem," see March 11, 1928, article.

Texas Guinan ran speakeasy saloons in the U.S. and became famous for her raucous greeting to customers, "Hello, sucker!"

Harlem Renaissance writer Zora Neale Hurston is best known for her novel "Their Eyes Were Watching God."

Duke Ellington was among those who set the standard for jazz in the 1920's, moving the music from black to white America.

Actress Marlene Dietrich seen here in her role as Lola in the film "The Blue Angel," about a German nightclub entertainer of the 1920's life in Europe.

Ernest Hemingway and his wife, Pauline Pfeiffer, aboard a ship as they arrive in New York.

Dancer and jazz singer Josephine Baker was the toast of the town thanks to her appearance in nightclubs in Paris.

The Jazz Age waned with the sobering decades of the Depression and then World War II. Fitzgerald left for Europe. But when he sat in Parisian cafes drinking with Hemingway, he wasn't wearing a derby. Those tales of the freewheeling jazz age were tales of a cultural revolution, and they left a mark on American life and art as enduring as Gatsby's dreams.

CARYN JAMES *was a critic at large for The New York Times where she wrote about a wide range of cultural subjects, including film, books, theater and television. At The Times, she previously served as an editor on the Book Review, a film critic and chief television critic. She is the author of several novels including "Glorie" and "What Caroline Knew." She also was a co-author of "The Best DVDs You've Never Seen, Just Missed or Almost Forgotten: A Guide for the Curious Film Lover."*

"All the News That's Fit to Print."

The New York Times.

THE WEATHER
Fair and warmer today and tomorrow; moderate south winds.
Temperature yesterday—Max., 60; Min., 39.
For weather report see Page 50

VOL. LXXV....No. 24,939. **** NEW YORK, THURSDAY, MAY 6, 1926. TWO CENTS in Greater New York | THREE CENTS Within 200 Miles | FOUR CENTS Elsewhere in the U. S.

NORGE BEGINS FLIGHT FOR SPITZBERGEN; DUE AT VADSO TODAY

She Will Refuel There and Then Continue On to Kings Bay.

HAS HEAD WINDS AT START

But Picks Up Speed After Sunset and Makes 75 Kilometers an Hour.

CIRCLES OVER LENINGRAD

Crowds in Streets Cheer as Dirigible Departs—No Trouble in Leaving Hangar.

By FREDRIK RAMM,
The New York Times Correspondent Aboard the Norge.

Copyright, 1926, by The New York Times Co and The St. Louis Globe-Democrat.
By Wireless to THE NEW YORK TIMES.

ON BOARD THE DIRIGIBLE NORGE, on Way to Vadso, May 5, 9:30 P. M. Russian Time (3:30 P. M., New York Daylight Saving Time).—Our speed is now 75 kilometers. It is after sunset and the temperature is sinking. In spite of furs and warm clothes we feel rather cold. The Norge has now covered half the distance from Rome to Point Barrow. Provided no unforeseen circumstances arise, the Norge is due at Vadso before noon tomorrow.

ON BOARD THE DIRIGIBLE NORGE OVER LAKE ONEGA, Russia, on Way to Vadso, May 5, 5:40 P. M Russian Time (11:40 A. M. New York, Daylight Saving Time).—We have now reached the west coast of Lake Onega. Our average speed since we left Gatchina has been fifty kilometers hourly. This means an average head wind for the first eight hours of thirty kilometers.

The ship moves now more slowly but rolls all the time. We had most of the heavy rolling halfway between the two great lakes of Ladoga and Onega when the ship in a few seconds was lifted 300 meters over the ground.

From seventy kilometers north of Petrozavodsk, where the Norge reached Lake Onega, we follow the Murmansk railway to the White Sea. All are well.

ON BOARD THE DIRIGIBLE NORGE, OVER LAKE LADOGA, May 5, 3 P. M. Russian Time (9 A. M. New York Daylight Saving Time).—After six hours of flight the Norge had passed the eastern coast of Lake Ladoga, 225 kilometers northeast of Leningrad, and was steering for Petrozavodsk on the western coast.

Owing to the fresh head winds, the ship makes only 45 kilometers an hour, the wind being 35. If this wind continues to Northern Finland, we can hardly reach Vadso before noon tomorrow. The ship rolls much. There is fine sunshine and all are well.

Lake Ladoga, 7,000 square miles in area and the largest lake in Europe, is eighty-five miles from Lake Onega. which is next to it in size.

Petrozavodsk is on Lake Onega, and is 185 miles northeast of Leningrad.

DEPARTS AMID CHEERS.

By WALTER DURANTY.

Copyright, 1926, by The New York Times Co and The St. Louis Globe-Democrat.
Special Cable to THE NEW YORK TIMES.

TROTSK AIRDROME, May 5.—The dirigible Norge of the Amundsen-Ellsworth-Nobile expedition made an excellent start for Vadso, in northernmost Norway, at 9:40 o'clock this morning. Despite a twenty-mile-an-hour wind which, it was feared, would make manoeuvring difficult, the ship was drawn out of the hangar rapidly and successfully and immediately sailed away from Leningrad on the penultimate lap of her Polar flight.

At midnight yesterday Colonel Nobile received a meteorological report that the weather was improving, sky likely to clear this morning and that the wind was milder from northeast, but likely to freshen as the day passed. At 5:30 this morning the members of the expedition jolted away to Gatchina Palace in an army motor truck. There were ten degrees of frost and deep mud puddles along the road coated with ice, but the wind was hardly perceptible and hopes ran high that the ship would be able to leave. Fortunately, also, the hangar faces northeast, so that there was little danger of a side current injuring the delicate fabric as it was drawn out of the hangar.

Gets Report From Vadso.

At 7:30 the wind was stronger, and Colonel Nobile received a cable message from Vadso that a thirty-mile-an-hour northerly wind was blowing there. He decided, nevertheless, to start, and by 8:30 o'clock the final stock of hydrogen and gasoline was aboard. The crew took their places at 8:45, and half an hour was spent in adjusting the balance of the ship. At 9:17 Colonel Nobile ordered the work of drawing the Norge from her hangar to begin.

At the bow there were a number of guide ropes, six others along the body and a number more at the stern. Two hundred and eighty Red soldiers took

Continued on Page Six.

New Ericsson Memorial Stamp Will Be Put on Sale May 29

Special to The New York Times.

WASHINGTON, May 5.—The issue of 15,000,000 five-cent stamps as a memorial to John Ericsson, builder of the Monitor, has been authorized by Postmaster General New in connection with the unveiling of the John Ericsson memorial statue in Potomac Park, this city, on May 29 by the Crown Prince of Sweden.

The stamp will be an upright rectangle, with a narrow white border line all around, with the exception of American and Swedish shields in the upper corners. Connecting these shields is a panel carrying the words "U. S. Postage."

The base is a gray panel inscribed John Ericsson Memorial." Resting on this base is a picture of the memorial statue.

The stamp will be placed on sale in New York, Chicago, Minneapolis and Washington on May 29.

LEWIS REFUSES PULITZER PRIZE

Author, in Declining $1,000, Declares Such Awards Are Objectionable, Dangerous.

ASSAILS MORAL STANDARD

Says Terms Are Misrepresented and They Really Demand a Compliance With 'Good Form.'

Sinclair Lewis has refused the 1925 Pulitzer Prize of $1,000 awarded on Monday to his novel, "Arrowsmith," it was announced yesterday by his publishers, Harcourt, Brace & Co., who made public a letter he has written to Columbia University from Kansas City, where he is writing a new novel. Mr. Lewis is the first person ever to refuse a Pulitzer Prize, but he urged other novelists to follow his example. His letter follows:

Hotel Ambassador,
Kansas City, Mo.

To the Pultizer Prize Committee, courtesy of Mr. Frank D. Fackenthal, Secretary, Columbia University, New York City.

Sirs:

I wish to acknowledge your choice of my novel "Arrowsmith" for the Pulitzer Prize. That prize I must refuse and my refusal would be meaningless unless I explained the reasons.

All prizes, like all titles, are dangerous. The seekers for prizes tend to labor not for inherent excellences but for alien rewards; they tend to write this, or timorously to avoid writing that, in order to tickle the prejudices of a haphazard committee. And the Pulitzer Prize for Novels is peculiarly objectionable because the terms of it have been constantly and grievously misrepresented.

Those terms are that the prize shall be given "for the American novel published during the year which shall best present the wholesome atmosphere of American life, and the highest standards of American manners and manhood." This phrase, if it means anything whatever, would appear to mean that the appraisal of the novels shall be made not according to their actual literary merit but in obedience to whatever code of good form may chance to be popular at the moment.

That there is such a limitation of the award is little understood. Because of the condensed manner in which the announcement is usually reported, and because certain publishers have trumpeted that any novel which has received the Pulitzer Prize has thus been established without qualification as the best novel, the public has come to believe that the prize is the highest honor which an American novelist can receive.

Award Becoming Tradition.

The Pulitzer Prize for Novels signifies, already, much more than a convenient thousand dollars to be accepted even by such writers as smile secretly at the actual wording

Continued on Page Seventeen.

SEVEN CONVICTS KILL A WARDEN, SUBDUE GUARDS AND ESCAPE

New Prison at Stateville, Ill., Supposed Delivery Proof, Is Scene of the Outbreak.

5 CORNERED HOURS AFTER

One Is Shot Dead in Pitched Battle With Deputies, Two of Whom Are Wounded.

OTHER DESPERADOES TAKEN

After Slaying Deputy They Kidnapped Guard and Trusty and Fled in Auto.

Special to The New York Times.

STATEVILLE, Ill., May 5.—Seven convicts, armed with knives, scissors and an iron bar, killed a deputy warden of the new "escape-proof" penitentiary here, locked up a guard and two trusties in a cell, wounded another trusty and "kidnapped" a guard and a trusty, whom they forced to drive them to freedom today outside the prison walls.

The guard and the trusty who drove the convicts from the prison were found three hours later handcuffed to a tree eighty miles away, beyond which trace of the convicts was lost, for the moment, although every available sheriff's deputy, policeman, bailiff and constable, with hundreds of armed citizens and State police searched throughout eight counties for the desperadoes.

Late tonight a Sheriff's posse encountered five of the convicts near Leonore, about fifty miles from here, and a pitched battle followed.

In the fight, one of the convicts, Bernardo Roa, was killed and two deputies, Harry Miller of Streeter and George Kaznic of Leonore, were wounded. The other four convicts were captured.

The escape from the penitentiary was made shortly after 11 o'clock this morning. The seven prisoners were working in the yard outside the building, and they asked permission, it was said, to see Deputy Warden Peter M. Klien, who is in charge of the new prison, which was completed a year ago after a study of such institutions all over the world and which was intended to make impossible an escape.

Deputy Warden Murdered.

They were told to wait in an anteroom until Mr. Klein could see them a few minutes later. Presently the summons came for the first man. Instead, three men stepped forward and as they reached the deputy warden they fell upon him with a knife, a pair of scissors and an iron bar. He was stabbed in the breast and struck on the head and killed instantly. The body was found later thrown behind a desk.

Next the seven men stepped into a corridor outside Mr. Klein's office and running in front of a solitary confinement cell. Inside the cell was Jacob Judnich, a guard, who kept the keys to the prison building. They demanded the keys of Judnich, but he refused to give them us, and since he was in the cell and the door was locked the convicts could not reach him.

But the door leading to the jail yard was open The seven men stepped outside and ran into John Keeley, Captain of the Prison Guard. They grasped him, he said later, brandished their weapons at him and told him he would be killed unless he obeyed instructions.

They forced Keeley into the prison building, led him past the Warden's office, where the man's dead body could be seen through the open door, and into the corridor outside the cell occupied by Judnich for safety. Here they held Keeley and told Judnich that unless he gave them the keys Keeley would be killed before his eyes. Terrified, yet feeling sympathy for Keeley, the guard, Judnich, handed the keys through the bars and the convicts were in command of that part of the building.

Slash Trusties and Guard.

Several of the convicts attracted the attention of Charles Odom and Charles

Continued on Page Eight.

Byrd Plane Flies Successfully at Kings Bay; Talk of Speedy Departure Across the Pole

By WILLIAM BIRD.

The New York Times Correspondent With the Byrd Expedition.
Copyright 1926 by the New York Times Co. and the St. Louis Post-Dispatch.
By Wireless to THE NEW YORK TIMES.

KINGS BAY, Spitzbergen, May 5.—The test flight today was entirely successful, Floyd O. Bennett piloting the plane for two hours. The population was thrilled and a spontaneous cheer arose at the take-off. Hats were tossed in the air. Commander Byrd watched with ill-concealed apprehension, but the landing was perfect, the plane bounding gently up a slope. Preparations are being speeded for the flight across the Pole.

Spirits rose with the Fokker plane Josephine Ford late this afternoon when the great plane was lifted in a cloud of powdery snow and accomplished a two-hour flight, landing perfectly in the appointed place, a half mile up the hill from the Norge's hangar.

An overcast sky throughout the day had added to the depression caused by repeated mishaps, and the expeditioners were straining themselves to maintain optimism. With the last adjustments finished at 6 o'clock, the course was cleared and Bennett, Novalle, Parker and Petersen entered the plane, Byrd remaining on the ground to give the others the coveted chance to fly.

The Josephine responded beautifully and her skis, slickened by a special preparation, slid smoothly down the slope, gathering momentum rapidly, and took off within 250 yards. She could have lifted sooner but Bennett was taking no chances. When the skis left the snow the whole population of Kings Bay came running from their dinner tables, hearing the whirring of the motors, and joined Byrd's men and the Norge's landing crew, then at the hangar for landing drill, in a spontaneous cheer, tossing their hats in the air.

Amundsen and Ellsworth, who were indoors, rushed out like the others just in time to see the Josephine rise. They expressed admiration of the plane's perfect work. Byrd never took his eyes off so long as the plane was in sight. Twice Bennett disappeared behind distant mountains for a quarter of an hour, causing some anxiety in the fear that he might lose his way among the low-hanging clouds.

The purpose of the test was to learn how the oil system worked in arctic conditions. It was entirely satisfactory; in fact, the only mishap was the breaking loose of a wireless generator fastened outside the fuselage and dangling on wires which caused vibration and some uneasiness among those on board until they discovered the trouble and hauled in the generator.

When the plane alighted, all rushed to congratulate the fliers, Byrd grasping Bennett's hand with emotion.

BOTH SIDES STILL HOLD FIRM IN BRITISH STRIKE, BUT MORE MEN ARE AT WORK, MORE TRAINS RUN; THREAT OF TROOPS TO GUARD VITAL SERVICES

LONDON CONDITIONS BETTER

Traffic Congestion Is Less—Now Under Control of Police.

PUBLIC BUSES APPEAR

Mail Service Is Maintained and Milk Delivery Functions With Fair Efficiency.

SCHOOLS REMAIN OPEN

Several Theatres Close, but Those Giving Performances and Movies Are Well Patronized.

Copyright, 1926, by The New York Times Company
By Wireless to THE NEW YORK TIMES.

LONDON, May 5.—London's streets became a bit more like themselves today when the bus service, which was almost entirely eliminated yesterday, began to be resumed. Not only were there more "pirate" buses—as those operated by small private companies are called—but the big General Omnibus Company put a few of its vehicles back on the streets.

The appearance of the first "Generals" created quite a sensation. Chauffeurs of taxicabs called the attention of their passengers to them, or else while caught in traffic jams exchanged observations with fellow chauffeurs about the great topic.

By the early hours of the afternoon "Generals" were by no means an uncommon sight, though the pirates still greatly outnumbered them, thus reversing the usual rule in London, where one sees about ten buses belonging to the General Company go by to one operated by pirate concerns. It was noticeable that the "Generals" visible today were almost all the older type of bus. The handsome large new buses were conspicuous by their absence.

Less Traffic Congestion.

The traffic congestion today was far less than the first day of the strike. Fewer vehicles tried to enter London and the drivers of those venturing into the city had learned valuable lessons yesterday. They did their best to keep off the principal thoroughfares and make better speed by worming their way through less important ones. The traffic police, too, had profited by yesterday's unprecedented congestion and handled the emergency traffic far better.

Big charabancs again poured into London this morning packed with workers and left this afternoon and evening conveying men and women clerks to their suburban homes. Some charabanks were run along the principal bus routes, picking up passengers exactly like the regular buses.

On the Embankment long lines of huge charabanks commandeered by the Postoffice Department stood in readiness to transport the mails along the roads throughout Britain, now that mail trains are unavailable. These vehicles were carefully guarded by special police posted all along the Embankment.

The Central London Underground Railway managed to run trains on a six-minute headway during the rush hour this morning between its suburban termini and way stations.

The tremendous run on the hotels continues. Rooms are being eagerly snapped up by those unwilling to try to get to their suburban and out-of-town homes after business hours. The Charing Cross Hotel, which is directly above the Charing Cross Railway Station, has been practically, entirely reserved by the railway management for its emergency railway staff. Volunteer trainmen kept coming in there today with slips of paper which, upon production, entitled them either to a room or a meal.

Restaurants Do Big Business.

The restaurants report that many lunchers who usually have a frugal midday meal—sometimes only a bun and cup of coffee—now have developed ravenous appetites as a result of being forced to walk miles to their jobs. Yesterday and today they ordered chops, steaks and all sorts of substantial fare—to the great satisfaction of the management.

Deliveries of letters are being made in London thrice daily. In some suburbs there had been no mail for two days, but the situation is improving.

School boys and girls who had looked forward to an enforced holiday because of the strike may be disappointed. At all schools in the London County Council area they are being urged to continue their attendance, but owing to transport exigencies modifications have been made whereby teachers will attend the schools nearest their own homes.

The theatre managers met yesterday to decide whether to close or remain open. William Gaunt, who is associated with the Shuberts in the management of His Majesty's, the Winter Garden, the Shaftesbury, the Apollo and the Adelphi, decided to close down. Five other theatres followed suit, but the rest gave the usual evening performances and some gave matinees today, reporting good houses. Most of the cinemas remain open and one of the largest reports that it will not close in any circumstances.

Many Mushroom Newspapers Spring Up to Amuse London

Copyright, 1926, by The New York Times Co.
Special Cable to THE NEW YORK TIMES

LONDON, May 5.—London journalism has reverted to the days of its infancy. Newspapers like those of Daniel Defoe, published in the eighteenth century, are now London's main source of news. Numerous sheets have sprung into existence now that anybody with a typewriter or a mimeographing machine has all the equipment necessary to become a newspaper publisher.

The most amusing newspapers are those published by the amateurs. Such is The Strand Gazette, whose price varies according to the intensity of the demand. One of its items reads: "Our correspondent has it on good authority that there is no immediate cause for worry about the liquid supply, one house in the vicinity having as many as fifteen barrels in the cellar."

Another is: "Not on strike—our tax bill has just come in. Is it a good omen?"

Some of the new mushroom sheets are printed, some mimeographed, while others are merely typewritten.

RAILWAY SERVICE SHOWS A GAIN

Volunteer Workers Run Many Trains Between London and Its Suburbs.

ROADS MUCH ENCOURAGED

Signalmen's Return to London & Midland Line Regarded as a Good Sign.

Copyright, 1926 by The New York Times Company.
Special Cable to THE NEW YORK TIMES.

LONDON, May 5.—More trains were running today to and from the Liverpool Street station here on the suburban section of the London & Northeastern Railway than there were passengers for them. It took THE NEW YORK TIMES correspondent an hour and a half to cover a distance of fourteen miles, it is true, but that was due to the overzeal of the volunteer train workers. They were so eager to get trains along that at times they congested the track.

At one spot tonight three trains were traveling toward London within a space of two miles. Four trains coming from London passed, but there were very few passengers in them. This was because of the uncertainty of the time when trains would run. Earlier in the evening, however, trains from London were crammed to suffocation with people. The passengers had the laugh on those who had traveled homeward by motor.

Some of the latter had unpleasant experiences. Strikers in the Bethnal Green district in the East End of London stopped several private motor buses and motor trucks and cleared off the passengers under threat of overturning the vehicles. In one case at least the police were on the spot in taxicabs within a few minutes and restored order for the time being.

Reports from all parts of the country show more trains running yesterday than on the first day of the last railway strike, and the services were improved today.

All essential food services were maintained on the railways and ample supplies of milk and fish were brought to London.

Difficulty in moving food was reported at Milfordhaven, where large quantities of fish were held up without means of rail or road transport, with the result that 2,000 willing workers were thrown out of employment.

The Great Western Railway announces that eleven services from London to various towns in the provinces have been arranged for and also good local service between provincial centres. Beginning today, the Metropolitan Railway, one of the principal underground systems of London, started services to London suburbs.

Continued on Page Two.

PREMIER SAYS DOOR IS OPEN

Tells Commons He Will Negotiate the Moment Strike Is Called Off.

WALES AND YORK PRESENT

They Hear Home Secretary Appeal to the Country to Stand Firm.

LLOYD GEORGE FOR CABINET

Labor Leaders Deny Strike Is Directed Against Government—Say Action Surprised Them.

Copyright, 1926, by The New York Times Company.
Special Cable to THE NEW YORK TIMES.

LONDON, May 5.—Prime Minister Baldwin announced in the House of Commons tonight that the moment the general strike was called off the Government would be prepared to resume negotiations.

The House had met to pass the emergency regulations asked for by the Government. The galleries were packed. Among the most interested spectators were the Prince of Wales and his brother, the Duke of York. Both had seats in the peers' gallery.

The Home Secretary, Sir William Joynson-Hicks, in moving a resolution embodying the regulations, announced that 7,900 special constables were on duty and more than 3,000 others had been enrolled in the last two days. He assured the House that the Government would continue to use its utmost endeavors to protect all those who desired to do their work and he appealed for the services of any able-bodied men who could help protect the community in time of danger.

Asks Country to Stand Firm.

He asked the country, in the words of the Prime Minister, to "stand firm." The people would hear all sorts of alarmist rumors, he said, but they were not to be worried by them. Whenever there was any real matter of importance he pledged his word that he would not keep back anything from the House.

Continuing, he said he had been in communication with the railway world and the House might like to know that though the position was serious the railways were improving.

This statement evoked ironical Opposition cheers and laughter, and there was renewed laughter when the Home Secretary said the omnibus services were better.

The great bulk of the electric light and power stations in London, he went on, were working well. The Government was employing naval ratings and was asking for volunteers, but it had only used 33 per cent. of the naval ratings and only 12 per cent. of the volunteers.

Five stations run by municipal companies had decided that no power or light should be permitted during the day—only at night. The London Hospital had had all its power cut off during the day.

This statement brought cries of "shame."

There was a grave possibility, the Home Secretary added, that meat in cold storage might go bad. He trusted and hoped arrangements would be made which would obviate these difficulties, but the Government realized its responsibility, and if necessary he would ask the House to support the Government in whatever steps it might take. Meanwhile the food supply was going on quite satisfactorily and milk distribution was efficiently conducted.

Henderson Pleads for Peace.

Arthur Henderson, formerly Home Secretary in the Labor Government, renewed his plea for a resumption of negotiations and declared the Government might have taken advantage of the first number of The British Gazette to state that they were still open to negotiate instead of attacking trades union leaders like Mr. Thomas, all of whom had never ceased to hope for further negotiations.

He disclaimed responsibility for the

Continued on Page Two.

Baldwin Appeals to People To Stand by the Government

Copyright, 1926, by The New York Times Co.
Special Cable to THE NEW YORK TIMES.

LONDON, May 5.—Premier Baldwin today issued the following appeal to the British people:

Constitutional Government is being attacked. Let all good citizens whose livelihood and labor have thus been put in peril bear with fortitude and patience the hardships with which they have been so suddenly confronted. Stand behind the Government, who are doing their part, confident that you will cooperate in the measures they have undertaken to preserve the liberties and privileges of the people of these islands.

The laws of England are the people's birthright. The laws are in your keeping. You have made Parliament their guardian. The general strike is a challenge to Parliament, and is the road to anarchy and ruin.

STANLEY BALDWIN.

SPORADIC CLASHES IN MANY SECTIONS

Attacks on Buses Continue in the Rougher Areas of London.

SMALL AFFAIRS ELSEWHERE

Smashing of Windows and Other Interference With Transportation.

LONDON, May 5 (AP).—Crowds in the various rougher sections of London showed a menacing attitude, especially toward police, this afternoon.

In the Limehouse district, which is one of the roughest districts in the city, taxicabs were driven off and other demonstrations were held.

At King's Cross the unfriendly crowds were so large that many of the big shops closed.

A crowd at Southwark chased three mounted policemen who were forced to flee.

Fighting occurred in the Shepherd's Bush district also. When a tramcar running under police protection broke down, a crowd gathered and began flinging missiles through the windows.

A motorbus was stoned and finally overturned. Then a free fight broke out in which women participated. Many were injured by broken glass. The police used their clubs freely.

Police Deal With Many Cases.

Copyright, 1926, by The New York Times Company.
Special Cable to THE NEW YORK TIMES.

LONDON, May 5. — Several charges arising out of the strike were heard in the Thames Police Court today.

One man, accused of placing himself in front of a charabanc and shouting "Get out and walk, you blacklegs," was followed to the police station by large crowds. He shed tears in the dock and was remanded, as was another man accused of throwing pieces of iron through plate glass windows.

A striking printer was fined at Bow Street Police Court for standing in the Strand and attempting to overturn an automobile carrying copies of the Government official newspaper.

The police denied a rumor that a man was killed in trouble last night in the East End of London. They admitted, however, that a special constable was injured in a mêlée with strikers seeking to damage motor cars.

At Canning Town, a tough East End district, the police were forced to make a charge with their clubs which they wielded with much effect.

At Poplar, another tough region, the police were also forced to use their clubs on the crowd, who had adopted a threatening attitude. As a result several strikers and sympathizers were treated at the Poplar Hospital.

Provinces Report Clashes.

The quiet produced by the general strike continued for the most part in the provinces. Violence flared up at Newcastle, where a mob attacked the Civil Commissioner's office. The rioters broke two windows before the police drove them off.

Special constables are being recruited in all parts of the country, but so far it has not been necessary to call on the territorials to aid the police. Detachments of soldiers and sailors have been moved to strategic points. One train carrying soldiers and sailors was stopped temporarily at Fratton this morning when the engineer left his engine. An officer took his place and drove the train to its destination.

Police dispersed a large demonstration of strikers in Albert Square, Manchester, this afternoon. The first prosecution at Manchester under the emergency regulations took place today when William Richard Stoker, a Manchester business man, was sent to prison for two months on the charge of attempting to do an act calculated to cause disaffection among his Majesty's forces. The police allege that his car was ready to carry seditious literature to Glasgow. An empty milk train, en route for Stafford, was

Continued on Page Three.

GOVERNMENT PLANS WIDEN

Aim to Maintain Regular Life of Community in Spite of Strike.

UNION CHIEFS CONFIDENT

Assert the Walkout Is Going On According to Schedule, With Tie-Up Almost Complete.

FOOD SUPPLIES ARE AMPLE

People Get Plenty of Milk, Fuel and Light, While Thousands Still Volunteer to Help Out.

Taxi Drivers Ordered Out; About 80 Per Cent. Strike

Copyright, 1926, by Chicago Tribune Co.

LONDON, May 6, 3:45 A. M.—About 80 per cent. of the London taxi drivers obeyed a midnight order to join the strike.

Several who refused were attacked by strikers and hauled off their vehicles, which were smashed up.

By T. R. YBARRA.

Copyright, 1926, by The New York Times Company.
Special Cable to THE NEW YORK TIMES.

LONDON, Thursday, May 6.—The greatest industrial strike in British history enters upon its third day with both sides confident, defiant and unshaken. Premier Baldwin declared last night that the Government is willing to negotiate with the strikers just as soon as the strike is called off. But the strikers show no signs of flinching. They are meeting the tremendous Government efforts to keep the regular life of the community going by equally vigorous endeavors to keep up the spirits of the strikers.

Already signs of an uglier temper are becoming apparent. As I write these words there is a lively row going on under the windows of THE NEW YORK TIMES offices, where The London Times staff is hustling bundles of its second strike-breaking issue into automobiles for distribution. The sentence I am writing was interrupted a few minutes ago by the noise of an angry scuffle in the street outside. I reached the window in time to see several bundles of copies of The London Times hurled into the slippery street by the strikers as fast as they were brought out from the presses.

The assistant foreign editor, Mr. Peterson, objected strenuously and got into a furious fist fight in the middle of the roadway, with three or four strikers sending smashing blows at his face and body. They finally knocked him into the mud, but not before he got home with some savage blows.

Then the police waded in and automobiles laden with bundles of The London Times dashed away at full speed.

Knots of angry strikers and determined groups of London Times men are still standing on the sidewalk outside the window, some bareheaded and without overcoats, despite the cold, damp weather, quite ready for more fisticuffs.

Fire in London Times Office.

The London Times office was the scene of another exciting incident last evening. Suddenly the fire gongs rang and the entire staff, together with numerous foreign correspondents housed in the big building, including THE NEW YORK TIMES staff, poured into the corridors to learn what was up. It transpired that a striker had sneaked into the building and poured some gasoline among the rubbish in a corridor and applied a match, whereupon a lively little blaze started.

It was soon extinguished, but the excitement continued long after the danger was past. Pools of water and the smell of smoke in corridors mystified the newcomers into the building and made them demand explanations from those who had seen the fire.

Disturbances on a large scale occurred tonight in Old Kent Road in the East End of London, where a large crowd of strikers held up motor trucks and private automobiles, many of which were overturned.

A motor truck taking beds to Hyde Park, which is the centre of the milk supplies, was set afire. Frequent charges were made by mounted police and seven arrests were made. Extra police from the Peckham and Camberwell districts rushed to the scene in tenders and the disturbances were quelled.

Baldwin Remains Calm.

Premier Baldwin remained calm today in the midst of Britain's tremen-

Germany Would Sell Coal to England As a Charge Against Reparations

Copyright, 1926, by The New York Times Company.
By Wireless to THE NEW YORK TIMES.

BERLIN, May 5.—That England could obtain large quantities of coal from Germany should a continuation of the general strike make this step advisable and charge the same against reparations as payments in kind is a possibility admitted by a spokesman for the Agent General for Reparations.

At least there is no insurmountable obstacle in the path of such a procedure, although it would mean a complete reversal of the policy maintained by England so far.

England has received no coal as payment in kind of annuities. The English have accepted $1,000,000 worth of dyes, but all other sums obtained through reparations have come under the head of the Recovery act, through which England collects a duty of 26 per cent. ad valorem on imports into the British Isles from Germany.

Should such a step be deemed advisable by London it is intimated by the German Ministry of Commerce here that it would be well received and no objections made. Although Germany cannot be required to deliver coal, it is hinted that available bottoms could be found in the German merchant marine to effect the trans port of large quantities. The German Government would not want to profiteer on any such transaction, but on the other hand, it could not meet the prices fixed for English coal before the strike set in.

"All the News That's Fit to Print."

The New York Times.

THE WEATHER
Showers today and tonight, followed by clearing and cooler tomorrow.
Temperatures yesterday—Max. 70, min. 62.
For weather report see Page 46.

VOL. LXXVI....No. 25,080. NEW YORK, FRIDAY, SEPTEMBER 24, 1926. TWO CENTS in Greater New York | THREE CENTS Within 200 Miles | FOUR CENTS Elsewhere in the U. S.

TUNNEY WINS CHAMPIONSHIP, BEATS DEMPSEY IN 10 ROUNDS; OUTFIGHTS RIVAL ALL THE WAY, DECISION NEVER IN DOUBT; 135,000 PAY MORE THAN $2,000,000 TO SEE BOUT IN THE RAIN

FLORIDA CONSCRIPTS ALL ITS UNEMPLOYED TO CLEAR WRECKAGE

Police, Militia and Legion Round Up Men in Streets and Set Them to Work.

CALL ISSUED FOR LABORERS

Miami Wants 25,000 Men and Hollywood and Fort Lauderdale 2,000 Each.

LOSS PUT AT $165,000,000

Known Dead Now 365, With 1,100 Injured, 500 Seriously—Fight on Disease Goes On.

By WARREN IRVIN,
Staff Correspondent of The New York Times.

MIAMI, Fla., Sept. 23.—Conscription of all unemployed persons to aid in clearing away wreckage and to speed the work of rehabilitating the Florida storm-swept area was adopted everywhere in that area today. Militiamen and police, aided by several hundred members of the American Legion who have been specially deputized, patrolled all streets and highways, apprehending all persons who could not show that they were employed and putting them immediately to work.

At the same time the city of Miami sent out a call for 25,000 laborers, and officials of Hollywood and Fort Lauderdale announced that they would employ 2,000 laborers in each city.

Mayor E. C. Romfh of Miami predicted this afternoon that within sixty days every trace of the storm's ravages will have been removed from Miami and the city will be as prosperous as ever.

Death Lists Called Inadequate.

Many here believe that the death list lacks scores of names of persons killed. A local newspaper man declared today that he made a check-up of bodies in the city and temporary morgues last Monday, at which time there were 175, but orders were given, he said, to bury the dead as quickly as possible, and many bodies were buried or shipped North for burial without any record being kept of them.

Even now it is almost impossible to get definite information as to the number of dead. The Police Department in Miami keeps no record of dead or injured and persons who inquire there are directed to the newspaper offices for information. Bodies are being taken to half a dozen different undertaking establishments and the only means of keeping a record is by constant checking up at undertaking establishments.

At Miami Beach the situation is still worse. No record was kept there for several days but yesterday the Publicity Director of the Chamber of Commerce was instructed to compile a list of dead and injured.

Hollywood and Fort Lauderdale are the only cities in which accurate records have been kept from the start.

Four new cases of typhoid at Davie, a village of 300 population five miles west of Fort Lauderdale, were reported today and caused health authorities to order the village evacuated. Sanitary conditions at Davie are very bad. The water there is still several feet deep in spots.

Doctor Rows to Patients.

One doctor who was on duty there without rest for seventy-two hours was compelled to row to a house in which a woman and three children were marooned. He said the demand for medicine liquor in the stricken area has caused the warehouse in Miami jail, where seized liquors are kept, to be emptied for the first time since this city became the bootleg distributing point for Florida.

In other sections, such as Hollywood, the police were sent out to raid all speakeasies and bootleg places, with orders to bring in seized liquors for the sick. A storm of protest arose from the church people when word got out that the doctors were using liquor for medicine.

The same doctor at Davie who rowed out to the home of the marooned woman was reported for "drunkenness," because a woman there said sh smelled liquor on his breath, and in another case when he prescribed liquor for a woman who had been exposed to the wind and rain for several hours the woman's husband threatened to shoot him if "he dared give my wife a drop of liquor."

A flotilla of destroyers arrived today from the navy base at Charleston, bringing all the anti-typhoid serum available in that district. This amounted to several thousand units.

While City Health Officer Claxton of Miami reported an adequate supply on hand today, health officials at Miami Beach said they needed about 3,000 more units of anti-typhoid serum and about 500 units of anti-tetanus serum. Nearly 10,000 persons have been vaccinated in the Miami area.

One case of tetanus developed yesterday in Miami Beach and two in Hollywood. All available tetanus serums

Continued on Page Eleven.

North Carolinians Weave Homespun Suit for Walker

North Carolina mountaineers, reputed by novelists to be a hard-drinking and generally rough lot, are now sitting peacefully in their hillside homes spinning a new suit for Mayor Walker.

The addition to the Mayor's wardrobe will be made of gray homespun and will be presented to him by citizens of Asheville, who arrive on the "Land of the Sky" special train on Oct. 6 on a boosting tour. The color will be gray—chosen by the Mayor himself.

When the delegation reaches the city it will go directly to the City Hall, where, with appropriate ceremony, the suit will be presented.

GENEVA CONFERENCE ADOPTS COURT PLAN

Right of Powers to Withdraw Approval of American Reservations Is Recommended.

NEW PROTOCOL NEXT STEP

United States Will Be Invited to Help Draft It—President's Action in Doub

By Wireless to THE NEW YORK TIMES.

GENEVA, Sept. 23.—With a single modification, the conference of signatories of the statute of the Permanent Court of International Justice adopted unanimously the conclusions concerning the American reservations which were presented this morning by its committee.

These conclusions were incorporated in "the final act of the conference," which was submitted for signatures.

The single modification concerned the fourth American reservation. The first part of the reservation provided for the withdrawal by the United States of adherence. The committee, to assure equality of treatment to all members, made the provision that the signatory States acting together and by not less than two-thirds majority should have a corresponding right to withdraw consent to the American reservations.

Modified by New Zealander.

On the proposal of Sir Francis Bell of New Zealand this provision was modified so as to extend only to the second paragraph of Reservation 4—by which statute the Court could not be amended without the consent of the United States—and Reservation 5, dealing with advisory opinions. The modification was made after a long debate in which it was agreed that any difficulties which might arise would be confined to the provisions covered by these reservations.

As it stands adopted, a decision by a two-thirds vote against the last points of the American reservations would not in any manner affect America's membership in the Court but only her prerogatives. The United States remains a full member, participating in the election of the Judges, paying her share of Court expenses and possessing the right to withdraw from the Court.

This modification followed a long series of compromises made between national dignity and resentment at the American demands on the one hand and the general desire to extend the influence and jurisdiction of the Permanent Court on the other. The effort made to meet the American demands was stressed by the President tonight in dissolving the conference.

The American reservations, he said, quoting Sir George Foster of Canada, comprised a legislative act by a State outside the League and Court and it would be very easy to say "no." But the conference had considered the difficulties were there to be overcome and nothing had been left undone to give satisfaction to the United States and assure her participation in the Permanent Court.

As to the fate of the conference's work nobody could know what this would be. But the spirit and manner in which the work had been done had proved in obvious manner its sincere desire to find a solution. The only thing that remained to be done was for the Governments to hasten their replies to the United States Government.

This spirit mentioned by the President and which had been evident on the part of the great majority of the delegations persisted in the debates today, though Canada and Sweden stood out against giving the United States more than equality.

Sir Francis Bell at the opening of the reading of the committee's conclusions this morning asked that all the provisions for withdrawing consent to American adherence be dropped. This was not the personal demand of a delegate, he said, but a motion by a Government signatory of the statute of the Court. His Government wanted to see the United States come into the Court and stay in it.

Question of Samoa Raised.

Western Samoa, which was now under the flag of New Zealand, was

Continued on Page Sixteen.

CROWD ARRIVES SMOOTHLY

Throngs Ushered Into Philadelphia Stadium Without Confusion.

MANY NOTABLES ATTEND

Governors of Six States and Mayor Walker Among Long List of Officials.

OVER 75,000 FROM HERE

Trains Alone Carry That Number and Others Make the Trip by Automobile.

Special to The New York Times.

PHILADELPHIA, Sept. 23.—One hundred and thirty-five thousand persons, the largest crowd which ever attended a sports event in America, let out a roar when the referee placed the heavyweight crown on the head of Gene Tunney, which must have made the old Liberty Bell at Independence Hall quiver once more.

As the battle began and the heavyweights set to exchanging their jarring blows which rang with a "plop" audible many rows back of the ring, they followed it with a roaring enthusiasm that only the greatest prize-fight crowd in history could produce.

Shortly before the main bout it was announced that the stadium had been completely sold out, breaking both attendance and receipt records. The paid admissions exceeded 130,000 and the gate receipts were over the two-million mark.

In addition to the paid admissions there were unpaid admissions amounting to $30,000 money value. Tex Rickard announced that he had purposely understated the crowd expected in order not to discourage possible last-minute purchasers of seats.

Crowd Is Well Handled.

Old-timers at the ringside who had seen every big fight since Fitzsimmons defeated Corbett said it was the most perfectly handled bout they had ever seen, for the huge concourse was ushered into the stadium without confusion.

The crowd, which had been cheering the preliminary fighters as hey mauled each other to while away the spectators' time, broke into their first real frenzy when Gene Tunney appeared in the path alongside the ring and began climbing up to the square. T e cheering was continuous from the moment he appeared. It broke into a single great outburst of yells, with shrill whistles from the thousands of lips sharpening it, as he entered the ring and went to his corner, smiling. In the ovation for Tunney there was perhaps a note of sympathy.

Dempsey entered a moment after Tunney, and another great roar went up. Rain began falling but nobody seemed to notice it, least of all the fighters as they squared away and the blows began to fly.

They were yelling madly for Gene as he began swinging into the champion with a force they had not dreamed the young challenger possessed. And when the first round ended with Tunney so unmistakably in the lead there was a minute of sheer delirium.

Women Shout Dismay.

They were at it again, and the voices of the women spectators now and again sounded out over all the clamor as Tunney staggered under the blows of the infuriated champion. There were feminine shouts of dismay as well when Tunney shot a hard one at Dempsey.

As the fight settled down into a give and take and the surprise at Tunney's showing waned, the cries of encouragement and warning became an intermittent hum, punctuated by shouts as the blows landed or missed. The crowd was watching for the fine points now.

As one of the thinly padded fists struck its target of flesh with a whack a concerted groan went through the rows of onlookers.

"The nose, the nose," the crowd yelled as one of Gene's uppercuts brought blood on Dempsey's right cheek. "That fancy nose is a goner. Hit that and he's through."

The fourth round passed and the fifth began. The clamor of the crowd quieted a little, for it gave place to admiration that Tunney had lasted so long. The crowd was yelling for a knockout each time Tunney pushed Dempsey into the ropes.

Dempsey was fighting an unexpectedly good man and the crowd was with his enemy. Then the sixth round began, the round which had been set by the experts as the last one possible for Tunney to fight. The crowd was hushed as Tunney went confidently from his corner.

A sigh of relief swept the stadium as Tunney emerged from it shaken but still strong, and there was a burst of applause as he took his seat. The old-time fight followers wagged their heads. "It's not the same old Dempsey," they said.

"He missed his chance right there," said somebody as Dempsey drove with all his dreadful strength at a point in space which Tunney had just left. "If that had landed we'd been on our way home."

And then a burst of women's cries

Continued on Page Three.

Dempsey's Share $850,000; Tunney to Receive $200,000

Special to The New York Times.

PHILADELPHIA, Sept. 23.—The receipts of the Dempsey-Tunney fight tonight were in excess of $2,000,000. On the basis of $2,000,000, the receipts were divided as follows:

Dempsey	$850,000
Tunney	$200,000
Federal Tax	$200,000
State	$100,000
Sesquicentennial	$200,000
Preliminary fights	$40,000
Tex Rickard, promoter	$410,000

AIRPLANE CARRIES TUNNEY TO SCENE

Challenger Is First to Make Way to Heavyweight Title Bout Through Air.

RISK DEPLORED BY MANY

Tunney, However, Is Calm Throughout—Calls Flying Least Trying on Nerves.

Special to The New York Times.

PHILADELPHIA, Sept. 23.—Not content with the prospect of facing Dempsey and destiny, Gene Tunney had to defy death, too. For the first time in the history of heavyweight championships, the challenger flew forth to the field of battle in an airplane.

From Stroudsburg, Pa., where Tunney trained for the three weeks, to Philadelphia the challenger took the shortest route. He winged above the silvery course of the Delaware River, winding through the Pocono Mountains, and landed at the navy yard in plenty of time to weigh in before the astonished eyes of the Pennsylvania State Boxing Commission.

Gene traveled in a red Curtiss Oriole plane, piloted by the expert hands of Casey Jones, noted for his feats of daring. The only other passenger was Wade Morton, driver of racing cars, who finished fourth in the last five-hundred mile classic at Indianapolis.

Challenger Disdains Danger.

The utter distain Tunney displayed for the battle at hand, with the golden goal for which he has striven seven years in the balance, was unusual in itself. He disregarded entirely the fact that a tremendous gate, the greatest financial success in the history of sports, depended upon his appearance in the ring at the proper time. He laughed at the suggestion of danger which he was tempting. He continued in the same unperturbed, undisturbed, confident mood he had displayed from the start.

When the news spread that the challenger had taken to the air with the chance of his life only a few hours away there was a general outcry of disapproval. But there was no opportunity in which to make the challenger change his course. He had decided on his means of travel a week before and he kept it secret from every one, including his manager, Billy Gibson, and Tex Rickard.

The challenger slept late on his morning of destiny, facing the beckoning call of opportunity with the calmness of a child. He arose at 8 o'clock and relished a special breakfast at the Glen Brook Country Club in Stroudsburg, specially prepared by George Ransberry, his private chef. When he came forth into the misty morning he greeted th small crowd waiting to bid him farewell and godspeed in his quest for the coveted crown with the announcement that he was going to fly to Philadelphia

Cheer Sends Him on Way.

There was gasps of amazement, and after a moment of surprised silence a cheer broke forth from the little knot of well-wishers.

Morton, the race driver, was waiting for the challenger with the motor running in a high-powered Duesenberg. Tunney climbed in beside the driver's seat and was speeded to the Shawnee Country Club at Buckwood Inn, about five miles away. There Jones and his Oriole awaited the coming of the precious passenger.

On arriving at the Buckwood Inn Gene was greeted by Reggie Worthington.

"Where's Casey?" asked the challenger.

"Oh, he's out playing golf," Worthington informed him.

"Say, I might play a couple of holes myself before I leave," Gene suggested in his matter-of-fact way, still calm and unexcited.

However, it was decided that the aerial expedition had better get under way, and Casey Jones was summoned from a bunker. He went over to a near-by shed and in a short time taxied out in a blood red sky chariot. Gene walked over to the third tee on the golf course, accompanied by a few friends and a few strangers who had been playing golf but had deserted their game on hearing that the chal-

Continued on Page Two.

TUNNEY ALWAYS MASTER

Challenger Bewilders His Opponent With His Speed, Accuracy.

AGGRESSIVE IN ALL ROUNDS

Sends Rain of Whiplike Lefts Which Champion Cannot Avoid.

OUTCOME IS A SURPRISE

Dempsey Lacks All Evidence of His Old Aggressiveness—Victor Is Acclaimed.

By JAMES P. DAWSON.
Special to The New York Times.

RINGSIDE, SESQUICENTENNIAL STADIUM, Philadelphia, Sept. 23.—Gene Tunney is the new world's heavyweight champion. The ex-marine fought like a marine here tonight in the Sesquicentennial Stadium, when he carried off the decision over Jack Dempsey, once known as the Manassa Mauler and the ring's man-killer, in a ten-round bout which saw the first passing of a heavyweight championship title on a decision.

Through every round of the ten, Tunney battered and pounded Dempsey. He rained rights on the tottering champion's jaw and he bewildered Dempsey with his speed and the accuracy of a whip-like left hand which Dempsey could not evade. When the decision was announced, the crowd let loose a roar of acclaim for "the man of destiny," who had conquered the man-killer, and the countryside sent the roar echoing back.

Confidence Aids Tunney.

The transfer of the title, the ascension of Tunney to the pinnacle in boxing, surprised the majority of those who witnessed the fight and experienced followers of boxing form. It surprised everybody, almost, but Tunney, whose confidence, more than anything else, perhaps, carried him on to a height which the vast majority thought unattainable for him.

He was complete master, from first bell to last. He out-boxed and he out-fought Dempsey at every turn. Where it had been expected that Tunney would break and run before the vicious attack of Dempsey, the tiger man, Tunney, the fighting marine, not only failed to back up, but he went forward all the time with the instinct of the true leatherneck and hammered Dempsey in a driving attack which brooked no restraining effort on the part of the champion.

There was no question of the victor at the finish. There was no question even of the winner of each round as the battle progressed, and Dempsey, instead of flashing the fighting fury which was expected of him, instead of surging forward with the tigerish, vicious rushes he has exhibited in previous and more favorable ring engagements, proved himself instead a floundering, weakened, almost helpless fighting machine from which the spark had gone.

All the evidences of the old Dempsey were merely that; only faint evidences, indications, unexpressive flashes save for their expression of futility of helpless hopelessness, of utter ineffectiveness.

They fought this battle in the rain—a driving, torrential downpour which started when the men entered the ring and which increased in fury as the fight progressed. The ring was flooded, the spectators drenched and the gladiators were drenched, but as the fury of the storm increased so did the fighting of Tunney, and Dempsey had nothing with which to meet this Marine attack.

Knockdown Is Lacking.

It was a disappointing transfer of a heavyweight title in one respect. The battle did not end in a knockout. Indeed, through its ten rounds the struggle held not even a knock down. This was due to the fact that Tunney is a weak hitter in the sense that he is not a finishing or destructive hitter.

He is not of the old Dempsey hitting school. But the New York lad is a punishing hitter, a cruel, tantalizing, tormenting puncher and a cool, unruffled boxer at all times. He did about everything else to Dempsey but knock the defending champion down and out. He battered Dempsey to a pulp, until the beaten champion at the finish was a close resemblance to the giant Jess Willard, whom Dempsey pounded and hammered into a helpless hulk out on the shores of Maumee Bay seven years ago when he won the title.

For the first time in his career

Continued on Page Two.

Times Wide World Photo.

GENE TUNNEY, THE NEW CHAMPION

Champion Tunney Praises the Loser; "I Have No Alibis," Asserts Dempsey

Special to The New York Times.

SESQUICENTENNIAL STADIUM, PHILADELPHIA, Sept. 23.—The following statements were made after the bout tonight:

By GENE TUNNEY.

Dempsey fought like the great champion that he was. He had the kick of a mule in his fists and the heart of a lion in his breast. I never fought a harder socker nor do I hope to meet one. Dempsey fought like a gentleman and never took an unfair advantage in the ring. Once or twice he may have hit me a little low, but always it was by accident. He never meant it.

"I'm sorry," he always said following anything close to a foul blow. When the gong rang at the end of the fight he threw his arm over my shoulder and said: "Great fight, Gene; you won." I don't care what they may say about him he is certainly a man in the ring. The hardest blows I felt were two socks on the Adam's apple. That's why I'm so hoarse. I have no plans for the future, but am content to rest a while with the ambition I have nourished for seven years at last realized. The marines, you know, are always first to fight and last to leave. No matter how heavy the going may be you will always find them there in the end.

By JACK DEMPSEY.

I have no alibis to offer. I lost to a good man, an American—a man who speaks the English language. I have no alibis.

Story of the Fight by Rounds

Special to The New York Times.

RINGSIDE, SESQUICENTENNIAL STADIUM, PHILADELPHIA, Sept. 23.—The round by round detail of the Tunney-Dempsey bout fought here tonight follows:

First Round.

Dempsey was attired in blue trunks and Tunney in purple. Dempsey looked rather thin as he stepped forward for a consultation.

As the round started Dempsey, with a scowl on his face, rushed out and drove Tunney to his own corner. Dempsey again rushed. Jack sent a terrific left to the jaw. Dempsey kept rushing in and drove Tunney into his own corner. Dempsey went in and Tunney swung a hard right to Dempsey's chin. Dempsey weaved in again and Tunney was short with a right. They boxed in the centre of the ring for a moment, then Tunney missed a right for the head but ripped two rights to the body. Dempsey jabbed Tunney away, and then Dempsey lunged over the ropes after missing a left swing. Tunney rushed in again and sent a heavy right to the chin. In a terrific exchange Tunney showered left and right swings to Dempsey's jaw and Dempsey was groggy. Gene's only mark in the exchange was a bleeding mouth.

Between rounds Dempsey appeared very tired and his seconds worked hard over him.

Second Round.

Dempsey rushed over to Tunney's corner, trying to get his man. Dempsey swung his right to the jaw, but Tunney got out of the way. They stepped out in the middle of the ring and Tunney swung right and left to the jaw. Dempsey came through with a right to the body and drove Tunney to his corner. Jack drove Gene to a neutral corner and punished him about the head. Tunney sent two lefts to Jack's head. They wrestled across the ring, Dempsey pounding the body. Gene sent short rights and lefts to the jaw. It was now raining heavily. Jack drove Tunney into his own corner with a terrific right to the heart and dazed Tunney. Tunney put over a left and right to the jaw at the bell and the crowd was in an uproar.

Third Round.

Dempsey came out slowly for the third and they met in the middle of the ring. Jack tried a terrific right for the jaw but missed. Gene stood up straight and jabbed lefts and rights to Jack's jaw. Gene put over a heavy right to the head and wrestled Jack back to the ropes. Tunney swung terrific rights and lefts to Jack's jaw. Tunney repeated with a right and had the champion staggering in midring. He graced the champion's jaw and then landed a good right to Jack's jaw. Tunney jumped away and sparred cleverly, but Dempsey kept boring in. Jack came in only to be sent back to the ropes with rights and lefts to the jaw. Tunney sent another left jab to the head, but Jack punished him heavily to the body in return. As Jack came in Tunney ripped lefts and rights to the body at the bell.

Fourth Round.

Dempsey came out with a terrific rush and with a wild right sent Tunney almost over the ropes. Tunney was in bad shape, but he continued to jab Jack away with a left. Jack's eye was cut with one of these lefts. Dempsey went in and sent two lefts to the jaw. Dempsey continued to weave in, trying to land a heavy body blow. Dempsey missed a left to the jaw. Tunney stabbed a left, then swung a heavy right to Jack's jaw. Dempsey's eye was in bad shape and

Continued on Page Three.

VICTORY IS POPULAR ONE

Ex-Marine Gets Ovation as He Enters Ring—Crowd 'Boos' Foe.

BIGGEST IN SPORT HISTORY

Rickard's Luck Turns, However, and Distinguished Gathering Is Thoroughly Drenched.

DEMPSEY'S NOSE SUFFERS

Rebuilt for Movies, It Is Target of Challenger as He Piles Up Points for Victory.

By ELMER DAVIS.
Special to The New York Times.

RINGSIDE, SESQUICENTENNIAL STADIUM, PHILADELPHIA, Sept. 23.—While the rain poured down on the greatest crowd that ever saw a sporting event, Gene Tunney beat Jack Dempsey, and captured the world's heavyweight championship in a ten-round fight here tonight.

The champion, in the phrase of one of the ringside critics, lost his title by a synthetic nose. It was by steady pounding away at the built-in beak which Dempsey acquired a couple of years ago that Tunney piled up a heavy lead on points in the early rounds.

Dempsey rallied toward the middle of the fight, but his effort to come back in a last round finish failed. The ex-marine, against whom the experts were betting three and four to one this afternoon, walked off with the title.

Crowd Is With Tunney.

It was the first time in history that the heavyweight championship of the world has changed hands on points, but there was never the slightest doubt after the start that if there were a decision Tunney would get it. The champion's only chance was to win by a knockout, and here his old power had deserted him. He was in somewhat better shape after three years of idleness than when he fought Tom Gibbons at Shelby, Mont., after a two-year layoff in 1923. The swings and hooks that always missed Gibbons occasionally landed on Tunney. But they never landed hard enough. The young fighter from Greenwich Village could stand up and take it.

Though the experts and the gamblers thought, by a heavy majority, that Dempsey would walk off with the fight, about 90 per cent. of the 130,000 people who saw the encounter were for Tunney. There was an uproarious cheer when the challenger entered the ring. He wore the scarlet trimmed blue dressing gown, with the Marine Corps emblem on the back, which was presented to him by old comrades of the Marine Corps. He climbed through the ropes at 9:30, and stood up to let the crowd see him.

Two minutes later the champion of the world came in. There was a scattering round of applause as he entered the ring, but when Joe Griffo, announcer, introduced him as "the heavyweight champion who has defended his title for the past six years," there was a roar of boos that rocked the whole amphitheatre. If ever a fighting champion, as yet undefeated and favored by all the experts to remain undefeated, had such a reception from a crowd, the episode is buried in the obscurity of the past.

The rain began to fall on the crowd in the Sesquicentennial Stadium just as the big fight started. Hitherto the proverbial Rickard luck had held, even against the weather. Though it rained in Philadelphia early this morning and heaps of dark clouds obscured the sky at nightfall when the crowd began to gather in the stadium, the rain held off.

A dozen fight programs have rained out in New York alone this Summer, but it looked as if Rickard, with the biggest fight of the past three years and the biggest fight crowd and biggest gate of all time, was going to get away untouched.

Five preliminary bouts had gone on and the ring had been cleared for the entrance of the principals to the big event when the rain began at last. The amplifier announcers who relayed Joe Griffo's statements to the farthest edges of the huge stadium had just announced, three or four times, that all persons in the audience were requested to keep their seats.

Crowd Came Prepared.

Suddenly all over the huge U-shaped cup of the permanent amphitheatre and the broad wooden expanse of the temporary seats, people stood up by thousands struggling into rain coats. Then they sat down again, grimly determined to stay to the finish, whatever the weather.

At the end, when the bleeding champion and the eager challenger were exchanging wallops before the bell, the ring was splashed and puddled, the crowd was drowned out, but everybody but Dempsey and his friends was happy.

All the predictions and expectations about this fight were upset. Dempsey had hoped to finish his opponent in one punch and expected to do it within two rounds.

The comparatively few last ditch supporters who expected Tunney to win

"All the News That's Fit to Print."

The New York Times.

THE WEATHER
Rain and warmer today; tomorrow rain and colder.
Temperature yesterday—Max., 45; min., 40.
For weather report see Page 24.

VOL. LXXVI....No. 25,200. **** NEW YORK, SATURDAY, JANUARY 22, 1927. TWO CENTS In Greater New York | THREE CENTS Within 200 Miles | FOUR CENTS Elsewhere in the U. S.

HARMONY ON BUSES NOW UP TO OLVANY, SAY PARTY LEADERS

Tammany Chief Only One Who Can End Estimate Board Deadlock, They Assert.

FACES FIRST REAL CRISIS

He Must Sustain Walker in Fight for Tri-Borough Award, Mayor's Friends Hold.

MILLER LIKELY TO BE KEY

Borough President's Votes Expected to Be Demanded to Support the Party's Pledge.

In George W. Olvany, leader of Tammany, rests the hope of a speedy award of bus franchises, indefinite delay on which is indicated by the present deadlock in the Board of Estimate unless Judge Olvany, the only Democratic leader believed to have sufficient power and influence to force an agreement, brings about harmony between the warring factions in the Board.

This was the political reaction yesterday to Mayor Walker's speech at the dinner of the Tammany Hall Speakers' Bureau Thursday night, at which the Mayor, with Judge Olvany present, referred to the deadlock and reiterated his intention of adhering to his campaign pledge to maintain the five-cent fare and declared he knew he had the Tammany leader's support.

Mr. Olvany, in the opinion of many Tammany men, is facing his first real crisis as leader of the New York County Democratic organization, which traditionally carries with it leadership of the city. In the opinion of friends of Mayor Walker, he must now sustain the Mayor, whose nomination he brought about, or have his political prestige impaired.

Supported Mayor on Fare.

So far as can be learned, Mr. Olvany has supported Mayor Walker on the five-cent fare, which has not yet come to a definite issue, but has not supported him in the bus franchise matter to the extent to which some of the Mayor's friends believe he should have done.

Mayor Walker favors the award of the bus franchise for Manhattan, Brooklyn and Queens to the Equitable Coach Company, backed by J. G. White & Co. and General Electric Company and American Car and Foundry Company interests, and of the Bronx franchise to the Surface Transportation Corporation, a Third Avenue Railway subsidiary. So far, Judge Olvany, it was said, has refrained from expressing a preference for any particular applicant. He maintained this non-committal attitude at the so-called secret conferences of the Board of Estimate which he attended, it was said, listened to the arguments, but said nothing to indicate that he favored the award to the Equitable or any other company.

Mayor Walker expects to win a preliminary victory in his fight to award a tri-borough franchise to the Equitable Company at next Thursday's meeting of the Board of Estimate when the vote is taken on his resolution to direct the preparation of franchise contracts with the Equitable Company and the Surface Transportation Corporation. Only a majority of the sixteen votes in the board are necessary to carry this resolution, and the Mayor expects to add the one vote of Borough President Maurice E. Connolly of Queens to the eight votes he obtained on a similar motion on Thursday. Controller Charles K. Berry, with three votes, and Borough Presidents Julius Miller of Manhattan and James J. Byrne of Brooklyn, with two votes each, are expected to vote against the resolution or to refrain from voting, which would have the same effect.

Mayor Needs Four Votes.

These nine votes will carry the resolution, but twelve will be necessary for the actual award of the franchises. With Controller Berry believed to be definitely opposed to any award to the Equitable, the Mayor must get the votes of both Mr. Miller and Mr. Byrne to obtain the necessary number of votes.

Unless he changes his mind, Mayor Walker will leave for Cuba soon after Thursday's meeting. The law requires the advertising of the franchise contracts for four weeks and a public hearing before action can be taken. During the Mayor's absence and immediately after his return, efforts will be made, it was said, to get the Manhattan and Brooklyn Borough Presidents into line for the award to the Equitable Company, or at least to reach an agreement on the award to some other applicant or applicants other than the B. M. T. and the Fifth Avenue Coach Company-New York Railways Corporation group, which Mayor Walker has declared he will not consent to in any circumstances.

According to friends of the Mayor Borough President Miller is the member of the board who is likely to be the key to the entire bus situation. The Mayor's threat of political reprisals against those who do not support his bus program might be effective against Borough President Connolly and Borough President Byrne, a brother-in-law of John H. McCooey, Brooklyn Democratic leader, for both Mr. Connolly and Mr. McCooey are constantly seeking patronage for members of their respective organizations. The threat of deprivation of patronage, it was said, would have no terrors for Mr. Miller.

Mr. Miller, however, is a member of Tammany, and it is understood to be one of the Mayor's chief grievances that he has not had the support of the

Continued on Page Three.

Clifford's Inn Hall of London Sought for Erection at Yale

Copyright, 1927, by The New York Times Co. By Wireless to THE NEW YORK TIMES.

LONDON, Jan. 21.—A graduate of Yale has offered to buy Clifford's Inn Hall, one of London's most famous structures, for re-erection at Yale. The Hall will soon be dismantled to make way for a modern building. During its long history it has sheltered many famous men, including William Makepeace Thackeray and Samuel Butler.

Announcing the Yale graduate's offer today, the owners of the Hall said:

"If we let it go in this way, failing any British welcome for it, we should demand $100,000, or some such sum, to go to the British Treasury. We ourselves have no right to benefit from the sale."

Another possibility mentioned is that the Hall might be taken to Canada as a shrine for the Canadian Bar Association.

10,000,000 HEAR OPERA OVER RADIO

"Garden Scene" From Faust Is Sent Out Over the Nation Through 25 Stations.

15 MICROPHONES ON STAGE

Applause in Chicago Auditorium Heard Distinctly in Widest Broadcast From a Theatre.

Radio grand opera, broadcast from the stage of its actual performance for a generation long since grown callous to these miracles of modern life, was heard by more millions in American homes last night than ever before listened to opera at one time.

In the widest broadcast yet attempted directly from a theatre, the Chicago Civic Opera Company's singing of "Faust," for the space of fifty-five minutes in a regular $10,000 subscription night of opera at the famous auditorium by the shore of Lake Michigan, was linked up through twenty-five different radio stations while the waiting listeners all over the nation tuned in. It was expected that many return messages would tell the results today.

Those who caught the opera "on the air" in and around New York from 10.30 to 11:25 o'clock last night were hearing the third act or favorite "garden scene" of Gounod's classic. This, the central episode of "Faust," and containing in almost unbroken series some of its best known melodies, was timed to the Western audience an apparent hour earlier, just as Rocky Mountain time made it an hour before that. Any hearers further out on the Pacific Coast must perforce have let their dinners grow cold until the first "national opera" experiment was over.

Charles Hackett as Faust.

Some of the local music critics listened as invited guests in the studio of Station WJZ, atop of the Aeolian Hall Building, in Forty-second Street. Of the Western stars, only Richard Bonelli, the American baritone, singing Valentine in the opera's earlier and later acts, was not in the action during the portion that was broadcast. Those in the garden scene were Charles Hackett as Faust, Edith Mason as Marguerite, Irene Pavloska as Siebel, Maria Claessens as Dame Marthe and Vanni Marcoux as Mephistopheles.

Fifty-five minutes of broadcasting, ending a half-hour before midnight, by Eastern clocks, passed without a hitch or mishap of any kind to 13,000 miles of telephone wire and all the free air in the United States.

Static, the foil of best laid radio plans, was wholly absent till the last few moments of the scene, when the final raptures of Faust and Marguerite on the Auditorium stage were mingled with faint sighing, as of the lightest wind in high treetops.

Mr. Marcoux's superb French diction as Mephisto was as robust and clear as if spoken in the homes of those who heard him here.

When the curtain fell to slow music under Mr. Polacco's baton, a group of the Radio Corporation's guests in Forty-second Street, New York, applauded, and then listened five minutes more to the applause and curtain calls out in the theatre a thousand

Continued on Page Two.

BAUMES LAWS FAIL, BANTON TELLS BAR; TOO SEVERE, HE SAYS

Prosecutor Finds Juries Free Guilty Rather Than Subject Them to Cruel Punishment.

BACKS THEORY OF STATUTE

But Urges Return to Policy of Having Penalty Fit Criminal, Not the Crime.

DEBATE ON WORLD COURT

State Association Reiterates Its Approval of Our Adherence Under Senate Reservations.

The Baumes laws have been nullified by their own severity in cases where juries have acquitted obviously guilty defendants and where witnesses have changed their testimony to perjure themselves, rather than subject men to "cruel and unusual punishment," declared District Attorney Joab H. Banton yesterday. He spoke at the fiftieth annual meeting of the New York State Bar Association at the headquarters of the Association of the Bar of the City of New York.

Mr. Banton cited several cases—including that of the negro, Harry Simmons, convicted as a first rather than a fourth offender by a jury before County Judge Taylor in Brooklyn the other day—involving the new laws that prisoners convicted as fourth offenders must be sentenced to life imprisonment; that prisoners convicted as second offenders must be sentenced to the maximum punishment for the crime committed; that prisoners convicted of crimes when armed must be sentenced to five or ten years' additional imprisonment, and that prisoners convicted of first degree robbery must be sentenced to at least fifteen years' imprisonment. The District Attorney pointed out that the decision of the jury was final, since a defendant could not be placed in jeopardy twice for the same crime.

Mandatory Clauses Weaken Laws.

Asserting that the theory of the new laws for segregation of habitual offenders was correct, Mr. Banton said their weakness was in their mandatory provisions, which deprived the courts of discretion in imposing sentences. He declared that in some cases first offenders were so dangerous to society that they should be sentenced to life imprisonment, and in other cases fourth offenders could receive short sentences with safety to society. He advocated the theory that punishment should fit the individual criminal rather than the crime, and it should be fixed after a scientific study of the individual.

Mr. Banton argued in favor of leaving the courts in possession of the privilege of accepting pleas of guilty to lesser charges than those on which defendants were indicted. He justified this practice as economical in that it spared the expense of trials and imprisoned criminals who otherwise might be acquitted.

Urges Speed in Arrest and Trial.

Certainty of arrest and speed of prosecution and trial, Mr. Banton went on, would be more effective than severity of punishment in diminishing crime. He recommended that police work be made more effective, and that the criminal courts be so organized that prosecutors could bring prisoners to trial within three weeks of their arrest. Mr. Banton said:

"What is the effect of increased penalties? A decrease in the number of convictions. After all, we must depend upon the verdict of the jury. In order to convict, the jury must say 'guilty.' Jurors are human beings and they balk at pronouncing a defendant guilty when he is to receive a sentence which, in their minds, is too severe.

"Recently, in Brooklyn, juries in two cases refused to convict defendants as fourth offenders, although each defendant had a known criminal record of three previous convictions. Fingerprints and other evidence showed the identity of the defendants as fourth offenders, and yet the juries declared they were only first offenders.

"The jury returned a verdict of not guilty in New York County recently

Continued on Page Four.

Fascisti to Regulate Schools and Colleges; Professors to Take Oath to Teach Loyalty

Copyright, 1927, by The New York Times Company. By Wireless to THE NEW YORK TIMES.

ROME, Jan. 21.—Fascist supervision of Italian colleges and universities is foreshadowed by a decree, published today, empowering the Cabinet to dismiss any professor for political manifestations not in line with the general policy of the Government.

"Professors in royal universities, royal institutes of superior instruction, and other professors of similar rank," says the decree, "are to be dispensed from service when for manifestations in connection with their office, or even outside their office, they do not give full assurance of faithful fulfillment of their duties, or if they place themselves in a condition of incompatibility with the general political aims of the Government."

All professors are, furthermore, by the same decree, required to take the following oath on assuming office:

"I swear to be faithful to the King and the royal successors, loyally to observe the Constitution and other laws of the kingdom, to exercise my office of teaching and all my academic duties with the object of forming hard-working, upright citizens devoted to their country. To that end I do not belong and will not belong to any association or political party whose activities are irreconcilable with the duties of my office."

ROME, Jan. 21 (AP).—Schools, colleges and universities may be abolished by the Italian Government if their teachings show disrespect of the institutions and principles of Italy's existing social system. This is provided for by decrees published this evening.

One measure empowers the Government to dismiss administrative magistrates whose official or personal activities or opinions are incompatible with the general political tendency of the State authorities.

The decrees issued today provide that persons not possessing "the requisite moral and political regularity" shall not be admitted to competitions for posts as teachers or professors. If they should happen to be admitted and should qualify they are not to be appointed anyway.

Chefs Fight Kitchen Fire in Athletic Club; Diners in Ignorance Until Told Meal Is Off

A fire in the kitchen of the New York Athletic Club, Central Park South and Sixth Avenue, just before the dinner hour last night, put the kitchen out of commission temporarily and caused members and their guests to go elsewhere to dine. J. C. Clyde, the manager, said he would be able to serve breakfast this morning.

Flames appeared in one of the flues over a big range as chefs and a score of helpers were preparing to serve dinner. Knives and dishes were dropped hastily in the rush for fire extinguishers. Some of the staff unlimbered an emergency hose, but the fire shot out into the room and across the ceiling, driving the amateur fighters back. An alarm was sent in and two fire companies responded. The fire was put out in a few minutes, but the dinner was ruined.

The flames were confined to the kitchen, which is on the seventh floor and in the centre of the building, with no rooms directly above. Members in the dining room below did not know what was going on until the fire was out. Water seeped through later and caused some damage.

As soon as the firemen left, workmen began repairs which were carried on through the night. Mr. Clyde estimated the damage at between $500 and $1,000.

ACCUSE 13 TROOPERS OF MEANEY MURDER

Coroner's Jury Calls the Siege in New Jersey Which Caused Woman's Death 'Atrocious.'

WARRANTS FOR THREE MORE

Two Brothers Testify Police Fired First—Constabulary Chief to Keep the Men on Duty.

Special to The New York Times.

FLEMINGTON, N. J., Jan. 21.—Warrants for the arrest of thirteen State troopers on a charge of murder were issued immediately after a Coroner's jury found them responsible for the fatal shooting of Beatrice Meaney on the night of Dec. 21, during a siege of her brother's farm at Jutland. Warrants were also issued for one trooper and two agents of the Society for the Prevention of Cruelty to Animals, charging them with being accessories to the murder.

Twelve of the thirteen troopers admitted during the inquest they had fired on the Meaney farmhouse during the battle. The thirteenth was the officer in command who issued the orders for the use of gas bombs and the laying of the siege.

The warrants were issued by Coroner William F. Charles. The jury of six decided that Miss Meaney had died as the result of "an unwarranted, atrocious and unlawful attack upon the home of Timothy Meaney."

Those Named in Warrants.

Those named in the warrants will be arraigned before the Coroner tomorrow morning at 10:30 o'clock. Charged with murder are: Lieutenant Daniel F. Rogers, who commanded the attacking force; Sergeants Daniel J. Dunn, Thomas Cunningham and George Wilton; Corporals Matthew A. Daly and August Albrecht; troopers Peter J. Smith, William Lang, Charles Schwartz, Lewis E. Kubler, Robert Johnson, Frederick Schwartz and Cyril Dalton. Trooper Alfred K. Larsen and Agents Harry Hanoway, 193 Weequahic Avenue, Newark, and Leslie Dusenbury of Irvington were charged as accessories. The two agents of the S. P. C. A. were arrested at their homes last night and turned over to Sheriff Anderson Y. Kinney.

Trooper Larsen precipitated the battle and siege when with the agents he went to the Meaney farm to investigate a complaint that cattle were being underfed. He shot James Meaney in the knee because, he said, James had threatened him with a stick, which he had mistaken for a shotgun.

The jury was out a little more than an hour after Timothy and James Meaney had concluded their testimony. Each had said that the troopers had fired first, and that at no time during the night had they heard the attacking force identify itself as the State Constabulary.

Timothy Meaney said as his sister had lain dying on the floor, troopers had beaten him as they searched him for weapons. He charged that about $3,000 was taken from him and never returned.

James Meaney testified that he had given Larsen no provocation for the shooting. He described how his sister, Beatrice, had hidden in a closet after the troopers had commenced firing. He said a bullet fired by a trooper had hit his sister "some time after midnight," as he had heard her fall inside the closet.

Applause Greets Verdict.

Neither former Judge George K. Large nor County Prosecutor Marshall Miller addressed the jury after James Meaney had left the stand. Foreman Green and Jurymen J. P. Reardon, Walter Agans, Thomas Hill, Otis Pimm and Frederick Bird took some exhibits in the case and retired to deliberate.

When they returned the verdict was delivered in a hushed court room. It was followed by instant applause, which was checked by Coroner Charles only after prolonged pounding of the gavel. None of the men named in the warrants was in the court room.

The Meaney brothers, who were present, did not take any part in the demonstration. They sat quietly surrounded by relatives with tight lips and set faces, listening intently as the Prosecutor asked that the warrants be issued.

When order had been restored in the court room Major Mark O. Kimberling, Deputy Superintendent of the State Police, walked over to the Prosecutor and said, "I will have the men here whenever you want them."

Prosecutor Miller said he would oppose any motion for bail and the Coroner said none would be granted.

The prosecutor was informed that an attempt would be made to have Supreme Justice Thomas W. Trenchard order the troopers released in bail. To this Mr. Miller said, "I know of only one case where a defendant on a murder charge was admitted to bail. That was Mrs. Hall, the wife of the Rev. Edward Wheeler Hall. This is not the

Continued on Page Six.

CHAPLIN NOW FIGHTS TO FREE HIS ASSETS

Funds Tied Up, He Couldn't Ride in Taxi Without Friends, Says Lawyer—To Post Tax Bond.

NEEDS CASH FOR COMPANIES

Withdrawal of $500,000 Here Was for Payroll—Actor Out for First Time Since Illness.

The difficulties in New York of Charlie Chaplin are to be adjusted within a few days, according to his attorneys, who continued their negotiations yesterday to free from Government tax liens more than $800,000, which represents the film comedian's wealth here, as well as that of the two motion picture companies in this city controlled by him.

Nathan Burkan, the actor's counsel and friend, with whom he is living, said at his office at 1,451 Broadway last night that to get the companies operating normally again he and his associates were arranging to post a bond equal in amount to the Government's claim, so as to release the actor's assets.

"Chaplin has no desire or design to treat the Government unfairly," said Mr. Burkan. "He has always paid his taxes and the companies have always paid theirs. But the Government thinks back taxes are due and we are perfectly willing to insure it against loss by posting of securities."

Chaplin, according to Mr. Burkan, would be absolutely penniless and "unable to hire a taxicab" if it were not for the fact that he has friends here. This same temporary poverty, he said, was causing considerable loss to the two picture companies, the activities of which were curtailed by lack of operating funds.

$500,000 Withdrawal Explained.

Payrolls must be met, he said, and the expense of conducting a studio must be met, but the actor was unable at present to touch a cent of his money. It was to meet these expenses, Mr. Burkan said, that Chaplin drew $500,000 from one account here a few days ago and not because he had any intention of forestalling the Government's liens.

Mr. Burkan admitted Chaplin recently transferred sums of money to banks here from California, where his estranged wife has tied up the rest of his funds, but this was explained by the statement that "substantial" sums had to be brought here to pay for the completion of Chaplin's new picture, "The Circus."

Chaplin always kept funds in New York banks, he said, and there was a transfer of money from time to time. It was announced some weeks ago, he said when the activities of the Chaplin Film Corporation on the West Coast stopped, that the corporation was to pursue all its activities in New York, and it was natural that the corporation should transfer its capital to continue its business. There was nothing unusual about it, he added.

Mr. Burkan strenuously denied a report circulated yesterday afternoon that Chaplin had agreed to pay in full the $1,135,000 claimed by the Government to be due in back income taxes. He said, in connection with the income taxes, that the comedian had no personal knowledge of taxes or even of liens, and that matters concerning taxes both for himself and the corporation were in the hands of expert accountants.

Chaplin Won't Work Here.

Mr. Burkan also said he did not think the comedian personally would do any work while here, as he had planned. Instead, he said, Chaplin would return to California to defend his suit and to fight for his two children and clear their names as soon as he was sent for by his Western attorneys.

The attorney took occasion to deny that he had discussed the California proceedings or criticized the court in any way. He will accompany Chaplin to California, he said.

Chaplin is recuperating from a nervous breakdown at the home of Mr. Burkan, 1,136 Fifth Avenue, and for the first time since his illness he went for a ride yesterday afternoon through Central Park in a friend's automobile.

Thousands of letters are being received by Chaplin, it was learned, from well-wishers "clamoring for fair play," according to Mr. Burkan.

It was said unofficially at the Custom House yesterday that Chaplin's difficulties with the Government, at least so far as this district was concerned, probably would be adjusted by Monday. This was learned following a conference between Frank K. Bowers, District Collector of Internal Revenue, and Mr. Burkan in Mr. Bowers's office.

Government Seeks Big Sum.

Special to The New York Times.

LOS ANGELES, Jan. 21.—The Federal Government's income tax liens of $1,133,778.31 against the property of Charlie Chaplin represents not only original differences between Chaplin's returns and the Government's estimates, but increases caused by penal-

Continued on Page Three.

COOLIDGE OPPOSES ARBITRATION MOVE IN MEXICAN DISPUTE

He Makes Known His Position After Senate Committee Declares for Step.

ACTION NOW IS UNLIKELY

President Holds Real Issue With Mexico Is Confiscation of American Property.

NORRIS ASKS FOR OIL FACTS

His Resolution Calls on Kellogg to Give Names of Concessionaires and Their Stand on Mexican Law.

Special to The New York Times.

WASHINGTON, Jan. 21.—President Coolidge made known today that he was opposed to arbitration of the controversy between the United States and Mexico. The President feels that if the American people fully realized the meaning of the issue between the two Governments, which, as the President sees it, is whether property legally owned by American citizens in Mexico is to be confiscated, they would uphold the attitude of the United States Government.

The statement of the President's position made at the White House this afternoon was a quick reaction from the action of the Senate Committee on Foreign Relations earlier in adopting the revised Robinson resolution, declaring it to be "sound policy" to submit the differences of the United States and Mexico to an arbitral tribunal.

It became obvious from what was said in behalf of the President that the Administration holds that the question at issue between the two Governments is whether property owned outright by American citizens in Mexico and acquired by them under Mexican laws shall be confiscated.

Construed in one way, the attitude of the Administration is that there is nothing to arbitrate.

President's Stand Is Explained.

An explanation of the President's views, included in what was said to newspaper men at the White House, stressed that the recognition of the late Obregon Government in Mexico by the United States Government was based on a written agreement between the two Governments that the new Mexico land and petroleum laws should not be retroactive; that is, they should not be applied so as to confiscate American property in Mexico acquired prior to the adoption of the Mexican Federal Constitution of 1917, which provided that all lands containing subsoil products and all other lands within certain areas owned by foreigners should become the property of the Mexican Government.

The arbitration resolution, as amended in committee, will be reported to the Senate tomorrow. In view of the White House statement, a clear issue is drawn between the President and the majority of the Foreign Relations Committee. Should the Senate adopt the resolution, the President would be within his rights in ignoring it.

Point to his unofficial rejection of the arbitration proposal is given by the formal announcement of the Mexican Government last night that "it is ready to accept in principle that its difficulties with the United States should be decided by way of arbitration."

President Sees Nothing to Gain.

In the opinion of President Coolidge, nothing helpful could be gained by a discussion of arbitration of the dispute. Although he had not read the text of the revised Robinson resolution, the President thought, it was said at the White House, that this would give the people at home and abroad information as to the attitude of the United States Senate and perhaps might lead to complication of the situation.

Taken broadly, the President appears to see no hope in arbitration and no question that should be arbitrated.

In view of certain statements that have been made about Mexico, the President was said to doubt whether the American people fully realized that there was only one question at issue.

He holds that there are some collateral things, but if the proposed confiscation of property were out of the way, the other questions between the United States and Mexico could be settled without much difficulty.

In his opinion, action that has been

Continued on Page Two.

CHINA CRISIS MORE GRAVE; OUR ENVOY ORDERED BACK; MARINES SENT TO MANILA

Shanghai Labor Urges Revolt, Honoring Day of Lenin's Death

Copyright, 1927, by The New York Times Co. Special Cable to THE NEW YORK TIMES.

SHANGHAI, Jan. 21.—The General Labor Union has issued a circular commemorating the anniversary of Lenin's death and calling on the workers to continue fighting for his principles and the furtherance of the revolution in China and throughout the world.

Despite the fact that the tramway strike has been settled, no cars are running, owing to a disagreement within the union over minor issues. The workers of the cotton mill demanded extra pay tonight for the Chinese New Year. When refused, they demonstrated and set fire to the mill.

NORRIS, AMID SOBS, TELLS OF KILLING

Pastor on Stand Asserts Chipps Threatened and Cursed Him Before Visit to Study.

SAYS HE FEARED FOR LIFE

And Shot Only When Lumber Man Was Nearing Him, His Hand in His Pocket.

Special to The New York Times.

AUSTIN, Tex.—Jan. 21.—With tears streaming down his face, the Rev. J. Frank Norris, Pastor of the First Baptist Church of Fort Worth, took the stand in his own defense today and told how he shot and killed D. E. Chipps, wealthy lumberman. Norris sobbed as he answered questions, his head buried in his hands. At times he would bow his head and meditate before replying to questions.

The accused pastor testified that he only shot Chipps when the lumberman had turned and was approaching him with his hand in his hip pocket. Chipps, he said, had threatened him over the telephone before visiting his study because of his sermon attacking Mayor H. C. Meacham of Fort Worth.

"In answer to the telephone call," the minister testified, "I said, 'Hello,' and a woman's voice answered back at the other end and said, 'Hello, Dr. Norris.' There was a pause and a man's voice came over the line and said, 'Hello.' I answered back, 'Hello, this is Dr. Norris' and then I couldn't understand what the other party was saying: I said, 'Who is this, this is Dr. Norris, what do you want?' and I still could not understand him and I shook up the telephone and I said, 'Hello' and kept repeating it, and then I heard this in a louder voice, in words and substance like this: 'We are coming over there to settle with you on that sermon.' And then I asked 'Who is this' and a voice came back, 'It don't matter. I am not going to stand it any longer, I am coming over there to kill you, you ——.'

Insisted on Name, He says.

"I says, 'Who is this.' He said, 'Never mind my name, you will find out when I get there.' I insisted on his name and then he said, 'My name is D. E. Chipps.'

"I said, 'I don't want you coming over here, you are mad, I don't want any trouble.' He said, 'By God, I am coming anyhow.'

"About that time I called my stenographer, a few feet awy, and said, 'Get this conversation.' Then I asked him again what was his name. He said, 'That doesn't matter.' I says, 'What do you want to come over here for, I don't want any trouble with you.' Then he ripped out another oath and said, 'You will find out when I get there.' I says, 'You are mad, I don't want to talk to you.' Then he got another sentence about half out and I hung up the receiver."

Mr. Norris's account of the scene in the study when Chipps arrived follows:

"When he first entered he announced his name by saying, 'This is D. E. Chipps.' Closing the door behind him, he stood there an instant, a few sec-

Continued on Page Seven.

Grief Over Bank's Troubles Kills President, Who Sold Out to Protect His Depositors

The death of Frank Williams, banker, at his home, 995 Fifth Avenue, on Thursday, became known yesterday and was ascribed by members of his family to worry and disappointment over the recent run on the Broadway Central Bank, of which he was President. The run caused the sale of the institution.

Since 1914 all Mr. Williams's interests had been closely bound up with those of the Broadway Central Bank. He was a Vice President and director of the Chelsea Exchange Bank when he and a group of associates, deciding there was need for an independent uptown bank, formed the Broadway Central, taking over a branch of Chelsea Exchange at Broadway and Ninety-seventh Street.

The bank prospered. On Jan. 8 of this year three trusted employes were arrested charged with embezzling funds of the institution. One newspaper printed what the officials termed a greatly exaggerated report of the amount of the thefts, and the next morning swarms of depositors besieged the doors of the bank.

Upward of $1,000,000 was paid out that day—a Saturday—and when the run continued on Monday the officials, fearing that the liquid assets would be exhausted before the run ended and that the bank would have to close its doors, sold the institution to the Central Mercantile Bank and Trust Company to protect the depositors.

The closing of the bank was a severe blow to Mr. Williams. He became ill and weakened rapidly. His death, however, came as a surprise to friends and associates.

Mr. Williams was born in Pierrepont Manor, Jefferson County, N. Y., in 1865. He was a hay and straw dealer here before entering the banking field. He is survived by his widow, whose first husband was Max Anderson, founder of the Hippodrome; one brother and four sisters. Mr. Williams was a member of the Columbia Yacht Club, the New York Athletic Club and the Round Table Club.

Funeral services will be held at the Campbell Funeral Church Broadway and Sixty-sixth Street, at 2 o'clock Monday afternoon. Burial will be in Woodlawn Cemetery.

RIOTS ALARM WASHINGTON

Spreading of Disorders Menaces Americans and All Foreigners.

55 OF OUR WARSHIPS THERE

Admiral Williams Has a Free Hand to Take All Protective Measures.

BRITAIN TO SEND MARINES

But London Declares Against Coercion, Expressing Sympathy With Nationalist Movement.

Special to The New York Times.

WASHINGTON, Jan. 21.—Confronted by the increasing seriousness of the anti-foreign demonstrations in China, the State Department has halted J. V. A. MacMurray, American Minister, on his way home to confer on the situation with Secretary Kellogg in Washington, and ordered him to return to his post in Peking. Mr. MacMurray was reached by cablegram at Seoul, Korea.

Officials did not minimize the gravity of the situation impelling this move, referring to it as the worst that has developed in China since the anti-foreign uprising of the Boxers in 1900. Official dispatches told of interior provinces being evacuated by foreigners and naval vessels "standing by" at Yangtse River points prepared to expedite the withdrawal of American and other foreign nationals.

Orders were issued by the Asiatic Fleet for 250 marines at Guam to proceed to Manila to be closer to the scene.

President Coolidge let it be known that in face of this situation the policy of this Government would continue to be the protection of American citizens and fulfilment of its treaties with China. There was no word from the White House to indicate that military measures would be taken at danger points to defend foreign settlements. This will be determined by events. The Government is extremely hesitant to strike any blow that might cause an explosion dangerous to all foreigners in China.

Situation Called Menacing.

If the State Department was actuated by any other consideration than to have the American Minister at his post in view of the acute situation that has developed so rapidly, it was not disclosed today. The order was sent two nights ago, but the announcement was withheld because of the uncertainty of its reaching Mr. MacMurray.

The situation was described as menacing because of the onward march of the Cantonese forces from South China toward Shanghai, and increasing anti-foreign demonstrations at Foochow, Hankow and Amoy. The Cantonese forces are concentrating at Hankow, six days from Shanghai, but some are at much closer points, even within sixty miles of Nanking, or 200 miles from Shanghai.

Much will depend, it was said, on whether they can be held back by the forces of General Sun Chuan-fang, in control of Shanghai, but whose allegiance is uncertain.

Admiral C. H. Williams, commanding the Asiatic Fleet, now at Shanghai, reported a general and speedy evacuation of interior Yangtse River points by foreigners. Rear Admiral Hough, commanding the Yangtse patrol, reported that the evacuation of Szechwan Province was progressing. Fifty Americans and thirty-five British have evacuated Chung King, ninety-six British will go to Kiu Kiang from Chengtu and twenty-five Americans from Chengtu to Chung King.

Missionaries Urge All to Flee.

The missionaries passing through Chung King, he added significantly, were sending word back to foreigners they had left behind to flee immediately.

Admiral Williams said he had ordered the marine detachment of 250 men at Guam to proceed to Cavite, the naval base near Manila, on the cargo ship Gold Star so they would be closer to Chinese waters.

The destroyer Pillsbury left Foochow for Manila yesterday with three men, thirty-one women and thirty-one children, all but five of whom were missionaries or Y. M. C. A. workers.

Meantime, he reported, conditions at Shanghai are quiet, although the number of strikes is increasing.

The State Department received similar reports from Consul Price at Foochow, who in addition to reporting the sailing of the Pillsbury said a similar number of refugees had gone by steamer from Foochow to Shanghai, Hongkong and other places, and American citizens were leaving interior points for Foochow.

What steps will be taken to meet the situation will depend on events. As things stand, the American naval forces are standing by at Shanghai and other points to speed the task of evacuation, and naval officers are confident they will be able to take care of questions as they arise. Many merchant ships undoubtedly would be available to them in an emergency in the work of evacuation.

Officials announced that the reported action of the Peking Legation in arranging a system of signals to sum-

"All the News That's Fit to Print."

The New York Times.

THE WEATHER
Increasing Cloudiness today; rain with rising temperature tomorrow.
Temperatures yesterday—Max., 50; min., 38.
For weather report see Page 30.

VOL. LXXVI....No. 25,276. * * * NEW YORK, FRIDAY, APRIL 8, 1927. TWO CENTS In Greater New York | THREE CENTS Within 200 Miles | FOUR CENTS Elsewhere in the U. S.

FAR-OFF SPEAKERS SEEN AS WELL AS HEARD HERE IN A TEST OF TELEVISION

LIKE A PHOTO COME TO LIFE

Hoover's Face Plainly Imaged as He Speaks in Washington.

THE FIRST TIME IN HISTORY

Pictures Are Flashed by Wire and Radio Synchronizing With Speaker's Voice.

COMMERCIAL USE IN DOUBT

But A. T. & T. Head Sees a New Step in Conquest of Nature After Years of Research.

Herbert Hoover made a speech in Washington yesterday afternoon. An audience in New York heard him and saw him.

More than 200 miles of space intervening between the speaker and his audience was annihilated by the television apparatus developed by the Bell Laboratories of the American Telephone and Telegraph Company and demonstrated publicly for the first time yesterday.

The apparatus shot images of Mr. Hoover by wire from Washington to New York at the rate of eighteen a second. These were thrown on a screen as motion pictures, while the loudspeaker reproduced the speech. As each syllable was heard, the motion of the speaker's lips and his changes of expression were flashed on the screen in the demonstration room of the Bell Telephone Laboratories at 55 Bethune Street.

When the television pictures were thrown on a screen two by three inches, the likeness was excellent. It was as if a photograph had suddenly come to life and begun to talk, smile, nod its head and look this way and that. When the screen was enlarged to two by three feet, the results were not so good.

Phone Hides His Face.

At times the face of the Secretary could not be clearly distinguished. He looked down, as he read his speech, and held the telephone receiver up, so that it covered most of the lower part of his countenance. There was too much illumination also in the background of the screen. When he moved his face, his features became clearly distinguishable. Near the close of his talk he turned his head to one side, and in profile his features became clear and full of detail.

On the smaller screen the face and action were reproduced with perfect fidelity.

After Mr. Hoover had spoken, Vice President J. J. Carty of the American Telephone and Telegraph Company and others in the demonstration room at Washington took his place and conversed one at a time with men in New York. The speaker on the New York end looked the Washington man in the eye, as he talked to him. On the small screen before him appeared the living face of the man to whom he was talking.

Time as well as space was eliminated. Secretary Hoover's New York hearers and spectators were something like a thousandth part of a second later than the persons at his side in hearing him and in seeing changes of countenance. The faces and voices were projected from Washington by wire. It was shown a few minutes later, however, that radio does just as well.

Similar Test by Wireless.

In the second part of the program the group in New York saw and heard performances in the Whippany studio of the American Telephone and Telegraph Company by wireless. The first face flashed on the screen from Whippany, N. J., was that of E. L. Nelson, an engineer, who gave a technical description of what was taking place. Mr. Nelson had a good television face. He screened well as he talked.

Next came a vaudeville act by radio from Whippany. A. Dolan, a comedian, first appeared before the audience as a stage Irishman, with side whiskers and a broken pipe, and did a monologue in brogue. Then he made a quick change and came back in blackface with a new line of quips in negro dialect. The loudspeaker part went over very well. It was the first vaudeville act that ever went on the air as a talking picture and in its possibilities it may be compared with the Fred Ott sneeze of more than thirty years ago, the first piece of comedy ever recorded in motion pictures. For the commercial future of television, if it has one, is thought to be largely in public entertainment—super-news reels flashed before audiences at the moment of occurrence, together with dramatic and musical acts shot on the ether waves in sound and picture at the instant they are taking place at the studio.

The next number from the studio at Whippany was a regular radio program piece—a short humorous dialect talk by Mrs. H. A. Frederick of Mountain Lakes.

Before and between the acts the announcer of the Whippany studio made

Continued on Page Twenty.

Voorhis Hopes When He Is 100 To Visit Smith in White House

Hope that he might celebrate his one hundredth birthday with Governor Smith in the White House was expressed yesterday by John R. Voorhis, veteran Grand Sachem of the Tammany Society and President of the Board of Elections. Mr. Voorhis will be ninety-eight years old next July and, if Governor Smith should be nominated for and elected President, his one hundredth birthday would occur in July, 1929, a few months after the inauguration.

"As near as I can determine, it looks as though Governor Smith would be nominated," Mr. Voorhis said. "The opposition to him is diminishing and the general sentiment for him is increasing. So far as his election is concerned, it is too far ahead to tell much about it."

Mr. Voorhis, who is still remarkably active, was seen at Tammany Hall. He stopped there on his return from a trip to Brownsville, where he went to inspect quarters sought by the Board of Elections for the storage of voting machines.

$840,000 FUR STRIKE AUDIT WAS HOPELESS

Accountants at Bribe Inquiry Testify Meagre Data Failed to Show Where Money Went.

REIGN OF TERROR KEEPS UP

Pickets Still Make Trouble, Says Frayne, Although There Is No Strike Now.

Accountants engaged by the American Federation of Labor's special committee to check up the expenditure of $840,000 by the Communist-led Joint Board of Furriers during last year's strike testified yesterday at the John Doe inquiry into allegations of police bribery that they could not find a single original voucher which specifically stated the use to which the money was put. Instead of original vouchers they said a forged cash book was furnished to them and not the book of original entry, as well as a large number of checks made out to "bearer," endorsed by the late Abraham Goodman, the Joint Board's counsel, and others.

The General Strike Committee handling the funds of the union checked out the money to counsel and to chairmen of various committees such as hall and picket committees, and the furthest the accountants were able to penetrate into the tangle of checks was to obtain some of the "receipts" for the money signed by subcommittee officers who received it from the Strike Committee, they asserted. They told Magistrate Joseph E. Corrigan, presiding at the inquiry, that they were never able to learn to whom the committee chairmen paid the money or whether some of it went for relief and court fines and how much was expended in this way.

Says Audit Was Hindered.

Every obstacle was placed in the way of the accountants by the Joint Board officers, according to the witnesses, until finally the union demanded individual receipts for every scrap of paper supplied for examination, with the understanding that

Continued on Page Nine.

THEFT OF 300 PAPERS ON MEXICO REVEALED BY FORGERY INQUIRY

Secret Military Reports Among Documents Stolen in Wholesale Diplomatic Robberies.

SOME WERE "DOCTORED"

Calles Turned Them Over to Us When It Became Known That We Knew He Had Them.

SUBJECT OF MYSTERY NOTE

Many Papers Believed Stolen From Our Embassy in Skillful Plot—Washington Disclaims "Leak."

By RICHARD V. OULAHAN.
Special to The New York Times.

WASHINGTON, April 7.—Pilfering of the United States Government's confidential correspondence relating to Mexico has been established through investigation which dovetails with the subject matter of the "mystery note" delivered to the Mexican Foreign Office recently by James R. Sheffield, the American Ambassador in Mexico City.

This pilfering was conducted on a wholesale scale, as nearly or quite 300 documents belonging to the United States Government were stolen. These documents were turned over to President Calles of Mexico, who, when the fact that he had them became known to the United States Government, delivered them to the State Department.

Included in this large batch of confidential papers was a considerable number of reports of a military nature, most of them supposed to have been taken from the office of the military attaché of the embassy in Mexico City.

Some time ago rumors were circulated in Washington that a "leak" in the State Department had been discovered and that an employe of the department had been dropped from the rolls in connection with the alleged "leak."

No "Leak," Officials Believe.

It is now being asserted that the alleged "leak" was associated with the established fact that confidential documents of the United States Government relating to Mexico had come into the possession of the Mexican Government.

While Government officials today maintained their attitude of silence concerning the pilfering of confidential diplomatic and military papers, it was indicated that there had not been any leak in the State Department. The denial took the form of a statement, in answer to inquiries, that it was not believed that any such leak had existed.

Officials showed a disinclination to discuss the matter and would not go further than to express that belief, with the additional information that they had not heard of any leak.

Other reports are that confidential military papers of the United States relating to Mexico had been offered for sale for $50,000. Another report is that official documents, presumably belonging to the Mexican Government, had been offered for sale to the American Embassy in Mexico City.

Signs of Skillful Plotting.

From what is known of the matter it is evident that a skillfully arranged effort to obtain confidential documents pertaining to the relations of the United States and Mexico has been in progress for some time. There are features of it as intriguing as elements of a fantastic novel having to do with international plotting.

It has been established, according to information obtained, that some of the stolen documents were "doctored" by having forged words and phrases inserted in them with the suspected intention of making it appear that the Coolidge Administration had hostile in-

Continued on Page Four.

Caruso Convicted of First Degree Murder; Killed Doctor After Death of Little Son

A jury in the Kings County Court late last night brought in a verdict of guilty of murder in the first degree against Frank Caruso for the killing of Dr. Casper S. Pendola of Maspeth in February.

Caruso, 36 years old and the father of five children, killed the physician when he found his 9-year-old son, Joseph, who was being treated by Dr. Pendola for diphtheria, had died.

The jury returned to the court room at 11:51 o'clock, after most of those who had listened all day to the trial had left the room. The defendant heard the foreman's announcement with little visible concern. He arose at the call of the clerk, walked a few steps forward and gave his pedigree in an even tone.

Caruso said he had been sixteen years in this country. He was a native of Italy. He lived at 36 Third Street, Brooklyn, and had been convicted and fined $100 eight years ago for having a pistol.

The case went to the jury at 6 P. M. Twice the jury returned to the court room, once to inquire about the different degrees of murder, and again to have a part of Judge McLaughlin's charge read. In the first hour of its deliberation a report reached the Court that it stood 7 to 5 for first degree murder.

After the verdict was announced Judge McLaughlin, turning to the jury, said: "I thank you for the careful consideration you have given to this case. The verdict will make for law and order. Any other finding would have been a miscarriage of justice."

In summing up George Voss, attorney for Caruso, declared that the defendant was moved to the frenzy that resulted in the killing because Dr. Pendola laughed when he heard that Caruso's son had died following treatment for diphtheria. He told the jurors that under the same circumstances they would have felt the urge to kill. He asked them not to class Caruso with the cold-blooded gangsters who murder with deliberation. He raised the technicality that the doctor had been killed by strangulation instead of stabbing, as charged in the indictment.

In his summing up Chief Assistant District Attorney Joseph V. Gallagher said that the testimony of a Holy Family Hospital ambulance surgeon and the autopsy report of Assistant Medical Examiner Gregory Robillard showed that Dr. Pendola had been stabbed to death. He said that the two knife wounds indicated that the murder was premeditated.

County Judge McLaughlin, in his charge to the jury, said the murder was neither legally justifiable nor excusable. After explaining the distinction between first and second degree murder he cautioned the jury to abandon all sympathy and sentiment in deciding the case.

Caruso will be sentenced on April 18.

HUGE POTASH 'TRUST' UNDER FEDERAL FIRE

Tuttle Sues French and German Groups, Alleging Scheme to Monopolize Markets Here.

$50,000,000 ANNUAL TRADE

American Concern Also Named in Complaint—Case Second Under Wilson Tariff Act.

Acting under instructions from the Department of Justice, United States Attorney Charles H. Tuttle began yesterday an injunction suit against a German syndicate called the Deutsche Kalisyndikat Gesellschaft, to restrain it from carrying out an alleged plan to create in the United States a monopoly in the sale of potash. It is charged that the plan violates the Sherman Anti-Trust law and the Wilson Tariff act and that a group of German and French producers of potash are now in this city to complete arrangements with certain American distributing agencies to make the monopoly complete and effective.

It is charged that the German companies have an exclusive selling agency in this city which operates under the name of the Potash Importing Corporation of America, that the French companies have a similar agency, and that these two groups have agreed to divide the business in this country and to handle the product with a single agency at prices to be agreed upon between them.

Danger to Our Interests Seen.

The danger of such a monopoly to the interests of the people in this country is indicated by Alexander B. Royce, a special assistant to the United States Attorney, in charge of trust cases, who said:

"The Government petition charges that beginning May 1, 1927, the French and German companies have agreed to continue the division of the United States business. It is also charged that these two groups have been dividing the sales of potash in this country since August, 1924. The complaint alleges that because the mines of the French and German companies constitute the only source of a large supply of potash, users in the United States are almost wholly dependent upon them."

It is explained that the syndicate is a combination of the owners of all the potash mines in Germany, that their headquarters and principal office is in Berlin, and that associated with them are the French companies which own potash mines in Alsace, the greater part of the product being shipped to the United States. From the close of the war until 1924 the French companies, it is asserted, sold potash to importers in this country independently of each other and free from agreements on prices, quantities, or conditions.

The Defendants Named.

The corporate defendants are the German syndicate, the Société Commerciale de Potasses d'Alsace, Mines Domaniales de Potasse d'Alsace, the Société Anonyme des Mines de Kali Sainte-Thérèse and the Potash Importing Corporation of America. The individual defendants are Dr. Maximilien Kempner, Dr. Oskar Eckstein, A. Diehn, Robert Kunze, Dr. Ernst Frohnknecht, all of whom are officers and employes of the syndicate; le Cornee, whose Christian name is not known, and Rene Gide, who are described as active in the control of the French potash industry; E. K. Howe, H. A. Forbes, Walker B. Howe and René Gide, a resident of this city, especially interested in the product of the Société Commerciale des Potasses d'Alsace. The latter is evidently a son or other relative of the René Gide first mentioned.

That the Government has been aware of the alleged negotiations by the defendants to monopolize the potash trade in the United States is indicated by the fact that it has been known that all the German defendants are guests at the Hotel Plaza, and all of the French defendants have quarters at 25 West Forty-third Street, and because certain movements of representatives of the two factions are known.

Mr. Royce said 1,000,000 tons of pot-

Continued on Page Three.

WARNS NIGHT CLUBS OF COMING CLEAN-UP

Banton Declares New Theatre Padlock Measure Also Applies to Them.

SURE OF PUBLIC SUPPORT

He Will Act on Complaints, He Says—Playhouse Owners Are Perturbed Over New Bill.

Governor Smith's approval of the Wales Theatre Padlock bill caused District Attorney Banton to announce yesterday that the bill was as directly applicable to night clubs and cabarets as to theatres, and to declare that "women in night clubs had better put on clothes, too." Mr. Banton, who drew the bill and enlisted the support necessary for its passage, said it was backed by the public, which would make convictions easy.

The District Attorney, while denying that he would spy on either the theatres or the night clubs, intimated strongly that the public as well as the police would report violations, said he would act promptly upon complaints of private citizens or policemen, and that clean entertainments would soon result. He added that, "as in all cases where a moral principle is involved, the Governor was found on the side of right-thinking people."

Theatrical producers and managers, for the most part, expressed disappointment over Governor Smith's action in signing the bill. Arch Selwyn, declaring that it had been a "very, very foolish thing for the Governor to do" expressed the opinion that the bill would mean "new graft in various departments of the city." An exception was A. L. Erlanger, who expressed approval of the Governor's action.

Banton Issues Statement.

In a statement issued soon after he had learned that Governor Smith had signed the bill, District Attorney Banton said:

"The producers and managers of plays now before the public had better go through them (the plays) and cut out their dirty lines and scenes. Authors of plays yet to be produced had better keep in mind this new law.

"We now have the right kind of law and the law is backed by the public. Public sentiment, when aroused, makes it easy for us to get convictions against indecent shows. Without it we find it hard to get convictions. Under this new law we shall find that theatre owners will be the best kind of censors of plays produced in their theatres—and that, after all, is what is effective in keeping the stage clean.

"This new law increases efficiency in the administration of the statute against obscenity in the theatres in the following particulars:

"First—Heretofore it has been necessary to proceed against the play as a whole. The amendment permits the arrest of those who interject into the play an obscene act.

"Second—All plays, or parts thereof, which depict or in any way deal with the subject of degeneracy are prohibited.

"Third—Therefore the owner of the theatre, like the ostrich, could hide his head in the sand and pretend not to know what was going on about him, and conviction of the owner or lessee of a theatre has been next to impossible, as in the case of John Cort, who for eleven months was one of the principal owners of the theatre in which 'Sex' was produced. From now on the owner or lessee of the property will be held responsible for a violation on his property, and on conviction of the actors or producers, the licensing authority may revoke the license and refuse to issue a new license for a period not exceeding one year."

Law Called Unconstitutional.

Commenting on a statement by William H. Klein, attorney for the Shuberts, that the new law was unconstitutional, Mr. Banton said:

"The license granted by a public official is only a privilege and the power to grant such license implies the power to revoke it. It is within the legislative power to define just what that official power is. This new law places the licensing power, in the case of the theatrical performance, on a par with any other licensing power in ex-

Continued on Page Eight.

2 Boys Killed, 5 Hurt, When Truck Hits Auto On Which 10 Were Riding Home From School

Two school boys were killed and five others were injured yesterday when a truck crashed into a coupe on which they were riding at Beverly and Rugby Roads, Brooklyn.

The boys killed were Lawrence Moen, 11 years old, of 360 East Seventh Street, and Caesar Saiya, 10 years old, of 698 Coney Island Avenue. Attilio Saiya, 14, brother of Caesar, received internal injuries and was sent to the Kings County Hospital, with Nicholas Demarinio, 13, of 239 East Ninth Street, whose right leg was fractured, and Timothy Barlow, 11, of 240 East Ninth Street, who was badly cut and bruised. John Ledischi, 13, of 260 East Ninth Street, was cut and bruised. After being treated at the hospital he was sent home. Columbus Saiya, another brother of the dead boy, received similar injuries, but ran home before a doctor reached the scene. He was treated at home last night.

The boys, with three others, were leaving Holy Innocents Parochial School, at Beverly Road and East Seventeenth Street shortly after 4 o'clock, when one of them hailed a friend driving past in a coupe. The boys had attended a confirmation class for confirm on next Sunday.

In the coupe were Stephen J. Collins of 1,042 Flatbush Avenue, and his wife. Asked if he could give them a ride home Mr. Collins told the boys to climb on. Those who could not find places on the running board clambered on the back of the car.

When the coupe reached Rugby Road, a short distance away, the boys' shouts of pleasure changed suddenly to screams of fright. As the coupe started across Rugby Road a truck driven by Frank Whalen of 646 Seventy-fourth Street, bore down on it and before Collins could get the coupe out of the way the truck crashed into it, striking Moen and Caesar Saiya, who were standing on the running board. Moen was instantly killed. The coupe was whirled around and hurled across the street. As it slammed against the curb five of the boys were thrown off. Collins, his wife and the other boys were only slightly injured.

The Saiya boy was hurried to the hospital, but was dead when he got there. Collins and Whalen were questioned by Assistant District Attorney Bernard Becker, who directed that both men be held for the action of the Brooklyn homicide court this morning. Collins said he did not see the truck coming because his vision was obscured by the boys standing on the running board of his car.

SMITH APPROVES THEATRE PADLOCKS; VETOES GAS CUT-OFF

Governor Declares Majority of the People and Producers Desire a Clean Stage.

APPLIANCE BILL A PUZZLE

Tempted to Sign It Because of Graft Talk, He Finally Rejects It as Too Broad.

30-DAY BILLS CLEANED UP

Port Authority, Sewage Plant and Salary Measures Approved—One Baumes Proposal Vetoed.

By W. A. WARN
Special to The New York Times.

ALBANY, April 7.—Although less than two weeks have elapsed since the Legislature adjourned sine die, Governor Smith today finished work on the huge mass of legislative measures the lawmakers sent to his desk for veto or approval, for the consideration of which the Governor is allotted thirty days under the law. The speed with which the thirty-day bills were disposed of is thought to establish a State record.

The Governor left this evening for New York City, where he will remain until Monday, when he will go to the Sea View Golf Club at Absecon, N. J. for an indefinite stay, accompanied by Mrs. Smith and other members of his family. He is badly in need of rest, having worked under high pressure for weeks.

Among the bills approved by the Governor today were the Theatrical Padlock bill, on which a hearing was held yesterday; the bill giving the Governor veto power over New York State members of the Port Authority Commission; the bill authorizing the State to surrender the northern end of Ward's Island to the New York City authorities as a site for a modern sewage disposal plant; a bill approving the New York-New Jersey-Pennsylvania compact for developing new water supply facilities on the Delaware River and a number of bills providing salary increases to be paid out of the New York City treasury to judges and some other county officials within the city.

Important Bills Vetoed.

Governor Smith vetoed the Thayer bill, which would have repealed the aldermanic ordinance under which a certain patented gas cut-off appliance must be installed in all buildings above a certain height and which was denounced by spokesmen for New York City realty interests at a hearing yesterday as prolific in graft to the promoters. The Governor said this measure had been so loosely drawn and would have such far-reaching disastrous effects that he felt compelled to withhold his approval.

Among other measures vetoed were a bill that would have enabled the Montauk Riding and Driving Club in Brooklyn to disregard vital provisions of the Tenement House law in the erection of a "club apartment" structure in Brooklyn, designed to have on the ground floor a huge arena for horse shows and driving meets; a bill which would have permitted osteopaths to perform minor operations and one which would have conferred the title of doctor on optometrists.

In all 3,401 bills were introduced at the recent session of the Legislature. Of these 861 reached the Governor's desk. Out of this number he approved 731, which now will take their place on the statute books. He vetoed 130. Approximately 400 bills were among the thirty-day lot.

Of forty-six bills permitting claim suits to be brought against the State in the Court of Claims, Governor Smith vetoed twenty-four and approved twenty-two. Some pension and retirement bills affecting New York City were among the measures which the Governor failed to give his approval. In a so-called omnibus veto were included forty bills rejected by the Governor as unnecessary or faultily drawn.

About the most important measure in this batch was one of the Baumes Crime Commission measures, providing for the establishment of bureaus of criminal identification in all cities with

Continued on Page Twelve.

Earl Carroll's Friends Will Seek a Parole; No Pardon Is Asked; Term Starts Tuesday

Special to The New York Times.

WASHINGTON, April 7.—Inquiries at the Department of Justice today indicated that friends of Earl Carroll, New York theatrical producer, who was sentenced to a term of a year and a day at Atlanta for perjury in connection with the famous bath tub case, will attempt to obtain a parole for Mr. Carroll at the appropriate time if executive clemency is refused before the sentence begins, as now seems assured.

Up to date no application for the exercise of executive clemency in behalf of Mr. Carroll has been received at the Department of Justice, which handles such matters before they are sent to the President for consideration. It was explained to friends of Mr. Carroll that executive clemency is rarely extended before the execution of a sentence, and then only in cases where precarious health or facts tending to throw doubt on the guilt of persons accused are cited.

In most instances the Attorney General will not consider recommending a pardon until at least one-third of the sentence of a person convicted has been served. A prisoner likewise is not eligible for parole until he has served one-third of the time for which he has been sentenced.

Under the mandate of the New York Court Mr. Carroll's sentence will begin on April 12, and as things now stand he will have to surrender himself to the custody of the authorities on that date.

SOVIET OFFICES IN TIENTSIN RAIDED BY CHINESE POLICE; NOW CUT OFF IN SHANGHAI

MORE DOCUMENTS SEIZED

Permission for Tientsin Search Is Given by French Consul.

THREAT TO MOVE EMBASSY

Soviet Consul General, Before Isolation at Shanghai, Says It May Go to Hankow.

PEKING EXPECTS RUPTURE

Wellington Koo Resigns as Premier in North—American Missionary Is Missing.

Special Cable to THE NEW YORK TIMES.

TIENTSIN, China, April 7.—The Chinese police, with the sanction of the French Consul, raided today the Soviet bank [the Dahl Bank] and also the offices of the Chinese-Eastern Railway and other Soviet offices, all in the French concession, and seized documents.

The raid was prompted by the discoveries in the Soviet buildings at Peking yesterday.

TIENTSIN, April 7 (AP).—Chinese police this afternoon entered the French concession, with permission of the Consul, and searched the Dahl Bank and various Soviet trade missions. The Chinese detained all persons pending the search and removed documents for examination.

French police took no direct part in the raid, but maintained order outside.

Shanghai Consulate Under Guard.

SHANGHAI, April 7 (AP).—Police, assisted by White Russian volunteers, late today surrounded the Soviet Consulate in the international settlement with orders to prevent any one from entering or leaving the premises.

No reason for this action was given but it was stated that there was no present intention to raid the Consulate.

Among the visitors whom the police held up was the Chinese Commissioner of Foreign Affairs, who was informed that he would not be allowed to enter unless he consented to be searched. The Commissioner refused to permit this and left.

The possibility of the removal of the Soviet Embassy at Peking to Hankow, the seat of the Cantonese or Nationalist Government, was suggested today by Wilhelm F. Linde, Soviet Consul here, as a result of yesterday's raid by Northern soldiers on buildings attached to the Russian Embassy.

Mr. Linde said that such a removal was not impossible in discussing the incident with newspaper men after he had called upon the Norwegian Consul General, Dean of the consular corps in Shanghai, to announce that he would hold the consular body responsible if the Soviet Consulate here were raided also.

The Soviet Consul General also declared that if the Peking raid was carried out with the approval of the diplomatic corps, it would set a precedent that would endanger the foundation of diplomatic prerogatives. In this connection he said that he understood that permission for the entry of the Chinese troops and police into the legation grounds at Peking had been granted solely by the Dean of the diplomatic corps and not from all the members.

Yangtse Evacuation Goes On.

While interest continued to centre here on the international possibilities of the Peking raid in so far as it may cause serious repercussions in Moscow, foreigners in various sections of China are steadily evacuating the areas where anti-foreign agitation has been spreading.

Hankow, scene of a growing tenseness, was the centre of riotous anti-foreign outbreaks over last week-end, resulting in further plans for a rapid departure of the comparatively few remaining foreigners.

"Situation growing worse steadily" was a wireless message received from there today.

With lawlessness in the city apparently increasing, the commander of the United States Yangtse River patrol is urging Americans still in the city to leave as soon as possible. Japanese are leaving the city in increasing numbers, while German and Russian nationals are preparing to leave soon.

Dr. C. P. Triberg of St. Peter, Minn., a member of the Augustana Synod Mission of the American Lutheran Church, was reported missing today and it is feared he has been captured by bandits. All the members of the mission, which was centred in the Province of Honan, are leaving China, fifty-four of the ninety-four members leaving tomorrow on the President Pierce.

In line with the decision to bring all British gunboats out of the upper Yangtse area, the British consuls and the remainder of the British communities at Chung-king, I-chang,

Court Banishes Man for Life From State of North Carolina

Special to The New York Times.

DANVILLE, Va., April 7.—J. H. Anderson of this city was banished from the State of North Carolina for life today by Judge W. E. Haring, sitting at Yanceyville. Anderson also was told by the Court that if he was found within 200 miles of Danville henceforth he would be arrested and required to serve two years on the roads.

A jury had convicted him after twenty-four hours' deliberation of an assault on a young woman. Anderson was permitted to choose between sentence or exile, and he chose the latter.

DAWES CONTINUES REED COMMITTEE

Declares It Has Legal Authority to Function During the Recess of Congress.

FESS TAKES GOFF'S PLACE

Naming of Ohio Senator Instead of Shortridge of California Surprises Washington.

CHICAGO, April 7 (AP).—Vice President Dawes, guided by a Supreme Court decision, today held that the Senate Campaign Fund Investigating Committee retains its powers although Congress has adjourned, and appointed Senator Simeon Fess, Republican, Ohio, to succeed Senator Guy D. Goff, Republican, West Virginia, who resigned as a member of the committee.

The Vice President followed the opinion of the high court in the recent case against Mal Daugherty, whose testimony was wanted by a Senate committee.

The filibuster in the expiring hours of the Senate of the Sixty-ninth Congress and the failure of the resolution of Senator James A. Reed of Missouri, the Chairman, to continue the committee, and the resignation of Senator Goff, left the decision to the Vice President.

Senators Goff, Borah, Republican, Idaho, and Walsh, Democrat, Montana, all expressed opinions that the committee continued legally to exist. Senator Keyes, Republican, New Hampshire, Chairman of the Committee on Audit and Control of the Contingent Fund of the Senate, held that the committee was dead and that he should not approve further expenditures from the fund by the committee.

Gives Reasons for Decision.

Vice President Dawes returned here yesterday from a vacation trip to Panama and late today advised Senator Fess of his selection to the Goff vacancy on the committee. At the same time the Vice President made public his action and basis for it in a statement in part as follows:

"In my judgment the Supreme Court of the United States in the case of John J. McGrain, Deputy Sergeant-at-Arms of the United States Senate, appellant, v. Mal S. Daugherty, rendered Jan. 17, 1927, conclusively disposes of the question in the affirmative. The Supreme Court was passing on the question of the powers of a Senatorial committee authorized by a resolution 'to sit and perform its duties at such times and places as may be deemed advisable or necessary by said committee.'

"It held that this language of the resolution extended the powers of the committee beyond the Congress which passed the creating resolution. Senate resolution 195, Sixty-ninth Congress, creating the present Senatorial Investigating Committee, contains the following language:

" 'Said committee is hereby empowered to sit and act at such time or times and at such place or places as it may deem necessary.'

"The holding of the Supreme Court,

Continued on Page Two.

"All the News That's Fit to Print."

The New York Times.

THE WEATHER
Cloudy with probable showers today; tomorrow partly cloudy.
Temperature Yesterday—Max. 72; Min. 63.
For weather report see Page 30.

VOL. LXXVI....No. 25,413. NEW YORK, TUESDAY, AUGUST 23, 1927. TWO CENTS In Greater New York | THREE CENTS Within 200 Miles | FOUR CENTS Elsewhere in the U. S.

SACCO AND VANZETTI PUT TO DEATH EARLY THIS MORNING; GOVERNOR FULLER REJECTS LAST-MINUTE PLEAS FOR DELAY AFTER A DAY OF LEGAL MOVES AND DEMONSTRATIONS

COOLIDGE PERCHES GOVERNMENT'S SEAT ON PEAK IN ROCKIES

He Reaches Yellowstone Park and Begins at Once His Sight-Seeing Trips.

VISITS CAMP ROOSEVELT

President Passes First Night in a Cottage Surrounded by Snow-Clad Mountains.

CROWDS EXTEND GREETINGS

Mrs. Coolidge and John Share in Ovations at Stations Where Special Train Halted.

From a Staff Correspondent of The New York Times.

MAMMOTH HOT SPRINGS, Yellowstone Park, Wyo., Aug. 22.—The seat of Government tonight is established on a high peak in the Rockies, the furthermost point west to which it has ever gone, in the majestic scenery of Yellowstone Park. With the arrival of President and Mrs. Coolidge into the national playground through the Gardiner entrance the Presidential flag was unfurled over a gray rambling cottage, the home of H. W. Child, President of the Yellowstone Transportation Company.

Here for one night the President will remain but in the next four days he will pass each night in a different place as he travels over the park.

The Presidential special train reached Gardiner in a Summer rainstorm. The mountain tops were covered with snow and through the clouds the sun was shining, presenting a rainbow that added to the first view the President and Mrs. Coolidge had of the national playground. A large station crowd followed the President's party through the five miles to the cottage, where hundreds had gathered to greet the visitors.

In less than three quarters of an hour Mr. and Mrs. Coolidge set out on their first expedition, visiting Camp Roosevelt, where they saw the greatest collection of wild game in the United States.

Five-Hour Auto Trip.

As the Presidential party started out on their afternoon auto trip the clouds disappeared, and the President and Mrs. Coolidge had sunshine throughout a five-hour journey through the northern end of the park. Their trip took them over forty-four miles to Camp Roosevelt, along the small canyon road to Tower Falls and to the petrified tree.

H. M. Albright, superintendent of the park, rode in the President's car, in which were the President, Mrs. Coolidge and John. He explained the scenery, delivering a most informative lecture, so the President said later. His recital held the attention of the President, who sat in silence for most of the trip, thrilled by the panoramic scenes unfolded to him at every turn of the road.

The park now is at the height of its beauty, the mountainsides are green, the roads brilliant in early Fall wild flowers and animal life astir as the cold nights approach.

The President not only saw bears at Camp Roosevelt, but antelopes jumping from the crags in Gallatin Range and deer feeding in the pools that indent the lowlands not far from the present Summer White House, opposite the Mammoth Hot Springs Hotel.

On the way to Camp Roosevelt the Forest Rangers had to cut away a tree that the high wind had thrown across the road. All along the roads motors bearing the licenses of distant States and park buses drew aside to give the President right of way, cheering the President as he passed. The drives seemed thronged with travelers. Nearly 10,000 are estimated now to be within the park area.

Camp Roosevelt is a rustic lodge that was built in 1906 to commemorate President Roosevelt's trip to the park in 1903 in company with John Burroughs. There Colonel Roosevelt pitched his camp, fished for many days and studied the wild life so abundant in this region. Today hundreds of tourists' tents, supplied with many modern comforts, surround the lodge.

A mother bear and three cubs ate and frolicked about undisturbed by the visitors. President and Mrs. Coolidge and John stood in the background watching them. This gave the movie men a good setting and the first real picture of the President's day in the park.

Visitors Greeted in Song.

On the porch were assembled a bevy of pretty girls and young men, known as the "Savages," composed of college students who work in the park. They formed a solid mass through which the President and

Continued on Page Fifteen.

Coins Word 'Avigation' For Directing of Aircraft

Special to The New York Times.

WASHINGTON, Aug. 22.—The suggestion that the word "avigation" be used in connection with aeronautics has been made by Lieutenant Lester J. Maitland, who piloted an army plane in the first successful non-stop flight from California to Hawaii. The idea has found favor with officers of the Navy Bureau of Aeronautics

Lieutenant Maitland suggested that "we use the term 'avigation' for the directing or operating of aircraft from one place to another."

The combination of the Latin roots avi (to fly) and agere (to move) is not only etymologically correct, the bureau officers argued, but the word will serve to differentiate navigation and avigation, very different arts. It is not too much to believe, officers of the bureau said, "that in years to come a skilled navigator may be entirely useless in an airplane, while 'avigators' will be in great demand for long-distance commercial flying."

WILBUR PREDICTS STUNT FLIGHT CURB

Naval Secretary Says Federal Law Must Stop Loss of Life as in Pacific Race.

TAKES STAND WITH EBERLE

Navy Extends Search for Dole Fliers by Two Days, but Has No Clues.

By The Associated Press.

SAN FRANCISCO, Cal., Aug. 22.—While navy ships and planes searched under an extended "zero hour," Secretary of the Navy Curtis D. Wilbur, a San Francisco visitor, and officials in Washington agreed today that some Federal move must be made to prevent a recurrence of the disasters that have befallen the Dole air race entrants the seven missing fliers of the Golden Eagle, the Miss Doran and the Dallas Spirit.

Admiral Eberle, Acting Secretary of the Navy, in Washington, predicted the enactment by Congress of a law to prohibit long-distance airplane "stunt flights" except under rigid conditions.

At the same time Admiral Eberle ordered the forty naval vessels searching the Pacific for the missing fliers to continue their efforts until Thursday. The original plans were that the hunt should officially terminate tomorrow night, a week from the date of the start of the Miss Doran and the Golden Eagle.

The extension was made as the result of the disappearance of the Dallas Spirit, piloted by Captain William Erwin of Dallas, Texas, and navigated by A. H. Eichwaldt of Hayward, Cal., which apparently dived into the sea nearly 700 miles west of San Francisco on Friday night after flashing an S O S call on its radio.

Secretary Wilbur was quoted as agreeing that "some step must be taken by the Federal Government to prevent future loss of lives in long-distance stunt flights."

He declined to comment on Admiral Eberle's prediction. He said that the President had some power in this respect, but added he was not sure that this was sufficient to cover the situation.

He declared it was inevitable that some action would be taken "to prevent needless loss of life."

Wide Hunt Lowers Hope for Erwin.

That navy men conducting the hunt for the missing men in the Dallas Spirit held little hope for their rescue was reflected by Lieut. Commander William C. Tooze of the destroyer Hazelwood, who said:

"I do not think there is one chance in a thousand that the Dallas Spirit will ever be found. The Hazelwood, in command of Commander E H. Connor, covered an area of 3,200 square miles about a point where she gave us her last position and in that space there was not a piece of flotsam—not even an oil spot."

The destroyers Hazelwood, Hull, Kidder, Farenholt and Corry were in San Francisco restocking their larders and refueling, preparatory to proceeding back out to sea to rejoin the airplane carrier Langley, some 500 miles off shore. The Langley has been dispatching observation planes over as wide area for searching purposes.

Reports from Honolulu bore no more hope. The Associated Press correspondent at the island headquarters declared that "another day

Continued on Page Seventeen.

WALKER JOKES WITH BEEFEATER GUIDE IN TOWER OF LONDON

Thinks He Could Find Use for Headsman's Block in New York.

RECEIVES STATE WELCOME

Rides With Mrs. Walker From Station to Hotel in Lord Mayor's Gilded Coach.

TENEMENTS IMPRESS HIM

As Guest of Lord Mayor He Sees Greyhounds Race—Leaves for Berlin Today.

Special Cable to THE NEW YORK TIMES.

LONDON, Aug. 22.—Mayor Walker's last day in London was a busy one. He visited the Tower of London, received a delegation of advertising men, inspected model tenements and after a quiet dinner at his hotel attended the greyhound races at White City tonight as the guest of the Lord Mayor of London.

Mayor and Mrs. Walker plan to leave tomorrow morning at 8:30 for Berlin, where they are due to arrive Wednesday evening at 8 o'clock.

The Mayor on arriving from Dublin on the boat train just after 7 o'clock this morning found, although he had not expected it to meet him, the state coach of the Lord Mayor of London waiting at the railroad station. The coach, an ornate, gilt encrusted affair, with two coachmen on the box and two footmen behind, was drawn by a span of beautifully groomed horses.

At the invitation of the Lord Mayor's representative who met them the Mayor and Mrs. Walker entered it and were driven to their hotel.

Immediately after breakfast the Mayor announced that he wanted to see the Tower of London. Mrs. Walker had planned a shopping tour and could not accompany him. The Mayor's secretary telephoned the Governor of the Tower and made an appointment for 11:30.

Mayor Walker was greeted on his arrival by the Governor, who appointed a stalwart "Beefeater" to conduct him through the Tower. The route led through the Bloody Tower down dark, winding stairs to dungeons, execution rooms of the past, gibbets and all manner of terrifying relics until the Mayor faced the execution block.

The Beefeater pointed to the block and began droning the names of those who perished on it. Mayor Walker stepped forward, the better to examine the block.

"A pretty nifty chin-rest those fellows had," he murmured. "It's nice to inspect close up things you missed. But say," he continued, addressing himself to the Beefeater, "I'd like to see this thing working. Can you arrange it?"

The Beefeater apparently didn't see the humor of the Mayor's remark. He continued explaining that the block was once used as a summary answer to political opponents.

"Then a demonstration's easy," observed the Mayor. "I can provide you material from New York."

He declined to say whom he had in mind, but examined the block closely.

"There are marks which make it look as if the axeman missed and got into the rough," he said.

As the party left the execution chamber the Mayor remarked:

"And no one ever asked for an encore."

Wanted to Meet Gog and Magog.

With the faintest trace of a smile Mayor Walker suggested to the guide that he would like to meet Gog and Magog, the giants whose statues he

Continued on Page Ten.

Society Gets Old Irving Home For Centre of Patriotic Work

The old home of Washington Irving at Seventeenth Street and Irving Place became the property of the National Society of Patriotic Builders of America yesterday when, in the living room, Mrs. William Cumming Story, President of the society, received the title from Algernon S. Bell, the former owner.

The dwelling will be the headquarters of the society. It was selected because it was a type consistent with the aims of the society, which, according to Mrs. Story, are "to preserve historic places, support the Constitution and maintain old American ideals."

Mrs. Story said the society would engage in propaganda for the dissemination of American ideals and culture, asserting that there are "many who come to this country and live and yet remain ignorant of American customs and ideals."

MRS. CHAPLIN WINS DIVORCE AND $825,000

She Gets $625,000 for Herself and $200,000 in Trust for the Two Children.

SUIT BASED ON CRUELTY

Actor Is Not in Los Angeles Court to Hear Her and Friends Tell of Alleged Neglect.

Special to The New York Times.

LOS ANGELES, Aug. 22.—Mrs. Lita Grey Chaplin received an interlocutory decree of divorce from Charles Spencer Chaplin, custody of their two small children and $825,000 in Superior Court today. The film comedian did not appear in court. A year must elapse before a final decree is granted.

When the case was called before Judge Walter Guerin, Edwin T. McMurray, uncle of the plaintiff and chief of her counsel, announced the terms of the property settlement under which Mrs. Chaplin is to receive $625,000, said to be in cash, and $200,000 in trust for the children.

Coming to a sudden and undramatic conclusion, the divorce action, based on charges of cruelty and neglect, was devoid of sensation at its quiet ending, very little different from routine cases. All charges referring to premarital relations of the couple made in the complaint were ruled out by the Judge, who stated that such evidence might be introduced later through testimony, but nothing further was offered.

Chaplin's chief attorney, Gavin McNab, asked the Court to dismiss the comedian's cross-complaint, asserting that his client agreed to the settlement "as an indication of the love of a father for his children, with a desire to keep the taint of scandal from their names."

Only a few sensation-hunters attended the trial, in contrast to the crowds which usually haunt the courts when film colony divorces are on the docket. They heard Mrs. Chaplin testify that her husband had taken her out but twice during the first two months of their married life, and then only for the sake of appearances, and that he never came home before 1 o'clock in the morning. Denying that she interfered with his career, she declared that she hardly ever saw him at all.

The witness described alleged incidents immediately prior to their

Continued on Page Eight.

Dawes Declares He Is Not a Candidate, Declining Young America Union's Support

Special to The New York Times.

CINCINNATI, Aug 22.—Vice President Dawes has informed Douglas T. Atkinson, Judge Advocate of the Young America Union, a secret nonsectarian political organization, that he is not a candidate for the nomination for the Presidency.

Mr. Atkinson received Mr. Dawes's reply at his home here today to a letter sent on behalf of the Young America Union pledging support to Mr. Dawes if he should run. The Vice President wrote as follows:

"I wish you to accept my thanks for your letter and the clipping which you enclosed. Also for your kindly words. They are all much appreciated. I am, however, not a candidate for the nomination."

The Young America Union was founded at Columbus, Ohio, last February. Its chief aim is stated to be to arouse the interest of the younger citizens of the country in civic affairs and to awaken in them a civic pride which it is hoped will be felt in the national issues of the day. The union now has chapters in Cincinnati, Columbus, Youngstown, Cleveland and other large cities in Ohio and is organizing them in other States.

Special to The New York Times.

WASHINGTON, Aug. 22.—The statement by Vice President Dawes in his letter to Mr. Atkinson, that he was not a candidate for the nomination for the Presidency, is viewed by political leaders who are in Washington as merely a reiteration of the position he is said to have taken when approached by others who have sought to sound him out.

The Vice President, it is understood, has not only told friends that he is not seeking the nomination, but that he will not enter the primaries in Illinois or other States. It is not felt, however, that this eliminates him from the race.

The strategy of the leaders who would like to see Mr. Dawes nominated, it is said, is to have him keep out of the primaries in the Middle West and leave the field open for former Governor Lowden of Illinois. Under this arrangement Dawes would fall heir to the Lowden delegates in the event that Mr. Lowden failed to obtain the nomination.

FULLER HEARS PETITIONERS

Governor Is Under Steady Pressure Until the Final Hour.

WOMEN LAST TO APPEAL

Mrs. Sacco and Miss Vanzetti Leave Him and at 11:03 P. M. He Gives Decision.

DEFENSE TRIED EVERY PLEA

Stone, Taft, Holmes and Other Federal as Well as State Judges Refused to Act.

From a Staff Correspondent of The New York Times.

BOSTON, Aug. 22.—Governor Fuller, at the end of a day marked by rapid and continuous action of the defense for Nicola Sacco and Bartolomeo Vanzetti, told Michael A. Musmanno of defense counsel at 11:03 o'clock tonight that he would not interfere in the execution.

The Governor made his decision after a series of extraordinary events. Counsel for the men, augmented by new and distinguished arrivals from New York and Washington, made eight ineffectual attempts to obtain a stay in the Federal courts and in the Superior and Supreme Courts of Massachusetts.

Chief Justice William Howard Taft refused to cross the border from his Summer home in Canada to act on the case. He referred the lawyers to his associates. Subsequently Harlan F. Stone likewise refused. Another effort to get Justice Oliver Wendell Holmes proved futile and other Federal and State Judges likewise declined to take jurisdiction.

A final and dramatic appeal by Mrs. Rose Sacco and Luigia Vanzetti to Governor Fuller at the State House tonight preceded the refusal of the Governor to take any further action to stay the carrying out of the death penalty.

Women Make Family Appeal.

Mrs. Sacco and Miss Vanzetti remained with the Governor for an hour and a half at the State House. In the presence of present and past counsel and State officials, the women begged for a respite. Mrs. Sacco appealed to the Governor as the father of children. She urged her motherhood as an argument that should carry some weight with him.

Miss Vanzetti begged for mercy on behalf of her brother. She urged the Governor to act at once and his name would be blessed. She gave Governor Fuller a message from her brother, saying:

"Some day you will realize my innocence."

To both pleas, Governor Fuller replied:

"I am sorry. My duties are outlined by law."

The women had appeared at the State House at 9:05 P. M. and were at once ushered before the Governor.

They left his office at 10:35 P. M. Their eyes were dry. They had wept almost all day and they were bereft of tears at the end.

Effort Is Made to the End.

Among those who pressed into the Governor's office until the last hour before the execution were Francis Fisher Kane, former United States attorney in Philadelphia; State Attorney General Arthur K. Reading, William G. Thompson and Herbert B. Ehrmann, former counsel for the men; Gardner Jackson and Aldini Felicani, members of the Sacco-Vanzetti Defense Committee, and Mr. Musmanno.

The Governor remained at his office until the executions were reported to him before retiring. He had continued to hear the importunities of defense counsel until nearly midnight.

A few minutes before the time for the executions the Governor said good-bye to Mr. Thompson, who had defended Sacco and Vanzetti for many years. When he left Mr. Thompson said:

"Briefly, I outlined to the Governor against the important aspect of the case and did what I considered my duty to my former clients, because, despite the fact that I withdrew from the case, I believe them innocent and they did not have a fair trial."

Fuller Receives Editor's Plea.

Governor Fuller reached his office at the State House at 11:40 A. M. from his Summer residence at Rye Beach, N. H. He greeted newspaper men with "It's a beautiful morning, isn't it." The Governor smiled and seemed in excellent health and spirits.

The Governor was preceded by the first of the day's delegations. Waldo L. Cook, editor of the pringfield Republican; John F. Moors, a Boston banker, and the Rev. Edward Staples Droun of the Episcopal Theological School at Cambridge had called at the Executive offices at 10:15. They left and returned in an hour.

When Mr. Cook and his associates returned they were accompanied by John Lovejoy Elliott of the Hudson Guild, New York City, and Paul U.

Continued on Page Two.

Four Final Legal Pleas Made to the Governor That Failed to Delay Execution of Death Sentence

From a Staff Correspondent of The New York Times.

BOSTON, Aug. 22.—Four final appeals to Governor Fuller for delay in the execution of the death sentences on Sacco and Vanzetti were based on the following grounds:

1. Willingness of the Department of Justice to open its files to the Commonwealth authorities.
2. The official docketing of the appeal for a writ of certiorari in the United States Supreme Court, which could not be acted on by the court until October.
3. A specific request from Arthur D. Hill, chief defense attorney, to allow alienists to examine Sacco and Vanzetti.
4. A request from Mr. Hill, dated last Friday, to delay until the matter of the Supreme Court and the Department of Justice files had been cleared up.

Governor Fuller, after a full day's consideration of these pleas, announced that he would take no further action.

CITY CROWDS SILENT ON NEWS OF DEATHS

Sacco Sympathizers Disperse After Many Protest Meetings Earlier in Night.

POLICE DOUBLY VIGILANT

Force Guards All Vital Points, While Warren and Inspectors Stay on Duty All Night.

The news that the death sentence had been carried out on Sacco and Vanzetti was received in mournful silence by their sympathizers here, who had assembled at various points in the city last night to follow the events in the case to the end. Realizing that their protests had been of no avail, the sympathizers broke up into groups and headed for their homes when the final word came. Some booed as they moved off, but there was no real disorder.

Interest in the fate of the two men was keen throughout the city. Newspaper offices were called by thousands seeking the latest development. Telephone operators of THE NEW YORK TIMES handled 1,755 calls for information from early evening to 1:15 A. M. Crowds gathered in the midtown section for first editions of the newspapers giving the details of the carrying out of the sentence.

Although there had been no reports of disorder up to an early hour this morning, the police guard on transit lines, prominent persons and public and semi-public buildings became doubly vigilant and Police Commissioner Warren announced that he would remain at headquarters throughout the night.

5,000 Wait in Streets.

A crowd of approximately 5,000 persons had stood patiently through the hours leading to the execution outside the offices of The Daily Worker at 30 Union Square East. Brief bulletins told of the approach of the death hour and of demonstrations staged throughout the world. Now and then a cheer would go up at announcement of a foreign protest. A bulletin telling how Sacco's wife and the sister of Vanzetti had arranged to plead with Governor Fuller was received in silence.

As the hour of death grew near the crowd knew that all hope had fled and even the murmur of conversations was stilled. When the final announcement was made to the thousands in the square the murmur of exclamations, blended into one noise, leaped up again, but soon died away. Reinforcements of police had been hurried down to support several hundred patrolmen, under command of Captain William H. Ward, who had patrolled the fringes of the meeting. But the reinforcements were not needed.

Motorcycle Police Ride By.

At 12:25 A. M., a sign was put up in a second floor window of the newspaper building warning the crowd that the end was nearing. Just at that moment fourteen motorcycle policemen, with sirens screeching, rushed down Fourth Avenue, dashed through the square and continued down without a halt. The advance of the motorcycle detachment caused an uneasy stir in the crowd, many apparently thinking that the meeting was about to be dispersed.

A few minutes after the detachment had roared its way by a sign appeared in the window. It read:

"Sacco murdered."

A few moans from women were heard and here and there some one hissed. The crowd, however, was curiously undemonstrative. Another sign came into the window. It said:

"The Workers' Party must not forget its martyrs."

This inscription stared out into the square for a moment and then was replaced by another, which read:

"Vanzetti murdered."

As this went up the police began

Continued on Page Three.

BOSTON BESIEGED; SCORES ARRESTED

Thousands Watch Squad After Squad of Sacco Picketers March Into Police Hands.

CHEERS AND JEERS MINGLE

Advances on State House Last Till Bail Gives Out—Night Move on Bunker Hill Fails.

From a Staff Correspondent of The New York Times.

BOSTON, Aug. 22.—Boston, most of whose citizens went calmly about their business twelve days ago when the execution of Nicola Sacco and Bartolomeo Vanzetti was stayed until midnight tonight, lost its indifference today and thousands stood in perspiring masses, blackening the northwest corner of Boston Common, while group after group of picketers, displaying placards and waving banners, were arrested by the police. The number arrested before the State House alone exceeded 150.

A lull came in the picketing at nightfall when bail funds were exhausted, but it started up again at 11 o'clock when two more arrests were made at the State House and two out of sixteen picketers were arrested on Main Street, Charlestown, near the prison.

The first two were Paulla Halliday, arrested for the third time in two days, and Frank Shay, actor, author and bookseller, both coming from Provincetown. They staged a small-scale demonstration in the glare of searchlights from the State House roof and were promptly picked up and jailed. Miss Halliday was deprived of her "Is Justice Dead?" slicker.

The two in Charlestown were not identified. The other fourteen who had been marching up and down with banners and placards for twenty minutes mingled with the crowd of curious and escaped.

Police Stop March on Bunker Hill.

Immediately afterward police were dispatched to stop a procession of 300 sympathizers marching from the Defense Committee's headquarters on Salem Street out to the Bunker Hill Monument in Charlestown, a distance of nearly two miles. This was the suggestion of Miss Ruth Hale, who suggested a silent demonstration after a session of prayers had been vetoed on the ground that Sacco and Vanzetti were atheists and would resent being prayed over.

When the marchers reached City Square, Charlestown, the police and their auxiliaries, 800 in all, barred the way. Mounted men charged. No one was seriously hurt. Nine were arrested.

Although there had been no outbreak of violence until the Charlestown expisode, Beacon Street, Tremont Street, the Common and Rutherford Avenue near the State Prison in Charlestown gave the picture of a town captured and placed under martial law. Police in uniforms and plain clothes, afoot, mounted on horses and motorcycles, and still others packed into automobiles, were everywhere in evidence.

On the streets approaching the prison and the State House every citizen was under suspicion and warned to take himself elsewhere.

Members of the State Constabulary from all parts of Massachusetts arrived in Boston in two and threes throughout the day till 100 of the total force of 158 were concentrated here. In addition to them and the regular police, squads of railroad and other private patrolmen have been drafted, armed and posted about the city. Surrounding the State House alone 300 were on duty and 500 others were assigned to the vicinity of the prison in Charlestown.

Police Go Into Action at Noon.

The police were first called into action in connection with Sacco and Vanzetti today at noon when the vanguard of sympathizers arrived before the gates of the State House grounds. There were forty-nine of them, men and women, and some

Continued on Page Four.

WALK TO DEATH CALMLY

Sacco Cries 'Long Live Anarchy'; Vanzetti Insists on His Innocence.

WARDEN CAN ONLY WHISPER

Much Affected as the Long-Delayed Execution Is Carried Out.

MADEIROS FIRST TO DIE

Machine Guns Bristle, Searchlights Glare During Execution—Crowds Kept Far From Prison.

From a Staff Correspondent of The New York Times.

CHARLESTOWN STATE PRISON, Mass., Tuesday, Aug. 23.—Nicola Sacco and Bartolomeo Vanzetti died in the electric chair early this morning, carrying out the sentence imposed on them for the South Braintree murders of April 15, 1920.

Sacco marched to the death chair at 12:11 and was pronounced lifeless at 12:19.

Vanzetti entered the execution room at 12:20 and was declared dead at 12:26.

To the last they protested their innocence, and the efforts of many who believed them guiltless proved futile, although they fought a legal and extra legal battle unprecedented in the history of American jurisprudence.

With them died Celestino F. Madeiros, the young Portuguese, who won seven respites when he "confessed" that he was present at the time of the South Braintree murder and that Sacco and Vanzetti were not with him. He died for the murder of a bank cashier.

Defense Works as They Die.

The six years legal battle on behalf of the condemned men was still on as they were walking to the chair and after the current had been applied, for a lawyer was on the way by airplane to ask Federal Judge George W. Anderson in Williamstown for a writ of habeas corpus.

The men walked to the chair without company of clergy, Father Michael Murphy, prison chaplain, waited until a minute before twelve and then left the prison.

Sacco cried, "Long live anarchy!" as the prison guards strapped him into the chair and applied the electrodes. He added a plea that his family be cared for.

Vanzetti at the last made a short address, declaring his inocence.

Madeiros walked to the chair in a semi-stupor caused by overeating. He shrugged his shoulders and made no farewell statement.

Warden William Hendry was almost overcome by the execution of the men, especially that of Vanzetti, who shook his hand warmly and thanked him for all his kindnesses.

The Warden was barely able to pronounce above a whisper the solemn formula required by law:

"Under the law I now pronounce you dead, the sentence of the court having been legally carried out."

The words were not heard by the official witnesses.

After Governor Fuller had informed counsel for the two condemned radicals that he could take no action, their attorney, Michael A. Musmanno, made a dash to the prison in an automobile and tried to make another call on Sacco and Vanzetti, but Warden Hendry refused, as the legal witnesses were just about to pass into the execution chamber.

The Witnesses Gather.

The witnesses gathered in the Warden's office an hour before midnight. They were instructed as to the part they would take.

W. E. Playfair of The Associated Press was the only reporter permitted to attend the execution, as the State law designated one representative of the press as a witness. The assignment was handed to him six years ago after Sacco and Vanzetti had been convicted in Dedham for the murder of William Parmenter and Alexander Berardelli.

At 11:38 all but the official witnesses were asked to leave the Warden's office. Led by Warden Hendry the official witnesses walked toward the rotunda of the prison. He rapped three times on the inner door. A key grated in the lock. Just then Mr. Musmanno dashed in breathlessly.

"Please, Warden," he said, touching Mr. Hendry on the arm. "A last request."

His voice was faint and broken.

"No, no," the Warden said, sternly, slightly unnerved at the last-minute interruption. Mr. Musmanno turned away, weeping. He had refused to accept as a farewell gift a book

"All the News That's Fit to Print."

The New York Times.

THE WEATHER
Clear and much colder today; tomorrow cloudy and warmer.
Temperature yesterday—Max. 39, min. 31.
U. S. Weather Forecast—For details see Page 22.

VOL. LXXVIII....No. 25,921. * * * * NEW YORK, SATURDAY, JANUARY 12, 1929. TWO CENTS in Greater New York | THREE CENTS Within 200 Miles | FOUR CENTS Elsewhere in the U. S.

MOSES BLOCKS VOTE ON PEACE TREATY; REED CONDEMNS IT

Borah Vainly Seeks Limit on Debate to Get Ratification by Monday.

FARM BILL REAL MOTIVE

Filibuster on Treaty and Cruiser Program Is Expected From Extra Session Foes.

REED ATTACKS PACIFISTS

"At Whose Heart Are the Cannons of Bermuda Aimed?" He Asks the Senate.

By RICHARD V. OULAHAN.

Special to The New York Times.

WASHINGTON, Jan. 11.—Developments in the Senate today produced a pessimistic outlook on the effort to bring about quick action on the international pact renouncing war. An attempt to limit debate with a view to voting on the treaty by Saturday evening or not later than Monday met with a rebuff. This opposition was a reflection of the desire of a group of Senators to have a farm relief bill passed at the present session so as to avoid an extra session in the Spring.

Nevertheless, the ratification of the anti-war pact is regarded as inevitable, and Senator Borah expressed confidence tonight that it would be ratified Monday. Whether this confidence is justified will depend chiefly on Senators Moses and Reed.

Senator Moses of New Hampshire put the spoke in the wheel of progress on the treaty. When Senator Borah sought an agreement to limit debate, Senator Moses objected on the ground that Senator Reed of Missouri, one of those who insist that ratification of the pact shall be accompanied by an interpretative declaration, was not in the chamber. He said he would consult Senator Reed about it, but when the Senate had adjourned for the day no progress toward consummating the proposed agreement had been made.

One Senator Blocks Progress.

Nearly every Senator who desires to discuss the treaty publicly has said his piece. Of the few remaining none cares to make an extended speech, according to the statement made by Senator Borah when the proposal for limiting debate was being discussed. It was his view that under an agreement to limit debate to half-hour speeches a vote on ratifying the pact could be had tomorrow. Senator Johnson of California suggested that Monday noon be fixed as the time to vote. Senator Moses then said that he would have to consult Senator Reed.

A rule of the Senate permits a limited degree of closure, but its machinery is complicated and many Senators object to its application. On that account Senator Borah asked approval by unanimous consent for his proposal that, starting at 3 o'clock Saturday afternoon, each Senator who desired to speak on the anti-war treaty should be limited to thirty minutes. The objection of Senator Moses was sufficient to defeat the request.

This was an object lesson in showing that the crusade for reforming the Senate rules, begun by Vice President Dawes on his inauguration nearly four years ago, has not progressed.

Reed Assails Pacifists.

Senator Borah's move followed a two hours' speech by Senator Reed of Missouri, denunciatory of the pact. He attacked pacifist proponents of the treaty with much of his old-time vigor. "Pacifists," he said, "conceive that safety is to be found in helplessness. They want to leave the door unlocked."

He was especially critical of what he portrayed as the attitude of Great Britain toward the United States. "At whose heart are the cannons of Bermuda aimed?" he asked. He declared that were the American fleet divided between the Atlantic and Pacific oceans, the British could destroy the Panama Canal in five hours. He declared for an interpretative declaration so as to safeguard the rights of the United States.

In speaking in favor of ratifying the treaty, Senator Brookhart gave an interesting reason for supporting it.

He argued that the treaty constituted recognition of the Government of Soviet Russia by the Government of the United States, which he has been advocating for a long time. The assertion has been made that as the pact was negotiated by the United States Government and the Soviet Government was a party to it, this constituted recognition of the Soviet Government by the United States. This contention has been denied by Secretary Kellogg and also by Senator Borah, who, like Senator Brookhart, advocates Soviet recognition.

Position of Moses and Reed.

Senators Moses and Reed appear to be determined to fight for an interpretative declaration. This attitude of Senator Moses and some

Continued on Page Four.

Senate as Unit Passes Bill To Pension Marshall's Widow

Special to The New York Times.

WASHINGTON, Jan. 11.—By unanimous vote, the Senate today passed a bill introduced by Senator Ashurst, granting an annual pension of $5,000 to Mrs. Lois L. Marshall, widow of former Vice President Marshall.

PHOENIX, Ariz., Jan. 11 (AP).—Mrs. Thomas R. Marshall spent a restful night at the hospital here, where she is an influenza patient. Physicians' bulletins this morning indicated that Mrs. Marshall was able to take nourishment and that her condition was not alarming.

HOUSE PASSES BILL FOR REAPPORTIONING

Fenn Measure Adopted Without Record Vote, but Test Shows 226 For, 134 Against.

BLACK ASSAILS THE DRYS

Measure Sets Up Machinery for Shifting Representation of States in 1930.

Special to The New York Times.

WASHINGTON, Jan. 11.—After two days of stormy debate the House late this afternoon voted down all proposals to shelve the reapportionment and passed the Fenn bill without a record vote. Opponents of the measure lost heart when their motion to recommit the bill to the census committee was defeated by vote of 134 ayes to 226 nays, the only record vote of the day.

The Fenn bill does not provide for immediate reapportionment, but sets up machinery for that procedure after each census in the event that the House itself fails to act. It would first take effect after the 1930 census and would be responsible for a rearrangement of the House membership in the Seventy-third and succeeding Congresses.

Seven-Year Fight Ended.

The passage of the bill ended a seven-year fight to get through the House a measure that would limit its membership to 435, its present size. The House passed a reapportionment bill based on the census of 1920, but it was allowed to die in the Senate, and all legislative effort in this direction since has failed. As a result a formidable reapportionment bloc was organized under the leadership of Representative McLeod of Michigan.

Party lines were cast aside as the House voted on the various amendments.

New York members, Republicans and Democrats alike, supported the bill, although the State probably will lose one member after 1930. The measure gained more friends as its consideration proceeded, and the final votes against it were made up largely of a few from New England, those of Southern States which would have fewer members, and others from Middle Western States where the population is decreasing.

Republican leaders made special efforts to obtain the passage of the bill, and Speaker Longworth; the majority leader, Mr. Tilson, and Representative Snell of New York, chairman of the Rules Committee, were on the floor continuously during the two days of debate.

Foes Near Victory.

At one time the opposing group came within four votes of attaching an amendment which would have nullified the bill and made it necessary for Congress again to pass on the subject. This amendment changed the method of apportionment prescribed in the bill from

Continued on Page Ten.

BOOTH ASKED TO QUIT; WILL REPLY MONDAY; REFUSAL PREDICTED

Salvation High Council Deputation Calls on Leader, in Sick Bed, to Resign.

HE GREETS THEM BY PRAYER

He Will Decline to Retire and Carry Case to Courts, It Is Expected.

SISTER FAILS TO SEE HIM

Evangeline, After Swift Auto Trip From London, Is Not Permitted to Enter General's Room.

Special Cable to THE NEW YORK TIMES.

LONDON, Jan. 11.—General Bramwell Booth was asked today to surrender command of the Salvation Army. He will reply on Monday, but his retirement, if it comes, will not be of his own volition.

The aged son of the Army's founder, who helped his father to collect the first pennies for the regeneration of outcasts, will go down fighting, it was believed tonight by the delegation which called on him today to resign and by Commander Evangeline Booth, his sister, who tried in vain to see him.

The General, clad in a black dressing gown and propped up in bed, received calmly the six men and one woman whom he had appointed to high offices in the Army in distant parts of the world. He knew they had come to serve a virtual warrant of deposition upon him. Rain beat dismally upon the bay window of the General's bedroom overlooking the North Sea from the grumbling shore of Southwold, a village on England's east coast.

Nurse the Only Witness.

There was only one witness of the scene apart from the small group of the General's immediate family and followers who are fighting for his retention of power long enough to name his successor. That was "Brigadier" Smith, his chief nurse.

The delegation of the High Council had passed on the floor below the General's wife and two daughters, one of the latter of whom till recently was believed to be the heir apparent to his rule.

The councilors filed in singly, approaching the bedside, and each was greeted with a feeble word indicative that the old man knew them all. When they had all gathered, there was silence for a moment.

"Let us pray," said the General.

Then he offered a prayer for the families of each and for wisdom to guide them all through the coming fateful days of the Army.

Some one—members of the high council are pledged to secrecy—stepped forward and read soberly the resolution which the council passed yesterday at its meeting at Sunbury-on-Thames appreciative of the General's lifelong labors, but asking him to retire. It rejected his own previous suggestion of a temporary council of five to rule the Army till he recovers.

To the "reform" group the issue is not one of personalities. It is frankly whether the "Booth dynasty" is to continue or whether real command of the far-flung organization shall pass to an international council.

Delegates Deeply Moved.

But to the old man on the bed the issues are more complicated. There are persons near him involved. He pleaded for time. Relinquishing lifelong command, and thereby radically altering the whole government of the Army, he suggested, was not a decision to be taken lightly. It was asked when he wished to reply to the council's request. He said he would answer on Monday.

The delegation then filed out. It was said later that they had been "profoundly shocked" by the Gen-

Continued on Page Three.

$25,000,000 More for Dry Force Approved By Senate Appropriations Committee

Special to The New York Times.

WASHINGTON, Jan. 11.—The Senate Committee on Appropriations today recommended an increase of $25,000,000 in the funds allotted for prohibition enforcement. This action came at a time when another committee of the Senate has under consideration a proposal to create an independent citizens' committee to investigate enforcement.

The Appropriations Committee had before it an amendment to the deficiency bill offered by Senator Harris of Georgia, an ardent dry, calling for an additional $50,000,000 for dry law enforcement.

While the committee cut in half the sum he advocated, Senator Harris said he was gratified, adding that $25,000,000 would go a long way toward showing that the dry laws can be enforced.

Senator Harris said he had been informed that more than half of the regular appropriation of $13,000,000 for the Prohibition Bureau is absorbed by overhead expenses. This item, he said, is practically a fixed charge, and will not be materially increased by the expansion of activity which will be made possible if the $25,000,000 increase becomes law. It will be possible to use practically all of the $25,000,000 for additional field work, he said.

"The enemies of the law keep saying that the law cannot be enforced," Senator Harris said. "But they neglect to say that Congress has never appropriated enough money to give it a fair chance."

The question whether Congress is really trying to make adequate provision for enforcement of prohibition was raised recently by Senator Bruce of Maryland, a wet. When the treasury and postoffice appropriation bill was before the Senate Mr. Bruce obtained an amendment to increase the prohibition item from $13,000,000 to $270,000,000. After a conference report rejecting the great increase, it was defeated by a margin of only two votes in the Senate.

Adams Runs Aground, Captain Hurled in Sea; Liner's Master Swims for Help in Panama

Special Cable to THE NEW YORK TIMES.

COLON, Panama Canal Zone, Jan. 11.—The Dollar liner President Adams grounded on a reef near Toro Point, outside the breakwater at the Atlantic entrance of the Panama Canal at 5:45 o'clock this morning, throwing the vessel's master, W. C. Morris, overboard. He was not injured nor were other members of the crew or passengers. The vessel was pulled off tonight.

Captain Morris had gone to the rail to take soundings when the ship struck. The impact hurled him into the sea. He swam 400 yards to the breakwater, then walked a third of a mile along the breakwater to Fort Sherman, where he telephoned to the office of the port captain of Cristobal that his ship was aground and needed immediate assistance.

In the meantime, while Captain Morris was returning to his ship in an army launch, the grounding was reported direct from the vessel by wireless.

The President Adams sailed from New York Jan. 3 on a regular voyage around the world, via the Panama Canal. She had 90 passengers, 141 in the crew and 3,561 tons of cargo aboard.

The reason for the grounding is undetermined, but apparently it took place in darkness, and the Toro Point light seems to have been mistaken for the breakwater light at the entrance to the harbor.

Panama Canal and United States Navy tugs rushed to the vessel's assistance, but four of them were unable to pull off the ship, which was fast to a coral reef amidship, with twenty-nine feet of water astern and only fifteen forward. The tide is only twenty-two inches at maximum and was of little assistance. Due to a bulge in the bottom, displacing the boilers and breaking the fuel-oil feed pipes, the ship was unable to use its own power.

The passengers were brought ashore at noon and lodged at the Hotel Washington.

The President Adams displaces 10,558 tons and is 502 feet long with a 62.2-foot beam.

Special Cable to THE NEW YORK TIMES.

BALBOA, Jan. 11.—The President Adams was pulled off the reef by tugs of the wrecking and salvage division of the Canal at 9 P. M. and is now afloat. It is expected that the ship will be towed through the canal tomorrow and enter drydock at Balboa.

The extent of the damage to the bottom has not been determined, but the ship is not taking water.

SAN FRANCISCO, Jan. 11 (AP).—The passengers of the President Adams will continue their voyage on the steamer California late today, says a message from R. Stanley Dollar, vice president and general manager, to the San Francisco office of the Dollar Steamship Company.

EINSTEIN EXTENDS RELATIVITY THEORY

New Work Seeks to "Unite Laws of Field of Gravitation and Electro-Magnetism."

HE CALLS IT HIS GREATEST

"Book," Consisting of Only Five Pages, Took Berlin Scientist Ten Years to Prepare.

Wireless to THE NEW YORK TIMES.

BERLIN, Jan. 11.—Professor Albert Einstein, author of the theory of relativity, general and special, issued the following statement today explaining his new "book," consisting of five pages, upon which he has labored for the past ten years and which will be published next week:

"A few days ago I submitted to the Academy of Sciences a work that treats with a novel development of the theory of relativity. The purpose of this work is to unite the laws of the field of gravitation and electromagnetism under a uniform viewpoint."

The length of this work—written at the rate of half a page a year—is considered prodigious when it is remembered that the original presentation of his theory of relativity filled only three pages.

Naturally, it is awaited with extreme interest by the entire scientific world. The title is "New Field of Theory."

Professor Einstein himself considers it by far his most important contribution to mankind—scientifically more important than his original theory, its five pages containing the quintessence of a new theory in which the great physicist tries to create a bridge between classic mechanics and modern electro dynamics.

This, as explained by members of the Prussian Academy, is an attempt to bring human conception of power, which they said has become "anemic," into a mathematically understandable and "tangible" form.

Origin of Matter Theory Seen.

BERLIN, Jan. 11 (AP).—The new theory of Professor Einstein is embodied in a paper, "Einheitlichen Feldtheorie." Friends of the professor say it will be of far more importance to science than is his theory of relativity.

There is considerable speculation as to the nature of the new theory, but the view is held generally that it treats of a synthesis between classical mechanics and modern electrodynamics, sciences which it has hitherto been considered impossible to interrelate.

It is believed by some that Professor Einstein demonstrates mathematically that matter is of electromagnetic origin and that division into mechanic and electro-magnetic parts can only be artificial.

In its further extension, some say, the theory would with that of relativity, lead to the mathematical conclusion that matter simply cannot be formed without electricity—in other words, that electricity, or electrical energy, is the original source of all existence.

His Relativity Theory.

Although Dr. Einstein had developed his original theory of relativity over a period of fifteen years and had aroused much academic interest in his new conceptions of time and space, the doctrine thrust itself upon popular attention like the bursting of a bombshell when on Nov. 6, 1919, the Royal Society in London gave it the stamp of its official approval.

Column after column in the newspapers and magazines was devoted to explaining that only twelve men (sometimes the figure was set at seven or four) could fully understand the new theory, and then attempts were made to unfold the new ideas to the lay reader. Dr. Einstein himself laughed at the supposition that so few could grasp it, main-

Continued on Page Two.

YANG YU-TING SHOT BY CHANG'S ORDER

Manchurian Ruler's Summary Execution of Father's Chief of Staff Laid to Plot.

ALARMS TOKIO, STIRS PEKING

Gain for Nanking Seen by Its Minister in Death of Leader, "Doubtful Ally."

By HUGH BYAS.

Special Cable to THE NEW YORK TIMES.

TOKIO, Jan. 11.—Yang Yu-ting, for many years Chang Tso-lin's chief of staff and, next to the dictator, the most powerful man in Manchuria, has been arrested at Mukden by order of Chang Hsueh-liang and summarily executed. The reason given in the reports reaching Tokio is that he opposed the union with Nanking, but the best-informed Japanese consider that reason as altogether inadequate, though they are unable to suggest another motive.

The present régime in Manchuria was established through the support of Yang Yu-ting and General Chang Tso-chen, with Chang Hsueh-liang, the son of Chang Tso-lin, as a figurehead. Chang Tso-chen is reported to be behind young Chang in this matter, so the execution may be a sudden bloody coup intended to eliminate a rival from the contest for an insecure throne.

Military circles here are surprised and alarmed, for the execution of a man who had great influence and numerous adherents is held to be symptomatic of the most serious trouble. Though Yang opposed union with Nanking, he was anything but subservient to the Japanese and observers here cannot believe that his objections to unification were the cause of his execution.

The fragility of law and order in Manchuria is illustrated by the fact that six months after its last ruler, Chang Tso-lin, was assassinated by a bomb, his chief of staff was shot by Chang's son.

Yang Accused of Plot.

TOKIO, Jan. 11 (AP).—Discovery of a plot to overthrow Chang Hsueh-liang, present Governor of Manchuria, was stated in Mukden dispatches today as the cause of the execution of Yang Yu-ting last night.

The reports also stated that Yang Yu-ting had misappropriated $20,000,000 Mexican from the arsenal funds at Mukden, that he had opposed the hoisting of the Chinese Nationalist flag in Manchuria and that he had placed Chang Hsueh-liang in an awkward plight regarding negotiations with Japan over the administration of the South Manchurian Railway.

The reports added that the Chinese Nationalist Government at Nanking first scented the plot and requested Chang to deal with it appropriately.

Chang has informed the Japanese Consul General and the military authorities in control of the railway zone that the evidence of the plot was irrefutable. At the same time he assured them that the incident would in no wise imperil relations with Japan. The young Governor has also assured the widow of Yang Yu-ting that she would be afforded full protection.

Another Reported Executed.

Ramifications of the plot were said to be extensive. One account said that Yang Yu-ting was summoned to the Governor's palace and that when he arrived there in company with Chang Yin-huai both were arrested. The fate of the latter is in doubt, an early report that he, too, had been executed by a firing squad remaining unconfirmed tonight. Another rumor was that Weng Chin-lin, director of the Mukden Arsenal, had been taken into custody.

Here in Tokio the action of the Manchurian Government was described as a coup d'état. It was

Continued on Page Nine.

7 DIE, 1 HURT, IN FALL OF BIG ARMY PLANE NEAR HARRISBURG

The C-2, Sister Ship of the Question Mark, Crashes Down in Royalton Village.

LONE SURVIVOR MAY DIE

Cause of Accident Puzzles the War Department as a Rigid Inquiry Is Started.

PILOT AMONG THE VICTIMS

Lieutenant Angell Had Just Taken Off—Captain Dinger Left Plane a Few Hours Before.

Special to The New York Times.

HARRISBURG, Pa., Jan. 11.—Seven men met death and one was seriously injured today at Royalton, nine miles south of here, when the army transport plane C-2 for some reason as yet undetermined nose-dived to the earth soon after taking off from the army air depot at Middletown on a return flight to its base at Bolling Field, Washington. Only one of the occupants of the plane escaped with his life, and tonight he is in a critical condition.

The victims were:

Dead.

ANGELL, HENRY R., Second Lieutenant, of Birmingham, Ala.
McCARTHY, JOSEPH B., Master Sergeant, of Washington, D. C.
CRONAN, HENRY, Staff Sergeant, of 211 Cockerell Avenue, Takoma Park.
LE HUTTA, RUDOLPH J., Staff Sergeant, of Washington, D. C.
BUCK, CLARENCE E., Private, of Chicago.
KELLY, MIKE D., private, of Minersville, Pa.
JONES, SAMUEL P., private, of Bellbuckle, Tenn.

Injured.

CONROY, PATRICK, Sergeant, of Somerville, Mass.

Five of the men died almost instantly. Lieutenant Angell, Kelly and Conroy were brought to Harrisburg hospitals, where Angell and Kelly died an hour later. Conroy, in the Polyclinic Hospital here, was not expected to recover.

The Middletown airport is an intermediate depot of the United States Army and flights from Bolling Field and other army fields in the Eastern part of the country are daily occurrences. Plane supplies are kept here and many calls are made for spare parts. Today's trip of the C-2, a big Fokker machine, and sistership of the famous Question Mark, was made partially for experimental purposes and to give the enlisted men air experience.

Two Left the Transport.

The plane left Washington this morning, there being ten occupants on the way to Middletown. The transport was in charge of Captain Henry A. Dinger. The plane was inspected and tuned up at Middletown and a few hours later, just before 2 o'clock this afternoon, Lieutenant Angell and seven enlisted men took off for the return trip.

Captain Dinger and Sergeant Maylon, who was also on the transport on its way from Washington, did not intend to return on it. They left in an amphibian plane assigned to Secretary of War Davis, which had been sent to Middletown for repairs. They left about the same time as the Fokker and did not know of the fate of the big ship until they arrived at Washington.

The accident occurred while the plane was flying low over Royalton and the transport came down in the centre of the town, landing in the backyard of the residence of William Holland, near the postoffice. Royalton is a village of 1,200 population, separated from Middletown by the Swatara Creek, which enters the Susquehanna River near the airport.

Persons from near-by residences rushed to the scene of the crash. At first they were unable to render any assistance to the aviators. Then axes were obtained to cut away the tangle of wreckage and the victims were lifted out.

Most of the occupants of the plane were severely crushed in the fall. Both legs of Lieutenant Angell and Kelly were broken. Angell's skull also was fractured and his left arm

Continued on Page Seven.

GRAND JURY TO HUNT 'RING' IN BANKRUPTCY LOOTING; TUTTLE ASKS CITY BAR'S AID

REFORMS WILL BE DRAFTED

$17,000,000 Involved in Receiverships in Year to Be Checked Up.

ANOTHER LAWYER INDICTED

Merrill E. Gates, Classmate of Prosecutor, Accused of Theft From an Estate.

PATRONAGE SEEN IN POSTS

Hughes Is Called On to Assign Bar Committee to Investigation of Entire System.

The Federal grand jury's investigation of the entire bankruptcy situation, requested by the Federal judges of this district, got under way yesterday with a promise of a thorough inquiry into what is commonly considered one of the most lucrative sources of political patronage in New York.

Another attorney and receiver in bankruptcy was indicted for embezzlement. There were indications, it was said, of the possible existence of a "bankruptcy ring." United States Attorney Tuttle declared he would be disappointed if only two or three indictments were returned.

Mr. Tuttle wrote to Charles Evans Hughes, president of the City Bar Association, stressing the importance and wide scope of the investigation and asking Mr. Hughes if he did not consider it advisable to have the bankruptcy committee of the association take part in the inquiry, which might lead to recommendations for reforms in the bankruptcy statutes.

Demands Records of Receivers.

The United States Attorney wrote also to all referees in bankruptcy and trustees. He asked for the names of all receivers in bankruptcy and information as to their records and possible delinquencies. The magnitude of bankruptcy operations and the possibilities for illegalities, it was pointed out, were indicated by the fact that more than $17,000,000 was in the hands of receivers in bankruptcy for liquidation last year. The general allowance for receivers is said to be 6 per cent for the first $500, 4 per cent for the next $1,000 and 2 per cent of the value of remaining assets, based upon the sale price. Receivers' surety bonds, Mr. Tuttle said, were generally about 50 per cent of the assets of the bankrupt concerns.

The alleged $50,000 shortage in the receiverships of David Steinhardt, fugitive attorney under indictment for embezzlement, was not covered by the surety bonds, Mr. Tuttle declared. Asked if the investigation were not merely a disciplinary measure because Steinhardt had "gone too far," Mr. Tuttle replied:

"No, this is by no means a disciplinary measure. This is a criminal prosecution. The investigation has three purposes: First, to find out who are delinquents in their accounts, reports or payments in bankruptcy cases; second, we want to bring about constructive results looking to the reform of the bankruptcy laws themselves, if necessary. It was with this in view that I asked the cooperation of the Bar Association. Third, we want to stop the evident habit of some receivers in bankruptcy, as evidenced in May, 1927, of forgetting their obligations, and of course we want to bring to justice all who have been guilty of criminality."

Tuttle's Classmate Indicted.

The attorney and receiver indicted yesterday is Merrill E. Gates Jr. of 154 East Sixty-fourth Street. Mr. Gates, who was arrested at his home Thursday night, was indicted on a charge of embezzlement in having appropriated to his own use some of the assets of the $10,000 estate of J. Harold Rapp, for which he was receiver. Mr. Gates pleaded not guilty and was released in $2,500 bail by Federal Judge Thacher. He told friends he had been in a hospital for some time and had not kept up his duties in connection with the estate, but that he had done nothing of an illegal nature.

When Mr. Tuttle was asked if he intended to carry the investigation through, "no matter whom it may hurt," he said:

"Well, we indicted Mr. Gates today. He was a classmate of mine at Columbia Law School in 1902."

Mr. Gates, who is a son of the late Dr. Merrill Edward Gates, former president of Amherst and Rutgers colleges, was a staff officer of the Seventy-seventh Division throughout the World War. He was later commander of the Seventy-seventh Division Headquarters Post of the American Legion. He was also a

Columbus Born in Spain, Document Found There Says

By The Associated Press.

MADRID, Jan. 11.—A document found yesterday in the archives of Pontevedra parish mentioned that place as having been the birthplace of Christopher Columbus. It thus supports the claim that the discoverer of America was a Spaniard and not a native of Genoa.

The document contained a description of the burial of Columbus and said that the Duke of Veragua, descendant of the mariner, had sold in the eighteenth century the lands on which stood the building where Columbus was born.

THREE ARE TRAPPED IN STOCK SWINDLE

Members of Suspected Gang Arrested Here, in Chicago and in St. Louis in Singer Deal.

EXPOSED BY A "PROSPECT"

Defrauding of Brown Professor Out of $60,000 in 1927 Laid to the Prisoners.

A merchant in Cairo, Ill., prevented what is regarded as a scheme to swindle stockholders of the Singer Sewing Machine Company and brought about the arrest of a gang of alleged confidence men sought for nearly two years. Details were made known yesterday after Charles H. Clarahan, postal inspector in charge of the New York office, received a telegram telling of the arrest of a man in St. Louis. Another had been arrested in New York ten days ago, and still another in Chicago several days ago, but no information was given out regarding the arrest until the third man was in custody.

Two weeks ago an official of the Singer Sewing Machine Company came to Inspector Clarahan with copies of a forged letterhead of the company written to a stockholder in Cairo, Ill., telling him of a proposed readjustment involving a stock dividend. The letters said that a representative of the company would visit the Cairo merchant and explain the plan.

"Salesman" Explains Plan.

Soon after the letter was received in Illinois a suave, high-pressure salesman called to explain the plan of exchange of stock on the basis of two for one and told of the advantages of the plan. He requested that the stock certificates be mailed to a "Mr. Williams," in care of the Singer Company, to a room on the eleventh floor of the Singer Building. The stockholder became suspicious, however, and communicated with the company.

Inspector Clarahan recognized the methods of the confidence game as the same as those by which Professor Albert E. Rand of Brown University lost 600 shares of Hercules Powder Company stock valued at $60,000 in 1927. Inspectors Herbert Graham, H. W. Mahan and William Troensegaard were detailed to run down the gang.

Locate Office Here.

They learned that an office had been rented on the eleventh floor of the Singer Building expressly to receive the stock and that at least two other stockholders in small towns in Illinois had been approached. J. J. Sullivan of New Haven was arrested ten days ago as the New York member of the gang and lodged in the Tombs on a charge of using the mails to defraud. His arrest was

Continued on Page Eight.

Stewart Asks 16,000 Employes for Proxies In Fight to Avert Ousting by Rockefeller

Special to The New York Times.

CHICAGO, Jan. 11.—Robert W. Stewart, chairman of the board of directors of the Standard Oil Company of Indiana, today launched in Chicago his fight to hold the post from which John D. Rockefeller Jr. is seeking to oust him.

More than 16,000 employes of the company who are stockholders received during the day a request from Colonel Stewart that they fill in proxies to be voted at the annual meeting March 7 for his re-election as chairman of the board.

Reports were current today that employes who refused to sign the proxies sent out by the Stewart committee gained the impression that their jobs would be in jeopardy if they persisted in refusal.

The proxies, according to the letters sent out, were to be sent to a committee composed of Colonel Stewart himself, Edward G. Seubert, president of the company, and Felix T. Graham, secretary.

This was taken to indicate that Mr. Seubert, who heretofore has maintained neutrality, is now supporting Colonel Stewart.

It is expected that within a few days the Standard Oil Company of Indiana will send out a statement showing great prosperity last year under Colonel Stewart's direction.

Colonel Robert W. Stewart, chairman of the Standard Oil Company of Indiana, left yesterday afternoon for Chicago after further conferences here at which his differences with John D. Rockefeller Jr. were discussed.

It was reported yesterday that Colonel Stewart recently sent word to Mr. Rockefeller that if he were dissatisfied with the Standard of Indiana management Colonel Stewart would find a buyer for the Rockefeller stock.

Friends of the company's chairman were busy yesterday canvassing stockholders of the Standard of Indiana to learn their attitude in the dispute.

Ambassador Herrick had canceled the plans of the reception committee and, by unanimous consent, took the flier to the embassy in the Place d'Iena.

A staff of American doctors who had arrived at Le Bourget Field early to minister to an "exhausted" aviator found instead a bright-eyed, smiling youth who refused to be examined.

"Oh, don't bother; I am all right," he said.

"I'd like to have a bath and a glass of milk. I would feel better," Lindbergh replied when the Ambassador asked him what he would like to have.

A bath was drawn immediately and in less than five minutes the youth had disrobed in one of the embassy guest rooms, taken his bath and was out again drinking a bottle of milk and eating a roll.

"No Use Worrying," He Tells Envoy.

"There is no use worrying about me, Mr. Ambassador," Lindbergh insisted when Mr. Herrick and members of the embassy staff wanted him to be examined by doctors and then go to bed immediately.

It was apparent that the young man was too full of his experiences to want sleep and he sat on the bed and chatted with the Ambassador, his son and daughter-in-law.

By this time a corps of frantic newspaper men who had been madly chasing the airman, following one false scent after another, had finally tracked him to the embassy. In a body they descended upon the Ambassador, who received them in the salon and informed them that he had just left Lindbergh with strict instructions to go to sleep.

As Mr. Herrick was talking with the reporters his son-in-law came downstairs and said that Lindbergh had rung and announced that he did not care to go to sleep just yet and that he would be glad to see the newspaper men for a few minutes. A cheer went up from the group who dashed by Mr. Herrick and rushed upstairs.

Expected Trouble Over Newfoundland.

In the blue and gold room, with a soft light glowing, sat the conqueror of the Atlantic. He immediately stood up and held out his hands to greet his callers. THE NEW YORK TIMES correspondent being first to greet him.

"Sit down, please," urged every one with one voice, but Lindbergh only smiled again his famous boyish smile and said:

"It's almost as easy to stand up as it is to sit down."

Questions were fired at him from all sides about his trip across the ocean, but Lindbergh seemed to dismiss them all with brief, nonchalant answers.

"I expected trouble over Newfoundland because I had been warned that the situation there was unfavorable. But I got over that hazard with no trouble whatsoever."

Sleet and Snow for 1,000 Miles.

"However, it wasn't easy going. I had sleet and snow for over 1,000 miles. Sometimes it was too high to fly over and sometimes too low to fly under, so I just had to go through it as best I could.

"I flew as low as 10 feet in some places and as high as 10,000 in others. I passed no ships in the daytime, but at night I saw the lights of several ships, the night being bright and clear."

Everyone then wanted to know if the flier had been sleepy on the voyage.

"I didn't really get what you might call downright sleepy," he said, "but I think I sort of nodded several times. In fact, I could have flown half that distance again. I had enough fuel

Continued on Page Two.

Through no fault of his own, Clarence D. Chamberlin, who with Bert Acosta established a world's non-stop flying record a few weeks ago, will not fly the record-breaking monoplane in an attempt to establish a second New York-Paris non-stop flight.

G. M. Bellanca, designer of the plane, and Charles S. Levine of the Columbia Aircraft Company, owner of the ship, came to the parting of the ways last night and the designer finally severed his connection with the promoter. Then Levine issued a statement that the proposed flight, which has been talked of for weeks, was off.

The statement said:

"Due to the crowning blow of Mr. Bellanca's resignation, the plane will be placed in the hangar. Mr. Bellanca's resignation causes us to abandon plans for the New York-Paris flight for the present."

At the very moment that the statement was issued the plane was near the runway at Roosevelt Field with gas tanks filled and oil and equipment aboard ready for the start for Paris.

Plane Threatened by Fire.

A few minutes later, as it was being wheeled off, preparatory to being housed for the night, it narrowly escaped being destroyed by fire. When the word came to the field that the flight was definitely off mechanics were ordered to empty one gasoline tank to lighten the machine. The gasoline spilled on the ground and while the ship was being towed away a carcless spectator threw the stub of a lighted cigarette down.

In an instant there was a terrific flare and a dense burst of smoke as the gasoline blazed up.

"The Bellanca's gone," was the cry that rose from thousands of spectators who had gathered at the field.

Word was flashed to the army air station at Mitchel Field that there had been an accident and ambulances and fire-fighting apparatus were sent across the road. An ambulance from the Nassau County Hospital at Mineola was also sent to Roosevelt Field, as well as fire apparatus from Mineola.

The plane, however, was beyond the danger line and was not injured.

It had been announced that the Columbia would take off at 8 o'clock and Chamberlin was in his flying clothes ready to climb into the cockpit with the unnamed pilot who was to have accompanied him on the trip.

With the elimination of the Bellanca monoplane, only Lieut.

Continued on Page Four.

Times Wide World Photo

CAPTAIN CHARLES A LINDBERGH,
Who Flew Alone Across the Atlantic, New York to Paris in Thirty-three and One-half Hours.

New York Stages Big Celebration After Hours of Anxious Waiting

Harbor Craft, Factories, Fire Sirens and Radio Carry Message of the Flier's Victory Throughout the City—Theatres Halt While Audiences Cheer.

New York bubbled all day yesterday with excitement and expectancy, first yearning for word of Captain Lindbergh, then half-doubting, gaining confidence as the afternoon progressed and finally acclaiming the victory of the young aviator with street monstrations where the crowds were thickest, in which the ancient phrase, "I told you so," was often repeated. It was evident during the day that New York had confidence in the lad from the West.

On the streets and elsewhere Lindbergh was the one topic of conversation the whole day long. In the subway, on the elevated, in trains and cars, motion-picture houses, theatres, wherever a few had gathered, or even where one man could find another to talk to, one heard "Lindbergh — Lindbergh — Lindbergh."

And such expressions as this:

"He'll make it, all right."

"Some baby!"

"Well, if he's hit Ireland, he's safe anyway."

"He's away ahead of his time."

"What's the difference in time between here and there, anyway?"

Confused On Difference in Time.

To this latter question there were some amazing answers. One woman who had the aviator's running time mixed with the difference in time between New York and Paris solemnly informed her companion that there was thirty-six hours difference in time between the cities. She said it with an air which signified: "I don't mean maybe." A surprising number of persons insisted that the difference in time was three hours.

Early in the day, even before there was any good reason why there should be definite news, the interest of the people was demonstrated in two ways. At every news stand there were little groups scanning the headlines and buying newspapers. In every newspaper office the switchboards were literally swamped with inquiries. It was not sufficient that the operator said there was no word, or, later, that Lindbergh's plane had been seen over Ireland. The inquirers wanted specific information:

"Well, when will you get the first news?" they asked. And later:

"If he's over Ireland how long will it be before he gets to Paris?"

"Is he all right?"

The questions that were asked, considering that no news could possibly come direct from Captain Lindbergh before he landed, were as surprising as the guesses at the difference in time.

The Times Gets 10,000 Phone Calls.

The telephone inquiries came from all sorts of people and all directions. Not a few rang up THE TIMES office and apologetically explained that they were on golf links or elsewhere at a distance, and hence could not

Continued on Page Three.

Special to The New York Times.

WASHINGTON, May 21.—The triumph of Captain Charles A. Lindbergh in flying from New York to Paris without a stop created a tremendous sensation in the national capital and found immediate response in a host of official messages and statements congratulating the daring aviator upon his achievement.

President Coolidge expressed his admiration in a message transmitted through Ambassador Herrick in Paris for delivery to the young flier in person.

With a single possible exception, this city has never been more thrilled since the armistice, when Woodrow Wilson mingled with noisy thousands in celebrating the end of the war. The exception was when Walter Johnson arose from apparent defeat and won the deciding world series baseball game in 1924.

"The American people," the President said, "rejoice with me at the brilliant termination of your heroic flight. The first non-stop flight of a lone aviator across the Atlantic crowns the record of American aviation, and in bringing the greetings of the American people to France you likewise carry the assurance of our admiration of those intrepid Frenchmen, Nungesser and Coli, whose bold spirits first ventured on your exploit, and likewise a message of our continued anxiety concerning their fate."

Secretary Kellogg, in a message similarly transmitted, said:

"I heartily congratulate you on the success of your great adventure in accomplishing a non-stop flight from New York to Paris. It is a great step in the advancement of aviation. Every one in the United States is proud of your accomplishment."

Knew Lindbergh as a Boy.

In a statement issued here Mr. Kellogg referred to his personal friendship for Lindbergh, whom he has known for years through the young man's late father, a Representative in Congress from the Secretary's home State of Minnesota.

"News has just reached me," Mr. Kellogg said, "of the success of Lindbergh in completing his flight from New York to Paris. It is an achievement of which every American can justly be proud. I have known Lindbergh since he was a boy and rejoice at this culmination of his ambitions, which could only have been gained by scientific knowledge, superb courage and physique and sterling character. Our rejoicing in Lindbergh's success, however, is tempered by our continued ignorance of the fate of Nungesser and Coli, whose courage and valor have now been equaled, but cannot be surpassed."

Hanford MacNider, Acting Secre-

Continued on Page Four.

As he was lifted to the ground Lindbergh was pale, and with his hair unkempt, he looked completely worn out. He had strength enough, however, to smile, and waved his hand to the crowd. Soldiers with fixed bayonets were unable to keep back the crowd.

United States Ambassador Herrick was among the first to welcome and congratulate the hero.

A NEW YORK TIMES man was one of the first to reach the machine after its graceful descent to the field. Those first to arrive at the plane had a picture that will live in their minds for the rest of their lives. His cap off, his famous locks falling in disarray around his eyes, "Lucky Lindy" sat peering out over the rim of the little cockpit of his machine.

Dramatic Scene at the Field.

It was high drama. Picture the scene. Almost if not quite 100,000 people were massed on the east side of Le Bourget air field. Some of them had been there six and seven hours.

Off to the left the giant phare lighthouse of Mount Valerien flashed its guiding light 300 miles into the air. Closer on the left Le Bourget Lighthouse twinkled, and off to the right another giant revolving phare sent its beams high into the heavens.

Big arc lights on all sides with enormous electric glares were flooding the landing field. From time to time rockets rose and burst in varied lights over the field.

Seven thirty, the hour anounced for the arrival, had come and gone. Then 8 o'clock came, and no Lindbergh; at 9 o'clock the sun had set but then came reports that Lindbergh had been seen over Cork. Then he had been seen over Valentia in Ireland and then over Plymouth.

Suddenly a message spread like lightning, the aviator had been seen over Cherbourg. However, remembering the messages telling of Captain Nungesser's flight, the crowd was skeptical.

"One chance in a thousand!" "Oh, he cannot do it without navigating instruments!" "It's a pity, because he was a brave boy." Pessimism had spread over the great throng by 10 o'clock.

The stars came out and a chill wind blew.

Watchers Are Twice Disappointed.

Suddenly the field lights flooded their glares onto the landing ground and there came the roar of an airplane's motor. The crowd was still, then began a cheer, but two minutes later the landing glares went dark for the searchlight had identified the plane and it was not Captain Lindbergh's.

Stamping their feet in the cold, the crowd waited patiently. It seemed quite apparent that nearly every one was willing to wait all night, hoping against hope.

Suddenly—it was 10:16 exactly—another motor roared over the heads of the crowd. In the sky one caught a glimpse of a white gray plane, and for an instant heard the sound of one. Then it dimmed, and the idea spread that it was yet another disappointment.

Again landing lights glared and almost by the time they had flooded the field the gray-white plane had lighted on the far side nearly half a mile from the crowd. It seemed to stop almost as it hit the ground, so gently did it land.

And then occurred a scene which almost passed description. Two companies of soldiers with fixed bayonets and the Le Bourget field police, reinforced by Paris agents, had held the crowd in good order. But as the lights showed the plane

Think French Should Be Reassured.

The declaration of the Germans that they have no prime intention of bringing about revisions of the Versailles Treaty is seen here as a passage which should calm French fears, even though the Germans cling to the provision of the League covenant providing for a revision of antiquated treaty provisions.

Likewise, the German statement relative to changing conditions in Rhineland occupation are regarded here as very mild, in view of the report from Berlin that the Reich would demand quick evacuation of the Coblenz and Mayence bridgeheads as part of the compact arrangement.

It was expected that Germany would object to the provisions of M. Briand's note for exceptions and possible Allied crossing of the Rhine peace zone. London does not believe that Germany seriously means the suggestion that the allies should renounce any and all sanctions for possible violations of the Versailles Treaty, especially in regard to reparations, but it is recognized that Berlin has raised a disputable issue in questioning the French claim to the right to guarantee arbitration treaties between Germany and Czechoslovakia.

The only lack of cordial spirit the British see in the German note is the manner in which Berlin refers to Germany's entry into the League. Knowing all along that the allies regarded the Reich's joining the League as an essential part of the bargain, Berlin's condescending agreement to consider the proposal favorably is regarded as slightly in bad taste.

Germany's suggestion for a temporary arrangement of Article XVI until universal disarmament brings other nations' armies down to the level of Germany's is seen as a rather clever move to raise during the coming negotiations the issue of the strength of the French army. The disposition here is not to regard this part of the German note as stating any essential position but rather as intended to seek a bargaining position.

Mr. Chamberlain will at once discuss with M. Briand the conclusions to be drawn from the German note and in particular will consider whether arrangements should be made to invite the Germans to a security conference at Brussels on Aug. 15 or thereabouts. Mr. Chamberlain is anxious to have the security negotiations in shape to be able at Geneva in September to offer the League Assembly something to replace the Geneva protocol work of last year's assembly, which was killed by the unfavorable attitude of the present British Government.

British Press Divided on Note.

The morning papers differ pretty much over the note, according to their political stand. The pro-Government papers find it good and the Opposition press finds it bad.

The Daily Telegraph sees in the friendly tone of the note its chief value. In the arguments raised by the Berlin document this paper perceives an indication of difficult negotiations but fair prospects of success. In the German request for consideration of modifications of the Treaty of Versailles The Telegraph finds the chief stumbling block, but considers the tone of the note indicates a desire for a Rhine compact, and says

Continued on Page Six.

to remain twenty days in a hospital, it was said at Pistoia, where he went for first aid. He was later brought to Rome by rail accompanied by members of the Fascist railroad police, who guarded him from further attacks.

About half way between Montecatini and Pistoia Signor Amendola's motor car was obliged to halt by two other motor cars drawn up across the road. As soon as Amendola slackened speed fifteen or more individuals who had been hiding behind the hedge sprang up and rushed at the Opposition leader, striking at him with sticks they carried. They then re-entered their motor cars and headed toward Montecatini at a rapid pace.

Amendola, though bleeding from several cuts, was not seriously wounded and ordered the car driven to Pistoia.

Had Gone for Water Cure.

Signor Amendola had gone to Montecatini in order to take a water cure for which the town is famous, but no sooner was his presence known than the hotel was completely surrounded by thousands of Fascist citizens, some even having come from surrounding villages. The crowd booed and hissed lustily.

When that form of amusement began to become monotonous efforts were made to break through the cordons of carabineers which the police officials in order to forestall trouble had placed across each entrance to the hotel.

After several determined rushes had been stopped by the carabineers, the Fascisti succeeded in penetrating into the hotel and chased Deputy Amendola to the fourth floor of the building, where he took refuge in his room, bolting the door. His secretary, who had not been equally fleet of foot, had his eye blackened.

Further hostilities were prevented by the intervention of Fascist Deputies, who prevailed upon the Fascisti to leave the Deputy alone and to enjoin their companions outside the hotel.

The local Fascist leaders and several

Continued on Page Five.

brought about when Lieutenant Detective Louis Dittman recalled that on Oct. 26, 1923, four-year-old Irving Pickelny had disappeared just as mysteriously from in front of his home at 358 Grand Street, and his body had been found in the cellar of the tenement at 71 Suffolk Street a month later.

Detectives Comb Tenements.

The Pickelny home was less than a quarter of a mile from the homes of the parents of the missing Perles boy and his aunt. Detectives were assigned in pairs to comb thoroughly the neighboring tenements as well as the cellar of the public school and tenements in the vicinity of the Perles home in East Third Street, a short distance away.

When they reported after four hours that not a trace of the boy had been found Chief Inspector William J. Lahey then caused an order to be issued from Police Headquarters to all the uniformed men of the section between Fourteenth Street and the Battery to be especially vigilant and arrest any one of subnormal appearance found acting suspiciously.

While the hunt for the boy by the detectives was in full swing hundreds of children and grown-ups were questioned in the hope of obtaining a clue. Samuel Perles, father of the boy, took an active part in this questioning.

As in the hunt for the slain Pickelny boy, the excitement attendant on the police activity aroused the imaginations of many children and much time was lost running down reports of the missing boy's having been seen at various places in the neighborhood, even up to yesterday forenoon.

One witness, however, gave the police information which led them to believe that Robert was alive at 5 P. M. last Sunday. This witness was Max Slissen, who lives on the third floor of 91 Ridge Street, two doors north of the Levine home. Slissen was encountered by Detective Morgan Callahan of the Missing Persons Bureau, who had been assigned

Continued on Page Four.

Search All London for Wisconsin Professor; He Had $3,000 and Family Suspects Foul Play

Special Cable to THE NEW YORK TIMES.

LONDON, July 21.—Joseph Victor Collins, Professor of Mathematics at Wisconsin University and candidate in 1910 for the United States Senate, is missing in London and foul play is suspected by his wife and daughter.

Scotland Yard circulated a description and photographs of the missing man, and detectives spent yesterday combing London and hospitals are carrying out a systematic search for him.

Once during the day it was believed he was found and his daughter was called to St. George's Hospital and endured the ordeal of inspecting a suicide's body. It wasn't that of her father.

Professor Collins, when he disappeared, had in his pockets American Express checks and loose change of a value of over $3,000, and the suspicion is that he fell in the hands of sharpers.

With his daughter he boarded an omnibus which passed the corner of a street where his hotel is. The daughter alighted, but the father continued to the railroad station to secure sleeping accommodations for the journey to Edinburgh to the educators' sessions there. That was the last seen of him.

His daughter, in interviews, said she thought he was followed. There were several suspicious-looking men on top of the omnibus, she said. He was the last man in the world, she said, to go off voluntarily, for he had heard all about London gangsters and American visitors.

Mrs. Collins also said she was sure there was foul play behind the disappearance.

EDINBURGH, July 21 (AP).—Professor Collins has not arrived here for the sessions of educators, and no room has been reserved for him in Edinburgh.

Special to The New York Times.

STEVENS POINT, Wis., July 21.—Professor Joseph V. Collins is 66 years old and a member of the Faculty of the Stevens Point State Normal School. He is a widely known mathematician. He was a candidate for State Superintendent of Schools in 1903 and for the United States Senate in 1910.

Members of the Normal School Faculty suggest the disappearance of the professor was due to the fact that he is near-sighted and had wandered into an unknown quarter of London. They think he may have broken his glasses, without which he cannot distinguish a person a few feet away.

Professor Collins had $20,000 in his possession. He has been an instructor at the Normal School since it was organized in 1894.

the State of West Virginia to join with the United Mine Workers of America of the rest of country in a general strike."

At the same time Mr. Bittner, after conferring at the Hotel Ambassador with Thomas C. Townsend, chief counsel for the miners in Northern West Virginia, sent telegrams to John D. Rockefeller Jr. and Samuel Untermyer, alleging that eviction proceedings have been started against hundreds of miners and their families, and that armed guards have assaulted miners. Mr. Untermyer is appealed to because of his large interest in the Bethlehem Steel Corporation, in control of the Bethlehem Mines Corporation. Mr. Rockefeller is supposed to be interested in the Consolidation Company.

Warns of Nation-Wide Strike.

Here is the telegram sent by Mr. Bittner to Secretaries Hoover and Davis:

Several large coal companies in Northern West Virginia, among whom are the Bethlehem Mines Corporation, a subsidiary of the Bethlehem Steel Corporation, and the Consolidation Coal Company, which is controlled by the Rockefeller and Watson interests, have abrogated their wage contracts with the United Mine Workers of America and are attempting to put into effect a wage reduction approximating 50 per cent.

Defenseless miners, their wives and little children are being evicted from their homes by these coal companies because the miners will not agree to violate and abrogate the terms of the wage agreement which is effective until March 31, 1927. Hundreds of armed gunmen are being employed to intimidate, coerce and force our people to accept this reduction in wages.

In the interest of the coal miners and all the people of our country the time has arrived when the Government of the United States should take a definite position against abrogation of wage contracts by the coal operators of Northern West Virginia.

The miners do not propose to have their wage agreements broken down by this method of guerrilla warfare on the part of the Northern West Virginia operators, and unless something is done to prevent this abrogation of wage agreements it will be necessary for the miners of the entire State of West Virginia to join with the United Mine Workers of America of the rest of the country in a general strike.

The United Mine Workers of America are forced to take this position due to the action of the coal operators who have been so unfaithful to our wage agreements solemnly made to insure peace in the coal mining industry.

Ask Rockefeller's Aid.

The following telegram was sent to John D. Rockefeller Jr.:

I wrote you several days ago informing you that the statement made by President Lewis of the United Mine Workers of America that your company in Northern West Virginia, the Consolidation Coal Company, had abrogated its agreement with the United Mine Workers of America was absolutely correct and the Consolidation Coal Company is using every means known to corporate greed to make effective a wage reduction of approxi-

Continued on Page Three.

would disclose any part of their conversation, except to say that it had been wholly informal and that naturally no decision of any kind had been reached. Prior to meeting Mr. Olvany, the Democratic leader in Brooklyn had talked for almost an hour with James P. Sinnott, one of his district leaders and a high spokesman for Mayor Hylan himself.

Confer in McCooey's Office.

This conference was held in Mr. McCooey's office at the Hall of Records in Brooklyn. What they talked about can only be surmised, for there was no announcement after their meeting. It was presumed, however, that the sole topic was Mayor Hylan's chances to get a renomination for Mayor.

Mr. McCooey is likely to be subjected for the next few days to pressure from sources both friendly and unfriendly to the Mayor and his third term aspirations. An emissary of William R. Hearst arrived in this city yesterday, showing every desire that his presence on the scene of strife should not be bruited about.

The emissary was William A. De Ford, a member of Mayor Hylan's Board of Transportation, and head of the legal department of the Hearst publications in the East. Mr. De Ford had interrupted a vacation to return to the city at a time which may prove crucial to Mayor Hylan's political future. Word had preceded him from Atlantic City, where he has been spending part of his holiday, that he was coming to town for important political conferences. Mr. De Ford when questioned yesterday, declared that he was aware of no such conferences in which he was to be a participant, and that his return at this time was to attend a meeting of the Transportation Board.

Hearst Expected Soon.

That the visit of Mr. De Ford was occasioned by reasons purely political, however, was the general opinion among politicians who learned of his presence in the city. Mr. De Ford has been one of Mr. Hearst's political advisers for the last couple of years. He is conversant with all the plans of the editor-politician in relation to the candidacy of Mayor Hylan. Mr. De Ford declined

Continued on Page Fourteen.

Dr. E. Eliot Finds Him Dead in His Room While Wife Is Away Shopping.

George Griswold Haven, senior member of the banking firm of Strong, Sturgis & Co. of 11 Wall Street and President of the Metropolitan Opera and Real Estate Company, which controls the Metropolitan Opera House, committed suicide by shooting himself through the head with a revolver at his residence, 6 East Fifty-third Street, yesterday morning.

Mr. Haven, who was 59 years old, had been suffering from a nervous disorder for eighteen months. His mind was clear, but for a year and a half he had been inactive in business and had rested and traveled, seeking to regain his health.

Once or twice recently, according to friends of Mr. Haven, he had expressed himself as despairing of recovery and had shown that he had thoughts of ending his life. He gave no warning of any kind yesterday and left no note or statement explaining his act.

Married Five Months Ago.

Yesterday morning he rose at 8 o'clock and appeared his usual self. He had breakfast with his wife, formerly Miss Dorothy James, daughter of Henry A. James of this city. They were married last February at St. George's Church in this city. The first Mrs. Haven had died two years before.

After breakfast Mrs. Haven went shopping and her husband went to his room on the fourth floor. At 10:30 o'clock yesterday morning Dr. E. Eliot of 34 East Sixty-seventh Street called at the Haven residence. He was an old personal friend of Mr. Haven, but had not been treating him professionally. A servant informed Dr. Eliot that Mr. Haven was in his room.

"I'll go up and see him," said Dr. Eliot. He found Mr. Haven lying dead on his bed. There was a revolver beside him. He had shot himself through the jaw. The bullet had lodged in the brain, killing him instantly. He had been dead about half an hour when Dr. Eliot discovered the body. The revolver was one

Continued on Page Ten.

Girl, Saved by Dog, Shoots Her Assailant; Negro Again Shot by Posse Before Capture

Special to The New York Times.

NEW BRUNSWICK, N. J., July 21.—Shot twice, once by Miss Barbara Long, who lives with her brother Nicholas on a farm near the Lincoln Highway a few miles from here, and a second time by one of a posse which pursued him through the fields after he is alleged to have attacked Miss Long, Jess Williams, a negro, was arrested today on a charge of atrocious assault. After his wounds had been treated at the Middlesex General Hospital he was taken to the New Brunswick Jail.

Miss Long was saved from serious harm by the intervention of a large shepherd dog which made the negro take to his heels through the fields. The negro begged for food, and as Miss Long was preparing it he forced his way into the kitchen of the farmhouse and began to choke her. Miss Long managed to break his grasp on her throat. She screamed and the dog sprang at him. The negro ran from the place and Miss Long fired both barrels of a shotgun at him as he fled. The man was hit, but kept running.

Nicholas Long, the girl's brother, ran to the house when he heard his sister's screams and the shots. He took the gun and followed the negro, being joined by several men working in the fields near by. One man jumped into an automobile and intercepted the negro, who had been wounded a second time by a shot from one of his pursuers.

The negro was later arraigned before Justice of the Peace C. W. Sedam and committed to jail without bail. According to the police, he said he did not intend to harm the girl, but merely tried to rob the place.

Referee Files Report and Recommends That Leon Jacobs, Lawyer, Get $5,000 Fee.

The details of the settlement of the suit brought by Jerome Napoleon Bonaparte, great-grandnephew of the Emperor, against his wife, Blanche Bonaparte, to set aside an agreement transferring all of his property to her, became known in the Supreme Court yesterday, when a report was filed by Emanuel B. Cohen, appointed referee to determine the amount of the fee to be paid to Leon R. Jacobs, who acted as attorney for Mr. Bonaparte. The referee recommended that the fee be fixed at $5,000, although counsel for Mrs. Bonaparte contended that $250 should be enough.

The report of the referee states that on Dec. 23, 1922, Mr. Bonaparte entered the Craig House, a sanitarium at Beacon, N. Y., "to endeavor to restrain himself of a habit which he had unfortunately contracted." He was discharged as cured on April 21, 1923. Mr. Bonaparte alleged in the suit filed in his behalf by Mr. Jacobs that while he was ill his wife induced him to go to the office of her attorney, William M. K. Olcott, and sign an ageement putting all his property in her hands, and reserving only a small part of the income for himself.

The referee states that Mr. Bonaparte went alone to the office of Attorney Olcott and signed the assignment of his property dictated by Mr. Olcott, whereby he was to get only $5,000 of the income, and the remainder was to go to his wife. The agreement also set forth that he had made a will leaving all of his property inherited from his father and grandparents to his wife.

Value of the Property.

The instrument stated that the property consisted of a half interest in rents from Baltimore property owned by his grandmother, Suzane M. Bonaparte, valued at $1[illegible]5,000; an interest in rents from property owned by his great-grandmother, Elizabeth Patterson, valued at $30,000; a half interest in a deed of trust executed by his father, Jerome Napoleon Bonaparte, in 1877, amounting to $11,000; a life interest under the will of his father, from which the income in 1924 was $10,452; a half interest in property owned by his father in Baltimore valued at $3,000, and a claim for a further quarter interest in his father's property, in litigation, which, if successful, would add $30,000 to his income.

The referee states that Mr. Bonaparte, after being released from the sanitarium, made several requests to his wife for the return of his property, but that she refused to return it and also refused to pay his bills at the Craig House. Mr. Bonaparte then consulted Attorney Jacobs as to taking legal action, and in the course of ten weeks saw him twenty times. At these interviews he stated that the value of his property was $500,000. Mr. Jacobs accordingly brought suit to set aside the transfer on the ground that the plaintiff did not realize what he was doing at the time he signed the agreement.

The attorney last saw his client when they called at the Hotel St. Regis to see

Continued on Page Eight.

from the fight.

The end of the trial came as unexpectedly as everything else in this trial, in which nothing has happened according to schedule except the opening of court each morning with prayer. It was reached practically by agreement between counsel in an effort to end the case, which showed signs of going on forever, although all the testimony offered before the jury took only two hours.

Young Scopes, in his shirt sleeves, his collar open at the neck, his carrot-colored hair brushed back, stood up before the bar with a gold epauletted policeman beside him, and Judge Raulston had pronounced sentence before his counsel could suggest that Mr. Scopes might have something to say.

"Oh," exclaimed Judge Raulston. "Have you anything to say, Mr. Scopes, as to why the Court should not impose punishment upon you?"

Scopes Calls Statute Unjust.

Mr. Scopes, who is hardly more than a boy and whose pleasant demeanor and modest bearing have won him many friends since this case started, was nervous. His voice trembled a little as he folded his arms and said:

"Your Honor, I feel that I have been convicted of violating an unjust statute. I will continue in the future, as I have in the past, to oppose the law in any way I can. Any other action would be in violation of my ideal of academic freedom, that is, to teach the truth as guaranteed in our Constitution, of personal and religious freedom. I think the fine is unjust."

No one had expected such a quick ending. Mr. Darrow came into court full of the pleasant anticipation of another "go" at Mr. Bryan, whom he questioned to the delight of hundreds the day before. But the court had no sooner opened than Judge Raulston decided that there would be no further questioning, and then ordered Mr. Bryan's testimony expunged from the record.

Mr. Bryan, who had contented himself with the thought that he would have an opportunity to put Mr. Darrow on the stand and tear into him, was somewhat chagrined at this turn of the case, and announced that he would have to appeal to the fairness of the press to give prominence to the questions which he would have asked Mr. Darrow.

"I had not reached the point where I could give my statement to answer the charges made by the counsel for the defense as to my ignorance and bigotry," he said, bitterly.

Sparrow Poses as Dove of Peace.

But before the day's session was over a dove of peace hovered over the court room in the form of a frightened sparrow, which had strayed in through an open window, and everybody exchanged felicitations except Mr. Bryan and Mr. Darrow. Judge John Raulston declared that the Word of God, "given to man, that man may use it as a waybill to the other world," was an indestructible thing, and prayed God that he had decided right the questions raised in the trial. A minister pronounced a benediction and court adjourned.

The general gratification of the people at the end of a good show was shown by their applause whenever any member of either side, or the visiting spectators, rose to thank Dayton for its hospitality and kindness. And there was a further manifestation of the remarkable change in sentiment which has taken place since this trial began.

The defense faced a unitedly hostile audience when they started. There were

Section 1

"All the News That's Fit to Print."

The New York Times.

THE WEATHER
Generally fair today and tomorrow; moderate to fresh southerly winds.
Temperature yesterday—Max., 66; Min., 53.
For weather report see Page 31.

Section 1

VOL. LXXVI....No. 25,320. NEW YORK, SUNDAY, MAY 22, 1927. Including Rotogravure Picture Section in three parts—Magazine and Book Sections in Rotogravure. FIVE CENTS In Manhattan Bronx and Brooklyn | Elsewhere TEN CENTS

LINDBERGH DOES IT! TO PARIS IN 33½ HOURS; FLIES 1,000 MILES THROUGH SNOW AND SLEET; CHEERING FRENCH CARRY HIM OFF FIELD

COULD HAVE GONE 500 MILES FARTHER

Gasoline for at Least That Much More—Flew at Times From 10 Feet to 10,000 Feet Above Water.

ATE ONLY ONE AND A HALF OF HIS FIVE SANDWICHES

Fell Asleep at Times but Quickly Awoke—Glimpses of His Adventure in Brief Interview at the Embassy.

LINDBERGH'S OWN STORY TOMORROW.

Captain Charles A. Lindbergh was too exhausted after his arrival in Paris late last night to do more than indicate, as told below, his experiences during his flight. After he awakes today, he will narrate the full story of his remarkable exploit for readers of Monday's New York Times.

By CARLYLE MACDONALD.

Special Cable to THE NEW YORK TIMES.

PARIS, Sunday, May 22.—Captain Lindbergh was discovered at the American Embassy at 2:30 o'clock this morning. Attired in a pair of Ambassador Herrick's pajamas, he sat on the edge of a bed and talked of his flight. At the last moment

MAP OF LINDBERGH'S TRANSATLANTIC ROUTE, SHOWING THE SPEED OF HIS TRIP.

LEVINE ABANDONS BELLANCA FLIGHT

Venture Given Up as Designer Splits With Him—Plane Narrowly Escapes Burning.

BYRD'S CRAFT IS NAMED

Lindbergh Cheered at Ceremony—Commander, Now Last in Field, Waits on Weather.

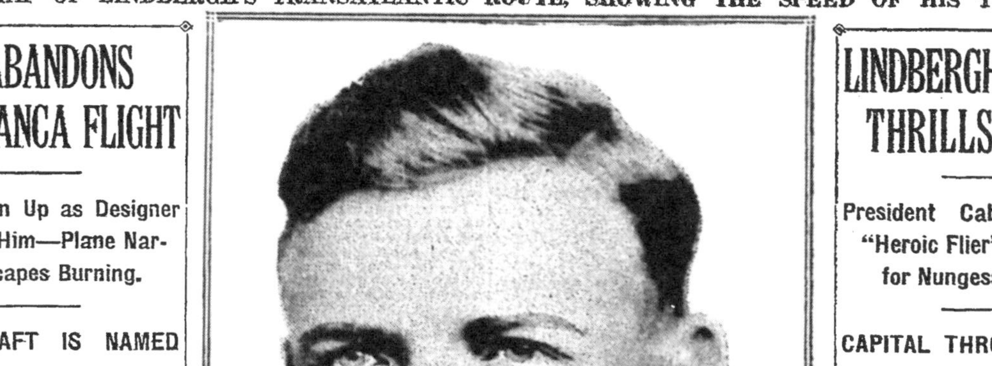

LINDBERGH TRIUMPH THRILLS COOLIDGE

President Cables Praise to "Heroic Flier" and Concern for Nungesser and Coli.

CAPITAL THROBS WITH JOY

Kellogg, New, MacNider, Patrick and Many More Join in Paying Tribute to Daring Youth.

CROWD ROARS THUNDEROUS WELCOME

Breaks Through Lines of Soldiers and Police and Surging to Plane Lifts Weary Flier from His Cockpit

AVIATORS SAVE HIM FROM FRENZIED MOB OF 100,000

Paris Boulevards Ring With Celebration After Day and Night Watch—American Flag Is Called For and Wildly Acclaimed.

By EDWIN L. JAMES.

Special Cable to THE NEW YORK TIMES.

PARIS, May 21.—Lindbergh did it. Twenty minutes after 10 o'clock tonight suddenly and softly there slipped out of the darkness a gray-white airplane as 25,000 pairs of eyes strained toward it. At 10:24 the Spirit of St. Louis landed and lines of soldiers, ranks of policemen and stout steel fences went down before a mad rush as irresistible as the tides of the ocean.

"Well, I made it," smiled Lindbergh, as the little white monoplane came to a halt in the middle of the field and the first vanguard reached the plane. Lindbergh made a move to jump out. Twenty hands reached for him and lifted him out as if he were a baby. Several thousands in a minute were around the plane. Thousands more broke the barriers of iron rails round the field, cheering wildly.

"All the News That's Fit to Print."

The New York Times.

THE WEATHER
Showers today and tomorrow; fresh south and southwest winds.
Temperature yesterday—Max., 73; min., 69.
☞ For weather report see Page 22.

VOL. LXXIV....No. 24,651. *** NEW YORK, WEDNESDAY, JULY 22, 1925. TWO CENTS In Greater New York | THREE CENTS Within 200 Miles | FOUR CENTS Elsewhere in the U.

LONG STEP TO PEACE IS SEEN BY BRITAIN IN GERMANY'S REPLY

Chamberlain to Consider With Briand Chances of a Parley in August.

WANTS COMPACT PRESSED

Meanwhile the French Think There Are Traps in the Berlin Note.

GERMANS LOOKING TO US

They Want Americans Made Members of the Arbitration Tribunal.

By EDWIN L. JAMES.

By Wireless to THE NEW YORK TIMES.

LONDON, July 21.—The British Government regards the German security note as a distinct step toward making the Rhine peace compact. While less favorable than London had hoped Dr. Stresemann's communication is seen as opening the way to early negotiations between the Allies and Germany.

Here one finds the belief that some of the most troublesome passages in the German Foreign Minister's note were written for home consumption, especially the section relating to article XVI. of the Covenant of the League. Following the action of the League Council notifying Germany that no special conditions could attend her entry, it is thought here that Dr. Stresemann wrote this part of the note with full knowledge that it was doomed to failure but in the hope of mollifying opposition in the Reich.

As the British see it, the last paragraph of the note is the most important one, in which Berlin says: "On essential points a significant rapprochement of the views of the two sides has already taken place," and in which the German Government hopes for a settlement of outstanding differences and expresses a wish for speedier discussions. That, the British say, really sums up what the Reich's note means, namely, that the

Party Goes South on Yacht To See Dredging by Beebe

The Vanadis, the yacht of Harrison Williams, 60 Broadway, left New York early yesterday morning for Cape Hatteras, where William Beebe and the New York Zoological Society Expedition on the Arcturus are expected Friday afternoon.

A party of friends of Mr. Williams are on board the Vanadis, and George Palmer Putnam, William Beebe's publisher, left New York by rail yesterday morning to join the party at Cape May at the invitation of Mr. Williams.

Beebe, returning from the Sargasso Sea, has notified the New York Zoological Society that he is on his way back to New York and will stop at a designated place off Hatteras to trawl and dredge. This point will be the rendezvous of the Arcturus and the Vanadis.

The Vanadis will also accompany the Arcturus on its return to New York on Saturday. Mr. Williams is chief patron of the zoological society's expedition.

MOB CLUBS DEPUTY, FOE OF THE FASCISTI

Giovanni Amendola, Leader of Aventine Opposition, Is Attacked on Country Road.

BOOED OUT OF MONTECATINI

Assault Follows Siege of Hotel, Peace Truce and Flight From Town of Water Cures.

By Wireless to THE NEW YORK TIMES.

ROME, July 21.—Deputy Giovanni Amendola, perhaps the most important leader of the Aventine opposition to the Fascist régime, was attacked and clubbed by unidentified persons presumed to have been Fascisti, while fleeing by motor car toward Pistoia from Montecatini, where a Fascist crowd, after besieging him in his hotel for several hours, eventually booed and hissed him out of town.

Deputy Amendola suffered several bruises and superficial wounds on va-

ALL POLICE BELOW 14TH ST. JOIN HUNT FOR A MISSING BOY

Comb East Side Tenements Aided by Forty Detectives for Robert Perles.

ABANDON DROWNING THEORY

Marine Division Fails to Find Clue in River—Lad Seen by Man at 5 P. M. on Sunday.

LITTLE GIRL ALSO SAW HIM

Says She Played With Him but Can Tell No More—Sewers and Intakes to Be Searched Today.

Forty detectives from lower east side precincts and all the uniformed patrolmen between the Battery and Fourteenth Street, on the east side, were brought into the hunt yesterday for Robert Perles, 4 years and 6 months old, who disappeared last Sunday after he had left his home at 272 East Third Street to visit a relative at 95 Ridge Street. Following the abandonment of their first theory that the boy had been drowned in the East River near the recreation pier at the foot of East Third Street, the police decided on an intensive search. Policemen from the Marine Division in launches had dragged the waters in the vicinity of this pier in the forenoon without uncovering any clue that might justify the theory.

A conference of detectives in charge of the quest in the Fifth Street Station at noon led to the issuance of an order to mobilize all detectives from the Old Slip, Beach Street, Oak Street, Mercer Street, Clinton Street and Fifth Street Stations in the block bounded by Delancey, Rivington, Attorney and Ridge Streets, in which lives Mrs. Annie Levine, aunt of the boy, and in which he was last seen playing in front of Public School 4. Mrs. Levine lives in a five-story tenement four blocks from the East River. At 11 A. M. Sunday, she said, she saw her little nephew playing with Daniel Blitz, a companion.

The decision to search every house

Buck M'Neil, Saver of 40 Lives, Gets First Honors on Tablet

"Buck" McNeil, the Battery Dock Master, who has saved more than forty persons from drowning off the sea wall at Battery Park, will be the first "Honor Man" to have his name engraved on a tablet to be placed in the office of Dock Commissioner Cosgrove, it was announced yesterday.

The tablet will be a memorial to the late Charles F. Murphy, who served as Dock Commissioner from 1898 to 1902. It will be presented by Charles F. Murphy, a nephew of the Tammany leader. Annually a Dock Department "Honor Man" will have his name engraved on the tablet. McNeil will also be presented with a medal by members of the department. He already has more than three dozen medals for saving life.

COAL STRIKE THREAT IS WIRED TO HOOVER

Miners' Official Warns of General Tie-Up Over West Virginia Wage Fight.

SEEKS ROCKEFELLER AID

Charges Assaults by Armed Guards—Anthracite Conferees Make Little Headway.

Special to The New York Times.

ATLANTIC CITY, N. J., July 21.—While the anthracite operators and miners spent an afternoon in fruitless bickering over a new wage agreement, representatives of the bituminous coal miners here today drew up plans for *an intensive campaign against soft coal* operators in Northern West Virginia. Van A. Bittner, chief representative of the United Mine Workers in that territory, sent an identical telegram to Secretary of Commerce Hoover and Secretary of Labor Davis denouncing the Bethlehem Mines Corporation, a subsidiary of the Bethlehem Steel Corporation, and the Consolidation Coal Company for their alleged violation of the Jacksonville agreement. He declared that "unless something is done to prevent this abrogation of wage agreements it will [illegible]

HYLAN REFUSES BAIT TO GO ON BENCH AND QUIT MAYOR'S RACE

Foes Realize Need for Keeping Him on Ticket to Block Third-Party Plan.

McCOOEY CALLS LEADERS

Brooklyn Chief Confers With Olvany, but Both Refuse to Tell What Was Said.

HEARST EMISSARY ACTIVE

Meeting of Borough Leaders on Mayoralty Situation Is Put Off Until Next Week.

In a final attempt to avert an open break and keep him in line for the ticket, Democrats who do not believe Mayor Hylan could make a winning fight for a third term, yesterday sent friendly emissaries to the Mayor, who now are bringing all their persuasive powers to bear with a view to inducing him to quit the Mayoralty race and accept a nomination for the Supreme Court in the Second Judicial District.

Up to last night these envoys of the anti-Hylan forces had not been able to budge Mayor Hylan from his determination to make a fight for the Mayoralty again. It was stated, however, that the pressure would continue, and that when the Mayor awakened to a realization of his loss of popularity with the voters there was hope that he would yield to their representations.

In the meantime the anti-Hylan forces are *sparring for time*. It was announced yesterday that the conferences of the five Democratic borough leaders, at which the Democratic city slate is to be decided upon, would be deferred until next week. This announcement was made after John H. McCooey, the Democratic leader in Brooklyn, which is Mayor Hylan's home borough, had met George W. Olvany, the Tammany chieftain, at the Hotel Vanderbilt, where they discussed the tangled Mayoralty situation for an hour or more over luncheon.

SCOPES GUILTY, FINED $100, SCORES LAW; BENEDICTION ENDS TRIAL, APPEAL STARTS; DARROW ANSWERS NINE BRYAN QUESTIONS

Both Sides Speed Procedure for Scopes Appeal; Defense Cost $25,000, With Lawyers Serving Free

Special to The New York Times.

KNOXVILLE, Tenn., July 21.—With the conviction of John Thomas Scopes, attorneys for the defense at Dayton began at once to formulate their plans for the appeal. The case will come before the Supreme Court when that tribunal sits in Knoxville in September. Attorneys for both sides today agreed to expedite the appeal procedure in order to assure a hearing of the issues at that session.

Clarence Darrow, chief of the defense staff, is expected to argue the case before the Supreme Court here. Frank Spurlock, prominent attorney of Chattanooga, assisting the defense, will also plead for Mr. Scopes, being well versed in the peculiarities of Tennessee law. John R. Neal of Knoxville also is expected to take an important part in the appeal proceedings.

For the State, Attorney General Stewart and Ben G. McKenzie doubtless will carry the burden.

The defense's appeal will consist of two main points: First, that the Anti-Evolution law is unconstitutional; second, that even though the law were valid, Mr. Scopes did not violate it, and that the defense was prohibited from proving this at the Dayton trial.

DAYTON, Tenn., July 21 (AP).—A misdemeanor case carrying as a penalty to the guilty offender a fine of $100 and costs of the trial brought an expenditure to the defenders of John Thomas Scopes of about $25,000.

The actual court costs are estimated at well over $300, or more than treble the fine assessed.

The greatest expense of the trial was the cost of bringing expert witnesses, who were not allowed to testify. Defense counsel estimated that cost to be $20,000 to $25,000.

Attorneys on both sides bore their own expenses and served without fees.

In addition several hundred dollars was paid out by the county in preparing the Court House for the trial.

G. G. HAVEN A SUICIDE, DUE TO ILL HEALTH

Banker and Opera Patron Shoots Himself After Vain Struggle to Recover.

FRIEND DISCOVERS BODY

BONAPARTE GIVES PROPERTY TO WIFE

Great-Grandnephew of the Emperor Signs Away All but $5,000 a Year.

AGREEMENT ENDS HER SUIT

FINAL SCENES DRAMATIC

Defense Suddenly Decides to Make No Plea and Accept Conviction.

BRYAN IS DISAPPOINTED

Loses Chance to Examine Darrow and His Long-Prepared Speech Is Undelivered.

HIS EVIDENCE IS EXPUNGED

Differences Forgotten in the End as All Concerned Exchange Felicitations.

Special to The New York Times.

DAYTON, Tenn., July 21.—The trial of John Thomas Scopes for teaching evolution in Tennessee, which Clarence Darrow characterized today as "the first case of its kind since we stopped trying people for witchcraft," is over. Mr. Scopes was found guilty and fined $100, and his counsel will appeal to the Supreme Court of Tennessee for reversal of the verdict. The scene will then be shifted from Dayton to Knoxville, where the case will probably come up on the first Monday in September.

But the end of the trial did not end the battle on evolution, for not long after its conclusion William Jennings Bryan opened fire on Clarence Darrow with a strong statement and a list of nine questions on the basic principles of the Christian religion. To these Mr. Darrow replied and added a statement explaining Mr. Bryan's "rabies." Dudley Field Malone also contributed a statement predicting ultimate victory for evolution and repeating that Mr. Bryan ran away

1929

New Deal, New Order

1939

FRONT PAGE NEWS 1929-1939

Hoover Says the Economy Is Sound

DECEMBER 4, 1929

In October 1929, Wall Street crashed and the Great Depression began. Two months later, President Herbert Hoover's crystal ball was still rosy. "The sudden threat of unemployment," he said, "created unwarranted pessimism and fear." After praising the Federal Reserve for keeping the credit system from breaking down, he proposed "systematic, voluntary measures of cooperation" with businesses and state governments. He also proposed a tax cut.

Lindbergh Baby Kidnapped

MARCH 2, 1932

The kidnapping and killing of Charles A. Lindbergh's infant son made headlines from the day it happened, and bigger headlines after a carpenter named Bruno Richard Hauptmann was arrested in 1934. The Lindberghs' nurse discovered the baby was missing. Ransom notes demanded $50,000, then $70,000. The Lindberghs delivered the money as directed, but the child was apparently already dead; the little boy's body was found near their New Jersey mansion. Later Hauptmann was caught spending some of the marked bills. Convicted after what was widely called the "trial of the century" and executed in 1936, he claimed until the end that he was innocent and that he had just been keeping the cash for a friend.

Hoover's Assault on Bonus Marchers

JULY 29, 1932

President Herbert Hoover had had it with the so-called "Bonus Expeditionary Force," a loose coalition demanding cash for the bondlike certificates the government had issued to World War I veterans—certificates which could not be redeemed until 1945. More than 17,000 veterans had descended on Washington in June and camped in shacks after demonstrating at the Capitol. They refused to leave after the Senate voted down a payment bill, and Hoover ordered federal troops, under the command of a rising young officer named Douglas A. MacArthur, to burn down the encampments and disperse the inhabitants.

New Leaders, New Powers

MARCH 21, 1933

In Washington and in Berlin, two new leaders—the leaders who would preside over World War II—expanded their powers with strikingly different tools. During the famous "first 100 days" of his administration, President Franklin D. Roosevelt staked out wide executive power to help shake off the Depression at home. He also pushed for a debt relief bill that would allow deferment of World War I–era loans to Europe. In Berlin, Hitler demanded dictatorial power until at least 1937.

The New Deal

MAY 8, 1933

The centerpiece of President Franklin D. Roosevelt's attack on the Depression was a massive government program whose very name promised a fresh start—the New Deal. It promised benefits to lower-income people who had not prospered in the twenties. That meant elevating the federal government's place in people's lives as never before—and setting up an alphabet soup of public works agencies like the Tennessee Valley Authority and the Civilian Conservation Corps.

Stock Market Crashes

OCTOBER 25, 1929

The Black Thursday sell-off was the beginning of the end—the end of the boom that had lifted the Twenties on a wave of stock speculation. Stockbrokers worried about meeting their margin calls as more than 12 million shares changed hands, triple what was then considered a busy day. The frenzy subsided after five leading bankers met at J.P. Morgan and Company. Then Morgan's floor-broker, who was also the president of the New York Stock Exchange, went to the trading floor, not to shut down the exchange, but to buy 10,000 shares of U.S. Steel. The price: $10 more per share than U.S. Steel had been selling for. Wall Street rode out the day, only to panic again the following week, on Black Monday and Black Tuesday—and drag the nation under. By the end of the year, stock losses exceeded $15 billion.

Roosevelt Takes Office

MARCH 5, 1933

Five short sentences into his inaugural address, Franklin D. Roosevelt spoke the words everyone would remember, the line that affirmed his optimism in the face of the Depression-fueled despair: "The only thing we have to fear is fear itself." As The Times reported, "'Action' was the promise of Mr. Roosevelt's speech, and action was immediately forthcoming"—with a bank holiday intended to stop the panic that had besieged financial institutions. Roosevelt also called a special session of Congress to push through his plan for dealing with the crisis.

Prohibition Ends

DECEMBER 6, 1933

The evangelist Billy Sunday had said "goodbye, John Barleycorn" when Prohibition began. But after 14 years of illicit drinking in speakeasies, the nation finally said goodbye to Prohibition. America had not stopped imbibing during Prohibition: in New York City alone, some 32,000 speakeasies sprung up, twice the number of saloons in business before the nation went "dry." Worse, Prohibition made for sham sanctimoniousness among officials like President Warren G. Harding, who preached temperance in public but enjoyed his whiskey in the privacy of the White House.

Hitler Consolidates His Power

JULY 1, 1934

Hitler ordered a purge of his own political party, tightening his hold on power as he laid the groundwork for his push across Europe. What became known as the "night of the long knives" came on the eve of a self-proclaimed month of peace. Hitler ousted Captain Ernst Roehm as head of the Nazi storm troops, which Hitler saw as a threat to his power. Roehm promptly committed suicide; more than 80 other Nazi officials were rounded up and killed.

Huey Long Assassinated

SEPTEMBER 9, 1935

Huey P. Long had left Louisiana state house for the United States Senate in 1932, ut he remained the dominant character in state politics—and some things could not be left to the hand-picked surrogates back home. So Long had returned to Baton Rouge to push through some important state legislation in person—specifically, bills that would enhance his already substantial power. Long, an enemy of President Franklin D. Roosevelt who had been talked about as a possible third-party presidential candidate, was leaving the Louisiana House chamber when a gunman opened fire. Long's assassin was the son-in-law of a district judge whom Long had driven from office.

The New York Times.

Jesse Owens Wins Four Medals

AUGUST 5, 1936

Jesse Owens, an American track and field star, won three gold medals on his own at the Olympics in Berlin and shared a fourth. The medal that Owens shared, in the 400-meter relay, was for a world-record-setting time. One of his individual medals was for the broad jump, in which he not only defeated a German athlete, but also set a record that stood until 1960. Hitler was furious that a non-German won, not to mention a non-white, and snubbed Owens. So the story went—until later biographies of Owens called it a myth, perhaps based on Hitler's snub of another black American medalist on the first day of the games.

The New York Times.
EDWARD VIII RENOUNCES BRITISH CROWN; YORK WILL SUCCEED HIM AS GEORGE VI; PARLIAMENT IS SPEEDING ABDICATION ACT

'The Woman I Love'

DECEMBER 11, 1936

Hemmed in by tradition and an unbending prime minister, King Edward VIII of Great Britain announced his abdication. After only 11 months on the throne, he said he could not carry on "without the help and support of the woman I love," the American socialite Wallis Simpson. As if it were not enough that she was a foreigner, she had been divorced twice. Prime Minister Stanley Baldwin turned down Edward's plan to allow the marriage but give her no title or rights to property. The Church of England also condemned the marriage. Edward and Mrs. Simpson went ahead with it in mid-1937. He died in permanent exile in 1972; she died in 1986.

The New York Times.
HINDENBURG BURNS IN LAKEHURST CRASH; 21 KNOWN DEAD, 12 MISSING; 64 ESCAPE

Hindenburg Explodes

MAY 7, 1937

The Hindenburg—a German zeppelin that made flying fast and luxurious for the thirties—caught fire, crashed and burned, all in less than half a minute, as it landed at a naval air station in New Jersey. "It's burst into flames! It burst into flames, and it's falling. It's crashing!" shouted a horrified radio announcer, on hand to cover what he had expected would be a routine arrival of a prestigious airship. "Four or five hundred feet into the sky and it—it's a terrific crash, ladies and gentlemen. It's smoke, and it's flames now. ... This is the worst thing I've ever witnessed." The flammable hydrogen used to float the giant craft was widely blamed for the catastrophe, though in the 1990s, researchers speculated that a more direct cause may have been lacquer used to waterproof the Hindenburg's fabric-covered skin.

The New York Times.

Amelia Earhart Disappears

JULY 3, 1937

America was crazy about aviators, and crazy about Amelia Earhart's daring solo flights, among them the first nonstop from Hawaii to California in 1935. She had logged 22,000 miles on a round-the-world flight and was heading from New Guinea to a refueling stop on a tiny Pacific island. She never got there. Radio operators reported hearing messages that she was far off course and short on fuel, but a massive search did not find her or her navigator, Frederick Noonan. Ever since, unconfirmed speculation has swirled that she was on an espionage mission for the U.S. and was captured by the Japanese, or that mechanical problems forced her down on some other island that her would-be rescuers failed to reach.

The New York Times.

George Gershwin Dies

JULY 12, 1937

In little more than 15 years, George Gershwin had gone from Tin Pan Alley song-plugger to respected composer who married jazz to what Jazz Age audiences considered "serious music." His "Rhapsody in Blue" had taken him into the concert hall; "Of Thee I Sing" had been the first musical comedy to win a Pulitzer Prize. More recently, he had moved to Hollywood, where he had complained of headaches and dizziness for some months. After he collapsed at a studio where he was writing the score for Samuel Goldwyn's first Technicolor movie, doctors discovered that he had a brain tumor. Gershwin, who was 39, died after surgery.

The New York Times.

Hitler Annexes Austria

MARCH 13, 1938

Hitler completed his first conquest with "Anschluss," a political union that annexed Austria. The takeover came two years after Hitler had forced Chancellor Kurt von Schuschnigg to declare Austria a "German state." But von Schuschnigg had strayed from Hitler's agenda by scheduling a vote on independence, only to exclude large numbers of Nazi sympathizers by limiting the balloting to Austrians over the age of 24. Hitler ousted von Schuschnigg, sent in more than 60,000 troops and went to Linz and Vienna in person, making clear who was now in charge.

The New York Times.

Spain Begs for Help

MARCH 16, 1938

The Spanish civil war that eventually carried General Francisco Franco to 39 years of dictatorial power in some ways raised the curtain for World War II. Franco's nationalists had help from Italy and Germany. Franco's opponents looked to the Soviet Union and to volunteers from the United States, who signed up with the International Brigades fighting Franco. Also lined up against Franco were such famous sympathizers as Pablo Picasso, Ernest Hemingway and W.H. Auden. By 1938, Franco's fascists controlled two-thirds of Spain, and with government troops in retreat, Premier Juan Negrin made an 11th-hour appeal to France. Paris was worried that Italy's alliances with Franco and with Hitler would prove overwhelming not just for Spain, but for itself.

The New York Times.

Joe Louis Wins

JUNE 23, 1938

Joe Louis—"champion of champions, the greatest of them all," in the words of the screenwriter Budd Schulberg—crushed the former heavyweight champion Max Schmeling in the first round at Yankee Stadium. It was a rematch with heavy political and racial overtones. Schmeling, a German who was a star Nazi athlete, had handed Louis the first loss of his professional career with a 12th-round knockout in 1936.

The New York Times.

A Scary 'War of the Worlds'

OCTOBER 31, 1938

It was only a Sunday-night radio program, but when Orson Welles said that Martians had landed in a rural corner of New Jersey, Americans believed him—and panicked. The broadcast sounded so real that thousands of listeners jumped in their cars, scrambling to escape the strange and terrifying creatures that Welles said were swarming toward Manhattan and zapping anything in their path with death rays.

The New York Times.

Kristallnacht in Germany

NOVEMBER 11, 1938

The first direct and widespread blast of Nazi violence against Jews began when German Propaganda Minister Joseph Goebbels called for the nationwide destruction of Jewish homes and businesses. Synagogues were also attacked in Baden-Baden, Frankfurt and Nuremberg, among other cities. In Berlin, the police stood by and huge crowds looked on as Nazi storm troopers and Hitler Youth went on a rampage that became known as Kristallnacht, "the night of broken glass," for the store windows the Nazis smashed in street after street. Nationwide, 91 Jews were murdered and 30,000 arrested and sent to concentration camps. Goebbels had ordered the pogrom, ostensibly as revenge for the shooting, in Paris, of a German diplomat by a Jewish student angry that his parents had been deported to Poland.

The New York Times.

1939 World's Fair Opens

MAY 1, 1939

The 1939 World's Fair showcased a "World of Tomorrow" that was bright and democratic, but America worried that the real world was increasingly threatened by fascism or communism. Crowds surged past the fair's futuristic centerpieces, the Trylon and Perisphere, and Ford's "Road of Tomorrow" had a cork-and-rubber surface and ramps that were stacked like platters of spinning records. But recordings had been around for a while. RCA introduced something that really was the future: commercial television.

"All the News That's Fit to Print."

The New York Times.

THE WEATHER
Cloudy, not quite so cold, today; tomorrow, partly cloudy.
Temperatures yesterday—Max. 35, min. 24.
U. S. Weather Forecast—For Details See Page 43.

VOL. LXXIX....No. 26,247. NEW YORK, WEDNESDAY, DECEMBER 4, 1929. TWO CENTS In Greater New York | THREE CENTS Within 200 Miles | FOUR CENTS Elsewhere Except 7th and 8th Postal Zones

BYRD TELLS OF SCENE AT SOUTH POLE WHERE HE DROPPED AMERICAN FLAG; 15 BELOW ZERO ON THE VAST PLATEAU

FLEW SIX MILES BEYOND AND AROUND BOTTOM OF WORLD

Commander Pictures Huge Ice Cap Fringed by Mountains, the Pole Itself in Centre of Uplifted Plain Hundreds of Miles in Diameter.

NO LANDING POSSIBLE ON CHAOTIC TERRAIN

"Devil's Ballroom," Mentioned by Amundsen, Seen in This Menacing Waste—Turned Back to Base Just in Time Ahead of Storm.

This is the third and final instalment of Commander Byrd's story. Yesterday he told of reaching the Plateau, with the Pole dead ahead. Today he describes the dash to the southernmost point and what he saw there.

By COMMANDER R. E. BYRD,
Leader of the Antarctic Expedition.

Copyright, 1929, by The New York Times Company and The St. Louis Post-Dispatch. All rights for publication reserved throughout the world.
Wireless to THE NEW YORK TIMES.

LITTLE AMERICA, Antarctica, Dec. 3.—There was now less than 300 miles between us and the Pole. If the sun remained, the sun compass and wind drift indicator should take us there as straight as a bee flies.

We would have to ride the engines all the way. The Plateau was so high that if one of the three engines should stop we would have to land on snow, which at places was nearly two miles above sea level, an uncertain thing at any time—more uncertain with a load aboard. The engines must keep going.

Engine Sputters, Then Resumes "Singing."

I was saying this to myself when the starboard engine began to sputter. Bernt Balchen nosed down. Harold June rushed to the gas tank valves and stood looking at the engine and listening to the jarring interruptions the missing cylinders caused in the rhythm.

Captain McKinley for once hesitated in his mapping work. After winning our hardest struggle, was our flight to be ended so near the objective? Bernt hurriedly manipulated the altitude control.

In the effort to economize on precious fuel the gasoline had been made too lean. The motor began to sing again. I say "sing," for its roar was music when it was not missing a beat. Flying on a flight of this kind is full of contrasts—everything perfect one minute and the next everything black.

Out Over the Plateau, Mountains on the Left.

All was well again. We looked around. Ahead was an apparently limitless plateau, glistening white in the sunshine. The great polar plateau at last! It was good to see it after the months we had wondered about it and the hundreds of times we had asked ourselves if we should ever be lucky enough to reach it.

To the left were great mountain masses looming high above our level. I would hesitate to estimate their altitude, but they are very high, since at this place the plateau itself was about 10,000 feet above sea level. Captain McKinley's photographs must tell the story.

Beyond this mass were separated peaks of many different shapes running to the southeastward. But could one say that they ran that way? For though they might continue in the same general line, so topsy-turvy is direction here that in 150 miles they would be running north of east. That is what happens near the Pole.

There was one great isolated peak completely snow-covered and looking like a great inverted white porcelain bowl. Back of us, running east and west along the rim of the plateau, were enormous peaks lifting their heads high into the air.

New Range North and South Rises on Right.

I looked over to the right and got one of those kicks that pull a man away from civilization, which repay him for his efforts.

There was a new mountain range in the distance, running north and south—a new bit of land to add to the map of the world. Mac would "shoot" it with his camera. We felt that it was worth while bringing him for that alone.

It occurred to me as I looked around at the mountains that they must fringe the whole plateau—nature's great dam holding the ice and snow there until in geological ages the period would lift itself from Antarctica; until the vast amount of snow melts and runs through outlets, the ocean that lies below it will not be revealed.

At present we can only guess what is beneath that great ice cap and what is its depth. It is one of the world's mysteries.

That imaginary point—the South Pole—is in the centre of an uplifted plain hundreds of miles in diameter, a magnificent edifice seemingly built to make more inviolable the tiny spot which we were seeking.

Lone Peak an Outpost on Polar Plain.

The plateau seems to range from 7,000 to 11,000 feet in altitude. Beyond the new mountain mass we saw a small peak sticking up through the great expanse of snow—a very lonely little black speck. It was hard to realize that it was the top probably of a mountain about 9,000 feet above sea level.

On we went, flying at the rate of 100 miles an hour through the air toward our goal. Our drift indicator showed a wind from the left. We had to head the Floyd Bennett a dozen degrees to the left in order to fly straight south.

It was impossible to tell our exact altitude above the plateau and, therefore, not easy to get our actual ground speed as it would have been over water or ice near sea level.

Head Wind and 10 Below Zero Nearing Pole.

But there was a way. With a stop-watch we got the time it took a crevasse, sastrugi or smoke bomb beneath to run the length of a twelve-inch wire in the bottom of the plane. And, turning north, we took the time over the same object in the same manner. Then with simple mathematics the speed could be calculated.

To do this we had to open a two-foot trap door. The strong wind coming up through it quickly numbed the face of the observer. It

Continued on Page Three.

Commons' Bars Offer Vodka; M. P.'s Prefer Beer and Whisky

Wireless to THE NEW YORK TIMES.

LONDON, Dec. 3.—Whether it was a bit of internationalism following the English-Russian rapproachment or just keeping up with the Joneses of the Mayfair hotels, vodka was recently added to the list of beverages available in the various bars in the House of Commons.

But there is no curiosity, let alone thirst, for it among the statesmen. The kitchen committee of the House reports that in the ten days vodka has been on sale there was not a single demand for it.

English beer still holds first place and Scotch whisky second, when members trickle out of the lobby to the bars to drink their private toasts.

FORD RAISES WAGES $19,500,000 A YEAR

Minimum Goes Up to $7 a Day, All American and Canadian Employes Sharing Increase.

PLAN IN EFFECT AT ONCE

New Economies Make Rise Possible, Edsel Ford Says—Linked With Hoover's Moves.

Special to The New York Times.

DETROIT, Mich., Dec. 3.—An annual increase in the pay envelopes of Ford Motor Company employes aggregating more than $19,500,000 was announced today by Edsel Ford, president of the company.

About $15,000,000 of the annual rise will be received by Detroit employes. The increases here are effective as of Dec. 2.

Mr. Ford's announcement reads:

"Ford Motor Company employes of every grade began working under an increase wage scale Monday. The minimum wage was increased from $6 a day to $7. All employes whose wage rate exceeded the minimum wage received an increase in their hourly rate.

Apprentice Wage $6 a Day.

"The probationary or hiring-in wage, which is paid to apprentice employes for the first two months, was raised from $5 a day to $6. In addition to these increases the salary roll was raised 5 per cent.

"It is the third time the Ford Motor Company has raised its minimum wage.

"On the basis of the October payroll, which registered 144,990 employes, the monthly increase will amount to $1,628,451, or slightly in excess of $19,500,000 a year. All Ford branches in the United States and Canada are included.

"Employes raised from $6 to $7 a day numbered 24,320 on the basis of the October payroll. Employes to the number of 113,643 have received increases which bring their daily wage between $7.20 and $10 a day.

"Of this number 27,410 men go to $7.20 a day; 33,396 go men to $7.60 a day; 22,971 go to $8 a day and 12,327 men go to $8.40 a day. Between that rate and $10 a day 17,539 men are affected."

Shares Gain With Workmen.

In a subsequent statement Mr. Ford said, in part:

"We are able to make this wage increase partly because of anticipated economies and the large volume of production which we have had over a period of months, and partly because of our excellent outlook for next year.

"Lately we passed on the benefits of some of our economies to our customers in the form of reduced prices on our cars; and now we share up with our workmen.

"It is our constant policy to do these two things.

"Wage increases cannot be collected from the public, nor can they be taken out of the quality of the production. They have to be made up by better management of the work. That is the way we intend to justify this increase.

"The wage increase from a minimum of $6 a day to $7 is the third major step of the kind taken by the Ford Motor Company since 1914."

No Rise in Car Prices.

"Will this increase in the wage scale involve increased price of Ford cars and trucks and other Ford products?" Mr. Ford was asked.

"Certainly not," he replied. "It is our policy to improve production methods so that along with improved quality of the output we may de-

Continued on Page Eighteen.

Says Liquor Was Found at Polls in Church; Voorhis Would Smell Pitcher to Settle Issue

Following a complaint made by Dr. H. W. Tiffany, pastor of the Baptist Church of the Redeemer at Ocean Avenue and Cortelyou Road, Brooklyn, that liquor had been taken into the basement of the church on election day when it was used as a polling place, the Board of Elections heard evidence on the charges for two hours yesterday and reserved decision.

Dr. Tiffany made his complaint by letter and asked that the Board of Elections remove the name of the church from its list of polling places. He appeared yesterday with Harry W. Maynard, president of the church's board of trustees; Arthur H. Bull and James Clendenning, trustees. All four said they had inspected the pitcher in which a quarter of an inch of liquid was found after election, and all said it was liquor of some sort. They judged it only by smelling it.

The local election board, consisting of Harold O'Connor, Harriet C. Spates, Angelina B. Ashley and Marie L. Kepler, were unanimous in denying that the pitcher contained an intoxicant. Asked to specify what it did contain, some thought it was ginger ale and others believed it was soda water.

The policeman stationed at the polling place, who is described as "Shield Number 13,555, Parkville Station," told the Board of Elections that the liquid was non-intoxicating. Mr. Bull, however, said he and the policeman had smelled it together and had agreed that it was liquor. John R. Voorhis, president of the board, asked for the pitcher, but found that it had not been brought to the hearing. Though not an expert, he remarked, his own sense of smell would settle the issue more quickly than any of the testimony he had heard. The board did not indicate when its decision would be made.

DENIES M'MANUS PHONED ROTHSTEIN ON MURDER NIGHT

Restaurant Cashier Says Voice That Called Gambler to Death Was Not the Defendant's.

ADMITS CHANGING STORY

Police Say They Disregarded All Guests at Hotel Who Heard No Disturbance.

Testimony concerning a voice over the telephone was offered yesterday in the trial of George A. McManus for the murder of Arnold Rothstein. It was the telephone call which the State contends lured the gambler to the Park Central Hotel where he was found fatally shot on the night of Nov. 4, 1928.

Al Scher, youthful, pale and nervous, told of the telephone call. He had been the cashier in Lindy's, a restaurant much frequented by Rothstein, on the night of the shooting. Between 9 and 10 o'clock that night, as nearly as Scher could recall it, he had been at his post.

One of the two telephones rang, Scher said, and he picked up the receiver. The witness was asked to tell the jury what was said, and Scher hitched around, away from General Sessions Judge Nott, toward the jury box. The crowd in the room in the Criminal Court Building stirred.

"Well," said the witness, twining and untwining long fingers, "the party wanted to speak to Arnold Rothstein. I said the 'party's' not in. I said would the party care to leave a message, I'd take it, if so. The party said it was George McManus."

Scher halted there. Assistant District Attorney George N. Brothers, twirling his spectacles, gently prodded him.

"What else?" he asked.

"Well," continued Scher, "the party said 'as soon as Mr. Rothstein comes in tell him to call up Room 349 of the Park Central.'"

Shortly before the witness took the stand James D. C. Murray, attorney for the defense, had conceded that McManus, under the name of George Richards, had rented Room 349. Scher, continuing his evidence, said he had delivered the message to Rothstein. Then Mr. Murray took the witness in hand.

Not McManus's Voice, Witness Says.

"This voice over the telephone," he asked, "did you recognize it as the voice of this defendant, George A. McManus?"

"No, I did not," replied Scher.

"If it had been the voice of George McManus, you would have recognized it, wouldn't you?"

"Yes."

"It was not the voice of McManus, was it?"

"No, it was not."

The lawyer beamed. He had had occasion to smile with satisfaction several times earlier in the session. These occasions had been during testimony which enabled the jury to catch a glimpse of the way the police functioned in the investigation of Rothstein's death. Detective Daly and Detective John F. Cordes had described the investigation.

Flood admitted that a newly married couple, who had occupied Room 347, had heard nothing on the night of the shooting. He said the couple had been in their room at the hour when Rothstein was wounded. Later testimony, however, indicated that the couple had not returned to their room until hours after the shot had been fired.

The defense sought to show that all of the guests on the third floor of the hotel had not been interviewed. Mr. Murray elicited the admission that guests who said they had heard nothing, and whose negative testimony would have aided the

Continued on Page Twenty-four.

SOVIET CANNOT SEE STIMSON NOTE AS A FRIENDLY ACT

Litvinoff's Answer Charges "Unjustifiable Pressure" and Expresses "Amazement."

RESENTS "INTERFERENCE"

Washington Astonished by the Sharp Reply—Stimson at First Gratified by Responses.

While Russo-Chinese negotiators reach an agreement in the Chinese Eastern Railway dispute, Moscow characterizes Stimson peace move as not a friendly act.

Stimson expresses gratification at responses of powers, but is silent on Soviet criticism.

Berlin reserves intervention until later, although expressing sympathy with our move. Paris press is divided in comment. Rome supports our stand and sends note to disputants. Tokio fears ill effects on direct efforts by China and Russia.

Revolt flares up again in Southern China with new drive on Canton, and mutiny in Pukow.

By The Associated Press.

MOSCOW, Dec. 3.—The American note to Russia and China reminding them of their obligations under the Kellogg pact for renunciation of war cannot be considered by the Soviet Government as a friendly act, according to a memorandum handed to Maurice Herbette, French Ambassador, tonight by Maxim Litvinoff, Acting Commissar of Foreign Affairs.

The memorandum was in answer to notes from both the United States and Great Britain, recently delivered to Moscow, the purport of which had found support with most of the nations signatory to the Kellogg pact, with the exception of Japan.

M. Litvinoff emphasized that the United States Government had appealed to that of the Soviet at a time when direct Mukden-Soviet negotiations were being carried on. By strength of this circumstance the American note to Russia was termed an unjustified attempt to influence Chinese-Russian negotiations and consequently could not be considered as a friendly act.

The memorandum said the Manchurian conflict could be settled only by direct negotiations on the basis of conditions already accepted by the Mukden Government and that the Soviet Government would not tolerate any outside interference.

The memorandum concluded with expressing surprise that the United States, which, by its own desire, does not have any official relations with the Soviet Union, should find it possible to give the Soviet Government advice and directions.

Text of Russian Note.

The text of the Russian memorandum follows:

The Union of Soviet Socialist Republics from the first day of its existence has pursued a policy of peace, and unlike other powers has never resorted to military action except as a necessary step for defense due to direct attack on the Union or armed intervention in its internal affairs. The Soviet Union has consistently pursued this policy and intends to pursue it independently of the Paris pact for abolition of war.

During recent years the Nanking Government, evading by its usual methods settlement of the conflict by diplomatic ways, has carried on toward the Soviet Union a provocative policy of violation of the customary rules and treaties, notwithstanding the fact that these treaties were not imposed on China by force, but were concluded on the basis of full equality and free will and that the Soviet Union voluntarily surrendered in these treaties extraterritorial consular jurisdiction and other privileges which the Chinese Government until now has been vainly trying to abolish in regard to other powers.

The climax of this policy was

Continued on Page Two.

PRESIDENT DECLARES BUSINESS SOUND; URGES SPEED ON TARIFF, PLEDGES TAX CUT; FAVORS STRONGER DRY LAW IN MESSAGE

Wall Street Well Pleased With Hoover Message; Stocks Rise Briskly as It Comes Over the Ticker

Wall Street appeared well pleased yesterday with President Hoover's message to Congress. The Street paid particular attention to the sections dealing with revision of the banking laws, the consolidation of railroads and supervision of public utilities. While bankers and industrial leaders declined to comment for quotation, it was quite evident, in banking parlors and brokerage offices, that the message, printed on the Wall Street tickers at midday, had been well received.

Stocks, which had been moderately firm all morning, started forward briskly during the reading of the message and continued their up-swing until the close.

The section of President Hoover's message dealing with the banking system was warmly seconded by members of the banking community, most of whom have felt for some time that an investigation into present-day banking conditions with a view to improving the present banking laws was to be desired.

Some bankers expressed the opinion that such an investigation might reasonably have been undertaken by the Federal Reserve Board, pointing out that that body is in close touch with the banking situation already, and in a position to gather all the necessary data expeditiously.

The suggestion of a Congressional committee, amplified by other "appropriate Federal officials," was looked upon as likely to achieve the same result, but with the possible injection of a political element into the investigation.

Mr. Hoover's approach to the subject was looked upon by bankers as typical of the President's sound attitude toward business and financial affairs. Bankers remarked that it was clear that the President was not attempting to formulate a stand upon the difficult question of group and branch banking, prior to the conduct of an investigation.

SENATORS REFUSE TO DELAY VARE CASE

Move by Reed Defeated, 43 to 31, and Norris Presses His Ousting Motion.

TALK OF GRUNDY FOR SEAT

Capital Circles Hear of Possible Appointment as Democrats Manoeuvre for Post for Wilson.

Special to The New York Times.

WASHINGTON, Dec. 3.—A motion to postpone consideration of the Norris resolution to deny a seat to Senator-elect William S. Vare of Pennsylvania met defeat by 43 to 31 in the Senate today, as the critical action on the Vare issue, which was the first business of the new session after the reading of the President's message.

Mr. Vare's supporters in the Senate privately concede that he has no chance of being seated, and the strategy of the organization Republicans from now on is, not to try to seat Mr. Vare but to unseat him in a way that will make it possible for Governor Fisher of Pennsylvania promptly to name his successor.

This would mean one more administration vote, as the Senate for three years has refused to receive Mr. Vare's credentials.

The test vote came soon after the Norris resolution was called up. Senator Norris said he was willing to postpone action on his motion until next Monday, provided the Senate would enter into a unanimous agreement to proceed that noon to the consideration of any report from the Committee on Privileges and Elections in the matter of the Vare-Wilson contest, the Norris resolution, which is based on the primary and not the general election of 1926, to be considered simultaneously.

Should the committee report be approved, the Senate thereafter would proceed without debate to dispose of the motion to unseat Mr. Vare.

Senator Reed of Pennsylvania, who is leading the Vare side of the fight, said the proposition met with his approval and for a brief time it seemed that the agreement would be entered into.

Borah Puts In Objection.

Senator Borah, however, said he was not ready to agree. Unless debate was limited and a date fixed for the final vote—he suggested Thursday of next week—he would have to object, said Mr. Borah. Unless this was done he could vision a debate that in all probability would continue until the holiday recess.

Senator Bratton of New Mexico, a Democratic member of the Committee on Privileges and Elections, supported Senator Borah. When it was apparent that no agreement was possible Senator Reed put the proposition to postpone before the Senate in the form of a motion.

Meanwhile reports from Harrisburg, Pa., that Joseph R. Grundy, who recently appeared before the committee that is investigating lobby activities on the tariff bill, would be appointed Senator by Governor Fisher of Pennsylvania in case Mr. Vare was ousted, attracted almost as much attention at the Capitol as the

Continued on Page Fifteen.

VIEWS ON MESSAGE DIVERGE SHARPLY

Insurgent Republicans Declare President Fails to Clarify the Tariff Situation.

REGULARS VOICE PRAISE

Drys Commend Stand on Law Enforcement—Wets See Admission of Failure.

Special to The New York Times.

WASHINGTON, Dec. 3.—Comment on President Hoover's message varied today according to the commentator's sympathy with the particular blocs or groups which have been striving either to gain or keep control of Congress. By members of each of these certain parts of the document were taken as complete vindication of the attitude of the group on the questions which have made the cleavage.

Insurgent Western Republicans of the Senate could see "nothing new" in the President's tariff views, while their opponents praised it as "a clear and concise statement" of the problems of the nation.

In the House the message was praised as a "statesmanlike" document by the administration's legislative leader, Speaker Longworth, but Representative Garner of Texas, the Democratic floor leader, interpreted it as a step toward a "commission form of government."

Wet leaders, such as Messrs. La Guardia of New York and Linthicum of Maryland, construed the reference to prohibition as an admission that the present law has failed, while drys of both parties cheered the remarks directed at law enforcement.

Among the comments were the following:

Speaker Longworth—It shows his wonderful grasp of affairs, both national and international, and his knowledge of pressing problems. His suggestions were sane and sound and I regard it as a great statesmanlike document.

Senator Watson—The President discusses the real, worth-while things in his annual message. I think that most of the items mentioned will receive the hearty approval of a majority of the members of Congress. His suggestions for reorganization of the executive departments are in accordance with recommendations on this subject made by some of his predecessors. His proposal to consolidate all activities of prohibition enforcement in one department is wise. The time has come when that should be done. It should have been done before. He asks for the creation of commissions to deal with a number of questions of importance. This feature of the message will receive earnest consideration. Without attempting to dictate, the President has outlined a program of legislation that is certain to make a good impression on Congress.

Senator Moses—The message is long, comprehensive and worth while.

Senator Robinson, Minority Floor Leader — With respect to the

Continued on Page Twenty-seven.

DOCUMENT HAS WIDE RANGE

Tells Congress Business Stability Parleys Gave New Confidence.

PRESSES FOR RAIL MERGERS

Transfer of Prohibition to the Attorney General Part of Reorganization Plan.

ROOT FORMULA ADVOCATED

On That Basis, the President Calls for Adherence to the World Court.

By RICHARD V. OULAHAN.
Special to The New York Times.

WASHINGTON, Dec. 3. President Hoover's first annual message to Congress, "on the state of the Union," read in the Senate and the House this afternoon, is crowded with recommendations and suggestions that will furnish the foundation of much controversy during the regular legislative session which was begun yesterday.

The President's first comprehensive survey of the domestic and international position of the United States since he entered the White House concerned himself principally with dealing with the problems of growth and progress which, he declared, confront the new session of Congress. Reviewing the recent White House conferences with leading financiers, railway presidents, business men, labor and farm leaders, the President referred to the country's sound economic position and the steps needed to maintain prosperity.

"I am convinced that through these measures we have re-established confidence," he said. "Wages should remain stable. A very large degree of industrial unemployment and suffering which would otherwise have occurred has been prevented. Agricultural prices have reflected the returning confidence. The measures taken must be vigorously pursued until normal conditions are restored."

Outstanding among his recommendations are an immediate tax reduction of 1 per cent on both individual and corporate incomes for the calendar year 1929, so as to cut $160,000,000 off the income taxes to be paid in 1930; legislation to expedite the consolidation of railroads and completion of the pending tariff bill in accordance with his recommendations for a "limited" revision.

For Revised Law on Chain Banks.

The President recommended a revision of the national banking laws to care for altered conditions growing out of chain banking; the expansion of the American merchant marine through the awarding of mail contracts on fourteen new routes, calling for 460,000 tons of new ships at a cost of $250,000,000; an immediate increase in the inland waterways appropriations from $50,000,000 to $55,000,000 annually, and a start on the reorganization of the government departments, including concentration of the prohibition enforcement machinery in the Department of Justice.

Among the other recommendations of the President were adherence to the World Court after the adoption of the "Root formula"; strengthening the administration of the prohibition laws; ratification of the settlement of the debt of France to the United States; and the establishment of a "full-time" Federal power commission.

Studies looking to reduction of a "continuously mounting" military outlay and a general revision of air mail rates "upon a more systematic and permanent footing" were urged.

Although Senators and Representatives have not had opportunity to give matured consideration to the President's proposals, already it is apparent that a spirited battle is to be waged over his recommendation that the investigation and enforcement functions of the prohibition unit be transferred from the Treasury to the Department of Justice.

Likewise, there will be opposition to the President's contention that the only practical way his desire to reorganize the government departments can be made effective quickly is to give him broad power, such as was conferred on President Wilson in the World War period, to transfer bureaus and other agencies from one department to another as

Continued on Page Twenty-six.

"All the News That's Fit to Print."

The New York Times.

LATE CITY EDITION
POSTSCRIPT
WEATHER—Fair today; tomorrow rain; not much temperature change.
Temperatures Yesterday—Max., 44; Min., 37.

VOL. LXXXI....No. 27,066. ***** + NEW YORK, WEDNESDAY, MARCH 2, 1932. TWO CENTS In New York City | THREE CENTS Within 200 Miles | FOUR CENTS Elsewhere Except 7th and 8th Postal Zones

JAPANESE ROUTING CHINESE IN FIERCE SHANGHAI BATTLE; DEATH TOLL EXCEEDS 2,000

WHOLE CHINESE LINE FLEES

Pressure From North of Fresh Japanese Troops Forces Quick Move.

PURSUERS LEFT BEHIND

Tachang, Miaoshin and Chapei Fall Before Advance Made Behind Smoke Screen.

TRUCE EXPECTED AT ONCE

Chinese Are Stunned by Sudden Blow—Say Retreat Meets Terms of Japanese.

By HALLETT ABEND.
Wireless to THE NEW YORK TIMES.

SHANGHAI, Wednesday, March 2.—The Chinese were routed this morning by the Japanese in the most sanguinary battle since the World War.

The Japanese killed and wounded before 10 o'clock admittedly exceeded 250. Yesterday's advance in this region totaled two kilometers (more than a mile) and the Japanese losses up to midnight officially were admitted to be slightly in excess of 300 killed and wounded, while the bodies of 1,800 Chinese soldiers were discovered this morning on the ground won yesterday.

Brief reports from General Kenkichi Ueda's headquarters report that the Chinese retreat is degenerating into an utter, panicky rout and the rapid Japanese advance is finding difficulty in maintaining contact with the fast fleeing Chinese soldiers.

The pall of smoke from burning Chinese villages and towns was thickening over Shanghai. Immense exultation was manifested in Japanese circles and the Chinese were stunned by the suddenness and magnitude of the military disaster.

The Japanese captured Tachang at 12:30 today.

Chinese in Pell Mell Retreat.

Early this afternoon the Japanese forces were rapidly approaching from beyond Taching and the Chinese were in pellmell retreat. There was great confusion at Nantao, where Chinese soldiers were attempting to evacuate in railway trains to Hangchow.

The Nineteenth Route Army has voluntarily withdrawn from Chapei, is abandoning other fronts and concentrating at Chenju, according to official oral notification given at 12:30 by the secretary of Mayor Wu Te-chen to United States Consul General Edwin S. Cunningham in his capacity as senior consul.

This withdrawal, the official notification said, also means the evacuation of all Chinese soldiers from Nantao ad Lunghua, but Mr. Cunningham was assured there was danger of disorders at Nantao because 2,000 regular police and 600 picked volunteers already have taken over the maintenance of law and order. It is understood that Chinese will not attempt to police Chapei, declaring "that is dependent upon the Japanese."

Truce Expected Soon.

Presumably the crumpling of the Nineteenth Route Army will be quickly followed by the signing of a truce and by further retirement of the Chinese forces, since Chenju is inside the twenty-kilometer zone which the Japanese insist must be evacuated.

Between 7:30 and 10 o'clock this morning the Japanese had pushed forward to within two kilometres of Tachang. A vast area was being bombed and shelled with unparalleled intensity and the region was dimmed with smoke from huge conflagrations.

The Chinese began the day's hostilities by using two batteries of big guns, firing from Chapei into the Japanese naval headquarters area in Hongkew Park, where many large fires are now burning. For an hour and a half the Chinese batteries kept the city rocking and the roar of their detonations made sleep impossible.

The Japanese had made exceedingly important gains at 10 o'clock toward Tachang, although the terrain is even more difficult than around Kiangwan, with a multitude of vertical banked creeks and sloughs

Continued on Page Twelve.

Settlement Stores Reopen And Shoppers Flock to Them

Special Cable to THE NEW YORK TIMES.

SHANGHAI, March 1.—Acting upon the request of General Tsai Ting-chai three of the largest Chinese-owned department stores on the Nanking Road of the International Settlement reopened today and many smaller stores and shops followed suit. This action contributed largely to a return to approximate normalcy in general business conditions.

SHANGHAI, March 1 (AP).—Stores and offices in the International Settlement reopened today and bargain hunters turned out in droves.

The three big department stores were crowded with shoppers, but the service staff was considerably depleted. Many of the clerks used to live in Chapei and Hongkew and nobody knows where they are now.

JAPAN WILL OFFER NEW TRUCE TERMS

Accepts League Proposal for Armistice at Shanghai With Reservations.

CHINA AFFIRMS AGREEMENT

Plans for Special Assembly at Geneva Tomorrow Await Outcome of Negotiations.

By CLARENCE K. STREIT.
Special Cable to THE NEW YORK TIMES.

GENEVA, March 1.—Naotake Sato this evening gave Joseph Paul-Boncour, President of the League Council, Tokyo's definite acceptance of the latter's so-called "President's plan" for a Shanghai truce and a round-table discussion. Mr. Sato added that the "details"—which is to say, the truce—were to be worked out in Shanghai. Later he confirmed his oral communication in a brief note.

The note merely said Japan was "happy to accept the plan the President has submitted. It mentioned none of the reservations which Mr. Sato gave M. Paul-Boncour orally regarding the details of the truce to be settled on the spot, apparently because Japan thought the terms of the "President's plan" included such reservations.

At any rate, these reservations not merely still stand, but it is understood Mr. Sato explained to M. Paul-Boncour that Japan, instead of accepting Admiral Kelly's armistice terms, was making a counter-proposal.

The United States delegation preferred to reserve comment on Tokyo's reply.

Diplomatic Move Seen.

There is a suspicion in Chinese and Soviet circles that, if Japan does really accept the truce terms, she will then try to win through diplomacy what she failed to win on the battlefield by seeking to have the boundaries of the International Settlement at Shanghai extended to include some districts largely populated by Japanese. There is nothing, certainly, in either the "President's plan" or Mr. Sato's declaration yesterday to prevent such a manoeuvre, for they bar merely any concession or move which exclusively favors the Japanese.

The wording of the second point of the president's plan" and the whole of Mr. Sato's declaration, especially the third point, appear to some to be designed to facilitate such a plan by their references to strengthening the international character of the Settlement.

The Chinese appear to regard the United States as the only one in the group on which they can count not to take advantage of the present situation to try to block China's old fight on the whole question of extraterritoriality.

New Settlement Status Hinted.

There is also some significant, although still vague, talk of the need of improving the status of the Shanghai International Settlement and possibly of putting it under League jurisdiction, like Danzig.

Although the skepticism here is pointed chiefly toward Japan, some are skeptical too of the Chinese Government being able to keep its troops to the terms of the armistice.

Pending definite developments with regard to the armistice and the

Continued on Page Thirteen.

145 in House Force Vote on Dry Law Test; Texan, Last Signer, Rolls Up in Wheelchair

Special to THE NEW YORK TIMES.

WASHINGTON, March 1.—An outright vote on whether the House shall consider a proposal to return liquor control to the States was assured today when the necessary 145 members had signed a petition to cite the Judiciary Committee for discharge from further study of the measure.

The vote probably will be taken on March 14, the first "discharge" day on the calendar.

The wets hailed it as the greatest day since prohibition when the last signature necessary was obtained soon after noon. The 145th member affixing his signature was Representative Mansfield, Texas Democrat. Mr. Mansfield, who is crippled, rolled up to the desk in his wheel chair, while Representative Blanton, Democrat, of Texas, a militant dry, was on his feet chiding the wets for their "failure" to get the required signatures.

The House was set into an uproar when at that moment it was found that Mr. Mansfield, from Mr. Banton's own State, had made the "wet failure" a literal "howling success." Some observers were quick to remark that March 2 is the Independence Day of Texas, the anniversary of its Declaration of Independence from Mexico.

Representative La Guardia of New York, a wet, was taking Mr. Blanton to task for his remarks when the news was broadcast that Mr. Mansfield had signed.

"Any time that this House has the experience of seeing the distinguished gentleman from Texas (Mr. Blanton) get unduly excited," Mr. La

Continued on Page Two.

SALES TAX ACCEPTED BY ADMINISTRATION, MILLS ANNOUNCES

Secretary Pledges Cooperation on New Bill Despite Changes in Treasury Plan.

$625,000,000 NOW IS GOAL

Basis for Manufacturers' Levy Is Widened as Subcommittee Completes Draft.

Special to THE NEW YORK TIMES.

WASHINGTON, March 1.—Acceptance by the administration of the new tax measure, including a general sales tax applicable to practically every manufacturing industry in the country, was assured today by Secretary Mills.

Mr. Mills told a Ways and Means subcommittee that, even though the original treasury plan had been changed at nearly every major point, the administration would cooperate to the fullest extent in setting in motion and administering the new tax increases.

The subcommittee completed the new tax bill, excepting one or two minor administrative features, this afternoon.

The manufacturers' tax provisions, as agreed on, exempt only a few articles, chiefly commodities for the "poor man's breakfast table" and his daily paper, and the farmer's products, his magazines and periodicals.

The final meeting of the subcommittee resulted in a decision to recommend an even wider base for the manufacturers' levy. Yesterday the subcommittee tentatively agreed to frame the tax so as to produce around $550,000,000 in additional revenue. Today it decided to extend the scope so as to produce $625,000,000.

The additions to the sales tax base were understood to have been made by adding commodities which were being held "in reserve" for special excises.

Members of the subcommittee declined to discuss details, but it was the prevailing idea that gasoline and industrial alcohol had been included in their definition of "manufactured products."

If this is true, gasoline and industrial alcohol would be subject to the 2 per cent general tax instead of the special excises of one cent a gallon as proposed originally.

Agree on Excess Levies.

Final decision on the special excise levies was reached today. Committeemen likewise declined to discuss these, holding that to mention them would be to let loose an "avalanche" of protests on members of Congress.

Other excises most prominently mentioned in discussions of the measure were a 5 to 10 per cent consumers' levy on electric energy and illuminating gas; a tax on oil, with a differential upward on oil imports, and an increase of 3 cents a share on stock transfers.

The bill probably will be presented to the full Ways and Means Committee tomorrow afternoon and may be offered to the House for action by Saturday night, according to Representative Crisp of Georgia, acting chairman.

Actual passage in the House by the end of next week was the confident hope of authors of the measure.

Representative Crisp, fatigued from his strenuous work on the bill, was buoyed in spirit today with the hope that it might even be introduced in the House tomorrow. He will offer the measure as soon as the Ways and Means Committee has agreed to it. It will then be referred back to the committee, which immediately will go through the routine of making a formal report.

Being a revenue bill, it will have priority in the House and, according to Mr. Crisp, will be called up as soon as possible for action.

He mentioned next Tuesday as a

Continued on Page Four.

SENATE BODY ACTS FOR BROAD INQUIRY ON SHORT SELLING

Banking Committee Will Go Beyond Hoover Idea in Stock Exchange Investigation.

EFFECTS ON TRADE SOUGHT

Subcommittee Named to Go Into Long and Short Sales and Interstate Phase.

Special to THE NEW YORK TIMES.

WASHINGTON, March 1.—An investigation of the New York Stock Exchange was recommended today by the Senate Banking and Currency Committee. A subcommittee, headed by Senator Walcott, Republican, of Connecticut, immediately began drafting a resolution requesting authority for such an investigation from the Senate.

The subcommittee was instructed by the full committee to include in the resolution authorizations covering studies of both long and short selling, the effect of speculation on interstate commerce, the use of interstate communications systems by speculators and the value of a proposed stock transfer tax as a check on speculation.

This decision went far beyond the action believed to have been requested by President Hoover Friday when he called Senator Walcott to the White House for a conference on "bear raiding." No intimation of an investigation of trading other than short selling has come from the White House.

The subcommittee was chosen after an executive session, during which the committee members argued the constitutional right of the Senate to investigate the Stock Exchange.

The full committee finally agreed generally that such authority does exist, and the subcommittee, charged with considering this point in more detail, reached the same conclusion late this afternoon.

Regulation Not Contemplated Now.

Leading members of the full committee, including Senator Walcott, indicated that no regulatory measure affecting the Stock Exchange is contemplated at this time. The committee intends to run to the ground rumors about the Stock Exchange and, if questionable practices are found, to suggest means of correcting them, preferably through the action of the governors of the Stock Exchange itself.

"I hope this will not result in Federal legislation," Senator Walcott told newspaper men. "We have no legislative plans. However, the committee feels that if we can by investigation persuade the Stock Exchange to draw such regulations as will abolish bear raids, bull raids and dangerous pool operations, then we will have done the country good service.

"There is not a man on that committee who wants the Stock Exchange abolished. But we want to see what abuses exist. There is so much talk about the Exchange, and we are just as anxious to clear the Stock Exchange of any unwarranted misrepresentations as we are to uncover abuses in security dealings."

The subcommittee was appointed by Senator Norbeck, Republican, of North Dakota, chairman of the full committee, who named Senators Steiwer, Republican, of Oregon, and Bulkley, Democrat, of Ohio, to serve with Senator Walcott.

What sides were taken by committee members on the question of constitutionality was not revealed, but Senator Norbeck said that eventually "almost every member agreed there is authority under some provision or other." The principal point at issue was whether the Stock Exchange could be considered as engaging in interstate commerce or whether its business should be considered as confined to New York.

The committee's executive session

Continued on Page Thirteen.

LINDBERGH BABY KIDNAPPED FROM HOME OF PARENTS ON FARM NEAR PRINCETON; TAKEN FROM HIS CRIB; WIDE SEARCH ON

FOUR STATES JOIN HUNT

Wire Systems Flash Out Alarm on First Word of Kidnapping.

NEW YORK CAR IS SOUGHT

Roads Are Scoured for Pair Said to Have Inquired Way to the Lindbergh Home.

AUTOS STOPPED ON ROAD

Hunt Here Is Led by Mulrooney—Underworld Haunts Visited in Scores of Cities.

The Baby's Description.

HOPEWELL, N. J., March 2 (AP).—A chubby, golden-haired boy closely resembling his famous father—that is the description given Charles Augustus Lindbergh Jr.

He is 20 months old, has blue eyes, curly hair, fair complexion. He is about normal size for a child his age. He has just begun to toddle and is learning to talk.

At 10:40 o'clock last night Colonel Charles A. Lindbergh telephoned the New Jersey State Police Headquarters at Trenton that his son had been kidnapped from the Lindbergh home in Hopewell, N. J. Within ten minutes every communication method of modern science had been utilized to broadcast the alarm and to mobilize the police systems of four States and scores of communities in the search.

Colonel Lindbergh had scarcely poured out his tale when the vast machinery of cooperating police systems began to function. While one man was calling the State police barracks at Lambertville, N. J., ten miles from Hopewell, on the telephone, another was writing out this message to be flashed over the police teletype system:

"Colonel Lindbergh's baby kidnapped from Lindbergh home at Hopewell between 7:30 and 10 P. M. Boy, 19 months, dressed in sleeping suit. Search all cars."

Pair in Stolen Car Hunted.

Shortly before 1 o'clock this morning the Princeton Police Department sent over the network of wires the first message containing anything approaching a definite clue. It read as follows:

"Information received that two men in blue or black sedan bearing New York license plates stopped a man working on highway and asked to be directed to the Lindbergh home in Hopewell."

Relayed to every outpost, this message gave the searchers their first indication of the possible description of the kidnappers' car. It was so vague, however, that they did not permit it to stop them from questioning the occupants of cars of other descriptions.

As the first alarm was being typed out the telephone connection with the Lambertville barracks had been established and Lieutenant Arthur Keaten, in command of that post, had been informed of the situation. With every man who could be spared, he started at once for Hopewell.

Upon their arrival Corporal Joseph Wolf, at Lieutenant Keaten's direction, telephoned back confirmation of the kidnapping, but he was not at that time able to add further details to the few which had been furnished by Colonel Lindbergh.

Meanwhile picked detectives were sent on the rounds of known underworld haunts to see if they could pick up any clues as to the identity of the kidnappers.

Window Found Open.

An open window in the nursery of the Lindbergh home at Hopewell indicated how the kidnappers had gained entrance to the house. A close watch has been kept on the baby since it was born, but apparently no member of the family dreamed of the possibility of a kidnapping and no one remained in the nursery last night after the nurse had placed the child in his crib and made sure he was asleep.

The small force under Lieutenant Keaten at once began a careful search of the woody areas surrounding the Lindbergh home, on the possibility of uncovering some clue to the

Continued on Page Three.

© The Misses Selby.

The Lindbergh baby photographed a year ago. Left to right are Mrs. Dwight W. Morrow, the baby's grandmother; Mrs. Charles Cutler Long, the great-grandmother; Charles Augustus Lindbergh Jr., and Mrs. Charles A. Lindbergh, his mother.

KIDNAPPING OF BABY SPEEDS FEDERAL LAW

Demand in Capital for Statute Providing Death Penalty Expected to Increase.

OFFICIALS HINDERED NOW

Can Act in Almost Any Other Interstate Crime—Patterson Assails "Filthy Act."

Special to THE NEW YORK TIMES.

WASHINGTON, Wednesday, March 2.—Immediate pressure for early passage of the measure making kidnapping a Federal offense is held certain to be the result of the kidnapping of Colonel Lindbergh's son.

Senator Patterson of Missouri recently introduced a bill to this effect. It provides a death penalty. The measure would give authority to the government when the kidnapped person is removed from one State to another. The bill was approved unanimously two weeks ago by the Senate Judiciary Committee and its supporters are confident that it will be adopted by the Senate.

A companion bill introduced by Representative Cochran of Missouri, chairman of the Committee on Expenditures, has been before the Judiciary Committee in that branch for about ten days. The hearings were scheduled for completion soon and the portents, before this morning's news, were for a favorable report.

Patterson Denounces Crime.

"It is a shock to me to hear of this outrage," said Mr. Patterson this morning when informed by THE NEW YORK TIMES. "I hope the child will soon be returned to its parents. This filthy act will aid us in passing the needed legislation, and I am sorry it will not be retroactive, so that the Lindbergh kidnappers can be dealt with by the Federal Government."

On Jan. 23 a telephone message was received by Senator Patterson from Chicago to the effect that there was a plot to kidnap General Charles G. Dawes, who had just been appointed president of the Reconstruction Finance Corporation. Mr. Patterson then said that this information came from a newspaper correspondent. It created excitement in Washington official circles, although the General refused to take it seriously. However, it spurred the efforts of those behind the legislation.

Action Urged in Chicago.

As a result, when the House Judiciary Committee began hearings, Colonel Isham Randolph of Chicago, head of the "Secret Six" of that city, and former Representative Cleveland A. Newton of St. Louis came to Washington to urge early action. Mr. Newton gave the following list of kidnappings which he said had

Continued on Page Three.

FATHER SEARCHES GROUNDS FOR CHILD

Lindbergh and Troopers Hunt With Flashlights for Clues on Big Estate.

NEWS ROUSES COUNTRYSIDE

Hundreds of Autos Rush to the Home in Lonely Woodland, Clogging Narrow Road.

Copyrighted, 1932, by The Associated Press.

HOPEWELL, N. J., Wednesday, March 2.—Charles Augustus Lindbergh Jr., 20-month-old son of the flying Colonel, was kidnapped last night from his nursery in the Lindbergh country home near here. The child, clad in a blue sleeping robe, was put to bed at the usual hour, 7:30 P. M. At about 10 P. M. someone peered into the nursery. The crib was empty.

Beneath the nursery window, footprints showed in the soft earth. These indicated that the kidnappers, moving with such stealth that the Lindberghs, although in the house, heard no sound, had removed their shoes before climbing a ladder to the window. The trail of the shoeless footprints was followed by The Associated Press reporter to the rutted lane, where police believe a waiting car was parked. Feminine footprints, as well as those of a man, were found.

The first news the Lindberghs had of the crime was when the frightened nurse ran downstairs, screaming that the baby had been kidnapped.

The first newspaper man to reach the home was an Associated Press reporter, who ran a mile over muddy, rut-cut roads to reach a phone to send the first direct news from the residence. This was at 12:40 A. M.

Colonel Lindbergh, bare-headed as usual, was pacing the grounds, while troopers and detectives went over the place with flashlights, seeking clues.

Mrs. Lindbergh, who telephoned the news to her mother, Mrs. Dwight W. Morrow, at the Morrow home in Englewood, N. J., was inside the house. A close friend of Mrs. Lindbergh said she was expecting another child within three months.

The house, glowing with lights from top to bottom, was the only bright spot in the wooded, gloomy district. Wishing to get complete privacy, the Lindberghs picked the site from the air and it is almost inaccessible to the outside world. A winding, muddy lane—their private property—leads to the new house from a country highway, called the Stoutsberg-Worstville Road. The entrance to the Lindbergh road is more than four miles from Hopewell and there are few neighbors near enough to be of any aid in time of

Continued on Page Three.

CHILD STOLEN IN EVENING

At 10 P. M. Nurse Finds Boy, 20 Months Old, Gone, in Nightrobe.

FOOTPRINTS IN THE ROOM

Muddy Trail Leads to Ladder in Wood and Half Mile to Highway, Where Car Waited.

WOMAN BELIEVED INVOLVED

Parents, Distraught, Guarded in Home—Police Deny Report of Ransom Note.

Charles Augustus Lindbergh Jr., 20-month-old son of Colonel and Mrs. Charles A. Lindbergh, was kidnapped between 8:30 and 10 o'clock last night from his crib in the nursery on the second floor of his parents' home at Hopewell, near Princeton, N. J.

Apparently the kidnapping was carried out either while Colonel and Mrs. Lindbergh were at dinner, or soon afterward. The baby's nurse, Miss Betty Gow, visited the nursery about 8:30 o'clock and found everything in order there. When she returned at 10 o'clock, however, the crib was empty.

Muddy footprints that trailed across the floor from the crib to an open window bore mute testimony as to how the baby had disappeared. Miss Gow dashed downstairs. "The baby's been kidnapped!" she shouted. Colonel Lindbergh raced to the nursery, followed closely by his wife. Mrs. Lindbergh recalled that earlier in the day she had tried to fasten a screen on the window that had been opened and had been unable to do so.

Satisfied that there was no mistake and that the baby actually was gone, Colonel Lindbergh telephoned Chief of Police Charles Williamson at Hopewell. Williamson drove to the house accompanied by another officer. Outside the door they met the Colonel. He was bareheaded, and wearing an old black leather jacket such as he frequently wears on his flights.

Footprints Under Window.

Briefly he told Williamson what had occurred. The chief telephoned first to State Police Headquarters at Trenton. Then he, his fellow officer and the Colonel began searching the grounds. Beneath the nursery window were marks where a ladder had stood and the footprints of one person. There were no shoe prints. The kidnapper, apparently, had worn socks or moccasins.

Sixty feet away in rocky ground at the edge of a wood the Colonel and Chief Williamson found a makeshift ladder. Its rungs were caked with mud. Colonel Lindbergh could not say whether it belonged on the premises. He thought it might have been left there by the builders while the house was being constructed during his flight to the Orient last Summer with Mrs. Lindbergh.

The searchers had no difficulty in following the footprints across the muddy ground. A second set of tracks joined them near the edge of the woods. They were much smaller. The two officers thought they might be those of a woman.

The search was interrupted by the arrival of a detachment of State Troopers sent from the barracks at Lambertville and the hunt began anew. The tracks were followed to the main highway, about half a mile from the house, where they disappeared. The kidnappers evidently had entered an automobile at that point.

Lindbergh Aids Search.

Carrying a flashlight, Colonel Lindbergh stayed with the searching party until long after midnight. Once or twice he returned to the house, but he declined to discuss the kidnapping with newspapermen. Instead, he referred them to Major Schoeffel of the State Police, who told the story in detail.

"I hope you boys will excuse me,"

Continued on Page Three.

"All the News That's Fit to Print."

The New York Times.

LATE CITY EDITION
WEATHER—Thunder showers and cooler today; tomorrow fair.
Temperatures Yesterday—Max., 86; Min., 69.

VOL. LXXXI....No. 27,215. Entered as Second-Class Matter, Postoffice, New York, N. Y. NEW YORK, FRIDAY, JULY 29, 1932. * * * *,+ TWO CENTS In New York City | THREE CENTS Within 200 Miles | FOUR CENTS Elsewhere Except in 7th and 8th Postal Zones

TROOPS DRIVE VETERANS FROM CAPITAL; FIRE CAMPS THERE AND AT ANACOSTIA; 1 KILLED, SCORES HURT IN DAY OF STRIFE

WALKER REPLY A DENIAL OF ALL SEABURY CHARGES; CALLS 10 OF 15 OUTLAWED

GOVERNOR TO ACT QUICKLY

Turns Answer Over to His Advisers—New Move Expected in Week.

POLITICAL PLOT IS CHARGED

Mayor Says He Is the Victim of a Campaign of Calumny to Aid Hoover Regime.

DEFENDS EQUITABLE DEALS

Declares Men Who Gave Him Cash Got No Favors—Denies Sherwood Was Agent.

The text of Mayor's reply to Gov. Roosevelt, Pages 6, 7 and 8.

Terming himself the victim of political misrepresentation, and insisting that his entire official life would bear the closest scrutiny, Mayor Walker filed with Governor Roosevelt yesterday his answer to the removal charges pending against him as the result of allegations first made by Samuel Seabury, counsel to the Hofstadter committee.

The Mayor's answer, a 27,000-word document, contained specific denials of wrongdoing in connection with the Equitable Bus franchise, the receipt of securities from brokerage firms interested in taxicab legislation, the "beneficences" of Paul Block, publisher, or the huge bank accounts of Russell T. Sherwood, missing accountant. The document came from the printers yesterday forenoon, and was given at once to Thomas F. McAndrews, the Mayor's secretary, who carried it by train to the Governor at Albany.

Mr. Roosevelt, after scrutinizing it briefly, released the reply for publication. A conference between the Governor and his two legal advisers, Martin Conboy of New York and John E. Mack of Poughkeepsie, will probably be held in the near future, it was indicated, to determine the next step in the removal case that, it is held, cannot but affect the political fortunes of Mr. Roosevelt as the Democratic Presidential nominee.

Seabury Is Denounced.

In form the Mayor's answer consisted of an attack upon Mr. Seabury and the Hofstadter committee, before which the evidence against the Mayor was developed, followed by a point-by-point reply to the allegations made by Mr. Seabury and subsequently embodied in charges filed with the Governor by William Jay Schieffelin, head of the New York Committee of One Thousand.

Two appendices contained an answer to the separate and supplementary charges filed by James E. Finegan, Brooklyn Democrat, and legal citations and details on financial transactions covered in the main body of the answer.

Most of the legal citations were to support the Mayor's assertion that ten of the fifteen allegations advanced by Mr. Seabury related to a previous term in office, and therefore could not be made the basis of action at present by the Governor. The answer, however, also replied in detail to these allegations.

Mayor Walker did not mention Mr. Seabury's statement that the Mayor had a "metallic receptacle" in his home, where he put cash received in stock and bond deals, nor did he mention the "unnamed person" said to have received payments from both the Mayor and from Sherwood.

The payments to the unnamed person were stressed at committee hearings as tending to prove a connection between the bank accounts of Sherwood and the Mayor. Mr. Walker in his reply denied Sherwood was his financial agent.

Calls Inquiry Political Plot.

The Mayor declared that the Hofstadter committee was organized and Mr. Seabury retained as counsel "to carry out a deliberate plan of calumny" in the hope of discrediting the Democratic administration of New York City. He accused Mr. Seabury of conducting a "manhunt," and declared the counsel would have fixed upon any Democratic Mayor of New York as a victim, in order to divert attention from the shortcom-

Continued on Page Eight.

Walker Hastens to Saranac; Gets Word Brother Is Worse

Mayor Walker left on a midnight train for Saranac Lake last night, after he had received a call at City Hall informing him that the condition of his brother, George F. Walker, had taken a sudden turn for the worse.

The brother, the youngest of the three Walker brothers, has been a patient at a Saranac sanitarium for several months, and in the past few days his condition has been a source of worry to the Mayor. A request had been made at City Hall, however, that no publicity be given to the illness of the Mayor's brother, until developments forced it.

George Walker is 48 years old, is married, and has two children. He is in the insurance business, being a member of the firm of Hughes & Walker of 27 William Street.

COOLIDGE EXPECTED TO AID HOOVER DRIVE

Sanders to Spend Week-End at Former President's Vermont Home for Political Talk.

NO EASTERN MANAGER YET

Senator Hebert Is Likely to Be Named to Run Campaign in This Section.

The probability that former President Calvin Coolidge will aid President Hoover in his campaign for reelection was indicated yesterday when Everett Sanders, chairman of the Republican National Committee, said that he would visit Mr. Coolidge Saturday and Sunday at the Coolidge homestead at Plymouth Notch, Vt., and expected to discuss the political situation with him.

Mr. Sanders, who was secretary to Mr. Coolidge when he was President, declined to be definite, because the invitation to visit his former chief came before he had been elected national chairman.

"I have no doubt he will take some part in the campaign," Mr. Sanders said, when asked if he expected Mr. Coolidge to make some campaign speeches for the President.

Mr. Sanders said that there had been no selection yet of an Eastern campaign manager and indicated that the choice was between Senator Felix Hebert of Rhode Island and Earl S. Kinsley, national committeeman from Vermont. From other sources it was learned that Senator Hebert probably would be named. Should Senator Hebert not be named for this post he will be the Eastern campaign manager for the Republican Senatorial Committee, Mr. Sanders said.

Mr. Sanders also indicated that General Edward Martin, who was under consideration for Eastern campaign manager, had found his duties in Pennsylvania too exacting to take on additional responsibility. General Martin, besides being active in military affairs, is the Pennsylvania State treasurer and chairman of the Republican State Committee.

Mr. Sanders had a luncheon conference with W. Kingsland Macy, New York State Republican chairman, and earlier in the day conferred with Charles D. Hilles, national committeeman, and former Governor Henry J. Allen of Kansas, publicity director of the national committee.

Asked to make a prediction on New York State, Mr. Sanders said:

"I am very confident that the President will be re-elected, but I do not wish to discuss his chance of carrying the different States."

One point of difficulty in the Republican campaign situation in this State has been cleared up by the recent visit to Washington of Mr. Macy and conferences here with Mr. Sanders, as a result of which it has been decided that the Republican State Committee will be in complete charge of the campaign in this State and that there will be no Hoover campaign committee as there was in 1928.

Sought to Supersede Macy.

Members of the so-called Hooverite group in this State suggested the reestablishment of the Hoover campaign committee and some members of the group went so far as to make suggestions which, if adopted, virtually would have put the officers of the proposed Hoover campaign committee in charge of the campaign and

Continued on Page Thirteen.

Thousands Crowding Into Los Angeles For Opening of Olympic Games Tomorrow

By ALLISON DANZIG.
Special to THE NEW YORK TIMES.

LOS ANGELES, July 28.—The biggest migration to California since the Forty-niners wrote an imperishable story of man's courage in braving the perils of the unknown has made Los Angeles the cosmopolitan capital of the world.

Not for a pot of gold at the end of the covered wagon trail has this world exodus to the jewel city of Southern California taken place, but for the tenth revival of the Olympic Games, which begin here on Saturday, with approximately 2,000 representatives of thirty-eight countries competing in an athletic plant that dwarfs the imagination, along with the coliseums and stadiums of the ancient Greeks and Romans.

Already, with the spectacular grand opening parade forty-eight hours away, there are thousands of visitors encamped in Los Angeles and its environs.

By railroad, plane, ship and motor car they continue to pour into the city and no one knows what sagas of enterprise and fortitude are being written on the national highways by athletic zealots who have seized upon the most desperately dilapidated means of conveyance to bring them to the games.

Los Angeles, festooned and bedecked with flags, streamers and banners of welcome to all within its domain, is assimilating this tremendous influx of people in the same ample fashion that it has prepared, over a period of nine years, to stage this tremendous athletic carnival, the first Olympiad to be held in this country since 1904.

With its enormous hotel capacity, it is well prepared to accommodate the great burden of humanity resting within its confines and thus far there is no overcrowding or dearth of reservations.

So far as it has been possible to ascertain, there has been no mark-up in the rates for rooms, nor have prices in the restaurants or else-

Continued on Page Nineteen.

BRITAIN ASKS EMPIRE FOR MORE PURCHASES TO BALANCE HER AID

Baldwin Says United Kingdom Imports Exceeded Exports by £95,700,000 in 1930.

RHODESIA FILES DEMAND

British In Drive at Ottawa to Capture United States Sales of Machinery in Canada.

The text of Britain's trade statement is on Page 10.

By CHARLES A. SELDEN.
Special to THE NEW YORK TIMES.

OTTAWA, July 28.—Two more cards were placed face-up on the Imperial Economic Conference table today when Stanley Baldwin, leader of the British delegation, presented a statement plainly intimating to the dominions that in his opinion they were lagging behind the United Kingdom in the mutual exchange of trade benefits and H. W. Moffatt, spokesman for Southern Rhodesia, filed a request that Britain help his country by buying more of its cattle.

The statement of the United Kingdom contained neither threat nor promise of what Great Britain would or would not do after the dominions have agreed upon what they can or cannot do for the mother country. It confined itself to what the United Kingdom already had done for the rest of the empire and showed by figures that she was buying from them annually £100,000,000 worth of goods in excess of what they were buying from her.

Advantages Are Contrasted.

Mr. Baldwin called attention to the fact that practically all of the dominion products were admitted to the ports of Great Britain free of duty, whereas British exports to the dominions had only the benefit of preferences. Although the preferences are much better than nothing, Mr. Baldwin considers them far less of a boon than free entry. He spoke particularly of the fact that even preferences may be based on tariffs so high that they restrict imports.

He did not refer to the fact, fully and painfully realized at Ottawa by all the dominion delegations, that after Nov. 15 the United Kingdom may deprive them of all the benefits of free entry which the empire countries now enjoy by simply applying to them the new British tariff act. That is England's trump card at this conference, which she may play to get from the dominions the trade concessions and preferences she thinks are just and fair.

Although no threats were made today nor even hinted, the British statement added nothing to the harmony of the conference and no doubt the dominions considered it as a rebuke, which they all think undeserved in spite of the figures that support it.

Denies Witholding Assistance.

Perhaps Stanley M. Bruce, leader of the Australian delegation, felt personally rebuked. He told the conference the other day that Great Britain had been tardy in recognition of all the preferences the dominions had given her. No doubt Mr. Baldwin had that remark definitely in mind today when he said:

"Any suggestion that the United Kingdom has been backward in developing or assisting dominion trade or that the concessions on the side of the dominions have not been fully reciprocated, both in the letter and

Continued on Page Ten.

HERRIOT PROTESTS SCHLEICHER SPEECH; EDITORS ATTACK IT

Premier Summons Germany's Envoy to Tell Him Arms Talk Disturbs France.

CITES HIS FRIENDLY POLICY

Description of French Stand as "Hypocritical" Results in Bitter Resentment.

By P. J. PHILIP.
Wireless to THE NEW YORK TIMES.

PARIS, July 28.—Premier Edouard Herriot summoned the German Ambassador, Dr. Leopold von Hoesch, to the Quai d'Orsay today to explain to him vigorously that the French people are considerably disturbed by the terms of Lieut. Gen. Kurt von Schleicher's radio speech Tuesday evening, in which he gave notice that Germany would arm, if necessary, contrary to the provisions of the Versailles treaty, and also attacked France.

M. Herriot's protest was the second the Reich Government has received in two days, for Ambassador André François-Poncet called at the Wilhelmstrasse in Berlin yesterday to make formal denial of some statements made by the German Defense Minister.

In the Paris press the substance of General von Schleicher's statement is the subject of strong comment today, but all that either Premier Herriot or the French Ambassador could do was to point out that its form was distinctly impolitic, not to say impolite.

Says He Went Too Far.

Even in the midst of the German electoral period, M. Herriot is believed to have told Dr. von Hoesch that it was going too far for a Minister of the Reich to make such a speech only a few weeks after the conclusion of the Lausanne agreement, in which France showed the utmost generosity to Germany and had abandoned all claim to further reparations payments.

It was even less opportune, it was pointed out, for the German Defense Minister to speak as he did within twenty-four hours of the time when

Continued on Page Eleven.

Stocks Rise Again in Year's Heaviest Trading; 2,735,635 Shares Sold, Leaders Up 1 to 4 Points

Invigorated by fresh optimism, the security markets made another broad advance yesterday. The day's transactions in stocks on the New York Stock Exchange totaled 2,735,635 shares, which represented the heaviest trading since Dec. 18 of last year. The net gains in market leaders ranged from 1 to 4 points, while there were scattered advances of 6 points or more.

In the bond market the net gains were widest among domestic corporation issues, running from 3 to 10 points in the conspicuously strong favorites. The extreme gain of 10 points occurred in Schulco 6½s, due in 1946, Series B. United Biscuit 6s, due 1942, were up 6½ points, Purity Bakeries 5s, due 1948, were up 6 points; Allis Chalmers 5s, due 1937, gained 4¼; Atchison, Topeka & Santa Fe bonds showed a maximum gain of 6 points; Atlantic Coast Line issues advanced as much as 7 points and Bethlehem Steel 5s of 1936 rose 4¾ points. Dealings in bonds were the heaviest in a month.

Aside from a further demonstration of strength in commodities, the development which contributed most to the cheerfulness in Wall Street was a spectacular rise of the dollar in terms of foreign currencies which reflected the further reinforcement of the gold position of the United States. Sterling fell 2¾ cents, while the French franc was off 7-16 point. All the other Continental currencies except the mark, which was unchanged, lost ground.

The upswing in stock prices was most striking in the forenoon. Profit-taking at midday and in the last hour reduced the early gains to some extent, but final prices showed substantial net appreciation in the average. For instance, Allied Chemical was up 3 points on the day; American Telephone, the market leader, closed with a net gain of 4⅝ points after falling more than a point from its high; Santa Fe preferred was up 4¼ points and the common 2⅜, Bangor & Aroostook 7½, Detroit Edison 10, du Pont 2¾, Norfolk & Western 3¾ and Eastman 1⅝. United States Steel common touched a high of 28½, but closed at 27⅝ with a small fractional gain. Steel preferred was up ¾ point after falling 2 points from its high.

Bank stocks again advanced vigorously, the bid price of First National showing a gain of 25 points and that of the Fifth Avenue 40 points.

ANACOSTIA CAMP NO MORE

Troops Move Into Last Bonus Army Refuge as Flames Start.

AND FINISH DESTRUCTION

Marchers Stream Away, Some in Broken-Down Autos, Some Trudging Afoot.

FEW KNEW WHITHER TO GO

At Midnight the Former Home of 20,000 of Bonus Army Is Held by the Military.

Special to THE NEW YORK TIMES.

WASHINGTON, July 28.—Flames rose high over the desolate Anacostia flats at midnight tonight and a pitiful stream of refugee veterans of the World War walked out of their home of the past two months, going they knew not where.

Cavalry stood guard at all the bridges leading across the river to the camp and thousands of onlookers gazed across the river at what had been the teeming residence of 20,000 persons.

The veterans were leaving at the behest of the military forces of the government, summoned by the President after collisions between the bonus marchers and the police. Some were departing in broken-down automobiles; some, on foot, dragged listlessly in search of new quarters.

Flames were raging in the camp. Many of the tents, numbering 2,100 and mostly belonging to the army, were ablaze and the infantry was busy trying to salvage as many as possible.

A heavy barrage of tear gas, laid down by the troops, penetrated to the houses for blocks around, and residents were forced to close their doors and windows in spite of the sweltering heat.

Had Thirty Minutes to Evacuate.

It was soon after 9 o'clock tonight that the troops, headed by General MacArthur, surrounded the main camp of the Bonus Expeditionary Force at Anacostia, wheeled their tanks into position, unlimbered their gas bombs and gave the thousands of veterans massed there thirty minutes in which to evacuate. They then sat down waiting for the order to be obeyed.

The spirit of the veterans seemed broken. Leaderless and aghast at the failure of their confident prediction that no soldier would go into action against them, they moved their women and children out of the camp and prepared to leave themselves.

General MacArthur and his staff followed the first troop of cavalry into the flat at Anacostia through a road leading off from the bridge.

Several veterans, as they heard the troops approach, set fire to improvised huts. The glow from the

Continued on Page Three.

Text of Hoover's Statement on Call for Troops To Put an End to Bonus Rioting in the Capital

Special to THE NEW YORK TIMES.

WASHINGTON, July 28.—The text of President Hoover's statement explaining his action in calling out troops to combat the bonus rioters is as follows:

For some days police authorities and Treasury officials have been endeavoring to persuade the so-called bonus marchers to evacuate certain buildings which they were occupying without permission.

These buildings are on sites where government construction is in progress and their demolition was necessary in order to extend employment in the district and to carry forward the government's construction program.

This morning the occupants of these buildings were notified to evacuate and at the request of the police did evacuate the buildings concerned. Thereafter, however, several thousand men from different camps marched in and attacked the police with brickbats and otherwise injuring several policemen, one probably fatally.

I have received the attached letter from the Commissioners of the District of Columbia, stating that they can no longer preserve law and order in the district.

In order to put an end to this rioting and defiance of civil authority, I have asked the army to assist the District authorities to restore order.

Congress made provision for the return home of the so-called bonus marchers, who have for many weeks been given every opportunity of free assembly, free speech and free petition to the Congress. Some 5,000 took advantage of this arrangement and have returned to their homes. An examination of a large number of names discloses the fact that a considerable part of those remaining are not veterans; many are Communists and persons with criminal records.

The veterans amongst these numbers are no doubt unaware of the character of their companions and are being led into violence which no government can tolerate.

I have asked the Attorney General to investigate the whole incident and to cooperate with the District civil authorities in such measures against leaders and rioters as may be necessary.

[The text of the letter from the District Commissioners to the President is printed elsewhere.]

BOMBS AND SABRES WIN CAPITAL BATTLE

Cavalry, Infantry and Tanks, Advancing as Gas Spreads, Swiftly Drive Veterans.

SHACKS BURN BEHIND THEM

Bayonets Clear the Section of Squatters, Who Are Ringed Finally by 1,500 Soldiers.

Special to THE NEW YORK TIMES.

WASHINGTON, July 28.—The Federal troops came out today and cleared Washington proper of the members of the Bonus Expeditionary Force. The contonments, the "forts" in the unused Federal buildings, the huts that the men themselves had built, were evacuated by the veterans when they found themselves faced with tear-gas bombs, bayonets and tanks.

The regulars had the equipment to do the job, the equipment that the Capitol Police had lacked and they had the orders to do it. The irregulars of the bonus army had only their stubborn sullenness in most cases and bricks, rocks and epithets in others and the fight did not last long.

Down Pennsylvania Avenue at 4:30 this afternoon the regulars came, cavalry leading the way, and after them the tanks, the machine-gunners and the infantry. For them the objective was the "fort" of the B. E. F., in the skeletonized building at Third Street.

There was a wait for maybe half an hour while the army officers talked it over with the police and the bonus marchers shouted defiance. They wanted action, and they got it.

Steady Sweep Down Avenue.

Twenty steel-helmeted soldiers led the way, with revolvers in their hands, and others advanced until about 200 were in position in front of the "bonus fort." Then the mounted men joined. They rode down street, clearing the path with their sabers, striking those within reach with the flat of the blades.

The action was precise, well executed from a military standpoint, but not pretty to the thoughtful in the crowd. There were those who resisted the troops, fought, cursed and kicked at the horses; there were those who scrambled for safety and those who tried to rescue their meager belongings from the fort.

Inch by inch, foot by foot, they were forced down Pennsylvania Avenue as the soldiers headed them toward Anacostia camp. They left in their path those who had been knocked over, and one passive resister, who sat down and waited unscathed while the storm blew over his head.

The success of the movement, the

Continued on Page Three.

B.E.F. TO CARRY ON, WATERS DECLARES

Men Will Organize Elsewhere if Driven From Capital, Commander Says.

WHITE HOUSE IS ASSAILED

'Political Interests' Cost a Life, He Charges, Admitting He Has Lost Control.

By The Associated Press.

WASHINGTON, July 28.—Walter W. Waters, titular commander of the "Bonus Expeditionary Force," declared tonight that "no matter what may happen from now on, the B. E. F. will carry on."

"If driven from Washington, it will organize elsewhere and continue the fight for justice for the veterans and the common people of the United States" he said in a statement. "We have gone too far now to quit."

The Waters declaration, telephoned to newspaper offices, included the assertion that a life was sacrificed "to serve the political interests of the administration."

The one-time dictator of the bonus army watched from the sidelines while the men who formerly paid him allegiance swept completely out of his control.

Before Federal troops arrived to push former service men off their encampments in front of a cloud of tear gas, "Commander" Waters threw up his hands in a gesture of defeat. He said frankly that he no longer had any control over the men.

Accompanied by a handful of his aides, Waters viewed from the sidewalks about the trouble-ridden area the swiftly breaking developments, which resulted in the death of a war veteran.

Just before arrival of the troops, he went to a small restaurant on Pennsylvania Avenue for a cup of coffee.

Asked about the day's happenings he replied:

"The men got completely out of control. There was nothing and is nothing I can do to control them."

In his statement later he said:

"Every drop of blood shed today or that may be shed in days to come as the result of today's events can be laid directly on the threshold of the White House.

"The B. E. F. had been organized on strictly American lines of respect for law and order and is pledged to uphold American institutions.

"They were under strictest orders to conduct themselves in orderly manner in the event of attempted

Continued on Page Two.

HOOVER ORDERS EVICTION

Blaming Reds, He Asserts Bonus Camps Included Many Criminals.

QUICK ACTION BY SOLDIERS

Eject Squatters After Police Fail and Then Burn Camps in and Near Capital.

BONUS ARMY SCATTERED

Demoralized by Soldiers' Gas Attack, Remnants Are Left Leaderless and Helpless.

Special to THE NEW YORK TIMES.

WASHINGTON, July 28.—Amidst scenes reminiscent of the mopping-up of a town in the World War, Federal troops late today drove the army of bonus seekers from the shanty village near Pennsylvania Avenue in which the veterans had been entrenched for months. Earlier in the day the police had fought and lost a battle there which resulted in the death of one veteran, possibly fatal injuries to a policeman and a long list of other casualties, many of them serious.

Ordered to the scene by President Hoover after the District of Columbia authorities confessed defeat, detachments of infantry, cavalry, machine-gun and tank crews laid down an effective tear-gas barrage which disorganized the bonus-seekers, and then set fire to the shacks and tents left behind by the veterans on the government land near Third and Pennsylvania Avenues, scene of the earlier clash with the police.

Begin to Clear Anacostia.

After the disputed area near the Capitol had been cleared, the troops moved late in the evening on Camp Marks, on the Anacostia River, the bonus army's principal encampment. At 10 o'clock this evening infantrymen with drawn bayonets advanced into the camp, driving the crowd before them with tear gas bombs. Then they applied the torch to the shacks in which the veterans lived.

Troops shortly afterward halted at the main bonus camp in response to what General Perry L. Miles, commanding the soldiers, said was a Presidential order. Theodore G. Joslin, the President's secretary, later denied positively that the President had issued any such order, and word came from the camp that the troops would resume operations within an hour.

At 11:15 P. M. the first troop of cavalry had moved into the disordered camp, now a mass of flames as the bonus-seeking veterans set fire to their own miserable shacks. At midnight practically all the veterans had left the place.

Warned that the soldiers would use tear gas the veterans had arranged to evacuate the 600 women and children earlier.

The normal population of Camp Marks was augmented by more than 2,000 veterans who had been evicted from other camps, bringing the total male population to 7,000.

Troops Avoid Bloodshed.

Soon after the khaki-clad regulars descended on the various camps along Pennsylvania Avenue this afternoon the bonus seekers were straggling sullenly away from the ominous blue mist of the tear gas, leaderless and apparently demoralized, seeking shelter in other open places scattered afar through the city. A few of them were sore from minor bruises, but on the whole the Federal troops had conducted their offensive without bloodshed. The veteran who was killed in the earlier clash with the police was identified tonight as William Hashka of Chicago.

The day's disturbances were blamed on the radical element among the bonus-seekers. Walter W. Waters, the young veteran from Oregon who led the unsuccessful bonus march to Washington, disclaimed responsibility for his followers' part in resisting the first eviction order of the police. Waters announced tonight that he was "through."

"The men got out of control. There was nothing and there is nothing that I can do to control them," he said.

With the bonus army in the city

Continued on Page Two.

"All the News That's Fit to Print."

The New York Times.

LATE CITY EDITION
WEATHER—Rain and warmer today; tomorrow fair and colder.
Temperatures Yesterday—Max., 40; min., 35.

VOL. LXXXII....No. 27,450. Entered as Second-Class Matter, Postoffice, New York, N. Y. NEW YORK, TUESDAY, MARCH 21, 1933. P TWO CENTS In New York City. | THREE CENTS Within 200 Miles | FOUR CENTS Elsewhere Except In 7th and 8th Postal Zones

REICHSTAG MEETING TODAY IS PREPARED TO GIVE HITLER FULL CONTROL AS DICTATOR

RULE TILL 1937 SOUGHT

Bill Bars Legislation by Deputies Unless They Are Invited to Act.

HITLER TO DRAW UP LAWS

Constitution Is Not to Apply to Them—Adjournment by the End of Week Is Likely.

EINSTEIN'S HOME IS RAIDED

Arms Search Brings Forth Only a Breadknife—Jewish Judges and Doctors Are Ousted.

By GUIDO ENDERIS.
Special Cable to THE NEW YORK TIMES.

BERLIN, March 20.—It was announced tonight, on the eve of the convocation of the new Reichstag, that the Hitler government would ask it for dictatorial powers lasting until April 1, 1937, or until the replacement of the present Legislature by another.

By the terms of the draft of an empowering act sent to the Reichstag tonight, that body is to be excluded from legislation entirely unless the Cabinet invites its cooperation and the government is to have the right to promulgate laws and decrees outside the channels prescribed by the Constitution, even if they conflict with its provisions.

As the government holds a majority, the passage of the bill is assured, and the Reichstag is expected to adjourn before the end of the week, the measure enabling the Cabinet to carry on without it for at least six months.

The bill contains five articles. The first empowers the government to make laws, including budget laws and loan-authorization laws, and the second says that these loans may deviate from the Constitution in so far as they do not affect the Reichstag and Reichsrat. The rights of the President remain unchanged.

Hitler to Draw Up Laws.

The third article provides that the laws made by the government shall be drawn up by the Chancellor, be promulgated in the Legal Gazette and take effect the following day.

Articles LXVIII to LXXVII of the Constitution are not to apply to these laws. These articles comprise the whole section of the Constitution specifying the manner of legislation, including the Reichsrat's power of caveat, the procedure for submitting bills to a national plebiscite, the requiring of a two-thirds majority of two-thirds of the Reichstag's membership for constitutional amendments, the President's duty of proclamation and his power of calling for a plebiscite, &c.

This article would exclude the Reichstag from legislative work entirely unless their cooperation were invited by the government, and also stipulates that Chancellor Hitler's signature shall suffice in future for the laws of the Reich, which have hitherto been signed by the President.

The fourth article declares that treaties with foreign States relating to objects of Federal legislation shall not require the consent of the legislative bodies for the period of the bill's validity, while the fifth provides that the bill is to take effect with its promulgation and lapse April 1, 1937, or before that, if the present Reichstag is replaced by another.

The Reichstag will be convoked at noon tomorrow in the old Church of the Garrison in Potsdam, where Frederick the Great is buried, and President von Hindenburg will attend the ceremony.

At 5 o'clock in the afternoon the Deputies will meet in the Kroll Opera House in Berlin to organize, as the chamber in the Reichstag Building has not yet been restored following the fire that gutted it a month ago.

Government Has 52% Backing.

This Reichstag is one chosen by popular suffrage, but under profoundly altered conditions from any obtaining in the numerous parliamentary elections in Germany since the World War. Its dominant National Socialist-Nationalist majority

Continued on Page Eleven.

Nazis to Put Bavarian Foes in Concentration Camp; 'Republican Army' Leaders to Be Held With Reds

Special Cable to THE NEW YORK TIMES.

MUNICH, March 20.—Chief of Police Himmler of Munich today informed newspaper men here that the first of several concentration camps will be established near this city soon for the detention of thousands of Communists, Marxists and leaders of the Reichsbanner organization.

He explained that in the long run it would be impossible to hold in jail those who would be arrested and to release them would only mean renewed agitation. Such measures as were planned, he added, must be carried out without any petty scruples.

He also announced that the Socialist press in Bavaria would remain suppressed until April 4.

In the process of putting Bavaria under the control of the government at Berlin there has been a sweeping campaign against all the leaders of the Left parties and reports have indicated that the arrests have run into thousands. In particular the new authorities undertook to break up the Reichsbanner, the army formed by the republican elements as an offset to the monarchists and the Nazi brown shirts. This organization has been ordered dissolved throughout Germany.

The problem of keeping the vast number of political prisoners led Dr. Wilhelm Frick, Minister of the Interior, to announce recently that they would be put in concentration camps and kept at hard labor.

JEWS HERE DEMAND WASHINGTON ACTION

National Leaders Ask "Proper Representations" to Berlin on Anti-Semitic Activities.

OTHER FAITHS TO PROTEST

Statement Being Drafted for Federation of Churches and Interfaith Committee.

The American Jewish Committee, of which Dr. Cyrus Adler is president, and the B'nai B'rith, Jewish fraternal organization headed by Alfred M. Cohen, announced last night that they had requested the United States Government "to make proper representations to the government of Germany" against the persecutions of Jews under the régime of Adolf Hitler.

The announcement was part of a statement signed jointly by Dr. Adler and Mr. Cohen after a meeting of the executive committee of the American Jewish Committee and representatives of the B'nai B'rith. The statement denounced the acts of oppression and persecution being practiced by Hitler bands against Jews as "medieval barbarism," and it appealed to enlightened public opinion in Germany and to "the conscience of the world" against "conduct unworthy of the traditions and ideals of the German people." The statement pledged the organizations behind it "to every possible measure" to ameliorate the sufferings of the Jews of Germany, but at the same time urged that such efforts "must be intelligent and reasonable."

"Prejudice must not be fought merely with appeals to passion and resentment," the statement declared.

It was reported also that efforts were being made by the American Jewish Committee to prevail upon Premier Mussolini of Italy to bring friendly pressure to bear upon the Hitler government to desist from further persecution of Jews and anti-Semitic propaganda. No confirmation regarding these efforts was obtainable, however. Neither Dr. Adler nor former Justice Joseph M. Proskauer, a member of the American Jewish Committee, would comment on this aspect of the situation.

Statement of Protest.

Following is the text of the statement of the American Jewish Committee and the B'nai B'rith:

The American Jewish committee and the B'nai B'rith express their horror at the anti-Jewish action in Germany which is denying to German Jews the fundamental rights of every human being in a spirit contrary to the traditions of American freedom of conscience, religion and liberty. The events of the past few weeks in Germany have filled with indignation not only American Jews, but also Americans of every other faith. The conscience of the civilized world is aroused against this reversion to medieval barbarism.

The pseudo-scientific race theories offered in support of this propaganda are a profound insult and offense to the entire Jewish people of the world, and the Jews

Continued on Page Ten.

BRITAIN SUSPENDS SOVIET TRADE TALKS

Halts Treaty Negotiations In Protest Against Arrest of Engineers.

TORIES CHEER THE MOVE

Shout Down Labor Leader in Parliament When He Tries to Put Questions.

By CHARLES A. SELDEN.
Wireless to THE NEW YORK TIMES.

LONDON, March 20.—There were cheers in the House of Commons today when Captain Anthony Eden, Under-Secretary for Foreign Affairs, made the expected announcement that the British Government had halted negotiations with the Soviet Government for a new trade treaty because of the arrests of British engineers in Russia.

The temper of the House was further indicated when George Lansbury, leader of the Labor Opposition, was shouted down by Conservatives when he asked questions implying that he thought there might be some justice in the Russian side of the case. Captain Eden had termed the charges against the British defendants unjustifiable, but he also said it had been impossible to learn from the Soviet authorities what the charges were.

Questions Put by Lansbury.

The Under-Secretary had also made the point that the four prisoners were not going to be allowed to have British lawyers to defend them if they were brought to trial. Mr. Lansbury asked, first, how the British Government could know the charges were unjustifiable if the government did not know what the charges were. His second question was:

"Would Russians arrested in England be allowed to have Russian lawyers in a British court?"

There was no answer to either of these questions.

But the chief point of interest in London tonight was that there might not be any trial at all. That much was implied not only by Captain Eden's expression in the House of Commons, "if a trial is held," but by his emphasis on those words. There seems to be ground for the belief in London that the British Government's actual carrying out of its threat to discontinue trade negotiations has had the desired effect upon the Soviet Government and that the Ogpu (Soviet political police) is getting ready to back down.

Eden Statement.

Captain Eden's statement in Parliament follows:

"The premises of the Metropolitan-Vickers Company in Leningrad were entered on the night of March 11 by Soviet authorities, who seized papers, mostly personal letters. I regret to state that, apart from Allan Monkhouse and Charles Nordwall, whose provisional release was announced in the House of Commons March 15, the other four British subjects arrested are still in custody, and, as far as I am aware, Ambassador Ovey has not been given an opportunity for a private interview with them.

"His Excellency has been in-

Continued on Page Twelve.

Sale of Billions in Baby Bonds to Public May Refund Treasury's Short Term Debt

Sweeping changes in the United States Treasury financing calculated to eliminate the great dependence on banks entailed by an unwieldy amount of short-term debt and to enlist the support of private investors, large and small, may be adopted at once by the Roosevelt administration, according to reports in financial circles yesterday.

In all probability bonds to be issued by the Treasury will include denominations as small as $20 and $50, a factor which can be counted on to aid materially in combating hoarding. In this connection it is pointed out that with a reawakening of national consciousness in time of adversity a proper response could be obtained if direct appeal were made by the new administration.

A nationwide drive, reminiscent of the Liberty Loan campaigns, is envisioned to have individuals displace banks as the principal creditors of the Treasury and to place the government's debt on a more permanent basis. Use of the postoffices, postal savings system and other governmental agencies to facilitate sales directly to investors is believed to be under consideration. The bonds would meet the requirements of the permanent investor and would be priced attractively.

During the last year or two the short-term debt of the Treasury has piled up at such a rapid rate that the refunding has been almost a weekly order of business. Little effort has been made in banking circles to gainsay the charge that this Treasury financing had been cut to order for the banks, as it dovetailed closely with the banks' need for liquidity. With the Treasury relying to a great degree on banks to

Continued on Page Three.

M'DONALD REVEALS ROME PEACE PLAN COVERS ALL EUROPE

British Premier Says Italian Proposal Would Not Use Force on Small Nations.

TREATY REVISION IS SEEN

French Are Divided on Move to Upset Their Policy—Cabinet Gets Details Today.

By ARNALDO CORTESI.
Wireless to THE NEW YORK TIMES.

ROME, March 20.—Prime Minister MacDonald of Great Britain revealed today, before departing for Paris, that the Mussolini peace plan will not be limited to the great powers of Europe, but will include all nations of Western Europe and perhaps Russia. He said the United States would be informed of all steps.

Mr. MacDonald discussed his week-end conference with the Italian Premier for half an hour with newspaper correspondents. Premier Mussolini was to have met the foreign correspondents in the morning, but cancelled the engagement. His views so far are limited to the official announcement yesterday that they "examined the project for an understanding on the larger political questions with the object of obtaining collaboration of the four Western powers."

Plan to Unite All Europe.

"No treaty was concluded, nor anything like a treaty," said Mr. MacDonald today. "Nor is there any truth in the report that a disarmament truce was decided. These are not intelligent anticipations.

"Our whole idea has been to open up the possibility of an enlightened agreement between all countries of Europe. We are not proceeding on the idea of making an agreement between four nations and then imposing it on the others. On the contrary, all the nations must participate in the elaboration of whatever agreement is reached and everything must be done in such a way that they will be satisfied with the results.

"What we have in mind is to create conditions necessary for real peace. This is, necessarily, an evolutionary process. What we are aiming at is not an imposed peace but a negotiated peace arising from the satisfaction of all countries that are in a position to disturb the peace.

"The change must be gradual. We cannot go like a bull at a gate, but must handle the European situation in such a way as to pacify Europe. This is very difficult because the various questions cannot be dealt with individually, but it is necessary to tackle the whole situation at the same time.

Considers Europe as Unit.

"It must be borne in mind that the situation of Europe must be considered as a unit, with all its dangers and also all its support as unities, for it must not be forgotten that though the situation holds many dangers it also holds many opportunities. The fundamental problem is to create a group of minds working for the common good and peace.

"We are fully aware of the tremendous difficulty in the task undertaken and are proceeding by degrees. We would like to make Europe a better, safer place tomorrow, but must reckon with human nature. We must take human nature as we find it.

"We must think of Europe as a whole and must think of the world. We must fit our several nationalisms into the picture of the whole world, of which we are a part.

"The change we have in mind will not be brought about rapidly. We will proceed as quickly as we

Continued on Page Eight.

MAYOR ACTS TO OUST SCHROEDER AT ONCE; M'KAY ALSO TO GO

Will Ask Action Friday on Bill to Put Sanitation Bureau Under One Man.

TO MERGE WEIGHTS OFFICE

Market Department Will Take Over Work of Official Undc. Fire as Lax.

Dr. William Schroeder Jr., chairman of the Sanitary Commission, and Joseph P. McKay, head of the Bureau of Weights and Measures faced loss of their positions yesterday as Mayor O'Brien moved for the reorganization of both agencies.

The Mayor, without referring to the criticism expressed last week by the City Affairs Committee and Alderman Joseph Clark Baldwin, Republican, on his delay in carrying out his campaign pledges, announced that he would take steps for the reorganization of both units of City Government this week.

He said he would introduce a bill in the Board of Aldermen branch of the Municipal Assembly today to merge the w^ights and measures bureau with the Public Markets Department. He added he would press for passage of a local bill this Friday reducing the Sanitary Commission from three members to one.

The elimination of Dr. Schroeder from city service has been forecast several times since Mayor O'Brien took office. The City Affairs Committee, in a letter last week to the Mayor, urged the removal of Commissioner McKay, basing its request on a report of James A. Higgins, Commissioner of Accounts, which showed many false reports to have been made by bureau inspectors.

McKay's Future in Doubt.

"What will become of Commissioner McKay after his bureau is merged with the Markets Department?" the Mayor was asked.

"There are no vacancies in the Markets Department carrying the rank of commissioner or deputy commissioner," he replied with a smile.

"Does that mean that Mr. McKay will be out of a position when the merger goes through?" was the next question.

"Well, I don't want to talk about that now," the Mayor said.

When it was suggested that Mr. McKay might accept a subordinate position in the Markets Department, the Mayor said:

"I do not know what Mr. McKay wants."

Mr. McKay is a resident of Staten Island and was appointed to his present post by former Mayor Walker in January, 1926. His salary was $9,000, later reduced by the Board of Estimate when general salary cuts were made. He had the support of David S. Rendt, Democratic leader of Richmond, when he obtained his appointment. In the 1930 primary fight he went over to John A. Lynch, Richmond Borough President, who was then opposing Mr. Rendt.

Schroeder Walker's Friend.

Dr. Schroeder, close friend and personal physician to former Mayor Walker, was named by him to head the Sanitary Commission at a salary of $22,500 soon after it was formed in December, 1929. Prior to that appointment, he had been named the first head of the Hospitals Department, reorganized by Mayor Walker in 1928. His salary in that post was $10,000 a year. From the Tammany standpoint, Dr. Schroeder's appointment was a personal appointment by the Mayor as distinguished from an organization appointment. As soon as Mayor Walker resigned, the general feel-

Continued on Page Five.

ROOSEVELT TO SEEK POWER TO DEFER DEBT PAYMENTS; 3.2 BEER PASSAGE ASSURED

Year's Moratorium on Home Foreclosures Voted for the State by the Senate, 44 to 1

Special to THE NEW YORK TIMES.

ALBANY, March 20.—The Senate passed tonight a bill declaring a one-year moratorium on foreclosure of mortgages on homes in the State. The vote was 44 to 1, Senator Walter W. Westall, Republican, of Westchester, voting in the negative.

The bill, introduced by Senator Joseph D. Nunan Jr. of Queens, applies the moratorium only to home-owners, and its only exception is for foreclosures for non-payment of taxes or assessments.

"It is practically the same language as that used in the bills passed by the Legislature giving broad powers on administration of the insurance and banking law," Senator Nunan said.

"It seems only fair to me that the Legislature should now turn its attention to that man who is striving to protect and maintain the savings he has put into his home for his family and himself. He needs relief and he is entitled to relief."

The Senate also passed the bill of President pro tem Dunnigan setting another one-year moratorium on the application of provisions of the multiple-dwelling law requiring changes in old-law tenements except those deemed necessary for fire protection.

Senator Byrnes, chairman of the Agriculture Committee, insisted that this committee would meet in the morning to consider drastic amendments to the Pitcher bill, for rigid State control of the milk industry, including price-fixing.

Senator Wojtkowiak, Democrat, of Erie, introduced a resolution for a Senate investigation of the Dairymen's League, but on objection of Senator Fearon, Republican leader, an attempt to gain immediate adoption failed and it was sent to committee.

3.2 PER CENT BEER PASSED BY SENATE

Conference Accord, Including Wine and Deleting Minors' Clause, Adopted, 43 to 36.

HOUSE TO APPROVE TODAY

Roosevelt Is Expected to Sign Bill by Night—Dry Leaders Appeal to Him for a Veto.

Special to THE NEW YORK TIMES.

WASHINGTON, March 20.—The return of the 4 per cent beer as known before prohibition (3.2 per cent by weight) and wine of the same alcoholic content by early next month seemed assured today when the Senate by a vote of 43 to 36 adopted the conference report on the Cullen bill.

The conference report represented a complete agreement on the three main points at issue. The Senate receded from its amendments reducing the alcoholic content from 3.2 to 3.05 and prohibiting sale to minors under 16 years of age and, in return, the House accepted the proposal to include wines.

The House is expected to approve the agreement early tomorrow, sending the bill to President Roosevelt for his signature. If the President signs tomorrow, the newly legalized beer and wine will be available for distribution on April 5.

Drys Urge a Veto by Roosevelt.

Meantime, an open letter to President Roosevelt urging him to veto the beer bill was sent to the White House by a committee representing the National Conference of Organizations Supporting the Eighteenth Amendment.

In the letter the leading drys of the country contended that Congress had gone further in adopting 3.2 per cent beer than the President had stipulated in his message recommending beer and other beverages "of such alcoholic content as is permissible under the Constitution."

Some dry leaders, however, expecting the measure to become law, indicated that they would wait for actual distribution of the beverages before appealing to the courts for injunctions against sale.

Swift Action in the Senate.

The day's legislative procedure was one of steady progress. The Senate stood by in temporary recess while the conferees worked for an accord. As soon as it had been reached, Senator Harrison took it into the Chamber and moved adoption, and action followed within a short time.

Leaders at first proposed to keep the House in session to vote on the report today. The usual rules require unanimous consent to take up a conference report, which otherwise must lie over a day. Realizing that one or two members surely would object to hasty consideration, and disliking to invoke any drastic procedure, the leaders postponed action until tomorrow.

Only two voices were raised in the Senate against adoption of the report, those of Senator Borah, author of the amendment barring gift or sale of the beverage to

Continued on Page Two.

ROOSEVELT INSISTS ON LONGER SESSION

Tells Congress Leaders Farm, Unemployment and Rail Measures Must Be Passed.

PARLEY AT WHITE HOUSE

Some Senators Demur, but Rainey Says Program Will Be Enacted Before Recess.

Special to THE NEW YORK TIMES.

WASHINGTON, March 20.—President Roosevelt, in conference with Congressional leaders tonight, insisted that farm relief, unemployment relief and railroad consolidation should be the chief additional legislation enacted in the present special session.

His program is to complete these and some minor measures without a recess of Congress in the expectation that an adjournment may be obtained early in May.

This statement was issued by the White House after the conference:

"A most interesting discussion was held between the President and a number of Senators and members of the House of Representatives. The discussion covered many phases of the economic problem.

"The subjects discussed included, among others, farm relief through efforts to raise crop prices and legislation to prevent the foreclosurs of mortgages on both homes and farms; a program to improve and coordinate railroad operations; another program relating to the general problems of transportation, and the immediate unemployment relief efforts divided into three parts—immediate work in national and State forests, government aid to States and a future program of public wor s.

"In the field of banking, correction of existing abuses was discussed."

Those at the Conference.

Those participating in the conference were Vice President Garner, Speaker Rainey, Senators Robinson of Arkansas, the majority leader, McNary, the minority leader; Wheeler, chairman of the Interstate Commerce Committee; Pittman, President pro tempore, and chairman of the Foreign Relations Committee; Harrison, chairman of the Finance Committee Borah and Norris; Representatives Byrns of Tennessee, the majority House leader; McDuffie of Alabama, Snell of New York, the minority House leader; Jones of Texas, chairman of the House Agriculture Committee; Buchanan of Texas, chairman of the Appropriations Committee; Ragon of Arkansas of the Ways and Means Committee, and Lewis Douglas, Director of the Budget.

Representative Doughton of North Carolina is chairman of the Ways and Means Committee, but because of his absence in his home State Representative Ragon represented the committee.

Senators at the conference told the President that it would be impossible to complete such a program by May. Strong opposition, they reported, existed against the farm bill. It was the opinion of the

Continued on Page Two.

TRADE DEALS PLANNED

The President Would Get Right to Negotiate For Debt Cuts.

CONGRESS WOULD 'ADVISE'

Joint Mandate From Senate and House Is the Proposal Under Consideration.

FRENCH PAYMENT NEARER

Daladier Aims to Let Chamber Reverse Course Without Partisan Influences.

By ARTHUR KROCK.
Special to THE NEW YORK TIMES.

WASHINGTON, March 20.—As June 15 approaches, with separate debt discussions with other nations not yet begun or definitely scheduled by the administration, a plan to avert the prospects and consequences of British and French default on that date is taking definite form in the inner councils of the United States Government.

The plan is that the Senate perform the seldom-used constitutional function of "advising" the President in advance of his final war debt and related economic settlements with other powers. On this occasion the House would participate in the passage of a joint or concurrent resolution of "advice," because debt payments relate to the budget, taxation and other aspects of domestic revenue-raising in which the House has initiatory rights.

The advisory Congressional resolution would, of course, be framed by the President, the Secretary of State and administration leaders in Congress, and it would be preceded by an official inquiry from the President, asking for specific advice from Congress on how to deal with the questions of debt-payment deferment and the like.

Would Add Presidential Powers.

It is argued by advocates of this plan—and Mr. Roosevelt is said to be impressed with their reasoning—that the effect of the procedure would be to give the President a broad grant of power in debt negotiations, including the right to suspend payments and prepare a scale of adjustments in exchange for concessions of an economic character from the debtor nations.

A constitutional form would have been scrupulously followed, even though it is one which has been used only in exceptional circumstances. The dignity of Congress would have been preserved. While Congress would really be giving to the President the latitude he wants in terms devised by himself and his executive advisers, the grant would actually come from Congress itself, and it would be very difficult for opponents of the idea to form a strong bloc against the resolution.

The Constitution awards to the Senate joint treaty-making rights and defines its powers as those of "advice" and "consent." The debt settlements in a way are treaties, but, for the reasons stated, the House is a partner in these. When Congress approved the Hoover moratorium it specifically provided that the Executive might make no further concessions or alterations in the debts without the approval of Congress. The point in the new proposal is to get that approval in advance and in terms so broad that Mr. Roosevelt can do almost anything he wants by way of suspension and effective negotiation.

The method of getting advance advice from the Senate was first invoked by President Washington. His first idea was to discuss projected treaties with the Senate orally in advance. This was tried in 1789 with reference to a treaty with the Southern Indians. But the Senate found the procedure unsatisfactory.

Washington Asked Advice.

Therefore Washington began to send special messages asking for advice. Twice in 1790 and twice again in 1792 he sought the Senate's advice on Indian treaties, and in every case the subsequent articles were ratified.

Later in 1792 Washington asked the Senate whether it would approve a treaty with Algiers for the payment of ransom and peace money, not in excess of certain

Continued on Page Nine.

"All the News That's Fit to Print."

The New York Times.

LATE CITY EDITION

WEATHER—Fair today; showers tonight and tomorrow. Temperatures Yesterday—Max., 71; min., 46.

VOL. LXXXII....No. 27,498. Entered as Second-Class Matter, Postoffice, New York, N. Y. NEW YORK, MONDAY, MAY 8, 1933. P TWO CENTS In New York City. | THREE CENTS Within 200 Miles | FOUR CENTS Elsewhere Except In 7th and 8th Postal Zones

LINDBERGHS HELD ALL NIGHT IN WILDS BY A SANDSTORM

Fliers Descend in Swirling Dust to Camp Amid Coyotes in Texas Panhandle.

UNABLE TO SEE 100 FEET

'Better to Sit Down Than Go Through,' Colonel Says Later on Reaching Kansas City.

SLEPT AND DINED IN PLANE

Couple Unaware of Search by Planes and Vigil at Fields—Continue to St. Louis and Columbus.

By The Associated Press.

KANSAS CITY, May 7.—Forced down in a swirling sandstorm, Colonel and Mrs. Charles A. Lindbergh spent last night on the windswept plains of the Texas Panhandle, snuggly protected in their plane, while widespread fears were raised for their safety.

After the storm had subsided, the couple took off from their isolated landing place this morning and arrived in Kansas City at 12:45 P. M., Central Standard Time, dusty and slightly worn, en route to Washington, D. C., from California.

Their arrival brought relief to friends and airmen, who had started a search and kept a vigil at air fields throughout the Southwest.

"I'm sorry," Colonel Lindbergh said. "People shouldn't worry. It's liable to happen any time in the Western country."

After their plane was refueled here, the Lindberghs departed for the East at 2:08 P. M., reached St. Louis at 4 P. M. and then went on to Columbus, Ohio, where they arrived at 8:32 P. M., Eastern Standard Time.

"Better to Sit Down" in Storm.

Regarding the fierce sandstorms of the Southwest, like the one which forced them down "somewhere north of Amarillo," Colonel Lindbergh said:

"It's better to sit down than go through them."

He said the storm struck them with blinding fury two hours after they had headed his red and black monoplane eastward from Albuquerque, N. M., at 3:34 P. M., Mountain Standard Time, yesterday, with a fresh supply of gasoline in continuation of their flight from Glendale, Cal., to the national capital.

Explaining that he was flying far northward of the regular line of the Transcontinental and Western Air, Inc., on a direct hop toward Kansas City, Colonel Lindbergh said that he had hoped to cut southward into the wireless beacon, but that the strength of the storm prevented.

Plane Made Snug Refuge.

Picking the most likely area available, he said he dipped to a safe landing.

"I couldn't walk more than 100 yards from the ship without losing sight of it," he said.

Night fell with dust and sand whistling through the air. But the Lindberghs were ready for emergencies.

"We passed a very comfortable night," said the flier's wife.

The plane was equipped for sleeping, and they had aboard a supply of food sufficient to last thirty days.

The sleeping equipment included a mattress. This was unfolded and placed in the fuselage, the fuselage covering closed, and all was snug for the night. Equipment in the plane is so arranged there is plenty of room for the improvised bed.

Supper and breakfast were eaten at the grounded plane, far from human habitation. They shared the vast spaces with jack rabbits, coyotes and cattle.

Unaware of Anxious Search.

With the storm subsiding, the couple took off about 9:30 A. M., Central Standard Time, for Kansas City, unaware that at least six planes were searching for them, that friends along the way had waited up all night for word and that communication wires were burdened with messages concerning their safety.

Rumors and official reports alike proved groundless as Kansas City friends waited anxiously during the night for the sound of their plane from the Southwest.

Air-line officials received a host of telephone calls asking the whereabouts of the Lindberghs.

"Not a word, sorry, "was the reply most of the night.

Major A. D. Smith, the T. W. A. manager at Albuquerque, directing the New Mexico search for the Lindbergh plane, checked in vain to Amarillo, Texas.

Paul Richter, superintendent of

Continued on Page Three.

Quakers Ask League to Give Passports to German Exiles

Wireless to THE NEW YORK TIMES.

GENEVA, May 7.—The International Quaker Centre has appealed to the Council of the League of Nations to appoint, at its session May 27, a committee to draw up a plan under which all persons without nationality would be placed under the League's protection and would receive Nansen passports, which are now restricted to Russian and Armenian refugees.

The petition says that there are tens of thousands of these persons and their number is constantly increasing because of recent political events, showing that although Germany is not mentioned, the plan is clearly meant to apply to German pacifists and Jews.

Previous efforts to extend the League passports, notably to Italian exiles, have always failed because of the opposition of the Fascist Government.

4 GERMAN NOTABLES SUICIDES IN A DAY

Daughter of Scheidemann and Husband Had Brooded Over Fate of Ex-Chancellor.

WOMAN TENNIS STAR DIES

Former Aide of Hugenberg, Accused of Revolt Against Him, Also Ends Life.

Special Cable to THE NEW YORK TIMES.

LONDON, Monday, May 8.—The London Times this morning publishes the dispatch below which was telephoned last night by its correspondent in Berlin. A similar dispatch filed by the Berlin bureau of THE NEW YORK TIMES was stopped by the Berlin censor under Article VII of the international telegraph code, which permits a government to withhold information inimical to the interests of the State.

BERLIN, May 7.—Frau Katz, daughter of Philipp Scheidemann, the Socialist who proclaimed the German Republic and who is especially unpopular with patriots, was found with her husband dead of gas poisoning in her dwelling in Berlin this morning. They had been brooding over the action of the Nazis in cutting off the pension of Herr Scheidemann, who is ill and in serious financial straits.

Suicides Are Numerous.

Daily charges of corruption against people associated with the former régime are leading to a large number of suicides. The former Mayor of Leer, near Emden, who was the object of such a charge, shot himself this morning, as did a former Democratic town councilor at Stuttgart against whom a warrant of arrest on a charge of corruption had been issued.

Dr. Ernst Oberfohren, who was for three years until recently the parliamentary leader of Dr. Alfred Hugenberg's Nationalist party, committed suicide at his home in Kiel today. He was generally regarded as the leader of those Nationalists who felt that the Nazi allies they had helped into power were having things too much their own way. Apparently he had freely criticized Dr. Hugenberg's leadership of the party.

The ear of the Nazi intelligence

Continued on Page Five.

DEBT TRUCE SOUGHT BY BRITISH AS PRICE OF TARIFF HOLIDAY

London Seems Ready to Block Roosevelt's Plans Pending Action on War Loans.

COUNTER BY US IS DENIED

Davis's Delay of Geneva Trip Was Not to Obstruct Arms Accord, Washington Says.

HE PUSHES FOR DECISION

Will See Runciman Today—But Tories in the Cabinet Do Not Share MacDonald's World View.

By FERDINAND KUHN Jr.
Wireless to THE NEW YORK TIMES.

LONDON, May 7.—The British Government is now awaiting some assurance of a moratorium on war debts before committing itself on President Roosevelt's proposed tariff truce.

Although Prime Minister MacDonald deprecated "haggling" when he was in Washington, his government apparently is quite willing now to use the debts as a bargaining weapon. The British want the war debts brought back to the centre of the economic stage and seem prepared to block Mr. Roosevelt's international plans until that is accomplished.

So far Norman H. Davis, United States Ambassador at Large, has met nothing but polite evasions in his repeated attempts to learn the British attitude. He has met no refusal, but also no acceptance, even with reservations, and has been able to get no explanation of the government's hesitancy. Tomorrow he intends to see Walter Runciman, President of the Board of Trade, in a renewed effort to fathom the government's mind. Even an outright refusal, he feels, would be more enlightening than the present lack of information.

Nationalism in Saddle.

If Congress gives President Roosevelt the powers he seeks it may reassure the British somewhat, but their adherence to a tariff truce will still be doubtful. Deep-seated nationalist convictions going far beyond the debt question are governing the British Cabinet in its attitude toward tariffs and the world conference generally. There is little doubt in the minds of the American negotiators that tariff nationalism is firmly in the saddle here and that Mr. MacDonald's internationalism is not the spirit of those who dominate his government.

The Tories who form a majority of the Cabinet, including so-called Liberals like Sir John Simon, the Foreign Secretary, have little faith in the success of the world conference or in the efficiency of international action to end the depression. They fear the conference is doomed to many months of futility and are unwilling to take the risks that might make it a success. Consequently, they are fortifying Great Britain's independent position by trade agreements like those recently signed with Denmark and Argentina and about to be concluded with other nations in sterling's orbit. The powerful Federation of British Industries has just launched a determined campaign of propaganda to prevent any fur-

Continued on Page Four.

Microscopic Operation on Mosquitoes Yields Malaria Serum to Treat Paresis

By The Associated Press.

WASHINGTON, May 7.—A surgical operation on mosquitoes, so delicate that it must be performed under the microscope, is the latest step in treatment of a dreaded form of human insanity, known as paresis.

The mosquito operation, announced today by the Public Health Service, provides a new method of combating one disease with another. It was described as making possible a more efficient and less costly means of helping paresis sufferers by infecting them with malaria, a treatement used successfully for several years to combat this form of insanity.

Formerly, paresis patients were infected with malaria by allowing them to be bitten by mosquitoes which carried the disease. The malaria has the effect of arresting the progress of the insanity by acting on a blood disease that causes it, and statistics show it has cured 35 per cent of cases that were not too far advanced.

The operation on the mosquitoes consists of removing their salivary glands, which are so small that they cannot be seen until magnified at least twenty times. The malaria germs are carried by the mosquitoes in these glands, and surgeons can use the gland contents to give paresis patients "artificial mosquito bites."

The artificial bites are preferable to real ones, because the glands are made into a serum, easier to ship than live mosquitoes, which sometimes die in transit. The live insects were also difficult to handle and sometimes escaped, with consequent danger of spreading malaria.

The mosquito operation has been developed by Dr. Bruce Mayne of the Public Health Service laboratories at Columbia, S. C. The mosquitoes used are specially bred under sanitary conditions and then allowed to bite persons who have malaria. The mosquito picks up some malaria germs, and these develop in its salivary glands. Then the mosquito is placed under ether, and operated upon.

The glands are removed and made into a serum, which is injected into the veins of paresis patients. One mosquito's glands contain enough malaria germs to inoculate about twelve paresis cases.

The serum keeps well enough at a temperature of 40 to 50 degrees Fahrenheit to allow shipment all over the United States.

All Autos in State Must Have Safety Glass by Jan. 1, 1935

By The Associated Press.

ALBANY, May 7.—Non-shatterable glass will be required in the windows and windshields of all automobiles and buses registered in New York State after Jan. 1, 1935, under a bill signed by Governor Lehman Saturday, just before he left for a fishing trip to Boca Grande, Fla., the executive offices announced tonight.

The "safety glass" will be required in all buses after Jan. 1, 1934, and in both pleasure cars and buses after Jan. 1, 1935. The bill was sponsored in the last Legislature by Assemblyman Jasper W. Cornaire, Jefferson Republican.

A check-up on the bills approved or vetoed by the Executive shows that the Governor and the Legislature made 766 new laws this year. The Legislature left 1,050 measures on the Executive's desk. He signed 766 and vetoed 281. The three others were recalled.

WARFARE RENEWED IN NORTHERN CHINA

Japanese in Peitaiho, South of Great Wall—Native Forces Retreating.

MONARCHIST AGENT SHOT

Gen. Chang Ching-yao, Linked With Restorationists, Is Near Death in Peiping.

By The Associated Press.

PEIPING, Monday, May 8.—Combined Japanese and Manchukuoan forces have pushed Chinese troops eight miles south of Peitaiho, coastal town south of Shanhaikwan and Chinwangtao, foreign legations here were advised today.

Armored trains and heavy shelling of the Chinese were playing a prominent part in the Japanese-Manchukuoan advance. Fighting was reported going on at several points northwest of Peitaiho, where Japanese fliers were conducting bombing raids.

Chinese advices earlier in the day said the Chino-Japanese war south of the Great Wall had been resumed with Japanese troops occupying Peitaiho at 11 P. M. yesterday.

Chinese Warned by Japan.

Chinese forces east of the Lwan River were warned yesterday by the Japanese military authorities that they must evacuate to territory to the west of the Lwan, or the Japanese would launch renewed attacks on Lwanchow. This development in the Chino-Japanese warfare south of the Great Wall was reported in Chinese dispatches.

The general belief was that the impending Japanese offensive would not be confined to the area west of the Lwan, but would include major thrusts at Kupei and Hsifeng passes in the wall, with the aim of completely crushing Chinese forces along the entire wall.

Monarchist General Shot.

Special Cable to THE NEW YORK TIMES.

PEIPING, May 7.—An unidentified assailant entered the Wagons-Lits Hotel today, proceeded to the second floor and shot General Chang Ching-yao, former Governor of Hunan Province, who, the police report, was involved in a North China monarchist restoration movement. General Chang Ching-yao was removed to the German Hospital, where he is expected to die.

The Wagons-Lits Hotel is in the diplomatic quarter of Peiping, a section that hitherto has been considered safe for Chinese political refugees, and many of them have gone there for safety. In this case, however, General Chang's assailant left the hotel unmolested, walked to a waiting automobile and drove past the police of the legation quarter through the Tartar wall into the Chinese section of the city, where the man vanished.

In 1917 General Chang Ching-yao, under appointment from the then boy Emperor, who is now Henry Pu Yi, Regent of Manchukuo, commanded China's inland navy during Chang Hsun's abortive monarchist restoration movement. In 1918 General Chang was Governor of Hunan. At that time the present United States Minister to China, Nelson T. Johnson, was Consul General at Changsha. Some of General Chang's troops killed an American missionary, and Mr. Johnson summoned a gunboat. This alarmed the General and he fled. Later, as a result of United States representations, the Chinese Government removed Chang Ching-yao from the Governorship of Hunan.

The shooting today in the quiet diplomatic quarter of Peiping has created widespread speculation in Chinese circles as to the extent to which General Chang was succeeding in his monarchist restoration plans.

ROOSEVELT PROMISES A 'PARTNERSHIP' WITH BUSINESS, FARMERS AND WORKERS TO PROVIDE PROFITS AND HIGHER WAGES

CONGRESS SPEEDS WORK

Securities Bill Comes Up in Senate Today and Farm Aid in House.

RAINEY SETS SCHEDULE

Expects House to Wind Up by June 1, With Debt Talk and 30-Hour Bill Barred.

SENATE DELAYS FEARED

With Many Controversial Topics Ahead, Its Rules Are Not So Conducive to Haste.

Special to THE NEW YORK TIMES.

WASHINGTON, May 7.—The Roosevelt legislative program will have been approved in its entirety in the House by the end of May, Speaker Rainey declared today in reviewing the legislative situation. Foreign debts and the thirty-hour week were not on the program, said Mr. Rainey, and he had no reason to expect that they would be added.

The Roosevelt bills and resolutions now awaiting action have the seeds of controversy in them, so it is altogether likely that, while House action will be speedy, the Senate, will strike a considerably slower pace, that body's rules permitting unlimited debate unless closure is invoked.

Especially provocative of delays are the coming tariff resolution and the proposal to give authority to the President, in a "rider" to the independent offices bill, to cancel or modify government contracts, furlough officers of the national services on half pay and reduce or suspend the extra pay of military and naval aviators.

So even if the House is ready to quit around June 1 it may be days, or even weeks, afterward before the Senate is ready to adjourn.

"There has been a lot of loose talk these past few days about what the President is going to do, especially in the matter of the foreign debts," said Mr. Rainey. "All this talk about the President being ready to cancel or reduce the foreign debts is just so much 'ballyhoo.'

"I say, and I say it of my own personal knowledge, that there has been no conference of Democratic leaders, and none is in contemplation, involving a protest to the President on any other proposition involving a cancellation, a postponement or a reduction of the debts owed to the United States by our war-time Allies.

Still Opposed to Cancellation.

"All talk about Democratic leaders in Congress being ready to 'call the hand' of the President, of warning him that he is committing 'political suicide,' smacks very much of political propaganda. The President has never suggested the cancellation or reduction of these debts with any member or members of the House, and I am certain this is also true of the Senate.

"There is no debt proposition of any kind on the administration program. Of course, we are opposed to cancellation, and so is the President.

"We hear it solemnly whispered about that if the President sends in a message asking authority to cancel or reduce the debts a storm in Congress will follow. That's true, just as would be the case if President Roosevelt asked for authority to give Alaska back to Russia or to surrender to some other power control of the Panama Canal.

"But for the fact that in certain quarters these things are mentioned with solemn faces the whole thing would be too ridiculous to even mention."

"Have you, Mr. Byrns or any of the other administration leaders in Congress been called to the White House to discuss possible legislation at this session authorizing the President to enter into negotiations for a revision of the debts?" Speaker Rainey was asked.

"The answer is no," he replied.

Items on House Program.

Taking up the uncompleted part of President Roosevelt's program, Speaker Rainey said that the House would move quickly on the matters awaiting action. The Simpson cost-of-production guaranty amendment as voted into the farm bill by the

Continued on Page Two.

The President's Address

Special to THE NEW YORK TIMES.

WASHINGTON, May 7.—The text of President Roosevelt's radio address as broadcast was as follows:

Good evening, my friends: On a Sunday night a week after my inauguration I used the radio to tell you about the banking crisis and about the measures we were taking to meet it. In that way I made clear to the country various facts that might otherwise have been misunderstood and in general provided a means of understanding which I believe did much to restore confidence.

Tonight, eight weeks later, I come for the second time to give you my report—in the same spirit and by the same means—to tell you what we have been doing and what we are planning to do.

Two months ago, as you know, we were facing serious problems. The country was dying by inches. It was dying because trade and commerce had declined to dangerously low levels; prices for basic commodities were such as to destroy the value of the assets of national institutions such as banks, savings banks, insurance companies, and others. These institutions, because of their great needs, were foreclosing mortgages, they were calling loans, they were refusing credit. Thus there was actually in process of destruction the property of millions of people who had borrowed the money on that property in terms of dollars which had had an entirely different value from the level of March, 1933. That situation in that crisis did not call for any complicated consideration of economic panaceas or fancy plans. We were faced by a condition and not a theory.

Two Alternatives Faced.

There were just two alternatives at that time: The first was to allow the foreclosures to continue, credit to be withheld, money to go into hiding, thus forcing liquidation and bankruptcy of banks, railroads and insurance companies and a recapitalizing of all business and all property on a lower level. That alternative meant a continuation of what is loosely called "deflation," the net result of which would have been extraordinary hardship on all property owners and all bank depositors, and, incidentally, extraordinary hardships on all persons working for wages through an increase in unemployment and a further reduction of the wage scale.

It is easy to see that the result of that course would have not only economic effects of a very serious nature, but social results also that might bring incalculable harm. Even before I was inaugurated I came to the conclusion that such a policy was too much to ask the American people to bear. It involved not only a further loss of homes and farms and savings and wages but also a loss of spiritual values—the loss of that sense of security for the present and the future that is so necessary to the peace and contentment of the individual and of his family. When you destroy those things you find it difficult to establish confidence of any sort in the future.

And it was clear that mere appeals from Washington for confidence and the mere lending of more money to shaky institutions could not stop that downward course. A prompt program applied as quickly as possible seemed to me not only justified but imperative to our national security. The Congress, and when I say the Congress I mean the members of both political parties, fully understood this and gave me generous and intelligent support. The members of the Congress realized that the methods of normal times had to be replaced in the emergency by measures that were suited to the serious and pressing requirements of the moment.

"No Surrender of Power."

There was no actual surrender of power; Congress still retained its constitutional authority to legislate and appropriate and no one has the slightest desire to change the balance of these powers. The function of Congress is to decide what has to be done and to select the appropriate agency to carry out its will. That policy it has strictly adhered to. The only thing that has been happening has been to designate the President of the United States as the agency to carry out certain of the purposes of the Congress. This was constitutional and is constitutional and is in keeping with the past American tradition.

The legislation that has been passed or in the process of enactment can properly be considered as part of a well-grounded and well-rounded plan.

First, we are giving opportunity of employment to a quarter of a million of the unemployed, especially the young men who have dependents, to let them go into the forestry and flood-prvention work. That is a big task because it means feeding, clothing and caring for nearly twice as many men as we have in the regular army itself. And in creating this civilian conservation corps we are killing two birds with one stone. We are clearly enhancing the value of our natural resources and at the same time we are relieving an appreciable amount of actual distress. This great group of men, young men, have entered upon their work on a purely voluntary basis, no military training is involved and we are conserving not only our natural resources but also our human resources. One of the great values to this work is the fact that it is direct and requires the intervention of very little machinery.

Secondly, I have requested the Congress and have secured action upon a proposal to put the great properties owned by our government at Muscle Shoals to work after long years of wasteful inaction, and with this goes hand in hand a broad plan for the improvement of a vast area including the whole of the Tennessee Valley. It will add to the comfort and happiness of hundreds of thousands of people and the incident benefits will reach the entire nation.

Next, the Congress is about to pass legislation that will greatly ease the mortgage distress among the farmers and among the home owners of the nation, by providing for the easing of the burden of debt that now bears so heavily upon millions of our people.

Plans for Public Works.

Our next step in seeking immediate relief is a grant of half a billion dollars to help the States, and the counties, and the municipalities in their duty to care for those who need direct and immediate relief.

In addition to all this, the Congress also passed legislation, as you know, authorizing the sale of beer in such States as desired. That has already resulted in considerable re-employment and incidentally has provided for States and municipalities much-needed tax revenue.

As to the future: we are planning, in a few days, to ask the Congress for legislation to enable the government to undertake public works, thus stimulating directly and indirectly the employment of many others in well-considered projects.

Further legislation has been taken up which goes much more fundamentally into our economic problems. The farm relief bill seeks by the use of several methods, alone or together, to bring about an increased return to farmers for their major farm products, seeking at the same time to prevent in the days to come disastrous

Continued on Page Two.

HE TOUCHES ON INFLATION

Will Use New Powers Only When, and if, Need Arises.

FAIR WAGE RETURN HIS AIM

President Plans to Put a Curb on Cutthroat Competition and Overproduction.

SPEAKS TO NATION ON RADIO

Other Nations Must Prosper, Too, He Remarks on London Parley Negotiations.

Special to THE NEW YORK TIMES.

WASHINGTON, May 7.—President Roosevelt, in a radio speech to the nation tonight, said that he would use the wide currency powers granted him under the pending inflation legislation only "when, as and if" he considered it necessary in order to raise commodity prices to the extent that the dollar of today would equal in purchasing power the dollar of pre-depression times.

The administration's purpose, he said, was to permit debtors to repay "in the same kind of dollar which they borrowed." But he added that there would not be such cheapening of the dollar as to allow borrowers to pay back a great deal less than they borrowed. His exact words, the only reference he made to inflation in his fifteen-minute speech, were as follows:

"The administration has the definite objective of raising commodity prices to such an extent that those who have borrowed money will, on the average, be able to repay that money in the same kind of dollar which they borrowed. We do not seek to let them get such a cheap dollar that they will be able to pay back a great deal less than they borrowed. In other words, we seek to correct a wrong and not to create another wrong in the opposite direction. That is why powers are being given to the administration to provide, if necessary, for an enlargement of credit, in order to correct the existing wrong. These powers will be used when, as and if it may be necessary to accomplish the purpose."

Reveals New Measures.

The President announced new governmental measures, going more fundamentally into present economic problems, aimed to set up "a partnership between government and farming, industry and transportation."

This would not be a "partnership in profits, because the profits would still go to the citizens, but rather a partnership in planning and a partnership to see that the plans are carried out," the President explained.

The administration is planning to ask Congress in the next few days for legislation to enable the government to undertake public works to stimulate employment, Mr. Roosevelt said. It will also propose "well-considered and conservative measures" to give industrial workers a more fair wage return, prevent "cut-throat" competition and unduly long hours for labor and encourage each industry to prevent overproduction.

The President indicated by detailing the present ills of industry that the measures would initiate broad economic planning, not only by the government but by industry itself.

"Government ought to have the right, and will have the right, after surveying and planning for an industry, to prevent, with the assistance of the overwhelming majority of that industry, all unfair practice and to enforce this agreement by the authority of the government," he declared.

Views on Anti-Trust Laws.

The purpose of the anti-trust laws to prevent monopolies and monopoly exactions must be continued, he said, "but these laws were never intended to encourage the kind of unfair competition that results in long hours and starvation wages and overproduction."

The speech, which was carried to South America and Europe, outlined to some extent the President's plans for dealing with international questions. Permanent prosperity could not return to the United

Continued on Page Two.

facturers and the old Penrose machine in that State.

Raised Funds for Campaigns.

Mr. Grundy was examined at the outset upon the part that he had taken in the national campaigns of 1924 and 1928 in raising funds for the Republican organization. The ways and means committee of the Pennsylvania Republican State Committee, he stated, had collected $600,000 to further the Coolidge cause in 1924, and last year, with Mr. Hoover at the head of the party ticket, it obtained contributions of about $1,000,000.

The witness testified that at the beginning of the present fight over the tariff he had set up an office in this city and that in the direction of his campaign to uphold the protective principle, he had expended $20,000 out of his own pocket.

This money had been used, he said, in preparing literature for dissemination to the press and in assembling statistical material for manufacturers. He agreed to submit an itemized statement of disbursements.

The name of James Francis Burke, an aide in Mr. Hoover's office during the campaign last year, was brought into the discussion by Senator Walsh of the committee. Mr. Grundy had given the names of several men with whom he had conferred during the Senate Finance Committee's consideration of the tariff bill. Mr. Walsh asked if Mr. Burke was one of them. The witness replied in the affirmative.

"Where did you see Mr. Burke?" asked Senator Walsh.

"At the White House on a number of occasions," was the reply.

"When you went to see him did you always go to the White House?"

"Oh, no," said the witness. "I saw him at other places."

Witness Attacks Coalition.

In a statement which the committee refused to permit Mr. Grundy to read, but which was admitted to the record, the witness hit squarely at the Republican-Democratic coalition now fighting the Finance Committee bill in the Senate. Four of the members of the Lobby Committee, Senators Caraway and Walsh, Democrats, and Borah and Blaine, Republicans, are identified with the coalition.

Mr. Grundy was particularly pointed in his references to Senator Borah, who, he said, was a member of the resolutions committee of the Kansas City convention, and, as such, had endorsed the tariff plank promising "revision wherever necessary."

He quoted from a speech made by Mr. Borah in the Boston arena on Nov. 2, in which the Idaho Senator urged his hearers to keep the "tariff policy in the hands of those who have believed in it from the beginning" by electing Mr. Hoover to the Presidency. Mr. Grundy contrasted Senator Borah's campaign speeches on the tariff with his present course in opposing the finance committee bill.

Charges Borah With Shifting.

"What influences have caused the esteemed Senator from Idaho to completely reverse himself within a period of a few months; what changes of mind have prompted him

Continued on Page Twenty-five.

no[illegible] leaked from the jury [illegible] as to how the eight men and four women of the jury stood. There were all kinds of rumors about the court corridors, but there was not the least authority for any of them.

The former Secretary of the Interior returned to his hotel as soon as the jury left the court room. He had the court's consent to remain there until a verdict was reached. Mr. Fall made no comment of any kind after the case went to the jury. The silence that has been his policy since the oil cases started more than six years ago was maintained to the end.

Mr. Fall, it was understood, remained in bed while the jury deliberated.

Takes Exceptions to Justice's Charge.

Friends of the defendant admitted frankly that they were not overpleased with Justice Hitz's charge. That this was also the attitude of Mr. Fall's lawyers was indicated by the fact that Frank J. Hogan, chief counsel for Fall, entered ten exceptions to specific parts of the charge and a general exception to the complete utterance. Government counsel said they were entirely satisfied with the charge.

The court room was jammed to the doors during the delivery of the charge. Time and again Fall looked at his lawyers, and to some persons in the court room it looked as though he were making a silent appeal to Mr. Hogan to interrupt the charge with objections to the interpretation of the law as expounded by Justice Hitz.

Justice Hitz told the jury to leave sympathy out of the case so far as they were concerned. Clemency, he added, was for the judge or the President to exercise.

The "sunshine of New Mexico," to which Mr. Hogan had asked the jury to return Fall, was not evidence declared Justice Hitz.

Judge Speaks Hour and a Quarter.

The charge of Justice Hitz, to which the defense took ten specific exceptions and one general exception to the whole charge, required an hour and fifteen minutes to deliver. With the exception of the written prayers for instruction, submitted by the government and by the defense, Justice Hitz addressed the jury without notes or manuscript of any kind.

Frank T. Hogan, chief counsel for Fall, was kept busy from the moment the justice began his own part of the charge until the end, writing objections to the instructions. Mr. Hogan is a master of shorthand and had his specific objections ready the moment the charge was concluded.

"Mr. Fall is charged here with bribery," said Justice Hitz. "And the charge of bribery, as used in this case, is the betrayal of a public trust by a public officer. He is not charged with conspiring with Doheny to defraud the government of the United States. He is not charged with having defrauded the government of the United States, but he is charged with having betrayed his trust as Secretary of the Interior in that, on a certain day, he received certain money from

Continued on Page Twenty-two.

[illegible]gomaster Max, [illegible] Kessons, the Italian Ambassador, Marquis Durazzo and the Minister of War, Count de Broqueville, when the Prince arrived at 9:30 o'clock. The band was playing the Italian national anthem as he stepped from his automobile and started toward the tomb. For an instant Prince Humbert stopped to talk to Count de Broqueville.

At that moment a young man was seen running quickly through the police cordon toward the Prince. As he ran he fired. There was another flash and the bark of a shot. Leaping forward a Belgian gendarme beat down the young assassin's arm with his sword and felled him before he could fire again.

Prince Humbert heard the shot and saw the scuffle but scarcely turned his head.

When the crowd realized what had happened there was a great outburst of cheering. Those near the would-be assassin attacked and nearly lynched him before he could be rescued by the police.

Prince Completes Program.

The whole incident lasted only two minutes, there being scarcely time to complete the playing of the national anthem. At once, with slow and dignified steps, the Prince walked toward the tomb of the Unknown Soldier carrying a large horseshoe wreath of laurel leaves bound with blue ribbon on which was embossed the arms of the House of Savoy.

Every one except the Prince himself was in an intense state of excitement and nervousness. The assassin might not have been alone. Perhaps another attempt would be made. The suggestion was whispered that the ceremony should be cut short, but the Prince insisted on reviewing the guard of honor and he walked down the lines with the Italian Ambassador, Count de Broqueville and Burgomaster Max, who all kept as close to him as etiquette would permit, the three forming a kind of bodyguard.

Meanwhile the police had been fighting for five minutes with the crowd to prevent the assailant from being lynched. He was so bruised in the scuffle as to be all but unconscious. When he reached the police station, however, he had recovered sufficiently to be able to give his name and to declare that he alone was responsible and had been actuated by his hatred of Fascism, which he said was killing his country.

Firer of Shot a Socialist.

Di Rosa is 21 years of age and was born in Milan. He left Italy secretly for Paris, not having a passport, and continued his studies there. He came, two days ago, to Antwerp with a false Swiss passport and waited there for the Prince's visit to Brussels. Dressed as a tourist, it was not difficult for di Rosa to get near the royal party at this morning's ceremony and if he had not slipped on the edge of the curb of a street refuge as he ran toward the Prince, it is almost certain that he would have succeeded in his crime.

Di Rosa declared he was a Socialist and a member of the Second International. He said he at first thought of trying to kill the Prince yesterday at the station but that he was afraid he would miss because of

Continued on Page Eight.

the City [illegible] Company.

The prosecutor presented evidence tracing the withdrawal of the money from the Atlantic Avenue branch of the City Trust Company in Brooklyn, its delivery to Mr. Ferrari, president, at his sickbed in his home in Brooklyn and its transfer by Ferrari to Dell' Osso, his brother-in-law.

Hiram C. Todd, special assistant district attorney, told Dell' Osso to relate what happened on Sept. 21, 1928, the day the witness said he was called to Ferrari's sickroom to receive the money.

"He called me up there and gave me $10,000 in an envelope," Dell' Osso testified. At this point James I. Cuff, Warder's attorney, objected to the witness telling what Ferrari had said to him. Justice Tompkins sustained Mr. Cuff.

"What did you do then?" Mr. Todd asked.

"I put the money in my pocket," said Dell' Osso.

"After you received the money what did you do with it?"

Says Warder Counted Money.

"I took it in the night time to Mr. Frank Warder's house."

He related how he had gone to work at the Park Row building of which he was superintendent until 5 o'clock, taking the subway to 116th Street and Broadway and finally arriving at Warder's door. Mr. Warder sat immobile as Dell' Osso continued:

"Frank Warder's wife come and open the door. I says, 'I want see Mr. Warder, I got something for him.' He came, I gave him the envelope, he opened the envelope, counted the money, put him in his pocket and asks me, 'What did Mr. Ferrari say?' and I says, 'He says best regards to everybody.'"

Dell' Osso testified that he had met Warder at the Highstown (N. J.) farm of Ferrari and at Ferrari's home in Bay Ridge, Brooklyn.

The cross-examination of Dell' Osso was brief compared to that of other State witnesses. Mr. Cuff had

Continued on Page Sixteen.

[illegible] president of the Guaranty Trust Company.
SEWARD PROSSER, chairman of the Bankers Trust Company.
THOMAS W. LAMONT, senior partner of the Morgan firm.

Exclusive of the vast wealth of the house of Morgan this group of bankers represented more than $6,000,000,000 of massed banking resources.

Meeting Eases Tenseness.

As the word went out in Wall Street that these financiers had met the air of tense anxiety in the financial district was relieved. Almost at once the word was passed around the floor of the Stock Exchange that "they" were going to support stock prices and the down-rush of security quotations was halted. Outside the offices of the Morgan firm, at Broad and Wall Streets, a crowd quickly gathered, and on the steps of the Subtreasury Building opposite newspaper photographers and motion picture men took their stand.

After the conference Mr. Lamont spoke to reporters. The meeting of the bankers, he said, had been held largely to exchange information on the stock market situation and no plan of concerted action to support the stock market had been agreed upon.

Despite this assertion, Wall Street was convinced that the bankers had agreed to bring to bear upon the market the immense support of their buying power. Whether or not such an agreement was reached, it was reliably reported in brokerage circles later in the day that large orders emanating from these banking interests had been executed on the floor of the Exchange shortly after the conference ended.

"There has been a little distress selling on the Stock Exchange," Mr. Lamont said, "and we have held a meeting of the heads of several financial institutions to discuss the situation.

"We have found that there are no houses in difficulty and reports from brokers indicate that margins are being maintained satisfactorily."

Mr. Lamont stated that the group

Continued on Page Two.

Missing Lake Ferry Sank With Crew of 57; Four Bodies Found; All Hands Believed Lost

Special to The New York Times.

CHICAGO, Oct. 24.—All indications tonight pointed to the loss of fifty-seven lives when the car ferry Milwaukee sank Tuesday night in Lake Michigan.

The Milwaukee was definitely given up for lost today, after another ship reported it had recovered the missing ferry's pilot house and two bodies wearing its life belts. A watch found on one of the bodies had stopped at 8:35, indicating that the Milwaukee went down about that time Tuesday night, seven hours after leaving Milwaukee.

The steamship Steel Chemist, a freighter out of Three Rivers, Quebec, was half way between Racine and Kenosha at noon today when the second mate sighted a floating body. A lifeboat was lowered and a drowned seaman was lifted aboard.

The Steel Chemist steamed ahead and twenty minutes later sighted a second body.

Captain Brown flashed a wireless to the Grand Trunk car ferry office at Milwaukee. The message was intercepted by the Coast Guard station at Racine, Wis., the same station which on Tuesday night had vainly attempted to catch the sinking ferry's last S O S.

About 8:25 P. M. Tuesday, when the Milwaukee was about to founder, A. W. Pfeiffer, a Racine insurance salesman, was spinning his dials to pick up a Louisville program. His receiver suddenly cut in on the Morse code and Pfeiffer, who was a naval radio operator in wartime, tuned in. The message was an S O S.

Pfeiffer telephoned the Coast Guard wireless operator what he heard. The operator tuned in, but could hear nothing. Pfeiffer went back to his radio and deciphered three words, "Water up to"——. Then silence.

Two other bodies of the Milwaukee's crew were picked up later near Kenosha.

Twenty-three officers and seamen of the stranded steamer Maple Court of the Canada Steamship Lines were rescued by the Coast Guard cutter Seminole early today after the ship had been hard aground for 48 hours on a reef at Cockburn Island, Lake Huron.

After taking off the Maple Court's crew, the Coast Guard cutter proceeded to Gravel Island to stand by the ore carrier William B. Pilkey, whose crew refused to abandon ship.

Break of 12 Cents a Bushel to New Season Low and 8-Cent Rally Mark Wild Trading.

STOCKS TUMBLE IN CHICAGO

Selling Swamps Exchange in 1,200,000-Share Day—Part of Big Losses Recovered.

Special to The New York Times.

CHICAGO, Oct. 24.—Fortunes in paper values were wiped out for mid-Western investors and speculators today as prices for grain and securities on the Chicago Board of Trade and the Chicago Stock Exchange, reacting to the selling wave in Wall Street, recorded sensational declines.

Amid wild scenes in the wheat pit, quotations for all deliveries at the close were from 4⅜ to 5⅛ cents a bushel lower than the final prices of Wednesday, when a depreciation of 4 cents a bushel laid the basis for today's unprecedented peace-time grain market.

On the Chicago Stock Exchange the heavy selling shattered records both for volume of sales and the severity of the day's average decline.

1,220,000-Share Turnover.

For the first time in the history of the local stock market more than 1,000,000 shares changed hands today. The turnover was 1,220,000 shares, and prices crashed $1 to $85 a share.

The big Chicago banks came to the aid of the distressed stock market, the heads of these institutions expressing the opinion that selling had become panicky. A canvass of the chief downtown institutions led to an estimate that many millions of dollars were made available.

There never has been such a wheat market as that of today outside of wartimes. Chaos prevailed among the brokers in the pit and excitement ran high in La Salle Street brokerage offices as grain quotations dropped 11 cents a bushel in a short period. At one time a 7-cent drop in about as many minutes was registered in Chicago and Winnipeg.

December wheat broke from $1.24¾ to $1.13¾, with a rally of around 8 cents, closing at $1.20¼ to $1.20½. May wheat at the low point was $1.24½ and closed at $1.31¼ to $1.31½.

In Winnipeg December wheat broke from $1.37⅛ to $1.25, but rallied to close at $1.32½, a net loss of 6 cents a bushel. May wheat broke from $1.45 to $1.31 and was $1.39¼ at the close. Liverpool prices at the last were off 3¼ cents.

A message from Winnipeg reported that a well-known Chicago grain speculator had sold 10,000,000 bushels of wheat there, scattering it among the trade. In Chicago millions of bushels were unloaded indiscriminately. Many orders to sell 500,000 bushels came into the pit here during the first three hours of trading.

It was common gossip around the Board of Trade that New York speculators and Arthur W. Cutten, who have been credited with being the heaviest longs for several months, were dumping their holdings here and in Winnipeg and at the

Continued on Page Three.

Drastic Market Decline Found Not Due to Any Basic Business Weakness.

STILL PLAN TAX REDUCTION

Reserve Board Meets Twice in Day and Keeps in Constant Touch With Markets Here.

Special to The New York Times.

WASHINGTON, Oct. 24.—After two extended meetings, over the second of which Secretary Mellon presided, the Federal Reserve Board late today decided that the avalanche of selling on the New York stock market today had not resulted in a situation serious enough to call for any immediate formal declaration.

While the tremendous liquidation was at its height there were indications that the board would make an announcement, but such action was withheld when the closing hour on the Exchange showed a part recovery of values.

Throughout the day, however, there were scenes of unusual activity about the offices of the board in the Treasury Building and members were requested to keep constantly in touch with developments.

After the afternoon meeting, which lasted from about 3:30 until 5 o'clock, Mr. Young met all inquiries with the statement that there was nothing to say, except that the bill rate in New York had been reduced to 5 per cent. No action was taken in regard to the New York bank's 6 per cent rediscount rate.

Secretary Mellon also refused to make any formal comment.

Brokers' Loans Show Decline.

While the board was meeting in the afternoon the report of brokers' loans made by New York member banks was issued, showing a decline of $167,000,000 to a total of $6,634,000,000, as compared with $6,801,000,000 one week ago. This report covered the loans up to the close of the market Tuesday night, and represented only a part of the drop which must have occurred as a result of the liquidation yesterday and today.

The chief concern of the board over the situation admittedly came in the early afternoon when selling orders were pouring into the market in unprecedented volume. Minute and almost continuous reports were telephoned, it is said, not only by officials of the New York Reserve Bank but by other prominent banking leaders, but the identity of those who may have been in touch with the board was withheld.

The first meeting of the board began at 10:45 A. M., before the selling had gained full force, and continued until 1 P. M.

While officials of the treasury would not permit themselves to be quoted, a definite reflection of their opinion was made available. This was that the break was the result of undue speculation and could be laid at the door of unsound technical con-

Continued on Page Four.

3 o'clock bell, most stocks had gained a measurable part of their losses.

Losses at Close Not Excessive.

The break was one of the widest in the market's history, although the losses at the close were not particularly large, many having been recouped by the afternoon rally.

It carried down with it speculators, big and little, in every part of the country, wiping out thousands of accounts. It is probable that if the stockholders of the country's foremost corporations had not been calmed by the attitude of leading bankers and the subsequent rally, the business of the country would have been seriously affected. Doubtless business will feel the effects of the drastic stock shake-out, and this is expected to hit the luxuries most severely.

It was by far the biggest market day in the country's history. Total sales on the New York Stock Exchange were 12,894,650 shares, as compared with the 8,246,000-share record set on March 26, and on the Curb were 6,337,415 shares, as compared with the 3,715,400 record established Monday. A total of 974 separate issues were dealt in on the Exchange, this figure, of course, establishing a new record. Bonds, which were strong, reached a volume of $23,233,000, the biggest day in that market since April 23, 1926, and unlike stocks, the fixed investments were strong, with the exception of the convertible issues, whose fluctuations synchronize with the selling price of the stocks to which they are prior.

Thousands Sacrifice Holdings.

The total losses cannot be accurately calculated, because of the large number of markets and the thousands of securities not listed on any exchange. However, they were staggering, running into billions of dollars. Fear struck the big speculators and little ones, big investors and little ones. Thousands of them threw their holdings into the whirling Stock Exchange pit for what they would bring. Losses were tremendous and thousands of prosperous brokerage and bank accounts, sound and healthy a week ago, were completely wrecked in the strange debacle, due to a combination of circumstances, but accelerated into a crash by fear.

The ticker services maintained by the New York Stock Exchange and the New York Curb Exchange proved pitifully inadequate for the task of recording history's biggest market. By 10:30 o'clock the Exchange ticker had fallen 15 minutes behind and that of the Curb Exchange 16 minutes; by 11:30 this was stretched to 48 for the Exchange and 47 for the Curb; at 1 o'clock they were 92 minutes late; by 2 o'clock, 131 minutes late for the Exchange and 116 for the Curb tickers, and by 2:30 the Exchange quotations were 147 minutes late and the Curb tickers 130 minutes behind. The New York Stock Exchange tickers did not complete the task of printing the market until 8½ minutes past 7 o'clock last night, while the Curb tickers finished at 5:54.

Financial District in Confusion.

Under these circumstances of late tickers and spreads of 10, 20 and at times 30 points between the tape prices and those on the floor of the

on remedial plans for presentation by the President to this afternoon's legislative conference.

Scrip Being Rushed.

Clearing house certificates will be used instead of currency in New York when the banks reopen on Tuesday after the two-day holiday proclaimed by Governor Herbert H. Lehman, according to present plans of the New York Clearing House Association, it was learned last night.

This was confirmed by Mortimer N. Buckner, president of the New York Clearing House Association and chairman of the board of the New York Trust Company, following a meeting of the clearing house committee at the clearing house, 77 Cedar Street.

Bankers from New York and other centres have been called to Washington to confer with William H. Woodin, Secretary of the Treasury, at 10 o'clock this morning on plans for meeting the emergency. George W. Davison, chairman of the Central Hanover Bank and Trust Company and head of the Clearing House Committee, left for Washington yesterday afternoon; and George L. Harrison, governor of the Federal Reserve Bank of New York was scheduled to go last night. Charles S. McCain, chairman of the board of the Chase National Bank, was in Washington yesterday and it was thought likely that he would remain for the conference.

In the event that the discussions of the bankers with Mr. Woodin develop a plan which can be put into effect through Congressional action, the proposals will be laid before President Roosevelt this afternoon and presented by him to a conference of legislators. It is expected that the results of the conference may have a bearing upon how quickly the new Congress is called into session.

In addition to the New York bankers, representatives from the banking communities of Philadelphia, Chicago, Baltimore and Richmond are expected to attend the conference

Act to Meet Payrolls.

It was indicated last night that arrangements would be made whereby payrolls due yesterday or tomorrow would be met by the withdrawal from the banks of sufficient amounts of currency to pay all or part in cash. Concerns accustomed to paying by check would be permitted to withdraw cash, it was predicted, or the banks would make special provision for cashing pay checks. Governor Lehman is expected to give his approval to a payroll plan being worked out by the banks and business houses.

The banking holiday ordered by Governor Lehman in a proclamation issued at his apartment, 820 Park Avenue, at 4:20 o'clock yesterday morning, was effective yesterday, and will expire at the

Continued on Page Twenty-five.

By FREDERICK T. BIRCHALL.

Special Cable to THE NEW YORK TIMES.

BERLIN, March 4.—In a countrywide blaze of bonfires and torchlight parades the allied National Socialist and Nationalist parties tonight closed the electoral campaign, which tomorrow is expected to entrench them securely in power not only throughout Germany as a result of the Reichstag elections but throughout Prussia, where the electorate will vote simultaneously for a separate State ticket.

Tonight, on every eminence along Germany's borders, not excluding the Polish Corridor, a bonfire flamed to signalize the Nazi ideal of an awakening nation. In Köenigsberg, East Prussia, Chancellor Adolf Hitler himself made his closing appeal to aroused patriotic fervor.

In every city and every town of considerable size uniformed Nazis marched to some centre, where amid the blare of brass bands playing partiotic songs, in which the whole assemblage joined, Nazi orators proclaimed the dawning of a new day.

In Berlin alone there were twenty-four parades to an equal number of meeting places, where through loud-speakers the voice of Herr Hitler was heard and acclaimed.

No Counter-Demonstrations.

There were no counter-demonstrations from the opposition. They were "verboten," for this is a one-way election. Nor, late tonight, despite the dire predictions sent to the outside world, had any serious disturbance been reported. All that is over, for what is the use of inviting inevitable and overwhelming reprisals when all the authority and all the weapons are monopolized by the other side?

In Thuringia, the only State in which a few Socialist newspapers remain unsuspended, they were all compelled by the Nazi State government today to reprint Chancellor Hitler's recent speech against "Marxism" on the front page.

The utmost left for those opposed to an all-Nazi régime is to vote against it silently and secretly tomorrow—if they dare—and to hope for the best.

So confident today are the government leaders of a verdict in their favor that even before the polls are open they are already announcing the first act of the new Reichstag. It will be to retire the Republican flag of black, red and gold under which Germany has fought her way out of the difficulties in which the World War left her and to replace it with the black-white-red banner of the former imperialism.

"We shall be happy to get rid of that emblem of 'Marxism,'" declared Captain Hermann Wilhelm Goering, Minister Without Portfolio and the spokesman of militant na-

Continued on Page Twenty.

extra session of Congress, no decision has been reached tonight, but probably will be by tomorrow night.

"The Secretary of the Treasury will begin tomorrow a series of discussions called at the request of President Roosevelt, looking to prompt action in the banking situation. He is calling a number of individuals and Reserve Bank officials to Washington. Some have already been invited and more will be called tonight."

Bankers from New York, Philadelphia, Chicago, Baltimore and Richmond were invited to the conference with Secretary Woodin at 10 o'clock tomorrow morning.

After they have discussed the banking situation, whatever plan may be adopted will be transmitted to President Roosevelt for presentation to the legislative conference in the afternoon.

Four Proposals Advanced.

While President Roosevelt was reviewing the parade from the stand in front of the White House this afternoon, members of his Cabinet and two former Secretaries of the Treasury, David F. Houston and William G. McAdoo, were engaged in discussion of a program which will be laid before the conference tomorrow.

The main points advanced but not finally decided upon at this informal conference, in which Secretary Woodin participated for a few minutes, were:

1. The organization of a corporation to which banks must subscribe to guarantee bank deposits.

2. The issue of scrip, as was resorted to in the banking emergency in 1907, to be put out by the banks to the amount of frozen deposits.

3. A tax on hoarded gold, as high as 15 per cent.

4. Other measures to protect our gold holdings.

Secretary of State Hull said, however, that a tax on hoarded gold did not seem practicable, and probably would not be resorted to in the hope of raising any considerable amount of money, but merely as a move to force hoarders to put gold into circulation and restore confidence in the banks.

These suggestions with others will come before the conference tomorrow and the new administration leaders were confident tonight that a program could be agreed upon for submission to and prompt action by Congress by the middle of next week.

Problem Is to Allay Fear.

"The main thing right now," said Secretary Hull, "is to allay the unreasonable and unreasoning fear in the public mind. That in itself would be a long step in the direction toward restoration of confidence. Nothing right now is more unjustifiable than attempts to hoard money."

Former Secretary of the Treasury

Continued on Page Twenty-four.

Spends Evening in Seclusion in Hotel After Seeing His Successor Take Office.

SEEMS GLAD TO GET AWAY

Bids Genial Farewell to Old Friends in Capital After Morning of Heavy Cares.

By RUSSELL OWEN.

Herbert Hoover entered private life yesterday after a day of foreboding, in which his successor addressed the nation as though it were entering upon a war. With downcast eyes and a diffident manner, Mr. Hoover went to the Capitol to see Mr. Roosevelt inaugurated as President, and left hurriedly, as if glad to throw from his shoulders the mantle of responsibility for the affairs of a country desperately distressed.

Immediately after the ceremony he left the Capitol and drove to the railroad station to take a train for New York, where he arrived at 5:50 o'clock last night. He went to the Waldorf-Astoria and spent the evening in seclusion, avoiding visitors.

Until half an hour before he stepped into the automobile that was to bear him and President Roosevelt to the inaugural ceremonies in Washington, he was busy with affairs of state. As no other man who has stepped from the office of Chief Executive, he was beset with complex problems until the end of his term. The last bills he signed were those to aid the country through the present crisis. He signed them grimly, with a grave face, realizing to the full the difficulties which he was bequeathing.

Raises Hat Only Once.

The drive from the White House to the Capitol was through lines of people who watched with serious, rather than enthusiastic faces. A sense of depression had settled over the capital so that it could be felt. The two men, side by side, were looked upon as symbols of a government trying to cope with dangers which were as subtle as they were treacherous. The few cheers were for Roosevelt rather than Hoover. He realized that, and only raised his hat once during the trip, although the new President smiled and doffed his hat frequently in response to the faint cheers from the stands and sidewalk.

But once in the railroad station to take the train to New York after the inauguration, Mr. Hoover came into his own again. There were people who firmly believed in him,

Continued on Page Four.

"This Is Pre-eminently the Time to Speak the Truth," He Says, in Demand That "the Temple of Our Civilization Be Restored to the Ancient Truths."

Special to THE NEW YORK TIMES.

WASHINGTON, March 4.—President Roosevelt's inaugural address, delivered immediately after he took the oath, was as follows:

President Hoover, Mr. Chief Justice, my friends:

This is a day of national consecration, and I am certain that my fellow-Americans expect that on my induction into the Presidency I will address them with a candor and a decision which the present situation of our nation impels.

This is pre-eminently the time to speak the truth, the whole truth, frankly and boldly. Nor need we shrink from honestly facing conditions in our country today. This great nation will endure as it has endured, will revive and will prosper.

So first of all let me assert my firm belief that the only thing we have to fear is fear itself—nameless, unreasoning, unjustified terror which paralyzes needed efforts to convert retreat into advance.

In every dark hour of our national life a leadership of frankness and vigor has met with that understanding and support of the people themselves which is essential to victory. I am convinced that you will again give that support to leadership in these critical days.

In such a spirit on my part and on yours we face our common difficulties. They concern, thank God, only material things. Values have shrunken to fantastic levels; taxes have risen; our ability to pay has fallen; government of all kinds is faced by serious curtailment of income; the means of exchange are frozen in the currents of trade; the withered leaves of industrial enterprise lie on every side; farmers find no markets for their produce; the savings of many years in thousands of families are gone.

More important, a host of unemployed citizens face the grim problem of existence, and an equally great number toil with little return. Only a foolish optimist can deny the dark realities of the moment.

Yet our distress comes from no failure of substance. We are stricken by no plague of locusts. Compared with the perils which our forefathers conquered because they believed and were not afraid, we have still much to be thankful for. Nature still offers her bounty and human efforts have multiplied it. Plenty is at our doorstep, but a generous use of it languishes in the very sight of the supply.

Charges "Money Changers" Lack Vision.

Primarily, this is because the rulers of the exchange of mankind's goods have failed through their own stubbornness and their own incompetence, have admitted their failure and abdicated. Practices of the unscrupulous money changers stand indicted in the court of public opinion, rejected by the hearts and minds of men.

True, they have tried, but their efforts have been cast in the pattern of an outworn tradition. Faced by failure of credit, they have proposed only the lending of more money.

Stripped of the lure of profit by which to induce our people to follow their false leadership, they have resorted to exhortations, pleading tearfully for restored confidence. They know only the rules of a generation of self-seekers.

They have no vision, and when there is no vision the people perish.

The money changers have fled from their high seats in the temple of our civilization. We may now restore that temple to the ancient truths.

The measure of the restoration lies in the extent to which we apply social values more noble than mere monetary profit.

Happiness lies not in the mere possession of money; it lies in the joy of achievement, in the thrill of creative effort.

The joy and moral stimulation of work no longer must be forgotten in the mad chase of evanescent profits. These dark days will be worth all they cost us if they teach us that our true

Continued on Page Three.

Their Spirits Are Lifted by His Smile of Confidence as They Watch Parade.

MANY ON ROOFS, IN TREES

Throng Waiting for Ceremony Is Solemnly Silent Until New President Appears.

Special to THE NEW YORK TIMES.

WASHINGTON, March 4.—The quadrennial pageant which traditionally accompanies the inauguration of a new President was enacted here today with all the pomp and panoply of more prosperous years and with all solemnity.

Before the august Capitol, in an inadequate and windswept forty acres, 100,000 of his countrymen saw Franklin D. Roosevelt swear on the ancient Bible of his Dutch fathers to cherish and defend the Constitution of his country.

Five hundred thousand others saw his reassuringly confident smile as he rode from Capitol to White House at the head of a parade of 18,000 marching men and women, among whom were such of his formidable rivals for the nomination as Alfred E. Smith and Governor Albert C. Ritchie of Maryland.

Mr. Roosevelt became the thirty-second President of the United States on a day that was cloudy and chill, with an occasional ray of sunlight piercing the clouds below which rode majestically the navy airship Akron and ninety-six military airplanes from Bolling and Langley Fields.

Flags flew at half-taff on the Senate and House Office Buildings in memory of Senator Walsh, who was to have been Attorney General in the new Cabinet.

Over the vast throngs there hung a cloud of worry, because of the economic and business outlook. The new President's recurrent smile of confidence, his uplifted chin and the challenge of his voice did much to help the national sense of humor to assert itself.

Reviews Parade for Three Hours.

Again, standing throughout the afternoon while legions of men of all degrees and colors marched past his glass-enclosed reviewing stand in the Court of Honor, the new President, advocate of a new deal, set an example of resolute fortitude and cheerfulness as he doffed his hat in deference to the colors and in greeting to old friends and supporters.

He stood between Admiral William V. Pratt, Chief of Naval Operations, and General Douglas Mac-

Continued on Page Two.

[illegible] also the inaugural address which Mr. Roosevelt then delivered in the presence of at least a hundred thousand persons who gathered in the Capitol grounds.

The sense of the administration's burden was apparent, too, in the manner and speech of Vice President Garner, who, an hour before the President took the oath, laid down his gavel as Speaker of the House of Representatives and was inducted into his new office in the Senate chamber, where he will henceforth preside.

Keeps Pledge of Action.

"Action" was the promise of Mr. Roosevelt's speech, and action was immediately forthcoming. The first moment after the ceremonies were over, the President swore in his Cabinet, summoned the party leaders to a Sunday conference to work out the plan for banking relief and arranged to call an extra session of the Seventy-third Congress, probably on Wednesday, to legislate the plan into law.

"This nation asks for action, and action now," he said on the steps of the Capitol. Within a few hours, he acted.

The President had consistently maintained his attitude that he would not accept responsibility without power in the period between his election and his inauguration. Powerful and subtle suasions could not move him. But when authority came he moved at once as he had said he would.

Atmosphere Is Grim.

Though the city was gay with flags and lively with the music of bands and cheers for the marchers in the inaugural parade which followed the oath taking, the atmosphere which surrounded the change of government in the United States was comparable to that which might be found in a beleaguered capital in war time.

The President in his address told the people that they were at war with the forces of depression and offered them leadership and action in the new campaign to be raged against these forces.

In words that burned and scourged he denounced the financial leaders of the nation, declared that these "money changers" should be driven from the temple and that they should not be allowed to return to their high places. No more, he declared, should those entrusted with other people's money be permitted to misuse it.

The inaugural address was a Jacksonian speech, a fighting speech, implicit with criticism of the lack of leadership and the philosophy of government which the President imputed to his predecessor, who sat there, listening. He would lead, he said, as the people expect, within the confines of the Constitution, and he will demand that Congress follow this leadership.

But if his present powers prove insufficient to win the war to which he pledged his full mind and

Continued on Page Three.

Section 1

"All the News That's Fit to Print."

The New York Times.

LATE CITY EDITION
WEATHER—Fair today and tomorrow; temperature unchanged.
Temperatures Yesterday—Max., 42; Min., 34

Section 1

VOL. LXXXII....No. 27,434. Entered as Second-Class Matter. Postoffice, New York, N. Y. NEW YORK, SUNDAY, MARCH 5, 1933. F Including Rotogravure Picture, Magazine and Book Sections. TEN CENTS | TWELVE CENTS Beyond 200 Miles. Except in 7th and 8th Postal Zones.

ROOSEVELT INAUGURATED, ACTS TO END THE NATIONAL BANKING CRISIS QUICKLY; WILL ASK WAR-TIME POWERS IF NEEDED

PLAN TO USE SCRIP HERE

Bankers Ready to Issue Clearing House Paper at End of Holiday.

WILL MEET WOODIN TODAY

Eastern Financiers to Join Parley at Capital on Plans to Permit Reopenings.

STOCK EXCHANGES CLOSED

Drain on the Gold Reserve Is Halted — Cash Being Set Aside to Meet Payrolls.

The Banking Situation.

The New York Clearing House Association prepared to print and issue certificates to be used by the public as substitute money.

In every State of the nation, including the District of Columbia, banking was wholly or partly suspended.

In London, Paris and other European capitals, dollar transactions were suspended.

Bankers from New York and other financial centres will confer with Secretary of the Tre[illegible]

Checks Still Accepted Here For Federal Income Taxes

Collectors of Internal Revenue in New York City were still accepting checks yesterday in payment of Federal income taxes, and it was said that checks would continue to be accepted during the bank holiday.

No consideration was yet being given to possible postponement of payments, due on March 15. This could only be granted by the Secretary of the Treasury or Commissioner of Internal Revenue in Washington, although the law allows individual applications for extension of time.

Walter E. Corwin, Collector in Brooklyn, said clearing-house certificates would not be accepted, if issued as a medium of exchange. The law permits payment in cash, checks, Treasury notes or Liberty bonds.

VICTORY FOR HITLER IS EXPECTED TODAY

Repression of Opponents Held to Make Election Triumph for Regime Inevitable.

FIRES BLAZE ON BORDERS

Nazis Light Them as Sign of "Reawakening"—Imperial Flag to Be Restored.

READY TO CALL CONGRESS

President Probably Will Summon Extra Session for Wednesday.

WORKS ON LEGISLATION

Cabinet Ordered to Meet With Him Today to Draft Banking Reform Measures.

AID LIKELY IN A WEEK

Steps Considered Include Deposit Guarantee, Use of Scrip and Tax on Hoarded Gold.

Special to THE NEW YORK TIMES.

WASHINGTON, March 4.—President Roosevelt plunged immediately into the banking situation tonight by summoning members of his Cabinet and leaders of Congress to meet tomorrow afternoon to decide upon a program to deal with it.

As soon as the program is agreed upon, Congress will be called into special session, probably on Wednesday, and it is the expectation of administration advisers that legislation will be enacted within another week.

The White House issued the following statement at 7:20 P. M.:

"Respecting the [illegible]

THE NEW PRESIDENT TAKING THE OATH OF OFFICE.

Associated Press Photo.

Franklin D. Roosevelt, With Hand Raised, Being Sworn by Chief Justice Charles Evans Hughes on the Rostrum in Front of the Capitol at 1:08 P. M. Yesterday. At the Right Are His Son, James Roosevelt, and Former President Hoover.

HOOVER, AS CITIZEN, HERE ON WAY HOME

Text of the Inaugural Address; President for Vigorous Action

500,000 IN STREETS CHEER ROOSEVELT

100,000 AT INAUGURATION

President, Grim, Terse, Pledges 'Adequate but Sound Currency.'

SCORES 'MONEY-CHANGERS'

In Fighting Speech He Demands Supervision of Credits and Investments.

STICKS TO CONSTITUTION

Calls on People and Congress to Follow Him as Leader in War on Depression.

By ARTHUR KROCK.
Special to THE NEW YORK TIMES.

WASHINGTON, March 4.—With solemn mien, Franklin D. Roosevelt of New York took the oath of office and became the thirty-second President of the United States on the main steps of the Capitol at eight minutes after 1 o'clock this afternoon.

A deep consciousness of the task before him was patent in his unusual demeanor as, his face stern, his voice grave, he repeated after Chief Justice Hughes the historic words of the oath. [illegible]

"All the News That's Fit to Print."

The New York Times.

Copyright, 1929, by The New York Times Company.

THE WEATHER
Cloudy and continued cold today; tomorrow fair and warmer.
Temperatures yesterday—Max. 59, min. 47.
U. S. Weather Forecast—For details See Page 30.

VOL. LXXIX....No. 26,207. * * * * NEW YORK, FRIDAY, OCTOBER 25, 1929. TWO CENTS In Greater New York | THREE CENTS Within 200 Miles | FOUR CENTS Elsewhere Except 7th and 8th Postal Zones

GRUNDY SAYS LOBBY IS NEEDED TO UPHOLD PARTY TARIFF VOWS

Pennsylvanian at Senate Inquiry Asserts Hoover Platform Demands the Rates in Bill.

TELLS OF CAMPAIGN FUNDS

Veteran Lobbyist Active in Raising $600,000 in 1924 and $1,000,000 Last Year.

HITS AT SENATE COALITION

Borah Assailed as Having Reversed Himself From Stand Taken in Campaign.

Special to The New York Times.

WASHINGTON, Oct. 24.—Joseph R. Grundy, head of the Pennsylvania Manufacturers' Association and a conspicuous figure for years in the Republican organization of that State, told the Senate Lobby Investigating Committee today that the rates in the pending tariff bill had been adopted in accordance with pledges in the Kansas City platform upon which Herbert Hoover made his successful run for the Presidency. The witness declared that 23,000,000 voters had endorsed the protective principle, and that if the consumers had wanted lower tariff duties they would have shown it by electing Alfred E. Smith to the Presidency.

Mr. Grundy has been identified with "tariff lobbies" since 1897, and frankly said so, insisting that only by alert watchfulness on the part of those concerned could "protected" interests get the kind of legislation that they needed at the hands of Congress.

A big crowd was in attendance to hear the testimony of Mr. Grundy, whose appearance was awaited with

Plane Lost in Channel Gale; 5 Aboard Fail to Reach Paris

Special Cable to THE NEW YORK TIMES.

LONDON, Oct. 24.—The English Channel was being swept by searchlights tonight in a hunt for three British airmen with two passengers who left Croydon airdrome in a new three-engined airplane to fly to East Africa.

A sixty-mile-an-hour gale was raging over the Channel when the airplane crossed the cliffs near Dover and disappeared into a mist.

The airplane, intended for passenger service in Kenya Colony, was piloted by Captain Campbell Black and carried G. D. Fletcher, an East African journalist, and R. Rowthorne as passengers.

Owing to low visibility and bumpy conditions the airplane returned once to Croydon and dropped another passenger who preferred to travel on the surface.

JURY IN FALL TRIAL LOCKED UP FOR NIGHT

No Word Comes After 11½ Hours' Deliberations of 8 Men, 4 Women in Bribe Case.

DEFENDANT STAYS ABED

Exceptions Were Taken by the Ex-Secretary's Counsel to the Judge's Charge.

Special to The New York Times.

WASHINGTON, Oct. 24.—The jury trying the case of Albert B. Fall, former Secretary of the Interior, who is charged with accepting a bribe of $100,000 from Edward L. Doheny, was locked up for the night at 11 o'clock tonight. It had deliberated since 11:30 o'clock in the morning without reporting a verdict. Court was recessed until 10 o'clock tomorrow morning.

I... hours that had elapsed

HUMBERT ESCAPES ANTI-FASCISTI'S SHOT AT BRUSSELS TOMB

Student Slips as He Tries to Assassinate the Italian Crown Prince.

HEIR CONTINUES PROGRAM

He Places Wreath on Unknown Soldier's Grave and Reviews Guard of Honor.

CROWD MOBS ASSAILANT

Italian Came From Paris to Kill Prince During Celebration of Royal Betrothal.

Special Cable to THE NEW YORK TIMES.

BRUSSELS, Oct. 24.—Within a few hours of the official announcement of his engagement to Princess Marie José and only a few feet from the tomb of Belgium's unknown soldier, an attempt was made this morning to assassinate Prince Humbert, heir to the Italian throne.

A young Italian law student, Fernando di Rosa, who had come to Brussels from Paris expressly to kill the Prince, confessed that he fired a revolver at him from a distance of twelve feet. Fortunately the assassin slipped just as he fired and the shot went wide.

Prince Humbert had wished, as his first act in the country of his future bride, to lay a wreath on the tomb of the Unknown Soldier. His engagement to the Princess being official, an elaborate ceremony had been arranged. There was a big crowd in the square around the Colonne de Congrès and two companies of infantry were lined up with their flags and the flag of the Italian veterans.

Gendarme Fells Assailant.

A' the official world had ... 'hered

Loud-Speaker Can Be Nuisance, McAdoo Advises Magistrates

The opinion that a radio loud-speaker, under certain conditions, may be classed as a nuisance was expressed by Chief Magistrate William McAdoo in a letter sent to the forty-six magistrates of the five boroughs yesterday. His letter declared:

"As you know, there is a wide-spread complaint all over the city by people who are annoyed and kept from sleeping by the loud-speaking radios in apartments, tenement houses and other buildings. Many complaints come to this office urging me to ask you gentlemen to treat these cases seriously.

"The person who starts a loud-speaker under conditions where it is found to annoy and disturb other people and keep them from proper rest, in my opinion, is guilty of a disorderly act, and where it is persistent and annoys a considerable number of people, he or she can be charged under Section 1,530 with maintaining a nuisance."

TESTIFIES HE HANDED $10,000 TO WARDER

Dell' Osso Asserts Former State Banking Head Counted Alleged Bribe in Home.

SENT BY FERRARI, HE SAYS

Memorandum on Withdrawal of Cash From City Trust Is Held From Jury Temporarily.

Gennaro Dell' Osso testified yesterday that he handed $10,000 "in large bills" to Frank H. Warder when the latter was State Superintendent of Banks. Dell' Osso, key witness for the State at Mr. Warder's trial for bribery, said he took the money to Mr. Warder's home for the late

WORST STOCK CRASH STEMMED BY BANKS; 12,894,650-SHARE DAY SWAMPS MARKET; LEADERS CONFER, FIND CONDITIONS SOUND

FINANCIERS EASE TENSION

Five Wall Street Bankers Hold Two Meetings at Morgan Office.

CALL BREAK 'TECHNICAL'

Lamont Lays It to 'Air Holes' —Says Low Prices Do Not Depict Situation Fairly.

FINDS MARGINS BEING MET

Sees Market 'Susceptible of Betterment'—Mitchell, Potter, Wiggin, Prosser at Talks.

Wall Street gave credit yesterday to its banking leaders for arresting the decline on the New York Stock Exchange at a time when the stock market was being overwhelmed by selling orders. The conference at which the steps were taken that reversed the market's trend was hurriedly called at the offices of J. P. Morgan & Co.

The five bankers who met at the headquarters of the famous private banking house at noon yesterday and again at 4:30 P. M., following the meeting of the board of the Federal Reserve Bank of New York, were:

CHARLES E. MITCHELL, chairman of the National City Bank.
ALBERT H. WIGGIN, chairman of the Chase N...

Wall Street Optimistic After Stormy Day; Clerical Work May Force Holiday Tomorrow

Confidence in the soundness of the stock market structure, notwithstanding the upheaval of the last few days, was voiced last night by bankers and other financial leaders. Sentiment as expressed by the heads of some of the largest banking institutions and by industrial executives as well was distinctly cheerful and the feeling was general that the worst had been seen. Wall Street ended the day in an optimistic frame of mind.

The opinion of brokers was unanimous that the selling had got out of hand not because of any inherent weakness in the market but because the public had become alarmed over the steady liquidation of the last few weeks. Over their private wires these brokers counseled their customers against further thoughtless selling at sacrifice prices.

Charles E. Mitchell, chairman of the National City Bank, declared that fundamentals remained unimpaired after the declines of the last few days. "I am still of the opinion," he added, "that this reaction has badly overrun itself."

Lewis E. Pierson, chairman of the board of the Irving Trust Company, issued last night the following statement:

"Severe disturbances in the stock market are nothing new in American experience. The pendulum always swings widely and it would seem as though the long-expected break should bring about an equilibrium.

"The position of the Federal Reserve Bank is unusually strong and the borrowings of member banks are moderate.

"Considering the record-breaking earnings in many industries, we may well remember that whenever fundamental values are lost sight of by the unthinking majority it is time for courage on the part of those investors who have a real sense of basic worth."

Because the clerical facilities of brokerage houses are overtaxed as a result of the recent phenomenally heavy trading, an agitation was started yesterday in favor of a suspension of trading on the New York Stock Exchange tomorrow.

It is thought possible that the governing committee will take action today, without waiting for a petition from the membership. In many brokerage houses the posting of books has fallen far behind and some relief will have to be afforded, according to brokers, unless the market quiets down shortly.

BIG DROP IN WHEAT; PIT IN A TURMOIL

TREASURY OFFICIALS BLAME SPECULATION

LOSSES RECOVERED IN PART

Upward Trend Starts With 200,000-Share Order for Steel.

TICKERS LAG FOUR HOURS

Thousands of Accounts Wiped Out, With Traders in Dark as to Events on Exchange.

SALES ON CURB 6,337,415

Prices on Markets in Other Cities Also Slump and Rally —Wheat Values Hard Hit.

The most disastrous decline in the biggest and broadest stock market of history rocked the financial district yesterday. In the very midst of the collapse five of the country's most influential bankers hurried to the office of J. P. Morgan & Co., and after a brief conference gave out word that they believe the foundations of the market to be sound, that the market smash has been caused by technical rather than fundamental considerations, and that many sound stocks are selling too low.

Suddenly the market turned about, on buying orders thrown into the pivotal issues, and before the final quotations were tapped out, four hours and eight minutes after the

CENTRALIZING THE POWER

SAM TANENHAUS

The 1930's were bracketed by two disasters: the stock market crash of October 29, 1929, which wiped away billions in fortunes built on rampant speculation, and Nazi Germany's invasion of Poland on September 1, 1939,[1] which hurtled Europe into war.

"I sit in one of the dives/On Fifty-second Street," W. H. Auden[2] wrote soon after that second catastrophe, "Uncertain and afraid/As the clever hopes expire/Of a low dishonest decade." The clever hopes were those of extremist ideologies—communism, fascism and Nazism—which promised to give enduring new shape to nations and peoples, but instead brought forth unimagined techniques of brutality and mass extermination. This grim truth exposed the dishonesty of many public activists, above all the leaders of the world's great democracies, who did so little, at times nothing at all, to halt the growing totalitarian threat.

The United States, protected by an ocean, was initially spared the worst. But the distance was rapidly shrinking. One of the most vivid Times headlines from 1930 was bannered atop the front page on September 3: "COSTE DOES IT IN 37 HOURS, 18½ MINUTES! FIRST TO MAKE PARIS-NEW YORK FLIGHT." The French aviator's journey reversed the route Charles A. Lindbergh had taken three years earlier[3] and also revised its meaning. As Lindbergh's flight had dramatized the boundless reach of American ingenuity, so Coste's implied that the furies of European turmoil were winging westward.

The Great Depression, following swiftly on the crash of 1929, conveyed a similar message, at least to President Herbert Hoover. As the slump worsened, and some 15 million Americans were thrown out of work and onto relief rolls, Hoover, though plainly distressed by the plight of the jobless and the hungry, staunchly insisted that the mercies

Crowds fill the street outside the New York Stock Exchange on October 24, 1929, as heavy trading on the stock exchange spreads panic among investors.

The Spirit of St. Louis is surrounded by well-wishers after it lands at Le Bourget airfield near Paris in 1927.

FURTHER READING

1 "Hostilities Begun," see September 1, 1939, front page.
2 "W. H. Auden Dies in Vienna," see September 30, 1973, front page.
3 "Lindbergh Triumph Thrills Coolidge," see May 22, 1927, front page.

The classic photo shows a farmer and children making their way across a dusty field in 1936 Arkansas during the Depression.

President Hoover organized largely unsuccessful voluntary measures to attempt to combat the Depression.

Shantytowns, such as this one, set up by thousands of unemployed and homeless Americans, were nicknamed "Hoovervilles."

of "systematic voluntary organizations" offered a sounder remedy than government measures tinged, however faintly, with foreign socialism.

But his optimism bordered on delusion. "We have now passed the worst," he declared six months into the Depression. Seven months later his party was repudiated in Congressional elections, a landslide victory for the Democrats. Defeat only calcified Hoover's resolve. In his Memorial Day address of 1931, delivered at Valley Forge, where George Washington's soldiers "suffered privation and death in the darkest hours of the War of Independence," as the Times story put it, the president pleaded with a nationwide radio audience to maintain faith in America's "great traditions," and reject the notion that "any one strategy sprung from the mind of any single genius" held the hope of fresh prosperity.[4]

But on Election Day 1932 the voters chose a new president, the governor of New York, Franklin D. Roosevelt, in a lopsided victory that The Times's Arthur Krock (not usually given to hyperbole) termed a "political cataclysm, unprecedented in the nation's history" since it also delivered the Democrats a huge majority in Congress and in statehouses across the land.[5]

At the time few suspected Roosevelt, the Dutchess County squire with his blue-blood's accent, his uptilted head and rumored dilettantism, might be a "genius" of any kind. In truth he possessed political nerve unmatched since the presidency of Abraham Lincoln. Promising a "New Deal for America," Roosevelt enacted a sequence of regulatory reforms and created a string of agencies, "the alphabet soup" conceived by a circle of policy intellectuals, his "brain trust," all of it climaxing with the Social Security Act, written into law in August 1935.[6] By then, Roosevelt was more than an effective president. He was ubiquitous, the single dominant figure in American life, bonding to the people of the nation through his innovative radio "fireside chats."

"The only will left in the national government is his will," the influential columnist H. L. Mencken wrote. "To all intents and purposes he is the state."

And yet, great though Roosevelt's power seemed, he was repeatedly stymied, to some extent by Congress but chiefly by the Supreme Court, which ruled, time after time, that his programs, including the far-reaching National Industrial

Recovery Act, were unconstitutional.[7] After his re-election in 1936—one of the most emphatic in history; he captured 46 states and almost 61 percent of the vote—Roosevelt announced a scheme of breathtaking audacity "prepared in a small group and with deepest secrecy," as The Times reported, to "permit an increase in the membership of the Supreme Court from nine to a minimum of fifteen if judges reaching the age of 70 declined to retire."[8]

The Court-packing plan, denounced on all sides, summoned up for many the very dangers Hoover, who equated the New Deal with "fascism," had warned against. The plan was rejected overwhelmingly, and Roosevelt, always a realist, obeyed the public will, even as his critics still drew ominous parallels with rising dictatorships abroad.

These alarms were exaggerated, not to say ideologically inflected, as was clear from events unfolding overseas. In the Soviet Union, Joseph Stalin was tightening his iron grip with purges and show trials of old revolutionary comrades, the victims routinely executed or sentenced to join the tens of millions languishing in the gulags.

In Germany too, Hitler, though legally elected, governed by murder. In 1934 he orchestrated the assassinations of onetime colleagues, including General Kurt von Schleicher, who had preceded him as chancellor.[9] This was the prelude to other brazen aggressions: Germany's occupation of Austria and its "liberation" of ethnic Germans in Czechoslovakia. Each international crime was met with protest. Each protest dwindled into appeasement, even in London, the seat of the globe's greatest empire. Hitler pressed on, finally formalizing a partnership with Stalin[10] on August 23, 1939, that dismembered Poland and set the stage for World War II a week later.

The majority of Americans wanted no part of it. F.D.R.'s support of Great Britain, through arms and aid, provoked outrage in Congress and among the public. Isolationism was another of America's longstanding faiths, and the president who challenged it invited repudiation. Roosevelt knew this from experience: He had served in the administration of Woodrow Wilson, who two decades earlier had led the nation into war, proclaiming a new global democratic order, only to see his presidency reduced to ashes.

A long line of jobless men wait outside a New York City lodging house for a free dinner during the winter of 1932–33.

President Roosevelt conducting an outdoor press conference from his car in Warm Springs, Georgia.

F.D.R. signs the Social Security bill on August 14, 1935, one of the many major accomplishments of the New Deal.

4 "Hoover Urges Nation to Be Steadfast in This 'Valley Forge' of Depression," see May 31, 1931, front page.
5 "Sweep Is National," see November 9, 1932, front page.
6 "Social Security Bill Voted; Will Benefit 30,000,000," see August 10, 1935, front page.
7 "Court Is Unanimous," see May 28, 1935, front page.
8 "Surprise Message; Asks Authority to Name New Justices if Old Do Not Quit at 70," see February 6, 1937, front page.

Hitler receives a standing ovation after announcing the annexation of Austria before the Reichstag in Berlin on March 13, 1938.

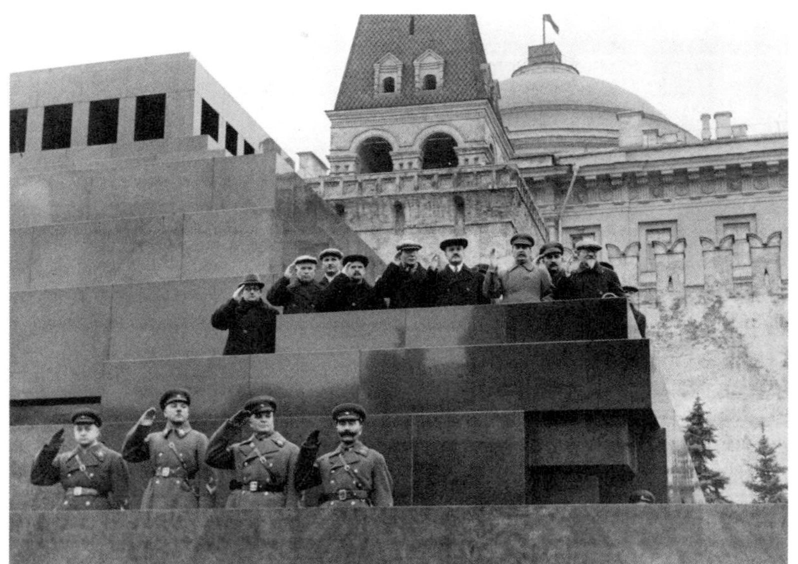

Joseph Stalin, second to the left on the top tier, reviews the Soviet armed forces.

Precedent had not stopped Roosevelt before. It didn't this time, either. The decade ended with his decision—kept secret as always—to defy yet another of America's "great traditions" by seeking a third presidential term. Again he was called a dictator. Again he went forward, creating a new and lasting role for the federal government in political and public life. And again the people would follow him, seeing in him not a dictator but a leader who had calmed a desperate nation when it was uncertain and afraid and instilled it with hopes that were not merely clever.

SAM TANENHAUS *is editor of The New York Times Book Review and The Week in Review. He was an assistant editor on the Op-Ed page in 1998–1999. Tanenhaus was also a contributing editor at Vanity Fair from 1999 until 2004 and has written for many other publications, including The New York Times Magazine, The New Republic, and The New York Review of Books. Tanenhaus is the author of "Whittaker Chambers: A Biography," a finalist for the Pulitzer Prize and the National Book Award, and winner of the Los Angeles Times Book Prize.*

9 "Schleicher Rites Barred By Police," see July 5, 1934, front page.
10 "Germany and Russia Agree on Non-Aggression," see August 22, 1939, front page.

Franklin Roosevelt and Winston Churchill meet secretly in the summer of 1941 aboard a British warship off the coast of Canada where they committed to common goals of U.S.-U.K. cooperation.

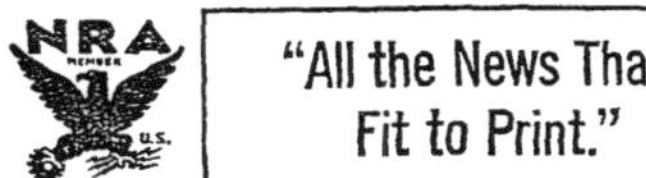

"All the News That's Fit to Print."

The New York Times.

Copyright, 1933, by The New York Times Company.

LATE CITY EDITION
WEATHER—Rain and warmer today; tomorrow fair and colder.
Temperatures Yesterday—Max., 44; min., 34.

VOL. LXXXIII....No. 27,710. Entered as Second-Class Matter, Postoffice, New York, N. Y. NEW YORK, WEDNESDAY, DECEMBER 6, 1933. MP TWO CENTS In New York City. | THREE CENTS Within 200 Miles | FOUR CENTS Elsewhere Except in 7th and 8th Postal Zones

LINDBERGHS AT SEA ON BRAZIL FLIGHT; 'O.K.' SHE REPORTS

630 MILES FROM AFRICA

Breeze Starts Fliers After Twenty Attempts in Dead Calm.

MOON LIGHTS THEIR WAY

10,000 Natives See Take-Off as Motor's Roar Stirs Them From Slumber.

RIDE THROUGH SQUALLS

Wife Radios Every Fifteen Minutes of Progress on 1,800-Mile Flight.

Colonel and Mrs. Charles A. Lindbergh were flying across the South Atlantic from Africa to Brazil this morning, reporting their progress by radio every fifteen minutes and their location every half hour.

At 2:20 A. M., New York time, five hours and twenty minutes after taking off from Bathurst, Gambia, in bright moonlight, they were 630 miles on their way across the Southern Ocean.

The first message from the plane was picked up by the Miami, Fla., station of Pan American Airways soon after 9:02 P. M. last night, New York time. It reported that the plane had taken off from Bathurst at that time. At 10 P. M., New York time, another message picked up by the Bahia, Brazil, station of Pan American Airways advised that the plane was flying Course 224 true, and gave its position, which Pan American officials estimated to be about 115 miles southwest of Bathurst. At 10:40 P. M. another message, also picked up by the Bahia station, reported "everything O. K.," and said the plane's position would be given every half hour and a progress O. K. sent out every fifteen minutes. The first progress O. K. was received by the Pan American station at Miami at 11 P. M., New York time.

Made 240 Miles in Two Hours.

At 11 P. M., the Bahia station also picked up a message. It gave for the plane a position approximately 240 miles southwest of Bathurst and right on her course. The operators at Bahia said that in her first message, Mrs. Lindbergh reported considerable static. But her messages, they said, were coming into Bahia strong, fast and clear, as if they were being sent by an experienced wireless operator.

The next message was received by the Pan-American station at Para, Brazil, at 11:50 P. M., New York time. It reported that the plane was flying at an altitude of 2,000 feet and making about 100 knots. There was unlimited visibility, the message said, with the sky about one-tenth overcast, and a quartering ten-knot tail wind.

At 12:30 this morning, the Pan American radio station at Miami and the Chatham, Mass., station of the Radiomarine Corporation each picked up a message from the plane giving a position approximately 446 miles southeast of Bathurst. The message said the plane was flying at an altitude of 1,200 feet, that there was visibility of about ten miles, that the sky was nine-tenths overcast, and that there was a quartering tail wind of 10 knots.

Squalls Met at Daybreak.

A message was received at 1:27 this morning at Pará, Brazil, reporting "skies eight-tenths overcast, scattered squalls, visibility three miles, daybreak; all's well."

At 1:50 A. M. the Bahia station picked up a message, "All's well."

At 2:20 A. M. a message was received at the Pará station reporting the plane's position as 630 miles southwest of Bathurst, flying at 1,000 feet, the skies nine-tenths overcast, frequent squalls, calm seas and no wind. That position indicated the Lindberghs had covered about one-third of the distance to Natal.

Natives Awaken for Start.

Special Cable to THE NEW YORK TIMES.

BATHURST, Gambia, Wednesday, Dec. 6.—With bright moonlight turning the waters around the little island of St. Mary, on which

Continued on Page Twenty-six.

Lindbergh Flight to Fame Twice as Long as New Hop

On the morning of May 20, 1927, six years and six months ago, Captain Charles A. Lindbergh, a mail pilot, left Roosevelt Field for Paris.

He flew alone, and veteran pilots shook their heads when they saw him take off. His silver plane, dripping with rain, lumbered slowly—too slowly—down the muddy runway. It gathered speed, bounced from the ground and settled back again. It barely cleared a tractor at the end of the runway and just climbed over low telephone wires at the end of the field.

Thirty-three and a half hours later the young mail pilot brought his gray plane down at Le Bourget. That famous flight covered 3,610 miles. The present flight, also in a single-engined plane, is about 1,875 miles.

PWA READY TO BAR CITY SUBWAY LOAN

Security for $25,000,000 Advance to Finish System Is Held Inadequate.

BANKERS' PACTS A FACTOR

Officials Here Say Attitude of Washington Is Based on a Misunderstanding.

Special to THE NEW YORK TIMES.

WASHINGTON, Dec. 5.—Inability of New York City to furnish security satisfactory to the Public Works Administration has caused the latter to abandon the allotment of $25,000,000 for completion of the Eighth Avenue subway.

New York officials have not been notified, but it was learned from reliable sources that the application for the loan would be refused.

At his press conference today Secretary Ickes said there was "nothing new" to report on the loan. He added, however, that the matter was held up by the question of security.

Senator Wagner announced virtual assurance of the loan more than two weeks ago. Since then the matter has been before the Special Board of Public Works, while PWA engineers and lawyers were investigating.

Application Signed by Mayor.

The application, for $25,000,000, signed by Mayor O'Brien, was on a loan and grant basis, 30 per cent of the cost of materials and structure to be an outright grant and the rest a loan on security furnished by the city.

The amount of money which completion of the subway would require is indefinite. Public Works Administration officials have scaled the sum down to some $22,500,000 under one estimate.

The money would be applied to equipping, tracking and finishing some eighteen miles of subway already dug, mainly in Brooklyn and Queens, and to the building of stations. Seven thousand men would obtain work through the Winter, it was estimated, and large supplies of capital goods would be purchased.

The allotment was discussed at the recent conference between Secretary Ickes and Mayor-elect LaGuardia, but it was not gone into in any detail.

The attitude of the PWA, it was learned, is that the city has tied up the revenues of the subway by its financing agreements with the banks, and would be operating on a margin too slender to enable it to guarantee any return on the investment, even if the PWA funds allowed the subway to open miles of route and thus tap new sources of revenue.

Unification Another Problem.

The PWA feels that the situation is further complicated by the competition of the other New York subway lines. If the other lines were taken over by the city under the unification plan, a campaign promise of the Mayor-elect, the PWA feels that there would be a general scaling down of the demands of creditors and a consequent loss to the government on its investment. The question of the 5-cent fare is not worrying the administration, Secretary Ickes has said.

While Mr. Ickes has already ex-

Continued on Page Twenty-seven.

TAX PLAN OFFERED TO CURB EVASIONS, RAISE $237,000,000

House Subcommittee Urges a Check on Personal Holding Concerns by 35% Levy.

WOULD INCREASE SURTAX

Normal Income Tax of 4% and Revision of Capital Gains Are Also Proposed.

Special to THE NEW YORK TIMES.

WASHINGTON, Dec. 5.—Broad tax reforms designed to increase the Federal revenue $237,000,000 a year and prevent "the avoidance and evasion of the internal revenue laws" were recommended today in a report submitted to the House Ways and Means Committee by a subcommittee.

The full committee immediately began study of the suggestions, and Representative Doughton, the chairman, said a completed bill would probably be ready for presentation soon after Congress meets next month.

Changes sought are aimed principally at persons whose incomes are in the higher brackets, as well as at corporations now legally permitted to take advantage of what committee members said were "unfair but legal" provisions of the revenue laws.

Some discord was apparent within the committee, but no member would publicly express his feelings.

"It isn't law yet, and it is not even past the committee," said one member. "It must go to the House and Senate."

Nine Changes are Urged.

Nine phases of the present law were recommended for modification as follows:

1. Establishment of a normal income tax rate of 4 per cent, instead of the present 4 per cent on the first $4,000 and 8 per cent on the remainder of net income, and revision of the surtax rate on a graduated scale, with the brackets reduced from 53 to 27; estimated to increase revenue $36,000,000 annually.

2. Change for three years in the depreciation and depletion section of the 1932 Revenue Act by reducing allowances by 25 per cent; estimated to add $85,000,000 for each of the three years.

3. Revision of the capital gains and losses section by revising the method of adjustment and prescribing a scale-length of ownership; estimated to add $30,000,000.

4. Amendment of the personal holding companies' section to prevent persons with large incomes from forming companies to evade taxes; estimated to add $25,000,000.

5. Abolition of certain sections of the "exchanges and reorganization" provisions to "close the door to one of the most prevalent methods of tax avoidance"; estimated to add $18,000,000.

6. Imposition of a tax on dividends paid out of corporation earnings accumulated before March 1, 1913; estimated to add $6,000,000.

7. Amendment of the foreign tax credit sections of the 1932 act; estimated to add $10,000,000.

8. Withdrawal of permission for corporations which are affiliated through 95 per cent stock ownership to file consolidated returns; estimated to add $20,000,000.

9. Revision of the partnership losses section of the 1932 Revenue Act; estimated to add $7,000,000.

Eager to expedite the "major problems," the subcommittee passed over a group of minor matters, according to the chairman, Representative Sam B. Hill of Washington. He said the subcommittee would continue study of these problems,

Continued on Page Fourteen.

PROHIBITION REPEAL IS RATIFIED AT 5:32 P. M.; ROOSEVELT ASKS NATION TO BAR THE SALOON; NEW YORK CELEBRATES WITH QUIET RESTRAINT

State House Bootlegger Is Barred in Maryland

Special to THE NEW YORK TIMES.

ANNAPOLIS, Md., Dec. 5.—Wet legislators here will patriotically support legal liquor. The State House bootlegger received formal notice today to discontinue his trade. The notice was served by a policeman on duty at the Capitol.

Throughout this session, the bootlegger has conducted a thriving business; a business which, he says, has been especially arduous because of the sudden demands made on him by legislators and their desire for prompt service.

While his services were cut off eight hours before post-prohibition stuff could be bought, the bootlegger thought the legislators had obtained a sufficient reserve to carry them through until evening and legal liquor.

RATIFYING BY UTAH ENDS PROHIBITION

With Impressive Ceremony, the 36th State Follows Ohio and Pennsylvania in Day.

CONVENTIONS ALL SOLEMN

Moderation Pleas Are Made at Columbus—Hush Greets Vote at Harrisburg.

Special to THE NEW YORK TIMES.

SALT LAKE CITY, Dec. 5—The Eighteenth Amendment to the Constitution of the United States passed out of existence officially at 3:32½ o'clock this afternoon, Mountain standard time (5:32½ New York time) with the ratification of repeal by the convention of Utah, the thirty-sixth required State.

The passing of national prohibition was marked by impressive ceremony in the hall of the House of Representatives in the State Capitol here.

To Delegate S. R. Thurman, a repeal leader of Salt Lake City, whose father was a member of the State's constitutional convention in 1895 before Utah was admitted to the Union, fell the honor of being the last to record his vote, the roll being called in alphabetical order.

His "Yea," placing the Twenty-first Amendment to the Constitution in effect, was greeted by enthusiastic applause from the audience of a few hundred persons.

About ninety seconds later Ray L. Olson of Ogden, president of the convention, who had been manager of the repealists' campaign, brought down his gavel and announced that the repeal amendment had been ratified. Notification was transmitted immediately to the White House by a special wire from the Capitol.

At the same time Delegate A. S. Brown, former president of the Salt Lake Chamber of Commerce, sent out word to President Roosevelt over the Columbia Broadcasting System. He congratulated the President on the successful culmination of the repeal movement.

The whole proceedings were in keeping with the historic aspect of the occasion. Besides high officials

Continued on Page Five.

Italy to Quit League Unless It Is Reformed; Demands Altered Aims and Set-Up at Once

By ARNALDO CORTESI.

Wireless to THE NEW YORK TIMES.

ROME, Wednesday, Dec. 6.—At the end of a long sitting lasting far into the night, the Fascist Grand Council, which had been convoked to decide on Italy's relations with the League of Nations, passed a suspended sentence on Geneva.

After having discussed every aspect of the probable effect of Italy's withdrawal, the Grand Council decided "to render Italy's further participation in the League dependent on radical changes in that organization to be brought about within the shortest possible time, which changes must affect the League in its constitution, in its methods and in its objectives."

At the same time the Grand Council reached a temporizing decision also in the matter of payment to the United States of the debt instalment due on Dec. 15. In view of the impossibility of conducting negotiations on the debt problem, the Grand Council decided "to effect on Dec. 15 a token payment of $1,000,000 as renewed proof of Italy's good-will, while awaiting a final settlement of this whole question."

Since the breakdown in the disarmament negotiations Premier Mussolini has been advocating efforts outside Geneva and the League of Nations. He has favored action under the Four-Power Pact initiated by Great Britain, France, Italy and Germany, or at any rate negotiations by the leading powers, including the United States.

As to reforms in the League, the press has suggested that the League be divorced from the Versailles Treaty, and that its constitution be revised to give the larger powers a freer hand in directing its affairs.

CITY TOASTS NEW ERA

Crowds Swamp Licensed Resorts, but the Legal Liquor Is Scarce.

CELEBRATION IN STREETS

Marked by Absence of Undue Hilarity and Only Normal Number of Arrests.

MANY SPEAKEASIES CLOSE

Machine Guns Guard Some Liquor Trucks—Supplies to Be Rushed Out Today.

Slowly gathering momentum from the time when the news began to spread just at nightfall that national prohibition was no more, the public rejoicing at the end of the long dry reign was carried on last night with restraint and absence of undue hilarity.

Throngs of New Yorkers ventured into Times Square and other centres of the metropolis and many of the thousand restaurants, hotels and clubs fortunate enough to have received their licenses for the sale of alcoholic beverages were swamped.

But gay as were their spirits, they were well-behaved. With the city's entire police force of 19,000 men mobilized to guard against overexuberant celebrants, arrests did not exceed the normal number for any day of the last five years. Incidentally, official word that repeal was a fact did not go out to the police until 9:20 P. M., just about four hours after Utah acted.

Stores Fail to Get Stocks.

The thronging to places of public entertainment was enhanced by the fact that only a handful of New Yorkers was able to drink a toast to the occasion with lawful liquor in their own homes. Because Utah did not make repeal effective until 5:32½ P. M., retail liquor stores with only two exceptions were unable to obtain wines and whiskies from the warehouses in the brief time left.

Indeed, the supply of lawful liquor even in the licensed places was woefully scant. Only fifty-four truckloads of bonded liquor were released from the warehouses before they closed last night, and the two largest warehouses shut their doors before the Twenty-first Amendment displaced the Eighteenth.

With 3,000 places licensed to dispense the newly legalized beverages in the metropolitan area and 2,000 more up-State, hardly one in a hundred was able to move in a stock in the few hours available. Some of the others, of course, had had the foresight to lay in supplies under medicinal permits during the dying days of prohibition.

Bootleggers and speakeasies came to the rescue, however, despite a stern warning from Police Commissioner Bolan that his men would not tolerate any such activity. They operated with a little more caution than usual, but nevertheless they took advantage of the occasion to dispose of a large part of their unlawful stocks. The raids threatened by Mr. Bolan proved few and on little known places.

Many Cordial Shops Close.

Cordial shops and other neighborhood dispensaries during the long drought showed fear of police activity last night for the first time in years. Hundreds of them closed their doors, others dealt only with long-known and trusted customers, and only a scattering number, principally in downtown Manhattan, carried on business as usual. Some of them carried signs promising to open as licensed liquor stores in a few days.

There was every indication, however, that New York's long reliance on contraband cheer was near its end. The warehousemen promised deliveries on a large scale would begin today, with 400 trucks licensed to speed legal liquors throughout the city and its suburbs.

A cargo of 6,200 cases of assorted wines and spirits worth about $170,000 arrived on the White Star liner Majestic from France and England late in the afternoon, but the ship was delayed five hours by

Continued on Page Two.

The Repeal Proclamation

Special to THE NEW YORK TIMES.

WASHINGTON, Dec. 5.—The text of the proclamation by William Phillips, Acting Secretary of State, certifying to the adoption of the Twenty-first Amendment repealing prohibition, follows:

WILLIAM PHILLIPS,

Acting Secretary of State of the United States of America.

To all whom these presents shall come, greeting:

KNOW YE, That the Congress of the United States, at the second session, Seventy-second Congress, begun and held at the city of Washington on Monday, the fifth day of December, in the year one thousand nine hundred and thirty-two, passed a joint Resolution in the words and figures as follows:

To wit—

JOINT RESOLUTION.

Proposing an amendment to the Constitution of the United States.

Resolved by the Senate and House of Representatives of the United States of America in Congress assembled (two-thirds of each House concurring therein), That the following article is hereby proposed as an amendment to the Constitution of the United States, which shall be valid to all intents and purposes as part of the Constitution when ratified by conventions in three-fourths of the several States:

ARTICLE.

Section 1. The Eighteenth Article of Amendment to the Constitution of the United States is hereby repealed.

Section 2. The transportation or importation into any State, Territory, or Possession of the United States for delivery or use therein of intoxicating liquors, in violation of the laws thereof, is hereby prohibited.

Section 3. This article shall be inoperative unless it shall have been ratified as an amendment to the Constitution by conventions in the several States, as provided in the Constitution, within seven years from the date of the submission hereof to the States by the Congress.

And, further, that it appears from official notices received at the Department of State that the amendment to the Constitution of the United States proposed as aforesaid has been ratified by conventions in the States of Arizona, Alabama, Arkansas, California, Colorado, Connecticut, Delaware, Florida, Idaho, Illinois, Indiana, Iowa, Kentucky, Maryland, Massachusetts, Michigan, Minnesota, Missouri, Nevada, New Hampshire, New Jersey, New Mexico, New York, Ohio, Oregon, Pennsylvania, Rhode Island, Tennessee, Texas, Utah, Vermont, Virginia, Washington, West Virginia, Wisconsin and Wyoming.

And, further, that the States wherein conventions have so ratified the said proposed amendment constitute the requisite three-fourths of the whole number of States in the United States.

NOW, therefore, be it known that I, William Phillips, Acting Secretary of State of the United States, by virtue and in pursuance of Section 160, Title 5, of the United States Code, do hereby certify that the amendment aforesaid has become valid to all intents and purposes as a part of the Constitution of the United States.

In testimony whereof, I have hereunto set my hand and caused the seal of the Department of State to be affixed.

Done at the city of Washington this fifth day of December in the year of our Lord one thousand nine hundred and thirty-three.

WILLIAM PHILLIPS.

Roosevelt Proclaims Repeal; Urges Temperance in Nation

President's Announcement Is in Accordance With the Instruction of Congress Contained in the Recovery Act—Declares Social Evils of Liquor Shall Not Be Revived.

Special to THE NEW YORK TIMES.

WASHINGTON, Dec. 5.—President Roosevelt's proclamation of the repeal of the Eighteenth Amendment was as follows:

By the President of the United States of America.

A Proclamation.

Whereas the Congress of the United States in the second session of the Seventy-second Congress, begun at Washington on the fifth day of December in the year one thousand nine hundred and thirty-two adopted a resolution in the words and figures following: to wit—

JOINT RESOLUTION.

Proposing an amendment to the Constitution of the United States.

Resolved by the Senate and House of Representatives of the United States of America in Congress assembled (two-thirds of each House concurring therein), That the following article is hereby proposed as an amendment to the Constitution of the United States, which shall be valid to all intents and purposes as part of the Constitution when ratified by conventions in three-fourths of the several States:

ARTICLE.

Section 1. The Eighteenth Article of amendment to the Constitution of the United States is hereby repealed.

Section 2. The transportation or importation into any State, Territory or possession of the United States for delivery or use therein of intoxicating liquors, in violation of the laws thereof, is hereby prohibited.

Section 3. This article shall be inoperative unless it shall have been ratified as an amendment to the Constitution by conventions in the several States, as provided in the Constitution, within seven years from the date of the submission hereof to the States by the Congress.

Declares Amendment Repealed.

Whereas, Section 217 (a) of the Act of Congress entitled "An act to encourage national industrial recovery, to foster competition and to provide for the construction of certain useful public works, and for other purposes," approved June 16, 1933, provides as follows:

Section 217 (a) The President shall proclaim the date of ———

(1) the close of the first fiscal year ending June 30 of any year after the year 1933, during which the total receipts of the

Continued on Page Two.

FINAL ACTION AT CAPITAL

President Proclaims the Nation's New Policy as Utah Ratifies.

PHILLIPS SIGNS DECREE

Orders 21st Amendment in Effect on Receiving Votes of Three Final States.

RECOVERY TAXES TO END

$227,000,000 a Year Automatically Dropped—Canadian Whisky Quota Is Raised.

Special to THE NEW YORK TIMES.

WASHINGTON, Dec. 5.—Legal liquor today was returned to the United States, with President Roosevelt calling on the people to see that "this return of individual freedom shall not be accompanied by the repugnant conditions that obtained prior to the adoption of the Eighteenth Amendment and those that have existed since its adoption."

Prohibition of alcoholic beverages as a national jolicy ended at 5:32½ P. M., Eastern Standard Time, when Utah, the last of the thirty-six States, furnished by vote of its convention the constitutional majority for ratification of the Twenty-first Amendment. The new amendment repealed the Eighteenth, and with the demise of the latter went the Volstead Act which for more than a decade held legal drinks in America to less than one-half of 1 per cent of alcohol and the enforcement of which cost more than 150 lives and billions in money.

Earlier in the day Pennsylvania had ratified as the thirty-fourth State and Ohio as the thirty-fifth.

Proclamation by President.

President Roosevelt at 6:55 P. M. signed an official proclamation in keeping with terms of the National Industrial Recovery Act, under which prohibition ended and four taxes levied to raise $227,000,000 annually for amortization of the $3,300,000,000 public works fund were repealed.

But the President went further. Accepting certification from Acting Secretary of State Phillips that thirty-six States had ratified the repealing amendment, he improved the occasion to address a plea to the American people to employ their regained liberty first of all for national manliness.

Mr. Roosevelt asked personally for what he and his party had declined to make the subject of Federal mandate—that saloons be barred from the country.

"I ask especially," he said, "that no State shall, by law or otherwise, authorize the return of the saloon, either in its old form or in some modern guise."

Makes Personal Plea.

He enjoined all citizens to cooperate with the government in its endeavor to restore a greater respect for law and order, especially by confining their purchases of liquor to duly licensed agencies. This practice, which he personally requested every individual and every family in the nation to follow, would result, he said, in a better product for consumption, in addition to the "break-up and eventual destruction of the notoriously evil illicit liquor traffic" and in tax benefits to the government.

The President thus announced the policy of his administration—to see that the social and political evils of the preprohibition era shall not be revived or permitted again to exist. Failure of citizens to use their new freedom in helping to advance this policy, he said, would be "a living reproach to us all."

He expressed faith, too, in the "good sense of the American people" in preventing excessive personal use of relegalized liquor. "The objective we seek through a national policy," he said, "is the education of every citizen toward a greater temperance throughout the nation."

As a means of enforcing his policy, the President has the Federal Alcohol Control Administration ready to take control of the liquor traffic and regulate it at the source of supply.

In its first major step today, the

Continued on Page Two.

"All the News That's Fit to Print."

The New York Times.

LATE CITY EDITION
WEATHER—Showers today; tomorrow fair, somewhat cooler.
Temperatures Yesterday—Max., 91; Min., 78.

Section 1

VOL. LXXXIII....No. 27,917. | Entered as Second-Class Matter. Postoffice, New York, N. Y. | NEW YORK, SUNDAY, JULY 1, 1934. | Including Rotogravure Picture, Magazine and Book Sections. | F | TEN CENTS | TWELVE CENTS Beyond 200 Miles. Except in 7th and 8th Postal Zones.

HITLER CRUSHES REVOLT BY NAZI RADICALS; VON SCHLEICHER IS SLAIN, ROEHM A SUICIDE; LOYAL FORCES HOLD BERLIN IN AN IRON GRIP

EXCHANGE, LABOR BOARDS NAMED; FARM BILL SIGNED

KENNEDY IN 'CHANGE POST

The Others Are Mathews, Landis, Healy, Pecora for Varying Terms.

WIRE BOARD IS CHOSEN

Members Are Sykes, Brown, Case, Stuart, Payne, Gary and Walker.

RAIL PENSIONS APPROVED

Clark Howell Heads Air Study —Moffett Made Administrator of the Housing Act.

President Clears His Desk

On the eve of his departure this evening on the cruiser Houston for a month's cruise, President Roosevelt cleared his desk last night.

He named the two commissions to regulate the Stock Exchanges and the operations of telegraph, telephone and radio companies.

He signed the Frazier-Lemke bill setting up new methods for the compromising of agricultural indebtedness.

He signed the railroad employes' pension bill.

He appointed James A. Moffett of New York, prominent oil executive, Administrator of the Housing Act.

He appointed an Aviation Commission, with Clark Howell as chairman.

He created an impartial Labor Relations Board, abolishing the old one and eliminating the NRA from a rôle in settling labor disputes.

Picks Exchange Board

Special to THE NEW YORK TIMES.

WASHINGTON, June 30.—As his last act tonight in cleaning up essential business before sailing from Annapolis for a month's holiday today, President Roosevelt named the personnel of the Securities and Exchange Commission.

He did not designate a chairman, there being some doubt as to his authority to do so, but it was understood in well-informed quarters that responsibility for the commission's work under the sweeping Stock Exchange Control Act would fall upon Joseph P. Kennedy, New York financier, who was designated to serve for five years. Four other commissioners were named for periods varying from one to four years.

The personnel of the commission follows:

JOSEPH P. KENNEDY of New York, five-year term.

GEORGE C. MATHEWS of Wisconsin, four-year term.

JAMES M. LANDIS of Massachusetts, three-year term.

ROBERT E. HEALY of Vermont, two-year term.

FERDINAND PECORA of New York, one-year term.

Messrs. Mathews and Landis are members of the Federal Trade Commission. Mr. Pecora was counsel for the Senate Banking and Currency Committee during the period in which it aired publicly for the first time in twenty years the manifold operations of securities exchanges and investment banking houses. As committee counsel he played a large part in shaping the law under which the commission will operate.

The naming of the Securities and Exchange Commission came after President Roosevelt, in a day of intensive work, had also named the Communications Commission and a commission to plan coordination of aircraft development, and had issued statements announcing the signing of the Frazier-Lemke Farm Mortgage Bill and the Railroad Pensions Bill.

Kennedy Close to Farley.

The membership of the Securities and Exchange Commission had been pretty generally forecast, but even so its composition was full of surprises, particularly the obvious placing in line for the chairmanship of Mr. Kennedy.

This is the first emergence of the New Yorker from what seemed to be political eclipse since the campaign of 1932, when he was distinguished both as a heavy contributor and important raiser of campaign funds, and because of his

Continued on Page Twenty-one.

Major Sports Results

Track—Bill Bonthron of Princeton broke the world's record for the 1,500-meter run in the national A. A. U. championship meet at Milwaukee. Timed in 3:48.8, he beat Glenn Cunningham by two feet. It was the fifth meeting between the stars and the triumph gave Bonthron the edge with three victories.

Tennis—Four Americans advanced at Wimbledon. Frank Shields defeated Christian Boussus of France and George M. Lott Jr. halted Harry Hopman of Australia. Miss Helen Jacobs conquered Mlle. Jacqueline Goldschmidt of France and Miss Sarah Palfrey beat Miss J. Jedrzejowska of Poland.

Baseball—Routing Carl Hubbell, the Dodgers stopped the Giants, 8—4, before 12,000 at the Polo Grounds. At Washington the Yankees were leading the Senators, 4—1, when rain caused the game to be called off in the fifth inning.

(Full details in Sports Section.)

JOHN JACOB ASTOR WEDS ELLEN FRENCH

Notables Fill Newport Church for Ceremony Climaxing Weeks of Social Activity.

ONLOOKERS PACK STREETS

Crowd Delays Both Bride and Bridegroom—Astor's Mother Sits in a Front Pew.

By RUSSELL B. PORTER.

Special to THE NEW YORK TIMES.

NEWPORT, R. I., June 30.—Two of America's oldest families, prominent in both landed wealth and in social position, were united in marriage here today at the wedding of John Jacob Astor 3d and Miss Ellen Tuck French.

The bridegroom is the third of his name in American life. The first John Jacob Astor, fur trader, founded the family in early American days. The second lost his life in the sinking of the Titanic, and the third John Jacob Astor, today's bridegroom, was born a few months later. He is a half-brother of Vincent Astor, and inherited with the latter the great Astor fortune.

The bride is a granddaughter of Amos Tuck French and is related to the Vanderbilt family.

These young members of old families, the bridegroom only 21 years old and the bride 18, were joined together in a setting repiete with symbols of early American traditions.

They were married according to the ancient simple ritual of the Protestant Episcopal Church, whose worshipers came to New England with the first settlers, in old Trinity Church, a long, narrow, weather-beaten white clapboard building with a towering white steeple and gilded spire and weather vane. It was all just as it was when the church was built more than two centuries ago, in 1726, eighty-seven years after the founding of Newport in 1639.

Shading the high steeple was a fine, old elm tree, as tall as or taller than the spire itself, with its great spreading branches almost speaking aloud the story of New England. The tree itself was as old or nearly as old as the church.

Church Recalls Colonial Days.

On the other side of the church, so that the wedding procession walked between it and the old tree to enter the building, was the old burying ground with its plain weather-beaten granite headstones bearing the names of men and women who played leading parts in shaping the history of the colonies and of the first days of the Republic.

All around the church, which is right in the centre of this fine old city, old frame buildings of Colonial architecture, with Grecian columns, steeply slanting roofs and gables, crowding close to the building line of the street, bespoke Newport's history.

The time joined with the place in celebrating the event with appropriate ceremony, for not only was it in the midst of the Summer season, when Newport's social colony is always in full swing, but it was coincident with a visit of a large part of the United States fleet. From time immemorial the navy has been associated with Newport, and

Continued on Page Eighteen.

FORD WILL ACCEPT NRA AND ITS CODE, JOHNSON IS TOLD

General Announces He Awaits Signed Certificate From Auto Maker.

SAYS HE ASKED CHANGES

Recovery Head Asserts His Suggestions Have Been Approved in Detroit.

Special to THE NEW YORK TIMES.

WASHINGTON, June 30.—General Johnson believed tonight that he was nearing such a settlement of his ten months feud with Henry Ford as would let the NRA put another feather in its cap and at the same time allow the automobile maker to re-enter the fertile field of government business.

General Johnson today read a copy of an unsigned letter purporting to be from the Ford Motor Company to a local dealer, setting forth the claims that that firm had been complying and would continue to comply with "pertinent" provisions of the Automobile Code.

The Recovery Administrator said that if the letter, with certain revisions which he suggested, were returned to him signed by Henry Ford or any other authorized executive of the Ford Motor Company, he would consider it a certificate of compliance, would call off his "crack-down" campaign against the company and recommend to President Roosevelt that it be allowed to resume bidding on government contracts.

A large order of motor trucks for the army, which War Department officials prefer should be Ford products, is said to be the immediate stake in negotiations between the NRA and Mr. Ford. Harry H. Woodring Assistant Secretary of War, has made overtures to General Johnson within the last thirty-six hours to learn what the Ford company would have to do to qualify to bid.

Representative Kvale of Minnesota, active in the House Military Affairs Committee investigating War Department purchases, accompanied the Ford dealer when he called to show the unsigned letter to General Johnson this afternoon.

Talks To Ford Adviser.

General Johnson believed the letter to be entirely authentic and to have originated at the Detroit offices of the Ford Company despite the circumstances under which it was shown to him. This belief was intensified by a telephone conversation which he had with William J. Cameron, editorial adviser to Mr. Ford, regarding the suggested revisions.

The letter, according to General Johnson, was addressed to the Northwest Motor Company of Bethesda, Md., the local dealer that has tried so consistently to keep in contractual relations with the governmental departments regardless of Mr. Ford's refusal to sign a compliance certificate for his code.

In its original form the letter said that although the company had complied and would continue to comply with the provisions of the automobile compact, it reserved its "constitutional rights" as guaranteed by the fundamental law.

This was the section to which General Johnson objected. He told R. P. Sabine, president of the Northwest Motor Company, and Representative Kvale that President Roosevelt would not stand for

Continued on Page Twenty-two.

POLICE FILL THE STREETS

Goering's Forces Keep Curious Throngs on Constant Move.

MACHINE GUNS MOUNTED

Public Buildings on Unter den Linden and Wilhelmstrasse Are Heavily Guarded.

NEWS IS AT A PREMIUM

Rumors Are Rampant as Only a One-Sheet Paper Provides Authentic Information.

Copyright, 1934, by The Associated Press.

BERLIN, June 30.—With the peaceful cool of a Summer evening made strangely tense by squads of armed police and the presence of machine guns, this capital city was facing tonight the possibility of a new unnamed, undefined political event.

Crowds of curious spectators, only partly informed as to events through limited press dispatches, surged up and down Wilhelmstrasse, where public buildings were massed with police ever ready to keep them on the move.

In front of the home of Captain Ernest Roehm, suicide deposed leader of the storm troops, were bristling truckloads of Prussian Premier Hermann Goering's special police. They formed an impressive barricade separate from the thousands who dragged their feet in slow response to demands that streets and sidewalks be kept clear.

Show of Force Excites Crowds.

The presence of police everywhere one turned was a direct stimulant to the excitement of the street and thoroughfare. Never in the history of Berlin, it was pointed out, had so many police appeared in the streets at one time with such obvious readiness for action. In addition to the regular police force, augmented by armed reserves, there was the steel-helmeted, green-clad police of Premier Goering.

The sudden appearance of a police machine gun detachment, with ammunition ready, in historic Potsdammer Platz brought a final touch to the grimness of the situation. The sight of another similar detachment riding up and down Unter den Linden left no doubt in the public mind as to the nature of the emergency.

Men and women rushed like hounds on the scent wherever carriers appeared with copies of one newspaper which had printed one page only for free distribution. This carried a brief account of Captain Roehm's discharge by Chancellor Hitler.

Reactions to the news were various and could be read at will on the faces of newspaper readers. Persons obviously of a conservative mind wreathed their faces in smiles as they read what had happened.

Continued on Page Three.

THREE OF THE LEADERS WHO DIED IN THE REICH MUTINY.

Times Wide World Photo.
Captain Ernst Roehm, ousted Storm Troop head, who committed suicide.

Associated Press Photo.
Karl Ernst, Berlin Storm Troop leader, arrested and later shot.

Times Wide World Photo.
General Kurt von Schleicher, slain by arresting officers.

HITLER COMMANDS NAZI ABSTINENCES

Forbids the Troopers to Spend Money on Banquets and Bans Moral 'Debauches.'

WANTS 'MEN, NOT APES'

Chancellor Asserts All Must Be on Best Behavior or Be Expelled From Ranks.

Wireless to THE NEW YORK TIMES.

BERLIN, June 30.—Chancellor Adolf Hitler issued these eleven commands today to Viktor Lutze, new Chief of Staff of the Storm Troops:

In naming you Chief of Staff of the Storm Troops I expect that you will accept the series of duties that I herewith inform you of.

1—I demand of a Storm Troop leader, just as from a Storm Trooper, blind obedience and unquestioning discipline.

2—I demand that every Storm Troop leader recognize, like every other political leader, that his behavior and reputation must be an example for his organization and for our whole body of followers.

3—I demand that Storm Troop leaders, exactly as in the case of political leaders, be expelled from the Storm Troops without hesitation as soon as their behavior disgraces them in the eyes of the public.

Demands Simplicity.

4—I demand specially from the Storm Troop leader that he be an example of simplicity, not of display. I do not desire Storm Troop leaders to give costly dinners or that they attend such dinners. There was a time when we were not invited to such affairs, and we have nothing to seek there now. Millions of our fellow citizens have not even the necessaries of life. They are not oblivious of those whom fortune has favored, but it is unworthy of a National Socialist to increase the gulf between fortune and misery, which is already great enough.

I prohibit the use of Storm Troop or party funds for festivals and the like. It is shameless to stage debauches with the pennies of our poorest citizens. The luxurious headquarters in Berlin, in which it has now been discovered that some 30,000 marks monthly were spent for banquets, is to be done away with immediately.

State Dinners Excepted.

I prohibit for all party groups banquets and dinners paid for with any variety of public funds. I forbid all party and Storm Troop leaders to partake of such banquets. The only exceptions are functions necessary for reasons of State, notably those for which the Reichspresident and the Reich Foreign Minister are responsible. I forbid all party leaders and Storm Troop leaders to give so-called diplomatic dinners. A Storm Troop leader does not need to engage in representation, but simply to do his duty.

5—I do not desire Storm Troop leaders to undertake business trips in expensive limousines or cabriolets, or to employ public funds for such trips. The same

Continued on Page Two.

Hitler Alone Had Power To Order Shooting of 7

Special Cable to THE NEW YORK TIMES.

BERLIN, June 30.—Over its report of the deaths of seven storm troop leaders who yesterday were in power in German, the Völkischer Beobachter, Chancellor Hitler's own newspaper, carried the headline, "Seven Storm Troop Leaders Shot. End of Convicted Traitors."

The German words used for the verb and adjective taken together in this connection carry a wider meaning than the English equivalent, as is the case with so many German words. They imply that the men were proved guilty and executed.

These men were shot on the spot without trial on the mere allegation of their guilt by order of a higher authority. The only authority which could give an order for their execution unchallenged was Adolf Hitler, who, according to the same article in this newspaper, "is the supreme conscience of the German people."

GOERING POLICE NET CATCHES LEADERS

Suicides and Killings Follow Raids on Homes of Notables in Berlin and Vicinity.

By OTTO D. TOLISCHUS.

Wireless to THE NEW YORK TIMES.

BERLIN, June 30.—General Kurt von Schleicher, former Premier, was killed with his wife while "resisting arrest with a weapon in his hand," according to an official communiqué.

The communiqué was one of a long series issued throughout the day as the criminal police of Premier Hermann Goering of Prussia rushed about Berlin and its vicinity, leaving a heavy wake of arrests, suicides and killings among prominent persons.

General von Schleicher met death at his villa in Neubadelsberg, between Berlin and Potsdam. His wife, Frau Elizabeth von Schleicher, it is stated, fell while trying to shield him with her body during an exchange of shots.

From that point tragedy quickly spread. One squad of General Goering's police rushed to the office of Vice Chancellor Franz von Papen in Vos Strasse, next to the Chancellery, and asked the Vice Chancellor to accompany them to his home. There they kept Colonel von Papen under house arrest, and questioned him regarding his relations with General von Schleicher. The amenities were preserved, and later it was stated Colonel von Papen was "at liberty."

Von Papen Visitors Barred.

Visitors to Colonel von Papen's house, however, were not allowed to see him. His secretary and a Reichswehr officer assured every one that Colonel von Papen was in good spirits, had just finished tea and was smoking his afternoon cigar.

His office meanwhile had been occupied by black uniformed special guards, men with field equipment, rifles and hand grenades. To inquirers they insisted they were merely Colonel von Papen's regular guard, placed there to protect him. Visitors noted, however, that all doors of the building stood open, as if a whirlwind had swept through.

In the face of this action, Colonel

Continued on Page Eight.

NAZI CHIEFS TELL OF ENDING REVOLT

Hitler and Lutze Appeal to the Storm Troops to Be Faithful to Their Movement.

RAID DESCRIBED BY PARTY

Leader of War Veterans Urges Them to Be Calm and to Be Loyal to Government.

Wireless to THE NEW YORK TIMES.

BERLIN, June 30.—A series of statements was issued today by German leaders on their success in crushing the radical Nazi revolt.

NAZI PARTY STATEMENT.

A communiqué from the National Socialist party read:

Munich, June 30.

For many months individual elements have been trying to drive a wedge and produce conflicts between the Storm Troops and the party, as well as between the Storm Troops and the State. Suspicions of this became more and more confirmed, but it was also plain that these endeavors were to be charged to a limited clique of certain leanings.

Chief of Staff Roehm, in whom the leader placed an exceptional amount of confidence, not only did not oppose these endeavors but undoubtedly sponsored them. His well-known unfortunate characteristic gradually led to intolerable burdens which drove the leader of the movement and the Highest Leader of the Storm Troops [Hitler] into most serious conflicts of conscience.

Chief of Staff Roehm established contacts with General von Schleicher without the knowledge of Der Fuehrer [the Leader]. His go-betweens were another Storm Troop leader and an obscure person well known in Berlin, to whom Der Fuehrer had always strongly objected.

Since these negotiations also led —of course without the knowledge of Der Fuehrer—finally to contacts with a foreign power, or rather to its representative, it was not possible to avoid intervention both from the standpoint of the party and the State.

Provocative incidents brought about according to the plan caused Der Fuehrer to fly from Bonn to Munich at 2 o'clock this morning, after visiting labor camps in Westphalia, in order to remove and arrest the most seriously compromised group of leaders. Der Fuehrer himself went with only a few companions to Wiessee in order to still any attempts at resistance.

The execution of the arrests revealed such immorality that any trace of pity was impossible. Some of these Storm Troop leaders had taken male prostitutes along with them. One of them was even disturbed in a most ugly situation and was arrested.

Der Fuehrer gave orders for this plague to be done away with ruthlessly. In the future he will not permit millions of decent people to be compromised by a few of such sick men. Der Fuehrer instructed Premier Goering of Prussia to take similar action in Berlin and especially to arrest the reactionary accomplices of this political plot.

At noon today Der Fuehrer

Continued on Page Four.

STORM TROOP CHIEFS DIE

Killed or Take Own Lives as Chancellor and Goering Strike.

REACTIONARIES ALSO HIT

Wife Shot With Schleicher as He Resists Police—Head of Catholic Action Slain.

HITLER FLIES TO MUNICH

Tears Off Rebels' Insignia and Arrests and Ousts Roehm —Papen Held but Freed.

By FREDERICK T. BIRCHALL.

Wireless to THE NEW YORK TIMES.

BERLIN, June 30.—On the eve of a self-proclaimed month of peace Germany has passed today through the throes of a violent purging that must profoundly affect her future. It is neither a revolution nor a coup d'état nor a counter-revolution but authoritative action intended to head off any of the three.

Chancellor Hitler in Munich, backed by General Hermann Wilhelm Goering, Premier of Prussia, in Berlin, has struck simultaneously at the rebel elements in his own Storm Troops and at certain reactionary elements temporarily allied with them or suspected of being so allied for their own ends in an attempt to upset the present régime in Germany.

When the day was over many Storm Troop leaders had been shot to death or had committed suicide.

In addition, General Kurt von Schleicher, Herr Hitler's predecessor as Chancellor, had been slain while resisting police who attempted to seize him as one of the plotters.

[Captain Ernst Roehm, chief of staff of the Storm Troops, committed suicide after having been ousted by Chancellor Hitler, according to The Associated Press, while Heinrich Klausener, chief of the Catholic Action, was shot to death by a Nazi special guard.]

The Official Version.

The official version is that the attempt was a joint effort "to bring pressure" on the government with a threat of violent action behind it. There is mention of a "foreign power" as being involved. The discerning interpret this reference as being to Russia and the ultimate aim of the rebels as a new national bolshevism.

Whatever the cause, Chancellor Hitler has acted swiftly and decisively. Flying to Munich in the early hours of this morning from Bonn, where he had been ostensibly inspecting work camps, he assembled his trusted special guards in that city and proceeded to gather in the suspected leaders, who had already proceeded to preliminary action.

Captain Roehm, the leader of the conspiracy, was arrested in his bedroom in his country house outside Munich by Herr Hitler himself and then and there deposed from all his offices. His fellow-conspirators were gathered in by the dozen in Munich and around it.

The official story told to foreign correspondents by General Goering this afternoon says that some of them, both in Munich and in Berlin, committed suicide and others were shot while resisting.

Goering Acts Swiftly.

Almost simultaneously in Berlin General Goering, by arrangement with Chancellor Hitler, was taking similar action. It came swiftly and unexpectedly just before noon. But here the members of the reactionary group believed to be acting with the rebel Storm Troop leaders were equally the objects of the assault.

Karl Ernst, group leader of the Berlin Storm Troops, was traced to a house near Bremen and surrounded there. He is dead and the official version is that he was shot while resisting arrest. The unofficial version is that he was brought by airplane to Berlin and executed on his arrival.

Police and special guards at the very outset sought to put General von Schleicher under arrest at his villa outside Potsdam. It is said that he attempted to draw a pistol. A volley of shots brought him down and his wife died with him.

Vice Chancellor Franz von Papen, who seems to have been under sus-

Continued on Page Two.

Dillinger Raids Bank in South Bend, Ind., Reported Shot; Officer Slain, Loot $28,000

By The Associated Press.

SOUTH BEND, Ind., June 30.—A bandit quintet with John Dillinger reported to be in command, stormed the Merchants' National Bank today, scooped up $28,439 and fled in a wild barrage of bullets, leaving a slain policeman and four wounded men in their wake.

The ruthless raiders engaged in gun battles with a detective, two officers and a jeweler as they fled from the bank and made their way to the escape car a half block away. More than fifty shots raked the street in the heart of the city.

Detective Harry Henderson, who identified the bandits' leader as Dillinger, said he believed that he had shot the long-sought gunman as the quintet's car sped away.

Patrolman Harold Wagner encountered the three gangsters who carried out the actual robbery as they were hurrying from the bank. He was fatally wounded before he could reach his pistol.

Those wounded were P. G. Stahley, manager of the Birdsell Manufacturing Company; Jake Soloman, Delos N. Coen, a cashier, and Samuel Toth. At Epworth Hospital it was found that a bullet had struck Soloman in the hip and coursed upward. His condition was described as critical. Toth was wounded in the eye as a bullet smashed the windshield of his automobile.

Leaving an outpost, believed to be John Hamilton, on guard at their automobile, and another bandit closer to the bank, the man identified by a police detective as Dillinger, with two henchmen, one of them believed to be "Baby Face" Nelson, rushed into the bank about noon. Cowing the twenty-five customers with a machine gun, the man identified as Dillinger took up a strategic post and sent a score of slugs into the ceiling while his confederates snatched up $28,439. C. W. Coen, vice president of the institution, who took cover under a desk three feet from the gunner, declared he was positive the leader was the desperado Dillinger.

Bundling their loot, the three commandeered Stahley, Coen and several other patrons and used them as human shields as they marched out the door. Wagner ran toward them from across the crowded street. The machine gunner shot him down, three bullets entering the policeman's body.

"All the News That's Fit to Print."

The New York Times.

LATE CITY EDITION

WEATHER—Rain today, temperature unchanged; tomorrow rain.
Temperatures Yesterday—Max., 77; min., 59.

Copyright, 1935, by The New York Times Company.

VOL. LXXXIV....No. 28,352. Entered as Second-Class Matter. Postoffice, New York, N. Y. NEW YORK, MONDAY, SEPTEMBER 9, 1935. PPP TWO CENTS In New York City. | THREE CENTS Within 200 Miles | FOUR CENTS Elsewhere Except in 7th and 8th Postal Zones.

ITALY SEEN PLAYING FOR TIME IN GENEVA AND INTENT ON WAR

League's Efforts May Turn on Making Peace Rather Than Preventing Conflict.

ROME IS STILL NOT BOUND

Assembly Meets Today, but Is Not Expected to Consider the African Problem.

'ON THE MARCH,' SAYS DUCE

Mussolini Asserts Italy Wants 'Peace With Justice'—Rome Raises Rediscount Rate.

The Italo-Ethiopian Crisis.

GENEVA—War seems probable in Africa before the League can achieve any settlement, as Italy apparently is playing for time. International police control for Ethiopia is one proposal being considered. The League Assembly convenes today but is not expected to take up the Ethiopian problem at this time.

ROME—Premier Mussolini in one speech yesterday said Italy wanted "peace and justice" and in another said "Italy is now definitely on the March." The Bank of Italy for the second time in a month raised the rediscount rate, this time from 4½ to 5 per cent.

ADDIS ABABA—Ethiopian troops were dispatched to the south to be ready for any Italian offensive from Italian Somaliland. The Emperor's advisers counseled firmness in the face of various proposals broached at Geneva. The Italian Minister protested against alleged arrests and annoyances of consulate members.

Sparring by Italy Seen.

By FREDERICK T. BIRCHALL.

Wireless to THE NEW YORK TIMES.

GENEVA, Sept. 8.—In the lull that has fallen upon the Italo-Ethiopian negotiations here it is possible to take account of the progress that has been made so far. It is impossible to escape the conviction that this progress has been more apparent than real.

The Italians, it should be emphasized, have not agreed to the formation of a new conciliation committee, set up by the League of Nations Council. By refraining from voting they have merely consented to ignore its establishment. Whether they will negotiate with the committee as a whole still remains to be seen.

They have said their sole object in remaining here is to pay to the great powers remaining in the League the courtesy of talking with them. But they take the position that their proposed war on Ethiopia is justified by their citation of Ethiopian shortcomings and that the League will exceed its prerogatives if it attempts to prevent that war, because, the Italians assert, Ethiopia is unworthy of membership and ought to be thrown out.

Italy Held Playing for Time.

However, it is quite obviously to Italy's advantage to prolong the negotiations here until the time is ripe to attack in East Africa. There are six divisions of Italian troops and half of the proposed equipment and airplanes still on their way to their base or only newly arrived there.

Eritrea and Italian Somaliland are still waterlogged from rains and in no condition for the movement of troops. It will be at least a fortnight before this condition changes. The probability is that the Italian advance in force may be delayed almost to October.

There must, however, be quick action in Geneva if an Italian invasion of Ethiopia proper is to be prevented. So the coming week will doubtless witness an intensification of the efforts to reach a settlement.

The first problem will be to find a basis on which to negotiate. The only basis in sight is that of the Paris proposals, which Italy has already rejected. It is contended by Rome that those proposals were presented as the maximum that could be obtained. The British and French assert, on the other hand, that they were offered merely as a basis for negotiation. The one certain fact is their rejection.

Obviously, therefore, the proposals must be expanded if they are to become even a basis for further talk. It is also pretty clear that they must be expanded in the direction of giving Italy greater political and military control over Ethiopia than the original proposal contemplated.

How that can be brought about while preserving even a remnant of Ethiopian sovereignty and independence is not clear at present. That will be the committee's problem.

The one thought in the minds of some members—it is said, inciden-

Continued on Page Four.

Thieves Free 'Gas' Flood, Imperil Chicago Area

Special to THE NEW YORK TIMES.

CHICAGO, Sept. 8.—Thieves took an automobile and a tank truck at the plant of the Red Flash Petroleum Corporation early today. In filling the tank truck from an electric gasoline pump they broke the pump, thereby endangering hundreds of lives and millions in property.

Sixteen thousand gallons of gasoline flooded streets and alleys, six inches in depth in many places, over a wide area. A spark from a locomotive or from an automobile, or a lighted cigarette stub, would have started a conflagration.

The petroleum company has many tanks at its plant. Abutting the plant are many homes and factories.

The police, hastily summoned, shut off the broken pump, and diverted all traffic until the gasoline had been washed into the sewers with fire hose.

DOHENY, OIL MAN, DIES IN WEST AT 79

Figure in Teapot Dome Case Had Spectacular Rise From Poverty to Wealth.

PROSPECTOR FOR 20 YEARS

Then He Turned From Gold to Petroleum and Started the Los Angeles Boom.

By The Associated Press.

LOS ANGELES, Sept. 8.—Edward Laurence Doheny, who wrested one of the world's largest fortunes from the oil fields of California and Mexico, died at 8 o'clock tonight at his home here. He was 79 years old.

Mr. Doheny's death was caused by age and complications after an illness that kept him bed-ridden for almost three years. At his bedside were his widow, Estelle, and five grandchildren.

Discoverer with the late Charles A. Canfield of one of the first oil fields of California, Mr. Doheny had a career that was one of the most picturesque in the history of American industry. In Tampico, Mexico, he reared a vast industrial empire that came to be known as one of the greatest concentrated oil holdings of private capital in the world.

Tragedy and sorrow stalked him at the very zenith of his career, however, because of his operations in Elk Hills, Calif. He was indicted in 1924 in connection with naval reserve leases. Albert B. Fall, former Secretary of the Interior, also indicted in this case, was convicted, but Mr. Doheny was acquitted.

Only recently a Doheny-controlled corporation here foreclosed on the New Mexico ranch of Mr. Fall, who disclosed that he had received orders to vacate. Mr. Doheny and Mr. Fall were reported to have remained close friends through the years, but Doheny made no comment on the foreclosure.

Waited Years for 'Strike.'

Edward Laurence Doheny left home when 16 years old to be a muleteer. He spent the next twenty years tramping plains, deserts and mountains as a prospector, with the "big strike" always just around the corner. In 1892, while walking the streets of Los Angeles, a mere chance caused him to shift his quest from gold to petroleum, and a few years later he was one of the greatest oil operators in the world. He spent his youth in hardship, his middle age in a phenomenal rise to wealth, power and fame, and much of his old age in grief and humiliation through the notorious oil scandals of the Harding administration.

Mr. Doheny came of Irish pioneers. He was born on Aug. 10, 1856, to Patrick and Eleanor Elizabeth (Quigley) Doheny at Fond du Lac, Wis., which was then in frontier territory. His boyhood surroundings were similar to those described in the old dime novels. He knew plainsmen and Indians, and at the early age when he left home to take charge of the mules in a government surveying expedition in Indian territory he already knew how to fend for himself.

No Future as Muleteer.

He saw no future in caring for mules but his trip to the Southwest gave him a taste for the sort of work to which he was to devote his youth. He had no technical training, but he observed the government surveyors, picked up the elements of their trade, and practiced for a while, but soon decided that it offered little better chances for wealth than did mule-driving, and it was wealth that Doheny wanted. He talked to prospectors and decided that prospecting was the life for him.

He spent twenty years looking for gold. Sometimes he found it. Repeatedly he built up mines, knew temporary affluence, "went broke" and started out again. The Black

Continued on Page Thirteen.

BIGGEST BUSINESS SINCE '30 FORESEEN THIS FALL BY LABOR

A. F. of L. Asserts Upswing Is Healthiest So Far and Is Not Due to Federal Spending.

FINDS STEEL 'OUT OF RED'

Higher Buying Power Created by NRA and AAA Has Been Felt at Last, Says Report.

Special to THE NEW YORK TIMES.

WASHINGTON, Sept. 8.—In the most optimistic statement on the recovery movement it has yet made, the American Federation of Labor today said that business was showing greater vitality than in any upswing since 1933 and that "the last four months of 1935 may well bring the highest level of industrial operations and earnings for any similar period since 1930."

"The present business upswing," the federation said, "is the healthiest thus far; it is the first not due to government spending or currency action; the first which seems due chiefly to inherent economic strength. Dividend payments in August exceeded last year by $11,000,000, or 4 per cent; the steel industry is out of the red for the first time since 1930. With these signs of increased industrial earnings, much depends upon the workers making a new drive now for higher incomes."

Buying power of the workers, lifted to higher levels in 1934 by the NRA, and the income of farmers, raised by the AAA, the report said, "at last have made themselves felt in sufficient degree to stimulate production."

The federation stated that orders for automobiles in the first half of 1935 were 75 per cent above last year and that, "as a result of increased buying and production and growing confidence, industry is beginning to order new machinery. Machine-tool orders in the first half of 1935 were 47 per cent above last year."

Big Expansion Outlays Cited.

"All these lines of activity," the survey continued, "have continued through July and August. The automobile industry is spending $100,000,000 on production equipment; the steel industry, $130,000,000, it is estimated. This new life in the heavy industries should mean more jobs where unemployment has been particularly severe."

The federation said that the trend had started strongly upward after a five months' waiting period, and that from the week of July 6 to Aug. 24 THE NEW YORK TIMES index recorded a gain of 8 per cent to 88 per cent of normal.

"This striking gain," it said, "was made in the short space of seven weeks; it leaves business well over half-way back to normal. Employment, however, has not kept pace with gains in business."

Stressing that the income of wage-earners had lagged, the survey quoted Department of Commerce figures in contending that workers lost three-fifths of their income from 1929 to 1933, and had regained a little over one-tenth by 1934.

The only important increase in employment since recovery started, the survey said, came in 1933, this being due largely to the shortening of work hours under NRA.

"In the Summer of 1933, 1,800,000 men and women were put to work by dropping five hours from the work week," the survey continued. "Since September, 1933, there have been no further significant gains in employment in spite of increasing production. This has been especial-

Continued on Page Two.

A. F. du Ponts Race by Air To Daughter Ill in Jamaica

By The Associated Press.

WILMINGTON, Del., Sept. 8.—A. Felix du Pont Jr. said tonight he had received word from his parents that they had arrived at Kingston, Jamaica, after a 2,000-mile airplane dash, to be at the bedside of their daughter, Miss Lydia du Pont.

Mr. du Pont said his parents informed him Miss du Pont was ill with tonsilitis in a Jamaica hospital. It was at first reported she was suffering with tropical fever.

The elder du Pont, who is vice president of E. I. du Pont de Nemours & Co., and Mrs. du Pont were taken from Wilmington to Washington yesterday in an airplane piloted by their son. At Washington they boarded a transport plane to Miami. The trip from Miami to Jamaica was made in another transport. Young du Pont said his parents arrived at Jamaica late today.

Miss du Pont was taken ill while working with a Philadelphia scientific expedition in the Colombia jungles.

$200,000 IN LIQUOR SEIZED ON VESSEL

British Ship and 3 Speedboats Captured by Coast Guard Near Atlantic City.

20 PRISONERS ARE TAKEN

Cutters Halt the Transfer of Cargo With Shot—Largest Haul Since Repeal.

Special to THE NEW YORK TIMES.

CAPE MAY, N. J., Sept. 8.—Three American boats, a British ship, twenty men and a cargo valued at $200,000—one of the largest captures since prohibition was repealed—were seized by Cape May Coast Guards shortly before last midnight ten miles southeast of Atlantic City.

Led by Lieutenant R. L. Burke, in charge of the Coast Guard air base here, three cutters on regular patrol observed the British oil schooner Popocatepelt anchored. Alongside of the 103-foot craft were the three American boats, with liquor aboard.

The smaller boats were listed as the Theresa of Margate, N. J.; Nampahc of Point Pleasant and the Dreadnaught. All the boats, about forty feet long, are equipped with high-powered motors.

Eight members of the crew were on the British boat, which was listed as a "British oil screw," equipped with a Diesel driving engine. Its capacity is 153 tons.

One shot was fired by the Coast Guards when they approached the schooner. This, the officials said, was the regulation warning. The rum-runners did not put up a fight, Lieutenant Burke said. The four boats and the prisoners were brought to the local base. The prisoners were segregated and questioned.

The Dreadnaught, Coast Guards said today, was leaking badly and every effort was being made to keep her afloat.

Liquor seized on the three American boats, it was reported, already had been unloaded from the British craft. When the American boats caught sight of the Coast Guardsmen an attempt was made to make for shore, but the cutters were soon alongside and the crews surrendered.

The cargo, consisting of 5,000 cases, was estimated to be worth $200,000. It was composed of British liquor, alcohol and assorted brandies.

The capture, Coast Guards

Continued on Page Two.

Panama Assemblyman Holds Police at Bay; Wanted Following Theft of U. S. Army Guns

Special Cable to THE NEW YORK TIMES.

PANAMA CITY, Sept. 8.—A member of the National Assembly, Victor Florencia Goytia, is holding at bay at his residence policemen who have an order for his arrest in connection with the recent theft of machine guns and other arms and of ammunition from the United States Army at Corozal.

Detectives have been guarding his house since yesterday, but Goytia refuses to leave and has announced that he will not be taken alive and will shoot the first man who touches him.

A former Chief of Police, Homero Ayala, who had been held by the Canal Zone police after his arrest by the Panama police yesterday and delivered to the Canal Zone authorities, was released in $1,500 bail today. He was one of the leaders of the revolt of 1931. After the overthrow of President Arosemena he became Chief of Police, but resigned later and joined the opposition to the present government.

The theft from the United States Army post included four machine guns, valued at $4,000; four automatic rifles, valued at $1,000, and small arms and ammunition valued at $400, all of which were believed to have been taken for possible revolutionary use.

Both Goytia and Ayala are prominently identified with the reformed Liberal party, which has been attacking the Arias government through the newspaper Panama American, edited by Goytia.

An investigation into the theft by Canal Zone police and the army, assisted by the Panama police, has resulted in the arrest of three Americans—Eddie Payne, a former soldier and former Canal Zone policeman; Ellis M. Stevens, an employe of the Panama Railroad, and Sergeant Carl Dumpke, a soldier of the Corozal Ordnance Depot—two Nicaraguans and two Panamanians.

The stolen arms have not yet been found, but the police say they have clues that are expected to lead to discovery of the cache.

'TOTAL REST CURE' IS BUSINESS NEED, SAY REPUBLICANS

'Breathing Spell' From Roosevelt Only Breeds Fear, National Committee Asserts.

CITES PLANS FOR NEW NRA

Howard Letter 'Stunt' Evaded Budget Balancing and Inflation Issues, It Charges.

Special to THE NEW YORK TIMES.

WASHINGTON, Sept. 8.—The Republican National Committee declared today that the business, financial and industrial interests of this country do not want "merely a breathing spell" from President Roosevelt's régime—"they want a complete rest cure."

In its weekly "Facts and Opinions" the committee, commenting on the exchange of letters last week between the President and Roy W. Howard, said that the Roosevelt-Howard correspondence failed to state the administration's position on inflation of the currency, balancing the budget and getting the government out of business.

"The Howard-Roosevelt question-and-answer stunt has changed no one's opinion of the Roosevelt administration or the policies and program of the New Deal," the committee asserted.

"It probably was not expected to do so. More likely it was designed to afford Mr. Howard a freshly laundered alibi for keeping his newspaper chain narrowly partisan in its support of the President and furnish an excuse in advance for advocating his renomination and re-election.

Charges 'Partisan Propaganda.'

"It was a good piece of partisan propaganda, even though perfectly transparent. The collaboration was perfect. The President did not dare run the risk of having such a prominent publisher publicly ask him any embarrassing questions to which he was expected to make a public reply. For that reason Mr. Howard avoided bringing up questions about inflation, return to a sound currency, balancing the budget, getting the government out of private business and, particularly, about the President's determination to make the United States Constitution conform to his socialistic program rather than abandon that program because it runs contrary to the United States Constitution. In other words, the political significance of Mr. Howard's letter is measured not by what it asked but by what it conspicuously failed to ask.

"On the other hand, Mr. Howard had something to protect. He could not afford to take his newspaper chain out on a limb by blindly hazarding a reply from an administration that had been as erratic as a weather vane in a whirlwind.

"Ghost writer No. 1 of the New Deal may not have composed both the letters, but he must be given due credit for a good job of editing. The President knew in advance the questions that would be asked. Mr. Howard knew in advance the answers that would be made.

Business Man 'Not Reassured.'

"Other than easing Mr. Howard's journalistic conscience and furnishing the President opportunity to offer a very abridged and very lame defense of his policies and motives, the correspondence has accomplished nothing.

"It is obvious the 'frightened business men,' out of solicitude for whom the correspondence was ostensibly initiated, are not going to be reassured regarding the Roosevelt program until they obtain some definite and dependable answer to the questions which Mr. Howard did not ask.

"There is nothing in the President's letter to which the confidence of men of affairs can make fast. He reiterates the fundamental fallacy of the New Deal—that it is impossible to distinguish between recovery and reform.

"Because of that blind obsession the Roosevelt administration in the name of reform unloosed forces destructive of our sound and legitimate economic structure, which made it impossible to have business recovery and which are justifiably accountable for the hostility and fright which Mr. Howard himself admits now pervade the world of business, finance and industry.

Holds Situation Aggravated.

"The President's letter aggravates the very situation it is supposed to alleviate by insisting that the policies of the New Deal are 'in conformity with the basic economic purposes which were set forth three years ago.'"

Some of the alleged rejections of his promises and of the party's platform pledges cited by the committee are:

Failure to maintain a sound currency.

Going off the gold standard contrary to predictions in his speech

Continued on Page Fifteen.

DOCTOR SHOOTS HUEY LONG IN LOUISIANA STATE CAPITOL; BODYGUARDS KILL ASSAILANT

Times Wide World Photo.

SENATOR HUEY P. LONG.

HELD IN 8 MURDERS, ENDS LIFE IN CELL

Gang Leader Hangs Himself After Confessing Murder of a Patrolman.

BETRAYED BY ASSOCIATES

Habit of Having Accomplices Slain Led Ex-Aides to Put Police on His Trail.

Anthony Cugino, Philadelphia desperado, sought for many months in connection with eight murders, committed suicide shortly before midnight last night in his cell at police headquarters.

Cugino had been subjected to fifteen hours of relentless questioning and, according to the police, had finally confessed to one of the eight murders—the killing of a policeman.

The gunman, known as the Stinger, whose arrest, according to the police, was brought about by the fear and hatred he had inspired in his own former associates, apparently had been resting quietly in his cell in the basement of the headquarters building. Patrolman Hugh O'Connell had seen him a few minutes earlier as he paced the lighted corridor in front of the cell group.

The next time the patrolman saw the prisoner Cugino was hanging from a water pipe in his cell.

He had torn his shirt into strips, fashioned a rope with the skill of a sailor, tied one end around the pipe and the other about his own throat and then had jumped from the edge of a wash bowl.

Cugino also used his necktie in fashioning his hangman's noose. The police investigation centred last night around the question as to why Cugino was allowed to keep an article with which he so easily improvised a rope.

O'Connell at once called for help, and Inspector James McGrath hurried to the cell. A few minutes later a police emergency squad arrived with pulmotors and then Dr. Wright, a police surgeon, and Dr. Louis Liccirdi from Columbus Hospital.

Both oxygen and adrenalin were administered in vain. The prisoner was pronounced dead at 2:25 A. M. after the police and physicians had worked nearly an hour over him.

O'Connell went on duty at 11:15 he informed Inspector McGrath and at that time Cugino seemed to be all right. At 11:30 two other prisoners in cells across the narrow aisle from that of Philadelphia's "Public Enemy No. 1," called to the policeman and asked for a drink of water. When he brought it they pointed out that Cugino seemed to be standing in a peculiar position.

"I called to him to get down," O'Connell said, "and there was no answer."

The patrolman then saw that the gangster had hanged himself.

Among the effects found on the

Continued on Page Two.

LONG PREDICTED HE WOULD BE SHOT

He Told Senate Aug. 9 That Plot to Kill Him Had Been Overheard in New Orleans.

ALWAYS HAD A BODYGUARD

Thomas Recalls Inquiry in Louisiana Revealed Hate and 'Almost Mob Desires.'

By The Associated Press.

WASHINGTON, Sept. 8.—News of the attempted assassination of Senator Huey Long in Baton Rouge startled the capital late tonight, with officials recalling instantly that only a month ago tomorrow he told the Senate a plot to kill him was afoot.

As word spread through the city, telephone calls to newspaper offices for information increased with the minute.

Until details of the shooting and his condition were known, officials and political leaders had little to say.

Senator Thomas, Democrat, of Utah, attributed the shooting of Senator Long to "an irresponsible and thoughtless person."

Recalls Overton Hearing.

Mr. Thomas is familiar with the Louisiana political situation, having presided at hearings there on the seating of Senator Overton of the Long faction.

"It is most unfortunate," Mr. Thomas's statement said. "I had first had acquaintance with the tense feelings and almost mob desires expressed by partisans on both sides when I presided in the Overton hearing two years ago.

"I cannot help but feel that the act was one of an irresponsible and thoughtless person, because no matter how hateful controlled government may become in the minds of its antagonists, the minute force is used confusion is instant.

"Shooting always invites more shooting. It cannot bring better conditions by shooting. The American system of recall is to use ballots and not bullets."

Others Took His Fears Lightly.

The committee of which Mr. Thomas was a member excoriated some of the methods involved in the conduct of Louisiana elections, but Mr. Overton kept his seat.

Many of the Senate, at the time of Long's speech, had taken the Louisianan's fears lightly.

The Louisianan, on Aug. 9, took the floor during a dull afternoon and said two of his supporters had sat in a hotel room in New Orleans adjoining an apartment where the reported plot was discussed. Some

Continued on Page Three.

SENATOR'S WOUND GRAVE

Pistol Pressed to Body, Bullet Goes Through His Abdomen.

ATTACKER A POLITICAL FOE

Would-Be Assassin a Relative of a Judge Whose Defeat Long Was Planning.

OPERATION IS PERFORMED

Follows Transfusion in Which Lieutenant Governor Gives Blood to the Senator.

Surgeons' Bulletin on Long.

Special to THE NEW YORK TIMES.

BATON ROUGE, La., Monday, Sept. 9.—The surgeons attending Senator Long issued the following bulletin at 2 o'clock this morning (4 A. M. New York time):

"Senator Long was wounded by one bullet entering the upper right side, emerging from the back. The colon was punctured in two places.

"The first blood transfusion has been given the Senator, with good results.

"The condition of Senator Long is thoroughly satisfactory. It will be seventy-two to ninety hours before further developments can be expected.

"Another bulletin will be issued at 7 A. M."

In an emergency operation the surgeons sutured veins to stop internal bleeding and cleansed the wound to prevent infection.

Special to THE NEW YORK TIMES.

BATON ROUGE, La., Sept. 8.—United States Senator Huey P. Long was shot through the stomach and gravely wounded tonight as he walked from the chamber of the Louisiana House of Representatives, where he had been directing the passage of bills aimed to strengthen his grip upon the politics of the State and to fight the New Deal and Roosevelt policies.

It was about 9:30 o'clock (11:30 New York daylight saving time), and the Legislature had just recessed until morning.

The would-be assassin, shot down and killed instantly by three members of the State police acting as bodyguards for Louisiana's senior Senator, was identified as Dr. Carl A. Weiss, an eye, ear, nose and throat specialist of Baton Rouge.

Dr. Weiss, who was 29, was the son-in-law of Judge B. H. Pavy of Opelousas, a leader of an anti-Long faction in St. Landry Parish.

One of the bills scheduled for passage at this special session of the Legislature was designed to gerrymander Judge Pavy's judicial district so that his re-election next January would have been well-nigh impossible.

The bill would have added the parishes of Acadia, Lafayette and Vermilion, where Long majorities are heavy, to Judge Pavy's home parish.

Lieut. Gov. Noe Gives Blood.

The most skilled surgeons in the State were summoned to the Senator's side at Our Lady of the Lake Sanitarium, to which he was rushed by automobile, conscious but bleeding profusely.

A blood transfusion was decided upon, and scores of friends volunteered to give their blood. Ten volunteers were selected for tests. Lieut. Gov. James A. Noe, a close friend of Senator Long, was accepted and the transfusion was made an hour and a half after the shooting occurred.

"Go ahead and clean it," Senator Long said through gritted teeth to the surgeon when they informed him that his wound would have to be cleaned. Tests were being made, physicians said, to determine whether the bullet which pierced Senator Long's abdomen was poisoned.

Soon after the transfusion was made it was reported that surgeons had decided to perform an emergency operation.

About an hour later the operation was carried out.

While the House gallery was crowded with spectators, there were few witnesses to the actual shooting. Senator Long had been strid-

Continued on Page Three.

"All the News That's Fit to Print."

The New York Times.

LATE CITY EDITION
Mostly cloudy, moderate temperature today. Tomorrow mostly cloudy, temperature unchanged.
Temperatures Yesterday—Max., 93; Min., 75

VOL. LXXXV.....No. 28,683. Entered as Second-Class Matter, Postoffice, New York, N. Y. NEW YORK, WEDNESDAY, AUGUST 5, 1936. P TWO CENTS In New York City. | THREE CENTS Within 200 Miles. | FOUR CENTS Elsewhere Except in 7th and 8th Postal Zones.

LEWIS UNIONS FACE DRASTIC PENALTIES IF C. I. O. GOES ON

A. F. of L. Ultimatum Today Is to Order Dissolution or Suspension of Units.

PEACE MOVES ABANDONED

Neither Side Acts to End the Dispute and Compromise Is Opposed at Hearing.

'REBEL' LEADERS SCORED

Lewis Is Called a 'Mussolini' and Howard a 'Machiavelli' by Frey at Labor Trial.

By LOUIS STARK
Special to THE NEW YORK TIMES.

WASHINGTON, Aug. 4.—Suspension of some of the unions affiliated with the Committee for Industrial Organization by noon tomorrow was indicated as a strong possibility tonight at the close of the second day's session of the executive council of the American Federation of Labor, which has been considering charges that the C. I. O. unions are seeking to build up a rival labor organization.

Unless last-minute developments intervene to brighten the prospects of peace between the craft and industrial groups within the Federation—and there were no peace feelers out tonight on either side—the dissident unions will be told to disband the C. I. O. in a month or to incur the penalty of continuing to remain suspended.

"The executive council will be prepared to render a decision tomorrow morning," said President William Green tonight. "It will decide whether the charges are justified by the weight of evidence and, if the charges are sustained and the unions found guilty, it will decide the penalty to be applied."

Loss of Charters Involved

Temporary suspension would carry with it exclusion from the next convention of the A. F. of L., and if a motion were made there to revoke the charters of the dissident unions it would win overwhelmingly and they would be read out of the federation. This is the assumption if the C. I. O. unions were not allowed to vote at the convention.

If the suspension action is taken, it is unlikely that all the twelve unions which have been summoned to trial would be involved. The International Typographical Union, of which Charles P. Howard is president, has informed the council that Mr. Howard affiliated himself as an individual as a member of and as secretary of the C. I. O. Thus the council would not be expected to punish the entire union for a personal act of its president.

The Hat, Cap and Millinery Workers Union, of which Michael F. Green is president, will also probably not be suspended, for it was only the millinery division, said to comprise most of the union's members, which officially decided to join the C. I. O.

A maximum of ten unions is said to be marked for suspension, but one or two besides the typographical and hat makers' unions may be excepted.

Lewis Unperturbed at Outlook

The unions associated with the C. I. O., of which John L. Lewis is president, may have until about Sept. 1 to signify whether or not they will obey the ruling of the executive council that they dissolve the committee.

That the council has prepared every step of its way, after thoroughly canvassing the legal aspects of the situation, was indicated by the presence of Charlton Ogburn, counsel to the federation, who conferred with Mr. Green at the close of yesterday's and today's sessions.

Mr. Lewis, in his office across the street from the hotel in which the council met today, appeared unperturbed by the possibility of his union's suspension from the federation. He declined to comment on the situation other than to say that he would have to confer with his associates as the council's action may make it necessary.

John P. Frey, president of the metal trades department, completed presentation of his evidence against the C. I. O. unions this morning, assisted by Edward Bieretz, vice president of the International Brotherhood of Electrical Workers.

Mr. Bieretz recalled that the council had voted last Winter that all radio employes should be enrolled in the International Brotherhood of Electrical Workers, which is a craft union. The radio employes had belonged to Federal unions organized on the industrial principle.

He went on to say that the United Radio and Electrical Workers had called a strike at the R. C. A. plant at Camden, N. J. The latter union,

Continued on Page Ten

U. S. Captures 4 Events; Owens Sets Jump Record

Negro Beats 26 Ft. 5 In. to Win 2d Olympic Title—Woodruff, Hardin, Helen Stephens Score—American Team Far in Front.

By ARTHUR J. DALEY
Wireless to THE NEW YORK TIMES.

BERLIN, Aug. 4.—The United States stole away what to date had been distinctly a German show by winning four of the five championships contested this bleak afternoon, as the greatest Olympic Games of them all swung through their third day.

Once again a huge crowd of 90,000 gathered for the morning preliminaries, and once again another capacity throng of 110,000 later packed the Reich Sports Field Stadium. They came to cheer for more German victories, but remained instead to turn their hosannas in the direction of the Americans.

The invincible Jesse Owens won the broad jump at the Olympic record distance of 8.06 meters (26 feet 5 21-64 inches). Miss Helen Stephens walked off with the women's 100-meter final in world record time. Glenn Hardin slammed to victory in the 400-meter hurdles, and John Woodruff, University of Pittsburgh Negro freshman, gave America its first 800-meter triumph in twenty-four years. And topping off the achievement of the Star-Spangled brigade, Owens twice broke the world 200-meter mark around a turn, as well as the Olympic standard, hitting the identical figures of 21.1 seconds in both trials.

Point Score

U. S.	95	Netherlands	4
Germany	76¾	Philippines	4
Finland	30¼	Austria	3
Poland	17	Brazil	2
Japan	16½	Great Britain	2
Canada	9	Argentina	1
Italy	7½	Greece	1
Sweden	6		

Table includes only men's and women's track and field.

Points are unofficial, based on 10 for first place and 5, 4, 3, 2, 1 for the next five places respectively.

The only championship to evade the eager Americans' grasp was the women's discus crown. And that went to Germany as Miss Gisela Mauermayer broke the Olympic record with a toss of 47.63 meters amid the exuberant shouts of her compatriots.

But Germany's share in the harvest was relatively a minor one. The United States closed so far ahead in the race for the men's track and field team championship that every one else already is lapped at least a full circuit behind. The

Continued on Page Twenty-five

LANDON GOES HOME TO VOTE IN PRIMARY; CALLS IT PRIVILEGE

Casts Ballot in Independence and Urges All to Use the Right of Suffrage.

FRIENDS GATHER AT POLLS

Nominee Attends a Women's Luncheon and Stag Dinner, Then Returns to Topeka.

By JAMES A. HAGERTY
Special to THE NEW YORK TIMES.

INDEPENDENCE, Kan., Aug. 4.—Governor Landon came back to his home town today and cast his ballot in the State primary election in the same district in which he was beaten for precinct committeeman six years ago. It was his first *visit here since his nomination for* the Presidency.

In accordance with the Governor's wish there was no demonstration on his arrival, but more than a hundred persons, most of whom were his friends and acquaintances, gathered at the polling place and saw him cast ballot No. 205 in the First precinct of the Third ward.

The first person to greet the Governor as he arrived at the polling place in the agency of the Arnold Motor Company in West Main Street was Charles H. Smith, who defeated him for precinct committeeman and still holds that post.

Mr. Landon's defeat for committeeman was attributed to the influence of the Prairie Oil Company, the heads of which were at that time opposed to Mr. Landon's political advancement because of his activity in seeking legislation to protect independent oil producers, of whom he is one. By party rule the Republican State chairman is selected from the county chairmen and only precinct committeemen are eligible for election as county chairmen. Thus Mr. Landon's defeat blocked a movement to make him State chairman.

Old Opposition Vanishes

This old opposition to Governor Landon among members of his own party in his home city is said to have vanished and the Republicans of Independence are now unanimous in support of their Presidential candidate. Mr. Smith is now an employe of the State Highway Department by appointment of the Governor.

Half a dozen newspaper photographers and one motion picture photographer had their cameras ready when Governor Landon appeared at the polling place soon after 1 o'clock. The judges of the precinct board—for they have two election boards in each precinct in Kansas, one to supervise the voting and the other to count the ballots—were ready for him.

Mr. Landon received his ballot from Mrs. Forriest Wyrick, a judge, who asked: "Which party?"

This question was repeated by Mrs. James Paton, a clerk of the election board.

"The Republican party," Governor Landon replied with a chuckle.

"I see that the old ward is right on the job," he added.

He was registered as "A. M. Landon," with residence at 300 West Maple Avenue, two blocks from the polling place.

The Governor took his ballot and

Continued on Page Twelve

PRESIDENT REBUKES FOES WHO CHARGE 'DROUGHT POLITICS'

Linking of Partisanship to 'Misery' Is Called 'Great Disservice' to the State.

CONFERS ON RELIEF COST

He Finds Increased Outlays in West Partly Offset by Cuts in Industrial Areas.

By CHARLES W. HURD
Special to THE NEW YORK TIMES.

HYDE PARK, N. Y., Aug. 4.—President Roosevelt turned momentarily today from a detailed study of drought relief and its cost to criticize sharply those who have pictured his proposed inspection trip into the West as a political tour.

"It is a very great disservice to the proper administration of any government to link up human misery with partisan politics," the President said at a press conference.

While his statement was a general one, it constituted a reply to charges made yesterday by John D. M. Hamilton, Republican National Chairman, that the Roosevelt administration was making political capital out of its drought-relief program. Mr. Hamilton made this statement in a speech at Bismarck, N. D.

The President's statement, dictated during a talk with newspaper men in the library of his mother's home here, followed a long conference with officials of the Treasury and of the bureaus immediately concerned with relief work.

They had been called here for what Mr. Roosevelt described as a routine conference on fiscal affairs in relation to the new commitments required by the unexpected acceleration of relief activities in the West.

He said that while there had been increases in such expenditures, these were partly offset by savings in industrial areas where a pick-up in business had cut down relief costs. He gave no comparative figures.

The Conferees on Finances

Mr. Roosevelt had called in for the drought study Secretary Morgenthau, Daniel W. Bell Jr., Acting Director of the Budget; Rexford G. Tugwell, Resettlement Administrator, who has just returned from a tour of the drought area; Aubrey Williams, Deputy Works Progress Administrator; Corrington Gill, Assistant Works Progress Administrator, and a group of statistical experts.

All left Hyde Park this afternoon except Mr. Tugwell, who missed his train and returned to join Mr. Roosevelt for a swim at the cottage.

The President received these callers, as he did newspaper men also, attired only in shirt, trousers and slippers, due to the heat, and he invited his guests also to take off their coats.

The fiscal conference supplemented one yesterday with Secretary Wallace and Chester C. Davis, member for agriculture of the Federal Reserve Board.

Replying to questions later at the press conference, the President told newspaper men that the financial condition of the government was

Continued on Page Thirteen

Madrid Terror Is Described In an Uncensored Dispatch

Observer Sees Long, Sanguinary Rebellion if Fascists Prevail and End of Liberal Republic if Government Crushes Them.

Wireless to THE NEW YORK TIMES.

LONDON, Aug. 4.—The following is the first full, uncensored account of events in Madrid to reach London since the Spanish civil war began:

MADRID, Aug. 2 (London Times Dispatch).—A fortnight has passed since the first flash of revolt started a conflict that is shaking this republic to its foundations. All is turmoil and strife.

The outlook is a cloud through which two alternatives loom like cliffs. Should the revolt triumph—and, viewed from Madrid, it cannot win without foreign intervention—a Fascist régime would be the result, against which rebellion would continue until drowned in blood. Should the sedition be suppressed—and that certainly will be a long business—the liberal republic of 1931 must perish in the process.

Two extremes are at each other's throats. One must succumb. There is no central force strong enough to separate them. The story of the rising thus far bears out that conviction.

A synopsis of events will show what is occurring. On Saturday night, July 18, as reports came in showing a revolt was spreading to province after province, Premier Santiago Casares Quiroga resigned. The head of the Popular Front government had failed to see and forestall a deep plan of the Union Militar Española. He was "fracasado" (broken); his prestige was gone, and therewith the confidence of the President.

President Manuel Azaña called in the Speaker of the Cortes, Diego Martinez Barrio, who easily formed a Cabinet representing a moderate tendency within republicanism.

The inclusion of Sanchez Roman in this Cabinet was a further guarantee for those who disapproved of the "Bolshevist" associations of the Quiroga Cabinet. Mr. Roman had refused to sign the pre-election Popular Front pact.

The new Cabinet was torpedoed immediately. The Marxist groups would have none of it, and their veto was absolute.

For some fateful hours the ship of state drifted without a helm until President Azaña, proud high priest of pure republicanism, bowed his head to the storm and constitutional prerogative foundered. The Quiroga Cabinet was recalled, but the Prime Minister and Juan Moles, the Minister of the Interior, both

Continued on Page Two

REBELS DEFEATED BY 80,000 LEFTISTS IN MADRID PASSES

Fascists Driven to Northern Side of Mountains, Where Rout Is Expected.

PREMIER STRESSES GAINS

Plane Bombing of Saragossa Aids Four Loyalist Columns, Advancing on City.

LONDON FOR NEUTRALITY

Britain's Full Acceptance of the French Plea Awaits Italy's Reply—Germans See Franco.

Developments in Spain

Madrid Leftists claimed important victories north of that city in an attack launched by 80,000 men. One advanced rebel force was said to have been trapped in Leon Pass by the drive.

Airplanes bombarded Saragossa as four Leftist columns converged on that city and heavy losses were reported on the insurgent side. They, however, reported victories at two points thirty miles from the city.

German naval officers paid a formal call on General Franco at Ceuta. A German ship was forced to leave Larache to escape a government bombardment and was forbidden to land its cargo.

Britain accepted in principle France's plea for neutrality in the civil war, but withheld full acceptance until Italy had acted. Rome's position was still uncertain. Germany was willing to be bound if Russia also would give pledges.

Secretary Hull instructed United States agents in Spain to watch carefully seizures of American property so claims could be presented later.

Drive Goes Past Mountains

By WILLIAM P. CARNEY
Wireless to THE NEW YORK TIMES.

MADRID, Aug. 4 (Passed by the Censor).—Premier José Giral told newspaper men this evening that the government forces had broken through to the other side of the Guadarrama mountains in a new battle against the rebels threatening Madrid.

San Rafael was captured in a drive by the loyalists, he said. This place is forty miles from Madrid.

"A militia column entered the town today," he added. "Some hand-to-hand fighting is still going on with small groups of rebels in the streets or barricaded in ruined buildings, but these will soon be dominated."

[San Rafael is on the road to Segovia, about ten miles from that city, which has been the forward base of one of the columns marching toward Madrid. It is at the northern end of the Leon Pass, the capture of which was announced by the rebels last week. They said they had penetrated to the southern end of the hills and the road to Madrid would no longer be so difficult.

[A dispatch to The Associated Press said officials declared 80,000 men were engaged in a new offensive, that it had been successful and that the drive of the loyalist forces had isolated the rebel defenders of Leon Pass.]

Other Government Gains

Premier Giral also announced that the government forces had had a good day.

"At Huesca [north of Saragossa]," he said, "our forces are at the city gates. The rebel artillery at Cordoba has been silenced since the early morning. We are closing in on Cordoba tonight."

On the Guadarrama heights tonight the forest is afire. Artillery shells and airplane bombs started this blaze.

The correspondent of the newspaper La Libertad with the government forces on the northwestern front reported that from Villalba and from El Escorial to the firing line he had not seen a horse. All transport is motorized. Artillery and other fighting equipment is moved by heavy trucks. The cavalry is outdated, the correspondent believes.

Commander Valderrama of the rebel forces was killed yesterday in fighting on the Somosierra front. An automatic pistol found on him is now the property of one of the leaders of the government army, General Riequelme. Jaime Cobedo, syndicalist leader, was killed yesterday on the same front while inspecting the proletarian militia with Deputy Angel Pestana, also a syndicalist. Deputy Pestana was wounded slightly.

Today's newspapers published a

Continued on Page Two

RA PLANS GRANTS TO 125,000 FARMERS

Tugwell Expects That Many in Drought Area to Need Aid Before the Next Crop.

CATTLE BUYING INCREASED

Move Begins to Block Feed Speculation and to Assure Sufficient Seed Supplies.

Special to THE NEW YORK TIMES.

WASHINGTON, Aug. 4.—The Resettlement Administration has put at 125,000 the number of rural families which it expects to aid before another crop can be raised. It is now financing about 32,000 families and the large majority of these have been receiving grants.

Disclosure of these estimates strengthened a belief of some officials that the RA, rather than the WPA, would be the chief drought relief agency. As first outlined by President Roosevelt, the relief program was to be handled by the WPA, which agency was to provide jobs on roads and water conservation projects for needy farmers.

It was estimated by the WPA today that about 40,000 farmers were now employed in the worst drought States of the Middle and Northwest areas. It has authorized the employment of 89,000 men, and although it has indicated that this quota will have to be increased, there has been no guess at what the total employment eventually will be.

With the continued hot weather and general lack of rain gradually diminishing hopes for successful planting of late forage crops for livestock feeding, the AAA added thirty more counties to the emergency area that now embraces 756 counties in nineteen States.

More Cattle Buying Ordered

It also ordered field representatives to speed up the cattle buying program. Purchasing agents at the five principal terminal markets gave immediate effect to the order to buy 2,110 cattle and 225 calves as the day's quota.

Reports to the AAA from its field representatives said that only a little over a fourth of the more than 4,000 head of cattle authorized to be bought yesterday had been actually acquired. This gave rise to suggestions that the agency may have been "bulling the market" for the benefit of farmers with cattle to sell, in announcing the 4,000 head purchase authorization.

The agency ran into difficulty today on its plan to spend $10,000,000 to buy 8,000,000 bushels of wheat, oats, barley and flax to be sold to farmers to be certain of ample seed for Fall and Spring planting. A question arose in the minds of some AAA lawyers as to whether the operation could properly be financed through the Reconstruction Finance and Commodity Credit Corporations.

The RA estimate of 125,000 farm families expected eventually to find their way on its list of clients was believed not to include thousands of Indians on Dakota reservations that the agency has decided to aid. Reports have been coming in to the Bureau of Indian Affairs of appalling conditions on the reserva-

Continued on Page Nine

2,000 IN WILD FIGHT RUSH FOR CITY JOBS

Clothing Torn, Policemen Felled and Desk Smashed in Melee in Municipal Building.

50 RESERVES HALT CRUSH

Futile Hurry for Applications Reflects Huge Demand for Low-Paid Public Posts.

The lure of city jobs with their assured income and promise of pensions incited a crowd of 2,000 men and women to wild disorder yesterday morning in the north lobby of the Municipal Building. The mêlée was so serious that police reserves had to be called to restore order.

When the violent episode was over, the lobby floor was strewn with scraps of clothing and hats. A desk at which James J. McMahon, clerk in charge of the Municipal Civil Service Commission's Application Bureau, had been seated was smashed beyond repair.

The disturbance marked the opening of a fourteen-day period for obtaining applications to take a civil service examination for places on an eligible list for jobs as watchman-attendant and attendant-messenger, which pay $1,200 to $1,800 a year. Applicants must pass written and medical examinations.

The Civil Service Commission had made it plain that early filing of applications was not necessary, but this statement failed to register with the job-seekers, who evidently felt that early filing would be an advantage.

1,000 There at Opening Time

In any event, a group of job-seekers, estimated at 1,000 or more, was outside the Municipal Building at 9 o'clock. They thronged into the elevators and were carried to the commission's offices on the fourteenth floor, where they formed in lines outside the application bureau.

Traffic on the elevators became so congested that the elevator starter urged the commission to transfer the handing out of applications to the north lobby.

For a time, the shift in the scene of operations was effective, although the application-seekers interfered with the arrival and departure of city employes and with WPA workers on a scaffold polishing marble in the lobby.

A few minutes later, however, about 1,000 more applicants suddenly appeared. Building attendants and a few patrolmen attempted in vain to keep order, assuring the crowd, which included about 100 women, that there was no hurry to obtain applications.

Police Felled in Crush

This effort failed. There was a surge of job-seekers, some men climbing over the shoulders of those ahead of them in the densely packed throng. McMahon's desk was crushed to bits. The stock of newspapers of Charles Ginsberg, crippled news dealer in the building, was ripped to pieces. The few patrolmen on duty went down under the crowd.

McMahon broke free and tele-

Continued on Page Six

WPA Worker Discovers $1,060 in 'Gold,' Takes Coins From East River Near Park Wall

On his first day of work in two months, Aleck Krunocky, 22-year-old WPA laborer, picked what appeared to be $1,060 in gold coins out of the waters of the East River yesterday.

Krunocky, who is unmarried and lives with his parents at 431 East 122d Street, is employed on work in Carl Schurz Park, which extends along the river front near East Eighty-sixth Street and is separated from the river by a twenty-foot bulkhead. Near this retaining wall yesterday Krunocky saw a Chinese waving excitedly. He investigated and the Chinese pointed to a shiny object on a rocky ledge glittering through about ten inches of murky water.

The tide was low and the East River was down several feet. Aided by another laborer, John Martin, and a stout rope, Krunocky climbed down the retaining wall to a precarious footing on the ledge. He picked up the shiny object.

"It looked like a half dollar, only gold," he said.

He looked further and found two packages wrapped in tarred paper, one of which had soaked through and had broken open. In it he found two more coins and scattered along the ledge a score more, all somewhat dulled with river dirt. Then he opened the second package and discovered enough more to bring the count up to fifty-three, all $20 pieces.

He hurried home with his find, getting away from the growing crowd of spectators as fast as possible, changed his clothes and went to the East 126th Street police station, where he laid the coins in rows before the astonished gaze of Lieutenant William Reidth. They looked like gold to the police officer, but to make sure he called in a pawn broker, who said emphatically that they were genuine.

A dozen policemen examined the money and some said they thought it was good and others declared that it was "light" and must be counterfeit. Today the money will be taken to the Federal experts in the Treasury Building for test.

Lieutenant Reidth called police headquarters and the marine division sent a launch to the point where the money was found. Detectives from the East 102d Street station joined the hunt and the news spread through the neighborhood that gold has been discovered in the WPA diggings in Carl Schurz Park. Hundreds of searchers spent the evening kicking through fresh dirt in the park, but no more gold was found.

Krunocky's discovery will be placed today in the vault of the property clerk at police headquarters to await claimants. If at the end of six months no one has proved ownership the money will be turned over to Krunocky.

U. S. BIDS GERMANS REVEAL SUBSIDIES

New Treasury Order Requires Full Data on Invoices of the Imports From the Reich.

BERLIN IN A COMPROMISE

Drops the Special Benefits to Shippers—Further Cut in Trade With U. S. Is Seen.

Special to THE NEW YORK TIMES.

WASHINGTON, Aug. 4.—Collectors of customs and American consular officers in Germany were instructed by the Treasury today to give information on invoices of exports from that country as to whether any subsidies or other benefits had been paid on goods shipped to the United States.

The instructions were prepared several days ago and prior to the announcement by the German Government that "aski" marks, which were a special subsidy to German shippers, had been abolished. Abolishment of the "aski" marks, in the opinion of American officials, probably prepared the way for unrestricted trade relations with the United States.

This action by Germany followed a conference of German officials with the State and Treasury Departments which was designed to improve trade relations.

The new orders required that the shipper should specially set out any benefits paid or furnished by the German Government to him on any products exported.

Germany Sent Delegation

On account of the payment of these benefits, which were held to have given an advantage to German exporters to the United States, this government placed certain countervailing duties on products from that country. As a result Germany sent a delegation to confer with the State and Treasury Departments. It was understood that a satisfactory arrangement was made and that the usual trade practices would be resumed.

The regulations issued today require that on goods shipped to the United States the master of the vessel involved should indicate "any benefits or privileges, including marks subject to special exchange" or marks not subject to "any special exchange regulations of the German Government or a department, office or agency thereof."

They further require that the invoices indicate foreign exchange to be converted into marks and the rate of exchange; permission to acquire scrip for redemption at the Konversionskasse; permission to acquire bonds for redemption in Germany and marks acquired from the German Government or any of its agencies in connection with the shipment of goods to the United States "otherwise than in payment of the purchase price of such goods."

"The declaration must be complete, and if any sum, benefit or privilege indicated by the form has not been received or is not to be received, that fact should be indicated in the appropriate place," the

Continued on Page Seven

GREECE IS PLACED UNDER ARMY RULE

Order for a General Strike Is Called a Communist Plot—Chamber Is Dissolved.

WIDE MOVEMENT FEARED

Labor Trouble in Bulgaria, Laid to Russia, Seen as Plot to Upset the Balkans.

By The Associated Press.

ATHENS, Aug. 4.—The Greek Government, confronted by "a Communist plot," tonight proclaimed martial law and dissolved the Chamber.

A twenty-four-hour general strike, scheduled to begin at midnight, was called by Leftist trade unions in protest against a recent law that fixed minimum-wage scales and subjected workers' claims to obligatory arbitration.

The Federation of Conservative Workers declared opposition to the strike in a manifesto.

Labor Meetings Banned

Wireless to THE NEW YORK TIMES.

ATHENS, Aug. 4.—In the face of a call for a twenty-four-hour general strike by the Greek Labor Federation, protesting against a recent government bill instituting compulsory arbitration of labor disputes and forbidding strikes, the authorities have prohibited all workers' meetings, fearing serious disorders.

Tonight, after a long audience with the King, Premier John Metaxas repudiated the government's alleged intention to set up a dictatorship. He insisted the measures the government had taken had no other aim but the maintenance of order.

Economic Unrest Growing

Economic unrest, resulting in strikes and bloody clashes between strikers and the army and police, has been growing steadily in Greece for several months. The strike movement, originating with tobacco workers, started in May and has been marked by attempted general strikes in various cities. The guidance of the campaign has been attributed to Communists, with Deputy Tinakos, a Red, reported as one of the leaders.

Throughout the series of Greek strikes the Greek Government watched the situation in neighboring Bulgaria, where a Communist strike had been sweeping the country. Greek political circles believed that the Bulgarian strike was directed from the Soviet Union and they feared its extension to other parts of the Balkans.

On May 11, after the settlement of a tobacco workers' strike in Saloniki that became a general one and threatened a food shortage, the Greek Labor Federation called a general protest strike of twenty-four hours to start at midnight on May 12. At that time Premier John Metaxas contemplated proclaiming martial law.

Strikes continued in different cities in the ensuing weeks but in the latter part of May it was reported that the movement in Thrace and other parts of Greece

Continued on Page Four

"All the News That's Fit to Print."

The New York Times.

LATE CITY EDITION
Cloudy, mild, with occasional rain today; clearing, colder tonight. Tomorrow colder.
Temperatures Yesterday—Max., 53; Min., 38

Copyright, 1936, by The New York Times Company.

VOL. LXXXVI....No. 28,811. Entered as Second-Class Matter, Postoffice, New York, N. Y. NEW YORK, FRIDAY, DECEMBER 11, 1936. P TWO CENTS In New York City. | THREE CENTS Within 200 Miles. | FOUR CENTS Elsewhere Except in 7th and 8th Postal Zones.

EDWARD VIII RENOUNCES BRITISH CROWN; YORK WILL SUCCEED HIM AS GEORGE VI; PARLIAMENT IS SPEEDING ABDICATION ACT

CODE FOR INDUSTRY VOTED HERE TO BACK AIMS OF NEW DEAL

Association of Manufacturers Pledges Cooperation for 'Era of Good Feeling.'

ASKS FOR CENSUS OF IDLE

Moley Urges Business Join in Federal Planning—McCarl for Industrial Board.

LABOR GIVES 30-HOUR PLAN

Industrial Progress Council in Washington Hears Program for a Shorter Week.

Industry and New Deal

The National Manufacturers Association meeting here adopted a code for industry pledging "era of good feeling" and cooperation with social aims of New Deal. The text of the code is on Page 30.

The Council for Industrial Progress in Washington heard labor's plan to promote employment by a thirty-hour week and Federal regulation of working conditions. Employers did not oppose new labor laws, but spokesmen insisted that they should conform to the Constitution. Page 33.

Code Is Adopted Here

A declaration of principles for American industry, calling for an era of good feeling both at home and abroad, pledging cooperation with the government in the national interest and embracing, at least in principle, some of the most important social reforms of the New Deal, was adopted yesterday afternoon at the final session of the forty-first annual convention of the National Association of Manufacturers, held in the Waldorf-Astoria Hotel.

The declaration was in harmony with the keynote speech delivered at Wednesday's session by Colby M. Chester, chairman of the General Foods Corporation and president of the association, and in striking contrast to the bitter criticisms of the New Deal uttered by industrialists at previous meetings.

In closing the convention Mr. Chester asserted his belief that it had "written a new, sound and progressive note in the industrial life of this nation in its declaration of principles," and predicted that it would have the support of "a united industry" within the year.

Census of Idle Is Urged

Resolutions were adopted urging a government census of unemployed and opposing governmental ownership of the railroads or any transportation system.

Addresses were made by Raymond Moley, editor of the magazine Today; John R. McCarl, former Controller General; George H. Mead, president of the Mead Corporation and chairman of the business advisory council to the Department of Commerce, and James A. Emery, general counsel of the association.

Mr. Moley urged joint economic planning by the government and business. He warned industry that it must recognize the meaning of the election returns—that the people voted for security of wages and living standards—and offer them a rational plan to attain these ends if it does not wish to be compelled to submit to impractical and drastic legislation.

A balanced budget through the reduction of relief expenditures and other government spending was advocated by Mr. McCarl. He urged industry to accept the responsibility for reducing the need for relief by giving more jobs. He also suggested that business organize a National Industrial Board to cooperate with the government in the "collective" solution of social and economic problems.

According to Mr. Mead, business wants "constructive regulation," contrary to a general public impression, although it is opposed to "government ownership or control." Business also believes in economic security, he said, adding that a "practical" economic security and

Continued on Page Thirty-one

4,336,000,000 Francs Set As French Budget Deficit

Wireless to THE NEW YORK TIMES.

PARIS, Dec. 10.—There will be a deficit of 4,336,000,000 francs in the French budget during the coming year, according to figures put before the Chamber of Deputies this morning by the finance commission.

The ordinary expenditure under the budget is estimated at slightly more than 48,000,000,000 francs and the income at 43,685,000,000 francs. With these figures before them, the Deputies began to vote in rapid succession for most of the 140 articles in the law having to do with the collection of revenue despite the protest of one Right Deputy who argued that to vote revenues before expenditures was contrary to all good sense and logic.

JAPAN WITHDRAWS DEMANDS ON CHINA

Indicates Dropping of Moves for Anti-Red Cooperation and Autonomy of North China.

ARMY IS UNDER CRITICISM

Foreign Office Wants Public to Know the Military Interfere With Major Policies.

By HUGH BYAS

Wireless to THE NEW YORK TIMES.

TOKYO, Dec. 10.—Withdrawal of all the Japanese demands regarding North China autonomy and of that for cooperation against communism was implied in a statement issued to the press today by Eiji Amau, Foreign Office spokesman.

Japan asks Nanking to fulfill the agreements already reached on lesser points, but the request is not accompanied by a threat or warning except that if Japanese lives or property are endangered or Japanese rights violated the government will take "adequate measures."

Ambassador Shigeru Kawagoe's failure to obtain satisfaction from China, even in minor matters, is explained as due to Chinese indignation over the invasion of Suiyuan Province by Mongols and Manchukuoans.

Mr. Amau said nothing to connect the Japanese Kwantung Army with these events, but the public was already aware that Manchukuo's Premier had proclaimed sympathy with the Mongolian rising and knew he would not have taken such a step without being prompted.

Mr. Amau's statement, read in conjunction with Foreign Minister Hachiro Arita's answer to the Privy Council yesterday, suggested that the Foreign Office wants the public to know how the Kwantung army interferes with major policies on which all branches of the Tokyo government have agreed.

The statement claims that a definite agreement was reached with China regarding suppression of anti-Japanese movements—including revision of the control of the press and of Kuomintang (Nationalist party) branches—engagement of Japanese advisers, control of Korean exiles and reduction of tariffs.

Consulate Involved

China further agreed to reopening of the Chengtu Japanese Consulate and accepted most of Japan's demands for settlement of recent incidents.

A hitch occurred over air services. No agreement was reached regarding joint defense against communism though both sides concurred on several items.

Economic cooperation in North China was agreed on in principle. This stage having been reached, the Chinese, "taking advantage of the Suiyuan affair," broke off negotiations, threatened to repudiate all the concessions already made and evaded Ambassador Kawagoe's repeated requests for a further interview with Foreign Minister Chang Chun. Mr. Kawagoe was said to have handed Mr. Chang a note embodying the agreed points, requesting that they be put into effect.

"Japan is now watchfully waiting for China's response and is prepared to take adequate measures if China fails to control anti-Japanese movements or if Japanese life and property interests are jeopardized," said the statement.

It is pertinent to recall that Mr.

Continued on Page Twelve

CROWDS IN LONDON CALM

News Is Received With British Reserve as Thousands Gather.

QUEEN MARY IS CHEERED

Many Break Through Police Lines When She Calls at Home of Duke of York.

TENSION OF WEEK ENDED

People Sad at Losing Edward but Relieved the Suspense at Last Is Over.

Wireless to THE NEW YORK TIMES.

LONDON, Dec. 10.—As the news of King Edward's abdication sped to the far corners of the empire this afternoon Britain received confirmation of her worst fear with mixed emotions, sadness at losing so popular and beloved a sovereign and relief that the gnawing suspense of the last week at last had drawn to an end.

Massed thousands stood silently outside the towering iron gates of Parliament while the terse, restrained statement of the first monarch in England's history ever to renounce the throne voluntarily was read to the House of Commons. Presently, as the twilight shadows of Westminster Abbey lengthened over Parliament Square, word sped from mouth to mouth that the reign of Edward was coming to an end.

Although the atmosphere a few minutes before had been highly charged with tension and anxiety the news was received calmly and with typical British reserve. There was no demonstration and no show of feeling save for the serious, strained faces in the crowd and the flutter of women's handkerchiefs here and there.

Crowds Gather Throughout Day

Throughout the day, from dawn until after midnight, crowds of varying proportions gathered outside all the buildings associated with the historic happenings of the day. People clustered about No. 10 Downing Street, the Houses of Parliament and all the royal residences, standing stolidly and silently when allowed or moving along without protest if required. If any emotion was perceptible that could be described as a corporate reaction, it was one of bewilderment and incredulity that such a thing ever could actually happen.

A throng composed mostly of women, which at times reached 10,000 or more, stood on the pavement before Buckingham Palace forming

Continued on Page Twenty

Edward Plans Radio Talk To British Empire Tonight

Special Cable to THE NEW YORK TIMES.

LONDON, Dec. 10.—King Edward will broadcast to the empire tomorrow night at 10 o'clock, immediately after he has signed the Abdication Act and ceased to be King, in the character of a private person. It is expected Parliament will have disposed of its business by then.

[American networks will broadcast the message at 5 P. M., Eastern Standard Time.]

The British Broadcasting Corporation has arranged for a worldwide hook-up.

Many persons feel the King's decision to broadcast is not wise. He has already sent a message to Parliament with a penciled note to the Prime Minister, commending the Duke of York to the support of the whole empire. These will be broadcast four times tonight and printed in every British newspaper.

MRS. SIMPSON CRIES LISTENING AT RADIO

Shaken and Exhausted by the Climax in Career of King Who Forsook Throne for Her.

WILL REMAIN AT CANNES

Edward Will Not Visit Her Now—Britons in France Question Her Course.

Wireless to THE NEW YORK TIMES.

CANNES, France, Dec. 10.—With tears streaming down her face, Mrs. Wallis Warfield Simpson, for whose sake Edward VIII has abdicated as King and Emperor of the greatest empire the world has ever known, listened today as did all the rest of the world to the news over the radio from the scene in the British Parliament.

She heard the words announcing that the King Emperor of whom so much had been expected had laid down his scepter and crown so as to be free to marry her some months hence and live the life of an ordinary mortal.

Says King Won't Go to Riviera

At 1 o'clock this afternoon the following statement was made by Herman L. Rogers, at whose villa Mrs. Simpson is staying:

"There is definitely no change so far as Mrs. Simpson's plans are concerned. She will stay here until after Christmas. She is now at the villa and in the best of health. There has been no change in the household.

"It cannot be stated if she has

Continued on Page Twenty

Soviet Orders Militia Punished for Arrests Without Warrants in Spite of New Charter

Special Cable to THE NEW YORK TIMES.

MOSCOW, Dec. 10. — The first charges of violating the new Constitution were brought at Kazan today in connection with the arrests of eleven persons there by the militia on its own initiative.

According to the new Constitution, "no one may be subjected to arrest except upon the decision of a court or with the sanction of the prosecutor." Apparently no such authorization was obtained, and Moscow authorities have called the Kazan militia's action an "outrageous violation" of the Constitution and ordered that the guilty be suitably punished.

According to an investigation in Kazan, a doorman at a restaurant was arrested this week purely on suspicion. When he failed to arrive home his father made inquiries, and on finding his son in jail complained to the public prosecutor. The latter showed little interest. A correspondent of the Moscow newspaper Izvestia then took up the matter and spurred the prosecutor to visit the jail, where he found eleven persons arrested without warrants.

Today also the first Soviet death sentence for the infringement of private ownership and personal property and the murder of a private individual was imposed in a Moscow court.

Two employes of a State antique shop had been selling valuable old books to two highly paid ballet dancers. Thus the employes had learned their clients had money and valuables. They invaded the young dancers' home in their absence, killed their mother and cook with a brass pestle and looted the apartment. The criminals were traced, arrested, convicted and tonight they will be shot.

Hitherto the death penalty has been imposed in murder cases only where the safety or welfare of the State was involved, the normal penalty for an ordinary murder being not more than ten years.

Nikolai V. Krylenko has assumed his duties as head of the All-Union Commissariat for Justice, newly created under the Constitution. Today he began reorganizing the whole legal profession of the country into voluntary associations, which will give legal aid to any accused persons demanding their services. Any accused person is entitled to free legal counsel if he desires. Legal aid offices are also being established by trade unions.

Because of the new legal guarantees many more lawyers than hitherto will be needed. Accordingly steps are being taken to enroll thousands more students in the law schools already established, and plans are being formed for the creation of many more schools in the various republics.

BALDWIN TELLS OF EVENTS

Relates to the Commons How He Warned King Against Marriage.

DENIES ANY BITTERNESS

Says Ruler, Far From Feeling Resentment, Had Become a Firmer Friend to Him.

LEGAL ISSUE IS REFUTED

Churchill Declares It Is Now Clear That There Was Never a Constitutional Crisis.

By CHARLES A. SELDEN

Special Cable to THE NEW YORK TIMES.

LONDON, Dec. 10.—The momentous session of Parliament that received today King Edward's message of abdication was best described by Prime Minister Stanley Baldwin himself when he said near the close of his narrative of the crisis:

"This House of Commons today is a theatre which is being watched by the whole world."

Never since the first British Parliament was called by Simon de Montfort 672 years ago had it been the theatre for such an impressive tragedy as that enacted today.

There have been greater political issues, perhaps, and more fateful struggles between Crown and Commons. There have been long Parliaments, short Parliaments and rump Parliaments. But there has been no precedent for today's enactment of the tragedy in which a monarch signed away his sovereignty over an empire of 500,000,000 people for his love of a woman.

And while the play was on, the wars of one hemisphere and the efforts in the other hemisphere to end wars were merely side shows.

Extra Police on Hand

Standing room only was the situation in the legislative chamber itself, while there was not even standing room left in the acres of lobbies and for many blocks outside on the streets that lead to the Houses of Parliament.

So many extra companies of police were assigned to duty around the buildings that it was feared serious disorder was anticipated by the authorities, but nothing could have been further from the fact. There was as much decorum in witnessing this self-effacement of Edward VIII as there was last January when the multitudes gathered to mourn for his father and to proclaim him.

Needless to say, the House itself was filled as it had not been since the session at which war was declared in 1914. In the diplomatic gallery, every seat was taken by Ambassadors and Ministers from nearly all nations.

What little daylight sometimes seeps into the Commons chamber on a Winter afternoon was completely shut out by a dense fog, so there was nothing but mellow illumination from the lights above the stained glass ceiling.

House Is Ill at Ease

The House was ill at ease during the hour's interval prior to the great moment when Prime Minister Baldwin entered with the King's message of abdication. The familiar cry, "Prayers are over," after the customary, brief devotional exercise with which every session opens, was followed by many involuntary, at least unusual, "Amens," suggestive of a devout wish that for this once they might be answered quickly.

There were no "King's men" in this House. But it was equally true there were no anti-King men.

The King's own message was received with sorrow and sympathy. When Mr. Baldwin made his long statement of the events that preceded the decision to abandon the throne, there vanished the last trace of the bitterness that had developed in the last week from fear that the Crown might try to override the Commons.

"We are not judges," said Mr. Baldwin, and it was one of his utterances to which members gave their warmest assent.

"While there is not a soul among us who will not regret this from the bottom of his heart," said the

Continued on Page Sixteen

Associated Press Photo.

SUCCESSOR TO THE BRITISH THRONE
The Duke of York

YORK GETS OVATION AT HOME IN LONDON

Cheering and Singing Theatre Crowds Surge About His Car While Auto Horns Salute.

HE DOFFS HAT TO THRONG

New Monarch Expected to Use Name 'George' as Symbol of Strength and Steadiness.

Special Cable to THE NEW YORK TIMES.

LONDON, Dec. 10.—Thousands of Londoners shouted a welcome tonight to a shy and awkward young man who was ready to step into the dazzling light of the greatest throne on earth.

With the abdication of King Edward VIII, the 41-year-old Duke of York was about to take his place on the world wide stage as the latest in the long line of English sovereigns. And tonight, in front of his town house at 145 Piccadilly, the crowds had their first chance to show him that they were glad.

A surging throng of theatre-goers on the way home surrounded his car as he returned after having dinner with Edward at Fort Belvedere. Cheering and waving hats, they filled the wide roadway in front of the house and blocked traffic so completely police were powerless to keep it moving.

Before the Duke entered the house he turned to the crowd and raised his hat several times. That was the signal for a great demonstration. Hundreds of motorists set up a deafening salute with their horns, while the crowd began singing the national anthem and "For He's a Jolly Good Fellow."

Popular Reign Indicated

It was a demonstration of some importance in the story of the British throne, for it showed that the Duke may be a popular King even without any of the brilliant qualities of his elder brother.

Tomorrow night he will become King, and Saturday morning his accession will be proclaimed with the stately pageantry that has come down unchanged from medieval times. For individual kings may come and go, but the British monarchy that has survived many shocks before this will keep its place as the keystone of the vast and loosely jointed empire.

Heralds in uniforms of gold will

Continued on Page Eighteen

EDWARD CHEERFUL AFTER TAKING STEP

Reported Like Man Who Has Had Crushing Load of Worry Lifted From Shoulders.

PACKS FOR HIS DEPARTURE

Knowledge That He Will Not Be Barred From Returning to England Relieves Him.

By FERDINAND KUHN Jr.

Wireless to THE NEW YORK TIMES.

LONDON, Dec. 10.—The blue and white flag of the Duchy of Cornwall fluttered slowly to the foot of its mast at 10 o'clock this morning on the high turret over Fort Belvedere.

It was a signal that made history, for at that moment King Edward was renouncing the greatest throne on earth so that he could marry the woman he loved. With his three brothers as his only witnesses, he signed the instrument of abdication as his "final and irrevocable decision" to retire into private life.

He will remain King until tomorrow afternoon, when the Abdication Bill is expected to reach him from Parliament. As soon as he signs it, however, his unhappy days as King will come to an end after the shortest reign in 453 years. The Duke of York will come to the throne as George VI and Edward will leave England as the first man in all the 1,000 years of the British monarchy to have left the throne of his own accord.

Edward Again Cheerful

Although he has not shown himself to the public for almost a week, it was reported on good authority tonight that he was like a man who had had a crushing load of worry lifted from his shoulders.

The depression and jumpiness of the last few days had vanished and the King was said to be cheerful and purposeful, superintending the packing of his belongings, dealing with State papers, which arrived incessantly from London, and looking forward to more happiness than he has known in a long time.

Workmen and tractors were busy all day on Edward's private flying field at Smith's Lawn in Windsor Great Park, apparently preparing it for the take-off of an important airplane. Four police cars were on duty and a cordon of police and

Continued on Page Sixteen

KING MAKES HIS DECISION

Chooses Woman Over Throne After 'Long and Anxious' Thought.

FINALE LIKELY TOMORROW

New Reign, Expected to Bring Back Calm of George V's, Is to Be Proclaimed Then.

CROWNING PLAN MAY HOLD

Edward Can Use Either of Two Titles, Earl of Rothesay or Baron of Renfrew.

Edward's letter, the Abdication Bill, Baldwin's speech, Page 17.

By FREDERICK T. BIRCHALL

Special Cable to THE NEW YORK TIMES.

LONDON, Dec. 10.—Some time Saturday morning, perhaps even as soon as tomorrow night, Edward VIII will cease to be a King and Emperor. He has made his choice between a woman and a throne and the woman has won.

Today at Fort Belvedere, his country home near Windsor Castle, and in the presence of his three brothers, the Dukes of York, Gloucester and Kent, the King signed a message to his Ministers announcing his determination "after long and anxious consideration" to renounce the throne to which he had succeeded on the death of his father. This, said the message, is "my final and irrevocable decision."

The message was carried by Prime Minister Stanley Baldwin this afternoon to a crowded session of the House of Commons and there read, not without emotion, by the Speaker.

Bill Introduced in House

There is no question of whether the House should accept it. Under the British Constitution there can be none, for it was an expression of the King's will and the King rules, though he does not govern, Britain and the empire. But immediately afterward, as soon as the Prime Minister in a speech that will be memorable for the restrained feeling it expressed and the leaders of the Opposition each after his fashion had voiced their regret, a bill was introduced that will implement the monarch's decision.

Tomorrow this formal bill of abdication will be rushed through all its stages in both houses, Commons and Lords. It will then be carried to the King for his royal assent. The moment he signs it he ceases to be King and his brother, the Duke of York, who is nearest to him, will reign in his stead.

The new King will take the throne, according to the best information available tonight, as George VI and for that choice there is a reason. It is desired, now that this storm is over and the skies are clearing, to get back to the ordered peace and quiet stability of the monarchy under the last King George, to leave behind this brief era of conflict between will and duty and to concentrate anew on the empire and its common destiny.

Proclamation Likely Tomorrow

Another era will begin probably at noon on Saturday when the accession of the new King is proclaimed from the balcony of St. James's Palace, again at old gray Charing Cross and finally from the steps of the Royal Exchange in the City of London, each time with all the pomp and ceremony that the monarchy has upheld here throughout a thousand years Kings may change but the old order remaineth; that is to be Britain's watchword still.

And thus, in circumstances that will arouse wonder and pity as long as history continues to be written, ends the brief reign of King Edward VIII. It has lasted ten months and twenty-two days before this strange storm that love of woman created has brought it to a close, and the empire still endures. Even a newcomer can

Continued on Page Sixteen

"All the News That's Fit to Print."

The New York Times.

LATE CITY EDITION
Fair today, temperature unchanged. Tomorrow fair, little change in temperature.
Temperatures Yesterday—Max., 71; Min., 54

VOL. LXXXVI....No. 28,958. Entered as Second-Class Matter. Postoffice, New York, N. Y. NEW YORK, FRIDAY, MAY 7, 1937. P TWO CENTS In New York City. | THREE CENTS Within 200 Miles. | FOUR CENTS Elsewhere Except in 7th and 8th Postal Zones.

HINDENBURG BURNS IN LAKEHURST CRASH; 21 KNOWN DEAD, 12 MISSING; 64 ESCAPE

ANARCHISTS RENEW BARCELONA STRIFE; 5,000 LEAVE BILBAO

Revolters, Regaining Part of Catalan Capital, Demand Shock Troop Dissolution

SOCIALIST MINISTER SLAIN

Insurgents Reported Gaining Unresisted in Aragon as Foes Withdraw 12,000

EVACUATION IN NORTH SPED

British Warships Protect Craft Taking Women and Children From Bilbao to France

The Spanish Situation

PERPIGNAN—Anarchists were reported to have regained positions in Barcelona and to have demanded the dissolution of the government's shock troops. Withdrawal of 12,000 men from the Aragon front, to deal with the situation, was also reported, leading to an advance by the Rebel armies. Page 1.

ROME—A heavy concentration of Rebels, including Italians, to rescue the Italians cut off at Bermeo, was under way on the Bilbao front. Page 10.

BILBAO—Five thousand women and children were taken from the city, and vessels carrying them to France were guarded by British warships. More refugees were preparing to leave. (Follows the above.) Page 10.

LONDON—Foreign Secretary Eden revealed that the British Government had evidence that Guernica was destroyed by airplanes. He favored a neutral inquiry. Page 10.

Anarchists Give Ultimatum

Special Cable to THE NEW YORK TIMES.

PERPIGNAN, France, May 6.—The Anarchists are reported to have regained control in parts of Barcelona this afternoon after the Catalan Generalidad believed it had dominated the situation.

The Anarchists issued an ultimatum to the government demanding the dissolution of the shock troops patroling the city, the government's chief support, within twenty-four hours and declaring that otherwise they would take matters into their own hands and use every means in their power to suppress the shock troops.

The Anarchists also have obtained the upper hand at Junquera in addition to Figueras, according to news received here, and threaten, it is alleged, to use asphyxiating gas unless their ultimatum is obeyed.

Anarchist broadcasts have been picked up here stating that the casualties in the disorders in Barcelona since the Anarchist rebellion Tuesday amounted to 400 dead and 2,000 wounded. Declaring that "enough blood has flowed," the broadcasts continue to appeal for calm every ten minutes, and it is therefore believed that trouble still persists in Barcelona.

French Consulate Menaced

The French Consulate was threatened by Anarchists, who asserted that Rightist sympathizers had taken refuge there. The consul appealed to French warships in the harbor and 200 armed sailors reinforced the consulate guard.

Telephonic communication with Barcelona is still cut off tonight, and telegraphic and telephonic communication with the interior of Catalonia, which was re-established yesterday, was again interrupted this morning.

The Spanish Consul at Perpignan has recommended that Frenchmen and others should not go further than Figueras, and trains do not proceed beyond Gerona.

Francisco Ascasso, leader of the Anarchists in the Aragon Government, is reported to have been murdered.

Rebels Gain on Aragon Front

By The Associated Press.

PERPIGNAN, France, May 6.—Reports of an unresisted Insurgent advance along the whole Aragon front of Northeastern Spain and of the withdrawal of 12,000 government troops from it to keep the peace in troubled Barcelona, put a new and serious face on the Catalan Anarchist insurrection tonight. The reports emanated from Insurgent

Continued on Page Ten

Judge Sentences Himself By Signing Papers Unread

Wireless to THE NEW YORK TIMES.

MOSCOW, May 6.—A judge on one of the most important benches of the Moscow District Court who has the bad habit of signing unread any document placed before him has just sentenced himself to jail.

The court clerks, deciding he needed a lesson in "Bolshevik vigilance," presented to him a sheaf of papers including one reading: "To the chief of Butyrky prison: Under Magistrate Abramson is sent to you for further detention." Judge Abramson signed all the papers and picked up his newspaper again.

The clerks, of course, extracted the sentence and were passing it around laughingly when the judge found out about it. He destroyed it in a rage, declaring such jokes tended to undermine Soviet justice.

The government learned about it, however, and today Izvestia delivered to Judge Abramson a stinging rebuke for perfunctoriness, reminding him that he dealt not in inanimate goods but in human fate.

HUGHES SEES CHOICE IN LAW OR TYRANNY

Courts Must Be Maintained, He Tells Law Institute, or We Replace Reason by Force

TEST OF BAR TO ROOSEVELT

Stewardship Is Questioned by Laymen, He Writes in Warning of 'Critical Audience'

Text of Chief Justice Hughes's address is on Page 17.

Special to THE NEW YORK TIMES.

WASHINGTON, May 6.—Chief Justice Hughes made what his hearers construed as a reference to the Supreme Court when he told the American Law Institute today that if society is to choose the processes of reason as opposed to the tyranny of force, "it must maintain the institutions which embody those processes." It was the second time that the Chief Justice of the United States has broken his silence since the controversy over reorganization of the Supreme Court started three months ago.

Vigorous applause, lasting more than a minute, followed the Chief Justice's words, with which he concluded a speech in which he avoided any direct reference to the court issue.

President Roosevelt in a message to the institute likewise refrained from any positive statement about the Supreme Court, but remarked that "law interpreters," among other legal experts, are facing a sometimes critical audience.

President on Lawyers' Position

"I am happy to greet you members of the bench, the bar and the law school faculties who have assembled for the fifteenth annual meeting of the American Law Institute," the President stated.

"I have followed with interest your accomplishments within recent years in the restatement of the law and your proposals for improvement in the administration of criminal justice.

"Today our stewardship as lawyers is being questioned. The laymen of America are not, perhaps, quite so disposed to make a complete delegation of law matters to law men. At least the layman asserts his right to evaluate us.

"Law scholars, law practitioners, lawmakers, law administrators and law interpreters have the stage today. But more significant, they must play their rôles before an intense and sometimes critical audience.

"But this is well. The virtue of the common law was its adaptability to growth and improvement. In generations present and future the lawyer likewise will be measured by the same test.

"It is encouraging today that so many outstanding leaders of the profession assemble to give service in the important and worth-while task to which the American Law Institute is dedicated. I extend again my warm and cordial greetings to your membership and my best wishes for continued success."

Only at one other time since President Roosevelt made his recommendations to Congress on Feb. 5 has the Chief Justice made any

Continued on Page Seventeen

NOTABLES ABOARD

Merchants, Students and Professional Men on the Dirigible

LEHMANN IS A SURVIVOR

Veteran Zeppelin Commander, Acting as Adviser on Trip, Is Seriously Burned

CAPT. PRUSS IS ALSO SAFE

C. L. Osbun, Sales Manager, Who Survived a Plane Crash, Escapes Second Time

Notables from many walks of life were among the passengers on the ill-fated Hindenburg. They included merchants, students and business and professional men and women.

Many of the survivors owed their lives to the fact that they were apparently near windows in the dirigible when the accident happened and were able to leap through them to the ground in safety.

Among the survivors listed were Captain Ernst Lehmann, veteran Zeppelin commander; Captain Max Pruss, the new Hindenburg commander; Herbert O'Laughlin of Chicago, employed by the Consumers Company of Elgin, Ill.; Clifford L. Osbun, export sales manager of the Oliver Farm Equipment Company of Chicago, and Ferdinand Lammot Belin Jr. of Washington, D. C.

Lehmann's Condition Grave

Early this morning Dr. E. G. Herbener, staff surgeon at the Paul Kimball Hospital in Lakewood, said that Captain Lehmann was on the doubtful list. Captain Lehmann is *suffering from shock and second* and third degree burns of the face and body. Captain Pruss is suffering from second and third degree burns of the face, forehead and arms and will probably recover, Dr. Herbener said.

Among the passengers who were still unaccounted for were John Pannes, passenger traffic manager of the Hamburg-American Line and North German Lloyd at New York, and his wife; Ernst Rudolf Anders, partner of the firm of Seelig & Hille, tea merchants of Dresden, Germany, and his son, R. Herbert Anders, and Hermann Doehner of Mexico, D. F.

Captain Lehmann and Captain Pruss were in the control gondola when the crash occurred. Both officers, together with several other members of the crew, leaped through the gondola windows to safety.

Lehmann an Adviser

Captain Lehmann, who was serving as adviser aboard the Hindenburg, had been commander of the ship until this year. He has had long experience with the lighter-than-air craft, and has been associated with Hugo Eckener, world-famous authority on Zeppelins, since 1931.

He was born March 12, 1886, at Ludwigshafen, on the Rhine, the son of a chemist. He became a naval cadet in 1905 and later entered the Polytechnic Institute at Charlottenburg, a borough of Berlin.

During the World War Captain Lehmann received the German Iron Cross award. After the war, as second in command to Eckener, he brought the dirigible Los Angeles to Lakehurst in 1924. When the Hindenburg was completed in 1936 Captain Lehmann was placed in command, a position he held until recently, when Captain Pruss was elevated as commander of the ship.

Mr. Osbun's escape from the disaster marked the second time that he had narrowly missed death as the result of a flying accident. Last year he was aboard a transport plane when it was forced down en route from Puerto Rico to Buenos Aires. Soon after he was transferred to a motorboat with other passengers and the motorboat blew up. Mr. Osbun escaped injury, but two other passengers were seriously burned.

Mr. Osbun declared that he was talking to fellow passengers in the dining salon, looking down through the observation window watching the ship being moored, when the disaster occurred. He was apparently blown through the window and thrown to the ground, suffering injuries. He was taken to the Paul Kimball Hospital in Lakewood, where his condition was said to be not serious.

Mr. Osbun is 37 years old, the fa-

Continued on Page Nineteen

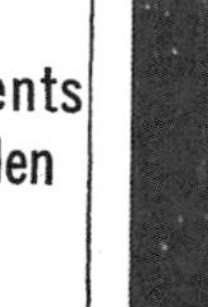

Associated Press Photo.

THE HINDENBURG IN FLAMES ON THE FIELD AT LAKEHURST

The giant airliner as she settled to the ground near her mooring mast at 7:23 o'clock last night

SHIP FALLS ABLAZE

Great Dirigible Bursts Into Flames as It Is About to Land

VICTIMS BURN TO DEATH

Some Passengers Are Thrown From the Blazing Wreckage, Others Crawl to Safety

GROUND CREW AIDS RESCUE

Sparks From Engines or Static Believed to Have Ignited Hydrogen Gas

A page of photographs of the disaster and survivors Page 20.

By RUSSELL B. PORTER

Special to THE NEW YORK TIMES.

NAVAL AIR STATION, LAKEHURST, N. J., May 6.—The zeppelin Hindenburg was destroyed by fire and explosions here at 7:23 o'clock tonight with a loss of thirty-three known dead and unaccounted for out of its ninety-seven passengers and crew.

Three hours after the disaster twenty-one bodies had been recovered, and twelve were still missing. The sixty-four known to be alive included twenty passengers and forty-four of the crew. Many of the survivors were burned or injured or both, and were taken to hospitals here and in near-by towns.

The accident happened just as the great German dirigible was about to tie up to its mooring mast four hours after flying over New York City on the last leg of its first transatlantic voyage of the year. Until today the Hindenburg had never lost a passenger throughout the ten round trips it made across the Atlantic with 1,002 passengers in 1936.

Two Theories of Cause

F. W. von Meister, vice president of the American Zeppelin Company, gave two possible theories to explain the crash. One was that a fire was caused by an electrical circuit "induced by static conditions" as the ship valved hydrogen gas preparatory to landing. Another was that sparks set off when the engines were throttled down while the gas was being valved caused a fire or explosion.

Captain Ernst Lehmann, who commanded the Hindenburg on most of its flights last year and was one of tonight's survivors, gasped, "I couldn't understand it," as he staggered out of the burning control car. Captain Max Pruss, commanding officer of the airship, and Captain Albert Stampf were also among the survivors.

Captain Lehmann was critically burned and injured; the other officers were also burned, but less seriously.

Experts in lighter-than-air operations who saw the accident said tonight that when the two landing lines were dropped by the dirigible at 7:20, they were immediately made fast to the mooring cars on the circular track about the mooring mast. The crew began to make the lines taut, but the ship had gathered too much momentum, according to these observers, and drifted several hundred yards past the mast. The starboard line pulled hard as the nose of the ship passed over the mooring mast at the top.

Order Not Heard

Captain Pruss, making his first trip in command of the dirigible, signaled and shouted, "Pay out!"

This order was heard by the operator on one mooring car, but not by the other, as the shout went against the wind and could not be heard. Consequently, one mooring car paid out and the other did not. The result was that the ship was thrown off its balance and lost the perfect equilibrium it had previously had.

Its nose dipped, forward ballast was dropped and the elevators were set to raise the ship. Instead the ship was held tight by one yaw line. The nose was pulled over and the elevators had an effect opposite to that which they were intended to have, according to this version. The tail dropped sharply and the bottom rudder hit the

Continued on Page Nineteen

DISASTER ASCRIBED TO GAS BY EXPERTS

Washington Sees Dangerous Combination of Hydrogen and Blue Gas as Cause

Special to THE NEW YORK TIMES.

WASHINGTON, May 6.—Washington airship experts and Congressional leaders received the news of the Hindenburg disaster with amazement and expressions of sorrow. But in every instance those who commented pointed out that the three disasters of the United States Navy were structural, while that of the German craft was due to the use of a combination of hydrogen and blue gas, the most dangerous of all gases for inflation of airships.

Dr. Hans Luther, the German Ambassador, said the disaster must not cause the world to lose faith in dirigibles and that it could not have been caused by technical defects.

"It is terrible," the Ambassador said. "I was horrified by the news, but it could not have been a technical matter. It must not cause us to lose faith in dirigibles because the Graf Zeppelin has operated safely and efficiently for eight years on the run from Europe to South America and elsewhere."

Secretary Hull sent the following message tonight to Konstantin von Neurath, the German Minister of Foreign Affairs:

"I extend to you and to the people of Germany my profound sympathy at the tragic accident to the dirigible Hindenburg and the resultant loss of life to passengers and crew."

"It is too terrible to believe," Admiral A. B. Cook, Chief of Naval Aeronautics, said. "From what I

Continued on Page Twenty-one

Airship Like a Giant Torch On Darkening Jersey Field

Routine Landing Converted Into Hysterical Scene in Moment's Time—Witnesses Tell of 'Blinding Flash' From Zeppelin

By CRAIG THOMPSON

Special to THE NEW YORK TIMES.

LAKEHURST, N. J., May 6—The Hindenburg, giant silver liner of the air, suddenly became a torch above the naval air station here tonight. What began as a routine landing of the transatlantic airship ended in a holocaust.

The ground crew, officials of the naval air base, spectators, reporters and press photographers were going about their customary business of aiding or watching the ship nose into the mooring mast.

Two ground lines had been dropped from the nose. These, attached to the cars running on a circular track around the mast, were holding the ship nose down at a thirty-degree angle, and helping it jockey into a position favorable with the wind for a mooring.

A thunderstorm had passed over the field a short time before and a drizzly rain was still falling. Twilight was beginning, although the visibility was still good.

So suddenly that it left spectators on the verge of hysteria for some time afterward, the ship burst into flame. Some one in the ground crew yelled "Run for your lives!" and the crew did. The stern of the ship settled and the photographers, squinting through the view finders of their cameras, ran toward the ship.

The occurrence sounded, witnesses said, like two explosions, one following the other about thirty seconds apart. Some said they saw one burst of flame, others two, but the noises they described as explosions gave way to the sounds of human screams.

In the "heavier-than-air" hangar, the pilot of an American Air Lines plane, waiting to ferry passengers from the airship into Newark, watched from a window.

"It seemed to happen so fast that I didn't think anybody could escape," he said afterward.

He was wrong, for about at that moment a man ran into the hangar.

"His face was black, but he seemed to be all right otherwise. He wanted to telephone his mother in Chicago."

The passenger was Herbert James O'Laughlin of Chicago.

On the field was an army detachment from Philadelphia, detailed there for just such an emergency. This detail promptly went to work, trucks scurrying over the field seeking the injured, while in the hangar telephone calls were being put through to all points in New Jersey and New York City calling for ambulances, doctors, nurses, medicine.

All this occurred while the flames spread toward the uptilted nose of the ship, while the stern sank to the ground to be followed shortly by the entire length, girder and strut, the bared ribs of the ship from which the skin had disappeared.

Robert Seelig, Murray Becker and Larry Kennedy, all newspaper camera men, related what they had seen.

"There was a noise that sounded like bullets coming out of the gondolas," Seelig said. "I saw nobody

Continued on Page Twenty-one

GERMANY SHOCKED BY THE TRAGEDY

At First Disbelieving, Line's Officials Tell of Receiving Message of Landing

Special Cable to THE NEW YORK TIMES.

BERLIN, Friday, May 7.—It was a few minutes after 1 o'clock this morning when the first news of the disaster to the Hindenburg reached Berlin by telephone from The New York Times Bureau in London. The bureau forwarded the brief bulletin to the effect that the airship had been destroyed while making its landing. No details were given.

At that hour the German newspapers were without news. Several first editions, in fact, had reported the Hindenburg's supposedly safe arrival on the strength of an erroneous telegram received by the company in Frankfort on the Main. It was almost two hours later before the news of the disaster with some few details reached the newspapers through the medium of the German official news agency.

Facts Difficult to Get

In the meantime such facts about the airship and its passengers proved difficult to obtain. The Frankfort and Berlin offices of the Zeppelin company were closed and no complete list of the passengers or crew was available. A list of twenty-one names comprising foreign passengers out of a total list of thirty-nine was obtained by telephone from Frankfort, where this correspondent had retained it since the sailing day.

Dr. Hugo Eckener, veteran chief of the Zeppelin service, was in Austria, where he had lectured last night in Vienna. The Vienna bureau of THE NEW YORK TIMES traced him to Graz and obtained his ad-

Continued on Page Nineteen

"All the News That's Fit to Print."

The New York Times.

LATE CITY EDITION
Showers early, generally fair and warmer today. Tomorrow generally fair, possibly thunder showers.
Temperatures Yesterday—Max., 76; Min., 58.

VOL. LXXXVI.....No. 29,015. Entered as Second-Class Matter. Postoffice, New York, N. Y. NEW YORK, SATURDAY, JULY 3, 1937. PP TWO CENTS In New York City. | THREE CENTS Within 200 Miles. | FOUR CENTS Elsewhere Except in 7th and 8th Postal Zones.

PHILADELPHIA DRIVERS STRIKE IN A.F.L. HOLIDAY AGAINST C.I.O.; BITTER LABOR ROW IN HOUSE

ALL TRUCKS HALT

Newspapers Suspend as the Strike Brings City Near Paralysis

MILK SHORTAGE IS FEARED

Mayor Ready to Add 10,000 Police—Other A. F. L. Groups Uphold Contracts

TAXI MEN REFUSE TO QUIT

C. I. O. Pacts Signed by Two Bakeries Cause Issue—NLRB Elections Demanded

Day's Strike Developments

Teamsters' council called a "holiday" for 25,000 drivers, halting the movement of food, freight, merchandise and newspapers in Philadelphia. Page 1.

Republic Steel mills at Massillon, Ohio, were reopened under protection of National Guardsmen. Page 6.

Johnstown remained quiet on eve of tomorrow's strike rally while Mayor and State police prepare for gathering of 40,000. Page 6.

A bitter attack by Representative Cox on Representative Maverick as defender of C. I. O. was vigorously applauded in the House. Page 1.

Members of Senate Civil Liberties Committee saw pictures of Chicago Memorial Day strike riot. Page 5.

Third Avenue system signed C. I. O. contract covering bus and trolley operators. Pay rises and preferential shop granted. Page 11.

Labor War in Philadelphia

Special to THE NEW YORK TIMES.

PHILADELPHIA, July 2.—A "general holiday" of 25,000 American Federation of Labor truckmen, called in a test of strength with the C. I. O., brought business activity in Philadelphia and its surrounding area to the edge of paralysis tonight.

The immediate occasion of the "holiday" was what the A. F. of L. leaders called an "invasion" of the truck union field by the C. I. O. through the signing of contracts with the Ward and Freihofer Baking Companies after the expiration of A. F. of L. contracts Wednesday night.

Eight hours after the "holiday" began at 2 P. M. today, virtually all deliveries were suspended. In the commission market district of the city between $1,500,000 and $2,000,000 worth of foodstuffs lay in warehouses, with little probability that they would be distributed before much of them spoil.

This evening at least a temporary milk shortage threatened. A statement by the Joint Teamsters Council, A. F. of L. organization which controls almost all the Philadelphia truckmen, promised that emergency milk and bread deliveries would be made tomorrow.

But parents who feared their children might go without food had bought up a large part of the milk supply immediately available.

Newspapers Suspend

At 10:30 this evening, after a conference of the publishers of all Philadelphia newspapers, it was agreed to suspend publication in line with the suggestion of Mayor Wilson "in order not to endanger the lives of citizens or policemen."

Conferences of the publishers were held in the office of Robert McLean, publisher of The Evening Bulletin, and the announcement was made after first editions of morning newspapers had been printed, though not generally distributed, because of the lack of trucks.

The suspension of publication, it was announced, will be indefinite. The Philadelphia newspapers affected are The Bulletin, The Daily News and The Evening Ledger, evening publications, and The Inquirer and The Record, morning newspapers. Their total circulation is about 1,500,000 copies. In Camden, N. J., The Camden Post and The Camden Evening Courier also suspended.

A statement released by the publishers and broadcast through radio stations and news services not affected by the "holiday" said that

Continued on Page Five

Cox Assails Maverick on the C.I.O. Amid Cheers of Representatives

Georgian Calls Texan More of a Buffoon Than a Public Servant and Asks if He Favors 'Terrorism'—Latter Angrily Defends Lewis and Warns 'Hysteria' Brought on Civil War

Special to THE NEW YORK TIMES.

WASHINGTON, July 2.—Supporters and opponents of the C. I. O. labor movement staged the bitterest debate of the session in the House today and suggestions were made that fist fights would result unless "these insulting remarks" were discontinued.

Representatives Maverick of Texas and Cox of Georgia were principals in the tussle, aided by Representatives Hill of Washington and Hoffman of Michigan.

After Mr. Maverick had answered Mr. Cox's speech of Wednesday attacking the C. I. O. movement as one which, if not halted, might plunge the country into civil war, the Georgia Representative took the floor for a speech in which language he used was bitterly objected to by Mr. Maverick.

The House, however, on a demand for a determination of the matter by Mr. Maverick, overwhelmingly voted to leave intact in the record Mr. Cox's words describing the Texan as "more interested in provoking amusement by his extravagance and buffoonery than in molding sound public sentiment."

In a parliamentary move rarely resorted to, Mr. Maverick had demanded that "the gentleman's words be taken down," after which it becomes the privilege of the House to determine whether the member's words reflect upon the integrity, character or standing of the offended colleague.

After the House, by a voice vote, had backed Mr. Cox, Mr. Maverick shouted that "a quorum is not present—they can put this on record if they want to." But Mr. Maverick withdrew his point of no quorum after Speaker Bankhead, striving to maintain order and enforce the rules, had observed that there obviously was no quorum present.

Mr. Maverick had defended the C. I. O. movement and had asserted Mr. Cox was "one of those" who sought to oppose the President in some points of his program.

"I want to think better than well of the gentleman (Mr. Maverick)," Mr. Cox said in reply. "However, it would be difficult for me to esteem him as highly as he might wish. I do want to believe, Mr. Speaker, that the gentleman loves his government and would not willingly lend himself as an instrument to its overthrow."

Quoting Andrew Jackson's words, "Our Federal Union, it must be preserved," Mr. Cox continued:

"Then I want him (Mr. Maverick) to join with me in asking the ques-

Continued on Page Six

PRIAL AND TAYLOR IN CONTROLLER RACE

Democrats Face Hard Fight in Primaries as Both Announce Candidacies in Day

LABOR COOL TO WAGNER

Party Reported to Be Loyal to La Guardia—Republicans Considering Smith

A primary fight for the Democratic nomination for Controller was indicated yesterday when former Deputy Controller Frank J. Prial announced his candidacy for that office and Controller Frank J. Taylor declared that he would be a candidate for re-election on his record.

Mr. Prial's announcement came just before the five Democratic county leaders, James J. Dooling, leader of Tammany; Frank V. Kelly of Brooklyn, Secretary of State Edward J. Flynn of the Bronx, James C. Sheridan of Queens and William T. Fetherston of Richmond, met in secret conference to prepare a slate for the Democratic city ticket. These five leaders were reported to be united on Senator Robert F. Wagner as the candidate for Mayor if he would consent to run.

There was no such unanimity on the candidate for Controller. Mr. Dooling was reported to favor the designation of Mr. Prial as the organization candidate in the interest of party harmony. Mr. Kelly was said to have insisted upon the designation of Controller Taylor. With agreement seemingly impossible, a bitter primary fight was in prospect with every indication that Mr. Prial would receive strong Tammany support.

The leaders made no definite decision. Mr. Sheridan insisted that the organization designate William F. Brunner, President of the Board of Aldermen, as its candidate for President of the new City Council.

Owen J. Brady, secretary of the Amalgamated Irish Societies, announced that this organization had sent a message to Mr. Dooling protesting against the nomination of Senator Wagner. The message read:

"Amalgamated Irish Societies of Greater New York strongly oppose nomination of Robert Wagner, consistent enemy of Irish race and leading advocate of American membership in League of Nations and World Court."

"I have decided to run for Controller," was Mr. Prial's laconic announcement, which he declined to amplify.

"Have you anything to add to this?" he was asked.

"No," he replied.

Mr. Taylor's declaration of his

Continued on Page Six

TREASURY DEFICIT IS $2,707,000,000 NET

Roosevelt Estimate In April Exceeded by $150,000,000 in Year-End Figures

DEBT ROSE $2,646,000,000

Receipts Up $1,178,000,000 —Outlay Exceeded Estimate by $220,000,000

Special to THE NEW YORK TIMES.

WASHINGTON, July 2.—The government ended the fiscal year on June 30 with a net deficit of $2,707,000,000 and a gross public debt of $36,425,000,000, according to final figures made public today by Secretary Morgenthau. The deficit was about $150,000,000 more than estimated by President Roosevelt on April 20. The debt was an increase of $2,646,000,000 for the fiscal year.

General receipts will be $5,294,000,000, exceeding those for 1936 by $1,178,000,000, and about $70,000,000 more than estimated in April. Total expenditures exclusive of $104,000,000 for statutory debt retirement were $8,001,000,000, or about $220,000,000 over the April estimate.

In addition to the gross public debt, Secretary Morgenthau said, the government has certain contingent liabilities in guarantees as to principal and interest on outstanding obligations of the Reconstruction Finance Corporation, Federal Housing Administration and the Home Owners Loan Corporation amounting as of June 30 to about $4,725,000,000, as compared with a total of $4,750,000,000 on June 30, 1936.

$3,889,000,000 of Assets Held

On May 31 the government held net assets in loans and other investments of governmental corporations and credit agencies of about $3,889,000,000, a decrease of $406,000,000 from May 31, 1936, the reduction representing mainly net recoveries by the government.

Daniel W. Bell, Director of the Budget, said he felt the government would come very close to the forecasts of a balanced budget in the year 1938 if revenues held up to estimates and Congress did not place any further burdens on the Treasury. The earlier forecasts had been for a deficit in 1938 of about $400,000,000, which it was hoped could be wiped out by economies.

Should that objective substantially be attained, it was estimated, with receipts of around $1,000,000,000 from social security legislation about $600,000,000 of outstanding government securities could be retired in the year. There would be issued, however, a like amount of special government securities which would be a charge against the public debt. Actual reduction of the

Continued on Page Twenty-six

NEW COURT BILL OFFERED IN SENATE TO END CONFLICT

Leaders Abandon President's Program in Effort to Save Him From Defeat

RETIRING AGE SET AT 75

Measure Limits Appointments to One a Year—Opponents Reject Compromise

The text of the new Court Bill will be found on Page 4.

By TURNER CATLEDGE

Special to THE NEW YORK TIMES.

WASHINGTON, July 2.—A substitute court bill, providing an addition of one justice a year to the Supreme Court to supplement those passing 75 years of age and refusing to retire, was introduced in the Senate today by Senate leaders, formally abandoning the President's original program.

It was presented by Senator Logan in the name of himself and Senators Ashurst and Hatch, but it represented the results of three weeks or more of negotiations by Senator Robinson, which he started when President Roosevelt gave him full authority to salvage what he could out of his judiciary reorganization plan and end the five-month controversy over the issue.

At the same time it started a drive to win such a compromise as might save Mr. Roosevelt from utter defeat on this most bitterly contested of all his measures to date.

Friends and foes of the proposal to enlarge the Supreme Court by the immediate addition of six new justices to replace or supplement those over 70½ years of age agreed that the new bill would be passed by a comfortable majority if it should ever reach a vote in the Senate.

This left a large "if," however, for opponents of the original six-justice bill vowed anew their determination to fight any increase in the membership of the high tribunal and boasted that they would filibuster for weeks to prevent the compromise plan from coming to a vote in the Senate.

Fighting "On Principle"

They said they were fighting the bill on a matter of principle, and that the principle was the same whether it increased the court by one or a dozen, *if to increase it* was to attempt to interfere with its line of decisions.

Whether the court-enlargement foes would attempt to make good on their threat, or whether, if they did, the administration leaders would try to ride out a filibuster were other unknown quantities in the equation. Any definite forecast of what might happen was, therefore, impossible.

The substitute bill will be brought up early next week, according to present plans. It may be debated for several days, possibly two or three weeks, without any suggestion of obstructionist tactics.

Should a filibuster then develop, however, it would be for the Senate leaders to determine whether they would attempt to ride it out, which most observers agreed they could do if they were willing to stay in session indefinitely, or whether, in the interest of early adjournment and greater harmony in the Democratic party, it would be better to postpone the matter indefinitely and recommit the bill to the Judiciary Committee for further study.

In view of all the circumstances

Continued on Page Four

SOVIET WITHDRAWS FORCE FROM AMUR AT SCENE OF FIGHT

Japanese-Manchukuoan Guard Also Gone, So Danger of New Clash Is Removed

PARLEYS WILL FIX BORDER

Tokyo Hails the Settlement as Evidence That Recent Purge Weakened Moscow

By HAROLD DENNY

Wireless to THE NEW YORK TIMES.

MOSCOW, Saturday, July 3.—The Commissariat of Defense issued an order early today for the withdrawal of Soviet armed patrols and naval cutters from Amur River islands, the ownership of which is in dispute between the Soviet Union and Japanese-controlled Manchukuo.

The islands were the scene of recent fighting with losses to both Soviet and Japanese forces. The ownership of the contested land will be determined by future negotiations.

Thus another threatening Far Eastern crisis appears to have blown over. The Soviet's order for withdrawal of its forces followed a half-hour conference at the Foreign Office late last night between Foreign Commissar Maxim Litvinoff and Mamoru Shigemitsu, the Japanese Ambassador, at which the envoy informed the Commissar that he had received telegraphic information from Tokyo that Japanese-Manchukuoan cutters had been withdrawn from the islands. He added that he expected the Soviet naval land and air forces would be promptly withdrawn also.

Both Statements Agree

According to the Soviet Foreign Office communiqué, the content of which was in harmony with the Japanese Ambassador's account of the conversation, Mr. Litvinoff agreed that the Japanese-Manchukuoan withdrawal met the suggestion he had previously made, that both sides withdraw and take up the sovereignty issue later. He promised immediately to inform military authorities so they could give the necessary orders.

The communiqué then continued:

"To the Ambassador's question as to whether the withdrawal would establish the status quo ante Mr. Litvinoff answered affirmatively. Explaining it would restore the status quo of both parties laying claim to the islands, he said that after the restoration of order it would be possible to start to review those claims.

"The Ambassador agreed that in the future it would be possible to begin demarcation of the border line on the Amur. Mr. Litvinoff made clear that such demarcation would determine the possession of the islands by one or the other party."

Border Issue Is Difficult

The solution, though it seems to dispose of the immediate danger, leaves the basic question of the Amur boundary unsettled. There are indications that will be a knotty problem. In the past two years the Soviet Union and Japan made proposals and counter-proposals for demarcation commissions without approaching agreement. The Japanese insisted the commission should be composed of three members, a Soviet citizen, a Manchukuoan and a Japanese. To this the Soviet objected that it would be tantamount to giving Japan two representatives to the Soviet's one.

Japanese Embassy officials asserted before Mr. Shigemitsu's confer-

Continued on Page Two

A. A. U. Declines Invitation to Germany; Religious Persecution Is Cited by Mahoney

Special to THE NEW YORK TIMES.

MILWAUKEE, Wis., July 2.—In the first rebuff given to a foreign nation in the half century of its existence, the Amateur Athletic Union of the United States tonight declined to permit a track and field team to compete in Germany this Summer.

The decision was made by the combined executive and foreign relations committee and the vote was unanimous. That part of the tour by a ten-man team that took it to Sweden, the Netherlands and Hungary was approved, but the athletic invasion of the Reich was banned.

In announcing the move, President Jeremiah T. Mahoney said.

"This is consistent with the stand that I have always taken. I do not believe that our American athletes should go to a country where freedom of speech, religion and action have been abolished. Since I first started the fight to keep our fine young boys out of a land that persecuted the Jews, the Nazis have begun to attack and stifle Catholicism and Protestantism as well. Nazi ideology cannot conform with American democracy."

The same leaders who made the unsuccessful fight to keep the United States out of the Olympic Games last Summer were behind tonight's move with reinforcements from other quarters.

Judge Mahoney was the *ex-officio chairman of the double committee meeting. Others there were* Jack Rafferty of Houston, Texas; Charles L. Ornstein of New York, Louis Di Benedetto of New Orleans, George W. Graves of Detroit, John J. Magee of Bowdoin College, Daniel J. Ferris of New York, Raymond N. Sellon of Milwaukee, Ward Haylett of Kansas State College and Charles F. Hunter of San Francisco.

The Houston convention last December saw this group come back into power in A. A. U. affairs after the Avery Brundage forces had held control in the Olympic year.

Mr. Ferris, as secretary-treasurer of the world's largest sport governing body, cabled to other inviting countries that their bids had been approved and to Germany that her offer had been declined.

MISS EARHART FORCED DOWN AT SEA, HOWLAND ISLE FEARS; COAST GUARD BEGINS SEARCH

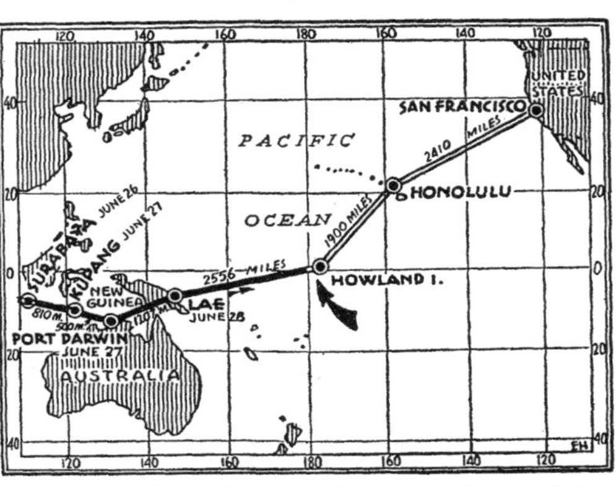

ROUTE OF EARHART PLANE IN PACIFIC

The flier took off from Lae, New Guinea, at 8 P. M., New York time, Thursday, and was in the vicinity of Howland Island at 4:43 P. M. Friday, when she was in communication with the Coast Guard cutter Itasca. She had intended to fly from this island to Honolulu and thence to the mainland for the completion of her world tour.

FUEL HAD RUN LOW

Fliers Were Near Goal When Last Reported but Saw No Land

PLANE EQUIPPED TO FLOAT

Has Sealed Gasoline Tanks and a Rubber Lifeboat for Emergency at Sea

RADIO BELIEVED HEARD

Los Angeles Amateurs Pick Up Weak Signals on Frequency Assigned to the Plane

By The Associated Press.

WASHINGTON, July 2.—Coast Guard headquarters was advised tonight that Amelia Earhart was believed to have alighted on the Pacific Ocean near Howland Island shortly after 5 P. M. Eastern daylight time today.

A message from the cutter Itasca, stationed in the vicinity of the island in the mid-Pacific, said:

"Earhart unreported at Howland at 7 P. M. [E. D. T.]. Believe down shortly after 5 P. M. Am searching probable area and will continue."

Admiral William D. Leahy, chief of naval operations, instructed the commandant of the naval station at Honolulu tonight to render whatever aid he may deem practicable in the search for Miss Earhart.

Plane Joins in Search

[A navy flying boat hopped off from Honolulu late last night for *Howland Island, 1,900 miles distant,* to join the cutter Itasca in hunting for Miss Earhart, The Associated Press reported. Two Los Angeles radio amateurs were said to have picked up weak signals on the frequency assigned to the Earhart radio.]

Coast Guard headquarters here received information that Miss Earhart probably overshot tiny Howland Island because she was blinded by the glare of an ascending sun. The message from the Coast Guard cutter Itasca said it was believed *Miss Earhart* passed *northwest* of Howland Island about 3:20 P. M. [E. D. T.], or about 8 A. M., Howland Island time. The Itasca reported that heavy smoke was bellowing from its funnels at the time, to serve as a signal for the flyer. The cutter's skipper expressed belief the Earhart plane had descended into the sea within 100 miles of Howland.

Husband Asks Assistance

In a message to Washington, the flier's husband, George Palmer Putnam, who is awaiting her return to this country at the Oakland, Calif., airport, said:

"Technicians familiar with Miss Earhart's plane believe, with its large tanks, it can float almost indefinitely. With retractable landing gear and smooth seas, safe landing (on the sea) should have been practicable.

"Request such assistance as is practicable from naval aircraft and surface craft stationed at Honolulu. Apparently plane's position not far from Howland.

"The plane's large wing and empty gasoline tanks should provide sufficient buoyancy if it came to rest on the sea without being damaged.

"There was a two-man rubber lifeboat aboard the plane, together with lifebelts, flares, a Very pistol and a large yellow signal kite which could be flown above the plane or the liferaft."

Mr. Putnam said his wife had planned to take emergency food rations and plenty of water on the hazardous flight, the most dangerous on her trip around the world.

Earlier the Coast Guard had ordered the cutter Roger B. Taney to proceed from Honolulu to Howland Island to aid the cutter Itasca in the search for Miss Earhart. A message from Honolulu, however, said the Taney was undergoing repairs and could not participate.

Amateurs Pick Up Signals

LOS ANGELES, July 2 (AP).—Two amateur radio operators claimed to have picked up signals tonight on frequencies officially assigned to the plane of Amelia Earhart.

Walter McMenamy said he picked up weak signals on 6210 kilocycles

Continued on Page Three

SOVIET 'LIQUIDATES' 120 MORE AS SPIES

Disclosure Indicates Others May Have Been Shot as the Agents of Estonia and Poland

AVIATOR IS AMONG THEM

Government Is Now Trying to Check Persecution of the Innocent in Campaign

Wireless to THE NEW YORK TIMES.

MOSCOW, July 2.—The detection and "liquidation" of two large groups of alleged spies—one of seventy members, said to be in the service of Estonia, and the other of fifty to seventy members, said to be in the service of Poland—were disclosed today by Leonid Zakovsky, chief of the Leningrad district of the Commissariat of Internal Affairs [the secret police department].

Mr. Zakovsky received the Order of Lenin on June 26 for "self-sacrificing fulfilment of most important orders of the government." The nature of the orders was not disclosed.

The detection of these groups apparently occurred in the past year, although many members were accused of having carried on activities for many years. Mr. Zakovsky did not say in so many words that all these 120 or more had been shot, but the plain inference is that they were.

Gives Details on Seizures

Mr. Zakovsky's disclosures, giving far more details than usual in such cases, are contained in an article he wrote for Komsomolskaya Pravda, Young Communist newspaper, instructing youth on the necessity of being on guard against foreign spies who invidiously worm their way into confidences.

He said the alleged Estonian group was led by the son of a Kulak [individualist farmer] in the Leningrad region and that that leader after training by the Estonian General Staff, returned to Russia and installed a secret radio station in a forest in the Leningrad region. By that means, it is said, he received and sent code messages.

Gradually, he recruited bands of saboteurs and spies in villages, factories and even in the Red army, but at length he was caught with the radio in the forest, resisted and was shot by secret police officers.

Mr. Zakovsky declared the Polish Intelligence Service organized bands in White Russia who, on the outbreak of war, were to become "Polish partisan rioters" commanded by Polish officers who would arrive on Soviet soil a few days before the outbreak of war.

Among other instances of alleged spying there was the case of a Soviet military aviator, who, Mr. Zakovsky said, became involved with a woman whose husband was a foreign spy. The husband and wife, after gaining important military information from him, blackmailed him into becoming a full-fledged spy and finally into organizing within his squadron a sabotage group that put planes out of repair, causing a number of accidents. The aviator was discovered and shot.

Indications that authorities are trying to check the distortion of the hunt for "spies" and wreckers

Continued on Page Three

VALERA FAR AHEAD IN IRISH ELECTION

His Return to Power in Dail Seems Assured by Early Count in Free State

VOTE ON CHARTER CLOSE

Heavy Adverse Sentiment Is Indicated—Larkin, Labor Leader, Wins Seat

Special Cable to THE NEW YORK TIMES.

DUBLIN, Irish Free State, July 3.—The first returns in the Free State general election received tonight indicate that the De Valera party, the Fianna Fail, is running ahead in many constituencies and the Cosgrave party faring badly.

Lord Mayor Alfred Byrne was the first candidate to gain election when he headed the poll in Northeast Dublin, far ahead of all other candidates. He received 12,068 votes. Next to him came Oscar Traynor, President Eamon de Valera's Minister for Posts and Telegraphs, with 9,693. The quota to insure election was 9,051.

Larkin Wins Seat

This constituency provided an election sensation when James Larkin, a labor leader, and once an inmate of Sing Sing prison in New York, won the third seat here by defeating General Richard Mulcahy, one of ex-President William Cosgrave's most effective front benchers. General Mulcahy was chief of staff of the Republican army during the fight against the British, and later was Minister for Defense in the Cosgrave administration. Subsequently he was a Minister in the local government. His defeat by Larkin is a big blow to the Cosgrave party.

Mr. de Valera easily headed the poll in Clare, where he was elected with 14,012 votes on the first count of a total of 63,000. This figure actually shows a decrease in de Valera's poll, compared to the 1933 election, when he received 18,000 votes of a total of 55,000. The decline is attributed to local dissensions over the selection of Fianna Fail candidates for this constituency.

In Cork City Mr. Cosgrave fared much worse than Mr. de Valera. Of a total of 53,019 votes the former President polled only 9,000-odd votes against the 14,863 he received in the 1933 election of a total of 68,000. Mr. Cosgrave headed the poll and was elected on the first count, but generally his party fared badly.

Results in Cork

His party's second candidate, Alderman William Desmond, polled only 2,008 and defeated the Labor candidate. On the other hand, the Fianna Fail held both its seats in Cork City with the return of Hugo Flinn, Parliamentary Secretary, and Thomas Dowdall. Already, before one-fourth of the results have been announced, the Cosgraveites have suffered two heavy defeats in Dublin and Cork.

In two other Dublin constituencies where results were available tonight the de Valera candidates headed the polls. Sean MacEntee, the Minister of Finance, was elected in Dublin Township on the first count with 10,124 votes.

Next to MacEntee came Cosgrave's former Attorney General, John Costello, with 8,418, who also was returned. In Dublin County

Continued on Page Two

"All the News That's Fit to Print."

The New York Times.

LATE CITY EDITION
Partly cloudy, showers, little change in temperature today. Tomorrow cooler, probably showers.
Temperatures Yesterday—Max., 88; Min., 70.

VOL. LXXXVI....No. 29,024. Entered as Second-Class Matter, Postoffice, New York, N. Y. NEW YORK, MONDAY, JULY 12, 1937. PP TWO CENTS in New York City. | THREE CENTS Within 200 Miles. | FOUR CENTS Elsewhere Except in 7th and 8th Postal Zones.

RIOTING BREAKS OUT AT MASSILLON MILL; 1 DEAD; 6 WOUNDED

Police Battle Republic Steel Strikers at Union Hall After an Officer Is Stoned

INDIANA WORKS TO OPEN

C. I. O. Acts to Withdraw Pickets on Basis of 'Agreement' With Governor Townsend

HE DENIES SIGNED PACT

Youngstown Sheet and Tube Spurns Any Deal With S.W.O.C. but Union Hails 'Victory'

Day's Labor Developments

Strike rioting broke out at gates of Republic Steel plant at Massillon, Ohio. Police fought rioters with tear gas. One man was reported killed. Page 1.

Youngstown Sheet and Tube's Indiana plant will be reopened today or tomorrow. S. W. O. C. moved to withdraw pickets. Company denied any agreement, but Governor Townsend said he had an "understanding" that ended the strike. Page 1.

Strike at Aluminum Company's Alcoa plant was ended by union on recommendation of representative of William Green. Page 4.

Republic Steel prepared to reopen more plants; Ohio will answer in Federal court today the C. I. O. suit to bar use of troops in strike. Page 4.

The Maritime Commission declared it would seek to end shipping strikes by setting new wage scales and training seamen. Page 4.

Agreements ending cloak trade stoppage will be signed today and 35,000 workers will return to 1,500 shops tomorrow. Page 5.

Subway motormen on the B. M. T. threatened to strike rather than submit to the referendum demanded by the Transport Workers Union, a C. I. O. affiliate. Page 5.

Rioting in Ohio

By The Associated Press.

MASSILLON, Ohio, Monday, July 12.—One man was killed and at least six others wounded late last night in an encounter between city police and strikers and sympathizers at a union hall near Republic Steel Corporation's Central Alloy division here.

City Patrolman Leo Kelley said the rioting broke out when Major H. O. Curley, former army officer named by Police Chief Stanley Switter to assist him during the C. I. O. steel strike, was stoned in front of the union local's headquarters.

Doctors pronounced an unidentified man in civilian clothes dead upon arrival at City Hospital.

Six others were rushed to the hospital, five of them suffering from bullet wounds and one a victim of tear gas.

Troops Rushed to Scene

Ohio National Guardsmen, Company I, 166th Infantry, arrived from near-by Canton as the Massillon police and police reinforcements from Canton massed at the scene.

Participants in the fierce fighting were estimated at 150 to 200.

Among the identified wounded were: Nick Vadias, 45, shot in abdomen and hip, condition critical; Jim Decan, 47, bullet wounds; Bill Netras, bullet wounds, and Ted George, buckshot wounds in right side.

The battle lasted for nearly an hour. The National Guardsmen from Canton arrived soon after order was restored. They were deployed about the mill area immediately.

Patrolman Kelley said that between sixty-five and seventy men were assembled in or near the steel union's "New Deal" lodge headquarters, 500 feet from the main entrance to Republic's property.

Curley, he added, was in charge of forty regular and special police assigned to the area. An automobile stopped in front of the hall and an occupant played a spotlight on the crowd of strikers or sympathizers.

"Curley walked toward the machine and the strikers began to stone him," the policeman said. "Then one man stepped out of the union hall doorway and fired five shots. The police then returned the fire."

Sheet and Tube to Reopen

Special to The New York Times.

CHICAGO, July 11.—Officials of the Youngstown Sheet and Tube Company announced tonight that they would reopen the company's

Continued on Page Four

Italy to Put $6,000,000 Into an Airport at Genoa

By The Associated Press.

GENOA, Italy, July 11.—Announcement was made today that Premier Benito Mussolini had approved plans for the construction of Italy's greatest combined seaplane and airport here, costing $6,000,000. The plans call for a long breakwater for the protection of shipyards and refueling docks along the waterfront.

A great air base at Genoa will be a danger to France. That port is only eighty miles from the French frontier and is only 200 miles from Marseilles.

This port is the chief French base for traffic with North Africa, and, according to present arrangements, most of the troops from Africa, on which France largely depends for defense, would be disembarked there.

3 RUSSIANS BEGIN NEW FLIGHT TO U.S.

Pilot Gromoff and 2 Comrades Take Off From Moscow for San Francisco via Pole

POOR WEATHER FORECAST

But Airmen Fear Worse Later and Start Second Record Attempt in Three Weeks

By HAROLD DENNY

Special Cable to The New York Times.

MOSCOW, Monday, July 12.—In the face of bad weather forecasts another Soviet airplane took off from Moscow at 3:23 this morning [8:23 P. M. Sunday, New York time] on the adventurous route over the North Pole.

The object of this ship is understood to be to set a world distance record and at the same time add another Polar victory for Soviet aviation. Although no announcement was made here, the plane's objective was said to be San Francisco.

It was also said unofficially that a third Soviet plane piloted by Sigismund Levanevsky would take off for the United States within the next month if the weather permitted.

Mikhail Gromoff, another of the Soviet's galaxy of "superfliers," was at the controls of the plane that took to the air this morning. He is the finest type of aviator—tall, handsome, quiet and calm.

His two associates in the plane are also unusually likable men. They are Andrei Yumacheff and Sergei Danilin. Danilin, besides being an expert navigator, is a sculptor, and Yumacheff is a painter.

Sister Ship of Other Plane

The plane in which they are now plunging toward the North Pole is a sister ship of the one in which Valeri Chkaloff, Georgi Baidukoff and Alexander Beliakoff thrilled the United States by their flight to Vancouver, Wash., three weeks ago. It is marked ANT 25-1. It is a single-motored monoplane with a slim fuselage and long tapering wings painted red—a huge dragonfly.

The plane took off from the mile-long concrete runway at the Sholkovo military airdrome twenty-five

Continued on Page Two

O'MAHONEY SCORES 'DEBATE THROTTLE' ON COURT MEASURE

'First Time' He Ever Saw Attempt to Pass a Major Bill 'Without Any Explanation'

BOTH SIDES UNYIELDING

Senate's 'Fight to a Finish' Dooms Other Legislation This Session, Some Hold

Special to The New York Times.

WASHINGTON, July 11.—The debate on the compromise Judiciary Reorganization Bill will enter its second week in the Senate tomorrow with both sides as determined to 'fight to a finish' as when they started. Senator O'Mahoney of Wyoming, who as a member of the Judiciary Committee opposed the President's original bill and who was one of the subcommittee of three which framed the majority's adverse report, expects to take the floor tomorrow morning to speak against the compromise measure.

Senator O'Mahoney said today that he did not expect to devote much of his argument to the political phases of the court situation, which have been emphasized by speakers during the past week, or to the majority report, which has brought the charge from administration supporters that it was as much an attack on the President himself as it was on the proposed legislation.

Will Discuss Bill Itself

The measure's opponents appear to be taking the attitude that Senators Wheeler and McCarran have answered pretty thoroughly the political arguments of the President's supporters and seek now to bring the discussion back to the merits or demerits of the measure itself.

"This is the first time in my experience that a major bill has been brought up and attempts made to pass it without a word of explanation," Senator O'Mahoney said today. "The measure itself hasn't been discussed by anybody yet, and that is what I am going to try to do."

Plainly irked by the administration strategy in invoking rules long in disuse to hinder a filibuster, Senator O'Mahoney said that it was "pretty hard to predict" what he would be allowed to do.

"It is difficult to predict what we can do," he said, "under these rules, which are obviously designed to throttle debate, but we will do what we can."

Bailey Ready to Take Place

On Saturday Senator O'Mahoney was ready to take the floor but could not speak because a cold had affected his voice. He is much improved today and expects to talk tomorrow.

If, however, Senator O'Mahoney's voice is still affected, Senator Bailey of North Carolina, who has been an opponent of both the original measure and any form of compromise since the plan was first broached by the President more than five months ago, plans to enter the debate. Senator B–ley likewise does not propose to touch on the political aspects, he said today.

"I shall address myself strictly to the merits of the proposals we are considering," he said. "My talk will

Continued on Page Two

Fifth Day of Heat Wave Kills 38 Before Thunderstorm Cools City

Heavy Rain Sends Mercury Down to 70° After It Had Reached High of 88°, but Only Temporary Relief Is Likely Before Thursday—295 Dead in Nation

A driving thunderstorm sent the mercury tumbling 12 degrees between 8:30 and 9 o'clock last night, giving the heat-oppressed the first real relief since the start of the five-day torrid wave that has scorched the nation from the West Coast to the Atlantic seaboard.

Thirty-eight persons died and thirty-three were prostrated in the metropolitan area alone on the fifth day. The death toll in the nation for the five days mounted to at least 295, many of them drownings, The Associated Press reported.

The temperature started dropping in the city as the storm approached, from 84 at 7 P. M. to 83 at 8, then to 82 at 8:30. As huge raindrops pelted the streets after 8:30 the mercury fell precipitately, touching 70 at 9 P. M.

The showers, the Weather Bureau said, would give only temporary relief. There was a possibility that there would be more showers today, but these, too, would give slight relief. Today's forecast is for partly cloudy weather with little change in temperature, except from possible showers. Tomorrow, however, is expected to be slightly cooler.

The Weather Bureau said it did not expect the heat wave to abate much before Thursday, adding, "even then the seasonal temperatures at that time will be rather warm." By the latter half of this week the government meteorologist thought New York City should come under the influence of a high-pressure area over the Middle West and Central Canada and possibly a low-pressure area off the Atlantic Coast. The combined effect should bring northerly winds and a consequent lowering of temperature.

The cumulative influence of the heat was shown by the twenty-five deaths on Saturday and the high number again yesterday. The death toll here for the five-day period has risen to sixty-six.

Although the temperature yesterday was not as high as on the preceding four days, the humidity was higher. The lowest percentage of moisture content in the atmosphere up until 6 o'clock last night was 56. This contrasted with an average of 38 and 40 per cent for the preceding four days.

The humidity, the Weather Bureau said, was about 20 per cent too high for the temperature. Hence the more acute physical discomfort.

Instead of being down to 35 per

Continued on Page Three

GEORGE GERSHWIN, COMPOSER, IS DEAD

Master of Jazz Succumbs in Hollywood at 38 After Operation for Brain Tumor

WROTE 'RHAPSODY IN BLUE'

Also Composed 'Porgy and Bess,' 'Of Thee I Sing' and Many Musical Comedies

Special to The New York Times.

HOLLYWOOD, Calif., July 11.—George Gershwin, 38-year-old composer, died today at 10:35 A. M. at the Cedars of Lebanon Hospital. He succumbed five hours after being operated on for removal of a brain tumor. The operation was decided upon when the composer's condition became critical at midnight.

Dr. Gabriel Segall of Los Angeles and Dr. Howard Nafsziger, University of California Professor of Surgery, performed the operation at 5 o'clock this morning.

Dr. Walter E. Dandy, Baltimore brain surgeon, turned back at Newark today upon learning that Mr. Gershwin's condition had changed suddenly and he would be operated on at once. Dr. Dandy had been summoned from Chesapeake Bay, where he was cruising over the week-end with Governor Harry W. Nice of Maryland.

Ira Gershwin, who wrote lyrics for his brother's music, was at his side when he died.

Two weeks ago Mr. Gershwin collapsed at the Samuel Goldwyn studios, where he had been working on nine compositions for "The Goldwyn Follies." He had completed five songs before his breakdown. Taken to the hospital for observation, the composer, when released last week, was in an extremely nervous condition. Yesterday he was returned to the hospital in a coma.

Also surviving are his mother, Mrs. Rose Gershwin; a sister, Mrs. Leopold Godowsky Jr. and another brother, Arthur.

He was a member of the American Society of Composers and Publishers, the Lambs Club and the Bohemians.

Child of the Jazz Age

George Gershwin was a composer of his generation. What he wanted to do most, he said, was to interpret the soul of the American people. Thus in the tempo of jazz he jabbed at the dignities of American life, while he won the plaudits of the musical élite with the classic qualities of "A Rhapsody in Blue." With his brother Ira and that master of gentle satire George S. Kaufman he set the nation laughing at the foibles of its government; but, in more serious mood, he found time to write music that the great conductors of his time were glad to present.

Mr. Gershwin was a child of the Twenties, the Age of Jazz. In the fast two-step time of the years after the war he was to music what F. Scott Fitzgerald was to prose. Four years after that mad decade began, Paul Whiteman sent the strains of his Rhapsody cascading far beyond Broadway and the music they called Jazz had come of age. Serge Koussevitzky of the Boston Symphony Orchestra played his work and the capitals of Europe called for more.

For the musical comedy stage, the vaudeville act, the Hollywood lot, he made his music. He had

Continued on Page Twenty

REPUBLICANS VIEW MAYOR AS NOMINEE

Leaders to Start Hunt This Week for a Rival, but Do Not Expect to Find One

'GO ALONG' RELUCTANTLY

Find Rank and File Resentful Toward La Guardia, but Hope for Fight Wanes

Republican leaders of the five counties are expected to start conferences this week on whether they should designate Mayor La Guardia as the party's candidate for re-election. It was considered unlikely that a decision would be made for another two weeks, however.

Republican leaders still are hopeful that a conservative Democrat, such as George V. McLaughlin, can be persuaded to make the race as the official Republican candidate, but they now do not really expect that to happen, and the redesignation of Mayor La Guardia by default is conceded to be a probability.

It is possible that the Brooklyn and Queens organizations will decline to go along with Kenneth F. Simpson's New York County organization, should New York County swing in line for the Mayor, and in that event any one running against the Mayor in the primaries would have organization support in some districts, but not in others.

Friends of the Mayor claim a majority of the members of the Kings County Executive Committee, but this is disputed by friends of John R. Crews, Republican leader of Brooklyn.

Find Republicans Resentful

Republican leaders now disposed to "go along" with the Mayor declared yesterday that at the same time they were convinced that the sentiment of the rank and file of the organization was against the Mayor's renomination. He may be a good Mayor, and he may be reelected, one leader declared, but the Republicans do not like his policies.

It is regarded as possible that the Republican leaders may pass the responsibility for designating or rejecting the Mayor to the members of the county committee. Mr. Crews has indicated that he intends to have the matter taken up at such a meeting, and the same may be done in Queens, where the county committee will meet on July 29. Leaders in the other boroughs may follow suit.

A definite decision by the Republican leaders probably will await a decision by the Democrats on their candidate. Nomination of either Jeremiah T. Mahoney or Samuel Levy by the Democrats probably would insure the Republican nomination for Mr. La Guardia, it was said, but if the Democrats nominated Senator Royal S. Copeland or James A. Foley the Republicans would be inclined to endorse the Democratic nominee.

The third course of action the Republicans had considered, the nomination of a third candidate, a conservative, died with the withdrawal of Senator Robert F. Wagner from the race, it was said. Had Senator Wagner been the Democratic nominee and Mayor La Guardia the Labor candidate, nomination of a third candidate, run-

Continued on Page Five

Fliers Quit Phoenix Hunt for Miss Earhart; Chance of Saving Her Held One in Million

By The Associated Press.

HONOLULU, July 11.—Aviators from the battleship Colorado tonight abandoned hope of finding Amelia Earhart and her navigator, Captain Frederick J. Noonan, in the Phoenix Island area after four days of scanning the islands from their three catapult planes.

As Captain Wilhelm H. Friedell of the Colorado tentatively ended the ship's search of the Phoenix area and left the island group astern to head for a rendezvous with the destroyers Drayton, Lampson and Cushing about 350 miles northeast of Howland Islands, however, navy fliers aboard the aircraft carrier Lexington prepared for a spectacular effort.

Heading in the approximate direction of Howland Islands but with their exact destination undetermined, the Lexington's 1,299 officers and men concentrated their immediate energies on detailed plans for a high speed 200,000-square mile aerial sweep of the Equatorial Pacific. The ship has sixty-two planes.

"There is only a chance in a million for a rescue," said naval officers directing the search.

They declared the main possibility remaining was that Miss Earhart's globe-girdling plane had alighted in the water and was still floating, in on which case it could be sighted from the Lexington's air fleet.

The Lexington's armada was expected to begin the search tomorrow afternoon or Tuesday, probably first scouting west and south of Howland Island and extending the search to the Gilbert Islands, toward which the equatorial currents in that area run.

Searchers said, however, that there was only an outside chance that the lost plane had descended as far short of Howland Island, its goal, as the Gilbert Islands, 600 miles east of Howland.

Until the Colorado's fliers confessed that they had lost hope, the Phoenix group had been regarded as the most likely place of finding Miss Earhart, missing since July 2.

The Colorado still was in position to send out her planes, however, and it was said they might make a final flight Monday.

The planes searched virtually the whole Phoenix area, but found nothing to bolster hopes for the missing fliers' safety. One of the planes, flying over Sydney Island in the group, reported sighting letters scooped in the sand spelling dozens of Polynesian words. The navy aviators, however, said there was no sign of life and they discounted the possibility that the markings in the sand could have related to the lost plane.

LOYALISTS TRIUMPH ANEW NEAR MADRID AS DRIVE IS PUSHED

Occupy Villanueva del Pardillo in Their Biggest Offensive and Seize 600 Prisoners

WAR IS IN CRUCIAL PERIOD

Great Open Battle in View as Government Adds to Gains—Rebels Dispute Foe's Claims

By HERBERT L. MATTHEWS

Wireless to The New York Times.

MADRID, July 11.—Spanish Government troops early today occupied Villanueva del Pardillo, about twelve miles west of Madrid, and took 600 more prisoners. This operation widened their salient and carried one step further the greatest government offensive of the civil war.

Since Monday the Loyalist forces have been making wide gains in a supreme effort to break the siege of Madrid, and this drive is regarded here as even stronger than the Rebel offensive against Bilbao. It is, therefore, no exaggeration to say that the war has reached its most crucial period.

It is hoped by the Loyalists that the race against time that the Negrin Government lost in the case of Bilbao will be won for Santander and Asturias.

In less than two months the government has worked a complete reorganization of the army and air forces, speeded up the war industries, made heavy purchases abroad and built up a great fighting machine. For weeks men, guns and materials of all sorts have been pouring up, choking roads with thousands of trucks. Planes by the dozens are filing the air over the Rebel lines, bombing towns, concentrations and trenches at will and again demonstrating that in Central Spain the Loyalists still dominate the air.

Equipment Is Extensive

Details of equipment cannot, of course, be given, but it can be said that there are many tanks, many guns and more troops than have yet been employed in this conflict.

The government is playing for the greatest of stakes, since, if it wins, the siege of Madrid will have been lifted. It is too soon to make any predictions. The Insurgents are naturally preparing a counter-offensive and, since the action is now in open territory, one must suppose that the first great open battle of the war will occur soon.

The offensive, whose first phase has ended with the capture of Villanueva del Pardillo, is conceded by foreign military experts here to be of particularly brilliant conception. Apparently the whole general staff worked it out, and those of us who have been watching its development see no reason to doubt that its direction has been entrusted to two Spanish officers—General José Miaja and Lieut. Col. Vicente Rojo, chief of the general staff.

The plan of campaign was and still is an intricate one. Its first part was successfully kept secret until it was launched, and its further development remains a mystery, except that it can clearly be seen from the map that the main thrust is in the direction of Navalcarnero, eighteen miles southwest of Madrid, and presumably intended to cut the Estremadura Road,

Continued on Page Six

Mussolini Expels Austrian Soccer Team; Vienna, Match Banned, to Protest to Rome

Wireless to The New York Times.

VIENNA, July 11.—A diplomatic protest will be made to Italy concerning the expulsion of an Austrian soccer team from that country, this correspondent learns.

The incident is a sequel to the free-for-all fight last Sunday in the Vienna Stadium between the Austrian Admira team and the Genoa eleven, which were competing for the Central European Cup. Four Italians were severely hurt.

The match, which ended in a tie, was to have been replayed in Genoa today, and the Admira team left Vienna Thursday, but Friday it was learned that the Italian soccer authorities refused to allow the match to take place.

The Admira players returned to Vienna tonight, announcing that they had been expelled from Italy by order of Premier Benito Mussolini.

"We telegraphed Il Duce yesterday," a member of the team declared, "to ask him to intervene with the Italian football authorities and allow the match to occur. Mussolini's reply was to order us to leave Italy within twenty-four hours. We wished to stay on in Venice to appeal to the committee of the Central European Cup contests, which is meeting tomorrow."

Dr. Geroe, the president of the Vienna Football Association, left tonight for Venice to enter an energetic protest at the meeting. One representative each of Italy, Austria, Czechoslovakia and Switzerland constitute the committee under a Hungarian president.

Baron Hornbostel, permanent head of the Austrian Foreign Office, tonight telephoned the Italian Minister of the Interior to ask for an explanation of the expulsion. He also spoke with Francesco Salata, the Italian Minister to Austria. The Austrian Minister in Rome, Egon Berger-Waldenegg, has been instructed to make representations to the Italian Government.

A fight among the players, carried on to the accompaniment of shouts of defiance from spectators who were held in check by strong police cordons, marked the closing moments of play in the European Soccer Cup match between the Genoa team and the Austrian Admira team at Vienna July 4, according to cabled dispatches.

The free-for-all began after a young Austrian player, who had tied the score by conversion of a penalty, thumbed his nose at his opponents, and was knocked down by one of the Italian players.

Hero of Shanghai Fight Ready for Call to War

By The Associated Press.

MANILA, July 11.—General Tsai Ting-kai, former commander of the Chinese Nineteenth Route Army, which withstood a Japanese attack at Shanghai in 1932, said today he was preparing to return to China because of the tense Chino-Japanese situation. He said China was almost unanimous for war against Japan.

"Chinese nationalism," he said, "is now strong enough to resist Japanese aggression."

He said Generalissimo Chiang Kai-shek would urge immediate resistance should the Japanese "force China's hand." He added that his country was confident of its ability to repulse Japanese in Chinese territory.

SYRIAN ARABS RIOT FOR NEW MANDATE

Between 6 and 20 Are Slain in Upper Jezireh Area in Clash of Natives and Troops

DISTRICT GOVERNOR KILLED

Premier of Iraq Demands That All Moslems Combat Plan to Partition Palestine

By The Associated Press.

JERUSALEM, July 11.—Between six and twenty persons were killed and wounded in the upper Jezireh district Friday in a clash between troops and demonstrators demanding a separate mandate and dissociation from the Syrian Republic, advices reaching here today said.

The reports, received from Damascus, said troops attempted to break up demonstrations held in mosques.

The mosques were emptied as crowds stormed government offices. The district governor was believed to have been killed. Troops were forced to fire into the crowd to break up the attack.

In Jerusalem, the Arab National Defense party issued a manifesto tonight severely condemning the recommendations of the British Royal Commission for splitting Palestine into separate Arab and Jewish States and the creation of a new British mandate controlling the holy cities of Jerusalem, Bethlehem and Nazareth.

Iraq Expresses Sympathy

Bagheb Bey Nashashibi, former Mayor of Jerusalem, presided at an executive party meeting. The manifesto said his party was interested in a "noble Arab nation" and could not see the partition scheme as a solution. The proposal has been supported by Emir Abdullah of Trans-Jordan and opposed by the Muftist party.

More than 500 telegrams of protest were received from various societies and religious committees by the Arab High Committee.

Hikmet Suleiman, Premier of Iraq, also cabled the High Committee, asserting his sympathy for Palestone Arabs in opposition to partition.

The High Committee will meet there tomorrow to discuss replies from Arab princes and kings on future policies.

Nashashibi's party is holding a conference later this week.

Provisional distribution candidates elected from Palestine Jewry to the Zionist Congress to be held in Switzerland in August indicated

Continued on Page Nine

HOSTILITIES RAGE ON PEIPING'S EDGE; CHINA WARNS FOES

Nanking Rules Out Increase of Tokyo Troops in North—Insists Fighting End

NANKING MOVES FOR WAR

Clash Is Believed Part of Plan to Seize Hopei Province for 'Another Manchukuo'

TOKYO SENDS MORE MEN

Japanese Foreign Office Sees Peace on Basis of Revised Demands to Chinese

The Chinese Situation

SHANGHAI—China warned Japan she would not tolerate increase of alien troops on her soil and infringement of her sovereignty, saying such actions would cause her to take "defensive measures." Large contingents of troops were moved northward. Page 1.

TOKYO—While war preparations were hastened the Foreign Office announced Japan's demands for settlement of the Peiping fighting had been revised and it hoped the matter would be confined to a local incident. Previously, after many councils of governmental army and navy chiefs, determination had been expressed to force a showdown on anti-Japanese agitations in North China. Page 8.

PEIPING—Fighting was renewed west of the city. Previously Chinese and Japanese had told of a settlement of the affair, but the Twenty-ninth Army was believed to have rejected its terms. Heavy Chinese guards were posted in the city, and its streets were prepared for defense. Page 8.

HEAVY FIGHTING RENEWED

Special Cable to The New York Times.

SHANGHAI, Monday, July 12.—The heaviest Chino-Japanese fighting since the initial outbreak last Wednesday began this morning on the outskirts of Peiping, according to telegrams received at the Chinese Government offices here.

TOKYO, Monday, July 12 (AP).—The Japanese War Office announced today that the vanguard of a Chinese army advancing from the south had opened fire on Japanese positions west of Peiping.

By HALLETT ABEND

Wireless to The New York Times.

SHANGHAI, Monday, July 12.—Japan was officially warned yesterday that China would not tolerate any foreign nation's arbitrarily increasing its garrison on Chinese soil and infringing on China's territorial sovereignty.

In a vigorous oral protest to the Japanese Chargé d'Affaires at Nanking, the Vice Minister for Foreign Affairs asserted that if such acts continued, China would be forced to take defensive measures. The Chinese official demanded that the Chargé immediately cable Tokyo to tell the government to order a cessation of Japanese military activities in the Peiping area.

The Chinese Government is reported to have telegraphed three orders to the Hopei-Chahar Political Council at Peiping:

First, the council must not accept the demands of the Japanese.

Second, the Twenty-ninth Army must not be permitted to retreat in any sectors.

Third, if necessary any and all sacrifices must be made to repel Japanese attacks.

The Hopei-Chahar Council in reply sent a telegram to the Nanking government emphatically denying having signed any agreement with the slightest political implications, although the Japanese Embassy in Peiping claims to have received a signed document accepting four terms at 8 o'clock last night.

Likened to 1932 Crisis

"The situation has assumed proportions more serious than anything that has arisen between China and Japan since the Shanghai hostilities early in 1932," said a high government spokesman in Shanghai. "Even the invasion and seizure of Jehol, previous incursions into North China, the fighting which resulted in the Tangku truce and last year's Suiyuan clash did not begin to approach in gravity today's crisis."

The Japanese report that several large contingents of Chinese troops, including some Central Government units, are moving northward. One force, commanded by General Wan Fu-lin, is advancing from

Continued on Page Eight

"All the News That's Fit to Print."

NEWS INDEX, PAGE 39, THIS SECTION

The New York Times.

LATE CITY EDITION
Mostly cloudy, slightly warmer to-day; Tomorrow rain and colder.
Temperatures Yesterday—Max., 54; Min., 34

Section 1

VOL. LXXXVII....No. 29,268. | Entered as Second-Class Matter, Postoffice, New York, N. Y. | NEW YORK, SUNDAY, MARCH 13, 1938. | Including Rotogravure Picture, Magazine and Book Review. | PP | TEN CENTS | TWELVE CENTS Beyond 200 Miles Except in 7th and 8th Postal Zones.

HITLER ENTERS AUSTRIA IN TRIUMPHAL PARADE; VIENNA PREPARES FOR UNION, VOIDS TREATY BAN; FRANCE MANS BORDER; BRITAIN STUDIES MOVES

HARRISON DEMANDS END OF PROFITS TAX TO HELP BUSINESS

Levy on Undistributed Gains, Modified by House, Should Be Killed Entirely, He Says

SENATOR ASKS FLAT RATE

He Would Revamp Excise on Capital Increases Also Under the Same Principle

CHAMBER IS 'ENCOURAGED'

It Asserts Federal Attitude to Business Is Improving, but Manufacturers Disagree

By The Associated Press.

WASHINGTON, March 12.—Chairman Harrison of the Senate Finance Committee proposed today that tax relief to "encourage new investments and melt much frozen credit" go far beyond the administration-approved provisions of the House tax bill.

In a statement issued while his committee arranged to begin study of the House measure on Monday, Mr. Harrison declared that the undistributed profits tax should be killed in its entirety.

"While the House retained only the skeleton of the undistributed profits tax," he said, "the remains will haunt business, and its complete removal and return to a sufficient flat corporation tax is preferable. It is simpler and more understandable."

Mr. Harrison declared also that the capital gains provisions of the bill which the House approved yesterday should be revamped to substitute a flat rate for the present sliding scale.

Administration leaders were expected generally to fight abandonment of the principle of the undistributed profits tax, which many business spokesmen have blamed for the current economic slump. The House bill, which must be acted upon by the Senate before it can become law, would modify this levy substantially but retain its principle.

Hints at Broader Tax Base

Mr. Harrison also mentioned the possibility of broadening the tax base to bring new taxpayers under the income levy, and of cutting some of the surtax rates on higher bracket individual incomes.

"If I interpret the sentiment of the Senate correctly, it desires to do justice and give encouragement to business in every provision of the pending tax bill, within government revenue requirements. I know that is the sentiment of the Finance Committee. So far as I am concerned, whatever influence I may possess, as chairman of the committee, I shall exert toward raising the required revenue, removing some complicated provisions, and, as far as possible, restoring confidence to business.

"If we can improve the capital gains provisions of the House bill, by taking capital gains out of the general income provisions and applying a flat rate of about 15 per cent on all capital gains from sales of property held over one or two years, it will, in my opinion, encourage new investment and melt much frozen credit.

"The undistributed profits tax, beautiful in theory, has not worked. Business does not like it, and would prefer a flat rate.

Wants Cut in High Surtax Rates

"I shall make an effort to strengthen Section 102 of the present law, imposing a penalty upon the unreasonable accumulation of reserves for the purpose of evading taxation.

"I do not know whether it is possible to be done, and I can give no one any encouragement that it will be done; but if I could write the tax bill at this time, I would reduce some of the high surtax rates. Tax laws should be written for revenue purposes; and when the surtaxes are as high as they are now, the Treasury observes diminishing returns, and realizes less revenue. I have come to the conclusion that, if we are forced to continue an exceptional spending policy, the income tax base should be broader, resulting in an increased tax consciousness upon the part of the people.

"I have a conviction, if there is a sit-down strike upon the part of capital because of fear or the uncertainties of investment, that we should break it up, if possible, and that effective work should be done toward removing some of the barriers that are checking the flow of capital and credit into new investments and new industries."

Special to THE NEW YORK TIMES.

WASHINGTON, March 12.—The United States Chamber of Com-

Continued on Page Two

California Senate Kills Pardon for Tom Mooney

By The Associated Press.

SACRAMENTO, Calif., March 12.—The California Senate tonight killed by an almost unanimous voice vote an Assembly-approved resolution "pardoning" Tom Mooney, convicted of the 1916 San Francisco Preparedness Day parade bombing.

The Senate debated the measure only a few minutes. Chairman W. P. Rich of the Rules Committee, which reported the resolution unfavorably, then moved that it be tabled. Only a few "nays" were heard.

The action at least temporarily disposed of the question as to whether the Legislature had the power to pardon. Senate concurrence was necessary to technical enactment.

Remaining before the Assembly, however, was a resolution asking Governor Merriam to pardon Mooney. The Assembly also passed a resolution of that nature a year ago, but the Senate likewise voted not to concur.

5 JERSEY FIREMEN DIE AS WALL FALLS

Deputy Chief in Paterson and Four Others Crushed After Quelling Warehouse Blaze

MANY SHOPPERS ROUTED

Damage of $250,000 Reported as Smoke Fills Store in Heart of Business District

Special to THE NEW YORK TIMES.

PATERSON, N. J., March 12.—A deputy fire chief and four other firemen were killed instantly and another was slightly hurt tonight when a three-story brick wall toppled on them while they were wetting down the smoldering ruins of the Quackenbush Company department store's warehouse, which was ruined by a spectacular fire of undetermined origin this afternoon.

The dead:

Deputy Chief James Sweeny, 58 years old, of 95 Lexington Avenue.

Captain John Davenport, 44, of 132 Franklin Street.

Fireman Louis Rodesky, 49, of 404 East Twenty-sixth Street.

Fireman Mathew O'Neil, 45, of 931 Ward Street.

Fireman John Lynch, 37, of 330 Buffalo Avenue.

Captain Paul Schaub, 44, of 72 Eighteenth Avenue, who was with the group at the time, escaped miraculously with bruises, the debris falling in such a manner as to knock him out of the way.

Fire Chief Collapses

Fire Chief Thomas L. Coyle collapsed when he saw his men buried under the avalanche of stone and had to be taken away from the scene.

Tonight's casualties brought the total to eleven. About 2 P. M., soon after the fire started, an employe trapped in the building suffered a broken leg when he jumped from a second floor window. A fireman was felled by smoke. Both were taken to the hospital.

Only two or three fire crews were at the scene when tonight's tragedy occurred, their job being not only to wet down the ruins but also to remove debris that might endanger public safety. At the time the wall collapsed, the firemen were devising a means to pull it down because they knew it was in danger of falling.

When the blaze was at its height this afternoon, dense clouds of smoke forced fifty families in the vicinity to leave their homes, shoppers to flee from the department store and a motion picture theatre audience to disperse, and damaged the store.

Damage $250,000

Chief Coyle estimated the damage at $250,000 but Robert W. Pyke, president of the Quackenbush Company, said that figure was a conservative one and added that in addition to the loss of the warehouse and its contents the smoke damage to the store proper might be "almost 100 per cent."

Mr. Pyke said he doubted that the store, one of the largest in Paterson, would be open for business on Monday. The concern was celebrating its fifty-third anniversary with a sale that attracted several hundred shoppers, all of whom were forced to leave as well as the 500 employes in the store, situated at Main and Ellison Streets.

The fire was in progress from a little before 2 P. M. until 4:30 P. M., when it was put under control by the city's entire Fire Department force of 125 men summoned on a general alarm, assisted by fifty volunteer firemen from Prospect Park, Haledon and Little Falls.

John Turri of 224 Hamilton Avenue, an employe in the warehouse, received a broken leg when he

Continued on Page Four

18 RUSSIANS TO DIE FOR TREASON PLOT; RAKOVSKY SPARED

Escapes With a Sentence of 20 Years—Bessonoff Gets 15, Physician 25 Years

HEART SPECIALIST SAVED

Dr. Pletneff Alone Among Three Doctors Wins Mercy —Bukharin Shows Fight

By HAROLD DENNY

Special Cable to THE NEW YORK TIMES.

MOSCOW, Sunday, March 13.—Eighteen of the twenty-one defendants in Moscow's third great public treason trial within two years were sentenced to be shot at the final session of the military court at 4:30 this morning.

The only defendants in this most dramatic of all Soviet trials whose lives are to be spared are S. A. Bessonoff and Christian G. Rakovsky, for both of whom mercy was recommended by Prosecutor Andrey Y. Vishinsky in his closing address, and Professor D. H. Pletneff, renowned as one of the foremost heart specialists in Europe, who confessed having helped to kill Maxim Gorky and others under coercion from Henry G. Yagoda, one-time terror of the Ogpu.

Mr. Rakovsky received a sentence of twenty years in prison. Professor Pletneff, twenty-five; Mr. Bessonoff, fifteen. Professor Pletneff and Mr. Rakovsky, who are elderly men, are unlikely to survive such terms.

Those Sentenced to Die

Nikolai Bukharin, Alexis I. Rykoff, Mr. Yagoda and Gregory T. Grinko, whose names have loomed so large in Soviet history, will die probably within the next twenty-four hours. The others sentenced to death are:

Nikolai N. Krestinsky, former First Assistant Foreign Commissar.

A. P. Rosengoltz, once Commissar of Foreign Trade.

Vladimir I. Ivanoff, former chief of the Soviet timber industry.

Akmal Ikramoff, a former leader of the Uzbek Soviet Republic.

Faysulla Khodjaieff, former President of Uzbek.

Mikhail A. Chernoff, former Commissar of Agriculture.

I. A. Zelensky, former head of Consumers Cooperatives.

Dr. I. N. Kazakoff, noted endocrinologist.

Dr. L. G. Levin, former chief of the Kremlin Hospital.

P. P. Kruchkoff, who was Gorky's secretary.

V. F. Sharangovitch, P. T. Zubareff, P. P. Bulanoff and V. A. Maximoff-Dikovsky.

Under the terms of the law governing terrorist cases, decreed after the assassination of Sergei M. Kiroff in 1934, there is no appeal except to the Presidium of the Supreme Soviet, which must act within three days, but which in preceding treason cases has acted much more swiftly.

There were no outcries, no faintings, no demonstrations of any sort on the part of the defendants as Judge Vassidy V. Ulrich finished his dreadful words. Most of the

Continued on Page Thirty

Graz Crowds Pull Down Memorial to Dollfuss

By The Associated Press.

GRAZ, Austria, March 12.—Yelling throngs pulled down the memorial statue to the late Chancellor Englebert Dollfuss in the main street of Graz tonight.

As the populace, soldiers and police shouted the Nazi greeting of "Heil, Hitler!" a crowd gathered around the Dollfuss memorial and brought the figure of the little Austrian Chancellor, who was murdered in the abortive Nazi putsch of 1934, crashing to the street.

Uninterrupted demonstrations and jubilation swept through the town, with 6,000 persons awaiting the arrival of German troops. The burgomaster of Graz telegraphed an invitation to Chancellor Adolf Hitler to visit the city.

FOREIGN EXCHANGE TUMBLES IN CRISIS

Chief World Currencies Break Sharply in the Flight of Capital to Safer Centers

FRANC IS ONLY EXCEPTION

Rush to Buy Dollars Brings New Lows for Year—Rise in Gold Shipments Due

Conditions bordering on near panic swept the money markets of the world yesterday as Europeans rushed to purchase American dollars and gold after Germany's conquest of Austria. The flight of capital, particularly from the smaller Continental nations, assumed gigantic proportions and brought an unprecedented volume of trading in the foreign exchange markets, both here and abroad.

Coincident with these conditions in the money markets, all the principal foreign currencies broke sharply in relation to the dollar with the exception of the French franc.

Guilders were dumped overboard in such heavy amounts that the price of the unit was forced down 14 points to a new low for the year. All other Continental currencies except the franc likewise touched new low levels for 1938, while the pound sterling dipped to its lowest quotations since last Dec. 1.

Despite the political tangle in France the franc moved forward as a result of the heavy influx of capital from Switzerland, Holland and Belgium. At the close of the market the French unit registered a net gain for the day of 2¼ points to 3.19¾ cents. The pound sterling fell 11/32 cent to $4.99¾ after dipping at one time to $4.98 11/16, which re-

Continued on Page Thirty-five

Mrs. H. D. Gibson Hurt in Long Island Hunt; Wife of Banker Crushed by Falling Horse

Special to THE NEW YORK TIMES.

GLEN COVE, L. I., March 12.—Mrs. Harvey D. Gibson, wife of the banker, received five broken ribs and back injuries when she was thrown from her dappled gray gelding Coq d'Argent during the Meadow Brook Hunt near Syosset this morning.

She was taken to the North Country Community Hospital here for X-ray examination by Dr. Garrett Duryea. Dr. John Morris of the surgical staff of Bellevue Hospital and Dr. H. C. Fleming of 535 Park Avenue came from New York for a consultation with Dr. Duryea and Dr. Opho Hudson of the Meadowbrook Hospital, Hempstead. Though no diagnosis was announced, it was learned she was "injured badly but not critically."

The accident occurred while the field was moving slowly in single line through a narrow and muddy path on the estate of George P. Mann. Mrs. Gibson's mount fell heavily without warning, pinning her before she had any chance to leap aside, according to riders near her.

It was assumed the animal stepped in a hole or tripped on a hidden root. Coq d'Argent, a thoroughbred hunter, won the lightweight division championship at Piping Rock last October. Mrs. Gibson rode sidesaddle as usual.

Mr. Gibson, co-master with Harry Peters of Islip, summoned his chauffeur, who had kept track of the riders from near-by roads. He remounted, unaware of her condition, after she left for the hospital four miles away.

The hunt started auspiciously with fifty riders meeting at the Thistleton Kennels on the Robert E. Tod estate in Syosset. Several jumps were taken without mishap as the riders swung across property owned by Louis J. Horowitz. Then they turned into the lane.

Three foxes were run to ground by the pack of forty hounds. Mr. Gibson dropped out a half hour after the accident. None of the field believed Mrs. Gibson, a veteran horsewoman, had been hurt seriously.

She was married to Mr. Gibson, president and chairman of the board of the Manufacturers Trust Company, in Bern, Switzerland, thirteen years ago. She had been married to George Galt Bourne in 1913. They were divorced eleven years later. She has a daughter, Whitney Bourne, the actress.

Mrs. Gibson's parents were Mr. and Mrs. Charles E. Whitney of Boston. She assisted her husband by radio appeals in 1933 when he was directing the Emergency Unemployment Relief Committee. The Lenox Hill Settlement House has been among her steadfast interests. A benefit entertainment for it attracted 2,000 persons to Land's End, the Gibson Summer home, Fox Point, L. I., on July 4, 1936. The affair was described as the most elaborate ever attempted on the North Shore.

PRAGUE NOW CRUX

London Considers Aid to Czechoslovakia if She Is Put Under Threat

EMPTY MOVES SHUNNED

Stunned Britons See End of Anglo-German Talks and Blow to Rome Accord

By FERDINAND KUHN Jr.

Special Cable to THE NEW YORK TIMES.

LONDON, March 12.—Under the pressure of Germany's shock tactics against Austria the British Government began seriously and anxiously today to consider what it would do if the German mailed fist descended soon upon Czechoslovakia.

There is little doubt among British Ministers now that Germany intends to go farther in Central Europe. Prime Minister Neville Chamberlain and his colleagues today found many of their illusions gone and their hopes destroyed, but their awareness of German aims and methods suddenly was made brutally clear.

The spectacle of "coercion backed by force," as it was described in the British protest to Berlin yesterday, appears to have shocked even those British Conservatives who have trusted until now in Germany's underlying peacefulness and good intentions. It remains to be seen how this changed outlook will be reflected in British policy.

Halifax Is Astonished

The story is told that last night when German troops had crossed the frontier, Viscount Halifax, British Foreign Secretary, paced up and down his huge room at the Foreign Office, holding his forehead like a man distracted and exclaiming:

"Horrible! Horrible! I never thought they would do it!"

This was the room where Sir Edward Grey one fateful Summer day in 1914 looked out of the window at lamplighters in the street below and said:

"The lamps are going out all over Europe; we shall not see them lit again in our lifetime."

The leaders of the British Government now wonder whether other lamps may be extinguished in Prague, Czechoslovakia, as in Vienna unless something can be done. The British Cabinet met for two hours in emergency session this morning, listening to reports and reviewing the Austrian situation, but it was significant that the Ministers talked more of the immediate future than of the past, which neither they nor any one can revoke.

The German conquest of Austria was accepted as an accomplished fact. There was no talk in London today of a spectacular post mortem, such as the session of the League of Nations Council, which met in London after the German re-occupation of the Rhineland and which arraigned Germany as a violator of solemn pledges.

Perhaps if Italy had been willing to join there might have been a concerted protest, but in the present circumstances the British feel that empty gestures would be humiliating and futile.

Naturally the Ministers were indignant. A photographer stopped Leslie Hore-Belisha, War Secretary, on the doorstep of 10 Downing Street and asked him to smile.

"Why should I smile?" was his grim reply.

Shortly after the Cabinet meeting Clement R. Attlee, leader of the Labor party, and Sir Archibald Sinclair, leader of the opposition Liberals, called at Mr. Chamberlain's invitation to discuss the situation with him.

Ministers to Be on Call

The sense of a crisis was deepened by the announcement that the Ministers were staying within reach of London over the week-end and that the Cabinet would meet again Monday morning in any case to approve a statement to be made before the House of Commons later in the day.

A communiqué issued after the Cabinet meeting said the British Government was keeping in closest touch with the French Government and was "giving continuous consideration to the situation."

"It was felt," said the communiqué, "that the action of the German Government was bound to have the most disturbing effect on Anglo-German relations and upon

Continued on Page Thirty-five

The Austrian Situation

Adolf Hitler entered Austria yesterday and in a speech before a great throng at Linz proclaimed the unity of that country with Germany. He will enter Vienna in triumph today. He was preceded by large forces of troops, which occupied important cities, a detachment going to the capital and another to Brenner Pass on the Italian frontier. Many bombing planes also appeared at Vienna. Heinrich Himmler organized the police of that city and many arrests were made. Ex-Chancellor Schuschnigg was under guard. Anti-Nazi newspapers were suppressed. Exodus attempts were balked by closing of neighboring frontiers.

Munich reported that at least 65,000 troops had gone into Austria, with much artillery, including heavy guns and tanks. Some 40,000 more moved toward the frontier and reinforcements were brought up. Men up to 38 were mobilized.

France suspended leaves of absence in the forces guarding the Maginot line and a high military council was held in Paris. Leon Blum again failed to gather a National Union Cabinet, but sought one of the Left. In London the Cabinet met and, while accepting the Austrian situation, considered what would be done in case Czechoslovakia was endangered. [The above dispatches on Page 1.]

The Fascist Grand Council at Rome, after a meeting on Austria, issued a vague communiqué neither approving nor disapproving of Germany's action, but conceding it was "an open expression of the sentiment and will of the Austrian people." It had before it a letter from Hitler to Mussolini explaining the former's course and pledging that the German troops would not go south of Brenner Pass. [Page 36.]

In Berlin Propaganda Minister Goebbels broadcast a proclamation by Hitler declaring the unity of the two German countries and warning that no nations could drive them apart. There were indications that a new Danubian settlement would be sought with Rome. [Page 34.]

PARIS ENDS LEAVES OF BORDER TROOPS

Defenders of the Maginot Line of Forts Opposite Germany Are Ordered to Stand By

BLUM'S EFFORTS BLOCKED

Unable to Get Consent for a National Union Cabinet, He Tries a New Popular Front

By The Associated Press.

PARIS, March 12.—Troops manning the powerful Maginot Line defenses facing the German border were held to their posts tonight as France took an increasingly grave view of the European crisis.

French officials meanwhile sought to convince Great Britain it was necessary for mutual safety to take a joint stand to discourage any German encroachment on Czechoslovakia. They considered the war-created democracy on the Reich's border the real powder barrel, because of alliances with France and Soviet Russia.

Premier-designate Leon Blum at the same time gave up attempts to form a national union government of all parties and sought desperately to set up another Popular Front Cabinet to give the country a Ministry. His proposal to include Communists in a Cabinet had brought almost united disapproval from Center and Right groups in the Chamber of Deputies.

Ministers Stay at Posts

The Ministers of Camille Chautemps's government, which resigned Thursday, remained at their posts immersed in the international developments.

Edouard Daladier, Minister of National Defense and War in that Cabinet, ordered the troops in the Maginot Line to remain at their posts without leave until further notice after he had conferred with military chiefs. The line is the famous barrier of steel and concrete and heavy guns that was constructed after the World War to halt any new German invasion. It is a vast underground system stretching virtually from Switzerland to Belgium.

The full import of the order canceling leave was not disclosed, but it was agreed generally that it was a sign of grave apprehensions. M. Daladier conferred at length with army and air commanders.

France definitely is committed by treaty to aid Czechoslovakia in the event of aggression; Britain's hands are free.

The Foreign Office pointed out, however, that there were no juridical grounds on which to base a charge of violation of a neutral State's territory in the case of Germany's Nazification of Austria. The Franco-Czechoslovak treaty, it was said, was not intended to cover a similar situation.

By this it was meant that Austria's new Chancellor, Dr. Arthur

Continued on Page Thirty-six

65,000 REICH TROOPS MOVE INTO AUSTRIA

40,000 More Mass Near Border as Planes and Artillery Join the Forces Driving Across

FRONTIER ROADS CLOGGED

Effort Made to Disguise the Movements as Anxiety of the People Persists

By STANLEY SIMPSON

Wireless to THE NEW YORK TIMES.

MUNICH, Germany, March 12.—With troops moving throughout the countryside, with innumerable planes roaring overhead and with men called as reservists taking hurried farewell of their families, Bavaria presented today an even more war-like atmosphere than yesterday.

It became obvious that many more units than Munich's Seventh Army Corps had been mobilized and equipped for possible war duty. In well-informed quarters it was estimated that about 65,000 German soldiers were on the way into Austria today—30,000 bound for Vienna and 35,000 for the Austrian provinces.

In place of the Bavarian troops thrown into Austria, reinforcements came into Bavaria from other parts of Germany. About 40,000 were transported today to Rosenheim, Traunstein and other points between Munich and the Austrian frontier.

Stream Into Austria

All day troops continued to march into Austria. Heavy artillery and tanks from Ingolstadt and Coburg were observed as late as 3 o'clock this afternoon moving out on the road to Kufstein, while light artillery was being brought up from Bamberg and Regensburg. In fact, local residents insist that Southern Bavaria is seeing more troops on the move than it ever saw during the World War.

Extraordinary activity was seen all along the road to Simbach, Bavarian frontier town separated from Braunau, Chancellor Hitler's Austrian birthplace, by a river bridge, and on roads to every other point on the Austrian frontier. Every small town within thirty miles of the frontier has the appearance of a garrison city.

In Muehldorf, about twenty miles from Braunau, large numbers of recruits were leaving in motor buses to join their units at the frontier. Some districts have been denuded of all able-bodied men. In some cases 38-year-old men—of the 1900 class—have been mobilized.

Some of the planes flying overhead, it was learned, carried loads of leaflets to Vienna and other Austrian cities.

Germans' Anxiety Persists

Residents of villages and towns in the frontier district have recovered from the acute alarm of yesterday morning, but there is still considerable anxiety. Although reassuring broadcasts were sent all day from the Munich station, that anxiety is subsiding only gradually. Classes in schools were interrupted

Continued on Page Thirty-six

LINZ HAILS HITLER

He Defies World to Part Two Peoples—Will Go to Capital Today

GERMAN TROOPS POUR IN

Reach Vienna and Brenner Pass—Himmler Rounds Up Nazis' Foes—Border Shut

Hitler Proclamation, Page 35; his speech at Linz, Page 32.

By G. E. R. GEDYE

Wireless to THE NEW YORK TIMES.

VIENNA, Sunday, March 13.—For the first time in twenty-four years, save for one or two fleeting visits, Chancellor Adolf Hitler of Germany at 4 o'clock yesterday afternoon set foot in Austria, his native land, as the victor at the head of a triumphal procession of jubilant Nazis.

He crossed the frontier, the River Inn, at Braunau, his birthplace, followed by a long motor column.

Both the German and Austrian banks were lined with enormous crowds to witness the historic moment when the Nazi leader should enter into possession—for it is clear that after the formality of a plebiscite under Nazi control Austria will become part of a new, great Germany—of the country where he was born and raised and where he acquired the political philosophy that has brought him greater power than any German has had in history.

It is the country that ever sinc his accession to power had formally rejected his doctrines and where his followers until a few weeks ago had been outlawed as members of an illegal movement.

Goes From Braunau to Linz

Amid the deafening cheers of the Nazis both in Germany and in Austria and the pealing of church bells, the Fuehrer's car slowly crossed the bridge over the Inn into Braunau, which was a mass of swastika banners. Then he proceeded to Linz, his first extended halt.

There, amid scenes of the wildest enthusiasm, he made a speech from the balcony of the City Hall in which he proclaimed the unity of Germany and Austria and warned the world that any effort to part the two peoples would be in vain.

In greeting Hitler at Linz, Dr. Arthur Seyss-Inquart, the new Austrian Chancellor, proclaimed the annulment of the peace treaty of St. Germain, which stipulated that the Austrian republic must remain independent and forbade union with Germany except with the consent of the League of Nations.

Hitler spent the night at the Wolfsgrubert Hotel in Linz and will make a triumphal entry into Vienna at about 11 o'clock this morning [5 A. M. Eastern standard time].

Meanwhile large forces of German troops had moved into Austria. According to German statements, the first ones did not cross the frontier until 5:30 yesterday morning and the movement was made simultaneously at all the main points of entry.

At Salzburg the troops were preceded by 100 tanks and marched in with bands playing and the men singing Nazi songs. Immediately after their arrival the commandant at the Salzburg garrison was ordered to report at the prefecture to the German commanding officer, General Kiebler.

The Austrian officer was told that he and his troops—including the 1915 class called to the colors by former Chancellor Kurt Schuschnigg Friday morning in defense of Austrian independence—would henceforth be under General Kiebler's orders and ranked as German troops.

Advance Proceeds Smoothly

The whole German advance proceeded according to an obviously prearranged and well-coordinated plan. A procedure similar to that at Salzburg was followed wherever the Germans crossed the frontier.

Early yesterday afternoon the Italian frontier guards at Brenner Pass had the pleasure of seeing armed forces of the other end of the Berlin-Rome axis arrive at their border.

Formal greetings were exchanged between the German and Italian commanders. At the head of the German troops was a column of machine gunners and motor cycle scouts with anti-tank guns. The

Continued on Page Thirty-one

"All the News That's Fit to Print."

The New York Times.

LATE CITY EDITION
Rain, warmer today and tonight. Tomorrow rain and colder.
Temperatures Yesterday—Max., 46; Min., 33.

VOL. LXXXVII....No. 29,271. Entered as Second-Class Matter, Postoffice, New York, N. Y. NEW YORK, WEDNESDAY, MARCH 16, 1938. PP TWO CENTS In New York City. | THREE CENTS Within 200 Miles. | FOUR CENTS Elsewhere Except in 7th and 8th Postal Zones.

LOYALIST SPAIN BEGS HELP OF FRANCE, ADMITTING SITUATION NEARS COLLAPSE; PARIS SEES NEW NAZI-FASCIST MENACE

ROOSEVELT CLINGS TO MERGER BY FIAT AS RAIL SOLUTION

Such a Course May Be Resort, He Indicates After Parley on Carriers' Predicament

NO CONCLUSIONS REACHED

But Agreement Is Voiced That Care Would Need to Be Taken of Displaced Employes

FINANCIAL AID NOW AN AIM

Morgenthau Present—Senator Wheeler Takes Stand Against Rail Holding Companies

Special to THE NEW YORK TIMES.

WASHINGTON, March 15.—President Roosevelt indicated today that consolidation of railroads might be compelled by the government as a way out of the carriers' predicament. It this were done, he said, a way would have to be found to take care of employes displaced as a result.

The President mentioned the possibility at a press conference after a conference with representatives of the railroad management, security holders and workers and Federal officials concerned. Many subjects were discussed, but only about half of the agenda had been covered, he explained, and the discussions will be resumed on Thursday.

The conference was agreed, however, that if the government encouraged or urged railroad consolidations which meant laying off men by government action, it could not take the position that it had no responsibility to the men and their jobs.

Obviously, said President Roosevelt, the government would have to do something for displaced employes where it forced the railroads to economize by consolidating existing lines or facilities. While the separation of workers on account of death, disability or old age would amount to about 3 per cent a year, the government might want to consolidate carriers at a faster pace.

Harrison Opposes Wage Cut

Apparently there was little discussion at the railway conference of reports that the roads are discussing a 15 per cent wage cut. Walter M. W. Splawn, chairman of the Interstate Commerce Commission, said afterward that while the subject was not referred to specifically, discussion of related subjects indicated a consensus that both wages and employment should be maintained at present levels if possible.

From others present at the conference it was learned that a vigorous stand against wage-cut proposals was voiced by George M. Harrison, president of the Railway Labor Executives Association, who also suggested that before such a course was taken the government should put the railroads "through the wringer" financially and then rent them and take over the management.

By taking over the roads on a rental basis, Mr. Harrison is said to have explained, they could be modernized and provided with new equipment and the need of laying off workers entirely avoided.

In addition to Messrs. Splawn and Harrison, those at the White House conference included Secretary Morgenthau, Interstate Commerce Commissioners Eastman and Mahaffie, Chairman Jesse H. Jones of the RFC, Henry Bruere, president of the Bowery Savings Bank of New York; Carl Gray of the Union Pacific Railway, Senator Wheeler, chairman of the Senate Interstate Commerce Committee, and Senator Truman and Chairman Lea of the House Interstate and Foreign Commerce Committee.

Against Holding Companies

Senator Wheeler is understood to have taken a stand against railroad holding companies. The President later confirmed that the meeting was agreed that the holding company as a device for influencing the operations of the roads should go, but he did not credit the position to any participant.

The Senator also was represented as having taken a strong stand for railroad consolidation by the compulsory method, if necessary, to achieve vital economies, but as having insisted on protection of displaced workers.

President Roosevelt emphasized that the conference was a "diagnostic" session, a general discussion of the ills confronting the $26,000,000,000 industry. There were many who thought that on the more basic phases of the problem it would be advisable to obtain legislation at the present session of Congress, the President said, although his mind was open on the subject and there had been no decision.

Continued on Page Thirty-nine

Barkley Would Bet Head On Forest Service Status

Special to THE NEW YORK TIMES.

WASHINGTON, March 15.—During Senate debate today on a provision in the Reorganization Bill to transfer the Forest Service from the Department of Agriculture to the Interior Department, Senator Barkley said:

"I'd bet my head against the hole in a doughnut that he (the President) will not make the transfer if he is given the power."

"The comparison is not fair," Senator Borah smilingly replied.

"Well," retorted Senator Barkley, laughing, "I hope the Senator does not minimize the odds I am offering."

AIM AT A TAX BILL TO HELP BUSINESS

Senators on Finance Committee Indicate Many Changes in the House Measure

NEW ESTIMATES ARE ASKED

Harrison Wants Treasury Figures on Straight Corporate and Capital Gains Levies

Special to THE NEW YORK TIMES.

WASHINGTON, March 15.—A tax measure which will restore business confidence and still yield the necessary revenue to the government is the aim of the Senate Finance Committee, Chairman Harrison stated today. As steps toward that objective he favored substituting for the undistributed profits tax, even in its modified form as passed by the House, a straight corporate tax and for the present graded capital gains levy and the intricate formula in the House bill, a straight 15 per cent tax on capital gains on assets held for two years.

To this end he has asked the Treasury to furnish him with estimates of the revenue to be derived from a corporate tax of 17, 18, 19 and 19½ per cent on corporate income.

"Of course we must get the needed revenue, especially if the government is to keep up its spending program," Senator Harrison said, "but to my mind a tax bill that would contain a little encouragement to business would be as fine a gesture as it would be possible for the government to make at this time."

Surtax Cut Favored

In addition to specific figures on substitutes for the capital gains levy and the undistributed profits tax, Senator Harrison has asked for an estimate of what the effect on revenues would be if the highest surtax was cut from 75 per cent to 60 per cent. A reduction of this sort is favored by other members of the committee.

Both Senator Gerry and Senator Bailey said that they felt that the extreme surtax had resulted in diminishing returns. They believed lower taxes might result in freeing wealth for investment, thus stimulating enterprise and re-employment.

Few members of the committee would express themselves as favoring the broadening of the income tax base to include lower brackets that are now exempt. Senator La Follette, however, said that he would introduce an amendment to cut exemptions of single persons from $1,000 to $800, of persons with one dependent from $2,500 to $2,000 and to extend the exemptions to include dependents up to twenty years of age.

He also plans to propose an extension of the surtax downward to include net incomes above $4,000 instead of above $6,000 as at present.

While not in favor of this, Senator Harrison and several of his colleagues admitted that its passage might be necessary to raise the required revenue unless government spending was curtailed.

"It would have the advantage of making a large part of our citizenry tax-conscious," Senator Harrison said.

Want Business Stimulation

A tax program to stimulate business along the lines suggested by the committee's chairman is favored by fifteen of the twenty-one members of the committee and while they individually were not prepared to be explicit until they had studied the House measure further, their attitude indicated that the committee would report a bill differing in many particulars from the measure passed by the House.

They expect to report their bill speedily. Senator Harrison today sent telegrams to fifty persons who wish to appear at the hearings which are scheduled to start Thursday afternoon. He asked those desiring to testify to file briefs and be prepared to restrict their remarks.

Continued on Page Forty

TORNADOES STRIKE TOWNS IN 7 STATES; AT LEAST 19 KILLED

Eight Dead, Many Injured and Damage Estimated at $1,000,000 at Belleville, Ill.

HOMES, FACTORIES RAZED

Communities in Near-by Missouri Are Hit—Storms in Five Southern States

Special to THE NEW YORK TIMES.

BELLEVILLE, Ill., March 15.—A tornado struck this city and other communities in Southwestern Illinois and Northeastern Missouri this afternoon, killing sixteen persons, injuring more than 100, some probably fatally, and destroying buildings and other property. Mayor George Remnsnider estimated at $1,000,000 the damage in the city of 30,000, fourteen miles southeast of St. Louis.

Eight were killed here, one in Glenview, a small community to the northeast, and one in O'Fallon, another town northeast. Near Kennett, Mo., six persons were killed.

Roaring northward parallel with the Mississippi, the storm struck near Kennett, wrecked farm houses twenty miles north of Cape Girardeau, Mo., leveled barns in Jefferson County, Mo., near St. Louis, crossed the Mississippi and swung toward Belleville.

This city was the hardest hit as the black, funnel-shaped wind struck at about 5 P. M. and swept everything in its 100-yard-wide path. It tore its way most disastrously on West Main Street, about a mile from the business center, following that thoroughfare for about six blocks. Nearly 200 buildings here were damaged and one was crushed into pulp.

The twister ripped the roof off the Union Grade School, which pupils had left at 3:15 P. M. The $1,000,000 Belleville High School, only 200 yards away, escaped untouched.

Factories Are Wrecked

Scores of houses were reduced to kindling wood or unroofed. Several factories, including that of the Suppiger Canning Company, were wrecked, the canning plant's second story being sliced off as if by a gigantic knife. A huge smokestack was toppled.

Telephone poles and trees were leveled, the debris clogging streets and adding to the widespread confusion. Light service was cut off and most of the telephone system was put out of commission.

The storm lasted only a few moments, but peril stalked the city for hours after it had gone. Those hurrying through the streets in frantic search for the dead and injured were menaced by broken high-tension wires. Fumes from severed gas mains poured into the streets.

The only illumination available tonight to rescue crews was moonlight and that from automobile headlights and pocket flashlights. With these insufficient aids the relief workers had to dig under piles of bricks or the smashed lumber of frame houses.

Mayor Remnsnider appealed to United States Army authorities for help and a detachment of 125 sol-

Continued on Page Twenty-four

GOV. LEHMAN ACTS TO FORCE PASSAGE OF INSURANCE BILL

Lines Up More Democrats and Measure Reaches Third Reading in Senate

DUNNIGAN PRESSES VOTE

Hopes for Final Decision Today as Republicans Ponder Quick Move in Assembly

By WARREN MOSCOW

Special to THE NEW YORK TIMES.

ALBANY, March 15.—Governor Lehman, irked by the evidence that his intention not to keep the Legislature in session to pass the Savings Bank Life Insurance Bill had been interpreted as a weakening on his part toward the measure, cracked the whip again today and drove into line three more Democratic Senators, making a total of twenty of the twenty-nine Democratic members now pledged to it.

In discussing the bill Mr. Lehman said:

"I am just as anxious as I ever was to secure the passage of the bill, and I will continue my efforts to do so."

Acting for the Governor, John J. Dunnigan, majority leader, won another victory on the bill, the only real controversial one of the current session, when, at a party conference, he gained the votes to advance the measure to a third reading.

Carrying out the agreement, the Senate tonight advanced it without debate or a record vote.

Mr. Dunnigan said he hoped to bring the bill up for a final vote tomorrow and have the necessary twenty-six Democrats on hand and pledged, by that time, to pass it. However, he did not have the twenty-six votes tonight.

The three who swung were Senators Feld and Burchill from Manhattan and Crawford from Brooklyn.

In addition to these, Senator Dunnigan counted on the vote of Senator Rogers of Monroe, who has not committed himself definitely, and three others not named. This would bring the total up to 24.

At least two Republicans were counted upon by the majority leader to give the bill a majority.

Assembly Passage First Is Aim

The bill will come up in the Assembly either tomorrow or Thursday, and there is some pressure on the Republicans, from within the party, to get the Assembly to pass the bill first and claim credit for it.

In the Assembly the Democrats at a party conference this morning found that they had fifty-two of the sixty-one Assembly Democrats lined up for the Insurance Bill. They can count on the five Laborites and need only nineteen Republican votes to have a majority for it.

The bill, in its present form, would permit the establishment by savings banks of insurance departments in which policies would be sold, on a weekly payment plan, with a maximum of $1,000 a policy in any one bank, and a total of $3,000 maximum to any policy-holder in any group of banks.

The aim of the bill is to reduce the cost of industrial life insurance

Continued on Page Sixteen

Contractor's Wife Pickets Union Offices; Jostled Backing Husband's Cause in Row

Mrs. Sylvia Penner, wife of Isaac Penner, head of the Penner Electric Company, contractors, was badgered and pushed about by a hostile crowd yesterday when she picketed the offices of Local 3 of the Electrical Workers Union, 130 East Twenty-fifth Street, in support of her husband's cause in a dispute with the union.

Mr. Penner has locked out members of the organization whom he had employed on a number of municipal construction jobs.

Carrying two placards in sandwich fashion calling upon the union to "drive out racketeering officers of Local 3" and announcing that "the company wants the right to hire members of Local 3 who are willing to work," Mrs. Penner was set upon by an irate group, said to have been composed of members of the union, who tore the signs from her and hurled them into the street after breaking them into bits.

Mrs. Penner was unable to identify her assailants after a police radio car from the East Twenty-second Street station had arrived. Picking up the fragments of her signs, she walked to Twenty-fourth Street and Lexington Avenue, to pose for a picture for Murray Becker, a photographer for The Associated Press. Several men who followed her from in front of the union's office attacked the photographer. They punched him, hurt his wrists and damaged his camera.

From his office at 200 West Seventy-second Street Mr. Penner issued a statement explaining that he was compelled to dismiss members of Local 3 employed by him on several municipal construction jobs, including public schools, because there were "sabotage, wasted time, theft of tools and equipment, and the piling up of costs of labor and material with the one thought of driving the Penner Electric Company out of business."

"The reason for this," Mr. Penner said, "is that the Penner Electric Company has taken these jobs away from the ring and thereby saved the city and State of New York hundreds of thousands of dollars."

The "ring" referred to by Mr. Penner is an alleged combine held responsible for arbitrary setting of wages and excluding contractors who are not members of the "ring."

The Penner Electric Company is not a member of the Electrical Code, subscribed to by contractors having agreements with Local 3. Mr. Penner had appeared as a witness in the suit of the National Electrical Manufacturers Association against Local 3 before Special Master John Kirkland Clark, charging illegal combination in violation of conspiracy laws. Frederick Katz, a brother-in-law of Mr. Penner, said the latter was willing to give all the details of his difficulties with Local 3 to District Attorney Thomas E. Dewey, who has had Local 3 under investigation for some time.

HITLER HAILS COUP

Tells Vienna Throng His Greatest Task Is Done—Reviews Big Parade

JOURNALISTS 'IMPRISONED'

Fuehrer Flies to Munich—Austria Now a District—Anti-Semitism Spreads

By G. E. R. GEDYE

Wireless to THE NEW YORK TIMES.

VIENNA, March 15.—After wreathing the Austrian heroes' monument, addressing another enormous crowd of his supporters to announce to them Austria's formal incorporation into Germany and witnessing a great military parade, Chancellor Adolf Hitler flew back to Munich tonight.

His speech was delivered in the Heldenplatz, outside the Hofburg, the former palace of the Habsburgs, to a wildly cheering Nazi crowd. Once again a public holiday was proclaimed and employers were ordered to foot the bill.

Throughout the day Nazi crowds gathered around the Hotel Imperial to cheer their triumphant leader. He drove in his car to the Hofburg amid further scenes of Nazi enthusiasm. Dr. Arthur Seyss-Inquart, who has been created Reich Statthalter [Governor] of Austria after having been Chancellor since the fall of the Schuschnigg government, addressed him in terms almost of adoration.

Declaring that "today all Germans greet for eternity" the leader who has created "the national German Reich," Dr. Seyss-Inquart concluded:

"My leader, we know only one thing: we thank the leader with intense devotion and unconditional loyalty. My leader, wherever the way may lead, we follow. Heil my leader!"

Hitler States New Mission

Hitler, replying, declared that the mission of an independent Austria had been to "prevent the creation of a really great German Reich, thus blocking the way for the future of the German people."

"Now I proclaim for this land its new mission," he continued. "Henceforth the oldest Eastern boundary of the German people shall be the youngest bulwark of the German nation and thus of the German Reich.

"For centuries in uneasy times past Eastern storms broke on the frontiers of the old Reich. For centuries in the future it will be an iron guard for the security and freedom of the German Reich and thus for the peace of our great people."

Thanking Dr. Seyss-Inquart and the other Austrians who had made the Nazi conquest possible in so short a time "with God's help," the Fuehrer concluded:

"At this hour I can report to the German people the completion of the most important act of my life; as leader and Chancellor of the German nation and the Reich I report before history the entry of my homeland into the German Reich!"

Correspondents Threatened

Unfortunately the impressive scene was witnessed only from a considerable distance by the entire foreign press corps, including many special correspondents who had come to Vienna for this historic occasion, because we were all confined to the Chancellery under a threat by the German officer commanding the guard there that he would give the order to shoot if any one tried to leave.

Austrian Nazi officials of the Chancellery were embarrassed but powerless to obtain our release and it was not until after the lapse of one hour that some of us discovered a telephone and rang up various legations and we were set free.

The imprisonment of the foreign correspondents was due to their having accepted an invitation from the new press chief, Joseph Hans Lazar, to confer with him between 9 and 10 A. M. regarding special passes. Those who arrived at 9 were held up in the courtyard by German Elite Guards, who hectoringly refused to allow them to go to the press room.

Eventually the journalists were allowed to go up to Herr Lazar, but when the permits had been issued the first who attempted to leave were stopped by the German guards and told to return.

After protesting to Herr Lazar,

Continued on Page Nine

Spanish Loyalists in Full Flight Before Rebel Sweep Toward Coast

Franco's Legions, Unresisted, Now Within Thirty Miles of Mediterranean—Two Are Killed as British Ship Is Bombed

By The Associated Press.

HENDAYE, France (at the Spanish frontier), March 15.—Shattered Government troops were in full retreat tonight before 100,000 Insurgents bent on tearing Government Spain apart and forcing a quick end to the Spanish civil war.

Encountering only feeble rearguard resistance, the Insurgents pushed forward ten miles from Alcaniz to capture Val de Algora, eight miles southeast, and the strategic village of Raimundo, controlling the main inland highway from Valencia to Barcelona. From that point only the rugged coastal sierras stood between Generalissimo Francisco Franco's army and the Mediterranean, a little more than thirty miles from Raimundo.

Since General Franco started his overwhelming Spring offensive a week ago from Villanueva, on the Aragon front between Saragossa and Teruel, his troops have advanced about sixty-five miles, conquering nearly 2,000 square miles of territory.

Rapidly consolidating his strength along a new twenty-mile line from Caspe to Alcaniz today, General Franco struck out again toward new objectives—Nonaspe, fifteen miles due east of Caspe; Candesa, twenty-five miles east of Alcaniz, and Valderrobres, on the Matarrana River, twenty-five miles southeast of Alcaniz.

Italian Black Arrow brigades, Foreign Legionnaires, Moorish cavalry and infantry and native Navarrese troops swept forward along the wide front, unchecked by fleeing government units. Their objective was to separate Catalonia, Spain's northeastern corner, from the rest of government territory.

Since the civil war started on July 18, 1936, General Franco has captured two-thirds of Spain, including the Biscayan coast on the north and virtually all of Western Spain.

Dispatches from the front said government forces thus far had been unable to organize effective resistance and their only chance to prevent dismemberment of Government Spain was to stop the Insurgent offensive in the coastal sierras. Broad highways leading out of Alcaniz opened the way for General Franco's mechanized and motorized units, but they might have more trouble with the inferior

Continued on Page Two

U. S. HAS DILEMMA OVER RECOGNITION

Acceptance Would Sanction Force, Raising Issue as to Ethiopia, Manchuria

TRADE PACTS A PROBLEM

If We Hold Austria an Entity, Reich, Now on the Blacklist, May Flood Us With Goods

By BERTRAM D. HULEN

Special to THE NEW YORK TIMES.

WASHINGTON, March 15.—President Roosevelt and Secretary of State Cordell Hull have taken under active consideration legal questions involved in the extinction of Austria, which it is fully realized pose a major diplomatic problem for the United States.

Neither was prepared to make an announcement today, but answers to several immediate questions promise to be given soon. These will define basic policy which may shape the position of the United States for the future, for they will show whether the United States recognizes German sovereignty over Austria.

If, as is generally expected, recognition is given, the implications may be far-reaching, for no one here apparently believes that the coup of Chancellor Hitler was made possible other than by military force. In this respect views entertained here are similar to those given by Prime Minister Neville Chamberlain to the House of Commons yesterday.

Only one move affecting Austria was taken here today, and that was not necessarily significant. President Roosevelt proclaimed the reciprocal trade agreement of March 7 between the United States and Czechoslovakia to be provisionally effective on April 16, pending approval by the Czechoslovak National Assembly, and in so doing treated Austria as an entity by continuing her on the list of nations to which the benefits of reciprocal trade agreements will be generalized.

No "Announcement" From Austria

Germany is on the blacklist, not enjoying these benefits because of economic policies discriminating against the United States. However, the Presidential action with respect to Austria may be changed after questions concerning Germany's relations to Austria have been decided. Had he removed Austria from the list it would have constituted recognition of Germany's domination.

Asked at his press conference whether the United States considered that Austria had ceased to exist as an independent State, the

Continued on Page Ten

THOUSANDS ENROLL IN BRITISH 'SERVICE'

Appeal for Anti-Air Raid Duty Gets Quick Response as Scope of Reich Threat Is Realized

ELECTION ISSUE IS HINTED

Public Opinion May Force Eden's 'Firmness' Policy in Reply to Request From France

By FERDINAND KUHN Jr.

Special Cable to THE NEW YORK TIMES.

LONDON, March 15.—Thousands of men and women enrolled all over Great Britain today in response to Home Secretary Sir Samuel Hoare's appeal last night for 1,000,000 anti-air raid volunteers.

Applicants stood waiting outside the town halls in London's boroughs before the doors were opened this morning. Housewives, servant girls and stenographers were among the women who outnumbered the men in many districts in signing up for what Sir Samuel described as "exacting and dangerous" duties in case of war.

Those who know European realities—among them at least three of Prime Minister Neville Chamberlain's Cabinet colleagues—are aghast at the extent of the Fascist triumph and the likelihood that these triumphs will spread in the near future. Slowly the realization is dawning that Germany has achieved the strategic domination of Central and Southeastern Europe and that Hungary, perhaps Rumania, and even Italy lie at her mercy.

Moreover, there is a growing awareness that the impending victory of the Spanish Fascists will involve at least a temporary German-Italian domination of an area that in Napoleonic times was so vital to Great Britain that she fought to keep it free of her enemies.

It would be an odd twist if the pressure of events forced Mr. Chamberlain back to the policy of "firmness" which Anthony Eden, former Foreign Secretary, tried in vain to get from him only four weeks ago.

Industrial Mobilization

Mr. Chamberlain hinted again today that Great Britain might be compelled to mobilize her industrial structure for war purposes if the international situation continued to grow more serious. Answering Labor critics in the House of Commons, he said:

"I do not know whether you would like us to imitate Germany in the methods she has employed in regimenting her country for the production of armaments. We may have to. But we will not do it until we are convinced that nothing else will serve our purpose."

Despite partial denials there was

Continued on Page Ten

NEGRIN IS REBUFFED

Premier Flies Back to Spain After an Urgent but Futile Appeal

TALK OF SURRENDER HEARD

Refugees Tell of Demoralized Effort by Barcelona—French Fear Direct Threat to Them

Loyalist Spain's situation became desperate yesterday when the Insurgents pressed their offensive to within thirty miles of the Mediterranean. [Page 1.] As Barcelona denied rumors of unrest [Page 2], Premier Negrin made a flying visit to Paris to submit an eleventh-hour appeal for French assistance. France was disturbed by what she saw as a Nazi-Fascist success in Spain, and this, combined with the events in Austria, caused Premier Blum to hold anxious conferences on finances and armaments. [Page 1.]

Meanwhile Chancellor Hitler, with an aggressive speech in Vienna, pressed the absorption of Austria into the Reich. [Page 1.] The country's status was revealed to be that of a district and as part of its co-ordination Jews were disfranchised and the number of arrests mounted hourly. [Page 8.]

As Britain pushed forward her rearmament program at greater speed, thousands responded to Sir Samuel Hoare's appeal for aid for air raid volunteers. [Page 1.]

The Austrian events confronted Washington with a problem of whether to throw overboard the Stimson non-recognition doctrine in favor of a more realistic foreign policy. [Page 1.]

France Is Worried

By P. J. PHILIP

Wireless to THE NEW YORK TIMES.

PARIS, March 15.—To the piled-up anxieties and dangers that confront the new French Government was added today news from Spain that despite the brave front that is still being kept up the situation of the republican government at Barcelona is becoming desperate.

Premier Juan Negrin arrived by plane from Barcelona and made urgent demands to the French Government for immediate aid in the name of Spanish democracy. He is reported to have said that the Loyalist cause was doomed otherwise.

It is declared that Dr. Negrin's appeal was unsuccessful, and after his talks he flew back to Barcelona. The French attitude is represented as being that the Loyalist cause is already lost.

Refugees from across the frontier brought accounts of demoralization, of factional strife within the Loyalist ranks, of continuous pressure by the Insurgents and of talk of surrender.

Late tonight the Toulouse airdrome received notice of the imminent arrival of President Manuel Azaña of Spain and Defense Minister Indalecio Prieto on "a mission to France."

Threat to France Is Seen

What is most disturbing here is the confirmed news that it is not Insurgent Spain that is winning, but the onward sweep of Nazi and Fascist airplanes and tanks manned by Germans and Italians. It appears that it is not Insurgent Spain that is going to be France's neighbor, but, in the French view, another Nazi-Fascist air, land and sea base.

For the French, the Spanish civil war is no longer a question of rival ideologies, but the vital matter of their own national security. It is known that German planes in great numbers have recently been added to Generalissimo Francisco Franco's forces, and it is known that several airfields near the French frontier are entirely manned and operated by Germans.

This news, even more than the German annexation of Austria, even more than the possibility of a threat to Czechoslovakia, has caused deep uneasiness. For twenty months France has kept out of the Spanish war because, with her own people divided, she did not wish to take sides. Now she is face to face with the fact that Nazi Germany

Continued on Page Three

"All the News That's Fit to Print."

The New York Times.

LATE CITY EDITION
Partly cloudy, possibly scattered showers today and tomorrow; little change in temperature.
Temperatures Yesterday—Max., 80; Min., 66

VOL. LXXXVII....No. 29,370. Entered as Second-Class Matter, Postoffice, New York, N. Y. NEW YORK, THURSDAY, JUNE 23, 1938. P THREE CENTS NEW YORK CITY and Vicinity | FOUR CENTS Elsewhere Except in 7th and 8th Postal Zones.

LOUIS DEFEATS SCHMELING BY A KNOCKOUT IN FIRST; 80,000 SEE TITLE BATTLE

FIGHT ENDS IN 2:04

Rights Drop the Loser Thrice and Trainer Tosses In Towel

1936 SETBACK AVENGED

Challenger Says He Was Fouled With a Kidney Punch —The Gate Tops $900,000

By JAMES P. DAWSON

The exploding fists of Joe Louis crushed Max Schmeling last night in the ring at the Yankee Stadium and kept sacred that time-worn legend of boxing that no former heavyweight champion has ever regained the title.

The Brown Bomber from Detroit, with the most furious early assault he has ever exhibited here, knocked out Schmeling in the first round of what was to have been a fifteen-round battle to retain the title he won last year from James J. Braddock. He has now defended it successfully four times.

In exactly 2 minutes and 4 seconds of fighting Louis polished off the Black Uhlan from the Rhine, but, though the battle was short, it was furious and savage while it lasted, packed with thrills that held three knockdowns of the ambitious ex-champion, every moment tense for a crowd of about 80,000.

A Representative Gathering

This gathering, truly representative and comparing favorably with the largest crowds in boxing's history, paid receipts estimated at between $900,000 and $1,000,000 to see whether Schmeling could repeat the knockout he administered to Louis just two years ago here and be the first ex-heavyweight champion to come back into the title, or whether the Bomber could avenge this defeat as he promised.

As far as the length of the battle was concerned, the investment in seats, which ran to $30 each, was a poor one. But for excitement, for drama, for pulse-throbs, those who came from near and far felt themselves well repaid because they saw a fight that, though it was one of the shortest heavyweight championships on record, was surpassed by few for thrills.

With the right hand that Schmeling held in contempt Louis knocked out his foe. Three times under its impact the German fighter hit the ring floor. The first time Schmeling regained his feet laboriously at the count of three. From the second knockdown Schmeling, dazed but game, bounced up instinctively before the count had gone beyond one.

On the third knockdown Schmeling's trainer and closest friend, Max Machon, hurled a towel into the ring, European fashion, admitting defeat for his man. The towel sailed through the air when the count on the prostrate Max had reached three.

Ignored in Boxing Here

The signal is ignored in American boxing, has been for years, and Referee Arthur Donovan, before he had a chance to pick up the count in unison with knockdown timekeeper Eddie Josephs, who was outside the ring, gathered the white emblem in a ball and hurled it through the ropes.

Returning to Schmeling's crumpled figure, Donovan took one look and signaled an end of the battle. The count at that time was five on the third knockdown. Further counting was useless. Donovan could have counted off a century and Max could not have regained his feet. The German was thoroughly "out."

It was as if he had been poleaxed. His brain was awhirl, his body, his head, his jaws ached and pained, his senses were numbed from that furious, paralyzing punching he had taken even in the short space of time the battle consumed.

Claims Blurred Vision

Following the bout, Schmeling claimed he was fouled. He said that he was hit a kidney punch, a devastating right, which so shocked his nervous system that he was dazed and his vision was blurred. To observers at the ringside, however, with all due respect to Schmeling's thoughts on the subject, the punches which dazed him were thundering blows to the head, jaw and body in bewildering succession, blows of the old Alabama Assassin reincarnate last night for a special occasion.

Louis wanted to erase the mem-

Continued on Page Fourteen

Bill Introduced in Cuba To Make July 4 a Holiday

Special Cable to THE NEW YORK TIMES.

HAVANA, June 22.—A bill declaring the coming Fourth of July a national holiday was introduced in the House of Representatives last night by Paul de Cardenas, Representative from Havana Province.

The bill is designed to suspend all commercial, industrial and governmental activities to permit attendance at a demonstration being organized for the Fourth of July as homage to the United States.

Plans for the demonstration, which will be held under the auspices of the cultural, social, economic and patriotic groups of the island, were launched last week.

The committee has asserted that homage is being paid to the United States "solely to cultivate and strengthen the sentiment of friendship and close relations that have always existed between the two peoples."

HAUGWITZ DISPUTE RISES OVER CHILD

Former Barbara Hutton Gets Police Guard for Son, 2, but Count Denies Kidnap Threat

Special Cable to THE NEW YORK TIMES.

LONDON, June 22. — Countess Haugwitz-Reventlow, the former Barbara Hutton, Woolworth heiress, broke into the news again today as London buzzed with rumors that her 2-year-old son Lance was under guard against kidnapping.

Late tonight Count Court Haugwitz-Reventlow, who is in Paris, acknowledged in a telephone talk with The Daily Mail that a sharp difference of opinion had arisen between him and the Countess over the future education of their son. According to The Daily Mail, the Danish nobleman also disclosed that the police were anxious to interrogate him should he land in Britain, but he strenuously denied any attempt or threat to kidnap his son.

The gates of Winfield House, the huge Haugwitz-Reventlow mansion, which stands in its own park within Regent's Park, were locked against all comers and policemen patrolled the grounds. Inquirers were referred to a statement issued by W. M. Mitchell, solicitor for the Countess.

Silent for "Legal Reasons"

"I am sure that the press will appreciate that for legal reasons it is impossible for the Countess to make any statement at the present time," he said. "If at a later stage she has anything to say, you may be sure that the press will be informed."

Mr. Mitchell made the statement at the gates of Winfield House, which was a center for reporters and photographers all day. Interest in the statement was heightened by a memorandum from Scotland Yard to the effect that the police had no information about any plot to kidnap the child, although the Countess acknowledged that she had "taken certain precautions."

Later, while Lance was being taken for an airing in the twelve-and-a-half-acre park, the Countess was driven rapidly with Sir Patrick

Continued on Page Ten

REPUBLICANS PLAN CONFERENCE RULE ON CONVENTION VOTE

Party Delegates Agree on a Program to Assure Unity on All Proposals

FIRST SESSION ON MONDAY

Leaders Indicate They Will Welcome Wiretapping as Campaign Issue

By W. A. WARN

Special to THE NEW YORK TIMES.

ALBANY, June 22.—Before the Constitutional Convention adjourned today for the week-end the Republicans took action to insure a firmer control over decisions reached in that body. There will be frequent conferences of all Republican delegates on important pending proposals.

The decision to assure cohesive party action and a united Republican front against the Democratic minority was reached after a discussion held last night at a private dinner given to Chief Judge Frederick F. Crane of the Court of Appeals, president of the convention, by the chairmen of standing committees. All Republican delegates had been invited and all but two or three attended. The conference plan, it was said today, was unanimously approved by all present.

The proposed creation of a steering committee, after having been discussed by Republican delegates for many days, has been definitely dropped.

The conferences, under the plan decided upon, will be held on call from State Senator Perley A. Pitcher, Republican floor leader in the convention. In the event that Senator Pitcher should fail to call a party conference on some important measure, a petition signed by ten of the ninety-two Republican members would compel him to issue the call.

Use of Caucus Barred

Mr. Pitcher stressed the distinction between conferences and caucus action. Where caucus action would bind all participants, conference action would leave a delegate free to vote according to his own convictions, even where that would be in conflict with a decision reached at a conference.

The practice resorted to sometimes at legislative conferences to turn them into a caucus at some critical stage was pronounced taboo by him.

The new plan will have its first application when the convention resumes next week. Senator Pitcher has already issued a call for the first conference, to be held at 4 P. M. Monday. The subject to be discussed is the Dunnigan search and seizure proposal, with its clause forbidding the use in court of evidence obtained through wiretapping or through search and seizure without a court warrant.

The party convention leaders oppose this clause and hope to bring enough persuasive arguments to bear to insure a solid front against the proposal.

Plan Used in the Senate

In establishing its conference plan and its taboo on the caucus, the party has virtually adopted a method which it has followed in the State Senate for fifteen years. It was recalled today that such conferences have demonstrated their effectiveness in keeping party members in line, even though on occasion a Senate leader has had at his command not more than twenty-six Senators, a bare majority.

The Dunnigan search and seizure proposal, and the one favorably re-

Continued on Page Six

Walker Calls on La Guardia at City Hall; Dapper Ex-Mayor Says Visit Is for Clients

Debonair and dapper as ever, former Mayor James J. Walker visited Mayor La Guardia at City Hall yesterday. He said his call was in the interest of several clients who have business dealings with the city.

Tanned and looking healthier than he has in years, Mr. Walker emerged from the Mayor's office after a half-hour chat. Cornered by the City Hall reporters, many of whom he knew, he was asked the nature of his call.

"I could tell you," he smiled, "but why should I? It wasn't anything much—just that I wanted to see the Mayor in the interest of a few clients of mine. Amicus curiae, you might call it—a friend of the court."

The former Mayor hotly denied a hint that he was late for his 2:45 appointment. He swore that he had been in City Hall at 2:40, and had spent the time chatting with Stanley Howe, the Mayor's secretary, until 3 o'clock when Mayor La Guardia was ready to see him. He wore a dark blue suit, a white shirt with a blue tie, Panama hat with the brim turned down, and cornflowers in his buttonhole.

Because there was a hearing going on upstairs on a proposed tax on bookmakers, Mr. Walker was asked if he had any clients who were bookmakers.

"Unfortunately, no," he said with the same eye-crinkling smile. "Taxation," he went on with mock seriousness in his tone, "is a very, very comprehensive subject."

A photographer broke in to ask him to pose "coming through the gate" and shaking hands with Patrolman Charles Stoffers, a veteran police aide in the building.

"Uh-uh," he demurred. "I don't like that coming-through-the-gate business. That picture has been made too many times."

Nevertheless he assumed the pose to satisfy the photographer. Asked if he had discussed a possible successor to the late Senator Copeland with the Mayor, Mr. Walker said:

"Politics? Now what would I know about politics?"

Labor Board Gives C. I. O. Control Of All West Coast Longshoremen

A. F. L. Loses to Bridges Union in Sweeping Decision Setting Up Nation's First Major Geographical Bargaining Agency

By LOUIS STARK

Special to THE NEW YORK TIMES.

WASHINGTON, June 22.—The C. I. O. won a major victory over the A. F. of L. today when its affiliate the International Longshoremen's and Warehousemen's Union, District No. 1, was certified by the National Labor Relations Board as the exclusive bargaining agency for all longshoremen in thirty-one Pacific Coast ports.

The Pacific Coast longshoremen led by Harry Bridges, Australian-born radical leader against whom deportation proceedings have been started on a charge of membership in the Communist party, seceded from the A. F. of L.'s International Longshoremen's Union last year and set up the organization.

In certifying the Bridges union the NLRB made an unprecedented decision in establishing the first major geographical bargaining unit in the marine industry.

The board found that 9,557 of the 12,860 longshoremen on the Pacific Coast had designated the Bridges union as their representative for purposes of collective bargaining.

The decision will affect all longshoremen and warehousemen employed by the Ship Owners Association of the Pacific Coast, Waterfront Employers Association of the Pacific Coast, the Waterfront Employers of Seattle, the Waterfront Employers of Portland, the Waterfront Employers Association of San Francisco and the Waterfront Employers Association of Southern California.

In the course of the hearings, the A. F. of L. protested against the request by Mr. Bridges that his union be designated as the exclusive bargaining agency on the ground that the board had no power to designate a bargaining unit larger than employes of one company.

The board's jurisdiction was protested by the A. F. of L. and its affiliate, the International Longshoremen's Union, because the contract between the employer and the Pacific Coast longshoremen was still in the name of the A. F. of L. organization on behalf of the employes.

The companies also argued that the appropriate bargaining unit for longshoremen must be one restricted to those working for a particular employer at a particular port.

Overruling these objections, the board held that, under the Labor Relations Act, it expressly received authority to decide that the "employer" unit shall be that most appropriate unit for purposes of collective bargaining. The act includes within the term employer "any person acting in the interest of an employer, directly or indirectly," and the term person "includes one or more associations."

The present contract between the employers' associations and the longshoremen is held by the A. F. of L. union, and the board ruled that it was not necessary for it to decide whether the contract now passes to the Bridges organization, because a majority of members had voted to leave the A. F. of L. and to join the C. I. O.

The board declared, however, that

Continued on Page Four

TURROU SPY STORY BARRED IN PRESS

Hardy Gets Writ Halting First Installment—Show-Cause Order Up Today

United States Attorney Lamar Hardy obtained yesterday a court order preventing The New York Post from publishing the revelations of Leon G. Turrou, special agent of the Department of Justice, chief investigator in the German espionage inquiry.

The action was taken about 4:30 P. M., but was not verified in New York City until shortly before 8 P. M. The news had been flashed from Washington about 6:30 P. M., however, which indicated that Mr. Hardy's unusual move had the approval of his chief, Attorney General Homer Cummings.

The effect of the order was to halt scheduled publication today of Mr. Turrou's first installment of a series of articles which were intended to run for about twenty-one days. The show cause order served upon J. David Stern, publisher of The Post, and Mr. Turrou, will be argued this morning before Judge Murray Hulbert at 10:30 A. M., in Room 506 of the Federal Court House in Foley Square.

Seeks to Wait on Inquiry

It was understood that Mr. Hardy's chief objection to the projected articles was that agents have not yet completed investigation of incidents listed in the advertisements and which later must be presented to the grand jury, whose proceedings are secret.

Several items listed for publication, it was learned, for a long time have been a source of grave concern to the War and Navy Departments. If proved true they would overshadow in importance any defense secret thus far known to have been obtained by the spy ring. Officials of the two services had nothing to do with Mr. Hardy's action, but early in the investigation they requested secrecy until the truth was established.

The aim of Mr. Hardy's proceeding is to obtain an injunction which would prevent publication of anything by Mr. Turrou concerning the case until the grand jury, which will be reconvened on Monday, has completed its work.

From Mr. Stern the proceeding drew a challenge to fight for the right to publish the series under sanction of constitutional principles.

"By endeavoring to enjoin this paper from printing the news," declared Mr. Stern, "the government is making an unprecedented attempt to erase the freedom of the press from the Constitution.

"The law places responsibility upon the publisher for news which does any injury. The Constitution protects against the restraint in anticipation of such injury because the exercise of such anticipatory

Continued on Page Two

PRESIDENT NAMES 9 FOR BRITISH SURVEY

He Also Includes Sweden in Investigation of Employer-Employe Conditions

By FELIX BELAIR Jr.

Special to THE NEW YORK TIMES.

HYDE PARK, N. Y., June 22.—President Roosevelt today completed the selection of a study group of nine members representing business, industry, labor, the general public and the law to investigate industrial-labor conditions in Great Britain, and added employer-employe relationships in Sweden to the group's field of inquiry.

The reason for including Sweden in the agenda of the investigation was not explained in the announcement of the personnel of the study group, and suggestions that the President might have in mind a legislative redefinition of labor's responsibility to the public and to management in this country were met with a flat denial by Presidential aides.

Mr. Roosevelt has not the slightest intention of attempting to duplicate in this country the well-defined methods of adjusting industrial disputes practiced in either Great Britain or Sweden, nor does he contemplate a combination of the methods of the two as a means of lessening interruptions to business and industrial operations here, it was explained.

Personnel of the Group

To conduct the inquiry, the President named the following group, for which no chairman was chosen, with each member having an equal voice in the preparation of a final report to the Secretary of Labor:

Lloyd K. Garrison, dean of the University of Wisconsin Law School and former head of the Labor Relations Board.

Robert Watt, representing the American Federation of Labor.

Gerard Swope, president of the General Electric Company.

Henry I. Harriman, former president of the Chamber of Commerce of the United States.

William H. Davis, New York attorney and former NRA deputy administrator.

Mrs. Anna M. Rosenberg, regional director of Social Security for New York.

Charles R. Hook, president of the American Rolling Mills Company.

Marion Dickerman, principal of the Todhunter School for Girls, New York City.

William Ellison Chalmers, assistant United States Labor Commissioner at Geneva, who is to act as general secretary and liaison officer of the group.

Conspicuously absent from the personnel list was a representative for the Committee for Industrial Organization. John L. Lewis, its head, had refused to designate such a representative on invitation of Secretary Perkins. He had agreed to do so but withdrew his agreement when it was hinted several weeks ago that one of the purposes of the inquiry was to pave the way

Continued on Page Three

CUT IN STEEL WAGE BROACHED TO LEWIS AS RECOVERY SPUR

U. S. Corporation Opens Talks on Plan to Make Jobs and Aid Trade by Reducing Pay

PRICE DROP IS EXPECTED

C. I. O. Likely to Face Choice Between Granting Request and Losing Contract

Tentative discussions have been held recently between officials of the United States Steel Corporation and of the Steel Workers Organizing Committee, C. I. O. affiliate, on the possibility of a readjustment of wages that would promote increased production and employment in the steel industry.

These discussions, which thus far have been informal and exploratory, involve the complicated relationships of prices, labor costs and operating volume. Officials of the United States Steel Corporation declined yesterday to comment on the situation beyond saying that conferences had been held at frequent intervals, usually in Pittsburgh, ever since a contract was signed with the C. I. O. affiliate early last year.

John L. Lewis, head of the Committee for Industrial Organization, who personally negotiated the union's contract with Myron C. Taylor, former chairman of the Steel Corporation, declined to comment on the reports that a wage reduction was being discussed.

Corporation Losing Money

United States Steel is operating at about 28 per cent of capacity and is losing money rapidly. Although it has officially maintained its published scale of prices unchanged, price-slashing is rampant in the steel industry and Big Steel is reported in financial circles to be giving serious consideration to the advisability of reducing its published price schedules.

According to the belief in well-informed Wall Street quarters, the corporation has suggested or is about to put up to Mr. Lewis and other C. I. O. officials the proposal that the organized workers and the company should agree to take a cut —one in basic wage rates, the other in prices—in the expectation that this adjustment would lead to larger orders, increased production and employment and a gain in total income for both the workers and the corporation.

The alternative, according to steel experts in the financial district, is likely to be a further diminution of the corporation's business and a further reduction in the amount of employment it can provide.

Should the Steel Workers Organizing Committee agree to a reduction in the basic wage rates, it is probable that some understanding would be reached simultaneously providing that the original wage rates would be restored after a substantial recovery in the corporation's business.

Lewis Faces Dilemma

It is recognized in financial circles that Mr. Lewis and other C. I. O. officials would find it peculiarly difficult to agree to a wage reduction. Organized labor in general has taken the stand that reduction of wages cannot contribute to prosperity.

Philip Murray, chairman of the S. W. O. C., in a speech delivered in Cleveland on Feb. 20, described how the committee in renewing its contract with United States Steel had turned back an effort to link wage rates with operating rates, and he declared that, as a result of the contract, the committee had

Continued on Page Four

Relief Pickets Ride to WPA Office in Autos; Somervell Wonders How They Can Afford It

Lieut. Col. Brehon B. Somervell, local Works Progress Administrator, has watched scores of picketing demonstrations without comment, but when he saw relief workers driving up to his office in automobiles yesterday to picket against wage cuts he decided it was time to do a little protesting on his own account.

"This is the first time I ever saw relief people come up here with automobiles loaded with banners to protest a wage cut," Colonel Somervell told reporters. "If there is anything that would justify a wage cut, it is that."

It all started when the administrator, returning to the WPA building at 70 Columbus Avenue late in the afternoon, found the WPA Teachers Union, Local 453, an A. F. of L. affiliate, organizing a picket line on the block between Sixty-second and Sixty-third Streets.

As he watched, two cars full of signs and pickets appeared. Asked later whether they were WPA cars, Colonel Somervell replied laughingly that he hoped they were not.

The demonstration brought out 610 persons, but most arrived under their own power, according to the police. Most of them were from WPA educational projects, but a sizable delegation represented the five Federal arts projects, which are outside Colonel Somervell's jurisdiction.

Signs carried by the marchers denounced the wage reductions, which range from $4.70 to $14.95 a month. "Up With Recovery—Down With Wage Cuts," one placard said. More than 26,000 clerical and professional workers are included in the groups affected by the cuts.

Deputy Inspector John Challan and thirty patrolmen watched the picket line for two hours. At one point a bag of water came hurtling from an upper window of the WPA building. There was no other incident.

LABOR PARTY THREATENS 3-CORNERED STATE RACE UNLESS TERMS ARE MET

Yield of Cigarette Tax Likely to Be $9,000,000

New York City's one-cent tax on each package of cigarettes appeared likely to bring in $9,000,000 a year, three times the estimate of the original yield, when collection figures made public yesterday showed that $1,525,305 had been collected since the tax went into effect on May 1.

City Treasurer Almerindo Portfolio said the city had collected $1,369,224 on the sale of penny stamps, $23,745 on the sale of three-cent stamps, $132,200 from the certification of stamping machines and $135 from various penalties.

The City Council will vote on continuance of this tax, along with others in Mayor La Guardia's program, at its meeting in City Hall tomorrow.

LEHMAN DECLINES TO NAME SENATOR

Says He Will Act on Copeland Vacancy Only If Extra Session Is Called

Special to THE NEW YORK TIMES.

ALBANY, June 22.—Governor Lehman will not appoint a United States Senator to succeed Royal S. Copeland, who died last week, unless President Roosevelt should call a special session of Congress before the vacancy can be filled by election.

The Governor, who yesterday announced his willingness to accept the Democratic nomination for the "short" term of two years which remains of Senator Copeland's six-year term, made this announcement soon after his return to his desk early this evening.

In response to questions by the news correspondents Governor Lehman said he had received a number of messages approving his decision and wishing him well in his venture as a Senate candidate. He said also that he had received no word from President Roosevelt, nor had he an appointment to see the President in the near future.

Mr. Lehman, who, in his capacity as Lieutenant Governor while Mr. Roosevelt was Governor, was looked upon as Mr. Roosevelt's right hand man in the State administration, broke with the President over the latter's proposal to enlarge the Supreme Court.

Denies Talk With Roosevelt

The Governor in reply to questions said he had not discussed with President Roosevelt his proposal to become a Senate candidate. He disclosed his intention to Postmaster General Farley who is State as well as National Democratic chairman, and some other party leaders whom he failed to name.

"What did Mr. Farley say when you told him?" the Governor was asked.

"I am not going to say anything about that; in fact, I have nothing to add to the statement I made yesterday."

"Was former Governor Smith one of the party leaders you told that you were going to run for the Senate?" he was asked.

"No comment," was his reply. Then he added: "I am not going to say with whom I did discuss my plans."

Asked if he had discussed the matter with leaders of the Amer-

Continued on Page Six

ASKS TWO OFFICES

Would Pick Senator and Lieutenant Governor in Coalition

REPUBLICAN TIE POSSIBLE

Copeland Post for Hillman Is Proposed by Critics of the Democratic Slate

By JOHN L. UNDERHILL

Unless the American Labor party is permitted to name its candidates for the rest of the term of the late Royal S. Copeland in the United States Senate and for Lieutenant Governor in coalition with one of the two major parties, the Labor party will go it alone and name its own slate this Fall.

This was decided yesterday, it was learned, by the board of strategy of the Labor party, meeting to consider the political developments brought about by the announced candidacies of Governor Herbert H. Lehman for the Senate and Attorney General John J. Bennett Jr. for the Governorship.

The Labor party leaders, it was said, are far from satisfied with the tentative Democratic slate of Senator Robert F. Wagner and Governor Lehman for the Senate and Mr. Bennett for Governor. It was indicated that the Labor party leaders feel that Sidney Hillman, president of the Amalgamated Clothing Workers of America, is eminently fitted for the short-term Senate nomination.

Republicans Are Interested

There is a possibility, it was indicated, that if the Democrats fail to come to terms with the Labor party the Republican will. Republican leaders, it was learned, have been in close touch with Labor party heads within the last few days. As yet, however, there has been no formal conference.

Should the Labor party fail to win either major party to a coalition ticket it can support—and the party insists that the whole ticket must be acceptable, even if it wins its two places — consideration will be given to the naming of a separate slate. In any event the party leaders insist that party independence must be maintained on a stronger basis than ever.

Just where Mayor La Guardia, who is dissatisfied with the Lehman candidacy, stands in the Labor party situation was not clear. He did not take part in yesterday's conference of the Labor party leaders and they have, it was learned, heard nothing directly as to his plans. Whether they would be willing to name him as their candidate for the Senate to run against the major party nominee, leaders were not prepared to say. In any event, he is not considered to be in the inner circles of the party.

In connection with the revelation of the Labor party stand, it was recalled that Alex Rose, executive secretary of the Laoor party and its official spokesman, announced earlier in the week that the party would insist on representation before a coalition could be effected. The party choices for Lieutenant Governor, it was learned, are Langdon W. Post, former Tenement House Commissioner, and Frederick F. Umhey, executive secretary of the International Ladies Garment Workers Union.

Mayor Defers Comment

Mayor La Guardia, obviously displeased with the tentative Democratic slate, commented cryptically at City Hall that he would have something to say soon.

"The essential need is for persons who will support good, sound, progressive policies in Washington, Albany and New York," the Mayor said. "I will have something to say on the subject within a few days."

David Dubinsky, president of the International Ladies Garment Workers Union, who had been mentioned as a possible Senate choice, withdrew his name from consideration.

"I am not a candidate for any political office," he said. "I do not believe that the American Labor party will or should make blanket commitments for the support of a slate of candidates of any other political party, Democratic or Republican. The American Labor party is in sympathy with the New Deal and is ready to support outspoken New Dealers, but this is a/

Continued on Page Six

"All the News That's Fit to Print."

The New York Times.

LATE CITY EDITION
Fair today, little change in temperatures. Tomorrow partly cloudy and warmer.
Temperatures Yesterday—Max., 56; Min., 47

VOL. LXXXVIII...No. 29,500. Entered as Second-Class Matter, Postoffice, New York, N. Y. NEW YORK, MONDAY, OCTOBER 31, 1938. PP THREE CENTS NEW YORK CITY and Vicinity | FOUR CENTS Elsewhere Except in 7th and 8th Postal Zones.

BOTH PARTIES SEE VICTORY IN FIGHT FOR GOVERNORSHIP

Democrats' Predictions of 865,000 Plurality in the City Viewed as Overoptimistic

REPUBLICAN HOPES GROW

Tremaine and Bennett Face Defeat if Lehman Wins by Only a Small Margin

By JAMES A. HAGERTY

With eight days left before the election, Democratic leaders are confident, probably overconfident, of the re-election of Governor Herbert H. Lehman, and Republican leaders are hopeful, increasingly hopeful, of the election of District Attorney Thomas E. Dewey to the Governorship.

The main interest of the party leaders has been in the contest for the Governorship and no definite estimates have been made of the probable vote for other State-wide candidates.

It is generally admitted that a close vote on the Governorship may result in defeat of Controller Morris S. Tremaine and Attorney General John J. Bennett Jr., who lack the American Labor party endorsement that their running mates on the Democratic State-wide ticket have, and the election of Julius Rothstein and Colonel Arthur V. McDermott, their Republican opponents. Informed Democratic leaders have estimated that Governor Lehman must have about 250,000 plurality to insure the re-election of Messrs. Tremaine and Bennett.

Chances of Poletti

Governor Lehman's re-election by a very small plurality, one not in excess of 100,000, might also result in the defeat of former Supreme Court Justice Charles Poletti, Democratic nominee for Lieutenant Governor, against whom a campaign has been waged by disgruntled Democrats, and the election of State Senator Frederic H. Bontecou, Republican.

There have been few guides to probable results of the contests for United States Senators and Representatives-at-Large. Because of the widespread and favorable publicity that Mr. Dewey has received from his work as a prosecutor, it has been assumed, without definite information to that effect, that he will get a larger vote than the Republican Congressional candidates, although Edward Corsi, candidate for the short Senatorial term, has undoubted strength in New York City, and John Lord O'Brian, candidate for the full Senatorial term, has general strength throughout the State.

Leaders of both major parties agree that it will take a Dewey victory to elect Mr. O'Brian, Mr. Corsi and Mrs. Helen Z. M. Rodgers and Richard B. Scandrett Jr., Republican candidates for Representatives-at-Large, and that Governor Lehman, if re-elected, will carry with him Senator Robert F. Wagner, Representative James M. Mead, candidate for the short Senatorial term, and Mrs. Caroline O'Day and Matthew J. Merritt, Democratic candidates for re-election as Representatives-at-Large.

Farley Estimates the Vote

Postmaster General James A. Farley, Democratic State chairman, bases his expectation of Governor Lehman's re-election on reports from up-State county chairmen that indicate that Mr. Dewey's plurality outside of New York City will be held to 350,000 and reports of the New York City Democratic leaders that Governor Lehman's city plurality will reach 865,000.

William S. Murray, Republican State chairman, has estimated Mr. Dewey's up-State plurality at 600,000. In New York City the local Republican leaders hope to hold Governor Lehman's plurality to 450,000 or even below that figure. The Republicans have been greatly encouraged by polls that show Governor Lehman and Mr. Dewey running neck and neck.

The probability is that Mr. Farley is much too high in his estimate of Governor Lehman's plurality in New York City and Mr. Murray is too high in his estimate of Mr. Dewey's plurality up-State.

In their estimate presented to Mr. Farley, the New York City Democratic county leaders predicted 200,000 plurality for Governor Lehman in Manhattan, 210,000 in the Bronx, 340,000 in Brooklyn, 100,000 in Queens and 15,000 in Richmond. Some of these estimates were regarded as far too high, and a revised Democratic estimate is understood to be as follows:

Manhattan, 150,000; Bronx, 210,000; Brooklyn, 320,000; Queens, 75,000; Richmond, 15,000; total estimated New York City plurality for Lehman, 770,000.

Even these revised estimates seem much too high, particularly in Queens and Manhattan. The Re-

Continued on Page Five

Central American Bloc Likely at Lima Parley

Special Cable to THE NEW YORK TIMES.

SAN SALVADOR, El Salvador, Oct. 30.—A solid Central American bloc at the Pan-American Conference in Lima, Peru, in December was foreshadowed today by the newspaper Diario Nuevo. It declared that "it is very likely that the five Central American delegations will present a solid front in the deliberations and voting."

"On the initiative of our Foreign Office," the newspaper added, "negotiations of such importance have started that their success may be taken for granted. From extra-official sources it is reported that the government of Guatemala is in accord with the plan."

ROOSEVELT LETTER ENDORSES EARLE

President Says He Has Right to Speak in Local Campaigns When Name Is Misused

Special to THE NEW YORK TIMES.

PHILADELPHIA, Oct. 30.—In a letter interpreted as an endorsement of the Democratic candidates in Pennsylvania's State-wide election, President Roosevelt has assailed Republican charges that he had refrained from giving formal support to the party's nominees in this State because he was unwilling "to put his hands in that muddy water."

The letter, addressed to Michael Francis Doyle, Democratic lawyer, under date of Oct. 26 but not made public until today, endorsed the State administration of Governor Earle, the Democratic candidate for United States Senator, as one that had always been eager to help forward a program of social and economic justice.

The President reiterated that he had not been asking voters to support Democrats as against Republicans in State and local contests, but added that he had the right to speak out in cases where his name "had been misused," as in Pennsylvania.

The President's statement was hailed in Democratic circles as evidence of Mr. Roosevelt's full support of Governor Earle for the Senate and of Charles Alvin Jones for Governor. Mr. Jones's name was not mentioned in the letter, but its concluding statement was declared by Democrats to make the President's endorsement of the whole party ticket sufficiently clear.

Criticizes "Reactionaries"

This particular statement read:

"It seems to me that liberals in Pennsylvania, irrespective of party, can scarcely place their trust in the liberalism or desire for social justice of any candidates who are sponsored by such obvious reactionaries as the well-known Messrs. Annenberg, Grundy and Pew. So much for that."

His reference was to Mr. L. Annenberg, publisher of The Philadelphia Inquirer; Joseph N. Pew Jr., oil man, and Joseph R. Grundy, industrialist, all of whom are active in the Republican drive to elect Judge Arthur H. James as Governor and re-elect Senator James J. Davis.

The Roosevelt letter was regarded as the President's answer to repeated pleas made to him by the State Democratic leadership for some action on his part that would serve to convince Pennsylvania voters, who gave him a 600,000 ma-

Continued on Page Eight

MEAD STANDS PAT AS A NEW DEALER IN BID FOR SENATE

Democratic Candidate Opposes Any Except Minor Changes in Labor and Security Laws

UPHOLDS THEORY OF TVA

Wants Budget Balanced, but Not if This Means 'Misery,' He Tells The Times

Text of Representative Mead's reply is printed on Page 6.

From a Staff Correspondent

BUFFALO, N. Y., Oct. 30.—Representatives James M. Mead, Democratic candidate for the short-term Senatorial seat in the election Nov. 8, today answered in a statement the six questions on campaign issues propounded by THE NEW YORK TIMES to the four New York nominees of the two major parties in an editorial Oct. 20.

Mr. Mead's answer, in the main, was a broad and little qualified defense of the New Deal legislation which he, as a member of the House of Representatives, had a part in formulating and passing.

The principles of the Social Security and National Labor Relations Acts he defended stoutly, seeing need only for revisions to extend the benefits of the former, a correction of technical defects and a tightening of administration.

Principal opposition to the Social Security Act he saw inspired by those who fear that it will "become too important a monument to the Democratic party and to men like President Roosevelt and Senator Wagner."

Opposes "Pay-as-You-Go" Policy

He unqualifiedly opposed a revision of the law to make social security payments on a "pay-as-you-go" basis.

"Such policy," he declared, "would destroy the reserve funds which are the protection of the future in so far as future benefits are concerned. The Social Security Act is, in simple language, a form of national insurance designed to provide for the well-being of individuals who meet with economic calamities.

"I will favor strengthening amendments to the law and where weaknesses in its administration may become evident they will be met with remedial legislative action which will likewise command my support. I agree with Senator Wagner that we will never return to the way of the poormaster and to the pauper's home."

The principle of the Labor Relations Act, he said, is one that "must be recognized in a democracy such as ours" and as a union man—he was formerly a railroad worker—he unqualifiedly endorsed that, denying that the law was in any way partisan.

"I wish to make it clear, however," he continued, "that I am not blanketing under complete approval every technical phase of the law. It is new. It can almost be termed to be in its experimental stage. It requires the continued concern and legislative assistance of Congress. My eyes are open to the helpful suggestions of business and of labor in the perfection of this legislation."

The main attacks on the measure,

Continued on Page Six

Radio Listeners in Panic, Taking War Drama as Fact

Many Flee Homes to Escape 'Gas Raid From Mars'—Phone Calls Swamp Police at Broadcast of Wells Fantasy

A wave of mass hysteria seized thousands of radio listeners throughout the nation between 8:15 and 9:30 o'clock last night when a broadcast of a dramatization of H. G. Wells's fantasy, "The War of the Worlds," led thousands to believe that an interplanetary conflict had started with invading Martians spreading wide death and destruction in New Jersey and New York.

The broadcast, which disrupted households, interrupted religious services, created traffic jams and clogged communications systems, was made by Orson Welles, who as the radio character, "The Shadow," used to give "the creeps" to countless child listeners. This time at least a score of adults required medical treatment for shock and hysteria.

In Newark, in a single block at Heddon Terrace and Hawthorne Avenue, more than twenty families rushed out of their houses with wet handkerchiefs and towels over their faces to flee from what they believed was to be a gas raid. Some began moving household furniture.

Throughout New York families left their homes, some to flee to near-by parks. Thousands of persons called the police, newspapers and radio stations here and in other cities of the United States and Canada seeking advice on protective measures against the raids.

The program was produced by Mr. Welles and the Mercury Theatre on the Air over station WABC and the Columbia Broadcasting System's coast-to-coast network, from 8 to 9 o'clock.

The radio play, as presented, was to simulate a regular radio program with a "break-in" for the material of the play. The radio listeners, apparently, missed or did not listen to the introduction, which was: "The Columbia Broadcasting System and its affiliated stations present Orson Welles and the Mercury Theatre on the Air in 'The War of the Worlds' by H. G. Wells."

They also failed to associate the program with the newspaper listing of the program, announced as "Today: 8:00-9:00—Play: H. G. Wells's 'War of the Worlds'—WABC." They ignored three additional announcements made during the broadcast emphasizing its fictional nature.

Mr. Welles opened the program with a description of the series of

Continued on Page Four

B. C. VLADECK DIES; CITY COUNCILMAN

American Labor Party Chief Here Was Manager of The Jewish Daily Forward

B. Charney Vladeck, American Labor party member of the City Council and general manager of The Jewish Daily Forward, died at Mount Sinai Hospital last night at 8:15. He was 52 years old.

Mr. Vladeck was stricken in his office of The Forward Friday night. Dr. I. W. Held of 2 East Ninety-fifth Street diagnosed his illness as coronary thrombosis and ordered him taken to the hospital that night.

Mr. Vladeck is survived by his widow, Mrs. Clara Richman Vladeck, and three children, May, William and Seymour Vladeck. His home was at 2 Horatio Street, Greenwich Village.

Fled From Russia

Soft-spoken, gray-haired and scholarly, Baruch Charney Vladeck looked neither like one who had been through the Russian revolution nor like one who would aspire to the rough-and-tumble atmosphere of New York City politics. Yet he had spent time in Czarist prisons for his revolutionary utterances and he was a member of the old Board of Aldermen years before he became leader of the labor caucus in the new City Council.

Born in the poverty-stricken town of Dookorah, Minsk, Russia, Mr. Vladeck early became identified with revolutionary groups. Radicalism was in the air then, he said many years later, and he "joined the movement as casually as a boy on the West Side might join the Democratic party—the alternatives for us were to emigrate or fight."

Mr. Vladeck's parents were Wolf and Broche Horowitz Charney and Charney was his family name. But in Russia Vladeck was as popular a name as John is here and he was called that by his early revolutionary associates. They feared that reference to his real name might be overheard by a police spy and his family might suffer.

His only formal education was that which he received at Yeshivah, where his devout Jewish parents sent him. When he was 18 years old he was caught by the police recommending "liberal books" to school children and he was sent to prison.

Barely Escaped Siberia

Mr. Vladeck's first prison term lasted eight months, but he was seized again in 1905, and this time narrowly escaped being sent to Siberia. He was saved only by the amnesties granted in that year of revolt. His father died when he was a young boy and his mother struggled hard to provide for her six children. But young Vladeck was in the midst of poverty—because of that poverty—and was hounded by the Czar's police. They pierced through all his pseudonyms. Jailed again, he participated in a hunger strike until released.

In 1908, feeling he was approaching a dead end, he left Russia and landed at Ellis Island. He spent his first days in this country studying the provisions of the United States Constitution and learning American history.

In Russia Mr. Vladeck had achieved considerable reputation as

Continued on Page Fifteen

DALADIER PREPARES TO RULE SEVERELY

Calls Cabinet Meeting to Talk Over Decrees to Promote Recovery in Industry

By P. J. PHILIP

Wireless to THE NEW YORK TIMES.

PARIS, Oct. 30.—With his own Radical Socialist party solidly behind him and with the Communists definitely shaken from his ranks, Premier Edouard Daladier returned to Paris this morning. He will attempt to complete the preparation of what promises to be a long and severe series of decrees for the restoration of industry and national finance.

One of the reassuring features of the situation is that since the crisis of last month the treasury has been able to meet all demands without difficulty. There has been a steady recovery in the purchase of national bonds and there has been little or no need to use the exchange stabilization fund to defend the franc.

Just what will be contained in the decree laws is being kept a close secret. The Cabinet has been called to meet at 5 o'clock tomorrow evening for its first formal discussion of the situation.

The decrees will receive final approval at a full Ministerial Council presided over by President Albert Lebrun later in the week. Both of these meetings will be, in a sense, formal, for the work of preparing the decrees has been carefully done during the past month by Premier Daladier himself in close concert with a selected few of his Ministers.

Especially concerned are Paul Marchandeau, Minister of Finance; Raymond Patenotre, Minister of National Economy; Paul Reynaud, Minister of Justice, and Georges Bonnet, Foreign Minister. The last two are also financial experts.

To Follow Marseille Plans

There is little doubt that what will be proposed will follow the plans that were outlined by the Premier and Minister of Commerce Fernand Gentin in speeches at Marseille. These will deal principally with the restoration of production and commerce. It is France's 18,000,000,000-franc adverse trade balance that is considered a primary weakness and also one that can be most easily remedied.

There are certain to be distinguishable traces of that "steered economy" at which M. Gentin hinted in Marseille. There will also certainly be provisions for the extension of the forty-hour-week with reduced rates for overtime. It is probable that there will be some amendment to the five-day-week schedule since this, even in key industries, results in idleness at great plants for many more hours than they produce.

M. Daladier's argument is that it will be slow work to reduce the burden of national charges, which he set at 102,000,000,000 francs for the next year. The only way to make this burden seem lighter is to increase the national income from its present low figure of 220,000,000,000.

Of that 102,000,000,000, which the Treasury will have to pay out, only about 65,000,000,000 will be recovered by ordinary taxation. The rest must be raised by other means. To increase the present taxation rates would be, it is argued, to put a new handicap on business and fur-

Continued on Page Two

La Guardia in Detroit Tells Labor to Unite Or Lose by a Fly Ball Between Green, Lewis

Special to THE NEW YORK TIMES.

DETROIT, Oct. 30.—If the fly ball of anti-labor falls between Center Fielder William Green and Right fielder John L. Lewis, then the ball game of progressivism is lost by a home run, Mayor La Guardia of New York told a cheering audience of 6,000 at a rally this afternoon.

The Mayor's imaginary world series was presented, complete with gestures, before a stageful of Democratic and Labor leaders, including Homer Martin, president of the United Automobile Workers of America, and Frank X. Martel, president of the Detroit and Wayne County Federation of Labor.

"Franklin D. Roosevelt is the pitcher and Frank Murphy, Governor of Michigan, is catcher," said Mr. La Guardia. "George Norris is at third base, La Follette at second, and I'm shortstop; Bill Green's in center and John Lewis is right field.

"Anti-labor comes to bat and Frank signals for a fast one. The pitcher shakes his head. Then he lets one go, and anti-labor knocks a fly right between Green and Lewis. Both of them shout, 'It's mine!' The ball falls between them, and anti-labor wins."

"Let's start right now healing the breaks in the ranks of labor," the Mayor urged, "so we can all start cooperating with the heads of government. I'm proud to be at a meeting where Homer Martin and Frank Martel sit side by side.

"I hope the example set by the working people of Detroit today in coming out here to endorse the cause of good government will be followed throughout the country.

"I see the dawn of peace in the labor movement right here. We should have a united front in the ranks and I think there could be no better place to begin than in Detroit right now. Labor must have government and industry must have stability, but industry cannot expect to have stability until the needs of its workers are satisfied.

"Frank Murphy and New York's Senator Wagner are real friends of labor. They will help bring peace in the family."

Attention was drawn to the presence of C. I. O. and A. F. of L. leaders together by Mr. Martel as one to the speakers.

"Homer Martin and I have been putting on this Damon and Pythias act in several places," he said. "We hope we can get through the camouflage this way without getting orders from our home offices reminding us that we're supposed to be enemies."

OUSTED JEWS FIND REFUGE IN POLAND AFTER BORDER STAY

Exiles Go to Relatives' Homes or to Camps Maintained by Distribution Committee

REVEAL CRUELTY OF TRIP

Others Sent Back to Germany Pending Parleys on Issue by the Two Governments

Wireless to THE NEW YORK TIMES.

WARSAW, Poland, Oct. 30.—The evacuation from frontier areas of thousands of Polish Jews—8,000 according to official reports and 12,000 according to an estimate by the Jewish Relief Committee—deported from Germany began today after they had been massed at frontier stations up and down the border for twenty-six hours. Their terrible ordeal is nearing its end.

Polish authorities have permitted officials of the Joint Distribution Committee to send the victims to relatives' homes in Poland or to special camps the committee maintains. The refugees spent a sleepless night in barracks, crowded station buildings or empty freight cars; many spent the night in the open in the no man's land between the frontiers.

The Joint Distribution Committee supplied food and will also pay specially reduced railway fares into the interior.

It is believed that the evacuation will last another day or so. Many refugees desire to remain in the frontier area pending the outcome of the Warsaw-Berlin negotiations, which may result in the repeal of the deportation order, enabling them to return to their homes in Germany.

Suffering Is Described

Reports from various points along the frontier describe the terrible suffering. The worst situation existed at the Zbaszym frontier station on the Paris-Berlin-Warsaw-Moscow line. There nearly 3,000 men, women and children arrived yesterday morning and were ordered by the Polish authorities to remain within sight of the station building. A large group—estimated at 1,000—was unloaded by the Germans in the open on the border between German Neu-Bentschen and Zbeszym and was not admitted into Poland until this morning. There were many children without parents in this group. They were taken from schools in Berlin and driven directly to the frontier.

Eight Polish Red Cross doctors are attending the refugees at Zbaszym. All Jewish physicians in the frontier areas have been mobilized to care for many of the sick and aged. Four deaths have been reported.

From Radzionka, near Beuthen, a birth was reported in a refugee camp. Deportees taken there by road were left in the open fields. Three hours passed before a telephone could be found to ask medical assistance for the mother.

In Chojnice, near Danzig, 1,500 arrived yesterday, most of them from Berlin. A long German train suddenly pulled into the Polish station and its German locomotive ran off before Polish authorities had time to inspect the train. The refugees were forbidden to leave the station so they remained inside a small building with many in the open until the evacuation began at noon today.

A group of fifteen children from

Continued on Page Three

Panama Limits Doctors To Citizens of Country

Special Cable to THE NEW YORK TIMES.

PANAMA, Oct. 30.—The nationalistic attitude of the National Assembly is indicated by the recent enactment of a law that prohibits the licensing of physicians and surgeons unless they are citizens of Panama.

The professions of oculist, dentist and pharmacist are also limited to citizens. Foreigners engaged in these professions at the time of the passage of the law are permitted to continue.

COL. FRANCO, FLIER, IS KILLED IN CRASH

Brother of Spanish Insurgent Chief Is Victim of a Storm Mishap Near Palma Base

By The Associated Press.

BURGOS, Spain, Oct. 30.—Lieut. Col. Ramon Franco, brother of the Insurgent Generalissimo, Francisco Franco, and former air attaché at the Spanish Embassy in Washington, was killed Friday in an airplane off Palma, Majorca, an Insurgent airplane base.

A statement issued here at Insurgent headquarters said:

"Lieut. Col. Franco left Majorca piloting a seaplane, with another plane following his. Soon after leaving the base a heavy storm arose and the second plane was obliged to return to its base.

"The bodies of Ramon Franco and three other occupants of the plane were found nine miles northwest of Cape Formentor and were conveyed to Palma, where they are lying in state in the Town Hall.

"The body of one occupant is missing. The watch of one of the officers had stopped at 5 minutes past 6, Oct. 28.

"Lieut. Col. Franco was chief of the Majorca base, which he organized."

Was Spain's Leading Aviator

Colonel Franco's fame was divided between rebellious political activities and heroic airplane flights that made him Spain's leading aviator.

He had a leading part in the revolution that resulted in the overthrow of the Spanish monarchy in 1931.

In January, 1926, he became the first to span the South Atlantic by air, flying from Cadiz, Spain, to Buenos Aires, Argentina.

Another chapter of his career in the air was his attempted flight from Spain to the United States in 1929. His plane was forced down in the vicinity of the Azores and it drifted helplessly with him for a week before he was rescued.

Colonel Franco's political theories were based on the assumption that Spain was not in need of a king as a ruler. He believed that almost any kind of capable government, except that of a monarchy, would be acceptable to the Spanish people. After the outbreak of the present war in Spain he decided that a strong dictatorship would solve the problems of the country.

In 1926, during the dictatorship of Miguel Primo de Rivera, he was thrown into jail for working against the regime. He was jailed again in 1930, this time for "breach of discipline," but he escaped to lead the famous Cuatro Vientos airdrome revolt of 500 aviation officers and enlisted men.

Under his leadership airplanes circled Madrid for two hours, raining handbills proclaiming that a successful republican movement had taken place. The field guns of the

Continued on Page Four

Japan Denies Right of Others to Interfere In 'Sacred War' to Create New East Asia

Wireless to THE NEW YORK TIMES.

TOKYO, Monday, Oct. 31.—An apparently inspired press campaign, which is becoming more violent as it proceeds, is pressing on the Japanese people the idea that Japan is now in a position to pursue her policy in East Asia independently of all other powers. Britain and France are particularly mentioned and they are bitterly attacked in editorials.

It is also asserted that even the United States is no longer in a position to suggest what Japan's conduct should be in this sphere.

The comment has given every indication of a spirit of jingoism running wild. The press, including Domei, the more than semi-official news agency, is becoming tenacious in its assertion that Japan's "sacred war" entitles the empire "to make full headway for the reconstruction of a new East Asia."

Domei asserts that the chief question before the country is how to minimize the frictions with foreign powers which will be a consequence of such a policy.

"It is believed," says the news agency, "that the United States and Britain henceforth will approach the imperial government oftener and more tenaciously than is generally supposed in connection with the Open Door in China."

It adds that Hachiro Arita, who has been made Foreign Minister, is expected to make these nations understand "the real intentions of Japan."

[The new press campaign has followed the revelation by the State Department in Washington that the United States early this month delivered a note to Japan demanding observance of the Open Door and cessation of attacks on American rights in China. The note was not published in Tokyo but its nature became known and indication was given that Japan, in a reply to be delivered soon, would insist that a new situation had been created in the Far East.]

Coincidentally with this campaign it is generally accepted here that all clauses of the national mobilization bill will soon be invoked and implemented, which would give the government powers closely resembling those of the regimes in Berlin, Rome and Moscow. It is understood the bill will probably be utilized for the forcible colonization of Manchukuo by young Japanese.

RAIL PAY PROBLEM UP TO ROOSEVELT AT PARLEY TODAY

Head of Carrier Executives and Leader of Labor Group to Meet President

HIS WORD TO GUIDE ACTION

Eastman Urges Enactment of I. C. C. Plan—Billion-Dollar Loan Talk Discredited

Special to THE NEW YORK TIMES.

WASHINGTON, Oct. 30.—President Roosevelt will meet tomorrow at the White House with George M. Harrison, head of the Railway Labor Executives Association, and John J. Pelley, president of the Association of American Railroads, in an effort to avert a general strike of the nation's 900,000 railroad employes.

The President's emergency fact-finding board recommended yesterday that the railroads withdraw their demand for a 15 per cent wage reduction and, unless railroad management complies with the board's suggestion or some compromise is reached, the strike will follow in thirty days.

Mr. Pelley said this afternoon that there had been no meeting of railroad executives over the week-end and he had not been in consultation with his colleagues on a program to meet the board's demands.

The carriers' conference committee, headed by H. A. Enochs, which planned the railroads' case before the fact-finding board, will meet tomorrow morning.

Situation Coming to a Head

It is expected that railroad management will not act officially until after Mr. Pelley learns what the President has in mind. After his conference at the White House, it is likely that Mr. Pelley will confer with railroad executives. By that time the Enochs committee may have some recommendations of its own.

The prospect for a strike was regarded here as the most serious since 1916, when President Wilson averted what might have been a general strike by obtaining passage of the Adamson Eight-Hour Law.

It seemed to be the view of Federal transportation experts that the report of the fact-finding board had put the railroad situation right back where it was last Spring when the urgent financial needs of the carriers commanded the attention of the President and of Congress but produced no action.

Blocking of Legislation

It was recalled that the President appointed a special committee of three members of the Interstate Commerce Commission to draft an emergency plan for the railroads, and that when the committee had made its recommendations the President asked Congress to act.

But, instead of recommending a concrete railroad program to Congress, Mr. Roosevelt sent the legislators not only the plan of the I. C. C. commissioners but also a group of other recommendations.

Although the President failed to make specific recommendations, Congress seemed well on the way to adopting the plans for immediate relief proposed by the three commissioners when the railroads announced their intention of asking labor to accept a 15 per cent wage reduction. This announcement resulted in blocking remedial legislation.

Joseph B. Eastman, I. C. C. Commissioner, former Federal Coordinator of Transportation and a member of the President's railroad committee last Spring, said today he believed that one of the most important things to be done regarding the transportation problem would be to carry out the committee's proposal for creation of a Federal Transportation Authority for two years to eliminate waste and aid railroad consolidation and coordination.

Liberal Loan Policy

While Congress failed to adopt the committee's recommendations for immediate action, which consisted, in the main, of extending further government credit to the railroads, both the Reconstruction Finance Corporation and the I. C. C., since last Spring, have followed as lenient a railroad lending policy as the law permits.

The committee's recommendation that during the emergency period the RFC be empowered to make railroad loans without I. C. C. certification that the borrower did not require judicial reorganization was not acted upon by Congress.

Nevertheless the I. C. C. approved a number of such loans without the concurrence of Commissioner Charles D. Mahaffie, who said in several such cases that he believed the railroads in question required reorganization.

Indicating the extent to which the I. C. C. has cooperated to facilitate financing of railroad equip-

Continued on Page Sixteen

"All the News That's Fit to Print."

The New York Times.

LATE CITY EDITION
Fair, slightly warmer today. Tomorrow cloudy, warmer, probably rain. Sunday much colder.
Temperatures Yesterday—Max., 60; Min., 42

VOL. LXXXVIII...No. 29,511. Entered as Second-Class Matter, Postoffice, New York, N. Y. NEW YORK, FRIDAY, NOVEMBER 11, 1938. P THREE CENTS NEW YORK CITY and Vicinity | FOUR CENTS Elsewhere Except in 7th and 8th Postal Zones.

GAIN OF 81 BY G. O. P. LEAVES HOUSE FATE TO 48 DEMOCRATS

They Can Block Any Roosevelt Measures if Minority Stands Firm in a Coalition

VAN NUYS FINALLY WINS

Contest Possible in Indiana—Gillette, Democrat, Victor on Total Iowa Count

By The Associated Press.

Republican party chieftains, flushed by their party's victories at the polls, expressed confidence last night that by combining with Democrats critical of many Roosevelt policies they could block President Roosevelt if he insisted on following a "leftward" course.

Returns from Tuesday's election showed 81 Republican votes added to that party's roster in the House and 8 in the Senate. The House figure was based on the assumption that the last contest remaining in doubt was won by the incumbent, Representative Knute Hill, Democrat, of the Fourth district in the State of Washington. With several precincts and absentee ballots still not tabulated, Mr. Hill was ahead by 630 votes.

In the Indiana Senatorial race, which was so close that it was decided only yesterday afternoon, Senator Frederick Van Nuys, Democrat, finally defeated Raymond E. Willis, Republican. In Iowa, scene of another nip-and-tuck contest, Senator Guy M. Gillette, Democrat, was the apparent winner over former Senator Lester J. Dickinson, Republican.

How the Two Parties Line Up

On this basis the Republican party held 170 seats in the House out of a total membership of 435 and 23 seats in the Senate out of a total of 96. Thus a coalition of 48 anti-New Deal Democrats with the Republican membership of the House would give such forces a majority. On some past issues many more than 48 Democrats have deserted the Administration. In the Senate the Republicans would have to pick up 26 Democratic votes to assume command.

In the light of this situation, Washington's most popular game was to speculate on what would happen when Congress meets again. To most minds the alternatives were some measure of capitulation to conservative opinion on the part of the President or two years of governmental deadlock.

A Republican member of Congress said that if the President should insist upon following an unchanged course he would be beaten badly in Congress. At the same time, should the Republicans seek to undo major New Deal legislation already enacted, the possibility of a Presidential veto, with the consequent necessity of mustering a two-thirds majority against Mr. Roosevelt in both houses, was regarded as hanging over the conservative forces.

Thus, many observers thought that the result depended upon Mr. Roosevelt's interpretation of what the election meant and his decision as to what course he would follow. According to such opinion he could seek compromise and cooperation or lay down the gauntlet and battle it out for the two years leading up to the 1940 Presidential election.

Van Nuys Ahead by 6,535

Special to The New York Times.

INDIANAPOLIS, Nov. 10.—Senator Frederick Van Nuys, Democrat, held a 6,535 vote lead tonight over his Republican opponent, Raymond E. Willis, on the final returns. The vote stood: Van Nuys, 784,155; Willis, 777,620.

Republicans were watching closely what they called an "unwarranted delay" in counting of the ballots in Terre Haute. Some possibility existed that should Mr. Van Nuys be certified as elected, the Republicans would start a contest.

Should the evidence warrant, Republicans may allege that many votes were cast illegally in Terre Haute, that legal votes were improperly counted, and that an unsuccessful challenge of 5,000 registrations should have been sustained.

Mr. Willis and Senator Van Nuys ran a see-saw race in early returns and then the Republican jumped into a 7,000 vote lead. More than half this margin was sliced abruptly by the count from forty-six of the ninety-three precincts in Vigo County (Terre Haute). Additional Terre Haute returns placed Senator Van Nuys 3,000 votes ahead, and his vote continued upward with each new report. Terre Haute citizens balloted by voting machines.

Republicans were elated over their substantial gains in the Indiana House delegation. In 1936 the lone Republican Representative Indiana sent to Washington was Charles Halleck of Rensselaer. On Tuesday the Republicans elected seven

Continued on Page Nineteen

Ickes Says Roosevelt Won in Vote; Wallace Calls It a New Deal Defeat

Former Asserts Third-Term 'Draft' May Be Necessary—AAA Head Hits Expression as Improper for a Cabinet Member

Special to The New York Times.

WASHINGTON, Nov. 10.—Secretaries Ickes and Wallace discussed the election with the press today but while they started from similar premises they arrived at different conclusions.

Mr. Ickes held that the results were an endorsement of President Roosevelt's policies, and said that the President would have been reelected if he had been running.

Mr. Wallace accepted the results as a defeat for the New Deal and said that the outcome, displacement of Northeastern Democrats by Republicans in Congress, "would be a hard blow to agriculture."

Both agreed that depression had a good deal to do with the result, Mr. Ickes asserting that what the country had seen was "a reaching out for security," while Mr. Wallace said that the "outstanding conclusion is that people do not like business depression."

They diverged again, however, on the question of a third term for Mr. Roosevelt. Mr. Ickes said that inasmuch as the President was "the liberal leader in the country" he had long thought it might be necessary to "draft" him for a third term.

Informed of this expression, Mr. Wallace, who is believed to have presidential aspirations himself, replied:

"I think it is altogether outside the province of any Cabinet member to express an opinion on that subject."

Elaborating his "victory" views, Mr. Ickes said that "the sentiment of the people of this country is a liberal sentiment and when it has a chance to express itself, the answer will be clear and unmistakable.

"Look at New York, for example. A candidate for Governor was endorsed by the estimable New York Times because he wasn't a rubber stamp, and because he helped save our glorious institutions. And what happened? He just squeaked through and the liberals ran far ahead of him.

"This election means to me that people are interested in individual security. How many Republicans were elected on the strength of promises of support of old-age pensions, even of the Townsend plan? When people become impatient promises are made, and some successful candidates have made promises they can't deliver on."

The Secretary said the Progressive party defeat in Wisconsin was due to a division of the liberal vote in that State. Of Pennsylvania he remarked cryptically:

"They wound up the clock on primary day and it went off on the minute."

Mr. Wallace said that the people

Continued on Page Twenty

LEHMAN RENEWS FULL-TERM PLEDGE

Hopes for Cooperation by the Republicans—Budget Work Already Started

Governor Lehman, in his first general press conference since his re-election on Tuesday, reiterated yesterday his pledge to serve out his full four-year term. The Governor, at the end of that time, will have been in Albany fourteen years, four as Lieutenant Governor under Franklin D. Roosevelt, and ten as Governor.

The question of his serving a full four years which came up immediately after his reluctant acceptance of the nomination at the Rochester Democratic State Convention, was answered by him in his first campaign address, and the new pledge came yesterday in response to a question from newspaper men.

When the question was asked, the Governor, sitting back in an arm chair, smiled, and said,

"Of course I will, there is simply no question about it."

Hopes for Cooperation

Asked if he had any comment on the Republican control of both branches of the Legislature, the Governor said:

"I hope they will cooperate with me as much as possible, and expect that they will."

Later, he was asked if he had any reason for expecting cooperation, beyond the fact that the Republican-controlled Assembly, under Speaker Oswald D. Heck and Ways and Means Chairman Abbot Low Moffat had done so at the last session. The Governor answered:

"They know that whatever legislation I will suggest will be in the interest of the people and I can not conceive that they are going to oppose sound and progressive legislation."

In response to questions as to whether extensive legislative changes would be required as a result of the approval of six of the nine constitutional convention proposals at the polls, the Governor said that he believed most of the changes would be administrative in nature, such as the changes in the budget-making procedure called for in the finance article, incorporated in the omnibus proposal.

Will Suggest Legislation

Asked whether he regarded the task ahead as chiefly administrative or requiring extensive reform legislation, the Governor said:

"I regard it as requiring careful administration. I will have a legislative program to suggest and I will continue to scrutinize all bills passed by the Legislature to make sure that none of them is against the interests of the State."

He reminded his listeners that not the least important part of his tasks in Albany had been the vetoing of some 2,000 of the 7,000 bills that had been presented to him during his tenure thus far.

Asked about the election of Charles Poletti, his personal selection, as Lieutenant Governor, Mr. Lehman said that he was sure that Mr. Poletti "is going to be a great help to me and to the people of the State."

The Governor's only comment on

Continued on Page Twenty-one

BIDS INDUSTRY 'GO' IN PENNSYLVANIA

Judge James Says His Election Was Signal for Forward Movement in Business

Special to The New York Times.

PHILADELPHIA, Nov. 10.—Judge Arthur H. James, Republican Governor-elect, urged Pennsylvania industry today to start its program of rehabilitation "right now" and not wait until he took office.

"The people gave the go-ahead signal at Tuesday's election," he said. "Those industries which had threatened to leave the State if the Democratic organization elected its candidates can unpack their trunks and stay at home."

Judge James came here to confer with James F. Torrance, Republican State chairman, and started tonight for a vacation in Texas with Colonel Carl L. Estes, a newspaper publisher in that State.

In an interview, the Governor-elect, who during the campaign accused Governor Earle's "little New Deal" administration of driving industry from Pennsylvania by levying high taxes on corporations, repeated his charges and defined his own attitude toward industry.

Reports Signs of Upturn

"Although it will be regulated," he asserted, "industry must be given a little more than a breathing spell. It must be given an opportunity to be restored to its feet. We still have the potential possibilities and resources that the State always had and with an eye to the problems of the people, instead of an eye for votes, we can bring Pennsylvania back to its place as a leader in industry."

Judge James asserted that he had had "definite evidence" that confidence was returning to industry.

"Right here in Philadelphia," he added, "I have been advised by a building concern that it plans to build 300 homes at an expenditure of $1,500,000, of which 70 per cent will represent weekly payrolls."

He said that during his vacation he would not consider Cabinet appointments, but would "eat, sleep and rest and do a little fishing and hunting in between."

The plurality by which he defeated Charles A. Jones, Democratic nominee for Governor, was almost 290,000, with the count virtually complete. The plurality of Senator James J. Davis, who won re-election over Governor Earle in the Republican sweep of Pennsylvania, was just short of 400,000.

With the Republicans assured of control of the State House of Representatives by a comfortable margin, interest continued to center on the manoeuvring which is to determine whether Judge James will have support of the State Senate, as well as to put over his legislative program early next year.

Should Senator Weldon B. Heyburn of Delaware County, an Independent Republican holdover elected in 1936 on the Democratic ticket, enter the caucus of Republicans instead of Democrats on the eve of the 1939 legislative session, a deadlock would result over the election of a president pro tem of the State Senate.

If Senator Heyburn stays with the Democrats during the next

Continued on Page Nineteen

ATATURK DIES AT 58; TURKS WILL ELECT A SUCCESSOR TODAY

National Assembly Expected to Name Gen. Inonu, Former Premier, as President

NATION GOES IN MOURNING

Peaceful Transition to New Era Seen—Unity Is Stressed Under Ideal of Founder

Wireless to The New York Times.

ISTANBUL, Turkey, Nov. 10.—Kemal Ataturk, President and creator of modern Turkey, died today at Dolma Baghche Palace at the age of 58. He had survived thirteen wounds received in battle and a number of assassination attempts, but succumbed to cirrhosis of the liver.

It is expected that General Ismet Inonu, former Premier and President Ataturk's comrade-in-arms, will be chosen tomorrow morning by the Republican People's party to succeed the dictator-soldier, hero of the reborn nation.

The bulletin announcing the death of Ataturk and signed by eight doctors read:

"The President's general condition, the gravity of which was announced in a bulletin published last night, grew steadily worse. On Nov. 10, 1938, at 9:05 A. M., our great chief, in a deep coma, breathed his last."

Three minutes after his death Salih Bozuk, former aide and one of the President's closest friends, unsuccessfully attempted suicide by shooting. He was seriously wounded.

Premier Stays at Bedside

Throughout the night Ali Fethi Okyar, Ambassador to London; Ataturk's sister and his adopted daughter, Sabihi Gueukschehn Honoum, the latter a famous airwoman, remained near the bedside. The first indication of the President's death came at 11:30 A. M., when it was noticed that the flags on government buildings were at half-staff. Soon the flags of ships in the harbor were at half-mast, and gradually all shops and houses exhibited similar signs of mourning.

Later, however, the authorities requested the withdrawal of flags except those on government buildings. Although the flags were at half staff the appearance of so much color gave the impression that Istanbul was en fete. All places of public entertainment were closed and no intoxicants will be sold in Turkey until further notice.

The government's communiqué issued this morning states:

"By Ataturk's death Turkey has lost her great creator, a nation its great Chief and humanity a great son. We offer our people deepest condolences in their great loss. Our only consolation in our affliction is our attachment to his great work and our service to our dear country. We declare that before all things his immortal work is the Turkish Republic.

"Your government is at its post at this grave time through which we are passing. The great Turkish nation will, without doubt, work as one body with the government to preserve order.

"In accordance with the Consti-

Continued on Page Eighteen

Pearl Buck Wins Nobel Literature Prize; Third American to Get the Swedish Award

Wireless to The New York Times.

STOCKHOLM, Sweden, Nov. 10.—The Swedish Academy today awarded the 1938 Nobel prize for literature to Pearl Buck, American, author of "The Good Earth" and other novels about China.

The Academy of Science awarded the Nobel prize for physics to Professor Enrico Fermi of Rome University "for his discovery of new elementary radioactive substances produced by irradiation of neutrons" and for other research on reactions created by neutrons.

Thanks to his discovery of the great explosive power of slow neutrons, Professor Fermi and his associates have been able to produce radio-activity in most elements, including the heaviest ones. Professor Fermi, who is 37 years old, is the discoverer of chemical element 93. Educated at Pisa, Goettingen and Leyden Universities, he was at one time Professor of Physics at the University of Florence.

A member of the Italian Academy since 1929, he is a corresponding member of the Turin and Leningrad academies of science.

The Nobel chemistry prize will probably be reserved until 1939.

Pearl Buck, in private life Mrs. Richard J. Walsh, said yesterday morning, one hour after learning of her triumph, that she was taken aback with the totally unexpected honor. Speaking in the office of her publisher, John Day Company, 40 East Forty-ninth Street, she recalled her first words as follows:

"I said, 'That's ridiculous,' and I suppose a great many others will say the same thing. Did Chinese expressions of gratitude come to mind? Certainly, I thought—though probably not aloud: 'O pu sing sin' (I don't believe it), but 'kung shi-kung shi' (congratulations)."

The author of "The Good Earth" and ten other books, numerous short stories and articles since 1930 was grateful that the Nobel Prize for literature was based on the sum of a writer's work rather than any single product. In a broadcast to Sweden yesterday at noon she defined one successful book as a sign of growth and was hopeful that her development would continue.

Theodore Dreiser merited the honor, the author said over the air, continuing:

"I don't know him and he doesn't know me, but I feel diffident in accepting the award just the same."

She told of having visited Stockholm on a pleasure trip in 1932 and said she would try to be there on Dec. 10 to accept the medal, scroll and check from the hands of King Gustaf. The money will amount to between $40,000 and $50,000, it was learned.

Mrs. Buck, as she prefers to be known publicly, was dressed in a

Continued on Page Five

BRITAIN WILL SPEND HUGE SUM TO PUSH AIR ARMING PLANS

£200,000,000 Will Go to Build Up Force Next Year—5,000 to 6,000 Planes Ordered

EDEN ASKS BIG REFORMS

Plea for Reorganization of National Life Is Viewed as a Bid for Power

By FERDINAND KUHN Jr.

Special Cable to The New York Times.

LONDON, Nov. 10.—The British Government will spend £200,000,000 on its Air Force in the next financial year, Air Minister Sir Kingsley Wood told the House of Commons today. This will be a 75 per cent increase over the budget estimate of £120,000,000 for the present financial year, which ends next March 31.

The new figure does not include a vast additional expenditure upon civilian defenses and anti-aircraft equipment, which the government has already promised without revealing the amount of money needed.

Sir Kingsley also announced that Britain's first-line air strength would be increased by 30 per cent over the present program, which provides for 2,750 first-line planes for home defense, 500 for defense of the empire and an unspecified number of reserves by March, 1940. Without giving away the secret of the reserve strength, Sir Kingsley told the House that fighting planes "now on order or to be ordered" number between five and six thousand.

Intensity Is Indicated

This was at least some indication of the intensity of the British rearmament program six weeks after Prime Minister Neville Chamberlain predicted "peace in our time" as a result of the Munich agreement.

Employment in aircraft factories, said Sir Kingsley, has jumped 15 per cent in two months and many factories are now working double shifts. He surprised the House by disclosing that 3,500 concerns were engaged on sub-contracting work for aircraft production at the present time.

The output of planes in October, he said, was 50 per cent above that in May and by next May would be three times the figure of last Spring. But he did not give a hint as to how British production or British strength at the moment compared with Germany's. Instead, he disclaimed any intention of a race with Germany, and he did not mention Earl Baldwin's famous pledge of an air force equal to that of the strongest power within striking distance of these shores.

"The more I study the matter the more difficulty I find in exactly defining or measuring parity," said Sir Kingsley.

"We cannot just take the number of aircraft one country possesses and compare it with the number in any other country. Each country has its own necessities in reference to its own particular position and responsibilities."

This was oddly like the argument used in German newspapers recently in attempting to justify a continuance of Germany's present enormous superiority over Britain in the

Continued on Page Eleven

NAZIS SMASH, LOOT AND BURN JEWISH SHOPS AND TEMPLES UNTIL GOEBBELS CALLS HALT

All Vienna's Synagogues Attacked; Fires and Bombs Wreck 18 of 21

Jews Are Beaten, Furniture and Goods Flung From Homes and Shops — 15,000 Are Jailed During Day—20 Are Suicides

Wireless to The New York Times.

VIENNA, Nov. 10.—In a surge of revenge for the murder of a German diplomat in Paris by a young Polish Jew, all Vienna's twenty-one synagogues were attacked today and eighteen were wholly or partly destroyed by fires and bomb explosions.

Anti-Jewish activities under the direction of Storm Troopers and Nazi party members in uniform began early this morning. In the earlier stages Jews were attacked and beaten. Many Jews awaiting admittance to the British Consulate-General were arrested, and according to reliable reports others who stood in line before the United States Consulate were severely beaten and also arrested.

Apartments were raided and searched and gradually some 15,000 arrested Jews were assembled at police stations. Some were released during the day. Tonight arrests were continuing.

Many of those arrested were sent to prisons or concentration camps in buses. Mobs of raiders penetrated Jewish residences and shops, flinging furniture and merchandise from the windows and destroying wantonly.

In their panic and misery about fifty Jews, men and women, were reported to have attempted suicide; about twenty succeeded.

Scores of bombs were placed in synagogues, blowing out windows and in many cases damaging walls. Floors that had been soaked with kerosene readily caught fire.

Fire brigades were summoned to fight fires in eighteen synagogues, and the fire engines remained in their neighborhood all day. Two of the synagogues were not being used for religious purposes.

Those wholly or partly destroyed were the synagogues in Schiffamtsgasse, Steingasse, Muellnergasse, Neue Welt-Gasse, Tempelgasse, Franz Hochedlinger-Gasse, Stumpergasse, Unter Viadukt-Gasse, Huber-Gasse, Schmalzhofgasse, Siebenbrunnengasse, Kluckegasse, Turnergasse, Neudeggergasse, Palnamitengasse, Schmelzgasse, Schopenhauerstrasse and Humboldtplatz.

At 9 A. M. the first fires broke out in the Hernalser and Hietzinger synagogues. The Hietzinger synagogue, which was in Moorish style and was the largest and finest synagogue in Vienna, was gutted.

At 11:30 A. M. several explosions took place in the Second District, and a number of synagogues were

Continued on Page Two

BATISTA SEES HULL AND TOURS CAPITAL

Tells Press Cuba Will Soon Adopt a Constitution and Elect a President

Special to The New York Times.

WASHINGTON, Nov. 10.—Cuba will shortly proceed with the adoption of a permanent Constitution and the election of a constitutional President "in accordance with the principles of a free people," Colonel Fulgencio Batista, Chief of Staff of the Cuban Army and the leading figure in his country, said here today.

He arrived this morning on a visit to General Malin Craig, Chief of Staff of the United States Army. *It is his first visit to this country.*

Colonel Batista's statement came in response to a question at the only press interview he gave today. He said that a constitutional convention would be elected as soon as possible, probably next May. He added that the elections might be held on May 20, Cuban independence Day.

Calls on Hull and Woodring

He paid courtesy calls on Secretary of State Cordell Hull, Secretary of War Harry H. Woodring and Assistant Secretary of War Louis Johnson and devoted the remainder of his day to sight-seeing under the guidance of Dr. Pedro Martinez Fraga, the Cuban Ambassador. Colonel Batista and Señora de Batista are staying at their embassy while they are here.

The Cuban Chief of Staff and former sergeant at Camp Columbia was in an affable and apparently pleased frame of mind today. From the time he arrived at the Union Station at noon through the rest of a tiring day he preserved a friendly and cordial demeanor toward all he saw.

Asked as to the object of his visit here, he said that it was purely a ceremonial visit in response to the invitation of General Craig. However, he said that he would be glad to discuss with interested American officials any problems the solution of which would help the two countries. He made it clear that he had not as yet been asked to take part in any such discussions. By implication, he included among the subjects he would be willing to discuss the American sugar tariff, extension of the existing trade agreement, and arrangements for mutual defense in time of threat from abroad.

General Craig met his guest at the station, and had arranged a fitting military display for him. He was accompanied by Colonel John A. Crane, head of the military attaché and foreign liaison branch of Military Intelligence, and Major Carnes Lee. Sumner Welles, Under-Secretary of State, George T. Summerlin, chief of protocol, and Ellis

Continued on Page Six

ITALY INTENSIFIES CURBS UPON JEWS

Cabinet Decrees Exclude Them From Official Employment, Limit Property Holdings

By ARNALDO CORTESI

Wireless to The New York Times.

ROME, Nov. 10.—The Italian Cabinet met again today under Premier Benito Mussolini's chairmanship and approved two important decrees in which the principles that the Fascist Grand Council laid down Oct. 6 for maintaining the "purity of the Italian race" are codified and promulgated in the form of organic laws.

These decrees closely follow the Grand Council's decisions of last month except that in a number of details they tend to increase the severity of the measures taken against the Jews.

The main points of difference between the decrees and the Grand Council's decisions are:

First, in the definition of a Jew it is added that he is a Jew who has a Jewish mother and an unknown father.

Second, Jews are required to announce that they belong to the "Jewish race" and all personal certificates and papers must mention the fact.

Third, to the disabilities to which Jews are subjected the following are added: They may not be guardians of "Aryan" minors or deficient persons; they may not own or manage industries or interests connected with the national defense, and they may not own land valued at more than 5,000 lire or houses whose taxable value exceeds 20,000 lire, whereas the Grand Council said that they were not to own more than 125 acres of land and made no mention whatever of houses.

Jews who have children not professing the Jewish religion may be deprived of the guardianship of their children if they give them instruction not attuned to the religious principles of the children or to "national ends."

Can't Employ "Aryan" Servants

Fourth, no Jew will be allowed to employ Italian "Aryans" as servants.

Fifth, the Council did not explicitly say that no Jews would be allowed to remain in the employ of the State and State organizations, though it was implicit in the declaration that no Jew could be a member of the Fascist party. The decrees, however, remove all uncertainty on this point, listing the careers closed to Jews.

Henceforth Jews will be excluded from the civil and military adminstrations of the State, the Fascist party and all the organizations connected with it, provincial and municipal administrations and all dependent organizations, all semi-

Continued on Page Two

BANDS ROVE CITIES

Thousands Arrested for 'Protection' as Gangs Avenge Paris Death

EXPULSIONS ARE IN VIEW

Plunderers Trail Wreckers in Berlin—Police Stand Idle —Two Deaths Reported

By OTTO D. TOLISCHUS

Wireless to The New York Times.

BERLIN, Nov. 10.—A wave of destruction, looting and incendiarism unparalleled in Germany since the Thirty Years War and in Europe generally since the Bolshevist revolution, swept over Great Germany today as National Socialist cohorts took vengeance on Jewish shops, offices and synagogues for the murder by a young Polish Jew of Ernst vom Rath, third secretary of the German Embassy in Paris.

Beginning systematically in the early morning hours in almost every town and city in the country, the wrecking, looting and burning continued all day. Huge but mostly silent crowds looked on and the police confined themselves to regulating traffic and making wholesale arrests of Jews "for their own protection."

All day the main shopping districts as well as the side streets of Berlin and innumerable other places resounded to the shattering of shop windows falling to the pavement, the dull thuds of furniture and fittings being pounded to pieces and the clamor of fire brigades rushing to burning shops and synagogues. Although shop fires were quickly extinguished, synagogue fires were merely kept from spreading to adjoining buildings.

Two Deaths Reported

As far as could be ascertained the violence was mainly confined to property. Although individuals were beaten, reports so far tell of the death of only two persons—a Jew in Polzin, Pomerania, and another in Bunzdorf.

In extent, intensity and total damage, however, the day's outbreaks exceeded even those of the 1918 revolution and by nightfall there was scarcely a Jewish shop, cafe, office or synagogue in the country that was not either wrecked, burned severely or damaged.

Thereupon Propaganda Minister Joseph Goebbels issued the following proclamation:

"The justified and understandable anger of the German people over the cowardly Jewish murder of a German diplomat in Paris found extensive expression during last night. In numerous cities and towns of the Reich retaliatory action has been undertaken against Jewish buildings and businesses.

"Now a strict request is issued to the entire population to cease immediately all further demonstrations and actions against Jewry, no matter what kind. A final answer to the Jewish assassination in Paris will be given to Jewry by way of legislation and ordinance."

What this legal action is going to be remains to be seen. It is known, however, that measures for the extensive expulsion of foreign Jews are already being prepared in the Interior Ministry, and some towns, like Munich, have ordered all Jews to leave within forty-eight hours. All Jewish organizational, cultural and publishing activity has been suspended. It is assumed that the Jews, who have now lost most of their possessions and livelihood, will either be thrown into the streets or put into ghettos and concentration camps, or impressed into labor brigades and put to work for the Third Reich, as the children of Israel were once before for the Pharaohs.

Thousands Are Arrested

In any case, all day in Berlin, as throughout the country, thousands of Jews, mostly men, were being taken from their homes and arrested—in particular prominent Jewish leaders, who in some cases, it is understood, were told they were being held as hostages for the good behavior of Jewry outside Germany.

In Breslau they were hunted out even in the homes of non-Jews where they might have been hiding.

Foreign embassies in Berlin and consulates throughout the country were besieged by frantic telephone calls and by persons, particularly weeping women and children, begging help that could not be given them. Incidentally, in Breslau the United States Consulate had to shut

Continued on Page Four

"All the News That's Fit to Print."

The New York Times.

LATE CITY EDITION
Generally fair and continued cool today. Tomorrow fair, slowly rising temperatures.
Temperatures Yesterday—Max., 60; Min., 45

VOL. LXXXVIII...No. 29,682. Entered as Second-Class Matter, Postoffice, New York, N. Y. NEW YORK, MONDAY, MAY 1, 1939. PP THREE CENTS NEW YORK CITY and Vicinity | FOUR CENTS Elsewhere Except in 7th and 8th Postal Zones.

PRESIDENT OPENS FAIR AS A SYMBOL OF PEACE; VAST SPECTACLE OF COLOR AND WORLD PROGRESS THRILLS ENTHUSIASTIC CROWDS ON THE FIRST DAY

POLES CONSIDERING COUNTER DEMANDS IN REPLY TO HITLER

Military Circles Say Claim on Danzig Should Be Dropped Before Further Parleys

BALTIC OUTLET STRESSED

Reich Specification of Width of Right of Way in Corridor Said to Be 15.5 Miles

In Warsaw there were indications yesterday that the Polish reply to Germany might call for a dropping of the Nazi demands regarding Danzig and the replacing of the League of Nations link to the Free City by a new Polish one. It was also reported that Chancellor Hitler in a detailed demand had asked a fifteen-and-a-half-mile motor road right-of-way across Pomorze. [Page 1.]

Both Paris and London seemed to be hopeful that a Polish-German compromise on Danzig could be reached. Reports from the two capitals indicated a disinclination to be forced to fight on this issue. [Page 12.]

The question of peace or war, however, was considered by Nazi spokesmen to have been put up to the democracies and their partners. [Page 13.]

With the arrival of the German Army commander in Rome it was believed new pressure was being put on Italy by Germany for a full-fledged military alliance. But it was significant that according to all reports the Brenner Pass between the two countries was being fortified on both sides. [Page 11.]

Poles to Use Hitler Tactics

By JERZY SZAPIRO

Wireless to THE NEW YORK TIMES.

WARSAW, Poland, April 30.—The German memorandum delivered to the Polish Foreign Office on Friday while Chancellor Adolf Hitler was attacking Poland will be answered in the same manner. A Polish memorandum, repudiating the German accusation and rejecting Danzig's incorporation into Germany and a highway across Pomorze [the Polish Corridor], but leaving the door open for further negotiations, will be delivered at the Berlin Foreign Office while Foreign Minister Josef Beck and Premier Felicien Slawoj-Skladkowski are addressing the Sejm [Parliament], probably on Friday.

[It was reported in Poland that Chancellor Hitler had demanded a German motor road right of way across Pomorze 15.5 miles wide, The Associated Press stated.]

Certain influential military circles hold that Warsaw should not enter into new negotiations with the Nazis unless the Germans withdraw their demands regarding Danzig. This view is expressed in the military journal, Polska Zbrojna, which published one of the strongest criticisms of Herr Hitler's speech and of German policy generally.

"Danzig is at the mouth of a great Polish river," it says, "and we cannot give it up. The Polonization of Danzig is notable; wherefore, why should the Germans show so much interest in what to them is but one of their provincial towns?"

Poland to Make Demands

The Gazeta Polska, official organ of the Polish Government, tomorrow will publish a noteworthy statement concerning the position of Danzig.

"Germany," it will say, "has shown her regard for international engagements by her recent occupation of Memel, by her denunciation of solemn treaties. She has demonstrated quite clearly that German policy aims at separating Poland from her outlet on the Baltic Sea, the importance of which to Poland needs no emphasis.

"The policy of Berlin thus creates a situation that forces Poland to go further in her demands concerning the status of Danzig than she did formerly when concluding with Germany the pact of 1934.'"

Although it is not explicitly stated, there is reason to believe that Poland's demands will include the transference of the functions of the League Commissioner to the Polish Government.

Will Close Exchanges

The Polish official answer to the German memorandum, it is believed, will close German-Polish exchanges for the time being. The Poles expect to delay the negotiations until there is a general clarification of the European situation.

No chances are being taken, however. All the military precautions ordered last month are still in force and the army is strengthened by

Continued on Page Twelve

Rider Will Ask Pensions For Congress Members

By The Associated Press.

WASHINGTON, April 30.—A quiet campaign to give pensions to members of Congress has materialized into a legislative proposal.

Chairman Ramspeck of the House Civil Service Committee said today that he intended to add provisions for the pensions to a bill making amendments to the Civil Service Law which has just been passed by the Senate.

Under the proposal, the government and the members would bear about equal shares of the cost. Five per cent of the salary of each member would be deducted monthly and would go toward the purchase of an annuity to be added to the amount to be paid by the government.

Civil service workers receive pensions which increase with length of service. They contribute 3½ per cent of their salaries.

Mr. Ramspeck reported that almost every member he had talked to favored the pension idea.

"They're getting security-minded," he added, laughing.

PARI-MUTUEL VOTE AGAIN UP IN STATE

Republicans Plan Assembly Test on Betting System—Democratic Split Reported

Special to THE NEW YORK TIMES.

ALBANY, April 30.—The question of pari-mutuel betting on horse-racing is returning to plague the 1939 session of the Legislature.

Pressure from pari-mutuel advocates has resulted in a decision on the part of Republican leaders to put the matter to a vote on the Assembly floor. If the proposed constitutional amendment should be passed by both Houses this year, it would be submitted to the people for approval in the Fall, as the 1938 Legislature approved the system.

Despite considerable support on the Republican side, there is no guarantee that the pari-mutuel proposal will pass in either House. The Democrats, who have blown hot and cold on the measure for years, are again reported to be divided on the subject.

In one recent year the proposed amendment was passed by the Senate, and when it came up a second time, as is required by the Constitution, its original sponsor voted against it. Last year John J. Dunnigan, the Democratic leader of the Senate, pushed the proposal through the Upper House, and it gained approval in the Republican controlled Assembly as well.

Senate Sponsor Now Lacking

With the intervening elections, the Republicans gained control of the Senate as well and Senator Dunnigan has made no move to introduce the proposal in the Senate. In fact, it has yet to have an official sponsor there. However, John D. Bennett and Norman F. Penny, Nassau County Republican Assemblymen, have introduced in the Assembly resolutions identical with the Dunnigan resolution of the year before, and passage this year by both Houses would constitute the required second action by the Legislature, even if the sponsors are not the same.

In the Assembly the practice of the Republican leadership, under Speaker Heck, is to refuse to throttle in committee any bill of the type of the pari-mutuel proposal, because of rumors always circulated about bookmakers' lobbies. Putting the bill out for a vote leaves it up to the individual membership. The Republicans will seek passage of the measure in the Assembly, but its final fate would appear to rest on the number of Democratic votes it can command.

Whether the matter will be brought to a vote this week, or the following week, was not disclosed today.

Sales Tax Vote Awaited

Tomorrow night the Legislature is expected to adopt the rest of the budget bills, and either then, or the next day, adopt the tax program which will be used to finance the Republican budget. The new taxes on this program are the increase in the liquor tax, effective on May 1, and the two-cent-per-package cigarette tax, effective on July 1.

Later in the week the sales tax probably will come up for a vote, with its eventual fate still depending on the support the Republicans can muster for it in the Senate, where they control by a margin of only two votes. The political aspects of the battle over the budget itself appear to make it unlikely that the Republican sales tax idea can gain any Democratic votes on the Senate side.

Local bills have been cleaned up to a large extent in both houses, and after the enactment of the tax bills, the settling of the sales tax problem, the revision of the unemployment insurance law, and the enactment of a housing measure, the Legislature will be in a position to quit and go home, to await a possible special-session call.

CONGRESS FACING SEVEN BIG ISSUES AS TIME SHORTENS

None Is on Week's Calendars, But All Except Taxes Are in Legislative Process

WAY CLEARED FOR ACTION

Routine Money Bills Passed, Reporting of Vital Measures to Floor Is Expected

By LUTHER A. HUSTON

Special to THE NEW YORK TIMES.

WASHINGTON, April 30.—Congress has been in session nearly four months and has disposed of only two of the major controversial items on its calendar. At least seven important issues remain to be settled in the two months that remain of the session if present plans are followed and a late Summer sitting is avoided by adjournment around July 1.

None of the major measures is on the calendar of either chamber for this week. The most progress that can be expected is that one or more of these measures may come from committees to the floor of the House or Senate.

The two issues that have been settled are the limited authorization for the President to reorganize executive agencies and the expansion of national defense, for which necessary appropriation bills have been passed. The decks also have been cleared of considerable of the routine, most of the important departmental appropriation bills having been disposed of.

Major Questions Outstanding

The following matters remain to be dealt with:

Amendments to the Social Security Act, the National Labor Relations Act and the Wages and Hours Law.

Revision or extension of existing neutrality laws.

The amount of the appropriation and the method of disbursement for relief during the 1940 fiscal year.

A farm program including the highly controversial question of export and domestic subsidies on farm products.

Legislation to repeal, modify or continue in effect certain provisions of the tax laws that are estimated to yield an annual revenue of around $2,000,000,000 even if general tax revision is not attempted.

Except for tax proposals, all of these measures are in the legislative mill. On some of them committee hearings are in progress; on others committee action has ended.

There is a possibility that proposed amendments to the Wages and Hours Law may come up in the House tomorrow. Representative Mary Norton, chairman of the Labor Committee, has indicated that she will try to bring up under suspension of the rules the proposals which her committe has approved. If this is not done, the proposals must lie over at least a week.

To Hear Green on C. I. O. Charges

On Capitol Hill tomorrow, however, interest probably will center in the hearing by the Senate Education and Labor Committee on proposed amendments to the National Labor Relations Act, where William Green, president of the American Federation of Labor, will be the witness.

Mr. Green is expected to reply to

Continued on Page Twenty-four

Times Sq. May Be Closed To Autos During Fair

Times Square may be turned over as a playground for World's Fair visitors if their numbers become great enough to warrant special police arrangements in the theatrical area.

Police Commissioner Valentine said yesterday that the Fair crowds may approximate the number of American Legion members who came to New York for their national convention in September, 1937. If that should develop, Mr. Valentine said, it would be advisable to turn over Times Square to the city's guests.

Automobile traffic would be routed north and south on either side of the Square, as it was during the Legion convention. For the last two weeks heavy police details have handled the crowds in Times Square, directing pedestrians to the right to obtain the maximum amount of order.

RUSSIAN AVIATORS, RESCUED, ARRIVE

Two Who Crashed in Canada Here in American Plane—One Fainted During Flight

Brig. Gen. Vladimir Kokkinaki and Major Mikhail Gordienko, the two Soviet airmen who crashed Friday night in a swamp off the coast of New Brunswick were landed in a rescue plane last night at Floyd Bennett Field at 10:31 o'clock.

The two men were brought to New York in the plane of Commodore Harold Vanderbilt, which was chartered by Soviet and American officials for the rescue work, which took more than thirty hours.

They and the rescue party, which left here Friday night after word of the crash of the Moscow-New York non-stop flight came through from Miscou Point, N. B., were "ferried" to the end of the scheduled flight in an American airplane.

Their own craft, in which they sped toward New York from Moscow in 23 hours and 40 minutes, still lay in the frozen morass where Major Gordienko squashed it in an emergency landing. He landed it because General Kokkinaki had fainted at an altitude of more than 27,000 feet, it was learned yesterday when the party first brought the two men as far south as Moncton, N. B.

In recounting last night the events which led up to the forced landing at the field General Kokkinaki said the main difficulty of flying in the substratosphere was at 27,000 feet, where his compass liquids froze and his radio reception was so poor that he could not tune in the directional beams. He offered this explanation as a reason why the ship apparently lost its course, having been reported in the same area for nearly four and a half hours prior to its final landing.

In the plane were the two Russian aces; Russell Thaw, pilot, and his co-pilot, John Revely; V. P. Butosov, Dr. Louis S. Spector and Peter Baranov, all of the Am-

Continued on Page Twenty-four

Hague Ignores Own Plea for Patriotic Rally; Skips Americanization Fete for Ball Game

Special to THE NEW YORK TIMES.

JERSEY CITY, N. J., April 30.—Mayor Frank Hague, who issued a proclamation yesterday calling on residents of Jersey City to "show your Americanism" by attending the city's tenth annual celebration today of Americanization Day, did not appear at that event this afternoon. Instead he attended the double-header baseball game between the Jersey City and Toronto teams of the International League at Roosevelt Stadium.

"As Mayor of Jersey City, I earnestly and respectfully invite all the people of our city to participate actively in the Americanization Day exercises, Sunday, April 30, 2 P. M., at Pershing Field," declared the Mayor's signed proclamation, published yesterday in newspaper advertisements.

"Show your Americanism by parading or being present Sunday afternoon. It is my request that the American flag be displayed on all homes and buildings Sunday. Every citizen should remove his hat as the colors pass by."

The proclamation listed Mayor Frank Hague among the speakers at Pershing Field, from which representative Jerry O'Connell, Montana Democrat and foe of the Jersey City Mayor, was whisked away by police several months ago when he attempted to speak there.

A crowd estimated at 4,000 persons assembled in the field today and 10,000 others marched there. During the parade and speechmaking, however, the Mayor was one of 29,362 baseball fans who did not take part in the Americanization celebration. He occupied a box at the baseball stadium with his nephew and private secretary, former Judge Frank Hague Eggers.

The Jersey City team won both games.

Commissioner Arthur Potterton, who spoke at Pershing Field, declared that "Jersey City takes the lead to show the world that nothing un-American will creep into our lives in this part of the State." Referring to other parts of the State and the nation, he said that "we have given them the courage they did not possess."

Representative Edward J. Hart, Democrat, was another speaker. Governor A. Harry Moore was present, but did not speak.

The Americanization Day celebration is sponsored by Captain Clinton Fisk Post, Veterans of Foreign Wars.

ROOSEVELT SPEAKS

He Sees Nations of This Hemisphere United in Desire for Peace

U. S. DEMOCRACY STRONG

Exposition Here and in West Born of Singleness of the American Ideal, He Says

By FELIX BELAIR JR.

In his first public utterance since Chancellor Hitler's virtual rejection of his plan to assure the peace of Europe for another ten years, President Roosevelt served notice on the world yesterday that the nations of the Western Hemisphere were "united in a desire to encourage peace and good-will among all nations" and voiced their hope that time would break down the barriers to tranquillity on the Continent.

In a brief address dedicating the New York's World's Fair to the cause of international amity and declaring it "open to all mankind," the President said that the American wagon was hitched to the star of peace, and asked that the months ahead "may carry us forward in the rays of that hope."

Avoids Any Direct Reference

For those who had expected a more direct reference by President Roosevelt to the state of affairs in Europe or something that might be interpreted as a reply to the German Chancellor's all but complete throwdown of his peace guarantee proposal there was disappointment, for his attitude regarding that had to be inferred from what he said of the traditional aspirations of the American republics.

Of recent years American historians would write that "sectionalism and regional jealousies diminished and that the people of every part of your land acquired a national solidarity of economic and social thought such as had never been seen before," the President said.

He added that "wise tolerance" almost as much as the American form of government had made possible this unity of sentiment in a nation made up of so many different creeds and national derivations. The President recalled that democratic government had endured unchanged in this country longer than in any other country on the globe at any period of history, a circumstance he attributed to the wisdom of the framers of the Constitution.

He Sees Aim Accomplished

"That this has been accomplished," the President added a little later, "has been due first to our own form of government itself and, secondly, to a spirit of wise tolerance which, with few exceptions, has been the rule.

"We in the United States, and, indeed, in all the Americas, remember that our population stems from many races and kindreds and tongues. Often, I think, we Americans offer up the silent prayer that on the continent of Europe, from which the American hemisphere was principally colonized, the years to come will break down many barriers to intercourse between nations—barriers which may be historic, but which so greatly, through the centuries, have led to strife and hindered friendship and normal intercourse."

From the distant reaches of the Court of Peace, at the head of which he spoke in front of the Federal Building, the President's voice came echoing back. The spectators sat motionless on folding chairs down the long concourse ending with the Trylon and Perisphere as Mr. Roosevelt slowly spoke the principal address of the day.

Not until the completion of his remarks, which carried for at least half a mile through the amplifiers arranged for the occasion, was there a suggestion of applause. The President deliberately had phrased his speech so as not to play upon the emotions and he received none of the clapping that punctuated a preceding address by Mayor La Guardia until he finished what he had to say.

The throng that came to hear him was apparently too much absorbed in his remarks to give any outward demonstration of approval until he was done. But cheering and applause was as spontaneous as it was general when Mr. Roosevelt stepped from the microphones after his concluding pronunciation:

"I hereby dedicate the New York

Continued on Page Four

Crowds Awed by Fair's Vastness And Medley of Sound and Color

Opening Day Has Everything, Including All Kinds of Weather—Spirit of Gayety Wanes When Pelting Rain Menaces Finery

The Fair had everything for its opening yesterday, including all kinds of weather. Early trains rolled to the Flushing Meadows under skies clear and blue, flooded with rich sunlight, carrying thousands come to look upon the miracle wrought by Grover Whalen's armies in the last three years.

Silk-hatted dignitaries, sailors on shore leave, men and women of all ages, dressed for fair weather and a great holiday. They came in hordes down the railroad and subway ramps, forty and fifty abreast, to gaze upon the wonders, to buy guide books from the shouting peddlers and to scramble for the observation cars.

Wealthier fairgoers climbed into motor-driven and man-powered chairs for their first tour of the grounds. Hundreds of thousands preferred to make it on foot, all a little bewildered and puzzled by the tremendous sweep of grounds, by the dazzling color, almost blinding in the bright sun. Guides, ushers, policemen and policewomen were breathless the first hour trying to keep up with the flood of questions.

Men and women, rank amateurs at reading maps, assembled in the walks or took over the benches, to puzzle out the direction of the various exhibits. Thousands were misled by the dazzling sun into thinking that the destinations they had marked off were close at hand. In most cases they learned that this was an illusion. The strong light had something of the effect of a mirage.

Above the grounds, despite notice that aircraft were to be kept from the Fair zone until the President's address, silver ships careened and darted, like gilded gnats. Two lazy blimps, reflecting the sun from their sides, came over the reviewing stand and crossed to the outer borders of the Fair. The crowds craned their necks to watch this activity in the sky, and drivers of observation cars kept sounding their musical horns to warn them to safer spots.

Everywhere, far as the eye could see, men in blue, gray, green and yellow uniforms assembled in military formations and headed toward the parade ground in the Court of Peace. Bugle notes, brassy and thin, sounded and echoed from all corners of the field. Drums rolled and fifes piped sharp marching tunes. The non-military visitors were in a dither, racing from one group to another.

Groups representing the foreign nations caught the eye as they

Continued on Page Two

CITY AND THE FLEET TAKE TURN AS HOST

1,000 Officers and Men Under Admiral Johnson Help Open Fair—Ships Draw Crowds

By HANSON W. BALDWIN

The city played host to the navy yesterday and the navy played host to the city.

It was—all things considered—an even exchange. Some 1,000 officers and men of the thirty-five visiting men-of-war, led by Rear Admiral Alfred W. Johnson, commanding the Atlantic Squadron, took part in the opening ceremonies for the World's Fair, and thousands of others rolled along Broadway and throughout the five boroughs with that walk peculiar to sailors home from the sea.

But the boats that brought the parties ashore took crowds of visitors back to the ships, while other thousands climbed the gangways of ships berthed at piers and stared with absorbing interest at turrets, the burnished muzzles of guns, the ranks of planes aboard the aircraft carrier Ranger, the ominous black hulls of the submarines and the torpedo tubes of the destroyers.

It was the visiting squadron's second day—and first Sunday—in port, and the public took full advantage of it. The men-of-war were a rival attraction, and a stellar one, to the World's Fair, and the crush of visitors was more than the navy could handle.

Estimates of Throng Vary

The crowd estimates varied widely. The police said 23,000 got aboard, while the navy thought 56,000 had crowded onto the battleships, cruisers, destroyers, submarines and auxiliaries in the few hours of the afternoon that the ships received the public. Perhaps 10,000 to 15,000 others were turned away—some of them after several hours in line—when ships' officers and the beach guard said the men-of-war were unable to accommodate any more visitors.

The visiting hours were supposed to have been from 1 to 5 P. M., but at the Ninety-sixth Street landing no more visitors were permitted to leave shore after 3:25 P. M. Naval officials explained that it took some time to clear the ships of visitors, especially when the vessels were lying out in the stream and all visitors had to be transported by small boats.

They explained that it was necessary at times to allow no visitors to leave the shore landing places later than 4 P. M. There was, however, despite the navy's announcement that all ships would be open daily from 1 to 5 P. M., considerable variation on individual ships.

The Ranger, aircraft carrier berthed alongside a pier at Canal

Continued on Page Ten

LIGHT AUTO TRAFFIC SURPRISE TO POLICE

Elaborate System to Cope With Expected Snarls on Roads Goes Unused

Although Police Department traffic experts were ready for the worst, streams of automobiles flowed evenly along principal Queens highways yesterday and not a single accident involving a serious injury was reported.

An elaborate system for emergency communications, worked out to cope with expected road snarls, went unused as 3,300 patrolmen, 523 of the traffic division, and 300 detectives—a total of 4,123—worked overtime to assure a safe and orderly opening to the World's Fair.

By 11 P. M. most of the motorists had either gone home or were on their way there and reports to police centers indicated there was no more congestion than there had been on the way out.

The only mishap on the record—spoiling what otherwise would have been a virtually incredible perfect mark—occurred at 1:10 P. M. just outside the Fair Grounds, at Lawrence and Sanford Avenues.

Louis Hoffman, 70 years old, of 1,266 Spofford Avenue, the Bronx, suffered lacerations of the left leg when struck by a car that the police said was driven by Louis Anzelone of 37-41 108th Street, Corona. Mr. Hoffman went home after treatment by an interne from Flushing Hospital. The driver was not held.

Policeman Is Injured

A patrolman was hurt inside the grounds a little later, when a crush developed outside the French Building. There were seven children lost, a man had an epileptic fit, and fifty peddlers were arrested for operating on the ramp leading from the combined I. R. T.-B. M. T. subway terminal, but otherwise, the first day was as safe as a lawn party.

A false fire alarm was turned in at the box in the R. C. A. building shortly before the opening parade, while the walks near the theme center were cluttered with people. Fire Chief Thomas F. Dougherty said it was "malicious."

Patrolman Bartholomew Nicastro, 35 years old, of 113-02 175th Street, St. Albans, was the man injured. The accident occurred at about 2 P. M. when the resurgent crowd he was trying to keep back threw him against a wooden "horse," which had been used in construction work. He was treated for a cut right leg by one of the Fair surgeons under Dr. Joseph Peter Hoguet, and remained on duty. In general, the Fair's six first aid stations had a dull day.

A checkup by the Fair police at 10 P. M. indicated that the stations,

Continued on Page Four

NATIONS IN PARADE

Mayor and the Governor Voice Welcome to the 'World of Tomorrow'

WEATHER REDUCES THRONG

Attendance Reported Above 600,000—Centers of Religion and Freedom Dedicated

By RUSSELL B. PORTER

The biggest international exposition in history was officially opened at 3:12 o'clock yesterday afternoon when President Roosevelt formally dedicated the New York World's Fair 1939 in an address before a gathering of 60,000 persons in the open-air Court of Peace.

Governor Lehman, Mayor La Guardia, Sir Louis Beale, British Commissioner General to the Fair and spokesman for the nearly sixty foreign nations that have exhibits, and Grover A. Whalen, president of the Fair Corporation, also made speeches at the opening ceremonies. They joined the President in emphasizing the message of peaceful progress that the Fair brings to mankind in an era when the whole world is troubled by war and threats of war.

When the President officially declared the Fair open he brought to a climax ceremonies that included a parade of 20,000 uniformed soldiers, sailors and marines, foreign groups in picturesque native costumes from nearly all the countries of Europe, Asia and the Americas, and the workmen who built the Fair, in their overalls and white caps.

Starting at the Trylon and Perisphere, the Theme Center of the Fair, the parade passed down Constitution Mall to the Court of Peace with flags waving, bands playing and spectators applauding until it ended with a colorful pageant in the Court of Peace.

Spectacle Impresses Visitors

Although the official exercises were the important part of the day from a formal viewpoint, actually the Fair itself made the greatest impression upon the visitors, judging from their comments as they strolled through the 1,216-acre Fair Grounds and as they journeyed homeward last night.

What they saw was a spectacle of surprising beauty and magnificence, especially last night when the whole Fair and the heavens above it were bathed in soft, glowing colors with the most modern lighting effects, and when fireworks combined with flame, water and color displays on the Lagoon of Nations, the pools in Constitution Mall and the surface of Fountain Lake.

In the daytime also the Fair is a beautiful sight, with the whole scene dominated by the 700-foot Trylon and the 200-foot Perisphere, from which radiates a rainbow of many-colored buildings of modernistic, functional architecture, some bizarre in shape and hue, others strikingly handsome and impressive in their suggestion of strength and use.

Green trees, shrubbery and lawns, playing fountains, shady benches and restful spots on all sides make a garden spot of this artificial city within a city which has been constructed within the past three and one-half years on what was formerly the ash dumps of the Flushing Meadows, and will be a great city park after the Fair is over.

See "World of Tomorrow"

In the huge crystal ball of the Perisphere, visitors peered to see what "the World of Tomorrow" would be like, finding it to be a conception of more and more progress in democracy and in the advance of science, industry, commerce, transportation, communication, the arts and the professions to bring peace and happiness to mankind. They found the same ideas expressed in the streamlined, futuristic dimensions of the buildings, statues, murals, dioramas, landscapes and exhibits of the Fair as a whole.

Like the worlds of yesterday and today, and also like the City of New York, which has the reputation of never being finished but of always changing, the "World of Tomorrow" has a great deal of unfinished business before it. The heart of the Fair, the half-mile stretch between the Theme Center and the Court of Peace where the official ceremonies were held, was virtually complete yesterday, but many other sections,

Continued on Page Three

1939

The World at War

1945

FRONT PAGE NEWS 1939-1945

The New York Times.

GERMANY AND RUSSIA SIGN 10-YEAR NON-AGGRESSION PACT; BIND EACH OTHER NOT TO AID OPPONENTS IN WAR ACTS; HITLER REBUFFS LONDON; BRITAIN AND FRANCE MOBILIZE

Stalin-Hitler Non-Aggression Pact

AUGUST 24, 1939

The treaty, signed in Moscow by the German foreign minister, Joachim von Ribbentrop, and the Soviet foreign minister, Vyacheslav Molotov, was an ominous prelude to war amid Nazi salutes and heel-clicking. Premier Joseph Stalin, perhaps bargaining for time before Germany attacked Russia, already had sent most of the Red Army high command to firing squads on bizarre charges of being spies for the Nazis. The pact was a deafening shock to a world that had stood by as Hitler re-armed Germany and bellowed about conquering Europe—a world that had never expected Nazis and Communists to be allies but irreconcilable enemies. Equally traumatic, especially for Communist parties abroad, was Stalin's cynicism in matching Hitler's aggression by signing secret articles for Poland to be partitioned by the two dictators.

The New York Times.

GERMAN ARMY ATTACKS POLAND; CITIES BOMBED, PORT BLOCKADED; DANZIG IS ACCEPTED INTO REICH

Germany Invades Poland

SEPTEMBER 1, 1939

"From now on, bomb will be met by bomb," Hitler declared as Germany launched its blitzkrieg against Poland after weeks of pressuring Warsaw to hand over territory. The invasion was the beginning of World War II: Britain and France immediately declared war on Germany. In less than a month, German tanks and infantry attacking from the west had overrun the Polish cavalry; German bombers had largely destroyed Poland's highways and railroads; Krakow, Danzig and Warsaw had fallen. And, as per their week-old agreement, Germany and Russia divided up the victim, with Soviet forces invading across Poland's eastern borders.

The New York Times.

NAZIS INVADE HOLLAND, BELGIUM, LUXEMBOURG BY LAND AND AIR; DIKES OPENED; ALLIES RUSH AID

Nazis Invade the Low Countries

MAY 10, 1940

Hitler invaded neutral Belgium, the Netherlands and Luxembourg and pushed through the Ardennes forest in northeastern France, outflanking the supposedly invulnerable Maginot Line (and ignoring advance intelligence). "The fight beginning today decides the fate of the German nation for the next thousand years," Hitler declared. The Dutch opened the dikes, but German paratroopers waded in anyway. Britain and France rushed troops to Belgium, but could not stop the onslaught. Soon German tanks rumbled into France, and before long paraded down des Champs-Élysées.

The New York Times.

JAPAN WARS ON U.S. AND BRITAIN; MAKES SUDDEN ATTACK ON HAWAII; HEAVY FIGHTING AT SEA REPORTED

Japan Attacks Pearl Harbor

DECEMBER 8, 1941

Soon after dawn, Japanese planes descended on the big American naval base at Pearl Harbor, where most of the Pacific Fleet was anchored. When the last of the bombers headed home, they had sunk four battleships, crippled nearly 200 airplanes and killed more than two 2,000 soldiers and sailors. President Franklin D. Roosevelt called December 7 "a date which will live in infamy," and Congress quickly declared war on Japan. Hitler believed the war would not last much longer, thanks to the Japanese attack—"Now it is impossible for us to lose," he said—and hastily declared war against the United States, giving F.D.R. the clinching justification he had sought for aiding the European allies.

The New York Times.

FIRST ATOMIC BOMB DROPPED ON JAPAN; MISSILE IS EQUAL TO 20,000 TONS OF TNT; TRUMAN WARNS FOE OF A 'RAIN OF RUIN'

Atom Bomb Destroys Hiroshima

AUGUST 7, 1945

A B-29 Flying Fortress named the Enola Gay dropped its payload on the Japanese city of Hiroshima—the first atomic bomb used in war. In a few seconds, Hiroshima was destroyed in a blinding explosion that packed the force of 20,000 tons of TNT. Within a week (and after another A-bomb dropped on Nagasaki) the Japanese would agree to allied terms for unconditional surrender. In Washington, President Harry S. Truman said the attack on Hiroshima signaled the beginning of the "age of atomic energy," a tremendous new force that could be used to advance civilization, or destroy it.

The New York Times.

75% OF B.E.F. REPORTED SAFELY OUT OF FLANDERS; ALLIES ATTACK ON SOMME, WIN ABBEVILLE AREA; ROOSEVELT WARNS WAR IMPERILS WHOLE WORLD

'Deliverance' at Dunkirk

JUNE 1, 1940

Hermann Göring had convinced Hitler that the Luftwaffe could destroy the retreating allied forces trapped on the coast at Dunkirk, near the border between France and Nazi-occupied Belgium. But the 300,000 soldiers on the beaches got away, thanks to civilian fishing boats and yachts the British called in because their destroyers were overloaded. Prime Minister Winston Churchill of Great Britain said, "there was a victory inside this deliverance," and Dunkirk cemented Churchill's resolve, expressed in one of his most famous wartime speeches: "We shall fight on the seas and oceans. . . . We shall fight in the fields and in the streets; we shall fight in the hills; we shall never surrender."

The New York Times.

ITALY AT WAR, READY TO ATTACK; STAB IN BACK, SAYS ROOSEVELT; GOVERNMENT HAS LEFT PARIS

Italy Joins the War

JUNE 11, 1940

With France crumpling under the Nazi assault, Mussolini joined the attack. The two dictators had formed an alliance in the spring during a strategy session in the Alps at which Mussolini persuaded Hitler that the Italian military was up to the job. But after stabbing the allies in the back, as President Franklin D. Roosevelt put it, Mussolini blundered in search of conquests to equal Hitler's. An Italian campaign in southern France gained little territory; the Italians far outnumbered the British in an assault in Somaliland but sustained far more casualties; and Mussolini invaded Greece without clearing the decision with Hitler—a misstep that forced Germany to begin a second offensive there after the allies held on to the strategic island of Crete.

The New York Times.

ROOSEVELT TRADES DESTROYERS FOR SEA BASES; TELLS CONGRESS HE ACTED ON OWN AUTHORITY; BRITAIN PLEDGES NEVER TO YIELD OR SINK FLEET

Roosevelt's Lend-Lease Plan

SEPTEMBER 4, 1940

As Germany pushed across Europe, America dithered and dawdled. Isolationists in Congress resisted stepping in to avert disaster in Britain and France. So President Franklin D. Roosevelt simply bypassed Congress and issued an executive order giving 50 all-but-obsolete destroyers to Britain in return for British-controlled air bases in Newfoundland, Bermuda, the Bahamas, Jamaica and a string of smaller islands off South America. In less than six months, Congress would approve the Lend-Lease Act, which would allow Roosevelt to do more for the allies—specifically, send more than $50 billion worth of arms their way.

The New York Times.

HITLER BEGINS WAR ON RUSSIA, WITH ARMIES ON MARCH FROM ARCTIC TO THE BLACK SEA; DAMASCUS FALLS; U.S. OUSTS ROME CONSULS

Germany Invades Russia

JUNE 22, 1941

Britain had not yielded to the blitz, as Hitler admitted when he said he could not mount a final attack without the German units that were posted in Eastern Europe. So he scrapped the 1939 nonaggression pact, saying Russia had betrayed it, and focused his attention on capturing the Soviet Union. By the end of the year, the Germans were on the doorstep of Moscow and Leningrad, and Premier Joseph Stalin's Union of Soviet Socialist Republics seemed to be on its knees.

The New York Times.

JAPANESE CAPTURE BATAAN AND 36,000 TROOPS; SINK TWO BRITISH CRUISERS; ITALIANS LOSE ONE; INDIA REPORTED AGREEING ON NATIVE COUNCIL

Japanese Capture Bataan

APRIL 10, 1942

The United States suffered one defeat after another in the months following Pearl Harbor. In the Philippines, where the Japanese routed General Douglas MacArthur's impossibly undermanned Filipino-American force, MacArthur began the humiliating, months-long retreat that became known as the Bataan death march. At Corregidor, the island controlling Manila Bay, the Americans finally gave up. But the long-expected defeat did not dampen MacArthur's determination. "I shall return," he famously promised—and he did, about 30 months later.

The New York Times.
AMERICAN FORCES LAND IN FRENCH AFRICA; BRITISH NAVAL, AIR UNITS ASSISTING THEM; EFFECTIVE SECOND FRONT, ROOSEVELT SAYS

Operation Torch

NOVEMBER 8, 1942

Operation Torch had opened a second front in the war, in North Africa, where German Field Marshal Erwin Rommel's much-feared Afrika Korps had once been thought to number 140,000 soldiers. It also stretched Vichy France's neutrality to the breaking point, with Marshal Henri Philippe Petain giving orders to fight the allies. But Vichy's supreme commander angered the Nazis by announcing a cease-fire when it became clear that some units were ready to abandon Petain for General Charles de Gaulle and his Free French army.

The New York Times.
ALLIES SEIZE SYRACUSE AND NINE OTHER TOWNS IN DRIVE FOR MESSINA, KEY DEFENSE OF SICILY; JAPAN LOSES 4 WARSHIPS IN NEW KULA BATTLE

Allies Invade Sicily

JULY 13, 1943

The code name for the large-scale amphibious assault was Operation Husky. The goal was ambitious: to take Sicily and open the door to an allied invasion of Italy. The allies had focused on Sicily as a landing target because they did not believe they could invade France—not yet, anyway—and some tragic lessons learned in Sicily were not repeated at Normandy, particularly a "friendly fire" incident—British gunners opened fire on an American parachute drop.

The New York Times.
'BIG 3' CHARTS TRIPLE BLOWS TO HUMBLE REICH AND AGREES ON A PEACE TO ELIMINATE TYRANNY; CARRIERS ATTACK MARSHALLS, 5TH ARMY GAINS

'Big Three' Plan Strategy

DECEMBER 7, 1943

The allied forces in Italy had distracted the Germans, but their progress had been painfully slow and their casualties high. At the Teheran conference, President Franklin D. Roosevelt, Prime Minister Winston Churchill of Great Britain and Premier Joseph Stalin of Russia (on his first foreign trip in 34 years) agreed on a new and wider strategy: "No power on earth can prevent our destroying the German armies by land, the U-boats by sea and their war plants from the air," they declared. That laid the foundation for a massive landing in France launched across the English Channel.

The New York Times.
ALLIED ARMIES LAND IN FRANCE IN THE HAVRE-CHERBOURG AREA; GREAT INVASION IS UNDER WAY

D-Day Invasion Begins

JUNE 6, 1944

D-Day was, for most Americans, an emotional turning point that drove home a message that was at once frightening and reassuring: Hitler could be stopped, but only with an all-out invasion that made use of the ships, bombers and jeeps that had been rolling off U.S. assembly lines. D-Day caught the Germans off guard along the coast of France, where the allies had given the beaches distinctly American code-names like Gold, Utah and Omaha. The soldiers poured out of their flat-bottom landing craft; only at Omaha did they run into serious resistance and heavy casualties. The allies had the toehold in Europe that they needed.

The New York Times.
U. S. DEFEATS JAPANESE NAVY; ALL FOE'S SHIPS IN ONE FLEET HIT; MANY SUNK; BATTLE CONTINUES

U.S. Defeats the Japanese Navy

OCTOBER 26, 1944

General Douglas MacArthur made good on his promise at Corregidor and stormed back to the Philippines. What followed was the largest air and naval battle in history. The Japanese command gambled that it could trap the allied transport ships that had brought MacArthur's troops to Leyte, the southernmost island of the Philippines. That led to three simultaneous confrontations in the Gulf of Leyte that left the Japanese navy all but destroyed, with four carriers, three battleships and eight destroyers lost.

The New York Times.

Americans Capture Iwo Jima

FEBRUARY 25, 1945

The famous Associated Press photograph of marines in combat helmets planting the American flag on Iwo Jima was taken on the fifth day of the battle on the heavily fortified Japanese Island. Another 30 days of fighting followed before the Americans took control of two Japanese airfields there, and moved on to Okinawa.

The New York Times.
PRESIDENT ROOSEVELT IS DEAD; TRUMAN TO CONTINUE POLICIES; 9TH CROSSES ELBE, NEARS BERLIN

Roosevelt Dies

APRIL 13, 1945

Vice President Harry S. Truman was having a late-afternoon drink with House Speaker Sam Rayburn when the White House switchboard tracked him down with the news. President Franklin D. Roosevelt, who had gone to Warm Springs, Georgia., for a few days, had died while posing for a portrait. Roosevilt, barely three months into his fourth term, was the only president millions of Americans had known; they had been unaware of how his health had declined as World War II dragged on. He was sixty-three.

The New York Times.
HITLER DEAD IN CHANCELLERY, NAZIS SAY; DOENITZ, SUCCESSOR, ORDERS WAR TO GO ON; BERLIN ALMOST WON; U.S. ARMIES ADVANCE

Hitler's Suicide

MAY 2, 1945

With Nazi Germany in ruins as the allies closed in from the east and the west, Hitler received news that Mussolini had been captured, shot and hanged. Hitler was determined to not die in the hands of his enemies and decided to commit suicide, ordering aides to burn his body after he was dead. He retreated to his bunker, where he first married Eva Braun and then dictated his will. Aides heard a gunshot; he had apparently shot himself in the temple. Braun had taken cyanide.

The New York Times.
THE WAR IN EUROPE IS ENDED! SURRENDER IS UNCONDITIONAL; V-E WILL BE PROCLAIMED TODAY; OUR TROOPS ON OKINAWA GAIN

Germany Surrenders

MAY 8, 1945

After President Franklin D. Roosevelt's death, the remaining Nazi leaders had hoped for a deal with President Harry S. Truman that would call for something less than the unconditional surrender that Roosevelt, Churchill and Stalin had demanded at the Yalta Conference. But Truman wanted exactly the same terms—no breaks because Hitler was gone. The Germans ultimately signed the surrender agreement the Americans wanted at a little schoolhouse in France that served as General Dwight D. Eisenhower's headquarters. Soon crowds were celebrating in Times Square, but the fighting went on in the Pacific.

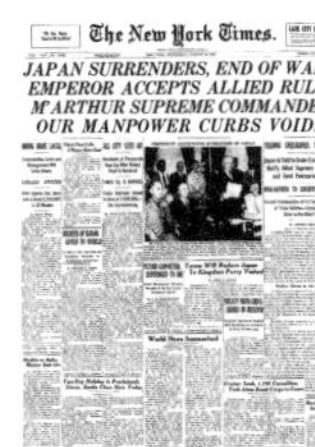
The New York Times.
JAPAN SURRENDERS, END OF WAR! EMPEROR ACCEPTS ALLIED RULE; M'ARTHUR SUPREME COMMANDER; OUR MANPOWER CURBS VOIDED

Japan Surrenders

AUGUST 15, 1945

In the aftermath of Hiroshima, Japan's Emperor Hirohito had little choice but to agree to the allies' demand for unconditional surrender. Hirohito had made peace overtures through the Russians before Hiroshima but had hedged on the terms. The allies had sent their message by the wrong medium, using a radio broadcast aimed at Japan to repeat that the allies would accept nothing short of unconditional surrender. Hirohito, who had expected a formal diplomatic reply, had not paid attention to the broadcast. Now, at last, the war was ending, a fact The Times emphasized with an exclamation point at the end of the headline.

The New York Times.
JAPAN SURRENDERS TO ALLIES, SIGNS RIGID TERMS ON WARSHIP; TRUMAN SETS TODAY AS V-J DAY

V-J Day

SEPTEMBER 2, 1945

"We are gathered here, representatives of the major warring powers," General Douglas MacArthur began. The most destructive war in human history was officially over with a round of signatures less than 20 minutes later. It had been almost exactly six years since Hitler invaded Poland. Some 16 million soldiers (300,000 of them American) and 40 million civilians had died as the conflict reached from Europe to the Pacific. President Harry S. Truman said Japan's surrender promised "a new and better world of peace."

"All the News That's Fit to Print."

The New York Times.

LATE CITY EDITION
Partly cloudy and warm with scattered showers today and tomorrow.
Temperatures Yesterday—Max., 88; Min., 70

VOL. LXXXVIII...No. 29,797. Entered as Second-Class Matter. Postoffice, New York, N. Y. NEW YORK, THURSDAY, AUGUST 24, 1939. PP THREE CENTS NEW YORK CITY and Vicinity | FOUR CENTS Elsewhere Except in 7th and 8th Postal Zones.

GERMANY AND RUSSIA SIGN 10-YEAR NON-AGGRESSION PACT; BIND EACH OTHER NOT TO AID OPPONENTS IN WAR ACTS; HITLER REBUFFS LONDON; BRITAIN AND FRANCE MOBILIZE

U.S. AND ARGENTINA PLAN TRADE PACT, WELLES DISCLOSES

Our Commerce Will Get Full Equality With That of All Foreigners, He Asserts

BEEF NOT TO BE INCLUDED

Long Preliminary Talks Ease Difficulties, With Offset Seen to Our Recent Losses

Special to THE NEW YORK TIMES.

WASHINGTON, Aug. 23.—The United States intends to negotiate a reciprocal trade treaty with Argentina as a move to put American commerce with that republic on a footing of equality with that of European competitors, Sumner Welles, Acting Secretary of State, stated today. There have been more than four years of preliminary discussion.

The State Department, making public a list of products upon which this country would make tariff concessions, set Oct. 4 as the closing date for submission of briefs by interested Americans and Oct. 16 for the opening of public hearings.

It was emphasized that fresh, chilled or frozen Argentine meats, the entry of which into this country is banned by the Tariff Act of 1930, and fine wools would not be a subject of discussion in the negotiations. This was expected by officials to remove the most serious objections which might have been advanced to conclusion of a reciprocal agreement. Barring of the entry of Argentine fresh beef here has long been a subject of some friction between the two countries in their commercial relations.

"It may be noted that during the fifteen-year period 1924-38 our exports to Argentina have exceeded our imports from that country by $486,900,000," Mr. Welles said in a statement.

Trade Cut by Foreign Pacts

"Our trade with Argentina has suffered in recent years for lack of a trade agreement. The trade of certain European countries with Argentina has been developing at our expense under the influence of their commercial agreements with Argentina. The placing of American commerce in Argentina on a footing of full equality with that of our European competitors was a subject which was gone into fully in preliminary discussions leading up to the present announcement.

"The agreement will enable us to maintain our competitive position in a market of great present and prospective importance.

"On our side we must, of course, offer reciprocal benefits. The products of interest to Argentina with respect to which consideration will be given in the course of the negotiations, with a view to seeing what concessions could be granted, are listed in connection with the announcement of the proposed negotiations. The concessions, which will in due course be formulated, should, of course, permit an increase in Argentina's exports to this country, but will not have injurious effect upon American production.

"The types of wool included in the list are the coarser types, of which there is only a very small production in this country."

Barter Agreement With Germany

It was presumed that in referring to European competitors Mr. Welles was speaking principally of Germany, which concluded a barter agreement with Argentina after the Pan-American Conference in Lima last December. England has long been a large trader with Argentina, however, and is a heavy buyer of Argentine beef.

Among the products upon which the United States will consider lowering duties in favor of Argentina are:

Tallow, oleo oil and oleo stearin, extract of meat, including fluid, pickled or cured beef packed or not packed in air-tight containers; dead turkeys, dead birds, chicken eggs, corn or maize, including cracked corn; asparagus in its natural state, and some wools.

With the possible exception of that made with Brazil, a reciprocal trade treaty with the Argentine would be the most important yet consummated with a Latin-American country, officials indicated. Be-

Continued on Page Thirty-five

BRITAIN ACTS FAST

Air Force Is Ready for Hostilities—Warships Mass in Skagerrak

EXPORT EMBARGO IS FIXED

Parliament Meets Today in an Emergency Session—King to Convene Privy Council

By FERDINAND KUHN Jr.

Special Cable to THE NEW YORK TIMES.

LONDON, Aug. 23.—The British Government prepared for action today with every indication that it was ready to go to war with Germany whenever a call for help from Poland should come.

Warning notices went out to reservists in all departments of the armed and civilian services; the King was returning to London to hold a meeting of the Privy Council tomorrow; Londoners were ordered to darken their windows until further notice; the air force was poised for instant action, and a concentration of an undisclosed number of British warships was reported in the Skagerrak, between the Norwegian and Danish coasts, as if to remind Germany of the blockade that she had to endure during the World War.

The emergency was underlined by a Board of Trade announcement placing an immediate embargo on unlicensed exports of essential war materials "in order to conserve the stocks in this country." The list included copper, nickel and rubber, which the Germans have been buying in large quantities in the past week or two, and also aluminum, lead, iron and steel scrap and raw cotton.

Parliament Session Today

Tomorrow both houses of Parliament will meet in emergency session to give the government sweeping powers of a sort unknown in democratic England since World War days. The new law will be something like the old Defense of the Realm Act, enabling the government to issue Orders in Council, without prior or subsequent Parliamentary sanction, for any purpose that the national interest may require.

Trade-union leaders were invited to examine the bill today and they came away satisfied that all possible safeguards of individual liberty would be included.

The real business of the Parliamentary session, however, will be to hear a complete review of the international situation by Prime Minister Chamberlain in the House of Commons and by Viscount Halifax, the Foreign Secretary, in the House of Lords. All indications are that the Prime Minister's words and the subsequent debate will be more sombre in tone than anything heard in the Commons chamber since Aug. 3, 1914, when Sir Edward Grey made his famous speech on the eve of the World War.

Everywhere it was agreed that a crisis of the utmost gravity now confronts Britain, a crisis far more serious than that of last Autumn, when this country was not committed as it is now. The British determination to carry out all the pledges to Poland was reaffirmed in the government message handed to Chancellor Hitler today by Sir

Continued on Page Five

The Developments in Europe

The signing of the Russo-German non-aggression pact, which many world capitals feared might be Chancellor Hitler's "go-ahead signal," took place in Moscow early this morning, half a day after German Foreign Minister von Ribbentrop had arrived in the Russian capital. The pact, which runs for ten years, in addition to prohibiting attack by either party against the other, forbids either to join any association of powers aimed at the other. Moreover, it provides that if one party is an "object of warlike acts" the other will not support such acts. [Page 1; text of the treaty, also Page 1.]

Signature of the pact followed a day that seemed to bring Europe closer to the brink. When the British Ambassador to Germany conveyed to Chancellor Hitler a warning that Britain would fight for Poland he was bluntly rebuffed. In Berlin word freely circulated that the German Army would march at 6 P. M. today (noon in New York). [Page 1.]

In the face of Herr Hitler's rebuff Britain went ahead with war preparations, including the sending of notices to reservists, poising of the air force and concentration of warships in the Skagerrak, north of Denmark. Parliament prepared to meet today to grant the government sweeping emergency powers. [Page 1.] Reinforcements were reported being sent to the Mediterranean, where the bases at Gibraltar and Malta were on the alert. [Page 3.] The dominions, led by Canada and Australia, were beginning to swing into line behind Britain. [Page 6.]

France, convinced that Germany intends to invade Poland within a few days, called up further reservists after a meeting of the Permanent Committee on National Defense. [Page 1.]

Poland remained outwardly calm, still doubting that Herr Hitler would risk precipitating a general war. [Page 2.]

In Turkey allegiance to the coalition powers was affirmed, although German Ambassador von Papen was flying to Angora from Germany, presumably to try to break that allegiance. [Page 1.] But in Rumania, another State guaranteed by France and Britain, informed circles said that country would strive to remain neutral [Page 7.]

Only in Rome were signs of war lacking. Although the press continued to attack Poland, no unusual defense preparations were evident. [Page 1.]

In an attempt to head off disaster King Leopold of the Belgians, speaking for the seven Oslo powers, appealed for peace. [With the text of the appeal, Page 5.]

President Roosevelt, disturbed by the outlook, was speeding back to Washington [Page 1], where officials were clearing the decks for action if it became necessary to safeguard United States neutrality and help Americans to escape from danger zones. [Page 3.] The State Department advised citizens not to go to Europe [Page 3] and those who were trying to return home found ships still running normally from foreign ports. [Page 3.]

In the Far East the army and navy leaders in Japan were understood to have shaped a policy to be followed in view of the new situation arising from the Russo-German treaty. [Page 4.] In China some observers believed the treaty would mean increased Soviet aid in resisting Japan. [Page 4.]

FRANCE MOBILIZES; NOW EXPECTS WAR

People Confident of Strength to Meet Aggressor as Hopes of Peace Diminish

By P. J. PHILIP

Wireless to THE NEW YORK TIMES.

PARIS, Thursday, Aug. 24.—Convinced by a report from French Ambassador Robert Coulondre at Berlin and by a reply that Chancellor Adolf Hitler gave yesterday to Prime Minister Neville Chamberlain's message through British Ambassador Sir Nevile Henderson at Berchtesgaden that an invasion of Poland is intended by the German Government within the next few days, the French Government last night decided to call up a further contingent of reservists today.

This decision was communicated to the press in an official statement from Premier Edouard Daladier's office as follows:

"On account of the international situation the French Government has decided to complete military measures already taken by calling up an additional contingent of reserve soldiers."

During last night notices were

Continued on Page Two

TURKEY REAFFIRMS PLEDGES TO ALLIES

Will Honor Pact With France and Britain—German Envoy Flies to Woo Her

Special Cable to THE NEW YORK TIMES.

ISTANBUL, Turkey, Aug. 23.—No official pronouncement has yet been made about the Russo-German non-aggression pact. In official quarters the position of Turkey is said to be unchanged; she has made agreements for mutual assistance against aggression with France and Britain and stands by them.

The Turkish people are still bewildered over yesterday's news, but less alarm about its possibilities is noticeable since last night's official British communiqué was published.

Until the Turkish Government has authentic information about the terms of the pact Turkish newspapers will be reticent. Cumhuriet, only Turkish newspaper with an editorial on the subject today, assumed the Soviet Union would stipulate that if Germany was guilty of aggression against any of her Western neighbors, the pact would become null and void.

In this case, the newspaper said, it should act as a deterrent against war in Europe, for the newspaper could not believe the Soviet Government will remain indifferent to the fate of its neighbors on the Baltic and Black Seas simply because it signed a pact of non-aggression with Germany.

Cumhuriet added that although a pact of non-aggresison was not an alliance, it implied friendly feelings, and it believed, therefore, that the anti-Comintern pact was political, not ideological, and that the Russo-German pact may be regarded as a truce.

Von Papen Flies to Turkey

BUDAPEST, Hungary, Aug. 23 (AP).—Franz von Papen, Germany's Ambassador to Turkey, passed by plane through Budapest today, en route from Salzburg to Angora.

Diplomatic circles conjectured his mission now was to renew attempts to draw Turkey out of the British-French bloc. They recalled German and Italian claims that Turkey's alliance with Britain and France was dependent upon Russia's not joining the opposition camp.

Wireless to THE NEW YORK TIMES.

BUDAPEST, Hungary, Aug. 23.—The international situation was dis-

Continued on Page Five

Sidney Howard Killed by Tractor on Estate; Playwright Is Crushed in Berkshire Garage

Special to THE NEW YORK TIMES.

TYRINGHAM, Mass., Aug. 23.—Sidney Coe Howard, playwright, was crushed to death today by a two and a half ton tractor in his garage on his 700-acre estate here.

Mr. Howard had put in a morning of hard work on a new play based on Carl Van Doren's "Benjamin Franklin" and, as was his custom, was going to seek relaxation in physical work on his estate, which included one of the most modern dairy farms in this part of the State. The chore he had set for himself was harrowing a twenty-eight-acre field which he had recently bought to extend his property.

Driving alone to the garage a quarter of a mile from his studio in the fields, Mr. Howard entered, turned on the ignition switch of the tractor and cranked it. The machine lurched forward, pinning the playwright against the wall of the structure. The tractor, put in the garage the night before by an employe, was believed to have been left in high gear.

Fred L. Fairbanks, superintendent of the estate, discovered Mr. Howard while on an inspection trip. The garage, a former Shaker schoolroom, is set off by itself on the estate and is seldom visited by any one except by those on business.

Mr. Fairbanks found his employer in an upright position, his head bent over his chest. He was pinned at the chest by the hood of the tractor, which had stalled after crushing him against the wall.

After starting the tractor and moving Mr. Howard's body, Mr. Fairbanks ran to the nearest telephone on the estate to notify Mrs. Howard and summon aid. Mrs. Howard was shopping in Lee, five miles away. When she returned

Continued on Page Nineteen

QUICK ACTION SEEN

Berlin Talks of 6 P. M. Deadline for Move Against Poland

DICTATOR WARNS BRITISH

Henderson So Wrought Up on Leaving Parley With Hitler That He Is Speechless

By OTTO D. TOLISCHUS

Wireless to THE NEW YORK TIMES.

BERLIN, Thursday, Aug. 24.—While Foreign Minister Joachim von Ribbentrop was in Moscow discussing, in the view of some German quarters, not so much a new non-aggression pact as "Poland's fourth and final partition," Chancellor Hitler yesterday received Sir Nevile Henderson, the British Ambassador, for a fifteen-minute conference.

According to reliable information, the conference ended on a rather blunt note that is interpreted in diplomatic quarters as possibly Herr Hitler's last word. The communiqué, issued last night, reads:

"Complying with the wish of the British Government, the Fuehrer received Sir Nevile Henderson at the Berghof today. The Ambassador delivered a letter from the British Prime Minister addressed to the Fuehrer, which was drawn up in the same sense as yesterday's British communication regarding the Cabinet session.

"The Fuehrer left no doubt in the mind of the British Ambassador that the obligations assumed by the British Government could not induce Germany to renounce the defense of her vital national interest."

Hitler's Tone Reported Blunt

Actually Herr Hitler's tone to Sir Nevile was reported to have been even more blunt than the communiqué indicates. In effect, Herr Hitler told the Ambassador that Britain had no business in Eastern Europe and that her guarantee of Poland merely encouraged Polish resistance to German demands, therefore it was up to Britain to persuade the Poles to yield or face the consequences.

Sir Nevile left the conference so wrought up he was speechless. Not trusting his memory to repeat the exact shadings of Herr Hitler's answer, he asked that it be put in writing and he returned for it a half hour later. He got it couched in the same strong terms that Herr Hitler used to him before.

At the same time there are also well-authenticated reports that, in addition to Prime Minister Chamberlain's letter, Sir Nevile also delivered to Herr Hitler an oral message that if Herr Hitler would give the Poles time Britain would try to induce Poland to come forth with new proposals. In that connection some circles launched—perhaps not unintentionally—the suggestion that Foreign Minister Josef Beck of Poland might after all ask to see Herr von Ribbentrop and even Herr Hitler. A preliminary meeting with the former might be arranged at Riga, Latvia, on Herr von Ribbentrop's return from Moscow. But Polish circles declare the suggestion was "extremely unlikely" because it spelled surrender.

As during the last few days the word in Berlin is that the zero hour, which will set the German Army on the march, will come today, and these rumors are supplemented with the additional detail that the exact hour is 6 P. M. [noon, New York time], which might mean "contact with the enemy" some time tomorrow. Furthermore, orders to postpone action, issued after Herr von Ribbentrop's departure for Moscow, have been canceled again.

Germans Elated by News

How much all that is merely a part of the "war of nerves" and how much is bitter reality remains to be seen. In fact the tension developing in Germany, at least in an atmosphere of fantastic unreality, is made no more real by the delayed Summer heat that lures the populace to the woods and beaches, and, together with the elation over the Russian pact and renewed confidence in Herr Hitler's diplomatic superiority over the democratic statesmen, helps to hide the war clouds.

However, the rebuff to Britain yesterday, which in some quarters is compared with the rebuff administered to the French Ambassador by King William of Prussia just preceding the Franco-Prussian War

Continued on Page Two

Text of the Berlin-Moscow Treaty

By The Associated Press.

MOSCOW, Thursday, Aug. 24.—The text of the German-Russian non-aggression pact announced here today follows:

The German Reich Government and the Union of Soviet Socialist Republics, moved by a desire to strengthen the state of peace between Germany and the U.S.S.R. and in the spirit of the provisions of the neutrality treaty of April, 1926, between Germany and the U.S.S.R., decided the following:

Article I

The two contracting parties obligate themselves to refrain from every act of force, every aggressive action and every attack against one another, including any single action or that taken in conjunction with other powers.

Article II

In case one of the parties of this treaty should become the object of warlike acts by a third power, the other party will in no way support this third power.

Article III

The governments of the two contracting parties in the future will constantly remain in consultation with one another in order to inform each other regarding questions of common interest.

Article IV

Neither of the high contracting parties will associate itself with any other grouping of powers which directly or indirectly is aimed at the other party.

Article V

In the event of a conflict between the contracting parties concerning any question, the two parties will adjust this difference or conflict exclusively by friendly exchange of opinions or, if necessary, by an arbitration commission.

Article VI

The present treaty will extend for a period of ten years with the condition that if neither of the contracting parties announces its abrogation within one year of expiration of this period, it will continue in force automatically for another period of five years.

Article VII

The present treaty shall be ratified within the shortest possible time. The exchange of ratification documents shall take place in Berlin. The treaty becomes effective immediately upon signature.

Drawn up in two languages, German and Russian.

MOSCOW, 23d *of August*, 1939.

For the German Government:
RIBBENTROP.

In the name of the Government of the U.S.S.R.:
MOLOTOFF.

NO MILITARY MOVES APPARENT IN ITALY

Country Remains Tranquil as Regime Fails to Whip Up Any War Fervor Among People

By HERBERT L. MATTHEWS

Wireless to THE NEW YORK TIMES.

ROME, Aug. 23.—The Italian ship of state sailed tranquilly on the edge of the European tornado today. There have been no conferences, communiqués, evacuation orders, special mobilization or troop movements.

There have been only some diplomatic visits to Count Ciano, the Foreign Minister, including those of the British and French Ambassadors. This is the fourth time since last Thursday that Sir Percy Loraine saw Count Ciano, which shows the degree of pressure the British are bringing to bear as well as their anxiety to make the Italian leaders realize Britain's determination to support Poland. Presumably, Sir Percy delivered a copy of the same note that was presented to Chancellor Hitler, although that has not been admitted.

André François-Poncet's visit was his first since returning to Rome last Friday. He has tried steadily to see the Foreign Minister but hitherto without success. It is believed he also impressed on Count Ciano France's intention to abide by her pledges.

The Hungarian Minister, Baron Frederick Villani, also saw Count Ciano today, reviving reports about Germany's demands on Budapest.

Italian People Are Calm

The Italian people are not being whipped up to the fervor that would be required to enter a war in the next few days. Nowhere do you see air shelters being hastily dug or gas masks being distributed.

Only in the newspapers do the commentators warn their readers that a conflict seems near, while relatively full accounts of the developments in various capitals are given. The British Cabinet's statement last night is published fully in all newspapers here, whereas the German press ignored it. If readers trusted their Italian newspapers this evening they would have a biased but reasonably correct appreciation of the dangers of the present situation.

On the other hand, so far as they know their country is making no last-minute efforts to meet the

Continued on Page Four

PRESIDENT SPEEDS TO ACT ON CRISIS

Disturbed by War Threat, He Will End Cruise Today and Board Train at Red Bank

By FELIX BELAIR Jr.

Special to THE NEW YORK TIMES.

RED BANK, N. J., Aug. 23.—Admittedly disturbed by the European war crisis, President Roosevelt is hurrying here aboard the navy cruiser Tuscaloosa after scrapping plans for a more ceremonious landing at Annapolis in order to be back at the White House in the event of an outbreak of hostilities.

A small White House secretarial staff is awaiting the arrival of the President off Sandy Hook early tomorrow to give him a bundle of official diplomatic reports on the latest developments abroad. Mr. Roosevelt plans to study the reports aboard his special train en route to Washington.

After debarking from the Tuscaloosa about 8 A. M. tomorrow the President will motor here with Brig. Gen. Edwin M. Watson, his secretary, and Rear Admiral Ross T. McIntire, White House physician. He is expected to stop long enough before entraining for the capital to telephone Secretary of State Cordell Hull, as well as to the embassies in London and Paris about overnight developments.

To Get War Supplies Report

Back at the White House in the early afternoon the President will have before him a report of the War Industries Committee on the status of the nation's munitions and other heavy industries. The committee has been canvassing the aviation and other industries in the past few days with a view to American preparedness.

Prior to the departure of the White House staff late today it was understood the War Industries Committee had drafted a report informing the President that the aviation and several other industries were prepared for any emergency that might arise and that aircraft manufacturers were ahead of schedule on orders of military planes from France and Great Britain.

Among Presidential intimates as well as the capital's political observers interest centered during the day on the question of whether Mr. Roosevelt considered the situation abroad sufficiently grave to call a

Continued on Page Three

BARS HOSTILE UNION

Treaty Forbids Either to Join Any Group Aimed at Other

ESCAPE CLAUSE OMITTED

Von Ribbentrop's Car, Flying Swastika, Passes Beneath Red Flag at Kremlin

By The Associated Press.

MOSCOW, Thursday, Aug. 24.—Germany and Soviet Russia early today signed a non-aggression pact binding each of them for ten years not to "associate itself with any other grouping of powers which directly or indirectly is aimed at the other party."

By the pact they also agreed to "constantly remain in consultation with one another" on their common interests and to adjust differences by arbitration.

The non-aggression clauses bound each power to refrain from any act of force against the other and if either party is "the object of warlike acts by a third power" to refrain from supporting that third power.

The pact did not include the usual escape clause providing for its denunciation in case one of the contracting parties attacked a third power. This provision has been written into most non-aggression agreements signed in the past by Moscow.

Arrives by Plane

By G. E. R. GEDYE

Special Cable to THE NEW YORK TIMES.

MOSCOW, Thursday, Aug. 24.—With the meticulous punctuality of a perfectly staged arrival, two huge Focke-Wulf Condor planes conveying Joachim von Ribbentrop, the German Foreign Minister, and his thirty-two assistants, landed at the Moscow airdrome on the stroke of 1 P. M. yesterday.

Adequate but not excessive police precautions were taken at the airdrome. For the first time the Soviet authorities displayed the swastika banner, five of which flew from the front of the airdrome building, but were placed so as not to be visible from the outside.

Vyacheslaff M. Molotoff was not present to welcome Herr von Ribbentrop, probably because he is not only Commissar of Foreign Affairs but also Premier, and therefore higher in rank than Herr von Ribbentrop. Instead the visitor was received by Vladimir P. Potemkin, Vice Commissar of Foreign Affairs; Mr. Barkoff, protocol chief; Mr. Merkuloff, Vice Commissar of Internal Affairs, under whom falls the NKVD, formerly the GPU; Mr. Alexandroff, chief of the Central European Department of the Foreign Office, and General Suvoroff, commander of the Moscow garrison.

Almost the entire staff of the huge German Embassy, headed by the Ambassador, Count Friedrich Werner von der Schulenburg, with the military, naval and air attachés in uniform, was present. The German civilians mostly wore top hats and cutaway coats.

The Italian Ambassador, Augusto Russo, with his military attaché in uniform, also was present. The feature of the reception most commented upon was the absence of any Japanese representative.

The German Embassy staff stood lined up like troops on parade. As each was presented to Herr von Ribbentrop he sprang to attention, clicked his heels, gave the Hitler salute and shook hands, again saluting and heel-clicking.

In Old Austrian Embassy

From the airdrome the party drove to the city through streets where police in their white Summer jackets stood every ten paces. For Herr von Ribbentrop the Soviet Government provided a large American car from the Kremlin car park, flying the swastika flag.

The party drove directly to the former Austrian Embassy, where they are being housed. Subsequently Herr von Ribbentrop and leading members of his mission had luncheon at the embassy with Count von der Schulenburg.

At about 3:30 P. M. Herr von Ribbentrop, accompanied by Count von der Schulenburg and an expert translator whom the Germans brought from Berlin, drove through the gates of the Kremlin with its

Continued on Page Six

"All the News That's Fit to Print."

The New York Times.

EXTRA

Partly cloudy and somewhat warmer today. Tomorrow generally fair with moderate temperatures.

Temperatures Yesterday—Max., 67; Min., 61

Copyright, 1939, by The New York Times Company.

VOL. LXXXVIII...No. 29,805. Entered as Second-Class Matter, Postoffice, New York, N. Y. NEW YORK, FRIDAY, SEPTEMBER 1, 1939. THREE CENTS NEW YORK CITY and Vicinity | FOUR CENTS Elsewhere Except in 7th and 8th Postal Zones.

GERMAN ARMY ATTACKS POLAND; CITIES BOMBED, PORT BLOCKADED; DANZIG IS ACCEPTED INTO REICH

BRITISH MOBILIZING

Navy Raised to Its Full Strength, Army and Air Reserves Called Up

PARLIAMENT IS CONVOKED

Midnight Meeting Is Held by Ministers—Negotiations Admitted Failure

By The Associated Press.

LONDON, Friday, Sept. 1.—The British Parliament was summoned to meet today at 5 P. M. [12 noon in New York].

British Call Up Forces

By FERDINAND KUHN Jr.

Special Cable to THE NEW YORK TIMES.

LONDON, Friday, Sept. 1.—All attempts to bring about direct negotiations between Germany and Poland appeared to have broken down tonight as Great Britain mobilized her fleet to full strength, stretched her other defensive preparations close to the limit and began moving 3,000,000 school children and invalids from the crowded cities into the safety of the countryside.

Censorship was established over cables after London had been cut off for hours from communication with the Continent.

It was the peak of the crisis, but a day of rumors had not shifted the fundamental issue nor given a conclusive answer to the question of peace or war.

At midnight the British Government was not yet convinced that Germany really intended to attack Poland and provoke a world war.

Terms Called Smoke Screen

All that had happened during yesterday, including the sudden broadcasting of Chancellor Hitler's sixteen-point demands, was interpreted here as a smoke screen rather than as the flash of guns.

After hearing Herr Hitler's "terms" officials here quietly announced tonight that "the government mainly interested in the proposals is, of course, the Polish Government."

Until the Polish Government has had time to consider them, it was said in Whitehall that "it would be highly undesirable for any comment to be made."

It was fully expected that Poland would reject them later today; indeed, Polish circles here were describing them tonight as "utterly unacceptable," for they would involve dismemberment of Poland and loss of Poland's capacity to defend her independence. In any event, there was no sign of any intention here to put pressure on Warsaw to accept.

Much might have been said about the German "proposals" here tonight if the government had not been so anxious to leave the first decision to Warsaw without any prompting. That the British regarded them as artful went without saying, since they conveyed a first impression of reasonableness that was not borne out by the terms themselves.

Until the announcement on the German wireless tonight, the British Government had not been told about them officially, and the Polish Government was not informed until Josef Lipski, Polish Ambassador to Berlin, visited Foreign Minister Joachim von Ribbentrop a few minutes before the broadcast took place.

Shortly after midnight last night, Sir Nevile Henderson, the British Ambassador in Berlin, had heard the "points" read to him by Herr von Ribbentrop, but the reading was so fast that the Ambassador could not even take notes of them in detail. In any event, he was told Herr Hitler's "points" were not being given to him or his government officially, on the ground that it was already too late.

Time Limit Expired

On Tuesday Herr Hitler had asked that a Polish negotiator should arrive in Berlin within twenty-four hours; and as nobody had arrived from Warsaw when the time limit expired, Sir Nevile was told that the "points" could not even be communicated officially to London.

The German time table with the

Continued on Page Four

Bulletins on Europe's Conflict

London Hears of Warsaw Bombing

LONDON, Friday, Sept. 1 (AP).—Reuters British news agency said it had learned from Polish sources in Paris that Warsaw was bombed today.

French Confirm Beginning of War

PARIS, Friday, Sept. 1 (AP).—The Havas news agency said today that official French dispatches from Germany indicated that "the Reich began hostilities on Poland this morning."

The agency also reported that the Polish Embassy here had announced that "Germany violated the Polish frontier at four points."

"German reports of pretended violation of German territory by Poland are pure invention, as is the fable of 'attack' by Polish insurgents on Gleiwitz," the embassy announcement said.

Attack on Entire Front Reported

LONDON, Friday, Sept. 1 (AP).—A Reuters dispatch from Paris said:

"The following is given with all reserve: According to unconfirmed reports received here, the Germans have begun an offensive with extreme violence on the whole Polish front."

First Wounded Brought Into Gleiwitz

GLEIWITZ, Germany, Friday, Sept. 1 (AP).—An army ambulance carrying wounded soldiers arrived at the emergency hospital here today at 9:10 A. M.

The men, carried in a wagon, were on stretchers. One had on a first-aid field bandage. It could not be ascertained where the ambulance came from.

At about 9:30 a half-mile long truck train manned by the engineering corps drove through the heart of the city with pontoon bridge building material. In the train were caterpillar tread, twenty-passenger motor vans.

Obviously the train had been on the road for a considerable time. All equipment was thickly covered with gray mud.

A scouting plane of the air force was patrolling an area over Gleiwitz.

Early today Gleiwitz residents reported that artillery fire

Continued on Page Four

DALADIER SUMMONS CABINET TO CONFER

News of Attack on Poland Spurs Prompt Action—Military Move Thought Likely

By The Associated Press.

PARIS, Friday, Sept. 1.—Edouard Daladier, Premier and War Minister of France, informed that German troops crossed the Polish frontier today, summoned an urgent meeting of his Cabinet for 10:30 A. M.

It was probable that Parliament would be called tomorrow.

Reports of the German invasion came from Berlin and from the Polish Embassy here. The Ministers were called to the Elysee Palace to meet with President Albert Lebrun.

Upon receipt of word of the German operations M. Daladier rushed to the War Ministry and called General Marie Gustave Gamelin, supreme commander of land, sea and air forces, into consultation.

A little later Daladier summoned Foreign Minister Georges Bonnet.

The Polish Embassy said that Germans violated the Polish frontier at four points and at the same time it characterized German charges that Poles had crossed into Germany as "pure invention."

Havas, French news agency, announced that "a German declaration of war against Poland probably will lead France and Great Britain to take new military measures."

Britain and France are committed to aid Poland in any fight to save her independence.

Ministers Stand Firm

By P. J. PHILIP

Wireless to THE NEW YORK TIMES.

PARIS, Aug. 31.—The Cabinet met with President Albert Lebrun for more than two hours this evening at the Elysée Palace. At the close of the meeting Minister of the Interior Albert Sarraut handed the press the following communiqué:

"MM. Edouard Daladier, President of the Council, and Georges Bonnet, Minister of Foreign Affairs, laid before the Cabinet a detailed account of the international situation as a whole.

"The Cabinet was unanimous in formally maintaining the engagements taken by France."

Later M. Daladier had further conversations with M. Bonnet, Fi-

Continued on Page Four

BRITISH CHILDREN TAKEN FROM CITIES

3,000,000 Persons Are in First Evacuation Group, Which Is to Be Moved Today

By FREDERICK T. BIRCHALL

Special Cable to THE NEW YORK TIMES.

LONDON, Friday, Sept. 1.—The greatest mass movement of population at short notice in the history of Great Britain is under way. It is an evacuation, under government order, of little children, invalids, women and old men from congested areas.

From London, Birmingham, Manchester, Liverpool, Edinburgh, Glasgow and twenty-three other cities the great exodus is going on as this dispatch is being written. The numbers are stupendous. More than 3,000,000 of these helpless human beings are being taken out of danger of German bombs.

Nothing like it has ever been attempted anywhere; yet it is going on without mishap—so far, indeed, without serious confusion.

Scenes everywhere were much the same whether in the aristocratic West End or the proletarian East Side, but one that this correspon-

Continued on Page Three

HOSTILITIES BEGUN

Warsaw Reports German Offensive Moving on Three Objectives

ROOSEVELT WARNS NAVY

Also Notifies Army Leaders of Warfare—Envoys Tell of Bombing of 4 Cities

By JERZY SZAPIRO

Wireless to THE NEW YORK TIMES.

WARSAW, Poland, Friday, Sept. 1.—War began at 5 o'clock this morning with German planes attacking Gdynia, Cracow and Katowice.

At Gdynia three bombs exploded in the sea.

The regular German Army started an offensive in the direction of Dzialdowka—in Upper Silesia and Czestochowa. The German plan apparently is to cut off Western Poland along the line of Dzialdowka-Lodz-Czestochowa.

The offensive is developing, from East Prussia, toward Silesia and northwards from Slovakia.

At 9 o'clock an attempt was made to bombard Warsaw. The planes, however, did not reach even the suburbs.

A military attack on the garrison at Westerplatte in the Danzig area was repulsed.

The Foreign Office at 8:45 A. M. issued a communiqué saying that military action had begun in Westerplatte in the Danzig area as well as in Buschkowa near Gdynia, and in Dzialowka, Chojnice and Lowa.

Hostilities have begun and Poland has been attacked, said the communiqué.

Three cities in Upper Silesia suffered artillery bombardment, particulars of which are lacking, it was said.

While this dispatch was being telephoned, the air-raid sirens sounded in Warsaw.

Danzig Fighting Reported

WARSAW, Poland, Friday, Sept. 1 (AP).—It was reported today that Tczew and Czestochowa were bombed by German airplanes early this morning.

There was no official confirmation of the bombing.

Fighting was reported at Danzig. It was reported officially that German troops had attacked Polish defenses near Mlawa, bordering the southern part of East Prussia. There was no announcement of the damage resulting from the bombing.

Mist and clouds were overhanging the city. A light drizzle apparently afforded momentary protection against air raids. Warsaw went to work as usual.

Roosevelt Warns Navy

WASHINGTON, Friday, Sept. 1 (AP).—President Roosevelt directed today that all naval ships and army commands be notified at once by radio of German-Polish hostilities.

The White House issued the following announcement:

"The President received word at 2:50 A. M. Eastern standard time

Continued on Page Five

Soviet Ratifies Reich Non-Aggression Pact; Gibes at British and French Amuse Deputies

By G. E. R. GEDYE

Special Cable to THE NEW YORK TIMES.

MOSCOW, Aug. 31.—With Premier and Foreign Commissar Vyacheslaff M. Molotoff, working under high pressure—so suddenly applied without any previous indication and contrasting so sharply with earlier delaying tactics this week as to suggest German insistence that the matter be finally settled—the Supreme Soviet [Parliament] tonight unanimously ratified the Russo-German non-aggression pact.

Ratification, which was first foreshadowed at midday, was preceded by a speech by Mr. Molotoff so precise in its definition of Soviet obligations to refrain from participating on the side of Great Britain and France in any war against Germany, so voluble in its defense against charges of inconsistency against Communist Russia for embracing Fascist Germany, and so insistent on the inevitability of friendship between "not merely the governments but also the peoples" of Germany and Russia as to extinguish the last faint hopes of the western democracies that Moscow might yet find loopholes or excuses for joining them at some subsequent date in resisting German aggression against Poland.

Mr. Molotoff's speech contained nothing to justify constantly repeated suspicions of the existence of a secret German-Soviet pact entitling the latter to participate in a partition of Poland.

The Premier's speech contained much trenchant and seemingly irrefutable evidence of blunders by the British and French Governments in handling the question of Soviet cooperation. It was not diffi-

Continued on Page Eight

FREE CITY IS SEIZED

Forster Notifies Hitler of Order Putting Danzig Into the Reich

ACCEPTED BY CHANCELLOR

Poles Ready, Made Their Preparations After Hostilities Appeared Inevitable

Special Cable to THE NEW YORK TIMES.

DANZIG, Friday, Sept. 1.—By a decree issued early this morning Albert Forster, Nazi Chief of State, proclaimed the annexation of the Free City to the Reich, thus settling by a fell stroke the original point of contention in the international crisis.

In a telegram to Chancellor Hitler Herr Forster explained his action as necessary to remove "the pressing necessity of our people and State." Herr Forster also issued a proclamation to the people of Danzig saying the hour awaited for twenty years had arrived because "our Fuehrer, Adolf Hitler, has freed us."

[A NEW YORK TIMES dispatch from Berlin this morning said Herr Hitler telegraphed Herr Forster today thanking him and all Danzigers, and stating:

"The law for reannexation is in effect immediately."

The Chancellor stated, furthermore, that Herr Forster was appointed head of the civil administration of the Danzig area.]

In a four-article decree Herr Forster declared the Constitution of Danzig no longer valid. He declared himself sole administrator of the Danzig part of the German Reich, and he declared that until the Reich's legal system had been introduced by command of Herr Hitler all laws except the Constitution remained in effect. Then Herr Forster immediately wired Herr Hitler of his action, begged the Chancellor to give his approval of the move and through Reich law complete the annexation.

The German flag is now flying everywhere over Danzig, Herr Forster said, and all church bells resound to the event. "We thank God," he declared, "that He gave the Fuehrer the strength and the possibility to free also us from the evil Versailles treaty."

Hitler Accepts Danzig

By The Associated Press.

BERLIN, Friday, Sept. 1.—The German official news agency, D. N. B., announced today that Albert Forster, Nazi Chief of State in Danzig, had proclaimed the reunion of the Free City with the Reich.

Herr Hitler today accepted the Free City of Danzig into the Reich.

"I acknowledge your proclamation of the return of the Free City of Danzig to the Reich," Herr Hitler's telegram said. "I thank you, Gauleiter Forster, and all Danzig men and women, for your loyalty which you have displayed for so many years.

"Greater Germany welcomes you with joy in her heart.

"The law of reunion will be enacted forthwith. I appoint you, Herr Forster, chief of the civil administration in the Danzig territory."

Forster's telegram to Herr Hitler read:

My Fuehrer.

I have just signed and then put into effect the following basic law, concerning the reunion of Danzig with the German Reich.

The basic State law of the Free State of Danzig and the reunion of Danzig with the German Reich is effective Sept. 1, 1939.

To lift the immediate distress of the people and State of the Free City of Danzig, I decree the following basic State law:

ARTICLE I

The Constitution of the Free City of Danzig has been suspended effective immediately.

ARTICLE II

All legal and administrative power will be executed exclusively by the head of State.

ARTICLE III

The Free City of Danzig with its territory and its peoples forms

Continued on Page Five

Hitler Acts Against Poland

The port of Gdynia, north of Danzig (toward top of map), was blockaded this morning. At Gleiwitz (shown by cross) artillery fire was heard after a Polish-German skirmish had been reported there. Cracow, to the east, was among Polish cities said to have been bombed.

Hitler Tells the Reichstag 'Bomb Will Be Met by Bomb'

Chancellor Vows 'Fight Until Resolution' Against Poland—Gives Order of Succession As Goering, Hess, Then Senate to Choose

Chancellor Adolf Hitler of Germany, in a world broadcast this morning, opened "a fight until the resolution of the situation" against Poland, announcing that "from now on bomb will be met by bomb."

At the same time he announced, to face any eventuality, that if anything "happened" to him, Field Marshal Hermann Goering was to be in charge; if to Marshal Goering, Rudolph Hess; if to Herr Hess, the Senate, which he proposes to appoint, will select a successor.

The Chancellor, after attempting to narrow the conflict with Poland by assuring the Western powers that he had no designs on their frontiers, by assuring the neutrality of the sideline powers and by acknowledging the friendliness of Italy and the new relations with Russia, issued a defy to Poland's allies.

Says He Will Carry on

"I shall carry on this fight regardless of against whom I may come," he declared.

At the same time he held the door open for Poland to capitulate to his demands, declaring that he did not intend to make war against women and children. He said that if a solution did not come from the present Polish Government, it would come from a future Polish Government.

The Chancellor expressed confidence, toward the close of his address, that his decision, which was being broadcast over amplifiers hastily erected by electricians at the last moment in the streets of Berlin and the provincial capitals, would be accepted by the German people.

The scene enacted in the Kroll Opera House in Berlin was carried over sound waves to most of the nations of the world. From Berlin hook-ups had been arranged with the three major networks of the United States, and, according to the announcer for the German broadcasting system, over the Italian, Hungarian, Spanish, Norwegian, Swedish, Danish, Yugoslav, British and French national networks.

The summons to the Reichstag, ordered by Herr Hitler himself, had been sent out only a few hours before the meeting. Most of the members had been awaiting the signal, and when the opera house opened shortly before 10 o'clock [5 o'clock, New York time] this morning, they were dressed in the uniforms of their military formations.

After Herr Hitler finished speaking the deputies enacted a law incorporating Danzig into the Reich, declaring Danzig citizens were now Germans, voiding the Constitution of the Free City and extending to its territory the jurisdiction of German law.

At 5:10 A. M., Marshal Goering opened the meeting and turned the floor over to the Chancellor.

In the early part of his address, Herr Hitler electrified his audience with this declaration:

"We have all been suffering under the tortures that the Versailles treaty has been inflicting upon us."

Then, speaking with measured deliberateness of Germany's claims to the pre-war German areas, he announced, as he had on a previous occasion:

"The Treaty of Versailles is, for us Germans, not a law."

Anticipating what the announcement's reiteration would lead to, the deputies roared applause. Then Herr Hitler, his indignation rising as he proceeded, set about building up the German case, asserting that his proposals for a peaceful solution of the problem of Danzig and the Polish Corridor had been rejected, and charging that the Poles had visited atrocities on Germans, especially women and children, "killing many of them."

SUMMARY OF SPEECH

A summary of Herr Hitler's speech was translated as follows:

"For months we have been suffering under the burdens of the Treaty of Versailles. Danzig was and is a German city. All these regions have only Germany to thank for their cultural development.

"Minorities in the Polish Corridor have been shamefully mistreated. Here, as in other respects, I have tried to solve the problems by peaceful means. In the fifteen years of National Socialism we have been

Continued on Page Three

HITLER GIVES WORD

In a Proclamation He Accuses Warsaw of Appeal to Arms

FOREIGNERS ARE WARNED

They Remain in Poland at Own Risk—Nazis to Shoot at Any Planes Flying Over Reich

By OTTO D. TOLISCHUS

Special Cable to THE NEW YORK TIMES.

BERLIN, Friday, Sept. 1.—Charging that Germany had been attacked, Chancellor Hitler at 5:11 o'clock this morning issued a proclamation to the army declaring that from now on force will be met with force and calling on the armed forces "to fulfill their duty to the end."

The text of the proclamation reads:

To the defense forces:

The Polish nation refused my efforts for a peaceful regulation of neighborly relations; instead it has appealed to weapons.

Germans in Poland are persecuted with a bloody terror and are driven from their homes. The series of border violations, which are unbearable to a great power, prove that the Poles no longer are willing to respect the German frontier. In order to put an end to this frantic activity no other means is left to me now than to meet force with force.

"Battle for Honor"

German defense forces will carry on the battle for the honor of the living rights of the re-awakened German people with firm determination.

I expect every German soldier, in view of the great tradition of eternal German soldiery, to do his duty until the end.

Remember always in all situations you are the representatives of National Socialist Greater Germany!

Long live our people and our Reich!

Berlin, Sept. 1, 1939.

ADOLF HITLER.

The commander-in-chief of the air force issued a decree effective immediately prohibiting the passage of any airplanes over German territory excepting those of the Reich air force or the government.

This morning the naval authorities ordered all German mercantile ships in the Baltic Sea not to run to Danzig or Polish ports.

Anti-air raid defenses were mobilized throughout the country early this morning.

A formal declaration of war against Poland had not yet been declared up to 8 o'clock [3 A. M. New York time] this morning and the question of whether the two countries are in a state of active belligerency is still open.

Reichstag Will Meet Today

Foreign correspondents at an official conference at the Reich Press Ministry at 8:30 o'clock [3:30 A. M. New York time] were told that they would receive every opportunity to facilitate the transmission of dispatches. Wireless stations have been instructed to speed up communications and the Ministry is installing additional batteries of telephones.

The Reichstag has been summoned to meet at 10 o'clock [5 A. M. New York time] to receive a more formal declaration from Herr Hitler.

The Hitler army order is interpreted as providing, for the time being, armed defense of the German frontiers against aggression. The action is also suspected of forcing international diplomatic action.

The Germans announced that foreigners remain in Polish territory at their own risk.

Flying over Polish territory as well as the maritime areas is forbidden by the German authorities and any violators will be shot down.

When Herr Hitler made his an-

Continued on Page Three

"All the News That's Fit to Print."

The New York Times.

LATE CITY EDITION
POSTSCRIPT
Fair, not much change in temperature today. Tomorrow cloudy.
Temperatures Yesterday—Max [illegible]

VOL. LXXXIX...No. 30,057. Entered as Second-Class Matter, Postoffice, New York, N. Y. NEW YORK, FRIDAY, MAY 10, 1940. THREE CENTS NEW YORK CITY and Vicinity | FOUR CENTS Elsewhere Except in 7th and 8th Postal Zones.

NAZIS INVADE HOLLAND, BELGIUM, LUXEMBOURG BY LAND AND AIR; DIKES OPENED; ALLIES RUSH AID

U.S. FREEZES CREDIT

President Acts to Guard Funds Here of Three Invaded Nations

SHIP RULING TODAY

Envoy Reports to Hull on Germany's Attacks by Air and Land

Special to THE NEW YORK TIMES.

WASHINGTON, Friday, May 10—President Roosevelt early today ordered the freezing of all credits held by Belgium, the Netherlands and Luxembourg in this country.

He called a conference for 10:30 A. M. of heads of the State, War and Navy Departments to consider pressing problems of neutrality.

The President acted swiftly after news of Germany's invasion of the three European neutral countries reached Washington and galvanized high officials into action. His order with regard to the freezing of all the invaded countries' credits and cash balances here was a counterpart of the action taken after Germany invaded Norway and Denmark.

Congress this week completed action on legislation that specifically authorizes the President by decree to freeze all such cash and credits of any belligerent. The object is to prevent these resources from falling into the hands of the invading power.

Ships to Be Considered

The President's order directed Secretary of the Treasury Henry Morgenthau Jr. to freeze all Belgian, French and Luxembourg credits before the markets open this morning.

It was announced also that the conference to be held at 10:30 will consider the question of Belgian and Netherland ships that may be in United States ports. Attorney General Robert H. Jackson also will attend this conference.

The White House, meanwhile, indicated some skepticism of the official explanation of the invasion given by German Propaganda Minister Joseph Goebbels, who was reported to have said that the Germans moved because of information that Great Britain and France intended to invade the countries involved.

"Nevertheless," said Stephen T. Early, Presidential secretary, after he had quoted the Goebbels statement, "it remains to be seen who invaded who."

It was announced that the President would remain awake throughout the night, if necessary, to receive reports and consult with officials. Sumner Welles, Under-Secretary of State, at 1:45 A. M. joined the group of State Department officials who remained on duty at the department.

Report From Ambassador

A general invasion of the three neutrals by heavy German land and air forces was reported to the State Department and Mr. Roosevelt early today by Ambassador John J. Cudahy at Brussels.

After trying vainly to re-establish telephone connection with Secretary of State Cordell Hull, over which he had relayed a "blow-by-blow" description of developments several hours earlier, the Ambassador got through the following terse message:

"German planes continue to cross the border and are bombing the airport near Brussels. It seems to be a general attack on all three countries."

A State Department press liaison officer who was relaying latest diplomatic bulletins to reporters as they came in by transatlantic telephone, dropped the cryptic remark: "As the American Ambassador spoke from Brussels, an embassy military attaché stood at his elbow."

After relaying the information to the President that the Belgian Government had ordered all hands to stand by, Ambassador Cudahy again called Secretary Hull between 10 and 11 o'clock and said he had been informed by officials in Brussels that one German and

Continued on Page Two

The International Situation

In the midst of Britain's Cabinet crisis Germany struck another powerful blow early this morning by invading the Netherlands, Belgium and Luxembourg.

After swarms of planes had engaged in air fights over Amsterdam, parachute troops, some of them clad in Netherland uniforms, descended at strategic points while planes bombed air fields. The Netherlands resisted the incursion and promptly opened the dikes that are part of her water defense system. [Page 1.]

Parachute troops likewise made surprise landings in Belgium and bombs from 100 planes blasted the Brussels airport. [Page 1.]

Appeals for help were dispatched to the Allies by the invaded countries and it was understood that machinery of assistance was being set in motion. Queen Wilhelmina in a proclamation issued at The Hague declared, "I and my government will do our duty." [Page 1.]

As in the case of Norway, Berlin explained that the German action had been taken to forestall the Allies; an announcement said that an attack on Germany had been planned through the territory of the Low Countries. What the Reich was doing, it was declared, was safeguarding the neutrality of those countries. [Page 1.]

President Roosevelt lost no time in acting on the new situation. After night conferences he ordered the freezing of credits of the three invaded countries. Further measures are to be taken today. [Page 1.]

London, meanwhile, announced that British troops had occupied Iceland to prevent a possible German seizure of that former Danish possession. [Page 1.]

Before all these happenings Neville Chamberlain had appeared to be on his way out as Prime Minister, but today it was expected the new developments might save him.

Following upon his relatively narrow escape in the House of Commons vote on Wednesday night, Mr. Chamberlain set about yesterday to see what could be done to satisfy his critics. He offered Cabinet posts to two leaders of the Labor Opposition, but they refused to serve under him. As to whether they would serve under another Conservative, they delayed their reply. If Mr. Chamberlain steps out of office, it is thought probable his place will be taken by the present Foreign Secretary, Viscount Halifax, with Winston Churchill acting as government spokesman in the Commons, from the floor of which the peer would by tradition be barred. [Page 1.]

A new offset to the Norwegian reverses was a London announcement that British submarines had attacked three German convoys and scored eleven torpedo hits, in addition to destroying two ships sailing home. [Page 6.]

Moreover, the Allies' Narvik campaign seemed to be making progress. From that far northern area it was reported that two Allied columns closing in on the railway to the port were within ten miles of each other near the Swedish border; their intention apparently was to join and drive westward along the railroad to Narvik itself, which is held by the Nazis. The Germans, in their effort to thwart the besiegers, were said to be landing parachute troops and supplying them by air. [Page 4.]

In the aftermath of the campaign in the south of the country Foreign Minister Koht disclosed that four of Norway's six divisions had been lost—killed, wounded or captured by the Nazis or interned by Sweden. [Page 6.]

Bombs Drop on Swiss Soil

By The United Press.

BERNE, Switzerland, Friday, May 10—The army staff announced today that foreign airplanes had dropped bombs in the Berne Jura Alpine district between Delemont, near the frontier, and Mount Terr, damaging a railroad.

Traffic continued over the road, the army staff said. It added that other foreign planes were flying over Swiss territory near Basle but that no details had been received.

MUSSOLINI TO LET 'ONLY FACTS' SPEAK

Press Assures Yugoslavia, but Reminds Her of Fate of Poland and Norway

By HERBERT L. MATTHEWS

By Telephone to THE NEW YORK TIMES.

ROME, May 9—The fourth anniversary of the founding of the new Italian Empire was celebrated today in an atmosphere of warlike preparation. The army was honored, Italian armed strength was glorified and the country was told by its leading commentators that the empire would soon earn that "freedom of the seas" which to Italians means domination of the Mediterranean.

Rome, like every other city in the empire, resounded today to martial music while thousands of soldiers paraded through streets from whose buildings hung innumerable flags. The great ceremony was at the Piazza Venezia this morning. Premier Mussolini awarded gold and silver medals to the kin of soldiers fallen in Fascismo's three wars in Ethiopia, Spain and Albania. Later, responding to the insistent appeal of the thousands of men massed below his balcony, he spoke very briefly, only to say that he was resuming his cloak of silence.

"May 9, 1936, was a great day in the history of the country, a day of solar victory," he said. "After my speeches, you must accustom yourself to my silence. Only facts will break it."

Small groups in the crowd thereupon began yelling "Tunisia!" and "Malta!" but the cries were not general.

At the same time this morning

Continued on Page Seven

ICELAND OCCUPIED BY BRITISH FORCE

Secret Expedition Is Justified as Thwarting Action There by Germany

By JAMES MacDONALD

Special Cable to THE NEW YORK TIMES.

LONDON, Friday, May 10—Forestalling a possible German swoop on the strategically valuable former Danish dominion of Iceland, the British have landed an expeditionary force there, it was announced this morning by the Foreign Office here.

Neither the size of the British contingent, which was sent out in the deepest secrecy, nor its place of landing was revealed in the official communiqué.

The landing of the expeditionary force was still going at an early hour this morning. Observers guessed that the landing place must be Reykjavik.

TEXT OF COMMUNIQUE

The official announcement read as follows:

Since the German seizure of Denmark it has become necessary to reckon with the possibility of a sudden German descent on Iceland.

It is clear that in the face of an attack on Iceland, even on a very small scale, the Icelandic Government would be unable to prevent their country from falling completely into German hands.

His Majesty's Government have accordingly decided to preclude this possibility which would de-

Continued on Page Three

ALLIED HELP SPED

Netherland and Belgian Appeals Answered by British and French

TACTICS ARE WATCHED

London Thinks Move an Effort to Get Bases to Attack Britain

Italians Reported Massing

By The United Press.

BUENOS AIRES, Argentina, Friday, May 10—The Madrid radio was heard broadcasting today that the British had closed the Strait of Gibraltar and that Italy was massing troops on the French frontier.

Special Cable to THE NEW YORK TIMES.

LONDON, Friday, May 10—The British Government received appeals for help early today from both the Netherlands and Belgium.

The British and French reply to the Netherland-Belgian appeals was prompt. Representatives of the respective governments here were told by 8:30 A. M. (3:30 A. M. New York time) they could expect all the help Britain could give them.

The Netherland Legation here received assurance that its country and Belgium were now regarded as Allies of Britain and France.

Within a few minutes after receipt of official news of the invasion of the Low Countries, the British Cabinet was called to 10 Downing Street and was in session with Prime Minister Neville Chamberlain.

According to information here, the Belgian Cabinet was in Brussels and Premier Hubert Pierlot conferred with King Leopold.

The German invasion of the Low Countries had been expected in London, and it must be presumed the Allies were ready for it to some extent.

Allies Visible to Planes

The biggest handicap to the British and French was in the timing of the German thrust at dawn. This prevented the Allies moving troops under cover of darkness, and since hundreds of German planes already had flown over practically all of Netherland and Belgian territory for some hours, the disposition of Allied troops and their every movement must have been known to the German High Command.

While the Netherlanders and Belgians had taken every precaution

Continued on Page Four

BRUSSELS IS RAIDED

400 Reported Killed—Troops Cross Border at Four Points

PARACHUTE INVASION

Mobilization Is Ordered and Allied Aid Asked—Luxembourg Attacked

Wireless to THE NEW YORK TIMES.

BRUSSELS, Belgium, Friday, May 10—The invasion Belgium had feared since the outbreak of the European war came before dawn this morning. About a hundred German planes flew over this city and bombed the airport.

The airfield at Antwerp also was bombed. Parachute troops were landed at Hasselt in Eastern Belgium. Artillery fire was reported heard along the German and Luxembourg frontiers.

Anti-aircraft guns at the airport commenced firing with the appearance of the first invaders and kept up a steady barrage. Those in the center of the city went into action at 5:30 A. M.

Above the drone of airplane engines could be heard the staccato of machine guns. Bombs wrecked many houses in the vicinity of the airport and caused some loss of life. [Exchange Telegraph (British news agency) said 400 persons had been killed in the first raid.]

Reports from Antwerp and other parts of the country said German planes had flown constantly over since 4:30 A. M., keeping anti-aircraft batteries steadily in action.

Premier Hubert Pierlot and Foreign Minister Paul-Henri Spaak conferred with King Leopold and then called an emergency meeting of the Cabinet. The radio broadcast repeated summonses to all soldiers to join their units at once. A "state of alarm" was decreed throughout the country with the appearance of the first planes.

The Belgian radio also stated German parachute troops had fluttered down at Nivelles, less than twenty miles south of Brussels, and at Saint Trond, about thirty-five miles east of the capital.

The broadcast stated that Germany had made no demarche in Brussels before the invasion.

Wireless to THE NEW YORK TIMES.

LONDON, Friday, May 10—The Germans crossed the Belgian frontier at four points this morning, according to an announcement over

Continued on Page Two

Chamberlain Saved by Nazi Blow In Low Countries, London Thinks

By RAYMOND DANIELL

Special Cable to THE NEW YORK TIMES.

LONDON, Friday, May 10—The first effect of the German attack on the Low Countries is expected to be that Prime Minister Chamberlain will be saved just when it looked as if he was sure to fall.

It was believed that the Labor party, which so far has refused to serve under him in a truly national government, and only yesterday rejected a formal offer to do so, will now close ranks, forget political difficulties and take any Cabinet job offered to its leaders. Furthermore, the Labor party conference, which was supposed to start at Bournemouth on Monday, now will probably be called off.

There is just a possibility that Mr. Chamberlain may quit immediately and turn his seals of office over to First Lord of the Admiralty Winston Churchill. This was a strong but unconfirmed rumor as a Cabinet meeting held this morning came to an end.

In addition, it was said that under Mr. Churchill, Alfred Duff Cooper would receive the Admiralty post, Anthony Eden the War Office and that Viscount Halifax would remain at the Foreign Office.

Until the invasion of the Low Countries was known, the consensus of political observers here had been that the end of the Chamberlain Government could not be long delayed.

The two questions uppermost were how soon it would take place and who would succeed him at No. 10 Downing Street. The betting had been that it would be sooner rather than later and that Foreign Secretary Viscount Halifax would be the next Prime Minister, with Mr. Churchill serving as his spokesman in the House of Commons, from whose floor the present Foreign Secretary, as a peer, is barred by tradition.

The troubles of the 71-year-old Prime Minister, who struggled vainly to maintain Europe's peace by appeasement and who was accused in the House of Commons of bungling the business of war-making, increased rather than diminished during the day. However, the House, despite the gravity of the internal crisis and perils abroad, decided to take its usual twelve-day Whitsuntide holiday, subject to recall in the event of major developments, which followed promptly.

Mr. Chamberlain's efforts to broaden the base of his Cabinet by

Continued on Page Five

NAZIS SWOOP ON THE LOW COUNTRIES

By land and air German troops descended this morning upon the Netherlands, Belgium and Luxembourg. The principal land incursion into the Netherlands was at Roermond.

Ribbentrop Charges Allies Plotted With the Lowlands

By GEORGE AXELSSON

Wireless to THE NEW YORK TIMES.

BERLIN, Friday, May 10—Foreign Minister Joachim von Ribbentrop at 9 o'clock this morning announced that Reich forces had launched military operations against Holland, Belgium and Luxembourg to "protect their neutrality."

Earlier it was reported that German troops had occupied Maastricht, the Netherlands, and had "landed" contingents in Brussels, probably meaning parachute troops.

Herr von Ribbentrop said that Germany had received unimpeachable proof that the Allies were engineering an imminent attack through the Lowlands into the German Ruhr district wherefore the Germans felt compelled to take corresponding measures. He said the time had come for settling the final account with the "Franco-British leaders."

And thus the war to a decisive finish has at last started in the West. This was the assumption when Herr von Ribbentrop informed the world through newspaper men that the German action meant that she had decided to settle all accounts with the Allies.

"France and Britain dropped their mask," said Herr von Ribbentrop. "The alarm in the Mediterranean was a feint behind which the Allies were preparing an onslaught on German territory which the Reich could not tolerate."

The notes—handed to The Hague and Brussels simultaneously with a shorter note to the Grand Duchy of Luxembourg just prior to their invasion by Germany—accused the Lowlands with having been overwhelmingly partial toward the Allies, adding that the attitude of the press was objectionable to the Reich.

A memorandum similar in tone to that handed to Denmark and Norway last month stated:

"In the life-and-death struggle thrust upon the German people, the government does not intend to await an attack by Britain and France inactively allowing the war to be carried through Belgium and Holland onto German soil. The government, therefore, has issued orders to safeguard the neutrality of the two countries with all the military means of the Reich."

Ribbentrop Reads Statement

In eight points the memorandum outlines the German argument that Belgium and Holland had not observed the strictest neutrality upon which German respect for their territories was founded. The document accuses them with having even supported Germany's enemies in their hostile intentions. Belgium fortified exclusively her Eastern frontier against Germany, leaving the French frontier unfortified, one argument reads.

Berlin slept peacefully unaware

Continued on Page Four

HOLLAND'S QUEEN PROTESTS INVASION

Wilhelmina Vows She and the Government Will Do Duty—Bars Negotiation With Foe

By The United Press.

THE HAGUE, the Netherlands, Friday, May 10—Queen Wilhelmina said today in a statement on the German invasion of the country that "I and my government will do our duty."

The Queen, in a proclamation addressed to "my people," said:

"After our country, with scrupulous conscientiousness, had observed strict neutrality during all these months, and while Holland had no other plan than to maintain strictly this attitude, Germany last night made a sudden attack on our territory without any warning.

"This was done notwithstanding a solemn promise that the neutrality of our country would be respected so long as we ourselves maintained that neutrality.

"I herewith direct a flaming protest against this unprecedented violation of good faith and violation of all that is decent in relations between cultured States.

"I and my government now will do our duty.

"Do your duty everywhere and under all circumstances. And let every one go to the post to which he has been appointed and, with the utmost vigilance and with that inner calm and serenity which comes from a clear conscience, do his work."

The Netherland general military headquarters in a communiqué said:

"Never will the High Command or government enter into negotiations with the enemy."

Dispatches from Europe and the Far East are subject to censorship at the source.

AIR FIELDS BOMBED

Nazi Parachute Troops Land at Key Centers as Flooding Starts

RIVER MAAS CROSSED

Defenders Battle Foe in Sky, Claim 6 Planes as War Is Proclaimed

First Bombing in France

Special Cable to THE NEW YORK TIMES.

PARIS, Friday, May 10—The Bron airdrome, a big airport near Lyon, was bombed by German planes today. One German aircraft was shot down. The alarm was first given at 4:25 A. M. The all-clear signal was given at 6:45 A. M.

WASHINGTON, Friday, May 10 (AP)—United States Ambassador William C. Bullitt telephoned the State Department from Paris at 4 A. M. today that the Germans had bombed a number of fortified towns in France, "such as Dunkerque and Calais."

By The United Press.

AMSTERDAM, The Netherlands, Friday, May 10—Germany invaded the Netherlands early today, land troops being preceded by widespread air attacks on airdromes and by the landing of parachute troops.

The Netherlands resisted and announced she was at war with Germany. Anti-aircraft batteries and fighter planes engaged swarms of German aircraft when they appeared simultaneously over a score of Netherland cities.

An official proclamation said:

"Since 3 A. M. German troops have crossed the Netherland frontier and German planes have tried to attack airports. Inundations are effective according to plans. The army anti-aircraft batteries were found prepared. So far as is known six German planes have been shot down."

[French, Belgian and British planes were sighted over the Netherlands this morning, a Reuters (British news agency) dispatch said in quoting the Netherland radio station at Hilversum, near Amsterdam.

German troops were first reported crossing the Netherland frontier near Roermond, eight miles north of the Belgian frontier. German planes landed troops by parachute at strategic points near Rotterdam, The Hague, Amsterdam and other large cities.

A large number of the German troops landed by parachute were said to be dressed in Netherland military uniforms.

Other Germans crossed the Maas River in rubber boats to Netherland territory. They were said to be reaching the Netherland side in "considerable numbers."

A fierce air battle raged over Amsterdam as Netherland fighter planes dived repeatedly on German bombers and troop transport planes with chattering machine guns.

Schiphol Airdrome outside Amsterdam, the nation's largest, was heavily bombed. Military authorities immediately threw a heavy guard around the airdrome in an effort to defend it against German parachute troops.

Planes identified as German Heinkels bombed Schiphol Airdrome repeatedly, loosing some thirty heavy caliber bombs on the landing field between 5:15 and 5:30 A. M.

Reports poured in of planes in great numbers over a score of Netherland cities. Netherland authorities, hurriedly organizing defense, flashed orders to the whole country to be on the alert against parachute troops.

Fifty planes were over Nijmegen, sixty miles southeast of Amsterdam on the German border.

A number of parachute troops reportedly landed at Sliedrecht, Delft and several other points. Delft is twelve and a half miles from The Hague. About 100 parachute troops

Continued on Page Three

"All the News That's Fit to Print."

The New York Times.

LATE CITY EDITION
Increasing cloudiness with rising temperature today. Tomorrow cloudy, somewhat colder.
Temperatures Yesterday—Max., 34; Min., 25

VOL. XCI No. 30,634. Entered as Second-Class Matter, Postoffice, New York, N. Y. NEW YORK, MONDAY, DECEMBER 8, 1941. THREE CENTS NEW YORK CITY and Vicinity

JAPAN WARS ON U. S. AND BRITAIN; MAKES SUDDEN ATTACK ON HAWAII; HEAVY FIGHTING AT SEA REPORTED

CONGRESS DECIDED

Roosevelt Will Address It Today and Find It Ready to Vote War

CONFERENCE IS HELD

Legislative Leaders and Cabinet in Sober White House Talk

By C. P. TRUSSELL
Special to THE NEW YORK TIMES.

WASHINGTON, Dec. 7—President Roosevelt will address a joint session of Congress tomorrow and will find the membership in a mood to vote any steps he asks in connection with the developments in the Pacific.

The President will appear personally at 12:30 P. M. Whether he would call for a flat declaration of war again Japan was left unannounced tonight. But leaders of Congress, shocked and angered by the Japanese attacks, were talking of a declaration of war on not only Japan but on the entire Axis.

The plans for action tomorrow were made tonight in a White

TOKYO ACTS FIRST

Declaration Follows Air and Sea Attacks on U. S. and Britain

TOGO CALLS ENVOYS

After Fighting Is On, Grew Gets Japan's Reply to Hull Note of Nov. 26

By The Associated Press.

TOKYO, Monday, Dec. 8—Japan went to war against the United States and Britain today with air and sea attacks against Hawaii, followed by a formal declaration of hostilities.

Japanese Imperial headquarters announced at 6 A. M. [4 P. M. Sunday, Eastern standard time] that a state of war existed among these nations in the Western Pacific, as of dawn.

Soon afterward, Domei, the Japanese official news agency, announced that "naval operations are progressing off Hawaii, with at least one Japanese aircraft carrier in action against Pearl Harbor," the American naval base in the

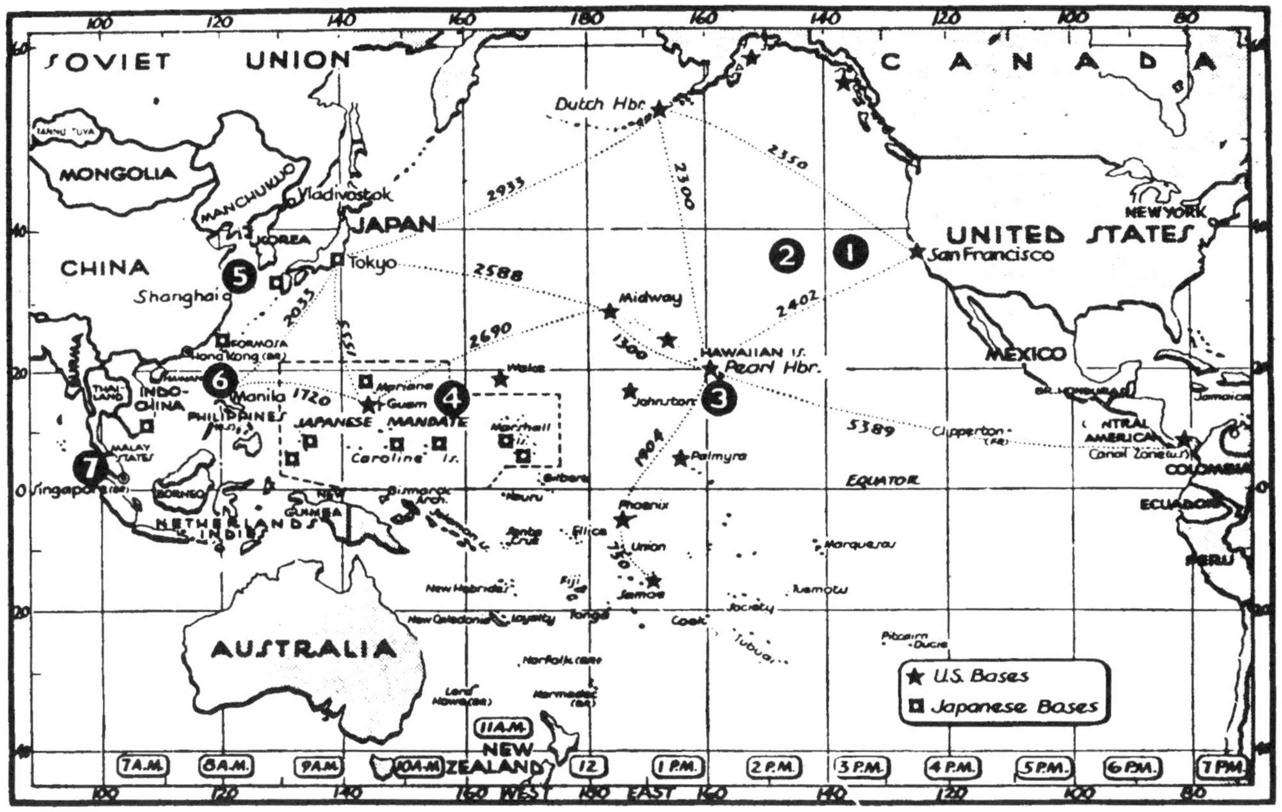

PACIFIC OCEAN: THEATRE OF WAR INVOLVING UNITED STATES AND ITS ALLIES

Shortly after the outbreak of hostilities an American ship sent a distress call from (1) and a United States Army transport carrying lumber was torpedoed at (2). The most important action was at Hawaii (3), where Japanese planes bombed the great Pearl Harbor base. Also attacked was Guam (4). From Manila (6) United States bombers roared northward, while some parts of the Philippines were raided, as was Hong Kong, to the northwest. At Shanghai (5) a British gunboat was sunk and an American gunboat seized. To the south, in the Malaya area (7), the British bombed Japanese ships, Tokyo forces attempted landings on British territory and Singapore underwent an air raid. Distances between key Pacific points are shown on the map in statute miles.

GUAM BOMBED; ARMY SHIP IS SUNK

U. S. Fliers Head North From Manila—Battleship Oklahoma Set Afire by Torpedo Planes at Honolulu

104 SOLDIERS KILLED AT FIELD IN HAWAII

President Fears 'Very Heavy Losses' on Oahu—Churchill Notifies Japan That a State of War Exists

By FRANK L. KLUCKHOHN
Special to THE NEW YORK TIMES.

WASHINGTON, Monday, Dec. 8—Sudden and unexpected attacks on Pearl Harbor, Honolulu, and other United States possessions in the Pacific early yesterday by the Japanese air force and navy plunged the United States and Japan into active war.

The initial attack in Hawaii, apparently launched by torpedo-carrying bombers and submarines, caused widespread damage and death. It was quickly followed by others. There were unconfirmed reports that German raiders participated in the attacks.

Guam also was assaulted from the air, as were Davao, on the island of Mindanao, and Camp John Hay, in Northern Luzon, both in the Philippines. Lieut. Gen. Douglas MacArthur, commanding the United States Army of the Far East, reported there was little damage, however.

[Japanese parachute troops had been landed in the Philip-

President, surrounded by his Cabinet and by Congressional leaders of both parties, went through reports, some official, some unconfirmed, of the continued assaults of the Japanese upon American Pacific outposts.

Meet Far Into Night

The conference lasted until after 11 o'clock and at its close an official statement was issued. This said that the President had reviewed for his conferees the latest advices from the Pacific and declared:

"It should be emphasized that the message to Congress has not yet been written and its tenor will, of course, depend on further information received between 11 o'clock tonight and noon tomorrow. Further news is coming in all the time."

Congressional leaders asserted as they left the White House that they did not know what the President would say tomorrow.

"Will the President ask for a declaration of war?" Speaker Rayburn was asked.

"He didn't say," answered the Speaker.

Asked whether Congress would support a declaration of war, Mr. Rayburn observed:

"I think that is one thing on which there would be unity."

Politics Declared Dropped

"There is no politics here," said Representative Joseph W. Martin Jr., Minority House Leader. "There is only one party when it comes to the integrity and honor of the country."

"The Republicans," said Senator Charles L. McNary of Oregon, the Senate minority leader, "will all go along, in my opinion, with whatever is done."

Unless international developments and plans changed overnight, it was indicated, the Presidential recommendations would be directed for the present, at least, at Japan only. This was asserted authoritatively in the face of widespread expectation that any

Continued on Page Six

Japanese bombers were declared to have raided Honolulu at 7:35 A. M., Hawaii time [1:05 Sunday, Eastern standard time].

Premier-War Minister General Hideki Tojo held a twenty-minute Cabinet session at his official residence at 7 A. M.

Soon afterward it was announced that both the United States Ambassador, Joseph C. Grew, and the British Ambassador, Sir Robert Leslie Craigie, had been summoned by *Foreign Minister Shigenori* Togo.

The Foreign Minister, Domei said, handed to Mr. Grew the Japanese Government's formal reply to the note sent to Japan by United States Secretary of State Cordell Hull on Nov. 26.

[In the course of the diplomatic negotiations leading up to yesterday's events, the Domei agency had stated that Japan could not accept the premises of Mr. Hull's note.]

Sir Robert was summoned by

Continued on Page Five

LANDS IN MALAYA

First Attempt Is Repulsed—Singapore Is Bombed and Thailand Invaded

By The Associated Press.

SINGAPORE, Monday, Dec. 8—The Japanese landed in Northern Malaya, 300 miles north of Singapore, today and bombed this great British naval stronghold, causing small loss of life among civilians and property damage.

About 300 Japanese troops landed on the east coast of Malaya and began filtering through jungle-fringed swamps and rice fields toward Kota Bahru airdrome, which is ten miles from the northern terminus of a railroad leading to Singapore.

An official report from the

Continued on Page Two

The International Situation

MONDAY, DEC. 8, 1941

Yesterday morning Japan attacked the United States at several points in the Pacific. President Roosevelt ordered United States forces into action and a declaration of war is expected this morning. [Page 1, Columns 7 and 8.] Tokyo made its declaration as of this morning against both the United States and Britain. [Page 1, Column 2.] The first Japanese assault was directed at Pearl Harbor Naval base in Hawaii. Many casualties and severe damage resulted. [Page 1, Columns 4 and 5; Map, Page 13.] United States Army aircraft took off from the Philippines this morning and some points in the Archipelago were bombed. [Page 8, Column 2.] Singapore and Hong Kong were bombed and a Japanese landing in Northern Malaya and a move on Thailand were reported. [Page 1, Column 3.] In Shanghai, Japanese marines occupied the waterfront; a British gunboat was sunk, a United States gunboat seized. [Page 9, Column 1.]

Factional lines dissolved as an angered Congress prepared to meet this morning. [Page 1, Column 1.] Secretary of State Hull accused Japan of having made a "treacherous and utterly unprovoked attack" after having been "infamously false and fraudulent." [Page 1, Column 6.] He released the text of diplomatic exchanges with Japan [Page 10], while the President gave out the text of his fruitless appeal to the Japanese Emperor. [Page 12.] The White House was the hub of Washington activity and news bulletins were released there. [Page 12, Column 3.]

The Federal Bureau of Investigation was ordered to begin a round-up of some Japanese in this country. [Page 6, Column 8.] As New York City went on a war footing and public precautions were taken, the FBI began the detention of Japanese nationals. [Page 1, Column 4.]

The unification of the country under the impact of the attack was swift. [Page 6, Column 6.] Formerly conspicuous isolationists indicated full support for the war effort. [Page 6, Column 4.]

Prime Minister Churchill notified Tokyo that a state of war existed. [Page 4, Column 1.] Declarations were made last night or early today by Australia, Canada [Page 14 Column 1], the Netherlands Indies [Page 7, Column 2] and Costa Rica. [Page 15, Column 1.]

Libya was the scene of a renewed tank battle and the Tobruk corridor was reported again clear of Axis forces. [Page 20, Column 2, with map.] On the Moscow front the German line was broken at two places, said Soviet sources. [Page 17, Column 2.]

At Our Main Bases on Oahu

By The United Press.

HONOLULU, Dec. 7—War broke with lightning suddenness in the Pacific today when waves of Japanese bombers attacked Hawaii this morning and the United States Fleet struck back with a thunder of big naval rifles. Japanese bombers, including four-engined dive bombers and torpedo-carrying planes, blasted at Pearl Harbor, the great United States naval base, the city of Honolulu and several outlying American military bases on the Island of Oahu. There were casualties of unstated number.

[The United States battleship Oklahoma was set afire by the Japanese attackers, according to a National Broadcasting Company observer, who also reported in a broadcast yesterday that two other ships in Pearl Harbor were attacked.

[The Japanese news agency, Domei, reported that the battleship Oklahoma had been sunk at Pearl Harbor, according to a United Press dispatch from Shanghai.

[Governor Joseph B. Poindexter of Hawaii talked with President Roosevelt late yesterday afternoon, saying that a second wave of Japanese bombers was just coming over, and the Gov-

Continued on Page Thirteen

ENTIRE CITY PUT ON WAR FOOTING

Japanese Rounded Up by FBI, Sent to Ellis Island—Vital Services Are Guarded

The metropolitan district reacted swiftly yesterday to the Japanese attack in the Pacific. All large communities in the area, including New York City, Newark, Jersey City, Bayonne and Paterson, went on immediate war footing.

One of the first steps taken here last night was a round-up of Japanese nationals by special agents of the Federal Bureau of Investigation, reinforced by squads of city detectives acting under FBI supervision. More than 100 FBI men, fully armed, were assigned to the detail.

The prisoners were sent to Ellis Island, where they will be held pending action at Washington. It was indicated hundreds would be detained.

Earlier Mayor La Guardia had convened his Emergency Board and directed that Japanese nationals be confined to their homes pending decision as to their status and had their clubs and other meeting places closed and put under police guard.

A police sergeant and five policemen immediately went to the Japanese Consulate at 630 Fifth Avenue in Rockefeller Center where the Consul General, Morito Morishima, and his staff were preparing to leave, and posted a guard there. The Consul General and his staff were escorted to their homes when they left. They were not to move about the city without police in attendance.

Rear Admiral Adolphus Andrews, commander of the North Atlantic Squadron, told reporters at a conference in the Federal

Continued on Page Three

TOKYO 'INFAMY'

Brands Japan 'Fraudulent' in Preparing Attack While Carrying On Parleys

Texts of Secretary Hull's note and Japan's reply, Page 10.

By BERTRAM D. HULEN
Special to THE NEW YORK TIMES.

WASHINGTON, Dec. 7—Japan was accused by Secretary of State Cordell Hull today of making a "treacherous and utterly unprovoked attack" upon the United States and of having been "infamously false and fraudulent" by preparing for the attack while conducting diplomatic negotiations with the professed desire of maintaining peace.

But even before he knew of the attack, Mr. Hull had vehemently brought the diplomatic negotiations to a virtual end with an outburst against Admiral Kichisaburo Nomura, the Japanese Ambassador, and Saburo Kurusu, special envoy, because of the insulting character of the reply they deliv-

Continued on Page Eleven

Lewis Wins Captive Mine Fight; Arbitrators Grant Union Shop

The three-man arbitration board appointed by President Roosevelt to arbitrate the union shop dispute in the captive coal mines last night reversed the decision of the National Defense Mediation Board and ruled that all workers in the captive mines should be required to join John L. Lewis's United Mine Workers as a condition of employment.

The decision was made by a two to one vote, with Benjamin F. Fairless, president of the United States Steel Corporation, dissenting. Dr. John R. Steelman, who took a leave of absence from his post as director of the United States Conciliation Service to serve as chairman of the arbitration panel, and Mr. Lewis voted in favor of extension to the captive mines of the union shop provision of the standard Appalachian agreement.

Despite his dissent, Mr. Fairless promised that the coal mining subsidiaries of United States Steel would put the ruling into effect. All eight steel companies operating captive mines had given formal assurances before the decision was reached that they would accept it as binding.

The arbitration award ended a dispute in which Mr. Lewis had repeatedly defied the President by calling strikes that menaced the production of steel and that had had its repercussions in the enactment by the House of the Smith anti-strike bill.

In explaining his vote for the union shop, Dr. Steelman pointed out that 95 per cent of the 53,000 captive miners had voluntarily assumed membership in Mr. Lewis's C. I. O. union and that 99.5 per cent of all the miners in the nation were now members of the union.

Since the bulk of the industry, including many owners of captive mines, was already operating under the union shop, it could not be argued that the United Mine Workers was endeavoring to take

Continued on Page Forty-three

pines and native Japanese had seized some communities, Royal Arch Gunnison said in a broadcast from Manila today to WOR-Mutual. He reported without detail that "in the naval war the ABCD fleets under American command appeared to be successful" against Japanese invasions.]

Japanese submarines, ranging out over the Pacific, sank an American transport carrying lumber 1,300 miles from San Francisco, and distress signals were heard from a freighter 700 miles from that city.

The War Department reported that 104 soldiers died and 300 were wounded as a result of the attack on Hickam Field, Hawaii. The National Broadcasting Company reported from Honolulu that the battleship Oklahoma was afire. [Domei, Japanese news agency, reported the Oklahoma sunk.]

Nation Placed on Full War Basis

The news of these surprise attacks fell like a bombshell on Washington. President Roosevelt immediately ordered the country and the Army and Navy onto a full war footing. He arranged at a White House conference last night to address a joint session of Congress at noon today, presumably to ask for declaration of a formal state of war.

This was disclosed after a long special Cabinet meeting, which was joined later by Congressional leaders. These leaders predicted "action" within a day.

After leaving the White House conference Attorney General Francis Biddle said that "a resolution" would be introduced in Congress tomorrow. He would not amplify or affirm that it would be for a declaration of war.

Congress probably will "act" within the day, and he will call the Senate Foreign Relations Committee for this purpose, Chairman Tom Connally announced.

[A United Press dispatch from London this morning said that Prime Minister Churchill had notified Japan that a state of war existed.]

As the reports of heavy fighting flashed into the White House, London reported semi-officially that the British Empire would carry out Prime Minister Winston Churchill's pledge to give the United States full support in case of hostilities with Japan. The President and Mr. Churchill talked by transatlantic telephone.

This was followed by a statement in London from the Netherland Government in Exile that it considered a state of war to exist between the Netherlands and Japan. Canada, Australia and Costa Rica took similar action.

Landing Made in Malaya

A Singapore communiqué disclosed that Japanese troops had landed in Northern Malaya and that Singapore had been bombed.

The President told those at last night's White House meeting that "doubtless very heavy losses" were sustained by the Navy and also by the Army on the island of Oahu [Honolulu]. It was impossible to obtain confirmation or denial of reports that the battleships Oklahoma and West Virginia had been damaged or sunk at Pearl Harbor, together with six or seven destroyers, and that 350 United States airplanes had been caught on the ground.

The White House took over control of the bulletins, and the Navy Department, therefore, said it could not discuss the matter or answer any questions how the Japanese were able to penetrate the Hawaiian defenses or appear without previous knowledge of their presence in those waters.

Administration circles forecast that the United States soon might be involved in a world-wide war, with Germany supporting Japan, an Axis partner. The German official radio tonight attacked the United States and supported Japan.

Axis diplomats here expressed complete surprise that the Japanese had attacked. But the impression gained from their attitude was that they believed it represented a victory for the Nazi attempt to divert lease-lend aid from Britain, which has been

Continued on Page Four

"All the News That's Fit to Print."

The New York Times.

LATE CITY EDITION
Partly cloudy today and tomorrow with little change in temperature.
Temperatures Yesterday—Max., 63; Min., 52

VOL. LXXXIX..No. 30,079. Entered as Second-Class Matter, Postoffice, New York, N. Y. NEW YORK, SATURDAY, JUNE 1, 1940. THREE CENTS NEW YORK CITY and Vicinity | FOUR CENTS Elsewhere Except in 7th and 8th Postal Zones.

75% OF B.E.F. REPORTED SAFELY OUT OF FLANDERS; ALLIES ATTACK ON SOMME, WIN ABBEVILLE AREA; ROOSEVELT WARNS WAR IMPERILS WHOLE WORLD

PLEA TO CONGRESS

President Asks Power to Call Out National Guard if Needed

BILLION MORE FUNDS

All Continents May Be Involved, Says New Defense Message

Text of the President's defense message is on Page 6.

By FELIX BELAIR JR.
Special to THE NEW YORK TIMES.

WASHINGTON, May 31—Warning that "all continents may become involved in a world-wide war," President Roosevelt in a special message today asked Congress for "over $1,000,000,000" in supplemental appropriations for preparedness, and for specific authority to call the National Guard and Army Reserves to active duty if needed to safeguard neutrality and for the national defense.

Further enlargement of the defense forces, for which outlays of more than $3,300,000,000 are pending in Congress, were necessary, the President said, in view of the success of blitzkrieg tactics on the Flanders Front.

He did not mention Germany, but referred to the "almost incredible events of the past two weeks in the European conflict."

The message contained no analysis of the way the money would be spent, but the President said he had instructed War and Navy Department experts to appear for this purpose before Senate and House committees. Representatives of other agencies were ordered to explain Administration plans for a 1,000,000-man Army for noncombat work incident to military and naval operations.

Immediate Orders in View

War Department plans, which were not described by the President, call for placing immediate orders for 2,800 bomber and pursuit planes, 1,700 tanks, about 500 heavy artillery units and larger quantities of anti-tank and anti-aircraft guns and other weapons perfected in War and Navy Department laboratories but not yet in actual production. The airplane cannon is an example of the latter.

Meanwhile, it was apparent that President Roosevelt had continued until today his correspondence with Premier Mussolini in an effort to forestall Italy's entry into the war. White House aides refused to say whether the President sent another appeal to the Italian dictator yesterday, but said such correspondence had been on a continuing basis.

Congressional reaction to the President's message was generally favorable, but two Republican Senators attacked his request for authority to call out the National Guard and the Army Reserves. Senator Vandenberg described the proposal as "shocking," and suggested that if an emergency was imminent Congress should remain in session.

Committee Takes Up Tax Bill

While the Senate put off consideration of two big Navy bills to debate the proposed transfer of the Immigration and Naturalization Bureau of the Labor Department to the Department of Justice, the Ways and Means Committee of the House took up the taxation bill by which it is hoped to raise $656,000,000 a year to finance the unprecedented peacetime defense program.

In the executive branch, the Advisory Defense Committee was organizing its administrative machinery in an effort to realize President Roosevelt's purpose of gearing the nation's industrial capacity to full defense production at the end of six months.

President Roosevelt assigned Attorney General Jackson to cooperate with State Governors in setting up State Defense Commissions. The White House said that the Federal Government was not sponsoring such commissions, but was interested principally in avoiding conflicts in their activities.

Edsel Ford conferred with Secretary Morgenthau at the Secretary's request, and with Dr. George J. Mead, in charge of coordinating the department's aeronautical activi-

Continued on Page Six

The International Situation

On the Battle Fronts

Unofficial estimates in London last night placed the number of British Expeditionary Force troops safely removed from the Flanders pocket at three-quarters of the original forces there. The action was regarded as one of the greatest military and naval feats of all time. [Page 1.]

With the battle in the north in its final stages, the French main army and the new B. E. F. in France went resolutely ahead with their preparations to meet and checkmate the next German offensive.

French tanks pounded at the Nazi positions along the Somme, straightening the new defense line that stretches east and north from Abbeville on the Channel coast along the Somme, Aisne and Chiers Rivers to the Luxembourg border. Success was reported in all local actions. Behind the natural and man-made defenses along the French rivers was an army whose morale appeared to have been strengthened instead of broken by the reverses in Flanders. The Blitzkrieg had achieved only a half victory in four weeks of desperate fighting, it was said by the Allies, and they were now prepared to meet and repel any German attempt to overrun France and bring a quick end to the war. [All the foregoing on Page 1.]

The British Air Force continued its fight against odds in protecting the evacuation from Flanders and the Channel crossing. Between flights the young pilots of the R. A. F. calmly sipped tea at their home fields. [Page 3.]

The German High Command said the Flanders and Artois campaigns were virtually over. The three French armies in the pocket had been either captured or destroyed, a German communiqué said, with only isolated groups still offering resistance. Fog, which grounded German planes, aided the evacuation of the Allied armies from Dunkerque and the other coastal debarkation points. The completion of operations in Flanders, the High Command said, had released the German troops there "for other tasks" and the stage was set for the second phase of the war. [Page 1.]

Repercussions Elsewhere

President Roosevelt warned Congress in a special message that the war may spread to all continents and asked an additional billion dollars for Army, Navy and civilian training programs. He requested special legislation empowering him to call any part or all of the National Guard into active service, and authority to hire "dollar-a-year" men to speed defense appropriations. Congressional reaction to the new requests was generally favorable. [Page 1.]

Tension heightened in Italy as the hour of decision neared; Premier Mussolini was said to be so busy making preparations for all eventualities that he had no time to receive United States Ambassador Phillips with another message from President Roosevelt. One of the preparations made, it was reported, was negotiation of a pact with Japan for the latter country to supply Ethiopia with food and raw materials in event Italy should go to war. [Page 1.]

A Uruguayan Government investigation of fifth column activities indicated widespread Nazi penetration in South America. The estimated 3,000 Germans in that small South American nation are highly organized along Nazi lines, complete with a secret police, the investigation has revealed. The local Germans are taxed not only for the expenses of their own organization but for the Nazi party in Germany. Their organization and propaganda work has been aided by the German Legation in Montevideo, it was charged. [Page 1.]

The liner President Roosevelt arrived at Galway, Ireland, last night to bring home more than 900 Americans, warned out of the British Isles by the danger of invasion. Their baggage was carefully examined to guard against any explosion at sea that might be blamed on Britain by Germany, as was the sinking of the Athenia Sept. 3. [Page 1.] Twenty-two other vessels were en route to America from Mediterranean ports, each of them also loaded to capacity with Americans fleeing the war. [Follows Galway story.]

U. S. Cruiser Is Sent South; Uruguay Finds Nazis Plotting

Quincy Hastily Dispatched on 'Good-Will' Mission to South America—Fear of Fifth Column Is Growing

Ready to Give Aid

By FRANK L. KLUCKHOHN
Special to THE NEW YORK TIMES.

WASHINGTON, May 31—The 10,000-ton cruiser Quincy, carrying two airplanes, is rushing tonight toward the east coast of South America on what is briefly announced by the Navy to be a "good-will" cruise, but on what is reliably reported to be the special mission of aiding several Latin-American countries, if necessary, in meeting Nazi fifth column activities.

The Quincy's first stop will be Rio de Janeiro, but it is believed that the cruiser may proceed on to Montevideo, where Uruguayan officials are frankly alarmed over organized Nazi activities and where President Alfredo Baldomir has sent to Congress a bill modifying constitutional provisions dealing with freedom of assembly.

The projected cruise to Rio de Janeiro of three battleships, the New York, Texas and Arkansas, was canceled coincidentally. While no official reason for the cancellation was given, it was believed possible here that the Quincy was better suited to the needs of the situation since she is one of the Navy's later ships and extremely fast. Moreover, the battleships planned to carry midshipmen on a cruise, and the middies are not usually taken to areas where action may develop.

The Quincy was on her shakedown cruise when the Spanish Civil War started in 1936 and was immediately rushed to Spain in order

Continued on Page Five

Organization Revealed

By JOHN W. WHITE
Wireless to THE NEW YORK TIMES.

MONTEVIDEO, Uruguay, May 31—The Uruguayan investigation of fifth column activities is disclosing an almost unbelievable Nazi political penetration into South America.

Conclusive evidence has been accumulated by police raids and other investigating methods to show that the Nazi party has established a perfectly organized branch party in Uruguay known as the Uruguayan District Group of the German National Socialist Party. It is under the leadership of a "little Fuehrer" and acknowledges dependence on and allegiance to the Nazi party headquarters in Germany.

Diplomatic and other observers consider the Uruguayan Government's investigation of the utmost importance because it is uncovering the details of Nazi methods throughout Latin America.

Argentina's investigation last year showed that the Germans there had organized as the Argentine District Group Party. Newspapers in several other republics, including Chile, Colombia and Bolivia, have charged that similar organizations exist in their countries. Latin-American diplomats here are informing their governments, therefore, that the details of Nazi operations in Uruguay are indicative of what can be expected in all other South and Central American nations.

These details show the existence of a general Nazi party organiza-

Continued on Page Five

GERMANS CAPTURED

Nazi War Material Also Taken Near Abbeville in Mopping-Up Drive

ALLIES CONTROL AIR

French Planes Dropping Food to Trapped Army Battling to Coast

By The Associated Press.

PARIS, May 31—French tanks supporting a second British Expeditionary Force being formed in France pounded at the Germans along the Somme front tonight.

They mopped up the Abbeville sector and reported they had regained unbroken command south of the Somme.

The Abbeville bridgehead was taken, but the capture of the town itself—lying to the north of the river—was not claimed. It remained in No Man's Land. Hundreds of Nazi prisoners and a mass of German war material were declared seized.

In the north, where the rearguard of the Allied armies of Flanders were struggling to force a passage through the Germans—who sought to cut them off in the mountains southeast of Dunkerque -- French bombers defied anti-aircraft fire and low visibility to drop food and munitions for the isolated forces.

More than twenty tons of bombs were launched by two flights of French bombers in heavy attacks on German concentrations north of the Somme and German anti-aircraft batteries and other objectives near Abbeville.

Bridgeheads Wiped Out

The tanks which led the Allied attack in the Abbeville sector were mostly of medium weight, twenty-three tons.

This apparent prelude to large-scale action on a new front—a front protecting Paris—was reported by the War Ministry spokesman along with a declaration that the flood waters spouting through locks opened by the French were holding back the German effort to smash Dunkerque, the port of exit for the retreating northern Allies.

These men were moving in retreat in a rectangle that earlier had been reported holding generally firm under the assaults of the greatest mechanized German Army ever to take the field.

Two muddy and weary divisions of the command of General René-Jacques-Adolphe Prioux—originally totaling about 30,000 men—led the march into Dunkerque, the Allied port of exit to the sea.

The Allied corridor of escape stretched from near Lille to Dunkerque.

Illustrating the cost to Germany of the massive offensive that began with the invasion of the Low Countries on May 10, the semi-official Telefrance Agency declared that since then the Nazis had lost 500,000 men—a figure which the agency asserted "finds itself writ-

Continued on Page Two

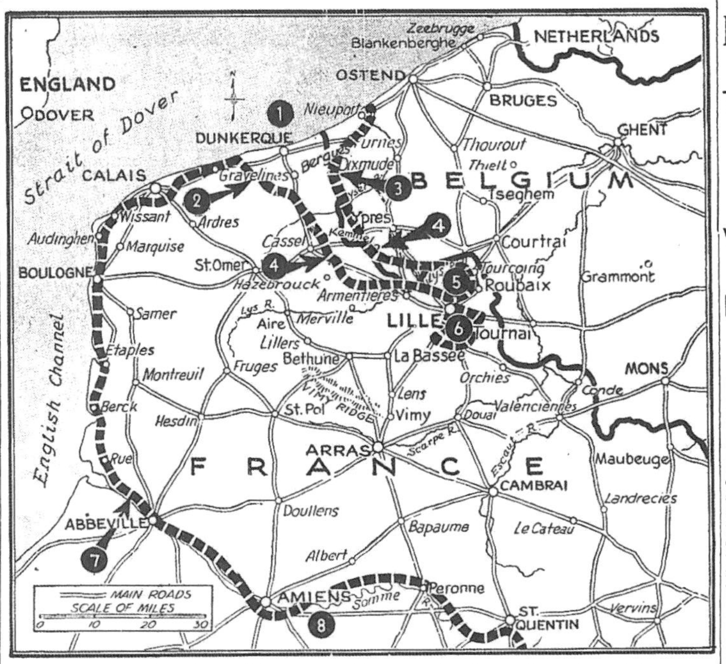

ALLIES ATTACK ON SOMME AND PUSH FLANDERS RESCUE

Large additional forces of British and French troops were embarked from Dunkerque (1) as foggy weather hampered German bombing of their retreat. The Nazis pressed against the sides of the pocket from the direction of Gravelines (2) and between Furnes and Bergues (3), but floodwaters from opened locks helped the hard-fighting withdrawing army hold them back. The Germans claimed to have wiped out a British force in the Mont Cassel area (4) and severe fighting raged between there and Mont Kemmel. The Nazis said French groups were isolated in two pockets north and south of Lille (5) and (6). The French announced the mopping up of the sector south of Abbeville (7) as French tanks pounded at the Germans along the Somme front (8).

MUSSOLINI TOO BUSY TO HEAR U. S. PLEA

Envoy Unable to Hand Him Roosevelt Note—Nation Tense With War Fever

By HERBERT L. MATTHEWS
By Telephone to THE NEW YORK TIMES.

ROME, May 31—Events seem to be approaching the grand and terrible climax for Italy.

For the first time since the tension started here, the feeling is that it is a question of days, rather than weeks; and one sign of it is that Premier Mussolini would not accept in person a message that United States Ambassador William Phillips tried yesterday to deliver to him on behalf of President Roosevelt.

The refusal was in no sense a rebuff to the United States or to Mr. Roosevelt. If it were only that there would be less anxiety about the immediate future. The reason Signor Mussolini did not receive Mr. Phillips is that there is no longer any time for such audiences.

[Italy has broken off negotiations with Britain through which the British planned to ease in behalf of Italian shipping the Allied

Continued on Page Four

'Kidnap Hitler' Prize Passes Over Deadline

Special to THE NEW YORK TIMES.

PITTSBURGH, May 31—One of those "once in a lifetime" opportunities, a chance to make $1,000,000, passed into discard at midnight, when Dr. Samuel Harden Church's offer of that sum for the kidnapping of Adolf Hitler expired.

Whether or not any one made a serious attempt to get the money is perhaps known only to Dr. Church, who refused to comment as his offer concluded, but he did admit that he would make a statement for publication Sunday.

Reporters who tried to reach the president of Carnegie Institute at his home or by phone were told by his secretary that a statement was forthcoming.

Dr. Church originally made the offer in behalf of fifty unidentified Pittsburghers, who put up $1,000,000 for the safe deliverance of Germany's leader to a League of Nations court.

FRENCH AT FRONT SEE FINAL VICTORY

War Has Shown the Germans Inferior, They Say, Despite Great Weapons

By P. J. PHILIP
Wireless to THE NEW YORK TIMES.

WITH THE FRENCH ARMIES IN THE EAST, May 31—Nothing of all the terrible things that have happened in these past three weeks since the German offensive began has shaken the amazing, one might almost say sublime, confidence with which the still intact bulk of the French Army regards the future. Coming again into this district just three weeks from the day when the first intimation of the German attack came to me and others in the shape of bombs crashing down on houses around us, it seems incredible that so much has changed.

Then the Maginot Line was an imposing barricade. The French and British Armies in the north lay behind what were believed to be the strong defenses and powerful armies of the Netherlands and Belgium and with defenses of their own. The only warfare that was going on was the Indian warfare of night skirmishing parties.

Now in these three weeks the German Army has completely overrun and conquered the Netherlands and Belgium, it has pushed through Northern France to the sea, forced,

Continued on Page Three

Liner Roosevelt at Galway for Americans; 900 Set to Sail; Others Dash From London

Wireless to THE NEW YORK TIMES.

GALWAY, Ireland, May 31—All alight and with the United States flag prominently displayed, America's refugee ship, the President Roosevelt, arrived at the outskirts of Galway Bay at 10 o'clock tonight.

A pilot boat water tender conveying shipping officials set out from the harbor here at 9 o'clock. Police Superintendent Thomas Collins, Commander Norman Hitchcock, Naval Air Attaché of the United States in the London Embassy, and an Irish Army representative were also on the tender.

The first batch of about 900 passengers is going out by tender at noon tomorrow. The last tender is going out at midnight tomorrow night and the President Roosevelt is expected to depart for the United States at an early hour on Sunday morning.

The boom which the hotel business has experienced here as a result of the big influx of American refugees was enhanced this afternoon when 200 more arrived by special train from Dublin. But the trek of the weary and luggage-laden Americans was hastened. Since the President Roosevelt's departure is not likely to take place until Sunday, about fifty more Americans, it was stated here, are making a dash from London tonight to make the homeward trip.

In addition to the hotels, the Galway stores are reaping much extra business from the influx, and there are brisk sales on such goods as Irish linen, lace, pottery, handicrafts and souvenirs.

Stringent precautions are being taken with regard to the examination of passengers and luggage and there is a rigid exclusion of all but passenger officials from the boat, due, it was learned today, to a special request of the United States Government, with which the Irish Government is in thorough agreement. Every precaution is being taken to insure that neither undesirable persons nor property will get on the ship. The augmented

Continued on Page Two

NEW GERMAN DRIVE NEAR, BERLIN HINTS

Push Toward Paris Expected as Flanders Battle Ends—Hitler Sees Rome Envoy

By PERCIVAL KNAUTH
Wireless to THE NEW YORK TIMES.

BERLIN, May 31—The battle in Artois and Flanders is over. The French First, Seventh and Ninth Armies engaged in these sectors, the Germans report, now are either captured or destroyed, with only isolated handfuls still offering flickering resistance in woods and villages. Between Dunkerque and Nieuport, a British rear guard is covering the evacuation of the final remnants of the British Expeditionary Force, which is escaping under cover of a thick Channel fog.

"The main bodies of the German divisions in Artois and Flanders are now free for other duties," today's communiqué of the German High Command declares. The stage is set for the second and possibly final phase of the big offensive.

At this critical hour, when Germany claims to have driven a wedge between the Allied armies, the dramatic entrance on the scene of her allied partner, Italy, is believed to be imminent. Italy's entrance in the war, in the opinion of neutral diplomatic circles here, probably will be synchronized with the launching of the second German drive.

Ribbentrop at Meeting

In his headquarters "somewhere in the West," Chancellor Hitler today received Count Dino Alfieri, the new Italian Ambassador to Germany. It was the second time that Premier Mussolini's envoy had been to the Chancellor's general headquarters, and the significance of this audience was enhanced by the fact that Joachim von Ribbentrop, German Foreign Minister, also was present.

[Authorized quarters, meanwhile, refused to confirm or deny reports that Dr. Joseph Goebbels, German Propaganda Minister, had been summoned to Herr Hitler's field headquarters from Berlin to prepare an "important announcement," according to The United Press.]

The German troops that swept

Continued on Page Four

Dispatches from Europe and the Far East are subject to censorship at the source.

BRITAIN HAILS MEN

Thousands More Arrive in Port to Receive a Frenzied Welcome

YACHTS, BARGES USED

Navy Praised Highly for Its Brilliant Feats in Evacuation

By HAROLD DENNY
Wireless to THE NEW YORK TIMES.

LONDON, May 31—About three-quarters of the British Expeditionary Force thus far has been evacuated from Dunkerque and brought to England, it was estimated unofficially in well-informed quarters late tonight. Military authorities would not confirm or deny this estimate, the actual figures being kept secret.

[The United Press reported that it was estimated that 75 to 80 per cent of the British Expeditionary Force and some of its Allies trapped by the Germans in Flanders had been snatched from what had appeared to be the certain annihilation of more than 500,000 men. Original estimates of the strength of the B. E. F. ranged from 300,000 to 350,000.

["At least one Belgian army corps is still fighting side by side with the Allies," the British Broadcasting Corporation said early today in a news broadcast picked up in New York by the National Broadcasting Company. The corps was said to be under the command of the former commander of the Liége district who had refused to obey King Leopold's capitulation order.]

Ragged and battle-weary British and French soldiers who fought their way out of the shambles of Northern France and Belgium continued to stream into port during the day, still dazed but happy as they hurried inland for brief leaves at home.

They were greeted with almost delirious enthusiasm by the populace as they disembarked from the motley collection of large and small boats which had ferried them across the Channel and by cheering crowds all along the railway lines.

They were welcomed not sadly as a beaten army but proudly as the heroes in one of the bravest chapters in Great Britain's military annals.

Earlier this week high army officers had expressed the fear that almost the entire British Expeditionary Force would be lost. To date a far larger number has been returned safely to England than any one had dared to hope.

The primary reason for this result is said to have been the skillful coordination with the troops by the British Navy assisted by elements of the French Navy and by the Royal Air Force in conjunction with French aviators.

Troops' Conduct Praised

The behavior of the soldiers under a pounding by a vastly superior force such as no troops ever had had to withstand before is praised without measure by commanders returning with them, who have seen much of the war. These soldiers stood their ground and retired always in perfect order under admirable discipline. So these fine battalions, among them some of the best in the British Army, were not destroyed after all, but their survivors after a rest will be able to re-form with additions and take the field again better than they were before, because now they are used to the most terrible engines the Germans can hurl against them.

Part of the B. E. F. and a considerable force of French still are holding a narrow strip of coast behind Dunkerque covering the withdrawal. This strip now is being called the "Corunna line" in memory of Sir John Moore's classic withdrawal from Spain in 1809, when his army had been placed in a similarly hopeless situation by the defection of the Spanish. French troops are in this line with the British, while more are with General Rene Prioux among those who are fighting their way to the coast.

The part played by the British fleet is so brilliant that today's returning soldiers shouted to the crowds along the beach: "Thank God for the navy" and cheered sailors on shore whenever they

Continued on Page Three

"All the News That's Fit to Print."

The New York Times.

LATE CITY EDITION
Cloudy with showers and little change in temperature today and tomorrow.
Temperatures Yesterday—Max., 65; Min., 57

VOL. LXXXIX..No. 30,089. Entered as Second-Class Matter, Postoffice, New York, N. Y. NEW YORK, TUESDAY, JUNE 11, 1940. THREE CENTS NEW YORK CITY and Vicinity | FOUR CENTS Elsewhere Except in 7th and 8th Postal Zones.

ITALY AT WAR, READY TO ATTACK; STAB IN BACK, SAYS ROOSEVELT; GOVERNMENT HAS LEFT PARIS

NAZIS NEAR PARIS

Units Reported to Have Broken Through Lines to West of Capital

SEINE RIVER CROSSED

3 Columns Branch Out From Soissons—Enemy Held, French State

By The Associated Press.

PARIS, June 10—Marauding German tanks were reported tonight to have reached the Paris region itself as the government left the capital.

While some German armored advance guards were said to have penetrated to the environs of Paris in isolated raids through the French lines, the main front was about thirty-five miles west and northeast of the capital. Although steadily approaching, the battle's roar still could not be heard here.

[The German High Command has no knowledge that Nazi tank units have reached the Paris region, The United Press reported.]

The battle, which had been waged heretofore on familiar World War territory for the most part, swung into virgin soil as the Germans advanced west of Paris.

In the triangle bounded by Amiens on the Somme, Rouen, seventy miles west of Paris on the Seine, and Vernon, forty miles west on the Seine, the Germans redoubled their attacks, crossing the river at several points. An armored column, which crossed the Bresle last week, led the assault.

The French took their main stand west of Paris all along the Seine in an effort to prevent the Germans from effecting further passages and taking the capital from the rear.

In the central sector of the Oise Valley, directly north of Paris where the Germans had suffered tremendous losses, they held back their infantry and sent out dive bombers in an effort to break down French resistance.

They broadened their salient, however, farther east, where they had crossed the Aisne. Three columns fanned out from Soissons through La Ferte Milon and Fere en Tardenois and toward Fismes.

Hold Firm on East Flank

They were just north of Chateau-Thierry and the Marne, where they were stopped in their 1918 thrust by Americans fighting with the French.

On the east flank, where the French have been holding firm, fresh German infantry, tanks and planes battered the French lines, but with small gains.

But France, besieged on two sides by Germans driving on Paris from the north and the Italians entering the war on the south, proclaimed her grim determination to carry on the fight.

The main combats were centered in the Seine Valley to the west of Paris, with the High Command declaring that some German elements had crossed the Seine River at certain points, and in the Ourcq River Valley to the northeast of the capital.

The communiqué, however, said the "enemy is held everywhere by vigorous counter-attacks."

The French communiqué was filed from Paris, but was issued "Somewhere in France." The regular press conference of the War Office was not held this morning, as only a few attachés were in the office.

The High Command reported that the German break-through to the Seine resulted from increased pressure applied by the Nazis between the route from Amiens to Rouen and from Amiens to Vernon as far as the lower Seine.

In the other principal area of combat, east of the Oise River, German columns coming down from the region of Soissons have resumed their attack toward the Ourcq River.

The German offensive in the

Continued on Page Two

The International Situation

On the Battle Fronts

Italian guns will speak today in Europe. Italy's declaration of war against France and Britain became effective at 12:01 A. M., Rome time. Before 100,000 men and women, packed in the Piazza Venezia and near-by streets, Premier Mussolini yesterday announced his decision. It was war against "the plutocratic and reactionary democracies of the West." For the present that does not include the United States, but Rome reports that few Italians, from Signor Mussolini down, believe they will see the end of this war without having America against them.

The Italian Premier specifically excluded Turkey, Switzerland, Yugoslavia, Greece and Egypt from his military designs. Rome hoped Turkey would fail to keep her agreement to support the Allies in a Mediterranean war.

Demonstrators in Rome carried placards naming Italian objectives in the war—Tunisia, Jibuti, Corsica, Suez, Malta, Cyprus. There were reports that action against some of these places already had started. But Rome was convinced that nothing big would get under way until today. [All the foregoing, Page 1, Column 8.]

The sixth day of the Battle of France brought the German invaders still closer to Paris; at one point—south of Beauvais—they were said to be within twenty-five or thirty miles of their goal. On the French left wing the Germans crossed the Seine at several points in a dangerous advance that threatened to envelop the capital. In the center, they pushed through to the Ourcq Valley, a movement that similarly threatened to flank Reims. On the French right wing the German pressure was furiously increased; but the French said no great gains had resulted. Information from the French side was less complete than usual because the government press bureau was evacuated from Paris and had not yet established a stable headquarters. [Page 1, Column 1.]

The French Government moved, apparently to the neighborhood of Tours. An exodus of civilians from Paris got under way. [Page 1, Column 2.]

Berlin analyzed the front thus: A semicircle had been thrown around Paris, from which three wedges were being driven into the defense lines. The first, in the lower Seine Valley, succeeded in cutting off the extreme left of the French Army, which can now be pushed to the coast. The second was progressing toward the Marne from the Aisne below Soissons. The third, on the French right, had pierced the Aisne and was headed toward Reims. [Page 1, Column 5.]

London admitted the loss of the airplane carrier Glorious, two destroyers, a transport and an oil tanker—totaling 50,706 tons—in an engagement in the North Sea. King Haakon of Norway arrived in Britain with his government. Some Norwegian troops also were carried off and will continue the war on the Western Front. [Page 16, Column 3.]

Repercussions Elsewhere

President Roosevelt, in a broadcast speech, termed Italy's entry into the war a threat to the American way of life. "The hand that held the dagger has struck it into the back of its neighbor," he said. Declaring it an "obvious delusion that we of the United States can safely permit the United States to become a lone island in a world dominated by the philosophy of force," he advocated all possible material aid to the Allies. [Page 1, Column 4.]

The Canadian Parliament declared war against Italy; Prime Minister Mackenzie King denounced Premier Mussolini as "a carrion bird waiting for brave men to die." [Page 4, Column 5.]

Premier Reynaud, broadcasting to the French people after Italy's announcement, said France had won out over greater difficulties in the past. He asserted France always had been willing to negotiate Italian demands peaceably. [Page 12, Column 1.]

Berlin, jubilant over the entry of the Italians, expressed the belief that Premier Mussolini's military effort would be concentrated in the Mediterranean. It was said that no immediate Italian land attack on France was expected. [Page 5, Column 1.]

Switzerland reported much military activity, but no rumble of guns, in mountain passes between France and Italy. The Swiss were concerned about rumors that there were new German troop concentrations on the country's northern frontier. [Page 5, Column 5.]

Turkey stood ready to fulfill her engagements to the Allies under the mutual-assistance pact of last October. It was believed that the first step, once Italy made that pact operative by an aggressive move in the Mediterranean, would be the placing of Turkish ports and air fields at the disposal of the Allies. [Page 1, Column 7.]

Belgrade heard reports that the Italians had landed troops and much mechanized equipment at the Italian-owned port of Zara, which is on the Yugoslav coast, and on the Italian-owned island of Lagosta, near by. [Page 1, Column 6.]

FRENCH MINISTRIES MOVED SOUTHWARD

Tours Is Believed New Capital, but Reynaud Goes to Army —No Civilian Panic

By The Associated Press.

PARIS, June 10—The French Government left Paris tonight.

"Paul Reynaud, Premier, has gone with the armies," said a communiqué, which also declared:

"The High Command asked the Ministers to effect their withdrawal to the provinces in conformity with established dispositions. This withdrawal has been effected."

The announcement of the departure of the Ministers was made only after they were safely installed "somewhere in France" in the southern provinces.

The government transfer at General Maxime Weygand's request was approved last night at a Cabinet meeting.

Under cover of darkness the Ministers drove to their new offices

Continued on Page Ten

BRITISH NAVY GUNS HAMMER AT NAZIS

Shelling From Sea, Rushing of Troops and Planes Mark London's Share in Battle

By HAROLD DENNY
Special Cable to THE NEW YORK TIMES.

LONDON, June 10—Britain was rushing all available forces today into the battle in France, which was officially called here the "Battle of Paris and London" because of the Nazi threat to England. This reinforcement across the English Channel will continue, it was stated, "despite the imminent danger of German invasion of the United Kingdom."

The guns of British warships pounded the Germans to support Allied troops near the coast.

"Important contingents" of new troops have already gone to France, it was announced.

Even closer cooperation of the

Continued on Page Twelve

OUR HELP PLEDGED

President Offers Our Full Material Aid to Allies' Cause

AMERICA IN DANGER

Fate Hangs on Training and Arms, He Says at Charlottesville

The text of the President's speech will be found on Page 6.

By FELIX BELAIR Jr.
Special to THE NEW YORK TIMES.

CHARLOTTESVILLE, Va., June 10—"On this 10th day of June, 1940, the hand that held the dagger has struck it into the back of its neighbor." In these words tonight President Roosevelt condemned the decision of Premier Mussolini which took Italy into the war on the side of Germany.

The remark was interpolated by the President in an address at the graduation exercises of the University of Virginia here. There could be no missing the depth of his feeling, since he put into the words all the emphasis at his command.

Italy's intervention was denounced furthermore as a definite threat to the way of life and the trade and commerce of the Americas. This government, he said, would give all material aid to France and Great Britain as "opponents of force."

The Chief Executive of the United States spoke to the nation and to the world only a few hours after Premier Mussolini announced his decision to join hands with Chancellor Hitler and unleashed his fascist legions against France and Great Britain. More details were revealed by Mr. Roosevelt of his correspondence with the Italian dictator in an effort to keep Italy at peace and to prevent the spread of war to the Mediterranean basin.

"To the Regret of Humanity"

"Unfortunately—unfortunately, to the regret of all of us and to the regret of humanity—the chief of the Italian Government was unwilling to accept the procedure suggested, and he has made no counter proposal," the President said.

And a moment later:

"The Government of Italy has now chosen to preserve what it terms its freedom of action and to fulfill what it states are its promises to Germany. In so doing it has manifested disregard for the rights and security of other nations, disregard for the lives of the peoples of those nations which are directly threatened by the spread of this war, and has evidenced its unwillingness to find the means, through pacific negotiation, for the satisfaction of what it believes are its legitimate aspirations."

The President bespoke the prayers and hopes of this nation for those peoples beyond the seas who were battling for their freedom.

"In our American unity," he

Continued on Page Six

Nazi Tide Laps at Paris as Italy Joins War

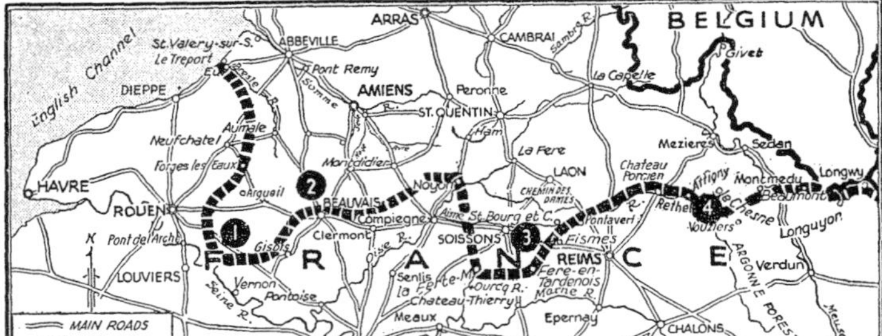

On the western end of the line the Germans pushed a wedge to the Seine southeast of Rouen (1) and struck mighty blows in the region of Beauvais (2). In the center they reached the Ourcq River below Soissons (3). To the east they crossed the Aisne at two points near Vouziers (4).

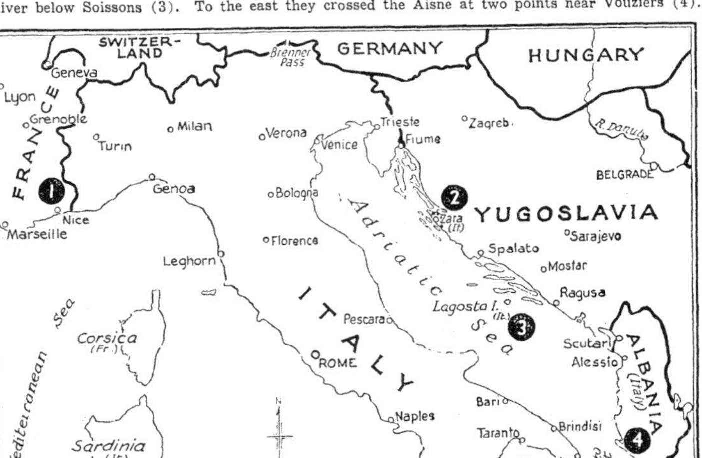

Italy's announcement of her entry into the war was accompanied by no attack anywhere. One report had Italian troops invading the French Riviera (1), but this was unsupported. Rome's troops landed at two Italian-owned points on the Yugoslav coast: Zara (2) and Lagosta (3). In Albania (4) Italian military preparations were accelerated.

NAZIS CLAIM BREAK IN SUPPLY ARTERY

Paris Cut Off From Havre by Thrust to Seine East of Rouen, Berlin Says

By C. BROOKS PETERS
Wireless to THE NEW YORK TIMES.

BERLIN, June 10—German forces in Northern France were fighting tonight to shorten the radius of a semicircle they are drawing about Paris, according to reports received here. Apparently they are attempting to drive three wedges into the remaining French territory north of the capital.

The first is on the Germans' extreme right wing, which is reported to have reached the lower Seine east of Rouen and therewith cuts off Paris from Havre. Mass tank formations, assisted by light motorized units, are claimed here to have made more than a sixty-mile ad-

Continued on Page Eleven

La Guardia Warns of Strict Neutrality Here; Consuls Told to 'Adhere to Consular Duties'

Mayor La Guardia went on the air over WNYC, the city broadcasting station, yesterday afternoon with a strong plea to the million persons of Italian blood in this city to preserve strict neutrality in the face of Italy's declaration of war.

Moving with characteristic rapidity, the Mayor telephoned the city broadcasting studio in the New York City Building at the World's Fair and said he would be on the air ten minutes later. He thought over the message he wanted to deliver while driving over from the World's Fair City Hall, and was prepared to speak immediately upon his arrival. Meantime, Morris S. Novik, director of the station, had made arrangements to rebroadcast the Mayor's talk over five commercial stations at intervals later in the day.

Speaking slowly and impressively, the Mayor stated his policy that the European war must be fought on the battlefields of Europe and not on the sidewalks of New York.

Recalling his war service as an ally of the Italian forces in Italy, the Mayor said he fully realized that the Italian entry into the war on the opposite side must be as painful to others of Italian blood as it was to him. Nevertheless, he insisted that the national policy of neutrality must be observed in the city. While he pledged full protection to consular officers of various European governments in the city, the Mayor made clear that these officials must stay within the bounds of their consular duties.

The Mayor's speech follows:

This is F. H. La Guardia, Mayor of the City of New York, talking.

On Sept. 2, 1939, when the Nazi

Continued on Page Eight

Three Italian Freighters Are Scuttled by Crews

By The Associated Press.

LA LINEA, Spain, Tuesday, June 11—Two Italian merchant ships, the 10,000-ton Chelina and the 2,000-ton Numbolia, were scuttled by their crews in Gibraltar waters late yesterday [Monday] when their crews heard the radio news that Italy had gone to war.

RIMOUSKI, Que., June 10 (UP)—The 3,921-ton Italian freighter Capo Noli was set afire by her crew tonight as she proceeded down the St. Lawrence, but the scuttling attempt failed.

The Marine Department said the Canadian pilot grounded the freighter near the Father Point pilot station. A naval control boat extinguished the flames.

The government salvage boat Lord Strathcona left Quebec tonight for the site with a large derrick in tow. The Capo Noli will be taken over by the Canadian Government and her crew probably will be interned.

ITALIANS REPORTED ON YUGOSLAV COAST

Said to Have Landed at Two Places Controlled by Rome—Mass on Greek Border

By The United Press.

BELGRADE, Yugoslavia, Tuesday, June 11—Large numbers of Italian troops were reported early today to have been landed along the Yugoslav coast at two Italian points as the Yugoslav Government prepared to fight in defense of its territory if necessary.

[It was reported from Berlin yesterday that Italian forces had invaded France through the Riviera, but this was denied in Rome, and German military quarters said later that they had no knowledge of any such movement.]

Reports from Split on the Adriatic coast said that large forces of Italian troops had been landed at

Continued on Page Four

TURKEY PREPARES UNDER ALLIED PACT

Partial Mobilization Expected Today—Troops Are on Move —Precautions in Balkans

By J. W. KERNICK
Special Cable to THE NEW YORK TIMES.

ISTANBUL, Turkey, June 10—Turkey, speeding her military preparations as a result of Italy's entry into the war, stood ready tonight to fulfill her obligations under her mutual-assistance agreement with Britain and France.

That accord, concluded last October, stipulates that Turkey will lend the Allies every assistance in her power in the event of hostilities in the Mediterranean as a result of aggressive action by a European power. Hence Turkish aid can be invoked as soon as the first shot is fired.

The Italian action has already resulted in the calling of several classes to the colors by the Turkish Government. It is believed that the next move will be to place ports and airfields at the disposal of the Allies.

[The Turkish Cabinet met last night to consider the question of war or peace, The Associated Press reported, but it was believed that Turkey's entrance into the war would be by gradual steps, not immediately.]

Italy's declaration of war caused neither surprise nor excitement in Turkey. The Turks had suspected for some time and lately became certain that Premier Mussolini could not forever remain an onlooker while Chancellor Hitler marched.

Premier Mussolini's assurances that he did not intend to attack Yugoslavia, Turkey, Greece, Switz-

Continued on Page Two

Dispatches from Europe and the Far East are subject to censorship at the source.

DUCE GIVES SIGNAL

Announces War on the 'Plutocratic' Nations of the West

ASSURES 5 NEUTRALS

Bid Is Made to Russia, But Rome Has No Pledge of Aid

'Hostilities' Are Reported

"Hostilities were started four hours ago, Central European time," Radio Roma, the official Italian short-wave radio, said last night at 11 o'clock Eastern daylight time in a broadcast recorded by Columbia Broadcasting System's short-wave listening station.

"The first Italian war bulletin is expected to be issued within a few hours."

At 2:18 A. M. today, however, the official British wireless said that "there have been no reports as yet of any engagements growing out of Italy's entrance into the war," Columbia's listening station reported.

By HERBERT L. MATTHEWS
By Telephone to THE NEW YORK TIMES.

ROME, Tuesday, June 11—Italy declared war on Great Britain and France yesterday afternoon, to take effect at one minute past midnight. The land, air and sea forces of the Italian Empire were already in motion.

It is a war, as Premier Benito Mussolini announced to the people from his balcony at the Palazzo Venezia at 6 in the evening, against the "plutocratic and reactionary democracies of the West." For the moment that does not include the United States, but few Italians believe that they will see the war to a finish without having the Americans against them.

Signor Mussolini expressly excluded Turkey, Switzerland, Yugoslavia, Greece and Egypt as enemies unless they attacked Italy or the Italian possessions.

Turkey provides the burning question of the day. Italians are absolutely convinced that the Turks will not move against them and will not honor their agreement with the Allies. It is hoped to confine Italian activity to France, Great Britain and the Mediterranean and to keep the Balkans tranquil. If that can be done, Italians think, the Turks will remain quiet.

Soviet Action Discounted

Russia has washed her hands of the struggle. The Italians know that any disturbance in the Balkans will immediately bring her in; but as long as the struggle is confined to the west and south the Soviet will do nothing either to hinder or help. This was told to your correspondent a few hours ago by a very authoritative source.

It was emphasized there were no agreements about furnishing material or anything else, nor any threats or promises.

The Italian Ambassador, Augusto Rosso, left in the morning for Moscow and Ivan Gorelkin, Soviet Ambassador, is coming back to Rome, thus ending a long period without such representation. The Italians were anxious to restore full diplomatic relations in this critical period, according to this writer's informant, and the Russians agreed, but without compromising themselves.

It thus appears that Premier Mussolini has embarked on this dangerous venture without really knowing what Soviet Russia will do in the long run.

President Roosevelt's speech clearly has come too late. There was nothing that the United States could do to halt this conflict, the Italians say. Whatever brake Mr. Roosevelt may have exercised was overcome by the momentum of the whole Fascist policy. Once it was set in motion, nothing could stop it.

The Italians do not believe that the United States can affect the issue, whatever it does. They are

Continued on Page Four

"All the News That's Fit to Print."

The New York Times.

LATE CITY EDITION
Fair, with little change in temperature today and tomorrow.
Temperatures Yesterday—Max., 80; Min., 63

Copyright, 1940, by The New York Times Company.

VOL. LXXXIX..No. 30,174. Entered as Second-Class Matter, Postoffice, New York, N. Y. NEW YORK, WEDNESDAY, SEPTEMBER 4, 1940. THREE CENTS NEW YORK CITY and Vicinity | FOUR CENTS Elsewhere Except in 7th and 8th Postal Zones.

ROOSEVELT TRADES DESTROYERS FOR SEA BASES; TELLS CONGRESS HE ACTED ON OWN AUTHORITY; BRITAIN PLEDGES NEVER TO YIELD OR SINK FLEET

R. A. F. REPELS RAIDS

Fliers Turn Back Three Drives on London—Reich Perfecting Technique

PLANES REACH BERLIN

2½-Hour Alarm in City —British Hit Hard at French Coast

By JAMES B. RESTON
Special Cable to THE NEW YORK TIMES.

LONDON, Wednesday, Sept. 4—German bombers started ringing that big London doorbell early yesterday morning. They rang it again in the afternoon while Prime Minister Winston Churchill and his Ministers were commemorating the first anniversary of the war, and they kept ringing it right up till last midnight, when the third "all clear" of the day was sounded over the capital.

It was a day of fierce air battles, fought at great height in blue and silver sky all over Southeast England, and at the end, though Reich Marshal Hermann Goering's night shift was still operating all over the island, the British Air Ministry announced that twenty-five Nazi planes had been shot down to fifteen of Britain's planes. Eight British pilots were said to be safe, though it is not known whether they are in condition to fly.

[British bombing planes flew high over Berlin shortly after last midnight. Berlin spokesmen were quoted as saying that most of the Royal Air Force planes were turned back by severe anti-aircraft fire between Wittenberg and Magdeburg, but several planes escaped through the anti-aircraft barrage and reached Berlin, where they were again met with anti-aircraft fire.]

These German bombers, which have already overwhelmed five countries in the past twelve months, have now perfected a technique in attacking this vast, sprawling city, and they tried to work it again yesterday morning in the first raid.

Two Formations Meet

Just at 10 o'clock, timed to perfection, one wave of bombers approached the Thames Estuary from their bases in Belgium. Simultaneously, another formation, flying high through a light haze, came up from bases in France and met them over the Kentish coast. Altogether there were about 250 of them, and defying anti-aircraft batteries at first they started along the banks of the Thames toward London.

As they came inland, however, they met first one, then a second squadron of British fighters, who dived through Nazi fighter patrols into the bombers, broke up the formation and then attacked them singly and drove them back over the coast.

Some German bombers dropped their dynamite in Kent and Essex, but all that is said about the effect of these bombs is that they caused few casualties and little damage.

What can be said is that, if these bombers were trying to get into the heart of London to attack objectives here, they certainly failed, for while sirens were sounded everywhere in Greater London nobody in the heart of the city saw any fighting.

There was an interesting sidelight to the second mass raid of the day. At 2:45 P. M. Mr. Churchill, who somehow contrives to look more confident every day, walked into Westminster Abbey to attend the special service in commemoration of the day a year ago when Britain declared war on Germany. Alongside him walked tall, gaunt Viscount Halifax, Foreign Secretary; dapper Arthur Greenwood, Minister without portfolio; Sir Kingsley Wood, Chancellor of the Exchequer; Anthony Eden, War Secretary, and Joseph P. Kennedy, United States Ambassador to Great Britain.

They took their places in the cool church beside a great audience. At 2:50 P. M., as they were sitting there waiting for the service to start, air-raid sirens started echoing through the great cathedral.

Mr. Churchill got up, walked over to the cloisters and had a long talk with the Dean. In a few minutes he returned and took his place beside his Ministers in the chancel. It was announced that the service would proceed.

Around the city the British fight-

Continued on Page Three

The International Situation

Destroyer-War Base Deal

Completion of a deal by which the United States will transfer to Britain fifty over-age destroyers and obtain ninety-nine-year leases on eight shore and island bases stretching from Newfoundland to British Guiana was announced by President Roosevelt yesterday in a message to Congress. Coincidentally, the British Government pledged not to scuttle or surrender its fleet under any conditions. [Page 1, Column 8.]

The objective of the arrangement with Britain is to build a 4,500-mile iron fence in the Atlantic to assure this country's safety for a century, an authoritative State Department source said. To attain this, any interpretations of international law and parts of treaties in conflict must be subordinated, he said. Since this country's purpose is its defense, no well-intentioned nation can call the move a hostile act, he declared. [Page 1, Column 7.]

President Roosevelt, en route to Washington, disclosed that he looked upon the agreement as a means of keeping an enemy from the country's front door. Listing it as in some ways more important for defense than Jefferson's Louisiana purchase, he hinted there might be other similar arrangements. [Page 1, Column 6.]

The President had acted on an opinion from Attorney General Jackson, who held that the Executive had the right to negotiate the transfer without Senate consent and the constitutional power to dispose of the vessels. [Page 1, Column 5.]

Wendell L. Willkie, Republican Presidential nominee, said the country would undoubtedly approve the arrangement, but criticized Mr. Roosevelt's failure to obtain Congress's approval. [Page 1, Column 3.]

London rejoiced. A Foreign Office spokesman described the agreement as a practical method for each nation to contribute to the other's defense requirements. [Page 1, Column 4.]

Axis spokesmen did not challenge the deal's legality under neutrality laws. In Berlin it was belittled as unlikely to affect the war's outcome. It was said to be a bargain for the United States and evidence that Britain was "cracking up." In Rome it was expected the Italians would be embittered. [Page 15, Column 1.]

Developments in Congress

The House opened debate on the Selective Service Training Bill, the discussion following the lines of the Senate's deliberation. Indications were that the bill would pass by a good margin, the principal controversy centering on the question of industrial conscription. Leaders planned for final action Friday. [Page 17, Column 1.]

The Senate Finance Committee opened hearings on the excess profits tax and defense expansion amortization bill. The probability of changes in the measure increased as witnesses hit at its effects on business. [Page 10, Column 1.]

The War in Europe, Asia and Africa

German bombers hammered at Britain's airfields, harbors and naval bases, engaging the Royal Air Force in battles all over Southern England. Three raids on London were repelled. [Page 1, Column 1.]

Several R. A. F. bombers reached Berlin early today to provoke violent anti-aircraft fire after the British had loosed a powerful aerial counter-offensive in which their planes had bombed German industrial centers, the French coast and Italian power stations. [Page 3, Column 1.]

In the central Mediterranean, new type Italian bombers scored a victory, damaging a British battleship, an aircraft carrier, a cruiser and a destroyer, the Rome High Command announced. The R. A. F. again pounded Assab, port in Italian Eritrea. [Page 4, Column 6.]

Led by Tahiti, France's most important colony in Oceania, the French-protected Society Islands have voted to throw in their lot with Britain, repudiating Vichy, it was reported. [Page 6, Column 1.]

A virtual Japanese ultimatum demanding a military base and passage for troops was reported to have been rejected by French Indo-China and conflict there was believed inevitable. [Page 6, Column 3.]

In an attempted Iron Guard coup three gunmen broke through King Carol's palace guard and fired several shots into the air. Others equally vainly besieged a radio station, fought with troops. [Page 1, Column 2.]

A clash between Hungarian and Rumanian troops over the occupation of Transylvania was reported at Bucharest. [Page 4, Column 1.]

BRITISH JUBILANT

Destroyers Strengthen Their Fleet at Point of Greatest Strain

MORAL EFFECT GREAT

But Press Warns People Gesture Does Not Mean U. S. Will Enter War

By RAYMOND DANIELL
Special Cable to THE NEW YORK TIMES.

LONDON, Sept. 3—It would be impossible to overstate the jubilation in official and unofficial circles caused today by President Roosevelt's announcement that fifty United States destroyers were coming to help Great Britain in her hour of peril. They will be manned by British crews and will fly the white ensign of the Royal Navy, it is true, but they are coming, nevertheless.

It was tangible proof that American talk of giving "all aid short of war" was more than idle chatter and that this country's friends across the Atlantic, despite German propaganda and the heavy bombardment of British cities and towns, had decided there was still lots of fight left in the British lion and that it was not too late to help turn the tide against totalitarian domination of Europe.

Destroyer Losses Offset

Under the arrangement, it was pointed out by authoritative sources, the United States gained security against future aggression, while the British fleet at one stroke acquired fifty 1,200-ton destroyers as an offset to the thirty lost since the beginning of hostilities.

These destroyers are badly needed at this stage of the war with British seapower engaged in a death grapple with the German Empire. Since the French were knocked out as an ally, the whole job of protecting convoys and maintaining the lifelines of the Empire against the new enemy in the Mediterranean has fallen upon the British fleet, while the air force has concentrated chiefly on destroying the enemy's supplies and defending the homes of the people of this island, which is under repeated bombardment from the air throughout its length and breadth.

Added to this multiplication of the navy's duties has been the necessity of blockading the whole Continent of Europe while standing by to resist the very real threat of a German invasion which, as War Secretary Anthony Eden warned today, still hangs over this country.

As great as was Britain's need the material gain by today's transaction was matched in British minds by the intangible implications of most open indication yet of Anglo-American cooperation for defense against the Nazi threats.

The Times, London, will point out editorially tomorrow that such cooperation between a belligerent and a neutral is "a new departure" but one that is dictated by the necessities of modern war. The editorial goes on to say:

"The tragic fate of some of the smaller peoples of Europe might have been averted if they had not been restrained from planning for

Continued on Page Fifteen

RULING BY JACKSON

Opinion Holds Transfer by President Needs No Senate Action

AN 'EXECUTIVE' DEAL

Opponents in Congress Seek to Find Means of Obstructing It

Attorney General Jackson's opinion is printed on Page 16.

By LEWIS WOOD
Special to THE NEW YORK TIMES.

WASHINGTON, Sept. 3—President Roosevelt has unqualified power to exchange fifty over-age destroyers for British naval and air bases in the Western Hemisphere without Senate consent, in the opinion of Attorney General Jackson, made public today, but, while Mr. Jackson asserted the Executive's right to dispose of naval vessels, he again refused to sanction the legality of delivery of "mosquito boats" now under construction.

Under a World War law the Attorney General ruled that it would be entirely proper to transfer the destroyers, since these were not built "with the intent that they should enter the service of a belligerent," but turning over the uncompleted mosquito boats, he argued, would be impossible, as this would legally mean that they were intended for a belligerent.

Opponents of the British-American deal sought tonight to find means of obstruction and delay, but this seemed to hinge upon the extent to which the direct interest of a taxpayer could be proved and the general opinion here was that the adversaries were blocked from court action and could depend only upon sufficient massing of public opinion. Apparently the Administration felt legally secure.

Writing his opinion to President Roosevelt last Tuesday, Mr. Jackson went into detail as to constitutional power and especially stressed the responsibility of the Executive to use every authority for national defense at a time when "present world conditions forbid him to risk" any constitutionally avoidable delay.

"No Future Commitments"

The Attorney General conceded that the wide Presidential power over foreign relations was not unlimited, but in this case, Mr. Jackson contended, there were no promises or future commitments by the United States which would require Senate consent or, indeed, any Congressional action. The agreement provided an opportunity to establish naval and air bases for coastline defense, he maintained, but needed no appropriation of money. Thus it was unnecessary for the Senate to ratify "an opportunity that entails no obligation," he declared.

Alluding to precedents, Mr. Jackson remarked that the "proposition falls far short" of the acquisition of the Louisiana Territory by President Jefferson from a belligerent during a European war. Outside of constitutional power, he went on,

Continued on Page Sixteen

UNITED STATES ACQUIRES DEFENSE BASTIONS

Bases at the places indicated by circled dots are being leased by Great Britain to this country for ninety-nine years. The leases for those in Newfoundland and Bermuda are in effect outright gifts; the leases for the others are in exchange for fifty over-age United States destroyers. The bases in the Caribbean area will supplement present American defense centers (black diamonds) in guarding approaches to the Panama Canal.

ROOSEVELT HAILS GAIN OF NEW BASES

Exchange of Over-Age Ships for British Leases Offers Outer Defense Line, He Says

By CHARLES HURD
Special to THE NEW YORK TIMES.

ON BOARD ROOSEVELT TRAIN, Sept. 3—President Roosevelt indicated that the chief value of the trade with Great Britain of fifty over-age destroyers for naval and air base sites in British crown colonies in the Western Hemisphere lay in the fact that this outer line of defenses would keep any enemy away from this country's front door.

For that reason, he said, his agreement with the British Government was more important for the defense of this country than anything since the Louisiana Purchase in 1803, which assured American military control over the Mississippi River.

There may be other similar negotiations, he added, but he cautioned newspaper reporters not to try to guess where they would be, listing the odds at 10 to 1 that such guesses would be wrong.

The President did not deny a suggestion made by a reporter that perhaps Greenland might be the site for another base. He merely renewed his caution against speculation.

The President's view of the agreement, which has been known to be in progress for several weeks, was given at a special press conference on his private train at the same hour that his offices in Washington sent to Congress a message that the exchange was accomplished.

A dozen newspaper reporters heard Mr. Roosevelt read the text of the message to Congress, which he completed during a trip from Hyde Park, N. Y., to Tennessee, North Carolina and West Virginia. He read the message, after laughingly telling them that there was no story. While the document, with supporting papers, was being made public in Washington at noon, he began his press conference at 11:50 A. M. Eastern time.

Mr. Roosevelt called the press conference to meet in the tiny vestibule of his private car forty-five minutes after he departed from South Charleston, W. Va., where he inspected work being done to restore to high productivity a long abandoned Navy ordnance plant built in 1917-18 to construct armor plate and shells.

Among the statements he made

Continued on Page Ten

SHIP TRADE IS HELD NOT HOSTILE ACTION

State Department Stresses Defense Phase of Exchange of Vessels for Bases

Special to THE NEW YORK TIMES.

WASHINGTON, Sept. 3—No country could consider the transfer of fifty United States destroyers to Great Britain and the obtaining by this country of naval and air bases in British New World territory as a hostile act, an informed State Department source said today.

Only a nation seeking world conquest could use this as a pretext for belligerent action, the source asserted.

The intention of this government in completing the agreement was merely to strengthen its own defenses and no other considerations were entertained, State Department officials said, in insisting that the United States had the opportunity to obtain a 4,000 or 5,0000 mile ring of steel around the eastern part of the hemisphere on terms unequaled since the Louisiana Purchase. They added that the protection would last for 100 years.

It was made clear that it was no time to consider any technical provisions which might be sought in international law by opponents of the agreement but that in these dangerous days, when the world is almost literally on fire, defense considerations must come first.

This view was expressed in answer to questions of correspondents about the Second Hague Convention of 1907, of which the United States and Germany are signatories, but Great Britain is not.

Hague 1907 Convention Is Quoted

Article VI of this convention asserts:

"The support in any manner, directly or indirectly, by a neutral power of a belligerent power, by warships, ammunition or war materials of any kind whatever, is forbidden."

Article VIII says:

"A neutral government is also bound to display the same vigilance to prevent the departure from its jurisdiction of any vessel intended to cruise, or menace in hostile operations, which had been adapted entirely or partly within the said jurisdiction for use in war."

Article XXVIII, however, states: "The provisions of this present convention do not apply except to the contracting powers and then only if all the belligerents are parties to the convention."

One could accurately visualize a

Continued on Page Sixteen

LINE OF 4,500 MILES

Two Defense Outposts Are Gifts, Congress Is Told—No Rent on Rest

FOR 50 OLD VESSELS

President Holds Move Solely Protective, 'No Threat to Any Nation'

Texts of messages on leasing of naval bases, Page 10.

By FRANK L. KLUCKHOHN
Special to THE NEW YORK TIMES.

WASHINGTON, Sept. 3—President Roosevelt informed Congress today that he had completed an arrangement by which the United States will transfer to Great Britain fifty over-age destroyers and obtain from Britain ninety-nine-year leases for sea and air bases at eight strategic continental and island points in the Western Hemisphere.

The new American defense line thus established will stretch 4,500 miles from Newfoundland to British Guiana and include other bases on the islands of Bermuda, the Bahamas, Jamaica, St. Lucia, Trinidad and Antigua.

It is intended to make difficult, if not impossible, naval and air attacks upon the United States and much of the New World. The exact sites of the bases will be determined later by the two governments.

A solemn pledge by the British Government to the United States not to scuttle or surrender the British fleet under any conditions was revealed coincidentally by the State Department's publication of correspondence between Secretary Hull and the British Ambassador, the Marquess of Lothian.

Secretary Hull was informed that it represented the "settled policy" of His Majesty's Government not to "surrender or sink" the British fleet.

Reshaping of Naval Defense

The deal, carrying with it farflung international as well as domestic defense implications, was hailed by President Roosevelt as the most important since the Jefferson Administration completed the Louisiana Purchase in 1803.

Informed official circles contended that it assured the British Fleet as an Atlantic sea-screen for the United States and made it possible for the American Fleet to remain in the Pacific.

Some thought it might lead to an informal defensive alliance between this country and Australia similar to the arrangement recently completed administratively with Canada, although others disagreed on this point.

President Roosevelt informed Congress that the British Government had given the right to bases in Newfoundland and Bermuda as an outright gift, "generously given and gladly received," but that "the other bases mentioned have been acquired in exchange for fifty of our over-age destroyers."

Previously, the President had insisted that the destroyer and base deals were separate.

Legal Basis for Procedure

Mr. Roosevelt explained in his message that he had acted upon a legal opinion by Attorney General Jackson which held that the Chief Executive had the right to dispose of the destroyers and complete the deal without consultation with the Senate and without its approval.

The President made clear that he would not seek the Senate's endorsement by remarking that he sent his statement merely "for the information of Congress."

Chairman Walsh of the Senate Naval Affairs Committee and several other Senators publicly condemned the proposed deal as illegal under domestic and international law when it was reported in the press some weeks ago that President Roosevelt had agreed to give Britain fifty destroyers after pleas from Prime Minister Winston Churchill.

In view of Senator Walsh's stand, some Senators privately expressed the opinion that there might be an attempt to have the Naval Affairs Committee open an investigation of the whole transaction.

After the President's message was

Continued on Page Twelve

BUCHAREST CHECKS IRON GUARDS' COUP

Shots Fired in Front of Royal Palace—Handbills Call On Carol to Abdicate

By EUGEN KOVACS
Wireless to THE NEW YORK TIMES.

BUCHAREST, Rumania, Sept. 3—A group of the Iron Guards, dissatisfied with the conduct and policy of other Iron Guards who are Ministers and who participated in the Crown Council, organized and carried out several attempts tonight against different public buildings in Bucharest. All these attacks failed.

A small group consisting of three persons appeared in an automobile this evening at 8:30 before the Royal Palace and one of them fired two shots in the air. A policeman on duty in front of the gates of the palace fired at the car but failed. The man who fired the shots tried to escape, however, but was arrested, while the car disappeared.

The regular news bulletin broadcast at 10 o'clock was canceled.

A second group, consisting of young men wearing military uniforms and disguised as Iron Guards, attacked the Bucharest radio station. The guard fired and succeeded in repelling the attacking group.

At the cabin of transmission of the Central Telephone Exchange a man was found who cut off some lines so that the telephone connection with abroad was cut off for a while. At the State Railway repair works in the suburb of Grivitza an-

Continued on Page Four

WILLKIE FOR PACT, BUT HITS SECRECY

Regrets President Did Not Put Deal With Britain Before Congress and People

By JAMES A. HAGERTY
Special to THE NEW YORK TIMES.

RUSHVILLE, Ind., Sept. 3—Asked today to comment on President Roosevelt's announcement of the agreement to turn over to Great Britain fifty over-age destroyers in return for air and naval bases in British Western Hemisphere areas, Wendell L. Willkie, Republican nominee for President, declared that the country undoubtedly would approve the program, but criticized the President's failure to obtain prior approval of Congress as smacking of totalitarianism.

In a statement prepared with care and with realization that it might have important foreign repercussions, Mr. Willkie said:

"The country will undoubtedly approve of the program to add to our naval and air bases and assistance given to Great Britain. It is regrettable, however, that the President did not deem it necessary in connection with this proposal to secure the approval of Congress or permit public discussion prior to adoption.

"The people have a right to know of such important commitments prior to and not after being made. We must be extremely careful in these times when the struggle in the world is between democracy and to-

Continued on Page Fourteen

Writer on British Destroyer Sees U-Boats in Raids and One Sunk

By BRYDON TAVES

ABOARD A BRITISH DESTROYER, in the North Atlantic, Sept. 3 (UP)—Germany is shooting the works to make good the threat of total blockade of the British Isles, but after eight days aboard a little British flotilla leader I can say that hundreds of ships are entering and leaving British ports each week.

German submarine and air attacks marked my voyage. Not one day passed without action. The British crew was either manning gun and depth-charge stations to fight off a U-boat or manning anti-aircraft stations to fight attacking planes.

I saw one British merchantman take a long-range torpedo squarely amidships and sink within a half hour. The next day our destroyer evened the score.

A "tin fish," meant for us, missed by a scant thirty feet as we whipped around. Then we rocked from the concussion of our own depth charges and I saw an oil patch spread slowly over the surface, marking that U-boat's end.

The destroyer was engaged in a typical convoy job, and its duties were something between those of a conscientious sheep dog and a sister of charity leading a bunch of orphans across Times Square.

We were one destroyer and one smaller warship escorting a thirty-ship convoy spread over fifteen square miles of ocean. Watching the line of hulls stretching out behind us, I remembered what a naval officer in a convoy control room in a West coast port told me just before I sailed.

"Give me fifty over-age American destroyers," he said, "and I will

Continued on Page Four

"All the News That's Fit to Print."

NEWS INDEX, PAGE 35, THIS SECTION

The New York Times.

LATE CITY EDITION
Partly cloudy and continued warm today and tomorrow.
Temperatures Yesterday—Max., 91; Min., 75

Section 1

VOL. XC..No. 30,465. Entered as Second-Class Matter, Postoffice, New York, N. Y. NEW YORK, SUNDAY, JUNE 22, 1941. Including Rotogravure Picture, Magazine and Book Sections. TEN CENTS New York City and Vicinity

HITLER BEGINS WAR ON RUSSIA, WITH ARMIES ON MARCH FROM ARCTIC TO THE BLACK SEA; DAMASCUS FALLS; U.S. OUSTS ROME CONSULS

MUST GO BY JULY 15

Ban on Italians Like Order to German Representatives

U. S. DENIES SPYING

Envoys Told to Protest Axis Charges—Nazis Get 'Moor' Text

By BERTRAM D. HULEN
Special to THE NEW YORK TIMES.

WASHINGTON, June 21—The Italian Embassy was directed by the State Department in a note published today to close all its consular offices and other agencies in this country having connections with the Italian Government by July 15. This was the reply to the Italian demand for the closing of all American Consulates in Italy.

At the same time Sumner Welles, Under-Secretary of State, announced that he had sent to Dr. Hans Thomsen, the German Chargé d'Affaires, the text of President Roosevelt's message to Congress yesterday denouncing the sinking of the American freighter Robin Moor in the South Atlantic on May 21.

This message, which accused Germany of being an international outlaw, engaging in piracy and attempting to intimidate the United States by the sinking and to drive American commerce from the seas, contained notice that this country would not yield before such measures and stated that compensation would be sought for the sinking.

It was transmitted "for the information" of the German Government, but constituted in effect a note of protest. A further communication will be sent asking damages when a final determination has been reached of the extent of damages that should be sought.

Will Deny Improper Acts

In addition, the State Department instructed the American Embassies in Berlin and Rome to inform the respective governments that the United States objects to all allegations of improper acts by American consular officials in those countries and to complete arrangements for the withdrawal of the consular officials and their staffs by July 15, the limit set by the German and Italian Governments.

The Axis governments had charged that the American Consuls had spied for the British. No reply has been made by the State Department to the German protests against the order closing Nazi consulates in this country, but the protest will be rejected. The United States alleged subversive activities as the reason for the demand for them to be closed by July 10.

The notes to the German and Italian Embassies were sent by messenger last night. However, no direct charge of improper activities was made against the Italian consuls in the note Mr. Welles sent to Don Ascanio dei principi Colonna, the Italian Ambassador. He merely stated that the continued functioning of Italian consular establishments within United States territory "would serve no desirable purpose."

In addition, the closing of Italian agencies having connections with the Rome government was requested. The Italian Embassy, as in the earlier case of the German Embassy, was exempted, but the closing of the office of the Italian Commercial Counselor in New York was demanded, along with the consulates.

Welles Note to Colonna

The note from Mr. Welles to Prince Colonna follows:

June 20, 1941

His Excellency
Don Ascanio dei principi Colonna
Royal Italian Ambassador
Excellency:

I have the honor to inform Your Excellency that the President has directed me to request that the Italian Government promptly close all Italian consular establishments within United States territory and remove therefrom all Italian consular of-

Continued on Page Two

Hope Dims for Submarine; Diver Balked at 370 Feet

Knox Believes All 33 Are Dead on the O-9 and Expects Rites at Scene for Navy 'Heroes'—Pressure Halts Descent

By RUSSELL PORTER
Special to THE NEW YORK TIMES.

PORTSMOUTH, N. H., June 21—As hope faded rapidly for the crew of the Submarine O-9, which failed to rise after submerging yesterday morning twenty-four miles east of this city, it became known tonight that the Navy might be unable to complete its salvage operations, and might be compelled to leave the bodies entombed where they lie—440 feet below the surface of the Atlantic.

This theory was based upon the assumption that the two officers and thirty-one men must already be given up as lost, but that assumption has become stronger with every new development since the submarine was reported missing.

Last night cork insulation from the interior of the hull was picked up, showing that at least part of the submarine had collapsed, and early today, after fourteen hours of dragging, grapnels located an object believed to be the sunken craft. Since then no signals from the O-9 have been received on the sensitive sound-detection devices on the salvage ships in response to their repeated messages.

The view that the O-9's fate was sealed was strengthened this afternoon when reporters and photographers, visiting the scene in a Navy press boat, saw one of the Navy's most experienced divers fail in an attempt to reach the O-9 after descending 370 feet, or within seventy feet of where the Navy believes it has located the submarine with grapnel lines.

The diver, George Crocker, 30 years old, of Seattle, asked to be hauled up when he became convinced that he was not getting enough air pressure from his life lines of helium-oxygen mixture to overcome the increasing sea pressure as he went lower and lower.

A message from the Falcon said: "Diver descended 370 feet. Had difficulty in breathing. Brought to surface. Will continue attempts by varying diving techniques."

On the salvage ship the dive was called "the most dangerous in submarine history." It was pointed out that no one had ever made a successful "working" dive at 440 feet and that any diver who went down so far, where he would have to grope his way in complete darkness under terrific sea pressure, 195.8 pounds to the square inch, could do so only at extreme risk to his life.

Colonel Frank Knox, Secretary of the Navy, returning tonight on

Continued on Page Thirty

R. A. F. BLASTS FOE

Bags 26 Nazi Planes in Record Day Raids on Invasion Coast

GERMANY IS BOMBED

British on 11th Straight Night Offensive Into Western Reich

Special Cable to THE NEW YORK TIMES.

LONDON, Sunday, June 22—Twenty-six Nazi fighter planes were destroyed in daylight yesterday by Royal Air Force fliers on their fifth straight day of raiding the Germans' invasion coast and air bases in Northern France.

Twice before dark, waves of R. A. F. warcraft—reportedly numbering at least 150 planes each—swept over the Channel in offensive operations.

Bombers attacked the Nazi's airdromes on each occasion while strong forces of fighters blasted the way for the big planes through formations of German defense fighters. While the major raids were going on, other strong R. A. F. units patrolled over the French coast and battled Messerschmitts.

Attack Goes On; Big Bombs Used

Last night and early this morning the R. A. F. was still attacking the invasion coast, using some of the latest type of high-powered bombs.

Explosions rolled across the Channel like peals of thunder, shaking the ground and rocking buildings for miles along the Kentish coast, observers there reported.

A night curtain of fog hung over the Strait of Dover and little could be seen of the raids. The latest British attacks were apparently being made in the Boulogne area, where some of the heaviest daylight bombing was carried out.

Meanwhile R. A. F. bomber forces were again attacking Western Germany, officials here said briefly early today. The attacks marked the eleventh consecutive night in which the British have bombed industrial centers and war bases in the Reich.

Two Nazi bombers were shot down during the night in small scattered enemy raids on the east and southeast coasts of England. A few German bombs were reported dropped there; there were no accounts of casualties or damage.

The R. A. F. coastal patrol squadrons reported destroying at least two enemy planes and one Nazi

Continued on Page Eighteen

SYRIAN CITY TAKEN

French Withdraw After a Hard Fight—British Closer to Beirut

TADMUR PUSH IS ON

Allied Planes Harassing Vichy Troops, Whose Defense Falters

By C. L. SULZBERGER
By Telephone to THE NEW YORK TIMES.

ANKARA, Turkey, June 21—French troops evacuated the city of Damascus today after a persistent bombardment by British artillery and withdrew to new positions outside the Syrian capital, according to official advices from Beirut. Early in the afternoon it was learned that the Allied vanguard was already beginning to enter the city. This evening the British reported complete occupation.

The Damascus airport at Mezze has been taken by Indian detachments of the Allied forces and one of the key points east of Damascus has been surrounded by Druz tribesmen fighting on the side of the British.

The Beirut radio announced tonight that a British motorized column pushing westward from Iraq was now heading toward Tadmur. The British column, it was said, has been bombed constantly by the French Air Force, which has just been reorganized and reinforced by French squadrons coming from North Africa. Some German planes also were said to have arrived in Syria.

Advance in High Gear

It is clear that the Allied advance is beginning to move into high gear. Unconfirmed reports that the British forces have reached Beirut indicate that it may also fall soon. Beirut's fate depends largely on whether the British will call in their superior naval forces to shell the city proper. So far this has been avoided in order to keep damage and casualties at a minimum.

[A dispatch from Cairo said that Australian forces had been progressing toward Beirut for two days and had passed Ras Damour.]

The Allies, convinced of the seriousness of the French resistance, evidently have begun to fight this undeclared war in earnest and intend to get it over with fast at any cost. The main center of French resistance in the east has been Damascus, and the capture of the city is of great importance.

The Allied counter-move to the French attack in the south, which developed earlier in the week, is now proceeding with dispatch in the Merdjayoun district. The fortress of Merdjayoun is in Allied hands and it is obvious that the region is being rapidly cleared, since the coastal advance is dependent to a large degree on a corrollary advance in the center.

Considerable concentrations of French artillery had been brought up around Damascus. The French dug in and placed batteries in many of the villas and gardens in the outer sections of the city. These batteries were slowly picked off by British gunners with Royal Air Force support, but the principal British effort was artillery shelling. The British sought to avoid excess damage by aerial bombardment, which is less accurate than artillery fire.

Tadmur Believed in Peril

The French admission that a British column is pressing toward Tadmur would seem to indicate that perhaps the town is endangered. Several days ago reliable sources here reported the existence of the column, but this was steadfastly denied by Beirut.

While there have been new reports that the trouble for the British in Iraq is far from over, the fact that they are able to spare considerable forces from there would indicate that everything is under control. It is known that British forces also are working westward along the North Syrian frontier toward Aleppo, but the exact strength of these units is not known here.

British military circles admit that the Syrian adventure can no longer

Continued on Page Twelve

WHERE GERMAN ARMIES MARCH ON RUSSIA

Shown on the map is the western frontier of the Soviet Union, a battle line of more than 2,000 miles. Berlin indicated an attack from Norway to Rumania.

The Hitler Proclamation

The text of Adolf Hitler's proclamation, as recorded here by Columbia Broadcasting System, follows:

It was a difficult step for me to send my Minister to Moscow in order to attend to work against the policy of encirclement of Britain.

I hoped that at last it would be possible to put away tension.

Germany never intended to occupy Lithuania. The defeat of Poland induced me to again address a peace offer to the Allies. This was declined because Britain was still hoping to bring about European coalition.

That is why Cripps [Sir Stafford Cripps, British Ambassador] was sent to Moscow. He was commissioned under all circumstances to come to an agreement with Moscow. Russia always put out the lying statement that she was protecting these countries [evidently Lithuania, Estonia and Latvia, the Baltic States].

The penetration of Russia into Rumania and the Greek liaison with England threatened to place new, large areas into the war. Rumania, however, believed she was able to accede to Russia only if she received guarantees from Germany and Italy for the remainder of the country. With a heavy heart, I did this, for if Germany gives guarantees, she will fulfill them. We are neither Englishmen nor Jews.

I asked Molotoff [Soviet Foreign Commissar V. M. Molotoff] to come to Berlin, and he asked for a clarification of the situation. He asked, "Is the guarantee for Rumania directed also against Russia?"

I replied, "Against every one."

And Russia never informed us that she had even more far-reaching intentions against Rumania.

Molotoff asked further, "Is Germany prepared not to assist Finland, who was again threatening Russia?"

My reply was that Germany has no political interests in Finland, but another attack on Finland could not be tolerated, especially as we do not believe that Finland is threatening Russia.

Molotoff's third question was, "Is Germany agreeable that Russia give guarantees to Bulgaria?"

My reply was that Bulgaria is a sovereign State and I did not know that Bulgaria needed guarantees. Molotoff said Russia needed a passage through the Dardanelles and demanded bases in the Bosporus.

A few days later she [Russia] concluded the well known friendship agreement which was to incite the Serbs against Germany. Moscow demanded the mobilization of the Serbian Army.

When I still was silent, the men in the Kremlin went one step further. Russia offered to deliver war material against Germany. This was at the same time that I advised Matsuoka [Japanese Foreign Minister Yosuke Matsuoka] to bring about a lessening of the tension with Russia.

Serbian officers flew to Russia, where they were received as allies. Victory of the Axis in the Balkans at first foiled the plan to involve Germany in a long war and then, together with England and with the hope of American supplies, to throttle Germany.

Now the moment has come when I can no longer look at this development. Waiting would be a crime against Germany.

For weeks the Russians have been committing frontier violations. Russian planes have been crossing the frontier again and again to prove that they are the masters. On the night of June 17 and again on June 18 there was large patrol activity.

The march of the German Armies has no precedent. Together with the Finns we stand from Narvik to the Carpathians. At the Danube and on the shores of the Black Sea under Antonescu [Rumanian Dictator Ion Antonescu], German and Rumanian soldiers are united.

The task is to safeguard Europe and thus save all.

I have therefore today decided to give the fate of the German people and the Reich and of Europe again into the hands of our soldiers.

BAD FAITH CHARGED

Goebbels Reads Attack on Soviet—Ribbentrop Announces War

BALTIC MADE ISSUE

Finns and Rumanians Are Called Allies in Plan of Assault

Statement by von Ribbentrop is printed on Page 6.

By C. BROOKS PETERS
By Telephone to THE NEW YORK TIMES.

BERLIN, Sunday, June 22—As dawn broke over Europe today the legions of National Socialist Germany began their long-rumored invasion of Communist Soviet Russia. The non-aggression and amity pact between the two countries, signed in August, 1939, forgotten, the German attack began along a tremendous front, extending from the Arctic regions to the Black Sea. Marching with the forces of Germany are also the troops of Finland and Rumania.

Adolf Hitler, in a proclamation to the German people read over a national hook-up by Propaganda Minister Dr. Joseph Goebbels at 5:30 this morning, termed the military action begun this morning the largest in the history of the world. It was necessary, he added, because in spite of his unceasing efforts to preserve peace in this area it had definitely been proved that Russia was in a coalition with England to ruin Germany by prolonging the war.

Saw Stalemate in West

Herr Hitler, in his proclamation as reported here, made one vitally interesting statement, namely, that the supreme German military command did not feel itself able to force a decisive victory in the West—apparently on the British Isles—when large Russian troop concentrations were on the Reich's borders in the East.

The Russian troop concentrations in the East began in August, 1940, Herr Hitler asserted. "Thus, there occurred the effect intended by the Soviet-British cooperation," he added, "namely, the binding of such powerful German forces in the East that a radical conclusion of the war in the West, particularly as regards aircraft, could no longer be vouched for by the German High Command.

[The German radio announced early today that documentary proof would shortly be given of a secret British-Russian alliance, made behind Germany's back.]

Designed "to Save Reich"

The German action, Herr Hitler explained to his fellow-National Socialists, is designed to save the Reich and with it all Europe from the machinations of the Jewish-Anglo-Saxon warmongers.

The German Foreign Minister, Joachim von Ribbentrop, followed Dr. Goebbels on the air with a declaration of the Reich Government read before the foreign correspondents in the Foreign Office. Herr von Ribbentrop said he received V. G. Dekanosoff, the Russian Ambassador, this morning and informed him that in spite of the Russian-German non-aggression pact of Aug. 23, 1939, and an amity pact of Sept. 28, 1939, Russia had betrayed the trust that the Reich had placed in her.

"Contrary to all engagements which they had undertaken and in absolute contradition to their solemn declarations, the Soviet Union had turned against Germany," the Reich note asserted. "They have first not only continued, but even since the outbreak of war intensified their subversive activities against Germany in Europe. They have second, in a continually increasing measure, developed their foreign policy in a tendency hostile to Germany, and they have third massed their entire forces on the German frontier ready for action."

The Soviet Government, it was charged, had violated its treaties

Continued on Page Seven

ARMY ASKS GUARD BE KEPT IN SERVICE

Recommends Congress Act to Hold State Troops, Reserve Officers Indefinitely

By HALLETT ABEND
Special to THE NEW YORK TIMES.

WASHINGTON, June 21—Members of the National Guard and Reserve Officers Corps will be kept in active service beyond the single year planned when they were called, if a recommendation made today by the War Department is approved by President Roosevelt and Congress.

Instead of a return to civilian life, starting Sept. 15, their terms of service in uniform may be extended indefinitely, or at least until the Army selectees have been sufficiently trained in ample numbers to permit the Guardsmen to be demobilized. The recommendation to the President does not specify any limit to the proposed extension of service.

At present there are 289,800 National Guardsmen, including their 21,800 officers, on active duty with the Federal Army. They were inducted into service in increments beginning Sept. 15 of last year. Some went into uniform as late as March of this year. Their terms of service, at time of induction, were limited to twelve months, which may not be extended except by act of Congress.

341,300 Would Be Affected

In addition to the National Guardsmen, who comprise eighteen divisions and one cavalry brigade now on active service, the government has called up 51,500 Reserve officers under the same terms, making collectively 341,300 officers and men who would be affected.

Today's War Department recommendation to the President that steps be taken to retain in the service these Guardsmen and Reserve officers was taken, according to the official announcement, because "the War Department has been flooded with queries from the field" as to whether or not the specified one-year limit of service would hold good or be changed.

"These queries are to be expected," continues the announcement, "because whatever the decision, there are many adjustments which the citizen-soldier must make in his affairs."

As yet no decision has been reached in the War Department whether or not to seek authority to retain selectees in the Army beyond the one-year training period specified in the Selective Service Act, but presumably such a step

Continued on Page Nineteen

NAVY MAY REPLACE SHIPYARD STRIKERS

Weighs Putting Own Machinists to Work to End Long Tie-Up in San Francisco

By The Associated Press.

SAN FRANCISCO, June 21—Striking A. F. L. machinists in a $300,000,000 defense program have come to a showdown with the United States Navy and their own international officers.

Reliable reports, not officially denied, indicated that the Navy might install its own machinists in the huge Bethlehem shipyards Monday if the local union did not heed the order of its international president to call off the strike by that time.

The same reports indicated that the Army also might be on hand

Continued on Page Twenty-eight

The International Situation

SUNDAY, JUNE 22, 1941

At 5:30 o'clock this morning, Berlin time, two statements were read over the German radio that constituted a declaration of war upon the Soviet Union by Germany. A proclamation of Adolf Hitler, read by Propaganda Minister Goebbels, said that Russia, with Britain and the United States, had sought to "throttle" Germany and that he had therefore decided to put the fate of the German people in the hands of the army. A statement by Foreign Minister von Ribbentrop contained the actual declaration of war. The Finns and the Rumanians were mentioned as allies. Berlin reported subsequently that troops were on the march in East Prussia. [Page 1, Column 8; with map.]

Yesterday was a good day for British arms.

In the Syrian campaign Damascus was occupied. The British announced its capture and Vichy reported its evacuation to avoid street fighting and destruction of the city. Another British force was pushing nearer Beirut, supported by the fleet and the air arm, while a third column was moving toward Tadmur. [Page 1, Column 5; Map on Page 12.]

No less encouraging to the British was a victory much closer to home in the largest British daylight air attack of the war. In a sweep two waves of 150 planes each pounded the French Channel coast, going particularly for airdromes, and engaged German air defenses. The British reported downing twenty-six Nazi planes in these attacks for a loss of five of their own. Late last night the British were continuing their attacks across the Channel. [Page 1, Column 4; Map, Page 18.]

The Libyan theatre was quiet, but British pressure in East Africa was indicated by a protest from Vichy against what was declared to be a virtual ultimatum from General Wavell to French Somaliland to join the Free French or suffer an intensified blockade. London confirmed the representations of General Wavell. [Page 14, Column 1.]

Washington continued the accelerated pace of its anti-Axis diplomatic offensive. The Italian Embassy was instructed to close the forty-nine Italian consulates and seven agencies in this country before July 15. President Roosevelt's message to Congress on the Robin Moor was handed to the German Embassy while the State Department instructed the United States embassies in Berlin and Rome to inform those governments that the United States objected categorically to any allegations of improper acts by United States consuls. [Page 1, Column 1.]

Italian consular circles here were silent concerning the Washington order, but Italian anti-Fascist quarters expressed jubilation. [Page 3, Column 1.]

"All the News That's Fit to Print."

The New York Times.

LATE CITY EDITION
Rain today and not much change in temperatures.
Temperatures Yesterday—Max., 53; Min., 35

VOL. XCI. No. 30,757. Entered as Second-Class Matter, Postoffice, New York, N. Y. NEW YORK, FRIDAY, APRIL 10, 1942. THREE CENTS NEW YORK CITY and Vicinity

JAPANESE CAPTURE BATAAN AND 36,000 TROOPS; SINK TWO BRITISH CRUISERS; ITALIANS LOSE ONE; INDIA REPORTED AGREEING ON NATIVE COUNCIL

SENATOR AND JONES CLASH OVER ATTACK ON WAR PLANT DEAL

Bunker Charges DPC Condones 'Unconscionable Profits' for Nevada Magnesium Plant

UNTRUE, SAYS SECRETARY

Fees Paid to 9 Contractors, He Adds, Will Be Less Than 2% of Cost of 70 Millions

Special to THE NEW YORK TIMES.

WASHINGTON, April 9—Senator Bunker, Democrat, of Nevada, today attacked the Defense Plant Corporation, an RFC subsidiary, charging that the terms of its contract with Basic Magnesium, Inc., for a plant at Las Vegas, Nev., meant "unconscionable profits." Secretary Jones, as head of the RFC, immediately replied that the charges were misleading and untrue, and, in effect, challenged Senator Bunker to press them without benefit of Senatorial immunity.

The Secretary of Commerce replied to Senator Bunker in a statement.

"Senator Bunker's statements accusing RFC officials of wrongdoing," he said, "are unworthy of a United States Senator and cannot go unchallenged. The Senator must know these statements are untrue.

"The magnesium plant that is being built by the government near Las Vegas, Nev., will cost approximately $70,000,000 and have an estimated annual capacity of 112,000,000 pounds of metallic magnesium.

Says Fees Total Less Than 2%

"Nine separate contractors are participating in the construction. The fees to be paid the nine contracting and engineering firms, together with the fee to Basic Magnesium, Inc., for its engineering plans, supervision and 'know-how,' will aggregate less than 2 per cent of the total cost of the plant.

"The operating or management fee of the plant is to be half cent per pound of magnesium produced, which is approximately 2 per cent of the estimated cost.

"The royalty for the ores will not exceed ¼ cent per pound of magnesium metal produced.

"No irregularities have been discovered in the construction of the plant that would warrant the irresponsible statements made by Senator Bunker. The plant is wholly owned by the government and will be operated for its account. All expenditures in connection with the construction of the plant as well as its operation are carefully audited as the work progresses.

"Defense Plant Corporation contracted with Basic Magnesium, Inc., for the construction of this plant at the request of OPM and the War Department, and the government's interest is fully protected.

"Senator Bunker's speech contains many false and misleading statements, which it takes no courage to make under his cloak of immunity."

"Sinister," Bunker Contends

In his speech in the Senate the Nevada Senator said:

"Those individuals who have participated in unconscionable profits in America and who have slowed down our war production are worthy of the disgust and contempt of every American."

He contended that the data he presented were sufficient "to warrant the conclusion that the Defense Plant Corporation has entered into an agreement that is so sinister as to indicate that some officials in our government are guilty of malfeasance in the performance of their duties."

"If the agreement between the Defense Plant Corporation and Basic Magnesium, Inc., represents a cross-section of conduct on the part of the Defense Plant Corpora-

Continued on Page Eighteen

Cripps Said to Have Accord On National Regime in India

Plan Is Reported to Envisage Rule by a Council With Briton Directing Army and Native in Defense Ministry

By The United Press.

NEW DELHI, India, April 9—Great Britain and India are in general agreement on a self-government plan that will establish the first all-Indian national government in two centuries and provide for an executive council of fifteen members, all but one of them to come from the various political parties, it was learned tonight.

The plan was reported to be acceptable, with the exception of a few minor adjustments, to the two major political groups—the All-India Congress party and the Moslem League.

Under the plan a native government minister will handle all Indian defense matters except war strategy and tactics, which a British military chief will control.

With only final details to be smoothed out, formal announcement of the settlement was predicted for late tomorrow or Saturday.

Inquiries late tonight revealed that under the agreement reached between the Congress party and Sir Stafford Cripps, British negotiator, the new national government would be directed not by a Cabinet but by the Executive Council of the Viceroy of India, the Marquess of Linlithgow.

The importance of that point in the agreement, it was said, was the fact that a Prime Minister would not be appointed and asked to form a Cabinet—the usual constitutional procedure—but that the Viceroy would appoint members to the council, after receiving the names of nominees by the various Indian parties.

Under the new government, the country will be mobilized to resist the Japanese, who are pressing closer.

It was learned that an executive

Continued on Page Six

2 Police Officials Suspended On Amen's Charges of Graft

In an unexpected move that may present a test case of far-reaching effect in the Police Department, Special Prosecutor John Harlan Amen's two extraordinary grand juries returned supplemental presentments yesterday against two high-ranking police officers who had sought retirement while under investigation in connection with alleged police protection of a $100,000,000 city-wide gambling racket.

The two, Inspector Camille C. Pierne of the Tenth Division in Brooklyn and Lieutenant Terence J. Harvey of the Brooklyn Borough headquarters squad, were named in Wednesday's presentments that bared the existence of police graft estimated at more than $1,000,000 a year, but no specific charges were lodged against them on the theory that a mere application for retirement was sufficient to preclude the prosecution of departmental charges against them.

However, Police Commissioner Valentine, after conferring behind closed doors with his aides and later in the afternoon with Mayor La Guardia, issued a statement Wednesday night asserting that he had notified Mr. Amen that inasmuch as the retirement applications of several police officers had not been acted upon by the Police Pension Fund he regarded them as members of the uniformed force and would like to be advised if the grand jury had made any charges against them so that he could be "guided accordingly."

Mr. Amen's reply yesterday was to send a letter to Commissioner Valentine asserting that it was because of his understanding of Mr. Valentine's earlier advice that he had not filed charges against men

Continued on Page Thirty-eight

GASOLINE SUPPLIES CUT AGAIN BY WPB

Deliveries to East and 2 States in Northwest Will Be Reduced From 80 to 66⅔% Per Cent

Special to THE NEW YORK TIMES.

WASHINGTON, April 9—The War Production Board issued today an order further curtailing gasoline deliveries to filling stations and bulk consumers in seventeen Eastern States, the District of Columbia and Oregon and Washington.

Effective April 16, deliveries of gasoline to filling stations and bulk consumers in curtailment areas will be cut to 66 2-3 per cent of average deliveries in December, January and February, adjusted for seasonal variations. Deliveries have been reduced 20 per cent since March 19.

Secretary Ickes, Petroleum Coordinator, discussing the WPB order, said at his press conference:

"If this curtailment proves satisfactory, we may go to Leon Henderson and tell him we see no need for rationing."

Mr. Ickes added that the matter

Continued on Page Twenty-six

Jesse Jones Shakes Eugene Meyer; Eye-Glasses Broken in Encounter

Special to THE NEW YORK TIMES.

WASHINGTON, April 9—Jesse Jones, Secretary of Commerce, and Eugene Meyer, editor and publisher of The Washington Post, were participants in a fistic encounter at the annual dinner of the Alfalfa Club at the Hotel Willard tonight.

A sharp verbal exchange arising from resentment by the Secretary of an editorial in which his testimony before the Senate's Truman committee investigating the rubber situation was criticized preceded the encounter, club members said.

As told by eyewitnesses, Secretary Jones was approached by Mr. Meyer, a long-time critic of the banker, as Mr. Jones entered the small ballroom of the hotel. Accounts of witnesses vary as to the words which immediately preceded the encounter, but most members agreed that Secretary Jones grasped Mr. Meyer by the coat and started to shake him. As Mr. Meyer wrenched himself free his eyeglasses fell to the floor and were smashed.

Mr. Meyer, the accounts continue, swung at the Secretary but friends, including John J. O'Connor, former New York Representative, pushed them apart. Secretary Jones left immediately after the fight, while Mr. Meyer stayed for a time chatting with friends.

The men have been frequent adversaries since the Hoover Administration, when both served with the Reconstruction Finance Corporation, of which Mr. Meyer was then chairman. Mr. Jones is also a publisher, owning The Houston Chronicle.

Today's editorial asserted that Mr. Jones had shielded himself behind the President, the British and the Netherlanders in defending his handling of the rubber situation.

PLANES GET SHIPS

Japanese Sink Big Naval Units in Bay of Bengal, Blast Base in Ceylon

BRITISH RAID CARRIER

Score Near-Misses, Get 4 Aircraft—2 Fleets Massing for Battle

By RAYMOND DANIELL
Wireless to THE NEW YORK TIMES.

LONDON, April 9—The Japanese have struck a heavy blow against the British Navy in the struggle for mastery of the Bay of Bengal, which is the key to the Indian Ocean, in sinking by air attack the heavy cruisers Dorsetshire and Cornwall. In return, near-misses were scored by bombers in an attack on a Japanese aircraft carrier in the Bay of Bengal.

Full enemy control of the Bay of Bengal, the eastern half of which the Japanese command already, would lay the eastern coast of India open to invasion. Renewed aerial attacks today on Trincomalee, the main British naval base on the island of Ceylon, off the south coast of India, made it more apparent than ever that the Japanese were seeking to extend their domination westward.

1,100 Are Rescued

News of the sinking of the 10,000-ton Cornwall and 9,975-ton Dorsetshire was given in an Admiralty communiqué, which placed the encounter with the Japanese planes in the Indian Ocean. The announcement said 1,100 survivors, —including the commanders, Captain A. W. S. Agar of the Dorsetshire and Captain P. C. W. Manwaring of the Cornwall—had been picked up. The Dorsetshire was the ship whose torpedoes administered the coup de grace to the German battleship Bismarck in the Atlantic last year.

The attack on the Japanese aircraft carrier was announced in a communiqué received tonight from Colombo, Ceylon. In the action, which followed today's attack on Trincomalee, four Japanese planes were shot down. Some of the attacking planes did not return, but their number was not disclosed. While Trincomalee was being raided a couple of Japanese planes appeared over Colombo, but dropped no bombs.

[The Colombo communiqué also revealed that in the attack on Trincomalee the Japanese damaged harbor and airdrome facilities and caused a few casualties among dockyard personnel, The Associated Press reported. Six of the Japanese planes were shot down, six others were probably destroyed and two were listed as damaged. The Japanese, who attacked with "a large force of bombers and fighters," caused no damage in the town of Trincomalee.]

Allied Cargo Ships Sunk

The loss of the Cornwall and the Dorsetshire, coupled with an official statement from New Delhi, India, that several merchantmen have been sunk in recent enemy air and naval attacks in the Bay of Bengal, represents a serious blow not only at British naval strength in that area but against United Nations lines of communication.

The number of merchant vessels lost was not announced, but the total of survivors from them—between 400 and 500, who have landed on the coast of Orissa in India—indicates a considerable number. Tokyo said today that the number of ships sunk was twenty-one, with twenty-three others so severely damaged that they must be regarded as lost.

The Japanese naval force in the Bay of Bengal area is operating hundreds of miles from its presumed base in the Andaman Islands. The distance from the Andamans to Ceylon is more than 1,000 miles. Before the occupation of

Continued on Page Six

IN THE FOX HOLES OF BATAAN

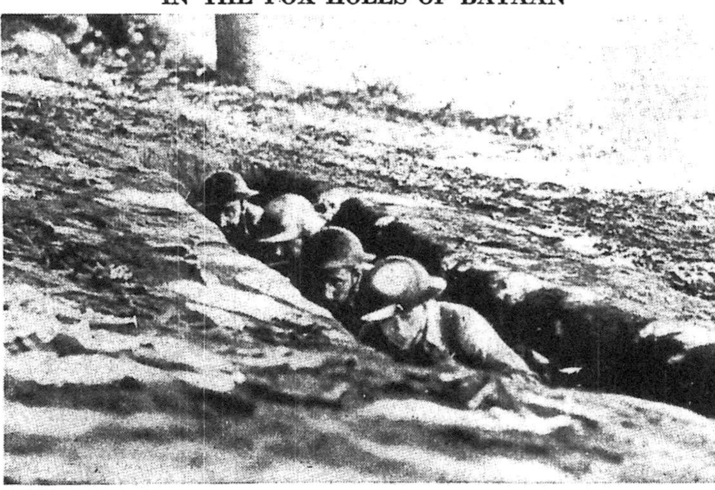

U. S. Troops in action on the Philippine peninsula, the fall of which was announced yesterday
Associated Press Wirephoto (U. S. Army Signal Corps)

ITALIAN CRUISER SUNK BY BRITISH

10,000-Ton Vessel Destroyed by Submarine—Foes Spar in Libyan Fighting

By ROBERT P. POST
Wireless to THE NEW YORK TIMES.

LONDON, April 9—A 10,000-ton eight-inch-gun Italian cruiser has been sunk in the Central Mediterranean by torpedoes from a British submarine, the Admiralty announced today.

The cruiser, which may have been convoying reinforcements for Marshal Erwin Rommel in Libya, was accompanied by destroyers and aircraft when Lieut. Comdr. E. P. Tomkinson, who received the Distinguished Service Order with bar in December for his work on submarine patrol, ordered the attack. Eight minutes after his torpedoes struck home, the commander risked attack by the cruiser's escort to show his periscope. The cruiser was heard to break up and sink while the destroyers picked up survivors.

Lieut. Commander Tomkinson's earlier exploits were carried out with the Urge, one of the smallest British submarines. Last April he sank a heavily laden oil tanker of more than 10,000 tons. For this he

Continued on Page Eight

Sacred Saffron of Priests Aids Foe's Burma Advance

By HARRISON FORMAN
Wireless to THE NEW YORK TIMES.

CHUNGKING, China, April 9—Clad in the sacred saffron robes of the Poongee—literally meaning "great glory"—the fifth column in Burma is taking advantage of the historic sanctuary provided by Burmese Buddhism. In the past the Poongees have included, besides the genuinely devout, many thieves, bandits and general malcontents, and they have always been a major problem for British administration.

Unlike most other priesthoods, the Poongees require no special training or lifelong vows. Any man may in practice become a Poongee for any period desired, days or years, by the simple procedure of shaving his head, donning a saffron robe, formally renouncing all things worldly before a temple and thereafter living solely by begging, which is not permitted for more than daily needs.

In practical example, a business man may welch on a contract or a debt by simply becoming a Poongee, and he thereby is cleansed of all worldly obligations and responsibilities. The Poongees are arrogant and a sacrosanct in so far as the police are concerned. The Poongees are publicly regarded as holy men who can do no wrong, and the British military confess they are practically helpless in the face of such fanaticism.

An eyewitness on the Burma front reports that at a certain supposedly secret airport there ap-

Continued on Page Five

War News Summarized

FRIDAY, APRIL 10, 1942

Rocky Bataan Peninsula, the finger of land that still defied the Japanese after they had conquered most of the Southwest Pacific, finally succumbed yesterday. Its 36,853 remaining American and Filipino defenders —drained by hunger, exhaustion and disease—could no longer rally to beat off an enveloping movement that broke their lines on the east flank. For three months they had fought against ever-growing odds. Although Corregidor Island and the other forts in Manila Bay stayed in American hands, it was questionable how long they could hold out. [1-8; map, P. 2.]

The United Nations suffered a probably greater strategic setback in the Bay of Bengal. Japanese planes sank two British 10,000-ton cruisers, the Dorsetshire and the Cornwall, and a great naval battle loomed with the coast of India at stake. Allied bombers attacked a Japanese naval squadron and scored near-misses on an aircraft carrier. In this Allied attack and in a raid on the Ceylon naval base of Trincomalee, the Japanese lost at least ten planes. [1:4; map, P. 6.]

Allied aerial successes were reported from Burma and Australia. Reinforced American volunteer pilots in the Burma theatre shot down ten enemy fighters and damaged two others without a loss of their own. [1:7.] United Nations bombers blasted planes and military targets in a surprise raid on Rabaul, New Britain. [3:1.]

With the threat to India growing daily, the drawn-out negotiations in New Delhi appeared nearing a successful compromise —the establishment of an Indian national government in which the defense minister would share responsibility with General Wavell. [1:2-3.]

The naval defeat in the Indian Ocean was offset somewhat by the sinking of a 10,000-ton Italian cruiser by a British submarine in the Mediterranean. In Libya, the British were jockeying for position against strong Axis forces, whose movements no longer seemed to indicate a large-scale offensive. [1:5.]

Germany flung large units of tanks and planes into the Russian front to feel out the Red Army's strength in virtually every sector, Moscow reports said, but the reinforced Soviet forces broke up their attacks and clung to the initiative. [11:1, with map.]

In occupied Europe, the embittered Norwegian people observed the second anniversary of the German invasion with a "strike" of silence as Quislingists and German troops marched in the streets. [9:1.]

AMERICANS BAG TEN IN BURMA AIR FIGHT

A.V.G. Routs Twenty of Foe Without One Loss—Lull in Land Fighting Continues

By The United Press.

CHUNGKING, China, April 9—Reinforced American Volunteer Group fliers have roared back into the Battle of Burma, destroying ten planes and damaging two others in a mass dogfight with twenty Japanese Zero fighters in which one American plane was lost but its pilot saved, an A. V. G. communiqué announced tonight.

The battle was fought over the Burmese town of Loi-Win, the communiqué said. [An Associated Press dispatch from Chungking, based on the same official source, said the encounter took place Wednesday over Leiyun in the south of China's Yunnan Province. Neither Loi-Win nor Leiyun appears on available maps.]

Week of Inaction Ended

This was the first challenge to Japanese air superiority over Burma battlegrounds since the invaders launched their all-out offensive against cities and airports in that theatre early last week. The strength of the A. V. G. force —American-made and American-flown planes fighting under the Chinese banner—was not disclosed.

Official Chinese dispatches disclosed that German officers were mapping the Japanese drive against Chinese lines north of Toungoo in Central Burma. One German officer was reported captured by the defenders and reconnaissance revealed that the Japanese were massing troops in Thailand to the east for a possible envelopment move against the Chinese on the Nazi model.

Chinese spokesmen said the Japanese concentrations in the Chiengmai area across the Thailand border not only menaced the Toungoo front but enabled the invaders to threaten a diversion drive into China's Kwangsi and Yunnan Provinces.

The Toungoo front—one-third of the way to bombed-out Mandalay from captured Rangoon—has been fairly static for a week. A belated Chinese communiqué reported the Japanese attacked south of Yedashe, eighteen miles north of Toungoo, on Monday and that fighting continued after dark that night. Subsequent communiqués

Continued on Page Five

DEFENSE CRUSHED

Stimson Reveals Defeat Followed Failure to Get in More Food

CORREGIDOR IS HELD

Wainwright on the Isle Free to Set Course, Roosevelt Tells Him

What Tokyo Reports

By The Associated Press.

TOKYO, Friday, April 10 (From Japanese broadcasts recorded in New York)—The Domei news agency said today that "60,000 Filipino and American troops resisting the Japanese on Bataan Peninsula have begged for a halt in hostilities after six days of fierce Japanese assault."

"Details of the conditions of surrender are not yet disclosed," said the Domei dispatch, "nor is it known yet whether the Japanese forces have decided to accept the terms."

Corregidor was raided twice yesterday by Japanese bombers and tons of explosives were unleashed on military installations, Domei reported.

By CHARLES HURD
Special to THE NEW YORK TIMES.

WASHINGTON, April 9—An overwhelming Japanese Army, aided by the allies of hunger, fatigue and disease, today crushed the small mixed force that had held Bataan Peninsula since December.

Japanese forces, heretofore estimated at 200,000 men, including fresh assault troops, and supported by tanks, artillery, bombers and attack planes in profusion, enveloped an exhausted defending army of 36,853 men, as counted officially yesterday afternoon.

The defeat of the American and Filipino forces was officially announced as a "probability" in a War Department communiqué issued as of 5:15 A. M. today. A few hours later Secretary of War Henry L. Stimson announced the defeat at his regularly scheduled weekly press conference. He already had carried the word to President Roosevelt.

Reveals Supplies Were Sent In

When Secretary Stimson met reporters in his conference room he paid the highest praise to the spirit of the defenders in a fight recognized as hopeless from the beginning had pledged that the Philippines would be reconquered. In the same talk he described extraordinary efforts made to provision the garrison, saying that "several shiploads of supplies" were sent into the Philippines, "but for every ship that arrived safely we lost nearly two."

As far as was known here today the rocky fortress of Corregidor Island still held its own astride the entrance to Manila Bay and other troops held adjacent fortified islands. The decision as to whether they should continue fighting was laid squarely on Lieut. Gen. Jonathan M. Wainwright, to whom President Roosevelt dispatched yesterday a message giving him absolute authority to continue the fight or make terms, as he might see fit.

Army Records Position

This promising is a heavy one for General Wainwright, for it is assumed here that he lacks transport to take more than a handful of the Bataan forces across the four miles of water that separates Bataan Peninsula from Corregidor. Even so his food is desperately short, Secretary Stimson having said this morning that every man in Bataan had been on short rations since Jan. 11. This was a primary reason for the collapse of the defense after five days of savage hand-to-hand fighting.

The long-expected defeat, which by its deferment wrote an epic in American military history, was officially indicated in War Depart-

Continued on Page Two

"All the News That's Fit to Print."

The New York Times.

LATE CITY EDITION
Continued cool today with light winds.
Temperatures Yesterday—Max.,57; Min.,45
Sunrise, 7:34 A. M.; Sunset, 5:45 P. M.

Section 1

NEWS INDEX, PAGE 55, THIS SECTION

VOL. XCII—No. 30,969. Entered as Second-Class Matter. Postoffice, New York, N. Y. NEW YORK, SUNDAY, NOVEMBER 8, 1942. Including Magazine and Book Sections. TEN CENTS New York City and Vicinity

AMERICAN FORCES LAND IN FRENCH AFRICA; BRITISH NAVAL, AIR UNITS ASSISTING THEM; EFFECTIVE SECOND FRONT, ROOSEVELT SAYS

U.S. DRIVES ON BUNA

American Troops Flown to Area Closing In on Big Japanese Base

PAPUA IS OVERRUN

All Except Beachhead of Buna-Gona Seized in New Guinea Push

By The Associated Press.

AT UNITED NATIONS HEADQUARTERS, Australia, Sunday, Nov. 8—American combat troops are in action near Buna, vital Japanese base on the north New Guinea coast, General Douglas MacArthur disclosed today.

Simultaneously, General MacArthur disclosed that the Allies have occupied Goodenough Island to the northeast of New Guinea, off Collingwood Bay, in an obvious flanking movement.

[American Army troops on Guadalcanal advanced on Friday (Solomons time) in the area to the west of Henderson airfield, the Navy reported yesterday. They crossed the Malimbui River a few miles south of Koli Point, where the Japanese recently landed reinforcements, but met little opposition.]

It was from Buna, in midsummer, that the Japanese began a drive across tortuous trails of the Owen Stanley Mountains which carried to within thirty-two miles of Port Moresby, Allied base on the south coast, before it was stalled. Late in September the Allies began encircling and infiltration movements which rolled the Japanese back and yesterday's communiqué had mentioned bitter fighting at Oivi, which is fifty-five miles south of Buna.

Japanese Resist at Oisi

"American ground troops in force, transported by air from Australia during the last month, have penetrated Central and Northern Papua to the vicinity of Buna," a communiqué stated.

"The Allied forces now control all of Papua except the beach head in the Buna-Gona area."

The surprising development came as a thrust around the eastern end of New Guinea from Milne Bay where Japanese troops landed in July only to be pinned against the sea and slain or forced to their ships.

"Units from Milne Bay," the communiqué said, "have now completed clearing remnants of hostile forces from the islands to the north and have occupied adjacent strategic points."

While this disclosure was being made, Australian ground forces still were meeting fierce resistance at Oivi where the retreating Japanese are making a stand. Today's communiqué said the Australians maintained constant pressure and were resorting to their hitherto successful tactics of local encircling movements in efforts to dislodge the defenders.

The Allied air force continued to support the overland drive with strafing attacks on the Japanese troops.

Island Attacked Oct. 22

AT UNITED NATIONS HEADQUARTERS, Australia, Sunday, Nov. 8 (UP)—*The announcement of sweeping Allied gains in New Guinea came as a surprise to observers here, although an Australian offensive through mountainous central New Guinea had been making steady progress toward the north coast for the past five weeks.*

[Delayed dispatches from Harold Guard, United Press staff correspondent in New Guinea, revealed that the Americans had

Continued on Page Forty-five

LEADS IN AFRICA

Lieut. Gen. Dwight Eisenhower
Associated Press

R. A. F. ROCKS GENOA; U. S. RAID ON BREST

Bombers From Britain Pound North Italy 2 Nights in Row —Hit Nazis on Coast

Special Cable to THE NEW YORK TIMES.

LONDON, Sunday, Nov. 8—Bombers from Britain struck a heavy blow at Northern Italy over Friday night, blasting the port of Genoa again in support of the Eighth Army's battling of the Nazis and Italians in the African desert.

Again last night the Royal Air Force sent its big bombers over Northern Italy, British officials reported briefly early today. The announcement meant that the R. A. F. from here was seeing to it that the Axis forces in Africa got no help from home.

American heavy bombers, both Flying Fortresses and Liberators, escorted by Allied fighters, carried out a smashing attack on the docks and U-boat pens at Brest in occupied France yesterday afternoon, United States Army headquarters here announced.

Bombs were seen to strike the targets at Brest. The communiqué stressed that sharp Nazi antiaircraft fire and enemy fighter opposition were encountered over the coast of Brittany.

The Brest raiders shot down four Nazi fighters. All the United States bombers returned, but one Allied fighter was lost.

The R. A. F.'s fighter squadrons

Continued on Page Twenty-one

NAZIS NEAR LIBYA

British Drive Out to Bar New Stand by Enemy or Reinforcements

FOE BOMBED ALL NIGHT

Pursuers Reported to Be Within 40 Miles of Halfaya Pass

By The United Press.

CAIRO, Egypt, Nov. 7—The British Eighth Army under Lieut. Gen. Bernard L. Montgomery hurled armored forces, motorized infantry and swarms of planes tonight at the remnants of German General Field Marshal Erwin Rommel's once-proud Afrika Korps—possibly only 25,000 out of an original 140,000—now trying to brace for a stand at Halfaya [Hellfire] Pass on the Libyan frontier, 240 miles west of the Alamein battleground.

The main body of the British forces was reported to be well west of Matruh, 110 miles west of El Alamein, and advance striking forces were believed to be as far as 200 miles west of El Alamein, or close to the Egyptian-Libyan frontier, 240 miles west of El Alamein.

How many men Marshal Rommel had left in the Halfaya area could not be established. Already 20,000 prisoners have been counted in British hands. Marshal Rommel's desert casualties were estimated at approximately 20,000 more. In addition, 75,000 Italian troops had been left far behind the swirling battleground, ready to surrender when the British could find time and men to round them up.

Marshal Rommel entered the battle with a maximum of 140,000 troops in the forward area. It was doubted whether he had more than one or two divisions left to attempt another stand at Halfaya unless he had been able to rush large reinforcements from the rear.

It appeared possible tonight that the Axis forces might not even attempt to stand at Halfaya, but would, instead, continue their headlong flight as deeply as possible into Libya in an effort to open a gap between themselves and the Eighth Army.

Such a manoeuvre, however, may already be doomed to failure. General Montgomery has ordered that every attempt be made to cut off Marshal Rommel's retreat. It was believed that he might have sent a hard-hitting, fast-moving

Continued on Page Four

SHOCK TROOPS LEAD

Simultaneous Landings Made Before Dawn at Numerous Points

PLANES GUARD SKIES

An Armada Pours Men on the Beaches—Early Actions Satisfactory

By WES GALLAGHER
Associated Press Correspondent

ALLIED HEADQUARTERS IN NORTH AFRICA, Sunday, Nov. 8—American soldiers, marines and sailors from one of the greatest armadas ever put into a single military operation swarmed ashore today on the Vichy-controlled North Africa shore before dawn, striking to break Hitler's hold on the Mediterranean.

[Reports reaching Allied headquarters in North Africa today disclosed that successful landings had been made by American assault parties on beaches of North Africa near two main objectives outlined in operational plans, an Associated Press dispatch stated.

[British forces reported attempting a landing at Algiers after a bombardment were said by the Vichy radio to have been "beaten off."]

Tall, decisive Lieut. Gen. Dwight D. (Ike) Eisenhower, supreme commander of the huge forces involved in the operation, worked throughout the night directing the first great American blow at the Axis.

Included in the forces were crack combat troops, Rangers (airborne units) and the cream of America's airmen.

British naval and air force units supported the American landing forces, who were preceded by a snowstorm of leaflets and a radio barrage promising the French that the United States had no intention of seizing French possessions and only sought to prevent Axis infiltration.

It undoubtedly was the longest over-water military operation ever attempted, with hundreds of ships in great convoys coming thousands of miles under the protection of British and American sea and air might.

I came on one of these big convoys.

Fighting-fit American soldiers

Continued on Page Five

WHERE THE UNITED STATES PREPARES FOR NEW FRONT

As the survivors of Marshal Rommel's beaten German legions fled westward toward the Libyan border (1), powerful American land, sea and air forces landed behind them at various places in Vichy France's colonies along the Mediterranean (2) and on the shores of the Atlantic, apparently in Morocco (3). British naval and aerial units are assisting them. There was no indication of military action against Vichy's possessions on the western bulge of the Atlantic (4). A large and comprehensive map of the African and Mediterranean theatre of war will be found on Page 1 of Section 4 of this issue of THE TIMES. However, Section 4 had gone to press before the announcement last night of the landing of American troops.

LANDING PLAN KEPT SECRET BY WRITERS

Americans Selected for Duty, Bureaus Sworn to Silence—Eisenhower Slipt Away

By RAYMOND DANIELL
Special Cable to THE NEW YORK TIMES.

LONDON, Sunday, Nov. 8—For weeks American newspaper men have been the custodians of one of war's biggest secrets. It was not an easy secret to keep because through all that time they had to improvise excuses for the absence of a large number of the members of their London staffs to conceal the fact that they had gone with the expeditionary forces.

Most London offices of Amer-

Continued on Page Fourteen

President's Statement

Special to THE NEW YORK TIMES.

WASHINGTON, Nov. 7—President Roosevelt's statement announcing the opening of a second front in French North and West Africa follows:

In order to forestall an invasion of Africa by Germany and Italy, which, if successful, would constitute a direct threat to America across the comparatively narrow sea from Western Africa, a powerful American force equipped with adequate weapons of modern warfare and under American command is today landing on the Mediterranean and Atlantic coasts of the French colonies in Africa.

The landing of this American Army is being assisted by the British Navy and air forces, and it will, in the immediate future, be reinforced by a considerable number of divisions of the British Army.

This combined Allied force, under American command, in conjunction with the British campaign in Egypt is designed to prevent an occupation by the Axis armies of any part of Northern or Western Africa and to deny to the aggressor nations a starting point from which to launch an attack against the Atlantic coast of the Americas.

In addition, it provides an effective second-front assistance to our heroic allies in Russia.

The French Government and the French people have been informed of the purpose of this expedition and have been assured that the Allies seek no territory and have no intention of interfering with friendly French authorities in Africa.

The government of France and the people of France and the French possessions have been requested to cooperate with and assist the American expedition in its effort to repel the German and Italian international criminals, and by so doing to liberate France and the French Empire from the Axis yoke.

This expedition will develop into a major effort by the Allied Nations and there is every expectation that it will be successful in repelling the planned German and Italian invasion of Africa and prove the first historic step to the liberation and restoration of France.

Blow to Knock Italy Out of the War Called Goal of American Invasion

Special Cable to THE NEW YORK TIMES.

LONDON, Sunday, Nov. 8—Allied Army, Navy and air forces commanded by Lieut. Gen. Dwight D. Eisenhower, commander of all American forces in the European theatre, have struck a powerful blow to free the Mediterranean from Axis control and knock Italy out of the war. That, in the opinion of military observers here, is the meaning of the movement of United States forces that now become part of the gigantic pincers with which it is expected that the last vestiges of the German and Italian forces in North Africa will be annihilated.

The movement now under way called for the finest timing. It was essential that, before that huge armada of whose presence at Gibraltar the Nazis were aware got under way, Britain's Eighth Army in Egypt should break through Marshal Erwin Rommel's defenses and start the westward push that is fast becoming a rout. Now United States soldiers swarming ashore at many points in French North Africa are closing Marshal Rommel's back door.

The first stage of the battle just beginning will be a struggle for the control of roads, railways and airfields in Algeria and the neighboring colony of Tunisia. Once the control of these has been won, Allied reinforcements and supplies will be able to dispense with the long journey around the Cape of Good Hope that has been one of

Continued on Page Thirteen

U.S. MEETS 'THREAT'

Big Expeditions Invade North and West Africa to Forestall Axis

EISENHOWER AT HEAD

President Urges French to Help, Calls Move Aid to Russia

Roosevelt's appeal to French people and Eisenhower's message to North Africans, Pg. 8.

By C. P. TRUSSELL
Special to THE NEW YORK TIMES.

WASHINGTON, Nov. 7—Powerful American forces, supported by British naval and air forces, landed simultaneously tonight at numerous points on the Mediterranean and Atlantic coasts of French North Africa, forestalling an anticipated invasion of Africa by Germany and Italy and launching effective second-front assistance to Russia, President Roosevelt announced tonight.

Lieut. Gen. Dwight D. Eisenhower is in command.

The President made the announcement even as the American forces, equipped with adequate weapons of modern warfare, he emphasized, were making the landings.

President Speaks to France

Soon he was speaking direct to the French Government and the French people by short-wave radio and in their own tongue, giving assurances that the Allies seek no territory and have no intention of interfering with friendly French, official or civilian. He called upon them to cooperate in repelling "the German and Italian international criminals."

By doing so, he said, they could help liberate France and the French Empire.

[United States and British planes dropped leaflets in France and French Africa containing messages to the people from President Roosevelt and General Eisenhower, London reported.]

General Eisenhower himself, the White House let it be known, also spoke by radio to the French people, explaining the purposes of the invasions.

His proclamation, delivered while the American troops were making their landings, gave specific directions to French land, sea and air forces in North Africa as to how they could avoid misunderstanding and prevent action against them by a system of signals. This is a military operation, General Eisen-

Continued on Page Three

Petain Says Vichy Will 'Defend' Lands

By The Associated Press.

LONDON, Sunday, Nov. 8—The Vichy radio said today that Marshal Henri Philippe Pétain had sent President Roosevelt a message expressing his "astonishment and sadness" at learning of "the aggression of your troops against North Africa."

Marshal Petain said that the reasons given by the President for the landings failed to justify them and added:

"France and its honor are involved. We are attacked and we will defend ourselves."

The Vichy government issued a communiqué opening with an "appeal to Frenchmen not to allow yourselves to be swayed by foreign broadcasts."

War News Summarized

SUNDAY, NOVEMBER 8, 1942

The White House announced last night that powerful American forces were landing on the Atlantic and Mediterranean coasts of French North Africa to forestall a German invasion. The announcement stated that the landing was to prevent the creation of an Axis threat to the Atlantic coast of the Americas across the narrow sea in Western Africa. France has been assured that the Allies seek no territory. [1:8.]

American correspondents with the African expeditionary force told of simultaneous landings by the United States troops at many points hundreds of miles apart. [1:4.]

Britain's Eighth Army continued its pursuit in North Africa of Marshal Rommel's shattered army. Twenty thousand prisoners had been taken, according to Cairo. British columns were said to be 200 miles west of El Alamein, close to the Libyan border. [1:3; map, P. 4.]

London announced that British heavy bombers had launched a "concentrated and effective" attack on Genoa Friday night and again raided Northern Italy last night. United States bombers attacked the U-boat base at Brest, France, and other planes from Britain pounded Nazi targets from the Netherlands to the Bay of Biscay. [1:2; map, P. 21.]

Moscow reported that the Soviet armies held on all fronts and killed some 1,800 of the enemy on the Stalingrad and Caucasus fronts. The German advances in the Nalchik region had apparently been halted. [38:4-5.]

General Douglas MacArthur's headquarters announced that American troops in force had been transported by air to New Guinea and had penetrated to the vicinity of Buna, Japanese base on the north coast. [1:1; map, P. 45.]

The United States Navy announced that Army forces on Guadalcanal Island in the Solomons had attacked Japanese troops to the east of the airfield Nov. 6 and had encountered little opposition. Announcement was also made that at least 5,188 Japanese had been killed in land fighting on Tulagi and Guadalcanal since the United States occupation Aug. 7. [46:1 with map.]

United States bombers attacked successfully the docks at Rangoon, Burma, and returned to their bases in India. [46:8.]

Major Sports Yesterday

FOOTBALL

Making both touchdowns in the second half, Notre Dame defeated Army before 75,142 spectators at the Yankee Stadium. With a scoring pass in the first period and several goal-line stands, Navy thrilled 74,000 fans at Philadelphia by upsetting Penn. Both Fordham and Columbia lost free-scoring contests here and the Big Three—Princeton, Yale and Harvard—all went down to defeat. Iowa toppled hitherto unbeaten Wisconsin. Scores of leading games:

Alabama	29	So. Carolina	0
Amherst	35	Trinity	6
Boston Coll.	28	Temple	0
Brown	20	Holy Cross	14
Colgate	35	Columbia	26
Cornell	13	Yale	7
Dartmouth	19	Princeton	7
Duke	42	Maryland	0
Duquesne	7	St. Mary's	7
Georgia	75	Florida	0
Ga. Pre-Fl.	41	Auburn	14
Ga. Tech	47	Kentucky	7
Great Lakes	42	Purdue	0
Illinois	14	Northwestern	7
Indiana	7	Minnesota	0
Iowa	6	Wisconsin	0
La. State	26	Fordham	13
Michigan	35	Harvard	7
Miss. State	7	Tulane	0
Missouri	26	Nebraska	6
Moravian	32	C. C. N. Y.	0
Navy	7	Penn.	0
Notre Dame	13	Army	0
Ohio State	59	Pittsburgh	19
Oklahoma	76	Kan. State	0
Oregon	14	U. C. L. A.	7
Penn State	18	Syracuse	13
Rice	40	Arkansas	9
So. Calif.	21	California	7
Stanford	20	Washington	7
Texas	20	Baylor	0
Tex. A. & M.	27	S. M. U.	20
Texas Tech	13	T. C. U.	6
Vanderbilt	19	Mississippi	0
Wash. State	25	Mich. State	13
Williams	31	Wesleyan	6

HORSE RACING

Good Morning won the Florence Nightingale Purse by half a length from Too Timely on the war-relief program before 22,099 racegoers who bet $1,550,089 at Belmont Park. Aonbarr defeated Riverland by a neck in the Grayson Handicap at Pimlico.

HOCKEY

The New York Rangers downed the Montreal Canadiens, 4—3, in the overtime opening game at Madison Square Garden.

(*Complete Details of These and Other Sports Events in Section 5.*)

"All the News That's Fit to Print."

The New York Times.

LATE CITY EDITION
Continued sultry today with winds becoming moderate.
Temperatures Yesterday—Max.,87; Min.,71
Sunrise, 5:35 A. M.; Sunset, 8:27 P. M.

VOL. XCII...No. 31,216. Entered as Second-Class Matter, Postoffice, New York, N. Y. NEW YORK, TUESDAY, JULY 13, 1943. THREE CENTS IN NEW YORK CITY

ALLIES SEIZE SYRACUSE AND NINE OTHER TOWNS IN DRIVE FOR MESSINA, KEY DEFENSE OF SICILY; JAPAN LOSES 4 WARSHIPS IN NEW KULA BATTLE

MEAT TRADE'S PLAN ON CATTLE SURPLUS NOW HELD DOOMED

Industry Leaders Attack OPA Proposal to Buy Stock, Pay Packers for Processing

HOSPITALS HERE PROTEST

Private Institutions Assert They Can't Get Supplies—Fishing Fleet Idle

By JEFFERSON G. BELL

The plan of the War Meat Board, set up recently by the industry to provision the nation out of America's record-breaking cattle surplus, seemed on the verge of collapse last night. Leading members of the livestock and packing industry admitted that Washington had ignored their proposals and, according to report, was about to come forward with a plan to buy cattle and to pay the packers for processing.

Cattle raisers and slaughterers asserted that this proposal would be "just another order," would make for "regimentation," and would require "an army" of new Government employes. Spokesmen for the livestock industry visiting New York City recently forecast the collapse of the War Meat Board.

Meanwhile the shortage of beef in New York City continued acute, and most of the Western and locally dressed meat was taken by Federal Government priority purchasing or by the preferred hotel and restaurant market, which yields a larger profit than other branches of the trade.

Hospitals Wire Protest

Spokesmen for New York City's voluntary hospitals, orphanages and homes for the aged declare that these have become the forgotten institutions. By telegraph their purchasing agents again sent a request to Washington for the adoption of a priority system for the sick, aged, handicapped and children.

The telegram, signed by H. P. Schwarzman, director of purchases of the non-profit cooperative Joint Purchasing Corporation, which buys for 115 voluntary hospitals and other charitable institutions, follows:

"Today's meat orders for our institutions are 80 per cent unfilled and some vital institutions, including the huge Montefiore Hospital for chronic diseases, which has the largest number of tuberculosis cases of any voluntary hospital in the country, aren't getting a single pound.

"Add to this sorry mess the fact that our egg suppliers are today cutting our egg orders by 50 per cent and you will recognize the makings of a real crisis in this sadly overlooked institutional food situation.

"Months ago we urged upon the Food Distribution Administration the adoption of a priority system to insure adequate feeding of the sick, aged, handicapped and children. We now repeat that some system of priorities is needed so that the institutional food problem is removed from the category of a day-to-day speculation."

Four Officials Get Appeal

The telegram was addressed to Judge Marvin Jones, Director of the War Food Administration; Prentiss M. Brown, head of the Office of Price Administration; Roy F. Hendrickson, Food Distribution Administrator, and James F. Byrnes, head of the Office of War Mobilization.

Dr. Edward M. Bernecker, Commissioner of Hospitals of New York City, reported that municipal hospitals had ample meat supplies.

Members of a committee of the Livestock and Meat Council that went from Chicago to Washington last Saturday to ask for support of the War Meat Board's plans reported yesterday the failure of their mission as they returned home. The committee went to the

Continued on Page Fifteen

Heat and Humidity Make City Swelter

The deadly combination of high humidity and high temperatures gave New York an uncomfortable day yesterday.

The day, which saw a high mark of 87 degrees at 3 P. M., began with a humidity reading of 98 at 6 A. M., or within 2 per cent of saturation. The humidity then dropped somewhat, but the temperature rose 10 degrees in five hours, from 76 at 9 A. M. to 86 at 2 P. M. At 4 P. M. the humidity was 75 per cent and the temperature had dropped to 84 degrees.

The Weather Bureau, which reported that the record high for July 12 was 93 degrees in 1908, said today would continue to be sultry with moderate winds. No rain is in sight.

RETURN OF MINERS TO AFL FOLD SEEN

Tobin Committee to Meet With Lewis in Capital Next Tuesday —Green Indicates Support

By JOSEPH SHAPLEN

Early return of John L. Lewis' United Mine Workers to the American Federation of Labor was foreseen yesterday with the announcement by Daniel J. Tobin, chairman of the committee appointed by the AFL executive council to confer with Mr. Lewis on the miners' application for reaffiliation, that he had called a meeting of the committee in Washington for next Tuesday. Mr. Tobin said he had sent an invitation to Mr. Lewis to attend.

The two other members of the AFL committee are Matthew Woll, AFL vice president, and George Harrison, president of the Brotherhood of Railway Clerks. Mr. Tobin is president of the International Brotherhood of Teamsters.

Mr. Tobin's action yesterday became known in a telegram from his office in Indianapolis addressed to THE NEW YORK TIMES in response to an inquiry following publication of his recent declaration that he would support acceptance of the miners' application by the AFL. Similar support has been expressed by Mr. Woll. Mr. Harrison has declared that any statement on the matter would have to come from Mr. Tobin.

Jurisdiction to Come Up

Mr. Tobin's committee will discuss with Mr. Lewis various technical matters of jurisdiction before making its recommendation to the executive council when it meets in Chicago next month. One of the problems will be the question of District 50 of the United Mine Workers, whose jurisdiction was confined originally to chemicals and coal byproducts but which has been expanded by Mr. Lewis to include workers coming within the jurisdiction of other organizations.

Mr. Lewis, it was learned, will be requested to confine the activities of District 50 to its original limits and to adjust whatever jurisdic-

Continued on Page Ten

ROOSEVELT SIGNS SIX BIG FUND BILLS AND CRITICIZES ONE

Hopes Congress Will Restore Crop Insurance as Risks of Farmers Rise With Output

YIELDS TO RESTRICTIONS

Accepts War Agency Cuts and Limit on Own Outlay—Total Approved Is $5,400,000,000

By C. P. TRUSSELL
Special to THE NEW YORK TIMES.

WASHINGTON, July 12—President Roosevelt signed today half a dozen appropriation bills, releasing for obligations of the current and last fiscal year funds totaling about $5,400,000,000, most of which had been delayed by controversies in Congress.

In approving one, the $848,295,000 supply bill for the Department of Agriculture, he expressed the hope that when the Senate and House return from the summer recess they would provide funds to continue the crop insurance program, which Congress ordered liquidated by Jan. 1.

"Certainly in these times when the farmer is being urged to produce more and assume greater risks, we should not stop a program which is of tremendous potential value to them," the President said in a statement.

As for ending crop insurance because "it was too expensive," he remarked that the same thing was said about rural free delivery of mail and rural electrification. He said he did not feel that crop insurance had had a fair trial.

Other Major Measures Signed

As he signed five other bills, the Chief Executive accepted a series of restrictions imposed by Congress, one of which applied to the use of his own $86,000,000 special emergency fund. Other major bills signed were:

The $142,430,000 Urgent Deficiency Bill which contained the emergency fund restriction and also a requirement that three Government employes, accused of "subversive" association, be reappointed by the President and confirmed by the Senate by Nov. 15 to hold their posts.

The $1,137,167,000 supply bill for the Labor Department and the Federal Security Agency, which orders the liquidation by Jan. 1 of the National Youth Administration.

The $2,911,697,000 War Agencies Bill, in which operating funds for the Office of Price Administration were held to $155,000,000 and the appropriation for the Office of War Information was cut.

The $253,256,000 Second Deficiency Bill, which became involved in a controversy through an attempt in the Senate to repeal the order in the Agriculture Department measure for liquidation of the crop insurance program.

The $105,000,000 Interior Depart-

Continued on Page Twenty-six

AMERICAN SOLDIERS RACE ASHORE FOR SICILY INVASION

With their rifles ready, they leap off landing barges into the surf at the Italian island
Associated Press Wirephoto, from U. S. Signal Corps Radiophoto

GERMAN ASSAULTS IN RUSSIA DIMINISH

Nazis Stopped All Along the 165-Mile Front—Counter-Blows Gain Power

By The Associated Press.

LONDON, Tuesday, July 13—The great eight-day-old German offensive in central Russia, after costing the Nazis "tremendous losses" in men and matériel, has begun to diminish in power, the Russians announced today.

All along the 165-mile Orel-Kursk-Belgorod front Monday the Nazis attempted repeatedly to smash through to new positions, but each time were ground down by Soviet defenders, said the Russian midnight communiqué, recorded by the Soviet monitor.

Finally, at many points the attackers apparently despaired of their hopes of crashing the Red Army lines and set about bolstering their initial positions, while the

Continued on Page Five

Cruiser and 3 Destroyers Sunk by Allies in Solomons

By TILLMAN DURDIN
By Wireless to THE NEW YORK TIMES.

ALLIED HEADQUARTERS IN THE SOUTHWEST PACIFIC, Tuesday, July 13—In the second naval engagement of the battle for the New Georgia Islands American warships last night sank a Japanese light cruiser and three destroyers, and probably sank two more destroyers. Announcing the engagement, today's communiqué said that only fragmentary reports had been received. Whether there were any American losses is not known.

The engagement took place off the northwest New Georgia Islands in or near Kula Gulf, where American warships last week sank nine enemy vessels in a night battle. It is probable that last night's Japanese force was another Tokyo attempt to supply and reinforce the garrisons on the New Georgia Islands.

The force was spotted early Friday evening between Bougainville and Vella Lavella and after midnight was northwest of Vella Lavella.

The naval clash came after an-

Continued on Page Five

400 SUPPLY TRUCKS SMASHED BY ALLIES

Planes Destroy Foe's Vehicles Rushing Men and Arms to Front in Sicily

By HERBERT L. MATTHEWS
By Wireless to THE NEW YORK TIMES.

ALLIED HEADQUARTERS IN NORTH AFRICA, July 12—As the battle of Sicily moved nearer to the decisive phase yesterday, the tempo of air fighting and bombing was increased.

The Axis sought vainly to interfere with the advancing Allies and to support its own counter-attacks, but the effort cost the enemy forty-five planes to nine of ours. At the end of a day of great activity, 400 Axis troop and supply vehicles littered the roads of Sicily and Catania had got one of the worst bombings of its career. United States Liberators from the Middle East attacked southern Italy.

[Spitfires from Malta accounted for half the enemy planes knocked down, while losing only two of their own number, The Associated Press reported.

[A British reporter at an Al-

Continued on Page Three

EISENHOWER SEES ADVANCE IN SICILY

Destroyer Takes Commander in Chief for Short Visit to Find All Is Going Well

By EDWARD GILLING
Representing the Combined Allied Press.

SOMEWHERE IN SICILY, July 12—Gen. Dwight D. Eisenhower, Allied Commander in Chief, landed in Sicily today from a British destroyer and drove to the front, where he visited Lieut. Gen. George S. Patton Jr., commanding the American invasion forces. General Eisenhower found, on the basis of action reports, that all was going well.

As General Eisenhower's destroyer skirted the coast an Axis battery turned its guns on the ship but its shells fell a mile astern.

General Eisenhower watched a big Allied cruiser shelling inland targets as his destroyer neared the coast of Sicily, saw the blasts of the land guns dueling with enemy batteries, made his way up a beach crowded with half-naked men loading supplies and sped to the front along hastily-built roads through the vineyards.

At General Patton's headquarters General Eisenhower heard of the progress of American troops, was told how the Allied forces had taken 4,000 prisoners on Saturday and had almost wiped out an Italian coastal regiment. It was then that he said that he was quite satisfied with the progress made by the Allied troops and that all was going well.

During a drive around the front areas General Eisenhower talked

Continued on Page Four

RAGUSA IS MENACED

Americans, British and Canadians Advancing on Key Junction

6,000 MEN CAPTURED

Most Towns Taken on First Day—Syracuse Fell in 18 Hours

By DREW MIDDLETON
By Wireless to THE NEW YORK TIMES.

ALLIED HEADQUARTERS IN NORTH AFRICA, July 12—Ten Sicilian towns, including the vitally important port of Syracuse, have fallen to the Allied armies, which are battering their way steadily northward today after having rebuffed seven Axis counter-attacks yesterday.

American, British and Canadian troops have smashed through the Axis defenses and are driving toward Ragusa, it was learned late tonight. Ragusa, a key rail and road junction, is a vital point for a junction between the Anglo-American armies.

[The Algiers radio, quoted in a British broadcast recorded by The United Press, said that a fierce battle was raging for Ragusa, seventeen miles inland from Pozzallo, between Allied troops and 30,000 Germans.]

Advances Meet Success

Syracuse was taken at 9 P. M. Saturday, eighteen hours after the first sea landings. Rosolini, a junction on the road from Syracuse to the southern coast, was taken by Canadian infantry, desperately eager to avenge the dead and the manacled prisoners of Dieppe. Ispica also fell to them. Noto was captured at 11:25 P. M. Saturday.

The Allied position had improved immensely, although official news of any important gain beyond those announced in today's communiqué was wanting.

The Canadians and British troops who linked up north of Pachino are meeting with considerable success in their advance. The situation is encouraging all along the front from Licata on the west to Syracuse on the east, although the Axis field army appears to be gathering for a counter-attack in force in the neighborhood of Agrigento, about twenty miles west of the American left flank.

The general opinion at headquarters tonight was that the enemy resistance was stiffening all along the line and that sharp counter-attacks, probably delivered by German as well as Italian units, could be expected.

Prisoners May Total 6,000

About 2,000 prisoners, most of them Italians, have been captured by the Allies thus far.

[Available information indicated that at least 6,000 Axis prisoners were in hand by tonight, The Associated Press said —2,000 of them said by Allied Headquarters to have been taken yesterday and 4,000 reported in front dispatches to have been seized on Saturday.

[Reuter reported that the Allies were attacking Agrigento, four miles west of Porto Empedocle, on the extreme left flank, and also roads and communications that fan out into the central Catania plain on the British Eighth Army's front on the right. There were unconfirmed reports, The Associated Press added, that both the airport at Catania, midway between Syracuse and Messina, the key to the island's defense, and Floridia had fallen to Allied arms.

[British forces were reported to have made new landings near Catania, The United Press said.]

The Eighth Army, under Gen. Sir Bernard L. Montgomery, is astride the most important road in the southeastern corner of the island. The storming of Syracuse by a tempered British division wins for the Allies the use of one of the best harbors in the Mediterranean

Continued on Page Two

War News Summarized

TUESDAY, JULY 13, 1943

Ten Sicilian towns have been captured by the Allied forces. From Licata on the west, to Syracuse, on the east, British, Canadian and American troops extended and consolidated their holdings along the coast. Enemy resistance was stiffening, and seven counter-attacks with tanks, the brunt of which was borne by American troops, were beaten back. More than 6,000 Axis prisoners were taken, while our losses continued to be light.

But there was evidence that the Axis was getting ready to strike. Its field army was being concentrated for a counter-attack near Agrigento about twenty miles west of the United States flank at Licata. American troops had pushed inland about ten miles. [All the foregoing 1:8; map, P. 2.]

In capturing Syracuse the British gave the Allies a much-needed harbor with landing facilities for heavy equipment and reinforcements regardless of weather conditions. [2:2.] The Americans lost only four men in capturing Licata and taking more than 300 prisoners. [3:1.]

The Allied air forces, in maintaining their ceaseless cover of the invading army, shot down forty-five Axis planes and lost only nine. In a spectacular fight over the beaches Spitfires destroyed twenty-four enemy fighters. Other planes wrecked more than 400 loaded troop and supply trucks, while still others attacked Catania, airfields in Sicily and Reggio Calabria and Vibo Valentia in southern Italy. [1:6.]

General Eisenhower made a tour of the bridgeheads won by his army. The same commanders who led the victorious Tunisian campaign are directing the fight in Sicily, with General Patton in charge of United States land forces and General Montgomery heading the British and Canadian Armies. [1:7.]

An Allied spokesman broadcasting to the Italian people from Algiers said the peace terms were unconditional surrender of the Fascist regime and Axis Armies and a free choice by the people of a non-Fascist Government. [5:1.]

American naval forces in the Central Solomons sank a Japanese cruiser and three destroyers in a new naval battle in the Kula Gulf. Two more destroyers were probably sunk. [1:5-6.] In the North Pacific American airmen sank a Japanese cargo ship, left one sinking and damaged two more trying to run supplies to Kiska. [5:6.]

The German armies in Russia went into their second week of the offensive on the Orel-Kursk-Belgorod front with minor gains and heavy losses to show for their efforts. The Red Army held everywhere, Moscow reported, and described the latest enemy thrusts as being made with "weaker forces." [1:4.]

Survey of Rents Under Way Here, Forecasting OPA Control if Needed

Further evidence that the Office of Price Administration is serious in its intention to enforce rent control here if the situation warrants came to light yesterday with the discovery that 200 employes of the Bureau of Labor Statistics have been checking rents in the city for the last two weeks.

Robert E. Behlow, regional price economist of the bureau, in charge of the survey, insisted that it "has nothing to do with rent control." An official of the OPA, however, admitted that the study was being made at the request of its Washington office, which would issue any order to freeze rents here.

Mr. Behlow said his employes were asking apartment house tenants for information on rent rates and services. "They are endeavoring to find out," he said, "what rent rates and services prevail now as against rents and services in previous periods." He said he could not define the term "previous periods." Results of the survey are expected to be made public shortly.

At a meeting of owners and managers of 100,000 rental units in Queens at the Queens Chamber of Commerce, Crescent Plaza Building, Long Island City, voluntary cooperation with the "spirit of rent control" was pledged by the 150 persons present.

These included A. E. MacDougall, vice president of the Queensboro Corporation, which developed and operates extensive holdings in Jackson Heights, and George

Continued on Page Fifteen

Giraud Arrives as French in City Prepare to Mark Bastille Day

Gen. Henri-Honoré Giraud, commander of the French forces in North Africa and with Gen. Charles de Gaulle co-President of the French Committee of National Liberation, arrived at La Guardia Field at 8:10 o'clock last night, the War Department disclosed.

Greeted by a number of high-ranking Army officials, the general stepped at once into an automobile stationed at the door of the plane. Half an hour later he arrived at a hotel in the city.

Extraordinary precautions were taken by Army authorities and the police to safeguard the distinguished visitor both at the airport and the hotel. The area near the hangar at which his plane alighted was guarded by a large detail of uniformed policemen and detectives. The public and reporters were kept at least 500 feet from the hangar.

At the hotel there was a cordon of military policemen, secret service operatives, detectives and uniformed policemen under the command of Deputy Chief Inspector John J. Di Martino.

En route from the airport to the hotel, General Giraud was escorted by thirty motor-cycle patrolmen and seven police cars. These were interspersed among five Cadillacs that conveyed the party from the field.

The general had come here virtually on the eve of Bastille Day from Fort Benning, Ga., where he had reviewed troops. Bastille Day, celebrated much as Americans do

Continued on Page Seven

"All the News That's Fit to Print."

The New York Times.

LATE CITY EDITION
Showers in forenoon; clear in afternoon; fair at night.
Temperatures Yesterday—Max., 50; Min., 35
Sunrise, 8:06 A. M.; Sunset, 5:29 P. M.

Copyright, 1943, by The New York Times Company.

VOL. XCIII...No. 31,363. Entered as Second-Class Matter, Postoffice, New York, N. Y. NEW YORK, TUESDAY, DECEMBER 7, 1943. THREE CENTS IN NEW YORK CITY

'BIG 3' CHARTS TRIPLE BLOWS TO HUMBLE REICH AND AGREES ON A PEACE TO ELIMINATE TYRANNY; CARRIERS ATTACK MARSHALLS; 5TH ARMY GAINS

MAYOR PORTRAYED AS SCHOOL RULER BY OUSTED OFFICIAL

Kuper, Former Law Adviser to Board, Tells NEA Inquiry Appointments Were Blocked

SEES MORALE IMPAIRED

Fear of Having Funds Held Up Kept the Members From Asserting Rights, He Says

Charges that Mayor La Guardia has interfered with the city school system, causing educational officials to bow to his will and robbing the Board of Education of its independence by threatening to withhold funds, were made at the National Education Association school inquiry, which began public hearings here yesterday.

A behind-the-scenes version of how the board operates, and of the role of the Mayor in deciding matters of school policy, was presented by Theodore Fred Kuper, law secretary of the board for eleven years until he was dismissed recently by order of the Mayor. Mr. Kuper took the witness stand at 10 A. M. and did not complete his testimony until the hearing adjourned late in the afternoon.

Hearing in Bar Building

Held in the trial room of the Bar Association Building, 42 West Forty-fourth Street, the open sessions are the culmination of three months of investigation and study by the National Education Association's panel of educators appointed to determine the charges of City Hall interference with school issues.

Dr. Ernest E. Cole, former New York State Commissioner of Education, who is acting as counsel for the inquiry, is conducting the hearings. Members of the panel include Dr. Orville C. Pratt, past president of the NEA and superintendent emeritus of schools at Spokane, Wash.; Dr. Ernest O. Melby, chancellor of the University of Montana; Miss Mabel Studebaker, president of the NEA's department of classroom teachers, and Dr. Donald DuShane, past president of the NEA and secretary of its commission for the defense of democracy through education.

Representatives of various school, civic and parents' groups appeared at the opening session. The investigation was requested by the New York High School Teachers Association and the Kindergarten-6B Teachers Association, two of the city's largest educational bodies. Mrs. Johanna M. Lindlof, president of the kindergarten group and former member of the Board of Education, sat through the entire session; she is to take the stand this morning.

Testimony by Kuper

Mr. Kuper marshaled a parade of statements and figures to support his contention that Mayor La Guardia interfered with local school independence and "frightened" board officials into submission. He cited incidents to illustrate the many points he raised. Members of the panel or Dr. Cole interrupted frequently to ask questions.

As a result of the Mayor's control over the school board 100 appointments to clerical and administrative positions, for which funds were provided in the budget, have been blocked, Mr. Kuper declared. This has resulted in decreased efficiency as well as a lowering of morale among the employes, he testified.

Important administrative positions, which the board sought to fill and for which money was present in the budget, remain vacant because the city Budget Director does not give the necessary certificates, it was brought out. One instance was cited in which the Superintendent of Plant Operation and Maintenance requested a supervising custodian; the position was approved by the Board of Education, but it took 404 days before the Mayor gave his consent.

"Bear in mind that the Board of Education has the inherent legal power and, in my opinion, the duty to fill these positions," Mr. Kuper

Continued on Page Twenty

Stalin Says U. S. Aid Saved the Allies

By Cable to THE NEW YORK TIMES.

CAIRO, Egypt, Dec. 6—The greatest tribute possibly ever paid American industrial production came from Premier Stalin during the Teheran talks.

In a toast at a dinner party the Soviet Premier said:

"Without American machines the United Nations never could have won the war."

He should know.

It is understood Premier Stalin said Russia was manufacturing 3,000 planes monthly against 3,500 British and 10,000 American.

FROZEN FOOD SPACE IS TO BE EXPANDED

Warehouses Here Are to Add Million Cubic Feet—Row Brews Over U. S. Hoards

By JEFFERSON G. BELL

Major warehouse interests of New York City disclosed yesterday that they already had taken steps to expand freezer capacity at least 1,000,000 cubic feet. This move is part of a program to ease storage, transportation and other problems caused by the Federal Government's vast hoard of food.

The Government stockpiles have so taxed the capacity of warehouses, notably freezer space, that the Office of Defense Transportation last week appealed for help to the War Food Administration and the Office of Price Administration.

The refrigeration expansion program was revealed by local WFA and warehouse spokesmen as chilly relations between national WFA and OPA on one side and ODT on the other threatened to develop into an interdepartmental row over charges that foods needed by civilians are being allowed to deteriorate or spoil because of improper warehousing.

Release of Supplies Suggested

In view of the explanation by warehouse interests here that they could not increase their freezer capacity sooner than sixty to ninety days, food-trade circles were unable to see what would be the solution of warehouse congestion unless supplies were released.

When Joseph B. Eastman, director of the Office of Defense Transportation, confirmed last week reports that he had asked WFA and OPA to take steps to ease the congestion of freezer facilities, he disclosed that he had received a letter promising "immediate" action. Neither Mr. Eastman nor any member of the ODT staff was reached yesterday for comment on the disclosure that plans for freezer expansion here held no promise of relief for another two or three months.

The local office of the Food Distribution Administration, WFA, 150 Broadway, disclosed that a survey of storage facilities here had showed that New York City warehouses are operating at 89 per cent of capacity.

"When we are operating at 90 to 95 per cent of capacity," explained

Continued on Page Twenty-three

BATTLING IN ITALY

3 More Camino Peaks Are Taken Despite Fierce Resistance

COUNTER-BLOW FAILS

Germans Beaten Back at Venafro—Eighth Army at Moro River

By MILTON BRACKER

By Wireless to THE NEW YORK TIMES.

ALGIERS, Dec. 6—The battle of the mountains continued yesterday in Italy as Lieut. Gen. Mark W. Clark's Fifth Army wrested three more peaks of the Mount Camino group from the Germans, who are putting up a fanatic battle for every inch of the rocky ground.

The slow and tortuous envelopment of the numberless ridges and peaks proceeded in an epic of difficult fighting in which the individual soldier had to combine the technique of the jungle fighter with that of the mountain goat. More rain tended to retard the four-day-old offensive as German gunfire swept the slopes and crevices from deeply dug-in positions. But the British and American infantry ground steadily forward and mopped up the isolated resistance strong points by-passed by the Allies' spearheads.

There is at least one ridge that our forces have pressed beyond and flanked without being able to silence the German fire from its crest. The entire tone of the struggle is one of a fierce will to resist. Despite severe losses, the German Tenth Army is setting a standard of savage defensive fighting that its opponents will never forget.

[American artillery has begun shelling Cassino, The United Press reported.]

Counter-Attack Repulsed

In the Venafro sector of the Fifth Army's front, above the Via Casilina, the Germans flung in another sharp counter-attack against American units. As they have done several times before, the Americans hurled back the attack, leaving the positions in this sector about the same.

On the British Eighth Army's front, too, the weather was bad. The Germans poured in reinforcements as the battles for Orsogna and Guardiagrele raged unabated. Both points remained in the enemy's hands.

The Eighth Army has, in general, pressed nearer to the Moro River from San Vito Chietino, however, and, at Casone, some four miles inland, three miles above Lanciano and 1,000 yards from the Moro's south bank, the Allies' infantry and tanks crushed several advanced German machine-gun posts in their drive to the bank.

The Eighth Army captured at least one German tank that proved to be without question a flame-thrower. This settled the dispute that began here on Nov. 29, when a flame-throwing tank was first

Continued on Page Sixteen

THE LEADERS OF THE 'BIG THREE' MEET IN TEHERAN

Marshal Stalin, President Roosevelt and Prime Minister Churchill on the porch of the Russian Embassy

The New York Times (U. S. Twelfth Air Force)

HEAVY TASK FORCES STRIKE IN PACIFIC

Blow at the Marshall Islands Comes as Allies Step Up Air Drive Against New Britain

By GEORGE F. HORNE

By Telephone to THE NEW YORK TIMES.

PEARL HARBOR, Dec. 6—Strong carrier task forces and heavy Navy bombers have attacked a number of bases in the Japanese-held Marshall Islands in the last few days, indicating a new development in the central Pacific offensive, which was touched off by our invasion of the Gilbert Islands.

[In the southwest Pacific, Allied fliers struck with increasing violence against invasion-menaced New Britain Island, on which lies Rabaul, main Japanese base in that war theatre. Our airmen poured 155

Continued on Page Seventeen

New Cairo Talks Reported To Get Turkey to Join War

By JAMES B. RESTON

By Wireless to THE NEW YORK TIMES.

LONDON, Dec. 6—The conversations that Prime Minister Churchill and, presumably, President Roosevelt had with President Ismet Inonu of Turkey in Cairo after the Teheran parleys have led to considerable speculation about the possibility of Turkey's entering the war. The background of these conversations would seem to justify this speculation. The question for Turkey, as an ally of Britain, now seems to be not whether but when and how she will help the Allies. This, it is presumed, is the question being discussed by Messrs. Churchill and Inonu.

[Reports that Messrs. Churchill, Roosevelt and Inonu were conferring in Africa have come from enemy and neutral sources.]

The basis of these conversations is the Anglo-French-Turkish treaty of alliance of Oct. 19, 1939. Article II stated: "In the event of an act of aggression by a European power

Continued on Page Seven

UKRAINE RAILWAY IS CUT BY RUSSIANS

Huge German Forces Are Split—Red Army Is Only 23 Miles From Kirovograd

By The Associated Press.

LONDON, Tuesday, Dec. 7—Russian troops smashed the enemy's Smela-Znamenka line in the central Ukraine yesterday, splitting huge German forces guarding those vital junctions on railways leading to Rumania and putting the Red Army within twenty-three miles of the Axis bastion of Kirovograd.

A Moscow communiqué and a midnight supplement announced the capture of Tsybulevo, eight miles northwest of Znamenka on the double-track railway leading to Smela, and the fall of Alexsandriya, twenty miles east of Znamenka. Twenty other towns and villages were swept up, said the bulletin, recorded by the Soviet monitor from a Moscow broadcast.

[The crossing of the Znamenka-Smela line probably took place in the Krasnoselye-Tsybulevo sector. Each village is two miles from the railroad line and represents the farthest penetration in yesterday's advance.

Continued on Page Twelve

WASHINGTON HAILS UNITY AT TEHERAN

Hull Stresses 'Concerting' of Plans to Crush Axis Forces—Congress Leaders Pleased

By BERTRAM D. HULEN

Special to THE NEW YORK TIMES.

WASHINGTON, Dec. 6—Opinion in the executive branch of the Government concerning both the Teheran and the Cairo conferences was set forth by Secretary of State Cordell Hull today in a statement declaring that the concerted plans adopted "will undoubtedly result in making effective to the fullest extent the fighting strength of all of the United Nations."

Opinion in general in the capital was that the communiqué issued on the Teheran conference showed that the three Chiefs of Government, President Roosevelt, Prime Minister Churchill and Premier Stalin, had had a meeting of minds and had reached detailed decisions for destroying the German Army, even though the declaration, perhaps significantly, did not use the phrase "unconditional surrender."

All in all, the announcement gave grounds for encouragement at a time when America is entering the third year of the war.

Way Open for Small Nations

It was of first importance that the three leaders had met, it was felt. And in meeting they had agreed to cooperate in the war and in the peace, and to invite the collaboration of small nations.

There were conjectures as to whether this collaboration might include the German people, if they sought it as a chastened people free of nazism and militarism.

Military details, obviously, could not be revealed, it was realized, but

Continued on Page Eleven

War News Summarized

TUESDAY, DECEMBER 7, 1943

President Roosevelt, Premier Stalin and Prime Minister Churchill announced to the world yesterday that "no power on earth can prevent our destroying the German armies by land, their U-boats by sea and their war plants from the air."

The three leaders, in a declaration dated Teheran, Dec. 1, said they had "reached complete agreement as to the scope and timing of operations which will be undertaken from the east, west and south."

"We came here with hope and determination," the three men said. "We leave here friends in fact, in spirit and in purpose." One of the purposes is to "work together in the peace" that will follow the war. All countries, large and small, were invited into "a world family of democratic nations" pledged to eliminate tyranny, oppression and intolerance and to "banish the scourge and terror of war for many generations."

In a second declaration the conferees pledged the independence and territorial integrity of Iran as a token of their determination to protect small nations. [All the foregoing 1:8; map P. 5.]

The meetings were held in the Soviet Embassy at Teheran about a round table ten feet in diameter. It was the first time Mr. Roosevelt had ever met Premier Stalin and the first time the latter had left his country since 1909. [3:1.]

A third international meeting was reported to have followed in North Africa, where, it was said, Mr. Roosevelt and Mr. Churchill conferred with President Inonu of Turkey regarding his country's entrance into the war. [1:5-6.]

The military plans laid at Teheran were expected to be in full effect by March or April of next year, when invasion from Britain would follow the Russian winter drive and an all-out aerial offensive against Germany. [1:6-7.]

Secretary of State Hull declared that the fighting strength of the United Nations could now become fully effective [1:7] and London opinion held that the Teheran announcement was designed to conceal more than was revealed. [9:2.] The people of Moscow were delighted that agreement on timing all blows against Germany had ended the "second-front" issue. [10:1.]

Allied troops continued to make progress on all fronts. Both the Eighth and Fifth Armies in Italy pushed forward against bitter opposition, reaching the Moro River and bringing Cassino under artillery fire. [1:3; map, P. 16.] The Red Army, smashing southwest of Kremenchug, was only four miles from Znamenka as it cut the Smela-Znamenka rail line. [1:6; map, P. 12.]

In the Pacific 155 tons of bombs were showered on Cape Gloucester as the assault on the western end of New Britain was maintained. [17:2-3.] A strong American carrier force attacked Japanese positions in the Marshall Islands [1:4] and United States submarines sent eleven more enemy ships to the bottom. [16:6.]

2d Brooklyn Jury Scores Mayor For Failing to Hire Enough Police

Already under censure by the August grand jury in Kings County for alleged failure to suppress crime in the Bedford-Stuyvesant section of Brooklyn, the administration of Mayor La Guardia was accused yesterday by the holdover July grand jury of inadequately policing the entire borough.

"We charge," the July panel declared in a presentment to County Judge Franklin Taylor, "that the present administration over a long period of years has utterly failed to take adequate measures to promptly fill the vacancies regularly occurring in the department, and also to provide additional patrolmen during this time."

At the same time County Judge Nathan R. Sobel was charging the December grand jury and pointing out, for the guidance of the August panel, that its presentment was faulty in that it had the effect of "indicting" an entire people for the crimes of a very few and "stirring up resentment, hatred and fear."

The August panel reconvened yesterday, continuing its inquiry into what it declares to be widespread and unchecked lawlessness in Brooklyn's "Little Harlem." It heard the testimony of several witnesses, then adjourned without disclosing when it would meet again.

In its presentment the July grand jury, whose term had been extended to permit it to investigate police protection in the city's most populous borough, attributed the critical police situation to the "short-sighted, improvident policies of this administration," which it said "have in large part contributed to the development of a situ-

Continued on Page Twenty

First Quarter of 1944 Likely to See Fruition of the Teheran Strategy

By DREW MIDDLETON

By Cable to THE NEW YORK TIMES.

LONDON, Dec. 6—Military plans for the defeat of the Wehrmacht drawn at Teheran, Iran, by President Roosevelt, Prime Minister Churchill and Premier Stalin, will probably be fully activated in the first three months of 1944.

During that period the strategic aerial offensive against Germany will assume its maximum proportions, the winter offensive of the Red Army should have brought it to the Dniester in the south and into Poland in the north and the Anglo-American invasion of northern Europe from Britain will be ready to start, with the tactical air forces already operating against the defenses in Western Europe and the lateral communications on which those defenses rely.

One of the first tangible results of the Teheran conference should be the arrival of Gen. George C. Marshall, United States Army Chief of Staff, in Britain to take up his position as Commander in Chief of all Allied invasion forces.

Once the invasion leader is settled into his job it is considered likely that the long-awaited announcement of the formation of an Allied Tactical Air Force and the appointment of American and British commanders to lead Allied Army groups involved in the invasion, will follow.

It may well be that the southern Europe front, now represented by a slow, painful advance in Italy may

Continued on Page Five

ATTACK PLANS SET

Dates Fixed for Land Drives From the East, West and South

IRAN TO BE FREED

Allied Leaders Say 'No Power on Earth' Can Balk Our Victory

The texts of the three-power declarations appear on Page 4.

By C. L. SULZBERGER

By Cable to THE NEW YORK TIMES.

CAIRO, Egypt, Dec. 6—Final concord on a campaign to destroy the German military power by land, sea and air and to erect an enduring peace in which all nations, both great and small, shall participate, was agreed upon in the momentous Teheran meeting between President Roosevelt, Premier Stalin and Prime Minister Churchill.

Simultaneously, the three leaders, as a sign of their faith in each other and as proof of the validity of their intentions toward little nations, guaranteed the post-war independence, sovereignty and territorial integrity of Iran.

These Allied agreements were announced to the world today in two joint declarations signed in order by President Roosevelt [the only titular Chief of State among the three], Premier Stalin and Prime Minister Churchill. They were issued in Teheran Dec. 1 after a long final sitting of the leaders and their innermost circles of advisers in the magnificent Soviet Embassy where President Roosevelt lived as a guest.

3-Pronged Attack Pledged

Their military promises can be summed up accordingly: the three powers will work together throughout the war; their military staffs have concerted plans for the destruction of German forces; these staffs have reached a "complete agreement as to the scope and timing of operations which will be undertaken from the east, west and south."

Guarantees satisfactory to the three chiefs now exist that the final victory will rest with the United Nations. "No power on earth can prevent our destroying the German armies by land, their U-boats by sea and their war plants from the air," says one of the joint declarations. "Our attacks will be relentless and increasing."

Seal Doom of Hitler

Thus in four days of deliberation in the romantic Iranian capital the "Big Three" laid the second half of the plans for ending the global war and establishing lasting peace for the benefit of all in its ruins. The Asiatic talks in North Africa between Mr. Roosevelt, Mr. Churchill and Generalissimo Chiang Kai-shek already had drawn up the program for accelerating the defeat of Japan and for building up a new Asia.

Now European talks of exactly the same length have rounded off the final plans for smashing Hitler which obviously must precede the destruction of Japan in the over-all scheme of the Allied grand strategy planners. Britain and America have clearly coordinated their ultimate schedule for the invasion of Europe from several points from the west and south with a program for new Russian offensives against the Reich.

It may be assumed that once the fulfillment of these plans comes about and Moscow's long pleas for a second front are entirely answered that the Soviet Union might conceivably alter its present neutral attitude toward Japan. This certainly was discussed at Teheran but the outcome of these discussions is not known.

It would seem a fair assumption from a complete survey of both the present wartime and future post-war problems indicated in the latest declarations that the three powers must now have agreed on

Continued on Page Four

"All the News That's Fit to Print"

The New York Times.

Copyright, 1944, by The New York Times Company.

6 A. M. EXTRA

Partly cloudy and warmer today; moderate to fresh winds.
Temperatures Yesterday—Max., 67; Min., 51
Sunrise, 5:25 A. M.; Sunset, 8:24 P. M.

VOL. XCIII. No. 31,545. Entered as Second-Class Matter, Postoffice, New York, N. Y. NEW YORK, TUESDAY, JUNE 6, 1944. THREE CENTS IN NEW YORK CITY

ALLIED ARMIES LAND IN FRANCE IN THE HAVRE-CHERBOURG AREA; GREAT INVASION IS UNDER WAY

ROOSEVELT SPEAKS

Says Rome's Fall Marks 'One Up and Two to Go' Among Axis Capitals

WARNS WAY IS HARD

Asks World to Give the Italians a Chance for Recovery

The text of President Roosevelt's address is on Page 5.

By CHARLES HURD

Special to The New York Times.

WASHINGTON, June 5—President Roosevelt hailed tonight the capture of Rome, first of the three major Axis capitals to fall, as a great achievement on the road to ward total conquest of the Axis. Rome, he said, marked "one up and two to go."

The President spoke for a quarter-hour on the radio, as had been announced yesterday, but his speech was notable for its lack of heroics. It was in no sense a speech of triumph, but rather a tribute to the United Nations forces and leadership that drove the Germans from Rome.

With this tribute he combined a solemn warning that much greater fighting lies ahead before the Axis is defeated, as well as high tributes to the Italian people, whom he again welcomed as a people into the family of nations opposed to the Axis.

"Italy should go on," Mr. Roosevelt said, "as a great mother nation, contributing to the culture and the progress and the good-will of mankind, developing her special talents in the arts, crafts, and sciences, and preserving her historic and cultural heritage for the benefit of all peoples.

"We want and expect the help of the future Italy toward lasting peace. All the other nations opposed to fascism and nazism ought to help to give Italy a chance."

Shrines Should Live, He Says

President Roosevelt saw considerable significance in the fact that Rome should be the first Axis capital to fall. He remarked its shrines, "visible symbols of the faith and determination of the early saints and martyrs that Christianity should live and become universal," and added that "it will be a source of deep satisfaction that the freedom of the Pope and of Vatican City is assured by the armies of the United Nations."

There is significance, too, he added, in the fact that Rome was liberated by a composite force of soldiers from many nations.

Reviewing the military picture, the President pointed out that "it would be unwise to inflate in our own minds the military importance of the capture of Rome." He cautioned his auditors that while the Germans have retreated "thousands of miles" across Africa and back through Italy "they have suffered heavy losses, but not great enough yet to cause collapse."

"Therefore," he added, "the victory still lies some distance ahead. That distance will be covered in due time—have no fear of that. But it will be tough and it will be costly."

Turning to the relief problem in the newly liberated portion of Italy, Mr. Roosevelt noted that some persons thought of the financial cost, but he maintained that the work would pay dividends "by eliminating fascism" and any future desire by Italians to "start another war of aggression." Relief has been planned, he added, but transport demands are so great that "improvement must be gradual."

He warned Italy that it "cannot grow in stature by seeking to build up a great militaristic empire,"

Continued on Page 5

Conferees Accept Cabaret Tax Cut

By The Associated Press.

WASHINGTON, June 5—A House-Senate conference committee agreed today to cut back the cabaret tax from 30 to 20 per cent, but eliminated a provision exempting service men and women from the levy.

The group decided to put the national debt limit at $260,000,000,000 as originally requested by the Administration.

The action is subject to House and Senate votes. The conferees met informally today, but members said that the decisions probably would stand as their final recommendation.

The House, at the insistence of a group of Republicans, passed a bill raising the debt ceiling only from $210,000,000,000 to $240,000,000,000. The Senate then put the figure at $260,000,000,000 and attached a rider reducing the cabaret tax from 30 to 20 per cent and exempting men and women in uniform from paying the tax on their checks.

Some tax experts argued that this exemption would make administration of the excise on night clubs impossible.

FEDERAL LAW HELD RULING INSURANCE

Supreme Court, 4-3, Decides Business Is Interstate and Subject to Trust Act

Special to The New York Times.

WASHINGTON, June 5—The Supreme Court, by a four-to-three decision today, held that the insurance companies of the country, with assets of $37,000,000,000 and annual premium collections in excess of $6,000,000,000, are in interstate commerce and thus subject to the Sherman Anti-Trust Law.

The decision upset precedents which began with a contrary decision by the court more than seventy-five years ago and have been reaffirmed repeatedly since the adoption of the anti-trust law in 1890.

The majority decision, written

Continued on Page 13

PURSUIT ON IN ITALY

Allies Pass Rome, Cross Tiber as Foe Quits Bank Below City

PLANES JOIN IN CHASE

1,200 Vehicles Wrecked —Eighth Army Battles Into More Towns

By The Associated Press.

ROME, June 5—The Allies' armor and motorized infantry roared through Rome today without pausing, crossed the Tiber River and proceeded with the grim task of destroying two battered German armies fleeing to the north.

Fighter-bombers spearheaded the pursuit, jamming the escape highways with burning enemy transport and littering the fields with dead and wounded Germans. The enemy was tired, disorganized and bewildered by the slashing assault, which in twenty-five days had inflicted a major catastrophe on the Germans and liberated Rome almost without damage.

Railway Yards Bombed

Five hundred American heavy bombers blasted railway yards at five points in northern Italy between Venice and Rimini along which the Germans might attempt to move reinforcements and equipment to bolster their beaten armies. Hour after hour, the Allies' planes swept down on highways leading northward and tore the fleeing enemy apart. Twelve hundred combat vehicles were destroyed from dawn to dark yesterday, and hundreds more today. Farther north, medium bombers smashed bridges and rail facilities.

[The Germans have abandoned the entire left bank of the Tiber from Ostia, at its mouth, to Rome, according to a Vichy broadcast quoted by The Associated Press.

[The Germans are already entrenched in mountain positions

Continued on Page 2

FIRST ALLIED LANDING MADE ON SHORES OF WESTERN EUROPE

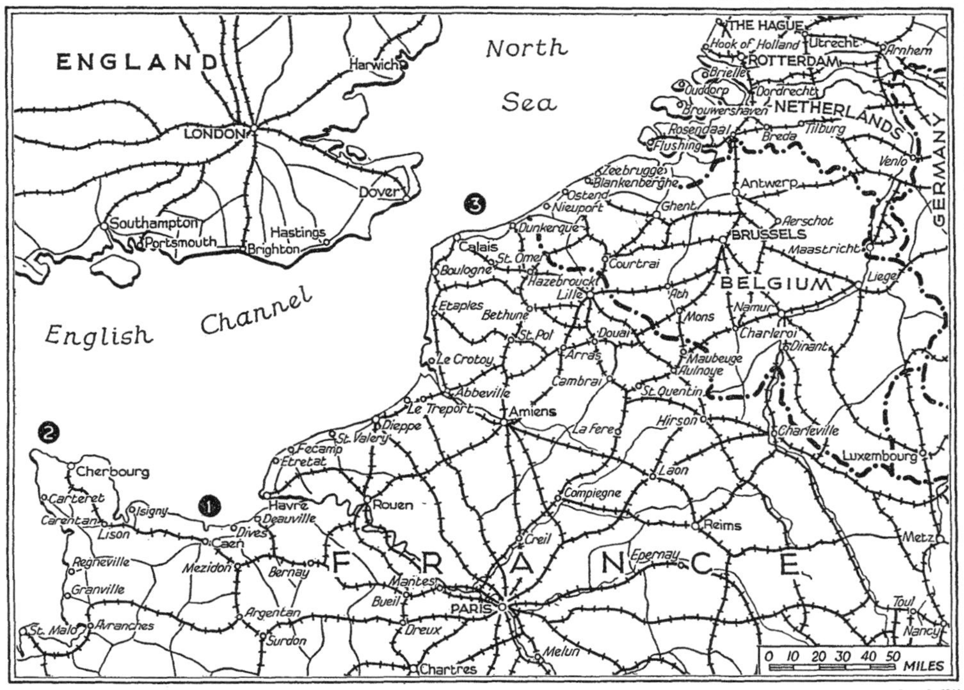

June 6, 1944

General Eisenhower's armies invaded northern France this morning. While the landing points were not specified, the Germans said that troops had gone ashore near Havre and that fighting raged at Caen (1). The enemy also said that parachutists had descended at the northern tip of the Normandy Peninsula (2) and heavy bombing had been visited on Calais and Dunkerque (3).

POPE GIVES THANKS ROME WAS SPARED

Voices Appreciation to Both Belligerents in Message to Throng at St. Peter's

By Wireless to The New York Times.

VATICAN CITY, June 5—Pope Pius XII appeared on the balcony of St. Peter's at 6 P. M. today to thank God that Rome had been spared from the ravages of war while before him in the densely packed square of St. Peter's and the new broad Via Della Conciliazione tens of thousands of Romans cheered themselves hoarse.

It was the third time today that the Pontiff had showed himself to cheering crowds, as he had appeared twice at a window of his office this morning. But this was a solemn, sacred occasion and no one knowing anything about Pius XII can doubt the fervor of his thankfulness that Rome had been saved.

The Pontiff seemed strong and well and his voice carried far, though it was difficult to hear every word he said because of the crowd.

"We must give thanks to God for the favors we have received," said the Pope. "Rome has been spared. This day will go down in the annals of Rome."

He went on to say he hoped that Italians would be worthy of the grace shown them and put aside hatred and all personal vendettas. He then thanked both belligerents —the Allies and Germany—for having left Rome intact.

After a prayer of thankfulness to the Blessed Virgin and Saints Peter and Paul, guardians of Rome, the Pontiff gave his blessing, "urbe et orbis," as the immense crowd knelt before him.

[The Associated Press estimated the crowd was between 250,000 and 500,000.]

The world has changed for Rome but the Vatican goes on imperturbably as it has through so many other conquests in centuries gone by. It is neutral in fact and spirit. The Pope and all high officials went about their daily routine today as in the past. Except for the tanks and armored cars running along the street in front of St. Peter's one could never know what had happened today.

Continued on Page 5

Italy's Monarch Yields Rule To Son, but Retains Throne

By The Associated Press.

NAPLES, June 5—Victor Emmanuel III stepped aside as King of Italy today, as he previously had said he would do upon the liberation of Rome, and handed to his 39-year-old son, Crown Prince Humbert, all "royal prerogatives." Italian political pressure had been brought to bear against him since the occupation of Naples.

In a decree signed by himself and countersigned by Premier Pietro Badoglio, head of the Italian Liberation Government, the King named his son Lieutenant General of the Realm. The monarch, however, retained his title as head of the House of Savoy and remains as King without power.

[The first act of the Council of Ministers after the transfer of royal powers was a formal denunciation of the 1940 armistice treaty inflicted on France, The United Press said.]

Victor Emmanuel, who became King July 29, 1900, had announced last April 12 his "irrevocable" decision to withdraw from public life "on the day on which Allied troops enter Rome."

Little more than a figurehead since Benito Mussolini assumed the dictatorship of Italy, Victor Emmanuel had won a reputation in the first years of his reign as a sympathetic monarch, interested in his people and their problems.

Prince Humbert, tall and erect, opposed fascism in Italy at the start, but later made a truce with Mussolini. In effect, Humbert becomes the King's regent.

TEXT OF ROYAL DECREE

The King's withdrawal decree:

I, Victor Emmanuel III, by the grace of God and by the will of the nation King of Italy, in collaboration with the President of the Council of Ministers and with the agreement of the Council, have ordered and order as follows:

My beloved son, Humbert of Savoy, Prince of Piedmont, is nominated our Lieutenant General. In collaboration with responsible Ministers he will in our name superintend all matters of administration and exercise all royal prerogatives without exception, signing royal decrees which will be countersigned and authenticated in the usual way.

We order all concerned to observe this decree and to see that it is observed as the law of the State.

Given at Ravello June 5, 1944.

VICTOR EMMANUEL.

(Countersigned) PIETRO BADOGLIO.

The withdrawal was presented to

Continued on Page 4

ALLIED WARNING FLASHED TO COAST

People Told to Clear Area 22 Miles Inland as Soon as Instructions Are Given

By Cable to The New York Times.

LONDON, Tuesday, June 6—The British Broadcasting Corporation began its 8 A. M. news bulletin this morning with quotations from a Supreme Headquarters' "urgent warning" to inhabitants of the enemy-occupied countries living near the coast.

Gen. Dwight D. Eisenhower has directed that whenever possible in France a warning shall be given to towns in which certain targets will be intensively bombed.

This warning, the broadcast said,

Continued on Page B

PARADE OF PLANES CARRIES INVADERS

Witness Says First 'Chutists Met Only Light Fire When They Landed in France

The first eyewitness account of the Allies' invasion of Europe was given in a pool broadcast from London this morning by Wright Bryan of the National Broadcasting Company, who accompanied the airborne troops in their landings.

His account said the first spearhead of Allied forces landed by parachute in northern France in the first hour of D-day.

"In the navigator's dome in the flight deck of a C-47, I rode across the English Channel with the first group of planes from the United States Ninth Air Force Troop Carrier Command to take our fighting men into Europe," Mr. Bryan said.

He added that just before he left French soil for the return trip he saw seventeen American paratroopers, led by a lieutenant colonel, jump with their arms, ammunition and equipment into German-occupied France."

He declared that his group at the head of the leading wing was met with "only scattering small

Continued on Page B

EISENHOWER ACTS

U. S., British, Canadian Troops Backed by Sea, Air Forces

MONTGOMERY LEADS

Nazis Say Their Shock Units Are Battling Our Parachutists

Communique No. 1 On Allied Invasion

By Broadcast to The New York Times.

LONDON, Tuesday, June 6—The Supreme Headquarters of the Allied Expeditionary Force issued this communiqué this morning:

"Under the command of General Eisenhower, Allied naval forces, supported by strong air forces, began landing Allied armies this morning on the northern coast of France."

By RAYMOND DANIELL

By Cable to The New York Times.

SUPREME HEADQUARTERS ALLIED EXPEDITIONARY FORCES, Tuesday, June 6—The invasion of Europe from the west has begun.

In the gray light of a summer dawn Gen. Dwight D. Eisenhower threw his great Anglo-American force into action today for the liberation of the Continent. The spearhead of attack was an Army group commanded by Gen. Sir Bernard L. Montgomery and comprising troops of the United States, Britain and Canada.

General Eisenhower's first communiqué was terse and calculated to give little information to the enemy. It said merely that "Allied naval forces supported by strong air forces began landing Allied armies this morning on the northern coast of France."

After the first communiqué was released it was announced that the Allied landing was in Normandy.

Caen Battle Reported

German broadcasts, beginning at 6:30 A. M., London time, [12:30 A. M. Eastern war time] gave first word of the assault. [The Associated Press said General Eisenhower, for the sake of surprise, deliberately let the Germans have the "first word."]

The German DNB agency said the Allied invasion operations began with the landing of airborne troops in the area of the mouth of the Seine River.

[Berlin said the "center of gravity" of the fierce fighting was at Caen, thirty miles southwest of Havre and sixty-five miles southeast of Cherbourg, The Associated Press reported. Caen is ten miles inland from the sea, at the base of the seventy-five-mile-wide Normandy Peninsula, and fighting there might indicate the Allies' seizing of a beachhead.

[DNB said in a broadcast just before 10 A. M. (4 A. M. Eastern war time) that the Anglo-American troops had been reinforced at dawn at the mouth of the Seine River in the Havre area.]

[An Allied correspondent broadcasting from Supreme Headquarters, according to the Columbia Broadcasting System, said this morning that "German tanks are moving up

Continued on Page A Following Page 3

War News Summarized

TUESDAY, JUNE 6, 1944

The invasion of western Europe began this morning.

General Eisenhower, in his first communiqué from Supreme Headquarters, Allied Expeditionary Force, issued at 3:30 A. M., said that "Allied naval forces supported by strong air forces began landing Allied armies this morning on the northern coast of France."

The assault was made by British, American and Canadian troops who, under command of Gen. Sir Bernard L. Montgomery, landed in Normandy. London gave no further details but earlier Berlin had broadcast that parachute troops had landed on the Normandy Peninsula near Cherbourg and that invasion forces were pouring from landing craft under cover of warships near Havre. Dunkerque and Calais were being heavily bombed, the Germans said.

Later announcements from Berlin said that there was fighting between Caen and Trouville and that shock troops had swung into action to halt the invasion. [All the foregoing, 1:8.]

General Eisenhower, in an order of the day to each member of the "great crusade," told his men the enemy would fight savagely and added: "We will accept nothing less than full victory. Good luck." In a broadcast to the "Peoples of Western Europe," he said the day would come when he would need their full help. A special word to France added that Frenchmen would rule the country. [1:6-7.] Almost simultaneously it was announced that General de Gaulle had arrived in London. [6:2.]

The liberation of Rome in no way slowed the Allied pursuit of the tired and disorganized German armies in Italy yesterday. Armored and motorized units sped across the Tiber River to press hard upon the retreating enemy's heels. Five hundred heavy bombers joined with lighter aircraft to smash rail and road routes leading to northern Italy and to add to the foe's demoralization. The Eighth Army, despite heavy opposition, especially northeast of Valmontone, captured a number of strategic towns. [1:3; map P. 2.]

General Clark said that parts of the two German armies had been smashed. He doubted the ability of the German Fourteenth to put up effective opposition and declared that the Tenth had taken a bad beating. [3:1]

King Victor Emmanuel fulfilled his promise and turned over all authority to his son, Crown Prince Humbert. [1:5-6.]

President Roosevelt warned the people of the United States in a radio talk last night not to over-emphasize the military significance of the liberation of Rome. "Germany has not yet been driven to surrender," he said. "Victory still lies some distance ahead. * * * It will be tough and it will be costly." The President appealed to the world to give Italy a chance to contribute her share to a lasting peace. [1:1]

In the Pacific theatre Americans were converging on the Biak airfields. Allied planes sank one and damaged two Japanese destroyers and shot down at least eighteen aircraft. [8:1.]

Eisenhower Instructs Europeans; Gives Battle Order to His Armies

Following are the texts of a statement by Gen. Dwight D. Eisenhower broadcast to the people of western Europe and his Order of the Day to the Allied Expeditionary Force as recorded by The New York Times and the Columbia Broadcasting System:

People of western Europe! A landing was made this morning on the coast of France by troops of the Allied Expeditionary Force. This landing is part of the concerted United Nations plan for the liberation of Europe, made in conjunction with our great Russian Allies. I have this message for all of you. Although the initial assault may not have been made in your own country, the hour of your liberation is approaching.

All patriots, men and women, young and old, have a part to play in the achievement of final victory. To members of resistance movements, whether led by national or outside leaders, I say: "Follow the instructions you have received." To patriots who are not members of organized resistance groups I say, "continue your passive resistance, but do not needlessly endanger your lives until I give you the signal to rise and strike the enemy. The day will come when I shall need your united strength. Until that day, I call on you for the hard task of discipline and restraint."

Citizens of France! I am proud to have again under my command the gallant forces of France. Fighting beside their Allies, they will play a worthy part in the liberation of their

Continued on Page 3

FROM BLITZKRIEG TO GENOCIDE

RICHARD BERNSTEIN

A scene from the controversial German film "Der Untergang," which portrayed some sympathetic aspects of Adolf Hitler's life.

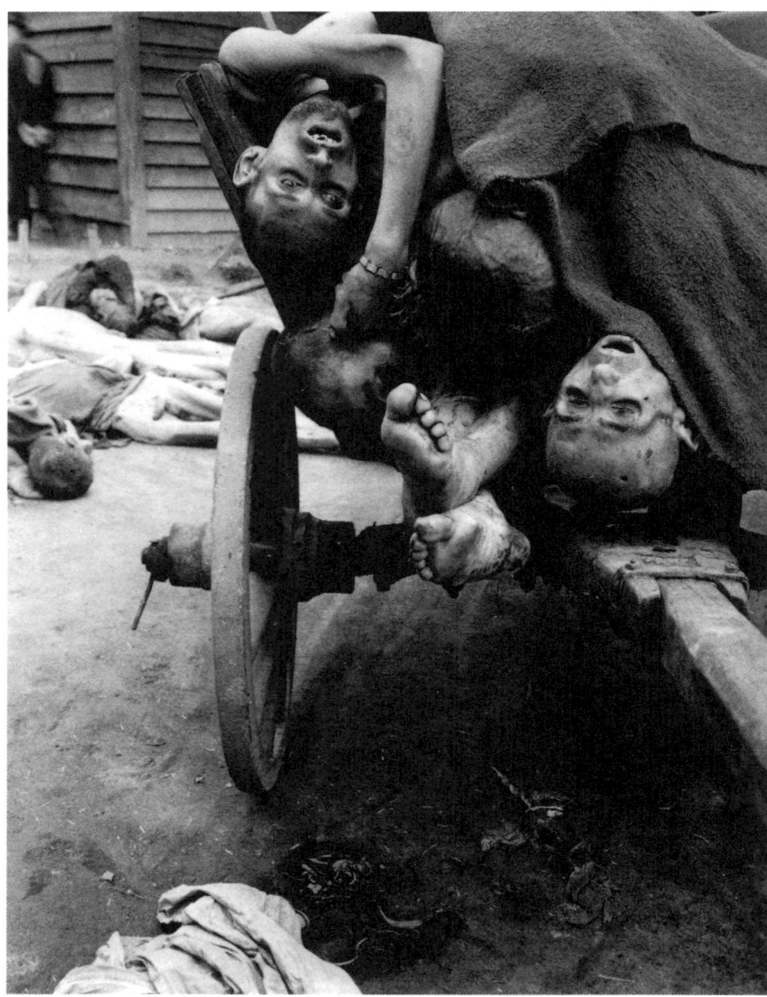

Bodies are stacked on wagons and removed from the Nazi concentration camp at Muhlhausen in Austria after the camp was liberated in 1945.

In 2004, nearly 50 years after the end of World War II in Europe, a sharp controversy having to do with the most painful and searing of national memories broke out in Germany over nothing seemingly more significant than a mere movie, "Der Untergang," or "The Downfall," a drama showing the final days of Adolf Hitler in his bunker beneath the streets of Berlin.[1]

The movie was highly praised by critics and audiences alike, who were transfixed by the stunning reincarnation of Hitler achieved by the well-known German actor Bruno Ganz.

But there was controversy nonetheless, because at certain moments in the film Mr. Ganz showed what was called "the human side" of Hitler, even some moments when the dictator showed tenderness to those close to him. Given what most Germans accept as Hitler's monstrous role in history, that seemed to some of them grossly inappropriate and even dangerously misleading.

The controversy faded after a short time, but that it took place at all illustrated an ongoing reality: Germany's actions in World War II, which ended on the battlefield three generations ago, have never stopped being fought in other ways than by force of arms, and the continuing battles are at times reminiscent of the ferocity of the war itself.

The residual issues include what might be seen as nettlesome details. An example is Poland's unhappiness over the word "Polish camp" commonly used to describe Auschwitz and Poland's campaign to change its name to Former Nazi Germany Concentration and Extermination Camp Auschwitz-Birkenau.[2] And there are larger, and thornier, issues, among the most important of them Japan's refusal to admit full responsibility for some of the wartime atrocities it committed in the war.

The issues reflect a great deal about how the war has come to be seen by postwar generations as a largely and intensely moral conflict, a mortal battle against a pure sort of evil and often unacknowledged complicity in it. In other words, the effort to fix blame and to avoid blame goes on, with sometimes deeply emotional consequences for nations and peoples.

Of the two main aggressors, it is surely Germany that has grappled most intensely and forthrightly with its past. Germans have spent years in fierce inner scrutiny stretching three postwar generations, the result of which has been a largely unqualified recognition of the country's responsibility for starting the war and causing incalculable suffering to tens of millions of victims, first and foremost the Jews, an entire people targeted for annihilation. But while Germany has long officially accepted its special and unique responsibility, an often angry debate has raged, not so much over what the Nazis did as over what their coming to power and staying there for 12 years says about the German nature.

The sharpest and most revealing debate in this regard is what the Germans call the Historikerstreit, or Historians' Quarrel, that engulfed what was then West Germany, especially its intellectuals, for several years in the mid and late 1980's.[3]

The Quarrel began when a respected historian, Ernst Nolte, writing in a long newspaper article, argued that the Holocaust was what he called a "defensive reaction" to the "class murder" taking place under Stalin in the Soviet Union. "The so-called annihilation of the Jews during the Third Reich," Mr. Nolte wrote, raising hackles by his use of that phrase so-called, "was a reaction or a distorted copy and not a first act or an original."

Mr. Nolte's theory introduced a whole new concept into the German scene. Before him, Nazism tended to be interpreted in one of two ways. It was seen either as the work of a small criminal clique that took power by means of demagogy and clever propaganda and then imposed a terrifying dictatorship on the rest of the population, or as an expression of something deep and enduring in the German national character.

Nazis Herman Göring, Rudolf Hess and others at the war crimes trial in Nuremberg, Germany, 1945–46.

Dr. Fritz Klein and other Nazi officers were ordered to bury concentration camp victims after the British liberated the camp in 1945.

FURTHER READING

1 "The Last Days of Hitler: Raving and Ravioli," see February 18, 2005, article.
2 "In Poland as in Iraq, History's Web is Tangled," see January 27, 2007, article.
3 "German Book Sets Off New Holocaust Debate," see September 6, 1986, article.

Daniel Jonah Goldhagen, author of "Hitler's Willing Executioners," with a copy of his book, in 1996.

Dresden after a two-day Allied bombing raid in 1945 that left 35,000 dead and more than 75,000 dwellings destroyed.

Now, Mr. Nolte was advancing the idea that the Nazis' most notorious act of evil may not have been all that evil after all, but was a rational and understandable if also excessive response to the very real danger of Soviet totalitarianism.

The theory, denounced by many other historians, has not withstood the test of time, and few Germans today seem to believe it. Indeed, if anything the Germans seem more receptive to views that attribute responsibility to the entire German people than to views that seem to exonerate them.

In 1996, for example, the American political scientist Daniel Jonah Goldhagen stirred controversy in his own country with a book, "Hitler's Willing Executioners," in which he contended that most Germans knew about and supported the Holocaust, which was the end result of a pervasive and uniquely virulent anti-Semitism with deep roots in the German psyche.[4] That view was heavily criticized in the United States as exaggerated, but the German translation became a best seller and Goldhagen was offered a warm welcome when he visited Germany for a series of lectures on his thesis.

But the debate has broadened over the years, with new subjects constantly appearing and showing some German impatience over being portrayed solely in evil terms for so many years. In the early 2000's demands were made to recognize German suffering in the war. In 2003, for example, a new, much read book, "The Fire" by Jörg Friedrich, contended that the Allied firebombings of cities like Hamburg and Dresden were war crimes that should be condemned as such.[5]

Meanwhile, in Asia, relations among Japan and some of its neighbors—notably China and Korea—also have been roiled by matters left over from the war. Among the most important in recent years has been Japan's refusal to admit responsibility for having forced Korean, Filipino and Chinese women into brothels that serviced Japanese soldiers during the war.[6]

Troubling Japanese-Chinese relations has been the insistence of some prime ministers, most notably Junichiro Koizumi, to pay annual homage at Tokyo's Yasukuni Shrine, which houses the remains of some Japanese war criminals.[7]

As these issues continue to be debated, a pattern has emerged. Germany has accepted the ineradicable stain of responsibility for modern history's greatest evil. It has built numerous monuments attesting to its criminal role in World

War II and in 2008, it announced that it would build two new memorials in Berlin to Nazi victims, one to murdered Gypsies and the other to gays and lesbians. Japan has, in the view of its critics, stubbornly resisted being put into the same category, and this reflects something essential about the way World War II is remembered in each country.

"The difference has to do with the prevailing metaphors of the war," Richard C. Holbrooke, a former American ambassador to the United Nations, has said. "In Germany the metaphor is Auschwitz," Mr. Holbrooke said. "In Japan it is Hiroshima, and that makes all the difference."

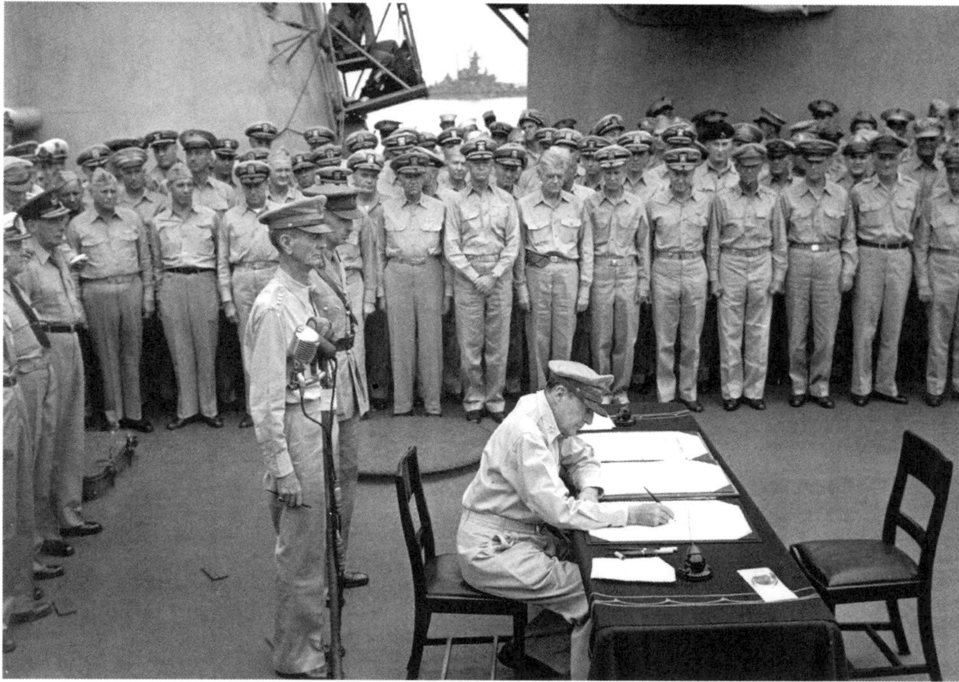

General Douglas MacArthur signs the treaty ending World War II aboard the U.S.S. Missouri in Tokyo Harbor, September 2, 1945.

RICHARD BERNSTEIN *is currently a columnist for the International Herald Tribune. He previously worked at The New York Times as bureau chief in Paris, Berlin, at the United Nations, and as national cultural correspondent. Bernstein has written several books including "Asia: From the Center of the Earth," "Out of the Blue," about the 9/11 terrorist attack on the World Trade Center towers, and "Fragile Glory: A Portrait of France and the French." Before joining The Times, he opened the Time magazine bureau in Beijing.*

4 "The Antagonist as Liberator," see January 26, 1997, magazine article.
5 "Germans Revisit War's Agony, Ending a Taboo," see March 15, 2003, article.
6 "In Japan, a Historian Stands by Proof of Wartime Sex Slavery," see March 31, 2007, article.
7 "Koizumi Exits Office as He Arrived: Defiant on War Shrine," see August 16, 2006, article.

Japanese Prime Minister Junichiro Koizumi bows at Yasukuni Shrine in 2004 to honor Japanese soldiers killed during World War II.

Captured U.S. Soldiers surrender to the Japanese at Corregidor in May of 1942.

"All the News That's Fit to Print"

The New York Times.

LATE CITY EDITION
Sunny, cool and windy; fair and becoming cooler tonight.
Temperatures Yesterday—Max., 69; Min., 51
Sunrise, 7:19 A. M.; Sunset, 6:01 P. M.

VOL. XCIV..No. 31,687. Entered as Second-Class Matter, Postoffice, New York, N. Y. NEW YORK, THURSDAY, OCTOBER 26, 1944. THREE CENTS IN NEW YORK CITY

U. S. DEFEATS JAPANESE NAVY; ALL FOE'S SHIPS IN ONE FLEET HIT; MANY SUNK; BATTLE CONTINUES

SPECIAL PRIVILEGE SOLD BY NEW DEAL, DEWEY CHARGES

Says Roosevelt Backs Plan for 1,000 to Put '$1,000 on the Line' to Aid Campaign

PARTY LETTER IS QUOTED

Governor Declares in Chicago Administration Lacks 'Honesty' to Solve Post-War Problems

The text of Mr. Dewey's speech will be found on Page 13.

By ALEXANDER FEINBERG
Special to The New York Times.

CHICAGO, Oct. 25—Governor Dewey declared tonight that "for $1,000 laid on the line to finance the fourth-term drive, this Administration boldly offers for sale 'special privilege.'" which includes the "assisting in the formulation of Administration policies."

Attacking the "rudimentary honesty" of the New Deal, Mr. Dewey, in a major campaign address preceding the appearance of President Roosevelt here Saturday, charged that the Chief Executive himself was the sponsor of the fund raising idea.

The Chicago Stadium, which accommodates 25,000 persons, was packed to capacity, with several thousand others clamoring to obtain admittance. Gov. Dwight H. Green of Illinois presented Mr. Dewey, who was received with tumultuous acclaim. He kept pointing to the microphone to still the demonstration, but it was just short of five minutes before he could begin his speech.

Governor Dewey said that the fund raising plan was disclosed in a letter signed by H. L. McAlister and Sam J. Watkins, State finance chairman, and written on the letterhead of the National Democratic Campaign Headquarters, Little Rock, Ark.

Dewey Quotes Letter

Mr. Dewey quoted the letter as follows:

"This is an invitation to you to join the One Thousand Club.

The idea of such a club originated at a recent conference at the White House between the President, Robert E. Hannegan, chairman of the Democratic National Committee, and Edwin W. Pauley, treasurer of the committee. At this meeting the President commented:

"'I think it would be a good idea to have a list of one thousand persons banded together from all over the United States to act as a liaison to see that facts relating to the public interest are presented factually to the President and members of Congress.

"Members of this organization undoubtedly will be granted special privilege by party leaders. These members will be called into conference from time to time to discuss matters of national importance and to assist in the formulation of Administration policies.

"To be eligible for membership in the One Thousand Club will require a contribution of $1,000 to the National Democratic campaign fund."

Mr. Dewey declared that "there in crude, unblushing words is the ultimate expression of New Deal policies," adding:

"And the sponsor of this idea is frankly stated in that letter to be the President himself. The man who holds the highest office within the gift of the American people at a conference in the White House sponsors an idea to sell 'special privilege' and a voice 'in the formulation of Administration policies' for one thousand dollars on the barrelhead."

The Governor said that New

Continued on Page 13, Column 1

No Extra Gasoline For Trip to Polls

By The Associated Press.

WASHINGTON, Oct. 25—Chester Bowles, OPA head, in a letter to Senator Davis, Republican, of Pennsylvania today stated that the OPA could not allow extra gasoline rations for private automobiles to take voters to the polls if other means of transportation are available.

Pennsylvania has no absentee voting law and Senator Davis contended that many persons from his State working elsewhere would be unable to return to cast their ballots unless they received extra gas rations.

"A special ration may be granted to carry persons to and from the polls for the purpose of voting in public elections (including primary elections), provided reasonably adequate alternative means of transportation are not available," Mr. Bowles wrote.

Where no other form of transportation is available those wishing to use cars for voting may apply to their local ration boards on special forms which the boards have available.

WAGNER ACCLAIMS PARTY FARM POLICY

He Says That Dewey Is Vague on Agriculture—Calls His Platform 'Double Talk'

By CLAYTON P. KNOWLES
Special to The New York Times.

SYRACUSE, N. Y., Oct. 25—The farm plank in the Republican platform offers nothing but "double talk" and Governor Dewey, rather than clarifying the issue, puts forward proposals "as vague and airy as a wisp of smoke," Senator Robert F. Wagner declared tonight as he carried his campaign for re-election into this city in the heart of the farm area.

"Mr. Dewey ridicules the so-called alphabetical agencies," he declared. "But how could low-interest loans have been provided without the Farm Mortgage Corporation? How could farm prices have been supported without the Agricultural Adjustment Administration? How could the number of farms with central electric service have been multiplied three times without the Rural Electrification Administration?

"These programs are not perfect. They need to be improved, but they are solid, they can be seen, they can be felt. When Mr. Dewey talks about the farmer, what he proposes is as vague and airy as a wisp of smoke."

His address, broadcast over a State-wide hook-up by the Columbia Broadcasting System, said that Governor Dewey's Commissioner of Agriculture last spring set minimum milk prices "far above

Continued on Page 12, Column 4

PRESIDENT ELATED

Gives News From Halsey That Foe Is 'Defeated, Damaged, Routed'

TEST IS ON, KING SAYS

Practically All Japanese Fleet in the Battle, Admiral Believes

By LEWIS WOOD
Special to The New York Times.

WASHINGTON, Oct. 25—President Roosevelt exultantly announced late today the receipt of a report from Admiral William F. Halsey saying that the Japanese Navy in the Philippine area had been "defeated, seriously damaged and routed" by our forces.

Two hours earlier Admiral Ernest J. King, Commander in Chief of the United States Fleet and Chief of Naval Operations, had disclosed that virtually all of the long elusive Japanese Fleet had been engaged at last in the furious sea battle of the Philippines.

These two startling revelations, exciting Washington as nothing has done since the European invasions, were taken here to mean that the vaunted Japanese naval power had been seriously crippled and the road to Tokyo made much easier. At last, it was presumed, the principal part of Japanese naval strength had been nettled out of hiding and then decisively beaten.

Announcement Is Dramatic

The circumstances of the President's statement were thrilling. When only a half dozen newsmen remained in the White House press room at 5:20 P. M., Press Secretary Stephen T. Early appeared at the door.

"Come quick," he cried, slapping his palms together for emphasis.

Rushing to the President's oval-shaped office, the reporters found him seated at his desk, smiling broadly. Obviously he had been interrupted in his late afternoon dictation. Before him lay scattered papers, but directly in front of him was a single sheet of paper, inscribed apparently with his own handwriting.

He had, said the President beamingly, a "real flash," just telephoned to him by Admiral William D. Leahy, Chief of Staff to the President as Commander in Chief of the Army and Navy. Picking up the paper, Mr. Roosevelt slowly and distinctly read:

"The President received today a report from Admiral Halsey that the Japanese Navy in the Philippine area has been defeated, seriously damaged and routed by the United States Navy in that area."

For a moment there was a pause. No one said a word. Then

Continued on Page 3, Column 3

SEA POWER OF LAND OF THE RISING SUN SHATTERED IN BATTLE

Piecing together the statements of Admiral Nimitz and General MacArthur gives this picture of the battle around the Philippines: One Japanese force, including four battleships, ten cruisers and thirteen destroyers, first sighted south of Mindoro (1) steamed east, across the Sibuyan Sea, through San Bernardino Strait and down the coast of Samar (2), where Admiral Kinkaid's combined force (5) attacked it and forced it to retire northward with perhaps ten ships damaged. It was apparently in this action that the American light carrier Princeton was sunk. A second enemy force, first sighted southwest of Negros (3), included two battleships, one or two cruisers and four destroyers. It moved east across the Sulu Sea and through Surigao Strait (4). Admiral Kinkaid attacked this group and it lost one battleship and several cruisers and destroyers; the rest of the force retreated west through the strait. This whole battle scene is at (A) on the inset. A third Japanese force was engaged southeast of Formosa (B).

BATTLESHIP IS SUNK

Seventh Fleet Smashes Two Japanese Forces Converging on Leyte

REMNANTS IN FLIGHT

They Are Hotly Pursued —Third Enemy Force Is Hit Off Formosa

The Imperial Japanese Fleet has been brought to battle. It is suffering a crushing defeat. Two of its divisions have been routed. One has been almost destroyed. Contact has been made with the main force southeast of Formosa by Admiral William F. Halsey's Third Fleet. That engagement is continuing, said the last communiqué.

Two strong Japanese naval forces converged on Leyte Gulf through the San Bernardino Strait in the Philippines to the north and the Surigao Strait to the south. Vice Admiral Thomas C. Kinkaid's Seventh Fleet smashed these two forces and put the remnants to flight after sinking or heavily damaging every ship in the southern enemy force.

One big Japanese carrier has been sunk. Two more have been heavily damaged and undoubtedly are out of action. One Japanese battleship of the Yamasiro class has been sunk. At least four others have been heavily damaged. Several enemy cruisers and destroyers have been sunk. Many others have been hit, both by bombs and torpedoes.

Enemy Defeated and Routed

The only announced American loss is the converted cruiser-carrier Princeton sunk. Other escort carriers were damaged by fire from one of the enemy battleship forces.

Gen. Douglas MacArthur reported triumphantly that "the Japanese Navy has suffered its most crushing defeat of the war." Admiral Ernest J. King, in Washington, said that "practically all" of the Japanese fleet was engaged and that he was confident of the outcome. President Roosevelt called a special press conference to announce receipt of a message from Admiral William F. Halsey reporting that the enemy has been "defeated, seriously damaged and routed."

Pending official word from Pearl Harbor, it appeared the greatest surface and naval air action in the history of naval warfare was being fought and won by the Pacific Fleet, the greatest naval force that ever went down to the sea.

Fate of Leyte Decided

SEVENTH FLEET HEADQUARTERS, Philippines, Thursday, Oct. 26 (AP)—Japan lost the first, and possibly the decisive, round in an all-out battle to halt on the Philippines line the American advance toward her home islands.

This occurred early yesterday morning when Admiral Kinkaid's outnumbered fleet battered and put to rout Japanese battle forces converging on Leyte Gulf.

Complete results are lacking as the action is continuing, with planes from Admiral Kinkaid's hurt but still fighting carrier force hitting the surviving enemy warships as they are retiring. [General MacArthur said the Japanese force that came through Surigao Strait fled back through it to the west and the other was in flight in a northerly direction.]

[Gordon Walker in a Mutual broadcast from the Philippines said "a Navy spokesman here claimed that practically every

Continued on Page 3, Column 2

ALLIES CUT UP FOE IN WEST HOLLAND

British Hammer Germans in One Area of 's Hertogenbosch —Canadians Tighten Traps

By CLIFTON DANIEL
By Wireless to The New York Times.

SUPREME HEADQUARTERS, Allied Expeditionary Force, Oct. 25—The Germans were rapidly losing their grip tonight on their strongholds between the North Sea and the British Second Army's salient in the Netherlands.

British forces converging from three sides drove them out of all

Continued on Page 7, Column 2

'17 Hours of Hell' Raised In Sea Battle Off Leyte

By RALPH TEATSORTH
United Press Correspondent

ABOARD ADMIRAL KINKAID'S FLAGSHIP, off the Philippines, Thursday, Oct. 26—The Tokyo Express rammed into the American Navy Limited today. The pride of Japan was wrecked so badly it may never make another long run. It was the day our Navy had dreamed about for considerably more than a year.

It was seventeen hours of concentrated hell and the most amazing thing about the battle was that our Pacific Flight Carrier Force—which nobody thought could deliver such a terrific punch—held off the bulk of the Japanese fleet all day and had it on the run all afternoon.

When evening came and most of

Continued on Page 4, Column 7

AIR PLANT IN JAPAN SMASHED BY B-29'S

Omura Target Is 'Perfectly Patterned,' Pilots Say—Foe Lists 100 Planes in Attack

Special to The New York Times.

WASHINGTON, Oct. 25—While the remnants of the demoralized Japanese Fleet were fleeing from Admiral William F. Halsey's forces in Philippine waters, United States Army Superfortresses today were carrying the war another step closer to the heart of Japan by carrying out a successful mission against the key aircraft assembly plant at Omura on the island of Kyushu.

Twentieth Air Force Headquarters here announced that a medium-sized task force of the mammoth bombers, operating from Twen-

Continued on Page 4, Column 4

AMERICANS MAKE BIG LEYTE JUMPS

Troops Push Westward on Isle —Southern Coast of Samar to the North Now Held

By The United Press.

ADVANCED HEADQUARTERS ON LEYTE, Thursday, Oct. 26—American dismounted cavalry troops have invaded Samar, third largest of the Philippines and last island barrier on the road to Luzon and Manila, while forces fighting on Leyte have punched nine miles inland to seize the key road junction of Burauen.

Gen. Douglas MacArthur also announced in a special communiqué that Field Marshal Count Juichi Terauchi's Japanese defenders of the northern Leyte front were "disintegrating" under the American hammer blows.

The three-mile American advance that occupied Burauen, southern terminus of an inland highway, split the Japanese lines in northern Leyte and threw the enemy back toward the hills, where Filipino guerrillas were reported in action.

The new American triumphs pushed our lines nine miles inland and raised to thirty-one the number of towns and villages captured. Six airfields also have been seized.

The invasion of Samar, with an

Continued on Page 4, Column 5

War News Summarized

THURSDAY, OCTOBER 26, 1944

The Japanese Navy came out to fight in the waters off the Philippines and was severely mauled. One force of four battleships, ten cruisers and thirteen destroyers moved up south of Mindoro into the Sibuyan Sea. Every battleship and at least one cruiser was hit. This flotilla rounded Samar and fled north. We lost an escort carrier.

A second force of two battleships, two cruisers and four destroyers came into the Sulu Sea from southwest of Negros Island. After all the ships had been hit it turned tail and retreated.

A third force, this one with carriers, came down from home waters and the battle was still going on. Most of the engagements were fought from the air and the enemy suffered heavily in plane losses. Our light carrier Princeton was hit and its magazine subsequently exploded. Most of the crew were saved. The Third Pacific Fleet took on the enemy carrier force and the Seventh turned back the two others. [All the foregoing 1:8.]

President Roosevelt, in an impromptu press conference, said that Admiral Halsey, commanding the Third Fleet, had just reported that the Japanese Navy had been "defeated, seriously damaged and routed." Earlier Admiral King had said that almost the entire enemy naval strength was involved in the Philippines battle. Fighting covered an area 600 miles north and south and 250 east and west. Navy officials were elated and felt the whole course of the war might be speeded. [1:3.]

On Leyte American troops had pushed twenty miles north of Tacloban and nine miles inland from Dulag. Additional landings on the northern part of Leyte and the southern part of Samar won control of San Juanico Strait, which separates them. [1:7; map P. 2.]

Superfortresses delivered a smashing assault on Japan's key aircraft plant at Omura on the island of Kyushu. One B-29 was missing. [1:6.]

German positions in the Belgium-Netherland pocket were becoming increasingly untenable as Canadian and British troops drew closer and menaced the enemy's escape line. [1:4; map P. 7.] More than 2,200 American and British bombers lashed rail and oil targets in the Reich. Six bombers and one of a great fighter escort were missing. [9:1.]

Russian forces captured the German port and U-boat base of Kirkenes in Norway and thirty other Norwegian villages. [1:6-7; map P. 11.] To the south the Red Army renewed its drive on Warsaw, gained more ground in East Prussia and liberated all of Transylvania by capturing Satu-Mare and Carei. [12:1, with map.]

Mount Belmonte, guarding the southern approaches to Bologna, was captured by Americans of the Fifth Army in Italy. The British Eighth Army gained three miles in the Adriatic sector. A German withdrawal was indicated. [10:7.]

The United Nations have resumed diplomatic relations with Italy, the first former enemy state to receive recognition. [1:2-3.]

U. S. and Britain Recognize Italy; Action Is First With an Ex-Enemy

By BERTRAM D. HULEN
Special to The New York Times.

WASHINGTON, Oct. 25—Diplomatic relations with Italy were resumed by the Allies tonight.

Recognition is being accorded by the United States, the other American republics in the United Nations and Britain. The Soviet Union had previously extended recognition to the Government of Premier Ivanoe Bonomi.

Our action was announced by Edward R. Stettinius Jr., acting Secretary of State, who said that Alexander C. Kirk, who has been serving as our diplomatic representative in Rome with the personal rank of Ambassador, would now be accredited to the Italian Government with the rank of Ambassador.

It is expected that Italy will now send an Ambassador here. The appointment of Count Carlos Sforza, long a friend of the United States, to the post, has been forecast since it became evident that recognition would not long be delayed.

Announcement of the recognition has been made at London and is expected at the Latin-American capitals, except for Buenos Aires. Argentina never severed relations with Italy, although she did with Germany and Japan.

The announcement by Mr. Stettinius follows:

"After consultation with the other American republics, as provided in the Resolutions of Rio de

Continued on Page 10, Column 5

Russians Invade North Norway; Take Kirkenes in Wide Advance

By W. H. LAWRENCE
By Wireless to The New York Times.

MOSCOW, Oct. 25—Entering their ninth country in less than seven months, Red Army forces smashed across the Norwegian frontier today and liberated the Barents Sea port of Kirkenes and thirty other Norwegian villages just fifty-four months and twenty-one days after the beginning of Adolf Hitler's treacherous invasion of the Scandinavian country.

This new expedition of Russian troops outside the Soviet Union was announced by Premier Joseph Stalin in a special order of the day and was saluted by Moscow's massed guns and highlighted in tonight's communiqué.

The Soviet Union's Norwegian campaign brings Allied armies back on the soil of that restless country for the first time since June 15, 1941, when the British had to withdraw their poorly equipped forces in the face of numerically superior German forces.

[On its European front the Red Army reopened the battle for Warsaw by outflanking the Polish capital on the north, drove farther into East Prussia against desperate resistance and completed the liberation of Transylvania.]

It would be wrong to assume from this dash across the Norwegian frontier at its northernmost point that the liberation of

Continued on Page 11, Column 4

"All the News That's Fit to Print"

The New York Times.

LATE CITY EDITION
Sunny with moderate winds.
Temperatures Yesterday—Max., 44; Min., 34
Sunrise today, 7:10 A. M.; Sunset, 6:41 P. M.

Section 1

NEWS INDEX, PAGE 39, THIS SECTION

VOL. XCIV..No. 31,809. Entered as Second-Class Matter, Postoffice, New York, N. Y. NEW YORK, SUNDAY, FEBRUARY 25, 1945. Including Magazine and Book Sections. TEN CENTS New York City and Suburban Area (15c Elsewhere)

AMERICANS DRIVE FOUR MILES BEYOND THE ROER; OUR CARRIER AIRCRAFT SLASH AT TOKYO AGAIN; MARINES WIN HALF OF IWO'S CENTRAL AIRFIELD

WMC DASHES HOPES OF EASED CURFEW; MAYOR ACTS TODAY

He Is Expected to Announce Order to Guide Cafes—Latter to Drop 25,000

LICENSE REFUND PLEA SET

Clubs Packed by Many Having Last Fling and Big Crowds Are Due Tonight

Hopes fostered by operators of night clubs and other amusement places that tomorrow night's midnight "curfew" might be eased to 1 A. M. received a jolt yesterday when the War Manpower Commission, in Washington, decreed that the "request" for midnight closing as originally announced by War Mobilization Director James F. Byrnes would not be altered.

Meanwhile, as night spots were packed and prepared for larger crowds tonight for last-minute flings, Mayor La Guardia stood his ground on the position he took Friday that the closing time for New York City places would remain the same until he had an opportunity to study the WMC edict.

The Mayor will confer with Mrs. Anna M. Rosenberg, regional director of the WMC, at 11 o'clock this morning in City Hall and is expected to make some definite announcement in his weekly broadcast over WNYC, city-owned station.

A survey of midtown night clubs, both in the Broadway area and on the East Side, showed they were doing a capacity business, but the managers were unanimous in declaring that capacity business had been the rule on Saturday night for some time past. All said, however, that reservations and telephone queries indicated larger crowds than usual tonight.

Tavern Owners Accuse Drys

Tavern owners throughout the city lined up with Billy Rose, owner of the Diamond Horseshoe, who had charged that the "curfew" was an "insidious move on the part of the drys to force prohibition back on the country."

Joseph Maguire, president of the United Liquor Dealers of Manhattan, tavern owners' group, said last night that at least 25,000 persons employed in the city's 7,500 taverns will get "pink slips" tonight.

After a meeting of his organization and the Bronx Tavern Owners Association, headed by John Kyle, at 257 Broadway, Mr. Maguire said a resolution was adopted characterizing the Byrnes order as "discriminatory" and declaring that "no increased war effort will be justifiably accomplished through its operation."

Tavern owners in New York City, he said, will send a committee to call upon the New York State Liquor Authority tomorrow morning to "demand a refund" on the $1,200 license fee they pay for operating until 4 A. M. six days a week and 3 A. M. on Sundays.

Says Men Can't Do War Work

"The men who will be thrown out of work as a result of this order are definitely unsuitable for any important part in the war effort," Mr. Maguire said. "Our industry has been gone over with a fine toothcomb by the Army and those now employed would be of little use in any war plant.

"Speaking for the tavern owners in this city and throughout the country, we cannot make too emphatic our feeling that this is just another move on the part of the million-dollar dry lobby in Washington to use the war as an instrument for forcing prohibition back on us."

Mr. Maguire said that his organization was sending a letter to Governor Dewey demanding that he "declare himself in keeping State rights intact." The Byrnes order, he asserted, is a direct violation of State rights in that it

Continued on Page 36, Column 2

Germans Are Gloomy About U.S. Offensive

By The Associated Press.

LONDON, Feb. 24—Amid unconfirmed reports that the Russians were crossing the final German defense lines before Berlin, German commentators said today that the "greatest mass of men and material ever assembled since the Normandy invasion" was forcing open the historic gate between the Maas [Meuse] River and the Eifel Mountains.

The German commentator, Capt. Ludwig Sertorius, declared that the Allies had hurled at least forty divisions at the Maas-Eifel sector alone and he predicted still greater blows to the south. Cologne was reported to be aflame after an aerial hammering and Berlin admitted that "many" bridgeheads had been merged across the Roer River between Linnich and Dueren in the past twenty-four hours as the Americans wedged deeper into the German defenses.

JOINT ARMS BOARD SHAPED IN MEXICO

Inter-American Parley Likely to Set Up Defense Council —U. S. Backs Proposal

By CAMILLE M. CIANFARRA
Special to The New York Times.

MEXICO CITY, Feb. 24—The Inter-American Conference on Problems of War and Peace is expected to create a permanent military board to draft and develop joint plans for the defense of this hemisphere, it was learned today.

This step, which is supported on the whole by the United States, is proposed in a resolution that Mexico will submit next week. It will call for the creation of a body composed of representatives of the general staffs of all the American nations represented at the Chapultepec conference.

Its aim is to build machinery for unified military action against any power outside or on this continent that attacks an American nation. One objective will be the standardization of military equipment and training methods throughout the hemisphere.

Latin-American delegates said that, if approved, Mexico's suggestion would represent a highly important development in the evolution of inter-American collaboration. Fundamentally it is designed to implement and strengthen the plans submitted by many nations here, including the United States, Colombia and Uruguay, for a regional security system within the framework of the Dumbarton Oaks proposals.

Some of these plans advocate the use of force in the event of aggression against an American nation, and the Mexican resolution would provide for machinery to implement that principle. The view of the Mexican delegation is that its suggestion would be not only in harmony with the Dumbarton Oaks plan for dealing with threats to the peace or acts of aggression, but also a valuable addi-

Continued on Page 17, Column 4

BIG FORCE STRIKES

Tokyo Indicates 1,600 Planes Hit in Waves—Sky Fights Swirl

5TH FLEET OFF COAST

Military, Naval and Air Bases Are Targets, Nimitz Announces

By Wireless to The New York Times.

ADVANCED HEADQUARTERS, Guam, Sunday, Feb. 25—Our fleet is at it again. A great force of carriers and battleships is steaming along close to Japan's shore while hundreds of carrier aircraft, perhaps as big a force as that which hit the same territory nine days ago, are striking again at the same target, the industrial center of Tokyo.

[Tokyo broadcasts estimated that the attacking force numbered as many as 1,600 planes, about 400 more than were believed to have taken part in the previous smash at the Japanese capital on Feb. 16 and 17.]

Remnants of the Japanese air force, which lost 500 planes positively destroyed and 150 damaged in the previous American attack on the Japanese capital, were presumed to be rising to the defense of its homeland as our Hellcats strafed military objectives, airfields and naval installations.

[Enemy broadcasts recorded by the Federal Communications System said Japanese planes were battling the attackers over the Tokyo area.]

Spruance in Command

The attack was announced briefly in a communiqué from Admiral Chester W. Nimitz reading as follows:

"Carrier aircraft of the Fifth Fleet are attacking military, naval and air installations in and around Tokyo. Admiral Raymond A. Spruance is present in command of the Fifth Fleet and Vice Admiral Marc A. Mitscher is in tactical command of the fast carrier task force making the attack."

Admiral Mitscher's force, the famous Task Force 58, is presumed to include fifteen to twenty of the fastest carriers and swiftest battleships, protected by a screen of destroyers, cruisers and minesweepers.

When the force struck on Feb. 16 and 17 we escaped without a single Japanese plane's having hit the floating bases from which the Hellcats had come, despite the fact that the attack lasted two days. In that strike the Hellcats bore the burden the first day, hitting the airfields. Helldivers and Grumman Avengers struck aircraft factories, engine, power and electronic plants the second day. This attack may be following the same pattern, although no information on this is available here.

The Tokyo radio was off the air most of the morning. The enemy

Continued on Page 25, Column 5

JAPANESE OVERRUN

Marines Smash Through Maze of Defenses in Bloody Iwo Battle

REACH PLATEAU'S TOP

Drive to Strip's Center, Widen Beachhead, Mop Up on Volcano

By WARREN MOSCOW
By Wireless to The New York Times.

ADVANCED HEADQUARTERS, Guam, Sunday, Feb. 25—Despite bazooka-type weapons and new 1,100-pound rocket bombs used by fiercely fighting Japanese in a mass of powerful interlocking defenses, the marines on Iwo Island pushed northward 300 to 500 yards to overrun half of the fighter airstrip in the center of the island on Saturday.

In a general push they widened the beachhead on the eastern coast by 600 yards, overcoming a maze of connecting pillboxes, blockhouses and fortified caves. They passed through heavily mined areas to make the advances, the greatest in one day since the landing on Monday.

[Secretary of the Navy James V. Forrestal is at Guam for conferences with Admiral Nimitz after having gone ashore at Iwo, The Associated Press reported.]

In a single area of 400 by 600 yards on the east coast, the marines had to neutralize about 100 caves, thirty to forty feet deep, indicating clearly why the seventy-four-day aerial bombardment of the island and the three-day ship shelling prior to our landing failed to decimate the garrison or its supplies.

Supplies Pouring Ashore

The marines are benefiting from the capture of Mount Suribachi, volcano at the southern end of the island, and the advance northward. Enemy artillery fire no longer is dominating the terior area under American control. The mortar fire on the marines' landing places has been reduced and supplies are pouring ashore.

Apparently the Japanese on Iwo are using new techniques developed from lessons of previous American

Continued on Page 28, Column 4

OLD GLORY GOES UP OVER IWO

Marines of the Fifth Division hoist the American flag atop Mount Suribachi
Associated Press Wirephoto (Navy radio from Guam)

EGYPTIAN PREMIER SLAIN IN CHAMBER

Extremist Lawyer Shoots Him After Reading of Decree Putting Nation in War

By SAM POPE BREWER
By Wireless to The New York Times.

CAIRO, Egypt, Feb. 24—Premier Ahmed Maher Pasha was shot and killed in Parliament tonight after he had read a royal decree declaring war against Germany and Japan.

Critically wounded by four revolver shots, the Premier was carried to a first-aid room in the

Continued on Page 10, Column 2

Eisenhower Points New Push At Knockout Blow in West

By Wireless to The New York Times.

SUPREME HEADQUARTERS, Allied Expeditionary Force, Feb. 24—Gen. Dwight D. Eisenhower asserted today that the offensive on the western front was expected "to destroy every German" in its path west of the Rhine and that, if necessary to quell German resistance, the Allied armies would drive on into the center of the Reich to meet the Russian armies.

"Our liaison with the Russians has always been as close and as intimate as was necessary to meet the situation at a particular moment," he told a press conference here. "The Russians have furnished me with all the information I have needed to know and they have done it willingly and cheerfully."

The Supreme Commander seemed entirely satisfied with the progress so far made in the resumed advance toward the Rhine and indicated that he expected that the offensive would be carried through without unusual losses. However, he held out no hopes for a quick and final victory over Germany and, with a laugh at the sourness of his own previous prediction, declined to forecast the date of the end of the war.

For the first time, officially, he disclosed that the American Ninth Army, one of the two that attacked across the Roer River yesterday, had remained under the control of Field Marshal Sir Bernard L. Montgomery, after it had been trans-

Continued on Page 4, Column 2

SOVIET FORCES GAIN IN 'POLISH CORRIDOR'

Red Army Stabs Up to 3 Miles on Wide Front—15 Blocks Captured in Breslau

By The United Press.

LONDON, Sunday, Feb. 25—Red Army troops, advancing up to three miles on a sixty-five-mile front up the "Polish Corridor" and across eastern Pomerania, yesterday hacked to within thirty-three miles south of Danzig and sixty-four miles of the Pomeranian coast in a drive to seal off the former free city and its twin Baltic port of Gdynia.

Troops of Marshal Konstantin K. Rokossovsky's Second White Russian Army threatened the German stronghold of Preussisch Friedland in Pomerania, and in the "Polish Corridor" drove to a point nine

Continued on Page 21, Column 1

War News Summarized

SUNDAY, FEBRUARY 25, 1945

The American drive toward the Rhine smashed four miles beyond the Roer River, its first major obstacle, and engulfed at least twenty-one towns as it achieved its preliminary objectives on schedule and with light casualties. The American Ninth Army, under Marshal Montgomery, was crashing through a string of villages beyond Juelich and Linnich, while the First, under General Bradley, was fighting through Dueren, main bastion of the Germans' Roer defenses. All enemy counter-attacks were beaten off, and it was believed the American drive had yet to reach its peak. [1:8; maps P. 3.]

First Army troops battering their way through Dueren already had occupied half of that industrial town in house-to-house fighting and reinforcements and supplies were reaching them over several bridges flung across the swollen river by engineers. [5:1.] Enemy resistance along the Ninth Army front was described as moderate and some Germans captured were youths of 15, but opposition was expected to become more intense as we penetrate deeper. [4:1.]

General Eisenhower spurred on his men by telling them the goal of the offensive was the destruction of every German west of the Rhine. He termed the progress of the First and Ninth Armies "certainly satisfactory" and said the Allied forces, if necessary, would drive into central Germany to meet the Russians moving in from the east for the kill. [1:6-7.]

The most devastating aerial offensive of the war continued in its twelfth day with fleets of heavy bombers blasting submarine yards and oil refineries in northwestern Germany. [3:1.]

The Red Army rolled toward the Baltic on a sixty-five-mile front, reaching within thirty-three miles of Danzig and sixty-four of the Pomeranian coast. [1:7.]

Hitler called on the German people to fight to the bitter end, warning them that "whoever is weak must perish." [13:1.]

Admiral Mitscher's naval task force again moved into the waters off Tokyo and its carrier planes renewed their attack on the Japanese capital. [1:3.]

The marines on Iwo captured half of the island's central airfield in the face of fierce resistance. [1:4; map P. 28.]

Manila's liberation was completed after a three-week battle as the last remnant of the Japanese garrison was destroyed. [1:6-7.] American troops in the Philippines achieved another signal success when they seized the Japanese internment camp at Los Banos, thirty-five miles southeast of Manila, freeing 2,146 prisoners. [26:3, with map.]

Just after he had read a decree declaring war on the Axis, Egypt's Prime Minister was shot and killed in the Chamber of Deputies in Cairo. [1:5.]

A permanent military board to plan for the defense of this hemisphere is expected to be set up at the Inter-American conference in Mexico City. [1:2.]

More Men, 30 to 34, to Be Drafted Unless Necessary to Industry

By JOSEPH A. LOFTUS
Special to The New York Times.

WASHINGTON, Feb. 24—Men up to the age of 34 will have to meet more rigid specifications to be eligible for occupational deferments under new regulations announced today by Selective Service headquarters.

Asserting that demands for the armed forces are rapidly depleting the younger age groups, a memorandum to local boards told them to dig deeper into the age brackets of 30 through 33. Registrants of those ages to be eligible for deferment must be "necessary to and regularly engaged in" an activity in war production or in support of the national health, safety or interest.

Previously the only requirement was that registrants in this age group, to be eligible for deferment, must be "regularly engaged in" an activity in support of the national health, safety and interest or in an activity in war production.

The memorandum also states that "if all other factors are equal, a father should be given greater consideration for occupational deferment than a non-father in this age group."

Concerning registrants of the ages thirty-four through thirty-seven, the memorandum states that "merely the determination is required that the registrant is

Continued on Page 31, Column 2

Foe's Manila Garrison Wiped Out; 2,146 Civilians Freed in Camp Raid

By The Associated Press.

MANILA, Sunday, Feb. 25—The three-week-old fight for Manila ended Saturday with the complete destruction of the Japanese garrison. Already more than 12,000 enemy dead have been counted.

Skyborne troops, infantrymen and Filipino guerrillas rescued 2,146 civilians from the Japanese internment camp at Los Banos, thirty-five miles south of Manila, at dawn Friday after killing the entire Japanese guard contingent of 243.

The internees, mostly Americans, were evacuated from the camp in amphibious tractors across Laguna de Bay before an estimated 8,000 enemy troops in the district could interfere with more than patrol fire. Two internees were hurt, and two rescuers were killed and two wounded.

Gen. Douglas MacArthur announced the conclusion of the slow, bloody street-by-street fight in Manila brought to a climax by overwhelming of enemy troops in Intramuros, the old walled city. Three thousand civilians of many nationalities were liberated in the final onslaught.

"Troops of the Thirty-seventh Infantry and First Cavalry Divisions of the Fourteenth Corps overwhelmed the enemy's final positions in South Manila and completed the destruction of the trapped garrison," General MacArthur announced. "More than 12,000 enemy bodies have already

Continued on Page 23, Column 3

21 TOWNS ENTERED

1st Army Captures Half of Dueren as 9th Drives On East of Juelich

4,000 CAPTIVES TAKEN

Third Army Clears 21 More Places in 5-Mile Gain Along Saar

By CLIFTON DANIEL
By Wireless to The New York Times.

SUPREME HEADQUARTERS, Allied Expeditionary Force, Feb. 24—The all-out American offensive to reach the Rhine and destroy the German forces west of it has rolled four miles beyond the Roer River in its first two days, overrunning twenty-one German towns and villages, penetrating four more and bringing in more than 4,000 prisoners.

Battling the racing flood of the Roer, the American First and Ninth Armies established a bridge and ferry system last night to move a steady flow of troops across the stream and now have a series of firm and well-manned lodgments on the east side of the Roer along a twenty-two-mile front. From the river, Lieut. Gen. William H. Simpson's and Lieut. Gen. Courtney H. Hodges' troops were fanning out onto the Cologne Plain "according to schedule," which means the Allies' Supreme Command is thoroughly satisfied.

Patton Gains Five Miles

Both the Canadian First and the American Third Armies took advantage of the German fluster over the powerful Roer assault to step up gains north and south of the new attack.

British infantry and armor swept through the Scottish troops south of Goch to resume the attack on Gen. H. D. G. Crerar's front. Along the line General Crerar's forces were thrusting toward Weeze and closing in around Uedem and Calcar. In the Uedem district there was slight evidence of a German withdrawal.

With advances up to five miles today, Lieut. Gen. George S. Patton's Third Army captured twenty-one towns and squeezed the tip of the German salient along the Luxembourg border down to a space three miles long and two miles wide. The tip is expected to be sliced off momentarily. Up to this morning the Third Army had dragged more than 1,000 prisoners out of the area. Resistance was becoming disorganized.

First Wins Half of Dueren

While the Ninth Army was ripping through a series of villages around and beyond Juelich and Linnich, the American First Army, only twenty miles from Cologne, drove the enemy out of half of Dueren, the largest of the Roer River towns and the main hinge of the German line. The First Army also swept out villages on both sides of Dueren, and the Ninth Army was reported from the front to have pushed on four miles beyond the Roer in the maximum advance. Together, the armies already are well established beyond the main road paralleling the east bank of the Roer and are approaching the edges of the thick forest lands east of Juelich, which are the first great natural obstacles in their path.

The two armies—the Ninth under the operational command of Field Marshal Sir Bernard L. Montgomery's Twenty-first Army Group and the First under Lieut. Gen. Omar N. Bradley's Twelfth Army Group—were disclosed by Supreme Commander Dwight D. Eisenhower to have crossed the Roer in strength—that is, on a major scale and with the intention of a strong, steady advance. Berlin reports said that the full force of the offensive had yet to be reached and that Generals Simpson and Hodges had massed twenty divisions, in

Continued on Page 3, Column 5

"All the News That's Fit to Print"

The New York Times.

LATE CITY EDITION
Clearing and warm today.
Fair, continued warm tomorrow.
Temperatures Yesterday—Max., 74; Min., 54
Sunrise today, 6:21 A. M.; Sunset, 7:32 P. M.

VOL. XCIV...No. 31,856. Entered as Second-Class Matter, Postoffice, New York, N. Y. NEW YORK, FRIDAY, APRIL 13, 1945. THREE CENTS IN NEW YORK CITY

PRESIDENT ROOSEVELT IS DEAD; TRUMAN TO CONTINUE POLICIES; 9TH CROSSES ELBE, NEARS BERLIN

U. S. AND RED ARMIES DRIVE TO MEET

Americans Across the Elbe in Strength Race Toward Russians Who Have Opened Offensive From Oder

WEIMAR TAKEN, RUHR POCKET SLASHED

Third Army Reported 19 Miles From Czechoslovak Border—British Drive Deeper in the North, Seizing Celle—Canadians Freeing Holland

By DREW MIDDLETON

By Wireless to The New York Times.

PARIS, April 12—Thousands of tanks and a half million doughboys of the United States First, Third and Ninth Armies are racing through the heart of the Reich on a front of 150 miles, threatening Berlin, Leipzig and the last citadels of the Nazi power.

The Second Armored Division of the Ninth Army has crossed the Elbe River in force and is striking eastward toward Berlin, whose outskirts lie less than sixty miles to the east, according to reports from the front. [A report quoted by The United Press placed the Americans less than fifty miles from the capital.] Beyond Berlin the First White Russian Army has crossed the Oder on a wide front and a junction between the western and eastern Allies is not far off.

[The Moscow radio reported that heavy battles were raging west of the Oder before Berlin, indicating that Marshal Gregory K. Zhukoff had launched his drive toward the Reich's capital. The Soviet communique announced further progress by the Red Army forces in and around Vienna.]

Paris is wild with excitement tonight. A special edition of the newspaper France-Soir carries a report by the radio station "Voice of America" that places American forces fifteen and five-eighths miles from Berlin after an airborne landing that had linked up with Lieut. Gen. William H. Simpson's forces advancing eastward from the Elbe. This would put American forces only seventy-five miles from the Red Army vanguard.

No Confirmation at Headquarters

There was no confirmation of this report at Allied Supreme Headquarters, which by its own admission was thirty-six hours behind developments on some sectors of the front.

Resistance was continuing only on the northern and southern flanks. The center had burst wide open. Weimar fell to Lieut. Gen. George S. Patton's infantry, and reports from the front said Erfurt also had been cleared. Schweinfurt and Heilbronn, two German bastions on the south, had fallen to United States Seventh Army forces, who were driving on Bamberg, while farther north Third Army forces were about thirty-five miles from the Czechoslovak frontier in the area east of Coburg.

[The German radio reported American Third Army forces at Lichtenberg, nineteen miles from the Czechoslovak border, The United Press said.]

The offensives to liberate the Netherlands and reduce the Ruhr

Continued on Page 12, Column 2

OUR OKINAWA GUNS DOWN 118 PLANES

Japanese Fliers Start 'Suicide' Attacks on Fleet, Sink a Destroyer, Hit Other Ships

By W. H. LAWRENCE

By Wireless to The New York Times.

GUAM, Friday, April 13—Japanese attempting to halt the American march to Tokyo, have started "desperate, suicidal" aerial attacks upon our ships and men in the Okinawa area, losing 118 planes on Thursday alone, Fleet Admiral Chester W. Nimitz announced today.

The Japanese succeeded in sinking a destroyer and damaging several other surface units, the communiqué said. All of the damaged vessels remained in action.

It was the first time that the Navy had revealed the suicidal nature of the Japanese air missions against our ships and men. The Japanese radio has been saying that this type of assault was being carried on by a "special attack corps" known in Japanese as "kamakazi," which, translated literally, means "divine wind."

Attack at Low Levels

The Japanese fliers launched their attacks upon our ships and men at a high speed and from low levels, diving directly into a ship or troop concentration to explode their bombs as they crashed.

There was no official estimate of the total number of enemy aircraft engaged in the Okinawa area attack other than the report of the 118 enemy planes destroyed.

Admiral Nimitz reported that the attacks began early on April 12 (Eastern Longitude time) with seven enemy planes shot down during the morning in the vicinity of the Hagushi beaches.

The tempo of the attack was stepped up in the afternoon as the Japanese bore in on our ships in wave after wave. Admiral Nimitz said that ships' guns, carrier aircraft and shore-based anti-aircraft shot down 111 of the attackers.

The revelation of the suicidal Japanese air attacks was the highlight of Admiral Nimitz' regular morning communiqué, which also disclosed the identity of two Marine and two Army divisions that have gone into action on Okinawa. These included the Twenty-seventh Army Division, formed from New York National Guard units, which are seeing action for the first time since the Saipan campaign and previously had engaged in the Gilbert Islands assault. It is com-

Continued on Page 13, Column 3

Army Leaders See Reich End at Hand

By The Associated Press.

WASHINGTON, April 12—High Army officials told Senators today that the end of organized fighting in Germany probably would come within a few days.

Describing the pell-mell dash of American Armies across Germany, General Staff officers expressed the opinion to members of the Senate Military Committee that a collapse of German arms was imminent.

Those who attended said the army chiefs declared that they were so sure of the results that orders had been drawn for a drastic reduction in shipments of durable equipment to Europe.

Franklin Delano Roosevelt

1882-1945

© Perskie

SECURITY PARLEY WON'T BE DELAYED

State Department Urges That World Be Shown We Plan No Changes in Policy

By JAMES B. RESTON

Special to The New York Times.

WASHINGTON, April 12—The United Nations Security Conference will open in San Francisco on April 25, despite the death of President Roosevelt, Secretary of State Edward R. Stettinius Jr. announced tonight.

Mr. Stettinius said that he had been authorized by President Harry Truman to make this announcement after a meeting of the Cabinet at the White House.

Most of the overseas delegations to the San Francisco conference have either arrived in this country or are now on their way, but while this was said to have been a factor in the decision to proceed with the conference, State Department officials urged that every attempt be made to give immediate evidence to the world that President Roosevelt's foreign policy would be sustained by the new Administration.

President Roosevelt had planned to address the San Francisco conference. His interest in an international organization of nations to maintain peace and security had gone back to his service in the Wilson Administration, when he sat in the gallery of the Senate and listened to the debate that resulted in the rejection of the League of Nations Covenant. He had expressed to friends his desire to participate in the San Francisco conference and to see the United States enter the new league during his term in office.

The sudden elevation of Presi-

Continued on Page 2, Column 1

War News Summarized

FRIDAY, APRIL 13, 1945

President Roosevelt died yesterday afternoon, suddenly and unexpectedly. He was stricken with a massive cerebral hemorrhage at Warm Springs, Ga., on the eve of his greatest military and diplomatic successes—the impending fall of Berlin and the opening of the San Francisco Conference to set up a World Security Organization that would make the world free from martial and economic strife [1:7-8.]

Mr. Roosevelt had been sitting in front of the fireplace of his Little White House, having gone to Warm Springs on March 30 for a three-week rest. About 2:15 Eastern war time he said, "I have a terrific headache," lost consciousness in a few moments and died at 4:35. He was 63 years old. [1:6.]

The tragic word spread quickly around the world. Expressions of sorrow poured in from all sections. [4:5.] American soldiers and sailors refused to believe the reports until there was no longer doubt that their Commander in Chief had gone. [4:2-3.]

Harry S. Truman was sworn in as President at 7:09 o'clock last night, and a few minutes later Mrs. Roosevelt left for Warm Springs. [1:7.] The new President immediately called a Cabinet meeting and declared that Mr. Roosevelt's policies would be continued, that the war would be carried on until Germany and Japan surrendered unconditionally and that the San Francisco Conference would open April 25 as scheduled. [1:3.]

Some 500,000 American soldiers of the Third and Ninth Armies, and thousands of tanks, sped along a 150-mile front toward Berlin and Leipzig. The Ninth, surging across the Elbe, according to delayed reports was less than fifty miles from the German capital and 115 from the Russians along the Oder. The Third Army captured Weimar, home of the late German Republic, and was twenty-three miles below Leipzig, with the First closing a pincers from the north. [1:1-2; map P. 2.]

The Moscow radio reported that the Red Army was waging fierce battles east of Berlin, indicating resumption of the drive on that city. Elsewhere Russian troops scored wide gains and cut the last escape railroad from Vienna. [13:1.]

Open cities were ruled out and every German was ordered by Himmler to fight to the death, although Goebbels said "the war cannot last much longer." [12:6-7.]

The Ninth Air Force destroyed at least 117 more German planes yesterday. [11:8.]

In Italy the Eighth Army advanced along a thirty-mile front toward Bologna and the Po Valley; the Fifth Army also made good gains and was eleven miles from La Spezia. [13:8, with map.]

Japanese planes resumed their suicide attacks on American ships off Okinawa, sinking a destroyer and damaging several other vessels. One hundred and eighteen enemy planes were shot down. [1:2.] The Americal Division invaded Bohol, last of the enemy-held central Philippines. [18:6.] The B-29 attack on Koriyama, 110 miles north of Tokyo, set a new Superfortress distance record. [18:2.]

Secretary of State Stettinius and Secretary of War Stimson, denouncing Germany's "steadily increasing" mistreatment of American prisoners, said those responsible would be brought to justice. [13:6-7.]

Clashes between Right and Left wing elements in Iran were reported from Moscow. [13:2.]

LAST WORDS: 'I HAVE TERRIFIC HEADACHE'

Roosevelt Was Posing for Artist When Hemorrhage Struck —He Died in Bedroom

By The Associated Press.

WARM SPRINGS, Ga., April 12—President Franklin D. Roosevelt's last words were:

"I have a terrific headache."

He spoke them to Comdr. Howard G. Bruenn, naval physician.

Mr. Roosevelt was sitting in front of a fireplace in the Little White House here atop Pine Mountain when what was described as a massive cerebral hemorrhage struck him.

The President's Negro valet, Arthur Prettyman, and a Filipino messboy carried him to his bedroom. He was unconscious at the end. It came without pain.

Dr. Bruenn said that he saw the President this morning and he was in excellent spirits at 9:30 A. M.

"At 1 o'clock," Dr. Bruenn added, "he was sitting in a chair while sketches were being made of him by an artist. He suddenly complained of a very severe occipital headache (back of the head).

"Within a very few minutes he lost consciousness. He was seen by me at 1:30 P. M., fifteen minutes after the episode had started.

"He did not regain consciousness, and he died at 3:35 P. M. (Georgia time)."

The artist sketching Mr. Roosevelt was N. Robbins of 520 West 139th Street, New York.

Only others present in the cottage were Comdr. George Fox, White House pharmacist and long an attendant on the President; William D. Hassett, Presidential secretary; Miss Grace Tully, con-

Continued on Page 4, Column 3

END COMES SUDDENLY AT WARM SPRINGS

Even His Family Unaware of Condition as Cerebral Stroke Brings Death to Nation's Leader at 63

ALL CABINET MEMBERS TO KEEP POSTS

Funeral to Be at White House Tomorrow, With Burial at Hyde Park Home—Impact of News Tremendous

By ARTHUR KROCK

Special to The New York Times.

WASHINGTON, April 12—Franklin Delano Roosevelt, War President of the United States and the only Chief Executive in history who was chosen for more than two terms, died suddenly and unexpectedly at 4:35 P. M. today at Warm Springs, Ga., and the White House announced his death at 5:48 o'clock. He was 63.

The President, stricken by a cerebral hemorrhage, passed from unconsciousness to death on the eighty-third day of his fourth term and in an hour of high triumph. The armies and fleets under his direction as Commander in Chief were at the gates of Berlin and the shores of Japan's home islands as Mr. Roosevelt died, and the cause he represented and led was nearing the conclusive phase of success.

Less than two hours after the official announcement, Harry S. Truman of Missouri, the Vice President, took the oath as the thirty-second President. The oath was administered by the Chief Justice of the United States, Harlan F. Stone, in a one-minute ceremony at the White House. Mr. Truman immediately let it be known that Mr. Roosevelt's Cabinet is remaining in office at his request, and that he had authorized Secretary of State Edward R. Stettinius Jr. to proceed with plans for the United Nations Conference on international organization at San Francisco, scheduled to begin April 25. A report was circulated that he leans somewhat to the idea of a coalition Cabinet, but this is unsubstantiated.

Funeral Tomorrow Afternoon

It was disclosed by the White House that funeral services for Mr. Roosevelt would take place at 4 P. M. (E. W. T.) Saturday in the East Room of the Executive Mansion. The Rev. Angus Dun, Episcopal Bishop of Washington; the Rev. Howard S. Wilkinson of St. Thomas's Church in Washington and the Rev. John G. McGee of St. John's in Washington will conduct the services.

The body will be interred at Hyde Park, N. Y., Sunday, with the Rev. George W. Anthony of St. James Church officiating. The time has not yet been fixed.

Jonathan Daniels, White House secretary, said Mr. Roosevelt's body would not lie in state. He added that, in view of the limited size of the East Room, which holds only about 200 persons, the list of those attending the funeral services would be limited to high Government officials, representatives of the membership of both

Continued on Page 3, Column 3

TRUMAN IS SWORN IN THE WHITE HOUSE

Members of Cabinet on Hand as Chief Justice Stone Administers the Oath

By C. P. TRUSSELL

Special to The New York Times.

WASHINGTON, April 12—Vice President Harry S. Truman of Missouri, standing erect, with his sharp features taut and looking straight ahead through his large, round glasses, became the thirty-second President of the United States in a ceremony lasting not more than a minute in the Cabinet Room of the White House at 7:09 o'clock tonight.

The oath was administered by Chief Justice Harlan F. Stone two hours and thirty-four minutes after the sudden death of President Roosevelt at Warm Springs. Mr. Truman had picked up a Bible from the end of the big Cabinet conference table, held it with his left hand and placed his right hand upon the upper cover. After repeating the oath, he bowed his head, lifted the Bible to his lips and kissed it.

Even before he had taken the oath Mr. Truman had asked President Roosevelt's Cabinet to continue in service. He also authorized Edward R. Stettinius Jr., Secretary of State, to announce that the United Nations Conference for International Organization would go on as scheduled.

To the newsmen at the White House he sent this word, through Stephen Early, press secretary:

"For the time being I prefer not to hold a press conference. It will be my effort to carry on as I believe the President would have done, and to that end I have asked the Cabinet to stay on with me."

Soon after he became President, Mr. Truman left the White House for the five-room Connecticut Avenue apartment where he has resided with Mrs. Truman and their 20-year-old daughter, Mary Margaret, for four years. He said he was "going home, to bed."

It was shortly after he had finished presiding over the Senate debate on the United States-Mexican Water Treaty late this afternoon that Mr. Truman received word from the White House of President Roosevelt's death. This was at about 5:15 P. M., a half hour before the news was made public. Reaching for his hat, he dashed out of the office, calling back to his staff that he was going to the White House.

Arriving at the White House, the

Continued on Page 3, Column 6

Byrnes May Take Post With Truman

Special to The New York Times.

WASHINGTON, April 12—James F. Byrnes, recently resigned as Director of War Mobilization and Reconversion, known to be one of President Truman's warmest friends in official Washington, is expected to be called to the White House for consultation, and possibly to take an important post in the Cabinet, in the immediate future.

President Truman's admiration of former Justice Byrnes is well known here. He undoubtedly would have been Mr. Truman's choice as a successor to Cordell Hull as Secretary of State.

"All the News That's Fit to Print"

The New York Times.

LATE CITY EDITION
Clearing and warmer today. Cloudy with moderate winds tomorrow.
Temperatures Yesterday—Max., 51; Min., 44
Sunrise today, 5:54 A. M.; Sunset, 7:53 P. M.

Copyright, 1945, by The New York Times Company.

VOL. XCIV. No. 31,875. Entered as Second-Class Matter, Postoffice, New York, N. Y. NEW YORK, WEDNESDAY, MAY 2, 1945. THREE CENTS IN NEW YORK CITY

HITLER DEAD IN CHANCELLERY, NAZIS SAY; DOENITZ, SUCCESSOR, ORDERS WAR TO GO ON; BERLIN ALMOST WON; U. S. ARMIES ADVANCE

MOLOTOFF EASES PARLEY TENSION; NEW MOVES BEGUN

Russian Says Country Will Cooperate in World Plan Despite Argentine Issue

4 COMMISSIONS SET UP

They Will Deal With Council, Assembly, Court and Some General Problems

By JAMES B. RESTON
Special to The New York Times.

SAN FRANCISCO, May 1—The United Nations Conference on International Organization has survived its first basic crisis and after six days of political maneuvering on secondary issues, it began to move at rapid tempo today toward its primary task—the creation of a world organization which would stop what Field Marshal Jan Christiaan Smuts called "this pilgrimage of death."

The test came last night. Rebuffed by the conference on his attempts to keep Argentina out of the conference and bring the Warsaw Poles in, Soviet Foreign Commissar Vyacheslaff M. Molotoff went late last night to Secretary Stettinius' penthouse at the Fairmont Hotel. He immediately made his position clear.

He still disapproved the conference actions on the Poles and the Argentine, but he wanted the conference to succeed; he would cooperate in its labors, and while he was under urgent pressure by the events in Europe to return to Moscow, he would remain at least for a few days until the major issues on the charter were thrashed out among the four sponsor powers. Then, he said, he would have to leave, probably at the week-end or early next week.

"Friendly Meeting" Is Held

Immediately, in what the Foreign Ministers of the United States, Great Britain and China described to their colleagues as "the most friendly meeting of the conference," the big four approved the formation of the working commissions and committees of the conference, and other committees began discussing, not the personalities or procedures of the conference, but the basic questions of creating an organization which would win the support, with the power, of the great nations without violating the rights and principles of all nations.

The three main developments of the day were as follows:

First, the conference approved four commissions to deal with the security council of the proposed organization, the general assembly, the judicial agency and general problems, and established twelve committees to study specific problems under these four commissions.

The heads of the four commissions were: Trygve Lie of Norway, Security Council; Field Marshal Smuts, General Assembly; Carraciolo Parra Rez of Venezuela, judicial organization; and Paul Henri Spaak of Belgium, general provisions.

Second, Field Marshal Smuts called on the four major powers to accept the special responsibilities which flow from the special authority given them under the Dumbarton Oaks proposals and urged all the nations here to pay more attention to the spiritual and economic aspects of the new charter than they had in the past.

Third, the Russians began studying in some detail the sixteen amendments to the Dumbarton Oaks proposals which were submitted by the United States. The other delegations started circulating amendments and exchanging views on proposals already circulated.

The facts on the crisis among the Big Three over Poland, Argentina, White Russia and the Ukraine can now be put down with assur-

Continued on Page 13, Column 6

Allies Invade North Borneo; Fighting Fierce, Tokyo Says

Australia Informed of Landing by Treasury Minister—MacArthur Reports Only Air Attacks and New Gains on Luzon

By The United Press.

MANILA, Wednesday, May 2—An official Australian announcement said yesterday that Allied troops had invaded Borneo, the world's third largest island, but Gen. Douglas MacArthur's communiqué early today reported only that heavy bombers were neutralizing enemy bases and airdromes on the oil-rich island.

Tokyo also reported the landings and said they had been made on the ten-square-mile island of Tarakan on the northeast coast, a region rich in oil wells, which the Netherlanders destroyed before the Japanese captured them in 1942. The enemy broadcast said "fierce fighting" was in progress.

[A later Japanese broadcast, picked up in San Francisco, reported that Allied units had landed on Tarakan Island at 6:30 A. M., Tuesday, Tokyo time. The broadcast said "the enemy had been bombarding the island since April 27, and on Monday morning began approaching the island in their landing attempts." It reported the landing force consisted of "about 5,000 soldiers" and said Japanese forces on the island "are holding secure their positions, obstructing the enemy's advance."

General MacArthur announced that heavy bombers in attacks on Borneo had struck Kuching, Macassar and Kendari, while medium units and fighters had attacked Japanese gun positions on Tarakan.

General MacArthur announced that on Mindanao Island the Twenty-fourth Division, in another swift drive, had advanced eleven miles

Continued on Page 16, Column 2

NEW CIGARETTES FACE PRICE INQUIRY

OPA Calls on Manufacturers of 21-Cent Brands to Prove Quality Merits Charge

By JAMES E. POWERS

Manufacturers of hitherto unheard of brands of cigarettes that have appeared on the market in recent weeks and are being retailed at four or more cents a package higher than ceiling prices for scarce popular brands will be called upon by the Office of Price Administration to show that the new products are of a quality rating the prices charged, it became known yesterday.

Daniel P. Woolley, regional OPA administrator, said an investigation was in progress as a result of complaints by smokers who said they had paid 21 cents a package for cigarettes "they had previously never heard of."

The United Wholesale Tobacco and Cigarette Distributors Association, a sub-jobbers' group, in a telegram to Senator William Langer of North Dakota, who recently introduced a resolution to set up a committee to look into the "black market" in cigarettes, demanded an immediate investigation of the entire cigarette shortage.

Mr. Woolley declared that as a result of OPA prosecution of violators of price ceilings, the black-market condition largely had been corrected here. He said he was centering on the pricing of the new cigarette brands.

Mr. Woolley added that studies were being made to determine

Continued on Page 40, Column 4

HARD COAL 'HOLIDAY' BRINGS WLB BAN

New Order by Board Asserts Output Is Urgent—Seizure Action Is Postponed

By JOSEPH A. LOFTUS
Special to The New York Times.

WASHINGTON, May 1—The War Labor Board issued a new order tonight to the United Mine Workers and the operators to resume the production of hard coal. To give the UMW leaders an opportunity to act on the order it decided to defer for twenty-four to forty-eight hours a recommendation to President Truman for Government seizure of the mines.

The miners went on a holiday today after expiration of their contract at midnight.

Dr. George W. Taylor, WLB chairman, in a telegram to both parties took cognizance of the miners' traditional "no contract, no work" policy.

"The board's order provides for a continuing contract," he said. "It is urgent that production should be immediately resumed."

As in acting on the soft coal dispute a month ago, the WLB provided in the new order that any legal wage adjustment agreed upon or finally ordered be retroactive to the expiration date of the old contract.

Union spokesmen told the WLB at a brief hearing that the Tri-District Scale Committee had voted to advise the miners to return to work when the operators accepted the settlement proposal made by Secretary of Labor Perkins.

Dr. Taylor, in questioning John Owens of the UMW, noted that

Continued on Page 40, Column 3

Eisenhower Halted Forces at Elbe; Ninth Had Hoped to Storm Berlin

By The Associated Press.

WITH THE UNITED STATES NINTH ARMY, in Germany, April 26 (Delayed by Censorship) — A direct order from Supreme Allied Headquarters halted the United States Ninth Army's drive to Berlin at the Elbe River at a time when the most pessimistic officers were predicting that Lieut. Gen. William H. Simpson's forces could reduce the German capital in ten days, "even if the Germans fought hard."

General Eisenhower's order said the Ninth would halt on the Elbe and await the arrival of Russian forces from the east, thereby leaving the capture of the capital to the Red Army. It also was understood that the American First and Third and British and Canadian armies received similar orders to halt at the Elbe.

It was not clear whether General Eisenhower's order was dictated by political policy agreed upon by the Great Powers or in a belief that it was a military necessity.

It was felt by high staff officers in the field, however, that the Ninth and other American forces could push on to the capital without great difficulty. While the order disappointed some staff officers, it was not altogether unexpected. It was known that the Ninth Army had pushed past the eventual British-American occupation area when it crossed the Weser River.

While the staff officers were disappointed, the American doughboys and tankmen who had to do the fighting and dying to get to Berlin expressed no regret. Almost to a man, they felt they could do with-

Continued on Page 4, Column 4

REDOUBTS ASSAILED

U. S. 3d, 7th and French 1st Armies Charging Into Alpine Hideout

NEAR BRENNER PASS

British in North Close About Hamburg—Poles Gain in Emden Area

Von Rundstedt Caught

By The Associated Press.

WITH UNITED STATES SEVENTH ARMY, Wednesday, May 2—Field Marshal Karl von Rundstedt has been captured by United States Seventh Army troops.

The Seventh Army caught the former German commander in the west in its drive into the Nazis' southeastern redoubt area.

By DREW MIDDLETON
By Wireless to The New York Times.

PARIS, May 1—The last defenses of the Third Reich were crumbling as Allied tanks and infantry swept almost unopposed into the northern and southern redoubts.

Gen. George S. Patton's United States Third Army has resumed its offensive into Austria, crashing to within twenty miles of Linz, and is only fifty-four miles from Amstetten, where Marshal Fedor I. Tolbukhin's Third Ukrainian Army was last reported. According to reports from the front, radio contact has been established between tanks of the Third Army's Eleventh Armored Division and the vanguard of the Soviet armies.

Other armored columns of the

Continued on Page 14, Column 1

NAZI CORE STORMED

Russians Drive Toward Chancellery Fortress, Narrowing Noose

BRANDENBURG TAKEN

Stralsund Port Swept Up in New Baltic Gains—Vah Valley Cleared

By C. L. SULZBERGER
By Wireless to The New York Times.

MOSCOW, Wednesday, May 2—Street battles within smoldering Berlin today entered their twelfth day since the Russians first broke into the city, with Nazi die-hards still holding grimly to the central part of the town, whittled down by yesterday's fighting, in which Marshal Gregory K. Zhukoff's First White Russian Army group completely occupied Charlottenburg and Schoeneberg and more than 100 blocks in the capital's central region.

Some 14,000 prisoners were taken within the city on Monday, the Russians announced. At the same time, the remnants of a hold-out group south of Berlin, part of which had been annihilated at Wendisch Buchholtz, was split in two and the survivors are being ground to death by Marshal Zhukoff's men.

Curiously enough, the midnight communiqué does not mention Marshal Ivan S. Koneff's First Ukrainian Army group, which has been working from the southwestern sector of the city toward the desperately defended Tiergarten.

Marshal Zhukoff's forward spearheads meanwhile struck deep into Brandenburg Province, capturing the city of Brandenburg, halfway to Magdeburg from Berlin.

While Gen. Andrei I. Yeremenko proceeded apace in his lightning

Continued on Page 3, Column 3

War News Summarized

WEDNESDAY, MAY 2, 1945

Hitler is dead, according to the Hamburg radio, and on Monday, the day before he allegedly fell at his command post in the Chancellery in Berlin, he appointed Admiral Karl Doenitz to be the new Fuehrer. The head of the German Navy, who had made his mark directing the enemy's U-boats campaign, pledged continuance of the war. [1:8.]

Washington received the news, as did London, with some skepticism and a desire to see the body. Selection of Admiral Doenitz was considered logical in view of his strong Nazi feelings. [1:7.]

The new development was interpreted in London as a move to counteract Himmler's reported peace bids, but Prime Minister Churchill broadly intimated in the Commons that he might have "information of exceptional importance" to impart before Saturday. Peace will probably come before all enemy forces have surrendered, he said. [1:6-7.] Germany was reported to have begun evacuation of Denmark and to be ready to leave Norway. Count Bernadotte said in Sweden he had no new Himmler proposals, and the Nazis' Scandinavian withdrawals were related there to a prospective general capitulation. [11:1.]

Meanwhile, general Allied progress on the battlefields against slight resistance continued. The United States Third Army, on the day Hitler was declared to have died, captured Braunau, his birthplace. The drive into Austria was resumed and had reached to within twenty miles of Linz and fifty-four of the last known Russian position. The Seventh Army smashed through the Tyrol on a broad front and cleared Munich. The British Second Army, by-passing Hamburg, raced to within eighteen miles of the Baltic port of Luebeck. [1:4; map P. 14.]

General Eisenhower, it was revealed, personally ordered the halt of the Allied drive on Berlin from the west to permit the Russians to take the capital. [1:2-3.]

The Russians greatly cut down the German holding in Berlin, capturing the districts of Charlottenburg and Schoeneberg. West of the city they occupied Brandenburg and along the Baltic they seized Stralsund. [1:5; maps Pages 2 and 14.]

New Zealand troops in Italy made contact with Yugoslav Partisans at Monfalcone near Trieste and the British entered Udine. While the Eighth Army was closing a trap along the Swiss border, the Fifth neared France. [1:6-7; map P. 14.]

Mussolini and his mistress were buried in unmarked paupers' graves in Milan. [13:1.] Admiral Horthy, former Regent of Hungary, was captured. [4:3.]

Invasion of Borneo was officially disclosed in Australia, although no word of the break into the Japanese-held Netherlands East Indies had come from General MacArthur. On Mindanao in the Philippines, Americans were within six miles of the city of Davao. [1:2-3; map P. 16.]

Seventh Division troops on Okinawa resumed their southward advance, entering the village of Kuhazu. [15:1.] More than 400 starved, naked Allied prisoners of war were liberated by the British as they drove on Rangoon in Burma. [15:3.]

Good progress was made at the San Francisco Conference. Foreign Commissar Molotoff, after assuring Secretary of State Stettinius of his desire that the conference succeed, announced that pressure of events would compel his return to Moscow within a few days. [1:1.]

ADOLF HITLER The New York Times, 1938

Clark's Troops Meet Tito's In General Advance in Italy

By VIRGINIA LEE WARREN
By Wireless to The New York Times.

AT ADVANCED ALLIED HEADQUARTERS, in Italy, May 1—After advancing fifty-five miles in less than a day along the coastal road rimming the Gulf of Venice, units of one division of the Fifteenth Army Group made contact this afternoon with Marshal Tito's forces at Monfalcone while other troops under Gen. Mark W. Clark continued to sweep German remnants from the valleys of north Italy and to seal off the few remaining escape routes through the Alps.

No details of the meeting at the small seaport northwest of Trieste between Marshal Tito's men, who had driven fourteen miles from Trieste, and leading elements of the Eighth Army's Second New Zealand Division were given in tonight's communiqué.

On the other side of Italy another historic meeting was imminent as Fifth Army troops, continuing their drive along the Gulf of Genoa, advanced on the Aurelian Way to within sixty miles of the French border, which has already been crossed by French troops heading this way.

General Clark announced yesterday that the military power of Germany had virtually collapsed, but there still are drives for his two armies to make and engagements still to be won. The Germans, trying to regroup for their flight across the Alps, were deprived of two key road junctions leading to mountain passes west of Brenner when Belluno and Udine were occupied this afternoon by units of the Eighth Army.

Udine, which was taken by the British Sixth Armored Division, is twenty-eight miles southwest of Caporetto, the scene of the Italian disaster in World War I. The forces that entered Belluno went on five miles to Ponte nell 'Alpi, guardian of the approach to Italy's

Continued on Page 13, Column 5

DOENITZ' ACCESSION VIEWED AS A BLIND

Capital Lays His Designation to General Ignorance of His Allegiance to Party

By The Associated Press.

WASHINGTON, May 1—If Adolf Hitler really designated Grand Admiral Karl Doenitz his successor, military men here believe, he did so for the following reasons:

1. Doenitz is a Nazi supporter who could be counted on to keep German resistance going if possible.

2. But he is not associated in the Allies' minds with German atrocities and the extreme policies of the Nazi party. Therefore, Hitler probably figured that he might be able to get better treatment from the Allies when the hour of surrender came.

3. He is immensely popular with the German people.

There was a disposition here tonight to look for continued organized resistance whose core would now be centered in the Baltic and North Sea port areas. Those places are the homes of the German Navy and especially of the U-boat fleet that Doenitz commanded from 1936 until he succeeded Grand Admiral Erich

Continued on Page 5, Column 1

Churchill Hints Peace This Week; 2-Day Celebration Is Authorized

By CLIFTON DANIEL
By Wireless to The New York Times.

LONDON, May 1—The general belief that peace with Germany will be announced this week persisted in Britain today, encouraged by Prime Minister Churchill himself and by Grand Admiral Karl Doenitz's announcement of the death of Adolf Hitler.

The War Cabinet again held a session tonight but so far as was known did not have any concrete proposal to consider. The chances that Heinrich Himmler ultimately will deliver an acceptable peace are now held in some official quarters to be only "fifty-fifty."

Nevertheless the buoyant Prime Minister told the House of Commons today that he might have "information of importance" to announce before Saturday.

The public's hopes were raised still further by a long Home Office circular giving the Government's views on how Britain should observe V-E Day, which the British, it appears, will be expected to celebrate strictly according to form.

[Stockholm reported, with the return there of Count Bernadotte, the "imminent liberation" of Denmark and Norway—already taking effect locally in Denmark—as a phase of a prospective general German capitulation that must be acceptable to the Allies' military commands.]

The hurrahing will begin with the announcement of the cessation of hostilities by Mr. Churchill over a nation-wide radio network. The King will speak at 9 o'clock that evening. And throughout that day

Continued on Page 10, Column 4

ADMIRAL IN CHARGE

Proclaims Designation to Rule—Appeals to People and Army

RAISES 'RED MENACE'

Britain to Insist Germans Show Hitler's Body When War Ends

By SYDNEY GRUSON
By Cable to The New York Times.

LONDON, May 1—Adolf Hitler died this afternoon, the Hamburg radio announced tonight, and Grand Admiral Karl Doenitz, proclaiming himself the new Fuehrer by Hitler's appointment, said that the war would continue.

Crowning days of rumors about Hitler's health and whereabouts, the Hamburg radio said that he had fallen in the battle of Berlin at his command post in the Chancellery just three days after Benito Mussolini, the first of the dictators, had been killed by Italian Partisans. Doenitz, a 53-year-old U-boat specialist, broadcast an address to the German people and the surviving armed forces immediately after the announcer had given the news of Hitler's death.

[The British Foreign Office said that it would demand the production of Hitler's body after the end of hostilities, The Associated Press reported.]

First addressing the German people, Doenitz said that they would continue to fight only to save themselves from the Russians but that they would oppose the western Allies as long as they helped the Russians. In an order of the day to the German forces he repeated his thinly veiled attempt to split the Allies.

Radio Prepares Germans

Early this evening the Germans were told that an important announcement would be broadcast tonight. There was no hint of what was coming. The stand-by announcement was repeated at 9:40 P. M., followed by the playing of excerpts from Wagner's "Goetterdaemmerung."

A few minutes later the announcer said: "Achtung! Achtung! In a few moments you will hear a

Continued on Page 5, Column 4

Copenhagen Writer Again Phones Story

By Cable to The New York Times.

STOCKHOLM, Sweden, May 1—For the first time in more than five years THE NEW YORK TIMES correspondent in Copenhagen, Svend Carstensen, tonight telephoned a story from the Danish capital. The Nazi-imposed censorship there has been lifted. Mr. Carstensen said:

"The Danes are overjoyed at their imminent liberation, but it is not noticeable on the Copenhagen streets.

"Anxious to avoid trouble on May Day, Copenhageners have been staying indoors. The blackout is still enforced and it is pitch dark in Copenhagen tonight. All Copenhageners are glued to radios listening to broadcasts on Hitler's death.

"We expect King Christian will resume his functions and name a new Cabinet any day now. In the meantime the strictest discipline is being observed so as not to give the Germans any excuses for starting more trouble."

On April 9, 1940, Mr. Carstensen was the first to give the world the news of the German invasion of Denmark in a wireless dispatch to THE NEW YORK TIMES. His dispatch was cleared less than an hour before the Nazis seized the radio station and was the last to be sent.

"All the News That's Fit to Print"

The New York Times.

LATE CITY EDITION
Cloudy with showers today. Partly cloudy and cooler tomorrow.
Temperatures Yesterday—Max., 64; Min., 47
Sunrise today, 5:46 A. M.; Sunset, 7:59 P. M.

VOL. XCIV..No. 31,881. Entered as Second-Class Matter, Postoffice, New York, N. Y. NEW YORK, TUESDAY, MAY 8, 1945. THREE CENTS IN NEW YORK CITY

THE WAR IN EUROPE IS ENDED! SURRENDER IS UNCONDITIONAL; V-E WILL BE PROCLAIMED TODAY; OUR TROOPS ON OKINAWA GAIN

ISLAND-WIDE DRIVE

Marines Reach Village a Mile From Naha and Army Lines Advance

7 MORE SHIPS SUNK

Search Planes Again Hit Japan's Life Line—Kyushu Bombed

By WARREN MOSCOW
By Wireless to THE NEW YORK TIMES

GUAM, Tuesday, May 8—In an island-wide American advance on Okinawa yesterday the First Marine Division drove south to the edge of Dakeshi Village, about a mile from Naha, the capital, straightening out the line on our right flank. In the center the Seventy-seventh Army Division used flame-throwing tanks for considerable advances, while the Seventh Army Division moved forward on the left flank.

[Airfields on Kyushu, southern Japan, were bombed Monday and Tuesday by Superfortresses, two of which were lost in heavy air opposition.

[Allied fliers started operating from the Tarakan airfield although fighting continued on that island off Borneo, and in the Philippines American troops made advances on Mindanao and Luzon.]

Japanese Dead at 36,535

As the United States forces on Okinawa resumed their drive, Fleet Admiral Chester W. Nimitz revealed that Japanese killed on the island had mounted to 36,535 on Monday, showing that the Americans were maintaining their rate of 1,000 a day.

The Americans have not yet taken the main Japanese artillery emplacements on Okinawa, which were the principal targets of the fleet off the island. The fleet's guns continued yesterday, along with carrier aircraft, to support the ground movements.

Meanwhile search bombers of Fleet Air Wing 1 continued to give an impressive demonstration of what the tightening air blockade of Japan will mean. Attacking at mast-head height with bombs and machine guns, these long-range aircraft, based in the Okinawa area, sank four more ships in waters off Korea and damaged five others.

The ships sunk were a large cargo ship, a medium cargo ship, a medium oiler and a large fleet tanker. Two small freighters were

Continued on Page 12, Column 2

Leopold Rescued By 7th Army Troops

By The Associated Press.

WITH THE UNITED STATES SEVENTH ARMY, Tuesday, May 8—Léopold III, King of Belgium, and his wife, Princess Rethy, have been liberated by the Seventh Army, it was announced today.

They were found near Strobl, eight miles east of Salzburg. The Americans had been told of their whereabouts by civilians.

With the King and his wife were eighteen members of their staff and four children. All were in good health.

Elements of the American 106th Cavalry Group had to overpower German Elite Guards to make the rescue. Seventh Army troops are now closely guarding the royal party.

The Pulitzer Awards For 1944 Announced

The Pulitzer Prize awards announced yesterday by the trustees of Columbia University included: For a distinguished novel, to "A Bell for Adano," by John Hersey; for an original American play of the current season, to "Harvey," by Mary Chase.

Among the newspaper awards were those to Hal Boyle, Associated Press war reporter, for distinguished correspondence; to James B. Reston of THE NEW YORK TIMES for his reporting of the Dumbarton Oaks Security Conference; to Joe Rosenthal, Associated Press photographer, for his photograph of marines raising the American flag at Iwo and to The Detroit Free Press for "distinguished and meritorious public service" in its investigation of legislative corruption at Lansing, Mich.

Further details of the awards will be found on Page 16.

MOLOTOFF HAILS BASIC 'UNANIMITY'

He Stresses Five Points in World Charter, but His View on One Is Questioned

By JAMES B. RESTON
Special to THE NEW YORK TIMES.

SAN FRANCISCO, May 7—The major allies who forced Germany's unconditional surrender have reached "unanimity" on the kind of world security organization which should be created at the United Nations conference to protect their newly won victory, Vyacheslaff M. Molotoff, Russian Foreign Commissar, said today.

While the delegates at the conference celebrated the end of the European war, and three Foreign Ministers, T. V. Soong of China, Paul Henri Spaak of Belgium and Trygve Lie of Norway left the conference to deal with urgent official business elsewhere, Mr. Molotoff told the press that the Soviet Union attached the "greatest importance" to five agreements reached by the heads of the Big Four delegations.

First, he said, these leaders agreed to support the principles of justice, international law, human rights and fundamental freedom for all.

Second, he added, the Big Four agreed not to make provision in the security charter for the revision of treaties.

His statement on this point was ambiguous and led to some speculation as to the unanimity of all four on the question.

Revision Power Called Danger

A reference in the United Nations charter to the necessity of revising treaties, Mr. Molotoff stated, "would play into the hands of enemy countries, which would certainly like to undermine and emasculate these treaties." Furthermore, he declared, to give the new League of Nations authority to consider revision of treaties would be a violation of national sovereign rights, which are guaranteed in the Dumbarton Oaks Charter.

For these reasons, he concluded, "the idea of revising treaties was rejected as untenable."

Third, Mr. Molotoff said, it was agreed among the Big Four that treaties directed against Germany, such as Russia's twenty-year alliances with Britain, France, Czechoslovakia, Yugoslavia and the Warsaw Poles, "should remain in force until such time as the Government concerned felt that the international security organization was really in a position to undertake the accomplishment of the tasks of

Continued on Page 15, Column 2

GERMANY SURRENDERS: NEW YORKERS MASSED UNDER SYMBOL OF LIBERTY

Thousands filling Times Square in spontaneous celebration yesterday

The New York Times

PRAGUE SAYS FOES ACCEPT SURRENDER

Czechoslovak Radio Reports All Fighting in Bohemia Will Be Ended Today

By The Associated Press.

LONDON, Tuesday, May 8—The Czechoslovak-controlled Prague radio announced today that the Germans in Prague and throughout Bohemia, a last major holdout pocket of German resistance, had accepted unconditional surrender.

The announcement came as the United States Third Army was reported to have advanced to the outskirts of the Czechoslovak capital, and three Russian armies hammered toward the same goal from the east and north.

"The German military plenipotentiary is negotiating with the Czechoslovak National Council on the modalities of unconditional surrender," said the broadcast, detailing what purported to be the

Continued on Page 11, Column 2

Wild Crowds Greet News In City While Others Pray

By FRANK S. ADAMS

New York City's millions reacted in two sharply contrasting ways yesterday to the news of the unconditional surrender of the German armies. A large and noisy minority greeted it with the turbulent enthusiasm of New Year's Eve and Election Night rolled into one. However, the great bulk of the city's population responded with quiet thanksgiving that the war in Europe was won, tempered by the realization that a grim and bitter struggle still was ahead in the Pacific and the fact that the nation is still in mourning for its fallen President and Commander in Chief.

Times Square, the financial section and the garment district were thronged from mid-morning on with wildly jubilant celebrators who tooted horns, staged impromptu parades and filled the canyons between the skyscrapers with fluttering scraps of paper. Elsewhere in the metropolitan area, however, war plants continued to hum, schools, offices and factories carried on their normal activities, and residential areas were calmly joyful.

One factor that helped to dampen the celebration was the bewilderment of large segments of the population at the absence of an official proclamation to back up the news contained in flaring headlines and radio bulletins. With the premature rumor of ten days ago fresh in everyone's mind, and millions still mindful of the false armistice of 1918, there was widespread skepticism over the authenticity of the news.

By mid-afternoon loudspeakers were blaring into the ears of the exulting thousands in the amusement district the news that President Truman's proclamation was being held up by the necessity of coordinating it with the announcements from London and Moscow, and that the formal celebration of the long-awaited V-E Day would be delayed until today.

This sobering note gradually

Continued on Page 7, Column 6

SHAEF BAN ON AP LIFTED IN 6 HOURS

Action Comes After Protests From Newspapers and Public —Writer Still Barred

Suspension of filing facilities of The Associated Press in the European theatre was clamped on by Supreme Headquarters, Allied Expeditionary Forces (SHAEF), yesterday in an unprecedented action and was lifted six hours and twenty minutes later.

The ban was continued, however, on all copy submitted for clearance by Edward Kennedy, chief of the press association's staff on the Western Front, who sent the momentous story announcing Germany's final surrender in a dispatch from Reims, France, which was received in New York over the AP wires at 9:35 A. M. (EWT).

It was not until seven hours and fifty-five minutes had elapsed aft-

Continued on Page 4, Column 2

Summary of News of the War and German Surrender

TUESDAY, MAY 8, 1945

The war ended in Europe yesterday after five years, eight months and six days of the bloodiest conflict in history. Grand Admiral Karl Doenitz surrendered unconditonally to the Allies in a little red schoolhouse at Reims, France. At 8:41 P. M. Sunday, New York time, Col. Gen. Gustav Jodl signed for the enemy and Lieut. Gen. Walter Bedell Smith, General Eisenhower's Chief of Staff, for the Allies. In the absence of any official announcement there was some confusion as to the compliance with the surrender. Fighting had been going on in Czechoslovakia and nothing had been heard from German pockets along the French coast. [1:7-8.]

President Truman planned a broadcast from the White House at 9 o'clock this morning. Washington, gratified that the war in Europe was over, was confused by lack of confirmation. [2:2.]

Prime Minister Churchill will also broadcast at 9 A. M. from London and Premier Stalin is expected to make a simultaneous announcement in Moscow. King George will talk over the radio six hours later. [2:8.] London will celebrate V-E Day today, but, unable to restrain its joy, staged many impromptu celebrations yesterday. [2:7.]

Most New Yorkers took the news calmly and thankfully, sobered by realization that the war in the Pacific was far from over. There were, however, noisy outbursts in such centers as Times Square and Wall Street. Scrap paper showers fluttered from roofs and windows. [1:4-5.]

German Foreign Minister Lutz Schwerin von Krosigk broke the news to his people. The future will be difficult, he warned, and then added: "We must make right the basis of our nation. In our nation justice shall be the supreme law and the guiding principle. We must also recognize law as the basis of all relations between the nations." This sudden, complete reversal in German policy was received with skepticism by the Allies. [3:1.]

Perhaps one reason for this was the announcement from Moscow that 4,000,000 men, women and children had been done to death by gas, shooting, famine, poisoning and torture in the German extermination camp at Oswiecim, Poland. [12:5.]

The actual situation in Czechoslovakia was obscure. Late last night a Patriot broadcast said the Germans were negotiating with the Czechoslovak National Council details of surrender in Prague and Bohemia. Fighting had continued throughout yesterday and German planes had bombed public buildings and hospitals. [1:3; map P. 11.].

The United States Third Army continued its general advance into Czechoslovakia and the Fifth and Seventh Armies joined again in the Alps. The British Second Army moved to Denmark and Poles entered the shattered port of Wilhelmshaven. [11:1.] Breslau fell to the Red Army after an eighty-four-day siege; 40,000 Germans were captured. [11:5.]

Japan accepted the surrender of her Axis partner with a statement that she never had expected German aid and would go on to victory without the Reich. [13:1.]

Infantry and marines on Okinawa scored another general advance after naval bombardment had pulverized Japanese strong points. Pacific Fleet planes sank or damaged thirteen more ships off Korea and Japan. [1:1; map, P. 12.] B-29's maintained their assault on Kyushu airfields. Two of the big planes were shot down. [14:3-4.]

On Tarakan Allied troops were within a mile and a half of the eastern shore. Americans gained on Mindanao and Luzon in the Philippines. [12:3-4.]

Foreign Commissar Molotoff said in San Francisco that unanimity on amendments to Dumbarton Oaks assured success of the conference. He declared that the Big Four consultations had ended. [1:2.]

GERMANS CAPITULATE ON ALL FRONTS

American, Russian and French Generals Accept Surrender in Eisenhower Headquarters, a Reims School

REICH CHIEF OF STAFF ASKS FOR MERCY

Doenitz Orders All Military Forces of Germany To Drop Arms—Troops in Norway Give Up —Churchill and Truman on Radio Today

By EDWARD KENNEDY
Associated Press Correspondent

REIMS, France, May 7—Germany surrendered unconditionally to the Western Allies and the Soviet Union at 2:41 A. M. French time today. [This was at 8:41 P. M., Eastern Wartime Sunday.]

The surrender took place at a little red schoolhouse that is the headquarters of Gen. Dwight D. Eisenhower.

The surrender, which brought the war in Europe to a formal end after five years, eight months and six days of bloodshed and destruction, was signed for Germany by Col. Gen. Gustav Jodl. General Jodl is the new Chief of Staff of the German Army.

The surrender was signed for the Supreme Allied Command by Lieut. Gen. Walter Bedell Smith, Chief of Staff for General Eisenhower.

It was also signed by Gen. Ivan Susloparoff for the Soviet Union and by Gen. Francois Sevez for France.

[The official Allied announcement will be made at 9 o'clock Tuesday morning when President Truman will broadcast a statement and Prime Minister Churchill will issue a V-E Day proclamation. Gen. Charles de Gaulle also will address the French at the same time.]

General Eisenhower was not present at the signing, but immediately afterward General Jodl and his fellow delegate, Gen. Admiral Hans Georg Friedeburg, were received by the Supreme Commander.

Germans Say They Understand Terms

They were asked sternly if they understood the surrender terms imposed upon Germany and if they would be carried out by Germany.

They answered Yes.

Germany, which began the war with a ruthless attack upon Poland, followed by successive aggressions and brutality in internment camps, surrendered with an appeal to the victors for mercy toward the German people and armed forces.

After having signed the full surrender, General Jodl said he wanted to speak and received leave to do so.

"With this signature," he said in soft-spoken German, "the German people and armed forces are for better or worse delivered into the victors' hands.

"In this war, which has lasted more than five years, both have achieved and suffered more than perhaps any other people in the world."

LONDON, May 7 (AP)—Complete victory in

Continued on Page 3, Columns 2 and 3

"All the News That's Fit to Print"

The New York Times.

LATE CITY EDITION
Thunderstorms, warm, humid; clear and cooler tonight. Fair tomorrow.
Temperatures Yesterday—Max., 84; Min., 71
Sunrise today, 6:06 A. M.; Sunset, 7:55 P. M.

VOL. XCIV..No. 31,980. Entered as Second-Class Matter, Postoffice, New York, N. Y. NEW YORK, WEDNESDAY, AUGUST 15, 1945. THREE CENTS IN NEW YORK CITY

JAPAN SURRENDERS, END OF WAR! EMPEROR ACCEPTS ALLIED RULE; M'ARTHUR SUPREME COMMANDER; OUR MANPOWER CURBS VOIDED

HIRING MADE LOCAL

Communities, Labor and Management Will Unite Efforts

6,000,000 AFFECTED

Draft Quotas Cut, Services to Drop 5,500,000 in 18 Months

By LEWIS WOOD

Special to THE NEW YORK TIMES.

WASHINGTON, Aug. 14—All manpower controls over employers and workers were abolished tonight, the War Manpower Commission announced, enabling employers to hire men where and when they pleased.

The end of the war threw on the Government the difficult task of trying to readjust perhaps 6,000,000 war workers into new employment. Nevertheless, the WMC said, all its facilities would be used to help workers find new places, with preference going to veterans, displaced migratory war workers and other preferentials.

At the same time President Truman announced that monthly inductions into the Army would be immediately slashed from 80,000 to 50,000, and said 5,000,00 to 5,500,000 men probably would be released from the service within the next year or eighteen months.

The induction rate of 50,000 monthly, the President said, would be sufficient to maintain the occupation forces and allow men of long service overseas to return to their homes.

Under the WMC program, the manpower controls are to be lifted at once and voluntary community action to hurry reconversion will be substituted. In every community, the number of displaced workers and returning veterans will be ascertained in cooperation with local management-labor groups. Full facilities of the United States Employment Service offices will be made available to all employers. Service for veterans will be enlarged.

The WMC program embraced these seven points:

1. All manpower controls are to be lifted at once and in their place voluntary community action to

Continued on Page 13, Column 3

Third Fleet Fells 5 Planes Since End

By The Associated Press.

GUAM, Wednesday, Aug. 15—Japanese aircraft are approaching the Pacific Fleet off Tokyo and are being shot down, Admiral Chester W. Nimitz announced today.

Five enemy planes have been destroyed since noon today, Japanese time, or 11 P. M. EWT.

Gen. Douglas MacArthur has been requested to tell the Japanese that American defense measures require the Third Fleet to destroy any Japanese planes approaching United States warships.

GUAM, Wednesday, Aug. 15 (U.P.)—When Admiral Halsey received word of Japan's capitulation today ,he sent this message to his fliers:

"It looks like the war is over, but if any enemy planes appear shoot them down in friendly fashion."

SECRETS OF RADAR GIVEN TO WORLD

Its Role in War and Uses for Peacetime Revealed in Washington and London

By WILLIAM S. WHITE

Special to THE NEW YORK TIMES.

WASHINGTON, Aug. 14—The great drama of radar, the war's most powerful "secret weapon" until the atomic bomb was devised, was displayed before a world audience today.

The Joint Board on Scientific Information Policy permitted the Office of Scientific Research and Development, the War Department and the Navy Department to tell the story of a device of which millions had known vaguely for two years, a device which at least three times stood between survival or defeat by the Axis powers for the United States and Great Britain.

It was radar, short for "radio detection and range," that helped the small surviving British air squadrons to beat the German blitz of 1940, thus not only saving the home islands but preserving them as the essential Anglo-American base from which the continental invasion went forward on June 6, 1944.

It was radar which "sees through the heaviest fog and the blackest night," that more than any other factor broke in 1942 the German submarine which was threatening to starve and strangle the British homeland.

And it was radar that permitted the remnants of the blasted United States Pacific Fleet to stay alive

Continued on Page 14, Column 3

ALL CITY 'LETS GO'

Hundreds of Thousands Roar Joy After Victory Flash Is Received

TIMES SQ. IS JAMMED

Police Estimate Crowd in Area at 2,000,000—Din Overwhelming

By ALEXANDER FEINBERG

Five days of waiting, of rumor, intimation, fact, distortion—five agonizing days following the first indication of a Japanese surrender, days of alternately rising hopes and fears—came to an end for New York, as for the nation and the world, a moment or two after seven o'clock last night. And the metropolis exploded its emotions, harnessed for the most part during the day, with atomic force.

"Official—Truman announces Japanese surrender."

These were the magic words, flashed on the moving electric sign of the Times Tower, at 7:03 P. M. that touched off an unparalleled demonstration in Times Square, packed with half a million persons.

The victory roar that greeted the announcement beat upon the eardrums until it numbed the senses. For twenty minutes wave after wave of that joyous roar surged forth.

Restraint was thrown to the winds. Those in the crowds in the streets tossed hats, boxes and flags into the air. From those leaning perilously out of the windows of office buildings and hotels came a shower of paper, confetti, streamers. Men and women embraced—there were no strangers in New York yesterday. Some were hilarious, others cried softly.

By 7:30 P. M. the crowd in the Square had risen to 750,000 persons; by 8:45 it had swelled to 800,000 and the number continued to rise. People were packed solidly between Forty-third Street and Forty-fifth Street. Individual movement was virtually impossible; one moved not in the crowd but with it.

At 10 P. M. Chief Inspector John J. O'Connell estimated that 2,000,000 persons were in the Times Square area from Fortieth to Fifty-second Street, between Sixth and Eighth Avenues. This constitutes an all-time record, police officials said. At that hour people were still pouring into the Square from subways, buses and on foot.

Those at the north end of the

Continued on Page 5, Column 1

PRESIDENT ANNOUNCING SURRENDER OF JAPAN

Mr. Truman reading the message in the White House. Seated are Admiral William D. Leahy, Secretary of State James F. Byrnes and former Secretary of State Cordell Hull. Standing (left to right) are Maj. Gen. Philip Fleming, head of the Federal Works Administration; William H. Davis, Economic Stabilizer; John W. Snyder, Reconversion Director; James Forrestal, Secretary of the Navy; Fred Vinson, Secretary of the Treasury; Tom Clark, Attorney General, and Lewis Schwellenbach, Secretary of Labor.

Associated Press Wirephoto

PETAIN CONVICTED, SENTENCED TO DIE

Jurors Recommend Clemency Because of His Age—Long Indictment Upheld

By G. H. ARCHAMBAULT

By Wireless to THE NEW YORK TIMES.

PARIS, Wednesday, Aug. 15—Marshal Henri-Philippe Pétain was convicted at 4:15 A. M. today of intelligence with the enemy and sentenced to death. Because of his age—the former head of the Vichy regime is 89—the jury expressed the hope that the death sentence might not be carried out.

Guards had to arouse Pétain in

Continued on Page 15, Column 5

Terms Will Reduce Japan To Kingdom Perry Visited

By JAMES B. RESTON

Special to THE NEW YORK TIMES.

WASHINGTON, Aug. 14—The Allied terms of surrender will not only demobilize and demilitarize Japan but also deprive her of 80 per cent of the territory and nearly one-third of the population she held when she attacked Pearl Harbor. Thus these terms, already approved by President Truman and our major Allies, will not only destroy the vast empire she conquered in the first eighteen months of this war but also reduce her to little more than the territory she occupied when Commodore Perry introduced her to the western world in 1853.

The main terms of surrender, as

Continued on Page 11, Column 2

TREATY WITH CHINA SIGNED IN MOSCOW

Complete Agreement Reached With Chungking on All Points at Issue, Russians Say

By Cable to THE NEW YORK TIMES.

LONDON, Aug. 14—The Soviet Union and China have signed a treaty of friendship and alliance, the Moscow radio announced tonight, and have reached "full agreement on all other questions of common interest."

The broadcast said the treaty and "other agreements" would be published shortly after they had been ratified by the two countries.

These are the first fruits of the talks that have been proceeding in

Continued on Page 6, Column 3

World News Summarized

WEDNESDAY, AUGUST 15, 1945

World War II became a page in history last night.

President Truman announced at 7 P. M. that he had received the Japanese reply to the Allied note of last Saturday and that he deemed it full acceptance of the Potsdam declaration of July 26. The Chief Executive said that the Japanese surrender would be made to Gen. Douglas MacArthur in his capacity as Supreme Allied Commander in Chief. Allied military commanders were ordered to stop fighting, but the proclamation of V-J Day will await the signing of the peace treaties. [1:7-8.]

Simultaneously with the President's announcement, Admiral Nimitz flashed "cease fire" orders to all units under his command. [8:3-4.]

The official announcement that the Japanese sneak attack on Pearl Harbor had resulted three years and 250 days later in the inglorious end of the Japanese Empire touched off unrestrained celebrations throughout the Allied world. Here in New York the flash on the moving electric sign on the Times Tower, "Official—Truman announces Japanese surrender," signaled a wild demonstration. [1:3.]

Emperor Hirohito announced the Japanese surrender to his people in his first broadcast to the nation. Weeping Japanese gathered outside the Emperor's palace to bow to the ground in their shame because their "efforts were not enough." [3:2.]

The fury of Allied military might continued to strike the Japanese up to the very last. Even as the Tokyo radio announced that the Japanese reply to the Allied note of Saturday was on its way, our Superfortresses were winging from the Marianas to the Japanese homeland. More than 1,000 planes struck Honshu with 6,000 tons of bombs in a fourteen-hour assault ending early yesterday. [8:1.]

In the midst of rejoicing it was disclosed that the heavy cruiser Indianapolis had been sunk, presumably by an enemy submarine, shortly after she had delivered an atomic bomb cargo to Guam. All men aboard were casualties. [1:6-7.]

The Red Army unleashed fierce new attacks. Russian armored forces raced ninety-three miles unchecked across western Manchuria toward Harbin and other Soviet columns scored new gains all along the 2,300-mile front. [8:6; Pacific area map P. 8.]

The Soviet Union signed "a treaty of friendship and alliance" with China after an agreement had been reached between the two nations on all questions of common interest. [1:6.]

Chinese Communists informed the Generalissimo that they refused to accept his command to remain at their posts. [6:1.]

A French jury sentenced Marshal Pétain to death. [1:4.]

Two-Day Holiday Is Proclaimed; Stores, Banks Close Here Today

By The Associated Press.

WASHINGTON, Aug. 14—Tomorrow and Thursday are days off for Government workers and holidays for pay purposes for workers in general.

And V-J Day, when it comes, will be a premium pay day, too.

President Truman announced both rulings tonight.

He directed agency heads throughout the Government to cut their forces down to a bare skeleton staff Aug. 15 and 16 and not to charge the two days against the employes' annual leave. He said it was in "inadequate" recognition of the four-year efforts on "one of the hardest working groups of war workers."

For other workers under wage control, Wednesday and Thursday count like Christmas and the few other accepted holidays for purposes of overtime pay and in figuring the number of days worked in a week. Many employers already have obtained approval for regular time pay to workers who take the day off.

Postal service for the next two days will "approximate holiday service," the Postoffice Department said.

Local postmasters will have wide discretion in carrying out the President's wishes, it was indicated, and those postal employes required to work tomorrow and next day will have compensating time off at a later date.

It was presumed, but not specifically stated, that Government workers generally will be off on V-J Day, too.

The White House said that the next two days are to be regarded as legal holidays.

Preston Delano, Controller of the

Continued on Page 6, Column 7

Cruiser Sunk, 1,196 Casualties; Took Atom Bomb Cargo to Guam

Special to THE NEW YORK TIMES.

WASHINGTON, Aug. 14—The American heavy cruiser Indianapolis was sunk by enemy action in the Philippine Sea with 1,196 casualties, every man aboard, the Navy announced today.

The 9,950-ton ship left San Francisco on July 16 on a special, high-speed run to deliver essential atomic bomb materials to Guam. The cargo was delivered. The cruiser was lost after having left Guam.

The sinking, which took one of the Navy's heaviest tolls of lives since Pearl Harbor, was disclosed a few minutes before President Truman announced Japan's surrender.

Casualties included five Navy dead, including one officer; 845 Navy missing, including sixty-three officers; 307 Navy wounded, including fifteen officers; thirty Marine missing, including two officers, and nine enlisted Marine wounded. Next of kin have been notified.

The skipper, Capt. Charles B. McVay 3d, 47, of Washington, was wounded.

The Navy Department also reported for the first time that in a previous action on March 31 the Indianapolis, flagship of the Fifth Fleet, was damaged by a suicide plane off Okinawa. She had been at the Mare Island, Calif., Navy

Continued on Page 10, Column 6

YIELDING UNQUALIFIED, TRUMAN SAYS

Japan Is Told to Order End of Hostilities, Notify Allied Supreme Commander and Send Emissaries to Him

MACARTHUR TO RECEIVE SURRENDER

Formal Proclamation of V-J Day Awaits Signing of Those Articles—Cease-Fire Order Given to the Allied Forces

By ARTHUR KROCK

Special to THE NEW YORK TIMES.

WASHINGTON, Aug. 14—Japan today unconditionally surrendered the hemispheric empire taken by force and held almost intact for more than two years against the rising power of the United States and its Allies in the Pacific war.

The bloody dream of the Japanese military caste vanished in the text of a note to the Four Powers accepting the terms of the Potsdam Declaration of July 26, 1945, which amplified the Cairo Declaration of 1943.

Like the previous items in the surrender correspondence, today's Japanese document was forwarded through the Swiss Foreign Office at Berne and the Swiss Legation in Washington. The note of total capitulation was delivered to the State Department by the Legation Charge d'Affaires at 6:10 P. M., after the third and most anxious day of waiting on Tokyo, the anxiety intensified by several premature or false reports of the finale of World War II.

Orders Given to the Japanese

The Department responded with a note to Tokyo through the same channel, ordering the immediate end of hostilities by the Japanese, requiring that the Supreme Allied Commander—who, the President announced, will be Gen. Douglas MacArthur—be notified of the date and hour of the order, and instructing that emissaries of Japan be sent to him at once—at the time and place selected by him—"with full information of the disposition of the Japanese forces and commanders."

President Truman summoned a special press conference in the Executive offices at 7 P. M. He handed to the reporters three texts.

The first—the only one he read aloud—was that he had received the Japanese note and deemed it full acceptance of the Potsdam Declaration, containing no qualification whatsoever; that arrangements for the formal signing of the peace would be made for the "earliest possible moment;" that the Japanese surrender would be made to General MacArthur in his capacity as Supreme Allied Commander in Chief; that Allied military commanders had been instructed to cease hostilities, but that the formal proclamation of V-J Day must await the formal signing.

The text ended with the Japanese note, in which the Four Powers (the United States, Great Britain, China and Russia) were officially informed that the Emperor of Japan had issued an imperial rescript of surrender, was prepared to guarantee the necessary signatures to the terms as prescribed by the Allies, and had instructed all his commanders to cease active operations, to surrender all

Continued on Page 2, Column 3

MacArthur Begins Orders to Hirohito

By Wireless to THE NEW YORK TIMES.

MANILA, Wednesday, Aug. 15—Gen. Douglas MacArthur in his first action as Allied Supreme Commander today directed Emperor Hirohito and the Japanese Government to furnish a radio station in the Tokyo area for "continuous use in handling radio communications between this headquarters and your headquarters." The message, sent in the clear, called for "the earliest practicable" arrangements to end hostilities.

Hirohito on Radio; Minister Ends Life

The Japanese Domei agency said at 11 o'clock last night that Emperor Hirohito had been "graciously pleased to personally read an imperial rescript accepting the Potsdam declaration."

The Domei English-language wireless dispatch, directed to the United States and recorded by the Federal Communications Commission, said that the Emperor had read the rescript over a nation-wide broadcast at noon Wednesday, Tokyo time.

Previously Domei had reported that weeping people had gathered before the Imperial Palace and "bowed to the very ground" in shame.

Japanese War Minister Korechika Anami committed suicide, Domei reported this morning. The wireless dispatch, directed to the American zone, said Anami had taken his life at his "official residence" to "atone for his failure in accomplishing his duties as His Majesty's Minister."

A complete story appears on Page 3.

"All the News That's Fit to Print"

The New York Times.

LATE CITY EDITION
Clearing early today; cooler. Clear and cool tomorrow.
Temperatures Yesterday—Max., 88; Min., 72
Sunrise today, 6:23 A. M.; Sunset, 7:28 P. M.

Section 1

NEWS INDEX, PAGE 33, THIS SECTION

Copyright, 1945, by The New York Times Company.

VOL. XCIV..No. 31,998. Entered as Second-Class Matter, Postoffice, New York, N. Y. NEW YORK, SUNDAY, SEPTEMBER 2, 1945. Including Magazine and Book Review. TEN CENTS New York City and Suburban Areas (15c Elsewhere)

JAPAN SURRENDERS TO ALLIES, SIGNS RIGID TERMS ON WARSHIP; TRUMAN SETS TODAY AS V-J DAY

HOLIDAY TRAFFIC NEAR 1941 LEVEL; 'GAS' IS PLENTIFUL

Exodus From City Is Greatest Since Pre-War Days but Congestion Is Avoided

GOOD WEATHER PROMISED

Near-by Resorts Do Capacity Business—3 Persons Die in Queens Accidents

America's millions, deprived since 1941 of the chance to cruise the highways of their nation, hit the road in traditional Labor Day week-end style yesterday.

There was a plentiful supply of gasoline, the sun shone warm out of blue skies, and everyone felt free from war worries. This combined to roll up traffic that continued heavy all day.

New York City's heat-ridden population took to car, train, bus and plane. The exodus to near-by mountain and seashore resorts was the greatest since that of 1941.

The weather formed a perfect lure. Not even the thunder showers predicted by the Weather Bureau for late afternoon took place. Today's prediction is for clearing weather early, followed by cooler, with the highest temperature around 80 degrees, and with fresh to strong northwest winds. A clear and cool Monday is forecast by the bureau. The temperature yesterday reached 88 degrees at 3:30 P. M. with the humidity at 52 per cent. The all-time high for the date was set in 1924 with 92.5 degrees and the low in 1872 with 51.

Many Cars Come Into City

Travel in the city was two-way. As cars streamed out of the city over bridges, on ferries and through tunnels, out-of-towners poured in. The main idea for Labor Day seemed to be change of scenery.

Thousands of automobiles, many of them looking as though they had just been taken off the jacks for the first time in years, formed a continuous procession along the main highways leading up-State, out on Long Island and to the South Jersey shore.

The Port of New York Authority reported that 69,400 automobiles had crossed the George Washington Bridge into New Jersey. Forty-five thousand cars passed through the Holland Tunnel during the sixteen hours preceding 6 o'clock last night. Lincoln Tunnel police said traffic was heavier than usual.

Few serious accidents were reported. "Maybe it's because the cars just don't have the pep," remarked a Westchester County parkway policeman.

Sights along the parkways bore out his contention. Many cars became pathetically silent as their drivers resignedly hauled them over to the side of the road to patch up tires or to fume over engine repairs.

Gasoline Supplies Abundant

Assured of as much gasoline as they wanted, motorists traveled leisurely and did not cause congestion. Filling station pumps received their heaviest workout in years. Station operators estimated that demands for gasoline ranged from 10 to 20 per cent over last week-end, but they reported there was no difficulty in obtaining supplies.

The Cities Service Oil Company said it was having difficulty in meeting orders for premium gasoline, ordinarily accounting for 25 per cent of sales, as the supply was limited, but no company reported shortages of non-premium gasoline. No motorist was forced to stay in town because of lack of fuel.

Trains, buses and airlines were crowded, as they have been all through the war. The airlines re-

Continued on Page 30, Column 2

Times Sq. Takes V-J News Quietly

Times Square throngs, which had greeted Japanese capitulation explosively last month, took the formal signing of terms in much calmer fashion last night.

Two hundred policemen, including twenty-five mounted patrolmen, who had been assigned to the area in case of another outburst of feeling, reported that the street crowds took the flashing of the bulletin from Times Tower at 10:04 P. M. with a few cheers and good-natured remarks, and did not attempt to start a celebration.

In numbers the crowd was no larger than an average Saturday night, and of the persons present perhaps half or more were out-of-town visitors here for the Labor Day week-end, the police estimated. Other parts of the city were similarly quiet.

Mayor La Guardia had said earlier that the people "have had their big time and are satisfied." He decided not to hold a celebration in Central Park today as had been planned.

PRESIDENT STRESSES LABOR DAY OF PEACE

But He Warns That After Six Holidays of Hostilities Great New Problems Lie Ahead

Special to The New York Times.

WASHINGTON, Sept. 1—President Truman hailed the first Labor Day of peace in six years today and declared a grateful world would always remember the workers of all free nations for their contribution to victory.

Secretary Forrestal and J. A. Krug, chairman of the War Production Board, also lauded the men and women of labor, and Philip Murray, chairman of the Congress of Industrial Organizations, told a radio audience that America's vast war plant must be put to work on peacetime products which would give prosperity unlimited to this country.

Mr. Truman's statement said that six years ago today the workers of the United States, and of the world, awoke to a Labor Day in a world at war, and added:

"We in the United States had two years of grace, but the issue was squarely joined at that hour, as we now know. There was to be no peace until tyranny had been outlawed.

"Today we stand on the threshold of a new world. We must do our part in making this world what it should be, a world in which the bigotries of race and class and creed shall not be permitted to warp the souls of men.

"We enter upon an era of great problems, but to live is to face problems. Our men and women did not falter in the task of saving freedom. They will not falter now in the task of making freedom

Continued on Page 24, Column 3

HAILS ERA OF PEACE

President Calls On U.S. to Stride On Toward a World of Good-Will

SALUTES HEROIC DEAD

Cautions Jubilant Nation Hard Jobs Ahead Need Same Zeal as War

Text of the President's address proclaiming V-J Day, P. 4.

By WILLIAM S. WHITE

Special to The New York Times.

WASHINGTON, Sept. 1—President Truman, in remembrance of all who have fallen and in an appeal to all Americans to go forward now in hope and fraternity toward "a new and better world of peace and international good-will," tonight solemnly proclaimed tomorrow to be V-J Day.

The moment that he began to speak was, in the official and historical sense, the first moment of peace this country had known since a December day nearly four years ago, when, at a sudden, a harsh and an incredible blow the whole of the Pacific world went into flames.

Into the human calendar of great American holidays, like the Fourth of July and the Eleventh of November, the President thus entered another date, the Second of September, although it does not technically signify the end of the "duration" and will have no basis as a legal end of the war. The termination of hostilities, for purposes of computing military service, for setting the limit to war agencies and for all other like formalities, will be set only by final decision of Congress.

Japanese Surrender Signaled

But Mr. Truman's speech was a speech to the heart of a country that had had the skill to make the atomic bomb and could now "use the same skill and energy and determination to overcome all the difficulties ahead," rather than to the keepers of its books of law.

It was notice from the White House, so long awaited, that nearly four years of war, a struggle of sacrificial grandeur such as the United States had never known, had at last come to an end, and that the terrible ledger opened at Pearl Harbor had now been balanced and closed.

The President spoke in this mood, a mood of valedictory and of dedication, as he proclaimed "this . . . victory of more than arms alone . . . this . . . victory of liberty over tyranny." He had just received the signal from across the world that the Japanese had signed, aboard the great battleship Missouri, the last, humiliat-

Continued on Page 4, Column 1

JAPANESE FOREIGN MINISTER SIGNING SURRENDER ARTICLES

Mamoru Shigemitsu (right, seated), on behalf of Emperor Hirohito, affixes his signature to document as Gen. Douglas MacArthur (left) and Lieut. Gen. Richard K. Sutherland (center) look on during ceremony aboard the Missouri in Tokyo Bay.

Associated Press Wirephoto (via Navy Radio from U. S. S. Iowa)

BYRNES FORESEES A PEACEFUL JAPAN

Says People Are Expected to Force Development—World Amity Vital, Hull Warns

Special to The New York Times.

WASHINGTON, Sept. 1—Secretary of State James F. Byrnes declared tonight that with Japan's surrender we have entered the second phase of our war—"what might be called the spiritual disarmament of that nation, to make them want peace instead of wanting war."

The intention of this Govern-

Continued on Page 5, Column 1

Japan's Surrender Ordered Over Militarist Opposition

By FRANK L. KLUCKHOHN

By Wireless to The New York Times.

TOKYO, Sept. 1—In the rubble of this once-proud imperial capital the story of how the Japanese Army opposed the surrender and how the Emperor made the final decision to capitulate after having heard the opinions of all his advisers, and how War Minister Korechika Anami had committed suicide was unfolded today by one of a handful of those in a position to know without bias what occurred.

It was also learned how the Japanese reacted step by step to wartime developments and how propaganda that Japan could win had been continued to the last moment, thus leaving the industrious long-

Continued on Page 7, Column 1

TOKYO AIDES WEEP AS GENERAL SIGNS

Imperial Staff Chief Hastily Scrawls His Signature—Shigemitsu Is Anxious

By The Associated Press.

ABOARD U. S. S. MISSOURI in Tokyo Bay, Sunday, Sept. 2—The solemn surrender ceremony, on this battleship today, marking the first defeat in Japan's 2,600-year-old semi-legendary history, required only a few minutes as twelve signatures were affixed to the articles.

Surrounded by the might of the United States Navy and Army, and under the eyes of the American and British commanders they so ruthlessly defeated in the Philippines and Malaya, the Japanese representatives quietly made the marks on paper that ended the bloody Pacific conflict.

The Japanese delegation came aboard at 8:55 A. M., 7:55 P. M. Saturday, E. W. T., as scheduled. They reached the Missouri in personnel speed boats flying the American flag.

Foreign Minister Mamoru Shigemitsu led the delegation. He climbed stiffly up the ladder and limped forward on his right leg, which is artificial. He was wounded by a bomb tossed by a Korean terrorist in Shanghai many years ago.

On behalf of Emperor Hirohito, Mr. Shigemitsu signed first for

Continued on Page 9, Column 1

U. S. CHIEFS DIVIDED ON ITALY'S COLONIES

State Department Split Over Russia and Influence Zones Is Projected by Issue

By JAMES B. RESTON

Special to The New York Times.

WASHINGTON, Sept. 1—A fundamental issue has developed in the Department of State over the future of the Italian colonies, particularly Eritrea, Libya and Italian Somaliland.

The issue is whether these colonies should go back to Italy as part of her sovereign territory, be taken from her and administered by the United States, Britain, France and the Soviet Union under the United Nations Organization or be administered by a neutral international commission under the United Nations.

The major powers that defeated Germany are soon to start draft-

Continued on Page 15, Column 1

World News Summarized

SUNDAY, SEPTEMBER 2, 1945

The rulers of Japan, who set the Pacific ablaze nearly four years ago with their surprise attack on Pearl Harbor and hoped to culminate that assault with a peace dictated in the White House, formally signed their unconditional surrender to the Allied powers in Tokyo Bay. Foreign Minister Shigemitsu signed the historic document for his country in the shadow of the sixteen-inch gun muzzles of the battleship Missouri. General MacArthur, who signed in behalf of the Allies, said mankind hoped a better world would result from the solemn occasion. [1:8; map P. 12.]

President Truman proclaimed today as V-J Day. He urged the nation to observe the day of victory over Japan in a spirit of dedication and as a symbol of "victory of liberty over tyranny." He also asked his countrymen to remember "our departed gallant leader, Franklin D. Roosevelt." [1:3.]

Japan's decision to surrender was dictated by Emperor Hirohito after he had overruled a strong faction within the Cabinet and the army that wanted to keep on with the war in the belief that the Japanese could defeat an invasion of the homeland, according to well-informed observers in Tokyo. [1:5-6.]

Medical "experiments" recalling medieval sadism were carried out on dying American prisoners of war by young Japanese Army doctors, two American physicians interned with their compatriots said aboard a United States hospital ship. [1:6-7.]

With the Foreign Ministers' Council scheduled to meet in London next week to begin consideration of peace terms, it was learned that a serious division of opinion over the disposition of the Italian colonies had developed in the State Department. [1:6.]

Former Secretary of State Stettinius said in London that the development of the atomic bomb emphasized the need for "the speedy creation of the United Nations Organization to keep the peace of the world" and predicted that as soon as the organization began functioning it would appoint a military staff to deal with the use of atomic bombs, as well as all other types of force in preserving peace. [18:2.]

"ALL THE NEWS THAT'S FIT TO PRINT"

In the first eight months of this year, The Times published 6,092 more columns of news than any other newspaper. With World Peace still to be won, and reconversion a topic of daily import, The New York Times continues to print the complete news.

Public Gets Big Army Food Stocks; Whipping Cream Is Freed of Bans

Special to The New York Times.

WASHINGTON, Sept. 1—The national food situation continued its steady improvement today as the Department of Agriculture, with four orders, increased the supplies of butter, canned salmon and ice cream and signalled the return of whipping cream.

This action was a direct consequence of the sharp reduction of military requirements of these foods. With the discontinuance of butter purchases by the armed forces, the Department explained, it is now possible to revoke the limitations on the sale of heavy cream and the use of butter fat in the production of all frozen desserts. Both these rulings will make whipping cream and ice cream of a higher butter fat content readily available.

In a simultaneous direction, the agency ordered released for civilian use all butter currently held by creameries and receivers for the armed forces and other Government buyers. Although as much as 20,000,000 pounds of butter may be returned to civilian consumers under this ruling, ration values will not be changed, it was indicated.

"At the time ration point values were established for September, the Office of Price Administration recognized the possibility of these

Continued on Page 33, Column 1

Enemy Tortured Dying Americans With Sadist Medical 'Experiments'

By ROBERT TRUMBULL

By Wireless to The New York Times.

ABOARD THE HOSPITAL SHIP BENEVOLENCE, in Tokyo Bay, Sept. 1 — Seriously ailing American prisoners at Shinagawa, the only hospital serving 8,000 prisoners of war held in the Tokyo area, were guinea pigs for fantastic experiments recalling the sorcery and sadism of the middle ages, Drs. Mack L. Gottlieb and Harold W. Keschner, both of New York, told this correspondent today.

Both doctors are recuperating aboard this ship after their rescue from Shinagawa on Wednesday by a special Navy evacuation mission headed by Comdr. Harold A. Stassen, former Governor of Minnesota and now Assistant Chief of Staff and Flag Secretary to Admiral William F. Halsey, commander of the Third Fleet.

[In an interview in Tokyo the Japanese Army doctor to whom some of these practices were charged confirmed the cruel treatment of American prisoners.]

Dr. Gottlieb, who had his home and office at 307 East Forty-fourth Street, was a Naval officer captured at Guam. Dr. Keschner, of 451 West End Avenue, was taken with an Army force in the Philippines. Both are in good physical

Continued on Page 14, Column 1

WAR COMES TO END

Articles of Capitulation Endorsed by Countries in Pacific Conflict

M'ARTHUR SEES PEACE

Emperor Orders Subjects to Obey All Commands Issued by General

The texts of the surrender documents and statements, P. 3.

By The Associated Press.

ABOARD THE U. S. S. MISSOURI in Tokyo Bay, Sunday, Sept. 2—Japan surrendered formally and unconditionally to the Allies today in a twenty-minute ceremony which ended just as the sun burst through low-hanging clouds as a shining symbol to a ravaged world now done with war.

[A United Press dispatch said the leading Japanese delegate signed the articles at 9:03 A. M. Sunday, Tokyo time, and that General MacArthur signed them at 9:07 A. M.]

Twelve signatures, requiring only a few minutes to inscribe on the articles of surrender, ended the bloody Pacific conflict.

On behalf of Emperor Hirohito, Foreign Minister Mamoru Shigemitsu signed for the Government and Gen. Yoshijiro Umezu for the Imperial General Staff.

MacArthur Voices Peace Hope

Gen. Douglas MacArthur then accepted in behalf of the United Nations, declaring:

"It is my earnest hope and indeed the hope of all mankind that from this solemn occasion a better world shall emerge out of the blood and carnage of the past."

One by one the Allied representatives stepped forward and signed the document that blighted Japan's dream of empire built on bloodshed and tyranny.

First was Admiral Chester W. Nimitz for the United States, then the representatives of China, the United Kingdom, the Soviet, Australia, Canada, France, the Netherlands and New Zealand.

The flags of the United States, Britain, the Soviet and China fluttered from the veranda deck of the famed superdreadnaught, polished and scrubbed as never before. More than 100 high-ranking military and naval officers watched.

Pledges Justice and Tolerance

"As Supreme Commander for the Allied powers," General MacArthur told the Japanese, "I announce it my firm purpose, in the tradition of the countries I represent, to proceed in the discharge of my responsibilities with justice and tolerance, while taking all necessary dispositions to insure that the terms of surrender are fully, promptly and faithfully complied with."

All through this dramatic half hour, only those aboard the battleship knew of what was taking place, because the Missouri has no broadcasting facilities.

But recordings were rushed to the near-by communications ship Ancon, and the solemn words of General MacArthur beginning the ceremony—"We are gathered here, representatives of the major warring powers"—were flashed around the world.

The Japanese representatives were present at the command of Emperor Hirohito contained in a proclamation issued by order of the Supreme Allied Commander.

The Emperor further commanded his officials "to issue general orders to the military and naval forces in accordance with the direction of the Supreme Commander

Continued on Page 2, Column 3

1945

Postwar Struggles

1953

FRONT PAGE NEWS 1945-1953

United Nations Opens

JANUARY 11, 1946

The new United Nations was, James Reston wrote in The Times, "another chapter in man's melancholy search for peace and security." But it was a chapter the U.S. was intent on writing, and before long, the U.N.'s home would be in New York, on a striking modern campus on Manhattan's East River. The U.S. also shouldered the largest share of U.N. dues, though in the 1980s Washington registered disapproval with some U.N. policies by withholding the money—more than $140 million in all. But President Ronald Reagan changed his mind shortly before he left office, and arranged to pay up.

The 'Iron Curtain' Descends

MARCH 6, 1946

Winston Churchill gave a name to the Soviet domination of Eastern Europe that so worried the west, declaring that an "iron curtain" had descended from the Baltic to the Adriatic. With President Harry S. Truman on the dais at a small college in Missouri, Churchill said, "This is certainly not the liberated Europe we fought to build up. Nor is it one which contains the essentials of permanent peace." Within a year, the Truman Doctrine, aimed at "containing" Communism, was U.S. policy.

Verdicts at Nuremberg

OCTOBER 2, 1946

The chief American prosecutor at the Nuremberg war-crimes trials, Supreme Court Justice Robert H. Jackson, made a novel legal argument: Germany had waged an illegal war of aggression, making the Nazi leaders guilty of "crimes against peace" as well as crimes against humanity. Of the defendants, Hermann Göring, who had been Hitler's second in command, and Joachim von Ribbentrop were to be hanged in two weeks. Göring committed suicide in prison first. Rudolf Hess, a former deputy Fuhrer who was sentenced to life in prison, strangled himself with an electrical cord in 1987.

India, Pakistan Win Fredom

JUNE 4, 1947

Under a partition plan formulated by Lord Mountbatten, the colony that London considered the jewel of the British Empire was split into two independent nations, India (where Jawaharal Nehru became the first prime minister) and Pakistan (under Ali Jinnah as the first governor-general). Mountbatten hoped the division would avert civil war, but the new boundaries did not mollify Hindus, Sikhs and Muslims. Violence erupted and spread widely as Hindus and Sikhs forced Muslims out of India and Muslims forced Hindus and Sikhs out of Pakistan. By the time the United Nations arranged a cease-fire in 1948, more than 10 million uprooted refugees had fled in what amounted to a forced exchange of populations.

The Marshall Plan

JUNE 6, 1947

Still too devastated to rebuild itself, Europe was floundering amid what Secretary of State George C. Marshall described as "hunger, poverty, desperation and chaos." So the U.S. offered, in effect, to finance the recovery with billions of American dollars and as much behind-the-scenes expertise as it could muster. The Marshall Plan promised money for allies and former enemies alike, but there were strings attached: the U.S. tied its billions to the principles of democracy and, at least by implication, to the containment of Communism. In four years, the U.S. spent more than $12 billion on the Marshall Plan; the gross national product of western European nations rose at least 15 percent beyond the prewar total.

State of Israel Proclaimed

MAY 15, 1948

The United Nations had cleared the way to establish Israel as the Jewish state in 1947 when it approved dividing the British colony of Palestine into separate Jewish and Arab territories. That was a triumph for Zionists like David Ben-Gurion, who became Israel's first prime minister. But the partition provoked the Arab League into war, and it went on the offensive as soon as British control ended. The fighting—interrupted by two short cease-fires—continued until 1949, when a U.N.-brokered settlement gave Israel the territory it had won, including Galilee and the Negev desert.

Breaking the Sound Barrier

JUNE 11, 1948

In the cockpit, Air Force Captain Chuck Yeager watched the gauge that showed how fast his rocket-powered plane was streaking through the atmosphere seven and a half miles above the earth—0.83, 0.88, 0.92. And that was with only two of the four burners going. Yeager fired a third burner, and the needle jumped to 0.98. Then, at 43,000 feet, it nudged past Mach 1—the fastest it could measure. Yeager had broken the sound barrier, and then some. His top speed was Mach 1.06, about 700 miles an hour. Yeager's fame, eclipsed when other test pilots were chosen for the space program (he was out of the running because he lacked a college degree), was revived in the 1980s by Tom Wolfe's bestseller, "The Right Stuff."

Truman Orders Military Integrated

JULY 27, 1948

President Harry S. Truman's executive order to desegregate the armed forces came two weeks after a floor fight at the 1948 Democratic National Convention and two years after an Army commission had recommended it. At the convention, Truman had favored a go-slow approach that appeased Southerners, but convention delegates voted it down in favor of a platform plank that called for rapid desegregation. Truman went back to the White House and issued the order; by the end of the Korean War in 1953, 95 percent of black soldiers were assigned to integrated units.

Truman Launches 'Fair Deal'

January 21, 1949

"Every segment of our population and every individual has a right to expect from our government a fair deal," President Harry S. Truman declared in his inaugural address. To provide it, he proposed what amounted to an extension of President Franklin D. Roosevelt's New Deal, withr federal aid to education, federal medical insurance and federal civil rights protection. Truman also looked abroad, denouncing Communism and outlining a four-point plan for U.S. leadership in world affairs. But with Congress controlled by southern Democrats, his domestic agenda languished.

Berlin Blockade Ends

May 5, 1949

In mid-1948, Stalin cut the access routes to West Berlin, at least by land and sea. But he did not control the skies, and the Berlin Airlift ferried more than two million tons of supplies, from ammunitions for allied military units to food, medicine and other civilian essentials. The airlift was, The Times observed, the West's most decisive victory in the struggle for divided Germany, and after 320 days, Stalin called off the blockade. But East Germany remained a Moscow satellite for four more decades.

Russia Explodes an A-Bomb

September 24, 1949

President Harry S. Truman delivered the news after his weekly cabinet meeting: "We have evidence that within recent weeks an atomic explosion occurred in the U.S.S.R." Secretary of State Dean Acheson said he assumed the blast meant the Russians had built an actual atomic bomb. But he and the chairman of the joint chiefs of staff, General Omar N. Bradley, said there was no need to revise U.S. strategy. "We have anticipated it for four years"—ever since Hiroshima—"and it calls for no change in our basic defense plan," General Bradley said.

Truman Authorizes Hydrogen Bomb

February 1, 1950

As the cold war deepened and the Pentagon fretted about losing military superiority to the Soviets, President Harry S. Truman ordered a crash program to manufacture a hydrogen bomb. He said the weapon, a thousand times more powerful than the atomic bombs that had decimated Hiroshima and Nagasaki, would bolster national security. But first it had to be designed and built, a tall order for the U.S., which had done only limited theoretical work on such weapons since World War II. Still, within a year, two physicists, Edward Teller and Stanislaw Ulam, had completed the first workable design. The bomb was detonated in 1952 in a test at Eniwetok Atoll in the Pacific.

Korean War Begins

June 28, 1950

Russian-made tanks rumbled across the 38th parallel, leaving their positions in Communist North Korea for the non-Communist South, from which U.S. forces had withdrawn less than a year before. Now President Harry S. Truman ordered U.S. air and navy units back, this time under General Douglas MacArthur as head of a 16-nation United Nations force. Their mission was to stop Kim Il Sung, who, with heavy support from the Soviet Union, aimed to seize the south and unify the two countries under its control.

Truman Fires MacArthur

April 11, 1951

After hundreds of thousands of Chinese troops joined the fighting in North Korea, forcing the allied force into retreat at the Yalu River and recapturing Pyongyang, President Harry Truman worried that the Korean conflict would widen into a world war. Truman had been preparing to announce that the United Nations was ready to discuss conditions for settlement in Korea when General Douglas MacArthur issued a statement calling for an "expansion of our military operations"—he wanted to bomb supply areas across the border in China. The risk of war with Peking was obvious, so Truman promptly relieved MacArthur of his command, a decision that cost Truman in the public opinion polls. MacArthur came home for the first time since World War II and told a joint session of Congress, "Old soldiers never die—they just fade away."

C.I.A. Coup in Iran

March 1, 1953

Premier Mohammed Mossadegh was deposed in a coup orchestrated by the C.I.A., whose director, Allen Dulles, was the brother of John Foster Dulles, the secretary of state. Washington, allied with the British, worried that Mossadegh would seize control of the British-owned Anglo-Iranian Oil Company and deliver Iran to the communists. C.I.A. operatives organized a revolt that drove Mossadegh to flee, brought Shah Mohammed Reza Pahlavi back from exile in Rome and planted the seeds of anti-American anger.

"All the News That's Fit to Print"

The New York Times.

LATE CITY EDITION
Sunny with moderate temperatures today. Tomorrow cloudy.
Temperatures Yesterday—Max., 52; Min., 42
Sunrise today, 7:20 A. M.; Sunset, 4:48 P. M.
Full U. S. Weather Bureau Report Page 37.

VOL. XCV...No. 32,129. Entered as Second-Class Matter, Postoffice, New York, N. Y. NEW YORK, FRIDAY, JANUARY 11, 1946. THREE CENTS IN NEW YORK CITY

UNO OPENED; ATTLEE ASKS WORLD UNITY

SPAAK IS ELECTED

Belgian Is President of the General Assembly After Floor Fight

SOVIET LEADS OPPOSITION

U.S. Votes on Russian Side for Norwegian—Session Contrasts With League Meeting in 1920

Addresses at the opening of the UNO in London, Page 3.

By JAMES B. RESTON
By Cable to THE NEW YORK TIMES.

LONDON, Jan. 10—The fifty-one nations of the greatest war-time coalition in history, representing four-fifths of the people in the world, started today another chapter in man's melancholy search for peace and security.

One hundred and forty-seven days after the close of the war that cost more than 20,000,000 casualties and left countless millions homeless and on the twenty-sixth anniversary of the ratification of the ill-fated League of Nations Covenant, the nations met this afternoon in the blue and gold auditorium of the Central Hall of Westminster for the first meeting of the United Nations General Assembly.

Greeting them on behalf of Britain, which served as the springboard for the final conquest of Germany, Prime Minister Attlee told them frankly that they would succeed in their new venture only if they brought "the same sense of urgency, the same self-sacrifice and the same willingness to subordinate sectional interests" with which they fought the war.

Spaak Elected President

Then, with a little less dignity than marks the balloting at a political convention at home, they proceeded to elect Paul-Henri Spaak, Belgian Foreign Minister, as President of the first General Assembly, despite a determined effort by the Soviet Union to replace him with the Norwegian Foreign Minister, Trygve Lie.

This election produced the only extraordinary incident of the day. When Dr. Eduardo Zuleta Angel of Colombia, chairman of the UNO Preparatory Commission and temporary president of the General Assembly, announced the balloting for the Presidency, the deputy chairman of the Soviet delegation, Andrei Gromyko, Russian Ambassador to Washington, asked to be recognized and strode to the microphone on the improvised modernistic blue and gold stage.

It was known at this point that the candidacy of M. Spaak would win, but Mr. Gromyko, assured that he was supported by the United States, told the General Assembly that his delegation attached great importance to the election and favored the Norwegian Foreign Minister because of his personal capacities and the active movements of his country in the war.

Pole and Ukrainian Back Lie

As soon as Mr. Gromyko had left the rostrum, Foreign Minister Wincenty Rzymowski of Poland asked to be recognized and he then seconded the Russian nomination. When he had finished, D. Z. Manuilsky, the Ukrainian People's Commissar for Foreign Affairs, a striking, white-maned figure with a booming voice, moved that Dr. Lie be elected by acclamation despite the fact that the rules of the Assembly call for elections by secret ballot.

After another short speech for Dr. Lie by Gustav Rasmussen, Danish Foreign Minister, the temporary president called for a vote on whether to decide the issue by secret ballot, but immediately Mr. Gromyko rose again and asked for a vote on the motion to elect Dr. Lie by acclamation.

Some confusion attended those motions during which Mr. Manuilsky voted both for the secret ballot and for the election of Dr. Lie by acclamation, but finally fifteen delegations voted for a secret ballot and only nine voted in favor of putting Dr. Lie in by acclaim. The

Continued on Page 3, Column 2

Delegates Welcome Copies of The Times

By Wireless to THE NEW YORK TIMES.

LONDON, Jan. 10—Copies of yesterday morning's issue of THE NEW YORK TIMES were distributed to delegates to the United Nations Organization's General Assembly this evening and they received an enthusiastic reception from all, particularly the American representatives.

"This is about as useful, informative and happy a thing as has happened to an exiled American in a long time," Adlai Stevenson said. He has been here for four months working on the establishment of the UNO.

King George will be among the recipients. Buckingham Palace officials said that he was very happy to have the paper.

Copies are being sent to prominent Britons, including former Foreign Secretary Anthony Eden, Prime Minister Attlee and leading members of the Cabinet, and to the heads of each of the fifty-one delegations to the Assembly. The papers are being flown across the Atlantic.

PRESS STILL BESET IN 'FREE' RUMANIA

Russian and Union Censors Bar Liberal Chief's Effort to Use Grant Given by Moscow

By SAM POPE BREWER
By Wireless to THE NEW YORK TIMES.

BUCHAREST, Rumania, Jan. 10—Even before United States Ambassador W. Averell Harriman took off for London at dawn today to report to Secretary of State James F. Byrnes at the United Nations Organization meeting on the Allied commission's work here, the great difficulty of getting a loyal execution of the Moscow communiqué's terms in this test case of Allied cooperation showed itself.

Though press freedom was promised and Rumanian censorship of the domestic press was officially dropped yesterday, first a Russian censor and then an unofficial typographical union censorship clamped down last night on an apparently inoffensive statement by Liberal Party Chief Constantin (Dinu) Bratianu on his party's conception of a "free press."

Mr. Harriman and Sir Archibald Clark Kerr, British Ambassador to Moscow, had a three-hour conversation last night with Premier Petru Groza in which the question of restoring the freedoms was discussed, among other things, but if the Premier's ideas on freedom are still the same as those expressed in the previous night's communiqué there is little likelihood that his "assurances" will be acceptable to the United States Government.

The outstanding flaw in M. Groza's statement was the assertion that the present Ministers of Justice, the Interior and Propaganda could be expected to protect such freedom, when it was under their aegis that flagrant abuses

Continued on Page 6, Column 2

CHIANG PROCLAIMS TRUCE AND REFORM AS COUNCIL BEGINS

Marshall Ends Deadlock With Early Meeting, Sends Word to Delegates' Session

TROOP MOVEMENT FROZEN

Civil Liberties, End of Police Abuses, Amnesty, New Voting Basis Promised China

Chiang's announcement of the truce appears on Page 10.

By TILLMAN DURDIN
By Wireless to THE NEW YORK TIMES.

CHUNGKING, Jan. 10—Only a few moments before President Chiang Kai-shek proclaimed a sweeping series of political and democratic reforms in China, a formal truce order, hammered out by Gen. George C. Marshall and representatives of the Chinese Government and the Chinese Communist party, brought a cease-fire order to the civil war fronts.

The agreement provided for an immediate halt to hostilities, full restoration of all war-blocked communications and the establishment of a control organization, with American participation, to supervise the carrying out of the armistice compact. The continued movement of Government forces in Manchuria and south of the Yangtze River is not prejudiced under the terms of the agreement.

This agreement highlighted a day of historic happenings in Chungking, all tied together with dramatic timing and with close political relationship.

Conference Assembles

The Political Consultation Conference, an assemblage of party leaders and non-party persons, dedicated to working out a program of political unity and democratization for China, met in its first session. The truce accord was reached after an emergency early morning meeting of the three negotiators just in time for President Chiang to reveal the agreement in his opening address to the conference.

In his speech President Chiang announced these far-reaching Government measures in the field of civil rights:

Steps to insure freedom of person, of conscience, of publication and of assembly.

Abrogation of secret police activity in assuring that rulings were being made under which only proper judicial and police authorities would be permitted to arrest, try or punish individuals.

Equality of "all legal parties before the law" and their right to open activity "within the law."

Release of all political prisoners "except traitors and those found to have committed definite acts injurious to the Republic."

Promotion of local self-government everywhere, with popular election to be held "according to law" and from "the lowest strata upward."

The supreme achievement of bringing at least an armistice and perhaps permanent peace to China came to fruition after a hitch in the discussion yesterday threatened to prolong if not seriously to endanger the negotiations. It is clear that the masterly mediation of General Marshall was a major factor in producing the final success.

Last night the three-man conference brought up a disagreement

Continued on Page 10, Column 2

Japanese Cabinet Has Resigned; Interest of Emperor Is Indicated

By Reuter.

TOKYO, Friday, Jan. 11—The Japanese Cabinet has resigned.

Japan's seven-day political crisis broke when ailing Prime Minister Baron Kijuro Shidehara, who is still confined to bed, informed the Cabinet through Foreign Minister Shigeru Yoshida that he had decided that the Cabinet should resign en masse as a result of General MacArthur's "political purge" directives of Jan. 4.

Mr. Yoshida, who earlier this morning called on the Emperor at the Royal Palace to inform him of the Premier's decision, is expected to make another call this afternoon, when it is believed that Hirohito will again give the resigning Baron Premier an imperial command to form a new Government.

The Premier's personal secretary stated that it would be several days yet before the Premier would be able to attend to state duties, but that the Cabinet would carry on in the meantime to give the Baron time to select a list of names of proposed new members to submit to General MacArthur's headquarters for approval.

By LINDESAY PARROTT
By Wireless to THE NEW YORK TIMES.

TOKYO, Jan. 10—Emperor Hirohito will take a hand to break the cabinet deadlock that has paralyzed Japan since General MacArthur's directive of Jan. 4 outlawed from public office all but two members of the Government of Baron Kijuro Shidehara, it was said in informed circles tonight.

Although the bulk of the Cabinet's members have been ordered ejected as members of former ultra-nationalist societies, it continues to cling tenaciously to its position. Faced with this situation, the Emperor, it is stated, will summon his personal advisers to ask them to find a solution, since the Japanese Government during the past week has, in effect, continued to func-

Continued on Page 10, Column 6

17.5% GM PAY RISE URGED BY BOARD; PHONE TIE-UP OFF UNTIL MONDAY; STEEL AND UNION PACT INDICATED

Appeal to Strikers By Union Leaders

Following is the text of the statement issued last night by the Association of Communication Equipment Workers asking its members to delay picketing until Monday:

"This is a special message to the members and officers of the Association of Communications Equipment Workers in all locals throughout the United States.

"Ernest Weaver, national president, and the bargaining committee composed of Messrs. Thornton, Massey and Barry request the officers to comply with a special request made by Secretary of Labor Schwellenbach not to establish picket lines at any location until Monday morning, Jan. 14.

"The Secretary of Labor has arranged a conference of the union and the company at 4 P. M., Friday, Jan. 11, in Washington, D. C. The members and officers of the ACEW are urged to comply with the request of the Secretary of Labor in consideration of the public, the long lines and other telephone workers. ACEW members will remain on strike."

PICKETING DELAYED

Union Calls on Locals to Change Plans After Schwellenbach Plea

PARLEY IN CAPITAL TODAY

Negotiations With Western Electric End Here After Rejection of Offer

By LAWRENCE RESNER

A postponement until Monday of picket lines that had threatened the disruption this morning of the nation's telephone service was ordered last night by leaders of striking telephone installation workers after a last minute appeal by Secretary of Labor Lewis B. Schwellenbach.

Despite this decision, which was announced at 11:20 P. M. by Ernest Weaver, president of the Association of Communications Equipment Workers, a certain amount of difficulty was anticipated in reaching all locals of the union to prevent all picketing.

To expedite a widespread announcement of the order, Mr. Weaver enlisted the aid of the nation's press and radio to publish and broadcast a message to the members of his union to delay action pending results of conferences with Secretary Schwellenbach scheduled to start at 4 P. M. today in Washington.

Leaders Urged to Comply

This message urged the members and officers of the ACEW "to comply with the request of the Secretary of Labor in consideration of the public, the long lines and other telephone workers."

Officials of Western Electric, against whom the installation workers' strike is directed, also agreed to join in the discussions

Continued on Page 13, Column 2

GOVERNMENT TO USE ALUMINUM PATENTS

Alcoa Cedes Rights to RFC for Licensing to Reynolds Metals, Leasing Federal Plants

By WALTER H. WAGGONER
Special to THE NEW YORK TIMES.

WASHINGTON, Jan. 10—The Aluminum Company of America agreed today to grant the Government free use of its patents for the production of aluminum together with the right to license them to its competitors acquiring Government-owned plants.

The decision by the country's

Continued on page 15, Column 5

World News Summarized

FRIDAY, JANUARY 11, 1946

Fifty-one nations met in the first General Assembly of the UNO in London, yesterday, and heard Dr. Eduardo Zuleta Angel of Colombia, temporary president, and Prime Minister Attlee plead for international unity. Paul-Henri Spaak, Belgian Foreign Minister, was elected President of the Assembly. The only incident arose when Soviet delegate Gromyko unexpectedly sought the election by acclamation of Norway's Foreign Minister Lie, but M. Spaak, backed by Britain, won on a secret ballot, 28 to 23. [1:1.]

Canada, Brazil and Poland are slated for two-year terms as non-permanent members of the Security Council, and the Netherlands, Mexico and Egypt for one-year terms. [3:1.]

The UNO Site Committee listened to a broadcast of the London proceedings in the library of the home of President Roosevelt. The members were impressed with Hyde Park. [2:6.]

Despite the Moscow parley's free press demand the Russian censors in Rumania emasculated a statement by Liberal leader Bratianu and the local typographical union, on some papers refused to print what was left undeleted. [1:2.]

Fighting between Iranian patriots and "autonomy" partisans broke out in the Russian-occupied zone between Azerbaijan and Teheran. Five persons were killed. [11:2-3, with map.]

A verbal tilt between Rabbi Stephen S. Wise and Chairman Hutcheson enlivened the Anglo-American Committee hearing. Non-Zionists said Palestine could not absorb all Jews seeking refuge. [2:2.]

The Cabinet in Japan resigned after getting word from Premier Shidehara. [1:2-3.]

In China following upon the Chungking - Communist truce, Generalissimo Chiang Kai-shek guaranteed equality for all political parties, freedom of speech and person, local elections, political amnesty and end of one-party government. [1:3.]

Korea, too, moved toward unity when the five major parties issued a joint statement praising the Moscow decision for self-government. [10:1.]

"We want to go home" demonstrations continued throughout the Pacific area. [4:1.] In Germany a soldier committee seemed satisfied with explanations offered at a conference with officers, but their comrades continued loud protests. [4:2-3.]

The Senate Military Affairs Committee appointed a subgroup to investigate demobilization. Hearings will start Monday and General Eisenhower may be called. [1:6-7.]

A general wage increase of 19½ cents an hour was recommended by the General Motors fact-finding board. This is six cents more than the company offered and 13½ less than the union demanded, but union acceptance is anticipated. The board said the increase was not inflationary. [1:8.]

Leaders of the United Automobile Workers were hastily summoned to a meeting in Detroit tomorrow. General Motors is expected to resume negotiations. Dealings with the other motor companies seemed to be making progress. [1:6-7.]

The General Motors decision added optimism to the resumed negotiations in this city between United States Steel and the union, the first time both sides had met since October. There was great hope that a strike might be averted. [1:6-7.]

What happens in the steel deliberations will largely determine whether 200,000 electrical workers walk out Tuesday. [12:2.]

The threatened disruption of the nation's telephone service scheduled for this morning was delayed until Monday on Labor Secretary Schwellenbach's plea to the Western Electric strikers. [1:5.] Cable operators refused to handle messages and money for soldiers reaching them through Western Union. [1:7.]

Meat packers rejected a Government offer to pay more for its meat without raising retail prices. There seemed little hope of halting a strike. [13:1.]

UAW to Consider Report During Week-End in Detroit

Executive Board and GM Union Committee Are Expected to Accept Federal Findings —General Motors Officials Silent

By WALTER W. RUCH
Special to THE NEW YORK TIMES.

DETROIT, Jan. 10—Leaders of the United Automobile Workers, CIO, were summoned hastily today to come to Detroit for two week-end meetings to consider the report of President Truman's General Motors fact-finding board.

As soon as it became known that the report would be released today, R. J. Thomas, international president, requested members of the international executive board of the UAW to come here for a special meeting on Saturday morning.

Almost simultaneously, Walter P. Reuther, vice president of the UAW, and director of its General Motors division, sent out telegrams to the national General Motors committee of the union, scheduling a meeting for Sunday afternoon.

Recommendations were expected to flow from the Saturday meeting into that set for Sunday, with the ultimate outcome likely to constitute a new overture on the part of the UAW toward settlement of the fifty-one-day-old General Motors strike. The UAW, it was learned, was almost certain to take the report of the fact-finding commission as an acceptable compromise of its wage differences with General Motors.

The corporation, however, remained silent on the Washington report. This was not as disquieting as it might have been had the company not withdrawn from the proceedings rather than argue with the UAW over the "ability to pay" issue. One company official explained that the concern could hardly be expected to comment upon the result of a proceeding from which it had withdrawn as a party.

According to the best available sources here, the company now will proceed to sit down with the UAW, as in the past, to negotiate private-

Continued on Page 15, Column 7

REPORT TO TRUMAN

Fact-Finders Proposing Increase 12½% Short of Union Demand

FIRM OFFERED 13½ CENTS

President Lauds Board, Asks Adoption of Recommendation and End to Walk-Out

The text of the Fact Finding Board's report, Pages 14, 15.

By LOUIS STARK
Special to THE NEW YORK TIMES.

WASHINGTON, Jan. 10—President Truman's fact-finding board in the General Motors dispute recommended today a general wage increase of 19½ cents an hour, or 6 cents more than the company offered.

The increase is about 17.5 per cent above present hourly rates as compared with the union demand for a 30 per cent rise.

The average wage in General Motors was estimated as $1.119 an hour. The proposed increase would bring this up to $1.314. The union requested $1.45 an hour.

Last November the Commerce Department estimated that the corporation was able to pay a wage increase of 15 per cent now and a further 10 per cent next year.

The President received the 12,000-word document from the board, headed by Lloyd K. Garrison, at noon and later issued a summary of the findings.

President Lauds Report

Praising the report as "a thorough and reasoned document," Mr. Truman said that he believed "it will commend itself to the good judgment of the American public." He added:

"I sincerely hope that the parties will follow the recommendations and bring about a speedy end to this most costly conflict. I am satisfied that if such a settlement is made the industrial skies will rapidly clear and American industry and labor will go forward to new heights of achievement in the interests of the whole country."

Outstanding in the report is the statement that the proposed wage increase is non-inflationary; that it will not require a price increase, and that it is well within the national stabilization policy.

R. J. Thomas and Walter P. Reuther, president and vice president of the CIO United Automobile Workers, hurried to New York to lay the board's findings before Philip Murray, CIO president, who resumed wage negotiations with the United States Steel Corporation today.

They issued no statement here, but it was said unofficially that the auto workers would accept the recommendations, which were also signed by the other board members, Milton E. Eisenhower, president of Kansas State Agricultural College, and Judge Walter P. Stacy of the Supreme Court of North Carolina.

There was no comment here from General Motors officials.

Report Tied to Steel Dispute

The report, coming as it did with renewal of the steel wage negotiations, caused speculation here to continue to be optimistic on the early settlement of the steel dispute, which threatens a strike of 700,000 workers Monday.

This union requested a wage increase of $2 a day, or 25 cents an hour. Steel union sources have indicated that the organization was prepared to accept $1.60, or 20 cents an hour, which would be slightly in excess of the General Motors recommendation.

Besides the wage recommendation, the Garrison Board proposed that "in line with the customary practice of American industry in similar situations," the status quo prevailing before the strike be restored by reinstatement of the 1945 contract which the company has canceled ("as it had a right to do").

After the contract is reinstated, the board suggested, the parties

Continued on Page 15, Column 1

Averting of Steel Strike Expected in Parley Here

By RUSSELL PORTER

Possibility of a settlement of the wage dispute in the steel industry without a strike increased yesterday afternoon when representatives of the United States Steel Corporation and the United Steel Workers of America, an affiliate of the Congress of Industrial Organizations, resumed collective bargaining negotiations in a three-hour conference, apparently held in a friendly atmosphere, and adjourned until 2 P. M. today for further discussion.

The conference is being held at the headquarters of the corporation at 71 Broadway.

The negotiations were interrupted last October, when the company refused any concessions to the union's demand for a $2-a-day wage increase unless a compensatory price increase was allowed by the Government. They were resumed after a price increase of about $4 a ton was authorized. The company had asked for $7.

Effect on Other Strikes Seen

Both sides refused comment on the progress of the negotiations after yesterday's meeting, but it was evident they were hopeful of an agreement that would avert the strike, scheduled to begin Monday, which would call out 700,000 workers throughout the industry.

Observers, meanwhile, felt a peaceful settlement of the steel dispute also would head off threatened CIO strikes in the electrical and packing-house industries and might influence compromise solutions of existing strikes in the automobile and other industries.

The recommendations of President Truman's fact-finding board for an increase of 19½ cents an

Continued on Page 12, Column 3

WIRE STRIKE STOPS MESSAGES TO GI'S

Funds Also Held Up Here as Pressure Becomes Severe—No Moves for Settlement

By A. H. RASKIN

Messages and money orders intended for soldiers and sailors overseas were piling up in cable offices here yesterday as the strike of 7,000 Western Union telegraph workers in New York, Long Island and northern New Jersey went into its third day.

With no moves for settlement of the strike in prospect, the pressure of the telegraph tie-up on business activity became increasingly severe. Many large companies, already handicapped by the virtual suspension of normal telegraphic service, reported that mechanical failures were interfering with the operation of inter-office communications between the home offices here and branches in other cities.

The Western Union management and the strikers differed as to the volume of traffic that was being kept up in the face of the

Continued on Page 12, Column 6

Senators to Inquire Into All Phases Of Demobilization of Armed Forces

By C. P. TRUSSELL
Special to THE NEW YORK TIMES.

WASHINGTON, Jan. 10—Under pressure from Senators and the War Department, a special Senate Military Affairs subcommittee was created today to investigate the entire question of demobilization of the armed forces. It will begin work as soon as witnesses are available.

Public hearings, said Senator Edwin C. Johnson of Colorado, chairman of the subcommittee, would start Monday if either Kenneth C. Royall, Acting Secretary of War, or General Eisenhower, the first scheduled witnesses, was able to appear then.

Appointed to the subcommittee by Senator Elbert D. Thomas, chairman of the Military Affairs Committee, were, besides Mr. Johnson, Senators Frank P. Briggs, Democrat, of Missouri, and Chapman Revercomb, Republican, of West Virginia.

Senator Johnson, in a letter to Senator Thomas, urged the entire Military Affairs Committee to call General Eisenhower before it for public discussion and interrogation.

"It is distressing and humiliating to all Americans to read in every newspaper in the land accounts of near mutiny in the Army," Senator Johnson said. "The causes for this deplorable situation must be brought out in the open. No American Army must ever be permitted by the Congress to degenerate into a mob."

Senator Revercomb is the author of a resolution which would effect the immediate discharge, on application, of any of an estimated 1,000,000 fathers who are still in the services here and overseas. He said today that he believed Congress should take over the demobilization program.

As plans for the investigation

Continued on Page 4, Column 4

"All the News That's Fit to Print"

The New York Times.

LATE CITY EDITION

Cloudy and mild today. Cloudy with occasional rain tomorrow.

Temperatures Yesterday—Max., 63; Min., 50
Sunrise today, 6:24 A. M.; Sunset, 5:52 P. M.
Full U. S. Weather Bureau Report Page 47

VOL. XCV..No. 32,183. Entered as Second-Class Matter, Postoffice, New York, N. Y. NEW YORK, WEDNESDAY, MARCH 6, 1946. THREE CENTS IN NEW YORK CITY

U. S. SENDS 2 PROTESTS TO RUSSIA ON MANCHURIA AND IRAN ACTIONS; CHURCHILL ASSAILS SOVIET POLICY

SPELLMAN CHEERED BY CROWDS IN CITY, URGES TRUE PEACE

New Cardinal's Return From Rome Evokes a Series of Ovations by Faithful

4,300 PACK OPERA HOUSE

Hope for Warless World 'Can Be Found in God Alone,' He Declares at Reception

By FRANK S. ADAMS

Peace cannot arise in this atomic age of discord and decay; it will not come until men "awaken to the simple, ageless truth that peace can be found in God alone," Francis Cardinal Spellman told an audience of 4,300 persons who filled the Metropolitan Opera House to capacity last night to welcome him on his return from Rome.

Mayor O'Dwyer, Governor Dewey and Postmaster General Robert E. Hannegan, representing President Truman, paid glowing tributes to the new prince of the church at the reception, which was the climax of a day of greeting in which many thousands of the faithful expressed their jubilation at the great new honor that had come to the Archbishop of New York.

From the time that he stepped from the Constellation plane Star of the Vatican at La Guardia Field at 2:30 P. M., to be greeted by the welcoming hand of Mayor O'Dwyer and a deafening roar from a crowd of 10,000 persons, until the close of the reception late last night Cardinal Spellman received one ovation after another.

Route Covers 15 Miles

The Cardinal was cheered as he was driven in an open car from the airport on a fifteen-mile trip through parts of Queens, the Bronx and Manhattan to St. Patrick's Cathedral, where a waiting throng raised a fresh burst of applause as he entered for the formal ecclesiastical ceremony marking his safe home-coming from the Eternal City.

The City Council in the course of the day adopted a resolution expressing "our deep appreciation and satisfaction" at the honor paid to Cardinal Spellman by his elevation. The resolution was adopted by a vote of 20 to 2, with the dissenting votes cast by the two Communist members, Peter V. Cacchione and Benjamin J. Davis Jr. Councilman Michael J. Quill was among those who voted for the resolution.

Thousands of the Cardinal's admirers were waiting inside and outside the Metropolitan Opera House when he arrived there at 8:17 P. M. for the reception. Flashlights illuminated the scene as the crowd outside milled as close to his car as a large police detail would permit. Within, another huge throng gave him a mighty burst of applause when he came into view.

Through it all the new prince of the church carried himself with the simple dignity that New York has come to expect of him on all occasions. His face beamed with happiness at the obvious joy of the thousands of his parishioners who paid such unstinting tribute to him, but it grew solemn as he emphasized the message he had brought back from his old friend, Pope Pius XII.

Opera House Is Packed

The great auditorium was filled as it has seldom been filled before. Not only were the 3,800 permanent seats filled but temporary seats had been installed on the stage and in the orchestra pit, while the maximum number of standees permitted by the fire regulations—499—were present at the rear of the orchestra and the balconies.

Seventeen Bishops were present, as follows: the Most Rev. William R. Arnold, Military Ordinariate; the Most Rev. Louis Kelleher, Auxiliary Bishop of Boston; the Most Rev. Joseph P. Donahue, Auxiliary Bishop of New York; the Most Rev. Bryan J. McEntegart, Ogdensburg, N. Y.; the Most Rev. William T. McGarty, Military Ordinariate; the Most Rev. J. Francis A. McIntyre, Auxiliary Bishop of New York; the Most Rev. John F. O'Hara, Buffalo; the Most Rev. Thomas A. Connolly, Auxiliary Bishop of San Francisco; Calif.; the Most Rev. William A. Griffin, Trenton, N. J.; the Most Rev. Raymond A. Kearney, Auxiliary Bishop of Brooklyn; the Most Rev. Gerald T. Bergan, Des Moines, Iowa; the Most Rev. Stephen J. Donahue, Auxiliary Bishop of New York; the Most

Continued on Page 16, Column 2

Worker's Shotgun Breaks Picket Line

Special to THE NEW YORK TIMES.

GRAND RAPIDS, Mich., March 5—Lawrence Squires, a recently discharged war veteran, went to work today with a shotgun under his arm and had very little trouble passing through a picket line at the Michigan Wheel Company foundry.

A line of fifteen pickets blocked the plant entrance when he arrived, but it quickly dissolved when he leveled his 16-gauge shotgun. The man directly in front of the muzzle dropped to the ground instantly.

Mr. Squires then seized the gun by the barrel and swung it about him like a club and pickets scampered out of his way. But when he got inside the plant company guards called city police and he was arrested on a charge of felonious assault with a dangerous weapon preferred by a union picket.

When arraigned Mr. Squires demanded formal examination. A hearing was scheduled on March 14 and bond was set at $500.

16-HOUR TALK FAILS TO END PHONE ROW

Conciliators Adjourn Parley—Still Hope to Avert Strike—Meeting Resumes Today

By A. H. RASKIN

Clinging to their hope for averting the nation-wide telephone strike called for 6 A. M. tomorrow, Federal conciliators adjourned a sixteen-hour conference with company and union negotiators in Washington at 2 o'clock this morning, without establishing a basis for settling the controversy. The conciliators announced that the talks would be resumed at 10 A. M.

As the red-eyed representatives of the long-lines department of the American Telephone and Telegraph Company and the Federation of Long Lines Telephone Workers left for their hotels, Edgar L. Warren, chief of the United States Conciliation Service, expressed the belief that some progress had been made. Secretary of Labor Lewis B. Schwellenbach and John Gibson, Assistant Secretary, took a hand in the Government's all-out effort to break the wage deadlock between the company and the union.

Despite the continuance of the conciliation efforts, Joseph A. Beirne, president of the National Federation of Telephone Workers, which has a membership of 250,000 in all parts of the Bell System, told reporters that he believed a strike was inevitable. He said the A. T. & T. and its affiliated companies had made no concessions that could be considered as offering any hope for averting the walkout.

Western Electric Parleys Here

In this city negotiations to settle the two-month-old strike of 17,200 Western Electric workers, who are affiliated with the federation, were broken off, but the Western Electric management promised to deliver a new wage proposal today to J. R. Mandelbaum, a Federal conciliator. He expressed the hope that it might provide a basis for renewed attempts to end the strike, but the union said it would take part in no more meetings unless the company offered an average increase of 18½ cents an hour.

At the Washington conference, which officials had hoped would

Continued on Page 20, Column 5

NEW GM DEADLOCK AS COMPANY SPURNS UAW BALLOT TERMS

Union Declares Corporation by Action Has Turned the Walkout Into a Lockout

DEWEY DESPAIRS OF POLL

Union Insists on Inclusion of Two Questions—Company Sticks to First Plan

Text of General Motors letter to UAW strikers, Page 20.

By WALTER W. RUCH

Special to THE NEW YORK TIMES.

DETROIT, March 5—The General Motors Corporation refused today to qualify the phraseology of its original proposed secret poll of 175,000 striking workers, now idle for 105 days, and was promptly accused by the United Automobile Workers, CIO, of having transformed the walkout into a lockout.

During a session of the negotiators filled with rancor, the corporation representatives held that the return proposal made yesterday by the union to submit in the poll two questions to the strikers was "without merit." The corporation also supplied details of the final terms upon which it wished to poll the strikers to determine their willingness to remain on strike.

The UAW, which wished to pose its final offer against that of the corporation, turned down the renewal of the General Motors suggestion that the workers be polled secretly as to whether they wished to accept or reject the offer of an increase of 18½ cents an hour in wages and other suggestions for settlement of national and local issues.

His usual buoyancy gone, James F. Dewey, special mediator, told reporters at 7 o'clock that the situation had reached "dead center" and that there was no hope of a secret poll of any kind. He knew as well as any in the room that there was current a fresh crop of rumors that failure to adjust the strike today would mean that the situation would be taken from his hands and shifted to Washington.

Union Reply Is Read

Forcing a smile, Mr. Dewey said as he departed that the parties would "probably" be meeting again tomorrow afternoon under his leadership. If this was the breaking point, it marked the first time in thirty-six years as a mediator that he had failed in his mission.

No one on either side tried to make light of the situation. It was a new low in the strike that has cost workers, the company and indirect producers well over a billion dollars.

After Mr. Dewey had gone Frank Winn, who usually wears a grin, strode solemnly into the press room. His hand trembling as he read, Mr. Winn, who is public-relations representative for Walter P. Reuther, vice president of the UAW and head of the General Motors department, dictated to reporters the following joint statement from Mr. Reuther and R. J. Thomas, international president:

"The refusal by the corporation to arbitrate the issues or to poll

Continued on Page 20, Column 3

Japan Atom Bombing Condemned In Federal Church Council Report

By ROBERT W. POTTER

Special to THE NEW YORK TIMES.

COLUMBUS, Ohio, March 5—A grim picture of a world threatened by the destructive forces of atomic energy, torn by national and racial rivalries and power politics, facing moral collapse and with many areas devastated and many peoples slowly starving, was presented today to the Federal Council of the Churches of Christ in America, in special session here. But throughout the reports and discussions strong faith was expressed in the power of God to lead man to make a better world.

"Only a new-born spiritual intensity can orient the world in a new direction," John Foster Dulles declared in summarizing the great need of the present.

A report on atomic warfare and the Christian faith, by a commission on the relation of the church to the war composed of twenty-one religious educators, strongly condemned the use of atomic bombs against the Japanese and saturation bombings of German cities.

The report, which will be expounded to the session tomorrow by Dr. Robert L. Calhoun, chairman of the commission and Professor of Historical Theology at Yale, warned that the uses of atomic weapons that could now be foreseen would make war not only more destructive and treacherous but more irresponsible than ever.

"In an atmosphere of general suspicion, atomic war would have, more than any previous form of combat, the characteristics of universal madness," it said.

Deploring the "irresponsible" bombings of Hiroshima and Nagasaki, the report proposed the rebuilding of the two cities as a token of repentance and that the churches of the United States undertake to provide a special aid for the survivors of the "two murdered cities."

It also proposed that the churches call upon the American Government immediately, to allay

Continued on Page 15, Column 7

BRITON SPEAKS OUT

Calls for Association of U. S., British to Stem Russian Expansion

APPEASEMENT IS OPPOSED

'Iron Curtain' Dividing Europe Is Not What We Fought For, Churchill Says at Fulton, Mo.

Text of Churchill's address on world problems, Page 4.

By HAROLD B. HINTON

Special to THE NEW YORK TIMES.

FULTON, Mo., March 5—A fraternal association between the British Empire and the United States was advocated here today by Winston Churchill to stem "the expansive and proselytizing tendencies" of the Soviet Union.

Introduced by President Truman at Westminster College, Great Britain's wartime Prime Minister asserted that a mere balance of power in the world today would be too narrow a margin and would only offer "temptations to a trial of strength."

On the contrary, he added that the English-speaking peoples must maintain an overwhelming preponderance of power on their side until "the highroads of the future will be clear, not only for us but for all, not only for our time but for a century to come."

Says Curtain Divides Europe

Mr. Churchill painted a dark picture of post-war Europe, on which "an iron curtain has descended across the Continent" from Stettin in the Baltic to Trieste in the Adriatic.

Warsaw, Berlin, Prague, Vienna, Budapest, Belgrade, Sofia and Bucharest are all being subjected to increasing pressure and control from Moscow, he said, adding:

"This is certainly not the liberated Europe we fought to build up. Nor is it one which contains the essentials of permanent peace."

Even in front of the "iron cur-

Continued on Page 5, Column 1

DISTINGUISHED VISITORS AT WESTMINSTER COLLEGE

President Truman and Winston Churchill in the procession with Dr. Franc McCluer, head of the school at Fulton, Mo.

Associated Press Wirephoto

HOOVER TO EXAMINE FOOD NEEDS ABROAD

Anderson Says His Survey May Cut Estimates but 'World Shortage Is Very Real'

By BESS FURMAN

Special to THE NEW YORK TIMES.

WASHINGTON, March 5—Herbert Hoover with a committee of experts will go to Europe, probably next week, to investigate food conditions at the request of President Truman.

Secretary Anderson made the announcement after a breakfast conference with Mr. Hoover. He named Dr. F. R. Fitzgerald, food allocations officer of the Department, as one of the experts to accompany the former President.

Testifying later before the House Special Committee investigating food, Mr. Anderson said:

"The Department of Agriculture contends the world food shortage

Continued on Page 19, Column 2

Franco Defied Allied Step Day Before It Was Made

Special to THE NEW YORK TIMES.

WASHINGTON, March 5—General Francisco Franco protested to Secretary of State James F. Byrnes twenty-four hours in advance of the three-power appeal to the Spanish people to oust him and his regime in Spain. Franco protested against any effort to apply "foreign pressure" on his Government.

The note, delivered Sunday by Spanish Ambassador Juan Cardenas, said that Spain considered "the question of its interior regime" a matter exclusively for its own sovereignty, and it said that "any further foreign intervention" would only heighten Spanish national feeling.

The warning from Franco to Secretary Byrnes was as follows:

"I have been instructed by my Government to communicate to Your Excellency the following:

"In view of the repeated announcement in the press and radio of this country of the publication of a joint statement of the Governments of France, Great Britain and the United States in connection with the Spanish situation, and in the eventuality of its being true that it contains a threat to Spain to force her to change her regime, the Spanish Government wishes to inform the Government of the United States in advance that Spain repudiates any foreign pressure put upon her, since it considers that the question of its interior regime concerning exclusively its own sovereignty.

"Any further foreign intervention that might appear as a threat to their independence would only serve to heighten the national feelings of the Spanish people, always zealous of the integrity of their sovereignty, the Spanish Government being, therefore, sure that national opinion shares unanimously this repulsing attitude.

"Furthermore, in following this precedent, Spain is convinced that she is lending a positive service to the international community in defending the principle of mutual

Continued on Page 17, Column 1

BRITISH SCIENTIST ADMITS ATOM LEAK

Dr. Alan N. May, Remanded for Trial, Refuses to Give Name or Nation of Accomplice

By SYDNEY GRUSON

By Wireless to THE NEW YORK TIMES.

LONDON, March 5—Dr. Alan Nunn May, 34-year-old British scientist, was remanded in custody for two weeks today after the prosecution told the court that he had admitted disclosing atomic energy secrets but had refused to divluge the name or nationality of the other person involved.

The court was told that investigations concerned with the case were continuing both here and in Canada.

The charge against Dr. May, under the Official Secrets Act of 1911, was that "on a day in 1945 you did, for purposes prejudicial to the safety and interest of the State, communicate to some person unknown certain information which was calculated to be, or might be, directly useful to an enemy."

Dr. May sat silent throughout the proceedings. The small Bow Street courtroom was jammed with many of Dr. May's students from King's College where he is a lecturer in physics.

Dr. May was arrested at the college yesterday by officers of Scotland Yard's special branch. He was

Continued on Page 3, Column 3

World News Summarized

WEDNESDAY, MARCH 6, 1946

A new, stiffened policy toward Russia became apparent in Washington last night. The United States sent two notes to Moscow, one expressing displeasure over Soviet actions in Manchuria, the other protesting against retention of Red Army troops in Iran.

As to Manchuria, we had asked Moscow and Chungking on Feb. 9 for information on their negotiations and reiterated our traditional Open-Door policy. Moscow did not answer, but Chungking replied that China had rejected Russian claims to Japanese Manchurian enterprises as "war booty" and had ruled out a subsequent proposal to share this "booty" and operate other enterprises jointly. Talks still were going on, Foreign Minister Wang said, in China, but he saw no reason for Russia to delay withdrawal of her troops, now more than a month overdue. [1:8.]

After the Iranian Ambassador had informed Secretary of State Byrnes that Russia had made new demands as a condition for evacuating the Red Army from Iran and that these had been rejected, a note on that subject was dispatched and will be made public as soon as it reaches Moscow. Russian troops were supposed, by treaty, to have been out of Iran last Saturday. [3:1.]

The State Department disclosed it had again urged Russian-dominated Bulgaria to obey the Moscow agreement and admit freely chosen opposition members to the Cabinet. [2:2.]

Moscow also provided the theme for Winston Churchill's address at Westminster College in Missouri. "Nobody knows what Soviet Russia and its Communist international organization intends to do in the immediate future," he said, "or what are the limits, if any, to their expansive and proselytizing tendencies." He strongly criticized Russian actions and said that what went on behind and in front of the "iron curtain" that spread across Europe from Stettin to Trieste was "certainly not the liberated Europe we fought to build up."

Russia, Mr. Churchill was convinced, does not want war, but there is nothing she admires "so much as strength."

The former Prime Minister admitted he felt less hopeful than he had about Versailles after the last war. The UNO must be built up into a powerful force for peace, "but time is short." He again urged an Anglo-American union as the surest safeguard for democracy. [All the foregoing 1:4.]

Dr. Alan May, a young British scientist, confessed that he had disclosed atomic energy secrets, but refused to reveal the name or nationality of the recipient. [1:7.]

In an advance protest delivered Sunday against the three-power note calling for his removal, Generalissimo Franco insisted that his continuance in power was a Spanish internal affair and did not call for "foreign intervention," the State Department disclosed. [1:6-7.]

Former President Hoover and a committee of experts will visit Europe to examine the extent of the food shortage and the need of assistance. [1:5.]

Attempts to settle the General Motors strike by a vote of the workers broke down when the company rejected the union's suggestions for the wording of the question and the union leaders assailed the company. [1:3.]

Soft coal operators agreed to meet with union representatives on a new contract and asked for cooperation to save the industry. [21:1.] Railroad engineers and trainmen received orders to start a nation-wide strike on Monday. [20:2.] Negotiators fail to agree and adjourn 16-hour conference in telephone dispute, but still hope to avert strike. [1:2.]

Kaiser Accuses Steel Companies Of Denying Metal for Autos to Him

By KENNETH AUSTIN

Henry J. Kaiser and Joseph W. Frazer, chairman and president, respectively, of the recently formed Kaiser-Frazer Corporation, declared at Mr. Kaiser's offices here yesterday that the steel industry was "discriminating" against their new automobile enterprise by refusing tonnage commitments for steel with which to make cars.

They made public telegrams addressed to Attorney General Tom Clark and Economic Stabilizer Chester Bowles in which they said:

"This situation not only jeopardizes our 30,000 stockholders with over $50,000,000 invested, but also our 4,000 distributors and dealers with an investment of more than $100,000,000.

"It completely stifles competition for which provision is made in the act authorizing OWMR and your office. We, therefore, request allocation by your office of cold rolled sheet steel. Have you any suggestions as to what procedure under the law your office can take to protect Kaiser-Frazer against this situation which, in our opinion, amounts to discrimination?"

Mr. Frazer said he had been told in Florida last week that "there was a plan by vested interests to bleed Henry Kaiser to death and get us piece by piece by withholding steel from Kaiser-Frazer Corporation while furnishing it to its competitors."

He added that Tom M. Girdler, chairman of Republic Steel, had told him recently that Mr. Kaiser's signing of a wage contract for his Fontana, Calif., steel works when virtually all other steel plants were closed by strike, had affected the attitude of the steel industry toward the Kaiser interests; and that he regarded as unfair the signing of a wage contract by the Kaiser-Frazer Corporation at the time when the General Motors Corporation was struck.

Mr. Girdler, in Cleveland, denied "emphatically" that he ever had

Continued on Page 21, Column 5

BYRNES AIDS CHINA

Insists That All Allies Have Manchurian Role, Based on Open Door

NEW FIRMNESS IS SHOWN

U. S. Opposes the Removal by Russians of 'War Booty' and Control of Industry

Text of interchange of notes on Manchuria, Page 2.

By BERTRAM D. HULEN

Special to THE NEW YORK TIMES.

WASHINGTON, March 5—Strong support is given China in her resistance to Russian demands in Manchuria through a note dispatched tonight to the Soviet Government by James F. Byrnes, Secretary of State.

While the contents of the note are not revealed, it was evident that our position was based on insistence upon consideration for Allied interests where they are involved and in the principle of the Open Door where economic rights are at stake.

Taken in conjunction with the Chinese resistance to the Russian demands and a firm note that Mr. Byrnes also sent tonight to Moscow on the continued presence of Russian forces in Iran, the diplomatic moves provided evidence that a new policy of firmness is being applied to Russia in sharp contrast to what has been branded by critics as a policy of appeasement.

It would take a long search of the records of our diplomatic history to find two protest notes addressed to a single power—and a friendly one at that—on two different questions and at the same time.

Based on Manchurian Issues

Our note on Manchuria was based on two developments reported officially to us in a note from the Chinese Foreign Office. One concerned Russian removal to Siberia of industrial equipment on the grounds that it was "war booty" of the Red Army. The other was a proposal by the Russians to the Chinese for their joint operation of industries in Manchuria. China rejected both ideas.

The Chinese note was sent in response to a request made by Secretary Byrnes in notes to Chungking and Moscow on Feb. 9 for reports on their discussions concerning Manchuria. In his note Mr. Byrnes based our position on the Open Door. It is a principle we have advocated ever since it was enunciated by John Hay in 1899 and especially during the years in which Japan was in the ascendancy in Manchuria.

The Chinese reply stated that the Soviet Government, in a memorandum on Jan. 21, declared that all Japanese enterprises in the Chinese Northeastern Provinces that had been of service to the Japanese army were regarded "as war booty of Soviet forces." China refused to take this view.

In another memorandum to the Chinese, Moscow proposed to hand over to China a part of the Japanese enterprises that it regarded as war booty and to have the remaining enterprises, including specified coal mines, power plants, iron and steel industries, chemical industries and cement industries, operated jointly by the Chinese and Russians. China again refused.

Russian Seizures Opposed

Our attitude, as set forth in the note of Feb. 9, was one of opposition to the Russian seizure of industries in Manchuria and that negotiations on this subject by the Chinese and Russians would be contrary to the Open Door policy.

Not only would such arrangements go beyond the Sino-Russian treaty of Aug. 14, 1945, we contended, but the matter of Japanese assets in Manchuria was one for determination by an inter-Allied reparations commission.

China did not mention reports of Russian removal of Japanese soldiers from Manchuria to Siberia for forced labor, and Secretary Byrnes said he had no official confirmation of the reports. However,

Continued on Page 2, Column 5

"All the News That's Fit to Print"

The New York Times.

LATE CITY EDITION
Mostly sunny today. Fair and warmer tomorrow.
Temperatures Yesterday—Max., 54; Min., 45
Sunrise today, 5:52 A. M.; Sunset, 5:35 P. M.
Full U. S. Weather Bureau Report, Page 59

VOL. XCVI...No. 32,393. Entered as Second-Class Matter. Postoffice, New York, N. Y. NEW YORK, WEDNESDAY, OCTOBER 2, 1946. THREE CENTS IN NEW YORK CITY

12 NAZI WAR LEADERS SENTENCED TO BE HANGED; GOERING HEADS LIST OF THOSE TO DIE BY OCT. 16; HESS GETS LIFE, SIX OTHERS ORDERED TO PRISON

SHIP OFFICERS QUIT, PARALYZING PORT 2D TIME IN MONTH

Never Before Have Masters Been Called From Bridges —Engineers Also Strike

WASHINGTON PLEAS FAIL

But Efforts to Settle Dispute Over Wages and Working Conditions Are Continued

By GEORGE HORNE

The cogs of the nation's merchant marine slowed to a standstill yesterday for the second time in a month as the unprecedented strike of licensed officers got under way.

It was unprecedented because never before in the country's shipping history have shipmasters—captains earning as much as $500 and $600 a month—been called from their bridges in a union action to enforce wage and working demands. But they were leaving their ships on order, along with brother engineer officers of the Marine Engineers Beneficial Association.

Reaction among the captains was mixed, and the situation affecting them at a late hour last night was obscure, after a welter of messages to and from the negotiating headquarters in Washington, where Government authorities were still trying to effect a settlement before the walkout could settle down to a long-term affair.

Many Captains Not in Union

Many captains are not members of the National Organization of Masters, Mates and Pilots (AFL), even on such ships as have MMP contracts. Shipping operators said the captains, who are the owners' supreme representatives aboard, and as such considered beyond the call of strike action, were "being threatened."

They declared that Capt. Harry Martin, East Coast president of the MMP, had agreed in Washington yesterday to leave security watches aboard all ships, including a captain and a day and night mate for stand-by duty. But they said the pledge was not being honored.

At a special meeting of the AFL Maritime Trades Department at the office of the International Longshoremen's Association last night it was announced that "the status quo" remains. That meant that captains were being called off, whether they agreed or not. The AFL spokesman said the response among all MMP officers was excellent.

Ship operators took the position that the masters were "in the middle" and "behind the eight-ball," and they agreed that many would have to leave their ships at the union's call.

The MMP leaders have stood by their original conception of the walkout as being no strike. It was, the union leaders said, simply a case of the men not working in

Continued on Page 4, Column 3

Cards Beat Dodgers In First Game, 4-2

Despite a muscle ailment, Howie Pollet pitched the Cardinals to a 4-2 victory over the Dodgers at St. Louis yesterday in the first of a three-game play-off series for the National League pennant. The Cards meanwhile routed Ralph Branca, first of five Brooklyn pitchers, with three runs in as many innings.

Howie Schultz momentarily tied the score for the Dodgers with his homer in the third and also batted in their second run with a single in the seventh.

The play-offs, first such in the history of major league baseball, will be resumed tomorrow at Ebbets Field, and the third contest, if necessary, will be played there Friday.

(Complete details on Page 35.)

12 Inches of Snow Blanket Several Up-State Areas

Flurries Are Reported as Far South as the Pennsylvania Line—Temperature Here Is Near Record Low for Date

By The Associated Press.

ALBANY, Oct. 1—Canadian-border areas of upper New York dug out tonight from more than a foot of snow as high winds churned the tail-end of the season's first storm into near-blizzard fury.

It was still snowing early tonight, but a United States weather forecaster described the pre-winter blast as a one-day storm. He predicted low temperatures for another 48 hours.

The storm, whipping across the Adirondack area from Canada, forced some schools to close, blocked secondary highways and disrupted power and communications lines in northern New York.

Although the brunt of the storm was felt in the upper Adirondacks, its effect was State-wide. Temperatures plummeted toward the freezing mark and snow flurries were reported in western and southern New York, along the Pennsylvania line.

Syracuse, reporting its earliest snow in forty-four years of official records, had a half-inch.

New York City's 45-degree temperature early this morning was within three degrees of the 1916 record low for the date.

Some up-State areas without snow had steady rain. Saratoga Springs reported a twenty-four-hour fall of 1.5 inches and Schenectady had 2.08 inches in the thirty-six hours ending at 8 A. M.

The villages of Malone in Franklin County and Potsdam in St. Lawrence apparently were hardest hit, with traffic crippled and heavy damage caused by falling trees and branches. Malone had 13 inches of snow and Potsdam a foot. Both were without electric power.

Malone's gas service was cut partly when a falling tree damaged a main. The Alice Hyde Memorial Hospital was without electricity all morning and gas most of the day. Power was re-

Continued on Page 27, Column 2

LEHMAN 'STRADDLE' CHARGED BY IVES

Says Rival Evades Wallace Foreign Policy Issue With Aim to Placate Left

Special to The New York Times.

ALBANY, Oct. 1—Irving M. Ives, Republican candidate for United States Senator, charged tonight that former Governor Herbert H. Lehman, his Democratic opponent, had issued a "shadow doctrine" on foreign policy designed to placate both old-line Democrats and left-wing groups.

Mr. Lehman, he declared, straddled the issue and took a "vague and insecure" stand which had something to please "each of the political organizations and splinter parties he represents in this campaign."

In a State-wide radio broadcast he challenged Mr. Lehman to tell the people whether he agreed with Secretary of State James F. Byrnes or with former Secretary of Commerce Henry A. Wallace. He declared it impossible to side with both.

Challenge on "Enslavement"

"Mr. Wallace believes in drawing an iron curtain across eastern Europe," he said, adding:

"We have seen that wars arise when people are enslaved and the truth kept from them. Does my opponent favor a policy which would permit this condition to ex-

Continued on Page 8, Column 3

City's Search for Meat Supplies Fails to Uncover Any Hoarding

A meat search by three city departments was three-quarters finished yesterday and disclosed holdings in local slaughterhouses, storage plants and railroad cars of 13,312,880 pounds—not much compared to New York's normal consumption of 3,800,000 pounds a day.

With fewer than fifty of the city's 400 major repositories of meat still to be visited by the task force of 225 policemen and inspectors of the Health and Market departments, Mayor O'Dwyer said he saw nothing in the findings so far to warrant municipal action.

Meat supplies in retail stores, meanwhile, continued to shrink, and the Office of Price Administration reported that the black market was shrinking even faster than the supply of available meat. This did not seem any great victory to housewives, since the race was in the direction of a zero supply.

OPA enforcement agents, continuing their daily check on prices and, incidentally, supply, found only one out of ten butcher shops with meat to sell. Many were shut and many others sold only poultry. There was more sausage meat than any other kind. Last week the district OPA had reported one shop out of five selling meat.

Yesterday's report by the district enforcement staff was to the effect that only 5 per cent of the meat being offered for sale was at black market prices, whereas the same office had estimated last week that 20 to 35 per cent of the local sales were at over-ceiling prices.

The City Council, in a majority resolution sent to its rules committee, called upon the Federal Government to seize all cattle and meat in the country and blamed the meat industry for "open defiance to the American people by the creation of a meat famine." The resolution, which also urged that the Government make available to the public as an emergency health measure the meat so

Continued on Page 33, Column 3

11,236-MILE RECORD SET AS NAVY PLANE LANDS IN COLUMBUS

Truculent Turtle Smashes Old Mark by 3,300 Miles in Non-Stop Flight From Australia

UP 55 HOURS 15 MINUTES

Four-Man Crew, Fresh Despite Rough Hop, Is Disappointed at Not Finishing in Washington

By FREDERICK GRAHAM
Special to The New York Times.

COLUMBUS, Ohio, Oct. 1—A non-stop flight distance record that surpassed the previous mark by more than 3,300 miles was set today when the Truculent Turtle, the Navy's new twin-engine, land-based patrol bomber, landed here to complete an 11,236-mile flight that started Sunday morning in Perth, Australia.

The plane touched down here at 12:25 P. M., Eastern standard time.

The time for the flight, which started in the warm spring weather of Australia and ended in chilly winds here, was 55 hours 15 minutes. Despite a heavy load of fuel and constant headwinds that averaged 11.5 miles an hour for the entire trip, the average speed of the plane was 203.4 miles an hour.

The old distance record, set by the four-motored Dreamboat, a Superfortress, in a flight from Guam to Washington, was 7,916 miles.

Like "Long Patrol Mission"

"You might say it was no tougher than a good, long patrol mission," Comdr. Thomas D. Davies, chief of the four-man crew that manned the flat-sided Lockheed plane, said when he dropped from the exit hatch in the belly of the fuselage and greeted Navy officers at the municipal field.

"We had turbulent air, headwinds and some instrument weather," Commander Davies con-

Continued on Page 12, Column 3

HULL, 75, STRICKEN AFTER PEACE PLEA

United Nations' 'Father' Calls on Powers to Renew Zeal—His Condition Serious

Text of Mr. Hull's statement appears on page 18.

By BERTRAM D. HULEN
Special to The New York Times.

WASHINGTON, Oct. 1—Cordell Hull, former Secretary of State, suffered a stroke in the United States Naval Hospital at Bethesda, Md., last night, a few hours after he had completed a statement appealing to the Great Powers to compose their differences for the sake of world peace.

The stroke was officially described at first as "light," but the hospital announced later that Mr. Hull's condition had become "more serious during the day." Friends meanwhile had described him as extremely weak and had expressed grave concern. They considered his condition to be critical.

A hospital bulletin issued at 10 o'clock tonight said Mr. Hull remained in serious condition. "No improvement has been noted in his condition since the last bulletin," it said. "No change" was reported at midnight.

Nevertheless, the former Secretary's statement for world peace was issued on his behalf tonight, carrying out his instructions. It

Continued on Page 18, Column 5

RECEIVING THEIR FREEDOM FROM NUREMBERG COURT

Col. Burton C. Andrus, who headed the prison where the defendants were confined during their trial, handing out letters certifying their liberty to Hans Fritzsche (left), Franz von Papen (second from right) and Hjalmar Schacht (right). Associated Press Radiophoto

GERMANY NOT FREE, SCHACHT COMPLAINS

Von Papen Says He Has Given Up Politics—Austria Seeks Extradition for Trial

By DANA ADAMS SCHMIDT
Special to The New York Times.

NUREMBERG, Germany, Oct. 1—Franz von Papen said that his political career was "absolutely ended," Hans Fritzsche asked to be tried again by a German court and Hjalmar Schacht asked for chocolate for his two children today when the three men acquitted by the International Military Tribunal appeared before 200 representatives of the world press.

Schacht got his candy bars and all reaped a harvest of cigarettes

Continued on Page 20, Column 3

Russian and Jackson Object; Schacht Called a Swindler

By The Associated Press.

NUREMBERG, Germany, Oct. 1—Soviet Justice J. I. Nikitchenko tonight assailed the acquittal of three high Nazis by the International Military Tribunal, asserting that the opinion freeing Hjalmar Schacht, banker, was in "obvious contradiction to the evidence." [Justice Nikitchenko also declared Schacht a "swindler," according to a Reuters dispatch.]

The Russian Major General also dissented from the acquittal for the German General Staff, the Reich Cabinet and the decision imprisoning Rudolf Hess for life instead of giving him the death penalty.

Justice Robert Jackson of the United States, speaking for what he called the prosecutors of all nations, declared the decisions on individuals were of secondary importance compared to the fact that the principle was established making aggressive war a crime punishable by death. However, Justice Jackson also assailed the Schacht verdict.

Justice Nikitchenko said Fritzsche, as a radio propagandist, "had a most basic relation to the preparation and conduct of aggressive warfare." The most detailed dissent was in the case of the German General Staff and High Command, of which Justice Nikitchenko said:

"Without their advice and active cooperation, Hitler could not have solved [his] problems. In the majority of cases their opinion was decisive. * * * The General Staff issued most brutal decrees and orders for relentless measures against unarmed, peaceful population and prisoners of war."

Justice Nikitchenko said bluntly

Continued on Page 24, Column 6

World News Summarized

WEDNESDAY, OCTOBER 2, 1946

Twelve high Nazi conspirators were sentenced by the International Military Tribunal in Nuremberg yesterday to death by hanging for the supreme crime of aggressive war; three received life sentences in prison, four received lesser terms and three were acquitted.

The men who will be executed not later than Oct. 16 are Goering, von Ribbentrop, Kaltenbrunner, Rosenberg, Frank, Frick, Streicher, Sauckel, Seyss-Inquart, Keitel and Jodl. Bormann was sentenced to death in absentia. Hess, Funk and Grand Admiral Raeder received life sentences, von Schirach and Speer twenty years, von Neurath fifteen years and Grand Admiral Doenitz ten years. Schacht, von Papen and Fritzsche were acquitted. [All the foregoing 1:8.]

The verdicts on Hess, von Papen and Schacht and the exoneration of the General Staff, Cabinet and Storm Troops as organizations brought a strong dissent from the Russian Justice, Maj. Gen. Nikitchenko. The chief American prosecutor, Justice Jackson, said he was "disappointed" in the liberation of von Papen and Schacht because it would adversely affect further prosecution of industrialists and militarists. [1:6-7.]

Russia accused the United States at a commission meeting of the Conference of Paris of attempting to change agreements reached by the Foreign Ministers Council on Trieste, and the Slav bloc succeeded in delaying a vote. [1:7.]

Former Secretary of State Hull, who is 75 years old today, was stricken in Bethesda Naval Hospital shortly after completing a statement urging the Great Powers to compose their differences for the sake of peace. His condition is serious. "Incalculable disaster" would follow any irreconcilable division in this "most perilous juncture in history," Mr. Hull said. [1:3.]

A House committee, it was disclosed, has been quietly laying the basis to ask Congressional approval for this country's first integrated, permanent world-wide espionage and counter-espionage service. [13:1]

Iran, rejecting Britain's disavowals, has asked for the recall of a British Embassy secretary accused of conspiring to bring about a revolt of southern tribesmen. [11:1.]

Dmitri Shostakovich's new Ninth Symphony has been condemned in the Soviet press for ideological weakness and failing to reflect the true spirit of the Russian people. [31:3-4.]

Bernard M. Baruch characterized as "either misinformation or complete distortion" charges at a political rally by supporters of former Secretary Wallace that the United States expected other nations to give up their atomic energy secrets while this country withheld all information. [1:6-7.]

The American Merchant Marine was almost completely tied up by the strike of engineers and deck officers that began at midnight yesterday. Federal conciliation efforts continued without result. [1:1.]

No progress was made toward ending the Pittsburgh power walkout that has halted production on vital materials [2:2], and a strike of CIO warehouse and office workers threatens to paralyze the dress manufacturing industry in New York. [2:4.] Thirty-seven persons were injured in a picketing riot at Hollywood studios. [3:1.]

The Navy bomber Truculent Turtle landed at Columbus, Ohio, establishing a new world distance record of 11,236 miles in its non-stop flight from Perth, Australia. [1:4; map P. 12.]

Baruch Rebukes Wallace Groups For Distorting U. S. Atom Plan

By A. M. ROSENTHAL
Special to The New York Times.

LAKE SUCCESS, N. Y., Oct. 1—In a sharp reply to followers of former Secretary of Commerce Henry A. Wallace, Bernard M. Baruch, American representative on the United Nations Atomic Energy Commission, categorically denied tonight that this country was asking the rest of the world to stop nuclear research and reveal its uranium resources while the United States retained complete freedom of action.

Mr. Baruch's strongly worded denial was the result of statements made in Chicago on Saturday at a conference of the National Citizens Political Action Committee, Independent Citizens Committee of the Arts, Sciences and Professions, and the Congress of Industrial Organizations' Political Action Committee. It was sent as a telegram addressed to Henry Morgenthau, Harold Ickes and Philip Murray, president of the CIO, who were speakers at the conference.

After noting that the conference had gone on record as saying that the United States was trying to have other nations accept "binding agreements" while keeping its technical knowledge to itself as long as it saw fit, Mr. Baruch declared:

"I say without reservation that this is either misinformation or complete distortion. Nowhere does any such statement occur in the American proposal."

Mr. Baruch followed his denial with a pointed request for a correction.

"I am sending this to you," he said in the telegram, "in order that you may see that this is corrected immediately."

The Baruch statement was issued by the American delegation at 7 P. M., on the eve of a meeting tomorrow morning of the Atomic Energy Commission's Committee 2, which will discuss the

Continued on Page 16, Column 3

SLAV BLOC STALLS VOTING ON TRIESTE

Connally Disputes Vishinsky's Charge That U. S. Seeks to Violate Big Four Accord

By LANSING WARREN
Special to The New York Times.

PARIS, Oct. 1—Making use of procedural entanglements in an atmosphere of raw nerves, the Slav States succeeded tonight in blocking a vote on the United States proposal to implement the Italian draft treaty's general clauses on a statute for Trieste.

During a tense discussion in the peace conference's Italian Political and Territorial Commission, Senator Tom Connally of the United States and Andrei Y. Vishinsky, Soviet Vice Foreign Minister, exchanged accusations and retorts. Other leading delegates made contradictory suggestions on procedure, and finally the lateness of the hour forced adjournment.

Mr. Vishinsky charged that the United States proposal was an adroit and deliberate effort to evade an agreement by the Big Four's Council of Foreign Min-

Continued on Page 17, Column 2

50-MINUTE SESSION

Tribunal Dooms Keitel, Ribbentrop, Streicher, Rosenberg, Jodl

SIX SAID TO APPEAL

Allied Council in Berlin Last Resort—Doenitz Gets Lightest Term

Verdicts in the Nuremberg trials are on pages 22, 23, 24.

By KATHLEEN McLAUGHLIN
Special to The New York Times.

NUREMBERG, Germany, Oct. 1—Death by hanging was decreed this afternoon for twelve of the original twenty-four defendants indicted in the Nuremberg war crimes trials. Three others—Dr. Hjalmar Schacht, Franz von Papen and Dr. Hans Fritzsche—were acquitted by the International Military Tribunal over the dissent of the Soviet member of the court, Maj. Gen. Iola T. Nikitchenko.

Those who will die by the noose within fifteen days, unless reprieved through an appeal within four days to the Allied Control Council in Berlin, are Hermann Goering, Joachim von Ribbentrop, Field Marshal Gen. Wilhelm Keitel, Ernst Kaltenbrunner, Dr. Alfred Rosenberg, Hans Frank, Wilhelm Frick, Julius Streicher, Fritz Sauckel, Col. Gen. Alfred Jodl and Arthur Seyss-Inquart.

Martin Bormann, who succeeded Rudolf Hess as Deputy Fuehrer and who was tried in absentia, owing to the lack of conclusive evidence that he is dead, also was sentenced to death by hanging if and when he ever is apprehended.

Mitigation in von Neurath Case

Life imprisonment was meted out to Hess, Walther Funk and Grand Admiral Erich Raeder. General Nikitchenko dissented likewise from his colleagues' judgment on Hess, expressing the opinion that he had merited death by hanging.

Baldur von Schirach, formerly supreme leader of the Hitler Jugend, and Albert Speer, Reich Minister for Armament and Munitions and chief of the Todt Organization, received twenty-year terms.

Possibly in consideration of his advanced years, Baron Constantin von Neurath, former Foreign Minister, although adjudged guilty on all four counts, received the comparatively mild sentence of fifteen years' imprisonment. He is 73. The Tribunal said in mitigation that he had been dismissed by Adolf Hitler for having been too lenient in his administration as Protector for Bohemia and Moravia and that he had intervened to obtain the release of many Czechoslovaks who had been arrested.

The mildest punishment of all fell to Grand Admiral Karl Doenitz, once Commander in Chief of the German Navy and, during the last days of the war, successor to Hitler as head of the German Government. He must serve ten years in prison.

[Six of those convicted—von Ribbentrop, Frank, Seyss-Inquart, von Schirach, Speer and Doenitz—have appealed their sentences, the British Broadcasting Company said, quoting official sources. The BBC broadcast was recorded by the National Broadcasting Company.]

Pattern Is Similar

In the courtroom, which over the last ten months has echoed unceasingly to the testimony of the unprecedented horrors precipitated upon the world through the Nazi hierarchy, the profound drama of the concluding phase of the trial lasted only fifty minutes. Lord Justice Sir Geoffrey Lawrence, as presiding jurist, announced all the sentences to the eighteen convicted men as they were summoned singly before the tribunal. An atmosphere of utter solemnity prevailed throughout this grim interval.

Beginning with Goering, former

Continued on Page 31, Column 3

"All the News That's Fit to Print"

The New York Times.

LATE CITY EDITION
Sunny and mild today. Partly cloudy and mild tomorrow.
Temperatures Yesterday—Max., 72; Min., 56
Sunrise today, 5:26 A. M.; Sunset, 8:22 P. M.
Full U. S. Weather Bureau Report, Page 55

VOL. XCVI..No. 32,638. Entered as Second-Class Matter, Postoffice, New York, N. Y. NEW YORK, WEDNESDAY, JUNE 4, 1947. THREE CENTS IN NEW YORK CITY

BRITAIN ACHIEVES SOLUTION IN INDIA; LEADERS ACCEPT IT

Procedure for Partition Is Made Public and Dominion Status Is Offered

SHIFT DUE THIS SUMMER

Parliament to Act Speedily—Churchill Praises Attlee and Mountbatten

Text of Attlee's statement on India situation, page 3.

By HERBERT L. MATTHEWS
Special to THE NEW YORK TIMES.

LONDON, June 3—The procedure for dividing India, an offer of dominion status and the transfer of British power this summer, and the fact that the Indian leaders had accepted these proposals were all announced today in New Delhi and London.

It was one of the most momentous days in India's long history. But overshadowing all details of the new plan is the astonishing fact that India, and almost certainly Burma—has been kept, at least temporarily, within the framework of the British Commonwealth.

It may well be necessary for the world to reverse its belief that the British Empire is melting away, since India is for all practical purposes, the heart and guts of Britain's Empire. This development seemed impossible only four months ago. Today, there is exultation in London.

Even Winston Churchill, sometimes called the most die-hard of all British believers in the Empire and its historic links to India, got up in the House of Commons and congratulated Prime Minister Attlee and the Viceroy Viscount Mountbatten, on their accomplishment. He conceded that they had succeeded in doing what he had sent Sir Stafford Cripps to India in 1942 to do: to keep India within the British Commonwealth and to get the consent of the major Indian communities to an agreed procedure for the transfer of power.

History Being Made

History was being made fast and furiously today. First, the great news came from New Delhi that the Indian leaders had agreed to work within the new plan. Then came the simultaneous announcements and the reading of the British Government's White Paper containing the details of the plan to both Houses of Parliament.

Meanwhile, the Viceroy, Pandit Jawaharlal Nehru, Mohammed Ali Jinnah and Sardar Baldev Singh were all making broadcasts in India, while here this evening Mr. Attlee also made a brief radio introduction to a rebroadcast of the Viceroy's radio talk. Press conference headlines and stories spread the news like wildfire.

The text of the plan is contained in a brief Government White Paper. It begins by referring to past hopes that the Indians would agree among themselves and by giving credit to the Hindus and Sikhs for setting up a Constituent Assembly in New Delhi and trying to make the Cabinet mission's plan work. It is pointed out that the Moslem League and the Moslems generally refused to participate in the Constituent Assembly.

Won't Frame Constitution

Hence "the task of devising a method by which the wishes of the Indian people can be ascertained has devolved on His Majesty's Government," says the White Paper. It adds that there is no intention to frame an ultimate Constitution for India or to prevent unification in the future.

It goes on to say that present Constituent Assembly will continue, but that its decisions cannot apply to those regions unwilling to accept its jurisdiction.

Hence a plan is offered to ascertain whether the people in those other regions want to form a separate Constituent Assembly.

The procedure is then suggested for getting the Legislative Assemblies of Bengal and the Punjab to decide whether those provinces should be divided, with western Punjab and eastern Bengal going to Pakistan. Rough boundary divisions are suggested for voting purposes, but the final boundaries, if there is partition, would be settled by boundary commissions.

The Legislative Assembly of the Province of Sind will make its decision whether to join Pakistan. The North-West Frontier Province, which although overwhelmingly Moslem has a Congress party Government and participates in the

Continued on Page 3, Column 6

THE BRITISH PLAN FOR THE PARTITION OF INDIA

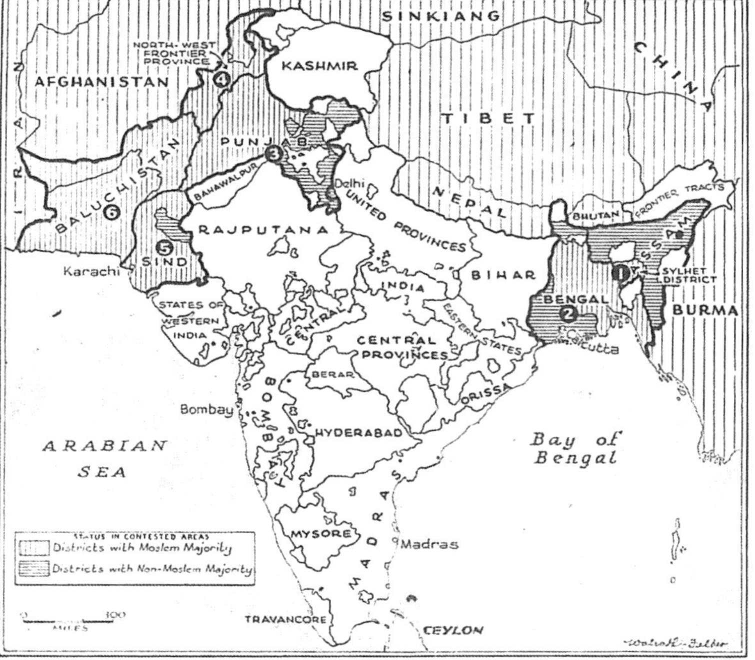

June 4, 1947

The shaded regions within the heavy black borders comprise the area from which the Moslem nation of Pakistan is to be evolved; the unshaded territories within these borders are Princely States. Under the British program, the Sylhet district in Assam (1) will hold a referendum to decide whether to join Moslem eastern Bengal if Bengal (2) is partitioned. The Provincial Legislatures of Bengal and the Punjab (3) will meet in Moslem and non-Moslem sections to decide on partition. A referendum in the North-West Frontier Province (4) is provided for, contingent upon the action taken in the Punjab; the Legislature of Sind (5) will make its decision at a special meeting, and Baluchistan (6) will have an opportunity to consider its position. The unshaded areas in the rest of India are states conceded to be Hindu or Princely States.

U.S., Argentina End Dispute; Hemisphere Parley Speeded

By WALTER H. WAGGONER
Special to THE NEW YORK TIMES.

WASHINGTON, June 3—The United States is satisfied with Argentina's compliance with the anti-Nazi provisions of the Act of Chapultepec and is now willing to resume discussions of a Western Hemisphere defense pact with the Latin-American nations, President Truman disclosed today.

The Government's new readiness for pan-American solidarity in general and American-Argentine amity in particular was revealed by the President in a statement issued immediately after a visit from Oscar Ivanissevich, the Argentine Ambassador. The meeting, when announced earlier today, was widely interpreted as a key conference in the long-delayed rapprochement. The President's statement was accepted by well-informed observers as the confirmation of this view. It read:

"The Argentine Ambassador, who has just returned from Argentina, reviewed with the President and the Secretary of State the steps which his Government has taken and is continuing to take in fulfillment of its commitments undertaken in the Final Act of the Inter-American Conference on Problems of War and Peace. He expressed the view of his Government that no obstacle remained to discussions looking toward the treaty of mutual assistance contemplated by the Act of Chapultepec. The President indicated his willingness to renew the consultations with the Governments of the other American republics initiated by the United States memo-

Continued on Page 14, Column 6

RUSSIA NOW ASKING LESS ATOM CONTROL

Gromyko in U. N. Would Limit Inspection, to Follow the Outlawing of Bomb

By A. M. ROSENTHAL
Special to THE NEW YORK TIMES.

LAKE SUCCESS, N. Y., June 3—Andrei A. Gromyko sharpened Russia's demand today for a high-priority treaty to outlaw the atomic bomb and announced that he would again carry the fight through to the United Nations Security Council.

The Soviet Deputy Foreign Minister presented a new resolution to the working committee of the Atomic Energy Commission, placing the necessity for prohibition of the bomb at the top of the list of atomic problems. International control of atomic energy, the Russian motion said, should come as a "complement" to outlawing the bomb.

Faced with immediate opposition from Britain, Canada, Australia, Belgium and Brazil, Mr. Gromyko conceded that he could not win a majority, and said he

Continued on Page 7, Column 4

Floods Flow Over Up-State Area; Rutland, Vt., Evacuating Families

By The Associated Press.

SYRACUSE, N. Y., June 3—The Gould Paper Company's dam at McKeever went out tonight, threatening new floods along the Moose and Black Rivers as rain-swollen streams receded elsewhere in flooded upstate areas.

The Moose river tore through the 300-foot lumber mill dam and swirled toward Lyons Falls, the first town on its 18-mile wilderness route. State police warned that Lyons Falls might be flooded by morning. The Black River already had inundated valley farm lands to the north. In a day of floods that drove families from their homes, closed roads, washed out bridges and railroad tracks and disrupted electric power in many parts of the state.

Flood conditions extended from the northern Adirondacks, through the Mohawk River valley and Finger Lakes region to the Pennsylvania border.

The rain let up generally today after overnight falls of from 2.5 to 3.81 inches. Overflowing streams inundated parts of Moravia and Ithaca, both of which were flooded two weeks ago; Elmira, devastated a year ago by a flash flood, and Syracuse, Watkins Glen, Moravia Falls, Barneveld, Wellsville, Scio, Watertown and Crown Point.

The Weather Bureau predicted fair skies for tomorrow.

Close to 300 families in a six-block area of Oneida were virtually isolated. Boats were utilized to move some to higher ground and carry workers to and from their jobs, after Oneida Creek had risen nearly eight feet. The water began receding tonight.

About thirty-five families were moved from the Ithaca College veterans housing project, as Six-Mile Creek crept up. By nightfall, the creek had receded and opening of a dam forestalled dam-

Continued on Page 30, Column 6

VANDENBERG SEES NEED FOR U. N. TRIAL ON HUNGARIAN COUP

Scores 'Apparent Treacherous Conquest' and Questions the Role Played by Russia

PACT RATIFICATION ASKED

Delay Would Prolong Soviet's Control, Senator Declares—Vote on Treaties Is Set

By C. P. TRUSSELL
Special to THE NEW YORK TIMES.

WASHINGTON, June 3—Senator Arthur H. Vandenberg, denouncing the "apparent treacherous conquest" of Hungary by the Communists, told the Senate today that it might become the duty of the United States to bring Hungary's case "to trial" before the United Nations.

The Republican President pro tempore of the Senate and chairman of the Foreign Relations Committee presented this view while calling upon his colleagues to ratify speedily the peace treaties with Italy, Hungary, Rumania and Bulgaria.

Taking vigorous leadership as the long-pending treaties underwent floor consideration, Mr. Vandenberg said the United States could not condone "by way of silence" what had happened in Hungary in the last ten days.

He charged that the autonomy of a people "appears to have been destroyed within a few short months by those same minorities which were overwhelmingly repudiated at the Hungarian polls."

"Call to Trial" Discussed

Then Senator Vandenberg declared:

"This may become, Mr. President, a clear call, if the facts justify these presumptions—a clear call to trial in the forum of the United Nations; and, I repeat, if the facts justify these presumptions, it will become America's duty to sound that call."

Mr. Vandenberg also declared that the Communists' actions in Hungary had raised "definite implications of Moscow's influence in these unholy events."

But Mr. Vandenberg contended that the Communist coup in Hungary did not provide reason for delay or rejection of the treaties, including the pact with Hungary.

These treaties, he reminded the Senate, represent "the consensus" of twenty-one nations. While they are not all that the United States

Continued on Page 8, Column 4

HUNGARIAN PURGE OF VOTERS PUSHED

Ministry Urges the Exclusion of 'Enemies of Democracy'—Envoy to U. S. Recalled

By ALBION ROSS
Special to THE NEW YORK TIMES.

BUDAPEST, Hungary, June 3—Hungarian Minister of Justice Istvan Ries announced today that he would meet tomorrow or Thursday with the Communist Minister of the Interior and head of the police, Laszlo Rajk, to work on a new election law.

"All who without a doubt are enemies of democracy must be excluded from the franchise," he said. "Democratic rights can be

Continued on Page 12, Column 3

Congress Would Override Labor Veto, Truman Is Told

Hatch Visits White House; Says He Believes Chances President Will Sign Bill Are Stronger—Final Vote Today Sought

By WILLIAM S. WHITE
Special to THE NEW YORK TIMES.

WASHINGTON, June 3—President Truman was directly informed today by an old Democratic Senatorial colleague of a prevailing Capitol opinion that a veto of the Republican labor bill would be overridden, if by a rather thin edge.

Senator Carl A. Hatch of New Mexico, an Administration follower and a close friend, called on the President on the eve of foregone—and heavy—House approval of the measure, a composite of the original bills separately passed by Senate and House.

As is protocol in these cases, Mr. Hatch declined to discuss any of the details of his conference with Mr. Truman. All the circumstances nevertheless made it wholly plain that the Senator had put the position to the President as it is viewed by many in Congress.

This forecast was that the House would brush aside a veto in the most decisive terms, and that the Senate would do likewise, but by a far closer vote.

Laying great stress upon the statement that he was giving an opinion wholly unconnected with any talk with the President, Senator Hatch observed:

"In normal times I think—from all I know of the President's convictions and record—that a veto would be the answer. Now, with more labor trouble threatened (in coal) one has somewhat to revise his thinking. Certainly, in my opinion, the chances are stronger than they would have been otherwise that the President will now approve this bill."

Meanwhile, a minority group of House Democrats standing at the thinly manned barricades against the bill asked, and received, leave from the President to go down to the White House tomorrow to urge their case for a veto.

The list of those proposing to

Continued on Page 18, Column 2

Obedience to 'Book of Rules' Slows Up Two Subway Lines

By CHARLES GRUTZNER

A subway slowdown on the city's IRT division hit the West Side line at the start of the evening rush hour yesterday, resulting in sluggish operation for a full hour. The evening slowdown and one in the morning on the IND division, which retarded sixty trains from Queens by five to eight minutes, were ascribed last night by Austin Hogan, president of Local 100, Transport Workers Union, CIO, to a decision by subway workers to "live up to the book of rules."

The TWU is trying to persuade Mayor O'Dwyer to oust Charles P. Gross, chairman of the Board of Transportation, because of Mr. Gross' rejection of the plan favored by the Mayor for negotiations between the board and its employes. The union also has charged Mr. Gross with making punitive assignments, in violation of seniority, of motormen and conductors on IND train runs.

Mr. Hogan said workers on the BMT subway had joined those on the IND and IRT in "living up to the book of rules," but a spokesman for the Board of Transportation denied last night that there had been any unusual incidents in BMT operation. John Wiley, night trainmaster of the BMT, said that "one or two trains were three or four minutes late," which made it an average night.

The IRT slowdown started, according to the Board of Transportation, with a train that left New Lots Avenue, Brooklyn, at 5:01 P. M. and was due at Van Cortlandt Park at 6:21 P. M. The train reached Van Cortlandt Park twenty-nine minutes late, with the result that succeeding trains were slowed up.

The motorman of the 5:01, James Lanigan, a subway veteran of many years of service, was questioned last night by Charles Russo, IRT night trainmaster. Mr. Russo said Mr. Lanigan told him he had had no mechanical trouble, but had kept his train in some stations as long as two minutes before all the waiting passengers boarded it. Mr.

Continued on Page 20, Column 4

MAYOR DENOUNCES TAFT-HARTLEY BILL

In Radio Talk for AFL He Calls It 'a Stab in Back of Our Free Labor Movement'

Mayor O'Dwyer, speaking last night on a national radio network under the auspices of the American Federation of Labor, vigorously opposed the Taft-Hartley revision of the Wagner Labor Relations Act as class legislation, sponsored by Republicans and "others who "fear the working man."

The Mayor, who had already indicated his opposition to the measure by a proclamation setting today as a day of city-wide protest against the measure, called it "a stab in the back of our free labor movement."

"Those of us who sincerely believe in free private enterprise also believe in free collective bargaining," the Mayor declared. "Freedom cannot be apportioned on a class basis. If the Republicans want the freedom for capital to own and operate businesses, as I do, they must also recognize the right of the working men and women to own and operate their unions.

"Now let me make this perfectly clear. I'm prepared to have it out both ways. I am against any kind of state control—for business or labor. I have an intense loathing and hatred for the Fascist and Communist glorification of the state at the expense of the individual.

"Let me also make this clear. Government has a job to do in cor-

Continued on Page 20, Column 6

World News Summarized

WEDNESDAY, JUNE 4, 1947

The Senate yesterday passed the Republican income tax reduction bill, 48 to 28, three votes less than the two-thirds majority required to override President Truman's expected veto. [1:8.] Federal Reserve Chairman Eccles said a tax cut now would be inflationary and would deepen and prolong an inevitable business recession. [25:1.]

A drop in production, sales and prices during the last half of this year was predicted in a report handed to a Senate-House committee that will open hearings June 23 on the nation's general business outlook. [41:1.]

Senator Hatch told President Truman that Congress would override a veto of the Taft-Hartley Labor Bill, scheduled for passage in the House today. House Democrats will call on the President to urge him to disapprove the measure. [1:6-7.] AFL unions in this city will hold a "veto rally" today. Mayor O'Dwyer, who will be one of the speakers [20:3], attacked the Republican bill in a radio talk. [1:7.]

Disquieting labor news came from Detroit, where the Briggs contract negotiations were called off by the company, which charged a "wildcat" strike, and Ford workers at one plant voted overwhelmingly for a strike. [21:4.] In Washington Southern coal operators offered an 85-cent daily wage increase, but insisted on an eight instead of a seven-hour day. Union rejection was forecast. [21:5.]

A House committee will open hearings next week on compulsory universal training. [19:6.] "War is mankind's most tragic and stupid folly," General Eisenhower told the West Point graduating class. The particular role of the professional soldier, he added, is to preserve "our American heritage of human dignity and justice for all" to the end that the nation become "a leader in the ways of peace." [19:2.]

President Truman announced that he was satisfied with Argentina's compliance with the Act of Chapultepec and was prepared to resume discussions on a hemisphere defense pact with all American republics. [1:2-3.] The President should have authority to send military missions to any countries requesting them, Secretary Marshall declared. [8:1.]

The "apparent treacherous conquest" of Hungary by the Communists may be "a clear call to trial in the forum of the United Nations," Senator Vandenberg said during Senate debate. He declared it made even more urgent speedy ratification of the peace treaties with Italy and the former Axis satellites. [1:5.] In Budapest, Hungary's Justice Minister said the election law must be "fully" changed and the vote withheld from "enemies of democracy." [1:4.]

Premier Ramadier accused French Communists of fomenting labor troubles for political purposes. [9:1.]

International inspection and control of atomic energy must wait until the atomic bomb is outlawed by covenant, Russia insisted again before a committee of the United Nations Atomic Energy Commission. [1:2.]

Britain's plan for turning India over to the Indians was announced in London and New Delhi. The proposal for separate Hindu and Moslem states, with dominion status, was received with joy in London, as evidence that the British Empire was not dissolving. [1:1.] Hindu, Moslem and Sikh leaders accepted the proposal, although far from satisfied. [3:1.]

The slowdown on this city's subway system spread during the evening rush hour from the IND to the West Side line of the IRT Division. [1:6-7.]

Jersey Charter Revision Favored By Large Majority in Light Voting

New Jersey voters approved overwhelmingly yesterday the holding of a constitutional convention to revise the 103-year-old state charter. Voting throughout the state was exceedingly light as no high public positions were at stake.

Incomplete compilations showed that in 1,716 election districts out of a total of 3,678 there were 116,742 votes authorizing a constitutional convention and 18,240 against.

In primary elections, also held yesterday, the voters nominated county officials and legislative representatives as well as Mayors in sixty municipalities.

By yesterday's will of the majority, the eighty-one successful delegates will hold the first session of the convention on June 12 in the gymnasium at Rutgers University in New Brunswick.

Gov. Alfred E. Driscoll said he could see no need for a special session of the Legislature to certify the results of the balloting on the charter revision proposal and the election of delegates. Formal requirements that the Legislature be informed of the results, the Governor indicated, probably would be fulfilled by notifying the officers of the Senate and Assembly and possibly by written formal notice to all legislators.

In the Paterson Democratic primary Michael De Vita, organization candidate, defeated John Delaney for the mayoralty nomination. With all 101 election districts in, Mr. De Vita received 5,883 votes to 1,597 for Mr. Delaney. Mayor William P. Furrey, Republican incumbent, though unopposed for his party's nomination, received 3,512 votes.

In Union County, Kenneth C. Hand seemed certain of designation for the Senate seat formerly held by Herbert J. Pascoe, who resigned. Mr. Hand, who was opposed by three candidates in the

Continued on Page 24, Column 4

TAX BILL IS PASSED BY SENATE, 48-28; TRUMAN TO DECIDE

Republican Leaders Concede Upper Chamber Will Sustain Veto if He Exercises It

TAFT HITS SUCH ACTION

Says President's Disapproval Would Put Him on Side of the 'High Spenders'

By JOHN D. MORRIS
Special to THE NEW YORK TIMES.

WASHINGTON, June 3—The Senate completed Congressional action on the tax reduction bill today amid persistent reports that President Truman would veto it.

The measure, calling for cuts ranging from 10.5 to 30 per cent in personal income taxes beginning July 1, was approved in its final form by a vote of 48 to 28.

That was three votes short of a two-thirds majority, which would be required to override a veto, but the apparent narrowness of the margin was somewhat misleading because of a large number of absentees.

On passage of the bill May 28, before it went to a joint conference for adjustment of differences with the House, the Senate's majority of 52 to 34 lacked six votes of two-thirds.

The action today, completing the redemption of a major Republican campaign pledge, put the fate of tax reduction this year into the hands of the President, who has announced his opposition to it.

No Substitute Bill Planned

Conceding the probable lack of sufficient strength in the Senate to override a veto, Republican leaders have served notice that they will institute no substitute measure if President Truman kills the approved bill.

The measure will be sent to the White House as soon as it is signed by Speaker Joseph W. Martin Jr., who was out of the city today. He is expected to affix his signature tomorrow, in which case Mr. Truman will have until midnight June 17 to act or allow the bill to become law without his approval.

Mr. Truman has repeatedly expressed his opposition to tax cuts this year on the ground that any surplus should be applied to the national debt. When the time comes for a reduction, low-income groups should have priority, he has asserted. His supporters in Congress argue that small taxpayers would not be helped sufficiently under the Republicans' bill.

A number of members predicted that Mr. Truman would veto the bill quickly, but most of them acknowledged that they did not have the word directly from the President.

Roosevelt's Veto Recalled

If their forecasts come true, it will be the second veto of a general tax bill in the country's history. The first, by President Roosevelt in 1944, was promptly overridden.

Traditional Congressional jealousy of its tax-writing prerogatives, a condition pointed up in a statement today by Senator Robert A. Taft, Republican, of Ohio, was considered to have had less influence on the 1944 action, however, than the strong language in which Mr. Roosevelt couched his veto message.

"The determination of tax policy always has been peculiarly the function of Congress and the House of Representatives, just as foreign policy is peculiarly the function of the President," said Mr. Taft, who is chairman of the Senate Republican Policy Committee.

"The President ought not to veto this bill," the Ohioan asserted, "unless he regards it as a dangerous threat to the welfare of the country, which it obviously is not."

A free economy cannot operate successfully under the present tax burden, and once inflation stops, a burden of this kind might turn a slight recession into a serious depression, Mr. Taft said, adding:

"All the spenders want to keep the tax receipts up to $40,000,000,000 in order to maintain a high standard of Government spending. The quicker we can revise our sights downward, the lower we can keep the expenditures.

"I don't believe the President can afford to veto this bill, because it would put him definitely on the side of high taxes and high expenses."

It was unanimously believed here that the Senate would sustain a veto and thus kill the bill, should the President disapprove it. Votes

Continued on Page 25, Column 2

COLLAPSE OF COLONIALISM

HELENE COOPER

Members of the Kikuyu tribe in native dress attend a reception in 1963 to welcome home Kenyan Prime Minister Jomo Kenyatta from a visit to London.

Suspected members of the Mau Mau are questioned by the British military for the murder of Europeans.

I grew up in West Africa with dreams of Mau Mau rebels filling my head, imaginary pangas clutched in my hand.

It was the 1970's, and the Mau Mau, those fearsome Kikuyu who fought for land and freedom and helped bring about the end of British colonial rule in Kenya, had lived a continent away and two decades before me. But my cousins and I, playing on the beach in Liberia, pretended we were Mau Maus, fighting to reclaim our Africa from the Europeans.

The Mau Mau rebellion in 1952 was really the final nail on Britain's colonial empire.[1] Sure, by the time the Kikuyu rose against the white settlers in Kenya, Britain was out of India, Pakistan, Egypt and Palestine. But Africa, where a hardened core of white settlers believed strongly that the red earth and violent sunsets were their own birthright, was still in play. And in Kenya, there was still the certainty among the ruling whites that this was a white man's country.

The Mau Mau rebellion changed that, and curiously, it did so not by achieving any of its goals—the Kikuyu, after four intense years of fighting, lost to the British military.

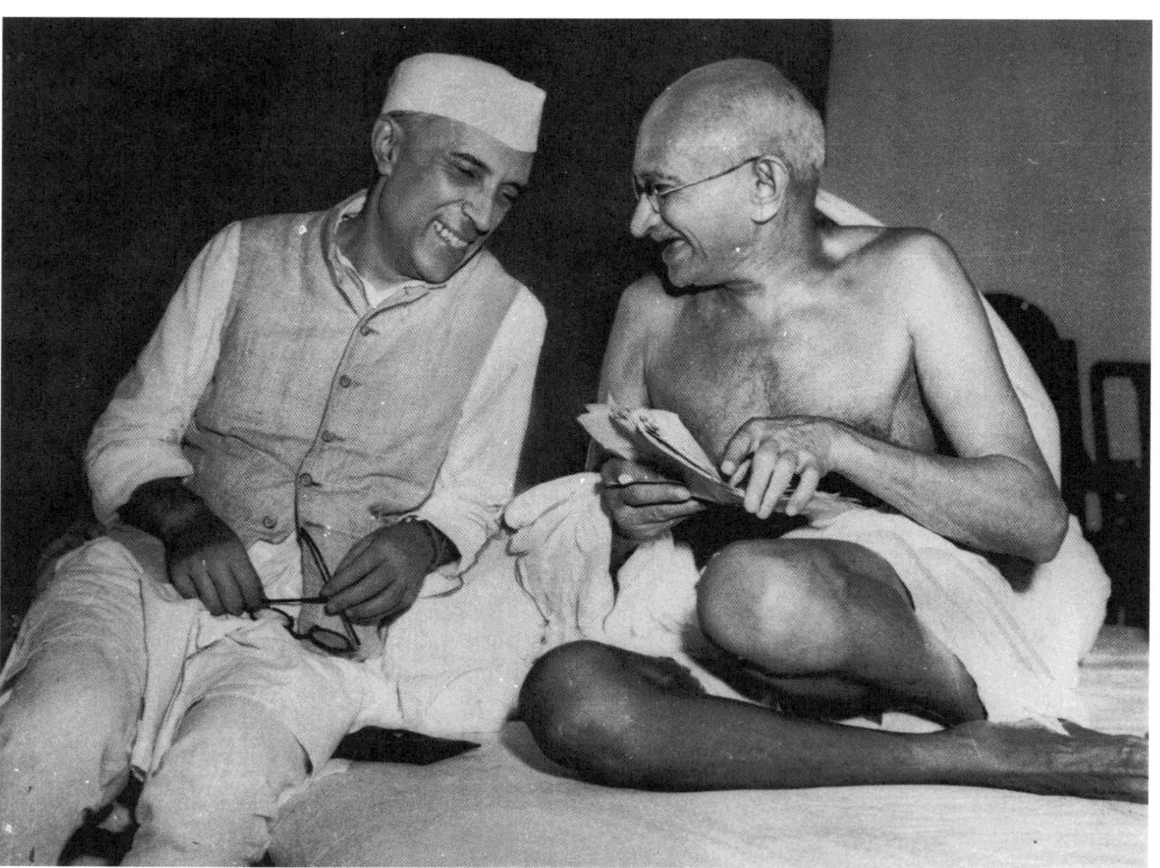

Mohandas Gandhi and Jawaharlal Nehru, the leaders of India's independence movement, meet in Bombay in 1946.

"When the fighting ended in 1956, white settlers still owned their farms in the highlands," writes Robert B. Edgerton in "Mau Mau: An African Crucible." "By 1956, most of Kenya's Africans had repudiated the Mau Mau. The rebellion was over, its goals unmet, its legacy uncertain."

At least, that's what many Mau Mau rebels and their supporters initially thought. What they didn't realize, at first, was that even though the rebellion had been crushed, its lasting impact would be to change the face of those who would rule Kenya. Britain had already begun to withdraw from its colonies around the world, but in Kenya, the white settlers were determined to stay, and to rule, in some form, separate from the British government if necessary.

The Mau Mau revolution forced those white settlers to rethink their plans, in large part because they weren't able to hold off the Mau Mau on their own. They were forced to call up British forces to bail them out—a bad omen for their future plans of running the country once Britain left Kenya.[2]

Unlike some other independence movements in Africa, the Mau Maus, besides hitting government targets, also went after what we would today call "soft targets"—what the Pentagon war planners euphemistically call "strikes against counter-population" targets. In plain English, that means they attacked white farms and families, even, at times, children.

I interviewed Ugandan President Yoweri Kaguta Museveni[3] during a 2007 visit to Washington. After a few

FURTHER READING

1 "British Worried by Kenya Terror," see October 20, 1952, article.
2 "British Put Troops in Kenya To Halt a Reign of Killings," see October 21, 1952, front page.
3 "Uganda's President Wins Third Term," see February 26, 2006, article.

Jomo Kenyatta became the first President of Kenya in 1964 after being imprisoned by the British for nine years.

This cat was found strangled next to a note written in blood threatening death to anyone who worked with the white population in Kenya.

British soldiers inspect the credentials of Kikuyu tribesmen to determine whether they might be members of the Mau Mau.

Suspected Mau Mau prisoners sit in the roadway of a prison camp in Kenya in 1952.

A Mau Mau stands in a dock in a British colonial court surrounded by Kenyan guards who were part of the British military.

minutes of small talk, Mr. Museveni quickly sidetracked to a favored topic among African heads of state: the mid-20th-century fight against colonialism in Africa.

"When we were all fighting colonialism, we fought and defeated the colonialists but we never resorted to terrorism," he said.

"What about the Mau Mau?" I asked him.

A smile and a sigh. "Okay, except the Mau Mau," he allowed. "The Mau Mau was not as disciplined as the other groups."

This seeming ambivalence toward the Mau Mau is prevalent among many Africans who want to appear politically correct. The Mau Mau did some pretty horrible things. On January 24, 1953, several Mau Mau raiders, aided by family servants, lured a white farmer, Roger Ruck, out of his farm and killed him with African machetes, called pangas. When his wife, Esme, ran out to her husband, they killed her too, and when their 6-year-old son, Michael, called out, frightened, from his room, he too was killed.[4]

The killings shocked Kenya—especially since the man who confessed to killing Michael was a Kikuyu servant who, just days before, had reportedly carried the little boy home tenderly after he fell from a horse. That, along with other Mau Mau attacks against settlers, fed the belief among the white settlers in Kenya that Africans were savages capable of unspeakable cruelty.

The contradiction, of course, is that far more Africans were killed during the Mau Mau revolution than white settlers, but few people at the time talked much about those killings, leaving many Africans convinced that the value of their lives did not equal the value of the lives of white settlers.[5]

My cousins and I, playing on the beach as children in West Africa and dreaming of the Mau Mau, were proud of the idea that Africans actually stood up to white colonialists to demonstrate that their lives were just as fragile as the lives of the hundreds of thousands of Africans who died during the struggles that raged as Europe colonized Africa. It's a perverted thought now—certainly we weren't proud of the Mau Mau for killing the Ruck family. We were just proud of them for giving the white settlers something to fear, just as Africans feared the whites.

The British government poured enormous resources into helping the white settlers defeat the Mau Mau, and by

1956, the rebellion was over and the British had won.[6] But by then, Britain's battles against Africans were a political embarrassment. The economic cost of holding on to the colonies no longer made sense, which meant that the next time there was a rebellion in Kenya, the white settlers couldn't count on the British to bail them out.

I understood little of this as a child, yelling my "Mau Mau!" war cry as I jumped on my brother's back on the beach. All I knew was that that scream meant that I was African, and ready to fight to keep my land my own.

HELENE COOPER *is diplomatic correspondent for The New York Times. Previously, she was the assistant Washington bureau chief of The Wall Street Journal. In 2000 Cooper won the Raymond Clapper Award for stories on China's entry into the World Trade Organization. In 2001, she won the Sandy Hume Memorial Award for Excellence in Political Journalism and in 2004, a National Association of Black Journalists' Salute to Excellence Award. A memoir, "The House at Sugar Beach," was published in 2008.*

4 "Kenya Terrorists Slay a Family of 3," see January 26, 1953, article.
5 "Mau Mau Massacres 150 Natives In Night Raid Near Kenya Capital," see March 28, 1953, front page.
6 "Mau Mau Campaign is Ended by Britain," see November 14, 1956 front page.

Kikuyu tribesman gather on the eve of Kenyan independence from England in 1963.

Former Mau Mau guerillas and their families commemorate the 50th anniversary of their movement in 2000.

"All the News That's Fit to Print"

The New York Times.

LATE CITY EDITION
Fair and warmer today and tomorrow.
Temperatures Yesterday—Max., 65; Min., 54
Sunrise today, 5:26 A.M.; Sunset, 8:23 P. M.
Full U. S. Weather Bureau Report, Page 45

VOL. XCVI...No. 32,640. Entered as Second-Class Matter. Postoffice, New York, N. Y. NEW YORK, FRIDAY, JUNE 6, 1947. THREE CENTS IN NEW YORK CITY

TRUMAN CALLS HUNGARY COUP OUTRAGE, DEMANDS RUSSIANS AGREE TO INQUIRY; MARSHALL PLEADS FOR EUROPEAN UNITY

PRESIDENT HOLDS TAFT'S ECONOMICS FALSE, DANGEROUS

BOOM-BUST IDEA HIT

Truman Attacks a View That Demand Justifies Keeping Prices High

INSISTS THEY CAN BE CUT

Decline From April Peak Noted in Formal Reply to Charge High Levels Are Wanted

Truman's statement criticizing Taft's economic views, Page 18.

By HAROLD B. HINTON
Special to THE NEW YORK TIMES.

WASHINGTON, June 5—President Truman, in a highly unusual step, denounced today as "fallacious and dangerous" certain economic views he attributed to Senator Robert A. Taft, Republican, of Ohio, one of the leaders of the majority party in Congress. A year ago he condemned Mr. Taft's economics in his message vetoing the first bill for the extension of price control.

In a long prepared statement which he read at his news conference today Mr. Truman took the position that the Ohio Senator stood for the theory that "high demand justifies or necessitates high prices." The President said that this view could only rely on "the old idea of boom and bust."

The Chief Executive included in his statement a table, prepared by the Bureau of Labor Statistics, which showed that prices of all commodities, taken together, had declined by two points by May 31 from the peak reached on April 30. The figure was 147.4 for the end of May, as compared with 149.4 for the end of April. These figures are based on 1926 levels as equaling 100.

Calls Again for Price Cuts

Still showing resentment at the virtual abandonment of price controls last summer, the President repeated his belief that the danger of collapse in the national economy could be averted by voluntary price reductions, now that price controls no longer existed. This has been his principal suggestion throughout his price-reduction campaign of the past few months.

The Presidential statement was a reply to a remark Senator Taft was said to have made to the effect that "the President and the Administration are abandoning talk of keeping prices down in favor of heavy spending abroad that will keep them up." Mr. Truman took this as an allusion to the Greek-Turkish aid program, which he considered the foundation of the Truman Doctrine.

He conceded that all foreign aid programs would put a strain on the American economy, but he said their abandonment would be as unintelligent as would have been the renunciation of the war effort because it created national economic problems.

The President took the position that these added burdens should stimulate the thinking of business and industrial leaders to exercise voluntary price restraint, "in their own interests as well as the interest of the American economy and the world situation."

Taft Delays His Reply

Senator Taft was busy all day on the Senate floor, piloting the labor bill. At the end of the session he said he would have no statement to make tonight, preferring to prepare at a later time what he will consider to be an adequate reply to the Presidential statement.

The President said that the administration's program to "aid starving millions and restore their economies was designed to promote world prosperity, and to enable them to resist totalitarian aggression until such time as they could stand on their own feet. The fact that this program entailed economic problems in the United States, he added, "makes it all the more important that we handle these domestic problems with vigor and common sense."

He accused Senator Taft of advocating reduction in demand as the only way of lowering prices.

Continued on Page 18, Column 3

'Death to Peron' Cry Interrupts His Talk

By The Associated Press.

BUENOS AIRES, June 5—A mysterious voice, shouting "Death to Perón!" interrupted a broadcast by President Juan D. Perón tonight. An Argentine Nationalist is believed to have been responsible.

President Perón was broadcasting over a national hook-up at a public farewell for his wife, Eva Duarte Perón, who is to leave tomorrow on a European tour.

The Argentine News Agency said authorities were examining the theory that a clandestine radio transmitter had broken into the Presidential broadcast.

When the President's speech was broken off, the unidentified broadcaster made a short speech denouncing "those who proclaim themselves supporters of a false social justice" and ending, "Death to Perón!"

VETO TACTIC DELAYS SENATE LABOR VOTE

Foes Assail Bill to Set Case for Rejection—Tell Truman Signing Means '48 Defeats

By WILLIAM S. WHITE
Special to THE NEW YORK TIMES.

WASHINGTON, June 5—President Truman was put under powerful pressure today, direct and oblique, to veto the Hartley-Taft labor bill as the Senate opened its last grand detailed debate on that measure.

Senate action on the bill was hoped for by tomorrow by its principal author, Senator Robert A. Taft, Republican, of Ohio.

The minority opposition plainly was not in the mood for any rapid decision and began a running attack on the bill almost from the moment Mr. Taft had taken the floor in the afternoon to open the debate. It was still possible that tomorrow might not bring the end.

The Taft forces had believed it possible to get a vote today, but this prospect vanished quickly.

The strategy of the opposition, in its efforts to bring about a veto, was in dual movements.

One of these was a direct personal appeal to Mr. Truman, made during the day by three Democratic callers from the House, who suggested to the President in effect that unless he disapproved the legislation the Democratic party would lose in 1948 some of the great metropolitan areas, and specifically New York City.

Representative Arthur G. Klein, Democrat, of New York, asserted to Mr. Truman flatly that the city was lost without a veto, and submitted to the President the photographs of a Madison Square Garden veto rally published in this morning's NEW YORK TIMES.

Representative John Lesinski, Democrat, of Michigan, was understood to have exhibited similar pictures of a recent unionist demonstration in Detroit.

Representative Ray J. Madden,

Continued on Page 18, Column 7

SUBWAY SHUT-DOWN AS SAFETY MEASURE ENVISAGED BY QUILL

Union Leader Charges Laxity of Car Inspection on City-Operated System

EMERGENCY ACTS SCORED

Transit Board Denies Neglect of Safety—Sees Slow-Down Virtually Overcome

By CHARLES GRUTZNER

The possibility of a shut-down of the subway system, today or Monday, on the ground that operation is unsafe under present conditions, was raised yesterday by City Councilman Michael J. Quill, international president of the Transport Workers Union, CIO.

Mr. Quill said at City Hall that the union would "stand by the workers in their refusal to operate any subway cars which are not fully inspected." He added that the union was compiling a list of Board of Transportation supervisors who were "trying to force motormen to take out cars without brake inspection."

The allegedly unsafe conditions, according to TWU officials, are the result in part of emergency operational measures taken by the board to counteract effects of the "book of rules" slowdowns in subway service during the last week. They are due also, according to the union, to a relaxation of safety requirements over a longer period.

"Unsafe" Cars Listed

Austin Hogan, president of TWU Local 100, and Barney Heslin, TWU official assigned to shops of the IND subway, made public a list of allegedly unsafe conditions. Mr. Hogan charged that safeguards against overheating of armature bearings had been removed last week upon order of the shop superintendent. Mr. Heslin said a squad of road car inspectors, whose job was to check on proper application of hand brakes, had been whittled down gradually. The union officials also listed many cars that they said had run beyond the required time without safety check-ups.

The union announced that 150 car inspectors from IRT yards in Manhattan, Brooklyn, the Bronx and Queens had sent to Mayor O'Dwyer a telegram complaining of allegedly inadequate inspection practices adopted by the board in the last few days.

A denial of the union's charges of neglect of safety requirements was made by a board spokesman who said:

"The New York City transit system is still the safest railroad in the world. It is as safe today as it was last month or last year, unless some of these people who are talking know about some things that haven't been reported to us."

Inspection in Barns

The board spokesman added that the road car inspection squad had been discontinued last fall because it was found more efficient to make the same inspections in the car barns. He insisted that there had been no lessening of inspections.

A reward of $500 was authorized by the board for information leading to the arrest and conviction "of the person or persons found guilty of violating Section 1991 of the Penal Law." The section cov-

Continued on Page 17, Column 1

City Seeks 'Authority' to Finance $25,000,000 Parking Program

The use of some form of "authority" to finance, construct and operate the thirty-three municipal parking lots and nine parking garages recommended on Wednesday by Mayor O'Dwyer's Special Traffic Committee will be considered by the Board of Estimate in executive session next week, it was indicated last night.

Direct city financing of the $25,000,000 program or any substantial part of it now seems unlikely because of the limitations of the capital budget, some of the projects of which already face curtailment because of increased costs of labor and materials.

It has been suggested that either the Triborough Bridge and Tunnel Authority or the World Trade Corporation undertake the $25,000,000 traffic relief program.

The former organization already has declared that it does not care to tackle the problem. It prefers to confine its activities in the parking garage field to the structure now planned at the Manhattan approach to the Battery-Brooklyn Tunnel and the proposed 2,000-car parking garage proposed in connection with the new Madison Square Garden project in the Columbus Circle area.

It has been suggested at City Hall, however, that the authority might be induced to alter its stand.

The charter granted by the state to the World Trade Corporation is broad enough to empower that agency to handle the proposed parking lot and garage program, but its entry into that field is doubted.

The corporation is about to start a $150,000 survey of the city's waterfront properties, both public and private, as a preliminary to presentation to the Board

Continued on Page 21, Column 7

SENATE APPROVES 4 PEACE TREATIES, REJECTING DELAY

Ratifies Italian Pact, 79 to 10, and Then Accepts Others Without Recorded Vote

FEAR FOR ITALY IS VOICED

Connally and McMahon Warn of Communist Dangers After U. S. Leaves Area

By C. P. TRUSSELL
Special to THE NEW YORK TIMES.

WASHINGTON, June 5 — The Senate ratified the long-disputed peace treaty with Italy today by a nearly 8-to-1 vote of 79—10. A two-thirds majority was all that was required for formal approval.

This test made, the Senate abandoned roll calling and in rapid succession shouted virtually unanimous ratification of the accompanying treaties with the three former Axis satellite states, Hungary, Rumania and Bulgaria, generally agreed to be now under Soviet domination.

Senate action was thus completed on the first treaties with former enemy nations of World War II. Great Britain already has ratified them. The Soviet Union and France still are to act on the Italian instrument, though France is in technical process of ratification now. France is not an enacting power concerning the treaties with Hungary, Rumania and Bulgaria.

Motion for Delay Defeated

The way for the Senate's fast and decisive action was cleared by a record vote which defeated, 67—22, a motion by Senator J. William Fulbright, Democrat, of Arkansas, that further consideration of all four treaties be postponed until next Jan. 25. Mr. Fulbright, as a member of the House, sponsored in 1943 the first resolution to express Congressional favor for the creation of international machinery, such as developed into the United Nations, for the maintenance of peace.

Voting for the ratification of the Italian treaty were forty-two Republicans and thirty-two Democrats.

Opposing ratification were three Democrats—Senators James O. Eastland of Mississippi, Pat McCarran of Nevada and W. Lee O'Daniel of Texas—and seven Republicans—Senators Styles Bridges of New Hampshire, C. Wayland

Continued on Page 3, Column 3

AS 'CURE' FOR ILLS

Only Then Can Our Aid Be Integrated, Says the Secretary

HITS 'PIECEMEAL' BASIS

He Tells Harvard Alumni Our Policy Is Not Set Against 'Any Country or Doctrine'

Marshall's speech calling for European unity, Page 2.

By FRANK L. KLUCKHOHN
Special to THE NEW YORK TIMES.

CAMBRIDGE, Mass., June 5—The countries of Europe were called upon today by the Secretary of State, George C. Marshall, to get together and decide upon their needs for economic rehabilitation so that further United States aid could be provided upon an integrated instead of a "piecemeal" basis. This was important to make possible a real "cure" of Europe's critical economic difficulties, he asserted in an address to Harvard alumni this afternoon after he had received the honorary degree of Doctor of Laws at this morning's commencement exercises.

General Marshall supported President Truman's statements in Washington earlier today that United States aid abroad was necessary. He declared that Europe "must have substantial additional help or face economic, social and political deterioration of a very grave character."

"There must be some agreement among the countries of Europe as to the requirements of the situation," he warned, adding that no American aid would be given to "any government which maneuvers to block the recovery of other countries." The Secretary emphasized that governments or parties or groups, seeking to make political capital by perpetuating human misery, would encounter "the opposition of the United States."

General Marshall was the recip-

Continued on Page 2, Column 3

World News Summarized

FRIDAY, JUNE 6, 1947

President Truman yesterday denounced the Communist coup in Hungary as an outrage and said the United States did not intend to stand idly by. He approved a sharp note to the Soviet commander in Budapest charging the Russians with implication in the ousting of Premier Nagy in violation of the Yalta Agreement. The note asked for a tripartite investigation and suggested an appeal to the United Nations if no satisfactory reply was received. [1:8.] Leftists in Hungary were busily trying to convince the people that the United States was responsible for Hungary's troubles. [1:6-7.]

Although many Senators were fearful of Italy's fate when American troops were withdrawn, the Senate ratified the Italian peace treaty, 79 to 10, and by voice vote approved the pacts with Hungary, Rumania and Bulgaria. [1:4.]

Dwight Griswold, former Republican Governor of Nebraska, was named to direct the Greek aid program and Richard F. Allen to be Field Administrator of the $350,000,000 post-UNRRA foreign relief fund. [4:1.]

Europe's economic ills can be cured only by an integrated Continental program and not by "piecemeal" palliatives, Secretary Marshall declared in accepting an honorary degree from Harvard. The United States will help, he said, but the European countries themselves must adopt a joint program. Aid, however, will be withheld from "any government which maneuvers to block the recovery of other countries" or, directly or indirectly, seeks "to perpetuate human misery to benefit therefrom." [1:5.]

In reaction to the Marshall address, British opinion held that the United States must relieve the world dollar shortage if Europe is to be revived [3:1] and the French also were uncertain how to reach unified action. [3:8.]

Senator Taft's economic views were characterized by President Truman as "fallacious and dangerous" and "the old idea of boom and bust." [1:1.] Within the Democratic ranks, Henry A. Wallace said he could not support Mr. Truman for another term. [15.1.]

A determined minority prevented the Senate from voting on the Taft-Hartley labor bill. Veto pressure on the President increased. [1:2.] Mr. Truman said he would act on the Republican income-tax reduction measure as soon as it reached him. [12:4-5.]

The House passed and sent to the Senate an Army military fund bill after restoring $40,000,000 for aircraft eliminated in committee. [9:4.] A Senate committee favorably reported, 9 to 1, a compromise bill to create a Cabinet post of Health, Education and Security. [1:7.]

Friendly relations with Argentina have been restored, President Truman announced. Ambassador Messersmith has completed his mission and resigned. [8:4-5.] The United States is not "disposed" to deal with the Nicaragua regime set up by the Somoza coup pending further developments. [8:4.]

President Truman, in a proclamation, asked citizens and residents to avoid action that might "tend to inflame the passions" of Palestine inhabitants during the United Nations inquiry. [1:6-7.]

More British officials received "explosive letters," believed sent from Italy by Zionist sympathizers. [1:6-7.]

Chinese Communists were reported closing in on Mukden, in Manchuria. [11:2.]

In this city, Councilman Quill accused the Board of Transportation of permitting unsafe subway operation and intimated that his men might refuse to run the trains. [1:3.]

U. S. Called Enemy by Reds In Rallies All Over Hungary

Socialists, Now Working With Communists, Believed Next Target of Latter—Soviet-Controlled Banks Not Nationalized

By ALBION ROSS
Special to THE NEW YORK TIMES.

BUDAPEST, June 5—Hundreds of speakers daily at hundreds of meetings throughout Hungary are engaged in agitating against Western nations and in particular against the United States. Communists and Socialists are speaking in the propaganda campaign, which began last Monday and is to last until a week from Sunday. It is now based on the clear-cut theme that the enemy is the United States and the West.

The so-called conspiracy is now presented as essentially a Western "conspiracy" and the victory over former Premier Ferenc Nagy as a victory over the United States. Every effort is being made to convince the Hungarian people that America is the root of evil, representing belligerent imperialism, reaction, Fascist tendencies, monopoly and every other severe epithet that can be found.

Joseph Revai, editor of the Communist organ Nepsava, has announced that Mr. Nagy arranged when he went to the United States to set up a counter-government in America to "betray the Hungarian democracy." The same speaker said:

"America wanted to eliminate Communists merely to save the rich classes [of Hungary] from the capital levy and to prevent nationalization of the banks.

"The reactionaries want to intimidate Hungary by saying she will not receive the $15,000,000. The $15,000,000 would mean eighteen forints for each Hungarian. I am sure there is not a worker who will sell the salvation of his soul to the stockjobbers of Wall Street for eighteen forints."

Communist speakers also are beginning to interpret more openly the purpose of the overthrow of

Continued on Page 3, Column 6

Halt in Palestine Agitation Here Requested by Truman

Special to THE NEW YORK TIMES.

WASHINGTON, June 5—By proclamation today, President Truman called on citizens and residents of the United States to refrain from undermining law and order in Palestine and from promoting violence there. The proclamation was blanket in form and named no organizations or individuals as having engaged in such activities.

The British Government has repeatedly protested the activities of organizations in the United States raising funds to facilitate the entry of Jewish immigrants, styled "illegal" by the British, into Palestine. One such note expressed inability to understand how such organizations could advertise that contributions to such funds may be deducted from personal income for taxation purposes in the same manner as gifts to charitable institutions.

Further complaints have charged that some of the most vigorous instigations of Jewish immigration into Palestine, despite British regulations, have been carried on by non-citizens of the United States who are here on visitors' visas.

TEXT OF STATEMENT

Mr. Truman's statement said:

The General Assembly of the United Nations in special session on May 15, 1947, unanimously adopted the following resolution:

"The General Assembly calls upon all Governments and peoples, and particularly on the inhabitants of Palestine, to refrain, pending action by the General Assembly on the report of the special committee on Palestine, from the threat or use of force or any other action which might create an atmosphere prejudicial

Continued on Page 5, Column 2

TAFT HEALTH BILL REPORTED TO FLOOR

Aiken Group Backs Creation of New Cabinet Post, 9 to 1—Enactment Held Likely

By BESS FURMAN
Special to THE NEW YORK TIMES.

WASHINGTON, June 5—A compromise bill on a Cabinet post for health, education and security was reported favorably today by a 9 to 1 vote of the Senate Committee on Expenditures in the Executive Departments.

Chairman George D. Aiken of Vermont said that this vote, which had surprised him in its expression of strong favorable sentiment, indicated that the bill would become law.

"What it really does is to raise the human being to the level of dignity already enjoyed by the Holstein cow through the Department of Agriculture," he said.

The bill as reported would set up an executive department of health, education and security, with a secretary of Cabinet rank and a $15,000 annual salary.

It would provide for three undersecretaries, one for each field, as

Continued on Page 12, Column 6

Bevin and Eden Get 'Letter Bombs'; Stern Gang Asserts It Sent Them

By MALLORY BROWNE
Special to THE NEW YORK TIMES.

LONDON, June 5—More explosive letters from Italy were handed over to Scotland Yard today, including one addressed to Foreign Secretary Bevin.

At least two other postal bombs arrived today but the police refused to identify their recipients. One is reported to have been Colonial Secretary Arthur Creech Jones but this is unconfirmed.

[The Stern gang claimed the responsibility for the explosive letters, according to a Jerusalem dispatch to THE NEW YORK TIMES. It said they had been sent by its "branch in Europe." Similar envelopes have been found in Palestine in the past. The gang's spokesman said recently that some of its major figures "may have left the country," but he did not say why.]

Former Foreign Secretary Anthony Eden carried a letter bomb in his briefcase for more than twenty-four hours. It was addressed to him at the London offices of The Yorkshire Post and forwarded to the House of Commons on Tuesday. He put it in his briefcase with other letters. "It looked very dull, just like a circular; otherwise I might have opened it on the way home," he said.

Yesterday he went to Eton College for the June celebrations, and when he got home received a warning from Scotland Yard. Even then, however, he did not look, but his secretary pounced on the letter bomb today.

The police have now exploded

Continued on Page 5, Column 4

YALTA BREACH SEEN

U. S. Note Prods Russia—A Terrible Situation, the President Says

U. N. APPEAL IN RESERVE

State Department Cites Terms of Occupation Pact—Vague Reports Accuse Nagy

By JAMES RESTON
Special to THE NEW YORK TIMES.

WASHINGTON, June 5—President Truman denounced the Communist coup in Hungary today as an outrage and approved the dispatch of a sharp note of protest to the Soviet commander in Budapest.

Nothing was said officially in the capital about the note, but responsible officials at the State Department confirmed that it did these things:

(1) Implicated the Soviet authorities in Hungary in the exile and resignation of the Hungarian Premier, Ferenc Nagy, and characterized this as a serious intervention in the internal affairs of Hungary.

(2) Called on the Russians to agree to a United States-Soviet-British investigation of the situation in Hungary.

(3) Charged the Soviet officials in Hungary with breaking the terms of the Yalta agreement, and

(4) Suggested that unless a satisfactory reply was obtained to this communication, the United States might submit the case to the appropriate division of the United Nations.

The President Speaks Out

Without waiting for either the investigation or the reply, however, President Truman spoke out in brisk and general terms in his news conference this morning about the charges that the Communist minority in Hungary, with the aid of Russian Army officials, had forced changes in the Hungarian Government.

Asked for comment on the Hungarian situation, the President replied that it was an outrage. It was a terrible situation, he added, and the United States did not intend to stand idly by under the circumstances. The State Department, he concluded, was making a full investigation.

The direct judgment of the President on the Hungarian situation was the subject of some speculation in diplomatic quarters this evening, in view of certain vague reports that have been reaching here from embassies in the Hungarian capital. These reports do not make any direct charges against former Hungarian Premier Nagy and the former President of the Hungarian Assembly, Bela Varga, but they do suggest that there is reason for believing that the Russians have some concrete evidence that both these officials were engaged in unconstitutional activities.

These reports do not suggest what these "unconstitutional activities" were, but they counsel caution in jumping to conclusions about the internal situation in Hungary until more details are obtained.

State Department Is Milder

Whether or not President Truman was aware of these vague words of caution from Budapest when he commented on the Hungarian situation this morning is not known, but the State Department has seen them, and the official note to Hungary, drafted at the State Department, evidently took them into account.

This note is written in milder terms than the President used. It does speak of the aggressive measures of the Communist minority; and it charges the Russians with interfering in Hungary's internal affairs; but it does not speak about outrages or terrible situations.

Indeed, it states that the United States does not want to engage in recrimination in this matter, but it points out that the Soviet officials in Hungary have certain obligations to the American and British members of the Allied Control Commission in Hungary, and it

Continued on Page 3, Column 2

"All the News That's Fit to Print"

The New York Times.

Copyright, 1948, by The New York Times Company.

LATE CITY EDITION
Fair and warmer today and tomorrow.
Temperature Range Today—Max., 65; Min., 48
Temperatures Yesterday—Max., 53; Min., 46
Full U. S. Weather Bureau Report, Page 31

VOL. XCVII. No. 32,984. Entered as Second-Class Matter, Postoffice, New York, N. Y. NEW YORK, SATURDAY, MAY 15, 1948. Times Square, New York 18, N. Y. Telephone LAckawanna 4-1000 THREE CENTS IN NEW YORK CITY

ZIONISTS PROCLAIM NEW STATE OF ISRAEL; TRUMAN RECOGNIZES IT AND HOPES FOR PEACE; TEL AVIV IS BOMBED, EGYPT ORDERS INVASION

NAVY PUSHES PLAN FOR CONSTRUCTION OF MISSILE VESSELS

Sullivan Asks House Committee to Approve Halting Work on Battleship, Destroyer Types

WANTS 65,000-TON CARRIER

Floating 'Submarine Killers' Are Also Stressed in Plea for Diverting $300,000,000 Fund

By C. P. TRUSSELL
Special to THE NEW YORK TIMES.

WASHINGTON, May 14—The Navy asked Congress today for authority to shift sharply its construction of fighting craft from battleship, cruiser and destroyer types to guided missile vessels, a 65,000-ton carrier able to base, far at sea, planes with an operating radius of 1,700 miles, better submarines and floating "enemy submarine killers."

Such new ships, John L. Sullivan, Secretary of the Navy, told the House Armed Services Committee, must have a higher priority "because of the more immediate need for them in the event of an emergency." The immediate reaction of the committee appeared to favor prompt action.

For such a shift in construction, Secretary Sullivan brought out, the Navy wanted to halt the building of thirteen naval vessels, including the battleship Kentucky, the large cruiser Hawaii, seven destroyers, two destroyer escorts and two submarines. To date about $197,000,000 has been spent on them.

However, this money was not to be abandoned, Mr. Sullivan emphasized. These craft could be converted now to the new program, he explained, or be put aside for a fitting-out later as new weapons were developed.

New Aims for $300,000,000 Fund

What the Navy wanted, Secretary Sullivan asserted, was Congressional permission to divert some $300,000,000 remaining in the present ship construction account to these purposes:

Starting the 65,000-ton aircraft carrier (the biggest ones now are the two of the Midway class, at 45,000 tons), which might cost around $124,000,000.

Building, for reproduction later, of a "submarine killer." (Hearings on the defense program have indicated that Russia has made great progress in the submarine field.) A "killer" machine, it is indicated, is developing in new work on the cruiser type of seacraft.

The construction of four submarines of types advanced beyond those now building.

In addition, there was under plan a conversion in an unidentified way of a carrier and two submarines.

Secretary Sullivan told the committee that the Kentucky and the Hawaii would not have to stand by for the development of new weapons. It is planned, he disclosed, that they be converted into guided missile ships. Apparently to allay fears in Congress that larger aircraft carriers make easier targets for enemy bombers, Mr. Sullivan drew upon experience in the second World War and the results of atom-bomb tests at Bikini.

Speed Held Bomb Defense

"The experiments at Bikini," Mr. Sullivan said, "have proved that a fast-moving fleet is an unprofitable target for an atomic bomb."

Members of the committee interpreted this as a Navy Department conclusion that even though a potential enemy might acquire the atomic bomb, the revised construction program proposed today promised a maximum of safety. Mr. Sullivan recalled that the Navy lost three large and two light carriers in the Pacific, but none was sunk by aircraft land-based. He indicated that mobility of a fleet, equipped to latest model, would discourage the spending of atomic bombs, even if an enemy had some.

Today, the Senate Republican

Continued on Page 7, Column 4

Heaviest Trading in 8 Years Marks Stock Market Spurt

3,840,000 Shares Change Hands as Wave of Bullish Enthusiasm Increases Securities 1 to 7 Points

The hectic days of the Nineteen Twenties were re-enacted yesterday on the floor of the New York Stock Exchange when the most turbulent session in recent years produced increases of 1 to 7 points in the share list. Accompanied by a burst of bullish enthusiasm not witnessed in almost a decade, the deluge of buying orders so taxed the facilities of the Exchange that the reporting ticker tape lagged behind floor transactions by five minutes.

The cracking of the 1947 high level at the approach of mid-day served as the signal for a buying rush. Public participation suddenly enlarged and buying orders pressed floor traders to the utmost. This condition existed for forty-five minutes in the final hour when 1,350,000 shares were traded.

Accompanied by the broadest market on record with a total of 1,151 issues dealt in, volume on the Stock Exchange spiraled to 3,840,000 shares, the largest since May 21, 1940, in contrast to the Thursday turnover of 2,030,000 shares.

Brokers termed it the "wildest" bull market in twenty years on the premise that at no time in the interval had the industrials and rails advanced with such a unity of force.

While the ground had been well laid for a movement of such scope earlier this week, it was the piercing of the 1947 resistance point that confirmed the presence of a bull market to those who act by the charts, or averages. Early in the day, telegrams were sent by several advisory services to their clients urging the purchase of securities. The response to this advice showed primarily in the late

Continued on Page 23, Column 4

Truman Sees His Election; Calls GOP 'Obstructionist'

By ANTHONY LEVIERO
Special to THE NEW YORK TIMES.

WASHINGTON, May 14—President Truman asserted tonight that there would be a Democrat in the White House during the next four years and that he would be the man. He made the statement to a cheering audience of 1,000 young Democrats at their meeting here.

The President's speech was a fighting one in the new Truman manner. He spoke extemporaneously, resorting to whimsy and irony and using forceful gestures of his arms to underscore his points.

Mr. Truman accused the Republican party of stealing Democratic platform planks. "You know," he said, "it has been their habit since 1936 of taking a few planks out of the old Democratic platforms and building a platform and then saying, 'Me, too.'"

[*The text of President Truman's speech is on Page 7.*]

"What have the Republicans done in the last fifteen and a half years?" Mr. Truman asked, then said:

"They have been obstructionists. They spent most of their time while I was in the Senate—and I was there for ten years—in obstructing progressive legislation that was for the welfare of the common man, and throwing bricks and mud at the greatest President that ever sat in the White House."

Mr. Truman was interrupted by applause at this obvious allusion to President Roosevelt.

"That has been their record," he continued, "and they haven't changed a bit. They were against Social Security. They were against TVA. They were against wages

Continued on Page 7, Column 2

MINNESOTA'S GUARD OUT IN MEAT STRIKE

Governor Acts After 200 Raid Cudahy Newport Plant, Attack 60 Workers and Abduct 25

Special to THE NEW YORK TIMES.

ST. PAUL, Minn., May 14—National Guard troops were ordered to South St. Paul and Newport, towns on opposite banks of the Mississippi River near here, by Governor Luther Youngdahl today following violent disorders at strike-bound packing plants in the area and the statement of the local sheriffs that their forces could not maintain law and order.

The Governor did not proclaim martial law but said the troops would take their orders from the civil authorities.

The Governor's action followed a serious outbreak at the Cudahy packing plant in Newport shortly before last midnight in which a group of about 200 men raided the plant with clubs, knives and hammers. In South St. Paul on Thursday strikers forced back police who tried to open a way through picket lines at the Swift & Co. plant in

Continued on Page 16, Column 3

Princess Elizabeth, in Paris Talk, Asks Common Effort of 2 Nations

By LANSING WARREN
Special to THE NEW YORK TIMES.

PARIS, May 14—Speaking in faultless French with just the touch of a British accent to delight French ears, Princess Elizabeth today asked France and Britain to make a common effort to lead Europe to moral and intellectual as well as economic reconstruction.

Her well-worded and discerning speech was cheered, but she went straight to the hearts of the Parisian throng when, with disarming frankness, she avowed her joy that her first foreign trip since her marriage had brought her here to Paris.

"For a long time," she said, "I have wanted to come to France. More fortunate than I, my husband already knew your admirable capital and he is all the happier to return. This trip is all the more important and agreeable for the warmth of your welcome which has touched us both."

From the time they stepped down from the train at the Gare du Nord early today, Princess Elizabeth and Prince Philip, Duke of Edinburgh, were the center of admiring attention from the throngs that lined the streets and from all the French officials who received them throughout the day.

President Vincent Auriol voiced the general feeling when in a statement issued tonight he said:

"I have been personally struck by her grace, her charm, her modesty and her nobility. I feel sure that the sentiments that she has expressed went straight to the hearts of all the French."

Elizabeth's address, broadcast to the French nation, was delivered from the top of the monumental entry to the Galliera Museum, where she came to open the British Government's exhibition of relics and souvenirs of famous Brit-

Continued on Page 6, Column 3

AIR ATTACK OPENS

Planes Cause Fires at Port—Defense Fliers Go Into Action

BORDER IS BREACHED

Cairo Vanguard Takes Colony—Trans-Jordan Reports a Movement

By The Associated Press.

TEL AVIV, Palestine, Saturday, May 15—Air raiders bombed this all-Jewish city at about dawn today.

First reports said there were "some casualties' 'near the power and light station.

[Cairo reported that Egyptian armed forces had been ordered to enter Palestine. Arab armies moved from Trans-Jordan at 12:01 A. M. Saturday to "liberate the Holy Land from Zionism," said a Trans-Jordan communiqué reported by The United Press from Amman.]

Tel Aviv was under complete blackout all night but no sirens were sounded during the raid. Civil guards were alerted and fifteen to twenty ships in the port area moved out to sea.

The planes swooped over Tel Aviv little more than twelve hours after Jewish leaders proclaimed the existence of a new Hebrew state of Israel.

Some bombs fell in the vicinity of the power station along the Yarkum River near Tel Aviv.

Persons at the scene said there was one hit on or near the power station, causing "some casualties."

TEL AVIV, Saturday, May 15 (UP) — Some ten bombs were dropped on Tel Aviv by two aircraft described as bombers and accompanied by two small fighters. One Jew was killed and three were hospitalized. Jewish Army aircraft took to the skies a few minutes after the enemy planes whizzed over rooftops at an estimated altitude of 300 feet.

Several fires could be seen north

Continued on Page 2, Column 3

U. S. MOVES QUICKLY

President Acknowledges de Facto Authority of Israel Immediately

TRUCE AIM STRESSED

Soviet Gesture to New Nation Anticipated—Others Due to Act

By BERTRAM D. HULEN
Special to THE NEW YORK TIMES.

WASHINGTON, May 14—President Truman announced early tonight recognition by the United States of the new Jewish State of Israel. The President acted instantly upon being informed that the new nation had been proclaimed.

"This Government," he announced, "has been informed that a Jewish state has been proclaimed in Palestine and recognition has been requested by the provisional government thereof.

"The United States recognizes the provisional government as the de facto authority of the new State of Israel."

These two paragraphs constituted the text of the President's statement.

Coupled with the announcement was an expression of hope for peace in Palestine. This was made known through a separate White House statement issued by Charles G. Ross, Presidential press secretary.

"The desire of the United States to obtain a truce in Palestine," this said, "will in no way be lessened by the proclamation of a Jewish state.

"We hope that the new Jewish state will join with the Security Council Truce Commission in redoubled efforts to bring an end to the fighting—which has been throughout the United Nations' consideration of Palestine a principal objective of this Government."

[Pending stabilization of the Palestine situation and indications that the State of Israel

Continued on Page 3, Column 2

World News Summarized

SATURDAY, MAY 15, 1948

Several hours after the state of Israel, the first Hebrew nation in 2,000 years, had been proclaimed in a Zionist declaration of independence in Tel Aviv, [1:8.]. President Truman announced that the United States recognized the "provisional government" of Israel as "the de facto authority of the new state." A second White House statement expressed the hope that the new regime would cooperate with United Nations efforts to bring about peace in Palestine. [1:5.] The British High Commissioner departed from Palestine and boarded a cruiser at Haifa as Britain's rule over the Holy Land formally ended. [1:7.]

The special session of the United Nations General Assembly ended last night after it had agreed to send a mediator to Palestine to try to arrange a truce. [1:6-7.] The trusteeship plan for Jerusalem sponsored by the United States was rejected by the Assembly, with the Arab states and the Soviet opposed to the measure. [1:6-7.]

Tel Aviv was bombed at dawn. Egypt ordered her troops to invade Palestine. Trans-Jordan reported her army on the move also. [1:4.] Haganah claimed that its forces captured Acre in the north. [2:8.]

In Moscow the newspaper Pravda, in the first editorial comment on the recent exchange between Washington and Moscow, accused the United States of double-dealing. [4:8.]

Paris crowds gave an enthusiastic welcome to Princess Elizabeth and the Duke of Edinburgh when they arrived for a visit. [1:2-3.]

Congress received a request from the Navy for authority to shift the emphasis in its construction of fighting craft to guided-missile vessels. [1:1.]

President Truman predicted that he would be re-elected next November. [1:2-3.]

Minnesota National Guard troops were rushed to South St. Paul and Newport after 200 persons had raided the Cudahy meat packing plant at Newport, where a strike is in progress, attacking about sixty workers and abducting twenty-five of them. [1:2.]

The New York Stock Exchange enjoyed one of its biggest days in recent years as an avalanche of buying orders sent stocks up from 1 to 7 points. Trading reached a total of 3,840,000 shares, the largest since May 21, 1940. [1:2-3.]

Winston Churchill's War Memoirs

See Page 17 for today's installment, in which Mr. Churchill describes the invasion of Norway and the clash of the British and German fleets.

AT HELM OF THE JEWISH STATE

David Ben-Gurion, *Premier* — Moshe Shertok, *Foreign Minister*

The New York Times

U. N. Votes for a Mediator; Special Assembly Is Ended

By THOMAS J. HAMILTON

After hearing both the Soviet Union and the Arab delegates denounce the United States for its sudden recognition of the new Jewish state in Palestine, the United Nations General Assembly decided last night to send a Mediator to the Holy Land to do what he could to arrange a truce and carry on public services.

The vote was 31 to 7, with sixteen abstentions and four delegates absent, and the General Assembly, which was called into special session at Flushing Meadow on April 16 at the request of the United States, adjourned for good at 8:32 P. M.

The failure of the General Assembly either to repeal the partition resolution of last November or to provide military force to keep the peace means that the fate of Palestine will be decided by the impending war between Jews and Arabs, not by any United Nations action.

The mediation resolution conforms substantially with a United States proposal announced last Wednesday, after it had become obvious that the General Assembly would not accept the original United States plan for a temporary trusteeship.

However, the General Assembly refused to accept a United States plan for a temporary trusteeship over Jerusalem, which was rejected earlier in the evening by a vote of 20 to 15, less than the necessary two-thirds majority.

Two other proposals regarding Jerusalem were rejected, but presumably the provisions of the partition resolution on Jerusalem, which was to have been established as an international enclave under the administration of the Trusteeship Council, still stand.

In addition, the Assembly de-

Continued on Page 4, Column 4

CUNNINGHAM GOES AS MANDATE ENDS

British Commissioner Boards Cruiser Off Haifa—Jews Take Down Union Jack

By The Associated Press.

HAIFA, Palestine, Saturday, May 15—Britain ended her mandate over the Holy Land last midnight. Lieut. Gen. Sir Alan Cunningham, the last British High Commissioner, sailed from Haifa port, finishing British mandate guidance.

Sir Alan's departure from Palestine's richest port caused little excitement among the Jews, who control most of the city.

The British fired a few rockets and searchlights spotlighted the cruiser as it steamed from the harbor.

Wearing the uniform of a British Army general, Sir Alan walked down a few steps of dock into a launch that took him to the cruiser Euryalus.

Upon getting into the launch, he turned and looked soberly up across the docks. There stood an honor guard of the King's Company of Grenadier Guards and Royal Marine commandos.

The launch pulled away amid the

Continued on Page 2, Column 7

U. N. Bars Jerusalem Trusteeship; Vote Follows Mandate Deadline

By MALLORY BROWNE

The United Nations General Assembly rejected yesterday the United States plan for a temporary trusteeship regime in Jerusalem.

Solidly opposed by the Arab States and the Russian bloc, the plan to set up a United Nations Commissioner authorized to protect the Holy City and its holy places failed to obtain the necessary two-thirds majority at the closing session at Flushing Meadow.

The vote, which came just after the bombshell of the United States recognition of the new Jewish State had burst in the Assembly, was 20 in favor, 15 against and 19 abstentions. The balance was turned by the hostility of Britain and most of the Dominions.

The United States fought hard all day, first in the Political and Security Committee of the Assembly, sitting at Lake Success, and then in the evening session of the Assembly, to get the trusteeship plan adopted before the end of the mandate at 6:01 P. M., New York time.

An Arab filibuster, aided by the Soviet bloc, defeated this effort. It was well past the zero hour when a roll-call vote showed that the Assembly preferred to leave Harold Evans, newly appointed Jerusalem municipal Commissioner, in sole charge of the Holy City and its treasures.

As one Arab after another filed up to the tribune and took up the maximum five-minute period allowed in repeating the arguments against a trusteeship plan, 6:01 o'clock went by.

At once Awni Khalidy of Iraq, who had led the Arab fight against the trusteeship plan, rushed up to the tribune and exultantly proclaimed that the time had passed; that the mandate was at an end, and that, since, as Francis B. Sayre of the United States had said, the measure must

Continued on Page 3, Column 5

THE JEWS REJOICE

Some Weep as Quest for Statehood Ends—White Paper Dies

HELP OF U. N. ASKED

New Regime Holds Out Hand to Arabs—U. S. Gesture Acclaimed

Text of declaration setting up new Jewish state, Page 2.

By GENE CURRIVAN
Special to THE NEW YORK TIMES.

TEL AVIV, Palestine, Saturday, May 15—The Jewish state, the world's newest sovereignty, to be known as the State of Israel, came into being in Palestine at midnight upon termination of the British mandate.

Recognition of the state by the United States, which had opposed its establishment at this time, came as a complete surprise to the people, who were tense and ready for the threatened invasion by Arab forces and appealed for help by the United Nations.

In one of the most hopeful periods of their troubled history the Jewish people here gave a sigh of relief and took a new hold on life when they learned that the greatest national power had accepted them into the international fraternity.

Ceremony Simple and Solemn

The declaration of the new state by David Ben-Gurion, chairman of the National Council and the first Premier of reborn Israel, was delivered during a simple and solemn ceremony at 4 P. M., and new life was instilled into his people, but from without there was the rumbling of guns, a flashback to other declarations of independence that had not been easily achieved.

The first action of the new Government was to revoke the Palestine White Paper of 1939, which restricted Jewish immigration and land purchase.

In the proclamation of the new state the Government appealed to the United Nations "to assist the Jewish people in the building of its state and to admit Israel into the family of nations."

The proclamation added:

"We offer peace and amity to all neighboring states and their peoples, and invite them to cooperate with the independent Jewish nation for the common good of all. The State of Israel is ready to contribute its full share to the peaceful progress and reconstitution of the Middle East."

World Jews Asked to Aid

The statement appealed to Jews throughout the world to assist in the task of immigration and development and in the "struggle for the fulfillment of the dream of generations — the redemption of Israel."

Plans for the ceremony had been laid with great secrecy. None but the hundred or more invited guests and journalists was aware of the meeting until it started, and even the guests learned of the site only ten minutes before. It was held in the Tel Aviv Museum of Art, a white, modern-design two-story building. Above it flew the Star of David, which is the state's flag, and below, on the sidewalk, was a guard of honor of the Haganah, the army of the Jewish Agency for Palestine.

As photographers' bulbs flashed and movie cameras ground out reels of the scene, great crowds gathered and cheered the Ministers and other members of the Government as they entered the building. The security arrangements were perfect. Sten guns were brandished in every direction and even the roofs bristled with them.

The setting for the reading of the proclamation was a dropped gallery whose hall held paintings by prominent Jewish artists. Many of them depicted the sufferings and joys of the people of the Diaspora, the dispersal of the Jews.

The thirteen Ministers of the

Continued on Page 2, Column 6

"All the News That's Fit to Print"

The New York Times.

LATE CITY EDITION
Mostly sunny and mild today and tomorrow.
Temperature Range Today—Max.,79; Min.,55
Temperatures Yesterday—Max.,67; Min.56
Full U. S. Weather Bureau Report, Page 47

VOL. XCVII..No. 33,011. Entered as Second-Class Matter, Postoffice, New York, N. Y. NEW YORK, FRIDAY, JUNE 11, 1948. Times Square, New York 18, N. Y. Telephone LAckawanna 4-1000 THREE CENTS IN NEW YORK CITY

SENATE VOTES 2-YEAR DRAFT OF 19-26 MEN; HOUSE IN DOUBT; 2,201 WAR PLANES ORDERED

$1,345,165,000 Allocated For Air Force Additions

Purchases to Be Made in the Coming Fiscal Year Include Trainers, Transports, Jet Fighters and Heavy Bombers

Special to THE NEW YORK TIMES.

WASHINGTON, June 10—The Air Force will place orders in the fiscal year starting July 1 for 2,201 new airplanes costing $1,345,165,000, Secretary W. Stuart Symington said today. This total is in addition to $653,635,000 already allocated by the Air Force for purchase of new airplanes for the Navy.

Delivery of the 2,201 planes will begin about a year later, will reach a peak in the second year and be completed within the third year, said Mr. Symington.

The orders to be given are about 500 less than the estimated annual purchases required to build up a 70-Group Air Force, Mr. Symington said. He added that the announced list was subject to change in periodic review if newer experimental types became available for replacement.

The purchase list represented every type of post-war "production plane" from trainers and transports through the range of jet fighters to heavy bombers of both the propeller and jet types. It did not include experimental types such as the XS-1, announced today as having exceeded the speed of sound, or various other types such as the giant B-36 bomber, a propeller aircraft with extreme range.

Mr. Symington said 100 B-36's had been ordered, but that he believed the order had been reduced to ninety-four to compensate for added costs. This airplane is being developed in competition

Continued on Page 3, Column 4

BILL WINS, 78 TO 10

Moves to Delay Start of Induction or Curb Program Crushed

HOUSE STALEMATE HOLDS

Rules Group to Vote Monday on Freeing Measure for a Decision on the Floor

By C. P. TRUSSELL

Special to THE NEW YORK TIMES.

WASHINGTON, June 10—The Senate passed the stop-gap selective draft bill today by a 78-to-10 vote. The measure calls for the induction, for two years of military service, of up to 250,000 men, 19 through 25 years of age, during the fiscal year starting July 1.

The bill, sent to the House for its decision, also contains a first step toward the objectives of the universal military training program, which, as such had been rejected, at least for this election year. This step would permit up to 161,000 youths 18 years of age to enlist voluntarily in the armed services for one year for training as future reserves and thus escape liability for a two-year draft when they became 19.

Whether the House would act on the draft was still uncertain.

Speaker Joseph W. Martin Jr. expressed hope that the House's own (Andrews) draft bill would undergo floor consideration next week, which is scheduled to be the last one of the Eightieth Congress.

Allen to Call Committee

Representative Leo E. Allen of Illinois, chairman of the House Rules Committee, declined to predict whether that body would permit the draft question to go to whole House consideration. He said he would call his committee together next Monday for a decision.

Mr. Allen opposes the proposed draft. So, apparently, does a majority of his committee. In past voting tests the decision has been seven to five to keep the Andrews Bill locked up at least until after the Senate had acted. Mr. Allen conceded that the 78-10 vote of the Senate this afternoon might prevent a blocking of the measure by his committee. He announced at the same time, however, that he would vote not to let the House consider it.

In the Senate, passage of the draft bill after six days and three nights of hot controversy came with that body divided as follows:

For passage—Republicans, 37; Democrats, 41.

Against passage—Republicans, 8, including Bricker of Ohio, Brooks of Illinois, Butler of Nebraska, Langer of North Dakota, Moore of Oklahoma, Wherry (the acting majority leader) of Nebraska, Wilson of Iowa and Young of North Dakota, and Democrats, 2, including Chavez of New Mexico and Taylor of Idaho, running mate with Henry A. Wallace on the third-party ticket.

Delay Is Voted Down

Before taking its decisive final vote, the Senate spent an hour passing on a flurry of amendments that had been rushed in for decision. In most part, the voting reflected Senate mood toward efforts to delay the draft, cut down its service time, inject civil rights involvements and let small, as well as large business, participate in production for the defense program.

Principal decisions included these:

By a vote of 69-20, the Senate rejected a proposal by Senator Chapman Revercomb, Republican, of West Virginia, that the drafting be withheld pending another six months of trial of the voluntary enlistment system. To spur enlistments, he proposed an easing of aptitude tests for qualification from the present mark of 80 points to 59, which obtained during a part of World War II.

It had been argued previously that any man 19 through 25 years of age who had passed the fifth grade in grammar school could make at least 80 points.

Although the Senate early today had rejected in a voice vote a proposal of Senator Wayne Morse, Republican, of Oregon, that the ac-

Continued on Page 2, Column 2

PALESTINIAN TRUCE GOES INTO EFFECT; 2 SIDES WATCHFUL

Ben-Gurion Says Any Israel Violator Will Be Treated as Foe—Arabs Skeptical

LEBANON TO SEIZE GOODS

Orders Halting of Shipments to Israel at Beirut—Bernadotte Puts Off Trip to Amman

By The Associated Press.

CAIRO, June 11—The order to cease firing in Palestine was broadcast to Egyptian troops today at a few moments before the deadline 2 A. M., New York time.

Trans-Jordan troops had received a similar order earlier and presumably the four-weeks armistice arranged by the United Nations mediator, Court Folke Bernadotte, and agreed to by both Israel and the Arabs, brought a stop to the shooting at the appointed hour.

Israel's Premier Warns

By GENE CURRIVAN

Special to THE NEW YORK TIMES.

TEL AVIV, Israel, June 10—Premier David Ben-Gurion today issued a warning to anyone in the state or occupied areas who violated the truce.

"The Government will not suffer any attempt to be made by anyone in our midst to break the truce and bring to naught the undertaking given by the Government to the United Nations," he said. "Anyone who attempts to break the discipline of the state at this hour will be considered an enemy of Israel, and the Government will mete out to him the treatment accorded in time of emergency to an enemy within the ranks."

This warning obviously is intended for Irgun Zvai Leumi and the Stern group, both of which are operating independently outside the State of Israel and do not consider themselves bound by any of its political commitments.

Will Hold Conquered Areas

At the same time, the Prime Minister disclosed that Israel has no intention of giving up any of the areas outside the state conquered during the war. This would include the coastal ports of Jaffa and Acre, which were granted to the Arabs in the partition plan but later were occupied by Israel.

[The secretary general of the seven-nation Arab League said in Cairo that any violation of the terms of the truce would result in its cancellation, and he expressed a conviction of "Zionist ill-will" as to the truce.]

"All areas, cities and villages, conquered by our armies will remain in our hands," Premier Ben-Gurion declared." During the truce period we shall develop our government services with greater energy, we shall strengthen our economy in town and country, we shall increase immigration, we shall expand settlement activities; nor shall we forget the needs of our armies."

Shertok Discounts Irgun

When asked at a press conference yesterday whether he had received any assurance from Irgun Zvai Leumi forces in Jerusalem that they would accept the truce, Foreign Minister Moshe Shertok answered:

"We do not consider them a decisive factor."

Soon afterward Irgun Zvai Leumi went on the air accusing the Foreign Minister of submitting "to shame rather than continuing the struggle." In all his inflammatory oratory on the air waves the Irgun Zvai Leumi spokesman did not indicate that the dissidents would accept or reject the truce. He accused Count Folke Bernadotte, United Nations Mediator, of being a "British servant" and he charged that the Israeli Government had made a great blunder in accepting the terms unconditionally when it should have demanded withdrawal of all foreign troops from Palestine.

Irgun Zvai Leumi held that acceptance of the truce would result in deterioration of the political and military position, while Arabs would have the benefit of uncontrolled, unsupervised movement of troops and arms through their many borders. Irgun, which has its own army—an army responsible for the capture of Jaffa—is considered an important factor in the defense of Jerusalem and, according to military observers, cannot be discounted at this point. If Irgun violated the cease-fire or did not accept it, they pointed out, there could be no truce in Palestine.

Regarding supplies to Jerusalem,

Continued on Page 8, Column 4

Russia Insists U. N. Send Soviet Group to Palestine

U. S. and Canada in Security Unit Oppose Moscow Military Observers—Discord Puts a Blight on Truce Hopes

By THOMAS J. HAMILTON

Special to THE NEW YORK TIMES.

LAKE SUCCESS, N. Y., June 10—Andrei A. Gromyko today renewed the Soviet Union's fight to have the United Nations Security Council send Russian military observers to help carry out the cease-fire and truce in Palestine, which is scheduled to begin at 2 A. M. tomorrow, New York daylight time.

Mr. Gromyko suggested that the Soviet Union send a "very small" number and indicated that he would be satisfied with fewer than the twenty-one military observers each, to be furnished by the United States, Belgium and France.

The Soviet request was opposed by Dr. Phillip C. Jessup and Gen. A. G. L. McNaughton, representatives of the United States and Canada. A decision was deferred until next Tuesday, when the Council will again take up the Palestine question. The disagreement cast a blight on the restrained hopes of Council members that the four-week truce, which will expire on July 9, will be followed by a lasting peace in Palestine.

[Secretary General Lie in a speech at Harvard urged the formation "very soon" of a small armed guard force to back up Security Council decisions. He advised such a force pending the formation of a larger body as envisaged in the Charter of the United Nations.]

At the beginning of the Council meeting Dr. Jessup paid tribute to Count Folke Bernadotte, United Nations Mediator, declaring that "his wisdom, his fairness, his energy and his firmness have won the respect of all" and that "he has succeeded in one of the most difficult tasks known to statesmanship, namely, that of securing a truce in a situation in which active war had already begun."

Dr. Jessup praised both Israel and the seven members of the Arab League for accepting the

Continued on Page 8, Column 7

Texts of Egyptian and Israeli replies on truce, Page 8.

Stassen Urges Full ERP Fund To Maintain National Honor

By FELIX BELAIR Jr.

Special to THE NEW YORK TIMES.

WASHINGTON, June 10—Harold E. Stassen, Republican Presidential contender, demanded today full restoration of the legislative authorization for the European Recovery Program as "a question of the national honor of the United States." The former Minnesota Governor went before the Senate Appropriations Committee at his own request to appeal to its Republican majority "not to tarnish the national honor of our country at this late hour in the session." He remained to take sharp issue with President Truman for his description of the present Congress as "the worst" in history.

All the ingredients of a star-spangled political debate were available when Mr. Stassen entered the crowded hearing room, and only a spark of partisanship was needed to set off another Presidential campaign display. It was supplied by Mr. Stassen when he said:

"With all of the difficulties that are naturally present with a Congressional majority of one party and a President of another, you have nevertheless made one of the most constructive two-year records in foreign policy of any Congress in the history of our nation."

Chairman Styles Bridges, Republican, of New Hampshire, quickly capitalized on the partisan significance of the remark by asking:

"Then you don't agree with the statement of the President of the United States out West where he said this was the worst session of Congress since the first one?"

Mr. Stassen said that he considered the Presidential utterance "an ill-considered, ad lib remark that will have unfortunate results for the President in his relations with Congress." He said that members of both political parties had responsibilities higher than those owed their organizations, and added:

"Even in the tensions of political debate public officials should not lose sight of their higher responsibilities to the nation."

Senator Joseph C. O'Mahoney,

Continued on Page 13, Column 4

BRITISH ISSUE BAN ON GERMAN TRAVEL

Bar Interzonal Permits After Soviet Extends Its Curbs Even to Coal Shipments

By EDWARD A. MORROW

Special to THE NEW YORK TIMES.

BERLIN, June 10—The split between the Eastern and Western zones of Germany was intensified tonight when the British Military Government announced it had stopped issuing permits for interzonal travel because of "inexplicable Soviet restrictions."

All German travelers who held such permits were advised to return to their homes in the Western zones until the situation created by the new Soviet regulations had been clarified.

The British action was the first sweeping move in which German nationals were caught in the web of the interzonal travel restrictions being imposed by the Soviet administration. A British spokesman said that reports from the British-Soviet zonal boundary showed that passes that heretofore had been honored by all four occupying powers were no longer being accepted by special Russian teams placed at all entry points into the Soviet zone.

"Consequently many German men, women and children are undergoing considerable inconvenience and suffering as a result of this inexplicable action," the spokesman added. "Until the situation is cleared up, German nationals are advised no applications for interzonal travel will be accepted."

Continued on Page 14, Column 3

Lewis Schwellenbach Dies at 53; Secretary of Labor Since 1945

Special to THE NEW YORK TIMES.

WASHINGTON, June 10 — Secretary of Labor Lewis B. Schwellenbach died in Walter Reed Hospital at 4:40 A. M. today after several weeks of illness. His age was 53.

At Olympia, Wash., President Truman received the news of the death of his friend and former Senate associate "with the deepest regret."

Tributes to the late Secretary poured in to the Department of Labor from Cabinet officers, labor and industrial leaders and men and women in many walks of life.

Secretary of State George C. Marshall, in a formal announcement, stated that "as a mark of respect to the memory of Secretary Schwellenbach the President directs that the national flag be displayed on all public buildings in the City of Washington until the interment shall have taken place."

Secretary Marshall added that "the death of this respected member of the President's Cabinet comes as a great shock and a great sorrow to his friends and as a national bereavement to the Government and the people of the United States."

Frustrated in his ambition to extend the confines of the Labor Department, which has been successively narrowed year after year by Congressional action, Mr. Schwellenbach is understood to have taken the disappointments to heart.

Brooding over the diminished prestige of his post, the Secretary, according to some intimates, figuratively died of a broken heart, despite whatever other physical symptoms directly caused his demise.

Mrs. Schwellenbach, the former Anne Duffy, was at the bedside when her husband died.

The Secretary had been in the hospital since May 29, shortly after his return from a siege of ill-

Continued on Page 24, Column 2

MUSTARD ASKS CITY TO STOP POLLUTION OR CLOSE BEACHES

Sewage Disposal Plants Must Be Rushed, He Warns Mayor, Citing Rise in Germ Count

$79,000,000 HELD NEEDED

$84,000,000 More for Long-Range Program—O'Dwyer Expected to Seek Action

By PAUL CROWELL

The city must decide "very soon" whether to spend enough money for the rapid construction of planned sewage disposal plants or prohibit bathing at all beaches within its limits, Health Commissioner Harry S. Mustard declared yesterday in a memorandum to Mayor O'Dwyer.

The warning was a repetition of one issued by Dr. Mustard in April, but fortified this time with a tabulation of the results of 600 samplings of water at various city beaches to determine their content of bacilli coli. These organisms are frequently responsible for the incidence of typhoid fever and other intestinal diseases contracted because of bathing in polluted waters.

Mayor Expected to Act

It was indicated that the Mayor, as a result of Dr. Mustard's memorandum, soon would renew efforts to set up an immediate and a long-range program of sewage disposal plant construction to prevent the closing of all city beaches to bathers and make possible the rehabilitation of those already closed.

The Mayor said last fall that an immediate $79,000,000 was imperatively needed, and a secondary program of $84,000,000 desirable to eliminate existing pollution of city waters by raw sewage. A proposal to make $135,000,000 available through exemption of city bonds from the debt limit was put forward, but made no progress in the Legislature.

Dr. Mustard's memorandum and the accompanying tabulations on bacillus counts were the results, up to June 1, of a survey begun by the Health Department on April 19. The survey, to be continued until Oct. 1, eventually will cover an estimated 2,600 samplings of city beach waters. Samplings will be made at ninety-five points, or forty-three more than last year.

Noting that no restrictions had been placed as yet against bathing at Coney Island, Rockaway

Continued on Page 46, Column 2

PRESIDENT PRESSES UTILITIES ATTACK; CONGRESS HIT ANEW

He Visions a Great Network of River Projects, but Declares Private Groups Will Fight It

USES ROOSEVELT'S WORDS

He Pleads at Seattle for People After Saying the Legislators Work for 'Better Classes'

President's address criticizing water power companies, Page 4.

By ANTHONY LEVIERO

Special to THE NEW YORK TIMES.

SEATTLE, Wash., June 10—President Truman offered today the vision of a great network of river control projects but declared its realization would demand "the toughest kind of fight" against private interests and their friends in Congress.

Hewing again to the issue of public versus private power projects, the Chief Executive used phrases reminiscent of the late Franklin D. Roosevelt. And for the second time in two days he invoked the name of his predecessor on his side of the issue.

The "men of little faith," the "private power lobby" all were denounced as opponents of projects which would enrich all the West.

Continuing his sharp assaults on Congress, President Truman earlier told a throng of about 5,000 persons at Bremerton that it was "interested in the welfare of the better classes."

Reply to Southerners Seen

And again the chief executive reiterated that he had been misrepresented and that he had come out to let the people see what he was like. Mr. Truman has been pressing this theme stronger and stronger as he gets deeper into this pre-convention speaking tour.

It is believed he is serving notice on all in his party that he is the titular leader and that he means to remain "the boss." It is interpreted aboard his train as the answer to those Southern Democrats and some others who would like to draft Gen. Dwight D. Eisenhower at the Democratic convention next month. The President follows up the argument by saying that he wants to come back later in the year to talk politics on a full basis.

The reason for Mr. Truman's increasingly bitter attacks on Congress, it was learned from a source

Continued on Page 4, Column 2

World News Summarized

FRIDAY, JUNE 11, 1948

A stop-gap selective draft bill was passed by the Senate yesterday, 78 to 10, and sent to the House. The measure makes men 19 to 26 liable to draft and permits 18-year-olds to avoid a later draft by enlisting for one year. [1:8.]

The Air Force will start on its seventy-combat-group set-up by placing orders in the year beginning July 1 for 2,201 new planes to cost $1,345,165,000, Air Secretary Symington announced. [1:6-7.] He disclosed that the experimental rocket plane XS-1 had flown "much faster than the speed of sound many times." [1:6-7.]

Congress, whose Republican leaders have again agreed to strive for adjournment a week from tomorrow [18:2], rushed to clear its slate. Harold E. Stassen urged a Senate committee to restore cuts made by the House in Marshall Plan funds. [1:2-3.] Senate Republicans decided to support a single-year extension of the Reciprocal Trade Act. [18:4.] The House opened debate on a bill to admit 200,000 displaced persons into this country [3:1] and in committee three Republicans joined Democrats to approve a liberalized housing bill. [19:1.]

Secretary of Labor Schwellenbach died at Walter Reed Hospital. He was 53 years old. [1:2-3.]

Negotiations on a new soft-coal contract reached an impasse as operators and miners clung to their divergent views on pensions. [16:5.] Justice Goldsborough continued the temporary injunction against a railroad strike. [16:2.]

New York waters are so dangerously polluted that the city must choose "very soon" between prohibiting bathing and building sufficient sewage-disposal plants, Health Commissioner Mustard reported. [1:5.]

Palestine at 2 A. M. today, New York time, had a truce in warfare under the four-week plan of the United Nations Mediator, although both sides were wary and Premier Ben-Gurion admonished any restless elements in Israel. [1:1.] Fighting had been intensified on the eve of the cease-fire. [10:3; with map.] The Haganah ordered a halt in all overseas recruiting. [10:4-5.] The International Ladies Garment Workers Union here decided on a loan of $1,000,000 to the State of Israel. [10:6.]

Restrained optimism in the United Nations was checked when Russia renewed her demand in the Security Council for the inclusion of Soviet military observers in supervising the truce. Andrei A. Gromyko suggested that Russia would be satisfied with a "very small" number, fewer than the twenty-one furnished by the United States, France and Belgium. [1:2-3.]

A small armed-guard force should be formed "very soon" to enforce Security Council decisions until differences between the major powers make an international army possible, Secretary General Lie said in receiving an honorary degree from Harvard University. [7:1.]

Britain has suspended the issuance of permits for interzonal travel by Germans until the "inexplicable Soviet restrictions" have been cleared up, Russia imposed new curbs and halted Berlin coal trains. [1:2.] The French Cabinet patched up differences over religious education and will enter the Assembly debate with a prospect of winning qualified approval of the six-power London accord on Western Germany. [14:7.]

German officials argued for a "reasonable" delay in calling a Constituent Assembly, which the London conferees had hoped would meet by Sept. 1. [14:3-4.]

Speed of Sound Is Exceeded By XS-1 in Repeated Tests

By CHARLES HURD

Special to THE NEW YORK TIMES.

WASHINGTON, June 10—An experimental airplane operated by the Air Force "has flown much faster than the speed of sound many times" in recent months, Secretary W. Stuart Symington disclosd today. The plane, known as the Bell XS-1, was piloted by a wartime ace, Capt. Charles E. Yeager, at the Muroc Air Force base.

This is the first recorded instance of piercing the sonic barrier in level flight, the Secretary added. Some other airplanes may have achieved such speed in dives.

The speed of sound varies with altitude, temperature, humidity and other conditions. It is figured by the Air Force, however, at 763 miles an hour at sea level under "standard conditions," when the temperature is 59 degrees Fahrenheit above zero. In the stratosphere, when the temperature drops to 67 degrees below zero, the speed of sound decreases to 662 miles an hour.

Whatever speed the XS-1 attained, a closely guarded secret, undoubtedly was registered at a very high altitude, since the plane was designed to operate most efficiently at high levels.

This plane, one of two of its type in existence, is carried aloft under the belly of a heavy bomber and released high in the air for flights which at high speed last only between two or three minutes, despite fuel capacity almost twice the weight of the airplane.

The XS-1 has a wing span of twenty-eight feet, is thirty-one feet long and eleven feet high, with a recorded empty weight of 4,892 pounds. It carries 8,000 pounds of fuel for its rocket mechanism. It was designed to reach a speed of more than 1,000 miles an hour at 40,000 feet and a theoreti-

Continued on Page 3, Column 2

RENT GOUGER GETS CITY PRISON TERM

Greenwald Called 'Ruthless Chiseler'—Maximum of 3 Years in Jail Imposed

Six weeks after his arrest for gouging payments of $2,000 to $4,000 each from eleven war-veteran doctors seeking professional apartments in Stuyvesant Town and Peter Cooper Village, Meyer Greenwald, former tenant selector, started yesterday to serve a City Prison term up to three years. He is the second convicted rent gouger to receive a jail sentence.

The 45-year-old attorney had been convicted in Special Sessions on June 3 of extorting $24,000 while serving as investigator of professional applicants at the two East Side housing projects operated by the Metropolitan Life Insurance Company. In his $9,000-a-year position, Greenwald was to select qualified persons from the more than 2,000 applications for thirty-two medical and dental offices available in the developments.

Yesterday, the probation report on Greenwald, who also had been active in other business ventures, revealed he was bankrupt. For

Continued on Page 19, Column 4

Test of Sound Truck Ban Is Noisy Despite Polite Police and Pickets

The first test of the city ordinance regulating the use of sound trucks after the decision of the United States Supreme Court that upheld their use as part of the "free speech" guarantee of the Constitution, was staged here yesterday by left-wing groups.

The result was the issuance of summonses, for making too much noise, to a group of nine left-wing speakers headed by City Councilman Eugene P. Connolly, who spoke in front of the National Democratic Club at Thirty-seventh Street and Madison Avenue, and the sound-truck operator.

The second, and larger demonstration, in front of the National Republican Club at 54 West Fortieth Street, brought no summonses to the speakers, some of whom already had been "tagged," but the operator of the sound truck received his, quietly, and after the meeting had broken up.

The net effect of the two meetings was that the demonstrators had two and one-half hours of uninterrupted oratory in the heart of Manhattan's midtown, and the police had two test cases to carry up through the courts in their contention that the Lockport case, in which the Supreme Court acted, had no bearing on the New York regulations that require persons who want to use a sound truck to apply for a permit five days in advance.

The point to this, according to the police, is that it permits investigation of whether the sound truck would cause hardship to businesses or institutions in the vicinity.

It was made clear that in the case of the meeting in front of the National Republican Club no permit would have been issued because of the meeting's proximity to the Public Library half a block away, and also that the committee conducting the meeting had not applied for a permit.

The police and the demonstra-

Continued on Page 16, Column 3

"All the News That's Fit to Print"

The New York Times.

LATE CITY EDITION

Showers this morning; partly cloudy later. Sunny, mild tomorrow.

Temperature Range Today—Max.,83; Min.,71
Temperatures Yesterday—Max.,83; Min.,66
Full U. S. Weather Bureau Report, Page 45

VOL. XCVII..No. 33,057. Entered as Second-Class Matter, Postoffice, New York, N. Y. NEW YORK, TUESDAY, JULY 27, 1948. Times Square, New York 18, N. Y. Telephone LAckawanna 4-1000 THREE CENTS IN NEW YORK CITY

U.S., BRITAIN BAR RAIL TRAFFIC WITH RUSSIAN GERMAN ZONE; SOVIET'S POLICE CHIEF OUSTED

OTHER NATIONS HIT

Retaliation for Blockade of Berlin Denied by Western Allies

ACTION CALLED TECHNICAL

Suspension of Police Head by Berlin Council Reversed by Russian Commandant

By EDWARD A. MORROW
Special to The New York Times.

BERLIN, July 26—All international railway traffic to and from the Soviet zone through the Western zones of Germany was halted today by order of the United States and British Military Governments.

Col. Hans Holmer, chief of the United States Military Government's Transport Group, explained that the order had been issued because of "technical difficulties." He estimated that approximately 300,000 tons of material was being moved annually over the tracks of the Western zones into the Soviet zone.

While some observers considered this move to be the first step in a counter-blockade, United States and British spokesmen asserted emphatically that it was in no way to be considered a retaliatory move to the Russian blockade of the Western sectors of the city. To prove their point, they cited a list of technical difficulties in allowing such traffic to continue.

This move against the Soviet administration by the United States and British Military Governments was matched by one taken by the City Council. Dr. Ferdinand Friedensburg, Deputy Mayor, announced the suspension of Paul Markgraf, Communist police chief, and the appointment of the Socialist Johannes Stumm in his place.

Soviet Commandant Takes Action

Late tonight the Russians announced that Maj. Gen. Alexander G. Kotikov, the Soviet Commandant in Berlin, had sent specific instructions to the Acting Lord Mayor that Herr Stumm be dismissed from the police force and not be made police chief. Herr Stumm, he charged, has been active in a move to split the force.

[An official British statement said that General Kotikov had gone "entirely beyond his powers" in ordering the dismissal of Herr Stumm, press services reported.]

In a sternly worded letter, he ordered that Herr Markgraf be instructed to carry on an investigation of all those engaged in such activity "regardless of the positions and offices they hold."

At a press conference, Dr. Friedensburg pointed out that the Council on several occasions had asked the Kommandatura to dismiss Herr Markgraf because of the allegedly unsatisfactory management of the police force, stating that the force had given protection only to Communists. Recently Herr Markgraf was said to have dismissed illegally more than 100 non-Communist men on the police force and to have permitted Communists to attempt to break up a meeting of the City Assembly.

Other Nations Affected

The ban on railway traffic, which will cut off Switzerland, Italy, France, the Low Countries and the Scandinavian nations from trade with the Soviet zone, is the first large-scale action in the East-West struggle over Berlin that affects countries other than the four occupying powers. The Governments of the countries affected were informed a few days ago that the Western zones would no longer accept such transit traffic, a British spokesman said. International transit traffic for Poland and Czechoslovakia will continue to be routed through the Western zones.

It is expected that Switzerland will be the greatest loser in traffic. Military government transport officials said that the Soviet zone had exported approximately 15,000 tons of brown coal and timber to that country.

Transport officials were unable

Continued on Page 6, Column 3

Molotov to Be Approached For Parley on Berlin Crisis

Allied Envoys to Make Proposal Orally in Hope of Ending Impasse—Truman Has No Bid for Talk With Stalin

By HERBERT L. MATTHEWS
Special to The New York Times.

LONDON, July 26—The next approach to Moscow on the Berlin situation will most likely be an oral one by envoys of the United States, Britain and France directly to Foreign Minister Molotov, it was learned from an authoritative source here today.

It is hoped that by making their demarche in this way instead of by formal notes it will be possible to break down the barriers that have prevented any real diplomacy on an issue that involves war or peace. Foreign Minister Molotov might be in a position to say something or react in some way and in that case the envoys would be able to talk things over with him and perhaps make progress.

[President Truman has received no official proposal for a conference with Premier Stalin on Germany, according to the White House. The President would be glad to see the Soviet leader in Washington, it was said.]

Each of the envoys, according to present plans, will receive a written aide memoire that will be the formal basis of what the Western Allies want to say about Berlin.

The idea for this form of approach is American, it is understood, but the State Department originally felt that the envoys should seek to deliver their messages to Premier Stalin. This was put up to the British and French by United States Ambassador Lewis W. Douglas on Saturday when the Standing Committee consisting of himself, René Massigli, French Ambassador to Britain, and Sir William Strang, British

Continued on Page 6, Column 5

Western German Leaders Agree to Launch New State

By JACK RAYMOND

FRANKFORT ON THE MAIN, Germany, July 26—The Minister-Presidents of Western Germany formally accepted today the responsibility of initiating a Government for the eleven states of non-Soviet Germany, and agreed with the United States, British and French Military Governors to begin their task at once.

Certain observations of the German leaders are to be forwarded to the Governments of the three occupying powers, but no reservations or conditions were placed on German acceptance.

The significance of today's action was regarded as two-fold:

First, although the Western Allies in the last few days had emphasized their willingness to negotiate with the Russians on the German problem, they are not countenancing any delay in carrying out the London agreement on Western Germany that precipitated the Berlin crisis.

Second, although the Germans had attempted to modify the impact of their participation in a "splitting" of Germany, they are accepting in full the authorization to proceed with the central regime that they have sought all along.

After a conference of more than three hours, the following communiqué, drafted by the participants, was issued:

"As a result of the final meeting between the Military Governors and the Minister-Presidents of the three Western zones, held under the chairmanship of General Koenig [Lieut. Gen. Joseph-Pierre Koenig, French Military Governor], an agreement was reached that the organization of the three

Continued on Page 6, Column 2

U. S. TO HELP BRITAIN IMPROVE INDUSTRY

Cripps, Hoffman Agree on a Joint Employer-Union Council —Chancellor Denies Rifts

By HAROLD CALLENDER

PARIS, July 26—After a three-hour talk today with Paul G. Hoffman, United States Economic Cooperation Administrator, Sir Stafford Cripps, Britain's Chancellor of the Exchequer, announced that they had agreed upon a joint undertaking to improve British methods of industrial production by utilizing United States technical advice.

Sir Stafford said that as a result there soon would be established a joint council composed of representatives of British and United States employers and trade unions to advise the London Government how the efficiency of British industry might be increased. He suggested that British engineers might be sent to the United States to study methods there.

Referring to a recent statement by Mr. Hoffman that the United

Continued on Page 9, Column 1

Israel Claims Rule in Jerusalem; Will Name Governor of New City

By GENE CURRIVAN
Special to The New York Times.

TEL AVIV, Israel, July 26—The New City in Jerusalem, with a population of 100,000 Jews, has been declared Israeli-occupied territory.

In an announcement to this effect a spokesman for the Provisional Government of Israel declared tonight that the Israeli Administration would take into account the "special Jewish character of the city" and that a military governor would be appointed for the city.

This move is in conformity with a previously announced principle that any territory occupied by Israeli forces would come under the jurisdiction of the state.

Jerusalem is outside the Israeli boundaries defined by the United Nations General Assembly and, along with the metropolitan area, which includes the Old City and Bethlehem, was proclaimed an international zone.

The decision was disclosed a few hours after Count Folke Bernadotte, United Nations Mediator for Palestine, had left for Rhodes. He had conferred with Foreign Minister Moshe Shertok on the proposed demilitarization of Jerusalem. United Nations observers and officials have been gathering in Jerusalem to supervise the truce and prepare the ground for the city's demilitarization.

It is believed the Israeli decision on Jerusalem was influenced by the presence in the city of the dissident Irgun Zvai Leumi and Stern Group, which defied the command of the Israeli Army because they were functioning in an area outside the jurisdiction of the Provisional Government.

The Israeli maneuver may set up a barrier to the proposal to demilitarize Jerusalem, a recommendation put forth by Count Bernadotte. With Jerusalem under

Continued on Page 11, Column 2

Housing Shortage to Ease In Year, Survey Indicates

Moses Calls on Savings Banks and Congress to Aid—Ross Urges Public Projects, Real Estate Group Backs Private Industry

By WILLIAM M. FARRELL

The housing shortage here will ease appreciably in the next year, but earnest efforts on the part of Government, financiers and builders are necessary if the improvement is to continue. This is the consensus of experts, including Robert Moses, who see the situation from a variety of viewpoints.

The bright aspects of the picture, Mr. Moses pointed out, are apparent to anyone who travels about the city and neighboring Long Island, Westchester and New Jersey. Rows of tiny bungalows are going up, and larger one-family homes are under construction everywhere, while big apartment houses and garden-apartment communities are being erected in the city and in suburban communities where once they were rare or unknown.

The brightness dims noticeably when rentals and prices are considered, but nevertheless the new construction will provide for thousands of families.

With available sources of materials and labor it would be hard to speed the present rate of housing construction, the City Construction Coordinator said. But he pointed to large-scale moves that are necessary to improve the city's ability to win the constant battle against obsolescence and to meet the needs of the growing population.

Savings banks, Mr. Moses said, have failed badly to contribute to the construction of new housing. Excepting the Bowery Savings Bank, he asserted, they have refused to meet an obligation to help in the development of the community they serve.

"They are public institutions," Mr. Moses said, "and of course they ought to protect the dimes and dollars of the poor who are their depositors, but they ought to invest locally. I believe it is almost time to have public representation on their boards of directors—by the State Banking Commissioner, perhaps."

The Veterans Administration also should devote more of its re-

Continued on Page 44, Column 4

U. N. BODY PUTS END TO TALKS ON ARMS; SOVIET VOTED DOWN

Better International Feeling Awaited—Issue Goes Back to Assembly Session

By A. M. ROSENTHAL
Special to The New York Times.

LAKE SUCCESS, N. Y., July 26—The last phase of United Nations disarmament work—the negotiations in the Commission on Conventional Armaments — was abandoned today and the whole arms reduction controversy made ready for full debate in the General Assembly.

Meeting in closed session, the commission's working committee voted, 9 to 2, against the Soviet Union and the Ukraine, to adopt a British resolution stating that arms reduction could be accomplished only in an atmosphere of international confidence and security.

Technically, the committee must meet once more to approve its report to the Assembly and the parent commission will have to hold another session before the end becomes formal. But delegates agreed

Continued on Page 10, Column 4

CITY RELIEF ROLLS CUT 1,064 IN MONTH TO TOTAL OF 139,521

June Drop Is First Substantial Post-War Decline—Stress on Job-Finding Credited

By DORIS GREENBERG

The first substantial post-war decrease in the city's relief rolls was reported yesterday by Commissioner of Welfare Raymond M. Hilliard.

At the end of June, the number of recipients of some form of public assistance had dropped 1,064 under the total at the beginning of the month, Mr. Hilliard said.

He also noted that preliminary figures pointed toward a July decline of possibly 2,000 more.

This reversal of a trend that started in September, 1945, and continued virtually unchecked, has resulted largely from new stress on the finding of jobs for relief applicants who are capable of working, the Commissioner said.

In a resume of Welfare Department operations during June—the initial report of a monthly series planned by Mr. Hilliard—the financial saving accompanying the

Continued on Page 17, Column 2

World News Summarized

TUESDAY, JULY 27, 1948

President Truman ordered the armed forces to put an end to discrimination "as rapidly as possible," and decreed a fair employment practices policy throughout the civil branches of the Government in which "merit and fitness" would be the only qualifications for a job. He put the double-barreled policy into effect by executive orders issued yesterday. [1:8.] Southern Democrats were further angered by the President's action, but had little hope of defeating civil rights bills in the special session of Congress. [4:2.]

When the President delivers his message to Congress at 12:30 today, he will ask the special session to act on eleven matters, among them anti-inflation legislation, the Taft-Ellender-Wagner Housing Bill, Federal aid to education, a 75-cent minimum legal wage, extended Social Security, reform of Federal pay schedules and the civil rights program. Congress met briefly yesterday and party leaders mapped their strategy. [1:6-7.] Republicans and Democrats blamed each other for living costs. [1:7.]

While retail meat prices continued high and milk was scheduled to rise one cent a quart in this city on Sunday and another cent on Oct. 1, industry leaders remained divided over renewed rationing and price controls. [1:6-7.] Experts predicted easing of the housing shortage here if the Government, industry and finance cooperated. [1:4-5.]

This city's relief rolls showed the first substantial post-war drop last month; the trend continued in July. [1:5.]

Right-wing candidates swept all Communist sympathizers out of office in the National Maritime Union, CIO, council. [45:1.]

International rail traffic through the Western zones of Germany into the Soviet zone was halted by United States and British occupation chiefs. This action was taken, it was explained, because of "technical difficulties" and was not in retaliation for the Russian blockade of Berlin. [1:1; map, P. 6.] It was learned in London that the Western powers probably would make their next approach to Moscow orally to Foreign Minister Molotov. The White House said no official proposal had been received for a Truman-Stalin meeting. [1:2-3.]

The Minister-Presidents of the eleven German states in the Western zones agreed to assume responsibility for a Western German government. [1:2-3.]

Sir Stafford Cripps announced that a joint United States-British council representing labor and industry would be established soon to help increase the efficiency of British industry. [1:2.]

A new French Cabinet was formed by Premier Marie after he had surmounted a left-wing Socialist rebellion. [5:1.]

A United Nations committee voted to suspend activities on conventional disarmament until international confidence and security had returned. [1:4.] The Little Assembly approved a program to facilitate the peaceful settlement of disputes. [13:1.]

Indonesia's economic revival has been prevented by the Netherlands' blockade, a United Nations group reported. [14:2.]

The New City of Jerusalem was declared Israeli-occupied territory by the Israeli Government, which said a military governor would be named. [1:2-3.]

TRUMAN ORDERS END OF BIAS IN FORCES AND FEDERAL JOBS; ADDRESSES CONGRESS TODAY

CONGRESSIONAL LEADERS CONFER

Joseph W. Martin Jr., Speaker of House, and Arthur H. Vandenberg, President pro tempore of Senate. The New York Times (by Tames)

PRESSES FOR RIGHTS

President Acts Despite Split in His Party Over the Chief Issue

LITTLE 'FEPC' IS CREATED

'Merit, Fitness' Set as U. S. Employment Guides—Military Equality Is Demanded

Texts of the President's two executive orders are on Page 4.

By ANTHONY LEVIERO
Special to The New York Times.

WASHINGTON, July 26—President Truman ordered today the end of discrimination in the armed forces "as rapidly as possible" and instituted a fair employment practices policy throughout the civil branch of the Federal Government.

On the eve of his appearance before Congress, the President issued two executive orders to carry out his sweeping aims. He said that men in uniform should have "equality of treatment and opportunity" without regard to race, color, religion or national origin.

Similarly, he decreed that "merit and fitness" should be the only application for a Government job, and that the head of each department "shall be personally responsible for an effective program to insure that fair employment policies are fully observed in all personnel actions within his department."

The two orders were expected to have a thunderbolt effect on the already highly charged political situation in the Deep South, a situation which is expected to be aggravated further tomorrow when Mr. Truman makes his omnibus call on Congress for action. The message, in one of its eleven major elements, is expected to go down the line for his ten-point civil rights program, which last February started the deep fissures in the Democratic party.

Enforcement Machinery Set Up

The Presidential orders, which require no Congressional sanction, specified in detail the machinery that would be employed to monitor both anti-discrimination programs.

In the National Military Establishment, Mr. Truman created an advisory panel, called the President's Committee on Equality of Treatment and Opportunity in the Armed Services. It will consist of seven members, none of whom was named today.

It was said, however, that one man who probably would be recommended for membership is Dr. Frank Graham, president of the University of North Carolina. It was believed he would be acceptable to North and South, Negro and white.

The civilian employe order directed that a Fair Employment Board be formed from among members and employes of the Civil Service Commission. This, too, is to be a seven-member board, as yet unnamed.

The committee of the armed forces received the mission of determining how present practices might be altered to carry out the Presidential order. In stipulating rapid application of the policy, Mr. Truman said that it should be done with due regard to "the time required to effectuate any necessary changes without impairing efficiency or morale."

Hearings, Appeals Provided

In the civil departments, the head of each was directed to designate an official as "Fair Employment Officer," who was charged with full operating responsibility for the non-discrimination program. Provision was made for hearings of complaints, appeals and disciplinary action.

As the top agency in this program, the Fair Employment Board in the Civil Service Commission received a six-point program providing for review of decisions, drafting of regulations, advice on problems to all departments, publication of information relating to the program, coordination of the policy in the departments and re-

Continued on Page 4, Column 3

Republican Chiefs Cautious, Awaiting President's Word

By C. P. TRUSSELL

WASHINGTON, July 26—The Eightieth Congress returned to work today in response to the July 15 call of President Truman. It did not come back happily. The first flashes of smiling greetings on reassembly soon wore off.

The Senate sat for twelve minutes, just long enough for the opening prayer, a quorum call to which sixty-five members answered "present" and for the naming of a committee to notify the White House formally that Congress was back in business.

In the House, 310 members answered to their names. Many of them immediately set out to give oral previews of the extra session and the campaigns. It appeared that the nearly two hours of debate on many subjects covered about the whole eleven-point program which Mr. Truman will deliver in person to a joint Senate-House session at 12:30 P. M. (EDT) tomorrow.

Late today, while Republican leaders were in a huddle over prospective programs and the question of just where the GOP stood as the extra session opened, Democratic leaders paid a call at the White House. Mr. Truman read to them lengthy passages from the speech he will make to the whole Congress tomorrow. There were suggestions for change, it was reported later. The President made notes and indicated, it was said, that the suggestions would be followed.

A "score card," made public later by Charles G. Ross, Presidential secretary, disclosed that Mr.

Continued on Page 3, Column 2

HOUSE SKIRMISHES ON LIVING COSTS

Opposing Parties Shunt Blame for Inflation — Selective Curbs Held Truman Aim

By SAMUEL A. TOWER
Special to The New York Times.

WASHINGTON, July 26—Congressional skirmishing over the blame for the high cost of living and the housing shortage broke out between the Republicans and the Democrats today, virtually immediately after the opening prayers had marked the convening of the recalled Congress.

While many legislators remained silent, awaiting tomorrow's message from President Truman, a number of Representatives were unable to withhold their fire and exchanged oratorical salvos across the aisle in attempts to pin the onus for the situations on the opposition.

The White House listed anti-inflation legislation and enactment of the long-range Taft-Ellender-Wagner Housing Bill among the points that would be covered in

Continued on Page 3, Column 5

Meat Men Here Split on Controls As Prices Stay High; Milk Going Up

As retail meat prices continued high yesterday, with little promise of any marked reductions in the next six to eight months, sharp differences over renewing rationing and price controls arose in the industry. Meanwhile, milk price advances of 1 cent a quart, scheduled here for Aug. 1, and a similar increase on Oct. 1, received official sanction of the Department of Agriculture in Washington.

Only the American Meat Institute held forth the hope that a seasonal increase in meat production by fall and winter "should tend to modify prices in some degree, unless offset by further increased consumer income." Joining with the institute in opposing controls was the New York State Association of Retail Meat Dealers.

Favoring controls, with a ceiling price on livestock at the source, was the National Industry Meat Council, representing 25,000 shops in eight Eastern states. In a complete reversal of its 1946 stand, the New York Retail Appetizers Association, representing 250 grocery and delicatessen shops, requested President Truman to reinstate the Office of Price Administration.

Milk prices to consumers here will advance as the result of the minimum fluid milk prices established for the New York area by the Department of Agriculture. The alternate formulae for minimum prices set by the department were identical with those recommended on July 6, the department specifying as follows:

"Minimum prices, per hundredweight for milk of 3.5 per cent butterfat content are: (1) $5.68 for August and September, and $6.12 for October through December; or (2) a New York price for the August-December, 1948 period comparable to that established under the Boston Federal milk order for Class 1 milk of 3.7 per cent butterfat content. The higher of the alternate minimums will be the effective price."

Department officials said that

Continued on Page 3, Column 7

"All the News That's Fit to Print"

The New York Times.

LATE CITY EDITION
Mostly sunny and cool today; cloudy tonight and tomorrow.
Temperature Range Today-Max.,34; Min.,15
Temperatures Yesterday—Max.,42; Min.,31
Full U. S. Weather Bureau Report, Page 43

VOL. XCVIII..No. 33,235. Entered as Second-Class Matter, Postoffice, New York, N. Y. NEW YORK, FRIDAY, JANUARY 21, 1949. Times Square, New York 18, N. Y. Telephone LAckawanna 4-1000 THREE CENTS NEW YORK CITY

TRUMAN, 32D PRESIDENT, IS INAUGURATED; CALLS ON U. S. TO LEAD DEMOCRATIC WORLD; DENOUNCES COMMUNISM, PLEDGES U. N. AID

COMMUNISTS WIN RIGHT TO WITNESSES AGAINST U. S. JURY

Will Call First Today in Effort to Prove Illegality of Body That Indicted Them Here

MIGHT SUMMON 12 JUDGES

Medina Permits Defense Step While Studying Motion to Strike Out Challenge

By RUSSELL PORTER

The right to call witnesses against the grand jury that indicted them was won yesterday by the eleven Communist leaders. Defense lawyers announced they would present their first witnesses this morning. They have contended the jury was illegal and its indictment void, because it was selected by methods that excluded certain minority groups.

Defense counsel said also they might put Judge John C. Knox, senior jurist of this Federal district; Judge Harold R. Medina, who is trying this case, and the ten other judges in this district, on the witness stand.

Jurors and jury officials also may be subpoenaed. A defense agent applied for 100 subpoenas from the clerk of the court and received fifty, all that were on hand.

The defendants were indicted by a special grand jury on charges of organizing the Communist party to teach and advocate overthrow and destruction of the Government by force and violence.

Jury Indicted Hiss Also

The same jury later indicted Alger Hiss, former State Department official, on charges of perjury to conceal evidence of espionage in the transmission of official secrets to Russian Communist agents.

Presumably, if the Communists succeed in voiding their indictment on the ground that the grand jury was improperly constituted, this would set a precedent for voiding the Hiss indictment.

Judge Medina opened the door to the grand jury challenge when he decided to "take proofs" while reserving decision on a prosecution motion to strike out this challenge.

"My disposition has been to grant the prosecution's motion," he said, "but this will give me time to study it further."

George W. Crockett Jr. of Detroit then stood up at defense counsel table. He is attorney for Carl Winter, Michigan State chairman, and Jacob Stachel, "educational" director of the Communist party.

Mr. Crockett announced he might have to call all the Federal judges of this district to the witness stand to testify regarding discrimination against Negroes and other minorities in selecting juries. Mr. Crockett himself is a Negro.

Says He Might Call Medina

Looking over his glasses at Judge Medina, Mr. Crockett said grimly:

"I might have to call your honor."

Judge Medina leaned back in his big red leather chair behind the bench and smiled amiably.

"That's been done before," he said.

The judge then asked United States Attorney John F. X. McGohey and the five chief defense lawyers to submit memoranda as to the competence of a judge as a witness in a proceeding before himself.

Mr. McGohey suggested the need to find out whether the judge would be disqualified by law from continuing to sit in a case after appearing as a witness.

"It would be an extraordinary thing," the judge added, "if a maneuver of that kind could disqualify the judge. I doubt that could be the law, because if it were, and if counsel were repeatedly seeking delay for various

Continued on Page 9, Column 1

North Ireland Votes On Eire Tie Feb. 10

By The United Press.

BELFAST, Northern Ireland, Jan. 20—A general election that is expected to determine whether Northern Ireland will remain part of the United Kingdom will be held Feb. 10, it was announced today.

It will be the first general election since Eire's declaration of independence from the British Commonwealth.

Observers here agree that the chief election issue would be Britain's plan for the establishment of federal Ireland. Under this plan, Northern Ireland and Eire would have their own parliaments but would send representatives to an All-Ireland Assembly at Dublin that would control vital matters such as defense and taxation. Both of these matters now are controlled by Britain in Northern Ireland.

CHIANG HELD READY TO LEAVE NANKING

Farewell Statement Reported Being Drafted in Move to Ease Parley With Reds

By HENRY R. LIEBERMAN
Special to The New York Times.

NANKING, Jan. 20—Generalissimo Chiang Kai-shek's speech-writer, Tao Hsi-sheng, was again reported at work tonight on a farewell statement for the Generalissimo in the midst of a dynamic political situation that has reached a new stage for ups and downs, even in China.

According to the Generalissimo's plans, as they were said to have existed just before midnight, he is now preparing to depart for Formosa over a route that may include stop-overs of undisclosed duration at Fenghwa, his old home in Chekiang Province, and Foochow on the coast of Fukien.

Several times before this the Generalissimo is known to have told his intimates that he was planning to leave Nanking, only to alter the plan soon thereafter. Now that Premier Sun Fo's Cabinet has formally decided to propose a cease-fire order to the Communists, however, his leaving Nanking seems to have become a more pressing matter for the peace-makers, anxious to make their sincerity plain to the Communists.

Even if the Generalissimo leaves Nanking, his departure for South China, where the Government is shifting its capital, is still regarded as leaving open the possibility of the anti-Communist bloc operating under his leadership from a series of new bases in Fukien, Kwangtung and Formosa.

It is considered almost inevitable that if the Generalissimo leaves, the step will be accompanied by some face-saving formula.

With the capital no longer

Continued on Page 12, Column 3

ASIAN LANDS URGE FREE INDIES IN '49; NEHRU INVITES BLOC

New Delhi Delegates Agree to Bid U. N. Order Dutch Back to Pre-'Police Action' Lines

COLONIAL RULE ASSAILED

Indian Premier Issues Call for Permanent Gathering to Guard Area Interests

By The United Press.

NEW DELHI, India, Jan. 20—Delegates from nineteen Asian countries decided at a secret meeting tonight to ask the United Nations Security Council to order the complete independence of Indonesia by the end of this year.

They decided also to recommend to the Council that the Dutch be ordered to withdraw immediately to the lines they occupied before the Dutch "police action" last Dec. 18 and that this withdrawal be completed by March 18.

The Asian delegates met here at the request of the Indian Prime Minister, Pandit Jawaharlal Nehru, to protest the Dutch military action in Indonesia and to study the possibilities of aiding the Indonesian Republic.

At the opening plenary session this morning, Prime Minister Nehru proposed the creation of a permanent organization of Asian states to guard the interests of the Far East.

He said that the immediate aim of the conference would be to find a solution to the Indonesian problem. But he added that the delegates also should consider the creation of a "permanent arrangement for effective mutual consultation and concerted effort in the *pursuit of common aims.*"

His statement was a clear call for a regional organization of *Asian states within the frame*work of the United Nations. It will be discussed Saturday by the full conference.

During the secret meeting today at Hyderabad House, the Asian delegates decided also to ask the Security Council to insure the re-establishment of a recognized Indonesian interim government by March 18, the deadline for troop withdrawals.

Tomorrow the delegates will discuss the question of applying *sanctions against the Netherlands*, and it appeared today that such sanctions would be approved by most of the nations represented.

Prime Minister Nehru, who was elected chairman, sounded what may be the only controversial note in this conference with his proposal for a permanent Asian organization.

His plea was supported by Brig. Gen. Carlos P. Romulo of the Philippine Republic. General Romulo

Continued on Page 11, Column 5

PRAISE IN CONGRESS

Members Hail Truman's Bold Stand, but Are Wary on New Aid

DETAILS ARE ASKED

Non-Partisan Questions Raised on Extent of Loan Guarantees

By C. P. TRUSSELL
Special to The New York Times.

WASHINGTON, Jan. 20—The principles and objectives enunciated by President Truman in his inaugural address today drew warm comment from members of Congress. But no guarantees were given that he would escape controversy over his "bold new program" for making American scientific advances and industrial progress available for the improvement and growth of underdeveloped areas of the world.

While the partisanship that stems usually from first reaction was almost absent, questions were raised at key points, and fuller explanation was demanded as to the proposed scope and application of the program, its possible cost and the means of financing it.

There was widespread call from members of both parties that there be a "spelling out" of details, especially that phase of the program that was interpreted by many as proposing a guaranteeing of investments in foreign countries.

Praise of U. N. Acclaimed

Mr. Truman's declaration of continuance of unfaltering support to the United Nations and its related agencies appeared to have won universal approval within both major parties. So did his pledge of continuing programs for world economic recovery, with reservations as to the new plan.

A strengthening of freedom-loving nations against the dangers of aggression seemed to have such widespread approval that predictions were made in some quarters that the proposed North Atlantic Collective Defense Pact would get through Congress "without trouble."

It was stated, in varied phrasing through many voices, that the President's analysis of democracy as compared with communism, and the force with which he had made the comparison, had done great

Continued on Page 5, Column 2

HARRY S. TRUMAN TAKING THE OATH AS PRESIDENT

The Chief Executive being sworn by Chief Justice Fred M. Vinson. In the center, holding Bibles, is Charles E. Cropley, clerk of the United States Supreme Court, and at the right of Mr. Truman is Vice President Alben W. Barkley.

The New York Times (by Ernest Sisto)

SPEECH SEEN AS AID TO WESTERN WORLD

Capital Observers Hold It Step to Expand Economic and Military Defenses Abroad

By JAMES RESTON
Special to The New York Times.

WASHINGTON, Jan. 20—President Truman's inaugural address was generally interpreted in the capital as one of the most ambitious pronouncements on foreign affairs ever made by an American President.

Mr. Truman said so much about what the United States was prepared to do about opposing communism, building a collective security system and restoring the economic strength of Western Europe, however, that some of his principal advisers on foreign affairs felt that he did not put enough emphasis on the reciprocal

Continued on Page 7, Column 1

More Than a Million Roar In Approval of Inauguration

By WILLIAM S. WHITE
Special to The New York Times.

WASHINGTON, Jan. 20—The roar of a great crowd—over a million persons were here as the unofficial delegates of the people of this country—rose and fell today in broken, happy cadence for Harry S. Truman's inauguration as President of the United States.

There was elation and aggressive triumph in the voices of these men and women, the triumph of the many whose man somehow had won against all the probabilities.

In their struggling, staring mass they overran the aloof green and marble reaches of Washington; they swarmed over cold official lawns hardly used year in and year out; they struggled, sometimes angrily, for places before the great, stern façades of the Supreme Court, the Capitol, the Library of Congress, the Treasury.

For many blocks they filled the lateral streets running into Pennsylvania Avenue, the traditional way here for pageants, and a great many thousands of them never really saw the parade for which they had come so far.

Their voices, making a hoarse medley of all the accents of the United States of America, beat strongly against the endless brass thumping of the endless bands.

The streets were filled and running with their noises, and the

Continued on Page 4, Column 6

BARKLEY SWORN IN AS VICE PRESIDENT

'Happy to Be Backing Up the President,' He Says—Day Marks Turn in Career

By CLAYTON KNOWLES
Special to The New York Times.

WASHINGTON, Jan. 20—With thirty-six years of continuous service in Congress behind him, Alben W. Barkley embarked upon a new career of service to the nation today as he took the oath of office as the thirty-fifth Vice President of the United States.

Erect and seemingly sturdy as an oak, the 71-year-old Kentuckian was sworn into his new office at 12:23 P. M. by Associate Justice Stanley F. Reed, a few minutes before Harry S. Truman took the

Continued on Page 3, Column 5

PEACE A MAJOR AIM

Truman Says America Will Not Waver From Fight on Aggressor

TO STRENGTHEN FREE

Proposes Sharing U. S. Scientific Gains With Undeveloped Areas

The text of the President's Inaugural Address, Page 4.

By ANTHONY LEVIERO
Special to The New York Times.

WASHINGTON, Jan. 20—Harry S. Truman denounced communism as a false doctrine and outlined a four-point program for American world leadership, and peace, as he assumed the Presidency in his own right in the most impressive inaugural of American history.

Thus with a positive statement of American aspirations, the thirty-second President of the United States concluded the traditional ceremony on Capitol Hill which reached a tremendous global audience on the radio waves.

He took the oath of office before a throng of more than 100,000 of his fellow countrymen at 12:29 P. M., a few minutes after Senator Alben W. Barkley of Kentucky took a similar oath and became the Vice President.

Unlike many of his predecessors, whose inaugural addresses were in the nature of philosophical discourses, the plain-spoken Missourian delivered a major policy statement. It was replete, like virtually all his speeches, with concrete statements and proposals.

Calls for Just Settlement

Mr. Truman drew a sharp, straight line between democracy and communism, without the slightest trace of the softening toward Russia which some observers had been suspecting recently.

The Chief Executive asserted that democracy was a vitalizing force, sustaining the initiative which was in our hands, and that we would not be moved from our faith by the Soviet political philosophy.

President Truman explained he was not making his strongly contrasting definitions of democracy and totalitarianism merely to be argumentative. He saw communism as a threat to world recovery and lasting peace, he said, and he was offering what he proclaimed to be a constructive program for all nations.

He did not leave Russia and her satellites out of his hopes. Although he mentioned none of them by name, as he neared the end of his address he expressed a belief that the countries under Communistic regimes would "abandon their delusions and join with the free nations of the world in a just settlement of international differences."

Would Share Progress

The heart of his aims Mr. Truman set forth in one, two, three, four fashion. First he reiterated unwavering support of the United Nations and here he made a friendly gesture to such nations that are aborning, as Israel, Korea and Indonesia. He said they would strengthen the United Nations as they themselves became strong with the nourishment of democratic principles.

As his second point, Mr. Truman reiterated this country's determination to work for world recovery by giving full measure to the European Recovery Program and promoting trade for all the world's markets.

On the North Atlantic Security Plan, which is now crystallizing, Mr. Truman focused his third point. He said, "We will strengthen freedom-loving nations against the dangers of aggression," but only within the recognized framework of the United Nations Charter and

Continued on Page 2, Column 4

Jerusalem's Fate Held Main Issue In Settlement of Palestine Question

By ANNE O'HARE McCORMICK
Special to The New York Times.

JERUSALEM, Jan. 20—The best place to study both sides of the Palestine conflict is in Jerusalem. Here are two distinct cities, as far apart in aspect, time, outlook and way of life as they are near in space.

Across a narrow No Man's Land, cluttered with the debris of a passionate war—for to both sides this is an intensely desired and holy place—the New City looks upon walls of the Old and the Old City looks back on the open streets and modern buildings of the New. They are in constant sight of one another, separated only by a small guard and a few strands of barbed wire 100 feet apart, but no citizen of one town ever sets foot in the other.

Not a Jew remains in the Old City and only a few hundred Arabs, strictly confined in a small section, are left in the New City. Each community is under military rule and each lives a separate, restricted life in a world of its own so different from the other that it is hard to remember that they ever mingled.

What will happen to Jerusalem is the central question in the Palestine settlement. Control of the Negeb, desert area to the south, now an international issue, is the foremost material objective of Israel. Her determination to own this empty area and to people it with 2,000,000 settlers shows how the ideas of the new state regarding both territory and population have expanded as a result of military conquests.

A leading Zionist statesman remarked the other day with the accent of regret that Israel's problems would be simpler if she were the smaller state envisioned in the United Nations partition plan. "But too much has occurred since to make it possible for any Govern-

Continued on Page 11, Column 4

World News Summarized

FRIDAY, JANUARY 21, 1949

Harry S. Truman, the thirty-second President of the United States, was inaugurated yesterday. He delivered a major address on foreign policy, assailing communism in a sort of parallel-column contrast of what he called communist vices with democratic virtues. He outlined a four-point program of American world leadership for peace: unfaltering devotion to the United Nations and its economic agencies, determination to carry on international recovery programs, creation of a North Atlantic security group within the United Nations framework to strengthen the democracies, and sharing of American scientific and technological progress with the rest of the world. [1:8.]

Observers called the speech the most ambitious pronouncement on foreign policy ever made by a President. They endorsed the principles but questioned some of the details. [1:5.] Congressional reaction was somewhat the same. Objection to what was felt to be a guarantee of American investments abroad was voiced. [1:4.]

President Truman started his day at an early breakfast with World War I comrades of Battery D [1:6-7] and went to the Capitol, where he and Vice President Barkley were sworn in. [1:7.] He reviewed the inaugural parade, which took nearly three hours to pass the stand [5:1], and then attended a reception at the National Gallery of Art. [6:3.] It was estimated that 1,000,000 persons had witnessed the ceremonies. [1:6-7.]

Some changes in the Taft-Hartley Law were advocated by the Chamber of Commerce of the United States. [35:6.] The United Automobile Workers will demand pensions of at least $100 a month. [16:4.] A strike caused New Jersey to cut off the supply of gas to industries in the Camden area. [16:2.]

Lawyers for the American Communist leaders on trial won the right to call witnesses against the grand jury that brought the indictments. [1:1.]

Generalissimo Chiang Kai-shek was reported ready to quit Nanking to smooth the way for peace talks with the Communists. [1:2.]

The New Delhi conference of Asiatic countries decided to ask the United Nations to order full independence for Indonesia. [1:3]

Disagreement on "important points" delayed an Israeli-Egyptian armistice. [11:2-3, with map.]

Big Four talks on an Austrian treaty will be resumed in London Feb. 7. [10:5.]

The new Greek Cabinet was sworn in. [14:2.]

Index to other news appears on Page 22.

Captain Harry, Not Mr. President, Starts Day of Days With Battery D

By CHARLES HURD
Special to The New York Times.

WASHINGTON, Jan. 20—From noon until late tonight President Truman's life blended into the panoply and formality of an inaugural history-making in its size, but this morning—and the morning began before sunrise—the time was his own and the man was Harry S. Truman or plain "Captain Harry."

The dividing line in the day occurred at 12:29 P. M. At that minute Mr. Truman took the oath as President of the United States and stepped into the pattern of his day of triumph. Behind him, however, even at noon, lay almost half a dozen active hours arranged as he had planned them.

He had, in those hours, spanned activities ranging from jocular chiding at a breakfast of his old companions in Battery D to attending divine services in St. John's Episcopal Church, together with doing a little work. Only two other personal intervals were left in his crowded day: one, a lunch in the office of his old friend, Leslie L. Biffle, Secretary of the Senate, and the other a private dinner late this evening with his family at Blair House.

Otherwise, Mr. Truman's time divided itself into four official parts that taxed many younger persons in his entourage, but in which he participated despite the fact that he had had less than five hours' sleep last night.

On this official schedule, he first took his oath of office and delivered an inaugural address at the Capitol in ceremonies starting at noon. At 2 P. M. he belatedly led his own inaugural parade to the White House, to stay there for more than three hours watching it march past. Long after the scheduled hour of 5 P. M. he hastened to the National Gallery of Art to

Continued on Page 3, Column 2

"All the News That's Fit to Print"

The New York Times.

LATE CITY EDITION
Mostly sunny, warm and humid today and tomorrow.
Temperature Range Today-Max.,82; Min.,62
Temperatures Yesterday-Max.,82.7; Min. 61
Full U. S. Weather Bureau Report, Page 55

VOL. XCVIII..No. 33,339. Entered as Second-Class Matter, Postoffice, New York, N. Y. NEW YORK, THURSDAY, MAY 5, 1949. Times Square, New York 18, N. Y. Telephone LAckawanna 4-1000 THREE CENTS IN NEW YORK CITY

BERLIN BLOCKADE TO END MAY 12; BIG FOUR MEETING IS SET FOR 23D; NOTE OF CAUTION SOUNDED BY CLAY

WOOD'S DRAFT OF LABOR BILL DIES IN HOUSE

TAFT LAW STANDS

Issue Is Sent Back to Committee, With Action at Session in Doubt

SHELVING VOTE IS 212-209

10 Southerners Switch to Bring Upset—Three of GOP File New Senate Measure

By JOSEPH A. LOFTUS
Special to The New York Times.

WASHINGTON, May 4—The House killed the Wood labor bill today in a hairline reversal that gave to the Democratic leadership and the labor chieftains little more than a chance to fight another day. The vote was 212 to 209.

Ten reconstructed Southern votes gave the major assist to an Administration drive which sent the bill back to committee after a coalition of Republicans and Southern Democrats seemed to have victory in its grasp.

Last night a vote of 217 to 203 had given preliminary approval to the Wood bill, which would have modified the Taft-Hartley Act while retaining its basic features.

Jubilation today among the Administration Democrats and labor leaders was tempered by a realization that the original Administration bill was, in effect, also killed in the crush and their target, the Taft-Hartley Act, is still the law of the land.

Burden on Backers of Change

Whether the two extreme views on the issue can be reconciled in time to pass any labor relations bill at this session of Congress is a real question. The burden of answering it is placed largely on those demanding a change in the present law.

The question is likely to be affected by what happens in the Senate. There a new labor bill was introduced today by three Republicans, Senators Robert A. Taft of Ohio, H. Alexander Smith of New Jersey and Forrest C. Donnell of Missouri.

Senator Taft, who is co-author of the Taft-Hartley Law, said that the bill would "retain the best features" of that law.

If the Administration and labor leaders fail to win legislation which suits them they will rely, as some quickly said today, on another political campaign, fortified by their contention that they have made substantial gains over their showing in the Eightieth Congress.

Representative Albert Gore, Democrat, of Tennessee, was cited by some Northern Democrats as the key to the switch of Southern votes. Mr. Gore supported the leadership in the vote against the Wood bill last night. He declined any credit for today's reversal and insisted it was a victory for Speaker Sam Rayburn.

Mr. Gore, nevertheless, summarized what happened before the decisive vote today.

Decries Inadequate Hearings

"I told these fellows I thought they ought to have another chance," he said, referring to Democrats on the Education and Labor Committee. "I asked for one commitment: Take the bill back and give it thorough consideration and report a bill back that the party could support. They said yes. I passed the word around and they (a group of Southern Democrats) said yes.

"They know pretty well what the majority of this Congress will support. They have had enough tests. We have had two demonstrations of the trouble a committee runs into when it doesn't give full consideration to a bill."

This was a reference to the Rankin veterans' pension bill and the Lesinski (Administration) labor bill.

Mr. Gore was asked if he thought a motive for today's vote-switching was to keep the Taft-Hartley Law.

"I don't think so," he replied.

The following Democrats voted for the Wood bill last night but supported the Administration today: Representatives William P. Bolton and George H. Fallon of Maryland, Oren Harris, Brooks Hays, W. F. Norrell and Boyd Tackett of Arkansas; Porter Hardy Jr. of Virginia, Joe L. Evins of

Continued on Page 30, Column 2

Military View Black; Pentagon Lights Fail

Special to The New York Times.

WASHINGTON, May 4—The nation's military leaders were temporarily incommunicado today as a power failure intermittently put the lights out and stalled the Pentagon switchboard.

Generals, admirals, lesser officers and civilian personnel were suddenly wrapped in darkness while they ate their lunch or sat at their desks.

The first blackout began at 12:10 and halted eating and other activities for more than ten minutes. A second and third were of shorter duration but just as effective.

Failure of a control cable and the resulting overload of another were blamed for the breakdown.

THRONGS HERE HAIL ISRAEL, WEIZMANN

Head of New State Exchanges Telegrams With Truman on First Anniversary

By IRVING SPIEGEL

The first anniversary of the establishment of Israel as a nation was celebrated with demonstrations yesterday at Madison Square Park and Carnegie Hall and by a dinner at which Governor Dewey urged the admission of Israel to the United Nations.

The day's highlight was an exchange of felicitations between Dr. Chaim Weizmann, Israel's first president, and President Truman. In a telegram, President Truman said:

"On this first anniversary of the independence of Israel it gives me great pleasure to convey to Your Excellency and to the people of Israel the hearty congratulations and sincere good wishes of the people of the United States."

In reply, Dr. Weizmann wired:

"Your message of greetings and congratulations on the occasion of the first anniversary of the independence of Israel is most warmly and gratefully appreciated. The people of Israel will never forget the part played by your great country as well as your personal sympathy and helpful attitude at all times in the achievement of their national independence."

The Madison Square Park meeting in the afternoon, marked by the appearance of Dr. Weizmann, his wife and his son Benjamin, attracted a crowd estimated at 125,000 persons. The throng, waving thousands of Israeli and American flags, filled all available space between Twenty-third and Twenty-sixth Street, overflowed on Fifth Avenue and into side streets.

Time and again, the crowd surged toward the flag-draped platform at Twenty-fourth Street and Madison Avenue. About a dozen persons were knocked down in the crush; three of them requiring hospitalization at Bellevue for minor injuries. Loudspeakers carried the addresses.

Spontaneous outbursts of "Hat-

Continued on Page 3, Column 3

DULLES CALLS WAR POSSIBLE IF TREATY IS KILLED IN SENATE

Calls on Group to Serve Notice Pact Does Not Imply World Division by U. S., Russia

CUT IN ARMS COST IS SEEN

Clayton and Carey Also Back Accord—Wallace Will Lead Off for Opponents Today

By WILLIAM S. WHITE
Special to The New York Times.

WASHINGTON, May 4—John Foster Dulles urged the Senate today to ratify the North Atlantic treaty and also to issue warnings that this country's concern with Europe's safety certainly would not leave the Soviet Union a free hand elsewhere in the world.

Senate rejection of the covenant, he said, without indicating that he looked for such a generally unexpected result, would be "an inexpressible disaster" that "quite possibly" might be followed by war.

Mr. Dulles, a United States representative to the United Nations General Assembly and one of the most influential voices on foreign policy in the Republican party, testified before the Senate Foreign Relations Committee.

The first witness in its six days of hearings to use such a term, he asserted that there were "dangers" in the covenant.

"The greatest single danger," he testified, "was the possibility that the drawing of a geographic security line around the twelve member countries of the treaty might permit erroneous inferences that it was 'a tacit offer to divide the world' with Russia.

Would Issue Declarations

While he did not suggest that the Senate actually attach specific reservations, he said that it would be "useful" if it issued declarations of American intentions on this point and on two others.

He indicated that he believed this could be done simply by clear language written into the text of the report that the committee will make when it formally recommends the treaty to the Senate for ratification. This latter action will require two-thirds of those Senators voting.

Apart from saying that the Senate ought to make it clear beyond "miscalculation" that this country was deeply interested not only in the security of the Western Hemisphere and the North Atlantic area but also in Asia and the rest of the world, Mr. Dulles proposed Senate declarations to the following effect:

1. That the United States did not intend that the consultations among treaty partners which Article IV of the treaty would permit should go into matters beyond the North Atlantic area or in any way provide a rival forum to the United Nations.
2. That the United States hoped and expected that the covenant would be operated "not as a military instrument but as a step in a political evolution that has behind it a long and honorable history and, before it, a great and peaceful future."

In colloquies with Senators Tom Connally, Democrat, of Texas, committee chairman, and Arthur H. Vandenberg of Michigan, its ranking Republican member, Mr. Dulles indicated that he was profoundly concerned about the possible "implications" of Article IV. That

Continued on Page 10, Column 3

GENERAL WORRIED

Believes That Agreement With Russians Can Be Only Temporary Truce

URGES A LONG OCCUPATION

Does Not See War Inevitable —Governor Gets Impressive Farewell of 11,000 Troops

By JACK RAYMOND
Special to The New York Times.

GRAFENWOEHR, Germany, May 4—Gen. Lucius D. Clay received an impressive farewell salute from his command today in a giant army and air force review at this former Wehrmacht training center. Then in an unusually frank interview he commented on the German scene, stressing publicly for the first time his belief that the impending agreement with Russia could be only temporary.

He denied, however, that this implied that war was inevitable. War could be avoided, he said, by faith in American ideals and aid to the rest of the world. He said that this technique for avoiding hostilities had not gone "too badly" in the Berlin situation.

The retiring Military Governor also gave his view that a unified Germany, which he believed inevitable, would not include restitution of all Polish-held territories. He emphasized that German territory had been promised to Poland in compensation for that taken by the Russians.

As far as the people of Germany were concerned, General Clay said that upon their adoption of democratic ways depended the length of the occupation period. The Allies must stay to make sure that the Germans abide by a new democratic constitution, he said, and this could take five to twenty years.

The fifty-two-year-old army commander spoke philosophically to the press in the club car of his private train. He said that he had learned "humility" during his tenure as Military Governor. Dealing with the lives of 45,000,000 people —even if they were former enemies—had meant dealing with intangibles and a constant concern whether decisions were right or wrong, he said. Earlier in the day

Continued on Page 6, Column 2

GENERAL CLAY GREETS ONE OF HIS SUCCESSORS

The retiring military governor of Germany and Lieut. Gen. Clarence R. Huebner.
Associated Press Radiophoto

CURRENCY A TOPIC

Berlin Money Is Put Up to Foreign Ministers, Meeting in Paris

PEACE MAY BE ON AGENDA

Briton and Frenchman Join U.S. and Soviet Representatives to Reach the Accord

By THOMAS J. HAMILTON
Special to The New York Times.

LAKE SUCCESS, May 4—The United States, Britain, France and the Soviet Union have agreed that the Soviet blockade of Berlin, together with counter-measures imposed by the Western powers, is to be raised and that the Council of Foreign Ministers shall take up "questions relating to Germany and the problems arising out of the situation in Berlin, including also questions of currency in Berlin," it was announced today.

Authoritative sources said that representatives of the Big Four agreed that restrictions on communications with Berlin should be lifted on May 12, to be followed by a Council of Foreign Ministers in Paris on May 23. The conference, which lasted an hour, convened at 10:30 A. M. today at the headquarters of the United States delegation to the United Nations at 2 Park Avenue.

Jacob A. Malik, Soviet representative to the United Nations, and Dr. Philip C. Jessup, United States roving Ambassador, were joined today by Sir Alexander Cadogan and Jean Chauvel, British and French representatives to the United Nations. Mr. Malik informed Dr. Jessup late last night that he would agree to their taking part.

West Gave Statement

This reply was in response to a written statement drawn up by the three Western power representatives Monday stating that they were ready to participate in the discussions, which until today had been conducted between the Soviet and United States representatives, with Dr. Jessup acting in behalf of the three Western powers.

The timetable, as presented in the statement of the Western representatives, is understood to have called for the resumption of normal communications with Berlin on May 9, with the Council of Foreign Ministers to convene on May 23, two weeks later. However, Mr. Malik, both in his reply last night and at the conference today, was said to have explained that it would be difficult to draw up and transmit the necessary detailed orders to Soviet occupation authorities so soon, and proposed May 12 instead.

This was accepted without objection by the Western representatives, and Mr. Malik in his turn agreed promptly that the Council of Foreign Ministers should meet on May 23, it was understood. The text of the Big Four agreement will be delivered tomorrow morning to Secretary General Trygve Lie for submission to the President of the Security Council, which still has the Berlin dispute on its agenda.

Details Are Not Stated

The three Western powers submitted the Berlin dispute to the Security Council on Sept. 26, 1948, and Andrei Y. Vishinsky, now Soviet Foreign Minister, vetoed a compromise resolution, offered by the six members not directly concerned, on Oct. 25. The Soviet Union afterward agreed to accept as a basis for consideration a currency plan drafted by Security Council experts, but this was rejected by the Western Powers on the ground that the Soviet Union had split the administration of Berlin, and it was no longer possible to establish a single currency in both the Soviet and Western sectors.

The Soviet Union, however, afterward dropped its demand for a settlement of the currency question before raising the blockade, and Mr. Malik's prompt acceptance of the Western powers' conditions today was interpreted here as another proof that the Kremlin was anxious to end the blockade and con-

Continued on Page 6, Column 4

TEN NATIONS ADOPT STATUTE OF EUROPE

It Is to Be Signed in London Today—Churchill Likely to Sit in the Parliament

By BENJAMIN WELLES
Special to The New York Times.

LONDON, May 4—Nine Foreign Ministers and the Belgian Ambassador reached full agreement here today on a Statute of the Council of Europe, which will now carry into effect the long-cherished ideal of a democratic European Parliament.

A three-hour session was held this morning in St. James's Palace by the representatives of Britain, France, Belgium, the Netherlands, Luxembourg, Italy, Ireland, Norway, Denmark and Sweden. They completed the review of the draft Statute, which had been laboriously

Continued on Page 8, Column 5

Berlin Greets End of Siege With Relief, Apprehension

By DREW MIDDLETON
Special to The New York Times.

BERLIN, May 4—The battle for Berlin is over. The battle for Germany is about to begin. As the long, bitter struggle for this city moved swiftly toward a triumphant conclusion for the United States, Britain and France tonight, the people of Berlin, half in relief and half in apprehension, greeted the news that an accord had been reached by the Big Four on lifting of the Berlin blockade.

They were conscious that they had contributed to the most decisive victory yet scored by anti-Communist forces in the struggle for Germany. But that that victory was only one battle in the long struggle for Germany to come, few Germans or Americans, British or French would deny tonight.

After 320 days of complete blockade, which had brought with it shortages of food and fuel, and unemployment, a vast sigh of relief rose from the average Berliner at the thought that the end of Soviet restrictions was in sight.

But the city's political leaders, headed by Mayor Ernest Reuter, who remarked that lifting of the blockade was "all very well" but that Berlin's future status was still in doubt, were apprehensive over the outcome of the battle for Germany which they believe will open at the meeting of the Council of Foreign Ministers.

What might have been a night of wild rejoicing was overlaid with gloomy forebodings of what the future might bring for zealous anti-Communists in Berlin if the city government was reintegrated.

Gen. Sir Brian Robertson, British Military Governor, assured the people of the city in a special mes-

Continued on Page 5, Column 1

U. S., BRITAIN TO ACT SOON IN RIGHTS CASE

Acheson Says New Move Is Set Against Bulgaria, Hungary, Rumania for Violations

By BERTRAM D. HULEN
Special to The New York Times.

WASHINGTON, May 4—Secretary of State Dean Acheson announced today that the United States and Britain would move shortly against Bulgaria, Hungary and Rumania on charges of violating the human rights clauses of their peace treaties by religious and political persecutions, suppression of freedom of speech and assembly, and ruthless measures against political opposition. Action is imminent, he declared.

It will be the first time that these provisions of the peace treaties have been invoked. The move will result from the trial of Joseph Cardinal Mindszenty in Hungary, the imprisonment of Protestant clergymen Bulgaria, and oppressive measures in general in all three countries violative of human freedoms.

The United States and Britain early this month protested to the three governments, only to have

Continued on Page 9, Column 4

World News Summarized

THURSDAY, MAY 5, 1949

Representatives of the Big Four yesterday agreed to end the Soviet blockade of Berlin and the Western counter-blockade and to convene the Council of Foreign Ministers in Paris to discuss the entire German question, including Berlin currency. It was said the blockades would be lifted one week from today and the Paris meeting would start on May 23. [1:8.] Determination of the date on which the Berlin airlift should end will be left with General Clay. [4:3.] After a farewell review of his forces in Frankfort, General Clay said the pending agreement could be only temporary, but he added that war was not inevitable. [1:4.]

Relief and skepticism marked the reaction to the news. Berlin felt that while the battle for the city was over, the battle for Germany was about to begin. [1:6-7.] London observers saw a change of tactics by Moscow, but not a change of heart. [8:2.] At a farewell luncheon in Paris Ambassador Caffery, pointing to Soviet propaganda on "capitalist warmongering," said peace could not "bloom in the poisoned atmosphere of lies and distortions." [7:3.] A Moscow journal called the United States press the tool of "warmongers" [7:5.] Washington opinion held that the economic squeeze on Russia and her satellites was the real reason for Moscow's changed attitude. [4:5-6.]

Action by the United States and Britain to invoke the human rights clauses of peace treaties with Bulgaria, Hungary and Rumania over religious and political persecutions is imminent, Secretary Acheson said. [1:7.]

He confirmed that Yugoslavia was seeking a World Bank loan and Spain a credit from the Export-Import Bank. [9:2.]

Failure to ratify the North Atlantic treaty, John Foster Dulles told a Senate committee, might "quite possibly" be followed by war. [1:3.]

House Democratic leaders mustered just enough strength to bury the Wood bill, approved on Tuesday as a substitute for the Administration labor bill. A vote of 212 to 209 sent the Wood bill back to committee, removing all labor legislation from the calendar. A new measure can be reported by the Labor Committee or the House can concur in any bill the Senate may pass. Meanwhile, the Taft-Hartley Act remains the law. [1:1.] Three Senate Republicans introduced a bill Senator Taft said included the best features of the Wagner Act and the Taft-Hartley Act. [31:1.]

A package of fourth-round demands said to represent a 30-cent hourly wage increase was completed by CIO steel union officials. [31:5.]

Governor Dewey named Keith Lorenz chairman of the State Labor Relations Board. [19:1.]

Rallies, dinners and meetings in this city marked the first anniversary of the establishment of Israel as an independent nation. [1:2.] Governor Dewey urged admission of Israel to the United Nations and a "satisfactory solution" in Jerusalem. [3:1.] Israel will state her position on internationalizing Jerusalem and on Arab refugees to a General Assembly committee today. [2:3.]

Chinese Communists were believed concentrating on a drive toward Fukien Province. [16:1.]

Index to other news appears on Page 28.

7,845 Here Seek Rent-Rise Forms; Attacks on Woods' Ruling Continue

By WILLIAM M. FARRELL

The number of landlords obtaining rent-rise application forms increased here yesterday, with the six area rent offices handing out or mailing 7,845 sets. Thirty-three applications for rent increases were filed by landlords who were among the 5,000 who had obtained the blanks on Tuesday.

Meanwhile, spokesmen for both landlords and tenants continued to denounce the formula for "fair net operating income" issued on Tuesday by Tighe E. Woods, the Federal Housing Expediter.

In Washington members of Mr. Woods' staff said property owners had hastened to obtain the application blanks in all places under rent control. Many cities have distributed all their supplies and more are being rushed to them. Officials predicted that 200,000 applications would be filed by the end of the week.

But most property owners here seemed to be less precipitate than the Washington statements would suggest. Employes who opened the Bronx Area Rent Office, at 1910 Arthur Avenue, found eighty landlords waiting in line outside at 8:45 A. M. During the day 1,750 sets of blanks were distributed. No more than four sets of two each were allowed to any one applicant. Eleven applications were filed.

In mid-Manhattan 2,700 sets were distributed and eleven applications were received. In upper Manhattan 625 sets were given out, no applications were filed. In Brooklyn 1,412 sets were distributed, five applications were received. In Queens 1,258 sets were handed out, six applications

Continued on Page 20, Column 3

Italy's Ace Soccer Team Perishes In Air Crash; 20 Bodies Recovered

By The Associated Press.

TURIN, Italy, May 4—Italy's national championship soccer team perished in the crash of a three-engine plane during a rainstorm here tonight.

Rescuers brought twenty partly charred bodies out of the tangled wreckage, but it was believed that the death toll would be between twenty-nine and thirty-one.

Aboard the plane were at least twenty-two players, coaches and managers of the team, three sports writers and a four-man crew. They were returning from an international match in Lisbon, and the team may have included two more players.

The disaster wiped out a team that had held Italy's championship for the past four years and had just about clinched this year's title.

News of the tragedy spread quickly in Rome. Lovers of soccer were shocked. The announcement of the plane crash caused Parliament to halt debate. Defense Minister Randolfo Pacciardi announced to the Chamber of Deputies:

"With extreme sorrow I announce the grave blow that has struck the 'Torino.'" Torino is the name of the team, which had its base in Turin.

The plane hit Superga Hill in the center of Turin. It brushed the cathedral that stands on the hill and fell in flames in its court yard.

The dead included British coach Leslie Lievesley, who trained British parachute and commando troops during the war.

TURIN, May 4 (UP)—For soccer-loving Italy, the crash was a tragic blow—comparable to the shock that United States sports fans would feel if a major league baseball team that had won the

Continued on Page 15, Column 2

"All the News That's Fit to Print"

The New York Times.

LATE CITY EDITION
Fair and quite cool today and tomorrow.
Temperature Range Today-Max.,62; Min.,49
Temperatures Yesterday—Max.,66; Min.,59
Full U. S. Weather Bureau Report, Page 27

VOL. XCIX..No. 33,481. Entered as Second-Class Matter. Postoffice, New York, N. Y. NEW YORK, SATURDAY, SEPTEMBER 24, 1949. Times Square, New York 18, N. Y. Telephone LAckawanna 4-1000 THREE CENTS IN NEW YORK CITY

ATOM BLAST IN RUSSIA DISCLOSED; TRUMAN AGAIN ASKS U.N. CONTROL; VISHINSKY PROPOSES A PEACE PACT

SMALL STEEL MILL SETS PENSION PLAN, A POSSIBLE PATTERN

Proposal by Employer of 1,200, With Workers Sharing Costs, Is Held Poser for Union

LIMITS CAUSE FOR STRIKE

Murray Is Firm for 'Package' Urged by Panel — Wildcat Walkout Hits Another Plant

By A. H. RASKIN

Special to THE NEW YORK TIMES.

PITTSBURGH, Sept. 23—The first hint at the strategy the steel industry may employ to head off a threatened strike of 500,000 steel workers Oct. 1 came today from one of the smallest companies in the industry.

While the United States Steel Corporation and other big companies marked time on the first day of their renewed negotiations with the United Steel Workers of America, CIO, the Follansbee Steel Corporation made a proposal to the union that was widely regarded here as the forerunner of similar offers to be made by the rest of the industry.

The company, which has 1,200 employes at plants in Follansbee, W. Va., and Toronto, Ohio, informed the union that it was prepared to commit itself to pay 6 cents an hour for pensions, provided its workers put up an additional 3 cents an hour.

Employes Pay for Insurance

The company already has a contributory program of social insurance, to which it gives about 4 cents an hour and the workers 2 cents.

The proposal would bring the company's outlay for pensions and welfare into line with the 10-cent "package" recommended by President Truman's fact-finding board. At the same time it would make an end run around the union's insistence that employers pay the whole cost of industrial social security.

The Truman panel endorsed the idea that employers should meet the bill for pensions and social insurance, but opened the door for supplementary payments by workers to increase the amount of protection that could be provided. The board said such arrangements could be effected through collective bargaining.

If other steel companies subscribe to the 6-cent figure for pensions and 4 cents for health, hospital and other forms of social insurance, on condition that their workers also contribute, the union would be maneuvered into the position of having to decide whether or not to strike solely for establishment of the non-contributory principle.

Philip Murray, president of the union, has stressed the union's belief that the most important element in the Truman board's report was its recommendation that care for the "human machine" should be as much a charge on industry as care of plant equipment. The union has barred any compromise on that issue.

Murray Again Threatening Strike

At a two-hour conference with representatives of United States Steel this afternoon, Mr. Murray reiterated the union's determination to strike unless the company agreed to shoulder the full cost of pensions and welfare on the 6-cent and 4-cent basis suggested by the fact-finders.

The company made no immediate reply. Subcommittees were set up by both sides to continue negotiations Monday, five days before the strike deadline.

There was nothing to indicate that "Big Steel" had abandoned the opposition it expressed in public statements last week to exemption of workers from any direct share of financial responsibility for their own pensions and insurance.

The company has committed itself to give 4 cents an hour for welfare, provided workers made an additional payment on their own, but it has declined to set any specific figure for pensions until a joint study of retirement benefits is completed next March 31.

Negotiations between the union and other large steel companies took place today in a dozen cities, but none of the companies gave any new indication of its position. In virtually all cases the talks were recessed until Monday without any sign of a break in the deadlock that has existed since the first negotiations got under way in June.

Union negotiators warned that the patience of the men in the steel mills was wearing thin at the lack of progress toward employer-

Continued on Page 28, Column 1

Cancer Patient Slain; Daughter Detained

Special to THE NEW YORK TIMES.

STAMFORD, Conn., Sept. 23—Carol Paight, 20 years old, was placed under police guard in Stamford Hospital tonight pending investigation of whether she shot her police-sergeant father in pity after learning that he had an inoperable cancer.

The father, Carl Paight, 52, died seven hours after he was shot with his own service pistol at 5:45 P. M. He had been in the hospital since Sept. 15, suffering from the effects of an operation that showed he had cancer.

The daughter, who had been alone with him, became hysterical. Sedatives were administered before she could be questioned by the police and a psychiatrist.

Father and daughter had been deeply attached, friends said. Police who knew both because of Sergeant Paight's twenty-eight years of service here, said that she had declared upon being told of the cancer that she did not want her father to suffer.

RED DEFENSE RESTS; REBUTTAL WAIVED

Jury in 9-Month Trial Excused Till Summaries Begin Oct. 4, May Get Case Week Later

By RUSSELL PORTER

The defense rested in the nine-month Communist trial yesterday, and the Government waived its right of rebuttal. Federal Judge Harold R. Medina gave counsel until 2 o'clock Tuesday afternoon to submit requests for instructions to be included in his charge to the jury and announced that arguments on closing motions would be heard at 10:30 o'clock Wednesday morning.

Judge Medina excused the jury until Tuesday morning, Oct. 4, when, if he denies the usual defense motions to throw out the case, summaries will begin. In the absence of unexpected developments, the case should go to the jury by the week beginning Monday, Oct. 10.

Eleven members of the Communist party's American Politburo or national board have been on trial since January 17, for criminal conspiracy to teach and advocate overthrow of the Government and destruction of American democracy by force and violence. Government witnesses have testified that the defendants reorganized the party for this purpose in 1945 on orders from Moscow.

The defense took roughly six months to present its case, including a two-month preliminary challenge to the Federal jury system. The Government introduced its evidence in two months.

The defense called thirty-five witnesses and the Government fifteen. The defense offered 429 exhibits, the Government 332.

Of the 158 trial days, the defense used 109—eighty-two in the trial proper and twenty-seven in the jury challenge. The Government used forty-nine days in the presentation of evidence. Ten days were devoted to picking the jury and two days to opening statements by opposing counsel.

The Government called its first witness on March 23 and rested on May 19. The defense began to present evidence on May 23, four months ago yesterday.

Nearly 20,000 pages of testimony

Continued on Page 7, Column 2

CIO SEES LEFTISTS QUITTING TO FORM OWN ORGANIZATION

High Officers Say Such Action Is Called for by New Line of Communist Party

FIGHT AT CONVENTION DUE

National Body Plans to Set Up Rival Right-Wing Unions if Pro-Red Groups Depart

By LOUIS STARK

Special to THE NEW YORK TIMES.

WASHINGTON, Sept. 23—High officers of the Congress of Industrial Organizations expressed the view today that the new Communist party line was to split all pro-Communist unions from the CIO and to form a new labor federation. This belief is supported by the following developments:

1. A factional struggle within the CIO Teachers Union in New York, in which the pro-Communists are demanding that the union leave the CIO, though their opponents proclaim loyalty to the parent body.
2. The decision of pro-Communist unions to carry the fight on autonomy and wage policies to the right wing, led by Philip Murray, president of the CIO.
3. The "impossible" demands decided on several days ago by the convention of the United Electrical Radio and Machine Workers that will be served on Mr. Murray.
4. Refusal of the Farm Equipment Workers Union to obey the CIO mandate to merge with the United Automobile Workers.

The Murray forces are prepared for a possible split. If it occurs, they will charter right-wing groups to form the nucleus of new organizations supplanting the dissidents.

Eleven Affiliates Involved

Eleven CIO affiliates may be affected by the possible schism. While they have been generally credited with a membership of 1,000,000 members, informed officials say that their total is more nearly 600,000.

The largest of the dissidents is the UE, which says it bargains for 600,000 members. This union, however, is reported by right-wing officers to be paying to the CIO on about 350,000 members. Some of the leftist-led unions have been in arrears in payments to the national organization for some months.

The largest nut that the CIO has to crack is the UE, its third largest affiliate. This union, well entrenched in General Electric, Westinghouse and other large radio and electrical manufacturing companies, is a strong, well-disciplined organization.

Despite its strength, CIO officials indicated that they would meet any challenge of the UE's re-elected officers. If the union should decide to leave the CIO, the latter's officers feel confident of winning adherence of the workers in the big General Electric and Westinghouse plants as the nucleus of a new electrical union.

Mr. Murray's associates are impatient for the battle because daily evidences of leftist dissidence convinces them that the latter have made up their minds to split the CIO and to put the blame on the right wing.

The latest aspect of the leftist attack on the CIO leadership is

Continued on Page 28, Column 7

ADDRESSING U. N.

Andrei Y. Vishinsky
The New York Times

VISHINSKY SAYS U.S. PLOTS ATOMIC WAR

Calls for Great Power Treaty to Strengthen World Peace in Assembly Speech

Text of Vishinsky address to U. N. Assembly is on Page 4.

By THOMAS J. HAMILTON

Andrei Y. Vishinsky, the Soviet Foreign Minister, accused the United States and Britain yesterday of planning an atomic war, and introduced a resolution at Flushing Meadow proposing that the United Nations General Assembly request the five Great Powers to conclude "a pact for the strengthening of peace."

The resolution also would call on all nations to settle their disputes without resorting to the use or threat of force, and would take note "of the unbending will and determination of peoples to ward

Continued on Page 4, Column 1

CAPITOL FOR ACCORD

Lucas Says 'Future of Civilization' May Rest on Atom Control

AIRING OF VIEWS URGED

McMahon Holds U. S. Should 'Demand Right' to Put Case Before Russians Via Radio

By WILLIAM S. WHITE

Special to THE NEW YORK TIMES.

WASHINGTON, Sept. 23—In a great anxiety that passed soon into a positive response—demands for fresh tries at international control of the atomic bomb—Congress heard today the news that an atomic explosion had occurred in the Soviet Union.

The atmosphere at the Capitol almost everywhere was consciously quiet and restrained. Some of the most responsible members of Congress issued statements saying that the American people could have confidence, in any possible crisis, in the military leadership and the military power of this country.

Beyond this, Administration Congressional spokesmen said in substance that the implications of the President's disclosure of what had happened in Russia were beyond the scope of any Congressional action. They looked toward the United Nations as the forum for this matter.

Senator Scott W. Lucas of Illinois, the Democratic leader of the Senate, and Senator Brien McMahon, Democrat, of Connecticut, the principal Congressional authority on atomic energy, came out almost at once for another attempt at bringing the bomb under the world's seal.

"I believe," said Senator Lucas, "that nothing could give the world greater confidence in survival than for the delegates at the United Nations to reconsider the question of atomic energy control, and arrive at an agreement acceptable to all.

"The world knows that our rep-

Continued on Page 3, Column 5

Truman Statement on Atom

By The United Press.

WASHINGTON, Sept. 23—The text of President Truman's statement today announcing a recent atomic explosion in the Soviet Union:

I believe the American people to the fullest extent consistent with the national security are entitled to be informed of all developments in the field of atomic energy. That is my reason for making public the following information.

We have evidence that within recent weeks an atomic explosion occurred in the U.S.S.R.

Ever since atomic energy was first released by man, the eventual development of this new force by other nations was to be expected. This probability has always been taken into account by us.

Nearly four years ago I pointed out that "scientific opinion appears to be practically unanimous that the essential theoretical knowledge upon which the discovery is based is already widely known. There is also substantial agreement that foreign research can come abreast of our present theoretical knowledge in time." And, in the three-nation declaration of the President of the United States and the Prime Ministers of the United Kingdom and of Canada, dated Nov. 15, 1945, it was emphasized that no single nation could, in fact, have a monopoly of atomic weapons.

This recent development emphasizes once again, if indeed such emphasis were needed, the necessity for that truly effective and enforceable international control of atomic energy which this Government and the large majority of the members of the United Nations support.

Soviet Achievement Ahead Of Predictions by 3 Years

By WILLIAM L. LAURENCE

President Truman's announcement that we have evidence of the occurrence of an "atomic explosion" in the Soviet Union within recent weeks ranks only next to his original announcement of the explosion of the first atomic bomb over Hiroshima on Aug. 6, 1945. It marks the end of the first period of the atomic age and the beginning of the second.

The momentous event is bound to have profound repercussions the world over. Though the scientists have predicted its coming, it came at least three years sooner than was expected. This was largely the result of an erroneous assumption that Russian scientists did nothing about developing an atomic bomb until after we informed them about it following Hiroshima. The fact of the matter is that scientists everywhere recognized the tremendous potentialities of atomic energy for war and peace as soon as the discovery of uranium fission was announced to the world in January, 1939.

While it is likely that Soviet scientists tested the first and only bomb they had, it would be dangerous to assume that they are four years behind us and that it would take them that long to catch up with us. It would be much more reasonable to assume that they have geared their plants to produce at the rate of one bomb a week, so that they will have a stockpile of at least fifty bombs a year from now, enough to destroy fifty of our cities with 40,000,000 of our population.

On the other hand, it is also likely that the latest event will make possible a better understanding between us and Russia, leading toward an agreement for the international control of atomic energy. Bargaining between equals is more likely to produce desirable results than bargaining between two principals, one of which holds

Continued on Page 2, Column 6

ACHESON RULES OUT SHIFT IN U. S. PLANS

Western Diplomats and Atomic Experts at U. N. Agree to Uphold Control Program

Text of Secretary Acheson's statement is printed on Page 2.

By A. M. ROSENTHAL

Secretary of State Dean Acheson said yesterday that he assumed the explosion in Russia reported by President Truman had been caused by an actual atomic weapon. He insisted, however, that the news had come as no shock and would not change the United States-sponsored plan for international control of atomic energy.

Other Western diplomats and atomic control specialists at the United Nations Assembly at Flushing Meadow took the same line. Unanimously, they said that the majority of the members of the United Nations would stick to the plan that had been fought by the Soviet Union for more than three years.

United Nations officials took it for granted that the President's announcement had pushed the world organization back into the center of the atomic picture despite the long deadlock on control negotiations. Secretary General Trygve Lie summed up the Secretariat attitude by saying that the

Continued on Page 2, Column 5

U. S. REACTION FIRM

President Does Not Say Soviet Union Has an Atomic Bomb

PICKS WORDS CAREFULLY

But He Implies Our Absolute Dominance in New Weapons Has Virtually Ended

By ANTHONY LEVIERO

Special to THE NEW YORK TIMES.

WASHINGTON, Sept. 23—President Truman announced this morning that an atomic explosion had occurred in Russia within recent weeks. This statement implied that the absolute dominance of the United States in atomic weapons had virtually ended.

"We have evidence that within recent weeks an atomic explosion occurred in the U.S.S.R.," President Truman said.

These words stood out in red-letter vividness in a brief undramatic statement in which the Chief Executive said that the United States always had taken into account the probability that other nations would develop "this new force."

He pleaded once again for adoption of the system of international control of atomic energy promulgated by the United States and supported by the large majority of countries now assembled in the United Nations General Assembly at Flushing Meadow.

McMahon Reveals News

Mr. Truman announced the discovery to the Cabinet, assembled in the White House at 11 A. M. for the usual Friday meeting. Simultaneously on Capitol Hill Senator Brien McMahon, Democrat, of Connecticut, stood before the members of the Joint Congressional Atomic Energy Committee and gave them the news, which Mr. Truman had passed on to him at 3:15 P. M. yesterday.

White House correspondents had their usual conference with Charles G. Ross, the President's secretary, at 10:30 A. M. It was routine, but as they filed out his secretary, Miss Myrtle Bergheim, advised them not to go away. A moment before 11 A. M. Miss Bergheim entered the press room and said: "Press!"

The news men filed into Mr. Ross' office. He said he wished the door closed, and a secret service man took his post there. Then Mr. Ross said that he would pass out an announcement and that nobody was to leave the room until everyone present had a copy. Then he began passing around the President's mimeographed statement.

Tass Correspondent Attends

One of the first reporters to scan his copy exclaimed, "Russia has the atomic bomb!" There was a wild rush through the door and to the telephones in the near-by press room. One of the news men who sprinted out was the correspondent of Tass, the official Soviet news agency.

"The President has just given it to the Cabinet," said Mr. Ross as they went.

Thus the President did not personally appear, and there was no opportunity then or later to put questions to him.

Secretary of Defense Louis Johnson came out of the Cabinet meeting soon afterward. He began shaking his head as the questions came. Reporters literally clutched his arms as he headed for his limousine.

"Have we made any change in the disposition of our forces since this happened?" This question was asked twice.

"No," Mr. Johnson finally said.

"Does the Cabinet know any more about this than is contained in the President's statement?"

"The Cabinet knows all about it," Mr. Johnson replied to this. "It was fully informed."

"Do you have reason to believe this was the first atomic explosion in Russia?" asked another reporter.

This time Mr. Johnson smilingly shook his head, negatively.

"Don't overplay it," remarked Mr. Johnson, departing. In the cir-

Continued on Page 2, Column 3

Auto Crash Kills Publisher's Wife As He Reaches for Spilling Cup

Special to THE NEW YORK TIMES.

HARRISON, N. Y., Sept. 23—Marvin Pierce, president of the McCall Corporation, magazine and fashion publishers, at 230 Park Avenue, New York, was driving to the Rye railroad station this morning when he tried to prevent a cup of coffee from spilling on his wife's clothes. In an accident that followed, his wife, Mrs. Pauline Robinson Pierce, 53 years old, was killed and Mr. Pierce was injured.

The couple left their Purchase Street home, adjoining the Westchester Country Club, soon after 8 A. M. Mr. Pierce, who is 56, was at the wheel and his wife was beside him, ready to drive home from the station after her husband had boarded a commuters' train for New York.

Mrs. Pierce held in her hands a cup of coffee that she had carried from the breakfast table. After sipping the fluid, she placed the cup for a moment on the seat between her husband and herself. From a corner of his eye Mr. Pierce saw the cup tipping toward his wife.

As Mr. Pierce reached for the cup, the auto swerved to the left side of the road, hit a soft shoulder, plunged 100 feet down a moderate embankment, slid between a pole and a tree and crashed into a tree and a stone wall. Striking the windshield, Mrs. Pierce died of a fractured skull. The accident occurred on Highland Road near Purchase Street.

Taken to the United Hospital in Port Chester, Mr. Pierce told his story to the police. Detectives found the coffee cup, bone China of English manufacture, unbroken in the wreckage of the car and took it to police headquarters. Physicians listed Mr. Pierce's injuries as a cerebral concussion, fractured nose, four broken ribs and several bruises. His condition tonight was improving.

Besides her husband, Mrs. Pierce leaves two sons, James R. and Scott Pierce of Rye, and two daughters, Mrs. Walter G. Rafferty of West Hartford, Conn., and Mrs. G. H. W. Bush of Bakersfield, Calif.

World News Summarized

SATURDAY, SEPTEMBER 24, 1949

President Truman issued yesterday a terse statement containing this dramatic disclosure: "We have evidence that within recent weeks an atomic explosion occurred in the U. S. S. R."

His announcement, indicating that United States monopoly in atomic weapons had ended, added that "ever since atomic energy was first released by man, the eventual development of this new force by other nations was to be expected." He said this "probability" had always been "taken into account" by this nation, and he renewed his plea "for that truly effective and enforceable international control of atomic energy which the Government and the large majority of the members of the United Nations support." [1:8.]

Secretary of State Acheson said he assumed that it was an atomic weapon that had been exploded in the Soviet Union. He said the news would not lead to any shift in the United States position on international atomic control. [1:7.]

New efforts to achieve an acceptable plan for international control of atomic weapons were urged in Congress, where Mr. Truman's announcement was received with restrained anxiety. [1:5.] Reassuring statements were made by General Eisenhower and Maj. Gen. Leslie R. Groves, wartime chief of the atomic bomb project. General Eisenhower said he saw no reason why "a development that was anticipated years ago should cause any revolutionary change in our thinking or in our actions." [2:2.] One result expected by Washington observers was a spur to the North Atlantic defense program. Closer cooperation among the United States, Britain and Canada in atomic development was also seen. [2:3-4.]

Scientists who had generally predicted that the Russians would eventually succeed in discovering the secret of setting off an atomic explosion saw the Russian development as having come at least three years earlier than had been expected. [1:6-7.]

Soviet Foreign Minister Vishinsky said nothing about Russian possession of an atomic bomb in his eagerly awaited address to the United Nations General Assembly. He accused the United States and Britain of planning an atomic war. Mr. Vishinsky introduced a resolution calling for "the unconditional prohibition of atomic weapons" and another asking the five major powers to make "a pact for the strengthening of peace." [1:4.]

Renewed negotiations by the Big Four Foreign Ministers' deputies on an Austrian state treaty got off to a bad start. Russian refusal to reconsider the controversial issues forced an indefinite adjournment. [6:2.]

The British Labor Government will ask for a vote of confidence after Parliament convenes next week to debate the Government's devaluation of the pound. [6:3.]

In China the battle for the important seaport of Amoy reached new intensity. [5:1; with map.]

In a move that might set the pattern for the big companies in the steel industry to stave off a threatened strike by 500,000 steelworkers, the Follansbee Steel Corporation offered a pension plan under which the company would pay 6 cents an hour and its employes an additional 3 cents an hour. [1:1.]

High CIO officials were reported to believe that the new Communist party line was to try to split all pro-Communist unions from the CIO to organize a new labor federation. [1:3.]

Index to other news appears on Page 14.

Couple Held in Quebec Air Crash; Woman Said to Have Planted Bomb

By The Associated Press.

QUEBEC, Sept. 23—Police reported tonight that a drug-dazed woman confessed to carrying a package, believed to have contained dynamite, which was placed aboard an ill-fated Quebec Airways plane that blew up Sept. 9, killing all twenty-three persons aboard.

Police said the woman, identified as Mrs. Arthur Pitre, admitted taking the package to the Quebec Airport where it was placed aboard the plane, but she insisted that she did not know the contents of the package.

Royal Canadian Mounted Police said the woman was recovering from sleeping pills she took at the suggestion of her lover, whose wife was aboard the plane.

Provincial police detained as a material witness J. A. Guay, a young Quebec jeweler, whose 28-year-old wife was one of the passengers who lost their lives when the plane was ripped open by a blast in its luggage compartment. The plane smashed into a mountain near Sault au Cochon, forty miles northeast of Quebec.

Mrs. Pitre was also being held as a material witness.

Police also are reported to have questioned a third person in connection with the case.

Police described the third person as a 26-year-old "pretty waitress." They said she was a close acquaintance of Guay.

The crash took the lives of three New York executives of the Kennecott Copper Corporation. They were President E. T. Stannard, President-designate Arthur D. Storke and Vice President R. J. Parker.

Quebec Provincial police detained Mrs. Pitre at her home in Quebec. Persons living near by saw police enter the woman's Gauvreau Street home, an apartment. Crowds gathered outside and police were called to keep the curious on the move.

Police Inspector René Belec told newsmen:

"We have definite proof that explosives were aboard the plane to

Continued on Page 26, Column 2

"All the News That's Fit to Print"

The New York Times.

LATE CITY EDITION
A little rain and cold today. Cloudy, continued cold tomorrow.
Temperature Range Today—Max.,38; Min.,31
Temperature Yesterday—Max.,37; Min.,32
Full U. S. Weather Bureau Report, Page 51

Copyright, 1950, by The New York Times Company.

VOL. XCIX...No. 33,611. Entered as Second-Class Matter. Postoffice, New York, N. Y. NEW YORK, WEDNESDAY, FEBRUARY 1, 1950. Times Square, New York 18, N. Y. Telephone LAckawanna 4-1000 FIVE CENTS

TRUMAN ORDERS HYDROGEN BOMB BUILT FOR SECURITY PENDING AN ATOMIC PACT; CONGRESS HAILS STEP; BOARD BEGINS JOB

PRESIDENT SEEKS 70-DAY COAL TRUCE, FACT-FINDING BOARD

He Ignores Taft Law in Asking 5-Day Week at Old Wages Pending Study of Dispute

AVOIDS WORD 'EMERGENCY'

Operator Acceptance Is Seen Likely, but the Plan Holds Disadvantages for Lewis

Text of announcement by White House on coal, Page 22.

By JOSEPH A. LOFTUS
Special to THE NEW YORK TIMES.

WASHINGTON, Jan. 31—President Truman moved into the soft coal dispute today with a proposal that John L. Lewis and the operators call a seventy-day truce and submit their arguments to a fact-finding board. He asked for an answer by 5 P. M. Saturday.

Under the truce "normal" production of coal would be resumed. This was understood to mean a return to the five-day work week by the members of the United Mine Workers, headed by Mr. Lewis. The wage scale of the expired union contract would be paid. A board of three would make recommendations in sixty days, but the recommendations would not be binding.

President Truman thus used the approach he used in the steel dispute last summer. This avoids use of the Taft-Hartley Law and its injunctive authority, although the President said in November that if he acted in the coal case he would use that law.

"Grave Concern" Voiced

The President's message to Mr. Lewis and the operators spoke of the "grave concern" about the dispute, but avoided Taft-Hartley words, such as "emergency" and "health and safety."

The dispute in the anthracite industry was omitted from the proposal.

The President said that in the final analysis the parties themselves must write their own agreement. "Voluntary action, not compulsion, in these matters is not only my personal conviction but the national policy," he declared.

Aware that the miners and operators were to meet at 2 P. M. tomorrow to try bargaining again, the President said he did not want to interfere with that. He told them that if they could reach an agreement to resume full production next Monday they should disregard his proposal and let him know about it by noon Saturday.

Mr. Lewis' attorneys are due in court at 10 A. M. tomorrow to answer a petition for an injunction filed by Robert N. Denham, general counsel of the National Labor Relations Board. Mr. Lewis and the other officers of the union filed affidavits in the case today. They denied violating the Taft-Hartley Law in the coal negotiations which began last May and accused the operators of refusing to bargain.

Surmise on Board Make-Up

The make-up of the fact-finding board, if the President's truce proposal goes into effect, is a matter of conjecture. When the proposal was under consideration at the White House in November the three men who had been asked if they were available were David L. Cole, who was a member of the fact-finding steel panel; John Dunlop, Harvard economics professor, and Willard Wirtz of Northwestern University, former chairman of the National Wage Stabilization Board.

Neither side would say tonight

Continued on Page 22, Column 2

Melchior Threatens To Quit Opera Here

Lauritz Melchior stepped into the Metropolitan Opera dispute last night by saying that he would not return next season "unless indicated plans change materially." He would make no comment on the possible return of Kirsten Flagstad, but, like Helen Traubel, he indicated resentment at not being approached sooner by Rudolf Bing, who will be the general manager for 1950-1951.

"I would have assumed," Mr. Melchior said, "that the natural courtesy of the management for the Metropolitan would dictate a call to any leading artist who had appeared regularly with the company for twenty-four years to determine his position with

Continued on Page 24, Column 2

By Winston Churchill: *The Second World War*

Volume III—The Grand Alliance

Book I—Germany Drives East

INSTALLMENT 6:

THE JAPANESE ENVOY

THE New Year had brought disturbing news from the Far East. The Japanese Navy was increasingly active off the coasts of Southern Indo-China. Japanese warships were reported in Saigon harbour and the Gulf of Siam. On January 31 the Japanese Government negotiated an armistice between the Vichy French and Siam. Rumours spread that this settlement of a frontier dispute in South-east Asia was to be the prelude to the entry of Japan into the war. The Germans were at the same time bringing increased pressure to bear upon Japan to attack the British at Singapore.

* * *

About this time several telegrams arrived from our Commander-in-Chief in the Far East urging the reinforcement of Hong Kong. I did not agree with his views.

Prime Minister to General Ismay 7 Jan 41

This is all wrong. If Japan goes to war with us there is not the slightest chance of holding Hong Kong or relieving it. It is most unwise to increase the loss we shall suffer there. Instead of increasing the garrison it ought to be reduced to a symbolical scale. Any trouble arising there must be dealt with at the Peace Conference after the war. We must avoid frittering away our resources on untenable positions. Japan will think long before declaring war on the British Empire, and whether there are two or six battalions at Hong Kong will make no difference to her choice. I wish we had fewer troops there, but to move any would be noticeable and dangerous.

Later on it will be seen that I allowed myself to be drawn from this position, and that two Canadian battalions were sent as reinforcements.

* * *

IN the second week of February I became conscious of a stir and flutter in the Japanese Embassy and colony in London. They were evidently in a high state of excitement, and they chattered to one another with much indiscretion. In these days we kept our eyes and ears open. Various reports were laid before me which certainly gave the impression that they had received news from home which required them to pack up without a moment's delay. This agitation among people usually so reserved made me feel that a sudden act of war upon us by Japan might be imminent, and I thought it well to impart my misgivings to the President.

Former Naval Person to President Roosevelt 15 Feb 41

Many drifting straws seem to indicate Japanese intention to make war on us or do something that would force us to make war on them in the next few weeks or months. I am not myself convinced that this is not a war of nerves designed to cover Japanese encroachments in Siam and Indo-China. However, I think I ought to let you know that the weight of the Japanese Navy, if thrown against us, would confront us with situations beyond the scope of our naval resources. I do not myself think that the Japanese would be likely to send the large military expedition necessary to lay siege to Singapore. The Japanese would no doubt occupy whatever strategic points and oilfields in the Dutch East Indies and thereabouts they covet, and thus get into a far better position for a full-scale attack on Singapore later on. They would also raid Australian and New Zealand ports and coasts, causing deep anxiety in those Dominions, which have already sent all their best-trained fighting men to the Middle East. But the attack which I fear the most would be by raiders, including possibly battle-cruisers, upon our trade routes and communications across the Pacific and Indian Oceans. We could by courting disaster elsewhere send a few strong ships into these vast waters, but all the trade would have to go into convoy and escorts would be few and far between. Not only would this be a most grievous additional restriction and derangement of our whole war economy, but it would bring altogether to an end all reinforcements of the armies we had planned to build up in the Middle East from Australasian and Indian sources. Any threat of a major invasion of Australia or New Zealand would of course force us to withdraw our Fleet from the Eastern Mediterranean, with disastrous military possibilities there, and the certainty that Turkey would have to make some accommodation, for reopening of the German trade and oil supplies from the Black Sea. You will therefore see, Mr. President, the awful enfeeblement of our war effort that would result merely from the sending out by Japan of her battle-cruisers and her twelve 8-inch-gun cruisers into the Eastern oceans, and still more from any serious invasion threat against the two Australasian democracies in the Southern Pacific.

Some believe that Japan in her present mood would not hesitate to court or attempt to wage war both against Great Britain and the United States. Personally I think the odds are definitely against that, but no one can tell. Everything that you can do to inspire the Japanese with the fear of a double war may avert the danger. If however they come in against us and we are alone, the grave character of the consequences cannot easily be overstated.

The agitation among the Japanese in London subsided as quickly as it had begun. Silence and Oriental decorum reigned once more.

Former Naval Person to President Roosevelt 20 Feb 41

I have better news about Japan. Apparently Matsuoka is visiting Berlin, Rome, and Moscow in the near future. This may well be a diplomatic sop to cover absence of action against Great Britain. If Japanese attack which seemed imminent is now postponed, this is largely due to fear of United States. The more these fears can be played upon the better, but I understand thoroughly your difficulties pending passage of [Lend-Lease] Bill on which our hopes depend. Appreciation given in my last Personal and Secret of naval consequences following Japanese aggression against Great Britain holds good in all circumstances.

* * *

Behind the complex political scene in Japan three decisions seem to emerge at this time. The first was to send the Foreign Secretary, Matsuoka, to Europe to find out for himself about the German mastery of Europe, and especially when the invasion of Britain was really going to begin. Were the British forces so far tied up in naval defence that Britain could not afford to reinforce her Eastern possessions if Japan attacked them? Although he had been educated in the United States, Matsuoka was bitterly anti-American. He was deeply impressed by the Nazi movement and the might of embattled Germany. He was under the Hitler

Continued on Page 31.

FRANCE PROTESTS SOVIET RECOGNITION OF HO CHI MINH RULE

Note to Russia Asserts Action Could 'Gravely Impair' Paris-Moscow Ties

U. S. AND BRITAIN INFORMED

Government of North Korea Announces Acceptance of Viet Nam Rebel Regime

By LANSING WARREN
Special to THE NEW YORK TIMES.

PARIS, Jan. 31—France tonight delivered to the Soviet Embassy here a vigorous protest against Soviet recognition of Ho Chi Minh, the enemy of France in Indo-China. The note charged that the Soviet action was of a nature "gravely to impair French-Soviet relations."

In diplomatic circles here the Soviet Union's action was considered as a threat not only to the French position in Indo-China but as an effort to prevent the United States from building a policy of containment in Asia such as has been successful in Europe.

The text of the French note follows:

The French Government has learned through publication of a communiqué by the Tass Agency that the Government of the U.S.S.R. has taken the decision of recognizing as the Government of the Viet Nam the insurrectional government of Ho Chi Minh. Such a decision violates the principles of international law, since the only regular government of the Viet Nam is the government constituted by His Majesty Bao Dai, to whom the French Government has transferred the rights of sovereignty which it previously held.

In encouraging, as is the obvious intention of the Soviet Government, the insurrectional movement of Ho Chi Minh, this decision can only render more difficult the restoration of peace in Viet Nam. In taking the initiative which it has just announced, the Government of the U.S.S.R. is committing with regard to France an act whose character and consequences cannot be underestimated.

For all these reasons the French Government raises a solemn protest against a decision which is of a nature gravely to impair Franco-Soviet relations.

The note was delivered by Alexander Parodi, general secretary of the French Foreign Ministry, after Soviet Ambassador Alexandre Bogomolov, who was invited to the Quai d'Orsay, had replied he could not come today but would present himself tomorrow.

Copies of the French protest to

Continued on Page 11, Column 1

DISCUSSING PLANS FOR MAKING HYDROGEN BOMB

Members of the Joint Congressional Atomic Energy Committee talk with Sumner T. Pike, right, acting head of the Atomic Energy Commission, after President Truman gave his approval. Seated are Chairman Brien McMahon, Representatives Carl T. Durham, Chet Holifield and W. Sterling Cole. Standing are Senator John W. Bricker, Representatives Paul J. Kilday, Melvin Price, Carl Hinshaw and Charles H. Elston.

The New York Times (by George Tames)

HISTORIC DECISION

President Says He Must Defend Nation Against Possible Aggressor

SOVIET 'EXPLOSION' CITED

His Ruling Wins Bipartisan Support on Capitol Hill—No Fund Request Due Now

By ANTHONY LEVIERO
Special to THE NEW YORK TIMES.

WASHINGTON, Jan. 31—President Truman announced today that he had ordered the Atomic Energy Commission to produce the hydrogen bomb.

The Chief Executive acted in his role of Commander in Chief of the Armed forces, ordering an improved weapon for national security. Thus, from the domestic standpoint, he removed the question of producing the super-weapon as an issue that might be argued on moral grounds.

As for international statecraft, Mr. Truman, by treating the hydrogen bomb as an addition to the American armory, also removed it as an issue that might be interpreted as an advanced threat or inducement in seeking international control of atomic weapons.

Nevertheless, Mr. Truman said that his perseverance in providing for national defense would be matched by his efforts to seek international control of atomic weapons.

New Phase of Atomic Age

In his announcement, Mr. Truman regarded the hydrogen bomb as a progressive outgrowth of United States production of the uranium-plutonium atomic bomb. He put it this way: the commission was "to continue its work on all forms of atomic weapons, including the so-called hydrogen or super-bomb."

His use of the word "continue" was understood to imply that with national security the over-riding consideration, the chief factor guiding his decision was whether it was practicable to make the weapon. Scientists have said that it is.

In effect, the President's decision, which won wide acclaim in Congress, marked the advent of a new phase of the atomic age and a surge ahead of Russia in the race to retain military ascendancy.

The bombs that visited destruction on Hiroshima and Nagasaki split the atom. The new bomb would fuse atoms instead, but with a power 100 to 1,000 times greater than the improved fission bombs that have been developed since the Japanese cities were struck.

The President's Statement

The President made his decision known in the following brief statement:

"It is part of my responsibility as Commander in Chief of the armed forces to see to it that our country is able to defend itself against any possible aggressor. Accordingly, I have directed the Atomic Energy Commission to continue its work on all forms of atomic weapons, including the so-called hydrogen or super-bomb.

Continued on Page 3, Column 2

STIKKER IS NAMED E. R. P. CONCILIATOR

Council in Paris Accepts Dutch Leader Supported by Britain —E. C. A. Goals Unmet

By HAROLD CALLENDER
Special to THE NEW YORK TIMES.

PARIS, Jan. 31—Dr. Dirk U. Stikker, Foreign Minister of the Netherlands, was named today to the post of "political conciliator" of the European Marshall Plan Council instead of Paul-Henri Spaak, former Premier of Belgium, whose appointment was vetoed by the British Government. Paul G. Hoffman, Economic Cooperation Administrator, and W. Averell Harriman, ECA Ambassador in Europe, had desired that M. Spaak be chosen.

Dr. Stikker was elected by the Council. He was the candidate of the British who had first suggested Dr. Halvard M. Lange, Nor-

Continued on Page 14, Column 4

Truman Asks Utility Leader To Head Top Research Body

By JAMES RESTON
Special to THE NEW YORK TIMES

WASHINGTON, Jan. 31—President Truman has offered the Government's top scientific job—chairmanship of the Research and Development Board in the Department of Defense—to William Webster of Boston, a vice president of the New England Electric System, it was learned today.

Mr. Webster, 49 years old, a graduate of the United States Naval Academy and former chairman of the Defense Department's Military Liaison Committee with the Atomic Energy Commission, would be largely responsible for preparing an integrated military research and development program so that weapons such as the new hydrogen bomb would take their proper place in a well-balanced defense policy.

The chairmanship of the Research and Development Board was held by Dr. Vannevar Bush from 1947 to 1948 and by Dr. Karl T. Compton, former president of Massachusetts Institute of Technology, from 1948 until Nov. 3, 1949. Since then the work of the board has been supervised by Dr. Robert F. Rinehart as deputy chairman.

Coincidental with his offer of the Government's principal scientific position to Mr. Webster, President Truman was reported to be working actively on selection of a successor to David E. Lilienthal as chairman of the Atomic Energy Commission. One person said to be under consideration is Carroll Wilson, present general manager of the AEC.

Mr. Lilienthal is reliably reported to have proposed that control of

Continued on Page 5, Column 3

IT'S A TRITON BOMB, MIGHTIEST POSSIBLE

Would Release Energy More Than Seven Times '45 Type —No Critical-Mass Limit

By WILLIAM L. LAURENCE

What President Truman referred to yesterday as "the so-called hydrogen bomb" is not a hydrogen bomb at all in the true scientific meaning of the term.

This, the most powerful super-bomb that can be built on earth, it can now be revealed, actually is the triton bomb, in which the basic element used is tritium, a hydrogen isotope (twin) of atomic mass 3. It is an element hardly known to the public but well known to nuclear physicists. A triton is the nucleus of tritium, composed of one proton and two neutrons.

The term hydrogen, as used by scientists, refers strictly to the common form of hydrogen of atomic mass 1, a mass that cannot be made into a bomb.

While the process responsible for the vast amounts of energy released by the sun every second is

Continued on Page 4, Column 4

World News Summarized

WEDNESDAY, FEBRUARY 1, 1950

President Truman, acting in his capacity of Commander in Chief of the Armed Forces, yesterday directed the Atomic Energy Commission "to continue its work on all forms of atomic weapons, including the so-called hydrogen or super-bomb." The work, he said, would go forward "on a basis consistent with the over-all objectives of our program for peace and security" and "until a satisfactory plan for international control of atomic energy is achieved." [1:8.]

Congressional opinion heavily supported the President, and demands for speeding the work were made. The Atomic Energy Commission reported to Congress that atomic weapons now were being made by the "industrial type" of production and stockpiles were growing rapidly. [3:5.]

New defense safeguards were thrown about the atomic plants at Oak Ridge, Tenn.; Los Alamos, N. M., and Hanford, Wash. Any plane approaching within 100 miles of the plants without prior identification and clearance will be intercepted by Air Force fighters. [1:8.]

The hydrogen bomb, it was disclosed, is really a triton bomb, the basic element of which is tritium, a hydrogen isotope. [1:7.]

William Webster has been asked to head the Research and Development Board of the Department of Defense as successor to Dr. Karl T. Compton, who resigned. [1:6-7.]

Dealing with the major domestic problem of coal, President Truman asked John L. Lewis and the operators to call a seventy-day truce and to submit the issues to a nonstatutory fact-finding board such as he had named in the steel dispute. The President asked for a full five-day week in the soft-coal mines during the truce. [1:1.] Leaders of more than 100,000 striking miners were divided over urging the men to return. Operators indicated an inclination to accept the plan. [22:5.]

This state paid $357,000,000 in jobless benefits last year, nearly twice the 1948 total, Albany reported. [21:1.]

A House committee reported, 17 to 1, a bill for economic aid to Korea and Nationalist China. [13:2.] The brutality of South Korean police was seen as a major problem of the Seoul Government. [13:4.]

France, in a strong note of protest, told Moscow that Soviet recognition of Ho Chi Minh in Indo-China "gravely" impaired French-Soviet relations. Washington called Moscow's action proof that the Ho regime was Communist. [1:4.]

Senator Connally said Britain's policy of extending her embargo on dollar oil to the Commonwealth was "an act of hostility to our economy." [15:2.]

Britain won a victory in the European Marshall Plan Council when Foreign Minister Stikker of the Netherlands was elected "political conciliator." [1:5.]

French Premier Bidault won five close votes of confidence on the budget. [14:3.]

This city's tentative realty value for tax purposes was set at $18,493,559,079. [1:6-7.]

Index to other news appears on Page 30.

City Realty Values Up for 6th Year; Assessment Total $18,493,559,079

By LEE E. COOPER

New York's taxable realty wealth has increased on the city's books for the sixth consecutive year, with the result that property owners are due to pay levies on the highest aggregate valuation in seventeen years, according to official figures made public yesterday.

In a report to Mayor O'Dwyer's office, William E. Boyland, president of the Tax Commission, set the total tentative assessed valuation of real estate in the five boroughs for 1950-51 at $18,493,559,079. This is $381,327,900 above the final valuation for 1949-50, which was $18,112,231,179.

The high mark in realty valuations here, including utility property and special franchises, was reached in 1932, with $19,616,935,429.

The report showed a net rise for this year of $316,525,750 in "ordinary" real estate, to $16,120,113,875, and of $64,802,150 in the holdings of utility corporations, which were listed tentatively for the new tax year at $1,655,893,290.

Added to these sums was $717,551,914 for special franchises, the exact amount of which will not be set by the State Tax Commission for another month. The figure used by the city officials is based on the 1949-50 records.

Although no particular area was found by the field assessors to have increased generally in value —in contrast to last year when sharp gains were listed for the land around Stuyvesant Town and the United Nations site—there were three times as many rises as there were decreases in the city as a whole.

Largely for purposes of "equalization," to bring properties in line with neighboring valuations, in-

Continued on Page 20, Column 4

Air Defense Mapped For Atom Projects

By AUSTIN STEVENS
Special to THE NEW YORK TIMES.

WASHINGTON, Jan. 31—The Air Force disclosed tonight that it planned to throw a protective aerial "wall" around key atomic installations of the country.

Under a plan worked out today at the Pentagon, the Air Force will insist on the positive identification of any airplane flying within 100 miles of three atomic plants and, failing to be advised of an aircraft's identity will send fighter planes aloft to observe its character and course.

The plan in effect is a revival of a wartime measure whereby in combat zones any aircraft picked up by radar or other means of detection was consid-

Continued on Page 3, Column 6

TRUMAN AND THE COLD WAR

CARLA ANNE ROBBINS

American G.I.s and Russian troops shake hands near the end of World War II. Their handshakes quickly turn cool with the Cold War.

"Red Rule" sounds archaic and Greece and Turkey's allegiances have long been settled. Aside from that, the headline stripped across the front page of the March 13, 1947, New York Times could have been written any day and about any American president for much of the following 45 years.

> Truman Acts to Save Nations From Red Rule;
> Asks $400 Million to Aid Greece and Turkey;
> Congress Fight Likely But Approval Is Seen

There was, however, nothing inevitable about President Harry Truman's decision to ask Congress for money—about $3.7 billion in 2007 dollars—and military advisers to bolster the two pro-Western, but less than democratic, governments. So soon after the end of World War II, many Americans were wary of being drawn into another European conflict, even by proxy. Nor were they certain that the Soviet Union—America's ally in the fight against the Nazis—was such an implacable enemy.

A three-way handshake brings together Winston Churchill, Harry Truman and Joseph Stalin at their historic meeting in Potsdam, Germany, after the surrender of Germany in World War II.

In his address to a joint session of Congress, President Harry Truman never mentioned the Soviets by name but, as Felix Belair Jr. wrote in the next day's Times, "there could be no mistaking his identification."[1] Reporters, especially those covering presidents and writing for the front page, have a tendency to overstate the drama and significance of such moments. Mr. Belair got it right when he wrote that "President Truman outlined a new foreign policy for the United States today" when Mr. Truman declared that the United States must "support free peoples who are resisting attempted subjugation by armed minorities or by outside pressures."[2] Commentators and historians would go further, annointing the president's declaration as the Truman Doctrine and describing it both as the day when the United States accepted the responsibilities of world leadership and the beginning of the Cold War.[3]

According to his biographer David McCullough, President Truman's thinking and American policy had been moving toward challenging the Soviet Union since his first meeting with Joseph Stalin at the Potsdam summit nearly two years earlier.

Still, the decision whether to draw the line at Greece and Turkey was thrust upon Mr. Truman just a few weeks before his message to Congress, when the British ambassador to Washington informed the Americans that Great Britain could no longer afford to prop up the two governments.[4] By the end of March, 40,000 British troops stationed in Greece would be withdrawn and all economic aid to Greece and Turkey would be cut off. It was London's hope that the United States would now shoulder the burden.

The Greek government, a center-right coalition, was battling Communist guerrillas for control of the country.[5] President Truman and his advisers believed the rebels were Moscow's tool. Today we know that Stalin was far more interested in protecting his spoils in Eastern Europe. He not only denied the rebels aid but had ordered Yugoslavia's Josip Tito to cut off all his support. Stalin was pressing Turkey to provide bases and access to the Mediterranean for the Soviet navy.[6]

A Greek peasant woman walks amongst the ruins after Greek Communists captured her village.

President Truman tells a joint session of the U.S. Congress that aid to Greece and Turkey was essential to halt the spread of Communism.

FURTHER READING

"New Policy Set Up," see March 13, 1947, front page.

2 "Text of President Truman's Speech on New Foreign Policy," see March 13, 1947, article.

3 "Peace Is Explored; Big Three Leaders at First Meeting in Berlin," see July 18, 1945, front page.

4 "Truman Asks Aid to Greece; British Unable to Bear Cost," see February 28, 1947, front page.

5 "U.S. Weighs Aid to Greece Of 350 Millions in 3 Years," see March 1, 1947, front page.

6 "British Bid to U.S. on Turks Foreseen," see March 9, 1947, front page.

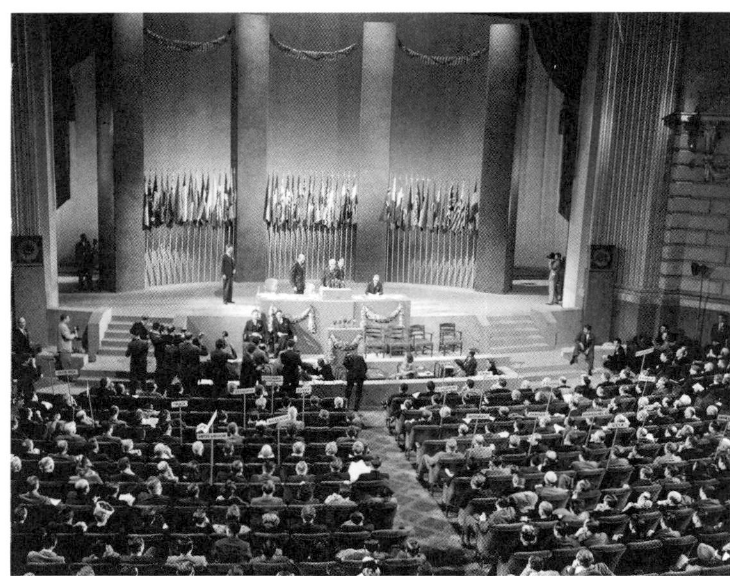
A conference of world delegates unanimously adopted the United Nations Charter in San Francisco, California, on June 26, 1945.

James B. Steinberg, dean of the Lyndon B. Johnson School of Public Affairs at the University of Texas, says that President Truman could have decided that Greece and Turkey weren't America's fight and tried to find some diplomatic accommodation with Russia or passed the problem on to the nascent United Nations. Or he could have decided that the United States had already ceded too much territory to Moscow—as some critics were charging—and declared that it was now America's policy to roll back Soviet control of Eastern Europe. Instead, Mr. Steinberg says, the President settled on the middle course: "He was not going to roll back, but he was also saying that he would not concede another inch."

There is no doubt that President Truman made the right choice. Given their strategic location, Greece and Turkey were too important to hand over to the Soviets. Western Europe's war-battered governments were also watching intently to see if the United States would stand up to Stalin.

A group of German children watch a U.S. freight plane delivering supplies during the Berlin Blockade in June of 1948.

The speech still made many in Europe uneasy. A Times reporter wrote from Paris that many European diplomats and analysts considered American protection obviously preferable to the alternative. But they also wondered if this would be the beginning of new American imperialism, with Europe's governments becoming new American protectorates.[7] All of Europe "is financially feeble and feels the pressure of Soviet Russia," the reporter wrote, adding that the difference with Greece and Turkey, "is merely that they are somewhat further out on a limb."

At home, the influential columnist Walter Lippmann writing in the New York Herald Tribune, warned of American overreach and an "ideological crusade" with "no limits." A few months later—after Foreign Affairs magazine published George Kennan's famously anonymous "X" article, calling for the containment of the Soviet Union—Mr. Lippmann launched a fusillade, warning of the strategic folly of taking on dependencies ("a weak ally is not an asset," he wrote) in areas not central to America's security. He also warned that the United States was not fitted militarily, nor Americans temperamentally, for a struggle of indefinite duration, and that such a policy would lead to the neglect and the ultimate alienation of America's European allies. "We must not deceive ourselves by supposing that we stand at the head of a world-wide coalition of democratic states in our conflict with the Soviet Union," Mr. Lippmann wrote.

A workman places a new tier of bricks on the Berlin Wall, which was erected in 1961.

The Times's Washington columnist, Arthur Krock, would lay out some of the most troubling questions he was hearing a few days after Truman's message.[8] "What is meant by 'support'? The President used the word without any hint of reservation as to money or method," he wrote. He also asked for Mr. Truman's definition of "free peoples." Did it cover the Palestine Arabs and the Chinese nationalists? And, "Are the American people prepared to take on a global obligation at an eventual cost which can only be guessed at?"

As it turned out, Americans had far more patience than either Mr. Lippmann or Mr. Krock could imagine for what became a 45-year competition, and much more stomach for global obligations of unimaginable costs. The United States took on the responsibility of rebuilding Europe and created institutions and a community of democracies that have outlasted the Soviet Union. The question still being debated is whether Mr. Truman's pledge inevitably also led to the next 45 years of proxy wars—in areas, as Mr. Lippmann warned, peripheral to America's strategic interest—most self-destructively in Vietnam.

Korean citizens, desperate to escape advancing North Korean troops in 1950, crawl across a bombed-out bridge over the Taedong River.

CARLA ANNE ROBBINS *is the deputy editorial page editor for The New York Times. Before joining the editorial board in 2006, Robbins was the chief diplomatic correspondent for The Wall Street Journal, where she won Georgetown University's Edward Weintal Prize for diplomatic reporting and shared in two Pulitzer prizes and other reporting prizes. Robbins also covered Latin America and the State Department for U.S. News & World Report. She began her career at Business Week magazine.*

Newspaper columnist Walter Lippmann and his wife, Helen, in September 1942.

7 "Europeans Uneasy on New U.S. Policy," see March 17, 1947, article.
8 "Some Questions Arising Over the 'Truman Doctrine,'" see March 20, 1947, article.

"All the News That's Fit to Print"

The New York Times.

LATE CITY EDITION
Sunny with pleasant temperatures today. Fair tomorrow.
Temperature Range Today-Max.,80; Min.,60
Temperatures Yesterday-Max.,90.3; Min.,69
Full U. S. Weather Bureau Report, Page 55

Copyright, 1950, by The New York Times Company.

VOL. XCIX..No. 33,758. Entered as Second-Class Matter, Post Office, New York, N. Y. NEW YORK, WEDNESDAY, JUNE 28, 1950. Times Square, New York 18, N. Y. Telephone Lackawanna 4-1000 FIVE CENTS

TRUMAN ORDERS U. S. AIR, NAVY UNITS TO FIGHT IN AID OF KOREA; U. N. COUNCIL SUPPORTS HIM; OUR FLIERS IN ACTION; FLEET GUARDS FORMOSA

114 RESCUED HERE AS LINER GROUNDS AFTER COLLISION

Excalibur, With Hole 15 Feet Wide in Side, Settles on Mud Flat Off Brooklyn

FIRES START ON FREIGHTER

One Person Slightly Injured—Responsibility for the Crash Still to Be Decided

By WILLIAM R. CONKLIN

Thirty-five minutes after a gay departure for a Mediterranean cruise, the American Export Line's Excalibur was disabled in a collision yesterday with a Danish freighter in the Narrows, but all her 114 passengers were taken off safely.

The confetti-speckled cruise ship left Pier 4, Jersey City, at noon for a forty-three-day voyage. At 12:35 P. M. the collision with the inbound Colombia occurred off Sixty-ninth Street, Brooklyn.

The impact crushed the bow of the freighter and tore a hole fifteen feet wide in the port side of the Excalibur forward of the bridge. Fire broke out in the Colombia's forepeak in a paint storeroom.

While passengers and both crews remained calm, water quickly flooded the forward holds of the cruise ship. The Excalibur settled with her bow on a midstream mud bank, with her screw lifted in the air.

Passengers Taken Off by Tugs

Passengers on the sinking ship donned bright orange life preservers and were taken off by two tugs of the Moran Towing Company. Except for one woman who bruised three fingers of her left hand, all passengers were uninjured. They were returned to Pier 4, and the ship line arranged for hotel accommodations for them.

No official on the scene would assess responsibility for the collision. The Coast Guard required both captains to file written reports on the crash today. Under usual procedure, a Coast Guard board of inquiry hears evidence and fixes blame. Unofficially, it was said that a misunderstanding of whistle signals was the probable cause of the accident.

Capt. S. N. Groves of Brooklyn, a veteran of twenty-five years at sea, commanded the Excalibur, a ship of 9,644 gross tons with a top speed of seventeen knots. The Colombia, owned by the United Steamship Lines of Denmark, was commanded by Capt. Christian Mikkelsen of Copenhagen. The freighter was operated by the Scandinavian-American Steamship Company of 25 Broadway. Carrying cotton, wool and lubricating oils, she was bound from Philadelphia to Pier 24 at Congress Street, Brooklyn.

When the collision occurred there was good visibility despite a light haze over the lower bay. Persons in Shore Road Park saw the collision clearly, half a mile off the Brooklyn waterfront.

As the Excalibur's forward holds filled, her nose dropped into a mudbank and she swung to face upstream on the incoming tide.

2 Fireboats Help Freighter

The fireboats William J. Gaynor and Firefighter put lines on the 5,146-ton freighter to fight the fire on board. With the help of the ship's forty-two crewmen they subdued a fire in the forward hold. A collision bulkhead between that point and the forecastle prevented them from tackling another fire in the peak.

With Army, Navy, Coast Guard and Moran tugs helping, the burning vessel was moved into the north side of the Sixty-ninth Street ferry pier. John L. Holian, Deputy Fire Chief commanding the Marine Division, summoned a hook and ladder company to pour streams into the burning peak from the pier. Within an hour, the fire was extinguished.

Joseph H. Boggs, senior assistant purser of the Excalibur, said it was fortunate that the collision had occurred in shoal water.

"Immediately after the crash we

Continued on Page 29, Column 2

SANCTIONS VOTED

Council Adopts Plan of U. S. for Armed Force in Korea, 7 to 1

THE SOVIET IS ABSENT

Yugoslavia Casts Lone Dissent—Egypt and India Abstain

Mr. Austin's statement to the United Nations is on Page 6.

By THOMAS J. HAMILTON
Special to THE NEW YORK TIMES.

LAKE SUCCESS, June 27—The Security Council adopted tonight a United States resolution recommending that members of the United Nations use armed force in repelling the invasion of southern Korea and restoring international peace and security.

The vote on the resolution, which amounted to Security Council authorization for President Truman's decision to send United States naval and air units to the defense of the Republic of Korea, was 7 to 1, with Yugoslavia voting against.

The representatives of India and Egypt did not vote because they had not received instructions from their Governments. The Soviet Union was absent.

Representatives of Britain, France, Nationalist China, Cuba, Ecuador and Norway announced this afternoon that they would vote for the United States resolution without change. However, the Council recessed at 5:12 P. M. to permit Sir Benegal Rau and Mahmoud Bey Fawzi, the representatives of India and Egypt, to try to reach their Governments by telephone.

The vote was finally taken at 10:45 P. M. after both said they had been unable to establish communication with responsible authorities. With Egypt and India again not participating, the Council then rejected, seven to one, a Yugoslav resolution proposing that the Council renew its appeal for compliance with the cease-fire resolution it adopted Sunday, and request the two sides to agree to United Nations mediation.

The Council then recessed again while Sir Benegal and Fawzi Bey again attempted to obtain instructions. Apparently Fawzi Bey did so, but neither he nor Sir Benegal made any further statement, and the Council adjourned at 11 P. M.

Both Security Council members and other delegates who crowded around their table showed their realization that a historic decision for the United Nations and the world was being taken tonight. Warren R. Austin, the United States representative, was determined to avoid postponing a decision until tomorrow, and the Indian and Egyptian representatives cooperated by not requesting a postponement because of their failure to receive instructions.

Mr. Austin said after the meeting that the immediate effect of the resolution "should be to stop

Continued on Page 7, Column 1

President Takes Chief Role In Determining U. S. Course

Truman's Leadership for Forceful Policy to Meet Threat to World Peace Draws Together Advisers on Vital Move

By ARTHUR KROCK
Special to THE NEW YORK TIMES.

WASHINGTON, June 27—Some of those who participated in the meetings Sunday and Monday nights, at which the momentous decisions were taken to resist further Communist aggressions, beginning in the Far East, with the combat air and naval power of the United States, described the President to associates today as determined from the outset to adopt the forceful policy which was announced this morning.

As soon as the first meeting assembled, they said, Mr. Truman made it plain that these were to be the bases of his decision:

1. The situation created by Communist tactics at various points of the world, culminating in the attack of North Korea on South Korea, had been allowed to drift too long.
2. The entire Far East was deteriorating in a manner to threaten the peace of the world, a line had to be drawn at once, and the United States had to draw it.
3. National security was the primary interest, but embedded in this were world peace and the prestige and future effectiveness of the United Nations, which was the architect of the South Korean Government.
4. It was a time for courage, even boldness, and calculated risk, which other members of the United Nations would be invited to share as they saw fit.
5. It was not a time to give the slightest consideration to previous policies or to individuals associated with those policies. If, for example, the fundamental change in the Far Eastern sit-

Continued on Page 4, Column 3

U. S. FORCE FIGHTING

MacArthur Installs an Advanced Echelon in Southern Korea

FOE LOSES 4 PLANES

American Craft in Battle to Protect Evacuation—Seoul Is Quiet

By LINDESAY PARROTT
Special to THE NEW YORK TIMES.

TOKYO, Wednesday, June 28—The United States is now actively intervening in the Korean civil war, an announcement from Gen. Douglas MacArthur's headquarters here made clear this morning.

[Gen. Douglas MacArthur announced Wednesday that the forces of South Korea now were holding the Communist Korean invaders, a United Press dispatch from Tokyo said. At the same time he reported that United States fliers had begun bombing and strafing missions against North Korean forces. Seoul was reported quiet.]

General MacArthur revealed that a "small advanced echelon" from his headquarters had been established in Korea, presumably cooperating with the United States Military Advisory Group, which has been in Korea since the republic was established there under President Syngman Rhee two years ago.

The MacArthur announcement stated that Far East air forces and elements of the naval forces under the general's command were "conducting" combat missions south of the Thirty-eighth Parallel—the dividing line between Communist North Korea and the United States-recognized Korean Republic. These operations, it was officially stated, are "in support of the Korean Republic," whose Government has now been reinstalled in the capital, Seoul, after isolation of the Northern armored spearheads that had penetrated to the outskirts of the city yesterday.

The announcement said that United States planes, which were providing air cover for the evacuation of women and children dependents of various United States missions, had shot down four North Korean fighters that were interfering with the operation of

Continued on Page 17, Column 3

Statement on Korea

By The Associated Press.

WASHINGTON, June 27—The text of President Truman's statement today on Korea:

In Korea the Government forces, which were armed to prevent border raids and to preserve internal security, were attacked by invading forces from North Korea. The Security Council of the United Nations called upon the invading troops to cease hostilities and to withdraw to the Thirty-eighth Parallel. This they have not done, but on the contrary have pressed the attack. The Security Council called upon all members of the United Nations to render every assistance to the United Nations in the execution of this resolution.

In these circumstances I have ordered United States air and sea forces to give the Korean Government troops cover and support.

The attack upon Korea makes it plain beyond all doubt that communism has passed beyond the use of subversion to conquer independent nations and will now use armed invasion and war.

It has defied the orders of the Security Council of the United Nations issued to preserve international peace and security. In these circumstances the occupation of Formosa by Communist forces would be a direct threat to the security of the Pacific area and to United States forces performing their lawful and necessary functions in that area.

Accordingly I have ordered the Seventh Fleet to prevent any attack on Formosa. As a corollary of this action I am calling upon the Chinese Government on Formosa to cease all air and sea operations against the mainland. The Seventh Fleet will see that this is done. The determination of the future status of Formosa must await the restoration of security in the Pacific, a peace settlement with Japan, or consideration by the United Nations.

I have also directed that United States forces in the Philippines be strengthened and that military assistance to the Philippine Government be accelerated.

I have similarly directed acceleration in the furnishing of military assistance to the forces of France and the associated states in Indo-China and the dispatch of a military mission to provide close working relations with those forces.

I know that all members of the United Nations will consider carefully the consequences of this latest aggression in Korea in defiance of the Charter of the United Nations. A return to the rule of force in international affairs would have far-reaching effects. The United States will continue to uphold the rule of law.

I have instructed Ambassador Austin, as the representative of the United States to the Security Council, to report these steps to the Council.

BID MADE TO RUSSIA

President Asks Moscow to Act to Terminate Fighting in Korea

CHIANG TOLD TO HALT

U.S. Directs Him to Stop Blows at Reds—Will Reinforce Manila

By ANTHONY LEVIERO
Special to THE NEW YORK TIMES.

WASHINGTON, June 27—President Truman announced today that he had ordered United States air and naval forces to fight with South Korea's Army. He said this country took the action, as a member of the United Nations, to enforce the cease-fire order issued by the Security Council Sunday night.

Then acting independently of the United Nations, in a move to assure this country's security, the Chief Executive ordered Vice Admiral Arthur D. Struble to form a protective cordon around Formosa to prevent its invasion by Communist Chinese forces.

Along with these fateful decisions, Mr. Truman also ordered an increase of our forces based in the Philippine Republic, as well as more speedy military assistance to that country and to the French and Vietnam forces that are fighting Communist armies in Indo-China.

After he had started these moves that might mean a decided turn toward peace or a general war, the President sent Ambassador Alan G. Kirk to the Russian Foreign Office in Moscow to request the Soviet Union to use its good offices to end the hostilities. This was an obvious proffer of an opportunity for Russia to end the crisis before her own forces might get involved.

Door Opened for Russia

In the capital this was regarded as being at once a possible face-saving device for Russia in a showdown crisis and a feeler to determine her intentions.

The decisions amounted to a showdown in the "cold war" with Russia, in which this country has at last decided to begin shooting in a limited area. Yet all the decisions followed a carefully worked out formula of action within the framework of the United Nations, as well as unilateral moves that avoided any direct provocation of the Soviet Union.

Mr. Truman based the decision to fight for the South Koreans entirely on the Security Council resolution which called upon all members of the United Nations to help carry it out. And at the Pentagon it was explained that our air and naval forces would fight only below the Thirty-eighth Parallel line that divides South Korea from the Russian-sponsored North Korea.

"The Security Council called upon all members of the United Nations to render every assistance to the United Nations in the execution of this resolution," Mr. Truman stated. "In these circumstances I have ordered United States air and sea forces to give the Korean Government troops cover and support."

Russia Is Not Mentioned

Mr. Truman carefully avoided mentioning Russia in his statement. He pivoted today's great shift in United States foreign policy on a conclusion that the "cold war" had passed from an uneasy passive stage to "armed invasion and war." He blamed "communism."

"The attack upon Korea makes it plain beyond all doubt that communism has passed beyond the use of subversion to conquer independent nations and will now use armed invasion and war," he said. "It has defied the orders of the Security Council of the United Nations issued to preserve international peace and security. In these circumstances the occupation of Formosa by Communist forces would be a direct threat to the security of the Pacific area and to United States forces performing

Continued on Page 2, Column 2

MAINLAND ATTACKS ENDED BY FORMOSA

Chinese Nationalists Halt Air, Navy Forays in Accordance With Request by Truman

By The Associated Press

TAIPEI, Formosa, Wednesday, June 28—The Chinese Nationalists today ordered their Air Force and Navy to cease attacks on the Communist mainland in accordance with a United States request.

President Truman had ordered United States warships to protect Formosa against Communist attack and at the same time asked the Nationalists to cease offensive operations.

Nationalist Foreign Minister George Yeh hailed the President's order for warship protection as "a most welcome sign of comradeship in the fight against communism."

Generalissimo Chiang Kai-shek and his Cabinet had met after the United States note was delivered to the United States Embassy. It was understood the note carried with it instructions to see that it was brought personally to Generalissimo Chiang's attention.

Mr. Yeh translated the text to the Generalissimo last night in the presence of United States Charge d'Affaires Robert Strong.

Mr. Strong was with Generalissimo Chiang for about twenty minutes. After his departure the latter consulted with Mr. Yeh, Premier Chen Cheng and other officials.

The decision was announced after Generalissimo Chiang conferred with Gen. Chou Chih-jou, Chief of the Joint General Staff, and other top Nationalist commanders.

The Nationalists were believed to have agreed to Washington's re-

Continued on Page 3, Column 4

HOUSE VOTES 315-4 TO PROLONG DRAFT

Korea Crisis Breaks Deadlock—Bill Expected to Be Sent to White House Tonight

Special to THE NEW YORK TIMES.

WASHINGTON, June 27—The House of Representatives today passed, by a vote of 315 to 4, an extension of the draft for another year.

The bill added authority for President Truman to call to active duty members of the National Guard and the reserve forces for periods not exceeding twenty-one months.

The Senate agreed to vote on the bill tomorrow afternoon. Swift passage is expected there so that the bill may reach President Truman for his signature tomorrow night.

As recently as yesterday the Senate and the House appeared to be in a hopeless deadlock over the manner in which the selective service system could be kept alive without much leeway for the President to put it to use. Today when

Continued on Page 16, Column 5

World News Summarized

WEDNESDAY, JUNE 28, 1950

United States air and sea forces were ordered by President Truman yesterday to give Korean troops "cover and support." Moving directly to meet Communist "armed invasion and war" in Asia, the President instructed the Seventh Fleet to "prevent any attack on Formosa," called on the Chinese Nationalists to halt all attacks on the mainland, ordered United States forces in the Philippines strengthened and moved to speed military assistance to those islands and to Indo-China. He instructed Ambassador Kirk in Moscow to urge the Soviet Union to help end hostilities. [1:8; map P. 2.]

Naval and air elements are "conducting combat missions south of the Thirty-eighth Parallel of Korea in support" of the Seoul Government, General MacArthur announced. An advance echelon of his General Headquarters has been set up in Korea, he added. Conflicting reports of the fighting showed positions little changed during the day. [1:5; maps P. 17.] In Washington it was said that General MacArthur had sufficient forces to give the South Koreans air and sea preponderance. [13:3.]

This country's new Far East policy was set at conferences during which the President's positive program and leadership convinced his top aides that his decisions "were both inevitable and right." [1:3-4.] He brought unity to an Administration that had been split on many vital policy issues. [4:6-7.]

Governor Dewey, speaking as head of the Republican party, pledged full support to the President [4:3] and Congress was almost unanimous in its endorsement. [1:7.] The House, 315 to 4, passed a one-year extension of the draft with broad new powers for the President; the Senate will vote today. [1:4.] Senate Republicans, however, blocked a vote today on the foreign arms-aid bill. [14:3.] The National Security Resources Board has ready for introduction a sweeping bill authorizing the President to freeze prices, wages, manpower and materials. [15:2.]

The United Nations Security Council, with Russia absent and Yugoslavia voting no, approved a United States motion to permit member nations to send armed forces to help repel the Korean invasion. [1:2.]

British parties united in supporting President Truman's program. The Labor Government won confidence votes on its refusal to join talks on pooling Europe's steel and coal industry. [19:4.]

John S. Service, a key figure in Senator McCarthy's charges of communism in the State Department, has been cleared by the department's Loyalty Security Board. [22:3.]

Index to other news appears on Page 28.

City, T.W.U. in 2-Year Peace Pact; Mayor Signs Fare Rise Resolution

Officials of the Transport Workers Union, C. I. O., the members of the Board of Transportation and Mayor O'Dwyer signed at City Hall yesterday a memorandum of understanding seeking to guarantee two years of peace in the city-owned rapid transit system.

The accord closely followed recommendations made on May 31 by the Mayor's Transit Fact-Finding Board, granting an 11-cent-an-hour increase to 35,929 operating employes, a third week of vacation after ten years and an additional holiday each year. The cost of the changes recommended by the fact-finders amounts to $13,188,515 a year.

The union bound itself not to engage in any strike or other interference with transit operations and not to seek any basic changes in the accord before July 1, 1952. It agreed to resolve all disputes in accordance with the grievance machinery set up in the pact. The union obligated itself also to recognize the board's managerial authority and to "cooperate in the attainment of efficient operations."

The Board of Transportation agreed to retain competent industrial engineers to report on a program for achieving a five-day, forty-hour week for all employes now having a scheduled work-week in excess of forty hours.

Mayor O'Dwyer also signed yesterday afternoon a resolution of the Board of Transportation, effective Saturday, increasing fares on the city-owned surface lines

Continued on Page 28, Column 4

NORTH KOREA CALLS U. N. ORDER ILLEGAL

Declares Security Council's 'Cease Fire' Invalid Without Assent of China and Russia

Special to THE NEW YORK TIMES.

HONG KONG, June 27—The North Korean Government issued a statement today saying that it regarded the cease fire order of the United Nations Security Council illegal for two reasons. It said these were, one, because the Democratic Peoples Republic of North Korea was not represented when its affairs were discussed and, two, because the Soviet Union and (Communist) China did not participate.

On the latter point it cited the United Nations Charter, which requires unanimity of five permanent members of the Security Council on questions of substance. China and Russia are both permanent members. [But the Communist rulers of China have not been recognized by the United Nations as representing that country.]

Drastic measures were taken in North Korea yesterday to organize

Continued on Page 18, Column 5

LEGISLATORS HAIL ACTION BY TRUMAN

Almost Unanimous Approval Is Voiced in Congress by Both Sides—House Cheers

By HAROLD B. HINTON.
Special to THE NEW YORK TIMES.

WASHINGTON, June 27—President Truman's announcement today that United States air and sea power would be employed to expel the Communist invaders from South Korea evoked almost unanimous support in Congress. His statement was read by the majority floor leaders in both houses.

In the House of Representatives, the members rose to their feet and cheered as the reading was completed by Representative John W. McCormack, of Massachusetts. In the Senate, the reading by Senator Scott W. Lucas, of Illinois, brought immediate declarations of support from several Republican Senators.

Showing the same spirit of solidarity in the face of crisis, as the present situation was frequently described, Senate and House conferees agreed on legislation to ex-

Continued on Page 5, Column 1

Stocks Rally After Big New Losses In War Scare; Sales Near 5 Million

By ROBERT H. FETRIDGE

Securities markets the world over were subjected yesterday to wide fluctuations as the Korean situation approached a crisis of universal concern.

Calmer thinking emerged successful on the New York exchanges, but only after prices encountered terrific battering. Losses that at one time ranged to 5 points and even more in standard issues on the New York Stock Exchange were either trimmed or eliminated. Quotations were definitely on the recovery side at the close, with the final composite rate down only 0.75 point. As pictured by THE NEW YORK TIMES index, the market was midway between the highs and lows of the day at the final bell.

London was the worst sufferer among the major exchanges, while the Canadian markets followed the lead of New York.

It was a wild day on the trading floor of the Stock Exchange. Business almost reached the 5,000,000-share mark, the reporting ticker tape was constantly thrown behind actual transactions and at one time was twenty-seven minutes late. This necessitated "flash" prices on the ticker to keep brokerage offices at least abreast of the price changes in the key stocks.

The trend changed with such rapidity that selling orders were still being executed after the price direction changed for the better.

Continued on Page 41, Column 6

100TH ANNIVERSARY
"All the News That's Fit to Print"
1851 1951

The New York Times.

Copyright, 1951, by The New York Times Company.

LATE CITY EDITION
Fair today, increasing cloudiness tomorrow and mild both days.
Temperature Range Today—Max., 60; Min., 45
Temperatures Yesterday—Max., 65; Min., 48
Full U. S. Weather Bureau Report, Page 18

VOL. C..No. 34,045. Entered as Second-Class Matter, Post Office, New York, N. Y. NEW YORK, WEDNESDAY, APRIL 11, 1951. Times Square, New York 18, N. Y. Telephone LAckawanna 4-1000 FIVE CENTS

TRUMAN RELIEVES M'ARTHUR OF ALL HIS POSTS; FINDS HIM UNABLE TO BACK U. S.-U. N. POLICIES; RIDGWAY NAMED TO FAR EASTERN COMMANDS

HOUSE VOTES U. M. T. ONLY AS A PROGRAM; MARSHALL WORRIED

Chamber Accepts Compromise Setting Up Commission to Draft Details of Plan

FUTURE LAW IS REQUIRED

Congress' Approval Is Needed to Start Universal Training—General Sees Risk in This

By JOHN D. MORRIS
Special to The New York Times.

WASHINGTON, April 10—Concessions offered by advocates of Universal Military Training to save the program from outright rejection were approved today by the House of Representatives, but it remained to be seen whether the aim had been achieved.

General of the Army George C. Marshall, Secretary of Defense, meanwhile voiced the fear that current maneuvering in the House might "largely emasculate" the training features of the pending draft and training bill.

It was not clear, however, whether he was concerned over the main fight, expected later this week, over a proposal to eliminate all Universal Military Training provisions from the bill.

It was to head this off that the bill's managers headed by Representative Carl Vinson, Democrat of Georgia, offered the concessions that were approved today. The House accepted them on a voice vote.

Further Action Necessary

Consequently, as the bill now stands, little more than the principle of Universal Military Training is retained. A commission to draw up a detailed U. M. T. plan would be created. A "National Security Training Corps" would also be established, at least on paper.

But before anyone could be drafted to serve in the proposed corps, there would have to be another formal act of Congress, subject to Presidential approval or veto like any other bill, authorizing details of the training program.

At the same time, however, the revised bill retains safeguards against future pigeon-holing of U. M. T. in the House Rules Committee or elsewhere. The planning commission, which also would administer the program once Congress had authorized its institution, would be required to submit a detailed training plan to Congress within six months. The House and Senate Armed Services Committees would be required to report out a bill or resolution within forty-five days of receiving the plan. The measure then could be called up at any time.

Opponents Withhold Attack

In the House, bills ordinarily must be cleared by the Rules Committee before they can be considered on the floor. The Rules Committee bottled up a Universal Military Training Bill in the Eightieth Congress.

Opponents of any form of U.M.T. legislation did not fight the concessions approved in the House today, explaining that the proposals would make the bill less obnoxious although still unacceptable to them.

They were still hoping for approval of a substitute sponsored by Representative Graham A. Barden, Democrat of North Carolina, that would retain only what they regard as the "emergency" features of the pending draft measure. These include a three-year extension of authority to draft men 19 through 26 years of age for actual military service.

The Barden bill would eliminate authority to lower the draft age to 18½ as well as all long-range training features of the pending measure.

The Senate has already passed a draft and training bill adhering closely to the Administration's recommendations. It would authorize the drafting of men at the age of 18 and permit the President to put Universal Military Training

Continued on Page 18, Column 4

Tobey Asserts He Recorded R. F. C. Talks With Truman

President Said to Withdraw Fee Accusation—Niles Held Attempting to Aid Dawson

By C. P. TRUSSELL
Special to The New York Times.

WASHINGTON, April 10—Senator Charles W. Tobey, Republican of New Hampshire, was represented tonight as having told the Senate (Fulbright) subcommittee investigating the Reconstruction Finance Corporation that President Truman had charged in a telephone conversation with him that members of Congress had accepted fees for obtaining R. F. C. loans for constituents.

The Senator was said to have reported also that in a later telephonic communication the President had said that he had been mistaken.

Both telephonic conversations were said to have been recorded on disks in Mr. Tobey's possession. The date, or dates, were not made public. The Senator declined to discuss the matter and members of the investigating group also were silent.

In another development in the R. F. C. inquiry, former Senator Burton K. Wheeler, Democrat of

Burton K. Wheeler
Associated Press

Montana, said today that he had asked Senator Tobey to "go easy on" Donald S. Dawson, White House aide, during the Senate investigation of the agency. Mr. Wheeler asserted that he acted at

Continued on Page 25, Column 3

Sterling Hayden Was a Red; 'Stupidest Thing I Ever Did'

Special to The New York Times.

WASHINGTON, April 10—Sterling Hayden, motion picture actor and decorated former United States Marine, told the House Committee on Un-American Activities today that he had been a member of the Communist party from June to December of 1946.

"It was the stupidest and most ignorant thing I ever had done in my life," he said. "I went into it with an emotional and very unsound approach, but I don't mean to imply that I was dragged into it. I went in voluntarily."

Mr. Hayden, a native of Montclair, N. J., said there were thousands of others like him, who should come in and tell their stories.

He added that shortly after the invasion of South Korea his attorney had written to J. Edgar Hoover, director of the Federal Bureau of Investigation, giving his Communist case history and seeking a means of eliminating any prejudice against his recall to the service.

Under questioning for more than three hours, the former husband of Madeleine Carroll, screen star, told of a restless life that started with his quitting high school at the age of fifteen and going to sea, and winding up in Hollywood. A Capt. Warwick Tompkins, described by him as an "open and avowed Communist," ran through his story.

He identified Captain Tompkins as an employe of Amtorg, the of-

Continued on Page 14, Column 5

PRICE AIDE RESIGNS, CONDEMNS DI SALLE

M. E. Thompson, Ex-Governor of Georgia, Hits 'Kansas City Crowd' in Administration

Special to The New York Times.

WASHINGTON, April 10—With bitter words for Price Stabilizer Michael V. DiSalle, and for the "Kansas City crowd" he said was in the saddle in the national Administration, M. E. Thompson, former Governor of Georgia, resigned today as a consultant to the Office of Price Stabilization.

Mr. Thompson, once a power in Georgia politics, and who asserted that he battled successfully against the States Righters there who tried to keep President Truman's name off the ballot in 1948, declared that he would not support the Democratic party in 1952 if the "Kansas City crowd" still held control.

"If this be political treason,

Continued on Page 20, Column 1

Navy Suspends Explosives Expert; State Department Then Bars Wife

Special to The New York Times.

WASHINGTON, April 10—The Navy Department suspended Dr. Stephen Brunauer today as a "security risk," giving the 47-year-old high explosives expert thirty days in which to answer the charges.

The State Department meanwhile, suspended Mrs. Esther Caukin Brunauer, wife of the Navy scientist, pending the outcome of the investigation of her husband. The State Department made it plain in a statement that the action against Mrs. Brunauer was based not on information about her, but only as a result of the Navy suspension.

Both of the Brunauers were named by Senator Joseph R. McCarthy, Republican of Wisconsin, in the course of his charges last year of Communist infiltration of the Government.

The announcement of Dr. Brunauer's suspension, effective immediately, was made while he was on a trip to New England for the Navy. Questioned by reporters at LaGuardia Field, on his way back to the capital, he said:

"I do not know for what reason I was suspended. I think some one made a mistake. I telephoned Washington and a Navy spokesman said he did not know the reason for the suspension. I do not want to comment further on anything."

Mrs. Brunauer issued a stout denial of the McCarthy charges on March 13, 1950, defending herself and her husband against the allegations they were Communists.

The Navy announcement of its suspension of Dr. Brunauer followed the disclosure by the State Department that the action had already taken place. The Navy gave no details of the charges, but said that Dr. Brunauer would have thirty days to answer the charges and request a hearing.

The decision of Francis P. Matthews, Secretary of the Navy will be final, it was said.

Asked whether the suspension of Mrs. Brunauer in response to charges against her husband was

Continued on Page 16, Column 3

RISE IN SALES TAX EXPECTED TO PASS CITY COUNCIL TODAY

Finance Committee Studies Bill at Length—Fight Against Measure Goes On

RUML A FISCAL ADVISER

Mayor Declines Challenge to Debate With Hoving—Joseph Suggests State-Wide Levy

The finance committee of the City Council spent an inconclusive three-hour executive session at City Hall yesterday afternoon weighing the merits of the proposed increase in the retail sales tax from 2 to 3 per cent, but when the meeting ended nothing had changed the prospect that the tax rise would be approved.

It was indicated that today the committee, after further behind-closed-doors deliberations, would favor the sales impost rise by a vote of 8 to 2, or possibly 7 to 3, and that later today the full City Council would adopt the measure by something like 19 to 6.

If the tax bill clears the Council hurdles today, as is indicated, it is expected that the Board of Estimate, whose members are committed to it, will give its approval at tomorrow's regular meeting.

Ruml to Advise Controller

Meanwhile, Controller Lazarus Joseph announced the appointment of Beardsley Ruml, business consultant, financier and economist, as a special deputy controller to advise Mr. Joseph on fiscal matters. Mr. Ruml, whose appointment was for an "indefinite" tenure, will serve without pay.

Mr. Ruml was at one time connected with the Federal Reserve Board and also with the New York Stock Exchange. He is a

Continued on Page 32, Column 4

U. S. PRODS NATIONS

Suggests U. N. Members Send More Troops to Fight in Korea

3 AVENUES ARE LISTED

Contributions Sought From Nations Not Yet Committed

By A. M. ROSENTHAL
Special to The New York Times.

UNITED NATIONS, N. Y., April 10—The United States has been quietly suggesting that members of the United Nations increase, or at least maintain, their contributions of troops for the Korean war effort.

Informed sources here report that for some time the United States has been keeping in touch with members of the world organization to see if non-United States representation in the international army could be increased.

[Chinese Communist troops in Korea clung to their positions along the Hwachon Reservoir in the face of daylong United Nations attacks. Eighth Army headquarters clamped a stringent security blackout on news from the front as a major battle seemed to impend in the reservoir area.]

So far there has been no general appeal to the United Nations members to contribute more troops; it has all been on a country-to-country basis. Diplomats said that there was no indication that a new general request for troops in Korea was in the making for the time being.

But on a longer-range basis, the question of more troops may be considered by the committee set up by the General Assembly on Feb. 1 to plan possible sanctions

Continued on Page 5, Column 3

World News Summarized

WEDNESDAY, APRIL 11, 1951

President Truman relieved General of the Army MacArthur of his command in the Pacific because the United Nations commander had been unable to give his "wholehearted support" to United States and United Nations policies. The Presidential ouster has forced the general from all his commands, including his role in the occupation of Japan. Lieut. Gen. Matthew B. Ridgway has been designated to take over all the Far Eastern commands. [1:8.]

The United States has been asking other United Nations members to increase, or at least maintain, their forces fighting in Korea and asking for troops from countries that have sent none. [1:5.]

Enemy resistance increased in the Hwachon Reservoir area of Korea. The Communists still held the dam although Hwachon itself appeared deserted. [3:1; map P. 2.] Mao Tse-tung was said to have been officially reported ill and Liu Shao-chi was said to be acting in his place at the head of the Chinese Communist regime. [9:2.]

Britain has suggested that the United States invite Communist China to the discussions on a Japanese peace treaty and send Peiping a draft of the proposed pact. The treaty, Britain holds, should include the return of Formosa to China. [1:6-7.]

The days of "easy and automatic" relations between the United States and Canada are over, Canada's External Affairs Minister declared. "There will be frictions" that can be settled easily, he said, if the United States recognizes that Canada's acceptance of Washington leadership does not mean she is "willing to be merely an echo of somebody else's voice." [1:6-7.]

A "severe, but not crippling" budget was presented to Britain by the Labor Government, which chose to increase taxes, already heavy, rather than cut social welfare funds. [1:7.]

The bill giving West German labor equal rights with management in the operation of the steel and coal industries was passed by the lower house. [14:2.]

The House passed and sent to the Senate a supplemental defense money bill 43 per cent below Administration requests [29:1] and cut from the draft bill a provision for Universal Military Training in favor of a Presidential commission to draw detailed plans. [1:1.] Defense Secretary Marshall ordered all three armed services to share equitably draftees of superior standing. [19:3.]

Mobilization Director Wilson called for an end to complacency, selfishness and partisanship if we are to beat down the "dreadful shadow" of history's most "absolute and ruthless" dictatorship. [23:1.] M. E. Thompson resigned as consultant to the Price Stabilizer in protest against "political" control and general wastefulness. [1:2.]

Organized baseball was ordered not to raise players' salaries above a club's 1950 highest. [33:2-3.] The Army halted certain pay rises for nonoperating rail workers until a special panel ruled in the case. [33:1.]

Senator Tobey was said to have disclosed that he had recorded telephone talks with President Truman about the Senate R. F. C. inquiry. [1:2-3.] The Navy suspended Dr. Stephen Brunauer, a scientist, as a "security risk" and the State Department dropped his wife, Esther, until the husband's case was settled. [1:2-3.]

Index to other news appears on last page of this section.

DISMISSED BY THE PRESIDENT

General of the Army Douglas MacArthur

Britain Asks That Red China Have Role in Japanese Pact

By WALTER H. WAGGONER
Special to The New York Times.

WASHINGTON, April 10—Britain has suggested to the United States that Communist China be brought into the negotiations for a Japanese peace treaty. The British proposal also specifically asked that the United States send a copy of its treaty draft to the Peiping regime for its consideration, and, further, that the treaty provide for the ultimate if not immediate return of Formosa to "China."

By "China" the British mean the regime of Mao Tse-tung, since that is the China now recognized by London.

These suggestions have been made in the course of recent conversations between the two Governments. They represent another difference of opinion that has developed between London and Washington on both the procedure for negotiating a Japanese treaty and the form the settlement should have.

The basis for the British request that Peiping be given a look at the United States treaty draft is to enable the Chinese Communists to reject the proposal if they want to, as the Soviet Union is expected to do.

At the same time, it is vigorously denied here that Britain will refuse to sign any treaty draft that Communist China rejects. Reports that such an "or else" position has

Continued on Page 8, Column 5

BUDGET INCREASES BRITONS' TAX LOAD

Income, Profit, Purchase, Auto and Gasoline Imposts Rise—Social Services Uncut

By RAYMOND DANIELL
Special to The New York Times.

LONDON, April 10—The already heavily burdened British people were called upon today to pay even higher taxes to preserve their welfare state. Hugh Gaitskell, Chancellor of the Exchequer, introducing his first budget, told the House of Commons that there were only two ways of meeting the extra cost of rearmament. One, which brought cheers from the Conservative Opposition, was by reducing expenditures for social welfare.

The alternative he offered was a sharp rise in both direct and indirect taxes. This brought cheers

Continued on Page 10, Column 3

Canada Bars a 'Yes' Role to U. S.; Pearson Sees Unity Despite Friction

By The United Press

TORONTO, April 10—Lester B. Pearson, Canadian Secretary for External Affairs, said today that "easy and automatic" relations between Canada and the United States were a thing of the past.

In a speech apparently aimed at United States consumption, Mr. Pearson said that Canada was not willing to be "merely an echo of somebody else's voice" and reserved the right to criticize "our great friend, the United States."

Mr. Pearson said that Canada intended to prevent the United Nations from becoming "too much the instrument of any one country" and that it was time for the United States to stop telling Canada "that until we do one-twelfth or one-sixteenth, or some other fraction as much as they are doing, we are defaulting."

He said that there might be "angry waves which may weaken the foundation of our friendship" but that Canada would march forward with the United States "in the pursuit of objectives which we share."

"Nevertheless, the days of relatively easy and automatic relations with our neighbor are, I think, over," he added.

Mr. Pearson indicated that one of the "angry waves" that could weaken relations between Canada and the United States was the controversy over General of the Army Douglas MacArthur's statement on the war in Korea.

Later, in a second speech, Mr. Pearson made an indirect reference to General MacArthur when he said that a successful foreign policy must work toward goals accepted by the majority of the people, and it would have a better chance of "reaching these goals if we abandon what has been called 'hoop-la diplomacy' at Lake Success, at Ottawa, or, I hasten to add, at Tokyo."

He said that the free nations stood in danger of "nothing less

Continued on Page 6, Column 3

PRESIDENT MOVES

Van Fleet Is Named to Command 8th Army in Drastic Shift

VIOLATIONS ARE CITED

White House Statement Quotes Directives and Implies Breaches

Texts of statements and orders in MacArthur dispute, Page 8.

By W. H. LAWRENCE
Special to The New York Times.

WASHINGTON, Wednesday, April 11—President Truman early today relieved General of the Army Douglas MacArthur of all his commands in the Far East and appointed Lieut. Gen. Matthew B. Ridgway as his successor.

The President said he had relieved General MacArthur "with deep regret" because he had concluded that the Far Eastern Commander "is unable to give his wholehearted support to the policies of the United States Government and of the United Nations in matters pertaining to his official duties."

General MacArthur, in a message to House Minority Leader Joseph W. Martin Jr. of Massachusetts, made public by Mr. Martin last Thursday, had publicly challenged the President's foreign policy, urging that the United States concentrate on Asia instead of Europe and use Generalissimo Chiang Kai-shek's Formosa-based troops to open a second front on the mainland of China.

The change in command is effective at once. General Ridgway, who has been in command of the Eighth Army in Korea since the death in December of Gen. Walton H. Walker, assumes all of General MacArthur's titles—Supreme Commander, United Nations Forces in Korea, Supreme Commander for Allied Powers, Japan, Commander-in-Chief, Far East, and Commanding General U. S. Army, Far East.

Commanded in Greece

The Eighth Army command will pass to Lieut. Gen. James A. Van Fleet whose most recent important command was as head of the American military mission in Greece, when that country was repelling a Communist-directed guerrilla attack under the Truman doctrine.

In ousting General MacArthur for his public disagreement with American policy designed to localize the Asiatic war, the President said:

"Full and vigorous debate on matters of national policy is a vital element in the Constitutional system of our free democracy.

"It is fundamental, however, that military commanders must be governed by the policies and directives issued to them in the manner provided by our laws and Con-

Continued on Page 3, Column 1

News Stuns Tokyo; MacArthur Is Silent

By The Associated Press.

TOKYO, Wednesday, April 11—A small brown envelope with "flash" printed on it in red carried to General MacArthur today the news that he had been discharged from his commands by President Truman.

It was delivered by a special aide, Col. Sid Huff, who said that the General received the news without comment. Colonel Huff indicated that the General had no forewarning that he was being relieved.

The General announced that he would have no statement immediately.

The message came as a Signal Corps communication about the time and Army radio announced the news.

General MacArthur got the word while at lunch with his wife, Senator Warren G. Mag-

Continued on Page 8, Column 4

"All the News That's Fit to Print"

The New York Times.

LATE CITY EDITION
A few snow flurries early today. Partly cloudy, cold tomorrow.
Temperature Range Today—Max., 35; Min., 28
Temperatures Yesterday—Max., 42; Min., 30
U. S. Weather Bureau Report, Sect. 5, Page 8

Section 1

NEWS SUMMARY AND INDEX, PAGE 95

VOL. CII..No. 34,735. Entered as Second-Class Matter. Post Office, New York, N. Y. NEW YORK, SUNDAY, MARCH 1, 1953. Including Magazine and Book Review. TWENTY CENTS New York City 50 Mile Zone | Elsewhere Twenty-five Cents

MOSSADEGH FLEES HIS HOME AS TEHERAN MOB ATTACKS IT IN DEMONSTRATION FOR SHAH

Principal Figures in Iranian Unrest

The Shah of Iran

Associated Press

Premier Mohammed Mossadegh

PREMIER IS UNHURT

Finds Haven, in Pajamas, in U. S. Point 4 Bureau, Then in Parliament

MONARCH CANCELS VOYAGE

Changes Mind About Leaving as Supporters Hail Him—Guards Fire on Crowds

By The Associated Press.

TEHERAN, Iran, Feb. 28—Mobs screaming loyalty for Shah Mohammed Riza Pahlevi drove Premier Mohammed Mossadegh out of his home today while Government guards held off the demonstrators with gunfire.

Dr. Mossadegh took refuge first in the adjoining offices of the United States Government's Point Four Program and then in the usually invincible Parliament building.

In rapid order, Dr. Mossadegh held an emergency Cabinet meeting during his flight, Parliament met in extraordinary session with Dr. Mossadegh present in pajamas, and the Shah broadcast to all Iranians his determination to stay in his country.

After Dr. Mossadegh reached the sanctuary of Parliament, it was reported late tonight that he had ordered his bed and food brought in. This usually indicates an extended stay during political upheavals.

The attack on his house was considered a threat to his safety; Iranian public figures under threat traditionally can camp in Parliament until the situation cools off.

Differences Become Acute

The Shah and Dr. Mossadegh have differed in the past over the Shah's post-war campaign for land redistribution, including royal family holdings and the abrupt manner of Dr. Mossadegh's expulsion of the British in his now-stymied national oil development project. The differences became more tense than ever this week.

At the palace, the demonstrators had persuaded the 33-year-old Shah not to leave for Europe today. He had announced that he planned to go away for reasons of health.

[There were reports abroad that the Shah had intended to abdicate, but Teheran dispatches did not say so directly. The Foreign Office in London, according to The Associated Press, said without amplification that it had received from the United States Embassy there a report "dealing with the future of the Shah."

[It was believed in London that the result of the events in Teheran might be to restore some of the Shah's prestige and diminish the authority of Premier Mossadegh. Iran's most recent internal troubles may also interrupt the negotiations for a settlement of the dispute with Britain over the nationalization of the British-owned oil concession in Iran, it was said.]

Today's mob action disrupted the Shah's travel plans, which apparently had resulted from meet-

Continued on Page 24, Column 3

HOUSE UNIT STUDIES CHARGE OF PERJURY AT POLICE INQUIRY

'Square Conflict' Pointed Out in Monaghan Contradiction of Greenberg Testimony

SOME DENIALS QUALIFIED

Keating Orders Police Head to Stop 'Making Speeches,' Threatens to Oust Herwitz

By RUSSELL PORTER

Police Commissioner George P. Monaghan contradicted Assistant United States Attorney Daniel H. Greenberg yesterday on the alleged agreement to let the police investigate themselves and exclude the Federal Bureau of Investigation from Federal civil rights cases here.

Testifying before a Congressional committee, the Commissioner denied he had once told Mr. Greenberg there was such an agreement. He denied that there had ever been such an agreement, that he had refused to let the F. B. I. question accused policemen, or that a departmental report on a police brutality case in the West Fifty-fourth Street station had been a mere "whitewash."

Representative Kenneth B. Keating, Republican of upstate New York, chairman of the House judiciary subcommittee before which Mr. Monaghan appeared, stressed the "square conflict" in testimony between the commissioner and the prosecutor. Mr. Keating told reporters the committee would consider whether to recommend perjury proceedings against anyone, but would first hear everybody concerned.

Monaghan Sometimes Indefinite

Mr. Monaghan qualified some of his denials. Asked if he had flatly said "no" to F. B. I. agents who asked permission to question accused policemen, he replied, "I don't think I did."

"Is that as strong as you can make it?" he was asked.

"I'd say I didn't say no. I have no recollection of saying no," replied the commissioner.

"Is that as strong as you're able to put it?"

"Yes."

Asked whether, in a talk with F. B. I. agents, he had referred to an agreement between the Police Department and the Justice Department, the commissioner said:

"I have no recollection that that came up."

"Is that as strong as you can put it?"

"Yes."

In his testimony he twice accused Representative Adam Clayton Powell, Democrat of Harlem, of "lying" in statements made to the committee about the Commissioner. Once Mr. Monaghan turned toward Mr. Powell, who was a spectator, shook his finger at him, and shouted:

"That was a lie, Clayton, and you know it."

Hearing Resumes Tomorrow

After Mr. Monaghan had been on the witness stand at the United States Courthouse in Foley Square for three and three-quarter hours and Chief Inspector Conrad H. Rothengast had testified for twenty minutes yesterday, the subcommittee adjourned until 10 A. M. tomorrow in Washington. Mr. Keating announced that Mr. Rothengast would be questioned further at that time, together with officials of the Department of Justice.

Mr. Keating also pointed out a

Continued on Page 53, Column 1

The New York Times (by Arthur Brower)

AT POLICE BRUTALITY HEARING: Police Commissioner George P. Monaghan, right, talks with Chief Inspector Conrad H. Rothengast before they testified at Congressional inquiry.

Hungary Suggests Trading Briton for Doomed Malayan

By RAYMOND DANIELL

Special to The New York Times.

LONDON, Feb. 28—Britain has received an unusual offer from one of the Soviet Union's satellites for an exchange of prisoners of the "cold war." Some weeks ago the Hungarian Government informed the British Minister in Budapest, Robert M. A. Hankey, that it would be interested in a trade. Hungary Britain was told, would release Edgar Sanders, who is serving a prison term for "espionage," if Britain would free Lee Meng, a woman leader of the Malayan Communist rebels, who is awaiting execution.

A Foreign Office spokesman said no peacetime precedent for such an exchange could be recalled.

Mr. Sanders, a 48-year-old British business man, was sentenced to thirteen years' imprisonment by Hungary three years ago at the same time as Robert A. Vogeler, United States business man, who has since been released.

Lee Meng was sentenced to death last September by the High Court at Ipoh, Malaya, following her conviction on a charge of having been in possession of a hand grenade. Last Feb. 17, the Judicial Committee of the Privy Council, in London, denied her appeal.

Last August, when Lee Meng first stood trial at Ipoh, two Asian Assessors on the bench found her innocent, and the British judge ordered retrial.

Captured Malayan Communists had testified at this hearing that Lee Meng was a high-ranking Communist jungle gang leader, who had ordered the murder of several Europeans and at least one Chinese in the tin-rich North Malayan state of Perak. According to police evidence, Lee Meng was one of Perak's leading Communists.

Lee Meng's defense, which seems to conflict with Hungary's subsequent interest in her fate, was that she was a victim of mistaken identity and that she was in fact Lee Tian-tai, a working girl, who did not even know what a hand grenade was.

It was said today at the Foreign

Continued on Page 4, Column 6

2 'VOICE' OFFICIALS HIT PROGRAM RULE AS BOON TO SOVIET

Say Bid for Hebrew Language Broadcast Curb Came While Red Anti-Semitism Grew

HEARINGS ARE TELEVISED

Witness Tells McCarthy Inquiry Some Information Employes Failed in Security Tests

By WILLIAM R. CONKLIN

Two officials in the Voice of America headquarters here testified under oath yesterday that Hebrew language broadcasts had been ordered stopped last December, at the time when open Soviet anti-Semitism could have made them most effective. However, the order later was suspended before its effective date.

A third witness told the Senate subcommittee investigating the State Department's broadcasting agency that Ed Schechter, a State Department employe who had failed to pass security loyalty tests, had received a key assignment under the United States High Commissioner to Germany.

James F. Thompson, facilities manager for the Voice of America here, swore that Theodore Kaghan, another who failed to clear security tests, had been chief of the press section under the High Commissioner in Germany until one year ago. In Bonn, Mr. Kaghan denied he had been turned down by the Voice for security reasons.

Mr. Thompson testified that Charles Lewis, Mr. Schechter's predecessor in Bonn as chief of the radio section, also had failed to pass the security-loyalty requirements.

The subcommittee hearing, with Senator Joseph R. McCarthy, Republican of Wisconsin, presiding, was televised nationally by the National Broadcasting Company between 2 and 4 P. M. From 3 to 4 it was carried here on WNBT, Channel 4. The hearing in Room 318 of the United States Courthouse in Foley Square drew an attentive "studio audience," which filled every seat inside.

Harris Order Cited

After a morning executive session at which eight witnesses testified in private, Senator McCarthy called Dr. Sidney Glazer, chief of Hebrew service for the Voice, and Gerald Dooher, his superior, who is acting chief of the Near East, South Asian and African Division of the broadcasting agency.

Under questioning by Roy M. Cohn, chief counsel, the witnesses testified that their proposed expansion of Hebrew language broadcasts to Israel and other parts of the world had been ordered stopped by Reed Harris, acting administrator of the United States International Information Administration in Washington.

Both quoted Mr. Harris as saying that the decision to abandon the Hebrew broadcasts had been based upon a budget decision in Washington. However, both protested that the estimated $30,000 saving would not have amounted to half that amount because of the requirement for paying specialists employed under contracts. They declared that the Harris order was suspended indefinitely after they had telephoned a protest to Wilson S. Compton, then

Continued on Page 28, Column 3

GREATER AID URGED TO AVERT COLLAPSE OF BRITAIN AS ALLY

C. E. D. Report Bids America Pay More of NATO Costs and Liberalize Trade

'NEW APPROACH' STRESSED

Wider Market Here Advocated but Deal for Convertibility of Sterling Is Opposed

By FELIX BELAIR Jr.

Special to The New York Times.

WASHINGTON, Feb. 28—The Committee for Economic Development asserted in a report today that continued financial aid to Great Britain was the alternative to collapse of the Anglo-American alliance and diplomatic and economic isolation for the United States.

The report urged a liberalization of this country's commercial policy to make it easier for Britain to market her products in this country. It said that the rearmament program of the North Atlantic Treaty Organization imposed too great a burden on the British economy and suggested that if the program could not be slowed down, the United States should increase its contribution for Britain's benefit.

Nevertheless, the committee cautioned against entering into any stabilization arrangement with the British Government to make its currency convertible into dollars within the sterling area as a stimulant to trade. It expressed belief that any such effort had little chance of success unless and until there was a vast improvement in Britain's balance of payments position with the United States.

Troubles Go Too Deep

The committee is a private and nonprofit research organization of representatives of business, banking, industry, agriculture, education and other fields devoted to adult schooling in economic questions. Its present findings are expected to have no little bearing on the official talks beginning here Wednesday with Anthony Eden, British Foreign Secretary, and Richard Butler, Chancellor of the Exchequer.

It has become increasingly apparent, the report said, that the nature of Britain's economic woes is too deep-seated to respond to the kind of money grant assistance on which Anglo-American economic cooperation has been based.

A "new approach" founded on increasing productivity in British export industries and a more aggressive effort at competitive penetration of world markets in return for a more liberal commercial policy in this country was proposed. The report acknowledged that "continuing aid on the present basis would be self-defeating," since it would encourage postponement of needed economic adjustments.

The report urged that the United States undertake to:

¶Assume a larger part of NATO rearmament costs, so that Britain could apply part of her corresponding expenditure to modernizing her industrial plant and management thinking.

¶Stabilize the United States' raw material purchases in the sterling area to help end wide fluctuations

Continued on Page 37, Column 1

Eisenhower Calls Chief Aides To Hear Van Fleet on Korea

By W. H. LAWRENCE

Special to The New York Times.

AUGUSTA, Ga., Feb. 28—President Eisenhower today summoned the nation's top military leaders and a bipartisan Congressional group to a White House luncheon on Tuesday to hear Gen. James A. Van Fleet's reasons for believing an all-out United Nations offensive in Korea now would certainly succeed.

General Van Fleet, who retired recently as commanding general of the Eighth Amy in Korea, is due in Washington by airplane at 12:15 P. M. on Tuesday and will go to the White House immediately for a thirty-minute private conference with the President in advance of the luncheon.

Out of the conferences may come new steps in the Administration's program to bring the Korean conflict to an early and honorable conclusion. The President pledged efforts for this when he was a candidate last October.

The President, who is here on a brief golfing vacation, will return to Washington tomorrow.

This afternoon the President played another eighteen-hole round and then paid his own tribute to one of golfing's all-time greats, Robert T. (Bobby) Jones Jr. of Atlanta, who won the amateur and open championships of the United States and Great Britain in 1930 to score golf's only "grand slam."

Poses With Jones Picture

Mr. Jones came to the Augusta club's trophy room to receive his portrait, painted by the President.

President Eisenhower talked with reporters before and after the presentation of his painting. He stood with Mr. Jones in front of the trophy room before a battery of cameras and newsmen with the 40-by-32-inch oil, which had been made from a photograph of Mr. Jones when he was at the peak of his game. The painting showed Mr. Jones following through with a wood.

"It's marvelous," was Mr. Jones' reaction.

"That's a boy, Bob," the President responded, with a pleased smile.

Then the golfer's father, Robert T. Jones, stepped forward to glimpse the painting. He told the President:

"I didn't believe you could do it, but you have."

General Eisenhower smiled his thanks.

Mrs. Jones Attends

The painting had caught well the fairway scene. The colors seemed especially well done. Only one thing about the picture bothered the President, and he gestured with his glasses to show Mr. Jones and the reporters "the one thing about it I don't like." He pointed to the left eye, which had smudged, and had the appearance of being black.

In the right-hand corner of the picture were the small initials "D.E.," but the President told Mr. Jones to look on the back if he ever forgot where he got it. On the back was printed:

"Bob—from his friend—D. D. E.—1953."

Mr. Jones was asked what he intended to do with the picture.

"Whatever he tells me," he re-

Continued on Page 74, Column 2

INVASION NEARER, CHIANG PROCLAIMS

Generalissimo Calls on People to Rally for Early Recovery of China From the Reds

By The Associated Press.

TAIPEI, Sunday, March 1—Generalissimo Chiang Kai-shek called on Formosa and the rest of free China yesterday to mobilize all their manpower and resources and speed united efforts for recovery of the Communist-held Chinese mainland in the near future.

In his first message since President Eisenhower lifted the restrictions imposed by the United States Seventh Fleet on operations by Nationalist military forces against the Reds, Generalissimo Chiang said:

"The moment of our counterattack is drawing nearer and nearer. Hundreds of millions of our compatriots are suffering from oppression at the hands of Russian puppets and are eagerly looking to us to deliver them at an early date."

[In Korea, the United States cruiser Los Angeles entered Wonsan Harbor and shelled the Red port. Patrol clashes marked the fighting on the front.]

The veteran Chinese Nationalist leader issued a 7,000-word statement on the eve of the third anniversary today of his reassumption of the Presidency of the Republic of China.

During the height of the Chinese civil war, Generalissimo Chiang

Continued on Page 3, Column 3

CITY HEADS UNITED FOR ALBANY TALKS

Mayor and Board Will Try Tomorrow to Save Major Items in Fiscal Plan

By PAUL CROWELL

Mayor Impellitteri and his seven colleagues on the Board of Estimate will go to Albany tomorrow in an effort to salvage some of the major items in the city's $218,700,000 fiscal program for 1953-54, which was rejected last Monday in a memorandum issued by Lieut. Gov. Frank C. Moore and State Controller J. Raymond McGovern.

The Mayor, the Board of Estimate members and the Mayor's advisory staff headed by Budget Director Abraham D. Beame will discuss the city's program with Mr. Moore, Mr. McGovern and the technical staff that drafted the memorandum issued by the two state officials. The meeting will constitute a resumption of the city-state conference that began last May and ended in November. The city's representatives will be present in response to an invitation extended by Mr. Moore and Mr. McGovern last Friday, setting the time of tomorrow's parley at 1 P. M.

Second Trek to Capital

The Mayor and his party will leave Grand Central Terminal at 9 A. M. tomorrow on the Empire State Express. It will be their second trek to the state capital since the Legislature convened on Jan. 6. The first expedition took place on Feb. 11, when the Mayor and his associates made their losing argument for $62,700,000 of additional state aid at a joint meeting of Assembly and Senate committees.

The conference with Mr. Moore and Mr. McGovern will be the first city-state parley on municipal finances in which the Board of Estimate will take part. Hotel reservations in Albany have been made for the Mayor and his group in the event it becomes necessary for them to stay over for another day of discussion.

Despite the apparent rejection in the Moore-McGovern memorandum of the city's entire 1953-54 program, the Mayor and his associates will go to Albany hopeful that some of the plan's major items can be salvaged. They have indicated strongly that they will not be "pressured" into proposing either a transit authority mandated to raise the fare on the city lines to meet operating deficits, or any type of city income tax.

The Mayor and his colleagues will enter the conference unanimous in the view that the state, having rejected the city's entire program, is under obligation to propose a substitute. The state group still contends, however, that it is up to the city to put forward alternative methods of providing revenues to balance its 1953-54 budget.

Recent exchanges of formal documents between the city and state groups have expressed the belief of

Continued on Page 56, Column 4

Auto Union Rejects G.M. Pay Rise Offer

By ELIE ABEL

Special to The New York Times.

DETROIT, Feb. 28—The United Automobile Workers, C. I. O., announced today that the General Motors Corporation had agreed to reopen its five-year "escalator" contract with the union, but that the management's offer of wage improvements had been rejected as inadequate.

In a statement disclosing the terms proposed by General Motors, the union noted with gratification the corporation's acceptance of the principle that long-term collective bargaining agreements were "living documents," subject to revision when abnormal economic conditions raised unforeseen problems.

The union contended, however, that the company's wage proposals fell short "of the equity to which the General Motors workers are entitled."

Management countered with the statement that its offer was "con-

Continued on Page 55, Column 3

Associated Press Wirephoto

FROM ONE GOLFER TO ANOTHER: President Eisenhower presenting to Robert T. (Bobby) Jones Jr. at Augusta, Ga., a portrait the Chief Executive painted of the "grand slammer."

Magsaysay, Defense Chief, Resigns In Split With Philippine President

Special to The New York Times.

MANILA, Sunday, March 1—Ramón Magsaysay, under mounting political pressures as Secretary of Defense, resigned last night from his post in the Cabinet of President Elpidio Quirino.

His action cleared the way for his candidacy as the Opposition Nacionalista party's standard bearer to oppose Mr. Quirino in next November's Presidential elections.

Mr. Magsaysay made his resignation known in a statement to the press after having sent a formal note to Mr. Quirino at Malacanan Palace by Army courier. The statement referred to the "difficulties and obstructionism" under which he had been trying to fulfill his duties in recent months and said, "I have reached the point where my continuing in office would be futile."

"Having reached the conclusion that peace and progress cannot be achieved under the present Administration, I can take no other course than to resign," Mr. Magsaysay added.

He indicated that the President had restricted his functions to killing Communist Hukbalahaps. The Defense Secretary's policies had given equal importance to rehabilitation of surrendered rebels and correction of the social conditions giving rise to rebellious tendencies.

Mr. Quirino, who made no immediate reply to the Magsaysay resignation, is prepared to leave early today for northern Luzon, where he is scheduled to open an interscholastic athletic meet. The rapid political developments of the last several days left no doubt that the leaders of the President's Liberal party, who have long encouraged and sought Mr. Magsaysay's

Continued on Page 3, Column 4

1953

America the Superpower

1960

FRONT PAGE NEWS 1953-1960

The New York Times.

STALIN DIES AFTER 29-YEAR RULE; HIS SUCCESSOR NOT ANNOUNCED; U.S. WATCHFUL, EISENHOWER SAYS

Stalin Dies

MARCH 6, 1953

Once World War II ended, the mutual determination to defeat Hitler that had bound the U.S. and the Soviet Union was replaced by a mutual suspicion that was perhaps even deeper. The U.S. came to see the Kremlin as a belligerent, godless dictatorship that threatened democratic Europe and America itself. But with Stalin dead, President Dwight D. Eisenhower remarked, "The slate is clean. Now let us begin talking to each other." Nikita Khrushchev, who jockeyed to succeed Stalin, repudiated Stalinism in 1956 in an electrifying secret speech that revealed Stalin's brutality—even against prominent comrades—but otherwise left the cold war in place.

Conquering Everest

JUNE 2, 1953

The target was the highest place on Earth, more than five miles up. Mount Everest had defeated earlier generations of mountaineers. This time, a sizable British team started up the south face, but only Sir Edmund Hillary and his Nepalese guide, Tenzing Norkay, went the last 3,000 feet. They spent 15 minutes at the top of the world, shaking hands and taking photographs. Hillary called it "a great moment," and it was a moment celebrated 4,500 miles away in London, where Queen Elizabeth II was about to be crowned.

Rosenbergs Executed as Spies

JUNE 20, 1953

A Soviet defector had stunned intelligence officials in 1945 by exposing an atomic spy ring. After the espionage trial of the century, Julius Rosenberg, an engineer who had served in the Army Signal Corps in World War II, and his wife, Ethel, were convicted of conspiring to hand over the secrets of the atomic bomb. Irving R. Kaufman, the federal judge who presided over the trial, called their crime "worse than murder" and sentenced them to death. The case became a cause célebre for many on the left, some of whom still maintain that the Rosenbergs were railroaded.

The Power of the H-Bomb

APRIL 1, 1954

The dialogue at a presidential news conference was fearsome. President Dwight D. Eisenhower had summoned reporters to hear Rear Admiral Lewis L. Strauss, the chairman of the Atomic Energy Commission, describe a new secret weapon, a hydrogen bomb, more powerful than the atomic bombs dropped on Hiroshima and Nagasaki. It had been detonated in a test that all but vaporized Bikini Atoll in the Pacific. Admiral Strauss called the explosion "large enough to destroy a city," and when reporters persisted, he said he meant "any city." New York? Yes: the destruction from an H-bomb dropped on Manhattan could reach 50 miles.

Senate Censures McCarthy

DECEMBER 3, 1954

The Army-McCarthy hearings, convened in mid-1954 to investigate what Senator Joseph R. McCarthy insisted was subversion in the military, turned into a 36-day tirade—and McCarthy's undoing. The turning point came when the Army's lawyer, Joseph N. Welch, asked McCarthy, "Have you no sense of decency, sir, at long last?" When the Senate censured McCarthy, he said he just wanted to get back to "the job of digging out Communists in government." But McCarthy's moment had passed.

Arthur Miller Won't Name Names

JUNE 22, 1956

The McCarthy era's anti-Communist crusade continued when the House Un-American Activities Committee subpoenaed Arthur Miller, whose 1953 hit play "The Crucible" had drawn parallels to the Salem witch trials in colonial Massachusetts. Miller said later that Chairman Francis Walter offered to cancel the hearing if his photograph were taken with Miller's fiancée, Marilyn Monroe. Walter didn't get his picture, and when Miller went before the committee, he didn't name names. He testified about his own encounters with Communist-front groups, but refused to identify others he had seen at meetings. For that, Miller was later found guilty of contempt of Congress. A federal appeals court overturned his conviction in 1958.

The New York Times.

ANDREA DORIA AND STOCKHOLM COLLIDE; 1,134 PASSENGERS ABANDON ITALIAN SHIP IN FOG AT SEA; ALL SAVED, MANY INJURED

Andrea Doria, Stockholm Collide

JULY 26, 1956

The S.O.S. said the luxurious Andrea Doria was in trouble off Nantucket—the sharp-nosed prow of the Swedish ocean liner Stockholm had sliced into the Andrea Doria's hull amidships. Both were equipped with radar, but as they approached in dense fog, officers on each bridge had guessed wrong about how the other would maneuver. The Andrea Doria's crew ordered the 1,134 passengers into lifeboats as the 29,000-ton vessel began to list. Like the Titanic, it had been billed as unsinkable, but it too went down within a few hours.

The New York Times.

HIGH COURT BANS SCHOOL SEGREGATION; 9-TO-0 DECISION GRANTS TIME TO COMPLY

School Segregation Outlawed

MAY 18, 1954

It took Chief Justice Earl Warren 30 minutes to get to the point as he read the 1,800-word opinion aloud at the Supreme Court: segregated schools are unconstitutional. The unanimous ruling repudiated an 1896 decision that had sanctioned "separate but equal accommodations" on railroad trains. That principle had spread to much of American life before World War II, but now the justices concluded that it had "no place" in public schools. In the South, the reaction was immediate and angry. Some Virginia districts shut down their schools rather than integrate; Governor Herman Talmadge of Georgia promised "a program to insure continued and permanent segregation."

Soviets Launch Sputnik

OCTOBER 5, 1957

It had a name—Sputnik, Russian for "fellow traveler"—and a place in history. This 184-pound satellite, whirling around the Earth at 18,000 miles an hour, was the first man-made object launched into orbit. America was stunned by the Soviets' edge in technology—and their indisputable advantage in propaganda. Suddenly "can do" American engineering couldn't. At the December blast-off of a satellite that weighed only three pounds, the rocket blew up on its Florida launch pad.

Crises in the Suez and Hungary

NOVEMBER 5, 1956

The crisis had been building since General Gamal Abdel Nasser of Egypt had moved to nationalize the Suez Canal. The response from Britain and France (which had its own issues with Nasser, over Egyptian support for rebels in Algeria) was an attack plan that made use of Israeli commandos, but after the United Nations intervened the assault was stopped. Thirteen hundred miles away in Budapest, Hungarians rose in rebellion against their Communist rulers, interpreting Soviet Premier Nikita Khrushchev's repudiation of Stalinism as a green light to demand freedom and independence from the Kremlin. During the brief uprising a new government was formed, but the Soviets decided on a crackdown as Hungarian leaders discussed something that was unthinkable in Moscow—withdrawing from the Warsaw Pact. As Soviet troops and tanks took over against the vastly outnumbered Hungarian freedom fighters, Washington condemned the invasion but otherwise took no action to lift the Iron Curtain.

Rock 'n' Roll Is Here to Stay

FEBRUARY 23, 1957

For the grown-ups who never quite understood Elvis Presley's appeal, the throng that lined up in Times Square for a rock 'n' roll throng was another question mark. Why wait 18 hours to see performers like Frankie Lymon and the Teenagers and the Platters? For the grown-ups who ran the city's Buildings Department, that same throng was a troubling exclamation point in a sentence with words like "dangerous conditions." Inspectors ordered them out of the Paramount Theater's balcony, worried that it would collapse amid their foot-stomping. The show eventually went on, and was seen by some 15,000 fans.

Siege in Little Rock

SEPTEMBER 25, 1957

The most chilling civil rights clash of the 1950's erupted around nine black students who tried to register at a white high school in Little Rock, Arkansas. Governor Orval Faubus deployed the National Guard, not to uphold their right to attend classes but to block the door at Central High. The black students were finally admitted after a three-week standoff, only to be sent home when whites went on a rampage. President Dwight D. Eisenhower ordered the 101st Airborne Division to take up positions at the high school—the first time since Reconstruction that the Army had been sent to restore order in the South.

Castro in Power

JANUARY 9, 1959

Fidel Castro overthrew the Cuban dictator Fulgencio Batista and swept into Havana, a charismatic guerrilla leader trailed by supporters who commandeered tanks that Batista's government had bought to use against them. Castro soon aligned Cuba with the Soviet Union; seized a billion dollars in American-owned property; survived the Bay of Pigs invasion and a trade embargo; and denounced the U.S. for 39 years. Among national leaders, only Queen Elizabeth II of Great Britain outlasted him.

Commuter Headaches

MARCH 4, 1959

Harrison E. Salisbury, a Times foreign correspondent reassigned to New York, took a fresh look at how New Yorkers got around. Drivers wasted hours in daily traffic jams; commuters were packed into overcrowded subways and buses. Salisbury found that mass transit solutions existed, but over the years, New York tried few of them, and the headaches only grew.

The Kitchen Debate

JULY 25, 1959

"You are a lawyer for capitalism and I am a lawyer for communism—let's compare," Soviet leader Nikita S. Khrushchev told Vice President Richard M. Nixon. And so they did, in an impromptu debate during a walk-through of an American-style house that had been built for an exhibition in Moscow. Nixon said it was an average American house; Khrushchev said the average American could not possibly afford it. Nixon explained how the washing machine worked; Khrushchev made fun of appliances that never work. On they argued, in an unscripted exchange that eventually turned philosophical, touching on capitalism and summit meetings.

Soviet Spacecraft Hits Moon

SEPTEMBER 14, 1959

The U.S. fell another step behind in the space race when an unmanned Soviet spacecraft slammed into the moon. The 860-pound craft, which looked like a diver's helmet with spikes sticking out, was the first from Earth to land on the lunar surface. It had taken a day and a half to go from a secret launch pad to the edge of the Sea of Serenity. When Premier Nikita Khrushchev visited Washington the following week, he gave President Dwight D. Eisenhower a replica of the Soviet pennant it carried.

Soviets Down U.S. Spy Plane

MAY 6, 1960

American spy planes had flown high over the Soviet Union since the mid-1950s—so high, at up to 70,000 feet that they were untouchable. Or so Washington believed, until a new-generation Soviet missile struck the U-2 piloted by Francis Gary Powers over a Soviet industrial center in the Urals. Washington initially denied that Powers had been on an espionage mission, but Moscow countered that he had confessed. The Soviets threw Powers in prison, but freed him two years later in exchange for a Soviet spy who had been caught in the U.S. Powers became a traffic-helicopter pilot for a Los Angeles television station. He was killed in a midair collision in 1977.

"All the News That's Fit to Print"

The New York Times.

LATE CITY EDITION
Fair, little temperature change today. Mostly fair tomorrow.
Temperature Range Today-Max., 42; Min., 29
Temperatures Yesterday—Max., 44; Min., 33
Full U. S. Weather Bureau Report, Page 47

VOL. CII..No. 34,740. Entered as Second-Class Matter. Post Office, New York, N. Y. NEW YORK, FRIDAY, MARCH 6, 1953. Times Square, New York 36, N. Y. Telephone LAckawanna 4-1000 FIVE CENTS

STALIN DIES AFTER 29-YEAR RULE; HIS SUCCESSOR NOT ANNOUNCED; U.S. WATCHFUL, EISENHOWER SAYS

WORST CITY CRISIS SINCE 1933 IS SEEN IN STATE TAX PLAN

Moore and McGovern Demand Payroll Levy and Transit Unit Mandated to Raise Fares

MAYOR CALLS DEMOCRATS

Estimate Board to Get Report on Views of County Leaders —Bus Reduction Directed

By PAUL CROWELL

The city Government is facing the most serious financial and political crisis to confront any Administration since 1933, when leading banking houses rescued a Democratic regime from fiscal disaster.

This was the consensus last night of top city officials to whom Lieut. Gov. Frank C. Moore and State Controller J. Raymond McGovern had indicated earlier in the day that a sound fiscal program for 1953-54 and succeeding years should include both a city payroll tax and a transit authority with a duty to increase fares to meet operating deficits of the municipal lines.

That the city Administration realized the political dangers inherent in the adoption of the suggested fiscal program was indicated later in the day when Mayor Impellitteri, without consulting the Board of Estimate, asked the five Democratic county leaders to confer with him at noon today at City Hall. Among those invited was Tammany leader Carmine G. DeSapio, the only member of the group who is at loggerheads with the Mayor on matters of patronage.

Leaders' Views Important

After a two-hour conference with Mr. Moore and Mr. McGovern at Mr. McGovern's office, 270 Broadway, the Mayor and Board of Estimate held an even longer closed meeting at City Hall, which will be resumed at 3 o'clock this afternoon. At today's session an important factor will be the attitude of the five Democratic county leaders, as reported by the Mayor, toward the proposals upon which the two state officials apparently are insisting.

In another municipal development, the Mayor's Transit Advisory Commission demanded that the eight privately owned bus companies involved in the recent bus strike and Michael J. Quill's Transport Workers Union, C. I. O., take immediate steps to wipe out excess bus lines and to reduce the number of buses on lines that were needed. City tax relief was made dependent on such action.

The conference with Mr. Moore and Mr. McGovern was a continuation of last Monday's talks at Albany on the city's $218,700,000 fiscal program, which in effect already had been rejected by the two state officials in their joint memorandum of Feb. 22.

At the outset of the meeting the

Continued on Page 19, Column 1

Eisenhower Plans to Pare Policy-Level Civil Service

Directive Will Repeal 2 That Truman Issued Anchoring Some Democrats in Their Jobs —Organization of Administration Object

By PAUL P. KENNEDY
Special to THE NEW YORK TIMES.

WASHINGTON, March 5—Several hundred persons face the possibility of losing Civil Service status and probably their Government jobs under an Executive Order to be issued by President Eisenhower next week.

In announcing the forthcoming order, James C. Hagerty, White House press secretary, said that all those affected would not necessarily lose their jobs. The announcement was generally interpreted, however, to mean that the Administration was preparing to clear out holdover Democrats in high policy-making and administrative positions in order to replace them with personnel of the Administration's own choosing.

President Eisenhower's order, which he directed to be drafted immediately, will repeal two Executive Orders of former President Truman in 1947 and 1948 in which certain persons on Schedule A of Civil Service rules would receive Civil Service protection against separation from the Government.

The President's order will emphasize that the rights of veterans, specified in the Veterans Preference Act of 1944 would be respected.

Schedule A is a list of positions to which appointments may be made without reference to Civil Service rules or regulations. The appointees may assume their positions without Civil Service examinations and their classifications are not subject to review by Civil Service Boards.

Mr. Hagerty said the "several hundred" persons to be affected by the order were employed in all departments and agencies of the Government. The order, he said, applied to people who had been put under Civil Service in the last twenty years.

The new Administration, since coming into office Jan. 20, Mr.

Continued on Page 15, Column 2

President May Take a Hand If Inquiries Imperil Amity

By C. P. TRUSSELL
Special to THE NEW YORK TIMES.

WASHINGTON, March 5—President Eisenhower indicated today that if the Senate investigation into the Voice of America, being conducted by Senator Joseph R. McCarthy, or other Congressional inquiries, reached a point of inviting international misunderstandings and difficulties he might intervene.

This, he emphasized at a news conference, would mean that he would have to desert his long-held conviction that the Congress had an inherent right to investigate as it pleased. He was still hoping, he said, to avoid a situation in which a spokesman for the Executive Branch of the Government would have to take issue with actions of the coordinate Legislative Branch.

The question that prompted these responses was based upon the hearings being conducted, largely before television, by the Judiciary subcommittee headed by Senator McCarthy, Republican of Wisconsin.

The group is inquiring into the management and personnel of the Voice, the Government's radio program for telling the story of America. Broadcasts are beamed to eighty-seven countries in nearly forty languages.

At yesterday's hearing Reed Harris, deputy director of the State

Continued on Page 14, Column 6

EISENHOWER PRAISES RESTRAINT IN PRICES

Asserts There Has Been Little Evidence of Gouging—More Controls Are Removed

By CHARLES E. EGAN
Special to THE NEW YORK TIMES.

WASHINGTON, March 5—President Eisenhower today complimented business for what he termed the admirable restraint it had shown in pricing policies since the removal of most price controls.

General Eisenhower said at his news conference that since the program of removing major segments of the economy from price regulation got under way Feb. 6, there had been little discernible evidence of attempts to gouge consumers.

The President's observations came immediately before an announcement from the Office of Price Stabilization that it had removed price ceilings on another wide range of items, including bread and bakery products, new and used cars, major household appliances, dry cleaning and diaper services.

Hopes for a New Climate

Another development was a Senate committee hearing at which Charles R. Sligh Jr., president of the National Association of Manufacturers, attacked proposals to establish stand-by controls authority. With such authority, the President could declare a ninety-day "freeze" of all prices and wages in event of all-out war or other critical emergency.

About the only major price increase that has occurred since the Office of Price Stabilization began implementing his orders for relaxation of price ceilings, the President said, has been an expected rise of 6 to 7 cents a pound in copper.

The absence of price gouging, the President added, confirms his belief that the American people are ready to be considerate and moderate. He added that he hoped a climate might be established—in labor-management relations, for instance—that would minimize harmful pressures on the economy

Continued on Page 15, Column 3

F.B.I. Agents Depict Rebuff by Monaghan

By LUTHER A. HUSTON
Special to THE NEW YORK TIMES

WASHINGTON, March 5—Leland V. Boardman, special agent in charge of the New York office of the Federal Bureau of Investigation, asserted today that Police Commissioner George P. Monaghan had notified him that he would not make New York City policemen available to any Federal law enforcement agency for questioning and that they would respond only to summonses from a Federal grand jury.

This policy, Mr. Boardman said, was founded upon a purported agreement between the New York Police Department and the Criminal Division of the Department of Justice to block out F. B. I. investigators from cases involving police brutality in civil rights cases.

Another agent quoted Commis-

Continued on Page 16, Column 2

VISHINSKY LEAVING

Foreign Minister Called to Moscow to Report —Will Sail Today

U. N. TO LOWER FLAG

Lie Praises Premier as Statesman—Pearson Hails Fight on Nazis

By THOMAS J. HAMILTON
Special to THE NEW YORK TIMES.

UNITED NATIONS, N. Y., March 5—Soviet Foreign Minister Andrei Y. Vishinsky, who was reported to have been informed of the death of Premier Stalin before the public announcement by the Moscow radio, plans to leave for Moscow tomorrow.

Mr. Vishinsky and a party of Soviet officials are scheduled to sail aboard the French liner Liberté tomorrow at 4 P. M. Plans for the sailing were disclosed at Police Headquarters. The police said they had been informed that the party would travel in seven automobiles from Glen Cove, L. I., where the Soviet delegation to the United Nations has headquarters, to Pier 88, Hudson River at Forty-eighth Street. The liner will call at Plymouth and Le Havre.

Mr. Vishinsky has a heart condition and therefore avoids air travel whenever possible.

Valerian A. Zorin, Soviet representative to the United Nations, revealed this afternoon Mr. Vishinsky's plans to leave tomorrow. Mr. Vishinsky's decision was taken after he had received a telephone call from Moscow earlier in the day.

Disclosure by Consulate

There was no indication whether this telephone call had given any indication of Mr. Stalin's death. The news that Mr. Vishinsky had been informed prior to the public announcement came from a telephone inquiry at the Soviet Consulate at 680 Park Avenue.

Earlier inquiries at the headquarters of the Soviet delegation to the United Nations had brought repeated denials that Mr. Vishinsky was there. The consulate revealed, however, not only that Mr. Vishinsky was actually at the delegation headquarters but also that he had been informed of the news earlier.

According to United Nations protocol, the only flag that will fly at the United Nations flagpole tomorrow is the banner of the United Nations itself, and it will be at half-staff. The same procedure will be followed during the day of the funeral of Premier Stalin.

Informed of the death of Mr.

Continued on Page 13, Column 2

CONDOLENCES SENT

President Orders Terse Formal Note on Stalin Dispatched to Soviet

TRIBUTE IS OMITTED

Eisenhower Still Ready to Confer on Peace With the Kremlin

By JAMES RESTON
Special to THE NEW YORK TIMES.

WASHINGTON, March 5—President Eisenhower authorized John Foster Dulles, Secretary of State, tonight to send the United States' "official condolences" to the Soviet Government on the death of Premier Stalin.

Earlier the President had told reporters at his press conference that he could not tell what effect the illness of the Premier would have on the "cold war." A definite watchfulness is our policy for the moment, the President added.

The President announced the statement of condolences less than an hour after he had been informed of Mr. Stalin's death by James C. Hagerty, press secretary, at 8:25 P. M. The statement was as follows:

> The President authorized the Secretary of State to send the following message to the American Embassy in Moscow: The Government of the United States tenders its official condolences to the Government of the Union of Socialist Soviet Republics on the death of Generalissimo Joseph Stalin, Prime Minister of the Soviet Union.

Dulles Informed by Hagerty

Mr. Hagerty notified Mr. Dulles, who was a guest at the British Embassy, immediately after the President had been informed.

The press secretary said the President's message would be transmitted to the Soviet Government by Jacob D. Beam, Chargé d'Affaires in Moscow.

The terse wording of the message was noted here, especially the phrase "official condolences." Diplomatic circles suggested that the wording was about as brief and formal as possible under diplomatic protocol.

They recalled, however, that the President previously had expressed condolences. In the first White House statement issued after word had been received of the serious illness of Mr. Stalin, General Eisenhower directed his words to the Soviet people rather than the Premier or the Government.

Indications were that the President's official condolences would stand in so far as the Government

Continued on Page 12, Column 5

PREMIER JOSEPH STALIN
A portrait released by Sovfoto, Soviet picture agency

Soviet Fear of an Eruption Discerned in Call for Unity

By HARRY SCHWARTZ

The fact that appeals for "monolithic unity" and "vigilance" have now become the main theme of Soviet domestic propaganda appears to be a clear indication that the present Soviet rulers fear Premier Stalin's death may result in an explosive resolution of the major tensions now repressed in the Soviet Union.

The unity theme dominates the official announcement of Stalin's death. It was first voiced in the initial communiqué regarding Stalin's illness issued by the highest Government and Communist party authorities. Unity and vigilance were the central ideas in the long leading editorials that appeared yesterday morning on the front pages of both Pravda and Izvestia.

Yesterday's Pravda editorial may also have given the first hint that Georgi M. Malenkov is leading in the succession race, but this hint seemed far from conclusive. The editorial mentioned by name only Lenin, Premier Stalin, and Mr. Malenkov, quoting the latter's speech last October when he said, "The prospects and ways of our progress are based on the laws of the national economy, on the science of the Communist social structure which have been evolved by Comrade Stalin."

The fact that Moscow has announced that Nikita S. Khrushchev will head the committee preparing

Continued on Page 12, Column 2

AMMUNITION SHORT, VAN FLEET ASSERTS

He Affirms Scarcity in Korea and Byrd Writes to Wilson Demanding Explanation

By HAROLD B. HINTON
Special to THE NEW YORK TIMES.

WASHINGTON, March 5—Gen. James A. Van Fleet, former Commander of United Nations ground forces in Korea, told the Senate Armed Services Committee today that he had been handicapped during the entire twenty-two months he had had the command by shortages of ammunition and manpower. He specified hand grenades, and mentioned "other types" of ammunition as having been seriously short all the time and critically short on occasions.

The apparent contradiction of the General's testimony today with that of yesterday, in which he indicated there were no serious shortages of anything in Korea, was unexplained, except for the interpretation that yesterday he had been speaking for the present, whereas today he had been speaking for the past.

Praised by Symington

So much the general said before a public meeting of the committee. Senator Stuart Symington, Democrat of Missouri and former Secretary of the Air Force, praised General Van Fleet for his intelligence and courage in reporting these matters to the public. If other military figures would emulate the example, he declared, "we won't send our youth out to fight with these shortages, even if we have fewer television sets."

[In the Korean war action, Air Force Thunderjet fighter-bombers made a record 1,000-mile raid on a Communist industrial center on the northeast coast sixty miles from Siberia. Navy carrier bombers made heavy attacks in North Korea. Ground action was light.]

In a later closed session with the committee, General Van Fleet apparently amplified his discussion of the shortages. The amplification prompted Senator Harry F. Byrd, Democrat of Virginia, to write a letter to Charles E. Wil-

Continued on Page 2, Column 6

PREMIER ILL 4 DAYS

Announcement of Death Made by Top Soviet and Party Chiefs

STROKE PROVES FATAL

Leaders Issue an Appeal to People for Unity and Vigilance

Text of official announcement of Stalin's death, Page 8.

By HARRISON E. SALISBURY
Special to THE NEW YORK TIMES.

MOSCOW, Friday, March 6—Premier Joseph Stalin died at 9:50 P. M. yesterday [1:50 P. M. Thursday, Eastern standard time] in the Kremlin at the age of 73, it was announced officially this morning. He had been in power twenty-nine years.

The announcement was made in the name of the Central Committee of the Communist party, the Council of Ministers and the Presidium of the Supreme Soviet.

Calling on the Soviet people to rally firmly around the party and the Government, the announcement asked them to display unity and the highest political vigilance "in the struggle against internal and external foes." [No announcement was made of a successor to Premier Stalin.]

The Soviet leader's death from general circulatory and respiratory deficiency occurred just short of four days after he had been stricken with a brain hemorrhage in his Kremlin apartment.

Accompanying the death announcement was a final medical certificate issued by a group of ten physicians, headed by Health Minister A. F. Tretyakov, who cared for Mr. Stalin in his last illness under the direct and closest supervision of the Central Committee and the Council of Ministers.

Pulse Rate Was High

The medical certificate revealed that in the last hours Mr. Stalin's condition grew worse rapidly, with repeated heavy and sharp circulatory and heart collapses. His breathing grew superficial and sharply irregular. His pulse rate rose to 140 to 150 a minute and at 9:50 P. M., "because of a growing circulatory and respiratory insufficiency, J. V. Stalin died."

[The news of Mr. Stalin's death was withheld by Soviet officials for more than six hours.]

Pravda appeared this morning with broad black borders around its front page, which was devoted entirely to Mr. Stalin. The layout included a large photograph of the Premier, the announcement by the Government, the medical bulletins and the announcement of the formation of a funeral commission

Continued on Page 8, Column 2

Treaties Manifesto Shelved in Congress

By WILLIAM S. WHITE
Special to THE NEW YORK TIMES.

WASHINGTON, March 5—President Eisenhower's proposed United States declaration against "perversion" of the wartime Yalta and Potsdam agreements into instruments for enslaving peoples was put on the shelf in Congress today.

The announced Congressional reason was that the manifesto would be inopportune now in view of Premier Stalin's fatal illness, though the President himself indicated at his news conference that he thought this need not delay action. The Congressional developments came before the announcement of Mr. Stalin's death.

The Republican leaders in Congress could not take the resolution to the floor of either house

Continued on Page 6, Column 5

Pole Flies to Denmark in First Intact Russian MIG-15 to Reach West

Associated Press Radiophoto

A young Polish pilot seeking political asylum flew this Soviet-made MIG-15 into a Danish airport at Bornholm yesterday, making it the first fighter plane of its type acquired undamaged by the West. Name of pilot (center figure) was withheld.

Special to THE NEW YORK TIMES.

COPENHAGEN, Denmark, March 5—The first intact Russian-built MIG-15 jet fighter—the newest known type of Russian jet fighter—to land west of the Iron Curtain came down this morning at Roenne Airport on the Danish island of Bornholm. It came from a Polish Baltic base.

The 21-year-old Polish lieutenant who fled with the fighter gave himself up to Danish authorities as a political refugee and asked for asylum. Very little is known about his story. Danish authorities are keeping it secret for the time being.

The young Pole performed a fantastic maneuver in landing the jet fighter on the grass-covered airstrip at Roenne, only 1,200 meters (3,937 feet) long. Jet fighters normally require a 3,000-meter (9,843 feet) concrete runway to start and land.

At the farther end of the air-

Continued on Page 3, Column 2

"All the News That's Fit to Print"

The New York Times.

LATE CITY EDITION
Fair with little change in temperature today and tomorrow.
Temperature Range Today—Max., 72; Min., 52
Temperatures Yesterday—Max., 70; Min., 53
Full U. S. Weather Bureau Report, Page 59

VOL. CII..No. 34,828. Entered as Second-Class Matter, Post Office, New York, N. Y. NEW YORK, TUESDAY, JUNE 2, 1953. Times Square, New York 36, N. Y. Telephone LAckawanna 4-1000 FIVE CENTS

2 OF BRITISH TEAM CONQUER EVEREST; QUEEN GETS NEWS AS CORONATION GIFT; THRONGS LINE HER PROCESSION ROUTE

AUTHORITY LEASES CITY TRANSIT LINES; FARE RISE IN SIGHT

Estimate Board Votes, 11-5, for 10-Year Pact Including Terms Asked by Joseph

EFFECTIVE DATE IS JUNE 15

New Agency Seeking Tokens From Mint, Indicating New Charge May Not Be 15c

Digest of lease signed by city and Transit Authority, Page 32.

By LEO EGAN

The Board of Estimate voted 11 to 5 yesterday to lease the city's $1,700,000,000 transit system to the newly created New York City Transit Authority for a period of ten years, during which the authority will be obligated to raise enough revenue from fares and incidental charges to meet operating costs.

By approving the lease, the board made it almost certain that the authority will raise transit fares by July 30 in an amount sufficient to overcome a prospective operating deficit of $47,000,000 for the fiscal year beginning July 1. A first step in this direction was taken by the authority within a few hours after the board acted when it decided to explore the possibility of obtaining from the United States Mint at Philadelphia an emergency supply of tokens, to be used on all three divisions of the rapid transit lines in the collection of a higher fare.

Casey Tells of Token Plans

The decision to request the Federal Government's help in obtaining enough tokens to put a fare change into effect by July 30, the statutory deadline, was announced by Maj. Gen. Hugh J. Casey, authority chairman, after a special authority meeting at the offices of the Board of Transportation, 370 Jay Street, Brooklyn.

Sidney H. Bingham, chairman of the Board of Transportation, will confer with the Director of the Mint at Philadelphia today on the possibility of obtaining 20,000,000 tokens, General Casey said. Subsequent additions to the supply would be obtained from private suppliers, he added.

To speed the negotiations with the Mint, the authority has requested Governor Dewey to intervene with the Secretary of the Treasury, General Casey said.

A design for the token was officially approved by the authority yesterday. It is a perforated coin, somewhat smaller than a dime.

By exploring the possibility of obtaining enough tokens for use on all three divisions, the authority indicated it might reject Mr. Bingham's recommendation for a 15-cent fare in favor of a smaller charge, perhaps 12 or 12½ cents a ride. The present fare is 10 cents.

A major justification for the Bingham recommendation was that it would involve use of tokens on only the I.R.T. division, which has electrically operated turnstiles. On the B.M.T. and IND divisions, which have mechanical turnstiles, two coins—a dime and a nickel—would be used to pay the fare.

General Casey emphasized in announcing the authority action that no decisions on a fare increase had been reached. It will not be possible to arrive at a conclusion, he said, until all pertinent facts are studied.

City Fiscal Problem Eased

The Board of Estimate's decision yesterday automatically relieved the city of the necessity of meeting the prospective operating deficit out of tax revenues in the new fiscal year that starts July 1. It likewise vested the city with power to collect $50,000,000 a year in additional taxes from real estate for general municipal purposes plus, for the next four years, enough to liquidate an accumulated deficit of $39,000,000 in the transit pension system.

Moreover, in accordance with special laws enacted by the Legislature earlier this year on the recommendation of Governor Dewey, transfer of the deficit-ridden transit system to the authority gives the city power at any time in the future to impose a one-half of 1 per cent payroll tax, payable in equal parts by employers and employes, estimated to raise $60,000,000 a year.

The city's budget for the new fiscal year, already approved by the Board of Estimate and City Council, contemplates full use of the additional real estate taxing powers, but no use of the payroll tax.

As had been forecast, Rudolph

Continued on Page 33, Column 2

Eisenhower Moves to Limit State Department to Policy

New Reorganization Plans Would Transfer Present Operating Functions to 2 Special Agencies, Information and Foreign Aid

By ANTHONY LEVIERO
Special to The New York Times.

WASHINGTON, June 1—President Eisenhower proposed today to restore the State Department to its traditional pre-war policy-making role and to transfer virtually all its operating functions to new organizations—the United States Information Agency and the Foreign Operations Administration.

A far-reaching reorganization of the State Department was projected by the President in two plans submitted to Congress today, with a promise of further changes to be sought early next year.

Today he stressed two objectives:

1. To divest the department of the functional tasks that had involved it in political controversy during the post-war era.
2. To make the Secretary of State supreme, next to the President, in the policy supervision of all foreign information and aid programs.

The controversial Voice of America and other information programs would be swept out of the State Department, the Mutual Security Agency and other agencies and concentrated in the new Information Agency. The Mutual Security Agency itself would become the nucleus around which would be built the new Foreign Operations Administration to take over various other programs for technical, economic and military assistance.

Of operating programs, all that would be left in the State Department would be the programs for the educational exchange of persons.

The two new agencies would have administrative autonomy, just as the Mutual Security Agency has today. But a new idea in Government organization was introduced. The directors of the two agencies not only would be subject to close

Continued on Page 24, Column 4

Text of message on propaganda and aid plans, Page 24.

MRS. HOBBY WARNS DOCTORS ON TASKS

Social-Economic Problems in the Field Must Be Solved by A.M.A. or Others, She Says

Mrs. Oveta Culp Hobby, Secretary of Health, Education and Welfare, declared at the annual meeting of the American Medical Association, which opened yesterday, that organized medicine must find solutions to the social-economic problems facing medicine today or the solution would be taken out of its hands. She expressed confidence that the American Medical Association "will meet this challenge."

Addressing the House of Delegates, policy-making body of the association, at the Waldorf-Astoria Hotel, Mrs. Hobby said the social and economic demands on the medical profession "are only the continuing challenge in this long history of constant adaptation to a changing society, but never have these problems been more onerous and critical than today."

The association opened its 102d annual meeting yesterday. For five days progress in all branches of medicine will be reviewed in 400 reports by leaders in their fields.

The sessions are being held in seven hotels and in Town Hall while 635 scientific and technical exhibits are being displayed on four floors of Grand Central Palace. The exhibits are open only to doctors and their guests.

Mrs. Hobby in her speech to the delegates said she agreed fully

Continued on Page 26, Column 5

HUMPHREY OPPOSES REVENUE LOSS NOW

He Calls Cut Gamble With U.S. Security—Asks House Unit to Extend Excess Profit Tax

By JOHN D. MORRIS
Special to The New York Times.

WASHINGTON, June 1—George M. Humphrey, Secretary of the Treasury, told Congress today that only "full mobilization" would justify tax increases to produce any more revenue than the Administration was now seeking.

The Government's chief fiscal officer so testified in opening the Administration's case before the House Ways and Means Committee for a six-month extension of the excess profits tax and the cancellation of automatic cuts in regular corporation and excise (sales) levies slated for next April 1.

The Administration, he said, wants those three phases of its tax program carried out in a single bill this year, though the committee has limited its present deliberations to extension of the excess profits law, which is due to expire June 30.

The Secretary asserted that losses in Federal revenue now would be an unsafe gamble with the country's security.

Mr. Humphrey also made the following points:

¶ That he was "very strongly opposed" to any change in the excess profits tax during the extension period.

¶ That he would fight any continuation of the levy beyond Dec. 31.

¶ That tax relief starting next

Continued on Page 47, Column 2

Harvard Elects Dr. N. M. Pusey, Midwest Educator, as President

Lawrence College Head, 46, Has 3 Degrees From University—Favors Humanities Study

By JOHN H. FENTON
Special to The New York Times.

CAMBRIDGE, Mass., June 1—Dr. Nathan Marsh Pusey, president of Lawrence College in Appleton, Wis., was elected the twenty-fourth president of Harvard University today by the Harvard Corporation today.

Dr. Pusey, who is a native of Council Bluffs, Iowa, and 46 years old, is a scholar in Greek history, and holds three degrees from Harvard: Bachelor of Arts, magna cum laude, 1928; Master of Arts, 1932, and Doctor of Philosophy, 1937. He prepared for college at Abraham Lincoln High School in Council Bluffs.

The Iowa educator will succeed Dr. James Bryant Conant, who will become president-emeritus of Harvard University on Sept. 1. Dr. Conant, now on leave, is serving as United States High Commissioner for Germany.

Dr. Pusey's election by the Harvard Corporation is subject to the confirmation of the Board of Overseers. This confirmation, customarily a formality, is scheduled to be voted on June 10, the day before the Harvard commencement. On only one occasion, in 1868, have the overseers refused the corporation permission to elect a president.

Associated Press
Dr. Nathan M. Pusey

The occasion of the only refusal was in the election of Dr. Charles W. Eliot, the original choice of the corporation, as the twenty-first president. The corporation prevailed after a delay of six months, and Dr. Eliot became president in 1869.

Dr. Pusey, reached by telephone at Appleton, said that he considered the corporation's action "a tremendous honor." But he de-

Continued on Page 27, Column 5

RHEE BOWS TO U.S.; SAYS KOREA AGREES TO EISENHOWER AIMS

Statement on Message From Washington Hints Opposition to Truce Plans Is Easing

By The Associated Press.

SEOUL, Korea, June 2—President Syngman Rhee disclosed today he had received a three-point message from President Eisenhower, and added: "We must accept anything that the United States President wants."

"Common sense and wisdom require that we cooperate with the United States at any cost," Dr. Rhee said, without saying what President Eisenhower had told him.

The statement of the 78-year-old leader of the Republic of Korea indicated that South Korean opposition to the secret proposal by the United Nations Command for bringing an armistice in Korea was lessening.

Dr. Rhee also said he was looking for some one to take the place of Maj. Gen. Choi Duk Shin as the South Korean delegate on the United Nations armistice negotiation team.

Dr. Rhee declined to elaborate on his apparently conciliatory statement. He spoke to correspondents at a parade of the British Commonwealth Division honoring the Coronation of Elizabeth II.

Nor did he make it precisely clear whether he was ready now to accept the Allied truce proposal, to which he and his Government had expressed vigorous opposition.

South Korea's acting Premier, Pyun Yun Tae, threatened yesterday a break with the Allies and a go-it-alone policy for South Korea but deferred action until after next Thursday's critical truce session.

The Communists are expected to reply to the Allied proposal at Thursday's meeting.

Rhee Said to Seek Treaty

By JAY WALZ
Special to The New York Times.

WASHINGTON, June 1—The Eisenhower Administration was reported today to have had a new request from President Syngman Rhee of South Korea for the pledge of a mutual defense pact and of military and economic help as a basis for the Seoul Government's support of present Allied truce proposals.

These conditions were said on good authority to be important features of a four-point program outlined in a letter forwarded to President Eisenhower through Ellis O. Briggs, United States Ambassador at Seoul.

The principal point in the still-secret United Nations proposal to the Communists for disposition of Korean war prisoners who refuse to return home was understood to be that final determination of the captives' fate would be up to the General Assembly of the United Nations.

Officially, the White House and State Department were silent on developments on Korea, and offered "no comment" even on reports that a letter from President Rhee might have been received.

Had Asked Pledge in Writing

The South Korean request for a mutual defense pact with the United States is not new. Dr. You Chan Yang, the Korean Ambassador here, has made repeated representations to the State Department for such a pledge of defense help in the event of future Communist aggression.

He has made the point that, while President Eisenhower has said publicly that the United States will never desert Korea, it would be more satisfying from the Korean standpoint to have "something down in black and white."

President Rhee's four points were reported to be (1) a pledge to sign a mutual defense pact with Korea; (2) a promise by the United States to provide military and financial help to Korea on a large scale; (3) withdrawal of all foreign troops on both sides as soon as a truce has started and prisoners have been exchanged, and (4) agreement that the United States would not stand in the way of South Korea in efforts to unite that country at some future time.

As far as the last point is concerned, sources felt South Korea did not have in mind the use of military force to bring together North and South Korea.

Meanwhile, some Capitol Hill leaders spoke out on recent Korean developments.

Senator William F. Knowland of California, who is chairman of the Senate Republican Policy Committee, said the United States should "risk" war with Russia to expand the fighting, if truce negotiations with the Communists collapsed at [illegible]

In anoth[illegible] Senator H. Alexand[illegible] Republican of New Je[illegible] he thought

Continued [illegible] Column 5

CROWDS DEFY RAIN

Face a Day of Showers After All-Night Vigil to Hail Their Sovereign

By RAYMOND DANIELL
Special to The New York Times.

LONDON, Tuesday, June 2—This is the day that all London, all Britain, all the Commonwealth and half the world have been awaiting. It is the day on which the crown of her forefathers is placed upon the head of this old country's radiantly lovely young Queen Elizabeth II whose reign, it is hoped, will usher in another golden age.

The weather for the day was uncertain. By early morning the wind still blew, but rains that fell during the night had ceased, at least temporarily. The weather forecaster, however, was not optimistic about the prospects for the day, which was chosen originally because rain had not fallen on June 2 for many years. The forecast was for cool weather and showers, with sunny intervals.

Last night's gusts and rain discomfited the hundreds of thousands of persons who squatted the whole length of the royal way but if these hardships dislodged any it was unnoticeable because there were others waiting to take their places.

Some of these squatters, lacking reserved seats in the stands to accommodate 250,000 persons, began staking out their claims as early as midnight Sunday.

Squatters Sit on Curbs

By noon yesterday they were sitting on the curbs at Trafalgar Square and were packed two and three deep on the sidewalks along the Mall leading from Admiralty Arch to Buckingham Palace. By dinner time last night the East Carriage Drive in Hyde Park was filled with men, women and even young children with raincoats, blankets, lunch baskets and inflatable mattresses prepared to defend their little vantage points until the Queen's ornate gilded coach, with its eight gray horses, one named Eisenhower, had passed late in the afternoon.

During the day Queen Mother Elizabeth, accompanied by Princess Margaret, visited the palace to see the Queen on the eve of her coronation. By the time they left, an hour later, the crowd outside Buckingham Palace numbered nearly 50,000. The police, who had let the crowd swarm over the roadway, had to make strenuous efforts to clear a path for their car.

Later Princess Margaret made a visit to Westminster Abbey, where she was received by the Earl Marshal. Again the police had trouble clearing a way for her to return home.

Even Oxford Street, that busy shopping center, was taken over by sidewalk squatters almost as soon as the big stores closed. Trafalgar Square, through which the Queen will pass three times on her way from Buckingham Palace to Westminster Abbey, out again and back to the palace, was filled with curbstone sitters even at midday. Some of them had been there twelve hours then with an additional twenty-four in front of them.

The litter they made of sodden

Continued on Page 8, Column 1

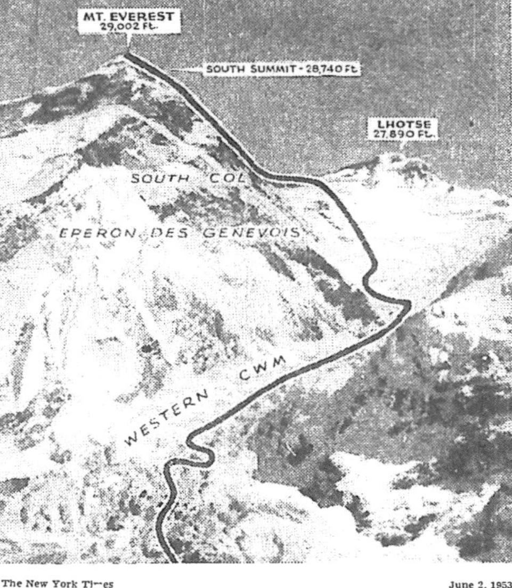

The New York Times June 2, 1953
AT THE TOP: Solid black line shows route of British expedition, the first to reach Mount Everest's summit.

HIGHEST PEAK WON

New Zealander and a Guide Made the Final Climb to Top Friday

By Reuters.

KATMANDU, Nepal, Tuesday, June 2—The British expedition has conquered Mount Everest, a radio message flashed from Namche Bazar to the British Embassy here said today.

The message said Edmond Hillary, a New Zealand beekeeper and mountaineer, and Tensing Norkay, the famous Sherpa guide, had reached the hitherto unscaled summit from Camp Eight last Friday.

The news of this success had to be rushed by runner from the British expedition's base camp on Khumbu Glacier to the radio post at Namche Bazar.

It is understood here that this was the expedition's third attack on the last slopes leading to the summit, a first double attempt having failed.

Experts here said the success was largely due to the fine weather, combined with properly acclimatized climbers and the excellent organization and leadership of Col. H. C. J. Hunt.

Full details of the exploit are not expected to reach here for some days.

It is believed here that the news was transmitted specially to London by diplomatic channels so Queen Elizabeth could be told.

Queen Told at Palace

LONDON, Tuesday, June 2 (Reuters)—The Times of London reported the news of the scaling of Mount Everest in a copyrighted message today.

The news was published in a special edition of The Times on early sale among coronation crowds in London.

Queen Elizabeth, resting at Buckingham Palace, was told on the eve of her coronation that the British expedition had conquered the mountain. The news was brought to her as she spent a quiet evening "at home." The British climbers had succeeded in their plan to give her a world-shaking coronation present.

Mount Everest, the 29,002-foot giant, was the last main outpost of the world unknown to man.

The thirteen members of the expedition formed the eleventh team to try to conquer the mountain in the past thirty years. Many climbers have died in the high ice and snow of the Himalaya giant.

The Sherpa guide, Tensing Norkay, is a 42-year-old native veteran of more assaults on Mount Everest than any other man.

With 362 porters, twenty Sherpa guides and 10,000 pounds of baggage the expedition left the Nepalese base of Katmandu on March 10. Thus it took eighty days from start to finish.

The climbers carried three flags—the Union Jack, the United Nations flag and the Nepalese flag—to plant on the summit.

They made an approach to the "Goddess Mother of the Snows" from the south, or Nepalese, side.

It was the route reconnoitered by Sir Eric Shipton, who led a British

Continued on Page 14, Column 7

Abbey, Bedecked and Aglow, Awaits the Coronation Hour

By TANIA LONG
Special to The New York Times.

LONDON, Tuesday, June 2—As one enters Westminster Abbey, where Elizabeth II is to be crowned in a few hours, a magnificent scene greets the eye. The austere gray interior has been converted into a rich and glowing setting for the young Queen's coronation. Carpeting and hangings in warm tones of blue and gold, banners of white embroidered with the royal coats of arms, and the deep rose of the throne and the royal chairs blend into a splendid symphony of color.

In the pale light of early morning a hush lies over the Abbey. Only a few of the great assemblage of 7,000 guests have arrived, and there is little movement in the vast edifice.

From the great west door, where the Queen will enter, a thick carpet of deep azure blue reaches through the nave to the choir stalls. Hangings of blue silk with royal emblems embroidered in gold are draped over the edges of the stands and balconies, giving warmth to the gray fabric of the church.

From the choir to the altar in that area known as the Coronation Theatre the floor is covered in rich gold pile, against which the deep rose-covered throne and chairs, and the opulent blue hangings on the walls stand out in sharp contrast.

Under a huge chandelier in the center of the Coronation Theatre and raised on a dais stands the throne. Five steps lead up to it. It faces the altar, and because the Queen will be facing away from the majority of the guests, its back is low so that they too may see the Queen's crowned head during the latter part of the ceremony.

The throne chair is late seven-

Continued on Page 6, Column 3

DULLES SAYS U.S. AIM IS TO GAIN FRIENDS

Report on Near East-Asian Trip Urges 'Impartial' Approach to Arab-Israeli Dispute

Text of Secretary Dulles' talk about recent trip, Page 4.

Special to The New York Times.

WASHINGTON, June 1—John Foster Dulles, Secretary of State, said tonight that it was the policy of the Eisenhower Administration to develop goodwill among the nations of the Near East and South Asia to thwart the Kremlin's desire to exploit their many differences.

To this end, he urged an "impartial" approach to Israeli-Arab disputes so as to win the support of both sides against the "common threat"—communism. He said the United States must make clear to all nations concerned with independence that the North Atlantic Treaty alliance was in no way related to a desire to help colonial powers keep or win back their colonies.

In a country-wide radio and television report on his twenty-day tour of the Middle East and South Asia, Mr. Dulles urged the strategic importance of that rich and populous area and said its problems could not be ignored without dangerous consequences.

'Primary Purpose' Stressed

The Secretary's half-hour address was carried over the radio and television networks of the American Broadcasting System and by the Du Mont television network, and the National Broadcasting Company radio network rebroadcast it. The Secretary gave a country-by-country account of the trip, on which he was accompanied by Harold E. Stassen, Director for Mutual Security. They made stops all the way from Egypt to Pakistan and India.

Mr. Dulles declared that the "primary purpose" of the trip "was to show friendliness and to develop understanding," and he added: "These people we visited are all proud peoples who have a great tradition and, I believe, a great future."

The Eisenhower Administration, he continued, plans to make "friendship—not fault-finding—the basis of its foreign policy."

Addressing himself to problems of the troubled Holy Land, Mr. Dulles said he had come back to Washington convinced that the Arabs were "more fearful of Zionism than of communism."

On the other hand, he added,

Continued on Page 5, Column 6

Notables File Past Empty Thrones On Way to Offer Homage to Queen

By C. L. SULZBERGER
Special to The New York Times.

LONDON, Tuesday, June 2—At 6 o'clock this morning the most distinguished men in Britain began filing past an empty throne. Within a few brief hours, seated upon it and wearing the heavy crown of St. Edward the Confessor, a young Queen will receive their homage.

For Britain and for her still vast empire, this is a significant moment. A new Elizabethan age of challenge and uncertainty has started.

Westminster Abbey, in its fullest splendor, with gold plate and regalia spread out on the altar, contains two thrones today. The first is that of King Edward I, a gnarled oaken chair having beneath it the Stone of Scone from the Scotland he had conquered.

Upon it the Queen is crowned. From it she will hear the acclaim of her subjects, the distant booming of her cannon and the solemn prayer of her primate, the Archbishop of Canterbury, exhorting:

"God crown you with a crown of glory and righteousness, that, having a right faith and manifold fruit of good works, you may obtain the crown of an everlasting kingdom by the gift of Him whose Kingdom endureth forever. Amen."

Only then, when she is fully consecrated and acclaimed, will the Queen, assisted by her lay and clerical peers, mount the royal throne on its dais.

Since the early dawn crept over the stirring city of London, pushing its light across gray Whitehall and through the soft rose and amber windows of this Holy Church of St. Peter, which is its rightful name, the Abbey has stood ready for one of those great occasions when it nurtures monarchs.

Finely attired lords and ladies are sweeping to their places, bear-

Continued on Page 12, Column 3

Tito Abolishes Rank Of Army Commissar

By JACK RAYMOND
Special to The New York Times.

BELGRADE, Yugoslavia, June 1—President Tito abolished today the system of political commissars in the Yugoslav armed forces, asserting that present conditions no longer required them.

Not mentioned in Marshal Tito's order was the fact that this will undoubtedly make it easier for Yugoslavia to carry on with growing plans for integrating her military establishment with Western defense projects.

"It will be much easier to deal with Yugoslav military leaders now," said a Western military liaison expert here.

The political commissars, who wore uniforms and were equal in rank with military commanders in the Yugoslav Army, were introduced in imitation of Soviet military practice in the early days of partisan warfare against Germany.

Even after the break with the

Continued on Page 18, Column 3

"All the News That's Fit to Print"

The New York Times.

LATE CITY EDITION
Fair and quite warm today. Hot and humid tomorrow.
Temperature Range Today—Max., 89; Min., 66
Temperatures Yesterday—Max., 85; Min., 63
Full U. S. Weather Bureau Report, Page 21

VOL. CII . No. 34,846. Entered as Second-Class Matter. Post Office, New York, N. Y. NEW YORK, SATURDAY, JUNE 20, 1953. Times Square, New York 36, N. Y. Telephone Lackawanna 4-1000 RAG PAPER EDITION SEVENTY-FIVE CENTS

REDS INSIST U.N. RECAPTURE ALL RELEASED PRISONERS; TRUCE TALKS RECESS AGAIN

FOE WRITES CLARK

Questions if Allies Can Control South Korean Leaders and Army

Text of the Communist note to General Clark is on Page 3.

By LINDESAY PARROTT
Special to The New York Times.

TOKYO, Saturday, June 20—Communist armistice delegates at Panmunjom demanded today that the United Nations recapture all 25,000 anti-Communist prisoners of the Korean war released by the order of Dr. Syngman Rhee, South Korean President.

The demand was made in the course of a twenty-five-minute meeting of the full truce delegations called for this morning by the senior Communist truce representative, Lieut Gen. Nam Il of North Korea.

The Communist high command sent a strong protest to Gen. Mark W. Clark, United Nations commander, asserting that the Allies, equally with Dr. Rhee, must bear "serious responsibility" for the incident. The message was signed by the top enemy commanders, Marshal Kim Il Sung, North Korean Premier, and Chinese Gen. Peng Teh-huai.

The Communist protest was an angry one, and it was significant that it was made directly to the Allied commander, not to the truce delegation. Yet it seemed to indicate that the enemy was not prepared to completely end the negotiations for an armistice.

The letter to General Clark repeated many of the old charges of American coercion and duplicity, but did not slam the door to further conversations.

[The Associated Press said that Pyun Yun Tae, Acting South Korean Premier, demanded Saturday in a letter to General Clark that all anti-Communist North Korean prisoners remaining in Allied stockades be turned over to the Republic for immediate release.

[Soon afterward, in Tokyo General Clark's United Nations headquarters made public a scorching letter to the South Korean President, saying General Clark could "not at this time estimate the ultimate consequences" of President Rhee's "precipitous and shocking" release of the 26,000 anti-Communist Korean war captives. General Clark accused Dr. Rhee of breaking a "persona. commitment" not to take action.]

At the armistice conference, the Communists in effect demanded that the Allied command promise to control the fiery South Korean President from acting on his own. Pointedly, the Communists asked:

"Is the United Nations Command able to control the South Korean Government and Army? If not, does the armistice in Korea include the Syngman Rhee clique.

"If it is not included, what assurance is there for implementation of the armistice agreement on the part of South Korea?

"If it is included, then your side must be responsible for recovering immediately all the 25,952 prison-

Continued on Page 3, Column 4

Associated Press Wirephoto via Radio from Tokyo

HIS ATTEMPT TO ESCAPE FAILS: A U. S. Marine, right, escorts a wounded prisoner in the prisoner-of-war camp at Ascom City, near Inchon, where about 500 anti-Communists escaped. Marines and other troops prevented a larger break-out.

U. S. SEES POSITION IN KOREA AS GRAVE

Dulles Meets With Both Parties and Envoys of U. N. Allies in Atmosphere of Urgency

By WILLIAM S. WHITE
Special to The New York Times.

WASHINGTON, June 19—The United States Government worked in haste today to save a Korean truce that some responsible men regarded as all but lost through South Korea's angry defiance of the United Nations.

The position was described authoritatively as grave, since June 25, 1950—the day the Communists invaded the Republic of Korea.

There was hope, however, that if the Communists genuinely wanted peace they would not make capital of the defiance shown by Dr. Syngman Rhee, President of South Korea, to the United States and to its allies in the United Nations force that went to the rescue of his country three years ago.

All the possibilities seemed in the end to narrow to this one, even though there was some speculation that it might be feasible to take some sort of action to replace Dr. Rhee. Senator Walter F. George of Georgia, the senior Democratic member of the Senate Foreign Re-

Continued on Page 2, Column 5

U. N. OFFICERS FELT RHEE WAS BLUFFING

Warnings Unheeded, Prisoner Command Took No Steps to Prevent Mass Escape

By ROBERT ALDEN
Special to The New York Times.

SEOUL, Korea, June 19—The United Nations Command was not prepared for the precipitate action taken by Dr. Syngman Rhee, President of South Korea, in freeing non-Communist prisoners of war.

According to an authoritative source in the Prisoner-of-War Command here, officials in Tokyo had been warned that such a measure might be taken by the Government of the Republic of Korea. However, the Prisoner-of-War Command was assured by higher headquarters that Dr. Rhee was "bluffing."

As a result, South Korean security guards were not replaced by American soldiers and other precautionary measures were insufficient.

However, the freeing of the prisoners came as no surprise to those who have been close to President Rhee these last few weeks. Nor was it a surprise to diplomatic circles in Pusan, the temporary South Korean capital.

They knew how defiant the President's attitude has been from the start, and they regard him as a rather unpredictable individual, apt to go off on a desperate tangent at almost any time.

Some Americans farther away from the scene, however, have had a tendency to underestimate what Dr. Rhee might do and to grasp at any straw that indicated that he was yielding ground in his fight. That was why the repeated threats to free the prisoners on the spot and the ample information available indicating that the South Korean Government was taking concrete steps along these lines were virtually ignored by those in a position to do something about it.

One reason for this reluctance to recognize the facts in the matter is that it is difficult for an American to understand Dr. Rhee's reasoning. The Korean leader feels that to accept a truce agreement as drawn is tantamount to inviting self-destruction.

He is not only worried about the question of complete unification of the country. He has a great fear, for example, of allowing into the country Communist representatives and "pro-Communist" Indian guards.

President Rhee and those close

Continued on Page 3, Column 2

West Asks Soviet to Bar Firearms In Keeping Order in East Berlin

By WALTER SULLIVAN
Special to The New York Times.

BERLIN, June 19—The three Western powers in Berlin urged the Soviet Union today to forbid the use of firearms by its troops and by the East German police in the Soviet sector of the city to prevent further bloodshed.

An announcement said Brig. Gen. Pierre Manceaux-Demiau, French Commandant in Berlin and this month's chairman of the Allied Kommandatura, had made repeated vain attempts to see high Soviet authorities to discuss the problem. It added that finally he had gone to Soviet headquarters in East Berlin to deliver in person a note stating the point of view of the Western Commandants.

Meanwhile, as the eastern part of the city continued to appear quiet, United States authorities delivered Otto Nuschke to Soviet officers. Herr Nuschke, East German Deputy Premier, was forced into the United States sector of Berlin by the rioters Wednesday.

Herr Nuschke, 70 years of age, was questioned thoroughly by both United States and West Berlin officials before being returned to the Soviet sector. According to an official announcement by the United States mission, he was asked whether he wanted political asylum in the West and said no.

The West Berlin police sought to determine whether he could be linked with "a kidnapping." Possibly this referred to the case of Dr. Walter Linse, anti-Communist leader, who was abducted from the United States sector last year.

East Germany's leading Communist newspaper, Neues Deutschland, conceded today that the work stoppages and disorders of the last few days had reached into the remotest corners of that region. It expressed

Continued on Page 4, Column 4

AID BILL APPROVED AS DEMOCRATS SAVE MEASURE IN HOUSE

G.O.P. Split on Cutting Funds, but 280-108 Vote Prevails —4.9 Billion Authorized

By FELIX BELAIR Jr.
Special to The New York Times.

WASHINGTON, June 19—The House of Representatives authorized today an appropriation of $4,998,732,500 for military, economic and technical aid to fifty-six free governments and dependencies resisting communism. The vote sending the measure to the Senate was 280 to 108, with one Representative merely voting "present."

Throughout the afternoon, a smoothly functioning bipartisan majority shouldered down repeated attempts to cut the authorization items below the recommendations of the Foreign Affairs Committee. But it was the Democrats under Representative Sam Rayburn of Texas, the minority leader, who provided the margin of victory.

Republicans by the score deserted the leadership of Speaker Joseph W. Martin Jr. to vote for economy amendments. There was no record vote on any of the attempts to slash the measure and, although the foreign policy prestige of President Eisenhower had been thrown into the debate by the Republican leadership, it was the Democrats who gave him his vote of confidence.

On the final vote, 160 Democrats joined with 119 Republicans and an Independent, Frazier Reams of Ohio, to provide the 280 majority for the bill. A total of eighty-one Republicans and twenty-seven Democrats voted against the measure. Representative Harold A. Patten, Democrat of Arizona, was the one who voted "present."

Members Rally to Vote

The high tide of opposition to the authorization—which is $476,000,000 less than the Administration had requested—came shortly before the final vote. Representative Hamer H. Budge, Republican of Idaho, offered an amendment to cut all the items by 10 per cent, but it was rejected by a standing vote of 152 to 101.

The same amendment had lost by a narrower margin a few minutes earlier when, on a count, the vote was put at 133 to 102. But when a vote by tellers was demanded, members burst from the cloakrooms on either side of the House to provide the extra votes.

An even earlier attempt to accomplish the same result and cut the authorization by $498,000,000 was made when Representative William M. Colmer, Democrat of Mississippi, sought to place a ceiling on the total authorization of $4,500,000,000. This move was rejected, 104 to 83.

The pattern of unrecorded voting on the amendments had been set shortly after the House met for business an hour before noon.

Representative Lawrence Smith, Republican of Wisconsin, proposed to cut $329,186,000 from the section providing military aid to Western Europe. The amendment would have eliminated military aid totaling $216,906,000 for Yugo-

Continued on Page 18, Column 4

ROSENBERGS EXECUTED AS ATOM SPIES AFTER SUPREME COURT VACATES STAY; LAST-MINUTE PLEA TO PRESIDENT FAILS

SIX JUSTICES AGREE

President Says Couple Increased 'Chances of Atomic War'

Texts of related documents in case are printed on Page 7.

By LUTHER A. HUSTON
Special to The New York Times.

WASHINGTON, June 19—President Eisenhower and the Supreme Court refused today to save Julius and Ethel Rosenberg from death in the electric chair.

The high court vacated the stay granted to the atomic spies on Wednesday by Justice William O. Douglas. It upheld the legality of the death sentence imposed by Federal Judge Irving R. Kaufman.

Less than an hour after the court had announced its verdict, President Eisenhower refused Executive clemency for the second time. He had denied a similar petition on Feb. 11.

"I can only say that, by immeasurably increasing the chances of atomic war, the Rosenbergs may have condemned to death tens of millions of innocent people all over the world," the President said. "The execution of two human beings is a grave matter. But even graver is the thought of the millions of dead whose deaths may be directly attributable to what these spies have done."

He was convinced, the President said, that the Rosenbergs had received "the fullest measure of justice and due process of law."

"When in their most solemn judgment the tribunals of the United States have adjudged them guilty and the sentence just, I will not intervene in this matter," the President declared.

Vinson Reads Court's Ruling

The prevailing opinion setting aside Justice Douglas' stay of execution was read by Chief Justice Fred M. Vinson and was concurred in by Associate Justices Stanley F. Reed, Robert H. Jackson, Harold H. Burton, Sherman Minton and Tom C. Clark.

Justices Douglas and Hugo L. Black dissented. Justice Felix Frankfurter announced neither a concurrence nor a dissent. In a brief separate opinion he said the questions raised were "complicated and novel" and that he felt the application of the Attorney General for revocation of the stay should not be disposed of until more time had been afforded for study and argument. He promised to set forth more specifically in due course the ground for this position.

Also read from the bench were a concurring opinion by Justice Clark, in which he was joined by Justices Vinson, Reed, Jackson, Burton and Minton, and a concurring opinion by Justice Jackson.

Continued on Page 8, Column 5

Their Death Penalty Carried Out

Julius Rosenberg — Ethel Rosenberg
Associated Press

Eisenhower Is Denounced To 5,000 in Union Sq. Rally

Sympathizers of Julius and Ethel Rosenberg bombarded judges with new appeals last night and staged rallies in a desperate last-minute flurry of efforts to save the condemned atom spies from the electric chair.

As time ran out for the doomed couple, lawyers and sympathizers tried every avenue of appeal and protest in a feverish evening that included:

¶An order by Police Commissioner George P. Monaghan to all police commands to maintain a special city-wide vigil against any disorder or violence in connection with the execution.

¶Three separate appeals to Federal Judge Irving R. Kaufman, who sentenced the Rosenbergs, to stay their execution. He rejected all.

¶Two separate appeals to two Federal Circuit Court judges to grant a stay. These also were denied.

¶A rally by an estimated 5,000 persons in Seventeenth Street, west of the north end of Union Square, where members of the New York Clemency Committee of the National Committee to Secure Justice in the Rosenberg Case denounced President Eisenhower as "bloodthirsty."

Final Pleas to Kaufman

Judge Kaufman, for whom the police ordered a reinforced fifteen-man guard at his Park Avenue apartment, was importuned by attorneys making frantic new legal maneuvers to save the Rosenbergs.

Daniel C. Marshall, a Los Angeles lawyer who had pleaded with the Supreme Court for a stay, begged Judge Kaufman to telephone the prison and delay the execution for one hour so that Mr. Marshall could elaborate his argument. But Judge Kaufman refused about twenty minutes before the executions began.

Milton H. Friedman, a lawyer representing the Rosenberg defense counsel, asked Judge Kaufman to stay the scheduled executions on the ground that they would constitute "an outrageous insult to world Jewry" if they were carried out on the Jewish Sabbath. Judge Kaufman rejected the plea, saying he had been assured the executions would not be within the Sabbath period.

Frank Scheiner, another lawyer representing the defense, asked Judge Kaufman to throw out the convictions of the couple on the same grounds argued yesterday before the Supreme Court. Judge Kaufman rejected this motion without any opinion.

Another defense lawyer, Arthur Kinoy, went to New Haven, Conn., in an unsuccessful effort to induce Judges Jerome N. Frank and Thomas W. Swan of the Federal Court of Appeals to block the executions.

'Prayer Meeting' Denunciations

In Seventeenth Street, more than 5,000 persons assembled for "a prayer meeting" for the Rosenbergs heard President Eisenhower denounced as "bloodthirsty."

A speaker at the rally was one who was linked with Attorney General Herbert Brownell Jr., Senator Joseph R. McCarthy, Republican of Wisconsin, and Senator William E. Jenner, Republican of Indiana, in "a plot" to destroy the rights and liberties of the American people.

A premature announcement at 8 P. M. that the Rosenbergs had been put to death created such a wave of hysteria at the

Continued on Page 6, Column 6

7 IN HAWAII GUILTY OF RED CONSPIRACY

Director of Bridges' Union and Six Others Convicted of Violating the Smith Act

Special to The New York Times.

HONOLULU, June 19—A Federal jury today found Jack W. Hall, regional director in Hawaii for the International Longshoremen's and Warehousemen's Union, and six other defendants guilty of a Communist conspiracy to teach and advocate the overthrow of the United States Government by force and violence.

Immediately after the verdict, stevedores halted work on all island docks in the possible forerunner of a general protest strike. The United Press reported. Within two hours after the verdict was announced Hall's union suspended negotiations on a new contract and longshoremen began walking off the job at Castle and Cook Pier 32. By 3:30 P. M., Hawaii time, all Honolulu docks were abandoned and stevedores had walked off the only two ships in the port of Hilo on the island of Hawaii.]

The all-male, multi-racial jury returned its verdict shortly before 1 P. M. Hawaii standard time (7 P. M. Eastern daylight time) after having deliberated for sixteen hours. Six men defendants clad in sports or aloha shirts and one woman heard the verdict read without any show of emotion as they stood behind the defense counsel's table.

A defense request for a poll of the jury revealed that the verdict was unanimous in each case.

The defense attorney, Richard

Continued on Page 5, Column 3

PAIR SILENT TO END

Husband Is First to Die —Both Composed on Going to Chair

By WILLIAM R. CONKLIN
Special to The New York Times.

OSSINING, N. Y., June 19—Stoic and tight-lipped to the end, Julius and Ethel Rosenberg paid the death penalty tonight in the electric chair at Sing Sing Prison for their war-time atomic espionage for Soviet Russia.

The pair, first husband and wife to pay the supreme penalty here, and the first in the United States to die for espionage, went to their deaths with a composure that astonished the witnesses.

Julius, 35 years old, was first to enter the glaringly lighted, white-walled death chamber. He walked slowly behind Rabbi Irving Koslowe, a chaplain at Sing Sing, who was intoning the Twenty-third Psalm, "The Lord is my shepherd, I shall not want." As Rosenberg neared the brown-stained oak chair he seemed to sway from side to side.

Guards quickly placed him in the chair. He was clean-shaven, no longer wearing his mustache, and wore a white T-shirt. At 8:04 o'clock the first shock of 2,000 volts, with its ten amperes, coursed through his body. After two subsequent shocks his life ended at 8:06½ P. M.

Dr. H. W. Kipp and Dr. George McCracken applied stethoscopes to his chest, and Dr. Kipp said:

"I pronounce this man dead."

Wife Kisses Matron

Ethel Rosenberg, the 37-year-old wife, entered the death chamber a few minutes after the body of her husband had been removed. She wore a dark green print dress with white polka dots, and, like her husband, was shod in loafer-type cloth slippers. Her hair was close-cropped on top to permit contact of an electrode.

Just before she reached the chair the five-foot, 100-pound woman held out her hand to Mrs. Helen Evans, a matron. As Mrs. Evans grasped her hand, Mrs. Rosenberg drew her close and kissed her lightly on the cheek. Rabbi Koslowe, standing about ten feet from the chair, was intoning the Fifteenth and Thirty-first Psalms.

Mrs. Evans choked up at the final farewell and left the room quickly. Mrs. Lucy Many, a former matron who is now a prison telephone operator, also shook hands with the doomed woman.

Mrs. Rosenberg sat in the electric chair "with the most composed look you ever saw," one witness said.

She winced a bit as the electrode came in contact with her head, but her arms remained relaxed under their binding straps. Silent, she waited while the guards dropped a leather mask over her face. To her right stood Joseph P. Francel, the state executioner, in an alcove.

The first of three successive shocks was applied at 8:11½ P. M. After the third shock the two doctors applied their stethoscopes and found she was still alive. After two more applications of the cur-

Continued on Page 6, Column 3

4-Day Seamen's Strike Ends As Wage Demands Are Met

By GEORGE HORNE

The four-day-old seamen's strike, which immobilized 125 vessels and threatened to paralyze one-half of the nation's fleet of 1,500 ships, came to an end at 12:45 A. M. today.

National Maritime Union seamen, who struck on Tuesday when the operators refused to accede to wage demands, signed with the dry-cargo shipping employers at the headquarters of the Federal Mediation and Conciliation Service. The union won its demands on winning wage rises ranging from 2 to 6 per cent. The settlement terms constituted a complete capitulation by the operators.

A few minutes earlier, the striking American Radio Association, also an affiliate of the Congress for Industrial Organizations, signed for a 6 per cent wage increase with a group of tanker operators.

Surrender of the employers in both cases had been foretold earlier in the day when a group of leading tanker operators submitted to the demands of the N. M. U. on the basis of similar wage rises and other terms. After this agreement was reached, it was a foregone conclusion that the rest of the industry would follow.

The mediators brought the N. M. U. into contact again with the Committee of Companies and Agents, Atlantic and Gulf Coasts, and it was apparent the costly hold-out of the companies was crumbling.

In its bargaining, the radio officer association also won its demands to gain full control over all radio telephones at sea, removing this equipment from the control of captains and other bridge officers. This was a major issue with the radio men.

All details of the fringe issues won by the seamen in their negotiations with the dry-cargo operators were not available, but mediators said they had matched those won earlier by the tanker men.

The new contract for the dry-cargo men will run for only a year, with a wage reopening in the fall. Union leaders called the wage terms "the best increases won by any industry this year." They were preparing to send out telegrams releasing the immobilized ships throughout the nation, including the superliner United States, tied up in New York.

Commissioners Harry Winning and Sidney Sheiner, who have been serving under Frank Brown, regional director of the Federal Mediation and Conciliation Service, in seeking to settle the costly walk-

Continued on Page 32, Column 2

Professor Loses Fulbright Award After Wife Balks at Red Inquiry

By FREDERICK GRAHAM

A Fulbright award granted last April to Dr. Nachtali Lewis of Brooklyn College to study in Italy during the next academic year has been canceled by the State Department. Senator Joseph R. McCarthy, Republican of Wisconsin, said here yesterday.

"I think it [the cancellation] is an excellent idea," the Senator asserted at the end of a thirty-seven-minute hearing of the Senate Permanent subcommittee on Investigations into the background of Dr. Lewis and his wife, Helen E. Lewis, who once held a teaching post at Brooklyn College.

The formal title of Fulbright award is the United States Educational Exchange Award. The awards are granted to educators and students for study abroad under the Fulbright Act, which is named for Senator J. William Fulbright, Democrat of Arkansas, who pioneered the program.

Senator McCarthy, who sat as a one-member subcommittee at the Federal Courthouse in Foley Square, said that the purpose of the inquiry was to learn whether Mrs. Lewis was now or ever had been a member of the Communist party.

Because she planned to go abroad with her husband for the study year at the expense of the Federal Government, Senator McCarthy declared that he believed it was very important to know if she was or had been a Communist. Unable to elicit an answer on that score from Mrs. Lewis, Senator McCarthy asserted that her refusal to answer on the ground it might tend to incriminate her was the same as saying that "I am a member of the party."

Mrs. Lewis steadfastly refused to answer questions as to whether she had held Communist cell meet-

Continued on Page 5, Column 4

"All the News That's Fit to Print"

The New York Times.

LATE CITY EDITION

Clearing and continued cold today; fair tonight and tomorrow.

Temperature Range Today—Max., 45; Min., 32

Temperatures Yesterday—Max., 44; Min., 32

Full U. S. Weather Bureau Report, Page 63

VOL. CIII . No. 35,131. Entered as Second-Class Matter. Post Office, New York, N. Y. NEW YORK, THURSDAY, APRIL 1, 1954. Times Square, New York 36, N. Y. Telephone Lackawanna 4-1000 FIVE CENTS

H-BOMB CAN WIPE OUT ANY CITY, STRAUSS REPORTS AFTER TESTS; U. S. RESTUDIES PLANT DISPERSAL

SOVIET IN BID TO JOIN NATO; U. S. SAYS 'NO'

OFFER BY MOLOTOV

He Urges West to Enter All-European Pact—Deplores 'Cold War'

Text of Soviet note to West on European security, Page 4.

By HARRISON E. SALISBURY

Special to The New York Times.

MOSCOW, March 31—The Soviet Union has proposed that the United States and West European states join a Soviet-sponsored general European security treaty. In return the Soviet Union is prepared to examine the question of assuming membership in the North Atlantic Treaty Organization.

The Soviet diplomatic move was contained in a note Vyacheslav M. Molotov, Soviet Foreign Minister, handed to Charles E. Bohlen, United States Ambassador, and his British and French diplomatic colleagues, Sir William Hayter and Louis Joxe.

There were qualifications and provisos, both written and implied, in Mr. Molotov's proposal, which was transmitted by the Western Ambassadors to Washington, London and Paris.

But the essence of what Mr. Molotov suggested was plain—that as soon as possible the "cold war," should be called off.

[The United States rejected the Soviet proposals. A State Department spokesman said the Soviet Government simply was continuing its effort to block the development of West European security. Paris sources called the Soviet note an attempt to spread confusion on the European Defense Community Treaty and to undermine the Atlantic alliance. British sources termed the Soviet suggestion of joining the alliance "just a Trojan horse."]

Defense Plan Main Target

The Soviet Foreign Minister made it plain that his immediate target was the European Defense Community.

But Mr. Molotov said the Atlantic alliance was another matter.

Mr. Molotov suggested that his proposed all-European organization and the Atlantic alliance be placed in balance. He proposed that all European powers, plus the United States, could join the Soviet - sponsored organization while the Soviet Union might become a member of the Atlantic alliance.

Mr. Molotov noted that the world was facing the peril of war in which atomic and hydrogen bombs threatened "incalculable disaster," including the annihilation of peaceful peoples, the wiping out of whole cities, of contemporary industry, culture and science, of "ancient centers of civilization" as well as "the great capitals of the states of the world."

Mr. Molotov asserted that in this moment all the world powers bore an especially great responsibility and said the Soviet Union

Continued on Page 5, Column 3

France Ousts Juin For Anti-Pact Talk

The New York Times

Marshal Alphonse P. Juin

Special to The New York Times.

PARIS, Thursday, April 1—Marshal Alphonse-Pierre Juin was disciplined by the French Cabinet at a special meeting early this morning for his speech against the European army treaty and for a snub to Premier Joseph Laniel. The

Continued on Page 7, Column 3

PRESIDENT BACKS FIRM ASIA POLICY

Supports 'United Action' Plan of Dulles—Senator Douglas Urges Facing War Risk

By WILLIAM S. WHITE

Special to The New York Times.

WASHINGTON, March 31—President Eisenhower made it plain today that this Government was deeply committed to "united action" against any Communist effort to overrun Southeast Asia.

He underwrote every word uttered by his Secretary of State, John Foster Dulles, in proclaiming that policy in a speech two nights ago.

[The Soviet Foreign Ministry in Moscow denied Mr. Dulles' assertion that Foreign Minister Molotov had agreed the Geneva conference would not be a five-power meeting.]

The President defined "united action" as primarily the responsibility of the free peoples directly under threat. He declared also that, speaking generally, the United States could put itself under no greater disadvantages than by spreading its ground forces and other forces about the

Continued on Page 12, Column 4

I. L. A. INSURGENTS REJECT PAY RISE, STALL PIER PEACE

Eisenhower, Putting Local Action First, Says U. S. Is Prepared to Cooperate

By A. H. RASKIN

Insurgent elements in the old International Longshoremen's Association yesterday killed a union-inspired move to end their strike, the longest and costliest in the port's history.

The union's sixty-two-member wage-scale committee spurned an employer pay offer and demanded a contract that would make the I. L. A. sole bargaining agent for the 24,000 workers on New York and New Jersey piers.

The shipping industry retorted that it could not legally sign such an agreement until the National Labor Relations Board decided whether the old union or its American Federation of Labor rival was entitled to speak for the dock workers.

The only remaining hope for a quick end to the twenty-seven-day tie-up was the possibility that the union might order the strikers back to the piers after the labor board in Washington had ruled on a new election. A ruling is expected before the end of this week.

At a City Hall conference with Deputy Mayor Henry Epstein, I. L. A. leaders authorized a statement that the sooner the board handed down its ruling the sooner the men would be back on the job. However, they shied away from any clear-cut promise that the strike would be called off as soon as the board acted.

President Watching Strike

In Washington, President Eisenhower said the Government was alert to the strike situation and was prepared to take whatever action might be necessary to cope with it, in cooperation with state and city authorities. The President added that the White House would be guided by this rule: Everything is handled locally as long as it can be.

The collapse of the back-to-work effort here speeded Federal plans to obtain a blanket injunction banning pickets and "loiterers" from the waterfront. Charles T. Douds, regional director of the National Labor Relations Board, laid the groundwork for such an injunction by issuing a sweeping complaint against the I. L. A. last night.

The complaint, described by members of Mr. Douds' staff as the most drastic ever issued by the board, accused the old union and its locals of having intimidated dock workers through mass picketing, blocking pier entrances, physical assaults, overturning automobiles, slashing tires and congregating in large groups" to harass non-strikers.

Labor board attorneys are expected to go into Federal Court today to ask for an injunction based on the Douds complaint. Its purpose would be to halt all picketing and other interference

Continued on Page 47, Column 4

NEW PLANS NEEDED

Defense Experts to Go to Work at Once on Factory Shifts

Special to The New York Times.

WASHINGTON, March 31—Dispersal plans for defense production plants in major cities will have to be redrawn in the light of today's hydrogen bomb disclosures.

Plans for dispersing defense production plants to date have been based upon a ten-mile radius of "immediate danger," which officials conceded was outdated.

Reliable sources indicated the Administration's defense planners were scheduled to go to work at once to draw a new set of criteria for plant dispersal.

The aim of the plant dispersal program is to get new key production plants outside probable target areas. To make this attractive, the Government offers builders of such plants accelerated tax amortization certificates permitting them to write off the cost of the plants for tax purposes in five instead of the normal twenty or more years.

Another plan, effective tomorrow, to insure control of materials and production in event of atomic or hydrogen-bomb attack, was announced by the Government today. Nominal account will be kept of available materials and production facilities so that an orderly but rapid expansion for military atomic production and construction will be possible in an emergency.

Eighty-nine Surveys Undertaken

The industry dispersal program is under the supervision of the Office of Defense Mobilization but is handled by the Area Development Division of the Business and Defense Services Administration within the Department of Commerce.

The Area Development group so far has organized committees to make dispersal plans in many key communities. Of eighty-nine committees that have undertaken such surveys, thirty-five have reported and their plans have been approved by the Office of Defense Mobilization. Among these is the committee for the New York City metropolitan area, which completed its work last month.

Officials predicted that the New York City survey, as well as the others, probably would have to be redone in the light of the facts learned about the destructiveness of the hydrogen bomb.

In announcing the new Defense Materials System, the Business and Defense Services Administration explained it would

Continued on Page 28, Column 2

The New York Times April 1, 1954

Extent to which a hydrogen bomb explosion could devastate New York and its environs

VAST POWER BARED

March 1 Explosion Was Equivalent to Millions of Tons of TNT

Text of Strauss statement and conference transcript, Page 20.

By WILLIAM L. LAURENCE

Special to The New York Times.

WASHINGTON, March 31—The United States can now build a hydrogen bomb big enough to destroy any city.

In revealing this today, Rear Admiral Lewis L. Strauss, chairman of the United States Atomic Energy Commission, hinted that such a bomb could be delivered by plane.

The bomb tested at the Eniwetok proving grounds on March 1, Admiral Strauss announced, provided "a stupendous blast in the megaton range." He said it was "double that of the calculated estimate." A megaton is equivalent to 1,000,000 tons of TNT.

The explosive power attained in the test was reported by a member of the Joint Congressional Committee on Atomic Energy as twelve to fourteen megatons. This represents an explosive force 600 to 700 times that of the bombs that destroyed Hiroshima and Nagasaki.

No Limit to Bomb Size

Admiral Strauss made his statement at the President's news conference. He declared that the hydrogen bomb could be made as large as desired—"large enough to take out a city, to destroy a city."

"How big a city?", he was asked.

"Any city!"

"New York?"

"The metropolitan area, yes," he replied.

Admiral Strauss explained later that by "metropolitan area" he meant the heart of Manhattan and not the actual metropolitan area, which covers 3,550 square miles.

[Prime Minister Churchill, yielding to Opposition pressure, agreed to debate the Government's policy on the hydrogen bomb in the House of Commons Monday.]

Despite the hydrogen bomb's enormous power, Admiral Strauss said, the test was "at no time out of control." Furthermore, he gave the nation and the world the assurance given to him by scientists that it was "impossible for any such test or series of tests to get out of control."

Admiral Strauss' appearance at the President's press conference was at President Eisenhower's request. He made available to the American people portions of the report he had made to President Eisenhower yesterday on the hydrogen bomb tests in the Pacific.

The tests of hydrogen weapons on March 1 and 26, he said, have "added enormous potential to our military posture." He later amplified this remark with a statement that "the results of these

Continued on Page 21, Column 4

Senate Unit Votes Changes President Asked in Taft Act

By JOSEPH A. LOFTUS

Special to The New York Times.

WASHINGTON, March 31—The Senate Labor Committee approved a Taft-Hartley revision bill today with the Democrats crying "steamroller." The vote was 7 to 6 along party lines.

The bill deals only with President Eisenhower's recommendations, minus an Administration proposal to require Federally conducted elections among workers before a strike could be called.

Another Administration proposal, for standards to conserve union welfare funds, will be dealt with separately after an inquiry.

The House Labor Committee expects to report a bill on the same subject next week. It will contain many more revisions than the Senate bill.

Two provisions dealing with state powers were added to the Senate committee draft today just before the final vote to report a bill. They are certain to be fought vigorously.

One of these new sections deals with state emergencies. As finally approved, it reads:

"Nothing in this act shall be construed to interfere with the enactment and enforcement by the states of laws to deal in emergencies with labor disputes which, if permitted to occur or continue, will constitute a clear and present danger to the health or safety of the people of the state; provided, that no state shall be authorized by this subsection to take action in any labor dispute in which the Federal Government is acting pursuant to Sections 206 to 210, inclusive, of this act."

Sections 206 to 210 are the national emergency provisions of the Taft-Hartley Act. When these were invoked, state action would be superseded, but the

Continued on Page 34, Column 3

HOUSING BAN FOES CLAIM A 'VICTORY'

G.O.P. House Chiefs Foresee 33,000 Units in Fiscal '55—Eisenhower 'Delighted'

Special to The New York Times.

WASHINGTON, March 31—What had been intended as a defeat for the Eisenhower Administration developed as a probable victory today as a parliamentary tangle over public housing legislation began unraveling.

President Eisenhower himself said he was delighted at the outcome.

Republican leaders of the House of Representatives already had claimed a victory by interpreting the mix-up, which occurred in the House yesterday, as meaning that the Public Housing Administration is free to go ahead with plans for construction of 33,000 to 35,000 new low-rent public housing units.

Today, the leaders moved to provide authority for an additional 35,000 units in the year starting July 1, 1955, by supporting an amendment to a general housing bill that comes before the House tomorrow.

Their aim is to give the President a legislative green light to carry out the first two years of his four-year program for 35,000 new units a year.

Action by Opposition

Yesterday's confusion in the House resulted from the attempt of public housing opponents, led by Representative Howard W. Smith, Democrat of Virginia, to kill the entire program by striking from a pending appropriations bill a "rider" allowing construction of 20,000 new units in the year starting next July 1.

The rider was eliminated from the bill on a point of order raised by Mr. Smith, who successfully challenged it as legislation on an appropriations bill in violation of House rules.

Killing the rider, according to Mr. Smith, would leave the Government without authority to start any new projects after next July 1. He based this position on an existing law, enacted as a rider on the same appropriations bill last year, limiting new construction to 20,000 units in the present fiscal year and prohibiting any further commitments without Congressional authorization.

As soon as Mr. Smith had com-

Continued on Page 34, Column 4

EISENHOWER SIGNS TAX CUT MEASURE

Excise Reductions Effective Today—President Voices Hope of Business Gain

By JOHN D. MORRIS

Special to The New York Times.

WASHINGTON, March 31—President Eisenhower signed the $999,000,000 excise tax reduction bill into law today. He voiced hope that the damage to Federal revenues would be offset to some degree by the resulting stimulation of business.

Federal sales taxes on a long list of items, from pocketbooks to household appliances, consequently will be reduced sharply as of 12:01 A. M. tomorrow. The savings are expected to be passed along to consumers, at least in part, by most of the industries affected. On a majority of the items covered, the tax cut amounts to 50 per cent.

Enactment of the bill adds an estimated $999,000,000 to the Federal deficit of $2,928,000,000 projected by President Eisenhower for the 1955 fiscal year, which starts next July 1.

On the ground that the Government could not afford such revenue losses in addition to those involved in other recent and pending tax cuts, the Administration had opposed any broad-scale reduction of excises at this time.

The President told his news conference that, nevertheless, he was accepting the bill wholeheartedly. From the beginning, he explained, there was a difference of opinion on the revenue effects. One school of thought, he noted, believes that the reductions can stimulate business to

Continued on Page 16, Column 7

10 Pupils Burned to Death in School Near Buffalo

Associated Press Wirephoto

Smoke and flames billow from frame annex of an elementary school in Cheektowaga, N. Y.

Special to The New York Times.

BUFFALO, March 31—Ten sixth grade pupils in the Cleveland Hill elementary school died today in a fire that trapped them in a room of the school's one-story frame annex on Mapleview Drive in suburban Cheektowaga. Twenty-two other persons, nineteen of them children, were burned or injured and taken to hospitals. The school has an enrollment of more than 1,200. Hundreds of pupils of the adjoining Cleveland Hill High School were sent home. The fire followed a blast that was described variously as an explosion and as "a

Continued on Page 34, Column 8

Reds in Mass Attack Against Dienbienphu

By TILLMAN DURDIN

Special to The New York Times.

SAIGON, Vietnam, March 31—Vietminh forces last night launched a new mass attack against the French defenses at Dienbienphu.

[The French High Command in Hanoi said three Vietminh divisions were assaulting Dienbienphu, The United Press reported.]

During a night of savage fighting the Communist-led Vietminh troops established a foothold within the French positions. However, they were pushed back this morning at some points by desperately resisting French Union contingents.

A late bulletin from French headquarters here said violent combat continued today. Bad weather yesterday facilitated the beginning of the Vietminh assault, but as the clouds cleared

Continued on Page 7, Column 1

Calm in Middle East Urged by President

By The United Press.

WASHINGTON, March 31—President Eisenhower called on Israel and the Arab states today to restrain their extremists and permit other nations to help them settle their disputes.

He declined to answer a question at his news conference as to whether he believed the bitter Arab-Israeli feud, which recently erupted into new violence, should be referred to the United Nations Security Council. However, he said the United Nations had the full support of the United States in its plan to seek harmony in the Middle East.

General Eisenhower said the United States had been giving strong support to the plan to develop the resources of the area, including the water resources of the Jordan River, and hoped the plan would be successful.

He said the Israeli-Arab issue was so charged with emotional-

Continued on Page 2, Column 3

Color Film of First H-Bomb Test Is Previewed by Press in Capital

Special to The New York Times.

WASHINGTON, March 31—The world's most fearsome weapon, the fusion bomb, was shown in action for the first time here in public today before an audience of representatives of the press and other information media.

They saw a reproduction on color film of the phenomena that followed the explosion of the first full-scale hydrogen weapon on the Pacific proving grounds in the Marshall Islands in November, 1952.

The event marked the entry of mankind into the Hydrogen Age, taking the fateful step from the kiloton (thousands of tons) to the megaton (millions of tons) of explosive power in terms of TNT.

The film was released by the Atomic Energy Commission and the Department of Defense for public issuance by the Federal Civil Defense Administration. It was intended for general release at 6 P. M. April 7, and reviews of it were to be embargoed until then.

However, a descriptive review by a syndicated columnist appeared in newspapers a few hours after the showing. Because of this The Times is publishing its review now.

The test in November, 1952, was known as Operation Ivy and the device tested was known as Mike. At the time it was made the explosion was the greatest in history. Since then, however, it has been greatly exceeded by the test explosions on March 1 and 26.

The film opens with an introduction by President Eisenhower, who recites an excerpt from his historic address before the United Nations on Dec. 8, 1953, relating to the need of the peoples of

Continued on Page 23, Column 2

"All the News That's Fit to Print"

The New York Times.

LATE CITY EDITION
Fair and cold today and tonight.
Fair and milder tomorrow.
Temperature Range Today—Max., 40; Min., 25
Temperatures Yesterday—Max., 37.4; Min., 28.5
Full U. S. Weather Bureau Report, Page 51

VOL. CIV..No. 35,377 Entered as Second-Class Matter, Post Office, New York, N. Y. NEW YORK, FRIDAY, DECEMBER 3, 1954. Times Square, New York 36, N. Y. Telephone LAckawanna 4-1000 FIVE CENTS

FINAL VOTE CONDEMNS M'CARTHY, 67-22, FOR ABUSING SENATE AND COMMITTEE; ZWICKER COUNT ELIMINATED IN DEBATE

POPE IN COLLAPSE, BUT REST FOLLOWS A DIFFICULT NIGHT

Morning Announcement Tells of the 78-Year-old Pontiff's Battle Against Illness

KIN CALLED TO BEDSIDE

Trouble Laid to a Perforated Ulcer and Physicians Study Possibilities of Operation

By The Associated Press.

ROME, Friday, Dec. 3—The Vatican announced this morning that Pope Pius XII, gravely stricken, had survived the night. A spokesman said a more detailed bulletin would be issued later today.

The Pope suffered a severe collapse yesterday.

The first word this morning on his condition was given by Dr. Luciano Casimiri, spokesman for the Vatican press office, at 8:05 o'clock [2:05 A. M., Eastern standard time.]

"After a difficult night, the Holy Father is now resting," the spokesman said.

There were unconfirmed reports that the Pope had suffered a heart attack in the night, accompanied by more of the intense gastritis, nausea and hiccups for which he has been under treatment. There were indications also that the Pope's condition may be aggravated by a gastric ulcer.

His personal physician, Dr. Riccardo Galeazzi-Lisi, spent the entire night at his bedside, after making emergency X-rays yesterday and calling in a surgeon for consultation.

Grave Fears Felt

By ARNALDO CORTESI

Special to The New York Times.

ROME, Friday, Dec. 3—Pope Pius XII suffered a collapse at 3:30 o'clock yesterday afternoon due, it is believed, to a perforated ulcer.

The Pope fell into a coma and the gravest fears for his life were felt. He is 78 years old and has been weakened because for the last four days his feeding has been by artificial means.

Extreme unction was administered and Pius' nearest relatives —three nephews—were called to his bedside.

Five hours later, the Pope had overcome the crisis and his archiater, or chief physician, Prof. Riccardo Galeazzi-Lisi, said there was no immediate cause for alarm.

The Pope was stated to be resting as easily as could be expected under the circumstances, although breathing heavily and reduced to exhaustion.

It was learned that the possibility of an abdominal operation sometime today or in the next few days was being considered. The exact nature of the operation under consideration was not stated but it is understood that a noticeable swelling of the Pope's abdomen developed yesterday afternoon, accompanied by cramps and excruciating pain. Radioscopic and clinical tests were made late in the evening to ascertain both the exact nature of the Pope's ailment and whether he is in condition to undergo surgery.

From the time he fell seriously ill in January of this year, Pope Pius had refused to take the barium meal necessary if full X-ray examination of his stomach

Continued on Page 4, Column 1

Rio Conference Ends With Major Accords

By SAM POPE BREWER

Special to The New York Times.

PETROPOLIS, Brazil, Dec. 2—The twenty-one American republics ended tonight their first general economic conference with agreements on many major points and plans to hold another such meeting within two years.

Antonio Carrillo Flores, Minister of Finance of Mexico, said in the principal address at the closing session that public opinion of this hemisphere would find on studying results of the conference that its work "was not sterile."

Carlos Lleras Restrepo of Colombia introduced a dissenting note into the general air of agreement. He said at this final session that his country did not feel the conference had gone far enough toward increasing international banking facilities and stabilizing commodity prices. An

Continued on Page 10, Column 5

President Rejects Blockade Of China Now as Act of War

But He Pledges No Let-Up in Efforts to Free 13 Americans Jailed by Peiping—Holds Truce Obligates U. N. to Act

By JOSEPH A. LOFTUS

Special to The New York Times.

WASHINGTON, Dec. 2—President Eisenhower asserted today he was not going to be pushed emotionally into an act of war—such as a naval blockade of Communist China.

Neither, he said, is he going to let Peiping get away with the imprisonment of thirteen Americans on spy charges.

He insisted that the United Nations act for the release of at least eleven of the Americans because they were uniformed veterans of the Korean war and as such the United Nations was obligated to act in their behalf.

[At the United Nations, the United States said it wanted the world body to condemn the imprisonment by Red China of eleven American airmen shot down during the Korean war.]

"We are yet far from exhausting all of our resources" to liberate these men, the President said at his news conference: "I mention only one of those that is available to us."

He asserted that Red China deliberately timed its announcement of the imprisonment to divide the people of the United States as well as the United States from its allies. He added that the United States must be forever on its guard against this divide-and-conquer technique.

His personal feelings of anger, resentment and frustration were as great as any American's, he said, but he believed that restraint in public expression was the wiser course. To respond with patience rather than with truculence does not mean appeasement, he declared.

The President was clearly reading a lesson in the behavior of public officials to Senator Wil-

Continued on Page 2, Column 4

East Bloc Says Joint Army Will Counter Bonn in NATO

By CLIFTON DANIEL

Special to The New York Times.

MOSCOW, Dec. 2—In a declaration signed in the Kremlin tonight, eight European Communist regimes gave notice that if the Atlantic powers enlisted West Germany in their alliance, an East European defense organization would be created.

Representatives of eight governments concluding a four-day conference here said another meeting would be called to plan defense measures should the London and Paris agreements for West German armament and sovereignty be finally ratified.

The envisioned defense organization would have combined military forces under a joint command like that of the North Atlantic Treaty Organization. It would be in addition to the existing framework of treaties concluded long ago among the eight powers.

Communist China's complete approval of the declaration and the measures envisioned in it was signified at the final meeting of the representatives of the eight European powers today. China's endorsement was given by Chang Wen-tien, Peiping's Deputy Foreign Minister and Ambassador to Moscow.

Having in mind the combined strength of Communist China, the Soviet Union and seven other units in the East bloc conference, the delegates declared:

"Never before have the forces of peace and socialism been so mighty and so consolidated as now. Any attempts to attack, launch a war and interfere with the peaceful life of our peoples will meet with a shattering rebuff."

The declaration, bound in a red Morocco folder with ribbons

Continued on Page 5, Column 5

ATOM POWER SEEN AS COMMON IN 1976

Half of All Electric Plants Then Building Will Use It, G. E. Head Tells N.A.M.

By A. H. RASKIN

By 1976 atomic energy will be used to fuel half of all the electric generating plants then being built, it was predicted yesterday. This forecast was put before the National Association of Manufacturers by Ralph J. Cordiner, president of General Electric.

His estimate of the speed with which nuclear power would come into widespread use as a source of electric power was considerably more optimistic than most official calculations. Mr. Cordiner made his prediction as part of a plea to industrialists to shun "creeping conservatism" in their approach to business planning.

The head of the country's biggest electrical manufacturing company advised his fellow-executives to make their plans on a twenty-year basis, instead of limiting themselves to the ups and downs of the immediate sales market.

West Called Stronger

Other highlights at the second session of the association's fifty-ninth annual Congress of American Industry in the Waldorf-Astoria Hotel included:

¶An assertion by Gen. Walter Bedell Smith that the United States and its allies had built up a sufficient superiority over the Communist countries to "deter aggression and maintain peace." The former Under Secretary of State emphasized, however, that the balance of power was still "rather tenuous."

¶A report by a Dutch industrialist that five of his employes, who spent three months working in a Pennsylvania linoleum factory, had come home convinced that "America is a working man's world."

¶An attack by Charles R. Sligh Jr., N. A. M. board chairman, on union proposals for a guaranteed annual wage. He contended that wage guarantees would destroy business, rather than stabilize employment.

¶An assertion by Prof. Leo Wolman of Columbia University that the Taft-Hartley Act represented no substantial improvement over the old Wagner Act in curbing union power and preventing encroachment on management rights.

¶Election as N. A. M. president of Henry G. Riter 3d of Montclair, N. J., president of Thomas A. Edison, Inc., and chairman of the board of Copperweld Steel. Mr. Riter, who was an investment banker before he became an industrialist, succeeds H. C. McClellan of Los Angeles.

General Smith, who quit the State Department two months

Continued on Page 24, Column 3

'Copter Saves 5 Plane Survivors Down 45 Hours on Mountainside

Two Perish in Crash of DC-3 in New Hampshire—Work of Stewardess Praised

By JOHN H. FENTON

Special to The New York Times.

BOSTON, Dec. 2—Five survivors of the crash of a Northeast Airlines plane were plucked by helicopter today from a bleak mountainside near the Maine-New Hampshire border. They had spent forty-five hours on the snow-covered spot in bitter cold.

The two others aboard the DC-3 died of injuries a few hours after the plane had fallen into a stretch of pine woods.

The dead were George McCormick, 37 years old, of Kingston, N. Y., co-pilot, and John McNulty, 39, of Boston, flight supervisor.

First to be rescued was the pilot, Capt. W. Peter Carey, 37, of Swampscott, Mass. He suffered severe head injuries. He and Miss Mary McEttrick, 23, of Boston, the stewardess, were flown here for medical treatment. Miss McEttrick suffered from shock and exposure.

The survivors praised Miss McEttrick for her coolness throughout the ordeal during which they huddled in the wrecked plane for nearly two days. Her cheerful attempts to make them com-

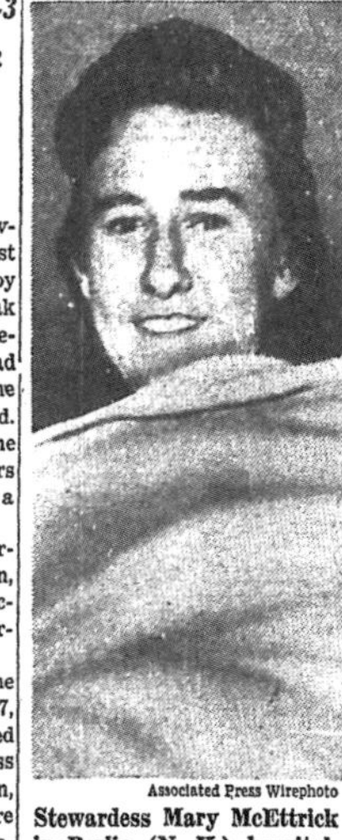

Associated Press Wirephoto

Stewardess Mary McEttrick in Berlin (N. H.) hospital.

fortable and her care of the injured prompted them to agree that "she's quite a girl."

Seventy-five Northeast employes, who were flown to Berlin,

Continued on Page 29, Column 4

EISENHOWER WARNS G. O. P. RIGHT WING; CHIDES KNOWLAND

Insists Party Must Follow a Progressive Course or Face Loss of Influence

Transcript and summary of the news conference, Page 18.

By WILLIAM S. WHITE

Special to The New York Times.

WASHINGTON, Dec. 2—President Eisenhower, reasserting leadership for his concept of a progressive Republican party, rebuked today the Senate Republican floor leader, William F. Knowland of California, and the party's right wing generally.

The President did not seek to disclaim the existence of a split in the party. He said instead that the party would not long be a force in American life unless it followed a course of progressivism.

As before, he defined this progressivism as a liberal attitude in the Government's relationship with the individual and a conservative attitude concerning the national economy and the individual's pocketbook.

It was the first time since he entered the White House two years ago that General Eisenhower publicly and without apology had criticized a leading member of his party in Congress. Always before, he had avoided such criticisms, relying frequently on the fact that the Constitution made Congress an independent branch of Government.

Even this time, the President somewhat softened his language toward the end, with the comments that while Senator Knowland sometimes made statements that certainly did not conform with the Administration's approach these normally affected method rather than principle.

China Blockade Urged

He made it clear, nevertheless, that distinctions in methods were important, suggesting that the methods of Senator Knowland might mean the difference between peace and war in Asia.

Senator Knowland, in the face of rejections from John Foster Dulles, Secretary of State, and the President himself, has been calling for a blockade of Communist China to force the liberation of United States citizens in Communist prisons.

Yesterday, moreover, Mr. Knowland broke with the Administration on another sensitive issue, coming out against a Senate censure of Senator Joseph R. McCarthy, Republican of Wisconsin.

The President said little about his differences with Senator Knowland over the McCarthy issue, observing only that it was up to the Senate to determine what was required for the preservation of its dignity.

On the point of the profound division within the Republican party over policy toward Red China, however, the President spoke extensively and voluntarily.

He took up Senator Knowland's

Continued on Page 18, Column 5

RANCOR CONTINUES

Welker Refuses to Let Flanders Apology Go Into the Record

By JAMES RESTON

Special to The New York Times.

WASHINGTON, Dec. 2—The McCarthy debate ended as it began in a spasm of rancor and vindictiveness that will divide the Senate and the country for a long time to come.

Though there were some lighthearted semantics at the close over whether Senator Joseph R. McCarthy was "censured" or "condemned," the underlying feeling among the principals ranged from uneasiness to sullen anger.

The junior Senator from Wisconsin himself produced almost the only hint of humor all day. Asked whether he thought the Senate had passed a resolution of "censure" or "condemnation," he replied:

"I wouldn't say it was a vote of confidence."

He then announced that he was "very happy to get this circus over" and would get back to "the job of digging Communists out of the Government" on Monday.

Controversy Continues

Even after the vote was over, the controversy went on.

Senator Ralph E. Flanders, Republican of Vermont, arose and said he wanted to apologize to the Senate for some remarks he had made about Senator McCarthy some months ago. He added that he had told the Wisconsin Senator that he proposed to do so and had asked him to remain in the chamber, but Senator McCarthy had declined.

Then Senator Flanders asked for unanimous consent to have the Congressional Record amended to show that he had apologized for some of his remarks. This was blocked by Senator Herman Welker, Republican of Idaho, who angrily refused to give consent.

The usual lavish courtesy of the upper chamber gave way to biting sarcasm at the close. When Senator J. William Fulbright, Democrat of Arkansas, said he would try to answer a question by Senator Welker, the latter remarked that he would be "very surprised if a distinguished Rhodes scholar could not answer any question."

The End of a Phase

The main significance of the special session was that it ended that phase of the McCarthy controversy in which the Senate of the United States was hesitant to take action against the Wisconsin Senator.

For most of the five years since Senator McCarthy launched his anti-Communist crusade, the Senate of the United States has led a double life—critical of the Senator in private, and afraid of his political power in public.

During most of this period there has been a kind of political paralysis among the anti-McCarthy faction, and it was never entirely clear who was for him and who was against him. This doubt has now been removed.

The Senator from Wisconsin will remain for a month as chairman of the Government Operations Committee. He will lose none of his rights. He will have the power of subpoena and he will wield his gavel.

What has changed is not Mr. McCarthy but his opponents. They are in the open now, willing and in some cases eager to match his criticisms with their own. In short, the balance of criticism, dominated for so long by Senator McCarthy, has been restored.

Behind this, too, is a decision by the Executive Branch of the Government to take a firmer position against his efforts to persuade Federal employes to give him documents they are not authorized to disclose.

So long as Congress hesitated to take action against Mr. McCarthy, the Executive itself was divided about how to defend its own classified files, but today's vote—regardless of what it is called—has stiffened the anti-McCarthy element in the Administration.

Thus, while he can exercise all

Continued on Page 16, Column 7

Associated Press Wirephoto

CONDEMNED ON TWO COUNTS: Senator McCarthy as he left the Senate floor last night after members adopted a resolution condemning his conduct. The vote was 67-22.

PRESIDENT ALERTS MAYORS ON ATTACK

Cities Are Front-Line Targets, He Warns—Asks Teamwork in Federal-Local Defense

By ELIE ABEL

Special to The New York Times.

WASHINGTON, Dec. 2—President Eisenhower warned today that United States cities were front-line targets for modern weapons "capable of such destruction as to appall the imagination."

The President called for closer municipal-Federal cooperation in civil-defense planning as he welcomed about 240 mayors, city manager and other local officials to a two-day conference in the State Department auditorium.

Val Peterson, Federal Civil Defense Administrator, expanded on the President's warning in a guarded discussion of radioactive "fall-out," a phenomenon that adds a new dimension to the terror of thermonuclear (hydrogen) bombs.

The idea that only city dwellers need to worry about bombing is obsolete today, Mr. Peterson said. If a hydrogen bomb is detonated on or close to the ground, he explained, tremendous amounts of earth and debris are sucked up into the fireball and made radioactive.

Although the heavy particles will not travel far, he said, the lighter ones may be swept along by winds of the upper air, at alti-

Continued on Page 19, Column 1

SENATORS CLEARED ON M'CARTHY MAIL

Inquiry Indicates Request for Check Was Handled by Staff as Routine Matter

By WILLIAM M. BLAIR

Special to The New York Times.

WASHINGTON, Dec. 2—A special Senate committee apparently will report to the Senate that a check of Senator Joseph R. McCarthy's mail in 1952 was handled as a routine matter by a subcommittee's staff members.

Senator Walter F. George, Democrat of Georgia, indicated as much to Senator McCarthy this afternoon as the special two-member committee completed its overnight inquiry into how the mail check was authorized.

"There's nothing to be gained from pursuing the matter further," Senator McCarthy told Senator George, who replied, "I don't think so."

Senator George and Senator Homer Ferguson, Republican of Michigan, spent the day in closed session to hear testimony from persons on the staff of the Senate subcommittee on Privileges and Elections, which had inquired into Senator McCarthy's finances in 1952.

Mr. Ferguson said that a written report would be filed with the Senate. The report is expected to be filed with the secretary of the Senate tomorrow. The two Senators were named by the Senate last night to in-

Continued on Page 15, Column 3

G.O.P. Weighs End of Rent Curb Outside of the Metropolitan Area

By LEO EGAN

Republican legislative leaders are giving serious consideration to relaxing state rent controls outside of the New York metropolitan area, which includes Nassau and Westchester counties as well as New York City.

Such a proposal could set the stage for a major clash between Governor-elect Averell Harriman, Democrat-Liberal, and Republican majorities in the Senate and Assembly.

The Democratic platform on which Mr. Harriman was elected favors tightening rather than relaxing rent control. Moreover, Mr. Harriman affirmed his full support of this position on several occasions during the campaign.

One proposal favored by some Republicans calls for decontrolling all rents outside the New York metropolitan area. If this is politically impossible or unacceptable they favor decontrolling all one and two-family houses outside of the metropolitan area, leaving controls in effect only on apartments and tenements.

Both suggestions were formally advanced at a recent closed-door meeting of the Temporary State Commission on Rents and Rental Conditions, headed by Assemblyman Joseph F. Carlino of Long Beach, L. I.

As a result, Joseph D. McGoldrick, State Rent Administrator, was instructed by the commission to prepare a report and recommendations on both proposals covering the probable effect of such a relaxation of controls, the number of dwelling units involved, and the ratio of vacancies to dwelling units affected at present.

Major up-state cities that would be affected by such a

Continued on Page 24, Column 5

REPUBLICANS SPLIT

Democrats Act Solidly in Support of Motion Against Senator

Excerpts from transcript of Senate debate, Pages 12, 13

By ANTHONY LEVIERO

Special to The New York Times.

WASHINGTON, Dec. 2—The Senate voted 67 to 22 tonight to condemn Joseph R. McCarthy, Republican Senator from Wisconsin.

Every one of the forty-four Democrats present voted against Mr. McCarthy. The Republicans were evenly divided—twenty-two for condemnation and twenty-two against. The one independent, Senator Wayne Morse of Oregon, also voted against Mr. McCarthy.

In the ultimate action the Senate voted to condemn Senator McCarthy for contempt of a Senate Elections subcommittee that investigated his conduct and financial affairs, for abuse of its members, and for his insults to the Senate itself during the censure proceeding.

Lost in a day of complex and often confused parliamentary maneuvering was the proposal to censure Senator McCarthy for his denunciation of Brig. Gen. Ralph W. Zwicker as unfit to wear his uniform.

This proposal was defeated by a parliamentary device that avoided a direct vote on the merits of the issue. Inquiry among influential Senators indicated they considered the Zwicker proposal a dilemma they wished to avoid.

Amendment Substituted

They said they wished to censure because the facts warranted it. If they failed to do so, they believed large elements of the public would feel the Senate took notice of offenses only against itself and not against ordinary citizens.

But also if they did censure for this, then Senator McCarthy could exploit the decision, contending he was being punished for his effort to expose former Maj. Irving Peress, the Army dentist who was promoted and honorably discharged, and who was denounced by Mr. McCarthy as a "Fifth Amendment Communist."

Mr. McCarthy's denunciation of General Zwicker, who was commanding officer at Camp Kilmer, N. J., when Dr. Peress was discharged, occurred when the Senator interrogated General Zwicker on the question of who had promoted Dr. Peress.

The direct test on the Zwicker issue was avoided by the substitution of the amendment to condemn Senator McCarthy for having insulted the Senate during his censure trial.

McCarthy Loses Three Tests

Thus in its final form the resolution of condemnation was in two parts, covering the offenses against the Elections subcommittee and its members in the first part, and against the Senate in the second. Three test votes were all lost by Mr. McCarthy before the final condemnation.

First was a motion to table the Zwicker proposal, made by Senator Styles Bridges, Republican of New Hampshire, the president pro tem of the Senate, who assumed the leadership of the effort to save Mr. McCarthy yesterday.

Such a motion, if it had succeeded, might have led to a situation that would have prolonged the debate.

But amid signs that the Zwicker issue would have tough sledding, Senator Wallace F. Bennett, Republican of Utah, served notice that if Mr. Bridges' move were defeated he would attempt to substitute for the Zwicker issue his amendment for abuse of the Senate. The significance of this was that an amendment by substitution would require no time out for debate.

Then the voting proceeded. The motion to table was defeated 55 to 33. Mr. Bennett's motion to substitute passed by 64 to 23 and in the next vote his amendment was adopted by the same tally.

The final vote placing Mr. Mc-

Continued on Page 14, Column 3

"All the News That's Fit to Print"

The New York Times.

LATE CITY EDITION
Condensation of U.S. Weather Bureau forecast:
Partly cloudy and warm today tonight and tomorrow.
Temperature range today: 85-65.
Temperature range yesterday: 70.0-60.5.
Full U. S. Weather Bureau Report, Page 46.

VOL. CV..No. 35,944. Entered as Second-Class Matter, Post Office, New York, N. Y. NEW YORK, FRIDAY, JUNE 22, 1956. Times Square, New York 36, N. Y. Telephone LAckawanna 4-1000 FIVE CENTS

SENATE EXPECTED TO VOTE INCREASE IN AIR FORCE FUND

Democrats Ask Billion Above President's Goal—Wilson Calls Rise Plans 'Phony'

MOVE LINKED TO AID CUT

Foreign Program Reduction Indicated Despite Urgings of the Administration

Special to The New York Times.

WASHINGTON, June 21—The Senate set out today to increase Air Force appropriations. The prospect was that foreign aid outlays would be simultaneously cut.

Debate was opened on a Democratic effort to enlarge the allocation for the Air Force by nearly $1,000,000,000 above President Eisenhower's request.

Although a decisive vote will not come until next week, there was no question tonight that a great deal more Air Force money would be ordered.

The Republicans were not offering all-out opposition to the Democrats. They themselves were marshaling behind a proposed increase of $500,000,000.

[At Quantico, Va., Charles E. Wilson called efforts in Congress to increase defense appropriations "phony." The Secretary of Defense opened a four-day meeting of top defense officials and field commanders.]

The real issue was: Would the Senate give to the Administration about $1,000,000,000 more for airpower than it had asked, or would this unsought grant be scaled down?

Knowland Gives View

The Senate Republican leader, Senator William F. Knowland of California, observed that half a billion would be "more acceptable" to the Administration than a billion.

He did not actually commit the Administration to condone the smaller rise. But he observed that the White House was "fully conversant" with the proposal and recognized the right of Congress to exercise its own judgment on the defense budget.

It was increasingly probable, meanwhile, that the foreign-aid program would suffer reductions related to the increase for the air arm.

Private nose-counting strongly indicated that the Administration would be turned back in its continuing attempts to persuade the Senate to approve at minimum the $1,457,575,000 for foreign aid that its Foreign Relations Committee had recommended.

Nevertheless, the fight went on. Gen. Alfred M. Gruenther,

Continued on Page 11, Column 3

SENATE OUTRAGED BY HUNT FOR 'BUG'

Security Check on Lehman's Office Is Protested

By RUSSELL BAKER
Special to The New York Times.

WASHINGTON, June 21—The Pentagon's security check on Senator Herbert H. Lehman's refrigerator closet raised Senate tempers today to a rare pitch of outrage.

For two hours, Senator after Senator took the floor to express "horror," "disgust," "shock," "amazement," "resentment" and "outrage."

The storm was produced by the visit of two Pentagon security agents yesterday to the New York Democrat's office in the Senate Office Building. They checked the possibility that a "bug" might have been planted to eavesdrop on top secret testimony on defense in an adjacent committee room.

Senator Lehman demanded an explanation from Charles E. Wilson, Secretary of Defense.

Senator Stuart Symington, Democrat of Missouri, demanded a Pentagon apology.

Senator Lyndon B. Johnson of Texas, the Democratic floor leader, accused the Pentagon's agents of "typical bureaucratic flatfoot stupidity." He called for an immediate report from the Capitol's politically appointed police force. A Capitol policeman accompanied the agents.

Senator Paul H. Douglas, Democrat of Illinois, proposed a

Continued on Page 10, Column 4

U. S. and Venezuela Open Inquiry in Plane Disaster

Cause of Crash That Killed 74 Is Sought Here in Records and Wreckage—Search Continues Off Jersey

By PETER KIHSS

Experts searched yesterday for the cause of the crash of a flaming Venezuelan airliner in the Atlantic Ocean Wednesday. All seventy-four persons aboard were killed.

Representatives of Venezuela and the United States conferred at New York International Airport, Idlewild, Queens, and studied documents. They agreed to use United States Navy diving operations for a possible attempt to locate significant pieces of the shattered plane.

The disintegrating impact of the crash, which occurred thirty-two miles off Asbury Park, N. J., left grave doubts about the effort. The airliner fell from an altitude of 8,000 feet in the crash—the worst in scheduled airline history. The Missing Persons Bureau here estimated yesterday that parts of bodies recovered Wednesday represented perhaps eight victims instead of six.

Manufacturers who were involved offered full cooperation. They stressed faith in the safety of the propeller, engine and fuel equipment, about which questions had been raised through the course of the tragic flight.

Lieut. Comdr. Frederick J. Hancox, a Coast Guard pilot, said it was his "impression" that the four-engine Super Constellation's running lights were on when it started dumping gasoline to lighten its load before landing. Commander Hancox had been flying an escort for the airliner on an attempted return to Idlewild after the Venezuelan craft reported an "overspeeding" propeller.

The plane's flight manual, issued by the Lockheed Aircraft

Continued on Page 47, Column 2

President Takes First Walk Out of His Hospital Room

By EDWIN L. DALE Jr.
Special to The New York Times

WASHINGTON, June 21—President Eisenhower walked out of his hospital bedroom today for the first time since his operation June 9. He walked about forty feet into the hospital corridor and sat in an armless desk chair before returning.

The President spent more time on business today than at any time since he entered the hospital. In the morning he had his regular forty-five-minute session on routine White House business with members of his staff. In the afternoon he had a forty-five-minute visit from Gen. Alfred M. Gruenther, Supreme Commander of the North Atlantic Treaty Organization forces in Europe.

James C. Hagerty, the White House press secretary, said the two had discussed general NATO problems and specifically General Gruenther's testimony this morning at a closed meeting of the Senate Appropriations Committee. The general was known to have urged cancellation of House fund cuts in the military portion of the foreign aid bill.

The Administration has taken the position that NATO in particular would suffer heavily if the cuts were approved. Mr. Hagerty said again today that the President was "vitally concerned" about the fund reductions.

Mr. Hagerty said he thought he could affirm that politics had not been discussed with General Gruenther. The press secretary repeated today that the President had not talked politics with any of his visitors.

Mr. Hagerty also declared "there is absolutely nothing" to a story appearing in this afternoon's papers to the effect that word had come out of Walter Reed Army Hospital that the President again would run for office.

The President's physicians

Continued on Page 14, Column 4

STEEL UNION SEES PLOT BY CONCERNS

Says There Is a Joint Effort to Force Acceptance of 5-Year No-Strike Pact

By A. H. RASKIN

The United Steelworkers of America charged yesterday that the country's eleven biggest steel producers had entered into a "conspiracy" to force union acceptance of a five-year no-strike contract.

David J. McDonald, president of the union, asserted that the industry leaders had concocted a plot "months ago" to compel a shutdown of steel production June 30 unless the union bowed to their terms.

Mr. McDonald based his charge on the filing by the companies two months ago of formal notices of contract termination, effective June 30. The steel producers explained that these notices were required under the Taft-Hartley Act.

However, the union head asserted that this was the first year the companies had submitted such notices in the nine years since the law was passed.

"The events which have occurred since these notices were sent make their purpose clear," Mr. McDonald said. "Obviously, the eleven companies, acting in concert from the start, determined, even prior to the beginning of negotiations with the union, to present a 'take it or leave it' offer and to force a shutdown in the event the union would not submit to their ultimatum.

'Not a Strike-Happy Union'

"The union, therefore, is today transmitting to all affected local unions appropriate instructions for use in the event a shutdown in the steel industry takes place midnight, June 30. These instructions are equally applicable to a strike or a lockout. The United Steelworkers of America is not a strike-happy union. We must, however, make responsible advance preparations for a shutdown in the event the industry persists in its preconceived plan."

Mr. McDonald made his accusation in a formal statement issued at the end of another fruitless bargaining session with a joint committee representing the three principal steel-making companies at the Roosevelt Hotel. The companies had no comment.

The union traditionally follows a "no contract, no work" policy, under which its 650,000 members in the basic steel mills quit work if no settlement has been reached at contract-expiration time.

By filing cancellation notices this year, the companies put themselves in a position for the first time to take affirmative action to shut down their mills in the event that the union chose to follow a selective strike policy under which workers would be

Continued on Page 24, Column 2

TRUMAN CAUTIONS WEST ON DANGERS IN SOVIET TACTICS

Tells Pilgrim Dinner British-U. S. Unity Is Vital—Doubts Reds 'Cast Out Old Adam'

Text of Truman's speech will be found on Page 2.

By DREW MIDDLETON
Special to The New York Times.

LONDON, June 21—The danger to the United States and Britain rarely has been greater, Harry S. Truman warned tonight.

The former President appealed to the British and to his countrymen to banish illusion and to remember they had to face nations striving to increase their powers to threaten, overawe and absorb.

Although Mr. Truman did not identify the Soviet Union or its new leaders by name, he is known to have had Moscow's gestures of friendship toward the West in mind. He said he himself was not prepared to believe that those who claimed to have been converted had, in fact, "cast out the old Adam."

The setting for Mr. Truman's speech was the Pilgrims Dinner. Selwyn Lloyd, British Foreign Secretary, who made the other principal speech, and a number of other political, religious and military leaders heard Mr. Truman's warning.

To this the former President coupled a plea for the "closest concert" of United States and British policy. He urged that "out of common prudence" the two nations should preserve their strength and unity.

A candid and honest appraisal of the world shows "that the common danger has rarely been greater," Mr. Truman emphasized.

Truman Gets Warm Welcome

Mr. Truman received a welcome surpassing that given any visiting American in the last three years.

The Earl of Halifax described Mr. Truman as a "person we would go tiger-hunting with." Earl Attlee said that the survival of the United Nations was largely due to the "courageous" action of Mr. Truman in the defense of Korea. Mr. Lloyd lauded the former President's "constructive faith" in United States-British relations.

Robert Gordon Menzies, Prime Minister of Australia, hailed the former President as "a great man" whose personal courage was equaled only by his loyalty to his subordinates.

The former President evoked a great burst of applause by informing the audience of his happiness that President Eisenhower was "well on the road to recovery."

Mr. Truman's warning on the Soviet moves came at an appropriate time.

The Foreign Office and other British Government departments have abundant evidence that the Soviet Union's professions of friendship are making an impression on the Continent. The North Atlantic Treaty Organization, a product of the Truman

Continued on Page 2, Column 4

Arthur Miller Admits Helping Communist-Front Groups in '40's

But Playwright Denies Being Under 'Discipline'—To Wed Marilyn Monroe Soon

By ALLEN DRURY
Special to The New York Times

WASHINGTON, June 21—Arthur Miller, playwright, disclosed today a past filled with Communist-front associations and a future filled with Marilyn Monroe. He said he would marry the film star before July 13.

The 40-year-old dramatist, a Pulitzer Prize winner, told the House Committee on Un-American Activities that he had signed many appeals and protests issued by Red front groups in the last decade. But he denied that he ever had been "under Communist discipline." He risked a possible contempt citation by refusing to give the committee names of those he had seen at Communist-run meetings.

Mr. Miller revealed his plans to marry Miss Monroe during a recess in the committee hearing. He said they would be wed before she left for England on July 13 to make a film with Sir Laurence Olivier.

In response to questions by Richard Arens, committee counsel, the playwright testified that

Associated Press Wirephoto

Arthur Miller at a recess yesterday of House hearing.

"in those days"—referring principally to the late Nineteen Forties—"I did sign a lot of things." He said he was not denying that he had also joined in sponsoring many Communist-backed causes.

He said that in recent years he had "ceased issuing statements right and left except where I personally was involved."

"I found I was getting tangled

Continued on Page 9, Column 2

Associated Press Wirephoto

RAINY DEPARTURE: Gen. Nathan F. Twining, left, Air Force Chief of Staff, boarding plane yesterday in Washington in the rain. With him is Lieut. Gen. C. S. Irvine, one of nine officers accompanying General Twining to the Russian air show to be held Sunday.

TWINING AND AIDES OFF FOR MOSCOW

U.S. Air Force Group to View Soviet Aviation Show—Will Make 10-Day Tour

Special to The New York Times.

WASHINGTON, June 21—Gen. Nathan F. Twining, Chief of Staff of the Air Force, left for Moscow today with nine other Air Force officers. They are scheduled to see a Soviet air show Sunday and visit the Soviet countryside.

General Twining said as he boarded his plane that his itinerary made it "clear" that the group would travel outside the immediate Moscow area after the air show. The trip will last ten or twelve days.

Asked whether he carried an invitation for Soviet Air Force officials to make a return visit to the United States, he replied, "I do not."

General Twining said he and his colleagues were "going to see and to listen." He said he would like to ride in Soviet planes, and added that he would report on his return to President Eisenhower, his superiors in the Pentagon and then perhaps "to the American people."

'Very Best Men' on Trip

The Air Chief said he "probably" would learn things he did not now know about Soviet air strength. He declared that the generals accompanying him were "the very best men in the Air Force for a trip of this nature," and all could fly Soviet planes.

General Twining and his aides left National Airport in an Air Force DC-6 transport for an unnamed base in Europe. He said the group would spend twenty-four hours at the base and arrive in Moscow about 4 P. M. on Saturday.

Accompanying General Twining were:

Lieut. Gen. Frank F. Everest, Deputy Chief of Staff for Operations; Lieut. Gen. Donald Putt, Deputy Chief of Staff for Development; Lieut. Gen. Thomas S. Power, commander, Air Research and Development Command; Lieut. Gen. Clarence S. Irvine, Deputy Chief of Staff for Matériel.

Others were Maj. Gen. Albert Boyd, deputy commander, Air Research and Development Command; Brig. Gen. William H. Blanchard, deputy director of operations, Strategic Air Command; Col. Thomas W. Wolfe, air attaché designate to the Soviet Union; Col. James C. Sherrill, General Twining's executive officer, and Lieut. Col. William H. McVey, General Twining's aide.

To Be Shown Air Sites

MOSCOW, June 21 (AP)—General Twining will get to see some of the Soviet Union's hitherto secret air installations.

It was learned today that the Soviet authorities will take him on a tour of aircraft factories in the Moscow area and show him at least one military airfield. They will also show him the noted Zhukovsky air engineering academy, top Soviet air research center.

The United States Air Chief also will be shown military installations in Stalingrad and Leningrad.

East Germans Free 19,000 And Assail 2 Justice Chiefs

By HARRY GILROY
Special to The New York Times.

BERLIN, June 21—The East German Government asserted today it had released more than 19,000 persons from prison in recent weeks. The action was said to have followed re-examination of their cases.

The announcement stated that by this step the East German regime was making "a decisive contribution to alleviation of the German situation and to a broadening of the possibilities of understanding between the two German states."

Perhaps by purposeful timing, the East German Communist party's Central Committee published criticisms today of the state's chief justice officials. Justice Minister Hilde Benjamin and Ernst Melsheimer, the Prosecutor General, came under fire.

They were said to have "applied schematically and rigidly in practice the Marxist maxim that crimes are an expression of the class struggle."

Meaning Is Disputed

The criticism of the justice officials continued with the statement: "They let themselves be told by out-of-the-world theoreticians that even a minor traffic accident was an expression of an aggravated class struggle."

The Government's announcement of the release of prisoners suggested that this should be viewed as of large political significance in West Germany. But an anti-Communist group in West Berlin, the Free Jurists Organization, promptly challenged this.

It said the majority of the prisoners who had recently been released from East German jails had committed ordinary crimes. It added that the only political prisoners released were members of the Social Democratic party, and that this was being done to affect this party in West Germany.

The East German Government said that it had granted an amnesty to 691 Social Democrats.

The Communist party criticisms against the justice officials indicated that important changes might be forthcoming in

Continued on Page 5, Column 6

Questionnaire Is Set On Widening NATO

By W. GRANGER BLAIR
Special to The New York Times.

PARIS, June 21—The North Atlantic Treaty Organization's Committee of Three was reported today to have prepared a list of questions on how to carry out the alliance's non-military aims.

It is understood that the questions will be sent to each of the Foreign Ministers of the fifteen NATO nations. It is hoped that the questionnaires will produce clear-cut answers to the problem of how to advance and unify the economic, social, cultural and political objectives of the West.

The Committee of Three, or "three wise men," was created last May by the alliance's Council of Ministers. The committee was charged then with finding an acceptable system that would bring a unity of purpose to the alliance's policies that so far has been conspicuously absent. Its members

Continued on Page 3, Column 2

BRITISH REDS ASK MORE STALIN DATA

Join the Criticism of Soviet Leaders for Putting Entire Blame on Dictator

Special to The New York Times

LONDON, June 21—The British Communists followed their Italian and French comrades today in protesting against aspects of the Kremlin's downgrading of Stalin.

They demanded "a profound Marxist analysis of the causes of degeneration in the functioning of Soviet democracy and party democracy."

The Political Committee of the British Communist party published a statement that made the following points:

¶Stalin alone cannot be blamed for all the evils of the regime he headed.

¶Communists outside the Soviet Union have been forced to depend on "enemy sources" for information about Nikita S. Khrushchev's denunciation of Stalin because no official texts of the Soviet party leader's speech have been received from Moscow.

¶The Soviet regime is still using the death penalty.

¶Despite the abuses of the Stalinist regime, the Soviet Union achieved "historic successes" in establishing socialism, defeating the Nazis and repairing its war devastation.

¶"A more adequate estimate of the role of Stalin, both in its positive and negative aspects, will be necessary."

Agrees With Other Reds

The Political Committee expressed its agreement with the French Communists and Palmiro Togliatti, Italian Communist leader, who questioned the anti-Stalin campaign and demanded greater autonomy for Italian Communists.

British Communists have appeared to enjoy a considerable degree of autonomy, mainly because they were generally ignored by Moscow.

Today's statement was foreshadowed last month when Rajani Palme Dutt, who is regarded as the "brains" of the British Communist party, defended Stalin in his magazine Labor Monthly.

The British Communist leader, John Gollan, is now in Moscow.

LONDON, June 21 (Reuters)—The British Communist chiefs said the Soviet leaders had been "correct in condemning the cult of the individual and in endorsing the return to Leninist principles of collective leadership and inner party democracy."

Special to The New York Times.

BERLIN, June 21—Walter Ulbricht, East German Communist leader, said today that criticism of the personality cult and of Stalin's mistakes "had made a deep impression on the [East

Continued on Page 5, Column 2

DULLES CHARGES PEIPING NEGLECTS TO DISOWN STALIN

Asserts Chinese Reds Outdo Dictator in Brutality and Reject Ban on Force

WELCOMES SOVIET BIDS

Urges Moscow to Let People Under Its Rule Vote Freely on Communism's Merits

Text of Secretary's address is printed on Page 4.

By LAWRENCE E. DAVIES
Special to The New York Times.

SAN FRANCISCO, June 21—Secretary of State Dulles chided the rulers of Communist China today for not having joined their Russian comrades in repudiating Stalin.

Mr. Dulles also suggested guardedly that forces at work within the Soviet Union and its satellites might offer the world much hope, provided the free nations stayed alert.

He credited the Soviet Communist leaders with having shown at least some signs of hoping to avoid a repetition of the "misrule" of the late Soviet dictator. But the Chinese Red rulers have not gone even this far, the Secretary of State told more than 5,000 at a convention of Kiwanis International.

The Chinese leaders have been "the most dedicated imitators of Stalin," he declared.

Chinese Reds Criticized

"The Chinese Communists have, indeed, sought to outdo Stalin in brutality," the Secretary went on. "And while the Soviet successors to Stalin at least profess to have renounced the use of force in international affairs, the Chinese Communists still refuse this.

"We have been, and are, patiently trying to get them to make a meaningful renunciation of force, particularly in the Taiwan [Formosa] area, but so far without success."

Mr. Dulles noted that Mao Tse-tung, Chinese Communist leader, wrote of Stalin after the dictator's death: "We rallied around him, ceaselessly asking his advice, and constantly drew ideological strength from his works."

[A major editorial in the People's Daily, leading Chinese Communist newspaper, April 5, denounced Stalin and his tactics.]

Speaking of the speech assailing Stalin Nikita S. Khrushchev made at the Twentieth Congress of the Soviet Communist party, Mr. Dulles noted that the Chinese Communist delegate had "applauded 'the firmness and invincibility of the Soviet Commu-

Continued on Page 5, Column 1

PEIPING CONVICTS 17 TOKYO P.O.W.'S

8-to-20-Year Terms Imposed Under New 'Lenient' Policy

By HENRY R. LIEBERMAN
Special to The New York Times.

HONG KONG, June 21—Communist China announced today it had sentenced seventeen Japanese to prison terms of eight to twenty years on war crimes charges.

The Peiping radio said that the Japanese, all former military men and administrators, had pleaded guilty while being tried by special military courts during the last eleven days under a "policy of leniency."

This policy also involves the imminent release of a so-called "first group" representing about one-third of the Japanese that Peiping says it is holding as war criminals.

It was reported earlier from Tokyo that 335 Japanese held in China as war criminals were about to be repatriated. The Hsinhua (New China) news agency said tonight the Japanese ship Koan Maru was expected to arrive in Tangku harbor in North China on Saturday to take these men home.

Last August the Foreign Ministry in Peiping said 1,069 Japanese war criminals were being detained in China.

Eight Japanese were tried in Mukden, in Manchuria, and nine at Taiyuan, capital of Shansi Province, in the delayed war crimes proceedings. The eight sentenced in Mukden and their

Continued on Page 5, Column 4

"All the News That's Fit to Print"

The New York Times.

7:30 A. M. EXTRA

Condensation of U. S. Weather Bureau forecast: Mostly sunny and warm today. Mostly fair and warm tomorrow. Temperature range today: 84—69. Temperature range yesterday: 85.2—67. Full U. S. Weather Bureau Report, Page 50.

VOL. CV No. 35,978. Entered as Second-Class Matter, Post Office, New York, N. Y. NEW YORK, THURSDAY, JULY 26, 1956. Times Square, New York 36, N. Y. Telephone LAckawanna 4-1000 FIVE CENTS

ANDREA DORIA AND STOCKHOLM COLLIDE; 1,134 PASSENGERS ABANDON ITALIAN SHIP IN FOG AT SEA; ALL SAVED, MANY INJURED

STASSEN SUGGESTS EISENHOWER STATE IF HE IS FOR NIXON

Aide to End Pro-Herter Drive If the President Gives Nod to the Vice President

GETS NO G.O.P. BACKING

Says Hall Tries to Foreclose Choice of Delegates in Advance of Convention

By JAMES RESTON

Special to The New York Times.

WASHINGTON, July 25 — Harold E. Stassen, the loneliest man in Washington, said today he would abandon his anti-Nixon campaign if President Eisenhower personally expressed a preference for Vice President Richard M. Nixon as the 1956 election ticket.

In the absence of such a statement from the President, the White House disarmament aide made it clear that he would continue to advocate the Vice-Presidential nomination of Gov. Christian A. Herter of Massachusetts.

The President has let it be known he was "delighted" that Mr. Nixon was available for the Vice-Presidential nomination. But he has not expressed a clear preference for him over other possible candidates.

Takes Aim at Hall

However, a reliable source informed The New York Times today that Governor Herter agreed to nominate Mr. Nixon for the Vice Presidency yesterday after a telephoned message from the White House saying that it was the President's wish that he do so.

Mr. Stassen was left today without the cooperation of Governor Herter or the public support of a single influential Republican politician.

Nevertheless, he took dead aim both at Mr. Nixon and the chairman of the Republican National Committee, Leonard W. Hall.

The 43-year-old Vice President, Mr. Stassen said, ran last in a private poll he (Stassen) conducted on eight potential Republican Vice-Presidential candidates. He did not say who was polled, or who did the polling, or what questions were asked—only that Mr. Nixon, Governor Herter and Mr. Stassen himself were among the eight.

He also wrote a letter in the middle of last night to Repre-

Continued on Page 8, Column 5

Jordanian Group Attacks U. N. Palestine Truce Unit

Villagers' Fire Wounds One Observer —Burns Scores Incident—Amman Puts the Blame on Israelis

By HOMER BIGART

Special to The New York Times.

JERUSALEM, July 25—Jordanian villagers attacked a team of United Nations military observers today near Jerusalem. Lieut. Col. E. H. Thalin of Sweden was seriously wounded by the Jordanian fire, United Nations sources said.

They reported that the villagers "went berserk" after an exchange of fire with Israelis in which several Jordanians were wounded. During the engagement the Israelis employed mortar fire. There were no Israeli casualties.

[Jordanian sources in Amman said Israeli fire had been responsible. The Amman reports said ten Jordanians were wounded.]

Colonel Thalin was the third United Nations casualty in two days. Yesterday two Canadian officers were seriously wounded in a mine explosion on Mount Scopus.

Maj. Gen. E. L. M. Burns of Canada, United Nations truce supervisor, said tonight that he was "astonished and deeply concerned by the attack by the Jordanian villagers."

He had already made arrangements to confer tomorrow with Maj. Gen. Ali Abu Nuwar, Chief of Staff of the Jordanian Army, on measures to be taken by Jordan to reduce the number of provocative incidents along the Israeli frontier. Israel's Premier, David Ben-Gurion, has threatened punitive action unless the provocations cease.

The current trouble spot on the frontier is in the Judean hills only five miles from Jerusalem where raw, new houses

Continued on Page 2, Column 3

DOWNTOWN TO GET 4TH NEW BUILDING

25-Story Structure Is Slated on Broad Street Site of R. C. A. Communications

By GLENN FOWLER

Another large office building is soon to rise in the downtown Manhattan financial district.

The building, the fourth large structure to be planned in the area within the last two years, will be twenty-five stories high. It will cover the block front on Beaver Street between Broad and New Streets, near Bowling Green.

It will stand on a plot of 48,000 square feet, running back 215 feet along Broad Street and 200 feet along New Street.

To be known as 60 Broad Street, the building will have an aluminum facade and a beacon light atop the roof. It will be fully air-conditioned, will have acoustic ceilings and will be equipped with operatorless elevators. Garage space will be provided in the basement. There will be 650,000 square feet of floor space above the ground floor.

The property on which the structure will be built is owned by R. C. A. Communications,

Continued on Page 41, Column 2

CONFEREES VOTE 3.7 BILLION IN AID

Reappropriated Fund Lifts Total to $4,006,570,000—Curb on Tito Supported

Special to The New York Times.

WASHINGTON, July 25—Conferees from the Senate and House of Representatives agreed today on a compromise foreign aid appropriation of $3,766,570,000.

This sum to carry the Mutual Security Program for another year would be increased by $240,000,000 of reappropriated money to a total of $4,006,570,000.

The bargain struck by the conferees amounted to a substantially even split between the $4,110,920,000 in new money originally allocated by the Senate and the $3,425,120,000 provided originally by the House.

President Eisenhower initially had asked for $4,900,000,000 for the fiscal year that opened July 1, although the appropriation for the fiscal year just ended was only $2,700,000,000.

Retained by the conferees was a rider in the Senate bill directing President Eisenhower not to give new military assistance funds to Communist Yugoslavia except for spare parts and replacements.

This stipulation was primarily the work of the Senate Republican leader, William F. Knowland of California. It did not affect $100,000,000 in military aid to Yugoslavia that already is "in the pipeline," nor did it

Continued on Page 12, Column 3

Eisenhower's Four Years

An Analysis of Agriculture Policy And Steps Taken to Meet Problems

This is the fifth of a series of articles analyzing the record of the Eisenhower Administration at the start of the Presidential election campaign.

By WILLIAM M. BLAIR

Special to The New York Times.

WASHINGTON, July 25—President Eisenhower has faced a number of stubborn dilemmas in the last four years but no other problem on the home front has been comparable to the one on farms.

Like the Communist problem overseas, it has absorbed his attention. From time to time it has been mitigated by his policies. Always, however, it has returned to plague him in one form or another.

In his home town of Abilene, Kan., in mid-1952 the President began formulating his program to reconcile freedom and prosperity for the American farmer. As he put it later, "full parity in the market place" and a minimum of Government regulation were his aims.

It has been a long, perplexing struggle for the President. But despite a notable effort, success has eluded him. The farmer still is tied up in Government controls and has considerably less cash in his pockets.

Every new Administration inherits the past. Thus twenty years of Democratic and often bipartisan farm policies have failed, despite high Federal subsidies, to solve the boom and bust ills that have beset agriculture in the midst of an expanding industrial economy and national prosperity.

Indeed, President Eisenhower and his embattled Secretary of Agriculture, Ezra Taft Benson, have blamed these policies and the last two wars for the surpluses that have resisted their remedies and have depressed farm prices.

From a peak of $15,943,000,000 in 1948, farm income fell to $12,851,000,000 in 1950, before the Korean war. It climbed to $14,801,000,000 in 1951, slipped to $14,051,000,000 in the Presiden-

Continued on Page 12, Column 1

Ailing Millikin Plans To Leave the Senate

By WILLIAM S. WHITE

Special to The New York Times.

WASHINGTON, July 25—Senator Eugene D. Millikin of Colorado, a powerful member of the Republican leadership, said a farewell today in the Senate.

He was compelled by long and agonizing illness to announce that he would not seek re-election in the fall.

The decision was a heavy blow to the Republican party generally, and to its conservative wing in particular.

Mr. Millikin as a well campaigner would have been a formidable favorite to keep his seat safe for the Republicans. Even as an ailing prospective campaigner he had been greatly feared by the Democrats.

His retirement seemed plainly to forward Democratic prospects for retaining control

Continued on Page 10, Column 3

CRAFT RUSH TO AID

Terse Radio Messages of the Rescue Vessels Depict Operations

Help for the stricken liners Andrea Doria and Stockholm flowed almost instantly from all points of the compass to the spot at which they collided last night.

Ships large and small, Coast Guard vessels, luxury liners, Gloucester fishing boats, coastal steamers, all headed for the spot off Nantucket Lightship where the lives of some 2,500 persons were in danger.

It was 11:22 last night when the ships collided in a dense fog. The Andrea Doria, luxury liner of the Italian Line, shaken dangerously despite a double hull and other special safety features, sent out the first SOS less than a minute later.

The Coast Guard, with stations at Cape Ann, Cape Cod, Boston and other near-by points, sent out every available craft as soon as the position of the crash had been determined. Then came reassuring promises of help from the Ile de France and other craft, within quick reach of the spot.

The Search and Rescue Division of the Coast Guard in New York received its first alert at 11:25 last night. It was then that the Coast Guard radio station at East Moriches, L. I., notified New York headquarters:

"Andrea Doria and Stockholm collided 11:22 local time Lat. 40:30 N., Long. 69:53 W."

Coast Guard Cutters Aid

The East Moriches radio had picked up simultaneous SOS messages from the ships a minute or two before. The next hour was spent verifying positions and notifying all Coast Guard and merchant ships of the disaster and calling on them for help. The Coast Guard sent out ten cutters from New York, Boston and New London, Conn., and diverted three other ships cruising in that area.

The stark drama being played on the open ocean in darkness and fog was pictured in tense, taut radio messages recorded by the wireless room of The New York Times. They read:

12:21 A. M.—S. S. Stockholm says: Badly damaged. The whole bow crushed and No. 1 hold filled with water. Have to stay in our position. If you [Andrea Doria] can lower your lifeboats we can pick them up.

12:21 A. M.—S. S. Andrea Doria replied: You have to row to us.

12:38 A. M.—S. S. Cape Ann reports: Now between the two ships and her boats are ready. Has two lifeboats.

12:45 A. M. Coast Guard boat says: Ten miles away; have eighteen boats.

1:12 A. M. Andrea Doria says: Needs more lifeboats still.

1:13 A. M. Unidentified ship, when queried, says: We have twelve lifeboats.

Stricken Ship's Boats Useless

1:21 A. M. Cape Ann asks Doria: How close do you want our ship to come to you?

1:24 A. M. Cape Ann reports: We have two boats for Andrea. Now proceeding to get close to her.

1:26 A. M. Andrea Doria reports: Danger immediate, need lifeboats, as many as possible. Can't use our lifeboats.

1:30 A. M. Stockholm gives position: Lat. 40:34 N; Long. 69:45 W.

1:33 A. M. Cape Ann asks Andrea: Want Cape Ann to move in any closer than Cape Ann is now?

1:34 A. M. Ile de France says: We are nine miles from you. Will launch as many boats as possible.

1:43 A. M. Doria repeats earlier message: Here danger immediate. Need lifeboats, as many as possible. Can't use our lifeboats.

1:46 A. M. Unidentified ship radios Andrea: Two lifeboats on way over to you.

1:53 A. M. S. S. Manaqui radios both ships: Will arrive yours at 0900 G. M. T. (5 A. M., E. D. T.) Have two lifeboats.

1:54 A. M. Andrea replies: O. K. Thanks.

1:56 A. M. Unidentified Nor-

Continued on Page 15, Column 1

The New York Times

The 29,000-ton Italian Line vessel, the Andrea Doria, which carried 1,134 passengers

The 12,644-ton Swedish American liner Stockholm, largest liner ever built in Sweden

SHIPS' PIERS QUIET IN NEW YORK PORT

Crowds Expected at Andrea Doria's Docks—Relatives Begin Calling Lines

The sea disaster had not early today awakened the pier at West Forty-fourth Street where the Andrea Doria had been scheduled to dock later in the morning.

This pier, as well as the terminal at West Fifty-seventh Street, where the Stockholm had left just before noon yesterday in a gala sailing, remained dark and quiet.

However, unaccustomed night lights began blinking on at the Italian Line's office at 24 State Street before 4 o'clock when members of the company's staff began arriving.

They had been rounded up from their scattered homes around the Metropolitan area by officials of the line under Rosmino Pernigotti, assistant general manager of the company here.

The company officials were making plans to handle expected crowds at West Forty-fourth Street during the morning. Several thousand visitors were expected to begin gathering there by 8 o'clock, some not knowing about the collision.

It is an axiom in the harbor that every arriving passenger attracts five or more relatives and friends as welcomers, and the Italian Line officials were preparing to give them the tragic news and to forestall a rush by worried relatives on the line's downtown office.

Many of the relatives already knew of the crash at sea, and the office and pier of the com-

Continued on Page 14, Column 3

Many Notables Are Listed Aboard the Andrea Doria

Persons prominent in business, the theatre, politics, journalism and government were among the passengers aboard the Andrea Doria when she collided last night with the Stockholm. Two directors of the Standard Oil Company (New Jersey) were on the passenger list. They were Stewart Coleman, traveling with his family, and Marion W. Boyer, accompanied by his wife. Mr. Coleman, 57 years old, lives at 365 Barrett Road, Cedarhurst, L. I. Mr. Boyer, 54, lives in Greenwich, Conn.

Another passenger was Richardson Dilworth, Mayor of Philadelphia, and his wife. Mr. Dilworth, a lawyer by profession, is 57. He served as a Marine in both World Wars, and received the Purple Heart in World War I and the Silver Star in World War II.

Ruth Roman, Hollywood motion picture star, and her son, Richard Hall, were on the Andrea Doria. Miss Roman recently divorced Mortimer Hall, owner of a Los Angeles radio station.

Two refugees from behind the Iron Curtain, the dancers Istvan Rabovsky and his wife Nora Kovach, also were passengers. They are natives of Hungary. In May, 1953, they fled to the West from East Berlin, where they had gone for a dancing engagement. In 1954, they came to this country.

Also on board were Camille M. Cianfarra, Madrid correspondent of The New York Times, and his family. A native of New York, Mr. Cianfarra joined The Times in 1935 in Rome. He became a specialist in Vatican affairs, and has written two books about the Vatican. He became Madrid correspondent in 1951.

Others on board included Ferdinand M. Thieriot, circulation manager of The San Francisco

Continued on Page 15, Column 5

SHIP BUILT TO TAKE COLLISION SAFELY

Andrea Doria Hull Divided to Give Stability—Lifeboats Could Carry 2,000

The Andrea Doria was specially built to give her more stability in case of just such a collision as she had last night with the Stockholm.

The hull was subdivided into eleven watertight compartments extending the entire length of the ship. Bulkheads parallel with her engine rooms were designed to lessen the effect of a collision.

The ship carried lifeboats with a capacity of 2,000 persons. Some of these boats were made of light metal alloy and were hung from davits operated by motor-driven winches. Two of the boats were motor-driven and fitted with radios.

Luxurious to the last detail, the ship was completely fireproofed and radar-equipped.

The ship has two groups of turbines capable of generating 50,000 horsepower to turn its three blade propellors, each weighing sixteen tons. They are nineteen feet in diameter and turn 143 revolutions a minute.

The Andrea Doria and the Stockholm had been the prides of the Italian and Swedish merchant marines.

The Stockholm, when launched in 1948, was the largest passenger vessel ever to have been built in Swedish yards. The Andrea Doria, when launched in 1951, was the last word in modern design and comfort. Each was flagship of its line until supplanted by new vessels a few years later.

When she went into service as flagship of the Swedish American Line, the Stockholm had a capacity of 364 passengers and 150 officers and crew. Alterations in 1953 increased the capacity to nearly 600 passengers with a proportionate increase in the size of the crew.

The Stockholm had an over-all length of 510 feet and a beam of

Continued on Page 15, Column 6

The New York Times July 26, 1956

SCENE OF THE COLLISION: The liners Andrea Doria and the Stockholm stricken off Nantucket Island (cross).

2D VESSEL IS SAFE

Ile de France In Today With Survivors From Crash Off Nantucket

By MAX FRANKEL

The trans-Atlantic liners Andrea Doria and Stockholm collided in a heavy Atlantic fog at 11:22 o'clock last night, forty-five miles south of Nantucket Island.

The Andrea Doria ordered her 1,134 passengers aboard to abandon ship. All were reported to have been rescued at 4:58 A. M. There was no immediate word, however, on the fate of her crew of 575.

At 5:15 A. M. today, however, the Ile de France reported from the scene that no more help was needed.

The French Liner estimated at 7 A. M. that she would arrive in New York shortly after 6 o'clock this afternoon with 1,000 survivors from the Andrea Doria. It was not clear to which ports the other survivors would be taken.

The Stockholm, although it had taken water through a crushed bow, was able to keep her 550 passengers and crew of 200 aboard. She was waiting for an escort to attempt to return to New York at a slow speed.

Many survivors of the Italian ship were said to have been seriously injured. The Stockholm said she had five "critical" cases aboard. Desperate and repeated calls for medical assistance were radioed from the score of rescue vessels in the area.

Deck Dips into Water

The Andrea Doria lay helpless in the thick fog. The black-and-white ship reported she was listing "very badly." She gave no other indication of the extent or nature of her damage nor was there word whether she could remain afloat.

The Stockholm reported at 6 A. M. that the Andrea Doria's main deck was dipping to the surface of the water.

The 29,000-ton Italian Line vessel apparently was listing so severely that she could launch no more than two of her lifeboats. Her lifeboats can carry 2,000 persons.

The French Ile de France, largest of the rescue vessels on hand, and the Stockholm apparently recovered the bulk of the Andrea Doria's passengers. At one time as many as 100 lifeboats probably were in the area. It was not clear how the passengers were loaded into the lifeboats.

At 4:58, the master of the Ile de France told the Stockholm:

"All passengers rescued.

"Proceeding to New York full speed."

The Ile de France left New York yesterday bound for Le Havre.

Since shortly after the collision, the Andrea Doria had run her lights and radio on emergency power and said she did not how much longer she could keep in touch with rescue craft. Her radio was so weak the Stock-

Continued on Page 14, Column 5

Cause of the Crash Puzzles Radar Men

Experts on radar said today they could not explain how the collision between the Andrea Doria and the Stockholm could have taken place because both vessels were equipped with radar equipment.

They said that even with the "visibility nil" conditions reported in the vicinity each ship should have been able to observe the other for distances up to fifty miles.

The experts declared that, even without knowing precisely what systems the vessels carried, they almost certainly were flexible installations such as are standard on large passenger vessels. They should have been capable of two types of operation—generalized scanning all about the vessel, and a narrower type of observation of a restricted sector of the horizon. They should also have been

Continued on Page 14, Column 6

"All the News That's Fit to Print"

The New York Times.

LATE CITY EDITION

Fair and cool today. Mostly sunny, continued cool tomorrow.
Temperature Range Today—Max., 68; Min., 52
Temperatures Yesterday—Max., 69; Min., 61
Full U. S. Weather Bureau Report, Page 51

VOL. CIII ... No. 35,178. Entered as Second-Class Matter. Post Office, New York, N. Y. NEW YORK, TUESDAY, MAY 18, 1954. Times Square, New York 36, N. Y. Telephone LAckawanna 4-1000 FIVE CENTS

HIGH COURT BANS SCHOOL SEGREGATION; 9-TO-0 DECISION GRANTS TIME TO COMPLY

McCarthy Hearing Off a Week as Eisenhower Bars Report

SENATOR IS IRATE

President Orders Aides Not to Disclose Details of Top-Level Meeting

President's letter and excerpts from transcript, Pages 24, 25, 26.

By W. H. LAWRENCE

Special to The New York Times.

WASHINGTON, May 17—A secrecy directive by President Eisenhower resulted today in an abrupt recess for at least a week of the Senate's Army-McCarthy hearings.

Democratic and Republican Senators, some publicly and some privately, predicted that the investigation might never resume in earnest. However, there were other Senators who insisted that the investigation would go on to completion.

The recess was voted after Herbert Brownell Jr., the Attorney General, disclosed formally that criminal prosecutions might be instituted against those involved in the "preparation and dissemination" of an altered, condensed but still confidential Federal Bureau of Investigation report. This was offered in evidence last week by Senator Joseph R. McCarthy, Republican of Wisconsin.

Republicans outvoted Dem-

Communist Arms Unloaded in Guatemala By Vessel From Polish Port, U. S. Learns

State Department Views News Gravely Because of Red Infiltration

Special to The New York Times.

WASHINGTON, May 17—The State Department said today that it had reliable information that "an important shipment of arms" had been sent from Communist-controlled territory to Guatemala.

It said the arms, now being unloaded at Puerto Barrios, Guatemala, had been shipped from Stettin, a former German Baltic seaport, which has been occupied by Communist Poland since World War II. The Guatemalan regime has been frequently accused of being influenced by Communists.

"Because of the origin of these arms, the point of their embarkation, their destination and the quantity of arms involved, the Department of State considers that this is a development of gravity," the announcement said.

A freighter arrived at Puerto

The New York Times — May 18, 1954

Site of arms arrival (cross)

Embassy Says Nation of Central America May Buy Munitions Anywhere

Barrios last Saturday, the State Department reported, carrying a large shipment of armament consigned to the Guatemalan Government.

The State Department did not divulge the exact quantity of the arms, their nature or where they had been manufactured.

Reliable sources told The New York Times, however, that ten freight car loads of goods listed in the manifest as "hardware" had been unloaded from this ship and sent to the city of Guatemala since Sunday. Guatemala is 150 miles from Puerto Barrios. The

Continued on Page 10, Column 5

REACTION OF SOUTH

'Breathing Spell' for Adjustment Tempers Region's Feelings

By JOHN N. POPHAM

Special to The New York Times.

CHATTANOOGA, Tenn., May 17—The South's reaction to the Supreme Court's decision outlawing racial segregation in public schools appeared to be tempered considerably today.

The time lag allowed for carrying out the required transitions seemed to be the major factor in that reaction.

Southern leaders of both races in political, educational and community service fields expressed comment that covered a wide range. Some spoke bitter words that verged on defiance. Others ranged from sharp disagreement to predictions of peaceful and successful adjustment in accord with the ruling.

But underneath the surface of much of the comment, it was evident that many Southerners recognized that the decision had laid down the legal principle rejecting segregation in public education facilities.

They also noted that it had left open a challenge to the region to join in working out a program of necessary changes in the present bi-racial school systems.

Three of the most illustrative

Associated Press Wirephoto

LEADERS IN SEGREGATION FIGHT: Lawyers who led battle before U. S. Supreme Court for abolition of segregation in public schools congratulate one another as they leave court after announcement of decision. Left to right: George E. C. Hayes, Thurgood Marshall and James M. Nabrit.

1896 RULING UPSET

'Separate but Equal' Doctrine Held Out of Place in Education

Text of Supreme Court decision is printed on Page 15.

By LUTHER A. HUSTON

Special to The New York Times.

WASHINGTON, May 17—The Supreme Court unanimously outlawed today racial segregation in public schools.

Chief Justice Earl Warren read two opinions that put the stamp of unconstitutionality on school systems in twenty-one states and the District of Columbia where segregation is permissive or mandatory.

The court, taking cognizance of the problems involved in the integration of the school systems concerned, put over until the next term, beginning in October, the formulation of decrees to effectuate its 9-to-0 decision.

The opinions set aside the "separate but equal" doctrine laid down by the Supreme Court in 1896.

"In the field of public education," Chief Justice Warren said, "the doctrine of 'separate but equal' has no place. Separate educational facilities are inherently unequal."

He stated the question and

SOVIET BIDS VIENNA CEASE 'INTRIGUES'

Envoy Warns Austrian Chief on Inciting East Zone—Raab Denies Charges

City Colleges' Board Can't Pick Chairman

The Board of Higher Education was unable to elect a chairman at its annual meeting last night at Hunter College.

A spokesman said it was the first time "within memory of board officials" that such a situation had occurred.

Nineteen of the twenty-one

2 TAX PROJECTS DIE IN ESTIMATE BOARD

Beer Levy and More Parking Collections Killed—Payroll Impost Still Weighed

MORETTIS' LAWYER

RULING TO FIGURE

manent Subcommittee of Investigation to recess the hearings until 10 o'clock next Monday morning. They acted amid charges and denials that the way was being prepared for a "whitewash."

Constitutional Division Cited

President Eisenhower cited the constitutional separation of powers between the Executive and Legislative branches in directing that details and conversations at a "high level" Administration meeting on Jan. 21 must be withheld from the committee.

Testimony already has been given that top White House, Justice and Defense officials had made plans at that conference to deal with Senator McCarthy.

The Presidential order served effectively to seal the lips of John G. Adams, the Army's regular counselor, about what Sherman Adams, the chief Presidential assistant, said to him in advising that a written report be prepared on how Senator McCarthy and his chief counsel, Roy M. Cohn, persistently sought preferential treatment for Pvt. G. David Schine.

Before his induction, Mr. Schine was an unpaid consultant to the McCarthy subcommittee, the same group that is now conducting the hearings under the temporary chairmanship of Senator Karl E. Mundt, Republican of South Dakota.

Senator McCarthy angrily denounced today's Eisenhower order as "an Iron Curtain." His ire was shared, but in more restrained terms, by all the Republican and Democratic members of the investigating committee.

The week's postponement of

Continued on Page 24, Column 1

Special to The New York Times.

VIENNA, May 17—The Soviet Union warned Austria today to put an end to "hostile and subversive intrigues" against the Soviet occupation forces, or Soviet authorities would do it themselves.

Ivan I. Ilyichev, Soviet High Commissioner, reverted to a practice of early post-war days by summoning Chancellor Julius Raab and Vice Chancellor Adolf Schaerf to give them this warning. The Chancellor denied the Soviet charges.

Mr. Ilyichev said the Austrian Government had been guilty of staging actions hostile to the Soviet while the Austrian press had published daily slanderous and inciting announcements about the Soviet Union and Soviet occupation troops.

The cessation of Soviet control over the movement of freight, said the High Commissioner, was abused to smuggle militarist literature and provocative incitements into the Soviet zone with the connivance of the Austrian Minister of Interior.

When Soviet authorities ordered the removal of anti-Soviet placards in their zone, the minister instructed his subordinates to disregard the order and the Government approved his action, said Mr. Ilyichev.

He added that the Government, and particularly the Minister of Interior, had tolerated militarist propaganda by former soldiers' organizations and dissemination of propaganda for another Anschluss (union) with Germany.

The High Commissioner reminded the Government leaders that since Austria had not ob-

Continued on Page 9, Column 3

governs the four municipal colleges, attended.

Two members nominated for the one-year-term were unable to attain the required majority of eleven votes. They were Joseph B. Cavallaro, who was up for re-election as chairman, and Dr. Harry J. Carman, who was restored to the board on March 2 by Mayor Wagner.

The election was laid over until June 15.

INDO-CHINA PARLEY WEIGHS TWO PLANS

French and Rebel Peace Bids Will Be Studied Jointly as a Basis for Settlement

By THOMAS J. HAMILTON

Special to The New York Times.

GENEVA, May 17—The Far East conference decided today to take up French and Vietminh proposals jointly as a basis for settlement of the war in Indo-China.

The secret session, which lasted three and a half hours, was generally recognized as the opening round in what may turn out to be a long process of negotiation. Another secret meeting will be held tomorrow.

Western delegates felt that Vyacheslav M. Molotov, Soviet Foreign Minister, was continuing to give the impression that in the end he might throw Moscow's influence on the side of an agreed settlement.

However, the West failed to obtain answers to the two fundamental questions that are expected to determine whether the negotiations here will have any chance of success: Will the Communists agree to a separate settlement for Laos and Cambodia, and will they agree to an armistice in Vietnam without at the same time requiring a political settlement?

The conference will address itself tomorrow to the issue of Laos and Cambodia. The two Indo-Chinese states are relatively free from Communist infiltration, and their leaders contend, with the support of the French, that the only thing that needs to be done is the withdrawal of the Communists.

The Laos-Cambodia and Vietnam issues were discussed inconclusively today after the delegates had devoted the first part of their meeting to the intricate dispute over evacuation of French Union wounded from Dienbienphu, seized by the Communist-

Continued on Page 2, Column 2

Two possible new revenue sources were definitely eliminated yesterday by the Board of Estimate in executive session. They were the proposed 1-cent-a-glass tax on beer and the suggestion to extend metered parking into hours now "free."

In a three-hour City Hall parley the board failed once more to decide on a new impost or imposts to balance the 1954-55 budget of $1,639,438,325. Mayor Wagner said after the meeting that the highly controversial 3 per cent sales tax on commercial services was "still one of the taxes at the top of the list."

Saying he felt the Board of Estimate was close to a decision on the knotty tax question, the Mayor added that "there's no decision to discard any tax" except the two mentioned above, and that at the same time "no tax is inevitable."

The board will wrestle with the tax question again in executive session on Thursday at 2:30 P. M. The Mayor said the City Council, which is holding up a bill to impose the sales tax extension, would be invited to send a delegation to the Thursday session.

Mr. Wagner asserted that he would like to see the Board of Estimate decide the tax question

Continued on Page 32, Column 5

viewpoints were those expressed by Govs. James F. Byrnes of South Carolina and Herman Talmadge of Georgia, and Harold Fleming, a spokesman for the Southern Regional Council, the most effective interracial organization in the South.

Byrnes Sees Reversal

Governor Byrnes, who has vigorously defended the doctrine of separate but equal facilities in education, said that he was "shocked to learn that the court has reversed itself" with regard to past rulings on that doctrine.

However, Governor Byrnes, a former Associate Justice of the Supreme Court, noted that the tribunal had not yet delivered its final decree setting forth the time and terms for ending segregation in the schools.

Pointing out that South Carolina, a party in the litigation before the court, had until October to present arguments on how the Supreme Court should order the implementation of the decision, Governor Byrnes declared "I urge all of our people, white and colored, to exercise restraint and preserve order."

Governor Talmadge repeatedly has vowed there "will never be mixed schools while I am Governor" and has warned that school integration would lead to "blood-

Continued on Page 20, Column 1

MUST BARE TALKS

Jersey Court Orders Counsel to Racketeers in Bergen to Divulge Data to Grand Jury

By GEORGE CABLE WRIGHT

Special to The New York Times.

TRENTON, May 17—The New Jersey Supreme Court today ordered a lawyer who once had represented top Bergen County racketeers to divulge to a grand jury the substance of confidential talks with those clients.

The four-to-three decision reversed the rulings of two lower courts. Involved was the refusal more than a year ago of John E. Selser, Hackensack attorney, to answer four questions put to him by the Bergen County grand jury.

Mr. Selser told the jury that one of his clients, Willie Moretti, slain gambler, had given him the names of persons connected with Walter G. Winne who had received protection money from syndicate gamblers. Mr. Winne, superseded prosecutor of Bergen County, was acquitted last week of nonfeasance in office.

But the attorney balked when asked to reveal these and the names of other persons who, his clients alleged, had been paid protection money or who had received political contributions on the state and county level. He pleaded that his lips were sealed by the duty of "nondisclosure of confidential communications between client and attorney."

Represented Morettis, Others

Mr. Selser had represented Moretti, who was murdered in Cliffside Park in October, 1951, and his brother, the late Salvatore Moretti, for many years. He also was the attorney of record for Joe Adonis, Arthur Longano and James (Piggy) Lynch. The last four were among five men convicted and sent to prison in May, 1952, as the leaders of the Bergen gambling syndicate.

Mr. Selser appeared before the grand jury in February, 1953. The present court action was brought by the state after his refusal to answer the above questions on that occasion and two other questions. The latter pertained to testimony by John J. Dickerson, former Republican state chairman, before the same grand jury.

Mr. Dickerson had testified that Adonis and the two Morettis visited his home in November, 1950, and that Willie told him then that $225,000 in protection money had been paid to Harold

Continued on Page 36, Column 2

IN '54 CAMPAIGN

Decision Tied to Eisenhower —Russell Leads Southerners in Criticism of Court

By WILLIAM S. WHITE

Special to The New York Times.

WASHINGTON, May 17 — Congress as a whole grappled gingerly today with the profound political implications of the Supreme Court's anti-segregation decision.

It became clear at once—and by both parties was accepted in private as inevitable—that the court's action would figure importantly in the coming Congressional election campaigns.

Publicly, however, the Republicans and the non-Southern Democrats, on the whole maintained silence. The Southerners, all angry or sorrowing in one degree or another, were quickly articulate and split among themselves into at least three factions.

¶One Southern group, by all the indications not a large one, was openly defiant of the court, as typified by the comment of Senator James O. Eastland of Mississippi.

"The South," Mr. Eastland said, "will not abide by nor obey this legislative decision by a political court."

¶A second Southern group, while not openly challenging the court, began to threaten efforts to force an alteration of its view, as illustrated by the comment of

Continued on Page 20, Column 2

"We come then to the question presented: Does segregation of children in public schools solely on the basis of race, even though physical facilities and other 'tangible' factors may be equal, deprive the children of the minority group of equal educational opportunities? We believe that it does."

States Stressed Rights

The court's opinion does not apply to private schools. It is directed entirely at public schools. It does not affect the "separate but equal doctrine" as applied on railroads and other public carriers entirely within states that have such restrictions.

The principal ruling of the court was in four cases involving state laws. The states' right to operate separated schools had been argued before the court on two occasions by representatives of South Carolina, Virginia, Kansas and Delaware.

In these cases, consolidated in one opinion, the high court held that school segregation deprived Negroes of "the equal protection of the laws guaranteed by the Fourteenth Amendment."

The other opinion involved the District of Columbia. Here schools have been segregated since Civil War days under laws passed by Congress.

"In view of our decision that the Constitution prohibits the states from maintaining racially segregated public schools," the Chief Justice said, "it would be unthinkable that the same Constitution would impose a lesser duty on the Federal Government.

"We hold that racial segregation in the public schools of the District of Columbia is a denial

Continued on Page 14, Column 6

Churchill Asks Negotiated Peace With Guarantees for Indo-China

By DREW MIDDLETON

Special to The New York Times.

LONDON, May 17—Britain will seek effective international guarantees for any peace settlement in Indo-China, Prime Minister Churchill declared today.

Negotiation of an "acceptable" settlement at the Geneva conference remains the immediate task of the British Government, Sir Winston emphasized in a statement to the House of Commons.

Until the outcome of that conference is known, he added, "final decisions" cannot be taken by the Government about the establishment of a collective defense system in Southeast Asia and the Western Pacific.

Peace by negotiation emerged from Sir Winston's cautious statement as the only policy that the Cabinet was ready to apply to the problem of Indo-China. Observers were struck by the fact that, aside from the Prime Minister's reference to the necessity of backing a settlement there with guarantees, the British position was substantially the same as when the Geneva conference began.

[Indonesia is considering asking India and Burma to join her in a nonaggression treaty with Communist China as a means of offsetting United States plans for a Southeast Asian alliance.]

Sir Winston's adherence to negotiation is acceptable to both major parties in the Commons,

Continued on Page 4, Column 3

Costello Is Sentenced to 5 Years, Fined $30,000 in U. S. Tax Case

By EDWARD RANZAL

Frank Costello was sentenced yesterday by Federal Judge John F. X. McGohey to five years in jail and fined $30,000 for income tax evasion.

The dapper, 61-year-old gambler was remanded immediately. Later Judge Harold R. Medina in the United States Court of Appeals refused to set bail pending appeal. Costello, who listened to the sentencing in icy-calm manner, was taken to the Federal House of Detention, 427 West Street.

Besides the jail sentence and the fines, Judge McGohey also assessed Costello for court costs. Lloyd F. MacMahon, chief assistant United States Attorney, said the costs would be about $5,000, only a fraction of what it cost the Government in its investigation, which began in earnest in 1952.

Costello was convicted Thursday night by a Federal court jury of five women and seven men of three counts of a four-count indictment. They found the gambler guilty of evading a total of $51,095 in taxes from 1947 through 1949.

In 1947 Costello evaded $22,563; in 1948, $13,786, and in 1949, $14,746. He was acquitted of the charge of evading taxes in 1946. Costello's attorney, Leo C. Fennelly, told Judge McGohey that the acquittal on this count meant that the gambler was entitled to a refund for that year.

Before the sentencing Mr. MacMahon said that for years Costello had schemed to cheat the Government out of taxes. He added that the gambler had concealed at least $140,000 of his income from 1947 through 1949, more than half his income.

Mr. MacMahon contended that Costello, by devious means, had concealed the receipt of his income as well as the source by using cash in every transaction where it was possible.

Evidence at the six-week trial, the prosecutor said, showed that from 1937 through 1945 Costello deliberately underestimated his income by at least $202,000. The statute of limitations, he added, bars prosecution for the earlier tax evasions.

"Costello has spent a lifetime making money on the shady side

Continued on Page 36, Column 4

'Voice' Speaks in 34 Languages To Flash Court Ruling to World

Within an hour after the Supreme Court decision on school segregation yesterday afternoon, the Voice of America sent a news broadcast by shortwave to Eastern Europe.

The decision came in time for the regularly scheduled "World-wide English Broadcast" at 2 o'clock. The broadcast was written in English on the Voice's central desk and was sent by teletype to the thirty-four language desks.

There it was translated and sent out in various foreign tongues all over the world as broadcast time arrived for each.

"The Supreme Court has ruled unanimously," the Voice said in its broadcast, "that racial segregation has no place in American public education. It held that separation of students on a racial basis denies equal educational opportunities.

"Chief Justice [Earl] Warren, reading the court's findings, said that the doctrine of providing separate but equal facilities has no place in public education. Separation of children solely because of race, he said, generates feelings in their hearts and minds which might never be undone. * * *

"The ruling in effect outlaws all segregation in public schools throughout the United States. The court held that to separate students is a denial of the due process of law guaranteed by the Fifth Amendment to the Constitution and equal opportunity

Continued on Page 15, Column 4

"All the News That's Fit to Print"

The New York Times.

LATE CITY EDITION
Condensation of U. S. Weather Bureau forecast:
Fair and mild today and tomorrow.
Temperature range today: 67—44.
Temperature range yesterday: 67.4—50.8.
Full U. S. Weather Bureau Report, Page 62.

VOL. CVI . . . . No. 36,080. Entered as Second-Class Matter, Post Office, New York, N. Y. NEW YORK, MONDAY, NOVEMBER 5, 1956. Times Square, New York 36, N. Y. Telephone Lackawanna 4-1000 FIVE CENTS

BRITISH AND FRENCH INVADE EGYPT BY AIR; U. N. APPROVES A POLICE FORCE FOR MIDEAST

Russians Crush Hungarian Rebels; U.N. Inquiry Voted; Eisenhower Note to Bulganin Urges Troop Withdrawal

PRESIDENT SEEMS NEW YORK VICTOR; JAVITS IS FAVORED

Connecticut and New Jersey Trends Are Also to G. O. P. —Cut in '52 Margin Seen

By LEO EGAN

All signs point to a victory for President Eisenhower in New York State tomorrow.

This conclusion is the result of an examination of the straws normally used by political leaders and forecasters to ascertain the direction and velocity of electoral currents.

But opinion is divided as to the strength of the tide apparently running in the President's favor. One question Republicans and Democrats are asking themselves is:

Will it be strong enough to carry Attorney General Jacob K. Javits to victor in his Senatorial contest with Mayor Wagner, the Democratic candidate?

The preponderant but by no means unanimous view is that it will be. The only phase of the question on which there is any unanimity is that Mr. Javits' margin, if he wins, will be far smaller than had been indicated prior to the outbreak of hostilities in the Middle East.

Parallel Trend in 3 States

In New Jersey and Connecticut, where the political currents usually run parallel to New York's, the same type of straws indicate that both states will be found in the Eisenhower column again this year. The only serious unresolved question in each is the size of the expected victory of President Eisenhower.

As in New York some forecasters and leaders are of the opinion that the margins for the Republican Presidential ticket in both New Jersey and Connecticut will approach and possibly surpass that of 1952. But the preponderant view is that they will be somewhat smaller.

In all three states Republicans are anxiously scanning weather forecasts and warning each other against overconfidence. Their forecasts and hopes rely heavily on a large vote in Tuesday's elections. Either the weather or complacency, by re-

Continued on Page 28, Column 5

HUNGARIANS TELL OF FINAL ASSAULT

Cry for Aid Heard by World in Last-Hour Broadcasts

By The Associated Press.

VIENNA, Nov. 4—Dramatic appeals for Western aid and firm avowals of intentions to fight to the end marked the news from Hungarian rebels as they fought the Russians today.

Premier Imre Nagy, who is reported to be a prisoner, led off with a broadcast over the Budapest radio:

"Soviet troops have opened an attack on Budapest at dawn with the clear intention to overthrow the lawful, democratic Government of the Hungarian people.

"Our troops are fighting the Soviets for right and freedom. The Government is at its place.

"This we bring to the information of the Hungarian people and the entire world."

Then came a series of messages by various routes:

The Budapest radio:

"Russian officers, Russian soldiers, stop shooting! Avoid a blood-bath! We are your friends and will remain so."

A Hungarian news agency message by teletype line to the Associated Press bureau in Vienna:

"Russian gangsters have be-

Continued on Page 22, Column 4

Stevenson Proposes U.N. Satellite Watch

Text of Stevenson's telegram is printed on Page 26.

By HARRISON E. SALISBURY
Special to The New York Times.

CHICAGO, Nov. 4—Adlai E. Stevenson proposed to President Eisenhower today that the United Nations Peace Observation Commission fly watchers into Hungary and other satellite nations such as Poland.

Mr. Stevenson's proposal was the fruit of night-long study of the rapidly mounting European crisis. He telegraphed his suggestion to the White House soon after 7 A. M.

Mr. Stevenson assured the President of his desire to "be as helpful as I can." He then proposed a course of action that he suggested might "offer protection or relief to the satellite nations which are now under

Continued on Page 26, Column 4

EISENHOWER SEES HIS TOP ADVISERS

Tells Soviet Premier West Is Shocked by Re-entry of Forces in Hungary

By DANA ADAMS SCHMIDT
Special to The New York Times.

WASHINGTON, Nov. 4—President Eisenhower, in an eleventh-hour move to save the freedom of Hungary, sent an urgent and personal message today to Marshal Nikolai A. Bulganin, Premier of the Soviet Union.

The President conferred with his top advisers on "ways and means" by which the United States could bring about a Soviet withdrawal and gain for Hungary the right to choose her own Government.

Then the President sent what he himself called an "urgent message" to Premier Bulganin. The President's statement read as follows:

"I feel that Western opinion, which was so uplifted only a few days ago by the news that the Soviet Union intended to withdraw its forces from Hungary, has now suffered corresponding shock and dismay at the Soviet attack on the people and Government of Hungary.

Meetings of Day Outlined

"I met today with the Secretary of State at Walter Reed Hospital and later with the Acting Secretary of State [Herbert Hoover, Jr.] and some of his staff, the Director of the Central Intelligence Agency, and some of my staff, to discuss the ways and means available to the United States which would result in:

"1. Withdrawal of Soviet troops from Hungary.

"2. Achieve for Hungary its own right of self-determination in the choice of its Government.

"I have sent an urgent message to Premier Bulganin on these points.

"There was likewise a thorough review of the Middle East situation and the measures now under way in the United Nations to restore peace in that area and to lay the groundwork for constructive solutions of its problems."

The President's feelings of shock and dismay were echoed at all levels of official Washington.

Some officials had suggested several days ago that the United States could have exerted some deterrent influence on the Soviet Union by some demonstrative movements of the Strategic Air Force, and by cancellation of military leaves. But these ideas did not gain Administration favor, and there was no evidence that they were discussed at

Continued on Page 23, Column 6

NEW RED REGIME

Kadar Heads a Cabinet Loyal to Moscow— Nagy a Prisoner

Program of new Hungarian regime is on Page 20.

By ELIE ABEL
Special to The New York Times.

VIENNA, Monday, Nov. 5—Hungary's brave hopes for independence lay crushed by the mailed fist of Soviet power.

Eight Soviet divisions, seven of them armored, and squadron after squadron of bombers overwhelmed the revolution against Soviet domination in its twelfth day, reports from Budapest said.

The end came with all the suddenness of modern war as dawn broke yesterday over Budapest.

Daylight found Premier Imre Nagy and most of his Cabinet prisoners of the Russians. No word about their whereabouts has leaked through the communications blackout so far.

A new Communist dictatorship presumably loyal to Moscow has been installed under the protection of the Soviet Army.

It is headed by Janos Kadar, First Secretary of the Hungarian Working People's (Communist) party.

Moscow Broadcasts Program

According to the Moscow radio, his colleagues in the regime are Antal Apro, a Deputy Premier under Mr. Nagy; Ferenc Munich, Hungarian Ambassador to Yugoslavia who in the turmoil of the last fortnight served briefly as Mr. Nagy's Minister of Interior, and Istvan Kossa.

[President Tito of Yugoslavia expressed approval of the new Kadar Government in Hungary.]

It seemed fitting that a fifteen-point program of the new Kadar Government should be broadcast first by the Moscow radio. The main points of that program, reminiscent of Marshal Tito's in Yugoslavia, are:

¶Unconditional independence and full sovereignty for Hungary.

¶Defense of the Communist system to preserve the "achievements of the last twelve years."

¶Cooperation with other Communist countries "on the basis of absolute political and economic equality."

¶Peaceful cooperation also with all other countries regardless of their "social systems or forms of government."

¶Improved living standards and better housing for the workers.

¶Elimination of bureaucracy

Continued on Page 21, Column 1

LABORITES PROTEST IN LONDON: The scene yesterday in Trafalgar Square as Britain's Labor party held a rally to protest against the handling of the Middle East situation by the government of Prime Minister Eden.
Associated Press Radiophoto

U. N. BODY ORDERS STUDY IN HUNGARY

Assembly Votes 50-8 to Send Investigators—Calls for Troop Withdrawal

Text of resolution, excerpts from debate, Pages 16, 17

By LINDESAY PARROTT
Special to The New York Times.

UNITED NATIONS, N.Y., Nov. 4—The General Assembly voted today for a United Nations investigation in Hungary.

The seventy-six-nation body deplored the use of force by the Soviet Union to crush the Hungarian revolt and called on the Soviet Government to desist from intervention in Hungarian affairs. The Soviet Government was asked to withdraw its forces "without delay."

The Assembly balloted in special session on a resolution introduced by Henry Cabot Lodge Jr. of the United States. It requested Secretary General Dag Hammarskjold to send his representatives into the central European state.

The resolution instructed the international investigators to look into the situation brought

Continued on Page 15, Column 3

U. N. Votes Police Force To Keep Peace in Mideast

By KATHLEEN McLAUGHLIN
Special to The New York Times.

UNITED NATIONS, N. Y., Monday, Nov. 5—The General Assembly voted early this morning to create an international United Nations Command Force, with the duty of supervising the cessation of the fighting in the Middle East. The vote was 57 to 0, with eighteen abstentions.

Maj. Gen. E. L. M. Burns of Canada, chief of the United Nations Truce Supervision Organization, was named Chief of Staff of the new unit, under the provisions of a resolution sponsored by Canada, Norway and Colombia.

Dag Hammarskjold, Secretary General, set out in the plan that none of the personnel of the international force should be drawn from the five countries that hold permanent membership

Hammarskjold's reports and debate excerpts, Pages 10, 11.

on the Security Council. The permanent members are the United States, Britain, France, the Soviet Union and Nationalist China.

Rudecindo Ortega of Chile, president of the Assembly, adjourned the meeting at 12:30 A. M. Delegates had left the headquarters before the news arrived that British-French forces had landed in Egypt.

Although United States personnel will not be included in the command force, the nation will support and help "in important ways," Henry Cabot Lodge Jr., United States delegate, assured the Assembly.

To facilitate the success of its

Continued on Page 10, Column 3

LONDON AND PARIS SET SUEZ TERMS

Agree to Truce as Soon as Egypt and Israel Accept U. N. Buffer Force

Special to The New York Times.

LONDON, Monday, Nov. 5—Britain announced this morning that she and France would cease all military action against Egypt as soon as the Israeli and Egyptian Governments signified acceptance of the United Nations plan for an international police force.

The British and French stand was contained in a reply to Dag Hammarskjold, Secretary General of the United Nations, made public by the Foreign Office today. The reply dealt with United Nations resolutions calling for a cease-fire in Egypt and for an international force to bring this about.

[Israel in her reply to the United Nations indicated that she would make a cease-fire conditional on immediate peace talks with Egypt, end of the Egyptian blockade of Israeli shipping and recall of the fedayeen (commando) gangs.

[Egypt had replied earlier that she agreed to a cease-fire provided Israeli troops withdrew behind the 1949 armistice lines.]

The British reply said that the French and British governments warmly welcomed the idea that an international police force be used as a shield between Israel and Egypt pending a Palestine settlement and a settlement of the question of the Suez Canal.

"But according to their information, neither the Israel nor the Egyptian Government has accepted such a proposal," the reply said.

"The two Governments continue to believe that it is neces-

Continued on Page 3, Column 1

Blockade of Canal Protested by Soviet

By WILLIAM J. JORDEN
Special to The New York Times.

MOSCOW, Nov. 4—The Soviet Union delivered sharp notes to Britain and France today protesting their closing of parts of the Mediterranean Sea and Red Sea to commercial shipping.

The Soviet Union called the British-French action an "act of aggression" and violation of international agreements. The Soviet protest said the action by the two Western powers in effect closed the Suez Canal to other nations. It added that both nations were committed to keep that waterway open in peace and war under the Constantinople Convention of 1888.

The Moscow Government said the action was "certain to result

Continued on Page 8, Column 3

THRONG IN LONDON DENOUNCES EDEN

Demonstrators Demanding His Resignation Over War Clash With Police

By DREW MIDDLETON
Special to The New York Times.

LONDON, Nov. 4—Mounted policemen charged a crowd of cheering, jeering demonstrators demanding the resignation of Prime Minister Eden tonight.

Goaded by Aneurin Bevan's polemics against the Government's intervention policy in Egypt, thousands of persons left a mass meeting in Trafalgar Square and swept down Whitehall toward Downing Street.

The crowd was checked short of the Whitehall entrance to Downing Street. Setting their horses at a brisk trot, the police drove the crowd down Whitehall toward the Cenotaph that honors Britain's dead in two world wars.

The crowd chanted "Eden must go!" and shrieked "Fascist bullies!" at the policemen. Red banners proclaimed "Law not war." The Trafalgar Square meeting may have been the wildest political demonstration Britain has known since the uproar over unemployment in the Thirties. Scotland Yard said at least eight policemen had been injured and more than twenty-seven persons arrested.

Gaitskell Makes Appeal

Hugh Gaitskell, leader of the Labor party, promised Conservative members of Parliament tonight that if they would oust the Prime Minister and halt the invasion of Egypt he and his followers in the Commons would support a new Conservative Government.

This shrewd incitement to rebellion in the Conservative ranks, made in a national broadcast, came at the close of one of the most tumultuous days in Britain's modern political history.

Mr. Bevan welcomed the "spontaneous" demonstration. The mass meeting in fact was arranged by the National Council of Labor.

Contingents from the constituency labor parties of the London area marched to the meeting, singing and shouting. It was the largest popular demonstration against the Government and its policy that the Labor party has yet organized.

The demonstration was one of a number held in the nation.

There are good judges of British political behavior who be-

Continued on Page 2, Column 3

Gomulka Asks 'Iron Discipline'; Cardinal Backs Polish Leader

By SYDNEY GRUSON
Special to The New York Times.

WARSAW, Nov. 4—Wladyslaw Gomulka told the Polish people today that "iron discipline" was necessary to avoid the "terrible fate" that had befallen Hungary.

The appeal of the United Workers (Communist) party leader was backed by Stefan Cardinal Wyszynski, Roman Catholic Primate of Poland, in his first public sermon since he was freed last week after three years' detention.

The news from Hungary cast no less a shadow over the meeting addressed by M. Gomulka than over the thousands of people who crowded inside the Church of the Holy Cross, and on the street outside, to hear Cardinal Wyszynski.

Not taking back one word of the Polish party's publicly expressed support for the Hungarians, M. Gomulka said "it depends only on us" whether Poland would suffer Hungary's fate. The way to avoid it, he added, was "to obey strictly the party and the Government."

"For the good of the Fatherland and the safety of our homes no rioting or demonstrations will be tolerated," M. Gomulka said.

Cardinal Wyszynski spoke less harshly but equally clearly. "We appeal to the heart of the nation, which is famous for its willingness to sacrifice in the name of the Fatherland," Cardinal Wyszynski said.

"But today even more important than a willingness to make the supreme sacrifice is a willingness to work for the good of our country," he added.

The two men's words reflected the feeling of tremendous responsibility that now weighs upon every Pole. The attitude here is that the survival of Poland is at stake and all other questions must be put aside. That is why the head of the Polish Communist party and the head of the Catholic Church in Poland have the same message for the nation today.

This morning's news of the

Continued on Page 19, Column 5

PARATROOPERS IN

Operation to Capture Suez Zone Begins— Fleet at Hand

By THOMAS P. RONAN
Special to The New York Times.

LONDON, Monday, Nov. 5—British and French forces invaded Egypt early today.

The British Defense Ministry said British and French parachutists had landed on Egyptian soil.

The people of Port Said, the port on the Mediterranean or northern end of the Suez Canal, had been warned by the Voice of Britain, radio station in Cyprus, to ensure the safety of the paratroops.

A dispatch from Cyprus said that the radio station was warning Egyptians to keep off the streets and to take cover immediately.

The paratroopers took off from the floodlit Cyprus airfields in dozens of Royal Air Force Hastings and Valetta transports just before dawn. Ninety minutes later the first wave was on the ground in the canal zone.

An Egyptian communiqué, broadcast by Cairo, reported the British-French drops. It said the parachutists had been "completely annihilated."

Take-offs from Cyprus

The Cyprus radio said the planes carrying the airborne troops had been taking off from Cyprus airfields. Troops of the British and French armies sailed from Cyprus yesterday for the invasion.

The start of the invasion carries on the British and French Governments' joint intention of taking control of the Suez Canal Zone by force.

A communique from British-French headquarters in Cyprus reported that men of the Allied parachute battalion were dropped over the Port Said area. Port Said provided the necessary facilities for the large-scale landing of troops and military equipment. [No further details of the landings had been reported up to 5 A. M., New York time.]

It was expected that some landings would also be made at the southern end of the canal, probably at Port Tewfik, and the two forces would drive to-

Continued on Page 4, Column 4

DULLES' SURGERY REMOVED CANCER

No Malignant Spread Found —His Condition Is 'Good'

By ALVIN SHUSTER
Special to The New York Times.

WASHINGTON, Nov. 4—The intestinal section removed from John Foster Dulles was cancerous, the State Department said today.

It emphasized that a thorough examination revealed "no evidence" that the malignancy had spread. The 68-year-old Secretary of State underwent an emergency operation yesterday.

Lincoln White, department press officer, said the Secretary was in "good" condition and was expected to return to his office in about six weeks.

Mr. Dulles was taken to Walter Reed Army Hospital yesterday after having awakened with sharp abdominal pains. The original diagnosis was appendicitis.

Today's medical bulletin described the tissue removed from the large intestine as adenocarcinoma, a malignant tumor. "Complete removal of the diseased tissue was accomplished," it added.

Mr. White declined to say whether the Secretary had been informed of the malignancy. Mr. Dulles' temperature was re-

Continued on Page 26, Column 1

THE AGE OF TELEVISION

FRANK RICH

By the mid-1950's nearly every American household owned a television.

If America in the 1950's could be summed up by a single word, it might be television. A novelty at the decade's dawn, TV was ubiquitous before it was over, the appliance that radically remade America's culture, politics and families alike. In the iconic Kodak snapshot of the era, a happy pair of young and hopeful postwar American parents and their beaming children gathered in their comfortable new suburban living room, all eyes glued to the majestic electronic box in their midst. Chances are they were watching families who more or less mirrored their own: Lucy and Desi,[1] Ozzie and Harriet, the Cleavers. The audience and their most popular entertainers all shared the same gleaming bubble: a tranquil, white, middle-class America where father could be counted on to know best.

This America had its political correlative in Washington, where Ike, a genial father figure, had put away his uniform to preside calmly over a decade of peace and runaway prosperity. New homes were rolling off the assembly line as fast as TV sets. So were Detroit's cars, which exchanged their monochromatic wartime utilitarianism for voluptuous bodies and hopped-up engines that managed to convey both the curves of the decade's premiere sex symbol, Marilyn Monroe, and the soaring futurism of jet travel. To accommodate these hot

The suburban life style was part of the American dream in the decade that followed World War II.

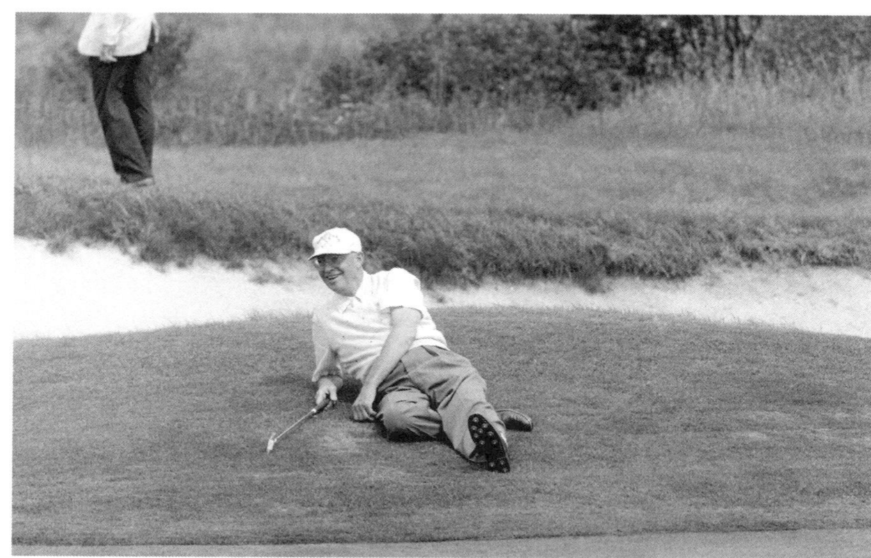

President Eisenhower, a father figure to many Americans, loved golf and spent many an hour on the links.

new vehicles, superhighways rolled out like ribbons over the American landscape, dotted by new pit stops called Holiday Inns. Now everyone could drive easily to the promised paradise of California. That state's dizzying growth was epitomized by the newly constructed Disneyland,[2] the first tourist mecca to be named after a hit network TV show. Maybe America's aging towns were about to be rendered obsolete by all those highways passing them by; maybe the Wild West had vanished forever into an endless procession of clichéd Hollywood westerns. But the idyllic trace memories of that vanished American past were preserved in Walt's spotless Main Street USA, where every day was the Fourth of July, and in the giddy re-enactments on tap in the subdivision of Frontierland.

Yes, there were some storm clouds over this contented America, but nothing to deter the president from playing golf. By mid-decade Joe McCarthy and the most hysterical symptoms of Red Panic had started to fade, and the Soviet threat, while worrisome, showed few signs of evolving from a Cold War into a hot one. To Americans, the Viet Minh's routing of the French at Dien Bien Phu seemed a million miles away, if it registered at all.[3] There were just too many miracles testifying to the inexorable march of progress, from the Salk vaccine[4] to Univac, Polaroid, Xerox, CinemaScope, fluoride, Tang, Saran Wrap and the fast-food revolution spawned by McDonald's. (Eating in a wide-finned car was nearly as exciting a novelty as making out in one.)

When the 1950's passed into memory, this buoyant, nostalgic image of the decade endured. After all hell broke loose in the 1960's, the 50's were increasingly mythologized as the last time when Americans were all on the same page, marriages were happy, teenagers could be depicted by Norman Rockwell, and everyone could smoke longer and sexier cigarettes without having to worry about their health. The grown-ups had Lawrence Welk to beguile them, and America's youth were more than content with the gentrified dance parties of Dick Clark. The No. 1 song on "Your Hit Parade" could still be as reassuring as Doris Day's "Que Sera, Sera."

FURTHER READING

1 "Radio and Television; Return of 'I Love Lucy,'" see September 17, 1952, article.
2 "Disneyland Gets Its Last Touches," see July 9, 1955, article.
3 "10,000 In Redoubt," see May 9, 1954, front page.
4 "Vaccine for Polio Successful," see March 27, 1953, front page.

The Federal-Aid Highway Act of 1956 paved the way for the rapid construction of superhighways all over the country.

Crowds walk through the gate of Sleeping Beauty's Castle at Walt Disney's theme park, Disneyland.

Senator Joseph R. McCarthy attending a special committee to investigate labor racketeering in 1957.

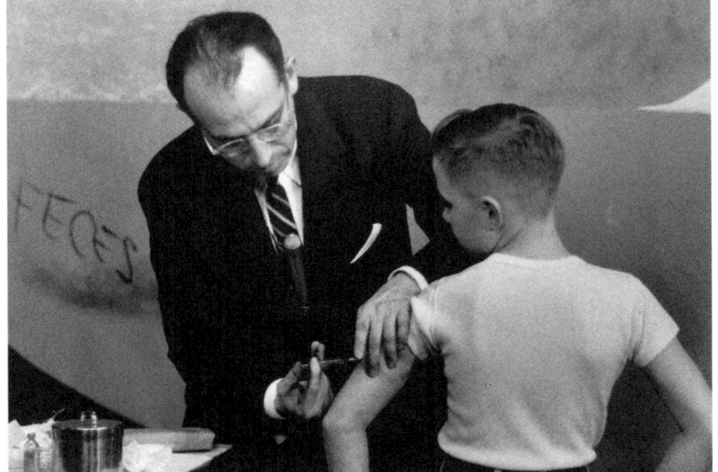

Dr. Jonas Salk inoculates a young boy with his new polio vaccine. Cases of the disease dropped by 85 percent just two years after the vaccine was put into use.

In 1955 entrepreneur Ray Kroc began franchising McDonald's restaurants, like this drive-in, all over the country.

The works of Tennessee Williams gave theatergoers a vision of life in the South in the 1940's and 1950's.

But of course it was all a fantasy. There was a rebellion brewing, visible in the pages of The New York Times and elsewhere, even if airbrushed out of most popular culture and public behavior. The fissures of sex, race and political and international conflict were just below the placid surface; the earthquakes to come were already on their way.

The year 1953 alone brought three harbingers of that future: the publication of James Baldwin's "Go Tell It on the Mountain"[5] and William Burroughs's "Junkie: Confessions of an Unredeemed Drug Addict" as well as the first issue of Hugh Hefner's Playboy, an alternative utopian fantasyland to Disney's created by another Middle American entrepreneur. The sexual anxiety lurking beneath the squeaky-clean families apotheosized on TV would rise to the surface in such cultural phenomena as Vladimir Nabokov's "Lolita"[6] (1955), the stage (1955) and film (1958) incarnations of Tennessee Williams's "Cat on a Hot Tin Roof" and Alfred Hitchcock's "Vertigo" (1958). Throughout the decade, new novelists as various as Grace Metalious ("Peyton Place," 1956), Philip Roth ("Goodbye, Columbus," 1959) and John Updike ("Rabbit, Run," 1960) would join J. D. Salinger ("Catcher in the Rye," 1951) in puncturing the complacent cliches of the postwar American dream. The youth revolt of the 60's was also on its way, given embryonic voice by artists as different as Elvis Presley[7] and Jack Kerouac ("On the

"American Bandstand" was the longest-running musical show in television history.

Road," 1957). Parents found their fears of the next generation realized as larger-than-life nightmares in mainstream entertainments from Hollywood ("The Blackboard Jungle," 1955) and Broadway ("West Side Story," 1957[8]).

Even so, many Americans were unaware that the Supreme Court's 1954 Brown v. Board of Education, decision was only the beginning, not the end, of a tumultuous new chapter in America's long-running racial drama.[9] Not even most progressives imagined that some American housewives would evolve into Betty Friedans instead of Donna Reeds. Only at the end of the decade would the shooting down of an American U-2 spy plane over the Soviet Union light the fuse of nuclear terror that would explode in the Cuban missile crisis of 1962.[10]

By then Americans had elected their first television president, the first American leader with the charisma of a Hollywood star. When the entire country gathered as one to watch J.F.K.'s final tragic chapter play out as a marathon television drama a year later, whatever remained of the deceptively tranquil America of the 1950's was decisively swept away.

FRANK RICH *has been an Op-Ed columnist for The New York Times since 1994. He had been The Times's chief drama critic since 1980 and has written about culture and politics for many other publications. His books include "Ghost Light" (2000), a childhood memoir set in the 1950's and '60's, and "The Greatest Story Ever Sold: The Decline and Fall of Truth From 9/11 to Katrina" (2006).*

5 "Guilt Was Everywhere," see May 17, 1953, article.
6 "The Tragedy of Man Driven by Desire," see August 17, 1958, article.
7 "TV: New Phenomenon," see June 6, 1956, article.
8 "Theatre: The Jungles of the City," see September 27, 1957, article.
9 "Editorial Excerpts From the Nation's Press on Segregation Ruling," see May 18, 1954, article.
10 "'Confession' Cited; Khrushchev Charges Jet was 1,200 miles from the border," see May 8, 1960, front page.

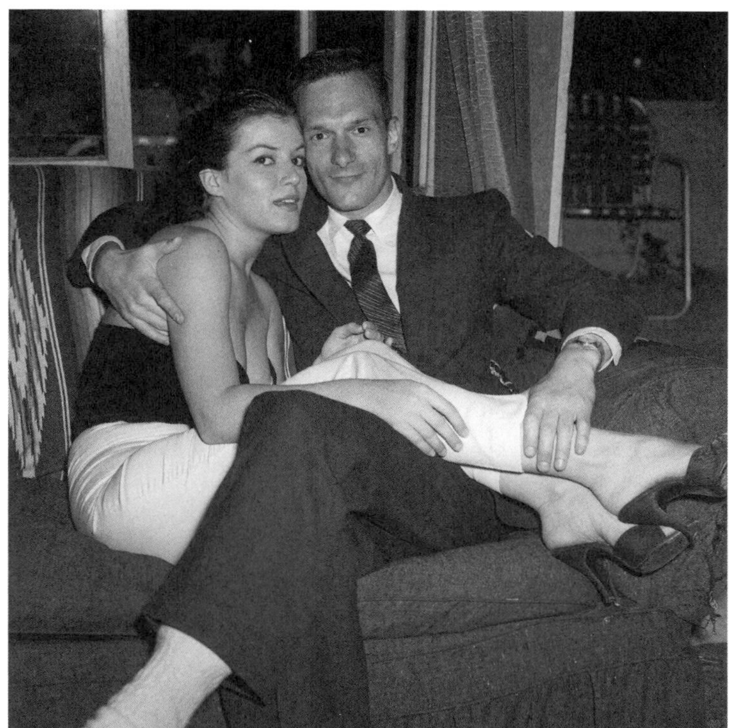

Hugh Hefner, seen here with Joan Bradshaw in 1957, published the first issue of Playboy in 1953, which featured Marilyn Monroe as its centerfold.

The plaintiffs in Brown vs. Board of Education. Oliver L. Brown, the named plaintiff, was a parent and welder from Topeka, Kansas.

"All the News That's Fit to Print"

The New York Times.

LATE CITY EDITION

Condensation of U.S. Weather Bureau forecast: Cloudy, mild, chance of rain late today. Clearing, cold tomorrow.

Temperature range today: 47—35.
Temperature range yesterday: 47-30.7.
Full U. S. Weather Bureau Report, Page 34.

VOL. CVI..No. 36,190. | Entered as Second-Class Matter, Post Office, New York, N. Y. | NEW YORK, SATURDAY, FEBRUARY 23, 1957. | Times Square, New York 36, N. Y. Telephone LAckawanna 4-1000 | FIVE CENTS

TUG MEN REJECT 6-YEAR CONTRACT BY 5-TO-1 MARGIN

22-Day Walkout to Continue —Proposal Had Included Wage Increase of 11%

EMPLOYERS 'DISGUSTED'

Future Negotiations to Revert to Original Terms—Dock Work to Resume Today

By GEORGE HORNE

The port's tugboat workers turned down overwhelmingly yesterday a proposed six-year contract offered by their employers.

Their action, taken at a mass meeting of the 4,000-man union at Manhattan Center, was a startling development in the twenty-two-day-old strike.

The employers, confident of the terms they had offered, including an immediate pay rise of 11 per cent, expressed themselves as being "shocked and disgusted."

Many of the strikers appeared to share this point of view. At the end of the vote, taken about 3 P. M., some of the crews of tugs and other harbor craft protested at the form in which the vote was conducted.

No Ballot Is Taken

There was no ballot. Capt. Joseph O'Hare, head of Local 333, United Marine Division, instructed the hundreds of men in the hall to move to the sides of the big room, with the "nays" on one side and the "ayes" on the other.

The meeting was closed to the press. However, according to union officials, the vote was about 5 to 1 for rejecting the terms of the contract, which had been ground out in a long series of caucuses and joint sessions under mediation auspices.

James P. McAllister, chairman of the Marine Towing and Transportation Employers Association, was out of the city, but members of his committee were standing by, some of them at the association's headquarters at 17 Battery Place. They were dumfounded by the development.

Federal and city mediators, who had all but led the disputants by the hands in recent weeks, were notified of the rejection. They were considering the next moves, but no resumption of negotiations had been arranged last night.

Dock Strike Appears Over

As the tug men decided to carry on their strike, another major waterfront dispute appeared to be settled. After the counting of a ratification vote here, Capt. William V. Bradley, head of the International Longshoremen's Association, ordered East Coast dockers back to the piers at 8 A. M. today. The vote was 6,829 to 4,017 for acceptance of the new stevedoring contract.

The tug strikers have frustrated normal operations in the country's premier port. But they have not, as they had expected, throttled the area's supply of fuel oil. Throughout the strike, a special fuel oil set-up has been functioning under City Administrator Charles F. Preusse, acting as fuel oil emergency coordinator. This apparatus has kept the city's fuel supplies above the critical level.

There was some speculation

Continued on Page 36, Column 4

Queen Gives Philip The Title of Prince

By KENNETT LOVE

Special to The New York Times.

LONDON, Feb. 22—Queen Elizabeth today bestowed the title of a Prince of the United Kingdom on her husband, the Duke of Edinburgh.

The new title was proposed to the Queen by Prime Minister Harold Macmillan and his senior Cabinet colleagues. They felt that the 35-year-old Duke should receive some significant mark of recognition for the services he had rendered to Britain and the Commonwealth, culminating in the four-month world tour of British territories he has just completed.

A Government announcement of the honor was published tonight in The London Gazette. In a notice dated "Whitehall, Feb. 22, 1957," it said:

"The Queen has been pleased by letters patent under the Great Seal of the realm bear-

Continued on Page 9, Column 4

HARRIMAN BALKS AT 'GAS' TAX RISE

Refuses to Back 1c Increase He Supported in '56—Calls Road Plan Conservative

By WARREN WEAVER Jr.

Special to The New York Times.

ELMIRA, N. Y., Feb. 22—Governor Harriman refused today to endorse an increase in the state gasoline tax from 4 to 5 cents a gallon.

The Governor said he supported the recommendations of the Temporary State Commission on Highway Finance regarding the construction of $4,500,000,000 of new roads in the next twelve years. He called the amount conservative, however.

He emphasized, too, that his support did not extend to the "financial implications" of the report made by the commission earlier this week. He said he would have to study this problem further and discuss it with the Republican legislative leaders.

Avoids Stand on Rise

In past weeks the Governor has avoided taking any position on a gasoline tax increase by saying he was waiting for the commission report. This group, which was appointed by Thomas E. Dewey when Governor, is headed by Charles Diefendorf, a Buffalo banker.

When the commission made a similar report last year, calling for an increase of 1 cent in the gasoline tax and 1½ cents in the Diesel fuel tax, the Governor endorsed both the highway program and the suggested tax increases.

But all Mr. Harriman would say today as he arrived for a

Continued on Page 36, Column 6

U. N. COMPROMISE ON CYPRUS URGES NEW NEGOTIATION

Indian Proposal for Greek, British and Turkish Talks Voted Without Dissent

By LINDESAY PARROTT

Special to The New York Times.

UNITED NATIONS, N. Y., Feb. 22—The United Nations, in a conciliatory move, called today for a resumption of negotiations on Cyprus between the governments concerned with the rebellious British crown colony.

The countries concerned are Britain, Greece and Turkey.

The action was taken by the adoption in the General Assembly's powerful Political Committee of a compromise resolution introduced by India. The vote was 76 to 0, with 2 abstentions, those by Panama and Afghanistan.

Earlier Motions Withdrawn

As a result of the balloting, Greece, Britain and Panama withdrew resolutions they had submitted earlier. Two Greek resolutions would have called for a declaration in favor of self-determination—home rule looking to union with Greece. The Mediterranean island has a mixed population of about 80 per cent Greek and 20 per cent Turkish extraction.

Greece also had asked that a seven-nation commission of investigation take up the Cyprus question. Panama had made a parallel proposal. Britain had asked the United Nations to deal with alleged Greek support of terrorism on Cyprus, which is an eastern base of the North Atlantic Treaty Organization.

The Indian compromise resolution was introduced this morning by V. K. Krishna Menon after attempts had been under way for several days to find a formula upon which the contending nations might agree.

This formula, it had been suggested, might follow that adopted in the case of Algeria. The Assembly, in that case, expressed a hope that a peaceful solution might be found between the French interests and those of the Algerian nationalists.

The Resolution Adopted

The Indian resolution follows:

"The General Assembly,

"Having considered the question of Cyprus,

"Believing that the solution of this problem requires an atmosphere of peace and freedom of expression,

"Expresses the earnest desire that a peaceful, democratic and just solution will be found in accord with the principles and purposes of the Charter of the United Nations, and the hope that negotiations will be resumed and continued to this end."

The move still was required to

Continued on Page 4, Column 4

The New York Times (by Sam Falk)

DISCUSS PROPOSAL FOR SANCTIONS: At conference before U. N. General Assembly session yesterday were, from left, at table: an aide; Dr. Fadhil al-Jamali of Iraq, Omar Loutfi of Egypt, Abdel Monem Rifai of Jordan, and Dr. Charles Malik of Lebanon. Dr. Malik later read at Assembly session a proposal for sanctions against Israel.

South Vietnam Head Escapes as Gunman Fires at Him at Fair

By FOSTER HAILEY

Special to The New York Times.

BANMETHUOT, South Vietnam, Feb. 22—An attempt was made to assassinate President Ngo Dinh Diem this morning as he was presiding at the opening of an exposition here. He was not injured.

The assailant fired from not farther than ten feet away with an automatic pistol of Austrian make. The Presidential party was nearing the exposition center after a ribbon-cutting ceremony.

A bullet ripped through the back of the coat of a Vietnamese reporter and struck the Minister of Agricultural Reform in the right arm and side, penetrating the right lung.

Assailant Not Identified

The name of the attacker was not immediately revealed by the police. One report was that he had identified himself as being from Communist North Vietnam. The country was divided by the armistice of 1954.

The assailant's face was bleeding from blows struck by policemen, Presidential aides and bystanders. He seemed to be not badly hurt.

The pistol shot was so muffled and the prisoner and the wounded minister were taken out of the area so quickly that many in the crowd were unaware that anything unusual had happened.

The wounded official is Do Van Cung. After treatment at the Banmethuot Hospital, he was flown to Saigon, where his

Continued on Page 8, Column 5

JAPAN'S PREMIER, LONG ILL, RESIGNS

Press Hails Ishibashi Step —Foreign Minister Kishi Slated as Successor

By ROBERT TRUMBULL

Special to The New York Times.

TOKYO, Saturday, Feb. 23—Premier Tanzan Ishibashi announced his resignation today.

Physicians had advised the ailing conservative leader he would be unable to resume the duties of his office for two more months. He has been confined to his home with a bronchial disorder diagnosed as pneumonia since Jan. 25.

Foreign Minister Nobusuke Kishi is expected to become the new Premier. [A later Reuters dispatch said the ruling Liberal-Democratic party had confirmed Mr. Kishi for Premier.]

Mr. Kishi, who has been acting Premier in the absence of his 72-year-old chief, has made a point of friendship with the United States. Mr. Ishibashi, on the other hand, had been expected to steer the Government on a more independent line had he remained in office.

Formal nomination of the new Premier in the Diet (Parliament) is expected Monday or Tuesday.

Meanwhile, the Socialist party, seeking to strike while the conservative forces are disrupted by factionalism, is demanding dissolution of the Diet and new national elections.

It was partly because of Leftist clamor and partly because of disunity in his own

Continued on Page 11, Column 2

U. N. Plan Proposed To Help Arab Exiles Pay Their Own Way

Special to The New York Times.

UNITED NATIONS, N. Y., Feb. 22—The United States and five other nations proposed today that the Arab refugees in Egypt, Syria, Jordan and Lebanon receive help to make them self-sufficient.

The proposal came in a resolution introduced in the General Assembly's Special Political Committee by Mrs. Oswald B. Lord of the United States delegation. The co-sponsors are Argentina, Britain, the Netherlands, New Zealand and the Philippines.

The resolution would authorize the director of the United Nations Relief and Works Agency for Palestine Refugees, Henry R. Labouisse, to disburse funds to the host nations for the purpose of setting up programs to permit the refugees to earn their way.

Prerequisite Cited

In presenting the resolution Mrs. Lord said such disbursements to host nations would be predicated on agreement that they would eventually accept financial responsibility for a certain number of refugees.

The six-power draft includes the proviso that any such help to refugees would not prejudice their rights to eventual repatriation or compensation.

The Arab states have been insisting that the refugees, variously estimated to total 900,000 to more than 1,000,000, be given the choice of returning to their original homes or accepting compensation. Israel contends it

Continued on Page 4, Column 7

BEN-GURION SENDS EISENHOWER NOTE

Israeli Message to President Said to Be 'Constructive' —White House Is Firm

By SETH S. KING

Special to The New York Times.

JERUSALEM (Israeli Sector), Feb. 22—Another personal message was sent to President Eisenhower late last night by the Israeli Premier, David Ben-Gurion.

"It was written in a constructive tone," a Foreign Ministry official said today.

This morning Ambassador Abba Eban started back to the United States for more conferences with Secretary of State Dulles. He was scheduled to arrive in New York Sunday, and was expected to confer with Mr. Dulles and other United States officials that afternoon.

[President Eisenhower and Secretary Dulles remained insistent on the immediate withdrawal of Israeli forces behind Israel's border. The United States' leaders will see Ambassador Eban before taking further steps.]

Mr. Ben-Gurion's message was transmitted through the United States Embassy after his speech last night.

Further Talks Requested

In this speech, the Israeli Premier rejected President Eisenhower's demand that Israel's troops be withdrawn at once from the Gaza Strip and Sharm el Sheikh in the Gulf of Aqaba area. However, at the same time he requested further discussions with the United States. He said he hoped the door was still open for a solution to the deadlock.

It was noted that the tone of Mr. Ben-Gurion's speech was more conciliatory than others he recently had made. This was particularly true when he discussed the Gaza Strip.

There were indications that Israel might be willing to drop her demands for an Israeli civil administration in this area after her troops had been pulled back.

Some observers now believed that Mr. Ben-Gurion was prepar-

Continued on Page 3, Column 3

SIX NATIONS ASK SANCTIONS BY U.N. AGAINST ISRAELIS

Asians and Africans Propose World-Wide Curbs in View of 'Continued Defiance'

U. S. PLANS SUBSTITUTE

Milder Resolution, Due Next Week, Would Again Urge Withdrawal by Israel

Documents and excerpts from Malik speech, Page 2.

By THOMAS J. HAMILTON

Special to The New York Times.

UNITED NATIONS, N. Y., Feb. 22—Six Asian and Arab states urged the General Assembly today to recommend that the world impose economic sanctions against Israel.

A resolution proposed by them would call upon "all states to deny all military, economic or financial assistance and facilities to Israel in view of its continued defiance" of seven resolutions calling for unconditional withdrawal behind the Israeli-Egyptian armistice line.

Henry Cabot Lodge Jr., who has led the fight within the Eisenhower Administration to have the United States support a sanctions resolution, did not speak during the brief Assembly session this afternoon. Other delegates said it was because the United States had not yet taken a decision.

Dr. Malik Reads Resolution

A United States spokesman declined to comment on the six-power draft resolution, which was read to the Assembly by Dr. Charles Malik, Foreign Minister of Lebanon, but not formally introduced. Aside from Lebanon, the only Arab co-sponsor is Iraq. The other co-sponsors are Afghanistan, Indonesia, Pakistan and the Sudan.

Authoritative sources revealed that the United States was now working on a milder resolution calling on Israel to withdraw, which it hoped would be ready when the Assembly resumed the debate Monday.

President Eisenhower, in his televised address Wednesday night, endorsed moral "pressure" on Israel to withdraw but did not use the word "sanctions."

Other delegates said they understood that the State Department and the United States delegation were discussing a resolution to exert such moral pressure. The decision would depend in part on whether Israel was now willing to make new proposals.

Third Approach Is Likely

There is a possibility that the Assembly will have before it next week a third approach to the problem of obtaining Israel's withdrawal from the Gaza Strip and the Gulf of Aqaba area.

Lester B. Pearson, Canadian Secretary of State for External Affairs, again sounded out British Commonwealth and Western European delegations today on a motion that would also call for Israel's withdrawal. However, it would be intended to provide more dependable assurances than the United States had mentioned against a revival of hostile acts by Egypt.

The suggested resolution would affirm the right of ships of all nations to use the Gulf of Aqaba. It would also provide that the Assembly establish a commission, which could consist of one man, to go to the Gaza Strip and report recommendations on its future status to the Assembly.

U. N. Chief Hails U. S. Talks

Mr. Pearson had prepared a speech making these suggestions for delivery this afternoon. He remained silent, however, since the speeches today by Dr. Malik and Dr. Mahoud Fawzi, Egyptian Foreign Minister, called for the immediate withdrawal and did not take up the assurances on which Israel had been insisting.

At the start of the meeting, Dag Hammarskjold, the Secretary General, told the Assembly that he had been "kept well informed" on the negotiations between the United States and Israel on a final Israeli withdrawal. He added that "these serious efforts to break through the unfortunate impasse" were deserving of "warm appreciation."

Mr. Hammarskjold said he could state "with confidence" that Egypt was willing and

Continued on Page 2, Column 3

Rock 'n' Roll Teen-Agers Tie Up the Times Square Area

Line Up at Theatre 18½ Hours—175 Police Called

By EDITH EVANS ASBURY

Teen-age rock 'n' roll enthusiasts stormed into the Times Square area before dawn yesterday and all day long they filled sidewalks, tied up traffic and eventually required the attention of 175 policemen.

They began lining up at 4 A. M. to see the show at the Paramount Theatre. It wasn't until eighteen and a half hours later—at 10:30 P. M.—that the last of the line entered the theatre. Late arrivals continued buying tickets, however, until the box office closed shortly after 1 A. M. The show featured Alan Freed, a disk jockey who takes credit for coining the phrase rock 'n' rol.

The rock 'n' rollers stamped their feet so vigorously in the theatre that firemen became alarmed and sent for inspectors from the Fire and Buildings Departments at 5 P. M. The management cleared three-fourths of the 1,600 youngsters from the second balcony as a precautionary measure.

All but the first four rows, seating 206, were refilled at 7:30 after a preliminary report by a building inspector, and at 8 o'clock occupancy of the entire second balcony was approved by Nicholas Lanese, chief construction inspector of the Building Department.

A theatre spokesmen said that 15,220 patrons had attended the six stage and seven movie shows between 8 A. M. and 1 A. M. The attendance figure and receipts of $29,000 set new records for the thirty-one-year-old theatre, the spokesmen said.

When the last stage show ended most of the crowd left leaving only a handful of persons watching the final showing of the movie.

"Rock 'n' roll is really swing with a modern name," Mr. Freed said in his backstage dressing room between performances. "It began on the levees and plantations, took in folk songs, and features blues and rhythm. It's the rhythm that gets the kids. They are starved for music they can dance to, after all those years of crooners."

Other experts described rock

Continued on Page 12, Column 2

The New York Times

Part of the holiday crowd waiting yesterday on West Forty-third Street for admittance to the Paramount Theatre

Mixed-Sports Ban Blocked in Georgia

By The Associated Press.

ATLANTA, Feb. 22—A small, determined band in the Georgia House of Representatives defeated today for at least a year a bill to prohibit interracial sports and social activities in Georgia.

Resisting heavy pressure from Gov. Marvin Griffin's Administration, the House bloc relied on parliamentary tactics to block passage of the measure during the final hours of the 1957 session.

In another action the Legislature called today for the impeachment of six members of the Supreme Court of the United States.

While the bill to outlaw interracial activities was still under consideration, the House shouted approval of a Senate resolution to adjourn at 5 P. M., and opponents talked out the final five minutes or so of the session.

The bill as passed by the Sen-

Continued on Page 35, Column 2

Pressure Bid Denied By Jewish Leaders

By IRVING SPIEGEL

A group of American Jewish leaders said yesterday that the Administration had not requested them to exert pressure on Israel to withdraw her troops from the Gulf of Aqaba area and the Gaza Strip.

Barney Balaban, president of Paramount Pictures, said that reports of such a request by Secretary of State Dulles were "incorrect." Mr. Balaban's statement was strongly endorsed by Philip M. Klutznick, president of B'nai B'rith, Jewish service organization.

Irving M. Engel, president of the American Jewish Committee, asserted that "there was absolutely no suggestion that we put pressure on the Israeli Government to require it to change its position."

Similar sentiments were expressed by Louis Novins, an officer of Paramount, and

Continued on Page 3, Column 3

"All the News That's Fit to Print"

The New York Times.

LATE CITY EDITION
U. S. Weather Bureau Report (Page 59) forecasts: Mostly fair and seasonable today and tomorrow. Temp. range: 70—57. Yesterday: 67.7—55.9.

VOL. CVII . No. 36,404. © 1957, by The New York Times Company. Times Square, New York 36, N. Y. NEW YORK, WEDNESDAY, SEPTEMBER 25, 1957. 10c beyond 100-mile zone from New York City FIVE CENTS

PRESIDENT SENDS TROOPS TO LITTLE ROCK, FEDERALIZES ARKANSAS NATIONAL GUARD; TELLS NATION HE ACTED TO AVOID ANARCHY

WEST AGAIN BARS SOVIET PROPOSAL ON MIDEAST TALK

U. S. Says Latest Moscow Note 'Cynically Distorts' American Actions

Text of U. S. note to Soviet will be found on Page 5.

By DANA ADAMS SCHMIDT
Special to The New York Times.

WASHINGTON, Sept. 24—The United States, Britain and France rejected today the latest in a series of Soviet bids for recognition of the Soviet Union's role in the Middle East.

A brief United States reply delivered in Moscow today said a Soviet note of Sept. 3 was "offensive in tone and cynically distorts United States objectives and actions in the Middle East."

It accused the Soviet Union of setting in motion "a chain of events leading to the present dangerous situation" by shipping large quantities of arms into the area.

U. S. Affirms Doctrine

The note warned the Soviet Union that the United States Government intended to carry out the national policy laid down in the Eisenhower Doctrine, which "regards the preservation of the independence and integrity of the nations of that region as vital to world peace and as vital, therefore, to its own national interests."

The doctrine, proclaimed in a Joint Resolution of the House of Representatives and the Senate on March 9, 1957, also affirmed the President's authority to use United States forces to aid any Middle East state that asked for help against aggression by a power controlled by international communism.

The Soviet Union's note had accused the United States of seeking to overthrow the Syrian Government and of generally fomenting trouble in the Middle East.

3d Rejection of Soviet Bid

It had proposed, for the third time, a four-power declaration renouncing the use of force in the area. Earlier Soviet proposals for such a declaration, all rejected by the West, were made Feb. 11 and April 19.

As interpreted by United States experts on the Middle East, these notes were meant to convey the idea that the four powers should meet to negotiate a settlement of their rivalries in the Middle East. The first of the notes even went into detail with a proposal for an embargo on shipment of arms to the area.

Because the Soviet Union has asserted its presence in Syria, and because there seems to be little the Western powers can do to reverse developments in

Continued on Page 5, Column 3

London and Bonn Rule Out Any Currency Revaluation

Britain Tells Monetary Fund Session She Will Draw $500,000,000 in Stand-By Credit From Export-Import Bank

By EDWIN L. DALE JR.
Special to The New York Times.

WASHINGTON, Sept. 24—British and West German spokesmen and the Managing Director of the International Monetary Fund said today that the question of exchange rates for the pound and the mark was "definitely settled." There will be no change.

At the same time, Britain, through Peter Thorneycroft, Chancellor of the Exchequer, announced she would draw "over the coming weeks" the $500,000,000 stand-by credit she arranged last winter with the United States Export-Import Bank.

In his speech at the annual meeting of the fund, Mr. Thorneycroft indicated that Britain was drawing the money to demonstrate to speculators that she had the resources to defend the pound.

Both the British and the West Germans emphasized that the recent huge flow of gold and dollars out of Britain and into West Germany had been based solely on speculation, not on basic factors in their foreign trading accounts.

Per Jacobsson, the Fund's Managing Director, said: "The growing knowledge that there will be no alteration in the value of either the Deutsche

Continued on Page 8, Column 5

SOVIET ASSAILED BY LLOYD AT U. N.

Briton Suggests Arms Sent Arabs May Be Stocks for Future Bases

Excerpts from Lloyd's speech are printed on Page 4.

By THOMAS J. HAMILTON
Special to The New York Times.

UNITED NATIONS, N. Y., Sept. 24—Britain denounced today Soviet arms shipments to Arab countries. Selwyn Lloyd, British Foreign Secretary, suggested that the purpose might be to "pre-stock forward bases for the Soviet Union itself."

Mr. Lloyd told the General Assembly that Soviet arms had been delivered "on such a scale as to give some color to this suggestion." He added that Britain viewed the Syrian situation "with grave concern." In addition, he criticized Soviet policy throughout the area.

Mr. Lloyd devoted most of his speech to the Middle East and to disarmament. He did not say what action the Assembly should take on either subject.

However, he declared that Secretary of State Dulles, in

Continued on Page 4, Column 3

City Approves Plan By Wiley to Build Midtown Garages

By JOSEPH C. INGRAHAM

The Board of Estimate has approved in principle the program of Traffic Commissioner T. T. Wiley for garage construction in the heart of lower and mid-Manhattan.

The decision clears the way for a start on $24,000,000 of garages. It also settles a three-year dispute between Mr. Wiley and other city executives that has stymied off-street parking relief.

As a result, the first of the projects—a garage in the Herald Square area—will be on the board's calendar on Oct. 9. Eight other garages are to be centrally located in Manhattan and two in the busiest parts of the Bronx.

The Herald Square garage will be east of the Avenue of the Americas between West Thirty-fifth and Thirty-sixth Streets with entrances and exits on both streets. There will be space for 610 cars on eight levels accessible by ramps. Rates will be geared to "meet the heavy unsatisfied demand for short-time parking," Mr. Wiley said.

Rates proposed by the Commissioner would be 25 cents a

Continued on Page 25, Column 1

SOLDIERS FLY IN

1,000 Go to Little Rock —9,936 in Guard Told to Report

The texts of Executive orders on troops are on Page 16.

By JACK RAYMOND
Special to The New York Times.

WASHINGTON, Sept. 24—The Army ordered all Arkansas National Guardsmen to report for Federal duty tonight and rushed 1,000 airborne troops of the Regular Army into Little Rock to preserve order.

The Regulars were members of the 101st Airborne Division, which won fame in World War II under the command of Gen. Maxwell D. Taylor, now Chief of Staff of the Army.

Maj. Gen. Edwin A. Walker, a much-decorated combat commander with a reputation for toughness, was put in command of the Regular Army contingent and the federalized Guardsmen in Arkansas. He is the commander of the Arkansas Military District.

General Walker's mission is to make sure that no one frustrates Federal Court orders that nine Negro pupils be admitted to Central High School.

Wilson Carries Out Order

Charles E. Wilson, Secretary of Defense, carrying out President Eisenhower's mandate, earlier had called the entire Arkansas Army and Air National Guard, totaling 9,936 men, into Federal service.

The Secretary of Defense and Wilber M. Brucker, Secretary of the Army, acted two hours after President Eisenhower's executive order authorizing "all appropriate steps" to make school attendance possible for the Negroes who had been admitted to the high school.

However, an Army spokesman said that it was planned to make "the absolute minimum demonstration of force necessary."

Immediately after Secretary Wilson signed the federalization call to the Arkansas Guard at 2:25 P. M., Secretary Brucker telephoned the office of Gov. Orval E. Faubus in Little Rock.

At the same time he sent a telegram to the Governor, explaining that President Eisenhower "desires" the personnel of the Arkansas Army and Air National Guard organizations

Continued on Page 14, Column 2

Associated Press Wirephoto

SOLDIERS IN LITTLE ROCK: Residents of Arkansas capital looking on last night as men of the 101st Airborne Division took positions outside the Central High School.

Troops on Guard at School; Negroes Ready to Return

By BENJAMIN FINE
Special to The New York Times.

LITTLE ROCK, Ark., Sept. 24—Troops from the Army's crack 101st Airborne Division, carrying carbines and billy clubs, took posts around Central High School tonight. They were here to see that court-ordered integration is carried out.

With police sirens wailing and headlights flashing, Army trucks loaded with soldiers roared into position. The soldiers represented about a quarter of the contingent of 1,000 crack troops of the division that was ordered to Little Rock by President Eisenhower to prevent mob riots and violence.

The first group of 500 airborne soldiers came to the city this afternoon from Fort Campbell, Ky., and a second group of 500 arrived by plane this evening. The bulk of the two groups bivouacked for the night in areas away from the school.

General Issues Order

Maj. Gen. Edwin A. Walker, commander of the Arkansas Military District, issued a formal order to the people of Little Rock not to collect in crowds and to let Central High School be integrated peaceably.

With the arrival of Federal troops, including some Negro soldiers who were not expected to be on duty at the school, Negro students were ready to try again to enter the high school.

A mob of 1,000 persons yesterday forced the city and school authorities to withdraw nine Negro students who had attended integrated classes for 3 hours and 13 minutes. The students did not try to enter the school today.

Mrs. L. C. Bates, president

Continued on Page 15, Column 1

GOVERNORS URGE WHITE HOUSE TALK

Southerners Move to Set Up Mediation Machinery in Use of Federal Troops

By JOHN N. POPHAM
Special to The New York Times.

SEA ISLAND, Ga., Sept. 24—Southern Governors moved tonight to establish mediation machinery that would remove Federal troops from the South. The Governors acted a few hours after the President had federalized the Arkansas National Guard.

Gov. Luther Hodges of North Carolina, chairman of the Southern Governors Conference in session here, announced that two proposals would be submitted to the resolutions committee of the conference for formal consideration tomorrow.

One is a proposal of Gov. Frank G. Clement of Tennessee to establish an informal committee of Southern Governors to seek a meeting with President Eisenhower in a search for a solution to the Little Rock school integration crisis.

The other is a request to the President to hold off the use of Federal troops and to agree

Continued on Page 16, Column 2

U. S. Cutters Conquer Northwest Passage

3 Coast Guard Craft First of the Nation to Make Transit

By JOHN H. FENTON
Special to The New York Times.

BOSTON, Sept. 24 — Two Coast Guard cutters were saluted in Boston Harbor today at the end of a successful mission to find a practical Northwest Passage—a route around the top of the North American Continent.

A third cutter, the Spar, proceeded directly to her home port at Bristol, R. I., to be welcomed there as the first United States vessel to circumnavigate the continent.

The cutters Storis, from Juneau, Alaska, and the Bramble, from Miami, Fla., put in here for their welcoming. They will continue their homeward voyages later in the week.

The three cutters were the first United States vessels to make the passage.

The shrill sirens of water-spouting fireboats and the deeper-throated whistles of other craft sounded a "well done" as the two bulky cutters made their way up the harbor.

Ranking Coast Guard officers and civil officials joined with members of families of the crews in a dockside welcome as the cutters tied up at

Continued on Page 10, Column 1

U. S. Coast Guard

Coast Guardsmen on the stern of the Spar view her sister cutters, Bramble, left, and Storis, during the transit of Simpson Strait. This was a difficult part of the voyage.

Rebel Chief Seized In Algiers Gunfight

By THOMAS F. BRADY
Special to The New York Times.

ALGIERS, Algeria, Sept. 24—The chief of the nationalist terrorist organization in Algiers was in the hands of French parachute troops today. The rebel leader, Saadi Yacef, 29 years old, had eluded capture in the crowded Casbah for more than two years.

With him was 24-year-old Miss Zorah Drif, an Algerian revolutionary, who was condemned to death in absentia by a French military tribunal.

A parachute colonel told reporters this evening that Mr. Yacef and Miss Drif had surrendered at 5:30 A. M. after the terrorist chief had wounded a lieutenant colonel and a master sergeant of a Foreign Legion parachute regiment. The colonel then took reporters to a hideout high in the Casbah where he described how the

Continued on Page 4, Column 3

Price Index Up .2%; Sets Another High

By RICHARD E. MOONEY
Special to The New York Times.

WASHINGTON, Sept. 24—The United States Consumers' Price Index rose two-tenths of a per cent in August, setting another record. It was the twelfth consecutive monthly increase, but among the smallest of the twelve.

The Labor Department's Bureau of Labor Statistics reported today that the index rose in August to 121, using the price average in the 1947-49 period as a comparison base of 100. All the major categories of prices increased, but food and housing were the strongest factors.

The August index was 3.6 per cent higher than that of a year earlier. This meant that a typical city family paid $1.03 3/5 in August of 1957 for the goods and services that cost $1 in August of 1956.

The Commerce Department

Continued on Page 24, Column 3

CONGRESS IS SPLIT ON USE OF TROOPS

Johnston Calls for Faubus to Resist President but Others Hail His Move

By JOHN W. FINNEY
Special to The New York Times.

WASHINGTON, Sept. 24—Congressional reaction to President Eisenhower's decision to use troops in the Little Rock integration crisis ranged from angry denunciation to outright praise today.

Southern Senators sharply criticized the President and suggested he had exceeded his legal authority. Northern Senators supported the President, but some of them expressed reservations that the action was rather belated.

Expects Faubus to Act

Senator Olin D. Johnston, Democrat of South Carolina, suggested that Gov. Orval E. Faubus of Arkansas "stand up for states' rights" and force a showdown with the President by calling out the Arkansas National Guard on his own.

Senator Johnston, a former Governor of South Carolina, said if he were Governor Faubus, "I'd proclaim a state of insurrection down there, and I'd call out the National Guard, and I'd then find out who's going to run things in my state."

Asked by reporters whether he believed Governor Faubus would take such steps, Senator Johnston said, "I think he will and I hope he will."

Aiken Defends Move

Senator John L. McClellan, Democrat of Arkansas, said he believed such use of military force by the Federal Government was "without authority of law."

He said he was "very apprehensive that such action may precipitate more trouble than it will prevent."

Senator Richard B. Russell, Democrat of Georgia and leader of Southern opposition to the Civil Rights Bill in the last session, said that President Eisenhower's use of troops might "put Negro children in the white schools," but that it would "have a calamitous effect on race relations and on the cause of national unity."

On the other side of the issue, Senator George D. Aiken, Republican of Vermont, said the President "is undoubtedly with-

Continued on Page 17, Column 3

EISENHOWER ON AIR

Says School Defiance Has Gravely Harmed Prestige of U. S.

Text of President's address appears on Page 14.

By ANTHONY LEWIS
Special to The New York Times.

WASHINGTON, Sept. 24—President Eisenhower sent Federal troops to Little Rock, Ark., today to open the way for the admission of nine Negro pupils to Central High School.

Earlier, the President federalized the Arkansas National Guard and authorized calling the Guard and regular Federal forces to remove obstructions to justice in Little Rock school integration.

His history-making action was based on a formal finding that his "cease and desist" proclamation, issued last night, had not been obeyed. Mobs of pro-segregationists still gathered in the vicinity of Central High School this morning.

Tonight, from the White House, President Eisenhower told the nation in a speech for radio and television that he had acted to prevent "mob rule" and "anarchy."

Historic Decision

The President's decision to send troops to Little Rock was reached at his vacation headquarters in Newport, R. I. It was one of historic importance politically, socially, constitutionally. For the first time since the Reconstruction days that followed the Civil War, the Federal Government was using its ultimate power to compel equal treatment of the Negro in the South.

He said violent defiance of Federal Court orders in Little Rock had done grave harm to "the prestige and influence, and indeed to the safety, of our nation and the world." He called on the people of Arkansas and the South to "preserve and respect the law even when they disagree with it."

Guardsmen Withdrawn

Action quickly followed the President's orders. During the day and night 1,000 members of the 101st Airborne Division were flown to Little Rock. Charles E. Wilson, Secretary of the Defense, ordered into Federal service all 10,000 members of the Arkansas National Guard.

Today's events were the climax of three weeks of skirmishing between the Federal Government and Gov. Orval E. Faubus of Arkansas. It was three weeks ago this morning that the Governor first ordered National Guard troops to Central High School to preserve order. The nine Negro students were prevented from entering the school.

The Guardsmen were gone yesterday, withdrawn by Governor Faubus as the result of a

Continued on Page 14, Column 6

Textile Union Gets 30 Days to Reform

By A. H. RASKIN

A scandal-tainted textile union was ordered yesterday to oust its two chief officers within thirty days or face possible suspension from the merged labor federation.

The ultimatum was given to the 40,000-member United Textile Workers by the executive council of the American Federation of Labor and Congress of Industrial Organizations.

It foreshadowed the fixing of a similar clean-up deadline today for the 1,400,000-member International Brotherhood of Teamsters and the 140,000-member Bakery and Confectionery Workers International Union.

The federation's Ethical Practices Committee has found all three unions guilty of violating the anti-racketeering provisions of the A. F. L.-C. I. O. constitution. The findings were based

Continued on Page 13, Column 3

"All the News That's Fit to Print"

The New York Times.

LATE CITY EDITION
U. S. Weather Bureau Report (Page 53) forecasts: Mostly fair and cold today, tonight and tomorrow.
Temp. range: 30—19. Yesterday: 36.2—21.

VOL. CVIII..No. 36,875. © 1959, by The New York Times Company. Times Square, New York 36, N. Y. NEW YORK, FRIDAY, JANUARY 9, 1959 10c beyond 100-mile zone from New York City. Higher in air delivery cities. FIVE CENTS

DE GAULLE TAKES THE PRESIDENCY; DEBRE IS PREMIER

General's Entry Into Office Marks Start of Fifth French Republic

SOUSTELLE IS SELECTED

Post of Minister-Delegate Indicates He Has Second Top Spot in Cabinet

De Gaulle's statement will be found on Page 3.

By ROBERT C. DOTY
Special to The New York Times

PARIS, Jan. 8—Gen. Charles de Gaulle was proclaimed today the first President of the new Fifth Republic and the French overseas community.

His first official act as President was to name former Minister of Justice Michel Debré, a loyal Gaullist certain to accept Presidential leadership, as his successor as Premier.

M. Debré's Government, announced tonight, includes most of the ministers who have served General de Gaulle since his return to power June 1, with the exception of the Socialists who withdrew in disagreement over policies of economic austerity.

Soustelle Gets High Post

Named Minister-Delegate with functions suggesting the role of Vice Premier was Jacques Soustelle, former Information Minister and architect of the victory of the neo-Gaullist party in the November legislative elections.

Stately ceremonies of transfer of power from the outgoing President, René Coty, marked the end of the eight-month transitional period opened by the May 13 revolt by Frenchmen in Algeria, which shook and finally brought down the Fourth Republic. The ceremonies signified the final launching of the Fifth Republic with what is in many respects a Presidential regime within parliamentary forms.

President de Gaulle reasserted in unmistakable terms his concept of his Presidential role as that of supreme guide and arbiter, rather than of the largely ceremonial figure French Presidents have been in the past.

His duty, he told 200 of France's dignitaries in the Grand Hall of the Elysée Palace at the inaugural ceremonies, is to assert, "even to impose" if necessary, the interests of the

Continued on Page 3, Column 3

BREAK WITH CAIRO IS HINTED BY BONN

Nasser Is Asked to Clarify Tie With East Germany

By SYDNEY GRUSON
Special to The New York Times.

BONN, Germany, Jan. 8—West Germany instructed its Ambassador in Cairo today to ask President Gamal Abdel Nasser for immediate clarification of the United Arab Republic's decision to establish consular relations with East Germany.

Spokesmen for the Bonn Government dropped strong hints that West Germany would consider breaking diplomatic relations with the United Arab Republic unless a satisfactory explanation was received from the Arab leader.

In the meantime the Foreign Ministry declared that there was no question of the Government's proceeding with its plans to send a delegation to Cairo to discuss West German participation in the building of the Aswan High Dam project on the Nile River. The Government has been considering guaranteeing a $50,000,000 investment in the project by private companies.

Government spokesmen used strong language to underline Bonn's displeasure with the agreement announced by Premier Otto Grotewohl of East Germany at the conclusion of his visit to Cairo yesterday. At the Foreign Ministry here it was said the agreement had "surprised and alienated" the West German Government. From

Continued on Page 6, Column 4

TRIUMPHANT ENTRY: Fidel Castro, Cuban revolutionary leader, waves to crowds as he rides down Havana's Malecón sea drive in a jeep at head of an armored column. Parade proceeded to Camp Columbia, Army Headquarters.

Associated Press Wirephoto

MIKOYAN APPEALS FOR A 'HOT PEACE'

Tells Detroit Dinner 'We're All Tired of Cold War'—President Asks Courtesy

By HARRISON E. SALISBURY
Special to The New York Times.

DETROIT, Jan. 8—Anastas I. Mikoyan told Detroit's top industrial leaders tonight that "we are all tired of the cold war and would very much like to have a hot peace."

Mr. Mikoyan made his plea for a new and friendly relationship between the United States and the Soviet Union before a group of Detroit business men including the chiefs of the Ford, General Motors and Chrysler automotive empires.

Those who heard the Soviet First Deputy Premier at the swank Detroit Club said they had been impressed by his frank talk and the straightforward way in which he discussed Soviet-American differences.

Mr. Mikoyan had entered the club through a shouting crowd of about 300 Hungarian and Ukrainian demonstrators, who threw eggs and snowballs.

Three of the crowd were arrested. Mr. Mikoyan was not touched by any of the missiles.

[President Eisenhower, having been told of the demonstrations, called on Americans to show courtesy to enable the Soviet visitor to take home an "accurate" picture of the United States.]

Visits Auto Plants

Mr. Mikoyan's address capped a day spent inspecting auto plants and speaking plainly on every occasion. At a luncheon at the Ford Administration Building, Mr. Mikoyan engaged in a no-holds-barred talk about Soviet-American conflicts with Henry Ford 2d and other auto executives.

It was apparent from comments by the auto executives that Mr. Mikoyan's campaign had made a positive impact.

Mr. Mikoyan said tonight that Soviet-American relations had passed through many stages: they had been good, they had been bad, they had been very, very bad. Now, he said, they are moving in the right direction.

"The wind is still cold but it is the wind of spring," he said.

Praises U. S. Aid in War

He recalled that Detroit sent the Soviet Union many trucks during World War II. He said this contribution was well remembered in the Soviet Union. The trucks gave great satisfaction. If they could speak, he said, they would express satisfaction with the people who have driven them.

"Gentlemen," Mr. Mikoyan said, "let us leave to the historians the question of who is to blame for the deterioration of our good wartime relations, and do all we can to improve our relationship now."

Mr. Mikoyan said he had great faith in the common sense of the American people. He said many barriers between the Soviet and the United States were "nonsense." He cited restrictions on trade and particularly the list of commodities of which ex-

Continued on Page 4, Column 2

Havana Welcomes Castro At End of Triumphal Trip

By R. HART PHILLIPS
Special to The New York Times

HAVANA, Jan. 8—Fidel Castro rolled into Havana this afternoon with 5,000 of his victorious rebels to receive a delirious welcome from the city's populace.

Riding in a jeep, the tall, 32-year-old leader received the cheers of thousands who jammed the streets. Looking exhausted but happy, he still wore the beard that has become a symbol of the revolution.

Señor Castro and his young rebels seemed to enjoy their triumphant entry into this capital city of 1,000,000 inhabitants after two long years of fighting in eastern Cuba against the military rule of Fulgencio Batista, who fled to the Dominican Republic New Year's Day.

Later, addressing 40,000 people at Camp Columbia, the army headquarters, Señor Castro appealed for unity among the various revolutionary groups and called for all rebel fighters to lay aside their arms. "No private armies will be tolerated," he warned.

Warships Fire Salute

Two Cuban warships steamed past the flag-decorated Morro Castle into the harbor and fired a salute as the Castro column passed along the Malecon sea drive on its way to Camp Columbia. Exuberant young rebels on guard duty throughout the city fired their weapons into the air.

The rebels rode in jeeps, trucks, automobiles and armored trucks and perched on Sherman tanks purchased by the Cuban Army for use against them.

The crowds showered them with confetti, waved the Cuban flag and the black and red flag of the Castro movement, and shouted greetings and cheers for Fidel, as the young leader is known throughout the island.

Some of the youthful fighters had already shaved off the beards they had vowed to keep until the dictatorship was overthrown, but others kept their hair and whiskers long.

Overhead flew army planes and the helicopter that had hovered over the vehicle of the rebel leader on his victory march to Havana from Santiago de Cuba, center of the revolution, where

Continued on Page 9, Column 5

Reds Here Suspend Touring Party Aide

By PETER KIHSS

One of the Communist party's top leaders, Charles Loman, has been suspended from his state party posts by New York State Communist leaders.

Mr. Loman, a member of the party's national committee and its Kings County chairman, is understood to have gone abroad last month. There are reports that he left without party permission and without rendering a required accounting.

There is an unconfirmed report that his Brooklyn organization refused to support the state board's suspension by sixteen votes to twelve.

Party leaders declined to confirm or deny that the Brooklyn group has had major party funds under its control. One estimate is that perhaps as much as $250,000 may have been built up in the last seven

Continued on Page 8, Column 5

U.S. BARS INCREASE IN MISSILE FORCES

Rejects Air Force Request for More ICBM Groups Despite 'Gap' Warning

By RICHARD WITKIN

In the face of warnings of a fast-developing "missile gap," the Administration has rejected Air Force recommendations for increasing the planned force of intercontinental ballistic missiles, informed sources revealed yesterday.

The proposed budget for the 1960 fiscal year is said to contain no money to expand the ICBM force beyond the thirteen squadrons previously authorized.

The Administration's over-all defense proposals have already provoked strong criticism from influential members of Congress in both parties.

Ammunition for Debate

The issue of the ICBM force promises to provide much of the ammunition in the defense debate now getting under way in Congress.

The proposed defense budget figure for 1960 has been held, in the interests of budget balancing, to $40,900,000,000. This is about $100,000,000 more than the expected total for the fiscal year that ends June 30.

Administration critics argue that, if inflation and military payrolls are considered, the 1960 proposal may provide less than the 1959 budget for military hardware.

The thirteen ICBM squadrons now authorized include nine Atlas and four Titan units.

The Atlas is a one-and-a-half stage missile expected to reach initial combat status this summer. All three rocket engines fire at take-off. Two of them drop away after expending their fuel.

Duty in Mid-1961

The Titan is a two-stage ICBM slated for operational duty about mid-1961.

Both missiles are designed to carry large thermonuclear warheads a distance of 6,325 miles in less than thirty minutes.

At about ten missiles a squadron, thirteen squadrons would give the nation a total ICBM force of 130 by 1962. A number of observers with limited access to intelligence data have warned repeatedly that the Soviet Union would, or at least could, have an ICBM force totaling 500 by 1961 and perhaps 1,000 by 1962.

These observers fear that the huge disparity between such a force and that planned by this country might tempt the Soviet Union either to launch an all-out attack or blackmail the

Continued on Page 10, Column 5

CENTRAL SPURNS PENNSY MERGER

Drops Studies to Determine Feasibility of Rail Plan—Symes 'Disappointed'

By ROBERT E. BEDINGFIELD

Directors of the New York Central Railroad called a halt yesterday to joint studies that had been under way thirteen months with the Pennsylvania Railroad as to the feasibility of a merger.

On learning of the Central's decision, James M. Symes, president of the Pennsylvania, issued the following statement:

"Quite frankly I am disappointed at the New York Central's announcement."

The two big rail systems first announced that they were embarking on the study on Nov. 1, 1957. Executives of both carriers have been guarded in all statements since then as to the progress being made.

Last fall, Alfred E. Perlman, Central's president, said that all stages of the study had been completed except those to be conducted in their special fields by the financial vice presidents of the roads. Late last month David Bevan, financial vice president of the Pennsylvania, said the financial stage, too, was near completion.

Central's directors announced their decision to break off the merger study following their regular monthly board meeting, which was held in Palm Beach, Fla. In a statement issued from the company's executive headquarters here, the directors indicated that rather than a

Continued on Page 33, Column 6

OFFICIAL AGENCY TO PLAN GROWTH OF REGION URGED

Report Asks Legal Status for Metropolitan Council as Government Adviser

Text of committee report is printed on Page 16.

By CLAYTON KNOWLES

A proposal that the Metropolitan Regional Council receive "full and effective" legal status was put before the Regional Plan Association yesterday.

The association's special committee on metropolitan government affairs urged in essence that the council, now a voluntary group, be transformed into the official planning and steering agency for all government in the region.

It warned that the future of the region hinged on the development of such an "official leadership institution with the capacity to foresee the region's difficulties, to develop alternative solutions and to lead the way for the region, step by step, from specific recommendations to official action to firm accomplishment."

The region embraces twenty-two counties in New York, New Jersey and Connecticut.

Congress Charter Urged

The report was produced after a three-month study by a committee of eight community leaders, headed by Prof. Wallace S. Sayre of Columbia. It found that no local or state government or ad hoc commission was equipped to provide the leadership the council could give.

But it stressed that the council, in which top elected officials of the area now cooperate informally, must be chartered by Congress and the respective state Legislatures "to make its proposals both authoritative and acceptable to the regional community."

In urging an official dual planning-steering role for the council, the Sayre Committee visualized recommendations emerging that would carry added weight at the national, state, regional and local levels.

Meeting Set for Today

It said that difficulties confronting the region were "already visible to many of its leaders, but the future dimensions of these problems, even within the coming decade, will be much greater, more complex and more critical than the present crisis in transportation."

Harold S. Osborne, president of the Regional Plan Association, has called a meeting of his board for noon today at the Century Club, 7 West Forty-third Street, to consider the report. The association is a voluntary citizen group.

If approved, the report will be presented by the association as its official position to the Metropolitan Regional Council

Continued on Page 16, Column 6

De Valera to Quit as Premier And Seek Ireland's Presidency

His Government Party Seeks to Abolish the Proportional Representation System

Special to The New York Times.

DUBLIN, Jan. 8—Eamon de Valera intends to resign as Premier of Ireland in the next few weeks and seek election as President. He made the decision known to close associates within the last few days.

The New York-born Premier, 76 years old, has been an Irish leader for more than half a century. He is expected to announce his decision to his party formally at the end of this month.

Already the machinery of his party, Fianna Fail, is being geared for the twin electoral battle of making him President and of abolishing the proportional representation system of parliamentary election.

John A. Costello's United Ireland party has chosen Gen. Sean MacEoin as its Presidential nominee.

In the early days of the war against the British the general was known as the doughty fighting "Blacksmith of Ballinalee." Between shoeing horses in the village of Ballinalee in County Longford, he led a column of the Irish Republican Army against the British troops.

It is generally conceded, how-

The New York Times
Eamon de Valera

ever, that no candidate has much chance against Mr. de Valera. His election as the next President, if he is nominated, is taken for granted here.

Fourteen years ago General MacEoin ran against President Sean T. O'Kelly, who is retiring in June, but was defeated.

Mr. de Valera has indicated that he would like Sean F. Lemass to succeed him. He is Deputy Prime Minister and Minister for Industry and Commerce. In the last year his po-

Continued on Page 2, Column 6

G.O.P. Aims to End 'Big Business' Label

By W. H. LAWRENCE
Special to The New York Times.

WASHINGTON, Jan. 8—Republican leaders are discussing plans for an extensive party face-lifting operation before the 1960 election. The principal aim would be to change the public's conception of the G. O. P. as the party of big business.

The Republican leaders are counting on President Eisenhower for a great deal of help, expecting more partisanship from him in his final months in office than he has shown since he has been in the White House.

Plans for the Republican come-back drive will be laid before the party's national committee at its meetings in Des Moines, Iowa, Jan. 22-23.

In analyses of the 1958 election reversals prepared for President Eisenhower, some

Continued on Page 14, Column 7

REPUBLICANS BACK MORE STATE TAXES

Leaders Predict Legislature Will Adopt Higher Levies and Withholding Plan

By LEO EGAN
Special to The New York Times.

ALBANY, Jan. 8—Republican leaders, following a canvass of their members in the Senate and Assembly, were confident tonight that they could muster the votes needed for Governor Rockefeller's tax-increase program.

The exact dimensions of this program remain to be determined. But it is expected to include putting state income taxes on a withholding basis, raising the gasoline tax from 4 to 6 cents a gallon and increasing the cigarette tax from 3 to 4 cents a package.

Senator Walter J. Mahoney of Buffalo, the Republican leader of the Senate, went on record today in favor of the change in the income-tax payment system. "I would certainly be in favor of it if a feasible plan is worked out," he said.

Plan to Blame Harriman

Republican leaders are planning to blame former Gov. Averell Harriman's Democratic administration for the tax increases. In this way they hope to make it easier, politically, for Republicans to muster the necessary strength to obtain approval of the program.

Well aware of the Republican strategy, Democrats are preparing to fight back. They are prepared to emphasize that all the expenditures made under Governor Harriman were authorized by the Republican-controlled Legislature.

They are likewise ready to demonstrate that Republicans, in many instances, went beyond Mr. Harriman's recommendations in voting appropriations.

But Controller Arthur Levitt, the only Democratic official holding elective office in the administration, has indicated that he will cooperate with Mr. Rockefeller in introducing the withholding system for income taxes.

Deficiency Funds Sought

The state's need for further revenues in the fiscal year starting April 1 was further emphasized today with the submission to the Legislature of an administration deficiency appropriation bill.

This measure would authorize the spending of $28,100,000 more than had been appropriated in Governor Harriman's last budget in the time remaining before March 31. It would likewise authorize loans amounting to $41,200,000 during the same period.

The bulk of the loans would be used to meet the Federal Government's share of state highway costs. These would be repaid as Federal funds become available.

A statement issued in connection with the bill said that $10,700,000 more than had been appropriated would be needed to meet the state's share of welfare costs. Caseloads since April 1 have been higher than anticipated and allowances to families have been raised.

A program for combating the legislative payroll abuses disclosed last year was also officially announced today. It involves making public the names, addresses, compensation and party sponsorship of all legis-

Continued on Page 17, Column 6

FILIBUSTER FOES FACE A SETBACK IN VOTING TODAY

Johnson Sets Up Showdown on Issue of Senate's Right to Adopt New Rules

HE ACTS TO KILL PLAN

Liberals Call Test Crucial for Success of Tighter Limitation on Debate

By RUSSELL BAKER
Special to The New York Times

WASHINGTON, Jan. 8—Senator Lyndon B. Johnson forced the filibuster battle toward a decisive stage today and confronted Senate liberals with the prospect of a major defeat in the first showdown vote.

The Senate Democratic leader, apparently commanding the votes to beat the liberals on the point they want most to win, scheduled this first test for 11:30 o'clock tomorrow morning.

The vote is scheduled to begin just one hour before President Eisenhower's State of the Union Message to a joint session of Congress.

Moving with surprising speed, Mr. Johnson cut through a parliamentary morass this morning, set up the showdown in relatively clear-cut outline and was confidently prepared to take on the liberals in a late-afternoon vote.

Vote Delayed for Morse Talks

The vote was postponed until tomorrow after Senator Wayne Morse, Democrat of Oregon, announced that he wanted to talk far into the evening on behalf of the liberal position.

Senator Morse did just that, speaking from 6:04 P. M. until 10:10 P. M., when the Senate recessed until 10 o'clock tomorrow morning. During his talk Senator Morse introduced his anti-filibuster proposal providing for limitation of debate by a majority vote of those present. Under it, with just a quorum of fifty Senators on hand, twenty-six votes could force closure.

Basically this is a three-way struggle over the fate of the old filibuster rule, which empowers a determined minority to block passage of controversial legislation through dilatory debate.

It was touched off by a group of Eastern and Northern liberals who want the rule drastically changed. The Southern bloc opposes any change. The leadership of both parties, behind Senator Johnson of Texas, is

Continued on Page 14, Column 4

16 NEW CITY TAXES BEING CONSIDERED

A Big One and Several Little Ones Likely to Be Picked

By PAUL CROWELL

The Board of Estimate is wrestling with the problem of picking one large nuisance tax and a combination of small ones to raise $145,000,000 for the next expense budget.

It considers that amount necessary to balance the budget, which is certain to go substantially above $2,000,000,000 for the fiscal year beginning July 1.

Informed City Hall sources let it be known yesterday that sixteen special taxes, including the proposed levy on legalized off-track betting on horse races, were under consideration.

Six of these are taxes the city already has authority to impose without action by the Legislature. The remaining ten would require action at Albany, either to permit the city to increase rates now in force or to impose entirely new levies, such as a tax of 5 or 10 cents on taxicab rides or an off-track betting levy.

Although it was expected that the Board of Estimate would not make even a tentative choice before the end of this month, it was strongly indicated that at least three of the revenue-producing steps under consideration would not be included in the final program.

These are a proposed tax on draught beer sales; a proposed 10-cent toll on the East River bridges and reimposition of the

Continued on Page 13, Column 1

"All the News That's Fit to Print"

The New York Times.

LATE CITY EDITION

U. S. Weather Bureau Report (Page 62) forecasts: Rain early today; fair tonight. Increasing cloudiness tomorrow. Temp. range: 48—35. Yesterday: 49.6—34.5.

VOL. CVIII. No. 36,929. NEW YORK, WEDNESDAY, MARCH 4, 1959. 10 cents beyond 50-mile zone from New York City except on Long Island. Higher in air delivery cities. FIVE CENTS

PIONEER IV SOARS NEARER THE MOON; SENDS BACK DATA

AIM SLIGHTLY OFF

Capsule Due to Pass Lunar Area Today After 38 Hours

By JOHN W. FINNEY

Special to The New York Times.

WASHINGTON March 3 — Pioneer IV, a small gold-plated capsule of instruments, soared toward the vicinity of the moon tonight, on the way to an orbital rendezvous with the sun.

After a year of planning and four failures, the United States finally succeeded in breaking the bonds of the earth's gravity and sending a rocket payload into outer space.

The 13.4-pound Pioneer IV was launched by a sixty-ton Army rocket from Cape Canaveral, Fla., early this morning. It was following a trajectory that was expected to take it past the moon at a distance of 38,000 miles and to go on into an elliptical orbit around the sun.

Meanwhile, Pioneer IV was sending a variety of scientific data back to earth.

By 6 P. M. today, the lunar capsule had completed half of its trip of nearly 250,000 miles to the vicinity of the moon.

Course Plotted

Administration scientists estimated that at 7 A. M. tomorrow, Eastern standard time, Pioneer IV would be traveling at 4,800 miles an hour and would be 188,931 miles from the earth at Lat. 22.18 degrees S. and Long. 314.8 degrees E.

The National Aeronautics and Space Administration, which sponsored the experiment, predicted that Pioneer IV would pass by the moon at 2 P. M. tomorrow — some thirty-eight hours after it left the launching pad.

[The rocket was launched from Cape Canaveral at 12:10:30 A. M. Tuesday and Washington announced two hours later that it was expected to pass the moon and go into orbit around the sun, as reported in late editions of Tuesday's New York Times.]

The actual firing of the rocket was in charge of an Army team from Redstone Arsenal, Huntsville, Ala., headed by Dr. Kurt H. Debus.

As a scientific experiment, Pioneer IV was pronounced "an unqualified success" by Space Administration officials. Its instruments and small, battery-

Continued on Page 14, Column 3

President For Study Of Radio Spectrum

Special to The New York Times

WASHINGTON, March 3—President Eisenhower asked Congress today to authorize his appointment of a five-member commission to make a thorough investigation of the Federal Government's role in the management of telecommunications.

In letters to Vice President Richard M. Nixon and House Speaker Sam Rayburn the President said the changing technology and changing needs in government and commercial areas posed problems in telecommunications that required examination. He said:

"The situation is becoming no less complicated by prospective developments in satellites and space vehicles, as well as in defense weapons systems." Possible reallocation of the entire radio spec-

Continued on Page 14, Column 5

HAWAII BILL WINS IN SENATE GROUP

Committee Vote Unanimous for Statehood—House Hearings Continue

By C. P. TRUSSELL

Special to The New York Times.

WASHINGTON, March 3—Statehood for Hawaii was approved unanimously today by the Senate Committee on Interior and Insular Affairs.

Supporters hoped to take the measure, strongly backed by the Administration, to the floor for action before the Easter recess, which begins March 26.

It appeared that the legislation had a large majority in both houses.

Meanwhile, the House Rules Committee, which serves generally as the traffic director of floor actions, resumed its hearings on the House statehood bill.

The measure was approved by the House Interior and Insular Affairs Committee last month.

Admission Is Opposed

The second rules hearing followed the pattern of the first, held last Thursday. It found key members expressing "concern" and ridicule at the prospective admittance of Hawaii.

Led by Representative Howard W. Smith, Democrat of Virginia and chairman of the panel, they held that the admission of Alaska had brought in a forty-ninth state that might not be able to carry the full responsibilities of statehood.

They charged that admission of Hawaii would expand the United States into Asia and give Communist propaganda a footing in accusing the United States of practicing colonial imperialism.

Charges that Communism had

Continued on Page 17, Column 4

REPUBLICANS TRIM STATE AID TO CITY AMID OBJECTIONS

Slash in Budget of 10 Million Stirs Democratic Charge of Shortchanging

By DOUGLAS DALES

Special to The New York Times.

ALBANY, March 3—The Republican majority in the Legislature decided today to reduce by $10,000,000 the new aid to the city proposed by Governor Rockefeller. The decision revived Democratic charges that the state regularly shortchanged New York City.

Some Republican legislators from the city joined the Democratic leadership in criticizing the cut, which would increase the city's need for new tax revenue from $141,000,000 to $151,000,000.

[In New York City, Mayor Wagner said only that he was "searching around" for possible new taxes and had ordered research done on some of them. A new big tax may be devised, the Mayor said, or a pair of middle-sized ones may be proposed.]

Proposed in Budget

In the budget submitted to the Legislature last month, Governor Rockefeller proposed that $15,000,000 in special aid be appropriated for New York City. The purposes of the aid have never been specified, but it is understood that some of it was to help with maintaining the four city colleges.

Senator Walter J. Mahoney of Buffalo, the Republican majority leader, said after a Senate conference today that he had led the fight to have the city aid reduced.

Senator Joseph Zaretzki of Manhattan, the Democratic leader, called the cut "criminal" and "shameful."

At the Republican's Assembly conference today, the voices of two New York City legislators were raised against the cut. They were Assemblyman John P. Brook of Manhattan and Luigi R. Marano of Brooklyn.

In a statement yesterday another city Republican, Assemblyman Anthony P. Savarese Jr. of Queens, asserted that reducing the special aid for the city would be "abandoning reason for expedience."

Payroll Tax Looms

Assemblyman Brook said he had "vehemently" protested the cut and would do his best to have it restored. He said he had warned the conference that if the $10,000,000 were deleted, the Legislature would be asked to vote for a rise in the New York City sales tax.

"None of us will vote for that," he declared. "There will be no alternative but a payroll tax."

Mr. Brook said he was certain there were other cuts that could be made more reasonably.

Senator Mahoney rejected the Democratic charge that the city was being shortchanged. "It's getting $32,000,000 more in the next fiscal year than it is receiving this year," he asserted.

Senator Zaretzki challenged this figure, declaring that New York City was getting only $24,000,000 of a total of $87,000,000 in new state aid for localities.

Mr. Zaretzki defended the Governor. "He has tried to be fair," he said. "These other fellows won't let him. They want to divide New York City from

Continued on Page 20, Column 2

G.O.P. in Assembly Balks at Tax Plan

Bloc Opposed to Leaders' Pact to Trim Income Levies and Budget

By LEO EGAN

Special to The New York Times.

ALBANY, March 3—A tax-conscious Republican majority in the Assembly balked tonight at approving a tax and budget compromise recommended by the Republican legislative leadership.

As a consequence the fate of Governor Rockefeller's proposals for increasing revenues from the income tax by $150,000,000 in the next fiscal year remained in doubt overnight.

Oswald D. Heck, Assembly Speaker, announced when a party conference of Assemblymen broke up at 8 P. M. that it would reconvene tomorrow and consider the program again.

In the meantime Republican holdouts will be under heavy pressure from both the Rockefeller Administration and from the legislative leadership to reverse their position.

After four hours of debate and explanation behind closed doors the leadership was still eleven votes short of the seventy-six needed in the Assembly for approval of the compromise.

The New York Times

Governor Rockefeller

Earlier, Senate Republicans in a two-hour conference behind closed doors had agreed to support the program. Only two of the thirty-four Republican Senators were listed as possible dissenters. This assured the thirty votes needed for Senate approval of the program.

The terms of the compromise, announced after the Senate Republican conference, called for increasing the income tax credits to be given married tax-

Continued on Page 20, Column 3

Existing Commuter Cures Found to Need Direction

This is the last of three articles on the growing commuter problem in the New York area and other major cities.

By HARRISON E. SALISBURY

A nation-wide survey indicates that every technological, economic and conceptual means needed to solve New York's commutation problems for the present and foreseeable future now exists. A canvass of technical experts, engineers, social scientists, public specialists and transport executives leaves no doubt that we possess an abundance of methods and forces capable of coping with the revolutionary consequences of the automotive age.

Why are they not applied? Why is the problem permitted each year to grow worse? Why has effort after effort at solution met failure—either partial or complete?

The answer to these questions seems to lie in the complex nature of modern society and a general failure to understand the substrata of its relations.

"New conditions," as Dr. Luther Gulick, president of the Institute of Public Administration, notes, "now require new thinking as a basis for new institutions and action."

Mass and Metropolis

In order to formulate a solution there must be a definition of what a city is about, what its purpose is in today's world and how we want to arrange these functions.

Are limits to be suggested for the concentration of individuals in narrow areas—such as the 10,940,000 total that the new zoning plan for New York City proposes? Or does democratic freedom imply growth without form or aim? Should a metropolis possess the power to direct or control the settlement of people in its environs?

A city, in most minds, is designed as a convenient and comfortable place to live and work in. People assemble in large numbers because these numbers make the conduct of economic and social life richer. A city is, with infinite elaboration, an extension of the old crossroads bazaar—a locale where people meet people, trade, work, rest, eat, entertain and engage in social contacts of endless variety.

Dual Dangers Feared

But if too many people gather in one place, sheer mass may adversely affect their contacts. Or if congestion thins out, the market may fail for want of buyers or sellers.

If too many or too few utilize some of the circulation systems and if some systems become engorged while others are attenuated the same result may occur.

As Lewis Mumford, dean of American social thinkers, puts it:

"Mechanical integration and social disruption have gone on side by side. Our capacity for effective physical organization has enormously increased; but our ability to create a harmonious counterpoise to these external linkages has not kept

Continued on Page 24, Column 1

JERSEY ROAD ASKS 60% RISE IN FARES

Central Telling 12,500 Daily Riders It Lost $3,250,000 in Fourteen Months

The Jersey Central Railroad is threatening its 12,500 daily passengers with a 60 per cent rise in all fares.

In a publication to be distributed today to all passengers, Earl T. Moore, president of the rail line, said the carrier had lost $3,250,000 in the last fourteen months. The fare rise would merely cover the "out-of-pocket cost of rendering passenger service," Mr. Moore asserted.

Officials of the road said requests for the fare increase would be sent late this month to the Interstate Commerce Commission and the New Jersey Public Utilities Commission. The only alternative to the higher fares is the abandonment of all passenger service, the president declared.

New Haven, Too

Last week-end the New York, New Haven and Hartford Railroad mailed warnings to its stockholders that it would soon have to ask another increase in fares. It did not say how much.

The Jersey Central carries passengers from a large part of middle New Jersey and part of Pennsylvania into Jersey City and Newark. Connections from these Hudson River terminals to New York are made by tube trains and ferries. Of the 12,500 daily passengers bound for New York each day, 10,000 are commuters.

Abandonment Threatened

"The Jersey Central, faced with a loss from all operations of about $1,360,000 for the first two months of this year, on top of a loss of almost $2,000,000 last year, can no longer," Mr. Moore wrote in The Commuter's Almanac, a monthly publication distributed to passengers.

"We must either abandon passenger service entirely or raise fares sufficiently to cover the out-of-pocket cost of service.

"We currently estimate that putting rail passenger service on a break-even basis will require an average rise of about 60 per cent in fares, excluding the 20c per trip ferry fare.

"If we did not have to pay approximately $1,000,000 in

Continued on Page 25, Column 4

NYASALAND STRIFE WIDENS AS 23 DIE; NATIONALIST HELD

Banda, Leader of Africans, Is Expelled as a Result of Emergency Decree

Special to The New York Times.

SALISBURY, Southern Rhodesia, March 3—Rioting spread throughout Nyasaland following the declaration of a state of emergency today. Twenty-three persons were reported to have been killed.

[News agencies said those killed were Africans. Reuters put the death toll at 26.]

The worst outbreak occurred at Nkata Bay on Lake Nyasa in the Northern Province, a center of the African National Congress' opposition to the Federation of Rhodesia and Nyasaland. Crowds of rioters stormed the prison there in an attempt to release persons detained under the emergency regulations and were fired on by security forces.

After the state of emergency had been proclaimed, security forces arrested Dr. Hastings Banda, leader of the Nyasaland branch of the African National Congress. He was flown out of Nyasaland in a Royal Rhodesian Air Force plane to an undisclosed destination in Southern Rhodesia.

Another Jail Stormed

At Nkata Bay an official report listed casualties as fifteen dead and "seven known wounded." But other reports reaching Zomba, the capital, put the death roll at seventeen, with thirteen injured.

At Fort Manning, on the Northern Rhodesian border, an African was killed when security forces opened fire on rioters who also were trying to free African Congress prisoners.

Troops, airmen and policemen were in action throughout the day in a round-up of African nationalists under the code name Operation Sunrise. Dr. Banda's rallying call has been "Kwaca"—the dawn (of freedom).

About 150 officers of the African Congress have been detained and a 6 P. M.-to-6 A. M. curfew has been imposed in the twin towns of Blantyre and Limbe.

Human Shields Used

At Mzimba there was another prison raid incident. A crowd of Negroes using women and children as shields defied a security patrol and freed some prisoners.

At Karonga a squad of policemen brought in from Tanganyika encountered a hostile crowd, it was reported. Two Negroes were killed and seven wounded. Later tonight air reconnaissance over Nkata Bay showed the area was quiet. Mzimba was also reported quiet.

A police squad opened fire on a crowd in Blantyre and three rioters were killed.

In the Blantyre and Limbe areas, more than 100 arrests of rioters were reported. Vehicles were stoned. Security forces in several areas arrested Negroes trying to block roads with trees and by digging ditches.

Schools in Blantyre, Limbe, Cholo, Lilongwe and Zomba were closed and parents have been warned to keep their children indoors.

Most of the Indian shops in Blantyre and Limbe closed. Hundreds of African workers

Continued on Page 6, Column 4

MOSCOW MEETING AGREES ON A NEED FOR BERLIN TALKS

Macmillan Foresees Joint Peace Avowal

By DREW MIDDLETON

Special to The New York Times.

MOSCOW, March 3—Prime Minister Harold Macmillan said today he believed that the continuing negotiations on a declaration of peaceful intent by the Soviet Union and Britain would be crowned by success.

Mr. Macmillan proposed a three-point declaration yesterday to counter Premier Nikita S. Khrushchev's suggestion of a British-Soviet nonaggression pact. This afternoon at a news conference he disclosed that discussion of such a declaration would continue and said he was hopeful about its result.

The disclosure indicated that on this point the British party gained more than its members had expected. Prime Minister Macmillan and Foreign Secretary Selwyn Lloyd

Continued on Page 2, Column 3

BRITONS END TRIP

Khrushchev and Guest Report No Accords on Major Issues

The texts of communiqué and cultural pact, Page 3.

By OSGOOD CARUTHERS

Special to The New York Times.

MOSCOW, March 3—Prime Minister Harold Macmillan and Premier Nikita S. Khrushchev reported today that they had failed to reach any agreement on key issues regarding Germany and West Berlin. They agreed, however, that early negotiations were urgently needed to try to settle these issues.

The two leaders also called for further study of the possibility of limiting armed forces and atomic and conventional weapons "in an agreed area of Europe" as a means of increasing European security.

They reported more specific agreement on strictly British-Soviet relations, particularly in the field of trade and cultural exchanges.

These were the main conclusions contained in a joint communiqué summing up the results of Mr. Macmillan's ten-day visit to the Soviet Union and his many hours of talks with Mr. Khrushchev and other Soviet leaders.

Leaders Sign Communiqué

The communiqué was signed by the British and Soviet leaders this morning in the Great Kremlin Palace not long before Mr. Macmillan and his party, including Foreign Secretary Selwyn Lloyd, left for their return flight to London.

Except for the acknowledgment of continuing differences over the German question, the communiqué recorded British-Soviet agreement on the principles, at least, of the need for disarmament and banning of nuclear weapons and establishment of "an effective system of international inspection and control" to achieve these ends.

The positive picture painted by the greater part of the communiqué was drawn in broad general terms and made no substantive disclosures. Thus it avoided, and in fact concealed, basic differences that still deeply divided the East and West on how these disputes should be settled.

Nevertheless, the two leaders said they were "resolved to continue their efforts to reach satisfactory agreement" on the

Continued on Page 3, Column 1

EISENHOWER SEEKS MACMILLAN VISIT

President Urges That He Come to Discuss Berlin—Talk in 2 Weeks Likely

By JACK RAYMOND

Special to The New York Times.

WASHINGTON, March 3—President Eisenhower invited Prime Minister Harold Macmillan today to come here to discuss the Berlin crisis at his convenience.

James C. Hagerty, White House press secretary, said that the time and details of the visit had not been decided. However, the British leader is expected to arrive in Washington in about two weeks.

[In London, where Mr. Macmillan returned Tuesday, it was reported authoritatively that he would promptly accept President Eisenhower's invitation. It was thought that he would leave for the United States soon after returning from Bonn March 13.]

Purpose of the Meeting

In reply to a question about the purpose of the meeting with Mr. Macmillan, Mr. Hagerty said:

"It certainly is to talk about the situation in Berlin and, I would assume, his trip to Moscow."

It will be Mr. Macmillan's third meeting with President Eisenhower since he succeeded Sir Anthony Eden as Prime Minister, following the Suez crisis of 1956. The last meeting was in Washington last June.

The discussions between the Prime Minister and the President are expected to cover the following:

¶Mr. Macmillan's impressions of Soviet policy, on the basis of his conversations in Mos-

Continued on Page 2, Column 5

CASTRO TO VISIT U. S. NEXT MONTH

Accepts Editors' Invitation —Capital Embarrassed

Special to The New York Times.

WASHINGTON, March 3—Premier Fidel Castro of Cuba has accepted an invitation to speak in Washington next month.

The invitation was extended by the American Society of Newspaper Editors, which will open its annual convention here April 16.

A formal acceptance was received in New Orleans tonight by George W. Healy Jr., president of the society and editor of The New Orleans Times-Picayune. Premier Castro said the Cuban Embassy in Washington would supply information about the persons who would accompany him.

The White House and the State Department are embarrassed by the prospective visit, officials indicated, because Premier Castro, a head of government, was invited by a private organization.

There would have been no such embarrassment if the revolutionary leader were still commander of the armed forces—the post he first assumed. Such a visit could have been represented as entirely unofficial.

Officials agreed that the Gov-

Continued on Page 11, Column 3

BUSES SEEK RIGHT TO PUT ADS ON SIDE

Mayor Asked to End Ban—$1,500,000 Gain Seen

By STANLEY LEVEY

The Transit Authority undertook yesterday to obtain the removal of Traffic Commissioner T. T. Wiley's ban on advertisements on the outside of its 2,000 buses.

Inspired by prospects of revenues of $750,000 to $1,500,000 a year for sale of this advertising space, the agency petitioned Mayor Wagner and the Board of Estimate to "use their good offices" in getting Mr. Wiley to change his mind.

Under Traffic Department regulations advertising is prohibited on the outside of all vehicles. Commercial vehicles, however, are permitted to carry it if they "are in use for normal delivery and not merely or mainly for the purpose of advertising." The result is that many trucks display ads for the products they deliver.

In some neighboring New Jersey and Long Island communities buses carry advertisements. Many of these, the authority noted, come into New York "plastered with ads," in the words of E. Vincent Curtayne, a member of the agency.

The Traffic Department has

Continued on Page 23, Column 3

U. S. Proposes National Listing Of Drivers Who Lose Licenses

By RICHARD E. MOONEY

Special to The New York Times.

WASHINGTON, March 3—The Federal Government has a plan to catch the driver who loses his license in one state but continues to drive on another state's license.

In a report to Congress, the Commerce Department's Bureau of Public Roads proposed to establish a national clearing house in a Federal agency that would list the names of drivers whose licenses had been suspended or revoked.

The Government's role would stop at the information stage. It would be up to the states to make use of it.

The report was submitted last week-end at the end of a highway safety study ordered by Congress in 1956. It included statistics on safe speeds that might surprise back-seat drivers.

Most states will not issue a license to a person who is known to have had his privileges suspended or revoked in another state, the report noted. It said the existing means for finding this out were "cumbersome and relatively ineffective." In other words, each state must check with the others.

Few bother to do so. Some that do are unable to get the information they seek. As a result most states are issuing licenses to those with revoked or suspended licenses.

The report estimated that 1,000,000 licenses were suspended or revoked at present, or more than 1 per cent of all drivers. It put the number of drivers at 82,000,000.

The clearing-house plan was not detailed, but the agency in

Continued on Page 19, Column 5

Capital Voices 'Grave Concern' On Anti-U. S. Violence in Bolivia

By E. W. KENWORTHY

Special to The New York Times.

WASHINGTON, March 3—The United States expressed to Bolivia today its "grave concern" about anti-United States violence in La Paz.

An angry crowd in the Bolivian capital stoned the United States Embassy and the office of the United States Information Service yesterday. Reports from La Paz said the crowd had been inflamed by an article in the Latin-American edition of the magazine Time.

[The police in La Paz fired to disperse demonstrators rushing toward the embassy Tuesday, The Associated Press reported. One Bolivian was killed.]

Lincoln White, State Department spokesman, said that Manuel Barrau, the Bolivian Ambassador, had been called to talk with Roy R. Rubottom Jr., Assistant Secretary of State for Inter-American Affairs.

"The purpose," Mr. White said, "was to express our grave concern with developments in La Paz and to tell him that we fully expect his Government to take all possible measures to safeguard the lives of American citizens and United States property."

Mr. White said that so far there had been no reports of injuries to United States citizens in La Paz. There are 700 in the capital, of whom about 200 are embassy employes and their dependents.

As a precaution, Mr. White said, all United States citizens in La Paz were being concentrated in suburban areas, where

Continued on Page 11, Column 1

"All the News That's Fit to Print"

The New York Times.

LATE CITY EDITION

U. S. Weather Bureau Report (Page 36) forecasts: Mostly fair and less humid today and tomorrow. Temp. range: 84—70; yesterday: 85.8—71.8. Temp.-Hum. Index: low 70's; yesterday: 79.

VOL. CVIII..No. 37,072. NEW YORK, SATURDAY, JULY 25, 1959. 10 cents beyond 50-mile zone from New York City except on Long Island. Higher in air delivery cities. FIVE CENTS

NIXON AND KHRUSHCHEV ARGUE IN PUBLIC AS U.S. EXHIBIT OPENS; ACCUSE EACH OTHER OF THREATS

PHONE RATE SLASH ON LONG DISTANCE ORDERED BY F.C.C.

Reduction Totaling 50 Million a Year Applies to Calls of More Than 300 Miles

A. T. & T. SCORES RULING

Sees 'Good Research, Good Management' Penalized—Revision Due in Fall

By RICHARD E. MOONEY
Special to The New York Times.

WASHINGTON, July 24—The Federal Communications Commission has ordered that long-distance telephone rates be cut by $50,000,000 a year.

The commission announced today that the Bell System would revise its rates effective about Sept. 15. The cut applies only to interstate calls of more than 300 miles.

Two months ago the commission was criticized by the House Antitrust subcommittee for failure to act on its own staff's recommendations for rate investigations and reduction. It was also under attack for failure ever to set standards for measuring the adequacy of telephone rates.

The subcommittee, whose chairman is Representative Emanuel Celler, Democrat of Brooklyn, based its report on an investigation last year into the 1956 settlement of the Government's telephone antitrust suit by consent decree.

'Penalty' Is Assailed

Frederick R. Kappel, president of American Telephone and Telegraph Company, which is the capstone of the Bell System, issued a statement here on the F. C. C. action. He said that his company was being penalized for "good research and good management."

"While earnings on our interstate long-distance business have improved in recent years," he said, "they are lower than they should be and well below earnings of business generally."

He attributed the improved earnings to "technical advances by Bell telephone laboratories, especially on very long circuits; efficient management, and more long-distance calls."

He said that the F. C. C. directive "ignores the long-range interests of the public," which require added investment by the system to improve the quality of service, and add facilities

Continued on Page 8, Column 2

SQUALL RIPS CITY, DISRUPTS POWER

Floods, Lightning and High Winds Strike in Rush Hour

By ROBERT CONLEY

A violent summer squall struck the city yesterday with flooding rain and winds that reached hurricane force.

The storm hit about 4 P. M. unleashing one of the heaviest concentrations of rain in years. More than a third of an inch fell within five minutes amid crashes of thunder and lightning.

It knocked out subway signals on the IND line in Queens and threw rush-hour service into turmoil.

Long-distance train service on the Pennsylvania Railroad was reduced to a trickle when lightning hit the Sunnyside passenger car yards in Long Island City. The bolt short-circuited generators and left six of the main trains to the South and West without power.

Building Is Battered

Winds roared into the city from almost every direction. Gusts of up to seventy-five miles an hour hit the Union Carbide Building, under construction at Park Avenue and Forty-eighth Street, tearing off sheets of aluminum sheathing on the lower floors and flinging debris and equipment into the streets from the still-exposed upper floors.

The lightning hit hardest in Queens. Hundreds of homes were left without electricity, the Fire Department lost its emergency radio for an hour, traffic lights went out on parkways and boulevards and motorists inched ahead with headlights on. One person was re-

Continued on Page 19, Column 4

Goldfine Is Spared Jail for Contempt

By WILLIAM M. BLAIR
Special to The New York Times.

WASHINGTON, July 24—Bernard Goldfine escaped jail today for contempt of Congress. At the same time, he was directed in Federal Court to answer the Congressional questions that led to the charge if recalled by House investigators.

Judge James W. Morris of the United States District Court imposed the maximum sentence for contempt of Congress but suspended both a one-year jail term and a $1,000 fine. Judge Morris also placed the Boston industrialist on probation for two years.

The brief court action here came shortly before the United States Court of Appeals in Boston upheld a three-month sentence imposed on Mr. Goldfine and a ten-day sentence against his bookkeeper, Miss

Continued on Page 37, Column 5

STRICT LABOR BILL OFFERED IN HOUSE

Substitute for Committee's Measure Expected to Get Administration's Backing

By The Associated Press

WASHINGTON, July 24—A labor controls bill much tougher than one approved yesterday by the House Labor Committee was unveiled today with apparent Administration approval.

It was drafted by Representatives Phil M. Landrum, Democrat of Georgia, and Robert P. Griffin, Republican of Michigan. They said it was generally in line with President Eisenhower's wishes.

Its introduction added complications to the floor battle now shaping up over the measure approved by the Labor Committee in a 16-14 division.

With the backing of Republicans and Southern Democrats, the substitute could be favored over alternatives to the all but friendless committee bill.

Hopes for Support

Mr. Griffin told newsmen he had discussed the bill with the White House staff and with aides of Secretary of Labor James P. Mitchell. He said:

"I am personally of the opinion it meets the recommendations of the Administration. I would hope and expect the Administration to support it."

The committee bill, denounced by its foes and praised faintly by its friends, faces floor efforts to junk it in favor of substitutes.

Members who contend that the committee bill is still too tough on unions—although generally less drastic than the measure voted by the Senate—are expected to back a measure in line with the demands of organized labor. Others, includ-

Continued on Page 38, Column 2

Fiancee Retracts Kidnapping Story

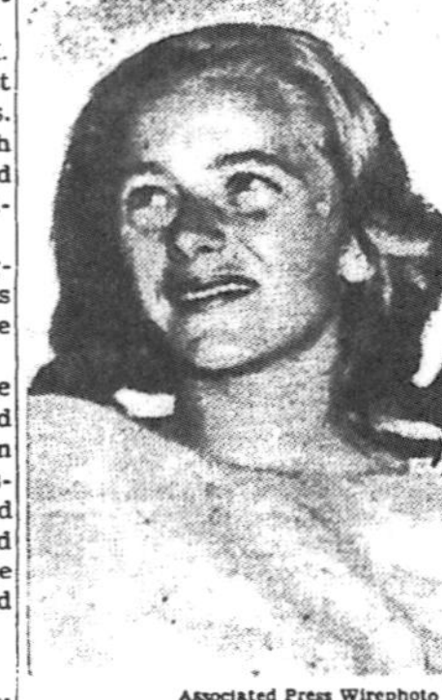

Associated Press Wirephoto

Miss Jacqueline Gay Hart in Chicago early yesterday.

Special to The New York Times.

CHICAGO, July 24 — Miss Jacqueline Gay Hart admitted to the Federal Bureau of Investigation tonight that she had not been kidnapped. She said she did not know how she had reached Chicago.

The 21-year-old Short Hills, N. J., woman admitted that her story of having been abducted at Newark Airport Tuesday night and having been driven to Grant Park here was false. She was found in the park early today.

The F. B. I. indicated it was

Continued on Page 37, Column 2

726-MILLION CUT IN AID BILL VOTED BY HOUSE GROUP

Eisenhower Deplores Move—Signs Measure Setting 3.5-Billion Ceiling

Special to The New York Times.

WASHINGTON, July 24 — Congress opened its second round of surgery on the foreign-aid bill today with a cut of $726,500,000 in President Eisenhower's request for funds for the fiscal year 1960.

The President, in a White House statement, was represented as "disappointed" by the size of the reduction but hopeful that a considerable amount could yet be restored.

Today's action was taken by the House Appropriations subcommittee, responsible for approving mutual-security spending.

The cuts that worried the Administration most were in the categories of military assistance and defense support.

President Signs Bill

In contrast to its past treatment in the House subcommittee, however, the Development Loan Fund fared comparatively well.

The subcommittee acted shortly after the President had signed a bill authorizing appropriations of $3,556,200,000.

The authorization bill sets ceilings on the amount of money Congress may vote for actual spending.

Normally, the appropriation is lower than the authorization and the House subcommittee recommendation is usually the deepest cut made during the legislative process.

The final figure is usually somewhat higher than the subcommittee recommendation.

'58 Cut Recalled

Today's cut by the subcommittee, though deep, nevertheless is about comparable to that made last year.

Thus, at this stage, this year's bill is in about as good a shape as last year's from the Administration viewpoint.

Following are the more significant cuts:

The President had requested $1,600,000,000 for military assistance. Congress authorized $1,400,000,000 The subcommittee cut it to $1,300,000,000.

The President had requested $835,000,000 for defense support. Congress authorized $751,000,000. The subcommittee cut to $700,000,000.

This item supplies economic aid for countries with which

Continued on Page 7, Column 3

BUTLER ENDS WAR ON PARTY'S HEADS

Truce Declared After Talks With Johnson and Rayburn

By RUSSELL BAKER
Special to The New York Times

WASHINGTON, July 24—A Democratic armistice was reached today between Paul M. Butler, National Chairman, and the party's Congressional leaders.

Peace was declared after an hour-long conference between Mr. Butler and the two Texans who make party strategy in Congress—Senator Lyndon B. Johnson and Speaker Sam Rayburn.

Ostensibly, the three-way chat ended three weeks of bitter public and private intraparty warfare between Mr. Butler and the Texans.

Harmony Reported

The substance of the armistice terms, as explained by all three combatants, was simple:

There had really been no fighting and no ill-will at all; impressions to the contrary were due to faulty press interpretations; therefore, it was only necessary to reassure the press that all was harmony.

The meeting took place in Speaker Rayburn's office just off the House floor. It was called at Mr. Butler's request.

Mr. Butler arrived alone and the three men were closeted without aides for an hour. After the meeting, Mr. Rayburn did most of the talking to newsmen. Mr. Butler confined himself to agreeing with the Speaker's account and expressing admiration for the Congressional leaders, Mr. Johnson talked sparingly.

Until their insistence today

Continued on Page 15, Column 5

Associated Press Radiophoto

INSIDE STORY: Vice President Richard M. Nixon describes operation of an automatic washing machine at the U. S. fair in Moscow to Premier Nikita S. Khrushchev of the Soviet Union. Mr. Nixon acted as host during tour of the fair.

NO TEMPERS LOST

Both Express Hopes for Agreement in Geneva Talks

The Eisenhower message and the Nixon speech; Page 2.

By HARRISON E. SALISBURY
Special to The New York Times.

MOSCOW, July 24—Vice President Richard M. Nixon and Premier Nikita S. Khrushchev debated in public today the merits of washing machines, capitalism, free exchange of ideas, summit meetings, rockets and ultimatums.

Mr. Nixon cut a symbolic red ribbon and formally opened the American National Exhibition. He said the fair was representative of the American way of life and called for peaceful competition, spiritual as well as material, between the United States and the Soviet Union.

Premier Khrushchev joined Mr. Nixon in expressing hope that the American exposition would promote understanding between the two countries. In a message read by Mr. Nixon, President Eisenhower extended his best wishes to the Soviet people and said he hoped one day to visit them.

"We should be glad if President Eisenhower found it possible to visit the Soviet Union," Mr. Khrushchev said.

Clashes Mark Day

But the day was highlighted by the sharp informal exchanges that took place between Mr. Nixon and Mr. Khrushchev.

The exchanges started in Mr. Khrushchev's quiet offices in the Presidium Building of the Kremlin. They reached a high point in an hour-long debate in the kitchen of a model house at the exhibition, and they wound up with laughs, finger-shakings and more argument at the formal opening of the exhibition.

In the course of the discussion, Mr. Khrushchev accused Mr. Nixon of trying indirectly to threaten the Soviet Union. Mr. Nixon rejoined that Mr. Khrushchev, by saying that the Soviet Union had better weapons than the United States, was also making an indirect threat. But both agreed that each nation wants peace.

Mr. Nixon appealed to Mr. Khrushchev not to let the Big Four Geneva conference of foreign ministers on Germany end in failure. He said it was now stalemated and that a way must

Continued on Page 2, Column 2

The Two Worlds: a Day-Long Debate

Nixon: 'I Am for Peace' Premier: 'Eliminate Bases'

Following is an account of the informal exchanges in Moscow yesterday between Vice President Richard M. Nixon and Premier Nikita S. Khrushchev. It was compiled from dispatches of The New York Times, The Associated Press, United Press International and Reuters.

Mr. Nixon was welcomed at the Premier's office in the Kremlin in the morning. There the principals exchanged greetings and handshakes, Mr. Nixon saying a few words in Russian.

Khrushchev: "You have learned some Russian."

Nixon (indicating with slightly separated fingers): "Just this much."

Khrushchev: "This is our first meeting. I welcome you. We hope your visit will be helpful in improving relations."

More pleasantries followed, Mr. Khrushchev remarking, "I hear you have been to the market place." Then reporters and photographers were ushered out and the statesmen had a private talk.

A Trade of Gibes About Trade

On arriving at the gate of the American National Exhibition later in the morning, Mr. Khrushchev voiced a gibe about the United States ban on the shipment of strategic goods to the Soviet Union.

Khrushchev: "Americans have lost their ability to trade. Now you have grown older and you don't trade the way you used to. You need to be invigorated."

Nixon: "You need to have goods to trade."

The statesmen went on to look at equipment for playing back recordings. Mr. Nixon took a cue from it.

Nixon: There must be a free exchange of ideas."

Mr. Khrushchev responded with a remark touching on the reporting of his speeches on his recent Polish tour.

Mr. Nixon said he was certain that Mr. Khrushchev's speeches and those of Frol R. Kozlov, a First Deputy Premier, had been fully reported in the West.

Khrushchev (indicating cameras recording the scene on video tape): "Then what about this tape?" (smiling). "If it is shown in the United States it will be shown in English and I would like a guarantee that there will be a full translation of my remarks."

Mr. Nixon said there would be an English translation of Mr. Khrushchev's remarks and added his hope that all his own remarks in the Soviet Union would be given with full translations in that country.

Khrushchev: "We want to live in peace and friendship with Americans because we are the two most powerful countries, and if we live in friendship then other countries will also live in friendship. But if there is a country that is too war-minded we could pull its ears a little and say: Don't you dare; fighting is not allowed now; this is a period of atomic armament; some foolish one could start a war and then even a wise one couldn't finish the war. Therefore, we are governed by this idea in our policy—internal and foreign. How long has America existed? Three hundred years?"

Nixon: "One hundred and fifty years."

They Will Wave As They Pass U. S.

Khrushchev: "One hundred and fifty years? Well, then, we will say America has been in existence for 150 years and this is the level she has reached. We have existed not quite forty-two years and in another seven years we will be on the same level as America.

"When we catch you up, in passing you by, we will wave to you. Then if you wish we can stop and say: Please follow up. Plainly speaking, if you want capitalism you can live that way. That is your own affair and doesn't concern us. We can still feel sorry for you but since you don't understand us—live as you do understand.

"We are all glad to be here at the exhibition with Vice President Nixon. I personally, and on behalf of my colleagues, express my thanks for the President's message. I have not as yet read it but I know beforehand that it contains good wishes. I think you will be satisfied with your visit and if—I cannot go on without saying it—if you would not take such a decision [proclamation by the United States Government of Captive Nations Week, a week of prayer for peoples enslaved by the Soviet Union] which has not been thought out thoroughly, as was approved by Congress, your trip would be excellent. But you have churned the water yourselves—why this was necessary God only knows.

"What happened? What black cat crossed your path and confused you? But that is your affair, we do not interfere with your problems. [Wrapping his arms about a Soviet workman] Does this man look like a slave laborer? [Waving at others] With men with such spirit how can we lose?"

Exchange of Ideas Urged by Nixon

Nixon (pointing to American workmen): "With men like that we are strong. But these men, Soviet and American, work together well for peace, even as they have worked together in building this exhibition. This is the way it should be.

"Your remarks are in the tradition of what we have come to expect—sweeping and extemporaneous. Later on we will both have an opportunity to speak and consequently I will not comment on the various points that you raised, except to say this—this color television is one of the most advanced developments in communication that we have.

"I can only say that if this competition in which you plan to outstrip us is to do the best for both of our peoples and for peoples everywhere, there must be a free exchange of ideas. After all, you don't know everything—"

Khrushchev: "If I don't know everything, you don't know anything about communism except fear of it."

Nixon: "There are some instances where you may be ahead of us, for example in the development of the thrust of your rockets for the investigation of outer space; there may be some instances in which we are ahead of you—in color television, for instance."

Khrushchev: "No, we are up with you on this, too. We have bested you in one technique and also in the other."

Nixon: "You see, you never concede anything."

Khrushchev: "I do not give up."

Appearances on TV Are Suggested

Nixon: "Wait till you see the picture. Let's have far more communication and exchange in this very area that we speak of. We should hear you more on our television. You should hear us more on yours."

Khrushchev: "That's a good idea. Let's do it like this. You appear before our people. We will appear before your people. People will see and appreciate this."

Nixon: "There is not a day in the United States when we cannot read what you say. When Kozlov was speaking in California about peace, you were talking here in somewhat different terms. This was reported extensively in the American press. Never make a statement here if you don't want it to be read in the United States. I can promise you every word you say will be translated into English."

Khrushchev: "I doubt it. I want you to give your word that this speech of mine will be heard by the American people."

Nixon (shaking hands on it): "By the same token, everything I say will be translated and heard all over the Soviet Union?"

Khrushchev: "That's agreed."

Nixon: "You must not be afraid of ideas."

Khrushchev: "We are telling you not to be afraid of ideas. We have no reason to be afraid. We have already broken free from such a situation."

Nixon: "Well, then, let's have more exchange of them. We are all agreed on that. All right? All right?"

Khrushchev: "Fine. [Aside] Agree to what? All right, I am in agreement. But I want to stress what I am in agreement with. I know that I am dealing with a very good lawyer. I also want to uphold my own miner's flag so that the coal miners can say: Our man does not concede."

Nixon: "No question about that."

Khrushchev: "You are a lawyer for capitalism and I am a lawyer for communism. Let's compete."

Vice President Protests Filibuster

Nixon: "The way you dominate the conversation you would make a good lawyer yourself. If you were in the United States Senate you would be accused of filibustering."

Nixon (halting Khrushchev at model kitchen in model house): "You had a very nice house in your exhibition in New York. My wife and I saw and enjoyed it very much. I want to show you this kitchen. It is like those of our houses in California."

Khrushchev (after Nixon called attention to a built-in panel-controlled washing machine): "We have such things."

Nixon: "This is the newest model. This is the kind which is built in thousands of units for direct installation in the houses."

He added that Americans were interested in making life easier for their women. Mr. Khrushchev remarked that in the Soviet Union they did not have "the capitalist attitude toward women."

Nixon: "I think that this attitude toward women is universal. What we want to do is make easier the life of our housewives."

He explained that the house could be built for $14,000 and that most veterans had bought houses for between $10,000 and $15,000.

Nixon: "Let me give you an example you can appreciate. Our steel workers, as you know, are on strike. But any steel worker could buy this house. They earn $3 an hour. This house costs about $100 a month to buy on a contract running twenty-five to thirty years.

Khrushchev: "We have steel workers and we have peasants who also can afford to spend $14,000 for a house." He said

Continued on Page 3, Column 1

RUSSIANS SCREEN BOOKS AT EXHIBIT

100 U. S. Volumes Removed From Show in Moscow

By MAX FRANKEL
Special to The New York Times.

MOSCOW, July 24—At Soviet insistence, more than 100 books were removed today from the shelves of the book show at the American National Exhibition.

A prolonged dispute over the display of books, through which Soviet visitors can browse, was the last major obstacle to the opening of the exhibit.

The wrangle was still not fully resolved tonight. About thirty books, including the 1959 World Almanac, were plucked out by Soviet inspectors this afternoon. These books await further appraisal and, no doubt, arguments.

Three Soviet officials continued screening the more than 8,000 volumes in the show today, even as Premier Nikita S. Khrushchev and Vice President Richard M. Nixon were trading verbal blows near-by over the problem of free information.

The Russians have protested with increasing vigor in the last week that the book show violated the ground rules for the exchange of Soviet and United States exhibitions. They maintained that only books

Continued on Page 4, Column 4

NEWS INDEX

News Summary and Index, Page 19

"All the News That's Fit to Print"

The New York Times.

LATE CITY EDITION
U. S. Weather Bureau Report (Page 58) forecasts: Fair and pleasant today; fair, cool tonight. Mostly fair tomorrow.
Temp. range: 75—56; yesterday: 77.0—57.6.

VOL. CVIII..No. 37,123. © 1959, by The New York Times Company. Times Square, New York 36, N. Y. NEW YORK, MONDAY, SEPTEMBER 14, 1959. 10 cents beyond 50-mile zone from New York City except on Long Island. Higher in air delivery cities. FIVE CENTS

SOVIET ROCKET HITS MOON AFTER 35 HOURS; ARRIVAL IS CALCULATED WITHIN 84 SECONDS; SIGNALS RECEIVED TILL MOMENT OF IMPACT

CONGRESS ENDING WITH EISENHOWER IN FIRM CONTROL

Early Democratic Initiative Gave Way to Moderation —Thrift the Key Issue

Record of voting during the session on Page 24

By JOHN D. MORRIS
Special to The New York Times.

WASHINGTON, Sept. 13—The Eighty-sixth Congress is bringing to a scheduled close tomorrow night a long session that produced substantial legislation shaped largely by a relatively conservative Republican Administration.

Its Democratic majorities, the largest in two decades, either compromised or yielded to a newly aggressive President Eisenhower on a broad range of economic and social issues.

The President was challenged on a few selected issues, but his free use of the veto and indirectly the veto threat forced frequent Democratic retreats and some surrenders.

In addition, the President was especially effective in rallying public opinion to his side. He did so with notable success in such major disputes as Federal spending and labor reform.

Appealed to Voters

With new-found vigor and articulation, he periodically sent strongly worded messages to Congress and repeatedly took his case directly to the voters in radio - television chats, speeches and news conferences.

At the Capitol, and particularly in the House of Representatives, the depleted Republican minorities fought his causes with effectiveness far beyond their numerical potential, often in coalition with conservative Democrats from the South.

When the new Congress came to Washington last January, fresh from a landslide victory for Democrats in the November elections, there were strong in-

Continued on Page 24, Column 1

SUSPECT IS SHOT AT PENN STATION

Youth Is Wounded in Chase —Bystander Is Grazed

A teen-aged suspect in a theft was shot and captured last night during a chase through Pennsylvania Station. One bystander was grazed in the neck by one of the five shots that were fired.

Two policemen pursued the suspect from the Greyhound Bus Terminal, on Thirty-third Street between Seventh and Eighth Avenues, across the street into the station. He was then chased along lower-level passageways to a railroad platform, where he was shot in the leg.

The station was not crowded when the chase started at 9:30 P. M., but about 200 persons in the station reacted with fear and consternation.

The pursuit began, the police said, with a telephone call from Robert E. Blackwell of 330 Oxford Street, Brooklyn. Mr. Blackwell, who phoned from the bus terminal, told the police that last Thursday a woman's pocketbook had been snatched in the terminal. He said that he had just spotted the thief.

When Patrolmen James Mierisch and Anthony Naglieri arrived in a radio car, Mr. Blackwell pointed to a man in the station. The police later identified him as Ronald Baxter, 19 years old, of 105 West 117th Street.

However, after questioning at the prison ward at Bellevue Hospital, the police said, Baxter admitted his name was James Talley, and he lived at 40-05 Twelfth Street, Astoria, Queens.

Continued on Page 58, Column 6

Schools Reopening In the City Today; 1,400,000 on Rolls

By LEONARD BUDER

After ten weeks of summer silence, school bells will signal the start of a new term here this morning.

Public, parochial and many private schools will reopen for more than 1,400,000 pupils.

The city's more than 800 public schools are expecting an enrollment of 985,000 youngsters, the largest number since 1941. Roman Catholic schools are expecting a record city-wide total of 369,950 pupils. Thousands of other pupils will attend Jewish and Protestant schools and nonsectarian private schools.

From kindergarten to senior high school, steps are being taken this year to improve what goes on in the classroom and to counteract some adverse influences that originate

Continued on Page 22, Column 4

STATE LABOR CUTS DEMOCRATIC TIES

Hollander Statement Praises G. O. P. Leaders but Also Bans All 'Entanglements'

Louis Hollander, chairman of the Committe on Political Education of the state A. F. L.-C. I. O., caustically criticized the Democratic leadership in Congress yesterday, while praising the records of Republican Governor Rockefeller and Senators Jacob K. Javits and Kenneth B. Keating.

The union chief, who headed the old state C. I. O. for ten years before the state merger last year, conceded that labor had been too close to the Democrats in past campaigns. He asserted that its future policy would be to shun entanglements with either party.

These views were given out after a joint meeting of the political education and executive committees of the state organization.

"I confess that the state C. I. O. made a mistake by allying itself solely with the Democrats," Mr. Hollander said in a statement. "They double-crossed us, and the Republicans ignored us because they felt sure we would be on the other side anyway. This drove even the more enlightened Republicans into the arms of the Dixiecrats on labor legislation, civil

Continued on Page 19, Column 4

CAPITAL FINISHING ITS PREPARATIONS FOR KHRUSHCHEV

President to Discuss Plans with Herter and Dillon— Premier Due Tomorrow

By DANA ADAMS SCHMIDT
Special to The New York Times.

WASHINGTON, Sept. 13—Washington was engaged this week-end in the most painstaking preparations ever made for the reception of an official visitor to the United States.

The preparations are for Premier Nikita S. Khrushchev, who is due at 11:30 A. M. Tuesday at Andrews Air Force Base, fifteen miles from Washington. He will be met there by President Eisenhower.

The President will discuss his part in dealing with Mr. Khrushchev at a White House meeting tomorrow morning with Secretary of State Christian A. Herter and Under Secretary Douglas Dillon.

Mr. Herter returned to Washington today from a vacation in Massachusetts and spent the afternoon going over plans for Mr. Khrushchev's visit with his aides.

Herter Visits Nixon

This evening he dined with Vice President Richard M. Nixon who, on the strength of his recent tour of the Soviet Union, is considered among the Administration's leading authorities on how to handle the Soviet dictator.

Vice President Nixon said today that the Soviet Premier had approved of Chinese Communist aggression, perhaps in the hope of getting "more action" out of his visit here. On a New York State radio hook-up, Mr. Nixon said that the absence of any disapproving note in Soviet statements about intrusions into India and Laos "would seem to indicate that they are encouraging, or at least approve, that action."

Meanwhile, the State Department was completing arrangements for handling more than 100 Soviet visitors, including thirty-four journalists; at least 300 American and foreign reporters who want to follow the whole tour, and about 2,000 others who will cover parts of it.

Plans were made for deploying about 15,000 military men, policemen, detectives, National Guardsmen and security agents to protect the Russians in Washington. About 40,000 men will be used to maintain security during the thirteen-day tour.

Coordinating the operation is

Continued on Page 10, Column 3

The New York Times — Sept. 14, 1959

AREA OF IMPACT: Cross near right center shows area where Soviet rocket hit surface of moon. Photograph is a composite picture of face of moon taken by camera of Lick Observatory near San José, Calif. Labeled are craters such as Copernicus at left center and three seas in area of the landing, Tranquillity, Serenity and Vapors.

FLAGS IN VEHICLE

Sphere Rams Surface at 7,500 M.P.H.— Moscow Jubilant

Text of Soviet announcement is on Page 16.

By MAX FRANKEL
Special to The New York Times.

MOSCOW, Monday, Sept. 14—The Soviet Union hit the moon with a space rocket early this morning.

The first object sent by man from one cosmic body to another bore pennants and the hammer-and-sickle emblem of the Soviet Government.

The announcement said steps had been taken to prevent the destruction of the pennants by the impact.

The object was a sphere of unknown size weighing 858.4 pounds. It crashed into the moon at a speed of about 7,500 miles an hour at 2 minutes and 24 seconds after midnight Moscow time. This was 5:02:24 P. M. Sunday in New York.

The time of impact was only 84 seconds later than Soviet scientists had predicted.

Instrument Sphere

The success of the Soviet's moon shot was made known in a jubilant Government announcement at 35 minutes after midnight over the Moscow radio.

The sphere was a hermetically sealed instrument container that had been ejected from the last stage of a multi-stage rocket.

The rocket was launched from Soviet territory at about one o'clock Saturday afternoon Moscow time (6 A. M. in New York).

The container covered a distance of 236,875 miles in about 35 hours.

The impact was not visible from the earth, but the strike was signaled by the sudden end to radio transmissions that were being received here from the container during its space voyage.

[Jodrell Bank in England reported that it had received the signals up to the time the rocket hit the moon.]

Fate of Sphere Unknown

The sphere was able to reach the moon's surface because there is little or no atmosphere that would produce friction and burn it up.

It is not known whether it shattered on impact or penetrated the dust that is thought to blanket much of the moon's surface.

Soviet scientists had estimated before the final announcement that the container would hit at a point about 270 miles from the center of the face among three large depressions in the moon's surface known as the Seas of Tranquillity, Serenity and Vapors.

There was no word here on the fate of the last stage of the rocket, which had been flying in space near the container. The container was separated from the rocket segment after they had safely escaped from the

Continued on Page 16, Column 1

Red China Charges Indians Are Using 'Two-Faced' Policy

By TILLMAN DURDIN
Special to The New York Times.

HONG KONG, Sept. 13—Marshal Chen Yi, Foreign Minister of Communist China, said today that the Indian Government "used two-faced tactics" in the border dispute between the two countries.

He added that Indian troops and administrative personnel "should withdraw from Chinese territory" and that "there does not exist a question of Chinese troops' withdrawing from anywhere."

For the first time Marshal Chen brought the Dalai Lama into the dispute between New Delhi and Peiping over the Chinese-Indian boundary.

Marshal Chen said the Dalai Lama's political activities in India against China and his move to raise the Tibetan question in the United Nations exceeded "by far what is allowed under the international practice of asylum." The Mar-

Continued on Page 3, Column 2

14th U.N. Assembly Begins Tomorrow

Proposed agenda for the U. N. Assembly on Page 8.

By LINDESAY PARROTT
Special to The New York Times.

UNITED NATIONS, N. Y., Sept. 13—The eighty-two-nation General Assembly will begin its fourteenth annual session here Tuesday with sixty-nine items on the agenda before it.

Some of the items are comparatively routine, such as elections of members of councils and committees. Others are potentially explosive politically.

Some of the most strenuous discussion this year was expected to center on the issues of French North Africa and disarmament. But Communist aggression in Tibet and Laos also is sure to get an airing, in the

Continued on Page 8, Column 6

NIXON SAYS SOVIET FAILED IN 3 SHOTS

Reports Moscow Attempted to Hit Moon With Rocket 'in the Last Two Weeks'

Vice President Richard M. Nixon said here last night that the Soviet Union had "failed three times in the last two weeks" to hit the moon with a rocket.

Mr. Nixon said he could not reveal the source of his information.

The Soviet Union has made no mention of any failures. Neither have there been previous disclosures by the United States that any had occurred.

The Vice President made his statement as he arrived at La Guardia Airport from Washington.

He also took the occasion to caution against "hysterical" reactions to the apparent success of the Soviet Union's moon shot.

"In science, sometimes we're ahead and sometimes they're ahead," he said.

Told to Expect Shifts

The Vice President said that the country should learn to expect such shifts in a highly complex endeavor of taking the first steps into outer space.

"But over-all, we are way ahead," he said.

Moreover, Mr. Nixon said, the excited reactions to the Soviet effort should not become the occasion for renewed attacks on the state of this country's science and education.

"It's nothing to get excited about," he cautioned. "Scientifically and educationally we are way ahead of the Soviets and there is no reason to junk our educational programs."

What the country should do, he said, is to "redouble" its efforts in an area where "someone else may be ahead."

The Associated Press reported that the Vice President's press secretary, Herbert Klein, had said "there is no official proof yet" of the Soviet success.

The Vice President nodded

Continued on Page 18, Column 4

Washington Praises Feat; Hopes for Sharing of Data

By JOHN W. FINNEY
Special to The New York Times.

WASHINGTON, Sept. 13—The Soviet achievement of placing the first man-made object on the moon was greeted here today with admiration and congratulations. But the reaction was tinged with regrets that once again the United States had been bested in the space race.

Within official Washington there was none of the near-hysteria that prevailed nearly two years ago with the launching of the first artificial earth satellite by the Soviet Union.

Rather, the Russian feat was regarded as another, if important, step in the exploration of space, in which the Soviet Union had the good fortune and the necessary rocket power to be first.

Statement by Dryden

The principal official reaction came from r. Hugh L. Dryden, deputy administrator of the National Aeronautics and Space Administration.

"We have followed with interest the travel of the Soviet lunar probe to its impact with the moon," he said in a statement.

"We wish to congratulate our fellow scientists and engineers on their success in this forward step in the exploration of space. We hope that the scientific data obtained in this flight will soon be available for study by the scientists of all countries."

There was no tendency to minimize the scientific importance of the Soviet lunar rocket in extending the frontiers of man's knowledge of space. But it was generally agreed that the most immediate importance of the feat probably lay in the diplomatic and psychological realms.

The timing of the launching just prior to Premier Nikita S. Khrushchev's heralded visit to the United States confirmed a belief within official circles that the space experiment had been designed as much for a psychological impact on American and world opinion as for an impact on the lunar surface.

On the basis of past Soviet practice of using technological triumphs as a psychological lever in diplomacy, there was every expectation that Mr. Khrushchev, on his forthcoming trip to this country, would proudly point to the Soviet moon rocket as evidence that the Soviet Union was the technological match of the United States.

Coming as it did on a sunny, fall-like afternoon when official Washington was more en-

Continued on Page 16, Column 7

NEWS INDEX

U.S Rejects Any Flag-Planting As Legal Claim to Rule Moon

By PETER KIHSS

The United States is taking the legal position that just planting flags on the moon—as the Soviet Union says it has done—will not give the Russians or anyone else any claim to rule over that body.

But John M. Raymond, deputy legal adviser to the State Department, said in Washington yesterday that the United States had "no views on how far you would have to go" to claim moon sovereignty, as yet. Mr. Raymond said one question was: "Is it subject to sovereignty?"

William A. Hyman, a New York international lawyer who has headed national and local bar association studies of space law and aeronautics, said here:

"Since consistency is not one of the Soviets' virtues, it would not be surprising to hear them say that if the satellite made physical contact with the moon, they would then claim they had extended sovereignty to the lunar sphere. But this would be in violation of their own position taken in September, 1958."

Mr. Hyman noted that at that time, the Soviet legal journal Sovetskoye Gosudarstvo i Pravo, in an article by Miss A. Galina, had urged that no government be permitted to incorporate any portion of interplanetary space under its jurisdiction. This was in an argument that rockets could be launched into space without asking permission of any other government.

The hope that any Soviet claim to moon sovereignty might be in the name of the

Continued on Page 16, Column 3

Khrushchev's Russia—7

Premier Tries a Pragmatic Approach Toward Soviet Arts and Literature

Following is the seventh of eight articles on the Soviet Union under Khrushchev by a correspondent who had extended tours of duty in Stalinist and post-Stalinist Russia and recently spent four months in the Soviet Union.

By HARRISON E. SALISBURY

Some people in Moscow are convinced that there was a plot last autumn in which a group of writers and editors allied themselves with powerful Communist party forces in an attempt to turn the ideological clock back to Stalin.

This, it is said, was an underlying reason for the savagery with which Boris Pasternak, Nobel Prize winner, and his novel "Doctor Zhivago" were attacked.

In the end Nikita S. Khrushchev turned against the cabal and repudiated the Stalinist implications of the literary-political intrigue and a new era of toleration in creative matters was decreed.

The Pasternak affair and its ramifications illustrate the dilemma of the Khrushchev regime in dealing with the intellectual. Mr. Khrushchev is deeply committed to greater creative freedoms. But Soviet writers, artists, musicians and poets move faster than the Communist party is prepared to go.

The ideological difficulties have been most severe in the realm of the printed word. In some artistic fields a quiet revolution has occurred with the aid and encouragement of Mr. Khrushchev. This is notably the case in architecture. Music is not far behind. Painting and sculpture are rapidly moving toward more modern Western concepts. Ballet stands on the threshold of new experimentation.

Only occasional echoes of the battles on the artistic front are heard in the West because the Soviet censorship often refuses to pass dispatches that touch on vital aspects of the controversies.

For example, the censors consistently eliminated all references to the fact that Mr. Khrushchev had sober second thoughts about the Pasternak case. The censorship also sup-

Continued on Page 14, Column 1

"All the News That's Fit to Print"

The New York Times.

LATE CITY EDITION
U. S. Weather Bureau Report (Page 61) forecasts: Fair today; mostly fair tonight. Partly cloudy and warm tomorrow. Temp. range: 74—54; yesterday: 69.1—52.5.

VOL. CIX..No. 37,358. © 1960, by The New York Times Company. Times Square, New York 36, N. Y. NEW YORK, FRIDAY, MAY 6, 1960. 10 cents beyond 50-mile zone from New York City except on Long Island. Higher in air delivery cities. FIVE CENTS

SOVIET DOWNS AMERICAN PLANE; U.S. SAYS IT WAS WEATHER CRAFT; KHRUSHCHEV SEES SUMMIT BLOW

CAPITAL EXPLAINS

Reports Unarmed U-2 Vanished at Border After Difficulty

Text of the U. S. statement on plane is on Page 7.

By JACK RAYMOND
Special to The New York Times.

WASHINGTON, May 5—The United States said today an American weather-observation plane flown by a civilian apparently went astray near the Turkish-Soviet border Sunday when the pilot's oxygen supply failed.

This was the official explanation of the incident described by Premier Khrushchev when he said an American "invader" had been shot down over the Soviet Union.

According to the official statement, the pilot was in a heavily instrumented U-2 single-engine plane, chartered from the Lockheed Aircraft Corporation by the National Aeronautics and Space Administration.

The pilot was identified later as Francis G. Powers, 30 years old, a Lockheed employe.

Plane Used in Research

The plane was flying at an altitude close to 55,000 feet, making weather observations over the Lake Van area of Turkey as part of a world-wide research program begun in 1956, a spokesman for the civilian space agency said.

The spokesman emphasized that the plane was unarmed and carried no military equipment of any kind. He said it was marked with the letters N. A. S. A. in black on a gold-yellow band and with an N. A. S. A. seal, a globe inside calipers. [Premier Khrushchev said the plane shot down bore no identification marks.]

Can Test Radioactivity

The U-2, in addition to its use for weather observation, was developed by Lockheed originally for the Air Force in a secret program initiated in 1954 to study radioactivity resulting from nuclear tests.

The U-2 can maintain flight at altitudes up to 55,000 feet for as long as four hours. It is powered by a single Pratt & Whitney J-57 turbojet engine.

In the high-altitude sampling program, U-2 aircraft have taken samples of radioactive fall-out by exposing filter paper to the atmosphere.

The agency spokesman denied that the U-2 missing in Turkey carried any radioactivity-detection instruments.

The incident occurred in one

Continued on Page 7, Column 1

Associated Press Radiophoto

ANNOUNCES DOWNING OF U. S. PLANE: Premier Khrushchev speaking yesterday during opening session of the Supreme Soviet (parliament) at the Kremlin in Moscow.

PREMIER IS BITTER

Assails 'Provocation Aimed at Wrecking' May 16 Parley

Excerpts from Khrushchev's remarks are on Page 6.

By OSGOOD CARUTHERS
Special to The New York Times.

MOSCOW, May 5—Premier Khrushchev said today that a United States plane on a mission of "aggressive provocation aimed at wrecking the summit conference" invaded Soviet territory May 1 and was shot down.

The Premier, in the most blistering speech against American policies he had made since his meetings with President Eisenhower last autumn, declared that the incursion, as well as declarations by United States policy makers, cast gloom on the prospects for the success of the summit meeting in Paris eleven days hence.

He expressed anger over the fact that President Eisenhower had supported declarations against Soviet foreign policies by Vice President Richard M. Nixon, Secretary of State Christian A. Herter, Under Secretary of State Douglas Dillon and others.

He Seems to Bar Nixon

He surmised, Mr. Khrushchev said, that General Eisenhower, while wanting peace, was a victim of tight restrictions by "imperialists and militarists" around him.

Mr. Khrushchev expressed regret that the President wanted to limit the summit meeting to one week and he virtually rejected a proposal to sit at the table with Mr. Nixon if the Vice President was elected to take over for General Eisenhower in case the session went over the time limit.

The most sensational section of Mr. Khrushchev's three-and-a-half-hour speech, made before the opening session of the Supreme Soviet, the nation's version of a parliament, was that concerning the charges of United States violations of Soviet airspace.

Foreign Policy to Fore

Mr. Khrushchev actually had been called upon to open the Supreme Soviet session to deal exclusively with sweeping new domestic policies that will affect every Soviet worker: gradual abolition of income taxes by 1965 and by next year, reduction of the work day to seven hours and an upward revaluation of the ruble.

However, the Soviet leader seized the occasion to discuss foreign policy and the summit conference. He apparently had determined to tell the Soviet people that recent Western actions and statements had darkened his previous optimism.

The Premier predicted to foreign diplomats earlier this week that his talk on foreign and domestic policies would contain major surprises. Indeed, his report of the plane incident came as a shock to Westerners and

Continued on Page 6, Column 4

A. M. A. DENOUNCES EISENHOWER PLAN FOR CARE OF AGED

Says Proposal Takes False Tack That Most Over 65 Are Medically Indigent

OTHERS JOIN IN ATTACK

Goldwater Sees 'Socialized Medicine'—Labor Assails Measure as Unsound

By AUSTIN C. WEHRWEIN
Special to The New York Times.

CHICAGO, May 5 — The American Medical Association assailed today the Eisenhower Administration's health - care plan for the aged.

A statement issued through the association's headquarters here in the name of its president, Dr. Louis M. Orr of Orlando, Fla., said the Administration plan was "based on the false premise that almost all persons over 65 need health care and cannot afford it."

"This is not a fact," the statement declared.

"The truth is that a majority of our older people are capable of continuing a happy, healthy, and in many cases, productive life.

"Of the more than 15,000,000 persons in the nation over 65 years of age, only 15 per cent are on old age assistance.

Rejects 2 Proposals

"An undetermined number, although able to finance other costs, find it difficult to withstand the additional burden of the cost of illness.

"It is for these people that something should be done. Neither the Forand advocates nor the Administration proposal is tailored to meet these problems."

[In Washington, the Administration's proposal was attacked by Senator Barry Goldwater as "socialized medicine" and by the merged labor federation as unsound and politically inspired.]

The medical association's reference to "Forand" alluded to a bill sponsored by Representative Aime J. Forand, Democrat of Rhode Island. It would extend the Social Security system, and increase Social Security taxes, to provide medical care for persons over 65.

The Administration's proposal, offered yesterday, calls for Federal and state subsidies of insurance systems to be set up by the states. The estimated annual cost of $1,200,000,000

Continued on Page 32, Column 3

O'DWYER'S NIECE NAMED TO BENCH

Mayor Appoints Her Despite Bar Groups' Opposition

By LAYHMOND ROBINSON

Mayor Wagner named Joan O'Dwyer O'Neill, 33-year-old niece of former Mayor William O'Dwyer, a city magistrate yesterday, despite the objections of two of the three bar groups to whom he had submitted her name.

He reported, however, that five bar groups, including the third one asked to pass on her, had given her "unanimous approval."

The Mayor also made it clear that he regarded Mrs. O'Neill as qualified for the $16,000-a-year post on the Magistrate's Court, which basically has jurisdiction over minor crimes.

10-Year Term Slated

The appointment, which needs no further approval, is to fill out two months of a term of a magistrate who resigned. Mrs. O'Neill will then be appointed for a full ten-year term.

In commenting on the division of the bar associations over the designation, the Mayor said he had "always sought bar association approval for bench nominees," but had "never intended or pretended that such support had to be unanimous."

He emphasized that he regarded Mrs. O'Neill, "whom I know quite well," as qualified for the position.

The opposition to her appointment had stemmed largely from the feeling by some lawyers that Mrs. O'Neill had not

Continued on Page 14, Column 5

West Virginia Poll Finds Kennedy Gain

By W. H. LAWRENCE
Special to The New York Times.

CHARLESTON, W. Va., May 5 — Substantial voting gains for Senator John F. Kennedy were reported today in West Virginia.

Politicians and polls alike brought reports of a strong, well-financed and well-organized Kennedy drive to wrest victory from Senator Hubert H. Humphrey of Minnesota, considered the favorite in next Tuesday's Democratic Presidential preferential primary here.

One politician, who classified himself as neutral but formerly pro-Humphrey, admiringly called the Kennedy effort "a blitz." But what he and other politicians, including many in the Kennedy camp, questioned was whether the indicated gains in the southern coal fields were

Continued on Page 13, Column 1

RIBICOFF ASSAILS NEW HAVEN LINE

'This Is Not the Way to Run a Business,' He Says in Calling 4-State Parley

By RICHARD H. PARKE
Special to The New York Times.

GREENWICH, Conn., May 5—Gov. Abraham A. Ribicoff accused the New Haven Railroad today of "shabby and shoddy" bookkeeping, of wasting "great sums" and of employing "scare words, false issues, emotional appeals and misrepresentations."

"Clearly," he said, "this is not the way to run a business and especially a business which must count so heavily on public goodwill, public support, public respect and, yes, even public affection."

Governor Ribicoff delivered his attack in announcing that he was inviting the Governors of New York, Rhode Island and Massachusetts and the Mayor of New York to confer with him on the New Haven's future. No date has been set for the conference.

Tax Relief Proposed

Mr. Ribicoff said he would ask them to consider taking action on the recommendations in the report issued on the New Haven yesterday by the Connecticut Public Utilities Commission.

The report, which was also critical of the railroad management, proposed several measures to aid the line. They included a joint tax-relief program by the four states and an interstate authority that would cooperate with the railroad in providing commuter service in the New York area.

Governor Ribicoff, who discussed the railroad at a meeting here of the First Selectman's Association of Fairfield County, also said he was prepared to recommend a railroad

Continued on Page 20, Column 1

DILLON CONSULTS A. F. L.-C. I. O. AIDE IN ARAB SHIP CASE

Seeks Way to End Picketing Here as Mideast Boycott of U. S. Vessels Spreads

By DANA ADAMS SCHMIDT
Special to The New York Times.

WASHINGTON, May 5—Under Secretary of State Douglas Dillon conferred today with Arthur J. Goldberg, special counsel of the American Federation of Labor and Congress of Industrial Organizations, on possible ways of ending the picketing of the United Arab Republic ship Cleopatra in New York.

Union and State Department officials spoke of the possibility of working out a statement of United States policy that would lead the Seafarers International Union to call off its pickets.

But State Department officials were emphatic in pointing out that they had no means of forcing the United Arab Republic to give up its practice of blacklisting ships that put in at Israeli ports. This boycott precipitated the picketing.

Meanwhile, concern grew at the State Department over indications that the blockade of the Cleopatra and the Arab counter-blockade were reversing the trend toward better United States relations with the Arab world.

Blockade May Spread

"From almost every post we have had laments that the diplomatic efforts of years are being upset by this affair," an official of the department said.

If the blockade continues the impact on commerce would deepen and might next spread to airlines, he added.

The reports included the following points:

¶In Khartoum, capital of the Sudan, the press for the first time in two years assumed an anti-United States tone.

¶The Bombay Port Workers Union telegraphed President Eisenhower protesting the blockade of the Cleopatra and declaring that its continuance would result in a boycott of United States ships seeking to enter the Bombay port. This was the first sign that the counter-blockade might spread beyond the Arab world.

¶A Libyan Government official suggested informally to United States diplomats that "it would be better" if United States ships avoided Libyan ports while the Cleopatra was being picketed.

¶Consulates in a number of Arab ports reported that as the result of a knifing incident in which the eye of a member of the Cleopatra crew was injured it might be unsafe for American crewmen in Arab ports.

¶The American Export liner Excalibur, due today in Alexandria, the United Arab Republic port, was diverted by its owners to a destination not yet disclosed. The United States freighter Exchequer began un-

Continued on Page 2, Column 3

U. S. ASKS DETAILS OF PLANE INCIDENT

Data Sought From Envoy in Moscow as Washington Reacts With Restraint

By WILLIAM J. JORDEN
Special to The New York Times.

WASHINGTON, May 5 — Washington reacted with restraint today to Premier Khrushchev's announcement that a United States plane had been shot down Sunday on Soviet territory.

There were some angry words on Capitol Hill—including a suggestion that President Eisenhower refuse to go to the summit meeting with Mr. Khrushchev in Paris May 16. But the Administration would say little more than that additional information was being sought from Moscow.

A message went to Ambassador Llewellyn E. Thompson Jr. in Moscow this afternoon instructing him to request more details from the Soviet authorities.

Text Made Available Late

The text of Mr. Khrushchev's long speech to the Supreme Soviet became available to officials only late this afternoon. Their first reaction was that he seemed to be preparing the way for placing the blame for a summit failure on the Western powers.

He also seemed to be giving advance warning that the Allied leaders could expect little softness from him at the Paris meeting. The consensus was that the Khrushchev address was the latest move in pre-summit maneuvering, but that it had not altered measurably the outlook for the summit meeting.

Mr. Khrushchev said that the Governments of the United States, Britain and France did not seem to be looking forward

Continued on Page 7, Column 6

Soviet Will Revalue Ruble; Income Tax to End by '65

By MAX FRANKEL
Special to The New York Times.

MOSCOW, May 5—Premier Khrushchev proclaimed a complex fiscal reform today. The changes will bring a new and more costly ruble into Soviet circulation next year and an abolition of most personal income taxes by 1965.

The Premier pledged greater take-home pay to lower-paid industrial workers and office employes and said that this would be matched by increased stocks of consumer goods in the stores.

In fact, he promised a great new drive for the production of consumer goods once his ambitious seven-year economic plan is fulfilled in 1965.

Mr. Khrushchev proposed the currency revaluation and tax revisions to the Supreme Soviet, the national Parliament. Enabling legislation as requested by the Soviet leader is expected after a day or two of comment from the Deputies. It is expected to be some time, however, before everyone here, including experts, understands the ramifications of the program.

Unanimous Adoption Seen

There is little doubt that the changes will be unanimously adopted essentially as outlined by Mr. Khrushchev in a broadcast speech. He asked that all the arithmetic complications of the new formulas be tirelessly explained to the Soviet people, together with assurances that the country will gain by the changes and that no one will suffer.

Premier Khrushchev also promised that the currency reform would not affect the Soviet Union's foreign economic dealings or contracts. The official value of the ruble is four to $1. American tourists in the Soviet Union, however, receive a premium payment that brings them a total of ten rubles a dollar.

There was no suggestion in Moscow that the reform was a prelude to free convertibility of

Continued on Page 3, Column 3

ANKARA STUDENTS JOSTLE MENDERES

Turkish Premier Is Caught in Street Demonstration —Escapes Amid Jeers

By JAY WALZ
Special to The New York Times.

ISTANBUL, Turkey, May 5—Premier Adnan Menderes was jostled and jeered in Ankara today when he was caught by surprise in a student demonstration.

Anti-Menderes students mingled with a crowd of the Premier's supporters. They crowded around him shouting "Freedom! Freedom!" as he walked among them on his way to a political club.

One student clutched Premier Menderes' arm and asked, "How long do we suffer at your hands?" The Premier angrily called a policeman to take the young man away.

After a few minutes Mr. Menderes escaped unharmed in a small car that had been parked near by. It pushed through the throng to his own waiting automobile. President Celal Bayar and two Ministers saw the disturbance but were not involved.

Police and Cavalry Busy

About 300 policemen and a troop of cavalry dispersed the crowd, which witnesses estimated at about 3,000. A Government spokesman maintained that only 250 were demonstrators. The rest were bystanders, he said.

A few shots were fired into the air but no one was reported injured. The disturbance lasted for about an hour and a half.

Before the demonstrations in Ankara, a group of students allied with Mr. Menderes' Democratic party were waiting to greet him as he drove to the political club in Kizilay Square in the new section of Ankara. Soldiers lined his route along Ataturk Boulevard.

The anti-Menderes students had passed the word to infiltrate the throng, using the watchword "Five, Five, Five, K.," meaning "Be at Kizilay Square at 5:55 P. M."

The outbreak marked the

Continued on Page 4, Column 5

London in Gala Mood for Princess' Wedding Today

Associated Press Radiophoto

Princess Margaret and Antony Armstrong-Jones as they arrived yesterday at Clarence House, the Princess' home, after rehearsing for their wedding in Westminster Abbey.

By DREW MIDDLETON
Special to The New York Times.

LONDON, May 5—The Church of England stressed the spiritual aspects of tomorrow's royal wedding in a brave but unavailing attempt to modify the carnival mood that has gripped the heart of this dignified capital tonight.

Outside Westminster Abbey crowds gaped at decorations hailing the marriage of Princess Margaret to Antony Armstrong-Jones. Inside, the Very Rev. Eric Symes Abbott, Dean of Westminster, emphasized that "here are two people—a man and a woman—for whom it is the greatest day of their lives." Westminster Abbey, the Dean observed,

Continued on Page 26, Column 3

23 Are Killed and Scores Injured As Twisters Hit East Oklahoma

By The Associated Press.

WILBURTON, Okla., May 5—At least twenty-three persons were killed by tornadoes that slashed across eastern Oklahoma tonight. At least eleven were killed and scores injured in this college town.

A witness, Mrs. Denny Jones, said the tornado hit Wilburton about 6:45 P. M. with a "freight-train" roar.

All communications were cut and travel and rescue efforts were hampered by torrential rains.

The highway patrol and newsmen listed the Wilburton victims as:

Gordon Mote, 70 years old; Mrs. James Reeves, wife of an instructor at Eastern Oklahoma A&M Junior College; a Mrs. Porter and a Mrs. McGee; James Parks, about 70; Mr. and Mrs. Mike Brady, both about 70; Truman Clark, about 45; Wildon Raines; Margie Bark, and one unidentified man.

Several of the older victims were killed when the twister leveled the Calvary Baptist Church where services were being held.

More than seventy-five persons were reported injured.

Ambulances raced over slick roads to hospitals at McAlester, Poteau, Hartshorne and Heavener.

A newsman on the scene said about 1,000 rescue workers rushed into the city of 2,000 in reply to a call for help.

Tornadoes killed five in the area around Moffett and Roland two small communities nestled against the Arkansas border near Fort Smith.

Sheriff Prentice Maddux of Fort Smith said four bodies

Continued on Page 62, Column 7

Harvey Firestone 3d Dies in Havana Fall

Special to The New York Times.

HAVANA, May 5—Harvey S. Firestone 3d plunged to his death from the twentieth floor of a Havana luxury hotel tonight, six hours after arriving here from Miami. The victim, who was 32 years old, was the son of Harvey S. Firestone Jr., chairman of the board of the Firestone Tire and Rubber Company.

[Cuban authorities ruled the death a suicide, The Associated Press reported.]

The Cuban police said David Morgan Firestone, 29, a cousin of the dead man, had told them that Harvey Firestone had attempted suicide on a previous occasion in the United States.

The victim had been crippled since birth by cerebral palsy.

Mr. Firestone arrived in Havana today accompanied by his

Continued on Page 62, Column 5

NEWS INDEX

1960

Turmoil and Triumph

1968

FRONT PAGE NEWS 1960-1968

A Farewell Warning

JANUARY 18, 1961

It was an unusual farewell speech from a president not known for sounding alarms. Dwight D. Eisenhower—West Point graduate, former commanding general and hero of World War II—warned against a dangerous "military-industrial complex" forged by the armed services, defense contractors and pork-barrel-loving lawmakers. The juggernaut was so far-reaching that it resisted reform, even when its missiles missed their targets and its fighter jets had to be grounded.

A Russian in Space

APRIL 12, 1961

The radio bulletin from Moscow was eight words long—"Russia has successfully launched a man into space." Cosmonaut Yuri Gagarin's flight was short, too—only an hour and 48 minutes—but it signaled another triumph for the Soviets and another embarrassment for the United States. President Kennedy's response, six weeks later, was to announce the goal that defined the space race: by the end of the decade, the United States would send an astronaut to the moon.

Ill-Fated Mission to Cuba

APRIL 18, 1961

The invaders hit the beach at a place called Bahia de Cochinos—the Bay of Pigs—hoping to overthrow the two-year-old government of Fidel Castro. The C.I.A., whose cadres had trained them in Florida and elsewhere, had won over President John F. Kennedy. But at the last minute he cancelled air support, worsening the odds against the already dubious mission. The failure humiliated the United States, planted the first doubts about U.S. intelligence and, some historians say, laid the groundwork for the Cuban missile crisis.

The Wall Was the Message

AUGUST 14, 1961

The Berlin Wall became an enduring symbol of the cold war and East-West tensions. Just a jumble of barbed wire at first, it began as Communism's answer to a population drain: more than 2.5 million East Germans had fled to the west during 11 years of Communist rule. As if such a formidable barricade were not enough to stop the exodus, the Communists posted guards with shoot-to-kill orders. "It pleases me," Soviet Premier Nikita Khrushchev declared.

American in Orbit

FEBRUARY 21, 1962

In five hours aboard Friendship 7, John H. Glenn Jr. circled Earth three times and made the space race competitive. The ride took Glenn 162 miles into space at a speed of 17,500 miles an hour, but the statistics hardly mattered after Glenn splashed down in the Atlantic. He was an instant hero who received congratulations from more than 30 world leaders (including Soviet Premier Nikita Khrushchev) and was treated to a ticker-tape parade in New York.

Death of a Sex Symbol

AUGUST 6, 1962

She was an American icon with a string of screen credits and a short list of ex-husbands that included Joe DiMaggio and Arthur Miller. She had sashayed into Madison Square Garden three months earlier in a show-stopping dress and sung "Happy Birthday, Mister President." That fueled rumors that Marilyn Monroe and John F. Kennedy were having an affair—rumors that continued long after her death, and his.

Integrating Ole Miss

OCTOBER 1, 1962

Federal marshals had to escort James H. Meredith to class after Governor Ross Barnett defied court orders to admit him as the University of Mississippi's first black undergraduate, touching off a federal–state showdown. By forcing Meredith's enrollment, President John F. Kennedy sent a message that Washington would enforce federal law if intransigent states stood in the way, a policy that drove the Deep South to the G.O.P.

On the Nuclear Brink

OCTOBER 23, 1962

It was a turning point in the cold war—a full-scale nuclear showdown—and, in the end, it cost Soviet Premier Nikita Khrushchev his job. The crisis began when spy-plane photos revealed Soviet missile installations in Cuba, ninety miles from the U.S., and President John F. Kennedy threatened a "full retaliatory response." After days of diplomatic exchanges, Khrushchev promised to dismantle the missiles. All that Washington said it had promised was not to attempt another invasion like the Bay of Pigs. Not quite. It turned out months later that Kennedy had also promised to remove American long-range missiles in Turkey which were aimed at the Soviet Union.

A Modernizing Pope

JUNE 4, 1963

He saw himself as a "good shepherd" whose mission was to rejuvenate the Roman Catholic Church. Pope John XXIII convened the Second Vatican Council, known as Vatican II, to approve liturgical reforms that included replacing the Latin mass with a rite that used everyday language. His last encyclical, "Pacem in Terris" ("Peace on Earth"), addressed cold war tensions, saying that peaceful coexistence between the West and the Communist bloc was essential.

A Second Death in Dallas

NOVEMBER 25, 1963

He slipped through a crowd of police officers and photographers awaiting a glimpse of Lee Harvey Oswald. Later Jack Ruby, a Dallas strip-joint operator who fired a single shot, said he had "tried to play the part of a hero." Conspiracy buffs speculated that Ruby was a hit man carrying out Mafia orders to kill Oswald. A jury sentenced him to death, but an appeals court overturned the conviction in 1966. Ruby, by then ill from cancer, spent his final days at the same hospital where Kennedy and Oswald had died.

Hazardous to Your Health

JANUARY 12, 1964

A scientific and medical broadside against the $8-billion-a-year tobacco industry affirmed the federal government's role in consumer protection. The surgeon general's report left no doubt that smoking caused cancer. Although tobacco lobbyists would dispute that conclusion for years, Congress soon required a warning on every pack—"Caution: Cigarette Smoking May Be Hazardous to Your Health"—and the Federal Communications Commission banned commercials for cigarettes on television and radio.

Behind the Beatlemania

FEBRUARY 17, 1964

Their so-cool frenzy looked spontaneous, but the Beatles' American tour was a product of carefully calculated promotion from start to finish. No matter. A screaming throng met the mop-haired British rock stars at the airport, jammed the sidewalk outside their New York hotel, watched their legendary appearance on "The Ed Sullivan Show" and snapped up their chart-topping single, "I Want to Hold Your Hand." And so it went, for decades, making them the most successful group in the history of show business.

Affirming Civil Rights

JUNE 20, 1964

"Let us close the springs of racial poison," President Lyndon B. Johnson declared as he signed the landmark civil rights bill that banned discrimination on the job and in public places like movie theaters and restaurants. The Senate passed it after an 83-day filibuster led by Southern Democrats who maneuvered to delay or derail it. Their "no" votes were joined by one from Senator Barry Goldwater, the Republican from Arizona who went on to run against Johnson in November—and lose in a landslide.

'I Have a Dream'

AUGUST 29, 1963

The crowd cheered the first time he said it, but the Rev. Dr. Martin Luther King Jr. did not stop: "I have a dream," he repeated, sounding "both militant and sad," as James Reston wrote in The Times. The setting was the historic march on Washington, a high point of the civil rights movement that affirmed Dr. King's strategy of nonviolent protest and his vision for a society that fulfilled the promises of the Constitution.

Death of a President
NOVEMBER 23, 1963

John F. Kennedy had been president for 1,036 days. Now he was on a fence-mending trip to Texas, where his popularity had waned. His limousine turned a corner, and a rifleman's bullets found their target. After Kennedy was pronounced dead, the speaker of the house, John W. McCormack, expressed the horror of a grieving nation: "My God! My God! What are we coming to?"

The Warren Commission's Conclusion
SEPTEMBER 28, 1964

The Warren Commission, appointed by President Lyndon B. Johnson to investigate the Kennedy assassination, found that Lee Harvey Oswald had acted alone. Conspiracy theorists have kept the controversy simmering ever since with explanations—some far-fetched, some seemingly less so—for possibilities the Warren Commission rejected: the C.I.A. was involved, they say. Or the Mafia, Fidel Castro, even the Soviet K.G.B.

Malcolm X Killed
FEBRUARY 22, 1965

Malcolm X had gone from teen criminal to jailhouse convert, championing Elijah Muhammad's Islamic beliefs and black separatism. But as the civil rights movement gained mainstream support, he abandoned Muhammad's Nation of Islam and moved toward advocating integration. Louis Farrakhan, a rising star of the Nation of Islam, denounced him, and Malcolm X knew he was courting danger. "I'm a marked man," he said a week before gunmen opened fire as he gave a speech in upper Manhattan.

The Watts Riots
AUGUST 15, 1965

Rage about joblessness and belligerent police in black ghettos were a simmering urban problem when a white patrolman stopped a black motorist in the Watts section of Los Angeles. Exaggerated accounts of their encounter soon spread, and hundreds of blacks poured into the streets, setting fires, vandalizing stores and shooting police officers. Eventually, 14,000 National Guardsmen were sent in. In six days of violence, 34 people were killed, nearly 900 injured and some 4,000 arrested.

The Six-Day War
JUNE 8, 1967

Israel's quick victory stunned the world, seizing the offensive after Egypt drove out United Nations peacekeepers, closed the strategically important Gulf of Aqaba and signed a military pact with Jordan. In less than a week, Israel destroyed the Egyptian air force, broke the gulf blockade, drove the Syrians from the Golan Heights, outmaneuvered the Jordanians in the West Bank and occupied ancient Jerusalem. Over the next 40 years, Israel successfully resisted pressure to withdraw to its prewar boundaries.

Pioneering Transplant
DECEMBER 4, 1967

"You promised me a new heart," Louis Washkansky, a grocer who had already survived three heart attacks, whispered in the recovery room. Dr. Christiaan Barnard whispered back that he had made good on the promise. In a five-hour operation, Dr. Barnard replaced Washkansky's diseased heart with a healthy one from a woman who had died in a car crash. Medically, the transplant was considered a success (though Washkansky died 18 days later of pneumonia). Ethically, it raised new concerns about acceptable standards for what amounted to experimental techniques.

Tet Offensive
FEBRUARY 2, 1968

A devastating North Vietnamese offensive, launched during the Tet lunar new year festival, caught the American military machine off guard. The attack on the big Marine base at Khe Sanh was accompanied by street fighting and even an assault on the American Embassy in Saigon. The North Vietnamese controlled Hue for more than three weeks. Eventually the Americans turned the tide, but back home, newspaper readers and television viewers were horrified by the images of bloodshed. President Johnson soon lost confidence in the top American general in Vietnam, William C. Westmoreland. Johnson promoted him to Army chief of staff—and denied kicking him upstairs.

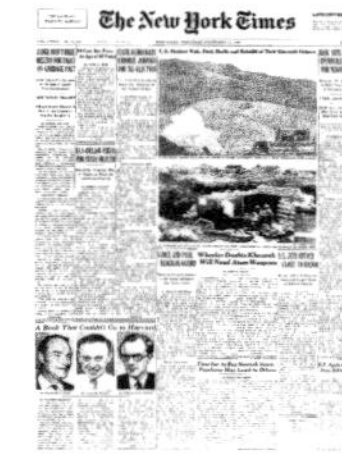

Dispute Over 'The Double Helix'
FEBRUARY 15, 1968

Some would call it a revealing footnote to scientific history. Some would call it mud wrestling in lab coats. The three scientists who won the Nobel Prize in medicine for deciphering the structure of DNA were at odds over a memoir by one of them, Dr. James D. Watson. Harvard's governing body overruled a panel of twelve professors and ordered the Harvard University Press not to publish the book, "The Double Helix," to which his Nobel co-winners, Dr. Francis H.C. Crick and Dr. Maurice H.F. Wilkins, had objected. Dr. Wilkins said he was especially displeased with the way Watson wrote about another researcher, Dr. Rosalind Franklin, who died before the Nobel was awarded (and was excluded, because Nobels go only to the living). Watson's book was published anyway—not by Harvard, but by a trade publisher, Atheneum.

L.B.J. Declines to Run Again
APRIL 1, 1968

President Lyndon B. Johnson had become an unpopular president weighed down by an unpopular war, and by the time he went on national television to announce a reduction in bombing raids on North Vietnam, he knew it too. The surprise came at the very end of his speech, when he said that he would not run for another term. Johnson, who lost the New Hampshire primary to the antiwar Democrat Eugene J. McCarthy by six percentage points, recognized that Vietnam had not only sapped his political strength, it had distracted the nation from domestic reforms he had hoped would be his legacy.

Assassination in Memphis
APRIL 5, 1968

A single shot at dusk brought down the Rev. Dr. Martin Luther King, Jr. on the balcony outside his motel room in Memphis. The gunman fired from inside a rooming house not far away and dropped the pump-action rifle on the sidewalk as he fled. The authorities apprehended an escaped convict named James Earl Ray in London several weeks later, following a trans-Atlantic manhunt.

'RFK Must Die'
JUNE 6, 1968

Robert F. Kennedy had just won the California primary, positioning himself as the front-runner for the Democratic presidential nomination and, for many, a personification of hope in a nation rattled by a far-off war and domestic race riots. Sirhan B. Sirhan, a Jordanian so angry over Kennedy's support for Israel that he had scrawled "RFK must die" in a notebook the police discovered later, opened fire as Kennedy headed through a hotel-kitchen passageway moments after his victory speech.

Crackdown in Czechoslovakia
AUGUST 21, 1968

During the "Prague Spring," Czech Communist leader Alexander Dubcek had taken the first steps toward democratic reforms. That was too much for Moscow's leader, Leonid Brezhnev, who first castigated Dubcek, then dispatched Red Army tanks and troops. Washington, preoccupied with its own problems in Vietnam, was not prepared for the invasion. The Soviets stripped Dubcek of his power but they had no one in line to replace him, and left him in office for eight more months.

Convention Battles
AUGUST 29, 1968

Inside the convention hall in Chicago, contentious Democrats nominated Vice President Hubert H. Humphrey and adopted a hard-line platform plank on the Vietnam War. Outside, the Chicago police clubbed antiwar demonstrators, sprayed tear gas and arrested hundreds. Inside, Senator Abraham Ribicoff told delegates there were "Gestapo tactics in the streets." While Chicago Mayor Richard Daley and his loyalists hollered obscenities from the floor, Ribicoff had the last word: "How hard it is to accept the truth."

"All the News That's Fit to Print"

The New York Times.

LATE CITY EDITION
U. S. Weather Bureau Report (Page 66) forecasts: Partly cloudy and cold today, tonight and tomorrow.
Temp. range: 48—20; yesterday: 45—31.

VOL. CX..No. 37,615. | © 1961 by The New York Times Company. Times Square, New York 36, N. Y. | NEW YORK, WEDNESDAY, JANUARY 18, 1961. | 10 cents beyond 50-mile zone from New York City except on Long Island. Higher in air delivery cities. | FIVE CENTS

EISENHOWER'S FAREWELL SEES THREAT TO LIBERTIES IN VAST DEFENSE MACHINE

VIGILANCE URGED

Talk Bids 'Godspeed' to Kennedy—Voices Hopes for Peace

Text of Eisenhower's address is printed on Page 22.

By FELIX BELAIR Jr.
Special to The New York Times.

WASHINGTON, Jan. 17—President Eisenhower cautioned the nation in a farewell address from the White House tonight to be vigilant against dangers to its liberties implicit in a vast military establishment and a permanent armaments industry unparalleled in peacetime.

In his speech, which brought down the curtain on fifty years of public service, the President also warned of a second threat —"the prospect of domination of the nation's scholars by Federal employment, project allocations and the power of money." He said this danger was "ever present and is gravely to be regarded."

The President concluded his televised speech with a prayer for the well-being of "all the peoples of the world."

Sees a 'Long Struggle'

He warned Americans that they faced a long struggle in the "cold war." He also cautioned the nation against being tempted by any "miraculous solution" to world problems.

President Eisenhower also spoke as an old soldier preparing to turn over the burdens of the Presidency to his much younger successor, President-elect John F. Kennedy. The two men will hold their second and final discussion of problems confronting the nation Thursday morning.

Foremost among these problems, the President listed the continuing Communist threat to the West and the need to combat it while striving for universal disarmament. It was "with a definite sense of disappointment" that he contemplated the failure to make greater progress toward a lasting peace.

Wishes Kennedy Well

He said that, with all Americans, "I wish the new President and all who will labor with him Godspeed" in working for solutions.

The President stressed the need to guard against "the acquisition of unwarranted influence, whether sought or unsought, by the military-industrial complex."

This warning against the political potential of the huge military-arms production apparatus by the President came as a surprise to many in the capital. A more sentimental leave taking had been expected from the old soldier.

He noted that the conjunction of an immense military establishment and a large arms industry—both essential to national and free world security—was something new in American experience.

"The total influence—economic, political, even spiritual, is felt in every city, every state house, every office of the Fed-

Continued on Page 22, Column 4

United Press International Telephoto

'A FEW FINAL THOUGHTS': President Eisenhower addresses the nation in farewell speech at the White House.

Prayer by President

Special to The New York Times.

WASHINGTON, Jan. 17—Following is the prayer with which President Eisenhower concluded the farewell address that he broadcast to the nation tonight:

We pray that peoples of all faiths, all races, all nations may have their great human needs satisfied, that those now denied opportunity shall come to enjoy it to the full; that all who yearn for freedom may experience its spiritual blessings; that those who have freedom will understand, also, its heavy responsibilities; that all who are insensitive to the needs of others will learn charity; that the scourges of poverty, disease and ignorance will be made to disappear from the earth, and that, in the goodness of time, all peoples will come to live together in a peace guaranteed by the binding force of mutual respect and love.

U. N.'S CONGO ROLE IS WORRYING U. S.; KENNEDY MAY ACT

Advisers Expected to Urge New Administration to Resolve Crisis Quickly

DAYAL CALLED HOSTILE

Reappraisal to End Trend Away From the West Is Weighed in Washington

By WALLACE CARROLL
Special to The New York Times.

WASHINGTON, Jan. 17—The United States is becoming increasingly uneasy over the trend in the Congo and the performance of the United Nations there.

It seems certain that the Kennedy Administration, which assumes its responsibilities Friday, will be told by its political and military advisers that it must act quickly to redress a bad situation.

There is no inclination here to "go it alone" in the Congo. The permanent officials of the Government are still convinced that the United States and its allies must continue to work through the United Nations to give the Congolese a chance to develop their nation.

Committed to U. N.

President-elect John F. Kennedy and all his principal advisers are committed to support the United Nations system.

What has developed here, however, is a feeling that United Nations operations as they affect the Congo should be subjected to a cold, hard reappraisal.

In the opinion of some high officials, events in the Congo have inverted the adage, "He who pays the fiddler calls the tune." The United States is paying a good part of the United Nations bill in the Congo, they observe, but forces hostile to the West are having more and more influence on what the United Nations does and what it does not do.

Causes of Unrest

These are some of the recent developments that have caused uneasiness in Washington:

¶President Joseph Kasavubu, Col. Joseph D. Mobutu, Chief of Staff of the Congolese National Army, and the army-appointed governing commission of young intellectuals, have been losing ground, both in a political and military sense.

¶Some of the United Nations representatives and military units in the Congo seem from here to have been favoring this trend. In particular, Rajeshwar Dayal of India, the personal representative of Secretary General Dag Hammarskjold, is regarded as hostile to the Kasavubu Administration and to Western influence. Mr. Hammarskjold, it is felt here, has been under such heavy pressure from the Communist and Asian-African powers that he has been unable or unwilling to correct the situation.

¶Forces supporting Patrice Lumumba, the imprisoned former Premier, have been gaining strength and extending their power by successful military operations. These forces have welcomed and enjoyed the support of the Communist powers both within the United Nations and in the Congo.

¶The United Arab Republic, possibly with the aid of the Soviet Union, is now reported to be sending military supplies by air to the Lumumba forces in

Continued on Page 2, Column 4

Harbor Pickets Tie Up Central Trains, But Fail to Block Other Rail Lines Here

Service Cut for 40,000 Commuters—New Talks Scheduled for Today

Texts of carrier and union statements on Page 25.

By A. H. RASKIN

A land offensive by striking marine workers halted all New York Central trains into and out of Grand Central Terminal yesterday.

The shutdown cut off service for 40,000 commuters and forced 2,000 long-distance passengers to use buses between New York and Albany.

Pickets representing 664 strikers on railroad ferryboats and tugs sought to spread their blockade of train movements to commuter operations on other metropolitan lines, but the immediate effect was slight.

Negotiations between the unions and railroad representatives were recessed at 2 A. M. today after seventeen consecutive hours. They were scheduled to resume at 9 A. M.

No progress was reported in the negotiations.

The New Haven, which carries 30,000 riders a day to and from Grand Central, got more

Continued on Page 24, Column 1

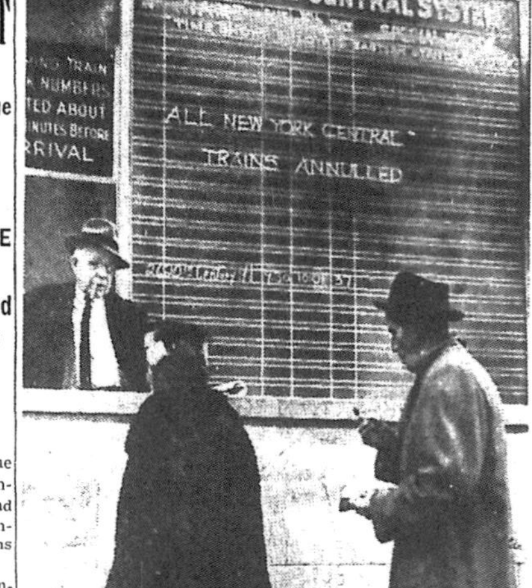

The New York Times

The arrival board at Grand Central Terminal tells the story of the canceled trains on the New York Central.

Regents Ask College Grant Of $200 for Each Student

By WARREN WEAVER Jr.
Special to The New York Times.

ALBANY, Jan. 17—The Board of Regents proposed today that the state give $18,200,000 a year to private colleges and universities to help them expand. The program would consist of a grant of $100 for each student enrolled in a private school for each semester.

It would be paid to colleges that are under religious sponsorship as well as to those that are nonsectarian.

To bypass the constitutional prohibition against giving public funds to private institutions, the plan, in theory, would award the $200 a year to each college student personally as a sort of across-the-board scholarship.

The money would be used to reduce the tuition being paid by the student. It would thus permit the private colleges to raise their tuition fees to increase their income without raising the cost of a college education to New York State residents.

Because the program would be supported by New York taxpayers, it would be limited to college students who were residents of the state.

Legislators Hear Details

The program was outlined by Dr. James E. Allen Jr., the state Education Commissioner, at a luncheon held today by the Regents for the Republican and Democratic legislative leaders. Edgar W. Couper, Vice Chancellor of the Regents, presided.

The leaders questioned Dr. Allen at length about the private college aid and other aspects of the Regents' recommendations for higher education. They expressed considerable interest in the proposal, but they did not go so far as to endorse it.

The program to grant $100 a semester would cost the state $9,200,000 in the 1961-62 fiscal year, opening April 1, because only one semester payment would be involved. Thereafter, the cost would be twice as high.

Dr. Allen also discussed with the legislative leaders the second Regents' program that would provide additional indirect financial assistance to the private colleges.

New Scholarship Plan

This is the recommendation that the number of Regent scholarships awarded each year be doubled to cover 10 per cent, rather than the present 5 per cent, of the number of high school graduates in the state. The board also proposes increasing the maximum grant from $700 to $1,500 and reducing the minimum from $250 to $100.

When this program is in full effect, four years after its start, it will cost the state $27,700,000 more a year. Thus the two forms of assistance would total $46,100,000 a year when fully in force.

It was reported at the meeting that a large majority of the private colleges in the state planned to increase their tuition beginning with the class entering next fall.

If the Regents' program is

Continued on Page 28, Column 2

LAOTIANS DEMAND SOME FRENCH GO

Relax Request for Complete Withdrawal of Advisers Under U. S. Urging

By WILLIAM J. JORDEN
Special to The New York Times.

WASHINGTON, Jan. 17—The Laotian Government of Premier Boun Oum has demanded that some French advisers be withdrawn from the country.

According to diplomatic sources, the Boun Oum regime originally insisted that all French advisers be removed, but modified its position under urging from some of its supporters, notably the United States.

The Government in Vientiane has agreed to accept less than total withdrawal and, instead, to have the French Government reassign the advisers whom the Laotian Government deems objectionable.

It is understood that one of those subjected to the Laotian Government's disapproval was Maj. Gen. Jean d'Arrivère, commander of the French military mission. The general has already left Laos, according to one report.

Anti-French feeling continues strong in the Government of Premier Boun Oum, diplomatic reports disclose. The French, in turn, are said to be irked in the extreme by Premier Boun Oum's position.

The Laotian-French dispute has complicated the already complex situation in Laos and has contributed to the inability

Continued on Page 4, Column 4

KENNEDY ADVISED TO PRESS GROWTH OF U. S. RESOURCES

Task Force Calls for 'New Leadership' for Program Including Atom Power

Excerpts from the resources report are on Page 16.

By TOM WICKER
Special to The New York Times.

WASHINGTON, Jan. 17—A task force on natural resources urged President-elect John F. Kennedy today to provide "vigorous new leadership" for a conservation and development program that would include federally produced nuclear power.

The report of the Kennedy-Johnson Natural Resources Advisory Committee said the group looked forward "to an Administration that will establish landmarks of achievement" in protecting "the rightful heritage of all Americans."

The committee also recommended increased water supplies, full development of major river basins through flood control and land reclamation, active starts on 2,000 watershed projects by 1968, improved waterways, some shoreline parks and a youth corps for conservation and other outdoor work.

Pollution Control Pressed

Mr. Kennedy ended his Florida vacation today and flew to Washington for two days of conferences here and in New York before his inauguration.

One of the earliest acts of the Eighty-seventh Congress, the task force declared, should be the passage of a stream pollution control bill, providing Federal assistance to communities in the construction of sewage treatment facilities.

This apparently referred to an increase in the present $50,000,000 yearly loan program. Last February, President Eisenhower vetoed a bill that would have provided $90,000,000 a year.

The report was based on the recommendations of members of the nation-wide advisory committee. It was prepared under the direction of Representative Frank E. Smith, Democrat of Mississippi.

200 Approve Report

About 200 committee members met here today, approved the report and heard two of the Kennedy Cabinet member-designates pledge their support to its purposes.

Representative Stewart L. Udall of Arizona, who will be Secretary of the Interior, said the new Administration had a "fresh opportunity to initiate new policies for the benefit of all generations to come."

Former Gov. Orville L. Freeman of Minnesota, the Secretary of Agriculture-designate, pledged his "personal attention" to a "sensible, practical, long-term program on use of natural resources." He also promised that interagency rivalries would not be allowed to interfere in administering such a program.

No cost estimates were included in the twelve-page re-

Continued on Page 16, Column 2

SPELLMAN ASSAILS A SCHOOL-AID PLAN

Proposal by Kennedy's Task Force Is Criticized for Not Including Church Pupils

By JOHN WICKLEIN

Cardinal Spellman last night assailed a proposal by President-elect John F. Kennedy's task force on education that Congress enact a $5,840,000,000 program of Federal aid to public schools.

No Roman Catholic schools or schools of other religious denominations were included in the proposal, the Cardinal pointed out.

"It is unthinkable," he declared, "that any American child be denied the Federal funds allotted to other children which are necessary for his mental development because his parents choose for him a God-centered education."

Cardinal Spellman expressed his views in a statement read at a final report meeting of his campaign for a $25,000,000 fund for the construction of educational facilities in the Archdiocese of New York. The pledges now on the books total $36,287,302.

The Cardinal, addressing a rally in Cardinal Hayes High School, the Bronx, said the task force's proposal, presented to the President-elect on Jan. 6, meant for many millions of Americans taxation for which they would receive no return.

"They will be taxed more than ever before for the education of their children," he said,

Continued on Page 16, Column 4

SOME DEDUCTIONS ON STATE TAX END

Conformity With U. S. Rules Cancels Several Claims Previously Allowed

By DOUGLAS DALES
Special to The New York Times.

ALBANY, Jan. 17 — Some New York State residents preparing their state income tax returns are discovering that they are unable to claim deductions for certain Federal taxes that were deductible in former years.

The reason is the enactment last year of a law designed to make state income tax procedures conform closely to Federal practice. Thus Federal levies that cannot be deducted on Federal tax returns cannot now be deducted on state returns.

For most taxpayers the inability to deduct the Federal taxes will cause little financial loss, and for some taxpayers, the changes resulting from conformity will mean net tax savings.

The Federal taxes that formerly could be listed on state returns are the 10 per cent telephone and telegraph tax; the 10 per cent transportation tax, scheduled to drop to 5 per cent on July 1; the 10 per cent tax on safety deposit box rentals; the 20 per cent tax on private club dues above $10 a year, and the 10 per cent tax on amusement admissions.

In cases where these taxes are part of deductible business expenses, they can still be deducted.

Despite the loss of these Federal tax deductions, the State Department of Taxation and Finance estimates that the net effect of conformity will result in a saving of $10,500,000 to resident taxpayers. In addition, Tax Commissioner Joseph H. Murphy estimates that conformity will cut to half the

Continued on Page 20, Column 4

M'NAMARA OFFERS FUND DISCLOSURE

Cabinet Selection Also Tells Senators He Is Willing to Amend $1,100,000 Trust

By JACK RAYMOND
Special to The New York Times.

WASHINGTON, Jan. 17—Robert S. McNamara offered today to amend a controversial $1,100,000 investment trust fund and to make "full disclosure" of his financial affairs.

The 44-year-old Mr. McNamara, who resigned as president of the Ford Motor Company to serve as Secretary of Defense in the Kennedy Administration, said he wanted to avoid "even a hint of conflict of interest."

Mr. McNamara was questioned at length about his finances as he appeared before the Senate Armed Services Committee, which must approve his nomination.

Roswell H. Gilpatric, named to be Deputy Secretary of Defense, and Dr. Elvis J. Stahr Jr., Secretary of the Army designate, had easier going as they testified on their backgrounds.

Committee members indicated privately that Mr. McNamara would be approved. The chairman, Senator Richard B. Russell, Democrat of Georgia, said the committee could not act un-

Continued on Page 16, Column 6

Canterbury Will Resign in May; Archbishop, 73, to Get Peerage

Dr. Fisher's Decision Startles Anglican Clergy—Selection of Successor Due Soon

By SETH S. KING
Special to The New York Times

LONDON, Jan. 17—Dr. Geoffrey Francis Fisher, ninety-ninth Archbishop of Canterbury and Primate of All England, will retire May 31.

The 73-year-old Archbishop read his statement of resignation to the startled leaders of the Anglican Church, assembled here today for the Convocation of Canterbury.

Although there had been hints that he was contemplating retirement, the announcement came as a surprise to most of the 200 clergymen who heard him.

The name of his successor, who will be nominated by Queen Elizabeth II on the recommendation of Prime Minister Macmillan, was not mentioned. It was believed that a new Archbishop would be named within the next two weeks.

A second announcement, from the Prime Minister's office, said that Dr. Fisher, who has been a member of the House of Lords while serving as Archbishop, would be given a life peerage. He would thus continue to hold a seat in the upper house of

Continued on Page 14, Column 4

The New York Times

Dr. Geoffrey F. Fisher, the Archbishop of Canterbury.

Merger Is Set by Hanover Bank And Manufacturers Trust Co.

By ALBERT L. KRAUS

Directors of the Manufacturers Trust Company and the Hanover Bank have approved plans to merge them to form the third largest bank in New York City and the fourth largest in the country.

Manufacturers Trust is one of the city's largest branch system banks. The Hanover is one of the few remaining institutions doing business chiefly with big corporations and smaller banks in other cities. Plans for the long-rumored merger were announced yesterday.

The new institution, to be known as the Manufacturers Hanover Trust Company, would have total resources of more than $6,000,000,000, deposits of nearly $5,500,000,000, and capital funds of $430,000,000. The merger must be approved by the stockholders of the two banks and state and Federal banking authorities.

Charles J. Stewart, president of Manufacturers Trust, would become chairman of the board of the combined institution, and Robert E. McNeill Jr., president of the Hanover, would become president. Gabriel Hauge, chairman of the finance committee of Manufacturers Trust and formerly economic adviser to President Eisenhower, would become vice chairman.

Horace C. Flanigan, chairman of Manufacturers Trust, would become chairman of the executive committee of the combined

Continued on Page 49, Column 1

Columbia Basin Treaty Signed By President and Diefenbaker

By The Associated Press.

WASHINGTON, Jan. 17—President Eisenhower and Canadian Prime Minister John G. Diefenbaker signed today a treaty for joint United States-Canadian development of the Columbia River resources. They hailed it as a milestone in international relations.

The pact is to run for at least sixty years and contemplates billions of dollars of construction.

As he affixed his signature, the President said it was "indeed a great personal gratification" for him "to be able to sign this treaty in the last few days" of his White House tenure.

Mr. Diefenbaker told the President, "The relationship between our two countries is a model for all mankind."

On a personal note, Mr. Diefenbaker told the President: "We wish you good health and long years of service in the cause of peace."

The ceremony was attended by representatives of the two Governments and several Senators.

Senator Mike Mansfield of Montana, the Democratic leader, said he hoped the treaty would receive Senate action in a month or two. Before going into effect, it must be approved by that body. Senator Mansfield expressed confidence that the treaty would be ratified.

Senator George D. Aiken of

Continued on Page 14, Column 4

NEWS INDEX

"All the News That's Fit to Print"

The New York Times.

LATE CITY EDITION

U.S. Weather Bureau Report (Page 81) forecast: Increasing cloudiness today; chance of rain tonight and tomorrow. Temp. range: 54—40; yesterday: 52—43.

VOL. CX..No. 37,699. © 1961 by The New York Times Company. Times Square, New York 36, N. Y. NEW YORK, WEDNESDAY, APRIL 12, 1961. 10 cents beyond 50-mile zone from New York City except on Long Island. Higher in air delivery cities. FIVE CENTS

SOVIET ORBITS MAN AND RECOVERS HIM; SPACE PIONEER REPORTS: 'I FEEL WELL'; SENT MESSAGES WHILE CIRCLING EARTH

HEAD OF RESERVE URGES PRICE CUTS TO RELIEVE SLUMP

Martin Asserts Reductions Would Mean More Jobs and Demand for Goods

By RICHARD E. MOONEY
Special to The New York Times.

WASHINGTON, April 11—The chairman of the Federal Reserve Board made a strong appeal today for price reductions as a means of solving the nation's economic problems.

"Throughout our country, we must not only increase our productivity but also pass some of the gains on to the consumer in the form of lower prices, rather than having all of it go exclusively to labor in higher wages or to management in higher profits," he said.

The chairman, William McC. Martin Jr., said that price cuts could stimulate buying demand that would "provide more jobs for those who are now unemployed, keep the economy moving to higher levels, and [provide] still greater job opportunities in the future."

Some Gains Reported

The Labor Department reported, meanwhile, a modest increase in the factory work week and factory pay for March.

Mr. Martin spoke at the annual meeting of the Association of Reserve City Bankers at Boca Raton, Fla. Copies of his talk were made available here.

It was not the first time that a voice from Washington had been raised in favor of price cuts. It is a point that gets lost, however, in the debates most often heard here, over what the Government should or should not do. In the form presented, it is simply an exhortation. Neither Mr. Martin nor the Kennedy Administration advocates price or wage controls.

Addressing himself to the domestic economy, Mr. Martin said that "at the moment we have pressing need to reduce unemployment and to promote economic growth at the maximum sustainable speed." The way to meet the need, he said, is "a judicious blend" of specific actions, monetary and fiscal policies, and wage-price policies.

Answers Critics of Policy

In such a setting, he said, interest rates need not rise so high nor fall so low as they have in past business cycles.

Mr. Martin used his speech to answer critics who have said that recent Federal Reserve strategy cannot work and has already failed. Seven weeks ago the reserve system abandoned its established policy of buying and selling only the shortest-term securities—Treasury bills—when it sought to impose its influence on credit conditions

Continued on Page 25, Column 5

Realtor Is Indicted In Expense Padding

By EDWARD RANZAL

The president of Pease & Elliman, Inc., a leading real estate concern here, was indicted yesterday on charges of income tax evasion through fraudulent claims for entertainment and travel expenses.

The indictment against the executive, Robert Neaderland, by a Federal grand jury was said to be the first of its kind in the Southern District of New York. It was expected to break ground for future prosecutions for overstatement of business expenses.

Mr. Neaderland, 53 years old, lives at 160 Central Park South. His company is one of the leading developers of apartments on the East Side. He is charged with attempting to evade $27,550 in income taxes in 1954 and 1955, according to

Continued on Page 30, Column 3

Wide College Aid Is Adopted by State

By WARREN WEAVER Jr.
Special to The New York Times.

ALBANY, April 11—A higher-education program that will make $12,300,000 in new financial assistance available to college and university students in New York State this year was approved by Governor Rockefeller today.

He said the program gave assurance that "no young man or woman with the ability and desire for a higher education need be deprived of that opportunity for lack of funds."

The seven higher education measures that were signed included a bill that gave New York City permission to establish a city university to consist of the four municipal colleges and the community colleges in the five boroughs.

One of the bills provides

Continued on Page 48, Column 3

COUNCIL APPROVES OWN CHARTER BILL

Rebuffs Mayor by Spurning State Law Under Which He Named Commission

By CHARLES G. BENNETT

The City Council passed its own bill yesterday calling for the appointment of a commission to draft a new City Charter. The vote was 21 to 3.

Council officers immediately prepared to send the measure directly to Mayor Wagner for his signature or veto. This would be based on a contention by the Council's high command that since the bill merely calls for the appointment of a commission, it does not require Board of Estimate action.

The Council's stand constituted a challenge to the new state law under which Mayor Wagner already has appointed an eleven-member commission to revise the Charter.

Majority Leader Joseph T. Sharkey, who is also Democratic leader of Kings County, repeated his charge that Governor Rockefeller and Mayor Wagner had been "playing together" on Charter revision. Mayor Wagner supported the state bill.

Mr. Sharkey also said he "hoped and expected" that there

Continued on Page 26, Column 3

ISRAEL DEFENDS TRIBUNAL'S RIGHT TO TRY EICHMANN

Ex-Nazi Is More Confident as Jerusalem Hearing Enters Its 2d Day

By HOMER BIGART
Special to The New York Times.

JERUSALEM (Israeli Sector), Wednesday, April 12—The Attorney General of Israel, Gideon Hausner, resumed this morning his defense of the right of his country to try Adolf Eichmann for the murder of millions of Jews.

The defendant, as he entered his bulletproof glass cage on the second day of his trial seemed more confident. For the first time, he looked out at the audience. Then he sat down and engaged in an animated conversation with his German lawyer, Dr. Robert Servatius through a microphone in the glass cage. Eichmann smiled at his lawyer and seemed at ease.

On the first day of the trial, Eichmann, stonily impassive, heard his lawyer challenge the court's right to try the former Nazi leader on charges of delivering millions of Jews to Nazi annihilation camps.

The debate over Israel's right to try Eichmann was expected to continue through today's session. The court will not meet tomorrow, Holocaust Day, a day of mourning in Israel for the victims of Nazi terror.

Indictment Is Read

For seventy minutes Eichmann remained standing while the presiding judge, Justice Moshe Landau of the Israeli Supreme Court, read in Hebrew a fifteen-count indictment charging him with crimes against the Jewish people and crimes against humanity. The indictment was translated into German for Eichmann's benefit.

Rigidly erect, his head tilted back and his thin lips tightly compressed, the one-time chief of the Gestapo's Jewish Affairs Section betrayed no emotion during the opening day of trial.

His thin, hawklike visage with its large, sharply pointed nose was fixed intently on the proceedings. Not once did Eichmann turn to gaze on the throng of newsmen, foreign observers and Israeli citizens in the 750 seats in the Beit Haam (House of the People), the converted

Continued on Page 16, Column 1

Population Center Moves West; Census Puts It at Centralia, Ill.

MILES · Detroit · MICHIGAN · Chicago · Lake Erie · Cleveland · Ft. Wayne · ILLINOIS · INDIANA · OHIO · Columbus · Indianapolis · Springfield · 1930 · 1910 · 1890 · 1920 · Cincinnati · 1880 · 1870 · 1860 · St. Louis · 1960 · 1950 · 1940 · 1900 · Portsmouth · Centralia · Evansville · Louisville · Charleston · Ohio R. · W. VA. · KENTUCKY · MO. · VA.

The New York Times · April 12, 1961

United States center of population, which was near Portsmouth, Ohio, a hundred years ago, has continued moving west and by 1960 was just northwest of Centralia, Ill.

By The Associated Press.

WASHINGTON, April 11—The population center of the United States has moved again.

Secretary of Commerce Luther H. Hodges announced today that the new center, based on the 1960 census, was near Centralia, Ill., fifty-seven miles west of its 1950 location.

In general, the population center is the point through which a straight line can be drawn in any direction dividing the country's population in half. As many people would live on one side of the line as on the other.

Mr. Hodges had another def-

Continued on Page 27, Column 3

Former Nazi Hears Indictment Read as Trial Begins in Jerusalem

Adolf Eichmann, charged with crimes against the Jewish people and against humanity, standing in special booth in Beit Haam courtroom yesterday. Justices at bench are, from left, Benyamin Halevi, Moshe Landau, Yitzhak Raveh.

Associated Press Radiophotos

Eichmann peers intently at tribunal during proceedings

U. S. IS DISTURBED BY DELAY ON LAOS

Soviet Lag on Cease-Fire and Increase in Supplies Regarded as Ominous

By WILLIAM J. JORDEN
Special to The New York Times.

WASHINGTON, April 11—Officials said today the United States Government was disturbed by Moscow's delay in accepting a Western plan for an immediate cease-fire in Laos.

A spokesman for the State Department said that continued delay would be regarded here as "a matter of very serious concern."

Adding to the worries of Administration leaders were intelligence reports of a general increase in the flow of Soviet-bloc military supplies to the Pathet Lao movement in recent days. This was regarded as an ominous sign of Soviet intentions in Laos.

Rusk Voices Hope

High officials continued to be hopeful, however, that Moscow would soon give a favorable answer to the cease-fire plan advanced by the British several weeks ago.

That hope was voiced on Capitol Hill today by Secretary of State Dean Rusk. The Secretary told Senators that he expected a Soviet answer "within a very few days."

The presumption here is that continued fighting in Laos contains the seeds of a possibly enlarged conflict and that the Soviet bloc does not want to

Continued on Page 12, Column 4

Centennial of War Rocked by Dispute

By The Associated Press.

CHARLESTON, S. C., April 11—New Jersey accused the National Civil War Centennial Commission of "pathetic mismanagement" tonight and asked that President Kennedy remove Maj. Gen. Ulysses S. Grant 3d as chairman.

Joseph Dempsey, vice chairman of the Jersey Centennial Commission, made the charge at a news conference after General Grant had turned down the state's request for time to rebut a dinner speaker who had criticized its civil rights practices.

General Grant and Donald Flamm, Jersey chairman, engaged in an unscheduled standing debate at the crowded dinner at the Charleston Naval Base. General Grant, in loud applause, insisted that New

Continued on Page 36, Column 3

BRITISH CONSIDER TRADE UNITY STEP

Kennedy Hopes London Will Enter Common Market

By JAMES RESTON
Special to The New York Times.

WASHINGTON, April 11—President Kennedy now has the impression that the British Government is seriously thinking about joining the European Economic Community, or Common Market.

This impression is based on the fact that during the President's conversations with Prime Minister Macmillan here last week the British leader asked what the United States Government would think if Britain decided to reverse her policy and join the Western European nations now working toward economic and political integration.

Administration to Cooperate

President Kennedy's reply was that the United States would regard this as a major advance toward the unity of the West.

The President did not in any way imply that the United States was thinking of joining the Common Market itself, but he did stress his Government's determination to cooperate fully with its allies in the Organization for Economic Cooperation and Development.

On a recent trip to London it is known that George Ball, United States Under Secretary of State for Economic Affairs, urged upon Viscount Hailsham, the British Lord President of the Council, that Britain give the most serious consideration

Continued on Page 2, Column 3

ADENAUER IN U. S. TO SEE KENNEDY

Arrives for First Talks With President—Stresses Unity

Special to The New York Times.

WASHINGTON, April 11—Chancellor Adenauer of West Germany arrived here tonight for his first meetings with President Kennedy.

He alighted at Andrews Air Force Base from the Lufthansa jet airliner that brought him without stop from Bonn.

In an arrival statement the 85-year-old Chancellor said the German people had already developed "great confidence" in the new President of the United States. He said he was looking forward to establishing personal contact with Mr. Kennedy.

Dr. Adenauer pledged that his country's considerable energy and ability would be devoted to the cause of peace and freedom. He said that his Government realized that its share of responsibility for the future of the world grew "in proportion with our efficiency and capacity."

"Our times are filled with threats and dangers," the Chancellor said, "but I feel sure that the free people of the world will overcome those dangers if they are united and resolute."

The West German leader and his party, including his daughter, Frau Libeth Werhahn, were

Continued on Page 4, Column 5

NEWS INDEX

FRANCE DECLARES ANTI-U.N. 'STRIKE'

De Gaulle Bars Any Role in Armed Ventures—Warns Algerians on Partition

By HENRY GINIGER
Special to The New York Times.

PARIS, April 11—France proclaimed today a virtual strike against the United Nations.

In one of the harshest indictments he has ever made against the organization, President de Gaulle said France "did not wish to participate either by her men or her money in any present or possible enterprise of this organization—or of this disorganization."

The President, in response to a question, confirmed his country's refusal to contribute to the costs of the United Nations force in the Congo. A Foreign Ministry spokesman said that in this context the President's statement referred to present or future military enterprises, although the word "military" did not occur in the text of the news conference.

On another issue, President de Gaulle offered a mixture of incentives for Algerian rebel cooperation with France. He warned anew that a "rupture" might result in the partitioning of Algeria to protect those Algerians who wished to remain under French control.

The President called for reform of the United Nations as well as of the Atlantic Alliance. He made it clear that the future of the alliance would be a major

Continued on Page 3, Column 5

187-MILE HEIGH

Yuri Gagarin, a Major Makes the Flight in 5-Ton Vehicle

Text of the Tass statement is printed on Page 22.

By United Press International.

MOSCOW, Wednesday, Apr. 12—The Soviet Union announce today it had won the race put a man into space. T' official press agency, Tass, a man had orbited the earth in spaceship and had been brough back alive and safe.

A brief announcement the first reported space mai had landed in what was scribed as the "prescribec area" of the Soviet Union afte a historic flight.

A Moscow radio announce broke into a program and sai in emotional tones:

"Russia has successfull launched a man into space. F' name is Yuri Gagarin. He wa launched in a sputnik name Vostok, which means "East."

Reports on Landing

Tass said that, on landing Major Gagarin said: "Please report to the party and Government, and personally to Nikit Sergeyevich Khrushchev, tha the landing was normal, I f well, have no injuries bruises."

He landed at 10:55 A. M. Moscow time [2:55 A. M. New York time].

Earlier, the major reported: "Flight is proceeding normally, I feel well."

After orbiting the earth '' major applied a braking device and the vehicle space landed the Soviet Union, Tass said.

Major Gagarin, 27 years old is an industrial technician, and married. He was reported have received pre-flight trainin similar to that of the astronauts who will man the United States' first space ships.

Soared to 187 Miles

The announcer said the Sputnik reached a minimum altitude of 175 kilometers (109½ miles and a maximum altitude of 302 kilometers (187⅝ miles)

He said the weight of the Sputnik was 10,395 pounds, o slightly over five tons.

The announcement of the launching came at 2 A. M. New York time.

It said everything functioned normally during the flight.

Constant radio contact was maintained between earth and the sputnik, the Moscow radio said.

The announcer said the duration of each revolution around the earth was 89.1 minutes.

The title of the announcement was "The First Human Flight into the Cosmos."

The radio, which was quoting a Tass press agency statement on the launching, said that Maj.

Continued on Page 22, Column 1

White House Confirms Firing; Feat Hailed by U. S. Scientists

By JOHN W. FINNEY
Special to The New York Times.

WASHINGTON, Wednesday, April 12 — Pierre Salinger, White House press secretary, announced early today that "American tracking stations have confirmed the fact that the Soviet Union has launched a satellite today."

"We are keeping in close touch with the situation but have no additional comment at this time," he said.

The Soviet success in sending the first man into space left United States officials in a resigned mood of congratulations.

The United States has no chance of equaling the Soviet feat until perhaps late this year.

The Soviet announcement did not take them by surprise, since there had been advance information from United States tracking stations that a satellite had been launched.

James E. Webb, head of the National Aeronautics and Space Administration, described the feat as "a significant accomplishment" that "demonstrates great technical capacity."

"I hope that they can find it possible to make the benefits of this event available to the rest of the world," he said.

Dr. Hugh L. Dryden, deputy administrator of the space agency, commented, "This is something we have been expecting for some time."

"It is only the beginning of man's continued effort of manned exploration of space," he said, "and I think we should continue as rapidly as we can with our own program."

In appraising the achieve-

Continued on Page 24, Column 1

"All the News That's Fit to Print"

The New York Times.

LATE CITY EDITION
U. S. Weather Bureau Report (Page 74) forecasts:
Mostly fair today.
Fair tonight and tomorrow.
Temp. range: 56—42; yesterday: 55—42.

VOL. CX. No. 37,705. | NEW YORK, TUESDAY, APRIL 18, 1961. | 10 cents beyond 50-mile zone from New York City except on Long Island. Higher in air delivery cities. | FIVE CENTS

ANTI-CASTRO UNITS LAND IN CUBA; REPORT FIGHTING AT BEACHHEAD; RUSK SAYS U. S. WON'T INTERVENE

The New York Times — April 18, 1961

CARIBBEAN STRIFE: Rebel forces attacking Cuba landed in Las Villas Province in the area of Bahia de Cochinos (1, and A on the inset map). Other anti-Castro landings were said to have taken place in area of Santiago de Cuba (2) and in Pinar del Rio (3).

SUPREME COURT UPHOLDS UNIONS AGAINST N. L. R. B.

It Upsets Board's Ruling That Contracts Illegally Force Membership

MAILERS' PACTS BACKED

New York Printers' Local and California Teamsters Win on Agreements

By ANTHONY LEWIS
Special to The New York Times.

WASHINGTON, April 17—A series of decisions by the National Labor Relations Board designed to prevent the compelling of union membership was struck down today by the Supreme Court.

The court disposed of a group of major labor cases that will affect dozens of others pending in the lower courts and before the labor relations board. The court did the following things in its principal rulings:

¶It upheld, 6 to 2, contracts of the International Typographical Union with newspapers that provided that the foreman of the composing room or mail room must be an I. T. U. member and must handle all hiring in his operation.

¶By the same vote, it upheld a provision in I. T. U. contracts that made the I. T. U. "general laws" applicable unless in conflict with Federal or state laws.

¶By the same vote, it held there was nothing illegal in bargaining agreements that provided that casual workers, both union and nonunion, be hired through a union-operated hiring hall.

¶It killed, 7 to 1, an N. L. R. B. ruling making labor and management refund to employes all union dues collected under an agreement found to constitute an illegal closed shop.

Douglas Writes Opinion

Justice William O. Douglas wrote the opinion of the court in all the cases. There was an eight-man court because Justice Felix Frankfurter took no part in the decisions.

Two cases settled long disputes over standard contracts sought by the typographical union. The first of these involved the New York Mailers' Union 6, which is affiliated with the I. T. U., and The New York Daily News and The Wall Street Journal.

The contract specified that mail room foremen must be members of the I. T. U. and must do the hiring. The N. L. R. B. had ruled that the foremen clause was a coercive device to make sure that only union members were hired and that it was thus a violation of the Taft-Hartley Law.

Justice Douglas wrote today that first, the contract said no foreman should be disciplined by the union for carrying out the publisher's instructions, and he concluded that the foreman remained the employer's agent despite his union membership.

Second, Justice Douglas said, the court would "not assume" that the foremen clause would produce discrimination in favor of union members in the absence of actual proof of discrimination.

The N. L. R. B. was thus left free to bring a case to show that

Continued on Page 27, Column 3

U. S. Finds Soviet's Reply On Laos Is Unsatisfactory

Rusk Says Note Is Unclear on Timing and Verification of Cease-Fire—Calls Issue 'Very Critical'

By E. W. KENWORTHY
Special to The New York Times.

WASHINGTON, April 17—Secretary of State Dean Rusk said today that the new Soviet note on Laos did not satisfy the United States on the timing and verification of a cease-fire.

This, Mr. Rusk said at his news conference, is a "very critical matter" in any attempt to bring "the situation to a peaceful and satisfactory conclusion." [Introductory statement, Page 18.]

The Soviet note "clarifying" Moscow's first reply to the British proposals of March 23 was delivered to Sir Frank Roberts, the British Ambassador, yesterday. The British Embassy informed Mr. Rusk of the contents of the reply last night.

The British had proposed a three-step procedure—a call for a cease-fire by Britain and the Soviet Union, the co-chairmen of the 1954 Geneva Conference that brought the Indochinese war to an end; verification of the cease-fire by the three-nation International Control Commission, which observed the carrying out of the Geneva accord in Laos, and a fourteen-nation conference to set up a neutral, independent Laotian Government.

It was the British intention that these steps should take place in quick order. But Britain and the United States had made clear that there could be no conference until a cease-fire was in effect.

In one respect the Soviet note represented an advance over the earlier response, according to informed sources here. Previously Moscow had indicated that the cease-fire and the conference must take place simultaneously—or very nearly so.

In yesterday's note, these

Continued on Page 2, Column 3

GIZENGA OFFICERS ACCEPT MOBUTU AS ARMY'S CHIEF

Kasavubu Agrees to Reform Troops—Signs Accord on Congo-U.N. Cooperation

By HENRY TANNER
Special to The New York Times.

LEOPOLDVILLE, the Congo, April 17—Congolese Army headquarters announced tonight that field commanders operating under the control of the Leftist regime of Antoine Gizenga had recognized the authority of Maj. Gen. Joseph D. Mobutu as military commander in chief.

General Mobutu is the commander of the Central Government's forces.

The announcement said officers of the Gizenga regime had recognized General Mobutu during a conference at Bundoki, on the border of Eastern Province. The province is controlled by Mr. Gizenga.

The announcement also said a cease-fire had been ordered all along the border of Eastern and Equator Provinces.

Here in Leopoldville President Joseph Kasavubu and representatives of Secretary General Dag Hammarskjold signed an agreement on reorganization of the Congolese Army and the withdrawal of some foreign advisers.

Resolution 'Accepted'

The Congolese President and his Government "accepted" the Security Council resolution of Feb. 21 with the "understanding" that the United Nations, in implementing the resolution, respected the sovereignty of the Congo Republic.

The announcement on the military agreement did not say whether Gen. Victor Lundula, who has been commanding Mr. Gizenga's forces, took part in the conference.

Despite rumors of rivalry between him and Mr. Gizenga, General Lundula has consistently stressed his loyalty to his civilian superiors in Stanleyville, capital of Eastern Province.

General Mobutu left Leopoldville a week ago for the border area where the military conference took place. Talks between the two sides had continued intermittently for several weeks with and without his participation.

Kasavubu Plan Backed

In accepting the Security Council resolution the Leopoldville Government "recognized" the necessity for reorganizing the Congolese National Army. It reaffirmed President Kasavubu's earlier proposal that the reorganization take place with United Nations assistance, but under his personal authority as chief of state.

The agreement called for the United Nations to give assistance to the President so that "all foreign civil officials, military and paramilitary mercenaries and political advisers who have not been engaged under his authority" will be re-

Continued on Page 4, Column 3

PREMIER DEFIANT

Says His Troops Battle Heroically to Repel Attacking Force

The texts of Castro appeals are printed on Page 14.

By TAD SZULC
Special to The New York Times.

MIAMI, Tuesday, April 18—Rebel troops opposed to Premier Fidel Castro landed before dawn yesterday on the swampy southern coast of Cuba in Las Villas Province.

The attack, which was supported from the air, was announced by the rebels and confirmed by the Cuban Government.

After fourteen hours of silence on the progress of the assault, the Government radio in Havana broadcast early today a terse communiqué signed by Premier Castro announcing only that "our armed forces are continuing to fight the enemy heroically."

The announcement, made shortly before 1 A. M., said that within the next few hours details of "our successes" would be given.

The communiqué came amid a wave of rebel assertions of victories, new landings and internal uprisings. The rebel spokesmen were acclaiming important progress in new landings in Oriente and Pinar del Rio Provinces, but none of these reports could be confirmed.

Government Reports Battle

The Government communiqué said a battle had been fought in the southeastern part of Las Villas Province, where yesterday morning's landings occurred.

Although the communiqué was signed by Premier Castro, the Cuban leader has not spoken to his nation since the attack began. An earlier communique, issued yesterday, reported the rebel landings.

In a communiqué issued last night, the Revolutionary Council, the top command of the rebel forces, said merely that military supplies and equipment were landed successfully on the marshy beachhead. The communique added that "some armed resistance" by supporters of Premier Castro had been overcome.

Premier Castro was reported to have escaped injury in an early-morning air raid yesterday near the beachhead.

The Revolutionary Council's announcement spoke of action in Matanzas Province, indicating that the rebels might have

Continued on Page 14, Column 1

HIGH COURT VOIDS CAFE'S NEGRO BAN

Holds Private Restaurant on State Land in Delaware Cannot Refuse Service

Special to The New York Times.

WASHINGTON, April 17—The Supreme Court held today that a privately operated restaurant situated in a publicly owned parking garage in Wilmington, Del., could not refuse to serve Negroes.

Six justices agreed on that result. The three others thought the case should have been sent back to the Delaware Supreme Court for clarification of its views on state law.

The decision is a significant one because of the light it throws on the established doctrine that only "official action" is covered by the Fourteenth Amendment. The Constitution does not prohibit racial discrimination by private persons or enterprises.

The court concluded that the Government of Delaware was sufficiently involved in this private enterprise, the restaurant, to bring it under the Constitution. In the view of observers here, the court broke at least some new ground in reaching that conclusion.

Justice Tom C. Clark wrote the opinion of the court. He was joined by Chief Justice Earl Warren and Justices Hugo L. Black, William O. Douglas and William J. Brennan Jr.

A separate concurring opinion, resting on quite different grounds, was filed by Justice Potter Stewart. Dissents suggesting that the court should

Continued on Page 26, Column 1

HAUSNER ATTACKS EICHMANN'S PLEA

Israeli Prosecutor Details His Charges After Ex-Nazi Says He Is Not Guilty

Text of decision and Hausner excerpts are on Page 23.

By HOMER BIGART
Special to The New York Times.

JERUSALEM (Israeli Sector), April 17—Attorney General Gideon Hausner began an attack today on Adolf Eichmann's plea of innocence at his trial for responsibility in the killing of millions of Jews.

Earlier in the day Eichmann lost a challenge to the court's jurisdiction and entered his not-guilty plea when the trial was resumed after the week-end recess. Eichmann's plea for a hearing on his kidnapping from Argentina was rejected by the court.

"In the sense of the indictment I am not guilty," Eichmann had told the three Israeli judges.

He made his statement of innocence in a precise but toneless voice in reply to charges that he had planned the annihilation of 6,000,000 European Jews for the Nazis during World War II.

From the qualified nature of his plea, it was clear that Eichmann's defense would be based on the contention that he was a mere cog in the machinery of genocide and that he was bound by higher orders when he delivered the Jews to death camps.

Standing rigidly erect and

Continued on Page 23, Column 7

ROA CHARGES U.S. ARMED INVADERS

Tells U.N. That C.I.A. Aided Attacks—'Aggression' Is Denied by Stevenson

Excerpts from Stevenson and Roa statements, Page 16.

By THOMAS J. HAMILTON
Special to The New York Times.

UNITED NATIONS, N. Y., April 17—Dr. Raul Roa, Foreign Minister of Cuba, charged today that his country had been invaded this morning "by a force of mercenaries, organized, financed and armed by the Government of the United States."

Dr. Roa told the General Assembly's Political Committee that the attack had been launched from points in Florida and Guatemala under the direction of the Central Intelligence Agency, which he called the "Gestapo." The Gestapo was the Nazi security police force.

He continued to use terms made familiar to nazism by calling Dr. José Miró Cardona, head of the anti-Castro Cuban Revolutionary Council, the "gauleiter." Gauleiters were regional party leaders under the Nazis.

Florida Launching Denied

Adlai E. Stevenson, chief United States delegate, said in reply that "the United States has committed no aggression against Cuba and no offensive has been launched from Florida or from any other part of the United States."

[In Guatemala, the Government denied that it had participated in any attack on Cuba.]

Just before the debate ended late this evening Dr. Roa charged that two jet planes from a United States carrier had escorted a Cuban rebel plane to safety this afternoon. He also alleged that forces from the United States Naval Base at Guantanamo had entered Oriente Province, where

Continued on Page 17, Column 1

Rusk Declares Sympathy Of Nation for Castro Foes

By JAMES RESTON
Special to The New York Times.

WASHINGTON, April 17—Secretary of State Dean Rusk expressed today the sympathy of the American people for those who struck against Castroism in Cuba, but emphasized "there is not and will not be any intervention there by United States forces."

The Administration did not deny that it was giving material support to the raiding parties, but this aid was undoubtedly on a much smaller

Transcript of Rusk's news conference is on Page 18.

scale than originally planned here and the landings in Cuba were much smaller than excited reports of "invasion" suggested.

No more than 200 to 300 men were involved in the week-end landings on the vast coastline of Cuba, according to reliable information reaching here.

In fact, the landings of the last forty-eight hours were not designed to get a lot of fighting men on the ground, but to provide supplies for the anti-Castro underground already operating there as a result of at least six other landings that have taken place over the last few months.

Refugees Assume Control

In the last ten days, the Cuban refugees have assumed control of the operations against Premier Fidel Castro. Accordingly, official Washington could not be sure of the fate of all the small parties that went ashore.

Secretary Rusk was extremely cautious in his remarks on the situation at his news conference this morning. What happens in Cuba, he said, is for the Cuban people to decide. He added, however, that the Administration was "not indifferent" to the intrusion of the "Communist conspiracy" into this hemisphere and promised to "work together with other governments of this hemisphere to meet efforts by this conspiracy to extend its penetration." [Opening statement, Page 18.]

On this point, considerable attention was being paid here

Continued on Page 18, Column 1

MOSCOW BLAMES U. S. FOR ATTACK

Izvestia Asserts 'American Hirelings' Invade Cuba—Khrushchev Confers

By SEYMOUR TOPPING
Special to The New York Times.

MOSCOW, April 17—The Soviet Union charged tonight that the United States was responsible for the landing in Cuba by what it described as "American hirelings."

Izvestia, the Soviet Government newspaper, contended that plans for landing anti-Castro forces in Cuba had been worked out and inspired by "American imperialists."

"On all continents voices now are crying out determinedly for an end to the armed aggression against Cuba and for the defense of the freedom and independence of the Cuban people," Izvestia said.

At his vacation retreat in Sochi on the Black Sea, Premier Khrushchev conferred on the Cuban crisis with Foreign Minister Andrei A. Gromyko. A formal Government statement is expected tomorrow.

Atmosphere Is Tense

An atmosphere of tension gripped the Soviet capital after the announcement at 4 P. M. by the Moscow radio that "an armed intervention against Cuba had begun."

It was felt by most Western experts that the Soviet reaction would be confined to strong diplomatic representations, complaints in the United Nations and a propaganda onslaught against the United States.

Some observers recalled that in a speech here July 10, Mr. Khrushchev had declared: "Figuratively speaking, if need be, Soviet artillerymen can support the Cuban people with their rocket fire, should the aggressive forces in the Pentagon dare to start intervention against Cuba."

The Soviet leader also had noted that the United States was no longer out of range of Soviet missiles.

Western experts said that Mr. Khrushchev's statement seemed to have more applicability to an invasion of Cuba by United States forces than to an attack of the type being under-

Continued on Page 17, Column 2

CHANTING CUBANS BACK CASTRO HERE

1,000 in Midtown March Dispersed by Police

Nearly 1,000 chanting, sign-bearing pro-Castro Cubans demonstrated last night outside the United Nations and the United States Mission to the United Nations and in the Times Square area.

Heavy police details had kept the crowds behind barriers most of the day and no violence erupted until a smaller group of pro-Castro Cubans blocked pedestrian traffic in Times Square. The police made two arrests and two policemen were injured during a brief scuffle with the demonstrators.

Many of the demonstrators carried Cuban flags and pictures of Dr. Castro as they marched from the United Nations Plaza along Forty-second Street to the corner of Eighth Avenue and Forty-third Street.

An emergency police signal brought ten radio cars and ten mounted policemen to that area. The crowd then broke up into four factions and departed in different directions.

A few minutes later, at 8 P. M., a smaller group of demonstrators formed on the sidewalk on Broadway between

Continued on Page 14, Column 5

Eisenhowers Are Welcomed Home to Pennsylvania

United Press International Telephoto

General and Mrs. Eisenhower in Harrisburg with Gov. David L. Lawrence of Pennsylvania

By The Associated Press.

HARRISBURG, Pa., April 17—Thousands of persons welcomed former President Dwight D. Eisenhower and Mrs. Eisenhower home to Pennsylvania today. The gathering was the state's official welcome for General Eisenhower, who left the White House Jan. 20. The former President, looking tanned and rested after a six-week vacation in California, was obviously touched. Gov. David L. Lawrence, a Democrat, headed the state and city officials on the platform. The Eisenhowers have a farm home in Gettysburg, thirty-five miles southwest of this capital city. It is the only home they have ever owned. They left for home by car after the ceremonies.

Jersey Votes Today In Primary Election

By GEORGE CABLE WRIGHT
Special to The New York Times.

TRENTON, April 17 — New Jersey residents will nominate major party candidates for Governor tomorrow, along with candidates for ten of twenty-one State Senate seats and for all sixty seats in the Assembly.

Also at stake will be the nominations for a number of county and local posts.

The polls will open at 7 A. M. and close at 8 P. M.

Interest will center on the balloting for the Republican nomination for Governor. A bitter three-way contest for the nomination came to a close tonight with television and radio appeals by the participants.

They are James P. Mitchell, the former Secretary of Labor, and State Senators Walter H. Jones of Bergen County and

Continued on Page 38, Column 1

Walker Is Relieved of Command While Army Checks Birch Ties

Special to The New York Times.

WASHINGTON, April 17—The Army said today that Maj. Gen. Edwin A. Walker had been relieved of his command in Germany while an investigation was made into reports that he had been indoctrinating his troops with the views of the John Birch Society.

The announcement said that Secretary of the Army Elvis J. Stahr Jr. had ordered General Walker transferred immediately from command of the front-line Twenty-fourth Division "pending the outcome of an official investigation."

The investigation will involve "certain published statements and actions of General Walker," the Army said.

General Walker was ordered transferred to the headquarters of the United States Army in Europe at Heidelberg, Germany, the Army said.

The announcement did not mention the Birch Society. However, officials acknowledged that the transfer and investigation had been prompted by allegations that the 51-year-old general had been urging the views of the Right-Wing group upon his troops for the last six months.

The Overseas Weekly, a privately owned newspaper distributed among American troops in Europe, reported last week that General Walker had instituted a special troop-indoctrination program using materials and publications of the society.

General Walker accused the newspaper yesterday of being "immoral, unscrupulous, corrupt and destructive." The newspaper stood by its original report and said that his charges

Continued on Page 24, Column 6

NEWS INDEX

"All the News That's Fit to Print"

The New York Times.

LATE CITY EDITION

U. S. Weather Bureau Report (Page 44) forecasts: Fair and cool today and tonight. Fair and milder tomorrow. Temp. range: 78—60; yesterday: 79—64. Temp.-Hum. Index: low 70's; yesterday: 75.

VOL. CX—No. 37,823. NEW YORK, MONDAY, AUGUST 14, 1961. FIVE CENTS

10 cents beyond 50-mile zone from New York City except on Long Island. Higher in air delivery cities.

SOVIET TROOPS ENCIRCLE BERLIN TO BACK UP SEALING OF BORDER; U.S. DRAFTING VIGOROUS PROTEST

SPECIAL SESSION SET FOR AUG. 21 ON SCHOOL ISSUE

Governor Expected to Seek to Limit Mayor's Power in Appointing Board

FISCAL CHANGES LIKELY

System May Get Right to Raise Funds—Residence Rules in Question

By WARREN WEAVER Jr.
Special to The New York Times.

ALBANY, Aug. 13—Governor Rockefeller today called a special session of the Legislature for Monday, Aug. 21, to provide fresh leadership and guidance for the New York City school system.

The Governor issued a one-sentence call for the Senate and Assembly to meet in the Capitol at noon a week from tomorrow to deal with "legislation pertaining to the structure, management, supervision and control" of the city's schools.

He provided no further information on the action he would urge upon the lawmakers. It was learned, however, that the administration proposals would include bills to do the following:

¶Strip the Mayor's office of its unrestricted power to appoint members of the Board of Education.

¶Abolish the requirement that members of the board live in certain boroughs and the practice of their having to get "clearance" from their county political leaders as a condition of eligibility.

¶Provide a reconstituted Board of Education with power to raise and spend funds without political interference.

¶Authorize the Board of Regents to supersede the present Board of Education with an interim board. The interim board would set education policy until a permanent unit, selected under a new system, could take office.

The Governor's chief adviser in his effort to reorganize the Board of Education is the state Education Commissioner, Dr. James E. Allen Jr. Their plan calls for legislation to set up an advisory committee or council of a dozen or more outstanding New York City educators, lawyers and laymen.

Membership on this council

Continued on Page 16, Column 1

8 CEZANNE WORKS STOLEN IN FRANCE

Art Valued at $2,000,000 Taken From Exhibition

By W. GRANGER BLAIR
Special to The New York Times.

PARIS, Aug. 13—Eight paintings by Paul Cézanne were stolen early today. The theft occurred at an exhibition of the postimpressionist's works at Aix-en-Provence, in southern France.

The value of the stolen canvases was unofficially estimated to be about $2,000,000.

The burglary thus equaled in value, if not in size, the theft twenty-eight days ago of fifty-seven modern art works from the Annonciade Museum in Saint-Tropez, on the French Riviera.

All the Cézannes taken had been lent to the Aix-en-Provence exposition by European and United States museums and private collectors.

'Card Players' Taken

The stolen works were:

"The Card Players," a version showing two figures, from the Louvre in Paris; a portrait of Marie Cézanne, sister of the painter, from the St. Louis Municipal Museum; a still life of a leg of mutton, from the Zurich, Switzerland, Museum, and a still life of a teapot, from the Cardiff Museum in Britain.

Also, a landscape near Aix, showing Caesar's tower, from a private collection; "Water Reflections," from a collector in Milan, Italy; "Seated Peasant," from Sidney Simon of New York, and "The Skulls [Les Crânes]," from Mme. Marianne Feilchenfeldt of Zurich.

The paintings were stolen, probably around 4 A. M., from the Vendôme Pavilion, a 287-year-old mansion built for the Duc de Mercoeur, who was Car-

Continued on Page 2, Column 3

Mayor Still Weighs Dismissal of Board

By GENE CURRIVAN

Deputy Mayor Paul R. Screvane said yesterday Mayor Wagner was committed to remove the members of the Board of Education if this was recommended by his newly appointed board of inquiry.

Mr. Screvane, who appeared on the "Searchlight" program on WNBC-TV, was asked if he thought the public had lost so much confidence in the board that it should either resign or be removed by the Mayor.

"If this is the decision of the three-man group we now have, and this decision can be made very quickly, the Mayor is already committed to do precisely that," he said.

Concerning a report that the

Continued on Page 16, Column 4

2 MAYORAL RIVALS ASK MORE JUDGES

Lefkowitz and Levitt Tell a Bar Group Congestion in Courts Must Be Eased

By LAYHMOND ROBINSON

Two aspirants for Mayor joined yesterday in calling for an increase in the number of judges in the city and state to ease court congestion.

In letters to a bar group that had solicited their views, State Controller Arthur Levitt, a Democratic contender, and Attorney General Louis J. Lefkowitz, Republican candidate, both urged more judgeships.

Neither, however, estimated how many more judgeships there should be. Their letters went to the New York State Association of Plaintiffs' Trial Lawyers.

Two Albany Attempts Fail

Bills to set up new judgeships in New York City were scuttled in the last two sessions of the Legislature when Republicans and Democrats could not agree on the number of posts or the persons who would fill them.

In his letter to Joseph Kelner, president of the 2,100-member bar association, Mr. Levitt called the court congestion problem a "serious menace" to justice.

Mr. Lefkowitz said the city and state deserved "a judicial system which provides an expeditious, economical and efficient administration of justice," and that "an increase in the number of judges is an important facet of this over-all program."

In releasing the Levitt and Lefkowitz statements, Mr. Kelner did not make clear whether he had also asked for Mayor Wagner's views on the subject.

A spokesman for the Mayor, who is running as an independ-

Continued on Page 17, Column 4

AID DEBATE DUE IN HOUSE TODAY; STIFF FIGHT SEEN

Mansfield Expects Senate to Approve Measure by Middle of the Week

By LLOYD GARRISON
Special to The New York Times.

WASHINGTON, Aug. 13—Senator Mike Mansfield, the majority leader, predicted today that the foreign-aid bill would pass the Senate by mid-week without any major changes.

But the bill, with its controversial request for $8,800,000,000 in long-term borrowing authority, is likely to meet much stiffer resistance in the House. The House is scheduled to take up the measure tomorrow and to continue debate on it for the rest of the week.

Senator Mansfield predicted that "the usual amendments" aimed at cutting the bill would be offered this week. But he contended that "we'll just about hold the amount of the bill as it now stands."

The Senate Foreign Relations Committee has cut $436,000,000 from the President's request for $4,762,500,000, leaving a total of $4,326,500,000.

Further Cut Doubted

It was this figure that Senator Mansfield predicted would pass without any significant change.

The heart of the bill is an Administration request for authority to borrow $8,800,000,000 from the Treasury over the next five years to finance long-term overseas loans.

Last Friday, by a seventeen-vote margin, the Senate defeated an amendment offered by Senator Harry F. Byrd, Democrat of Virginia. The amendment would have required the President to go to the House and Senate appropriations committees each year for the money.

The measure is likely to contain an amendment representing a compromise proposal made last week by Senator J. W. Fulbright in an effort to win liberal Republican votes against the Byrd amendment.

Review Plan Expected

The compromise by the chairman of the Senate Foreign Relations Committee would give Congress the right to review for a thirty-day period all loans over $10,000,000. But it would not give Congress the right to veto such loans.

The Administration wants the reviewing period shortened to fifteen days. It would also like to limit the review to loans above $15,000,000, to lessen the paper work.

However, the Arkansas Democrat's compromise is expected to go through unaltered.

Over the week-end the Administration sought to counter

Continued on Page 5, Column 1

ALLIES IN ACCORD

Britain and France Due to Join in Challenge on German Action

Text of Rusk's statement on Berlin appears on Page 7.

By TAD SZULC
Special to The New York Times.

WASHINGTON, Aug. 13—Secretary of State Dean Rusk charged today that the East German closing of the West Berlin border was a double violation of agreements between the Soviet Union and the Western powers.

In a statement issued with President Kennedy's approval, Mr. Rusk declared "these violations of existing agreements will be the subject of vigorous protest through appropriate channels."

Mr. Rusk said that the travel ban was in contravention of accords on free circulation within the city and of a decision by a four-power meeting of foreign ministers in 1949 assuring access to Berlin from what are now the former occupation zones.

Allied Access Unaffected

He noted, however, that the Communist measures did not "thus far" interfere with the access by the Western Allies to Berlin.

The threat that this may occur later has been raised by the Soviet Union's announcement that it will sign a peace treaty with East Germany and turn over to East Germany the control of routes to the disputed city.

[In London and Paris officials viewed the East German action with extreme concern. Britain denounced the new restrictions as a violation of Berlin's four-power status.]

According to a State Department spokesman, a protest is expected to be made tomorrow in similar notes to be handed by the United States, British and French military commanders in Berlin to their Soviet counterpart.

There was also the possibility, diplomatic sources indicated, that the protest delivered by the military commanders might promptly be followed with a direct protest to the Soviet Union by the Western Allies.

With the closing of the bor-

Continued on Page 7, Column 1

Associated Press Radiophoto

NO EXIT: An East German couple walks away from barbed-wire barrier on border between East and West Berlin. East German troops blocked their entry to West Berlin.

ADENAUER IS SURE ALLIES WILL REACT

Tells Germans Reds' Berlin Decree Will Be Countered—Economic Step Hinted

By GERD WILCKE
Special to The New York Times.

BONN, Germany, Aug. 13—Chancellor Adenauer assured Germans on both sides of the Iron Curtain tonight that Bonn "with its Allies will take the necessary measures" to counter the Communists' closing of the border between East and West Berlin.

In a statement issued after consultation with some of his top advisers, Dr. Adenauer said:

"It is the law of the hour to meet the challenge from the East firmly but calmly and to do nothing that can worsen the situation."

Although Dr Adenauer did not say what counter-measures the West was contemplating, it was generally felt here that economic sacntions might be high on the list.

Dr. Adenauer suggested at election rallies last week that the Communist bloc could be hurt economically if Western trade was cut off. Premier Khrushchev, he said, would use different language if the partners of the North Atlantic

Continued on Page 6, Column 8

Closing of Border Is Seen As First of Soviet Moves

By SEYMOUR TOPPING
Special to The New York Times.

MOSCOW, Aug. 13—The closing of the border between East and West Berlin was regarded by informed Western observers here today as the first in a series of acts the Soviet Union will take in respect to Berlin.

These observers also viewed the Berlin action as signifying that Premier Khrushchev had decided irrevocably to conclude a separate peace treaty with East Germany.

Mr. Khrushchev has been under pressure from East Germany for years to curb the westward flow of refugees by sealing the Berlin border. For reasons of broader policy, the Soviet Premier withheld his consent.

Mr. Khrushchev apparently felt that any one-sided abrogation of the four-power accord on free movement within Berlin would prejudice the chances of the West's joining in a peace treaty that would recognize the status quo in Eastern Europe.

Action Was Expected

It has been regarded as inevitable, however, that the border would be closed if a heavy flow of refugees continued from East to West Germany through Berlin.

The draining away of East German manpower through the West Berlin refugee centers was dislocating the economy of the Communist state.

According to well-informed sources, three factors counted in Mr. Khrushchev's decision to restrict the transit of Germans across the border at this time:

¶Mr. Khrushchev came to the conclusion that the West would not join in any peace treaty that would recognize the division of Germany and that he must sign a separate treaty with the East Germans.

¶There was concern that the flight of the refugees would reach dangerous and unmanageable proportions before the

Continued on Page 7, Column 4

MOOD OF BERLIN: CONTROLLED FURY

Sunday Motorists Flocking to Checkpoints Jarred by Sight of Guns

By HARRY GILROY
Special to The New York Times.

BERLIN, Aug. 13—At times today East Berlin looked like a new tourist attraction. Then it was a war camp. Next it was the picture of an ominous mob with a flicker of revolt in the air.

West Berlin was alternately a family strolling in its Sunday best, a woman crying.

It depended on where you moved and what you stumbled upon. The 3,300,000 people of this metropolis were put under sudden violent strain when the East German regime sealed the East-West Berlin border.

Churchgoers answered the call of church bells in the morning in what was described as the usual Sunday attendance. Some references were made from the pulpits to the "serious events." There was a large attendance at vesper services.

Communist Units Eyed

In the cool dawn only a dozen Berliners gathered on each side of the Brandenburg Gate and at other crossing points between East and West Berlin to look at the spectacle of Communist policemen, soldiers and "factory fighting groups" deploying as if to stand off an approaching army.

By noon, thousands of West Berlin motorists were jamming the approaches to the gateways with their cars and everyone seemed to be out for a look.

Hundreds of these cars drove through the East Berlin checkpoints, with the occupants receiving snappy salutes from the East German guards, and went on to make the main streets of East Berlin more crowded and lively than they are on ordinary days.

These motorists were in for a shock. In the Marx-Engels Platz stood twenty-seven big military trucks, most of them filled with troops holding submachine guns.

Continued on Page 7, Column 5

TEAR GAS IS USED

Reds' Police Disperse Crowds—Workers Kept From Jobs

Soviet bloc communiqué, East German decree, Page 6.

By SYDNEY GRUSON
Special to The New York Times.

BERLIN, Monday, Aug. 14—Two battle-ready Soviet Army divisions were reported to have ringed Berlin yesterday in support of East Germany's sudden and dramatic closing of the border between East and West Berlin.

The Soviet divisions were said to have armor and artillery with them. Other Soviet Army divisions among the estimated total of twenty in East Germany were reported on the move throughout the restive country

The new Communist measures shut off West Berlin to East Berliners and East Germans. They did not affect the movement from West Berlin into the Communist-controlled Eastern sector of the city or the vital communications linking West Berlin to West Germany.

Barrier Effective

According to preliminary reports to West Berlin authorities, none of the 53,000 East Berliners with jobs in West Berlin had crossed the border by 9 A. M. today. Also, it was reported, no refugees had reached West Berlin under the cover of darkness.

The East German action brought angry exchanges yesterday between East Berliners and the Communist People's Police near some of the thirteen border crossing points left open.

Smoke and tear-gas bombs and water hoses were used to disperse one crowd of several hundred youths who had taunted the police and armed Communist factory brigades trying to explain the necessity for the new measures.

Rope Barrier at Gate

At one border point, the East German police also hurled tear gas to break up a crowd of West Berliners facing them across the road. The crowd melted into side streets until the gas had cleared, but then most of them came back. The police then left them alone.

As the night wore on, the Berliners drifted to their homes. Along toward dawn, fewer than 100 young people stood behind the rope barricade put up about fifty yards from the Brandenburg Gate. Approximately 200 West Berlin riot policemen were on guard in parked trucks.

Today, there were no reports of early morning incidents from either side of the border, the West Berlin police reported, and both halves of the divided city began to come to life under a gray cloud-filled sky with no indication that trouble was in the offing.

Under an order of the East

Continued on Page 6, Column 1

'61 Ball May (or May Not) Account for Homers

Conclusion Reached Through Analysis Is Inconclusive

Engineers' report on baseballs used in majors, Page 19.

By HOWARD M. TUCKNER

Baseball fans, who are swiveling their heads like spectators at a tennis match as home-run balls fly by, are asking:

"Is the 1961 ball the same ball that Babe Ruth hit?"

Scientific tests show that maybe it is, and maybe it isn't.

With both Mickey Mantle and Roger Maris threatening Ruth's 1927 record of sixty home runs—and even 150-pound weaklings casually smashing the ball into the bleachers—the players, the fans and particularly the loyalists who do not want to see the Sultan of Swat dethroned are looking suspiciously at that little ball.

And after what Maris and Mantle did yesterday—Mantle hit his forty-fifth homer, Maris his forty-fourth and forty-fifth—these suspicions are bound to intensify. Both New York Yankee sluggers are comfortably ahead of Ruth's record pace.

By common consent of the romanticists of the "Golden Era" of baseball, the 1961 ball is "livelier" than the ones Ruth belted thirty-four years ago. But for the realists, those fans waiting eagerly for the Mantles and the Marises to get past that magic mark of sixty and who insist, like broken records, that "records are made to be broken," the ball is really no better; the players are better.

The New York Times decided to subject some baseballs—a total of seven, including a vintage ball of 1927, a 1936 ball and one from the current batch being launched at Yankee Stadium—to scientific analysis.

The tests, made by technicians who had no rooting interest in the outcome, were undertaken by Foster D. Snell, Inc., consulting chemists and engineers, at 29 West Fifteenth Street.

After subjecting two of the balls to surgical dissection, and all of them to battering by an explosive-driven Remington Arms Ram, to deformation measurements with a vernier caliper, to study by a rubber technologist and to similar probings, the technologists do not find anything in any of the balls to show clearly that a home run has been easier to hit in any one period of baseball than in any other period.

The two technicians who conducted the experiments, Robert W. Batey, the company's director of special evaluations, and Stephen E. Taub, the firm's acting director of engineering, reached this conclusion:

"The 1961 ball is slightly larger, slightly lighter and slightly livelier than one 1927 ball."

(The 1961 ball studied by the experts was donated by the New York Yankees and the 1927 ball was a treasure piece that Babe Ruth smacked for a homer at the Stadium.)

The technicians, adding a quick postscript to their "conclusion," went on to say that

Continued on Page 19, Column 1

The New York Times

Stephen E. Taub, an engineer, uses an explosive-driven ram in making baseball comparison tests in Central Park.

Baseball Hit by Ruth Not Unlike Those of '36 or Today

U. S. Is Preparing Disarmament Plan

John J. McCloy, President Kennedy's chief adviser on disarmament, disclosed yesterday that the United States was working on a "far-reaching" disarmament plan.

Mr. McCloy said the plan would be ready for presentation some time this fall and was being discussed with this country's allies. He asserted that it would be premature to reveal any of its details now.

Mr. McCloy was interviewed on the National Broadcasting Company's television program "Meet the Press."

Mr. McCloy, who recently talked privately with Premier Khrushchev at the Soviet leader's villa near Sochi on the Black Sea, also made the following observations:

¶His impression was that Mr. Khrushchev knew very well

Continued on Page 7, Column 7

Emergency Aid Plan Given Latin Parley

By EDWARD C. BURKS
Special to The New York Times.

PUNTA DEL ESTE, Uruguay, Aug. 13 — The United States today pledged prompt emergency aid to Latin-American nations and then reported that all significant issues of the Inter-American Economic and Social Conference had been settled.

Preliminary calculations showed that about $150,000,000 could be quickly available in existing foreign-aid funds for projects described as of an emergency nature.

But United States officials here said that considerably more could be earmarked for emergency projects out of the more than $1,000,000,000 that President Kennedy has promised in Latin-American aid under his Alliance for Progress programs

Continued on Page 3, Column 3

NEWS INDEX

News Summary and Index, Page 27

"All the News That's Fit to Print"

The New York Times.

LATE CITY EDITION
U. S. Weather Bureau Report (Page 90) forecasts: Increasing cloudiness today. Snow, rain tonight. Rain tomorrow. Temp. range: 38—26; yesterday: 37—30.

VOL. CXI. No. 38,014. © 1962 by The New York Times Company. Times Square, New York 36, N. Y. NEW YORK, WEDNESDAY, FEBRUARY 21, 1962. 10 cents beyond 50-mile zone from New York City except on Long Island. Higher in air delivery cities. FIVE CENTS

GLENN ORBITS EARTH 3 TIMES SAFELY; PICKED UP IN CAPSULE BY DESTROYER; PRESIDENT WILL GREET HIM IN FLORIDA

CARLINO CLEARED IN SHELTER CASE BY ETHICS PANEL

Lane Scored in Unanimous Report, Which He Calls 'Cynical and Callous'

Text of concluding sections of report is on Page 50.

By WARREN WEAVER Jr.
Special to The New York Times.

ALBANY, Feb. 20—The Assembly Committee on Ethics and Guidance exonerated Speaker Joseph F. Carlino today of charges of conflict of interest made by Assemblyman Mark Lane.

In a unanimous report submitted to the Legislature, the bipartisan committee said:

¶Mr. Carlino did not "betray the public trust" by serving as a director of a company manufacturing home fall-out shelters while helping to pass school-shelter legislation last November.

¶He did not draft or support the shelter legislation "in any improper manner" for the benefit of the company, Lancer Industries, Inc.

¶The Speaker was not influenced in his official actions in behalf of the bill by the fact that he was a member of the board of directors of Lancer.

¶He did not receive any special benefit from the passage of the legislation.

Charges Unsubstantiated

"The committee concludes with respect to each and every accusation contained in the charges filed," the report said, "that Assemblyman Lane and those who testified in their support failed to submit credible evidence to substantiate them."

In submitting the report, the Ethics Committee requested that the full 150-member lower house vote "with respect to the conclusions reached herein" in the light of the fact that "the charges were directed against its [the Assembly's] highest ranking official."

Assemblyman Donald A. Campbell, Republican of Amsterdam, who is chairman of the committee, said he would move in the Assembly tomorrow for acceptance of the report. Mr. Carlino is expected to be absent during the debate and vote.

Assemblyman Lane, a Democrat of Manhattan, had charged that the Speaker was guilty of

Continued on Page 50, Column 1

ROCKEFELLER BARS KOREA WAR BONUS

Voices Opposition in Face of Legislators' Backing

By LAYHMOND ROBINSON
Special to The New York Times.

ALBANY, Feb. 20—Governor Rockefeller expressed strong opposition tonight to a state bonus for veterans of the Korean war.

Mr. Rockefeller told the New York State Department of the American Legion that he could not "as a responsible leader of government" support the demand for a bonus. The veterans' group had been campaigning for a $100,000,000 bonus for the 482,000 Korean war veterans or their next-of-kin in the state.

The Governor said his stand was backed "unanimously" by the "Republican leadership of the state." This was a reference to the leaders of the Republican-controlled Legislature.

He said that demands for funds for education, mental health, narcotics control and other state services were too great to permit a diversion of money for a veterans' bonus.

Mr. Rockefeller thus took a position in direct opposition to that of most of the Republican and Democratic members of the Legislature, who have been pushing for the bonus. The issue

Continued on Page 51, Column 1

N.A.S.A. via Associated Press Wirephoto

READY: Lieut. Col. John H. Glenn Jr. walks to the van to take him to the launching site at Cape Canaveral, Fla.

N.A.S.A. via United Press International Telephoto

LIFT-OFF: The Atlas rocket booster bearing the Project Mercury spacecraft roars aloft with 360,000-pound thrust.

N.A.S.A. via Associated Press Wirephoto

RECOVERY: Crewmen of destroyer Noa secure capsule carrying astronaut before lifting it out of the Atlantic.

Jersey Bus Strike Settled; Service Is Due Tomorrow

By PETER KIHSS

An agreement to end the New Jersey bus strike was reached last night. The agreement, subject to ratification by the striking employes, was announced by Gov. Richard J. Hughes. The pact will be submitted to the union members at their garages starting at 7 A. M. today.

Union and management men expressed hope that buses could begin operating tomorrow at 4:30 A. M.

The strike against Public Service Coordinated Transport started at 12:01 A. M. Monday and halted 2,511 buses providing 1,000,000 rides a day. The company's 200 routes serve all of New Jersey's twenty-one counties except Warren and Hunterdon and go into New York City and Philadelphia. The Newark subway system was also shut.

Carlin Gets Credit

Governor Hughes credited Mayor Leo P. Carlin of Newark with having "sparkplugged" the successful negotiations. Mayor Carlin flew back from a Miami Beach vacation yesterday and arranged the talks with both sides and with Daniel F Fitzpatrick, a Federal mediator, and the Governor and himself. The meeting started in Newark at 8:30 P. M., and the agreement was announced at 11:28 P. M.

Earlier, David L. Yunich, president of Bamberger's New Jersey, had asserted that the strike was having a "devastating * * * almost catastrophic" effect on retail business in Newark and elsewhere in the state. A Camden department store reported sales had fallen nearly 50 per cent on Monday, although not that far yesterday.

Despite the drop in shopping, most commuters managed to get to work by alternate means and with a minimum of confusion.

The agreement reached last night provides for a wage increase of 10 cents an hour retroactive to Feb. 1 and extending to next Feb. 1; 4 cents more an hour from then until Aug. 1, 1963, and another 4 cents an hour from then until

Continued on Page 39, Column 3

ROSENTHAL WINS QUEENS ELECTION

But Democrat-Liberal Has Margin of Only 193 Votes —Machines Guarded

By CLAYTON KNOWLES

Benjamin S. Rosenthal, a Democrat-Liberal backed by President Kennedy, squeaked through to victory last night in a special Congressional election in Queens' Sixth District.

By the slim margin of 193 votes, Mr. Rosenthal, a lanky 38-year-old Elmhurst lawyer, edged past Thomas F. Galvin of Flushing, the Republican candidate, to win a three-way race. Emil Levin of Flushing, a Democrat running as an independent, finished far behind.

The unofficial final tally, delayed as the early vote was hastily rechecked for errors, was: Rosenthal, 16,032; Galvin, 15,839, and Levin, 4,216.

Republicans immediately challenged the result and, while Mr. Galvin did not immediately ask for a recount, he sent a telegram demanding that the voting machines be impounded. All voting machines, normally just

Continued on Page 48, Column 3

McNamara Reports Gains by Vietnamese

By JACK RAYMOND
Special to The New York Times.

WASHINGTON, Feb. 20—Secretary of Defense Robert S. McNamara returned to the capital today and reported improvement in the South Vietnamese effort against Communist insurgents.

He had presided at a meeting of United States military and civilian officials yesterday at the headquarters in Hawaii of Admiral Harry S. Felt, commander of United States forces in the Pacific. The meeting was the third in a series of monthly talks on the hostilities in South Vietnam.

A spokesman for Mr. McNamara said that the forces of South Vietnam, supported by the United States, "are hitting

Continued on Page 8, Column 5

NEWS INDEX

KENNEDY PRAISES 'WONDERFUL JOB'

Tells Glenn Nation Is 'Really Proud of You'—Welcome at White House Planned

By TOM WICKER
Special to The New York Times.

WASHINGTON, Feb. 20 — President Kennedy phoned Lieut. Col. John H. Glenn Jr. today immediately after the astronaut's successful orbital flight and arranged to meet him at Cape Canaveral Friday morning.

The President also set in motion plans for bringing Colonel Glenn to Washington on Monday or Tuesday, for receptions at the White House and the Capitol and a parade down Pennsylvania Avenue

A television set in his office and an open telephone line to Cape Canaveral had kept Mr. Kennedy informed of Colonel Glenn's progress all through the day.

The astronaut's three orbits around the earth, Mr. Kennedy said in a statement, have embarked the United States on a "new ocean"—that of space.

"I believe the United States must sail on it and be in a position second to none," the President said within minutes of Colonel Glenn's safe emergence from his Mercury capsule.

Colonel Glenn, he said, is the "kind of American of whom we are most proud." Mr. Kennedy also praised "all those who participated" in making the astronaut's flight successful.

Then, at 4:10 P. M., Mr. Ken-

Continued on Page 23, Column 7

Leaders of Algeria Back Peace Terms

By THOMAS F. BRADY
Special to The New York Times.

TUNIS, Feb. 20—The Algerian nationalist Provisional Government met today and gave full approval to peace accords negotiated with the French by four members of the rebel regime.

One Algerian said afterward: "All twelve members of the Government are in unanimous agreement." This was a reference to five ministers who are prisoners in France, the four negotiators and three ministers who remained in Tunis during the secret talks last week on the French-Swiss border.

The negotiators were Belkacem Krim, M'Hammed Yazid, Saad Dahlab and Lakhdar Ben Tobbal. They met here today

Continued on Page 11, Column 1

The President's Statement

Special to The New York Times.

WASHINGTON, Feb. 20—Following is the text of President Kennedy's statement on Colonel Glenn's flight:

I know that I express the great happiness and thanksgiving of all of us that Colonel Glenn has completed his trip, and I know that this is particularly felt by Mrs. Glenn and his two children.

A few days ago Colonel Glenn came to the White House and visited me, and he is—as are the other astronauts—the kind of American of whom we are most proud.

Some years ago, as a Marine pilot, he raced the sun across this country—and lost. And today he won.

I also want to say a word for all those who participated with Colonel Glenn in Canaveral. They faced many disappointments and delays—the burdens upon them were great —but they kept their heads and they made a judgment, and I think their judgment has been vindicated.

We have a long way to go in this space race. We started late. But this is the new ocean, and I believe the United States must sail on it and be in a position second to none.

Some months ago I said that I hoped every American would serve his country. Today Colonel Glenn served his, and we all express our thanks to him.

ADENAUER WANTS PARLEY ON BERLIN

Suggests Foreign Ministers of Big Four Meet 'Soon'

By SYDNEY GRUSON
Special to The New York Times.

BONN, Germany, Feb. 20—Chancellor Adenauer suggested today that a Big Four foreign ministers' conference on Berlin should be convened "soon." He was speaking to the Parliamentary group of the Christian Democratic Union.

He said that it might be "expedient" to "take a pause" in the Berlin talks now going on between Andrei A. Gromyko, the Soviet Foreign Minister, and Llewellyn E. Thompson Jr., the United States Ambassador to Moscow.

Ambassador Thompson should not continue "negotiating" endlessly, Dr. Adenauer added. There have been four meetings in the last seven weeks between Mr. Gromyko and Mr. Thompson without any advance toward a Berlin settlement.

[A warning by Izvestia, the Soviet Government newspaper, that Moscow was ready to push through a separate peace treaty with East Germany if the United States did not alter its position in the talks raised the possibility of a renewal of the Soviet deadline on a peace pact.]

Dr. Adenauer's advocacy of a new conference of the United States, British, French and Soviet foreign ministers reflected his unhappiness with the course of the Gromyko-Thompson talks.

He is known to believe that Mr. Thompson has made what

Continued on Page 2, Column 2

URBAN PLAN VOTE PUT OFF IN SENATE

Administration Rebuffed on Forcing Issue to Floor

By RUSSELL BAKER
Special to The New York Times.

WASHINGTON, Feb. 20 — President Kennedy affronted the Senate's dignity today and got a political rebuff for it.

In a surprising repudiation of the Administration's voting form sheets, the elders turned on the White House and rejected a leadership move to get a quick floor test of the President's urban affairs proposal. The vote was 58 to 42.

Thus, the White House lost its chance to get a favorable Senate vote on the plan before the House could vote to kill it. The Democrats also lost their chance to get the Senate's Republicans clearly on record for or against the plan to create a Cabinet-level Department of Urban Affairs and Housing.

Today's test came on the dusty parliamentary question whether the Senate should take the plan away from the Government Operations Committee and bring it to an immediate floor vote. This is known as "discharging" the committee. It is an extraordinary procedure that is rarely used because it is repugnant to Senate traditions.

Today it became the instrument of the President's defeat.

The move to discharge the Government Operations Committee was undertaken with misgivings yesterday by Mike Mansfield of Montana, Senate Democratic leader. The reason was a sudden threat by the

Continued on Page 16, Column 4

COL. GLENN FLOWN TO ISLE FOR CHECK

He Feels Tired but Elated —Goes to Grand Turk for Report and Examination

By JOHN W. FINNEY
Special to The New York Times.

GRAND TURK ISLAND, Feb. 20—An elated but tired John H. Glenn Jr. returned to earth tonight and reported that he "couldn't feel better."

The 40-year-old astronaut also reported that he had felt no sickness or discomfort during his five-hour, three-orbit flight around the earth, even during the extended period of weightlessness.

Colonel Glenn landed at this small British possession at 9:11 P. M. in a Navy S-2-F submarine patrol plane. He was clad in light blue coveralls. He had co-piloted the plane from the carrier Randolph, where he spent several hours after being retrieved from the Atlantic ocean.

Around his ears were the marks of the earphones that he had worn while piloting a plane that traveled at about one-hundredth the speed of his Friendship 7 space capsule. And on his face was an excited enthusiastic smile.

Asked how he felt, the red-headed marine replied: "Fine, wonderful, I couldn't feel better."

And he was also hungry. His first comment on stepping into the small hospital arranged for him was: "First I want something to eat—I am hungry." A steak dinner was promptly or-

Continued on Page 23, Column 2

Moscow, Unmoved, Gives News of Orbit

By THEODORE SHABAD
Special to The New York Times.

MOSCOW, Feb. 20 — The Russians voiced congratulations tonight on hearing of Lieut. Col. John H. Glenn Jr.'s orbital space flight.

But they showed no enthusiasm on the successful launching and landing of the spacecraft Friendship 7.

These reactions were reported from Moscow University by United States exchange students who had been listening with Russians to radio reports of Colonel Glenn's progress.

"They congratulated us in friendly fashion but were oddly reserved," an American said.

Soviet radio and television were unusually prompt in reporting the flight. The first bul-

Continued on Page 22, Column 5

81,000-MILE TRIP

Flight Aides Feared for the Capsule as It Began Its Re-Entry

Transcript of conversations with Glenn, Pages 25 and 26.

By RICHARD WITKIN
Special to The New York Times.

CAPE CANAVERAL, Fla., Feb. 20—John H. Glenn Jr. orbited three times around the earth today and landed safely to become the first American to make such a flight.

The 40-year-old Marine Corps lieutenant colonel traveled about 81,000 miles in 4 hours 56 minutes before splashing into the Atlantic at 2:43 P. M. Eastern Standard Time.

He had been launched from here at 9:47 A. M.

The astronaut's safe return was no less a relief than a thrill to the Project Mercury team, because there had been real concern that the Friendship 7 capsule might disintegrate as it rammed back into the atmosphere.

There had also been a serious question whether Colonel Glenn could complete three orbits as planned. But despite persistent control problems, he managed to complete the entire flight plan.

Lands in Bahamas Area

The astronaut's landing place was near Grand Turk Island in the Bahamas, about 700 miles southeast of here.

Still in his capsule, he was plucked from the water at 3:01 P. M. with a boom and block and tackle by the destroyer Noa. The capsule was deposited on deck at 3:04.

Colonel Glenn's first words as he stepped out onto the Noa's deck were: "It was hot in there."

He quickly obtained a glass of iced tea.

He was in fine condition except for two skinned knuckles hurt in the process of blowing out the side hatch of the capsule.

The colonel was transferred by helicopter to the carrier Randolph, whose recovery helicopters had raced the Noa for the honor of making the pick-up. After a meal and extensive "de-briefing" aboard the carrier, he was flown to Grand Turk by submarine patrol plane for two days of rest and interviews on technical, medical and other aspects of his flight.

The Noa, nearest ship to the

Continued on Page 20, Column 1

NEW YORK PAUSES TO 'WATCH' GLENN

Millions Rivet Attention on Astronaut in Flight

By NAN ROBERTSON

The thoughts of millions of New Yorkers were riveted for hours yesterday on one man alone in space.

Minute by minute, they followed the orbital flight of Lieut. Col. John H. Glenn Jr. three times around the earth, waiting in agonizing suspense for his safe return. The life of New York almost stood still during the dramatic countdown.

From then on until Colonel Glenn scrambled "hale and hearty" out of his capsule on the destroyer Noa, people carried on absent-mindedly and in spurts. Millions of working hours were lost during the day, but no one could have begrudged this. Employers and the employed alike were drawn irresistibly to radio and television sets.

The most spectacular display of interest occurred in Grand Central Terminal, where throngs of up to 9,000 persons massed before a huge television screen. The police described it as the largest static crowd in the station's history. The terminal manager said those who

Continued on Page 22, Column 6

"All the News That's Fit to Print"

The New York Times.

LATE CITY EDITION

U. S. Weather Bureau Report (Page 42) forecasts: Mostly fair, warm and humid today, tonight and tomorrow.
Temp. range: 86—69; yesterday: 85—65.
Temp.-Hum. Index: 78; yesterday: 78.

VOL. CXI . . No. 38,180. | NEW YORK, MONDAY, AUGUST 6, 1962. | 10 cents beyond 50-mile zone from New York City except on Long Island. Higher in air delivery cities. | FIVE CENTS

Marilyn Monroe Dead, Pills Near

Star's Body Is Found in Bedroom of Her Home on Coast

Police Say She Left No Notes—Official Verdict Delayed

Special to The New York Times

HOLLYWOOD, Calif., Aug. 5—Marilyn Monroe, one of the most famous stars in Hollywood's history, was found dead early today in the bedroom of her home in the Brentwood section of Los Angeles. She was 36 years old.

Beside the bed was an empty bottle that had contained sleeping pills. Fourteen other bottles of medicines and tablets were on the night stand.

The impact of Miss Monroe's death was international. Her fame was greater than her contributions as an actress.

As a woman she was considered a sex symbol. Her marriages to and divorces from Joe DiMaggio, the former Yankee baseball star, and Arthur Miller, the Pulitzer Prize playwright, were accepted by millions as the prerogatives of this contemporary Venus.

The events leading to her death were in tragic contrast to the comic talent and zest for life that had helped to make "Seven Year Itch" and "Some Like It Hot" smash hits all over the world.

Associated Press

Marilyn Monroe

Miss Monroe's physician had prescribed sleeping pills for her for three days. Ordinarily the bottle would have contained forty to fifty pills.

The actress had also been under the care of a psychoanalyst for a year, and had called him to her home last night. He had suggested she take a drive and relax. She remained home, however.

After an autopsy the Los Angeles coroner reported that Miss Monroe's "was not a natural death." He attributed it to a drug. He added that a toxicological study, to be completed within forty-eight hours, should yield more detailed information. He refused, until then, to list the death as a suicide.

Pending a more positive verdict by Dr. Theodore J. Curphey, the coroner, the Los Angeles police refused to call the death a suicide. They said they had no idea how many pills the actress might have taken, or whether any overdose might have been accidental. Miss Monroe left no notes, according to the police.

In addition to a physical autopsy, Los Angeles has a "psychological" autopsy. Two experts will look into the psychological history of Miss Monroe.

However, the non-physical

Continued on Page 13, Column 6

COMMON MARKET AND BRITISH VOICE HOPES IN IMPASSE

Both Sides Say Gains Were Made on Role for London Before Session Ended

OCTOBER MEETING SET

Failure to Settle Question of Commonwealth Exports Is Blow to Macmillan

By EDWIN L. DALE Jr.
Special to The New York Times.

BRUSSELS, Belgium, Aug. 5—Representatives of Britain and the European Economic Community expressed disappointment and some bitterness but no discouragement today over their failure to reach full agreement on the basis for British membership in the Community.

They stressed that substantial progress had been made on major issues.

The protracted negotiations, the present session of which lasted four days, will resume early in October.

After nearly twenty-two hours of continuous effort, the negotiators gave up this morning on the key matter still impeding agreement: Britain's effort to assure markets for the agricultural imports she receives from Canada, Australia and New Zealand.

New Tariff to Be Imposed

At the end, only a few points were still unsettled in a Common Market plan designed to give some assurance to the three Commonwealth countries. Their exports, now in large part duty-free in the British market, will be subject to a new common tariff and a variable levy system for farm products if Britain joins the six-nation Community.

The plan includes world commodity agreements, a pledge of a "reasonable" farm price policy aimed at preventing overproduction and a detailed arrangement to maintain preferential treatment for all British Commonwealth countries during a transition period up to 1970.

[The inconclusiveness of the negotiations was viewed in Britain as a setback for Prime Minister Macmillan. It is believed he will now find it more difficult to hold doubtful Conservatives in line and to get an unqualified reaction from the Commonwealth Prime Ministers when they meet next month.]

Key to the Failure

The key to the failure to conclude the matter appears to have been the last-minute introduction by France of a highly complex financial issue. While hundreds of millions of dollars are potentially involved, the issue has no connection with the Commonwealth. The French made agreement on the point a condition for an over-all settlement.

The result of the work of the last four days is that the British will have the "major part" of the terms of their entry to present to the Commonwealth Prime Ministers when they meet in London Sept. 10, but not a full outline, as had been wished.

The British Government must deal with the political as well as the economic consequences

Continued on Page 4, Column 5

N.A.A.C.P. to Ask Courts To End Union Racial Bars

By JOHN D. POMFRET
Special to The New York Times.

WASHINGTON, Aug. 5—The National Association for the Advancement of Colored People is planning a major legal assault on discrimination against Negroes by labor unions. The new effort is to begin in early fall. The aim will be to create a body of judge-made law equal to that now found in the field of public education.

The N. A. A. C. P. was instrumental in creating these laws following the 1954 Supreme Court decision outlawing segregation in public schools.

Much as the association attacked the doctrine of "separate but equal" in the school segregation case, its lawyers are preparing to make the doctrine of "voluntary association" a main target in the union field.

This doctrine holds that private voluntary groups have the right to decide whom they will admit. It has been advanced by some unions as a defense against legal efforts to compel them to take in Negroes.

Role of Unions Cited

The association will argue that the doctrine does not apply to unions because they are not voluntary associations. Their certification by the National Labor Relations Board as exclusive bargaining agents, their role in collective bargaining and their control in some situations of access to jobs distinguish them from social or fraternal groups, the association will contend.

Herbert Hill, the association's labor secretary, said that the N. A. A. C. P. was going into court as a "last resort." In the seven years since it was established, he declared, the merged labor federation has been "either unwilling or unable to eliminate discrimination" by its affiliated unions.

Mr. Hill asserted that the American Federation of Labor and Congress of Industrial Organizations had given the elimination of racial discrimination by affiliated unions "a low level of priority."

"They have no understanding of the problem," Mr. Hill said. "What is progress for them is not progress for us."

A federation spokesman said that the federation "has made progress in the fight against discrimination."

"We will not be satisfied until discrimination is completely eliminated and we will continue to make progress in a trade union way undeterred by outsiders," he asserted.

Animosity between the association and the federation dates from early 1959 when the association concluded that the federation was not going to move vigorously enough to end discrimination against Negroes.

Since then, the association has assisted in building Negro caucuses inside unions to exert internal pressure and has filed complaints with Federal and state anti-discrimination agencies against unions. The legal effort now in preparation is an extension of these efforts into a new field.

The first case, according to Mr. Hill, will begin as a petition to the National Labor Relations Board to decertify a union on

Continued on Page 22, Column 3

CITY ACTS TO PAY ITS BILLS FASTER

Economies Are Expected—Tenney Says Poor Liaison Is a Cause of Delays

By PAUL CROWELL

Steps are being taken to have the city pay its bills more quickly, city Administrator Charles H. Tenney reported yesterday.

Mr. Tenney said that delays were a result, in part, of inadequate liaison between the office of the Controller and the management offices of other city agencies.

His report was based on a study requested in January by Controller Abraham D. Beame. Mr. Beame said at the time that he was convinced many individuals and companies were reluctant to bid for city business only because there were long delays in the payment of bills.

Changes Already Made

More bidders, Mr. Beame said, would mean more competition and, probably, lower prices and savings for the city.

The Tenney study, in which Mr. Beame's office took part, found that the procedures of the Controller's office in processing venders', suppliers' and contractors' bills were "basically sound."

Mr. Tenney reported that bookkeeping and record-keeping changes had already been made to shorten and simplify the handling of bills in the office of the Controller.

Mr. Tenney, who sent copies of his report to Mayor Wagner and Mr. Beame, said he would

Continued on Page 10, Column 3

KENNEDY PRESSES FOR SAFER DRUGS

Asks Senate to Stiffen Bill to Improve Quality and Combat Health Hazard

By ALVIN SHUSTER
Special to The New York Times

HYANNIS PORT, Mass., Aug. 5—President Kennedy asked the Senate today to strengthen its pending new drug law to insure "safer and better" drugs for the American consumer.

The President proposed a series of "essential" amendments to the Senate bill. One would enable the Government to move faster to remove from the prescription market any new drug suspected of being a hazard to public health.

Safety Goal Stressed

The proposals were substantially the same as those requested in a special message the President sent to Congress earlier this year. They were renewed today in a letter to Senator James O. Eastland, Democrat of Mississippi, who is chairman of the Senate Judiciary Committee.

Last month the committee approved a bill embodying many of the earlier proposals. But, as the President told his news conference last week, it did "not go far enough."

Accordingly, he asked Senator Eastland to amend the bill to make sure the American people were protected "against

Continued on Page 28, Column 1

PRESIDENT NAMES DEAN AT COLUMBIA TO POST ON A. E. C.

John G. Palfrey Is Second Lawyer Picked for Agency in Resolution of Dispute

Special to The New York Times.

HYANNIS PORT, Mass., Aug. 5—President Kennedy announced today his intention to appoint John G. Palfrey, dean of Columbia College, New York, as a member of the Atomic Energy Commission.

He also announced his selection, reported yesterday, of James T. Ramey, executive director of the Congressional Joint Committee on Atomic Energy, to fill another vacancy on the A. E. C. Mr. Palfrey will succeed Loren K. Olson. Mr. Ramey will succeed John S. Graham.

Mr. Palfrey and Mr. Ramey are lawyers.

Mr. Palfrey, who has done research work on the political and legal aspects of atomic energy, served three years on the staff of the office of the general counsel of the A. E. C.

Dispute Over Posts

Since the resignations of Mr. Olson and Mr. Graham July 1, the Administration and some influential members of the Joint Committee on Atomic Energy have been arguing behind the scenes over candidates for the two $22,000-a-year posts.

Some Executive Branch officials, particularly in the Atomic Energy Commission itself, had rejected candidates, including Mr. Ramey, who had been put forward by the Democrats on the Congressional committee. The Democrats then refused to accept Administration candidates.

The resolution of the dispute was regarded as a compromise. The committee Democrats got Mr. Ramey, one of "their boys." The A. E. C. got Mr. Palfrey, who had been in the office of the general counsel of the commission from 1947 to 1950.

May Serve Short Terms

Besides settling the differences between the two parties, the Administration also had to find two men who would be willing to serve as short a term as one year.

Mr. Palfrey's term officially runs to July 30, 1967, and Mr. Ramey's to June 30, 1964. But it is understood that the Administration is planning to ask Congress next year to replace the five-man commission with a single administrator.

The selection of Mr. Palfrey and Mr. Ramey presumably will satisfy fears expressed by some members of the Joint Committee that the commission was falling into the hands of scientists.

The present three members of

Continued on Page 2, Column 4

The New York Times | Aug. 6, 1962

BLAST IN THE ARCTIC: The Soviet Union resumed tests of nuclear weapons in the air over Novaya Zemlya (cross).

RUSSIANS RESUME A-TESTING IN AIR; BLAST 2D BIGGEST

Explosion at High Altitude Over Arctic Island Is Put in 40-Megaton Range

U. S. DEPLORES ACTION

But Voices Hope Soviet Will Still Work for a Treaty—Stresses Pending Offer

By TAD SZULC
Special to The New York Times

WASHINGTON, Aug. 5—The Soviet Union resumed its nuclear tests in the atmosphere early today with a powerful high-altitude blast believed to have been in the forty-megaton range.

The blast, over Novaya Zemlya, in the Arctic, appeared to have been the second most potent nuclear explosion ever achieved. The record is held by the Soviet Union, which detonated last Oct. 30 a nuclear device with an explosive force estimated at the equivalent of fifty-eight megatons of TNT. A megaton is 1,000,000 tons.

The United States Government called the resumption a "somber episode," but expressed the hope that Moscow would nonetheless cooperate in working for an effective treaty prohibiting all tests of nuclear weapons.

This morning's test, at 5:08 A. M., Eastern daylight time, was first reported by Swedish and Japanese scientists. It was later confirmed, without details, by the Atomic Energy Commission here. News of the test was withheld from the Soviet people.

Issue Before Geneva Parley

The start of the Soviet test series, forecast by Moscow two weeks ago, came on the eve of the expected presentation before the seventeen-nation disarmament conference in Geneva of new and simplified United States proposals for a test ban treaty.

Moscow broke a three-year-old moratorium on nuclear testing last fall. The United States followed with an extensive series of tests underground and in the atmosphere.

In a statement made public this morning, the State Department commented that, "despite its resumption of atmospheric nuclear testing, we hope the Soviet Union will match our efforts to negotiate an effective nuclear test ban treaty."

It said that "the Soviet Union's initiation of yet another series of atmospheric tests — the second such series in less than a year—can only be regarded as a somber episode."

The statement stressed that "the series was started even as

Continued on Page 3, Column 5

Ben Bella Ally Is Named Chief of Political Bureau

By HENRY TANNER
Special to The New York Times.

ALGIERS, Aug. 5—Mohammed Khider, Mohammed Ben Bella's closest ally, was named today as Secretary General of the powerful Political Bureau. The position is the key post on the seven-man organ of the Algerian National Liberation Front.

Mr. Khider, envoy of Mr. Ben Bella in the negotiations last week that ended a month-long crisis in the nationalist leadership, was also given charge of financial affairs and information.

Hadj Ben Alla, another close collaborator of Mr. Ben Bella, was given control of military affairs.

Mr. Ben Bella himself was put in charge of "coordination of interior affairs" with the Transitional Executive. This, too, is regarded as a key position.

Executive Has Little Power

The Transitional Executive theoretically has responsibility for the country's administration under the cease-fire agreement signed in March with France. But it has no real power of its own and is taking instructions from nationalist leaders.

Mr. Ben Bella apparently will be the man through whom the Transitional Executive will have to work in the future. Some observers said he would act as Algeria's Interior Minister until the Constituent Assembly election set for Sept. 2.

Mohammed Boudiaf, one of Mr. Ben Bella's most determined opponents, was given charge of "guidance and external affairs." He is one of the principal ideologists of the nationalist movement.

The Political Bureau is the policy-making body of the National Liberation Front, the

Continued on Page 8, Column 6

SOVIET TEST STIRS REGRET AT GENEVA

Negotiators for Ban Hope New Series Will be Last —Dean and Zorin Meet

Special to The New York Times.

GENEVA, Aug. 5 — Western and neutralist delegates at the seventeen-nation disarmament conference here expressed regrets today that the Soviet Union had renewed nuclear tests. The test renewal had long been accepted here as inevitable.

Arthur H. Dean of the United States commented that the new round of testing begun by the Soviet Union was "particularly regrettable when we are trying our best to work out a test ban treaty."

"It makes our work all the more complicated," the United States negotiator said.

Arthur S. Lall of India said India was "against tests by anyone, anywhere, any time."

Renewed Effort Urged

"Although both sides are now testing," the Indian delegate said, "this should not be allowed to interfere with the efforts to get a test ban treaty. On the contrary, efforts must be redoubled because of the greater urgency of the problem."

Mr. Dean held an "inconclusive" discussion today on the test ban issue with Valerian A. Zorin, a Deputy Foreign Minister, who is Moscow's delegate at the talks.

Mr. Dean was understood to have emphasized that Moscow must agree to on-site inspections if Washington makes concessions on the controls to guarantee the observance of the projected treaty to end testing.

No arrangements were made during their ninety-minute private talk for a formal discussion of the test ban problem in full conference here.

Meeting Inconclusive

Mr. Dean and Mr. Zorin, who are co-chairmen of the conference, also failed to set a meeting of the three-power subcommittee in which the United States, Britain and the Soviet Union conduct negotiations for a treaty to outlaw atomic tests.

They met at the Soviet delegation's headquarters. No Soviet comment was immediately available. United States sources described the session as "inconclusive."

The hope among the neutralists in particular is that once the United States and the Soviet Union have completed their current tests they will consider their defense requirements satisfied and will be better prepared to compromise on a test

Continued on Page 3, Column 2

Jamaica Now Independent After Long British Rule

Associated Press Radiophoto

Prime Minister Sir Alexander Bustamante with Princess Margaret at National Stadium

By R. HART PHILLIPS
Special to The New York Times.

KINGSTON, Jamaica, Monday, Aug. 6—Jamaica became an independent nation with dominion status within the British Commonwealth today. Princess Margaret as representative of her sister, Queen Elizabeth II, witnessed the end of the 307 years of British colonial status. About 30,000 Jamaicans jammed the big new National Stadium and cheered the raising of the new flag. On the stroke of midnight, the huge spotlights were turned off and in silence and darkness, the British flag that had flown over the island was hauled down and the green, gold and black

Continued on Page 6, Column 2

TRIBES REASSERT POWER IN CONGO

Aim Is to Revise Provinces to Follow Ethnic Lines

By DAVID HALBERSTAM
Special to The New York Times.

LEOPOLDVILLE, the Congo, Aug. 5 — Tribal political power is reasserting itself strongly in the Congo. It is manifest in the powerful desire of the Congolese to form new provinces along basically tribal lines.

When the Congo won independence from Belgium on June 30, 1960, there were only six major provinces in this huge country. With the sanction of Parliament, seven new provinces have been approved. A total of nineteen provinces is foreseen shortly.

Observers view the trend as essentially federalist and traditionalist and thus anti-nationalist and against the mainstream of pan-African political development. It marks, in effect, these observers believe, the failure of the late Patrice Lumumba and his nationalist movement to make any deep inroads into the traditional tribal alignment in the Congo.

There are, the observers note, about forty ethnic groups in the Congo, of which about twenty are major groups. The new provinces are generally being developed along major ethnic lines.

The new province of South Kasai, for example, is essentially a Baluba tribal area,

Continued on Page 8, Column 4

Charter Change Urged to Keep Fiscal Power of Estimate Board

The Citizens Budget Commission urged yesterday an early revision of the new City Charter to preserve the Board of Estimate's authority to control capital projects from the time a site is chosen through the appropriation of funds.

The present Charter gives the board this authority. In exercising it the board has followed a time-consuming procedure of holding public hearings on each aspect of a given capital project, from the planning stage on.

The Citizens Budget Commission recommended a single public hearing on each project, covering all its phases. It proposed that the Mayor should not initiate any project unless the Board of Estimate then approved it.

The civic organization pointed out that the new Charter, which becomes effective Jan. 1, provides for a public hearing by the Board of Estimate on all capital projects before the Mayor initiates them, but gives the board no power to disapprove them since the hearing would be held after the budget was approved.

The public hearing, the civic group contended, would therefore be "farcical and deceptive."

It proposed that the Charter be revised through a local law giving the Board of Estimate authority to approve "the site, final plans, cost estimates, major construction contracts, proposed bond issues and necessary appropriations."

As it now stands, the new Charter provides for appropriation of funds for all projects in the city's capital budget when the budget is adopted by the Board of Estimate and the City Council. The Citizens Budget Commission contended this would leave actual initiation of any project listed in

Continued on Page 10, Column 6

NEWS INDEX

"All the News That's Fit to Print"

The New York Times.

LATE CITY EDITION

U. S. Weather Bureau Report (Page 61) forecasts: Sunny and mild today and tonight. Increasing cloudiness tomorrow. Temp. range: 73—52; yesterday: 72—50.

VOL. CXII. No. 38,236.

NEW YORK, MONDAY, OCTOBER 1, 1962.

10 cents beyond 50-mile zone from New York City except on Long Island. Higher in air delivery cities.

FIVE CENTS

NEGRO AT MISSISSIPPI U. AS BARNETT YIELDS; 3 DEAD IN CAMPUS RIOT, 6 MARSHALS SHOT; GUARDSMEN MOVE IN; KENNEDY MAKES PLEA

Khrushchev Invites Kennedy to Moscow; White House Studies Bid for Berlin Talk

Mrs. Kennedy Is Urged to Make Trip—Udall Carried Message

U.S. and British Officials Review Parleys With Gromyko on Crisis

By JAMES RESTON
Special to The New York Times

WASHINGTON, Sept. 30—Premier Khrushchev has sent a private invitation to President Kennedy to visit the Soviet Union.

It is understood that the message was delivered to the President by Secretary of the Interior Stewart L. Udall, who recently visited the Soviet Union.

The Soviet leader first made the suggestion in a five-hour talk with Mr. Udall, after he had stressed the need for another major effort to reach an accommodation on the Berlin problem.

Later, just as Mr. Udall was leaving, Mr. Khrushchev again said that he hoped it would be possible for the President to go to Moscow and take Mrs. Kennedy along. No date was mentioned, but the invitation was passed on to the President and is now the subject of discussion within the State Department and the White House.

The New York Times
Stewart L. Udall

No decision has been reached. The project is being studied in the light of increased tension over Berlin and the growing conviction here that the Soviet Union will sign a peace treaty with the Communist East German regime, probably in mid-November.

Recent conversations between Secretary of State Dean Rusk and the Soviet Foreign Minister, Andrei A. Gromyko, about Berlin have been courteous and correct. However, they have failed to indicate any new basis for a Berlin accommodation.

The President discussed the Berlin question at luncheon today with the Earl of Home, the British Foreign Secretary, Mr. Rusk, Under Secretary of State George W. Ball, David Bruce, the Ambassador to Britain, and the British Ambassador in Washington, Sir David Ormsby Gore.

It is not known whether the Khrushchev invitation was considered. A communiqué issued from the White House later

Continued on Page 2, Column 4

PRESIDENT MEETS WITH LORD HOME ON CURBING CUBA

They Agree on Peril in Rise of Communism—British Policy Shift Hinted

By TAD SZULC
Special to The New York Times

WASHINGTON, Sept. 30—President Kennedy and the Earl of Home, the British Foreign Secretary, discussed at the White House today ways of "containing further Communist expansion and subversion in the Caribbean."

The announcement in a joint statement that "they agreed on the serious nature of developments in Cuba" suggested that Britain may have altered her policy of regarding the Cuban affair as a matter of concern to the United States alone.

But it was understood that Mr. Kennedy and Lord Home were not able to work out a solution to the problem of the chartering of British and other Western Allied ships to the Soviet Union to carry petroleum and other strategic cargoes to Cuba.

Lord Home was reported to have repeated for Mr. Kennedy the standing British view that the Government had no control over privately owned shipping and that no official restrictions were possible while Britain maintained diplomatic relations with Cuba.

Role in Patrols Possible

However, diplomats indicated that Britain's possible cooperation with the United States could extend to her participation in the patrolling of the Caribbean against the movement of arms or agents from Cuba, particularly in the direction of British Guiana.

British Guiana's Prime Minister, Dr. Cheddi B. Jagan, is a Marxist and in recent months his Government has sought to increase economic and political ties with Cuba. The British Government is concerned by the situation.

President Kennedy and Lord Home also reviewed the questions of Berlin, the Congo, Laos and hopes of achieving a nuclear test ban. They were together for two hours and twenty minutes at luncheon and in an additional talk.

Lord Home and Secretary of State Dean Rusk flew here for the meeting from New York, where they were attending the sessions of the United Nations General Assembly. From the White House, British and Amer-

Continued on Page 3, Column 1

TEAR GAS IS USED

Mob Attacks Officers—2,500 Troops Are Sent to Oxford

By CLAUDE SITTON
Special to The New York Times

OXFORD, Miss., Monday, Oct. 1—James H. Meredith, a 29-year-old Negro, was admitted last night to the University of Mississippi campus and was scheduled to enroll today in the all-white institution.

A riot broke out shortly after his arrival, and marauding bands of students and adults, many of whom were from other states, were still ranging through the campus and the town early today.

At least three men were killed, one of them unidentified. Fifty persons were being treated for various injuries in the university infirmary. Six United States marshals were shot, one was critically wounded.

Although the riot started at about 7:30 P. M., Central standard time, Army troops did not arrive until five and a half hours later. About 200 military policemen arrived from Memphis shortly after 1 A. M. (3 A. M., E. D. T.)

[Army headquarters received word early today that about 200 more persons had joined the rioting mob and that the situation on the campus was "very bad," The Associated Press reported. About 2,500 regular Army military policemen and infantrymen were converging on Oxford. Army observers in Mississippi reported to headquarters that automatic weapons fire was being aimed at the registration building.]

Marshals Besieged

A small detachment of Mississippi National Guardsmen went to the aid of a besieged force of 300 deputy marshals in the university administration building. The marshals were under the command of top Justice Department officials, including Nicholas de B. Katzenbach, deputy attorney general.

For a time, it appeared that the marshals would not be able to hold the building, which is called the Lyceum. But barrage after barrage of tear gas discouraged the rioters, and they began to break up.

A number of other Mississippi National Guardsmen had arrived early today at the armory on the eastern outskirts of town. But there was considerable delay before they began a drive to the campus.

Automobiles loaded with roughly dressed whites, some of whom were from Alabama, began pulling into the campus shortly after the state highway patrol withdrew from the campus entrances early last night.

Clouds of tear gas billowed around the administration building.

The tree-dotted mall in front

Continued on Page 23, Column 6

United Press International Telephoto

U. S. MARSHALS USE TEAR GAS IN MISSISSIPPI: Two of the marshals, armed with riot clubs and wearing gas masks and helmets, move in on the rioters on University of Mississippi campus after Federal officers hurled tear gas at the demonstrators.

SHIPPING TIED UP IN PIER WALKOUT

Longshoremen Go on Strike From Maine to Texas—U. S. Action Expected

By EDWARD A. MORROW

Longshoremen struck in all ports from Maine to Texas at 12:01 this morning as their three-year contract expired.

Leaders of the International Longshoremen's Association, representing 75,000 members, said their action was the result of a lockout. Spokesmen for the New York Shipping Association, which sets the industry pattern for the Atlantic and Gulf Coasts, called it a strike.

A Sunday work record was set in the Port of New York yesterday, with 10 times the normal number of longshoremen employed. Fifty-four ships sailed before the midnight deadline.

The strike was not expected to cause any immediate hardship on the consumer public here, but thousands of trans-Atlantic passengers arriving here this week may be inconvenienced.

No strike negotiations were set, and it was apparent that both sides expected the problem to be put on President Kennedy's desk. His probable action will be to invoke the Taft-Hartley Act to bring the longshoremen back to work during an 80-day cooling-off period.

The President can request an injunction after a finding is made that a strike endangers

Continued on Page 14, Column 4

Dutch Control Ends In West New Guinea As U.N. Takes Over

By A. M. ROSENTHAL
Special to The New York Times

HOLLANDIA, New Guinea, Monday, Oct. 1—A brief and delicate United Nations experiment in a transfer of power began here today in a public square.

More than 350 years of rule in the East by the Netherlands had turned a small European country into a great colonial power. That rule ended without pomp, and quietly passed into history today, totally defeated by Asian nationalism.

Once the Dutch ruled over all the islands and riches of the East Indies. Thirteen years ago they gave up control to the new republic of Indonesia, keeping one territory, West New Guinea, which was known as Netherlands New Guinea.

About twenty Indonesians in civilian tunics watched today as a Guatemalan official of the United Nations read the proclamation ending Dutch rule in New Guinea, and began seven months of United Nations jurisdiction that will end in the transfer of authority to Indonesia on May 1.

500 Netherlanders Remain

Also in the square were representatives of Australia, which rules the eastern half of New Guinea and is watching with some nervousness the arrival of an Asian power on her frontiers.

No flags were raised at the public ceremony. The United Nation had planned to raise its banner and the Dutch flag. But Papuans demanded the raising also of a banner symbolizing the New Guinea independence movement.

To avoid antagonizing them or the Indonesians, the United Nations dispensed with the public flag ceremony and instead merely hoisted the Dutch and United Nations banner over United Nations headquarters.

There were a few score Netherlanders in the crowd. Only about 500 of the original 2,700 Dutch officials remain in New Guinea. Most Dutch women and children have left, and a Greek ship will carry others home next week.

From today until May 1 the United Nations will be in formal control of a territory three

Continued on Page 8, Column 3

CHOU IS ADAMANT IN SOVIET DISPUTE

Upholds Aid for 'Liberation' Wars—Speech Is Viewed as Rebuke to Moscow

Special to The New York Times

HONG KONG, Sept. 30—Premier Chou En-lai declared in Peking tonight that no one could force Communist China to change the "just stand it takes in international affairs."

His statement was interpreted here as a reply to a recent Soviet assertion that economic tasks must take precedence over political tasks in the Communist bloc. The Chinese Communists hold that the bloc should give priority to political tasks by actively aiding "liberation struggles" in various countries.

Premier Chou asserted that "imperialist reactionaries of various countries and modern revisionists" had, in collaboration with one another, "continually launched anti-Chinese campaigns in an attempt to isolate China and compel China to change the just" stand.

"But their attempt is completely futile," he said. "It is they themselves, not China, who

Continued on Page 4, Column 4

BARNETT GIVES IN; PLEADS FOR CALM

Declares Mississippi Was 'Overpowered' by U. S.—Vows a Court Fight

Text of Barnett's statement will be found on Page 23.

By PETER KIHSS
Special to The New York Times

JACKSON, Miss., Sept. 30—Gov. Ross R. Barnett, declaring that his state had been "physically overpowered" by the Federal Government, gave up his fight tonight to keep a Negro out of the University of Mississippi.

In a statement issued here, the Governor announced that Mississippi would keep up a struggle in the courts against the admission of James H. Meredith, who was placed in residence at the university tonight under escort of Federal marshals.

But with the Mississippi National Guard mobilized and Federal troops entering the state to enforce the Federal court's order for Mr. Meredith's admission, Governor Barnett declared that Mississippians "must at all odds preserve the peace and avoid bloodshed."

Crowds that had been rallied earlier by the White Citizens Council here to support the Governor in his fight against racial desegregation heard broadcasts of the Governor's statement on portable transistor radios.

Crowd Is Silent

They were silent. The state's position had been crumbling for an hour or more, since Mr. Meredith had been escorted on to the university campus at Oxford.

Just before midnight Governor Barnett issued a statement that he would continue his crusade. This apparently was to counter interpretation that he had backed down. However, it did not indicate any change in his projected legal tactics.

The statement said: "I will never yield a single inch in my determination to win the fight we are all engaged in. I call on all Mississippians to keep the faith and courage. We will never surrender."

Earlier, thousands of segregationists ringed the block on which the Governor's mansion stands. They had been called there by the Citizens Council to protect the Governor against a possible Federal effort to arrest him.

But inside the mansion, Gov-

Continued on Page 23, Column 1

President Asks Mississippi To Comply With U.S. Laws

By ANTHONY LEWIS
Special to The New York Times.

WASHINGTON, Sept. 30—President Kennedy appealed to the students and the people of Mississippi tonight to comply peacefully with Federal law and bring the desegregation crisis to an end. "The eyes of the nation and all the world are upon you and upon all of us," he said, "and the honor of your university and state are in the balance."

The President spoke to the nation on television less than an hour after Gov. Ross R. Barnett of Mississippi pulled back from his all-out defiance of Federal authority. The Governor indicated he would no longer attempt to block the enrollment of James H. Meredith, a Negro, at the University of Mississippi.

Kennedy's speech, proclamation, Executive order and wire to Barnett are on Page 22.

Mr. Kennedy expressed cautious hope that the great Federal-state conflict, the gravest since the Civil War, was coming to a peaceful end. He said Federal Court orders "are beginning to be carried out."

But he qualified his optimism most carefully, and indeed made clear that the Government was waiting anxiously to see how Mississippi officials and citizens behaved. There was still much concern here tonight about violence at the university in Oxford.

There were no recriminations in the President's talk, nor even a reference to Governor Barnett. It was addressed pri-

Continued on Page 22, Column 1

A.E.C. MAY CREATE ATOM-ROCKET CITY

Nevada Desert Site Studied as Nuclear Missile Work Encounters Setbacks

By GLADWIN HILL
Special to The New York Times

LOS ANGELES, Sept. 30—Unpublicized accidents, delays and disappointments in the development of a nuclear-propelled rocket are forcing the Atomic Energy Commission to consider, reluctantly, the creation of a new Oak Ridge in the Nevada Desert.

The objective of the new atomic company town would be to make the hazardous experimental work more palatable to personnel urgently needed to push along the lagging $4,000,-000-a-week Rover project.

Most of the 700 persons now involved in the work have to spend four hours a day commuting between the desert test site and Las Vegas, 100 miles to the south. Living in the gambling center is expensive and it has other adverse features that commission officials acknowledge have posed morale problems and have hampered the recruiting of scientific talent.

The talent is needed to overcome a succession of problems that have afflicted what a number of leading scientists assess as one of the most important programs in the international space race.

Project Begun in 1955

Just as atomic bombs are so much more powerful than conventional explosives, so nuclear propulsion could yield two to three times the payload lift physically possible with the biggest chemical-fuel rockets. This advantage is judged indispensable by many scientific observers to getting useful payloads — such as persons — anywhere beyond the close range of the moon.

At its inception in 1955 the Rover project was envisioned as the possible answer to the projected moon landing. But slippages in the project's schedule have put this out of consideration in favor of relatively small-lift chemical-fuel rockets.

Although $257,000,000 has

Continued on Page 13, Column 1

Giants and Dodgers End Season in a Tie

The Los Angeles Dodgers and the San Francisco Giants ended the National League season in a tie for first place yesterday and will play a two-of-three game series to determine the champion. The playoff will start today in San Francisco and move tomorrow to Los Angeles.

Two eighth-inning home runs set up the pennant tie. Willie Mays walloped one that lifted the Giants to a 2-1 victory over the Houston Colts. Gene Oliver of the St. Louis Cardinals belted the homer that defeated the Dodgers, 1—0.

The winner of the playoff will meet the New York Yankees in the World Series starting in the West Coast city on Thursday. The series games in New York will be played next Sunday and Monday and, if necessary, Tuesday.

Details on Page 48.

NEWS INDEX

New York Times Begins Printing Western Edition in Los Angeles

Special to The New York Times.

LOS ANGELES, Sept. 30—The New York Times began printing here tonight a Western edition for readers in thirteen Western states, including Alaska and Hawaii.

The innovation marks the first time in the United States that a daily newspaper of general readership has been printed in two cities simultaneously. The first issue was that of Monday, Oct. 1.

The operation is being accomplished by means of a speedy method of long-distance typesetting. Text coded onto punched paper tape in New York is transmitted over telephone lines across the continent at 1,000 words a minute. The electric impulses produce a duplicate tape here, which is fed into typesetting machines.

Perforating a single tape in New York simultaneously produces tape for use in Los Angeles, and in Paris for The New York Times's two-year-old International Edition.

The Western Edition will be essentially a duplicate of The New York Times, now 111 years old. The main differences will be the exclusion of news of purely local New York interest, and the additional Western advertising.

The new edition will be printed six days a week, Monday through Saturday. A morning newspaper, it will be distributed primarily by mail, arriving in cities of distribution throughout the area on the day of publication. It will also be sold on newsstands at 10 cents a copy.

Special dispatches and features from The New York Times's Sunday Edition will appear in the Western Edition. A four-page Review of the Week section will appear regularly on Mondays. The Western Edition will regularly include The New York Times's full business and financial report and market tables.

The New York Times's president and publisher, Orvil E. Dryfoos, explained that the new edition was being inaugurated "in direct response to readers' demand," as reflected in the suggestions of thousands of Western residents after the establishment of the simultaneous International Edition in Paris.

The Western Edition, Mr. Dryfoos added, "will seek to

Continued on Page 27, Column 1

Morgenthau Urges Off-Track Bet Vote

By CLAYTON KNOWLES

Robert M. Morgenthau, Democratic candidate for Governor, put himself on record twice yesterday in favor of a statewide referendum on off-track betting.

He acknowledged he had misgivings about the proposal, originally advanced by Mayor Wagner as a solution for city fiscal difficulties. But the candidate said his personal views would "have to be weighed against the need for additional revenues."

It has been widely estimated that legalized off-track betting would produce $100,000,000 a year in new revenue for the city and state.

In a second new stand, Mr. Morgenthau said it was his feeling that the proposal for a bonus for veterans of the Korean War was another "one of the things that should be put to the voters."

The Democratic platform,

Continued on Page 34, Column 2

TONIGHT at 8:45 P.M.! "Fiorello!" Complete Score. Radio Station WVNJ: 620 AM - 100.3 FM.

Congress Is Driving To Quit This Week

By JOHN D. MORRIS
Special to The New York Times

WASHINGTON, Sept. 30 — Congress moves into one of the busiest weeks of its session tomorrow, with leaders pressing for adjournment by Saturday night.

The size of the foreign aid program is the main issue still to be decided. Action on tax and trade bills, among other major elements of President Kennedy's legislative program, is expected to be completed without further time-consuming controversy.

A new fight over Federal aid to higher education is developing, however, as a result of an Administration decision to press for passage of a $972,000,000 program of aid for medical and dental schools.

A $4,422,800,000 foreign aid money bill, approved Friday by

Continued on Page 35, Column 3

AN EDUCATION IN DURHAM

GENE ROBERTS

By the winter of 1960, dismay was widespread among black Americans who had believed the Supreme Court's 1954 school desegregation decision would bring about significant racial change. While there had been real progress in the border states, the 11 states that made up the Confederacy were still resisting. Mississippi, Alabama and South Carolina had not admitted a single black pupil into white schools. Even in North Carolina, which was considered to be relatively progressive, only a handful of school districts had desegregated, and, even then, only with token black admissions. White politicians defended their resistance, in part, by saying most blacks wanted their own schools and were not interested in dismantling segregation.

George C. Hayes, Thurgood Marshall and James M. Nabrit led the fight to abolish segregation from the U.S. school system.

At North Carolina Agricultural and Technical College in Greensboro, four black freshmen, who had been in the seventh grade when the court decision was handed down, gave vent to their frustration by sitting at the whites-only lunch counter at Woolworth's five-and-ten-cent store and refusing to move until they were served.[1] They were joined the next day by other students. Then the movement quickly spread to Raleigh and Durham. Martin Luther King, delighted by the nonviolent protest, flew into Durham to give support to the students.[2]

Black and white students leaving school on the day that the U.S. Supreme Court ruled to end segregation in the nation's school system.

I was a state capital reporter for the News and Observer in Raleigh, but I was interested in the race story. I drove over to White Rock Baptist Church in Durham, expecting to see a student rally. When I arrived, I saw scores of students, but they were all milling about the churchyard. Middle-aged blacks had come more than an hour early and had filled all the seats, even standing so thickly at the back of the pews that no one else could squeeze in.

It was an unseasonably warm night, and a church deacon who wanted news coverage boosted me through an open window. I sat on the windowsill throughout the long event. While there were college professors and public school teachers in the audience, many of the women were clearly

Sit-ins at lunch counters were often initiated by students who believed desegregation was moving too slowly.

FURTHER READING

1 "Negroes in South in Store Sitdown," see February 3, 1960, article.
2 "Negro Sitdowns Stir Fear Of Wider Unrest in South," see February 15, 1960, front page.

maids, cooks and laundresses who were shut out by segregation from higher-paying jobs. Even small change was precious, and there was a custom among them to put their nickels, dimes and quarters into their pocket handkerchiefs and knot the handkerchiefs tightly to minimize the risk of losing the coins.

After Dr. King, in a spellbinding appeal, called for an end to segregation, his aides asked for contributions to the cause. From my perch I could see black women reach for their purses in unison, open them in their laps, and unknot their handkerchiefs. I left the church convinced, white politicians to the contrary, that there was going to be sweeping racial change. I had just seen how deeply the black commitment ran.

If I had been more experienced in racial coverage, I might have known earlier of the depth of black feeling. The black press had been conditioning black Americans for decades to demand sweeping racial change; and black readers had made it clear, in letters to the editors, that they were ready.

But I, like the great majority of white Americans, barely knew of the existence of black newspapers. Yet they had long been a part of the American scene.

Rev. Martin Luther King Jr. speaks at the March on Washington in front of more than 200,000 people on August 28, 1963.

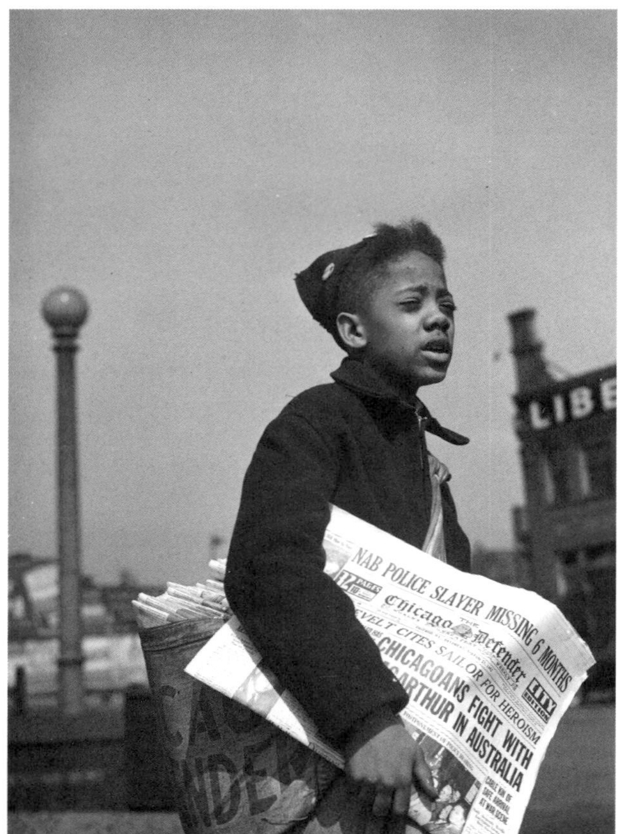

A newsboy sells copies of the Chicago Defender, one of the nation's leading black newspapers, in 1942.

The use of police dogs against civil rights demonstrators in Birmingham, Alabama, in 1963 brought nationwide reaction in support of the demonstrators.

The first black newspaper, Freedom's Journal, was published in 1827.[3] It proclaimed in its first issue: "Too long have others spoken for us." Eventually, other black newspapers began to appear. By the 1950's, more than 2,700 black newspapers had been founded. Yet by 1951, only about 175 black papers were still in publication. The average paper died after nine years. However, it was usually lack of advertising, not lack of readership, that led to these failures.[4]

Black papers commanded a devoted black readership in the 1930's, 40's and early 50's, reaching two million households at peak, for a simple reason: the mainstream press wasn't covering racial discrimination in America. The black press was—and aggressively. At the outbreak of World War II, black journalists debated whether blacks should fight for freedom abroad when they clearly did not have it in a broad swath of America. Ultimately, leading black newspapers coalesced around a "Double V" campaign—one V for victory over the axis powers abroad, and the other for victory over racial injustice in America.

Seeing themselves as an alternative press, most black papers unhesitatingly advocated racial equality in both their news and editorial columns. The Birmingham World, the Arkansas State Press in Little Rock and the Tri-State Defender in Memphis were among the black papers in the South that regularly condemned segregation and white supremacy. And Southern blacks could—and often did—subscribe by mail to Northern black newspapers.

The Afro-American in Washington and Baltimore had a lynching beat and sent reporters deep into the South whenever it got wind of mob atrocities. The Pittsburgh Courier assigned a full-time reporter to cover Jackie Robinson's desegregation of major league baseball in 1947.[5] The Amsterdam News and the Chicago Defender were among the papers that sent reporters to the Mississippi Delta in 1955 to cover the murder of Emmett Till, a 14-year-old Chicago boy who allegedly whistled at a white woman while visiting relatives in the Delta.

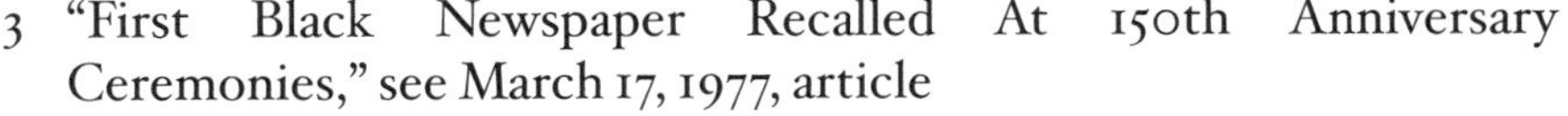

3 "First Black Newspaper Recalled At 150th Anniversary Ceremonies," see March 17, 1977, article
4 "Negro Press Urged to Clarify Image," see March 13, 1965, article.
5 "Robinson, Wright, Negro Players, Start Training at Sanford Camp," see March 5, 1946, article.

A copy of the Freedom Journal, the first black owned and operated newspaper in the United States, was displayed in Maryland in March of 2002.

A photo of Emmett Till, the 14-year-old Chicago boy whose weighted down body was found in the Tallahatchie River in Mississippi, in August 1955.

J. W. Milam and his brother Roy Bryant confer with their attorney before pleading innocent to the kidnapping and murder of Emmett Till.

Airborne troops guard students as they enter Little Rock Central High School in Arkansas in 1957.

White students crowd around two black students attempting to enter Little Rock Central High School on September 9, 1957.

The Till trial was a turning point for racial coverage by white Northern journalists, at least in part because the Supreme Court's desegregation decision had made racial discrimination a national issue. About 40 white journalists from the mainstream press joined a dozen black reporters in the courtroom to witness the quick acquittal of the accused white murderers.[6]

Mainstream coverage escalated in 1956, when white mobs gathered to block Autherine Lucy from desegregating the University of Alabama;[7] and it escalated again as the Montgomery bus boycott gathered momentum,[8] introducing Martin Luther King to racial protest.[9]

After the Little Rock school crisis in 1957, there was no longer any doubt that Northern newspapers and television networks would cover desegregation stories.[10] Blacks could now get racial news daily instead of waiting for news from the black newspapers, which, with few exceptions, were published weekly.

The black papers saw their circulations plummet, and most went out of business or became community publications. But they left an important legacy. Arguably, there would not have been a civil rights movement if the black press had not paved the way.

GENE ROBERTS *is a former managing editor of The New York Times (1994–1997). While he was executive editor of The Philadelphia Inquirer for 18 years (1972–1990), the paper was awarded 17 Pulitzer Prizes. He joined The Times in 1965 and served as chief Southern and civil rights correspondent, chief war correspondent in Vietnam and national editor. Roberts also taught journalism from 1991 to 1994 at the University of Maryland. Along with co-author Hank Klibanoff, he was awarded the 2007 Pulitzer Prize for their book "The Race Beat: The Press, the Civil Rights Struggle, and the Awakening of a Nation."*

6 "Mississippi Jury Acquits 2 Accused in Youth's Killing," see September 24, 1955 front page.
7 "Tuscaloosa: A Tense Drama Unfolds," see February 26, 1956 article.
8 "Negroes' Boycott Cripples Bus Line," see January 8, 1956 article.
9 "Negro Minister Convicted of Directing Bus Boycott," see March 23, 1956 front page.
10 "Students Unhurt; Negro Newspaper Men Are Attacked at High School in Little Rock, Ark.," see September 24, 1957 front page.

"All the News That's Fit to Print"

The New York Times.

LATE CITY EDITION

U. S. Weather Bureau Report (Page 74) forecasts: Partly cloudy, breezy, cool today. Fair and cool tonight and tomorrow. Temp. range: 54—45; yesterday: 66—44.

VOL. CXII..No. 38,258. NEW YORK, TUESDAY, OCTOBER 23, 1962. 10 cents beyond 50-mile zone from New York City except on Long Island. Higher in air delivery cities. FIVE CENTS

U.S. IMPOSES ARMS BLOCKADE ON CUBA ON FINDING OFFENSIVE-MISSILE SITES; KENNEDY READY FOR SOVIET SHOWDOWN

U. S. JUDGES GIVEN POWER TO REQUIRE VOTE FOR NEGROES

High Court Upholds Order Forcing the Registration of 54 in Alabama County

Special to The New York Times

WASHINGTON, Oct. 22 — The Supreme Court held today that Federal judges have the power to make state registrars put specific Negroes on the voting rolls.

Alabama had challenged an order by Federal District Judge Frank M. Johnson Jr. requiring the registration of 54 specific Negroes in Macon County, Ala. The order was upheld by the United States Court of Appeals for the Fifth Circuit.

Today the Supreme Court unanimously affirmed the disputed order. And it did so in a way that indicated once again its mood of impatience with Southern efforts to maintain denials of Negro rights.

One-Sentence Ruling

All that was before the court was an application for review of the Fifth Circuit decision. The usual alternatives would have been to deny the petition or to grant it and hear oral argument later.

Instead, the court granted review and then, summarily, affirmed the lower courts. It did so in a single sentence, with just one citation in the way of explanation.

The citation was to a decision in 1960 upholding a Federal Court order in a Louisiana voting case. There, a district judge had told Louisiana registrars to put back on their books 1,377 Negroes whose names had been removed in a purge by the segregationist Citizens Council.

Action by Congress

The Macon County case was one of the first brought by the Department of Justice under the Civil Rights Act of 1957. It is especially significant because the county is in the so-called Black Belt, with a predominantly Negro population.

In 1958, when the suit was started, virtually all of the 3,000 white persons of voting age in the county were registered. But only about 1,000 of the 12,000 potential Negro voters were actually eligible.

In a further move, the registrars resigned, and this was held to leave no defendants to be sued. Congress in 1960 handled this problem by providing

Continued on Page 24, Column 4

102 SAVED AT SEA AS PLANE DITCHES

Rescue Is Made off Alaska Minutes After Accident

By The Associated Press.

SITKA, Alaska, Oct. 22—A military-charter airliner ditched in the ocean near here today, but all 102 persons aboard were saved in a quick rescue operation.

The plane, a DC-7C of Northwest Airlines, was going from McChord Air Force Base in Washington to Anchorage, Alaska. It carried 95 passengers and a crew of seven.

The rescue was reported by Northwest and the Alaska Coastal-Ellis Airline at Sitka, which also reported that there apparently were no serious injuries.

The plane went down shortly after the Federal Aviation Agency at Anchorage got word that it was being ditched because of propeller trouble.

A Coast Guard plane alighted on the water nearby; the Air Force sent two rescue planes, and small boats from Sitka, about seven miles north of the

Continued on Page 8, Column 3

Chinese Open New Front; Use Tanks Against Indians

Nehru Warns of Peril to Independence —Reds Attack Near Burmese Border and Press Two Other Drives

Special to The New York Times

NEW DELHI, Oct. 22—Prime Minister Jawaharlal Nehru told the people of India tonight that the Chinese Communist attack was a threat to their liberty.

His grave warning followed word that the advancing Chinese had opened a third front in

Excerpts from Nehru's speech will be found on Page 2.

the Himalayas, near the Burmese border, and had used tanks for the first time. Five more Indian posts fell to the Chinese on the third day of savage fighting.

[A bid for negotiations for a peace accord was broadcast by the Chinese Communist radio early Tuesday, The Associated Press reported from Tokyo.]

In a broadcast, Mr. Nehru denounced the Peking regime as "a powerful and unscrupulous opponent, not caring for peace or peaceful methods."

"The time has come," he said, "for us to realize fully this menace that threatens the freedom of our people and the independence of our country."

Prime Minister Nehru said India would not abandon her economic development program and policy of nonalignment with international blocs, but called on the nation to switch "from the slow-moving methods of peacetime to those which produce results quickly."

"We must build up our military strength by all means at our disposal," he said.

The third front in the Himalayan fighting was opened early today when the Chinese attacked an Indian post at Kibitoo, on the border between

Continued on Page 3, Column 1

U.S. Bids U.N. Bar China; Denounces Attack on India

By SAM POPE BREWER

Special to The New York Times

UNITED NATIONS, N. Y., Oct. 22—Adlai E. Stevenson told the General Assembly today that Communist China's "naked aggression" against India was new proof that it was unfit for membership in the United Nations.

The chief United States representative at the United Nations spoke as the Assembly took up the perennial question of admitting Peking.

Mr. Stevenson told the members that by their actions on the Indian frontier the Chinese Communists "again show their scorn for the Charter of this organization."

The Vice President of the Philippines, Emmanuel Pelaez, told the Assembly that there were more than 40,000,000 Chinese living outside China who would become "a Trojan horse" if the United Nations accepted the Communist Government.

Mr. Pelaez said that the Chinese abroad, 1,000,000 of them in the Philippines, would be used for subversion by the Peking Government. He said they could now be controlled because the Communist Government did not have the means to get at them.

On the fighting in India, Mr. Stevenson declared: "Should there be some among us who think that perhaps the whole thing is a mistake that will right itself before long, let me point out that when a nation moves its troops with tanks and armor, it is no mistake. It is a premeditated act. It is naked aggression. And it has been going on with gathering momentum for some three years."

He quoted Prime Minister

Continued on Page 5, Column 3

U. S. SAID TO EASE KATANGA POLICY

Reported Willing to Put Off Any Economic Sanctions —Congolese Disturbed

By LLOYD GARRISON

Special to The New York Times

LEOPOLDVILLE, the Congo, Oct. 22 — Authoritative sources said today that the United States was no longer insisting that Katanga Province strictly meet the deadlines of the United Nations plan to end its secession from the Congo.

This has alarmed Congolese officials. They say that the United States shift is reflected in United Nations policy.

The United Nations plan, introduced Aug. 2 by U Thant, Acting Secretary General, was said to have been conceived largely by the United States.

As outlined by Mr. Thant, the plan's first stage called for the following timetable:

Within thirty days a program was to be decided on for the reintegration of Katanga's army into the Congolese National Army. Sixty days were to be allowed for the program to be carried out.

Recall of Missions

All Katangese foreign missions were to be recalled immediately, and all Katanga's foreign currency reserves were to be put under the control of the central Government, with 50 per cent of these reserves rebated to Katanga.

Unification of the Congo's currency was to have begun within 10 days.

Katanga was to have started immediately to share 50 per cent of her tax revenues with the central Government.

Not one of these conditions has been met.

Last week Cyrille Adoula, Premier of the central Government, declared that "the deadline for the first stage has passed." He said that it was now time for the United Nations to consider the second stage — economic sanctions.

A shift in United States policy became apparent over the weekend after the departure of George C. McGhee, Under Secretary of State for Political Af-

Continued on Page 3, Column 6

Stocks Plunge Early On Crisis, but Rally

By RICHARD RUTTER

An already badly battered stock market was hit by massive selling yesterday as talk of a new international crisis spread in Wall Street.

The selling was of dimensions reminiscent of late May when the market experienced its worst break in a generation. Yesterday, the tape ran as much as 19 minutes late before a half-hearted recovery set in that cut losses by about one-third.

Both tape lateness and volume were the greatest since July 10. Two million shares were traded in the first two hours.

Stock markets in London, Frankfurt and Brussels, following Wall Street's lead, also took large losses.

The selling was directly ascribed to news in the morning about an air of crisis in Wash-

Continued on Page 49, Column 6

SHIPS MUST STOP

Other Action Planned If Big Rockets Are Not Dismantled

By JAMES RESTON

Special to The New York Times

WASHINGTON, Oct. 22— President Kennedy drew the line tonight, not with Cuba, but with the Soviet Union. After almost a generation of trying to keep the "cold war" from reaching a direct confrontation between United States and Soviet power, a decision has been made to force Soviet missile bases from this hemisphere at the risk of war.

This is the official interpretation of President Kennedy's speech tonight, and the orders to American forces bear it out. On the highest authority, it can be said that these orders include the following:

¶Ships carrying to Cuba weapons capable of striking the continental United States must either turn back or submit to search and seizure, or fight. If they try to run the blockade, a warning shot will be fired across their bows; if they still do not submit, they will be attacked.

¶This applies not only to ships but to any planes suspected of carrying additional offensive weapons to Cuba. There is no evidence that there are nuclear warheads in Cuba, but long-range aircraft suspected of carrying these or any other offensive weapons, will be intercepted, and instructions have been issued to do everything possible to check all Communist-bloc planes en route to Cuba via Newfoundland or Africa.

Prepared to Risk War

Even this will not satisfy the new policy announced by President Kennedy. Not only must new offensive weapons be stopped, under the President's orders, but those already in Cuba must be dismantled, or the United States will take whatever additional action is necessary, beginning with a much more rigorous blockade of such things as Cuba's essential oil supplies, to force compliance.

If this leads to Soviet retaliation, such as a counter-blockade of Berlin, the United States is prepared to risk a major war to defend its present position in the former German capital. Accordingly, American forces, not only in Berlin and West Germany but all over the world, have been placed on emergency alert. The new policy has been defined in a private communi-

Continued on Page 19, Column 1

Canada Asks Inspection of Cuba; Britain Supporting Quarantine

Diefenbaker Comments

By RAYMOND DANIELL

Special to The New York Times

OTTAWA, Oct. 22 — Prime Minister John Diefenbaker of Canada declared tonight the time had come for an impartial inspection of what is happening in Cuba by eight of the "nonaligned nations."

Interrupting debate of the Canadian economic crisis in the House of Commons, Mr. Diefenbaker described President Kennedy's speech on Cuba as "somber and challenging."

"Naturally," he said, "there has been little time to give consideration to positive action that might be taken. But I suggest that if there is a desire—and I am sure there is on the part of the U.S.S.R.—to have the facts, if a group of nations, perhaps the eight comprising the unaligned members of the 18-nation disarmament committee, were given the opportunity of making an on-site inspection of Cuba to ascertain what the facts are, a major step forward would be taken."

Meanwhile it was disclosed that Canada has barred the use of her airfields, including that

Continued on Page 21, Column 2

British Note Peril

By DREW MIDDLETON

Special to The New York Times

LONDON, Oct. 22—Qualified sources said today that approval for President Kennedy's military quarantine of Cuba could be expected from the British government.

A Foreign Office spokesman declared, "Revelation of the Soviet build-up in Cuba will come as a shock to the whole civilized world."

Official comment cannot be given until after Prime Minister Macmillan and his Cabinet have discussed the President's statement.

Initial reaction among diplomats was that the President had taken the most reasonable course to frustrate what military circles regard as evident danger to the United States: a buildup of Soviet nuclear capacity in Cuba.

The danger that war might result from a Soviet attempt to break what amounts to a military blockade of Cuba is accepted. But one experienced airman expressed the general feeling this way: "War can come from any one of a number of causes,

Continued on Page 21, Column 1

Associated Press Wirephoto

ANNOUNCES HIS ACTION: President Kennedy speaking to the nation last night on radio and television. He told of moves to keep offensive equipment away from Cuba.

TRAFFIC DELAYED AT BERLIN BORDER

Reds Start Intensive Check of Civilian Trucks an Hour Before Kennedy Speech

By SYDNEY GRUSON

Special to The New York Times

BONN, Oct. 22—The East German police began to slow down civilian traffic between West Berlin and West Germany late tonight.

About an hour before President Kennedy announced the United States countermeasures against the Soviet build-up in Cuba, the police started intensive examination of the papers of trucks moving into East German territory.

The connection, if any, between the two actions was not immediately clear. Similar harassment of civilian traffic has occurred periodically over the years. The immediate reaction in West Berlin was to consider tonight's harassment as part of the regular order of things, rather than as an advance countermeasure to the American moves against Cuba.

Nevertheless, there was deep anxiety that the Soviet Union would retaliate by causing trouble on the West's access lines to the city.

The outcome of tomorrow's meetings between Andrei A. Gromyko, the Soviet Foreign Minister, and East German Communist leaders was awaited with concern. Mr. Gromyko

Continued on Page 17, Column 8

Moscow Says U.S. Holds 'Armed Fist' Over Cuba

By SEYMOUR TOPPING

Special to The New York Times

MOSCOW, Tuesday, Oct. 23—In a broadcast before President Kennedy's speech on the missile build-up in Cuba, the Moscow radio said that the unusual activity in Washington indicated that the United States "once again was raising its armed fist over Cuba." The broadcast said there was "real hysteria" in Washington.

A Soviet reply to the United States note on Cuba that was given last night to Anatoly F. Dobrynin, the Soviet Ambassador to Washington, was expected to be delivered in 24 hours. It was expected that the reply would take the form either of a diplomatic communication or a message to President Kennedy from Premier Khrushchev.

Western observers said it appeared inevitable in view of recent Soviet statements that the reply would be a denial of any offensive Soviet intent and a charge of United States aggression against Cuba.

Veracity Questioned

The veracity of the Soviet Government was directly questioned in President Kennedy's speech, which was given after delivery of the note. The President said evidence had been obtained that Moscow was constructing offensive missile bases on Cuban territory.

The Soviet Government statement of Sept. 11, which warned the United States that an attack on Cuba would mean war, contended that the Soviet weapons supplied to Cuba were of a defensive nature.

Western observers said the crisis over Cuba would enter a critical phase when and if United States war vessels sought to halt and search a Soviet ship bound for Cuba.

A number of Soviet vessels carrying civilian goods and pos-

Continued on Page 18, Column 3

All Military Forces Mobilized by Castro

By The Associated Press.

KEY WEST, Tuesday, Oct. 23 —All of Cuba's military forces have been mobilized as a result "of the news from the United States," the Havana radio said today.

The broadcast said the order was issued by Premier Fidel Castro, who will address the nation later today.

"Our combat units rapidly placed themselves on a fighting basis," said the Havana broadcast.

"Hundreds of thousands of men were mobilized in the course of a few hours," added the broadcast, which followed by some hours President Kennedy's announcement of a naval blockade against Cuba.

During the evening, Havana appeared slow to react to President Kennedy's broadcast and

Continued on Page 20 Column 5

BIG FORCE MASSES TO BLOCKADE CUBA

Armada Is Under Orders to Open Fire if Necessary— All Troops Are Alerted

By JACK RAYMOND

Special to The New York Times

WASHINGTON, Oct. 22— American ships and planes began preparing tonight to impose a blockade of Cuba. United States forces are under orders to thwart any attempt to deliver offensive weapons to Havana.

A Defense Department spokesman said that a large force of ships and planes concentrating in the Caribbean area had instructions to use force if necessary, including sinking of ships, to carry out President Kennedy's orders for a "quarantine" of Cuba.

The Pentagon said also that United States military units throughout the world, including the garrison in Berlin and the nuclear-armed Strategic Air Command, had been placed "on alert."

Dependents of servicemen at the Guantanamo Bay Naval Base in Cuba have been evacuated, the department said.

Forces at Base Doubled

It added that the military forces there, which were previously put at 3,300 naval officers and men and several hundred Marines, have been doubled.

Air defense units in the United States, particularly radar warning stations, interceptor aircraft and ground-to-air missiles, "have been redeployed," the department spokesman said.

The orders for additional defense precautions were taken the spokesman continued, on the basis of aerial photographic evidence of long-range ballistic missile bases and the arrival of Soviet Ilyushin-28 bombers in Cuba.

The spokesman displayed some of the aerial photographs and pointed to some missiles sites that, he said, had been established only in the last 10 or 15 days.

He said some of the missile

Continued on Page 20 Column 1

NEWS INDEX

PRESIDENT GRAVE

Asserts Russians Lied and Put Hemisphere in Great Danger

Text of the President's address is printed on Page 18.

By ANTHONY LEWIS

Special to The New York Times

WASHINGTON, Oct. 22 — President Kennedy imposed a naval and air "quarantine" tonight on the shipment of offensive military equipment to Cuba.

In a speech of extraordinary gravity, he told the American people that the Soviet Union, contrary to promises, was building offensive missile and bomber bases in Cuba. He said the bases could handle missiles carrying nuclear warheads up to 2,000 miles.

Thus a critical moment in the cold war was at hand tonight. The President had decided on a direct confrontation with — and challenge to — the power of the Soviet Union.

Direct Thrust at Soviet

Two aspects of the speech were notable. One was its direct thrust at the Soviet Union as the party responsible for the crisis. Mr. Kennedy treated Cuba and the Government of Premier Fidel Castro as a mere pawn in Moscow's hands and drew the issue as one with the Soviet Government.

The President, in language of unusual bluntness, accused the Soviet leaders of deliberately "false statements about their intentions in Cuba."

The other aspect of the speech particularly noted by observers here was its flat commitment by the United States to act alone against the missile threat in Cuba.

Nation Ready to Act

The President made it clear that this country would not stop short of military action to end what he called a "clandestine, reckless and provocative threat to world peace."

Mr. Kennedy said the United States was asking for an emergency meeting of the United Nations Security Council to consider a resolution for "dismantling and withdrawal of all offensive weapons in Cuba."

He said the launching of a nuclear missile from Cuba against any nation in the Western Hemisphere would be regarded as an attack by the Soviet Union against the United States. It would be met, he said, by retaliation against the Soviet Union.

He called on Premier Khrushchev to withdraw the missiles from Cuba and so "move the

Continued on Page 18, Column 1

KENNEDY CANCELS CAMPAIGN TALKS

He and Johnson Take Step to Concentrate on Crisis

By CABELL PHILLIPS

Special to The New York Times

WASHINGTON, Oct. 22—The White House announced tonight that President Kennedy and Vice President Johnson would make no further political appearances in the Congressional campaign because of the Cuban crisis.

The move by the Administration was considered evidence not only of the seriousness of the situation but also of the desire of the President to unify the country behind his blockade order and keep the issue out of partisan politics.

In this connection, the White House said the President personally informed former Republican Presidents Dwight D. Eisenhower and Herbert Hoover, as well as former Democratic President Harry S. Truman, of his decision.

And the White House announced that John J. McCloy, former disarmament adviser to the Kennedy Administration and a Republican, had been as-

Continued on Page 18, Column 7

"All the News That's Fit to Print"

The New York Times.

LATE CITY EDITION

U. S. Weather Bureau Report (Page 78) forecasts: Cloudy with chance of showers today; clear tonight. Fair, warm tomorrow. Temp. range: 80—63; yesterday: 69—58. Temp.-Hum. Index: high 60's; yesterday: 67.

VOL. CXII..No. 38,482. NEW YORK, TUESDAY, JUNE 4, 1963. TEN CENTS

POPE JOHN XXIII IS DEAD AT 81, ENDING 4½-YEAR REIGN DEVOTED TO PEACE AND CHRISTIAN UNITY

ARIZONA UPHELD OVER CALIFORNIA ON WATER RIGHTS

Supreme Court's 7-1 Ruling Caps 40-Year Fight on Use of the Colorado River

WIDE EFFECT FORESEEN

3 Justices Strongly Oppose Provision Allowing U. S. to Apportion Supplies

By WILLIAM M. BLAIR
Special to The New York Times

WASHINGTON, June 3 — Arizona won in the Supreme Court today its 40-year struggle with California over how much water each state can take from the Colorado River.

The Court, voting 7 to 1, upheld a special master's recommendations on division of the water. The decision is of great economic significance to the Southwest, for the Colorado and its tributaries are the major water sources in that rapidly growing area.

The Court split, 5 to 3, however, on the majority ruling that the Secretary of the Interior had the power to apportion mainstream water among users in the lower basin states, particularly in periods of shortage.

Oppose Federal Role

The dissenters on this issue were Justices John Marshall Harlan, William O. Douglas and Potter Stewart. They sharply challenged the majority view that Congress intended a "single appointed Federal official" to have the authority to apportion mainstream waters, whether in shortage or surplus.

They found this delegation of power "extraordinary." And they argued that state law was intended to control apportionment among users within a single state and that this principle had been established by the Court in earlier water rights cases.

The majority opinion said California was entitled to 4,400,000 acre feet of water annually from the mainstream of the Colorado, Arizona 2,800,000 acre feet and Nevada 300,000 acre feet. An acre foot is the amount of water that will cover one acre to a depth of one foot —about 325,850 gallons.

The division was confined to the area's mainstream. The Court rejected California's effort to include the Colorado's tributaries, principally the Gila in Arizona, in any water allo-

Continued on Page 23, Column 1

AGENCY SHOP WINS COURT'S APPROVAL

Ruled Permissible by U. S. Law, Optional in States

By JOSEPH A. LOFTUS
Special to The New York Times

WASHINGTON, June 3—A labor contract requiring nonmembers to pay service fees to a union is permissible under Federal law, but may be prohibited by state law, the Supreme Court ruled today.

The agency shop, as this type of contract is called, was reviewed in two decisions. There was no dissent. Associate Justice Arthur J. Goldberg did not participate.

Where the state's prohibition is enforceable—in state courts or before the National Labor Relations Board—was a question reserved for later decision. That point was set for argument in the next term.

In two other labor decisions, the Court reversed damage verdicts won by individuals against unions in the state courts of Texas and Ohio. The vote in each was 6 to 2. Justices William O. Douglas and Tom C. Clark dissented. Justice Goldberg did not participate.

The central point in all four cases was the extent of state jurisdiction in the field of labor-management relations. Under the Court's doctrine of Federal pre-emption, the states have no jurisdiction except where Congress has specifically conceded it, or where the N.L.R.B. can afford no remedy, or where there is an overriding state in-

Continued on Page 24, Column 5

Douglas Upbraids Black From Bench

Special to The New York Times

WASHINGTON, June 3 — Justice William O. Douglas made an unusually sharp attack today on a major opinion by his colleague on the Supreme Court, Hugo L. Black.

The tenor of Justice Douglas's extemporaneous remarks from the bench startled those in the courtroom. His strong language was the more surprising because the two men have served together for 24 years and have been regarded as extremely close in judicial philosophy.

Justice Douglas's dissent was in the Colorado River water case. Justice Black wrote the opinion of the court deciding generally against California's claims and in favor of Arizona's.

From the bench Justice

Continued on Page 22, Column 3

PRESIDENT DELAYS RIGHTS MESSAGE

Plans Conferences in Fight on Public Discrimination —G.O.P. Offers a Bill

By E. W. KENWORTHY
Special to The New York Times

WASHINGTON, June 3—President Kennedy decided tonight to delay for a week his civil rights message to Congress proposing legislation to outlaw discrimination in public accommodations.

He had hoped to get new legislative proposals to Congress tomorrow. He leaves on Wednesday for a Western trip and will stay out of Washington the rest of the week.

One factor in tonight's decision was that last-minute tinkering with the draft bills and the accompanying Presidential message was still going on. It was deemed wise not to rush so important a matter.

The President believed also that it would help the legislation to go ahead first with scheduled conferences. He will meet tomorrow, for example, with business executives with large holdings in the South. His brother, Attorney General Robert F. Kennedy, will meet other groups.

Democrats Briefed

The week will also be used to try to create a favorable climate at the Capitol. Democratic Congressional leaders, who were briefed on civil rights by the President today, will discuss the legislation with others in both parties.

The decision to delay the message was especially difficult for the President because 24 House Republicans introduced today their own legislation to bar racial discrimination in public accommodations. They were plainly intent on beating the Administration in offering a measure.

One of two main proposals in the Administration's legislation would deal with racial discrimi-

Continued on Page 27, Column 1

PUPIL TRANSFERS TO DIVIDE RACES VOIDED BY COURT

Supreme Bench Says Plan in Two Tennessee Areas Slows Desegregation

By ANTHONY LEWIS
Special to The New York Times

WASHINGTON, June 3 — The Supreme Court held unconstitutional today a school desegregation plan that allows pupils to transfer out of schools where their race is in the minority.

Justice Tom C. Clark said that the plan was invalid because it based transfers "solely on racial factors" and led to "perpetuation of segregation." He spoke for a unanimous Court.

The transfer plan was at issue in cases from Knoxville, Tenn., and from Davidson County, adjoining Nashville. Similar provisions are in use in Memphis and in some Virginia communities.

Five other Southern states have statutes saying that no child may be compelled to attend a school where he would be in a racial minority. They are Alabama, Arkansas, Florida, Louisiana and North Carolina.

Broad Impact Likely

Thus today's decision can be expected to have a major impact on the South. It will remove the legal basis for a device widely used to cushion the effect of school desegregation.

In practice, the Tennessee provisions — and those in other areas — worked as follows:

School boards, in response to the Supreme Court's desegregation decision, abolished the former separate school maps for whites and Negroes. New school districts were drawn for a single, nonracial system.

But any white student who thereupon found himself in the district of "a school previously serving colored students" could automatically transfer to another school. So could a Negro zoned into a school formerly serving whites.

Transfers Made Easy

The plan also, significantly, permitted automatic transfers "when a student would otherwise be required to attend a school where the majority of students of that school or in his or her grade are of a different race."

A student in such a minority situation had only to ask and he would be transferred. Others who wanted to switch schools had to persuade the school board there was "good cause."

The provision was generally regarded as a way of assuring white families that their children would not be placed in a mostly Negro school. It was defended as necessary to reduce opposition to desegregation.

Negroes, on the other hand, said the transfer provision had made true integration of the schools impossible. They especially criticized the fact that there was no automatic right of a pupil to transfer from a school entirely or mostly of his

Continued on Page 25, Column 3

DC-7 With 101 Lost in Alaska; 95 Military Men and Kin Aboard

Vast Air-Sea Hunt Pressed for Chartered Craft After Radio Contact Breaks Off

By The Associated Press

JUNEAU, Alaska, June 3—A military-chartered airliner carrying 101 persons—men, women and children — vanished off southeastern Alaska today under circumstances suggesting sudden disaster.

The Northwest Airlines DC-7, a piston-engined aircraft, last radioed 30 to 40 miles at sea off Prince of Wales Island, requesting a change of altitude from 14,000 to 18,000 feet. Air traffic men trying to reply minutes later got no answer.

The last confirmed message from the plane was at 10:06 A.M., about two and a half hours after it had left McChord Air Force Base, Wash., with 95 military passengers, including dependents, and a crew of six.

An intensive search by planes and vessels was made in deteriorating weather.

The Coast Guard said later tonight that a Canadian plane had reported sighting what appeared to be wreckage near

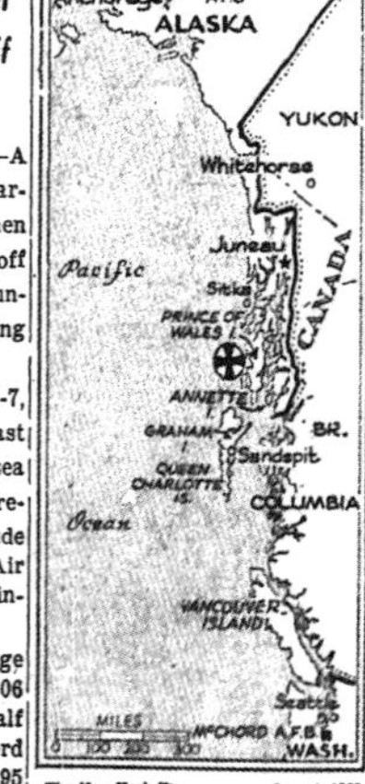

The New York Times June 4, 1963
Cross shows where plane last reported its position.

Graham Island, in northern British Columbia.

The only detailed information concerning the sighting came

Continued on Page 13, Column 1

Army May Release Ft. Tilden for Park

By CHARLES G. BENNETT

There is a "very, very good possibility" that the Army might make Fort Tilden available to the city for the Breezy Point park development, Mayor Wagner said yesterday.

"We learned last week," the Mayor said at an impromptu press conference, "that there is a good possibility that the Army might move its installations and Nike bases from there in the near future, and then we can start negotiations."

An Army spokesman said in Washington last night that the Army had been reviewing the situation but had not made any decision.

Fort Tilden is on 317 acres next to the 236-acre Jacob Riis Park. The city proposes ultimately to have in all 1,362

Continued on Page 43, Column 5

HAITIAN CONTACTS RESUMED BY U. S.

Duvalier Regime Regarded as Firmly in Power Even if Not Constitutional

By TAD SZULC
Special to The New York Times

WASHINGTON, June 3 — The United States resumed "normal diplomatic business" with Haiti today after nearly three weeks of a suspension of contacts intended to underline Washington's disapproval of President François Duvalier.

The decision to return to normal relations and to remove a Navy task force from the vicinity of Haiti appeared to reverse last month's undisguised policy efforts aimed at Dr. Duvalier's removal.

At the peak of the Haiti crisis, the Kennedy Administration is known to have convinced itself that President Duvalier's regime was on the brink of collapse because of mounting United States pressures.

It was then expected that Dr. Duvalier would voluntarily give up office and leave Haiti on May 15. The United States regarded that date as the end of his legal term.

Marine Landing Envisaged

Accordingly, the Administration secretly prepared with at least three Latin-American governments a plan that might have involved a landing in Haiti by United States marines, it has been disclosed. An inter-American "police action" in support of a new regime in Haiti was also envisaged.

The details of this planned operation were disclosed by diplomats who participated in its preparation last month.

The operation was abandoned on May 15, however, after an all-night vigil here by officials of the Organization of American States. It then became clear that Dr. Duvalier did not intend to leave Haiti.

The State Department later that day instructed Ambassador Raymond L. Thurston in Port-au-Prince to suspend immediately his contacts with the Haitian Government. The move was made secretly and the Administration confirmed it indirectly only after it was published in press dispatches from Haiti.

Regime Still Held Illegal

Today, Lincoln White, the State Department spokesman, announced that the United States chargé d'affaires in Port-au-Prince, Glion Curtis Jr., was being instructed "to resume normal diplomatic business with the Government of Haiti."

Administration officials insisted that the lifting of the short-lived diplomatic sanctions did not imply any change in the United States view that the Duvalier regime was unconstitutional. It was made clear, however, that the United States had concluded that the Haitian Government was firmly in power.

Therefore, officials said, a re

Continued on Page 6, Column 3

POST AWAITS VOTE

Archbishop of Milan a Possible Choice as New Pontiff

By PAUL HOFMANN
Special to The New York Times

ROME, June 3—Amid the drama of Pope John XXIII's final hours, Romans speculated whether his successor would be an Italian or a "foreigner."

At the same time, ecclesiastics and laymen debated whether the next Pontiff would show the conciliatory, progressive attitude of Pope John or lead the Roman Catholic Church back to a more conservative position.

An Italian prince of the church, Giovanni Battista Cardinal Montini, 65-year-old Archbishop of Milan, was widely mentioned as the leading candidate.

Cardinal Montini is regarded as a prominent representative of the "progressive" wing of the world episcopacy, which revealed its strength with the manifest encouragement of Pope John during the first session of the Ecumenical Council in the Vatican last autumn.

A Close Aide to Pius XII

As monsignor, the present Cardinal Montini was for many years a close aide to the late Pope Pius XII, Pope John's predecessor, in the Vatican Secretariat of State. The slim, ascetic-looking churchman, who is credited with a prodigious capacity for hard work, became Archbishop of Milan, one of the largest Catholic dioceses in the world, in 1954, but still was not a Cardinal when Pope Pius XII died in 1958.

The Archbishop of Milan then already had such a reputation that some commentators suggested that the Cardinals would depart from a 600-year-old tradition and elect a prelate who was not one of their number.

Instead the Cardinals elevated one of their number, Angelo Giuseppe Cardinal Roncalli, Patriarch of Venice. As Pope John XXIII he conferred on Archbishop Montini the red hat of Cardinal in his first consistory in December, 1958. Cardinal Montini was close to Pope John throughout his pontificate and if he is elected as his successor he is expected to continue his policies.

Cardinals Take Over Rule

Soon after Pope John died tonight, the Cardinals present in the Vatican started taking over the interim government of the church on behalf of the 82 members of the Sacred College of Cardinals. The Cardinals will rule jointly until their vote in conclave results in the election of the new Pope.

Prominent among conservative Italian Cardinals thought to be of papal timber is Giuseppe Cardinal Siri, Archbishop of Genoa. He is 57 years old.

The leader of the conservative wing at the Ecumenical Council, Alfredo Cardinal Ottaviani, a 72-year-old Vatican theologian and guardian of

Continued on Page 18, Column 6

Africans Complain Of Bias in Moscow

By SEYMOUR TOPPING
Special to The New York Times

MOSCOW, June 3 — A sharp controversy has arisen between Soviet authorities and African students here who have complained of discrimination fostered by a Moscow newspaper article.

The article, published by Komsomolskaya Pravda, the newspaper of the Communist Youth League, purported to tell the experiences of a Russian girl who was sold into a harem by a Moslem student she had married.

African students here interpreted the article as a warning to Russian girls against association with them. It was published on Oct. 27 after a number of Africans had complained of being attacked by Russians because they had appeared publicly in the company

Continued on Page 5, Column 1

Associated Press
POPE JOHN XXIII

Washington Mourns Loss Of Great Force for Peace

By M. S. HANDLER
Special to The New York Times

WASHINGTON, June 3—President Kennedy paid high tribute today to the statesmanship and moral leadership of Pope John XXIII. The President said of the Pontiff:

"His compassion and kindly strength have bequeathed humanity a new legacy of purpose and courage for the future."

Mr. Kennedy led official Washington in mourning the passing of Pope John as a great loss to mankind. Members of both houses of Congress and churchmen of various faiths joined in expressing the belief that the Pontiff had made an immense contribution to the reconciliation of all Christian faiths, to the reconciliation of his church with Judaism, and to the preservation of peace.

President Kennedy said the Pope had "brought compassion and understanding drawn from wide experience to the most divisive problems of a tumultuous age."

Statement by President

The President's statement said:

"The highest work of any man is to protect and carry on the deepest spiritual heritage of the race. To Pope John was given the almost unique gift of enriching and enlarging that tradition. Armed with the humility and calm which surrounded his earliest days, he brought compassion and an understanding drawn from wide experience to the most divisive problems of a tumultuous age. He was the chosen leader of world Catholicism, but his concern for the human spirit transcended all boundaries of belief or of geography.

"The ennobling precepts of his encyclicals and his actions drew on the accumulated wisdom of an ancient faith for guidance in the most complex and troublesome problems of the modern age. To him the divine spark which unites men would ultimately prove more enduring than the forces which divide. His wisdom, compassion and kindly strength have bequeathed humanity a new legacy of purpose and courage for the future."

The reference to Pope John's encyclicals marked the second time Mr. Kennedy had expressed such praise. At Boston College

Continued on Page 21, Column 7

WAGNER ORDERS FLAGS LOWERED

Leads City in Mourning and Picks 2 Representatives to Attend Pope's Funeral

Mayor Wagner yesterday ordered flags on all city buildings flown at half-staff until the burial of Pope John. The Mayor led the city in mourning the Pope.

"Pope John XXIII symbolized faith, goodness, courage and compassion," Mayor Wagner said, adding, "He appealed always to the best in the human heart and all humanity is uplifted by the noble example which he set."

Mayor Wagner also designated Commissioner of Public Events Richard C. Patterson Jr. and Thomas J. Deegan, chairman of the World's Fair executive committee, as official city representatives at the Pope's funeral.

Both are in Rome on other business.

Washington will not accord the Pope the flag tribute he will receive in New York. The State Department explained that flags in Washington are

Continued on Page 18, Column 4

St. Peter's Throng Silenced by Grief

Special to The New York Times

ROME, June 3—A vast throng in the piazza in front of St. Peter's Basilica heard the news of the death of Pope John this evening in sad and resigned silence.

Many knelt in quiet prayer and crossed themselves as other hundreds surged toward the bronze doors leading into Vatican City to watch as one of the two portals was swung shut as a traditional sign that the Pope was dead.

The Pope's death came only minutes after a choral offering brought to an end a mass celebrated for the Pontiff on the steps of the Basilica by Luigi Cardinal Traglia, pro-vicar of the Diocese of Rome.

More than 35,000 Romans, visitors, pilgrims, nuns and clergymen gathered to hear the mass, which started at 7 P.M. By the time the last sacred

Continued on Page 21, Column 2

NEWS INDEX

A LIBERAL PONTIFF

Church Council and Encyclical on Amity Marked Tenure

By ARNALDO CORTESI
Special to The New York Times

ROME, June 3 — Pope John XXIII, champion of world peace and a tireless fighter for the union of all Christian churches, died in the Vatican tonight while Cardinals and other prelates and several of his relatives prayed around his sickbed. He was 81 years old.

John XXIII was the 261st Pope to sit on the throne that was first occupied by the Apostle Peter.

In the four years, seven months and six days of his reign he conquered the hearts of people throughout the world. Few other Popes before him were so universally admired.

The Pope's death came at 7:49 P.M. (2:49 P.M. Eastern daylight time.)

After a long struggle the Pope developed peritonitis, brought on by a stomach tumor. The tumor was discovered last November.

Doctors Gave Up Hope

His doctors had given up hope at the onset of the peritonitis, an inflammation of the lining of the abdominal cavity. This was given as the cause of his death.

Much of the intervening period was passed in a state of coma or semicoma. The Pope was lucid most of yesterday, however, but in great pain, which he bore with remarkable fortitude. Early yesterday afternoon he suffered a "new crisis."

Before entering his last state of coma, he repeatedly said in Latin: "Into Thy hands, O Lord, I commit my soul."

The Pope had dedicated much of his pontificate to promoting Christian unity and the unity of all men as brothers with a common God.

Pope's Last Words

In his last words, addressed to the assembled Cardinals and prelates around his sickbed, the Pope said:

"Ut unum sint." They are Latin words meaning "That they may be one."

The words were originally spoken by Jesus after the Last Supper.

The night of May 25 the Pope suffered a hemorrhage that brought him close to death. A series of blood transfusions saved his life. He had been improving when peritonitis developed.

John XXIII was elected Pope Oct. 28, 1958. He was born in the village of Sotto il Monte in northern Italy Nov. 25, 1881. He was 81 years, six months and nine days old at his death.

Pope John passed his last days in his bedroom on the top floor of the Vatican Palace. A small crowd of ecclesiastics and laymen had congregated there when they were told that the Pope was near death.

Those at Bedside

Those around the bedside included Eugene Cardinal Tisserant, the bearded French dean of the Sacred College; Benedetto Cardinal Aloisi Masella, who as Cardinal Camerlengo, or Chamberlain, heads the interim administration of the Roman Catholic Church; the Pope's three brothers—Giuseppe, Alfredo and Zaverio Roncalli—and his widowed sister, Assunta; three nephews, several members of the Papal household, such as his sacristan, his confessor and his Master of the Chamber.

A larger crowd, including ambassadors and ministers, waited in an adjacent room.

Swiss guards kept all others out of the Papal apartment.

About 30 minutes before the Pope died it became clear from his labored breathing and his falling pulse rate that he was near death. The Pope's personal physician, Prof. Antonio Gasbarrini, warned Cardinal Aloisi Masella that the Pope had not long to live.

Mass for the Pope was said at an altar in an adjoining room

Continued on Page 18, Column 1

"All the News That's Fit to Print"

The New York Times.

LATE CITY EDITION

U. S. Weather Bureau Report (Page 38) forecasts: Sunny and cool today; fair, milder tonight. Cloudy, milder tomorrow.

Temp. Range: 46—32; yesterday: 53—37.

VOL. CXIII..No. 38,656.

NEW YORK, MONDAY, NOVEMBER 25, 1963.

TEN CENTS

PRESIDENT'S ASSASSIN SHOT TO DEATH IN JAIL CORRIDOR BY A DALLAS CITIZEN; GRIEVING THRONGS VIEW KENNEDY BIER

Associated Press Wirephoto

FAREWELL: Kneeling with her mother at John Fitzgerald Kennedy's coffin in the Capitol, Caroline touches the flag

CROWD IS HUSHED

Mourners at Capitol File Past the Coffin Far Into the Night

Texts of eulogies spoken in Washington, Page 4.

By TOM WICKER

Special to The New York Times

WASHINGTON, Monday, Nov. 25—Thousands of sorrowing Americans filed past John Fitzgerald Kennedy's bier in the Great Rotunda of the United States Capitol yesterday and early today.

Mr. Kennedy's body lay in state in the center of the vast, stone-floored chamber. Long after midnight the silent procession of mourners continued.

Some wept. All were hushed. As the two lines moved in a large circle around either side of the flag-covered coffin, almost the only sounds were the shuffle of feet and the quiet voices of policemen urging the people to "keep moving, keep moving right along."

By 2:45 A. M. today 115,000 persons had passed the bier.

Yesterday afternoon a crowd estimated at 300,000 lined Pennsylvania and Constitution Avenues to watch the passage of the caisson bearing the body of the 35th President of the United States, slain in the 47th year of his life by an assassin's bullet.

A Riderless Horse

Behind the caisson, following military tradition, came a riderless bay gelding, with a pair of military boots reversed in the silver stirrups.

The horse was Sardar, the thoroughbred that belongs to Mrs. John F. Kennedy.

Mrs. Kennedy, her two children, President and Mrs. Johnson and Mr. Kennedy's brother, Attorney General Robert F. Kennedy, rode in the first car of a 10-car procession that followed the caisson.

The procession moved at a funeral pace, to the sound of muffled drums, from the White House to Pennsylvania Avenue. It was a journey Mr. Kennedy had made formally four times.

At the Capitol, brief ceremonies of eulogy were held in the Rotunda before the admission of the waiting thousands who swarmed over the plaza and stretched in a long line up East Capitol Street.

At the conclusion of the cere-

Continued on Page 2, Column 1

World's Leaders to Attend Requiem Today in Capital

Mrs. Kennedy Will Walk Behind the Caisson to Mass at Cathedral

By JACK RAYMOND

Special to The New York Times

WASHINGTON, Nov. 24 — Mrs. John F. Kennedy, joined by world and national leaders, will walk behind the horse-drawn caisson that bears her husband's body from the White House to St. Matthew's Roman Catholic Cathedral tomorrow.

Following a requiem mass, John Fitzgerald Kennedy, the 35th President of the United States, will be escorted in a solemn state procession to Arlington National Cemetery to be buried with military honors.

The gravesite, on a beautiful grassy knoll, provides a sweeping view of the capital city and it is itself easily in view from the Memorial Bridge approach to the national burial ground.

The state funeral procession will begin at 10:30 A.M. at the Capitol, where the closed, flag-draped coffin of the President

Continued on Page 6, Column 8

Officials of Nearly 100 Lands in U.S.—They Will Meet Johnson

By MAX FRANKEL

Special to The New York Times

WASHINGTON, Nov. 24 — An emperor, a king, a queen, princes, presidents, premiers and ministers from every continent converged on Washington this evening to pay final tribute to

List of leaders expected at the funeral, Page 6.

President Kennedy and to make the acquaintance of President Johnson.

Representing nearly 100 nations, the foreign dignitaries will include the largest assembly of ruling statesmen ever gathered in the United States for any event.

Their arrival here, through the night, virtually overwhelmed an already tense and overburdened capital. Nonetheless, each visitor received the protocol deference and police protection of more normal

Continued on Page 6, Column 1

ONE BULLET FIRED

Night-Club Man Who Admired Kennedy Is Oswald's Slayer

By GLADWIN HILL

Special to The New York Times

DALLAS, Nov. 24 — President Kennedy's assassin, Lee Harvey Oswald, was fatally shot by a Dallas night-club operator today as the police started to move him from the city jail to the county jail.

The shooting occurred in the basement of the municipal building at about 11:20 A.M. central standard time (12:20 P.M. New York time).

The assailant, Jack Rubenstein, known as Jack Ruby, lunged from a cluster of newsmen observing the transfer of Oswald from the jail to an armored truck.

Millions of viewers saw the shooting on television.

As the shot rang out, a police detective suddenly recognized Ruby and exclaimed: "Jack, you son of a bitch!"

A murder charge was filed against Ruby by Assistant District Attorney William F. Alexander. Justice of the Peace Pierce McBride ordered him held without bail.

Detectives Flank Him

Oswald was arrested Friday after Mr. Kennedy was shot dead while riding through Dallas in an open car. He was charged with murdering the President and a policeman who was shot a short time later while trying to question Oswald.

As the 24-year-old prisoner, flanked by two detectives, stepped onto a basement garage ramp, Ruby thrust a .38-caliber, snub-nose revolver into Oswald's left side and fired a single shot.

The 52-year-old night-club operator, an ardent admirer of President Kennedy and his family, was described as having been distraught.

[District Attorney Henry Wade said he understood that the police were looking into the possibility that Oswald had been slain to prevent him from talking, The Associated Press reported. Mr. Wade said that so far no connection between Oswald and Ruby had been established.]

Oswald slumped to the concrete paving, wordlessly clutching his side and writhing with pain.

Oswald apparently lost con-

Continued on Page 10, Column 1

Mrs. Kennedy Leads Public Mourning

By MARJORIE HUNTER

Special to The New York Times

WASHINGTON, Nov. 24 — Mrs. John F. Kennedy, firmly holding the hands of her two children, followed the coffin bearing the body of her husband as it left the White House today for the last time.

Her eyes swollen, she moved quietly to the edge of the steps of the North Portico and paused to watch the coffin placed in the caisson by military bearers.

Her son, John Jr., tugged at her hand and pointed to a black, riderless horse, part of the ceremonial procession. She leaned down and spoke to him.

Mrs. Kennedy wore a simple black suit and black lace mantilla. John Jr., who will be 3 years old tomorrow, and Caroline, who will be 6 on Wednesday, wore similar pale blue coats, white anklets and red shoes.

As the three stood there, framed against the black-draped doorway, there was an eerie silence. It was broken only by the occasional sound of hoofs of the restless gray horses that were to pull the caisson up Pennsylvania Avenue to the Capitol.

Mrs. Kennedy was composed, but appeared to be on the verge of tears as she and the children stepped into a black limousine for the slow ride to the Capitol. In the car, too, were President and Mrs. Johnson and Attorney General Robert F. Kennedy.

Still holding the hands of her children, Mrs. Kennedy followed the flag-draped coffin into the Capitol Rotunda. She stared straight ahead as the coffin was placed on the catafalque, a simple funeral bier draped in black broadcloth.

John Jr., wide-eyed and bewildered, was restless. Clutching a tiny flag, he was led away by a military aide.

Later, after the tributes had been spoken, Mrs. Kennedy walked slowly to the coffin, touched it with her fingertips, knelt and kissed it. Caroline was by her side. They were rejoined by John Jr. at the door.

Shortly after 9 o'clock tonight Mrs. Kennedy returned to the Capitol and again kneeled before the coffin and kissed it.

Mrs. Kennedy walked into the Rotunda on the arm of her husband's brother, Robert, who stopped at the rope holding

Continued on Page 2, Column 8

JOHNSON AFFIRMS AIMS IN VIETNAM

Retains Kennedy's Policy of Aiding War on Reds—Lodge Briefs President

By E. W. KENWORTHY

Special to The New York Times

WASHINGTON, Nov. 24 — President Johnson reaffirmed today the policy objectives of his predecessor regarding South Vietnam. He called upon all Government agencies to support that policy with full unity of purpose.

This was disclosed by White House sources after a meeting between President Johnson and Henry Cabot Lodge, United States Ambassador to South Vietnam.

The meeting lasted nearly an hour. It was described as being devoted to a full review of the conclusions reached by participants in a strategy conference on South Vietnam held in Honolulu last Wednesday.

In another move today that emphasized the President's desire to convey at home and abroad the impression of continuity, Mr. Johnson asked all members of the White House staff to remain at their jobs.

This was announced by Pierre Salinger, White House press secretary.

Some Expected to Leave

Mr. Salinger said the President would leave up to the officials involved how long they wished to serve him.

Inevitably some of these officials—especially those from the universities and foundations—will decide to leave their posts after an interval.

But the President's request today would seem to insure that during the difficult days of adjustment and transition he would continue to have the benefit of the experience of key policy figures.

Attending the meeting between the President and Ambassador Lodge today were Secretary of State Dean Rusk, Secretary of Defense Robert S. McNamara, Under Secretary of State George W. Ball, John A. McCone, director of the Central Intelligence Agency, and McGeorge Bundy, special assistant to the President for national security affairs.

Secretaries Rusk and McNamara, Ambassador Lodge and Mr. Bundy all took part in the Honolulu conference.

As a result of the meeting, White House informants said, President Johnson laid down a

Continued on Page 5, Column 1

Millions of Viewers See Oswald Killing On 2 TV Networks

By JACK GOULD

The fatal shooting of Lee H. Oswald, who was held as the assassin of President Kennedy, was seen as it occurred yesday by millions of television viewers.

The National Broadcasting Company telecast the dramatic happening live. Less than a minute later the Columbia Broadcasting System telecast it by means of tape, made as the shooting occurred.

C. B. S. headquarters recorded the pictures from Dallas as they were received here over a closed circuit. Officials, upon seeing the contents of the Dallas relay, put the tape out over the network instantly.

The incident marked the first time in 15 years of television around the globe that a real-life homicide had occurred in front of live cameras. The closest parallel occurred in October, 1960, when Inejiro Asanuma, Japanese political leader, was knifed on a public stage in

Continued on Page 10, Column 8

JOHNSON SPURS OSWALD INQUIRY

President Orders F. B. I. to Check Death—Handling of Case Worries Capital

By ANTHONY LEWIS

Special to The New York Times

WASHINGTON, Nov. 24—President Johnson directed the Federal Bureau of Investigation tonight to look into "every aspect" of the murder of Lee H. Oswald.

He spoke with the director of the F.B.I., J. Edgar Hoover, and ordered the redoubled investigation.

The action came as official Washington was showing increasing concern about the entire handling of the aftermath of President Kennedy's assassination.

Officials were convinced that Oswald was the assassin. But their concern was over the public impression of the criminal proceedings.

Tonight they were consider-

Continued on Page 11, Column 3

BUSINESS OF CITY WILL HALT TODAY

Mayor Says Only Essential Services Will Be Provided

Changes in events here are listed on Page 9.

By LEONARD INGALLS

Normal public, business and social activity in the city will be almost completely suspended today out of respect for President Kennedy.

Mayor Wagner announced yesterday that the city would continue in full mourning throughout the day. Only essential city services will be maintained, he said.

"Those city employes not engaged in activities imperative to the health, safety and welfare of our citizens are to be released from duty and their offices closed through Monday," Mr. Wagner said at City Hall.

Proclamation of the day as a legal holiday by Governor Rockefeller in observance of Mr. Kennedy's funeral permits banks and other institutions to close.

Classes at schools and colleges will be suspended. Department stores and specialty shops will be shut. Securities exchanges and commodity markets will not operate. Most places of entertainment will be closed. There will be no deliveries of mail and post offices will be shut.

Special memorial services for the murdered President have been scheduled at churches and synagogues.

At St. Patrick's Cathedral

Continued on Page 9, Column 1

Pope Paul Warns That Hate and Evil Imperil Civil Order

Special to The New York Times

ROME, Nov. 24 — Pope Paul VI, alluding to the assassination of President Kennedy, said today that it showed how much "capacity for hatred and evil still remains in the world."

Without mentioning Mr. Kennedy by name, the Pontiff spoke of "the crime that has aroused in these days the deploration of the whole world." He said it illustrated "how great the threat to civil order and peace still is."

The Pope was addressing thousands of people gathered in St. Peter's Square for his usual Sunday-noon benediction.

"We cannot, at this moment of prayer together, take our thoughts from the crime that has aroused in these days the deploration of the whole world," he said.

"After dwelling upon the man who is no longer with us and after comforting those who still live in mourning and grief, our thoughts show us how much the capacity for hatred and evil yet remains in the world, how great the threat to civil order and peace still is, and how great is the need for the grace

Continued on Page 4, Column 7

NEWS INDEX

JOHNSON SCORED BY CHINESE REDS

Views Called 'Reactionary'—Taiwan Aid Attacked

By United Press International

TOKYO, Nov. 24—Communist China bitterly criticized President Johnson today and termed him a supporter of the late President Kennedy's "trickery policy."

"Since the emergence of the Kennedy regime," the Chinese Communist press agency Hsinhua said, "Johnson has positively supported various reactionary policies of the Kennedy Administration and participated in formulating and promoting such policies.

"Johnson has supported Kennedy's trickery policy and has called for the maintenance of such a policy in a series of his speeches."

The Chinese Communists reported the assassination of President Kennedy in a four-paragraph dispatch eight hours after it occurred. But they made no comment.

Hsinhua said Mr. Johnson "was one of the central figures in the Kennedy Government and has made frequent trips abroad."

The Chinese statement added that Mr. Johnson believed "the United States, in making two-faced antirevolutionary plots, must maintain a strong position on the basis of strong force."

"He also looks toward Cuba with animosity and has called for the elimination of the Cuban revolutionary Government," it

Continued on Page 7, Column 6

Copyright 1963—Dallas Times-Herald and Photographer Bob Jackson, from United Press International Telephoto

OSWALD IS SHOT: Lee Harvey Oswald cringes as Jack Ruby attacks him at Dallas jail. Policeman is J. R. Leavelle.

"All the News That's Fit to Print"

The New York Times.

LATE CITY EDITION

U.S. Weather Bureau Report (Page 95) forecasts: Snow, chance of sleet or rain today, tonight, then clearing tomorrow. Temp. Range: 37—28; yesterday: 36—23.

NEWS SUMMARY AND INDEX, PAGE 95

SECTION ONE

VOL. CXIII. No. 38,704. | © 1964 by The New York Times Company. Times Square, New York, N. Y. 10036 | NEW YORK, SUNDAY, JANUARY 12, 1964. | 40c beyond 50-mile zone from New York City, except on Long Island. 50c beyond 200-mile zone from New York City, higher in air delivery cities. | THIRTY CENTS

CIGARETTES PERIL HEALTH, U. S. REPORT CONCLUDES; 'REMEDIAL ACTION' URGED

CANCER LINK CITED

Smoking Is Also Found 'Important' Cause of Chronic Bronchitis

Committee's summary of its findings, Pages 64 and 65.

By WALTER SULLIVAN

Special to The New York Times

WASHINGTON, Jan. 11—The long-awaited Federal report on the effects of smoking found today that the use of cigarettes contributed so substantially to the American death rate that "appropriate remedial action" was called for.

The committee that made the report gave no specific recommendations for action. But health officials said that possible steps might include educational campaigns, the requirement that cigarette packages carry warnings and control of advertising.

The report dealt a severe blow to the rear-guard action fought in recent years by the tobacco industry. It dismissed, one by one, the arguments raised to question the validity of earlier studies.

Role of Smoking in Cancer

Combining the results of many surveys, the study panel found no doubt about the role of cigarette smoking in causing cancer of the lungs.

In men who smoke cigarettes, the death rate from that disease is almost 1,000 per cent higher than in nonsmokers, it said. Lung cancer has become the most frequent form of cancer in men.

Such smoking was also found to be "the most important" cause of chronic bronchitis, increasing the risk of death from that disease and from emphysema, a swelling of the lungs due to the presence of air in the connective tissues. Emphysema is a disease of increasing incidence.

As to coronary artery disease, a frequent cause of heart failure and the leading cause of death in this country, mortality is 70 per cent higher for cigarette smokers than for nonsmokers, the report said.

Relationship Assumed

The role of smoking as a cause of the disease, it said, "is not proved." However, it said, the study committee considers it "prudent" from the public health viewpoint to assume such a cause-and-effect relationship rather than wait until such a relationship has been established beyond doubt.

[The Tobacco Institute rejected the report, saying it was not the last word on smoking and health. The three major broadcasting networks said they would review their policies on tobacco advertising in the light of the report.]

The report was prepared on the initiative of President Kennedy to help the Government decide what to do about the smoking question. The committee was formed by Dr. Luther L.

Continued on Page 65, Column 6

Associated Press Wirephoto

DISCUSSES SMOKING REPORT: Dr. Luther Terry, the Surgeon General, at news conference held in Washington.

Johnson Chides the G.O.P. For Opposing His Budget

By WARREN WEAVER JR.

Special to The New York Times

WASHINGTON, Jan. 11—President Johnson made his first frankly partisan speech tonight to the first purely political group he has invited to the White House. Standing under a picture of Abraham Lincoln in the State Dining Room, the President grinned as he told members of the Democratic National Committee he could not understand why his budget had not gotten a warmer Republican reception.

"I always thought there could be nothing more satisfying to economy-minded Republicans than the reduction of the budget," he declared.

Then he quoted critical budget comments by such Republicans as Senator Thruston B. Morton of Kentucky, Governor Rockefeller of New York, Representative Charles A. Halleck of Indiana and Senator Everett McKinley Dirksen of Illinois.

Notes Arends Remark

He recalled that Representative Leslie C. Arends of Illinois had accused him of providing "something for everyone."

"He sounds kind of sorry, doesn't he?" Mr. Johnson asked, and his guests laughed.

The President quoted Senator Barry Goldwater as saying that the Johnson budget "out-Roosevelts Roosevelt, out-Kennedys Kennedy and makes Truman look like a piker."

"What finer compliment could anyone have?" Mr. Johnson inquired, and the Democratic leaders cheered.

These critical Republicans,

Continued on Page 55, Column 3

ATLANTA HOTELS DROP COLOR LINE

14 Leading Establishments Agree to Admit Negroes in Bid to Avert Protests

Special to The New York Times

ATLANTA, Jan. 11—Fourteen major Atlanta hotels and motels have publicly pledged to accept reservations regardless of race "in accordance with usual hotel practices."

Antisegregation demonstrations have appeared imminent in Atlanta. The hotels' announcement, made from the office of Mayor Ivan Allen Jr., was seen as an effort to forestall the protests.

The establishments in the agreement represent most of the city's main downtown hostelries and several on the fringes of the city. Six have been regarded as desegregated for some time. Others have been pledged to operate under the "Dallas plan," accepting some Negroes for conventions, but recently there had been word that they were quietly honoring Negro reservations.

The practices of most Atlanta hotels have been vague since last fall. The announcement today, listing the 14 participants, seemed to pin down their commitments more clearly and represented a liberalizing of policy for most.

A group of civil rights leaders, meanwhile, voted today to organize massive demonstrations against segregation in Atlanta. Immediately after the

Continued on Page 62, Column 5

SIX-PHASE INQUIRY ON ASSASSINATION CHARTED BY PANEL

Aides Chosen for Detailed Study of Kennedy Slaying and Security Agencies

By ANTHONY LEWIS

Special to The New York Times

WASHINGTON, Jan. 11—The staff of the commission investigating President Kennedy's assassination has divided its job into six broad areas of inquiry.

One covers every detail of Lee Oswald's activities on the day of the assassination, Nov. 22. Oswald was charged with the crime.

A second topic is the life and background of Oswald—an attempt to reconstruct his associations and ideas and psychology.

Oswald's career in the Marine Corps and his stay in the Soviet Union will be handled separately as a third.

His murder in the Dallas police station will be the fourth subject, including all the controversial questions of how it was allowed to happen.

Fifth will be the story of Jack Ruby, the nightclub operator who slipped into the police station and shot Oswald. This will be a particularly delicate subject because of possible conflict with Ruby's trial.

Study of Agencies

Finally, the staff will inquire exhaustively into the procedures used to protect President Kennedy. This will involve a scrutiny of the performances of the Secret Service, the Federal Bureau of Investigation and the Dallas police, as well as the influence, if any, of hate movements in the Dallas community.

The commission's counsel, J. Lee Rankin, outlined the plan in an interview.

He said it was clear to him now that the job could not be done in a matter of weeks, but he still hoped the inquiry could be finished three to six months from now. He recognized the importance of not letting it drag on.

"The commission realizes that the country wants to be sure of the facts," Mr. Rankin said. "The first thing is to do the job right. The second is to do it as quickly as possible."

New Name to Be Added

A senior lawyer assisted by a younger man will handle each of the six inquiry subjects. Mr. Rankin himself will have charge of one topic, and a group of distinguished lawyers from around the country has been gathered for the other senior posts.

The commission announced four of these senior appointments today, and a fifth is expected to follow shortly. The four named today, all men in active practice, are:

Francis W. H. Adams of New York, 59 years old. He was Police Commissioner in New York City in 1954-55.

Joseph A. Ball of Los Angeles, 61 years old, a leading criminal lawyer, a member of the Supreme Court's Advisory Committee on the Federal Rules

Continued on Page 46, Column 3

U.S. AND PANAMA AGREE TO CLEAR BORDERS IN STEP TO EASE TENSION; PLEDGE ON FLAG ISSUE IS OFFERED

Associated Press Wirephoto

FUNERAL PROCESSION IN PANAMA CITY: Thousands following the coffin yesterday bearing the body of a Panamanian student killed in Thursday's rioting near Canal Zone.

TROOPS CURB RIOTS

Chiari's Regime Finds Reds Infiltrating—Arms Search On

By HENRY RAYMONT

Special to The New York Times

PANAMA, Sunday, Jan. 12—The United States and Panama have agreed to take practical steps to ease the tensions along the borders of the Canal Zone.

After consultations with Assistant Secretary of State Thomas C. Mann and Secretary of the Army Cyrus R. Vance, the Canal Zone authorities agreed last night to remove troops that had been stationed along the border since the outbreak of violence Thursday.

For its part, the Panamanian National Guard undertook to clear its side of the border of snipers and those suspected of planning to provoke incidents.

In addition, the United States, in a conciliatory gesture, promised to make sure that the flags of both nations would henceforth fly side by side in the Canal Zone.

Link to Castro Alleged

The Government of President Roberto F. Chiari charged that the demonstrations had been infiltrated by Communists and supporters of Premier Fidel Castro of Cuba. It was stressed, however, that the majority of the demonstrators were engaged in a "purely civic movement."

During the night, cars in the city were being stopped and searched for arms.

Late last night, fighting between jeering Panamanians and United States soldiers with fixed bayonets erupted again on the Canal Zone border. Rioters stormed the barricade at the Tivoli guest house, and were forced back by the soldiers.

Bands Roam City

Bands of youth roamed the city, screaming anti-American slogans and hurling bottles and other missiles toward the border. One group praised President Chiari in the same slogans used by Castro sympathizers.

The pledges to ease the tensions were made at all-day meetings among Panamanian officials, the high-level United States mission, and the Inter-American Peace Committee, representing the Organization of American States.

The three-way talks began yesterday morning after the O.A.S. group arrived from Washington and moved to conciliate the deepening United States-Panamanian crisis.

The United States and Panama each named a permanent

Continued on Page 25, Column 1

MORRISON BEATEN IN LOUISIANA VOTE

Former Diplomat Loses to McKeithen in Democratic Gubernatorial Primary

By CLAUDE SITTON

Special to The New York Times

NEW ORLEANS, Jan. 11—John J. McKeithen, a militant segregationist, today won the Democratic gubernatorial nomination in Louisiana and almost certain election by upsetting deLesseps S. Morrison.

Unofficial returns from 2,187 of the state's 2,219 precincts showed these totals:

McKeithen 484,179
Morrison 437,994

The victory of the rural northern Louisiana lawyer may spell trouble in this state for the Democratic Presidential nominee in the November election, even if, as expected, it is President Johnson. Mr. McKeithen has refused to commit himself to support the party's choice.

Scattered rains that cut the turnout of voters in the populous southern section, a Morrison stronghold, helped to account for the margin for Mr. McKeithen, 45-year-old State Public Service Commissioner.

Far more important, however,

Continued on Page 59, Column 3

Long Panama Negotiation Expected by Washington

By TAD SZULC

Special to The New York Times

WASHINGTON, Jan. 11—The United States searched today for steps that it hoped could lead to a mutually acceptable political solution of the Panama crisis. But the Administration was aware that, in the highly charged emotional atmosphere of Panama, it might be difficult for the Government of President Roberto F. Chiari to enter immediately into what is considered here a reasonable basis for negotiations on the fundamental issues.

The United States, therefore, was preparing for what may be a prolonged and complicated negotiating process that may have to be conducted in part without formal diplomatic relations. Diplomatic ties were broken by Panama yesterday.

Mann Reports to Johnson

President Johnson received a written report from Thomas C. Mann, Assistant Secretary of State for Inter-American Affairs, who flew to Panama yesterday at the head of a high-level United States mission to try to resolve the crisis.

The crisis developed Thursday night in a battle between Panamanian and United States forces on the border of the Canal Zone, culminating a dispute over the flying of the Panamanian flag.

The report covered mainly Mr. Mann's 90-minute meeting last night with President Chiari. It is understood that Mr. Mann limited himself for the most part to listening to the Panamanian President's exposition of the situation.

The White House said later that, on the basis of the first report and of a telephone con-

Continued on Page 25, Column 3

SENATORS SCORE BALL'S AID PLAN

2 Democratic Chiefs Oppose State Department Control Urged by Rusk Aide

By FELIX BELAIR Jr.

Special to The New York Times

WASHINGTON, Jan. 11—Senate Democratic leaders rejected today a proposal that the State Department take over direction and control of the foreign aid program in place of the Agency for International Development.

The proposal, submitted by Under Secretary of State George W. Ball, was sharply criticized by the Senate majority leader, Mike Mansfield of Montana, and the assistant majority leader, Hubert H. Humphrey of Minnesota.

They said that President Johnson's interdepartmental committee now studying the aid program was "wasting its time" if it was seriously considering turning over A.I.D. to the State Department or scattering its functions among six or seven other departments and agencies.

"I can think of nothing that would foul up the foreign aid program more completely and effectively than to turn it over to a bunch of Foreign Service officers." Senator Humphrey declared.

'Scramble and Hide'

"And the 'scatteration' scheme," he continued, "is nothing more than a transparent attempt to scramble and hide the aid appropriation by breaking it down into its components and assigning a part of it to various agency budgets. It would only mean that the Senate and House Appropriations Committees would have to unscramble the items and put them back together in a single money bill again."

President Johnson has given the study group, which is headed by Mr. Ball, until next Wednesday to make recommendations for overhauling the aid program.

In his instructions to the eight-member panel, the President stressed the criterion of Congressional acceptance. For this reason, the position of the Senate Democratic leadership was viewed as spiking any

Continued on Page 31, Column 3

Mrs. Johnson Cheered in 'Poverty Pocket' Coal Towns

United Press International Telephoto

Mrs. Lyndon B. Johnson greets youngster who turned out to welcome her to Wilkes-Barre

By NAN ROBERTSON

Special to The New York Times

WILKES-BARRE, Pa., Jan. 11—Mrs. Lyndon B. Johnson visited today one of the "pockets of poverty" that President Johnson has declared war on—the Wilkes-Barre and Scranton area of Pennsylvania. It is part of that impoverished 10-state strip known as Appalachia. Here, in the anthracite mine area, the jobless rate is nearly double the nation's average. On the way from Washington, Mrs. Johnson was briefed on the region, its problems and some of the solutions that have been found by two Pennsylvania Representatives. They were Daniel

Continued on Page 42, Column 4

City Democrats to Restore Clubs As Job Centers for Minorities

By LEONARD INGALLS

The Democratic party in New York County is moving on a broad scale to restore to its neighborhood clubhouses some of their functions of the past in helping people find jobs and better housing.

Edward N. Costikyan, the Democratic county leader, has proposed that the county organization embark on such a program that also would include a special effort to improve public education in Harlem.

He has recommended to the county executive committee, made up of district leaders, that the party's 300,000 enrolled members and 35 district clubs in Manhattan be enlisted in an intensive effort to obtain pledges of nondiscrimination and to help members of minority groups find work.

He proposed that every Democratic district club solicit every Democrat and local businesses, labor unions and institutions like hospitals to obtain pledges that they would hire any person who met the qualifications for a job.

They also would be asked to agree to advise the Democratic county organization of vacancies and job qualifications. A full-time employment expert would be kept at Democratic county headquarters in the Chatham Hotel, 33 East 48th Street.

In submitting his proposals recently, Mr. Costikyan noted that many enrolled Democrats in Manhattan owned their own businesses and that others played key roles in labor unions. The committee is scheduled to

Continued on Page 32, Column 4

West Berlin Offered Emergency Passes

By United Press International

BERLIN, Jan. 11—East Germany has offered to permit West Berliners through the Communist-built wall to visit relatives in East Berlin in certain hardship cases, it was disclosed today.

The offer was made public as the East German Communist leader, Walter Ulbricht, returned from a two-day visit to Moscow and meetings with Premier Khrushchev.

West Berlin officials said that they were convinced that Mr. Ulbricht and Mr. Khrushchev had conferred on plans to revive the system of passes through the wall as a wedge to gain recognition for East Germany.

Under the terms of the hardship plan, passes would be issued to West Berliners in the event of the death or sickness

Continued on Page 9, Column 3

Today's Sections

Index to Subjects

"All the News That's Fit to Print"

The New York Times.

LATE CITY EDITION

U. S. Weather Bureau Report (Page 52) forecasts:
Mostly sunny today; fair tonight.
Partly cloudy, milder tomorrow.
Temp. Range: 40—25; yesterday: 36—27.

VOL. CXIII .·. No. 38,740. · © 1964 by The New York Times Company. Times Square, New York, N. Y. 10036 · NEW YORK, MONDAY, FEBRUARY 17, 1964. · TEN CENTS

CONGRESS EXPECTS ACCORD THIS WEEK ON TAX CUT BILL

Conferees Will Meet Today to Tackle the Remaining Conflicts Over Measure

HOUSING HEARING OPENS

Weaver to Explain Program to House Panel—College Proposal Up Thursday

By JOHN D. MORRIS
Special to The New York Times

WASHINGTON, Feb. 16—Quick agreement on the final version of the Administration's tax-reduction bill is expected this week as Congress resumes work after a six-day pause for Lincoln's Birthday.

Other major scheduled business includes the opening of hearings on housing and college student aid—programs that were submitted by President Johnson for action this session.

In addition, advocates of a strong manned-bomber force will again carry their fight to the House floor in debate on a $16.9 billion military procurement and research bill.

The tax bill, as passed by the Senate Feb. 7, provides $11.6 billion in annual tax relief for individuals and corporations through rate reductions coupled with structural revisions of the Revenue Code.

Conference Meets Today

The version passed by the House last September called for a net cut of slightly less than $11.1 billion.

A Senate-House conference committee meets tomorrow with the expectation of settling all differences in two or three days. Additional time will be required for staff work, however, and it is uncertain whether the final text will be ready for House and Senate approval before next week.

In any event the bill almost certainly will reach Mr. Johnson's desk for his prompt signature within 10 days or two weeks.

A lower income-tax withholding rate under such a schedule would go into effect early in March. The conference committee has already agreed on a provision for reduction of the 18 per cent withholding rate to 14 per cent, effective a week after the President signs the bill.

Two major issues face the conferees as they resume negotiations.

One involves a House-approved section, deleted by the Senate, for a $260 million cut in capital-gains taxes. Present indications are that the House

Continued on Page 11, Column 1

SEA UNIONS RESIST U.S. ON WHEAT BAN

Will Cease Loading Soviet Grain Today, Despite Pleas

By DAMON STETSON
Special to The New York Times

BAL HARBOUR, Fla., Feb. 16—The International Longshoremen's Association went ahead today with plans to stop loading wheat for shipment to the Soviet Union tomorrow despite urgent appeals from Washington.

There were indications that the longshoremen might be willing to relax their prohibition if given assurances that at least 50 per cent of the wheat shipments would be carried in United States vessels.

However, neither Thomas Gleason, president of the I.L.A., nor Paul Hall, head of the Maritime Trades Department of the American Federation of Labor and Congress of Industrial Organizations, seemed to be in a mood to accept such assurances without iron-clad guarantees that they would be enforced.

Mr. Gleason said the longshoremen had opposed the wheat deal in the first place and had agreed last fall to load ships only at the urging of President Kennedy.

But he contended that the Administration had "reneged" on an agreement to ship half of the grain in vessels of the Unit-

Continued on Page 52, Column 7

Roy Cohn Says U.S. Intercepts Mail

INDEFINITE — UNTIL CANCELED

POST OFFICE DEPARTMENT
ORDERS TO BOX SECTION OR OTHER SPECIAL ORDERS

DATE OF ORDER	NAME OF PERSON OR FIRM	OLD ADDRESS (or present street address)	NEW POST OFFICE BOX ADDRESS OR SPECIAL INSTRUCTIONS
3-29-63	THOMAS & MARIE BOLAN	238-07 121 AVE	CONFIDENTIAL — SUBMIT ALL FIRSTCLASS MAIL TO SUPERVISOR. DO NOT REVEAL THIS TO ADDRESSEE OR OTHER UNAUTHORIZED PERSON.

POD Form 3986 Aug. 1958

Exhibit that was attached to papers submitted to Federal Court last week by Roy M. Cohn

By EDWARD RANZAL

Roy M. Cohn has asked for dismissal of a perjury indictment against him on the ground that the Government has been intercepting his mail and that of his lawyer for almost a year.

A copy of a purported special Post Office Department order for the interception of mail addressed to the home of Thomas A. Bolan, Mr. Cohn's lawyer, was attached to papers submitted to Federal Judge Archie O. Dawson last week in connection with the dismissal request.

Mr. Bolan, who is a member of Mr. Cohn's law firm of Saxe, Bacon & O'Shea, lives in Cambria Heights, Queens.

Judge Dawson ordered the Government to show cause on Feb. 28 why the indictment should not be dismissed. The court order also directs the Government to show cause why any evidence obtained as a result of the alleged interception should not be suppressed, and directs that any interceptions cease immediately.

Judge Dawson, who is in charge of all aspects of the perjury case, has scheduled the trial for March 16.

Mr. Cohn, former chief counsel to the Senate committee under the late Senator Joseph R. McCarthy, and another lawyer, Murray E. Gottesman, have been charged with lying before a grand jury investigating the United Dye and Chemical Corporation stock swindle.

The defendants also are charged with conspiring to obstruct justice by attempting to prevent indictments in the case against four men.

On the purported Post Office Department order is the heading, "Orders to Box Section or Other Special Orders." Printed in pen or pencil are the words "indefinite—until canceled."

The document pertaining to Mr. Bolan is dated March 29, 1963, and states:

"Confidential: Submit all first-class mail to supervisor. Do not reveal this to addressee

Continued on Page 10, Column 6

Alabama Compiling Files On Civil Rights Advocates

By CLAUDE SITTON
Special to The New York Times

MONTGOMERY, Ala., Feb. 14—An intelligence network of state agencies and officials is amassing information on civil rights advocates and others at the direction of Gov. George C. Wallace. Its components, which generally have only informal ties with one another, sometimes work openly.

Far more frequently however, their activities and the results are secret.

Their interest extends beyond Alabamians. They have given considerable attention to Negro leaders, Justice Department officials, newsmen and others who have come into the state during racial crises.

Intimidation Seen

In this racial aspect the operation is similar to those found in Mississippi and Louisiana. But in terms of over-all scope and amount of activity the intelligence network seems to be unparalleled in this country.

State officials say that the information being obtained will not be misused to bring pressure, political or otherwise, on anyone.

Nevertheless, the investigations alone have served as a means of intimidation in some cases. And after one such inquiry a Negro student was expelled from the University of Alabama after having won admission under a Federal court order.

Governor Wallace controls all the agencies involved, either di-

Continued on Page 16, Column 1

MARCH IS PLANNED BY PUERTO RICANS

50 Leaders Schedule Protest for March 1 at City Hall to Seek Equal Schools

Puerto Rican organizations agreed yesterday to stage a silent march on City Hall on March 1 to dramatize their demands for equal educational opportunities in all of the city's schools.

A spokesman for the organizations said that the plan was for the marchers to assemble at 3 P.M. the day of the march in the vicinity of Varick and Canal Streets.

He said that invitations would be extended not only to Puerto Ricans but also to all Spanish-speaking residents of New York City.

The organizations made plans for the march at a meeting held at the La Ronda Cafe, 2689 Broadway, near 103d Street. About 50 leaders of the major Puerto Rican organizations here attended.

Gilberto Valentin, executive secretary for the National Association for Puerto Rican Civil Rights, was named president of the parade committee. He said that the proposed second school boycott was not discussed at the meeting.

"We went along with the first boycott because we felt it was a good method of highlighting the discrimination," he said. "We haven't decided on the second."

The Puerto Rican leaders said

Continued on Page 22, Column 1

17 Gershwin Songs Are to Be Released

By MURRAY SCHUMACH
Special to The New York Times

HOLLYWOOD, Feb. 16—Seventeen unpublished compositions by George Gershwin, who died in 1937, are to be made public by his brother, Ira.

Perhaps more important than the Gershwin music that is now being made available is the fact that there is a much larger storehouse of Gershwin compositions in the composer's notebooks, which date back to 1920.

Fourteen of the pieces have been sent to George Balanchine by André Kostelanetz, the conductor, with the permission of the composer's brother, who wrote the lyrics for most of the Gershwin songs in Hollywood and on Broadway. Three others will be used in a film.

Mr. Kostelanetz has asked the

Continued on Page 26, Column 4

GOLDWATER SAYS HE HAS 450 VOTES

Finds 125 More 'Practically Sure'—655 Are Needed for G.O.P. Nomination

Special to The New York Times

CHICAGO, Feb. 16—Senator Barry Goldwater today claimed 450 "sure" votes for the Presidential nomination at the Republican National Convention in July, plus 125 more "practically sure" votes.

The total, he said, does not include votes he hopes to win in primary elections in California, New Hampshire and Oregon.

To win the nomination, 655 votes are needed.

Mr. Goldwater also said that he did not believe any candidate could be nominated without winning the California primary, which will be held on June 2. It is the last primary in the nation and the largest, with its prize of 86 convention votes.

This is the first time Mr. Goldwater has said his nomination would be impossible if he lost in California. His only opponent there is Governor Rockefeller of New York.

The Senator declared that he also planned to fight for delegates in New York. He is known to feel privately that he has a chance to pick up as many as 22 of the state's 92 votes if he challenges Mr. Rockefeller there, an estimate considered very high by most observers.

Mr. Goldwater did not docu-

Continued on Page 19, Column 3

PANAMA INQUIRY SAID TO DISPUTE U.S. CONTENTIONS

Reported to Find Excessive Shooting During Rioting and Little Red Influence

Special to The New York Times

WASHINGTON, Feb. 16—An investigating committee of the Organization of American States was reported today to have found that Communist influence in last month's anti-United States riots in Panama was minimal.

It also found, after a week-long inquiry, that the firepower used by United States troops to keep Panamanian mobs from penetrating the Canal Zone was "disproportionate" to the threat posed to the security of the United States-occupied territory.

The five-nation committee also decided that the action of the United States forces, even if deemed excessive, did not justify Panama's charges of aggression.

Committee in Panama

The committee, still in Panama, was appointed by the Council of the inter-American organization to look into Panama's charges and to seek conciliation in the dispute.

[The head of the fact-finding group said in Panama that a formula for peace in the dispute would probably be presented to both sides Monday.]

A confidential account of the committee's investigation was received by Latin-American diplomats here over the weekend.

It conflicted on two basic points with the position taken by the United States. These were that "Castro Communist" agents trained in Cuba played a preponderant role in inciting the riots and that United States troops had acted with great discipline and restraint during the riots of Jan. 9 and 10. The disorders stemmed from a dispute over the flying of United States and Panamanian flags in the Canal Zone.

Sanctions Ruled Out

These differences were not considered, however, as giving validity to Panama's charges that the United States had turned the incidents into a "deliberate armed aggression."

It is understood, therefore, that the committee in its final report to the Council will declare that there is no ground to invoke any of the sanctions provided by the Rio de Janeiro Treaty of Reciprocal Assistance, under which the inquiry is being carried out.

Instead the investigating team will now concentrate on finding some formula acceptable to the two sides so that they can resume normal diplomatic relations and seek to remove the irritants that led to the trouble.

In reviewing the causes of the clashes, which left 24 persons dead and several hundred wounded, the committee will

Continued on Page 9, Column 1

4 Beatles and How They Grew

Publicitywise

By McCANDLISH PHILLIPS

The Beatles will fly back to England late this week, having accomplished exactly what they set out to do: stir up such a whirlwind in America as to heap tinder on the enormous bonfire they have lit in Britain.

The small British cultural expedition is now resting at Miami Beach, limp from adulation.

The Beatles are undisputed titans of American popular music, a high-yield, low-security occupation. Their fame has swept two continents, and they may yet become the vocal scourge of the whole Western world.

They and their attendant frenzy, Beatlemania, did not just happen. They were brought to their present pre-eminence in latter-day vaudeville by artful contrivance.

That is not the whole explanation. The world is full of promotional wizards who would do as well, if they could. However, if an act can be manipulated to a certain vogue, all the engines of publicity can then rush to its disposal.

That is what happened here. The Beatles could not have done what they did in America had they not done what they first did in Britain. There are so many acts here in the Rock

Continued on Page 20, Column 3

Moneywise

By MARTIN ARNOLD

Beatleggers are trying to grab a large share of the Beatle merchandising boom.

Paul G. Marshall, the group's American lawyer, said yesterday that he was investigating at least 60 cases of the use of the Beatle name without Beatle approval. Such Beatleware as shirts, hats, slacks, pajamas and wigs are involved.

Mr. Marshall said that on Saturday he obtained a State Supreme Court preliminary injunction stopping a Brooklyn company from manufacturing shirts with the name Beetles—as in bugs—stamped on front.

He also said that he was asking the New York District Attorney to investigate at least two cases of the criminal piracy of the Beatle name. Similar investigations are under way in California, Pennsylvania and Rhode Island, he said.

Nicky Byrne, president of Seltaeb (Beatles spelled backward), Inc., the Beatles' licensing agent, has predicted that Americans will spend about $50 million on Beatle products in 1964. He said yesterday that he hoped to have a Beatle motorscooter, manufactured in Europe, on the market in the United States soon.

A Beatlemobile (for adults)

Continued on Page 20, Column 3

Peoplewise

By JOHN A. OSMUNDSEN

Even before they return as promised to their native England, they have set minds across the United States to wondering what the uproar was all about.

They—the Beatles, of course—were seen and heard by, and conquered, millions of Americans.

How, people are asking, could four mop-headed, neo-Edwardian-attired, Liverpudlian-accented, guitar-playing, drum-beating, "little boys" from across the ocean come here and attract the immense amount of attention they did by stomping and hollering out songs in a musical idiom that is distinctly American?

Ask a typical Beatle fan—female, in her early teens—and she will say it is because:

"They're so keee-ooot."

Or because:

"They're different! They're just so different!"

Adults, some but not all of whom view the Beatles somewhat cynically, are likely to say that the craze sprang from the high-powered promotion that the performers received before their arrival and throughout their stay.

Social scientists agree with both the adult and teen-age views but note that, no matter

Continued on Page 20, Column 7

Papandreou Party Wins in Greece

United Press International Radiophoto

George Papandreou, leader of Center Union party, as he voted yesterday in Athens during Greek national election.

By DAVID BINDER
Special to The New York Times

ATHENS, Monday, Feb. 17—George Papandreou's Center Union party won an overwhelming victory in the national election yesterday. With about 90 per cent of the ballots counted, the Center Union had 2,260,052 votes against 1,415,884 for the conservative party, the National Radical Union. The pro-Communist United Democratic Left party, which backed the Center Union in 24 of 55 districts, had 499,611. Panayotis Canellopoulos, National Radical Union leader, said in a statement conceding defeat that his

Continued on Page 4, Column 4

3 Americans Die in Blast At Saigon Movie Theater

By PETER GROSE
Special to The New York Times

SAIGON, South Vietnam, Monday, Feb. 17—A terrorist bomb exploded in the lobby of a movie theater of the American community here last night. Three Americans were killed and at least 50 were injured.

Confusion and indignation spread among American residents of the capital as investigators studied the bold attack, the second bombing in a week apparently directed against American servicemen and dependents.

A week ago tonight a bomb exploded under the grandstand at an American softball park, killing two servicemen and injuring 23 other Americans.

Added Protection Sought

The United States chargé d'affaires, David Ness, scheduled an urgent meeting with the South Vietnamese Premier, Maj. Gen. Nguyen Khanh, later today. They will "discuss the security measures to be taken to offer the American community maximum protection," the United States Embassy said.

One of the dead in the theater blast was unidentified. The two others, one a marine captain and the other a military policeman, had been standing in the lobby.

A spokesman said there was some evidence that the policeman had died of a shot in the neck. Some witnesses reported that he was shot as the bomb was planted, but witnesses' versions were confused and could not be officially confirmed.

An unspecified number of women and children were injured, the embassy said. Most were treated at a hospital for superficial wounds and released. Seven persons, six

Continued on Page 5, Column 1

Churchmen Uphold Right to Be Atheist

By HENRY TANNER
Special to The New York Times

MOSCOW, Feb. 16 — The Executive Committee of the World Council of Churches, meeting in Odessa, has approved the principle that every man must have a legal right either to believe in religion or to be an atheist.

The Rev. Dr. O. Frederic Nolde of New York announced the committee's view at a news conference he held jointly here tonight with other members of the Executive Committee. Dr. Nolde is chairman of the Council's International Affairs Commission.

The Rev. Dr. W. A. Visser 't Hooft of the Netherlands, secretary general of the Council, and Dr. Franklin Clark Fry,

Continued on Page 2, Column 4

ETHIOPIA CHARGES TRUCE IS BROKEN

Says Somali Troops Attack Three Points at Frontier—Addis Ababa Accused

Special to The New York Times

ADDIS ABABA, Ethiopia, Feb. 16 — Ethiopia charged tonight that troops from Somalia attacked the Ethiopian border towns of Dolo and Yet two hours after a cease-fire became effective at noon today.

[Somalia charged that Ethiopian troops had penetrated Somali territory at 12 places, The Associated Press reported from Mogadiscio.]

The Ethiopian report said Somali attempts to occupy Dolo had been repulsed. Later another Ethiopian town, Ferfer, was shelled, it was reported.

Foreign Minister Ato Ketema Yifru described the attacks as a deliberate and serious breach of the cease-fire agreement. Ethiopia is informing the Organization of African Unity and U Thant, Secretary General of the United Nations.

The truce was called for by the Council of Ministers of the African group on Friday. Acceptance by both Somalia and Ethiopia was announced yesterday.

Artillery Fire Reported

ADDIS ABABA, Feb. 16 (AP)—The Ethiopian Information Ministry said today that Somali troops had attacked the towns of Dolo and Yet under cover of artillery fire.

A Somali attack yesterday, before the cease-fire went into effect, was repulsed with heavy losses, a ministry spokesman asserted.

The Somali radio in a countercharge said that Ethiopian shelling had killed three Somali civilians and destroyed half the village.

"The Ethiopians went all-out to wreak the maximum damage

Continued on Page 8, Column 5

NEWS INDEX

U.S. AND BRITAIN DRAFT NEW PLANS FOR CYPRUS PEACE

Ball and Officials in London Agree to Isolate Makarios With Diplomatic Effort

RESOLUTION PREPARED

U.N. Will Be Asked to Back International Patrol Force and Neutral Mediator

By LAWRENCE FELLOWS
Special to The New York Times

LONDON, Feb. 16 — The lines of a two-pronged approach to the Cyprus problem by London and Washington emerged today from talks between British officials and the American Under Secretary of State, George W. Ball.

First, according to diplomatic sources, there will be an effort to achieve, as completely as possible, the diplomatic isolation of Archbishop Makarios, the Cypriote President.

The second objective, taking shape on the horizon, is an attempt to end the island's communal fighting by administrative partition between the Greek and Turkish Cypriote factions, these sources said.

Britain Drafts Resolution

The first diplomatic step was taken last night when Britain, with the support of the United States, called for an early meeting of the United Nations Security Council "to consider the urgent problems raised by the deterioration of security in Cyprus."

Tonight final touches were put on a resolution that Britain plans to introduce in the Security Council tomorrow. It calls for a mandate to establish a peace-keeping force in Cyprus, and for the appointment of a neutral mediator to settle the quarrel between the communities.

[In Nicosia, President Makarios addressed Cyprus by radio for the first time since the fighting erupted Christmas week. He said internal anarchy and foreign intervention posed grave threats.]

Ball Voices Gratitude

Mr. Ball left for New York today after conferring with Foreign Secretary R. A. Butler. On his departure, he stressed that Washington and London were in complete accord on the Cyprus question.

The Under Secretary also praised the British troops who have been guarding the tenuous peace in Cyprus.

As he spoke, the Ministry of Defense prepared to establish intermediate military headquarters in several parts of Cyprus to permit quicker responses to local outbreaks of violence.

A further squadron of Life Guards prepared to leave for Cyprus to build up the force trained and equipped to use armored patrol cars.

In planning the Security Council action, London aimed to block an attempt by Archbishop Makarios to bring about a vote on a resolution of his own, which the United States and Britain regard as dangerous on several counts.

Within a few days Washington and London hope to move toward persuading the Greek and Turkish Governments to support a compromise solution

Continued on Page 3, Column 1

Soviet Family Law To Protect Children

By THEODORE SHABAD
Special to The New York Times

MOSCOW, Feb. 16—A Soviet law being drafted on marriage and the family will make an unmarried father responsible for his children.

The new legislation, to be published shortly, will also simplify present complicated and expensive divorce proceedings without returning to the "postcard" divorces of the early Soviet period—so called because either spouse could divorce the other simply by mailing a notice to the Bureau of Vital Statistics.

Details of a reform of the family law, long in preparation, were disclosed today by Olga P. Kolchina, a member of the Bills Committee of the

Continued on Page 2, Column 3

"All the News That's Fit to Print"

The New York Times.

LATE CITY EDITION

U. S. Weather Bureau Report (Page 52) forecasts: Fair and hot today and tomorrow. Chance of late showers each day.

Temp. Range: 91—71; yesterday: 80—65. Temp.-Hum. Index: 80 to 85; yesterday: 74.

VOL. CXIII . No. 38,864. NEW YORK, SATURDAY, JUNE 20, 1964. TEN CENTS

CIVIL RIGHTS BILL PASSED, 73-27; JOHNSON URGES ALL TO COMPLY; DIRKSEN BERATES GOLDWATER

U.S. STRESSING IT WOULD FIGHT TO DEFEND ASIA

WARNING TO REDS

Commitment to Laos and South Vietnam Called Unlimited

By MAX FRANKEL

Special to The New York Times

WASHINGTON, June 19—The Administration is saying more emphatically each day that North Vietnam and its closest ally, Communist China, must leave their neighbors alone or face a war with the United States.

In the minds of officials here the United States commitment to the security of Southeast Asia is now unlimited and comparable with the commitment to West Berlin.

In diplomatic terms this means the officials find themselves unable to negotiate with anything except the threat of force to persuade the Asian Communists to stop the efforts to "liberate" South Vietnam and Laos.

Thus far, the Administration is not sure that the Asian Communists have accurately interpreted the warning signals from Washington. It is not sure that its allies in Europe appreciate the gravity of the United States commitment. And it is not sure that the American people understand the reasons for it.

Decision Publicized

Accordingly, the word is being passed with increasing vigor to the Congress, to the Washington press corps and to the Western allies.

These official assertions suggest that the decision to deny Southeast Asia to Communism was, in effect, taken a long time ago through circumstance and a cumulative series of lesser decisions.

The view that Laos can somehow be handled separately from South Vietnam has been abandoned. The earlier emphasis on limited involvement in South Vietnam's guerrilla war has been replaced by unlimited pledges of support for the whole region.

The hope here is that Hanoi and Peking are alert to this hardening of attitudes and that they have been properly forewarned by the less direct as well as public utterances of Administration leaders and, particularly, by the recent involvement of United States military planes in Laos.

Compromise Doubted

The subtleties of the situation have made the Administration reticent to discuss future military moves beyond hints that every violation of past agreements in Southeast Asia and every change in the forms of contest will draw a firm response.

All the comments here stress that the choice between war and peace lies in the hands of the Asian Communists because Washington sees no way of negotiating a compromise. It will not sit down with Peking and Hanoi until recent violations of past agreements for Laos are redressed because it could have no confidence in any new agreement.

To some extent, the Adminis-

Continued on Page 7, Column 1

JOHNSON IS FIRM

Vows in California to Oppose Violators of Freedom in World

By TOM WICKER

Special to The New York Times

SAN FRANCISCO, June 19—President Johnson promised tonight to open an "offensive in the pursuit of peace" based on an overwhelming military power that "makes it possible to seek agreement without fearing loss of liberty."

The President, addressing an audience of nearly 2,500 at a Democratic party fund-raising dinner, also pledged stern American opposition to "those who believe they can violate their neighbor's borders and steal their neighbor's freedom."

At the end of a day in California during which he gave several indications that he expected to be President for at least four more years, Mr. Johnson said he wanted to double the size of the Peace Corps, pursue what he called the "great society" with "the vision and valor of pioneers" and achieve "full equality for all our people."

Earlier in the day, after an enthusiastic welcome from more than 300,000 San Franciscans who lined Market Street to see his motorcade, the President came as near as he ever has to predicting his election in November.

Predicts the Good Life

"A Government which can get things done and knows where it is going," he said, is "the kind of Government you have had for the past four years—and that is the kind of Government you are going to get for the next four years."

Mr. Johnson's remarks were made at the dedication of a new Federal office building in downtown San Francisco. Before coming here, he also spoke at Edwards Air Force Base in the Mojave Desert and broke ground for a new Oakland Bay area rapid transit system at ceremonies in Concord.

It was not until tonight, when he attended the $100-a-plate fund-raising dinner, that Mr. Johnson played an openly political role.

At every stop he voiced his prophecies of the good life for every American, promising Californians the lion's share.

At the party dinner, he shifted his emphasis somewhat, detailing the increases since 1960 in American military might. He declared:

"We have used that strength not to intimidate others, but to

Continued on Page 6, Column 4

SENATOR KENNEDY HURT IN AIR CRASH; BAYH INJURED, TOO

Both Are in Fair Condition in Massachusetts Hospital —Pilot of Plane Killed

By The Associated Press

SOUTHAMPTON, Mass., Saturday, June 20—Senator Edward M. Kennedy, younger brother of President Kennedy, and Senator Birch Bayh were injured in the crash of a private plane last night while on the way to the Massachusetts Democratic Convention.

The pilot was killed and two other persons were injured. Mr. Kennedy was semiconscious.

Both Senators were reported in fair condition at Cooley Dickinson Hospital in nearby Northampton.

Also injured were Mrs. Bayh, reported in good condition, and Edward Moss of Andover, administrative aide to Mr. Ken-

Associated Press

Senator Edward M. Kennedy

nedy, who was reported in critical condition.

The pilot was identified as Edwin J. Zimny, 48 years old, of Lawrence, a last-minute substitute for the regular Kennedy pilot.

Senator Kennedy, Democrat of Massachusetts, was treated in an emergency room for back and chest injuries. His wife, Joan, visited him after he was transferred to an intensive-care unit.

Senator Bayh, Democrat of Indiana, suffered a hip injury. Mrs. Bayh was reported suffering from shock.

Mr. Kennedy's parents, Mr. and Mrs. Joseph P. Kennedy, who were vacationing at their summer home in Hyannis Port, were not told of the plane crash.

Attorney General Robert F. Kennedy, brother of the Senator, boarded the family plane with an aide and was reported on the way to Boston.

Two Civil Aeronautics Board investigators were sent from

Continued on Page 54, Column 1

PRESIDENT'S PLEA

He Declares the Task Now Is to Change Law Into Custom

Special to The New York Times

SAN FRANCISCO, June 19—President Johnson called the Senate passage of his civil rights bill today a "challenge to men of good will in every part of the country to transform the commandments of our law into the customs of our land."

Mr. Johnson said it was now the nation's task "to reach beyond the content of the bill to conquer the barriers of poor education, poverty, and squalid housing which are an inheritance of past injustice and an impediment to future advance."

He said that he did not "underestimate the depth of the passions involved in the struggle for racial equality."

But he also spoke of "a large reservoir of goodwill and compassion, of decency and fair play which seeks a vision of justice without violence in the streets."

Johnson Statement

If these forces, the President said, "do not desert the field, if they can be brought to the battle, then the years of trial will be a prelude to the final triumph of a land 'with liberty and justice for all.'"

The President issued his statement on the rights bill here, while he was beginning a two-day tour of California. The full text of the statement follows:

"Senate passage of the civil rights bill is a major step toward equal opportunities for all Americans. I congratulate Senators of both parties who worked to make passage possible.

"I look forward to the day, which will not be long forthcoming, when the bill becomes law. That will be a milestone in America's progress toward full justice for all her citizens.

"No single act of Congress can, by itself, eliminate discrimination and prejudice, hatred and injustice.

Broad National Consensus

"But this bill goes further to invest the rights of man with the protection of law than any legislation in this century.

"First, it will provide a carefully designed code to test and enforce the right of every American to go to school, to get a job, to vote, and to pursue his life unhampered by the barriers of racial discrimination.

"Second, it will, in itself, help educate all Americans to their responsibility to give equal treatment to their fellow citizens.

"Third, it will enlist one of the most powerful moral forces of American society on the side of civil rights—the moral obligation to respect and obey the law of the land.

"Fourth, and perhaps most important, this bill is a renewal and a re-enforcement, a symbol and a strengthening of that abiding commitment to human dignity and the equality of man which has been the guid-

Continued on Page 11, Column 8

United Press International Telephoto

ON HAND FOR THE VOTE: Visitors waiting outside the Capitol yesterday for admittance to the Senate Chamber, before the vote on the civil rights bill was registered.

ACTION BY SENATE

Revised Measure Now Goes Back to House for Concurrence

By E. W. KENWORTHY

Special to The New York Times

WASHINGTON, June 19 — The Senate passed the civil rights bill today by a vote of 73 to 27.

The final roll-call came at 7:40 P.M. on the 83d day of debate, nine days after closure was invoked.

Voting for the bill were 46 Democrats and 27 Republicans. Voting against it were 21 Democrats and six Republicans.

Except for Senator Robert C. Byrd of West Virginia, all the Democratic votes against the bill came from Southerners.

Senator Barry Goldwater of Arizona voted against the bill, as he said yesterday he would. The five other Republicans opposing it all support Mr. Goldwater's candidacy for the Republican Presidential nomination.

They were Bourke B. Hickenlooper of Iowa, chairman of the Senate Republican Policy Committee; Norris Cotton of New Hampshire, Edwin L. Mechem of New Mexico, Milward L. Simpson of Wyoming and John G. Tower of Texas.

2 Pledge Acceptance

The bill will now go back to the House for concurrence in the changes that the Senate made in the measure the House passed last Feb. 10 by a vote of 290 to 130.

Tonight, Representatives Emanuel Celler, Democrat of New York, and William M. Mc Culloch, Republican of Ohio, who are the chairman and ranking minority member of the House Judiciary Committee, said that they would accept the Senate version of the bill.

"We believe that the House membership will take the same position," they said.

With the support of these two men, who were responsible for the House bill, acceptance of the Senate bill in the House is assured.

President Johnson hopes to have the bill on his desk by July 3 at the latest so that he can sign it on the Fourth of July.

Powers of the Bill

The bill passed by the Senate outlaws discrimination in places of public accommodation, publicly owned facilities, employment and union membership and Federally aided programs. It gives the Attorney General new powers to speed school desegregation and enforce the Negro's right to vote.

The Senate bill differs from the House measure chiefly in giving states and local communities more scope and time to deal with complaints of discrimination in hiring and public accommodations. It allows the Attorney General to initiate suits in these areas where he finds a "pattern" of discrimination, but does not permit him, as did the House bill, to file suits on behalf of individuals.

After the roll-call, several thousand people gathered in the plaza before the floodlit Capitol to applaud the Senate Democratic leader, Mike Mansfield of Montana, and the Republican leader, Everett McKinley Dirksen of Illinois. Mr. Dirksen was instrumental in shaping the compromise that the Senate passed.

Burke Marshall, the Justice Department's civil rights chief, said after the bill was passed tonight that the department would move promptly to enforce the measure.

"I think there is going to be compliance with this bill," Mr. Marshall said. "That's the first thing."

"But where there is a pattern

Continued on Page 10, Column 1

ARIZONAN TARGET OF G.O.P. LEADER

Illinoisan, in Speech on the Senate Floor, Scores View Bill Is Unconstitutional

By ANTHONY LEWIS

Special to The New York Times

WASHINGTON, June 19 — The Republican leader in the Senate, Everett McKinley Dirksen of Illinois, closed the civil rights debate tonight with a biting attack on his party's leading Presidential prospect, Senator Barry Goldwater.

Senator Goldwater's announced opposition to the bill brought on the attack. He said yesterday that he could not "in good conscience" vote for the bill because he thought it was "unconstitutional" and would lead to a "police state."

Earlier, it was reported that former President Dwight D. Eisenhower had indicated to Mr Goldwater that the general would not hold a negative vote on the bill against the Arizonan.

On the floor of the Senate, Mr. Dirksen ridiculed the Goldwater, constitutional argument and moral position.

Looking often at Senator Goldwater, though never mentioning him by name, Mr. Dirksen in effect challenged the likely nominee of his party on what may be the chief issue at the Republican National Convention next month.

Dirksen Cites Legislation

First, Senator Dirksen mentioned many past pieces of legislation that had first been denounced as "unconstitutional." He listed the child labor prohibition, the Pure Food and Drug Act, the Minimum Wage Law and Social Security.

"It required no constitutional amendment," Senator Dirksen said, "to bring about all these forward thrusts in the interests of the people.

"It leads me to one conclusion: in the history of mankind, there is an inexorable moral force that moves us forward.

"No matter the resistance of people who do not fully understand, it will not be denied."

At this point, Senator Dirksen turned and looked directly at Senator Goldwater, who sat at his desk at the side of the chamber. Thrusting his right arm in Senator Goldwater's direction, he said:

"Utter all the extreme opin-

Continued on Page 11, Column 6

Rights Bill Roll-Call Vote

By The Associated Press

WASHINGTON, June 19—Following is the 73-27 vote by which the Senate passed the civil rights bill tonight:

FOR PASSAGE—73

Democrats—46

Anderson (N.M.)	Hayden (Ariz.)	Monroney (Okla.)
Bartlett (Alaska)	Humphrey (Minn.)	Morse (Ore.)
Bayh (Ind.)	Inouye (Hawaii)	Moss (Utah)
Brewster (Md.)	Jackson (Wash.)	Muskie (Me.)
Bible (Nev.)	Kennedy (Mass.)	Nelson (Wis.)
Burdick (N.D.)	Lausche (Ohio)	Neuberger (Ore.)
Cannon (Nev.)	Long (Mo.)	Pastore (R. I.)
Church (Idaho)	Magnuson (Wash.)	Pell (R. I.)
Clark (Pa.)	Mansfield (Mont.)	Proxmire (Wis.)
Dodd (Conn.)	McCarthy (Minn.)	Randolph (W. Va.)
Douglas (Ill.)	McGee (Wyo.)	Ribicoff (Conn.)
Edmondson (Okla.)	McGovern (S. D.)	Symington (Mo.)
Engle (Calif.)	McIntyre (N.H.)	Williams (N. J.)
Gruening (Alaska)	McNamara (Mich.)	Yarborough (Tex.)
Hart (Mich.)	Metcalf (Mont.)	Young (Ohio)
Hartke (Ind.)		

Republicans—27

Aiken (Vt.)	Dirksen (Ill.)	Morton (Ky.)
Allott (Colo.)	Dominick (Colo.)	Mundt (S. D.)
Beall (Md.)	Fong (Hawaii)	Pearson (Kan.)
Bennett (Utah)	Hruska (Neb.)	Prouty (Vt.)
Boggs (Del.)	Javits (N. Y.)	Saltonstall (Mass.)
Carlson (Kan.)	Jordan (Idaho)	Scott (Pa.)
Case (N. J.)	Keating (N. Y.)	Smith (Me.)
Cooper (Ky.)	Kuchel (Calif.)	Williams (Del.)
Curtis (Neb.)	Miller (Iowa)	Young (N. D.)

AGAINST PASSAGE—27

Democrats—21

Byrd (Va.)	Hill (Ala.)	Russell (Ga.)
Byrd (W. Va.)	Holland (Fla.)	Smathers (Fla.)
Eastland (Miss.)	Johnston (S. C.)	Sparkman (Ala.)
Ellender (La.)	Jordan (N. C.)	Stennis (Miss.)
Ervin (N. C.)	Long (La.)	Talmadge (Ga.)
Fulbright (Ark.)	McClellan (Ark.)	Thurmond (S. C.)
Gore (Tenn.)	Robertson (Va.)	Walters (Tenn.)

Republicans—6

Cotton (N. H.)	Hickenlooper (Iowa)	Simpson (Wyo.)
Goldwater (Ariz.)	Mechem (N. M.)	Tower (Tex.)

Negro Leaders Hail Passage; Some Southerners Voice Anger

CORE Plans Tests

By MARTIN ARNOLD

Leaders of national civil rights groups last night hailed the Senate passage of the civil rights bill, and vowed that the measure would be quickly tested.

There was little indication that the Senate's action would reduce the number of demonstrations in the immediate future.

James L. Farmer, national director of the Congress of Racial Equality, said that CORE would press for implementation and enforcement of the bill's provisions.

"There will be no breathing spell on demonstrations," Mr. Farmer said. "We breathe easiest when the pressure is on."

"The passage of the civil rights bill may well be the single most important act of our Congress in several decades," Mr. Farmer said. "It gives hope to Negroes that the American people and Government mean to redeem the promise of the Declaration of Independence and the Emancipation Proclamation."

Mr. Farmer also saw the bill

Continued on Page 10, Column 4

Region's Reaction Varied

By United Press International

ATLANTA, June 19 — Deep South politicians and businessmen lashed out angrily at passage of the civil rights bill today and an elderly Negro said, "I'll believe it when I see it."

Gov. George C. Wallace of Alabama declared that "this is a sad day for individual freedom and liberty," but a Chattanooga housewife said, "I firmly believe in it."

Reaction differed sharply between stanchly segregationist areas and areas where there has been desegregation.

Many Negroes approached on the streets in the South had little, if any comment.

"I just don't know much about it. I'm afraid to say," said a Negro in Nashville.

"It is good. I am glad," said George Thomson, a 40-year-old Negro cab driver in Montgomery, Ala.

Jefferson Johnson, an elderly Negro selling ice cream on a street in Birmingham, Ala., said:

"I'll believe it when I see it. I hope it'll do good, but—well,

Continued on Page 12, Column 6

North Katanga City Is Seized By Rebels, the Congo Reports

Europeans Flee Albertville, Crossing Lake Tanganyika to Nearby Burundi

By J. ANTHONY LUKAS

Special to The New York Times

LEOPOLDVILLE, the Congo, June 19—Albertville, the capital of North Katanga Province, was reported today to have fallen to anti-Government rebels.

According to messages reaching here, rebels striking south along the shore of Lake Tanganyika entered the city about midday. It is not known here whether there was any resistance from Congolese soldiers there.

Many of the city's Europeans have fled in steamers across the lake. At least 150 women and children left on two steamers last night for Bujumbura, the capital of Burundi.

Another steamer, with 350 persons aboard, was scheduled to leave early this afternoon, but it was not whether it got away.

Meanwhile, the United States Embassy here said that two American civilian pilots who had been flying combat missions for the Congolese Army had voluntarily decided to cease the flights. An embassy official said the pilots made their decision after they learned that they might be subject to penalties under United States law.

Map: The New York Times, June 20, 1964

Rebels were said to have seized Albertville (cross).

The embassy spokesman added to the official United States position tht the two men were "individual Americans on contract to the Congolese Government."

He said the United States Government had neither authorized their contract nor directed their activities here.

The Americans, Ed Dearborn and Don Coney, also insisted in an interview here, as they had previously, that they were civilians under contract to the Congolese Government.

Mr. Dearborn said he had hepatitis and planned to return to the United States soon. However, he and Mr. Coney would answer no other questions.

Continued on Page 4, Column 3

Yanks Woo Cabbies With 20,000 Tickets

By ROBERT LIPSYTE

The New York Yankees, long lordly and aloof atop baseball's corporate standings, have gone down to the street to wage promotional warfare.

They have given away more than 10,000 reserved tickets worth $25,000 to more than 5,000 city cab drivers on the sidewalk along Broadway between 60th and 61st Streets in the last two days. Today, they expect to give away 10,000 more.

The Yankees' first mass give-away program is the latest in a series of gimmicks to raise lagging attendance and combat the Mets at the box office.

"The idea," said Robert O. Fishel, the Yankees' public relations director, "is to make

Continued on Page 18, Column 2

Erhard Bars Visit To the Soviet Union

Special to The New York Times

BONN, June 19 — Chancellor Ludwig Erhard turned down today an unofficial but urgent Soviet invitation to go to Moscow for an attempt at improving Soviet-West German relations.

He suggested instead that the Soviet Premier ask for an official invitation to Bonn if he thought the trip would be worthwhile.

At his first news conference here in six months, Dr. Erhard carefully held open the door for an eventual encounter with Premier Khrushchev while dashing cold water on the prospects of settling soon any of the fundamental questions that divide Bonn and Moscow.

As he spoke, Bonn's Western allies were putting the final

Continued on Page 2, Column 4

NEWS INDEX

"All the News That's Fit to Print"

The New York Times.

LATE CITY EDITION
U. S. Weather Bureau Report (Page 58) forecasts: Cloudy, windy, chance of showers today and tonight. Cold tomorrow.
Temp. Range: 62—54; yesterday: 64—51.

VOL. CXIII. No. 38,654. NEW YORK, SATURDAY, NOVEMBER 23, 1963. TEN CENTS

KENNEDY IS KILLED BY SNIPER AS HE RIDES IN CAR IN DALLAS; JOHNSON SWORN IN ON PLANE

TEXAN ASKS UNITY

Congressional Chiefs of 2 Parties Give Promise of Aid

By FELIX BELAIR Jr.
Special to The New York Times

WASHINGTON, Nov. 22—Lyndon B. Johnson returned to a stunned capital this evening to assume the duties of the Presidency.

The new President asked for and received from Congressional leaders of both parties their "united support in the face of the tragedy which has befallen our country." He said it was "more essential than ever before that this country be united."

Partisan differences disappeared in the chorus of assurances with which the Congressional leaders responded.

Mr. Johnson was described by those who talked with him as "stunned and shaken" by the assassination of President Kennedy.

Discusses U.S. Security

But he moved quickly from problems of national security and foreign policy to funeral arrangements for Mr. Kennedy.

Across the street from the West Wing of the White House, the President conferred with officials in his old Vice Presi-

Henry Grossman

"This is a sad time for all people. We have suffered a loss that cannot be weighed. For me it is a deep personal tragedy. I know the world shares the sorrow that Mrs. Kennedy and her family bear. I will do my best. That is all I can do. I ask for your help—and God's."—President Lyndon Baines Johnson.

PRESIDENT'S BODY WILL LIE IN STATE

PARTIES' OUTLOOK FOR '64 CONFUSED

LEFTIST ACCUSED

Figure in a Pro-Castro Group Is Charged—Policeman Slain

By GLADWIN HILL
Special to The New York Times

DALLAS, Saturday, Nov. 23—Lee Harvey Oswald, a 24-year-old warehouse worker who once lived in the Soviet Union, was charged late last night with assassinating President Kennedy.

Oswald was arrested at 2:15 yesterday afternoon, nearly two hours after the assassination of the President, as the suspected killer of a policeman on the street in the Oak Cliff district, three miles from where the President was shot.

Chief of Police Jesse Curry announced that Oswald had been formally arraigned at 1:40 A.M., Central standard time, today on a charge of murder in the President's death. The arraignment was made before a justice of the peace in the homicide bureau at Police Headquarters.

Capt. Will Fritz, head of the homicide bureau, identified Oswald as an adherent of the left-wing "Fair Play for Cuba Committee." But there were also reports that Oswald, apparently politically erratic, had

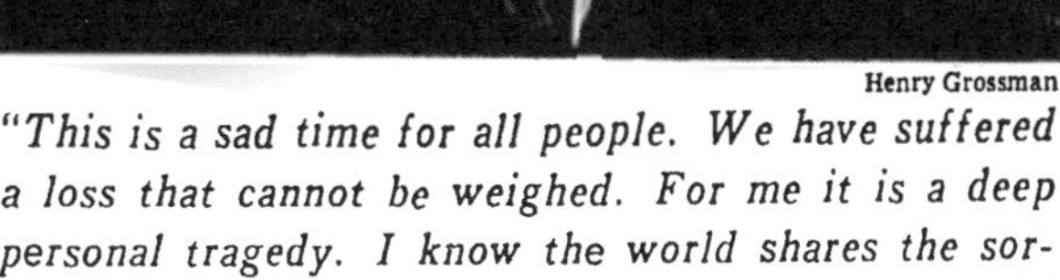

Henry Grossman

John Fitzgerald Kennedy
1917-1963

Why America Weeps

Kennedy Victim of Violent Streak He Sought to Curb in the Nation

Gov. Connally Shot; Mrs. Kennedy Safe

President Is Struck Down by a Rifle Shot From Building on Motorcade Route—Johnson, Riding Behind, Is Unhurt

By TOM WICKER
Special to The New York Times

DALLAS, Nov. 22—President John Fitzgerald Kennedy was shot and killed by an assassin today.

He died of a wound in the brain caused by a rifle bullet that was fired at him as he was riding through downtown Dallas in a motorcade.

Vice President Lyndon Baines Johnson, who was riding in the third car behind Mr. Kennedy's, was sworn in as the 36th President of the United States 99 minutes after Mr. Kennedy's death.

Mr. Johnson is 55 years old; Mr. Kennedy was 46.

Shortly after the assassination, Lee H. Oswald, who once defected to the Soviet Union and who has been active in the Fair Play for Cuba Committee, was arrested by the Dallas police. Tonight he was accused of the killing.

Suspect Captured

"All the News That's Fit to Print"

The New York Times.

LATE CITY EDITION
U. S. Weather Bureau Report (Page 55) forecasts: Cloudy with scattered showers today; partly cloudy tonight and tomorrow.
Temp. range: 77—62; yesterday: 81—61.
Temp.-Hum. Index: 70 to 75; yesterday: 72.

VOL. CXII. No. 38,568. NEW YORK, THURSDAY, AUGUST 29, 1963. TEN CENTS

200,000 MARCH FOR CIVIL RIGHTS IN ORDERLY WASHINGTON RALLY; PRESIDENT SEES GAIN FOR NEGRO

Associated Press

VIEW FROM THE LINCOLN MEMORIAL: The scene during the march looking toward the Washington Monument

ACTION ASKED NOW

10 Leaders of Protest Urge Laws to End Racial Inequity

Excerpts from talks at rally are printed on Page 21.

By E. W. KENWORTHY
Special to The New York Times

WASHINGTON, Aug. 28 — More than 200,000 Americans, most of them black but many of them white, demonstrated here today for a full and speedy program of civil rights and equal job opportunities.

It was the greatest assembly for a redress of grievances that this capital has ever seen.

One hundred years and 240 days after Abraham Lincoln enjoined the emancipated slaves to "abstain from all violence" and "labor faithfully for reasonable wages," this vast throng proclaimed in march and song and through the speeches of their leaders that they were still waiting for the freedom and the jobs.

Children Clap and Sing

There was no violence to mar the demonstration. In fact, at times there was an air of hootenanny about it as groups of schoolchildren clapped hands and swung into the familiar freedom songs.

But if the crowd was good-natured, the underlying tone was one of dead seriousness. The emphasis was on "freedom" and "now." At the same time the

KENNEDY SIGNS BILL AVERTING A RAIL STRIKE

PRECEDENT IS SET

Arbitration Imposed by Congress—Vote in House 286-66

Text of Kennedy's statement will be found on Page 13.

By JOHN D. POMFRET
Special to The New York Times

WASHINGTON, Aug. 28 — Congress passed today a bill that prevented a national railroad strike scheduled for midnight. President Kennedy signed it immediately.

The House completed the Congressional action. It adopted by a standing vote of 286 to 66 the same joint resolution passed yesterday by the Senate. The measure provides for arbitration of the two principal issues in the railroad work rules dispute and bars a strike for 180 days.

The action was without Federal precedent. Never before in the history of peacetime labor relations has Congress imposed arbitration in a labor-management dispute.

The failure of the railroads and the five train operating unions to resolve their dispute, and the Congressional action this made necessary, is considered by many to represent a major failure for the collective bargaining system.

Many Are Reluctant

Even many Congressmen who voted for the measure, convinced that the economic consequences of a national railroad strike made action to head it

8 Dead in Utah Mine; Fate of 15 Unknown

Special to The New York Times

MOAB, Utah, Aug. 28 — Eight men were known dead today and 15 were trapped a half-mile underground in a potash mine rocked yesterday by a severe explosion.

Two survivors hoisted to the surface today reported that three men were dead, at least five were alive and the fate of 15 was unknown. Later, however, rescue workers deep in the mine spotted five more bodies that officials said might be the men whom the survivors first believed alive.

Rescuers were being hampered by deadly gas, extreme heat, water and mechanical failures. A communications breakdown added to their frustrations.

Donald Hanna, 27 years old, of Price and Paul McKinney,

Continued on Page 14, Column 3

U.S. SPURNS DENIAL BY DIEM ON CRISIS

Absolves the Army Again in Vietnam Pagoda Raids and Points Toward Nhu

By TAD SZULC
Special to The New York Times

WASHINGTON, Aug. 28— The United States reaffirmed today its belief that the South Vietnamese Government had

U.S. PRESSES U.N. TO CONDEMN SYRIA ON ISRAELI DEATHS

Stevenson Deplores Killing of Youths—Thant Assures Council on Cease-Fire

Text of Stevenson statement appears on Page 2.

By KATHLEEN TELTSCH
Special to The New York Times

UNITED NATIONS, N. Y., Aug. 28 — Adlai E. Stevenson declared today that the recent slaying of two Israeli farmers by Syrians was "wanton murder" deserving the strongest condemnation by the Security Council.

The United States delegate, followed by the British representative, gave forceful support to Israel's charges arising from the Aug. 20 ambush killing of two 19-year-old Israelis at the Almagor farm settlement.

Mr. Stevenson rejected Syria's countercharges against Israel as "not corroborated" by United Nations investigations.

The United States policy statement drew a favorable reaction from Michael S. Comay of Israel, who said it encouraged him to expect the Council to take "firm and vigorous action."

Syrian Disapproves

However, there was disapproval from Dr. Salah el-Tarazi of Syria, who criticized Mr. Stevenson as "not particularly objective." He added that Mr. Stevenson in past years had not deplored Syrian losses with equal feeling.

The Council, resuming its airing of the new crisis, was told by the Secretary General, U Thant, that United Nations inspection showed "no evidence of a military build-up on either side" of the armistice line.

Mr. Thant reported that both parties were heeding the United Nations cease-fire achieved last

feared that their action might set a precedent detrimental to collective bargaining.

An arbitration board was created by Congress to consider the two key issues. These are whether diesel locomotive firemen are necessary in freight and yard service and the size of train-service crews.

Congress ordered negotiations on the remaining issues on the theory that with the two main issues disposed of, the presumably less important matters could be settled by traditional collective bargaining.

But some well-informed Government sources do not believe the remaining issues will be

Continued on Page 13, Column 1

LODI KILLER SLAIN; 2D MAN GIVES UP

Ex-Convict Is Shot 7 Times in a Midtown Hotel

One of the killers of two New Jersey policemen was shot to death early yesterday by New York detectives during a violent struggle in his midtown hotel room. Sixteen hours later, the second man wanted in the slayings quietly surrendered.

The slain killer, 25-year-old Frank Falco, was asleep in his underwear when the police, using a passkey, entered his room at the Manhattan Hotel, Eighth Avenue and 44th Street. Although awakened with a revolver pressed to his throat, he fought desperately before being killed by seven bullets. He died snarling at the police and cursing them.

Thomas (Rabbi Tom) Trantino, 27, the second man, walked into the East 22d Street station house at 9:10 P.M., accompanied by a lawyer. He was neatly dressed and clean-shaven.

The men, both ex-convicts, had been the object of a grim police hunt since Detective Sgt. Peter Voto and Gary Tedesco, a police appointee, were gunned down early Monday morning in the Angel Lounge on Route 46 in Lodi, N. J. Mr. Tedesco was to have officially joined the Lodi force today.

A tip led the New York detectives to the hotel, where Falco had checked in at 8 P.M. Tuesday under the name of J. Rello of Newport, R. I.

Lieut. Thomas Quinn, a 53-year-old police veteran with 16 citations for bravery, entered Falco's 23d-floor room first, his

Continued on Page 35, Column 2

violated pledges on the Buddhist crisis and that Vietnamese military chiefs were innocent of responsibility for assaults on pagodas.

This was the reaction of the Administration to communiqués issued in Saigon in the last 24 hours by the Government of President Ngo Dinh Diem in the name of the Vietnamese Joint General Staff.

The communiqués charged that Washington's public statements on the crisis reflected "totally erroneous information."

[In Saigon, youths loyal to the secret police were reported to be warning the population against anti-Government demonstrations.]

Change Is Held Vital

With the Vietnam crisis already regarded by the United States as extremely grave, this public dispute seemed to push it toward an unpredictable showdown.

The quarrel over who smashed pagodas and who arrested leaders of the Buddhist protest movement is understood to affect deeply the Kennedy Administration's evolving policy of encouraging Vietnamese military chiefs to reach for power.

This policy, still tentative, is that a fundamental change is required in the structure of the Saigon Government, Washington sources explain. They say the goal is national harmony that would let Vietnam concentrate again on the war against the Communist guerrillas of the Vietcong.

Specifically, Washington is said to deem internal peace out of the question as long as Ngo Dinh Nhu, chief of secret police and brother of the President, retains his vast power.

Mr. Nhu is considered almost a symbol of the friction between Vietnam's Buddhists and the Roman Catholic Ngo family, which dominates the Government.

It is reported that in searching for an alternative to the regime—a course that was unthinkable here before the Buddhist crisis—the United States has almost openly been ad-

Continued on Page 3, Column 4

NEWS INDEX

subsequent exchanges of shooting greatly increased tension in the area. Bullets collected at one shooting site were on exhibit in the Council chamber.

Both Mr. Stevenson and Roger W. Jackling of Britain urged Syria and Israel to accept the suggestion by the United Nations truce chief, Lieut. Gen. Odd Bull, for avoiding new eruptions along their border, including an exchange of prisoners. Mr. Comay indicated a favorable Israeli reaction.

Evidence Questioned

Dr. Tarazi, in his turn, insisted that Israel's allegations remained unproved and that some evidence could have been faked. He noted photographs of footgear found at the ambush scene and said Syrian soldiers did not wear such shoes.

He was supported by Sidi Baba of Morocco, who accused Israel of making a "great superficial fuss" over the Almagor incident to create a climate for pressuring the Arabs into signing a peace treaty.

The United States and Britain are understood to be drafting a resolution that would condemn the killings and rebuke Syria by implication, rather than by outright condemnation, as Israel has been asking. Similar formulas have been used in the past.

Such an indirect condemnation might be blocked by a veto from the Soviet Union, however, which in the past has rejected resolutions opposed by the Arabs.

Mr. Stevenson told the 11-nation Council that General Bull's information was admit-

Continued on Page 2, Column 3

2 Girls Murdered In E. 88th St. Flat

Two young women, one the daughter of a writer and the other of a prominent surgeon, were bound and stabbed to death yesterday in their apartment at 57 East 88th Street.

The victims, Janice Wylie, 21 years old, and Emily Hoffert, 23, had been slashed repeatedly. Three bloodstained kitchen knives were found in the five-room apartment, which the girls shared with another young woman. The suite had been ransacked.

The bodies were found on a bedroom floor by Janice's father, the writer Max Wylie, and by Patricia Tolles, 23, the third roommate.

Mr. Wylie, who lives nearby, at 55 East 86th Street, is a

Continued on Page 35, Column 5

United Press International Telephoto

VIEW FROM THE WASHINGTON MONUMENT: Marchers assembling around Reflecting Pool at the Lincoln Memorial

CONGRESS CORDIAL BUT NOT SWAYED

Leaders of March Pay Calls of Courtesy at Capitol

By WARREN WEAVER Jr.

Special to The New York Times

WASHINGTON, Aug. 28—The civil rights demonstration that swept more than 200,000 people through the capital today appeared to have left much of Congress untouched — physically, emotionally and politically.

In the morning, 13 demonstration leaders drove quietly up Capitol Hill and paid courtesy calls on Congressional leaders of both parties. The atmosphere was cordial, but there were no conversions.

In the afternoon, about 75 Senators and Representatives went from Capitol Hill to the Lincoln Memorial to be introduced, sit on the steps and listen to Gospel singing and speeches on civil rights.

A few demonstrators violated marching orders and went up to the Capitol to visit legislators in their offices. A few Senators welcomed trainloads and busfuls of constituents in person.

Otherwise, there was really very little contact between the marchers and the group they were working hardest to impress. And there was very little evidence that the demonstration, however large and fervent, would play a material role in advancing civil rights legislation.

Senator Hubert H. Humphrey, one of the most enthusiastic of

Continued on Page 17, Column 1

'I Have a Dream . . .'

Peroration by Dr. King Sums Up A Day the Capital Will Remember

By JAMES RESTON

Special to The New York Times

WASHINGTON, Aug. 28—Abraham Lincoln, who presided in his stone temple today above the children of the slaves he emancipated, may have used just the right words to sum up the general reaction to the Negro's massive march on Washington. "I think," he wrote to Gov. Andrew G. Curtin of Pennsylvania in 1861, "the necessity of being ready increases. Look to it." Washington may not have changed a vote today, but it is a little more conscious tonight of the necessity of being ready for freedom. It may not "look to it" at once, since it is looking to so many things, but it will be a long time before it forgets the melodious and melancholy voice of the Rev. Dr. Martin Luther King Jr. crying out his dreams to the multitude.

News Analysis

It was Dr. King who, near the end of the day, touched the vast audience. Until then the pilgrimage was merely a great spectacle. Only those marchers from the embattled towns in the Old Confederacy had anything like the old crusading zeal. For many the day seemed an adventure, a long outing in the late summer sun—part liberation from home, part Sunday School picnic, part political convention, and part fish-fry.

But Dr. King brought them alive in the late afternoon with a peroration that was an anguished echo from all the old American reformers. Roger Williams calling for religious liberty, Sam Adams calling for political liberty, old man Thoreau denouncing coercion, William Lloyd Garrison demanding emancipation, and Eugene V. Debs crying for economic equality—Dr. King echoed them all.

"I have a dream," he cried again and again. And each time the dream was a promise out of our ancient articles of faith: phrases from the Constitution, lines from the great anthem of the nation, guarantees from the Bill of Rights, all ending with a vision that they might one day all come true.

Find Journey Worthwhile

Dr. King touched all the themes of the day, only better than anybody else. He was full of the symbolism of Lincoln and Gandhi, and the cadences of the Bible. He was both militant and sad, and he sent the crowd away feeling that the long journey had been worthwhile.

This demonstration impressed political Washington because it combined a number of things no politician can ignore. It had the force of numbers. It had the melodies of both the church and the theater. And it was able to invoke the principles of the founding fathers to rebuke the inequalities and hypocrisies of modern American life.

There was a paradox in the day's performance. The Ne-

Continued on Page 17, Column 6

PRESIDENT MEETS MARCH LEADERS

Says Bipartisan Support Is Needed for Rights Bill

Rights statement and Labor Day proclamation, Page 16.

By TOM WICKER

Special to The New York Times

WASHINGTON, Aug. 28—President Kennedy served tea and sympathy and blunt political advice late today to the tired but proud leaders of the march on Washington.

In an hour-long conference, the President told the 10 leaders that "very strong bipartisan support" would be needed to get civil rights legislation enacted this year.

In a statement issued immediately after the conference, Mr. Kennedy said that "the cause of 20,000,000 Negroes has been advanced" by the orderly demonstration, "conducted so appropriately before the nation's shrine to the Great Emancipator."

Earlier, in a Labor Day statement released in advance of the holiday, the President called on the nation to speed up its efforts to achieve equal rights for all in jobs, education and voting.

The main discussion between the march leaders and the President concerned prospects for civil rights legislation, the leaders said after the White House meeting. They talked with Mr. Kennedy around the long table in the Cabinet Room, where the leaders were served tea, coffee,

Continued on Page 16, Column 7

leaders emphasized, paradoxically but realistically, that the struggle was just beginning.

On Capitol Hill, opinion was divided about the impact of the demonstration in stimulating Congressional action on civil rights legislation. But at the White House, President Kennedy declared that the cause of 20,000,000 Negroes had been advanced by the march.

The march leaders went from the shadows of the Lincoln Memorial to the White House to meet with the President for 75 minutes. Afterward, Mr. Kennedy issued a 400-word statement praising the marchers for the "deep fervor and the quiet dignity" that had characterized the demonstration.

Says Nation Can Be Proud

The nation, the President said, "can properly be proud of the demonstration that has occurred here today."

The main target of the demonstration was Congress, where committees are now considering the Administration's civil rights bill.

At the Lincoln Memorial this afternoon, some speakers, knowing little of the ways of Congress, assumed that the passage of a strengthened civil rights bill had been assured by the moving events of the day.

But from statements by Congressional leaders, after they had met with the march committee this morning, this did not seem certain at all. These statements came before the demonstration.

Senator Mike Mansfield of Montana, the Senate Democratic leader, said he could not say whether the mass protest

Continued on Page 16, Column 1

Capital Is Occupied By a Gentle Army

By RUSSELL BAKER

Special to The New York Times

WASHINGTON, Aug. 28—No one could remember an invading army quite as gentle as the 200,000 civil rights marchers who occupied Washington today.

For the most part, they came silently during the night and early morning, occupied the great shaded boulevards along the Mall, and spread through the parklands between the Washington Monument and the Potomac.

But instead of the emotional horde of angry militants that many had feared, what Washington saw was a vast army of quiet, middle-class Americans

Continued on Page 17, Column 7

dential offices in the Executive Office Building.

Senator George A. Smathers, Democrat of Florida, a personal friend of the dead President, was one of those who described Mr. Johnson as shaken.

"Everyone is," he added. "But the President is the more so because he was right there when the tragedy occurred."

While flying to Washington aboard the Presidential plane, Mr. Johnson arranged for a meeting with Cabinet members to ask that they remain at their posts. He made the same request of staff members in the executive office.

Meets With Harriman

"Calm and contained" was the way Senator J. W. Fulbright described the President's manner during a discussion of foreign-policy matters with Under Secretary of State W. Averell Harriman. The Arkansas Senator said the President had been working on "what looked like a statement"—presumably an assurance of continuity of the nation's foreign policy.

The new President's first conference was aboard the helicopter that flew him the 15 miles from Andrews Air Force Base

Continued on Page 11, Column 3

Funeral Mass to Be Monday in Capital After Homage Is Paid by the Public

By JACK RAYMOND

Special to The New York Times

WASHINGTON, Saturday, Nov. 23—The body of John F. Kennedy will lie in state in the rotunda of the Capitol tomorrow and then will be borne to St. Matthew's Roman Catholic Cathedral for a pontifical requiem mass at noon Monday.

The President's body was returned to Washington yesterday in the same Air Force jet that carried him to Texas Thursday.

The plane, with Mrs. Kennedy, the new President, Lyndon B. Johnson, and Mrs. Johnson aboard, arrived at Andrews Air Force Base at about 6 P.M.

It was announced later that Mr. Kennedy's body would lie in the East Room of the White House today from 10 A.M. to 6 P.M., during which time Government and diplomatic officials will pay their respects.

The coffin will be taken from the White House to the Capitol rotunda tomorrow morning,

Continued on Page 9, Column 3

Republican Prospects Rise—Johnson Faces Possible Fight Against Liberals

By WARREN WEAVER Jr.

Special to The New York Times

WASHINGTON, Nov. 22—President Kennedy's assassination threw the American political scene into turmoil today.

It removed at a single blow the man who would have been nominated for a second term in the White House by acclamation nine months from now.

It elevated into the Presidency and the leadership of the Democratic party an older, more conservative man still emerging from his Southern heritage.

It increased immeasurably for the leaders of the Republican party prospects of electing a President next November.

The shock of the President's death stilled the official voices of politics in the capital. But so profound was the potential effect on the Government and leadership that private consideration could not be silenced.

Before, there had been facts and strong probabilities on the

Continued on Page 6, Column 3

once tried to join anti-Castro forces.

Worked in Warehouse

Oswald was employed in the Texas School Book Depository, the warehouse from which the fatal shots were fired at the President's car.

The police said at least six witnesses placed Oswald in the building at the time of the assassination.

One was quoted as saying that Oswald had stayed behind on an upper floor when other employes went down to the street to see Mr. Kennedy pass by.

The defendant's only comment, shouted at reporters as he was led handcuffed through a police building corridor to be questioned, was "I haven't shot anybody." "He has not con-

Continued on Page 4, Column 1

NEWS INDEX

By JAMES RESTON

Special to The New York Times

WASHINGTON, Nov. 22—America wept tonight, not alone for its dead young President, but for itself. The grief was general, for somehow the worst in the nation had prevailed over the best. The indictment extended beyond the assassin, for something in the nation itself, some strain of madness and violence, had destroyed the highest symbol of law and order.

Speaker John McCormack, now 71 and, by the peculiarities of our politics, next in line of succession after the Vice President, expressed this sense of national dismay and self-criticism:

"My God! My God! What are we coming to?"

The irony of the President's death is that his short Administration was devoted almost entirely to various attempts to curb this very streak of violence in the American character.

When the historians get around to assessing his three years in office, it is very likely that they will be impressed with just this: his efforts to restrain those who wanted to be more violent in the cold war overseas

Continued on Page 7, Column 6

City Goes Dark

By ROBERT C. DOTY

Shock and sorrow for the murdered President darkened and silenced midtown Manhattan last night.

In early afternoon, when the first radio and television bulletins carried the news, the city began its mourning. By nightfall, the normal quick Friday night pace had slowed as near to a halt as it ever comes.

Many of the city's normal weekend commercial, social and sporting activities were canceled. Decisions for closings by many stores and other businesses were being debated.

Courts closed in the middle of hearings yesterday. Hundreds of public and private social functions and sporting events were interrupted or postponed. Most midtown legitimate and motion picture theaters, night clubs and dance halls locked

Continued on Page 5, Column 2

Oswald, 24 years old, was also accused of slaying a policeman who had approached him in the street. Oswald was subdued after a scuffle with a second policeman in a nearby theater.

President Kennedy was shot at 12:30 P.M., Central standard time (1:30 P.M., New York time). He was pronounced dead at 1 P.M. and Mr. Johnson was sworn in at 2:39 P.M.

Mr. Johnson, who was uninjured in the shooting, took his oath in the Presidential jet plane as it stood on the runway at Love Field. The body of Mr. Kennedy was aboard. Immediately after the oath-taking, the plane took off for Washington.

Standing beside the new President as Mr. Johnson took the oath of office was Mrs. John F. Kennedy. Her stockings were spattered with her husband's blood.

Gov. John B. Connally Jr. of Texas, who was riding in the same car with Mr. Kennedy, was severely wounded in the chest, ribs and arm. His condition was serious, but not critical.

The killer fired the rifle from a building just off the motorcade route. Mr. Kennedy,

Continued on Page 2

Capt. Cecil Stoughton via United Press International

THE NEW PRESIDENT: Lyndon B. Johnson takes oath before Judge Sarah T. Hughes in plane at Dallas. Mrs. Kennedy and Representative Jack Brooks are at right. To left are Mrs. Johnson and Representative Albert Thomas.

Associated Press

WHEN THE BULLETS STRUCK: Mrs. Kennedy moving to the aid of the President after he was hit by a sniper yesterday in Dallas. A guard mounts rear bumper. Gov. John B. Connally Jr. of Texas, also in the car, was wounded.

TODAY: TEXT OF WARREN COMMISSION REPORT—A 48-PAGE SECTION

"All the News That's Fit to Print"

The New York Times.

LATE CITY EDITION

U. S. Weather Bureau Report (Page 45) forecasts: Cloudy, then fair today; fair and cooler tonight. Fair tomorrow. Temp. Range: 70—55; yesterday: 73—59.

VOL. CXIV . No. 38,964.

NEW YORK, MONDAY, SEPTEMBER 28, 1964.

Today's Issue Contains 96 Pages in Two Sections

TEN CENTS

WARREN COMMISSION FINDS OSWALD GUILTY AND SAYS ASSASSIN AND RUBY ACTED ALONE; REBUKES SECRET SERVICE, ASKS REVAMPING

F.B.I. IS CRITICIZED

Security Steps Taken by Secret Service Held Inadequate

By FELIX BELAIR Jr.

Special to The New York Times

WASHINGTON, Sept. 27—A sweeping revision of the organization and basic operating practices of the United States Secret Service was recommended today by the Warren Commission.

The commission sharply rebuked the Secret Service for failure to make adequate preparation for the visit of President Kennedy to Dallas last November. It reprimanded the Federal Bureau of Investigation for failure to supply the Secret Service with information concerning the presence of Lee Harvey Oswald in Dallas.

The commission deplored the fact that "there was no fully adequate liaison" between the F.B.I. and the Secret Service before the Dallas trip. It noted that some improvements had occurred since then but it insisted that, ultimately, Presidential protection required improvement in working arrangements of all Federal agencies concerned, including the Central Intelligence Agency, the State Department and the military intelligence branches.

Scrutiny Is Urged

The State Department was admonished to scrutinize more carefully requests for return to the United States of defectors

The report's appendix on Presidential protection will be printed in tomorrow's Times.

like Oswald "who have evidenced disloyalty or hostility to this country or who have expressed a desire to renounce their citizenship."

The brunt of the commission's indictment was directed at the century-old agency responsible for the safety of the President and his family. Its chief charge was that the Secret Service had not checked buildings along the route of the Presidential motorcade in Dallas nor asked the local police to do so.

The commission called for the appointment of a new special assistant to the Secretary of the Treasury with general supervisory authority over the Secret Service.

The commission found, however, that the conduct of the Secret Service agents in the Presidential motorcade "demonstrates that the President and the nation can expect courage and devotion to duty from agents of the Secret Service."

It acknowledged that whatever the human and material resources at the command of the Secret Service, a President can only be made as safe as he wants to be.

The report declared that its recommendations were "compelled by the facts disclosed in this investigation." It noted that

Continued on Page 15, Column 1

Harris & Ewing

THE WARREN COMMISSION: President's Commission on the Assassination of President Kennedy at commission offices at Veterans of Foreign Wars Building, Washington. From left: Representative Gerald R. Ford, Representative Hale Boggs, Senator Richard B. Russell, Chief Justice Earl Warren, Senator John Sherman Cooper, John J. McCloy, Allen W. Dulles, and J. Lee Rankin, commission counsel. Portraits are of President Johnson, President Kennedy and Joseph J. Lombardo, head of Veterans of Foreign Wars.

JOHNSON NAMES 4 TO ACT ON REPORT

Commission Calls for Action to Increase the Security of the Presidency

By The Associated Press

JOHNSON CITY, Tex., Sept. 27—President Johnson appointed a four-man committee today to advise him "on the execution of the recommendations of the Warren Commission."

The commission, which investigated the assassination of President Kennedy, recommended action to tighten the protection of Presidents and to make the killing of a President or a Vice President a Federal crime.

[Mike Mansfield of Montana, the Senate majority leader, said in Washington that Congress, which has been aiming at adjournment at the end of this week, "should stay here and act, if the President sends us any recommendations."]

Members of the committee are Secretary of the Treasury Douglas Dillon, Acting Attorney General Nicholas deB. Katzenbach, John A. McCone, director of the Central Intelligence Agency, and McGeorge Bundy, Special Assistant to the President for National Security Affairs.

The President named no chairman for the committee, but it was understood that Secretary Dillon, as ranking member, would have general supervision over the group.

The group will presumably

Continued on Page 17, Column 3

A New Chapter Unfolds in the Kennedy Legend

By JAMES RESTON

Special to The New York Times

News Analysis

WASHINGTON, Sept. 27—The Warren Commission has fulfilled its primary assignment. It has tried, as a servant of history, to discover truth. But the assassination of President Kennedy was so symbolic of human irony and tragedy, and so involved in the complicated and elemental conflicts of the age, that many vital questions remain, and the philosophers, novelists and dramatists will have to take it from here.

The commission has not concluded the Kennedy mystery so much as it has opened up a whole new chapter in the Kennedy legend.

It has provided the greatest repository of Presidential political history, drama and fiction since the murder of Mr. Lincoln and since legend is often more powerful than history, this may be the commission's most significant achievement.

Now the central mystery of who killed the President has been answered by the commission only in the process of raising a new catalogue of mysteries. Now the main characters in the play have been surrounded by a host of new characters, each of whom appears briefly at a critical moment with some vital testimony, only to disappear without our really knowing much about who they are.

The whole story is full of the mystery of life. Lee Harvey Oswald's motive for murdering the President remains obscure. The distinguished members of the commission and their staff obviously gave up on it.

The "might-have-beens" are maddening. If only he had been given that visa to go to Cuba and thence to the Soviet Union just before the assassination! If he had not been allowed to come back from there in the first place! Who was "the neighbor" who got him the job in the Texas Book Depository, from where he shot the President? And what were the details of Oswald's attempted suicide in Moscow?

The wild accidents are equally intriguing. There is, for example, the case of Mrs. Bledsoe, who rented Oswald a room in Dallas and then, on a 10,000-to-1 chance, just happened to be on the bus he boarded when he was running away from the crime.

Then there are the consoling yearnings and kindnesses in the midst of tragedy: Ruth Paine, who was also "alienated" and "isolated," and frustrated like Oswald, but who nevertheless "befriended" Marina Oswald in her time of

Continued on Page 15, Column 6

'MYTHS' OF CASE DENIED IN DETAIL

Panel Says Misinformation on the Assassination Led to 'Distorted' Views

By PETER KIHSS

The Warren Commission rejected in detail yesterday a number of charges suggesting that Lee Harvey Oswald had not acted alone in the assassination of President Kennedy.

The commission said that "publicizing of unchecked information" had led to "myths" and "distorted" interpretations. While each inaccuracy could be explained, it went on, "the number and variety of misstatements issued by the police" in Dallas would have "greatly assisted a skillful defense attorney."

On the other hand, Mark Lane, chairman of a Citizens Committee of Inquiry here, contended that if the report contained all the available evidence, "Oswald would have been acquitted" of both the President's assassination and the murder of the Dallas patrolman, J. D. Tippit.

In a news conference, Mr. Lane, a former Assemblyman, said his group would continue its efforts to "answer the unanswered questions." He said it had more than 250 workers here, with other committees in England, France and Denmark, and interested groups on 20 college campuses. His group estimated that it had raised and

Continued on Page 16, Column 4

PANEL UNANIMOUS

Theory of Conspiracy by Left or Right Is Rejected

The text of the report begins on the first page of the second section.

By ANTHONY LEWIS

Special to The New York Times

WASHINGTON, Sept. 27—The assassination of President Kennedy was the work of one man, Lee Harvey Oswald. There was no conspiracy, foreign or domestic.

That was the central finding in the Warren Commission report, made public this evening. Chief Justice Earl Warren and the six other members of the President's Commission on the Assassination of President John F. Kennedy were unanimous on this and all questions.

The commission found that Jack Ruby was on his own in killing Oswald. It rejected all theories that the two men were in some way connected. It said that neither rightists nor Communists bore responsibility for the murder of the President in Dallas last Nov. 22.

Why did Oswald do it? To this most important and most mysterious question the commission had no certain answer. It suggested that Oswald had no rational purpose, no motive adequate if "judged by the standards of reasonable men."

A Product of His Life

Rather, the commission saw Oswald's terrible act as the product of his entire life—a life "characterized by isolation, frustration and failure." He was just 24 years old at the time of the assassination.

"Oswald was profoundly alienated from the world in which he lived," the report said. "He had very few, if any, close relationships with other people and he appeared to have had great difficulty in finding a meaningful place in the world.

"He was never satisfied with anything.

"When he was in the United States, he resented the capitalist system. When he was in the Soviet Union, he apparently resented the Communist party members, who were accorded special privileges and who he thought were betraying Communism, and he spoke well of the United States."

The commission found that Oswald shot at former Maj. Gen. Edwin A. Walker in Dallas on April 10, 1963, narrowly missing him. It cited this as evidence of his capacity for violence.

It listed as factors that might have led Oswald to the assassination "his deep-rooted resentment of all authority, which was expressed in a hostility toward every society in which he lived," his "urge to try to find a place in history" and his "avowed commitment to Marx-

Continued on Page 14, Column 1

High Clerics to Ask Stronger Statement By Council on Jews

Special to The New York Times

ROME, Sept. 27—A powerful array of Roman Catholic prelates, including at least three American Cardinals, are preparing to speak out for a strong statement by the Ecumenical Council on the Jews, clerical sources said today.

The sources said that Richard James Cardinal Cushing, Archbishop of Boston, is known to have prepared an address to be given at the Council when the issue is debated.

The draft of the declaration was introduced last Friday by Augustin Cardinal Bea, the German Jesuit, who heads the Council's Secretariat for the Promotion of Christian Unity. It is considered by many Council Fathers—the voting prelates — and observers to be a "watered down" version of an earlier draft.

Other Cardinals Named

The earlier statement, among other things, made plain that the Jews of Christ's time and of today bore no responsibility for the Crucifixion. The weakened declaration declares only that Jews of today cannot be blamed.

Among those expected to attack the newer version are two other American Cardinals—Joseph Elmer Ritter, Archbishop of St. Louis, and Albert Gregory Meyer, Archbishop of Chicago.

Cardinal Spellman of New York has also said that he favors the more forceful state-

Continued on Page 7, Column 1

2 CITIES DENY REIN ON POLICE IN RIOTS

Civilian Review Units Hold F.B.I. Criticism Unfounded

By FRED POWLEDGE

Officials of civilian police advisory boards in Rochester and Philadelphia disagreed yesterday with a statement by the Federal Bureau of Investigation that boards such as theirs had "virtually paralyzed" the police during the summer riots.

The Rev. William H. Gray Jr., executive secretary of Philadelphia's eight-member review board, said: "It's over-simplifying the situation to say that the board has an effect on the rioting or the police behavior."

Ross J. Guglielmino, the executive director and legal counsel of the Rochester board, said he did not feel the F.B.I. criticism applied to Rochester.

What the F.B.I. Found

The two men commented in telephone interviews on a report released Saturday by President Johnson. The President had asked the F.B.I. to collect its investigations of summer riots in New York City, Rochester, Dixmoor, Ill.; Philadelphia, Seaside, Ore., Hampton Beach, N. H., and Jersey City, Paterson, and Elizabeth, N. J., and advise him if there were any pattern in the outbreaks.

The report, submitted by F.B.I. Director J. Edgar Hoover, concluded that the riots were not basically racial, although large numbers of Negroes took part; that they were not organized on a national basis, and that none of them was planned by any one group or individual.

Among the several points

Continued on Page 48, Column 1

Congress Will Act On Appalachia Aid And Medical Care

Special to The New York Times

WASHINGTON, Sept. 27—The fate of two key Administration programs—health insurance for the aged and aid to Appalachia—may be decided this week as Congress pushes toward adjournment.

"We could finish up Saturday; that's my most optimistic guess," Senator Mike Mansfield of Montana, the majority leader, said today. "But I have my fingers crossed."

The health insurance issue, currently in House-Senate conference, could delay adjournment until the following week, some legislative leaders believe.

Prospects for conference approval of some form of health insurance for the aged under Social Security have ranged from bright to gloomy in recent days.

The House passed a bill this summer to increase Social Security taxes as well as cash

Continued on Page 18, Column 4

CAMPAIGN IMPACT BELIEVED LIKELY

'Kennedy Legacy' Could Aid Democrats at the Polls

By TOM WICKER

Special to The New York Times

WASHINGTON, Sept. 27—The effects of the Warren Commission's report are sure to extend far beyond its conclusion that Lee Harvey Oswald, acting alone, killed President Kennedy last Nov. 22.

The massive document could have repercussions in the 1964 elections, on the present conduct of President Johnson, and ultimately on the availability to the public of Mr. Johnson and future Presidents.

It may produce major changes for the Secret Service, the agency now assigned to protect the President.

Other Agencies Affected

The assignments and powers of other agencies such as the Federal Bureau of Investigation and even the Central Intelligence Agency might be revamped and independent review of their activities and efficiency might be increased.

In the field of legislation, the report might produce—as recommended by the commission—a law making it a Federal crime to kill or attempt to kill a President, a Vice President or any officer next in line to the Presidency and the President-elect and Vice President-elect. Other legislation, particularly relating to security and investigative agencies and to the protection of Presidents, could also grow from the report.

Although the State Department was generally cleared of

Continued on Page 15, Column 5

G.I.'s Rescue Vietnam Captives; Uprising Stirs Mistrust of U.S.

By PETER GROSE

Special to The New York Times

SAIGON, South Vietnam, Sept. 27 — United States Army helicopters rescued 60 Vietnamese hostages today from a camp of rebel tribesmen in the central highlands.

The release of the prisoners met a Government condition for negotiations with the armed mountain tribesmen. It appeared to reduce the danger of a violent clash.

Nevertheless the revolt is having serious political consequences, involving growing suspicion between the United States mission and the Premier, Maj. Gen. Nguyen Khanh. The rebellion has intensified Saigon's feeling that the United States, which has supported General Khanh, is undergoing a change of policy.

[About five persons were reported shot dead when security forces fired on a crowd in Quinhon, 270 miles northeast of Saigon. Later a mob stormed a radio station and troops were called in to evict the demonstrators, Reuters reported.]

Officials around General Khanh say he no longer believes he can count on American help to stay in power and he feels he must seek firmer support from

Continued on Page 2, Column 1

NEWS INDEX

In this issue editorials appear on Page 28, obituaries on Page 29, TV and radio news on Page 47, and the News Summary and Index on Page 2.

Scientific Police Work Traced Bullets to Rifle Oswald Owned

By JOHN W. FINNEY

Special to The New York Times

WASHINGTON, Sept. 27—The Warren Commission's conclusion that Lee Harvey Oswald killed President Kennedy rests in large part on scientific evidence painstakingly established through modern technology.

On the basis of the scientific evidence alone it was possible to establish that the shots were fired by a rifle owned and possessed by Oswald, that the shots were fired from the sixth-floor window of a building in which Oswald worked, and that the fatal wound could have been caused by the bullets from the high-powered rifle.

These crucial points were established through scientific detective work that combined the techniques of handwriting, ballistics, and fiber and wounds analysis. Among the devices used were microscopes, spectroscopes, X-rays, surveying instruments and skulls filled with gelatin.

Even nuclear science was employed. Paraffin casts from Oswald's hands and face were put into a nuclear reactor at the Oak Ridge (Tenn.) National Laboratory in an unsuccessful attempt to see if radiation would show up traces of gunpowder. One major question left

Continued on Page 16, Column 5

NEW NUMBER FOR ORDERING WANT ads in The New York Times. OXford 5-3311. Fast, direct-line service to want ad takers.—Advt.

"All the News That's Fit to Print"

The New York Times

LATE CITY EDITION

U.S. Weather Bureau Report (Page 40) forecasts: Fair, windy and cold today; clear and very cold tonight. Sunny tomorrow. Temp. range: 38—24; yesterday: 50—28.

VOL. CXIV. No. 39,111. © 1965 by The New York Times Company. Times Square, New York, N.Y. 10036 NEW YORK, MONDAY, FEBRUARY 22, 1965. TEN CENTS

Malcolm X Shot to Death at Rally Here

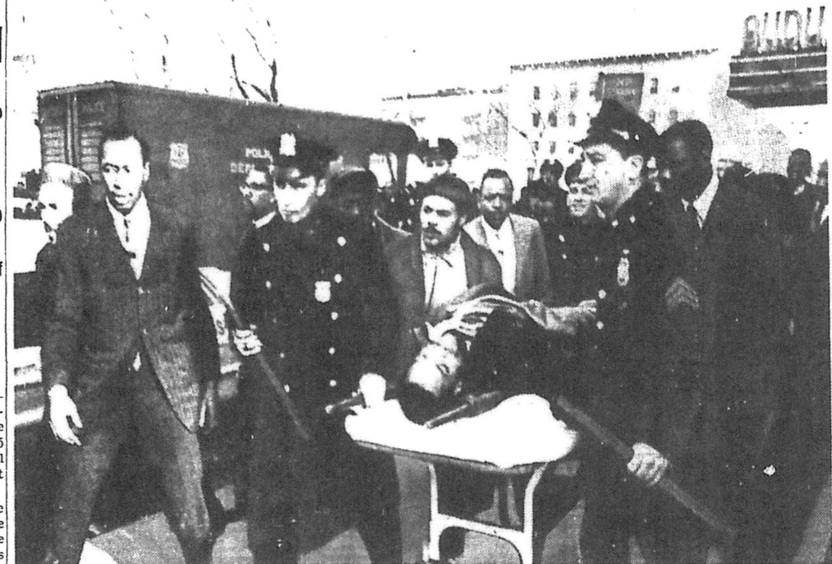

United Press International

Malcolm X being taken to hospital from Audubon Ballroom yesterday after he was shot while addressing a meeting

Three Other Negroes Wounded—One Is Held in Killing

By PETER KIHSS

Malcolm X, the 39-year-old leader af a militant black nationalist movement, was shot to death yesterday afternoon at a rally of his followers in a ballroom in Washington Heights.

Shortly before midnight, a 22-year-old Negro, Thomas Hagan, was charged with the killing. The police rescued him from the ballroom crowd after he had been shot and beaten.

Malcolm, a bearded extremist, had said only a few words of greeting when a fusillade rang out. The bullets knocked him over backward.

Pandemonium broke out among the 400 Negroes in the Audubon Ballroom at 166th Street and Broadway. As men, women and children ducked under tables and flattened themselves on the floor, more shots were fired. Some witnesses said 30 shots had been fired.

3 Weapons Fired

The police said seven bullets had struck Malcolm. Three other Negroes were shot.

About two hours later the police said the shooting had apparently been a result of a feud between followers of Malcolm and members of the extremist group he broke with last year, the Black Muslims. However, the police declined to say whether Hagan is a Muslim.

The Medical Examiner's office said early this morning that a preliminary autopsy showed Malcolm had died of "multiple gunshot wounds." The office said that bullets of two different calibers as well as shotgun pellets had been removed from his body.

One police theory was that as many as five conspirators might have been involved, two creating a diversionary disturbance.

Hagan was shot in the left thigh and his left leg was broken, apparently by kicks. He was under treatment in the Bellevue Hospital prison ward last night; perhaps a dozen policemen were guarding him, according to the hospital's night superintendent. The police said

Continued on Page 10, Column 1

Malcolm Knew He Was a 'Marked Man'

By THEODORE JONES

"I live like a man who's already dead," Malcolm X said last Thursday in a two-hour interview in the Harlem office of his Organization for Afro-American Unity.

"I'm a marked man," he said slowly as he fingered the horn-rimmed glasses he wore and leaned forward to give emphasis to his words. "It doesn't frighten me for myself as long as I felt they would not hurt my family."

Asked about "they," Malcolm smiled, shook his head, and said, "those folks down at 116th Street and that man in Chicago."

The references, Malcolm quickly confirmed, were to his former associates in the Black Muslim movement and to Elijah Muhammad, the organizer and head of the movement. Before Malcolm X left the movement 18 months ago, he was the minister of the Black Muslims' Harlem mosque at 116th Street and Lenox Avenue.

"No one can get out without trouble," Malcolm continued, "and this thing with me will be resolved by death and violence."

Why were they after him? "Because I'm me," he replied.

But realizing that was not enough to say, he pushed into an almost endless flow of sentences.

"I was the spokesman for the Black Muslims," he said. "I believed in Elijah Muhammad more strongly than Christians do in Jesus. I believed in him so strongly that my mind, my body, my voice functioned 100 per cent for him and the movement. My belief led others to believe.

"Now I'm out. And there's the fear if my image isn't shattered, the Muslims in the movement will leave. Then, they know I know a lot. As long as I was in the movement, anything he [Elijah Muhammad] did was to me by divine guidance."

Malcolm said that he knew many things that made him a

Continued on Page 11, Column 2

SCHOOL AID DELAY BRINGS A DEMAND FOR HOUSE ACTION

Administration Is Seeking to Get a Decision This Week From Powell Group

SHOWDOWN IS VOWED

Supporter Pledges Move if Measure Is Not Called Up at Thursday Session

By MARJORIE HUNTER

Special to The New York Times

WASHINGTON, Feb. 21 — The Administration is determined to get House committee action this week on the $1.25 billion school aid bill, a virtual legislative truant in the last few weeks.

This was to have been the week that the bill was to have come up for floor action in the House. Instead, the measure has not even been brought up before the full House Education and Labor Committee.

President Johnson and House leaders are "deeply concerned" over the failure of Representative Adam Clayton Powell, Democrat of Manhattan, to move the bill out of his committee, sources close to the President said today.

The bill, which has top priority on the President's legislative list, got off to a fast start early in the new Congress.

Met on Saturdays

Working day and night, a House subcommittee held 10 days of public hearings. The subcommittee even met on Saturdays, almost unheard of so early in a new session, in order to speed the bill.

The measure was approved Feb. 5 by the six subcommittee Democrats. The three Republicans boycotted the voting session in protest against failure to hold longer hearings.

"We were in good shape to move the bill right along," Representative Frank Thompson Jr., Democrat of New Jersey, a member of the subcommittee, said today. "But nothing happened."

Representative Powell failed to call the full committee into session the following week. And he did not call a meeting after the long Lincoln birthday holiday recess.

The committee is required under its own rules to meet next Thursday.

"If the chairman doesn't bring up the bill then, we'll have a showdown," Representative Thompson promised.

Linked to Travel Funds

Representative Powell could not be reached today to comment on whether he intended to call up the bill at the Thursday meeting.

Administration sources say that the delay over the education bill appeared to be tied in with Representative Powell's effort to win favorable House action on a resolution determining how much money will be authorized for his committee's travel and investigation this year.

The House is expected to vote this week on a number of such authorization measures, including one for the Powell committee.

Meanwhile, Republicans have used the more than two-week breather to draft proposed

Continued on Page 18, Column 1

POWELL OPPOSING NEW MOTLEY POST

Says Senator Can Be More Effective in Albany Than in Borough Presidency

By MARTIN GANSBERG

Representative Adam Clayton Powell asserted yesterday that the elected leaders of Harlem were opposed to the selection of State Senator Constance Baker Motley as Manhattan Borough President.

In a sharply worded telegram to Mayor Wagner, Mr. Powell, who heads the 12th District South, said that he also was speaking for Hulan Jack, Mark T. Southall and Percy Sutton in insisting that Mrs. Motley would "be much more effective as a Senator than as Borough President."

"Not one of the elected leaders representing the Harlem community has sponsored her," Mr. Powell asserted. "Unfortunately, and once again, the selection of a Negro is apparently being made by the white man."

Mr. Jack is leader of the 14th District North, Mr. Southall of the 12th District North and Mr. Sutton is a State Assemblyman from the 11th District. The other Harlem leaders are George Miller of the 11th District and J. Raymond Jones of the 13th District.

Mr. Powell's statement, released here by a spokesman for him, was issued at 1:30 yesterday morning after he had completed telephone conversations from Puerto Rico, where

Continued on Page 17, Column 7

Rise of 24 Million In U.S. Labor Force Is Forecast by 1980

By JOHN D. POMFRET

Special to The New York Times

WASHINGTON, Feb. 21 — The Labor Department issued new projections today indicating that the nation's labor force would grow to 86 million in 1970 and 101.4 million in 1980.

It was 77 million in 1964 and 73 million in 1960.

Although the projected increase between 1970 and 1980 —15.4 million—is 2.4 million higher than the projected increase between 1960 and 1970, the rate of gain would be about the same, 17.7 per cent from 1960 to 1970 and 17.9 per cent from 1970 to 1980.

An increase of 24 million workers between 1964 and 1980 would mean that 1.5 million new jobs would have to be created each year, on the average, merely to absorb the growth in the labof force. Still more jobs would be needed to offset gains in output per man-hour and to reduce the level of unemployment.

The projections were compiled by Miss Sophia Cooper and Denis F. Johnston of the Bureau of Labor Statistics.

According to their study, the rest of this decade will show

Continued on Page 19, Column 1

AGE IS A PROBLEM IN LABOR COUNCIL

Some in A.F.L.-C.I.O. Feel Older Chiefs Should Quit —Most Are Over 65

By DAMON STETSON

Special to The New York Times

BAL HARBOUR, Fla., Feb. 21—Some leaders of the American Federation of Labor and Congress of Industrial Organizations are beginning to worry about the superannuated character of the organization's executive council.

The 29-member council, which opens its winter meeting here tomorrow in the plush surroundings of an alabaster-white beachfront hotel, is getting along in years. Fifteen members—more than half—of the labor organization's top policy-making body are 65 years old or over, nine are 70 or over, and one is 82.

One of these elder statesmen of the labor movement, who is still playing an energetic role as leader of his own union, said that he did not feel age alone was any criterion of a labor leader's effectiveness. But he said that he was disturbed that some former union presidents were continuing as members of the council long after having given up active direction of their unions and going into retirement.

If the labor movement isn't careful, he said, the council will become little more than a fraternal organization of old men who like to come to Florida in the winter to play gin rummy.

Although some labor leaders here are willing to talk privately about the need for an infusion of new blood in the council, no one is saying much publicly about it at this time.

Among some of the younger council members, there is a feeling that the council and the merged labor organization ought to become more dynamic and aggressive. But there is a reluctance, at the same time, to push out old war horses of an earlier era.

George Meany, president of the A.F.L.-C.I.O., who is 70, is one member who has shown no

Continued on Page 19, Column 1

PANEL OF 7 NAMED TO TRY TO IMPROVE TRANSIT FINANCES

Governor and Mayor Join In Attempt to Avert a Rise in the 15-Cent Fare

By EMANUEL PERLMUTTER

The appointment of a seven-man citizens' committee to try to solve the financial problems of the city's transit system was announced yesterday by Governor Rockefeller and Mayor Wagner.

The naming of the committee followed a recent announcement by Joseph E. O'Grady, chairman of the Transit Authority, that the 15-cent fare might have to be increased in view of the system's growing deficit.

With the election of a Mayor coming up this fall, and that of a Governor next year, both Mr. Wagner and Mr. Rockefeller have been reported to be trying to avoid a fare rise. One has been avoided in the last few years by increases in financial assistance from the city, with the acquiescence of the Legislature.

Make-up of the Panel

The chairman of the citizens' study committee, named by Mr. Rockefeller and Mr. Wagner, will be J. Victor Herd, board chairman of the Continental Insurance Company.

Other members of the committee are John A. Coleman, former president of the New York Stock Exchange; J. Clarence Davies, former chairman of the city Housing and Redevelopment Board; Charles Garrahan, vice president of the Amalgamated Clothing Workers of America; George S. Moore, president of the First National City Bank of New York; Clifton W. Phalen, president of the New York Telephone Company, and Walter N. Rothschild Jr., president of Abraham & Straus.

The announcement said the committee had been appointed "to make recommendations for the immediate and long-term solution of the substantial financial problem presented by the city subway and surface lines."

Review Is Planned

It "will review the administration and economics of public mass transit in the city and its relationship with other forms of transportation serving New York City," the statement continued.

"The committee will report to the Governor and the Mayor as quickly as their recommendations can be developed."

Although no time limit was set within which the committee is to make its recommendations, it is virtually under obligation to make them before the end of the year. The authority would have to know where it could get additional revenues before it could make a contract offer to its union employes late this fall.

The committee was envisaged almost 14 months ago in the contract settlement between the Transit Authority and the Transport Workers Union.

Asked about the delay in its creation, a spokesman for Mayor Wagner said yesterday, "It was a question of getting the right men for the committee."

On Feb. 2, Mr. O'Grady said the authority expected a deficit of more than $33 million in the fiscal year starting July 1. He said this prospect made it doubtful that the 15-cent fare

Continued on Page 22, Column 7

MILITARY COUNCIL DISMISSES KHANH; HE BOWS TO EDICT

VOTE UNANIMOUS

Tran Van Minh Named Acting Commander of Armed Forces

By JACK LANGGUTH

Special to The New York Times

SAIGON, South Vietnam, Monday, Feb. 22—Lieut. Gen. Nguyen Khanh bowed today to a unanimous decision of the Armed Forces Council to replace him with Maj. Gen. Tran Van Minh as commander in chief.

After the council voted late yesterday to oust him, General Khanh spent the night telephoning military commanders throughout the country to rally support. Unsuccessful, he called the council's headquarters in Saigon early this morning from the resort of Dalat, northeast of the capital, to admit defeat.

Council members said they hoped to bring General Khanh into the capital later in the day for a news conference.

Earlier, Brig. Gen. Nguyen Chanh Thi, commander of the army's I Corps, said the South Vietnamese Air Force would bomb any troops or tanks that moved toward Saigon.

Saigon Wary About Firing

General Thi, who helped to keep General Khanh in power in the past, had become a leader in the movement to drop him.

Unusual troop movements and some mortar fire on the outskirts of the capital kept Saigon wary after the broadcast announcement of General Khanh's removal. But the mortar fire and flares dropped around Tansonnhut Airport were apparently connected with operations against the Vietcong.

The ouster came a day after General Khanh, aided by loyal paratroops and air units, defeated a brief and bloodless attempt at a military coup d'état. Some of the officers who backed him were among those who now voted for his dismissal.

Suu Agrees to Action

General Khanh did not attend the council meeting.

The council's announcement did not specify whether General Minh, who was named acting commander in chief, would also inherit General Khanh's second post, the chairmanship of the Armed Forces Council.

A council delegation called on the chief of state, Dr. Phan Khac Suu, to tell him about the vote. The new Premier, Dr. Phan Huy Quat, was present.

Dr. Suu readily agreed to sign an order to dismiss General Khanh and appoint General Minh.

In his order, Dr. Suu said General Khanh would be reassigned. The general's ambitions and his courting of Buddhist political support have long made him suspect among his colleagues.

Second Meeting Held

Council members met again near midnight to map a strategy that would keep General Khanh from regaining power.

Air Vice Marshal Nguyen Cao Ky first insisted that General Khanh be required to leave the country.

But General Khanh was not yet ready to give up. From his command post at the southeastern beach resort of Cap Saint-Jacques, he telephoned offers to junior officers, not on the council, who he thought might support him.

Brig. Gen. Nguyen Van Chuan, General Thi's deputy, was offered command of the I Corps if he would send troops to support General Khanh. General Thi countered the call with a message of his own, cautioning the deputy that General

Continued on Page 3, Column 1

French Official Asks Talks to Stop War

By JACK RAYMOND

Special to The New York Times

WASHINGTON, Feb. 21—Maurice Couve de Murville, the French Foreign Minister, urged before a nationwide American television audience today that negotiations for a settlement in Vietnam be attempted "as soon as possible."

His public advocacy of negotiations followed three days of private talks with President Johnson, Secretary of State Dean Rusk and other officials during which he was unable to win them over to the idea.

In reply to a question, Mr. Couve de Murville said: "We think that the negotiations [to end the fighting in Vietnam] should be engaged as soon as possible.

"A long time, in our

Continued on Page 3, Column 6

U.S. FINDS BACKING IN WORLD'S PRESS

Extent of Support for Action in Asia Surprises Capital, U.S.I.A. Director Says

By JOHN W. FINNEY

Special to The New York Times

WASHINGTON, Feb. 21 — Foreign editorial reaction to the United States air strikes in North Vietnam has been generally favorable—more so than some Administration officials expected, according to Carl T. Rowan, director of the United States Information Agency.

An analysis by the agency shows that the actions this month drew almost universal support in the South American press, strong support in Southeast Asia and guarded endorsement in some countries of the Middle East and South Asia.

The only strong opposition, except from the Communist press, came from Africa and some sections of the Middle East and South Asia.

World Reaction 'Good'

Summarizing the reaction, Mr. Rowan said in an interview: "The general world reaction to our actions in Vietnam has been good, and considerably better than I had expected."

Among newspapers supporting the United States air strikes they were viewed as a legitimate and necessary response to the Communist attacks on American installations in South Vietnam and as a demonstration of American firmness.

There was a nearly unanimous feeling that the United States should not widen the war in South Vietnam. But a majority of the newspapers accepted the repeated policy statements of the Johnson Administration that it was seeking only to press the Communists into ceasing aggressive activities in South Vietnam.

A majority of the editorial

Continued on Page 3, Column 5

Democrats in Legislature to End Duplicate Bill-Filing as Waste

By SYDNEY H. SCHANBERG

Special to The New York Times

ALBANY, Feb. 21—Democratic leaders disclosed today that they had decided to abolish the wasteful practice of duplicate bill-filing in the Legislature.

Senate Majority Leader Joseph Zaretzki said he and Assembly Speaker Anthony J. Travia reached the decision at a meeting last week.

Under present practice, sanctioned by existing rules, hundreds of times every year several different legislators—sometimes dozens—file the same bill.

The bills are printed separately, but the wording is identical. It costs the state $12.32 a page to print legislative bills, and the cost of the duplication runs into tens of thousands of dollars.

Senator Zaretzki said that from now on, if more than one legislator wanted to introduce the same bill they would have to sponsor it cooperatively. That is, instead of many bills on one subject there would be only one, with the names of the sponsors affixed, whether Republican or Democratic.

Mr. Zaretzki said that although the change was based so far solely on a leadership decision, a formal change would be proposed this week in the Legislature's rules. The Senate leader said he was assured of enough votes in both houses to carry the proposal.

The Manhattan Democrat said he had already asked Earl W. Brydges, the Republican minority leader in the Senate, not to introduce any bills on Governor Rockefeller's program without

Continued on Page 17, Column 5

Washington's Birthday

Today is Washington's Birthday, a Federal and state holiday, and following is a list of services and facilities that are or are not affected:

Public and parochial schools, banks, stock and commodity exchanges—Closed.

Department stores and retail business in the city and suburban areas—Some open, some closed.

Post offices—Special delivery only, no business transacted.

Parking—Alternate-side rules suspended, all others, including parking meter rules, in effect.

Sanitation—No refuse collection.

Congo Seeks Return Of Ousted Teachers

By JOSEPH LELYVELD

Special to The New York Times

LEOPOLDVILLE, the Congo, Feb. 21—The Congolese Government sent an urgent message to Athens today inviting the UNESCO teachers it expelled yesterday as subversives to return to their classes here as soon as possible.

Actually, a decision not to expel the teachers was taken last night before their plane departed from Leopoldville for Athens. But something went wrong with official communications and the security police at the airport insisted that the teachers and their dependents, a total of 35 persons, board the plane.

The snag in communications was eventually straightened out to the satisfaction of the security police, but not before the plane was airborne. Leopoldville

Continued on Page 6, Column 1

Moscow Announces a Relaxation Of Attitude Toward Intellectuals

By THEODORE SHABAD

Special to The New York Times

MOSCOW, Feb. 21 — The Communist party proclaimed today a relaxed attitude toward the Soviet Union's intellectuals.

An article that appeared in Pravda, the principal party newspaper, assailed what was described as a trend toward anti-intellectualism under the Khrushchev era and asserted that "genuine creativeness is possible only through search, experimentation, free expression and clashes of viewpoints."

The article, viewed here as a policy statement of Premier Khrushchev's successors on the party's attitude toward intellectuals, was signed by Aleksei M. Rumyantsev, who was named the paper's editor-in-chief after Mr. Khrushchev's downfall in October.

In an evident allusion to the former Premier, Mr. Rumyantsev condemned "attempts to impose one's subjective evaluations and personal tastes as the yardstick of artistic creation, especially when they are expressed in the name of the party."

The Pravda editor, a leading ideological spokesman of the administration, said party criticism of literature would be guided by a policy statement made in 1925, long before Stalin imposed rigid controls over the arts.

The 40-year-old pronouncement, which he quoted, said:

"Communist criticism must rid itself of the tone of literary command. The party must in every way eradicate attempts at homebred and incompetent administrative interference in literary affairs." Mr. Rumyan-

Continued on Page 2, Column 2

NEWS INDEX

"All the News That's Fit to Print"

The New York Times.

LATE CITY EDITION

U. S. Weather Bureau Report (Page 95) forecasts: Mostly sunny, hot and humid today; fair, warm tonight and tomorrow.
Temp. Range: 92—68; yesterday: 87—63.
Temp.-Hum. Index: high 70's; yesterday: 77.

NEWS SUMMARY AND INDEX, PAGE 95

SECTION ONE

VOL. CXIV—No. 39,285. | THE NEW YORK TIMES, SUNDAY, AUGUST 15, 1965. | 50c beyond 50-mile zone from New York City, except on Long Island, higher in air delivery cities | THIRTY CENTS

21 DEAD IN LOS ANGELES RIOTS; 600 HURT; 20,000 TROOPS CALLED; PRESIDENT CONDEMNS VIOLENCE

U.S. ADDING 6,400 TO MARINE FORCE IN SOUTH VIETNAM

Step Goes Beyond Increase Announced by Johnson—Advance Units Arrive

DANANG STRENGTHENED

Company There Carries Out Attack by Copter Against Vietcong-Held Village

By CHARLES MOHR
Special to The New York Times

SAIGON, South Vietnam, Sunday, Aug. 15—A few thousand more United States marines landed in South Vietnam today as advance elements for a total of 6,400 Marine Corps reinforcements expected within days.

A military spokesman said that headquarters units of the Seventh Regimental Landing Team of the First Marine Division, with a battalion of troops, had come ashore in landing craft at Chulai, 350 miles north of Saigon, yesterday. Another regiment of marines has been stationed there for several months.

The spokesman did not disclose the size of the newly arrived group, but a battalion landing team numbers 1,500 to 1,800 men.

Another Battalion Lands

This morning another battalion of marines began landing at Danang, north of Chulai. Danang is the main headquarters of the Marine forces in South Vietnam.

The spokesman said the full regimental strength of 6,400 would soon be on hand.

The Marine landings were not part of the planned increase of 50,000 American troops announced by President Johnson on July 28, the spokesman added. Instead, he said, they represent a "supplement."

As of Aug. 8, there were 82,400 American servicemen in South Vietnam, 25,700 of them marines. Mr. Johnson has said that the total will soon reach at least 125,000.

In the Danang area before dawn, United States marines engaged in an unorthodox night helicopter-assault operation. A rifle company was landed near the village of Phoan under the illumination of aerial flares of 1.5 million candlepower dropped

Continued on Page 2, Column 3

Sports News

GOLF

Dave Marr shot a one-under-par 70 yesterday to tie Tommy Aaron for first place in the Professional Golfers Association tournament in Ligonier, Pa. Each has 209 for 54 holes. Gardner Dickinson shot a 69 for 210 and Jack Nicklaus and Bill Casper shared fourth place at 211.

BASEBALL

Hector Lopez's single with the bases loaded in the ninth inning yesterday gave the New York Yankees a 3-2 victory over the Kansas City Athletics in the second Bat Day at the Stadium. The victory gave the Yanks a 59-59 won-lost mark, the first time they have been at .500 since they were 7-7. The Cleveland Indians beat the league-leading Minnesota Twins, 3-1, behind the three-hit pitching of Sam McDowell, who struck out 11 to run his total to 227, best in the league.

The New York Mets beat the Astros, 1-0, in 10 innings at Houston and ended an 11-game losing streak. The victory was the Mets' first in the Astrodome. The Los Angeles Dodgers beat the Pittsburgh Pirates, 1-0, in the 10th inning for Sandy Koufax's 21st victory.

FOOTBALL

The New York Giants opened their exhibition season by absorbing a 44-7 trouncing from the Packers at Green Bay.

HORSE RACING

What a Treat scored a neck victory in the 85th Alabama Stakes for 3-year-old fillies at Saratoga. Discipline was second and Terentia third in the $63,200 race, but their order was reversed after a foul claim by Larry Adams, Terentia's jockey. Eighteen fillies started. Mister Judge, $21, won the $22,950 Longport Handicap at Atlantic City by a neck.

Details in Section 5

Earl Brown Rejects Spot on Beame Slate

The New York Times

Earl Brown

By RICHARD L. MADDEN

Earl Brown, chairman of the city's Commission on Human Rights, declined yesterday to run for Manhattan Borough President on the slate of Controller Abraham D. Beame in the Democratic primary.

Mr. Brown said that "overriding personal considerations have left me no choice." He did not elaborate.

The Beame forces circulated petitions to put Mr.

Continued on Page 43, Column 1

MOSCOW REPORTS NEW MOON PHOTOS

Pictures of Far Side Said to Fill In the Gap of Earlier Survey by Spacecraft

By PETER GROSE
Special to The New York Times

MOSCOW, Aug. 14—An unmanned spacecraft has transmitted high-definition television pictures of hitherto unphotographed areas on the side of the moon opposite the earth, Tass, the Soviet press agency, said today.

The pictures were not made public.

Combined with the first photographs ever of the far side of the moon, taken in October, 1959, the new pictures give the Russians a complete pictorial record of the side of the moon that is never turned toward the earth, Tass said.

The pictures announced today were taken July 20 from a point much closer to the moon than the earlier series, less than 7,000 miles above the surface against about 40,000 in 1959.

The new pictures show surface features three miles or less across, according to Grigory Leikin, a senior researcher of the Astronomical Society at the Soviet Academy of Sciences.

A complete atlas of the

Continued on Page 41, Column 1

PAPANDREOU BLOC SPLIT BY WALKOUT IN HIS OWN PARTY

Two of Ex-Premier's Aides Claim Enough Support to Form New Greek Regime

Special to The New York Times

ATHENS, Aug. 14—Two of former Premier George Papandreou's principal aides announced today that they had decided to break away from his majority Center Union party at the head of an undisclosed number of Members of Parliament.

The declaration by Stephanos Stephanopoulos, Deputy Premier in the Papandreou Government ousted July 15, and Elias Tsirimokos, its Interior Minister, raised hopes that a Greek Government would be formed Monday.

A spokesman for the two leaders said they had "the support of more Center Union Deputies than is needed to swing a parliamentary majority in their favor."

Third Aide May Defect

A third Papandreou aide, Savros Papapolitis, who heads a group of 10 Center Union Deputies, asserted that he was reconsidering his allegiance to the former Premier and might join the defectors.

The spokesman for Mr. Stephanopoulos and Mr. Tsirimokos, both of whom were expected to be candidates for Premier, said a formal declaration of secession from the Papandreou party would be sent to Parliament Monday.

Today's development was a direct result of former Premier Papandreou's stiffening attitude in his conflict with King Constantine, who forced him out of power July 15 in a clash over political influence in the Greek army. The King was opposed to a Papandreou plan to replace the Defense Minister and to purge right-wing army officers.

Novas Cabinet Failed

Constantine promptly appointed a Papandreou aide, George Athanasiadis-Novas, Speaker of Parliament, to form a new government. But Mr. Athanasiadis-Novas managed to get the support of only 25 Center Union deputies.

He was overthrown in a stormy session of Parliament early on Aug. 5 by the combined Papandreou forces and 22 pro-Communist Deputies while Athens was in the grip of riots and street fighting between Papandreou supporters and the police.

A week ago, King Constantine asked another Papandreou aide, Mr. Stephanopoulos, to form a government. But the Premier-designate gave up the attempt after having been rebuffed at a Center Union caucus by a majority still loyal to Mr. Papandreou.

At a 90-minute audience at the palace Friday, Mr. Papan-

Continued on Page 42, Column 1

JOHNSON SHOCKED

He Calls Disturbances 'Tragic' and Appeals for Order on Coast

By ROBERT B. SEMPLE Jr.
Special to The New York Times

AUSTIN, Tex., Aug. 14—President Johnson described the Los Angeles riots today as "tragic and shocking." He warned the rioters that their rights could not be won and their grievances remedied "through violence."

The President appealed to "every person in a position of leadership" in Los Angeles to make "every effort to restore order."

He also instructed two high Administration officials to meet with Gov. Edmund G. Brown of California in New York and to place themselves at the Governor's disposal in an effort to stop the riots. Mr. Brown stopped in New York before returning to California from an interrupted overseas vacation.

The two officials were Lee C. White, special counsel to the President, and LeRoy Collins, Under Secretary of Commerce. Mr. Collins is former director of the Community Relations Service, which is charged with encouraging voluntary compliance with the Civil Rights Act of 1964.

Report on Troops Denied

A report from California said that the Administration had also promised to provide Federal troops if necessary to quell the disturbance. This report was quickly denied by a Presidential aide, Joseph A. Califano Jr.

Reached in Washington, Mr. Califano pointed out that California had 21,000 National Guardsmen on whom it could call and said that there was no need to involve Regular Army troops.

Mr. Johnson's appeal for speedy restoration of order was read to reporters by his press secretary, Bill D. Moyers. The President, spending the weekend at his ranch 65 miles west of Austin, has been keeping in close touch with the situation through the Justice Department and members of his staff in Washington.

The President's statement did not speculate on the causes of the disturbances and White House aides here were reluctant to do so. One aide said that the riots had happened so quickly there had been little opportunity to examine the reasons for them. He said that the

Continued on Page 77, Column 3

GUARDSMEN SWEEP AREA: Mobilized National Guardsmen move in convoy formation through Negro section of Los Angeles where looting and arson continued into fourth day.

United Press International Telephotos

SCENE OF DESTRUCTION: Deserted after another night of violence in the city, 103d Street is littered with debris. Estimates of damage ranged up to $100 million.

CURFEW ORDERED

Outbursts Spread to New Areas—Disaster Zone Is Proclaimed

By GLADWIN HILL
Special to The New York Times

LOS ANGELES, Aug. 14—Rioting, looting and burning spread today for the fourth day in the Negro district of southwestern Los Angeles. The disorders continued despite the rifle fire of National Guard troops and local peace forces.

The death toll from the hoodlum-instigated lawlessness rose tonight to 21. Nineteen of the victims were rioters, one was a sheriff's deputy and one a fireman. The last two were white men, as was one of the victims officially classed as a rioter.

The number of injured reached about 600, most of them rioters. Arrests totaled 1,400. Estimates of property damage ranged from $30 million to $100 million.

The number of California guardsmen called up rose to 20,000, according to Lieut. Gen. Roderick Hill, the state's National Guard adjutant. Some 4,000 were on patrol today. More than 1,000 policemen and deputies were in the area.

Curfew Hours

Tonight Lieut. Gov. Glenn Anderson proclaimed a curfew in a 35-square-mile area where the rioting has centered. From 8 P.M. to sunrise, he decreed, anyone on the streets except law-enforcement officers and newsmen will be seized.

Mr. Anderson, serving as acting Governor until Gov. Edmund G. Brown returned tonight from a European vacation, also proclaimed the riot zone a disaster area. This permitted policemen to be brought in as needed from surrounding cities in four counties.

Local authorities said help might have to be sought from the Federal Government.

"It's a mess, and it's getting progressively worse," General Hill said. "It started with a few square blocks, and today it was spreading over 21 square miles."

Sniping Increases

There were signs late tonight of some diminution in the disorders. Reports of new outbreaks of looting and fires were less frequent. But there was an increase in sniping from roofs and buildings.

Two sheriff's deputies were wounded in one exchange with snipers.

The depredations in the four-day rampage, triggered by the arrest last Wednesday night of a Negro on charges of drunken driving, spread despite a massive sweep operation. Block by block, the troops and civilian officers removed everyone from the streets who could give no

Continued on Page 79, Column 1

2,000 GUARDSMEN ON CHICAGO ALERT

Kerner Notifies Units After 2d Night of Racial Riots—Negroes Get Appeal

By DONALD JANSON
Special to The New York Times

CHICAGO, Aug. 14—Gov. Otto Kerner placed 2,000 National Guardsmen on stand-by alert at armories here today in the wake of two nights of Chicago's worst racial rioting in 13 years.

The action was taken at the request of Orlando W. Wilson, Chicago's superintendent of police, to forestall any resumption of the bottle-throwing violence that injured 60 persons last night.

Mr. Wilson warned residents of the largely Negro West Side neighborhood where the rioting occurred that unless they did "all in their power" to help the police prevent lawlessness the situation could deteriorate into uncontrolled strife such as Los Angeles has suffered the last few days.

He spoke at a solemn news conference in the office of Mayor Richard J. Daley. The Mayor, by his side, appealed to Chicagoans to stay off the street in the West Side neighborhood so that the police could isolate troublemakers and prevent any recurrence of last night's eight-hour riot.

The area, 40 blocks west of downtown Chicago, was quiet tonight. Taverns that ordinarily would have been jammed on a Saturday night were closed. Pulaski Road between Madison Street and the Eisenhower expressway was littered with broken glass, and store windows hit by rocks and bottles were boarded up to prevent looting.

By the time the police restored order shortly before dawn today 104 persons had been arrested, primarily on charges of disorderly conduct and resisting arrest. Most of

Continued on Page 76, Column 1

Discontent and Hate Viewed as Factors In Coast Violence

By WALLACE TURNER
Special to The New York Times

LOS ANGELES, Aug. 14—Negroes in a depressed area of Los Angeles were swept up into an emotonal tide of hate and bitterness that caused them to beat and burn, observers said here today.

One worker for the Congress of Racial Equality, Cornell Henderson, a Negro, declared, "There were a lot of young hoods and agitators. But there were a lot of others who were just discontented and took advantage of the situation for emotional release."

There also was a heavy overlay of hate preaching, said Mr. Henderson.

"I saw the Black Muslims in the area," he said. "They were preaching resistance and 'down with the police brutality' and the usual thing that they talk about. They wanted to have the white men driven away. They chanted 'go away, whitey' at any white people they saw."

Psychiatrists, examining and

Continued on Page 80, Column 1

Policeman Kills One, Shoots 2d in Beating

By THEODORE JONES

A 23-year old Brooklyn laborer was fatally shot and a 15-year-old youth was wounded early yesterday by an off-duty patrolman who went to the aid of a man being beaten and robbed by six youths.

The police said both the youth and the laborer had attacked the patrolman with knives after he had identified himself and sought to help the beaten man in front of a five-story apartment house at the corner of Nostrand and Vernon Avenues. The policeman and all others involved were Negroes.

However, a witness to the shooting gave a different version. He said the slain man, identified as Willie James

Continued on Page 77, Column 1

GOV. BROWN VOWS TO RESTORE ORDER

Arrives in Los Angeles Aboard White House Plane—Cut Short Holiday in Greece

Special to The New York Times

LOS ANGELES, Aug. 14—Gov. Edmund G. Brown returned to California tonight and pledged "to restore law and order in Los Angeles."

In a news conference alongside the White House jet that flew him from New York, he said that he did not plan to accept President Johnson's offer of Federal help now.

"I don't want to federalize the National Guard—that's a major step—unless I have to," Governor Brown said.

"But if I have to, I will. I intend to restore law and order to Los Angeles."

"I will go down to the area as soon as I can," he said.

In a brief stopover in New York, the Governor referred to the Negro rioting here as "a state of insurrection."

Governor Brown arrived at the Los Angeles international airport just before 10 P.M. Pacific daylight time (1 A.M. Sunday, Eastern daylight time.) He was met by Lieut. Gov. Glenn Anderson, who ordered the National Guard to riot control duty Friday afternoon.

The Governor appeared on the steps of the Air Force Jetstar after a four-minute conference inside the cabin. Other participants were the state Attorney General, Thomas Lynch; Hale Champion, the State Director of Finance, one of the Governor's chief advisers, and Jack Burby, the Governor's press secretary.

Mrs. Brown accompanied her husband.

The Governor said he had returned to California to "give what aid the Governor can give to the Mayor and police officials of Los Angeles."

He said: "I want to see this catastrophe ended."

The Governor sidestepped

Continued on Page 81, Column 3

164-Year-Old Brooklyn Navy Yard Launches Last Ship

The New York Times (by Jack Manning)

Mrs. Bruce Solomonson, daughter of Vice President and Mrs. Humphrey, christens the amphibious transport Duluth, the last ship to be launched at the Brooklyn Navy Yard.

By DOUGLAS ROBINSON

The 164-year-old Brooklyn Navy Yard launched its last ship yesterday amid the blare of martial music, the boom of cannon and the fluttering of flags. The installation, formally known as the New York Naval Shipyard, was one of 95 bases and facilities ordered closed last year by Defense Secretary Robert S. McNamara as part of an economy move. Despite the gay trappings of the launching, an air of sadness hung over the assembled workers and their families who joined Navy officers and officials to watch the amphibious transport Duluth float into the East River. "It's not a happy day, especially for the younger workers," commented Vincent DiNovi, who has been a machinist at the yard for 25 years. "It's not a happy launching and it's the last

Continued on Page 47, Column 4

Today's Sections

Index to Subjects

"All the News That's Fit to Print"

The New York Times

LATE CITY EDITION

Weather: Fair and warm today and tonight. Partly cloudy tomorrow. Temp. range: today 85-63; Wed. 81-62. Temp.-Hum. Index: mid-70's; Wed. 72. Full report on Page 93.

VOL. CXVI. No. 39,947 NEW YORK, THURSDAY, JUNE 8, 1967 — 10 CENTS

ISRAELIS ROUT THE ARABS, APPROACH SUEZ, BREAK BLOCKADE, OCCUPY OLD JERUSALEM; AGREE TO U.N. CEASE-FIRE; U.A.R. REJECTS IT

JOHNSON WILL USE CABINET TO COURT STATES' OFFICIALS

Aides Will Seek to Tighten Ties Between Governors and the White House

By WARREN WEAVER Jr.
Special to The New York Times

WASHINGTON, June 7—President Johnson has decided to use the members of his Cabinet as diplomatic agents in his campaign to improve relations between the Administration and state governments.

The President has approved a plan under which each member of the Cabinet would be assigned four or five states as his personal responsibility, with instructions to maintain personal contact between the Governors and the White House.

As part of the same effort, each of the 50 states will be given a "day" in Washington next fall and winter, when a planeload of its key officials will fly here to hold conferences all over the capital, capped by a meeting of the Governors with the President.

Bryant's Work Continued

Both projects reflect Mr. Johnson's continuing determination to build domestic as well as foreign bridges by working to sort out the tangled Federal-state relations that have been increasingly complicated by the administration of the Great Society programs.

Both are attempts to give some permanency to the contacts established during the last four months by Farris Bryant, the President's envoy to the states, on visits to 40 capitals with a squad of Federal experts.

Mr. Bryant, a former Governor of Florida who is now the director of the Office of Emergency Planning, plans to leave his White House post this summer, possibly to return to politics in his home state, and he is eager to help establish more permanent lines of communication before his departure.

As now envisioned, each Cabinet officer would visit all of

Continued on Page 29, Column 2

Rise in Debt Ceiling Rejected in House; Johnson Rebuffed

Special to The New York Times

WASHINGTON, June 7—The House of Representatives dealt the Johnson Administration a sharp setback today by rejecting a bill to increase the ceiling on the national debt $29-billion, to $365-billion.

The vote against passage was 210 to 197, with Republicans voting solidly to kill the bill. Enough Democrats, mostly Southerners, voted with them to turn the tide.

About six Northern Democratic "doves"—opponents of the war in Vietnam—also joined the opposition.

In all, 34 Democrats joined with 176 Republicans to defeat the measure.

Today's action raised the possibility—though a slim one—of financial chaos after June 30. At that time the debt limit reverts to its "permanent" ceiling of $285-billion, though the debt, at $330-billion, is already far above that level. The legal authority of the Treasury to pay its bills would be in doubt.

However, the Ways and

Continued on Page 30, Column 4

U.S. VOWS TO SEEK A DURABLE PEACE

Johnson Recalls Bundy for New Mideast Planning Unit—'Real Chance' Is Seen

By MAX FRANKEL
Special to The New York Times

WASHINGTON, June 7—President Johnson pledged today to do his best to help translate the new Middle Eastern situation into a more lasting settlement between Israel and her Arab neighbors.

Apparently hoping to exploit Israel's lightning military success—which has surprised but not displeased the White House—Mr. Johnson ordered the drafting of special policies for a "new peace" and set up new machinery to deal with the situation.

The President said that the United States, which had worked hard to avoid the war, felt that "there is now a real chance" to turn from "the frustrations of the past to the hopes of a peaceful future."

But Mr. Johnson said the handling of the crisis and the preparations for a lasting settlement would require the most careful consideration in the United States Government. To organize that effort he recalled McGeorge Bundy to temporary duty at the White House as executive secretary to a special subcommittee of the National Security Council.

Mr. Bundy will seek a temporary leave from the presidency of the Ford Foundation, which he assumed last year after serving as special assistant for

Continued on Page 19, Column 1

EBAN SEES THANT

Says Acceptance Is Based on Enemy's Reciprocal Action

Excerpts from debate at U.N. are printed on Page 18.

By DREW MIDDLETON
Special to The New York Times

UNITED NATIONS, N. Y., June 7—The Security Council unanimously adopted a Soviet resolution today calling on the combatants in the Middle East to "cease fire and all military activities" at 4 P.M., New York time today.

The Government of Israel shortly thereafter announced that she had accepted the call of the Council for a cease-fire, provided her Arab foes agreed.

In the evening, reports from the Middle East indicated rejection of the call by the United Arab Republic, Syria, Iraq, Saudi Arabia, Algeria and Kuwait. Jordan told Secretary General Thant that she would abide by the cease-fire, except in self-defense.

Says It's in Effect

Abba Eban, the Foreign Minister of Israel, told the Secretary General that a cease-fire was already in effect between Jordan and Israel.

In presenting the resolution, the Soviet delegate, Nikolai T. Fedorenko, made it clear that if Israel failed to heed the Security Council's demands, Moscow would consider severing diplomatic relations. The original Security Council resolution, adopted yesterday, simply called for a cease-fire.

But the reports from the Arab capitals indicate, diplomatic sources here said, that military operations will continue.

According to diplomats, the best hope lies in a draft resolution presented by George Ignatieff, the Canadian delegate. This proposes that the President of the Security Council and the Secretary General take measures to insure compliance with the resolutions.

Today's resolution demanded that the combatants "cease fire and all military activities on 7 June 1967 by 2000 hours Greenwich mean time." The resolution was adopted less than an hour before this time, which is 4 P.M. New York time, 10 P.M. in Jordan and Israel and 11 P.M. in the United Arab Republic and Syria.

The Council adjourned without voting on the Canadian draft largely because Milko Ta-

Continued on Page 18, Column 2

United Press International Radiophoto

OLD JERUSALEM IS NOW IN ISRAELI HANDS: Israeli soldiers in prayer at the Wailing Wall yesterday

Major Mideast Developments

On the Battlefronts

Israel claimed victory in the Sinai Desert after three days of fighting. Sharm el Sheik, guarding the entrance to the Gulf of Aqaba, fell after a paratroop attack, and the Israelis said the blockade of the gulf was broken. Other Israeli units were within 20 miles of the Suez Canal, and one Israeli report placed them in the eastern section of Ismailia, on the canal itself.

In Jerusalem, for the first time in 19 years, Israeli Jews prayed at the Wailing Wall as their troops occupied the Old City. Israeli troops captured Jericho, in Jordan, and sped northward to take Nablus, giving them control of the west bank of the Jordan.

The Egyptian High Command reported that its forces had fallen back from first-line positions in the Sinai Peninsula and were fighting fiercely from unspecified secondary positions. It announced that Egyptian troops had pulled back from Sharm el Sheik to join main defense units.

In the Capitals

In the United Nations, Israel accepted the call for a cease-fire, provided the Arabs complied. Jordan announced that she would accept and ordered her troops to fire only in self-defense. But Baghdad declared that Iraq had refused. There were indications that Syria, Algeria and Kuwait were also opposed.

In Cairo, an Egyptian official said the United Arab Republic would fight on.

In Moscow, the Soviet Union threatened to break diplomatic relations with Israel if she did not observe the cease-fire.

In Paris, the French proposed an international agreement for free passage in the Gulf of Aqaba similar to the one governing the Dardanelles in Turkey.

In Washington, President Johnson promised to seek a settlement that would assure lasting peace in the Mideast.

In London, the British urged the Israelis to halt before they aroused more turmoil in the Arab world and diminished the chances for a settlement.

Israelis Weep and Pray Beside the Wailing Wall

By TERENCE SMITH
Special to The New York Times

JERUSALEM, June 7—Israeli troops wept and prayed today at the foot of the Wailing Wall—the last remnant of Solomon's Second Temple and the object of pilgrimage by Jews through the centuries.

In battle dress and still carrying their weapons, they gathered at the base of the sand-colored wall and sang Hallel, a series of prayers reserved for occasions of great joy.

They were repeating a tradition that goes back 2,000 years but has been denied Israeli Jews since 1948, when the first of three wars with the Arabs ended in this area.

The wall is all that remains of the Second Temple, built in the 10th century before Christ and destroyed by the Romans in A.D. 70.

The Israelis, trembling with emotion, bowed vigorously from the waist as they chanted psalms in a lusty chorus. Most had submachine guns slung over their shoulders and several held bazookas as they prayed.

Among the leaders to pray at the wall was Maj. Gen. Moshe Dayan, the new Defense Minister. He told the troops:

"We have returned to the holiest of our holy places, never to depart from it again."

General Dayan, who was ap-

Continued on Page 17, Column 1

CAIRO ANNOUNCES A SINAI PULLBACK

Blames Foreign Aid to Foe, but Says Troops Fight On in Secondary Positions

By ERIC PACE
Special to The New York Times

CAIRO, June 7—An Egyptian military communiqué reported today that forces of the United Arab Republic had fallen back from some first-line positions on the Sinai Peninsula and were engaged in fierce fighting against Israeli troops from secondary positions.

Another statement of the High Command, broadcast four hours later by the Cairo radio, said Egyptian troops at Sharm el Sheik, guarding the entrance to the Gulf of Aqaba, had joined other Egyptian forces "now concentrated in the Sinai Peninsula."

There was no elaboration, but the communiqué, broadcast about 5:30 P.M., appeared to confirm Israeli reports that the Egyptians had been forced to retreat from Sharm el Sheik.

At night, the High Command reported that Israeli paratroops had dropped over the "second-line Egyptian front" but had been "completely wiped out."

The communiqué also said the Israelis had tried another drop at Sharm el Sheik after the

Continued on Page 17, Column 6

AQABA GULF OPEN

Dayan Asserts Israel Does Not Intend to Capture the Canal

By The Associated Press

TEL AVIV, June 7—Israel proclaimed victory tonight in the Sinai Peninsula campaign against the United Arab Republic. On the eastern front, both the Old City of Jerusalem and Bethlehem were captured from the Jordanians.

"The Egyptians are defeated," said Maj. Gen. Itzhak Rabin, the Israeli Chief of Staff. "All their efforts are aimed at withdrawing behind the Suez Canal, and we are taking care of that. The whole area is in our hands. The main effort of the Egyptians is to save themselves."

Israel Losses 'Not Great'

Describing the developments through the third day of this third Arab-Israeli war in 19 years, General Rabin made these claims:

¶Sinai, the Egyptian territory between Israel's Negev Desert and the Suez Canal, is taken.

¶Most of the Jordanian territory on the west bank of the Jordan River, including Jericho, is in Israeli hands, and most of Jordan's army has been captured.

¶Relative to what was done, the number of Israelis casualties was "not great."

The Israelis were reported to have swept to the Suez Canal.

[An Israeli delegation source at the United Nations said Israeli troops had seized that part of the canal city of Ismailia that is on the eastern side of the waterway. But this was denied by an army source in Tel Aviv, who said, according to Reuters, that the Israelis had not taken any point along the canal.

[Maj. Gen. Moshe Dayan, the Israeli Defense Minister, declared that there was "no intention" of taking the canal, United Press International reported.]

'Never to Depart'

After the fall of the Old City of Jerusalem, Defense Minister Moshe Dayan said there that the Israelis had reunited their capital and would never "depart from it again."

Israel reported that paratroops aided by naval units had captured Sharm el Sheik, commanding the entrance to the Gulf of Aqaba, and said the blockade that the Egyptians had mounted from that position had been broken.

"The Strait of Tiran is now open," General Rabin said.

Israel's chief of staff said his men had taken on the United Arab Republic, Jordan, Syria and Iraq, knocked out their air forces and overrun their armor and infantry.

"All this the armed forces of Israel did alone," he declared.

The general then turned over the briefing to Brig. Mordechai Hod, commander of the air force, who announced 441 Arab

Continued on Page 16, Column 1

CONFEREES BLOCK A DRAFT LOTTERY

Compromise Bill Continues Deferment of Students

By United Press International

WASHINGTON, June 7—Senate and House negotiators reached agreement today on a new military draft bill that rules out, for the present, any lottery-like random selection system to determine the order of induction.

The bill was a compromise of differing bills that the Senate and House had passed. It would guarantee the continuance of educational deferments for college undergraduates and students enrolled in apprentice and job training programs.

Senator Richard B. Russell, Democrat of Georgia, who is chairman of the Senate conferees, said the Senate might act on the four-year draft extension bill tomorrow. House action must await approval by the Senate.

Congressional action will clear the way for President Johnson, under current discretionary powers, to reverse the order of induction and take 19-year-olds first from the Selec-

Continued on Page 3, Column 1

NEWS INDEX

Dorothy Parker, 73, Literary Wit, Dies

By ALDEN WHITMAN

Dorothy Parker, the sardonic humorist who purveyed her wit in conversation, short stories, verse and criticism, died of a heart attack yesterday afternoon in her suite at the Volney Hotel, 23 East 74th Street. She was 73 years old and had been in frail health in recent years.

In print and in person, Miss Parker sparkled with a word or a phrase, for she honed her humor to its most economical size. Her rapier wit, much of it spontaneous, gained its early renown from her membership in the Algonquin Round Table, an informal luncheon club at the Algonquin Hotel in the nineteen-twenties, where some of

Continued on Page 38, Column 1

The New York Times — June 8, 1967

CONQUEST IN THE MIDEAST: Israeli troops took Sharm el Sheik (1), drove on to the Suez Canal (2) and seized control of the Old City in Jerusalem (3). Photo was taken in September, 1966, during the flight of Gemini II.

Pentagon Believes Israeli Jets Struck From Sea, Eluded Radar

By WILLIAM BEECHER
Special to The New York Times

WASHINGTON, June 7—At least a part of the Israeli Air Force that caught large numbers of Egyptian aircraft on the ground in the early hours of the war may have slipped through gaps in the United Arab Republic's radar net by flying in over the Mediterranean.

This possibility was raised today by Pentagon analysts. If correct it would help to explain how Israeli pilots were able to surprise so many Egyptian jets before they could get into the air.

It might also serve to provide part of the explanation behind insistent Arab assertions that carrier-based United States and British jets participated in the raids.

The early blows to Arab, and especially Egyptian, air strength is credited by most military analysts as having been a decisive factor in the Israeli successes on land that followed.

"We know that some of the Israeli planes returned to their bases by way of the sea," one ranking officer said, "and we assume they may have approached from the seaward too."

The officer said it was obvious that Israel had excellent intelligence on weaknesses in the Egyptian radar system and exploited them.

Shortly after the raids, he went on, the Jordanian radio charged that Jordanian radar

Continued on Page 18, Column 8

"All the News That's Fit to Print"

The New York Times

LATE CITY EDITION

Weather: Sunny and windy today; clear tonight. Milder tomorrow. Temp. range: today 42-35; Sunday 51-42. Full U.S. report on Page 93.

VOL. CXVII . . . No. 40,126 © 1967 The New York Times Company. NEW YORK, MONDAY, DECEMBER 4, 1967 10 CENTS

Thousands Mourn Spellman at St. Patrick's

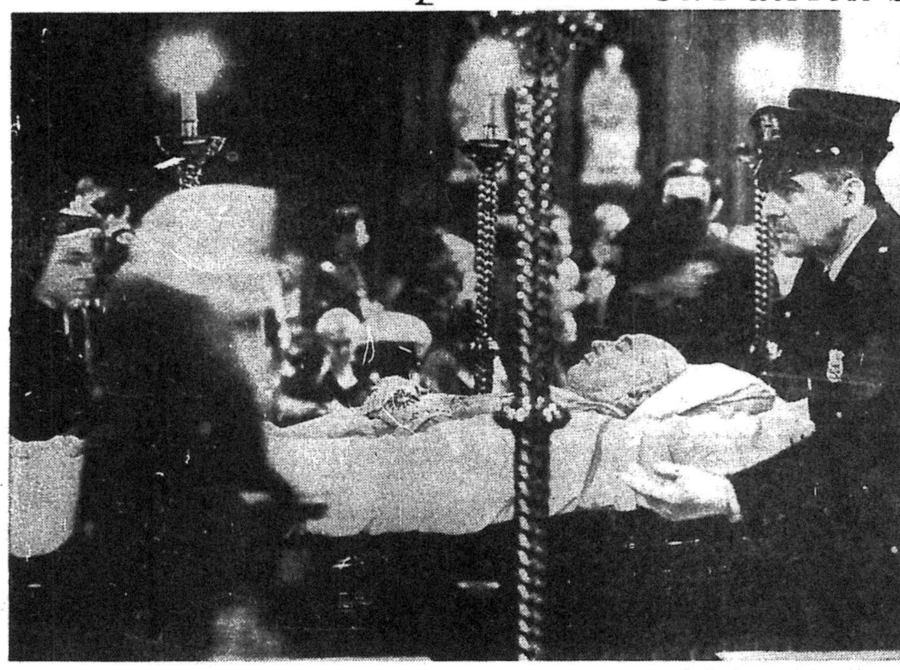

The New York Times (by Barton Silverman)

The bier of Cardinal Spellman at St. Patrick's Cathedral. Patrolman gestures to mourner to proceed past coffin.

By PAUL HOFMANN

In a somber rite, the body of Cardinal Spellman was taken to St. Patrick's Cathedral last night and placed on a catafalque in the center aisle for the first of a five-day series of requiem masses.

The Cardinal, who died Saturday morning at the age of 78, will be buried in a crypt of St. Patrick's on Thursday after a service that is expected to be attended by all seven American Cardinals.

The bronze-lined coffin of African mahogany arrived at the Fifth Avenue entrance of St. Patrick's at 6:15 P.M.

The coffin was taken into the cathedral under crossed swords held by 12 Knights of Columbus wearing white-plumed hats.

The Most Rev. John J. Maguire, who is temporarily administering the archdiocese, met the open coffin inside the church and opened the ceremonies by sprinkling the Cardinal's body with holy water and blessing it.

A procession formed, with clergymen in purple and black mourning vestments preceding the coffin and volunteer members of the city's Police and Fire Departments in an honor guard following it on its way down the cathedral's 186-foot long nave. A group of 60 relatives and friends of the Cardinal walked behind the coffin and then took seats in front pews.

Votive candles lighted by hundreds of mourners flickered along the church's walls. The cathedral was filled to capacity.

Cardinal Spellman's body was clad in white liturgical vestments and a scarlet skullcap. A golden cross lay on his chest and a bishop's ring was on his right hand.

The coffin was placed on a black-draped catafalque, surrounded by six tall candles, in the center aisle in front of the main altar.

At 6:30 P.M. the cathedral's bells tolled and eight bishops and ten other prelates gathered around the altar to concelebrate a requiem mass during which a choir chanted the responses.

Concelebration is a form of offering mass jointly by more than one priest. It is believed to have been common in early Christianity and has been revived in the recent reforms of Roman Catholic liturgy.

The main celebrant was Archbishop Maguire, who as newly named Administrator of the Archdiocese is its head until a successor, to be named by Pope Paul VI, takes over.

The 17 other celebrants were members of the Board of Consultors, a body appointed by Cardinal Spellman that conferred on Archbishop Maguire on Saturday the task of administering the archdiocese during the see's vacancy.

Outside the church, hundreds of persons were waiting in triple line behind police barricades along East 51st Street from Fifth Avenue to Madison Avenue. Rain that had fallen earlier in the day had stopped by now. After the end of the concelebrated mass, around

Continued on Page 51, Column 1

TAXICAB INDUSTRY SEEKS SHARP RISE IN FARE SCHEDULE

Cost of Long Trips Would Be Increased Most—$1 Ride to Go to $1.70 Under Plan

By PETER MILLONES

The taxi industry will ask the city today for a fare increase that would raise a ride that now costs 45 cents to 60 cents, a 60-cent ride to 90 cents and a $1 trip to $1.70.

The increases would be greater for passengers taking long-distance trips than for those who ride short distances.

Under the proposal, meters would be readjusted so that a rider watching the fare would see the meter click a dime at a time instead of a nickel.

The Metropolitan Taxicab Board of Trade, which represents all but three of the 74 taxi fleets here with 6,800 cabs, says in a letter to the city:

"A larger increase is requested on the longer rides to provide incentive to the driver to take such trips and enter outlying areas which have been trips where driver resistance has occurred up to now."

Problems of Return Trip

According to regulations of the Hack Bureau, drivers are not supposed to choose their customers but accept all orderly persons who want to go anywhere in the city. In fact, they spurn long-distance trips from Manhattan to Queens and Brooklyn, for example, because they often fail to get a passenger back to their normal area of operation.

The industry's remedy would, for example, increase the fare for a trip that now covers just over five miles to $2.90 from $1.60.

Whether these proposed increases will be acceptable to the City Council, the Mayor and the Board of Estimate was unclear yesterday. Both the Democratic-led City Council and Mayor Lindsay, a Republican, have stated their willingness to approve an adjustment in fares to help pay the costs of a new contract that gave cab drivers an increase in pay.

But whether they will approve increases of the size desired by the industry remains to be seen. The Lindsay administration is studying the finances of the $200-million-a-year industry now.

Getting Specific Proposals

It is understood that the Council prefers to wait for specific legislative proposals from the administration before holding public hearings on an increase.

The whole question of a fare increase is complicated because the new three-year contract between the industry and Local 3036 of the New York City Taxi Drivers Union is based on the assumption that the industry's requested increase will be approved.

Thus, if the increase proposed is not approved, the labor contract, arrived at after wildcat strikes by the 29,000

Continued on Page 54, Column 3

Associated Press Cablephoto

AFTER MEETING: President Makarios of Cyprus and Cyrus R. Vance, U.S. envoy, after talks in Nicosia yesterday.

3 NATIONS REPLY TO THANT APPEAL IN CYPRUS CRISIS

Greek Response Is Clearly Affirmative—Makarios Will Give Full Answer Today

TURKS RAISE U.N. ISSUE

U.S. and Britain Favor Plan to Increase Functions of International Force

By DREW MIDDLETON

Special to The New York Times

UNITED NATIONS, N. Y., Dec. 3—Greece, Turkey and Cyprus sent separate replies today to Secretary General Thant's appeal for peace on Cyprus.

All the replies could be considered as accepting his appeal for peace in the sense that they did not reject it.

This was considered a gain by Mr. Thant, the United States and Britain, which have interested themselves in trying to end the crisis from the United Nations.

The reply of Archbishop Makarios, President of Cyprus, relayed by Zenon Rossides, the Cypriote representative at the United Nations, was the least communicative of the three. President Makarios said only that he welcomed the constructive suggestion made by Mr. Thant and that his full reply would be sent in 12 hours.

Proposal Is Welcomed

Greece welcomed Mr. Thant's proposal and told the Secretary General that she would be willing to carry it out.

Premier Suleyman Demeril of Turkey, however, raised a more important point. He accepted Mr. Thant's appeal, but he gave his Government's support to that point in Mr. Thant's message that emphasized that an expansion of the United Nations forces on Cyprus might be necessary to oversee demilitarization of the island and to end communal fighting there.

Ambassador Arthur J. Goldberg and Lord Caradon of Britain had urged a favorable response upon the three Governments in messages issued shortly after Mr. Thant's appeal.

Mr. Thant's key paragraph, from the Cypriote standpoint, discusses enlarging the mandate of the 4,500-man United Nations force in Cyprus to give it "broader functions in regard

Continued on Page 3, Column 1

Enemy Shells Allied Posts; Vietcong Attack Repulsed

Special to The New York Times

SAIGON, South Vietnam, Dec. 3—The Vietcong unleashed a series of mortar and ground attacks against United States and South Vietnamese positions today. In one attack, against the Binhson government subsector headquarters 12 miles north of Quangngai City and 330 miles northeast of Saigon, 35 enemy soldiers were reported to have been killed.

A South Vietnamese spokesman said that the attack started at 1:30 A.M. with a heavy mortar barrage, followed by a charge by some 600 enemy troops, who fought until allied reinforcements arrived at 5 A.M.

[The Vietcong attacked the United States military headquarters base at Longbinh with small arms and mortars Monday. The raid touched off a fire in a storage area of the base. Page 5.]

U.S. and Korean Aid

A United States spokesman said that a cavalry troop from the American Division and South Korean marines near the Binhson post were rushed to help the headquarters compound. Army helicopters and AC-47 Dragonships fired at the enemy.

The Government spokesman said that an American military adviser and a South Korean adviser in the headquarters were killed and that six United States advisers were wounded. South Vietnamese casualties were described as moderate, which means that the defending force of some 200 troops was badly hurt.

Elsewhere, the Vietcong fired 40 mortar shells at a company of the United States First Infantry Division at Budop, which is near the Cambodian border and 88 miles north of Saigon.

A United States spokesman said that two American soldiers

Continued on Page 5, Column 3

TREASURY FEARS BIG INTEREST RISE

Lasting Harm to Economy Held Possible if Congress Delays on a Tax Increase

By EDWIN L. DALE Jr.

Special to The New York Times

WASHINGTON, Dec. 3 — There is a sense of quiet, but genuine, alarm in the Treasury over what might happen to interest rates in the coming weeks if Congress shows no movement on a tax increase before it adjourns.

No one is talking of financial collapse or panic. But at the top levels of the Treasury there is a deep fear that interest rates could rise so steeply as to do lasting damage—damage that could not be wholly repaired even if Congress did move on a tax increase next year.

"The markets still have some hope of action," said one high official. "If that hope goes, there is no telling how high rates will go."

Rates fell markedly on the news two weeks ago that the House Ways and Means Committee would resume consideration of the tax bill. They rose again last Thursday and Friday on the news that the committee chairman, Representative Wilbur D. Mills, Democrat of Arkansas, had still made no decision to act.

These interest rates are the

Continued on Page 38, Column 4

GROUP IN HARLEM ASKS MORE POLICE

Many Residents Say Crime Has Risen Sharply—Fear Keeps Some Off Streets

By EARL CALDWELL

A group of Harlem residents met last night to voice their concern about rising crime in their neighborhood and to seek methods of obtaining more police protection.

The residents, who live in the Lenox Terrace Apartments, a large, luxury complex in the area of 135th Street and Fifth Avenue, decided to petition the city for more police and to seek meetings with Mayor Lindsay, Borough President Percy E. Sutton and Police Commissioner Howard R. Leary.

"We've got to take some action," said Mrs. Virginia Bell of 45 West 132d Street, a resident of the six-building complex that houses more than 1,700 families.

Mrs. Bell was one of more than 100 Lenox Terrace residents to attend the meeting during the evening. The meeting was held in the apartment of Mr. and Mrs. John Meade of 2186 Fifth Avenue.

While residents of Lenox Terrace were meeting in the Meades' apartment, a group called Petitions for Protection circulated petitions for more policemen in the area from 110th to 116th Street in lower Harlem.

These Harlem residents, too, were concerned about a crime problem that has emptied the neighborhood's tenement-lined side streets at night, forced merchants to close their shops early and brought armed civilian patrols into the streets.

Residents and shopkeepers have no statistics to cite, but there is a widespread feeling that crime in the streets has risen sharply.

Many residents refuse to leave their homes at night. Some merchants close their

Continued on Page 61, Column 2

Heart Transplant Keeps Man Alive in South Africa

By The Associated Press

CAPETOWN, Dec. 3 — The world's first successful human heart transplant was announced today.

In a five-hour operation that began at 1 A.M., surgeons at the Groote Schuur Hospital removed the heart of a young woman who died after an automobile crash and placed it in the chest of a 55-year-old man dying because his own heart was damaged, the announcement said.

When the transplanted heart was in place, it was started beating by an electric shock.

Dr. Jan H. Louw, the hospital's chief surgeon, said:

"It was like turning the ignition switch of a car."

The hospital said that the man was in satisfactory condition but that the next few days would be a critical period.

The heart was removed from the body of Denise Ann Darvall, 24, an accounting machine operator, and transferred to Louis Washkansky, a businessman, the hospital said.

Mr. Washkansky was reported fully conscious, with blood pressure normal.

Doctors around the world hailed the transplant achievement but said the crucial question would be whether the man's body would accept the alien heart.

In the first stage of the operation, Mr. Washkansky and the body of Miss Darvall were put on heart-lung machines, each manned by a team of technicians.

In the second stage, the donor's heart was removed and kept going by a pump.

The third stage was the re-

Continued on Page 56, Column 1

$9-BILLION BUDGET FOR CITY FORECAST

Chamber, Looking to 1975, Urges Stricter Control —Cites Recent Gains

By RICHARD E. MOONEY

The New York Chamber of Commerce predicted yesterday that by 1975 the city's expense budget would have risen from the present $5.2-billion to $9-billion or more if current spending trends continued.

In an annual review of budget developments the chamber cited "substantial improvement" in the city's fiscal behavior, specifically the discontinuation of borrowing to pay for day-to-day operating costs in the last two years.

But it said that "the city must exercise more effective control over expenditures in the future if it is to achieve real fiscal stability."

The review showed that the city expense budget had doubled in 10 years. This does not include spending for long-range, capital projects. Spending for education and hospitals has almost tripled during the decade, and outlays for welfare have quadrupled.

"These increases are clear manifestations of the urban crisis," said G. G. Tegnell, the chamber's executive vice president. "The problems that have caused them are not easily solved, but we must strike a balance of needs and supportable local taxation."

Publication of the review coincided with the conclusion of

Continued on Page 22, Column 4

Public's Misuse of Ambulances Is Found to Cause Delays Here

By MARTIN TOLCHIN

Public abuses of the city's emergency ambulance services have led to excessive delays, including many of more than an hour, in transporting critically ill patients to hospitals, according to an analysis made public yesterday.

The report found that nearly 4,000 of 41,632 calls took more than 60 minutes, and included a significant number of patients who might have benefited from quicker action.

"A lot of people die," David C. Dimendberg, the author of the report and former director of the Emergency Ambulance Service, said in an interview.

The desirable time it should take to complete a call, he said, is about 30 minutes.

He noted that lengthy delays had been found in transportation of cardiac cases, asthmatics, unconscious persons and victims of traffic accidents.

The delays were caused neither by a shortage of ambulances nor heavy automobile traffic, but by false alarms, the use of ambulances by persons who could take other transportation, and other abuses that diverted the vehicles from their proper function, he said.

The study found that 37 per cent of those who called an emergency ambulance walked into it.

"If you can walk, usually you don't need two men to come with a stretcher," Mr. Dimendberg said. "In certain cities, if a patient is well enough to walk to an ambulance, the ambulance won't take them."

Of those with illnesses who called ambulances, only one in four were urgent cases, a group that included cardiacs, asthmatics and those found unconscious. The remainder had vague body aches, colds, fevers

Continued on Page 58, Column 3

NEWS INDEX

Rail Buses to Link Midtown to Kennedy Airport

45-Minute Runs Are Planned Next Year From East Side Over L.I.R.R. Tracks

By MARTIN GANSBERG

Buses that can travel on railroad tracks as well as highways will be put into service "sometime in 1968" to speed trips between mid-Manhattan and Kennedy International Airport.

They will run partly on roads and partly on tracks of the Long Island Rail Road.

The move, which will begin with 15 buses, is expected to reduce the traveling time from the East Side Airlines Terminal to the airport by at least half an hour, Austin J. Tobin, executive director of the Port of New York Authority, said yesterday.

"Despite severe traffic tie-ups" he said, "this will make it possible to get to the airport in 45 minutes." The same trip now takes as much as an hour and a half.

Mr. Tobin also predicted in announcing the new service that the cost of the trip would remain at the present $2. He said the buses would be able to carry 45 passengers.

He said that he and Dr. William J. Ronan, head of the Metropolitan Commuter Transportation Authority, would go to Kansas City this week to watch final tests of buses there developed by the W. T. Cox Company of Camdenton, Mo.

At a demonstration of such a bus last July in Floral Park L. I., Dr. Ronan was one of the

Continued on Page 94, Column 4

The New York Times Dec. 4, 1967

8 CHILDREN KILLED IN 2 BLAZES HERE

5 in Brooklyn Left Alone—3 Die on Lower East Side

Eight children, ranging in age from 4 months to 6 years, died yesterday in two fires, in Brooklyn and Manhattan.

Five of the children, left alone by their mothers, were asphyxiated in a bedroom of the Brooklyn apartment they shared. Desperate efforts by firemen — including mouth-to-mouth resuscitation and cardiac massage—failed to revive them.

In the other fire, earlier in the day on the Lower East Side, three children who had apparently been playing with matches were killed in their apartment at 620 East Sixth Street. Their crippled parents, Charles and Regina Scheibel, and two other children were injured.

The victims of the Brooklyn fire were the three children of Mrs. Louise Faulk—Angie, 3 years old; Keith, 2; and Kenneth, 4 months; and the two children of her sister Annie—John, 5; and Elizabeth, 4.

All were found unconscious in the smoke-filled bedroom of their mothers' three-room apartment. The families shared an apartment on the second floor of a three-story frame building at 1038 Broadway in the Bushwick section.

The alarm was turned in at 7:04 P.M. Firemen from three

Continued on Page 16, Column 4

"All the News That's Fit to Print"

The New York Times

LATE CITY EDITION

Weather: Rain, mild temperatures today, tonight. Showers tomorrow. Temp. range: today 42-35. Thurs. 36-32. Full U. S. report on Page 70.

VOL. CXVII . . . No. 40,186 © 1968 The New York Times Company. NEW YORK, FRIDAY, FEBRUARY 2, 1968 10 CENTS

STREET CLASHES GO ON IN VIETNAM, FOE STILL HOLDS PARTS OF CITIES; JOHNSON PLEDGES NEVER TO YIELD

GUERRILLA DIES: Brig. Gen. Nguyen Ngoc Loan, national police chief, executes man identified as a Vietcong terrorist in Saigon. Man wore civilian dress and had a pistol. A picture sequence of the execution is on Page 12.

PRESIDENT ASKS PAY-PRICE CURBS AND RISE IN TAX

INFLATION FEARED

Economic Report Says Failure to Act Risks a 'Feverish Boom'

Text of Johnson's Economic Report, Pages 20 and 21.

By EDWIN L. DALE Jr.
Special to The New York Times

WASHINGTON, Feb. 1—The Johnson Administration asserted today that there would be "no prospect" of slowing the pace of inflation this year unless negotiated union wage settlements were "appreciably lower" than the average 5.5 per cent increase last year.

The warning came in the Annual Report of the Council of Economic Advisers, which accompanied the Economic Report of the President, transmitted to Congress today. President Johnson, in his report, said:

"I must again urge—in the strongest terms I know—that unions and business firms exercise the most rigorous restraint in their wage and price determinations in 1968."

Speedy Action Urged

Apart from the appeal for restraint, and the 5.5 per cent bench mark for wage increases, the main thrust of both reports was an urgent further request for the Administration's proposed 10 per cent surcharge on income taxes.

Asking action on the bill "in the next few weeks," the President said:

"We must choose whether we will conduct our fiscal affairs sensibly; or whether we will allow a clearly excessive budgetary deficit to go uncorrected by failing to raise taxes, and thereby risk a feverish boom that could generate an unacceptable acceleration of price increases, a possible financial crisis, and perhaps ultimately a recession."

In discussing the outlook for

Continued on Page 19, Column 2

Associated Press

Richard M. Nixon in official campaign photograph.

NIXON ANNOUNCES FOR PRESIDENCY

Discloses Plans in a Letter to New Hampshire Voters —Opens Drive Today

By ROBERT B. SEMPLE Jr.

Richard M. Nixon formally announced yesterday, as expected, that he was a candidate for the Republican Presidential nomination.

The announcement, which Mr. Nixon had presaged by his energetic preliminary campaigning in the last few months, was in the form of a letter to the voters of New Hampshire.

Copies of the letter were handed to newsmen at Nixon campaign headquarters at 521 Fifth Avenue at about the same time that others were reaching the mailboxes of 150,000 New Hampshire homes—85 per cent of the state's households, Nixon aides said.

The New Hampshire primary, the first of a series of Presidential trial heats, will be held March 12. The former Vice President will begin his campaign with a news conference in Manchester today.

'Special Responsibility'

The letter, composed by Mr Nixon himself, told New Hampshire voters of their "special responsibility" as participants in the first Presidential primary in the nation.

Explaining why he had decided to become a candidate, Mr. Nixon suggested that his 14 years as a member of Congress and as Vice President and his eight years as a private citizen since then had given him the experience and the perspective necessary to provide the "new leadership" he said the nation required.

Mr. Nixon—who lost the Presidency to John F. Kennedy by a narrow margin in 1960—declared:

"Peace and freedom in the world, and peace and progress

Continued on Page 9, Column 1

LINDSAY REDUCES OUTLAY OF FUNDS FOR NEW SCHOOLS

Cites Unused Backlog as He Submits a 'Tight' Capital Budget of $996-Million

Excerpts from capital budget appear on Page 22.

By RICHARD E. MOONEY

Mayor Lindsay submitted a $996-million capital budget yesterday for the coming fiscal year—slightly reduced from the current year's record total, but sharply reduced in the sensitive area of schools.

"This is a tight budget," the Mayor said, adding that he had decided to keep it well under the legal limit for city borrowing. It is also "a realistic budget," he said, because it does not include funds for projects that are not moving fast enough to need money next year, such as school construction.

The cut in school funds brought an immediate charge from Alfred A. Giardino, president of the Board of Education, that the Mayor was recommending "retrogressive education."

Counteroffer by Mayor

The Mayor countered with an offer to set up a school construction task force to expedite school construction, and a pledge that there will be funds for every school project that is ready for them.

The new budget covers city spending for construction and other capital projects—new subway cars and buses, hospital renovation, and the like—in the fiscal year 1968-69, starting next July 1. The city's current operating expenses, which will run close to six times as large, will be covered in a separate message two months from now.

The Board of Estimate and the City Council, both controlled by Democrats, have until mid-March to act on the capital budget. They usually add a little to it.

Few New Programs

Thereafter the Mayor has two weeks to veto changes he does not like, and the Board and the Council then have two more weeks to override him if they can muster a two-thirds majority in each body.

One striking feature of yesterday's message was the almost total absence of new programs. There was only one, to subsidize vest-pocket industrial sites for factories that threaten to leave the city.

In the major categories, there was an eight-fold increase to

Continued on Page 22, Column 1

M'NAMARA SAYS SOVIET DOUBLED ITS ICBM'S IN '67

But Secretary, in Farewell Report, Tells Congress U.S. Force Is Bigger

Excerpts from the McNamara report are on Page 16.

By WILLIAM BEECHER
Special to The New York Times

WASHINGTON, Feb. 1—The Soviet Union took a giant step toward closing the nuclear missile gap last year by more than doubling its force of intercontinental ballistic missiles, Defense Secretary Robert S. McNamara disclosed today.

But the outgoing defense chief indicated he did not regard the development as particularly ominous. Each nation, he said, now possesses strategic forces capable of withstanding a surprise attack and retaliating overwhelmingly against the other.

Making it clear that he believed a nuclear stalemate had been achieved between the two superpowers, he declared:

"It is precisely this mutual capability to destroy one another, and conversely, our respective inability to prevent such destruction, that provides us both with the strongest possible motive to avoid a strategic nuclear war."

A Valedictory Message

In a voluminous farewell report to a joint session of the Senate Armed Services Committee and the Defense Appropriations subcommittee, a 220-page unclassified version of which was made public, Mr. McNamara delivered what amounted to a valedictory message covering his seven years as Defense Secretary.

Clark M. Clifford, whose nomination to succeed Mr. McNamara was approved by the Senate earlier this week, is expected to take over by the end of this month.

Senator John Stennis, Democrat of Mississippi, expressed concern as he emerged from the hearing at the scope of the Soviet strategic buildup and the American response. "I am not nearly as optimistic as the Secretary that the [defense] budget is adequate to meet all our needs," he said.

Noting a growing sense of disillusionment and war-weariness on the part of the American public, Mr. McNamara warned against the temptation to renounce growing burdens around the world in favor of a neo-isolationist "fortress America."

Such a move, he insisted,

Continued on Page 16, Column 4

A RESOLUTE STAND

President Won't Halt Bombing—Predicts Khesanh Victory

By MAX FRANKEL
Special to The New York Times

WASHINGTON, Feb. 1—President Johnson responded today to the new enemy challenges in South Vietnam with a vow that "the enemy will fail again and again" because "we Americans will never yield."

The enemy in South Vietnam has been met and matched, he said, and will be thrown back in the hills around Khesanh.

The enemy in North Vietnam will continue to be bombed "with a very precise restraint," he said, until there are "some better signs than what these last few days have provided" that he will not step up his terrorism or accelerate his aggression.

Mr. Johnson seized upon a previously scheduled ceremony of honor for an Air Force officer to give a reaction to the assaults on dozens of American installations in South Vietnam this week and to the major enemy build-up around Khesanh.

"Let those who would stop the bombing," he said, "answer this question: What would the North Vietnamese be doing if we stopped the bombing and let them alone?

"The answer, I think, is clear. The enemy force in the South would be larger. It would be better equipped. The war would

Continued on Page 13, Column 1

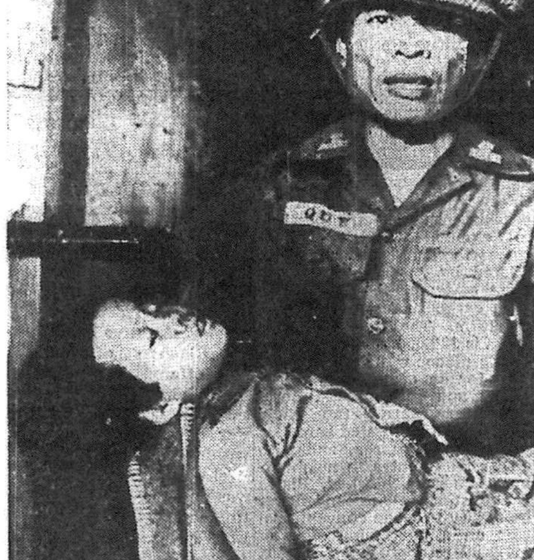

Associated Press

HIS FAMILY SLAIN BY VIETCONG: A South Vietnamese officer carries the body of one of his children from his home. Terrorists overran the base of his unit in Saigon, beheaded an officer and killed women and children.

ENEMY TOLL SOARS

Offensive Is Running 'Out of Steam,' Says Westmoreland

By CHARLES MOHR
Special to The New York Times

SAIGON, South Vietnam, Friday, Feb. 2—Vicious street fighting continued today in many South Vietnamese towns and cities, and the Vietcong attacked three more province capitals.

The United States military commander, Gen. William C. Westmoreland, said yesterday that there was some evidence that the enemy's general offensive was "about to run out of steam," but he also conceded that the enemy had the capability to continue "this phase of their campaign for several more days."

[The United States command announced that 10,593 enemy soldiers had been killed since 6 P.M. Monday—by far the heaviest losses ever inflicted by the allies in Vietnam, United Press International reported. American losses were put at 281 killed and 1,195 wounded and South Vietnamese losses at 632 killed and 1,588 wounded.]

Some Question Totals

The assertion today that more than 10,000 of the enemy had died in the outbreaks was viewed with reserve by some observers. One, a press release, said that in a fight near Pleiku in the central highlands, 208 of the enemy were killed and one Vietnamese militiaman wounded.

Since Monday, the Vietcong have attacked 26 of the country's 44 province capitals, penetrating some of them deeply.

New attacks were reported yesterday and today on the towns of Baria, Muchoa and Phucuong, all province capitals. Other important cities, such as Danang, have also been attacked in the Vietcong drive.

Five battalions of Vietcong and North Vietnamese troops were still fighting heavily within the walls of the ancient

Continued on Page 12, Column 1

Hanoi Says Aim of Raids Is to Oust Saigon Regime

Special to The New York Times

HONG KONG, Friday, Feb. 2—The Hanoi radio declared today that the latest attacks by the Vietcong were part of a general offensive aimed at overthrowing the Saigon Government.

The radio, monitored here, broadcast an appeal by the Vietcong to the people of South Vietnam to aid "in attacking and tracking down the U.S. and puppet forces and in capturing all their agents."

"Compatriots," the broadcast said, "the long-awaited general offensive against the Thieu-Ky puppet administration has come. The revolutionary armed forces, representing the will of the entire people, have opened fire at our archenemy.

"We would like to tell our compatriots that we are determined to overthrow the Thieu-Ky puppet administration."

The radio said the aim of the Vietcong struggle was to "win independence for the nation, peace for our country and democracy and happiness for the people" and to build a political power "entirely for the fatherland and the people."

The appeal was issued in the name of the South Vietnam Revolutionary Armed Forces Command.

A representative of the Vietcong's political arm, the National Liberation Front, said in Hanoi yesterday that the Vietcong had staged "the most all-out and widespread attacks ever known."

The representative, Nguyen Phu Xoai, said at a news conference reported by the Hanoi radio that in some places, such

Continued on Page 12, Column 8

Vietcong's Attacks Shock Washington

By TOM WICKER
Special to The New York Times

WASHINGTON, Feb. 1—Widespread Vietcong attacks on cities throughout South Vietnam dealt this city a hard blow, too.

From the State Department to Capitol Hill and the Pentagon, the well-coordinated and tenacious attacks were under discussion. They were recognized as costly but also as what Senator John Stennis, Democrat of Mississippi, called them—"embarrassing" and "humiliating" to the Johnson Administration and the South Vietnamese Government.

Doves tended to believe that their criticism of the war was

Continued on Page 13, Column 7

A.C.L.U. Bars Help To Draft Resisters

By JOHN LEO

The American Civil Liberties Union said yesterday it would not defend individuals who refuse to register for military service as a protest against war or the draft.

In a formal statement on civil disobedience, the union said: "We have assumed that the [draft] laws are constitutional, regardless of how unwise or unjust they may be from the viewpoint of the individual who violates them."

The A.C.L.U. thus opposes four of its own largest affiliates. The Civil Liberties Unions of New York, Southern California, Massachusetts and New Jersey do not consider the

Continued on Page 3, Column 6

CITY U. WILL BUILD IN BROOKLYN SLUM

Community College to Rise in Bedford-Stuyvesant

By M. A. FARBER

The City University will build its next community college in Bedford-Stuyvesant, a predominantly Negro and Puerto Rican section of Brooklyn.

It will be the first of the university's seven two-year institutions to be placed in a slum neighborhood and will be particularly designed for "equalizing educational opportunities" for minority-group youths.

In announcing the decision yesterday, the Board of Higher Education said the college would experiment with liberalized admissions policies and increased community service programs.

Dr. Albert H. Bowker, the university's chancellor, also disclosed that he would recommend a Southeast Bronx site for an eighth two-year institution in the municipal system.

The Bronx site, Dr. Bowker said, is in the neighborhood of the new Lincoln Hospital, which is to be bounded by Park and Morris Avenues and 144th and 149th Streets. This college would be modeled after the one planned for Bedford-Stuyvesant.

Like the central Brooklyn in-

Continued on Page 32, Column 1

WESTERNER GETS CITY HEALTH POST

Dr. Bucove of Washington Will Succeed Dr. Brown

By MARTIN TOLCHIN

A public health physician who advocates decentralization of the city's health services was named yesterday to head the Health Service Administration.

Mayor Lindsay announced the appointment of Dr. Bernard Bucove, director of health for the State of Washington, to the $37,500-a-year post. The 55-year-old physician will receive $2,500 a year more than Dr. Howard J. Brown, who resigned last December after 17 stormy months as the city's chief health officer.

In an interview from his Olympia, Wash., office, Dr. Bucove was asked:

"Are you amazed that somebody finally took the job?"

The physician said he agreed with a recommendation to create a public corporation to operate the city's health facilities, thereby freeing the facilities from municipal red tape. The recommendation was made by a committee led by Gerard Piel, publisher of Scientific American magazine.

"I would hope to be able to implement the major part of

Continued on Page 32, Column 4

Bond Issue Sought To Clean State Air

By PETER KIHSS

New York City's Air Pollution Control Commissioner called yesterday for a $1-billion state bond issue to pay for new clean-air facilities, including incinerators to burn refuse for heat and power.

The Commissioner, Austin N. Heller, said this would follow the precedent set by the state's $1-billion clean-water program. The water bond issue was approved by the Legislature and Governor Rockefeller and then by the voters in 1965 to pay for construction of sewage treatment and other water purification systems throughout the state.

Mr. Heller's proposal was

Continued on Page 18, Column 3

HOUSE, 382-4, VOTES HELP TO CONSUMER

'Truth-in-Lending' Measure Now Goes to Conferees

By JOHN D. MORRIS
Special to The New York Times

WASHINGTON, Feb. 1—The House passed today a comprehensive "truth-in-lending" bill designed to give consumers full and clear information on how much they pay in interest and other finance charges on loans and credit purchases.

The bill, which its supporters call an unusually strong consumer protection measure, was approved on a roll-call vote of 382 to 4.

The Senate unanimously passed a less comprehensive bill last year. A Senate-House conference committee will try to work out a compromise version.

President Johnson issued a statement praising the House for bringing "every American consumer another step closer to knowing the cost of the money he borrows."

"I urge the House and Senate to resolve their differences promptly and to give the American consumer a strong truth-in-lending bill," he added. "I hope this will be the first of many measures that will mark this Congress as the consumers' Congress."

The four votes against the bill today were cast by Representatives Thomas G. Abernethy and G. V. Montgomery, Democrats of Mississippi; Robert G. Stephens Jr., Democrat

Continued on Page 19, Column 1

I LOVE YOU SANDY—RL. —ADVT.

NEWS INDEX

"All the News That's Fit to Print"

The New York Times

LATE CITY EDITION

Weather: Sunny and seasonable today. Fair tonight and tomorrow. Temp. range: today 43-25; Wed. 35-18. Full U.S. report on Page 86.

VOL. CXVII...No. 40,199

NEW YORK, THURSDAY, FEBRUARY 15, 1968

10 CENTS

JUDGE WON'T FREE DELURY FOR TALKS ON GARBAGE PACT

Streit Rejects Plea by Union for Release of Leader From Imprisonment

NEGOTIATIONS RESUMED

O'Dwyer Asserts Absence of Chief of Sanitationmen Impedes Bargaining

By DAMON STETSON

State Supreme Court Justice Saul S. Streit denied yesterday a request of the sanitationmen's union that its jailed president, John J. DeLury, be released in the sheriff's custody to participate in contract talks with the city.

Paul O'Dwyer, a lawyer representing the Uniformed Sanitationmen's Association, had applied for Mr. DeLury's release from 9 A.M. to 5 P.M. daily, following a resumption of negotiations yesterday in the tangled sanitation dispute.

The resumption of the contract talks came after legislative leaders postponed action on Governor Rockefeller's plan for a temporary state take-over of the Sanitation Department to give Mayor Lindsay time to settle the dispute himself.

Legislature Adjourns

In Albany yesterday, the Legislature adjourned for the week without acting on the Governor's plan.

Striking sanitationmen returned to their jobs last Saturday night with the expectation that the Governor's plan would be adopted and that they would be paid at a rate recommended by a special mediation panel, accepted by the union but rejected by Mayor Lindsay.

In arguing for Mr. DeLury's release from Civil Jail, Mr. O'Dwyer said it was "extremely difficult" to conduct negotiations without the union president, whom he called the most knowledgeable union official involved in the current dispute.

Frederic S. Nathan, first assistant corporation counsel of the city, opposed Mr. DeLury's release. The union leader is serving a 15-day sentence for contempt of court for having defied an order to halt the nine-day strike of sanitationmen.

Mr. Nathan said that if Mr. DeLury were let out of Civil Jail, where he is imprisoned, it would be a "travesty on his jail sentence."

"The primary consideration is respect for law, particularly the orders of this court," he asserted.

Justice Streit, in making his ruling in his chambers, said:

Continued on Page 33, Column 5

10-Cent Bus Fares At Age of 65 Voted

By SETH S. KING

The Board of Estimate ordered the Manhattan and Bronx Surface Transit Operating Authority yesterday to allow elderly passengers to ride its buses for 10 cents during nonrush hours, holidays and weekends.

The order was included in the board's extension of the authority's lease to operate buses in Manhattan and the Bronx through Dec. 31, 1969. The board unanimously approved extension of the lease.

A Transit Authority source said, however, that it would take several months to establish a system for handling the half fares for passengers 65 years or older.

By the time such an arrangement could be worked out, the surface transit authority, as a subsidiary of the

Continued on Page 38, Column 2

$1.1-BILLION ASKED FOR STATE HEALTH

Rockefeller Proposes Plan to Modernize Municipal and Private Hospitals

By JAMES F. CLARITY

Special to The New York Times

ALBANY, Feb. 14—Governor Rockefeller proposed a $1.1-billion program today for the construction and rehabilitation of municipal and nonpublic hospitals, nursing homes and health centers.

Mr. Rockefeller, in a special message to the Legislature, coupled the billion-dollar program with proposals for increased research and treatment for heart and respiratory diseases. He also promised to ask "shortly" for passage of compulsory health insurance legislation "to insure that costs of this care will be met."

"Too many hospitals are obsolete, under-equipped, and unsuited to the demands of modern medicine," the Governor said in his message accompanying the proposed legislation. "Too many communities are without adequate nursing homes and other care facilities. Too often the cost of rectifying both these conditions exceeds present resources.

"This state leads the nation in the actions it has taken to expand the availability and the quality of health facilities. More remains to be done and the legislation I am urging will go far in that direction."

The proposed legislation, Mr. Rockefeller said, would "further improve the hospital and other health facilities available to our people and . . . promote research into the disease that

Continued on Page 12, Column 4

STATE DEMOCRATS ENDORSE JOHNSON FOR RE-ELECTION

Final Committee Resolution Omits Any Reference to His Conduct of War

By CLAYTON KNOWLES

Special to The New York Times

BUFFALO, Feb. 14—The New York State Democratic Committee voted overwhelmingly today an endorsement of President Johnson for re-election.

The action constituted a major gesture of support for the Administration even though the resolution, as finally adopted, omitted direct reference to the President's conduct of the war in Vietnam and progress at home toward his Great Society objectives.

A substitute resolution upholding Mr. Johnson's course in Vietnam was tabled, as was a resolution to withhold any Presidential endorsement at this time.

State's Convention Role

New York State will cast 190 of the 2,622 votes at the Democratic National Convention, or 14.4 per cent of the total a Presidential aspirant needs for nomination. The state has 43 electoral votes, the highest in the nation.

The State Democratic Chairman, John J. Burns, hailed the resolution as "a tangible evidence of unity within the Democratic party in New York State for the President."

In all, six dissenting votes were recorded on the final ballot after the hour-long debate at the Statler-Hilton Hotel, where the committee met. Only 57 of the 300 members were present, but they held 163 proxies.

Kennedy Backers Pleased

There was in the final outcome a measure of satisfaction for all elements of the party.

Supporters of Senator Robert F. Kennedy, who backs the President but has repeatedly challenged his course in Vietnam, were pleased that specific reference to the war had been omitted.

Backers of Senator Eugene J. McCarthy of Minnesota, the President's opponent in national primaries, also drew comfort from this omission. They had vainly sought to bar any Presidential endorsement at this time.

And elements favorable to the nomination of Representative Joseph Y. Resnick of Ellenville for the Senate nomination felt they had achieved a major point in having the resolution broadened to give the President "vigorous support in the forthcoming election. The resolution as passed

Continued on Page 24, Column 1

U.S. Marines Wait, Duck Shells and Rebuild at Their Khesanh Outpost

A U.S. Marine spotter, right, crouches behind a heavily sandbagged bunker as a North Vietnamese shell explodes

United Press International

A reinforced post office at the marine outpost was built underground to replace one destroyed by enemy shells

VANCE AND PARK REACH AN ACCORD

Agree on Moves to Counter North Korean Actions—War Threat Noted

By ROBERT TRUMBULL

Special to The New York Times

SEOUL, South Korea, Thursday, Feb. 15—The United States and South Korea agreed today on a joint program to counter aggressive moves by the Communist North Korean regime.

A communiqué issued jointly by President Chung Hee Park, of South Korea and Cyrus R. Vance, President Johnson's special envoy, declared that recent North Korean actions "seriously jeopardize the security of this area and if persisted in, can lead to renewed hostilities in Korea."

The agreement declared that "if such aggression continued" the two Governments would consult promptly on action to be taken under their mutual security treaty.

Earlier Stand Eased

South Korean official sources said that Seoul had reluctantly dropped its earlier insistence on an "automatic" military reaction by the United States forces here to any infiltration from the North by Communist commando units and armed agents.

Mr. Vance made a final 90-minute courtesy call on President Park this morning. The envoy was to leave for Washington in his special Air Force plane this afternoon.

Mr. Vance and the South Korean Foreign Minister, Choi Kyu Ha, formulated the agreement in a meeting that began at 9 last night and did not finish until 5 this morning.

They met in a two-room suite on the 16th floor of the Tower Hotel. The United States Ambassador, William J. Porter, was reported to have remained with the Foreign Minister until 6:30 A.M. working out the

Continued on Page 7, Column 1

Wheeler Doubts Khesanh Will Need Atom Weapons

By JOHN W. FINNEY

Special to The New York Times

WASHINGTON, Feb. 14—Gen. Earle G. Wheeler, Chairman of the Joint Chiefs of Staff, expressed confidence today that the Marine outpost at Khesanh in South Vietnam could be defended without the use of nuclear weapons.

When a reporter asked whether the use of nuclear weapons was being excluded in event the outpost was in danger of being overrun, the general replied: "I refuse to speculate any further." He then repeated his statement that he did not think nuclear weapons would be required.

The question of the use of nuclear weapons was raised by reporters after General Wheeler, along with Defense Secretary Robert S. McNamara, testified at a closed session of the House Defense Appropriations Subcommittee.

Noting that there were numerous rumors that consideration was being given to the use of nuclear weapons, a reporter asked the general whether he wished to make any comment.

While the question was phrased to apply to all of Vietnam, General Wheeler narrowed it when he said:

"I do not think that nuclear weapons will be required to defend Khesanh."

It seemed likely that General Wheeler's comments would only contribute to the widespread speculation, particularly among critics of the Administration, that consideration was being given to the use of nuclear weapons in Vietnam.

The concern being expressed by some Senators is that, faced with the alternative of losing 5,000 marines at Khesanh or using nuclear weapons, the Administration would choose to

Continued on Page 3, Column 7

U.S. JETS ATTACK CLOSE TO HANOI

Bridge and 2 Airfields Are Targets of Biggest Raids on North in 6 Weeks

By The Associated Press

SAIGON, South Vietnam, Thursday, Feb. 15—United States warplanes yesterday mounted their biggest assault on North Vietnam in six weeks, bombing a bridge just outside Hanoi and two airfields in the region of the capital, a military spokesman said today.

The raiders also wrecked four missile sites in the protective ring around Hanoi, the spokesman said.

Waves of planes swept through clearing skies. The United States command did not announce the total number of missions, but the strike was said to be the biggest since Jan. 4.

[United States Navy ships shelled the walled Citadel at Hue Thursday, United Press International reported, after American jets bombed the enemy stronghold. A Navy plane was downed off Hainan island by a Chinese MIG. Page 2.]

The raids on the Hanoi area centered on the Canal des Rapides Bridge, about three miles outside the city limits.

Pilots reported hitting the steel bridge with 3,000-pound bombs but said they could not assess the damage because of broken clouds.

The Hanoi radio said a populated area of the capital was rocket-bombed and asserted that six planes had been down-

Continued on Page 3, Column 1

Time Inc. to Buy Newark News; Purchase May Lead to Others

By HENRY RAYMONT

Time Inc. is acquiring its first newspaper, The Newark Evening News.

The move, which had been expected for several weeks, was announced yesterday by James A. Linen, president of Time Inc., and by Richard B. Scudder and Edward W. Scudder Jr., publisher and president, respectively, of The News.

The acquisition will be made through an exchange of stock planned for completion by July and subject to a ruling by the Internal Revenue Service that the transaction will be tax-free. The deal would involve more than $34-million.

The highest price paid for a single newspaper was the $50-million that S. I. Newhouse paid for The Cleveland Plain Dealer last March.

A Time Inc. official indicated last night that the purchase of the Newark paper could lead to a large-scale expansion in the newspaper publishing field.

Time Inc., the 46-year-old magazine and book publishing company that in recent years has expanded into a $500-million communications empire, had been studying the possibility of entering the newspaper field for almost a year.

After having turned down the idea of starting an afternoon paper in New York following the closing last May of The World Journal Tribune, Time executives decided some months ago to begin negotiations with The Newark Evening News.

The News is New Jersey's biggest daily, with an average

Continued on Page 32, Column 1

RUSK SAYS HANOI SPURNS U.S. TERMS FOR NEGOTIATION

Declares 'All Explorations to Date' Prove Rejection of Johnson's Position

2 NEW CONTACTS CITED

Washington Given Reports After Thant and Fanfani Meet North Vietnamese

Text of the Rusk statement is printed on Page 2.

By HEDRICK SMITH

Special to The New York Times

WASHINGTON, Feb. 14—Secretary of State Dean Rusk declared today that all explorations so far showed that North Vietnam had rejected United States terms for entering peace negotiations.

In a special statement, Mr. Rusk recalled that President Johnson promised, in his State of the Union Message on Jan. 17, to report to Congress on diplomatic soundings of North Vietnamese offers to talk.

"I must report that all explorations to date have resulted in a rejection of the President's terms for negotiating," Mr. Rusk said.

Soundings Are Reflected

American officials said the Secretary's remarks took into account contacts last week by the Italian Foreign Minister, Amintore Fanfani, with North Vietnamese representatives, as well as diplomatic soundings in India, Moscow and Paris by Secretary General Thant of the United Nations.

Mr. Thant met in Paris today with Mai Van Bo, Hanoi's chief representative in Europe.

Mr. Rusk, seeking to dampen what the Administration views as rising but false hopes for talks, issued his assessment late today through the State Department spokesman, Robert J. McCloskey.

This was the first time in the six weeks since intensive diplomatic exploration got under way that Secretary Rusk said that North Vietnam had "rejected" American terms. Previously he gave negative appraisals of North Vietnamese diplomatic and military actions, but avoided interpreting any of Hanoi's moves as a flat rejection.

Propaganda Charged

His shift to the more pessimistic appraisal seemed to signify that the Administration had given up hope of entering talks in the near future.

Officials said Mr. Rusk's statement could be read as meaning that the Government was inclined to interpret a series of North Vietnamese statements more as propaganda than as bids for serious negotiations.

The recent round of diplomatic soundings intensified after the North Vietnamese Foreign Minister, Nguyen Duy Trinh, said explicitly on Dec. 29 that Hanoi "will" hold talks if the United States uncondi-

Continued on Page 2, Column 3

U.S. Again to Send Arms Aid to Jordan

Special to The New York Times

WASHINGTON, Feb. 14—The United States announced today that it had decided to resume arms shipments to Jordan, which have been suspended since the six-day Israeli-Arab war last June.

The State Department, in making the announcement, said that detailed negotiations on a new military aid agreement with Jordan had begun.

The State Department coupled its announcement with another plea for "restraint on all arms shipments" to the Middle East. But officials acknowledged that the Soviet Union, the primary supplier for the militant Arab states, has shown no serious interest in curbing the arms race. As a result, they said, American sales to Jordan were necessary to protect

Continued on Page 9, Column 1

A Book That Couldn't Go to Harvard

The New York Times

Dr. Francis H. C. Crick

Rick Stafford

Dr. James D. Watson

Pix

Dr. Maurice H. F. Wilkins

By WALTER SULLIVAN

For the first time in at least two decades the Harvard Corporation has overruled the university's Board of Syndics and has ordered the Harvard University Press not to publish a book.

Harvard's Board of Syndics consists of 12 professors who advise the university press regarding books to be published. The name "syndic" was applied in the past to government officers, magistrates and agents of corporations. Syndics served in ancient trading companies, and still function at some universities as overseers of such activities as publishing.

The work in question is "The Double Helix," now by Dr. James D. Watson—now professor of biochemistry and molecular biology at Harvard—tells of the long struggle to decipher the structure of DNA (deoxyribonucleic acid). Within that substance is encoded the information of heredity.

The university halted plans for publication when the two men who shared the Nobel Prize with Dr. Watson for this work voiced protests.

The two men are Dr. Francis H. C. Crick, with whom Dr. Watson worked closely at Cambridge University in England, and Dr. Maurice H. F. Wilkins of the University of London.

The book tells the story in highly personal terms, describing the idiosyncrasies of the principals, their quarrels and friendships.

"The Double Helix" is being published Feb. 26 by Atheneum, where the man

Continued on Page 13, Column 1

NEWS INDEX

"All the News That's Fit to Print"

The New York Times

LATE CITY EDITION

Weather: Partial clearing today; fair, cool tonight and tomorrow. Temp. range: today 62-53; Sunday 68-48. Full U. S. report on Page 90.

VOL. CXVII..No. 40,245 | NEW YORK, MONDAY, APRIL 1, 1968 | 10 CENTS

JOHNSON SAYS HE WON'T RUN; HALTS NORTH VIETNAM RAIDS; BIDS HANOI JOIN PEACE MOVES

ROCKEFELLER URGES ALBANY LEADERS TO SPEED BUDGET

Ready to Work With Them to Provide Funds as Fiscal Year Opens Today

By PETER KIHSS

Governor Rockefeller urged Republican and Democratic legislative leaders yesterday to agree quickly on a new budget as the state moved into the 1968-69 fiscal year today without a budget.

The Republican - controlled Senate has passed one version of the budget, but the Democratic-controlled Assembly is pondering a counter-version. The Governor said in a statement he was "ready to work with the leadership in both houses" for "a budget that meets the needs of the people of our state and provides the revenues necessary to finance it."

After the Legislature does act, the Governor will presumably seek a supplemental appropriation to restore some of the spending cuts that both parties' legislative fiscal committees make in his proposed school, urban, crime and construction programs. This is a traditional technique.

Assembly May Act Today

Fiscal aides to Assembly Speaker Anthony J. Travia analyzed the Senate proposals through the night. Mr. Travia himself said he was considering two interim moves. One would have the Assembly approve the budget appropriations and cuts already agreed on; the other would seek a temporary authorization for state spending at the rate for the last quarter of the fiscal year just ended.

Joseph Zaretzki, Senate Democratic minority leader, charged here yesterday that the budget bills rammed through the Senate early Saturday by the Republican leader, Earl Brydges, and his party followers aimed only "to get by next November's election."

Senator Zaretzki asserted that two of its key elements—

Continued on Page 38, Column 3

Liberals Designate Javits; Nickerson Race Confused

Baron May Enter Race

By CLAYTON KNOWLES

The Liberal party State Committee designated Senator Jacob K. Javits for re-election late yesterday, but under conditions that confronted him with the prospect of waging a primary fight to gain the extra line on the voting machines.

A bloc of unionists in the party, contending that an endorsement of Mr. Javits would aid Richard M. Nixon in his Presidential bid, put up Murray Baron, a long-time Liberal leader. Although Mr. Baron lost, he rolled up enough votes to qualify to run in the June 18 primary.

The Liberals acted several hours before President Johnson's withdrawal. Mr. Baron came under heavy attack in the prevote debate as "more

Continued on Page 50, Column 1

Johnson Causes Upset

The contest for the Democratic Senate nomination in New York was thrown into confusion last night by President Johnson's announcement that he would not seek the party's nomination for re-election.

Eugene H. Nickerson, the organization's candidate for the nomination and a supporter of Senator Robert F. Kennedy, said of the Johnson announcement: "I was very surprised. It just comes as such a complete surprise to me that I think we have to sleep on it."

Representative Joseph Y. Resnick of Ellenville, a Senate candidate who supports President Johnson, sent a telegram to the President urging the President to reconsider his decision.

"Mr. President," the Resnick

Continued on Page 50, Column 5

TAX RISE PUSHED

Increase in War Costs Cited—No Specific Cuts Suggested

By EILEEN SHANAHAN
Special to The New York Times

WASHINGTON, March 31—President Johnson called on Congress tonight to "move from debate to action, from talking to voting" on a tax increase.

He pledged himself to accept any appropriate reductions in Federal spending that Congress voted, but he proposed nothing specific in the way of economy moves.

He announced, in fact, that there would be an increase in Government outlays because of the war. These, he said, would amount to $2.5-billion in the current fiscal year, which ends June 30, and $2.6-billion in the next fiscal year.

What effect the President's decision not to run for re-election might have on the long fight over the tax increase and Government spending was not immediately clear. A lame duck President is usually considered to have greatly diminished power to influence Congress, but the President's removal of himself from the campaign could also remove some of the partisanship from the tax and spending issue.

Deficit to Increase

The increases the President announced in defense spending would raise the deficit for the current year to $22.3-billion and for next year to $20.5-billion, if the 10 per cent tax surcharge is not enacted, and assuming that there are no other changes in spending from the official January estimates.

If the tax increase is enacted, with April 1 the effective date for individuals and Jan. 1 for corporations, as the President has asked, this year's deficit would be $20.4-billion and next year's, $10.6-billion.

"Enactment of a tax increase now, together with expenditure control, is necessary to protect our security, continue our prosperity and meet the needs of our people," Mr. Johnson said.

He said he believed there

Continued on Page 30, Column 3

DMZ IS EXEMPTED

Johnson Sets No Time Limit on Halting of Air and Sea Blows

By MAX FRANKEL
Special to The New York Times

WASHINGTON, March 31—President Johnson announced tonight that he had ordered a halt in the air and naval bombardment of most of North Vietnam and invited the Hanoi Government to join him in a "series of mutual moves toward peace."

The President said:

"Tonight, in the hope that this action will lead to early talks, I am taking the first step to de-escalate the conflict. We are reducing—substantially reducing—the present level of hostilities. And we are doing so unilaterally and at once."

The President said that attacks would continue only in the area just north of the demilitarized zone, which separates North Vietnam from South Vietnam, and where, he said, the "continuing enemy build-up directly threatens allied forward positions and where movements of troops and supplies are clearly related to that threat."

Hanoi's Stand Recalled

The President set no time limit for his restraint order. Until now, North Vietnam has demanded an "unconditional"—apparently meaning permanent—halt in the bombing of all its territory and all other acts of war against it.

North Vietnam's restraint and other unspecified events, the President indicated, can make possible an early end of "even this limited bombing."

The areas to be spared, he said, include almost 90 per cent of North Vietnam's population and "most of its territory."

The White House refused to give a more specific geographical delineation.

[In Saigon, the United States command said that the order went into effect at 9 P.M. Sunday, New York time, when President Johnson began his address, The Associated Press reported. Page 15.]

At the same time, Mr. Johnson used a televised address to the nation to urge the Soviet Union and Britain to do everything possible to move from his "unilateral act of de-escalation" toward a genuine peace.

He designated Ambassador at Large W. Averell Harriman and the American Ambassador to Moscow, Llewellyn Thomp-

Continued on Page 28, Column 1

Associated Press

ADDRESSES THE NATION: President Johnson last night

SURPRISE DECISION

President Steps Aside in Unity Bid—Says 'House' Is Divided

Text of Johnson's address will be found on Page 26.

By TOM WICKER
Special to The New York Times

WASHINGTON, March 31—Lyndon Baines Johnson announced tonight: "I shall not seek and I will not accept the nomination of my party as your President."

Later, at a White House news conference, he said his decision was "completely irrevocable."

The President told his nationwide television audience:

"What we have won when all our people were united must not be lost in partisanship. I have concluded that I should not permit the Presidency to become involved in partisan decisions."

Mr. Johnson, acknowledging that there was "division in the American house," withdrew in the name of national unity, which he said was "the ultimate strength of our country."

"With American sons in the field far away," he said, "with the American future under challenge right here at home, with our hopes and the world's hopes for peace in the balance every day, I do not believe that I should devote an hour or a day of my time to any personal partisan causes or to any duties other than the awesome duties of this office, the Presidency of your country."

Humphrey Race Possible

Mr. Johnson left Senator Robert F. Kennedy of New York and Senator Eugene J. McCarthy of Minnesota as the only two declared candidates for the Democratic Presidential nomination.

Vice President Humphrey, however, will be widely expected to seek the nomination now that his friend and political benefactor, Mr. Johnson, is out of the field. Mr. Humphrey indicated that he would have a statement on his plans tomorrow.

The President informed Mr. Humphrey of his decision during a conference at the latter's apartment in southwest Washington today before the Vice President flew to Mexico City. There, he will represent the United States at the signing of a treaty for a Latin-American nuclear-free zone.

Surprise to Aides

If Mr. Humphrey should become a candidate, he would find most of the primaries foreclosed to him. Only those in the District of Columbia, New Jersey and South Dakota remain open.

Therefore, he would have to rely on collecting delegates in states without primaries and on White House support if he were to head off Mr. Kennedy and Mr. McCarthy.

Former Vice President Richard M. Nixon is the only announced major candidate for the Republican nomination, although Governor Rockefeller has said that he would accept the nomination if drafted.

Mr. Johnson's announcement tonight came as a stunning surprise even to close associates. His main political strategists, James H. Rowe of Washington, White House Special Assistant Marvin W. Watson, and Postmaster General Lawrence F. O'Brien, spent much of today conferring on campaign plans.

They were informed of what was coming just before Mr.

Continued on Page 27, Column 1

3 Beachfront Hotels Destroyed by Fire In Rockaway Park

By LAWRENCE VAN GELDER

Flames spurred by howling ocean winds raged through the Rockaway Park section of Queens yesterday, destroying three beachfront hotels, damaging small stores and bungalows, charring police and fire equipment and forcing the evacuation of hundreds of residents.

As the number of alarms climbed swiftly to eight, more than 400 firemen and 60 pieces of equipment were pitted against the intense blaze, which sent up a column of gray smoke visible for more than a dozen miles in the afternoon sky.

Despite the fury of the fire and the menacing wind-whipped embers that flew through the neighborhood around Beach 116th Street and Ocean Promenade, no serious injuries were reported from the blaze, which was attributed by officials to three small children. Four firemen, however, were reported

Continued on Page 36, Column 4

HOUSE PLAN SPURS INVESTING ABROAD

Committee Asks Creation of Quasi-Public Corporation to Attract Private Capital

By FELIX BELAIR Jr.
By The Associated Press

WASHINGTON, March 31—The House Foreign Affairs Committee urged in a report today that the Federal Government consider creating a quasi-public corporation to promote private American investments in underdeveloped countries.

The report, originated by Representative Leonard Farbstein, Democrat of Manhattan, won the unanimous approval of the committee.

The gist of the report was that the investment guarantee program of the Agency for International Development was no longer able to attract sufficient private capital to spur economic growth in the poor countries of Latin America,

Continued on Page 8, Column 1

Political Chiefs Stunned; Kennedy Sets News Parley

By SYLVAN FOX

Political leaders across the country reacted with shock, surprise and—in some cases—admiration to President Johnson's announcement last night that he would not seek re-election in November. Some political leaders immediately focused attention on Vice President Humphrey as a possible contender for the Democratic Presidential nomination.

Others suggested that Mr. Johnson's withdrawal could alter the position of Governor Rockefeller, who pulled out of contention for the Republican Presidential nomination on March 21.

Neither Mr. Humphrey nor Mr. Rockefeller was commenting immediately on his political plans in the light of Mr. Johnson's withdrawal.

Senator Robert F. Kennedy, like many others, was left almost speechless by the President's announcement.

"I don't know quite what to say," Senator Kennedy commented when he got the word of the President's decision. The Senator, a leading contender for the Democratic Presidential nomination, scheduled a news conference for 10 A.M. today.

Continued on Page 27, Column 4

WISCONSIN WEIGHS IMPACT ON VOTING

Primary Excitement Turns to Surprise—McCarthy and Nixon Wind Up Campaign

By DONALD JANSON
Special to The New York Times

MILWAUKEE, March 31—Excitement over a spirited contest between Senator Eugene J. McCarthy and President Johnson in the Wisconsin Democratic Presidential primary turned to surprise tonight with the President's announcement that he was not a candidate for re-election.

Thousands of Wisconsin voters, who had expected to choose between the two on Tuesday, saw and heard the President on television take himself out of the contest.

The announcement ended speculation that the Wisconsin primary, the first in the nation to have the President's name on the ballot, would produce a record vote.

It left only Senator McCarthy as an active candidate on the Democratic ballot and only former Vice President Richard M. Nixon as a major candidate on the Republican side. It eliminated the urgency that thousands of Republicans had felt to cross over to the Democratic contest to vote against the

Continued on Page 48, Column 1

The New York Times (by William E. Sauro)

AT ROCKAWAY PARK BLAZE: More than 400 firemen were called out to fight eight-alarm fire that raged on Beach 116th Street in the Rockaway Park section of Queens. Jamaica Bay is in rear. Four firemen were slightly hurt.

Top Saigon Officials Confused By Refusal of Johnson to Run

By GENE ROBERTS
Special to The New York Times

SAIGON, South Vietnam, Monday, April 1—President Johnson's refusal to seek re-election plunged the top level of the South Vietnamese Government into confusion today and touched off a meeting of key American officials.

It was apparent, according to Americans who were at the presidential palace at the time, that President Johnson's announcement caught the South Vietnamese by surprise.

"Top advisers and officeholders began rushing toward the Vice President's office in obvious states of agitation," said one American who was waiting for a conference with Vice President Nguyen Cao Ky. "A few minutes later, Ky's military aide appeared and said all appointments had been canceled."

There was similar excitement at the United States Embassy. A receptionist said that no high officials were available for comment and explained that they were all in a top-level meeting.

There was also a rash of meetings at the headquarters of the military command here.

While many military officers and virtually all South Vietnamese officials are op-

Continued on Page 28, Column 5

NEWS INDEX

"All the News That's Fit to Print"

The New York Times

LATE CITY EDITION

Weather: Clearing today, turning cold tonight. Fair, cool tomorrow. Temp. range: today 62-44; Thurs. 73-52. Full U.S. report on Page 92.

VOL. CXVII. No. 40,249 NEW YORK, FRIDAY, APRIL 5, 1968 10 CENTS

MARTIN LUTHER KING IS SLAIN IN MEMPHIS; A WHITE IS SUSPECTED; JOHNSON URGES CALM

JOHNSON DELAYS TRIP TO HAWAII; MAY LEAVE TODAY

President Spends a Hectic Day Here and in Capital —Sees Thant at the U.N.

By MAX FRANKEL

Special to The New York Times

WASHINGTON, April 4 — President Johnson postponed his trip to Hawaii at least until tomorrow after he heard of the death of the Rev. Dr. Martin Luther King Jr. tonight.

The news, which visibly shocked the President, came at the end of one of the most extraordinary days in perhaps the most extraordinary week of his Administration.

Mr. Johnson was to have flown from Washington at about midnight for a weekend of strategy conferences with his military and diplomatic leaders stationed in South Vietnam. On the way, he had planned a breakfast meeting in California with former President Dwight D. Eisenhower.

Instead, the President telephoned Mrs. King in Atlanta, made a brief appeal for calm on television and went to his office to follow the reports of unrest and disturbance given him periodically by Attorney General Ramsey Clark.

Cancels Dinner Appearance

Mr. Johnson also canceled an appearance before a Democratic party fund-raising dinner here —the final event of a hectic schedule that became ever more hectic as the day unfolded.

The President began the day by making final arrangements for the Hawaii meeting. It had been tentatively planned before his order Sunday to curtail the bombing of North Vietnam and the news yesterday that Hanoi was interested in establishing direct contact.

[The new United States peace moves are producing a quiet but bitter reaction in the South Vietnamese Government that is causing increasing concern among United States officials in Saigon. Page 14.]

But the diplomatic development, though not the principal subject of the Honolulu meetings, added special weight to his conversations with Gen. William C. Westmoreland, the American commander in South Vietnam, and other officials.

Mr. Johnson was careful not to arouse false hopes of peace, but he appeared encouraged and in buoyant spirt as he decided before noon to fly first to New York to attend the investiture of the Most Rev. Terence J. Cooke as Archbishop of New York.

Then, while in New York,

Continued on Page 12, Column 1

Hanoi Charges U.S. Raid Far North of 20th Parallel

By EVERT CLARK

Special to The New York Times

WASHINGTON, April 4 — North Vietnam charged in a broadcast today that United States planes had bombed a "populated area" in northwestern Vietnam far north of the 20th parallel. The Defense Department said it knew of no such raid but was investigating.

President Johnson has ordered that there be no attacks on North Vietnam north of the 20th Parallel as a step toward de-escalating the war.

[In South Vietnam, United States marines beat off an attack by about 400 North Vietnamese soldiers charging up a hill near Khesanh, killing 93, The Associated Press reported. Meanwhile, an American relief column was nearing the besieged base. Page 15.]

The Hanoi radio, in a broadcast monitored and translated here, said three waves of United States planes dropped more than 50 bombs on a "populated area" about 30 miles west of Laichau, capital of Laichau Province, this morning.

The nearest village to that

Continued on Page 15, Column 1

The New York Times April 5, 1968

Hanoi said that area near Laichau (cross) was target.

HUMPHREY HINTS HE'LL ENTER RACE

Tells Unionists in Pittsburgh He Will Act Soon—Abel and Wirtz Back Him

By ROY REED

Special to The New York Times

PITTSBURGH, April 4—Two thousand labor representatives, including the head of the United Steel Workers union, clamorously urged Vice President Humphrey today to run for President.

The Vice President left little doubt that he would oblige them, but he indicated that he would wait until President Johnson returned from his Hawaii conference before making an announcement.

"I know what your request is, and I know what your thoughts are," he told the delegates to the Pennsylvania A.F.L.-C.I.O. convention. "I am most grateful. I am not one to walk away from a decision, and a decision will come in due time."

But nothing he does should interfere with President Johnson's peace mission, he said.

Several other political leaders urged Mr. Humphrey today to enter the race for the Democratic Presidential nomination. The most prominent among them was Secretary of Labor W. Willard Wirtz, who was addressing a union convention at Miami Beach.

I. W. Abel, president of the steelworkers Union, rose as Mr.

Continued on Page 32, Column 1

Johnson Shuns Role Of '68 'Lame Duck,' Kennedy Was Told

By JOHN HERBERS

Special to The New York Times

WASHINGTON, April 4—In his meeting with Senator Robert F. Kennedy yesterday President Johnson said he would remain out of the political fight this year because he did not believe it was appropriate for a "lame duck" President to try to pick his successor.

This and other details of the Johnson-Kennedy meeting were learned today from knowledgeable sources.

The meeting, which Senator Kennedy had requested in the interest of "national unity," was described as an extraordinarily friendly one, with both the Senator and the President speaking in a conciliatory manner.

President Johnson was pictured as the "elder statesman" of the party who had decided to remain aloof from this year's scramble for the Presidency in an effort to keep the party as strong as possible and retain his own dignity and effectiveness as President.

At one point, it was reported, the President said he did not want to make a spectacle of himself as a lame duck President attempting to dictate to the party who should be nominated at the national convention.

In this regard, he pointed out that in 1956 former President Harry S. Truman went to the

Continued on Page 31, Column 4

DISMAY IN NATION

Negroes Urge Others to Carry on Spirit of Nonviolence

By LAWRENCE VAN GELDER

Dismay, shame, anger and foreboding marked the nation's reaction last night to the Rev. Dr. Martin Luther King Jr.'s murder.

From the high offices of state to the man in the street, news of the moderate civil rights leader's violent death in Memphis yesterday drew, for the most part, stunned and sober statements.

Most major Negro organizations and Negro leaders, lamenting Dr. King's death, expressed hope that it serve as a spur to others to carry on in his spirit of nonviolence. But some Negro militants responded with bitterness and anger.

Roy Wilkins, executive director of the National Association for the Advancement of Colored People, said his organization was "shocked and deeply grieved by the dastardly murder of Dr. Martin Luther King."

"His murderer or murderers must be promptly apprehended and brought to justice," Mr. Wilkins said.

'A Man of Peace'

"Dr. King was a symbol of the nonviolent civil rights protest movement. He was a man of peace, of dedication, of great courage. His senseless assassination solves nothing. It will not stay the civil rights movement; it will instead spur it to greater activity."

Whitney M. Young Jr., executive director of the National Urban League, said:

"We are unspeakably shocked by the murder of Martin Luther King, one of the greatest leaders of our time. This is a bitter reflection on America. We fear for our country.

"The only possible answer now is for the nation to act immediately on what Dr. King has been fighting for—passage of the civil rights and antipoverty bills and a true and just equality for all men. Those of us who have remained loyal to his concept of nonviolence have been dealt a mortal blow."

Mayor Richard G. Hatcher of Gary, Ind., a Negro, termed the death of Dr. King "every man's loss."

"Men who care for humankind and struggle for its salvation through reason and faith have lost a leader of monumental stature," he said. "A man of his magnitude will not soon pass this way again."

At his home in Stamford, Conn., the former baseball star Jackie Robinson called the

Continued on Page 26, Column 1

PRESIDENT'S PLEA

On TV, He Deplores 'Brutal' Murder of Negro Leader

Statements by Johnson and Humphrey are on Page 24.

Special to The New York Times

WASHINGTON, April 4—President Johnson deplored tonight in a brief television address to the nation the "brutal slaying" of the Rev. Dr. Martin Luther King Jr.

He asked "every citizen to reject the blind violence that has struck Dr. King, who lived by nonviolence."

Mr. Johnson said he was postponing his scheduled departure tonight for a Honolulu conference on Vietnam and that instead he would leave tomorrow.

The President spoke from the White House. At the Washington Hilton Hotel, where Democratic members of Congress had gathered to honor the President and the Vice President, Mr. Humphrey, his voice strained with emotion, said:

"Martin Luther King stands with our other American martyrs in the cause of freedom and justice. His death is a terrible tragedy."

The dinner was canceled 10 to 15 minutes after the Vice President spoke. Mr. Johnson, who was scheduled to appear at the dinner, canceled his plans to attend.

F.B.I. Inquiry Ordered

Attorney General Ramsey Clark ordered an immediate inquiry by the Federal Bureau of Investigation into the shooting of Dr. King in Memphis.

He said the purpose of the investigation would be to determine whether any Federal law had been violated.

One provision of the law that could be invoked makes it a crime to engage in a conspiracy to deprive a person of his civil rights.

In addition to F.B.I. agents, Department of Justice civil rights representatives were on the scene in Memphis and were in touch with the Attorney General.

Military sources said that no National Guard units had yet been Federalized and no Regular Army troops had been alerted yet for possible movement to cities where violence had broken out.

National Guard troops, such as the 4,000 men who have been called into Memphis, remain under state control until the responsible Governor requests help and the President

Continued on Page 24, Column 7

Associated Press

THE REV. DR. MARTIN LUTHER KING Jr.

Scattered Violence Occurs In Harlem and Brooklyn

12 Are Arrested Here

By THOMAS A. JOHNSON

Sporadic violence erupted in Harlem and Brooklyn's Bedford-Stuyvesant section last night after news of Dr. Martin Luther King's assassination spread in the two predominantly Negro communities.

Mayor Lindsay, who went to Harlem in an effort to quiet the outbreaks, was caught in the midst of an unruly crowd and had to be hustled into a limousine by bodyguards.

Police reinforcements, including elements of the riot-trained Tactical Patrol Force, were rushed into both communities.

Two arrests were reported in Brooklyn and 10 in Harlem. A television crewman was said to have been injured by flying glass.

There were numerous instances of rock-throwing, looting and arson reported both in Brooklyn and in Harlem, starting around 11 P.M. and continuing early today.

Gangs of youth in both areas were reported roaming through the streets, now and then taunting policemen and firemen on duty.

The police fired several volleys of shots in the air to disperse crowds along Brooklyn's Fulton Street and Harlem's

Continued on Page 26, Column 2

Widespread Disorders

Disorders broke out in scattered parts of the nation last night after the slaying of the Rev. Dr. Martin Luther King Jr. The National Guard was called out or alerted in several cities.

In Washington, scattered but persistent looting and vandalism erupted, led for a time by Stokely Carmichael, former head of the Student Nonviolent Coordinating Commitee. All available policemen were being called to duty.

About 4,000 Tennessee National Guardsmen were ordered to duty in Nashville because of disorders.

In North Carolina, Gov. Dan K. Moore alerted the Guard in Greensboro at the request of Mayor Carson Bain. State Highway patrolmen were dispatched to Raleigh.

There were riotous outbursts

Continued on Page 26, Column 5

NEWS INDEX

GUARD CALLED OUT

Curfew Is Ordered in Memphis, but Fires and Looting Erupt

By EARL CALDWELL

Special to The New York Times

MEMPHIS, Friday, April 5—The Rev. Dr. Martin Luther King Jr., who preached nonviolence and racial brotherhood, was fatally shot here last night by a distant gunman who then raced away and escaped.

Four thousand National Guard troops were ordered into Memphis by Gov. Buford Ellington after the 39-year-old Nobel Prize-winning civil rights leader died.

A curfew was imposed on the shocked city of 550,000 inhabitants, 40 per cent of whom are Negro.

But the police said the tragedy had been followed by incidents that included sporadic shooting, fires, bricks and bottles thrown at policemen, and looting that started in Negro districts and then spread over the city.

White Car Sought

Police Director Frank Holloman said the assassin might have been a white man who was "50 to 100 yards away in a flophouse."

Chief of Detectives W. P. Huston said a late model white Mustang was believed to have been the killer's getaway car. Its occupant was described as a bareheaded white man in his 30's, wearing a black suit and black tie.

The detective chief said the police had chased two cars near the motel where Dr. King was shot and had halted one that had two out-of-town men as occupants. The men were questioned but seemed to have nothing to do with the killing, he said.

Rifle Found Nearby

A high-powered 30.06-caliber rifle was found about a block from the scene of the shooting, on South Main Street. "We think it's the gun," Chief Huston said, reporting it would be turned over to the Federal Bureau of Investigation.

Dr. King was shot while he leaned over a second-floor railing outside his room at the Lorraine Motel. He was chatting with two friends just before starting for dinner.

One of the friends was a musician, and Dr. King had just asked him to play a Negro spiritual, "Precious Lord, Take My Hand," at a rally that was to have been held two hours later in support of striking Memphis sanitationmen.

Paul Hess, assistant adminis-

Continued on Page 24, Column 1

Archbishop Cooke Installed; President Looks On

By EDWARD B. FISKE

The Most Rev. Terence J. Cooke was installed as the seventh Roman Catholic Archbishop of New York yesterday in a historic pageant attended by the President of the United States and highlighted by prayers for the success of his peace efforts in Vietnam.

"Let us pray with all our hearts that God will inspire our President," the 47-year-old Archbishop said in his homily at St. Patrick's Cathedral.

"In the last few days, we have all admired his heroic efforts in the search for peace in Vietnam. We ask God to bless his efforts with success. May God inspire not only our President, but also other leaders and the leaders of all nations of the world to find a way to peace."

Then the Archbishop, speaking from a white marble pulpit and surrounded by a blaze of purple, gold and scarlet robes, addressed himself directly to Mr. Johnson, who sat below him in a front pew.

The President, sitting with his hands clasped and his legs crossed, listened with obvious intensity to the Archbishop's words.

"Mr. President," he said, "our hearts, our hopes, our continued prayers go with you."

Mr. Johnson, accompanied by his daughter, Mrs. Patrick J. Nugent, led a festive congregation of about 5,000 cardinals, bishops, priests, laymen, nuns, civic leaders

Continued on Page 38, Column 1

The New York Times (by Neal Boenzi)

President Johnson and his daughter, Mrs. Patrick J. Nugent, right, listening during yesterday's ceremonies. At left are Mrs. John F. Kennedy and Lieut. Gov. Malcolm Wilson. Security personnel are in the row between them.

Archbishop Luigi Raimondi, Apostolic Delegate to the U.S., speaking after Archbishop Terence J. Cooke was enthroned

"All the News That's Fit to Print"

The New York Times

LATE CITY EDITION

Weather: Sunny, warm today; fair, continued warm tonight, tomorrow. Temp. range: today 88-62; Wed. 83-59. Temp.-Hum. Index 75; Wed. 74. Full U.S. report on Page 94.

VOL. CXVII..No. 40,311 NEW YORK, THURSDAY, JUNE 6, 1968 — 10 CENTS

KENNEDY IS DEAD, VICTIM OF ASSASSIN; SUSPECT, ARAB IMMIGRANT, ARRAIGNED; JOHNSON APPOINTS PANEL ON VIOLENCE

MARCUS TESTIFIES DE SAPIO HAD ROLE IN A CON ED DEAL

Says Itkin Sought Delay of Permit to Aid Own Scheme With Ex-Tammany Head

By BARNARD L. COLLIER

Former Water Commissioner James L. Marcus testified yesterday that he had been asked to delay approval of a permit to Consolidated Edison while the former Tammany Hall leader, Carmine G. De Sapio, was trying to make a deal with the utility company.

Marcus testified that the request came last September from his business partner, Herbert Itkin, who was in turn trying to negotiate a deal with Mr. De Sapio.

The testimony was elicited from Marcus under cross-examination on the third day of a Federal bribery conspiracy trial that has been marked by the mention in Marcus's testimony of several prominent members of both the Republican and Democratic parties.

Marcus was asked if there was a time when he, as Commissioner of Water Supply, Gas and Electricity, had "done business" with Con Edison. His answer was yes.

Says Itkin Asked Delay

"Itkin came to me," he said, "and said that Con Ed wanted a permit to increase the voltage on one of their power lines for 20 miles." He added that his approval as Commissioner was needed.

"Itkin said I should hold up for a while because he was negotiating with Carmine De Sapio, who was negotiating with Con Ed."

Marcus said that Mr. Itkin asked him to delay the approval for "a few weeks."

At that point in the trial, which came at about 4:40 P.M., Herman Zoloto, a lawyer representing Henry Fried, a contractor, and Mr. Fried's company, S. T. Grand, Inc., shouted:

"You're way ahead of your story, Mr. Marcus!"

Judge Edward Weinfeld broke in and scolded Mr. Zoloto for "a highly improper re-

Continued on Page 41, Column 1

TRANSIT PACKAGE SUBMITTED TO CITY

M.T.A. Seeks Approval of 8 New Subway Routes

By EMANUEL PERLMUTTER

A $1.27-billion package of subway and commuter railroad additions and improvements was submitted to the Board of Estimate and Mayor Lindsay yesterday.

The program was presented by the Metropolitan Transportation Authority and the New York City Transit Authority with a request for speedy city agreement on the new routes and engineering designs.

The over-all plan, which would take 10 years to complete, consists of eight new subway routes, including a Second Avenue subway, and Long Island Rail Road connections to the East Side of Manhattan and to Kennedy International Airport.

City approval of the routes and designs is a first step before application can be made for $60-million set aside by the Legislature for the engineering design of the mass transportation program presented by the Metropolitan Transportation

Continued on Page 55, Column 1

France Will Meet Tariff Deadline; Strikes Dwindling

By HENRY TANNER

Special to The New York Times

PARIS, June 5 — Maurice Couve de Murville told France's partners in the Common Market today that despite the nationwide strike now coming to a close, the Government would honor the July 1 deadline for the abolition of remaining tariffs in the European trade bloc.

Today workers in the nationalized railroad company, the Paris transit system, the post and telegraph offices and other public administrations voted to go back to work. Trains are expected to start running tomorrow on several major national lines and the Paris subways.

By the end of the week, it is expected, the nationwide strike, now in its 18th day, will be all but ended.

Mr. Couve de Murville, who is the new Minister of Economy and Finance, also reassured his countrymen

Continued on Page 15, Column 1

JERUSALEM POLICE CLASH WITH ARABS

Israelis Halt Procession on Anniversary of War—U.N. Council Meets on Fighting

Special to The New York Times

JERUSALEM, June 5—A silent Arab procession commemorating the first anniversary of the Arab-Israeli war erupted into a violent clash today when Israeli policemen intercepted the marchers at the edge of the walled Old City of Jerusalem.

The clash was the most violent aspect of a widespread protest in which Arabs shuttered shops and other businesses here and elsewhere on the west bank of the Jordan and in the occupied Gaza Strip. It came after a day-long battle yesterday across the Jordan between the Israelis and Jordanians, in which aircraft and artillery were used.

[The United Nations Security Council met Wednesday at the urgent request of Israel and Jordan to consider recurrent hostilities along their cease-fire line. It postponed debate, probably until Thursday. Page 3.]

In the west-bank towns of Nablus, Jenin and Tulkarm, all centers of Arab nationalism, the general strike was 100 per cent effective. All stores, cafes and offices were closed, public transportation ceased and the streets were virtually devoid of traffic and pedestrians.

Schools throughout the west bank and Gaza Strip had no

Continued on Page 2, Column 4

Italy's Cabinet Quits As Parliament Opens

By ROBERT C. DOTY

Special to The New York Times

ROME, June 5—Premier Aldo Moro and his center-left coalition Government, which has ruled Italy for four and a half years, resigned tonight with the convening of the new parliament, the fifth since World War II.

President Giuseppe Saragat asked Mr. Moro and his ministers to remain in office as a caretaker government while the search for a new government, which may be arduous, goes on.

Resignation of the government with the convening of a new parliament is automatic. But any hope that the Moro

Continued on Page 14, Column 3

6 IN RACE GUARDED

Secret Service Given Campaign Security Task by President

Text of the Johnson speech is printed on Page 23.

By MAX FRANKEL

Special to The New York Times

WASHINGTON, June 5—For the second time in five years, Lyndon B. Johnson undertook today, amid national shock and outrage, to offer protection, prayer, comfort and assistance to his political rivals in the Kennedy family and then to try to heal the country's political and psychological wounds.

The President's first reaction to the shooting of Senator Robert F. Kennedy this morning was that "there are no words equal to the horror of this tragedy."

But tonight, in an emotional and at times even angry statement on television, he pleaded with all Americans to end the violence in their midst once and for all, to tolerate neither hatred nor the preaching of violence and to resolve to live under the law.

A Guard for Candidates

Mr. Johnson said he was appointing a commission of distinguished citizens to investigate both the circumstances and the causes of physical violence of all kinds in the United States, in the hope that the nation can learn "how we can stop it".

Earlier he had moved swiftly to provide protective Secret Service details to the six announced Presidential candidates of major parties, other than Vice President Humphrey, who already has such protection because of his office.

Meanwhile, in the House of Representatives, a vote of 317 to 60 cleared the way for the House to accept the Senate version of an anticrime bill, including controls over the interstate sale of hand guns. The vote rejected a move to send the legislation to a Senate-House conference.

Members of Commission

To the commission Mr. Johnson named Milton Eisenhower, former president of Johns Hopkins University; Archbishop Terence J. Cooke of New York; Albert Jenner, Chicago lawyer who worked for the commission that investigated the assassination of President Kennedy; former Ambassador Patricia Harris; Eric Hoffer, the longshoreman-turned-philosopher; Senators Philip Hart, Democrat of Michigan, and Roman L. Hruska, Republican of Nebraska; Representative Hale Boggs, Democrat of Louisiana, majority whip in the House; Representative William M. McCulloch, Republican of Ohio, and Federal Judge Leon Higginbotham of Philadelphia.

The President described himself as shocked, dismayed and deeply disturbed, as he knew all Americans were, by the shooting, which he described as the "latest spectacular example" of lawlessness and violence.

"So let us, for God's sake, re-

Continued on Page 23, Column 1

NEWS INDEX

AFTER THE SHOOTING: Senator Kennedy's wife, Ethel, bends over him as a man checks pulse to determine condition

HANOI INSISTS U.S. HALT ITS BOMBING

Aides Call Talks Response to Johnson—Suspicion Voiced of a Plot Against Kennedy

By HEDRICK SMITH

Special to The New York Times

PARIS, June 5—North Vietnamese negotiators contended today that Hanoi had responded to President Johnson's restriction of American air attacks on the north by entering official talks here. They asserted that the next move, a total halt in bombing, was up to the United States.

The North Vietnamese argument, put forward in the seventh negotiating session between the two sides since May 13, produced one of the sharpest exchanges since the Vietnam talks began here.

The North Vietnamese made no direct comment on the shooting of Senator Robert F. Kennedy, but circles close to the delegation voiced suspicions in private, asking if the attack was not part of a conspiracy by the Johnson Administration. [Page 33.]

Near the end of today's session at the former Majestic Hotel, Hanoi's chief representative, Xuan Thuy, leaned across the negotiating table and asked the American delegates bluntly:

"When will the United States unconditionally cease the bombing and all other acts of war against the Democratic Republic of Vietnam so that other questions can be discussed?"

In response, W. Averell Har-

Continued on Page 8, Column 4

Big Board Weighs 4 Special Closings

By VARTANIG G. VARTAN

A securities industry panel recommended yesterday that the New York Stock Exchange, the American Stock Exchange and the over-the-counter market close down for four days over the next month to cope with the deluge of paperwork in brokerage offices.

The panel proposed closing the securities markets for three Wednesdays—June 12, 19 and 26—as well as Friday, July 5.

The board of governors of the New York Stock Exchange will meet this afternoon to consider the proposal. Wall Street sources said that in view of the critical situation the governors are expected to accept the pro-

Continued on Page 73, Column 1

The New York Times (by George Tames)

ROBERT F. KENNEDY

A Pall Over Politics

Murder Raises Grave Questions for Presidency Races Now and in Future

By TOM WICKER

Special to The New York Times

News Analysis

WASHINGTON, Thursday, June 6—The murder of Robert F. Kennedy shattered the 1968 Presidential campaign and lowered a pall of uncertainty over American politics now and in the years to come. For the immediate future, it may well have assured the nominations by the Democrats and Republicans of the present front-running candidates — Vice President Humphrey and Richard Nixon. It raised grave questions, however, about the personal dangers of political campaigning in the United States.

It added a tragic new dimension to the near-martyrdom of the Kennedy family, which has now lost two sons to assassins' bullets.

It removed forever one of the most promising young political leaders in recent American history, one with particular appeal for the poor, the downtrodden and the alienated inhabitants of the Negro slums. That appeal had been proved in all of Robert Kennedy's primary victories this year.

These elements of society also revered the Senator's brother, President Kennedy, who was assassinated on Nov. 22, 1963. How they would react to Robert Kennedy's murder—both in the immediate future and for the long political pull—was a crucial question.

The murder added sorrowful emphasis to one of Robert Kennedy's major political themes—the necessity for orderly and just redress of grievances, in place of violent action.

Ultimately, Mr. Kennedy's death—the first assassination of an American Presidential candidate—might lead to changes in campaigning practices, even to the fundamental manner in which the nation chooses its President.

The most immediate effect, however, was that for the third—and most harrowing—time a shock wave of unexpected events had completely altered the shape of the 1968 campaign.

The first came on March 12 when Senator Eugene J. McCarthy of Minnesota won 42 per cent of the Democratic vote in the New Hampshire primary, and Mr. Kennedy immediately thereafter became an active candidate.

The second transformation

Continued on Page 25, Column 6

NOTES ON KENNEDY IN SUSPECT'S HOME

Cite 'Necessity' to Murder Senator Before June 5, Anniversary of War

By PETER KIHSS

A notebook found in the Pasadena home of Sirhan Bishara Sirhan had "a direct reference to the necessity to assassinate Senator Kennedy before June 5, 1968," Mayor Samuel W. Yorty of Los Angeles said last night.

The date was the first anniversary of the six-day war, in which Israeli forces smashed those of the United Arab Republic, Syria and Jordan.

Sirhan, a 24-year-old Christian Arab, who has described himself as a Jerusalem-born Jordanian, is being held in the shooting of the New York Senator.

Justice Department records indicated that Sirhan came to the United States with his family in January of 1957 as immigrants, less than three months after the Suez war in 1956. Sirhan was 12 at the time.

The family quickly broke up in discord, the father staying in New York to work as a plumber and then going back to their former Palestine home, the mother taking five children to California, where a sixth child immigrated later.

Sirhan was described yesterday by Police Chief Thomas Reddin of Los Angeles as "very cool, very calm, very stable and quite lucid."

He was quoted as having said,

Continued on Page 21, Column 6

Father of Suspect 'Sickened' by News

By TERENCE SMITH

Special to The New York Times

ET TAIYIBA, Israeli-Occupied Jordan, Thursday, June 6—Bishara Sirhan's hands trembled as he talked about his son Sirhan Bishara Sirhan, the accused assailant of Senator Robert F. Kennedy.

Mr. Sirhan dwelled on the tragedy of the shooting. He became angry as he talked, and finally said: "This news made me sick when I heard it. If my son has done this dirty thing, then let them hang him."

Mr. Sirhan's memories of his five sons are those of 10 years ago, when he last saw them and their mother. After years of fierce family quarrels, Bishara

Continued on Page 21, Column 4

SURGERY IN VAIN

President Calls Death Tragedy, Proclaims a Day of Mourning

Texts of the medical reports appear on Page 22.

By GLADWIN HILL

Special to The New York Times

LOS ANGELES, Thursday, June 6—Senator Robert F. Kennedy, the brother of a murdered President, died at 1:44 A.M. today of an assassin's shots.

The New York Senator was wounded more than 20 hours earlier, moments after he had made his victory statement in the California primary.

At his side when he died today in Good Samaritan Hospital were his wife, Ethel; his sisters, Mrs. Stephen Smith and Mrs. Patricia Lawford; his brother-in-law, Stephen Smith; and his sister-in-law, Mrs. John F. Kennedy, whose husband was assassinated 4½ years ago in Dallas.

In Washington, President Johnson issued a statement calling the death a tragedy. He proclaimed next Sunday a national day of mourning.

The Final Report

Hopes had risen slightly when more than eight hours went by without a new medical bulletin on the stricken Senator, but the grimness of the final announcement was signaled when Frank Mankiewicz, Mr. Kennedy's press secretary, walked slowly down the street in front of the hospital toward the littered gymnasium that served as press headquarters.

Mr. Mankiewicz bit his lip. His shoulders slumped.

He stepped to a lectern in front of a green-tinted chalkboard and bowed his head for a moment while the television lights snapped on.

Then, at one minute before 2 A.M., he told of the death of Mr. Kennedy.

Following is the text of the statement from Mr. Mankiewicz:

"I have a short announcement to read which I will read at this time. Senator Robert Francis Kennedy died at 1:44 A.M. today, June 6, 1968. With

Continued on Page 20, Column 1

KUCHEL UNSEATED AS RAFFERTY WINS

Conservative Beats Senator in California's Primary

By LAWRENCE E. DAVIES

Special to The New York Times

LOS ANGELES, June 5—Dr. Max Rafferty, State Superintendent of Public Instruction, defeated Senator Thomas H. Kuchel in the Republican Senatorial primary in California yesterday, cutting short Mr. Kuchel's 15-year career in the Senate.

Returns from 20,714 of 21,301 precincts gave:

Rafferty ...	1,056,038	50%
Kuchel	985,097	47%

As the vote count continued today, it became apparent that the conservative Republicanism of Southern California had carried Dr. Rafferty to victory over the heretofore unbeatable Republican whip in the Senate.

Mr. Kuchel, an outspoken liberal-moderate who had made political extremists such as John Birch Society members his targets in recent years, was beaten by the voters in Los Angeles, San Diego and Orange Counties, after having led Dr. Rafferty last night and early today.

Dr. Rafferty, who has become

Continued on Page 28, Column 3

"All the News That's Fit to Print"

The New York Times

LATE CITY EDITION

Weather: Sunny, warm today; fair, seasonable tonight and tomorrow. Temp. range: today 89-73; Tuesday 91-72. Temp.-Hum. Index yesterday 81. Complete U.S. report on Page 90.

VOL. CXVII . No. 40,387 | NEW YORK, WEDNESDAY, AUGUST 21, | 10 CENTS

CZECHOSLOVAKIA INVADED BY RUSSIANS AND FOUR OTHER WARSAW PACT FORCES; THEY OPEN FIRE ON CROWDS IN PRAGUE

13 INDICTED HERE IN RIGGING OF BIDS ON UTILITY WORK

Contracts Worth 49-Million Involved—14 Construction Companies Also Named

By MARTIN TOLCHIN

Fourteen. major construction companies, 12 top corporate executives and one employe were indicted here yesterday on charges of rigging bids on utilities .contracts totaling $49.8-million.

The defendants were accused of deciding among themselves who would be low bidder in the contracts with Consolidated Edison, the Brooklyn Union Gas Company, and the Empire City Subway Company —the latter a subsidiary of the New York Telephone Company.

The indictments charge that the defendants then accommodated the selected low bidder by submitting higher bids.

The companies included such important contractors as Lipsett, Inc., a leading demolition company that razed Pennsylvania Station, the Savoy Plaza Hotel and the Third Avenue El; the Slattery Contracting Company, which held the general contract for excavating the site of United Nations Headquarters and built subway spurs and the Lincoln Center reflecting pool, and the Thomas Crimmins Contracting Company, which did the excavation for numerous skyscrapers.

1959 Activities Covered

The companies received contracts to dig trenches for electrical conduits and gas mains and for paving work. The contracts totaled $49,788,165.

The four indictments, with a total of 28 counts, were an outgrowth of the investigation of James L. Marcus, former City Water Commissioner, who pleaded guilty in Federal court to receiving a $40,000 kickback on a city reservoir cleaning contract.

"Our interest in Marcus and [Herbert] Itkin led us to the inquiry that led to these indictments," Frank S. Hogan, New York County District Attorney, said.

He noted that the indictments alleged activities that began in 1959, "before the community at large was aware of Marcus and Itkin," and

Continued on Page 35, Column 3

OUTLOOK GUARDED FOR EISENHOWER

His Condition Still Critical Despite 'Favorable Trend'

By FELIX BELAIR Jr.
Special to The New York Times

WASHINGTON, Aug. 20 — Former President Dwight D. Eisenhower clung resolutely to life today, but with a fragile grip that his doctors acknowledged could loosen at any time.

The condition of the 77-year-old General of the Army still was listed as "critical" and the outlook for his survival as "guarded." His doctors have used this term to mean uncertain or unpredictable.

A bulletin issued at Walter Reed Army Medical Center about 11 A.M. mentioned the development of a "favorable trend" in the pattern of abnormal heart rhythm.

The episodes of rapid irregularity in the heartbeat persisted, the doctors reported, but they were isolated and did not involve the sustained fibrillating, or fluttering, reported prior to last night.

At the time of the morning

Continued on Page 13, Column 1

Democrats Debate Position on the War in Vietnam

The New York Times

Secretary of State Rusk defended the Administration's policies at the hearing.

Associated Press

Senator George S. McGovern of South Dakota was critical of the Administration.

The New York Times (by George Tames)

Kenneth P. O'Donnell, left, who was an aide to President Kennedy, talks witn Senator J. W. Fulbright, standing right, at the platform hearing. The Senator spoke against the war.

NIXON INCREASES GALLUP POLL LEAD

Tops Humphrey, 45% to 29, and Maintains His Margin Over McCarthy, 42 to 37

Special to The New York Times

PRINCETON, N. J., Aug. 20 —Richard M. Nixon stretched a slim mid-July edge over Vice President Humphrey to a 45-to-29 per cent lead in voter preference immediately following the Republican National Convention, according to the latest Gallup Poll.

Against Senator Eugene J. McCarthy—Mr. Humphrey's chief rival for the Democratic Presidential nomination—Mr. Nixon held a 42-to-37 per cent lead, almost the same margin he had in the previous test in mid-July.

Mr. Nixon's improved advantage over the Vice President was caused more by Mr. Humphrey's losses than by gains by Mr. Nixon. The Republican nominee was 5 percentage points higher than the pre-convention survey, while Mr. Humphrey was 9 points lower.

Support for the independent candidacy of George A. Wallace of Alabama held up. He polled 18 per cent in the Nixon-Humphrey-Wallace test and 16 per cent in the Nixon-McCarthy-Wallace post-convention survey.

In interviewing between Aug. 8 and 11, the following question was asked of a representative sample of 1,526 adults in over 320 localities:

"Suppose the Presidential election were being held today. If Hubert Humphrey were the Democratic candidate, running against Richard Nixon, the Republican candidate, and George Wallace of Alabama were the candidate of a third party, which would you like to see

Continued on Page 34, Column 2

Guard Is Called Up To Protect Chicago During Convention

By DONALD JANSON
Special to The New York Times

CHICAGO, Aug. 20—Gov Samuel H. Shapiro called up the National Guard today to keep order in the city during the Democratic National Convention.

At the request of Mayor Richard J. Daley, the Governor ordered 5,649 Illinois National Guardsmen to round-the-clock duty in Chicago beginning Friday to head off threats of "tumult, riot or mob disorder."

Meanwhile, an Army spokesman in Washington confirmed in a telephone interview that about 6,000 regular Army troops received rigorous riot-control training at Fort Hood, Tex., last week as a precautionary measure.

That exercise, he said, was called Operation Jackson Park, after the park in Chicago

Continued on Page 32, Column 2

Democrats to Seat Mississippi Rebels

By MAX FRANKEL
Special to The New York Times

CHICAGO, Aug. 20—Mississippi's regular delegation to the Democratic National Convention was barred from its seats tonight by an overwhelming vote of the Credentials Committee on the ground that it had failed to meet national standards to assure the full participation of Negroes in the political process.

A biracial delegation including many members who have fought many years for this moment will be seated in place of the regulars.

At the same time, the Credentials Committee rejected by various votes the delegate

Continued on Page 32, Column 6

KENNEDY BACKERS OFFER WAR PLANK

But McCarthy Group Balks at Compromise—Rusk Is for General Statement

Text of plank and excerpts from statement, Page 33.

By JOHN W. FINNEY
Special to The New York Times

WASHINGTON, Aug. 20 — Supporters of the late Senator Robert F. Kennedy circulated in the Democratic platform committee today a compromise dovish plan on Vietnam calling for a halt in the bombing of North Vietnam, a cease-fire and negotiations between the Saigon Government and the National Liberation Front, the political arm of the Vietcong.

In the bitter fight developing within the platform committee, the proposed plank is designed to provide a common front for supporters of Senator Eugene J. McCarthy, Senator George S. McGovern and Senator Kennedy.

For the moment, however, some difficulty was being encountered in winning the approval of some McCarthy partisans, who were holding out for a plank that would be more critical of the Administration.

As the doves began to mount a concerted attack on the Administration's Vietnam policy, Secretary of State Dean Rusk was called in to defend the Administration position. Mr. Rusk,

Continued on Page 33, Column 2

NEWS INDEX

SOVIET EXPLAINS

Says Its Troops Moved at the Request of Czechoslovaks

By RAYMOND H. ANDERSON
Special to The New York Times

MOSCOW, Wednesday, Aug. 21 — Moscow announced this morning that troops from the Soviet Union and four other Communist countries had invaded Czechoslovakia at the request of the "party and Government leaders of the Czechoslovak Socialist Republic."

The announcement followed unofficial information here that Alexander Dubcek, the reform leader of the Czechoslovak party Presidium, had been overthrown.

In a statement authorized by the Soviet Government, the official press agency, Tass, declared at 7:30 A.M. Moscow time (12:30 A.M., New York time) that Czechoslovakia had come under a threat from "counterrevolutionary forces" involved in a collusion with foreign forces hostile to socialism.

Friendship Stressed

Tass said that troops from Bulgaria. East Germany, Hungary, Poland and the Soviet Union, acting from motivations of "inseverable friendship and cooperation," entered Czechoslovakia early this morning.

The troops will be withdrawn as soon as the threat to Czechoslovakia and neighboring Communist countries has been eliminated, according to Tass.

"The actions that are being taken are not directed against any state and in no measure infringe state interests of anybody," the statement said. "They serve the purpose of peace and have been prompted by concern for its consolidation."

"The fraternal countries firmly and resolutely counterpose their unbreakable solidarity to any threat from outside," the Soviet explanation continued. "Nobody will ever be allowed to wrest a single link from the community of Socialist states."

Polemics Resumed

The handwriting was on the wall for the Czechoslovak reform regime last Friday when the Soviet press abruptly resumed its bitter polemics against the country.

Czechoslovakia's seven-month-old experiment with democracy under Communist rule was explicitly doomed yesterday when the Soviet Communist party warned in an editorial that imperial intrigues must be "nipped in the bud."

Rumors swept Moscow yesterday that the Soviet party's Central Committee had met in secret session, presumably to endorse intervention. Official sources insisted, however, that

Continued on Page 14, Column 6

13 Points in Delta Are Shelled by Foe

By JOSEPH B. TREASTER
Special to The New York Times

SAIGON, South Vietnam, Wednesday, Aug. 21 — The Vietcong shelled 13 cities and military installations in the Mekong Delta this morning, extending their latest wave of attacks into South Vietnam's southern-most region.

Seven of the shellings were followed by ground attacks.

Initial reports were sketchy, but a United States military spokesman said that allied casualties and damage in all of the attacks appeared to be light.

To the north, allied troops are making an increasing number of forays into the southern

Continued on Page 4, Column 3

The New York Times — Aug. 21, 1968

FIVE-POWER INVASION: Soviet planes carried troops into Prague (cross). Ground forces of bloc crossed Czechoslovak borders that are indicated by heavy line.

Versions of the Two Sides

Following are the texts of the Prague radio announcement of the Soviet-bloc invasion of Czechoslovakia, as monitored in Washington, and of a Soviet statement distributed in New York by Tass, the Soviet press agency.

Czechoslovak Radio Broadcast

To the entire people of the Czechoslovak Socialist Republic:

Yesterday, on 20 August, around 2300 [11 P.M.], troops of the Soviet Union, Polish People's Republic, the G.D.R. [East Germany], the Hungarian People's Republic and the Bulgarian People's Republic crossed the frontiers of the Czechoslovak Socialist Republic.

This happened without the knowledge of the President of the Republic, the Chairman of the National Assembly, the Premier, or the First Secretary of the Czechoslovak Communist party Central Committee.

In the evening hours the Presidium of the Czechoslovak Communist party Central Committee [had] held a session and discussed preparations for the 14th Czechoslovak Communist party congress.

The Czechoslovak Communist party Central Committee Presidium appeals to all citizens of our republic to maintain calm and not to offer resistance to the troops on the march. Our army, security corps and people's militia have not received the command to defend the country.

The Czechoslovak Communist party Central Committee Presidium regard this act as contrary not only to the fundamental principles of relations between Socialist states but also as contrary to the principles of international law.

All leading functionaries of the state, the Communist party and the National Front: Remain in your functions as representatives of the state, elected to the laws of the Czechoslovak Socialist Republic.

Constitutional functionaries are immediately convening a session of the National Assembly of our republic, and the Presidium is at the same time convening a plenum of the Central Committee to discuss the situation that has arisen.

PRESIDIUM OF THE CZECHOSLOVAK COMMUNIST PARTY CENTRAL COMMITTEE.

Announcement by Moscow

Tass is authorized to state that party and Government leaders of the Czechoslovak Socialist Republic have asked the Soviet Union and other allied states to render the fraternal Czechoslovak people urgent assistance, including assistance with armed forces. This request was brought about by the threat which has arisen to the Socialist system existing in Czechoslovakia and to the statehood established by the Con-

Continued on Page 14, Column 2

Soviet Turns Back Clock

By JAMES RESTON

The Soviet invasion of Czechoslovakia has transformed world and American politics.

It occurred in the middle of the American Presidential election of 1968, as the Soviet invasion of Hungary took place during the Eisenhower-Stevenson Presidential election of 1956. The Soviet Union moved on Prague while the United States was preoccupied in Vietnam, as they moved on Budapest in 1956 while the British and French were preoccupied with the invasion of Suez. The latest move by Moscow startled Washington just as officials there were convening on new moves to reach an understanding with the Soviet Union on Vietnam.

News Analysis

Washington was prepared for a dramatic move by the Soviet Union against the new liberal regime in Prague, but not for anything quite so bold as an invasion by the Red Army.

It had been observing closely the increasingly violent attacks on the Czechoslovak Government in the Soviet press, and Under Secretary of State Charles E. Bohlen, former United States Ambassador to the Soviet Union and France, had warned of the possibility of a coup d'état, followed by Soviet military intervention in Czechoslovakia. But a direct invasion at this time was discounted.

In fact, the Johnson Administration, under attack on its Vietnam policy just before the Democratic Presidential nominating convention next week in Chicago, was discussing new moves to enlist the help of the Soviet Union for a compromise in Vietnam when the Red Army moved.

The first impression of the crisis was that this Soviet intervention in Czechoslovakia, like the first one at the end of World War II, would increase

Continued on Page 15, Column 1

TANKS ENTER CITY

Deaths Are Reported —Troops Surround Offices of Party

By TAD SZULC
Special to The New York Times

PRAGUE, Wednesday, Aug. 21—Czechoslovakia was occupied early today by troops of the Soviet Union and four of its Warsaw Pact allies in a series of swift land and air movements.

Airborne Soviet troops and paratroopers surrounded the building of the Communist party Central Committee, along with five tanks. At least 25 tanks were seen in the city.

Several persons were reported killed early this morning. Unconfirmed reports said that two Czechoslovak soldiers and a woman were killed by Bulgarian tank fire in front of the Prague radio building shortly before the station was captured and went off the air.

[Soviet troops began shooting at Czechoslovak demonstrators outside the Prague radio building at 7:25 A.M., Reuters reported. C.T.K., the Czechoslovak press agency, was quoted by United Press International as having said that citizens were throwing themselves in front of the tanks in an attempt to block the seizure of the city.]

Move a Surprise

The Soviet move caught Czechoslovaks by surprise, although all day yesterday there were indications of new tensions.

Confusion was caused in the capital by leaflets dropped from unidentified aircraft asserting that Antonin Novotny, the President of Czechoslovakia who was deposed in March by the Communist liberals, had been pushed out by a "clique." The leaflets said that Mr. Novotny remained the country's legal President.

At 5 A.M. the Prague radio, still in the hands of adherents of the Communist liberals, broadcast a dramatic appeal to the population in the name of Alexander Dubcek, the party

Continued on Page 14, Column 1

JOHNSON SUMMONS SECURITY COUNCIL

Calls Emergency Session After Seeing Soviet Envoy

By B. DRUMMOND AYRES JR.
Special to The New York Times

WASHINGTON, Aug. 20— President Johnson met with the National Security Council in an emergency session tonight to discuss developments in Czechoslovakia after he received a visit from the Soviet Ambassador.

The Council meeting, which was held in the Cabinet Room in the West Wing of the White House, began at 10:15 P.M. and lasted for 55 minutes.

It was followed by a 15-minute meeting at the State Department between the Soviet Ambassador, Anatoly F. Dobrynen, and Secretary of State Dean Rusk.

There was no indication after either of the meetings of what course the United States would take in the crisis, which clearly came as a stunning surprise here.

During the recent weeks of tension around Czechoslovakia, the Administration has insistently maintained a hand-off attitude, arguing that any gestures of support from Washington would only complicate the Prague regime's status in the Communist camp. Any move to exploit the Soviet di-

Continued on Page 15, Column 1

"All the News That's Fit to Print"

The New York Times

LATE CITY EDITION

Weather: Sunny, mild today; fair and milder tonight and tomorrow. Temp. range: today 77-56; Wed. 75-57. Temp.-Hum. Index yesterday 69. Complete U.S. report on Page 70.

VOL. CXVII . No. 40,395 | NEW YORK, THURSDAY, AUGUST 29, 1968 | 10 CENTS

HUMPHREY NOMINATED ON THE FIRST BALLOT AFTER HIS PLANK ON VIETNAM IS APPROVED; POLICE BATTLE DEMONSTRATORS IN STREETS

SOVIET TO LEAVE 2 BLOC DIVISIONS ON CZECHS' SOIL

Svoboda Tells the Cabinet Other Forces Will Depart in 'Several Months'

By TAD SZULC

Special to The New York Times

PRAGUE, Aug. 28—President Ludvik Svoboda told his Cabinet today that the withdrawal of the Soviet-led occupation troops from Czechoslovakia would take "several months and stages" and that at least two divisions would remain permanently stationed on the West German border.

Authoritative sources that provided the account of the Cabinet meeting at Hradcany Castle quoted the President as having informed the ministers that no exact date had been set to begin the withdrawal of the forces of the Soviet Union and the four other Warsaw Pact countries that invaded Czechoslovakia a week ago.

The National Assembly adopted an eight-point resolution asking that a firm date be set forthwith for removal of the occupying forces and declaring that the Czechoslovak Army of 200,000 men was capable of guarding its own frontiers.

Prague Back at Work

Meanwhile, Prague was back at work, but a curfew was maintained and Soviet armored scout cars and motorized infantry trucks with machine guns mounted on their cabs continued to cruise through the city's crowded streets.

In a speech to the nation tonight, Premier Oldrich Cernik announced that today's Cabinet session had drafted a proposal to the Soviet Union, Poland, Hungary, Bulgaria and East Germany to begin "soon" the actual negotiations for the departure of their armies.

He said that within two weeks economic talks with the Soviet Union were to begin "during which compensation for damages" caused by the invasion would be discussed among other topics.

Czechoslovakia has long been

Continued on Page 3, Column 1

Associated Press

John Gordon Mein

U.S. ENVOY SLAIN IN GUATEMALA

Terrorists Shoot Mein After Ambushing Car—Johnson and Rusk Ask Inquiry

By Reuters

GUATEMALA, Aug. 28—The United States Ambassador, John Gordon Mein, was slain here this afternoon by unidentified youths who had ambushed his limousine.

The 54-year-old career Foreign Service officer tried to put up a fight, but fell under a hail of pistol and machine-gun fire, dying instantly. At least nine bullets struck his body.

As the Ambassador was driving along Avenida Reforma to the embassy, several youths leaped out of two small Japanese-made cars and opened the limousine's rear door to force him out. He resisted and they opened fire.

[In Washington, President Johnson and Secretary of State Dean Rusk expressed shock and grief and called on Guatemala to investigate the assassination.]

Campaign of Terror

Mr. Mein is believed to be the first United States Ambassador assassinated at his post.

The kidnapping of prominent people has been an element of the terror campaign that has been waged by extremist political elements in this uneasy Central American country, which has a population of more than 4.6 million.

The shooting occurred three blocks from the Biltmore Hotel, where Mr. Mein had attended a luncheon given by the Foreign Minister, Emilo Arenales Catalán. The scene was about 10 blocks from the embassy.

The Ambassador's chauffeur,

Continued on Page 16, Column 3

HUNDRED INJURED

178 Are Arrested as Guardsmen Join in Using Tear Gas

By J. ANTHONY LUKAS

Special to The New York Times

CHICAGO, Thursday, Aug. 29—The police and National Guardsmen battled young protesters in downtown Chicago last night as the week-long demonstrations against the Democratic National Convention reached a violent and tumultuous climax.

About 100 persons, including 25 policemen, were injured and at least 178 were arrested as the security forces chased down the demonstrators. The protesting young people had broken out of Grant Park on the shore of Lake Michigan in an attempt to reach the International Amphitheatre where the Democrats were meeting, four miles away.

The police and Guardsmen used clubs, rifle butts, tear gas and Chemical Mace on virtually anything moving along Michigan Avenue and the narrow streets of the Loop area.

Uneasy Calm

Shortly after midnight, an uneasy calm ruled the city. However, 1,000 National Guardsmen were moved back in front of the Conrad Hilton Hotel to guard it against more than 5,000 demonstrators who had drifted back into Grant Park.

The crowd in front of the hotel was growing, booing vociferously every time new votes for Vice President Humphrey were broadcast from the convention hall.

The events in the streets stirred anger among some delegates at the convention. In a nominating speech Senator Abraham A. Ribicoff of Connecticut told the delegates that if Senator George S. McGovern were President, "we would not have these Gestapo tactics in the streets of Chicago."

When Mayor Richard J. Daley of Chicago and other Illinois delegates rose shouting angrily, Mr. Ribicoff said, "How hard it is to accept the truth."

Crushed Against Windows

Even elderly bystanders were caught in the police onslaught. At one point, the police turned on several dozen persons standing quietly behind police barriers in front of the Conrad Hilton Hotel watching the demonstrators across the street.

For no reason that could be immediately determined, the blue-helmeted policemen charged the barriers, crushing the spectators against the windows of the Haymarket Inn, a restaurant in the hotel. Finally the window gave way, sending screaming middle-aged women and children backward through the broken shards of glass.

The police then ran into the restaurant and beat some of the

Continued on Page 23, Column 1

The New York Times (by Neal Boenzi)

AT CONVENTION: Cheering in the amphitheatre after Vice President Humphrey's name was placed in nomination

United Press International

IN STREETS: Police attempting to clear demonstrators on Michigan Avenue outside Conrad Hilton Hotel last night

VICTOR GETS 1,761

Vote Taken Amid Boos For Chicago Police Tactics in Street

Excerpts from the nominating speeches are on Page 22.

By TOM WICKER

Special to The New York Times

CHICAGO, Thursday Aug. 29 — While a pitched battle between the police and thousands of young antiwar demonstrators raged in the streets of Chicago, the Democratic National Convention nominated Hubert H. Humphrey for President last night, on a platform reflecting his and President Johnson's views on the war in Vietnam.

Mr. Humphrey, after a day of bandwagon shifts to his candidacy, and a night of turmoil in the convention hall, won nomination on the first ballot over challenges by Senator Eugene J. McCarthy of Minnesota and George S. McGovern of South Dakota.

The count at the end of the first ballot was:

Humphrey	1,761¾
McCarthy	601
McGovern	146½
Phillips	67½
Others	32¾

Violence Draws Attention

There was never a moment's suspense in the balloting, and throughout a turbulent evening, the delegates and spectators paid less attention to the proceedings than to television and radio reports of widespread violence in the streets of Chicago, and to stringent security measures within the International Amphitheatre.

Repeated denunciations of Mayor Richard J. Daley from convention speakers and repeated efforts to get an adjournment or recess were ignored by convention officials and Mr. Daley.

He sat through it all, usually grinning and always guarded by plainclothes security men, until just before the roll call. Then he left the hall. A few miles away, the young demonstrators were being clubbed, kicked and gassed by the Chicago police, who turned back a march on the convention hall.

Watched From Hotels

Most of the violence took place across Michigan Avenue from the convention headquarters hotel, the Conrad Hilton, in full view of delegates' wives and other watching from its windows.

From the convention rostrum, Senator Abraham A. Ribicoff of Connecticut, denounced "Gestapo tactics in the streets of Chicago."

Julian Bond, the Negro insurgent leader from Georgia, in announcing his delegation's

Continued on Page 20, Column 1

PRAGUE'S LEADERS WARNED BY SOVIET

It Says It Will Be Vigilant—Hints Doubt on Outcome

By RAYMOND H. ANDERSON

Special to The New York Times

MOSCOW, Aug. 28—The Soviet Union warned today that the reform leaders of Czechoslovakia, although allowed to return to Prague and to retain their positions after the negotiations here, were on a short leash and under the vigilant eyes of the Kremlin.

Soviet commentators asserted that a counterrevolutionary threat continued to exist in Czechoslovakia, and they indicated that Moscow had doubts that the Prague leadership could or would cope with the dangers adequately.

[In Bonn, the West German Government called for a complete restoration of Czechoslovakia's sovereignty and a pullback of all Soviet invasion forces. Page 6.]

Pravda, the Communist party organ, expressed indignation that underground radio stations in Czechoslovakia had broadcast criticism of the agreement worked out in Moscow between the Soviet leadership and a Czechoslovak delegation headed by President Ludvik Svoboda.

Yuri Zhukov, the political

Continued on Page 4, Column 3

FIGHTING INTENSE IN SAIGON REGION

G.I.'s Battle Through Night With Foe on Infiltration Routes Near Capital

Special to The New York Times

SAIGON, South Vietnam, Thursday, Aug. 29—Sharp fighting flared around Saigon last night and this morning as United States infantrymen battled a sizable enemy force on flatland infiltration routes northwest of the capital.

The United States command said this morning that fighting had continued through the night with a company-size enemy unit 32 miles northwest of Saigon and 4 miles north of Trangbang.

So far, a total of 86 enemy soldiers have been killed in the fighting, American spokesmen said. Reports from the scene were sketchy, but United States spokesmen termed American casualties light.

101st Division Involved

According to the spokesman, the fighting began Tuesday after soldiers of the 101st Air Cavalry Division set up a cordon around an area and began moving in.

Fighting tapered in the evening, but by noon yesterday units of the division, trudging through muddy fields, came under sharp fire. Fighting continued into the morning.

Farther north, near another key infiltration route into Saigon, soldiers of the United States 25th Infantry Division fought two enemy companies seven miles southeast of Tayninh. During the four-hour bat-

Continued on Page 10, Column 1

Defeat for Doves Reflects Deep Division in the Party

By JOHN W. FINNEY

CHICAGO, Aug. 28 — A deeply divided Democratic National Convention, after a climactic floor clash between the Administration's supporters and its critics, adopted today a White House-dictated plank supporting President Johnson's policy in Vietnam. The whole platform was then approved.

By a vote of 1,567¾ to 1,041¼, the convention rejected a plank advanced by Democratic doves calling for an unconditional halt in the bombing of North Vietnam. Instead, it adopted a plank that called for a bombing halt but only on conditional terms.

Excerpts from the debate on platform, Page 22.

The vote reflected the deep, emotional division within the party over the Vietnam issue. The division manifested itself in nearly three hours of increasingly acrimonious debate, conducted against a backdrop of sporadic chants of "Stop the war!" from the galleries and the New York and California delegations.

It was a division that Vice President Humphrey, in his bid for the Presidential nomination, had hoped to avoid. But he could not avoid it when Mr. Johnson intervened behind the scenes to toughen the language of the plank so that it would correspond to Administration policy.

In the wake of the policy confrontation, the major question was whether Mr. Hum-

Continued on Page 25, Column 1

HUMPHREY AIDES LIST 4 FOR TICKET

Say Muskie, Harris, Alioto and Shriver Are Leading for the No. 2 Spot

By STEVEN V. ROBERTS

Special to The New York Times

CHICAGO, Aug. 28—Aides of Vice President Humphrey advanced four names today as leading candidates for the Vice-Presidential nomination: Senators Edmund S. Muskie of Maine and Fred R. Harris of Oklahoma, Mayor Joseph L. Alioto of San Francisco and Sargent Shriver, the Ambassador to France.

The list contained no surprises. All four men have figured in recent speculation.

However, Mr. Humphrey met in his hotel suite today with key political figures, including Mayor Richard J. Daley of Chicago, and aides said the Vice-Presidency was one topic of discussion. It was generally believed that the final decision would not be made until tomorrow.

It was considered a remote possibility that Mr. Humphrey would try to heal the deep breach in the party over the Vietnam war by choosing a prominent war critic. Senators Eugene J. McCarthy of Minnesota, George S. McGovern of South Dakota and Edward M.

Continued on Page 22, Column 2

Dubcek Was Put in Handcuffs: An Account of Confrontation

The following chronological account of the confrontation of Soviet and Czechoslovak leaders after the invasion of Czechoslovakia was written by Vincent Buist of Reuters.

PRAGUE, Aug. 28—Alexander Dubcek, the Czechoslovak Communist leader, was hustled out of his party headquarters last Wednesday, handcuffed and flown to a secret destination in Slovakia in a Soviet military aircraft.

All the way he sat on the plane's metal deck.

This was disclosed in an account of Mr. Dubcek's arrest and of the Moscow negotiations given to me today by an official of the Czechoslovak Communist party's Central Committee.

The official said Mr. Dubcek was in his private room speaking on the telephone when the Central Committee building was surrounded by Soviet paratroopers with light tracked vehicles last Wednesday morning.

The party leader was trying to find out details of the extent of the invasion as a Soviet security officer and two soldiers armed with light machine guns burst into the room.

They tore the telephone out of Mr. Dubcek's hands and ripped the wire out of the wall, the official said.

The party leader was taken away and locked in a room in

Continued on Page 2, Column 5

The Party and the Police

By JAMES RESTON

Special to The New York Times

News Analysis

CHICAGO, Aug 28 — The Democratic party was deeply hurt politically here tonight by the vicious clashes between demonstrators and the police in the streets of Chicago. Though the party itself had no direct responsibility for the incidents, it held its convention here knowing of the dangers of violence and counted on Mayor Daley and his police to handle the situation without embarrassment to the party. This gamble failed, despite all the barbed wire barricades, the police, secret agents and National Guardsmen. It was not only that Mayor Daley was condemned from the rostrum and stood in the aisles mocking Senator Abraham Ribicoff, who had condemned the police action, but tens of millions watched the incidents on television to the obvious detriment of the Democratic party.

By the end of the night, Daley had become a symbol in the convention of the opposition within the party to the turbulent conditions of American life. So strong was the feeling against Mayor Daley and his police that even the name of Illinois was loudly booed when the roll of the states was called for nominations for the Presidency.

Thus the convention pre-

Continued on Page 20, Column 3

NEWS INDEX

Gruening Defeated In Alaska Primary

By LAWRENCE E. DAVIES

Special to The New York Times

ANCHORAGE, Alaska, Aug. 28 — A dramatic, unexpected victory by a dark, good-looking, 38-year-old challenger has terminated the long political career of Senator Ernest Gruening, an 81-year-old warhorse known to his admirers as "Mr. Alaska."

Mike Gravel, a real estate developer from Anchorage and former Speaker of the state's House of Representatives, won the Democratic nomination for the Senate over Mr. Gruening in yesterday's primary election in Alaska.

Unofficial returns to Secretary of State Keith Miller in

Continued on Page 26, Column 5

1968

Passion, Pain and Progress

1976

FRONT PAGE NEWS 1968-1976

The New York Times

Woodstock Nation

AUGUST 17, 1969

Everything was groovy, from Jimi Hendrix playing a sarcastic, off-key arrangement of "The Star-Spangled Banner" to Pete Townshend of the Who smashing his guitar and lobbing it at the crowd. More than 350,000 hippies, flower children and curiosity-seekers jammed a muddy field in upstate New York for the rock concert that made the word "Woodstock" world famous. It was also a counterculture extravaganza, the make-love-not-war happening that defined a generation.

The New York Times

Anti-Vietnam Demonstration

NOVEMBER 16,1969

American involvement in Vietnam had swelled from a small number of "support troops" and advisers in 1961 to 190,000 combat-ready soldiers in 1966 to 550,000 in 1969. As President Richard M. Nixon neared the end of his first year in the White House, a quarter of a million protesters converged on Washington. Their message was blunt: bring the troops home. Nixon did not see them as he met with aides in the Oval Office because the White House was behind a cordon of police and tourist buses parked bumper to bumper, blocking from view the mostly peaceful demonstration on the Mall.

The New York Times

Killings at Kent State

MAY 5, 1970

It was one of the darkest moments in the American heartland during the Vietnam War—a 13-second volley that killed four students and wounded nine at Kent State University in central Ohio. They were among hundreds protesting President Richard M. Nixon's invasion of Cambodia; many students had been part of a melee earlier in the week, when Molotov cocktails were lobbed at the campus R.O.T.C. building. This time, Governor James A. Rhodes sent in National Guard troops who opened fire. Thirty-five years later, a student in the crowd who was injured made public an audio recording on which he said Guard commanders could be heard giving the order to shoot.

The New York Times

The Pentagon Papers

JULY 1, 1971

On June 13, The Times published the first in a series of articles based on a 7,000-page classified history of the Vietnam War that contrasted euphemistic government rhetoric with the actual history of U.S. escalation in a losing struggle. Scrambling to halt further publication, the Nixon administration invoked national security as a justification for prior restraint, but the Supreme Court ruled that publication could continue. The White House soon set up a "plumbers" unit, which was later involved in the Watergate break-in, to find the source of leaks like the one that had put the Pentagon Papers in The Times's hands.

The New York Times

Limiting Strategic Arms

MAY 27, 1972

President Richard M. Nixon's trip to Moscow was the culmination of three years of Strategic Arms Limitation Talks. The U.S. and the Soviet Union agreed to caps on their anti-ballistic missiles and on their land- and sea-based missile systems. Conservatives had long opposed any such deal with the Soviets, and in 2001, President George W. Bush gave notice that the U.S. was withdrawing from what he deplored as a "relic" of the cold war.

The New York Times

MEN WALK ON MOON

ASTRONAUTS LAND ON PLAIN; COLLECT ROCKS, PLANT FLAG

'One Small Step for Man'

JULY 21, 1969

Anyone with imagination had already gone to the moon—Jules Verne, in the 19 century, had envisioned a three-man crew, a Florida blastoff and a homeward flight ending with an ocean splashdown. When it really happened, there was a three-man crew and a Florida blastoff, and the history-making walk by Neil A. Armstrong and Edwin E. Aldrin capped a cold war crusade ordered by President John F. Kennedy when the Soviets seemed to be winning the space race. The third astronaut on the mission, Michael Collins, stayed in their space capsule, Columbia, orbiting the earth. Armstrong said his famous words as he emerged from the lunar module: "That's one small step for man, one giant leap for mankind."

The New York Times

NIXON RESIGNS

HE URGES A TIME OF 'HEALING'; FORD WILL TAKE OFFICE TODAY

Nixon Resigns

AUGUST 9, 1974

In only 17 months, President Richard M. Nixon went from winning re-election in a landslide to resigning in disgrace rather than face an impeachment trial. Nixon realized he could not survive the Watergate scandal after the Supreme Court ordered the release of the "smoking gun," a conversation tape-recorded in the Oval Office soon after the June 1972 break-in at Democratic headquarters in the Watergate office complex in Washington. The tape showed that Nixon had been directly involved in the cover-up from the beginning, ordering a halt to the F.B.I. investigation and offering hush money to the burglars.

The New York Times

'Cruel and Unusual Punishment'

JUNE 30, 1972

Was the death penalty constitutional? The answer, by a one-vote margin, was no. The Supreme Court said that most jury-ordered executions amounted to "cruel and unusual" punishment. That put some 600 death-row inmates in limbo. But more than 30 states soon rewrote their statutes, making death sentences mandatory for certain kinds of crimes (and thus taking decisions about execution out of the jury box) or spelling out rules for juries and judges. Over the next 30 years, the court diluted the restrictions, while keeping capital punishment legal under some circumstances.

The New York Times

9 ISRAELIS ON OLYMPIC TEAM KILLED WITH 4 ARAB CAPTORS AS POLICE FIGHT BAND THAT DISRUPTED MUNICH GAMES

Massacre in Munich

SEPTEMBER 6, 1972

Masked gunmen from Black September, a group with ties to Yasir Arafat's Palestinian Liberation Organization, invaded the Israeli dormitory at the Olympics in Munich. After killing two coaches and taking nine athletes hostage, they demanded freedom for more than 200 Palestinians held in Israeli jails. German authorities promised safe passage to Egypt, arranging for helicopters to fly the commandos and the captives to a nearby airport and a waiting jetliner. It was a setup. German sharpshooters took aim on the runway, setting off a bloodbath. They killed five Palestinians—but the commandos murdered all of the hostages.

The New York Times

LYNDON JOHNSON, 36TH PRESIDENT, IS DEAD; WAS ARCHITECT OF 'GREAT SOCIETY' PROGRAM

High Court Rules Abortions Legal the First 3 Months

A Right to Abortion

JANUARY 23, 1973

The Supreme Court declared that first-trimester abortions were a "fundamental right" after sidestepping the question of when life begins, at conception or later in a pregnancy. The decision in Roe v. Wade came less than a year after Congress had passed the Equal Rights Amendment, prompting some historians to observe that the women's movement had now achieved more than the civil rights movement had achieved in the 1960's. Roe also electrified the anti-abortion movement, propelling conservative Christians to political prominence as their tactics escalated.

The New York Times

VIETNAM PEACE PACTS SIGNED; AMERICA'S LONGEST WAR HALTS

'Peace With Honor'

JANUARY 28, 1973

Just before the 1972 election, Henry A. Kissinger, the national security adviser to President Richard M. Nixon, had declared that peace in Vietnam was "at hand." Nixon ordered extensive bombings at Christmastime, saying they were the only way to bring the North Vietnamese back to the negotiating table. Finally both sides signed the Paris peace accords, which Nixon promised would bring "peace with honor." Kissinger and his North Vietnamese counterpart, Le Duc Tho, won the Nobel Prize the following year but Le would not accept it, saying his nation was not at peace. He went on to direct the 1975 campaign that overthrew the South Vietnamese government and ultimately unified the country.

The New York Times

NIXON ACCEPTS ONUS FOR WATERGATE, BUT SAYS HE DIDN'T KNOW ABOUT PLOT; HALDEMAN, EHRLICHMAN, DEAN RESIGN; RICHARDSON PUT IN KLEINDIENST POST

Nixon Dismisses Top Aides

MAY 1, 1973

As Richard M. Nixon's presidency was being rocked by Watergate, he dismissed two top White House officials though he called them "two of the finest public servants it has been my privilege to know." Years later, H. R. Haldeman, Nixon's longtime chief of staff, said that Nixon himself had "initiated" the Watergate break-in and had been involved in the cover-up from the beginning. John D. Ehrlichman, Nixon's domestic policy adviser, did no finger-pointing, explaining, "I abdicated my moral judgments."

The New York Times

FEDERAL GRAND JURY INDICTS 7 NIXON AIDES ON CHARGES OF CONSPIRACY ON WATERGATE; HALDEMAN, EHRLICHMAN, MITCHELL ON LIST

The Unindicted Co-Conspirator

MARCH 2, 1974

Only seven high-ranking officials were named when a federal grand jury in Washington handed up conspiracy indictments in the Watergate scandal. Later it was revealed that there was an eighth, an "unindicted co-conspirator"—President Richard M. Nixon himself. Eventually 19 Nixon aides and associates went to prison. The grand jury also filled a briefcase with Watergate documents and asked Judge John J. Sirica to deliver it to the House Judiciary Committee for its impeachment investigation.

The New York Times

FORD GIVES PARDON TO NIXON, WHO REGRETS 'MY MISTAKES'

'A Full, Free and Absolute Pardon'

SEPTEMBER 9, 1974

A month after President Richard M. Nixon's resignation, his successor, Gerald R. Ford, issued "a full, free and absolute pardon." Ford maintained that pre-empting any prosecution of Nixon was "part of the healing process," but the pardon only seemed to reopen the wounds of Watergate. Ford's press secretary quit in protest, and Ford himself eventually admitted that the backlash was "far worse than I had anticipated."

The New York Times

MINH SURRENDERS, VIETCONG IN SAIGON; 1,000 AMERICANS AND 5,500 VIETNAMESE EVACUATED BY COPTER TO U.S. CARRIERS

Americans Flee Saigon

APRIL 30, 1975

North Vietnamese tanks rumbled into what had been the South Vietnamese capital, and Americans—diplomats, reporters, photographers—clambered aboard helicopters on the roof of the U.S. Embassy in Saigon. It was the final moment in America's costly intervention, and came two years after the U.S. had withdrawn its combat troops. But Washington had continued its support for the faltering South Vietnamese government, and did not establish diplomatic relations with Vietnam until the 1990's. In 2005, just before the 30th anniversary of the evacuation, Prime Minister Phan Van Khai said it was time to leave the past behind and look forward.

"All the News That's Fit to Print"

The New York Times

LATE CITY EDITION

Weather: Cloudy, warm and humid, showers likely through tomorrow. Temp. range: today 88-75; Saturday 89-74. Temp-Hum. Index yesterday 81. Complete U.S. report on Page 83,

SECTION ONE

VOL. CXVIII . . No. 40,748

NEW YORK, SUNDAY, AUGUST 17, 1969

60c beyond 50-mile zone from New York City, except Long Island. 75c beyond 200-mile radius. Higher in air delivery cities.

50 CENTS

The New York Times (by Jack Manning)

MUSIC WAS THE MAGNET for throngs at Woodstock Music and Art Fair. Towers near the stage hold loudspeakers.

300,000 at Folk-Rock Fair Camp Out in a Sea of Mud

By BARNARD L. COLLIER

Special to The New York Times

BETHEL, N. Y., Aug. 16—Despite massive traffic jams, drenching rainstorms and shortages of food, water and medical facilities, about 300,000 young people swarmed over this rural area today for the Woodstock Music and Art Fair.

Drawn by such performers as Joan Baez, Ravi Shankar, Jimi Hendrix and the Jefferson Airplane, the prospect of drugs and the excitement of "making the scene," the young people came in droves, camping in the woods, romping in the mud, talking, smoking and listening to the wailing music.

Looking out over 20 acres of youths squeezed body to body, the festival's organizers, the state police and officials of the Sullivan County Sheriff's office agreed that the crowd was over 300,000.

Participants Well-Behaved

The crowd, which camped on the 600-acre farm of Max Yasgur near here for the three-day festival, was well-behaved, according to both the sponsors and the police, even though about 75 persons in the area were arrested, mostly on charges of possessing narcotics.

Most of the hip, swinging youngsters heard the music on stage only as a distant rumble. It was almost impossible for them to tell who was performing and probably only about half the crowd could hear a note. Yet they stayed by the thousands, often standing ankle-deep in mud, sometimes paying enterprising peddlers 25 cents for a glass of water.

Roadways leading from the site were lined tonight with thousands of weary-looking youths who had had enough, and were trying to reach places where they could get food or transportation.

During the first 24 hours of the fair, festival medical officers said that a thousand people had been treated at first-aid stations for various ailments, including exposure and a few accident cases. About 300 were ill because of adverse drug reactions.

Doctors Fly to Scene

A dozen doctors, responding to a plea from the fair's sponsors, flew from New York to the scene, about 70 miles northwest of the city, near the Catskill Mountain resorts of Liberty and Monticello.

Michael Lang, the 24-year-old producer of the event, said that the medical help was summoned not because of any widespread illnesses, but because of the potential threat of a virus cold or pneumonia epidemic among such a large gathering.

Parked cars jammed roadways in all directions for up to 20 miles, and thousands of festival-goers, weary after long walks to get here, had to spend the night sleeping on the rain-soaked ground. They awoke to find food and water shortages.

But Mr. Lang said this afternoon: "It's about the quietest, most well-behaved 300,000 people in one place that can be imagined. There have been no fights or incidents of violence of any kind."

A state police official agreed. "I was dumfounded by the size of the crowd," he

Continued on Page 80, Column 1

Today's Sections

Index to Subjects

VARIED DRUG LAWS RAISING U.S. FEARS

Justice Agency Dismayed as Some States Crack Down While Others Ease View

By MARTIN ARNOLD

Many State Legislatures across the country, trying to come to grips with the nation's growing narcotic problems, this year are passing diverse and sometimes contradictory laws that are causing considerable dismay within the Justice Department.

"We are delighted with the concern over drug abuse but are afraid that the contradictory laws will hinder rather than help Federal narcotic enforcement," said Anthony J. Roccograndi, assistant chief counsel of the Justice Department's Bureau of Narcotics and Dangerous Drugs.

Actions by the States

Because of this concern, the Justice Department is trying to sell the various states on the idea of a model state drug control act, which would standardize narcotic and drug laws throughout the land and bring them into closer conformity with Federal laws.

But the department declines to specify precisely what it wants in the model act and is delaying intensive efforts to obtain support for one until Congress acts on the narcotic abuse proposals that President Nixon sent to Congress on July 14.

At least 20 states this year have either passed new laws on narcotic abuse or amended old laws while about 20 other states have seriously debated legislation.

Meanwhile, at least 10 states

Continued on Page 60, Column 1

Majority on Relief Are White on L.I. And in Westchester

By AGIS SALPUKAS

More than half the people receiving welfare money in Nassau, Suffolk and Westchester. Counties are white, many of them ironic victims of a search for a better life in the suburbs.

"It's a myth that welfare recipients in the suburbs are mostly black, living in ghettos," said Joseph Barbaro, the Commissioner of Social Services of Nassau County, in a recent interview.

The myth has been sustained, he added, because white welfare recipients generally try to hide their circumstances. They avoid protest demonstrations, surplus food centers and, in many cases, continue to live in the middle-class houses that started their financial difficulties.

Their mortage payments are often taken care of by welfare grants—because, according to welfare officials, most of the time it is cheaper than trying to relocate a family.

Instead of trying to "keep up with the Joneses" many now struggle to keep up minimal appearances out of fear that their immediate neighbors will dis-

Continued on Page 68, Column 3

MAYORS WELCOME NIXON'S AID PLANS BUT DOUBT IMPACT

Call Urban Proposals Steps in Right Direction, but Say Funds Are Inadequate

By ROBERT M. SMITH

Special to The New York Times

WASHINGTON, Aug. 16—The mayors of 11 major cities across the nation think the legislative approach that President Nixon has proposed might solve some of their problems, but they wonder what it will do for the major troubles that afflict their cities.

To a man, however, the mayors applaud the fact that the President has made new and concrete proposals to deal with the problems of the nation's urban areas.

As Atlanta's Mayor Ivan Allen Jr., a Democrat, put it: "The significance of President Nixon's welfare reforms is that they are the first real attempt to view the needs of the poor in light of current problems, not circumstances which existed in the Depression."

"They represent a change from an outmoded public assistance program to a flexible system for a rapidly changing society."

A Minimum Standard

The Mayor of Dallas, Erik Jonsson, said there were certain to be objections to the President's proposals, but they are "an intelligent, sincere approach to a beginning—the Administration has taken the position that they have to try."

As for the money that the proposals would bring in to the cities, Mr. Jonsson said, "The total may move a small mountain, but not a big one."

Mayors in several cities across the nation were asked by correspondents for The New York Times to give their views on President Nixon's urban package — the proposals on welfare reform and manpower training, revenue sharing and mass transit.

The mayors who commented were those of New York, Albany, Atlanta, Dallas, Baltimore, Houston, Jackson, Miss., New Orleans, Philadelphia, San Francisco, and St. Louis.

Some of the mayors said it was too early to gauge precisely how the new programs would affect their cities. However, most of them said the amount of money involved was inadequate to meet their problems.

For example, Baltimore's Mayor Thomas J. D'Alesandro 3d, a Democrat, noted that his

Continued on Page 69, Column 4

Associated Press

AT CHECKPOINT IN BELFAST: British soldiers check parcel before letting residents pass in a Catholic area.

SHOTS AND FIRES PLAGUE BELFAST FOR THIRD NIGHT

Two More Catholics Die—Blazes Engulf Textile Mill and Plastics Factory

BUT CAPITAL IS QUIETER

British Troops on Patrol—Wilson to Cut Vacation for Talks in London

By JOHN M. LEE

Special to The New York Times

BELFAST, Northern Ireland, Aug. 16—Several shooting incidents plagued riot-torn Belfast today as armed British soldiers patrolled barbed-wire barricades around militant Roman Catholic areas. Armored cars with mounted machine guns were stationed in narrow side streets.

Fire engulfed a textile mill and plastics factory in a Catholic district. Militant Protestant youths erected barricades of burned cars and oil drums in their streets, and small boys joined in the looting of a burned-out candy store.

But late tonight Belfast was quieter than it had been in two days. Just before midnight the police said there had been no casualties today.

Pub Crowds Missing

Dark streets in the downtown area and in the segregated riot areas were empty of the usual Saturday night pub crowds. Hardly any traffic was moving and nothing was open. Even the militant Protestant areas, patrolled by the part-time special policemen, often criticized as Protestant partisans, were deserted.

John McGrath, a Catholic asphalt contractor, had trouble getting through the troops and police to his home, and he stopped for a moment and said: "It looks like the troops are finally calming it down, but the divisions are greater than ever."

Earlier, additional units of British troops were requested and sent into Belfast to reinforce those sent yesterday. An army spokesman refused to disclose their numbers.

Death Toll Put at 8

Two more men died from gunshot wounds received earlier, bringing the total riot deaths since Thursday to eight. All have been Catholics. A 15-year-old boy died last night.

The latest police figures for injuries in the 24 hours ending at 8 A.M. were 236 persons, including 4 policemen. Of these, 66 had been shot, mostly by shotguns.

The continuing violence and the mounting intervention of British troops have precipitated a three-way political crisis touching the British Government, the locally autonomous Government of Northern Ireland, which is united with Britain, and the Republic of Ireland to the south.

The Prime Minister of Northern Ireland, which is commonly known as Ulster, Maj. James

Continued on Page 3, Column 1

Most Materiel in Vietnam To Go With U.S. Forces

By JAMES P. STERBA

Special to The New York Times

SAIGON, South Vietman, Aug. 16 — Plans for the Vietnamization of the war effort call for the turnover of only a small fraction of the equipment now being used by United States forces here.

High-level military planners in charge of reductions in American troops and supplies said recently that the largest part of the fighting equipment—such as helicopters, tanks, trucks and artillery—was expected to be distributed among other American military installations in Southeast Asia or sent to other military assistance programs in the Pacific.

These planners stressed that the "legitimate needs" of the Vietnamese armed forces would be filled. In other words, the South Vietnamese would not be left to carry on the war without sufficient equipment.

Much Would Be Useless

However, the planners said that since the training of the South Vietnamese forces was not expected to be upgraded to anywhere near the level of that of the United States forces, much of the advanced equipment used by Americans would be of no value to Saigon's forces.

According to one military official, 80 to 90 per cent of the "legitimate needs" of the South Vietnamese forces have already been filled. These needs include M-16 rifles, mortars and some light-artillery equipment carried by individual soldiers, jeeps, trucks and some aircraft.

Limited amounts of heavy, more advanced equipment can be expected to be turned over to the South Vietnamese in the next two years as operation and maintenance training programs are completed.

Only Part of Equipment

The key factor in the turnover program is the amount of time left for the Americans to train the South Vietnamese, the planners said. The longer the hostilities drag on, the more time there will be to train the South Vietnamese.

Both a peace settlement and a hastened American pullout would cause a curtailment in programs to upgrade the quality and increase the number of South Vietnamese specialists in the operation and maintenance of aircraft, radar networks, electronic-sensing gear, communications equipment and complicated vehicles such as diesel trucks and earth-movers and ships, these planners said.

But even if these programs are completed on schedule, they involve only a tiny fraction of the American equipment in South Vietnam.

The planners emphasized that United States military needs had first priority. Although priorities next on the list were not made known, officials said that teams from American military-assistance programs in

Continued on Page 8, Column 1

Survey Finds Public Concerned That Discipline in Schools Is Lax

By M. A. FARBER

A major Gallup survey has concluded that the chief complaint against public schools is that students do not receive enough discipline, that the nation is about evenly divided in its willingness to pay more for the schools and that Americans are "ill-informed about education itself."

Spokesmen for the Gallup organization in Princeton, N. J., said that the survey, "based upon a representative sampling of all adults in the country," was the "most extensive" it had conducted on the subject. Officials of the National Education Association in Washington said it was also the most comprehensive survey they knew of.

Another Gallup poll, made public today, reported that 44 per cent of those interviewed believed that racial integration in the public schools was going "too fast," while 22 per cent said it was "not fast enough" and 25 per cent said it was "about right." That poll also showed that the percentage of white parents who would object to sending their children to schools with Negro pupils was generally declining.

The survey of adult public opinion and knowledge of public schools was conducted last February for C.F.K., Ltd., of Denver, a nonprofit educational group headed by Charles F. Kettering 2d.

The Gallup organization said it had found that the teaching profession "has probably never been held in higher esteem" and that the public had accepted the right of teachers to join

Continued on Page 66, Column 3

Student and Puerto Rican, 25, Appointed Trustees of City U.

The New York Times

Jean-Louis d'Heilly — Maria Josefa Canino

By MAURICE CARROLL

A 28-year-old student at the City University and a 25-year-old graduate were appointed by Mayor Lindsay yesterday to the Board of Higher Education.

The appointments gave the board, whose members average about 60 years in age, its first student and its two youngest members.

The student, Jean-Louis d'Heilly, first met Mayor Lindsay when he was organizing a demonstration against Mayor Lindsay.

The graduate, 25-year-old Maria Josefa Canino, has been active in Puerto Rican community organizations since she was a teen-ager.

Miss Canino succeeds Dr. John E. Conboy, who, according to the Mayor's announcement, asked not to be reappointed. The recent retirement of Henry E. Schultz, whose term ran until 1971, leaves board membership at 20, including the two new appointees.

Early on Friday morning, each of the new appointees got a personal telephone call from Mayor Lindsay to tell them of their appointments to the 21-

Continued on Page 36, Column 1

Refugees Gather at 2 Camps in Ireland

By ALVIN SHUSTER

Special to The New York Times

GORMANSTON, Ireland, Aug. 16—A 75-year-old man, his hands shaking and eyes staring, sat on the wooden bench in front of the army barracks numbered 47-A.

The voice over the loudspeaker blared the announcement that "dinner for civilians will be served at half past one in the dining room."

Children, as if on vacation, climbed over fences and played in the dirt before the white brick building marked with a hastily prepared sign, "Civilian Rest Center," and furnished with lounge chairs and a television set.

Soldiers carried the metal frames of army cots past mothers pushing baby carriages.

This army camp, built by the Canadians in World War I, is now the home of the latest members of the world refugee population. And, like other refugees elsewhere in the world, they tell stories of fear, violence, bitterness and bewilderment.

The camp, which was occupied until last week by reservists in summer training, is the larger of the two refugee centers set up this week by Ireland for Roman Catholics fleeing the sectarian violence in Northern Ireland.

Yesterday 22 refugees had arrived. By this morning, 150 —about half of them children—were living in the austere and damp quarters as temporary refugees. They did not bring their worldly possessions, just enough for a few days. Their intention is to return to Northern Ireland when calm returns.

Moreover, they do not represent the total number of Catholics who have left their homes to come south during the crisis. Many others, perhaps hundreds, have traveled to Ireland to stay temporarily with relatives and friends.

For the moment there is little to do here. Dublin is 23 miles away, and the Irish Sea just a few minutes walk past the volleyball court and the officers' mess. But the weather was cloudy and cool today, and no one felt like swimming.

"The women here want to help," said an army officer. "They want to cook. But we are not used to that kind of help. We'll prepare their meals and help them all we can."

They came by car, train and bus, sometimes helped by Catholic civil rights workers. There are no restrictions at the border except for a routine check by Irish customs officials. British customs officials meet travelers from the south. There are similar checks at rail and air

Continued on Page 3, Column 1

"All the News That's Fit to Print"

The New York Times

LATE CITY EDITION

Weather: Fair and continued cold today, tonight. Fair tomorrow. Temp. range: today 41-26; Saturday 47-34. Full U.S. report on Page 95.

SECTION ONE

VOL. CXIX . No. 40,839 | NEW YORK, SUNDAY, NOVEMBER 16, 1969 | 60¢ beyond 50-mile zone from New York City, except Long Island. 75¢ beyond 200-mile radius. Higher in air delivery cities. | 50 CENTS

250,000 WAR PROTESTERS STAGE PEACEFUL RALLY IN WASHINGTON; MILITANTS STIR CLASHES LATER

The New York Times (by Barton Silverman)

Demonstrators at foot of the Washington Monument. Some wave flag of National Liberation Front of South Vietnam.

A RECORD THRONG

Young Marchers Ask Rapid Withdrawal From Vietnam

By JOHN HERBERS

Special to The New York Times

WASHINGTON, Nov. 15—A vast throng of Americans, predominantly youthful and constituting the largest mass march in the nation's capital, demonstrated peacefully in the heart of the city today, demanding a rapid withdrawal of United States troops from Vietnam.

The District of Columbia Police Chief, Jerry Wilson, said a "moderate" estimate was that 250,000 had paraded on Pennsylvania Avenue and had attended an antiwar rally at the Washington Monument. Other city officials said aerial photographs would later show that the crowd had exceeded 300,000.

Until today, the largest outpouring of demonstrators was the gentle civil rights march of 1963, which attracted 200,000. Observers of both marches said the throng that appeared today was clearly greater than the outpouring of 1963.

At dusk, after the mass demonstration had ended, a small segment of the crowd, members of radical splinter groups, moved across Constitution Avenue to the Labor and Justice Department buildings, where they burned United States flags, threw paint bombs and other missiles and were repelled by tear gas released by the police.

There were a number of arrests and minor injuries, mostly the result of the tear gas.

Exodus Begins

At 8 P.M., most of the demonstrators, who had come from all parts of the country, were on buses, trains and cars leaving the city. By 11 P.M., the police said all was quiet in the city.

About 3,000 youths were unable to get to their buses, which were parked by the Tidal Basin, because of the tear gas and heavy traffic, so the city operated an emergency shuttle service of sightseeing buses.

The predominant event of the day was that of a great and peaceful army of dissent moving through the city.

At midday, under clear skies and in the face of a cold north wind, a solid moving carpet of humanity extended from the foot of the Capitol, 10 long blocks up Pennsylvania Avenue to the Treasury Building, four blocks down 15th Street and out across the grassy hill on which the Washington Monument stands.

The crowds brought to Washington a sense of urgency about a Vietnam peace and impatience with President Nixon's policy of gradual withdrawal. This theme, which was repeated throughout the day in various forms, was expressed

Continued on Page 60, Column 1

APOLLO 12 SWINGS ONTO A WIDER PATH TOWARD THE MOON

Course Correction Is Made to Fulfill Requirements for Landing Wednesday

CRAFT PASSES MIDPOINT

Color TV Beamed to Earth —Clock Only Casualty of Power Lapse in Lift-Off

By JOHN NOBLE WILFORD

Special to The New York Times

HOUSTON, Nov. 15—With a short blast of its rocket, the Apollo 12 spacecraft swung out tonight on a wider, slower and somewhat riskier course toward the moon.

The three moonbound astronauts moved smoothly beyond the midpoint in their outward journey, transmitting a color telecast to the earth, checking out spacecraft systems and generally relaxing after their tense, rain-soaked launching yesterday at Cape Kennedy, Fla.

Flight controllers here reported that the 96,000-pound spacecraft was functioning almost flawlessly. An on-board clock was apparently the only casualty of the electrical failure that hit Apollo 12 shortly after lift-off.

Apollo 12, man's second mission to land on the moon, is aiming for lunar orbit Monday night. Then two of the astronauts are to ride the squat, four legged landing craft, dubbed the Intrepid, to a touchdown on the moon's Ocean of Storms early Wednesday morning for a 32-hour visit for scientific exploration.

Equipment Is Checked

At 5:43 P.M., Eastern standard time, today, Comdrs. Charles Conrad Jr., Richard F. Gordon Jr. and Alan L. Bean, all Navy pilots, began transmitting television from inside the cockpit as they checked out equipment and squared away for the rocket firing.

The three astronauts were wearing caps with long bills decorated in Navy braid. Commander Conrad's cap was topped with a small propeller, which he flipped into motion for the television audience 133,000 miles away on the earth.

A snowstorm of ice particles swirled outside the spacecraft window, the frozen debris from an earlier venting of waste water.

Inside the cabin, lights blinked rapidly on the DSKY—the display keyboard for the computerized guidance and navigation system.

Commander Conrad, the Apollo 12 command pilot, and his crew were setting the switches, closing circuit breakers and checking computer data

Continued on Page 66, Column 3

City's New Master Plan Calls Middle Class Vital

Asserts 'Crucial Challenge' Is to Keep Whites While Improving the Lot of Poor Blacks and Puerto Ricans

The "crucial challenge" facing the city is its ability to retain its largely white middle class, while elevating low-income blacks and Puerto Ricans, according to the first volume of the long-awaited Master Plan for New York.

The 90,000-word installment of the "Plan for New York City," made public yesterday by the City Planning Commission, proposes the strengthening of the city's role as a national center with a goal of "several hundred thousand more office workers in the business districts in the next 10 years."

Donald H. Elliott, the chairman of the City Planning Commission, described the nonbinding Master Plan as a "realistic and pragmatic" guide to urban policy for "the next five or ten years."

The comprehensive document discusses a broad range of city problems and attempts to outline a development strategy for dealing with them.

It envisions a city in which electrically powered taxicabs operate, private cars are restricted from some business streets, more recreational facilities are built to join housing and piers on the waterfront, and a new rail tunnel runs under the Hudson.

It urges more training and jobs for the underemployed, classes for 3-year-olds, a network of neighborhood medical services and mixed residential and industrial buildings.

The plan, much revised from portions of a first draft obtained by The New York Times last February, voices hope on some problems, pessimism on others.

For example, the plan states: "The plain fact is that no one yet knows how to make a ghetto school work." It also warns that the city's parochial schools are in "serious financial difficulties," and maintains that the city must choose between subsidizing them or ex-

Continued on Page 84, Column 3

Arms Parley in Helsinki Is Set to Open Tomorrow

By BERNARD GWERTZMAN

Special to The New York Times

HELSINKI, Finland, Nov. 15—The chief disarmament negotiators of the United States and the Soviet Union arrived here today and expressed guarded hope for success in the preliminary talks on limiting strategic arms, which begin Monday.

Both Gerard C. Smith, director of the Arms Control and Disarmament Agency, and Vladimir S. Semyonov, a Deputy Foreign Minister, stressed the preliminary nature of the Helsinki talks, which most diplomats expect to last about three weeks.

In these talks, the expected topic is the framework, time and place for further negotiations on halting the arms race in offensive and defensive systems of strategic weapons.

Both delegations arrived under dark gray skies in a cold drizzle, the usual weather in this northern capital at this time of year. It was already dark at 3:30 in the afternoon when Mr. Semyonov's train arrived.

Earlier, upon arriving aboard a United States Air Force jet, Mr. Smith repeated Secretary of State William P. Rogers's words that the purpose of the talks "is to have a free discussion about how the substantive negotiations will be conducted."

At the same time, Mr. Smith left open the possibility that the preliminary talks might move directly into specific issues. Lacking advance indication on what the Soviet Union might propose, Mr. Smith seemed careful to avoid foreclosing any options.

"We do not rule out the pos-

Continued on Page 14, Column 1

Parade Marshals Keep It Cool

By MAX FRANKEL

Special to The New York Times

WASHINGTON, Nov. 15—It was a campus crowd. It was chilled. It was huge. It was obviously proud of its size, tolerant about its diversity and almost smug about its self-control. It was parading a sense of right, and the most important thing for most of the marchers was simply to have been there.

Arms were thrust especially high, the fingers forming a V, outside the sealed portals of the Justice Department. You see, they were saying to nervous officialdom, peacefulness, it's easy. Was it worth arguing for a week whether to march along Constitution instead of Pennsylvania?

The radical minority that has been spoiling for a fight came back to Justice at dusk to bash in some windows and force this capital's efficient police to hurl out the tear gas again. Thousands milled around to watch the efforts to raise the Vietcong flag and hundreds here and dozens there sniffed the gas that pursued the looters and bottle throwers around town tonight.

But the mean or just plain rowdy here this weekend have been flotsam on a sea of serene people who frown upon all violence, in Vietnam or Washington. During the daylight activities, the marchers and their monitors in the police were all smiles.

Smiles were especially broad for the thousands of marshals along the route, young men and women indistinguishable from the marchers except for the armbands that made them the symbols of self-discipline.

"Keep warm by keeping cool, friends," the marshal in blond curls kept saying. He snapped pictures of his friends as they passed and swapped reassurances with the police sergeant whenever he came along.

The marshals evoked cheers. "What do we want?" "Peace." "When do we want it?" "Now." The marshals gave out advice. "Keep moving please." "Hold hands if you're chilly." "Just six more blocks, three of them in the sun."

The marshals locked arms to contain the militants, prancing in ranks of 15, thrusting Vietcong banners high above the much more common Stars and Stripes (and one hearts and stripes). When the Yippies chanted obscenities a chorus of marshals would sing out in counterpoint with the Beatle song "Give Peace a Chance."

The marshals modestly accepted the crowd's offerings—peanut butter and jelly on white and Fig Newtons.

The pace was that of a football crowd filing into the stadium. The age, too. The adults, alumni perhaps of other marches, in two's and three's, feeling very young and gay,

Continued on Page 62, Column 1

Nixon Sees 4 Aides During the Protest

By JAMES M. NAUGHTON

Special to The New York Times

WASHINGTON, Nov. 15—President Nixon talked about the Vietnam war with four key advisers today as the police and bumper-to-bumper buses isolated the White House from massed antiwar marchers.

As the talks took place, thousands of peace demonstrators filed up Pennsylvania Avenue to within one block of the White House. At 15th Street the marchers

Continued on Page 61, Column 5

TEAR GAS REPELS RADICALS' ATTACK

Capital Police Retaliate as Youths Hurl Bottles and Rocks at U.S. Buildings

By JOHN KIFNER

Special to The New York Times

WASHINGTON, Sunday, Nov. 16—Young radical demonstrators hurling rocks and bottles at Government buildings in the heart of the Capital were turned back last night by barrages of tear gas.

The District of Columbia police fired volley after volley of gas after a militant splinter group from the main antiwar march pelted the Justice Department and twice ran a Vietcong flag up the building's main flagpole.

Police officials reported that there had been at least 93 arrests, including three on felony charges. Hospitals reported that 97 demonstrators were treated for various causes, primarily the effects of the gas.

In nearly all of the encounters, the police did not use their clubs or make physical contact with the demonstrators, relying instead on gas.

After the demonstration at the Justice Department was broken up in a dense cloud of CS, a chemical gas used in Vietnam that causes burning sensations in the eyes and skin, choking and nausea, clumps of young people wandered through the main streets of Washington.

Some were shaken and distraught, but others ranged

Continued on Page 60, Column 6

Nixon Aide Says Agnew Stand Reflects White House TV View

By E. W. KENWORTHY

Special to The New York Times

WASHINGTON, Nov. 15—Vice President Agnew's speech charging the television networks with biased news reporting "reflected the views of the Administration," Clark R. Mollenhoff, special counsel to President Nixon, said today.

Controversy meanwhile, continued to swirl over the Vice President's remarks, both in the United States and abroad. Six former Government officials and 11 law school deans signed a statement expressing alarm over the "inflammatory" remarks attributed to Mr. Agnew and other high officials. [Details on pages 78 and 79.]

Mr. Mollenhoff said there had been discussion within the White House staff "for a long time" about the way network reporters and news commentators had dealt with various issues.

Mr. Mollenhoff was responding to questions about a Washington dispatch in today's issues of The Des Moines Register, for which Mr. Mollenhoff worked before he joined the

Continued on Page 78, Column 3

Today's Sections

Index to Subjects

*Included in all copies distributed in New York City and suburban area.

Irate Black Athletes Stir Campus Tension

By ANTHONY RIPLEY

Special to The New York Times

DENVER, Nov. 15—Rising militancy among black athletes is reaching out to touch most college campuses where blacks take part in intercollegiate sports.

Though much less explosive in their actions than their fellow black students, roused black athletes in increasing numbers are gambling their principles against their educations.

There is an element of self-destruction in this. It has led to dismissals and a cutback in recruiting, and for many blacks from poor families a college education means a football

Continued on Page 85, Column 1

Associated Press

A row of buses blocked access to the White House. Coffins held cards with names of Americans killed in South Vietnam.

More Than 100,000 on Coast Demonstrate in Moderate Vein

By WALLACE TURNER

Special to The New York Times

SAN FRANCISCO, Nov. 15—Upwards of 100,000 people from many walks of life and widely varying political persuasions staged today the biggest peace demonstration ever seen in the West.

They began to gather in the darkness last night, and some of them marched as far as seven miles through this cool, gray city to the rally in Golden Gate Park. Others drove, hitchhiked or rode buses hundreds of miles to reach here today.

In their talk, the speeches they heard and the signs they carried, they repudiated President Nixon's plea that they quietly follow his leadership toward ending the war in Vietnam. Many of them also specifically repudiated Vice President Agnew's criticisms of peace demonstrations.

Again and again throughout the day it was plain that the moderates in the diverse group that planned this demonstration had kept control. The marchers were chaperoned by upward of 1,000 monitors who kept them in line and made them wait at stop lights.

But the strongest indication that the moderates were in control came at the rally when David Hilliard, chief of staff of the militant Black Panther party, was booed. Mr. Hilliard at-

Continued on Page 61, Column 1

"All the News That's Fit to Print"

The New York Times

LATE CITY EDITION

Weather: Rain ending early today; clearing tonight. Fair tomorrow. Temp. range: today 66-49; Monday 62-53. Full U.S. report on Page 90.

VOL. CXIX . . No. 41,009 NEW YORK, TUESDAY, MAY 5, 1970 10 CENTS

HIGH COURT BACKS CHURCHES' RIGHT TO TAX EXEMPTION

Holds, 7 to 1, That Law Does Not Violate Ban on State Support of Religion

DOUGLAS CASTS DISSENT

Majority Rejects Plea of a Bronx Lawyer Over His Plot on Staten Island

By FRED P. GRAHAM

Special to The New York Times

WASHINGTON, May 4 — The Supreme Court ruled 7 to 1 today that laws that exempt church property from taxation do not violate the Constitution's prohibition against state support of religion.

The opinion was written by Chief Justice Warren E. Burger and was disputed only by Justice William O. Douglas. In it the Court upheld the constitutionality of New York State's exemption from real estate taxes of church property used solely for religious purposes.

The law had been challenged by Frederick Walz, a lawyer from the Bronx who purchased a 22-by-29-foot, weed-choked plot on Staten Island in 1967 and promptly sued the City Tax Commission over his $5.24 tax bill for a year.

'Establishment' Is Seen

Mr. Walz, who described himself as a "religious person, not a member of any religious organization," said that tax exemptions granted to church property raised his own tax bill and forced him to contribute to religious groups against his will.

He asserted that the result was an indirect state subsidy to churches, in violation of the First Amendment's prohibition against any "establishment of religion" by the Government.

The Supreme Court rejected that argument today, partly on the ground that no particular religion is singled out for favorable treatment and partly on the historical ground that church tax exemptions have been accepted almost without challenge in all states for most of the nation's history.

Chief Justice Burger's opinion conceded that the church exemption "necessarily operates to afford an indirect economic benefit." But he reasoned that the state might be less neutral toward churches if it taxed them and that it was faced with the delicate matter of deciding on each church's proper assessment.

Surprise and Concern

He concluded that some contact between churches and the state was inevitable and that it would be unfair to deny tax exemptions to religious groups while granting exemptions to nonsectarian charities that do similar good works.

The Supreme Court's decision to review Mr. Walz's appeal prompted widespread puzzlement in legal circles and concern among churchmen. The constitutionality of church tax exemptions was considered so well settled that the New York courts brushed off the challenge with brief orders declaring that it had no merit.

The American Civil Liberties Union backed Mr. Walz, and

Continued on Page 40, Column 5

4 Kent State Students Killed by Troops

8 Hurt as Shooting Follows Reported Sniping at Rally

By JOHN KIFNER

Special to The New York Times

KENT, Ohio, May 4—Four students at Kent State University, two of them women, were shot to death this afternoon by a volley of National Guard gunfire. At least 8 other students were wounded.

The burst of gunfire came about 20 minutes after the guardsmen broke up a noon rally on the Commons, a grassy campus gathering spot, by lobbing tear gas at a crowd of about 1,000 young people.

In Washington, President Nixon deplored the deaths of the four students in the following statement:

"This should remind us all once again that when dissent turns to violence it invites tragedy. It is my hope that this tragic and unfortunate incident will strengthen the determination of all the nation's campuses, administrators, faculty and students alike to stand firmly for the right which exists in this country of peaceful dissent and just as strongly against the resort to violence as a means of such expression."

In Columbus, Sylvester Del Corso, Adjutant General of the Ohio National Guard, said in a statement that the guardsmen had been forced to shoot after a sniper opened fire against the troops from a nearby rooftop and the crowd began to move to encircle the guardsmen.

Frederick P. Wenger, the Assistant Adjutant General, said the troops had opened fire after they were shot at by a sniper.

"They were under standing orders to take cover and return any fire," he said.

This reporter, who was with the group of students, did not see any indication of sniper fire, nor was the sound of any gunfire audible before the Guard volley. Students, conceding that rocks had been thrown, heatedly denied that there was any sniper.

Gov. James A. Rhodes called on J. Edgar Hoover, director of the Federal Bureau of Investigation, to aid in looking into the campus violence. A Justice Department spokesman said no decision had been made to investigate.

At 2:10 this afternoon, after the shootings, the university president, Robert I. White, ordered the university closed for an indefinite time, and officials were making plans to evacuate the dormitories and bus out-of-state students to nearby cities.

Robinson Memorial Hospital identified the dead students as Allison Krause, 19 years old, of

Continued on Page 17, Column 1

Tarentum Valley Daily News via Associated Press

A girl screams as fellow student lies dead after National Guardsmen opened fire at Kent State

Associated Press

Ohio National Guardsmen advancing over the campus of Kent State University yesterday behind a screen of tear gas

37 COLLEGE CHIEFS URGE NIXON MOVE FOR PROMPT PEACE

Warn Invasion of Cambodia Poses New Alienation Peril —Student Strikes Begin

By ROBERT D. McFADDEN

The presidents of 37 colleges and universities urged President Nixon yesterday to "demonstrate unequivocally your determination" to end promptly the United States military involvement in Southeast Asia.

In a letter to Mr. Nixon, the presidents said that "the American invasion of Cambodia" and the weekend bombing of North Vietnam had generated "severe and widespread apprehensions on our campuses."

"We share these apprehensions," the presidents said, adding:

"We implore you to consider the incalculable dangers of an unprecedented alienation of America's youth and to take immediate action to demonstrate unequivocally your determination to end the war quickly."

The signers, representing many of the nation's leading academic institutions, "urgently" requested a meeting with Mr. Nixon.

The letter was drafted by Dr. James M. Hester, the president of New York University, and bore the signatures, among others, of the presidents of Princeton University, Columbia University, the University of Notre Dame, Dartmouth College, the University of Pennsylvania and Johns Hopkins University.

Nationwide Strike Urged

In Washington, the leaders of the National Student Association and the former Vietnam Moratorium Committee called for a nationwide university strike of indefinite duration, starting today, to protest the war and to mobilize public opinion for a withdrawal of United States forces from Indochina. It would involve students, faculty members and administrators.

Antiwar groups at dozens of colleges and universities across the nation, meanwhile, began demonstrations and rallies to protest the Administration's policies.

There were strike pledges from at least 100 colleges and universities, and at some schools the strike began yesterday. Support for the strike was expressed in the editorials of many campus newspapers, along with a condemnation of what some called President Nixon's "illegitimate" decision to send troops into Cambodia.

At many schools, the strike was officially approved by college administrations. Most of

Continued on Page 18, Column 6

President Assailed By Fulbright Panel

By JOHN W. FINNEY

Special to The New York Times

WASHINGTON, May 4—The Senate Foreign Relations Committee complained today that the Nixon Administration, by sending American troops into Cambodia "without the consent or knowledge of Congress," was usurping the war-making powers of Congress.

The committee, which is headed by Senator J. W. Fulbright, also charged that over the years the executive branch had been "conducting a constitutionally unauthorized, Presidential war in Indochina." The charge was promptly rejected by the White House, which contended that President Nixon was relying upon his constitutional powers as Commander in Chief.

"The action which the

Continued on Page 4, Column 4

U.S. SAYS BIG RAIDS IN NORTH ARE OVER

Officials Stress That There May Be Smaller Strikes if Flights Are Periled

By WILLIAM BEECHER

Special to The New York Times

WASHINGTON, May 4—The Defense Department announced today it had "terminated" large-scale air raids mounted in recent days against three areas of North Vietnam.

But Pentagon officials stressed that smaller air strikes might be conducted in the future if American reconnaissance flights over North Vietnam were attacked.

For the first time, the Pentagon acknowledged that the raids north of the demilitarized zone over the weekend had been larger in scope than any since the bombing halt in November, 1968, and that so-called "logistics support" facilities for air defense had been struck in addition to antiaircraft gun and missile sites.

3 Areas Attacked

The Defense Department said that from 50 to more than 100 planes had been employed in each of the strikes near Barthelemy Pass, Bankarai Pass and in another area immediately north of the demilitarized zone. Barthelemy Pass, about 240 miles north of the demilitarized zone, is believed to be the farthest point north raided by American aircraft since November, 1968.

All three areas, officials said, are key conduits for the flow of men and matériel to enemy military units throughout Indo-

Continued on Page 15, Column 1

KOSYGIN ATTACKS NIXON FOR MOVING G.I.'S TO CAMBODIA

He Tells News Conference Action Raises Doubts on Bids for Negotiations

WARNS ON ARMS PARLEY

China Pledges Support to Indochinese People — U.S. in New Drive

Excerpts from Kosygin's text and Q. and A., Page 2.

By BERNARD GWERTZMAN

Special to The New York Times

MOSCOW, May 4—Premier Aleksei N. Kosygin today assailed President Nixon for having sent American forces into Cambodia. He warned that the action might lead to a "further complication" in the international scene and a worsening of Soviet-American relations.

[Communist China also denounced the United States on Cambodia and pledged support to the people of Indochina in their "patriotic struggle" against American forces. Page 3]

[The Associated Press reported that thousands of American and South Vietnamese troops launched a new offensive into northeast Cambodia Tuesday, according to an announcement by the United States command The command said the attack was launched from a base 50 miles west of Pleiku, in the Central Highlands, near the Laotian border.]

Reading from a statement at the start of his first news conference in the Soviet Union in more than five years in office, Mr. Kosygin said the Cambodia intervention raised doubts about Mr. Nixon's sincerity in seeking an "era of negotiation."

He Sees Contradictions

"Is it possible to speak seriously," Mr. Kosygin said, "about the desire of the United States President for fruitful negotiations to solve pressing international problems while the United States is grossly flouting the Geneva Agreements of 1954 and 1962 to which it is a party, and undertaking one new act after another undermining the foundations of international security?

"What is the value of international agreements which the United States is or intends to be a party to if it so unceremoniously violates its obligations? It is impossible not to give serious thoughts to the fact that President Nixon's practical steps in the field of foreign policy are fundamentally at variance with those declarations and assurances that he repeatedly made both before assuming the Presidency and when he was already in the White House."

Attack Shocks Envoys

Western diplomats, who had expected a Soviet Government statement against the Cambodian action, were surprised that it was delivered by Mr. Kosygin in person, and were shocked by the personal attack on Mr. Nixon. Although Mr. Kosygin spoke in calm tones, the diplomats were taken aback by his characterization of President Nixon as a man whose words could not be trusted.

This seemed to indicate to the diplomats that a violent campaign would be started to enlist world opinion against Mr. Nixon.

Although the news conference was called to discuss Cambodia, in answer to a question on the Middle East, Mr. Kosygin said that Soviet military advisers were attached to the armed forces of the United Arab Republic to combat Israeli "aggression" and had certain

Continued on Page 3, Column 1

WAR AND ECONOMY SPUR STOCK DROPS

Administration Economist Voices Apprehension as Market Falls 19.07

By TERRY ROBARDS

Uneasiness over the United States involvement in Cambodia and the bombing of North Vietnam, plus continuing uncertainty about the nation's business outlook, created a mood of deep pessimism on Wall Street yesterday and sent the securities markets into a tailspin.

Stock and bond prices fell sharply in response to selling by discouraged investors. The Dow-Jones industrial average, a gauge of price action on the New York Stock Exchange, plunged 19.07 points in its worst decline since the loss of 21.16 points Nov. 22, 1963, the day President Kennedy was assassinated.

In Washington, a leading Nixon Administration economist expressed apprehension about the situation. "The Administration is obviously concerned," he said, declining to be publicly identified.

"An emotional reaction triggered by the stock market decline may mislead people concerning the basic strength of the economy and its favorable prospects," he asserted, adding that "the facts in the economic sense are pretty good."

His statements represented the first clear indication of anxiety by the Nixon Administration with respect to the stock market's behavior. They were issued before the close of trading and before it was clear that yesterday's nosedive would be

Continued on Page 69, Column 2

Report of Songmy Incident Wins a Pulitzer for Hersh

By PETER KIHSS

A report on the alleged Songmy massacre of Vietnamese civilians by United States soldiers won the 1970 Pulitzer prize in international reporting yesterday for Seymour Hersh, a free-lance reporter whose article was circulated through the Dispatch News Service.

A black playwright, Charles Gordone, won the drama prize for an Off Broadway play, "No Place to Be Somebody"—the first Off Broadway production so honored.

A musical composition on an electronic synthesizer won the music prize for the first time, the award going to "Time's Encomium," by Charles Wuorinen.

Ada Louise Huxtable, architecture critic of The New York Times, became the winner of the first Pulitzer prize for distinguished criticism. This was a new category, set up for criticism or commentary, and was divided in the judging, with Marquis W. Childs of The St. Louis Post-Dispatch taking the award for distinguished commentary.

The gold medal for meritorious public service went to Newsday of Garden City, L. I., for a three-year investigation and exposé of secret land deals and zoning manipulations by public and political party officeholders.

With 17 individuals named Pulitzer prize-winners in the 54th year of the awards, the laurels for history were carried off by former Secretary of

Continued on Page 48, Column 1

ISRAELIS REPORT KILLING 21 ARABS

Toll in Guerrilla Battle at Jordan River Is Termed Largest Since '67 War

By RICHARD EDER

Special to The New York Times

JERUSALEM, May 4—Israeli military authorities announced today that an Israeli patrol surprised and killed 21 armed Palestinian infiltrators shortly after they crossed the Jordan River into Israeli-controlled territory last night.

At the same time the Israelis reported some tentative signs that intensive air strikes on Egyptian artillery positions west of the Suez Canal were beginning to ease the recent pressure on Israeli troops on the east bank.

Last night's encounter with the guerrillas involved the largest death toll reported by Israeli forces since the start of the struggle with Arabs infiltrating into territories occupied by Israel after the 1967 war.

According to the account provided by Israeli military authorities, the infiltrators, members of Al Fatah guerrilla organization, were pinned down by fire from the Israeli patrol just before midnight, not far from the banks of the Jordan River.

The infiltrators tried to take shelter in scrub and thornbushes, the account continued. Apart from firing one bazooka shot, it went on, they made no move to answer the Israeli fire, which went on heavily but intermittently all night and which, by sunup, had killed all but six of them.

When it began to grow light,

Continued on Page 8, Column 4

3 in Bombing Plot Plead Guilty Here

By ARNOLD H. LUBASCH

Samuel J. Melville, Jane L. Alpert and John D. Hughey 3d pleaded guilty yesterday as the self-styled revolutionaries were about to stand trial on charges of conspiring to bomb Federal buildings here last fall.

After the case was convened amid stringent security measures in Federal Court, Judge Milton Pollack asked the bearded 34-year-old Melville why he wanted to plead guilty to three charges against him.

"I plead guilty to count one because I did conspire with others to destroy Federal property," Melville replied as he stood erectly in blue jeans and

Continued on Page 34, Column 1

Study of LSD Spurs Suspicions Of Drug's Link to Birth Defects

By SANDRA BLAKESLEE

The first extensive, long-term study comparing the incidence of birth defects with parental use of LSD has concluded that the drug "must be seriously considered as a possible mutagen"—an agent that produces genetic changes in cells.

"Although we cannot rush in and say we have unequivocal evidence at this time that LSD use causes birth defects, we are on firmer ground, more suspicious, than ever before," said Dr. Cheston M. Berlin, a principal investigator in the study.

Dr. Berlin, a pediatrician at George Washington University School of Medicine, where the study was conducted, presented his findings at two recent scientific meetings. He elaborated on the results in an interview yesterday.

The issue of whether LSD (shorthand for lysergic acid diethylamide) is a mutagenic agent has not yet been resolved, Dr. Berlin said.

Such agents, or changers, act in some way to alter the normal configuration of the genetic material within the cells of an organism, often causing the organism to reproduce itself abnormally, producing birth defects.

If LSD is a mutagenic agent, Dr. Berlin said, evidence of its cellular interference might turn

Continued on Page 23, Column 1

U.S. Officials in Saigon Reduce Their Hopes in Cambodia Drive

Red Leaders Elude Sweep

By TERENCE SMITH

Special to The New York Times

SAIGON, South Vietnam, May 4—Senior United States military and civilian officials here are beginning to scale down their definitions of success for the four-day-old American-South Vietnamese sweep into the Fishhook area of Cambodia.

One of their preliminary conclusions is that the success or failure of the sweep will have to be measured in terms of supplies captured and facilities destroyed, since the top enemy command and the vast majority of the 7,000 Communist soldiers who were believed to have been in the area appear to have fled.

Another preliminary conclusion is that additional forays into other parts of eastern Cambodia are virtually inevitable if lasting damage is to be inflicted on the North Vietnamese supply system. Strikes into eastern Laos, the officials say, are not to be ruled out.

The officials consider that substantial withdrawals of United States combat troops from Vietnam will almost certainly have to be deferred to

Continued on Page 16, Column 3

Big Base Area Discovered

Special to The New York Times

LANDING ZONE NORTH ONE, Cambodia, May 4—Soldiers from this northernmost American outpost in the drive against enemy sanctuaries in Cambodia today reached the site of what is believed to be the largest North Vietnamese base area discovered in the operation, which began last Friday.

The base area, referred to on tactical maps as "The City," is situated in rolling hills and jungles near the northwestern tip of Binhlong Province of South Vietnam. The area is about two miles south of this outpost, which was hastily set up yesterday as a blocking position 20 miles north of where American tanks first plunged into Cambodia along the southern edge of the Fishhook area.

[As the American soldiers advanced, North Vietnamese and Vietcong troops increased their pressure against Pnompenh by cutting the Pnompenh - Saigon highway 29 miles from the Cambodian capital. Page 16.]

A company of soldiers from this base camp was waiting tonight for reinforcements and

Continued on Page 16, Column 3

NEWS INDEX

"All the News That's Fit to Print"

The New York Times

LATE CITY EDITION

Weather: Chance of showers today, tonight. Partly sunny tomorrow. Temp. range: today 74-94; Wed. 72-91. Temp. Hum. Index yesterday 82. Full U.S. report on Page 94.

VOL. CXX . . . No. 41,431 — NEW YORK, THURSDAY, JULY 1, 1971 — 15 CENTS

SUPREME COURT, 6-3, UPHOLDS NEWSPAPERS ON PUBLICATION OF THE PENTAGON REPORT; TIMES RESUMES ITS SERIES, HALTED 15 DAYS

Nixon Says Turks Agree To Ban the Opium Poppy

By JOHN HERBERS

Special to The New York Times

WASHINGTON, June 30—President Nixon announced today that Turkey had agreed to eliminate within a year her production of opium poppies, which account for about two-thirds of the illegal heroin reaching the United States.

Mr. Nixon, in a brief announcement delivered in the White House press room, said that as a result of negotiations between the United States and Turkish Governments, Premier Nihat Erim had agreed to ban altogether the cultivation of opium poppies by June, 1972.

He said the joint announcement, made simultaneously in Washington and Ankara, "represents by far the most significant breakthrough that has been achieved in stopping the source of supply of heroin in our worldwide offensive against dangerous drugs."

Two weeks ago, Mr. Nixon sent a message to William J. Handley, the United States Ambassador in Turkey, saying that the time for talk had passed and the United States must have action by the Turkish Government in ending poppy cultivation.

Today, the President praised Premier Erim for "courageous, statesmanlike action" and said the United States would provide money and technical assistance in helping Turkish farmers shift to other crops.

Officials would not say how much American money would be involved, but the United States has made a $3-million commitment to Turkey on the heroin problem.

Secretary of State William P. Rogers, who helped work

Continued on Page 22, Column 1

PRESIDENT CALLS STEEL AND LABOR TO WHITE HOUSE

He Asks Both Sides to Meet With Him Tuesday Before Contract Talks Start

By PHILIP SHABECOFF

Special to The New York Times

WASHINGTON, June 30 — President Nixon has called negotiators of the steel companies and steelworkers union to meet with him next Tuesday before they sit down to begin contract negotiations, a White House spokesman announced today.

It will be the first time that the President will have met with labor and management in any industry prior to nationwide contract negotiations, according to Ronald L. Ziegler, the White House press secretary.

Discussion Issues Listed

Mr. Ziegler said that the President had called the meeting to discuss general economic developments and trends in the world steel markets.

Earlier today, the chairman of the Federal Reserve Board, Arthur F. Burns, told a Congressional committee that the "first priority" should be given to a new Government move to try to moderate price and wage increases and expressed his concern over the spread of "inflationary psychology" in this country.

The Administration has repeatedly warned that excessive increases in steel wages and prices would severely retard efforts to control inflation. Hints have been dropped that import quotas that protect domestic steel from foreign competition will be cased or lifted if prices go too high.

President Nixon has been in-

Continued on Page 38, Column 1

Pentagon Papers: Study Reports Kennedy Made 'Gamble' Into a 'Broad Commitment'

By HEDRICK SMITH

The Pentagon's study of the Vietnam war concludes that President John F. Kennedy transformed the "limited-risk gamble" of the Eisenhower Administration into a "broad commitment" to prevent Communist domination of South Vietnam.

Although Mr. Kennedy resisted pressures for putting American ground-combat units into South Vietnam, the Pentagon analysts say, he took a series of actions that significantly expanded the American military and political involvement in Vietnam but nonetheless left President Lyndon B. Johnson with as bad a situation as Mr. Kennedy inherited.

"The dilemma of the U.S. involvement dating from the Kennedy era," the Pentagon study observes, was to use "only limited means to achieve excessive ends."

Moreover, according to the study, prepared in 1967-68 by Government analysts, the Kennedy tactics deepened the American involvement in Vietnam piecemeal, with each step minimizing public recognition that the American role was growing.

The expansion of that role, over three decades, is traced in the 3,000 pages of the Pentagon's study, which is accompanied by 4,000 pages of documents on the Vietnam era. Previous articles in The Times's presentation of this material have recounted President Johnson's movement to war in 1964 and 1965.

President Kennedy made his first fresh commitments to Vietnam secretly. The Pentagon study discloses that in the spring of 1961 the President ordered 400 Special Forces troops and 100 other American military advisers sent to South Vietnam. No publicity was given to either move.

Small as the numbers seem in retrospect, the Pentagon study comments that even the first such expansion "signaled a willingness to go beyond the 685-man limit on the size of the U.S. [military] mission in Saigon, which, if it were done openly, would be the first formal breach of the Geneva agreement." Under the interpretation of that agreement in effect since 1956, the United States was limited to 685 military advisers in Vietnam. Washington, while it did not sign the accord, pledged not to undermine it.

On May 11, 1961, the day on which President Kennedy decided to send the Special Forces, he also ordered the start of a campaign of clandestine warfare against North Vietnam, to be conducted by South Vietnamese agents directed and trained by the Central Intelligence Agency and some American Special Forces troops. [See text, action memorandum, May 11, 1961, Page 3.]

The President's instructions, as quoted in the documents, were, "In North Vietnam . . . [to] form networks of resistance, covert bases and teams for

Continued on Page 6, Column 1

The Times today resumes its series of articles on the Pentagon's secret study of the Vietnam war. The study was obtained through the investigative reporting of Neil Sheehan, and the articles were researched and written over three months by Mr. Sheehan and other staff members. The fourth and fifth articles, both by Hedrick Smith, are published today and form an account of decisions in the Kennedy Administration.

Three pages of documentary material covering the Kennedy policy begin on Page 3, and documents on the 1963 coup begin on Page 9. A summary of the three earlier articles, covering the Johnson Administration, appears on Page 15.

BURGER DISSENTS

First Amendment Rule Held to Block Most Prior Restraints

Decision, concurring opinions, dissents start on Page 17.

By FRED P. GRAHAM

Special to The New York Times

WASHINGTON, June 30 — The Supreme Court freed The New York Times and The Washington Post today to resume immediate publication of articles based on the secret Pentagon papers on the origins of the Vietnam war.

By a vote of 6 to 3 the Court held that any attempt by the Government to block news articles prior to publication bears "a heavy burden of presumption against its constitutionality."

In a historic test of that principle — the first effort by the Government to enjoin publication on the ground of national security — the Court declared that "the Government has not met that burden."

The brief judgment was read to a hushed courtroom by Chief Justice Warren E. Burger at 2:30 P.M. at a special session called three hours before.

Old Tradition Observed

The Chief Justice was one of the dissenters, along with Associate Justices Harry A. Blackmun and John M. Harlan, but because the decision was rendered in an unsigned opinion, the Chief Justice read it in court in accordance with long-standing custom.

In New York Arthur Ochs Sulzberger, president and publisher of The Times, said at a news conference that he had "never really doubted that this day would come and that we'd win." His reaction, he said, was "complete joy and delight."

The case had been expected to produce a landmark ruling on the circumstances under which prior restraint could be imposed upon the press, but because no opinion by a single Justice commanded the support of a majority, only the unsigned decision will serve as precedent.

Uncertainty Over Outcome

Because it came on the 15th day after The Times had been restrained from publishing further articles in its series mined from the 7,000 pages of material—the first such restraint in the name of "national security" in the history of the United States—there was some uncertainty whether the press had scored a strong victory or whether a precedent for some degree of restraint had been set.

Alexander M. Bickel, the Yale law professor who had argued for The Times in the case, said in a telephone interview that the ruling placed the press in a "stronger position." He maintained that no Federal District Judge would henceforth temporarily restrain a newspaper on the Justice Department's complaint that "this is what they have printed and we don't like it" and that a direct threat of irreparable harm would have to be alleged.

However, the United States Solicitor General, Erwin N. Griswold, turned to another lawyer shortly after the Justices filed from the courtroom and remarked: "Maybe the newspapers will show a little

Continued on Page 15, Column 1

Soviet Starts an Inquiry Into 3 Astronauts' Deaths

By BERNARD GWERTZMAN

Special to The New York Times

MOSCOW, June 30—The Soviet authorities appointed a special commission tonight to investigate the deaths of their three astronauts who perished this morning when their Soyuz 11 craft was returning to earth after the longest manned space flight in history.

News of the astronauts' deaths shocked many Soviet people. And Western specialists predicted that their deaths would retard development of the Salyut space station program. The three astronauts had spent more than three weeks working and exercising aboard the Salyut craft, described as the world's first space laboratory.

[In the United States, American officials said the Soviet space disaster had probably been caused by a failure in the oxygen supply. They also said the accident should not delay United States space flights. Articles on Page 30.]

Tonight, the Soviet people seemed caught up in the human aspects of the disaster and the mystery of what caused the deaths of Lieut. Col. Georgi T. Dobrovolsky, the flight commander; Vladislav N. Volkov, the flight engineer, and Viktor I. Patsayev, the test engineer.

Were their deaths caused by the weakened state of their bodies after nearly 24 days of weightlessness? Were they

Continued on Page 30, Column 3

U.S. and Diem's Overthrow: Step by Step

The Pentagon's secret study of the Vietnam war discloses that President Kennedy knew and approved of plans for the military coup d'état that overthrew President Ngo Dinh Diem in 1963.

"Our complicity in his overthrow heightened our responsibilities and our commitment" in Vietnam, the study finds.

In August and October of 1963, the narrative recounts, the United States gave its support to a cabal of army generals bent on removing the controversial leader, whose rise to power Mr. Kennedy had backed in speeches in the middle nineteen-fifties and who had been the anchor of American policy in Vietnam for nine years.

The coup, one of the most dramatic episodes in the history of the American involvement in Vietnam, was a watershed. As the Pentagon study observes, it was a time when Washington—with the Diem regime gone—could have reconsidered its entire commitment to South Vietnam and decided to disengage.

At least two Administration officials advocated disengagement but, according to the Pentagon study, it "was never seriously considered a policy alternative because of the assumption that an independent, non-Communist SVN was too important a strategic interest to abandon."

The effect, according to this account, was that the United States, discovering after the coup that the war against the Vietcong had been going much worse than officials previously thought, felt compelled to do more—rather than less—for Saigon. By supporting the anti-Diem coup, the analyst asserts, "the U.S. inadvertently deepened its involvement. The inadvertence is the key factor."

According to the Pentagon account of the 1963 events in Saigon, Washington did not originate the anti-Diem coup, nor did American forces intervene in any way, even to try to prevent the assassinations of Mr. Diem and his brother Ngo Dinh Nhu, who, as the chief Diem political adviser, had accumulated immense power. Popular discontent with the Diem regime focused on Mr. Nhu and his wife.

But for weeks—and with the White House informed every step of the way—the American mission in Saigon maintained secret contacts with the plotting generals through one of the Central Intelligence Agency's most experienced and versatile operatives, an Indochina veteran, Lieut. Col. Lucien Conein. The colonel, who is now in retirement, first landed in Vietnam in 1944 by parachute for the Office of Strategic Services, the wartime forerunner of the C.I.A.

So trusted by the Vietnamese generals was Colonel Conein that he was in their midst at Vietnamese General Staff headquarters as they launched the coup. Indeed, on Oct. 25, a week earlier, in a cable to McGeorge Bundy, the President's special assistant for national security, Ambassador Lodge had occasion to describe Colonel Conein of the C.I.A. —referring to the agency, in code terminology, as C.A.S.—as the indispensable man:

"C.A.S. has been punctilious in carrying out my instructions. I have personally approved each meeting between General Don [one of three main plotters] and Conein who has carried out my

Continued on Page 12, Column 1

CHOU TIES U.N. SEAT TO TAIPEI'S OUSTER

Also Says Peking Must Have Permanent Council Post if It Is to Be Member

By TAKASHI OKA

Special to The New York Times

TOKYO, June 30 — Premier Chou En-lai of China said in an interview published here today that for his country to join the United Nations it was necessary not only that all membership rights be "restored," including a permanent seat on the Security Council, but that the Nationalists be ousted from the United Nations.

Mr. Chou made the comment in a meeting with Yoshikatsu Takeiri, chairman of Komeito, the Clean Government party, who is visiting Peking with eight of his followers. The Premier's comments were published today in the party newspaper Komei Shimbun as well as in other major Japanese newspapers.

'What Steps Are Necessary?'

Mr. Chou's comments, which are consistent with the line Peking has taken on prospective United Nations membership, apparently weakened attempts by the United States, Japan and other interested members of the United Nations to safeguard at least a General Assembly seat for the Nationalists while admitting the Chinese Communists to the Security Council as well as the Assembly.

"What steps do you think are necessary in order to get China back into the United Nations?" Mr. Chou was asked,

Continued on Page 32, Column 4

Jim Garrison Is Arrested; U.S. Says He Took Bribes

By ROY REED

Special to The New York Times

NEW ORLEANS, June 30—District Attorney Jim Garrison was arrested by Federal agents today and charged with taking bribes to protect illegal pinball gambling in New Orleans.

The Justice Department said that the last payment, $1,000, was delivered to Mr. Garrison at his home last night in marked $50 bills. The payment, the department said, was handed to him by a once-trusted confidant who had secretly gone to work for the Government's agents.

Mr. Garrison, 50 years old, who attempted to prove a conspiracy in the 1963 assassination of President Kennedy, was taken into custody at his home. He was fingerprinted and placed under $5,000 bond by a Federal magistrate.

The Justice Department said that Mr. Garrison had taken up to $1,500 a month in bribes.

According to the Government, Mr. Garrison had received the bribes from pinball operators since 1962.

"I've never accepted a dollar in my life," the District Attorney told reporters as he walked into the French Quarter Courthouse to face the magistrate.

Mr. Garrison was one of 10 men arrested. The others in-

Continued on Page 55, Column 3

Cousin Asserts Jerome Johnson Told of Job With Italian League

By BARBARA CAMPBELL

A cousin of Jerome A. Johnson, who was shot to death at the site of a rally in Columbus Circle after allegedly firing three bullets into Joseph A. Colombo Sr., said yesterday that Johnson told him "several months ago" he was working for the Italian-American Civil Rights League as a photographer.

This was corroborated by a close friend of Johnson's, who said the 24-year-old slain man had also told him on a May 15 visit to California that he was working for the league.

About three months before the shooting, Johnson gave his cousin a telephone number where he could be reached, and a check by The New York Times disclosed yesterday that the number had been recently changed. The operator said the number had been switched to a new number, that of the Italian-American League.

This latest development raised a series of questions for investigators. If Johnson was working for the league, was he known there? Was he an employe or a hanger-on, perhaps a temporary called in on occasions?

Chief of Detectives Albert A. Seedman said last night only that the telephone-number switch, if true, "certainly puts

Continued on Page 53, Column 1

THE STATES RATIFY FULL VOTE AT 18

Ohio Becomes 38th to Back the 26th Amendment

By R. W. APPLE Jr.

Special to The New York Times

WASHINGTON, June 30—The 26th Amendment to the Constitution lowering to 18 years the minimum voting age in local and state as well as Federal elections, was ratified tonight.

Ohio became the 38th state to approve the Amendment when the state's House of Representatives, meeting in extraordinary evening session, gave its assent, 81 to 9. The Ohio Senate had approved the measure yesterday, 30 to 2.

The ratification of at least 38 states, or three-quarters of the total, is required for constitutional amendments.

An atmosphere of near-panic attended Ohio's climactic vote. The Republican Speaker of the House, Charles F. Kurfess, had planned to let a number of members, both Republicans and Democrats, speak on the issue before calling for a vote.

But after only three short speeches, the Republican floor leader, Robert E. Leavitt, interrupted to warn:

"I've just been informed that the Legislature of Oklahoma

Continued on Page 43, Column 1

Conferees Cut Military Pay Rise As Authority to Draft Runs Out

By DAVID E. ROSENBAUM

Special to The New York Times

WASHINGTON, June 30 — The Nixon Administration won a major budgetary victory today in the House-Senate conference on the draft extension bill.

The conference agreement also appeared to represent a setback for supporters of an all-volunteer Army, who had sought larger pay increases than those cleared by the conferees.

The conferees accepted a figure for military pay and allowances that was more than $900-million below what both the Senate and House had approved. The raises voted by the conferees would cost about $1.8-billion in the fiscal year starting tomorrow and would go into effect Oct. 1.

The figure approved by the conference was still $800-million above what President Nixon sought in his budget, but the House and Senate had passed increases of about $1.7-billion over the budget.

The Nixon Administration had argued that so large an increase would force severe and possibly dangerous reductions in other parts of the defense budget.

The Government's basic authority to draft men into the military expires at midnight tonight.

The conferees completed action on all provisions of the draft bill today except the Senate-passed amendment that calls for the withdrawal of United States troops from Indochina within nine months if prisoners of war are first

Continued on Page 29, Column 1

False Advertising Laid to H&R Block

By JOHN D. MORRIS

Special to The New York Times

WASHINGTON, June 30 — H & R Block, Inc., which says it prepares income tax returns for eight million American annually, was accused by the Federal Trade Commission today of false advertising and illegally using confidential information supplied by customers.

The commission published similar but separate citations against H & R Block and the Beneficial Corporation, which offers income tax services on a smaller scale through a subsidiary, the Beneficial Management Corporation. In radio and television advertisements, the name

Continued on Page 57, Column 2

ACTION BY GRAVEL VEXES SENATORS

But No Disciplinary Action Against Him Is Expected

By JOHN W. FINNEY

Special to The New York Times

WASHINGTON, June 30 — Many Senators privately expressed dismay, shock and chagrin today at Senator Mike Gravel's release of parts of the Pentagon's secret study of the Vietnam war. But it appeared that no disciplinary action would be taken against the Alaska Democrat.

Last night Senator Gravel tried to read the documents to the Senate in an all-night speech and, when he was blocked for lack of a quorum, proceeded to call an impromptu meeting of his Senate Public Works subcommittee. He read from the study for three and one-half hours, with his voice sometimes breaking into sobs, and tears occasionally rolling down his face.

His action incurred the displeasure of many of his colleagues, who felt that it reflected on the dignity and composure of the Senate. But in the clublike atmosphere of the Senate, there was a widespread reluctance, extending down from the leadership, to take any formal disciplinary

Continued on Page 16, Column 2

NEWS INDEX

"All the News That's Fit to Print"

The New York Times

LATE CITY EDITION

Weather: Mostly sunny, mild today. Fair and mild tonight, tomorrow. Temp. range: today 54-71; Friday 46-67. Full U.S. report on Page 58.

VOL. CXXI ... No. 41,762 | NEW YORK, SATURDAY, MAY 27, 1972 | 15 CENTS

U.S. AND SOVIET SIGN TWO ARMS ACCORDS TO LIMIT GROWTH OF ATOMIC ARSENALS; TRADE PACT DELAYED, TALKS TO GO ON

Joint Commission Set Up To Resolve Trade Issues

By ROBERT B. SEMPLE Jr.

Special to The New York Times

MOSCOW, May 26—The United States and the Soviet Union announced the formation of a joint commission today to devise a comprehensive trade agreement that has proved impossible to reach during President Nixon's visit to Moscow.

The announcement, not altogether unexpected, represented an admission by both sides that the two countries had been unable to reconcile differences on the trade issue, and it constituted the first disappointment of the Moscow summit meeting.

Under the terms of the agreement, announced to reporters here by Peter M. Flanigan, Assistant to President Nixon, the joint commission will have these assignments:

¶To negotiate an over-all trade agreement including reciprocal "most favored nation" treatment—meaning, essentially, that imports from the Soviet Union will receive the same tariff advantages given most other United States trading partners.

¶To devise arrangements under which credits will be provided to finance sales by each nation to the other.

¶To negotiate provisions for the establishment of business offices in each country by concerns in the other.

¶To set up an arbitration mechanism for settling commercial disputes arising from trade.

President Appears Tired

The President himself appeared tired yet exhilarated after his first five days in the Soviet Union. At a dinner he gave this evening for Leonid I. Brezhnev, general secretary of the Soviet Communist party, Mr. Nixon raised his glass, and said:

"We look forward to the time when we shall be able to welcome you in our country and in some way respond in an effective manner to the way in which you have received us so generously in your country."

In effect, today was Mr. Nixon's last day of official meetings with Soviet leaders. He will pay a ceremonial visit to Leningrad tomorrow, rest for most of Sunday before delivering a televised address to the Soviet people that evening, and will participate in a reception Monday before flying to Kiev.

Yet the final day ended on what was seen by both sides as an immensely positive note, reflected not only in the arms agreement but in the words of the dignitaries here.

Mr. Nixon, in his toast tonight, called the arms accord not only an "enormously important agreement" but also an "indication of what can happen in the future as we work toward peace in the

Continued on Page 9, Column 6

U.S. TRADE DEFICIT BIG AGAIN IN APRIL

Imports Exceeded Exports by $699-Million, Second Largest Gap on Record

By EDWIN L. DALE Jr.

Special to The New York Times

WASHINGTON, May 26—The United States recorded another huge deficit in its foreign trade in April, the Commerce Department reported today. Imports exceeded exports by $699-million, the second largest deficit for a month on record. The high was set last October, at $821-million.

In the first four months of the year the total trade deficit was $2.2-billion, almost guaranteeing that the year as a whole will see a larger deficit than last year's $2-billion, which was the first trade deficit in this century.

However, officials continue to expect some improvement as 1972 proceeds and the delayed effects of devaluation of the dollar begin to be felt.

Exports in April, seasonally adjusted, were $3.760-billion, down from $3.891-billion in March and the lowest export total of the year so far. A drop in exports of large jet aircraft was partly responsible.

Imports in April were $4.46-billion, down slightly from the figure of $4.475-billion in March. Both figures were above April a year ago—indicating a continued expansion of trade—but the rise in imports was much bigger than that for exports.

For the first four months of the year, exports were running

Continued on Page 35, Column 1

Lindsay Aide Says Council Must Raise Taxes on Property

By FRANCIS X. CLINES

Mayor Lindsay's office insisted yesterday that the City Council had no choice but to approve up to $89-million in higher property taxes to close an expected budget gap, regardless of the continuing opposition of Council members.

Councilman Matthew J. Troy Jr., the leader of the tax revolt, agreed with Deputy Mayor Edward K. Hamilton that there was such an obligation in the City Charter's mandate to approve real-estate taxes by June 25. But he said he would violate it rather than vote aye.

"I'm prepared to go to jail," Mr. Troy declared.

The Mayor's press spokesman, Thomas Morgan, immediately commented: "We've alerted the Corrections Department to prepare a padded cell with a view."

Thus, a farcical tone was added to the considerable confusion as the Mayor's office tried to decide what to do next in completing a balanced budget.

Continued on Page 12, Column 5

NEWS INDEX

AFTER SIGNING: President Nixon and Leonid I. Brezhnev exchange treaty copies at Kremlin. In center, Soviet President Nikolai V. Podgorny.

United Press International

FOE PUSHES FIGHT IN TWO KEY AREAS

Losses Heavy, but Enemy Clings to Small Gains at Kontum and Hue

Special to The New York Times

SAIGON, South Vietnam, Saturday, May 27—North Vietnamese soldiers hurled themselves against Government defenses in the Central Highlands city of Kontum and near the northern city of Hue through the day yesterday.

They suffered many casualties and lost 16 tanks, 13 at Kontum and three near Hue, according to American and South Vietnamese military spokesmen. But at nightfall they reportedly continued to hold small pockets of ground taken from the South Vietnamese.

In Kontum, North Vietnamese infiltrators still occupied pockets in the southeastern and northeastern parts of town and continued to keep the airport closed to traffic, according to American sources.

In the northernmost part of South Vietnam, Communist forces were said to hold small bulges of territory about 20 miles northwest of Hue, having penetrated Government defenses along the Mychanh River.

Informed sources said that at one point four North Vietnamese tanks rolled into a de-

Continued on Page 6, Column 2

A First Step, but a Major Stride

By MAX FRANKEL

Special to The New York Times

News Analysis

MOSCOW, Saturday, May 27—The nuclear age gained its first strategic arms limitation treaty in the Kremlin last night. Its awkward name—commonly shortened to SALT—is needed because the accord involves no disarmament. Its purpose is to freeze the balance of terrifying weapons and to make sure the terror works by preventing any effective defense against them.

It is a major step forward in the already long history of nuclear arms negotiation. But it is also only a beginning.

Both President Nixon and the Soviet Party chief, Leonid I. Brezhnev, vowed to press ahead toward further limitations and perhaps eventually even some reductions in arms. So this treaty is likely to be known as SALT I.

It is a beginning, achieved after seven years of effort and 30 months of negotiation in one of those fleeting moments when the two superpowers felt themselves strategic equals, despite inequality in the quality and number of their arms, and when their two leaders felt themselves strong enough politically to make the agreements stick.

The arms race will go on, not only in the regular army, navy and air force weaponry that is unaffected by the accord but also in the quality of nuclear warheads—that is, their size and accuracy and evasive skills—and in the arts of antisubmarine warfare and even in the technology of the missile defense systems that the treaty is to limit severely at inadequate levels.

Indeed, under certain conditions or political pressures, the treaty itself may stimulate further competition in these uncovered areas. And because the accord renounces those weapons that both sides think they now possess in sufficient number, it may not even save much money in future budgets.

The United States had no plans to augment the land and submarine missiles and antimissile installations covered by the treaty. The energetic Soviet build-up of recent years was presumably intended primarily to reach a comfortable level before the freeze.

The significance of the treaty lies in that it makes the freeze legally binding. It becomes an important weapon for political

Continued on Page 9, Column 7

LAIRD DISCOUNTS BIG ARMS SAVINGS

Reaction to Pact in Capital Mostly Favorable but Some Conservatives Are Critical

By JUAN M. VASQUEZ

Special to The New York Times

WASHINGTON, May 26—Defense Secretary Melvin R. Laird today hailed the United States arms agreements with the Soviet Union but warned against the expectation of major cost savings.

Returning to the capital after several days of discussions with Atlantic alliance defense ministers in Brussels, Mr. Laird declared that the agreements to limit strategic arms "will enhance the national security of the United States."

He asserted, however, that "we still need to keep up our guard" and that the United States must "maintain a technological superior position."

He added, "There will be no savings as far as the request for offensive strategic weapons which have been presented to the Congress in the 1973 budget."

Specifically, he cited the Air Force B-1 bomber program and submarine construction as areas in which Congress might seek reductions, according to reports he had heard. "That just cannot be," he said.

Mr. Laird, a former Congressman from Wisconsin, told

Continued on Page 10, Column 3

U.S. AND SOVIET NUCLEAR ARSENALS

THE ARMS RACE

LAND-LAUNCHED ICBM'S: Soviet 1,618; U.S. 1,054; 934; 224 ('65 '67 '69 '71)

SUB-LAUNCHED MISSILES: U.S. 710; Soviet 656; 464; 107 ('65 '67 '69 '71)

WHAT ACCORDS ALLOW (Basically present levels)

ICBM'S: U.S. 1,054; Soviet 1,618

SUB-LAUNCHED MISSILES: U.S. 656; Soviet 710

ANTIMISSILE MISSILES: U.S. (200); Soviet (200); 64

WARHEADS (Not covered by accords)

U.S. 5,700

Soviet 2,500

The New York Times/May 27, 1972

Photograph from Gamma/Photoreporters

MISSILE IN SILO: Above photograph, from a Czech source, is said to show a Soviet emplacement. Soviet arms totals on chart include weapons that are under construction.

Court Throws Out Jersey Law Barring Primary Cross-Voting

Special to The New York Times

NEWARK, May 26—New Jersey's primary election law prohibiting enrolled voters from casting ballots in other party contests was declared unconstitutional today by a three-judge Federal panel.

The decision specifically threw out the provisions that require enrolled voters to sit out two consecutive primary elections before switching parties. The court declared this waiting period "unreasonable and excessive."

The court directed Attorney General George F. Kugler Jr. to notify local election boards that they must permit voters to choose in which primary they want to vote on June 6 without reference to their party enrollment.

A spokesman for the Attorney General said he would not comment on whether the decision would be appealed until he had had time to study it.

If the decision stands for the coming primary, it could affect the outcome of the contests for 109 Democratic convention delegates between Senators Hubert H. Humphrey and George McGovern. Republican voters could tip the scales in favor of the man they consider the weaker candidate against President Nixon, who is unopposed on the Republican primary ballot.

The Democratic state chairman, Salvatore A. Bontempo, said he did not know how the decision would affect the primary balloting but said he was

Continued on Page 23, Column 2

CEILINGS ARE SET

Nixon and Brezhnev Pledge to Abide by Treaty at Once

By HEDRICK SMITH

Special to The New York Times

MOSCOW, Saturday, May 27—President Nixon and the Soviet Communist party leader, Leonid I. Brezhnev, signed two historic agreements last night that for the first time put limits on the growth of American and Soviet strategic nuclear arsenals.

In a brief televised ceremony in the Great Hall of the Kremlin, the two leaders put their

Arms accord texts, Page 8, and toasts on Page 9

signatures to a treaty that establishes a ceiling of 200 launchers for each side's defensive missile systems and commits them not to try to build nationwide antimissile defenses. The treaty, which is to run indefinitely, requires ratification by the Senate in Washington, but both sides pledged to abide by it at once.

Applause After Signing

They also signed an interim accord on offensive systems that freezes land-based and submarine-based intercontinental missiles at the level now in operation or under construction.

After signing the two accords, Mr. Brezhnev and Mr. Nixon walked toward each other, smiling broadly, and shook hands vigorously amidst applause from a gathering of senior officials, including negotiators who had worked through the day to put the final touches on the agreement.

Mr. Nixon then said:

"We want to be remembered by our deeds, not by the fact that we brought war to the world, but by the fact that we made the world a more peaceful one for all peoples of the world."

Can Improve Quality

Mr. Kosygin said in reply:

"This is a great victory for the Soviet and American peoples in the matter of easing international tension. This is a victory for all peaceloving people, because security and peace is the common goal."

Later, American officials reported that the two leaders had resolved several deadlocks in their talks here this week.

In a toast at a dinner he gave for the Soviet leaders at Spaso House, the American Ambassador's residence, the President hailed the agreements as "enormously important."

Gerard C. Smith, the chief American negotiator, told reporters that today's two agreements were "not the end of the road by any means, but they

Continued on Page 8, Column 1

Von Braun Will Leave NASA For Job in Aerospace Industry

By HAROLD M. SCHMECK Jr.

Special to The New York Times

WASHINGTON, May 26—Dr. Wernher von Braun, one of the chief architects of man's first landing on the moon, is retiring from the National Aeronautics and Space Administration.

The German-born rocket expert, who has worked for the United States Government since the end of World War II, will leave the space agency July 1 to become corporate vice president for engineering and development of Fairchild Industries, a major aerospace company.

"Dr. von Braun's decision to retire from NASA is a source of great regret to all of us at the agency," said Dr. James C. Fletcher, NASA's administrator.

"For more than a quarter of a century, he has served the United States as the leader in space rocket development," Dr. Fletcher said in the announcement. "His efforts first put the United States in space with Explorer I. As director of the Marshall Space Flight Center for over 10 years, he directed the development of the world's most powerful rocket, the Saturn 5—which has taken 10 American astronauts to the surface of the moon."

Two of those astronauts, Neil A. Armstrong, the first man to set foot on the moon, and Edwin E. Aldrin Jr., his companion on the historic Apollo 11 moon landing, have al-

Continued on Page 59, Column 1

THE SPACE RACE

JOHN NOBLE WILFORD

The "space race" loomed large in geopolitics and the public consciousness for a brief but intense period, mainly in the 1960's and early 70's. It was a riveting, often suspenseful new chapter, which unexpectedly expanded the nature of the cold war. Challenged in 1957 by the Soviet Union's Sputnik, the first artificial Earth satellite, and subsequent successes, the United States responded out of fear and anxiety by mobilizing its technology in a rare burst of shared purpose.[1]

The response was critical in a divided world in which the two superpowers stared each other down, armed with the menace of mass destruction. As President John F. Kennedy declared in 1961, committing the country to send a man to the moon by the end of the decade: "Now it is time to take longer strides—time for this nation to take a clearly leading role in space achievement which, in many ways, may hold the key to our future on Earth."[2]

There it was, the space race had a defining objective, distant but as clear and magical as the shining light in the night sky. No one at the start could be sure of exactly how the goal was to be attained or if it was reachable in the allotted years. But few Americans, shaken by the Soviet big lead in space, doubted that this adversary had to be "beaten" to re-establish to the world and themselves their reputation for superior technology.

Mobilization for the Apollo Project was breathtakingly swift.[3] Industries shifted to the production of rockets and spacecraft and advanced navigation systems. New launching complexes and a mammoth assembly building rose at Cape Canaveral, Florida. Astronaut training facilities and Mission Control transformed pasture land outside Houston. Hundreds of thousands of people who might otherwise have

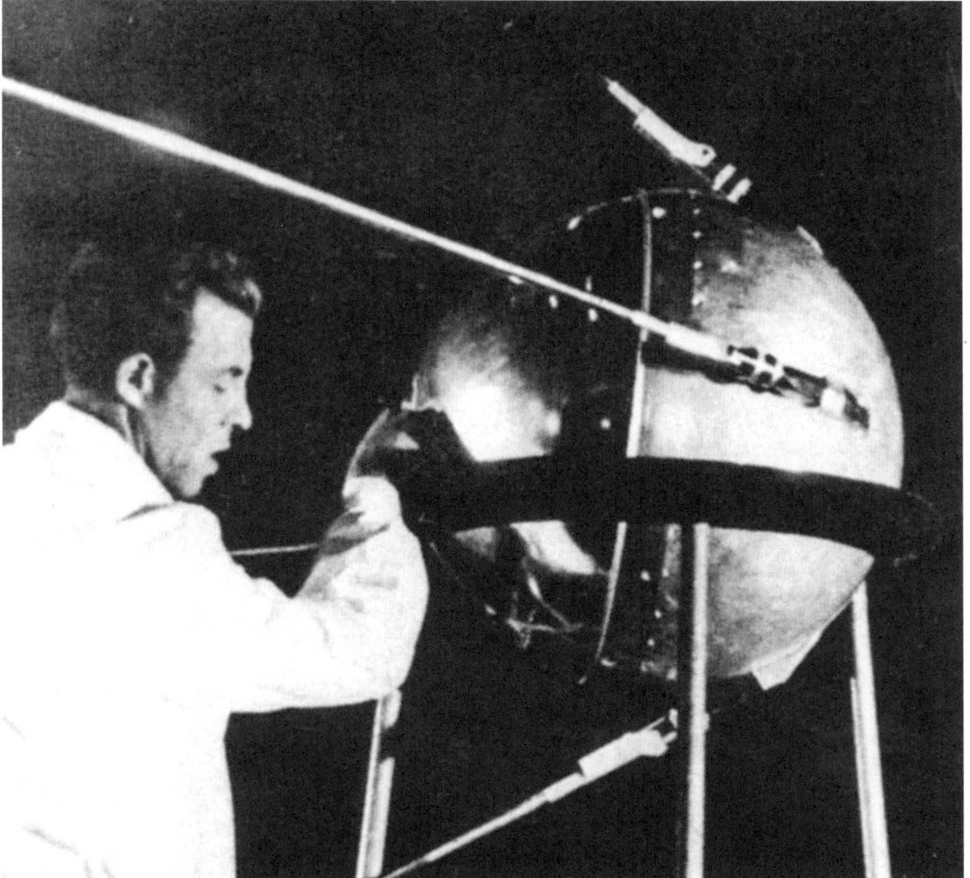

The massive effort by the U.S. to reach out into space was prompted in great part by this Soviet satellite called Sputnik I in 1957.

Soviet cosmonaut Yuri Gagarin's 108-minute orbit around the Earth gave the Russians a big lead in the space race in 1961.

FURTHER READING

1 "In the Nation: The Effects of the Sputnik Thus Far," see October 10, 1957, article.
2 "Kennedy Asks 1.8 Billion This Year to Accelerate Space Exploration, Add Foreign Aid, Bolster Defense," see May 26, 1961, front page.
3 "Project Apollo: Man's Race for Moon," see July 30, 1962, front page.

President John F. Kennedy signs a bill authorizing a vastly expanded effort in the development of space travel in July of 1961.

The U.S. space program suffered a serious setback in 1967 when the crew of Apollo 1 was killed in a flash fire during a training session.

spent their working lives outside the sweep of history joined in the prodigious effort. There were engineers and scientists, managers and test pilots, technicians and workers everywhere—even reporters who chronicled the endeavor.

Some $25 billion was spent in the 1960's on Apollo. With a few notable exceptions (communications and spy satellites, robotic probes to Venus and Mars), every aspect of the space program had a role in the lunar-landing undertaking. The Mercury flights, already under way, put American astronauts in low orbit for the first time.[4] Gemini followed, the two-seat capsules in which astronauts orbited for longer durations and practiced rendezvous and docking techniques required for lunar missions.[5] Several robotic vehicles circled the moon to map potential landing sites and landed to examine the composition and firmness of the surface.

Tragedy struck in January 1967. In a countdown rehearsal on the launching pad for the first Apollo flight, fire erupted in the cockpit, killing the three astronauts and casting serious doubt on the attainability of the lunar goal in the decade.[6] At the time, Soviet intentions were unknown as designs on the moon were shrouded in secrecy. (Subsequent testimony of Russian engineers and the release of documents have revealed their part in running the race to the moon, at least up to the launching failures in the late 1960's that beset their huge moon rocket.)

It was more than 18 months before the redesigned Apollo spacecraft was finally tested in Earth orbit. Meanwhile, the Saturn 5 moon rocket had passed rigorous launching tests.[7] So Apollo officials decided on a daring change of plans. They would send the next manned spacecraft to the moon—not for a landing, but a circumnavigation.

Astronaut John Glenn and President Kennedy inspect Friendship 7, the space vehicle Glenn rode in orbit.

In late December 1968, the three astronauts of Apollo 8 circled the moon 10 times. Out their windows they saw the achingly beautiful Earth, a blue-and-white marble against the darkness of space. On Christmas Eve, the men took turns reading verses from Genesis.[8] It was a gift from on high at a time of turmoil and despair in the year of political assassinations, rioting cities and a fiercely divisive war in Vietnam.

After two more flights, one in low orbit and the other to the moon in a non-landing exercise, Apollo 11 achieved the climax of the decade's space race. On July 20, 1969, Neil Armstrong stepped down the landing craft's ladder and took "one giant leap for mankind."[9] Buzz Aldrin then joined him for the first walk on the moon, on the "magnificent desolation" of the Sea of Tranquillity. In contrast to exploration's previous landfalls, the whole world was watching on television.

Apollo 11 essentially ended the race. Public interest in spaceflight was flagging by the time of Apollo 13, in April 1970. The optimism with which the country first committed itself to Apollo had given way to self-doubt. The Vietnam War, another chapter in the cold war, shoved space to the periphery of the national attention.

Apollo 13 was the mission that failed. On the way to the moon, an explosion in the rear compartment crippled the craft. There could be no lunar landing. There might be no safe return to Earth for the astronauts.[10] Over the next few days of despairing hope, engineers on the ground devised a rescue plan and talked the astronauts through improvised fixes to keep their craft going. The astronauts swung around the moon, using its gravity to turn them back toward Earth, and splashed down in the Pacific just before their oxygen ran out.

This near calamity reminded stay-at-homes that for humans, leaving Earth is no Sunday drive in the country. It made spaceflight seem both more exciting and dangerous. But by the end of 1972, the American attention span for

The first view of Earth from space on Apollo 8 as it rose above the horizon of the moon during its flight in 1968.

A footprint left by one of the astronauts shows in the soft, powdery surface of the moon.

The Apollo 11 lunar module rises off the moon after astronauts Neil Armstrong and Edwin E. Aldrin completed their lunar assignments landing in July 1969.

4 "81,000-Mile Trip," see February 21, 1962, front page.
5 "Gemini, in Its First Orbit, Docks with Agena Target in a 94-Minute Maneuver," see September 13, 1966, front page.
6 "Apollo Program Dealt Hard Blow," see January 28, 1967, front page.
7 "NASA Aides Fear Soviet Space Gain," see August 14, 1968, article.
8 "Excerpts From Radio Conversations Between the Apollo 8 Crew and Houston," see December 25, 1968, article.
9 "Voice From Moon: 'Eagle Has Landed,'" see July 21, 1969, front page.
10 "Power Failure Imperils Astronauts," see April 14, 1970, front page.

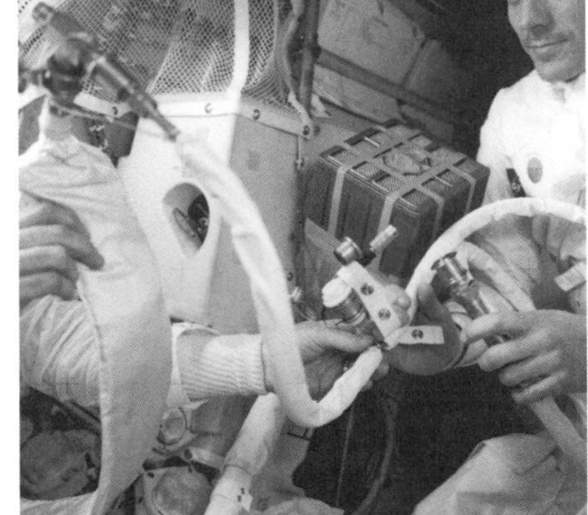

The astronauts of Apollo 13 link a hose to a device in order to eliminate deadly carbon dioxide in the ship's cabin.

The crew at the Manned Spacecraft Center in Houston celebrate the successful splashdown of Apollo 13 after its close call with disaster.

outer space had virtually evaporated. The last of the 12 men to walk on the moon packed up and returned home, and no one has been back since.[11]

At the conclusion of that flight, Apollo 17, the historian Arthur M. Schlesinger Jr. predicted that in 500 years, the 20th century would probably be remembered mainly for humanity's first ventures beyond its native planet.

JOHN NOBLE WILFORD *is a senior science correspondent for The New York Times. He covered all the Apollo missions for The Times, won a Pulitzer Prize in 1984 for articles on science and planetary exploration, and in 1987 shared another Pulitzer with colleagues for coverage of the aftermath of the space shuttle Challenger disaster. Before joining The Times in 1965, Wilford worked for The Wall Street Journal and Time magazine. He is the author of "We Reach the Moon," "The Mapmakers," "Mars Beckons," "The Mysterious History of Columbus," and co-author or editor of other books, including "Cosmic Dispatches."*

11. "The moon is more of a mystery than ever," see April 16, 1972 article.

Astronaut Bruce McCandless takes a "space walk" in 1984, without the tether that usually connects astronauts to the space craft.

"All the News That's Fit to Print"

The New York Times

LATE CITY EDITION

Weather: Rain, warm today; clear tonight. Sunny, pleasant tomorrow. Temp. range: today 80-66; Sunday 71-66. Temp.-Hum. Index yesterday 69. Complete U.S. report on P. 50.

VOL. CXVIII . No. 40,721

NEW YORK, MONDAY, JULY 21, 1969

10 CENTS

MEN WALK ON MOON

ASTRONAUTS LAND ON PLAIN; COLLECT ROCKS, PLANT FLAG

Voice From Moon: 'Eagle Has Landed'

EAGLE (the lunar module): Houston, Tranquility Base here. The Eagle has landed.

HOUSTON: Roger, Tranquility, we copy you on the ground. You've got a bunch of guys about to turn blue. We're breathing again. Thanks a lot.

TRANQUILITY BASE: Thank you.

HOUSTON: You're looking good here.

TRANQUILITY BASE: A very smooth touchdown.

HOUSTON: Eagle, you are stay for T1. [The first step in the lunar operation.] Over.

TRANQUILITY BASE: Roger. Stay for T1.

HOUSTON: Roger and we see you venting the ox.

TRANQUILITY BASE: Roger.

COLUMBIA (the command and service module): How do you read me?

HOUSTON: Columbia, he has landed Tranquility Base. Eagle is at Tranquility. I read you five by. Over.

COLUMBIA: Yes, I heard the whole thing.

HOUSTON: Well, it's a good show.

COLUMBIA: Fantastic.

TRANQUILITY BASE: I'll second that.

APOLLO CONTROL: The next major stay-no stay will be for the T2 event. That is at 21 minutes 26 seconds after initiation of power descent.

COLUMBIA: Up telemetry command reset to re-

Neil A. Armstrong moves away from the leg of the landing craft after taking the first step on the surface of the moon

A Powdery Surface Is Closely Explored

By JOHN NOBLE WILFORD
Special to The New York Times

HOUSTON, Monday, July 21—Men have landed and walked on the moon.

Two Americans, astronauts of Apollo 11, steered their fragile four-legged lunar module safely and smoothly to the historic landing yesterday at 4:17:40 P.M., Eastern daylight time.

Neil A. Armstrong, the 38-year-old civilian commander, radioed to earth and the mission control room here:

"Houston, Tranquility Base here. The Eagle has landed."

The first men to reach the moon—Mr. Armstrong and his co-pilot, Col. Edwin E. Aldrin Jr. of the Air Force—brought their ship to rest on a level, rock-strewn plain near the southwestern shore of the arid Sea of Tranquility.

About six and a half hours later, Mr. Armstrong opened the landing craft's hatch, stepped slowly down the ladder and declared as he planted the first human footprint on the lunar crust:

"That's one small step for man, one giant leap for mankind."

His first step on the moon came at 10:56:20 P.M., as a television camera outside the craft transmitted his every move to an awed and excited audience of hundreds of millions of people on earth.

Tentative Steps Test Soil

"All the News That's Fit to Print"

The New York Times

LATE CITY EDITION

Weather: Partly cloudy today; cool tonight. Fair, pleasant tomorrow. Temp. range: today 65-78; Thursday 64-85. Highest Temp.-Hum. Index yesterday: 75. Details on Page 66.

VOL.CXXIII..No.42,566 | NEW YORK, FRIDAY, AUGUST 9, 1974 | 20c beyond 50-mile radius of New York City, except Long Island. Higher in air delivery cities | 15 CENTS

NIXON RESIGNS

HE URGES A TIME OF 'HEALING'; FORD WILL TAKE OFFICE TODAY

'Sacrifice' Is Praised; Kissinger to Remain

By ANTHONY RIPLEY

Special to The New York Times

WASHINGTON, Aug. 8—Vice President Ford praised President Nixon tonight for "one of the greatest personal sacrifices for the country and one of the finest personal decisions on behalf of all of us as Americans."

Mr. Ford, who will take office as the 38th President at noon tomorrow, vowed to continue Mr. Nixon's foreign policy and announced that Secretary of State Kissinger had agreed to stay on in the new Administration.

"I pledge to you tonight, as I will pledge to you tomorrow and in the future, my best efforts in cooperation, leadership and dedication to what's good for America and good for the world," he said.

The Vice President, who never sought the nation's highest office and disclaimed any intention of seeking it after Mr. Nixon's term, will take the oath of office in a private ceremony at the White House.

Thus will he become the first man to serve as President without being chosen by the American people in an election. Tomorrow night he will address the nation on radio and television. It is expected that he will speak at 6 P.M.

All day today the signs of the historic change were in the air, sensed by the crowds that gathered along Pennsylvania

Text of Mr. Ford's remarks appears on Page 2.

SPECULATION RIFE ON VICE PRESIDENT

Some Ford Associates Say Selecting a Successor Could Take Weeks

The New York Times/William E. Sauro

Vice President Ford meeting with newsmen last night

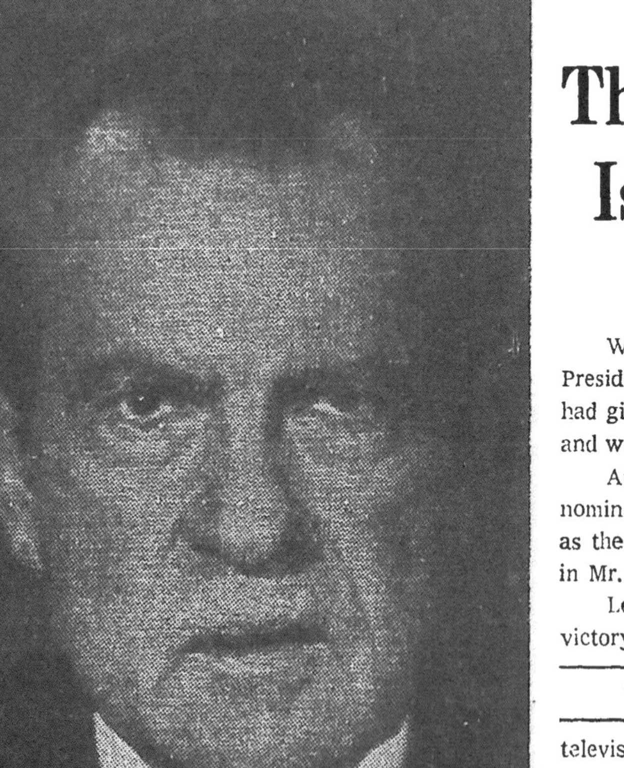

United Press International

President Nixon on TV as he announced his resignation

POLITICAL SCENE SHARPLY ALTERED

Rise and Fall

Appraisal of Nixon Career

JAWORSKI ASSERTS NO DEAL WAS MADE

The 37th President Is First to Quit Post

By JOHN HERBERS

Special to The New York Times

WASHINGTON, Aug. 8—Richard Milhous Nixon, the 37th President of the United States, announced tonight that he had given up his long and arduous fight to remain in office and would resign, effective at noon tomorrow.

At that hour, Gerald Rudolph Ford, whom Mr. Nixon nominated for Vice President last Oct. 12, will be sworn in as the 38th President, to serve out the 895 days remaining in Mr. Nixon's second term.

Less that two years after his landslide re-election victory, Mr. Nixon, in a conciliatory address on national television, said that he was leaving not with a sense of bitterness but with a hope that his departure would start a "process of healing that is so desperately needed in America."

Text of the address will be found on Page 2.

He spoke of regret for any "injuries" done "in the course of the events that led to this decision." He acknowledged that some of his judgments had been wrong.

The 61-year-old Mr. Nixon, appearing calm and resigned to his fate as a victim of the Watergate scandal, became the first President in the history of the Republic to resign from office. Only 10 months earlier Spiro Agnew resigned the Vice-Presidency.

HOUSTON: Copy. Out.

APOLLO CONTROL: We have an unofficial time for that touchdown of 102 hours, 45 minutes, 42 seconds and we will update that.

HOUSTON: Eagle, you loaded R2 wrong. We want 10254.

TRANQUILITY BASE: Roger. Do you want the horizontal 55 15.2?

HOUSTON: That's affirmative.

APOLLO CONTROL: We're now less than four minutes from our next stay-no stay. It will be for one complete revolution of the command module.

One of the first things that Armstrong and Aldrin will do after getting their next stay-no stay will be to remove their helmets and gloves.

HOUSTON: Eagle, you are stay for T2. Over.

Continued on Page 4, Col. 1

VOYAGE TO THE MOON

By ARCHIBALD MACLEISH

PRESENCE among us,

wanderer in our skies,

dazzle of silver in our leaves and on our
waters silver,

O
silver evasion in our farthest thought—
"the visiting moon" . . . "the glimpses of the moon" . . .

and we have touched you!

From the first of time,
before the first of time, before the
first men tasted time, we thought of you.
You were a wonder to us, unattainable,
a longing past the reach of longing,
a light beyond our light, our lives—perhaps
a meaning to us . . .

Now
our hands have touched you in your depth of night.

Three days and three nights we journeyed,
steered by farthest stars, climbed outward,
crossed the invisible tide-rip where the floating dust
falls one way or the other in the void between,
followed that other down, encountered
cold, faced death—unfathomable emptiness . . .

Then, the fourth day evening, we descended,
made fast, set foot at dawn upon your beaches,
sifted between our fingers your cold sand.

We stand here in the dusk, the cold, the silence . . .

and here, as at the first of time, we lift our heads.
Over us, more beautiful than the moon, a
moon, a wonder to us, unattainable,
a longing past the reach of longing,
a light beyond our light, our lives—perhaps
a meaning to us . . .

O, a meaning!

over us on these silent beaches the bright
earth,
presence among us

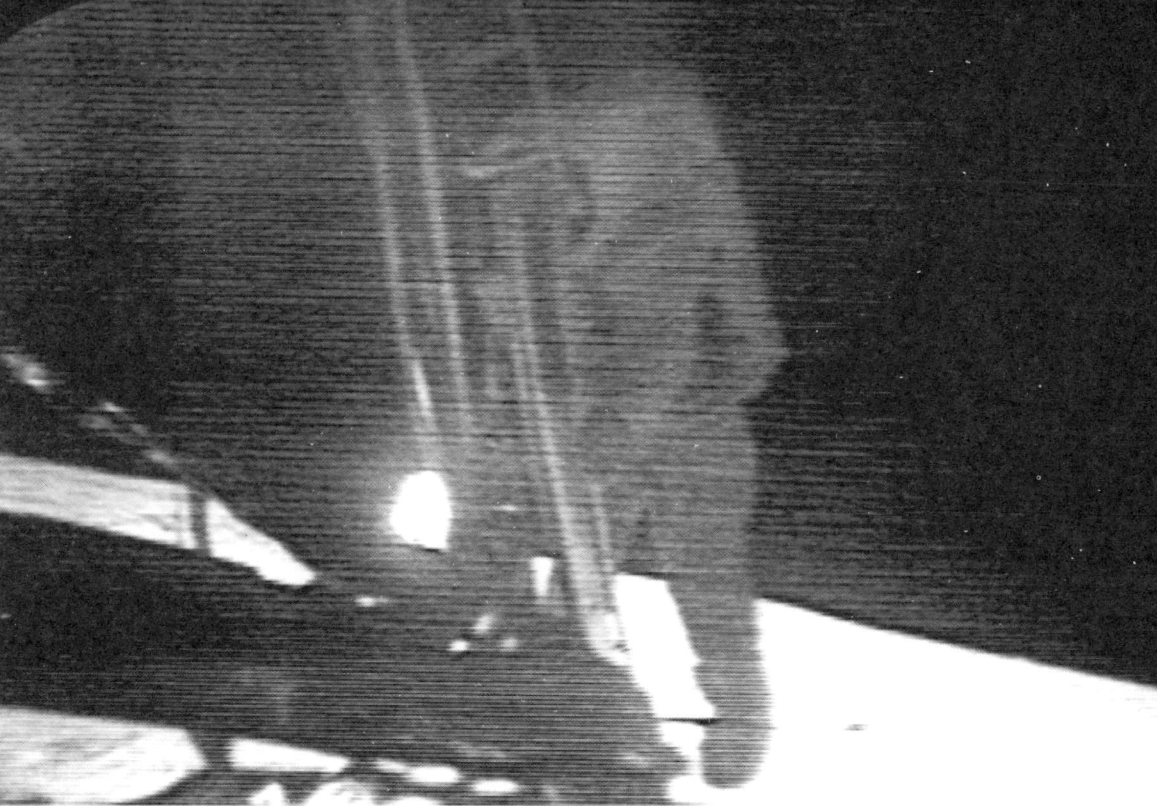

The New York Times from C.B.S. News

Col. Edwin E. Aldrin Jr. climbing down the ladder. The television camera was attached to a side of the lunar module.

Associated Press

Mr. Armstrong, right, and Colonel Aldrin raise the U.S. flag. A metal rod at right angles to the mast keeps flag unfurled.

the lunar soil's firmness and of his ability to move about easily in his bulky white spacesuit and backpacks and under the influence of lunar gravity, which is one-sixth that of the earth.

"The surface is fine and powdery," the astronaut reported. "I can pick it up loosely with my toe. It does adhere in fine layers like powdered charcoal to the sole and sides of my boots. I only go in a small fraction of an inch, maybe an eighth of an inch. But I can see the footprints of my boots in the treads in the fine sandy particles.

After 19 minutes of Mr. Armstrong's testing, Colonel Aldrin joined him outside the craft.

The two men got busy setting up another television camera out from the lunar module, planting an American flag into the ground, scooping up soil and rock samples, deploying scientific experiments and hopping and loping about in a demonstration of their lunar agility.

They found walking and working on the moon less taxing than had been forecast. Mr. Armstrong once reported he was "very comfortable."

And people back on earth found the black-and-white television pictures of the bug-shaped lunar module and the men tramping about it so sharp and clear as to seem unreal, more like a toy and toy-like figures than human beings on the most daring and far-reaching expedition thus far undertaken.

Nixon Telephones Congratulations

During one break in the astronauts' work, President Nixon congratulated them from the White House in what, he said, "certainly has to be the most historic telephone call ever made."

"Because of what you have done," the President told the astronauts, "the heavens have become a part of man's world. And as you talk to us from the Sea of Tranquility it requires us to redouble our efforts to bring peace and tranquility to earth.

"For one priceless moment in the whole history of man all the people on this earth are truly one—one in their pride in what you have done and one in our prayers that you will return safely to earth."

Mr. Armstrong replied:

"Thank you Mr. President. It's a great honor and privilege for us to be here representing not only the United States but men of peace of all nations, men with interests and a curiosity and men with a vision for the future."

Mr. Armstrong and Colonel Aldrin returned to their landing craft and closed the hatch at 1:12 A.M., 2 hours 21 minutes after opening the hatch on the moon. While the third member of the crew, Lieut. Col. Michael Collins of the Air Force, kept his orbital vigil overhead in the command ship, the two moon explorers settled down to sleep.

Outside their vehicle the astronauts had found a bleak

Continued on Pages 2, Col. 1

Today's 4-Part Issue of The Times

This morning's issue of The New York Times is divided into four parts. The first part is devoted to news of Apollo 11, and includes Editorials and letters to the Editor (Page 16). Poems on the landing on the moon appear on Page 17.

General news begins on the first page of the second part. The News Summary and Index is on the first page of the third part, which includes sports news, obituaries (Page 51) and transportation news and weather reports (Pages 50 and 52).

Financial and business news begins on the first page of the fourth part.

Following is the News Index for today's issue:

By CHRISTOPHER LYDON

Special to The New York Times

WASHINGTON, Aug. 8 — Potentially the most revealing and most important decision of Gerald R. Ford's Presidential debut — his choice of a successor in the Vice Presidency — was a much-discussed mystery here today.

Close friends of Mr. Ford continued to feed speculation about more than a dozen possible candidates. But none of the friends claimed to have discussed the Vice-Presidential question with Mr. Ford or to be speaking for him on it. A number of Ford associates thought he might hold off the decision for days or even weeks.

"Eveybody's on tenterhooks up here," a Senator remarked this afternoon in a telephone interview from the Republican cloakroom, "but I think they're wasting their time. It's going to be a week or two. So far I'd say he's a loner on this issue."

Former Defense Secretary Melvin R. Laird, a Ford counselor in the House for more than a decade, was being quoted again today as saying he believes that Nelson A. Rocke-

Continued on Page 4, Column 1

Avenue near the White House. Applause rang out from the crowds when Mr. Ford appeared briefly.

After watching Mr. Nixon on television tonight with his family, the Vice President stepped outside into a slight drizzle at his suburban split-level home in nearby Alexandria, Va., to face television cameras and photographers assembled in the street and about 100 cheering neighbors.

Speaks Outside Home

Speaking without notes or a prepared text, Mr. Ford pledged to continue the Nixon foreign policy and called the Secretary of State "a very great man" whom he has known for many years.

On domestic policy, he said that he had been "very fortunate in my lifetime" to have adversaries in Congress but said that he did not think he had "a single enemy" there.

President Nixon had cited in his resignation address his lack of support in Congress as one of the major reasons for his resignation.

Mr. Ford said, "The net result is that I think tomorrow I can start out working with Democrats and with Republi-

Continued on Page 4, Column 3

The Other Major News

Wholesale Prices Up

A new upward surge of farm prices joined a big jump in industrial prices to produce the year's largest monthly increase in the wholesale price index. The rise for July was 3.7 per cent, seasonally adjusted, and 3.9 per cent before adjustment. Page 45.

Election Bill Voted

The House approved by a vote of 355 to 48 a broad campaign-finance reform bill. The measure would set limits on political contributions, restrict candidate spending and provide subsidies for Presidential primaries, conventions and elections. The bill now goes to a House-Senate conference committee. Page 36.

Cyprus Talks Open

The foreign ministers of Greece, Turkey and Britain met in Geneva to try to work out an effective cease-fire on Cyprus and to tackle the political problems behind the fighting there. Page 16.

On Cyprus, acting President Glafkos Clerides named a moderate Cabinet stripped of any militant proponents of union with Greece.

Mr. Clerides, who will occupy the key posts of Foreign Affairs and Interior, left for Athens on his way to Geneva for the talks on a political settlement. Page 16.

10 Police Accused

Ten New York City police sergeants were arrested for allegedly participating in a "club" that collected more than $250,000 over a decade from legitimate businesses and illegal rackets operations in Queens. Page 68.

Meskill Named Judge

Gov. Thomas J. Meskill of Connecticut was nominated by President Nixon to a seat on the Federal bench. Mr. Meskill, a Republican, stunned the state Republican party earlier this year by declining to run for a second term amid reports that he had been offered a judgeship. Page 38.

SHARPLY ALTERED

G.O.P. Prospects Improved, Ford in Good Spot for '76 and Watergate Fades

By R. W. APPLE Jr.

Special to The New York Times

WASHINGTON, Aug. 8—President Nixon's resignation drastically altered the American political landscape.

It improved Republican prospects for the Congressional elections in November, thrust Vice President Ford into the favorite's role for the 1976 Presidential election, ended the Watergate agony that has served to bind together the heterogeneous Democratic party and removed from the political stage the man who was the dominant Republican for the last 15 years.

In a larger sense, it seemed to presage an era of more open government, of more cooperation and less antagonism between Capitol Hill and the White House and of decline of the White House staff as an independent power center.

Lives Are Altered

A kind of "honeymoon" between the executive and legislative branches was widely predicted by Congressional leaders today. Congressmen who knew Mr. Ford for years as a Capitol Hill colleague said that they expected to work closely with him.

At least in the beginning, pragmatic conservatism is expected to remain the dominant ideological tone in the executive branch.

How that will be translated into policies, and how those policies will shape the political dialogue, will not be clear for weeks. But experts in the two fields forecast an essentially unchanged foreign policy and a similar, but more carefully and consistently applied, economic policy.

By his decision, Mr. Nixon

Continued on Page 6, Column 4

Appraisal of Nixon Career

By ROBERT B. SEMPLE Jr.

The central question is how a man who won so much could have lost so much. How could a public figure who so well perceived the instincts of the majority of his countrymen have misused the powers and duties those same countrymen so eagerly ceded him?

The historians will be kept busy on these questions, but for those who spent their time observing Mr. Nixon for the last six years the answer may well be found in a phrase he often applied to himself. "At bottom," he used to say, "I am a political man."

By his own description, he was a man of action rather than contemplation, a tactician rather than a theologian, a student of technique who seemed always impatient with substance, a figure whose exceptional antennae seemed to dwarf and even hide what lay at the core.

To his enemies, he was both manipulative and synthetic; to his friends, a pragmatist unencumbered by inflexible principles; to those who watched him, a man who learned to run before he had learned to walk and who, on reaching his destination, was not always certain what to do when he got there—except, perhaps, to keep going.

That image has only been reinforced and deepened by the transcripts of three conversations with H. R. Haldeman on June 23, 1972, six days after the Watergate break-in, which were released on Aug. 5, and the edited transcripts of White House conversations published April 30. Whatever history's judgment of those tapes, this much was clear: Faced with mounting evidence of deception and wrongdoing in his own official family, he sought not to confront the issue but to manipulate it until he himself became part of the deception.

Mr. Nixon used the words "I am a political man" proudly, as if to challenge the moralists, but in the end they became his epitaph—a possible explanation for both his success and failure.

For if the words implied the presence of a talent for finding opportunities for political prof-

Continued on Page 11, Column 1

A Tiny G.O.P. Bastion Feels Loss and Relief

By PRANAY GUPTE

Special to The New York Times

SHELTER ISLAND, L.I., Aug. 8—Six years after he put it on his car, Evans K. Griffing sadly stripped off his bold, red-lettered bumper sticker today — the one that said "NIXON."

Mr. Griffing felt a sense of loss. So did hundreds of people in this conservative community 100 miles east of New York City.

In 1968 and 1972, Suffolk County gave Richard M. Nixon the largest single election plurality of any county in the United States. Today all that had changed on Shelter Island.

As the hour of the President's resignation announcement approached, many islanders expressed both a feeling of hurt at having been "betrayed" by Mr. Nixon and relief that he was leaving office.

"We tried to stay by him till the very end," said Thomas L. Jernick, the Town Supervisor. "But when he disclosed on Monday that he had covered up his role in Watergate, we couldn't support him any more. He lied to us, and for a President of the United States to lie is inexcusable."

"We really believed in Mr. Nixon" was a phrase used again and again by dozens of islanders today.

At the same time they spoke hopefully of the Ford Administration and of moving urgently to tasks long neglected—ending the nation's political turmoil and easing its economic distress.

Shelter Island has 1,800 year-round residents, most of whom are registered Republicans.

Only last June interviews with islanders indicated that whatever else Watergate had done, it apparently had not diluted Shelter Island's faith in Mr. Nixon. People said at the time that they felt the President was being vilified by the media

Continued on Page 7, Column 6

NO DEAL WAS MADE

Says Nixon Did Not Ask for and Was Not Given a Way to Avoid Prosecution

By RICHARD D. LYONS

Special to The New York Times

WASHINGTON, Aug. 8—Leon Jaworski, the special Watergate prosecutor, said tonight after President Nixon's resignation speech that no deals had been either made or offered that would have given Mr. Nixon immunity from prosecution on any charges that might stem from the Watergate scandal.

"There has been no agreement or understanding of any sort between the President or his representatives and the special prosecutor relating in any way to the President's resignation," Mr. Jaworski said in a statement issued by his office.

Mr. Jaworski's words, plus the fact that the President made no mention of the immunity issue in his address to the nation, left open the possibility, at least for the moment, that Mr. Nixon might be charged and stand trial.

No Immunity Sought

Mr. Nixon did not ask for any immunity assurances from Mr. Jaworski before the resignation speech, the prosecutor said, adding that none had been offered.

As Mr. Jaworski put it, "The special prosecutor's office was not asked for any such agreement or understanding and offered none."

"Although I was informed of the President's decision this afternoon, my office did not participate in any way in the President's decision to resign," the statement concluded.

Mr. Jaworski met earlier today with Gen. Alexander M. Haig Jr., the White House chief of staff, but that meeting was said to have been only for the purpose of informing the special prosecutor of what the President would say later in the evening.

The meeting did not take place in the White House, presumably because Mr. Jaworski would have been recognized there, and his visit would have excited speculation.

Earlier today, there were moves in both houses of Congress to grant Mr. Nixon immunity from prosecution, but

Continued on Page 2, Column 4

Mr. Nixon, speaking from the Oval Office, where his successor will be sworn in tomorrow, may well have delivered his most effective speech since the Watergate scandals began to swamp his Administration in early 1973.

In tone and content, the 15-minute address was in sharp contrast to his frequently combative language of the past, especially his first "farewell" appearance—that of 1962, when he announced he was retiring from politics after losing the California governorship race and declared that the news media would not have "Nixon to kick around" anymore.

Yet he spoke tonight of how painful it was for him to give up the office.

"I would have preferred to carry through to the finish whatever the personal agony it would have involved, and my family unanimously urged me to do so," he said.

Puts 'Interests of America First'

"I have never been a quitter," he said. "To leave office before my term is completed is opposed to every instinct in my body." But he said that he had decided to put "the interests of America first."

Conceding that he did not have the votes in Congress to escape impeachment in the House and conviction in the Senate, Mr. Nixon said, "To continue to fight through the months ahead for my personal vindication would almost totally absorb the time and attention of the President and the Congress in a period when our entire focus should be on the great issues of peace abroad and prosperity without inflation at home."

"Therefore," he continued, "I shall resign the Presidency effective at noon tomorrow. Vice President Ford will be

Continued on Page 3, Column 1

Only Nixon Is Serene At Sad White House

By PHILIP SHABECOFF

Special to The New York Times

WASHINGTON, Aug. 8—On his 2,027th and penultimate day as President of the United States, with his staff and family unable to conceal their anguish, Richard M. Nixon went composedly through the schedule of a busy President.

He met with his Vice President and the bipartisan leadership of Congress. He appointed Federal judges, accepted resignations from executive agencies and signed several laws.

He vetoed as inflationary an appropriation bill for the Department of Agriculture and the Environmental Protection Agency.

He also announced, over national television, that tomorrow he would resign his high office.

Mr. Nixon did not loosen his self control even when he talked of his "regret" and his "sadness" at leaving the Presidency. His delivery, with its familiar half-smiles, did not reflect the momentous message he had for his audience: that at noon tomorrow he would become the first healthy, living American President to leave office before his term expired.

At 12:30 this afternoon, the White House press secretary, Ronald L. Ziegler, announced that the President would address the nation at 9 P.M.

Mr. Ziegler did not say what the speech would be about. He did not have to. He choked on his words several times and was struggling visibly to keep himself under control as he left the rostrum of the packed but hushed briefing room at the White House.

The young women who work in the press office went through the motions of their jobs while tears streamed down their faces.

But the President himself, according to his appointments

Continued on Page 3, Column 8

"All the News That's Fit to Print"

The New York Times

LATE CITY EDITION

Weather: Rain today; showers likely tonight. Fair and milder tomorrow. Temp. range: today 68-74; Thursday 66-76. Temp.-Hum. Index yesterday 71. Full U.S. report on Page 70.

VOL. CXXI . No. 41,796 NEW YORK, FRIDAY, JUNE 30, 1972 15 CENTS

SUPREME COURT, 5-4, BARS DEATH PENALTY AS IT IS IMPOSED UNDER PRESENT STATUTES

Party Panel Strips McGovern of 151 California Delegates

SENATOR SET BACK

He Deplores Move by Coalition of Rivals—State Law Ignored

By WARREN WEAVER Jr.

Special to The New York Times

WASHINGTON, June 29—The Democratic National Convention's Credentials Committee stripped Senator George McGovern today of 151 delegates he thought he had won in the California primary, disregarding state law in a display of political power.

Accomplished by a coalition of his rivals for the Presidential nomination, the move abruptly slowed the momentum of the South Dakotan's campaign and heavily clouded his prospects for tying up the nomination before the convention meets July 10.

The committee ended nearly four hours of debate by voting, 72 to 66, to divide the 271-member California delegation among all the Presidential candidates who competed in the June 6 primary, instead of following the California statute, which allots all the delegates to whoever gets the most votes.

Move Called 'Outrageous'

In an unusually bitter news conference at the Capitol, Senator McGovern called the committee decision "an incredible, cynical, rotten political steal" and "an outrageous way to treat the American people."

Informed at a National Press Club luncheon about the committee action, Senator Hubert H. Humphrey said that his chances for the nomination had been "markedly improved."

"I'm not going to say any more—I've got the votes," the Minnesotan said.

Authoritative sources said, meanwhile, that Senator McGovern, if he ultimately won the nomination, viewed Senator Edward M. Kennedy of Massachusetts as his first choice for a running mate. [Details on Page 20.]

Appealed Is Planned

The Credentials Committee decision will be appealed to the convention when it opens in Miami Beach, but it may prove difficult for the McGovern forces to reverse because the 151 delegates at issue—or perhaps the entire 271 from California—will not be able to vote on their own case.

This dramatic reversal for Senator McGovern was achieved by a tight, well-disciplined coalition of committee members who were either uncommitted or favored Senator Humphrey, Senator Edmund S. Muskie of Maine, Senator Henry M. Jackson of Washington or Gov. George C. Wallace of Alabama.

The development provoked angry protests from Mr. McGovern's supporters, who main-

Continued on Page 20, Column 3

Press Loses Plea to Keep Data From Grand Juries

Special to The New York Times

WASHINGTON, June 29—The Supreme Court held 5 to 4 today that journalists have no First Amendment right to refuse to tell grand juries the names of confidential sources and information given to them in confidence.

The decision overturned a lower Federal court ruling on behalf of Earl Caldwell, a reporter for The New York Times

Excerpts from Supreme Court action are on Page 15.

in San Francisco, who had refused to enter a Federal grand jury room to be questioned on information given him by the Black Panther party.

In two related cases, the Court held that Paul M. Branzburg, an investigative reporter for The Louisville Courier-Journal at the time his case arose, and Paul Pappas, a television newsman in New Bedford, Mass., must tell state grand juries names and other information given them in confidence or face imprisonment for contempt.

The sweeping decision by Justice Byron R. White, supported by President Nixon's four appointees, contained a firm rejection of the theory that the First Amendment shields newsmen under certain circumstances from having to testify when the result would be to cut off news sources and deprive the public of news.

This theory has never been considered before today by the Supreme Court. But in recent years, as a wave of subpoenas issued from grand juries for newsmen's notes, radio stations' tapes and television companies' films, some lower courts began to construe the First Amendment as giving journalists some protection against being compelled to disclose confidences.

The courts usually reasoned that if forcing a newsman to testify would cut off future information, he should be excused unless the Government could show a compelling need for his testimony.

"We cannot accept the argu-

Continued on Page 15, Column 4

Gravel Is Denied Immunity In Case of Pentagon Papers

By ROBERT M. SMITH

Special to The New York Times

WASHINGTON, June 29—The Supreme Court ruled today, by a 5-to-4 vote, that Congressional immunity did not prevent a grand jury from asking Senator Mike Gravel or his aides certain questions about his version of the Pentagon papers—including the question where had he obtained the papers.

In a second case that turned on the same constitutional issue, the Court held, 6 to 3, that legislative privilege did not shield Daniel B. Brewster, a former Democratic Senator from Maryland, from prosecution on bribery charges.

Both decisions were handed down, with several others, on the last day of the Court's current term. The Gravel decision was written by Justice Byron R. White, who was joined by the four men President Nixon named to the Court—Chief Justice Warren E. Burger and Associate Justices Harry A. Blackmun, Lewis F. Powell Jr. and William H. Rehnquist.

Senator Gravel, Democrat of Alaska, reacted by issuing a

Continued on Page 16, Column 4

FUND MISUSE LAID TO 4 L.I. UNIONISTS

U.S. Says They Used Money in Labor-Industry Pool to Pay Ball Team's Debt

By DAVID K. SHIPLER

Four officials of a Long Island construction union were charged yesterday with using employer funds to pay off a union debt of $11,245.

The charges, filed by the Federal Organized Crime Strike Force in Brooklyn, came just hours after city officials discharged a veteran inspector in the Buildings Department who was accused of taking a $100 bribe from the owner of a Park Avenue cooperative apartment.

The two cases, while unrelated, continued to focus attention on the widespread corruption in the construction industry described early in the week by a New York Times report. According to the articles in The Times, based on a six-week investigation, builders pay at least $25-million a year here in bribes to inspectors, policemen, union

Continued on Page 28, Column 1

NIXON DISCLOSES VIETNAM PARLEY RESUMES JULY 13

He Says U.S. Is Returning on Assumption Hanoi Will Negotiate Constructively

By ROBERT B. SEMPLE Jr.

Special to The New York Times

WASHINGTON, June 29 — President Nixon disclosed tonight that the United States and North Vietnam would resume the Paris peace talks on the Vietnam war on July 13.

In a nationally televised news conference—his first in more

Transcript of Nixon news conference is on Page 2.

than a year—Mr. Nixon said the United States was returning to the negotiating table "on the assumption that the North Vietnamese are prepared to negotiate in a constructive and serious way."

He said that if both sides were prepared to engage in serious talks the war could be ended by next year. He also left open the opposite possibility—that the North Vietnamese might not proceed "on that basis," in which case he vowed to continue American bombing and other forms of military pressure. [Question 1, Page 2.]

Talks 'Without Conditions'

Though Mr. Nixon seemed pleased to anounce the resumption of the talks, which were suspended by the United States on May 4, he gave no hint in his remarks that his intense diplomacy in Moscow and Peking in recent weeks had produced assurances that Hanoi was now prepared to move closer to the American position. The most he could or would say was that both sides had agreed to resume negotiating "without conditions."

The President also used the news conference to offer an unusually strong defense of his bombing policy and to give that policy an expanded rationale. In previous statements he has described the bombing as an essentially military tactic designed to protect the shrinking American ground forces in Vietnam and to compensate for the North Vietnamese attacks launched at the end of March.

Tonight he emphasized that

Continued on Page 3, Column 5

U.S. Copters Ferry 1,000 To Quangtri Battleground

By MALCOLM W. BROWNE

Special to The New York Times

SAIGON, South Vietnam, Friday, June 30—About 1,000 South Vietnamese marines were flown by United States helicopters yesterday into an area between the city of Quangtri and the South China Sea to join in the drive to retake the Communist-held province.

With the South Vietnamese offensive in the northernmost part of the country broadened, heavy fighting was reported from the area today. The thrust was begun Wednesday by a task force of more than 10,000 South Vietnamese marines and paratroopers.

During the night, South Vietnamese troops reported that they killed 225 enemy soldiers in various enemy sectors. Two enemy tanks were reported destroyed by artillery fire near Hailang, in the southern part of Quangtri province, where the bulk of the South Vietnamese tank force was fighting.

The helicopter-borne assault yesterday brought two battalions of South Vietnamese marines into two landing zones in a region east of the city of Quangtri. That city was abandoned to Communist forces on May 1 and the present drive is intended to oust the North Vietnamese from the whole province within three months.

The main South Vietnamese force, which began a northward drive Wednesday from positions along the Mychanh river line, northwest of the city of Hue, consists of elements of South Vietnamese marine and airborne divisions.

A United States Navy spokesman said that American marine helicopters took four hours to complete the landings. While a South Vietnamese spokesman said there had been no enemy opposition, another American spokesman said enemy ground fire had been encountered in both of the landing zones east of the city.

After heavy naval bombard-

Continued on Page 3, Column 4

Senate Votes Antipoverty Bill, Including Plan for Legal Aid

By The Associated Press

WASHINGTON, June 29—The Senate passed a $9.6-billion antipoverty bill today that included a provision to put the Legal Services program for the poor under an independent corporation.

The bill, passed by a vote of 74 to 16 after a week of debate, authorizes funds for two additional years for programs designed to help 26 million Americans officially defined as poor.

The Senate vote sent the legislation back to the House, which passed a somewhat different version last February.

The conference to try to settle the differences between the two measures will be held after Congress returns July 17 from its recess for the Democratic National Convention.

The bill authorizes sums well beyond President Nixon's recommendations for many programs of the Office of Economic Opportunity, the antipoverty agency. And the bill does not give the President the completely free hand he sought in handling or transferring the programs.

In addition, Administration officials indicated that they still found unacceptable the form of the Legal Services Corporation set out in the bill.

For these reasons, there is reason to believe that Mr. Nixon

Continued on Page 10, Column 4

Associated Press

SPARED: Elmer Branch, 19, sentenced to die for nonfatal assault, in Huntsville, Tex., jail. He was one of condemned men whose sentences were upset by Supreme Court.

PRESIDENT WIDENS FOOD PRICE CURBS

Applies Controls to Produce After It Leaves the Farm —Seafood Also Covered

Special to The New York Times

WASHINGTON, June 29—President Nixon extended controls today to the retail and wholesale prices of such unprocessed food products as eggs, fresh vegetables, fresh fruits and all raw seafood products.

But he stopped short of the far more drastic step of placing direct controls on the prices farmers receive for these products.

The action was the President's second effort this week to impose some restraint on rising food prices, which could be a crucial issue next fall in the Presidential campaign. His reluctance to act directly on farm prices, however, appeared to reflect his concern about antagonizing the farm vote in an election year, as well as fears among some officials that direct controls might be difficult to enforce and might result in shortages.

Officials conceded at a White House briefing that the action might have little immediate effect on prices. But they expressed hope that it would exert pressure on mark-ups and profit margins at each stage of the food distribution chain that, in time, could stem the

Continued on Page 10, Column 2

$502,000 Hijacking Laid to Jobless Man

By JERRY M. FLINT

Special to The New York Times

DETROIT, June 29—Martin Joseph McNally, 28 years old, was arrested last night in front of his home in Wyandotte, Mich., outside Detroit, by agents of the Federal Bureau of Investigation and charged with air piracy in connection with an airline hijacking in the Midwest last week in which $502,000 ransom was paid. He was held today in $100,000 bond.

The hijacker bailed out over Peru, Ind., but dropped the money, which was later recovered.

Government attorneys said Mr. McNally, an unemployed

Continued on Page 9, Column 2

Nixon Backs Death Penalty For Kidnapping, Hijacking

By WILLIAM ROBBINS

Special to The New York Times

WASHINGTON, June 29—President Nixon said tonight he hoped that the Supreme Court's decision restricting the death penalty "does not go so far as to rule out capital punishment for kidnapping and hijacking."

Asked about the Court's 5-to-4 decision, issued today, Mr. Nixon said that "any punishment is cruel and inhuman which takes the life of man or woman." He added that the death penalty had actually saved lives by deterring such major crimes as kidnapping. [Question 15, Page 2.]

The President acknowledged, however, that he had not had time to study all nine opinions. He said that he had read only the opinion of Chief Justice Warren E. Burger, which was a dissent from the majority ruling.

The words of the Chief Justice as well as those of another dissenter, Justice Powell, clearly bar capital punishment under both Federal and state laws as presently written.

"Not only does it [the ruling] invalidate hundreds of state and Federal laws," Justice Powell wrote in his dissenting opinion, "it deprives those jurisdictions of the power to legislate with respect to capital punishment in the future, except in a matter consistent with the cloudily outlined views of those Justices who do not purport to undertake total abolition."

And Chief Justice Burger himself said: "It is clear that if state legislatures and the Congress wish to maintain the availability of capital punishment, significant statutory changes will have to be made."

On other domestic questions, the President did the following:

¶He declined to say whether Vice President Agnew would be his choice as a running-mate in the next election.

¶He voiced support for legislation specifically restricting the possession of handguns.

¶He said former Secretary of

Continued on Page 14, Column 5

Parole in Capital Offenses Less Likely, Officials Say

By MARTIN ARNOLD

Governors and high state officials said yesterday that the Supreme Court's ruling that capital punishment was unconstitutional could profoundly change the structure of criminal penalties in the country.

Officials in many areas said it might become much more difficult, if not impossible, to get parole in cases that were until yesterday capital offenses. Thus, when a person is sentenced to life in prison, it may mean just that, they said.

Gov. Preston Smith of Texas said that the state legislature would be called upon to pass mandatory life prison sentences for certain crimes, barring any parole.

Gov. Jimmy Carter of Georgia said:

"This decision clears the way for us to re-examine all our laws in Georgia. I still don't think seven years is long enough for a man to serve in prison who has committed premeditated murder and is given a life sentence."

Gov. Ronald Reagan of California said he believed that the ruling would allow his state to reinstate the death penalty in certain cases — "cold-blooded, premeditated, planned murder" —if the voters approved a death penalty referendum that will be on the ballot in November.

Brendan Ryan, St. Louis Circuit Attorney, said: "We will have to re-examine our statutes and perhaps make a life sentence really mean life. Perhaps we should now redefine our homicide laws so as to make some eligible for parole after a given time, but others only parolable through executive clemency, if at all."

Prof. Yale Kamisar of the University of Michigan Law School, considered one of the nation's leading constitutional authorities, expressed surprise and delight with the ruling, but was fearful that there would be a reaction against it.

"There will be increased attention given life sentencing,"

Continued on Page 15, Column 1

COURT SPARES 600

4 Justices Named by Nixon All Dissent in Historic Decision

By FRED P. GRAHAM

Special to The New York Times

WASHINGTON, June 29—The Supreme Court ruled today that capital punishment, as now administered in the United States, is unconstitutional "cruel and unusual" punishment.

The historic decision, came on a vote of 5 to 4.

Although the five Justices in the majority issued separate opinions and did not agree on

Excerpts from Court decision on death penalty, Page 14.

a single reason for their action, the effect of the decision appeared to be to rule out executions under any capital punishment laws now in effect in this country.

The decision will also save from execution 600 condemned men and women now on death rows in the United States, although it did not overturn their convictions. Most will be held in prison for the rest of their lives, but under some states' procedures some of the prisoners may eventually gain their freedom.

Eighth Amendment Cited

The decision pitted the five holdovers of the more liberal Warren Court against the four appointees of President Nixon, who dissented. The ruling came as the Supreme Court handed down its final decisions of the year and recessed until Oct. 2.

Three Justices in the majority, William O. Douglas, William J. Brennan Jr. and Thurgood Marshall, concluded that executions in modern-day America necessarily violate the Eighth Amendment's prohibition against "cruel and unusual punishments."

The other two in the majority, the two "swing men" of the Court, Justices Potter Stewart and Byron R. White, reasoned that the present legal system operates in a cruel and unusual way, because it gives judges and juries the discretion to decree life or death and they impose it erratically.

As Justice Stewart put it, the death penalty is "so wantonly and so freakishly imposed" that those who are sentenced to death receive excessively harsh treatment.

View of Chief Justice

"These death sentences are cruel and unusual in the same way that being struck by lightning is cruel and unusual," he said.

As the dissenters pointed out, this alignment means that no death sentence can pass muster before the present Supreme Court unless it satisfies the objections voiced by Justices Stewart and White.

Chief Justice Warren E. Burger suggested that legislatures could attempt to do this in two ways. One is to state in statute books in detail the conditions under which a judge or jury can impose the death penalty—such as rape accompanied by a vicious assault, or a convict's murder of a prison guard.

The second would be to revert to the practice of more than a century ago, and impose mandatory death sentences for

Continued on Page 14, Column 4

NEWS INDEX

"All the News That's Fit to Print"

The New York Times

LATE CITY EDITION

Weather: Sunny and milder today; fair and mild tonight, tomorrow. Temp. range: today 58-77; Tuesday 57-74. Temp.-Hum. Index yesterday 67. Full U.S. report on Page 90.

VOL. CXXI ... No. 41,864 NEW YORK, WEDNESDAY, SEPTEMBER 6, 1972 15 CENTS

9 ISRAELIS ON OLYMPIC TEAM KILLED WITH 4 ARAB CAPTORS AS POLICE FIGHT BAND THAT DISRUPTED MUNICH GAMES

MRS. MEIR SPEAKS

A Hushed Parliament Hears Her Assail 'Lunatic Acts'

By TERENCE SMITH
Special to The New York Times

JERUSALEM, Sept. 5—Her voice heavy and trembling with emotion, Premier Golda Meir today denounced "these lunatic acts of terrorism, abduction and blackmail, which tear asunder the web of international life."

Speaking to a hushed and somber parliament before the fate of the Israeli hostages held captive in Munich was known, she said, "It is inconceivable that the Olympic events should continue as long as our citizens are under the threat of being murdered in the Olympic Village."

She called on all the nations participating in the Olympics to do "whatever is necessary" to rescue the nine Israelis taken hostage by Arab guerrillas in an early-morning attack in which two other Israelis were killed.

[Official sources in Jerusalem said early Wednesday that the Cabinet would meet later in the morning and that there would be no statement on the deaths of the hostages until then.]

Cabinet Still Firm

Although she was not explicit, Mrs. Meir left the impression that Israel would continue to refuse the guerrillas' demands for the release of 200 Palestinian commandos held in this country. Cabinet sources said the Government remained committed to its hard-line policy of neither dealing with nor making concessions to the guerrillas.

Most Israelis seemed stunned by the news of the bizarre attack on the Israeli athletes, which was first reported here on a radio broadcast at 9 A.M. (3 A.M. Tuesday, New York time). Although Israeli citizens traveling abroad have been attacked by Palestinian guerrillas before, the Olympics seemed to many an unlikely setting.

"The games were going so well," one Jerusalem news dealer said, "and now this."

In parliament, where the members had gathered in an extraordinary session to confirm the Justice Minister, the attack was the sole topic of conversation.

Cabinet Ministers and members of parliament sat in the building's modern, sun-washed dining room waiting for additional news from Munich. Each hour on the hour, the large room grew silent and the ministers gathered four deep around a radio as the Israeli radio summarized the developments.

The tension was greatest at

Continued on Page 20, Column 2

United Press International

A copter making a test run before picking up Arabs involved in the attack on Israelis. At rear is the Olympic Tower. Sign in German says, "Olympic Village, Gate 6."

West German policemen talking with a spokesman, right, for Arabs who invaded Israeli quarters at Olympic Village

Associated Press

A West German Army ambulance passing through the heavily guarded gate at the military airfield in Fürstenfeldbruck, near Munich, after the commandos and the hostages landed in three helicopters.

A 23-HOUR DRAMA

2 Others Are Slain in Their Quarters in Guerrilla Raid

By DAVID BINDER
Special to The New York Times

MUNICH, West Germany, Wednesday, Sept. 6—Eleven members of Israel's Olympic team and four Arab terrorists were killed yesterday in a 23-hour drama that began with an invasion of the Olympic Village by the Arabs. It ended in a shootout at a military airport some 15 miles away as the Arabs were preparing to fly to Cairo with their Israeli hostages.

The first two Israelis were killed early yesterday morning when Arab commandos, armed with automatic rifles, broke into the quarters of the Israeli team and seized nine others as hostages. The hostages were killed in the airport shootout between the Arabs and German policemen and soldiers.

The bloodshed brought the suspension of the Olympic Games and there was doubt if they would be resumed. Willi Daume, president of the West German Organizing Committee, announced early today that he would ask the International Olympic Committee to meet tomorrow to decide whether they should continue.

Policeman Killed

In addition to the slain Israelis and Arabs, a German policeman was killed and a helicopter pilot was critically wounded. Three Arabs were wounded.

There were some reports that two of the hostages said to have been killed might still be alive. "It is a dim hope," said Dr. Bruno Merk, the Interior Minister of Bavaria, "but I am skeptical on this point."

The bloodbath at the airport that ended at 1 A.M. today, came after long hours of negotiaton between German and Arabs at the Israeli quarters in the Olympic Village where the Arabs demanded the release of 200 Arab commandos imprisoned in Israel.

Finally the West German armed forces supplied three helicopters to transport the Arabs and their Israeli hostages to the airport at Fürstenfeldbruck. From there all were to be flown to Cairo.

A Boeing-707 provided by the Lufthansa German Airlines was waiting.

Two of the terrorists, carrying their automatic rifles, walked about 170 yards from the helicopters to the plane. And then they started back to pick up the other Arabs and the hostages.

Positions Cited

As the Arabs were returning, German sharpshooters reportedly opened fire from the darkness beyond the pools of light at the airport. The Arabs returned fire.

The torment of the entire event was heightened by confusion created in the public mind by contradictory reports from German and Olympic officials after the gunfire erupted at the airport.

Dr. Merk, in a press conference at 3 o'clock this morning said:

"In this situation our task and goal to free the hostages was made more difficult by the lack of agreement from Israel to free prisoners or to get guarantees from the Arabs not to take action against the hos-

Continued on Page 18, Column 1

752 Air-Conditioned Cars Ordered for City Subways

By EDWARD RANZAL

Mayor Lindsay announced yesterday that 752 new air-conditioned subway cars had been ordered for $210.5-million. He said the contract was the largest ever signed in the country for the purchase of passenger railroad cars.

The first group of cars, which will be manufactured by the Pullman - Standard Company, are to be delivered by 1973.

The cars will provide a quieter ride than present equipment, according to Dr. William J. Ronan, chairman of the Metropolitan Transportation Authority.

The new equipment, which will be used on the IND and BMT lines, will enable the authority to phase out more than 1,200 pre-World War II cars, which are smaller than the new ones. A study is being made, Dr. Ronan said, to produce an air-conditioned unit that can be used in cars in the smaller tunnels of the IRT system.

20% of Fleet by '75

Each car will cost more than $273,000. The city will provide one-third of the total funds—the money has been provided in the city's 1972-73 capital budget—and the Federal Urban Mass Transportation Administration will supply the rest.

By 1975 more than 20 per cent of the city's fleet of nearly 7,000 subway cars will consist of new air-conditioned cars.

The first order under the contract will be for 454 cars at a cost of $127.4-million. Some of them will be delivered in

Continued on Page 91, Column 2

Berrigan and a Nun Get Prison Terms In Letter Smuggling

By JOHN KIFNER
Special to The New York Times

HARRISBURG, Pa., Sept. 5—The Rev. Philip F. Berrigan—cleared of charges that he led a plot to kidnap President Nixon's adviser on national security affairs, Henry A. Kissinger—was sentenced in Federal District Court here today to four concurrent two-year terms for smuggling letters out of the Lewisburg Penitentiary.

Sister Elizabeth McAlister, also cleared of the plot charges, was sentenced to one year in jail and three years' probation for smuggling letters.

Moments after the sentences were announced, Government attorneys moved to dismiss the first three substantive counts of their indictment, confirming that the Justice Department would not seek a retrial of the controversial "Harrisburg Seven" case.

The Government charged Father Berrigan, Sister Elizabeth, two other Roman Catholic priests, a former priest, a former nun and a Pakistani scholar with conspiracy to kidnap Mr. Kissinger as ransom to force a halt to the bombing in Viet-

Continued on Page 16, Column 1

PARLEY REJECTS HIJACKING TREATY

U.S.-Canadian Project for Penalizing Nations Aiding Air Pirates Rebuffed

By ROBERT LINDSEY
Special to The New York Times

WASHINGTON, Sept. 5—Delegates to a 17-nation conference here rejected today United States-Canadian efforts to negotiate an international anti-hijacking treaty based on a draft proposed by the two nations.

The move for nonacceptance was led by France and Britain and supported by the Soviet Union and Egypt.

Faced with what appeared to be certain defeat of the proposed treaty if it came to a vote, the two North American nations acquiesced in a French proposal to start writing a new treaty from scratch, after debates on what "principles" should be included.

The delegates have eight working days left before the conference is scheduled to end.

Today's rejection was a significant setback for the United

Continued on Page 91, Column 2

Nixon Tightens Security In U.S. Against 'Outlaws'

By TAD SZULC
Special to The New York Times

WASHINGTON, Sept. 5—President Nixon said today that 'extra security measures" would be taken in the United States to protect American citizens as well as visiting Israelis from possible attacks by Palestinian guerrillas.

Mr. Nixon, speaking to newsmen in San Francisco, left it unclear, however, whether he meant that this new protection would cover prominent American Jews or only those whom he described as "Americans of Israeli background, American citizens."

Speaking before the gunfight at a military airport in Munich, in which the Israeli hostages were killed, Mr. Nixon discussed the capture of Israeli Olympic team members by Palestinian guerrillas and the slaying of two Israelis. He said:

"Since we are dealing with international outlaws who are unpredictable, we have to take extra security measures to protect those who might be the targets of this kind of activity in the future. That might include Americans of Israeli background, American citizens."

Late tonight, after word was received in Washington of the death of the Israeli hostages and West German policemen, Secretary of State William P. Rogers issued this statement on behalf of the Administration:

"There are no words which can fully express our reaction to today's tragedy at the Olympic Games. I know I speak for all Americans in extending the deepest sympathies of the

Continued on Page 18, Column 4

Reports First Said Israelis Were Safe

Contradictory reports last night about the fate of the Israeli hostages seized by Arab terrorists in the Olympic Village threw the public into confusion all over the world.

Throughout the day, as the tragedy in Munich unfolded, millions of viewers throughout the world watched on live television, which employed circuits that had been intended for the Games. But in the evening, when the events reached their climax, viewers could get no definitive word for hours on how the hostages fared.

At first the West German Government's official spokesman, Conrad Ahlers, announced

Continued on Page 20, Column 1

GAMES SUSPENDED; RITES IN ARENA SET

Halt Is the First Since 1896, When the Classic Resumed —Egypt Team in Forfeit

By NEIL AMDUR
Special to The New York Times

MUNICH, West Germany, Wednesday, Sept. 6 — The Olympic Games were suspended yesterday for the first time since competition in the modern era began in 1896.

Late-afternoon and evening events were called off in the wake of an attack staged by Arab guerrillas before dawn on the Olympic Village in which two Israelis were killed and nine others taken hostage. The hostages were later killed.

After the attack, Mark Spitz, the American swimmer who won seven gold medals at the Munich Olympics and who is Jewish, flew hurriedly to London on his way back to the United States. There were fears before his departure that he too might become a victim. [Page 20.]

The announcement of the suspension, made by the International Olympic Committee, also said that a memorial service would be held for the victims

Continued on Page 18, Column 7

Elizabeth City Hall Under Investigation

By RONALD SULLIVAN
Special to The New York Times

TRENTON, Sept. 5—Law enforcement authorities reported here today that the administration of Mayor Thomas J. Dunn of Elizabeth was the target of a Union County grand jury investigation of alleged municipal corruption.

Mayor Dunn, a Democrat running for a third term, said in an interview that he had "no knowledge of any investigation involving me or my administration." But he said he volunteered last spring to go before a Union County grand jury.

According to official sources, the grand jury is investigating charges of payoffs and kickbacks involving city officials, contracts and businessmen. City license officials have already been subpoenaed, as have a number of city records and contracts.

Karl Asch, the county prosecutor, refused to comment on the nature of the reported investigation. He did say his staff had been instructed to seek indictments before the Nov. 7 elections.

Last week two of Mr. Dunn's three mayoral opponents were indicted in separate matters by a Union County grand jury.

Matthew J. Nilsen, a Republican freeholder in the county, was indicted on charges of atrocious assault in August in a case involving an alleged extortion.

In the other indictment, Michael J. DeMartino, a Democratic City Councilman in Elizabeth, was charged with misconduct in office in a case involving a $3,000 bribe in 1968.

Mayor Dunn recently endorsed President Nixon for re-election. Political observers in Union County noted that the indictments of two of his opponents were sought by a Republican prosecutor, and were seen as aiding the Mayor's re-election chances.

However, Mr. Asch, who has obtained indictments against prominent Union County political figures in recent months, contended today that his anti-corruption drive was "absolutely nonpolitical" and that the investigation of the Dunn

Continued on Page 49, Column 6

NEWS INDEX

"All the News That's Fit to Print"

The New York Times

LATE CITY EDITION

Weather: Partly sunny, mild today; fair tonight. Sunny, mild tomorrow. Temp. range: today 45-59; Monday 35-54. Full U.S. report on Page 76.

VOL. CXXII . No. 42,003 © 1973 The New York Times Company NEW YORK, TUESDAY, JANUARY 23, 1973 15 CENTS

LYNDON JOHNSON, 36TH PRESIDENT, IS DEAD; WAS ARCHITECT OF 'GREAT SOCIETY' PROGRAM

High Court Rules Abortions Legal the First 3 Months

State Bans Ruled Out Until Last 10 Weeks

National Guidelines Set by 7-to-2 Vote

By WARREN WEAVER Jr.

Special to The New York Times

WASHINGTON, Jan. 22 — The Supreme Court overruled today all state laws that prohibit or restrict a woman's right to obtain an abortion during her first three months of pregnancy. The vote was 7 to 2.

In a historic resolution of a fiercely controversial issue, the Court drafted a new set of

Excerpts from opinion and dissent are on Page 20.

national guidelines that will result in broadly liberalized anti-abortion laws in 46 states but will not abolish restrictions altogether.

Establishing an unusually detailed timetable for the relative legal rights of pregnant women and the states that would control their acts, the majority specified the following:

¶For the first three months of pregnancy the decision to have an abortion lies with the woman and her doctor, and the state's interest in her welfare is not "compelling" enough to warrant any interference.

¶For the next six months of pregnancy a state may "regulate the abortion procedure in ways that are reasonably related to maternal health," such as licensing and regulating the persons and facilities involved.

¶For the last 10 weeks of pregnancy, the period during which the fetus is judged to be capable of surviving if born, any state may prohibit

Continued on Page 20, Column 5

Cardinals Shocked —Reaction Mixed

By LAWRENCE VAN GELDER

Reaction to the Supreme Court decision on abortion fragmented yesterday along predictable lines, as leaders of the Roman Catholic Church assailed the ruling while birth control and women's rights activists praised it.

In the forefront of Catholic reaction were Cardinal Cooke of New York and Cardinal Krol of Philadelphia, who is also

Statements by Cooke and Krol appear on Page 20.

the president of the National Conference of Catholic Bishops.

Cardinal Cooke issued a statement calling the Court's action yesterday "shocking" and "horrifying." Cardinal Krol called the decision "an unspeakable tragedy for this nation."

But William Baird, a crusader for birth control and abortion, called the decision "a triumph" that culminated a long struggle.

"I'm delighted to see that our position—that women have the right to control their own bodies—has been vindicated," he said.

Dr. Alan F. Guttmacher, president of the Planned Parenthood Federation of America, called the decision "a wise and courageous stroke for the right to privacy, and for the protection of a woman's physical and emotional health."

"By this act," he said, "hundreds of thousands of American women every year will be

Continued on Page 20, Column 1

Ruling Seems to Forestall Abortion Debate in Albany

By WILLIAM E. FARRELL

Special to The New York Times

ALBANY, Jan. 22—The United States Supreme Court's abortion decision today appeared to quash the hopes of Right to Life and other antiabortion groups for a full-scale debate in the Legislature again this year on repealing the state's liberalized abortion law.

"No way," replied Assemblyman Constance E. Cook, a Republican of Ithaca and a sponsor of the liberalized abortion law, when asked if the issue of restoring the old state statute would be seriously discussed again.

The liberalized state law permits a woman to have an abortion on demand until the 24th week of pregnancy. The old law permitted abortions only when a woman's life was in jeopardy.

Rendered 'Useless'

The Supreme Court's 7-to-2 ruling, Mrs. Cook said, rendered efforts by antiabortion lobbyists to force it to the floors of the Senate and Assembly "a useless show of strength."

Similarly, Assembly Speaker Perry B. Duryea, Republican of Montauk, said he felt it would be "futile" to bring repeal legislation up for debate again.

Well-organized opponents of the liberalized abortion law succeeded in having it repealed in both houses last year despite a pledge by Governor Rockefeller that he would veto a repeal measure. The Governor kept his promise.

Mr. Rockefeller, who did not comment on the court decision today pending a review of it by his legal staff, reaffirmed that he would again veto a repeal measure this year, but the antiabortion groups were undaunted.

Today, the comments of abortion opponents contained some of the emotional comments that the issue has always elicited here.

From his newly opened lobbying office near the Capitol, Edward J. Golden, chairman of the New York State Right to Life Committee, said, "virtually all protection under law has

Continued on Page 22, Column 1

3.7 MILLION CARS RECALLED BY G.M. TO CORRECT FLAW

Shields Will Be Installed to Prevent Entry of Gravel Into Steering System

By JERRY M. FLINT

Special to The New York Times

DETROIT, Jan. 22 — The General Motors Corporation recalled today 3.7 million 1971 and 1972 cars, its full-size Chevrolet, Pontiac, Buick and Oldsmobile models.

G.M. said it would install a shield at the bottom of the car to keep gravel from bouncing into the steering mechanism, which could jam the steering.

The automaker insisted that the trouble was rare, and rejected the idea of a recall on this problem last year. But at the same time the company said it had received reports of 96 incidents allegedly tied to the trouble, with 23 turned into accidents in which 12 injuries were reported.

Criticism by Nader

The recall is one of the largest but does not match the recall for correction of safety defects of 6.7 million G.M. cars in 1971 or 4.4 million Fords last June.

Ralph Nader, the auto industry's major critic, has criticized G.M. for its failure to recall cars to correct this problem, and last August the Government's safety agency issued a consumer warning bulletin on the problem.

At that time, General Motors said that it did not believe the safety hazard was serious but offered to repair the cars without charge. Reports of the trouble kept appearing and the company has changed its position.

Steering May Jam

The condition, General Motors said, can become a problem only if a car "is driven over loose gravel, on extremely rutted roads at speeds which caused the car to pitch excessively." If the front frame cross-member, a cross bar similar to a step on a ladder, dips so low to the ground that it scoops up loose stones or gravel "it then is possible that stones of a certain size and shape may lodge between the steering coupling and the frame." The stones fall out of the car if turned to the right, G.M. said, but the steering may

Continued on Page 78, Column 2

KISSINGER IN PARIS; CEREMONIAL SITE CHOSEN FOR TALKS

Use of Conference Center Indicates Both Sides View Truce Round as Vital

By FLORA LEWIS

Special to The New York Times

PARIS, Jan. 22 — Henry A. Kissinger arrived here tonight, and it was announced that his talks tomorrow with Le Duc Tho of North Vietnam would be moved to the ceremonial setting of the International Conference Center.

Hanoi and Washington announced jointly last week that this next round of negotiations would complete a cease-fire agreement for Vietnam. Today there was still no official word on how long that task would take, but the choice of location — after months of meetings in secluded private quarters — suggested that the two sides considered tomorrow's session important.

The announcement that the talks would be moved to the center was made by the North Vietnamese here tonight, then confirmed by the American delegation.

The conference center is the old Hotel Majestic, on the Avenue Kléber, site of the formal four-sided Paris peace conference for over four years.

At the airport Mr. Kissinger said nothing more than "I am glad to be here." He went directly to the residence of the South Vietnamese Forign Minister, Tran Van Lam, though it was nearly midnight and he had left Washington early in the morning.

That was apparently a proto-

Continued on Page 6, Column 4

NATION IS SHOCKED

Citizens Join Leaders in Voicing Sorrow and Paying Tribute

By ROBERT D. McFADDEN

Shock, sorrow and the sense of a historic leader lost were the mourning themes of public officials and private citizens across the nation last night as word spread that Lyndon Baines Johnson was dead.

From the White House and the halls of Congress where he had served, and in cities and towns across the land where he had campaigned and made his policies felt, there was an outpouring of tribute to the former President, Senator and Representative from Texas.

Statement by Nixon

Many recalled Mr. Johnson's efforts to promote racial equality, to fight poverty and to improve education; others said that his deep commitment to the war in Indochina had prevented him from achieving all his domestic goals.

President Nixon, in a statement, declared: "To President Johnson, the American Dream' was not a catch phrase—it was a reality of his own life. He believed in America, in what America could mean to all its citizens and what America could mean to the world. In the service of that faith, he gave himself completely."

Mr. Nixon noted that in more than three decades of public life, Mr. Johnson "knew times of triumph and times of despair—he knew controversy and adulation. Yet, no matter what the mood of the moment, at the center of his public life—and at the center of his spirit—was an unshakeable convic-

Continued on Page 25, Column 1

Black Muslims Accused By Rival Sect in 7 Killings

Leader of Hanafis Calls for Muhammad Ouster

By PAUL DELANEY

Special to The New York Times

WASHINGTON, Jan. 22 — The leader of the Hanafi community of Moslems here today blamed the Black Muslims for the slaying last Thursday of seven of his followers, including three of his children, and he, in effect, declared war on the Black Muslims.

The leader, Hamaas Abdul Khaalis, called on other Moslem groups in this country and abroad to assist in deposing the Black Muslims and their leader, Elijah Muhammad.

The slayings and Mr. Hamaas's statement at a news conference evoked apprehension among law enforcement authorities and Islamic experts that more bloodshed would come.

Meanwhile, a team of Washington detectives went to New York today to investigate the possibility of a connection between the Moslem feud and the attempted robbery of a Brooklyn gun store that resulted in a 47-hour siege over the weekend. The belief is that the aborted robbery, which came one day after the mass killings here, was an attempt to obtain arms for the pending battle.

The slayings occurred at the headquarters of the Hanafi, a three-story stone mansion in the interracial "Gold Coast" section, where many of the city's black middle-class citizens reside. The seven victims included five children, four of whom were drowned, ranging in age from 9 days to 10 years old.

Mr. Hamaas revealed some

Continued on Page 77, Column 2

Four Held for Murder in Brooklyn Siege

By PETER KIHSS

The four men seized in the 47-hour weekend siege and shootout at a Brooklyn sporting goods store were held without bail yesterday on charges of murdering a policeman—which could lead to a death penalty—and of kidnapping 10 hostages.

Three were arraigned in Kings County Criminal Court with the proceedings virtually walled off by a tight guard of a dozen uniformed court officers ranged in front of the court railing.

The fourth was arraigned in Kings County Hospital, where he had undergone surgery for a bullet wound in the stomach.

District Attorney Eugene Gold told Judge Robert M. Haft that two of the defendants each had a previous arrest — one in 1964 and one in 1966. Both apparently were then about 16 years old, and Gerald Lefcourt, a defense lawyer, said the men told him the charges had been dismissed.

Outside of court, Robert M. McKiernan, president of the Patrolmen's Benevolent Association, demanded prosecution that could lead to electrocution for the fatal shooting of Patrol-

Continued on Page 77, Column 3

Pilgrims' Jet Crashes in Nigeria; 180 Are Feared Dead, a Record

By THOMAS A. JOHNSON

Special to The New York Times

LAGOS, Nigeria, Jan. 22 — A chartered jetliner carrying Nigerian Moslems home from a pilgrimage to Mecca crashed and burned today while landing in fog in northern Nigeria, and it was feared that 180 people had been killed.

Twenty-two of the 202 aboard survived, among them the pilot and several other crew members, according to reports from the airport at Kano, 525 miles north of here.

A death toll of 180 would make the crash the worst air disaster in history. Previously, the crash of a Soviet airliner near Moscow on Oct. 13, in which 176 people died, had been listed as the worst. The chartered jet, a Boeing 707 that belonged to Royal Jordanian Airways, was one of many planes involved in transporting Nigerian Moslems, as about

Continued on Page 10, Column 4

The New York Times/Jan. 23, 1973

The New York Times/George Tames

LYNDON BAINES JOHNSON, 1908—1973

Foreman Stops Frazier In 2d Round, Wins Title

By RED SMITH

Special to The New York Times

KINGSTON, Jamaica, Jan. 22 —Under Caribbean skies that had never witnessed anything remotely like it, big George Foreman smashed Joe Frazier to the floor six times tonight and won the heavyweight championship of the world in 4 minutes 35 seconds.

Arthur Mercante, the referee from New York, stopped the uneven match with Frazier on his feet but hardly in the contest.

A crowd of 36,000 paying $412,000, substantially more than had been expected, saw one of the most startling upsets in two and a half centuries of heavyweight title matches. Frazier, in his 10th defense of the title New York State conferred on him in 1968 and his third since he whipped the former champion, Muhammad Ali, in 1971, had been favored at 3 to 2 in the betting shops here.

Foreman, unbeaten in 37 fights and author of 34 knockouts since he won the Olympic heavyweight title in 1968, had been recognized as Joe's most formidable opponent since Ali but most boxing men doubted that he could stand up under the ceaseless pressure of a characteristic Frazier attack.

They'll never know now whether they were right or wrong, for Joe never got a chance to apply pressure. Looking rather thick in the middle at 214 pounds, the champion tried to "come out smoking" but Foreman used his greater size and longer reach to smother the fire. At 6 feet 3 inches, the challenger had three and a half inches in height and a five-inch advantage in reach.

Reaching out with both hands, he fended off Frazier's early rushes, turning the challenge aside. Then he sank a hook deep into Joe's body, and the crowd had the first hint of what was in store. In a moment Foreman was moving forward, using both hands with authority. Even so, there was an instant of shocked silence when an uppercut sent Joe sprawling.

The champion got to his feet immediately and resumed his jigging style, both hands high,

Continued on Page 33, Column 6

Iceland Evacuates 7,000 on Isle After an Ancient Volcano Erupts

By The Associated Press

REYKJAVIK, Iceland, Tuesday, Jan. 23—Seven thousand people were being evacuated from an offshore Icelandic island early today as a volcano that had been quiet for more than a thousand years erupted.

Police authorities on the tiny island of Heimaey, one of a group off the south coast of Iceland, said boats and planes were being used to get the inhabitants of the town of Vestmannaeyjar to safety on the mainland.

But, they said, a hail of ash from the belching volcano of Helgafell was making operations from the island's airstrip difficult. They said a stream of molten lava also threatened to seal off the harbor, trapping boats.

Telephoned reports to Reykjavik—70 miles northwest of Heimaey—said a fissure 2,000 to 3,000 yards long opened and was spewing out lava and ash.

Fiery explosions were hurtling molten debris more than 1,500 feet into the air.

One side of Vestmannaeyjar is only 150 yards from Helgafell.

The New York Times/Jan. 23, 1973

The police said the lava was flowing away from the town and into the Atlantic, but they said this could change at any time.

Women and children were being evacuated by air along with patients from the town's hospitals.

Others were boarding boats in the harbor. Iceland's big fishing fleet, Coast Guard vessels and other merchant ships were ordered to the island, the police said.

The United States Air Force base at Keflavik promised to

Continued on Page 10, Column 3

STRICKEN AT HOME

Apparent Heart Attack Comes as Country Mourns Truman

Special to The New York Times

SAN ANTONIO, Tex., Jan. 22 —Lyndon Baines Johnson, 36th President of the United States, died today of an apparent heart attack suffered at his ranch in Johnson City, Tex.

The 64-year-old Mr. Johnson, whose history of heart illness began in 1955, was pronounced dead on arrival at 4:33 P.M. central time at San Antonio International Airport, where he

An obituary article appears on Pages 26 through 29; an appraisal, Page 25.

had been flown in a family plane on the way to Brooke Army Medical Center here.

A spokesman at Austin said that Mr. Johnson's funeral would probably be held Thursday at the National City Christian Church in Washington. He said the body would lie in state at the Johnson Library in Austin from noon tomorrow until 8 A.M. Wednesday, with an honor guard, and then would be taken to Washington, where it will lie in state at the Capitol rotunda until the funeral. Mr. Johnson will be buried at the L.B.J. Ranch.

Death came to the nation's only surviving former President as the nation observed a period of mourning proclaimed less than a month ago for former President Harry S. Truman.

A Legacy of Progress

Although his vision of a Great Society dissolved in the morass of war in Vietnam, Mr. Johnson left to the nation a legacy of progress and innovation in civil rights, Social Security, education, housing and other programs attesting to his fundamental affection for his fellow Americans.

At Fort Sam Houston, where Brooke Army Medical Center is situated, flags were hoisted to full staff and then immediately lowered again in respect for the Texan who was thrust into the Presidency on Nov. 22, 1963, when an assassin's bullet took the life of President Kennedy in Dallas.

Ironically, Mr. Johnson died in what appeared to be the waning days of the Vietnam war. The man who won election in 1964 to a full term as President with the greatest voting majority ever accorded a candidate was transformed by that war into the leader of a divided nation.

Amid rising personal unpopularity, in the face of the lingering war and racial strife at home, Mr. Johnson surprised the nation on March 31, 1968, with a television speech in which he announced, "I shall not seek and I will not accept the nomination of my party as your President."

Stage Set for Defeat

He thus renounced an opportunity to cap with a second full term a career in public life that began in 1937 with his election to Congress as an ardent New Dealer and led to the majority leadership of the Senate and to the Vice-Presidency and the Presidency. His renunciation set the stage for Democratic defeat at the polls in 1968.

Two days before Mr. Johnson's death, Richard M. Nixon, the Republican who was elected in 1968, took the oath of office for his second term as President. Mr. Nixon telephoned Mrs. Johnson today at the hospital here to express his sympathy.

At a news briefing tonight in Austin at KTBC, the Johnson family's television and ra-

Continued on Page 25, Column 5

TODAY: ANNUAL ECONOMIC SURVEY OF WESTERN HEMISPHERE, SECTION 3

"All the News That's Fit to Print"

The New York Times

LATE CITY EDITION
Weather: Rain late today, tonight becoming light snow early tomorrow. Temp. range: today 40-45; Saturday 40-44. Full U.S. report on Page 59.

SECTION ONE

VOL. CXXII . . No. 42,008 | NEW YORK, SUNDAY, JANUARY 28, 1973 | 75¢ beyond 50-mile zone from New York City, except Long Island. Higher in air delivery cities. | 50 CENTS

VIETNAM PEACE PACTS SIGNED; AMERICA'S LONGEST WAR HALTS

Nation Ends Draft, Turns to Volunteers

Change Is Ordered Six Months Early—Youths Must Still Register

By DAVID E. ROSENBAUM
Special to The New York Times

WASHINGTON, Jan. 27—Defense Secretary Melvin R. Laird announced today that the military draft had ended.

As a result of the announcement, men born in 1953 and afterward will not be subject to conscription, and men born before 1953 but not yet drafted will have no further liability to the draft.

These men will be the first in two generations to have no prospect of being drafted. Except for a brief hiatus in 1947 and 1948, men have been conscripted regularly since 1940.

President Nixon's authority to conscript troops into the military expires June 30. Since no one has been drafted since December, the President achieved his goal of turning the military into an all-volunteer force six months ahead of the deadline.

The President and Mr. Laird had promised repeatedly that the June 30 deadline would be met. But Mr. Laird had held out the possibility that as many as 5,000 men would be drafted this year from March through June.

Message From Laird

But, in a message to senior defense officials that was made public today, Mr. Laird said:

"With the signing of the peace agreement in Paris today, and, after receiving a report from the Secretary of the Army that he foresees no need for further inductions, I wish to inform you that the armed forces henceforth will depend exclusively on volunteer soldiers, sailors, airmen and marines.

"The use of the draft has ended."

Although no one will be drafted, the Selective Service machinery will most likely remain on the books for standby use in an emergency. Men will continue to have to register for the draft when they turn 18, and young men will still be assigned lottery numbers based on their birthdays.

Congress has mandated, however, that the Government call up Reserves and National Guardsmen before it turns to a reinstatement of the draft to meet future emergencies.

A spokesman for the Selective Service System said that men who had refused to report for induction would still be subject to criminal prosecution. But, he said, men with induction postponements that were due to expire before June 30 will not be drafted.

"We will draft nobody," the spokesman said.

Hopes Senate Will Act

Mr. Laird's single qualification about ending the draft applied to doctors and dentists. The Nixon Administration has asked Congress to approve sizable bonuses for doctors and dentists in an effort to attract enough volunteers in those professions.

The House of Representatives passed such legislation last year, and Mr. Laird said in his message today:

"I am particularly hopeful that the Senate will promptly follow the lead of the House and enact legislation giving added incentives for service from members of the health professions, so that the requirements for health services personnel can also be put on a volunteer basis."

The House is almost certainly willing to pass the bill again this year, but Representative F. Edward Hébert, chairman of the House Armed Services Committee, has said that his committee will not act until the Senate passes the legislation.

Mr. Laird also urged Congress to approve bonuses to attract men to the National Guard and

Continued on Page 28, Column 1

In the morning ceremony at the Hotel Majestic in Paris were, from the left, the Vietcong, North Vietnamese, South Vietnamese and U.S. delegations

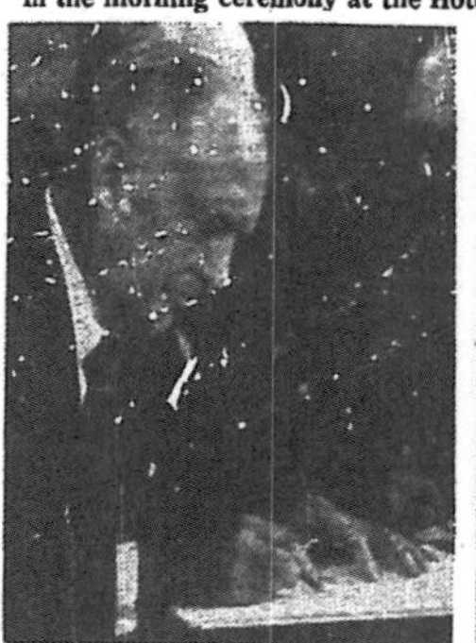

Associated Press, United Press International and C.B.S. News

Signing, from left, William P. Rogers for U.S., Nguyen Duy Trinh for Hanoi, Mrs. Nguyen Thi Binh for the Vietcong, Tran Van Lam for Saigon

CEREMONIES COOL

Two Sessions in Paris Formally Conclude the Agreement

By FLORA LEWIS
Special to The New York Times

PARIS, Jan. 27—The Vietnam cease-fire agreement was signed here today in eerie silence, without a word or a gesture to express the world's relief that the years of war were officially ending.

The accord was effective at 7 P.M. Eastern standard time.

Secretary of State William P. Rogers wrote his name 62 times on the documents providing—after 12 years—a settlement of the longest, most divisive foreign war in America's history.

The official title of the text was "Agreement on Ending the War and Restoring Peace in Vietnam." But the cold, almost gloomy atmosphere at two separate signing ceremonies reflected the uncertainties of whether peace is now assured.

The conflict, which has raged in one way or another for over a quarter of a century, had been inconclusive, without clear victory or defeat for either side.

Involvement Gradually Grew

After a gradually increasing involvement that began even before France left Indochina in 1954, the United States entered into a full-scale combat role in 1965. The United States considers Jan. 1, 1961, as the war's starting date and casualties are counted from then.

By 1968, when the build-up was stopped and then reversed, there were 529,000 Americans fighting in Vietnam. United States dead passed 45,000 by the end of the war.

The peace agreements were as ambiguous as the conflict, which many of America's friends first saw as generous aid to a weak and threatened ally, but which many came to consider an exercise of brute power against a tiny nation.

Built on Compromises

The peace agreements signed today were built of compromises that permit the two Vietnamese sides to give them contradictory meanings and, they clearly hope, to continue their unfinished struggle in the political arena without continuing the slaughter.

The signing took place in two ceremonies. In the morning, the participants were the United States, North Vietnam, South Vietnam and the Vietcong. Because the Saigon Government does not wish to imply recognition of the Vietcong's Provisional Revolutionary Government, all references to that government were confined to a second set of documents. That set was signed in the afternoon,

Continued on Page 24, Column 7

Hanoi Lists of P.O.W.'s Are Made Public by U.S.

By BERNARD GWERTZMAN
Special to The New York Times

WASHINGTON, Jan. 27—The State Department tonight released the list of American civilians acknowledged by North Vietnam as having been captured in South Vietnam during the Vietnam war. The list left about half the 51 American civilians believed missing or captured unaccounted for.

The list that the North Vietnamese turned over to American officials in Paris today named 27 American civilians as prisoners of the Vietcong, and listed seven other Americans as having died in captivity.

At the same time, the Defense Department began releasing, in batches, the names of the military prisoners in Communist hands who were on the list turned over in Paris along with the civilians.

2 Diplomats Listed

The United States, in Paris, provided a list of 26,000 Communist prisoners held by South Vietnam in exchange. The lists were turned over following the formal signing of the Vietnam cease-fire agreement.

Frank A. Sieverts, the State Department official charged with prisoner affairs, said that Hanoi apparently did not in-

Continued on Page 26, Column 1

The Toll: 12 Years of War

Military

United States—45,933 killed, 303,616 wounded, 587 captured, 1,335 missing (up to Jan. 13, 1973).
South Vietnam—183,528 killed and 499,026 wounded.
North Vietnam and Vietcong—924,048 (an estimate by Saigon; figures on wounded not available.)

Civilian

415,000 South Vietnamese killed and 935,000 wounded in combat (1965 through 1972).
31,463 South Vietnamese killed and 49,000 abducted as result of Vietcong actions against civilians.
20,587 killed by Saigon actions against civilian Vietcong.
North Vietnamese—Casualties not known.

BATTLES CONTINUE AFTER CEASE-FIRE

U.S. Copter Sent to Pick Up Vietcong Officers Said to Have Been Shot Down

By FOX BUTTERFIELD
Special to The New York Times

SAIGON, South Vietnam, Sunday, Jan. 28—A cease-fire officially went into effect throughout Vietnam at 8 A.M. today, but widespread fighting continued and there were reports that an unarmed American helicopter sent to pick up a Vietcong delegation and bring it to Saigon had been shot down over Tay Nin Ninh Province.

The helicopter, which was painted white and which is normally used for medical evacuation flight, was to bring the Vietcong's delegation to the four-power Joint Military Commission that will oversee the cease-fire. There was no immediate word on the fate of the crew.

[North Vietnam issued a statement Sunday informing its people of the cease-fire, saying, "Today, the 28th of January, war completely ends in both zones of our country," Reuters reported from Hong Kong.]

334 Incidents Reported

The South Vietnamese command reported this morning that in the 24 hours ending at dawn, North Vietnamese and Vietcong troops initiated 334 incidents throughout the country. According to Government officers, that is the highest number since they began keeping a record. However, more Communist troops were probably involved during the 1968 Tet offensive, they said.

Only an hour and a half before the cease-fire began, Communist gunners struck Tan Son Nhut airport on the outskirts

Continued on Page 18, Column 1

A Reluctant G.I.'s Life and Death

By JON NORDHEIMER
Special to The New York Times

ST. JOSEPH, Mo.—The house on Penn Street where Charley Stockbauer used to live sits near a historic crossroads of America.

It was from St. Joseph that the pioneers who won the West a century ago set out across the prairie in rough wagons drawn by mules and oxen and gritty conviction.

They came here by railroad and steamboat in the waning days of winter and huddled in muddy encampments on the gray bluffs above the Missouri River, waiting with mounting excitement for the floodwaters to recede from the Kansas plain.

As with most American school children, the seeds of patriotism were planted deep in Charley Stockbauer, and he grew to manhood in St. Joseph surrounded by the ghosts of 19th-century heroes and the legends of the days when men strode boldly toward an uncertain horizon, enduring hardship and fear on the impulse of duty or national destiny.

Values Questioned

These values are still enshrined, but they have been questioned as never before by Charley Stockbauer's generation during the turbulent years when the vagaries of the war in Vietnam challenged traditional American attitudes about sacred abstractions such as patriotism.

Charley Stockbauer was a confused and reluctant warrior in a conflict that almost nobody fully understands, and that confusion and reluctance are mirrored here in the town that was his home before he died in Vietnam. Patriotism has not died in St. Joseph, but here, as elsewhere across the country in these days when the war has at last come to an end, there is a reticence about it all, a nervous hesitance about parading the flag.

The myths and the legends persist. Buffalo Bill and Wild Bill Hickok were raw-boned riders from the Overland Pony Express, and the mail they carried westward started out from a brick building that still stands on Penn Street. Indian fighters purchased, with leather pouches

Continued on Page 24, Column 2

Nation Celebrates Peace In Prayer and Muted Joy

By MICHAEL KNIGHT

President Nixon, like millions of other Americans, watched the signing of the Vietnam cease-fire agreement on television yesterday and then, like many others, took part in a modest and somber celebration of the end of a tragic war.

The President, relaxing in his home at Key Biscayne, Fla., had proclaimed 7 P.M. yesterday as a "national moment of prayer and thanksgiving" and the 24-hour period thereafter as a day of prayer.

Throughout the country, in cities and in hamlets, church bells tolled, fire companies sounded their horns, and small, quiet gatherings were held in homes and in public places.

Some Voice Caution

Some of those who celebrated the end of the American war did so cautiously. The executive secretary of the Washington, D. C., Council of Churches said, "The reason many of us are not throwing our hats in the air is that we are just so stunned and ashamed because the war went on so long, so needlessly."

In Elmira, N. Y., Mrs. Lucielle Cesari did not turn on the lights of a Christmas tree in her yard, lights she had lit every night for five years in a "vigil" remembering the war.

In Longmeadow, Mass., a bell forged by Paul Revere, the silversmith and patriot, was sounded in its steeple at the First Church of Christ. The bell was first sounded to signal the end of the War of 1812.

In Key Biscayne, the President attended a special service at the Key Biscayne Presbyterian Church about a mile from his home.

The minister, the Rev. John A. Huffman, Jr., borrowed from a song by two antiwar activists,

Continued on Page 20, Column 3

United Press International

President and Mrs. Nixon and their daughter, Mrs. David Eisenhower, attending a memorial service in Key Biscayne Presbyterian Church, near the Florida White House.

Other News About Accords

CAMBODIA—The exiled Cambodian head of state said in Peking that his guerrilla forces would fight on despite the cease-fire in Vietnam. Cambodia announced a suspension of offensive activities tomorrow. [Page 26.]

TRUCE OBSERVERS—Teams of officers from Poland and Canada left for Vietnam to join with others expected from Hungary and Indonesia. [Page 24.]

INTERNATIONAL CONFERENCE—The United States proposed Feb. 26 as the date for 12-nation meeting on guaranteeing peace. [Page 16.]

LAOS—The head of the pro-Communist negotiating team returned from Hanoi and gave no indication that a cease-fire could be arranged quickly in Laos. [Page 21.]

Today's Sections

Index to Subjects

*Included in all copies distributed in New York City and the suburban area.

"All the News That's Fit to Print"

The New York Times

LATE CITY EDITION

Weather: Partly sunny today; fair tonight. Chance of rain tomorrow. Temp. range: today 50-64; Monday 45-68. Full U.S. report on Page 86.

VOL. CXXII ... No. 42,101 © 1973 The New York Times Company NEW YORK, TUESDAY, MAY 1, 1973 15 CENTS

NIXON ACCEPTS ONUS FOR WATERGATE, BUT SAYS HE DIDN'T KNOW ABOUT PLOT; HALDEMAN, EHRLICHMAN, DEAN RESIGN; RICHARDSON PUT IN KLEINDIENST POST

Biaggi Testimony to Jury Ordered Released in Full

U.S. Judge Criticizes Candidate's Petition —Delays Disclosure Pending Appeal —Troy Out as Campaign Chief

By JOHN CORRY

A Federal judge yesterday ordered the release of Mario Biaggi's testimony before a grand jury but held up the order when the mayoral candidate's lawyer said he would appeal to block disclosure.

In issuing the order, Judge Edmund L. Palmieri denied a motion by the Bronx Congressman for a panel of three judges to look over his testimony and state whether he had taken the Fifth Amendment "solely" on questions about his personal finances.

In the past, Mr. Biaggi had told leaders of the Conservative party that he had answered all the questions put to him by the grand jury.

Excerpts from court testimony appear on Page 35.

"Upon reflection," said Judge Palmieri in explaining why he ordered the minutes disclosed, "this court can only conclude that this blatantly unsanctioned petition [by Mr. Biaggi] was made with an expectation of its denial by the court, and for the purpose of publicly exploiting the court's denial of the motion."

Judge Palmieri said that he agreed with United States Attorney Whitney North Seymour Jr., who had asked for full disclosure of the testimony, that Mr. Biaggi's motion constituted an abuse of the court.

"What we have here is tantamount to a manipulation of legal procedures so that the truth can either be successfully concealed or at the very least made to appear different from the underlying facts," the judge said.

Appeal Set for Today

Mr. Biaggi's lawyer, Arthur H. Christy, said he would appeal the decision today to the United States Circuit Court of Appeals. Court sources reported that an appeal would probably be heard later this week or early next week.

Asked outside the court if Mr. Biaggi had told him to appeal, Mr. Christy said, "I follow the instructions of my client."

The political impact to the decision came quickly. Mr. Biaggi dismissed City Councilman Matthew J. Troy Jr. as his mayoral campaign manager. Mr. Troy said he had been preparing to quit anyway.

Simultaneously, leaders of the Conservative party, which has endorsed Mr. Biaggi for Mayor, were thrown into an argument.

Some of the leaders said they

Continued on Page 34, Column 5

ROGERS DEFENDS CAMBODIA RAIDS

Facing Fulbright Committee, He Says the Constitution Justifies the Bombing

By BERNARD GWERTZMAN

Special to The New York Times

WASHINGTON, April 30 — Secretary of State William P. Rogers said today that the continued American bombing in Cambodia was legally justified by the Constitution and was "a meaningful interim action" to force the Communist-backed insurgents there to agree to a cease-fire.

Mr. Rogers, testifying before the Senate Foreign Relations

Text of Rogers memorandum will be found on Page 10.

Committee, presented the Administration's long-awaited legal justification for the Cambodian bombing, an issue that has aroused considerable criticism from members of the committee, including its chairman, Senator J. W. Fulbright.

They have argued that President Nixon has no legal basis for the bombing, now that all American troops have been withdrawn from South Vietnam.

Though the committee members generally accorded Mr. Rogers friendly treatment, his arguments, both in his comments to the committee and in a 13-page legal memorandum, failed to sway the most vocal critics such as Senators Ful-

Continued on Page 11, Column 1

Egyptian Air Bases Reported Equipped For Libyan Planes

Special to The New York Times

BEIRUT, Lebanon, April 30— Diplomatic sources report that ground equipment has been installed at some Egyptian air bases for French-built fighter-bombers from Libya and British-built planes from other Arab countries, and that it has been tested by the aircraft during brief visits.

Israel has been charging that French-built Mirage jets from Libya and British-built Hunter interceptors from Iraq have been transferred to Egyptian bases, but there has been no comment in Cairo. A French Government spokesman said last week that French inquiries about the charges had brought denials from Libya and Egypt.

According to informed diplomats here, however, several embassies are known to have reported to their governments that ground equipment for Mirages was installed several weeks ago. These embassies are said to believe that the

Continued on Page 6, Column 1

Elliot L. Richardson, named Attorney General, yesterday

United Press International

President Nixon in White House press room after address

CONTROLS VOTED FOR ANOTHER YEAR

President Reluctantly Signs Compromise Bill Extending Wage and Price Curbs

By EDWARD COWAN

Special to The New York Times

WASHINGTON, April 30— With the reluctant support of the Administration, both houses of Congress approved today, and President Nixon signed, a compromise bill extending for another year the President's authority to regulate wages and prices.

Mr. Nixon signed the bill tonight, just after making a nationwide television and radio speech. The existing law, called the Economic Stabilization Act, was scheduled to expire at midnight.

The vote in the House was 267 to 115, a larger margin for passage than appeared likely before the Easter recess. The voice vote in the Senate was unrecorded.

Voting for the bill were 153 Democrats and 114 Republicans; opposed were 58 Democrats and 57 Republicans.

Meanwhile, the Department of Agriculture reported that prices received by farmers fell by 1.5 per cent in April, the first decline in a year. [Page 55.]

Mr. Nixon had sought a simple one-year extension of the act. But with the public frus-

Continued on Page 17, Column 1

Ellsberg Judge Demands Affidavits on Bugging Tie

By MARTIN ARNOLD

Special to The New York Times

LOS ANGELES, April 30 — The judge in the Pentagon papers trial today ordered four figures connected to the Watergate affair to produce affidavits concerning any link between that break-in and the trial here.

Federal District Judge William Matthew Byrne Jr. said that he was not foreclosing the possibility of summoning the four men here to testify, although he denied, for now, a defense request for an immediate hearing.

The affidavit order was directed to John W. Dean 3d, former special counsel to President Nixon; L. Patrick Gray 3d, former acting director of the F.B.I., and G. Gordon Liddy and E. Howard Hunt Jr., conspirators in the Watergate bugging.

Judge Byrne indicated that he also would probably require affidavits and perhaps testimony from former Attorney General John N. Mitchell, Richard G. Kleindienst, the present Attorney General; John D. Ehrlichman, until today the President's chief for domestic affairs; H. R. Haldeman, Mr. Nixon's chief of staff who also resigned today; Charles W. Colson, former Presidential special counsel, and Robert C. Mardian, former Assistant Attorney General.

Today's court session began with the judge announcing from the bench that about a month ago he met with Mr. Ehrlichman and President Nixon, "for approximately one minute or less," at Mr. Ehrlichman's suggestion.

At that time, he said, he was offered a new Government position, but he said he told Mr. Ehrlichman that he could not consider it "until this case is concluded." He did not say what the position was, but his name has been mentioned as a possible director of the Federal Bureau of Investigation.

Then, in response to demands from two defense lawyers,

Continued on Page 33, Column 6

SHAKE-UP LAUDED BY CONGRESSMEN

But Many Warn That Step Is Not Enough to Restore Faith in Administration

By JAMES M. NAUGHTON

Special to The New York Times

WASHINGTON, April 30 — Members of Congress joined in widespread, bipartisan praise today for President Nixon's shake-up of his Administration's high command.

But many Senators and Representatives coupled their commendations with warnings that a housecleaning of the White House staff would not be sufficient to restore faith in the Nixon Administration or the Government as a whole.

Furthermore, Representative John E. Moss of California urged House Democratic leaders to open a formal inquiry into the possible impeachment of President Nixon.

The suggestion by the longtime Democratic Congressman—which key leaders of both parties in the House described as "premature" — was the most severe reaction on Capitol Hill to the latest developments in the Watergate conspiracy case.

At Huron, Ohio, the nation's Democratic Governors joined in the call for appointment of a special prosecutor in the Watergate case.

Mark O. Hatfield, Republican

Continued on Page 33, Column 6

2 AIDES PRAISED

Counsel Forced Out —Leonard Garment Takes Over Job

By R. W. APPLE Jr.

Special to The New York Times

WASHINGTON, April 30— Four top Nixon Administration officials resigned today as a consequence of the Watergate case, one of the most widespread scandals in American Presidential history.

H. R. Haldeman, the austere and secretive White House

Texts of Nixon announcement and resignations, Page 30.

chief of staff, and John D. Ehrlichman, the President's chief adviser on domestic affairs, maintained their innocence in letters submitting their resignations. Both said their ability to carry out their daily duties had been undermined.

The President chose Elliot L. Richardson, the Secretary of Defense, to succeed Richard G. Kleindienst as Attorney General and placed Mr. Richardson in charge of the Watergate investigation.

Mr. Kleindienst said he had quit because close friends had become Watergate suspects and "impartial enforcement of the law" ruled out such "intimate relationships."

Dean's Departure Asked

Mr. Nixon also announced that he had "requested and accepted" the resignation of John W. Dean 3d, the White House counsel, who had threatened to implicate superiors. Leonard Garment, a special Presidential consultant, was named to replace Mr. Dean temporarily.

No replacements for the two key aides were named, and the President gave no hint as to whom he might choose.

In a related development, the United States Information Agency announced tonight that Gordon Strachan had resigned as general counsel "after learning that persons with whom he had worked closely at the White House had submitted their resignations today." The statement said Mr. Strachan "stressed that he had no complicity in the Democratic National Committee break-in or in any alleged attempt to cover it up."

Mr. Haldeman's and Mr. Ehrlichman's departures strip the White House of its central operating mechanism at a time when far-reaching decisions must be made on inflation, Indochina policy and American relations with Europe.

The actions were announced

Continued on Page 30, Column 1

NEW DATA CITED

President Tells How He Changed Mind About Charges

By JOHN HERBERS

Special to The New York Times

WASHINGTON, April 30 — President Nixon told the nation tonight that he accepted the responsibility for what happened in the Watergate case even though he had had no knowledge of political espionage or attempts to cover it up.

The President went on na-

The text of Nixon's speech is printed on Page 31.

tionwide television and radio to discuss the case after he received the resignations of three top staff members who have been implicated—H. R. Haldeman, John D. Ehrlichman and John W. Dean 3d. He also accepted the resignation of Attorney General Richard G. Kleindienst.

Wrongdoing Alleged

While the President accepted the responsibility and pledged every effort to achieve justice in the case, he alleged wrongdoing or cover-up attempts on the part of those he had delegated to run his 1972 Presidential campaign and those he appointed to investigate the matter during the campaign.

And he implied that his own election officials, in the Watergate espionage, were attempting to stop wrongdoing by the Democrats.

Mr. Nixon also said that hereafter the investigation of the Watergate matters would be delegated to his new Attorney General, Elliot L. Richardson, while he, the President, turned his attention to grave foreign and domestic matters. He added that he would leave it up to Mr. Richardson whether to appoint a special prosecutor.

Weeks of Tension

The speech, which came after weeks of growing tension at the White House as developments in the Watergate scandal implicated Administration figures, was an emotional appeal to save the integrity of the Presidency for the 1,361 days, by Mr. Nixon's count, that remain in his term. This was the 100th day of his second term.

"Tonight I ask for your prayers to help me in everything that I do," Mr. Nixon said at the end. "God bless America, and God bless each and every one of you."

He accepted responsibility for Watergate with these words:

"In any organization the man

Continued on Page 31, Column 5

Nixon Asks Tax Law Shift To Ease Filing on Income

By EILEEN SHANAHAN

Special to The New York Times

WASHINGTON, April 30 — The Nixon Administration proposed today changes in the tax laws and tax forms that would make it easier for millions of individuals to figure out their Federal income taxes.

The Administration's proposals contained little, however,

Summary of proposed changes is printed on Page 34.

that appeared likely to satisfy the demands of those who have been calling for reform of the tax laws.

All the basic provisions of the laws that reduce taxes for those who invest in business or property — the provisions relating to capital gains, depreciation, the depletion allowance and so on — would remain untouched under the Administration's plan.

The Administration did, however, recommend enactment of two new provisions that would limit the ability of wealthy individuals to combine different preferential sections of the tax laws in ways that permit them to escape all or most Federal income tax.

The proposals were submitted to the House Ways and Means Committee by the Secretary of the Treasury, George P. Shultz, in the form of a 175-page booklet called "Proposals for Tax Change."

The committee chairman, Wilbur D. Mills, Democrat of Arkansas, said he thought the proposals did not go far enough and criticized particularly the lack of any proposed changes in the taxation of capital gains and in the estate and gift taxes.

The plan for simplifying the

Continued on Page 35, Column 7

Kissinger Is Going to Moscow For Talks on Brezhnev's Visit

Special to The New York Times

WASHINGTON, April 30 — Henry A. Kissinger will fly to Moscow this week for talks with Leonid I. Brezhnev, the Soviet Communist party leader, on plans for Mr. Brezhnev's expected visit to the United States late in June.

While in Moscow with his top staff aides, Mr. Kissinger will also discuss Vietnam, arms control negotiations, trade questions and other matters with Mr. Brezhnev and other top officials, a senior Administration official said.

The White House, in making the announcement, limited itself to saying that Mr. Kissinger would leave Thursday for four to five days in Moscow "for an exchange of views on a wide range of bilateral problems and matters of mutual interest."

But a senior Administration official said that the primary mission of the President's adviser for national security would be to discuss the details and likely agenda for Mr. Brezhnev's visit to the United States, which will return Mr. Nixon's visit to the Soviet Union last spring.

No date for Mr. Brezhnev's trip has been announced, but an Administration official said that both sides were planning on late June—around June 25.

It will be Mr. Brezhnev's first journey to the United States and the first by a top Soviet

Continued on Page 4, Column 4

NEWS INDEX

End of Era in Nixon Presidency

By ROBERT B. SEMPLE Jr.

Special to The New York Times

WASHINGTON, April 30 — The resignations of H. R. Haldeman and John D. Ehrlichman from President Nixon's senior staff clearly mark the end of one era of the Nixon Presidency and the beginning of another. Things simply will not be the same. The question is how much different they will be.

News Analysis

The few men who remain in the President's suddenly shrunken entourage do not believe that the scandals of the moment will have much impact on Mr. Nixon's own personality. His habits are well entrenched, and any future White House operation will reflect the style of its master.

But there are some here now, in the White House and on Capitol Hill, who hope that Mr. Nixon will seize what they sense to be a rare opening to redesign his relationships with Congress, the bureaucracy, and even the press.

They hope to increase his access to others and theirs to him, to replace the closed corporation that the White House had become with the "open Presidency" to which he once aspired, and to return to his own first principles by decentralizing some of the power that has steadily flowed from the Government agencies to a few decision-makers in the White House.

Mr. Haldeman and Mr. Ehrlichman helped design that system, ran the system and, in time, came to symbolize the system. Their Teutonic names and mutual zeal for efficient execution gave rise to many jokes. Their enemies called them Hans and Fritz; their friends simply teased them.

In Mr. Ehrlichman's office on the second floor of the White House is a copy of Daniel P. Moynihan's "Understanding Poverty," which carries this inscription: "For John Ehrlichman. Achtung D.P.M."

But their power was no joke. They were men with long ties and easy access to the President, men of loyalty, men who transmitted Mr. Nixon's orders to the bureaucracy and to whom, with few exceptions, Mr. Nixon's Cabinet members were forced to report before winning humble access to the Oval Office.

In all areas other than for-

Continued on Page 33, Column 4

"All the News That's Fit to Print"

The New York Times

LATE CITY EDITION

Weather: Chance of showers later today, tonight. Milder tomorrow. Temp. range: today 36-46; Friday 43-49. Additional details on Page 62.

VOL. CXXIII...No. 42,406 · © 1974 The New York Times Company · NEW YORK, SATURDAY, MARCH 2, 1974 · 20¢ beyond 50-mile radius of New York City, except Long Island. Higher in air delivery cities. · 15 CENTS

FEDERAL GRAND JURY INDICTS 7 NIXON AIDES ON CHARGES OF CONSPIRACY ON WATERGATE; HALDEMAN, EHRLICHMAN, MITCHELL ON LIST

John N. Mitchell
Former Attorney General

H. R. Haldeman
Headed White House staff

John D. Ehrlichman
Was Presidential adviser

Charles W. Colson
Former White House lawyer

Robert C. Mardian
1972 campaign coordinator

Kenneth W. Parkinson
Lawyer for campaign unit

Gordon C. Strachan
Assisted Mr. Haldeman

COLSON IS NAMED

A Question of Veracity of the President Is Indirectly Raised

By ANTHONY RIPLEY
Special to The New York Times

WASHINGTON, March 1—A Federal grand jury today indicted seven men, all former officials of President Nixon's Administration or of his 1972 re-election campaign, on charges of covering up the Watergate scandal.

Never before have so many close and trusted advisers of an American President faced criminal accusations in a single indictment.

All were charged with conspiracy — a conspiracy, the grand jury said, that continued "up to and including" today; six were charged additionally with obstruction of justice; two with perjury and three with false statements to the Federal Bureau of Investigation, the grand jury or both.

Five pages of Watergate material with indictment text begin on Page 14.

The indictment accused one defendant, H. R. Haldeman, the former White House chief of staff, of lying when he quoted the President as saying "it would be wrong" to raise hush money for the perpetrators of the original Watergate burglary—a break-in June 17, 1972, at the Democratic National Committee headquarters.

Endorsed Statement

This indirectly raised a question about Mr. Nixon's veracity because he endorsed Mr. Haldeman at a news conference last Aug. 22. The President recalled a meeting at the White House at which clemency for the Watergate defendants and financial support for their families was discussed. Mr. Nixon said he had told his White House counsel, John W. Dean 3d, "John it, is wrong, it won't work."

With the indictment, the grand jury handed to Chief Judge John J. Sirica of the Federal District Court here a sealed report, accompanied by a bulky briefcase reportedly containing information about Mr. Nixon's role in the Watergate affair.

This information was presumably intended for the House Judiciary Committee, which is considering a motion to impeach the President and put him on trial before the Senate.

The defendants and the charges against them are as follows:

John N. Mitchell, former Attorney General and director of Mr. Nixon's 1968 and 1972 Presidential campaigns—conspiracy, obstruction of justice, false statements to the F.B.I., false statements to the grand jury and perjury.

Mr. Haldeman—conspiracy, obstruction of justice and perjury.

John D. Ehrlichman, former assistant to the President for domestic affairs—conspiracy, obstruction of justice, false statements to the F.B.I. and false statements to the grand jury.

Charles W. Colson, former special counsel to the President—conspiracy and obstruction of justice.

Robert C. Mardian, former aide to Mr. Mitchell in the 1972 campaign—conspiracy.

Kenneth W. Parkinson, attorney for the Committee for the Re-election of the President—conspiracy and obstruction of justice.

Gordon C. Strachan, former aide to Mr. Haldeman—conspiracy, obstruction of justice and false statements to the grand jury.

The key conspiracy count

Continued on Page 16, Column 1

Heath, Trailing Labor Party In Britain, Declines to Resign

Special to The New York Times

LONDON, March 1—Prime Minister Heath, deprived of his majority in Parliament by Britain's voters, declined to resign tonight. His action raised the prospect that Mr. Heath's Conservatives, outnumbered by the Labor party in the House of Commons, would try to remain in power.

Thus Britain faced one of the gravest crises in her modern political history. The last time when neither main party won an over-all majority was in 1929.

There was no official word. But sources close to Mr. Heath said that he had told Queen Elizabeth tonight that he wanted to stay in office despite his party's failure to win an over-all majority in the general election yesterday.

Wilson Prepared to Govern

A few hours earlier, Harold Wilson, the leader of the Labor party, said that he was prepared to form a new Cabinet. Labor also failed to win a majority, but it holds five more seats than the Conservatives.

With the virtual stalemate between the two big parties, the balance of power in the new House would be held by smaller ones, including the Liberals, Scottish and Welsh Nationalists and the Members from Northern Ireland.

If Mr. Heath carries on with a minority government, despite his campaign bid for a "fresh mandate" and a "strong" majority, the question is for how long. He could go down to defeat quickly in the new House of Commons if a majority voted "no confidence" on some issue that arose for debate.

If that occurred, it is expected that he would ask the Queen to call for Mr. Wilson to form a new Government. Any call for a new election is regarded as unlikely until sometime later after the party leaders have a chance to try to win support in the House.

It was Mr. Heath, on Feb. 7, who used his power as Prime Minister to order Parliament dissolved and to call yesterday's election.

His goal was a mandate to settle a strike in the Government-owned coal mines that had crippled the country's production and forced it onto a three-day work week. Yesterday that mandate from the voters eluded him.

Tonight this was the standing of the parties in the new House of Commons, compared with their standings in the old one:

	New	Old
Labor	301	287
Conservative	296	322
Liberal	14	11
Others	23	10
Undecided	1	..

Mr. Heath, after a day of meetings with his advisers at 10 Downing Street, emerged shortly after 7:30 P.M. local time (3:30 P.M., New York time) for his meeting with the Queen, who had interrupted a visit to Australia to return here.

Statement Is Issued

A statement from 10 Downing Street said:

"The Queen has granted the Prime Minister's request to her to grant him an audience at 7:45 P.M. so that he can report on the current political situation."

If Mr. Health had submitted his resignation, the announcement would have come quickly. But it was clear that he had

Continued on Page 10, Column 1

British Pound Plunges

The value of the British pound fell 1.85 cents and prices of stocks went down 24 points in hectic trading in London yesterday in reaction to the setback for Britain's Conservative Government. Details on Page 41.

MITCHELL JUDGE HALTS TRIAL HERE

Weighs Motion for Mistrial Over 'Apparent Excesses' in Prosecutor's Speech

By RALPH BLUMENTHAL

Federal Judge Lee P. Gagliardi abruptly suspended yesterday the conspiracy-perjury trial of John N. Mitchell and Maurice H. Stans for what he called "apparent excesses" by the chief Government prosecutor in his opening statement.

Judge Gagliardi said that he would rule Monday on demands by defense attorneys for a mistrial. He ordered the prosecutor, Assistant United States Attorney James W. Rayhill, to submit a "documented response" with his "excuses."

While neither side would comment on the surprising development, some observers in the court believed it unlikely that the judge would decide to discharge the newly picked jury, which had been carefully isolated from news of yesterday's Watergate indictments naming Mr. Mitchell along with six others.

Conspiracy Charged

The historic trial was interrupted just after the Government had told the jury that it would prove that the defendants had conspired to quash a Federal investigation of Robert L. Vesco, the fugitive financier, in exchange for his secret $200,000 cash contribution to President Nixon's re-election campaign, that the defendants covered up the scheme and lied, about it when questioned under oath.

At the close of his hour and 50 minutes presentation in the fifth-floor courtroom in the

Continued on Page 18, Column 6

Nixon Urges Quick Trials, Cautions on Prejudgment

By JOHN HERBERS
Special to The New York Times

WASHINGTON, March 1 — President Nixon expressed the hope today that trials arising out of the new Watergate indictments "will move quickly to a just conclusion." He also cautioned the nation to remember that the accused are presumed innocent unless proved guilty.

"The indictments indicate the judicial process is finally moving toward resolution of the matter," Gerald L. Warren, the White House deputy press secretary, said in a statement approved by Mr. Nixon. The statement, read to newsmen, added:

"It is the President's hope that the trials will move quickly to a just conclusion. The President is confident that all Americans will join him in recognizing that those indicted are presumed innocent unless proof of guilt is established in the courts."

The statement also declared that the President had "always maintained that the judicial system is the proper forum for the resolution of the questions concerning Watergate."

Two of the seven men accused in today's indictment, Charles W. Colson and Kenneth W. Parkinson, issued personal statements of innocence and predicted their eventual exoneration on the charges. The other five relied on their attorneys to issue brief statements of innocence. [Details, Page 16.]

Word of the Watergate indictments reached the Oval Office today via the news tickers, and the President—busy with policy meetings, ceremony and entertaining of Congressmen—reacted with his brief formal statement a short time later.

Gen. Alexander M. Haig Jr. and Ronald L Ziegler, the President's chief assistants, informed Mr. Nixon of the charges against his former high associates just as the President was ending a meeting with his economic and energy advisers and was preparing to welcome the Mayor of Meridian, Miss., Tom Stuart, who had gotten 20,000 names on a petition in

Continued on Page 17, Column 3

SIRICA SAID TO GET FINDINGS ON NIXON

Grand Jury Reported to Ask Him to Give Evidence on Watergate to House

By JAMES M. NAUGHTON
Special to The New York Times

WASHINGTON, March 1—The Watergate grand jury reportedly asked Chief Judge John J. Sirica of the United States District Court today to give the House impeachment inquiry evidence relating to President Nixon's role in the Watergate case.

The grand jury issued a sealed "report" to the judge, and investigative sources said that they understood the document contained a description of the grand jury's findings about Mr. Nixon's possible involvement in the Watergate cover-up.

Moments later, the special Watergate prosecutor's office gave Judge Sirica a large briefcase said to contain a mass of documents and other evidence sought by the House Judiciary Committee for its investigation of the President's conduct in

Continued on Page 17, Column 1

The Scene in Sirica's Court: A Historic 13 Minutes

By LINDA CHARLTON
Special to The New York Times

WASHINGTON, March 1—At 10 A.M. today, Judge John J. Sirica was sitting in his chambers, reminiscing about his 16 years on the bench, whiling away the time until he could put a black robe over his gray suit and walk into Courtroom 2 to preside over history.

He arrived to be greeted with the shuffle of a crowd rising to its feet as a court functionary intoned ceremonial phrases, ending with the prayer for the country and for "this honorable court."

Some 13 minutes and surprisingly few words later, it was over.

The small, wood-paneled courtroom, with a checkerboard cork floor, an American flag and seal and two maroon ceramic water pitchers as the only decorations, was filled—with lawyers, Watergate task force staff members and reporters. The long line of would-be spectators that had started forming two hours before the 11 A.M. hearing was exiled to the corridor.

The prosecution's table was crowded with lawyers and papers. At the defense table, on the right side of the courtroom, sat a lone figure, Paul Murphy of the law firm of Hundley & Gacheris, representing John N. Mitchell.

The focus of attention was a group of 21 distributed

Continued on Page 18, Column 3

The New York Times/Marilyn Church

Assistant U.S. Attorney James W. Rayhill, standing, making his opening statement to the jury in the trial of John N. Mitchell, seated foreground, and Maurice H. Stans. Judge Lee P. Gagliardi is at upper left.

RED CROSS VISITS 65 ISRAELI P.O.W.'S

Sees Prisoners in Syria—Kissinger Confers With Assad in Damascus

By BERNARD GWERTZMAN
Special to The New York Times

DAMASCUS, Syria, March 1—Israeli prisoners held by Syria, long the focus of a dispute that prevented troop-pullback negotiations, received their first visit from Red Cross inspectors today.

The visit was arranged as part of the latest round of Middle East diplomacy, which carried Secretary of State Kissinger today from Egypt to Israel and then to Syria. He immediately began talks here with President Hafez al-Assad to convey ideas on troop disengagements that he had just received from Premier Golda Meir and other top Israeli officials.

At the end of the session between President Assad and the Secretary of State, both American and Syrian spokesmen indicated that talks on the separation of forces would continue after Mr. Kissinger left here tomorrow on his way to return to the United States. There was no announcement that any firm agreement had been reached on how negotiations between Israel and Syria would take place.

The Syrian spokesman said that Mr. Assad had not accepted the Israeli ideas presented to him by Mr. Kissinger and had offered one in return, which Mr. Kissinger "will study

Continued on Page 4, Column 3

Two-Way Radios in Taxis To Help City Fight Crime

By WILL LISSNER

The city officially began a program yesterday to put on the streets thousands of cruising taxicab drivers trained in the observation and reporting of crime and who are in radio communication with the police.

The new auxiliary arm of the police is the Civilian Radio Motor Patrol, which, Mayor Beame said, already has 500 crime watchers at work — 350 in the Bedford Park section of the Bronx and 150 in communities in Brooklyn operating from a Sheepshead Bay base.

Many taxicabs are dispatched by radio, the dispatcher having the transmitter and the cab the receiver. These one-way systems cannot be used in this program. The patrol system in use links the dispatcher and the driver by a two-way radio.

Under the system, telephone lines link the dispatcher to the switchboard operator in the police station. When necessary, the desk sergeant can then talk directly to the taxicab driver.

Two similar networks are to be opened soon in Queens, one in Long Island City and one in Richmond Hill, according to Stanley Bakalar, president of the Associated Radio Metered Taxi Owners Council.

"Eventually Manhattan and Staten Island will be covered, too," he added.

"This is another example of how we can use the city's greatest asset—its citizens—in attacking its number one problem, crime," Mayor Beame said. He and Police Commissioner Michael J. Codd and a group of Bronx officials joined in inaugurating the system at a ceremony at the Bedford Park station in the Bronx.

The program costs the city only the services of the coordinator, Lieut. John Higgins, and the training officers. In the Bronx the cost of installing the tie-lines between the taxi dispatchers and the police was paid for by the First National City Bank and the $12 monthly service charge for the tie-line phones is paid by the taxi cooperatives—the All City Radio Taxi Association and the Bronx Two-Way Radio Metered Taxi Company. Each taxi will display a yellow and black decal announcing its participation in "Civilian Radio Patrol, Community Service."

The city's police have a number of programs in operation using civilians to supplement the department's professional manpower. A primary one is the Auxiliary Police, whose members patrol the streets and perform other police functions under the supervision of police officers.

Another is the Blockwatcher Program, in which civilians act as the eyes of the police on their own block.

NEWS INDEX

"All the News That's Fit to Print"

The New York Times

LATE CITY EDITION

Weather: Warm, partly sunny today; partly cloudy tonight, tomorrow. Temp. range: today 62-78; Sunday 58-77. Highest Temp.-Hum. Index yesterday: 72. Details on Page 66.

VOL. CXXIII..No. 42,597 © 1974 The New York Times Company NEW YORK, MONDAY, SEPTEMBER 9, 1974 Higher in air delivery cities. 20 CENTS

FORD GIVES PARDON TO NIXON, WHO REGRETS 'MY MISTAKES'

U.S.-Bound Plane With 88 Crashes in Sea Off Greece

All on T.W.A. Flight From Tel Aviv Are Believed Dead—Wreckage Is Sighted

By The Associated Press

ATHENS, Sept. 8 — A Trans World Airlines jet bound for the United States with 88 persons aboard crashed today in the stormy Ionian Sea off Greece. The Greek Civil Aviation Authority said there appeared to be no survivors.

T.W.A. said that the Boeing 707 fell from an overcast sky after the pilot reported that an engine had failed.

Flight 841 originated in Tel Aviv, stopped in Athens and was scheduled to make stops in Rome and New York.

The airline's Tel Aviv office said 49 passengers boarded the plane there for Rome and the United States. They included 17 Americans, including a baby, 13 Japanese, four Italians, four French, three Indians, two Iranians, two Israelis, two Sri Lankans, an Australian and a Canadian.

The nationalities of 30 other passengers and the nine crew members were not immediately known. [Reuters reported a total of 37 Americans aboard.]

[In Beirut, it was reported that a Palestinian youth organization said it had placed a guerrilla aboard the plane with a bomb. In New York, however, a spokesman for T.W.A. said sabotage was "highly unlikely."]

"All that can be seen by our overflying planes are remnants of the wreckage and bodies floating on the surface," said a Greek aviation official. "The stormy sea in the area is making it difficult for our ships to approach.

"Only when our ships can get nearer will we be able to

Continued on Page 6, Column 1

The New York Times/Sept. 9, 1974

State Panel Charges City Fails to Pursue Fugitives

By SELWYN RAAB

The State Commission of Investigation disclosed yesterday that the backlog of missing bail jumpers and probation violators in the city had risen during the last three years from 82,000 to 130,000.

After sifting through voluminous police and court records, the commission largely blamed the Police Department's warrant division for the 50 per cent increase since 1971 in unexecuted warrants for criminal defendants who fail to appear in court. The police division is primarily responsible for capturing such fugitives.

Sharply criticizing the performance of the division over the last three years, the investigation commission said in a report that it had found that warrant officers rarely worked at night or on weekends and that a typical attempt to track down a fugitive consisted of no more than one or two visits to an often fictitious home address given by the suspect.

The commission described the problem of fugitives here as "critical to the public safety" and called for a major reorganization of the warrant division.

"At the present time the people of New York City are unnecessarily subjected to the risk of grave harm from known criminals because of ineffective warrant enforcement," the commission declared in its report.

In response to the findings, Police Commissioner Michael J. Codd said he was "concerned" by the growing backlog, and he hinted there might be a reorganization of the warrant division.

He also announced the assignment of First Deputy Com-

Continued on Page 21, Column 1

'PAIN' EXPRESSED

Ex-President Cites His Sorrow at the Way He Handled Watergate

By EVERETT R. HOLLES

Special to The New York Times

SAN CLEMENTE, Calif., Sept. 8—President Ford's pardon for Richard M. Nixon evoked today from the former President an expression of "regret and pain at the anguish my mistakes over Watergate have caused the nation and the Presidency."

Within 10 minutes after the Presidential pardon was announced in Washington, Mr. Nixon's statement was released at his Casa Pacifica estate, citing his sorrow in allowing Watergate to become "a national tragedy."

"That the way I tried to deal with Watergate was the wrong way is the burden I shall bear for every day of the life that is left in me," he said.

Hopes Burden Is Lifted

In a subsequent statement, given in response to reporters' questions, an aide quoted Mr. Nixon as saying that, in gratefully accepting the Presidential pardon, he hoped Mr. Ford's "compassionate act would contribute to lifting the burdens of Watergate from our country."

When the Nixon statement was released by his adviser and former White House press secretary, Ronald L. Ziegler, Mr. and Mrs. Nixon were already on the way to a new haven of seclusion away from the heavily guarded Casa Pacifica.

They left at 7 A.M., Pacific Coast time, in a large black limousine accompanied by Secret Service agents and Mr. Nixon's military aide, Lieut. Col. Jack Brennan, reportedly for the Palm Desert estate of Walter H. Annenberg, Ambassador to Britain.

A close friend of the Nixons said the former President planned to play golf on the Annenberg private 18-hole course.

[In New York, Mr. Nixon's daughter, Julie Nixon Eisenhower, said that her father had gone to the Annenberg estate "for a rest," The Associated Press reported.]

Mr. Ziegler and Mr. Nixon's appointments secretary, Stephen

Continued on Page 24, Column 1

Sygma

Richard M. Nixon in a photo made earlier this year

Associated Press

President Ford speaking at the White House yesterday

The Statement by Nixon

I have been informed that President Ford has granted me a full and absolute pardon for any charges which may be brought against me for actions taken during the time I was the President of the United States. In accepting this pardon, I hope that his compassionate act will contribute to lifting the burden of Watergate from our country.

Here in California, my perspective on Watergate is quite different than it was while I was embattled in the midst of the controversy while I was still subject to the unrelenting daily demand of the Presidency itself.

Looking back on what is still in my mind a complex and confusing maze of events, decisions, pressures, and personalities, one thing I can see clearly now is that I was wrong in not acting more decisively and more forthrightly in dealing with Watergate, particularly when it reached the stage of judicial proceedings and grew from a political scandal into a national tragedy.

No words can describe the depths of my regret and pain at the anguish my mistakes over Watergate have caused the nation and the Presidency, a nation I so deeply love and an institution I so greatly respect.

I know that many fair-minded people believe that my motivation and actions in the Watergate affair were intentionally self-serving and illegal. I now understand how my own mistakes and misjudgments have contributed to that belief and seemed to support it. This burden is the heaviest one of all to bear.

That the way I tried to deal with Watergate was the wrong way is a burden I shall bear for every day of the life that is left to me.

Proclamation of Pardon

Richard Nixon became the thirty-seventh President of the United States on January 20, 1969, and was re-elected in 1972 for a second term by the electors of forty-nine of the fifty states. His term in office continued until his resignation on August 9, 1974.

Pursuant to resolutions of the House of Representatives, its Committee on the Judiciary conducted an inquiry and investigation on the impeachment of the President extending over more than eight months. The hearings of the committee and its deliberations, which received wide national publicity over television, radio, and in printed media, resulted in votes adverse to Richard Nixon on recommended Articles of Impeachment.

As a result of certain acts or omissions occurring before his resignation from the office of President, Richard Nixon has become liable to possible indictment and trial for offenses against the United States. Whether or not he shall be so prosecuted depends on findings of the appropriate grand jury and on the discretion of the authorized prosecutor. Should an indictment ensue, the accused shall then be entitled to a fair trial by an impartial jury, as guaranteed to every individual by the Constitution.

It is believed that a trial of Richard Nixon, if it became necessary, could not fairly begin until a year or more has elapsed. In the meantime, the tranquility to which this nation has been restored by the events of recent weeks could be irreparably lost by the prospects of bringing to trial a former President of the United States. The prospects of such trial will cause prolonged and divisive debate over the propriety of exposing to further punishment and degradation a man who has already paid the unprecedented penalty of relinquishing the highest elective office in the United States.

NOW, THEREFORE, I, Gerald R. Ford, President of the United States, pursuant to the pardon power conferred upon me by Article II, Section 2, of the Constitution, have granted and by these presents do grant a full, free, and absolute pardon unto Richard Nixon for all offenses against the United States which he, Richard Nixon, has committed or may have committed or taken part in during the period from January 20, 1969, through August 9, 1974.

IN WITNESS WHEREOF, I have hereunto set my hand this 8th day of September in the year of our Lord nineteen hundred seventy-four, and of the independence of the United States of America the 199th.

NO CONDITIONS SET

Action Taken to Spare Nation and Ex-Chief, President Asserts

By JOHN HERBERS

Special to The New York Times

WASHINGTON, Sept. 8—President Ford granted former President Richard M. Nixon an unconditional pardon today for all Federal crimes that he "committed or may have committed or taken part in" while in office, an act Mr. Ford said was intended to spare Mr. Nixon and the nation further punishment in the Watergate scandals.

Mr. Nixon, in San Clemente, Calif., accepted the pardon, which exempts him from indictment and trial for, among

Text of the Ford statement is printed on Page 24.

other things, his role in the cover-up of the Watergate burglary. He issued a statement saying that he could now see he was "wrong in not acting more decisively and more forthrightly in dealing with Watergate."

'Act of Mercy'

Philip W. Buchen, the White House counsel, who advised Mr. Ford on the legal aspects of the pardon, said the "act of mercy" on the President's part was done without making any demands on Mr. Nixon and without asking the advice of the Watergate special prosecutor, Leon Jaworski, who had the legal responsibility to prosecute the case.

Reaction to the pardon was sharply divided, but not entirely along party lines. Most Democrats who commented voiced varying degrees of disapproval and dismay, while most Republican comment backed President Ford.

However, Senators Edward W. Brooke of Massachusetts and Jacob K. Javits of New York disagreed with the action. [Page 25.]

Dangers Seen in Delay

Mr. Buchen said that, at the President's request, he had asked Mr. Jaworski how long it would be, in the event Mr. Nixon was indicted, before he could be brought to trial and that Mr. Jaworski had replied it would be at least nine months or more, because of the enormous amount of publicity the charges against Mr. Nixon had received when the House Judiciary Committee recommended impeachment.

This was one reason Mr. Ford cited for granting the pardon, saying he had concluded that "many months and perhaps more years will have to pass before Richard Nixon could obtain a fair trial by jury in any jurisdiction of the United States under governing decisions of the Supreme Court."

"During this long period of delay and potential litigation, ugly passions would again be aroused, our people would

Continued on Page 24, Column 4

Jaworski Won't Challenge Pardon, Spokesman Says

By JOHN M. CREWDSON

Special to The New York Times

WASHINGTON, Sept. 8 — Leon Jaworski, the Watergate special prosecutor, apparently has no plans to challenge the validity of the unconditional pardon that President Ford bestowed today on Richard M. Nixon, according to a spokesman for Mr. Jaworski.

The special prosecutor "accepts the decision," said John Barker, the spokesman. "He thinks it's within the President's power to do it. His feeling is that the President is exercising his lawful power, and he accepts it."

Mr. Barker added that Mr. Jaworski had not been consulted in advance on the decision by either Mr. Ford or White House lawyers, and learned of the President's position less than an hour before it was announced.

Some lawyers, including Senator Edmund S. Muskie, Democrat of Maine, questioned the legal and constitutional validity of a Presidential pardon conferred before an indictment had been brought or a conviction obtained.

"It could be challenged," declared Mr. Muskie, adding "there are those who say that it ought to be challenged, lest the precedent be established in an undesirable way."

But the remarks by Mr. Barker and by other lawyers familiar with the Watergate prosecutions indicated strongly that Mr. Jaworski was little inclined to test the pardon by seeking to indict Mr. Nixon, which one authority described as "the way to do it."

The principal Watergate grand jury voted earlier this

Continued on Page 25, Column 6

Nixon Tapes Must Be Kept 3 Years for Use in Court

By R. W. APPLE Jr.

Special to The New York Times

WASHINGTON, Sept. 8 — Richard M. Nixon and the Ford Administration have reached an agreement under which the former President will ultimately be permitted to destroy the White House tape recordings that led to his downfall.

The agreement, announced today by the White House, also provides that all of Mr. Nixon's Presidential papers and tapes will be preserved for three years for possible use in court cases arising out of the Watergate scandals.

Mr. Nixon signed the agreement in San Clemente, Calif., on Friday; it was countersigned yesterday by Arthur F. Sampson, head of the General Services Administration.

Philip W. Buchen, counsel for President Ford, said at a White House briefing this afternoon that Mr. Ford instructed him about 10 days ago to resolve the controversy over the White House files so the Administration would not find itself "enmeshed for a long time" in jurisdictional disputes.

Although Mr. Buchen denied

Continued on Page 26, Column 1

CANDIDATES SKIRT LAWSON FINANCING

Evidence Shows Big Money Played a Major Role—Voting Is Tomorrow

By FRANK LYNN

Big money—from family fortunes and large contributors—played a major role in the Democratic primary campaigns despite new state and Federal

Ballot and candidate list appear on Page 28.

campaign-finance laws that were supposed to have reduced its influence.

The question of how much money was spent and where it came from was being discussed as the primary campaigns drew to a close. The polls will be open tomorrow in the city from 6 A.M. to 9 P.M. and in the rest of the state from noon to 9 P.M.

Interviews with campaign aides and campaign financial reports show that there was considerable evidence of circumventing of the new laws in fact and in spirit, possible unrecorded cash contributions and spending and even "laundering" of campaign contribu-

Continued on Page 28, Column 1

Knievel Safe as Rocket Falls Into Snake Canyon

By JON NORDHEIMER

Special to The New York Times

TWIN FALLS, Idaho, Sept. 8—Evel Knievel failed today in an attempt to rocket 1,600 feet across the Snake River Canyon when a tail parachute deployed prematurely on the take-off of his vehicle.

The vehicle, which Mr. Knievel calls the Sky-Cycle X-2, went streaking to about 1,000 feet above the river before floating into the canyon to make a nose-down crash landing on a rocky bank at the river's edge.

Mr. Knievel was pulled from the craft several minutes later by a rescue team. He had superficial cuts and scrapes of the face and legs.

The flight aborted almost as soon as steam exploded from a rear nozzle of the 13-foot-long craft and propelled it along a 108-foot launching track aimed at the cloudless sky.

A drogue parachute designed to slow the rocket at an altitude of 2,800 feet deployed while the vehicle was still on the ramp, whipping in a blast of steam.

Once the vehicle lifted off the ramp, it turned belly up and the main chute, attached to the drogue, was automatically deployed at about 1,000 feet.

A large crowd along the canyon's south rim gasped as a 15-mile-an-hour wind blew the vehicle back toward them, rocking gently in the air nose-down like a red, white and blue Christmas ornament.

For several seconds, it appeared that Mr. Knievel, who could be seen struggling inside the open cockpit, might crash into the crowd on the rim of the canyon.

But the vehicle dropped onto a boulder-strewn ledge, bounced twice on its bottom and came to rest about 20 feet from the water's edge.

The vehicle was obscured from sight from the plateau 540 feet above, and some cries of anguish were heard in the crowd when several minutes went by and there was no sign of the stuntman.

But a helicopter picked him

Continued on Page 50, Column 5

Chris Evert Beaten

Evonne Goolagong of Australia defeated Chris Evert in the semifinals of the United States Open tennis at Forest Hills, Queens, yesterday, 6-0, 6-7, 6-3, and will meet Billie Jean King in the final today. Details, Page 45.

Some Mixed Reactions in Foley Square

By PAUL L. MONTGOMERY

A few hours after President Ford's pardon of his predecessor was announced yesterday, Mr. and Mrs. Wilson Wainwright of Olean, N.Y., were strolling in Foley Square in lower Manhattan, looking at the public buildings.

"It's going to make a lot of people mad, but I can see why he did it," Mr. Wainwright said. "It wouldn't look right to the rest of the world to have a President of the United States in jail."

Mr. Wainwright, here on a late-summer vacation, was asked if he had any doubts about former President Richard M. Nixon's guilt.

"None that I can see," his wife, Judy, replied. "I guess some people would say it would have been better to pardon him after the courts decided."

Nearby, at 100 Centre Street, the afternoon session of the arraignment part of Criminal Court was about to begin. In the dingy, crowded room, lawyers and policemen, and defendants and their families lounged on the oak benches, waiting for the judge to return from lunch.

Hal Mayerson and Peter Davis of the Legal Aid Society, which represents indigent defendants, had been discussing the pardon during the break.

"It's a bit unseemly to pardon someone before they're prosecuted," Mr. Davis said. "It doesn't do much for the concept of equal justice under law."

"How about all the young men who refused to serve in an illegal, immoral and vicious war?" Mr. Mayerson asked. "Is he going to pardon them, too? It's like Peter was saying, maybe they should give Nixon a pardon if he does 18 months of alternate service."

Mr. Mayerson looked around the room.

"Seriously, though, it's outrageous," he continued. "You get a lady here who's going to jail for stealing a blouse, or some guy in on assault because he got tired of living with the rats and hit somebody. And here's one of the biggest plun-

Continued on Page 25, Column 6

terHorst Quits Post To Protest Pardon

Special to The New York Times

WASHINGTON, Sept. 8—J. F. terHorst, whose appointment as White House press secretary was the first in President Ford's new Administration, resigned tonight in what he said was a protest over the granting of an unconditional pardon to former President Nixon.

In a statement released by the White House tonight, Mr. Ford said that he deeply regretted Mr. terHorst's decision.

"I understand his position," the statement said. "I appreciate the fact that good people will differ with me on this very difficult decision. However, it is my judgment that it is in

Continued on Page 25, Column 1

NEWS INDEX

"All the News That's Fit to Print"

The New York Times

LATE CITY EDITION

Weather: Continued mostly cloudy, cool today, tonight and tomorrow. Temperature range: today 46-58; Tuesday 45-53. Details on Page 81.

VOL. CXXIV. . No. 42,830 | © 1975 The New York Times Company | NEW YORK, WEDNESDAY, APRIL 30, 1975 | Price higher in air delivery cities. | 20 CENTS

MINH SURRENDERS, VIETCONG IN SAIGON; 1,000 AMERICANS AND 5,500 VIETNAMESE EVACUATED BY COPTER TO U.S. CARRIERS

U.S., GREECE AGREE TO END HOME PORT FOR THE 6TH FLEET

Air Base of Americans at Athens Is Also Closed, but Some Facilities Remain

By United Press International

ATHENS, April 29—United States and Greek officials announced today the termination of the home-port arrangement for Sixth Fleet ships at the port of Eleusis near Athens and the closing of the American air base at Athens airport.

The announcement came in a joint statement at the end of a second round of talks on the status of United States military facilities in Greece.

The Greek Government threatened to close all United States bases and it withdrew from the North Atlantic Treaty Organization's military command after the invasion of Cyprus by Turkey last July.

"Certain United States facilities which contribute to Greek defense needs will continue to operate on the Greek Air Force base at Hellenikon," today's statement said.

The statement said that the second phase of the talks, held April 7 to 29 by the two delegations under the United States Embassy Minister, Monteagle Stearns, and Ambassador Petros Kalogeras of Greece also discussed the status of other facilities.

"Agreement is also expected on the elimination, reduction and conservation of other United States facilities in Greece," it said.

The two delegations said that they made progress on the review of the privileges, immunities and exemptions of American personnel in Greece.

The two Governments said

Continued on Page 4, Column 4

United Press International

A crewman from an American helicopter helping evacuees to the top of a building in Saigon for flight to a U.S. carrier

FORD UNITY PLEA

President Says That Departure 'Closes a Chapter' for U.S.

By JOHN W. FINNEY
Special to The New York Times

WASHINGTON, April 29—The United States ended two decades of military involvement in Vietnam today with the evacuation of about 1,000 Americans from Saigon as well as more than 5,500 South Vietnamese.

The emergency helicopter evacuation was ordered last night by President Ford after the Saigon airport was closed

Ford statement and excerpts from Kissinger's, Page 17.

because of Communist rocket and artillery fire. The 1,000 Americans were the last contingent of a force that once numbered more than 500,000.

They were carried by a fleet of 81 American helicopters to carriers in the South China Sea.

The helicopters removed the 5,500 South Vietnamese citizens because their lives were presumed to be in danger with a Communist take-over of South Vietnam. Over the last two weeks, a total of about 55,000 South Vietnamese have been removed. Most of them will come to the United States. The helicopter flights ended the United States evacuation of South Vietnamese.

Last Marines Evacuated

The final withdrawal of Americans was completed at 7:52 P.M., about two hours after the White House had announced the evacuation was completed, when 11 marines were taken by helicopter from the roof of the American Embassy in Saigon. Officials said that the marines, the last of a security guard sent in to protect the evacuation, were safely removed although small-arms fire had broken out around the deserted embassy.

President Ford, in a statement issued by the White House, said the evacuation "closes a chapter in the American experience." In a plea for national unity in the post-Vietnam period, the President said:

"I ask all Americans to close ranks, to avoid recrimination about the past, to look ahead to the many goals we share and to work together on the great tasks that remain to be accomplished."

Appeal by Kissinger

At a news conference, Secretary of State Kissinger appealed to North Vietnam not to storm Saigon by force because the United States believed the new South Vietnamese Govern-

Continued on Page 17, Column 1

END OF DEFENSE

Troops Leave Posts in Capital and Turn in Their Weapons

By The Associated Press

SAIGON, South Vietnam, Wednesday, April 30—President Duong Van Minh announced today the unconditional surrender of the Saigon Government and its military forces to the Vietcong.

Columns of South Vietnamese troops pulled out of their defensive positions in the capital and marched to central points to turn in their weapons.

[In Washington, the White House said that President Ford had "no comment" on the surrender of Saigon, but a White House spokesman said the surrender was considered "inevitable." Page 16]

Troops Move In

Within two hours, Communist forces began moving into Saigon, and a jeep flying the Vietcong flag and carrying eight cheering men in civilian

The text of President Minh's statement is on Page 16.

clothes armed with an assortment of weapons could be seen driving near the United States Embassy compound.

The Vietcong flag was raised over the presidential palace at 12:15 P.M. (12:15 A.M. Wednesday, New York time), and soon after a detachment of Communist troops in a jeep arrived at the palace and asked General Minh to accompany them. He drove off with them, but their destination was not immediately disclosed.

Vietcong flags materialized on other buildings as well, and Vietcong soldiers soon walked along the main streets shaking hands with Saigon residents. The red, yellow-starred flag of North Vietnam could also be seen on trucks carrying soldiers in green helmets and uniforms.

Bursts of Fire

Sporadic bursts of firing could be heard, but the only resistance to the Communist take-over was reported to be from marines stationed at the zoo and public gardens.

The take-over followed by hours the ending of the American involvement in Vietnam through the evacuation of most of the approximately 1,000 Americans still here yesterday.

The surrender announcement, made in a broadcast to the nation, signaled the end of three decades of fighting. It came 21 years after the 1954 Geneva accords divided Vietnam into North and South and a little more than two years after the Vietnam cease-fire

Continued on Page 16, Column 1

Abram Offers Bills To Curtail Abuses Of Nursing Homes

By ALFONSO A. NARVAEZ
Special to The New York Times

ALBANY, April 29—Morris B. Abram proposed today a series of changes in the laws governing nursing homes to "deal with the most serious immediate problems" uncovered during his month-long investigation.

The proposals were contained in a package of 11 bills submitted to Governor Carey and legislative leaders by Mr. Abram, head of the Moreland Act Commission investigating the nursing-home industry.

Among other things, they would authorize nursing-home residents to file class-action suits for deprivation of their rights and would entitle them to receive a minimum of 25 per cent of the daily reimbursement rate paid by government regulations for each day of a violation.

[In Washington, Senator Frank Moss, Democrat of Utah and chairman of the long-term care subcommittee of the Special Committee on Aging, introduced a package of 36 bills for nursing home reform. Among them were measures to make long-term care more readily available to all older Americans, improve inspection and enforcement procedures and provide training for nursing-home physicians, nurses,

Continued on Page 81, Column 3

CAMBODIA ORDERS FOREIGNERS OUT

Planned 250-Mile Road Trip to Border Is Protested by Paris as Debilitating

By FLORA LEWIS
Special to The New York Times

PARIS, April 29—The French Government said today that the people who have been isolated in its Phnom Penh embassy since the Cambodian Communists took over two weeks ago had been ordered expelled "in the worst possible conditions."

There are 610 refugees in the embassy. They are to be sent out by truck to the town of Poipet on the Thailand border, beginning tomorrow.

Foreign Minister Jean Sauvagnargues told newsmen after having conferred with President Valéry Giscard d'Estaing;

"We fear these extremely precarious evacuation conditions will be beyond the strength of some whose health is poor."

"We continue to insist that the plane that we have held in Vientiane for evacuation of the ill be allowed to land in Phnom Penh."

However, a Foreign Ministry spokesman said that so far there has been no response to

Continued on Page 17, Column 6

74 Saigon Planes Fly 2,000 to Thailand

By DAVID A. ANDELMAN
Special to The New York Times

BANGKOK, Thailand, April 29—At least 74 South Vietnamese Air Force planes fleeing the country streamed into U Taphao air base in southern Thailand without warning this afternoon.

The pilots and passengers—2,000 people—requested asylum, American and Thai Foreign Ministry officials said.

About 30 of the planes were F-5 jet fighters and there were reports that at least one had crashed on a highway near the base as it was making its approach.

The planes began arriving at the huge naval and air base on the Gulf of Siam at about the time that the American evacuation of South Vietnam was ending and the planes were still landing as night fell.

The aircraft were said to include C-47 transports and the C-130 cargo planes that the American military has been using to ferry refugees from South Vietnam to Guam and the Philippines. However, all the aircraft were understood to be Vietnam Air Force planes, originally supplied by the United States.

A Thai Foreign Ministry spokesman said that American authorities at U Taphao had been asked to turn over the aircraft to the Thai Government, which would return them to "the new South Vietnamese government." The pilots and passengers, the Thai spokesman said, "must leave Thailand."

"They just landed first and asked permission afterwards," said an astounded Thai Foreign Ministry official. Other Government sources said that apparently no efforts were made to prevent the planes from landing and no aircraft went up to intercept the fighters as they roared in.

American Embassy officials in Bangkok declined to comment on the Thai request that the planes be returned and their status was unclear. An unresolved question here appeared to be whether the planes were still American property or belonged to whatever government continued in Saigon. The planes could be worth $200-million, one official said.

No details were available on the status of the refugees or

Continued on Page 16, Column 6

G.M.'s Profits Fall

First-quarter profits of General Motors declined 50.8 per cent from the depressed 1974 quarter. Page 53.

HEAVY USERS FACE CON ED INCREASE

P.S.C. Also Orders Cuts for Smaller Consumers

By WILL LISSNER

The state's Public Service Commission ordered the Consolidated Edison Company yesterday to raise its rates for those customers who accounted for the heaviest summer power demands and to cut the rates for customers whose usage did not create excess power demand.

The change — technically a revision of the rate structure approved last November to give the utility $338.7-million more a year — will not mean any extra revenue for the company. Nor will it affect the rates for the great majority of customers, the 2.5 million small residential and commercial users.

Instead, yesterday's order makes revisions in bills that will take less than $20-million from some customers and give it to others, a relatively small amount compared with its total annual billings for electricity of $2.10-billion. It affected less than 500,000 of its 2.9 million customers in New York City, Westchester County and part of Nassau County.

But the order was significant because it introduced into energy ratemaking the philosophy that the customers who are responsible for excess costs should be required to bear more

Continued on Page 34, Column 5

2d Key Met Museum Aide Quits In Dispute Over Hoving Methods

By GRACE GLUECK

With an attack on Thomas P. F. Hoving's administration at the Metropolitan Museum of Art alleging its inability to function "in any way that creates or preserves trust, confidence and decency," Anthony M. Clark, chairman of the museum's department of European paintings, has resigned.

Mr. Clark's resignation, one of several that have occurred among senior curatorial personnel at the museum in recent years, represents the first open challenge to Mr. Hoving's administration.

The resignation, effective June 30, follows that of John Walsh, the vice chairman and curator of this key department a month ago. Mr. Clark would not speak for Mr. Walsh, who is abroad, but it is understood that their basic grievances are similar.

"I can't work with or for the present administration at the Met," said Mr. Clark, who had been director of the Minneapolis Institute of Arts for 10 years before his appointment to the Metropolitan in 1973. "I believe that its relation to art has become incidental, wrong and even risky. It's also hell on professionals."

In a statement last night, Mr. Hoving said that he was

Continued on Page 24, Column 1

NEWS INDEX

United Press International

President Ford and Secretary of State Kissinger returning to White House to resume talks on Vietnam. They had just said good-by to King Hussein of Jordan after visit.

Saigon Copter Lands on Another In Stampede to U.S. Ship's Deck

By The Associated Press

ABOARD U.S.S. BLUE RIDGE, in South China Sea, April 29—Scores of South Vietnamese helicopters filled with military men and civilians fled Saigon today and headed out to sea to search for the carriers of the United States Seventh Fleet.

Seven of the helicopters arrived unexpectedly above this vessel carrying Americans and Vietnamese evacuated from South Vietnam. The seven copters made a dash for the helipad at the rear of the ship.

One pilot dropped his helicopter on the blades of another that had just landed and chunks of metal ripped through the air. The top helicopter, with its load of women and children, nearly toppled into the sea, but they were rescued and there were no injuries.

United States sailors heaved the two damaged choppers overboard to clear the landing pad. For the Vietnamese it was a last-ditch chance to survive.

As other Vietnamese helicopters landed their passengers were pulled free. American sailors ripped the doors off the craft to make them sink and the pilots then jettisoned them in the sea to make room for other arrivals circling overhead. Two small craft rescued the swimming pilots.

The American evacuation was reported orderly, although it was delayed several times because of weather and pilot fatigue.

The Blue Ridge is the command and communications vessel of the 40-ship Seventh Fleet armada waiting off the coast of South Vietnam to evacuate Americans and other foreigners

Continued on Page 17, Column 2

1976

Science and Hope

1981

FRONT PAGE NEWS 1976-1981

Celebrating the Bicentennial

JULY 5, 1976

Americans celebrated the 200th birthday of the United States for 18 months, long enough to re-enact major milestones like Paul Revere's ride and Washington's crossing of the Delaware. By the time the Fourth of July rolled around, the agenda called for more than the usual picnics and fireworks. New York welcomed a proud flotilla of square-riggers that looked like Revolutionary War–era vessels along with modern, motorized cruisers. Americans looked back to that first Fourth, which President Gerald R. Ford called "the beginning of a continuing adventure." They voiced relief that the government established then had withstood the recent crisis of Watergate. And they tried their luck with a New Jersey bicentennial lottery game, which promised an annual payout of $1,776.

'Son of Sam' Suspect Arrested

AUGUST 11, 1977

"Well, you got me," the suspect said—an understated ending to a terrifying string of cold-blooded murders that became a symbol, and then an enduring memory, of the crime-filled seventies in New York. His preferred targets were young women with shoulder-length hair in middle-class neighborhoods in Brooklyn, Queens and the Bronx. He shot them alone at first, and later in parked cars when they were out on a date (he also fired at their boyfriends). The gunman's nickname came from a note he had left beside the bodies of a couple he had killed in April 1977: "I am the Son of Sam. I love to hunt. Prowling the streets looking for fair game." The note also said, "The women of Queens are the prettyest (sic)." Detectives tracked down the suspect, a deranged postal worker named David L. Berkowitz, from parking tickets issued to cars on the street where he had shot another couple in July. Berkowitz pleaded guilty to six murders and seven attempted murders, and was sentenced to life in prison.

High Court Backs Affirmative Action

JUNE 29, 1978

Ruling on a landmark civil rights case, the Supreme Court hedged. Its five-to-four decision upheld affirmative action in principle but said university admissions quotas based solely on race violated federal law. The court insisted on less rigid racial preferences, describing race as one element among many that schools could consider. That standard was eventually applied to hiring decisions in the workplace.

Conceived in a Test tube

JULY 27, 1978

The newborn infant had an ordinary-sounding name but an extraordinary story. Louise Brown was the world's first baby born after in vitro fertilization. Some scientists discounted the achievement because her mother's doctors—who had experimented with fertilizing and implanting eggs for years—did not submit the details to a medical journal, they peddled them to a London tabloid. She was born as doctors in Boston isolated a single human gene for the first time, clearing the way for tests for birth defects. Louise Brown had a baby of her own in 2006: a boy, conceived naturally.

The Jonestown Massacre

NOVEMBER 21, 1978

Congressman Leo Ryan and an entourage that included a television correspondent went on a fact-finding mission that ended in their deaths—and the mass suicide of nearly a thousand others, ordered by their charismatic leader to drink Kool-Aid laced with cyanide. Ryan had been investigating a religious cult called the People's Temple and the Rev. Jim Jones, a onetime San Francisco activist who built a belief system around the notion that he was a reincarnation of Jesus and Lenin. Ryan and his group were shot as they tried to escape. Jones's followers quickly ladled out the poison; their leader shot himself to death on an altar.

Diplomatic Relations With China

DECEMBER 16, 1978

It had been more than six years since President Richard M. Nixon's history-making trip to China ended with a promise to work toward normalizing diplomatic relations. President Jimmy Carter revived the negotiations and agreed to more than new embassies in Washington and Beijing. He promised to scrap Washington's obligations under a mutual defense treaty with the Chinese nationalists of Taiwan. That angered conservatives like Senator Barry Goldwater, who said Carter's maneuvering "stabs in the back the nation of Taiwan."

The Camp David Accords

MARCH 27, 1979

"No more war, no more bloodshed," Prime Minister Menachem Begin of Israel declared after signing the first peace treaty between his nation and an Arab country. The treaty became known as the Camp David Accords, for the compound in the Maryland mountains where President Jimmy Carter installed Begin and President Anwar el-Sadat of Egypt in separate cabins. Carter shuttled back and forth, eventually convincing both to agree to historic concessions from both. The result was two agreements. One established the framework for the phased withdrawal of Israeli troops from the Sinai. The other called for eventual Palestinian self-government in the West Bank and Gaza.

The 'Thatcher Revolution'

MAY 4, 1979

"Free choice is ultimately what life is about," Margaret Thatcher declared after she was elected prime minister in Britain. The first woman to serve as the prime minister of a European country, she remained in power for 11 years, longer than any other British prime minister since Lord Salisbury stepped down in 1902. Mrs. Thatcher took office after a crippling winter of strikes shut down schools and left garbage piling up in the streets. She responded by limiting the power of trade unions, cut tingtaxes, privatizing social services and building up the military.

I.R.A. Kills Lord Mountbatten

AUGUST 28, 1979

To Britons, he was a hero of World War II, a confidant of Queen Elizabeth II and an influential adviser to prime ministers. To the Irish Republican Army, Earl Mountbatten of Burma had the misfortune of being the high-profile target of what the I.R.A.'s military wing called "an execution," even though he had not played a personal role in Britain's response to "the troubles" that had wracked Northern Ireland for decades. Lord Mountbatten was killed when his fishing boat exploded. "His death leaves a gap that can never be filled," Prime Minister Margaret Thatcher said.

Mount St. Helens Erupts

MAY 21, 1980

The deadliest volcanic eruption in United States history began with a mild earthquake in Washington State that touched off a frightening landslide. Volcanic debris rumbled down from near the top of Mount St. Helens, one of some 160 active volcanoes in what geologists call the Pacific Ring of Fire, killing 57 people and destroying 250 homes. The eruption left Mount St. Helens 1,300 feet shorter than it had been; its dome had given way to a U-shaped basin that reminded some of a lunar landscape. Not President Jimmy Carter. "The moon looks more like a golf course compared to what's up there," he said after flying over Mount St. Helens.

John Lennon Assassinated

DECEMBER 9, 1980

The doormen on West 72nd Street, steps from Central Park, had noticed the awkward-looking man in the black raincoat, but they figured he was just another Beatles fan making the pilgrimage to John Lennon's fortress-like apartment building. But Mark David Chapman, who already had Lennon's autograph, was looking for fame. Mentally ill, he thought he would find it by shooting Lennon, and when Lennon's limousine pulled up, he pulled out a revolver and fired at close range. Lennon's wife, Yoko Ono, screamed for help as Chapman paced back and forth, waiting for the police to arrive. Chapman was sentenced to 20 years to life in prison. More than 20 years later, he told a parole hearing that his fame gambit had failed: "I'm a bigger nobody than I was before, because, you know, people hate me now instead of, you know, for something positive." He has been denied parole four times and remains in Attica prison in upstate New York.

TODAY: SIX PAGES OF BICENTENNIAL ARTICLES AND PICTURES

"All the News That's Fit to Print"

The New York Times

LATE CITY EDITION

Weather: Partly cloudy and less humid today through tomorrow. Temperature range: today 64-80; Sunday 63-82. Details on page 30.

VOL. CXXV ... No. 43,262 NEW YORK, MONDAY, JULY 5, 1976 — 25 cents beyond 50-mile zone from New York City, except Long Island. Higher in air delivery cities. — 20 CENTS

Nation and Millions in City Joyously Hail Bicentennial

ISRAELIS RETURN WITH 103 RESCUED IN UGANDA RAID

Toll Is Put at 3 Hostages, 7 Hijackers, Army Officer and 20 of Amin's Men

FORD LAUDS OPERATION

Freed Captives Are Received Joyously at Airport After Their 7-Day Ordeal

By TERENCE SMITH

Special to The New York Times

JERUSALEM, July 4—An Israeli commando unit that last night conducted a daring raid on the Entebbe airport in Uganda flew home today with the hostages it released.

Military officials said that 103 hostages had been flown to Israel. They said that four Israelis, seven of the 10 hijackers and about 20 Uganda soldiers had been killed.

Text of the Rabin address will be found on page 2.

Some of the hostages arrived exhausted, some exuberant, to a noisy, joyous reunion here with family and friends. A majority of those freed last night were Israelis.

[President Ford sent a message of congratulation to Prime Minister Yitzhak Rabin, voicing "great satisfaction" that the passengers of the hijacked plane had been saved and "a senseless act of terrorism thwarted." Page 2. President Idi Amin of Uganda condemned the Israeli action.]

Back at Same Airport

A week to the day after they set off on an Air France airbus, the Israeli passengers and French crew members were back at the same airport where they had originally started their trip. They were weeping, laughing and literally falling into each other's arms with relief.

Their return here brought to an end seven days of terror that culminated in the spectacular rescue operation, in which Israeli airborne troops traveled 2,500 miles to pluck the hostages from the gunpoints of their captors at the Entebbe airport.

Rabin Addresses Parliament

The success of the operation, which surprised most Israelis, electrified the country. Flags were brought out, people rejoiced openly in the streets, and in the sky over Jerusalem, a skywriter wrote in Hebrew: "Kol hakavod zahal," or "All honor to the army."

Addressing a specially convened session of the Israeli Parliament, Prime Minister Yitzhak Rabin declared: "This operation will become a legend. It is Israel's contribution to

Continued on Page 3, Column 4

The New York Times/Edward Hausner

Preceded by a fireboat, the Coast Guard training ship Eagle leads the armada of ships past the Battery up the Hudson for the naval review

French Officials See Signs Amin, Hijackers Colluded

Special to The New York Times

PARIS, July 4 — Officials and released hostages said here today that they had substantial evidence that President Idi Amin had been in collusion with the hijackers of an Air France airbus in the seizure of the plane as well as after it landed in Uganda.

Although the officials refused to be quoted publicly, one said that negotiations got "much tougher" last night after President Amin returned to Uganda from a meeting of the Organization of African Unity in Mauritius.

A highly placed French source said that President Amin had refused to allow Pierre Renard, the French Ambassador to Uganda, or a special French envoy to deal with the hijackers directly.

While President Amin was out of the country, messages from Israel had to be passed by French Government representatives through the Somalian Ambassador, Hashi Abdullah Farah, to the hijackers. Messages back to the Israelis followed the same route.

Uganda Guards

When Gen. Amin returned from Mauritius yesterday, he resumed the role of mediator. He told the French Ambassador that demands for the release of 53 pro-Palestinian prisoners in Israel, Kenya and Europe must be met by early today or all the hostages would be killed.

Officials here pointed out that on the list of prisoners were five Ugandans held in Kenya on charges of attempting to assassinate President Jomo Kenyatta.

They also noted that during the first 24 hours after the aircraft reached Entebbe, the hijackers withdrew to rest and Ugandans guarded the hostages.

Other evidence pointing to the Uganda President's involvement with the terrorists was included in comments by French diplomats and the reports of hostages freed earlier by the terrorists. At the time of the Israeli rescue operation nearly all of the hijackers' captives were Israelis or dual nationals.

Among the passengers released last week were Michel Cojot and his 12-year-old son, Olivier. Mr. Cojot, a French management consultant, served as interpreter for the hostages, and negotiated on their behalf for small conveniences during the ordeal.

'Not Shadow of Doubt'

Mr. Cojot said that he had "not a shadow of a doubt" that the Uganda President knew of the hijack plan in advance and had prepared for the action.

He said that the airbus, a new European-built plane with a normal four-hour flying capacity, flew non-stop to Entebbe after a refueling stop in Benghazi, Libya — a six-hour flight. "We couldn't possibly have made any other airport by then," he said. "The hijackers were obviously certain they

Continued on Page 4, Column 2

CARTER TO BEGIN TALKS ON TICKET

Will See Muskie Today and Other Possible Running Mates Soon After

By CHARLES MOHR

Special to The New York Times

PLAINS, Ga., July 4—Jimmy Carter has asked Senator Edmund S. Muskie to visit him here tomorrow and discuss the Maine Senator's qualification to serve as Mr. Carter's running mate on the 1976 Democratic ticket.

Mr. Carter told reporters gathered at the driveway of his home in this small Georgia town this morning that he expected to talk to at least four other persons about the Vice-Presidential nomination between now and the Democratic National Convention, which convenes July 12.

The former Georgia Governor, who is assured of the Presidential nomination, said that it would be wrong to assume that there was any special significance in the fact that Senator Muskie was the first to be invited to meet with him. And, indeed, few political observers seem to feel that Mr. Muskie is a front-runner for the job. He was the Vice-Presidential nominee in 1968 and an unsuccessful candidate for the Democratic Presidential nomination in 1972.

A highly knowledgeable source said that the three men

Continued on Page 16, Column 4

A Day of Picnics, Pomp, Pageantry and Protest

By JOHN L. HESS

The nation celebrated its 200th birthday yesterday with pageantry and prayer, with games and parades, with picnics and fireworks, with the peal of bells and the chant of protests.

It began with a flag-raising atop Mars Hill Mountain in Maine, where dawn reached the continent, and moved on to Fort McHenry, in Baltimore Harbor, where it was greeted by the rocket's red glare of the national anthem. The activities were to end nearly a day later with an indigenous festival in American Samoa.

At 2 P.M., Eastern daylight time, descendants of the Revolutionaries laid hands symbolically on the Liberty Bell in Philadelphia, and bells rang in the 50 states and in American communities overseas. At Independence Hall, President Ford read the day's keynote address.

This being an American festival, many new records were claimed: the largest cherry pie (60 square feet), at George, Wash.; the largest cake (69,000 pounds), at Baltimore; the largest fireworks display, in Washington, D.C.; the largest gathering of sailing ships, in New York Harbor.

Yet many sponsors of celebrations were disappointed at the turnouts. The Philadelphia parade, planned for 70,000 marchers, drew about half that

Continued on Page 18, Column 1

PRESIDENT TALKS

Philadelphia Throngs Told U.S. Is Leader—Liberty Bell Rings

By JAMES T. WOOTEN

Special to The New York Times

PHILADELPHIA, July 4 — With its famous bells ringing, bands blaring, choirs singing and fireworks exploding, this city today staged a joyous, cacophonous commemoration of that day two centuries ago when the representatives of the 13 English colonies met here to renounce their allegiance to the British Crown.

At least one million people were in Philadelphia for the centerpiece of the Bicentennial observances.

President Ford came here from Valley Forge to recall that first Fourth of July as "the beginning of a continuing adventure," unfinished, unfulfilled, but still unchallenged as a model of social and political achievement.

"The world is ever conscious of what Americans are doing, for better or for worse," he said at Independence Hall, "because the United States remains today the most successful realization of humanity's universal hope.

Says Nation Leads

"The world may or may not follow, but we lead because our whole history says we must."

Then, after he left for New York City, the Liberty Bell, that faulted but venerated symbol, was softly sounded with a rubber mallet as millions across the nation watched on television. In clamorous response, hundreds of other bells rang out in Philadelphia's steeples and towers.

Meanwhile, several miles from the official observances, more than 30,000 other Americans, most of them members of two radical coalitions, staged their own peaceful Bicentennial celebration. Mayor Frank L. Rizzo had warned of potential disorders, but there were none.

At the main celebration, blue-shirted policemen cordially gave

Continued on Page 18, Column 5

PANOPLY OF SAILS

Harbor Armada Led by Tall Ships in Salute to Fourth

By RICHARD F. SHEPARD

Buoyed by panoramic spectacles that included a unique armada of tall-masted ships, a massive fireworks display and a series of festivals that took over downtown Manhattan, millions of New Yorkers and visitors in a happy mood observed the nation's Bicentennial yesterday.

It was a day of mammoth presentations.

Uncounted crowds lining the waterfront of the magnificent but underused harbor saw a virtually unbroken bridge of small craft that reached from the shores of Brooklyn to the coast of New Jersey.

More than 225 sailing ships under 31 flags paraded up the Hudson, a river that foretold their doom in 1807 when Robert Fulton's smoky little Clermont started steamboat service on it.

International Review

A 22-nation fleet of 53 naval units gray and grim—even ships festooned with pennants—lined the upper Bay and the Hudson for the International Naval Review, which had Vice President Rockefeller as the chief United States official present.

President Ford flew onto the hulking 79,000-ton aircraft carrier Forrestal, the host ship of the review, and later went by helicopter to the U.S.S. Nashville, anchored in mid-Hudson. He watched the sailing ships and was stranded for 40 minutes by a sudden squall before taking off again, headed for Washington, without having set foot ashore in the city.

As night fell, hundreds of thousands jammed onto the shore of lower Manhattan—some dangling from trees like so many Christmas decorations—to watch the dazzling fireworks explode over the harbor and the Statue of Liberty. When it was over, the tide of the departing throngs sometimes swept people out of con-

Continued on Page 20, Column 3

The New York Times/Teresa Zabala

President Ford waves to the crowd at Valley Forge, Pa., where he signed a bill making it a national historical site. He stands on a covered wagon that represented Michigan, his home state, in the Bicentennial wagon train.

Ethnic Diversity Adds Spice to the Holiday

The New York Times/[illegible] W. Strong

City Hall is the scene of street dancing and music in July 4th in Old New York Festival

By FRED FERRETTI

New Yorkers and their friends poured into lower Manhattan yesterday and compressed 200 years of their history and varied ethnic heritages into a day-long birthday party crammed with prayer, martial music, high spirits and good fellowship.

It was the tall ships and the warships that drew them there, but it was Dr. Quackenbush's Traveling Medicine Show, Delancy's Loyalist Red Coat Brigade, Fraunces Tavern, Oscar Brand, falafel and pizza and egg rolls, and John Philip Sousa that kept them there.

Not even a succession of torrential downpours late in the afternoon could drive them away. They watched George III beheaded at Federal Hall National Memorial, listened to Terence Cardinal Cooke pray at Castle Clinton, watched the Turks take over Wall Street for

Continued on Page 22, Column 4

O, Say, It Was a Glorious Patchwork-Quilt of a Fourth

By McCANDLISH PHILLIPS

The Fourth of July celebration in New York City yesterday was as American as a patchwork quilt—full of a joyous order-in-disarray and a series of brilliantly improbable juxtapositions.

It was an exercise in percussion, procession, demonstration, declamation, detonation, commemoration, vociferation, trivialization, solemnization and, for some, indigestion.

The free and independent citizens of New York City got themselves into a good many unusual postures as they scrambled for perspective on events, sometimes at the price of mild peril.

In parks and on piers, on fences, balconies, ramps, rooftops, chimneys, ledges, abutments and the ladders of water storage tanks, they sat, stooped, stood and clung, chiefly to watch great ships come sailing out of the distant past and go up the hazy Hudson like a vision.

It was a great day for family portraits to be taken with the most senior member of the American family. The process began early in the day in front of the Federal Hall National Memorial on Wall Street, on the site where George Washington took the oath as President on April 30, 1789.

Washington's statue dominates the steps leading up to the eight columns of the hall, and the base of the pedestal is a stage large enough for at least half a dozen persons to stand on.

As soon as one group posed and left, the next moved up to be photographed with the unblinkingly obliging founding father.

Seven small children in bright summer colors nearly ringed the great figure, standing under his outstretched right hand, their heads reaching to half the height of the pedestal. They looked very serious for the moment or so they stood there.

Though few noticed it, Christopher Columbus was in town. Not the old boy him-

Continued on Page 20, Column 5

NEWS INDEX

"All the News That's Fit to Print"

The New York Times

LATE CITY EDITION

Weather: Partly sunny today; mild tonight. Fair and warm tomorrow. Temperature range: today 72-89; yesterday 71-86. Details, page D19.

VOL. CXXVI . . No. 43,664 | © 1977 The New York Times Company | NEW YORK, THURSDAY, AUGUST 11, 1977 | 25 cents beyond 50-mile zone from New York City. Higher in air delivery cities. | 20 CENTS

U.S., PANAMA IN ACCORD ON TRANSFER OF CANAL BY END OF THE CENTURY

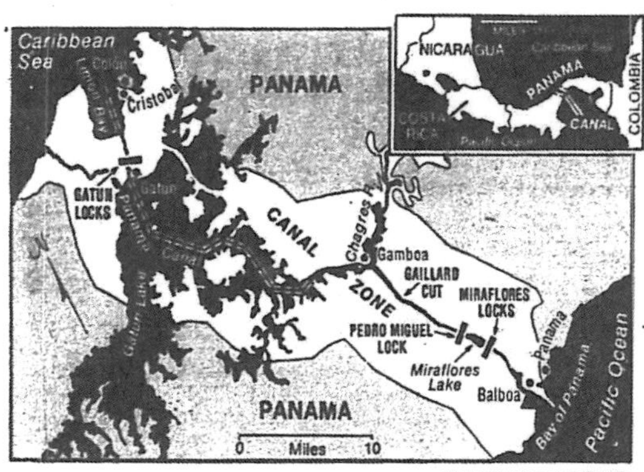

The New York Times/Aug. 11, 1977

By GRAHAM HOVEY
Special to The New York Times

PANAMA, Aug. 10—The United States and Panama announced today that they had reached "agreement in principle" on "the basic elements" of a new treaty that will call for transfer of the Panama Canal and the Canal Zone to Panamanian control by the year 2000.

The chief negotiators for the two Governments came to a crowded news conference in Panama City's Holiday Inn

Text of United States statement on the accord, page A12.

shortly before 6:30 P.M. (7:30 P.M., New York time) and announced an accord that they said would establish " a new relaship between our countries."

Ellsworth Bunker, the 83-year-old veteran of many diplomatic negotiations over three decades, spoke for himself and his co-negotiator, Sol M. Linowitz, who sat beside him.

Mr. Bunker said "legal specialists" would continue working to translate the basic elements into "formal treaties." He said he and her. Linowitz would fly back to Washington tomorrow and report immediately to President Carter.

American officials said later that, on their arrival at Andrews Air Force Base outside Washington, the two negotiators would be taken by helicopter to the White House for the conference with Mr. Carter.

Formidable forces in the United States are gearing up to resist any transfer of the canal or the zone to Panamanian control. Some of these groups claim to have more than the necessary 34 Senators lined up to block ratification.

As though anticipating a hard fight, Mr. Bunker said: "We are confident that this treaty will not only protect but strengthen our national security interests.

"It will also be a strongly positive element in our overall relationship with our Latin American neighbors, and preserve our vital common interest in an open, secure and efficient canal."

The Panamanian chief of government, Brig. Omar Torrijos Herrera, also faces severe testing in his efforts to win ratification and popular acceptance of a treaty that necessarily required compromises from both sides.

In a statement tonight, General Torrijos said that "the treaty is like a small stone in a shoe which one must suffer for 23 years in order to remove a nail from one's heart."

The new treaty would replace the 1903 pact under which Panama, then an independent country for only 15 days, gave the United States control in perpetuity and "as if it were sovereign" over the 533-square-mile Canal Zone and allowed it to build and operate the Panama Canal.

Dr. Romulo Escóbar Bethancourt, head of the Panamanian negotiating tea mand a close associate of General Torrijos, spoke for his delegation at the news conference. He was accompanied by Dr. Aristides Royo, Panama'. Minister of Education and his co-negotiator.

Referring to negotiations that have gone on intermittently since 1964, Dr. Escobar said Panama had fought for "13 arduous years" for a treaty that he believed would eliminate the "painful perpetuity" over the Canal Zone granted to the United States by the 1903 treaty and restore Panama's "full physiognomy as a nation."

Dr. Escobar then left to escort Mr.

Continued on Page A12, Col. 1

VANCE, ENDING VISIT, SAYS MIDEAST SIDES ARE STILL FAR APART

Indicates Arabs Are More Flexible Than the Israelis—Favors a U.N. Trusteeship Over West Bank

By BERNARD GWERTZMAN
Special to The New York Times

JERUSALEM, Aug. 10—Secretary of State Cyrus R. Vance, at the end of his Middle East mission, said today that although Israel and the Arabs seemed to want peace, wide gaps had to be bridged before a Geneva conference could be convened.

Mr. Vance will report to the Egyptian, Syrian and Jordanian leaders tomorrow, and the foreign ministers of those countries and Israel will assemble in New York next month for continued individual discussions with him on the issues that seem to frustrate American peacemaking efforts.

The Secretary of State told a group of West Bank Arab dignitaries today that a transition period under United Nations trusteeship was the most reasonable solution of the issue of a Palestinian homeland, members of the group reported. Mr. Vance met with them at the home of Foreign Minister Moshe Dayan in Tel Aviv. [Page A4.]

Refuses to Assign Blame

Earlier at a news conference in the King David Hotel, Mr. Vance refused to assign blame for the slow progress toward a Middle East settlement, but indirectly he seemed to credit the Arabs with greater flexibility than the Israelis.

In characterizing the continuing differences, he said:

"The parties remain divided on key issues which must be resolved if progress is to be made toward a settlement."

The two days of talks between Prime Minister Menahem Begin and Mr. Vance ended today without a sign of confrontation, just as Mr. Begin's talks in Washington with President Carter last month skirted a public dispute. Any crisis in Israeli-American relations appeared to have been deferred.

Foreign Minister Dayan and the Arab foreign ministers will go to New York for the United Nations General Assembly session that begins next month. Mr. Vance said he would move among the parties there to accelerate the pace of the negotiations. These talks could be significant or, as seems more likely, they could just keep the appearance of momentum.

Mr. Vance said the Israelis had agreed that Mr. Dayan was authorized to discuss not only procedural matters relating to a Geneva conference, but also substantive questions. In the past, the Israeli position has been that substantive issues would

Continued on Page A5, Col. 1

SUSPECT IN 'SON OF SAM' MURDERS ARRESTED IN YONKERS; POLICE SAY .44-CALIBER WEAPON IS RECOVERED

The New York Times/Paul Hosefros

Suspect in slayings, identified by police as David Berkowitz, being escorted into Police Headquarters this morning.

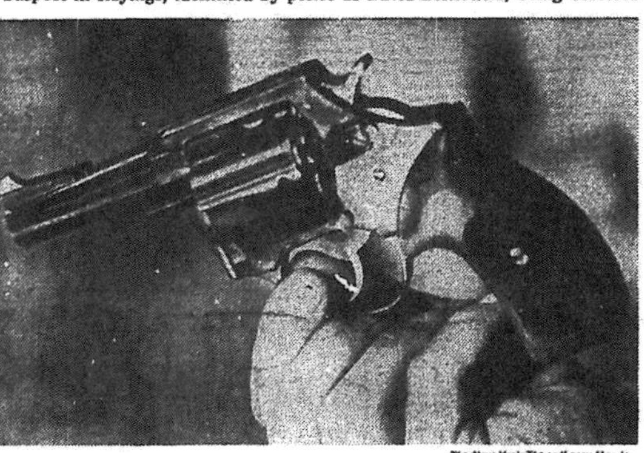

The New York Times/Larry Morris

Police officer holding .44-caliber gun police say was used by "Son of Sam."

Postal Worker Traced Through Car Believed Used in Getaways

By ROBERT D. McFADDEN

A 24-year-old postal employee said by the police to be the "Son of Sam," the .44-caliber killer who took the lives of six young people and wounded seven others in a year-long reign of terror in New York City, was taken into custody late last night in Yonkers, just north of the city.

The suspect was identified as David Berkowitz of 35 Pine Street in Yonkers.

He was said to have been traced through a car allegedly used in the getaways from eight attacks in the Bronx, Queens and, most recently, in Brooklyn.

When seized, according to the police, Mr. Berkowitz was advised of his rights by arresting officers and responded: "Well, you've got me."

The .44-caliber Charter Arms Bulldog revolver, which ballistics experts said had been used in all of the attacks, was recovered, the police said.

The suspect was rushed from Yonkers to New York City Police Headquarters after his arrest and authorities said he would be booked for the ambush murder of Stacy Moskowitz, 21, and the blinding of her date, Robert Violante, 20, in his latest alleged attack on July 31.

Motive Is Unclear

The police said early today that, although the suspect had made some admissions, the motive for the crimes remained unclear. The suspect was described by the police as a loner whose father, Nat, is retired and living in Miami and whose mother is deceased.

The police said the suspect was a graduate of Columbus High School in the Bronx, had attended the Bronx Community College for one year and had served with the Army in Korea.

Mayor Beame, during a 1:40 A.M. news conference in Police Headquarters in Lower Manhattan declared:

"I am very pleased to announce that the people of the City of New York can rest easy tonight because police have captured a man they believe to be the Son of Sam."

First Deputy Police Commissioner James Taylor earlier had said: "We have him."

Chief of Detectives John L. Keenan, at the headquarters news conference, said the suspect had been traced after detectives had looked into every summons given to cars parked in the vicinity of the last shooting, at Bay 14th Street and Shore Parkway in the Bath Beach section of Brooklyn.

Gun Found in Car

One ticket, for illegal parking at a fire hydrant, was given to a cream-colored Ford Galaxy sedan. The police traced the car, and yesterday found it parked in front of 35 Pine Street in Yonkers.

Detectives who found the car said they had looked inside and had seen the butt of a machine gun sticking out of a gunny sack. They said they had also found a letter with printing that resembled that on the two letters known to have been written by the killer, as well as a message later found in the suspect's apartment.

The written message contained the following passage:

"Because Craig is Craig, so must the streets be filled with crime (death) and huge drops of lead poured down upon her

Continued on Page D17, Col. 3

Yonkers Neighbors Believe Suspect Had Harassed Them

By RONALD SMOTHERS
Special to The New York Times

YONKERS, Thursday, Aug. 11—David Berkowitz, the suspect in the .44-caliber slayings, was described by neighbors here this morning as a quiet man who kept to himself yet one whom they suspected of harassing them and of setting a fire in the building.

"He just didn't say a lot," said Rachel Resto, 21 years old, who lives in the six-story building at 35 Pine Street where Mr. Berkowitz was apprehended. "He would just say hello and how are you."

The most revealing aspect of what the excited residents said early today was how little they knew of the man who a year ago had moved into a $230.50-a-month studio apartment on the top floor of the building, facing the Hudson River.

"Loner," "strange person" was how they described him. But they all agreed on one point. "He didn't look like the sketches," said one resident, Venus Balducci.

Frankie Resto, the building's paperboy, said that Mr. Berkowitz was not seen much at night, and when asked about it, he told some people that he was a night-time security guard. But others knew that he was a postal employee, as the police disclosed, and they thought that he worked in the Bronx.

The residents told of some anxiety in the building since Saturday, when a fire was set in front of the door to an apartment on the sixth floor. When it was extinguished, several .22-caliber bullets were found in the fire.

Residents said there were suspicions that the fire had been set by someone living in the building, and while they did not think of Mr. Berkowitz until yesterday, the residents were thinking of no one else today.

Beame Policy Lets Employees Share Productivity Gains

By STEVEN R. WEISMAN

Mayor Beame's office disclosed yesterday that Mr. Beame had agreed a week ago to a new policy enabling municipal employees to receive additional wage increases this year to be paid out of future productivity improvements in the work force.

The agreement was reached in negotiations with one municipal union—the Uniformed Sanitationmen's Association—and its surprise disclosure provoked an unusual flurry of protests from leaders of other municipal unions until they were assured the new policy would apply to all.

At one point, Samuel DeMilia, president of the Patrolmen's Benevolent Association, suspended the long-anticipated count of ballots on the controversial police contract until midafternoon—after he received his assurance from City Hall. Elsewhere, labor officials called a halt to trustee meetings of various municipal employee pension funds, which were convening to approve a crucial financing arrangement with the Municipal Assistance Corporation.

The new wage policy—which would have to be approved by the Emergency

Continued on Page B4, Col. 3

Lance's Former Bank Is Reported Under S.E.C. Inquiry on Securities

By JUDITH MILLER
Special to The New York Times

WASHINGTON, Aug. 10—The Securities and Exchange Commission is pursuing an inquiry into the securities activities of a bank that Bert Lance headed in Georgia, sources close to the commission inquiry said today.

The investigation is separate from the wide-ranging inquiry into Mr. Lance's banking and loan activities by the office of John Heimann, the Comptroller of the Currency. That inquiry has caused concern in the Carter Administration and put Mr. Lance under more scrutiny than any of the President's other senior advisers.

Word of the informal S.E.C. inquiry became known on a day when Mr. Lance, who is the director of the Office of Management and Budget, came under increased financial pressure. As expected, the National Bank of Georgia, in which he is a major stockholder, announced that it would not issue its usual 20-cent dividend for the second quarter of this year. Mr. Lance has about 200,000 shares of stock in the bank and the move will deprive him of about $40,000.

Mr. Lance is on vacation at Sea Island, Ga., and could not be reached for comment.

Spokesmen for the S.E.C. would neither confirm nor deny that the commission was investigating Mr. Lance's former bank. The agency's policy is never to announce investigations unless the commissioners vote to do so.

A source familiar with the inquiry, however, said that while "there is no formal investigation at this time," the S.E.C.'s enforcement division had been examining the Lance bank's securities transactions for some time.

The commission does not regulate

Continued on Page D11, Col. 5

Successes Cited On Virus Drug

By RICHARD D. LYONS
Special to The New York Times

BETHESDA, Md., Aug. 10 — Federal medical researchers reported today the first successful use of an antivirus drug against a disease that is usually fatal.

The drug, named adenine arabinoside, or ara-A, has been used successfully in treating a small number of cases of herpes virus encephalitis, a disease that destroys the brain.

Dr. Richard M. Krause, director of the National Institute of Allergy and Infectious Diseases, a branch of the National Institutes of Health, said that officials believed the finding to have more far-reaching significance than this successful application.

The broader possibility, Dr. Krause and six other scientists said at a news con-

Continued on Page B7, Col. 1

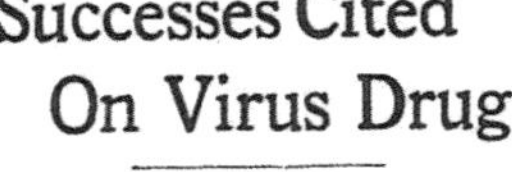

The New York Times/Hirotaka Yoshizaki

VOLCANO DAMAGES RESORT AREA: Volcanic ash and rocks from Mount Usu cover the streets of the evacuated resort of Toyako Onsen, Japan. Eruption caused extensive damage. Article, Page A10.

INSIDE

Riverside Nominates Coffin

The Rev. William Sloane Coffin, former Yale chaplain and well-known social activist, has been nominated as senior minister of Riverside Church. Page B10.

Jury Gets Mandel Case

After a seven-week trial, the conspiracy and corruption case against Gov. Marvin Mandel of Maryland went to the jury. Page A14.

"All the News That's Fit to Print"

The New York Times

LATE CITY EDITION

Weather: Sunny, warm today; fair tonight. Sunny, warm tomorrow. Temperature range: today 69-84; yesterday 75-90. Details, page B17.

VOL.CXXVII...No.43,986 Copyright © 1978 The New York Times NEW YORK, THURSDAY, JUNE 29, 1978 25 cents beyond 50-mile zone from New York City. Higher in air delivery cities 20 CENTS

HIGH COURT BACKS SOME AFFIRMATIVE ACTION BY COLLEGES, BUT ORDERS BAKKE ADMITTED

PRESIDENT TO ISSUE ORDER TO LIBERALIZE RULE ON SECRET DATA

Change in Procedure on Classified Documents Designed to Exhibit Interest in Open Government

By MARTIN TOLCHIN

Special to The New York Times

WASHINGTON, June 28 — President Carter plans a sweeping liberalization of the procedures governing the classification of Government documents.

He intends shortly to issue an executive order that will sharply limit the extent and duration of classifications, such as "confidential," "secret" and "top secret," and reduce the number of agencies that have classification authority.

The executive order will also provide that declassification procedures consider "whether the public interest in disclosure outweighs the damage to national security that might be reasonably expected from disclosure," according to the document, a copy of which was obtained by The New York Times.

The White House intends to present the executive order as a demonstration of the President's commitment to open government. Although civil liberty groups praised the new procedure, they said they did not believe the new policy would offset what they regarded as the Administration's commitment to secrecy in other areas.

Three Cases Cited

They cited the cases against Frank Snepp, a former agent of the Central Intelligence Agency who wrote a book critical of the agency, and the prosecutions of David Truong and Ronald Humphrey for theft.

"Nothing that they could do in the executive order could outweigh the harm to free debate on national security issues brought about by the Snepp and Truong cases," said Morton Halperin, director of the Center for National Security Studies, who helped to formulate the new procedures.

Mark Lynch, a staff attorney for the American Civil Liberties Union who specializes in government secrecy, said that the new procedures "could be very useful" because "they'll have to think harder about what they're doing."

He agreed with Mr. Halperin, however,

Continued on Page A16, Column 3

2 U.S. NEWSMEN GET SOVIET LIBEL CHARGE

TV Agency Files Suit Stemming From Dispatches About Dissident

By DAVID K. SHIPLER

Special to The New York Times

MOSCOW, June 28—Two American reporters were formally accused in a Moscow court today of having libeled Soviet state television by writing articles about an imprisoned dissident's televised "confession" that his friends and relatives believed had been fabricated.

It was the first time that Western diplomats and correspondents could remember the Soviet Government's taking legal action against foreign journalists for their dispatches.

The two reporters, Craig R. Whitney of The New York Times and Harold D. Piper of The Baltimore Sun, appeared in court in answer to a summons and were presented with copies of the claim against them by Lev Y. Almazov, chairman of the Moscow City Court.

Written Response Is Due Tomorrow

Judge Almazov set noon Friday as a deadline for a written response to the charge, and July 5 as a trial date. A guilty finding, according to Article 7 of the Civil Code, may result in a court order to publish a retraction and, failing that, a fine.

The claim, brought by the Soviet Government's broadcasting agency, asked that the two reporters "be held answerable for publishing in the foreign press slanderous information denigrating the honor and dignity of the members of the staff of the State Committee for Television and Radio of the U.S.S.R. and that they be caused to publish a retraction in the press."

It was not explained how a Soviet court could claim jurisdiction over newspapers

Continued on Page A13, Column 1

Associated Press

Gerard C. Smith

South Africans Reported Ready For Nuclear Ban

By JOHN F. BURNS

Special to The New York Times

JOHANNESBURG, June 28—American efforts to persuade South Africa to sign the treaty banning the spread of nuclear weapons reportedly reached an advanced stage today as high-level officials of the two Governments ended talks in Pretoria on the nuclear issue.

Sources close to the talks disclosed tonight that Gerard C. Smith, President Carter's ambassador at large in charge of efforts to prevent the spread of nuclear weapons, had been in the South African capital of Pretoria since Sunday for discussions with Foreign Minister Roelof F. Botha and other senior officials, including Abraham J. Roux, chairman of the South African Atomic Energy Board.

[Reports from Washington indicated, meanwhile, that South Africa was considering signing the treaty and was prepared to accept stricter international controls to prevent its atomic energy program from being used to develop weapons.]

Details Not Disclosed

Neither side in the Pretoria talks would divulge any details of what went on or say whether an agreement was in prospect. However, it is known that Mr. Smith, a 68-year-old veteran of arms-limitation talks, arrived here with the aim of gaining South African accession to the nuclear treaty in return for a pledge of continued cooperation between the two Governments in the peaceful applications of nuclear energy.

The talks in the South African capital are the culmination of secret negotiations that began last year, after a diplomatic flurry over fears that South Africa was preparing to test a nuclear explosive. The

Continued on Page A6, Column 3

BELL HAILS DECISION

Calls Ruling a 'Great Gain'— Plaintiff Is 'Pleased' and Others Express Relief

By LINDA GREENHOUSE

Special to The New York Times

WASHINGTON, June 28—Among the entire spectrum of people and groups with a stake in the Bakke decision, there were degrees of satisfaction and relief today.

From Allan P. Bakke himself, who will enter medical school next September at the age of 38, to the civil rights organizations that opposed his challenge to the special minority-admissions program, people drew from the 154 pages of Supreme Court language the conclusions they most wanted to find. Mr. Bakke said he was "pleased" with the decision.

Attorney General Griffin B. Bell told reporters at the White House that he and President Carter regarded the decision as "a great gain for affirmative action." "This is what we thought the law was," the Attorney General said.

Benjamin L. Hooks, executive director of the National Association for the Advancement of Colored People, called the decision a "clear-cut victory for voluntary affirmative action," not only in education but also in other areas.

'Quotas Are Flatly Illegal'

Arnold Forster, general counsel of the Anti-Defamation League of B'nai B'rith, said his organization was "comforted that, once and for all, the United States Supreme Court has held that racial quotas are flatly illegal."

Among educators, the reaction was almost one of relief that their worst fears had not come to pass and that most existing college admissions policies could continue unchanged. [Page A23.]

Whether the decisions in Regents of the University of California v. Bakke will go down in history as "an act of judicial statesmanship," in the words of Prof. Alan Dershowitz of Harvard Law School, the nine Justices in their six opinions did seem to be offering something for everyone in a case that has been scrutinized as closely and argued as bitterly as any to reach the Court in recent decades.

The Court both ordered Mr. Bakke's admission to medical school and upheld the use of race as a factor in university admissions programs.

Black Leader Sees Threat

At a news conference of black leaders in New York City, Jesse Jackson, chairman of Operation PUSH, warned that the part of the decision striking down the minority-admissions program at the medical school of the University of California at Davis might be received by other universities as a signal to cut back on even those affirmative action programs that quite clearly have the approval of a majority of the Supreme Court.

But other civil rights leaders chose to focus on the part of the opinion establish-

Continued on Page A23, Column 6

Associated Press

Allan P. Bakke returning to home in Los Altos, Calif., after work yesterday

A Plateau for Minorities

Most College Programs Expected to Continue, But Ruling Is Seen as Brake on Rights Efforts

By JOHN HERBERS

Special to The New York Times

News Analysis

WASHINGTON, June 28—The United States Supreme Court's split decision in the Allan P. Bakke case means, according to the consensus on both sides, that the great majority of affirmative action programs, public and private, will continue, as will the debate and lawsuits over what constitutes a proper racial balance.

For that, the leaders of the nation's minorities expressed pleasure and relief today at the 5-to-4 decision, which said that race may be considered in deciding who is admitted to colleges.

The rigid affirmative action program of the medical school of the University of California at Davis, which the Court struck down, was considered extreme in that it set aside 16 of 100 places for members of minority groups. Many other programs for enrolling minorities are more flexible and seem to fall within the boundaries set in today's decision.

A Retreat Is Seen

However, as Julian Bond, the Georgia civil rights leader and state legislator, said, affirmative action efforts reached a plateau today, and there was some fear that the decision would cause a decline in attempts to broaden educational and employment opportunities for blacks and other minorities.

Associate Justice Thurgood Marshall expressed the opinion, widely held among minority leaders, that the nation has been retreating from a commitment to racial justice made in the 1960's, in a parallel to what happened in the 19th century after the Reconstruction period.

"I fear that we have come full circle," he wrote, pointing out that "several affirmative action programs" were voided in that period by the Supreme Court. He cited the decision in Plessy v. Ferguson, which upheld segregation in public education, and said, "Now we have this Court again stepping in, this time to stop affirmative action programs of the type used by the University of California."

Although the majority decision appeared to please a broad spectrum of people on both sides of the issue, Justice Marshall put his finger on a deep division remaining in this country between blacks and whites.

The division concerns whether the nation should give special preference to a people who in a unique way were subjected to a basic denial of human rights, beginning with slavery.

"It must be remembered," he wrote, "that during most of the past 200 years, the Constitution as interpreted by this Court did not prohibit the most ingenious and pervasive forms of discrimination against the Negro. No, when a state acts to remedy the effects of the legacy of discrimination, I cannot believe that this same Constitution stands as a barrier."

Associate Justice Lewis F. Powell Jr., who wrote the main opinion, made it clear that special preference for blacks was not what the majority had in mind when it said race could be considered in an admissions policy. He spoke of the need for diversity, for Asians, Mexican-Americans, people from rural as well as urban areas.

"The file of a particular black applicant may be examined for his potential contribution to diversity without the factor of race being decisive when compared, for example, with that of an applicant identified as an Italian-American if the latter

Continued on Page A22, Column 3

GUIDANCE IS PROVIDED

Medical School Racial Quota Voided, but Advantage for Minorities Is Allowed

By WARREN WEAVER Jr.

Special to The New York Times

WASHINGTON, June 28—The Supreme Court by a 5-to-4 vote affirmed today the constitutionality of college admission programs that give special advantage to blacks and other minorities to help remedy past discrimination against them.

But the Justices also ruled that Allan P. Bakke must be admitted to the University of California Medical College at

Excerpts from opinions, Pages A20, A21.

Davis, determining that the college's affirmative action program was invalid because it was inflexibly and unjustifiably biased against white applicants like him.

In today's opinion, the Court provided some guidance for educators trying to insure that their programs will pass judicial muster, and future cases will almost certainly shed some more light on what constitutes permissible affirmative action.

Most Significant Since '54

Both decisions involved 5-to-4 votes, with Associate Justice Lewis F. Powell Jr. joining four other Justices to force the admission of Mr. Bakke, then shifting to join the four remaining Justices in support of the constitutionality of carefully tailored flexible affirmative action plans.

Although the two-sided ruling aroused some confusion and controversy, it was generally regarded as the most significant civil rights pronouncement the high court had made since it outlawed public school segregation in 1954.

It was not initially clear whether the Bakke decision would affect future Supreme Court rulings on affirmative action in employment. Such hiring plans tend to incorporate fixed arbitrary formulas for blacks, women and others, somewhat akin to the Davis admissions program that was invalidated today, but the high court has generally approved them in the past.

Two Groups in Voting

Generally, however, civil rights advocates felt they had won a major victory by preserving the constitutionality of admissions plans to professional schools that favor minority group members, who had been all but barred from such education until recent years.

One group of Justices—William J. Brennan Jr., Byron R. White, Thurgood Marshall and Harry A. Blackmun—maintained that the special Davis admissions program was permissible because the Government could use racial classifications as long as it has the benign purpose of remedying past discrimination. They voted, as a result, to deny Mr. Bakke entrance.

A second group of four—Chief Justice Warren E. Burger and Associate Justices Potter Stewart, William H. Rehnquist and

Continued on Page A22, Column

Boy, 15, Who Killed 2 and Tried To Kill a Third Is Given 5 Years

By CHARLES KAISER

A 15-year-old Harlem youth who admitted killing two subway passengers and attempting to kill a subway motorman in one eight-day period last March has been sentenced to a maximum of five years in prison.

Under the terms of the sentence, imposed by Judge Edith Miller in Family Court—it was the maximum she could impose for juvenile offenders under state law—the youth will be required to spend at least 18 months in a "secure facility." After that he could be moved to a "residential facility" or kept in the secure facility, at the option of the state's Division for Youth.

Robert H. Silberling, head of the District Attorney's juvenile offense bureau, said that the state could, at its discretion, choose to keep the youth confined beyond the court-imposed five-year sentence. But when he reached the age of 21, Mr. Silberling said, he would have to be released.

Morgenthau Comments

"We've urged longer sentences," said District Attorney Robert M. Morgenthau of Manhattan, who cited the case yesterday in renewing a call for revision of the state's juvenile-offender laws. "I don't think the present law provides for adequate sentences for violent offenders. There has to be a provision for longer sentences for unusual cases like this one."

According to police and court officials, what makes the case unusual is the violent nature of the slightly built youth who they say has threatened to kill the detectives who arrested him, the prosecutors assigned to the case and Judge Miller herself. The police said he had also stabbed a fellow inmate at the Spofford Juvenile Center in the neck with a fork, saying: "I'll kill you if you sit down next to me."

"He's a kid who showed no remorse whatsoever," said Detective Sgt. Thomas Brady, who helped supervise the investigation that led to the youth's arrest.

Special Units Formed

Crimes by youthful repeat offenders, especially against the elderly, have generated controversy over what have been called lenient sentences sometimes handed out by judges. A highly publicized series of such crimes two years ago led to the formation in November 1976 by the Police Department of senior-citizen robbery units in all five boroughs.

Last year Mayor Koch's advocacy of the death penalty for heinous crimes and of tougher anticrime measures in general was a major issue in the mayoralty campaign. Some people believe that Mr.

Continued on Page B7, Column 1

INSIDE

Blackout Cost Tallied

New York City's blackout last July cost at least $310 million, a study by the Library of Congress research service found. Page B9.

Levitt Disputes Vouchers

Arthur Levitt charged that the Port Authority let directors accused of falsifying expense vouchers alter them retroactively. Page B6.

News Summary and Index, Page B1

United Press International

WED IN MONACO: Princess Caroline and Philippe Junot during civil marriage ceremony at palace in Monaco. They exchanged vows in same room where Prince Rainier and Grace Kelly were wed in 1956. Page C10.

BIOMEDICAL BREAKTHROUGHS

GINA KOLATA

It was just five years, from 1976 to 1981, but in that short time, medical advances and new medical problems and ethical challenges fundamentally changed society. From cancer treatments to heart disease risk, from epidemiology to infertility, the discoveries and issues of that period turned out to be landmark events.

In breast cancer, for example, the results of a study, announced in 1981, spared millions of women disfiguring surgery.[1] The study involved women with early breast cancer who had been randomly assigned to have their entire breast removed or to have just the cancerous lump removed, followed by radiation to the area. Many surgeons and cancer specialists had resisted the study from the start because it flew in the face of prevailing wisdom about the spread of cancer. The notion had been that in order to be sure they eliminated all of the cancerous cells, surgeons had to remove the entire breast. Although there had been hints that women with early breast cancer could do just as well if the tumor alone was removed, sparing the breast, very few women were having the procedure.

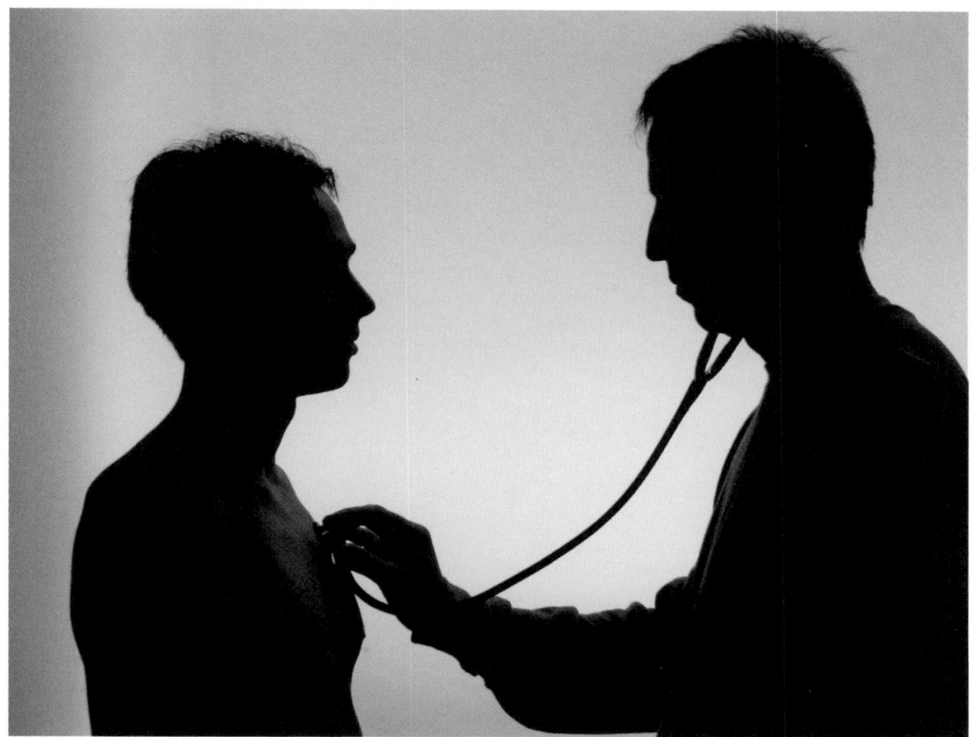

Silhouette picture of a physical examination.

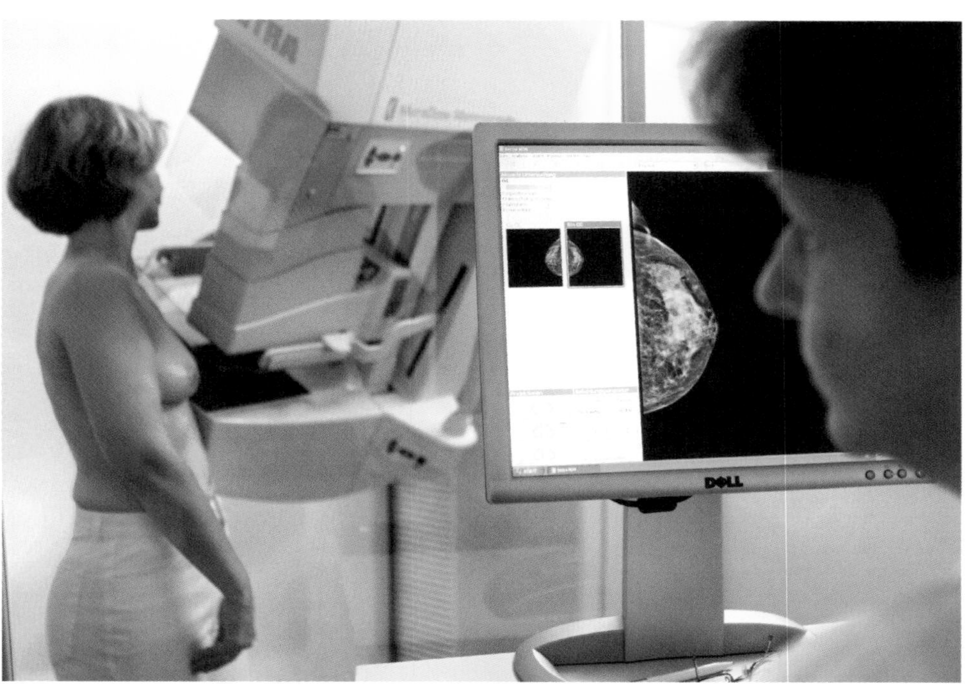

Modern mammography came to existence in 1969, and it became a standard practice by 1976.

FURTHER READING

1 "Study Supports Limited Surgery for Breast Cancer," see July 2, 1981, front page.

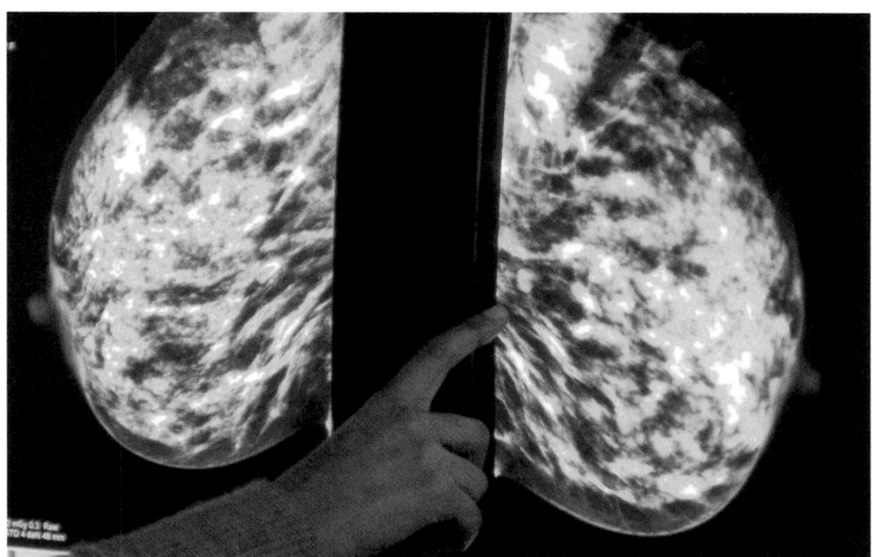

A technician checking a mammogram for signs of breast cancer.

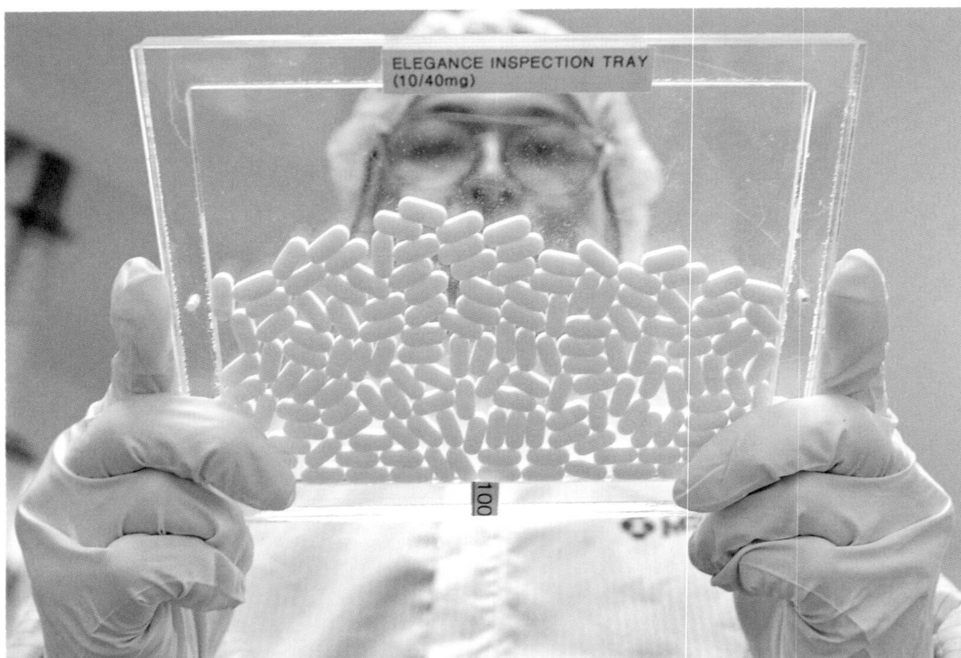

New medicines, such as these cholesterol-reducing pills, help protect people from heart disease.

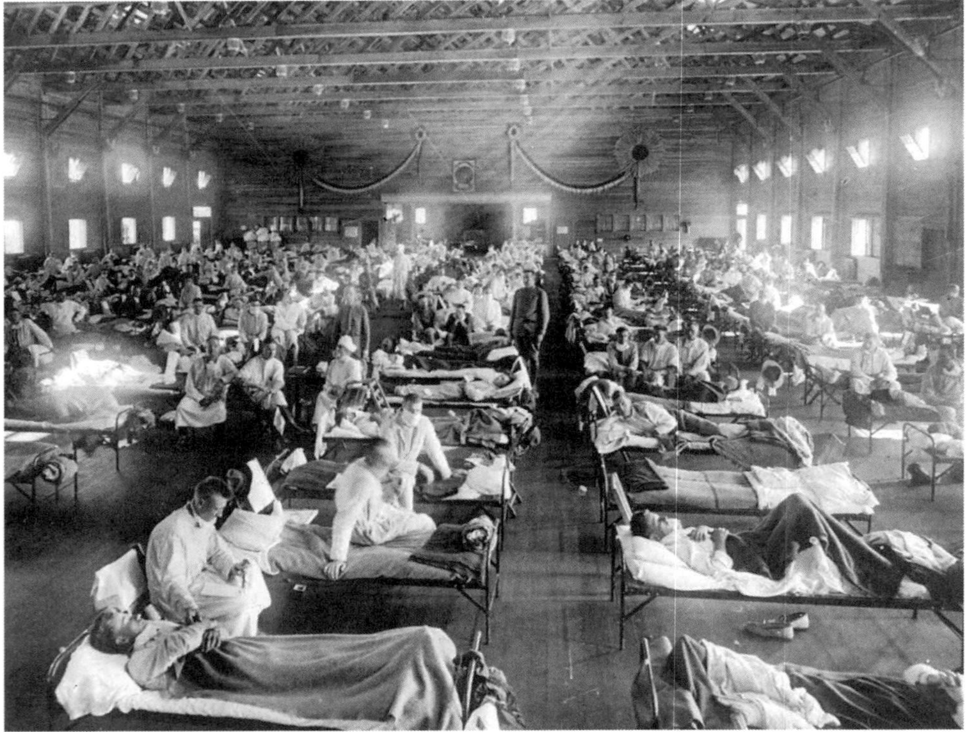

Influenza victims crowd a room at the emergency hospital in Camp Funston, Kansas, during a 1918 epidemic that killed an estimated 20 million people worldwide.

The new study changed all that. Women who had a lumpectomy followed by radiation to the breast were just as likely to remain cancer free as those who had had a mastectomy.

In heart disease, this was the time when scientists established the role of so-called good cholesterol, HDL. After following thousands of people for years, researchers reported in 1981 that the higher a person's HDL level, the lower the risk of heart disease. As a result, the cholesterol picture was fleshed out. There was a dangerous form of cholesterol, LDL, that increased heart disease risk. And there was the protective form, HDL.[2] That led to a new question: Is there a safe and effective way to raise HDL levels? And, if so, would raising HDL prevent heart disease? Those questions are still unanswered, although promising studies are under way.

With LDL, scientists discovered that they could lower levels and prevent heart disease with a new class of drugs, statins, that came on the market in the late 1980's.[3] Raising HDL has turned out to be much harder. But the HDL discoveries changed the way doctors assess cholesterol levels and decide whether patients need treatment. Today, every cholesterol test includes measures of HDL.

Epidemiologists look back on the era with a different perspective. It was the time of the great swine flu debacle and, coincidentally, a time when they saw the emergence of a new bacterial disease.

In 1976, infectious disease specialists were deeply worried that they had seen the first hints of a new influenza strain that, like the pandemic flu of 1918, could sweep across the nation, killing millions of people. They had to make a decision—should they persuade vaccine makers to develop a vaccine against that strain, the swine flu, or should they wait and see if it really was deadly? Since it takes six months for a vaccine to be produced, waiting could be disastrous. But there also were problems with vaccinating a nation against an epidemic if it turned out to be a false alarm.

Scientists advised the federal government to get the vaccine and immunize everyone immediately. The swine flu strain, however, turned out not to be dangerous or even especially infectious. And as the immunization campaign got started, doctors began reporting cases of a rare nerve disease, Guillain-Barré syndrome, in people who got the vaccine.[4] That led to lawsuits, an abrupt cessation of the swine flu immunizations, and a lasting fear of flu shots, even though the vaccines are actually extremely safe.

About the same time, infectious disease specialists were confronting a new problem. A mysterious epidemic had broken out at a convention of the American Legion that was meeting at a Philadelphia hotel in July 1976 to commemorate the bicentennial.

As many as 221 people fell ill and 34 died of a pneumonia that baffled medical investigators.[5] Finally, in January 1977, the cause was found, a previously unknown bacterium.[6] It was named Legionella pneumophila, and the disease was named Legionnaires' disease. The bacteria seemed to be living in the cooling tower for the hotel's air-conditioning system. From there, they were pumped through the building vents, entering rooms and infecting the lungs of hotel guests.

In medical ethics, the era was marked by the case of a young woman from New Jersey, Karen Ann Quinlan, who became the focus of a gripping, yearlong national debate. Ms. Quinlan, 21 years old, came home from a party and lapsed into a coma in April 1975. She was kept alive on a respirator, but after a few months, her parents asked that it be disconnected and that she be allowed to die. The hospital refused, setting off a legal battle over the right to die. Finally, in March 1976, the New Jersey Supreme Court ruled that the respirator could be disconnected.[7]

And, two years later, in a case that not only raised ethical questions but also launched a whole new medical specialty, world opinion was astonished by the birth in Britain of Louise Brown, the first baby to be born after being conceived in a petri dish.[8]

Two British doctors, Dr. Patrick C. Steptoe and Dr. Robert G. Edwards, got the technique to work, explaining that success came only after 100 failed attempts. Some

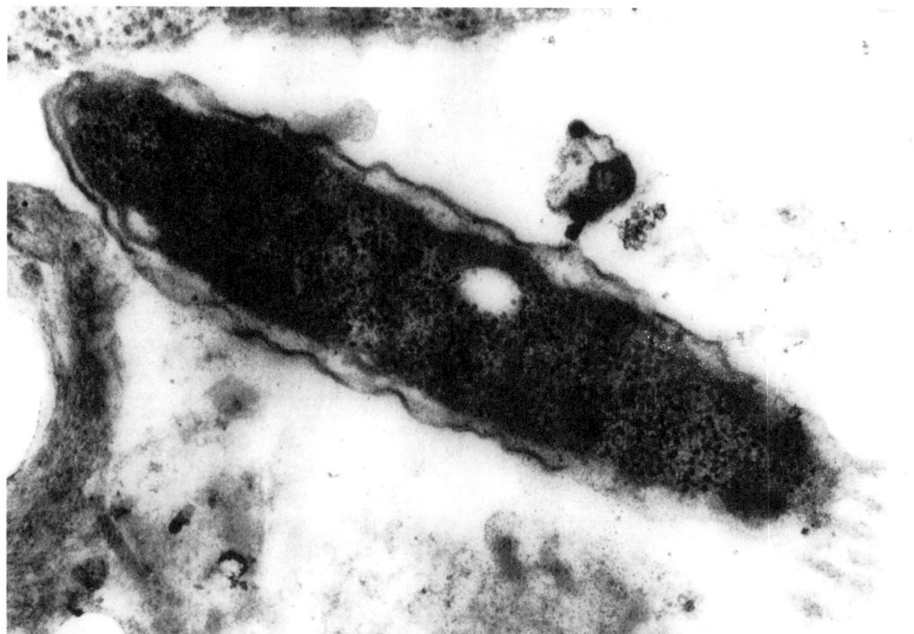

A microscopic image of a colony of the bacteria Legionella pneumophila, which causes the so-called Legionnaires' disease.

Karen Ann Quinlan lived in a coma for an additional 10 years after the courts allowed her parents to disconnect her respirator in 1976.

2 "High Levels of a Protein in Blood Linked to Heart Disease Prevention," see September 4, 1977, front page.
3 "Cholesterol: Drug Hailed as Treatment Breakthrough," see March 10, 1987, article
4 "Swine Flu Program Suspended in Nation," see December 17, 1976, article.
5 "Shift in Inquiry Into Legionnaires' Illness Raises Public Health Questions," see September 12, 1976, article.
6 "A Haunting Feeling of a Clue Overlooked Led to Legionnaires' Disease," see January 24, 1977, article.
7 "Court Rules Karen Quinlan's Father Can Let Her Die By Disconnecting Respirator if Doctors See No Hope," see April 1, 1976, front page.
8 "Woman Gives Birth to Baby Conceived Outside the Body," see July 26, 1978, article.

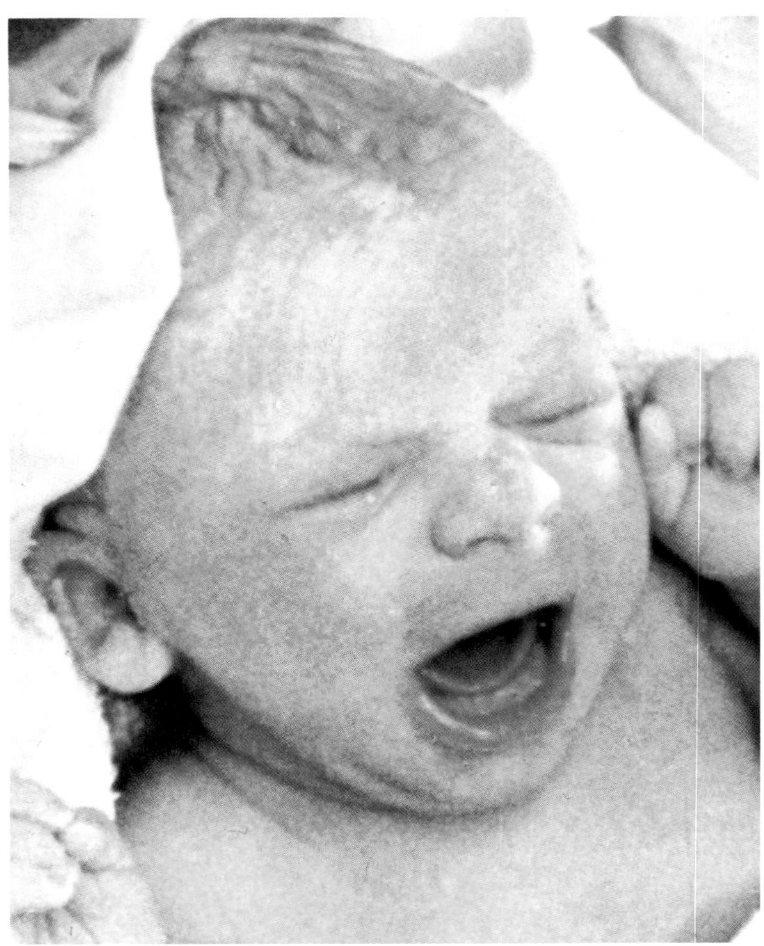

Louise Brown, the world's first test-tube baby, shortly after she was born at a London hospital in 1978.

charged that the feat was a hoax and that in vitro fertilization was biologically impossible.

But Lesley Brown, the mother of Louise, had no fallopian tubes, the hairlike tubes where eggs are normally fertilized and the structures that push the early embryo into the uterus. Without fallopian tubes, it would be impossible for Mrs. Brown to have a baby any other way than with in vitro fertilization, her doctors said.

Some critics said that in vitro fertilization violated natural laws and was an affront to the sacred act of procreation. Others feared that scientists would be creating babies with serious birth defects.

But soon, as demand for the method exploded, ethical qualms were mostly silenced and a new medical industry grew. Now, in vitro fertilization is commonplace although its commercialization, the expense—often reaching tens of thousands of dollars—and the problem of what happens to the unused embryos present difficult issues for ethicists and the lay public.

GINA KOLATA *is a senior medical writer for The New York Times. Before joining The Times in 1987, she worked at Science Magazine where she was a senior writer. Kolata is the recipient of numerous awards and was a finalist for the Pulitzer Prize in 2000. She is also the author of six books including "Clone: The Road to Dolly and the Path Ahead" and, most recently, "Rethinking Thin: The New Science of Weight Loss—and the Myths and Realities of Dieting."*

Louise Brown (front center) poses 25 years after her birth at a reunion in England with others who were born in vitro.

"All the News That's Fit to Print"

The New York Times

LATE CITY EDITION

Weather: Hazy, storms by evening; clearing tonight. Sunny tomorrow. Temperature range: today 87-67; yesterday 77-64. Details on page D15.

VOL.CXXVII . . . No.44,014

NEW YORK, THURSDAY, JULY 27, 1978

25 cents beyond 50-mile zone from New York City. Higher in air delivery cities.

20 CENTS

161 INSPECTORS HIRED BY KOCH TO COMBAT AGENCY CORRUPTION

INCOMPETENCE ALSO A TARGET

City's Employees Told They Must Report Any Malfeasance — Gotbaum Attacks Plan

By EDWARD RANZAL

Mayor Koch hired 161 new inspectors yesterday for an "overseer" program meant to root out corruption and incompetence in 30 New York City agencies.

In an executive order, he also strengthened employee guidelines for standards and discipline and made it obligatory for the agencies' 225,000 employees to inform superiors of corruption, criminal activity or conflicts of interest among fellow workers.

An employee who knows of criminal activity by another city employee, or people doing business with the city, but fails to report it, could be dismissed, said Stanley Lupkin, the Investigation Commissioner.

Gotbaum Is Critical

"While the overwhelming majority of city employees, who are honest and perform their duties competently, have nothing to fear from this program," the Mayor said, "I want to serve notice on the small number of employees who violate the public trust that they have no place in this administration."

Victor Gotbaum, head of District Council 37, the largest municipal union, promptly criticized the program as "destructive."

"Show and tell," he said of the informer requirement.

Lindsay Also Named Inspectors

The program is not new to the city. Former Mayor John V. Lindsay appointed inspectors general to monitor the conduct of city employees in major mayoral agencies. In 12 years the program has grown to cover 11 agencies.

Under Mayor Koch's program, 25 inspectors general, 17 deputies and 280 confidential inspectors will seek to end corrupt practices, misconduct and incompetence in the 30 agencies.

The Mayor announced his program at a news conference in the City Council Chamber after he swore in new inspectors general and their deputies.

After the announcement, Mr. Gotbaum called the Mayor's action "kind of sad," saying it was not going to "make for job satisfaction among employees."

During his election campaign Mr. Koch spoke out about ineptitude and dishonesty among municipal workers. In his first days in office he promised to adopt the program he put into action officially yesterday. Since then relations between Mr. Koch and some city labor leaders have been edgy.

Besides the conflicts that have been

Continued on Page D16, Column 6

Associated Press

ACTIVIST FREED: Mariya Slepak in Moscow after she received a suspended sentence. Page A3.

INSIDE

Trade Deficit Cut in June

The Commerce Department said the nation's trade deficit had been halved in June but had worsened sharply in the first half of the year. Page D1.

Water Supply Board Abolished

Governor Carey signed a bill abolishing the New York City Board of Water Supply, long criticized as a useless bastion of political patronage. Page B2.

Associated Press

Dr. Robert Edwards, left, and Dr. Patrick Steptoe at news conference yesterday in Manchester, England

Scientists Praise British Birth as Triumph

Early Insertion of Embryo Into Womb Is Linked to Successful Gestation

By ROY REED

Special to The New York Times

LONDON, July 26 — Scientists applauded, English churchmen nodded a qualified approval and the British press turned somersaults today to welcome the world's first baby born from an egg fertilized in a laboratory.

The 5-pound-12-ounce baby, a girl born slightly prematurely, was delivered by Caesarean section last night at the Oldham General Hospital in Lancashire. Dr. Patrick C. Steptoe was in charge of the delivery. A hospital spokesman said the baby was "quite normal."

At a news conference today, Dr. Robert G. Edwards, a Cambridge University specialist in reproductive physiology, who was one of the two physicians involved in the birth, said that the embryo was placed in the womb of Mrs. Brown two and a half days after fertilization. This was in contrast to the four and a half days that had elapsed before the embryo was placed inside the womb in earlier attempts, he said. When the embryo was placed in Mrs. Brown's womb, he added, it had only reached the eight-cell stage.

Supported Earlier Speculation

This supported earlier speculation that such early insertion, which was previously thought to endanger the embryo, had contributed to the procedure's success.

The baby was gestated in the normal manner, with placenta and umbilical cord linking it to the mother's blood supply. However, where unusual birth conditions are anticipated, Caesarean deliveries have become the practice to minimize the risk of harm to the baby.

The doctors had known the sex of the child for some time, but Mrs. Brown had insisted that she not be told. "After waiting for years for this wonderful thing to happen, I do not want to be cheated of the final thrill," she said.

Church leaders both here and in other countries generally welcomed the achievement, but with qualifications, especially from Roman Catholic leaders. [Page A16.]

Leo Abse, a Labor Party Member of Parliament, urged the regulation of

Continued on Page A16, Column 2

Doctors' Success in Conception in the Laboratory Intensifies the Debate Over Reproductive Control

By WALTER SULLIVAN

Special to The New York Times

LONDON, July 26 — The first authenticated birth of a baby conceived in a laboratory, an event that comes on the heels of other developments in reproductive control, has intensified debate among scientists that touches such issues as the sanctity of life.

Early in this decade, when the work of the two men responsible for the birth, Dr. Robert G. Edwards and Dr. Patrick C. Steptoe, first became widely known, it was denounced by a number of scientists, theologians and others. In Britain a winner of the Nobel Prize in chemistry termed the research a "stunt" and proposed that "the whole nation should decide whether or not these experiments should continue."

Some of the most vehement critics, warning of dire social consequences, have contended that procreation is sacred and that the performance of its most critical step in a laboratory degrades humanity.

Other critics have said that, in a world suffering from overpopulation, scientists should concentrate on how to prevent births rather than encourage them.

This is the last of three articles on the implanting of human embryos and its implications.

Questions about the medical procedures and the possibility of birth defects have been raised also. And there is considerable controversy involving the destruction of embryos that attempts at implantation could entail.

What Dr. Steptoe and Dr. Edwards did was enable Lesley Brown to become pregnant despite a defect in her oviducts. Mrs. Brown gave birth last night in Oldham, England, to a healthy girl that the Browns named Louise today. The pregnancy was reportedly achieved by

Continued on Page A16, Column 5

Doctors Isolate a Human Gene, Allowing Birth-Defect Detection

By United Press International

BOSTON, July 26 — For the first time, doctors have been able to identify a single gene among the millions in a human cell and can now see whether an unborn baby is missing certain parts of its genetic blueprint, a team of researchers reported today.

The report, in The New England Journal of Medicine, is the first example of applying some of the tools of gene-cutting, part of what is called recombinant DNA technology, to finding and understanding hereditary birth defects while a child is unborn.

Achievement Is Praised

Dr. Arthur W. Nienhuis of the National Heart, Lung and Blood Institute, who wrote an editorial in the journal on the implications of the achievement, said: "This is the first direct examination of the gene. The power of the technique is extraordinary, but the actual execution of it once mastered is not terribly difficult."

While the technique so far has allowed detection of only a rare group of genetic diseases, researchers predicted that within a few years they will have the genetic knowledge enabling them to detect more common ones, perhaps even cystic fibrosis.

Scientists estimate that there are three million to four million genes in each human cell. The team of researchers from Harvard and Yale Universities and the Haceteppe University in Turkey reported being able to produce an image of the gene that directs production of hemoglobin, which carries oxygen in the blood.

Thus, the team said, doctors can now detect certain debilitating and sometimes fatal forms of anemia, caused by

Continued on Page A16, Column 3

New York City Announces Moves To Halt Illegal Conversion of Lofts

By JOSEPH P. FRIED

New York City officials announced plans yesterday to prevent further illegal conversions of factory buildings to residential use and to bring "into compliance with fire, health and safety codes" the 1,000 structures that have already been illegally converted.

Under plans disclosed by Mayor Koch and City Councilman Thomas J. Manton of Queens, head of the Council's Housing and Buildings Committee, the city will not seek to evict people already living in lofts or other illegally converted space — except in a certain situation.

The exception is where city inspectors find "hazardous conditions," such as a "nonsprinklered building with an open, unenclosed stairway and without a second means of egress directly accessible by each dwelling unit." In such cases, an "immediate vacate order" will be issued.

In all the other cases, however, the city will use a combination of legal efforts and consulting aid to owners to remove whatever deficiencies prevent the structures from meeting health and safety standards, the Mayor and Mr. Manton said.

These and other steps to deal with problems stemming from the increasing number of conversions of lofts to residential use were outlined in an "action plan" on the issue that was drawn up by a Koch administration task force that was formed in March. Subsequently, the City Council urged the administration to act on the problems.

In an attempt to deal with a second problem stemming from the growing number of conversions — the reported displacement of manufacturing tenants to make way for residential tenants who pay higher rents — the plan envisions a program of relocation payments for manufacturing concerns displaced in legal conversions under the so-called J-51 tax-incentive program.

In addition to these local steps, the task-force report cited two bills passed by

Continued on Page D16, Column 4

Egyptians Order Israel's Mission To Leave Today

By WILLIAM E. FARRELL

Special to The New York Times

JERUSALEM, July 26 — Prime Minister Menachem Begin said tonight that Israel had been ordered by Egypt to withdraw, by tomorrow, its military mission based in Egypt since January.

The negotiation support group went to Egypt when talks opened on peace issues, after President Anwar el-Sadat's visit to Jerusalem. It remained in Egypt even though the peace talks quickly became stalemated.

The order for the withdrawal of the 10 middle-rank military technicians and communications specialists was made after a meeting of the National Security Council in Cairo.

[Egyptian War Ministry officials confirmed in Cairo that the Israeli mission had been ordered to leave the country. They said the action reflected a Cairo decision to avoid further direct contacts until Israel adopted a new position on peace talks.]

'We Shall Do So,' Begin Says

Mr. Begin, appearing on television, seemed unruffled by the Egyptian order, implying that it was part of a new war of nerves by Cairo in the strained peace maneuvering. He urged Israelis to be patient, saying: "I don't minimize anything. I advise all Israelis to have strong nerves."

Mr. Begin said he received the order for the recall of the Israeli group a few hours earlier. "We shall do so," Mr. Begin added.

"Welcome home," he said in reference to the small Israeli mission, whose members spent much of their time at a military base near Alexandria playing volleyball and cards. The mission had been a lingering symbol of direct Egyptian-Israeli contact in the uncertain period that

Continued on Page A3, Column 1

Justice Dept. Supports Detroit Police Quotas

By STEVEN V. ROBERTS

Special to The New York Times

WASHINGTON, July 26 — In its first official interpretation of the Supreme Court's Bakke decision, the Justice Department has urged approval of an affirmative action program that sets strict numerical quotas for the promotion of blacks in the Detroit police department.

The Court's decision last month did not require public agencies to be "colorblind," the department argued, and did not disturb previous rulings that required such agencies to take positive steps to remedy the effects of past discrimination.

The Justice Department's comments came in a brief as a friend of the court filed today with the United States Court of Appeals for the Sixth Circuit in a case called Detroit Police Officers Association v. Coleman A. Young. In that case, white police officers challenged an affirmative action plan that mandated the police department to promote one black to the rank of sergeant for every white promoted. Last February, the plan was ruled unconstitutional by Judge Fred W. Kaess of Federal District Court.

The department's brief had political as well as legal implications. Supporters of

Continued on Page B18, Column 1

CURBS ON RHODESIA UPHELD BY SENATE, BUT CONDITIONALLY

CARTER COULD LIFT SANCTIONS

He Must Determine Free Vote Has Occurred and New Regime Is Intent on Negotiations

By GRAHAM HOVEY

Special to The New York Times

WASHINGTON, July 26 — The Senate rejected a move to repeal economic sanctions against Rhodesia today, but then decisively adopted a compromise measure setting conditions under which the President could be required to lift the sanctions in the future.

The sponsors of the compromise amendment to the International Security Assistance Bill insisted that it was designed to keep the United States on a

Roll-call vote on Rhodesia, page A6.

"moderate middle course" between the current Rhodesian Government, led by Prime Minister Ian D. Smith, and the Patriotic Front, the nationalist group that is waging guerrilla war to bring down that Government. Tonight, the Senate passed the full aid bill, 73 to 13.

Despite the "moderate" nature of the amendment on Rhodesian sanctions, Administration officials fear that its language would make it appear that the United States is siding with Mr. Smith and the three black members of his transitional Government, who are committed to establishing majority rule after free elections planned for December.

Good Faith an Issue

In effect, the amendment would require President Carter to lift the sanctions, but only after he had determined that a Rhodesian government had been established through free elections under impartial international observation, and that it had committed itself to negotiate in good faith with the guerrilla leaders.

The sanctions, voted by the United Nations Security Council in 1966 and 1968, have the force of American law. They ban all trade with Rhodesia.

The sponsors of today's amendment, Senator Clifford P. Case of New Jersey and Jacob K. Javits of New York, both Republicans, argued that their proposal would eliminate fears in this country and in Africa that the United States was siding with the Patriotic Front guerrilla leaders, Joshua Nkomo and Robert Mugabe.

Reluctant to Negotiate

The transitional Government has equal numbers of white and black ministers and has promised to hold elections based on universal suffrage in December, but thus far have been unwilling to negotiate with the guerrillas.

The Case-Javits amendment was adopted today by 59 to 36, but the most critical test came on an earlier movement to table it, which the Senate defeated, 57 to 39. Its adoption sidetracked the amendment of Senator Jesse Helms, Republican of North Carolina, who proposed an immediate end of sanctions.

Senator Helms withdrew his amendment after a substitute proposal by Senator John C. Danforth, Republican of Missouri, had been defeated, 54 to 42, in the closest roll-call vote of the day.

Mr. Danforth had proposed that the

Continued on Page A6, Column 1

The New York Times/Teresa Zabala

GOLDBERG GETS FREEDOM AWARD: Arthur J. Goldberg speaking at White House yesterday after President Carter awarded him the Medal of Freedom, nation's highest civilian award. Also present were Mrs. Goldberg; his daughter, Barbara Goldberg Cramer; her three sons, and Secretary of State Cyrus R. Vance. Page C2.

TODAY AND EVERY WEEK: SCIENCE TIMES, THE NEW TUESDAY SECTION

"All the News That's Fit to Print"

The New York Times

LATE CITY EDITION

Weather: Mostly cloudy, chilly today; cloudy, damp tonight and tomorrow. Temperature range: today 27-38; yesterday 39-49. Details on page B10.

VOL. CXXVIII . . No. 44,043 | Copyright © 1978 The New York Times | NEW YORK, TUESDAY, NOVEMBER 21, 1978 | 25 cents beyond 50 mile zone from New York City. Higher in air delivery cities. | 20 CENTS

400 ARE FOUND DEAD IN MASS SUICIDE BY CULT; HUNDREDS MORE MISSING FROM GUYANA CAMP

United Press International

Chairman Hua Kuo-feng

2 Peking Wall Posters Raise New Questions On the Status of Hua

By FOX BUTTERFIELD

Special to The New York Times

HONG KONG, Nov. 20 — Two wall posters calling for a full public investigation into the suppression and cover-up of the major anti-Government demonstration in Peking in 1976 appeared in the Chinese capital today, raising questions about the status of Hua Kuo-feng, Chairman of the Chinese Communist Party.

The posters said an inquiry was necessary so that "those responsible for the suppression and cover-up could be brought to justice." According to diplomats in Peking, the posters demanded that the committee of investigation be made up of all major organs of the party and state.

Mr. Hua's present standing is closely linked to the incident, which took place in Tien An Men Square in central Peking on April 5, 1976 and was ostensibly in memory of the recently deceased Prime Minister Chou En-lai. At the time, Teng Hsiao-ping was blamed.

Two days later, "on the proposal" of Mao Tse-tung, Mr. Teng was purged and Mr. Hua was named party Chairman and Prime Minister. Mr. Teng, now again a Deputy Prime Minister, was reinstated in 1977 after the death of Mao and the arrest of his radical followers.

Yesterday, another poster put up in

Continued on Page A5, Column 1

SHORTAGES GROWING IN NO-LEAD GASOLINE OF HIGHER OCTANES

Although Overall Supply Appears Adequate, Some Companies Lag on Premium Grades

By ANTHONY J. PARISI

Shortages of premium unleaded gasoline are cropping up around the country, arousing fears among motorists of a general shortage of fuel for their automobiles.

Although supplies of gasoline appear adequate over all, some companies have been unable to keep up with the keen demand for high-octane unleaded gasoline, which provides superior performance for some automobiles. Some service stations have begun to turn away customers, who then find themselves waiting on longer and longer lines at stations that still have sufficient supplies on hand.

The Shell Oil Company, which has had to shut down two of its key refineries, was the first to report such shortages. Now Mobil stations are having problems, too, and other companies say their supplies are getting tighter by the day.

Some Rationing at Stations

To spread limited supplies among as many customers as possible, some stations have even begun to ration premium unleaded fuel — the first widespread example of gasoline rationing since the Arab oil embargo of 1973-74. The Bronxville Service Station in suburban Westchester County, for example, has been limiting purchases of Mobil Super unleaded to 10 gallons at a time — when it can get supplies. Yesterday it had no premium gasoline of any kind.

The shortages have appeared just as the Department of Energy is preparing to remove controls from gasoline prices. Yesterday, the department's Economic Regulatory Administration published an environmental impact statement on gasoline decontrol, recommending that the Government proceed with the plan despite concerns that the price of unleaded gasoline may skyrocket as a result.

One reason for the shortage is that motorists whose cars require unleaded gas have grown impatient with how their cars perform using regular grades of lead-free fuel. Almost a third of all the

Continued on Page D5, Column 4

Associated Press

Bodies lie strewn about vat containing drink laced with cyanide at the Jonestown headquarters of the People's Temple

LEADER OF SECT DIES

Parents Reported to Give Children Poison Before Dying Beside Them

By JON NORDHEIMER

Special to The New York Times

GEORGETOWN, Guyana, Nov. 20 — In a scene that dashed the senses, Guyanese forces today picked their way through an open-air pavilion choked with the bodies of 405 men, women and children in an American cult group who apparently commited suicide on the orders of their leader.

Wearing gaily colored clothes, the bodies were clustered in family groups, side-by-side in deathly embrace, all but three dead from drinking a concoction made of Kool-Aid and cyanide.

The setting was the jungle church of the People's Temple, the group that has been blamed for the slaying of Congressman Leo J. Ryan and four other Americans on Saturday.

Survivor Describes Scene

A surviving cult member gave the first newsmen to reach the scene today an account that was as incredible as it was filled with horror, a story of death plots and madness, of parents spooning a poisonous punch into the mouths of their babies before drinking it themselves.

And on the altar of the pavilion, surrounded in death by his followers as he had been surrounded by them in life, was the body of James Warren Jones, also known as the Rev. Jim Jones, the charismatic leader of the People's Temple, who had promised his racially integrated flock a utopia in the South American wilds. Instead, he gave them death.

"The time has come to meet in another place," he was said to have told the cultists he had assembled around him shortly after learning of the failure of a plan to kill the entire group of newsmen and parents of cultists who had flown deep into a lonely jungle airport with Congressman Ryan, according to the survivor, Odell Rhodes, 36 years old, from Detroit.

400 Are Still Missing

And then, according to the survivor's account, cyanide was dumped into a huge soup kettle, and the liquid was fed first to the babies, then to the children old enough to drink it themselves, and finally swallowed by the adults, many of whom were older people who had turned their Social Security checks and their lives over to the custody of Mr. Jones.

The leader, who at different times had described himself as the reincarnation of Christ and Lenin, died of a bullet wound in the head, according to the Guyanese police.

Nothing is known about the whereabouts of the remaining 400 or more cultists, who either fled into the jungle to escape death, or have elected to die deeper inside the canopied rain forest, where flesh-eating piranha and electric eels move in the murky jungle streams and insects swarm in the midday heat.

Cult Was Drilled in Suicide

It was learned that the cult was routinely drilled in suicide by Mr. Jones, who had a vision of a need to destroy the community if it was ever attacked.

Apparently, Mr. Ryan, who had been asked to investigate claims by his California constituents that members of the cult were being held in virtual bondage on the commune, and the party that accompanied him last Saturday, were seen as a grave danger.

Mr. Jones had decided to kill Mr. Ryan and the two dozen or so people who ac-

Continued on Page A17, Column 1

Defectors From Sect Depict Its Rehearsals for Suicide

By ROBERT LINDSEY

Special to The New York Times

LOS ANGELES, Nov. 20 — "He has mass suicide drills, where he tells all the people, hundreds of people, to drink a certain drink, and he says, 'That's fatal, you're all going to die in 45 minutes, I want to see how you feel about dying for socialism.'"

And, said Timothy Stoen, a San Francisco lawyer and former aide to the Rev. Jim Jones, the founder of the People's Temple, when Mr. Jones ordered his followers in his Guyana commune to drink the liquid, "everybody drank."

"It was like he wanted to believe he was God," said Anna Mobley, a member for four years. "He would get you so tired it would make you lose your mind."

"He had something they called the 'blue-eyed monster,' a thing they did to children," another former member said. "They took children into a dark room and attached electrodes to them and then shocked them and told them never not to smile at Jim Jones."

"He sent spies to our home and said that if we didn't sell all our property, we would die," said Wade Medlock, the owner of a Los Angeles maintenance company, who turned over two of his homes to the cult under threats.

The remarks were made at a meeting of a group called the Human Freedom Foundation, which was set up here last summer by two psychics, Maria Papapetros and Jenita Cargile, after former cult members had sought them out for counseling on how to "deprogram" themselves. A recording of the meeting was made available to The New York Times.

According to former members, the cult was run as a police state by Mr. Jones, who was said to have enforced discipline by beatings and death threats; pursued bizarre sexual activities, and indoctrinated members in his personal brand of agrarian socialism.

According to Mr. Stoen, Mr. Jones first enticed members with a doctrine of selflessness and a simple Christian faith of social equality that found support among blacks and upper middle-class whites who had become alienated in the 1960's.

Once he got "control of their minds, he would accept no dissent and told members that a defector had no right to live," Mr. Stoen said. He is a former deputy district attorney in Mendocino County who had been attracted by Mr. Jones's views in the late 1960's and became one of his lieutenants as the cult spread to San Francisco and Los Angeles and ultimately to the settlement in Guyana.

He said that as a sect official he had transferred more than $5 million to foreign bank accounts and said he believed the church's assets probably totaled much more.

Mr. Stoen said "people who disagreed would get phone calls at 3 A.M. with heavy breathing" or cult officials would find a drunk and pay him to read a script containing threats over the telephone. The children of parents who decided to leave the sect were often seized and kept in Guyana under guard.

Mr. Jones, he continued, had a "relationships committee" that had to approve

Continued on Page A16, Column 4

© 1978, The San Francisco Examiner

CULT LEADER: Jim Jones in Jonestown before shootings. Guyana revealed references from prominent Americans. Page A16.

© 1978, The San Francisco Examiner

Bodies of five Americans lie at ambush site in Port Kaituma, Guyana. From left, in foreground: Representative Leo J. Ryan; Don Harris, reporter for NBC: Gregory Robinson, photographer for The San Francisco Examiner, and Patricia Parks, believed to be a member of the commune. At rear is Robert Brown, an NBC cameraman.

Bally Corp. Plan to Build Casino On Historic Site Backed by Jersey

By DONALD JANSON

Special to The New York Times

ATLANTIC CITY, Nov. 20 — New Jersey officials indicated today that they would permit the Bally Manufacturing Corporation, the world's leading manufacturer of slot machines, to demolish the historic Blenheim Hotel rotunda on the Boardwalk to make way for a casino.

The "preliminary" finding by the State Department of Environmental Protection is the latest step in changing the face of Atlantic City, with the classic resort hotels of the city's heyday yielding to a new line of modern casino hotels. Keeping the Moorish rotunda of the Blenheim intact — the main wing has been demolished — is the focal point of a determined drive by preservationists.

Last May 26 Resorts International opened the city's first casino in the old Haddon Hall Hotel after radically altering the structure and renaming it the Resorts International Hotel.

Since then 32 companies, including most of the major concerns operating casinos in Nevada, have either acquired potential casino sites in Atlantic City or announced plans to do so.

One company, Caesars World, operator of Caesars Palace in Las Vegas, has acquired two Boardwalk sites and has a casino under construction on one of them. Steel girders are up on the site of the Howard Johnson Regency Hotel, which will be incorporated into the new casino hotel.

Caesars hopes to open the city's second casino by next Memorial Day. It has also acquired, for possible construction of another casino, the site of the Traymore Hotel, a Boardwalk landmark that was demolished six years ago.

Bally hopes to be third to open an Atlantic City casino. Its target date is July. It acquired three adjacent, historic hotels and wants to demolish all three eventually.

Last month Bally did demolish the Marlborough, a Queen Anne 1902 wooden structure that was one of first in the city to provide a private bath with every room.

In addition Bally is ripping out the interior of the Dennis, built in 1900 in the French Chateau style, and renovating it. The Dennis is the oldest hotel name on the beachfront today.

Last week 326 pounds of dynamite top-

Continued on Page B7, Column 2

INSIDE

Carter Aides Named in Inquiry

A grand jury is studying charges that White House aides considered dropping the Vesco extradition case in return for $10 million in stock. Page B11.

Trucking Restriction Dropped

The Interstate Commerce Commission dropped a 40-year-old rule that barred companies that truck their own goods from hauling goods of others. Page D1.

"All the News That's Fit to Print"

The New York Times

LATE CITY EDITION

Weather: Windy, mild today; blustery tonight. Sunny tomorrow. Temperature range: today 51-30; yesterday 45-30. Details on page 39.

VOL.CXXVIII . . . No.44,068 | NEW YORK, SATURDAY, DECEMBER 16, 1978 | 25 cents beyond 50-mile zone from New York City. Higher in air delivery cities. | 20 CENTS

U.S. AND CHINA OPENING FULL RELATIONS; TENG WILL VISIT WASHINGTON ON JAN. 29

LINK TO TAIWAN ENDS

Carter, in TV Speech, Says 'We Recognize Reality' After 30-Year Rift

By TERENCE SMITH
Special to The New York Times

WASHINGTON, Dec. 15 — President Carter announced a "historic agreement" tonight under which the United States and China will establish diplomatic relations on Jan. 1.

The President also said that Teng Hsiao-ping, the powerful Deputy Prime

Transcript of Carter statement, Page 8

Minister of China, would visit this country on Jan. 29. The visit here will be the first by a high-level Chinese Communist official since the end of the Chinese civil war in 1949. It will end what Administration officials described tonight as "a 30-year anomaly in international affairs."

In a dramatic and unexpected speech on national television, Mr. Carter also announced that the United States would terminate diplomatic relations and its mutual defense treaty with Taiwan. But in remarks addressed especially to the people of the island, he pledged that the United States would remain interested in the peaceful resolution of the issue.

[In Peking, a simultaneous announcement was made by the Communist Party Chairman Hua Kuo-feng. An official Chinese statement repeated the Chinese position that a reunification of Taiwan with the mainland was "entirely China's internal affair." Page 10.]

'New Vista of Relations'

"The United States of America recognizes the Government of the People's Republic of China as the sole legal Government of China," the President said, reading from a joint communiqué released in Washington and Peking.

Speaking to reporters in the White House press room after his speech, an ebullient Mr. Carter said that the new agreement would open "a new vista of trade relations with the almost one billion people of China."

He added his own feeling that "the security of Taiwan is adequately protected" under the agreement. The United States will withdraw its remaining military personnel from Taiwan within four months.

'Recognizing Simple Reality'

"We do not undertake this important step for transient, tactical reasons," Mr. Carter said. "In recognizing that the Government of the People's Republic of China is the single Government of China, we are recognizing simple reality."

The President conceded that the normalization of relations with China after nearly 30 years was a politically controversial act and said that it had received "mixed response" from Congressional leaders with whom he met earlier in the evening.

The move drew angry fire from moderate and conservative Republicans, however. Senator Barry Goldwater of Arizona denounced it as "a cowardly act," and charged that it "stabs in the back the nation of Taiwan."

Bill Brock, the Republican national

Continued on Page 8, Column 1

Israel Rejects New Peace Proposal; U.S., Irritated, Charges Distortion

Cabinet Backs Begin Stand

By PAUL HOFMANN
Special to The New York Times

JERUSALEM, Dec. 15 — The Israeli Cabinet decided today to reject the latest proposals by Egypt for a peace treaty as well as the "attitude and interpretation" of the United States regarding the proposals.

At the end of a special four-hour meeting, Prime Minister Menachem Begin,

Text of Israeli decision, page 5.

looking grim, said to reporters:

"The consultations, the negotiations will resume — we cannot say when."

[An official in the Egyptian Foreign Ministry denied Israeli charges that Cairo had made new demands during Secretary of State Vance's trip. Page 4.]

No Hope for Treaty by Deadline

The endorsement by the Cabinet of Prime Minister Begin's stand in talks with Secretary of State Cyrus R. Vance here Wednesday and yesterday quashed any remaining hope that the proposed Egyptian-Israeli peace treaty might be signed by this Sunday, the original deadline.

Foreign Minister Moshe Dayan warned in an interview broadcast tonight that there was a possibility the draft peace treaty might not be signed at all, and that negotiations between Israel and Egypt would have to start all over again.

The Cabinet's refusal to go along with the United States Government's view

Continued on Page 5, Column 1

Vance Reports to President

By BERNARD GWERTZMAN
Special to The New York Times

WASHINGTON, Dec. 15 — The Carter Administration accused Israel today of deliberately distorting the nature of new peace proposals taken to Jerusalem this week by Secretary of State Cyrus R. Vance in his effort to complete an Egyptian-Israeli treaty.

Obviously irritated by the Israeli Cabinet's decision to reject the proposals, announced today by Prime Minister Menachem Begin, officials accompanying Mr. Vance on his Air Force plane from Cairo to Washington, gave reporters a highly detailed briefing intended to rebut Mr. Begin's statements.

Vance Goes to White House

Mr. Vance, who arrived at Andrews Air Force Base late this afternoon, went by helicopter directly to the White House to report to President Carter on the trip to Cairo and Jerusalem.

There was no official statement by the White House after the Vance-Carter meeting. But the State Department was instructed to draft a "white paper" to put on record the complaints against the Israelis.

Relations between Washington and Jerusalem were again under severe strain, and Mr. Vance was described as "saddened" and annoyed by the Israeli Cabinet's decision, which left little room for any early progress.

The immediate reaction of American officials in the Vance party was that a

Continued on Page 3, Column 1

The New York Times/Teresa Zabala
President Carter at the White House last night

United Press International
Deputy Prime Minister Teng Hsiao-ping

Koch Gets 3 Billion School Budget; Smaller Classes Among Objectives

By MARCIA CHAMBERS

The New York City School Chancellor, Frank J. Macchiarola, submitted a $3 billion expense budget to Mayor Koch yesterday that calls for smaller classes, intensified remedial instruction and additional personnel to combat truancy, vandalism and internal mismanagement.

To finance these additional programs, the Chancellor said he had to find $130 million in the budget from sources not yet committed to the public school system's anticipated revenues. The system's costs are roughly a third of the city's overall expense budget. He said that following the Mayor's lead he intended to try to get the necessary funds from the state and Federal Governments.

The Chancellor plans to have an all-day meeting on Monday with Federal officials in an attempt to obtain changes in Federal law that would give the school system more say in how and where remedial funds can be spent. Then, Mr. Macchiarola said, he intends to talk to Albany lawmakers, who are under a court ruling to revise the state-aid allocation formula for the financing of public schools.

If the city school district — the biggest in the country, with nearly a million students — "gets its fair share of state funding," he said, "we would get triple the

The Mayor's consultant on the City University has endorsed $160 million in priority construction projects. Page 25.

amount we get now." He said that would be more than enough for the new programs.

In an obvious criticism of his predecessor, Irving Anker, Mr. Macchiarola said in his budget message to the Board of Education that "additional funds will be required in order to begin the programing that has been neglected — not without severe effect — in recent years." Mr. Macchiarola's proposed 1979-80 budget is virtually the same as the Anker budget proposal last year. The Board of Education will hold a public hearing on the

Continued on Page 28, Column 1

CITY OF CLEVELAND DEFAULTS ON LOANS

Council Adjourns Without Action as Midnight Deadline Passes

By REGINALD STUART
Special to The New York Times

CLEVELAND, Saturday, Dec. 16 — Fiscal default befell this city last night when its government failed to repay some $15.5 million in loans to a group of local banks and the city treasury.

As the midnight deadline for repayment of the loans passed, the City Council had not taken action on the fiscal rehabilitation plan proposed by Mayor Dennis J. Kucinich. Operating under parliamentary procedures that prohibited a formal vote on the Mayor's plan, the council adjourned at three minutes past midnight.

The council members had gathered at City Hall for an 11 P.M. emergency session called by the Mayor, who was seeking to surmount stiff council opposition before the deadline, which had been set by the banks.

The Mayor, in a confident but passionate speech before a chamber packed with about 500 people and highlighted by the cheers and applause of his supporters, said the council's failure to act on his plan meant that as of Monday there would be hundreds of layoffs of police, fire, garbage, street maintenance and snow removal workers.

After adjournment, Mr. Kucinich had no comment for reporters.

Despite the emergence of numerous plans and proposals, alternatives and op-

Continued on Page 11, Column 1

United Press International
Mayor Dennis J. Kucinich of Cleveland, foreground, was accused at City Council debate of not acting to prevent default

China Move Reflects Carter's Aim To Protect Arms Pact and Taiwan

By HEDRICK SMITH
Special to The New York Times

WASHINGTON, Dec. 15 — Administration officials said tonight that President Carter's announcement of American plans to establish diplomatic relations with China reflected a belief that such ties would not jeopardize a new arms agreement with the Soviet Union or expose Taiwan to an attack from the mainland.

To the Carter Administration, the opening with China — pushed vigorously in the last 10 days by the Chinese themselves — offered a chance, officials said, to bring diplomatic relations into line with political reality and give the United States a vast new market and political partner in Asia and elsewhere in the world. But it involved a calculated political risk at home.

By announcing that it was terminating the American defense treaty with Taiwan at the end of 1979, the Administration opened itself to immediate charges from political conservatives that it was abandoning Taiwan.

Senator Barry Goldwater, the Arizona Republican, sounded the first attack by calling Mr. Carter's move "a cowardly act." The President himself acknowledged to reporters that the move drew "a mixed response" from the Congressional leadership.

But Administration officials, seeking to head off a potential domestic political storm, asserted after the President's speech that the United States had vigorously and repeatedly informed the Peking leadership that this country had a

Continued on Page 8, Column 5

China: The Long Wait

By FOX BUTTERFIELD
Special to The New York Times

News Analysis

HONG KONG, Saturday, Dec. 16 — President Carter's announcement last night that the United States and the People's Republic of China are finally normalizing diplomatic relations comes nearly seven years after Richard M. Nixon pledged in the Shanghai Communiqué of February 1972 to work toward that goal.

The major obstacle to progress on establishing relations has been America's longtime military and diplomatic commitment to the Chinese Nationalist Government on Taiwan, a problem compounded by the continued strong support for Taiwan among many in the United States.

The two sides continued to disagree. Mr. Carter clearly is taking something of a political gamble. But China did not directly challenge the President's promise and avoided the using threats of armed liberation of Taiwan that it has in the past.

In the end, the resolution of this impasse was a simple but subtle tactic that some specialists had long suggested. In announcing the break with Taipei, Mr. Carter simultaneously pledged that the United States "will continue to have an interest in the peaceful resolution of the Taiwan issue."

For its part, China reasserted its often-stated position that "as for the way of bringing Taiwan back to the embrace of the motherland and reunifying the country, it is entirely China's internal affair."

After the initial euphoria that accompanied Mr. Nixon's epochal trip to China, relations between the two nations seemed to languish for several years as events gave Taiwan a series of reprieves. First, Mr. Nixon's plans to improve ties were hampered by the Watergate scandal. Then President Gerald R. Ford was caught by the debacle of Vietnam's col-

Continued on Page 10, Column 4

Taiwan's President Protests to U.S. Over Decision on Ties With Peking

Special to The New York Times

TAIPEI, Taiwan, Saturday, Dec. 16 — President Chiang Ching-kuo protested bitterly today against the United States' decision to establish diplomatic relations with Peking and sever ties, including the mutual defense treaty, with the Chinese Nationalist Government here.

He vowed that the Chinese Nationalists "shall neither negotiate with the Communist regime nor compromise with Communism." His Government, he said, will never give up its "sacred task of recovering the mainland and delivering the compatriots there." He accused the United States of "denying the hundreds of millions of enslaved peoples on the Chinese mainland of their hope to an early restoration of freedom."

Mr. Chiang made his protest to the United States Ambassador, Leonard Unger, on being informed at 2 A.M. (1 P.M., Friday New York time) that the step Taiwan had been expecting since the visit of President Richard M. Nixon to Peking in 1972 would finally take place on Jan. 1.

While the break had long been expected to occur eventually, the timing came as a surprise, and it was denounced here both in and out of government.

The Government announced that it was calling off the legislative elections that were due on Dec. 23 to lessen the possibility of violent reactions to the American decision.

Shen Chang-huan, the Foreign Minister, registered his protest by resigning, and the President asked the Prime Minister, Sun Yun-suan, to take over the Foreign Ministry as well.

President Chiang was notified eight hours before President Carter went on television to announce the decision. As President Carter spoke, President Chiang issued his statement here denouncing the American decision as seriously damaging the rights and interests of "the Republic of China," meaning Nationalist China.

Declaring that the United States had

Continued on Page 8, Column 1

INSIDE

Saudis Moderate on Oil Prices

On the eve of a meeting of oil-exporting countries, Saudi Arabia's delegate called for moderation in determining an increased price of oil. Page 29.

Shah Urged to Compromise

Washington is pressing the Shah to replace Iran's military Government with a civilian coalition, a step that would leave him with some power. Page 2.

PULLOUT SECTION ON SIGNING OF MIDEAST PEACE TRACT, PAGES A11 TO A18

"All the News That's Fit to Print"

The New York Times

CITY EDITION

Metropolitan area weather: Sunny today; mostly sunny, mild tomorrow. Temperature range: today 32-48; yesterday 41-49. Details on page C12.

VOL.CXXVIII No.44,169

—NEW YORK, TUESDAY, MARCH 27, 1979—

25 cents beyond 50-mile zone from New York City. Higher in air delivery cities.

20 CENTS

EGYPT AND ISRAEL SIGN FORMAL TREATY, ENDING A STATE OF WAR AFTER 30 YEARS; SADAT AND BEGIN PRAISE CARTER'S ROLE

OPEC PARLEY WEIGHS NEW OIL PRICE RISES AND CUTS IN OUTPUT

Saudis Say They Will Try to Resist Big Increases — Carter Puts Off Decisions on Energy

By PAUL LEWIS

Special to The New York Times

GENEVA, March 26—Pressure for another large increase in world oil prices built up today at the opening of a meeting of oil ministers of the 13 member nations of the Organization of Petroleum Exporting Countries.

The advocates of a sharp new oil price rise, of anywhere from 20 to 35 percent from current levels on April 1, also urged other oil producers to reduce output. The aim would be to keep world markets tight as Iran resumes exports to insure that the new price levels stick.

But Saudi Arabia, the world's largest oil exporter, resisted pressure for price jumps, pointing out that they could do severe damage to the economies of both the developing and the industrialized world. "There is worry particularly about the effects of price changes on developing countries," OPEC's secretary general, René Ortise, said.

Effort to Reduce Increases

Sheik Ahmed Zaki Yamani, Saudi Arabia's oil minister, interviewed after tonight's session, said the ministers faced a "deadlock," with the Saudis feeling that the increases demanded by Iran and Libya were "too steep." Observers here interpreted his stance as an effort to cut probable increases to more moderate levels.

The ministers have not yet voted themselves the power to take any pricing action at the current two-day session but are expected to do so tomorrow. A simple majority vote would grant the meeting such authority.

On the question of possible punitive cutbacks in supplies, reflecting displeasure with some consuming nations' positions on the Palestinian question, Iraqi representatives said such moves were possible, particularly against Egypt. But they carefully noted that no such moves were planned by OPEC, although the "oil weapon" could re-emerge if conditions returned to the situation of 1973.

Carter Decisions Deferred

In Washington, meanwhile, Administration officials said that President Carter's decisions on various energy proposals, expected Thursday, would be deferred, apparently because key White House officials had not been able to devote enough time to the controversial plans. [Page D12.]

When Sheik Yamani entered the OPEC

Continued on Page D12, Column 3

United Press International

Leaders join hands after signing pact. President Anwar el-Sadat signed first, followed by Prime Minister Menachem Begin. President Carter was witness.

Mood of Peace Seems Somber And Uncertain

By BERNARD WEINRAUB

Special to The New York Times

WASHINGTON, March 26 — Shortly after 6 A.M. today, President Anwar el-Sadat arose in the residence of the Egyptian Ambassador and began wandering around the five-bedroom house.

He scanned the morning newspapers, pedaled a stationary exercise bicycle, nibbled a slice of unbuttered toast, sipped a glass of orange juice and, by 7 A.M. turned on the television to watch the morning news.

Less than one mile away, in a guarded ninth-floor suite at the Washington Hilton Hotel, Prime Minister Menachem Begin of Israel peered out the windows at the traffic moving along Connecticut Avenue.

He turned away and, carrying a cup of tea, walked to a writing desk and began working on the emotional speech that he would deliver in mid-afternoon at the White House ceremony ending 30 years of war between Israel and Egypt.

It was the start of a day marked by paradox — a triumphal day of peace that seemed curiously somber, a day of celebration blurred by protests in the heart of Washington, a bright day shadowed by uncertainty.

"There is, you know, a sense of trepi-

Continued on Page A9, Column 1

Treaty Impact Still Unknown

'Hopes and Dreams' but 'No Illusions' for Carter

By HEDRICK SMITH

Special to The New York Times

News Analysis

WASHINGTON, March 26 — The elusive, unprecedented peace treaty that Egypt and Israel signed today has enormous symbolic importance and the potential for fundamentally transforming the map and history of an entire region, but the agreement faces an uncertain future.

Israel has now won what it has sought since 1948 — formal recognition and acceptance from the most powerful Arab state and the ultimate prospect of exchanging ambassadors and entering into a full range of normal relations.

For all the violent denunciations that this historic breakthrough aroused in the Arab world, the best diplomatic estimate here is that the treaty has markedly reduced the risk of a major war in the Middle East for a considerable time by removing Egyptian strength from the active Arab arsenal.

And it has demonstrated American capacity to influence events in the Middle East despite the setbacks Washington has suffered since the overthrow of the

Continued on Page A10, Column 5

CEREMONY IS FESTIVE

Accord on Sinai Oil Opens Way to the First Peace in Mideast Dispute

By BERNARD GWERTZMAN

Special to The New York Times

WASHINGTON, March 26— After confronting each other in a state of war for nearly 31 years, Egypt and Israel signed a formal treaty at the White House today to establish peace and open "normal and friendly relations."

On this chilly early spring day, about 1,500 invited guests and millions more watching television saw President Anwar el-Sadat of Egypt and Prime Minister

Transcripts of statements at signing are on page A11. Texts of treaty and Camp David accords are on pages A12, A13 and A14.

Menachem Begin of Israel put their signatures on the Arabic, Hebrew and English versions of the first peace treaty between Israel and an Arab country.

President Carter, who was credited by both leaders with having made the agreement possible, signed, as a witness, for the United States. In a somber speech he said, "Peace has come."

'The First Step of Peace'

"We have won, at last, the first step of peace—a first step on a long and difficult road," he added.

All three leaders offered prayers that the treaty would bring true peace to the Middle East and end the enmity that has erupted into warfare four times since Israel declared its independence on May 14, 1948.

By coincidence, they all referred to the words of the Prophet Isaiah.

"Let us work together until the day comes when they beat their swords into plowshares and their spears into pruning hooks," Mr. Sadat said in his paraphrase of the biblical text.

Mr. Begin, who gave the longest and most emotional of the addresses, exclaimed: "No more war, no more bloodshed, no more bereavement, peace unto you, shalom, saalam, forever."

"Shalom" and "salaam" are the Hebrew and Arabic words for "peace."

A Touch of Humor by Begin

The Israeli leader, noted for oratorical skill, provided a dash of humor in his speech when he seconded Mr. Sadat's remark that Mr. Carter was "the unknown soldier of the peacemaking effort." Pausing, Mr. Begin added, "I agree, but as usual with an amendment."

Since Mr. Begin was known through the negotiations as a stickler for details, much to the American side's annoyance, Mr. Carter seemed to explode with laugh-

Continued on Page A10, Column 1

Photographs for The New York Times by TERESA ZABALA

Judge Bars Hydrogen Bomb Article After Magazine Rejects Mediation

By DOUGLAS E. KNEELAND

Special to The New York Times

MILWAUKEE, March 26 — A Federal District Court judge here, acting only after his suggestion for an attempt at out-of-court settlement was turned down, granted the Government's motion for a preliminary injunction today to keep The Progressive magazine from publishing an article about the hydrogen bomb.

In so doing, Judge Robert W. Warren became the first Federal judge ever to issue an injunction imposing prior restraint on the press in a national security case.

The magazine's attorneys said they would file an appeal shortly with the United States Court of Appeals for the Seventh Circuit in Chicago. Before announcing his decision, Judge Warren, a former Wisconsin Attorney General, acknowledged that he considered his decision a "terrible" one to have to make. Declaring that he had "grappled long and hard with this difficult problem," he added that he did not wish to "achieve notoriety" in such a manner.

Scientists Sought Compromise

Before issuing the injunction, Judge Warren urged the Department of Justice and The Progressive to accept a proposal by the Federation of American Scientists

Continued on Page B12, Column 3

INSIDE

H.R.A. Administrator Quits

Blanche Bernstein, the Human Resources Administrator, resigned rather than accept Mayor Koch's offer to stay in the job without power. Page B1.

Vietnam Invasion Toll Heavy

A tour through the area of Vietnam invaded by China showed that the region is almost entirely in ruins with roads, bridges and towns destroyed. Page A3.

Palestinians, Reacting to the Pact, Go on Strike and Denounce Egypt

Special to The New York Times

BEIRUT, Lebanon, March 26 — Vowing revenge, staging strikes and protest marches and calling for punitive measures against Egypt, Palestinians and other Arabs reacted angrily today against the signing of the Egyptian-Israeli peace treaty in Washington.

Yasir Arafat, chairman of the Palestine Liberation Organization, vowed to chase Americans out of the Middle East and to "chop off the hands" of President Carter, President Anwar el-Sadat of Egypt and Prime Minister Menachem Begin of Israel. He spoke to a group of guerrilla recruits at the Sabra Palestinian camp here as effigies of the three signers were burned.

The inhabitants of Lebanon's 15 Palestinian camps protested the signing today by refusing to work, as did many Lebanese Moslems. Similar protests were staged in the occupied West Bank of the Jordan River and the Gaza Strip, and in the Arab Old City of Jerusalem a grenade exploded tonight, wounding five tourists.

Iran Government Condemns Pact

In Teheran, the Iranian Government condemned the treaty, and 30 Arab students took over the Egyptian Embassy there. Protesters also stormed the Egyptian Embassy in Kuwait, where 250,000 Palestinians live, forming the largest foreign community in that small country. In Damascus, Syria, demonstrators occupied the offices of the Egyptian airline, Egyptair.

Meanwhile, foreign and finance ministers of Arab League countries gathered today in Baghdad, Iraq, for a meeting tomorrow on possible economic and political measures against Egypt. The countries had vowed last November to hold such a meeting if. the Egyptian-Israeli peace treaty was signed, but Saudi Arabia, Egypt's principal foreign backer, has been trying to exercise a moderating influence.

King Hussein of Jordan flew to Damascus and Baghdad during the day in what was believed to be an effort to coordinate the positions of hard-liners and moderates at tomorrow's Arab meeting.

Gromyko Comments on Treaty

In Damascus, Foreign Minister Andrei A. Gromyko of the Soviet Union ended a three-day visit to Syria today by joining with President Hafez al-Assad in denouncing the peace treaty, saying it appeared bound to increase tension in the Middle East. A joint Soviet-Syrian communiqué said the treaty was aimed at perpetuating the Israeli occupation of Arab lands, the annexation of Arab East

Continued on Page A10, Column 3

"All the News That's Fit to Print"

The New York Times

LATE CITY EDITION

Weather: Mostly cloudy, mild today; showers tonight. Showers, tomorrow. Temperature range: today 52-68; yesterday 54-70. Details on page A27.

VOL.CXXVIII . . No.44,207 | NEW YORK, FRIDAY, MAY 4, 1979 | 20 CENTS

25 cents beyond 50-mile zone from New York City. Higher in air delivery cities

CONSERVATIVES WIN BRITISH VOTE; MARGARET THATCHER FIRST WOMAN TO HEAD A EUROPEAN GOVERNMENT

United Press International

Margaret Thatcher leaving polling station after casting her vote in London yesterday

BIG SHIFT FROM LABOR

Tory Leader Is Given Clear Mandate to Change the Country's Course

By R. W. APPLE Jr.

Special to The New York Times

LONDON, Friday, May 4 — Margaret Thatcher and the Conservative Party won a decisive victory in Britain's general election yesterday.

Mrs. Thatcher, an Oxford-educated chemist and lawyer who entered Parliament in 1959, won a substantial majority and a clear mandate to reverse the nation's course. She promised during her campaign to restrain the trade unions, to cut personal income taxes and to bolster the armed forces.

She will become Europe's first woman Prime Minister.

Voting Pattern Changes

Projections by the television networks and by the Press Association suggested that the Tories would hold a majority over all other parties of approximately 30 to 35 seats. But the voting pattern was not as uniform as in past elections, and the ultimate majority might therefore be somewhat smaller.

With results declared in 510 of 635 constituencies, the totals were as follows:

Conservatives	255
Labor	244
Liberals	7
Scottish Nationalists	2
Welsh Nationalists	2

The totals reflected a gain of 45 seats for the Conservatives, a loss of 37 for Labor and a loss of one for the Liberals. The Scottish Nationalists had lost six seats and the Welsh Nationalists had lost one.

British Analysts Baffled

For Prime Minister James Callaghan and the Labor Party, the brightest spots were in Scotland and northern England, where the Conservative tide was running far less strongly than in the London area. The irregular pattern baffled British analysts such as David Butler of Nuffield College, Oxford, who said, "The confident simplicities of past elections don't apply."

Before going to bed shortly after dawn, Mrs. Thatcher said she hoped "to announce victory about midday." The Prime Minister, still smiling despite the late hour and the adverse trend, commented, "I shall have something more to say when things are entirely clear."

The former Liberal Party leader, Jeremy Thorpe, who had represented North Devon for 20 years, was beaten by 8,000 votes. His highly publicized legal difficulties — his trial on charges of conspiracy and incitement to murder opens Tuesday — apparently proved too big an obstacle to overcome.

Although national trends suggested he would lose, Dr. David Owen, the Foreign Secretary, clung to his seat in Plymouth by 1,001 votes.

But a number of well-known Members of Parliament were swept away, including Hugh Jenkins, a former Arts Minis-

Continued on Page A10, Column 1

The New York Times / George Tames

Senator Abraham A. Ribicoff

Ribicoff Decides He Won't Seek A Fourth Term

By STEVEN R. WEISMAN

Special to The New York Times

WASHINGTON, May 3 — Senator Abraham A. Ribicoff of Connecticut announced today that he would retire from the Senate after his current term of office — his third — expires next year.

His decision startled his political colleagues, as well as his staff aides, and immediately set off a scramble to succeed him. At least three Democrats and three Republicans in Connecticut indicated their interest in running for his seat. [Page B4.]

Mr. Ribicoff, a 69-year-old Democrat, has become Connecticut's most influential elected official in modern times, and his departure from Washington would bring to a conclusion an extraordinary public career that has included service as a United States Representative, Governor, Cabinet member under President John F. Kennedy and, since 1963, United States Senator.

Today he dismissed any suggestion that he would accept either a Cabinet post or an ambassadorship after he retired.

"As Mike Mansfield said, 'There is a time to stay and a time to go,'" Mr. Ribicoff told reporters this morning, referring to the former Senate majority leader, who is now Ambassador to Japan. "I've watched them come and go," Mr.

Continued on Page B4, Column 1

PRODUCER PRICES UP BY 0.9% FOR APRIL; FOOD DOWN A LITTLE

Rises Expected to Keep Consumer Costs High and Further Harm Carter Fight on Inflation

By STEVEN RATTNER

Special to The New York Times

WASHINGTON, May 3 — Producer prices rose by nine-tenths of 1 percent in April, and, despite a slight slowing from March, signs pointed to at least another month of substantial increases, according to Labor Department figures released today.

The increase would have been greater if food prices had not fallen slightly last month. The overall increase in prices at the producer level was the smallest for any month since last November. Food prices have been rising rapidly, and Carter Administration officials were particularly relieved by last month's abatement.

The Government now computes producer prices for finished goods ready for shipment to retailers to compile a more accurate economic indicator than the former Wholesale Price Index, which has been abandoned. But producer prices are roughly equivalent to wholesale prices.

Period of Weeks or Months

Producer price increases do not directly affect consumers but gradually work their way over a period of weeks or months to the retail level. Accordingly, last month's rise in the Producer Price Index suggests that high rates of consumer price increases will continue.

The increases would, in turn, further jeopardize President Carter's anti-inflation program, which seeks to hold wage increases to 7 percent annually. Meanwhile, consumer prices rose at a 13 percent rate in the first three months of the year. The April rise in producer prices translated into a compound annual inflation rate of 11.5 percent.

The rises last month in wholesale prices were paced by sharply higher prices for fuel, plastics, cars and leather. Home-heating oil, for example, rose by 6.7 percent in the month alone. Gasoline prices increased by 4.4 percent. The increases in energy prices reflects the worldwide shortage of oil as a result of the shutdown earlier this year of Iranian oil production and the price increases imposed as a result by the Organization of Petroleum Exporting Countries.

Perhaps more worrisome was the news that the most recent increases in energy prices appeared to have begun to filter

Continued on Page D14, Column 5

Terrorists Bomb the Rome Offices Of the Christian Democratic Party

By HENRY TANNER

Special to The New York Times

ROME, May 3 — A group of urban guerrillas raided the Rome area headquarters of Italy's dominant Christian Democratic Party today, wrecked two floors with bombs, killed one policeman, wounded two others and escaped.

The attack, the largest terrorist operation since Red Brigade terrorists kidnapped former Prime Minister Aldo Moro last year, killing five bodyguards and subsequently Mr. Moro, came on the eve of a general election campaign.

The raiders spray-painted the walls of the party headquarters with the initials of the Red Brigades and with its emblem, a five-pointed star. They also left behind this inscription: "We shall transform the fraudulent elections into a class war."

Fears were expressed that there would be a wave of terrorist attacks during the campaign for the elections that are scheduled for June 3 and 4.

Shaken by the magnitude of today's attack, former President Giuseppe Saragat and other political figures called for stronger antiterrorist measures. Some suggested that martial law was needed, as they had done when Mr. Moro was abducted on March 16, 1978. His body was found nearly two months later.

"Political terrorism," Mr. Saragat said, "is turning into full-scale civil war and must be confronted not only by the police but also by the armed forces of the republic."

The Red Brigades, the most feared of Italy's terrorist groups, have as their aim the destruction of the Italian state and society as a step toward a revolutionary takeover. They accuse the Communist Party of having sold out to the bourgeoi-

Continued on Page A4, Column 3

'Genuine' Tory Taking Charge

Margaret Roberts Thatcher

By WILLIAM BORDERS

Special to The New York Times

LONDON, May 3 — To Margaret Thatcher, "free choice is ultimately what life is about," and she likes to illustrate what she means in political terms with this example: "If somebody comes to me and asks, What are you going to do for us small businessmen? I say, the only thing I'm going to do for you is make you freer to do things for yourselves. If you can't do it then, I'm sorry. I'll have nothing to offer you."

Woman in the News

Judging by what she has been saying over the years, in public and in private, that is the center of Mrs. Thatcher's political philosophy, — what she calls "a positive creed, to promote, not destroy, the uniqueness of the individual."

In the election campaign Mrs. Thatcher sketched a vision of a Britain that would be rebuilt, on the strong base of that kind of individualism, to the economic strength it used to know, "so that once again the products stream from our factories and workshops while the customers of the world scramble over each other to buy them." She also promised a government that "would stop trying to step in and take decisions for you that you should be free to take on your own."

Now, the British people, having chosen as their leader the first woman to head a modern European government, will have a chance to put to a practical test what she terms the genu-

Continued on Page A11, Column 1

The New York Times / John Sotomayor

Bird watchers stalking their "prey" early yesterday morning in Central Park

For Central Park Bird Watchers, Thrills Take Flight Every Spring

By ROBIN HERMAN

Why don't bird watchers get "warblers' neck" in Central Park? Why does the Police Department assign a patrolman to watch the bird watchers? And have you ever seen a rock dove?

Bird watchers don't get warblers' neck from craning to see warblers in the treetops because the hills in Central Park put bird watchers at eye level with the tops of the trees. The Police Department assigns an officer to watch bird watchers because many of them carry expensive field glasses that make them likely targets for muggers. And if you think you have never seen a rock dove you probably have because they are otherwise known as pigeons and Central Park is full of them.

Fifty New Yorkers who went "birding" yesterday at 7 A.M. along the Central Park Ramble spotted nearly 40 species of birds in an hour and a half, including multitudes of rock doves bobbing and cooing on the paths and outcroppings. The real prizes, however, were the visiting warblers who stop in Manhattan this month for a drink and a bite to eat on their way to summer

Continued on Page B3, Column 2

INSIDE

Giants Pick Quarterback

The Giants' first pick in the National Football League draft was Phil Simms, a quarterback from Morehead State in Kentucky. Page A21.

Islanders Tie Series

Bob Nystrom's goal in overtime gave the Islanders a 3-2 victory over the Rangers, tying their playoff series at two games apiece. Page A21.

News Summary and Index, Page B1

CALIFANO REASSESSES RADIATION HAZARDS

He Now Says Some Cancer Deaths From Accident Are Possible

By CHARLES MOHR

Special to The New York Times

WASHINGTON, May 3 — Joseph A. Califano Jr., Secretary of Health, Education and Welfare, said today that radiation exposure from the Three Mile Island reactor accident was higher than earlier measurements had indicated. As a result, he said, statistical probability indicates that at least one cancer death caused by radiation could be expected among the two million people living within 50 miles of the Pennsylvania power plant.

He also said that the radiation could be expected to cause as many as 10 additional nonfatal cancers.

Mr. Califano, who testified a month ago that no deaths would result from the exposure, said today that subsequent measurements showed radiation levels had been nearly twice as high as earlier estimates. He also said that the estimates were expected to rise further.

His testimony, before the Subcommittee on Energy, Nuclear Proliferation and Federal Services of the Senate Government Affairs Committee, took note of the contention of some scientists that assumptions about low-level radiation as a cause of cancer might be 10 times too low. Mr. Califano quoted some experts as saying that the increase in cancer deaths from the accident could be as high as 10.

Under normal conditions, the number of cancer deaths in a population of two million would be 325,000.

Meanwhile, the Nuclear Regulatory Commission reported that the Oyster Creek Plant at Forked River, N.J., was shut down automatically yesterday during a test of the reactor's pressure-reading instruments. [Page B3.]

And the Nuclear Regulatory Commission, considering the status of a Maine reactor that was among five closed in

Continued on Page A19, Column 4

In Her Own Words

Comments by Margaret Thatcher since taking the party leadership in 1975:

Limitation of government doesn't make for a weak government — don't make that mistake. If you've got the role of government clearly set out, then it means very strong government in that role. Very strong indeed. You weaken government if you try to spread it over so wide a range that you're not powerful where you should be because you've got into areas where you shouldn't be.

•

Overtaxation is transparently foolish. Most of us are willing to work for our families and neighbors but not for the Chancellor of the Exchequer. In a free country people will work hard if it pays them to do so. At present, taxes are so high that for many it is not worthwhile working hard, and for some it is not worthwhile working at all. The first step to recovery, therefore, is to lower taxes on earnings.

•

There are two ways of making a cabinet. One way is to have in it people who represent all the different viewpoints within the party, within the broad philosophy. The other way is to have in it only the people who want to go in the direction in which every instinct tells me we have to go. As Prime Minister I couldn't waste time having any internal arguments.

•

The power of trade unions over individual members is far too great. We shall have to stand up against those elements who are prepared to use their present freedom in society to destroy society. . . . A strong trade-union movement is an integral part of modern industrial society, but it must not ride roughshod over the rest of that society.

•

On immigration from the Commonwealth: Small minorities can be absorbed — they can be assets to the majority community — but once a minority in a neighborhood gets very large, people do feel swamped. They feel their whole way of life has been changed.

•

On male colleagues: I'm not conscious of them as men at all. Don't mistake me: I see A as taller than B; I see X as more handsome than Y. What woman wouldn't? What man wouldn't have such perceptions about women? But I don't see me and my colleagues in an "I'm a woman, you are men" relationship.

"All the News That's Fit to Print"

The New York Times

LATE CITY EDITION

Weather: Cloudy, humid, warm today; cloudy, late thunderstorms tomorrow. Temperature range: today 72-88; yesterday 73-88. Details on page C16.

VOL.CXXVIII . . . No.44,323

NEW YORK, TUESDAY, AUGUST 28, 1979

25 cents beyond 50-mile zone from New York City. Higher in air delivery cities.

20 CENTS

LORD MOUNTBATTEN IS KILLED AS HIS FISHING BOAT EXPLODES; I.R.A. FACTION SAYS IT SET BOMB

2 BOYS ALSO VICTIMS

In Ulster, 17 Soldiers Die in Worst British Loss in 10 Years of Strife

By WILLIAM BORDERS

Special to The New York Times

MULLAGHMORE, Ireland, Aug. 27 — Earl Mountbatten of Burma, one of the heroes of modern British history, was killed today when his fishing boat was blown up in the sea, apparently by terrorists of the Irish Republican Army.

The 79-year-old World War II hero died instantly in the explosion, which occurred a quarter mile off the coast, near his summer home here in the northwest of Ireland. A 14-year-old grandson and a 15-year-old passenger were also killed and four other passengers in the 29-foot boat, including a daughter, Lady Brabourne, were seriously injured.

Sailor, military strategist, political negotiator, adviser to Prime Ministers: An obituary is on page A10.

The explosion this morning reverberated like thunder through this peaceful little seaside village. A witness who saw it from the shore said, "The boat was there one minute and the next minute it was like a lot of matchsticks floating on the water."

I.R.A. Takes Responsibility

In Belfast, Northern Ireland, the Provisional wing of the Irish Republican Army issued a statement taking responsibility for the killing, which it called "an execution," and vowed to continue the "noble struggle to drive the British intruders out of our native land."

In a separate incident, at least 18 British soldiers were killed in a bombing in Northern Ireland. It was the single heaviest death toll for the British Army in the 10 years since it was sent in to quell fighting between Roman Catholic and Protestant militants. The I.R.A. also took responsibility for the incident. [Page A11.]

Lord Mountbatten, who never had any particular connection with the sectarian battle over Northern Ireland, was an uncle of Prince Philip, a cousin of Queen Elizabeth, and former chief of the British defense staff and the last Viceroy of India. His murder, probably the boldest and most dramatic act of the long terrorist campaign here, sent waves of shock and indignation across both Britain and Ireland.

Reaction of Nation's Leaders

"His death leaves a gap that can never be filled," Prime Minister Margaret Thatcher said in a statement from Chequers, the Prime Minister's country residence. "The British people give thanks for his life and grieve at his passing."

At Buckingham Palace, a spokesman said that Queen Elizabeth, who received the news at Balmoral Castle in Scotland, was "deeply shocked" at the loss of the elder cousin whom she and the rest of the

Continued on Page A11, Column 1

Camera Press/Norman Parkinson

Earl Mountbatten of Burma

Strike at British Nobility

Act Could Bring New Peace Initiatives in Ulster Or Toughen London's Resolve Against Terrorism

By R. W. APPLE Jr.

Special to The New York Times

News Analysis

LONDON, Aug. 27 — By choosing Earl Mountbatten of Burma as the latest target of their campaign against British rule in Northern Ireland, the terrorists of the Irish Republican Army struck at the symbolic heart of British society, the monarchy.

The 79-year-old Lord Mountbatten — "Uncle Dickie" to the royal family — was Queen Elizabeth's confidant and adviser as well as one of the few surviving heroes of Britain's finest hour, the victory over the Axis in World War II.

The killing was intended, in the view of analysts here, to focus the maximum possible public attention on the stalemate in Northern Ireland. If it was meant to shock, it succeeded. Britons, who admired Lord Mountbatten as much for his common touch as for his royal lineage and his public triumphs, were roused from the torpor of a holiday weekend into expressions of horror and outrage.

Full Impact of Death Unclear

It was not clear tonight, however, whether Lord Mountbatten's death would lead to new initiatives in Northern Ireland or would simply strengthen British resolve to crush the sectarian terrorists, something that neither Labor nor Conservative governments have been able even to approach during a decade of unbroken violence that has cost nearly 2,000 lives.

Prime Minister Margaret Thatcher led the nation in paying tribute to the man who had won more medals and honors than any living Briton. She said that his life "ran like a golden thread of inspiration and service" to his country throughout this century.

'War Against Terrorism'

Later, in a second statement following the death of 18 British soldiers in a separate incident, the Prime Minister added:

"The Government will spare no effort to insure that those responsible for these and all other acts of terrorism are brought to justice. The people of the United Kingdom will wage war against terrorism with relentless determination until it is won."

If Mrs. Thatcher maintains that resolute posture, she will have the support of the major figures in the key opposition parties. James Callaghan, the Labor leader, and David Steel, the Liberal leader, both denounced the terrorists. Mr. Steel said that "this cowardly attack" would "simply reinforce the determination of the British people and its united Parliament to destroy terrorism."

But the attack itself, like the murder in

Continued on Page A11, Column 4

Associated Press

The body of Earl Mountbatten being carried from the harbor at Mullaghmore, Ireland, after explosion aboard boat

Soviet Ballerina Goes Home After Meeting U.S. Officials

Miss Vlasova Says Her Decision to Return Was Not Coerced

By ROBERT D. McFADDEN

Lyudmila Vlasova, the wife of Aleksandr Godunov, the Bolshoi Ballet dancer who defected last week, spurned an offer to meet with her husband and left for Moscow yesterday.

Her departure ended a three-day deadlock between the United States and the Soviet Union over the conditions for allowing Miss Vlasova to express her wishes freely.

After three days aboard a Soviet jetliner grounded by the United States at Kennedy International Airport, Miss Vlasova stepped into a van that had been pulled up alongside the aircraft at midafternoon and declared her intentions in the presence of a dozen Soviet and American officials, an interpreter and Mr. Godunov's lawyer.

Immediately after the 20-minute interview with the 36-year-old Bolshoi ballerina, the Americans said they were satisfied that Miss Vlasova had spoken freely in a noncoercive atmosphere, conditions they had insisted upon in negotiations with Soviet officials all weekend.

Principle Believed Upheld

"We are satisfied that the principle involved in this incident has been upheld — that is, that she is leaving on the basis of her own preference," said Donald F. McHenry, the deputy United States representative at the United Nations, who led the American negotiators.

Specifically, Mr. McHenry said, Miss Vlasova was asked if there was anyone she wanted to see or give a message to before she returned to the Soviet Union, an obvious reference to her husband.

"Her answer," Mr. McHenry said, "was 'nyet.' "

At 6:39 P.M., after being held up by a thunderstorm, Miss Vlasova and 52 other Soviet citizens who had been on the blue and white, 138-seat Aeroflot jetliner since 5 P.M. Friday roared away on a homeward flight to Moscow and the incident, a human rights confrontation that had grown into an international test of wills, was officially closed.

Unofficially, however, a number of questions remained unanswered: Why, after Mr. Godunov's defection last Wednesday, was Miss Vlasova removed from the Bolshoi troupe by eight Soviet security men and put aboard the Moscow-bound jetliner? And why was Mr. Godunov given no opportunity to speak to her aboard the plane?

In Washington, President Carter's press secretary, Jody Powell, and the acting Secretary of State, Warren M. Christopher, said the American effort had not been in vain, but had established the principle that foreigners in the United States had a right to choose freely whether to remain or leave.

"In the end, it paid off, and the principle was established," Mr. Powell said at the White House. "Certainly it is not the first such incident, nor is it likely to be the last." Mr. Christopher, who had made the decision to halt the Soviet plane, called it "a victory for the principle of no forced repatriation." [Page B4.]

Yevgeny N. Makeyev, who had led the Soviet negotiators, said it had been "a victory for proletarian justice." He called Miss Vlasova "a patriot of her country" and said: "Certainly she will continue to tour with the Bolshoi."

Miss Vlasova's mother, Alexandra Gerasimovna, appeared on Soviet television and expressed indignation over the detention of her daughter. She had appealed twice to President Carter for her daughter's return.

Representative Lester Wolff, a Long Island Democrat, charged that the Immigration and Naturalization Service had "botched" its job by allowing Miss

Continued on Page B4, Column 5

United Press International/Joel Landau

Lyudmila Vlasova aboard plane

MONDALE DECLARES THAT A STRONG CHINA IS IN U.S. INTERESTS

In Speech on Peking TV, He Offers Credits and Gives an Apparent Warning to the Russians

By JAMES P. STERBA

Special to The New York Times

PEKING, Aug. 27 — Vice President Mondale told the Chinese people in a televised speech today that a "strong and secure and modernizing China" was in the American interest in the coming decade. He said the United States was prepared to extend $2 billion in trade credits over five years, and he warned that any nation seeking to weaken or isolate China would also be regarded as acting against the interests of the United States.

"Despite the sometimes profound differences between our two systems," the Vice President declared, "we are committed to joining with you to advance our many parallel strategic and bilateral interests.

Excerpts from address are on page A4.

"Thus any nation which seeks to weaken or isolate you in world affairs assumes a stance counter to American interests."

Apparent Warning to Moscow

This apparent warning to the Soviet Union came in what was said to be the first broadcast address by an American leader to the Chinese people. The speech, delivered to about 900 professors, teachers and students from several schools in the Peking area, was taped for televising later tonight, with parts of it carried by radio.

Mr. Mondale, who arrived Saturday for a week's visit to China, also announced in his speech that by the end of the year the White House would send to Congress the Chinese-American trade agreement that was signed in May. This accord would give China so-called most-favored-nation status, making it eligible for cuts in tariffs to the same levels as those applied to America's close trading partners.

"And its submission is not linked to any other issue," Mr. Mondale said in an apparent allusion to the debate in the United States over granting similar status to the

Continued on Page A5, Column 1

Kurds Report Agreement on Truce In Talks With Khomeini Associate

By Reuters

TEHERAN, Iran, Aug. 27 — Representatives of the Kurds, whose guerrilla forces have been hard pressed by Iranian Government troops, began preliminary peace talks here today and reported afterward that a cease-fire had been agreed on and that the state radio would proclaim it tomorrow morning. There was no official confirmation from the Government side.

With the Kurdish center of Mehabad expecting an attack following the fall of three other Kurdish towns, a five-member delegation arrived here today and said it had reached agreement on truce arrangements with an associate of Ayatollah Ruhollah Khomeini, Iran's de facto head of state.

A spokesman for the Kurds, Rahim Seif Ghazi, said that Teheran's spiritual leader, Ayatollah Mahmoud Taleghani, had promised that a cease-fire order would be broadcast in the morning and that formal negotiations for peace could then begin.

The current fighting between Kurds demanding autonomy and Iranian Government forces seeking to bring the Kurdish minority under Ayatollah Khomeini's Islamic rule began with a local uprising 12 days ago in the Kurdish area of Paveh. Government troops recaptured Paveh on Aug. 16 and subsequently put down violence in nearby Sanandaj, the capital of the province of Kurdistan, and Saqqiz.

Iraqi Officers Captured

The official Pars press agency said today that two Iraqi military officers had been captured during the fighting at Paveh and sent to Teheran for questioning. Iranian officials had charged earlier that civilian Kurds from across the Iraqi border might be involved in the fight for Kurdish autonomy in Iran.

Mr. Ghazi, the spokesman for the Kurdish peace delegation, said the group had asked during the preliminary talks

Continued on Page A3, Column 1

Critics Question Builder's Drive For U.S. Center Sought by Saudis

The following article is based on reporting by Philip Taubman and Judith Miller and was written by Miss Miller.

Special to The New York Times

IRVINE, Calif. — Fifteen months ago, executives of 40 of the nation's largest corporations gathered for an unusual breakfast at the Biltmore Hotel in Santa Barbara, Calif. They had one thing in common: business interests in Saudi Arabia.

The goal of the hosts at the breakfast was to raise a large share of the money for a proposed $22 million Middle East Studies Center at the University of Southern California in Los Angeles.

Interviews with participating executives and others indicate that the breakfast was part of an intensive effort by J. Robert Fluor to forge links between Arab officials, two American academic institutions and his own considerable business interests. Mr. Fluor is chairman of the U.S.C. board of trustees and president of the Fluor Corporation, a major construction and engineering concern that conducts billions of dollars of business in Saudi Arabia.

Method and Motive Questioned

Critics in academic circles and in foundations have asserted that Mr. Fluor's activities could have been intended to use the educational institutions as vehicles for Saudi attempts to influence attitudes and policies in this country.

While it is not unusual for corporations to contribute to academic institutions, what distinguished the effort on behalf of the proposed California center was the manner in which it was pressed. "We were sandbagged," said Michael Ameen, a Mobil official who described the fund-raising effort as "insulting and stupid."

There appears to be nothing illegal about what Mr. Fluor attempted to do, and he denies completely the accusations of any improper relationships or conflict of interest in his activities. However, his

Continued on Page A12, Column 1

The Los Angeles Times

J. Robert Fluor

INSIDE

Conrail Adds Commuter Seats

Conrail will provide 6,000 additional seats for its Harlem, Hudson and New Haven lines to relieve standing-room-only conditions in rush hours. Page B1.

U.S. Ends Fiscal Inquiry

The Federal inquiry into New York City's fiscal crisis came to an official end with a decision that no charges were warranted. Page B1.

"All the News That's Fit to Print"

The New York Times

LATE CITY EDITION

Weather: Cloudy, sporadic rain today; rain ending tonight. Sunny tomorrow. Temperature range: today 55-65; yesterday 62-74. Details on page B6.

VOL.CXXIX . . No. 44,590 | NEW YORK, WEDNESDAY, MAY 21, 1980 | 25 CENTS

30 cents beyond 50-mile zone from New York City. Higher in air delivery cities.

BUSH WINS MICHIGAN; REAGAN AND CARTER ARE OREGON VICTORS

CALIFORNIAN NEARS MAJORITY

Results Leave Him Just Shy of 998 Delegates Needed to Capture Republican Nomination

By ADAM CLYMER

George Bush checked Ronald Reagan's march to a delegate majority yesterday, defeating the former California Governor in the Michigan Republican primary and postponing Mr. Reagan's amassing the 998 convention votes needed for nomination.

Mr. Reagan easily defeated Mr. Bush in the Oregon primary yesterday. But the solid Bush margin in the Michigan contest, for 82 delegates, prevented Mr. Reagan's triumph in Oregon, with 29, from giving him the majority last night, according to The New York Times's count. However, he needs as few as six more, and is considered certain to win them within the next week.

President Carter soundly defeated Senator Edward M. Kennedy of Massachusetts in Oregon's Democratic primary, winning the bulk of the state's 39 delegates to the National Convention. There were no delegates at stake in Michigan's Democratic primary, and neither Mr. Carter nor Mr. Kennedy was on the ballot. That state's 141 delegates were selected in caucuses last month.

Key Reagan Aide Resigns

Even as Mr. Reagan lost in Michigan, his campaign also suffered the resignation of Anderson Carter, his field director, the politician on his staff with the most experience in recent campaigns. In announcing that he would leave in a few days, Mr. Carter gave no reason, but some campaign sources said that he was unhappy with the dominance of other aides whom he considered inexperienced.

In a very light turnout in Michigan, Mr. Bush ran well ahead of Mr. Reagan in all parts of the state, taking about 57 percent of the popular vote. It was clear from his strength across the state that the intensive campaigning for him by Gov. William G. Milliken had played a critical part in his triumph.

With more than half the returns in, Mr.

Continued on Page A26, Column 2

50,000 Warned of Volcano Flood Threat

Scientists See Danger In Overflow of Lake Dammed by Debris

By WALLACE TURNER

Special to The New York Times

VANCOUVER, Wash., May 20 — Officials said today that about 50,000 people living in Washington cities along the lower Columbia River were threatened by a flash flood that might develop in the aftermath of the eruption of Mount St. Helens.

"I think an overflow is imminent," said Dwight Crandell, one of the United States Geological Survey scientists monitoring the eruption. The threat of flooding was created when the outlet of Spirit Lake, on the mountain's shattered north flank, was plugged by dirt, rock, trees and volcanic ash from the explosion on Sunday morning. The outlet is the source of the Toutle River, the valley of which was the scene of mudflows, flooding, and flows of superheated volcanic ash.

"The best we would hope for," Mr. Crandell said, "is for the water to spill over the top and go quietly down the river. The worst would be for the whole thing to come crashing down."

Much of Valley in Path

A total, rapid deterioration of the earth plug, which scientists say is 200 feet high and 1.5 miles wide, would mean a disastrous flood that would careen down the Toutle River Valley to the Cowlitz River at Castle Rock, Wash., and then inundate much of Kelso and Longview, Wash., before pouring into the Columbia River.

The cloud of gas and particles of volcanic debris that resulted from the eruption moved east today, widening into an arc from Maine to Georgia. The cloud was not visible in New York, and environmental officials said it did not present any health hazard.

98 Reported Missing

Whether there will be any long-term health effects from the fallout is not known without more detailed analysis of the content of the cloud, but scientists say that the eruption is not likely to bring any significant changes in weather patterns, and they expect only negligible effects to be felt at ground level. [Page A20.]

The names of six persons killed in Washington were released today by the authorities, who also said that two unidentified bodies had been discovered and that they were trying to locate 98 other persons who had been reported missing.

Continued on Page A20, Column 2

©Everett (Wash.) Herald/Vern Hodgson via Associated Press

In what he called "a stroke of luck," Vern Hodgson, an amateur photographer of Lynnwood, Wash., was setting up his 35mm camera on a tripod when Mount St. Helens began to erupt Sunday morning. He took these pictures from a distance of 15 miles, using 400 ASA color print film. In all, he made 16 pictures in about four minutes, shifting from a 75-150mm zoom lens with an extender, making it the equivalent of a 300mm lens, to a 50mm lens and finally a 25mm wide-angle lens as the cloud from the eruption widened to about 20 miles.

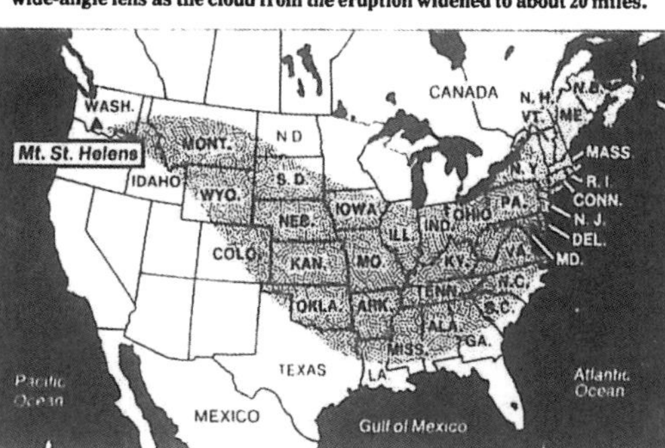

The New York Times/May 21, 1980

Dissipating cloud of fallout from eruption reached Eastern States last night

QUEBECERS DEFEAT SOVEREIGNTY MOVE BY DECISIVE MARGIN

A TRUDEAU VICTORY

Many French Canadians Join English-Speakers to Back Federalism

By HENRY GINIGER

Special to The New York Times

MONTREAL, May 20 — In a historic referendum, Quebec voted overwhelmingly today to reject a move to put this predominantly French-speaking province on the road out of the Canadian federation.

Federalist forces, led by Prime Minister Pierre Elliott Trudeau of Canada and Claude Ryan, leader of the Quebec Liberal party, who had cautioned against breaking up Canada and had promised constitutional changes, took 59 percent of the vote compared with 41 percent for the "yes" side led by the provincial Premier, René Lévesque.

Mr. Lévesque did not even obtain a majority of French speakers, who make up 80 percent of the province's 6.2 million people. About 54 percent of the Quebec French refused to heed his appeal for solidarity and joined with more than 80 percent of the non-French minority, mainly English-speakers, to produce the decisive federalist victory.

Lévesque Close to Tears

Close to tears, Mr. Lévesque appeared before his supporters tonight and promised "a next time." He said the vote, "an upsurge of old Quebec," had to be accepted, but he warned Mr. Trudeau that "the ball was in his court now" and that he had to make good his promises of constitutional change.

At a news conference in Ottawa, Mr. Trudeau renewed this promise. He said he did not wish to celebrate noisily because of all the wounds created by the campaign in Quebec, but added that both sides had shown they wanted change.

"Now that we have reaffirmed our will to live together, we must apply ourselves without delay to the task of rebuilding our home to conform to the present needs of the Canadian family," the Prime Minister said in appealing to Mr. Lévesque to join in the task of renewal of the federation. Joe Clark, the former Prime Minis-

Continued on Page A9, Column 1

Cabinet Resigns In South Korea As Riots Grow

More Deaths Reported in Huge Kwangju Protest

By HENRY SCOTT STOKES

Special to The New York Times

SEOUL, May 20 — The South Korean Cabinet of Prime Minister Shin Hyon Hwack resigned today "to take responsibility for failure to maintain domestic calm" as riots continued in the provincial city of Kwangju.

Reports from Kwangju, a stronghold of Kim Dae Jung, the arrested opposition leader, said that a television and radio station was burned as 30,000 demonstrators, mainly students and workers, marched in groups and that some battled a division-strength army unit that was rushed to the city when troubles began there.

[The Associated Press reported from Seoul that troops in Kwangju opened fire Wednesday on demonstrators who were trying to drive commandeered buses and armored personnel carriers at them, killing at least three, according to witnesses. The report said that as many as 200,000 people surged through the streets of Kwangju in the fourth straight day of protests against martial law. In rioting Tuesday, the agency said, up to 11 persons were killed, 13 buildings were wrecked and 50 vehicles burned.]

Seoul, situated only 25 miles from the strategic border with North Korea, was calm today. But the full martial law imposed Saturday night, which gave Lieut. Gen. Chon Too Hwan, the head of the country's intelligence apparatus, virtual control of the country, appeared shaky in other provincial cities such as Mokpo, Chongju and Yosu.

Political Liberalization Asked

The imposition of full martial law followed several days of protests by university students in Seoul demanding an end of the limited form of martial law previously in force and a more rapid rate of progress toward a democratic governmental structure.

After the student leaders called off the

Continued on Page A8, Column 2

Accord Is Reported on Evacuation Of Last 710 Love Canal Families

By ROBIN HERMAN

Special to The New York Times

ALBANY, May 20 — New York State and Federal officials were reported tonight to have reached agreement on evacuating 710 remaining families in the Love Canal area of Niagara Falls, but were snagged on whether the relocation should be permanent or temporary.

Governor Carey told Federal officials this afternoon — including Vice President Mondale and members of the New York delegation in Congress — that short-term assistance was unacceptable and that the Federal Government should offer the residents of the chemically polluted area the option of permanent relocation.

Love Canal was calmer yesterday after the release of two Federal officials held by protesters. Page B1.

A new study found nerve damage in some residents of the area. Page B7.

A deputy assistant to the President for intergovernmental affairs, Eugene Eidenberg, said in Washington early tonight that he had been in consultation with Governor Carey but that no final decision had been reached.

Sources close to the negotiations reported, however, that the decision to relocate had been made, and that an announcement awaited only a resolution of details. It was not immediately clear when the evacuation would begin.

State and Federal officials had not agreed on how the cost would be spread

Continued on Page B6, Column 1

CONFEREES' ACCORD ON BUDGET SNAGGED

5 Liberal House Democrats Balk at $6.1 Billion Rise for Military

By MARTIN TOLCHIN

Special to The New York Times

WASHINGTON, May 20 — House and Senate budget conferees reached a tentative agreement to resolve a "guns versus butter" dispute this evening but it quickly collapsed when five liberal House Democrats balked at accepting $154 billion in military spending for the fiscal year 1981.

"They made a firm offer and we accepted it," Senator Ernest F. Hollings, chairman of the Senate Budget Committee, said of the House conferees' proposal to increase military spending by $6.1 billion from the $147 9 billion proposed by the House.

"They reneged on it," the South Carolina Democrat told reporters.

Chairmen Meet for Hour

The Senate has passed a budget resolution calling for military spending of $155.7 billion. Although the Senate conferees had indicated earlier in the day that they would not accept any figure below $155.4 billion, they relented and agreed to the House conferees' proposal for spending of $154 billion, which would represent an increase of about 5 percent over 1980 after accounting for inflation.

The compromise proposal resulted from an hour-long meeting between Mr.

Continued on Page A33, Column 2

INSIDE

Decision on Cubans' Status

The White House said arriving Cubans would be treated as applicants for asylum, so Congress need not be consulted on the number admitted. Page A24.

New York to Get U.S. Funds

New York State will get the Federal money it needs to make $40 million in Medicaid payments to New York City hospitals and nursing homes. Page B3.

Miami Police Inquiry Is Set

The Attorney General announced that a team of Federal prosecutors and agents would study alleged abuses by the Miami police. Page A22.

U.S. Scolds France on Soviet Talks And Britain Over Sanctions on Iran

By BERNARD GWERTZMAN

Special to The New York Times

WASHINGTON, May 20 — The United States criticized France today for failing to consult before the French-Soviet meeting in Warsaw and criticized Britain for reneging on a Common Market commitment to block exports to Iran under contracts made since the takeover of the American Embassy.

After holding back on criticism of the French move for two days and expressing satisfaction with the Common Market steps to impose sanctions as of Nov. 4 — a move that nevertheless fell short of an earlier European pledge to cancel all trade except food and medicine — the Carter Administration found itself today in public dispute with two of its major allies.

Britain's abrupt decision against imposing the retroactive sanctions made the united front that Western Europe had presented on the Iranian crisis collapse. In Paris, French officials acknowledged that the talks yesterday in Warsaw between President Valéry Giscard d'Estaing and Leonid I. Brezhnev, the Soviet leader, had achieved no major breakthrough, but they insisted that the meeting had at least kept lines of communication open. [Pages A16 and A14.]

Muskie Criticizes France

Secretary of State Edmund S. Muskie said at a news conference that France, by failing to consult with its allies about the Warsaw talks, was reasserting its independence at the cost of allied solidarity and unity.

The criticism of Prime Minister Margaret Thatcher's Government was the first by the Carter Administration. It was issued by the State Department late in the day after Britain announced that it would not carry out the Common Market decision it had participated in making on Sunday.

That decision, a compromise between those who wanted sanctions to include only future contracts and those who wanted the embargo to include all existing trade, barred exports retroactively to Nov. 4, the day the embassy was seized.

"We are extremely disappointed to learn that the British Government has decided not to make British sanctions on exports to Iran effective as of Nov. 4," the department said.

"We expect the European community's nine members to honor the commitment made at Naples, which we welcome and in which the United Kingdom had joined," it said.

Mr. Muskie, in referring to France's

Continued on Page A16, Column 1

157 ELDERLY WOMEN DIE IN JAMAICA FIRE

14 Missing at Institution — Police Charge Arson Was Involved

By United Press International

KINGSTON, Jamaica, May 20 — Fire swept through a two-story wooden home for poor and elderly women here early today, and officials said at least 157 were killed and 14 others were missing.

Of the 204 women asleep in their beds when the fire broke out about 1 A.M., only 33 were reported safe and accounted for hours after the blaze had been brought under control.

Prime Minister Michael N. Manley told Jamaicans in a radio broadcast that security officials thought arsonists could have started the blaze.

A police spokesman said tonight that arson had certainly been the cause of the fire, citing a report that telephone wires to the 3-building complex had been cut shortly before the blaze started. Earlier, the city's fire chief had said there was no proof of arson, and suggested that an electrical short could have started the fire.

The fire chief, Allan Ridgeway, said the fire consumed the building so quickly that his men had to stand helplessly by,

Continued on Page A3, Column 1

"All the News That's Fit to Print"

The New York Times

LATE CITY EDITION

Weather: Cloudy, chance of showers today; rain tonight. Clearing tomorrow. Temperature range: today 40-48; yesterday 46-64. Details on page C12.

VOL.CXXX — No. 44,792 NEW YORK, TUESDAY, DECEMBER 9, 1980

30 cents beyond 50-mile zone from New York City. Higher in air delivery cities. 25 CENTS

Associated Press

Yoko Ono being escorted from hospital last night after John Lennon, her husband, was pronounced dead

A HIGH IRANIAN SAYS U. S. REPLY FOSTERS ACCORD ON HOSTAGES

He Says Issue 'Is Now Much Closer to Being Solved'—Comments Raise Hopes for Release

By JOHN KIFNER

Special to The New York Times

TEHERAN, Iran, Dec. 8 — The Speaker of the Iranian Parliament said tonight that the 13-month-old dispute over the American Embassy hostages "is now much closer to being solved."

As Iranian officials spent a fifth day considering the latest American response to Teheran's four demands for freeing the hostages, the Speaker, Hojatolislam Hashemi Rafsanjani, said on the state television, "The matter is much more clear now."

"The United States has, to an extent, clarified its position and it is now much closer to being solved," Hojatolislam Rafsanjani said. "I think that if the United States has good will and if it truly wants to solve the matter, it will be solved."

Earlier in the day, Hojatolislam Rafsanjani said at a news conference that the new American response had "almost made it clear that it is ready to meet these demands."

His relatively straightforward and consistent statements appeared to raise some hope of working out the release of the hostages.

Algerians Await Iran's Reply

A three-member Algerian delegation brought the latest American message here Thursday after meeting with Deputy Secretary of State Warren M. Christopher in Algiers. The Algerians have been waiting here to bring back the Iranian reply.

[In Washington, John H. Trattner, the State Department spokesman, said he had no comment on Iranian statements and said the United States was awaiting an official response to its latest clarifications. In a related matter, the families of the hostages have been invited to Washington for a briefing by officials on Friday. The meeting was scheduled some time ago.]

The conditions laid down by the Iranian Parliament on Nov. 2 were that the United States pledge not to interfere in Iran's internal affairs; that the United States unfreeze Iranian assets in American banks, which are estimated at $8 billion; that all American law suits against Iran be abrogated, and that the wealth of the late Shah be returned.

The American responses have not been made public, but the Carter Administration is understood to have said that it agrees to the conditions in principle but faces Constitutional and legal barriers to carrying out the last two. These problems

Continued on Page A12, Column 3

MOSCOW AND ALLIES ACTIVATE RESERVES; INVASION FEAR RISES

Poles Play Down Report by Soviet Of a Union Plot

By JOHN DARNTON

Special to The New York Times

WARSAW, Dec. 8 — The Polish Government and the independent trade union organization, Solidarity, sought today to counter a report in the Soviet press that "counterrevolutionaries " within the union movement were out to destabilize the country and were moving toward a confrontation with the Communist Party.

The Soviet article, a report from Warsaw carried by Tass, the official press agency, was regarded by Western diplomats and Polish party sources here as the strongest attack to date on the unions and the Polish party's ability to exert its authority.

Farmers Demand Meeting

Because it suggested that law and order was breaking down in Poland, some sources saw the article as a justification for intervention should Moscow decide to take action to end the three-month-old Polish liberalization.

[Private farmers in Poland demanded a meeting with Prime Minister Jozef Pinkowski and said they would consider strike action if the Government refused to legalize their independent trade union, Reuters reported.

[The farm unionists said that Agriculture Minister Leon Klonica refused to sign an agreement on legal status for an independent farmers' union that he initialed last week. Union leaders told reporters that Mr. Klonica had said he was not competent to sign such an agreement. A spokesman said all action was being closely cordinated with the leadership of the Solidarity movement, which had called for a moratorium on strikes in view of the country's tense political and economic situation.]

The Tass report came as the United States warned that Soviet troops had completed a military buildup across Poland's borders and were now in a position to launch an attack should the Soviet leaders choose to do so.

The information is available to most Poles, who listen regularly to Western radio broadcasts. But many did not seem to regard an invasion as imminent and instead interpreted the buildup as an intense form of psychological pressure and as a sign to the leadership here that it must demonstrate its control.

The Tass dispatch said that "counter-

Continued on Page A8, Column 3

SOVIET ASSAILS UNION

U.S. Aides Say a Move Into Poland May Be Masked as Military Games

By BERNARD GWERTZMAN

Special to The New York Times

WASHINGTON, Dec. 8 — Administration officials said today that some military reservists had been called up in the past few days in the Soviet Union, East Germany and Czechoslovakia, increasing the possibility of joint military intervention in Poland under the guise of Warsaw Pact maneuvers.

The State Department repeated that it had no evidence of a decision to intervene in Poland, but there was reported to be general agreement in the Administration that some kind of intervention might be only days away.

Adding to the concern here was a Tass dispatch from Warsaw that was broadcast in the Soviet Union and repeated in other East European countries charging that "counterrevolutionary groups" in the Polish labor movement were turning to "confrontation" with local Communists. The report by the official Soviet press agency also said there had been disorders in Kielce, 95 miles south of Warsaw. [Page A8.]

Groundwork for Intervention

Officials here said that the reports of disorders apparently were untrue and that the Russians and their allies were probably laying the groundwork at home for intervention in Poland.

The Soviet leader, Leonid I. Brezhnev, arrived in New Delhi on an official visit, but American officials said this did not necessarily mean that any intervention would have to await his return later in the week, although that was the assumption yesterday. [Page A10.]

A senior State Department official said a plan of action for intervening in Poland may have been worked out at Friday's Warsaw Pact summit meeting in Moscow. He said it appeared likely that Soviet, East German and Czechoslovak forces, perhaps with contingents from Bulgaria and Hungary, would be "invited" by Polish leaders to take part in exercises in Poland while Polish security forces cracked down on dissidents.

Troops Prepared to Move

The White House said yesterday that preparations for possible Soviet intervention in Poland had been completed, and State Department and Defense Department officials said today that some Soviet, East German and Czechoslovak forces were ready to enter Poland at a moment's notice. Poland shares borders with those three countries.

Ambassadors from allied and other friendly governments were invited to the

Continued on Page A8, Column 4

REAGAN PLANS DRIVE FOR TRANSITION AID

Republicans Need $1 Million More To Cover Record Operations

By DAVID E. ROSENBAUM

Special to The New York Times

WASHINGTON, Dec. 8 — President-elect Ronald Reagan is planning to raise hundreds of thousands of dollars in private donations to finance the most elaborate transition operation in history.

The $2 million Government appropriation under the Presidential Transition Act will not be nearly enough to pay for the salaries and expenses of the Reagan team, according to transition planners, who say at least $1 million more will have to be spent.

Verne Orr, who is in charge of administrative and budgetary matters for the transition, said that about $500,000 was available in unspent private contributions made to Mr. Reagan in the Republican primaries. The remainder, he said, would be solicited from "people who have contributed generously in the past" to Mr. Reagan and Vice President-elect George Bush.

Volumes of Information

Mr. Reagan's advisers say that the extensive operation, involving more than 1,000 people and teams of planners in every Government department and nearly every agency, will facilitate the work of Cabinet secretaries and other top officials once they are appointed. The teams are collecting volumes of informa-

Continued on Page B22, Column 2

John Lennon of Beatles Is Killed; Suspect Held in Shooting at Dakota

By LES LEDBETTER

John Lennon, one of the four Beatles, was shot and killed last night while entering the apartment building where he lived, the Dakota, on Manhattan's Upper West Side. A suspect was seized at the scene.

The 40-year-old Mr. Lennon was shot in the back twice after getting out of a limousine and walking into an entrance way of the Dakota at 1 West 72d Street, Sgt. Robert Barnes of the 20th Precinct said.

"Obviously the man was waiting for him," Sergeant Barnes said of the assailant. The suspect was identified as Mark David Chapman, 25, of Hawaii, who had been living in New York for about a week, according to James L. Sullivan, chief of detectives of the 20th Precinct.

Wife Reported Unhurt

Jeff Smith, a neighbor, said that he heard five shots fired shortly before 11 P.M. Other witnesses said they heard four when the shooting occurred at 10:45 P.M.

With the singer when he was shot was his wife, Yoko Ono, who was not hurt by the bullets that struck her husband as they entered an archway that led into the courtyard of the Dakota complex.

Witnesses said Mr. Lennon was wearing a white T-shirt and dungaree jacket when he was shot. They said Miss Ono screamed, "Help me. Help me."

They said the suspect paced back and forth in entrance way to the Dakota after shooting the musician, arguing with the doorman and holding the gun in his hand pointing downward.

One witness, Ben Eruchson, a cab driver from Brooklyn, said, "He could have gotten away. He had plenty of time."

There were bullet holes in the structure and blood on the bricks of the building.

Immediately after Mr. Lennon was

Continued on Page B7, Column 1

©1980, Jack Mitchell

John Lennon

Another $350 Million in U.S. Aid Is Needed Urgently, Chrysler Says

By EDWARD COWAN

Special to The New York Times

WASHINGTON, Dec. 8 — The Chrysler Corporation told the Government today that it must have $350 million in additional Federal loan guarantees within the next 30 days if it is to keep operating.

The three members of the Government's Chrysler Loan Guarantee Board reacted coolly during a two-hour meeting with Chrysler executives, indicating reservations about enlarging the Government's risk — $800 million of guarantees have been issued so far — but not refusing outright, Government sources reported.

Treasury Secretary G. William Miller, the loan board's chairman, suggested that the company had to raise additional capital funds to sustain itself for the next two years or so, the sources said.

"That's absolutely essential," one Federal official said after the meeting.

Two methods of raising additional capital were discussed, informants said. One way would be for Chrysler to join forces with another company, either through a joint venture or by sale of a fractional interest, such as the American Motors Corporation's agreement to sell a 46 percent interest to Renault of France.

Some officials speculated that Chrysler might be able to raise money from the Mitsubishi Motors Corporation, a Japanese car maker, or Peugeot-Citroën, the French auto company. Chrysler owns a minority interest in both.

A second way would be to persuade holders of Chrysler debt to exercise their option to convert the debt to equity — shares of ownership — for an additional cash payment. That, if done, would dilute the value of the Chrysler common stock outstanding.

Lee A. Iacocca, Chrysler's chair-

Continued on Page D7, Column 4

INSIDE

Stricter Fire Law Sought

The New York State Association of County Executives voted unanimously to ask the Legislature to enact a more stringent fire code. Page B1.

Stock Prices Drop Sharply

The stock market fell 22.53 points amid anxiety about Poland and rising interest rates. New six-month Treasury bills were sold at 15.07 percent. Page D1.

United Press International

President Leonid I. Brezhnev of the Soviet Union was flanked by President Sanjiva Reddy and Prime Minister Indira Gandhi after arriving in India. Police clashed with Afghan demonstrators protesting Mr. Brezhnev's visit. Page A10.

Soviet Armed Services Showing Weaknesses In Several Key Areas

The following article is based on reporting in Washington by Philip Taubman and Richard Halloran and in Moscow by Anthony Austin. It was written by Mr. Taubman.

The Soviet armed forces, like those of the United States, have formidable weaknesses in readiness and manpower. There are ethnic tensions within the ranks; there is a shortage of sophisticated weaponry, and there are deficiencies in battle-readiness in both the army and the navy.

At first glance, it may appear that a large proportion of the Soviet Army's 170 or more divisions are undermanned. Secretary of Defense Harold Brown spoke of

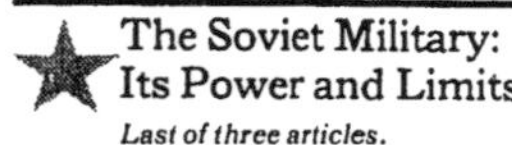

The Soviet Military: Its Power and Limits

Last of three articles.

such units earlier this year when he said, in a debate on the state of American military preparedness, that roughly two-thirds of the Soviet divisions were not ready for combat.

However, many of these problems are offset by the Soviet Union's basic military doctrine, which has led to a peacetime framework of forces and industrial and educational systems geared to swift and vast mobilization. Undermanned divisions that function as training units

Continued on Page A10, Column 1

THE COMPUTER AGE

STEVE LOHR

In hindsight, the prescient often seems obvious. It's a truism that certainly applies to an article in The Times on August 20, 1980, "Amid Stagnation, High Technology Lights a Path," by Peter J. Schuyten. When read today, its emphatic declarations of faith in the future of computing and telecommunications strike a tone that is both shrill and quaint. The industry executives and scientists seem to be hyperventilating to make points that today's reader knows to be true. High-technology fields, authorities said more than 25 years ago, are "the jewels of American innovation" that will deliver breakthroughs in efficiency and productivity, and become more important to the American economy than autos and steel. Well, yes, of course.

But a bit of context helps explain why this front-page piece was smart, even contrarian, for its day. The American economy was being battered by the second of two oil-price shocks and foreign competition.

Japan was the emerging economic superpower, not only humbling America's auto and steel industries, but also threatening the technology sector. A front-page article in 1981 from Tokyo cited the "overwhelming evidence that Japan, more than any other nation, has embraced advanced electronic and computer technology as a way to improve industrial productivity, save energy and, in theory, make day-to-day life more convenient, enriching and entertaining."[1] I believed it when I wrote it, and I was scarcely alone.

1 "Computer Technology Pervades Life in Japan," see September 5, 1981, article.

In the late 1970's Japan emerged as a major industrial power becoming a leading exporter of automobiles.

The Japanese stock exchange in 1987 marked its recognition as a world financial capital.

I.B.M. developed this "super computer" that ties together parallel processing units to provide vast amounts of information in quick time.

In the late 1970's mainframe computers like this one were used to handle information and documentation. These days, they are smaller, more powerful and still widely used.

Close-up of a main computer board in a desktop computer.

I.B.M. designed and unveiled its personal computer in the early 1980's aimed at use by businesses and in schools as well as for personal use at home.

The anxiety about the nation's economic future lasted for years. In the 1984 presidential campaign, Walter F. Mondale colorfully distilled the fear: "What are our kids supposed to do? Sweep up around Japanese computers and sell McDonald's hamburgers the rest of their lives?"[2]

In the 1980 Schuyten article, the succession of industry leaders and experts were not only celebrating the importance of high-tech industries but also appealing for help. The answer, according to many of those interviewed, was "a government industrial policy that nurtures the high-technology sector."

It didn't happen. And the United States, despite its anxiety, led the next two big waves of innovation, wealth generation and job creation in high technology, personal computing and, later, the Internet. The champions of industrial policy, Japan and Europe, trailed well behind.

The 1980 article proved remarkably perceptive about the long-term direction, even if it did not foresee the precise path toward a brighter future. Nor did just about anyone else. Consistently underestimated was the role of upstart entrepreneurs and lone tinkerers generating new ideas and products. By its very nature, such bottom-up ferment is unpredictable: a continuous process of trial and error fueled by venture capital and encouraged by a risk-taking culture. The ingredients are not unique to America, but they seem to find the most fertile ground here.

In the years between 1976 and 1981, a flagship electronic corporation took a step that accelerated the rise of the personal computer, and the sweeping changes it would bring in business and society. In August 1981, I.B.M., the mainframe giant, entered the personal computer industry and served notice that personal computers were no longer mere hobbyists' playthings but serious tools for business.

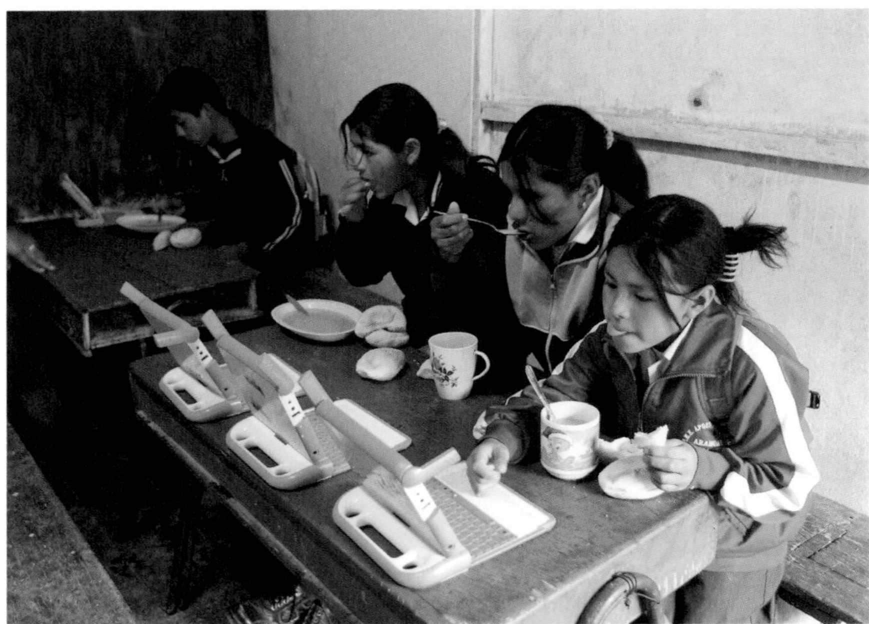

The organization One Laptop Per Child brought new technology to small communities like this village in Peru.

Computers moved into classrooms at all levels, providing students with vast quantities of information not previously available.

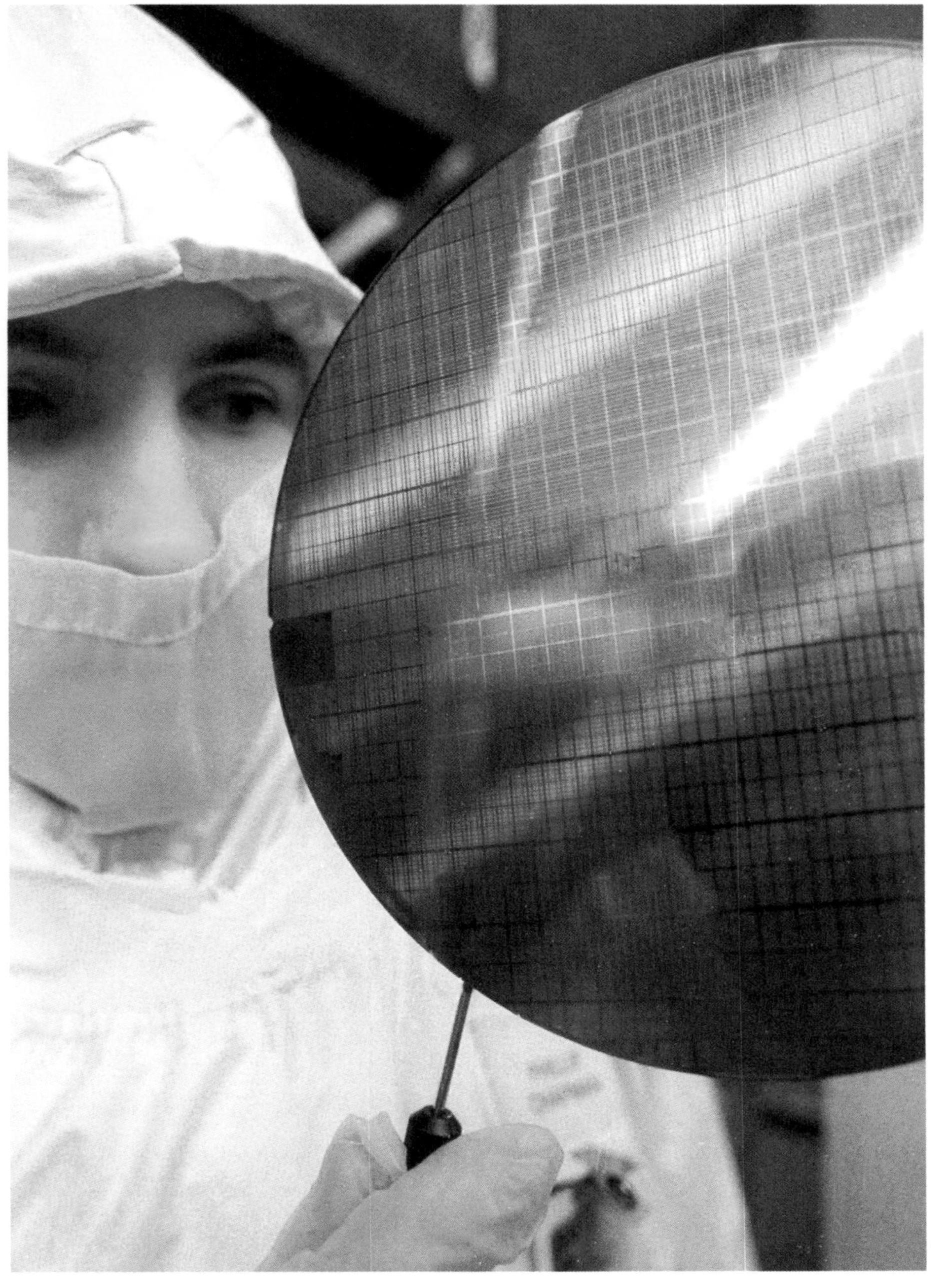

A production worker at an I.B.M. plant in Vermont checks a wafer of computer chips in 1995.

"Next, a Computer on Every Desk" read the headline on a long article in the Sunday business section of The Times on I.B.M.'s move.[3] One theme of the story was that the personal computer industry had become an arena for big companies and one company that was getting big fast, Apple Computer. One expert quoted in the article said that "if an Apple came along today, I don't think they would stand a chance." Yet three years later, in 1984, Michael Dell founded his namesake company in a dormitory room at the University of Texas with seed funds of just $1,000.

A big-company tilt, too, is reflected in The Times's coverage of that earlier computer era. Microsoft was founded in 1975, but in the 1976–81 span, Bill Gates is quoted only once, in the Sunday article on I.B.M. His is one of the few quotes from those years that suggest the changes made possible by putting computing power in the hands of individuals. He spoke of the personal computer in visionary, anthropomorphic terms. Someday, he said, the personal machines "will have as much stored knowledge of what you know, what you've said, what you've done than any friend would have the patience to learn."

In those years, the mainstream press had hardly a clue about the earthquake beneath our feet. It had not yet discovered, for example, the counterculture personal computer hackers of Silicon Valley's Homebrew Computer Club, who gathered to swap tips and software in the mid-1970's and

Bill Gates founded Microsoft in 1975 and developed an operating system for the I.B.M. personal computers introduced in the 1980's.

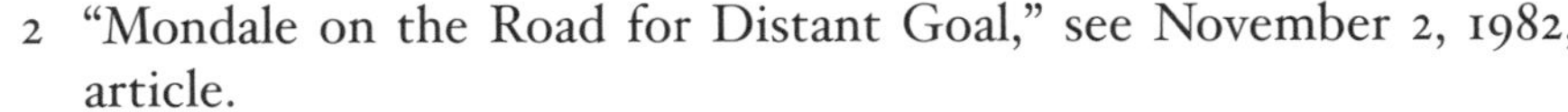

2 "Mondale on the Road for Distant Goal," see November 2, 1982, article.
3 "Next, a Computer on Every Desk," see August 23, 1981, article.
4 "A Strange Brew's Buzz Lingers in Silicon Valley," see March 26, 2000, article.

The Apple IIC was introduced in 1984 by the three founders of Apple Computer: Steve Jobs, John Scully and Steve Wozniak.

By the 21st century computers had become a vital part of the world's culture. Here, visitors to a 2008 technology fair in Germany play computer games.

early 1980's.[4] Two regulars, Steve Jobs and Steve Wozniak, founded Apple in the Jobses' family garage in 1976. And Jobs got four passing mentions in the Times from 1976 to 1981, and was not quoted—an oversight that would be more than made up for before long. (Within a few years, The Times, like other major newspapers and news magazines, took the new generation of technology whiz kids seriously indeed.)

The forerunner of the Internet, called Darpanet, was mentioned once, in an article by Peter Schuyten in November 1980.[5] The article discussed how telecommunications companies were looking at e-mail and online services as a potential "gold mine in the 80's." There was a lot of early enthusiasm for delivering all kinds of information over networks to computer terminals in homes and offices. In 1982, the French government introduced its ambitious videotext service, Minitel.[6]

Peter Schuyten, the perceptive analyst of computer power, himself got excited by the prospect. He left The Times in 1981 to join a rival company's electronic newspaper project. I remember needling him at his going-away party, remarking that the electronic newspaper concept sounded like a great idea, but not likely to become a reality anytime soon.

It did take a long time, but online publishing would eventually ruthlessly and creatively transform the media industry. And it came in a form no one predicted in the early 1980's, because it didn't exist then, the World Wide Web.

The pattern plays out again and again in the ever wider world of computers as the combination of human smarts, persistence and serendipity delivers startling breakthroughs that soon become woven into the fabric of everyday life, from the E mainframe to the personal computer to Google.

STEVE LOHR *is a technology reporter for The New York Times. He was a foreign correspondent during the 1980's for The Times, based in Tokyo, Manila and London. For more than a decade, he has covered technology and its impact on the economy and society. Lohr has written for many magazines, including the Atlantic Monthly and the Washington Monthly and is the author of "Go To: The Story Programmers Who Created the Software Revolution," as well as two other books about technology.*

5 "G.T.E.: The Promise of Electronic Mail," see November 2, 1980, article.

6 "Computer Linkups Spurred by France," see April 30, 1984, article.

1981

A Bloodless Revolution

1993

FRONT PAGE NEWS 1981-1993

Reagan Inaugurated, Hostages Freed

JANUARY 21, 1981

The two events were 6,300 miles apart: the inauguration of Ronald Reagan in Washington, and the release of 52 American hostages who had been held for 444 days in Tehran. Reagan, a B-movie actor-turned-politician, promised "national renewal" and a tough-minded conservative ideology as antidotes to Jimmy Carter's presidency. Carter had been unable to free the hostages—a rescue mission had failed, and subsequent secret negotiations had timed their release to his departure from the White House.

Reagan Survives Shooting

MARCH 31, 1981

Outside a Washington hotel where President Ronald Reagan had given a midday speech lurked a 25-year-old man who, one witness said, looked "fidgety—agitated—a little strange." John Hinckley Jr. had a goal: to impress the actress Jodie Foster. He believed that the way to do that was to assassinate Reagan. The president did not realize that he had been wounded until after Secret Service agents had shoved him into his limousine. A Secret Service agent and a Washington police officer were also hit, as was Reagan's press secretary, James Brady, who suffered brain damage. Brady went on to champion a policy that put him at odds with Reagan—handgun control. Hinckley was found not guilty by reason of insanity and was committed to a Washington mental hospital.

A Woman on the Court

JULY 8, 1981

President Ronald Reagan's nomination to succeed Associate Justice Potter Stewart on the Supreme Court was a surprise: Sandra Day O'Connor, an appellate judge from Arizona. Right-to-life groups mobilized, saying she was pro-abortion, but the Senate soon confirmed her. She became the crucial swing vote as the court turned to the right, reaffirming the 1973 Roe v. Wade decision that had legalized abortion. She resigned in 2006, saying she wanted to spend time with her family. Her husband had had Alzheimer's disease since the 1990's; in 2007, when his memory was long gone, their son said in a television interview about Alzheimer's patients who forget their spouses, that he "had a girlfriend" in the assisted-living center where he lived and was like a "teenager in love"—and that Ms. O'Connor was "thrilled" that he was "relaxed and happy."

Crackdown on Solidarity

DECEMBER 14, 1981

By late 1981, Solidarity had evolved from a labor movement to a powerful political force with Lech Walesa, an electrician in the Polish shipyard at Gdansk, negotiating more than wage concessions. That was too much for Poland's new Communist strongman, General Wojciech Jaruzelski, who imposed martial law as more than 100,000 Soviet soldiers ominously bided their time at the Polish border. Jaruzelski's decree targeted not only Solidarity "confrontationalists" but the Polish Communist officials who had accommodated its rise. Walesa was imprisoned as Pope John Paul II called on his fellow Poles to pray "to peacefully build a peaceful future." Walesa remained behind bars until 1983, when he won the Nobel Peace Prize.

Gorbachev's Rise

MARCH 12, 1985

To Kremlin watchers, Mikhail S. Gorbachev's promotion to succeed Konstantin U. Chernenko was a milestone as symbolic as the transition that had followed Stalin's death 32 years earlier. Inside the ruling Communist Party, power was being passed to a younger generation. Gorbachev, 54, pushed through reforms—perestroika, which changed the structure and function of the state-run economy, and glasnost, which thawed diplomatic dealings with the west. But the changes had vast and unintended consequences, including the economic and political collapse of the Soviet Union, the demise of communism everywhere except China and Gorbachev's own fall from power in 1991.

Space Shuttle Disaster

JANUARY 29, 1986

Little more than a minute after liftoff on a morning so clear that television cameras could easily follow its doomed journey, the space shuttle Challenger blew apart. All seven astronauts aboard died, among them Christa McAuliffe, a New Hampshire high school teacher who had won a contest to become the first private citizen to go on a NASA mission. The shuttle was firing its booster rockets when there was a flash and flaming debris began tumbling toward Earth. A presidential commission later blamed the disaster on rubber gaskets called O-rings—and on NASA officials who had overridden warnings about design problems and safety concerns in a cold-weather launch.

Meltdown at Chernobyl

APRIL 30, 1986

Soviet radio described it as a "disaster," an unusually strong word for state-controlled broadcasters. For once, they had not stopped short of the truth. What happened at the Chernobyl reactor, which generated about 10 percent of Ukraine's electricity, was a full-fledged nuclear meltdown that raised anxiety about health and safety thousands of miles away. An explosion and fire shot far more radiation into the atmosphere than had been released at Three Mile Island in Pennsylvania in 1979. The accident killed 56 people, including nine children with thyroid cancer, but a 2005 study estimated that 4,000 others could eventually die from exposure. Soviet officials blamed plant operators for the catastrophe. Later reviews pointed to design problems in the 1970's-era reactor.

Iran-Contra Scandal

NOVEMBER 26, 1986

The story, as explained by Attorney General Edwin Meese III, was mind-boggling: using Israel and an Iranian arms dealer as go-betweens, the Reagan administration had sold weapons to Iran in an effort to free American hostages in Lebanon. The money had come from profits of clandestine shipments to right-wing guerrillas in Nicaragua known as contras—even though Congress had blocked such aid in 1984. The administration arranged for Israel to send Iran weapons it already had on hand; then Washington sent replacements to the Israelis. The administration maintained that the arms deals were dreamed up and carried out by "a loose cannon," a National Security Council aide acting on his own. But Colonel Oliver North later told Congress, "I thought I had received authority from the president." National security adviser Robert McFarlane pleaded guilty to withholding information from Congress; he was pardoned by president George Bush in 1992. Vice Admiral John Poindexter, who had been the deputy national security adviser and had succeeded McFarlane in 1985, was found guilty of charges arising from Iran-contra; his conviction was later overturned.

Arms Reductions

DECEMBER 9, 1987

A far-reaching treaty signed by President Ronald Reagan and the Soviet leader, Mikhail S. Gorbachev, pledged that the superpowers would shrink their nuclear arsenals. It took two years of off-again, on-again negotiations, but in the end, the U.S. and Russia promised to dismantle and destroy more than 2,600 intermediate-range missiles. Gorbachev had dropped an earlier demand for the elimination of Reagan's so-called Star Wars missile-defense system. The treaty—and the warmth between the two leaders—marked another step in the evolution of Reagan's foreign policy, which had begun with tough talk and a deep suspicion of the Soviets.

Soviet Retreat in Afghanistan

APRIL 8, 1988

The Soviet war in Afghanistan, often called the Soviet Vietnam, cost Moscow some 15,000 lives and undermined the Soviet Army's once-invincible reputation. It turned out that the Afghan mujahedeen had help. Congress steered billions to the C.I.A., which funneled arms to the Afghans in the largest-ever C.I.A. covert funding operation. So, as one Times correspondent later wrote, the C.I.A. fought a deadly confrontation with the Soviets through a surrogate.

Lockerbie Bombing

DECEMBER 22, 1988

Pan Am Flight 103 was 47 minutes into its journey from Heathrow Airport in London to New York when it exploded 31,000 feet over Lockerbie, Scotland. The 258 passengers and crew members died, as did 11 on the ground who were struck by falling debris. Scottish police and the F.B.I. interviewed 15,000 witnesses in an investigation that led to indictments against two Libyans, apparently acting in retaliation for U.S. military action against Libyan fighter jets and vessels in the Gulf of Sidra. The suspects were turned over to Scottish officials 11 years later after long-running negotiations with the Libyan leader Muammar el-Qaddafi. One was found guilty in 2001 (an appeals court said in 2007 that he might have been wrongfully convicted). The other was acquitted.

Tiananmen Square Crackdown

JUNE 6, 1989

For westerners, the enduring image of the government crackdown on thousands of young pro-democracy demonstrators in Tiananmen Square in Beijing was a photograph of a single, unarmed man stopping a long column of tanks. He simply walked in front of the lead tank and raised his arm as if he were a traffic cop. The encounter symbolized the ambivalence of the government's position after days of touch-and-go maneuvering between determined, well-organized demonstrators and soldiers not sure when to press on and when to retreat. But this time, the demonstrators dispersed; their leaders were eventually arrested; and the Chinese leader Deng Xiaoping prevailed, avoiding the waves of unrest and the loss of state control that were dissolving the Soviet bloc.

The Fall of the Berlin Wall

NOVEMBER 11, 1989

Willy Brandt, who had been the mayor of West Berlin when the Berlin Wall went up in 1961, never expected to see it come down. But come down it did, and with it Communist rule. The once-feared guards stood by as hundreds of thousands of East Germans rushed across the once-forbidden border, tearing down the wall as they went. At the city hall in West Berlin—where President John F. Kennedy had delivered his famed "Ich bin ein Berliner" speech when the wall was new—Chancellor Helmut Kohl welcomed the newcomers, declaring, "We belong together."

Nelson Mandela Is Freed

FEBRUARY 12, 1990

"We have waited too long for our freedom," declared Nelson Mandela, the towering symbol of South Africa's struggle against apartheid. Mandela had just been freed from jail after 27 years as a political prisoner. Now he urged blacks—and the international community—to keep up the pressure on the white leader who had ordered his release, President F. W. de Klerk. Mandela maintained that easing the international boycott against South Africa would "run the risk of aborting the process toward ending apartheid." But Mandela's liberation was a major step toward that very goal, which would come in 1994, along with Mandela's election in biracial voting as de Klerk's successor.

Iraq Invades Kuwait

AUGUST 3, 1990

Iraqi tanks and ground forces poured into Kuwait, as Saddam Hussein set his sights on two ambitious goals, pre-eminence among Arab leaders in the Mideast and dominance in world oil markets. He was counting on the first to come with a shift in the balance of power away from Egypt, which he believed had been too willing to accommodate Washington and Israel. He believed the second would come with control of Kuwait, which he had accused of stealing Iraqi oil and ignoring OPEC output ceilings. Instead, he set the stage for the Persian Gulf War of 1991 and, eventually, for the American-led invasion of Iraq in 2003.

East and West Germany Unite

OCTOBER 3, 1990

German unification seemed all but inevitable after the Berlin Wall came down and Soviet-style Communism collapsed across Eastern Europe. The moment came in a jubilant ceremony after West German Chancellor Helmut Kohl had pushed through political and diplomatic changes with breathtaking speed. But he also accepted the burden of the absorbing East Germany into West Germany's wealthy economy—something that German investors (and foreigners) were reluctant to do.

War on Iraq

JANUARY 17, 1991

The United Nations had given the go-ahead for military action against Iraq if Saddam Hussein did not order his troops home from Kuwait by mid-January. He did not, and a coalition of American-led troops soon pounded Iraq. President George H.W. Bush said the goal was "not the conquest of Iraq, but the liberation of Kuwait." But he also said the coalition was determined to destroy Hussein's "nuclear bomb potential" and his chemical-weapons facilities. Hussein responded by setting Kuwaiti oil wells afire. The allied troops stopped short of Baghdad, and Hussein remained in power.

The Soviet Union Dissolves

DECEMBER 9, 1991

The Soviet Union, reassembled from the imperial Tsarist empire after the Russian Revolution of 1917, finally went into the dustbin of history, as Leon Trotsky might have said. It had been dying a lingering death, one Times correspondent wrote, and its death became certain with a three-way agreement between the leaders of Russia, Ukraine and Belarus that stripped Mikhail S. Gorbachev of what little authority he still had. Russian president Boris N. Yeltsin promised to cover the Soviet government payroll with Russian cash; he also took over the old Soviet Foreign Ministry and the K.G.B. Gorbachev resigned two weeks later; the Soviet parliament went out of business the following day.

Riots in Los Angeles

MAY 2, 1992

Rodney G. King had been viciously beaten by four white police officers who pulled him from his car after a chase through the San Fernando Valley—the videotape had been played over and over on television. But a jury acquitted the officers, and Los Angeles erupted in six days of violent riots that left 55 dead, blocks and blocks of burned-out, looted stores, and many puzzled Los Angeles officials who had underestimated the rage of blacks and Hispanics over the acquittals. President George H.W. Bush, who sent 5,000 troops to help restore order, said he was "stunned" by the verdict. King later agreed to a $3.8 million settlement with the police department and the city.

"All the News That's Fit to Print"

The New York Times

LATE CITY EDITION

Weather: Partly sunny today; mostly cloudy and cold tonight and tomorrow. Temperature range: today 28-38; yesterday 36-43. Details on page D21.

VOL.CXXX . . . No. 44,835

NEW YORK, WEDNESDAY, JANUARY 21, 1981

30 cents beyond 50-mile zone from New York City
Higher in air delivery cities

25 CENTS

REAGAN TAKES OATH AS 40TH PRESIDENT; PROMISES AN 'ERA OF NATIONAL RENEWAL'

MINUTES LATER, 52 U.S. HOSTAGES IN IRAN FLY TO FREEDOM AFTER 444-DAY ORDEAL

'ALIVE, WELL AND FREE'

Captives Taken to Algiers and Then Germany — Final Pact Complex

By BERNARD GWERTZMAN

Special to The New York Times

WASHINGTON, Wednesday, Jan. 21 — The 52 Americans who were held hostage by Iran for 444 days were flown to freedom yesterday. Jimmy Carter, a few hours after giving up the Presidency, said that everyone "was alive, was well and free."

The flight ended the national ordeal that had frustrated Mr. Carter for most of his last 14 months in office, and it allowed Ronald Reagan to begin his term free of the burdens of the Iran crisis.

The Americans were escorted out of Iran by Algerian diplomats, aboard an Algerian airliner, underscoring Algeria's role in achieving the accord that allowed the hostages to return home.

Transferred to U.S. Custody

The Algerian plane, carrying the former hostages, stopped first in Athens to refuel. It then landed in Algiers, where custody of the 52 Americans was formally transferred by the Algerians to the representative of the United States, former Deputy Secretary of State Warren M. Christopher. He had negotiated much of the agreement freeing them.

They then boarded two United States Air Force hospital planes and flew to Frankfurt, West Germany early this morning. They will stay at an American military hospital in nearby Weisbaden, where they will be visited by Mr. Carter, as President Reagan's representative, later today. They will stay in Wiesbaden for a week or less to "decompress," as one official described it.

The 52 Americans were freed as part of a complex agreement that was not completed until early yesterday morning, when the last snags holding up their release were removed by Mr. Carter and

Continued on Page A3, Column 5

Teheran Captors Call Out Insults As the 52 Leave

By JOHN KIFNER

Special to The New York Times

TEHERAN, Iran, Jan. 20 — The 52 American hostages began to roll down the runway to freedom today minutes as President Reagan was finishing his inaugural address.

As the Algerian 727 lifted off from Mehrabad Airport, ending 444 days of captivity for the Americans, they could see, most of them probably for the last time, a full moon picking out the sharp white peaks of the Elburz Mountains to the north. The time was 8:55 P.M., 12:25 P.M., New York time.

"God is great! Death to America!" cried the young Islamic militants who kept custody of the hostages to the last minute, hustling them to the stairs of the airplane.

They Soon Are 'Former Hostages'

The American diplomats, Marine guards and the other hostages stepped one at a time from a bus, whose windows were covered with checked curtains, into a clear cold night. As they touched the tarmac, two young militants, the hoods of their parkas up against the chill, took them just above the elbows and propelled them through the shouting crowd toward the Algerian plane with its red stylized bird emblazoned on the tail.

Looking dazed, some with long hair and beards that contrasted with the neat trims of their official days before the embassy takeover Nov. 4, 1979, they stumbled into the first-class section of the plane. Now they were what a bulletin on Pars, the state press agency, would describe later as "former hostages."

"They seem stunned, as if they cannot believe they are going free," Ahmad Azizi, the Government's director of hostage affairs, remarked to an Iranian state television crew covering the departure.

At 8:20, the doors were sealed, Pars reported, and the engines began to whine. A

Continued on Page A8, Column 1

United Press International

11:57 A.M.: Ronald Reagan being sworn in as 40th President by Chief Justice Warren E. Burger. Nancy Reagan held the Bible and Senator Mark O. Hatfield witnessed the ceremony.

FREEZE SET ON HIRING

Californian Stresses Need to Restrict Government and Buoy Economy

By STEVEN R. WEISMAN

Special to The New York Times

WASHINGTON, Jan. 20 — Ronald Wilson Reagan of California, promising "an era of national renewal," became the 40th President of the United States today as 52 Americans held hostage in Iran were heading toward freedom.

The hostages, whose 14 months of captivity had been a central focus of the Presidential contest last year, took off from Teheran in two Boeing 727 airplanes at 12:25 P.M., Eastern standard time, the very moment that Mr. Reagan was concluding his solemn Inaugural Address at the United States Capitol.

The new President's speech, however, made no reference at all to the long-awaited release of the hostages, emphasizing instead the need to limit the powers of the Federal Government, and to bring an end to unemployment and inflation.

'Government Is the Problem'

Promising to begin immediately to deal with "an economic affliction of great proportions," Mr. Reagan declared: "In this present crisis, government is not the solution to our problem; government is the problem." And in keeping with this statement, the President issued orders for a hiring "freeze" as his first official act. [Page B6.]

Wearing a charcoal gray club coat, striped trousers and dove gray vest and tie, Mr. Reagan took his oath of office at 11:57 A.M. in the first inaugural ceremony ever enacted on the western front of the United States Capitol. The site was chosen to stress the symbolism of Mr. Reagan's addressing his words to the West, the region that served as his base in his three Presidential campaigns in 1968, 1976 and 1980.

Oldest to Assume Presidency

The ceremony today, filled with patriotic music, the firing of cannons and the pealing of bells, marked the transfer of the Presidency back to the Republicans after the four-year term of Jimmy Carter, a Democrat, as well as the culmination of the remarkable career of a conservative former two-term Governor of California who had started out as a baseball announcer and motion picture star.

At the age of 69, Mr. Reagan also became the oldest man to assume the Presidency, and in five months he will become the oldest man to serve in the office.

Mr. Carter, looking haggard and worn after spending two largely sleepless nights trying to resolve the hostage crisis

Continued on Page B8, Column 2

Anxious Families and Towns Erupt Into Long-Postponed Celebrations

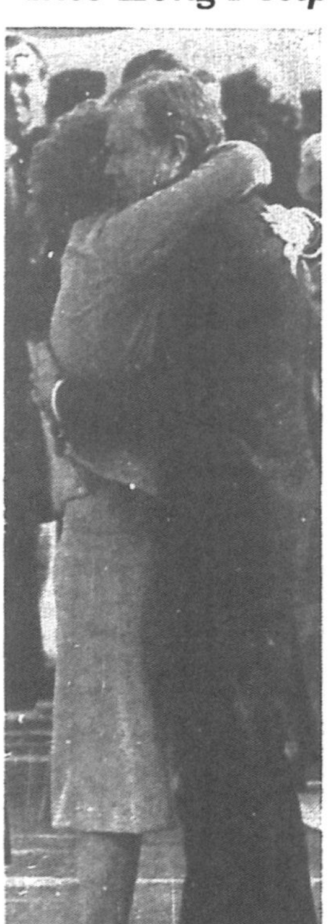

Black Star / John Troha for The New York Times

Anita Schaefer, wife of a hostage, embraced Mr. Carter at airport.

By JOSEPH B. TREASTER

Saying his final farewells at Andrews Air Force Base yesterday, Jimmy Carter spotted Anita Schaefer, the wife of one of the hostages, and exuberantly embraced her.

"Tom is in the air," Mr. Carter said, speaking of her husband, Col. Thomas E. Schaefer of the Air Force, who was the senior military officer at the United States Embassy in Teheran.

"Really, truly, Mr. President," she whispered.

"Really, truly — at long last," he said, "Tom is safe. I'll be with him tomorrow morning in Germany."

"Oh, thank God, Mr. President."

Then they both cried. And they embraced again.

The First Glimpse

As the hostages arrived in Algiers, relatives strained close to television screens for the first glimpse of their loved ones out of captivity in more than 14 months.

"There's Billy," cried Letezia Gallegos, as her brother, Sgt. William Gallegos of the Marines, stepped down the ramp. His mother, Theresa, broke into deep sobs.

News that the plane carrying the hostages had taken off from Teheran came to Penelope Laingen, the wife of L. Bruce Laingen, the embassy's chargé d'affaires, as she sat in a reserved seat at the inauguration of President Reagan. A military policeman shouted the word for everyone to hear.

Some had gotten the word from radio and television broadcasts, and still others, like Marjorie Moore, the wife of Bert C. Moore, the administrative consul, received phone calls from the State Department.

Most of the homes of the hostages' families, torn by doubt, fear and anger for so long, exploded with joy. They cried

Continued on Page A5, Column 1

Pars via Associated Press

12:25 P.M.: Sgt. Joseph Subic Jr. propelled by militants to waiting plane at airport in Teheran

A Hopeful Prologue, a Pledge of Action

By HEDRICK SMITH

Special to The New York Times

News Analysis

WASHINGTON, Jan. 20 — For a President who has promised Americans a new beginning, an era of national renewal at home and restored strength and stature abroad, the release of the American hostages in Iran was exquisitely timed.

The extraordinary deadline diplomacy that put the 52 captured Americans into the air over Iran minutes after the howitzers thundered a new leader into office provided a graceful exit for Jimmy Carter, a hopeful prologue for Ronald Reagan and relief for a nation weary from 14 months of humiliation and seeming impotence.

Almost unavoidably the human drama in Iran overshadowed an Inaugural Address that was less an inspirational call to national greatness than a plain-spoken charter of Mr. Reagan's conservative creed, less a sermon than a stump speech, less a rallying cry than a ringing denunciation of overgrown government and a practical pledge to get down to the business of trimming it at once.

For all the new President's vaunted reputation as one of the nation's most polished political orators, his Inaugural Address offered surprisingly few rhetorical flourishes beyond the populist tribute to ordinary Americans that "those who say that we are in a time when there are no heroes, they just don't know where to look."

Although Mr. Reagan made no direct mention of the hostages, their release was on everyone's lips. Moments before Mr. Reagan took his oath of office, word that the hostages were about to be flown out of Iran swept through the crowd stretched out before the Capitol, and though that news was premature, it provided the perfect symbolic backdrop for

Continued on Page B7, Column 1

More News And Pictures

The Inauguration

The Hostages

"All the News That's Fit to Print"

The New York Times

LATE CITY EDITION

Weather: Mostly sunny, mild today; fair tonight. Chance of showers tomorrow. Temperature range: today 48-72; yesterday 56-65. Details on page C9.

VOL.CXXX . No. 44,904 | Copyright © 1981 The New York Times | NEW YORK, TUESDAY, MARCH 31, 1981 | 40 cents beyond 50-mile zone from New York City. Higher in air delivery cities. | 25 CENTS

REAGAN WOUNDED IN CHEST BY GUNMAN; OUTLOOK 'GOOD' AFTER 2-HOUR SURGERY; AIDE AND 2 GUARDS SHOT; SUSPECT HELD

Bush Flies Back From Texas Set to Take Charge in Crisis

By STEVEN R. WEISMAN

Special to The New York Times

WASHINGTON, March 30 — Vice President Bush, cutting short a trip to Texas, returned to the White House this evening to take charge of the crisis in the Government and to assume the responsibilities of the Presidency if President Reagan's injuries prevented him from serving in the office.

It was unclear tonight how long Mr. Bush would remain in charge of Government functions, however. At George Washington Univerity Hospital, the dean of clinical affairs said that President Reagan was "alert" and that he "should be able to make decisions by tomorrow." But he said Mr. Reagan might have to remain in the hospital for two weeks.

"I can reassure this nation and a watching world that the American Government is functioning fully and effectively," Mr. Bush said this evening after presiding over a half-hour Cabinet meeting in the White House situation room, where participants also heard the televised news conference reporting on Mr. Reagan's condition.

'Officers Fulfilling Obligations'

"We've had full and complete communications throughout the day, and the officers of the Federal Government have been fulfilling their obligations with skill and with care," Mr. Bush continued. He added that "all our prayers" and "all our hope" were extended for the recovery of the two wounded law enforcement men and for James S. Brady, the White House press secretary.

White House spokesmen said this evening that no steps had been taken to install Mr. Bush as Acting President under the terms of the 25th Amendment to the Constitution, which provides for succession in case of Presidential disability.

Mr. Bush was scheduled to fill in for the President tomorrow, however, at a series of previously scheduled functions, including a Cabinet meeting, a session with Congressional leaders, and a lunch with the Prime Minister of the Netherlands, Andreas A. M. van Agt. He prepared to

Americans were saddened and outraged by news of the shooting of the President. In the business community, activity came to a standstill; stock trading was halted. Pages A5 and D1.

spend the night at his own official residence in northwest Washington, a few miles from the White House.

Contradictory Statements

There were contradictory statements in the afternoon and evening about who was in charge of the Government.

Shortly after 4 P.M., Secretary of State Alexander M. Haig Jr., who rushed to the White House minutes after the attack, announced he was in control pending the return of the Vice President to Washington. Mr. Haig also said he was in charge because the newly created system of "crisis management" was in effect, and he suggested that it was his role to serve as crisis-management coordinator until the

Continued on Page A5, Column 2

Suspect Was Arrested Last Year In Nashville on Weapons Charge

Associated Press

John W. Hinckley Jr. in photo made Jan. 21 for his driver's license.

By PHILIP TAUBMAN

Special to The New York Times

WASHINGTON, Tuesday, March 31 — The 25-year-old son of a Denver oil executive was overpowered by police officers and Secret Service agents yesterday at the scene of an attack on President Reagan. He was charged with the attempted assassination of the President and the shooting of three other persons.

The suspect was identified as John W. Hinckley Jr., who was said to have been in psychiatric care recently. He was arrested in Nashville last Oct. 9 for possession of concealed weapons, according to Nashville police records, and was released after paying a fine of $62.50. President Carter had arrived in Nashville a few hours earlier that night to speak at Opry Land.

Yesterday, in the tumult that followed the firing of a series of shots at Mr. Reagan's party, Mr. Hinckley was grabbed and pushed against a wall outside the Washington Hilton Hotel. Secret Service agents said that a Harrington Richards .22-caliber pistol was recovered from him, and he was quickly taken away in a District of Columbia police car.

Mr. Hinckley, described as a blue-eyed, sandy-haired man about 5 feet 10 inches tall, was turned over by the police to the Federal Bureau of Investigation and was arraigned early this morning in Federal District Court here.

He was ordered held without bail by Federal Magistrate Arthur L. Burnett on a charge that he "knowingly and intentionally" attempted to kill President Reagan and assaulted a Secret Service

Continued on Page A2, Column 4

Witnesses to Shooting Recall Suspect Acting 'Fidgety' and 'Hostile'

By RICHARD D. LYONS

Special to The New York Times

WASHINGTON, March 30 — "I spotted him walking rapidly up and down outside the back door of the hotel," John M. Dodson said. "He looked fidgety — agitated — a little strange, and I said to myself 'What if he takes a shot at the President?' "

Mr. Dodson, a computer specialist, was not the only person to take note of the behavior of the blond young man outside the Washington Hilton where President Reagan was making a speech. Walter C. Rogers, a reporter for Associated Press Radio, said the young man had been hostile to the group of reporters he had penetrated. And another witness, Samuel Lafta, an iron worker from Warren, Mich., said that a police lieutenant had stared at the young man several times.

But, nothing was done until the shots that wounded the President, his press secretary and two guards rang out. Then, the young man was overwhelmed by police officers and Secret Service agents.

Mr. Dodson, who works for the Pinkerton Detective Agency was standing on the seventh floor of the Universal North

Continued on Page A4, Column 3

Other News

Polish Strike Suspended

A nationwide strike threatened for today was averted after leaders of Solidarity reached a tentative settlement with the Polish Government. Page A9.

Indonesians Storm Hijacked Jet

Four of five hijackers were slain and 55 hostages freed when commandos in Bangkok retook an Indonesian airliner held since Saturday. Page A8.

ABC News

President Reagan leaving the Washington Hilton. At right is James S. Brady. As Mr. Reagan waved to the crowd . . .

Associated Press

. . . the gunman fired, hitting the President below his left arm. In photo made over roof of Presidential car . . .

Associated Press

. . . Secret Service agents are seen pushing Mr. Reagan into the vehicle, which immediately sped to a hospital.

NBC News

Circle at right shows gun held by suspect. Legs of Timothy J. McCarthy, the wounded agent, are visible at center.

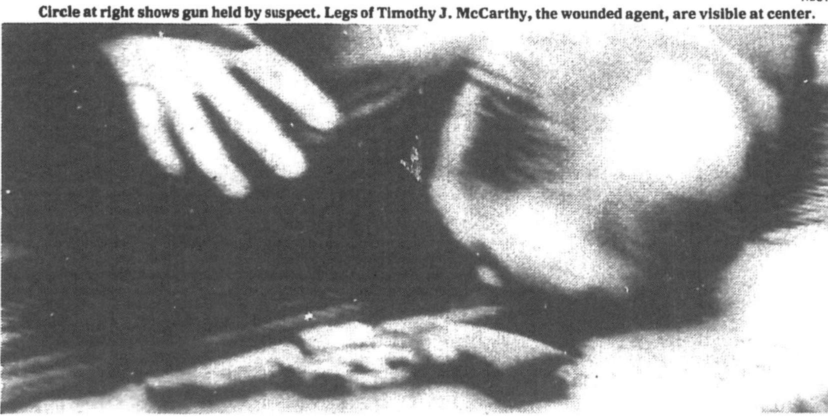

ABC News

James S. Brady lies on sidewalk. The pistol is believed to belong to a security agent, who put it down while helping.

LEFT LUNG IS PIERCED

Coloradan, 25, Arrested — Brady, Press Chief, Is Critically Injured

By HOWELL RAINES

Special to The New York Times

WASHINGTON, Tuesday, March 31 — President Reagan was shot in the chest yesterday by a gunman, apparently acting alone, as Mr. Reagan walked to his limousine after addressing a labor meeting at the Washington Hilton Hotel. The White House press secretary and two law-enforcement officers were also wounded by a burst of shots.

The President was reported in "good" and "stable" condition last night at George Washington University Hospital

Statements in capital, pages A5 and A7.

after undergoing two hours of surgery. "The prognosis is excellent," said Dr. Dennis S. O'Leary, dean of clinical affairs at the university. "He is alert and should be able to make decisions by tomorrow."

The hospital spokesman said surgeons removed a .22-caliber bullet that struck Mr. Reagan's seventh rib, penetrating the left lung three inches and collapsing it.

A rapid series of five or six shots rang out about 2:30 P.M. as Mr. Reagan left the hotel. A look of stunned disbelief swept across the President's face when the shots were fired just after he raised his left arm to wave to the crowd. Nearby, his press secretary, James S. Brady, fell to the sidewalk, critically wounded.

Eyewitnesses said six shots were fired at the Presidential entourage from a distance of about 10 feet. The assailant had positioned himself among the television camera crews and reporters assembled outside a hotel exit.

The authorities arrested a 25-year-old Colorado man, John W. Hinckley Jr., at the scene of the attack. He was booked on Federal charges of attempting to assassinate the President and assault on a Federal officer, and early this morning he was ordered held without bail by Federal Magistrate Arthur L. Burnett.

According to police records, Mr. Hinckley was arrested in Nashville last fall on weapons charges on a night when President Carter was speaking there.

Scene of Turmoil

Within minutes after the attack yesterday afternoon, Americans were witnessing for the second time in a generation television pictures of a chief executive being struck by gunfire during what appeared to be a routine public appearance. For the second time in less than 20 years, too, they watched as the nation's leaders scrambled to meet one of the sternest tests of the democratic system.

Mr. Reagan, apparently at first unaware that he had been wounded, was shoved forcefully by a Secret Service agent into the Presidential limousine,

Continued on Page A3, Column 3

A Bullet Is Removed From Reagan's Lung In Emergency Surgery

By ROBERT REINHOLD

Special to The New York Times

WASHINGTON, March 30 — President Reagan was treated for a partly collapsed lung today, but the bullet that entered his left side and lodged in the tissue of his left lung did not do much further damage, according to doctors who operated on him. Surgeons removed a .22-caliber bullet from the President's lower left lung.

Neither Mr. Reagan's heart nor such vital blood vessels as the aorta were affected, Dr. Dennis S. O'Leary, dean for clinical affairs at George Washington University, said at a briefing this evening. "The bullet was never close to any vital structure," he said. He called Mr. Reagan's prognosis "excellent."

Emergency surgical procedures, which took about two hours, found no bleeding or damage in the abdominal area. Mr. Reagan received five units, or two and a half quarts, of blood in a transfusion before surgery. His vital signs were stable throughout his ordeal.

The adult body contains five to six quarts of blood. The hazard of blood loss relates to how rapidly the blood is lost and whether the volume of the blood sup-

Continued on Page A7, Column 1

"All the News That's Fit to Print"

The New York Times

LATE CITY EDITION

Weather: Mostly sunny today; clear tonight. Mostly sunny tomorrow. Temperature range: today 76-99; yesterday 74-94. Details on page B8.

VOL.CXXX . . . No. 45,003 | NEW YORK, WEDNESDAY, JULY 8, 1981 | 30 cents beyond 50-mile zone from New York City. Higher in air delivery cities. | 25 CENTS

Rupturing of Reservoir Pipelines Imperils Newark's Water Supply

Chain Reaction Set Off as Valve Is Opened — Vandalism Suspected

By ROBERT HANLEY

Special to The New York Times

PEQUANNOCK TOWNSHIP, N.J., July 7 — A valve at an aqueduct was opened here today, apparently by vandals, starting a chain reaction that burst two huge pipelines and cut off Newark from its main water supply.

"It's an imminent catastrophe," said James F. Conley, the chief engineer of Newark's Division of Water Supply.

Mr. Conley said that unless the city could activate two existing pipeline interconnections with three other water supply systems and could build two new ones, parts of Newark "will be out of water" in five days.

The New York Times/July 8, 1981

Other Communities Affected

The pipelines that ruptured, he said, normally carry about 75 million of the 120 million gallons a day used by 600,000 people in Newark and parts of Elizabeth, Bloomfield, Belleville and Wayne.

Those four other communities, all of which purchase some of their water from Newark, began planning for alternative supplies.

Mayor Kenneth A. Gibson of Newark declared a water emergency in the early afternoon, prohibiting all nonessential uses of water, including lawn watering, car washing and opening of hydrants for any purposes other than firefighting.

Douglas Eldridge, a spokesman for the Mayor, said officials did not expect any declines in water pressure or other serious difficulties in the next day or two. He said some discolored water could come from taps because of adjustments being made on the distribution system following the huge loss of water.

But officials said that if the city could not restore a steady water source within five days, parts of Newark would run out of water. A heat wave that pushed temperatures today into the mid-90's and may see higher readings tomorrow is expected to increase water use and has heightened the officials' concern.

A 1,200-foot section of the two pipelines was torn away after they ruptured, sending tens of millions of gallons of water down a hillside here from about 4 A.M. today until the aqueduct's main supply valves at the Charlotteburg Reservoir were shut off sometime after 5 A.M., Mr. Conley said.

The cascading water, estimated at 40

Continued on Page B2, Column 4

U.S. FRAMES POLICY ON HALTING SPREAD OF NUCLEAR ARMS

American Reliability as Seller of Technology Stressed — Use Must Be Peaceful

By TERENCE SMITH

Special to The New York Times

WASHINGTON, July 7 — The Reagan Administration plans to announce shortly that while it is committed to halting the spread of nuclear weapons abroad the United States will be a "clearly reliable and credible" supplier of nuclear technology for peaceful purposes.

This policy is contained in an eight-point set of guidelines that has been prepared by the State Department and submitted to the White House. The White House is expected to issue the list before a meeting in Ottawa July 20-21 of the leaders of seven industrial nations. The spread of nuclear weapons will be one of the items on the agenda.

Although the guidelines are couched in the most general of terms, Administration officials say, they reflect a stronger commitment to halting the spread of nuclear weapons than was contained in Mr. Reagan's campaign statements last year and in a transition paper prepared by his advisers in December.

A Bigger Nuclear Umbrella

As described by Administration officials who have seen the guidelines, there are several principal points:

¶The goals of stopping the spread of nuclear weapons must be strongly reaffirmed.

¶A determined effort should be made to reduce the motivation of other countries to obtain nuclear weapons and an acknowledgement should be given that security considerations are often a basic factor in that decision. To this end, officials said, the United States would be prepared to sell conventional arms and consider extending its own nuclear umbrella.

¶The 1968 Nonproliferation Treaty, by which the nuclear powers undertook not to help others make or acquire nuclear weapons, and the 1967 Treaty of Tlatelolco, Mexico, which established a nuclear-free zone in Latin America, must be emphatically supported.

¶The International Atomic Energy Agency and its system of safeguards against the conversion of nuclear power and research facilities to weapons purposes should be strongly supported.

¶The United States should cooperate with other supplier countries to prevent the transfer of sensitive technology and material to nonnuclear countries where such transfers carry a risk of weapons production.

¶A high level of intelligence activities, including the possible upgrading of

Continued on Page A8, Column 1

REAGAN NOMINATING WOMAN, AN ARIZONA APPEALS JUDGE, TO SERVE ON SUPREME COURT

Associated Press

Judge Sandra Day O'Connor at news conference yesterday in Phoenix

REACTION IS MIXED

Senate Seems Favorable but Opposition Arises on Abortion Stands

By STEVEN R. WEISMAN

Special to The New York Times

WASHINGTON, July 7 — President Reagan announced today that he would nominate Sandra Day O'Connor, a 51-year-old judge on the Arizona Court of Appeals, to the United States Supreme Court. If confirmed, she would become the first woman to serve on the Court.

"She is truly a 'person for all seasons,'" Mr. Reagan said this morning, "possessing those unique qualities of temperament, fairness, intellectual

Remarks on Court post, page A12.

capacity and devotion to the public good which have characterized the 101 'brethren' who have preceded her."

White House and Justice Department officials expressed confidence that Judge O'Connor's views were compatible with those espoused over the years by Mr. Reagan, who has been highly critical of some past Supreme Court decisions on the rights of defendants, busing, abortion and other matters.

Some Quick Opposition

From the initial reaction in the Senate, it appeared her nomination would be approved. However, her record of favoring the proposed Federal equal rights amendment and having sided once against anti-abortion interests while she was a legislator provoked immediate opposition to her confirmation by the National Right to Life Committee, Moral Majority and other groups opposed to abortion.

At a brief news conference in Phoenix, Judge O'Connor declined to explain her views, saying that she intended to leave such matters to her confirmation hearings before the Senate Judiciary Committee. [Page A12.]

Mr. Reagan, himself an opponent of abortions, said in response to a question that he was "completely satisfied" with her position on that issue.

No Radical Shift Expected

White House officials were hopeful that Judge O'Connor's appointment could be historic not only because she is a woman but also because her presence on the Court, as a replacement for Associate Justice Potter Stewart, who was often a swing vote between ideological camps on the Court, could shift the Court's balance to the right.

However, an examination of the Court's voting patterns suggests no radical shift is likely even if she does vote with the more conservative Justices. [News analysis, page A13.]

It is the additional hope of Mr. Reagan's aides to make the Court even more conservative in the years ahead, when more vacancies are possible.

Judge O'Connor was appointed to

Continued on Page A12, Column 2

'A Reputation for Excelling'

Sandra Day O'Connor

By B. DRUMMOND AYRES Jr.

Special to The New York Times

Woman in the News

WASHINGTON, July 7 — Judge Sandra Day O'Connor's place in history is already secure, based on today's announcement that she will be President Reagan's nominee as the first woman on the United States Supreme Court.

But if her past is prologue, after her Senate confirmation Judge O'Connor might well go on to leave even larger "footprints on the sands of time," as Mr. Reagan, quoting Longfellow, described the mark of United States Justices. Thus far in her 51 years, Judge O'Connor has compiled an impressive list of academic, civic, political and legal achievements.

"She's finished at the top in a lot of things," said Mary Ellen Simonson of Phoenix, who was a legislative aide when Mrs. O'Connor was majority leader of the Arizona State Senate, the first woman in the nation to hold such a leadership position.

"She has a reputation for excelling," Mrs. Simonson continued. "As a result she's been one of the state's leading role models for women. Now she's a national role model."

Judge O'Connor, who currently sits on the Arizona Court of Appeals, the state's second highest court, refused this afternoon to discuss "substantative issues" when she met with reporters in Phoenix. And, because of her short, 18-month tenure on the appeals court and its somewhat limited docket, she has faced few of the nettlesome issues routinely taken up by the United States Supreme Court. Nevertheless, her past and her acquaintances provide some insights into her mind and personality.

She is said, by friend and foe alike, to be notably bright, extremely hard-working, meticulous, deliberate, cautious and, above all, a Republican conservative.

"But she has an open mind when it comes to her conservatism," said a longtime friend, Sharon Rockefeller, wife of Gov. John D. Rockefeller IV of West Virginia. "I can't conceive of her closing off her mind to anything."

A leading Democratic politician in

Continued on Page A13, Column 5

New Pact Ends 7-Day Strike Of Garbage Haulers in Jersey

By ALFONSO A. NARVAEZ

Special to The New York Times

WEST PATERSON, N.J., July 7 — A seven-day strike against private garbage haulers in 108 northern and central New Jersey communities ended today when 1,400 drivers and loaders accepted a three-year contract that gives them a 50 percent pay increase.

Garbage trucks in the 12 affected counties will begin rolling early tomorrow. and Picket signs that had blocked municipal sanitation employees will come down from entrances to landfills.

The new contract was accepted after a long and confusing day in which the union members first rejected an agreement hammered out by negotiators in an 18-hour session at the Sheraton Heights Hotel in Hasbrouck Heights.

$155-a-Week Raise

When that proposal was rejected, the negotiators immediately went into new talks.

The union then approved a proposal that gives the drivers the $155-a-week raise over three years that was contained in the proposal they rejected, but adds three days of sick leave a year and guarantees that double time for work on the sixth day will go to workers with seniority. The drivers currently earn $310 a week for an average six-day, 48-hour week, and the loaders get about $50 less.

The union also won an additional paid holiday, four weeks of vacation after 15 years and $56 in increased health and welfare benefits.

The agreement provides for an immediate increase of $55 a week, then $35 a week on Jan. 1, 1982, $20 a week on July 1, 1982, and $45 more on July 1, 1983.

The cost of the package to residents and communities in the affected area has not yet been calculated. However, during the negotiations, the State Attorney General, James J. Zazzali, assured the owners — members of the New Jersey State Municipal Contractors Association and the Solid Waste Industry Association — that their requests for rate increases would be handled expeditiously.

The membership did not vote on the final package. The leaders of the union,

Continued on Page B4, Column 1

Sun-Powered Airplane Crosses Channel

Special to The New York Times

MANSTON, England, July 7 — After several earlier unsuccessful attempts, the first solar-powered airplane succeeded today in crossing the English Channel.

It took an atypically sunny English summer afternoon and a five-and-a-half-hour flight, but late this afternoon, the Solar Challenger dropped slowly onto the concrete landing strip of Manston Royal Air Force Base, on the southeastern coast of England.

Designed by Paul MacCready, who also designed the first human-powered plane to cross the Channel, the 210-pound Solar Challenger is powered by 16,000 photovoltaic cells on the wings that convert solar energy to electricity, which drives the motor.

No Battery Power

Other airplanes have flown on solar power, but only the Solar Challenger has been able to do so without the help of storage batteries. The project was paid for largely by DuPont and employed many high-strength, low-weight materials made by that company.

Starting from an airport at Cormeilles-en-Vexin, 25 miles northwest of Paris, the spidery plane, which has a wingspan of 47 feet, made the 165-mile journey at an average speed of about 30 miles per hour and a cruising altitude of 11,000 feet.

Standing in the deep grass along the main east-west runway at Cormeilles, a small crowd of about 30 persons had gathered to cheer on the tiny, transparent aircraft and its pilot. They watched the delicate plane corkscrew slowly and almost silently into the sky above the airport. The 2.7 horsepower electric motor produced only a slight buzz.

At an altitude of about 2,000 feet, Stephen Ptacek, the 28-year-old pilot from Golden, Colo., headed northwest in the direction of the Channel. In two or three minutes, he disappeared from sight.

Mr. Ptacek was greeted at the Man-

Continued on Page B4, Column 1

Associated Press

French policemen watch as Solar Challenger begins flight to England

Baker Vows Support for Nominee

By FRANCIS X. CLINES

Special to The New York Times

WASHINGTON, July 7 — Anti-abortion groups today denounced President Reagan's decision to nominate Judge Sandra Day O'Connor to the Supreme Court, but initial reaction in the Senate, which will vote on confirmation, was favorable.

"I commend the President for the courage of his decision," said Howard H. Baker Jr., the Senate Republican majority leader. "I am delighted with his choice, and I pledge my full support for her confirmation by the full Senate."

The National Right to Life Committee, an amalgam of anti-abortion lobbying groups in the 50 states, said that it would mobilize its members to "prevail upon senators to oppose this nomination." The committee said that Judge O'Connor was "pro-abortion" as a member of the Arizona State Legislature.

Dr. Carolyn Gerster, a vice president of the National Right to Life Committee, said that the nominee, as a legislator, voted in 1974 not to allow an anti-abortion resolution out of caucus, thus killing it. The resolution asked Congress to pass a Constitutional amendment protecting the fetus except when the mother's life was in danger, and allowed abortions in the case of rape.

Dr. Gerster based her statement of Judge O'Connor's record on that and other votes, which were characterized as "pro-abortion," on newspaper accounts and the recollections of other legislators, she said. Before 1975, the State Legislature kept no records of

Continued on Page A12, Column 1

Prelate, 52, Chosen By the Pope to Lead The Polish Church

By JOHN DARNTON

Special to The New York Times

WARSAW, July 7 — Bishop Jozef Glemp of Warmia was named today by Pope John Paul II as Archbishop of Gniezno and Warsaw and the Primate of Poland, succeeding Stefan Cardinal Wyszynski, who died on May 28.

The new head of the Church in this overwhelmingly Roman Catholic nation said he would continue the policies begun by his predecessor of dialogue and cooperation with both the Government and the Solidarity labor union.

"I am convinced I must follow the road laid out by Cardinal Wyszynski," he said in an interview. "The work of the Primate is not political. It is pastoral. But if we in the church are to do our duty, we must not remain above social issues. If the Solidarity and other social movements want to follow the truth and the light, we will give them our protection. It is in line with the proper role of the church."

Archbishop Glemp, 52 years old and a specialist in both canon and civil law, said he believed in working closely with the Conference of Bishops and would strive for collegial rule. Cardinal Wy-

Continued on Page A6, Column 1

INSIDE

9 More Executed in Iran

Iran executed nine opponents in its drive against "counterrevolutionary" elements. It also ordered Reuters to close its Teheran bureau. Page A3.

Upset in Mississippi Vote

Wayne Dowdy, a Democrat, apparently won a Congressional election in Mississippi, beating a strong supporter of President Reagan. Page A18.

"All the News That's Fit to Print"

The New York Times

LATE CITY EDITION

Weather: Increasing cloudiness today; rain likely tonight, tomorrow. Temperature range: today 29-40; yesterday 28-38. Details, page C21.

VOL.CXXXI . . . No. 45,162 | NEW YORK, MONDAY, DECEMBER 14, 1981 | 25 CENTS

30 cents beyond 50-mile zone from New York City. Higher in air delivery cities.

POLAND RESTRICTS CIVIL AND UNION RIGHTS; SOLIDARITY ACTIVISTS URGE GENERAL STRIKE

Judge Reduces Westway Suits To Single Issue

Landfill's Effect on Fish Still to Be Considered

By ROBIN HERMAN

A Federal judge has whittled down the longstanding legal attacks on the Westway highway project to a single issue — the fate of fish in the Hudson River — and he will set a hearing date today for arguments on that obstacle.

The judge, Thomas F. Griesa of Federal District Court in Manhattan, has dismissed all objections to the highway contained in two remaining lawsuits except for questions on the effect the landfill for the project would have on aquatic life.

John Marino, the state's Assistant Transportation Commissioner for New York City, said that the judge's action was "a very positive development" and that it reflected the Carey administration's interest in seeing the highway built.

As for environmentalists' concern about aquatic life — especially striped bass — Mr. Marino said yesterday: "When was the last time you had striped bass from the Hudson? That's our comment on it. I don't expect that in the end this will be a serious issue. The way is clear for Westway. It's a go-ahead."

Most Objections Dismissed

The judge, meeting in private on Friday with both the plaintiffs and the state and Federal defendants, dismissed altogether a suit brought in 1974 by Action for Rational Transit, an anti-Westway group, which was attempting to block the project. The suit contended chiefly that the highway would violate Federal clean-air standards.

Also, according to both sides, Judge Griesa dismissed most objections made in a 1977 suit brought by the Sierra Club and other environmental and civic groups. That suit challenged the dredge-and-fill permit for the project granted by the Army Corps of Engineers.

The suit charged that the Government had not adequately examined alternative routes, the trade-in of the Federal Westway funds for mass-transit funds or the possibility that the landfill on which the highway would be built could threaten New Jersey with flooding. It also questioned whether the river's aquatic life had been considered in the environmental impact statement. The highway's official cost is $1.7 billion, but it is expected to exceed that figure by millions of dollars.

After a hearing, possibly next month, on the aquatic-life question, Judge Griesa has said he will issue a written decision on all claims. At that time, the two groups of plaintiffs can appeal the earlier dismissals, which the judge made orally.

Albert Butzel, the lawyer representing the Sierra Club, said yesterday that,

Continued on Page B10, Column 3

HAIG WARNS SOVIET

He Says U.S. Is 'Seriously Concerned' and Backs New Warsaw Talks

By BERNARD GWERTZMAN

Special to The New York Times

BRUSSELS, Dec. 13 — Secretary of State Alexander M. Haig Jr. said today that the United States was "seriously concerned" about the imposition of martial law in Poland, and he renewed the West's warning to the Soviet Union not to interfere in the crisis.

After talking by phone with President Reagan, who was then at Camp David, Md., Mr. Haig said at a news conference here that the United States was urging

News conference excerpts, page A19.

the Polish Government to resume negotiations and to pursue a policy of compromise with the Solidarity trade union to prevent an outbreak of civil strife that could worsen the situation.

Mr. Haig said Polish authorities had assured the United States Embassy this morning that "there will be no return" to the situation that existed in Poland prior to establishment of the independent union in 1980. In addition, he said Western intelligence agencies had not detected any Soviet military moves "which would be a source of alarm."

"But we continue to watch the situation very carefully," he said.

'Very Serious' Consequences

If the Soviet Union intervened in Poland, Mr. Haig said, "the consequences would be very serious and long lasting." Western officials have previously said that, in that event, all trade with the Soviet Union would be suspended and political relations would be sharply curtailed.

President Reagan, arriving back at the White House, was asked about the danger of Soviet intervention and said that the United States had several times "made it plain how seriously we would view interference" by the Soviet Union. The Polish Ambassador and the Soviet Deputy Chief of Mission were summoned to the State Department for discussions on the situation. [Page A15.]

Mr. Haig was scheduled to leave Brussels this morning for a seven-day trip to Israel, Turkey, Pakistan, India, Egypt and Morocco. But after talking by phone with Vice President Bush and with various foreign ministers, Mr. Haig decided at the last minute to scrap his travel plans. Reporters traveling with him

Continued on Page A19, Column 4

Sipa Press / Black Star

Police in Wroclaw surround the Solidarity offices and keep crowds away. Photo was made from inside the building. Wroclaw, formerly Breslau, is an industrial city 190 miles southwest of Warsaw, near the Czechoslovak border.

WALESA NEGOTIATES

New Army Council Bans Rallies and Sets Wide Grounds for Arrests

By JOHN DARNTON

Special to The New York Times

WARSAW, Dec. 13 — Poland's new military leaders issued a decree of martial law today, drastically restricting civil rights and suspending the operations of the Solidarity union. The union's activists reacted with an appeal for an immediate general strike to protest.

A proclamation broadcast by the newly formed Martial Council for National Redemption, now the top authority in the country, also banned all kinds

Premier's address, page A16.

of public gatherings and demonstrations and ordered the internment of citizens whose loyalty to the state was under "justified suspicion."

The military rule was announced in a dramatic broadcast at dawn by Gen. Wojciech Jaruzelski, the Prime Minister and Communist Party leader, who said a strict regime was necessary to save Poland from catastrophe and civil war. Hours before, Solidarity leaders meeting in Gdansk had proposed holding a national referendum on forming a non-Communist government.

No Reports of Violence

Following a provision in the constitution, General Jaruzelski, declared a "state of war," equivalent to a state of emergency in other countries.

There were no immediate reports of any violence, but opposition to the military move seemed in the offing. Union activists, in dozens of leaflets being circulated in the streets, called for an immediate general strike.

Many Solidarity activists were in detention following coordinated police raids across the country after midnight last night. So were several former leaders of Poland's Communist Party.

Among the detained were some of the top leaders and advisers of the Solidarity union who had assembled in Gdansk to work out strategy in the latest confrontation with the Government.

Walesa Flown to Warsaw

Lech Walesa, Solidarity's chairman, who became an international figure by his role in the workers' uprising of last summer, was meeting with Government officials at a site outside Warsaw today, Jerzy Urban, a Government spokesman, said at a news conference.

Mr. Walesa was flown to Warsaw in a Government plane at 4 A.M. to begin talks with Stanislaw Ciosek, the Minister of Trade Union Affairs, according to the Interpress information agency. Mr. Urban said that Mr. Walesa had not been detained at any point.

Mr. Urban also stressed that Soli-

Continued on Page A16, Column 1

Communism and Better Life: Poles Found Wait Too Long

John Darnton, who has been chief of The New York Times bureau in Warsaw since September 1979, reports in the following article on the problems underlying the crisis in Poland.

Special to The New York Times

WARSAW — Behind the workers' revolt that began with strikes in the summer of 1980 and grew to a revolution on the shoulders of the Solidarity union, the operation of which was suspended when martial law was declared, lies a story of failure. It is the failure of Communism, in the eyes of the workers, to deliver on its promise of a better life.

The revolt sprang from an unspoken consensus among Poles that despite more than three decades of sacrifice and toil, conditions of everyday life were scarcely improving and that the Communist system had failed most dramatically in precisely those areas, in the realm of social welfare, where its ideology called for greater exertion and improvement.

Appalling dirt and safety conditions in factories, cramped and unavailable apartments, substandard and sloppy health care, lines in front of meat shops — food shortages in general despite a stringent rationing system — these were the distinguishing traits of what the Government referred to as "people's Poland." They were glossed over, ignored or denied by successive governments that pressed instead for higher production statistics in heavy industry.

They certainly did not keep pace with expectations and, compared with the West, which more and more Poles were visiting when restrictions were loosened as the cold war period came to a close, Poland was failing behind.

'My Life Doesn't Count'

"All my adult life I've been told that my life doesn't count, that I'm sacrificing myself for my children," said one well-known Polish journalist, speaking privately. "Well, now I'm 48. My son is 19. His life is no better than mine and he's being told he must sacrifice himself for his children. What's life all about, anyway?"

Satisfying the basic needs of the population was given low priority when it came to allocating investment in the national budget, but it was given lip service in public propaganda and high-

Continued on Page A18, Column 1

Army's Rule: Two Targets

General Hits at Foes In Party and Solidarity

By DAVID BINDER

Special to The New York Times

WASHINGTON, Dec. 13 — Poland's soldier-leader, Wojciech Jaruzelski, has struck at what he perceives as the two main roots of his country's current troubles: the radical "confrontationists" of the Solidarity labor movement and the still influential members of the Communist Party's old guard.

News Analysis

His martial law decree, accompanied by the detention of Solidarity leaders and former party leaders and an internal communications blackout, has eliminated the cadres and the instruments that might have been used to rally supporters against his rule.

A 56,000-Member Force

The state of emergency was long in the making, in the estimate of Administration specialists on Polish affairs, and was foreshadowed not only by large-scale maneuvers of Soviet troops on Poland's borders earlier in the year, but also by the brief mobilization of the Polish Internal Defense Forces last September.

The Internal Defense Forces are heavily equipped paramilitary security troops with 56,000 members. They are trained for riot control, and are deployed in three contingents, one in War-

Continued on Page A19, Column 1

Budget Cuts, Weak Market Hurt Gasohol

By DOUGLAS MARTIN

Special to The New York Times

DES MOINES — Interest in gasohol, which has attracted more Government encouragement in recent years than any other energy source, has been fading — the result of an oversupply of crude oil and the Administration's efforts to curb Federal spending.

Enthusiasm for gasohol, a mixture of gasoline and alcohol, was born amid farmers' anger over the restrictions on grain sales to the Soviet Union and consumers' concern about the shutdown of Iran's oil fields. The fuel seemed a way for America to cultivate its way out of the energy crisis, drawing on this nation's unrivaled agricultural strength. Most commercial gasohol is a 90-10 mixture of refined gasoline and ethanol derived from corn.

Pledge of Subsidies

The Carter Administration and Congress responded to the apparent groundswell by pledging subsidies for gasohol exceeding $30 billion by 1992, making it, gallon for gallon, by far the most heavily subsidized fuel.

But over the past few months, the White House has moved vigorously to slash funding for gasohol plants, large

Continued on Page D5, Column 5

The New York Times / Dith Pran

Demonstrators marching past the Polish Consulate on 37th Street near Madison Avenue. Similar protests against the military takeover in Poland were held in Paris, Vienna, London, Rome, Brussels and other European cities.

Biotechnology: Better Breeds and Crops

By HAROLD M. SCHMECK Jr.

The first major products from the young industry using the techniques of gene-splicing are expected to go on world markets next year, a development that some experts believe will usher in a new era in the prevention and treatment of disease.

Agriculture will probably be the first to benefit from such products, including vaccines against foot-and-mouth disease and scours, two economically serious diseases that afflict cattle.

Two important medical products now undergoing extensive clinical tests are expected to follow, probably in 1983 in the United States: human insulin and human growth hormone produced in bacteria that have been adapted for the purpose by gene-splicing techniques. Animal growth hormone produced by the same techniques is also being developed for agricultural use.

The predicted uses of gene-splicing techniques include such diverse products as industrial enzymes, food additives, medical and veterinary test chemicals and drugs, as well as improved plant species.

The long-range potential uses for the chemical, mining, energy and forest products industries, and for agriculture, dwarf all the prospective uses for medicine. Except for products related to health and food, however, the emergence of competitive major industrial

Continued on Page D13, Column 1

The New Genetics

Biology at a Turning Point

Second of three articles

Other Developments

Warsaw mood — Every hour on the hour beginning at 6 A.M., Poles listening to their radios heard Prime Minister Wojciech Jaruzelski speak in solemn tones about having placed the country under martial law. The interludes were filled with music. More cars were on the streets than is usual for a Sunday, particularly in a period of acute gasoline shortage. All telephones had stopped functioning, presumably to keep those who might wish to resist from coordinating actions. Page A17.

Washington concern — The Reagan Administration called in the Polish Ambassador and the Soviet Deputy Chief of Mission for discussions. Several allied diplomats were also called to the State Department. President Reagan returned ahead of schedule from a weekend at Camp David to be briefed on Poland by Administration officials. Page A15.

Soviet silence — The Soviet Union made no official comment on the declaration of martial law in Poland. The Polish developments were reported in a series of brief and largely factual dispatches by the official news agency Tass. Page A19.

Papal appeal — Pope Paul John II asked his fellow Poles to pray for peace and to do everything in their power "to peacefully build a peaceful future." Page A14.

German reaction — Chancellor Helmut Schmidt of West Germany, visiting a small East German town, seemed intent on demonstrating through his presence that there was no reason for the West to dramatize the situation in Poland. Page A20.

Polish-American reaction — Tens of thousands of Polish-Americans across the nation voiced outrage and despair. In the New York metropolitan area and in Chicago, Philadelphia and other centers of Polish-American life, the outpouring was emotional but nonviolent as workers, scholars, writers, clergymen and diplomats spoke of their homeland. With a communications blackout severing their contacts with friends and relatives in Poland, there was also widespread concern over loved ones and acquaintances. Page A17.

INSIDE

U.S. Wins Davis Cup

John McEnroe defeated José-Luis Clerc in five sets to give the United States a victory over Argentina in the final of the Davis Cup. Page C1.

Sakharovs: Weak but Elated

The Soviet dissident Andrei D. Sakharov and his wife were said to be emaciated but in high spirits at the success of their hunger strike. Page A3.

"All the News That's Fit to Print"

The New York Times

Late Edition

Weather: Rain early today, tapering off to showers and ending in the afternoon; clearing tonight. Sunny tomorrow. Temperatures: today 41-49, tonight 33-37; yesterday 39-62. Details on page B2.

VOL.CXXXIV. . No. 46,346 NEW YORK, TUESDAY, MARCH 12, 1985 — 50 cents beyond 75 miles from New York City, except on Long Island. — 30 CENTS

CHERNENKO IS DEAD IN MOSCOW AT 73; GORBACHEV SUCCEEDS HIM AND URGES ARMS CONTROL AND ECONOMIC VIGOR

ISRAELI ARMY KILLS 24 IN RAID ON TOWN IN SOUTH LEBANON

Attack Across New Defense Line Follows Car-Bombing of a Military Convoy

By JOHN KIFNER

Special to The New York Times

ZRARIYAH, Lebanon, March 11 — Israeli troops stormed across their new defense line today and killed at least 24 people in a raid against this southern Lebanese village.

The raid, the fiercest of the current Israeli crackdown, came about 12 hours after a suicide car bomber crashed into an Israeli Army convoy, killing 12 Israeli soldiers.

The main street of this village was a scene of hysteria and chaos after the Israeli force withdrew just before dusk, with women shrieking and waving their hands in the air or sitting on the ground weeping.

The casualty figures were still in doubt tonight. An Israeli military announcement said 24 people it described as "terrorists" had been killed, but the Israeli radio later put the death toll at 30. The Lebanese police and local radio stations said 25 people had died.

Bodies in Burned-Out Cars

Western journalists saw six bodies in burned-out cars on the outskirts of the village and there were a number of others in the village itself.

The raid appeared to signal a determination by Israel that its "iron fist" policy would not be altered in the face of continued guerrilla resistance.

Today's raid, guerrillas and villagers said, actually began at about 11 P.M. Sunday when Israeli troops tried to infiltrate the village, which is a few miles north of their new second-stage defense line on the Litani River.

Members of the Amal Shiite militia, supported by a 30-man garrison that the Lebanese Army recently established here, fought back against the attack, militiamen and residents of the village said.

Israeli Force Put at 1,000

But at 6 A.M. today, after a heavy artillery barrage, the Israelis came from three directions in overwhelming force and pushed into the village of about 8,000 people, according to witnesses.

Militiamen and members of the local police force, who said they had been cuffed about by the Israelis, put the attacking force at as many as 1,000 soldiers and perhaps 200 to 300 vehicles.

Continued on Page A8, Column 4

Sygma/Regis Bossu; United Press International

Succession in Moscow

The announcement of the death of Konstantin U. Chernenko, above, the Soviet leader, was quickly followed by the naming of his successor, Mikhail S. Gorbachev. The move represents a shift to a new generation of Soviet leadership.

A Leader With Style — and Impatience

Special to The New York Times

MOSCOW, March 11 — Coming to power at the age of 54, Mikhail Sergeyevich Gorbachev, the peasant's son from southern Russia, is expected to bring a new style of leadership to the Kremlin. If the expectations prove correct, this leadership will be more open, perhaps, less obsessively suspicious, less burdened with memories of Stalin's terror and the war.

Man in the News

For the moment, Mr. Gorbachev seemed anxious to give fire to the program of economic change he had inherited from his mentor, Yuri V. Andropov.

He revealed his impatience in a major speech last December when he said, "We will have to carry out profound transformations in the economy and in the entire system of social relations."

'Intensive Development'

There was an echo of that today when he said, "We are to achieve a decisive turn in transferring the national economy to the tracks of intensive development."

He added, "A good deal is to be done."

What remained to be seen, however, was how Mr. Gorbachev (pronounced gore-bah-CHAWFF) would translate his impatience into action by the enormous bureaucracy that manages the Soviet Union's ponderous, creaky, centralized economy.

For all the fervor, style and obvious achievement he has displayed in reaching the highest position in the Soviet power structure, Mr. Gorbachev and the generation he represents remain an untested and largely unknown political force.

These are people who were reared after the war and after the Stalinist terrors, who grew up in a state more secure in its power and potential, men who got better educations than their predecessors and had more contact with the outside world.

Konstantin U. Chernenko was a dedicated Bolshevik but also a pragmatist. An obituary, page A14.

Yet these are also men who have made their careers in a Communist Party that has changed from an idealistic elite into an entrenched, privileged and self-perpetuating bureaucracy intolerant of too much independence or nonconformism among its members.

Under Mr. Andropov, Mr. Gorbachev worked under a seasoned politician who knew the power structure intimately from within as a consequence of his 15 years at the head of the K.G.B., the internal security and intelligence agency. And though he himself rose to the peak of Soviet power, Mr. Gorbachev's political biography did not conclusively prove his ability to wage the sort of brutal political struggle that is required to get change through the bureaucracy.

After a steady and apparently uneventful climb through the provincial party apparatus in the Stavropol region of southern Russia, north of the Caucasus, Mr. Gorbachev was brought to Moscow to take over as

Continued on Page A16, Column 1

BUSH SENT TO RITES

Reagan Decides Against Trip, but Says He Is Ready for Meeting

By BERNARD WEINRAUB

Special to The New York Times

WASHINGTON, March 11 — President Reagan decided today against attending the funeral of Konstantin U. Chernenko, but he said he was "more than ready" to meet the new Soviet leadership.

White House officials said Vice President Bush, who is in Geneva after a visit to drought-stricken African nations, would lead the American delegation to Mr. Chernenko's funeral in Moscow on Wednesday.

President's statement, page A17.

Mr. Bush also represented the United States at the funerals of Leonid I. Brezhnev in 1982 and Yuri V. Andropov in 1984. He is to be joined by Secretary of State George P. Shultz and the United States Ambassador to Moscow, Arthur A. Hartman.

'Looking Forward' to Meeting

Mr. Reagan, in his first public comments after Mr. Chernenko's death, said he was "looking forward" to meeting the new Soviet leader, Mikhail S. Gorbachev. But the President voiced doubt that Soviet policies would change in any substantive way as a result of the selection of Mr. Gorbachev.

White House officials indicated that Mr. Reagan had seriously considered flying to Moscow for the funeral to underscore American resolve to improve relations. But after a morning meeting with leading aides, Mr. Reagan decided against the trip, largely because he felt little would be accomplished by a brief visit.

"As of 4 A.M. this morning I started

Continued on Page A17, Column 1

Arms Talks Still On

The United States and the Soviet Union agreed that a new round of arms talks would go ahead as scheduled on Tuesday. Page A20.

TRANSFER IS SWIFT

New Leader, 54, Loses No Time in Offering His Own Program

By SERGE SCHMEMANN

Special to The New York Times

MOSCOW, March 11 — The Kremlin today announced the death of Konstantin U. Chernenko and, within hours, named Mikhail S. Gorbachev to succeed him as Soviet leader.

The announcement said Mr. Chernenko died Sunday evening after a grave illness at the age of 73. He had been in office 13 months, and had been ill much of the time, leaving a minor imprint on Soviet affairs.

The succession was the quickest in Soviet history, suggesting that it had been decided well in advance. Whereas the Central Committee had taken several days to name a successor to Leonid I. Brezhnev and Yuri V. Andropov, Mr. Gorbachev was confirmed in his new job 4 hours and 15 minutes after Mr. Chernenko's death was announced.

Youngest Leader Since Stalin

Mr. Gorbachev became, at 54, the youngest man to take charge of the Soviet Union since Stalin and the seventh to head the Soviet state.

"I am well aware of the great trust put in me and of the great responsibility connected with this," he said. "I promise you, comrades, to do my utmost to faithfully serve our party, our people and the great Leninist cause."

Kremlin statement and speech by Gorbachev, pages A15-A16. Autopsy report, page A19.

In his acceptance speech on being named General Secretary, he showed his impatience to start working.

"We are to achieve a decisive turn in transferring the national economy to the tracks of intensive development," he said. "We should, we are bound to attain within the briefest period the most advanced scientific and technical positions, the highest world level in the productivity of social labor."

Real Arms Cut Urged

In world affairs, he said he valued the "successes of détente, achieved in the 1970's." Referring to the Soviet-American arms talks starting Tuesday in Geneva, Mr. Gorbachev said the Soviet Union sought a "real and major reduction in arms stockpiles, and not the development of ever-new weapon systems, be it in space or on earth."

The speech was one sign that the leadership intended to pursue business as usual despite Mr. Chernenko's

Continued on Page A15, Column 1

Tass via Associated Press

Politburo members at the House of Unions in Moscow, where the body of Konstantin U. Chernenko lay in state. From the left were Vitaly I. Vorotnikov, Mikhail S. Gorbachev, the new Soviet leader, Prime Minister Nikolai A. Tikhonov, Foreign Minister Andrei A. Gromyko, Viktor V. Grishin and Grigory V. Romanov.

Young Team Takes Reins

Kremlin Starts Shift To a New Generation

By SETH MYDANS

Special to The New York Times

MOSCOW, March 11 — With the naming of Mikhail S. Gorbachev as its new leader, the Soviet Union has finally begun its long-awaited shift to a new generation of leadership.

News Analysis

The speed with which the announcement of his appointment was made and the fast pace of scheduled funeral rites suggested that plans for the succession had been firmly in place before the death of Konstantin U. Chernenko on Sunday.

The signposts of change contained in an address by the new leader, which was read immediately to the nation, showed that Mr. Gorbachev planned to take the Soviet Union forward toward changes in policy that have been on hold for the last year.

But Western and Soviet analysts here cautioned that although Mr. Gorbachev and his economic planners have been laying their plans for months, change in the Soviet Union comes slowly and with difficulty.

They said that although the new leader seemed to have stepped into his new role with vigor, it might take months or years for him to consolidate

Continued on Page A20, Column 1

Reagan's Doctors Find a Growth, But Stress His Health Is Excellent

By PHILIP M. BOFFEY

Special to The New York Times

WASHINGTON, March 11 — Doctors discovered a second small growth in President Reagan's intestinal tract in his annual physical examination Friday, but the growth was not a precursor of cancer, the White House announced today.

The doctors also detected signs of blood in the President's stool, Larry Speakes, the White House spokesman, told reporters at a briefing where the doctors were not present. He said they had not determined the cause but believed it to be from the polyp or a false reading caused by the President's diet.

Over all, the results of the physical, perfomed at the Naval Medical Center in Bethesda, Md., were excellent, according to Mr. Reagan's doctors.

Capt. Walter Karney, chief of internal medicine at the naval hospital, who led the examining doctors, was quoted by the White House as saying:

"President Reagan continues to enjoy good health. His overall physical and mental condition is excellent. I am especially impressed with the fact that his blood pressure is lower than a year ago — this is quite remarkable."

The President's blood pressure while lying down was measured at 130 over 74. His pulse while resting was reported as 57 beats a minute, which Mr. Speakes described as "probably lower than most of us."

Mr. Reagan, who is 74 years old, is the oldest person ever to be President. His health and ability to perform in office became an issue in last year's campaign after he appeared to stumble verbally in a debate with the Demo-

Continued on Page A25, Column 1

INSIDE

Jets Strike Cities in Gulf

Iranian planes attacked the outskirts of Baghdad and Iraqi planes hit Iranian cities as stepped-up fighting continued for an eighth day. Page A3.

Bid-Rigging Charged

Key contractors acted to bar competition for concrete work on all major projects in New York City since 1978, a Federal lawsuit charged. Page B1.

In U.S., Cautious Hopes for Better Relations

By HEDRICK SMITH

Special to The New York Times

WASHINGTON, March 11 — The shift to a new generation of Soviet leadership has raised cautious hopes in the Reagan Administration that in the long run it will bring new vigor and decisiveness in the Kremlin and could lead to improvements in Soviet-American relations.

News Analysis

But President Reagan and his top advisers expect no significant changes in Soviet foreign policy to emerge over the next several months from the new leadership of Mikhail S. Gorbachev, a 54-year-old party official with a reputation for interest in modest internal economic changes.

The Soviet decision to pursue arms talks in Geneva, with only a token ceremonial interruption, is seen by Government specialists as a deliberate Kremlin move to project both strength of leadership and continuity of policy despite the death of the third Soviet leader in 28 months.

"Preserving the image of continuity at this point is at least as important as the fact of continuity," a State Department official said. "They are embarrassed at the succession of infirm leaders they've had," another Government specialist said, "and they don't want Chernenko's death to look as though it's hampering them."

The speed with which Mr. Gorbachev was named the General Secretary of the Communist Party was taken as evidence by officials here that the ruling Politburo made the key decision to select him as the new leader in late February, if not before.

Moreover, they see evidence that Mr. Gorbachev had been performing as the effective leader of both the party and the Soviet Defense Council in the final months of Konstantin U. Chernenko's life. Each of those developments adds

Continued on Page A17, Column 4

THE FALL OF COMMUNISM

SERGE SCHMEMANN

There is no shortage of theories about why the Soviet Union collapsed so precipitously. The Poles will argue it was Solidarity, whose rise in 1980 and survival despite martial law and the threat of a Soviet invasion undermined the credibility of Communist power.[1] Germans claim it was their breach of the Berlin Wall that has come to define the collapse of Communism.[2] Fans of Ronald Reagan are convinced his "Star Wars" program and his "evil empire" taunt broke the Soviet Union's morale.[3] Cold warriors believe the trigger was the unbearable military and economic cost of the nine-year war in Afghanistan. Kremlinologists identify the root cause as the rise of a new generation of leaders, personified in Mikhail Gorbachev, who believed the system could be reformed without collapsing it.[4] To economists, it was the inevitable collapse of an inherently unsustainable system of central control. As for the Russians themselves, they like to think they rose up and overthrew a system that had oppressed them for 70 years.

I was there for the decline and fall—when many of these front pages were filled—mostly in the Soviet Union, but also in Germany, Poland and elsewhere in Eastern Europe, and I would not dispute any of these factors. In retrospect, I think the real mystery is not why the Soviet state collapsed, but how it managed to run so long on empty. When I arrived in Moscow as a reporter in 1980, the operative joke among Russians was "We pretend we work, you pretend you pay."

A piece of the Berlin Wall comes down at Berlin's Brandenburg Gate on November 11, 1989.

Supporters carry Lech Walesa, a leader of the Polish Solidarity movement, which was credited as contributing to the collapse of the Soviet Union.

FURTHER READING

1. "Poland's Leader Puts Military in Charge After Union Chiefs Call a National Vote on Future of the Communist Government," see December 13, 1981, front page.
2. "Clamor in the East; East Germany Opens Frontier to the West for Migration or Travel; Thousands Cross," see November 10, 1989, front page.
3. "Would a Space-Age Defense Ease Tensions or Create Them?" see March 27, 1983, article.
4. "The Fall of Gorbachev/A Special Report; A Russian Is Swept Aside by the Forces He Released," see December 15, 1991, front page.

A man hammers away at the Berlin Wall that divided West and East Berlin for 28 years.

President Ronald Reagan put pressure on Soviet leader Mikhail Gorbachev to use his influence to tear down the barriers between East and West.

A Russian military parade through Red Square in Moscow in November of 1963.

Vladimir Lenin and Joseph Stalin at Gorky, Russia, in 1922.

That cynicism applied to every endeavor, from the empty rituals of fealty on Red Square to the propaganda nobody believed. Perhaps it was the security the state provided after decades of some of the most murderous convulsions in history; perhaps it was a reluctance to acknowledge, after all that suffering, that the ideals and promises of Communism were illusions.

Perhaps it was the very audacity of an ideology that promised no less than a reinvention of mankind that made it so hard to write off, especially as right up until its collapse it remained as potent militarily as it was economically moribund. "Conceived in utopian promise and born in the violent upheavals of the 'Great October Revolution of 1917,' the Union heaved its last in the dreary darkness of late December 1991, stripped of ideology, dismembered, bankrupt and hungry—but awe-inspiring even in its fall," I wrote in an obituary for the U.S.S.R.[5]

But that is in retrospect. To be honest, in all those years working in the Soviet Union, and then in East and West Germany before the fall of the Berlin Wall, I must acknowledge that none of us who followed the Communist East—and the Cold War was a formidable industry, employing untold thousands of analysts, academics, diplomats, spies and reporters—anticipated how rapidly and relatively bloodlessly the Soviet empire would dissolve. If you lived in Moscow back in those days—or in Berlin, or Warsaw, Prague, Budapest, Bucharest or Sofia—the repressive machinery just seemed too massive, too ubiquitous to give up without a protracted death struggle. The K.G.B. (or Stasi,[6] or Zomo, or Securitate, or whatever name the political police went by) headquarters in even a provincial city was prominent and forbidding. Surveillance reached to every corner of life, assisted by legions of willing informers. By contrast, the ranks of committed dissidents seemed minuscule and impotent.

Yes, we knew the system was rotting from inefficiency, fatigue and cynicism, but we all spoke of reform, of change, of evolution—never of collapse, and certainly not tomorrow. Only a month before the Berlin Wall fell open, Erich Honecker was still parading thousands of torch-bearing youths through Berlin.[7] And almost a year after the Germanys were reunited and most of Eastern Europe had broken loose, President George H. W. Bush was still urging

Ukraine, in what is cruelly remembered as his "chicken Kiev" speech, against succumbing to "suicidal nationalism" and seceding from the Soviet Union.[8]

Yet there were moments where we caught glimpses of the impending collapse. It's just that they were not as dramatic as the great geopolitical dramas of the time. I remember an old woman walking up to a tank in central Moscow under a wet snow and handing the soldier an apple, saying, "What, little son, are you cold?" Those tanks were supposed to instill the old terror; all they did that sorry evening was to prompt elemental grandmotherly concern. The fear was gone.

That was really what happened. Ultimately, the only real foundation of Communist rule was fear: the great fear instilled by the Terror in the Soviet Union, the famine in Ukraine and the serial crackdowns in Eastern Europe—East Germany in 1953,[9] Hungary in 1956,[10] Czechoslovakia in

Thousands of Muscovites celebrating the failure of a three-day hard-line Communist coup attempt in the Russian capital.

5 "End of the Soviet Union; The Soviet State, Born of a Dream, Dies," see December 26, 1991, front page.
6 "East Germans Face Their Accusers," see April 12, 1992, magazine article.
7 "Gorbachev Lends Honecker a Hand," see October 7, 1989, front page.
8 "After The Summit; Bush, in Ukraine, Walks Fine Line on Sovereignty," see August 2, 1991, front page.

A Soviet tank is used in East Berlin to quell anti-Communist riots in June of 1953.

Pro-Solidarity workers on a pilgrimage in southern Poland in September of 1988.

Hungarian revolutionary forces take aim at Hungarian secret police during an uprising in Budapest in 1956.

1968[11]—and the brutal repressions that persisted throughout the entire life span of the Soviet system. Fear kept the Communists in power. And when it lifted—when Polish workers lost their fear of a Soviet invasion, when Hungarian border guards stopped shooting at fleeing East Germans, when Baltic marchers confronted security forces and when the Russians themselves declared enough—there was nothing left.

This is really why the collapse was so precipitous. Without fear, Communism was just a bunch of old men trying to hide the truth. And when they lost their stomach for dispensing blood and violence, they had nothing to offer. One of my finest memories is of a balmy night in August of 1991, wandering among Russians who had gathered around the "White House," Boris Yeltsin's bastion in Moscow, to defend it against an anticipated raid by leaders of a rearguard Communist.[12] As the sun rose, it became clear that no tanks were coming, that it was over. People stretched and smiled and began to quietly wander off, free—for that glorious moment, at least—of the chains of fear.

Statues of Lenin and Stalin are removed from a Czechoslovakian town in 1990, as the nations of the Soviet bloc move away from the Soviet Union.

Russian President Boris Yeltsin urging the Russian people to resist hard-line Communist attempts to take over the central government in 1991.

SERGE SCHMEMANN *is the editorial page editor of the International Herald Tribune. Previously, he worked for the Associated Press and served as bureau chief for The New York Times in Moscow, Berlin and Jerusalem. Schmemann won the Pulitzer Prize for international reporting in 1991 for his coverage of the reunification of Germany. He also won an Emmy Award (Outstanding Individual Achievement in a Craft: Writing) in 2003 for the Discovery Channel documentary "Mortal Enemies" and is the author of a memoir of his childhood, "Echoes of a Native Land: Two Centuries of a Russian Village."*

9 "Berlin: The Story of the Uprising; From Workers' Protest It Developed Into a General Revolt," see June 21, 1953, article.

10 "Nagy Quits Warsaw Pact, Declares Hungary Neutral," see November 2, 1956, front page.

11 "Czechoslovakia Invaded by Russians and Four Other Warsaw Pact Forces," see August 21, 1968, front page.

12 "After The Coup; Gorbachev Back as Coup Fails, But Yeltsin Gains New Power," see August 22, 1991, front page.

"All the News That's Fit to Print"

The New York Times

Late Edition

Weather: Partly cloudy and cold today, chance of snow; chance of snow tonight. Partly cloudy, cold tomorrow. Temperatures: today 27-30, tonight 13-19; yesterday 14-23. Details, page C19.

VOL.CXXXV . . . No. 46,669 NEW YORK, WEDNESDAY, JANUARY 29, 1986 — 60 cents beyond 75 miles from New York City, except on Long Island. 30 CENTS

THE SHUTTLE EXPLODES

6 IN CREW AND HIGH-SCHOOL TEACHER ARE KILLED 74 SECONDS AFTER LIFTOFF

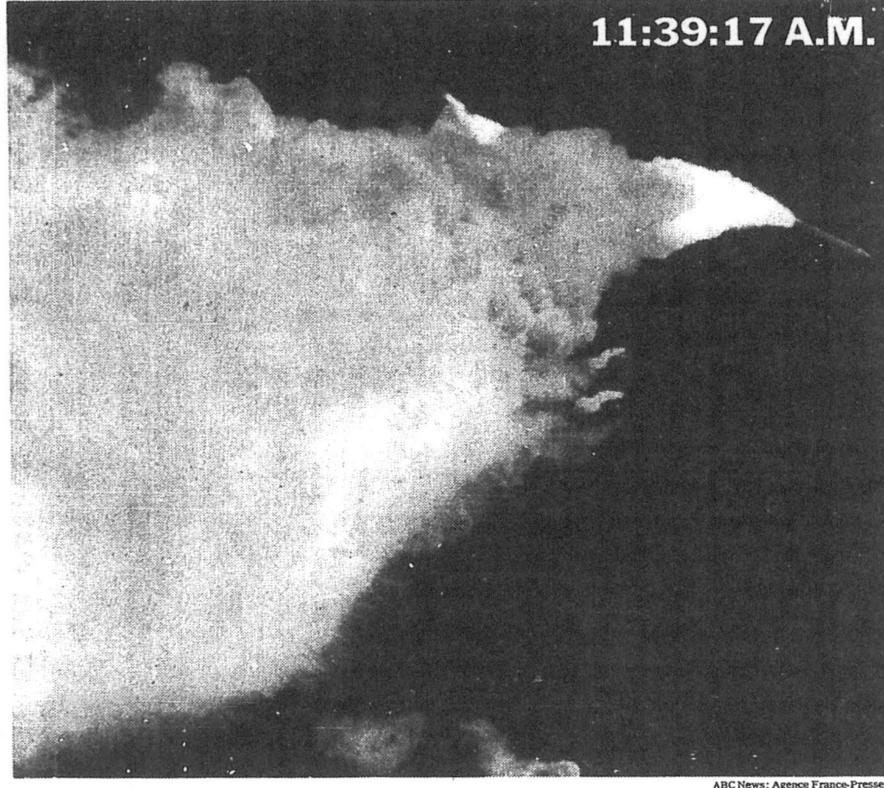

ABC News; Agence France-Presse

Thousands Watch A Rain of Debris

By WILLIAM J. BROAD

Special to The New York Times

CAPE CANAVERAL, Fla., Jan. 28 — The space shuttle Challenger exploded in a ball of fire shortly after it left the launching pad today, and all seven astronauts on board were lost.

The worst accident in the history of the American space program, it was witnessed by thousands of spectators who watched in wonder, then horror, as the ship blew apart high in the air.

Flaming debris rained down on the Atlantic Ocean for an hour after the explosion, which occurred just after 11:39 A.M. It kept rescue teams from reaching the area where the craft would have fallen into the sea, about 18 miles offshore.

It seemed impossible that anyone could have lived through the terrific explosion 10 miles in the sky, and officials said this afternoon that there was no evidence to indicate that the five men and two women aboard had survived.

No Ideas Yet as to Cause

There were no clues to the cause of the accident. The space agency offered no immediate explanations, and said it was suspending all shuttle flights indefinitely while it conducted an inquiry. Officials discounted speculation that cold weather at Cape Canaveral or an accident several days ago that slightly damaged insulation on the external fuel tank might have been a factor.

Americans who had grown used to the idea of men and women soaring into space reacted with shock to the disaster, the first time United States astronauts had died in flight. President Reagan canceled the State of the Union Message that had been scheduled for tonight, expressing sympathy for the families of the crew but vowing that the nation's exploration of space would continue.

Killed in the explosion were the mission commander, Francis R. (Dick) Scobee; the pilot, Comdr. Michael J. Smith of the Navy; Dr. Judith A. Resnik; Dr. Ronald E. McNair; Lieut. Col. Ellison S. Onizuka of the Air Force; Gregory B. Jarvis, and Christa McAuliffe.

Mrs. McAuliffe, a high-school teacher from Concord, N.H., was to have been the first ordinary citizen in space.

After a Minute, Fire and Smoke

The Challenger lifted off flawlessly this morning, after three days of delays, for what was to have been the 25th mission of the reusable shuttle fleet that was intended to make space travel commonplace. The ship rose for about a minute on a column of smoke and fire from its five engines.

Suddenly without warning, it erupted in a ball of flame.

The shuttle was about 10 miles above the earth, in the critical seconds when the two solid-fuel rocket boosters are firing as well as the shuttle's main engines. There was some discrepancy about the exact time of the blast: The National Aeronautics and Space Administration said they lost radio contact with the craft 74 seconds into the flight, plus or minus five seconds.

Two large white streamers raced away from the blast, followed by a rain of debris that etched white contrails in the cloudless sky and then slowly

Continued on Page A5, Column 4

From the Beginning to the End

The last flight of the shuttle Challenger lasted about 74 seconds. Here is the transcript, as recorded by The New York Times, of its final moments, before and after liftoff.

PUBLIC AFFAIRS OFFICER: Coming up on the 90-second point in our countdown. Ninety seconds and counting. The 51-L Mission ready to go. . . .

T minus 10, 9, 8, 7, 6, we have main engine start, 4, 3, 2, 1. And liftoff. Liftoff of the 25th space shuttle mission and it has cleared the tower. . . .

MISSION CONTROL CENTER: Watch your roll, Challenger.

PUBLIC AFFAIRS OFFICER: Roll program confirmed. Challenger now heading down range. [Pause.] Engines beginning throttling down now at 94 percent. Normal throttle for most of flight 104 percent. Will throttle down to 65 percent shortly. Engines at 65 percent. Three engines running normally. Three good cells, three good ABU's. [Pause.] Velocity 2,257 feet per second, altitude 4.3 nautical miles, down range distance 3 nautical miles. [Pause.]

Engines throttling up, three engines now at 104 percent.

MISSION CONTROL: Challenger, go with throttle up.

FRANCIS R. SCOBEE, CHALLENGER COMMANDER: Roger, go with throttle up.

PUBLIC AFFAIRS OFFICER: One minute 15 seconds, velocity 2,900 feet per second, altitude 9 nautical miles, down range distance 7 nautical miles. [Long pause.]

Flight controllers here looking very carefully at the situation. [Pause.]

Obviously a major malfunction. We have no downlink [communications from Challenger]. [Long pause.]

We have a report from the flight dynamics officer that the vehicle has exploded.

How Could It Happen? Fuel Tank Leak Feared

By MALCOLM W. BROWNE

Debris from the explosion of the shuttle Challenger was scattered so widely over the Atlantic Ocean that investigators may never recover enough of it to pin down the cause of the disaster. But suspicions quickly focused on the craft's huge external fuel tank, a potential bomb that carried more than 385,000 gallons of liquid hydrogen and more than 140,000 gallons of liquid oxygen at liftoff.

The most logical explanation is that a large leak must have occurred either in the tank itself or in the pipeline and pumping system that carried liquid hydrogen to the orbiter's three main engines.

Barbara Schwartz, a spokesman for the Johnson Space Center, acknowledged that pure liquid or gaseous hydrogen cannot burn; only if the pure hydrogen carried in the rear section of the shuttle's tank were allowed to come into contact with air, or with the liquid oxygen in the tank's nose section, could it have burned or exploded.

Potential Dangers of Hydrogen Gas

But what might have started the leak, and what could have ignited the explosion that followed?

Parallel questions, never fully answered, were raised after the fire that destroyed the German airship Hindenburg as it was landing at Lakehurst, N.J., on May 6, 1937. The shuttle Challenger, like the Hindenburg, had been releasing hydrogen gas into the air shortly before the disaster, and some of the gas might have remained aboard the craft, mixed with air and ready to detonate if exposed to the smallest spark.

Neither NASA nor Martin Marietta Aerospace, the manufacturer of the external fuel tank, would comment yesterday on possible causes of the disaster.

But the geometry of the shuttle's external fuel tank, as described by official manuals from NASA and the Rockwell International Corporation, a major shuttle contractor, suggest one potential danger point in particular: the "intertank," or midsection of the structure, which separates the liquid oxygen tank from the liquid hydrogen tank. The bulk of the hydrogen fuel is closest to the liquid oxygen at this point, and a rupture or leak in the plumbing or walls of the intertank could have flooded the two fluids together to create a gigantic bomb.

Suggestions that the unseasonably cold weather at

Continued on Page A4, Column 1

After the Shock, a Need to Share Grief and Loss

By SARA RIMER

The nation came together yesterday in a moment of disaster and loss. Wherever Americans were when they heard the news — at work, at school or at home — they shared their grief over the death of the seven astronauts, among them one who had captured their imaginations, Christa McAuliffe, the teacher from Concord, N.H., who was to have been the first ordinary citizen to go into space.

Shortly before noon, when the first word of the explosion came, daily events seemed to stop as people awaited the details and asked the same questions: "What happened? Are there any survivors?"

In offices, restaurants and stores, people gathered in front of television sets, mesmerized by the terrible scene of the shuttle exploding, a scene that would be replayed throughout the day and night. Children who had learned about Mrs. McAuliffe were watching in classrooms across the country.

It seemed to be one of those moments, enlarged and frozen, that people would remember and recount for the rest of their lives — what they were doing and where they were when they heard that the space shuttle Challenger had exploded. The need to reach out, to speak of disbelief and pain, was everywhere. Family members telephoned one another, friends telephoned friends.

"It was like the Kennedy thing," said John Hannan, who heard the news when his sister called him at his office, a personnel recruiting concern in Philadelphia. "Everyone was numb."

'I Felt Very Close to Her'

Florine Israel, a legal secretary at the New York Civil Liberties Union, echoed the sentiments of many who spoke of Mrs. McAuliffe not as an astronaut but as a friend. "I felt very close to her," she said. "She was ordinary people. She was a mother, a working woman. I felt like I was a part of it."

The image of the shuttle exploding flashed across 100 television sets in the electronics department of Macy's, in midtown Manhattan, where a crowd of workers from nearby offices and facto-

Continued on Page A3, Column 1

Reagan Lauds 'Heroes'

President Reagan, shaken by the explosion of the space shuttle, postponed his State of the Union Message. "We mourn seven heroes," he said in a talk broadcast from the White House after the disaster. "There will be more shuttle flights and more shuttle crews and, yes, more volunteers, more civilians, more teachers in space."

He also sought to console the nation's pupils, many of whom saw telecasts of the loss of the teacher who was to have been sent into space. Article and transcript, page A9.

Francis R. Scobee
Commander

Michael J. Smith
Pilot

Judith A. Resnik
Electrical Engineer

Ellison S. Onizuka
Engineer

Ronald E. McNair
Physicist

Gregory B. Jarvis
Electrical Engineer

Christa McAuliffe
Teacher

"All the News That's Fit to Print"

The New York Times

Late Edition

Weather: Mostly sunny, warm today; increasing cloudiness tonight. Mostly cloudy, chance of showers tomorrow. Temperatures: today 78-82, tonight 50-59; yesterday 52-71. Details, page A18.

VOL.CXXXV . . . No. 46,760 | Copyright © 1986 The New York Times | NEW YORK, WEDNESDAY, APRIL 30, 1986 | 60 cents beyond 75 miles from New York City, except on Long Island. | 30 CENTS

SOVIET, REPORTING ATOM PLANT 'DISASTER,' SEEKS HELP ABROAD TO FIGHT REACTOR FIRE

VIRTUAL CERTAINTY OF FAILURE SHOWN FOR SHUTTLE SEAL

New Tests Indicate That Cold and Design Flaws Doomed Challenger From Start

By DAVID E. SANGER

Special to The New York Times

WASHINGTON, April 29 — New and unpublished test results show that a failure of a safety seal on the space shuttle Challenger was virtually inevitable because of a combination of cold weather on the morning of the launching and serious design flaws.

The test results, conducted for the Presidential panel studying the accident and summarized for The New York Times, also determined that the joint would sometimes begin to fail at temperatures as high as 50 degrees Fahrenheit.

In the past, officials of the National Aeronautics and Space Administration have testified that they felt confident the shuttle could be launched at far lower temperatures without undue risk to the crew.

Failure Was Probable

The Challenger was launched Jan. 28 in 36-degree weather, but investigators estimate that the temperature of the joint that contained the failed seal was about 28 degrees, a temperature at which failure is more likely than not, the tests show.

The analysis of the accident, in which the seven crew members died, is expected to serve as the centerpiece of the Presidential commission's report, due in early June. On Monday panel members received a summary of the results, based on tests conducted in recent weeks primarily by NASA engineers and outside aerospace experts working for the commission's working group analyzing data and design.

'I Wouldn't Fly That Rocket'

"The bottom line is that temperature is the key variable, but temperature alone didn't cause it," Maj. Gen. Donald J. Kutyna, who led the working group, said in response to questions about the results. General Kutyna, a former fighter pilot, warned against a "quick fix" of the joint, saying that under the current design "even on a warm day I wouldn't fly that rocket."

The findings, when taken with testimony before the commission, strongly suggest that the middle-level NASA officials from the Marshall Space Flight Center who decided to go ahead with the launching, despite warnings about the low temperature from engineers working for the manufacturer of the booster rocket, acted with virtually no knowledge of the true performance limitations of the crucial joints and the synthetic rubber rings that were relied on to seal them.

Investigators say they are at a loss to

Continued on Page B7, Column 1

Agence France-Presse

AN IMPERIAL ANNIVERSARY: Emperor Hirohito reading a message at ceremony in Tokyo marking his 60th anniversary on the throne as well as his 85th birthday.

Indonesia Bars Two Journalists In Reagan Party

By GERALD M. BOYD

Special to The New York Times

DENPASAR, Bali, April 29 — President Reagan arrived today on this Indonesian island on the first major stop of his trip to the Far East, but the occasion was marred, White House officials said, when the Indonesian Government detained two Australian journalists in the President's party and barred them from the country.

In a separate incident, Indonesian authorities detained and expelled Barbara Crossette, a correspondent for The New York Times who was seeking to report on the Reagan visit. [Page A6].

Moments before Mr. Reagan was greeted at the island's airport by President Suharto, the Indonesian leader, and colorfully clad Balinese dancers, Indonesian authorities removed the two Australians from the White House press plane.

Ordered to Leave Country

The journalists, from the Australian Broadcasting Corporation, were ordered to leave the country in a move that White House officials said highlighted sharp differences between the United States and Indonesia over press and political freedoms.

The two correspondents, Jim Middleton and Richard D. Palfreyman, are based in Washington and had been told that they would not be allowed to enter, despite the protests of American officials, following unfavorable reports in

Continued on Page A6, Column 1

ASSESSMENT OF U.S.

Intelligence Sources Say Accident Began Days Ago and Continues

By PHILIP M. BOFFEY

Special to The New York Times

WASHINGTON, April 29 — United States intelligence sources said today that the nuclear disaster in the Soviet Union started as long as four or five days ago and was continuing to spread radioactive material into the atmosphere.

Most experts agreed that the graphite core of the Chernobyl reactor, at Pripyat in the Ukraine, had caught fire and was burning fiercely.

Details of the accident remained scarce today, the day after the Russians announced that an accident had taken place at the reactor. Without such details, experts found it difficult to speculate about the short- and long-term dangers the disaster posed to health and the environment.

Soviet Technology Faulted

But they faulted Soviet technology, which uses graphite, a form of carbon, to moderate nuclear reactions. In the United States, water is used as a moderator.

They also said the stricken reactor was not encased in a protective concrete containment dome, as is customary in the United States. The external shell could cut down on the radioactive material spewed into the atmosphere.

The experts warned that such graphite fires can be very difficult to extinguish, and that an unextinguished fire continues to release more radioactivity over the Soviet Union and other countries downwind of the reactor.

"The graphite is burning and will continue to burn for a good number of days," said Kenneth L. Adelman, the United States arms control administrator. He told Congress that, because the reactor is on a river, "there is concern over water contamination."

Europeans Are Critical

European officials and nuclear experts criticized the Soviet Union for not disclosing the accident as soon as it occurred. Some United States intelligence officials say they believe it happened Friday or possibly even Thursday. Moscow did not reveal the accident until Monday.

The Associated Press quoted a ranking information official, who was not identified, as saying that today "smoke was still billowing from the site" at the reactor.

"The roof had been blown off and large portions of the walls had caved in, and it seemed at the time that the nuclear unit just above it might still be in some danger," The A.P. said, adding that it was understood — but not officially confirmed — that much of the American intelligence information had been gathered by a KH-11 spy satellite.

Zhores Medvedev, the exiled Russian

Continued on Page A11, Column 2

Reuters

Photograph published in the February issue of Soviet Life magazine shows cooling system of a reactor at the Chernobyl nuclear power plant near Kiev.

The Nuclear Disaster

What Happened

In an unusual public admission, the Soviet state radio said a "disaster" had occurred at a nuclear power plant in the Ukraine. West German and Swedish officials said Soviet officials had asked for help in controlling a burning nuclear reactor. The nuclear accident, described by Swedish experts as potentially the worst ever at a power plant, sent a radioactive cloud across parts of the Soviet Union, Eastern Europe and Scandinavia. Moscow provided few details, but intelligence sources believe that the accident occurred last Thursday or Friday and that radiation was continuing to spew yesterday. Western experts say they believe graphite used to moderate the nuclear reaction in the plant caught fire. They disagree on whether the fire was associated with a meltdown, in which nuclear fuel rods burn out of control.

The Health Damage

The Russians reported that four nearby localities had been evacuated, two people had died and others had been treated. Western experts say they fear that a great many more, perhaps thousands, who lived near the plant may become ill or die from radiation poisoning in coming years or suffer cancers and genetic mutations later. So far, radiation levels reaching Scandinavia are not considered dangerous.

Could It Happen Here?

American commercial reactors use water rather than graphite, a flammable material, to moderate nuclear reactions. They also, unlike the Soviet reactor in the accident, have steel and concrete containment structures designed to prevent the escape of radiation. But experts say they do not have enough information to tell whether the accident holds any lessons for nuclear power safety here.

Unanswered Questions

These are among the unanswered questions: When did the accident begin? What caused the accident? How much radiation of what types has been released? How many people have been killed, injured or exposed to dangerous radiation? Have soils, crops, water and livestock in the Ukraine been dangerously contaminated?

2 DEATHS ADMITTED

Moscow, in Terse Report, Asserts the 'Radiation Situation' Is Stable

By SERGE SCHMEMANN

Special to The New York Times

MOSCOW, April 29 — The Soviet Government was reported today to have asked West Germany and Sweden for assistance in handling a fire in a nuclear reactor core.

The reports, from officials in those countries, came amid indications that a reactor accident reported Monday in the Ukraine, 70 miles north of Kiev, was a major disaster, perhaps the worst in the history of nuclear power.

[The United States formally offered humanitarian and technical assistance to the Soviet Union to help it deal with the accident. Page 6.]

'Radiation Situation' Stable

The developments came as the Soviet Government issued its second official statement on the accident in the Chernobyl nuclear power station at Pripyat, saying that the "radiation situation has now been stabilized."

The four-paragraph statement disclosed for the first time that the accident at the four-reactor plant had occurred in the No. 4 reactor, which went into service in 1983, and that the three others were in operating order, but had been shut down. Each of the four reactors had an electrical generating capacity of 1,000 megawatts.

[At one point, according to Reuters, the Moscow radio referred to the accident as "a disaster," but later dropped the word. United Press International quoted the radio as having said, "The disaster was the first one at a Soviet nuclear power plant in more than 30 years." There was a nuclear accident in the Urals in 1957 that the Soviet Government has never acknowledged.]

Four Localities Evacuated

The Soviet Government statement, which was read on the evening television news, said that two people had been killed in the accident and that the power-station settlement, an allusion to Pripyat, and three other nearby localities had been evacuated.

[Some Western officials questioned whether the death toll could be as low as two. In Washington, Kenneth L. Adelman, director of the Arms Control and Disarmament Agency, called the Soviet assertion "frankly preposterous."]

The reported Soviet request for assistance from West Germany and Sweden indicated to experts that the reactor's graphite core was burning uncontrollably, and therefore that the fuel rods in it might have melted down partly or completely. Some foreign scientists agreed that if this was the case, the accident was the worst nuclear-power disaster in history.

But the Soviet authorities provided

Continued on Page A10, Column 5

Casualties in Soviet Could Keep Rising, U.S. Experts Assert

By HAROLD M. SCHMECK Jr.

American experts said yesterday that deaths and injuries from the reactor accident in the Soviet Union may continue to mount for several weeks in the vicinity of the disaster if severe radiation has been released.

These experts on health and radiation said there appeared to be no danger for the Western Hemisphere and probably little in the Scandinavian countries, on the basis of what has been reported thus far.

When the Soviet Union announced that two people had been killed in the accident at the Chernobyl power plant in the Ukraine, there was no indication if the cause of death was radiation, fire or other nonnuclear effects.

There was an unconfirmed report from the area that many more may have died. If that report is confirmed, said Dr. Kenneth Mossman of Georgetown University Medical School, it would suggest extremely high levels of gamma radiation.

Two types of radiation exposure are likely to be involved in the damage at and near the reactor site.

The first and most immediately dangerous is external gamma radiation, which is similar to X-rays and equally penetrating. Gamma radiation can damage cells, genes and vital tissues,

Continued on Page A12, Column 1

The New York Times/Paul Hosefros

BODIES OF CHALLENGER'S CREW LEAVE FLORIDA: Coffin of Francis R. Scobee being carried from plane at Dover Air Force Base, Del. Remains of astronauts will be turned over to their families for burial. Page B7.

INSIDE

Dismissal in Secrets Case

Officials said a Pentagon aide was dismissed on the ground that he gave information about covert U.S. operations for a news article. Page A17.

Methodists' Nuclear Stand

The United Methodist Church's Council of Bishops voted to issue a pastoral letter declaring opposition to any use of nuclear weapons. Page A15.

Red Sox Pitcher Fans 20

Roger Clemens of Boston set a major league record by striking out 20 Seattle batters in the Red Sox 3-1 victory. He issued no walks. Page A27.

"All the News That's Fit to Print"

The New York Times

Late Edition
New York Today: Rain, heavy in afternoon. High 51-56. Tonight, rain changing to showers. Low 42-47. Tomorrow, gradual clearing. High 48-53. Yesterday: High 52, low 39. Details on page B9.

VOL.CXXXVI . . . No. 46,970 | Copyright © 1986 The New York Times | NEW YORK, WEDNESDAY, NOVEMBER 26, 1986 | 60 cents beyond 75 miles from New York City, except on Long Island. | 30 CENTS

IRAN PAYMENT FOUND DIVERTED TO CONTRAS; REAGAN SECURITY ADVISER AND AIDE ARE OUT

Friedman Is Guilty With 3 in Scandal

The New York Times/Jim Wilson

Stanley M. Friedman and his daughter, Betty, leaving courthouse in New Haven yesterday after guilty verdict. Rudolph W. Giuliani, below, prosecuted case.

ALL PLAN TO APPEAL

Charges of Corruption in New York Case Carry Long Prison Terms

By RICHARD J. MEISLIN
Special to The New York Times

NEW HAVEN, Nov. 25 — A jury today returned guilty verdicts against Stanley M. Friedman, the Bronx Democratic leader and long one of New York City's most powerful political figures, on all charges against him in the first Federal trial stemming from New York City's corruption scandal.

Three other defendants were also found guilty of charges including racketeering, conspiracy and mail fraud for their participation in a "racketeering enterprise" that transformed the city's Parking Violations Bureau into a tool for their corrupt personal profit.

The 12 jurors, their expressions grim, delivered the verdict at 11:11 A.M. after deliberating for three days on the eight weeks of testimony and argument in the case. The jury found Mr. Friedman and each of his co-defendants guilty of racketeering, conspiracy and mail fraud charges carrying lengthy prison sentences and heavy financial penalties.

Sentencing Set for March 1

In addition to Mr. Friedman, those found guilty were Lester N. Shafran, the former director of the Parking Violations Bureau; Michael J. Lazar, a real-estate developer and former city transportation administrator, and Marvin B. Kaplan, the chairman of Citisource Inc., a company chosen to manufacture hand-held computers to issue summonses for the parking bureau. Mr. Kaplan was also found guilty of having perjured himself while testifying before the Securities and Exchange Commission last February.

Judge Whitman Knapp, who presided over the trial, scheduled sentencing for March 1 at 10 A.M. Lawyers for all four defendants said they would file appeals at that time.

The trial of the four defendants was the first to stem from Federal investigations into corruption in the New York City government, and the United States Attorney in Manhattan, Rudolph

Continued on Page B3, Column 1

More Inquiries to Come

The verdicts in New Haven cleared the way for other inquiries into New York City corruption, perhaps lasting for several years. Page B3.

Manila and Rebels Say Cease-Fire Could Be Signed in a Day or Two

By BARBARA CROSSETTE
Special to The New York Times

MANILA, Nov. 25 — The Government of President Corazon C. Aquino said tonight that it might be within two days of signing a cease-fire agreement with Communist rebels.

Peace talks, broken off after the killing of a left-wing labor leader nearly two weeks ago, resumed this afternoon, less than 48 hours after the President said the talks would be called off if no accord was reached by Sunday.

Tonight, after eight hours of talks, the leader of the Government team, Agriculture Minister Ramon V. Mitra, told reporters, "I like to think we have just one more meeting, and then make an announcement."

He implied that the final meeting would take place Wednesday and that an agreement would be announced Thursday. "We are so close," he said.

'Technical Hitches' Cited

Declining to disclose the length of the cease-fire agreed on, Mr. Mitra said it was less than 100 days, the time sought by the Communists, but more than 30 days, the Government's proposal.

At the outset of the talks aimed at establishing a cease-fire, both sides said they hoped it would be a opportunity for more comprehensive negotiations to bring the insurgency to a formal end and bring guerrillas back into society.

It was not made clear today whether the Government had agreed to the rebels' preconditions, which included the scaling back of military deployment, the disbanding of certain paramilitary units and the restriction of the police to civilian law-enforcement duties.

The proposed truce, if begun early next month as planned, would extend through the Christmas season and pos-

Continued on Page A16, Column 1

INSIDE

Takeover Action Swings Up

A lull in merger activity abruptly ended, with billion-dollar offers for Chesebrough-Pond's, Borg-Warner and Carter Hawley Hale. Page D1.

Bumpurs Case Revived

New York State's top court reinstated charges against a policeman who killed a knife-wielding, emotionally disturbed woman in 1984. Page B1.

President Reagan deferring reporters' questions to Attorney General Edwin Meese 3d at news conference yesterday in Washington. With them were Donald T. Regan, left, White House chief of staff, and Larry Speakes, the White House spokesman, next to the President. Mr. Reagan had just announced the resignation of Vice Adm. John M. Poindexter, far right, as national security adviser and the dismissal of Lieut. Col. Oliver L. North, right, for his role in the Iranian arms affair.

The New York Times/Paul Hosefros

The Iran Affair: A Presidency Damaged

How Arms Funds Were Diverted: The Meese Version

Account is based on statements by Attorney General Edwin Meese 3d. He placed all transactions between January 1986 and the present.

The United States provides approximately $12 million worth of arms to Israel.

↓

Israelis sell the arms to "representatives of Iran."

↓

The amount of payment, including profits, is negotiated between "representatives of Israel" and "representatives of Iran," then transferred to the Israeli representatives.

↓

Israeli representatives transfer to the C.I.A. the full amount of money owed to the United States for the arms already supplied plus money for any transportation costs involved. The C.I.A. uses these funds to repay the Department of Defense.

Profits — estimated to be between $10 million and $30 million — are then deposited into Swiss bank accounts established by the rebels fighting in Nicaragua. These funds were not touched by any American.

Both Friends and Foes See Reagan as Isolated

By R. W. APPLE Jr.
Special to The New York Times

WASHINGTON, Nov. 25 — After six years of seeming invulnerability, President Reagan has been grievously damaged by the crisis over secret arms shipments to Iran.

News Analysis

With a unanimity rare in Washington, leading Republican and Democratic politicians agreed today that the disclosure of payments to the Nicaraguan rebels and the departure of two White House aides had probably hurt the Administration more than it helped. Some think the damage may be irreparable.

A week of almost unrelieved criticism of Mr. Reagan's secret decision to send arms to Iran, and of startling public bickering among senior Administration officials, has created the image of a President isolated, stuck with an unpopular policy and uncharacteristically defensive. The disclosures today produced a sensation in Washington unmatched, perhaps, since the days of the Watergate crisis.

'Probably No Smoking Gun'

"There is probably no smoking gun here," said a man who served in the White House during the Watergate years. "But there is a new mess in Washington, if not a new Watergate. There will be a whole string of fresh disclosures in the months to come, and that will throw the Administration off stride.

"It will hurt the effort in Nicaragua, it will hurt the campaign against terrorism and it will hurt Reagan — unless, of course, he gets lucky and something happens in Iran that shows he was right after all."

In the weeks to come, Mr. Reagan seems certain to find his credibility, his competence and his control under stern challenge.

On a personal level, Mr. Reagan remains the most popular President of modern times, and he has shown enormous resilience in the past. But he approaches the last two years of his Administration — a time when the strongest Presidents have seen their power slip slowly away — with the Senate and the House of Representatives under Democratic control, with severe budgetary problems demanding attention and now with months or perhaps even

Continued on Page A12, Column 5

More on the Policy Crisis

Legal questions were raised by the operation involving the Nicaraguan rebels, including whether criminal laws had been broken. Page A11.

•

The contra-aid mystery may be explained by the disclosure, Congressional investigators and Administration officials said. Page A13.

•

Israel said it sent arms to Iran at the "request" of Washington and did not know some payments were channeled to the contras. Page A12.

•

A Saudi arms dealer played a central role in financing the Iranian purchase of arms, Israeli and American sources said. Page A13.

•

Doubts were raised by intelligence experts, officials and lawmakers concerning the Administration's explanation of the arms shipments and assertions that only two American Government officials knew money was going to the contras. Page A11.

•

A sister of an American hostage held in Lebanon wrote to President Reagan in support of his Iran initiative and expressed "a deep sense of shame" that she had not spoken out sooner. Page A16.

•

Alton G. Keel Jr., the acting national security adviser, is described as an intelligent and hard-working man who has seldom taken a visible leadership role. Page A12.

•

Nancy Reagan dismissed the idea that the President had been badly damaged by the growing turmoil in his Administration. Page A10.

DISARRAY DEEPENS

Was Not 'Fully Informed' About Secret Moves, President Asserts

By BERNARD WEINRAUB
Special to The New York Times

WASHINGTON, Nov. 25 — President Reagan said today that he had not been in full control of his Administration's Iran policy, and the White House said that as a consequence up to $30 million intended to pay for American arms had been secretly diverted to rebel forces in Nicaragua.

At the same time, the President announced that two men he held responsible — Vice Adm. John M. Poindexter,

Statement by President Reagan and Meese's comments, page A10.

the national security adviser, and Lieut. Col. Oliver L. North, a member of the admiral's staff — had left their posts.

With the Administration already in turmoil over the earlier disclosure of clandestine arms shipments to Iran, and with speculation rampant about a major overhaul of the White House staff, the President's statement seemed to deepen a sense of disarray. By all accounts, Mr. Reagan now faces the most serious crisis in his six-year Presidency.

Shultz to Control Policy

The State Department, meanwhile, said Secretary of State George P. Shultz had been given control over future Iran policy, authority that apparently met his condition for remaining in office. State Department officials, including Mr. Shultz, have said they were left in the dark on much of the Iran operation. [Page A12.]

Mr. Reagan stunned legislators and ranking Administration officials by announcing in a televised session with reporters that he had not been "fully informed" of some details of the Iran operation and that Admiral Poindexter and Colonel North were leaving after "serious questions of propriety had been raised."

Inquiry Still Under Way

Mr. Reagan said that, "although not directly involved," Admiral Poindexter had "asked to be relieved of his assignment" and would return to Navy duties. Colonel North, the President said, "has been relieved of his duties on the National Security Council staff." Colonel North was widely reported to be the central figure in the Iran arms deal.

After Mr. Reagan's announcement, Attorney General Edwin Meese 3d said the Justice Department was still investigating how Nicaraguan rebel forces, known as contras, received "somewhere between $10 and $30 million"

Continued on Page A11, Column 1

TOP LEGISLATORS PROMISE INQUIRY

Likely Violations of Law Cited — Contra Aid May Suffer

By STEVEN V. ROBERTS
Special to The New York Times

WASHINGTON, Nov. 25 — Congressional leaders expressed astonishment today at the latest disclosures about United States dealings with Iran and vowed to investigate the Administration's actions.

The leaders asserted that several laws had probably been violated when funds paid by Iran for weapons were transferred to the Nicaraguan rebels.

The leaders also said Congress would probably approve legislation next year cutting off aid to the Nicaraguan rebels and would see to it that the head of the National Security Council would have to be confirmed by the Senate.

But the biggest question on Capitol Hill today was whether President Reagan and his chief aides had known about the operation.

Representative Jim Wright, the Texas Democrat who will become Speaker of the House in January, voiced skepticism about White House explanations that Vice Adm. John M. Poindexter, the national security adviser, was the highest ranking official to know about the operation.

It "defies logic," Mr. Wright told reporters, to believe that such a critical

Continued on Page A11, Column 1

"All the News That's Fit to Print"

The New York Times

Late Edition
New York: Today, partly sunny skies. High 48-58. Tonight, partly cloudy. Low 40-45. Tomorrow, variable clouds and sun, showers. High 50-55. Yesterday: High 48, low 32. Details, page C32.

VOL.CXXXVII . . . No. 47,348 NEW YORK, WEDNESDAY, DECEMBER 9, 1987 — 50 cents beyond 75 miles from New York City, except on Long Island. — 30 CENTS

REAGAN AND GORBACHEV SIGN MISSILE TREATY AND VOW TO WORK FOR GREATER REDUCTIONS

Associated Press

A.B.A. Rates Kennedy

Judge Anthony M. Kennedy, the Supreme Court nominee, has received the American Bar Association's highest rating. Page A29.

Estimate of Risk Of Dioxin Is Cut In Cancer Study

By PHILIP SHABECOFF
Special to The New York Times

WASHINGTON, Dec. 8 — The Environmental Protection Agency, in a new draft study with the potential for far-reaching policy implications, has sharply reduced its estimate of the cancer-causing potential of dioxin, a widespread chemical pollutant.

Dioxin has been described as among the most potent toxic substances known to man. But in a new risk assessment, the E.P.A. concludes that dioxin's potency as a cancer-inducing substance is one-sixteenth that of the agency's original estimate two years ago.

Agency officials said, however, that even considering the revised risk levels, dioxin is still the most toxic of the cancer-linked substances regulated by the agency.

Under the new risk assumptions, dioxin is 10,000 times more likely to cause cancer than PCB's, or polychlorinated biphenyls, at the same level of exposure, one agency official said. But the new assessment lowers the risk of dioxin by a significant amount and "brings it in out of left field," the official said.

Since dioxin appears in such minute quantities, the effect of the reassessment might be that previously troubling levels will be considered far less dangerous or even safe. The new report appears to strike a compromise between those scientists who see the alarm over dioxin as exaggerated and

Continued on Page D27, Column 1

ECONOMY REPORTED HOLDING UP WELL SINCE STOCK SLIDE

A Recession Is Unlikely Soon, Analysts Say, Despite Slip in Consumer Spending

By ROBERT D. HERSHEY Jr.
Special to The New York Times

WASHINGTON, Dec. 8 — Defying widespread predictions, the economy has held up well since the stock market collapsed in mid-October and an imminent recession appears quite unlikely, private and Government analysts maintain.

Many forecasters who had initially slashed estimates for growth next year have been nudging them upward of late, prompted by successive sets of data indicating that the stock market tremors have yet to shake the economy's foundations.

These improved forecasts come despite consumer spending that slowed before the market plunge and seems to have lost further impetus since.

Spending Tied to Incomes

But while consumer spending has slowed, it has not dropped as sharply as many economists had feared. As best as economists can determine, people have apparently decided to base their spending on their incomes, not on their assets. And so their losses in the stock market have not dramatically affected their buying habits.

While the housing sector has been slumping, the decline in construction of new homes and sales of homes stems from the rising interest rates that preceded the stock market's collapse, and much of those increases have been reversed.

"I have zero evidence of an '88 early recession," said Joseph W. Duncan, chief economist for Dun & Bradstreet, who has just completed surveys of business expectations and production and investment plans. "Corporate America so far is saying, 'We're just going to move ahead because we have strong orders.' "

G.N.P. Loss 'Added Back'

An economist for a large New York bank said that, of a dozen economists with whom he lunched today, more than half had "added back" much or all of the loss of 1988 gross national product they had subtracted from their late-October G.N.P. estimates.

And in a survey last week, 51 economists polled by Blue Chip Economic Indicators, an Arizona-based newsletter,

Continued on Page D2, Column 5

Associated Press

Mikhail S. Gorbachev being welcomed yesterday by President Reagan at the White House.

HOW TO DESTROY THE 2,611 MISSILES

Treaty Details Ways but U.S. Withholds Data on Sites

By MICHAEL R. GORDON
Special to The New York Times

WASHINGTON, Dec. 8 — The text of the treaty signed today by President Reagan and Mikhail S. Gorbachev spells out how hundreds of American and Soviet inspectors will insure that 2,611 American and Soviet missiles are smashed, exploded, crushed, burned or launched to be destroyed.

But at American insistence, the text released today to the press and television does not include a 73-page annex that describes exactly where the weapons are kept.

American officials said that because of the danger from terrorists, the information was too sensitive to publish. Soviet officials, who have it, said that there was no reason why the information should be withheld and that it would be published in Moscow.

Rights of Inspectors

Under the treaty provisions, inspectors will have the right to visit installations on each side to confirm information provided by the other side. And when bases and support installations are eliminated, officials from each side will conduct special "close out" inspections. Inspectors will also observe the destruction of missiles.

Each side will have an annual quota of short-notice inspections for 13 years after the treaty goes into force.

Inspectors can make use of a camera that instantly produces two photographs, one for each side. The photos will be be taken not by the inspectors but by escorts from the nation being inspected. But the escorts are to photograph what the inspectors want.

To carry out inspections in the Soviet Union, American officials will fly to Moscow or Irkutsk. Once there, they

Continued on Page A21, Column 1

A Tempered Optimism

At the End of an Unlikely Journey, Reagan And Gorbachev Are Mindful of Differences

By R. W. APPLE Jr.
Special to The New York Times

News Analysis

WASHINGTON, Dec. 8 — Even for this city, which long ago mislaid its sense of wonder, this was a thrilling day, bathed in a glow of satisfaction at what has been achieved and of optimism about what may lie just ahead.

Often Washington looks on the dark side, especially where the Soviet Union is concerned, but there were few in the capital who failed to feel a frisson of excitement as Mikhail S. Gorbachev stepped from his limousine and grasped Ronald Reagan's hand, few in the country who were immune to the drama of television pictures of the two leaders in profile with the red Soviet flag whipping in the wind behind them.

If, as Henry A. Kissinger once said, Americans oscillate between despair and euphoria in their attitudes toward the Soviet Union, today's emotions may be relatively short-lived. Certainly the hopes raised in June 1973, when Leonid I. Brezhnev was welcomed to the White House by Richard M. Nixon under steel-gray skies much like this morning's, proved ephemeral.

Both Mr. Reagan, with his call for "a heavy dose of realism," and Mr. Gorbachev, with his reminder of the "profound historical, ideological, socio-economic and cultural differences" that divide the superpowers, seemed to be warning of the limits of the process of accommodation they have begun.

But it is nonetheless remarkable that it has begun at all, and that these two men are those sponsoring it. For each, the moment at which they swapped pens after signing the treaty banning medium- and shorter-range nuclear arms represented the end of a long, im-

Continued on Page A20, Column 1

The Arms Treaty

The arms treaty and excerpts from the protocols to it are on pages A24-26. Additional coverage of yesterday's events, including remarks by President Reagan and Mikhail S. Gorbachev, appears on pages A20-23.

A MOOD OF WARMTH

As Summit Talks Begin, the Attention Shifts to Strategic Arms

By DAVID K. SHIPLER
Special to The New York Times

WASHINGTON, Dec. 8 — With fervent calls for a new era of peaceful understanding, President Reagan and Mikhail S. Gorbachev today signed the first treaty reducing the size of their nations' nuclear arsenals.

The President and the Soviet leader, beginning three days of talks aimed at even broader reductions, pledged to build on the accord by striving toward what Mr. Gorbachev called "the more important goal," reducing long-range nuclear weapons.

In their White House conversations, the leaders were said to have reviewed their previous proposals aimed at furthering those negotiations, and they established an arms-control working group of ranking officials to hold parallel sessions.

'Mine is Mikhail'

An immediate mood of warmth was established as the two leaders agreed this morning to call each other by their first names, a White House official said. He quoted the President as telling Mr. Gorbachev, "My first name is Ron."

Mr. Gorbachev answered, "Mine is Mikhail."

"When we're working in private session," Mr. Reagan reportedly said, "we can call each other that."

The new treaty, which provides for the dismantling of all Soviet and American medium- and shorter-range missiles, establishes the most extensive system of weapons inspection ever negotiated by the two countries, including placing technicians at sensitive sites on each other's territory.

The Mood for Talking

The signing, the fruition of years of negotiation, set the mood for two and a half hours of talks between the leaders. The talks were "very serious, substantive discussions," Secretary of State George P. Shultz said tonight before a formal dinner in the White House.

The visit to Washington by Mr. Gorbachev was the first by a Soviet leader since Leonid I. Brezhnev was here 14 years ago, and it took on immediate drama as Mr. Reagan, who entered office with deep suspicions of the Soviet Union, welcomed Mr. Gorbachev on the South Lawn of the White House.

"I have often felt that our people should have been better friends long ago," he told his guest as they stood

Continued on Page A20, Column 1

Air Crash Inquiry Is Said to Focus On Disgruntled Ex-Worker on Jet

By ROBERT REINHOLD
Special to The New York Times

TEMPLETON, Calif., Dec. 8 — The Federal Bureau of Investigation said today that criminal activity was strongly suspected in the crash of a jetliner that smashed into a cattle ranch here Monday after the pilot reported gunfire in the passenger cabin.

The crash killed all 43 people aboard the plane operated by Pacific Southwest Airlines, which last May was acquired by USAir.

Suspicion focused on a disgruntled former employee of USAir, dismissed last month on charges of stealing money from the company, who boarded the plane along with his former supervisor. The two men, together with all 36 other passengers and 5 crew members, died when the four-engine British Aerospace 146 Series 200 jet plunged into a green, oak-studded hillside near here in central California.

A Government official said he had been told that the employee, David A. Burke, had left a message on a friend's recording machine telling her that he was going to take care of the person who had dismissed him. But by the time she heard the message, the plane had crashed.

ABC News quoted unidentified officials as saying Mr. Burke left a suicide message indicating he intended to kill his former supervisor. The network said the authorities believed the former employee boarded the flight with a .44 magnum pistol.

Richard T. Bretzing, special agent in charge of the F.B.I.'s Los Angeles of-

Continued on Page D27, Column 3

The Emerging Candidate: Who Is Senator Simon?

By ROBIN TONER
Special to The New York Times

WASHINGTON, Dec. 8 — Senator Paul Simon of Illinois promises an administration of good deeds. He spins the vision of a nurturing Government.

If elected President, he says, he would give the unemployed an $8 billion-a-year job program. He would protect the elderly from the towering costs of nursing home care. The 11 books he has written bristle with Federal solutions to the nation's problems: a new program to rebuild the country's bridges and highways, a new Reconstruction Finance Corporation, a new drive to combat illiteracy.

"I want a Government that cares," he says. "I want a Government that helps people."

In a campaign dominated by tests of character, Mr. Simon's test has arisen not in his personal life but around his public policy. The issue is the cost of his unquestioned good intentions, the practicality of a politician who often affects a disdain for politics, the credibility of a man whose slogan is, "Isn't it time to believe again?"

In the simplest terms, his rivals for the Democratic nomination now demand that he explain how he would pay for it all and balance the budget in three years, as he promises.

"Paul, you're not a pay-as-you-go Democrat, you're a promise-as-you-go Democrat," Representative Richard A. Gephardt declared last week in a nationally

Continued on Page A28, Column 1

The New York Times/Paul Hosefros

Mr. Gorbachev applauding after he and Mr. Reagan signed copies of the treaty. At rear, staff members exchanged the copies so that each could be signed by the other leader.

News Summary, Page A2

INSIDE

Sandinistas Down American

An American pilot has been shot down over Nicaragua while "engaged in enemy activity," the Nicaraguan Defense Minister said. Page A3.

Reds Trade Dave Parker

The Cincinnati Reds traded Dave Parker, their aging but productive power hitter, to the Oakland Athletics for two young pitchers. Page A31.

Cardinal Krol to Retire

John Cardinal Krol, the Archbishop of Philadelphia, announced that he would retire on Feb. 11. Page A28.

$10 Million for Met Wing

Henry R. Kravis, a New York investor, has pledged $10 million to the Metropolitan Museum of Art to complete a new wing. Page C25.

Anti-Corruption Fund Asked

Top New York law-enforcement officials asked the Legislature for a $10 million fund to uncover corruption by officials and businesses. Page B1.

"All the News That's Fit to Print"

The New York Times

Late Edition
New York: Today, rain and fog. High 44-48. Tonight, rain ending, fog. Low 37-40. Tomorrow, clouds, fog, afternoon clearing. High 47-52. Yesterday: High 45, low 41. Details are on page A19.

VOL.CXXXVII . . No. 47,469 — Copyright © 1988 The New York Times — NEW YORK, FRIDAY, APRIL 8, 1988 — 50 cents beyond 75 miles from New York City, except on Long Island. — 30 CENTS

GORBACHEV AND AFGHAN LEADER SAY WAY SEEMS CLEAR TO START SOVIET TROOP PULLOUT BY MAY 15

Tass via Agence France-Presse
Najibullah, left, the Afghan leader, and Mikhail S. Gorbachev at meeting in Tashkent, U.S.S.R.

GENEVA PACT SEEN

Acceptance of U.S. Plan on Arms Aid Indicated in Joint Statement

By PHILIP TAUBMAN
Special to The New York Times

MOSCOW, April 7 — The Soviet Union and Afghanistan said today that they believed the last barriers to a negotiated settlement of the war in Afghanistan had been eliminated.

The two Governments indicated, but did not explicitly confirm, that they had accepted an American formula breaking the last remaining deadlock at the Geneva talks aimed at ending the eight-year-old war.

The compromise would permit Washington to continue providing military aid to the Afghan guerrillas during a withdrawal of Soviet forces at a level commensurate with the aid Moscow gives to the Afghan Government.

Signing Likely Next Week

Western diplomats here said the announcement appeared to clear the way for quick completion of the Geneva talks, with the signing of an agreement likely before the end of next week.

In Washington, Reagan Administration officials voiced cautious optimism that a settlement would soon be formally concluded and lead to a Soviet withdrawal. But they also said they were reserving final judgment until the United States received a formal response from the Soviet Union and reviewed the detailed Geneva accords. [Page A10.]

In a joint statement issued after a meeting today, Mikhail S. Gorbachev and the Afghan leader, Najibullah, said the Soviet Union would begin withdrawing its troops on May 15 if the Geneva accords were completed within the next few days. [Text of statement, page A10.]

Reagan Visit Seen as Factor

The departure date, originally set by Moscow for early February but postponed as the negotiations bogged down, suggested that Mr. Gorbachev wanted to start bringing Soviet soldiers home before President Reagan's visit to Moscow in late May.

Mr. Gorbachev and Mr. Najibullah met in the Soviet Central Asian city of Tashkent, 190 miles north of the Afghan border.

Mr. Gorbachev later told workers at two collective farms near Tashkent: "There is a certainty that an agreement will be signed on a political settlement. I think that Pakistan and Afghanistan will come to an agreement. And we with the Americans will agree to be guarantors, I think."

Resolution of the Afghan conflict, which Soviet forces entered in Decem-

Continued on Page A10, Column 3

MAJOR DEMOCRATS IN NEW YORK STATE BACKING DUKAKIS

AN INITIATIVE BY CUOMO

Urging Leaders to Choose, He Remains Neutral to Avoid Anger in Jackson Camp

By FRANK LYNN

Governor Cuomo yesterday urged top New York Democrats to choose a Presidential candidate to support, and, as he expected, most of them started lining up behind Gov. Michael S. Dukakis of Massachusetts.

The move, orchestrated through the Democratic state chairman, Laurence J. Kirwan, allowed the Governor to bow to the preference of most of the state's Democratic leaders. At the same time, it permitted him to maintain his own public neutrality and thus not offend New York supporters of the Rev. Jesse Jackson, with whom Mr. Cuomo will have to deal long after 255 delegates to the Democratic National Convention are picked in the state's Presidential primary April 19.

"The Dukakis campaign people have been complaining that they can't get anywhere in the state with the Governor hanging back," said a leading Democrat.

Dukakis a Clear Choice

He added, "They asked the Governor that if he did not endorse Dukakis, to at least release the Democratic leaders on the ground that Dukakis had played the Cuomo game, showing him respect and deference."

Mr. Cuomo gave no personal signal of his own preference, party officials said. But he was aware that Governor Dukakis was the clear favorite among county leaders, legislators and other public officials who make up the state's Democratic leadership, particularly after the sweeping Dukakis victory in the Wisconsin primary last Tuesday.

So he knew what to expect when Mr. Kirwan, saying that he was speaking for the Governor, urged the leaders yesterday to choose one of the party's three remaining active Presidential candidates: Mr. Dukakis, Mr. Jackson or Senator Albert Gore Jr. of Tennessee.

'I Want You to Pick'

Addressing about half of the 300-member Democratic State Committee at the New York Hilton in Manhattan yesterday afternoon, Mr. Kirwan said, "The Governor now feels that there are three candidates in this race, and 'I want you to pick one of the three.' "

The first party leader to take the advice was Joseph F. Crangle, the Erie

Continued on Page A18, Column 4

The New York Times/David Jennings
Governor Cuomo yesterday.

Hondurans Riot At U.S. Offices; Four Said to Die

By Reuters

TEGUCIGALPA, Honduras, Friday, April 8 — The United States Consulate was set afire Thursday night and at least four people were killed during a riot sparked by the expulsion of a suspected drug dealer to the United States, radio stations reported.

Witnesses said shots were fired from inside the consulate building and protesters responded with pistol fire. At least 4 students died and at least 2 were wounded as the crowd of 1,500 protesters scattered in panic, radio stations said. It was not clear who fired from inside the building.

The third floor of the consulate was reported burning fiercely and part of the outside of the main United States Embassy building across the street was also ablaze as firefighters arrived. Power was cut off, blacking out street lights and adding to the confusion as the shooting started, reports said.

20 Cars on Fire

The shots came after the protesters had set fire to part of the embassy, hurling rocks and flaming sticks, and had broken into the consulate building. At least 20 cars belonging to embassy personnel were burning in the street.

About 200 anti-riot officers and firefighters moved in to quell the violence, which was being called the worst anti-American riot ever in Honduras, traditionally a close American ally.

[The Associated Press quoted an embassy spokesman, Michael O'Brien, as saying that there was extensive damage to embassy buildings but that no American citizens had been injured. He said the Hondu-

Continued on Page A9, Column 1

Authorities Debate Increased Firepower For Narcotics Agents

By PETER KERR

A rise in the use of machine pistols by drug dealers in New York — and a decision to issue submachine guns this month to 300 Federal drug agents in the region — has officials arguing about the safest way to arm agents and the police in the densely populated city.

The growth of violent crack-dealing organizations in New York in the last two years has brought a new class of powerful handguns into general use in the underworld in the city, Federal officials said. The weapons hold 20 or more rounds and can be easily converted into machine guns that fire bursts of bullets with each pull of the trigger.

Crack organizations in Brooklyn and Queens are sending couriers, often by bus, to buy the guns in Texas, Georgia and Alabama, where firearms laws are more lax, according to the New York office of the Federal Bureau of Alcohol, Tobacco and Firearms.

Automatic weapons have been used by drug organizations in Florida and elsewhere in the country since the early 1980's. Drug dealers in New York have generally used cheaper less-powerful weapons, until recently.

The latest example of the danger posed by criminals armed with such weapons occurred Tuesday night, the police said, when four men sprayed a crowded Brooklyn intersection with

Continued on Page B5, Column 4

One Week of Killings

New York City police recorded 17 deaths by violence last week. Behind each police report is the story of a life. Page B1.

Tokyo's Surging Stock Prices Top Record Set Before October Crash

By SUSAN CHIRA
Special to The New York Times

TOKYO, Friday, April 8 — Prices on the Tokyo stock market continued today to rise above the peak reached before last fall's global market collapse. No other major stock market has returned to its pre-crash levels.

Yesterday, the Nikkei average of 225 stocks closed at 26,769.22 yen, well above the previous record of 26,646.43 yen reached on Oct. 14, five days before share prices around the world collapsed. That increase was 258.05 yen, or 97-hundredths of 1 percent. In trading today the Nikkei had risen another 141.68 yen, to 26,910.90, by the close of the morning session.

The surge in prices demonstrates the underlying strength in the Tokyo Stock Exchange, the world's largest in terms of money invested. While the Tokyo market has now exceeded pre-crash levels, the New York and London markets have posted comparatively modest advances and are well below their record levels.

[In a move to bolster investor confidence in the market, the New York Stock Exchange proposed a sharp increase in the level of capital required for specialist brokers to buy or sell stocks. Page D1.]

High corporate profits, low interest rates, continuing economic growth, and Government actions to prevent any drastic fall in stock prices have driven the Tokyo market's rebound, analysts here said.

Fears of Overheating

Some Japanese officials, notably Satoshi Sumita, governor of the Bank of Japan, have expressed fears that the Tokyo market could be overheating. Mr. Sumita told reporters yesterday that share prices were rising too fast in relation to the rate of economic growth.

Other analysts point out that any panic in other stock markets might spread to Tokyo, given the degree to

Continued on Page D6, Column 1

ACCORD INDICATED ON STABLE DOLLAR

Officials Expect Action When 7 Nations Meet Next Week

By PETER T. KILBORN
Special to The New York Times

WASHINGTON, April 7 — American and foreign officials indicated today that they expect the United States and six other leading industrial nations to agree next week to try to keep the dollar's value roughly at its current level for the foreseeable future.

The officials thus confirmed speculation in the financial markets that after a couple of weeks of currency turbulence the countries want a steady dollar and will do what they can to keep it steady. Some economists had suggested that the dollar, which closed today at 125.72 Japanese yen, should decline some more.

The officials also said the countries, known as the Group of Seven, could report some progress on a proposal by Treasury Secretary James A. Baker 3d to use prices of gold and other commodities in guiding their economic policies. But they said that while Mr. Baker favors the immediate adoption of such a price index in making Group of Seven policy, other nations could urge delay.

The anticipation by market traders of a renewed commitment to a stable

Continued on Page D2, Column 1

Robert T. Bakker

A comparative drawing showing the relative sizes of a pygmy tyrannosaur, center, a previously unknown species; a tyrannosaurus rex, a tiger and a polar bear.

It Would Seem T. Rex Had a Pygmy Cousin

By MALCOLM W. BROWNE

Paleontologists reported yesterday that a peculiar dinosaur skull, unearthed 46 years ago but erroneously identified at the time, is actually that of a previously unknown genus, a pygmy tyrannosaur possibly related to modern birds.

The announcement yesterday at the Cleveland Museum of Natural History culminated a yearlong study of the skull by three scientists who recognized it as a fossil of extraordinary importance.

Many paleontologists believe that the dinosaurs never entirely died out but merely evolved into birds, and the identification of the new genus supports that theory. Differences of opinion persist, however, as to which dinosaurs might have been the ancestors of birds.

The skull was found in Montana in 1942 but had never stirred particular scientific interest because it was assumed to have come from a gorgosaur, a large flesh-eating dinosaur of the late Cretaceous period, of which many specimens have been collected and studied.

Over the years several scientists questioned this assumption, but it was not until last year that Dr. Robert T. Bakker of the University of Colorado, on a visit to the museum, challenged the label on the skull and began an investigation.

He enlisted as collaborators Dr. Michael E. Williams of the Cleveland Museum and Dr. Philip Currie of the Tyrrell Museum of Paleontology in Drumheller, Alberta, Canada. Dr. Currie is an expert in theropod, or "beast-footed," dinosaurs, a category to which the two-foot skull belonged.

"We found that this animal was much more like a tyrannosaur than a

Continued on Page A16, Column 1

Guard's Bullet Reportedly Struck Israeli Girl Killed on West Bank

By JOHN KIFNER
Special to The New York Times

ELON MOREH, Israeli-Occupied West Bank, April 7 — As angry, armed Jewish settlers turned the funeral here for a teen-age girl into a passionate rally, an army investigation was reported today to have found a bullet from an Israeli guard's rifle in the victim's body.

The report raised questions about the emotionally charged reports on Wednesday that the 15-year-old girl, Tirza Porat, had been stoned to death by Palestinian villagers. Army spokesmen said late tonight that it was not clear what had caused the girl's death and that an investigation was under way.

Israeli soldiers shot and killed a Palestinian youth outside the village of Beita today as they searched the hills surrounding the site where Wednesday's confrontation took place. The army said the unidentified youth was a suspect who was trying to flee. There was no independent confirmation of this report, and the death raised the number of Palestinians known to have been killed in four months of protest here to 123.

The army also blew up five houses in the sealed-off village, saying they were the homes of people known to have taken part in the clash on Wednesday.

Palestinian accounts of the events in Beita were not immediately available because the village and the surrounding area were sealed off by the army. The military order to shut the Palestine Press Service, which maintained a

Continued on Page A3, Column 1

INSIDE

Eggs Linked to Illness

Clean, inspected Grade A eggs may be responsible for an increase in food poisoning in the Northeast, Federal researchers say. Page A16.

Speakes Roils the Capital

Larry Speakes, President Reagan's ex-spokesman, depicts him in a new book as inspiring but uninformed. Washington Talk, page A20.

News Summary, Page A2

"All the News That's Fit to Print"

The New York Times

Late Edition
New York: Today, mostly sunny, more seasonable. High 38-44. Tonight, clear, cold. Low 18-28. Tomorrow, becoming cloudy, showers. High 36-41. Yesterday: High 53, low 39. Details, page D20.

VOL.CXXXVIII . . No. 47,727 — NEW YORK, THURSDAY, DECEMBER 22, 1988 — 35 CENTS
50 cents beyond 75 miles from New York City, except on Long Island.

DREXEL CONCEDES GUILT ON TRADING; TO PAY $650 MILLION

CIVIL CASE REMAINS

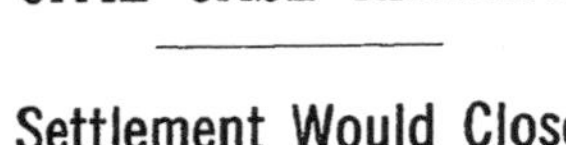

Settlement Would Close 2-Year Investigation Into Boesky Deals

The New York Times
Frederick H. Joseph

Black Star
Michael R. Milken

By STEPHEN LABATON

In the largest settlement ever of Federal securities law violations, Drexel Burnham Lambert Inc., the Wall Street powerhouse, agreed in principle yesterday to plead guilty to six felony counts and pay $650 million.

If the settlement is approved by officials in Washington, it would end an investigation lasting more than two years into Drexel's relationship with Ivan F. Boesky, the Wall Street speculator who settled insider-trading charges in 1986. He was the Government's main witness against Drexel.

Government lawyers have said the investment firm and Mr. Boesky traded on insider information and concealed the ownership of stock in more than a dozen deals from 1984 to 1986. Many were related to corporate takeovers and restructurings.

The settlement, which will include guilty pleas to charges of mail fraud, wire fraud and securities fraud, marked a stunning reversal by the firm. A day earlier, Drexel rejected a deal and seemed resolved to fight the charges.

A Dramatic Meeting

The agreement was reached after a dramatic meeting Tuesday evening between the firm's chief executive, Frederick H. Joseph, and United States Attorney Rudolph W. Giuliani, who gave the investment house until 4 P.M. yesterday to settle or be indicted. The charges would have included racketeering and obstruction of justice.

In a brief statement, Drexel said it had concluded that a settlement "is in the best interests of our firm and our employees."

Neither Mr. Giuliani nor Drexel mentioned Michael R. Milken, the central figure in the Government's two-year investigation. Mr. Milken, based in Beverly Hills, Calif., made Drexel the dominant Wall Street force in the business.

Continued on Page D4, Column 1

More on the Drexel Case

The Decision to Settle — An indictment of the investment firm appeared imminent until late Tuesday afternoon, when U.S. Attorney Rudolph W. Giuliani placed a call to Drexel's chief executive, Frederick H. Joseph. Page D5.

A Climactic Deal — The long Government investigation of trading abuses on Wall Street, leading to the Drexel settlement, raises serious questions about Wall Street's ability to police itself and serves notice that many innovative trading and takeover practices will be closely scrutinized. News Analysis, Page D5.

The Storm Around Milken — Michael R. Milken's name was not mentioned in Drexel's agreement to plead guilty, but the financial machine he created was clearly at the center of the Federal investigation. Page D4.

AGENCY DEFENDED IN DEATH OF CHILD

Official Says Custody Is Given Even With Known Neglect

By SUZANNE DALEY

New York City's top child-welfare official said yesterday that even if his agency had been aware that a Brooklyn mother had a history of child neglect, it still would have recommended that she retain custody of a 5-year-old girl who died in her care last week.

At the time of the custody battle in 1986, neither the judge in the case nor caseworkers were aware that the mother had been charged with neglect three years earlier and had lost custody of two other children.

But the official, William J. Grinker, said that despite this lack of knowledge, caseworkers investigating the family for the court had made the right choice in favoring the mother over the father in the custody battle.

The 25-year-old mother, Abigail Cortez, and her live-in companion, who is also 25, have been charged in the beating death of the girl, Jessica. Police officials have described the child-abuse case as one of the worst they have ever seen.

"From my total review of the case file, in my judgment, knowledge of any prior activities and facts that we have on the record would not have affected our recommendation," said Mr. Grinker, the city's Human Resources Administrator and Commissioner of Social Services.

Mayor Koch, in an interview, dif-

Continued on Page B6, Column 3

Pentagon Official Accuses 8 Concerns on Secret Data

By RICHARD HALLORAN
Special to The New York Times

WASHINGTON, Dec. 21 — The director of a Defense Department investigative agency said today that eight of the nation's leading arms makers face possible criminal prosecution for illegal possession of secret Government documents.

The planning and budget documents were used to prepare bids for Government contracts, Government officials said.

The official, John F. Donnelly, said in Congressional testimony that the companies were Boeing, the Amecon division of Litton Systems, McDonnell Douglas, Northrop, TRW Inc., Sanders Associates, General Dynamics and Martin Marietta.

A Congressional staff report said the names of four companies — Boeing, General Dynamics, Martin Marietta and Sanders — had been referred to the United States Attorney in the Eastern District of Virginia for possible prosecution.

'Black Market' Seen

In the testimony today, a senior official in the Pentagon Inspector General's office, Donald Mancuso, said the trafficking in secret documents was "insidious," corrupted the procurement process, undermined public confidence and endangered national security.

Asked by Senator William Proxmire, Democrat of Wisconsin, whether the trade in such documents continues, Mr. Mancuso said, "Absolutely; it is going on today."

The accusations today were separate from the Justice Department's well-publicized inquiry into possible improprieties by consultants to arms makers in which inside information was said to have been used to gain unfair competitive advantage in weapons sales.

After a flurry of activity and publicity last summer, that case has been quiet as grand juries in New York and Virginia have been considering the evidence out of the public eye. Officials close to the case have said for several weeks that indictments were expected

Reaction From Companies

Reaction from several of the companies named by Mr. Donnelly was mixed. A spokesman for Boeing said, "We are aware of the investigation and we are fully cooperating with the Government."

But a spokesman for Litton said: "We have no knowledge of any current investigation. We have no knowledge of anyone in this company trafficking in classified information."

Similarly, a spokesman for McDonnell Douglas said, "We are not aware of any such investigation." He said several employees had been interviewed earlier but that the company believed the matter to have been closed. A spokesman for Northrop said, "We are not aware of it."

In a hearing before Senators Proxmire and Senator Charles E. Grassley, Republican of Iowa,Mr.

Continued on Page A19, Column 1

Army Technician and a Civilian Are Held as Spies for Soviet Bloc

By MICHAEL WINES
Special to The New York Times

WASHINGTON, Dec. 21 — An Army intelligence specialist and a Turkish-born civilian living in Florida were arrested today, breaking what American officials said was a major espionage operation that funneled information about the West's eavesdropping capacity to the Soviet Union and East Germany for six years.

American officials said the operation appeared to have inflicted serious damage on the United States' electronic spying efforts in Europe but added that the extent of the damage was still being assessed.

On Tuesday an agent of the Federal Bureau of Investigation, posing as a Soviet spy, met for two hours with the central figure in the case, an Army warrant officer, James W. Hall, in a Savannah, Ga., hotel.

An F.B.I. affidavit made public today said that Mr. Hall, believing the Federal agent was a Soviet contact, "described in notable detail his espionage history against the United States" and "admitted his motivation to be greed." His annual salary from the Army is about $20,000.

["He was living far above his pay grade," a Pentagon official told Reuters.]

Mr. Hall, a native of New York City who is 30 years old, was a signals intelligence and electronic warfare technician who had served in West Berlin and Frankfurt. He was arrested by Army intelligence agents early today at his home in Richmond Hill, near Savannah.

Earlier today, Federal agents in Belleair, Fla., near Tampa, took into cus-

Continued on Page D22, Column 3

JETLINER CARRYING 258 TO U.S. CRASHES IN SCOTTISH TOWN

The New York Times/Dec. 22, 1988
Houses and cars near Lockerbie were set ablaze by the crash.

ALL BELIEVED DEAD

Syracuse University Had 36 People Aboard — Cause Is Unknown

By CRAIG R. WHITNEY
Special to The New York Times

LONDON, Dec. 21 — A Pan Am Boeing 747 on a flight from London to New York with 258 people aboard crashed tonight in a southern Scottish village, British military authorities reported. The airline said it knew of no survivors.

The passengers included at least 36 Syracuse University students of a group of 38 who purchased tickets for the flight. An unknown number of American military personnel flying home for the holidays were also reported to have been aboard.

The plane was flying at 31,000 feet when it suddenly disappeared from radar and crashed into two rows of houses, setting them on fire.

There was no immediate indication of the cause of the crash. British officials would not respond to speculation by some about a structural failure or an on-board explosion in the jumbo jet.

Flight Originated in Germany

Pat Coffey, a spokesman for the British Royal Air Force, said the plane, Pan American World Airways Flight 103, left Heathrow Airport outside London after originating at Frankfurt, West Germany, and was bound for Kennedy International Airport.

Among those on board was the chief administrative officer of the United Nations' Council for Namibia, Bernt Carlsson of Sweden, who was flying to New York for the signing of an accord on Namibian independence, aides to Mr. Carlsson said. Others were believed to include two executives of Volkswagen's United States affiliate — James Fuller, a vice president, and Lou Marengo, marketing director, and also executives of The Associated Press. There were also unconfirmed reports that six members of the State Department's Diplomatic Security Service were aboard.

Pan Am officials in New York said it was the worst single-plane disaster in the airline's history.

Disappears From Radar Screens

The plane left Heathrow about 25 minutes behind schedule at 6:25 P.M. (1:25 P.M., New York time). It disappeared from air controllers' radar scopes 52 minutes later, shortly before a series of explosions and fires were reported on the ground in the Scottish village of Lockerbie, according to witnesses and official accounts. [The Associated Press quoted authorities as initially saying that the plane may have hit a hillside in the hamlet of Corrie, six miles from Lockerbie, and that debris was strewn across the countryside.]

"The aircraft is reported to have hit two rows of houses, which have been

Continued on Page A16, Column 1

Armenia Opens To Show Capital Under Tight Lid

By BILL KELLER
Special to The New York Times

YEREVAN, U.S.S.R., Dec. 20 — At Yerevan University and at the Polytechnical Institute, where passions have run high during this year of Armenian self-assertion, soldiers with automatic rifles take attendance each morning.

Army tanks and armored personnel carriers straddle entrances to city squares that earlier this year teemed with tens of thousands of demonstrators. After midnight, armed soldiers stop any car not bearing a pass from the Ministry of Defense.

In the last week and a half, the authorities have methodically arrested many nationalist leaders, including a member of the Armenian legislature, and others have gone into hiding, emerging occasionally to give defiant interviews to Western reporters.

All the Markings of Martial Law

The authorities do not call it martial law, but the capital of Armenia has all the outward markings of a city under military rule.

The Soviet press briefly reported the imposition of military discipline after ethnic unrest broke out in the city last month. But the sense of occupation has been conveyed far more dramatically in the past two weeks, as Armenia has been opened to crowds of outsiders, both Soviet and foreign, in the relief effort mounted since the devastating earthquake north of here on Dec. 7.

For many of the visiting relief workers, journalists, doctors and diplomats, the emergency measures are a visible

Continued on Page A8, Column 3

Agence France-Presse

Relocation of Quake Victims Hampered by Bad Weather

In Leninakan, U.S.S.R., Armenians wait for trains to Yerevan and Moscow. Heavy snow and cold temperatures are causing difficulties in relocating survivors of the earthquake that devastated Armenia.

Homeless Addicts in Oregon Find Aid in Restoring Lives

By TIMOTHY EGAN
Special to The New York Times

Portraits Of the Homeless
Last of four articles.

PORTLAND, Ore. — When city officials here proposed putting homeless drug addicts and alcoholics under one roof with nothing but peer pressure to keep them clean, a chorus of skepticism could be heard all the way up the Willamette River.

Five years later, the program, begun by Mayor Bud Clark of Portland, has a demonstrated record of success in aiding a category of homeless people often considered beyond hope or rehabilitation.

A recent study by the city has found that about a third of all residents leave the program with a job, and 60 percent leave free of their chemical dependency.

The program has attracted the attention of officials in New York and San Francisco, among other cities. A representative of the Port Authority of New York and New Jersey recently visited Portland in search of solutions to the problem of homeless people sleeping in bus and train stations. San Francisco, meanwhile, adopted parts of the Portland program after looking at what the city had done.

The first step in the program is offering alcoholics and drug abusers a room in a residential hotel for up to six months on one condition: that they stay off drugs and alcohol. With the housing as an anchor, the program provides intensive counseling and therapy for up to 200 people a year, many of them addicted to both alcohol and crack, the smokable form of cocaine.

Recently all 29 residents of the Everett Hotel, one of three hotels in the program, were given surprise urine tests,

Continued on Page A18, Column 1

Probable Appointee Assures Lawmakers On Abortion Views

By ROBIN TONER
Special to The New York Times

WASHINGTON, Dec. 21 — Leading Congressional opponents of abortion met with Dr. Louis W. Sullivan today and later termed him an acceptable candidate to be Secretary of Health and Human Services, a sign that President-elect Bush might be able to proceed with the selection of his first black Cabinet appointee.

In the meetings, Dr. Sullivan promised he would have "strong pro-life people" under him in the department, one of the lawmakers said.

But leaders in the anti-abortion movement appeared to be unswayed.

"There are many questions remaining," Dr. John C. Willke, president of the National Right to Life Committee, said in a statement released tonight that repeated the group's opposition to the appointment. "The most immediate one is this: Either Dr. Sullivan has been totally misquoted or he has completely changed his position in the last few days, for he now says that is pro-life."

Officials handling the transition to a Bush administration said today that

Continued on Page D22, Column 6

INSIDE

Labor Backs Israeli Pact
After a stormy meeting, the Labor Party gave final approval to the new Israeli coalition government led by the Likud party. Page A14.

Panamanian in U.S.
Panama's ousted President arrived in Washington as the United States sought ways to remove Gen. Manuel Antonio Noriega. Page A3.

Action on 2 Nuclear Plants
The Nuclear Regulatory Commission took steps to allow the operation of the Seabrook and Pilgrim power plants in New England. Page A18.

"All the News That's Fit to Print"

The New York Times

Late Edition
New York: Today, sporadic rain. High 74. Tonight, patchy dense fog. Low 64. Tomorrow, hazy skies and afternoon thunderstorms. High 79. Yesterday: High 79, low 60. Details, page C20.

VOL.CXXXVIII . . . No. 47,893 NEW YORK, TUESDAY, JUNE 6, 1989 — 50 cents beyond 75 miles from New York City, except on Long Island. — 35 CENTS

ARMY RIFT REPORTED IN BEIJING; SHOOTING OF CIVILIANS GOES ON; BUSH BARS ARMS SALES TO CHINA

Associated Press

A Drama Within a Drama on the Streets of Beijing

An unarmed Chinese civilian halting the progress of a tank convoy heading for Tiananmen Square yesterday. He later climbed on the lead tank and spoke to its crew before being hustled away by friends. Page A16.

UNITS SAID TO CLASH

Troops in Capital Seem to Assume Positions Against an Attack

By NICHOLAS D. KRISTOF

Special to The New York Times

BEIJING, Tuesday, June 6 — Chinese troops took up what seemed to be defensive positions here on Monday that suggested they feared attack from other army units, and there were reports that clashes between units had already occurred on the outskirts of the capital.

The troops continued to fire on civilian protesters all day Monday. But the reported clashes between units, this morning in the city's western reaches and on Monday night at the military airport in southern Beijing and on the city's northern outskirts, seemed to refocus the troops' attention primarily on defensive measures rather than on attacks on demonstrators.

[In Washington, Bush Administration officials confirmed reports of an armed clash between army units on the outskirts of Beijing. Page A16.]

'Threat of Civil War' Seen

"The threat of civil war can no longer be excluded," a Western diplomat said.

Clashes between military units would probably reflect cleavages in the nation's political leadership. Different armies sometimes have loyalties to different political figures, and actual combat would represent a new dimension in the power struggle that has been under way for nearly three weeks between rival factions in the Communist Party leadership.

Some troops still fired on unarmed citizens on Monday and early this morning, but mostly they fired in the air. Fewer casualties were reported, with the number seeming to be in the dozens on Monday, well down from the figures on Sunday.

Several Hundred Believed Dead

The total number of fatalities may never be known, but it seems likely that a minimum of several hundred people were killed, and it is possible that the true number of deaths might be 1,500 or more. Thousands more are recovering from bullet wounds or beatings.

The forces that were responsible for most of the bloodshed are also the ones that now appear to be preparing against attack. They are from the 27th Army, which was summoned to Beijing from Inner Mongolia to quell the democracy movement. This army has a long association with the family of President Yang Shangkun, the 82-year-old military figure who has taken a hard line against student protests.

The attackers probably are from the the 38th Army, based in Baoding, 90 miles southwest of Beijing. The 38th Army is not clearly linked to any particular political leader, but it is widely reported to have refused to at-

Continued on Page A14, Column 1

PRESIDENT SPURNS OTHER SANCTIONS

Doesn't Want 'a Total Break in Relations,' He Declares

By BERNARD WEINRAUB

Special to The New York Times

WASHINGTON, June 5 — President Bush today ordered a suspension of American military sales to China in response to what he called the "violent and bloody" crackdown against demonstrators in Beijing.

After saying little during the weekend of bloodshed, Mr. Bush held a news conference this morning to take account of pressure which was mounting in Congress from both liberals and conservatives for a firm American reaction on behalf of the student "prodemocracy" movement.

While halting military sales and suspending visits of Chinese and American military delegations, the President resisted suggestions that he impose economic sanctions or withdraw the American Ambassador from Beijing.

Mr. Bush appeared to be seeking middle ground between Congressional calls for more severe penalties and his own instincts, based in part on his experience as head of the United States Mission in China, that Washington should not move abruptly to freeze relations with the Chinese leadership.

"I don't want to see a total break in this relationship and I will not encourage a total break," Mr. Bush said. [Excerpts from the news conference, page A15.]

"When you see these kids struggling

Continued on Page A15, Column 1

Communists Concede Victory by Solidarity And Call for Coalition

By HENRY KAMM

Special to The New York Times

WARSAW, June 5 — The Communist Party acknowledged tonight that the Solidarity movement had achieved a "decisive majority" of the popular votes in the Polish parliamentary elections, and it challenged the victors to join in a coalition government.

No official figures from the elections Sunday have been made public while counting continues, but the party spokesman, Jan Bisztyga, said in a nationally televised statement, "The elections were of a plebiscite character, and Solidarity has achieved a decisive majority."

The complex voting system resulted in a sweeping Solidarity victory in the popular vote, but this will not be fully reflected in the number of seats the opposition movement will hold in the new two-chamber Parliament.

Solidarity has apparently won an overwhelming majority in the 100-seat Senate, but under a pre-election agreement the Communists are guaranteed a majority in the lower house, called the Assembly.

Janusz Onyszkiewicz, Solidarity's national spokesman, said at a news conference that partial results showed almost all Solidarity candidates winning. He said all the movement's contenders for the 161 seats open to the opposition in the 460-seat lower house appeared to have obtained the clear majority needed for election in the first round of voting.

According to vote compilers in Solidarity's modest computer center in a dingy downtown cafe that was allotted to the movement as its Warsaw campaign headquarters, the opposition has captured perhaps as many as 96 seats in the new 100-seat Senate, whose powers will be limited to a veto over legislaton.

Leading Communists in Danger

Most significantly, perhaps, the Government was said in unofficial, preliminary results to be falling short of electing its 35 leading members, who had been placed on an unopposed list for the Assembly. Their only requirement for victory was to obtain more than half of the votes cast.

Solidarity compilers, relying on reports from their poll watchers at most of the voting places, said this national list's total vote was so far averaging 40 to 43 percent. The list includes 8 of the 17 members of the Communist Politburo. Among them are Prime Minister Mieczyslaw Rakowski, the Interior Minister, Gen. Czeslaw Kiszczak, and the Defense Minister, Gen. Florian Siwicki.

Diplomats here expressed doubt that Mr. Rakowski's Government could avoid tendering its resignation if the final results show these leaders to have been rejected by a majority of the voters, who could cast a negative vote by crossing off a candidate's name from the list. Such a move would present Gen. Wojciech Jaruzelski, the Communist Party chief and President, and the ruling party with their most embarrassing problem.

'Issue of Responsibility'

In what was seen by Poles as an ominous reminder of the imposition of martial law in 1981, Mr. Bisztyga said in his television statement, which was the Government's only comment on the voting, that neither the Government nor the opposition could allow a "triumphant mood and adventurism to cause anarchy that would endanger democracy and the social order."

"As a result of this election there arises the issue of responsibility for the Polish state," he said. "Somebody has to be responsible for its stability. The first step that the opposition should take toward co-responsibility is a common concern for order in the country."

Since last year the Solidarity movement has resisted Communist offers to share in government on the ground

Continued on Page A7, Column 1

Prime Drops to 11%

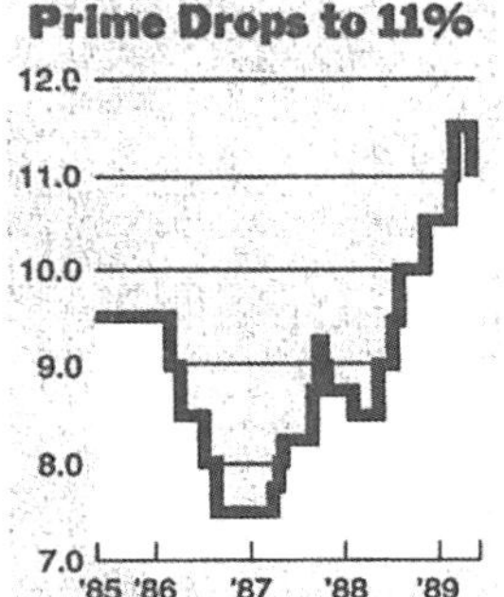

The reduction, led by Citibank, was the first since February 1988. The rate is used as a base for loans to small- and medium-size businesses and to individuals. Article, page D1.

Superconductors Showing a Flaw That Dims Hope

Recent discoveries have dimmed hopes that a new class of superconductors will ever find wide use, despite predictions two years ago that they could bring vast economic benefits.

New findings by AT&T Bell Laboratories, I.B.M.'s Thomas J. Watson Research Center and other research groups say that the substances, which conduct electricity with no loss to resistance, may be inherently incapable of carrying enough current to be very useful. And all of them cease to be superconductive when they are exposed to the large magnetic fields required for or created in most large-scale applications, including energy-storage systems, power-line transformers and medical imaging equipment.

Wary of Short-Term Projects

A recent survey by Coopers & Lybrand, accountants and management consultants, found that most of the most active investors in such ventures are already wary of short-term projects aimed at exploiting high-temperature superconductors.

Still, a handful of laboratories are developing the substances for uses not requiring large currents. Such applications potentially include sensitive devices needed by the armed forces to detect submarines and missile exhausts.

High-temperature superconductors might also find uses in special medical devices like machines that record electromagnetic emissions from the brain. But those devices are certain to be extremely expensive, analysts say.

It is too early to say that scientists will not be able to solve these problems, said Dr. David J. Bishop, of Bell Labs, "but right now, no one can say how."

Science Times, page C1.

Court, Ruling 5 to 4, Eases Burden On Employers in Some Bias Suits

By LINDA GREENHOUSE

Special to The New York Times

WASHINGTON, June 5 — In a major civil rights ruling, a sharply divided Supreme Court today made it substantially easier for employers to defend hiring and promotion practices that have an unfavorable impact on women and members of racial minorities.

The 5-to-4 decision redrew ground rules that for much of the last two decades had governed an important category of lawsuits under the Civil Rights Act of 1964. The cases use statistical evidence to demonstrate that, whether or not the employer intended to discriminate, employment policies have an impermissible discriminatory impact on women or minorities.

The key part of the ruling, in a 15-year-old discrimination suit against salmon canneries in Alaska, was to relieve employers of the burden of justifying, on grounds of "business necessity," practices that are shown to have a discriminatory impact.

The legal question of the burden of proof, while technical and sometimes elusive, can determine the outcome of a lawsuit.

The Court's majority, in an opinion by Justice Byron R. White, said the plaintiffs have the legal burden of proving that the employer had no objective, business-related justification for the challenged practices.

"We acknowledge that some of our earlier decisions can be read as suggesting otherwise," Justice White said, adding that such an interpretation was based on a misunderstanding of the Court's precedents of the last 18 years. [Excerpts from the opinions, page A24.]

Justice White's majority opinion was

Continued on Page A24, Column 4

Freelance Workers Gain on Copyrights

In an important legal victory for freelance artists and writers, the Supreme Court ruled that such artists ordinarily retain the right to copyright what they create. The Court held that the right applies as long as the artists were not in a conventional employment relationship with the organization that commissioned their work.

Article, page A24.

Agence France-Presse

The body of Ayatollah Ruhollah Khomeini in a glass case on view to hundreds of thousands of Iranians.

Final Tirade Heard as Throngs Mourn Khomeini

By JOHN KIFNER

Special to The New York Times

TEHERAN, Iran, June 5 — The body of Ayatollah Ruhollah Khomeini, the soul of Iran's Islamic fundamentalist revolution, lay surrounded by hundreds of thousands of weeping, chanting mourners today. Even in death, he managed one last denunciation of his enemies.

The United States and moderate Arab leaders are "terrorists" and "pirates," the Ayatollah declared in his last will and testament, read over the Teheran radio today.

"May God's curse be upon them," the Ayatollah said in his will.

So great was the crush to get close to the Ayatollah's body — displayed in a refrigerated glass box — that at least eight people were trampled to death in a stampede, according to the state-run press agency, and more than 500 injured.

"Sorrow, sorrow is this day," the huge throng chanted. "Khomeini the idol-smasher is with God today."

The streets of the capital were hung with black mourning banners as the death of the 89-year-old leader left the nation shaken and its future leadership uncertain, despite the selection on Sunday of the President, Hojatolislam Ali Khamenei, to replace Ayatollah Khomeini as supreme religious leader.

President Khamenei's appointment appears to be something of a stopgap measure until presidential elections are held on Aug. 18.

"We hope temporarily to be able to fill the leadership because the new terms of the Constitution are currently under review," President Khamenei said on state television Sunday after his appointment had been announced. He said the constitutional study would take several months and would probably go to a referendum during the presidential election.

For the moment, some analysts believe, power here rests in a triumvirate of President Khamenei; the Ayatollah's son, Ahmed Khomeini, who had

Continued on Page A11, Column 1

House Leadership Candidates Are Among Top Fund-Raisers

By RICHARD L. BERKE

Special to The New York Times

WASHINGTON, June 5 — Candidates vying to lead the House of Representatives into a new era of Congressional ethics and campaign financing are themselves among the lawmakers whose incomes and political funds have benefited most from the current system.

Democrats who are seeking election to important House posts, and Republican leaders already in place, have collected among the largest sums in speaking fees and campaign contributions from special interests, according to figures compiled by the Federal Election Commission and Common Cause, a lobbying group here that has called for tighter restrictions on contributions.

The most obvious examples are Representative Thomas S. Foley, who is virtually certain to succeed Jim Wright in the election of a new Speaker on Tuesday, and the current House Republican leader, Robert H. Michel. Both have pledged to move quickly to address questions of the financial and ethical practices of members.

Others seeking Democratic leadership positions include Representative Richard A. Gephardt of Missouri, a contender for minority leader who was attacked by competitors in last year's Presidential campaign for accepting large sums from political action committees, and Representative Beryl Anthony Jr. of Arkansas, a candidate for majority whip who, as chairman of the Democratic Congressional Campaign Committee, has been the driving force

Continued on Page D23, Column 1

INSIDE

Vodka Market Bucks Trend

When most of the liquor business has been stagnant, the vibrant $450 million premium vodka market has lured several new entrants. Page D1.

Lendl Suffers Upset

Seventeen-year-old Michael Chang suffered from cramps, but defeated top-seeded Ivan Lendl at the French Tennis Open. Page A25.

"All the News That's Fit to Print"

The New York Times

Late Edition
New York: Today, increasing clouds, windy, cool. High 54. Tonight, clearing, breezy. Low near 40. Tomorrow, mostly sunny conditions. High 57. Yesterday: High 55, low 44. Details are on page 32.

VOL.CXXXIX . . No. 48,051 NEW YORK, SATURDAY, NOVEMBER 11, 1989 — 50 cents beyond 75 miles from New York City, except on Long Island. — 40 CENTS

JOYOUS EAST GERMANS POUR THROUGH WALL; PARTY PLEDGES FREEDOMS, AND CITY EXULTS

D'AMATO BACKED SUPPORTERS' BID FOR H.U.D. MONEY

Senator's '84 Letter Appears to Contradict Assertions He Never Urged Grants

By MICHAEL WINERIP

Senator Alfonse M. D'Amato urged the Federal Housing Secretary to approve a grant worth several million dollars for a Buffalo housing-renovation project run in part by two of the Senator's supporters, according to a newly obtained document.

In a March 15, 1984, letter written on Mr. D'Amato's Washington office stationery, the Senator asked Secretary Samuel Pierce of the Department of Housing and Urban Development to use "deliberate speed" in approving the moderate-rehabilitation grant for the 65-unit Buffalo project. Within two months the grant was approved.

The letter, marked as having been hand delivered, appears to contradict repeated assertions by the Senator that he never asked department officials to approve specific moderate-rehabilitation projects. A statement issued to The New York Times last month by the Senator's office said, "The Senator has made no contact with any officials of H.U.D. on behalf of any development or developer as it relates to mod rehab."

Links to Projects

In May 1984, when the department's Buffalo office informed local officials of the moderate-rehabilitaton grants that had won approval that year, that letter was marked "cc: Sen. Alfonse M. D'Amato." He was the only elected official designated by the department to receive a copy of its letter about the Buffalo projects.

The Buffalo matter is the most recent in a series of disclosures that have linked the Senator with department projects that benefited his family members, friends and campaign contributors and that have stretched from his hometown, Island Park, L.I., throughout New York State and to Puerto Rico. Federal prosecutors and Congressional investigators are conducting inquiries into several of these programs although Mr. D'Amato has not been identified as a subject of any inquiry.

Allegations in '85

A spokeswoman for the Senator, Zenia Mucha, said last night that the Senator "can't be expected to remember every single letter over a nine-year period." She said that when Mr. D'Amato called on behalf of projects it was "based on merit and need, and no other factors were ever considered."

The moderate-rehabilitation program, which was intended to rebuild housing for low-income people, has been a central focus of inquiries into political favoritism by the department

Continued on Page 32, Column 1

Agence France-Presse

East Germans pouring through a gate leading to the newly opened Berlin wall and, beyond it, West Berlin.

Reuters

An East German border guard handing a flower back to West Berliners who sat atop the Berlin wall. (Detail from a scene that appears on page 7.)

Redefining Europe

As the Revelry Goes On, Politicians Ponder The Ramifications of Changes in Germany

By CRAIG R. WHITNEY
Special to The New York Times

News Analysis

WEST BERLIN, Nov. 10 — By the simple act of forcing their Communist rulers to open the Berlin wall and allow them to go wherever they wish, the people of East Germany have irrevocably changed the way Berlin, Germany and all of Europe have defined themselves for more than 40 years.

Thousands and thousands of East Berliners celebrated their triumph today by promenading up and down the elegant, tree-lined shopping boulevards of the western part of the city, which most of them had never before been allowed to see. They made the Kurfürstendamm into a street festival this evening as church bells pealed joyously into the night.

'A Different Relationship'

Willy Brandt, who was Mayor of West Berlin when the wall was built in 1961, said at a rally this evening, "The moving together of the German states is taking shape in reality in a different way than many of us expected." said . No one should act as if he knows in which concrete form the people in these two states will find a new relationship. But that they will find a relationship, that they will come together in freedom, that is the important point."

But the entire postwar European order has been based on the assumption that Germany, and Europe, would remain divided, and the countries of Eastern and Western Europe firmly anchored in their respective alliances.

In that assumption the United States, in the NATO alliance, guaranteed the security of Western Europe. And in that same assumption France, West Germany and the other major industrial countries of Western Europe began the economic and political unification of the European Community.

West German politicians, including Mr. Brandt and Chancellor Helmut Kohl, who interrupted an official visit to Poland today to fly to Berlin, all insist that West Germany's commitment to West European integration and the alliance remains.

But politicians, diplomats and business leaders all over Europe are considering new implications for both institutions now that the end of German partition is at last imaginable.

"Europe, though Europeans did not always appreciate it, has been a haven of order these past 44 years," The Economist wrote today. "For East Europeans the price of that stability has been high: a lifetime wasted under a government you loathed. For West Europeans the stability has been marvelous. They could get rich, and start to build a new unity, within a clearly defined zone which ended at the river Elbe and the Bohemian forest."

Now, a NATO diplomat in Brussels said, "The end of the wall raises questions of what's going to happen in Europe. The whole concept of the European Community now may have to change."

So would the concept of the NATO alliance, this diplomat conceded: "Our role will be to design a new role for the alliance — maintaining a balance of stability with the East while all this change is going on.

"There's a reassessment of the War-

Continued on Page 9, Column 4

U.S. ENTHUSIASTIC, BUT HAS CONCERNS

New Order in Eastern Europe Astonishes Washington

By THOMAS L. FRIEDMAN
Special to The New York Times

WASHINGTON, Nov. 10 — Like the rest of the world, Washington is scrambling to keep pace with the changes unfolding by the hour in Eastern Europe. But in contrast with the pivotal role the United States played 40 years ago in shaping the postwar European order that now seems to be coming apart, Washington finds itself more of a bystander — astonished, enthusiastic and concerned.

Twice in the last 24 hours, Secretary of State James A. Baker 3d found himself being slipped notes from aides informing him of major changes in Eastern Europe that only a week earlier no one had imagined, let alone predicted. Officials said a policy review that Mr. Baker ordered three weeks ago on how the United States should relate to changes in East Germany will have to be tossed out and begun anew.

The political changes reverberating across Europe, and the diminished threat of military conflict, also promised to stir new debate in Washington about the need for maintaining a large, expensive American military presence in Western Europe. Moving quickly to deflate such speculation, Defense Sec-

Continued on Page 8, Column 1

BERLIN A FESTIVAL

Communist Leadership Announces a Program of Radical Change

By SERGE SCHMEMANN
Special to The New York Times

WEST BERLIN, Nov. 10 — As hundreds of thousands of East Berliners romped through the newly porous wall in an unending celebration, West German leaders today proclaimed this the moment Germans had yearned for through 40 years of division.

At the same time, change continued unabated in East Berlin, where the Communist Party's Central Committee concluded a three-day session with the announcement of a program of radical changes. They included "free, democratic and secret elections," a "socialist planned economy oriented to market conditions," separation of party and state, parliamentary supervision of state security, freedom of assembly and a new law on the press and broadcasting.

'In the Midst of an Awakening'

"The German Democratic Republic is in the midst of an awakening," the Central Committee declared in the prologue to the newly adopted program. "A revolutionary people's movement has brought into motion a process of great change. The renewal of society is on the agenda."

Though the West Berlin police could give no estimate of the numbers of East Berliners who crossed over in the last 24 hours, the authorities said that only 1,500 so far had announced their intention to stay.

Beyond Berlin, only one of many points along the border between the two Germanys where people could cross, 55,500 East Germans crossed over the border between the two Germanys since the wall was opened on Thursday, and 3,250 remained in West Germany, the West German Interior Ministry said.

Chancellor Helmut Kohl, who interrupted a state visit to Poland to come to West Berlin, told an emotional crowd of East and West Berliners gathered outside the West Berlin city hall: "I want to call out to all in the German Democratic Republic: We're on your side, we are and remain one nation. We belong together."

Speaking on the steps of the city hall, from which President John F. Kennedy had made his "Ich bin ein Berliner" speech shortly after the wall was raised, Mr. Kohl declared: "Long live a free German fatherland! Long live a united Europe!"

Kurfürstendamm Is Packed

All through the night and through the day, East Berliners continued to flood into West Berlin in vast numbers, filling the glittering Kurfürstendamm until traffic came to a halt, forming long lines to pick up the 100-mark "welcome money" — about $55 — that West Germany has traditionally given East Germans on their first time in the West, gaping at shop windows and drinking in the heady new feeling of freedom.

A festival air seized the entire city. West Berliners lined entry points to greet East Berliners with champagne, cheers and hugs. Many restaurants offered the visitors free food. A television

Continued on Page 6, Column 1

Bush Offers Housing Plan to Aid Poor, Homeless and New Buyers

By ANDREW ROSENTHAL
Special to The New York Times

DALLAS, Nov. 10 — President Bush today proposed a $7 billion, three-year package of housing programs and tax breaks to aid low-income families, first-time home buyers and the homeless "who live a nightmare in the midst of the American dream."

"This initiative will address the full range of housing concerns," Mr. Bush said in a speech to the National Association of Realtors here. He termed the program "a comprehensive agenda to help bring basic shelter and affordable housing within reach of millions of Americans."

The three-year program would provide mortgage assistance for low-income families and tax breaks for first-time buyers, but it does not include money for building new public and low-income housing units, which some advocates for the homeless regard as essential. Instead, it seeks to generate additional housing units through a variety of means that Republicans have been urging.

For example, a major element of the proposal involves matching grants to local authorities and nonprofit organizations for the acquisition of property and the rehabilitation of housing units.

Democratic legislators, advocates of low-income housing and spokesmen for the housing industry praised it as signaling a new interest in housing problems after years of relative inattention during the Reagan Administration. But several said the level of financing was insignificant compared to the needs of the homeless or people in substandard housing.

Jack F. Kemp, the Secretary of Housing and Urban Development, said the program was directed more toward stimulating the low-income housing industry than directly subsidizing individual purchases.

In announcing the plan, Mr. Bush

Continued on Page 13, Column 1

INSIDE

Bulgarian Chief Quits After 35 Years of Rigid Rule

By CLYDE HABERMAN
Special to The New York Times

SOFIA, Bulgaria, Nov. 10 — Todor I. Zhivkov, Eastern Europe's longest-serving leader, resigned today as Bulgaria's President and Communist Party leader, after 35 years of guiding the country with old-line orthodoxy.

Mr. Zhivkov, 78 years old, was immediately replaced as the party's General Secretary by his longtime Foreign Minister, Petar T. Mladenov, who is viewed here as likely to take a somewhat more flexible approach toward economic and political restructuring. It will be up to the politically weak National Assembly to choose his successor as President.

Since Mr. Zhivkov and other top officials recently began to talk about the need to separate state and party roles, it seemed possible that someone other than Mr. Mladenov could be selected.

Mr. Zhivkov's resignation came as a surprise but not as a total shock to Western diplomats, who said that the Bulgarian leader had apparently fallen victim to the fast-paced changes elsewhere in Eastern Europe.

Bulgarian officials reportedly said in confidence that Mr. Zhivkov did not want to stay too long and risk being forced from power in disgrace, as were Janos Kadar of Hungary or Erich Honecker of East Germany.

There were strong rumors of more shifts to come in top party echelons, but the state press agency and television network made no announcements. The prospects for genuine change here, several diplomats said, are likely to be determined by the extent of any future shake-up.

Doubts on Rapid Change

Mr. Mladenov, who is 53 and was Foreign Minister for 18 years, wasted no time as the new leader in warning that "there is no alternative to restructuring" Bulgaria's struggling economy and tightly controlled political apparatus. The present system has "handicapped progress in our society in all spheres," he told the party Central Committee, adding: "We have to turn Bulgaria into a modern, democratic and lawful country."

Despite his words, however, many

Continued on Page 9, Column 4

Agence France-Presse

Todor I. Zhivkov

"All the News That's Fit to Print"

The New York Times

Late Edition
New York: Today, light snow, becoming partly sunny. High 38. Tonight, clear, breezy late. Low 30. Tomorrow, partly cloudy, windy. High 49. Yesterday: High 48, low 32. Details, page C8.

VOL.CXXXIX . . . No. 48,144 NEW YORK, MONDAY, FEBRUARY 12, 1990 — 50 cents beyond 75 miles from New York City, except on Long Island. — 40 CENTS

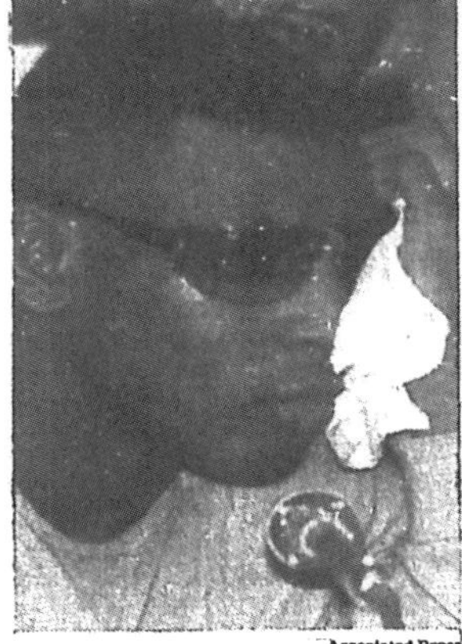

Associated Press
Mike Tyson applying a cold towel to his swollen eye during a news conference after the fight.

Boxing Officials Could Overturn Defeat of Tyson

By PHIL BERGER

James (Buster) Douglas knocked out Mike Tyson this weekend and won the world heavyweight championship in one of the greatest upsets in boxing history. But Douglas's victory in Tokyo may be undone by a rancorous dispute over a long count on Tyson's knockdown of Douglas in the eighth round.

Two of boxing's major governing bodies, the World Boxing Association and the World Boxing Council, suspended the result of the fight yesterday pending hearings into the controversy. The third major group that recognized Tyson as the champion, the International Boxing Federation, said it now considers Douglas to be the champion.

Tyson's corner had protested that Douglas received a long count, and, according to the W.B.C., a formal protest was later lodged by Japanese boxing authorities.

The result of the bout, fought Sunday in Tokyo (Saturday night in the United States), could ultimately be determined by the political and legal wrangling of the governing bodies as well as the considerable influence of Tyson's promoter, Don King.

Tunney-Dempsey Recalled

But this much is clear: By dominating the fight and knocking out the undefeated and seemingly invincible Tyson in the 10th round, Douglas, a relative unknown, shocked the sports world. And he also apparently upset the carefully laid plans for Tyson's boxing future, including a projected $22 million payday for a title defense against Evander Holyfield in June.

The knockdown in dispute, recalling the famous long count in the 1927 Gene Tunney-Jack Dempsey title fight, occurred after Tyson, battered by Douglas for most of eight rounds, connected on a right uppercut to Douglas's jaw that sent the challenger backward to the canvas.

Referee Octavio Meyran Sánchez leaped to Douglas's side and, after a pause, began counting with his fingers

Continued on Page C4, Column 5

INSIDE

Not Quite Watchdogs Yet
Across Eastern Europe, the once mighty official press is in even bigger trouble than the Communist parties it has praised for so long. Some papers have fallen into oblivion. Others are hoping for independence. Page A12.

A Turn in the Drug War?
In what experts hope is a turning point, the crime rate in and around Washington, D.C., is growing more slowly, and the number of suspects testing positive for cocaine use has dropped in recent months. Page B9.

Crisis Among Counselors
As the problems they confront grow more serious than those of 20 or even 10 years ago, guidance counselors in New York schools remain heavily overloaded. Page B1.

Checking-Account Bonus
Some banks are giving customers insurance that automatically protects goods bought by check against damage or loss and extends manufacturers' warranties. Page D1.

U.S. INVITES IDEAS FROM THE SOVIETS ON STRATEGIC CUTS

AN ADMINISTRATION SHIFT

Moscow's Earlier Suggestions on Reducing Nuclear Arms Have Been Spurned

By MICHAEL R. GORDON
Special to The New York Times

WASHINGTON, Feb. 11 — In a shift of position, the Bush Administration has told Moscow that it is now prepared to receive Soviet proposals about reductions in long-range nuclear arms that go beyond the emerging strategic arms treaty, Administration officials disclosed today.

Until recently, the Bush Administration has rebuffed Moscow's suggestions that the two sides open discussions on a possible second arms treaty that would make deeper reductions in long-range nuclear weapons, like ocean-spanning ballistic missiles, cruise missiles and bombers, than does the arms treaty now under negotiation.

But Secretary of State James A. Baker 3d told Soviet leaders in Moscow last week that the Administration is now ready to entertain new Soviet ideas on what sort of subsequent reductions in long-range nuclear arms should be carried out after the current Strategic Arms Reduction Talks are concluded.

Thinking of 'Next Phase'

"Up to now we have not been willing to discuss the Soviet ideas on Start-2 on the ground that we still have work to do on Start-1," said a senior Administration official. "Now we are saying you can raise your ideas if you want to. We are getting to the point where we need to think a little bit about the next phase."

The question of whether to seek further reductions in long-range nuclear weapons after an agreement is reached has been a contentious one for the Bush Administration. Some Administration officials, like the White House national security adviser, Brent Scowcroft, have argued that reductions in nuclear weapons should not be pursued for their own sake, and the Administration has yet to formulate a basic position of what additional cuts in long-range nuclear arms, if any, might be sought.

The treaty currently under negotia-

Continued on Page A11, Column 1

The Price of Peace

Movements that fought in the trenches of the cold war are flushed out as peace breaks out in Central and Eastern Europe. Page A10.

MANDELA, FREED, URGES STEP-UP IN PRESSURE TO END WHITE RULE

Reuters
Nelson Mandela leaving Victor Verster prison yesterday after spending 27 years in South African jails.

SPEECH IS RESOLUTE

He Asks Other Nations Not to Lift Sanctions Against Pretoria

By CHRISTOPHER S. WREN
Special to The New York Times

CAPE TOWN, Feb. 11 — After 27 and a half years in prison, Nelson Mandela finally won his freedom today and promptly urged his supporters at home and abroad to increase their pressure against the white minority Goverment that had just released him.

"We have waited too long for our freedom," Mr. Mandela told a cheering crowd from a balcony of Cape Town's old City Hall. "We can wait no longer."

"Now is the time to intensify the struggle on all fronts," he said. "To relax our efforts now would be a mistake which generations to come will not able to forgive." [Transcript of the address, page A15.]

First Speech Since '64

Mr. Mandela's 20-minute speech, which he prepared before leaving prison today, constituted his first remarks in public since before he was sentenced in June 1964 to life imprisonment for conspiracy to overthrow the Government and engage in sabotage.

He asked the international community not to lift its sanctions against South Africa, despite the recent changes introduced by President F. W. de Klerk, which culminated in Mr. Mandela's release.

"To lift sanctions now would be to run the risk of aborting the process toward ending apartheid," he said.

An Eloquent Militancy

Mr. Mandela's voice sounded firm and his words as eloquently militant as when he defended violence as the ultimate recourse at his political trial in 1964. Though he looked all of his 71 years and was grayer than artists' renditions over the years had depicted, he walked out of Victor Verster prison erect and vigorous.

In Washington, President Bush rejoiced over the release of Mr. Mandela, spoke to him by telephone and invited the anti-apartheid leader to visit the White House. [Page A17.]

Mr. Mandela gave no evidence that his militant opposition to apartheid had been tempered by the more than 10,000 days he spent in confinement. But he also said nothing that would have surprised the Government had he said it during his years of incarceration. Indeed, there appeared to be nothing in Mr. Mandela's initial remarks after his release to give the Government much consolation or encouragement.

Although he has been viewed as a potential leader for all South Africans, he stressed time and again that his loyalty lay with the African National Congress, for which he was working under-

Continued on Page A14, Column 1

On Mandela's Walk, Hope and Violence

By JOHN F. BURNS
Special to The New York Times

PAARL, South Africa, Feb. 11 — When Nelson Mandela made his walk to freedom today, he did it with the same simplicity and command of occasion that made him a leader among millions of South African blacks when his imprisonment began more than 10,000 days ago.

At 4:14 P.M. on a sun-warmed day — 27 years, six months and one week after his arrest on Aug. 5, 1962 — Mr. Mandela stepped from the car that drove him to the last guard post at the Victor Verster prison.

From there, smiling gently, he passed under a raised barrier and flicked his right hand quickly out from his body in greeting. He then raised his right arm several times in the bolder, black nationalist salute, his left hand holding the hand of his wife, Winnie, and walked to the point where the prison entrance road abuts the highway running through the undulating wine country of the Western Cape.

It was a walk of perhaps 70 yards, through a corridor of policemen, and as he made it, Mr. Mandela said not a word, at least none that could be heard by any in the crowd of 5,000 blacks and whites chanting his name. But to those who have come to know Mr. Mandela in the only way that was possible under the total ban that the South African Government threw around the black leader in prison — through his speeches and writings of a generation ago — there was no mistaking the symbolism involved in beginning his life outside jail on foot.

About the time in 1961 when President John F. Kennedy was spending his first summer in the White House, Mr. Mandela, then about the same age as Mr. Kennedy, used a phrase that became the title of a book of Mr. Mandela's speeches and writings. The book has been passed hand to hand in dog-eared copies among South Africans, who were forbidden until today under censorship laws and statutes governing political prisoners to own any book by or about the black leader. There was, Mr. Mandela said, "no easy walk to freedom" for South African blacks after three centuries of white domination and repression.

Dignified and Resolute

The Nelson Mandela who made his own walk to freedom today, after more than 22 years in the fortress prison on Robben Island, in the gale-swept mouth of Cape Town harbor, and five more years in a series of other prisons, had hair that had turned to gray. He looked at least 30 pounds lighter than he had at his last public appearance, in June 1964 when, with the physique of the heavyweight boxer he had been in his youth, he stood in the dock at the Rivonia Trial in Johannesburg and acknowledged that he was guilty as charged of sabotage and attempting to overthrow the Government.

But in other respects, the 71-year-old

Continued on Page A14, Column 1

Bush Homeless Plan: 'Godsend' or False Hope?

By JASON DePARLE

Federal Aid, New York Homeless
A special report.

On the night of Sept. 25, 1988, a previously obscure piece of Federal legislation was ushered onto political center stage before a television audience of millions.

During the season's first Presidential debate, a panelist asked George Bush what he would do for the homeless, "this voiceless segment of our society."

Mr. Bush answered without hesitation. "I want to see the McKinney Act fully funded," the Republican candidate said.

The McKinney Act?

The reference hardly resonated in the living rooms of America. Most viewers had never heard of the McKinney Act, and Mr. Bush's terse answer offered virtually no basis on which to judge it.

But Mr. Bush has kept his word. Last year, at his urging, Congress came close to fully financing most McKinney programs for the first time since the act was passed in 1987.

And the legislation remains a central provision of the Administration's plan for helping the homeless. As recently as last month, Mr. Bush pointed toward funds from the McKinney Act in telling a convention of home builders in Atlanta that "my Administration is going to do its part" in working to "solve the problems of the helpless and the homeless."

$67 Million for New York

The act itself is a quiver of 16 programs, each taking a different aim at homelessness. Some of the programs support shelters, with food or funds. Others provide services like job training, health care or treatment for alcohol or drug abuse.

The funds approved last year are likely to raise New York State's share to about $67 million, from $45 million. Because the money filters through a variety of governments and private organizations, it is impossible to determine how much of it is spent in New York City.

But despite the McKinney Act's broad aims and the recent increase in financing, many of those who provide shelter and services to the homeless say the McKinney Act falls short in at least these three respects:

¶It provides relatively little money.

¶It creates daunting bureaucratic obstacles.

¶And it provides almost no funds for low-income housing, which advocates argue must be part of a solution to homelessness.

"It's much ado about nothing," said Douglas H. Lasdon of the Legal Assistance Center for the Homeless in Manhattan. "It gives people the impression that something's being done, but it's not."

Measured in paint or plaster, protein or pajamas, the law has made a difference in the lives of dozens of New York organizations. Some money from the act, named for Representative Stewart B. McKinney, a Connecticut Republican

Continued on Page B8, Column 1

Rural Doctor's Struggle to Care for the Poorest

By PETER APPLEBOME
Special to The New York Times

TCHULA, Miss. — There aren't many doctors like Ronald Myers, a jazz-playing, Baptist-preaching family practitioner whose dream has always been to practice medicine in the kind of place most other doctors wouldn't even stop for a tank of gas.

But there are plenty of places like Tchula, a forlorn patch of Mississippi Delta poverty where it is hard to find a street that's not rutted, a sign that's not crooked, a paint job that's not peeling or a life that's not perched on the brink of economic ruin.

Dr. Myers's story — how hard it has been for him to get here and how hard it may be for him to stay — provides a dispiriting look at health care in rural America. The situation is worsening because the Government's program to provide doctors for the nation's neediest areas is being dismantled as health care needs continue to grow.

"Working in Tchula, Miss., is like working in a third world country," said Dr. Myers, who became Tchula's only doctor when he opened a clinic this month in an abandoned restaurant next to an empty liquor store. "The needs are that great. So how is it that here's a well-trained physician who wants to come to an area that's desperately poor, and I can't get any assistance? I can't get a loan. I'll take a tongue depressor if someone will give me one. There's a problem somewhere."

In poor rural areas, particularly in the South, regular medical care is seldom more than a distant dream. In areas like Tchula and nearby Belzoni, where Dr. Myers previously worked, infant mortality rates are three times the national average, most women receive little if any prenatal care and people usually see a doctor only when they have no choice.

"The health problems in this area

Continued on Page B11, Column 1

Agence France-Presse
A South African youth celebrating Nelson Mandela's release yesterday at an African National Congress rally in Soweto. Mr. Mandela urged supporters to increase their pressure against the white Government.

0 354713 07

"All the News That's Fit to Print"

The New York Times

Late Edition
New York: **Today,** sunny. High 89. **Tonight,** clear, not as cool. Low 70. **Tomorrow,** mostly sunny, very warm, more humid. High 91. **Yesterday,** high 89, low 65. Details are on page C22.

VOL. CXXXIX . No. 48,316 | NEW YORK, FRIDAY, AUGUST 3, 1990 | 50 cents beyond 75 miles from New York City, except on Long Island. | 40 CENTS

INVADING IRAQIS SEIZE KUWAIT AND ITS OIL; U.S. CONDEMNS ATTACK, URGES UNITED ACTION

The New York Times
Representative Floyd H. Flake

INDICTMENT NAMES QUEENS LAWMAKER IN MISUSE OF FUNDS

Rep. Flake Faces 17 Federal Counts Involving Church and Housing Complex

By ARNOLD H. LUBASCH

Representative Floyd H. Flake, a powerful Queens minister who rode his popularity into Congress four years ago, has been indicted on charges of diverting tens of thousands of dollars in church funds to his own use.

The 17-count Federal indictment, which was unsealed yesterday, charges that Mr. Flake and his wife, Margarett, engaged in a two-pronged conspiracy involving his church and the housing complex for the elderly that it built in Jamaica under his stewardship. They are accused of fraudulently obtaining $66,700 from the church, embezzling $75,000 from the housing complex and evading income taxes on both amounts.

Pastor Since '76

The Representative, a Democrat whose Sixth Congressional District covers southern Queens, issued a detailed statement denying the charges. His lawyer said he still intended to run for re-election in November, and Mrs. Flake's lawyer added that the charges would fuel "a perception that minority politicians are being unfairly targeted for prosecution."

Since 1976, the 45-year-old Congressman has been pastor of the Allen A.M.E. Church in Jamaica, one of the largest and oldest black churches in New York City, with 6,000 members and a history reaching back into the 1830's. During his tenure, Mr. Flake has built up the church, and his own influence, with a network of social-services for the largely poor and largely black Jamaica neighborhood.

3d Congressman to Be Indicted

And yesterday, under the warm afternoon sun, there was a wary feeling of racism at work and an insistence that the charges against the pastor had to be false. [Page B4.]

Mr. Flake is the third New York City Congressman indicted in the last three years. The others, Mario Biaggi and Robert Garcia, both Bronx Democrats, were convicted in the Wedtech racketeering case. Mr. Garcia's conviction was overturned in June.

In announcing the unsealing of the indictment, the United States Attorney

Continued on Page B4, Column 5

Covenant Report Is Said to Find Sex Misconduct

By M. A. FARBER

An investigation ordered by the Covenant House board of directors concludes that the Rev. Bruce Ritter, the charity's founder and longtime president, engaged in sexual misconduct with young men living at Covenant House shelters for runaway youths, according to people who have read the investigation's report.

They say the four-month investigation, headed by Robert J. McGuire, a former New York City Police Commissioner, finds that had Father Ritter not resigned last February, the board would have had to dismiss him.

A Secretive Personal Fund

The report, which is to be issued today, also says the Covenant House board, controlled by Father Ritter until this year, failed to exercise proper oversight. The report notes, for example, that the board did not know that Father Ritter was receiving a salary of $98,000, the bulk of which was going into a secretive personal fund.

The fund, called the Franciscan Charitable Trust, had accumulated close to $1 million. Plans now call for it to be liquidated, with the assets going to Covenant House, as Father Ritter says he intended all along.

Father Ritter, who has vehemently denied the allegations, calling them "garbage," has declined to be interviewed for months and is said to have refused to cooperate with Mr. McGuire's investigation. The 63-year-old

Continued on Page B4, Column 2

IRAQ · Umm Qasr · Shatt al Arab · IRAN · Fao · RAUDHATAIN OILFIELD · SABRIYA OILFIELD · BUBIYAN I. · KUWAIT · PIPELINE · Kuwait Bay · FAILAKA I. · Mutla · Jahra · AREA OF DETAIL · Kuwait City · INTERNATIONAL AIRPORT · Persian Gulf · Ahmadi · Fahaheel · Sea Island (Oil loading terminal) · MINAGISH OILFIELD · BURGAN OILFIELD · Miles 0 20 · SAUDI ARABIA

SYRIA · Teheran · Baghdad · IRAQ · IRAN · JORDAN · SAUDI ARABIA · KUWAIT · Persian Gulf · Riyadh · Yanbu · Red Sea · Jidda · Miles 0 400

Miles 0 2 · Kuwait Bay · Sief Palace · Dasman Palace · U.S. Embassy · British Embassy · Central Kuwait · Saudi Arabian Embassy · Salam Palace · SHUWAIKH · AIRPORT RD. · SECOND RING RD. · THIRD RING RD.

Jim Perry/The New York Times
Iraqi invaders quickly moved into Kuwait City, taking control of Government buildings and the airport.

'NAKED AGGRESSION'

Bush Suggests Action by U.N. — Emir Flees to Saudi Arabia Exile

By R. W. APPLE Jr.
Special to The New York Times

WASHINGTON, Aug. 2 — Iraqi troops stormed into the desert sheikdom of Kuwait today, seizing control of its capital city and its rich oilfields, driving its ruler into exile, plunging the strategic Persian Gulf region into crisis and sending tremors of anxiety around the world.

President Bush condemned the invasion as "naked aggression" and sought to enlist world leaders in collective action against Iraq.

Faced with a dire threat from the truculent Iraqi leader, Saddam Hussein, to a region containing much of the world's oil reserves and with world financial markets in turmoil, Mr. Bush banned nearly all imports from Iraq and froze the nation's assets in the United States. At a news conference in Woody Creek, Colo., the President and Prime Minister Margaret Thatcher of Britain raised the possibility of economic or even military action by the United Nations.

Iraq Suspends Payments

In response, Iraq, which had been accusing Kuwait for weeks of stealing its oil and violating production limits set by the Organization of Petroleum Exporting Countries, suspended debt payments to the United States. Western experts asserted that Iraq had been motivated by a financial squeeze that only more oil dollars could ease and by ambitions for regional dominance.

Although oil prices rose sharply today, analysts noted that world inventories are unusually high, and they saw no immediate threat to supplies.

Witnesses in Kuwait said that hundreds of people were killed or wounded today as Iraqi ground forces, led by columns of tanks, surged into the desert emirate at the head of the gulf. Other troops came by air.

For Mr. Bush, the invasion posed manifold problems: the difficulty of direct military action despite the huge commitment of money and resources to the gulf in recent years; fear of another surge in oil prices, which could hurt economic growth and rekindle inflation; the potential disruption of the fragile budget negotiations between the White House and the Congress, in which a gasoline tax has been considered, and possible damage to the Re-

Continued on Page A8, Column 1

IRAQ'S ADVANTAGE LIMITS U.S. OPTIONS

Lack of Warning or Proximity Hinders American Action

By MICHAEL R. GORDON
Special to The New York Times

WASHINGTON, Aug. 2 — The Bush Administration faced the sobering reality today that despite a longstanding commitment to defend America's vital interests in the Persian Gulf, there was no easy military means to compel Iraq to withdraw its forces from Kuwait.

With the forces of pro-Western Arab powers like Saudi Arabia no match militarily for Iraq's powerful army, and with only a token American military presence in the area, the Administration's immediate responses included condemning the invasion, freezing Iraqi assets in the United States and calling for international sanctions.

Pentagon officials said that the United States had undertaken some military preparations as a result of the Iraqi attack. One aircraft carrier, the Independence, was under way at high speed from the Indian Ocean toward the Arabian Sea, adjacent to the Persian Gulf. It is expected to reach the area in several days.

A 2d Carrier Is Shifted

Another aircraft carrier, the Eisenhower, was being shifted to the Eastern Mediterranean Sea to put its attack planes within range of Iraq. The modest fleet of American ships in the Persian Gulf was expanded from six to eight. And some Air Force aerial refueling tankers were said to have been dispatched to the Indian Ocean region.

Defense Secretary Dick Cheney canceled plans to go with President Bush to Aspen, Colo., for Mr. Bush's speech on military issues and instead monitored the Gulf crisis from the Penta-

Continued on Page A8, Column 4

A New Gulf Alignment

Iraqis, Bargaining on Anti-U.S. Sentiment, May Profit by Intimidating the Monarchies

By YOUSSEF M. IBRAHIM
Special to The New York Times

News Analysis

PARIS, Aug. 2 — Iraq's invasion of Kuwait ushers in a new alignment in which Iraqis, Iranians and Palestinian hard-liners appear to share an interest in subduing the oil-rich monarchies of the region and challenging United States influence in the Arab world.

In ordering his forces to attack Kuwait, President Saddam Hussein of Iraq calculated that the odds were largely in his favor.

Arab diplomats and military experts said the only serious risk for Iraq was swift retaliation from the United States military forces. But that is a move that Washington may not be ready to take, given that the Iraqi armed forces are widely considered the most tested and best equipped in the Gulf region.

The Iraqis have much to gain from their invasion of Kuwait. A successful offensive could establish Baghdad as the dominant power in the Middle East, giving it a much greater say in decisions on oil production and prices.

Beyond that, the attack could become a rallying point for those in the Arab world who resent United States influence in world affairs and who feel that some Middle Eastern nations like Egypt have gone too far in accommodating Washington. Lastly, it could finally settle Iraq's longstanding border disputes with Kuwait.

The prospects for an effective counter to the attack appear slimmer in view of evidence that the Iraqis coordinated their move with Iran, which helped exert diplomatic pressure on Kuwait and the United Arab Emirates to raise prices last month at a meeting of the Organization of Petroleum Exporting Countries.

Iran officially condemned the Iraqi move late today, but the suspicion remained that it had at the very least not discouraged Baghdad's action.

Sense of Powerlessness

In the wake of the invasion, the Arab world is discovering how powerless it is in countering an Iraqi attempt to assert its dominance.

Saudi Arabia is Kuwait's closest ally in the region and the founder of the Gulf Cooperation Council, the alliance to which both Kuwait and the United Arab Emirates belong. But it has hardly lifted a finger to halt the Iraqi invasion, giving the impression that it is powerless and ever more dependent on American assistance. Although the Saudis have spent billions of dollars on

Continued on Page A10, Column 3

Soviet Smokers Vow Strikes As Cigarettes, Too, Disappear

By CELESTINE BOHLEN
Special to The New York Times

MOSCOW, Aug. 2 — It happens like clockwork, all over the city. A truck pulls up to a boarded-up kiosk, unloads its wares, the sale window opens and within minutes smokers appear out of nowhere to take places in line, hopeful that for this day, anyway, their addiction can be fed.

Along with other ills, the Soviet Union is now in the throes of a nicotine fit, brought on by a painful and puzzling withdrawal of cigarettes from a nation of heavy smokers.

In many parts of the country, the cigarette shortage — caused by a series of typical economic lapses — has galvanized the patient, line-suffering Soviet consumer into action.

In the city of Perm last week, a demonstration that began in front of an empty tobacco shop spilled into downtown streets, ending in a rally outside City Hall, where 2,000 people chanted and waved banners, badgering the Communist Party for cigarettes. "Hey, you up there, your people have nothing to smoke as well as nothing to eat," one banner read. "Party, have you got a smoke?" asked another.

Aircraft Workers Threaten Strike

In Kuibyshev, smokers at an aircraft plant threatened a strike over the cigarette shortage and protesters mounted a daily vigil at a local tobacco plant that had been shut for repairs.

Warning strikes have also been reported in Ulyanovsk and Ufa, while in Voronezh and Orel, angry smokers have smashed the windows of tobacco kiosks. This month, at the height of the harvest in the Krasnador region, combine operators brought their machines to a stop with a nonnegotiable demand: "No tobacco, no work."

Such public vehemence has been absent during other shortages: when cheese, onions, lemons or sausages disappear from the stores, Soviet shoppers simply shift their queues from one

Continued on Page A4, Column 5

2 Teen-Agers Shot As Violence Persists On New York Streets

The tide of violence in New York City in the last two weeks — four children killed by stray gunfire, an advertising executive shot dead in the West Village, two cab drivers murdered, a young couple bludgeoned in Central Park — continued yesterday as officials struggled to respond to growing fears.

A 14-year-old Queens boy was shot and killed after he told another teenager to stop riding a friend's moped. In the Bronx, a 15-year-old girl standing with friends in a park was critically wounded when a youth fired a gunshot into her group. A homeless drifter was charged with Monday's fatal shooting of the ad executive at a phone booth.

And pressure grew on city officials to cope with the latest wave of violence. Mayor David N. Dinkins today will announce a crackdown on gun users. Police Commissioner Lee P. Brown, in an interview, contended that the police alone could not solve the problems of crime and violence.

Articles, pages B1 and B3.

Reuters
Iraqi gunners yesterday on the coast near Kuwait City, where they fired on Kuwaiti naval vessels offshore.

The Iraqi Invasion: Global Reverberations

OIL PRICES Spot market prices surged, with the American benchmark crude rising to $23.11 a barrel, up $1.57. The invasion stirred fears of slower economic growth, higher inflation and OPEC domination of the world oil market. But price increases should be limited by a near-record stockpile worldwide. Page A9.

FINANCIAL MARKETS The dollar rose, gold prices jumped and most stock markets fell. Japan, dependent on imported oil, was hard hit. As of today's close in Tokyo, its stock market had fallen 4.3 percent since the invasion took place. Page D1.

THE SOVIET UNION Moscow announced a suspension in the delivery of arms and military hardware to Iraq. The move interrupted Moscow's longtime role as Baghdad's chief arms supplier. Page A10.

UNITED NATIONS With Moscow and Washington in agreement, the Security Council voted 14 to 0 to condemn the invasion and demand an Iraqi withdrawal. Page A10.

DIPLOMACY Secretary of State James A. Baker 3d cut short a visit to Mongolia and plans to issue a joint statement about the crisis in Moscow today with the Soviet Foreign Minister, Eduard A. Shevardnadze. Syria condemned the invasion and called for an emergency Arab summit conference.

ISRAEL Israeli leaders condemned the invasion, but they also appeared relieved by the move. For months, President Saddam Hussein has been sharply threatening Israel. Officials in Jerusalem were openly frustrated that the rest of the world did not seem adequately concerned. Page A10.

THE EUROPEAN ALLIES Western European countries unanimously condemned the invasion, with Britain and France joining the United States in freezing billions of dollars worth of Kuwaiti assets. Page A10.

INSIDE

Why a Bishop Quit
The recent resignation of the Roman Catholic Archbishop of Atlanta came about after evidence of his "intimate relationship" with a woman, church officials said. Page A12.

A Troubled Savings Rescue
Almost a year after the Federal bailout of the savings and loan industry, economists see problems, including a danger to banks. Page D1.

Barry Case Goes to Jury
The drug case against Washington's Mayor is now in the hands of 12 of the city's residents. Page A12.

"All the News That's Fit to Print"

The New York Times

Late Edition

New York: **Today,** sunny, becoming windy. High 73. **Tonight,** breezy, mild. Low 62. **Tomorrow,** quite windy, sunny, warmer. High 77. **Yesterday,** high 69, low 56. Details are on page C7.

VOL.CXL . . No. 48,377 | NEW YORK, WEDNESDAY, OCTOBER 3, 1990 | 50 cents beyond 75 miles from New York City, except on Long Island. | 40 CENTS

TWO GERMANYS UNITE AFTER 45 YEARS WITH JUBILATION AND A VOW OF PEACE

DINKINS PROPOSES RECORD EXPANSION OF POLICE FORCES

Mayor Offers New Programs for Corrections and Youth to Help Combat Crime

By RALPH BLUMENTHAL

Seeking to take command of an issue that has shaken his leadership, Mayor David N. Dinkins announced a barrage of proposals yesterday to fight crime, including a record expansion of New York City's police forces and ambitious new corrections, youth and education programs. The total cost would be $1.8 billion over the next four years.

With New York City already in financial straits, the Mayor proposed paying for the initiatives through a rise in the real-property tax, a new city payroll tax to be shared by workers and employers and a 25-cent surcharge on state lottery tickets.

The taxes, which would rise from $138 million in what remains of the first fiscal year to $644 million in the fourth year, would require approval by the City Council and the State Legislature.

'Assault on All Fronts'

"We will not wage war by degree," Mr. Dinkins said, releasing a 535-page police manpower study and a 57-page mayoral report that began a day of briefings and culminated in a news conference timed for live television coverage on the evening news. "Our strategy calls for an assault on all fronts." [Excerpts, page B2.]

The anti-crime program was hailed by many community leaders, but reaction to the tax plan was mixed. The State Senate majority leader, Ralph J. Marino, voiced strong reservations about the potentially negative effect on commuters and businesses. Gov. Mario M. Cuomo said that if it were necessary for public safety, he "could" support the payroll tax, but that he had yet to review the plan in detail.

Assembly Speaker Mel Miller also urged caution. "We're going to have to go slowly in weighing the tax package," most of which, he noted, would not take effect until the fiscal year beginning next July. The City Council Speaker, Peter F. Vallone, voiced general support for the plan but seemed taken aback that it went so far beyond the Council's own proposal to hire more officers through a lottery surcharge.

Thomas Reppetto, president of the

Continued on Page B2, Column 1

In Appeal for Support for Budget, President Calls Plan Best for Now

By DAVID E. ROSENBAUM

Special to The New York Times

WASHINGTON, Oct. 2 — Faced with a revolt in his party's Congressional ranks and wariness around the country, President Bush appealed on television tonight for public support of the budget compromise he and Congressional leaders struck last weekend. He predicted "economic chaos if we fail to reduce the deficit."

In a show of bipartisanship that verged on coalition Government, the President was followed with a broadcast by Senator George J. Mitchell of Maine, the Democratic leader. He urged support for the President "because the nation is more important than partisan differences." [Transcripts of the Bush and Mitchell speeches appear on page D28.]

Tough Task for Bush

Mr. Mitchell was preaching to the converted for the most part. Despite considerable opposition among liberals, a majority of Congressional Democrats appear to support the agreement.

But Mr. Bush has the more difficult task of swaying enough dissident Republicans to win enactment of the plan.

The President said that neither he nor anyone else was completely satisfied with the compromise, but he said it was "the best agreement that can be legislated now."

In the strongest statement he has made about economic perils that might lie ahead, Mr. Bush emphasized: "If we fail to enact this agreement, our economy will falter, markets may tumble and recession will follow."

He called on the public to "tell your Congressmen and Senators you support this deficit-reduction agreement."

A Bipartisan Appeal

The President continued: "If they are Republicans, urge them to stand with the President. If they are Democrats, urge them to stand with their Congressional leaders."

"Those who dislike one part or another may pick our agreement apart," Mr. Bush said, "but if they do, believe me, the political reality is no one can put a better one back together again."

Senator Mitchell made almost identical points. He would have preferred "a budget that asks more from the wealthy and less from the elderly," he said. But as for the compromise, he

Continued on Page D27, Column 1

Pivotal Moment for Bush

By ANDREW ROSENTHAL

Special to The New York Times

News Analysis

WASHINGTON, Oct. 2 — With his speech tonight from the Oval Office, George Bush completed a fundamental transition: The President who succeeded for so long at giving Americans only good news is now telling them to prepare for economic pain at home and the possibility of war abroad.

With remarkable speed, Mr. Bush has moved from the most protracted honeymoon in recent White House history to twin crises that could determine the success of his Presidency.

The decision to confront the Republican rebellion on Capitol Hill over the budget agreement quickly and directly in a nationally televised speech represented a judgment that any delay could allow events to spin out of control. If the emerging prospects for passage of the budget package turn into defeat, Mr. Bush would immediately lose his calculated gamble that such an agreement would be good for the economy and thus bolster his re-election campaign in 1992.

For more than a year and a half, everything seemed to be going Mr. Bush's way, especially in Europe. Then on Aug. 8, six days after the Iraqi invasion of Kuwait, Mr. Bush went on national television to announce that he was sending troops to the Persian Gulf and to prepare the country for the possibility that American soldiers and civilians could die in a far-off war.

Tonight, less than two months later, Mr. Bush again spoke from the Oval

Continued on Page D27, Column 4

More on the Budget

A SECOND LOOK Some experts say the deficit will be cut less than predicted. Page D27.

TAX BREAKS Big companies may benefit from provisions aimed at small ones. Page D29.

PLANNING AHEAD How changes in deductions will affect some taxpayers. Page D29.

The German flag was unfurled in front of the Reichstag building in Berlin at midnight as the two Germanys were reunited. (Associated Press)

A MILLION IN BERLIN

Flag at Reichstag Marks Start of a New Era at Center of Europe

By SERGE SCHMEMANN

Special to The New York Times

BERLIN, Wednesday, Oct. 3 — Forty-five years after it was carved up in defeat and disgrace, Germany was reunited today in a midnight celebration of pealing bells, national hymns and the jubilant blare of good old German oom-pah-pah.

At the stroke of midnight Tuesday, a copy of the American Liberty Bell, a gift from the United States at the height of the cold war, tolled from the Town Hall, and the black, red and gold banner of the Federal Republic of Germany rose slowly before the Reichstag, the scarred seat of past German Parliaments.

Then the President, Richard von Weizsäcker, drawing on the words of the West German Constitution, proclaimed from the steps of the Reichstag: "In free self-determination, we want to achieve the unity in freedom of Germany. We are aware of our responsibility for these tasks before God and the people. We want to serve peace in the world in a united Europe."

Singing of Anthem

With that, a throng estimated at one million joined in the West German national anthem, now the anthem for united Germany: "Unity and justice and freedom for the German fatherland . . ." The words are from the third stanza of the prewar anthem, whose opening verses, now banned, began, "Deutschland, Deutschland über Alles."

The moment marked the return of a nation severed along the front line between East and West to the center stage of Europe, this time as an economic powerhouse vowing never again to bring grief to a continent it had so terribly ravaged in the past century.

It is the smallest unified German state to rise in the 119 years since Otto von Bismarck first gathered the Germans under the Prussian crown.

Beer and Revelry

Hundreds of German flags waved and firecrackers snapped in the chilly autumn night. Beer and sparkling wine flowed freely and the strains of divergent bands mingled in a rowdy cacophony. Soon bottles began smashing on the pavement and celebration turned to intoxication, and by early morning the center of the new capital was deep in smashed bottles and weaving revelers.

A force of about 5,000 police officers had been massed in case radicals tried

Continued on Page A17, Column 1

Germany by the Numbers

In some respects, the united Germany is less than the sum of its parts. The statistical tale is told in charts and a map on page A16.

Senate Confirms Souter, 90 to 9, As Supreme Court's 105th Justice

By RICHARD L. BERKE

Special to The New York Times

WASHINGTON, Oct. 2 — Ten weeks after President Bush nominated David H. Souter, a little-known New Hampshire judge, for the Supreme Court, the Senate voted overwhelmingly today to confirm him as the Court's 105th Justice.

The vote was 90 to 9, with only Democrats voting against confirmation. The balloting came after nearly four hours of speeches on the Senate floor in which supporters said they were confident Judge Souter would preserve fundamental constitutional values, while opponents said too much was not known about his positions on critical issues like abortion.

Case on Sensitive Issue

Chief Justice William H. Rehnquist will swear in Judge Souter at a relatively short ceremony at the Court on Tuesday morning, in time to sit for oral arguments later that day in the second week of the Court term.

On Wednesday, Judge Souter will be among the Justices hearing a major case on the lawfulness of corporate policies that exclude women from jobs that might endanger a developing fetus. Today the Court took up the major issue left unresolved from the era of official school segregation: what a school system that was segregated by law decades ago must do to free itself from Federal court supervision. [Education, page B8.]

With the Souter nomination behind him, Senator Joseph R. Biden Jr., the Delaware Democrat who is chairman of the Judiciary Committee, was looking to future vacancies on the Court. He said he hoped that the Administration "will not learn the wrong lesson" from the strong bipartisan support the nominee received.

"Our overwhelming approval is not a sign that the Senate intends to be lax about exercising its advise-and-consent power, or intends to use that power only to screen out extremist nominees," Mr. Biden said. "Rather, it is a sign that we take this power seriously, and that we intend to exercise it responsibly. And in doing so, Judge Souter falls within the sphere of candidates acceptable to the Senate."

Mr. Biden emphasized, however, that he and several other Democrats who supported the nomination had serious misgivings because Judge Souter

Continued on Page A24, Column 1

Top Soviet General Tells U.S. Not to Attack in Gulf

Gen. Mikhail A. Moiseyev, left, chief of the Soviet General Staff, discussing options in the Persian Gulf crisis yesterday in New York City. With him was Gen. Colin L. Powell, the Chairman of the Joint Chiefs of Staff. (Jack Manning/The New York Times)

By MICHAEL R. GORDON

The head of the Soviet military said yesterday that the economic sanctions against Iraq were working and that no force should be used in the Persian Gulf unless it was approved by the United Nations.

The remarks by the Soviet general, Mikhail A. Moiseyev, Chief of the Soviet General Staff, were the most explicit comments made so far by a Soviet official on the need to have United Nations approval for the use of force by the United States and other nations that have opposed the Iraqi invasion of Kuwait.

The Soviet general's comments — in an unusual joint interview with Gen. Colin L. Powell, Chairman of the Joint Chiefs of Staff — signaled a basic disagreement with Washington about the circumstances under which military force could be used in the Persian Gulf.

"We cannot view the resolution of any crisis like this by means of using arms," said General Moiseyev, who is on a tour of the United States as a guest of General Powell. But General Powell pointedly said President Bush had not ruled out any options.

The two generals were interviewed by writers and editors of The New York Times.

Suggesting that military force was not needed to force Iraqi troops out of Kuwait, General Moiseyev said the economic embargo was beginning to hurt Iraq.

"Saddam Hussein has really understood now finally how far he has gone," General Moiseyev said. "He is finding himself in economic and political isolation, and he can't survive very long that way."

General Moiseyev asserted that protests, uprisings and desertions in Iraqi were sapping the strength of the Iraqi military and impelling President Hussein to seek a diplomatic solution.

"You can't keep an army together

Continued on Page A12, Column 1

INSIDE

Air Crash Mystery in China

Did a cockpit struggle cause a hijacked Chinese plane to crash into a parked jet at Canton's airport, killing 127 people? Chinese officials would not confirm the report. Page A3.

South African Rift Persists

The leader of the Inkatha movement spurned a meeting with the African National Congress, dampening prospects for a reconciliation between the two warring groups. Page A3.

Melee in Pakistan

A mob stormed the courtroom where former Prime Minister Benazir Bhutto is to stand trial on corruption charges. Page A6.

Women in Locker Rooms

Three recent incidents in football have reopened the issue of access to locker rooms by women covering men's sports. Page D31.

Bitter Dispute Is Threatening Program for Marrow Donors

By GINA KOLATA

A program that has the lofty goal of finding altruistic people to donate bone marrow to save the lives of dying patients has become enmeshed in a dispute that threatens its ability to function.

The conflict involves charges that a former subcontractor in the federally financed program provided misleading information to dying patients and volunteers who wanted to help them; withheld the names of thousands of potential marrow donors, and failed to account to families for large sums of money raised in their names.

The subcontractor, the Life-Savers Foundation of America, has denied the allegations and accused the National Marrow Donor Program of overcharging patients and being inefficient in matching patients and donors.

Registry of Potential Donors

The national program has amassed a file of 200,000 people who are willing to donate marrow if their tissue is compatible with that of a patient with leukemia or another disease. Without transplants, the patients will die, and the demand for donors far exceeds the supply.

But Federal officials, transplant surgeons and ethicists are worried that allegations of questionable conduct in the treatment of dying patients and their families could cause the network of volunteer donors to fall apart. They say altruism is fragile at best, and any hint of misconduct is more than enough to make people shy away from donating.

The national program has asserted in court and in a letter to Senator Al Gore, Democrat of Tennessee, that Life-Savers caused patients unnecessary anguish by raising false hopes that there was a donor.

Officials of the national program, who say they have severed all ties with the subcontractor, say some families

Continued on Page A26, Column 1

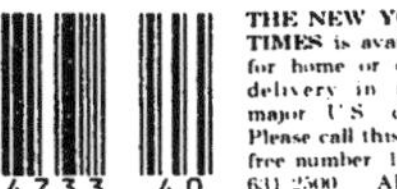

"All the News That's Fit to Print"

The New York Times

Late Edition
New York: **Today,** partly cloudy, windy. High 49. **Tonight,** clear, cold winds. Low 32. **Tomorrow,** variable clouds. High 40. **Yesterday,** high 55, low 38. Details are on page D22.

VOL.CXL . . . . No. 48,483 — NEW YORK, THURSDAY, JANUARY 17, 1991 — 50 cents beyond 75 miles from New York City, except on Long Island. — 40 CENTS

U.S. AND ALLIES OPEN AIR WAR ON IRAQ; BOMB BAGHDAD AND KUWAITI TARGETS; 'NO CHOICE' BUT FORCE, BUSH DECLARES

A TENSE WAIT ENDS

News of Attack Sweeps the Country, Stirring Profound Feelings

By JAMES BARRON

In one long moment yesterday, word that the United States had attacked Baghdad swept the country.

In split-level suburban homes on the East Coast where dinner was in the oven, in big-city restaurants in the Midwest where bars were jammed with the happy-hour crowd and in skyscraper offices on the West Coast where people were still at work, there was an odd mixture of apprehension, sadness and relief.

In malls, shoppers emptied out of stores and cried. In supermarkets, cashiers rushed to call relatives and share the news that after five months of waiting and wondering America was at war. In department stores, people crowded in front of television sets, with some saying they were stunned that President Bush had decided to act so soon after the United Nations deadline for Iraq to withdraw from Kuwait.

A Scene Out of World War II

Suddenly, in public places where cacophony is the norm, there was an unusual silence, eerie rather than giddy. Grand Central Terminal in Manhattan — where even whispers can take on an echoing, high-decibel intensity — was quiet. On trains to Connecticut, passengers gathered around people who had radios with headsets. "The people with the radios would listen to the news and then relay it to the other passengers," said Dan Brucker, a spokesman for the Metro-North Commuter Railroad, "kind of like World War II radio dispatchers delivering the news."

The word that waves of air attacks were striking Iraq silenced black-tie galas in Manhattan. And in a Houston hotel, the chatter around the bar stopped when the President began his speech from the Oval Office. Only the machine making frozen margaritas kept whirring.

Some people applauded Mr. Bush's decision to order the attack. "It was direct and to the point," Lester Alexander, a New Orleans real-estate investor, said of Mr. Bush's speech. "He did not try to sell me on his reasons, but he

Continued on Page A19, Column 4

TURKEY
SYRIA
JORDAN
IRAQ
IRAN
KUWAIT
SAUDI ARABIA
Persian Gulf
Miles 0 100
Possible air strike targets
Air bases
Oil refineries
Conventional weapons plants
Chemical, nuclear, biological warfare facilities
Al Kindi, Tall Afar, Mosul, Erbil, Qayyarah, Kirkuk, Bayji, Tikrit, Samarra, Al Qaim, Balad, Baghdad, Rashid, Al Asad, Falluja, Tuwaitha, Salman Pak, Shaik Mazhur, Rutba, Iskandariya, Ubaydah bin al Jarrah, Al Amarah, Euphrates, Tigris, Tallil, Jalibah, Basra, Shatt al Arab, Rumaila, Umm Qasr, Kuwait City
Miles 0 25
Tikrit, Tharthar Lake, Shari Lake, Samara, Balad, Tigris, Euphrates, SADDAM INTERNATIONAL AIRPORT, Falluja, Baghdad, Rashid, Al Taqaddum, Salman Pak, Shaik Muzar
The New York Times

No Ground Fighting Yet; Call to Arms by Hussein

By ANDREW ROSENTHAL
Special to The New York Times

WASHINGTON, Thursday, Jan. 17 — The United States and allied forces Wednesday night opened the long-threatened war to drive President Saddam Hussein's army from Kuwait, striking Baghdad and other targets in Iraq and Kuwait with waves of bombers and cruise missiles launched from naval vessels.

"The liberation of Kuwait has begun," President Bush said in a three-sentence statement confirming the start of the attack that was read by his spokesman, Marlin Fitzwater, shortly after the raids began.

Later, in a televised address to the nation from the Oval Office, a somber Mr. Bush said that after months of continuous diplomatic overtures had failed to produce movement by Iraq, the United States and its allies "have no choice but to force Saddam from Kuwait by force. We will not fail." [Transcript, page A6.]

No Planes Reported Missing

United States officials said shortly after midnight Wednesday that none of the planes that took part in the night-time raids were reported missing.

In Baghdad, Mr. Hussein said in a speech broadcast by the Iraqi radio that "the mother of all battles has begun," according to news service reports. He called Mr. Bush a "hypocritical criminal" and vowed to crush "the satanic intentions of the White House." It was unclear when Mr. Hussein had read his remarks, whether they had been pre-recorded, or where he was at the time. [Page A18.]

Mr. Bush said his goal "is not the conquest of Iraq, it is the liberation of Kuwait." But he also said, "We are determined to knock out Saddam Hussein's nuclear bomb potential. We will also destroy his chemical-weapons facilities."

3 Other Nations Take Part

Defense Secretary Dick Cheney and Gen. Colin L. Powell, Chairman of the Joint Chiefs of Staff, told reporters at the Pentagon Wednesday night that those targets had been among those assigned to the first wave of American F-117 Stealth fighter-bombers, F-15 fighter-bombers, British Tornado attack planes and Saudi and Kuwaiti F-15's that raided Iraqi military targets about 3 A.M. local time Thursday (7 P.M. Wednesday Eastern standard time.)

Administration officials also said United States Navy ships in the waters off the Arabian Peninsula had fired ground-hugging cruise missiles at targets that had been programmed into their guidance systems for months. The officials said the ships fired a total of 50 Tomahawk missiles in an assault on Iraqi command and communications centers.

Seeking to Avoid Civilians

Mr. Cheney said the initial targets were spread throughout Iraq and Kuwait and were chosen to "do everything possible to avoid injury to civilians." Both officials declined to say if there had been any American or allied losses, or to describe in any detail how badly they thought they had damaged Baghdad or the other Iraqi targets.

"The response of the Iraqi forces at this point has been limited," Mr. Cheney said, leading analysts to conclude that the allies may have succeeded in their goal of largely incapacitating Iraq's Air Force at the outset.

But Mr. Cheney said that the war was just beginning and that "it is likely to run for a long period of time."

Reports of New Attack

Cable News Network reported that antiaircraft fire resumed in Baghdad about 9:30 A.M. Iraqi time and that its correspondents heard explosions that sounded like bombs in the far distance from their central Baghdad hotel.

The network also reported the first sighting of President Hussein since the start of the attacks, by a Western television technician at a Baghdad television center this afternoon.

Mr. Cheney said the United States could not confirm reports that Iraq had fired Soviet-made Scud missiles at allied positions after the attack began. Reuters reported from Bahrain that the civil defense authorities there had detected missile launches but that the weapons fell short of their targets.

Assuring Americans that ground forces were not yet engaged in the battle, the President added: "Five months ago, Saddam Hussein started this cruel war against Kuwait. Tonight, the battle has been joined."

He said initial reports indicated that "our operations are proceeding according to plan."

"Our objectives are clear," he said. "Saddam Hussein's forces will leave Kuwait, the legitimate Government of Kuwait will be restored to its rightful

Continued on Page A14, Column 1

Raids, on a Huge Scale, Seek to Destroy Iraqi Missiles

ABC News
President Bush as he announced in a televised address last night that an air attack had been launched against Iraq.

By MICHAEL R. GORDON
Special to The New York Times

WASHINGTON, Thursday, Jan. 17 — The military campaign to evict Iraq from Kuwait began, as expected, with night air strikes on a huge scale at targets deep in Iraq and Kuwait.

According to early reports of the night operation from the Pentagon, no American aircraft were lost and grave damage appeared to have been done to Iraqi military forces. Cable News Network reported that another series of sorties began at midmorning Baghdad time.

American officials said the first onslaught against Iraqi air defenses, communications and weapons sites included the firing of Tomahawk sea-launched cruise missiles, as well as F-117 Stealth fighter-bombers, F-15E fighter-bombers and a wide variety of other Air Force and Navy planes.

British and Saudis Join In

The American aircraft were accompanied by British and Saudi Tornado fighter-bombers, Saudi F-15's and Kuwaiti combat planes.

The aims of the nighttime attack were to damage the Iraqi military establishment by destroying command and control centers, including those in Baghdad, and to establish air superiority by knocking out Iraqi air defenses and airfields.

Pentagon officials said that all Navy planes in the night operation were reported to have returned safely. There were no reported Air Force losses, though the return of some of the planes to an air base near Taif, Saudi Arabia, was being delayed by bad weather there. Britain reported that all of its planes had returned safely.

Pentagon officials said that its bomb-damage assessments were still being conducted, and they disputed reports that the attacks had decimated the Republican Guards, the elite of the Iraqi Army.

Satellite Reports Awaited

Pentagon officials said the attack on Iraq appeared to be very successful because the Iraqi Air Force had not challenged the attacking planes and because the United States has no confirmed reports of launchings of Iraqi Scuds, long-range surface-to-surface missiles that are considered a threat to the allies' bases and to Israel. But they added that they were still awaiting definitive satellite and other reconnaissance reports.

Gen. Colin L. Powell, the chairman of the Joint Chiefs of Staff, said at a Pentagon news conference that "there has been no air resistance" from the Iraqis. Pentagon officials said that they hoped to destroy the Iraqi planes in their hardened shelters.

The allied air forces also attacked Scud batteries, and, as President Bush emphasized, American planes struck at Iraqi nuclear and chemical-weapons production sites. No ground forces were used in the operation, the Pentagon said.

In mounting the air attack, the United States is also trying to make good on assurances to the Israelis that Washington would blast the Scud missiles that threaten Israel to make it unnecessary for Israel to enter the war, the American officials said. Defense Secretary Dick Cheney said that the Pentagon had no information to confirm that Iraqi Scud missiles had struck Saudi Arabia.

The timing of the attack was de-

Continued on Page A15, Column 1

Rumble in the Sky Ends a 5-Month Wait

By PHILIP SHENON

IN SAUDI ARABIA, Thursday, Jan. 17 — "It's absolutely awesome, I mean the ground shook and you felt it," said Col. Ray Davies, describing the takeoff of the first planes to attack Iraq from a big Saudi air base where he is chief maintenance officer.

The 44-year-old colonel said the first group of jets left at 12:50 A.M., about an hour before the first word of attack was broadcast by television reporters in Baghdad.

"We've been waiting here for five months; now we finally got to do what we were sent here to do," Colonel Davies told a group of American reporters who were brought to the base. "This is history in the making."

The F-15 fighter bombers, heavily loaded with bombs and supplemental underwing fuel tanks, thundered off in pairs into what had been a still desert night. The aircraft, which quickly became faint red dots, were also armed with cannon and air-to-air missiles to be used in their own defense.

The activity at the airfield, whose exact location cannot be identified under military reporting rules, was the first indication here that the assault was under way. All commercial traffic at the airport had been suspended a short time earlier.

Just before 4 A.M. Saudi time, hundreds of journalists and other guests at the Dhahran International Hotel, including many Filipino and Pakistani workers, were herded into the bomb shelter in the hotel basement and instructed to put on gas masks. Sirens started to wail throughout the city.

Waiting for the Signal

As the guests, primarily journalists, waited for the signal "gas clear," a hotel employee serving as warden directed guests to spread out in the area, which serves as a kitchen. The air conditioning had been turned off to prevent the spread of chemical agents in case the hotel in the eastern Saudi oil city was hit by Iraqi missiles. The room was quiet except for the sound of a radio on which a news announcer was saying that the attack had begun.

A British defense consultant who is working for the hotel, Philip Congdon,

Continued on Page A17, Column 6

MORE ON THE GULF

Bush Evokes Glory Of Past, Not Vietnam

To tell Americans that war with Iraq had started, President Bush harked back to one of the great days in American military history — D-Day, June 6, 1944. News analysis, page A16.

In Cairo, Jubilation Among Kuwaiti Exiles

Hundreds of Kuwaitis drove their cars through the Egyptian capital, honking and waving flags after hearing news of the American-led attack. "Thank God! Thank God!" was a cry heard over and over again. Page A18.

Israel on Alert

Israel declared a state of emergency minutes after word of the attack. There was no indication of an Iraqi attack on Israel. Page A18.

OTHER NEWS

Gorbachev Is Moving To Muzzle the Press

Faced with mounting condemnation of the assault by Soviet forces on demonstrators in Lithuania, President Mikhail S. Gorbachev moved to undermine a law guaranteeing freedom of the press — a hallmark of the era of openness that he himself ushered in. Page A8.

In a show of defiance in the Lithuanian capital, hundreds of thousands of mourners streamed through the streets to bury the dead. Page A8.

Dinkins Offers Budget With Layoffs and Cuts

Mayor David N. Dinkins presented a preliminary New York City budget of $29.3 billion for the next fiscal year. The announcement was met with a mix of pain and uncertainty. The plan includes thousands of layoffs and service cuts. Page B1.

Daily News Threatens To Close or Sell

The management of The Daily News threatened to close or sell the paper unless it stems heavy losses. Both sides in the 12-week-old strike agreed the move was an ultimatum to the unions to make major concessions or lose their jobs for good. Page B1.

The War Begins

"The liberation of Kuwait has begun. In conjunction with the forces of our coalition partners, the United States has moved under the code name Operation Desert Storm to enforce the mandates of the United Nations Security Council.

"As of 7 o'clock P.M. Operation Desert Storm forces were engaging targets in Iraq and Kuwait."

STATEMENT, PRESIDENT BUSH, 7:06 P.M.

"All the News That's Fit to Print"

The New York Times

Late Edition
New York: **Today,** limited sun, perhaps a shower late. High 62. **Tonight,** cooler. Low 40. **Tomorrow,** cloudy, a light shower. High 41. **Yesterday,** high 59, low 45. Details are on page D10.

VOL.CXLI . . . No. 48,809

NEW YORK, MONDAY, DECEMBER 9, 1991

50 CENTS

DECLARING DEATH OF SOVIET UNION, RUSSIA AND 2 REPUBLICS FORM NEW COMMONWEALTH

Frantic Moves Came to Light In Days Before Maxwell Died

As the Empire Was Crumbling

A special report.

The New York Times

Robert Maxwell

By STEVEN PROKESCH
Special to The New York Times

LONDON, Dec. 8 — At the time of his mysterious death on Nov. 5, Robert Maxwell almost certainly knew he was about to be caught.

He had drained hundreds of millions of dollars from his two flagship public companies and from employee pension funds in a frantic attempt to keep his heavily indebted publishing empire afloat.

The auditors of the Maxwell empire, Coopers & Lybrand Deloitte, were to conduct their next regular audit of the pension funds in a couple of months. And Coopers would have quickly discovered the transactions, said a person very familiar with the details of a special financial examination of the empire conducted for the banks after Mr. Maxwell's death. He agreed to discuss the report only if his identity was not disclosed.

'Basically Grabbing Cash'

The Coopers team also found evidence that some of the diverted money went to The Daily News in New York to cover its losses. That raises more doubts about the future of the newspaper, which Mr. Maxwell acquired in March.

The maneuvering by Mr. Maxwell to prop up the private companies that controlled his empire "was doomed to failure," the person familiar with the Coopers report said.

"It wasn't a sophisticated fraud like B.C.C.I.," he said, referring to the scandal surrounding the Bank of Credit and Commerce International. "The guy was basically grabbing cash, and Coopers found it out within days of going in." The Coopers team was led by Richard Stone, the partner in charge of the accounting firm's corporate finance division.

That discovery led the main holding companies of the Maxwell empire to file Thursday for the British equivalent of bankruptcy protection.

It is now apparent that the pressure on Mr. Maxwell to find money for the private companies was increasing sharply in the weeks before his death, according to the Coopers report, bankers, and directors and executives of the Maxwell empire.

"It would appear that there was a desperate need for cash from June

Continued on Page D3 Column 1

West Europeans Gather to Seek A Tighter Union

By ALAN RIDING
Special to The New York Times

MAASTRICHT, the Netherlands, Dec. 8 — In an atmosphere of great expectation tinged with no small apprehension, European Community leaders gathered here tonight for a crucial two-day summit meeting that should determine the region's place in the world well into the 21st century.

Their aim is to prepare the 12-nation community to compete with regional economic groups led by the United States and Japan and to exercise greater political influence in international affairs. To achieve this, they hope to speed up Europe's 34-year-old march toward political and economic integration.

They will therefore be taking up proposals to establish a single currency and a regional central bank, to move toward common foreign and security policies, to give more power to the European Parliament and to harmonize their approaches to social and environmental questions.

Nowhere Near Full Union

The measures fall far short of creating anything resembling a United States of Europe. While some politicians like to evoke the centuries-old dream of full union, it is at least decades away.

Yet if approved, the changes will significantly bolster the community's existing plan to form a single regional market of 340 million consumers on Jan. 1, 1993, eventually turning what is already the world's largest trading bloc into the world's dominant financial power.

Adoption of the Maastricht agenda is far from assured. Britain, long the

Continued on Page A10, Column 1

U.S. Seeks to Trim 'Friendly Fire' Toll

Alarmed by the number of American soldiers killed and wounded by "friendly fire" in the Persian Gulf war, the military has begun top-to-bottom changes to decrease the frequency of such incidents in future conflicts.

The changes in training, equipment and procedures will affect tens of thousands of soldiers, the Army said, and are the most significant shifts so far in American military practices resulting from lessons learned in the gulf war.

"We're committed to addressing this problem in an institutional and effective way," Gen. Gordon R. Sullivan, the Army Chief of Staff, said.

The changes are to be announced later this week, at which time senior Army generals are also expected to discuss new policies on notifying relatives of American soldiers who were accidentally killed by their own forces.

Article, page A12.

The New and the Old

LATVIA — ESTONIA — LITHUANIA — BYELORUSSIA — Brest — Minsk — UKRAINE — Kiev — Moscow — RUSSIA — MOLDAVIA — GEORGIA — ARMENIA — AZERBAIJAN — TURKMENIA — UZBEKISTAN — KAZAKHSTAN — KIRGHIZIA — TADZHIKISTAN

Miles: 0 — 1,000

Source: The Statesman's Yearbook, 1991-92; U.S.S.R. Facts and Figures Annual, 1991

POPULATION
January 1990
Others 70.6 million; Baltics 8 million; Russia 148 million; Ukraine 51.8 million; Byelorussia 10.3 million

CONSUMER GOODS
Share of production 1988
Other 28.2%; Baltics 6.8%; Russia 47.0%; Ukraine 16.4%; Byelorussia 1.5%

AGRICULTURE
Share of total output, 1988
Other 21.4%; Baltics 4.4%; Russia 46.7%; Ukraine 22.1%; Byelorussia 5.4%

The New York Times

"We, the republic of Byelorussia, the Russian Federation and Ukraine . . . state that the U.S.S.R., as a subject of international law and geopolitical reality, is ceasing its existence." — Brest declaration, Dec. 8, 1991

The Union Is Buried: What's Being Born?

By CELESTINE BOHLEN
Special to The New York Times

News Analysis

MOSCOW, Dec. 8 — Ever since the August coup d'état, the Soviet Union has been dying a lingering death, its final agony stretched over months of crisis and negotiations while it was kept alive largely by the frantic faith of one man, Mikhail S. Gorbachev, the Soviet President.

Today, the union died — if future historians will accept a death warrant signed by the patient itself as proof, which is how the leaders of Russia, Ukraine and Byelorussia intended their statement, signed in the Byelorussian border town of Brest, to be read.

Gorbachev's Vain Pleas Make His Eclipse Clear

The Brest statement does not reckon with Mr. Gorbachev; it simply ignores him, which only made his appearance tonight on Soviet television all the more poignant as he once again pleaded, cajoled and banged his fists, making the case that without a union the country will fall apart.

But for some time now, Mr. Gorbachev's warnings have had a hollow ring, since for most people, the collapse he keeps warning about has already happened. This is a fact they can confirm with their daily lives, as they go to factories that have run out of materials, to office jobs where they have stopped getting salaries or to shops where there are no goods.

A Fresh Start?

By sweeping the old structures out of the way, President Boris N. Yeltsin of Russia, President Leonid M. Kravchuk of Ukraine and the Byelorussian leader, Stanislav Shushkevich, have cleared the way for something new — assuming, of course, that the military or other conservative forces mount no effort to restore the center.

What exactly the new shape of things will be was not totally clear from today's statement, nor could it be, given the absence of some major players, most notably representatives of Kazakhstan and the Central Asian republics.

But the absence of Mr. Gorbachev seemed to make no difference one way or the other. Once the Houdini of Soviet politics, the man who could turn setbacks to his advantage, the master of the surprise move, the Soviet President had become a Johnny-one-note whose insistence on renovating old structures — the word perestroika means reconstruction — in the end got in the way of more radical but in the view of others more constructive approaches.

By bypassing him publicly, the lead-

Continued on Page A9, Column 1

TAKE OVER A-ARMS

Newborn Bureaucracy Is Inheriting Functions of Old Authority

By SERGE SCHMEMANN
Special to The New York Times

MOSCOW, Dec. 8 — The leaders of Russia, Ukraine and Byelorussia declared today that the Soviet Union had ceased to exist and proclaimed a new "Commonwealth of Independent States" open to all members of the former union.

In a series of statements issued after a two-day meeting at a Byelorussian government retreat, the leaders of the three Slavic republics declared void all efforts to create a new union on the ruins of the old one. But they called for the creation of new "coordinating bodies" for defense, foreign affairs and the economy that would have their seat in Minsk, the capital of Byelorussia, and decided to maintain the ruble as the common currency.

They declared that the "norms" and activities of the former union ceased as of the moment of signing, and that the new commonwealth assumed all international obligations of the Soviet Union, as well as control over its nuclear arsenal.

Gorbachev's Move

"The U.S.S.R., as a subject of international law and geopolitical reality, is ceasing its existence," the leaders declared. [Text, page A8.]

The action essentially stripped President Mikhail S. Gorbachev of his office and authority, and the immediate question was whether the tough and tenacious Soviet leader would resist — and if he did, whether the military or other levers of power would support him.

The three cofounders of the new commonwealth — President Boris N. Yeltsin of Russia, President Leonid M. Kravchuk of Ukraine and Stanislav Shushkevich, Chairman of the Byelorussian Parliament — were scheduled to meet on Monday with Mr. Gorbachev and with Nursultan A. Nazarbayev, the President of Kazakhstan and the unofficial spokesman for the Muslim republics of Central Asia.

Portents of Disaster

Mr. Gorbachev had no immediate reaction. But in a taped interview with French television broadcast today, he argued fervently that the consequences of dismantling the union would make the war in Yugoslavia "a simple joke by comparison."

The Central Asian republics had all indicated an interest in retaining some form of union, and it was not immediately clear why Mr. Nazarbayev was excluded from the Byelorussian declaration, or how he would respond. Arriving in Moscow today, he declared that he was still in favor of preserving an association, and at least in maintaining joint control over the nuclear arsenal.

The predominantly Slavic republics declared that they drew their authority to dissolve the union from the fact that they were its original cofounders. They and the Trans-Caucasus republic, later

Continued on Page A8, Column 3

Jim Estrin for The New York Times

Short on funds, long on tolerance, Ira Levine and his team at Lafayette High School try to stay positive.

A Team Plays On in a Search for Normalcy

Long Shots

A Bruising Season in Brooklyn

A periodic visit with the Lafayette High School basketball team.

By HARVEY ARATON

Dexter Wooten's eyes grew wide and bright as he watched Antonio Carrasquillo score layup after layup against Midwood High School's undersized and helpless defenders under the basket.

"I could get me a lot of assists playing with Antonio," Wooten said at the game early last week, a smile breaking out from under the brim of his black-and-red Chicago Bulls cap.

That's what Ira Levine, the basketball coach at Lafayette High School, was thinking last June when Carrasquillo's improved class attendance enabled him to pass his academic subjects: Finally, as a senior, Carrasquillo, an agile, 6-foot-9-inch basketball star-in-waiting, would make his debut in the New York City Public Schools Athletic League. He would arrive, unannounced, to make Levine's team a force in Brooklyn, a threat to the defending city champion and perennial divisional power, Lincoln.

But even the tallest and most gifted centers, as Patrick Ewing, the Knicks' $33 million man, knows, must be surrounded by complementary players, and one by one Carrasquillo's began to disappear.

In many ways, the losses were just events in the life of public high school sports. They might have happened as easily at any other New York City school. They might have happened at a school in Chicago, Los Angeles or Detroit. The situation was trying, but not debilitating. Short on funds, long on tolerance, the high school coach and his team play on.

Lafayette's team turned into an urban soap opera early this fall when

Continued on Page C8, Column 3

INSIDE

Oiling the Machinery

The challenge for the President's new chief of staff will be to revitalize a domestic policy apparatus that rusted while John Sununu and Richard Darman held sway. Page A12.

Another View in Japan

Japan's Socialists said the nation had "turned its back on the historical truth" by refusing to "sincerely apologize" for wartime conduct. Page A7.

Who Knows Who Nanny Is?

Parents often know little about the people caring for their children, a fact highlighted by an au pair's arrest in a girl's arson death. Page B1.

Dallas Times Herald Shuts

The city's oldest daily newspaper ceases publication today, after selling its presses and subscription lists to its rival, The Morning News. Page D1.

The New York Times, 1991

Focus of AIDS Debate Dies

Kimberly Bergalis, who stirred a national debate over AIDS testing of doctors and other health workers, died of AIDS at the age of 23. Page D9.

"All the News That's Fit to Print"

The New York Times

Late Edition
New York: **Today,** partly sunny, warm and breezy. High 77. **Tonight,** thunderstorms. Low 58. **Tomorrow,** turning sunny, windy. High 72. **Yesterday,** high 71, low 50. Details, page 41.

VOL.CXLI . No. 48,954 | NEW YORK, SATURDAY, MAY 2, 1992 | 50 CENTS

TOLL IS 38 IN LOS ANGELES RIOTS BUT VIOLENCE SEEMS TO ABATE; BUSH DISPATCHES FORCE OF 5,000

CALM IS TENUOUS

Most Fires Are Put Out — Rodney King Calls for Racial Peace

By RICHARD W. STEVENSON
Special to The New York Times

LOS ANGELES, May 1 — After witnessing two days of nearly unchecked rioting across vast swaths of the city, residents today began the excruciating process of getting on with life in ravaged neighborhoods, and the White House sent 5,000 Federal troops to help insure a growing but tenuous calm.

National Guard troops were sent to shopping centers that the police had cleared of looters. Children, their schools closed for the second day in a row, could be seen playing unsupervised. Families strolled along fire-scarred streets and gawked at the troops.

And Rodney G. King, in his first public appearance since just after police officers beat him 14 months ago, asked for the violence and lawlessness to end.

Cleanup Efforts Begin

But as an uneasy peace took hold, sporadic violence flared in several other cities around the country, among them Atlanta, Seattle, Miami and San Francisco.

In South-Central Los Angeles there were scattered shootings and stabbings, but the widespread looting of Wednesday night and Thursday gave way to spontaneous cleanup efforts by residents of some of the areas worst hit by the rioting. The Los Angeles Fire Department said that by early evening all but one or two of the 3,767 building fires that had raged throughout the city since Wednesday were doused and that few new fires were breaking out.

Officials said the dusk-to-dawn curfew imposed on Thursday had generally succeeded in keeping people off the streets and would remain in effect for at least another day.

1,419 Injured

By late afternoon the death toll from the violence stood at 38, surpassing the total of 34 who died during the seven days of the Watts riots here in August 1965. In addition, 1,419 people, along with two police officers this morning, had been reported injured and more than 4,000 arrested.

Of the 38 people known to have died in the unrest, 15 are black, 11 Hispanic, 5 white and 2 are Asian. The races of 5 had not been determined, the Los Angeles County Coroner's office said. And like the victims of the violence, those looting the stores across the city were of every race.

The coroner said 28 of the dead had been killed by gunfire, with 6 of them having been killed in gunfights with the police.

Five people were killed on Wednesday and most of the others were killed on Thursday, the coroner's office said. The coroner could not provide a figure

Continued on Page 6, Column 1

Jim Wilson/The New York Times

Los Angeles police officers and National Guardsmen patrolling yesterday in front of a razed building.

MORE ON THE UNREST

Waves of Anger Ripple From Coast to Coast

Across the nation, angry demonstrators protested the acquittal in the California case — peacefully in many cases, violently in others. The National Guard was called into Las Vegas; injuries and arrests were reported in several other cities. Page 10.

The Morning After

As relative calm was restored in much of South-Central Los Angeles, a growing sense of sadness and futility emerged there. Page 7.

When the Voters Speak

Race and crime have opened sores in American politics and changed its direction before, and there is little reason to doubt they will again this year. News analysis, page 9.

Bush Says Verdict 'Stunned' Him; He Vows to Put an End to Rioting

By ANDREW ROSENTHAL
Special to The New York Times

WASHINGTON, May 1 — President Bush said tonight that he had been "stunned" by the verdict in the Los Angeles police beating case, promised that the state court trial that touched off rioting and looting "was not the end of the process" and sent Federal troops into the ravaged city to restore order.

Seeking to diminish tensions and demonstrate that Mr. Bush is taking action, the Justice Department disclosed that a grand jury in Los Angeles has been reviewing evidence and issuing subpoenas to determine whether the four police officers acquitted of beating a black motorist should now be charged under Federal civil rights laws.

Mr. Bush, while expressing sympathy for the outrage of civil rights leaders over the acquittal, said he would use "whatever force is necessary" to stop the violence in Los Angeles. The President sent 1,000 marines and between 2,500 and 3,000 soldiers into the streets. They werearmed with light weapons and ordered to return fire if fired upon. Mr. Bush also put the California National Guard under Pentagon command and dispatched 1,000 riot-trained Federal law officers to reinforce the local police.

Troops on City Streets

His orders, issued at 9:20 P.M., put a total of between 6,500 and 7,000 soldiers, marines and National Guard troops into the streets of Los Angeles during the night.

Mr. Bush addressed an anguished nation from the Oval Office, surrounded by the symbols of the Presidential power that he has brought to bear in war and diplomacy and is now being forced to turn to in the biggest domestic crisis of his political career. [Excerpts, page 8.]

By mixing forceful calls for order with expressions of sympathy, he seemed to be moving to stabilize the situation before the violence that has touched Los Angeles and a number of other cities developed into a national

Continued on Page 8, Column 3

Fears and Rumors Roil a Nervous New York

Monica Almeida/The New York Times

New York seemed a city under siege yesterday as shops closed and office towers emptied early. A store near the Port Authority Bus Terminal on Eighth Avenue was sheathed in plywood as commuters rushed past.

By ALISON MITCHELL

Panicked by the stark television images of blazing blocks and rioting in Los Angeles, New York acted like a city under siege yesterday. Shopkeepers pulled down their metal shutters by early afternoon. Office towers in Rockefeller Center emptied by midday. And jumpy commuters created an early rush hour, jamming roads, railway stations and bus terminals to race back home before nightfall.

Scattered violence broke out in the city and in New Rochelle later in the day. In Harlem, two men were pulled from a truck and one was stabbed. At Madison Square Garden, hundreds of youths stormed into a hallway, smashing two glass doors and strewing schedules and programs. Then they set off down Seventh Avenue, their numbers swelling to 1,000, according to the police.

In New Rochelle, cars were overturned and a fast-food restaurant was set afire, and in upstate New York, a cabby was pistol-whipped and a police van overturned. [Page 10.]

Voicing Apocalyptic Fears

But throughout the day, even before any violence began, there was a flood of rumors, spread in office buildings and subway cars as if New Yorkers were giving voice to their most apocalyptic fears of racial unrest. Each hour brought a new cascade of false reports — that the Abraham & Straus store in Brooklyn was blazing, that the Port Authority Bus Terminal had been closed by riots and that the bridges were blocked, cutting off Brooklyn from Manhattan.

The shocking television film that was broadcast from Los Angeles replayed in people's minds, more vivid than what they saw in New York and causing a dread as intense as if the violence were occurring along Fifth Avenue. "I already told my wife to leave early," said Achmocat Jouloul, assistant manager of 44th Street Cameras and Electronics. "I've seen the violence on TV. I hope it doesn't happen to us."

Sporadically, crowds of several hundred black teen-agers marched through Brooklyn, by City Hall and through Manhattan in spontaneous protest rallies that had begun in their high

Continued on Page 10, Column 5

As Los Angeles Storm Swirls, Chief of Police Is Oddly Quiet

By JANE FRITSCH
Special to The New York Times

LOS ANGELES, May 1 — As Los Angeles sank into chaos the day after the acquittal of four white police officers charged with beating a black motorist, Chief Daryl F. Gates was contemplative through a strategy meeting at City Hall, a block from his headquarters at Parker Center.

Deferring to subordinates, he said little until the meeting on Thursday neared an end, an official who took part recalled today. Then Chief Gates seemed to come alive. "I don't want any demonstrations at Parker Center," the official quoted Mr. Gates as telling the group. "It's demeaning to me."

That was essential Daryl Gates, the self-assured police chief whose personality and outspokenness have always been as much an issue here as the conduct of officers on the street. A Police Department spokesman said Mr. Gates would not comment about the meeting because he was too busy running the department.

In his final weeks of leading the 8,000-officer force, Mr. Gates faces the most troubling crisis of his 14-year tenure as chief, a position he has said he will relinquish soon. Some supporters say he has handled the sudden unrest in Los Angeles as well as could be expected. But critics, and there are many, say that his vaunted abilities to lead the department have failed him at a crucial moment.

'Very Laid Back'

As the crisis unfolded in the streets and police officers looked on, helplessly outnumbered, supporters and detractors alike say it is clear that Mr. Gates underestimated the anger of black and Hispanic residents and the swiftness with which it was unleashed. And perhaps, like many who have seen the vivid videotaped beating of Rodney G. King, Mr. Gates had not really believed in the possibility of an acquittal.

"He's been very laid back," said City Councilman Zev Yaroslavsky. "He is certainly not doing what I'd be doing if I were in charge of keeping order in the city right now."

Since the verdicts were announced

Continued on Page 6, Column 6

The Chase After Cheaters On College-Entry Exams

By ANTHONY DePALMA

Most of the 350,000 high school students across the country who are taking their college entrance examination today will rely on hard work, concentration and a bit of luck to get through the two-and-a-half-hour test. But a few are likely to try cheating — from paying imposters to take the test for them to using different colored M&M candies to signal answers.

And the people who give the test are ready to track them down.

An elaborate system of checks used by the Educational Testing Service, which administers the Scholastic Aptitude Test, is intended to insure that the few who circumvent the rules — about 450 a year out of 1.8 million who take the test, the service estimates — are caught.

Much Is at Stake

But two recent cases, one just decided in Maryland and another about to go to trial in New York City, illustrate how difficult it is to flush out cheaters without infringing on the rights of students who legitimately improve their scores from one test sitting to another.

Such cases involve high emotions and bitter disappointment because so much rides on the S.A.T. Today's administration of the test, one of six during the year, will be held in testing centers across the country.

Test scores are used by most colleges to make admissions decisions. The scores are based on a scale of 200 to 800 for each of two sections, verbal and math. The difference between a combined score of, say, 1050 and one of 1450 could mean the difference between being accepted at a middle-ranked college and a top-flight university. .

"A great deal of pressure is placed on the students," said Shirley Kane-Orr, chairwoman of the Educational Testing Service's Board of Review, which examines all test challenges. "Students are sometimes pushed into taking actions they wouldn't otherwise take."

In Maryland, a high school student in the bottom quarter of his class scored a 1410 on the test last November. An anonymous letter from someone who believed that the student, Lawrence H. Adler of

Continued on Page 5, Column 1

Bonn's Shaken Leader

By CRAIG R. WHITNEY
Special to The New York Times

News Analysis

BONN, April 30 — Two years ago, Chancellor Helmut Kohl of Germany was the most powerful leader of a resurgent Europe, and acted as if he knew it. Today, a year and a half after German unification, he seems much less self-assured, his authority at home and abroad shaken by political and social turmoil.

With France and Italy also afflicted by malaise and Europe as a whole wondering whether it did the right thing in December in aiming for a common currency and closer political union by the end of the decade, it is the British, who were skeptical anyway, who seem strong.

Prime Minister John Major, who won a 20-seat majority for a new five-year government mandate on April 9, has said he is determined to push for a rapid expansion of the present 12-nation membership of the European Community when Britain takes the presidency for six months on July 1, rather than the closer political cooperation and coordination on social policy the others sought.

A Wave of Strikes

Everything is relative in Europe, of course, and to Germans the biggest wave of strikes in a generation has been quite unsettling. This week, it left millions of commuters stranded and the trash cans overflowing in a country where order and neatness are national obsessions.

The Government coalition seemed to be tottering after Monday's surprise announcement by Hans-Dietrich Genscher, who has been Vice Chancellor and Foreign Minister for a generation, that he would resign on May 17. Some diplomats and journalists here saw a parallel with earlier crises of 1974, when Chancellor Willy Brandt resigned, or 1982, when Mr. Genscher withdrew his Free Democratic Party's support from the Social Democrats of Chancellor Helmut Schmidt and put the Christian Democrats of Mr. Kohl in power instead.

British newspapers have been comparing the chaos in Germany today to the "winter of discontent" in Britain in 1979, when the economy virtually ground to a halt under relentless pressure from powerful British labor unions and voters put Margaret Thatcher and the Conservatives in power, where they have remained ever since.

But the trouble in Germany is very different. Long-distance trains ran normally most of last week, and the airports were unaffected except by the usual air traffic control delays. To spare the public undue unpleasantness over the May Day holiday weekend, the German public service employees' unions let up on the pressure, everywhere except in the most populous

Continued on Page 4, Column 4

INSIDE

Election Law Changes

Legislative officials said today that lawmakers have reached a tentative agreement on the first significant steps in years to revise New York's arcane election laws. Page 25.

Bickering on School Board

A year after efforts to unite a divided New York City Board of Education, mistrust persists, slowing action on almost any issue. Page 25.

Rangers Gain on Cup

The Rangers won Game 7 and eliminated the Devils, 8-4, to move into round 2 in their quest for their first Stanley Cup in 52 years. Page 29.

The New Kentucky Home

Bending with the times, the Kentucky Derby is mixing some modern tones with the mint juleps of a 118-year institution. Page 34.

1993

Emerging Frontiers

2001

FRONT PAGE NEWS 1993-2001

First World Trade Center Attack

FEBRUARY 27, 1993

The explosion—a car bomb in the garage of the World Trade Center—rocked Lower Manhattan and was felt at the Statue of Liberty. At least five people died and hundreds were injured; hundreds more raced down smoke-filled stairwells and escaped. The attack was planned by Ramzi Ahmed Yousef, a Muslim fundamentalist who was later arrested in Pakistan and tried in New York. After his conviction in 1996, the State Department said, ". . . the potential exists for retaliation by Yousef's sympathizers." In fact, it was his uncle, Khalid Shaikh Mohammed, who had earlier suggested using airliners to attack American targets, as the 9/11 hijackers did.

Handshake of Peace

SEPTEMBER 14, 1993

An unofficial Israeli-Palestinian dialogue in Norway led to formal negotiations between Prime Minister Yitzhak Rabin of Israel and Yasir Arafat, the leader of the Palestinian Liberation Organization. President Bill Clinton invited them to the White House to sign their preliminary treaty (and famously nudged a reluctant Rabin to shake hands with Arafat). Later Clinton pressed Rabin's successor, Benjamin Netanyahu, to continue negotiations. Later still, Clinton urged Arafat to agree to a framework outlined by Netanyahu's successor, Ehud Barak. But the two sides did not come to terms, despite Clinton's efforts.

Apartheid Ends, Mandela Elected

MAY 3, 1994

After many years as what Nelson Mandela called "the skunk of the world," South Africa ended apartheid and the injustice and racial persecution that had reigned under it. The change was a historic redefining that followed the negotiated surrender of white power and the completion of a new constitution. Under South Africa's first open election, with blacks free to vote, Mandela won the presidency with nearly two-thirds of the vote. And Mandela, who had spent 27 years as a political prisoner for demanding a nonracial parliament, went on to preside over that very thing. Election-night crowds danced in the streets, singing, "We have washed this land clean of apartheid."

Cease-Fire in Northern Ireland

SEPTEMBER 1, 1994

"It happened in the Middle East and South Africa, and now it is happening in Ireland," declared Gerry Adams, the leader of Sinn Fein, the political wing of the Irish Republican Army. What happened was a cease-fire that the I.R.A. promised would end a quarter-century of bloodshed, known by the Irish simply as "the troubles." Some Protestant paramilitary forces promised to disarm, but numerous hurdles obstructed peace negotiations—and Protestants and Roman Catholics remembered the short-lived cease-fires in the 1970's. Still, this hiatus recognized reality. Most of Northern Ireland's 900,000 Protestants and 600,000 Roman Catholics were tired of a vicious conflict fueled by ancient, all-but-forgotten hatreds.

Oklahoma City Bombing

APRIL 20, 1995

Timothy J. McVeigh and Terry Nichols, two misfits who had gravitated to the world of rightist militias after serving in the Army, took out their anger at government with a rental truck, 4,800 pounds of homemade fertilizer and a plan that was at once simple and lethal: park the truck on the street and blow up a federal office building in Oklahoma City. One hundred sixty-eight people died in the blast, including 19 children, and more than 500 were injured. It was the worst act of domestic terrorism on American soil. McVeigh was executed in 2001, the first person put to death for a federal crime in 18 years. Nichols was sentenced to life in prison.

Simpson Cleared

OCTOBER 4, 1995

It began as a murder case, but it exposed the wide and angry rift between blacks and whites. O.J. Simpson, a former pro football superstar, was charged after his ex-wife and her boyfriend were found murdered outside her home in Los Angeles. Defense lawyer Johnnie Cochran summarized Simpson's claim that the police had distorted the facts by having him try on a blood-stained glove detectives said they had found at the scene. Simpson's hands were too big, and Cochran told the jurors, "If it doesn't fit, you must acquit." They did just that. Simpson later lost what was widely seen as a retrial, a $33 million wrongful-death suit brought by his ex-wife's family. Simpson was arrested again in 2007, accused of storming a sports memorabilia dealer's hotel room in pursuit of items he insisted, on a tape recording punctuated by profanity, had been stolen from him.

Rabin Slain

NOVEMBER 5, 1995

Yitzhak Rabin's handshake with Yasir Arafat at the White House in 1993 so upset Yigal Amir, an Israeli religious extremist, that he went to a peace rally in Tel Aviv to carry out his self-appointed mission: gun down Rabin at close range. Rabin had ignored the personal risk of pushing ahead with peace negotiations; he never wore a bulletproof vest. The assassin maintained that he acted for all Israel, the land he believed God had given the Jews: "What pulled the trigger was not only my finger, but the finger of this whole nation, which for 2,000 years yearned for this land."

Peace Accord on Bosnia

NOVEMBER 22, 1995

In four devastating years, the conflict in Bosnia had become the worst in Europe since World War II, with more than 250,000 men, women and children (mostly Bosnian Muslims) massacred, raped and tortured in a brutal exercise of ethnic cleansing, and more than two million people uprooted. The Dayton peace accords, brokered by Washington, were signed by the leaders of Bosnia, Croatia and Serbia after 21 days of negotiations at an Air Force base in Ohio. The accords divided Bosnia along ethnic lines, with the new Bosnian Serb republic and Bosnian-Croat federal borders to be watched over by 60,000 NATO peacekeepers, 20,000 of them U.S. soldiers. But the accords contained no firm assurances that Serbian war criminals would be brought to justice.

Diana Killed in Crash

AUGUST 31, 1997

Diana, Princess of Wales—the ex-wife of Prince Charles, heir to the British throne, and darling of tabloids the world over—died after a car crash in Paris in which her boyfriend, Dodi al-Fayed, was also killed. There were claims and counterclaims about whether their chauffeur was drunk or high, and about whether it was even an accident. Al-Fayed's father, the billionaire owner of Harrod's department store, talked of a conspiracy to kill the couple. Diana's brother accused paparazzi who had long stalked her, adding that "every proprietor and editor of every publication that has paid for intrusive and exploitative photographs" bore some responsibility.

Al Qaeda Bombs U.S. Embassies

AUGUST 8, 1998

The bombings of American embassies in Kenya and Tanzania eventually drilled a new name into public consciousness—al Qaeda. But in the wake of almost simultaneous explosions that killed 224 people and wounded thousands, intelligence agencies scrambled to identify the bombers. Washington soon offered a $5 million reward for the capture of Osama bin Laden. In a Taliban-controlled tribal region of Pakistan, where he had lived for years in mountain strongholds, a court concluded that he was "a man without sin" after a three-week proceeding. But a White House spokesman called him "a proven threat to U.S. national interests."

Clinton Admits Adultery

AUGUST 18, 1998

For eight months, the nation had been transfixed by a White House soap opera: had President Bill Clinton had a sexual relationship with Monica S. Lewinsky, a White House intern? The president had denied it, saying publicly that he had not had sex "with that woman, Miss Lewinsky." But in the privacy of the grand jury room, he admitted to an Oval Office dalliance. Then he went on television, saying he had misled the nation (and his wife, Hillary Rodham Clinton). "It was wrong," he said, before attacking Kenneth W. Starr, the independent counsel who broadened his reach far beyond his original mandate, which was to investigate the Whitewater scandal.

NATO Assault on Serbia

MARCH 25, 1999

With strong American backing, NATO opened an assault on Serbia. President Slobodan Milosevic had been negotiating a peace treaty in France, but when the talks failed and the NATO campaign began, so did another round of ethnic cleansing, this time targeting mostly Muslim ethnic Albanians in Kosovo. Accusing Milosevic of fanning "flames of ethnic and religious division," President Bill Clinton said moral revulsion drove him to use force.

The Nightmare of Columbine

APRIL 21, 1999

The deadliest school massacre in American history began with noise in the hall, outside the choir room: the pop of a gun, the flash of a muzzle, a wounded teacher falling. Two students brought a frightening arsenal to Columbine High School in Littleton, Colorado, and unloaded the weapons as they worked their way through corridors, classrooms and the library. They killed more than 20 and wounded nearly 30 before they turned the guns on themselves. Copycat threats followed. Scores of students were suspended, including three in Cherry Hill, New Jersey, who wore black trench coats, as the Columbine killers had, but only pantomimed gunfire.

Trade With China

NOVEMBER 16, 1999

President Bill Clinton made the overtures that reopened stalled trade negotiations with China. The result was a watershed agreement that admitted China to the World Trade Organization and swept away restrictions that had kept American companies from doing business in China. American banks, auto manufacturers and agribusiness companies eagerly looked to a huge new sales territory. Clinton said the deal "creates a win-win for both countries." But Republicans accused him of pandering to China, and within a few years, critics said the deal had not helped the U.S. trade deficit.

Human Gene Decoded

JUNE 27, 2000

"Today, we are learning the language in which God created life," President Bill Clinton declared as two competing teams of scientists unraveled the human genetic code. And what a code it is: two sets of 23 giant DNA molecules, some three billion chemical letters loaded with contradictions and complexity. What an achievement this was: one of the teams relied on a supercomputer that compared some 500 million trillion letters of code; it also divided the genome into fragments as short as only 20,000 letters. Scientists talked of using genetics to fight illnesses like cancer.

Whitewater Inquiry Ends

SEPTEMBER 21, 2000

In the hands of a different prosecutor, the investigation that had led to impeachment proceedings retired to its original focus—and ended. Robert W. Ray, who had replaced Kenneth W. Starr as independent counsel, decided not to bring charges against President Bill Clinton or Hillary Rodham Clinton in connection with a land deal known as Whitewater that dated to 1978, the year Bill Clinton became governor of Arkansas. At issue was whether the other investors gave the Clintons preferential treatment. Ray's decision was a victory for Clinton, who had maintained all along that he had done nothing wrong, and for Mrs. Clinton, who was seven weeks away from being elected to the United States Senate from New York.

Court Declares Bush Winner

DECEMBER 13, 2000

Thirty-five days after Election Day, the Supreme Court effectively declared George W. Bush president. The five-to-four decision gave him the victory he had not won on Election Day, when he lost the popular vote to Al Gore by 338,000 votes. But Bush's allies challenged the election results in Florida, where the issue was whether ballots had been counted correctly, or counted at all. Florida officials had struggled to interpret voters' intentions despite poorly designed ballots and "hanging chads" on punch-card ballots that voters had not punched all the way through.

"All the News That's Fit to Print"

The New York Times

Late Edition
New York: **Today,** cold winds, mostly sunny. Clouds south of the city. High 33. **Tonight,** clear. Low 22. **Tomorrow,** mostly sunny, cold. High 35. **Yesterday,** high 27, low 21. Details, page 34.

VOL.CXLII . . No. 49,255 — Copyright © 1993 The New York Times — NEW YORK, SATURDAY, FEBRUARY 27, 1993 — 50 CENTS

BLAST HITS TRADE CENTER, BOMB SUSPECTED; 5 KILLED, THOUSANDS FLEE SMOKE IN TOWERS

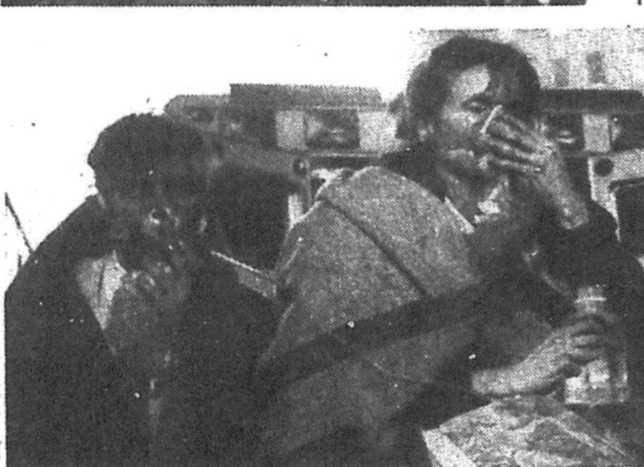

Associated Press; Carrie Boretz for The New York Times; Marilynn K. Yee/The New York Times

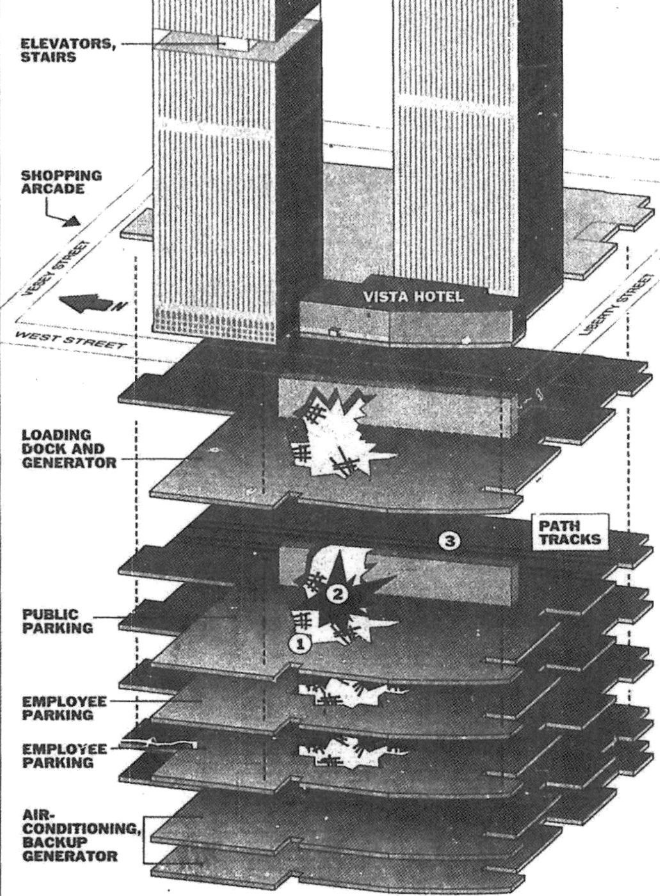
ELEVATORS, STAIRS
SHOPPING ARCADE
WEST STREET
VISTA HOTEL
LOADING DOCK AND GENERATOR
PATH TRACKS
PUBLIC PARKING
EMPLOYEE PARKING
EMPLOYEE PARKING
AIR-CONDITIONING, BACKUP GENERATOR
1 The blast occurred in a parking garage on the second level of the multi-level basement of the north World Trade Center tower.
2 It carved a 200- by 100-foot crater on the public parking level, blew through a ceiling and knocked a hole in a wall.
3 Cinder blocks and rubble from the collapsing wall fell to the tracks of the PATH station, and damaged lower levels.
This drawing is schematic and is based on information from reporters and officials at the scene.

Jean Rutter/The New York Times; Illustration by David Montesino and Julie Shaver

Many Are Trapped for Hours In Darkness and Confusion

By ROBERT D. McFADDEN

An explosion apparently caused by a car bomb in an underground garage shook the World Trade Center in lower Manhattan with the force of a small earthquake shortly after noon yesterday, collapsing walls and floors, igniting fires and plunging the city's largest building complex into a maelstrom of smoke, darkness and fearful chaos.

The police said the blast killed at least five people and left more than 650 others injured, mostly with smoke inhalation or minor burns, but dozens with cuts, bruises, broken bones or serious burns. The police said 476 were treated at hospitals and the rest by rescue and medical crews at the scene.

The explosion also trapped hundreds of people in debris or in smoke-filled stairwells and elevators of the towers overhead and forced the evacuation of more than 50,000 workers from a trade center bereft of power for lights and elevators for seven hours.

No Bomb Fragments Found

The blast, which was felt throughout the Wall Street area and a mile away on Ellis and Liberty Islands in New York Harbor, also knocked out the police command and operations centers for the towers, which officials said rendered the office complex's evacuation plans useless. [Page 23.]

James Fox, an assistant director of the Federal Bureau of Investigation in charge of the agency's New York office, said that no bomb fragments were found but that a joint terrorist task force of Federal agents and city detectives had examined the wreckage and believed that a car bomb had caused the explosion.

There was no warning of an impending explosion, Police Commissioner Raymond W. Kelly said. Jack Killorin, a spokesman in Washington for the Treasury Department's Bureau of Alcohol, Tobacco and Firearms, said that after the blast, authorities received at least nine telephone calls claiming responsibility.

Mr. Killorin said the first call was made 15 minutes after the blast to a non-emergency number of a New York Police Department precinct by an individual who mentioned the conflict in Bosnia. He said other claims were made between an hour and several hours after the event by callers who cited that and a variety of other reasons for the attack. He declined to elaborate.

Some law-enforcement officials said an explosion of such size, without a claim of responsibility in advance, might suggest that it went off accidentally.

Mr. Kelly was more oblique about the cause of the blast, saying only that a car bomb or other type of explosive device was not being ruled out.

Four hours after the explosion, a bomb threat forced the evacuation of the Empire State Building in midtown Manhattan, and there were numerous other bomb threats in the city, the police said. But it was unclear if any were related to the World Trade Center explosion or only the macabre work of pranksters.

As the day ended, a series of investigations began — into the cause of the explosion and its possible perpetrators, and into what went wrong in what many called a botched evacuation, with no alarms and no instructions for thousands caught in dark, smoky stairwells, in stark contrast to carefully laid plans.

Mayor David N. Dinkins, visiting in Osaka, Japan, was notified by City Hall and, in a telephone news conference, called the Fire Department response the largest for any non-natural disaster in the city's history. He said he had spoken with President Clinton and had thanked him for the cooperation of Federal investigators.

The effects of the blast radiated outward, disrupting most non-cable television transmissions throughout the metropolitan area, halting traffic in most of lower Manhattan and PATH train

Continued on Page 22, Column 1

Agence France-Presse

A man calling for help.

PRESIDENT URGES MORE RUSSIAN AID

In a Speech on World Trade, He Seeks a 2-Way Street

By R. W. APPLE Jr.
Special to The New York Times

WASHINGTON, Feb. 26 — President Clinton declared today that having spent trillions of dollars to win the cold war, the United States must summon the will to spend much more than planned in Russia and the other former Soviet republics "to support democracy's success where Communism failed."

Documents sent to Capitol Hill with the President's economic message last week, but little noticed at the time, indicated the President will ask for $700 million in aid next year for the former Soviet republics, nearly doubling the $417 million allotted for this year. Mr. Clinton, who plans to meet with President Boris N. Yeltsin of Russia on April 4, said "the world will suffer" if Russia's tottering economic reforms collapse. [Excerpts, page 6.]

Wants America to Compete

In a speech at American University consciously evocative of one delivered there 30 years ago by John F. Kennedy, the President endorsed the broad thrust of former President George Bush's trade policies. But at the same time, he sent two signals of change with his call for greater support for Russia and a suggestion that he would demand progress on human rights as the price for continued growth in trade with China.

The speech was devoted to international economics and trade and was not

Continued on Page 6, Column 1

First, Darkness, Then Came the Smoke

For Workers in Offices, the First Imperative Was to Get Outside

By N. R. KLEINFIELD

It depended on where you were in the towers when it came. For some the warning was a trembling underfoot or just a blank computer screen and flickering lights. For others, it was a shocking noise. One woman was blown out of her high heels. Another, desk chair and all, sank into the floor. And then, instantly it seemed, came the billowing smoke and the chilling realization that you had to get out of there.

The Face of Death

There were those who panicked, those who coolly absorbed it, those who got sick to their stomach and those who saw the face of death. No one was sure what had happened; did a plane hit the building, was it an earthquake, had lightning struck? Many wondered why there seemed to be no évacuation plan and no guidance — not realizing that the blast had knocked out the center's operations center.

But thousands of people in the World Trade Center yesterday afternoon knew they were in the grip of one of the most dreaded urban nightmares: they were in the city's tallest building and something was very wrong.

Joann Hilton was low. And, in this disaster, that was the worst place to be. A secretary working for the Port Authority of New York and New Jersey, she was at her desk in the command office on the B1 level of the building, musing about the weekend.

"All of a sudden, we heard this big boom," she said. "It sounded like an earthquake. And then the floor just collapsed and me and my chair sank into the floor. The ceiling started to come down, too, and I'm in my chair in the floor. Some of the lights went out. And then it was all dark. Like a cave. Somebody pulled me out of that floor and we beat it out of there."

Denise Bosco was high. She was on the 82d floor, where she too works as a secretary for the Port Authority. "The whole building shook," she said. "The lights flashed on and off. The computers went down. Then, instantly, there was smoke. I was terrified. People panicked. They started pushing and shouting to get out. Some of them were throwing up. I said, 'Oh dear God, what is it? What is it? Is it my time? Is this the way?' "

Wrapped in a Bath Towel

Her coat was still in her office and she was wrapped in a white bath towel as she stood outside. She broke down into tears. "It was horrible," she said. "There was this awful feeling that we might not be able to get out. We were in the mighty, tall tower but we weren't getting out."

They didn't know whether to stay put or flee, but instinct said to run.

Continued on Page 22, Column 4

Reuters

The explosion that shook the World Trade Center yesterday left a crater 60 feet wide below the building.

Manhattan Is Held in the Grip Of Traffic Snarls and Anxiety

By DEBORAH SONTAG

Traffic snarled to a standstill in lower Manhattan. Major arteries downtown closed, and a half-dozen subway lines were rerouted. Nervous relatives jammed the 911 emergency lines. And an anxiety that began in lower Manhattan at lunchtime yesterday grew infectious as the day grew long, generating a restless buzz throughout New York City.

As news spread that the explosion at the World Trade Center — which the F.B.I. said may have been caused by a car bomb — had been followed by a bomb scare at and evacuation of the Empire State Building, nerves began to fray. Drivers sitting bumper to bumper on Canal Street leaned on their horns, waiting over an hour to enter the Holland Tunnel. Subway riders jostled their way onto overcrowded trains, pondering their commuters' headaches as well as what seemed to be a different kind of urban terrorism.

An Eerie Quiet on Closed Streets

"It's frightening," said Charles Sampey, 34 years old, a building superintendent riding the IRT No. 3 downtown at 6 P.M. "You'd expect more to get robbed in New York than to get hit by a terrorist bomb."

After an underground explosion rocked the World Trade Center at noontime, the Franklin D. Roosevelt Drive, the West Side Highway, the Brooklyn Battery Tunnel and most side streets in lower Manhattan were closed to all but emergency vehicles. It grew eerily quiet — "like Sunday at dawn," said a Triborough Bridge and Tunnel Authority spokesman, Frank Pascual — but for the cry of sirens. With their antennae atop the Trade Center, all except one New York television station — WCBS, Channel 2 — went off the air.

As trading on five commodities exchanges was disrupted and thousands of employees were evacuated from the smoke-filled office complex, transportation officials immediately began making emergency plans for an imminent rush hour. They added buses, trains and ferries to New Jersey to

Continued on Page 22, Column 1

354613

INSIDE

Economy Ended 1992 With Robust Growth

The gross domestic product grew at the robust rate of 4.8 percent in the final three months of 1992, the best quarterly performance in five years and a full percentage point higher than initial estimates. Page 35.

Judge Rebuffs Gay Group On St. Patrick's Parade

A Federal judge ruled that New York City cannot order the Ancient Order of Hibernians to include a gay contingent in the annual St. Patrick's Day Parade up Fifth Avenue. The city will not appeal. Page 21.

Bosnia Sees a Turning Point

After hearing of American plans to airdrop relief supplies, many Bosnians said they sensed a major change in their plight. Page 5.

"All the News That's Fit to Print"

The New York Times

Late Edition

New York: **Today,** patchy fog, then mostly sunny. **High 86. Tonight,** clear. Low 72. **Tomorrow,** sunshine mixed with clouds, humid. **High 88. Yesterday,** high 84, low 65. Details, page C16.

VOL.CXLII . . No. 49,454 | | *NEW YORK, TUESDAY, SEPTEMBER 14, 1993* | 75 cents beyond the greater New York metropolitan area. | *50 CENTS*

RABIN AND ARAFAT SEAL THEIR ACCORD AS CLINTON APPLAUDS 'BRAVE GAMBLE'

Associated Press

"The children of Abraham . . . have embarked together on a bold journey." — President Clinton.

Old Warriors Now Face Task Of Building Upon Foundation

By THOMAS L. FRIEDMAN

Special to The New York Times

WASHINGTON, Sept. 13 — In a triumph of hope over history, Yitzhak Rabin, the Prime Minister of Israel, and Yasir Arafat, the chairman of the P.L.O., shook hands today on the White House lawn, sealing the first agreement between Jews and Palestinians to end their conflict and share the holy land along the River Jordan that they both call home.

At 11:43 A.M. on the sun-splashed South Lawn of the White House, Foreign Minister Shimon Peres of Israel and Mahmoud Abbas, the foreign policy aide for the Palestine Liberation Organization, signed a Declaration of Principles on Palestinian self-government in Israeli-occupied Gaza and the West Bank. Three thousand witnesses watched in amazement, including former Presidents Jimmy Carter and George Bush.

Mr. Rabin, whose face is etched with the memories of every Arab-Israeli war, captured in his remarks the exhaustion of all parties with the centuries-old conflict. "We the soldiers who have returned from the battle stained with blood," he said, "we who have fought against you, the Palestinians, we say to you today in a loud and clear voice: 'Enough of blood and tears! Enough!' "

Mr. Arafat, relishing his moment of acceptance on the White House lawn, strove to give Mr. Rabin the appropriate response, declaring in Arabic: "Our two peoples are awaiting today this historic hope, and they want to give peace a real chance."

An Awkward Moment

And President Clinton, who gracefully shepherded Mr. Arafat and Mr. Rabin through their awkward moment of public reconciliation, hailed them both for their "brave gamble that the future can be better than the past." [Transcripts of the leaders' remarks are on page A12.]

The agreement, which will eventually allow Palestinians to run their own affairs as Israeli troops pull back within months from the Gaza Strip and Jericho in a first step, was reached during secret negotiations over the past few months between Israelis and Palestinians, under the direction of Mr. Peres and Mr. Abbas, through the mediation of Norway.

The documents were signed on the same wooden table on which the Peace Treaty between Egypt and Israel was signed in 1979. That table stood today as a silent memorial to the assassinated Egyptian President, Anwar el-Sadat, whose path-breaking visit to Israel in 1977 and subsequent agreements at Camp David brought him denunciations as a traitor by Mr. Arafat.

But the audience in attendance, and perhaps the millions more watching back in the Middle East, seemed less interested in the formal signing than in the visual moment that would somehow make this tentative peace real: the handshake between the two old warriors who personified the conflict between their peoples.

A Nudge, a Hand, a Smile

Moments after the documents were signed, Mr. Clinton took Mr. Arafat in his left arm and Mr. Rabin in his right arm and gently coaxed them together, needing to give Mr. Rabin just a little extra nudge in the back. Mr. Arafat reached out his hand first, and then Mr. Rabin, after a split second of hesitation and with a wan smile on his face, received Mr. Arafat's hand. The audience let out a simultaneous sigh of relief and peal of joy, as a misty-eyed Mr. Clinton beamed away.

Two hands that had written the battle orders for so many young men, two fists that had been raised in anger at one another so many times in the past, locked together for a fleeting moment of reconciliation.

But much difficult work, many more compromises, will now have to be performed by these same two men to make it a lasting moment.

That reality was underscored by the fact that both Mr. Rabin and Mr. Arafat invoked their peoples' undying attachment to Jerusalem in their respective speeches.

[Later in Jerusalem, Israeli Radio reported that Mr. Rabin, accompanied by Foreign Minister Shimon Peres, was traveling to Morocco on Tuesday for a surprise meeting with King Hassan to discuss establishing diplomatic relations. The report said said Tunisia was among several Muslim and Arab countries now ready to establish ties with Israel.]

In an opening speech that was both eloquent and moving, Mr. Clinton described the history of the effort to make peace in the Middle East and paid tribute to Mr. Rabin and Mr. Arafat. He also pledged United States support for their effort.

"The United States is committed to insuring that the people who are affected by this agreement will be made more secure by it and to leading the world in marshaling the resources necessary to implement the difficult details that will make real the principles

Continued on Page A13, Column 1

MORE ON THE ACCORD

Arafat's Strategy: '2 Olive Branches'

Transforming one's image from guerrilla leader to statesman is not easy, but Yasir Arafat was trying hard to make it happen. Efforts in the past have had mixed results for all the countries involved. "This time," he said just an hour after making peace with Israel, "I am coming with two olive branches." Page A15.

Arabs and Jews Reflect

As many speak out about the events of recent days, there are new hopes, on both sides, but fears from years past remain. Page A16.

Divisions in Syria

Thousands marched in Syria, waving black flags in protest against Mr. Arafat, but elsewhere in the nation the response was more stunned, disbelieving, silence. Page A17.

Security Surprises

Security for the dignitaries was about what you would expect in the capital, but despite the hardware and planning, there were surprises. Page A14.

A 45-Year Struggle

Over the years since the birth of Israel in 1948, the Palestinian movement has drawn support from Palestinians inside Israel, in Israeli-occupied territories and in neighboring Arab countries while pressing for nationhood or self-rule. Page A15.

The Next Challenge for the U.S.

Peace Momentum Up to Washington

By R. W. APPLE Jr.

Special to The New York Times

News Analysis

WASHINGTON, Sept. 13 — As he himself said, this was not Bill Clinton's day. It was not he who brought together the sober old soldier and the grinning guerrilla fighter in the leafy calm of the South Lawn of the White House, far from the battlefields of the Middle East, for a paean to peace.

However deft, however sagacious, he was but the master of ceremonies. He thanked those who had labored to bring about the latest in a series of once-inconceivable changes that have remade the world in five short years. He bestowed the congratulations of the world's only superpower. And he gave Yitzhak Rabin a timely little nudge when he seemed reluctant to grasp the outstretched hand of Yasir Arafat.

Now, though, President Clinton will have to assume the central role if the momentum toward a comprehensive peace settlement is not to be lost. That is likely to be a long, messy job of diplomatic donkey work in the dark corners of history — a much less gratifying chapter than today's carefully scripted pageant of good intentions.

Israel and Jordan are poised to move forward tomorrow. But the other Arab nations whose representatives watched today's ceremony from the front rows know that only the United States can provide the impetus needed for the next round of negotiations. Mr. Arafat spoke for them, too, when he said his people "are relying on your role, Mr. President" to "usher in an age of peace."

So this President, who so longs to concentrate on problems at home, is thrust like so many of his predecessors into an international arena not of his choosing. Along with the rest of the world, the United States has a new ward, the inchoate entity called Palestine, and it has the main responsibility for fostering Israeli settlements with its other neighbors while deepening the one with the Palestinians.

It will be up to Mr. Clinton, who does not much like doing so, to butt heads between the Israelis and the Syrians, and perhaps take considerable heat from American Jews in the process, which he did not have to endure this time.

Neither Mr. Clinton nor any other American President has ever wanted to do business with Mr. Arafat and the Palestine Liberation Organization. As Mr. Rabin, the Israeli Prime Minister, said in one of his many moments of eloquence this morning, "It's not so

Continued on Page A13, Column 6

President's Tie Tells It All: Trumpets for a Day of Glory

By MAUREEN DOWD

Special to The New York Times

WASHINGTON, Sept. 13 — The President who loves to stay up late told his aides that he went to bed at 10 P.M. on Sunday, so he could be rested for the historic day.

They did not believe him, of course.

"No way," said Dee Dee Myers, the White House press secretary. "He got the big hand and the little hand mixed up."

"It was Jerusalem time," suggested Mark Gearan, the White House communications director.

But what happened next is not in contention: The President said he woke up at 3 A.M. and could not go back to sleep. He was worrying about the speech he would make to mark what was sure to be one of the most remarkable events of his Presidency: the moment when the two men who had been bitter enemies for so long, the Israeli Prime Minister, Yitzhak Rabin, and the Chairman of the Palestine Liberation Organization, Yasir Arafat, would recognize each other's existence on the South Lawn of the White House.

With his wife and daughter still asleep, Mr. Clinton put on a blue jogging suit and went into the study in the White House residence. He picked up a Bible. He read the entire Book of Joshua, wanting to review the part about the trumpets in Jericho that toppled walls and making sure he put a reference in his speech contrasting the victory of war and the victory of peace.

In another part of the White House, a team led by Jeremy Rosner, a National Security Council speechwriter, was scrambling to fulfill the President's last request: Mr. Clinton wanted a passage from the Koran to balance his Biblical allusions. The desperate White House staff members finally called Prince Bandar bin Sultan, the Saudi ambassador, who helped them pick out an appropriately soothing passage: "If the enemy inclines toward peace, do thou also incline toward peace."

Watching for the Dawn

At some point, Mr. Clinton moved from the study to the kitchen to read and drink coffee. He wanted to sit near the window, where he could keep track of when the dawn arrived and what the sky looked like.

The White House staff had worked over three days to compile a 26-page step-by-step log choreographing every movement that the leaders would make, and yet Mr. Clinton knew as well as anyone that, with this most delicate of all diplomatic meetings, a million things could go wrong — a look, a word, a handshake, the weather.

At dawn, as he later told aides, who

Continued on Page A14, Column 5

Jim Estrin/The New York Times

Palestinian women dancing with joy in Jericho, on the West Bank.

Palestinians: Glee And Flag-Waving

Special to The New York Times

JERICHO, Israeli-Occupied West Bank, Sept. 13 — Palestinians took to the streets of the West Bank and Gaza Strip today in rapturous and noisy celebrations of the Palestine Liberation Organization accord with Israel and what they said was the cornerstone of their future state.

In the sleepy city of Jericho, the seat of the future Palestinian self-governing authority, it looked as though every one of the 15,000 residents was in the streets.

Savoring a new reality few had dared to imagine just a few weeks ago, they danced all day and into the night. In the Gaza Strip they handed flowers to Israeli soldiers. In East Jerusalem they shouted "Shalom!" to Israeli well-wishers.

The accord also changed the face of the occupied territories and East Jerusalem, where Palestinian flags, which had technically been banned, flew with impunity.

Reuters

Israelis watching the signing on television on a Jerusalem street.

Israelis: Searching For New Bearings

Special to The New York Times

BEIT ZAYIT, Israel, Sept. 13 — When Yitzhak Rabin shook hands with Yasir Arafat, six Israelis watching it on television together on the western outskirts of Jerusalem might as well have been struck by lightning. They could only sigh deeply in disbelief before their thoughts and emotions unscrambled themselves.

The dominant feeling, in the room and across the country, is that there is no alternative to having Israelis and Palestinians come to terms with each other, as they are now trying to do.

Like many Israelis, Eliezer Shenhav, a surgeon who had friends into watch the ceremony, wrestled with religious convictions that taught him that God intended all of the biblical Land of Israel to be in Jewish hands.

Articles, page A17.

INSIDE

Primary Candidates Work on Voter Turnout

Appearing at subway stops and centers for the elderly and monopolizing the talk shows, candidates in the Democratic primaries for New York City offices played to their surest supporters in the closing hours of the campaign. The races could hinge on voter turnout. Page B1.

POLLING PLACES will be open from 6 A.M. to 9 P.M. today in New York City, Westchester and Nassau, and from 6 A.M. to 8 P.M. in Connecticut.

Fall Air Fares Cut by 45%

The nation's airlines cut fares by up to 45 percent on domestic flights through Dec. 16, but tickets must be bought by Saturday. Page D1.

"All the News That's Fit to Print"

The New York Times

Late Edition
New York: **Today,** sunny, pleasant. High 66. **Tonight,** becoming cloudy. Low 49. **Tomorrow,** cloudy, chilly, a few showers. High 58. **Yesterday,** high 65, low 44. Details, page B7.

VOL. CXLIII . . No. 49,685 NEW YORK, TUESDAY, MAY 3, 1994 — 75 cents beyond the greater New York metropolitan area. — 50 CENTS

MANDELA PROCLAIMS A VICTORY: SOUTH AFRICA IS 'FREE AT LAST!'

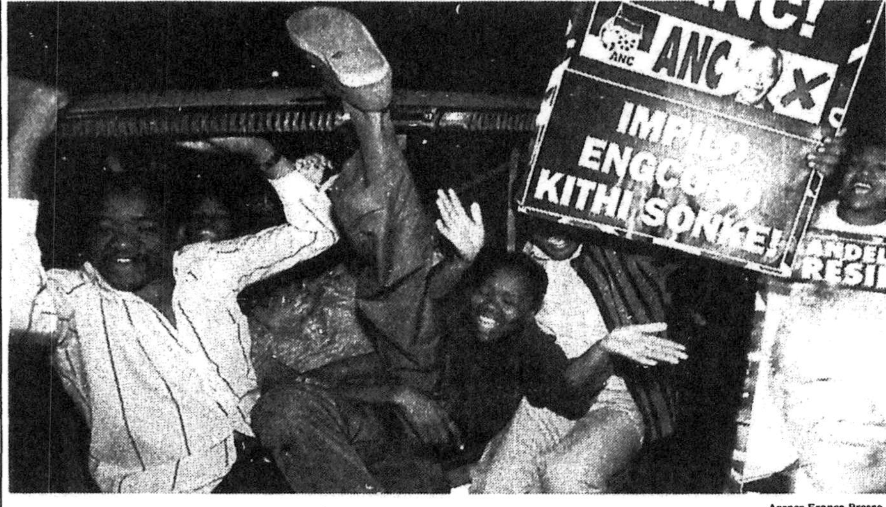

Agence France-Presse

Soweto residents celebrating yesterday after the African National Congress's election victory was announced.

DE KLERK CONCEDES

Victors Get Big Margin in Vote — Leaders Vow to Cooperate

By BILL KELLER
Special to The New York Times

JOHANNESBURG, May 2 — With a dignity that owed nothing to defeat, Frederik Willem de Klerk, the last white ruler in Africa, tonight conceded his presidency to Nelson Rolihlahla Mandela.

"Mr. Mandela has walked a long road, and now stands at the top of the hill," said Mr. de Klerk of the man he freed after 27 years in prison, and with whom he negotiated the surrender of white power. "As he contemplates the next hill, I hold out my hand to Mr. Mandela in friendship and in cooperation."

Mr. Mandela later seized his election mandate with matching grace before a rapturous crowd in a Johannesburg hotel ballroom. He welcomed Mr. de Klerk and other political rivals as partners in a new Government of national unity.

"I stand here before you filled with deep pride and joy," Mr. Mandela said. "Pride in the ordinary, humble people of this country — you have shown such a calm, patient determination to reclaim this country as your own. And joy that we can loudly proclaim from the rooftops: *free at last!*"

Acknowledging his political collaboration with Mr. de Klerk, Mr. Mandela said, "I also want to congratulate him for the many days, weeks and months and the four years that we have worked together, quarreled, addressed sensitive problems and at the end of our heated exchanges were able to shake hands and to drink coffee." [Excerpts from the Mandela and de Klerk statements are on page A15.]

Less than half the vote had been counted in the first South African election open to blacks, but the African National Congress majority was more than 60 percent, and both men were eager to keep to a timetable that leads to Mr. Mandela's being inaugurated as president on May 10.

Mr. de Klerk remains President until that day, and then assumes a subsidiary role as one of two vice presidents. A galaxy of world figures, including Hillary Rodham Clinton and Vice President Gore, are expected in Pretoria to witness the last and most orderly relinquishment of white dominion on the continent.

With more than 11 million votes counted of an eligible electorate estimated at nearly 23 million, the African National Congress had 62.8 percent, Mr. de Klerk's National Party 23.1 percent, the Inkatha Freedom Party of Chief Mangosuthu G. Buthelezi 6.7 percent, and the Freedom Front, which seeks a separate white homeland, 2.9 percent.

A two-thirds majority, which leaders of the congress dismissed Sunday as a faded hope, no longer seemed out of reach, since the later counts appeared to be coming more heavily from black townships that are African National Congress strongholds.

With two-thirds of the new Parliament, the congress would be able to write a new Constitution with few concessions to other parties, although Mr. Mandela has sworn that even with a landslide he would seek con-

Continued on Page A14, Column 1

A Joy Born in Pain Dances in the Street

By FRANCIS X. CLINES
Special to The New York Times

ALEXANDRA, South Africa, May 2 — An eruption of joy swept the vast black ghettos of South Africa tonight as Nelson Mandela claimed his presidential victory with a bit of boogie dancing on television that was instantly imitated by street throngs across the land.

Even the pool players dropped their cue sticks and poured out of the Lethabong barroom here in this landmark black township. They strutted and weaved with a spontaneous mass gathering that danced through the darkness enveloping their shanty hovels, singing: "We have have washed this land clean of apartheid."

Similar scenes were reported across the nation as the black majority of 30 million broke out in celebration at the evidence of what their balloting of last week had accomplished in the first democratic election of this racism-scarred land.

Mr. Mandela, the most revered of apartheid's black political prisoners, was before their eyes on television, one of their own confidently accepting the electoral leadership of a new South Africa and announcing to all, black and white: "I am your servant."

In scant minutes, dancing crowds illumined by fireworks snaked through the ghetto streets booming their response in song: "Nel-son Man-del-a! You're called to lead our na-tion!"

They converged at intersections, doubling in size and giddiness, and swept off in fresh directions, determined to make this the night for registering their political emancipation in the nation's streets.

Only minutes before, this valley of shanties widely called "Alex" rested sleepy and smoke-wreathed from the nightly fires that are the citizens' only form of garbage removal. Unofficial jitney buses cruised for passengers, but night life was well indoors, within some of the saddest jerry-built housing on earth, and within warm community gathering spas, too, like the Lethabong bar and restaurant.

"He never gave up on us," Madodo Mbalomba declared, raising his mug of cold Castle draft beer to toast Mr. Mandela on the TV above the bar. "This is a joyous night."

Farther down the bar, Johannesi Tloubatla put down his beer to applaud. "Mandela must make our place right," he said. "I want to see him govern."

The chef, Lot Baloy, came out from

Continued on Page A14, Column 1

Associated Press

Nelson Mandela dancing as he came on stage to claim victory.

Jury Acquits Dr. Kevorkian Of Illegally Aiding a Suicide

By DAVID MARGOLICK
Special to The New York Times

DETROIT, May 2 — Four years after Dr. Jack Kevorkian helped the first of 20 people end their lives, a Michigan jury today cleared him of charges that he had violated a state law prohibiting assisted suicide by helping a terminally ill man take his life last year.

The jurors cited uncertainties over Dr. Kevorkian's motive, the wisdom of the two-year-old law under which he had been prosecuted, and precisely where he had helped a 30-year-old man end the agony of his degenerative nerve disease.

The decision, by a jury of nine women and three men, came after nine hours of deliberations. The trial was the first for Dr. Kevorkian, a 65-year-old retired pathologist, under a 1992 law enacted specifically to stop his activities.

Though he faced four years in prison if convicted, the doctor, wearing a white windbreaker over a maroon cardigan sweater, appeared cocky, almost bemused, as the jury filed in. His expression did not change as the verdict of not guilty was read.

The verdict brought predictable responses from partisans in the debate over assisted suicide.

"It sends a message to prosecutors that juries in Michigan are not willing to convict a doctor who helps a terminally ill person implement a decision to hasten inevitable death," said Robert Sedler, a professor of constitutional law at Wayne State University in Detroit, who had argued the state Civil Liberties Union's challenge to the statute. "And it sends a message to politicians that if you vote out a new law criminalizing such conduct you may face political retribution."

Lynn Mills, a spokeswoman for Michigan Right to Life, which opposes assisted suicide, said: "That jury has just unleashed the floodgates. There is going to be no stopping him or other doctors who believe that they are God."

Dr. Kevorkian would not say after the verdict whether or when he would accede to dozens of requests from terminally ill patients to help them

Continued on Page A20, Column 1

Justices Decide Incinerator Ash Is Toxic Waste

7-2 Ruling Could Raise Municipalities' Costs

By LINDA GREENHOUSE
Special to The New York Times

WASHINGTON, May 2 — In a decision that could substantially increase the cost of waste disposal, the Supreme Court ruled today that any toxic residue created by burning household and industrial waste in municipal incinerators must be treated as hazardous waste and not dumped in ordinary landfills.

The 7-to-2 decision interpreted a Federal law governing hazardous waste, the Resource Conservation and Recovery Act of 1976. For years the law has been the subject of administrative and judicial confusion about its application to the ash left by the new generation of municipal incinerators that burn trash and produce energy.

Hazardous waste requires storage in specially constructed leak-proof sites and other handling that can be several times more expensive than that of conventional waste. Fearing such higher costs, a large coalition of municipal, county and state governments had urged the Court to interpret the law as exempting the ash from regulation as hazardous waste.

Many of these operators said that the ruling would not force the closing of any incinerators, and that they were trying to estimate how much their expenses would increase. The operators and groups that oppose the incinerators said that the ruling might derail plans for new incinerators, including one planned for the Brooklyn Navy Yard. [Page A18.]

Justice Antonin Scalia, writing for the majority, said Congress had not created an exemption for the ash. He noted that while Congress explicitly exempted municipal incinerators from Federal regulation under a variety of circumstances, the law did not mention ash and "simply cannot be read" to support the cities' argument.

Continued on Page A18, Column 1

AGENCY OFFERING AN AID BLUEPRINT FOR PALESTINIANS

KEY ROLE BY WORLD BANK

$1.2 Billion From 40 Nations to Be Economic Structure for Start of Self-Rule

By THOMAS L. FRIEDMAN
Special to The New York Times

WASHINGTON, May 2 — The World Bank unveiled a three-year, $1.2 billion program today, worked out with the Palestine Liberation Organization, to quickly lay an economic foundation for Palestinian self-rule in the Gaza Strip and Jericho.

Last Oct. 1, the United States organized a meeting of 40 donor countries, which pledged $2.4 billion to support the new Palestinian authority in the former Israeli-occupied areas.

Since then, the World Bank and economic experts from the P.L.O. have been working on a program that would take these diverse and often vague pledges and forge them into a coherent, detailed plan for economic development — identifying the major needs, specifying how the money should be spent, eliminating duplication and setting clear priorities.

This program is expected to begin almost immediately after the planned signing in Cairo Wednesday of the full Israeli-P.L.O. accord governing the transfer of Gaza and Jericho to Palestinian self-rule. The first steps in the economic program will involve the laying of sewers and construction of waste-disposal facilities in Gaza and Jericho.

Other projects — for improving housing, roads, health centers, telecommunications and water — will follow as soon as the engineering studies are completed.

"If the peace process has any hope of success, the Palestinians need to see improvements in their living conditions very quickly," said Caio Koch-

Continued on Page A6, Column 1

Driver With Suspended License Charged in Deaths of 3 in Family

1993

Cathy Vaccarello, center, and her daughters, Marie, right, and Concetta, top, were killed after being hit by a car. Giovanni Vaccarello, left, was in critical condition. John, above, was not with the family at the time.

By DAVID FIRESTONE

For 27 years he drove through New York without a license, accumulating an ominously long list of suspensions and arrests, including three for driving while intoxicated. Abraham Meyers, a 55-year-old janitor from Ozone Park, Queens, was obsessed with cars, his neighbors said, and nothing could stop him from getting behind the wheel.

Late Sunday night, Mr. Meyers climbed into his Lincoln Continental once again, the police said, despite a blood-alcohol level more than twice the legal limit. He tore down Cross Bay Boulevard in Howard Beach, Queens, they said, driving 71 miles an hour in a 40-m.p.h. zone, and hit four members of the Vaccarello family of Brooklyn as they crossed the street after leaving a family party. Three of them were killed and a fourth was critically injured.

Mr. Meyers, who last had a legal driver's license in 1967, has been arrested repeatedly since then on a number of offenses, including driving while intoxicated. But despite a recent crackdown on drivers with multiple offenses, the authorities were unable to prevent him from getting in a car and turning the key.

"Some people are not going to be deterred by anything," said George Filleau, a spokesman for the Department of Motor Vehicles. "That's why we will continue to have tragic accidents like this one. People who are not deterred by penalties of law — I guess that's the definition of a criminal."

The Vaccarellos, who lived in Bay Ridge, had just left a relative's anni-

Continued on Page B2, Column 1

On the Diamond, Something Is Going, Going, On!

By MURRAY CHASS

Seven years later, the mystery remains unsolved.

"There's no rhyme or reason to it that we've ever been able to identify," said Scott Smith, the Rawlings executive designated to tell the world no, the baseball has not been "juiced up." He uttered that refrain throughout the 1987 season, and has resurrected it again this season in fielding what has probably been a Rawlings record for the number of telephone calls in any April.

That's because major league baseball has another mystery on its hands. Baseballs are flying out of ball parks in record numbers, and people are searching for reasons why. This has become a whodunit because everybody's doing it.

There were 708 home runs in April, 210 more than were hit in the equivalent number of games at the start of last season. The average of 2.22 a game was much higher than last April (1.58) and higher even than the record-setting season of 1987, when batters hit 2.0 a game in April.

But it is not only the numbers that have managers, players, television commentators and fans talking about the long ball. It is also the sight of home runs from hitters not noted for power; of seemingly mis-hit balls soaring into the stands; of blasts to the opposite field, and of multiple-homer games by the likes of such relatively obscure players as Karl Rhodes and Todd Hundley.

Some say the ball is livelier, or "juiced up" to use the common baseball terminology, and that major league baseball wants it that way. Others cite the inferior quality of pitching, the warmer-than-usual April weather and the improved ability of hitters over all. Whatever the reason, the numbers are indisputable.

This year's April average projects to 5,035 home runs for the season,

Continued on Page B13, Column 1

INSIDE

Mrs. Clinton's Role Queried
In a Congressional report on the travel office affair, Hillary Rodham Clinton is quoted as having urged a White House official to replace workers with "our people." Page B8.

$5.3 Billion for Syntex
Roche Holding of Switzerland agreed to acquire Syntex, a troubled drug company, for $5.3 billion. Page D1.

U.N. Peace Force Sought
The United Nations is asking African nations whether they are willing to take part in a peacekeeping force for Rwanda. Page A3.

Sheik's Documents Seized
F.B.I. agents searched the home of one of Sheik Omar Abdel Rahman's aides and seized copies of the cleric's writings, lawyers said. Page B1.

"All the News That's Fit to Print"

The New York Times

Late Edition

New York: **Today,** becoming sunny, breezy. High 77. **Tonight,** clear, light winds. Low 58. **Tomorrow,** mostly sunny, light winds. High 74. **Yesterday,** high 77, low 64. Details, page C12.

VOL.CXLIII . . No. 49,806 NEW YORK, THURSDAY, SEPTEMBER 1, 1994 — 75 cents beyond the greater New York metropolitan area. — 50 CENTS

Pool photo by Wilfredo Lee

You Can't Get There From Here

Hillary Rodham Clinton and her daughter, Chelsea, checking a map during a bicycle ride yesterday on Martha's Vineyard. Page B12.

MEDIA GIANTS SAID TO BE NEGOTIATING FOR TV NETWORKS

2 SEPARATE DISCUSSIONS

Time Warner Is Reported to Be Seeking NBC, While Disney May Be Pursuing CBS

By GERALDINE FABRIKANT

In moves that could lead to a change of ownership for one and perhaps even two of the three major television networks, Time Warner Inc. is negotiating to buy the NBC Network and the Walt Disney Company has apparently contacted CBS Inc. about buying that company.

Time Warner, which already has extensive holdings in cable television, has held talks in recent weeks with the General Electric Company about buying its NBC Network subsidiary and some of NBC's cable services for about $2.5 billion in stock and cash, according to several people familiar with the negotiations. To hear its critics, NBC has never been a good fit for General Electric, which acquired the network in 1985 and has seen it slip to third place from first place in the prime-time ratings since then.

Meanwhile, Disney has expressed interest to CBS about a buyout, according to a person familiar with the talks. Earlier this summer, CBS nearly merged with QVC Inc., a cable-channel home-shopping company.

Owning a television network is appealing to Time Warner and Disney because they would be guaranteed a big, continuing market for their programming.

A senior industry executive familiar with NBC's side of the negotiations said: "It's all true. Time Warner has held talks both with Jack Welch and Bob Wright." He was referring to John F. Welch Jr., the chairman and chief executive of General Electric, and Robert C. Wright, the president of NBC. He added that as of the end of last week Time Warner had decided to "go to the next step and see what happens."

Representatives for General Electric and Time Warner declined to comment on any talks, as did Judy Smith, an NBC spokeswoman. And a person close to Time Warner noted that he would give the deal less than a 50-50 chance of happening.

In the case of CBS, the company's chairman, Laurence A. Tisch, denied that there were any discussions with Disney. Disney declined to comment.

Two executives with knowledge of

Continued on Page D18, Column 1

I.R.A. DECLARES CEASE-FIRE, SEEING 'NEW OPPORTUNITY' TO NEGOTIATE IRISH PEACE

Reuters

Some residents of Northern Ireland celebrated the cease-fire yesterday by waving Irish flags as they passed the I.R.A. political office in Belfast.

RELIEF IN BELFAST

But Most Protestants Are Skeptical — Next Step Is Still Vague

By WILLIAM E. SCHMIDT

Special to The New York Times

BELFAST, Northern Ireland, Thursday, Sept. 1 — After waging a 25-year campaign of bloodshed and terror, the Irish Republican Army declared Wednesday that it was ready to abandon warfare in favor of peace talks on the future of Northern Ireland, and at midnight its fighters lay down their arms.

In a five-paragraph communiqué declaring the unconditional cease-fire, the secret I.R.A. leadership described itself at "an historic crossroads."

It said the time had come to rely on political solutions rather than force to get the British out of Northern Ireland and unite the province with the Irish Republic to the south.

"We believe we are entering a new situation, a new opportunity," read the statement, which was released Wednesday morning after several days of eager speculation over its contents. [Text, page A12.]

In West Belfast's mostly Catholic neighborhoods, weary redoubts of support for the republican cause, the news brought vast crowds of people into the streets to wave Irish flags, honk horns and dance jigs.

"The struggle is not over," Gerry Adams, the head of Sinn Fein, the I.R.A's political arm, told hundreds outside his headquarters. "The struggle has entered a new phase."

But while many hoped the announcement was the beginning of the end of one of the most intractable political and sectarian conflicts, it also sowed doubt and foreboding, especially among the nearly one million Loyalists in Northern Ireland. This is the mostly Protestant majority who are deeply opposed to union with the mostly Catholic south and prefer to maintain their ties to Britain.

Among other things, it is not clear whether Loyalist paramilitaries in Northern Ireland, who have become more involved in bloody shadow warfare with the I.R.A., will abide by the cease-fire, or whether Loyalist politicians, the I.R.A.'s sworn enemies, will agree to talk with Mr. Adams.

While the communiqué on Wednesday called for "complete cessation of military operations," there was no mention of whether the I.R.A. would surrender its huge cache of weapons, and Mr. Adams quickly seized the offensive, saying it was up to Britain to begin reducing its military presence in the province.

Still, Prime Minister John Major, whose Government has waged war on the I.R.A. for decades, said he was "greatly encouraged," providing the announcement meant a permanent renunciation of violence. The Irish Prime Minister, Albert Reynolds, de-

Continued on Page A12, Column 3

End of 'The Troubles'?

Trying to Exchange Old Hatreds for Peace On a Battlefield With Little Middle Ground

By JOHN DARNTON

Special to The New York Times

News Analysis

LONDON, Aug. 31 — The cease-fire announced today by the Irish Republican Army is widely seen as the most hopeful step toward peace in Northern Ireland since what the Irish call "the troubles" began 25 years ago. But that does not mean that peace will be easily achieved.

Without wanting to detract from the historic moment of the occasion, analysts and diplomats point out that numerous hurdles remain before Sinn Fein, the political arm of the I.R.A., can actually sit down at the negotiating table with representatives of the British Government.

And once negotiations begin, it is difficult to imagine a solution that could square the ambitions of the Roman Catholic republicans, who want union with Ireland, with the fears of the Protestant Loyalists, who insist on remaining part of Britain.

Because the British Government's policy is that it will not do anything against the wishes of the majority of people in Northern Ireland — and the majority are Protestants who want the status quo to continue — a deep gulf looms between any British and I.R.A. negotiators.

In the 16 months that the idea of a peace proposal has been bandied about — mostly from the inchoate notion that if peace can come to South Africa and the Middle East, why not Ulster? — no one has put forward a credible idea of how a final settlement might be arranged or what kind of political entity might actually result.

Occasionally, people on the outskirts of the diplomatic maneuvering

Continued on Page A13, Column 2

For Those Hoping to Run in '96, New York's the Place to Be in '94

By KEVIN SACK

Special to The New York Times

ALBANY, Aug. 31 — By the time New York's gubernatorial race is decided on Nov. 8, President Clinton will have campaigned more in the state for Gov. Mario Cuomo than he did for himself in the 1992 general election.

On the Republican side, meanwhile, a number of prospective 1996 Presidential candidates, led by Senator Bob Dole, are eagerly assailing Mr. Cuomo and raising money for his opponents.

These are hardly selfless gestures. With the possible exception of California's gubernatorial race, no statewide election this year is drawing more attention from politicians with an eye on the 1996 Presidential election than the New York campaign, according to top Democratic and Republican officials.

In the last two months, Mr. Clinton has attended two fund-raisers for Mr. Cuomo, one in Manhattan and one in Washington, and has scheduled another appearance at a Manhattan event in October. He came to New York only once during the 1992 campaign after leaving the Democratic National Convention at Madison Square Garden, said John A. Marino, who was the state Democratic chairman at the time.

Despite Mr. Clinton's sliding approval ratings and his difficulties with Congress, the President, like any President, has incomparable value as a fund-raising attraction for state and local candidates.

On the Republican side, Mr. Dole, considered a possible frontrunner for his party's nomination, tapped his own contributors to raise an estimated $200,000 at a Manhattan fund-raiser on Tuesday night for State Senator George E. Pataki, a Republican candidate.

"There's no one else we're doing this level of activity for," said Joanne L. Coe, the director of Mr. Dole's Campaign America political action committee.

Another potential Republican candidate, Jack F. Kemp, former Secre-

Continued on Page B4, Column 1

Vatican Says Gore Is Misrepresenting Population Talks

By ALAN COWELL

Special to The New York Times

ROME, Aug. 31 — Six days before the United Nations population conference in Cairo, the Vatican made an unusual, personal attack today on Vice President Al Gore, accusing him of misrepresenting the gathering's intentions on abortion.

The accusations were a setback for the Clinton Administration's effort to lower the level of discord with the Vatican over the conference. They also signaled the Vatican's continued readiness to confront the United States over central moral issues.

Since preparations for the conference began in April, Pope John Paul II and his aides have taken the lead in condemning it as likely to legitimize abortion as a means of birth control, in direct contradiction of Roman Catholic doctrine on the sanctity of life from the moment of conception.

Today's broadside by Joaquín Navarro-Valls, the Pope's chief spokesman, was the first time that the Vatican had formally accused the United States of being the principal sponsor of pro-abortion policies and also the first time it had publicly attacked a high American official by name.

"Mr. Al Gore, Vice President of the U.S.A. and member of the American delegation, recently stated that 'the United States has not sought, does not

Continued on Page A8, Column 3

Reuters

After 49 Years, Russian Troops Bid Bittersweet Goodbye to Germany

With parades and speeches about fragile friendship, Russia ended its military presence in Germany yesterday. Singing "Farewell, Germany," soldiers marched past a Soviet war memorial in eastern Berlin. Page A3.

When Children Kill Children: Boy, 11, Is Wanted in Chicago

By DON TERRY

Special to The New York Times

CHICAGO, Aug. 31 — Someone stepped out of the shadows between two storefront churches on the city's far South Side the other night and started shooting wildly at a knot of teen-agers playing football.

When the gunfire stopped, a 14-year-old girl lay dead, killed by a bullet apparently meant for someone else. At first, the shooting appeared to be another senseless, though increasingly common, story of an innocent slaughtered in the street.

But the slaying of Shavon Dean has become more than that. It has shaken this city and made many here fear for the future, not because of the victim's tender years but because of the even younger age of her suspected killer, an 11-year-old boy.

The suspect, who police say belongs to a gang, stands 4-foot-8, sports a tattoo that says "I love mommy" and has an arrest record that could belong to a middle-age thug.

And ever since the shooting last Sunday night, the boy has eluded the police and their growing child-hunt.

"This is a tragedy for everybody on both sides," Shavon's aunt, Ida Falls, said today. "That boy is 11 years old. He don't know no better. The gangs tell him what to do and he does it. He's just a child, a child that killed a child."

The boy, who has not been identified by the police because of his age, lived around the corner from Shavon and is known in the neighborhood for causing trouble. He is also a suspect in the shooting and wounding of a teen-age boy earlier on Sunday in another skirmish in what seems like a never-ending gang war here.

But gunplay and funerals are not confined to big cities and their street gangs. In the apple-growing community of Wenatchee, Wash., about 160 miles east of Seattle, two 12-year-old

Continued on Page B10, Column 1

INSIDE

Repeat of Mariel Boatlift?

Clinton Administration officials say that they have evidence that Havana has released several dozen prisoners and encouraged them to join the flood of Cuban refugees. Page A6.

Ruling on Gay Navy Man

A Federal appeals court ruled that the Navy cannot discharge a flight instructor merely because he said that he is gay. Page A16.

Trying to Trace Deadly Drug

Seeking the supplier of a deadly blend of heroin that may have killed as many as 14 people, the police saturated the Lower East Side of Manhattan with undercover agents. Page B3.

Rockefeller Center Shooting

As tourists and workers scattered, a man with an assault rifle shot and killed a stagehand outside the "Today" show studio. Page B1.

"All the News That's Fit to Print"

The New York Times

Late Edition

New York: Today, sunny, mild, light winds. High 71. Tonight, increasing clouds. Low 50. Tomorrow, cloudy, cool, occasional rain. High 59. Yesterday, high 76, low 51. Details, page C13.

VOL.CXLIV . . No. 50,037 Copyright © 1995 The New York Times NEW YORK, THURSDAY, APRIL 20, 1995 $1 beyond the greater New York metropolitan area 60 CENTS

AT LEAST 31 ARE DEAD, SCORES ARE MISSING AFTER CAR BOMB ATTACK IN OKLAHOMA CITY WRECKS 9-STORY FEDERAL OFFICE BUILDING

CLUES ARE LACKING

U.S. Officials Scurry for Answers — Reno to Ask Death Penalty

By DAVID JOHNSTON

WASHINGTON, April 19 — The authorities opened an intensive hunt today for whoever bombed a Federal office building in Oklahoma City, and proceeded on the theory that the bombing was a terrorist attack against the Government, law-enforcement officials said.

President Clinton appeared in the White House press room this afternoon and somberly promised that the Government would hunt down the "evil cowards" responsible. "These people are killers," he said, "and must be treated like killers."

Attorney General Janet Reno, speaking to reporters at the White House in early evening, said that casualty figures from the scene were climbing and that of the 550 people who worked in the building, 300 were unaccounted for.

Ms. Reno said Federal prosecutors would seek the death penalty against the bombers. "The death penalty is available," she said, "and we will seek it."

But the authorities said they had no suspects, and questions about the identity of the bombers swirled around the case. The only solid fact was the explosion itself.

Some law-enforcement officials said the bombing might be linked to the second anniversary today of Federal agents' ill-fated assault on the Branch Davidian compound near Waco, Tex., an operation that ended in a fire that killed about 80 people, including many children. Among the offices housed by the Federal building in Oklahoma City was one quartering local agents of the Bureau of Alcohol, Tobacco and Firearms, the agency that Branch Davidians and their sympathizers blamed for the confrontation.

But other officials said that neither the Branch Davidians nor right-wing "militia" groups that have protested the Government's handling of the Davidians were believed to have the technical expertise to engage in

Continued on Page B8, Column 1

David Longstreath/Associated Press

12 Victims Were Children in 2d-Floor Day-Care Center

By JOHN KIFNER

OKLAHOMA CITY, April 19 — A car bomb went off with a thunderous explosion here this morning, ripping through a Federal office building, collapsing walls and floors, and killing at least 31 people. Many others were buried in the wreckage, and the death toll seemed certain to rise.

At least 12 children whose parents had just dropped them off at a second-floor day-care center were among those immediately known dead in the deadliest bombing in the United States in 75 years.

As dusk fell, scores of the more than 500 people who normally work in the building were still missing. John Hansen, an Assistant Oklahoma City Fire Chief, said it appeared that dead and wounded victims were underneath the piles of concrete, plaster and glass. Late tonight, rain fell from the gray clouds that had threatened for much of the day, adding hardship to horror and raising the possibility the wreckage would shift, imperiling the trapped injured and their rescuers.

The National Guard has been called in, and late tonight limited martial law was declared to keep the streets clear.

Reflecting on the early report of the death toll, Fire Chief Gary Marrs said, "We're sure that it will go up, because we've seen fatalities in the building."

At the White House, President Clinton convened an inter-agency task force to coordinate Federal assistance and called on Americans to pray for the dead and stricken. He also dispatched a small army of Federal investigators to Oklahoma and pledged a relentless hunt for the killers.

Attorney General Janet Reno, noting that the dead children ranged from 1 to 7 years old, and that some had been burned beyond recognition in the day-care center just above the curb where the bomb detonated, said the crime was a capital one and that the Government would seek the death penalty if those responsible were caught. She also said that there were 550 people working in the building and that about 300 were still unaccounted for.

By late tonight, no one had claimed responsibility for the bombing, which occurred on the second anniversary of the Federal raid on the Branch Davidian compound near Waco, Tex., in which David Koresh and scores of his followers perished. There was no evidence that today's bombing, which was similar in intensity to the World Trade Center bombing in New York two years ago, but far more deadly, was linked to the Davidians.

Associated Press

The Alfred P. Murrah building in Oklahoma City before its north side, facing left, was bombed.

Rescue teams, bringing in backhoes, bulldozers and other heavy equipment, dug in the rubble tonight in darkness, rain and a cutting wind, searching for victims in the flattened center of the nine-story Alfred P. Murrah Building.

Three survivors were pulled out of the wreckage by firefighers shortly after 9:30 P.M. There were cries from a woman in the basement, firefighters said, but they were having difficulty getting to her because there appeared to be bodies in the way. That vignette of horror was just one of hundreds played out all day long, from morning to dark.

Federal buildings in seven other cities were evacuated because of bomb threats, and security was tightened at Government buildings from coast to coast.

Shards of glass littered the street around the Federal building here, and much of the masonry was literally peeled away from the building, leaving a gaping nine-story hole. Federal Bureau of Investigation agents in bright yellow rain slickers,

Continued on Page B9, Column 1

OTHER NEWS

Gas Fumes Create Panic in Yokohama

In a chilling reminder of the gas attack last month in Tokyo, caustic fumes spread through Yokohama's railroad station and through a train, sending about 300 people to hospitals. No one took responsibility for release of the gas. Page A10.

Court Upholds Anonymity

In a decision threatening state election laws, the Supreme Court ruled the Constitution guarantees the right to distribute anonymous campaign literature. Page A20. Add two more lines of type in all.

Lugar Declares Candidacy

Saying he has an unblemished [illegible]cter, Senator Richard Lugar of Indiana announced that he would seek the Republican nomination for President in 1996. Page A16.

Mayor Wants to End Relief

A day after touting the success of new rules for a welfare program, Mayor Giuliani said he really favors abolishing the program. Page B1.

Charles H. Porter IV/Associated Press

Emergency workers remove a child injured in the explosion in downtown Oklahoma City, which occurred as employees began reporting for work yesterday. At least 31 were killed, including numerous children at a day-care center, and scores were injured or missing, some still buried in the rubble.

In Shock, Loathing, Denial: 'This Doesn't Happen Here'

By RICK BRAGG

OKLAHOMA CITY, April 19 — Before the dust and the rage had a chance to settle, a chilly rain started to fall on the blasted-out wreck of what had once been an office building, and on the shoulders of the small army of police, firefighters and medical technicians that surrounded it.

They were not used to this, if anyone is. On any other day, they would have answered calls to kitchen fires, domestic disputes, or even a cat up a tree. Oklahoma City is still, in some ways, a small town, said the people who live here.

This morning, as the blast trembled the morning coffee in cups miles away, the outside world came crashing hard onto Oklahoma City.

"I just took part in a surgery where a little boy had part of his brain hanging out of his head," said Terry Jones, a medical technician, as he searched in his pocket for a cigarette. Behind him, firefighters picked carefully through the skeleton of the building, still searching for the living and the dead.

"You tell me," he said, "how can anyone have so little respect for human life."

The shock of what the rescuers found in the rubble had long since worn off, replaced with a loathing for the people who had planted the bomb that killed their friends, neighbors and children.

One by one they said the same thing: this does not happen here. It happens in countries so far away, so different, they might as well be on the dark side of the moon. It happens in New York. It happens in Europe.

It does not happen in a place where, debarking at the airport, passengers see a woman holding a sign that welcomes them to the Lieutenant Governor's annual turkey shoot.

It does not happen in a city that has a sign just outside the city limits, "Oklahoma City, Home of Vince Gill," the country singer.

"We're just a little old cowtown," said Bill Finn, a grime-covered firefighter who propped himself wearily up against a brick wall as the rain turned the dust to mud on his face. "You can't get no more Middle America than Oklahoma City. You

Continued on Page B11, Column 1

More on the Blast

THE RESCUE When rescuers found the hundreds of cut, burned and terrified victims, it became a matter of grasping for the living while trying to ignore the dead. Page B10.

AROUND THE NATION Shocked and fearful, government officials at Federal, state and some local levels shut down offices in at least eight cities, including New York. Page B10.

THE BOMB The powerful bomb was very likely made of ingredients that are widely available from gardening centers, chemical suppliers and gasoline stations. Page B8.

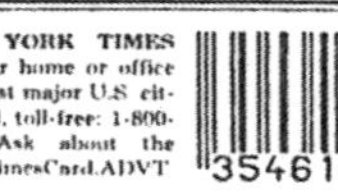

"All the News That's Fit to Print"

The New York Times

Late Edition
Today, cloudy, showers, more humid. High 75. **Tonight,** diminishing showers, patchy fog. Low 65. **Tomorrow,** showers. High 75. **Yesterday,** high 81, Low 60. Details are on page C10.

VOL.CXLV . No. 50,204

NEW YORK, WEDNESDAY, OCTOBER 4, 1995

$1 beyond the greater New York metropolitan area.

60 CENTS

Welcoming the Pope

TODAY

3 P.M. Arrival at Newark International Airport at restricted terminal. Welcoming ceremony, address and meeting with President Clinton.

Todav's Host Diocese
Archdiocese of Newark

5 P.M. Evening prayer at Sacred Heart Cathedral, Newark. Afterward, the Pope spends the night at the residence of the Vatican's representative to the United Nations on East 72d Street in Manhattan.

TRAFFIC Interstate 280 and New Jersey Turnpike closed as Pope and President pass; traffic barred from area around Sacred Heart Cathedral for much of the day. East 72d Street between Fifth and Madison Avenues closed to vehicles and pedestrians.

VIEWING ABC, NBC, WWOR, New York 1, FOX and CNN will provide live coverage of the arrival.

TOMORROW Addresses the United Nations and celebrates Mass and delivers homily at Giants Stadium.

FRIDAY Celebrates Mass and delivers homily at Aqueduct Racetrack in Queens. Leads evening prayer and delivers an address at St. Joseph's Seminary in Yonkers.

SATURDAY Celebrates Mass and delivers homily in Central Park. Recites rosary and delivers a brief address at St. Patrick's Cathedral.

Jury Clears Simpson in Double Murder; Spellbound Nation Divides on Verdict

At the words "not guilty," a tense O. J. Simpson uncoiled and breathed a sigh of relief.

Pool photo by Reuters

After 474 Days as a Prisoner, He Is Free

By DAVID MARGOLICK

LOS ANGELES, Oct. 3 — Orenthal James Simpson, a man who overcame the spindly legs left by a childhood case of rickets to run to fame and fortune, surmounted a very different sort of obstacle today, when a jury of 10 women and 2 men cleared him of charges that he murdered his former wife and one of her friends.

The verdict, coming 16 months after Nicole Brown Simpson and Ronald L. Goldman were slashed to death in the front yard of Mrs. Simpson's condominium and after 9 months of what often seemed like interminable testimony, sidebars and high-priced legal bickering, was reached in the end with breathtaking speed. When it was read, much of the nation, President Clinton included, stopped work to listen to it.

And with the Simpson verdict, as with the Simpson case, the nation once more divided — largely along racial lines. So, too, did defense lawyers, with the onetime chief of Mr. Simpson's legal team, Robert L. Shapiro, criticizing his successor.

"Not only did we play the race card, we dealt it from the bottom of the deck," Mr. Shapiro told Barbara Walters tonight in an interview on an ABC News special.

In a scene that lent a certain symmetry to the entire Simpson saga, Mr. Simpson immediately returned to the freeways of Los Angeles in a white van, and as fans waved from the streets he headed back to his home at 360 North Rockingham Avenue. While a dozen helicopters flew overhead, and fans festooned the fence with roses and balloons, he was met by A. C. Cowlings, who had been in the driver's seat of the white Ford Bronco on June 17, 1994, five days after the killings.

Mr. Simpson pursed his lips, gulped a few times and wore a forced, pained grin as Deirdre Robertson, the law clerk to Judge Lance A. Ito, read the verdict. Mrs. Robertson tripped over "Orenthal," but not over what came next: "not guilty." When she uttered those words, Mr. Simpson's body instantly uncoiled. He then breathed a sigh of relief, and a faint smile appeared.

As Mrs. Robertson's recitation continued — ". . . in violation of Penal Code Section 187A, a felony, upon Nicole Brown Simpson, a human being," Mr. Simpson waved at the panelists and mouthed the words "Thank you." The reading then unfolded again, with the name "Ronald L. Goldman" substituted for Mrs. Simpson. Mr. Simpson embraced his chief lawyer, Johnnie L. Cochran Jr., and silently thanked and rethanked the jury again.

"Ladies and gentlemen of the jury, is this your verdict, so say you one, so say you all?" Mrs. Robertson then asked. "Yes," the panel members — nine black, two whites and a Hispanic man — replied matter-of-factly. Critics of what the jurors did today maintained that they had been manipulated by a cynical defense team that talked more about the racism of the Los Angeles police than about the guilt or innocence of their client. Mr. Simpson's lawyers countered that prosecutors simply had not proven their case.

As he left court, one juror, a for-

Continued on Page A10, Column 1

Racial Split at the End, as at the Start

By MARTIN GOTTLIEB

The seven workers at the Pasqua Coffee Bar in lower Manhattan like to joke around with one another, to trade stories about family and regular customers, and to help one another out in jams.

But until the astonishingly abrupt culmination of the O. J. Simpson murder trial yesterday, they never seemed to get around to discussing what, for much of America, has been a prickly and divisive topic.

Then, as the voice of the court clerk intoning "not guilty" came over the restaurant's radio, Charmon Savage, a black man who works in the kitchen, jumped up, punched the air with both fists and exclaimed, "Yes! Yes! Yes!"

Geraldine Foney, the restaurant manager, who is white, lowered her head with disgust in her eyes. "I thought he should have rotted in hell," she said.

And several other women on the staff, including Debi Diaz, a counterwoman, grumbled in disbelief after hearing the verdict of the jurors, nine of whom are black. "They have to retry him," she said. "It's ridiculous, you know."

The scene at the Pasqua Bar was repeated in thousands of different settings across the country yesterday, with reactions that seemed often to be shaped by race — especially by race — sometimes by the person's sex and frequently by a jaded belief that personal wealth can triumph over just about anything.

At the Texas Bar-B-Q in downtown Dallas, a black-owned restaurant, a couple of black men greeted the verdict with eruptions of elation. Several white customers quietly left shortly afterward.

At Jocks n Jills Sports Bar at the CNN Center in Atlanta, the reaction was much the same as the verdict came over a bank of wall-to-wall television sets — black customers often embraced and cheered; whites sat in stony silence.

Over the Internet, the comments were often starkly racial.

Since it first began to transfix the country in June 1994, the Simpson murder case has been a combination soap opera, passion play and national Rorschach test laden with sex, celebrity, wealth, violence and, perhaps most sensitively, race.

The reactions to the verdict parallel the racial divide in every opinion poll taken since the trial began. Separated by a constant gap of about 40 percentage points, many whites seemed to hold fast to the belief that Mr. Simpson was guilty, while blacks believed as adamantly in his innocence. Several polls indicate that behind the response of many blacks is a deep suspicion of the police and the criminal justice system.

A poll taken by CBS News immedi-

Continued on Page A12, Column 1

Carrie Boretz for The New York Times

Ozier Muhammad/The New York Times

Passers-by watched the verdict with shock through the windows of the "Today" show studios at Rockefeller Center, left; at her restaurant in Harlem, Sylvia Woods cheered as she hugged her daughter and a waitress.

A Day (10 Minutes of It) the Country Stood Still

By N. R. KLEINFIELD

The country stopped.

Between 1 and 1:10 P.M. yesterday, people didn't work. They didn't go to math class. They didn't make phone calls. They didn't use the bathroom. They didn't walk the dog.

They listened to the O. J. Simpson verdicts.

Airplane flights had to wait. At Hartsfield International Airport in Atlanta, passengers and airport workers alike were so fixedly watching the television sets at the departure gates that several Delta Air Lines flights due to leave between 1:24 and 1:32 boarded late. When a Delta agent with poor timing tried to start her boarding instructions for a Louisville flight just as the verdicts were being read, a hundred passengers shouted her down.

Finance ceased. At the Barnett Bank branch on Biscayne Boulevard in Miami, tellers stopped counting bills and the lines of impatient customers evaporated as everyone turned, tantalized, to the television on the wall. Seeing the envelope containing the verdicts, a sales manager implored: "Open it. Open it."

It was an eerie moment of national communion, in which the routines and rituals of the country were subsumed by an unquenchable curiosity. Millions of people in millions of places seemed to spend 10 spellbinding minutes doing exactly the same thing.

The curiosity infected everyone, no matter what larger matters might be under consideration. President Clinton left the Oval Office at two minutes before 1 to catch the verdicts in his secretary's office with several of his aides.

The Supreme Court was hearing arguments at the big moment. Immediately after the verdicts were announced, two messengers appeared. One went to the side where Justice Ruth Bader Ginsburg sat, and the other to the side where Justice Stephen G. Breyer sat, and they

Continued on Page A12, Column 3

The Reidys, All 11, Reflect On a Faith Proudly Lived

One Catholic Family Awaiting the Pope

By FELICIA R. LEE

To William J. Reidy, an Irish-Catholic father of nine, Pope John Paul II operates in the world in much the manner Mr. Reidy operates his large household in the affluent Riverdale section of the Bronx: offering guidelines and hoping his flock will believe.

"It's like a father," said Mr. Reidy, who was educated in Catholic schools from kindergarten through college and attends Mass every Sunday. "He talks first, makes a lot of noise, and you have guidelines." As a father, Mr. Reidy knows well that it's not at all certain how the message will be received.

"There is the presumption that the central voice is the universal voice," said the 54-year-old Mr. Reidy, adding, "but I am not sure what Catholic means."

Still, every last Reidy child — from Tim, 20, to Gavin, 3 — is a proud Catholic, and all are looking forward to the Pope's arrival today, each in his or her own way.

Ask Marcia Reidy, their mother, who spends much of her time taking care of her 10-year-old handicapped son, what Catholicism means to her, and she says: "It's an impossible question. It means to be a Christian. It means taking care of the children."

To 12-year-old Michael Reidy, an altar boy at St. Gabriel's in the Bronx, the Pope represents "the closest thing we have to God on earth." But already, his 14-year-old brother, Owen, also an altar boy, isn't so sure. "He's the Pope," he said. "I sort of find that just a name. How closer to God can he be than lay people? It's not like God is going to walk into his living room."

And then there is the Reidy's oldest, Tim. From the church, he learned that homosexual acts are sinful, but at Princeton, where he is a junior, he met openly gay people for the first time and has tried to fit them in with his idea of Catholicism.

Like so many area Catholics, the Reidys will be personally touched by the Pope's visit this week. Owen and his sisters Marcia, 16, and Anne, 17, will attend his Mass on the Great

Continued on Page B6, Column 1

A.M.A. Says Plan Would Drive Many Doctors Out of Medicare

By ROBERT PEAR

WASHINGTON, Oct. 3 — After months of public silence, the American Medical Association expressed deep concern today about Republican proposals to redesign Medicare, saying that new limits on payments would make the program unattractive to many doctors.

James H. Stacey, a spokesman for the medical association, said that under the Republican plan doctors in the standard Medicare program were facing not only a cut in the growth of Medicare payments, but also an absolute reduction in payment for many services.

"This causes real problems for the A.M.A.," Mr. Stacey said in response to a question. "It would be a major blow to the traditional fee-for-service Medicare program."

The doctors' concerns echo comments from the Clinton Administration and Democrats in Congress, who say the Republicans would cut payments to doctors so severely that many doctors would decide not to treat Medicare patients. As a result, they say, patients would be forced to obtain care through health maintenance organizations and other private health plans, even though the Republicans insist that beneficiaries will always be free to keep traditional Medicare coverage.

Until today, the American Medical Association had generally refrained from criticizing the Republican proposals on Medicare. Indeed, it has praised some of those proposals, including one that would relax antitrust laws for doctors and another that would limit payments to victims of medical malpractice.

By contrast, in the battle over President Clinton's health care plan in 1993 and 1994, the medical association regularly made itself heard. It supported Mr. Clinton's goal of guaranteeing health insurance coverage for all Americans, and it initially supported his proposal that all employers be required to buy such insurance for their employees. But the association later urged Congress to consider alternatives to the "employer mandate," and many doctors said Mr. Clinton's health plan envisioned too big a role for Government.

The specific points raised today concerned the fee schedule Medicare has used since 1992 to pay doctors. Each physician service is assigned a numerical value, and this number is multiplied by a fixed amount of money, called a dollar

Continued on Page A22, Column 1

BASEBALL '95 PLAYOFFS

Mariners	6
Yankees	9
Red Sox	4
Indians	5
Braves	5
Rockies	4
Reds	7
Dodgers	2

SportsWednesday, pages B10-B15.

INSIDE

Giuliani's Plan for Schools
Mayor Giuliani outlined a specific proposal for City Hall to gain control over the school system. Page B1.

Veto With a Message
President Clinton vetoed a bill to pay Congress's administrative expenses, scolding lawmakers. Page A22.

NEWS SUMMARY A2

MORE ON THE TRIAL

A Free Man
O. J. Simpson left court free of criminal charges but not of the side effects of the case, from possible television deals to huge legal bills. Page A10.

The Cryptic Jury
Jurors who made an art form out of being unreadable finally showed a few small signs of emotion, but only for a moment. Page A11.

The Los Angeles Factor
The trial was a national event, but the dynamics of Los Angeles, particularly the Police Department's images, were crucial. Page A13.

Opinions Everywhere
There was rejoicing at a black college in Atlanta, cynicism at a health club in Massachusetts, disbelief at a bar in Michigan. Page A13.

"All the News That's Fit to Print"

The New York Times

Late Edition
New York: Today, sunny, not as windy, very cool. High 50. Tonight, clouds. Low 39. Tomorrow, becoming sunny, milder. High 59. Yesterday, high 55, low 38. Details, page 51.

VOL.CXLV . No. 50,236 | NEW YORK, SUNDAY, NOVEMBER 5, 1995 | $2.50

RABIN SLAIN AFTER PEACE RALLY IN TEL AVIV; ISRAELI GUNMAN HELD; SAYS HE ACTED ALONE

Associated Press

THE SPEECH Prime Minister Yitzhak Rabin addressing a peace rally yesterday in Tel Aviv before he was shot to death.

Reuters

THE ATTACK Mr. Rabin lying at the feet of security officers after he was shot before entering his car.

PERES TAKES OVER

Stunned Nation Asks if Talks With the P.L.O Are in Jeopardy

By SERGE SCHMEMANN

JERUSALEM, Nov. 4 — Prime Minister Yitzhak Rabin, who led Israel to victory in 1967 and began the march toward peace a generation later, was shot dead by a lone assassin this evening as he was leaving a vast rally in Tel Aviv.

Mr. Rabin, 73, was struck down by one or two bullets as he was entering his car. Police immediately seized a 27-year-old Israeli law student, Yigal Amir, who had been active in support of Israeli settlers but who told the police tonight that he had acted alone.

The police said Mr. Amir had also told them that he had tried twice before to attack the Prime Minister.

It was the first assassination of a prime minister in the 47-year history of the state of Israel, and it was certain to have extensive repercussions on Israeli politics and the future of the Arab-Israeli peace.

Mr. Rabin was to lead his Labor party in elections scheduled for November next year, and without him the prospects for a Labor victory, and of a continuation of his policies, were thrown into question.

In the immediate aftermath, Foreign Minister Shimon Peres, Mr. Rabin's partner in the peace negotiations, automatically became Acting Prime Minister. It was widely expected that he would be formally confirmed as Mr. Rabin's successor.

Mr. Rabin, who rose to national prominence as commander of the victorious Israeli army in the 1967 Six-Day War, became the second Middle Eastern leader, after President Anwar el-Sadat of Egypt, to be killed by extremists from his own side for seeking an Arab-Israeli peace. Mr. Sadat, the first Arab to make peace with Israel, was assassinated in 1984.

Mr. Rabin and his Labor Government have come under fierce attack from right-wing groups over the peace with the Palestinians, especially since the agreement transferring authority in the West Bank to the Palestine Liberation Organization was reached in September. Mr. Rabin has been heckled at many of his appearances in recent weeks and his security has been tight.

A gruff, chain-smoking career military man, Mr. Rabin led Israel both in its greatest military triumph and in one of its most dramatic bids for peace.

Shortly before his death, Mr. Rabin, obviously buoyed by the huge turnout of more than 100,000 supporters of the peace process, told the rally, "I have always believed that the majority of the people want peace and are ready to take a chance for peace." [Excerpts, page 16A.]

He then joined other participants in singing the "Song of Peace," a popular paean. Unfamiliar with the words, the prime minister followed from a text he tucked into his pocket.

Hours after the shooting, Mr. Peres said the blood-soaked sheet of music was found in his pocket and

Continued on Page 16A, Column 1

A Shaken Clinton Mourns Rabin, 'Martyr for His Nation's Peace'

By DAVID E. ROSENBAUM

WASHINGTON, Nov. 4 — President Clinton, who plans to leave on Sunday for the funeral of Prime Minister Yitzhak Rabin of Israel, went to the Rose Garden of the White House tonight and, his voice cracking, called Mr. Rabin "a martyr for his nation's peace."

"Peace must be and peace will be Prime Minister Rabin's lasting legacy," Mr. Clinton said.

The President and other officials here, though shocked and saddened by Mr. Rabin's assassination, said tonight that they expected the peace effort in the Middle East to continue uninterrupted.

Secretary of State Warren Christopher issued a statement in which he said, "History will record Prime Minister Rabin as one of the towering figures of this century."

As a political matter, Mr. Rabin was a crucial ally of Mr. Clinton's. The President's success in 1993 in bringing together Mr. Rabin and Yasir Arafat, the leader of the Palestine Liberation Organization, is the most important foreign policy success of the Clinton Presidency.

"Yitzhak Rabin was my partner and my friend," the President said. "I admired him, and I loved him very much."

To Israel's people, he said, "Just as America has stood by you in moments of crisis and triumph, so now we all stand by you in this moment."

The President was in his residence watching a college football game on television when Anthony Lake, his national security adviser, called about 3:20 P.M. to tell of the shooting, the White House said.

Other top officials rushed to the White House situation room to receive information from the United States Ambassador to Israel, Martin Indyk, who had gone to the hospital in Tel Aviv where Mr. Rabin died.

Around 4 P.M., Mr. Lake went to the President's office to tell him that Mr. Rabin had died.

Mr. Clinton then called Mr. Rabin's widow, Leah, and the new Acting Prime Minister, Shimon Peres, to express his sympathy.

Michael D. McCurry, the President's press secretary, said Mrs. Rabin and Mr. Peres had said they had never seen Mr. Rabin happier than he was tonight, right after his speech at the peace rally in Tel Aviv and just before he was shot.

Mr. McCurry said Mr. Clinton had invited leaders of Congress of both parties to join him at the funeral.

The President issued a proclama-

Continued on Page 16B, Column 1

Suspect Says He Tried to Kill Rabin Before

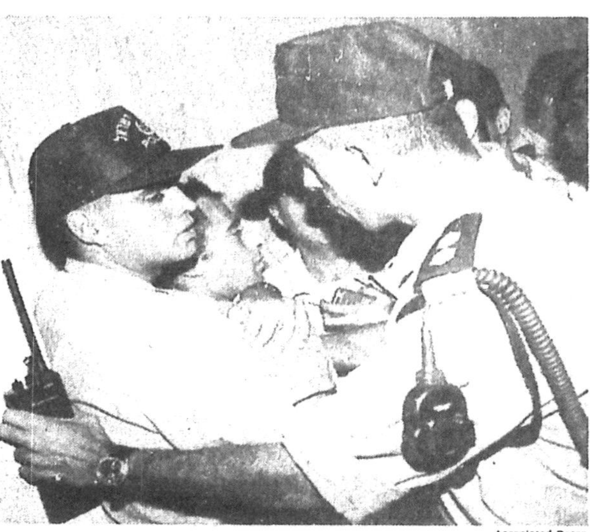

Associated Press

THE SUSPECT An Israeli police officer grabbed Yigal Amir, the suspected assassin, around the neck after the shooting.

Arrested Law Student Often Joined Protests Against Government

By JOEL GREENBERG

JERUSALEM, Nov. 4 — Yigal Amir, the 27-year-old law student who was arrested for the assassination of Prime Minister Yitzhak Rabin tonight, was described by acquaintances as a militant critic of the Government who regularly joined protests against Mr. Rabin's policies.

He told interrogators that he had carried out the killing on his own.

Under questioning by the police, Mr. Amir said he had been planning the assassination for a long time and had intended to kill Mr. Rabin on two previous occasions but was thwarted by tight security measures.

After his self-appointed mission tonight, Mr. Amir, a short, dark-haired man dressed in a blue shirt and light-colored pants, was pinned to a wall by police officers and rushed to a waiting police car.

"I have no regrets," he was quoted as telling investigators. "I acted alone and on orders from God."

According to some accounts, Mr. Amir had links to a small militant anti-Arab group known as Eyal that is virulently opposed to the Government's accords with the Palestine Liberation Organization.

A leader of the group, Avishai Raviv, acknowledged tonight that he knew Mr. Amir. But he denied that the assassin belonged to Eyal or that the group had anything to do with the shooting.

After the shooting, Israeli reporters received beeper messages signed Ain, a Hebrew acronym for the Israeli Avenging Organization, a previously unknown group. The group claimed responsibility for the killing, though it was not immediately known if it had any connection with Mr Amir.

The assassination was the second incident of extreme violence by right-wing Jewish militants since the 1993 signing of the Israeli-Palestinian accord.

In February 1994, Baruch Goldstein, an American follower of the anti-Arab group Kach, massacred 29 Muslims at prayer at the Shrine of

Continued on Page 16A, Column 4

Teachers' Union Reaches Accord That Protects Jobs

By STEVEN LEE MYERS

Mayor Rudolph W. Giuliani and the leaders of New York City's teachers union announced a tentative agreement yesterday on a contract that would increase wages and benefits by 13 percent over five years and offer an unusual written commitment protecting union members from layoffs through 1998.

But the agreement included no significant concessions from the union's rank and file, even though the Mayor and his aides had vowed to achieve them to pay for raises. And by that measure, it fell short of the goal Mr. Giuliani set for himself: to scale back generous benefits and force employees to work harder for what they already earn.

The contract, subject to ratification by the union's 90,000 members and the Board of Education, provides no wage increases in the first two years, giving the city time, the Mayor said, to find ways to pay for raises of 3 to 4 percent in each succeeding year.

By the end of the pact in September of the year 2000, the top salary for teachers with 25 years experience would rise to $70,000, from $60,000 now. In the final year, the city would also contribute $75 per worker to the union's welfare fund. In all, the salary of a starting teacher would increase to $31,900, from $28,700.

"This contract is a historic breakthrough for the school system and for labor relations in the City of New York," the Mayor said. "It provides for much more educational value and at the same time is fiscally sound."

For Mr. Giuliani, the Republican Mayor nearing the midpoint of his term, the contract with the United Federation of Teachers was the first in the first round of bargaining conducted entirely by his administration. And it sets, he said, the general parameters for contracts with all of the city's 83 municipal unions.

Although the Mayor entered office

Continued on Page 46, Column 4

NEWS SUMMARY 2

TODAY'S SECTIONS

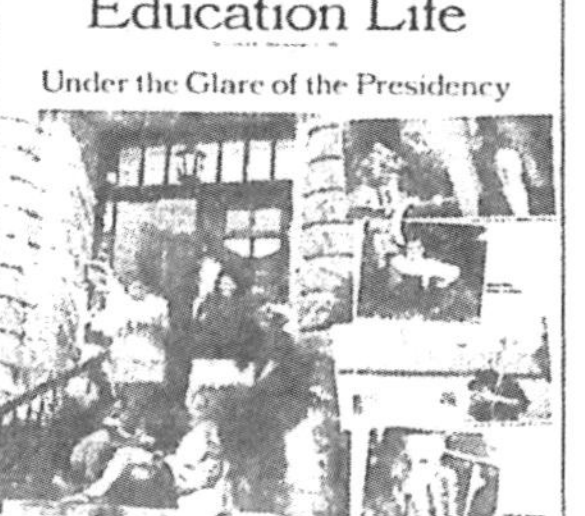

Education Life
Under the Glare of the Presidency

*In New York City and the metropolitan region.
(† Elsewhere, auto pages are in section 3.)
§ In most parts of New York City
¶ In Long Island, Westchester, Connecticut and central and northern New Jersey*

THE DEATH OF RABIN

Associated Press

A Soldier-Statesman

Yitzhak Rabin was a soldier turned peacemaker, a man who tried to end the bloodshed that had plagued his country. Obituary, page 16.

Israeli Politics Clouded

The assassination threw a question mark over Israeli politics just a year before elections that could decide the future of the Arab-Israeli peace. News analysis, page 16A.

Horror and Condolences

Leaders of American Jewish groups were horrified by the killing. The head of the Palestine Liberation Organization offered condolences, while some other Arabs celebrated the assassination. Page 16B.

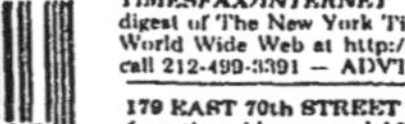

"All the News That's Fit to Print"

The New York Times

Late Edition
New York: **Today,** some sun, windy, a flurry. High 43. Tonight, part cloudy, chilly. Low 33. **Tomorrow,** mainly cloudy. High 46. **Yesterday,** high 54, low 43. Details are on page B16.

VOL.CXLV . . . No. 50,253 | Copyright © 1995 The New York Times | NEW YORK, WEDNESDAY, NOVEMBER 22, 1995 | $1 beyond the greater New York metropolitan area | 60 CENTS

ACCORD REACHED TO END THE WAR IN BOSNIA; CLINTON PLEDGES U.S. TROOPS TO KEEP PEACE

Reuters

SERBIA Slobodan Milosevic President — **BOSNIA-HERZEGOVINA** Alija Izetbegovic President — **CROATIA** Franjo Tudjman President — **UNITED STATES** Warren Christopher Secretary of State

All Sides Make Concessions To End 4 Years of Conflict

By ELAINE SCIOLINO

DAYTON, Ohio, Nov. 21 — The presidents of three rival Balkan states agreed today to make peace in Bosnia, ending nearly four years of terror and ethnic bloodletting that have left a quarter of a million people dead in the worst war in Europe since World War II.

The leaders — Alija Izetbegovic of Bosnia, Franjo Tudjman of Croatia and Slobodan Milosevic of Serbia — initialed the peace agreement and 11 annexes in a hastily-arranged ceremony in the same conference room at Wright-Patterson Air Force Base where they opened their talks 21 days ago.

The agreement is to take effect when it is formally signed by the parties in Paris in mid-December.

Unlike previous peace accords that have collapsed, this one was reinforced by widespread fatigue of a war that has uprooted two million people from their homes and appalled the world with scenes of harrowing atrocities, and by the promise of enforcement by 60,000 NATO troops. President Clinton, hailing the agreement in a White House Rose Garden ceremony, reiterated his pledge that the NATO force would include 20,000 Americans.

"The agreement is a victory for all those who believe in a multi-ethnic democracy in Bosnia," said Secretary of State Warren Christopher, who spent several exhausting days brokering the final details of the accord. "It offers tangible hope that there will be no more days of dodging bullets, no more winters of freshly dug graves, no more years of isolation from the outside world."

But underneath the self-congratulation of today's ceremony was a grim awareness that the basic questions the parties failed to settle before the war remain: Can Bosnia, with its mutually suspicious populations of Muslims, Serbs and Croats, survive as a single state? What degree of self-government should be given to the Serb minority within its borders? And does Mr. Milosevic have the power to force the Serbs of Bosnia to do what he says?

Today the Bosnian Serb representatives who served in a delegation headed by Mr. Milosevic did not show up for the ceremony to initial the various annexes that affect the Serbian part of Bosnia.

The Bosnian Serbs were particularly upset by the military annexes in the agreement, which they charged essentially made NATO an occupying force, American and European negotiators said.

Under the agreement, NATO will have the right to remove or relocate specific forces and weapons from any location in the country whenever it determines that they constitute a threat to its troops.

The Bosnian Serbs were even

Continued on Page A10, Column 1

HIGHLIGHTS

TERRITORY Bosnia would maintain its current borders, but be divided into two entities — a Bosnian-Croat federation and a Bosnian Serb republic.

A central government, with a parliament and presidency, would remain in a united Sarajevo.

WAR CRIMINALS Would not be allowed to hold office, but no requirement to arrest them was specified.

TROOPS Forces would be withdrawn to agreed positions and an international force sent in to keep the peace. NATO has outlined a plan for a 60,000 member force — one-third of it American — to act as peacekeeper.

REFUGEES Would have the legal right to return home; human rights would be monitored by an independent commission.

SLOVENIA, CROATIA, KRAJINA REGION, Bihac, VOJVODINA, SERBIA, Tuzla, Srebrenica, BOSNIA AND HERZEGOVINA, Sarajevo, Zepa, Gorazde, YUGOSLAVIA, MONTENEGRO, KOSOVO, MACEDONIA

ONE NATION, DIVIDED
Bosnian-Croat federation
Serb republic

The New York Times

Study Finds Doctors Refuse Patients' Requests on Death

By SUSAN GILBERT

After 25 years of public outcry over the right to die with dignity, doctors are still ignoring patients' last wishes, according to a new study of terminally ill patients.

The study, reported in today's issue of The Journal of the American Medical Association, has found that doctors often misunderstand or ignore the patients' requests, with the result that large numbers of people still die alone, in pain and tethered to mechanical ventilators in intensive care units. Twenty-five years since the living will movement began, the study's authors say they have discovered that the wills, which are supposed to give terminally ill patients legal safeguards against unwanted medical treatment, offer virtually no protection.

The study also found that increasing communication between doctors and patients did not help.

"People think advance directives are solving the problem," said Dr. William Knaus, one of the researchers who directed the study. "We have very good information that they aren't, that nothing has changed — the amount of pain at the end of life, the number of people dying alone attached to machines."

The $28 million study, financed by the Robert Wood Johnson Foundation, took place at six medical centers around the country. It was divided into two parts, each one lasting two years and involving similar groups of terminally ill patients.

In the first phase, the researchers gathered base-line information, including the percentage of patients who did not want aggressive medical care like cardiopulmonary resuscitation and mechanical ventilation, the percentage of doctors who knew their patients' wishes, how often aggressive treatment was used and how much pain patients were in before they died.

The researchers found large gaps between what the patients wanted and what they got. Thirty-one percent of patients said they did not want cardiopulmonary resuscitation, but 80 percent of the doctors misunderstood or ignored their patients' wishes.

Forty-nine percent of the patients who wanted to avoid cardiopulmonary resuscitation by having their doctors write do-not-resuscitate orders did not get their wish.

The patients who did had to wait a long time for the doctors' orders. Depending on their medical specialty, doctors took an average of 22 to 73 days to write the orders after the patients requested them, and 46 percent of the orders were written within two days' of the patient's death. Half the patients spent eight or more days in what the researchers de-

Continued on Page C7, Column 1

China Charges Leading Dissident With Trying to Overthrow Regime

By PATRICK E. TYLER

BEIJING, Nov. 21 — China formally charged the country's best-known dissident, Wei Jingsheng, today with trying to "overthrow the Chinese Government," a step that almost certainly will lead to conviction and a second, lengthy prison sentence for the 44-year-old democracy advocate.

Mr. Wei had been held incommunicado at an undisclosed police "guest house" without charge since April 1994, when he was seized by seven carloads of plainclothes policemen while driving into the Chinese capital from the nearby city of Tianjin.

At the time he was on parole after serving 14½ years of a 15-year prison sentence on charges of counter-revolutionary incitement and passing state secrets to foreigners for his activities during the 1978-79 Democracy Wall movement in Beijing.

Mr. Wei, an electrician turned political essayist, gained wide attention for his biting criticisms of the Communist Party leadership, particularly the Government's failure to pursue democratic reforms promised by Deng Xiaoping and other senior leaders during the years after the death of Mao in 1976.

Today's decision by the party leadership to bring criminal charges against Mr. Wei caught many of his supporters and family members by surprise and indicates a determined effort by the Government to prevent him from returning to Chinese society, where he has been a magnet for pro-democracy forces.

In one sense, the Government acted to ease the contradiction between its often-stated position that China seeks to become a nation ruled by law, and Mr. Wei's continued secret detention without charges in blatant violation of the country's own published criminal procedures.

The action against Mr. Wei went forward despite recent appeals by President Clinton and Chancellor Helmut Kohl of Germany. Mr. Kohl visited here this month seeking the release of China's political prisoners, especially Mr. Wei, who has now spent more than 16 years in detention, nearly half that time in solitary confinement.

Earlier this year, Mr. Wei's younger sister, Wei Shanshan, wrote a letter to Mr. Deng pointing out the illegality of his detention.

"No formal charges have been brought against him, nor is he being

Continued on Page A7, Column 1

An Imperfect Peace

By ROGER COHEN

DAYTON, Ohio, Nov. 21 — A cold Balkan peace was concluded today, one built over the graves of numberless victims by the very leaders who unleashed the Yugoslav wars, but still a peace that almost certainly offers the last hope for the stubborn vestiges of civilized life in Bosnia.

News Analysis

The American-brokered peace is necessarily imperfect and so could contain the seeds of future conflict. It divides Bosnia along ethnic lines, thus offering some endorsement to the racist politics of the Serbs who fought for secession. It offers no cast-iron guarantees that war criminals will be brought to justice. It will provide scant solace to the myriad bereaved and homeless of a long and savage conflict.

The possibility is real that the de facto division of Bosnia agreed upon today could prove permanent despite the establishment of central government institutions and the vows of the Bosnian, Croatian and Serbian presidents to work for the contrary.

For this peace remains to be defined. On paper, it is a bewildering, apparently unworkable jigsaw setting up two distinct self-governing units — a Muslim-Croat federation and a Serb republic — overseen by a rotating collective Bosnian presidency, a federal parliament, a constitutional court and other central institutions.

The Bosnian state laid out today has two armies — that of the Serbs and that of the federation. It has three administrations — that of the Serb republic, that of the federation, and that of the central Government. And it has an independent history made up entirely of a war whose legacy is one of deep mistrust and lingering anger.

Out of such confusion, it seems, a civil society could now grow; equally, a new and perhaps yet more savage conflict could erupt.

Even today, in an ominous sign, the Bosnian Serbs showed deep unhappiness with parts of the agreement, especially the establishment of a unified Sarajevo, and refused to initial all the documents.

For the Muslim-led Bosnian Government, it was another agonizing day. President Alija Izetbegovic showed no joy at the accord, shaking the hand of American officials and the Serbian and Croatian presidents in a distinctly perfunctory way. But

Continued on Page A11, Column 1

Education Chief in Trenton Asks Legislature to Set School Budgets

By NEIL MacFARQUHAR

TRENTON, Nov. 21 — New Jersey officials, under court order to equalize spending between rich and poor school districts, today proposed that the State Legislature, rather than local voters, set the basic school budget for all districts.

The New Jersey Commissioner of Education, Leo F. Klagholz, presented the plan — the latest development in a 25-year legal battle — without actual dollar figures. The Commissioner said it would take weeks to determine whether following the recommendation would mean an increase in the state budget for education and what effect it might have on local property taxes.

The 77-page report released unexpectedly today was developed from suggestions put forward in 70 public hearings and meetings over the last year, Dr. Klagholz said. It now goes to the State Legislature for consideration.

Once combined with curriculum standards, which the department said it would submit by January, the government will determine what the state will pay for in every classroom, defining for the first time the minimum level of education that the state guarantees.

New Jersey is one of a dozen states that are under court orders to close the disparity in spending among school districts. Spending for students in New Jersey ranges from a low of $5,900 per pupil to a high of $11,500 per pupil in districts with kindergarten through 12th grade students. In districts with just kindergarten through eighth grade, spending runs from $4,800 to $15,900.

New Jersey joins a small group of states seeking to address such court orders to establish equity between wealthy and poor districts through the quality of the education delivered rather than the dollars spent.

Presently, each district determines its own curriculum, applying to the state for relief if it needs more money. New Jersey spends $12 billion a year on education — more per pupil than any other state — but Dr. Klagholz said the spending was not reflected in overall student achievement.

Under the new plan, the state would both establish the curriculum and outline school spending levels. It would determine everything from the number of teachers needed by an

Continued on Page B5, Column 1

Back to Square One At Columbus Circle

After more than a decade of neighborhood battles, environmental studies and court fights over the fate of the New York Coliseum, New York State and New York City have decided to turn the clock back to 1984 and look for a new buyer for the valuable Columbus Circle site.

Requests for new development proposals are to be issued before the end of the year.

Article, page B1.

Clinton's Next Task Will Be to Sell Plan To the U.S. Public

By ALISON MITCHELL

WASHINGTON, Nov. 21 — Even as he triumphantly announced the Balkan accord, President Clinton today began the difficult task of convincing a skeptical public and a hostile Congress to support sending 20,000 American troops to enforce the peace in Bosnia.

"We are at a decisive moment," the President said in a mid-morning appearance in the White House Rose Garden. "The parties have chosen peace. America must choose peace as well."

Clearly aiming his remarks at the American public, Mr. Clinton spoke of the "senseless slaughter of so many innocent people that our fellow citizens had to watch night after night after night for four long years on their television screens."

White House advisers were keenly aware that Mr. Clinton will have to make a major personal investment in the effort to convince Americans that their country's leadership responsibilities require that their soldiers be sent to a chaotic region to patrol a peace that could yet revert to war.

With a NATO plan to enforce a Balkans peace expected to be submitted to the President within a week — and large-scale deployment of troops possibly only weeks away — Mr. Clinton and his foreign policy team were preparing to mount a quick and extensive campaign, including a televised presidential ad-

Continued on Page A11, Column 1

INSIDE

The Dow Surges Past 5,000
The extraordinary bull market in stocks shows no sign of letting up, with the Dow Jones industrial average surging past 5,000 for the first time. Market Place, page D1.

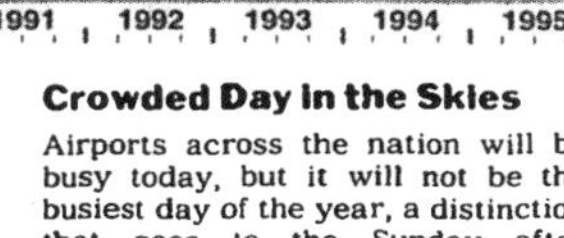

New Cabinet for Israel
Acting Prime Minister Shimon Peres of Israel announced his Cabinet, in which he will direct the Defense Ministry as troops leave parts of the West Bank. Page A3.

Crowded Day in the Skies
Airports across the nation will be busy today, but it will not be the busiest day of the year, a distinction that goes to the Sunday after Thanksgiving. Page A12.

"All the News
That's Fit to Print"

The New York Times

Late Edition
New York: Today, mostly sunny and pleasant. High 83. Tonight, tranquil. Low 69. Tomorrow, ample sun, warmer, more humid. High 88. Yesterday, high 79, low 63. Details, page 32.

VOL. CXLVI . . No. 50,901 NEW YORK, SUNDAY, AUGUST 31, 1997 — $3 beyond the greater New York metropolitan area. — $2.50

In Bronx Club, Welfare Mothers Prepare for Jobs, and Then Wait

By RACHEL L. SWARNS

Linda Bailey walked nervously into the world of work, smoothing the wrinkles in her cream pants suit, fiddling with the pearls around her neck, reading and rereading her crisp new résumé and imagining that she belonged in the crush of professional women in midtown Manhattan.

Then she swung back to reality and her brittle confidence cracked.

The suit was the only one she owned. The two dollars in her wallet had to last for two days. She had promised her sons 50-cent ice creams and the world "once Mommy has work." But Ms. Bailey has not worked in eight years. Ms. Bailey is on welfare. And on days like these, she fears she will never escape the dole.

"Sometimes I think these people got all the jobs," said Ms. Bailey, 33, dazed by the throngs of workers shoving past as she hawked her résumé from office to office. "Will there be any jobs for me?"

New York City is pushing thousands of anxious welfare mothers into the job market for the first time in years, sending them to job readiness programs to learn to dress professionally, to write résumés, to give an employer a firm, confident handshake and to believe in the prospect of financial independence and newfound self-respect.

But while the four-week programs, known as job clubs, have already sent nearly 8,000 women to pound the pavement with résumés and newly fired dreams, the vast majority of these women fail to find work, city officials say. Of the 13 women who participated in a Bronx job club with Ms. Bailey last month, 3 found jobs to push them off the welfare rolls. Ms. Bailey was not among them.

One year after the passage of the landmark Federal welfare law, the experiences of the women in the Bronx job club reflect the challenges confronting states as they struggle to move welfare recipients with little education and little work experience into jobs.

Most states offer job readiness programs for welfare recipients and some have demonstrated marked success. But until recently, New York City has focused more on placing women in six-month workfare assignments, where they work for their benefits, than on programs to place them directly in permanent jobs.

But this strategy has been criticized for simply shuttling some welfare mothers from workfare assignments to job clubs and back. And this summer, as the City Comptroller's office reported faltering job placement rates at several clubs, city officials decided to extend the contracts of the private agencies that run the programs only through December, while they consider a new plan.

"The problem was that job clubs

Continued on Page 30

Librado Romero/The New York Times

Linda Bailey, 33, seeking job leads in a work-readiness program.

U.S. Is Seeking More Influence Over Education

By PETER APPLEBOME

As vacations end and 52 million students return to school, their elders find themselves in a historic tug of war pitting the traditional local control of education against a growing national presence that is making Washington a bigger player in education now than at perhaps any other time in the nation's history.

When Congress convenes in September, President Clinton will try to win support for the first truly national performance tests in the schools, and Republicans in Congress will mobilize to kill the initiative.

In a radio address yesterday in which he promoted his testing plan, the President said he was encouraged by a report on long-term trends that showed student improvement in some subjects. [Page 18]

Republicans and a few Democrats will push for proposals to increase vouchers and school choice, a California Congressman will argue for a bill designed to upgrade teaching by linking Federal aid to improved state teaching standards, and other issues like national reading initiatives and development of a national curriculum will receive enormous attention.

Experts disagree on how much of what is happening reflects a long-term shift toward greater Federal involvement or is a result of a historical moment: a politically adroit President intensely focused on education, aging baby boomers who

Continued on Page 18

U.S.-MEXICO STUDY SEES EXAGGERATION OF MIGRATION DATA

JOINT SCRUTINY IS A FIRST

Elusive Statistic on Increase in Yearly Mexican Influx Lowered to 105,000

By SAM DILLON

MEXICO CITY, Aug. 30 — The first formal migration study to be sponsored by the American and Mexican Governments has concluded that the number of undocumented Mexican workers who have settled in the United States in this decade is far lower than some politicians have suggested, only about 105,000 a year.

Drawn from a two-year analysis of American and Mexican census and other data, the figure is the first authoritative estimate of the net annual flow of illegal Mexican workers into the United States, which has been an elusive statistic at the center of political and academic dispute on both sides of the border.

During the last Presidential campaign in the United States, some conservatives made immigration a powerful issue, with lurid portrayals of an America overrun by illegal Mexicans, a million of whom were said to pour across the border each year, taking jobs from Americans and driving up welfare costs.

The new estimate appears alongside a series of other groundbreaking conclusions in a new Binational Study on Migration. The document was commissioned by Presidents Clinton and Ernesto Zedillo in early 1995 and brought together 20 prominent demographers and scholars — 10 Mexican and 10 American — for two and a half years of research, field work and analysis.

"No controversy ever really ends, so it would be ingenuous for us to think this will resolve all the disputes over migration," said Francisco Alba Hernández, a demographer at the Colegio de México who took part in the study. "But this is our attempt to arrive at the most reasonable overview."

The study was circulated Friday to Secretary of State Madeleine K. Albright, Attorney General Janet Reno, Foreign Minister José Ángel Gurría of Mexico and other senior officials; it is to be made public Tuesday. A contributor to the study provided The New York Times with its executive summary and key chapters.

Migration is one of the most contentious issues dividing the countries, and for three decades each Government has molded policies to suit its own needs. The joint study is part of a shift toward increased co-operation, officials said.

Continued on Page 9

Diana Killed in a Car Accident in Paris

Pool photo by John Stilwell

Diana in May, at the opening of an arts center in Leicester.

In Flight From Paparazzi — Friend Dies

By CRAIG R. WHITNEY

PARIS, Sunday, Aug. 31 — Diana, the Princess of Wales, was killed shortly after midnight today in an automobile accident in a tunnel by the Seine. The accident also killed Emad Mohammed al-Fayed, the Harrods heir, and their driver, the police said.

Diana's death was announced this morning by the Interior Minister, Jean-Pierre Chevènement. She died after being hospitalized in intensive care at the Pitié-Salpêtrière Hospital in southeast Paris.

A bodyguard was seriously injured, according to a police spokesman.

"The car was being chased by photographers on motorcycles, which could have caused the accident," a spokesman for the Prefecture of Police said. Several motorcyclists were detained for questioning after the crash, Reuters reported, quoting police officials.

The Princess, 36, was divorced from Prince Charles, the Prince of Wales and heir to the British throne, last year. She had vacationed with Mr. al-Fayed, 41, the son of Harrods's owner, Mohammed al-Fayed, on the French Riviera earlier this month and had been expected to return to London today to be with her two sons, the Princes William and Harry. [Obituaries of Diana and Mr. al-Fayed appear on page 31.]

French radio stations reported that a spokesman for the British royal family in London expressed anger and said the accident was predictable because photographers relentlessly pursued the Princess wherever she went.

The crash occurred 35 minutes past midnight in the Alma Tunnel, on the right bank of the Seine under the Place de l'Alma, the police said.

The driver was hired from the Ritz Hotel in Paris. The Princess and Mr. al-Fayed had been pursued from the Ritz Hotel, where they were believed to be staying after spending time together on the Riviera.

The Paris police said that the Interior Minister, Jean-Pierre Chevènement, and the Prefect of Police, Philippe Massoni, had accompanied the British Ambassador in Paris to the hospital where the Princess was treated.

The police said the car was totally wrecked. The impact was so great, the car's radiator was hurled onto the knees of the front-seat passenger. The Princess was in the back seat.

The site of the accident, in the Eighth Arrondissement, is on a high-speed road along the Seine with a divided roadway as it passes under the Place de l'Alma to the Place de la Concorde.

On Aug. 21, Diana and Mr. al-Fayed, who is of Egyptian ancestry and is commonly called Dodi, flew to the French Mediterranean resort of St. Tropez for their third holiday in each other's company in five weeks.

Mr. al-Fayed's father said in an interview with The New York Times in London last week that the two were simply "young people getting

Continued on Page 10

Limerick, Burned, Also Finds A Salve in 'Angela's Ashes'

By WARREN HOGE

LIMERICK, Ireland, Aug. 24 — This sodden city in western Ireland has been such a hard-luck town that it cannot even lay claim to the form of verse everyone assumes was named after it.

"The truth is you can go into pubs here, and you'll hear yarns and doggerel and songs and parodies," said Brendan Halligan, editor of The Limerick Leader. "But I've never heard anyone recite a limerick."

H. D. Inglis, author of an early travel guide, came here in 1834 and found Limerick "the very vilest town" he had ever visited. Heinrich Böll, the German Nobel-Prize-winning novelist, saw it for the first time in 1950 and pronounced it a "gloomy little town" with "everything submerged in sour darkness."

More recently it has been made fun of in a popular television show as "stab city," a label — arising out of several muggings in the 1980's — that the Mayor, Frank Leddin, finds so objectionable he will not utter it. "You can mention it," he said in his office by the Shannon River, "but you won't be quoting Frank Leddin."

Long considered Ireland's most entrenched Catholic city — the author Conor Cruise O'Brien once called its bishop the "Mullah of Limerick" — it has suffered from stereotyping as "violent, intolerant, obscu-

Continued on Page 12

Economies in Asia Are Losing Some Zip

Has the Asian boom fizzled?

For years, Asian stock markets were the hottest in the world. But lately, currency and stock market turmoil is splashing throughout Asia. Just this week, Malaysia curbed the selling of stocks, setting off a convulsion that sent the Philippine market tumbling 9 percent on Thursday, and the Hong Kong index cascading 5 percent on Friday.

By now, the Thai market has plunged 70 percent from its peak in 1994, and some experts are questioning how secure the foundation might be under the Asian miracle.

Article, page 6.

Billion-Dollar Plan to Clean New York City Water at Its Source

Suzanne DeChillo/The New York Times

Scientists from New York City's Department of Environmental Protection testing for impurities at the Kensico Reservoir, near White Plains.

By ANDREW C. REVKIN

TROUBLED WATERS

A special report.

The flow of drinking water to New York City begins as far away as a damp spot under some leaves on a mountainside 120 miles north of Times Square. For 155 years, the city has maintained a complicated network of reservoirs and aqueducts to carry rain and melted snow from distant hills to bathtubs in Brooklyn and sinks on Staten Island.

Now the purity of that flow faces the gravest threats ever, from both old sewage systems and a new wave of unbridled development in the watershed. To combat those threats, a growing force of scientists, engineers, special police officers and others from the city's Department of Environmental Protection has fanned out this summer across suburbs and farmland to explain and enforce the first new pollution rules for the watershed in 44 years.

They have 10 years and a billion dollars to fix faulty sewage treatment plants, to rebuild barnyards and pastures to control the flow of manure, and to buy tens of thousands of acres of land to build a buffer zone against encroaching development. Cities across the nation are developing programs to prevent pollution of drinking water at its source, but nothing approaches the magnitude of the cleanup that has just begun in the 2,000 square miles of hills and river valleys funneling water to the nine million people who use New York City's system.

But the grand experiment has shaky underpinnings: scientists have only an embryonic understanding of the forces that keep water pure or allow pollution to accumulate. And the plan depends on a fragile political alliance between rural upstate communities and New York City that can be upset at any time.

In essence, the city's task is to control three distant, sprawling regions where, since 1911, it has had the right under New York State law to limit water pollution. But for decades the main goal of city water officials was to increase the supply of water; its purity was rarely at issue. Now, the bureaucracy is forced to reinvent itself and to put the emphasis on cleanliness.

The Federal Government has made the rules clear: if the city cannot insure purity by managing the far-flung watershed, it will have to spend billions on a filtering plant. And while all involved emphasize that there are no health problems today with the flow of what a succession of New York City mayors have called "the champagne of drinking water," the problems are mounting.

Already, 10 out of 19 reservoirs are

Continued on Page 28

THE NEW YORK TIMES is available for home or office delivery in most major U.S. cities. Call, toll-free: 1-800-NYTIMES. Ask about TimesCard. ADVT.

INSIDE

First Ladies of the Court

The Houston Comets defeated the Liberty to win the inaugural championship of the Women's National Basketball Association. Sports, section 8.

A Boycott in Mexico

The long-dominant party in Mexico boycotted the opening of Congress, the first in more than four decades that it does not control. Page 8.

TODAY'S SECTIONS

"All the News That's Fit to Print"

The New York Times

Late Edition

New York: **Today:** Hazy sun with increasing humidity, high 85. **Tonight,** cloudy, low 70. **Tomorrow,** sunny and humid, high 85. **Yesterday,** high 84, low 68. Weather map is on page C7.

VOL. CXLVII . . . . No. 51,243 | Copyright © 1998 The New York Times | NEW YORK, SATURDAY, AUGUST 8, 1998 | $1 beyond the greater New York metropolitan area. | 60 CENTS

BOMBS RIP APART 2 U.S. EMBASSIES IN AFRICA; SCORES KILLED; NO FIRM MOTIVE OR SUSPECTS

Khalil Senosi/Associated Press

Sayyid Azim/Associated Press

Sayyid Azim/Associated Press

Soon after a blast ripped Nairobi yesterday, workers, top, carried a woman rescued from the embassy over the rubble of a collapsed building next door. Ambassador Prudence Bushnell, left, was shielded by Rizwan Khaliq, a commercial officer, as she was evacuated, and a United States marine stood guard outside the embassy.

Kenya and Tanzania Attacks Are Nearly Simultaneous

By JAMES C. McKINLEY Jr.

NAIROBI, Kenya, Aug. 7 — Two powerful bombs exploded minutes apart outside the United States Embassies in Kenya and Tanzania this morning, killing at least 80 people, 8 of them Americans, in what officials said were coordinated terrorist attacks.

In Nairobi, an enormous explosion ripped through downtown shortly after 10:30 A.M., turning the busy Haile Selassie Avenue into a scene of carnage and destruction that left more than 1,600 people injured and dozens still missing long after night fell. The blast, which leveled a three-story building containing a secretarial school and gutted the rear half of the Embassy next door, dismembered more than a dozen people passing on foot and incinerated dozens of others in their seats in three nearby buses.

Just minutes before, a bomb apparently planted in a gasoline tanker detonated near the front entrance of the United States Embassy in the Tanzanian capital, Dar es Salaam, about 400 miles to the south. The blast destroyed the front of the building and toppled a side wall, throwing charred debris down the street, setting cars on fire and toppling trees. At least 7 people were killed and 72 injured, none of them American, officials said.

In Washington, President Clinton condemned the attacks as abhorrent and inhuman acts of cowardice. He vowed to bring those responsible to justice "no matter what or how long it takes." [Transcript, page A8.]

The bombings underscored how vulnerable American officials and diplomats remain in an age of global terrorism, particularly in some third-world capitals where borders are porous and security is not as tight as in the industrial world.

The blasts seemed to be coordinated attacks against the United States, and appeared to be unconnected to any local grievances or political currents in the two capitals, American officials said.

At least eight Americans and an unknown number of Kenyan employees of the Embassy died in Nairobi, which left the offices a honeycomb of burned-out rubble with bodies buried inside.

"It's going to take a couple of days to find out what's in there," Bill Barr, an Embassy spokesman, said. Mr. Barr said 15 American officials were hospitalized and six others were still missing.

Witnesses said the explosion, which shattered windows for several blocks and blew the roof off a building across the street, was preceded by a smaller blast, perhaps a grenade. Both appeared to emanate from a parking lot just behind the Embassy, the police said. Hundreds of people were cut by falling glass and ran bleeding from the area, flooding local hospitals.

"This is a real national disaster and we highly suspect it is a terrorist attack," said Otieno Osur, the director of police operations in Nairobi.

By nightfall, rescue workers and soldiers in Nairobi toiled under floodlights with backhoes to extricate dozens of bodies still buried in the rubble of the Ufundi House, which is located

Continued on Page A6

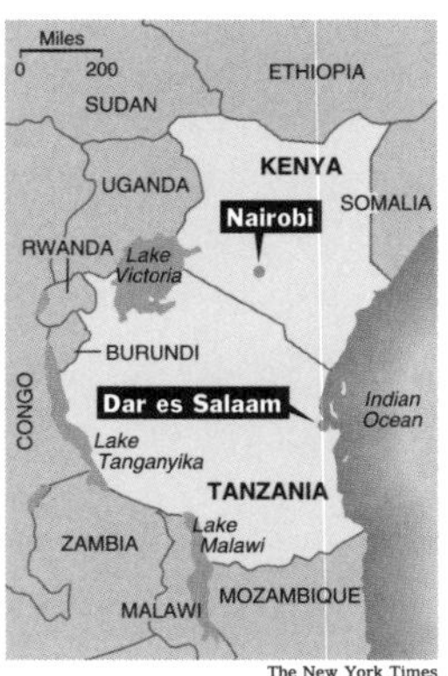

The New York Times

Just minutes, and 400 miles, apart, bombs struck American embassies in two East African capitals.

FOCUS ON SUSPECTS IN PAST ATTACKS

Clinton Sending F.B.I. Agents and Medical Aid to Scene

By PHILIP SHENON

WASHINGTON, Aug. 7 — Administration officials said the attacks on two American embassies in East Africa only minutes apart today probably were carried out by one of a small number of sophisticated terrorist groups presumed to have attacked American installations in the past.

President Clinton ordered teams of F.B.I. agents, medical military specialists and explosives experts to leave immediately for Africa to track down the bombers and aid the victims. Although few terrorism investigations overseas have ever borne fruit, Mr. Clinton vowed to bring the bombers to justice.

At a news conference at the State Department, Under Secretary Thomas R. Pickering said it was too early to single out suspects in the bombing or to speculate about why they had chosen to carry out the bombings in Kenya and Tanzania.

"If we can find them, we'll ask them," he said. "I don't believe at this stage that we are reading anything special into the choice of these until we get further down the investigative process. I don't have an answer. Terrorists tend to be unpredictable, and there may be some of that in this."

Secretary of State Madeleine K. Albright was reported to be rushing home from Italy, where she was to have attended the weekend wedding of her chief spokesman, Assistant Secretary of State James P. Rubin. She said in a statement that the Administration "will spare no effort to use all means at our disposal to track down and punish the perpetrators of these outrageous acts."

A senior American intelligence of-

Continued on Page A8

INSIDE

Job Growth Slows a Bit

The economy created jobs at a slower but still robust pace last month, and the unemployment rate held steady at 4.5 percent. Page D1.

Japan Proposes Tax Cuts

Japan's new Prime Minister called for tax cuts and increased public-works spending to revive the ailing Japanese economy. Page D1.

Glimpse of a Phone Strike

Millions of Bell Atlantic customers got a taste of the inconveniences of a full-fledged strike. Page B1.

Teaching the Holocaust

A debate on whether the Holocaust should be the defining focus of Jewish history. Arts & Ideas, page B7.

COMING ON SUNDAY

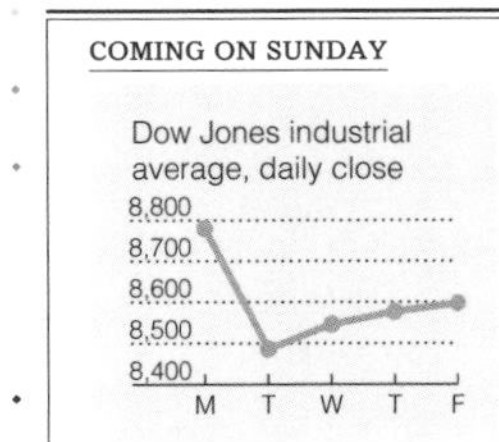

AND NOW WHAT?

The bulls stumbled badly on Tuesday and they failed to stampede back to Wall Street by week's end, as they had after other recent market drops. A new market psychology seems to be settling in. *Money & Business.*

Judge Cites Possible Breaches Of Ethics Guidelines by Starr

By JAMES BENNET

WASHINGTON, Aug. 7 — A Federal judge here has found that prosecutors investigating President Clinton's relationship with Monica S. Lewinsky may have violated Federal rules by providing protected grand jury testimony to journalists, according to court papers that were unsealed today.

In a rare ray of good news for the White House, Judge Norma Holloway Johnson of Federal District Court declared that Kenneth W. Starr, the Whitewater independent counsel, may have broken the ethical code governing criminal investigations in his remarks to reporters.

Finding that President Clinton's lawyers had compiled a persuasive list of potential violations by Mr. Starr's office, Judge Johnson said in her ruling on June 19 that the prosecutors now carry the burden of proof and must demonstrate their innocence in a hearing to avoid contempt citations and possible penalties.

Mr. Starr appealed aspects of the ruling. On Monday, the United States Court of Appeals here dealt a setback to Mr. Clinton. It ruled that, to prevent the disclosure of more secret information, the President's lawyers could not question prosecutors during the hearing, nor subpoena documents, as Judge Johnson had decreed.

The appeals court did not address the substance of the accusations against Mr. Starr, and its ruling will probably not affect the grand jury investigation. All the court motions and decisions related to the appeal of Judge Johnson's ruling were released today by the United States Court of Appeals for the District of Columbia Circuit.

Mr. Starr has repeatedly denied that his office illegally slipped grand jury secrets to reporters. Dozens of members of his office submitted affidavits to the judge declaring that they had not disclosed any protected information cited in a laundry list of news articles and broadcasts compiled by David E. Kendall, the President's private lawyer.

But in an opinion crackling with anger, Judge Johnson swatted aside the affidavits as defining the secrecy rules "too narrowly," and complained of "the serious and repetitive

Continued on Page A10

NEWS SUMMARY A2

On the Internet: www.nytimes.com

Rent Deregulation Has Risen Sharply Under 1997 Law

By RANDY KENNEDY

Since New York lawmakers scaled back rent regulations last summer, at least three times the number of apartments in New York City have been deregulated under the new laws as under the old ones, a new study has determined.

The rise — from 1,000 a year to more than 3,500 — has occurred almost exclusively in Manhattan, the study found, and is higher than either landlords or tenant groups predicted during the wrenching battle over rent laws. And it indicates that with the economy booming and real estate prices soaring, landlords in prime neighborhoods have taken full advantage of measures they won in Albany to bring about deregulation by increasing rents sharply when some apartments turn over.

Under the new laws, landlords were allowed to increase rents on vacant units by 20 percent, and all regulations were lifted when, upon vacancy, the rent rose beyond $2,000.

The survey by the city's Rent Guidelines Board, the first detailed look at the city's housing market since the new laws were passed, also found that while rents had risen steeply for newly occupied apartments south of 96th Street in Manhattan, the new laws appeared to have had only a small impact elsewhere, as many economists predicted.

"This really is a tale of two cities,"

Continued on Page B2

Bombed Embassies Did Not Meet Toughened Security Standards

By JAMES RISEN

WASHINGTON, Aug. 7 — The two United States embassies in East Africa that were bombed today did not meet security standards that had been ordered for the State Department's overseas posts after separate terrorist attacks against the American Embassy and Marine barracks in Beirut, Lebanon, in the 1980's, State Department officials acknowledged.

The embassies in Nairobi, Kenya, and Dar es Salaam, Tanzania, had never been modified to fully comply with the tougher security standards called for in 1985 by a panel headed by retired Adm. Bobby R. Inman, largely because the White House and Congress never provided enough funds to pay for a worldwide conversion of all United States embassies, officials said.

Over the years, the State Department was given less than one-third of the money that would have been required to modify or build embassies meeting the standards, which were imposed to prevent repetition of the bombing of the United States Embassy in Beirut in September 1984, in which at least 16 people died, and the October 1983 bombing of the United States Marine barracks in Beirut, which killed 241.

In fact, both the prohibitive costs, as well as a growing belief that compliance with the security standards directly conflicts with the public diplomatic functions of American overseas posts, have led Congress and the Administration to quietly drop the idea of modifying all embassies to comply with the Inman standards.

The United States Embassy in Nairobi, which was built in 1981, before the Inman standards were recommended, was scheduled to undergo a $3 million rehabilitation and security improvement in January 1999, the first major modification for security since its construction, a State Department official said today.

The planned alterations were to

Continued on Page A6

"All the News
That's Fit to Print"

The New York Times

Late Edition
New York: **Today,** hazy sun, some afternoon thunder. High 90. **Tonight,** clearing, less humid. Low 66. **Tomorrow,** sunny, breezy. High 76. **Yesterday,** high 79, low 73. Details, page C5.

VOL. CXLVII . . . . No. 51,253 NEW YORK, TUESDAY, AUGUST 18, 1998 — $1 beyond the greater New York metropolitan area. — 60 CENTS

CLINTON ADMITS LEWINSKY LIAISON TO JURY; TELLS NATION 'IT WAS WRONG,' BUT PRIVATE

JANUARY 26, 1998

"I want to say one thing to the American people. I want you to listen to me. I'm going to say this again: I did not have sexual relations with that woman, Miss Lewinsky."

AUGUST 17, 1998

"I did have a relationship with Miss Lewinsky that was not appropriate. In fact, it was wrong."

Reuters

Expresses Regret but Asserts It Is Now Time to Move On

By JAMES BENNET

WASHINGTON, Aug. 17 — Trying to wrest political forgiveness from profound personal embarrassment, President Clinton admitted in testimony today and in an extraordinary address tonight that he misled his wife and the public and conducted a relationship with a White House intern that was "not appropriate."

"It was wrong," he said, speaking in somber yet defiant tones from the same straight-backed chair from which, hours earlier, he carried on a far more contentious exchange with prosecutors. "It constituted a critical lapse in judgment and a personal failure on my part for which I am solely and completely responsible."

After seven months of emphatic denials of a sexual relationship with Monica S. Lewinsky, the former intern, Mr. Clinton also found himself addressing the most personally painful of matters — adultery — in the most public forum imaginable.

Speaking just after 10 P.., he tried to turn the very freakishness of the day to his advantage, issuing a proud, almost angry demand for his privacy back.

"Now, this matter is between me, the two people I love most — my wife and our daughter — and our God,'" he said. "It's nobody's business but ours. Even presidents have private lives."

To the grand jurors, Mr. Clinton declined to answer some questions from prosecutors about the details of his relationship with Ms. Lewinsky. Mr. Starr's team told the President that they might subpoena him again, and Mr. Clinton's lawyers said in return that he might fight such a subpoena. Mr. Starr also left open the possibility that he would recall Mr. Clinton to testify further.

Mr. Clinton acknowledged in his testimony having had "inappropriate intimate physical contact" with Ms. Lewinsky, according to one lawyer and adviser to the President knowledgeable about his appearance.

Mr. Clinton denied that he had obstructed justice and tried to cover up his relationship with the intern, Monica S. Lewinsky. "I told the grand jury today and I say to you now that at no time did I ask anyone to lie, to hide or destroy evidence or to take any other unlawful action," he said in his public address. He urged the public to put the matter behind it. "It is past time to move on," he said.

In testifying and then speaking to the public, Mr. Clinton tried the riskiest high-wire act of his career, trying to balance legal and political burdens. Two days short of his 52d birthday, he sought to protect his Presidency and elude legal jeopardy by acknowledging an intimate relationship in the White House with a subordinate less than half his age.

Mr. Clinton had been working on his speech for several days, aides said, trying to strike the right balance between disclosure and dignity, remorse and pride.

Kenneth W. Starr is investigating whether the President lied under oath in denying an affair with Ms. Lewinsky last January in his deposition during the Paula Corbin Jones sexual misconduct suit. Beyond the nature of Mr. Clinton's relationship with Ms. Lewinsky, Mr. Starr has been investigating whether Mr. Clinton tried to obstruct justice and suborn perjury, matters that the President did not address in detail tonight.

Mr. Clinton had been working on the speech himself for days, aides said, trying to strike the right balance between disclosure and dignity, regret and pride. His address followed by less than four hours the

Continued on Page A12

RUSSIA ACTS TO FIX SINKING FINANCES

Takes Drastic Steps on Loans and on Value of the Ruble

By CELESTINE BOHLEN

MOSCOW, Aug. 17 — The Russian Government moved hastily today to avert financial collapse with a series of drastic measures, including delaying payments for 90 days on foreign debt owed mostly by banks, restructuring Government bonds and sacrificing the ruble to market forces.

Holding tonight at 6.43 rubles to the dollar, off slightly from Friday's level, the value of the Russian currency is now free to float as low as 9.5, a risky step — tantamount to devaluation — that many fear could set off a new round of inflation. It could also wipe out as much as a third of the ruble's purchasing power in an economy heavily dependent on imports.

Letting the ruble float marks a major change in strategy for President Boris N. Yeltsin's Government, which after seven years of economic reforms could point to a stable currency and low inflation as its two major achievements. But that policy has been overwhelmed by a crisis brought on by Russia's other economic realities, including the insolvency of its banking system.

The decision came over the weekend after Russian officials had once again asked foreign backers for more financial aid. Coming one month after a major drive, spearheaded by Washington, to put together a $22.6 billion package of loans and credits to Russia, the request was denied, and top Russian officials today acknowledged that further help from the West was unlikely.

At a news conference this morning, Prime Minister Sergei V. Kiriyenko said the steps had been made necessary by the near-collapse of

Continued on Page A8

Strong at Politics, Weakened by Lapses

Bending Truth and Rules a Mark of His Political Life

By TODD S. PURDUM

WASHINGTON, Aug. 17 — On Jan. 20, 1997, as an ebullient Bill Clinton took the oath of office for the second term that he hoped would secure his place in history, he returned to a theme that had been at the core of his claim to be a new kind of Democrat, declaring: "Each and every one of us, in our own way, must assume personal responsibility, not only for ourselves and our families but for our neighbors and our nation."

Exactly one year later, Mr. Clinton learned that Kenneth W. Starr, the Whitewater independent counsel, was investigating accusations that the President had started a sexual relationship with a White House intern in 1995 and then tried to cover it up.

Had the man who won the Presidency by speaking out for the people who "play by the rules" once more surrendered to a lifelong compulsion to bend and break them? Tonight, in the most painfully personal statement of his life, and perhaps in American political life, Mr. Clinton was forced to acknowledge that he had.

How someone of such surpassing intellect and such protean political talents could indulge in such conduct at a time when he knew a special prosecutor was already scrutinizing his Administration and when his own re-election still hung in the balance remains the most puzzling question about William Jefferson Clinton. But it is not a new question, and in some ways it was entirely predictable that this President should have come to this pass, his promise once again shadowed by his shortcomings.

For Mr. Clinton has always been convinced that he could outsmart, out-talk, out-charm and outlast any adversary, and very often, enough to confirm that conviction, he has. In the darkest days of the 1992 primaries, he dared to campaign on a platform of personal responsibility, despite widespread questions about his own marital fidelity, marijuana use and draft record, and widespread doubt that his answers were candid or complete. In his first term, he shifted ground so many times that even his best friends sometimes said they did not know where he stood.

Time and again in the risky running melodrama of his public life, Mr. Clinton has treated the truth as an à la carte menu.

Last Jan. 21, as news of the accusations involving Monica S. Lewinsky came out, Mr. Clinton told National Public Radio: "I don't know any more about it than I've told you, and any more about it, really, than you do."

In the end, such sweeping elisions of reality lie far beyond the ken of conventional political analysis. But professionals who have studied the arc of Mr. Clinton's life and career have suggested some answers.

"Most people wish to think well of themselves," wrote Stanley A. Renshon, a political scientist and psychoanalyst at New York University in his 1996 study of Mr. Clinton, "High Hopes." "However, Bill Clinton appears to have come to believe the *best* of himself and, either to avoid or discount evidence from his own behavior, that all is not as he believes it to be. He attributes to himself the most sincere and best of motives. His errors, when acknowledged, are the result of basically correct efforts

Continued on Page A13

One by One, Clinton Told Aides Truth

By RICHARD L. BERKE and DON VAN NATTA Jr.

WASHINGTON, Aug. 17 — Before he addressed the grand jury and then the nation, President Clinton called in some of his closest aides over the weekend, associates said, and one by one, he told them that the accusation they had steadfastly denied for months was true: he had had an improper relationship with Monica S. Lewinsky.

The meetings, which took place on Saturday and Sunday, were described by close Clinton associates as informal and involving only some aides. And only in some cases, they said, did Mr. Clinton express regret for his conduct.

After seven months of public denials and private anguish over the inquiry by Kenneth W. Starr, it was those conversations that helped Mr. Clinton fully come to terms with the toll the sex scandal has wrought on his friends and on his Presidency, two people close to him said.

"It hit him hardest on Sunday," one close friend said. "This was a very, very difficult weekend for him. Nothing is more important to him than his place in history. He is worried that this investigation will eclipse everything else."

Even late last week while Mr. Clinton's associates were telling reporters that he might acknowledge having had sexual relations with Ms. Lewinsky, the friend said he was still "in denial."

"Four days ago," he said, "the President told me he never had sex with Monica."

Some who met with the President — and who had stood loyally by the President — expressed feelings of betrayal and humiliation, people close to Mr. Clinton said. One friend said that there was "a lot of disap-

Continued on Page A14

Justin Lane for The New York Times

News crews began setting up on the White House lawn at 5 A.M. yesterday for President Clinton's testimony before the Federal grand jury.

U.S. Says Suspect Won't Admit Role in Bombings or Ties to Saudi

By DAVID JOHNSTON

WASHINGTON, Aug. 17 — Law enforcement officials said today that a key suspect in the bombing of the American Embassy in Nairobi had been interviewed at length by American investigators, but had not admitted any role and had not implicated Osama bin Laden, the shadowy Saudi-born extremist thought to have inspired the bombings in Kenya and Tanzania.

Nevertheless, the officials said they believed that the suspect, Mohammed Saddiq Odeh — initially identified as Mohammed Sadik Howaida — was an important figure in the Nairobi bombing plot and had knowledge of most of the details.

The officials said they expected that Mr. Odeh would eventually cooperate with American authorities. Pakistani officials said he had cooperated when apprehended, shortly after landing in Karachi on a flight from Kenya on Aug. 7, the day of the nearly simultaneous bombings at the embassies.

Moreover, the officials did not dispute reports from Pakistan that Mr. Odeh had voluntarily confessed there, and that he had identified several collaborators, calling Mr. bin Laden the driving force behind the bombing and his spiritual guide in an Islamic holy war against the United States.

But a spokesman for the Taliban militia, which has protected Mr. bin Laden at a stronghold in Afghanistan, previously said he had pledged not to engage in terrorism while living under Taliban protection and had nothing to do with the embassy bombings.

Mr. Odeh was arrested when Pakistani immigration authorities found that his face did not match the photograph on his Yemeni passport.

The document, in the name of Abdull Bast Awadah, was apparently stolen. Afterward, Mr. Odeh took responsibility for the Nairobi bombing and said he had visited Kenya over the course of several years to plan the attack, Pakistani authorities said.

Today the Pakistani national newspaper, The News, said Mr. Odeh was a 34-year-old Palestinian engineer who had helped supervise technical details of the bombing plot.

According to other reports, he is married to a Kenyan and his home base during his visits to Nairobi was Mombasa, Kenya.

The newspaper said Mr. Odeh had told his Pakistani interrogators that

Continued on Page A7

INSIDE

5 Held in Ulster Bombing
The British police arrested five men near Omagh, Northern Ireland, in the bomb attack on Saturday that killed 28 people. Page A3.

Black Women Earning More
Pushed by welfare changes and pulled by a strong economy, the income of black women is up by 21 percent in three years. Page A10.

Alaska Is Thawing
The planet's northern tier is warming, in what many call a signal that the climate is changing. Page F1.

The Writer Julian Green Dies
The novelist, playwright and candid memoirist, who became the first American elected to the Académie Française, was 97. Page B8.

More on the Testimony

A PIVOTAL ROLE Hillary Rodham Clinton helped the President write his speech and plan his strategy. Page A15.

A MOMENTOUS DAY A confrontation setting the course of a Presidency plays out without an audience. Page A13.

A SHIFT FOR STARR As questioning ends, the independent counsel will focus on grounds for impeachment. Page A14.

"All the News That's Fit to Print"

The New York Times

Late Edition
New York: **Today**, sunny and breezy, high 48. **Tonight**, mainly clear and chilly, low 32. **Tomorrow**, sunny and cool, high 47. **Yesterday**, high 58, low 45. Weather map is on page D8.

VOL. CXLVIII . . . . No. 51,472 | NEW YORK, THURSDAY, MARCH 25, 1999 | $1 beyond the greater New York metropolitan area. | 60 CENTS

NATO OPENS BROAD BARRAGE AGAINST SERBS AS CLINTON DENOUNCES YUGOSLAV PRESIDENT

Early Attacks Focus on Web Of Air Defense

By STEVEN LEE MYERS

WASHINGTON, March 24 — Waves of NATO strikes today opened what officials said would be a protracted assault on the Yugoslav military, but one that would do little immediately to end the deadly crackdown in Kosovo.

The first barrage of several dozen cruise missiles started falling on air defenses across Yugoslavia, Pentagon and NATO officials said. They were fired from six B-52 bombers and four American ships, two American submarines and a British submarine.

After a brief lull, American warships fired another burst of cruise missiles at a target, not long before dawn in Yugoslavia. That strike — involving only a handful of missiles — was not part of the original plan but rather came after NATO commanders saw an opportunity to hit Yugoslav aircraft that had returned to one of their bases, Pentagon officials said.

NATO warplanes also pressed new attacks, the officials said, describing rolling waves of strikes. "It's a fairly continuous attack," one official said.

The offensive entailed scores of fighter jets and bombers from the United States and seven other NATO members, including Britain, Germany and the Netherlands, the officials said, speaking on condition of anonymity.

Today's strikes were not aimed at the Serbian troops and tanks that have been systematically destroying village after village in Kosovo with renewed fury since peace talks collapsed last week. The battering focused largely, though not entirely, on the air defenses and command network that pose the greatest threat to allied pilots crisscrossing Yugoslavia.

"You need a few days of this," a NATO official said, "before you can put in a larger number of the aircraft you need to go after the forces involved in the repression."

The attacks today included strikes by F-117 stealth fighters, as well as the combat debut of the B-2 stealth bomber, which at $2.1 billion apiece is the most expensive warplane ever built. Two of the B-2 bombers, flying from Whiteman Air Force Base in Missouri, each dropped 16 one-ton bombs.

As expected, Yugoslavia mounted a fierce defense, though not precisely the one expected. American and NATO officials said. The Yugoslav

Continued on Page A13

HUNGARY · Subotica · Sombor · CROATIA · Novi Sad · Sremska Mitrovica · Pancevo · Batajnica · Belgrade · Kovin · ROMANIA · Pozarevac · YUGOSLAVIA · Valjevo · SERBIA · BOSNIA AND HERZEGOVINA · Kragujevac · Titovo Uzice · Cacak · Sarajevo · Kraljevo · Savac · Kremna · Krusevac · KOSOVO · Raska · Prokuplje · Nis · Kursumlija · Novi Pazar · Leskovac · Bajgora · Podujevo · MONTENEGRO · Vucitrn · BULGARIA · Glogovac · Pristina · Decani · Volujak · Vranje · Danilovgrad · Komorane · Lapusnik · Junik · Podgorica · Dakovica · Dulje · Zjum · Adriatic Sea · ALBANIA · MACEDONIA · Skopje · Miles 0 50

NATO's Attack: Missiles from ships · Missiles from planes · Smart bombs from planes · BRITAIN · GERMANY · FROM MISSOURI · ITALY · YUGOSLAVIA · Black Sea · Mediterranean Sea

Sites attacked (According to Serbian officials) · Army bases · Yugoslav troops in Kosovo · Antiaircraft sites and air bases

Source: Periscope · The New York Times

With Flash in Sky, Kosovars Fear Ground Fighting

By CARLOTTA GALL

PRISTINA, Serbia, March 24 — Two enormous flashes filled the sky shortly after 8 P.M. Seconds later came the sound of the explosions as the first NATO missiles struck somewhere south of the city, possibly the airport, or one of the military bases.

Minutes later the electricity went off, pitching the city into blackness.

Under a bright moon, tracer fire from an antiaircraft gun tore upward into the sky.

A few lone cars roared through the streets, mostly deserted long before darkness fell. An hour later, ripples of powerful explosions resounded far off in the distance. Otherwise, Pristina, the Kosovo capital, lay dark and quiet.

The air raid sirens first sounded just after 1 P.M. over the city, as a test apparently, but raised tensions as people piled into buses to escape the province. Many of those who stayed behind prepared for a time of crisis.

Shoppers cleaned out the stores of basic supplies of sugar, flour and candles. Long lines of cars formed at gas stations. Buses pulled out of town, packed full with passengers and belongings, heading for neighboring Macedonia and Turkey.

Still other people were out walking the streets, soaking up the warm sunny weather.

Even before the bombing began today, the war being fought here — in villages, from the hills, and along the roads — was continuing in full swing.

With air strikes imminent, army and police units seemed to be pressing their offensive against the guerrillas in all parts of Kosovo and stepped up police activity in the city.

Heavy explosions sounded across the northern part of Kosovo as Serbian forces continued to shell positions held by ethnic Albanian rebels on either side of the Cicavica mountain range.

In southern Kosovo, near the main border crossing, the military was out in force and the village of Gajre, taken by Serbian forces almost two weeks ago, was on fire, reporters said.

Here, police officers and army sol-

Continued on Page A14

Missiles Rock Kosovo Capital, Belgrade and Other Sites

By FRANCIS X. CLINES

WASHINGTON, March 24 — The forces of NATO opened an assault on Serbia with cruise missiles and bombs today as President Clinton denounced the Yugoslav President, Slobodan Milosevic, for feeding the "flames of ethnic and religious division" in Kosovo and endangering neighboring countries.

The missiles began striking Serbian targets within minutes of Mr. Clinton's midday announcement that the long-threatened attack was under way. It was expected to be a broad, sustained barrage intended to stun the Yugoslav leader and punish the military for its yearlong onslaught against the ethnic Albanian separatists of Kosovo.

"Ending this tragedy is a moral imperative," Mr. Clinton declared in an address to the nation tonight from the Oval Office. "It is also important to America's national interests."

He spoke several hours after the first explosions of incoming missiles erupted in the night skies of Kosovo's capital, Pristina. The Yugoslav news agency Tanjug said the city's main commercial and military airport had been hit.

The biggest allied military assault in Europe since World War II occurred after a day in which Serbian forces maintained their military pressure against the ethnic Albanian majority in Kosovo. Steady streams of alarmed residents fled toward Kosovo's borders.

Sirens sounded, and the flash and thunder of explosions cut through the night sky of Belgrade and other scattered targets, including the northern Serbian town of Novi Sad and the main airport in the Yugoslav coastal republic of Montenegro. One explosion was reported near Batajnica, the main Serbian airport and military base near Belgrade.

As he explained the NATO attack — an initiative against a problem Serbia considers purely internal, not international in scope — Mr. Clinton sought to reassure the United States against a commitment to any large-scale ground war.

"I don't intend to put our troops in Kosovo to fight a war," he emphasized in reviewing the explosive history of the Balkans. He denounced Mr. Milosevic as a dictator "who has done nothing since the cold war ended but start new wars and pour gasoline on the flames of ethnic and religious division."

"We act to prevent a wider war, to defuse a powder keg at the heart of Europe that has exploded twice before in this century with catastrophic results," the President said gravely of the military attack by the 19-member NATO alliance.

In his afternoon announcement of the military attack, Mr. Clinton said: "President Milosevic, who over the past decade started the terrible wars against Croatia and Bosnia, has again chosen aggression over peace. He has violated the commitments that he himself made last fall to stop the brutal repression in Kosovo."

In Belgrade, a defiant Mr. Milosevic called for defense of his nation "by all means possible," terming Kosovo "only the door intended to allow foreign troops to come in and steal away our freedom."

The Belgrade Government, denouncing "neo-Nazism," called for the United Nations Security Council to condemn "NATO's criminal, ter-

Continued on Page A12

Paul Hosefros/The New York Times

President Clinton after his television talk on Serbia last night.

A Fresh Set Of U.S. Goals

By R. W. APPLE Jr.

News Analysis

WASHINGTON, March 24 — For half a century, the United States and other countries have pursued political goals through air power, bombing their adversaries in an effort to persuade them — force them, if possible — to change their policies.

It has seldom if ever worked, unless combined with resolute action on the ground.

That may be one reason why the Clinton Administration's explanation of its policies underwent a subtle shift today.

In the hours just before missiles began striking targets in Kosovo, there were vehement denials at the State Department and at the White House that NATO was trying to bomb Serbia back to the bargaining table and force President Slobodan Milosevic of Yugoslavia to sign a peace agreement.

"The threat of force was there to help him come to the conclusion that a peaceful solution was the best solution," said James P. Rubin, the State Department spokesman. But the use of force, as opposed to the threat of force, was completely different, he said.

What NATO was now trying to do, President Clinton said this afternoon, was "to stop the brutal repression" by the Serbs.

"Our strikes have three objectives," he said — to "demonstrate the seriousness of NATO's opposition to aggression," to deter President Milosevic "from continuing and escalating his attacks" in Kosovo, and to damage Serbia's capacity to wage war in the future.

A top Pentagon planner conceded, "We have no great expectations that Milosevic is going to back down and agree to a satisfactory peace settle-

Continued on Page A12

Mayor, Under Fire, Opens Door Wider To Black Officials

By DAN BARRY

After an hourlong meeting with C. Virginia Fields, the Manhattan Borough President, whom he had shunned for more than a year, Mayor Rudolph W. Giuliani said last night that he would meet again with her and with other leading black officials at a time when the aftershocks of the Amadou Diallo shooting continue to rumble through the city.

The Mayor's office also announced that he would finally meet with the state's highest-ranking black elected official, State Comptroller H. Carl McCall. The two men last met in November 1994; since then, the Mayor has refused several requests from Mr. McCall for another meeting.

The sudden decision to open his door marked a stark turnaround for the Mayor, who had previously dismissed Ms. Fields and Mr. McCall as being more interested in publicity than in substantive discussion.

But the Mayor has come under increasing pressure to appear more conciliatory, as the outcry continues over the death of Mr. Diallo, an unarmed black man killed in a hail of 41 bullets fired by four white officers.

The Mayor also said yesterday that he expected Police Commissioner Howard Safir to keep his job, though he declined to comment on whether it was appropriate for Mr. Safir to have accepted a free trip to Los Angeles for the Academy Awards ceremony from a cosmetics executive. Mr. Safir has been under fire for the trip and for the conduct of his officers in the Diallo case. [Page B12.]

Yesterday, Police Headquarters in

Continued on Page B12

U.S. Navy via Agence France-Presse

Srdjan Ilic/Associated Press

THE ATTACKERS, AND THEIR TARGETS A Tomahawk missile being launched yesterday from the U.S. Navy cruiser the Philippine Sea, in the Adriatic. Near Pristina, the capital of Kosovo, a Yugoslav Army barracks burned.

INSIDE

737 Rudder Action Advised

Changes should be made in Boeing 737's to bolster their rudder control, the National Transportation Safety Board said. Page A28.

Microsoft Offers to Settle

Microsoft has sent the Justice Department a proposal to settle its antitrust case, but it apparently falls short of expectations. Page C1.

Ruling on Pinochet

England's top court ruled that Gen. Augusto Pinochet could face extradition to Spain, but narrowed the charges against him. Page A6.

Updated news: www.nytimes.com

Russian Anger at U.S. Tempered by Need for Cash

By MICHAEL R. GORDON

MOSCOW, March 24 — Stung by NATO's decision to carry out air strikes against Yugoslavia, Russia tonight suspended cooperation with the Western alliance and denounced the attack as an act of brazen aggression.

Behind the words, however, was a tempering factor: Russia still needs billions of dollars in Western loans.

That need was underscored by Russia's announcement tonight that Michel Camdessus, the managing director of the International Monetary Fund, would arrive in Moscow this weekend for more talks. A senior American official said today that the visit was occurring with the encouragement of the United States.

Caught between the imperatives of its pro-Serbian policy and its pressing economic needs, Russia did its best today to head off a NATO attack. In a telephone conversation, President Boris N. Yeltsin urged President Clinton not to go through with the air strikes and made an impassioned television address carrying the same message.

"I am appealing to the whole world," Mr. Yeltsin said. "I am appealing to people who survived the war, to those who experienced the bombings, their children, to all political figures. As long as there remain some minutes, let's persuade Bill Clinton not to take this tragic, dramatic step."

Prime Minister Yevgeny M. Primakov, for his part, telephoned the Yugoslav President, Slobodan Milosevic, to encourage him to reach an accommodation on the Kosovo issue.

Washington's and Belgrade's rebuffs to the Kremlin appeals were taken here as a powerful blow to

Continued on Page A13

MORE ON THE BOMBINGS

Clinton Explains Decision

The President said he decided to use force because of moral revulsion at the killings in Kosovo and to serve American interests. Page A15.

Serbs Turn Back to Loyalty

Even the Serbs most bitterly opposed to President Slobodan Milosevic feel a surge of nationalism at a threat from the West. Page A14.

"All the News That's Fit to Print"

The New York Times

Late Edition
New York: **Today**, sunshine yielding to clouds. High 60. **Tonight**, cloudy, patchy rain. Low 49. **Tomorrow**, early showers, then sun. High 65. **Yesterday**, high 50, low 44. Details, page D5.

VOL. CXLVIII . No. 51,499 — Copyright © 1999 The New York Times — NEW YORK, WEDNESDAY, APRIL 21, 1999 — $1 beyond the greater New York metropolitan area. — 60 CENTS

2 STUDENTS IN COLORADO SCHOOL SAID TO GUN DOWN AS MANY AS 23 AND KILL THEMSELVES IN A SIEGE

George Kochaniec/Rocky Mountain News via Associated Press

Reuters

Emergency workers tended to the wounded yesterday in Littleton, Colo. Students ran from the school where, the authorities said, two young men killed up to 23 people and injured at least 20 before shooting themselves.

A 'SUICIDE MISSION'

Authorities Say Killers Also Used Bombs — at Least 20 Injured

By JAMES BROOKE

LITTLETON, Colo., April 20 — In the deadliest school massacre in the nation's history, two young men stormed into a suburban high school here at lunch time today with guns and explosives, killing as many as 23 students and teachers and wounding at least 20 in a five-hour siege, the authorities said.

The two students who are believed to have been the gunmen were identified as Eric Harris and Dylan Klebold, students at Columbine High School. They were found dead of self-inflicted gunshot wounds in the library, said Steve Davis, the spokesman for the Jefferson County Sheriff's Department.

Beginning about 11:30 A.M., the gunmen, wearing ski masks, stalked through the school as they fired semiautomatic weapons at students and teachers and tossed explosives, with one student being hit nine times in the chest by shrapnel, the authorities said. Gunshots continued to ring out at the school for hours. At least 13 bombs were found inside the school. One of them, set on a timer, exploded just before 11 o'clock tonight, officials said. There were no injuries. Three automobiles were rigged with bombs, one of which exploded.

About 3 P.M., hundreds of police officers evacuated the building and searched for the gunmen. Their bodies and those of several of their victims appeared to have been wired with explosives.

Mr. Davis said that as many as 25 people had been killed, both students and faculty members. He said most of the bodies had been found in the school's entrance, the library and the commons cafeteria. No precise death toll was available.

Kaleb Newberry, 16, said: "I was in class and one teacher came in and basically told us to run for our lives, I saw a girl maybe five paces behind me fall.She was shot in the leg."

Students said the gunmen were part of a group of misfits who called themselves the trench coat mafia, which expressed disdain for racial minorities and athletes. Members of the group found their way out of anonymity at the school by banding together, dressing in dark Gothic-style clothing, including long black coats. They became easy to notice among the 1,870 students, since every day, regardless of the weather, they wore their coats. [Page A17.]

Today the gunmen appeared to

Continued on Page A16

In a Violent Instant, Routine Gives Way to Panic

By JAMES BARRON with MINDY SINK

When he heard the noise in the hall, Adam Foss leaned out of the choir room, the room where the confident singers of Columbine High School in Littleton, Colo., rehearse the kinds of songs that student choruses have sung for generations.

Hours later, he remembered seeing the barrel of a shotgun. He remembered seeing a flash of fire. He remembered seeing a teacher go down. He realized he was trapped in a school under siege.

Mr. Foss, 18, scrambled back into the choir room, he said, and herded the other students into a closet, an 8-by-8-foot room, the kind of musty, stuffy place where robes or sheet music are stored. Not knowing whether the gunman was poised to blast the closet or had gone away, Mr. Foss and his friends barricaded the door with a filing cabinet and waited.

The boys peeled off their shirts — the closet was hot, and they dared not open the door. They lifted one or two classmates with asthma who had trouble breathing toward the ceiling, where the ventilation seemed better. Together, they waited as the minutes ticked by until the police swept through the school and shouted that it was safe to come out.

But in that terrifying moment late yesterday morning, the everyday routine of a suburban high school had given way to uncertainty, and then to panic, as two assailants familiar with the layout of the school moved through the halls, guns blazing. Later the authorities said they had every reason to know their way around the school: They were students there.

Bullets zipped through the walls of a science classroom. Glass doors burst in a shower of tiny fragments. Pipes ruptured as the gunmen set off explosions that penetrated the walls of the two-story building.

Some students froze where they were — by their lockers, in the cafeteria, at their desks. Others tried to make a quick getaway, hoping not to catch the attention of the gunmen.

"Me and my friends got to my car and drove off," said a student whom The Associated Press identified only as Janine. Eliza Madden, a 16-year-old sophomore, fled barefoot after

Continued on Page A17

Whitman Says Troopers Used Racial Profiling

Minority Groups Faced Bias on the Turnpike

By IVER PETERSON

TRENTON, April 20 — Gov. Christine Todd Whitman and her Attorney General conceded today for the first time that some state troopers singled out black and Hispanic drivers on the highway, and that once they were pulled over, they were more than three times as likely as whites to be subjected to searches.

Mrs. Whitman and Attorney General Peter G. Verniero made the acknowledgement, after years of denials from state officials, as Mr. Verniero released the results of a two-month study of selected motor vehicle stops by state troopers. The study concluded that racial profiling had been conducted by some troopers in their zeal to stop drug trafficking.

The Governor said that while no official policy permitting such racial profiling existed, management styles, coaching of state troopers by superiors and a system that rewarded both aggressive ticket-writing and drug seizures had combined to create an atmosphere that went beyond simple racism to "a problem that is more complex and subtle than we first realized."

She said she was surprised. "To see numbers that indicate that fully 77 percent or more of those asked to consent to a search of their vehicle during a stop are minorities is extremely disturbing," she said. "It is not something that any of us had any reason to anticipate, because they are numbers that none of us had seen before."

Yet black and Hispanic drivers and even some former state troopers have testified to the existence of a pattern of racial searches, and dozens of criminal cases resulting from arrests during highway stops are being contested by defendants on the ground that the stops were the result of racial profiling, which courts have ruled to be illegal under the Fourth Amendment's protections against unreasonable search and seizure.

Significantly, in releasing his report today, Mr. Verniero announced that the state would drop its appeal of a March 1996 State Superior Court ruling that dismissed criminal charges against 17 black defendants in Gloucester County. In that case

Continued on Page B8

SERBS REPORTED TO PUSH ALBANIANS FROM 2D REPUBLIC

NATO FEARS A WIDER WAR

Kosovars Seeking a Refuge in Montenegro Under Pursuit — Allies Press Attacks

By ERIC SCHMITT

WASHINGTON, April 20 — NATO and Pentagon officials said today that Serbian forces had begun driving ethnic Albanians from Montenegro, signaling a widening of the Balkan conflict.

The Serbs' actions appeared to be focused on Albanians who had fled to Montenegro. Serbia and Montenegro form what remains of the former Yugoslav federation.

But initial reports were sketchy and could not be confirmed on the ground, or by other agencies monitoring developments in Yugoslavia.

Describing the reports at his briefing in Brussels, NATO's civilian spokesman, Jamie P. Shea, said: "This is something rather new and distressful if this pattern is now spilling over elsewhere into Yugoslavia. It can only exacerbate the problem, which is already, as you know, of alarming proportions."

The Pentagon spokesman, Kenneth H. Bacon, said NATO officials had evidence suggesting for the first time that troops in Montenegro are driving out Albanian refugees who had escaped from the Serbian campaign in Kosovo. Neither he nor Mr. Shea indicated where the new refugees may be going.

Late tonight, NATO conducted its first air strike against Serbian television and radio stations, knocking several of them off the air. The building that was attacked by cruise missile, across from downtown Belgrade, also contained offices of two political parties linked to President Slobodan Milosevic. [Page A11.]

Allied officials also reported that NATO warplanes had flown 603 missions in the 24 hours through this morning, the highest number in the four-week bombardment.

Military officials said the planes had attacked ammunition depots, an ammunition plant near Belgrade, tanks, trucks and a high-level command post. For the first time, NATO

Continued on Page A11

Kosovo Family's Journey From Torment to Torment

By ANTHONY DePALMA

KUKES, Albania, April 20 — The moment he crossed into Albania and registered with the police at the shabby border station about 10 miles east of here, Ymer Behrami was given four blankets, a large green tarp and what he believed was a chance for him and his family to leave behind the madness in Kosovo.

But he had no idea that by passing into Albania he was now engaged in a new struggle — to provide for the seven children on his wagon.

As it turned out, the apartment he expected to be waiting for him in Albania never appeared. Obtaining food, even a piece of bread, forced him to fight and claw like an animal. The intimidation and humiliation he thought he had left behind with the Serbian forces in Kosovo found him again, only this time from his own side.

Within hours, he heard Albanian soldiers bark orders at him and saw Albanian children taunt him with the three-fingered Serbian salute. He watched his children shiver with cold and cry from hunger. And after surviving the threats and beatings of the Serbian police, he was rounded up by armed Kosovo Albanian rebels, who questioned him and frightened him so much that after he was released he took his family and fled yet again.

For every one of the more than 600,000 Kosovo Albanians expelled by Serbs in the last four weeks, the escape from Kosovo was but a single point in a long exodus of terror and pain, preceded by months of anxiety and followed by long days of disappointment and vulnerability. Their journey did not start at the border, nor end there.

Still, it was natural for Mr. Behrami, a stern and stoic 58-year-old of Albanian descent whose family had been in Kosovo for many generations, to feel the bright, warm sun of midafternoon and to think he was lucky to be alive.

The last nine months had been

Continued on Page A13

Edward Keating/The New York Times

Part of an extended family from Kosovo took shelter in a borrowed wagon at a refugee camp near Kukes, Albania.

China Stole Design Of Atom Warhead, A U.S. Report Finds

By JAMES RISEN and JEFF GERTH

WASHINGTON, April 20 — A comprehensive new analysis by United States intelligence officials has concluded that China stole design information related to America's most advanced nuclear warhead from a Government nuclear weapons laboratory, Government officials say.

The intelligence report is expected to be presented to the Clinton Administration and Congress on Wednesday. Previously the White House, citing other intelligence reports, had said that the evidence of Chinese atomic espionage was less conclusive.

Although Energy Department officials have raised alarms about evidence of Chinese espionage at the national weapons labs since 1996, a 1997 report by the Central Intelligence Agency was cited by the White House in playing down the Energy officials' conclusions in the matter, officials say. President Clinton also said as recently as last month that, "It is my understanding that the investigation has not yet determined for sure that espionage occurred."

In the new assessment, the intelligence community reports on damage done to national security from what it says is Chinese nuclear spy-

Continued on Page A7

Private School Choice Plan Draws a Million Aid-Seekers

By ANEMONA HARTOCOLLIS

A billionaire Wall Street financier who raised $170 million in scholarships to send low-income children to private schools said yesterday that more than a million families had responded to his offer, or nearly one out of every 50 schoolchildren in America.

The financier, Theodore J. Forstmann, better known for his leveraged buyouts of companies like Gulfstream Aerospace, Dr. Pepper and General Instruments, said he had turned his business savvy to helping thousands of children escape failing public schools and go to private and religious schools. But the response to his offer surprised even him, he said, and it has added fuel to the debate over efforts to use taxpayer money to send children to private schools.

Although the scholarships were open to students now enrolled in either public or private schools, the vast majority of applicants came from public schools, indicating a deep dissatisfaction among parents with the education their children are getting, Mr. Forstmann said. The 40,000 winners, chosen over the last few days by a computerized lottery, are to be announced today at simultaneous ceremonies in New York and Los Angeles.

In capturing public attention for his cause, Mr. Forstmann was armed with an obvious fervor, immense wealth, and a well-oiled public relations machine that generated public service announcements by the baseball star Sammy Sosa, the poet Maya Angelou and the actor Will Smith. In February, Mr. Forstmann benefited from a dollop of Oprah Winfrey, who instructed viewers to turn off their vacuum cleaners while she interviewed him. A Republican,

Continued on Page B4

INSIDE

Prayers for a Scarred City

About 1,500 people gathered at the call of Cardinal O'Connor for a prayer service to help ease tensions in the wake of the Diallo case. Page B1.

Trade Deficit Hits Record

The strength of the United States economy pushed the nation's trade deficit to a monthly high. Page C1.

Arizona Drug Program

Treating rather than imprisoning nonviolent offenders has saved $2.5 million, a report says. Page A14.

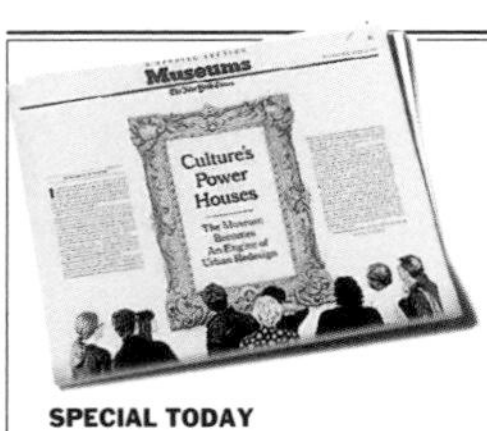

SPECIAL TODAY

Museums

No longer mere repositories of art and artifacts, museums have become the engines of urban transformation, helping cities from Spain to California to reinvent themselves. With articles on art vs. architecture, the museum expansion boom, the gray eminence of exhibition design, the Rock-and-Roll Hall of Fame and what's hot in the museum merchandise. **SECTION G.**

CHINA AND INDIA: THE NEW SUPERPOWERS

ROGER COHEN

The most significant event of the early 21st century was the rise of India and China and the consequent entry into the global economy of one third of humanity. Iraq stole the headlines but the revolutionary shift lay here. Hundreds of millions of people were lifted from poverty and given choices for the first time. Their passage from semi-feudal villages to a connected world affected everything from the price of goods at Wal-Mart to the quality of the air. It signaled a gradual shift of power toward Asia comparable to the rise of Europe in the 17th century or the emergence of the United States in the late 19th and early 20th centuries.

The hegemonic power the United States inherited at the cold war's conclusion proved a brief interlude. It ended with the framing of a distinct Chinese model backed by 10 percent annual growth and a limitless labor supply. American promises of democracy were met by Chinese pledges of "harmony." One-party China championed prosperity over the vote. It promised "no strings attached" assistance to providers of coveted raw materials from Africa[1] to South America.[2] With United States values of freedom and human rights increasingly questioned after the Iraq invasion, everyone knew what the "strings" were.

Countries had new strategic choices. They could opt for Washington's ideological interventionism or Beijing's development-first pragmatism. China's Market–Leninism found favor in Moscow, where Russia adopted its own version of economic opening allied to autocracy. The usefulness of democracy was questioned. It was depicted by the growing legions of American critics as no more than a camouflage for United States interests. In Iran and Sudan, as in Myanmar and Zimbabwe, the United States found its options for confronting repression limited by Chinese influence.

But the world was a long way from cold-war rivalry of the Washington–Moscow variety. Interconnectedness defined

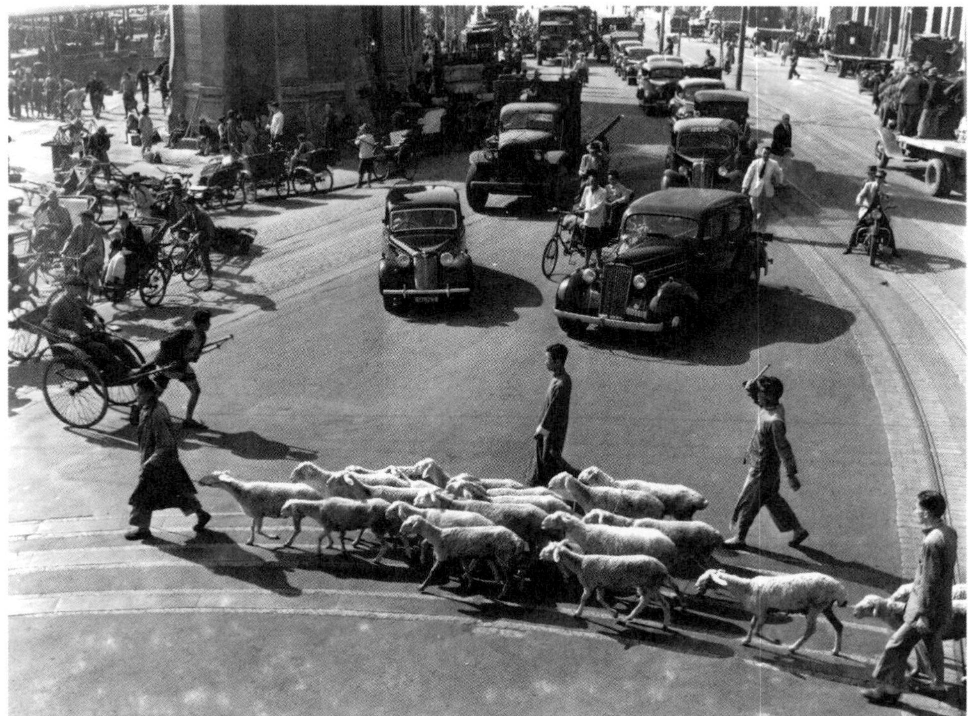

A flock of sheep crossing the heart of Shanghai's business district as rickshaws seek passengers in 1947.

Barges loaded with commercial products make their way through the polluted atmosphere in Suzhou, China.

Shanghai's dramatic cityscape illustrates the expanding role of China in world affairs.

FURTHER READING

1 "China Opens Summit for African Leaders," see November 2, 2006, article.
2 "China Widens Economic Role in Latin America," see November 20, 2004, front page.

China produces a large percentage of the world's toys, though their trade has been stung by recalls.

Vietnamese workers put the finishing touches on a production line making athletic shoes at a Nike factory in Ho Chi Minh City.

A peasant uses his water buffalo to plow a field in the shadow of an immense tower that will provide water for factories near Hanoi, Vietnam.

the early 21st century. Sometimes it was literal: Indian graduates answering 800-number United States customer calls about broken computers in Memphis or Honolulu.[3] Sometimes it was strategic: The United States–Chinese relationship became as symbiotic as it was confrontational.

Chinese manufacturing depended on the United States consumer; America depended on China to finance its deficits. The perennial smog over Hong Kong, drifting in from China's Guangdong Province, was tied to Americans' inexhaustible credit-driven thirst for cheap goods selling in Costco.[4] China's Communist Party leaders, anachronistic in name but pragmatic in deed, needed the United States economy to ingest a huge tide of imports—three-quarters of all toys and one-third of all shoes were made in China by 2007—and spur the growth necessary for political stability. The United States Treasury needed Chinese central bankers buying United States debt.[5] The two countries were tied at the hip.

Beyond the war on terror and nuclear proliferation fears, that bond strengthened prospects for 21st-century stability. But the question remained: How would the benefits of Asia's emergence be spread? Capitalists had many more cheap workers at their disposal—from China, Vietnam, India and the former Soviet bloc—not least because technology eliminated distance. The result was the rich thrived. Whether in America or the developing world, the distance between rich and poor grew, often in exponential fashion.[6] The tide of globalization raised yachts faster than boats.

Nguyen Hien, a 19-year-old Vietnamese woman, is still poor. But her life has been transformed. She grew up in isolated poverty on a rice paddy in the Mekong Delta. When I met her, she was working in a factory in Ho Chi Minh City hand-stitching an eye to Kermit the Frog or attaching a leg to Winnie the Pooh. The stuffed furry animals would end up in Disney and other Western stores, where pampered kids and their parents would not think for a minute of the faraway young women making them.

Her job earns her about $60 a month—not much but far more than she has ever known. Whether you view this as opportunity or exploitation depends on what you make of globalization. Certainly the peasants moving to factory jobs in cities, and the graduates pouring out of Indian and Chinese universities, posed a direct threat to developed-world jobs from Calais to Cleveland. A global economic shift was in progress on a scale comparable to the agricultural-industrial shift of the late 19th century.

The shift was disruptive, sometimes painful, but overwhelmingly hopeful. Much more of humanity, clutching cell phones, free to move, establishing networks beyond repressive governments, was in a position to attain a fundamental dignity beyond the enslavement of subsistence or political subjugation.

Technology terminated totalitarianism, or left only cranky North Korean vestiges. It took decades, and in China's case tens of millions of deaths, for the Chinese and Indians to move beyond a devastating communist experiment on the one hand and a paralyzing attachment to anti-Western socialism on the other. Just how much energy and creativity had been bottled up by these botched political experiments was clear in the extent of the wealth created at their demise.

But explosive growth brought attendant problems, not least ever-higher oil prices and devastating environmental damage. Filth-spewing, accident-prone Chinese factories meant polluted rivers and blighted air.[7] Tens of millions of health problems lay down the road. By 2025, the number of elderly people in China would increase to 280 million, or almost 20 percent of the population, from 130 million. In India, by 2025, the number of elderly (60 years old or more) would increase to 166 million, or 11.5 percent of the population, from 84 million in 2005. India's social problems, including the Brazil-like proximity of new wealth and enduring poverty, were also acute.[8]

Two things seemed certain in both countries. Continued economic growth and superpower status would not come without difficulty or crisis, and averting looming environmental disasters would only come through global cooperation.[9] Absent United States technology transfers and an accord between developed and developing countries on cutting carbon dioxide emissions, the unquenchable Indian and Chinese thirst for growth would not be reconciled with the need to confront global warming.

In its global implications the environmental crisis was a good paradigm for the interconnected 21st-century world. No longer, it seemed, could a single country dictate agendas

Fishermen using traditional nets in front of the modern, affluent skyline of a major Mumbai residential district.

Wealth and poverty exist side by side in many of the new Asian economies.

Employees stroll the grounds of Infosys, a major outsourcing company in India that writes software for American firms.

3 "30 Little Turtles," see February 29, 2004 article.
4 "Hong Kong Journal; Choking on China's Air But Loath to Cry Foul," see February 12, 1999.
5 "China's Milestone, Our Millstone," see October 21, 2006 article.
6 "Study Finds Wealth Inequality is Widening Worldwide," see December 6, 2006.
7 "As China Roars, Pollution Reaches Deadly Extremes," see August 26, 2007, front page.
8 "The Myth of the New India," see July 6, 2006, article.
9 "Economic Boom Fails to Generate Optimism in India," see August 16, 2006, article.

Building in India is speeding ahead as the nation deals with a rapidly expanding economy.

Call centers in India, such as this one in Bangalore, are symbolic of the quickly expanding economies of Asia.

or resolve problems alone. Even as Asia rose, America remained a necessary power. Just as the European Union could only prosper with the United States offsetting Franco-German rivalry, so the emergence of China and India was smoothed by America's Asian presence, which reassured Japan and others.

While a rapid transfer of political and industrial power from West to East seemed unlikely, the process appeared inexorable. But just what ideas China and India stood for on a global scale remained murky. Harmony had a ring to it. Yet it scarcely seemed compatible in the long term with Chinese repression and censorship. India's ideological position was unquestionably democratic, and involved emergent cooperation with the United States on nuclear issues,[10] but remained too shifting to identify with certainty.

What was clear was that openness, a core quality of the Internet age, was the key to the two countries' rise. Tortured prisoners in Abu Ghraib and Guantánamo notwithstanding, there was still no more open society in the early 21st century than a compromised but still vital United States. Its cooperation with China, notably on removing North Korea's nuclear threat,[11] and its broadening relationship with India constituted some of the most hopeful signs of the early 21st century.

They suggested that the forces pushing toward a more integrated and eventually peaceful world might be stronger in the long term than those pitting the West against extremist Islam. While the jihadists wanted to turn back the clock to the Caliphate and the dictates of theocracy, more than two billion Chinese and Indians were focused with released energy on technology and the future. In this they joined Americans—the world's forward-lookers par excellence—and a Chinese-Indian-American troika looked like the best hope for a century far better in its unfolding than in its bloody beginning.

ROGER COHEN, *who writes an Op-Ed column for The Times, became The International Herald Tribune's editor-at-large in 2006. A former foreign editor of The Times, he had been a correspondent and bureau chief for the paper in Berlin, Paris and the Balkans. Cohen was previously a foreign correspondent for The Wall Street Journal in Italy and the East Mediterranean and chief correspondent in Latin America, and for Reuters in London and elsewhere in Europe. He also has written several books including "Hearts Grown Brutal: Sagas of Sarajevo" and "Soldiers and Slaves: American POWs Trapped by the Nazis' Final Gamble."*

10 "In Its Nuclear Deal with India, Washington Appears to Make More Concessions," see July 28, 2007, article.
11 "China pushes North Korea and U.S. talks," see July 18, 2003, article.

"All the News That's Fit to Print"

The New York Times

Late Edition
New York: **Today**, partly sunny, cold and windy. High 43. **Tonight**, clear and breezy, low 32. **Tomorrow**, sunny with less wind, high 47. **Yesterday**, high 46, low 40. Weather map, Page D5.

VOL. CXLIX . . . . No. 51,708 — NEW YORK, TUESDAY, NOVEMBER 16, 1999 — $1 beyond the greater New York metropolitan area. — 75 CENTS

DEAL ON U.N. DUES BREAKS AN IMPASSE AND DRAWS CRITICS

Abortion Rights Advocates See 'Sellout' as Gore Splits With the White House

By ERIC SCHMITT

WASHINGTON, Nov. 15 — A fragile deal between the White House and House Republicans to end a fight over abortion and United Nations dues drew scathing criticism today from abortion rights advocates and cutting reviews from Vice President Al Gore and former Senator Bill Bradley.

In breaking an impasse that will free nearly $1 billion that the United States owes the United Nations, an issue that could undermine America's global reputation and a year-end budget agreement, both sides today claimed victory.

But the deal still has a few crucial loose ends, like the timing of the repayment of the back dues and a dispute over debt relief to the world's most impoverished nations.

But its central element would put into law a ban on United States money going to international organizations that promote abortion rights. Until the agreement is completed, the long-term impact of the measure remains uncertain.

For now, the compromise appears to pave the way to end a long-running dispute that has threatened to strip the United States of its vote in the United Nations General Assembly unless it pays before Dec. 31. The seat and vote in the Security Council are not affected.

The criticism from Mr. Bradley and Mr. Gore underscore Mr. Gore's desire to avoid giving his Democratic rival any opening to exploit. As Mr. Gore's presidential campaign heats up, he has been more willing to take positions that diverge from President Clinton's.

Speaking to employees at Microsoft in Seattle today, Mr. Gore would not directly answer whether he supported the deal brokered by a White House House deputy chief of staff, Steve Ricchetti. "I do not favor bargaining away any critical policy aspect of a women's right to choose," Mr. Gore said.

A senior Gore adviser said the vice president had expressed "strong reservations" about the deal, and while heaping most of the blame on Republicans said Mr. Gore "opposed what the White House ended up doing."

While Mr. Gore has tried to distance himself from Mr. Clinton on the issue of his personal conduct, this position is probably the one in which he most distanced himself from the president.

Under a compromise struck late

Continued on Page A24

F.B.I. MAY BE ASKED TO TAKE OVER CASE OF EGYPTAIR CRASH

CRYPTIC WORDS ON TAPE

After Review of Voice Recorder, Safety Board Is Concerned About Intent of Pilot

By MATTHEW L. WALD and DAVID JOHNSTON

WASHINGTON, Nov. 15 — Government officials said this evening that the National Transportation Safety Board was considering asking the F.B.I. to take over the case of EgyptAir 990 because of suspicions raised by a review of the plane's cockpit voice recorder.

The officials said they were focusing on a cryptic utterance, possibly a prayer. They said there were questions about exactly what was said and what it meant, but they were concerned that the statement might be the last words of a pilot determined to destroy himself and the airplane.

The plane crashed in the Atlantic, near Nantucket Island, two weeks ago, killing all 217 people on board.

The officials would not characterize the words beyond saying that they might have been a prayer. The crew's conversations, other than uneventful ones with air traffic controllers, were in Arabic, and senior officials of the safety board said this evening that even with the aid of additional interpreters brought in today, they did not understand some of what was said on the tape. The problems were apparently ones of language and culture, and of clearly hearing what people said in a noisy cockpit.

Transportation investigators also emphasized that they had not yet synchronized the voice tape with the flight data recorder tape, which recorded events occurring on the airplane and could put the statement in context. For instance, a prayer being said after the plane began plummeting so fast that passengers were weightless would not be suspicious.

But a senior law-enforcement official said tonight that he believed the tape showed that after one of the two pilots left the cockpit, another crew

Continued on Page A23

U.S. REACHES AN ACCORD TO OPEN CHINA ECONOMY AS WORLDWIDE MARKET

Agence France-Presse

Ending 13 years of on-again, off-again negotiations, the United States trade representative, Charlene Barshefsky, sealed a trade agreement yesterday with China's foreign trade minister, Shi Guangsheng.

White House and Business Groups To Push Congress on China Pact

By RICHARD W. STEVENSON

WASHINGTON, Nov. 15 — The Clinton administration and business groups prepared an intense campaign today to win approval in Congress for China's entry into the World Trade Organization, facing opposition from conservatives who object to almost any dealings with China and liberals who say the trade pact would be bad for workers.

Members of both parties said the deal would most likely be approved in the House, the more difficult of the two Congressional battlegrounds, based on the solid bipartisan majority that granted China a one-year extension of favorable trading terms earlier this year. The Senate tends to be more supportive of free trade measures than the House.

But neither the supporters nor the opponents were taking the outcome for granted, given the volatility of the relationship between the United States and China and the political sensitivity of trade issues heading into an election year.

"It's going to take an awful lot of work," said Representative David Dreier, a California Republican who is chairman of the House Rules Committee and a leading advocate of bringing China into the trade group.

Congress would not vote on the agreement itself, but on whether the United States should permanently grant China normal trading privileges, which is in effect a condition of the deal. Since 1974, Congress has had to vote annually on whether to retain a normal trading relationship with China, a process that critics of China have used to express their displeasure with Beijing.

Eager to win greater access to the huge market in China — and stung by criticism that they had been ineffectual in rallying support for past trade votes — business groups promised an all-out campaign to get the deal enacted.

"We were asked by the administration if we could deliver the votes," said L. Craig Johnstone, senior vice president for international economic and national security affairs at the United States Chamber of Com-

Continued on Page A16

A WATERSHED DEAL

Business Access for U.S. — A Foot in Trade Group for China

By ERIK ECKHOLM with DAVID E. SANGER

BEIJING, Nov. 15 — American and Chinese negotiators reached a landmark agreement today that would open the economy of China, the world's most populous nation, to foreign competitors and would also make it a full partner in the world's trading system.

After six days of arduous negotiations, the United States trade representative, Charlene Barshefsky, and China's trade minister, Shi Guangsheng, signed the papers at 3:50 p.m., shook hands and raised a Champagne toast to an agreement that capped 13 years of on-and-off negotiations on China's entry into the World Trade Organization.

Under the deal, Beijing would reduce tariffs on various industrial and agricultural products and lift many of the barriers that have been in the way of American banks and insurance and telephone companies that want to expand their operations in China or take controlling interest in Chinese companies.

In exchange, the United States agreed to support China's bid for membership in the global trade group, the 135-member organization that sets the rules for international commerce. China still must complete agreements with the European Union, Canada and some developing countries, including Brazil, before its application can be taken up by the group's member states.

"Let me just say that this is a profound and historic moment in U.S.-China relations," said a clearly exultant Ms. Barshefsky, adding that the agreement would not only aid the economies of both countries, but also serve as an anchor in their tumultuous political relationship.

The last six days of day-and-night negotiations were conducted in a "win-win spirit," Mr. Shi said, "and finally we reached an agreement that serves the interests of both China and the United States."

For all the rejoicing, the agreement faces tough resistance in the United States, where it is opposed by labor unions and some critics of China. Congress will not vote on the deal itself, but must vote to put an end to its annual review of Chinese trade and to establish normal — and permanent — trade relations with Beijing.

For China, membership in the

Continued on Page A17

MORE ON THE ACCORD

PACT DIVIDES REPUBLICANS The agreement to support China's membership in the World Trade Organization laid bare the deep divisions about China among Republican candidates for president. **PAGE A16**

IN CHINA, WELCOME NEWS Many Chinese were filled with disbelief that after many false starts, China had actually taken the plunge into the international economy. But Beijingers also seemed keenly aware that some would do better than others along China's new path. **PAGE A18**

HONG KONG STOCK SURGE Shares of Chinese and China-related companies surged in Hong Kong as investors concluded that the landmark trade agreement — and the increased competition it promises — would help Chinese companies more than it would hurt them. **PAGE C12**

FOR NEGOTIATOR, JUBILATION For the chief American trade negotiator, the pact is the capstone deal of her tenure in a once-backwater cabinet post — a post that, a decade after the cold war's end, has made its occupant a central player in American foreign policy. Woman in the news. **PAGE A16**

WINNERS AND LOSERS Many industries — including banking, auto manufacturing, and farming — hailed the agreement as an opportunity to expand rapidly into the Chinese market. The dissonant notes came mainly from textile makers. **PAGE C1**

City's Teachers Perform Poorly On State Exams

By ABBY GOODNOUGH

Not only does New York City have a disproportionate number of uncertified teachers, but those who do pass the state certification exams tend to score much lower than their counterparts in the suburbs and upstate, according to state data that is to be placed into evidence today in a landmark school-financing case.

The data shows that 31 percent of teachers in the city's public schools failed the main certification exam — the liberal arts and sciences test — at least once, compared with only 4.7 percent of teachers elsewhere in the state. About 47 percent of city teachers who took the state certification test for math failed at least once, compared with about 21 percent of teachers elsewhere. And 26.9 percent of city teachers who took the state test that measures elementary teaching skills failed, compared with 3 percent elsewhere.

The statistics suggest that prospective teachers who excel on the certification exams gravitate toward the more selective suburban systems, where they can command salaries much higher than city schools offer. The starting salary for New York City teachers is $30,807 — roughly 25 percent less than starting salaries in affluent suburban counties like Westchester and Suffolk.

The plaintiffs in the financing case cautioned yesterday that the data did

Continued on Page B12

School Prayer Case

The Supreme Court decided to hear a Texas school district's appeal of a federal court ruling that barred a student from leading others in prayer before a school football game.

Article, page A24.

New Battles Erupt In A.T.M. Fee War As Banks Retaliate

By ANDREW POLLACK

SANTA MONICA, Calif., Nov. 15 — Lashawanda McCullom, a 30-year-old nurse, put her credit union's cash card into a Bank of America automated teller machine here, punched in her secret code and requested a withdrawal. The machine spit out her card and flashed a message: "Due to a recent vote by the Santa Monica City Council, the convenience of this A.T.M. is now available to Bank of America cardholders only."

Ms. McCullom, who expressed mild frustration at being denied her cash, was caught in the cross-fire of a skirmish over A.T.M. surcharges that now seems to be breaking into a full-fledged war. Suddenly, the fact that it costs an extra $1.50 or so to get money out of a cash machine seems to have tapped into some deep well of public resentment — or at least politicians believe it has.

This oceanside suburb of Los Angeles last month passed the nation's first local ordinance banning banks from charging noncustomers for using their A.T.M.'s. San Francisco voters approved a similar measure earlier this month. California's two largest banks, Bank of America and

Continued on Page C6

After Med School, the A B C's of Insurance

By N. R. KLEINFIELD

The investigators came late last January, on a Thursday. They were deliberately cryptic. All they would tell St. Luke's-Roosevelt Hospital Center was that they were looking into a possible violation of the federal "anti-dumping" law, which prohibits hospitals from refusing to at least examine and stabilize patients who cannot pay. It was serious business. Only a handful of cases were investigated each year. Not until the investigators left did the hospital learn what it was all about.

The previous July, a French woman in her 40's had come to the emergency room with abdominal pain. Pelvic cancer was suspected, and she was admitted to the obstetrics and gynecology floor, where the diagnosis was confirmed. A private doctor, along with the house staff, attended to her. The doctor concluded that she needed surgery within several weeks followed by chemotherapy. The woman had no insurance. The senior physician discharged her, and left a note on the woman's chart saying she had instructed her to obtain health insurance or go to a public hospital.

Investigators determined that when the woman left the hospital, on Manhattan's West Side, she had barely been able to walk. That same day, she went to Bellevue Hospital Center, a city facility, where surgeons operated immediately. Officials there felt the woman had been treated unlawfully by St. Luke's-Roosevelt and complained to the State Health Department.

The agency's investigators spent five days at St. Luke's and issued a harsh report criticizing the care of the French woman but also identifying much else they didn't like — tardy treatment of patients in the E.R., poor recordkeeping, uninsured patients being told they would have to pay at least $400 and then leaving the E.R. without being examined. The hospital was ordered to put new policies into effect or be cut off Medicare, an action that, in effect, would close it down.

Hospital administrators felt their decision on the uninsured woman had been a judgment call — that she was not in imminent danger and had time to make arrangements to enter another hospital — although they acknowledged that doctors should have helped her transfer. And the docu-

Continued on Page B2

Angel Franco/The New York Times

Dr. Bryan Holland, an intern in pediatrics, examining Jerel Rauceo.

LIFE, DEATH AND MANAGED CARE

Third of four articles:
'Something Has to Give'

INSIDE

Gore Speaks at Microsoft
Facing Microsoft employees stung by the antitrust case, Vice President Al Gore told them competition is a good thing. **PAGE A22**

U.N. Admits a Bosnia Failure
The United Nations issued a self-critical report about a massacre that its peacekeepers failed to halt during the Bosnian war. **PAGE A3**

Shadow of a Planet
Astronomers say a drifting shadow on a distant star confirms the existence of planets around stars outside Earth's solar system. **PAGE A21**

G.E. Is Sued Over Pollution
New York Attorney General Eliot L. Spitzer linked economic damages to the company's dumping of PCB's into the Hudson River. **PAGE B1**

Hubble Telescope Turns Off
The Hubble Space Telescope has temporarily ceased operations because one of the gyroscopes that helps point it failed. **PAGE A21**

NEWS SUMMARY A2

Updated news: www.nytimes.com

"All the News That's Fit to Print"

The New York Times

Late Edition
New York: **Today**, afternoon thunderstorms, high 88. **Tonight**, showers end, low 67. **Tomorrow**, partly cloudy with showers late, high 81. **Yesterday**, high 88, low 74. Weather map, Page D8.

VOL. CXLIX . . No. 51,432 NEW YORK, TUESDAY, JUNE 27, 2000 — $1 beyond the greater New York metropolitan area. — 75 CENTS

Genetic Code of Human Life Is Cracked by Scientists

JUSTICES REAFFIRM MIRANDA RULE, 7-2; A PART OF 'CULTURE'

By LINDA GREENHOUSE

WASHINGTON, June 26 — The Supreme Court reaffirmed the Miranda decision today by a 7-to-2 vote that erased a shadow over one of the most famous rulings of modern times and acknowledged that the Miranda warnings "have become part of our national culture."

The court said in an opinion by Chief Justice William H. Rehnquist that because the 1966 Miranda decision "announced a constitutional rule," a statute by which Congress had sought to overrule the decision was itself unconstitutional.

Miranda had appeared to be in jeopardy, both because of that long-ignored but recently rediscovered law, by which Congress had tried to overrule Miranda 32 years ago, and because of the court's perceived hostility to the original decision.

The chief justice said, though, that the 1968 law, which replaced the Miranda warnings with a case-by-case test of whether a confession was voluntary, could be upheld only if the Supreme Court decided to overturn Miranda. But with Miranda having "become embedded in routine police practice" without causing any measurable difficulty for prosecutors, there was no justification for doing so, he said. [Excerpts, Page A18.]

Justices Antonin Scalia and Clarence Thomas cast the dissenting votes.

The decision overturned a ruling last year by the federal appeals court in Richmond, Va., which held that Congress was entitled to the last word because Miranda's presumption that a confession was not voluntary unless preceded by the warnings was not required by the Constitution.

The decision today — only 14 pages long, in Chief Justice Rehnquist's typically spare style — brought an abrupt end to one of the odder episodes in the court's recent history, an intense and strangely delayed refighting of a previous generation's battle over the rights of criminal suspects. Miranda v. Arizona was a hallmark of the Warren Court, and Chief Justice Rehnquist, despite his record as an early and tenacious critic of the decision, evidently did not want its repudiation to be an imprint of his own tenure.

There was considerable drama in the courtroom today as the chief justice announced that he would deliver the decision in the case, Dickerson v. United States, No. 99-5525. The announcement meant that he was the majority opinion's author. Given his statements over more than 25 years about Miranda's lack of constitutional foundation, there was the distinct possibility that he was about to announce that Miranda had been overruled.

The way Chief Justice Rehnquist chose to begin his announcement did little to clarify matters. "You have the right to remain silent," he intoned in a firm voice, moving on to the other familiar warnings without further introduction. Some in the courtroom audience wondered whether they might be hearing these phrases as the official words of the court for the last time.

By the time the chief justice fin-

Continued on Page A18

Multiple-Party Ballot Rejected in Primaries

The Supreme Court invalidated California's blanket primary, in which voters can cast ballots for candidates of any party. The 7-to-2 decision also cast serious doubt on the more common open primary, which allows voters in more than half the states to request a particular party's ballot.

Article, Page A19.

The Book of Life

The three billion **base pairs** ... ... of the intertwining double helix of **DNA** ... ... that make up the set of **chromosomes** in our cells, have been sequenced.

BASE PAIRS
Rungs between the strands of the double helix

BASES
A adenine
C cytosine
G guanine
T thymine

By ordering the base units, scientists hope to locate the genes and determine their functions.

The New York Times

Science Times
A special issue
- Putting the genome to work.
- Some information has already paid research dividends.
- Two research methods, two results.
- From Mendel to helix to genome.
- More articles, charts and photos of the genome effort.

Section F

Francis S. Collins, head of the Human Genome Project, left, with J. Craig Venter, head of Celera Genomics, after the announcement yesterday that they had finished the first survey of the human genome.

Paul Hosefros/The New York Times

A SHARED SUCCESS

2 Rivals' Announcement Marks New Medical Era, Risks and All

By NICHOLAS WADE

WASHINGTON, June 26 — In an achievement that represents a pinnacle of human self-knowledge, two rival groups of scientists said today that they had deciphered the hereditary script, the set of instructions that defines the human organism.

"Today we are learning the language in which God created life," President Clinton said at a White House ceremony attended by members of the two teams, Dr. James D. Watson, co-discoverer of the structure of DNA, and, via satellite, Prime Minister Tony Blair of Britain. [Excerpts, Page D8.]

The teams' leaders, Dr. J. Craig Venter, president of Celera Genomics, and Dr. Francis S. Collins, director of the National Human Genome Research Institute, praised each other's contributions and signaled a spirit of cooperation from now on, even though the two efforts will remain firmly independent.

The human genome, the ancient script that has now been deciphered, consists of two sets of 23 giant DNA molecules, or chromosomes, with each set — one inherited from each parent — containing more than three billion chemical units.

The successful deciphering of this vast genetic archive attests to the extraordinary pace of biology's advance since 1953, when the structure of DNA was first discovered and presages an era of even brisker progress.

Understanding the human genome is expected to revolutionize the practice of medicine. Biologists expect in time to develop an array of diagnostics and treatments based on it and tailored to individual patients, some of which will exploit the body's own mechanisms of self-repair.

The knowledge in the genome could also be used in harmful ways, particularly in revealing patients' disposition to disease if their privacy is not safeguarded, and in causing discrimination.

The joint announcement is something of a shotgun marriage because neither side's version of the human genome is complete, nor do they agree on the genome's size. Neither has sequenced — meaning to determine the order of the chemical subunits — the DNA of certain short structural regions of the genome, which cannot yet be analyzed.

With the rest of the genome, which contains the human genes and much else, both sides' versions have many small gaps, although these are thought to contain few or no genes. Today's versions are effectively

Continued on Page A21

A Pearl and a Hodgepodge: Human DNA

By NATALIE ANGIER

The human genome, the sum of all genetic material encased in nearly every cell of the human body, is very, very long — at least three billion chemical letters long, as many letters as you would find in a thousand copies of an entire Sunday issue of The New York Times.

The human genome is pithy. The English alphabet has 26 letters; the Russian, 33 letters; and the Japanese, 1,850 symbols. Yet, with just four distinct characters at its disposal, four nucleic acid bases, the human genome has given rise to the creators of every language uttered, every ballad sung, every Pokémon card traded.

The human genome is a pigsty, bulging with nongenes, ex-genes, freeloader genes, viral detritus, pocket lint and chewing gum. All but a few percent of it appears to be doing nothing at all.

The human genome is a pearl, a model of high performance and reliability. Millions of times a year, egg genome meets sperm genome, and the result is a human baby, its parts all in place, its brain a universe of love and meaning.

In short, the human genome exults in contradictions.

And scientists, with their announcement that they have completed a so-called working draft of the entire sequence of the human genome, must traffic in a few contradictions of their own. They rightly regard the sequencing of the genome as a major scientific landmark.

"This is a milestone in biology unlike any other," said Francis S. Collins, director of the National Human Genome Research Institute. "We only have to do this once, reading out the sequence of our own instruction book, and here we are on brink of it."

At the same time, scientists know that the bulk of their work in deciphering that sequence has yet to be done. "Complexity is the word on everybody's lips these days when they see what the genome really looks like," said David Baltimore, the molecular biologist and Nobel laureate who is president of the California Institute of Technology. "We've got another century of work ahead of us, to figure out how all these things relate to each other."

Though scientists underscore the importance of their accomplishment by calling the genome a "portrait of who we are," they quickly append that: people are not, and never will be, mere products of their genes.

"One of my concerns is that, as we begin to glimpse some of the biological contributions to certain personality traits, in people's minds those contributions will loom larger than they should," Dr. Collins said, "and the notion of genetic determinism will gather further momentum that it doesn't deserve."

Even in the case of a seemingly familial disease like schizophrenia,

Continued on Page A21

Clinton Raises Estimate of Surplus And the Stakes on How to Use It

By RICHARD W. STEVENSON

WASHINGTON, June 26 — President Clinton raised his projection of the federal budget surplus today by nearly $1.3 trillion for the next decade, putting a breathtaking sum of new money on the table as the two parties and their presidential candidates battle over tax cuts, spending and how to prepare for the nation's long-term challenges.

"How we use these surpluses in this moment of prosperity will determine America's future for decades to come," Mr. Clinton told reporters in the Rose Garden.

The new estimate put up for political grabs an amount of money two and a half times greater than what the White House had projected less than five months ago.

The robust forecast is the latest result of a strong economy that is rewriting the budget outlook on an almost continuous basis by recasting projections for years to come, even though events could easily undermine those projections.

And those assumptions are promoting an economy that has shown tentative signs of slowing in recent months.

The new estimate brought the total surplus projection to slightly less than $4.2 trillion for 2001 through 2010.

Of that, $2.3 trillion is projected to come from the Social Security system and is considered by both parties to be off limits for tax cuts or spending programs.

The rest — almost $1.9 trillion, up from $746 billion under the White House's last estimate, in February — is projected to come from general tax receipts, and is the pot of money that Democrats and Republicans are fighting over.

Seeking to frame the debate over how the money should be used, Mr. Clinton immediately proposed a deal to divide part of the windfall with the

Continued on Page A20

Sharansky in Eyes of Israelis: A Hero or Betrayer of Peace?

By DEBORAH SONTAG

JERUSALEM, June 26 — It has been 14 years since Interior Minister Natan Sharansky began making the transition from icon to man when he emigrated to Israel. It has been four since he morphed further from man to politician.

But his experience as a prisoner of conscience in the former Soviet Union not only stamped him forever; it also shaped others' expectations of him in unyielding ways.

To Israelis and to Jews worldwide, Mr. Sharansky is somewhat frozen in time behind the bars where he sat for nine years while they invested in him as a hero and fought for his freedom. And everything that he does is judged as a return on that investment, which means some amount of disappointment for everyone, left and right, secular and religious.

"Everybody marched for me," Mr. Sharankcy, 52, said in an interview today. "And everybody feels I owe them."

Right now, Mr. Sharansky is fighting an uphill battle to persuade Prime Minister Ehud Barak to join hands with the rightist Likud Party to form a national unity government. He portrays this, too, as an outgrowth of his days as a Soviet dissident. In his old punishment cell, he says, he did not distinguish between different kinds of Jews, and ever since meeting the divided reality of the Jewish nation, he has sought to forge a consensus.

Some lionize him for this, and contend that Mr. Sharansky would be an ideal national leader, much as he would break the mold with his thickly accented Hebrew and a military record that consists of three weeks in

Continued on Page A10

Buildings' Savior Now a Troubled Landlord

By AMY WALDMAN

This spring, the grievances at 1084-1086 Home Street in the South Bronx piled up like the garbage in the courtyard: sporadic heat and hot water, unpaid light bills, water-cracked walls, rats swaggering through like neighborhood bullies. Hallway graffiti cursed the landlord, who had not bothered to paint over it.

The building's state was not the handiwork of a profiteering landlord. Rather, the overseer of 1084-1086 Home Street is the Banana Kelly Community Improvement Association, a Bronx nonprofit community development corporation once praised as a national model for residents who want to restore failing housing and reclaim lost neighborhoods.

Today, its own properties are increasingly troubled, whether by periods without heat or by unrealized plans, as with a former synagogue, empty and encrusted with scaffolding, on Fox Street.

For a group that got its start rehabilitating abandoned buildings, there may be no symbol more dispiriting than 866 Beck Street, a Banana Kelly building that deteriorated so much that it was emptied of tenants and boarded up.

"Our savior has become a slumlord," said Marta Rivera, the chairwoman of the local community board and a tenant at 1084 Home Street since 1987.

The criticism, if harsh, is understandable, given what Banana Kelly, which drew its memorable name from the curve of the Bronx street where it was born, once meant in the South Bronx.

Two decades ago, foundations, reporters and government officials flocked to the Hunts Point-Longwood neighborhoods to see how Banana Kelly had transformed drug-infested, derelict tenements into livable spaces, and had created low-income housing co-ops that proved the salvation of

Continued on Page B8

The New York Times

A DREAM FORECLOSED
A special report.

Vote in Zimbabwe Shows Opposition Making Big Gains

By RACHEL L. SWARNS

HARARE, Zimbabwe, Tuesday, June 27 — Supporters of the opposition party cheered and danced on Monday as election results from the weekend's parliamentary elections showed their fledgling party making unprecedented gains on the governing party that has dominated Zimbabwe for 20 years.

The final result was unclear, but with more than three quarters of the vote in today from counting stations across the country, tallies quickly established that the nine-month-old party had become a powerful opposition force in Zimbabwe — a feat considered unimaginable just a year ago.

For years, President Robert Mugabe's governing party has controlled all but three seats in Parliament. But the new opposition party, the Movement for Democratic Change, easily surpassed that figure, winning 48 seats and claiming lopsided victories in urban districts, where voters have been squeezed by skyrocketing inflation and deepening unemployment.

Based on the early returns, it appeared that the governing party would likely maintain its majority as it carried 51 mostly rural districts, where the party's support has traditionally been strongest. Mr. Mugabe was also guaranteed 20 appointed

Continued on Page A6

INSIDE

Chechnya Assault to Resume
The day after a top commander announced a halt to Russian attacks in Chechnya, the Kremlin said that the attacks would continue. PAGE A9

A Move Ahead for Ulster
Two envoys have inspected a number of Irish Republican Army arms caches, a step in advancing Northern Ireland's peace pact. PAGE A3

Miami Relatives File Appeal
The Miami relatives of 6-year-old Elián González asked the Supreme Court to block his return to Cuba pending a formal appeal. PAGE A14

Fed Unlikely to Raise Rates
The Federal Reserve is expected to leave interest rates unchanged when it completes its two-day meeting tomorrow. BUSINESS DAY, PAGE C1

Updated news: www.nytimes.com

THE NEW YORK TIMES is available for delivery in most major cities. On the Web: homedelivery.nytimes.com, or telephone, toll-free: 1-800-NYTIMES. ADVT.

"All the News That's Fit to Print"

The New York Times

Late Edition
New York: **Today**, partly cloudy and warm, high 79. **Tonight**, clear, low 59. **Tomorrow**, sunny and cooler with light breezes, high 73. **Yesterday**, high 82, low 64. Weather map, Page D8.

VOL. CL . . No. 51,518 | Copyright © 2000 The New York Times | NEW YORK, THURSDAY, SEPTEMBER 21, 2000 | $1 beyond the greater New York metropolitan area. | 75 CENTS

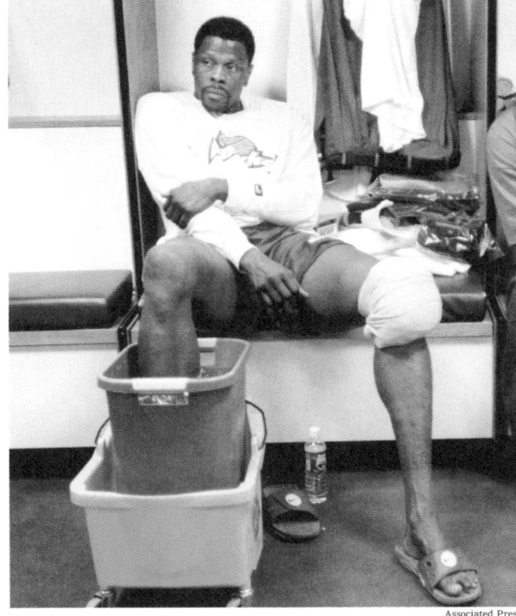

Associated Press

Patrick Ewing after his last game as a Knick, a loss on June 2 to the Indiana Pacers in Game 6 of the N.B.A. Eastern Conference finals.

Knicks Send Ewing to Sonics As 4-Team Deal Ends an Era

By CHRIS BROUSSARD

After one embarrassingly botched trade attempt and several other false starts, the Knicks last night finally parted with Patrick Ewing, the cornerstone of the franchise for the past 15 years.

A four-team, 12-player deal that was largely orchestrated by the Knicks and Ewing's agent, David Falk, will send the future Hall of Fame center to the Seattle SuperSonics, Knicks General Manager Scott Layden announced last night.

In return, the Knicks will receive the sharpshooting Los Angeles Lakers forward Glen Rice, the Lakers backup center Travis Knight and Phoenix Suns center Luc Longley.

In addition, they will receive several peripheral players — guard Vernon Maxwell, forwards Lazaro Borrell and Vladimir Stepania — and a first-round draft pick and two second-round picks in 2001 from Seattle, as well as the Lakers' first-round pick in 2001. The Knicks also sent Chris Dudley, their backup center, and a first-round pick in 2001 to Phoenix.

The Lakers will also receive Horace Grant, Greg Foster, Emanual Davis and Chuck Person from Seattle.

The blockbuster deal was Layden's first significant move with the Knicks, and it appeared that Ewing, who desperately wanted out of New York, forced his hand.

"It became clear that he was looking for a change, and when he requested a trade, we respected his request," Layden said in a statement last night. "It was important in doing so, however, that we had the ability to add value, and with Glen and his All-Star credentials, as well as two veteran big men and draft picks, we believe we have done that."

The trade represented the insuperable gap that had developed between the 38-year-old Ewing and the Knicks.

Ewing, the former Georgetown all-American who was the No. 1 draft pick in 1985, toiled admirably, if fruitlessly, for 15 years in search of a National Basketball Association championship.

It is not likely that he will win his elusive title with the Sonics, who have the superior Lakers and Portland Trail Blazers to conquer.

Nor is he likely to receive the two-

Continued on Page D2

Law Firm Charged In Aiding Smugglers Of Chinese to U.S.

By SUSAN SACHS

Federal prosecutors yesterday accused one of the city's busiest immigration law firms of working hand in hand with the smugglers who bring illegal immigrants from China and then keep them as virtual indentured servants in the United States until the price of their passage is repaid.

In a 44-count indictment filed in Federal District Court in Manhattan, the government described the Manhattan law firm of Robert E. Porges as a racketeering enterprise and accused Mr. Porges, his wife and six current and former employees of receiving $1.2 million in fees from unnamed smugglers over the last seven years.

Mary Jo White, the United States attorney, said that in return for that money, the firm acted as an adviser to smugglers, even suggesting the best points of entry into the country to avoid detection and arranging transportation to New York City for immigrants who succeeded in sneaking into the country by land or sea.

She also said some law firm employees, mainly under the direction of Mr. Porges's wife, Sheery Lu Porges, helped the smugglers seize the illegal immigrants upon arrival in the city and hold them as "hostages" until the $40,000 to $50,000 they promised to pay for their passage was paid.

After a brief hearing yesterday after the grand jury indictment was unsealed, Mr. Porges, 62, was released and given two weeks to post a $2 million bond on behalf of himself and his wife. She was ordered to be held until the bond was posted.

No pleas were entered at the hearing, and Mr. Porges did not speak to reporters. He appeared pale and shaken.

Nicholas Kaiser, his lawyer, said, "We're confident that after a speedy trial, Mr. Porges will be shown to

Continued on Page B11

CHINESE SEE PAIN AS WELL AS PROFIT IN NEW TRADE ERA

FEARS ABOUT JOB LOSSES

Many Worry That the Country Has Not Prepared Well for Global Competition

By CRAIG S. SMITH

SHANGHAI, Sept. 20 — China greeted its new prospects as a permanent American trade partner with official applause today, but there is growing trepidation as the country now shifts its focus to its future membership in the World Trade Organization.

Many Chinese worry that the country is ill-prepared to face the global competition that membership will bring. The global group's rules will force Chinese industries to become stronger in the long run, but many people are expected to lose their jobs along the way.

"It's a kind of double-edged sword," said Shen Dingli, an expert on China-United States relations. And people here are worried about the edge most likely to cut them.

The new trade status became a fait accompli when the Senate overwhelmingly passed a trade bill on Tuesday to end what China considered a humiliating annual debate about whether it deserved to be treated as a normal trade partner or warranted punishment for its shortcomings along with countries like Libya, Iraq and North Korea. The House already had approved the bill, and President Clinton is set to sign the law, which he considers a crowning achievement.

The new relationship will give both countries "a chance to start anew," a Foreign Ministry spokesman said in Beijing. But it is easy to find people here who worry about what that new beginning will bring. On Nanjing Road, Shanghai's busiest shopping street, two parking lot guards discussed the bleak prospects for Shanghai's auto industry, one of the town's biggest employers. "I think they'll die," one said.

And the manager of a cramped grocery store downtown shrugged with resignation when asked about the likely impact on his business.

"Already, medium-size shops like us can barely compete with the foreign megamarkets," said the gray-haired manager, who gave his name as Qiu. His prices are higher, the store's aisles narrower and its selection poorer than any of the sprawling Carrefours or Metros scattered around the city.

"We have high tariffs to protect us now, but after we join the W.T.O. there'll be no such protection," he said.

The trade bill has no direct bear-

Continued on Page A12

Cyclist Ends Long Wait for Gold

Marty Nothstein won the United States' first gold medal in cycling since 1984, defeating Florian Rousseau of France in the men's sprint finals yesterday in Sydney, Australia.

SWIMMING Pieter van den Hoogenband of the Netherlands earned his second gold medal of the Games, defeating the two-time Olympic champion Aleksandr Popov of Russia in the 100-meter freestyle.

GYMNASTICS Aleksei Nemov of Russia, motivated by his 18-day-old son, whom he has never seen, won the all-around competition. He has a chance to win seven medals in Sydney.

SportsThursday and Section S.

Reuters

Marty Nothstein after winning the two-of-three-race men's sprint finals in two rounds.

WHITEWATER INQUIRY ENDS; A LACK OF EVIDENCE IS CITED IN CASE INVOLVING CLINTONS

... referred to as Madison Guaranty/Whitewater. At this time, it is appropriate, in the public interest, and consistent with the law to inform the public of the findings and conclusions regarding the core matters within this Office's Madison Guaranty/Whitewater jurisdiction. Except for limited pending matters, the Madison Guaranty/Whitewater investigation is now closed.

An excerpt from the special counsel's statement saying he could not prove the Clintons had committed a crime.

In Poll, Mrs. Clinton Makes Gain Among Women From the Suburbs

Voters Say Lazio Came Across as Too Tough in Initial Debate

By ADAM NAGOURNEY with MARJORIE CONNELLY

Voter attitudes toward Rick A. Lazio have turned markedly more negative since June, with suburban women now moving solidly toward Hillary Rodham Clinton and many New Yorkers saying Mr. Lazio came across as harsh and inexperienced in his debate with Mrs. Clinton last week, according to the latest New York Times/CBS News poll.

The survey, which began last Thursday and was completed on Tuesday night, suggested deterioration in Mr. Lazio's standing at the time that most politicians believe that voters are beginning serious consideration of the choice before them in the race for Senate.

Mrs. Clinton now has a 9-point lead over her opponent, with 48 percent to Mr. Lazio's 39 percent. The remaining voters are undecided or are supporting minor-party candidates.

In the last Times/CBS poll, taken in June, Mrs. Clinton had a 5-point lead over Mr. Lazio, who had just entered the race.

When the undecided voters were encouraged to express which way they were leaning, and their probable votes were added to the totals, Mrs. Clinton broke the 50 percent barrier in the most recent poll, something of a milestone in this race, leading Mr. Lazio by 51 percent to 41 percent.

The poll was taken starting the evening after the debate in Buffalo, an encounter that seems to have enhanced Mrs. Clinton's standing, at least for the time being. Nearly half of the poll respondents who saw the debate pronounced Mrs. Clinton the winner, a perception that Mrs. Clinton's advisers acknowledged could fade with time.

Mrs. Clinton and Mr. Lazio are to meet in at least two more debates, and Mr. Lazio had, as of Aug. 23, the last federal reporting date, $10.2 million in campaign funds to finance television advertisements attacking an opponent who Mr. Lazio's advis-

Continued on Page B6

After the Debate

Voters who watched the Sept. 13 debate were asked:

Who won the debate?

	MEN	WOMEN
Clinton	43%	51%
Lazio	41	26

Was either of the candidates too aggressive in the debate?

	MEN	WOMEN
Clinton	4%	5%
Lazio	53	56
Neither	39	32

Those with other answers are not shown.

Source: New York Times/CBS News Poll

Military Backs Ex-Guard Pilot Over Pvt. Gore

By STEVEN LEE MYERS

WASHINGTON, Sept. 20 — Al Gore enlisted in the Army and went to Vietnam. George W. Bush joined the Texas National Guard and did not. But for many people in uniform, that makes little difference. It is Mr. Bush, not Mr. Gore, who seems to enjoy some automatic credibility with the military because of his party affiliation, his policy positions, his running mate, his advisers — and his father.

If Mr. Gore hoped his own military record would make him more palatable to the nation's 1.4 million men and women in uniform — and by extension the 24 million who are veterans — he might be disappointed.

Eight years after President Clinton's lack of a military record and his advocacy for gays in the military set the stage for his roiling relations with the Pentagon, Mr. Gore appears to have far less support in the military, especially among the officer corps, than his opponent. Mr. Bush, who did not serve in Vietnam but trained as a fighter pilot during his National Guard stint, has wide support.

In about 20 interviews in recent weeks, those in uniform or recently retired from service expressed overwhelming, though not universal, support for Mr. Bush — not only as the Republican presidential candidate, but as a veteran and the son of former President Bush, who many said served ably as commander in chief during the military's shining moment after Vietnam, the Persian Gulf war.

They cited Governor Bush's policy proposals, his accusations that the Clinton administration had overseen

Continued on Page A25

Congress Appears Set To Act on Rollovers

The 103 deaths attributed to defective Firestone tires have galvanized Congress to tackle the larger problem of vehicle rollovers.

Automakers have blocked federal action, but the last obstacle appeared to fall when Senator Richard Shelby of Alabama dropped his objections to a plan to begin providing consumers with information on the stability of many 2001 models.

Business Day, Page C1.

BEGAN 6 YEARS AGO

White House Sees Major Victory, Particularly for Mrs. Clinton

By NEIL A. LEWIS

WASHINGTON, Sept. 20 — An independent prosecutor today put an end to the six-year Whitewater investigation, saying he had concluded that there was insufficient evidence to show that either President Clinton or his wife, Hillary Rodham Clinton, had committed any crimes in connection with the Arkansas real estate venture that vexed his presidency through two terms.

Robert W. Ray, the prosecutor, said he could not prove that the president or Mrs. Clinton had been involved in any criminal behavior in connection with a set of complicated Whitewater-related financial and legal transactions in Arkansas. Nor, he said, could he prove that they had concealed information from investigators or obstructed justice in any manner related to Whitewater.

In saying he did not have evidence to charge either the president or Mrs. Clinton with a crime, Mr. Ray was notably spare in his language. On each of the accusations, he said only that "the evidence was insufficient to prove to a jury beyond a reasonable doubt" that they had committed any crime. [Text, Page A23.]

Nonetheless, Mr. Ray's statement was a definitive legal conclusion on the issue and thus was regarded by the White House and its supporters as a significant victory, especially for Mrs. Clinton, who is running for the Senate from New York.

The report's conclusions also appeared to largely undercut concerns that it was unfair to Mrs. Clinton for Mr. Ray to issue a statement only weeks before she faces Representative Rick Lazio, a Republican congressman from Long Island, in the Senate voting. The Ray statement seemed to provide little ammunition for Mrs. Clinton's opponents.

The Whitewater investigation began in January 1994 when President Clinton, under increasing pressure, asked for a special prosecutor to be named to investigate his Whitewater

Continued on Page A23

INSIDE

Explosion in London

Some form of small missile struck the headquarters of Britain's M.I.6 intelligence agency, but the explosion caused minimal damage and no casualties, the police said. PAGE A7

Crash Victims Coming to U.S.

Eight Cuban survivors of a plane crash in the Gulf of Mexico were being taken to Key West for medical evaluation, a move that would allow them to apply for residency in the United States. PAGE A23

Euro and Oil in Spotlight

The slumping single European currency and the soaring cost of fuel quickly took over as the dominant themes ahead of a meeting of some of the world's top finance officials in Prague. PAGE C1

Updated news: www.nytimes.com

S.E.C. Says Teenager Had After-School Hobby: Online Stock Fraud

By GRETCHEN MORGENSON

By day, Jonathan G. Lebed was just another 15-year-old high school student in Cedar Grove in northern New Jersey. But after school, securities regulators say, Mr. Lebed masterminded a stock manipulation scheme on the Internet that earned him almost $273,000 in illegal gains.

Yesterday, just days before Mr. Lebed's 16th birthday, the Securities and Exchange Commission accused the teenager of developing a scheme to increase the prices of nine obscure, low-price stocks he had bought by sending numerous optimistic messages to investing chat rooms on the Internet. As other investors read his messages and bought the shares, prosecutors said, Mr. Lebed sold his holdings at profits ranging from $11,000 to $74,000 a trade. The scheme began in August 1999, when Mr. Lebed was 14, prosecutors said, and continued until Feb. 4 this year.

Mr. Lebed settled with the S.E.C. yesterday, neither admitting nor denying the civil accusations but agreeing to pay the money he made plus interest, for a total of $285,000.

The S.E.C. did not require him to pay a fine or penalty. His lawyer, Kevin H. Marino, said, "The Lebeds feel that this is a reasonable settlement, and they are very happy to have the entire matter behind them." Neither of Mr. Lebed's parents was accused of wrongdoing by the S.E.C. Mr. Lebed was not available for comment.

Late yesterday afternoon, Gregory Lebed, Jonathan's father, stood outside the family's two-story brown-shingle house greeting reporters. Dressed in jeans and a gray T-shirt, he said he could not comment on his son's situation other than to say he was fine. "He's a good student," he said. Acknowledging that many people are trading stocks on the Internet these days, Mr. Lebed said: "So they pick on a kid."

Regulators said Jonathan Lebed was the first minor to be sued by the S.E.C. "Jonathan Lebed's conduct was essentially a pump-and-dump scheme, and it was every bit as serious as other Internet fraud cases we have brought," said David S. Horowitz, assistant district administrator at the S.E.C.'s Philadelphia district office. "What's different is his age."

Mr. Lebed conducted his trading in accounts set up for him in his father's name at two different broker-

Continued on Page C10

"All the News That's Fit to Print"

The New York Times

Late Edition
New York: **Today**, bright start, then cloudy, high 31. **Tonight**, snow arriving, low 28. **Tomorrow**, snow changing to rain, high 35. **Yesterday**, high 52, low 37. Weather map is on Page D8.

VOL. CL . . No. 51,601 | NEW YORK, WEDNESDAY, DECEMBER 13, 2000 | 75 CENTS

$1 beyond the greater New York metropolitan area.

BUSH PREVAILS

BY SINGLE VOTE, JUSTICES END RECOUNT, BLOCKING GORE AFTER 5-WEEK STRUGGLE

An Awareness of Hazards

By LINDA GREENHOUSE

WASHINGTON, Dec. 12 — The Supreme Court effectively handed the presidential election to George W. Bush tonight, overturning the Florida Supreme Court and ruling by a vote of 5 to 4 that there could be no further counting of Florida's disputed presidential votes.

The ruling came after a long and tense day of waiting at 10 p.m., just two hours before the Dec. 12 "safe harbor" for immunizing a state's electors from challenge in Congress was to come to an end. The unsigned majority opinion said it was the immediacy of this deadline that made it impossible to come up with a way of counting the votes that could both meet "minimal constitutional standards" and be accomplished within the deadline.

The five members of the majority were Chief Justice William H. Rehnquist and Justices Sandra Day O'Connor, Antonin Scalia, Anthony M. Kennedy and Clarence Thomas.

Among the four dissenters, two justices, Stephen G. Breyer and David H. Souter, agreed with the majority that the varying standards in different Florida counties for counting the punch-card ballots presented problems of both due process and equal protection. But unlike the majority, these justices said the answer should be not to shut the recount down, but to extend it until the Dec. 18 date for the meeting of the Electoral College.

Justice Souter said that such a recount would be a "tall order" but that "there is no justification for denying the state the opportunity to try to count all the disputed ballots now." [Text, Page A27.]

The six separate opinions, totaling 65 pages, were filled with evidence that the justices were acutely aware of the controversy the court had entered by accepting Governor Bush's appeal of last Friday's Florida Supreme Court ruling and by granting him a stay of the recount on Saturday afternoon, just hours after the vote counting had begun.

"None are more conscious of the vital limits on judicial authority than are the members of this court," the majority opinion said, referring to "our unsought responsibility to resolve the federal and constitutional issues the judicial system has been forced to confront."

The dissenters said nearly all the objections raised by Mr. Bush were insubstantial. The court should not have reviewed either this case or the one it decided last week, they said.

Justice John Paul Stevens said the court's action "can only lend credence to the most cynical appraisal of the work of judges throughout the land."

His dissenting opinion, also signed by Justices Breyer and Ruth Bader Ginsburg, added: "It is confidence in the men and women who administer the judicial system that is the true backbone of the rule of law. Time will one day heal the wound to that confidence that will be inflicted by today's decision. One thing, however, is certain. Although we may never know with complete certainty the identity of the winner of this year's Presidential election, the identity of the loser is perfectly clear. It is the nation's confidence in the judge as an impartial guardian of the rule of law."

What the court's day and a half of deliberations yielded tonight was a messy product that bore the earmarks of a failed attempt at a compromise solution that would have permitted the vote counting to continue.

It appeared that Justices Souter and Breyer, by taking seriously the equal protection concerns that Justices Kennedy and O'Connor had raised at the argument, had tried to persuade them that those concerns could be addressed in a remedy that would permit the disputed votes to be counted.

Justices O'Connor and Kennedy were the only justices whose names did not appear separately on any

Continued on Page A26

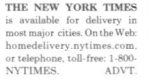

Associated Press

Thirty-five days after Election Day, the Supreme Court effectively handed George W. Bush the presidency.

A Shaky Platform on Which to Build

By R. W. APPLE Jr.

News Analysis

WASHINGTON, Dec. 12 — Whatever else it did tonight, the Supreme Court failed to speak with the kind of clarion political voice about the vexed 2000 presidential election that much of the nation had hoped for.

If, as seems sure, Gov. George W. Bush has won, he has won a narrow victory — narrow in Florida, narrow in the Electoral College and narrow in the Supreme Court. He will have only a shaky platform from which to begin his presidency in January, and it will require immense skill to remove the questions about his legitimacy that were left hanging by tonight's decision.

The court provided no clear, unanimous validation of the electoral process. Its extraordinarily complex ruling led to widespread confusion in the first few minutes after it was issued, and it may well provide ammunition in the months ahead for embittered supporters of Vice President Al Gore, whose chances seemed to have been sorely and in all probability fatally damaged.

Nor was there any certainty that the Democrats would refrain from further challenges, either in the courts or in the halls of Congress. One possible line of attack is the Florida Legislature's actions to choose electors. But there was no clear avenue for further legal maneuvering by the Gore team.

"I had hoped that the court would bring the country together," said Senator Dianne Feinstein, Democrat of California. "I had hoped that it would send a clear message, but that does not appear to have happened."

One of Mr. Gore's confidants described the court's opinion as "confusing but devastating." Some backers, including Edward G. Rendell, the general chairman of the Democratic party, and Laurence H. Tribe, one of Mr. Gore's top lawyers, said it was time for the vice president to concede, but some others disagreed.

James A. Baker III, Mr. Bush's chief spokesman in the Florida fight, confined himself to a statement of pleasure, without appearing triumphant and without putting any pressure on Mr. Gore to quit the contest.

In reversing the order of the Florida Supreme Court, the court came down on the side of Governor Bush. With less than a week remaining until the Electoral College is to cast its votes, the justices in the core ruling that the Florida court was wrong to order a recount found a way to speak with one voice, avoiding a contentious split, but no sooner had they done so than they started bickering again among themselves.

Still, beneath the welter of verbiage, the same five justices who had voted on Saturday to halt a partial recount ordered by the Florida Supreme Court remained convinced that the court's recount plan was unconstitutional.

As a formality, Washington

Continued on Page A24

The Tally

ELECTORAL VOTES (270 NEEDED)	
GEORGE W. BUSH	271
AL GORE	267
NATIONAL POPULAR VOTE	
AL GORE	50,158,094
GEORGE W. BUSH	49,820,518

Source: Associated Press

With a Victory Apparently His, Bush Plays the Strong, Silent Role

By DAVID E. SANGER

AUSTIN, Tex., Dec. 12 — For 35 days Gov. George W. Bush has insisted that he won Florida and with it the presidency. But when the Supreme Court appeared to seal his victory late this evening, there was silence from the Governor's Mansion here and Mr. Bush's aides quite deliberately avoided any claim of victory.

All day Mr. Bush had stayed out of sight, never venturing from his house. But just before 11:30 p.m., Mr. Bush's chief legal strategist, former Secretary of State James A. Baker III, said he had spoken with the Texas governor and Dick Cheney, his running mate, and described them as "very pleased and gratified" by the court's ruling, and he thanked the Bush legal team as well as the hundreds of volunteers in Florida for their efforts.

But Mr. Baker left it open to Vice President Al Gore to make the next move. Aides said they would wait to see whether Mr. Gore would make a concession announcement, but made it clear that under their reading of the court's opinion, that that was now inevitable.

The Gore camp was even more subdued, with no official announcement by the vice president or his staff. But aides and supporters were clearly downcast and in some cases stunned. "It makes you want to call 911 and report a burglary," said Greg Simon, a longtime Gore adviser who has been working in Florida on the recount.

Before Mr. Baker's brief comment, Mr. Bush's aides here were poring through faxes of the opinion and the lengthy dissents, trying to figure out whether their victory was, in fact, in hand. "We're just reading it like everyone else," said one top aide, speaking in the busy but surprisingly subdued campaign headquarters about eight blocks from Mr. Bush's residence. The governor is not expected to say anything in public until Wednesday, and even then, the aide said, may wait for Mr. Gore to act first.

Mindy Tucker, a Bush spokeswoman, said, "We are heartened it does mean the Florida Supreme Court has been reversed, and the recount they called for will not happen."

Tonight's decision appeared to mark the end of one of the most bizarre periods in American political history. Twice in that period, first on election night and then last Friday afternoon, Mr. Bush and his aides thought that the presidency would be his within moments. Twice those moments disappeared, only to come back tonight for the third — and it appeared the final — time.

The first time Mr. Bush thought he had been elected president was in the early morning hours of Nov. 8, as the networks put Florida's votes in his column. Mr. Bush received a congratulatory call from Mr. Gore, who told him he was about to go before his supporters in Tennessee and concede the election.

So the governor prepared to speak before a victory rally here, in front of the Capitol. He waited to see Mr. Gore's public concession, and waited

Continued on Page A25

G.O.P. IS CAUTIOUS

Camps Choose to Digest Ruling and Refuse to End Their Battle

By RICHARD L. BERKE

WASHINGTON, Dec. 12 — Exactly five weeks after one of the most unsettled presidential elections in American history, George Walker Bush appeared tonight to have swept away any lingering legal obstacles, gaining the right, at long last, to consider himself president-elect.

While the campaigns of Mr. Bush and Vice President Al Gore were still reading and digesting the Supreme Court's tangled and elaborate ruling as midnight approached, officials in both camps said it was now virtually impossible for Mr. Gore to reach the White House.

The post-election tumult overshadowed a spectacular political rise for Mr. Bush only eight years after his father was turned out of the White House.

In perhaps a fitting coda to a turbulent election night that never seemed to end, the court's verdict was not issued until about 10 p.m., and — as campaign officials pored over the ruling page by page — Gore aides said there would be no concession speech tonight.

Just the same, the Bush campaign proceeded with extreme caution, mindful that it appear presumptuous — or unduly triumphant. In a terse statement he read to reporters in Tallahassee, Fla., late tonight, James A. Baker III, the former secretary of state and Mr. Bush's top adviser in the case, said Mr. Bush and his running mate, Dick Cheney, were "very pleased and gratified" that the court agreed that "there were constitutional problems with the recount ordered by the Florida Supreme Court."

Careful not to declare victory, Mr. Baker added, "This has been a long and arduous process for everyone on both sides."

Mr. Bush's advisers said they wanted to give Mr. Gore room to concede before the governor, who was cloistered in the Governor's Mansion in Austin, Tex., publicly proclaimed victory.

Mr. Gore himself, who collected more popular votes than Mr. Bush, and who insisted that a full and accurate recount would show him to be the winner in Florida, remained in his home in Washington with his family.

His campaign chairman, William M. Daley, issued a statement describing the complicated ruling and not leaving any hint of a concession that other Gore aides said would be forthcoming.

"The decision is both complex and lengthy," Mr. Daley said. "It will take time to completely analyze this decision."

Mr. Daley said the Gore camp would comment further on Wednes-

Continued on Page A30

Once Again, the TV Mystery Prevails as Late-Night Fare

By PETER MARKS

Was the election over, or did Vice President Al Gore still have a chance? Had the United States Supreme Court sent the case back to Florida, or settled the matter once and for all? Was the vote 5 to 4, or 7 to 2? And what exactly had the justices voted on, anyway?

For the better part of an hour last night, correspondents, commentators and legal experts frantically tried to make sense on live television of a ruling that seemed about as easy to reduce to simple language as the assembly manual for the space station.

Viewers across the channels were given the opportunity to watch as anchors and reporters struggled mightily to digest and summarize a complex, voluminous decision. It was a task so confusing and rife with tension that at times, analysts sitting next to each other at the network anchor desks could not agree on even the most basic implications of the historic ruling.

Some were quick to declare it the definitive victory for Gov. George W. Bush; others thought it still held out some sliver of hope for Mr. Gore. But talking heads on every channel seemed to agree that the job of parsing it on the air was monumental.

"It may take an army of lawyers to translate this thing," Dan Rather said on CBS at 10:18 p.m., Eastern Standard Time, about 20 minutes after the opinion was released. To which his colleague Bob Schieffer, searching for the appropriate adjective, added, "'Complicated' is the understatement of the year."

A long day of network calm over the court's deliberations was broken just before 10 p.m., when the first word reached the anchors on cable that the opinion was about to be issued. MSNBC trained a camera on Bob Kur, an NBC correspondent who was posted on the Supreme Court steps like a member of a relay team, waiting for the baton to be passed.

"Tell me if you see any movement

Continued on Page A25

SPECIAL TODAY
E-Commerce
After a year in which the boldest Internet entrepreneurs soared and plunged, Saul Hansell finds that the Web has changed business in modest but still substantial ways. **SECTION H**

Part of Drug Battle: Keeping It in Stores

Critics of the Food and Drug Administration have argued that the agency has been allowing drugs to be rushed into use since a 1992 law enabled speedier reviews. A case in point is that of Odell Buggs, a 28-year-old counselor who suffered a stroke that her doctors attributed to an ingredient in her over-the-counter decongestant, Tavist-D. She sued the manufacturer, the pharmaceutical giant Novartis A.G., saying its cold pills had left her with brain damage. Novartis, based in Switzerland, had a strong defense: the ingredient, phenylpropanolamine, or PPA, was in dozens of cold remedies, as well as appetite suppressants, and had been taken in billions of doses with no ill effects. The Buggs case offers a glimpse into how companies marketing PPA worked aggressively to assuage concerns about the safety of a drug that for six decades was a staple in American medicine cabinets.

Article, page A31.

INSIDE

Fatal Crash Grounds Osprey
The Marine Corps grounded its V-22 Ospreys after another of the problem-prone aircraft crashed, killing four marines. PAGE A33

Clinton's Pledge to Ireland
President Clinton, on his third trip to Ireland, said he would keep working for reconciliation in Ulster even after leaving the White House. PAGE A8

Pressure to Free Pollard
A new push is being mounted to persuade President Clinton to free the convicted spy Jonathan Jay Pollard before leaving office. PAGE A14

McVeigh Drops Appeal
Timothy J. McVeigh, sentenced to die for the 1995 Oklahoma City bombing, has asked to be executed within four months. PAGE A18

Putin Nurturing Old Friends
President Vladimir V. Putin of Russia visits Cuba this week, part of an attempt to rebuild ties with client states of the Soviet era. PAGE A8

NEWS SUMMARY A2

Updated news: www.nytimes.com

2001

An Uncertain Future

2008

FRONT PAGE NEWS 2001-2008

Microsoft Wins on Appeal
JUNE 29, 2001

Back in the last century Microsoft was formed to write programs for a do-it-yourself computer that came in a kit. The year was 1975, and only 5,000 computers were sold in four months—hardly a monopoly. By the 1990's, with Microsoft's MS-DOS and Windows running on personal computers on nearly every desk, the Justice Department moved to break up what it said was an aggressively monopolistic giant. Judge Thomas Penfield Jackson agreed. But an appeals court ordered Microsoft left alone, rejecting the Justice Department's main claim—that Microsoft had tried to monopolize the market for Web browsers by forcing computer manufacturers to install its Internet Explorer.

Kyoto Protocol Signed
JULY 24, 2001

One hundred seventy-eight nations agreed to a compromise on the seven-year-old Kyoto Protocol limiting greenhouse gases. But the world's biggest polluter was not among them. President George W. Bush, in office for only six months, had earlier repudiated Kyoto as "fatally flawed." He said it made industrial nations responsible for too much of the cleanup and the U.S. responsible for too much of the cost. The president's approach troubled long-standing American allies, especially in Europe, where officials favored multinational accords.

Assault on Afghanistan
OCTOBER 8, 2001

President George W. Bush declared war on terrorism hours after the jetliners hit their targets on Sept. 11. He threatened a campaign against Afghanistan unless it turned over Osama bin Laden immediately. It did not. But the actual military response did not begin until the U.S. and Great Britain launched air strikes against bin Laden's training camps in mountainous border areas. Bin Laden proved elusive. So did another of the president's goals: building a stable Afghanistan after the military actions ended.

Anthrax Scares
OCTOBER 17, 2001

For an already jittery nation, there was a new worry: anthrax in the mail. Envelopes containing small but deadly quantities were delivered to news organizations in New York and to the office of the Senate majority leader, Tom Daschle, in Washington. There, after an aide opened the letter, the Capitol was evacuated; the House of Representatives shut down for four days. Federal officials made bioterrorism a new priority as two postal workers at a mail-processing center in Washington died of anthrax exposure. There was a rush for Cipro, an antibiotic used in treating anthrax, and disease investigators in "moon" suits were busy, though they chased many false alarms.

Anti-Terror Bill Enacted
OCTOBER 26, 2001

President George W. Bush, who had promised to bring "evildoers" to "justice" after the Sept. 11 attacks, wanted new law-enforcement powers to hunt them down. He got those powers in a bill that breezed through the House and the Senate. It expanded the government's authority to eavesdrop with wiretaps, to detain immigrants without charges and to prosecute banks that launder money. "We treat terrorism with kid gloves in the current criminal code—this bill stops that," declared Senator Orrin G. Hatch of Utah. But the public was not so sure. Only 18 percent of those questioned for a New York Times/CBS News Poll said they had a "great deal" of confidence in the federal government's ability to protect against future terror attacks.

The New York Times

U.S. ATTACKED

The 9/11 Attacks
SEPTEMBER 12, 2001

The plan was devastating but simple: commandeer four jetliners and fly them into quintessential symbols of American wealth and power—the World Trade Center and the Pentagon. (The fourth, apparently destined for the United States Capitol in Washington, crashed in Pennsylvania after the passengers banded together and fought back.) The twin towers of the trade center collapsed in less than two hours, leaving tons of smoldering debris at what came to be called "ground zero." The government soon laid responsibility on Osama bin Laden, naming nineteen al Qaeda–linked hijackers, some of whom had attended flight schools in the United States so they would know what to do after forcing their way into the cockpit and seizing the controls.

Invasion of Iraq
MARCH 21, 2003

President George W. Bush accused Iraq of developing weapons of mass destruction and of ties to the 9/11 terrorists. But one reason for taking action also sounded personal when he called Saddam Hussein "the guy who tried to kill my dad." That referred to a reported plot to assassinate former President George H.W. Bush in the 1990's, after the first Gulf War. The son's single-minded focus on ending Hussein's dictatorship—"regime change," in the lingo of administration policy makers—alienated many U.S. allies who wanted more time for U.N. inspectors to search for nuclear weapons. They refused to join what the president called the "coalition of the willing" that eventually went ahead with the invasion. Vice President Dick Cheney predicted Iraqis would welcome the troops, but the relentless religious struggles, the civilian casualties of the insurgency and the general chaos would continue for years.

Enron's Collapse
JANUARY 24, 2002

Enron, an energy-trading company that had once symbolized Texas-size power and wealth in the 1990's, was suddenly synonymous with corporate greed, fraud and corruption. The company collapsed in a Pandora's box of deals involving off-the-books partnerships, which would have been legal if Enron had followed accounting rules. It did not, and as they unraveled, they wiped out years of profits. Top executives including the chief executive, Jeffrey K. Skilling, and the chief financial officer, Andrew S. Fastow, went to prison. Enron's chairman, Kenneth L. Lay, was convicted on fraud and conspiracy charges but died of heart disease before he could be sentenced.

Domestic Security Agency
NOVEMBER 20, 2002

Fourteen months after the Sept. 11 attacks, Congress overwhelmingly approved an administration plan to create a huge new agency responsible for homeland security. The new department absorbed 170,000 employees from 22 other agencies. They added new responsibilities for fighting terror to their old jobs, which included managing the immigration process, protecting the nation's borders and even guarding the president himself. The public hoped for an agency that could respond rapidly to emerging threats. Skeptics worried that the Department of Homeland Security was little more than a giant bureaucracy, but defenders argued that the agency could not easily publicize its successes without jeopardizing secret countermethods.

Widening the Case for War
JANUARY 29, 2003

A year earlier, he had identified Iraq as a potential target for "regime change." Now President George W. Bush detailed his reasons for an attack. He said that intelligence showed that Iraq was aiding terrorists, and that only military action could avert an attack involving weapons of mass destruction. He cited British intelligence as the source of information that Saddam Hussein had "sought significant quantities of uranium from Africa." That turned out to be untrue, and later figured in the investigation of how a covert C.I.A. employee's name became public.

Laying the Groundwork
FEBRUARY 15, 2003

Appearing before the United Nations Security Council, Secretary of State Colin L. Powell put his reputation behind the Bush administration's efforts to win approval for an invasion of Iraq. Powell accused Saddam Hussein's regime of "endlessly" stringing out weapons inspections by denying U.N. teams access to Iraqi defense facilities. Powell did not persuade France, which suggested waiting a month for another report from the inspectors. But the British foreign secretary, Jack Straw, sided with the U.S., saying the Security Council needed to "hold our nerve in the face of this tyrant."

In Control of Baghdad
APRIL 10, 2003

The image that Americans remembered, especially after it had been played over and over on television, was of American marines toppling a larger-than-life statue of Saddam Hussein in Baghdad. That took but a few minutes on the day when they took control of the capital. The dictator himself was on the run, having escaped a coordinated attack by bunker-busting bombs earlier in the week. But Secretary of Defense Donald H. Rumsfeld cautioned that the three-week-old war "most assuredly is not over."

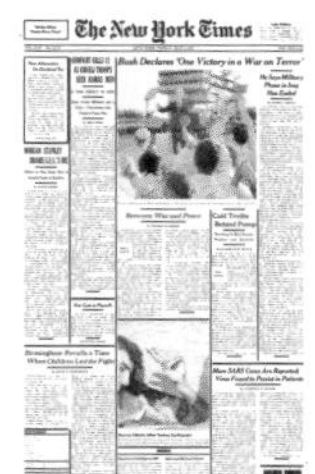

'Mission Accomplished'
MAY 2, 2003

President George W. Bush did something no president had done before—he landed on an aircraft carrier in a fighter jet riding in the co-pilot's seat. He climbed out of the cockpit after the picture-perfect touchdown and delivered a speech in which he declared that "major combat operations in Iraq have ended." But the violence continued, the troops remained on active duty and the casualties climbed as the insurgency showed no sign of winding down.

U.N. Headquarters in Iraq Destroyed
AUGUST 20, 2003

Amid the chaotic bloodshed in Iraq, where an increasingly bold insurgency made Western organizations worry they were a bull's eye, a huge suicide bomb blast demolished the United Nations compound in Baghdad. Among the 17 victims was the highly regarded chief U.N. representative in Iraq, Sergio Vieira de Mello. Later, Al Qaeda in Mesopotamia claimed responsibility for the blast, as well as for an unrelenting campaign of car bombings, mortar attacks, kidnappings and beheadings.

A Victory for Same-Sex Marriage
NOVEMBER 19, 2003

Declaring that the state constitution "forbids the creation of second-class citizens" who could not enter into the same kinds of state-sanctioned unions as heterosexual couples, Massachusetts' highest court legitimized same-sex marriage. The decision opened a new front in the battle over gay marriage, which had been simmering long before the United States Supreme Court had paved the way by overturning a Texas law criminalizing sodomy early in the year. That six-to-three decision did not deal directly with same-sex marriage, but the case, and especially Justice Antonin Scalia's angry dissent, galvanized both gay rights advocates and conservative opponents (who talked of a constitutional amendment defining marriage as a rite involving a man and a woman). In Massachusetts, the court underscored its original decision in 2004, saying that only full marriages, not civil unions, were constitutional.

'We Must Stay the Course'
APRIL 14, 2004

With a well-armed insurgency driving Iraq toward civil war, President George W. Bush said the U.S. would not change course, in part because the conflict was an important part of the broader fight against terrorism. "The defeat of violence and terror in Iraq is vital to the defeat of violence and terror elsewhere," he said, "and vital, therefore, to the safety of the American people."

The Shame of Abu Ghraib
MAY 9, 2004

When Saddam Hussein was in power, the Abu Ghraib prison in Iraq was infamous as a place where Iraqis were tortured. Abu Ghraib became much more widely synonymous with a new and deeper shame as an interrogation center run by American military and intelligence personnel. A general said that prisoners were victims of "sadistic, blatant and wanton criminal abuses." A handful of low-level guards eventually faced charges, including Pfc. Lynndie R. England and her former lover, Pvt. Charles A. Graner Jr., who testified that he had ordered her to lead a prisoner out of a cell on a leash. Some guards complained that they had just been following orders. But an Army judge refused their requests to call top-ranking officers and Pentagon officials including Secretary of Defense Donald H. Rumsfeld as witnesses.

No Ties to Al Qaeda
JUNE 17, 2004

One of President George W. Bush's firmest justifications for the Iraq war were his claims that Saddam Hussein had connections to the Islamic terrorists behind the Sept. 11 attacks. But a bipartisan commission appointed to investigate those charges concluded that there had been no "collaborative relationship" between Hussein and al Qaeda, Osama bin Laden's network of Islamic terror cells. The commission said al Qaeda emissaries had sought Iraq's help in the 1990's, but contrary to what the president and Vice President Dick Cheney had said, Hussein's government either rejected the overtures, or had simply ignored them.

Iraq Had No Illicit Weapons
OCTOBER 7, 2004

The Bush administration had justified its war on Iraq by saying that Saddam Hussein had secret stockpiles of weapons of mass destruction. But David A. Kay, the nuclear specialist who led the fruitless search for unconventional weapons in Iraq after the war began, said the government was "all wrong, probably." His successor as the top American weapons inspector, Charles A. Duelfer, concluded that Iraq had destroyed most of them after the Persian Gulf war in 1991. Duelfer said Iraq had done away with the last of its biological-weapons factories in 1996.

Towering Tsunami
DECEMBER 27, 2004

The earth rumbled deep under the Indian Ocean, creating devastating shock waves—a tsunami that surged toward land at 500 miles an hour. On the beaches in its path, there was no time to escape the 100-foot-high waves—and no warning that tragedy was on the way. More than a quarter of a million people were killed in 14 countries; at least that many were reported missing. Rapid relief operations prevented widespread outbreaks of disease. But as days and weeks went by, hard-hit areas like Aceh province in Sumatra remained a jumble of collapsed buildings and makeshift shelters. Scientists later reported that the earthquake that started it all had registered at least 9.1 on the Richter scale, making it one of the most powerful ever measured.

Pope for a Television Age
APRIL 3, 2005

Pope John Paul II was the first non-Italian pope in 455 years and, as a Times correspondent wrote, "transformed the papacy into a television-ready voice for peace, war and life." His was an abidingly conservative voice on social issues. But he went to unusual lengths to seek forgiveness for the church, apologizing for Catholics' failure to help Jews in the Holocaust and acknowledging sexual abuse by priests in the U.S. He also played a leading role in the fall of Communism. Lech Walesa, the leader of Poland's Solidarity opposition movement, said the pope deserved 50 percent of the credit; Solidarity, 30 percent; and the world situation, the other 20 percent. "He was like Moses," said Przemyslaw Kalicki, standing in the crowd in Krakow when John Paul II's death was announced. "He led us through the Red Sea of Communism."

Katrina's Destruction
AUGUST 31, 2005

Hurricane Katrina left much of New Orleans submerged when water broke through levees. But Katrina was soon remembered for the ineffectual government response; for the fault lines of race and class that were exposed; for the homeless, hungry crowd that sought refuge inside the Superdome; for the rescue helicopters that circled overhead as the water rose; for the camps where people spent long months in government-issued trailers that were supposed to be only short-term homes; and for President George W. Bush's compliment to the head of the Federal Emergency Management Agency: "Brownie, you're doing a heck of a job." The Bush administration soon replaced Michael D. Brown. But the rebuilding dragged on for years amid a population drain that left deep doubts that New Orleans would ever recover.

Libby Indicted
OCTOBER 29, 2005

As Vice President Dick Cheney's chief of staff, I. Lewis Libby Jr. was a trusted, powerful official who had a hand in planning the war in Iraq. But he resigned after he was indicted on charges of lying during an investigation of how the identity of a covert C.I.A. employee was leaked to reporters. Libby was later convicted, but President Bush commuted his two-and-a-half-year prison sentence in 2007.

The New York Times

Demonstrating for Immigrants' Rights

MAY 2, 2006

In a nation that once opened its doors wide to immigrant workers and citizens-to-be, immigration policy had become a divisive political issue—emotionally debated, confusing and sometimes infected by racially tinged rhetoric. Some demanded tighter borders and tighter rules for noncitizens already in the United States—and for employers who hired them. Grass-roots immigrant groups responded with a daylong boycott. Thousands of immigrants skipped work and school and marched in dozens of cities. But they did not bring the nation to a halt, as they had hoped.

The New York Times

Recommending a Shift on Iraq

December 7, 2006

Three and a half years after the American-led invasion of Iraq began, President George W. Bush insisted that the United States was making progress in Iraq. But a bipartisan commission sounded alarm bells, saying the situation there was "grave and deteriorating." The commission, led by former Secretary of State James A. Baker III and former Representative Lee H. Hamilton of Indiana, did not share Mr. Bush's often-repeated faith in Iraq as an eventual centerpiece for democracy in the Mideast. It recommended stepping up efforts to stabilize Iraq. It also recommended remaking the military's mission so the U.S. could "begin to move its combat forces out of Iraq responsibly."

The New York Times

SADDAM HUSSEIN HANGED IN BAGHDAD; SWIFT END TO DRAMA; TROOPS ON ALERT

Saddam Hussein Hanged

DECEMBER 30, 2006

He said he had been chosen by God to rule Iraq forever, and Saddam Hussein outlasted half a dozen American presidents—but not the soldiers who had rolled into Baghdad in 2003 and found him in an underground "hidey hole" near his hometown of Tikrit. Three years later, the Iraqi court established to review the brutalities of his ruthless regime convicted him. That brought a burst of anger from Hussein and his supporters among Iraq's Sunni minority. But the court announced a death sentence, and after he was hanged, people danced in the streets in the heavily Shiite Sadr City section of Baghdad. Declared Jawad Abdul-Aziz, whose father, three brothers and 22 cousins were killed as reprisals for an assassination plot in the 1980's: "Now, he is the garbage of history."

The New York Times

Global Warming Is 'Unequivocal'

FEBRUARY 3, 2007

"There's a lot of differing positions" on global warming, George W. Bush declared during a debate with Al Gore, his opponent in 2000. Seven years later, after the Bush administration had refused to join the emission-reducing Kyoto Protocol, the Intergovernmental Panel on Climate Change called the evidence of global warming "unequivocal." The panel, a United Nations–sponsored network of climate experts, tried not to sound alarmist in outlining its decidedly disturbing predictions: temperatures could rise by up to eight degrees by the end of the 21st century, and oceans would rise 12 feet or more.

The New York Times

Benazir Bhutto Assassinated

DECEMBER 28, 2007

Benazir Bhutto, a former prime minister of Pakistan, had returned from exile to marshal opposition to the increasingly unpopular President Pervez Musharraf, the Bush administration's ally in Islamabad. She was shot to death as she left a political rally in Rawalpindi. With her husband taking over her role as an opposition leader, Musharraf's party was crushed in parliamentary voting, and he soon found himself swearing in a cabinet that included opposition figures who had served prison sentences under his military regime.

The New York Times

After an Election, Bloodletting

FEBRUARY 15, 2008

In the weeks after a disputed election—President Mwai Kibaki defeated Raila Odinga, an opposition leader who claimed to have won the vote—ethnic violence rocked Kenya. Hundreds of thousands were driven from their homes in what had been tribally mixed areas as Kenya segregated itself along new ethnic lines. The government played a part, with police officers accompanying people to what the government called their "ancestral" homes. More than a thousand people, including entire families, were savagely killed with clubs, machetes and guns in clashes along the way. After several weeks the two politicians negotiated a power-sharing arrangement that left Kibaki in charge but made Odinga prime minister. The new cabinet had 20 ministers from each camp. All of them, including Odinga, pledged their loyalty to the president.

The New York Times

Castro Steps Aside

FEBRUARY 20, 2008

Fidel Castro had bedeviled American presidents for almost 50 years on everything from the failed Bay of Pigs invasion to a U.S. trade embargo. He had not been seen in public in more than a year, since he had been hospitalized for surgery that left him frail and weak. Castro did not announce that he was handing power to his younger brother Raúl with the kind of fist-waving, podium-pounding speech he was once famous for. Instead, he sent a brief written notice to a newspaper.

The New York Times

SPITZER RESIGNS

A Disgraced Governor Resigns

MARCH 13, 2008

Governor Eliot Spitzer of New York had made his reputation as a tough-as-nails prosecutor who chased corruption on Wall Street so ferociously that people nicknamed him Eliot Ness. As he threatened and bullied his way through the state capital, he was quoted calling himself a "steamroller" (with a vulgar flourish). But Spitzer, once thought of as having presidential potential, also steamrolled his own career in a way New Yorkers found almost impossible to believe. He was caught in a scandal involving high-priced prostitutes he had patronized and secretive money transfers he had made to pay for out-of-town trysts, not to mention cellphone calls and text messages that the F.B.I. had intercepted.

The New York Times

Bailing Out Bear Stearns

MARCH 15, 2008

It sounded like something out of the Great Depression—a run on tottering Wall Street brokerage house. Bear Stearns was facing crippling losses from mortgage-linked investments, and as the housing slump deepened and the credit crunch tightened, the Federal Reserve feared a chain reaction that would bring down other Wall Street firms. The Fed stepped in to broker a deal to sell Bear Stearns to JPMorgan Chase with a $30 billion line of credit. The bargain price of $2 a share (later sweetened to $10 a share) was a fraction of Bear Stearns' value just months earlier.

The New York Times

Obama's Speech on Race

MARCH 19, 2008

Commentators compared Senator Barack Obama's speech on race and race relations to some of the most celebrated oratory in American political history—John F. Kennedy's 1960 speech on his Catholicism and Franklin D. Roosevelt's inaugural address, for example. Obama, running for the Democratic presidential nomination against Senator Hillary Rodham Clinton, said that "the complexities of race in this country" had never really been "worked through"—and "if we retreat into our respective corners, we will never be able to come together" on other issues. Obama also distanced himself from his former pastor in Chicago, the Rev. Jeremiah A. Wright, whose anti-white and anti-American comments had been turning up on the Internet and on cable-news channels. Obama said Reverend Wright's remarks "rightly offend white and black alike." Still, Obama added, "imperfect as he may be, he has been like family to me."

"All the News That's Fit to Print"

The New York Times

Late Edition
New York: **Today**, partly sunny, high 85. **Tonight**, partly cloudy, low 73. **Tomorrow**, partly sunny, hot and humid, high 92. **Yesterday**, high 91, low 75. Weather map appears on Page D8.

VOL. CL . . No. 51,799 · Copyright © 2001 The New York Times · NEW YORK, FRIDAY, JUNE 29, 2001 · $1 beyond the greater New York metropolitan area. · 75 CENTS

MILOSEVIC IS GIVEN TO U.N. FOR TRIAL IN WAR-CRIME CASE

IN PRISON AT HAGUE

Quick Move by Serbs to Turn Him Over Shows Rifts in Belgrade

By MARLISE SIMONS with CARLOTTA GALL

THE HAGUE, the Netherlands, Friday, June 29 — Slobodan Milosevic, the Yugoslav leader blamed for starting four Balkan wars and impoverishing and isolating his country, was delivered early this morning to a prison cell and eventual trial by the United Nations war crimes tribunal here.

Mr. Milosevic, who was indicted during the 1999 war over Kosovo on charges that his security forces committed war crimes in that province, was the first former head of state delivered by a government to face an international war crimes court.

The decision to send him to trial abroad caused deep divisions in Belgrade, both among the democratic leaders elected to replace him last fall and Serbs in general.

The transfer was executed swiftly by the Serbian government without even informing Mr. Milosevic's successor as Yugoslav president, Vojislav Kostunica. On a downtown Belgrade square that had been the scene of many pro- and anti-Milosevic demonstrations through his violent 13 years of power, thousands of his supporters gathered to vent their anger.

On Thursday evening, as Prime Minister Zoran Djindjic of Serbia was announcing the surprising transfer, Mr. Milosevic was whisked in a police van from his Belgrade jail and flown on a Serbian government helicopter to an American air base in Tuzla, Bosnia, and from there to a military airfield near The Hague, the seat of the tribunal.

From there, a helicopter took him to a large jail compound, where hundreds of bystanders, many of them exiles driven by war from the former Yugoslavia, applauded outside the prison walls.

Mr. Milosevic was transferred exactly 10 years after the outbreak of war in Slovenia and Croatia, which had declared independence from the old Communist Yugoslavia, and on the fated Serbian holiday of Vidovdan, or St. Vitus's Day, the date in 1389 when Serbs lost a key battle in Kosovo. It was on the 600th anniversary of that battle, on June 28, 1989, that Mr. Milosevic addressed close to a million Serbs in Kosovo, promising to defend their interests, through war if necessary.

There was an immense international outpouring of relief that Mr. Milosevic was in the hands of those who hold him responsible for the

Continued on Page A12

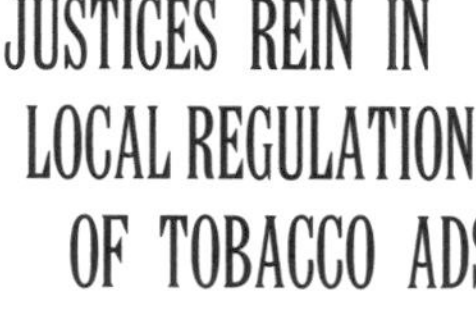

Associated Press

Challenge for a Tribunal
Slobodan Milosevic's trial will test a new system of international law. News analysis, Page A12.

Powell Backing Plan to Monitor Mideast Truce

By JANE PERLEZ

JERUSALEM, June 28 — Secretary of State Colin L. Powell said today that observers would be needed to monitor a cease-fire between Israelis and Palestinians. Then, as he prepared to end his 36-hour visit, Secretary Powell announced a seven-week timetable for the two sides to end hostilities and move toward political talks.

The timetable called on both sides to prevent all clashes for seven days, and, if that succeeded, to enter into a six-week "cooling off" period. The plan was effectively a combination of Israeli Prime Minister Ariel Sharon's insistence that Israel would not agree to any further measures until there had been a week without violence, and the notion that the two sides would need several weeks in which to retreat from the bitter hostility and bloodshed of the past nine months.

How the reduction of violence would be measured, however, remained unclear. Secretary Powell said only that it was "the two parties that will have to decide together." Mr. Sharon said he expected "complete quiet" during both the seven-day and subsequent six-week period.

The fragility of the plan was promptly demonstrated when a Jewish settler was shot dead on the West

Continued on Page A6

JUSTICES REIN IN LOCAL REGULATION OF TOBACCO ADS

SWEEPING BAN REJECTED

Court Invokes Federal Statute and Manufacturers' Rights to Commercial Speech

By LINDA GREENHOUSE

WASHINGTON, June 28 — The Supreme Court today placed significant limits on the ability of state and local governments to regulate tobacco advertising in a case from Massachusetts that also appeared to invalidate a similar law in New York City.

All nine justices agreed that smoking by children was a serious public health problem that government policies could appropriately address. But invoking an amalgam of statutory and constitutional reasons, all nine also found invalid the core of a sweeping tobacco advertising ban that was adopted two years ago in Massachusetts and was the most far-reaching of any state.

The decision was a victory for the tobacco industry as well as for the advertising industry, which had argued on behalf of the cigarette makers for a vigorous First Amendment protection for advertising.

The Massachusetts restrictions, for example banning all advertising, even in shop windows, that could be seen within a 1,000-foot radius of schools and playgrounds, went considerably beyond those in the 1998 settlement between 4 major cigarette manufacturers and 46 states.

While the ruling today does not threaten that settlement, it could complicate efforts to go further at the federal as well as state level. Although the industry has not challenged the 32-year-old federal ban on cigarette advertising on radio and television, the court's constitutional analysis of the industry's right to market its products to an adult audience would appear to make the ban vulnerable if it were attacked on First Amendment grounds.

With a majority opinion by Justice Sandra Day O'Connor, the decision today overturned a ruling issued last year by the United States Court of Appeals for the First Circuit, in Boston, which rejected challenges brought against the Massachusetts regulations by makers of cigarettes, smokeless tobacco and cigars. This array of plaintiffs complicated the case for the Supreme Court because federal pre-emption, one basis for the cigarette industry's challenge, did not apply to the other two branches of the tobacco industry.

The argument was that a 1965 federal law, the Federal Cigarette Labeling and Advertising Act, preempts state regulation by providing

Continued on Page A21

APPEALS COURT VOIDS ORDER FOR BREAKING UP MICROSOFT BUT FINDS IT ABUSED POWER

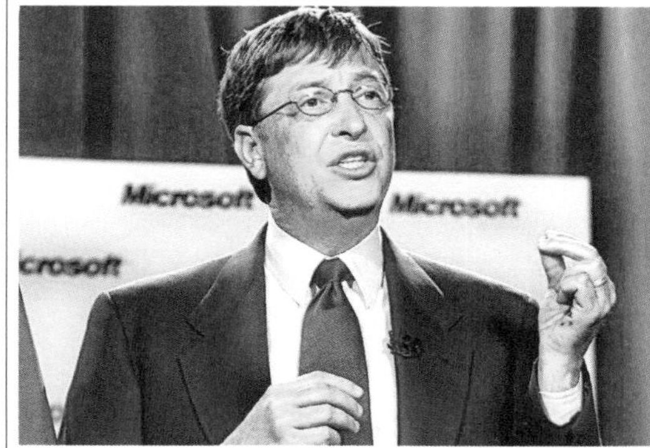

Reuters

William H. Gates said yesterday he hoped for new settlement talks.

WHAT THE APPELLATE COURT SAID ABOUT THE MONOPOLY . . .

"We uphold the District Court's finding of monopoly power in its entirety."

THE BREAKUP . . .

"The District Court must reconsider whether the use of the structural remedy of divestiture is appropriate . . . While we do not undertake to dictate to the District Court the precise form that relief should take on remand, we note again that it should be tailored to fit the wrong creating the occasion for the remedy."

. . . AND JUDGE JACKSON'S CONDUCT.

"The violations were deliberate, repeated, egregious and flagrant. . . . Public confidence in judicial impartiality cannot survive if judges, in disregard of their ethical obligations, pander to the press."

Excerpts from ruling, Page C8.

UNANIMOUS RULING

Sharp Rebuke Is Leveled at Judge in Charge of the Original Case

By STEPHEN LABATON

WASHINGTON, June 28 — A federal appeals court unanimously threw out a lower court's order today that the Microsoft Corporation should be broken up, although the appeals court found that the company had repeatedly abused its monopoly power in the software business.

The appeals court also sharply chastised the district judge who oversaw the Microsoft antitrust trial and removed him from any further involvement in the case because of derogatory comments he made to reporters about the company and its senior executives.

The unsigned opinion was welcomed by Microsoft, which is no longer under immediate threat of being split into two companies. The company is already preparing the release of a new version of the Windows software operating system, which has features that industry executives say could further consolidate Microsoft's dominance of the personal computer software market. [Page C1.]

But the opinion was also hailed by federal and state officials for affirming the principle that Microsoft had bullied smaller software rivals, computer makers and other large companies like the chip maker Intel, and had broken the law in ways that stifled competition.

Among other companies in the computer industry, reaction was muted, as many executives said they needed time to study the opinion.

Justice Department officials, some state attorneys general, and Microsoft executives said today that they had not decided what they would do next — although Microsoft's chairman, William H. Gates, said he hoped the ruling might open the way to new settlement talks.

The parties now have three options:

¶They can appeal to the Supreme Court.

¶They can proceed to a new trial before a different district judge to consider some of the unresolved antitrust liability questions and reconsider an appropriate remedy.

¶Or they can reopen settlement negotiations, which failed during the Clinton administration but which Microsoft executives hope can be rekindled with the new leadership at the Justice Department.

Ari Fleischer, the White House spokesman, said that President Bush had been told of the decision this morning and would now await guidance from the Justice Department about how to proceed.

Officials at the Justice Department said they were pleased but had not decided which avenue to pursue.

"We believe this is a significant victory in terms of the determination

Continued on Page C7

Supreme Court Limits Detention In Cases of Deportable Immigrants

By LINDA GREENHOUSE

WASHINGTON, June 28 — In its second decision this week affirming the rights of immigrants, the Supreme Court ruled today that the government may not detain deportable aliens indefinitely simply for lack of a country willing to take them.

The 5-to-4 decision rejected the government's view, as argued by both the Clinton and Bush administrations, that immigration law authorized and the Constitution permitted indefinite, even lifelong detention of immigrants adjudged deportable but unable to be repatriated.

Justice Stephen G. Breyer's majority opinion said that because interpreting the law in that way would present a "serious constitutional threat" under the Fifth Amendment's guarantee of due process, the court would construe the law to permit only "reasonable" detention. Justice Breyer said that after six months of detention, if deportation did not seem likely in the "reasonably foreseeable future," the government would have to come up with special reasons for keeping someone in custody. [Excerpts, Page A20.]

Justice Anthony M. Kennedy objected in dissent that the court was unwisely substituting "judicial judgment for the executive's discretion and authority," in effect establishing a rule that after six months, "foreign relations go into judicially supervised receivership."

The immigration decision, along with three others, came on the final day of the court's 2000-1 term, a quiet day devoid of the fireworks of the closing days in recent years that were marked by justices' reading angry dissents from the bench. Chief Justice William H. Rehnquist was not in court, instead attending a judicial conference in Hot Springs, Va.

Continued on Page A20

Jack Lemmon, Dark and Comic Actor, Dies at 76

By ALJEAN HARMETZ

Jack Lemmon, the brash young American Everyman who evolved into the screen's grumpiest old Everyman during a movie career that lasted a half century, died on Wednesday at a hospital in Los Angeles. He was 76 and lived in Beverly Hills.

The cause was complications from cancer, said a spokesman, Warren Cowan.

Through most of his more than 60 movies, Mr. Lemmon was the least glamorous and most approachable of movie stars — the good-natured, ordinary guy next door with a slightly skewed moral compass. He was a master of sardonic comedy and could convey urban frustrations so deftly that audiences identified with him and thus were able to laugh at themselves.

As C.C. Baxter in "The Apartment" (1960), Billy Wilder's Academy Award-winning film, he created the definitive comic hero for an age of anxiety, an office worker so eager to win a promotion that he lends his apartment to his married bosses for weekly trysts with their secretaries. As a lecherous landlord in "Under the Yum Yum Tree" (1963), he rented apartments only to pretty and, he hoped, compliant women.

As Ensign Pulver in "Mister Roberts" (1955), a performance that gained him an Oscar for best supporting actor, he was a callow but likable wheeler-dealer. As a policeman turned pimp in Mr. Wilder's "Irma la Douce" (1963), he was so bewitched by a prostitute that he tricked her by becoming her lover in disguise. And in one of his most memorable roles, as a musician forced to dress up as a woman to escape gangsters in Mr. Wilder's "Some Like It Hot" (1959), he got

Everett Collection

Jack Lemmon in "The Apartment," one of his Oscar-nominated roles.

engaged to another man (played by Joe E. Brown) because it was his only chance to marry a millionaire.

"Some Like It Hot" ended with a classic last line. When Mr. Lemmon, as Daphne, finally tells the millionaire that he is a man, Brown's response is, "Nobody's perfect."

Roles that would have been distasteful in the hands of another actor were redeemed by Mr. Lemmon's keen and agile clowning, bedrock affability, cherubic face and jaunty smile. The critic Pauline Kael found him "demoniacally funny" in "Some Like It Hot," while Stanley Kauffmann described him as "easily one of the most expert American actors

Continued on Page B7

Giuliani May Leave Mansion To Escape Marital Tensions

By ELISABETH BUMILLER

Mayor Rudolph W. Giuliani is considering moving out of Gracie Mansion to escape the tension in his failed marriage, a City Hall official said yesterday.

The official said it was not clear where Mr. Giuliani would live if he were to leave the 200-year-old Federal-style mansion, the mayor's official residence on the Upper East Side of Manhattan. But in recent weeks, the official said, Mr. Giuliani has been staying overnight at the East 57th Street apartment of Howard Koeppel, a political supporter and Queens car dealer, as well as at the homes of other friends.

The mayor's sleepovers at Mr. Koeppel's apartment were first reported in yesterday's Daily News, which had 17 reporters and interns working on the story, including a team that staked out Mr. Koeppel's high-rise morning and night for the last two weeks.

Donna Hanover, the mayor's estranged wife, continues to live in the relatively small family quarters of Gracie Mansion with the couple's two children, Andrew, 15, and Caroline, 11. The mayor had been using a guest room. His divorce lawyer, Raoul L. Felder, has said that Ms. Hanover's use of noisy exercise equipment has awakened the mayor as early as 5 a.m.

The mayor himself did not directly answer questions at a City Hall news conference yesterday about his sleeping arrangements. "I really am not going to discuss it," Mr. Giuliani said. "I think that relates to my personal life. I have to make choices about my personal life, like everybody does, in order to be healthy, and feel comfortable, and do what I think is the right thing."

Mr. Giuliani, who was barred by a judge last month from bringing his

Continued on Page B3

INSIDE

North Koreans Leave China
Seven North Koreans who were seeking asylum in a United Nations office in Beijing were allowed to leave China for a third country. PAGE A10

Retracing a Trail of Violence
School was out in Paterson, N.J., and tradition called for trouble. A man whom several youths described as a bum was beaten to death. PAGE B1

Curbing Price of Power
The federal government agreed to allow New York to limit spikes in electricity prices to prevent soaring rates this summer. PAGE B1

Marbury Traded for Kidd
In an exchange of point guards, the Nets sent Stephon Marbury to Phoenix for Jason Kidd. PAGE D1

Updated news: www.nytimes.com

"All the News That's Fit to Print"

The New York Times

Late Edition
New York: **Today**, hazy, hot and humid, high 93. **Tonight**, muggy, low 77. **Tomorrow**, hazy sunshine, late thunder possible, high 89. **Yesterday**, high 88, low 60. Weather map, Page D8.

VOL. CL . . No. 51,824 NEW YORK, TUESDAY, JULY 24, 2001 — $1 beyond the greater New York metropolitan area. — 75 CENTS

BUSH PANEL BACKS LEGALIZING STATUS OF SOME MIGRANTS

MEXICANS TO BE ELIGIBLE

Proposal May Aid One Million People but the Exact Terms Have Not Yet Been Set

By ERIC SCHMITT

WASHINGTON, July 23 — A cabinet-level panel has recommended that President Bush endorse a limited plan allowing some of the estimated three million Mexicans living in the United States illegally to apply for permanent legal status, a White House spokesman said today.

Some administration officials and outside experts said that perhaps one million to two million of the illegal Mexican immigrants might ultimately meet eligibility requirements, based on their job history and how long they have been here. The exact terms have not been determined, administration officials said.

Even so, such a program, if adopted by Congress, would be one of the largest attempts to legalize the status of illegal residents in American history. A 1986 law granted legal status to about three million illegal immigrants from several countries.

In a confidential one-page memorandum sent to the White House late on Friday, a working group headed by Secretary of State Colin L. Powell and Attorney General John Ashcroft addressed, at least for now, only unlawful Mexicans, who make up the bulk of the estimated seven million to eight million illegal immigrants in the United States.

Democrats and immigrant groups have urged the administration to expand any legalization plan to include illegal immigrants from other countries.

A White House spokesman, Scott McClellan, said no decisions had been made on that issue or on many other details of the proposal.

The stakes are high for Mr. Bush. He is trying to remake relations with Mexico and at the same time court Latino voters who would be crucial to any re-election bid in 2004.

The legalization plan is the most sensitive result of broader discussions on border and migration issues that Mr. Bush and President Vicente Fox of Mexico began in February. Secretary Powell and Mr. Ashcroft, and their Mexican counterparts, were delegated to develop recommendations before the two presidents meet in Washington in early September.

Allowing illegal immigrants to change their status would be a central component of a new, ambitious temporary-worker program that American and Mexican officials are discussing. It would let some unlawful Mexicans living in the United States legalize their status and also permit future migrants to earn legal residency.

"The panel recommends consider-

Continued on Page A14

Pool photo by Paolo Cocco via Associated Press

President Bush and Pope John Paul II meeting yesterday at the papal summer residence at Castel Gandolfo.

Indonesia Gets A New Leader; Ex-Chief Balks

By SETH MYDANS

JAKARTA, Indonesia, July 23 — In the most peaceful transfer of power in Indonesia's history, Megawati Sukarnoputri was sworn in as president today, moments after the nation's top legislative body voted to cut short the fractious and rudderless tenure of her predecessor.

But in a historical novelty, Indonesia, the world's fourth-most-populous nation, was left with two claimants to the presidency as Abdurrahman Wahid refused to recognize the action to remove him and remained isolated in his official residence.

With his power having vanished literally overnight, his ministers resigning one after another and the crowds of supporters he had counted on failing to materialize, Mr. Wahid, 61, made no public statement today. He appeared for a moment as evening fell, waving forlornly from the palace veranda, dressed in a pair of striped shorts and a white polo shirt.

His aides said he had no intention of making way for Mrs. Megawati, and government officials said there were no immediate plans to force him to leave.

Mrs. Megawati, the daughter of Indonesia's founding president, Sukarno, appears to have felt that it was her destiny eventually to inherit his mantle. But as a politician, she has remained detached from the fray. [Woman in the news, Page A9.]

Mr. Wahid is the first Indonesian president to cling to office once it became clear that his power was

Continued on Page A9

Bush Hears Pope Condemn Research in Human Embryos

By ALESSANDRA STANLEY

CASTEL GANDOLFO, Italy, July 23 — President Bush, facing a decision whether to allow federal financing for research using human embryo cells, heard an appeal today from Pope John Paul II to "reject practices that devalue and violate human life at any stage from conception until natural death."

The pope made his statement after meeting Mr. Bush at the papal summer residence here outside Rome, declaring that this path was the obligation of "a free and virtuous society, which America aspires to be." He specifically declared that the creation of human embryos for research purposes, which some American scientists have begun doing, was an evil akin to euthanasia and infanticide. [Excerpts, Page A8.]

Though the pope did not specifically address the decision that Mr. Bush is facing, the president said at a news conference that he would take the pope's words into "consideration," but stressed that he had no intention of being rushed into a decision.

Whether he should allow federal financing for some forms of embryonic stem cell research, a pledge Mr. Bush made during the campaign, is one of the most politically delicate decisions facing the president.

"I take this issue very seriously," Mr. Bush said, "because it is an issue that, on the one hand, deals with so much hope, hope that perhaps through research and development we'll be able to save lives. It's also an issue that has got serious moral implications, and our nation must think carefully before we proceed."

He added: "And, therefore, my process has been, frankly, unusually deliberative for my administration. I'm taking my time."

While research on embryonic stem cells usually involves the use of frozen embryos, some American scientists created a stir this month when they disclosed that they had mixed eggs and sperm for the express purpose of extracting stem cells from

Continued on Page A8

178 NATIONS REACH A CLIMATE ACCORD; U.S. ONLY LOOKS ON

A Compromise to Curb Emissions Linked to Global Warming

By ANDREW C. REVKIN

BONN, July 23 — With the Bush administration on the sidelines, the world's leading countries hammered out a compromise agreement today finishing a treaty that for the first time would formally require industrialized countries to cut emissions of gases linked to global warming.

The agreement, which was announced here today after three days of marathon bargaining, rescued the Kyoto Protocol, the preliminary accord framed in Japan in 1997, that was the first step toward requiring cuts in such gases. That agreement has been repudiated by President Bush, who has called it "fatally flawed," saying it places too much of the cleanup burden on industrial countries and would be too costly to the American economy.

Today, his national security adviser, Condoleezza Rice, said in Rome, where the president met with the pope, "I don't believe that it is a surprise to anyone that the United States believes that this particular protocol is not in its interests, nor do we believe that it really addresses the problem of global climate change." She reiterated that the president had created a task force to come up with alternatives.

The agreement by 178 countries was largely the product of give and take involving Japan, Australia, Canada and the European Union. But Japan's role was crucial because it is the largest economy after the United States and its opposition would have killed any agreement.

Largely as a result of concessions to Japan, the product is a significantly softened version of the Kyoto accord, allowing industrial nations with the greatest emissions of greenhouse gases, principally carbon dioxide, to achieve their cuts with greater flexibility. For example, Japan won a provision to receive credits for reducing the gases by protecting forests that absorb carbon dioxide.

Still, the agreement is a binding contract among nations — excluding the United States — under which 38 industrialized countries must reduce those emissions by 2012 or face tougher emissions goals. Those countries now account for close to half of the emissions. The agreement now moves to a complex ratification process that calls for approval from the biggest polluting countries, which can be achieved even with United States opposition.

Officials from the European Union exulted over the compromise. Olivier Deleuze, the energy and sustainability secretary of Belgium, said there were easily 10 things in the final texts that he could criticize. "But," he said, "I prefer an imperfect agreement that is living than a perfect agreement that doesn't exist."

The Kyoto accord calls for the 38 industrialized countries by 2012 to reduce their combined annual gas emissions to 5.2 percent below levels measured in 1990. It set a different, negotiated target for each, with Ja-

Continued on Page A11

Agency Eases Research Ban At University

By JAMES GLANZ

BALTIMORE, July 23 — A federal agency investigating the death of a volunteer in a research study at Johns Hopkins University announced today that it was easing its four-day-old suspension of research experiments involving human subjects at the university.

But because of strict conditions imposed by the agency, the Office for Human Research Protections, most of the thousands of studies that were suspended are unlikely to resume for weeks or months as they undergo comprehensive new reviews by panels at the university and officials at the agency.

Still, some studies involving either minimal risks to subjects or treatments of gravely ill patients — for example, those taking experimental cancer drugs — may go forward almost immediately, the agency said.

Although some of those exemptions already existed, Hopkins officials generally praised the decision.

"We're extremely glad this has been lifted," said Dr. Chi Van Dang, vice dean for research at Hopkins.

University officials had excoriated the agency for imposing the suspension last Thursday, calling that decision outrageous and excessive. Today, Dr. Dang said he hoped that negotiations would succeed in further loosening the restrictions.

"There should be additional dialogue," Dr. Dang said.

Despite the quick turnaround, Dr. Arthur Caplan, an ethicist at the University of Pennsylvania, said that the episode at Johns Hopkins, which followed recent suspensions of human research at Duke University, Penn

Continued on Page A14

Eudora Welty, a Lyrical Master Of the Short Story, Is Dead at 92

Thomas Victor

Eudora Welty in 1980.

By ALBIN KREBS

Eudora Welty, whose evocative short stories, notable for their imagery, sharp dialogue and fierce wit, made her a revered figure in contemporary American letters, died yesterday at a hospital near her home in Jackson, Miss. She was 92.

She was plagued by health problems and had been confined for some time to her home, where she had lived since high school and where she wrote most of her stories, novels, essays, memoirs and book reviews.

As a short-story master, Miss Welty is often mentioned by critics in the same breath as Chekhov, but she was dismissed early in her career as a regionalist and did not earn widespread critical respect until she was no longer young. When recognition came, she accepted it with the ease, modesty and grace that had become her hallmarks.

She was awarded a Pulitzer Prize in 1973 for her novel "The Optimist's Daughter." She also received the National Book Critics Circle Award, the American Book Award, several O. Henry Awards and the Gold Medal of the National Institute of Arts and Letters. She was inducted into the French Legion of Honor and received the Medal of Freedom in 1980, presented, she said happily, by "one of my great Southern heroes, President Jimmy Carter."

Late in 1998 Miss Welty said she

Continued on Page B8

Pool photo by Bill O'Leary, via Agence France-Presse

Paying Tribute to Katharine Graham

The Clintons were among those at the funeral yesterday at Washington National Cathedral. Vice President Dick Cheney and his wife, Lynne, bowed as her coffin passed. Gov. George E. Pataki, behind Senator Hillary Rodham Clinton, and Mayor Rudolph W. Giuliani, right, also attended. Page B9.

3 Girls, Trapped in Surf at Rockaways, Drown

By RICHARD LEZIN JONES

Four cousins wading in knee-deep water at a beach in Far Rockaway, Queens, were swept away yesterday by the fierce currents that have killed so many swimmers there. While their uncle and scores of other people watched helplessly from the shore, a boy struggled back to safety, but three girls were all pulled underwater and drowned.

The girls — two sisters, Jubeda and Shajeda Ahmed, ages 16 and 12, and their cousin Rahela Begum, 13 — had gone into the water with the boy, Rizwan Islam, 11, more than an hour before city lifeguards arrived for their 10 a.m. shift at the public beach, the authorities said.

The body of Miss Begum was recovered near the Atlantic Beach Bridge about a half-mile away from where they disappeared under the surf. The authorities said the other two girls were presumed to have also drowned.

A battalion of rescue workers in the water, in the air and along the shore searched all day and into the evening, but there was no sign of the other girls. The search was to resume at 9 a.m. today. One diver said the search was slowed by a strong current that churned underwater debris, making it difficult to see. "It's like a sandstorm down there," he said.

Every summer, city officials warn against swimming at public beaches without lifeguards, but three to five people die each year citywide, from Coney Island in Brooklyn to Orchard Beach in the Bronx. The stretch of Rockaway beach where the girls died was the same place where a Manhattan woman and her 6-year-old daughter drowned a year ago. Locals call it the death trap, and few dare to swim there, even with lifeguards.

The girls had gone to the beach

Continued on Page B3

INSIDE

Germ Arms Pact Revisited

European nations urged the completion of a draft agreement to enforce the 1972 ban on biological weapons. The Bush administration has concluded the accord is flawed. **PAGE A11**

Patients' Rights Showdown

House Republican aides said they did not yet have the votes to defeat a bipartisan patients' bill of rights supported by Democrats and opposed by President Bush. **PAGE A15**

A Mixed Picture of Police

City residents disagree on whether the relationship between the police and the communities they serve has improved since the torture of Abner Louima in 1997. **PAGE B1**

Working on New Life Forms

Scientists are taking the first steps toward creating alternative life forms that have genetic codes different from all other creatures on earth. **SCIENCE TIMES, PAGE F1**

Updated news: www.nytimes.com

"All the News That's Fit to Print"

The New York Times

Late Edition
New York: **Today**, sunny and very cool, high 54. **Tonight**, clear with light winds, low 39. **Tomorrow**, sunny and milder, high 60. **Yesterday**, high 56, low 46. Weather map, Page D10.

VOL. CLI . . No. 51,900 NEW YORK, MONDAY, OCTOBER 8, 2001 $1 beyond the greater New York metropolitan area. 75 CENTS

U.S. AND BRITAIN STRIKE AFGHANISTAN, AIMING AT BASES AND TERRORIST CAMPS; BUSH WARNS 'TALIBAN WILL PAY A PRICE'

Home Front: Edgy Sunday

Nagging Uncertainty About Consequences

By R. W. APPLE Jr.

News Analysis

WASHINGTON, Oct. 7 — When the word came that the waiting had ended, first from Kabul, then from officials at the Pentagon and finally from President Bush, it came on a pristine fall Sunday, "a perfect day for football," as the announcers like to say, just as many people were sitting down in front of their television sets for their weekly dose of gridiron glory.

The president looked stern and sounded resolute as he told the American people that "the battle is now joined on many fronts" and promised "sustained, comprehensive and relentless operations" to bring to justice those responsible for the Sept. 11 attacks. But it was not easy to grasp all the implications, even as the generals and the politicians talked of precision munitions and the suppression of enemy air defenses in Afghanistan, a little-known country 7,000 miles away.

So a superficial sort of normality quickly reasserted itself, as it did after the shocking news that came on another Sunday — Dec. 7, 1941. Shoppers resumed shopping, and the football telecasts went on as scheduled.

But as Americans turned their attention back to watching football this afternoon, much of the country was unsettled. No matter how hard they try not to, no matter how steadfast they may consider themselves, millions of Americans fear retaliation. Even before the bombs burst all across Afghanistan, they were busy buying gas masks and antibiotics. Promising to take every precaution, Mr. Bush still made the remarkable concession that "many Americans feel fear today."

Never before has the United States launched a military campaign against such an elusive and hydra-headed foe, with so little clarity about precisely how it will prevail. And not since the War of 1812 has a foreign threat to the American homeland been quite so palpable. It was "a moment of utmost gravity," as Prime Minister Tony Blair of Great Britain said, a moment for the

Continued on Page B2

Associated Press Television News

'To all the men and women in our military — every sailor, every soldier, every airman, every coast guardsman, every marine — I say this: Your mission is defined, your objectives are clear, your goal is just.'

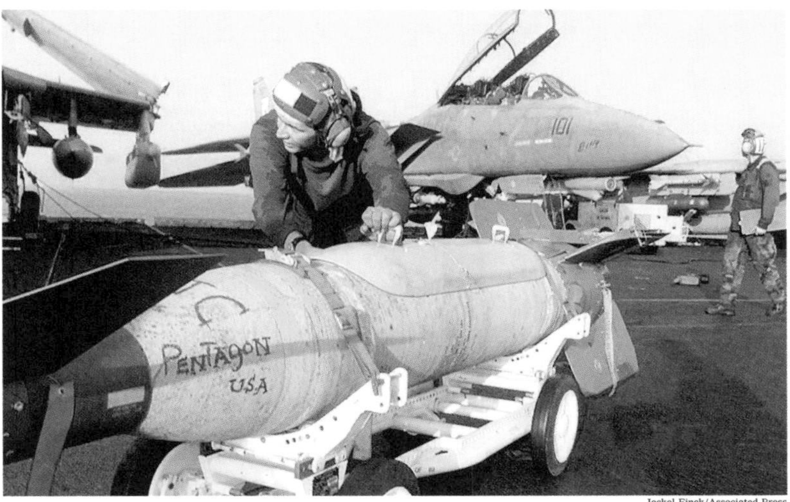

Jockel Finck/Associated Press

A bomb with a message was moved into position on the U.S.S. Enterprise in preparation for yesterday's strikes.

Bomb and Missile Attacks — Bin Laden Issues Threat

By PATRICK E. TYLER

WASHINGTON, Oct. 7 — Striking at night from aircraft carriers and distant bases, the United States and Britain launched a powerful barrage of cruise missiles and long-range bombers against Afghanistan today to try to destroy the terrorist training camps of Osama bin Laden's Qaeda network and the Taliban government that has protected it.

"On my orders, the United States military has begun strikes," President Bush said in a televised statement from the White House at 1 p.m., just more than half an hour after the first explosions were reported in Kabul, the Afghan capital.

"These carefully targeted actions are designed to disrupt the use of Afghanistan as a terrorist base of operations and to attack the military capability of the Taliban regime," Mr. Bush said.

The Taliban was warned, he said, to meet America's demands to surrender Mr. bin Laden, stop supporting terrorism and release foreign aid workers they hold. "None of these demands were met," he said. "And now, the Taliban will pay a price."

"Today we focus on Afghanistan," he added, but "the battle is broader." Alluding to the Sept. 11 terror attacks that destroyed the World Trade Center, damaged the Pentagon and killed more than 5,000 people, Mr. Bush again warned that nations that sponsor or protect "outlaws and killers of innocents" will "take that lonely path at their own peril."

The skies over Kabul lit up with flashes, and thunderous explosions rumbled through the night, witnesses said. The Taliban fired antiaircraft guns into the dark sky, and their tracers could be seen by residents of the capital and around the cities of Kandahar and Jalalabad, strongholds of the radical Islamic regime.

Mr. Bush's statement was followed by one from Prime Minister Tony Blair of Britain. Both leaders emphasized that the military campaign was not "a war with Islam," as Mr. Blair asserted, though no Muslim country took part directly in the attacks and many refused to allow offensive operations to be staged from their territory.

Mr. Bush said "we are the friends of almost a billion" people worldwide "who practice the Islamic faith."

Defense Secretary Donald H. Rumsfeld noted that the United States had sent its armed forces five times in the last decade to defend oppressed Muslim populations — in Kuwait, northern Iraq, Somalia, Bosnia and Kosovo.

Shortly after Mr. Bush spoke, Mr. bin Laden issued his own threat. On what appeared to be a recorded videotape beamed worldwide by CNN, he staked a claim to lead all Muslims in the fight against America, casting it as the murderer of Iraqis and of Palestinians oppressed by Israel, America's friend.

Mr. bin Laden blessed the hijack-

Continued on Page B3

Routine Start In Novel War

Trying to Tilt Balance Against Elusive Foe

By MICHAEL R. GORDON

Military Analysis

WASHINGTON, Oct. 7 — The principal aim of the airstrikes unleashed today is to tilt the balance of power within Afghanistan against the Taliban and give American-led forces unchallenged command of the skies for the difficult mission to come.

American and British forces attacked the standard targets: command posts, air defenses, aircraft, electrical plants and terrorist training bases in bombing and cruise missile attacks, which Pentagon officials indicated could last a week or more.

But this is the easy part.

The more difficult task will be hunting down Osama bin Laden and helping the anti-Taliban foes within Afghanistan install a new government. In effect, the airstrikes were a conventional start to an entirely unconventional conflict.

Defense Secretary Donald H. Rumsfeld signaled as much today when he told reporters that the "so-called war" was notably different from previous conflicts that American forces had fought with Iraq and Serbia.

As Mr. Rumsfeld put it, "In this battle against terrorism there is no silver bullet."

The United States' adversary is a hodgepodge of forces with unsophisticated arms and loose command and control. Nonetheless, they are a threat, and the Pentagon leadership is not assuming that its foes will

Continued on Page B2

Bin Laden Taunts U.S. and Praises Hijackers

By JOHN F. BURNS

ISLAMABAD, Pakistan, Oct. 7 — Within hours of the first American bombs' dropping on Afghanistan, the world's most wanted man, Osama bin Laden, appeared in a videotape broadcast worldwide in which he taunted the United States and celebrated the Sept. 11 terrorist attacks.

Sitting calmly in a rocky outcrop, Mr. bin Laden, the man accused of orchestrating the attacks, vowed that "America will not live in peace" as long as the goals of his extremist Islamic group remain unmet.

"Here is America struck by Almighty God in one of its vital organs, so that its greatest buildings are destroyed," Mr. bin Laden said, referring to the attacks in which hijacked airliners rammed into the World Trade Center and the Pentagon, killing several thousand people. "Grace and gratitude to God."

Although there was no date on the tape, and no immediate way of establishing where it was made, it appeared to have been carefully prepared so as to have the maximum effect the moment American military operations against Mr. bin Laden and the Taliban rulers of Afghanistan began. In this sense, it suggested a sophisticated enemy, well aware of how modern wars are fought.

Mr. bin Laden said: "America has been filled with horror from north to south and east to west, and thanks be to God. What America is tasting now is only a copy of what we have tasted. Our Islamic nation has been tasting the same for more than 80 years, of humiliation and disgrace, its sons killed and their blood spilled, its sanctities desecrated."

The reference to 80 years appeared to be invoking the Western colonization of Arab lands. The entire broadcast was infused with calls based on the argument that Islam has long been humiliated. "These events have split the whole world into two camps," he said. "The camp of belief and the camp of disbelief."

It amounted to an evident attempt to rally the entire Islamic world against the United States — an outcome that the Bush administration and its allies have sought to avoid by saying their argument is with terrorists, not with Islam, and by reaching out to Arab states.

In the tape, Mr. bin Laden, a Saudi-born fugitive, heaped praise on the 19 Arab men identified by American investigators as having hijacked the airliners used in the Sept. 11 attacks. "God has blessed a group of vanguard Muslims, the forefront of Islam, to destroy America," he said. "May God bless them and allot them a supreme place in heaven, for he is

Continued on Page B7

Al Jazeera via Associated Press

In a videotape, Osama bin Laden asked God to bless the hijackers.

FOR HOME DELIVERY CALL 1-800-NYTIMES

0 354613 9 41101

Tension and Secrecy on Warships As the Jets and Missiles Roar Off

By DOUGLAS JEHL

ABOARD U.S.S. ENTERPRISE, in the Arabian Sea, Monday, Oct. 8 — With crew members crowded onto the observation deck in nervous excitement, strike aircraft roared off the flight deck here at 10:20 on Sunday night, four hours after the first wave of the American attack began on Afghan targets.

Warplanes, including a pair of F-14's heavily laden with munitions, took off in a fiery thrust of afterburners and then disappeared into the night sky. Tomahawk cruise missiles soared into the sky from a nearby guided-missile cruiser, presumed to be the Philippine Sea.

On the Enterprise there was a mood of high tension, but also apprehension. The rear admiral who commands the Enterprise battle group, and is the senior officer aboard this ship, said he feared that his work could put at risk the safety of his family back home in Norfolk, Va., if his name were widely known.

Commanders on the Enterprise have adopted a posture of extraordinary caution in discussing the mission, declining even to allow their last names or those of their crew to be published. The admiral's fears are clearly widely shared. Not even during the Persian Gulf war did senior American officers seem so skittish.

Before the strikes, the ship's captain addressed his crew, consisting of 5,000 men and women, over the loudspeaker and recalled that in 1941, an aircraft carrier named Enterprise took part in the first retaliatory strikes on Japan after Pearl Harbor.

On Sunday night, this officer proclaimed that the latest Enterprise, like its namesake, had stepped in to avenge "a treacherous attack on our homeland."

"Like 1941, this war will be a little

Continued on Page B3

NEWS SUMMARY A2

Updated news: www.nytimes.com

A NATION CHALLENGED

Weeklong Campaign

The airstrikes on Taliban sites began what officials said would be a weeklong campaign, but Osama bin Laden was not a target. PAGE B4

Nation on High Alert

Fearing reprisals, officials tightened security at airports, train stations, sports stadiums and public buildings across the country. PAGE B1

Unease, but Also Support

Americans expressed profound unease about new terrorist attacks after the air strikes. But few questioned the necessity. PAGE B1

Thunderous Blasts And Bright Flashes Mark Kabul Strikes

By DAVID ROHDE

TOPDARA, Afghanistan, Monday, Oct. 8 — Under a clear sky lit by a three-quarters moon, a steady bombardment of Kabul began Sunday night, sending bright flashes of light and loud concussions rolling across this farming plain just 35 miles north of the Afghan capital.

The American strikes involved single heavy bombs thunderously detonating on targets. Each impact lit up small sections of the plain and sent concussions echoing off the surrounding mountains for 15 seconds.

American jets could not be seen or heard here, so the bombs fell silently from the sky, their detonations resounding with no warning and their flashes appearing unannounced.

The strikes, which began just before 9 p.m. Sunday here, prompted cheers and excited chatter from scores of Northern Alliance fighters manning mountainside positions in this village 2,000 feet above the strategic Shamali Plain that separates the main Afghan opposition force from Kabul.

Since the attacks in the United States on Sept. 11, the Northern Alli-

Continued on Page B5

"All the News That's Fit to Print"

The New York Times

Late Edition
New York: **Today**, windy and turning cooler, high 58. **Tonight**, clear but still breezy, low 43. **Tomorrow**, sunny, high 60. **Yesterday**, high 68, low 52. Weather map and details are on Page S2.

VOL. CLI . No. 51,909 | NEW YORK, WEDNESDAY, OCTOBER 17, 2001 | $1 beyond the greater New York metropolitan area. | 75 CENTS

ANTHRAX MAILED TO SENATE IS FOUND TO BE POTENT FORM; CASE TIED TO ILLNESS AT NBC

Sign of Escalating Threat

Daschle Letter Called First Use as Weapon Of Such a Sophisticated Form of the Germ

By STEPHEN ENGELBERG and JUDITH MILLER

News Analysis

The discovery of what government officials say is high-grade anthrax in a letter mailed to Congress is the most worrisome development yet in a series of bioterrorist attacks that has already rattled the nation.

The officials and weapons experts said yesterday that it suggested that somewhere, someone has access to the sort of germ weapons capable of inflicting huge casualties.

So far, the officials said, the attacker or attackers have used a rudimentary delivery system: the mail. Their intent and capabilities remain unknown, as does the amount of anthrax available to them. But what worries the officials in Washington is the possibility that an adversary with even a small quantity could easily find much more effective means of spreading the disease.

Until yesterday's preliminary analysis of the letter received by Tom Daschle, the Senate majority leader, the spate of anthrax-laced envelopes stirred considerable anxiety but posed a limited threat. Some experts assumed that the anthrax being sent around the country was crudely made, composed mostly of large particles that fell to the ground and thus endangered primarily those in the immediate area.

What government officials say arrived in Senator Daschle's office was significantly more threatening. Following the use of anthrax in Florida, it suggests that for the first time in history a sophisticated form of anthrax has been developed and used as a weapon in warfare or bioterrorism.

The key to understanding the danger, experts said, is in the size of the particles. The anthrax sent to Mr. Daschle, government officials said, was finely milled so that it would float a considerable distance on the smallest of air currents.

Producing germs that could be spread as a mist had been the main technical challenge facing germ warriors throughout the 20th century. Anthrax is what the Nobel laureate Joshua Lederberg calls a "professional pathogen," a hardy germ that could wreak havoc if inhaled. The trick was turning it into an aerosol that lingers.

Decades ago, Soviet and American scientists separately devised methods to dry and grind anthrax into the tiny particles — five microns or less — that could easily enter the nostrils and lodge in the lungs.

Experts say an adversary armed with anthrax in this form would have a host of possible targets for mass terrorism. Experiments by the United States in the 1960's showed that anthrax released in the New York City subway could spread widely underground, infecting large numbers of people. Federal officials used a benign germ related to anthrax to demonstrate the possible effects.

An enemy with large quantities of high-grade anthrax could mount a credible attack on a city or large office building. Dried anthrax could be spread using a crop-duster or

Continued on Page B4

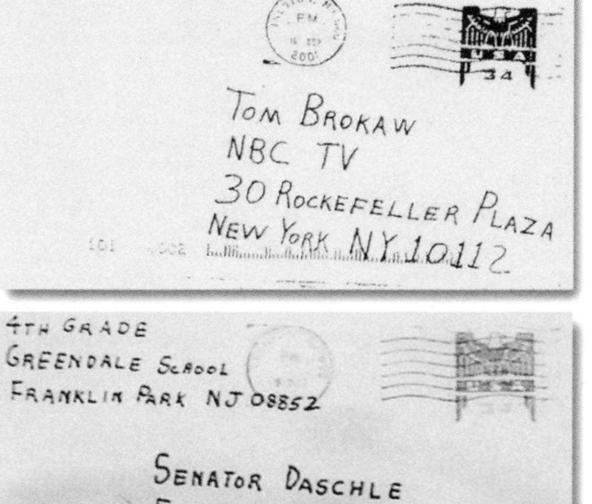

Reuters

These letters both contained anthrax. Government officials are worried that an enemy could find a more effective way of spreading the disease.

AIRBORNE THREAT

U.S. Says It Could Have Been Made by Expert, Adding to Concern

By DAVID JOHNSTON and ALISON MITCHELL

WASHINGTON, Oct. 16 — The anthrax mailed to the office of the Senate majority leader was pure and highly refined, consisting of particles so tiny that they could spread through the air without detection, government officials said tonight.

The officials said the potent grade of highly concentrated anthrax found in the letter sent to Senator Tom Daschle of South Dakota could have been made by an expert capable of producing large amounts of it, although it is not yet known who may have manufactured or purchased the anthrax sent to the senator.

The letter, which was opened on Monday morning in Mr. Daschle's office, bore strong similarities in language and handwriting to the one sent to the NBC anchor Tom Brokaw in New York and appeared to have been composed by the same person. Officials stopped short of explicitly linking the attacks to international terrorism, but the gravity of the threat instantly transformed the investigation into a major national security concern.

"We were told it was a very strong form of anthrax, a very potent form of anthrax which clearly was produced by someone who knew what he or she was doing," Mr. Daschle said after a briefing for senators by the F.B.I. and an Army epidemiologist. He said the sample that had been mailed to him "had a fairly significant degree of concentration of spores."

Senator Olympia J. Snowe of Maine said the strain was "very refined, very pure."

Heightened concern over the purity and concentration of the anthrax came as a Congressional official said there had been some intelligence warnings last week that suspicious packages would be sent to important places and people.

President Bush was scheduled to fly to California on Wednesday, a one-day stop on his way to an economic summit in China. White House officials said that the trip was still on "as of now" and that Mr. Bush was waiting for final test results on the anthrax found in the Senate. His trip could be curtailed if necessary, the officials said.

Former Gov. Tom Ridge of Pennsylvania, Mr. Bush's new chief of domestic security, met at the White House with senior federal law enforcement and health officials this afternoon.

In an interview with Mr. Brokaw on "NBC Nightly News," Mr. Ridge called the threat of bioterrorism "the No. 1 priority this week and for the weeks ahead" and suggested it was time to build up supplies of smallpox vaccine and resume routine vaccinations of children, a practice that was stopped nearly three

Continued on Page B5

Pool Photo by John McConnico, via Associated Press

Secretary of State Colin L. Powell and Gen. Pervez Musharraf, the Pakistan president, said moderate Taliban leaders might be part of a new Afghan government if the present one is ousted by the military campaign.

POWELL SUGGESTS ROLE FOR TALIBAN

U.S. Joins Pakistan in Seeking a Coalition Afghan Regime

By PATRICK E. TYLER

ISLAMABAD, Pakistan, Oct. 16 — The United States and Pakistan agreed today to work urgently for the creation of a new, broad-based government in Afghanistan that both sides said could include moderate elements of the Taliban movement whose present leadership is now a target for the American-led military campaign.

The agreement was the most visible achievement of Secretary of State Colin L. Powell's visit here today as bombs continued to fall in Afghanistan on Taliban troop concentrations and on targets associated with Al Qaeda, the terrorist organization of Osama bin Laden.

The bombing of frontline Taliban positions near Kabul, the Afghan capital, has been largely avoided pending agreement on what sort of government might replace the Taliban. But in the last 24 hours the bombardment of Taliban positions, including those near the capital, has intensified.

Secretary Powell said he had come to tell Pakistan that the United States — long chastised here as having abandoned its cold war ally following the collapse of the Soviet Union — was returning "to demonstrate our enduring commitment" to "a great Muslim nation."

The secretary said the revivified relations with Pakistan did not represent "just a temporary spike" in American focus, adding that Wash-

Continued on Page B3

Pressuring the Enemy

U.S. Is Counting on Unrelenting Firepower To Overcome Resistance in Afghanistan

By MICHAEL R. GORDON

Military Analysis

WASHINGTON, Oct. 16 — The intensified airstrikes now under way against the Taliban, a blitz of day and night operations, are intended to crack the leadership in its moment of weakness.

Not only are United States forces pouring on the firepower, but they are also expanding the list of targets and permitting pilots to fire at will within designated zones. Warplanes have begun to strike Taliban troops defending Kabul, the Afghan capital. And today the Pentagon hinted that the raids would soon be broadened to include Taliban front-line forces that have been battling the Northern Alliance, the anti-Taliban group. [Page B2.]

"Yesterday was a particularly heavy day," said Lt. Gen. Gregory S. Newbold, the director of operations for the Joint Chiefs of Staff. "Today is another intense day."

The waves of airstrikes — more than 100 warplanes, including two AC-130 gunships, were dispatched Monday against targets in Afghanistan — far exceed the expectations of many analysts who took to heart Defense Secretary Donald H. Rumsfeld's observation that Afghanistan is not a "target rich" environment.

But the Americans have every reason to keep the pressure on. Ever since the Vietnam War, United States military doctrine has called for unrelenting operations in the hope of breaking the enemy's resistance. And there are increasing signs that the Taliban are beginning to show the strain.

The Northern Alliance has pushed to the outskirts of Mazar-i-Sharif, a strategically important crossroads in northeastern Afghanistan. The fall of the city would not only strip the Taliban of a key logistics hub for their northern defense but it would also open up a supply line for the Northern Alliance. The city could also potentially provide a forward base of operations for any American special forces that might operate within Afghanistan.

There have been some Taliban defections in the north. Another indication that the pressure may have created internal fissures came when the Taliban foreign minister initiated secret talks in Pakistan in the hope of drawing Washington into negotiating a bombing pause.

This does not mean that the Taliban are on the verge of collapse. Pentagon officials say that American intelligence about the inner workings of the Taliban is so limited that Washington may not know if the government is about to topple until it actually begins to happen, but it

Continued on Page B2

A Fireball, a Prayer for Death, Then an Uphill Battle for Life

By LESLIE EATON

This is the story of a woman who decided to live. No one knows yet if she will.

Her name is Lauren Manning, and on the morning of Sept. 11 she had just walked into the north tower of the World Trade Center when the first plane hit. She was engulfed in a fireball.

"I heard a whistling sound and I was on fire," she told her husband, Greg, when he found her at St. Vincent's Manhattan Hospital that morning. "I prayed to die. Then I decided to live, for Tyler and for you." Tyler is their 11-month-old son.

The terrible calculus of the catastrophe at the trade center seems to have divided the people there into two neat categories: the thousands who escaped with their lives (and their nightmares) and the thousands who did not. But there is a small third group, the gravely injured, for whom the road from ground zero will be very long, if they get to walk it at all.

Mrs. Manning is a member of that group. She was transferred to the burn unit at New York Presbyterian Hospital. She was among 17 victims of the attack, all of whom had burns over 14 percent to 90 percent of their bodies; she was among the most seriously injured. Five of the others have died. Three have been released.

Lauren and Gregory P. Manning, in the spring of last year.

Others have been taken off the critical list. And seven, including Mrs. Manning, remain in a deep, drug-induced sleep while doctors tend to their wounds.

Her doctors would not talk, even in the broadest terms, about the treatment that she and the other patients were receiving. But the hospital confirmed that generally, a patient's

Continued on Page B10

A NATION CHALLENGED

A Close Call for Suspect

An incident at Miami International Airport on Dec. 26 nearly brought the hijacking planner, Mohamed Atta, to the attention of the Federal Aviation Administration. **PAGE B1**

More Bailouts Unlikely

Despite offering assistance to airlines and insurers, the Bush administration is refusing calls for bailouts from other industries hurt by the terrorist attacks. **PAGE C1**

A Family's Perilous Journey

Like many refugees, the family was trying to escape the hardships of Afghanistan. But plenty of new ones awaited in Pakistan. **PAGE B1**

Questions for bin Laden

CNN said it had agreed to submit questions to Osama bin Laden, putting the network in a potentially uncomfortable position. **PAGE B9**

ALSO INSIDE

Diamondbacks Win Opener

Arizona's Randy Johnson stopped Atlanta, 2-0, in Game 1 of the National League Championship Series. The Yankees-Mariners series starts today. **SPORTSWEDNESDAY, PAGE S1**

Updated news: www.nytimes.com

A Rush for Cipro, and the Global Ripples

By DONALD G. McNEIL Jr.

News Analysis

PARIS, Oct. 16 — America's demand for Cipro, an antibiotic for treating anthrax, could raise serious questions for the United States government, and poor countries seeking cheaper drugs to treat their own epidemics of AIDS and other diseases will be looking closely at the way they are answered.

Bayer, the German drug company that makes Cipro, said today that it was tripling production of the antibiotic in the face of growing public fears about anthrax. Bayer did not say how much of its increased production would come to the United States, and it was not clear exactly how much Cipro might be needed. [Page B7.]

Although a government official said doctors had assured him that patients exposed to anthrax can be treated with other antibiotics after an initial course of Cipro, it is not clear that the public will accept such assurances in what it perceives as a health emergency.

Shortages of Cipro — whether caused by a genuine anthrax emergency or by panic buying — may convince Bush administration health officials that they want the generic version, ciprofloxacin, more than Bush administration trade officials want Bayer's patent protected.

American budget officials could also decide to buy cheaper generic drugs.

Alternatively, American consumers might become outraged to learn that while Cipro has cost nearly $350 a month in the United States, a generic drug from reputable suppliers costs only $10 a month in India.

Senator Charles E. Schumer, Democrat of New York, proposed today that the government buy generic versions for its emergency stockpile, noting that such a step would reduce dependence on a single supplier and could significantly reduce the costs of getting the amount of ciprofloxacin needed.

If the United States were to purchase large amounts of cheaper generic drugs, it could open the floodgates for poor countries who want cheaper versions for their epidemics of AIDS, malaria, tuberculosis and other diseases.

The pharmaceutical companies — often backed by Western governments — have long defended the patent system as the only one that allows them to protect their products and recover the high costs of developing drugs.

But experts say that if the United States wants to purchase generic drugs to meet the sudden demand for ciprofloxacin, that presents no legal problem.

American law is very clear: when the United States government needs a patented product, any official authorized to make purchases can ignore the patent and license someone else to make it.

"Any employee of the United States government can authorize a compulsory license for the product without even holding a hearing," said James P. Love, director of the Con-

Continued on Page B7

"All the News That's Fit to Print"

The New York Times

Late Edition
New York: **Today**, sunny, a few afternoon clouds. High 77. **Tonight**, slightly more humid. Low 65. **Tomorrow**, sun then clouds. High 81. **Yesterday**, high 81, low 63. Weather map, Page C19.

VOL. CL . . No. 51,874 NEW YORK, WEDNESDAY, SEPTEMBER 12, 2001 — $1 beyond the greater New York metropolitan area. — 75 CENTS

U.S. ATTACKED

HIJACKED JETS DESTROY TWIN TOWERS AND HIT PENTAGON IN DAY OF TERROR

A CREEPING HORROR

Buildings Burn and Fall as Onlookers Search for Elusive Safety

By N. R. KLEINFIELD

It kept getting worse.

The horror arrived in episodic bursts of chilling disbelief, signified first by trembling floors, sharp eruptions, cracked windows. There was the actual unfathomable realization of a gaping, flaming hole in first one of the tall towers, and then the same thing all over again in its twin. There was the merciless sight of bodies helplessly tumbling out, some of them in flames.

Finally, the mighty towers themselves were reduced to nothing. Dense plumes of smoke raced through the downtown avenues, coursing between the buildings, shaped like tornadoes on their sides.

Every sound was cause for alarm. A plane appeared overhead. Was another one coming? No, it was a fighter jet. But was it friend or enemy? People scrambled for their lives, but they didn't know where to go. Should they go north, south, east, west? Stay outside, go indoors? People hid beneath cars and each other. Some contemplated jumping into the river.

President Vows to Exact Punishment for 'Evil'

By SERGE SCHMEMANN

Hijackers rammed jetliners into each of New York's World Trade Center towers yesterday, toppling both in a hellish storm of ash, glass, smoke and leaping victims, while a third jetliner crashed into the Pentagon in Virginia. There was no official count, but President Bush said thousands had perished, and in the immediate aftermath the calamity was already being ranked the worst and most audacious terror attack in American history.

The attacks seemed carefully coordinated. The hijacked planes were all en route to California, and therefore gorged with fuel, and their departures were spaced within an hour and 40 minutes. The first, American Airlines Flight 11, a Boeing 767 out of Boston for Los Angeles, crashed into the north tower at 8:48 a.m. Eighteen minutes later, United Airlines Flight 175, also headed from Boston to Los Angeles, plowed into the south tower.

Then an American Airlines Boeing 757, Flight 77, left Washington's Dulles International Airport bound for Los Angeles, but instead hit the western part of the Pentagon, the military headquarters where 24,000 people work, at 9:40 a.m. Finally, United Airlines Flight 93, a Boeing 757 flying from Newark to San Francisco, crashed near

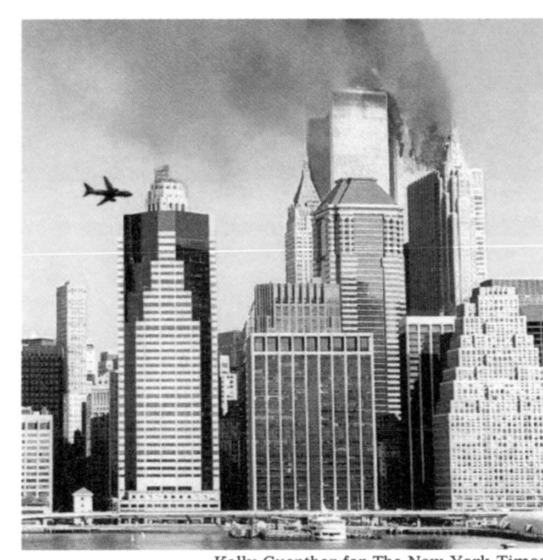

Kelly Guenther for The New York Times

SECOND PLANE United Airlines Flight 175 nearing the trade center's south tower.

For those trying to flee the very epicenter of the collapsing World Trade Center towers, the most horrid thought of all finally dawned on them: nowhere was safe.

For several panic-stricken hours yesterday morning, people in Lower Manhattan witnessed the inexpressible, the incomprehensible, the unthinkable. "I don't know what the gates of hell look like, but it's got to be like this," said John Maloney, a security director for an Internet firm in the trade center. "I'm a combat veteran, Vietnam, and I never saw anything like this."

The first warnings were small ones. Blocks away, Jim Farmer, a film composer, was having breakfast at a small restaurant on West Broadway. He heard the sound of a jet. An odd sound — too loud, it seemed, to be

Continued on Page A7

Steve Ludlum

Justin Lane for The New York Times

Paul Hosefros/The New York Times

AMERICAN TARGETS A ball of fire exploded outward after the second of two jetliners slammed into the World Trade Center; less than two hours later, both of the 110-story towers were gone. Hijackers crashed a third airliner into the Pentagon, setting off a huge explosion and fire.

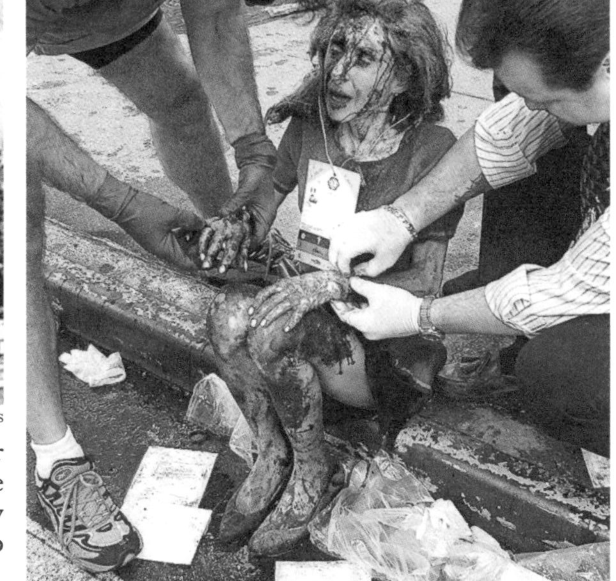

Ruth Fremsen/The New York Times

A Somber Bush Says Terrorism Cannot Prevail

By ELISABETH BUMILLER with DAVID E. SANGER

WASHINGTON, Sept. 11 — President Bush vowed tonight to retaliate against those responsible for today's attacks on New York and Washington, declaring that he would "make no distinction between the terrorists who committed these acts and those who harbor them."

"These acts of mass murder were intended to frighten our nation into chaos and retreat, but they have failed," the president said in his first speech to the nation from the Oval Office. "Our country is strong. Terrorist acts can shake the foundation of our biggest buildings, but they cannot touch the foundation of America."

His speech came after a day of trauma that seems destined to define his presidency. Seeking to at once calm the nation and declare his determination to exact retribution, he told a country numbed by repeated scenes of carnage that "these acts shattered steel, but they cannot dent the steel of American resolve."

Mr. Bush spoke only hours after returning from a zigzag course across the country, as his Secret Service and military security teams moved him from Florida, where he woke up this morning expecting to press for his education bill, to command posts in Louisiana and Nebraska before it was determined the attacks had probably ended and he could safely return to the capital.

It was a sign of the catastrophic

Continued on Page A4

Pittsburgh, raising the possibility that its hijackers had failed in whatever their mission was.

There were indications that the hijackers on at least two of the planes were armed with knives. Attorney General John Ashcroft told reporters in the evening that the suspects on Flight 11 were armed that way. And Barbara Olson, a television commentator who was traveling on American Flight 77, managed to reach her husband, Solicitor General Theodore Olson, by cell phone and to tell him that the hijackers were armed with knives and a box cutter.

In all, 266 people perished in the four planes and several score more were known dead elsewhere. Numerous firefighters, police officers and other rescue workers who responded to the initial disaster in Lower Manhattan were killed or injured when the buildings collapsed. Hundreds were treated for cuts, broken bones, burns and smoke inhalation.

But the real carnage was concealed for now by the twisted, smoking, ash-choked carcasses of the twin towers, in which thousands of people used to work on a weekday. The collapse of the towers caused another World Trade Center building to fall 7 hours later, and several

Continued on Page A14

Awaiting the Aftershocks

Washington and Nation Plunge Into Fight With Enemy Hard to Identify and Punish

By R. W. APPLE Jr.

News Analysis

WASHINGTON, Sept. 11 — Today's devastating and astonishingly well-coordinated attacks on the World Trade Center towers in New York and on the Pentagon outside of Washington plunged the nation into a warlike struggle against an enemy that will be hard to identify with certainty and hard to punish with precision.

The whole nation — to a degree the whole world — shook as hijacked airliners plunged into buildings that symbolize the financial and military might of the United States. The sense of security and self-confidence that Americans take as their birthright suffered a grievous blow, from which recovery will be slow. The aftershocks will be nearly as bad, as hundreds and possibly thousands of people discover that friends or relatives died awful, fiery deaths.

Scenes of chaos and destruction evocative of the nightmare world of Hieronymus Bosch, with smoke and debris blotting out the sun, were carried by television into homes and workplaces across the nation. Echoing Franklin D. Roosevelt's description of the attack on Pearl Harbor as an event "which will live in infamy," Gov. George E. Pataki of New York, a Republican, spoke of "an incredible outrage" and Senator Charles E. Schumer of New York, a Democrat, spoke of "a dastardly attack."

But mere words were inadequate vessels to contain the sense of shock and horror that people felt.

As Washington struggled to regain a sense of equilibrium, with warplanes and heavily armed helicopters crossing overhead, past and present national security officials earnestly debated the possibility of a Congressional declaration of war — but against precisely whom, and in what exact circumstances? Warships were maneuvering to protect New York and Washington. The North American Air Defense Command, which had seemed to many a relic of the cold war, adopted a pos-

Continued on Page A24

MORE ON THE ATTACKS

RESCUERS BECOME VICTIMS Firefighters who rushed to the trade center were killed. **PAGE A2**

SEARCH FOR SURVIVORS Some people trapped in the rubble for hours were rescued. **PAGE A2**

OFFICIALS SUSPECT BIN LADEN Eavesdropping intercepts after the attacks were cited. **PAGE A21**

TERRORISTS EXPLOIT WEAKNESS Investigators had criticized precautions against hijacking. **PAGE A17**

CASUALTIES IN WASHINGTON An unknown number of people were killed at the Pentagon. **PAGE A5**

"All the News That's Fit to Print"

The New York Times

Late Edition
New York: **Today,** sunny, windy and cold, high 54. **Tonight,** partly cloudy, low 41. **Tomorrow,** partly sunny, brisk and chilly, high 52. **Yesterday,** high 75, low 63. Weather map is on Page A16.

VOL. CLI . No. 51,918 — NEW YORK, FRIDAY, OCTOBER 26, 2001 — $1 beyond the greater New York metropolitan area. — 75 CENTS

Edward Keating/The New York Times

Twin Towers Job Fair Draws Thousands of Applicants

About 10,000 people showed up yesterday at Madison Square Garden for a job fair sponsored by New York City. The fair was aimed at helping those who lost their jobs after the trade center attacks. Page D11.

ANTITERRORISM BILL PASSES; U.S. GETS EXPANDED POWERS

After a Week of Reassurances, Ridge's Anthrax Message Is Grim

By SHERYL GAY STOLBERG and JUDITH MILLER

WASHINGTON, Oct. 25 — After a week of sending calming messages about the threat posed by the anthrax in a letter that was opened on Capitol Hill, Tom Ridge, President Bush's director of homeland security, said publicly for the first time today what others have said in private: the germs were very pure, very concentrated and very deadly.

"It is clear that the terrorists responsible for these attacks intended to use this anthrax as a weapon," Mr. Ridge said. "Clearly, we are up against a shadow enemy, shadow soldiers, people who have no regard for human life. They are determined to murder innocent people."

Mr. Ridge's remarks on the anthrax-tainted letter sent to Tom Daschle, the Senate Democratic leader, followed a two-and-a-half-hour meeting he held Wednesday night with law enforcement and public health officials, who have been at odds this week over whether proper sharing of information might have spared lives. His comments came as at least two more cases of anthrax were found today. [Page B6.]

At the closed-door session — held in the Roosevelt Room of the White House and attended by, among others, Tommy G. Thompson, the secretary of health and human services, and Robert S. Mueller III, the director of the Federal Bureau of Investigation — the Army scientists analyzing the Daschle letter detailed their latest findings. Mr. Ridge directed those in attendance to cooperate fully with one another, and, asserting his new authority as the president's point man on homeland defense, declared himself in charge of the government's response to bioterrorism.

"The point was, we are all going to get together on one message here," said one person who was not at the session but was briefed about it. The F.B.I. was a particular target for criticism, another official said.

Mr. Thompson, the health secretary, said the officials discussed "ways that we can circulate information faster between the laboratories and the principals" in the inquiry. While he said the agencies had been "cooperating very nicely," he acknowledged that he "was always concerned" about laboratories at the Centers for Disease Control and Pre-

Continued on Page B6

BUSH SET TO SIGN

Measure Provides Tools White House Sought, With Some Limits

By ADAM CLYMER

WASHINGTON, Oct. 25 — The Senate passed sweeping antiterrorism legislation today, sending President Bush a measure that would expand the government's ability to conduct electronic surveillance, detain immigrants without charges and penetrate money-laundering banks.

The measure also permits officials to share grand jury information to thwart terrorism and relaxes the conditions under which judges may authorize intelligence wiretaps.

The president's deputy press secretary, Claire Buchan, said, "The president is pleased that the Congress has acted quickly to provide additional tools in fighting the war on terrorism, and he looks forward to signing the bill into law tomorrow."

Attorney General John Ashcroft said that within hours of President Bush's signature he would distribute new directives to all federal prosecutors and F.B.I. agents telling them how to use the law. One step to be taken right away, senior law enforcement officials said, is to seek subpoenas to obtain information on computers used by any terrorist suspects.

The Senate vote was 98 to 1, after a 356-to-66 vote in the House on Wednesday. Only Senator Russell D. Feingold, Democrat of Wisconsin, voted against the bill, arguing that it would allow unconstitutional searches and punish individuals for vague associations with possible terrorists.

The bill provides most of the additional powers Mr. Ashcroft sought after the suicide attacks on the World Trade Center and the Pentagon.

But it added the money-laundering measures after a push by Senator Paul S. Sarbanes, the Maryland Democrat who is chairman of the Banking Committee. And the bill curtailed some of the tools Mr. Ashcroft sought, reflecting concerns in both parties and houses that the administration proposal went too far.

For example, it denied the administration the power to detain indefinitely and without charges immigrants suspected of involvement in terrorism. The bill does expand the limit to seven days of detention, from two days, though under some circumstances that could be repeatedly extended by six-month periods.

The bill denied the administration the power to use foreign wiretaps that would have been illegal in the United States. It also provides that authority for expanded surveillance of computers and telephones will expire after four years. The administration wanted permanent authority.

Senator Feingold, while praising his colleagues for denying Mr. Ashcroft some of the powers he sought, complained of "relentless" pressure to move quickly, "without deliberation or debate." He attacked the bill for enabling the government to ob-

Continued on Page B5

Bayer Halves Price for Cipro, But Rivals Offer Drugs Free

By KEITH BRADSHER

WASHINGTON, Oct. 25 — When Bayer agreed on Wednesday to sell 100 million tablets of its anthrax medicine, Cipro, to the government for 95 cents apiece, Bayer and the Bush administration said the deal assured an ample supply at a very low price.

But while Bayer nearly halved its previous price, three big pharmaceutical companies have since stepped forward to offer large quantities of their antibiotics free if the Food and Drug Administration will approve their use for the treatment of anthrax. Executives in the generic drug industry say Bayer is still at least breaking even and may even be making a large profit. And some infectious-disease experts warn that Bayer remains unable to supply enough Cipro if terrorists start releasing new strains of anthrax that are resistant to other antibiotics.

Tommy G. Thompson, the secretary of health and human services, strongly endorsed the Bayer deal today. "If you can get a company to reduce its price from $1.75, to 95 cents, for the first 100 million — and I hope that's all we'll need — then that's an excellent deal," he said.

Bayer officials did not return nearly a dozen calls for comment today, but said on Wednesday that they had happily made concessions for the good of the nation in their negotiations with Mr. Thompson.

"I was smiling going in because how often in your life do you and your company have an opportunity to make a difference," said Helge H. Wehmeier, Bayer's chief executive of American operations, who refused to discuss whether Bayer was making a profit on the deal.

Some executives in the generic drug industry, like Bruce L. Downey, the chairman and chief executive of Barr Laboratories, say Bayer's price is comparable to what they might charge to cover their costs and make

Continued on Page B8

U.S., Awaiting Putin, Delays Missile Defense Tests

By THOM SHANKER and DAVID E. SANGER

WASHINGTON, Oct. 25 — The Bush administration, moving to strike a deal on offensive and defensive strategic arms with Russia, has postponed three antimissile tracking tests that Defense Secretary Donald H. Rumsfeld said today might be interpreted as violating the 1972 Antiballistic Missile Treaty.

The announcement came only four days after President Vladimir V. Putin of Russia, speaking alongside President Bush in Shanghai, said the two nations had an "understanding that we can reach agreements," a comment widely interpreted to mean that they were headed toward a major amendment of the treaty.

President Bush and his senior national security advisers have maintained that the treaty is wildly out of date — Mr. Bush used the world "dangerous" in Shanghai — and must be drastically rewritten or scrapped. Mr. Rumsfeld's announcement today appeared to be intended to give Mr. Bush maximum negotiating flexibility in the days leading up to Mr. Putin's arrival here, on Nov. 12, for a three-day meeting that may result in an accord redefining the strategic relationship between the two countries.

On Wednesday, Mr. Bush met with the Joint Chiefs of Staff and his national security team on the other element of the equation: a review of the nuclear posture of America that may include proposals for large cuts in its arsenal of strategic weapons.

The White House will most likely describe that proposal to Russia in the next few days, to meet Mr. Putin's demand that missile defense be linked, at least loosely, with cuts in offensive arsenals.

At a Pentagon news briefing today, Mr. Rumsfeld said that three missile defense tracking tests — two that had been scheduled for Wednesday and one for Nov. 14 — were postponed while discussions between the two presidents are under way.

"We have said we will not violate the treaty while it remains in force," said Mr. Rumsfeld, regarded as the administration's most unwavering advocate of a policy to "move beyond" the treaty. "In recent days, to keep from having it suggested that we might not be keeping that commitment, we have voluntarily restrained our ballistic missile defense

Continued on Page A12

Not Yet Citizens but Eager to Fight for the U.S.

Ruby Washington/The New York Times

Alexandr Manin, who emigrated from Kazakhstan, has enlisted in the United States Marine Corps. He will leave for basic training next month.

By DAVID W. CHEN and SOMINI SENGUPTA

As a youth in Kazakhstan, Alexandr Manin had no interest in the war that the Soviet Union was waging in Afghanistan in the 1980's. But since arriving in New York three years ago, he has had a change of heart, and has joined the military.

The United States military, that is.

Mr. Manin, who is here as a legal permanent resident but is not yet a United States citizen, is scheduled to leave on Nov. 5 for basic training with the Marines. The law allows permanent residents like him — those who have a green card — to enlist.

"It doesn't matter that America is not my country; New York is my city, and what happened shook my life," said Mr. Manin, a fast-talking 25-year-old from Greenpoint, Brooklyn. "I feel patriotic, and I have this itch now to go sooner."

Particularly in New York, with its huge population of immigrants, many residents for years have been signing up to fight under the American flag, even though they do not carry an American passport. In fact, immigrant men and women seem more likely to enlist than their native-born peers.

In New York City, 13 percent of those under the age of 18 are immigrants, both legal and illegal. But in the Navy, 1,200, or 40 percent, of all New York City recruits were green-card holders in the last year. In the Marines, the number is 363, or 36 percent; in the Army, it is 589, or 27 percent.

On a national level, the percentage of green-card military recruits is relatively small, hovering around 5 percent for most services. Even so, the

Continued on Page B2

For the Asking, a $480 Seat

By JESSE McKINLEY

Saying they want to cut into the lucrative market dominated by ticket scalpers, the producers of "The Producers" are preparing to set aside at least 50 seats every performance and charge the unprecedented amount of $480 a ticket.

The sum is nearly five times the current cost of $100 for the most expensive seats, itself a Broadway high.

The plan is set to begin early next month with the sale of 50 premium orchestra and mezzanine seats at the St. James Theater, seats that have been almost impossible to attain since the show opened to rave reviews in April.

The move marks the first time in Broadway history that producers will withhold, and aggressively mark up, some of the best seats for those willing to pay for assured access, a practice already employed in luxury suites for teams like the Knicks and the Yankees, as well as in boxes for events like the U.S. Open and in special seating at rock concerts.

The producers said the decision was made after months of watching scalpers buy tickets for the show and then quickly resell them to hungry theatergoers at an enormous profit.

"What we're trying to do here is strike a blow at the heart of the scalping operation," said Rocco Landesman, one of the play's producers and the president of Jujamcyn Theaters, which owns the St. James. "The scalpers and their profits serve no one but the scalpers. Those monies belong to the people who created the show,

Continued on Page D11

A NATION CHALLENGED

U.S. Intensifies Its Bombing Of Front-Line Taliban Forces

For the first time, front-line Taliban forces were hit with cluster bombs. Addressing concerns that the bombing has not undercut the Taliban, a top general said, "We think we're having some success." PAGE B1

Report Details Arrests of 2

A newly released report and interviews with officials reveal suspicions about two men who are being held as material witnesses in the attacks. PAGE B4

Orphan Figures Questioned

While there is still no overall count of the bereaved children, early estimates of those left behind on Sept. 11, always high, now appear to be seriously out of line. PAGE B1

ALSO INSIDE

Israeli Raid Reconstructed

A reconstruction of an Israeli "police action," a 22-hour siege in which five Palestinians died, makes it seem more like war. PAGE A12

FOR HOME DELIVERY CALL 1-800-NYTIMES

0 354613 9 43501

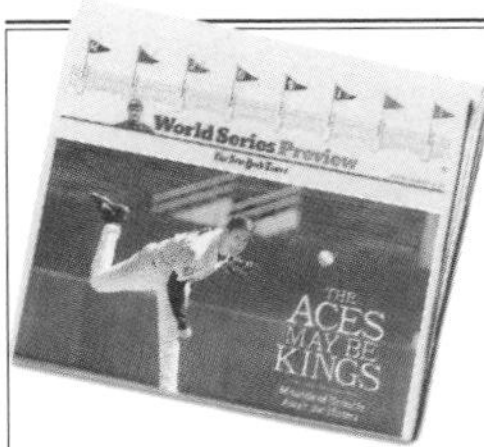

Game 1 Tomorrow

The Yanks' Mike Mussina faces the Diamondbacks' Curt Schilling in the World Series opener at Phoenix. SportsFriday, Page S1.

Updated news: www.nytimes.com

"All the News That's Fit to Print"

The New York Times

Late Edition
New York: **Today**, rain and mild, high 53. **Tonight**, breezy and drier, low 37. **Tomorrow**, partly to mostly sunny, high 45. **Yesterday**, high 48, low 42. Weather map appears on Page A20.

VOL. CLI . No. 52,008 | NEW YORK, THURSDAY, JANUARY 24, 2002 | $1 beyond the greater New York metropolitan area. | 75 CENTS

PRESIDENT TO SEEK $48 BILLION MORE FOR THE MILITARY

MOST SINCE REAGAN ERA

Bush Aides Say His Budget Will Focus on Fighting Terror and Reviving Economy

By RICHARD W. STEVENSON and ELISABETH BUMILLER

WASHINGTON, Jan. 23 — President Bush said today that he would seek $48 billion in additional spending on the military next year, a wartime increase that will be the centerpiece of the budget proposal he sends to Congress next month.

The request, which was larger than even some Pentagon officials had expected and the biggest since the Reagan-era military buildup, illustrated what administration officials said would be a focus by the president on two basic themes as he sets his agenda for the coming year: doing whatever it takes to win the war against terrorism at home and abroad and reviving the economy.

It came as Congress began its annual budget debate with a report from the Congressional Budget Office showing that the projected surplus for the next decade had dwindled to $1.6 trillion from $5.6 trillion a year ago and $3.4 trillion last summer.

The report renewed the partisan debate over the tax cut of about $1.3 trillion over 10 years, which Mr. Bush pushed through Congress last year. He did so over opposition from most Democrats, who argue that it will leave the nation short of money to address both its current needs and the long-run costs of paying Social Security and Medicare benefits to a rapidly aging population.

The budget office said the government would run deficits this year and next even in the unlikely event that Congress does not increase spending or cut taxes. And it said there does not appear to be any realistic hope of paying off the national debt within this decade, as both parties had pledged to do as recently as a year ago.

Administration officials forecast a deficit this year of $106 billion in the $2 trillion federal budget, followed by a deficit next year of $80 billion.

They said Mr. Bush's plan would call for outright cuts in some domestic programs, and would hold overall increases in spending outside of national security to very low levels.

But they said the president's budget, which will be sent to Capitol Hill on Feb. 4, would call for doubling spending on domestic security programs to more than $25 billion next year, and would set aside $90 billion in the current fiscal year and $75 billion next year for an economic recovery package built around tax

Continued on Page A24

U.S. Says Officials In Puerto Rico Stole For Party and Profit

By MIREYA NAVARRO

SAN JUAN, P.R., Jan. 23 — A wave of corruption scandals that has already led to dozens of arrests of officials and police officers crested today with the federal indictment of 17 people, including a former education secretary charged with stealing money for himself and for his political party.

Victor Fajardo, Puerto Rico's education secretary from 1994 to 2000 under the administration of Gov. Pedro J. Rosselló, is accused of extorting millions of dollars, a house worth nearly $1 million and a valuable painting from contractors. He was so flush with cash that he kept more than $300,000 hidden at home, law enforcement officials said.

Also indicted were Richard D'Acosta, president of the Puerto Rico Chamber of Commerce; his wife, Victoria Vargas; José O. Cruz, associate education secretary; a sister-in-law of Mr. Fajardo, María Ramos Matos; 10 contractors; a subordinate of Mr. Fajardo; and a man accused of setting up a sham company.

Beyond the charges, what has drawn analysts's attention and public indignation is the connection to the New Progressive Party, one of the two main parties here.

The indictment accuses Mr. Fajar-

Continued on Page A25

Shawn Thew/Agence France-Presse

Walker Arrives in Virginia

John Walker, second from left in the back seat with a security officer, arriving at Alexandria Detention Center last night after being flown from Afghanistan to Dulles International Airport. He is to appear in court this morning for a hearing on charges of conspiring to kill Americans as a member of the Taliban. Page A15.

A Panel Casts Doubt On Mammogram Use

An independent panel of experts said there was insufficient evidence to show that mammograms prevented breast cancer deaths.

The group, a screening and prevention editorial board for the National Cancer Institute, said that while it was possible that mammograms were beneficial, it was also possible that they were not.

Previously, the group had said the evidence showed that mammograms prevented breast cancer deaths starting at age 40. Yesterday it agreed that seven large studies of mammography had serious flaws, weakening the studies' validity. The new opinion clouds a continuing debate over whether women should have regular mammograms.

For its part, the cancer institute, which has recommended that women have regular mammograms starting in their 40's, has not announced any plans to reconsider the issue.

Article, Page A16.

U.S. Suspends the Transport Of Terror Suspects to Cuba

By KATHARINE Q. SEELYE with STEVEN ERLANGER

WASHINGTON, Jan. 23 — The Pentagon today suspended the transfer of Taliban and Al Qaeda prisoners from Afghanistan to its naval base in Guantánamo Bay, Cuba.

Officials said flights were suspended because the base had run out of space, for the time being. Washington is facing sharp criticism from its closest allies over its treatment of the prisoners, and officials said they did not want to overcrowd the stockade.

The United States also began to question prisoners today for the first time since they started arriving at Guantánamo two weeks ago, officials said, though some had been interrogated in Afghanistan. The sessions today were held in a tent by several United States agencies, officials said. No foreign governments are taking part at this time, nor do the prisoners have lawyers.

The compound is holding 158 prisoners and has 160 cages built of chain-link fencing. The military intends to construct 320 more temporary cages and then move all prisoners into cells with solid walls. Total capacity is planned for 1,000.

Maj. Stephen A. Cox of the Marines said in an interview from Guantánamo that the flights of prisoners were being halted only temporarily.

"Rather than put ourselves in the position of bringing them out here and doubling them up in two per unit, which is not good from a detainee perspective or from a security perspective, we said, 'Let's hold on for a second,' " he said. "But we will resume the flow soon."

Another military official in Washington said, "They don't necessarily want to put more people in those cells now," referring to the 8-foot by 8-foot cages. "They don't want it to be perceived that we're jamming them in there."

The United States' treatment of the prisoners has drawn especially blunt criticism from Europe, where it has raised fears that Washington may be applying international law selectively.

The decision by the Pentagon to keep the detainees outside the United States and not to classify them as prisoners of war under the Geneva Conventions has troubled European and other allies. The United States may be "making up the rules as it goes along," said a West European

Continued on Page A15

Record Label Pays Dearly To Dismiss Mariah Carey

By ALEX KUCZYNSKI with LAURA M. HOLSON

In one of the most spectacular and swift reversals of fortune in the entertainment industry, EMI Records said yesterday that it had ended its agreement with Mariah Carey, who has had more No. 1 songs than any musical artist except Elvis Presley and the Beatles.

EMI signed Ms. Carey only last April to one of the music industry's most lucrative contracts, guaranteeing a reported $80 million for five albums.

But after disappointing sales of the first album Ms. Carey delivered, "Glitter," released last fall, EMI's Virgin Records division decided to cut its losses. It will pay Ms. Carey $28 million to free itself from the high costs of producing and promoting any more albums, the company said.

The cancellation was the latest setback for Ms. Carey, the 31-year-old singer who has battled highly publicized emotional problems in the last year, including a breakdown that led to a stay at a rehabilitation center.

Her debut film, also titled "Glitter," bombed on its release. Her romance with a popular Latin singer collapsed. And the girlish charm that captivated fans and critics a decade ago hardened in recent interviews as she cast aspersions on rival performers.

Ms. Carey's dizzying trajectory from the Long Island suburbs to pop superstardom, and now back a few steps, is not merely a fable about the powers and detractions of fame. EMI's decision to part ways with Ms. Carey reflects the troubles in the recording industry at large, which is battling dwindling compact disc sales, the digitized universe of songs available on the Internet and increasingly demanding stars.

In an interview yesterday from Arizona, Ms. Carey, who is scheduled to sing the national anthem at the Super Bowl on Feb. 3, sounded rested, though her comments were not uncombative.

She quoted a lyric from a rap group, A Tribe Called Quest, to explain her reaction to being dropped by EMI.

"It goes like this," she said. "Something like, 'Industry Rule No. 480: Record company people are shady.'

"Jobs change, and people

Reuters

Mariah Carey at the Sundance Film Festival in Utah last week.

Continued on Page A22

WIDE EFFORT SEEN IN SHREDDING DATA ON ENRON'S AUDITS

Many Helped, Lawmaker Says — Hearings Beginning Today

By RICHARD A. OPPEL Jr.

WASHINGTON, Jan. 23 — Scores of people who worked at Arthur Andersen's Houston office were involved in the destruction of documents related to the Enron Corporation, the chairman of one of the Congressional subcommittees that will begin hearings Thursday on Enron's collapse said today.

The chairman, Representative James C. Greenwood, Republican of Pennsylvania, head of the House Energy and Commerce oversight subcommittee, said investigators for the subcommittee had determined that document shredding was widespread and that up to 80 people had received orders to destroy papers. He said it called into question Andersen's attempts to blame rogue employees for the episode.

The hearings on Thursday will be Congress's first public exploration into the Enron collapse, the largest corporate Chapter 11 bankruptcy filing in American history.

Tonight, Enron's chairman and chief executive, Kenneth L. Lay, announced his resignation, saying the many investigations into the company's collapse would require too much of his attention.

Last week, Andersen, one of the Big Five accounting firms, fired the lead partner on the Enron account, David B. Duncan, saying he orchestrated widespread document destruction shortly after learning of a government investigation into Enron's finances.

But Mr. Greenwood expressed skepticism about that account. "Do you believe that 80 Andersen employees were directed by Mr. Duncan to violate an express provision of policy by Andersen in the face of yet another investigation, and none of them picked up the phone and called their superiors and said, 'This doesn't seem right'?" he asked. "The question we need to get to is, Were there instructions from above."

Other people close to the investigation said they doubted that the number of Andersen employees was as high as Mr. Greenwood's estimate, but they said it was a much larger group than the company had suggested. Mr. Duncan is expected to appear under subpoena at the energy and commerce subcommittee hearing, but he plans to invoke his Fifth Amendment right against self-incrimination, his lawyer said today. Mr. Duncan, will "rely on his Constitutional right not to testify" unless he is given immunity, his lawyer, Robert Giuffra, told the committee in a letter today.

Also today, Congressional investigators made public a memo Mr. Duncan wrote last October saying he expressed concerns about the way in which Enron was about to disclose huge losses from controversial dealings that investigators believed played a significant role in the company's collapse. The disclosure, he said, was misleading to investors and possibly illegal.

On Oct. 16, Enron disclosed that it lost $618 million during the third quarter and that it would have to reduce its net worth by $1.2 billion, partly because of dealings with investment partnerships that had been headed by Andrew S. Fastow, who was then the company's chief finan-

Continued on Page C7

Enron Chief Quits Under Pressure And Calls Inquiries a Distraction

By JIM YARDLEY and JOHN SCHWARTZ

F. Carter Smith/Corbis Sygma

Kenneth L. Lay, Enron's ex-chief.

HOUSTON, Jan. 23 — Kenneth L. Lay resigned this evening as chairman and chief executive of the Enron Corporation under pressure from outside creditors, nearly two months after his company filed for one of the largest bankruptcies in the history of American business.

Mr. Lay, 59, suggested in a statement that he had decided to resign "in cooperation" with the court-appointed creditors committee that is overseeing the bankruptcy proceedings. He said the various federal inquiries into Enron's collapse were too large a distraction as he tried to resuscitate the company he has led since 1986.

"I want to see Enron survive, and for that to happen we need someone at the helm who can focus 100 percent of his efforts on reorganizing the company and preserving value for our creditors and hard-working employees," he said in a statement released by the company.

"Unfortunately," he added, "with the multiple inquiries and investigations that currently require much of my time, it is becoming increasingly difficult to concentrate fully on what is most important to Enron's stakeholders."

Mr. Lay will remain on Enron's board. The creditors committee is searching for a specialist in reorganizing companies to join Enron and serve as acting chief executive as soon as possible.

Thomas A. Roberts, a lawyer for Enron in New York, said that Mr. Lay had been discussing the possibil-

Continued on Page C7

Many Ride Out the Recession In a Graduate School Harbor

By YILU ZHAO

PHILADELPHIA, Jan. 17 — The sagging economy has created a bonanza of applicants for the nation's schools of business, law, journalism, education and many other graduate programs as laid-off workers and college seniors are deciding to wait out the recession by honing their skills.

College job placement offices may be in the doldrums, but admissions officers at many of the nation's professional schools and graduate programs say they are being inundated with applications.

The trend is striking. Admission officers at Emory University business school say applications were up 80 percent at the end of the first round in the admissions cycle in December in comparison to the same period last season; those at U.C.L.A. report a 90 percent increase and those at the University of Chicago report a 100 percent jump. Yale University Law School says applications are up 57 percent at this point in the season compared to the same point last year while Vanderbilt says its applications are up 47 percent. Engineering and education schools talk of similar surges. The bars for entrance have been raised.

Students at the University of Pennsylvania here give a simple explanation for the sudden enthusiasm for graduate education: the difficulty of finding jobs. Dave Feygenson, a senior, would have liked to work on Wall Street first and attend graduate school later if he could find a job. But after searching for a job in vain, he has applied to Ph.D. programs in finance at the nation's top schools.

"Why fight the economy?" he said. "Why not get it done now, since I cannot find a job anyway."

The only professional schools unaffected by this recession are schools of medicine. They are usually immune to economic cycles because the completion of a medical degree

Continued on Page A25

INSIDE

Sharon's Edge

With the peace accords opposed by Ariel Sharon and signed by Yasir Arafat all but dead now, Mr. Sharon has the upper hand. **PAGE A3**

Hingis Gains Australian Final

Martina Hingis defeated Monica Seles, 4-6, 6-1, 6-4, to advance to her sixth consecutive Australian Open final. **SPORTSTHURSDAY, PAGE D1**

Updated news: nytimes.com
Tomorrow in The Times: Page A20

"All the News That's Fit to Print"

The New York Times

Late Edition
New York: **Today**, mostly sunny, high 57. **Tonight**, a clear start, low 46. **Tomorrow**, cloudy with a risk of rain late, high 55. **Yesterday**, high 49, low 37. Weather map is on Page D8.

VOL. CLII . . No. 52,308 — NEW YORK, WEDNESDAY, NOVEMBER 20, 2002 — $1 beyond the greater New York metropolitan area. — 75 CENTS

SENATE VOTES, 90-9, TO SET UP A HOMELAND SECURITY DEPT. GEARED TO FIGHT TERRORISM

170,000 EMPLOYEES

U.S. Bureaucracy Faces Its Biggest Overhaul in Half a Century

By DAVID FIRESTONE

WASHINGTON, Nov. 19 — The Senate voted today to reorganize broad elements of a scattered federal government around a focused response to terrorism, approving the creation of a huge Department of Homeland Security in Washington's biggest transformation in 50 years.

Ending months of rancorous debate on the new department, the Senate approved the bill on a 90-to-9 vote that hid some misgivings many Democrats said they still harbored about President Bush's design for the agency. Only after urgent phone calls from the president and last-minute promises by Republican leaders to eliminate several special-interest business provisions did wavering moderates from both parties agree to the final vote.

The House approved the same bill last week, and after a few technical differences between the bills are resolved by House leaders on Friday the bill is expected to be on the president's desk before month's end. Even so, it will probably be years before the new department has fully assumed all its functions.

"We're making great progress in the war on terror," Mr. Bush told Senate Republicans in a conference call this afternoon. "Part of that progress will be the ability for us to protect the American people at home. This is a very important piece of legislation. It is landmark in its scope."

With a work force of nearly 170,000 employees around the world, the department will be led by a new cabinet secretary, who will almost certainly be Tom Ridge, now the director of the White House domestic security office.

Facing a need for the workers to discard their old loyalties and begin a new cooperation to prevent terrorist attacks and respond to those that occur, Mr. Ridge said, "We're going to look for advice and counsel from a lot of folks." [Page A14.]

Not since Congress and the Truman administration upended the nation's military apparatus to fight the cold war in 1947 has the government been reshaped so dramatically

Continued on Page A14

Byrd, at 85, Fills the Forum With Romans and Wrath

By JOHN TIERNEY

WASHINGTON, Nov. 19 — As his colleagues hurriedly tried to give the president a domestic security bill, Senator Robert C. Byrd took the floor this morning to tell them of a "truly great" senator from the first century A.D. named Helvidius Priscus. One day this Roman was met outside the senate by the emperor Vespasian, who threatened to execute him if he spoke too freely.

"And so both did their parts," Mr. Byrd said. "Helvidius Priscus spoke his mind; the emperor Vespasian killed him. In this effeminate age it is instructive to read of courage. There are members of the U.S. Senate and House who are terrified apparently if the president of the United States tells them, urges them, to vote a certain way that may be against their belief."

Mr. Byrd, of course, is not one of those timid souls, and his recent speeches have been extraordinary even for the maestro of senatorial rhetoric, who turns 85 on Wednesday. While his colleagues have debated the fine points of the domestic security bill, he has been virtually alone in asking the larger question: Why is this new department suddenly so necessary? What will the largest and hastiest reorganization of the federal government in half a century do besides allow politicians to claim instant credit for fighting terrorism?

"This mon-*stros*-ity," Mr. Byrd has been calling the bill, repeatedly lifting its 484 pages above his head with trembling hands and flinging them down on his desk with the fury of Moses smashing the tablets. Mr. Byrd used to be known less for his distaste of federal bureaucracy than for his love of federal aid — he once vowed to be West Virginia's "billion-dollar industry," while his critics crowned him the "prince of pork." But now he is riffing against big government.

"Osama bin Laden is still alive and plotting more attacks while we play bureaucratic shuffleboard," Mr. Byrd told the Senate. "With a battle plan like the Bush administration is proposing, instead of crossing the Delaware River to capture the Hessian soldiers on Christmas Day, George Washington would have stayed on his side of the river and built a bureaucracy." Mr. Byrd imagined Nathan Hale declaring, "I have but one life to lose for my bureaucracy," and Commodore Oliver Perry hoisting a flag on his ship with the rallying cry, "Don't give up the bureaucracy!"

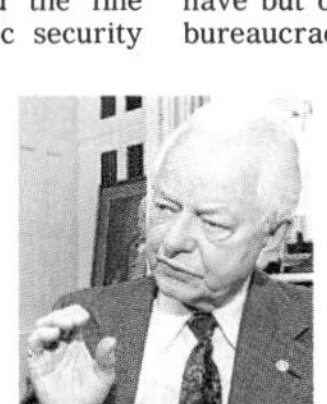

It would not be strictly accurate to say that Mr. Byrd's speeches have fallen

Continued on Page A15

Agence France-Presse

Oil Tanker Sinks Off Spanish Coast

The tanker Prestige split and sank yesterday off Galicia in northern Spain, threatening coastal areas with oil contamination. The tanker was carrying 20 million gallons of fuel oil when it began leaking. Page A6.

In Search of a Mission

At NATO's Summit Meeting, Chief Task May Be Saving Alliance From Obscurity

By PATRICK E. TYLER

News Analysis

PRAGUE, Nov. 19 — At any other time during the last 50 years, a summit meeting of the Western alliance would be a gathering radiating the unmistakable military power these leaders could throw against any security threat to Europe or the United States.

But after a year of American-led combat operations in Afghanistan, where NATO countries played a marginal role, and now with the prospect of war in Iraq, the grand alliance has never seemed more on the sidelines.

With President Bush here to meet with leaders from NATO's 18 other members and to welcome seven new ones, the most urgent task facing the assembly will be to rescue the alliance from obscurity.

"The fact of the matter is that the main threat is gone and NATO has become far less relevant," said James R. Schlesinger, the former American defense secretary who spent a cold war career burnishing a trans-Atlantic military machine designed to defend Europe and the West from the onslaught of Soviet and Warsaw Pact forces.

Nonetheless, a resuscitation package has taken shape in the wake of the Sept. 11 attacks, one that goes well beyond the retooling and reform that has been a work in progress at NATO's Brussels headquarters since the Soviet Union dissolved.

The effort is centered on creating a NATO rapid response force that could move swiftly with light, technologically advanced weapons around the world to strike at new threats from terrorists or rogue nations with weapons of mass destruction.

First broached by Secretary of Defense Donald H. Rumsfeld at a meeting of NATO defense ministers in Warsaw in late September, the new template would bring NATO closer into alignment with the Bush administration's military strategy. The reach would be more global than previously sketched plans for an all-European defense force.

In the new NATO, commanders would ease requirements that all members contribute proportionately to the common defense. Instead, contributions could be based on areas of specialization, which Mr. Bush referred to on Monday, an idea that allows the smaller and weaker members to find a niche in NATO's force.

One country could provide a unit trained for mountain warfare, another could contribute decontamina-

Continued on Page A8

G.I.'S HONE SKILLS ON IRAQ'S BORDER

Kuwait Has Given U.S. Army Vast Spaces for Maneuvers

By MICHAEL R. GORDON

CAMP NEW YORK, Kuwait, Nov. 19 — The United States Army has quietly doubled the number of its troops in Kuwait and is practicing offensive operations against Iraq close to the border with Saddam Hussein's forces.

In exercises over the past two days, Army combat engineers trained to blow paths through mine fields. They rehearsed erecting bridges under fire so armored forces can continue their thrusts into enemy territory. Troops conducted infantry assaults against mock strongholds. Army howitzers and Apache helicopters blasted targets at test ranges in terrain virtually identical to the desert American soldiers would confront if President Bush were to order an invasion of Iraq.

"Even though Saddam Hussein has accepted the U.N. resolution, we continue to maintain the mindset that we are going to war," said Capt. James Schwartz, the commander of Battery A, a unit of 155-millimeter howitzers from Fort Stewart, Ga.

"In order to keep ourselves mentally ready, that is the mindset that we use," he added. "When I talk to my soldiers, I tell them to take this training seriously because we are about 10 miles from Iraq."

The Army began training in Kuwait after the Persian Gulf war in 1991, when the United States and its allies evicted Iraqi occupation troops from Kuwait. The exercises were intended to deter Baghdad from attacking Kuwait again, an unlikely prospect. But the mood is tenser now that it is Washington that is considering whether to go on the offensive.

The Army has also quietly expanded its presence here. Over the past

Continued on Page A11

M.T.A. Gets Choice: Raise Transit Fares, Cut Service, or Both

By RANDY KENNEDY and MICHAEL COOPER

The chairman of the Metropolitan Transportation Authority will propose either raising transit fares and tolls, reducing service or a combination of both when the agency's board meets tomorrow, state officials said yesterday.

The officials said the board would be presented with three choices, each of them involving difficult trade-offs for riders. If the basic fare remains the same — $1.50 for subways and buses — "service cuts in all areas" will be necessary to repair the agency's budget, one official said. If the fare is increased to $1.75 — with similar increases in bridge and tunnel tolls, the Long Island Rail Road and the Metro-North Railroad — service cuts would still need to be imposed on nights and weekends, where transit ridership has increased markedly in recent years.

Or to keep service for riders at present levels, fares would be increased to $2 — a 33 percent increase that would also be applied to tolls and commuter rail.

The news that commuters could end up either paying more or facing service cuts comes in the wake of Mayor Michael R. Bloomberg's plans to impose higher property taxes in New York City and to tax commuters who work in the city. Yesterday, however, Gov. George E. Pataki repeated his opposition to the commuter tax plan, throwing into

Continued on Page B10

TV Memo

Forget the Sex and Violence; Shame Is the Ratings Leader

By ALESSANDRA STANLEY

The appeal of "The Bachelor" for women is hardly a mystery. This gauzy ABC dating competition is "Jackass" for women: a reality show that revels in emotional risk taking and rejection in the same way that "Jackass," the MTV series, celebrates men's foolhardiness and physical pain.

More than sex, more than violence, humiliation is the unifying principle behind a successful reality show, be it "The Real World," "Survivor," "Fear Factor" or "The Bachelor."

And there is much more ahead, from "The Will," an ABC reality show in which contestants compete for an inheritance, to "Exhausted," a Fox game show based on sleep deprivation. HBO is now hoping to top its rivals with a reality show as only HBO could do it: "Cathouse," which will be shown next month, put hidden cameras in a Nevada brothel. Viewers have shown an insatiable appetite for the queasy thrill that comes from watching an ordinary person suffer searing public embarrassment in exchange for 15 minutes of fame.

"Cathouse" proves, even more than "The Bachelor," that ordinary people want to be on television even if it means 15 minutes of shame.

Tonight, on the finale of "The Bachelor," Aaron chooses between the golden-haired ingénue Brooke and the sophisticated brunette Helene, who was cast as the brainy contestant. (In the land of the blond, the dark-eyed one is queen.) The ratings are expected to be among the highest of the year on any network.

ABC hopes to score again early next year with a distaff version: a Bachelorette will choose among 25 eligible men, but that does not have the same kick to it. Not, as the show's producers fret with ill-concealed glee, because viewers will brand her a slut for canoodling with several suitors, but because the sight of men competing over a woman is more accepted.

In our culture, there is still nothing particularly humiliating about a man pursuing unrequited love, but there is almost always something faintly ridiculous about a woman trying too hard. Cyrano de Bergerac was noble. Christi, the weepy, in-

Continued on Page C15

A Verdict of Guilty Is Uttered 20 Times In Wendy's Killings

By SARAH KERSHAW

Two and a half years after a massacre at a Wendy's restaurant in Queens, the man accused of staging the execution-style killings in a walk-in refrigerator was found guilty yesterday on all counts. The jury foreman's methodical reading of 20 guilty verdicts was punctuated by sobs and outbursts of rage from relatives of the victims.

Starting today, the jurors will begin to decide whether to sentence the man, John B. Taylor, 38, to death.

After deliberating for 11 hours over two days, the jury convicted him of killing two bound and gagged workers, then commanding his mentally retarded accomplice to kill five others in the restaurant's basement. Five of the workers died; two survived.

The jury's decision was a stunning blow to the defense: Mr. Taylor was found guilty of all 20 counts of murder and attempted murder. Six of the charges are punishable by death.

As the verdicts were delivered, Mr. Taylor's face was frozen in a grimace. His head hung low, as it had during most of the three-week trial in State Supreme Court in Queens.

Today that same jury of seven men and five women will focus on Mr. Taylor's punishment, after the judge interviews each to determine if he or she is prepared to go forward.

It is only the fourth jury in New York City since the state reinstated capital punishment in 1995 to grapple with whether a defendant should live or die. Only one New York City jury, in Brooklyn, has imposed the death sentence since 1995, and that sen-

Continued on Page B6

Stephen Crowley/The New York Times

Lt. Ryan Kuo commanding his tank during maneuvers by the United States Army this week in western Kuwait. The American military presence has doubled, and its posture is offensive rather than defensive.

INSIDE

A New Face in Israel

Israel's opposition Labor Party chose as its leader a former general who calls for opening peace talks with the Palestinians. **PAGE A3**

Health-Care Crisis Cited

The National Academy of Sciences urged the Bush administration to test solutions to what it said was a crisis in health care. **PAGE A20**

Plea Deal Set in Bet-Rigging

One of three charged with rigging a Breeders' Cup bet will reportedly plead guilty and provide details of another horse-race scheme. **PAGE D1**

NEWS SUMMARY A2

Updated news: nytimes.com
Tomorrow in The Times: Page D8

NOAH AND 9/11

THOMAS L. FRIEDMAN

Originally published in The New York Times on September 12, 2002

The sun rises over the empty space in the skyline where the Twin Towers stood on September 12, 2001.

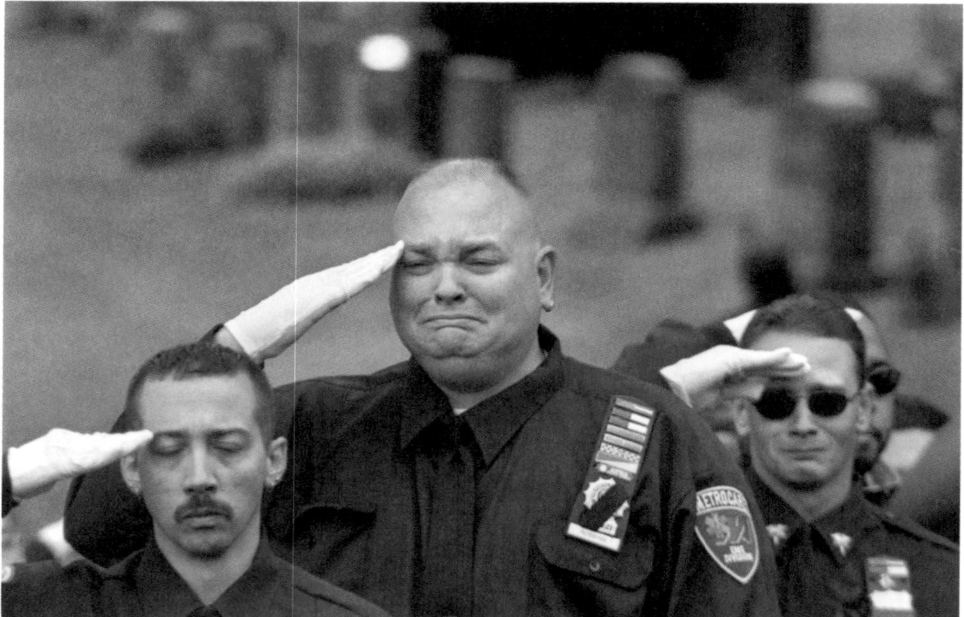

EMS workers salute their colleague, Yamel Jager Merino, who was killed when the World Trade Center collapsed.

Over the past year several friends have remarked to me how much they still feel a pit in their stomachs from 9/11. One even said she felt as if this was the beginning of the end of the world. And no wonder. Those suicide hijackings were such an evil act that they shattered your faith in human beings and in the wall of civilization that was supposed to constrain the worst in human behavior. There is now a big jagged hole in that wall.

What to do? For guidance, I turned to one of my mentors, Rabbi Tzvi Marx, who teaches in the Netherlands. He offered me a biblical analogy. "To some extent," said Tzvi, "we feel after 9/11 like we have experienced the flood of Noah—as if a flood has inundated our civilization and we are the survivors. What do we do the morning after?"

The story of Noah has a lot to offer. "What was the first thing Noah did when the flood waters receded and he got off the ark?" asked Tzvi. "He planted a vine, made wine and got drunk." Noah's first response to the flood's devastation of humanity, and the challenge he now faced, was to numb himself to the world.

"But what was God's reaction to the flood?" asked Tzvi. "Just the opposite. God's reaction was to offer Noah a more detailed set of rules for mankind to live by—rules which we now call the Noahite laws. His first rule was that life is precious, so man should not murder man." (These Noahite laws were later expanded to include prohibitions against idolatry, adultery, blasphemy and theft.)

It's interesting—you would have thought that after wiping out humanity with a devastating flood, God's first post-flood act wouldn't have been to teach that all life is precious. But it was. Said Tzvi: "It is as though God said, 'Now I understand what I'm up against with these humans. I need to set for them some very clear boundaries of behavior, with some very clear values and norms, that they can internalize.' "

And that is where the analogy with today begins. After the deluge of 9/11 we have two choices: We can numb ourselves to the world, and plug our ears, or we can try to repair that jagged hole in the wall of civilization by insisting, more firmly and loudly than ever, on rules and norms—both for ourselves and for others.

"God, after the flood, refused to let Noah and his offspring indulge themselves in escapism," said Tzvi, "but he also refused to give them license to live without moral boundaries, just because humankind up to that point had failed."

The same applies to us. Yes, we must kill the murderers of 9/11, but without becoming murderers and without simply indulging ourselves. We must defend ourselves—without throwing out civil liberties at home, without barring every Muslim student from this country, without forgetting what a huge shadow a powerful America casts over the world and how it can leave people feeling powerless, and without telling the world we're going to do whatever we want because there has been a flood and now all bets are off.

Because imposing norms and rules on ourselves gives us the credibility to demand them from others. It gives us the credibility to demand the rule of law, religious tolerance, consensual government, self-criticism, pluralism, women's rights and respect for the notion that my grievance, however deep, does not entitle me to do anything to anyone anywhere.

It gives us the credibility to say to the Muslim world: Where have you been since 9/11? Where are your voices of reason? You humbly open all your prayers in the name of a God of mercy and compassion. But when members of your faith, acting in the name of Islam, murdered Americans or committed suicide against "infidels," your press extolled them as martyrs and your spiritual leaders were largely silent. Other than a few ritual condemnations, they offered no outcry in their mosques; they drew no new moral red lines in their schools. That's a problem, because if there isn't a struggle within Islam—over norms and values—there is going to be a struggle between Islam and us.

In short, numbing ourselves to the post-9/11 realities will not work. Military operations, while necessary, are not sufficient. Building higher walls may feel comforting, but in today's interconnected world they're an illusion. Our only hope is that people will be restrained by internal walls—norms and values. Visibly imposing them on ourselves, and loudly demanding them from others, is the only viable survival strategy for our shrinking planet.

Otherwise, start building an ark.

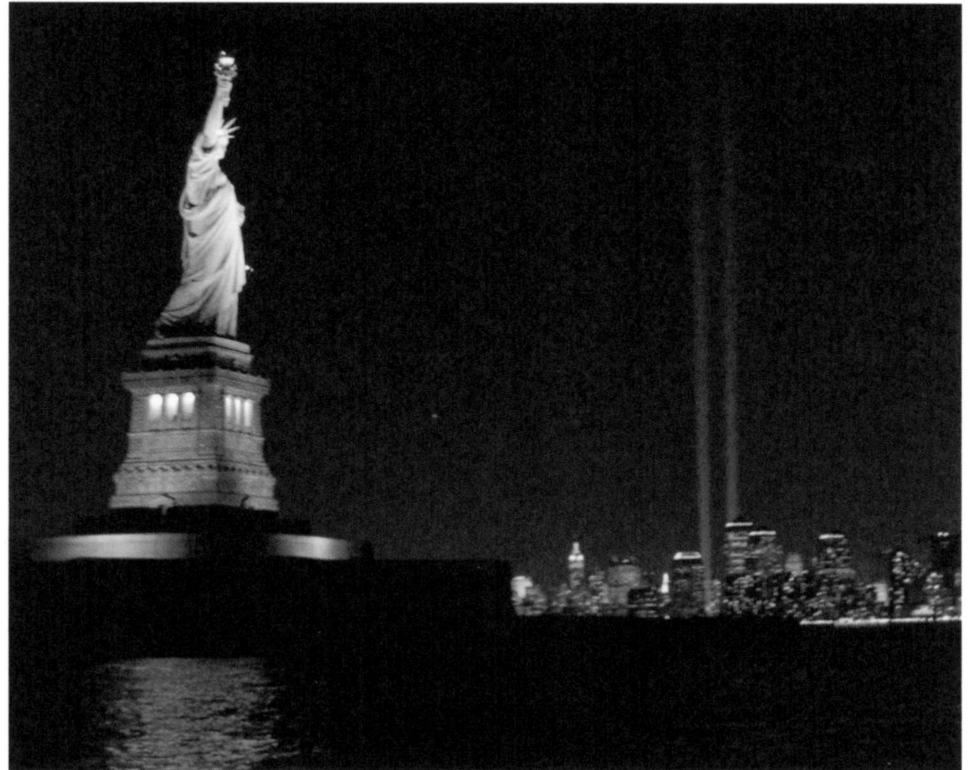

The "Tribute in Light" memorial, first installed on March 11, 2002, is visible for miles and has shone on every anniversary of the attacks.

Firefighters unfurl an American flag from the roof of the Pentagon on September 12, 2001, for the visit of President Bush.

THOMAS L. FRIEDMAN *spent three years in Beirut with United Press International before he was hired by The Times in 1981. After a year in New York as a financial reporter, he returned to Beirut as bureau chief, arriving six weeks before the Israeli invasion. After the war, in 1989, he published "From Beirut to Jerusalem," which won the National Book Award for non-fiction. Among many other awards, he has won three Pulitzer Prizes for his work in the Middle East. His latest book, due in the fall of 2008, is "Hot, Flat and Crowded: Why We Need a Green Revolution—and How It Can Renew America."*

"All the News
That's Fit to Print"

The New York Times

Late Edition
New York: **Today,** mostly cloudy, a rain or snow shower. High 38. **Tonight,** partial clearing. Low 25. **Tomorrow,** partly sunny. High 34. **Yesterday,** high 22, low 7. Weather map, Page D8.

VOL. CLII . No. 52,378 | NEW YORK, WEDNESDAY, JANUARY 29, 2003 | ONE DOLLAR

CALLING IRAQ A SERIOUS THREAT, BUSH VOWS THAT HE'LL DISARM IT, AND ALSO REBUILD U.S. ECONOMY

Getty Images

Prime Minister Ariel Sharon celebrated with supporters last night.

Israeli Voters Hand Sharon Strong Victory

By JAMES BENNET

TEL AVIV, Wednesday, Jan. 29 — Prime Minister Ariel Sharon and his rightist party, Likud, crushed Israel's Labor Party in parliamentary elections here Tuesday night, as voters vented their doubts about any prompt, secure end to the bitter conflict with the Palestinians.

Amram Mitzna, Labor's chairman, called Mr. Sharon to concede less than an hour after polls closed at 10 p.m. Israeli television projected that Likud could win almost twice as many seats as Labor in the 120-seat Parliament.

Based on results from 99.9 percent of the polling centers, Likud won 37 seats, and Labor only 19 — the fewest ever for the party with a mighty past.

Labor appeared still to be paying for Israelis' disillusionment with the Oslo accords, the all-but-dead 1993 agreement that was to have created a new era of peace and prosperity in the Middle East. Mr. Sharon, despite his as yet unfulfilled promise of peace and security, is widely viewed as the most dependable leader in a time of deep uncertainty.

Another clear winner was an anti-religious party, Shinui, which appears to have surged to 15 seats from 6 in the last Parliament.

The party's name means "Change," and its rise reflected in part a protest against Israel's status quo. It also reflected frustration with

Continued on Page A8

U.S. AND ITS ALLIES FIGHT REBEL FORCE ON AFGHAN PEAKS

BIGGEST CLASH IN MONTHS

Airborne Troops, Supported by Bombing and Gunships, Hit Followers of Warlord

By CARLOTTA GALL

KABUL, Afghanistan, Jan. 28 — Some 350 American, European and Afghan forces fought a fierce battle through the night against a large group of rebel fighters in a mountainous region of southeastern Afghanistan, in the heaviest fighting they have encountered in nine months, the American military spokesman said here today.

As many as 80 fighters aligned with the former mujahedeen commander Gulbuddin Hekmatyar, a warlord who once battled Soviet occupation but has now joined forces with the remnants of the Taliban to oust the Americans, were thought to be lodged in caves and mountain hideouts near the border with Pakistan, said the spokesman, Col. Roger King. Those forces fired on Apache helicopters that went to investigate their presence in the Adi Ghar, a mountain range just north of Spinbaldak, the border crossing between the southern Afghan town of Kandahar and the Pakistani city of Quetta.

American forces responding to the violence included a rapid reaction force of the 82nd Airborne Division, backed by air support from American B-1 bombers and AC-130 gunships and Norwegian F-16's, Colonel King said.

The bombers dropped 2 500-pound and 19 2,000-pound bombs on the area during 12 to 14 hours of fighting, he said.

The AC-130's and Apaches were repeatedly engaged too, he said. An estimated 18 enemy fighters were killed, while no coalition casualties were reported by tonight, he said.

The fighting, coming almost 16 months after the United States began its war against the Taliban and Al Qaeda forces and as United States forces prepare for a possible war in Iraq, underscores just how much unfinished business there is in the remote mountainous regions of Afghanistan and neighboring Pakistan.

For Norway, it was the first time its planes had carried out operational bombings since World War II, said a military spokesman, Per Hoeiby.

According to the military spokes-

Continued on Page A19

Doug Mills/The New York Times

President Bush made it clear that he would seek the support of the world in confronting Iraq, but would not wait.

A SOMBER ADDRESS

President Says America Is Not Afraid to Take Unilateral Action

By RICHARD W. STEVENSON and DAVID E. SANGER

WASHINGTON, Jan. 28 — In an assertive speech that covered the main themes of his administration, President Bush tonight combined an unflinching threat of military action against Saddam Hussein with sweeping proposals on the key domestic issues of health care and tax relief.

Mr. Bush, delivering his second State of the Union message before Congress, sought to assure Americans that he could deal with their economic troubles and foreign crises simultaneously and with compassion and resolve.

He spoke forcefully, purposefully and in somber tones of an America unafraid to take unilateral action, if necessary, against an Iraqi leader he portrayed as the personification of evil.

"Trusting in the sanity and restraint of Saddam Hussein is not a strategy, and it is not an option," Mr. Bush said. [Transcript, Page A12.]

He defended his doctrine of preemption as the necessary response to terrorism and sought to increase the pressure on his hesitant allies by announcing that he was sending Secretary of State Colin L. Powell to the United Nations on Feb. 5.

Moving to control the next part of the decision-making calendar, Mr. Bush said Mr. Powell would "present information and intelligence" to buttress White House contentions that Mr. Hussein had deceived United Nations inspectors and that he had secret links to Al Qaeda and other terrorist groups.

But the president tempered that message with a new agenda of international humanitarianism, built on a major new initiative against AIDS in Africa.

He promised his American audience tax relief for ordinary families and for investors in the stock market.

Addressing his determination to deal once and for all with Mr. Hussein, the president made it clear that while he would seek the world's support in confronting Iraq — and in liberating it — he would not wait. "We will consult, but let there be no

Continued on Page A10

Bush's Twin Challenges

As President Prepares the Public for War, He's Careful to Cover His Domestic Flank

By TODD S. PURDUM

News Analysis

WASHINGTON, Jan. 28 — With his sweeping, if unproven, charge that Saddam Hussein "aids and protects terrorists, including members of Al Qaeda," President Bush tonight delivered his strongest effort yet to convince doubting allies and anxious Americans that war with Iraq may be unavoidable, and the best way to protect the home front from "a day of horror like none we have ever known."

At the same time, by outlining an ambitious effort to reshape health care and build "an economy that grows fast enough to employ every man and woman who seeks a job," Mr. Bush sought to protect himself from the charges of political indifference that destroyed his father's presidency after the success of the Persian Gulf war in 1991. He spoke feelingly of the need for more drug treatment programs, mentors for children of prison inmates and new efforts to combat AIDS in Africa.

But the chief thrust of a speech aimed by turns at the American heartland and the heart of Europe was a methodical argument to build support for attacking Iraq to rid it of weapons of mass destruction, and to pressure traditional American allies to join the campaign. There were promises of detailed evidence to come from Secretary of State Colin L. Powell, coupled with a gruesome catalog of Iraqi torture methods and a warning that if Mr. Hussein "is not evil, then evil has no meaning."

Presidents have used their annual State of the Union messages to articulate broad doctrine, to shape debate in time of war and to confront and defuse political problems. Tonight, in what he called "a time of great consequence," President Bush tried to do all three.

A year ago, in his first State of the Union speech, Mr. Bush addressed a shaken nation that had recently been attacked and a public galvanized be-

Continued on Page A10

President Vows Steps to Handle Domestic Woes

By ROBIN TONER and ROBERT PEAR

WASHINGTON, Jan. 28 — President Bush vowed tonight that he would not burden future generations with the nation's pressing domestic problems: growing budget deficits, a lagging economy and a crisis in health care.

He offered few new specifics on how he would solve those problems, and Democrats asserted that some of his proposals could actually worsen them. But Mr. Bush, addressing one of the core critiques of his administration, argued that he "will not pass along our problems to other Congresses, other presidents and other generations."

He insisted that cutting taxes, spurring investment and re-igniting growth would be the best way to balance the budget in the future and to return the nation to sound economic footing. He also asserted that his economic proposal — a 10-year, $674 billion tax cut plan — would benefit all Americans, the working class as well as the rich.

"This tax relief is for everyone who pays income taxes," he declared.

Mr. Bush repeated his call to speed up tax cuts that are due to increase the child credit and reduce taxes on many married couples. "If this tax relief is good for Americans three, or five, or seven years from now, it is even better for Americans today," the president said.

In a State of the Union address intended to show his attentiveness to the home front, Mr. Bush reminded his audience of the "compassionate conservatism" that was at the core of his presidential campaign.

He also acknowledged the strains on the federal budget, the growing gaps in the health care system and the need to overhaul Medicare and

Continued on Page A16

Senior Officials Sent Packing In Overhaul of City's Schools

By ABBY GOODNOUGH

At the latest farewell party for a high-ranking Department of Education veteran, the guests smiled as Chancellor Joel I. Klein paid tribute to William P. Casey, who helped run the department's instructional division under two of Mr. Klein's predecessors and invested four decades of his life in the New York City school system.

But behind the ritual was tension so thick as to suffocate, according to several people who attended. Mr. Casey was following in the footsteps of at least a dozen other senior education officials who have departed since Mr. Klein took over last summer, some clutching pink slips, others choosing to go because they felt underappreciated or marginalized.

As the mayor and the chancellor publicly announce one major change after another, shaking the foundation of the nation's largest and most labyrinthine school system, there is a quieter, and some say just as far-reaching shuffle going on among the so-called educrats, some of whom have been in power for decades.

Leaving or losing influence en masse are people who, unlike a long line of short-lived chancellors, knew the system's complexities and tangled history cold. With their departure, years of business and political ties have been severed, and the list of people, companies and organizations with access to and influence over the system has changed overnight. Many of those leaving started as teachers and remained close to the teachers' union as they rose through the system, ensuring it a voice in decisions large and small.

Replacing them are outsiders recruited by Mr. Klein, including some who have never worked in a school system or even in New York. Many

Continued on Page B2

Mayor Outlines Plan To Close Budget Gap

Mayor Michael R. Bloomberg released his latest plan to balance the city budget, this time shifting the focus away from city actions and placing his trust largely in Albany and the city's labor unions to help close a $3.4 billion gap.

Mr. Bloomberg, whose approval rating has suffered as New Yorkers have accused him of failing to understand their burdens, called potential layoffs "in many senses a human tragedy," and departed from his usual emphasis on municipal responsibility when it comes to the city's budget-balancing. He placed the bulk of the responsibility for getting the city through the next fiscal year at the doorstep of Gov. George E. Pataki and municipal union leaders.

Articles, Pages B1 and B7.

Bush Enlarges Case For War by Linking Iraq With Terrorists

By MICHAEL R. GORDON

WASHINGTON, Jan. 28 — President Bush, enlarging the case for going to war with Iraq soon, said tonight that there was intelligence showing that Iraq was helping and protecting terrorists. He warned that Saddam Hussein could distribute weapons of mass destruction to terrorists who could use them against the United States.

Iraq's alleged terrorist connection is just one reason Mr. Bush cited for preparing for war. He also said Iraq could threaten the Persian Gulf region if it developed weapons of mass destruction, and he assailed its record on human rights.

To that end, he pointed to the example of North Korea, which is already suspected of having nuclear weapons and is, Mr. Bush said, "an oppressive regime" that rules by fear and starvation.

The allegation that Iraq is conspiring with terrorists seemed tailored to address the question of why it is important to act now.

In essence, Mr. Bush argued that military action is needed to avoid the risk of a Sept. 11-style attack using weapons of mass destruction. In last year's State of the Union address, Mr. Bush identified Iraq as a potential target. Tonight, he sought to make the case for why the United States needs to strike Iraq soon if it does not disarm.

With American forces massing in the Persian Gulf region and estimates that the United States and its allies could be ready to strike by late February or early March, Mr.

Continued on Page A11

Associated Press

President Bush receiving accolades on the House floor last night after his address. The speech was interrupted 77 times by applause.

INSIDE

African Refugees Trapped

New security checks for the thousands of people seeking entry into the United States are adding a layer of misery to a dismal Kenyan refugee camp. PAGE A3

Symphonic Troubles

Besides losing top executives, the Pittsburgh Symphony, one of the country's major ensembles, is facing a plunging endowment and tough labor negotiations. PAGE E1

"All the News That's Fit to Print"

The New York Times

Late Edition
New York: **Today**, clouds, unusually cold, high 24. **Tonight**, overcast, frigid, low 9. **Tomorrow**, cloudy with snow arriving, high 23. **Yesterday**, high 30, low 15. Weather map is on Page D8.

VOL. CLII . . No. 52,395 NEW YORK, SATURDAY, FEBRUARY 15, 2003 ONE DOLLAR

Powell Calls for U.N. to Act on Iraq and Meets Deep Resistance

From left: Ruby Washington/The New York Times; Reuters; James Estrin/The New York Times

In the United Nations Security Council chamber yesterday, a conflict over Iraq was mirrored in the main players' faces. From left, Dr. Mohamed ElBaradei and Hans Blix, chief weapons inspectors; Foreign Minister Dominique de Villepin of France; and Secretary of State Colin L. Powell.

NASA OFFICIAL SAYS HE HELD OUT HOPE IN FINAL MOMENTS

GRADUAL SENSE OF DOOM

Videotape Shows Response of Controllers as Signs Grew of Shuttle Disaster

By JOHN SCHWARTZ

HOUSTON, Feb. 14 — The NASA official in charge of shuttle Columbia's re-entry said today that despite the accumulating signs of trouble aboard the spacecraft as it crossed the southwestern United States, he had remained confident that it would land safely.

The official, LeRoy E. Cain, a veteran NASA flight director, acknowledged at a news conference today that some of the sensor readings showing elevated temperatures in parts of the shuttle's left wing — or no readings at all — made him nervous. But the realization that things were going badly wrong dawned on him only gradually.

Only when he heard reports of debris falling from the sky in East Texas did he know that the ship was lost.

"At that point we didn't know the details of the breakup," Mr. Cain said. "We didn't know the details of the situation and what it was. All we knew was we had a significant event that was potentially catastrophic."

Even then, he said, he held out hope that the module holding the seven astronauts had managed to withstand the breakup.

Mr. Cain spoke with reporters several hours after NASA released a videotape recorded in Mission Control on the morning of Feb. 1, as Columbia made its fatal re-entry. In the video, flight controllers are seen staring helplessly at their monitors and trying futilely to find the craft by radio or radar after communication with it had ceased.

Mr. Cain asked for more explanation for the rapid series of failures along the shuttle's left wing. Charlie Hobaugh, the capsule communications officer, tried over and over to raise the orbiter on the UHF radio.

Then Phil Engelauf, a senior flight director representing the mission operations directive at Mission Control,

Continued on Page A18

Envoys Abandon Scripts on Iraq And Bring Emotion to U.N. Floor

By FELICITY BARRINGER

UNITED NATIONS, Feb. 14 — It was supposed to be a moment for dueling bugles, with the French foreign minister, Dominique de Villepin, rallying his troops against the rush toward war in Iraq, and the American secretary of state, Colin L. Powell, rallying his against any delay in the disarmament of a dictator.

The bugles did indeed sound the prescribed notes — but with a spontaneity that gave uncommon depth and resonance to the confusion, division and anger over Washington's monumental war preparations.

Around the horseshoe table of polished Norwegian wood in the Security Council today, the debate sounded surprisingly personal.

Most of the diplomats transcended their scripts, bringing emotion and exasperation to an arena steeped in rote routines, and the audience responded in kind.

In a breach of decorum seldom witnessed in the protocol-conscious chamber, applause broke out as Mr. de Villepin concluded his bugle call by evoking the ideas and conscience of "La France."

"This message comes to you today from an old country, France," the translator of Mr. de Villepin's remarks intoned through the large white earpieces that gave the roomful of more than 400 people a vaguely alien appearance.

"It wishes resolutely to act with all the members of the international community. Faithful to its values, it believes in our ability to build together a better world."

Before the translation ended, the applause began in the gallery; on the Council floor, only the Syrian foreign minister tapped his hands together.

At the head of the table, to the right of the German foreign minister, Joschka Fischer, the secretary general, Kofi Annan, pushed the points of his fingers against each other, bend-

Continued on Page A9

U.S. TRIES TO EASE JITTERS ON TERROR

No Need to Seal Up Windows, Administration Aides Say

By PHILIP SHENON

WASHINGTON, Feb. 14 — The Bush administration tried today to calm a jittery public after a week of heightened terrorism warnings, with Homeland Security Secretary Tom Ridge saying that "we just don't want folks sealing up their doors or sealing up their windows." Senior administration officials said the government had received no new intelligence in recent days to suggest an imminent attack.

Clearly worried that some people had gone too far in responding to the government's recommendation this week that they buy duct tape and plastic sheeting to seal doors in the event of a biochemical attack, Mr. Ridge said he wanted to remind the public that the emergency supplies should be kept ready — but not used.

"I want to make something very, very clear," he said at a news conference. "God forbid there may come a time when the local authorities or national authorities or someone will tell you that you've got to use them."

President Bush also joined the effort to quell the anxiety created by last week's decision to raise the national terrorism alert level to "high" and the government's advice on Monday that families prepare a home disaster kit that included a flashlight, a can opener and bottled water.

In a speech at F.B.I. headquarters

Continued on Page A13

If, and When: War's Timing

Argument at the U.N. On How Long to Wait

By PATRICK E. TYLER

News Analysis

With the United States poised to launch a military strike against Iraq within a matter of weeks, the question of whether war should replace United Nations inspections as the primary instrument to disarm Saddam Hussein became one of timing yesterday.

When the French foreign minister, Dominique de Villepin, suggested yesterday that the Security Council give the inspectors a month more before convening again on March 14, he was not proposing a 30-day deadline for Iraq. Rather, there was an implication that however remote the possibility, there could still be a compromise if Iraq was more forthcoming by then.

Neither President Bush nor Secretary of State Colin L. Powell responded to the French time line yesterday, which also seemed significant since most military experts believe that it could easily take a month more to complete the transport of the required American and British troops to the front lines in Kuwait and Turkey. They need time to find their equipment, fire their weapons and get a taste of the Middle Eastern desert before Mr. Bush can push the button.

Some American military officials have focused on the moonless nights of early March as the time to begin a bombing campaign, but other mili-

Continued on Page A8

Clash Comes as Inspectors Tell of Progress

By JULIA PRESTON

UNITED NATIONS, Feb. 14 — The chief United Nations weapons inspectors today reported some progress in Iraq, and Secretary of State Colin L. Powell faced deep resistance to his call for a Security Council decision to authorize military force.

The clash was frontal and impassioned as Foreign Minister Dominique de Villepin of France spurned Mr. Powell's arguments, saying that the inspections had not failed and that there was no cause for armed action yet.

He proposed holding a new meeting of Security Council foreign ministers on March 14 to take stock of Iraq's cooperation.

Drawing a rare burst of applause from the audience in the Council chambers, Mr. de Villepin told Mr. Powell: "In this temple of the United Nations, we are the guardians of an ideal, the guardians of conscience. This onerous responsibility and immense honor we have must lead us to give priority to disarmament through peace."

Mr. Powell set aside his prepared remarks, speaking spontaneously and throwing his personal prestige behind his assertion that Iraq had failed decisively to comply with Council's demand that it disarm.

"We cannot allow this process to be endlessly strung out as Iraq is trying to do right now," Mr. Powell said. "My friends, they cannot be allowed to get away with it again," he added, referring to Iraq's effort to hide illegal weapons.

For some time, the Bush administration has been saying a decision on whether to go to war must come within weeks. Whether it would be prepared to wait until March 14, another four weeks, was unclear today.

Both the chief arms inspectors, Hans Blix and Dr. Mohamed ElBaradei, cited measures Iraq had taken to allow surveillance flights, provide new documents and open investigations of past arms stocks as indications that its cooperation had improved, even if it fell short of being unconditional.

Mr. de Villepin proposed extending and strengthening arms inspections, and Russia and China — both permanent Council members with veto power — rallied behind the proposal, as did Germany and many other nonpermanent members.

Faced with the unexpectedly reso-

Continued on Page A8

Reuters

America's Cup Race Begins, and Quickly Ends

Team New Zealand's crew struggled with a shredded headsail shortly after the start of its America's Cup defense. The boat withdrew from the race, which was won by Alinghi, the Swiss challenger. SportsSaturday.

Joy and Anger Greet List of Top City Schools

By ABBY GOODNOUGH and JENNIFER MEDINA

Public School 321 in Park Slope made the list, but the middle school that many of its graduates attend, M.S. 51, did not. Public School 87 on the Upper West Side made it, but not the Computer School, a small alternative school in the same neighborhood.

As Chancellor Joel I. Klein released the long-awaited list of schools he considered good enough to exempt from the new uniform curriculum yesterday, some parents, teachers and principals celebrated, while others huffily prepared to appeal their school's exclusion. A few furious parents even vowed to take their children out of the system.

Despite a complicated formula meant to produce an ethnically and geographically diverse list, a vast majority of the 208 schools are from the middle-class and wealthy neighborhoods of Manhattan, Brooklyn, Queens and Staten Island. District 5 in Harlem and most of the Bronx are not represented at all, nor are East New York or Ocean Hill-Brownsville sections of Brooklyn.

Many poor, minority neighborhoods, like Bedford-Stuyvesant and Bushwick in Brooklyn, have only one or two schools on the list. The test scores at those schools are generally lower than the scores of middle-class schools on the list. For example, at P.S. 33 in the central Bronx, whose students are overwhelmingly poor, less than half passed standardized reading tests last year. Yet in many of the Manhattan schools on the list, the number of students passing reading tests was more than 70 percent.

Mayor Michael R. Bloomberg announced last month that he would impose uniform reading and mathematics curriculums on all but 200 "successful schools" as part of a far-reaching overhaul of the troubled school system. The idea was to replace what had become a vast patchwork of academic programs, so that every student could be learning more or less the same lessons at the same time.

Mr. Bloomberg said the uniform curriculums would be of particular help to the many students and teachers who move often from school to school.

But he quickly realized that the idea of exempting schools was far more contentious than he had expected. Some parents and educators

Continued on Page B4

Republicans in Senate Preparing Agenda With a Surgeon's Touch

By DAVID FIRESTONE

WASHINGTON, Feb. 14 — Republican Senate leaders unveiled a legislative agenda today that mixed tax cuts with an unusually wide variety of health issues, showing the influence of Senator Bill Frist, the surgeon who is their new majority leader.

Of the Top 10 bills that Republicans plan to introduce, half reflect Dr. Frist's medical background, particularly a measure to combat the spread of AIDS, which has also been championed by President Bush, and one that bans a form of late-term abortion. Other medical bills would add a prescription drug benefit to Medicare, limit medical malpractice insurance costs and make it easier for drug companies to manufacture vaccines.

Party leaders also plan an energy bill that will probably include increased domestic oil drilling, an education bill that adds more local flexibility to federal requirements, and a bill matching one passed in the House on Thursday that adds stricter work requirements for welfare recipients. Another top-priority bill, already introduced, would repeal the estate tax.

Although issues like Medicare reform or limits on medical malpractice awards might have come up under the leadership of Dr. Frist's predecessor, Trent Lott, it is unlikely that so many health issues would have received such prominence.

The ceremonial unveiling of the list was about six weeks later than usual. The list of high-priority bills is normally presented by each party's leader on the first day of the Congressional session in January. But Dr. Frist took office after the turmoil of Mr. Lott's resignation and did not have time to assemble the agenda. Also, though they risked appearing tentative, several senators said they wanted to wait until after they received their "marching orders" from President Bush's State of the Union address, and the Senate then took a month to approve last year's unfinished spending bills.

Having helped shepherd the spending measure to approval late Thursday, Dr. Frist asserted that today was the first real day of the Congressional session.

"I am here today to declare that the 107th Congress is over," he said at a news conference, calling today a "pivot point" in the transition to a Congressional session led entirely by Republicans. Though he dutifully explained the party's belief that cutting taxes would create jobs, he reserved his most passionate language, as he always has, for the need to spend $15 billion to fight the spread of AIDS around the world.

"This little virus is only 22 years

Continued on Page A17

INSIDE

Associated Press, 1962

Walt Rostow Is Dead

An architect and defender of the Vietnam war as an adviser to Presidents John F. Kennedy and Lyndon B. Johnson, he was 86. PAGE A23

American Killed in Colombia

A United States government employee was shot dead, and three others are missing, after a plane crash in a rebel-dominated area. PAGE A3

Cloned Sheep Dolly Is Dead

Dolly, the sheep who made history as the first clone from a mammal, has died from a lung infection, her veterinarians said. She was 6. PAGE A4

Updated news: nytimes.com
Tomorrow in The Times: Page D8

"All the News That's Fit to Print"

The New York Times

Late Edition
New York: **Today,** partly cloudy, breezy, not as cold, high 47. **Tonight,** rain, low 38. **Tomorrow,** rain, chilly breezes, high 43. **Yesterday,** high 38, low 35. Weather map is on Page C13.

VOL. CLII . . No. 52,449 — Copyright © 2003 The New York Times — NEW YORK, THURSDAY, APRIL 10, 2003 — ONE DOLLAR

U.S. FORCES TAKE CONTROL IN BAGHDAD; BUSH ELATED; SOME RESISTANCE REMAINS

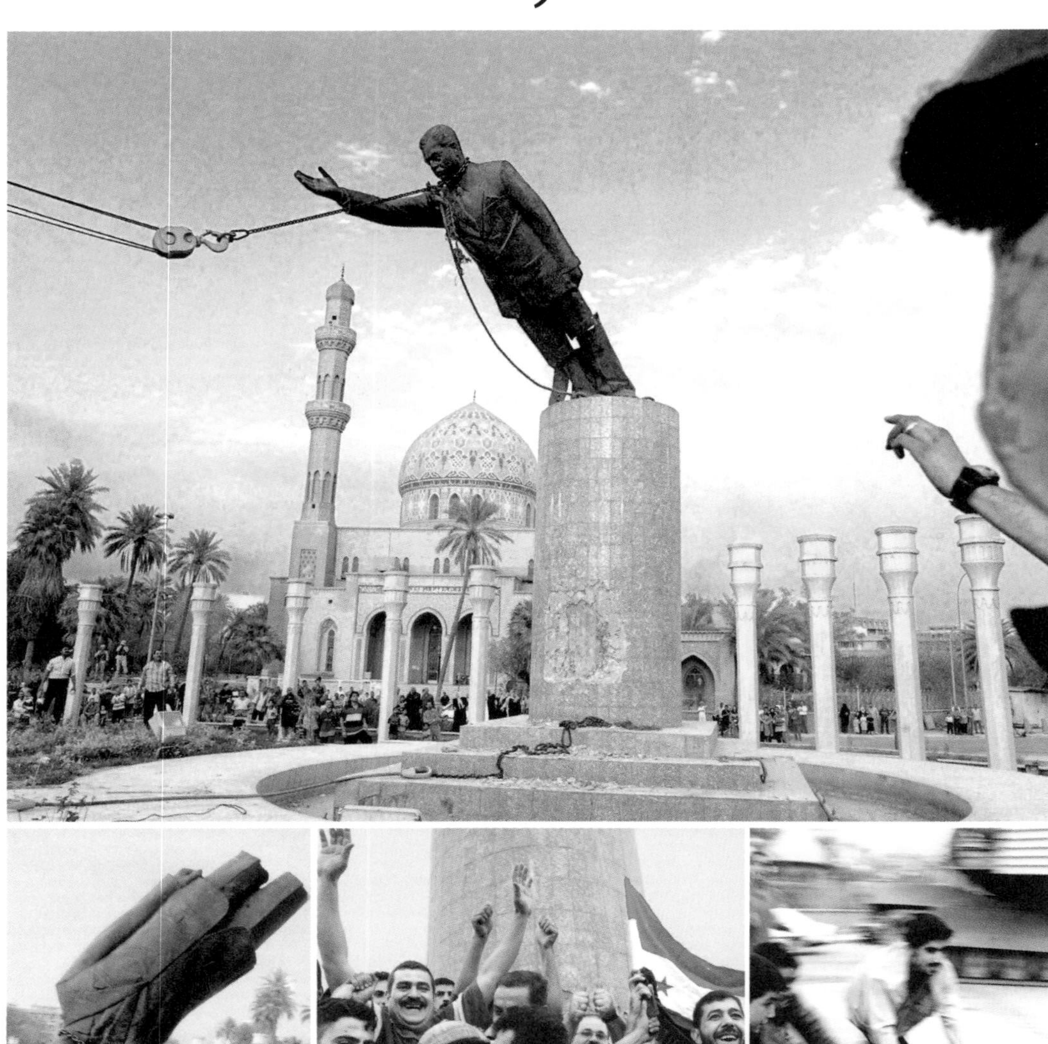

Top, Jerome Delay/Associated Press; bottom left, Ramzi Haidar/Agence France-Presse; bottom center and right, Tyler Hicks/The New York Times

A SYMBOL CRASHES DOWN In a square in central Baghdad, American marines lashed a towering statue of Saddam Hussein to their armored vehicle and pulled it down. Jubilant Iraqis, bottom center, kissed Lance Cpl. Shawn Hicks, while others dragged the statue's head through the streets.

Hussein Statue Is Toppled — Rumsfeld Urges Caution

By PATRICK E. TYLER

KUWAIT, Thursday, April 10 — Much of Baghdad tumbled into American hands on Wednesday as Saddam Hussein's image was pulled down from pedestals and portraiture in the city. But American and British commanders said the war in Iraq, including the battle for Baghdad, was not over and faced critical days ahead.

Marines entered the Iraqi capital in force from the east, linking up with an Army division that controlled the western and southern approaches, as well as the city center.

Early this morning, Marine units surrounded a house in north Baghdad where they believed Saddam Hussein had taken refuge, military officials said.

The officials said they believed Mr. Hussein had been wounded, and perhaps one of his sons killed, when an American bomber dropped four 2,000-pound bunker-busting bombs on the upscale west Baghdad neighborhood of Mansur on Monday.

In Washington Defense Secretary Donald H. Rumsfeld, while clearly pleased with events, noted that the war, just three weeks old, "most assuredly is not over."

Although he set no timetable, Mr. Rumsfeld framed the unfinished military task so broadly that it seemed certain that the military campaign could take weeks, if not months, as the Army and Marines confront what is left of the Iraqi army and as special operations forces and Central Intelligence Agency officers use a cash reward system to track down thousands of Hussein loyalists.

"We will not stop until Saddam Hussein's regime has been removed from every corner of that country," Mr. Rumsfeld said.

Bastions of Iraqi resistance were still holding out in north and central Iraq, military officials said. Mr. Hussein, his sons and his top aides, if alive, were still at large. The chemical and biological weapons and the laboratories for making them — the destruction of which the Bush administration cited as a prime motive for war — had yet to be located.

Even in Baghdad, fighting had not subsided entirely. An armored column of the First Brigade of the Third Infantry Division clashed Wednesday evening with at least two squads of Iraqi troops in western Baghdad after encountering land mines strewn across a highway cleared of Iraqi mines just hours earlier. That indicated a remnant of command control, an American officer said.

Ten or more Iraqi regular army divisions were still deployed in the field, military officials said, and though many others have collapsed without a fight, an enormous arsenal of conventional weapons was still hidden around the country where tens of thousands of Hussein loyalists, Baath Party officials and Iraqi soldiers have apparently gone home or underground.

Up and down the chain of American and British commanders, there was a sense of caution about the dramatic collapse of authority in Baghdad, largely because so many members of an extremely repressive government and its army, police force and intelligence services had simply turned into vapor. Their potential reappearance represented a threat that no prudent military commander could ignore, officials said.

It was also not clear the extent to

Continued on Page B4

Speed and Flexibility

By MICHAEL R. GORDON

CAMP DOHA, Kuwait, April 9 — If there is a single reason for the allied success in toppling President Saddam Hussein's government, it is the flexibility the American military demonstrated in carrying out its campaign.

Military Analysis

From the very start the American military had to adapt to fickle allies, changes ordered by superiors in Washington and new tactics by their foe.

American forces began the campaign without the northern front called for in the strategy and with fewer troops than had been planned. They were forced to advance the date of the land attack, and they fought battles in the southern cities of Iraq that had never been anticipated.

In the final analysis, the speed of the allied land assault, coupled with American airpower, enabled the military to arrive at the outskirts of Baghdad before the Iraqis could set up an adequate defense.

"We executed faster than they could react," a senior American military official said today.

American commanders caution, however, that the war is not over yet. Only a fraction of Baghdad has been searched by American forces. Troops have yet to move into some key areas that have long been dominated by members of the Hussein government and which have been defended by the paramilitary fedayeen.

American forces also have yet to enter Tikrit, Mr. Hussein's ancestral home, which is defended by portions of the Adnan Republican Guard Division. Kirkuk, the northern Iraqi city, remains under Iraqi control as do the country's northern oil fields, which American officials are concerned Iraq may try to destroy.

Thus, while the allies may have delivered a mortal blow to the Iraqi government, they still face some complex tasks.

From the very beginning, this was a lopsided contest.

Iraq had about a third as many tanks as it had during the 1991 Persian Gulf war. And the Iraqi Air Force was thoroughly intimidated by the allies. Iraqi warplanes never took to the skies in this war. The Iraqis even buried some of their planes to try to protect them against air attack.

But the Iraqis had some advantages, including their intention to make their main stand in the streets of Baghdad, confront the American armed forces with the prospect of urban warfare, high casualties and a drawn-out fight. There was also the potential threat of chemical and biological weapons, a danger that American officials say they fully expected to confront.

Addressing the American advance on Baghdad, Vice President Dick

Continued on Page B4

Bush Tunes In And Sees Iraqis In Celebrations

By ELISABETH BUMILLER and DOUGLAS JEHL

WASHINGTON, April 9 — An elated President Bush watched celebrating Iraqis drag a statue of Saddam Hussein through Baghdad today as Vice President Dick Cheney and Defense Secretary Donald H. Rumsfeld, barely disguised their glee and their disdain for critics of the Pentagon battle plan.

Although the official word from the White House was that there would be no gloating and that the battles were not yet over, Mr. Cheney and Mr. Rumsfeld seemed to treat cautionary notes about hubris as so much political politeness.

At the Pentagon, Mr. Rumsfeld compared the toppling of Saddam Hussein's government to the fall of the Berlin Wall, and said that Mr. Hussein had taken his place with Hitler, Stalin, Lenin and Nicolae Ceausescu "in the pantheon of failed, brutal dictators."

In New Orleans, Vice President Dick Cheney called the military campaign "extraordinary" and dismissed critics as "retired military officers embedded in T.V. studios."

At the White House, Mr. Bush, watching the Iraqi crowds topple the Saddam Hussein statue on a television set just outside the Oval Office, exclaimed, "They got it down!" according to an aide.

But the euphoria swiftly shifted to the problems of administering a perilous peace. By this afternoon the administration was dealing with questions of who would run Iraq, and

Continued on Page B10

Cheers, Tears and Looting in Capital's Streets

By JOHN F. BURNS

BAGHDAD, Iraq, April 9 — Saddam Hussein's rule collapsed in a matter of hours today across much of this capital city as ordinary Iraqis took to the streets in their thousands to topple Mr. Hussein's statues, loot government ministries and interrogation centers and to give a cheering, often tearful welcome to advancing American troops.

After three weeks battling their way north from Kuwait against Mr. Hussein's hard-core loyalists, Army and Marine Corps units moving into the districts of eastern Baghdad where many of the city's five million people live finally met the kind of adulation from ordinary Iraqis that American advocates of a war to topple Mr. Hussein had predicted.

Amid the celebration, many of Mr. Hussein's troops and officials simply abandoned their posts and ran away.

Much of Baghdad became, in a moment, a showcase of unbridled enthusiasm for America, as much as it metamorphosed into a crucible of unbridled hatred for Mr. Hussein and his 24-year rule.

American troops, but almost as much any Westerner caught up in the tide of people rushing into the streets, were met with scenes that summoned comparisons to the freeing of Eastern Europe 14 years ago.

There was no word on the fate of Mr. Hussein or his sons, Uday and Qusay, targeted by American bombs in a western residential area on Monday. But his whereabouts — even his very existence — seemed irrelevant as American Marines used an M88 tank recovery vehicle to topple a large statue of Mr. Hussein in the central Firdos Square.

Crowds surged forward to stomp on the downed statue, whose head had briefly been covered in an American flag, and several men dragged its severed head through the streets.

A burly 39-year-old man named Qifa, assigned by Mr. Hussein's Information Ministry to keep watch on an American reporter, paused at midmorning, outside the inferno that had been the headquarters of Iraq's National Olympic Committee, to ask the reporter to grip his hand. The building, used to torture and kill opponents of Mr. Hussein, had been one of the most widely feared places in Iraq.

"Touch me, touch me, tell me that this is real, tell me that the night-

Continued on Page B3

A High Point in 2 Decades of U.S. Might

By R. W. APPLE Jr.

WASHINGTON, April 9 — The collapse of government authority in Baghdad, dramatized by the toppling of a colossal statue of President Saddam Hussein, constitutes the high-water mark for a new American determination to use the nation's military might to project its power around the world.

News Analysis

The resurgence began in 1981 with the Reagan administration, which took office with the humiliation of the Iranian hostage crisis looming large in the national psyche. That had come to symbolize President Jimmy Carter's less robust approach to foreign affairs, and Ronald Reagan campaigned against him on promises to rebuild the military and pursue aggressive policies.

Since then, American troops have gone into full-fledged military action on four continents, using increasingly sophisticated weapons and a wide variety of tactics, usually but not invariably achieving their immediate goals in short order.

American intervention has not been automatic; Washington did nothing much to halt the slaughter in Rwanda and Burundi, for example. It has often been late, as in trying to stay out of Bosnia until 1995.

It has occasionally come to grief, as in Somalia in 1993. More often, though, it has succeeded, as in Grenada (1983), Panama (1989) and Kuwait (1991).

The norm, under three Republican presidents as well as a Democrat, has become markedly active.

But projecting strength is not the same as making friends or enhancing national security.

The standing of the United States has perhaps never been lower among Islamic nations and nations with restive Islamic minorities than it is today. American esteem has also fallen across much of Europe.

The Iraqi war itself, American alliances with Arab governments considered corrupt or tyrannical by their own people, strong American backing for Israel and perceived American indifference to the Palestinian cause have all combined to tarnish the American image, most

Continued on Page B4

NEWS SUMMARY A2

Updated news: nytimes.com
Tomorrow in The Times: Page C13

INSIDE

11 Die in Afghanistan Error

An American plane trying to hit escaping rebels in eastern Afghanistan accidentally bombed a family's house instead, killing 11 people, including 7 women. **PAGE B15**

Illness Count Questioned

The number of people hospitalized in China with severe acute respiratory syndrome has been sharply understated, a retired military physician said. **PAGE A8**

Murdoch Extends Empire

Rupert Murdoch's News Corporation agreed to buy control of Hughes Electronics and its DirecTV satellite unit from General Motors for $6.6 billion. **PAGE C1**

A Masters Like No Other

The tournament opens today with Tiger Woods chasing a record and the Augusta National Golf Club facing protests over membership rules. **SPORTSTHURSDAY, PAGE S1**

FOR HOME DELIVERY CALL 1-800-NYTIMES

"All the News That's Fit to Print"

The New York Times

Late Edition
New York: **Today**, humid with a late shower, high 76. **Tonight**, showers, cooler, low 52. **Tomorrow**, cloudy, a shower, high 57. **Yesterday**, high 71, low 51. Weather map is on Page D8.

VOL. CLII . . No. 52,471 NEW YORK, FRIDAY, MAY 2, 2003 ONE DOLLAR

Bush Declares 'One Victory in a War on Terror'

Associated Press

President Bush, on the Abraham Lincoln, off California, said last night that the major combat in Iraq was over.

He Says Military Phase in Iraq Has Ended

By DAVID E. SANGER

SAN DIEGO, May 1 — President Bush declared tonight that the military phase of the battle to topple Saddam Hussein's government was "one victory in a war on terror that began on Sept. 11th, 2001, and still goes on."

Speaking from the deck of the aircraft carrier Abraham Lincoln before thousands of uniformed sailors and aviators as the ship approached San Diego Harbor, he argued that by vanquishing Mr. Hussein's government, he had removed "an ally of Al Qaeda," and he vowed to continue to search for banned weapons in Iraq — a search that so far has been largely unsuccessful — and to confront any other nations that use such weapons to threaten the United States or could sell them to terrorists.

Mr. Bush's speech tonight, 43 days after he announced to the nation from the Oval Office that the war had begun with a surprise bombing of a compound where Mr. Hussein had been sighted, ended the combat phase of one of the swiftest wars in American military history, and one of the most dramatic chapters of Mr. Bush's presidency. [Text, Page A16.]

In the 20-minute speech to the men and women of the Abraham Lincoln, whose aircraft dropped nearly a third of the ordnance that rained down on Iraq, Mr. Bush made it clear that he considered the Iraq conflict just one major moment of a broader fight that he would pursue against Al Qaeda and other terrorists.

He spoke in emotional terms not only about the troops who toppled Mr. Hussein but also about the Sept. 11 attacks, melding the battle against terrorism with the battle against Iraq. "We have not forgotten the victims of Sept. 11th, the last phone calls, the cold murder of children, the searches in the rubble," he said. "With those attacks, the terrorists and their supporters declared war on the United States. And war is what they got."

The Bush administration has never linked the attacks on the World Trade Center and the Pentagon to Mr. Hussein, although senior officials did charge that Iraq had ties to the Qaeda network.

The president's stern words about governments that support terrorism and pursue illegal weapons programs appeared to be a direct warning to Iran and North Korea and "any outlaw regime that has ties to terrorist groups, and seeks or possesses weapons of mass destruction." Those states, he said, pose "a grave danger to the civilized world, and will be confronted."

Just in the last week, the State Department said Iran had the deepest ties to terrorism of any nation in the world, and North Korea boasted that it had already obtained nuclear weapons and was making more.

Mr. Bush did not declare final victory tonight as the sailors of the Lincoln, some in blue work uniforms and others in dress whites, assembled on the four-and-a-half-acre flight deck at dusk. Much remained to be done, he said, in rebuilding Iraq, and he promised that allied forces would stay as long as necessary.

White House officials said they did

Continued on Page A16

Between War and Peace

By MICHAEL R. GORDON

Military Analysis

BAGHDAD, Iraq, May 1 — Apache helicopter gunships zoomed toward a band of paramilitary fighters who were stealing crates of ammunition from an arms cache near Saddam Hussein's hometown, Tikrit. As the Iraqis tried to make their getaway, the Apaches opened fire, turning the Iraqis' truck into a hunk of twisted metal and killing 14.

This is not an old episode from the war. It took place Wednesday night, just a day before President Bush flew to the aircraft carrier Abraham Lincoln to announce the end of major combat operations in Iraq, and it illustrates the complicated mission American forces now face as they try to bring stability to Iraq.

American forces are operating in a netherworld between war and peace. One moment, they may be working on restoring electrical power, and the next they may be involved in a firefight. The foe is any of a broad array of forces that oppose the new order: hard-core members of Mr. Hussein's old government, criminal bands, Iranian agents, suicide bombers and power-hungry Iraqi factions determined to seize control.

"We are moving into stability operations, and stability operations are characterized by momentary flare-ups of violence," Brig. Gen. Daniel Hahn, the chief of staff for the Army's V Corps, said today. "It will look at times like we are still at war."

By conventional measures, the war in Iraq has been over for weeks. Allied forces have overthrown Mr. Hussein and his government, and 15 of the 55 most wanted men in that ruling circle are in American custody. The Americans and their allies have defeated his military, moved into his palaces and started to patrol the streets of Iraq's capital. American commanders renamed Saddam International Airport before they even got here: it is Baghdad International now and a major hub for military operations here.

From the start, however, the United States' declared goal was not just

Continued on Page A18

Cold Truths Behind Pomp

Tending to Key Issues, Politics and Security

By ELISABETH BUMILLER

News Analysis

WASHINGTON, May 1 — President Bush's made-for-television address tonight on the carrier Abraham Lincoln was a powerful, Reaganesque finale to a six-week war.

But beneath the golden images of a president steaming home with his troops toward the California coast lay the cold political and military realities that drove Mr. Bush's advisers to create the moment.

The president declared an end to major combat operations, White House, Pentagon and State Department officials said, for three crucial reasons: to signify the shift of American soldiers from the role of conquerors to police, to open the way for aid from countries that refused to help militarily and — above all — to signal to voters that Mr. Bush is shifting his focus from Baghdad to concerns at home.

Mr. Bush was careful, though, not to close the door completely on his greatest political strength, his role as the warrior president who struck back after Sept. 11. For the first time in months, he reprised his most emotional oratory from the attacks and directly tied it to Iraq and his battle against terrorism.

"The battle of Iraq is one victory

Continued on Page A17

New Alternative On Dividend Tax

House Republican leaders agreed to abandon President Bush's plan to eliminate all taxes on dividends, forging instead a new proposal that would reduce the taxes on both dividends and capital gains.

The proposal would lower the tax on dividends to equal that of capital gains and would cut the gains tax for most investors to 15 percent from 20 percent.

The new idea, which House leaders acknowledged was born of the Senate's refusal to accept Mr. Bush's full tax package, won lukewarm support from the White House, where a spokeswoman called it a "positive step."

Article, Page A26.

GUNFIGHT KILLS 12 AS ISRAELI TROOPS SEEK HAMAS MEN

A TANK ASSAULT IN GAZA

Dead Include Militants and a Child — Palestinians Cite Threat to Peace Plan

By GREG MYRE

GAZA, May 1 — Israeli tanks and troops charged into a densely packed neighborhood here before dawn today and killed 12 Palestinians, including wanted militants and a 2-year-old boy, according to Palestinian officials. The fierce gun battles took place hours after a major Middle East peace plan was introduced.

The timing of the raid, which the Israelis said was directed at a leading weapons smuggler with the militant Hamas movement, prompted angry Palestinian charges that Israel was trying to sabotage the international peace plan, known as the road map, before it began.

"The Israelis fired massively from tanks toward houses," said Abd al-Razak al-Majaydah, the Palestinian general security commander for Gaza. "The Israeli operation may result in the failure of the new government's mission."

That was a reference to the Palestinian government that was installed Tuesday with a pledge to halt violence against Israel.

The Israelis attacked a day after a suicide bombing killed three people in Tel Aviv. Israel said it would ensure its own security until the Palestinians prove that they are committed to reining in militants.

"How can anyone expect to advance when there continue to be attacks against Israelis?" said David Baker, an official in the office of Prime Minister Ariel Sharon. "This is an untenable situation."

The Israeli ground forces, backed by helicopters, surrounded the four-story cinder-block house of Yousef Abu Hein, a Hamas militant, at around 1:30 a.m. and called on loudspeakers for his surrender. But Mr. Abu Hein remained inside, and militants from nearby homes unleashed a barrage of automatic rifle fire and rocket-propelled grenades, setting off firefights that persisted for more than 12 hours.

With the Israelis firing from helicopters and tanks and with Palestinians shooting from inside houses, more than 60 Palestinians and 8 Israeli soldiers were wounded in the

Continued on Page A6

Nets Gain in Playoffs

The Nets eliminated the Milwaukee Bucks in the first round of the N.B.A. playoffs last night with a 113-101 victory. Kenyon Martin scored 29 points as the Nets won the series, 4-2, and advanced to play the Boston Celtics. Boston moved on by beating the Indiana Pacers, 110-90.

SportsFriday, Page D1.

MORGAN STANLEY DRAWS S.E.C.'S IRE

Efforts to Play Down Role in Scandal Seem to Backfire

By FLOYD NORRIS

Morgan Stanley's efforts to play down its role in the Wall Street research scandal appeared to backfire yesterday, as the chairman of the Securities and Exchange Commission released a blistering letter addressed to the firm's chief executive.

William H. Donaldson, the commission chairman, said in a letter dated Wednesday that he was "deeply troubled" by comments from Philip J. Purcell, the Morgan Stanley official, which he said "evidence a troubling lack of contrition."

He warned that Morgan Stanley could face further legal action if it continued to deny having acted badly in the research scandal, which was the subject of a $1.4 billion industry settlement.

At a conference of institutional investors on Tuesday, the day after the details of the settlement were announced, Mr. Purcell said: "I don't see anything in the settlement that will concern the retail investor about Morgan Stanley. Not one thing." A reporter from The New York Times attended the conference, and Mr. Purcell's remarks appeared in an article in the paper the next day. Mr. Donaldson's letter began with a reference to the Times article.

Mr. Purcell took a different tone yesterday, responding in writing to Mr. Donaldson. "Obviously, your concerns are troubling to me," Mr. Purcell said. "I deeply regret any public impression that the commission's complaint was not a matter of concern to retail investors."

Before and after the settlement's details were announced, Morgan Stanley sought to establish a public perception that it had behaved better than other major investment banking firms, even though it was required to pay $125 million in the settlement. At the conference on Tuesday, Mr. Purcell argued that Morgan shares were a good invest-

Continued on Page C4

Birmingham Recalls a Time When Children Led the Fight

By DAVID M. HALBFINGER

BIRMINGHAM, Ala., May 1 — Across 40 years in time, some memories do not fade.

Cardell Gay, now 56, can still feel the wallop of the water as Bull Connor, the feared public safety commissioner who embodied segregation in Birmingham, had city firemen aim their hoses at him.

Gwendolyn Sanders Gamble, 55, can still hear the police attack dogs snarling, the preaching that drew her out of school, and the praying and singing that carried her into the street day after day.

Sandra Berry Pratt, 52, can still see her mother in a bright yellow dress, yellow pumps, and yellow handbag, jumping for joy as Ms. Pratt, then 12, was carted off to jail by the police five minutes into a protest outside a department store.

Some 2,000 people are expected to commemorate this weekend the epochal battle they fought in the civil rights movement, when children as young as 6 years old marched, picketed, jammed the jails and juvenile halls, shut the city's shopping district down, and at last broke the back of segregation in Birmingham, the most segregated city in the nation.

The surviving leaders of those 1963 protests will be here, including the Rev. Fred L. Shuttlesworth, now of Cincinnati, then a Birmingham firebrand who brought Martin Luther King Jr. to town and prodded him into a no-holds-barred campaign of civil disobedience; and the Rev. James Bevel, who played Pied Piper to the city's black schoolchildren.

But if the hotels are not exactly filling up, the reason is that many of those countless youngsters, the self-described foot soldiers of the battle of Birmingham, the ones who did not become famous in their own right, have never left.

The four-day program, which began tonight, serves up history with

Continued on Page A28

Hurriyet, via Associated Press

Rescue Efforts After Turkey Earthquake

A boarding school student trapped in the wreckage from an earthquake that killed at least 100 in eastern Turkey talked to a rescuer. Page A10.

INSIDE

Surprise in Intelligence Bill

The Bush administration and Senate Republicans are seeking to extend domestic national security subpoena powers now held only by the F.B.I. to both the C.I.A. and the military.

PAGE A21

Episcopal Bishop Is Dead

Paul Moore Jr., the retired Episcopal bishop of New York who for more than a decade was the most formidable liberal Christian voice in the city and early advocate of women's ordination, was 83.

PAGE C11

More SARS Cases Are Reported; Virus Found to Persist in Patients

By LAWRENCE K. ALTMAN

Dismaying developments in three nations yesterday underscored the capriciousness of SARS, the respiratory virus that had seemed to be coming under control in many countries.

In Canada, health officials announced two new possible cases in Toronto, the first identified there in 11 days. The cases involved health care workers in two hospitals where the disease, severe acute respiratory syndrome, had spread in the past.

Officials of the World Health Organization said they were particularly disturbed to learn only yesterday that one Toronto case had been tentatively diagnosed Monday night, as senior Canadian health officials were traveling to Geneva to try to persuade the W.H.O. to reverse an advisory that people without urgent business avoid traveling to Toronto. The warning was lifted on Tuesday.

In Hong Kong, health officials said it now appeared that many patients who seemed to have recovered may still have some SARS virus in their bodies when they are discharged from a hospital, raising the disturbing possibility that they might still be able to spread the disease. Officials also confirmed that 12 patients, apparently recovered, had relapsed after their discharge from a hospital.

And scientists in Taiwan reported 11 new cases and 2 additional deaths yesterday. Taiwan's caseload, just 41 as recently as last Friday, has more than doubled, to 89. The scientists said there was new evidence of SARS both within hospitals and in the general community, and added that the local authorities were putting large numbers of people into quarantine.

With just 56 probable cases and no deaths, the United States has been largely spared, thanks in part to an aggressive public-health plan put into effect after the anthrax attacks of fall 2001. [Page A12.]

The epidemic continued to rage in

Continued on Page A14

"All the News That's Fit to Print"

The New York Times

Late Edition
New York: **Today**, mostly sunny, high 88. **Tonight**, mostly clear and muggy, low 75. **Tomorrow**, partly cloudy and humid, high 91. **Yesterday**, high 83, low 68. Weather map is on Page D8.

VOL. CLII . . No. 52,581 | NEW YORK, WEDNESDAY, AUGUST 20, 2003 | ONE DOLLAR

HUGE SUICIDE BLAST DEMOLISHES U.N. HEADQUARTERS IN BAGHDAD; TOP AID OFFICIALS AMONG 17 DEAD

Agence France-Presse

American soldiers and rescue workers searched for casualties yesterday in the rubble of the United Nations headquarters in Baghdad.

Associated Press

Israeli paramedics helped a victim of yesterday's suicide bombing.

BOMBING KILLS 18 AND HURTS SCORES ON JERUSALEM BUS

HAMAS IS A MAIN SUSPECT

Israel Breaks Off Security Talks With Palestinians and May Seal Towns in Response

By JAMES BENNET

JERUSALEM, Aug. 19 — A Palestinian suicide bomber killed at least 18 people, including children, when he detonated an explosive packed with ball bearings tonight aboard a city bus crowded with families, some of them returning from Judaism's holiest site, the Western Wall.

The blast resounded across Jerusalem as it peeled up the roof of the bus and blew out its windows, smearing human remains on a preceding tour bus and opening a deep wound in the American-backed peace effort.

More than 100 people were reported hurt, many seriously, in one of the deadliest attacks in almost three years of conflict. Men carrying blood-spattered children raced toward approaching ambulances. On a street strewn with broken glass and bloodied sheet metal, a man knelt near the shattered bus to perform mouth-to-mouth resuscitation on a toddler.

Later, in a hospital here, Yaacov Bahar, 35, held his hands in the air in front of him, as though he were still carrying an infant, as he described helping bring four children from the bus.

"In my eyes, I'm still seeing the nightmare," said Mr. Bahar, who was being treated for shock.

Breaking off security talks tonight, Israel froze all contacts with the Palestinian leadership after the bombing.

A senior Israeli official said Israel would probably seal Palestinians into their cities and towns again on Wednesday, reimposing tight travel restrictions that had been loosened somewhat as the peace effort took hold in recent weeks.

The attack tonight was claimed by members of both Hamas and Islamic Jihad. The Israeli police said the bomber was from Hamas.

Palestinian and Israeli officers had been discussing how Palestinian forces would assume responsibility from Israel for policing two West Bank cities, continuing an exchange of control called for by the peace plan, known as the road map.

But Israeli officials reacted to the bombing with fury tonight, and expressed frustration toward a peace plan they said was endangering their security.

"Israel cannot be the perpetual testing ground for peace proposals that the Palestinians fail to implement," said Dore Gold, an adviser to Prime Minister Ariel Sharon.

In Gaza City, the Palestinian prime minister, Mahmoud Abbas, told reporters, "I declare my strong condemnation of this horrible act that doesn't serve the interests of the Palestinian people." Mr. Abbas said

Continued on Page A6

Job on the Line, Davis Promises To Fight Recall

By JOHN M. BRODER with DEAN E. MURPHY

LOS ANGELES, Aug. 19 — In a fight for his political life, Gov. Gray Davis pleaded with Californians today to reject the attempt to recall him, describing it as part of a right-wing effort "to steal elections Republicans cannot win."

Mr. Davis, a Democrat elected to a second term only last fall, made a vigorous case for himself in a late-afternoon address at the University of California at Los Angeles that was carried live on several local television stations and cable news networks.

"There are many reasons to be against this recall," he said. "It is expensive, it's undemocratic, it's a bad precedent, and it almost certainly will breed more recalls." [Excerpts, Page A18.]

Mr. Davis's speech came at a critical juncture in which he is fighting a growing perception in his party that his ouster is inevitable. In a vivid illustration of the governor's difficulties, Lt. Gov. Cruz M. Bustamante, the only prominent Democrat on the recall ballot, in essence kicked off his own campaign today, appearing outside his home near Sacramento to present a plan raising $8 billion in new income, tobacco and commercial property taxes to solve the state's budget problems.

Mr. Davis's speech was his first full address on a recall election that threatens his political future. He offered apologies to voters for his handling of California's energy and

Continued on Page A18

Chaos as a Strategy Against the U.S.

Foes Aim to Stoke Iraqis' Frustration

By THOM SHANKER

News Analysis

WASHINGTON, Aug. 19 — The bombing of the United Nations headquarters in Baghdad today provided grisly evidence of a new strategy by anti-American forces to depict the United States as unable to guarantee public order, as well as to frighten away relief organizations rebuilding Iraq.

Military officers and experts on terrorism said the bombing fit a pattern of recent strikes on water and oil pipelines and the Jordanian Embassy, although they emphasized that it was too early to uncover any connections among the attacks.

In recent weeks terrorists have conducted almost daily attacks on the American military. But after the bombing today there is a growing belief that anti-American fighters, whatever their origin and inspiration, have adopted a coherent strategy not only to kill members of allied forces when possible, but also to spread fear by destroying public offices and utilities.

President Bush was defiant today. He said: "Every sign of progress in Iraq adds to the desperation of the terrorists and the remnants of Saddam's brutal regime. The civilized world will not be intimidated, and these killers will not determine the future of Iraq."

Speaking at his ranch in Crawford, Tex., he added that the assailants were "the enemies of every nation that seeks to help the Iraqi people."

But the problem now posed for American forces in Iraq is an acute one. Put simply, if Iraqis are afraid and unconvinced that their situation is improving, their hostility to the United States may grow.

The attacks on foreign embassies and the headquarters of international organizations, as well as water and oil pipelines, appear specifically devised to halt improvements in the quality of life for average Iraqis.

"The goal is to deny the American occupation force the ability to pacify Iraq, to prevent the Americans from winning the hearts and minds of the people," said Loren Thompson, a military affairs analyst with the Lexington Institute. "If Iraq is in constant chaos, the United States can never move on to the next stage."

It is unclear whether the fighters are remnants of the former government or foreign Islamic zealots who have crossed into Iraq to kill Americans.

No one claimed responsibility for the attack. But it seems clear that any improvement in the standard of living of Iraqis is viewed by opponents of the occupation as a victory for the United States and its efforts to create a stable, democratic Iraq.

Across the government today, officials said the tactics and procedures

Continued on Page A9

SCENE OF CARNAGE

Bomb in Cement Truck — Dozens Hurt and Many Are Missing

By DEXTER FILKINS and RICHARD A. OPPEL Jr.

BAGHDAD, Iraq, Aug. 19 — A suicide bomber drove a gleaming new cement mixer full of explosives into the side of the United Nations compound here today and blew it up, killing 17 people and wounding at least 100 in an attack on one of the principal agencies in charge of rebuilding Iraq.

The bomb demolished the three-story converted hotel that served as the United Nations headquarters, scattering the wounded and the remains of the dead. United Nations employees, many of them recently flown in from Europe and the United States, crawled and ran from the wreckage, their clothes torn and splattered with blood. Many were delirious, calling out to friends and colleagues left in the rubble behind.

Among the dead was Sergio Vieira de Mello, 55, the United Nations secretary general's special representative in Iraq. Mr. Vieira de Mello's body was pulled from the wreckage tonight by American soldiers.

L. Paul Bremer III, the chief American civilian administrator here, said there were indications that Mr. Vieira de Mello had been the target of the attack. The truck bomb crashed into the compound just beneath Mr. Vieira de Mello's third-floor office.

The suicide bombing marked a brazen assault on the American occupation here, apparently calculated to destroy any sense of security for people charged with reviving Iraq in the aftermath of the war. If anarchy was the goal today, it was anarchy that unfolded.

Screams and moans rose from the dozens of bloodied United Nations workers who lay across the courtyard, as American soldiers yanked and pulled the living from ruins. Bodies lay about, some missing limbs, others covered with white sheets.

Susan Manuel, a United Nations spokeswoman, said the bombing marked the deadliest attack on the

Continued on Page A8

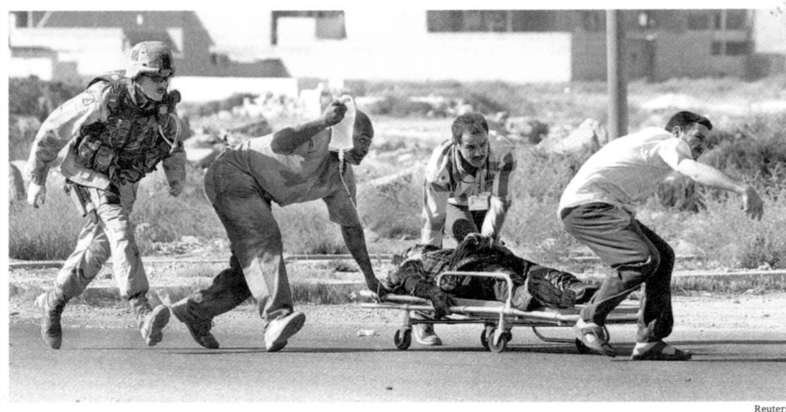

Reuters

Medical workers evacuated a man wounded in the bombing to a United States Army helicopter yesterday.

U.S. Backs Colombia on Attacking Drug Planes

By JUAN FORERO

BOGOTÁ, Colombia, Aug. 19 — Defense Secretary Donald H. Rumsfeld, on a one-day visit to Colombia, said today that the United States would support Colombia in resuming a policy that allows Colombian fighter pilots to shoot down planes suspected of ferrying drugs or force them to land.

Such a policy, which has been criticized by human rights groups, was suspended in Colombia and Peru after a Peruvian jet fighter mistakenly shot down a private plane carrying American missionaries, killing two people, one an infant, in 2001.

A White House statement said President Bush had determined that Colombia had since "put in place appropriate procedures to protect against loss of innocent life."

The announcement did not specify those safeguards, but American officials said they would include radio or visual contact, first trying to force suspect planes to land, and then firing warning shots. Only as a last resort, American officials said, would a plane be downed.

"Some of these procedures existed in the old program," one American official said, "but they were not enforced."

A much more limited program, still being developed, may be put in place in coming months in Peru, officials said.

The announcement was timed as part of a visit to Colombia by Mr. Rumsfeld, who arrived in Bogotá, the capital, this morning under tight security to underscore American support for President Alvaro Uribe.

The Uribe government has received $2.5 billion from Washington, largely in military aid, since 2000 as it battles leftist rebels and drug traffickers. Colombia is likely to get $700 million more this year.

The Colombian drug trade, which supplies most of the cocaine entering the United States, has been increasingly tied to both the leftist insurgency and right-wing paramilitary groups. To move the drug, traffickers have often relied on private aircraft.

"There are plenty of ways that illegal trade can move — land, sea or air — and if you're not attentive to the air, it becomes a preferred method," said Mr. Rumsfeld, who was traveling with reporters.

As in the past, the American role in the drug interdiction plan will consist of working closely with Colombian officials to identify suspect planes, American officials said.

Under the new policy, coordinates

Continued on Page A4

Energy Dept. Will Take Control Of Investigation Into the Blackout

By JAMES GLANZ and ANDREW C. REVKIN

The Department of Energy has agreed to lead a sweeping investigation to determine precisely how a huge swath of the nation's electrical system collapsed last week, draining power from tens of thousands of miles of high-voltage electrical lines, leaving millions in the dark and inflicting widespread damage on local economies from Detroit to New York.

Energy Department officials said that the investigation would employ hundreds of experts from federal agencies, national laboratories and the organizations that control the flow of electricity on the nation's power grid, and would take responsibility for discovering an answer outside an industry organization that had been leading the initial inquiry.

"The electric transmission grid is quite possibly the most vital piece of infrastructure which we have," said the secretary of energy, Spencer Abraham, in Washington yesterday afternoon. "We owe ourselves an explanation of this incident and an assurance that steps will be taken to address the cause."

Mr. Abraham promised explicitly that the investigation would make no attempt to shield the electric power industry from responsibility for the blackout, the largest in the nation's history. But Mr. Abraham also made clear that he took a dim view of early speculation on the causes of the blackout. Some experts have pointed to failures in high-voltage transmission lines controlled by FirstEnergy Corporation, in Ohio, as the first of a cascade of failures in the catastrophe.

"We have already seen many theories abound," Mr. Abraham said, adding that the evidence — though still sketchy — would be pursued no

Continued on Page A16

INSIDE

The Roots of a Bond Fight

The court battle between Albany and New York City over a state aid package to help the city balance its budget is one for the history books. A series of political decisions led to the current standoff. **PAGE B1**

Florida Revisits Class Size

Florida's top education officials are seeking a partial repeal of a plan to reduce class size that was approved by voters last fall. The move could cost state taxpayers billions of dollars. **PAGE A10**

Updated news: nytimes.com
Tomorrow in The Times: Page D8

"All the News That's Fit to Print"

The New York Times

Late Edition
New York: **Today**, showers yield to steady rain, heavy at times. High 61. **Tonight**, rain. Low 51. **Tomorrow**, cloudy, cooler. High 54. **Yesterday**, high 52, low 45. Details, Page D8.

VOL. CLIII . . No. 52,672 | Copyright © 2003 The New York Times | NEW YORK, WEDNESDAY, NOVEMBER 19, 2003 | ONE DOLLAR

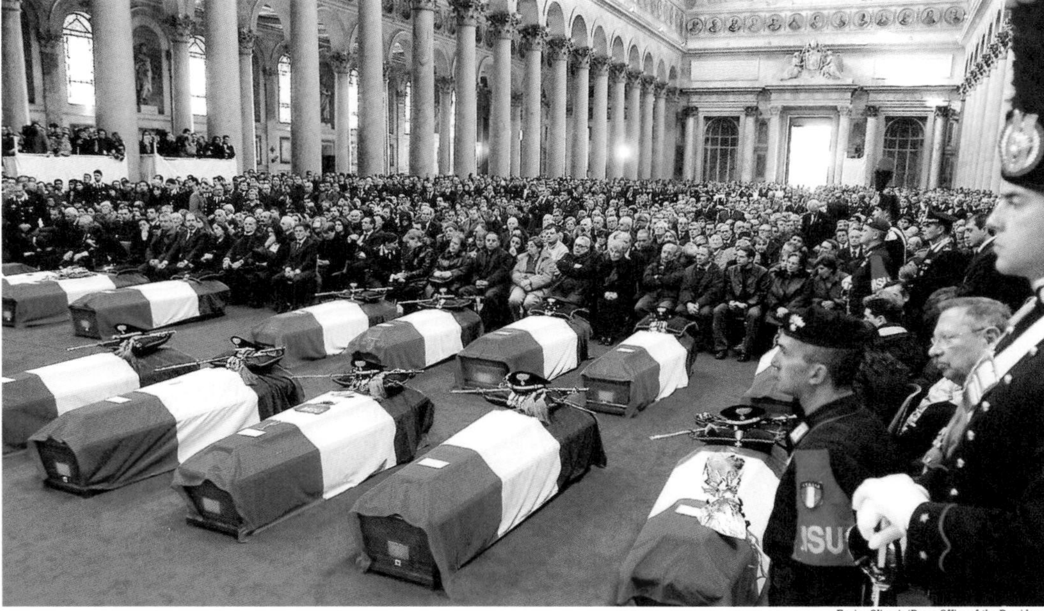

Enrico Oliverio/Press Office of the Presidency

19 Italians Killed in Iraq Are Laid to Rest

At St. Paul's Basilica in Rome, a state funeral was held yesterday for 17 Italian servicemen and 2 civilians who were killed on Nov. 12 when their headquarters in Nasiriya was hit by a car bomb. Fourteen Iraqis also died in the attack. It was the worst military loss for Italy since World War II.

MARRIAGE BY GAYS GAINS BIG VICTORY IN MASSACHUSETTS

Legislature Told to Clear Way — Court Cites State Constitution

By PAM BELLUCK

BOSTON, Nov. 18 — Massachusetts' highest court ruled on Tuesday that gay couples have the right to marry under the state's Constitution, and it gave the state legislature 180 days to make same-sex marriages possible.

The 4-to-3 decision was the first in which a state high court had ruled homosexual couples are constitutionally entitled to marry, and legal experts predicted it would have ramifications across the country.

"The question before us is whether, consistent with the Massachusetts Constitution, the commonwealth may deny the protections, benefits and obligations conferred by civil marriage to two individuals of the same sex who wish to marry," wrote Chief Justice Margaret H. Marshall of the state's Supreme Judicial Court. "We conclude that it may not. The Massachusetts Constitution affirms the dignity and equality of all individuals. It forbids the creation of second-class citizens." [Excerpts, Page A24.]

The decision, which did not explicitly tell the state legislature how to carry out the ruling, sent lawmakers and legal experts scrambling to determine what options exist short of legitimizing gay marriage. Other experts said that the court appeared determined to extend full marriage rights to gay men and lesbians.

The decision ignited a storm of reaction throughout the nation, with gay groups and some liberals heralding the ruling, and conservatives and some religious groups denouncing it.

"We're thrilled and delighted the highest court in the state of Massachusetts confirms that our community has the right to enter into civil marriage the same as other couples," said David Tseng, the executive director of Parents, Families and Friends of Lesbians and Gays, who noted that three of the four justices in the majority were appointed by Republican governors. "This is a tremendous victory for fairness and for families."

Tony Perkins, president of the Family Research Council, a conservative group, said "it is inexcusable for this court to force the state legislature to 'fix' its state constitution to make it comport with the pro-homo-

Continued on Page A24

Echoes of a June Ruling

A Supreme Court ruling on sodomy paved the way for yesterday's decision, experts said. Page A24.

At Sniper Trial, A Chilling Tape Is Heard by Jury

By ADAM LIPTAK

CHESAPEAKE, Va., Nov. 18 — Last November, during questioning, a homicide detective gave Lee Malvo a chance to show that his heart was not entirely cold.

The detective asked Mr. Malvo, accused of shooting 13 people last fall in the sniper attacks in the Washington region, whether he might not have, for a moment at least, hoped that some of the people whom he shot would survive.

"I intended to kill them all," Mr. Malvo replied in soft, calm voice.

Ten people died, and Mr. Malvo is now on trial here on charges that he had a role in what prosecutors call a terrorist rampage.

An hourlong audiotape of the questioning played for the jury on Tuesday provided the first extended look at Mr. Malvo's thought processes and demeanor. On the tape, Mr. Malvo spoke in clipped, cogent, bloodless phrases. "I marveled at how intelligent he was," the detective, Samuel Walker, said. "At one point, I kind of chuckled to myself to try to decide how to counter a question or statement that he made."

In trying to persuade Mr. Malvo to talk, Detective Walker suggested that his age could help him avoid the death penalty. Mr. Malvo was 17 at the time of the shootings.

"They are going to charge me as an adult," said Mr. Malvo, who is now 18. "I know they are."

Mr. Malvo is indeed being tried as

Continued on Page A20

Veil Lifts on Finalists for 9/11 Memorial Design

By DAVID W. DUNLAP

It would be a luminous place, a verdant place.

The outlines of the twin towers might rise like islands from a watery setting. Or they might be preserved in some fashion all the way down to bedrock. Visitors might find themselves under a kind of structural cloud, while family members could gather in their own sanctuary. It would be a quiet place.

Everywhere, there would be names. Alphabetically. Chronologically, by age. Collegially, alongside fellow workers. Geographically, by tower. But all accounted for: those who struggled and died at the Pentagon, in a Pennsylvania field and on that very spot in Lower Manhattan.

And on that spot, along with the pools and the trees and the points of light like votive candles, there would also be a tomb for those who are still nameless — the unidentified dead — so they might at last come to rest.

These are some of the ways New York may choose to memorialize the terrorist attacks of Sept. 11, 2001, and Feb. 26, 1993, at the site of the World Trade Center.

After four months of extraordinary secrecy, the veil started to lift last night, fold by fold, on the eight finalists chosen by the jury in the memorial design competition. Many designers are young; one is French, one Israeli.

The descriptions came from relatives of those who were killed in the terrorist attacks as they emerged last night from a preview of the exhibition at the Winter Garden in Battery Park City. The show will open to the public today.

Neither the jurors nor the entrants will be present today when the plans are formally announced. This is meant to guarantee that the 13-member jury can keep deliberating in some isolation from politics and public-relations as it narrows the choices to a winner, probably by the end of the year.

The family members had been asked not to talk with reporters by the Lower Manhattan Development Corporation, which is sponsoring the competition, but some said they had refused to sign confidentiality agreements. Most of those who spoke requested anonymity.

They used words like "reverential" and "respectful" to describe the designs. And "overwhelmed" when speaking of their own feelings. But some expressed disappointment that the plans did not set aside more of the twin towers' foundations as a setting for the memorial.

In one design are glass memorial columns, one for each victim, divided by the footprints of the two towers. They would be placed chronologically by the age of the victims when they died, with the names of the

Continued on Page B4

Big Shift on Housing

In New York City, where for generations government has played an ambitious role in helping people pay their rents, a fundamental shift is taking place. Three major programs, originally intended as temporary relief measures, are winding down.

Article, Page B1.

Remains Thought to Be Dean's Missing Brother

By JODI WILGOREN and MICHAEL SLACKMAN

BEDFORD, N.H., Nov. 18 — Every day on the campaign trail, Howard Dean wears an unfashionable black belt that belonged to his younger brother Charlie, a silent memorial to the man who vanished while traveling the Mekong River 29 years ago.

On Tuesday, Dr. Dean, who rarely mentions his family on the stump, interrupted his schedule to announce that a search team had found his brother's remains buried in a rice paddy in central Laos.

"This has been a long and very difficult journey for my mother and for my brothers Jim, Bill and myself," Dr. Dean, the former governor of Vermont, said after a Democratic presidential candidates' forum at a hotel here. "We greet this news with mixed emotions, but we're gratified and grateful that we're now approaching closure on this very difficult episode in our lives."

The Pentagon will not try to make an official identification until after the remains are flown to a forensic laboratory in Hawaii next week, but personal items found with the bodies — shoes, a sock and a P.O.W.-M.I.A. bracelet with the name of a Texan, all similar to those worn by the 23-year-old Charles Dean — strongly suggest the crude grave was his. Remains believed to belong to his traveling companion, Neil Sharman of Australia, were also recovered at the site.

Charles Dean is one of 1,875 Americans, including 35 civilians, still missing in connection with the Vietnam War.

Lt. Col. Jerry O'Hara, a spokesman for the Joint P.O.W./M.I.A. Accounting Command of the Defense Department, said the remains were found on Nov. 8, and that James Dean, a brother of the candidate, was told on Thursday.

Dr. Dean said he and his two brothers shared the news with their mother on Monday night at a fund-raiser in Washington marking his 55th birthday. The brief, stoic announcement on Tuesday was scheduled only after wire services picked up on Australian news reports about the recovery.

Last year, Dr. Dean, who sought grief counseling in the 1980's after suffering anxiety attacks, made a pilgrimage to Southeast Asia to look into his brother's mysterious 1974 disappearance and witness the military's recovery operations.

Dr. Dean has worn the black

Continued on Page A22

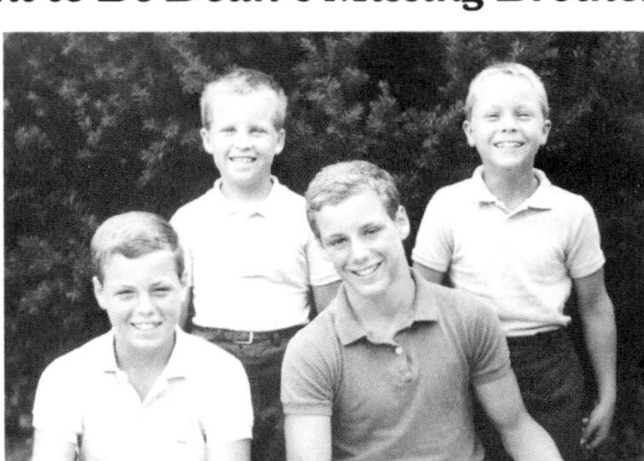

Associated Press

The Dean brothers in an undated photograph. Charlie, left, whose remains may have been found in Laos; James; Howard; and Bill.

A Thorny Issue For 2004 Race

By ADAM NAGOURNEY

News Analysis

WASHINGTON, Nov. 18 — The Massachusetts Supreme Judicial Court decision on gay marriage Tuesday forced President Bush and his Democratic opponents onto difficult political ground, as they struggled to deal with a polarizing issue that is critical to their most fervent supporters but that has confused and divided much of the nation.

The decision galvanized conservatives. Led by Representative Tom DeLay, the House majority leader, denouncing what he called a "runaway judiciary," they vowed to seek a constitutional amendment prohibiting marriage between gays. "This is not going to stop here — this is going to be in the forefront for a long time to come," said Roberta Combs, president of the Christian Coalition.

For Democrats, such declarations raise the unwelcome prospect that next year's presidential contest will be fought, at least in part, on the kind of cultural issues that have repeatedly put them at a disadvantage over the last 20 years. And it seems certain to add to the burden they are already carrying as they contemplate competing with President Bush in the once solidly Democratic South, aides to several Democrats said.

Most of the Democratic presidential candidates went to great lengths on Tuesday to emphasize that they opposed gay marriage, even as they restated their support for some forms of legal rights for same-sex couples. But the candidates also voiced strong opposition to any constitutional amendment barring gay marriage; supporting it would be nothing short of suicide in a Democratic primary. But that stance provides what even Democrats said

Continued on Page A24

Letter From Asia

Japan Heads to Iraq, Haunted By Taboo Bred in Another War

By NORIMITSU ONISHI

TOKYO, Nov. 18 — Not one Japanese soldier has been killed, or has killed, in combat since the end of World War II.

That remarkable fact is being repeated here often these days, precisely because, as Japan prepares to send ground forces to Iraq, things could change in the near future. The death of a soldier, a sad though common reality for most nations, would be a pivotal point in Japan's postwar history.

The government twice pushed back the date of deployment because of mounting violence in Iraq, evidently wary of the public's reaction to any casualty. But the government's hesitation runs deeper than that. While Japan's wartime leaders sent more than two million soldiers to their deaths, its postwar leaders are proud of having avoided a single combat fatality. A single casualty would tarnish that record and, some fear, reopen the Pandora's box of ultranationalism, which thrived more than a half-century ago.

Especially toward the desperate final stages of World War II, Japan used its men as if they were mere ammunition, dispatching countless numbers on suicide missions. "Duty is heavier than a mountain, while death is lighter than a feather," went the imperial rescript to soldiers.

Contrast that to the saying that came to symbolize postwar Japan's official attitude toward death.

In a 1977 hijacking of a Japan Airlines plane, the government gave in to demands in order to win the release of the 156 passengers. As the prime minister at the time explained, "Human life is weightier than the earth."

Now, Japan seems to be groping its way somewhere between these two extremes, cautiously, hesitatingly.

"The legacy and trauma of World

Continued on Page A4

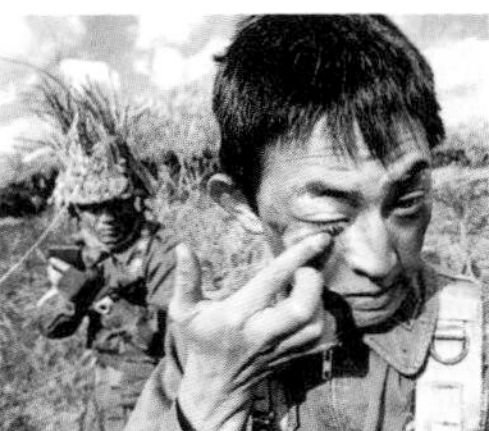

Ko Sasaki for The New York Times

Japanese soldiers applying camouflage paint during an exercise.

U.S. Moves to Limit Textile Imports From China

By EDMUND L. ANDREWS

WASHINGTON, Nov. 18 — The Bush administration moved on Tuesday to severely restrict the growth of a half-billion dollars' worth of Chinese textile imports and immediately found itself caught between battle cries from the industry for more protectionism and anxiety among global investors who fear it.

Invoking special "safeguard" clauses in its trade agreements with China, the Commerce Department said it would begin discussions to impose new quotas that could sharply reduce China's rapidly growing exports of knit fabrics and a handful of other products.

In themselves, the actions affect only a sliver of China's exports to the United States. But textile companies and unions are putting heavy pressure on President Bush to expand the agenda to cover nearly all of the $10.3 billion in imports of Chinese clothing and fabric.

"We have 12 months between now and when our elected officials go and face the people," said Auggie Tantillo, Washington coordinator for the American Manufacturing Trade Action Coalition. "If we are going to get relief, we're going to have to get it in the next 12 months."

Under pressure from lawmakers in both parties, and alarmed by the loss of manufacturing jobs from steel states like Pennsylvania to textile states like North Carolina — both political battlegrounds — administration officials have become increasingly strident in demanding that China play "by the rules."

But the administration has staunchly opposed Congressional proposals to impose sweeping new tariffs on Chinese imports, in part because they have brought lower prices to consumers and in part because trade restrictions have a chilling effect on investor confidence.

Retailing organizations immediately denounced the administration's decision, saying it would produce a spiral of new protectionism that would lead to higher prices of products ranging from bedroom furniture to television sets.

"The administration is balancing

Continued on Page C2

INSIDE

Few Signs of Iraq Infiltration

The commander of the Army division on Iraq's eastern borders said his troops had encountered only a handful of foreign fighters trying to sneak into the country. **PAGE A10**

Bonds Wins Sixth M.V.P.

Barry Bonds of the San Francisco Giants became the first player to win the award for a third straight year. He deflected questions about an inquiry into steroids. **PAGE D1**

Updated news: nytimes.com
Tomorrow in The Times: Page D8

"All the News That's Fit to Print"

The New York Times

Late Edition
New York: **Today**, showers end, cloudy, mild, high 62. **Tonight**, clouds diminish, low 44. **Tomorrow**, some sun, breezy, high 56. **Yesterday**, high 48, low 41. Weather map, Page D8.

VOL. CLIII . . No. 52,819 — NEW YORK, WEDNESDAY, APRIL 14, 2004 — ONE DOLLAR

Bush Asserts 'We Must Not Waver' on Terror or Iraq

Stephen Crowley/The New York Times

President Bush said last night that he still intended to turn over control to a government in Iraq by June 30.

Says He'll Send More Troops if Needed

By RICHARD W. STEVENSON and DOUGLAS JEHL

WASHINGTON, April 13 — President Bush vowed on Tuesday night that the United States would not bow to the surge of violence in Iraq, saying that to change course in the face of mounting attacks would betray the Iraqi people and embolden America's enemies around the world.

Mr. Bush strongly reiterated his commitment to transferring sovereignty in Iraq back to Iraqis on schedule on June 30 despite the spike in resistance there.

Seeking to tamp down concern that Iraq is spinning out of control, Mr. Bush said he would provide the military with whatever forces it needed to quell the insurgency and come up with whatever money is necessary to rebuild Iraq.

"Now is the time and Iraq is the place in which the enemies of the civilized world are testing the will of the civilized world," Mr. Bush said to a prime-time audience from the ornate setting of the White House East Room. "We must not waver."

Appearing somber but relaxed as he confronted what he called tough weeks — and what his advisers acknowledge has been one of the most trying periods of his presidency — Mr. Bush cast the conflict in Iraq as an integral part of the broader fight against terrorism and suggested that any failure to follow through would be unthinkable and have dire consequences for Americans.

"A free Iraq will confirm to a watching world that America's word, once given, can be relied upon even in the toughest times," Mr. Bush said in a 17-minute statement that opened what was only his third news conference in prime time, the last being on the eve of the war.

"Above all, the defeat of violence and terror in Iraq is vital to the defeat of violence and terror elsewhere, and vital, therefore, to the safety of the American people." [Transcript, Page A12.]

In what was apparently a response to critics who have called on him to give the United Nations a greater role, particularly his Democratic rival in the presidential race, Senator John Kerry, Mr. Bush said he would like another U.N. resolution, to make it easier for other countries to help in Iraq. He noted that the U.N. envoy, Lakhdar Brahimi, was taking a central role in seeking to establish a transitional government.

He also cited the presence in Iraq of a U.N. team planning for elections

Continued on Page A14

F.B.I. IS ASSAILED FOR ITS HANDLING OF TERROR RISKS

9/11 PANEL'S DRAFT REPORT

Ashcroft and Ex-Officials Testify That Combating Threat Was Priority

By PHILIP SHENON and ERIC LICHTBLAU

WASHINGTON, April 13 — The F.B.I. came under withering criticism on Tuesday from the independent commission investigating the Sept. 11 attacks, with its chairman describing new staff reports on the bureau's performance before and after the attacks as an "indictment of the F.B.I."

"It failed and it failed and it failed and it failed," the chairman, Thomas H. Kean, a former Republican governor of New Jersey, said of the bureau at a public hearing of the 10-member panel. "This is an agency that does not work. It makes you angry. And I don't know how to fix it."

As the commission released a pair of interim staff reports that offered extensive and agonizing new details about how the F.B.I. and the C.I.A. may have bungled opportunities to thwart the Sept. 11 attacks, Mr. Kean said he welcomed President Bush's comments this week that the White House would consider an overhaul of the nation's intelligence agencies, including the F.B.I.

Mr. Kean's criticisms of the bureau were echoed by others on the bipartisan commission on Tuesday and came as the panel conducted sometimes harsh questioning of Louis J. Freeh, director of the F.B.I. from 1993 until he retired three months before the Sept. 11 attacks; Thomas J. Pickard, who was the bureau's acting director during the summer of 2001; Attorney General John Ashcroft and his predecessor, Janet Reno. [Excerpts, Page A16.]

In their testimony, all four insisted that they had no higher priority than counterterrorism before Sept. 11.

Mr. Freeh said the bureau had performed heroically in dealing with terrorist threats for years despite an inadequate budget. Mr. Pickard said that in his three months as head of the F.B.I. he repeatedly ordered his deputies to be ready for a possible domestic attack. Mr. Ashcroft suggested that the failings of the Justice Department and the F.B.I. before Sept. 11 were largely the fault of the Clinton administration. Ms. Reno said that she was aware of the F.B.I.'s faults but she believed that

Continued on Page A17

Agence France-Presse — Getty Images

Attorney General John Ashcroft at the Sept. 11 panel hearing.

BUSH MAY ACCEPT WEST BANK PLAN

In U.S. Shift, Some Support for Israeli Settlements

By STEVEN R. WEISMAN

WASHINGTON, April 13 — President Bush is planning to issue a declaration on Wednesday that his aides say will recognize Israel's right to retain some Jewish settlements in the West Bank as part of any peace accord with the Palestinians.

The declaration, to be made when Prime Minister Ariel Sharon visits the White House, would represent a subtle but substantial shift in American policy, which has viewed the settlements as obstacles to peace and asserted that final borders must be arrived at through negotiations solely between Israel and the Palestinians.

Administration officials also said Mr. Bush would assert that Palestinian refugee families that once lived in Israel should live in a future Palestinian state in the West Bank and Gaza Strip, rather than in the Israeli lands they continue to claim.

The officials said the declarations — planned for Wednesday as part of a carefully scripted visit by Mr. Sharon — are similar to peace proposals put forward in private in 2000 by President Clinton, and represent a shift to a position where Washington would help set specific terms of any agreement.

They appear to fall short of what Mr. Sharon had been seeking — an acceptance of five specific settlement blocs and an outright rejection of the Palestinian "right of return" to Israel. The exact language and form of the assurances, and their timing, were being discussed Tuesday night. An Israeli official said aides to Mr. Sharon were also study-

Continued on Page A8

Price of AIDS Drug Intensifies Debate On Legal Imports

By GARDINER HARRIS

The recent decision by Abbott Laboratories to quintuple the price of its crucial AIDS drug Norvir will be at the center of a federal hearing today in which AIDS groups and consumer advocates plan to argue that the government should begin allowing the import of cheaper drugs.

The hearing, which will be conducted by the Department of Health and Human Services, is a result of last fall's Medicare drug legislation, in which Congress called for a general inquiry into the import question. But the escalating protest over Norvir, whose average annual dosage cost rose to about $7,800 in January from $1,500, has suddenly given the import issue unexpected urgency.

Norvir is a vital ingredient in many of the drug "cocktail" regimens prescribed for tens of thousands of AIDS patients. Abbott, which cannot raise its prices overseas where governments control drug markets, says it has had to raise prices in the United States to continue financing its research into H.I.V. and other diseases.

Norvir will also be the focus of a hearing that has yet to be scheduled. At that session, the National Institutes of Health will hear arguments over whether federal health authorities should take the unusual step of allowing generic versions of Norvir years before Abbott's patents expire.

In the cases of drugs that were developed with federal money — as

Continued on Page C14

U.S. Workers, Lured by Money And Idealism, Face Iraqi Reality

By ANDREW JACOBS and SIMON ROMERO

They were driven by the promise of six-figure salaries or a powerful sense of patriotism. For others, the decision to sign up for a job in the cauldron of Iraq was motivated by desire to help ordinary Iraqis improve their lives. Among the tens of thousands of American citizens working in Iraq, few could have imagined how dangerous their jobs would become.

But in the last two weeks, many of the simplest tasks have carried extraordinary danger, as civilian workers have become targets of kidnappings and murder. Yesterday, there were reports that bodies were found mutilated in a shallow grave but the findings could not be confirmed. The news came just days after seven civilians working for the Halliburton Company of Houston and two soldiers disappeared in an ambush near that site last Friday.

Wendy Hall, a spokeswoman for Halliburton, said the company had been notified of the bodies' discovery, but she said she could not confirm that they were those of missing employees. "Our workers in Iraq are courageous volunteers in service to their country and their loved ones," Ms. Hall said in a statement last night.

There are no concrete figures on the number of civilians who have been killed or wounded in Iraq, but Halliburton has acknowledged that 30 of its employees and contractors have died since the war began last year. Several workers from the United States and other countries were still missing last night — like Thomas Hamill, a former dairy farmer who worked for Halliburton as a fuel truck driver and was captured last week on a highway outside Baghdad.

In interviews yesterday, several civilian workers who have spent time in Iraq said the experiences

Continued on Page A11

Making a Case For a Mission

Freedom in Middle East As Model for the World

By DAVID E. SANGER

News Analysis

WASHINGTON, April 13 — Facing a moment of political peril unlike any in the more than one thousand days of his presidency, George W. Bush made the case on Tuesday night for staying the course in Iraq with the language and zeal of a missionary and combined it with a stark warning that failure would embolden America's enemies around the world.

"We're changing the world," Mr. Bush said halfway through a speech and news conference that was largely an hourlong justification for holding fast in Iraq, no matter how the casualties mount, no matter how chaotic the process of forming a new government.

Drawing later on a line he often slips into his campaign speeches, he reminded a global audience that "freedom is the Almighty's gift to every man and woman in this world. And as the greatest power on the face of the Earth, we have an obligation to help the spread of freedom."

With those words, Mr. Bush drove home the singlemindedness that has become the hallmark of his presidency, his greatest strength in the eyes of his admirers and a dangerous, never-change-course stubbornness in the eyes of his detractors. He could have simply talked Tuesday evening about the crimes of Saddam Hussein or the fear that chaos in Iraq would

Continued on Page A14

MORE ON IRAQ

A CLERIC REMAINS DEFIANT A rebel cleric resisted disbanding his militia as American troops moved in to confront him, but there were reports a deal had been struck. **PAGE A10**

ENVOY TO IRAQ TO BE NAMED John D. Negroponte, a veteran American diplomat, is expected to be appointed ambassador to Iraq. **PAGE A11**

A FLIGHT FROM POVERTY For poor workers from China, getting jobs outweighed any risks in Falluja, Iraq. **PAGE A11**

Lynsey Addario/Corbis, for The New York Times

CLASHES IN FALLUJA Capt. Shannon Johnson calling in a mortar strike yesterday against an Iraqi sniper firing on the marines' rooftop position. The attacks and responses go on despite a declared cease-fire. Page A10.

City's Small Schools Uneasy Inside the Big Ones

By ELISSA GOOTMAN

At Bronx Aerospace Academy High School, all 161 students wear blue uniforms and well-shined black shoes. They have 13 laptop computers and, thanks to private money, a $40,000 flight simulator to spice up lessons. They take field trips to places like the New England Air Museum and have classes of no more than 28.

But the tiny Bronx Aerospace is inside the vast Evander Childs High School, population 3,100, recently named one of the city's most unruly schools. There, classes generally have 34 students, the maximum allowed by the teachers' contract. There are no laptops. Field trips are rare. Jeans, tight for girls and baggy for boys, are the preferred dress.

So it is not surprising that tensions have developed between the two schools. Evander Childs students have banged on classroom doors at Aerospace, torn down posters in its hallways and teased the Aerospace students, mocking their uniforms and their marching, students and faculty members said. A few times, the friction turned physical.

"It's like the bathroom in a big family: one bathroom, but there are five members in the household," said Mónica Ortiz-Ureña, the principal of Evander Childs. "The biggest challenge is addressing the needs of the small schools and my school with a balance."

Next year, the balance is likely to be even more elusive across the city, as dozens of new small schools take root within their large schools, each with its own culture, philosophy about discipline, private financing and dress code.

New York City has been a nationwide leader in the small schools movement, and replacing large high schools is a centerpiece of Mayor Michael R. Bloomberg's efforts to overhaul the school system. He has vowed to create 200 small schools in three years using private money, including $58 million from the Bill and Melinda Gates Foundation, which has been underwriting small schools for several years.

About 50 small schools predate the

Continued on Page B9

INSIDE

Jewish Targets in Spain

Terrorists believed to be behind the Madrid train bombings last month also considered attacks on Jewish sites, an investigator said. **PAGE A6**

Lung Cancer Gender Gap

Women with lung cancer survive longer than men and respond differently to at least one drug, researchers will report today. **PAGE A20**

New Coach for St. John's

St. John's hired Norm Roberts, an assistant at Kansas who has strong Queens roots, as the basketball coach. **SPORTSWEDNESDAY, PAGE D1**

China's Troubled Economy

Economic worries intensified in China as bank lending climbed and the central bank failed to sell all treasury bills at current rates. **PAGE C1**

Fox

Money Talks for 'Simpsons'

Actors who give voice to "The Simpsons," the long-running television series, want to share in the show's profits. **THE ARTS, PAGE E1**

Updated news: nytimes.com

Tomorrow in The Times: Page D7

"All the News That's Fit to Print"

The New York Times

Late Edition
New York: **Today,** some showers, mostly cloudy, high 65. **Tonight,** an evening shower, low 58. **Tomorrow,** clouds, some sun, high 68. Yesterday, high 64, low 51. Weather map, Page 35.

VOL. CLIII . . No. 52,844 | NEW YORK, SUNDAY, MAY 9, 2004 | $4.50 beyond the greater New York metropolitan area. | $3.50

In Abuse, a Portrayal of Ill-Prepared, Overwhelmed G.I.'s

By DOUGLAS JEHL and ERIC SCHMITT

WASHINGTON, May 8 — The orders that sent most of the 320th Military Police Battalion to Iraq came on Feb. 5, 2003, as part of the tide of two-week-a-year soldiers being called up from the National Guard and the Army Reserve in preparation for war.

In theory, the battalion's specialty was guarding enemy prisoners of war, a task that was expected to be a major logistical problem. In fact, an Army report said few of the 1,000 reservists of the 320th had been trained to do that, and fewer still knew how to run a prison. They were deployed so quickly from the mid-Atlantic region that there was no time to get new lessons.

"You're a person who works at McDonald's one day; the next day you're standing in front of hundreds of prisoners, and half are saying they're sick and half are saying they're hungry," remembered Sgt. First Class Paul Shaffer, 35, a metalworker from Pennsylvania. "We were hit with so much so fast, I don't think we were prepared."

The battalion — including insurance agents, checkout clerks, sales people and others — ultimately would follow a grim trajectory into the episodes of prisoner abuse that have shocked the nation. The soldiers found themselves in charge of Abu Ghraib prison in Iraq at a time when the increasing rage of the anti-American insurgency, along with the desperation of American commanders to glean intelligence, magnified the pressures on the unit. This account of the troubled battalion is based on interviews with soldiers, their relatives, military commanders and Army reports.

Within days of the American invasion of Iraq, the 320th was in Kuwait, and the unit moved swiftly into southern Iraq, first to a prisoner of war camp overseen by Brit-

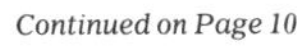

Continued on Page 10

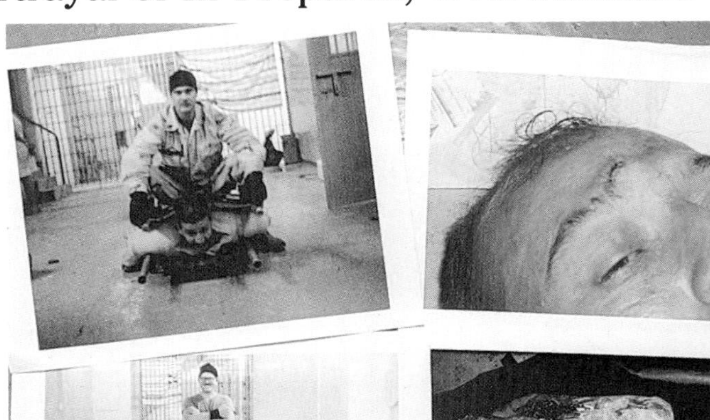

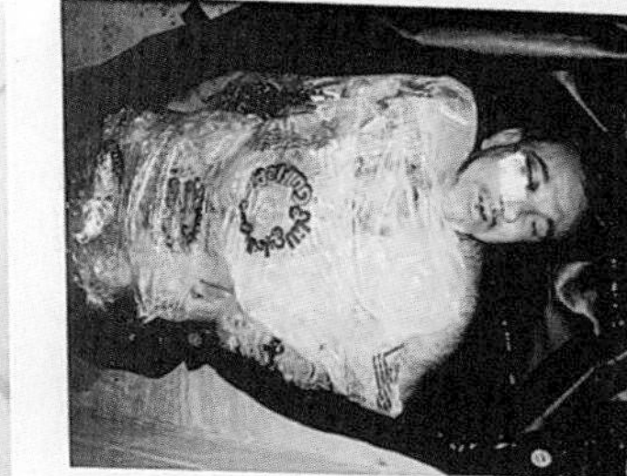

Photographs of prisoners who were abused, and some who are dead, at Abu Ghraib prison in Iraq.

War and Abuse Do Little Harm To U.S. Brands

Most Products Escape Rising Anger Abroad

By SIMON ROMERO

FRANKFURT, May 8 — When American troops moved into Iraq last year, European executives at the Ford Motor Company braced for an adverse consumer reaction.

"Our sales and image and market share are things we monitor extremely closely," said Niel Golightly, a Ford spokesman in Cologne, Germany. "So the potential fallout risk from Ford being perceived as a symbol of America's foreign policy is something we're always looking at."

But aside from a single incident at a dealership in Italy last year, the company has seen no evidence that widespread anti-Americanism abroad has been aimed at the well-known Ford brand. In Europe, Mr. Golightly said, Ford's market share has remained steady, and sales are expected to improve slightly this quarter. And the business outlook remains upbeat despite recent developments in Iraq, including the revelation of photographs depicting the humiliation of Iraqi prisoners by American soldiers.

For a variety of reasons, American companies that sell globally say that they have so far experienced little if any disruption from discontent over the war in Iraq. For the most part, consumers around the world seem as likely to be influenced by economic conditions as by politics. And, in a display of the growing sophistication in marketing big American brands in global markets, many people see products originating from the United States as firmly rooted in their own home nations.

Even Muslims in the Middle East and Southeast Asia do not seem to translate their anger into a boycott of American products. For example, as Hidayat bin Ismail, 19, emerged Friday from midday prayers at the Sultan Mosque in Singapore, he acknowledged that he was still patronizing places like McDonald's and KFC even after seeing the pictures of American soldiers abusing Iraqi prisoners.

"When Americans do these things, I don't think all Americans are bad," he said. "And if one Muslim is bad, it

Continued on Page 11

U.S. PRESSES U.N. ON ROLE IN IRAQ FOR POLITICIANS

A MIX WITH TECHNOCRATS

Members of Iraqi Council Seek to Maintain Their Power After June 30

By STEVEN R. WEISMAN

WASHINGTON, May 8 — The Bush administration is pressing the United Nations envoy to change his proposal for a transitional Iraqi government once self-rule is returned on June 30, Iraqi and administration officials say.

Instead of a government that is nonpolitical, the administration is pushing for one that gives prominent roles to people with ties to political parties, the officials say.

The officials said the new thinking in Washington reflected doubts that a transitional government of technocrats would be strong enough.

Leading Kurdish and Shiite political figures, many of them members of the American-appointed Iraqi Governing Council, have pressed for the change, administration officials said. These figures are clamoring to hold on to power after the council is dissolved June 30.

In particular, the administration is said to be wedded to a large role for Adnan Pachachi, the former foreign minister who has guided the process of writing Iraq's transitional constitution, and to figures tied to political groups loyal to Grand Ayatollah Ali al-Sistani, the Shiite cleric.

"The government is going to have both technocrats and people of political stature," said a senior administration official. "It's important to have both sides in the government."

In Iraq on Saturday, insurgents backing a rebel Shiite cleric took the offensive in two southern cities against British forces, acting to seize government buildings and striking at convoys. The move suggested that a new front was opening in the confrontation between the militias of the cleric, Moktada al-Sadr, and American and British troops, after days of American attacks. [Page 12.]

Only two weeks ago, the administration embraced the proposal of

Continued on Page 12

In Vast Philanthropy, Kerry's Wife Wields Sway

By STEPHANIE STROM

When the newly widowed Teresa Heinz took over the stewardship of one of the country's largest philanthropic organizations more than a decade ago, all she had to guide her was a soggy, charred legal pad of handwritten notes that had been found in the debris of the plane that crashed in 1991, killing her husband, Senator H. John Heinz III.

Mr. Heinz had been jotting down plans for a sweeping overhaul of the organization that would put it on sounder financial footing by diversifying its holdings out of H.J. Heinz Company shares and changing its management structure.

"When Jack died and we had to diversify, I had to learn about everything," recalled Teresa Heinz Kerry, who in 1995 married John Kerry, the Democratic presidential contender, "and I knew nothing about money and investments."

Thirteen years later, she is the guiding force behind the Heinz Endowments, which control $1.3 billion in assets and gave away $54.5 million last year. She also runs the Heinz Family Philanthropies, an umbrella for a $70 million family foundation she created after her husband's death and the two non-tax-exempt charitable trusts that finance it.

As a result, the city of Pittsburgh is in many ways a monument to Mrs. Heinz Kerry's philanthropy. It is home to more environmentally sound buildings, certified as green buildings, than any other city in the country, thanks in large part to the Heinz Endowments. The city's riverfronts are undergoing a renaissance, led by the endowments. Its school administration has changed in response to the endowments' concerns. Even the look of a bridge over the Allegheny River bears the endowments' influence.

Mrs. Heinz Kerry says that she does not have political ambitions like Hillary Rodham Clinton. At the same time, she has made it clear that she intends to carry on her philanthropic activities should she get to the White House. "I checked it out with lawyers before the campaign began," she said in a recent one-hour interview about her philanthropy. "There is nothing that says I cannot do it."

Yet the idea of a first lady who gives out $50 million to $70 million a

Continued on Page 18

Shift on Salmon Reignites Fight On Species Law

By TIMOTHY EGAN

SEATTLE, May 8 — Three years ago, Mark C. Rutzick was the timber industry's top lawyer trying to overturn fish and wildlife protections that loggers viewed as overly restrictive. Back then, he outlined to his clients a new strategy for dealing with diminishing salmon runs. By counting hatchery fish along with wild salmon, the government would help the timber industry by getting salmon off the endangered species list, Mr. Rutzick wrote.

Now, as a high-ranking political appointee in the Bush administration who is a legal adviser to the National Marine Fisheries Service, Mr. Rutzick is helping to shape government policy on endangered Pacific salmon. And in an abrupt change, the Bush administration has decided for the first time to consider counting fish raised in hatcheries when determining if some species are going extinct.

The new plan, which officials have said is expected to be formally announced at the end of the month, closely follows the position that Mr. Rutzick advocated when he represented the timber industry.

Mr. Rutzick, a Portland lawyer who was suggested for the fisheries job by Senator Gordon H. Smith, Republican of Oregon, would not comment on his role in shaping government salmon policy. Officials at the fisheries service say Mr. Rutzick was part of a working group that shaped the new plan, but would not give further details.

The policy shift has caused a furor among some members of the scientific community and has touched off a fresh battle over what may be the nation's most powerful environmental law.

To most biologists, salmon that are born and raised in a cement tank

Continued on Page 22

When Students' Gains Help Teachers' Bottom Line

Kevin Moloney for The New York Times

Valeri Kershaw, a teacher in Denver, says she likes the added motivation provided by performance-based pay.

By DIANA JEAN SCHEMO

DENVER — As a teacher of emotionally disturbed children, Jeremy Abshire sets goals for each of his students. Geronimo, 14, an American Indian who knew only the letters for "Jerry," will read and write, and sign his true name. Shaneesa, a meek 12-year-old reading at a first-grade level, will catch up to her middle-school peers and attend regular classes in the fall.

Under a proposal approved by teachers here and to be considered by voters next year, if Mr. Abshire's students reach the goals he sets, his salary will grow. But if his classroom becomes a mere holding tank, his salary, too, will stagnate.

"The bottom line is, do you reward teachers for just sitting here and sticking it out, or for doing something?" said Mr. Abshire, who has been teaching for four years. "The free market doesn't handle things that way, so why should it be any different here?"

In March, Denver's teachers became the first in a major city to approve, by a 59 percent majority, a full-scale overhaul of the salary structure to allow "pay for performance," a controversial approach that rewards teachers for the progress of their students.

At a time when more and more superintendents are supporting moves away from the traditional salary structure for teachers, and finding their efforts stymied in an atmosphere of suspicion and financial austerity, Denver teachers' vote is a major breakthrough.

Under the city's plan, teachers and other school employees would earn raises if students meet academic tar-

Continued on Page 21

MORE ON IRAQ

SUPPORT FOR RUMSFELD Condoleezza Rice said Defense Secretary Donald H. Rumsfeld still had "the strongest possible support" from President Bush. PAGE 4

NOW WHAT FOR U.S.? How will America exert moral authority in foreign policy? WEEK IN REVIEW

MILITIAMEN GO ON OFFENSIVE After days of American attacks, insurgents backing a rebel Shiite cleric took the offensive. PAGE 12

EUROPE GLUM ON BUSH Most Europeans, even conservatives, find little good to say about the American president. PAGE 4

INSIDE

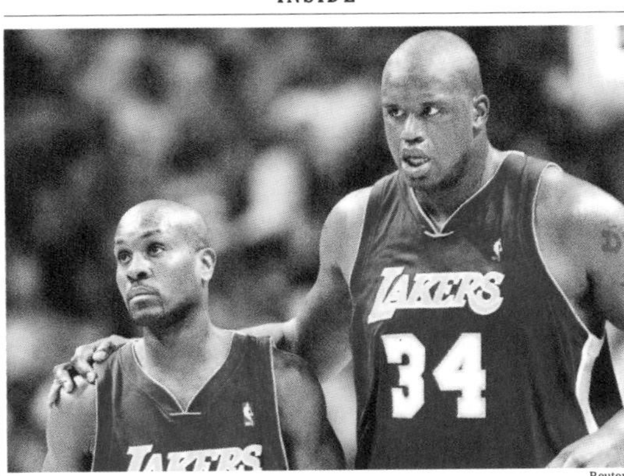

Reuters

Why the Lakers Are in Trouble

Gary Payton, left, joined Shaquille O'Neal in hopes of winning a title. But discord among the Lakers has them teetering in the playoffs. SPORTSSUNDAY

Venting in Cyberspace

Japanese are turning to a Web site founded by a former college student to get things off their chests. PAGE 3

Force Against Gay Marriage

From an unmarked warehouse in Longwood, Fla., Liberty Counsel pursues its agenda: stopping same-sex marriage across the nation. PAGE 14

Flaws at New Youth Center

Connecticut's new juvenile center, built to remedy failed policies, was poorly planned and cost too much, critics say. PAGE 25

Attack of the Blockbusters

In a Summer Movies special section: togas are back; the well-adjusted Will Ferrell; Alfonso Cuarón's "Harry Potter"; and all the season's films. ARTS & LEISURE, PART 2

Buying Art, Avoiding Taxes

On the periphery of the excitement over Sotheby's and Christie's auctions are galleries and dealers whose customers are at the center of a tax-evasion inquiry. SUNDAYBUSINESS

NEWS SUMMARY 2

International 3-12
Metro 25-32
National 14-22

Obituaries 34 | TV Update 33
Radio 33 | Weather 35

Job Market/Section 10
In New York City and the metropolitan region.

Updated news: nytimes.com

"All the News That's Fit to Print"

The New York Times

Late Edition
Today: Mainly cloudy, an afternoon shower, high 83. **Tonight,** a shower, fog, low 71. **Tomorrow,** turning partly sunny, high 82. **Yesterday,** high 87, low 74. Weather map is on Page B11.

VOL. CLIII . . No. 52,883 | NEW YORK, THURSDAY, JUNE 17, 2004 | ONE DOLLAR

PANEL FINDS NO QAEDA-IRAQ TIE; DESCRIBES A WIDER PLOT FOR 9/11

European Pressphoto Agency

The 9/11 commission at a hearing yesterday that included photographic evidence projected onto screens. The commission released two reports.

G.O.P. Nearing Money Record For Convention

New York Panel Aims to Collect $64 Million

By MICHAEL SLACKMAN

The New York City Host Committee for the Republican National Convention is expecting to raise a record amount of money, and already has tens of millions of dollars in contributions and commitments from donors ranging from an Indian tribe that runs a casino in Connecticut to real estate agents, financiers and drug manufacturers.

The list of major contributors includes corporations like Pfizer and Citigroup but also individuals like Mayor Michael R. Bloomberg and David Rockefeller, who each gave $5 million of their own money toward the $64 million goal, the committee said.

The committee's aggressive fund-raising is expected to exceed the record $36.1 million collected by Los Angeles officials for the Democratic convention in 2000, and will effectively signal an end to the effort to make conventions publicly financed, campaign finance experts said.

After the Watergate scandal of the 1970's, Congress legislated that conventions were to be publicly financed to help avoid corruption and to limit the influence of corporate cash on politics, campaign finance experts said. The furious fund-raising pace illustrates how conventions have become the chief means that corporate donors have found to make large contributions to organizations benefiting political parties since new restrictions were imposed on such donations, known as soft money, campaign finance experts said.

At first, the committee refused to divulge the names until later, saying that by law it did not have to make them public until after the convention, which is scheduled Aug. 30 to Sept. 2. After receiving inquires, the committee released a partial list of its major donors to The New York Times and said it would post that list today on its Web site, nyc2004.org.

The committee continues to withhold the amounts donated, saying only that the list includes contributors who gave from $2,500 to $5 million, and it has held back the names of 20 contributors who have asked not to be identified now, committee officials said. Some of the contributors donated services, like Disney, which contributed tickets to "The Lion King," officials said.

While the list of major donors is in-

Continued on Page B8

RUMSFELD ISSUED AN ORDER TO HIDE DETAINEE IN IRAQ

KEPT HIM FROM RED CROSS

Officials Concede a Lapse — Inmate Is Still Held Seven Months Later

By ERIC SCHMITT and THOM SHANKER

WASHINGTON, June 16 — Defense Secretary Donald H. Rumsfeld, acting at the request of George J. Tenet, the director of central intelligence, ordered military officials in Iraq last November to hold a man suspected of being a senior Iraqi terrorist at a high-level detention center there but not list him on the prison's rolls, senior Pentagon and intelligence officials said Wednesday.

This prisoner and other "ghost detainees" were hidden largely to prevent the International Committee of the Red Cross from monitoring their treatment, and to avoid disclosing their location to an enemy, officials said.

Maj. Gen. Antonio M. Taguba, the Army officer who in February investigated abuses at the Abu Ghraib prison, criticized the practice of allowing ghost detainees there and at other detention centers as "deceptive, contrary to Army doctrine, and in violation of international law."

This prisoner, who has not been named, is believed to be the first to have been kept off the books at the orders of Mr. Rumsfeld and Mr. Tenet. He was not held at Abu Ghraib, but at another prison, Camp Cropper, on the outskirts of Baghdad International Airport, officials said.

Pentagon and intelligence officials said the decision to hold the detainee without registering him — at least initially — was in keeping with the administration's legal opinion about the status of those viewed as an active threat in wartime.

Seven months later, however, the detainee — a reputed senior officer of Ansar al-Islam, a group the United States has linked to Al Qaeda and blames for some attacks in Iraq — is

Continued on Page A12

In Detail: How bin Laden Set Plan in Motion in '99

By DOUGLAS JEHL and DAVID JOHNSTON

WASHINGTON, June 16 — In early 1999, Osama bin Laden summoned Khalid Shaikh Mohammed to his well-guarded compound in Kandahar, Afghanistan, to confide to the lieutenant that his long-discussed proposal to use aircraft as terror weapons against the United States had the full support of Al Qaeda.

That meeting, described for the first time by the independent commission investigating the Sept. 11, 2001, attacks, set in motion an extraordinary series of events. But the path from Kandahar to the World Trade Center was anything but a straight line.

Described in vivid detail by two captured Qaeda operatives who helped plan the attacks, the plot was more troubled and improvisational than had been previously understood.

As late as August 2001, one commission report says, Mr. Mohammed fretted about infighting between Mohamed Atta, the mission leader, and a Lebanese pilot, Ziad al-Jarrah. With his frosted hair and his fondness for Beirut nightclubs, Mr. Jarrah seemed so close to choosing a girlfriend over Al Qaeda that the plotters scrambled to line up a replacement pilot. But in the end, Mr. Jarrah was at the controls of United Flight 93 when it crashed in Pennsylvania.

Of the four Qaeda operatives first assigned to the plot in 1999, only two ended up among the final 19 hijackers who carried out the attacks. Both of them — Khalid al-Midhar and Nawaq Alhazmi — washed out as student pilots and were relegated to lesser roles. To take their place as pilots, Mr. Mohammed turned to other recruits spotted at the camps in Afghanistan.

Mr. Atta, the Egyptian pilot who was at the center of the core group, did not join the team until after the plot was well under way. The lineup of hijackers was changing throughout the two years of preparations. Meanwhile, an impatient Mr. bin Laden began pressing for an attack as early as 2000, even if it meant using untrained pilots to crash into the ground instead of into buildings.

At the start, though, Mr. bin Laden and Mr. Mohammed envisioned attacks even more audacious than the one that was ultimately carried out, the report said.

Mr. Mohammed, the American-educated Kuwaiti from Pakistan who emerges in the commission's account as a main partner of Mr. bin Laden, at one point planned an attack involving 10 planes. Mr. Mohammed wanted to hijack the last plane himself, then kill every man on board and land to deliver an anti-American diatribe. Another version,

Continued on Page A14

CHALLENGES BUSH

A Chilling Chronology Rewrites the History of the Attacks

By PHILIP SHENON and CHRISTOPHER MARQUIS

WASHINGTON, June 16 — The staff of the commission investigating the Sept. 11 attacks sharply contradicted one of President Bush's central justifications for the Iraq war, reporting on Wednesday that there did not appear to have been a "collaborative relationship" between Al Qaeda and Saddam Hussein. The assertion came in staff reports that offer a chilling, richly detailed chronology of the Sept. 11 plot and rewrite much of the history of the attacks.

The chronology, based on the panel's review of highly classified accounts of interrogations of captured Qaeda leaders, shows that Osama bin Laden was far more intimately involved in the planning of the attacks than previously known and approved the selection of each of the 19 hijackers. It also shows that the original plot called for attacks that would have been even larger and more deadly.

The commission's investigators said in a pair of reports released at a public hearing that Mr. bin Laden and his deputies discussed target lists as early as 1999 that would have included the White House, the Capitol, C.I.A. and F.B.I. headquarters, nuclear power plants and skyscrapers in California and Washington State. The plot involved hijacking 10 jets instead of 4 and, the commission's staff said, originally included a plan for simultaneous hijackings of American passenger planes in Southeast Asia. [Excerpts, Page A16.]

The reports say that Mr. bin Laden, who has been depicted in the past as being far less involved in the logistics of the operation, ordered the Sept. 11 attacks over the opposition

Continued on Page A15

Account of Plot Sets Off Debate Over Credibility

By DAVID JOHNSTON and DON VAN NATTA Jr.

WASHINGTON, June 16 — In the Sept. 11 commission reports released Wednesday, the striking portrait of Al Qaeda as a wobbly but determined organization lurching toward its catastrophic strike against America was built largely on the two plot leaders' own words.

In a series of interrogations in secret locations with United States officials, two of the plot masterminds, Khalid Shaikh Mohammed and Ramzi bin al-Shibh, have provided the most detailed account yet of the origins of the Sept. 11 attacks and the challenges faced by the group's top lieutenants.

But their accounts have stirred an unresolved debate about their credibility. Mr. bin al-Shibh, who was captured in 2002, and Mr. Mohammed, who was apprehended in 2003, have been the subjects of highly coercive interrogation methods authorized by the Bush administration for use against high-level Qaeda detainees, senior government officials say. Those methods, some officials said, cast doubt on the reliability of the accounts.

In interviews earlier this year, some counterterrorism officials in the United States and Europe said that Mr. Mohammed had begun to cooperate and that important breakthroughs were being made in the understanding of the Sept. 11 plot and Al Qaeda's strengths and limitations. "He's singing like a bird," a senior European counterterrorism official said in a recent interview.

Mr. bin al-Shibh has also proven to be cooperative with interrogators, several senior officials said. But they said his cooperation also did not be-

Continued on Page A14

Fred R. Conrad/The New York Times

Amy Sabbatini, wife of the golfer Rory Sabbatini, bathing their son, Harley, in the sink of their motor home.

Some Pro Golfers Now Take Homes on the Road

By WILLIAM L. HAMILTON

At the United States Open, which begins today at the Shinnecock Hills Golf Club on Long Island, there's a lot of talk about driving distance.

Mobile-home-on-the-highway driving distance.

Players in increasing numbers have hit the road this year in custom coaches more associated with country and western singers or movie stars. But unlike the singers and the stars, the golfers are pulling into town with their families — wives, babies, dogs and in-laws.

The players say they avoid the headaches of hotels, guest housing and extensive airport security searches. And they get to go home in the evening after they play, an advantage they say helps stabilize their games.

Six players, including Davis Love III, ranked fourth in the world, drove the 100 miles to Southampton from last week's Buick Classic in Harrison, N.Y., arriving on Sunday night and Monday morning like an itinerant circus, setting up camp and calling it a neighborhood.

"I've got my bed, my pillows, my satellite card, my underwear and socks on the bus," said Love, who helped pioneer the recreational-vehicle movement three years ago. Now there are 19 players traveling in motor homes, including the 10 who parked their vehicles on a bluff by Peconic Bay in Southampton.

"You don't have maids knocking on your door at 10 o'clock in the morning," said Kim Johnson, the wife of Zach Johnson, a rookie playing his first Open. She was sitting in the living room of their new, half-million-dollar custom coach, a fireplace at one end, a dashboard at the other. She microwaved popcorn as the wind off the bay buffeted her home. The Johnsons chose a 45-foot Travel Supreme Select, long enough to accommodate a king-size bed.

A neighbor, Amy Sabbatini, the wife of Rory Sabbatini, stopped by to share a restaurant recommendation. The Sabbatinis, who were parked behind the Johnsons, are traveling with their 9-month-old son, Harley, who is bathed by his mother in the coach's kitchen sink.

No more golf widows, but instead, screen-door visits, potluck barbecues and the occasional caddy sleeping on the couch.

Continued on Page D9

Tee Time at Shinnecock

All eyes in golf will be on the United States Open today, but many players' eyes will be on the challenging seventh hole at Shinnecock Hills. SportsThursday, Page D1.

INSIDE

Iraqi Cleric Orders Militia to Stand Down

Moktada al-Sadr, the Shiite cleric whose militia has tormented Americans for nearly three months, ordered his fighters to disarm and go home. In Najaf, his loyalists appeared to be heeding the order. But north of Baghdad, two Americans died in an attack. PAGE A12

U.S. Latin Envoy Quits

Otto J. Reich, President Bush's special envoy to Latin America, resigned and took with him a lifetime of experience fighting Fidel Castro and other foes of American foreign policy. PAGE A3

Liposuction's Bad News

Having fat removed by liposuction provides none of the protection from heart disease and diabetes that would result from weight loss through diet and exercise, researchers are reporting. PAGE A24

Improving on Star Trek

Two scientific teams reported that for the first time they have teleported individual atoms, a process that could someday help in solving complex problems using quantum computers. PAGE A22

High Seas Jamming

For jazz and rock fans who enjoy their comforts, music cruises are like floating festivals. And when the jam sessions are over, the stars, like Les Claypool, left, can't escape into S.U.V.'s. THE ARTS, PAGE E1

MORE ON 9/11 PANEL

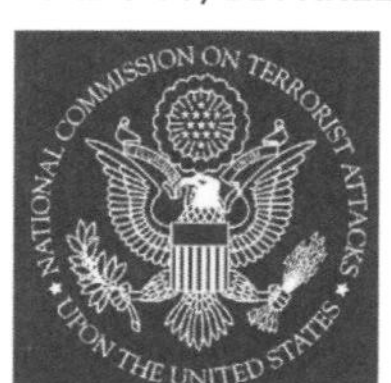

KEY EVIDENCE DISCREDITED A meeting often cited as proof of a Qaeda-Iraq link never happened, the commission found. PAGE A14

QUESTIONS FOR BUSH The administration is on the defensive over an issue it once expected to be a political plus. NEWS ANALYSIS, PAGE A15

FAMILIES WANT OPEN BOOK For family members of those who lost their lives in the Sept. 11 attacks, the detailed report is not nearly detailed enough. PAGE A18

FOR HOME DELIVERY CALL 1-800-NYTIMES

"All the News That's Fit to Print"

The New York Times

Late Edition
New York: **Today,** mainly sunny and warmer, high 72. **Tonight,** patchy fog, low 59. **Tomorrow,** continued sunny and warm, high 73. **Yesterday,** high 63, low 46. Weather map, Page B11.

VOL. CLIV . . No. 52,995 + | NEW YORK, THURSDAY, OCTOBER 7, 2004 | ONE DOLLAR

CITY TRASH PLAN FORGOES TRUCKS, FAVORING BARGES

4 TRANSFER STATIONS SEEN

Bloomberg Tries to Limit Hauling Garbage Over Borough Lines

By IAN URBINA

Three years after the closing of the mammoth Fresh Kills landfill on Staten Island, the Bloomberg administration has drawn up a 20-year plan to deal with the city's residential waste by shipping the bulk of it elsewhere by barge, officials who have been briefed on the plan said yesterday.

The city has struggled for years with how to handle the 11,000 tons of waste per day that used to go to Fresh Kills, and since it was closed the city has been relying on trucks to cart most of its garbage out of state, a costly solution that generates pollution and traffic congestion. In an announcement planned for today, Mayor Michael R. Bloomberg was expected to address those concerns by proposing renovation of four waste transfer stations along the city's waterfront: two in Brooklyn, one in Queens and one on the Upper East Side of Manhattan.

The plan is the culmination of a wider strategy that includes committing the city to recycling more of its garbage and shipping its commercial refuse away through a pier on the West Side of Manhattan — proposals announced over the last two weeks.

The city did not release any estimates of what the plan would cost or when it would take effect.

One goal appears to be to keep one borough's garbage from becoming another's burden, as is the case now, when garbage trucks rumble throughout the city carting trash mainly to points west of New York. While Manhattan, Queens and Brooklyn would have marine transfer stations, where trash can be dumped onto barges, Staten Island and the Bronx would rely on trains to cart trash away.

In recent years, the cost of handling waste has skyrocketed, as the city has depended on private transfer stations and private out-of-state haulers. By reopening its own transfer stations, the city hopes to reduce

Continued on Page B9

Emilio Morenatti/Associated Press

Afghans to Vote on Saturday, Once the Ballot Boxes Arrive
A donkey carried ballot boxes yesterday up a mountain path in northeastern Afghanistan. The election is on Saturday; yesterday, a vice presidential candidate survived a bomb attack in the northeast. Page A3.

U.S. REPORT FINDS IRAQIS ELIMINATED ILLICIT ARMS IN 90'S

Weapons Capability Had Eroded Before War, Inspector Says

By DOUGLAS JEHL

WASHINGTON, Oct. 6 — Iraq had destroyed its illicit weapons stockpiles within months after the Persian Gulf war of 1991, and its ability to produce such weapons had significantly eroded by the time of the American invasion in 2003, the top American inspector for Iraq said in a report made public Wednesday.

The report by the inspector, Charles A. Duelfer, intended to offer a near-final judgment about Iraq and its weapons, said Iraq, while under pressure from the United Nations, had "essentially destroyed" its illicit weapons ability by the end of 1991, with its last secret factory, a biological weapons plant, eliminated in 1996.

Mr. Duelfer said that even during those years, Saddam Hussein had aimed at "preserving the capability to reconstitute his weapons of mass destruction when sanctions were lifted." But he said he had found no evidence of any concerted effort by Iraq to restart the programs.

The findings uphold Iraq's prewar insistence that it did not possess chemical or biological weapons. They also show the enormous distance between the Bush administration's own prewar assertions, based on reports by American intelligence agencies, and what a 15-month inquiry by American investigators found since the war.

Mr. Duelfer said he had concluded that between 1991 and 2003, Mr. Hussein had in effect sacrificed Iraq's illicit weapons to the larger goal of winning an end to United Nations sanctions. But he also argued that Mr. Hussein had used the period to try to exploit avenues opened by the sanctions, especially the oil-for-food program, to lay the groundwork for a plan to resume weapons production if sanctions were lifted.

In addition, the report concluded that Mr. Hussein had deliberately sought to maintain ambiguity about whether it had illicit weapons, mainly as a deterrent to Iran, its rival. [Page A28.]

The American inspector presented his conclusions to Congress on Wednesday, including highly charged public testimony before the Senate Armed Services Committee.

With Iraq figuring prominently in the last dash toward the presidential election, Democrats argued that the report had undermined the administration's case for war, while the White House and its Republican allies called attention to elements in the report that highlighted potential dangers posed by Mr. Hussein's gov-

Continued on Page A28

Stump Speech Retooled, Bush Goes on Attack

By RICHARD W. STEVENSON and DAVID E. SANGER

FARMINGTON HILLS, Mich., Oct. 6 — President Bush delivered a scathing, point-by-point critique on Wednesday of Senator John Kerry's stands on national security and the economy, giving no ground on either his decision to go to war or growing questions about mistakes in the occupation of Iraq.

In a retooled and highly combative stump speech delivered on the day when a new report raised questions about his rationale for going to war, Mr. Bush seemed to be trying to make up ground that polls show he lost during last week's debate. He accused Mr. Kerry of "proposing policies and doctrines that would weaken America and make the world more dangerous" and of pursuing a "strategy of retreat" in Iraq.

"Last week in our debate, he once again came down firmly on every side of the Iraq war," Mr. Bush said of Mr. Kerry, to ripples of laughter from a partisan audience in Wilkes-Barre, Pa. "He stated that Saddam Hussein was a threat and that America had no business removing that threat. Senator Kerry said our soldiers and marines are not fighting for a mistake — but also called the liberation of Iraq a 'colossal error.' He said we need to do more to train Iraqis, but he also said we shouldn't be spending so much money over there. He said he wants to hold a summit meeting, so he can invite other countries to join what he calls 'the wrong war in the wrong place at the wrong time.' "

Mr. Bush's new speech signaled that he would stand firm between now and Election Day over his handling of Iraq and appeared to be an

Continued on Page A30

For Flu Shots, Smaller Supply, More Concern

By KIRK JOHNSON

DENVER, Oct. 6 — Suzanne Walker arrived at a suburban grocery store near here Wednesday afternoon for the annual ritual of a flu shot.

So she filled out the forms and stood in line, but when she got to the front was told that while there was plenty of vaccine for others, there would be none for her. As a healthy 58-year-old, she was not among the groups on the priority list: infants, elderly, chronically ill and front-line medical workers. Ms. Walker understood, but still found herself annoyed.

"I just wish they would have called and told me," she said.

The flu season is not here yet, but with the nation suddenly facing a profound vaccine shortage, an uncertain triage of prevention — who will get a shot and who will not — began in earnest on Wednesday.

The British government halted vaccine shipments to the United States on Tuesday because of concerns about contamination at a factory owned by the Chiron Corporation, a major vaccine supplier, and health officials estimated that as much as half of the expected American supply could be affected. The flu season typically begins in late fall.

An equally profound wrinkle, health officials said, is that the vaccine supply is uneven, and in most cases largely unknown as well, since

Continued on Page A33

After Convictions, the Undoing Of a U.S. Terror Prosecution

By DANNY HAKIM and ERIC LICHTBLAU

TRIAL AND ERRORS
The Detroit Terror Case

DETROIT, Oct. 6 — Publicly, federal prosecutors declared in the summer of 2002 that they had thwarted a "sleeper operational combat cell" based in a dilapidated apartment here.

Privately, senior Justice Department officials had doubts about the strength of the case even as they were moving to indict four Middle Eastern immigrants on terrorism charges. The evidence was "somewhat weak," an internal Justice Department memorandum obtained by The New York Times acknowledged. It relied on a single informant with "some baggage," and there was no clear link to terrorist groups. But charging the men with terrorism, the memorandum said, might pressure them to give up information.

"We can charge this case with the hope that the case might get better," Barry Sabin, the department's counterterrorism chief, wrote in the memorandum, "and the certainty that it will not get much worse."

But the case did get worse. After winning highly publicized convictions of two suspects on terrorism charges in June 2003, the Justice Department took the extraordinary step five weeks ago of repudiating its own case and successfully moving to throw out the terrorism charges. In a long court filing, the government discredited its own witnesses and found fault with virtually every part of its prosecution.

The blame, the department suggested in its filing, lay mainly at the feet of the lead prosecutor in Detroit, Richard G. Convertino, whom it portrayed as a rogue lawyer. But documents and interviews with people knowledgeable about the case show that top officials at the Justice Department were involved in almost every step of the prosecution, from formulating strategy to editing the draft indictments to planning how the suspects would be incarcerated.

President Bush himself said the

Continued on Page A32

Howard Stern Signs Rich Deal in Jump To Satellite Radio

By BILL CARTER and JEFF LEEDS

Howard Stern, one of the most popular but polarizing personalities in radio, has proclaimed his emancipation from the decency czars of the F.C.C.

Mr. Stern announced on his show yesterday morning that he had signed a lucrative contract that will move him from commercial broadcast radio to Sirius Satellite Radio starting in January 2006. His listeners there will have to pay $12.95 a month but he will no longer be bound by government strictures.

The deal is a risky bet by Sirius that the addition of Mr. Stern will help the concept of pay radio gain national acceptance — and quickly bring the company to profitability. And it is a blow to Viacom, whose struggling Infinity broadcasting unit produces and syndicates the show.

But for Mr. Stern, the jump to satellite is worth trading his regular audience of about 12 million people for Sirius's 600,000 current listeners. While the new deal will pay him more than he currently makes, Mr. Stern said in a telephone interview yesterday that his biggest motiva-

Continued on Page C4

Eddie Malluk/WireImage.com

Howard Stern says his move is more about freedom than money.

DeLay Admonished By Panel a 2nd Time

For the second time in a week the House ethics committee admonished Representative Tom DeLay, the House majority leader, this time finding that he engaged in fund-raising activities that created the appearance of impropriety. The panel also found that Mr. DeLay had wrongly used his influence in exhorting the Federal Aviation Administration to search for Texas state legislators who fled to Oklahoma last year to avoid a vote on redistricting.

Mr. DeLay moved quickly to defend himself.

"For years, Democrats have hurled relentless personal attacks at me, hoping to tie my hands and smear my name," he said in a statement. "All have fallen short, not because of insufficient venom, but because of insufficient merit."

Article, Page A24.

INSIDE

Senate Passes a 9/11 Bill At Odds With the House

The Senate voted to approve a reorganization of intelligence gathering, enacting the major recommendations of the Sept. 11 commission, including the creation of a national intelligence director and a national counterterrorism center. The overwhelming vote, 96 to 2, is likely to increase pressure on House Republican leaders to adopt a similar measure. PAGE A22

New Corporate Tax Cuts

In an act of pre-election largess, House and Senate negotiators approved a corporate tax bill that would provide corporations and farmers in politically sensitive states with about $145 billion in new tax cuts. BUSINESS DAY, PAGE C1

Protest Cases Dropped

The Manhattan district attorney's office said it would not prosecute 227 protesters arrested during the Republican convention, saying it would be hard to prove that they had deliberately defied orders. PAGE B1

G. Paul Burnett/The New York Times

The Yankees Tie It Up

Derek Jeter scored the winning run in the bottom of the 12th inning last night on a sacrifice fly by Hideki Matsui as the Yankees staged a two-run rally to beat the visiting Minnesota Twins, 7-6, and tie their division series at one victory apiece. In Anaheim, the Red Sox beat the Angels, 8-3, to take a 2-0 lead in their series. In Atlanta, Roger Clemens pitched the Houston Astros to a 9-3 victory over the Braves in Game 1 of their series. SPORTSTHURSDAY, PAGE D1

3 Win Nobel in Chemistry

An American and two Israelis won the Nobel Prize in Chemistry for their study of the way cells break down proteins that have outlived their usefulness. PAGE A20

New Controversy Over Gaza

Prime Minister Ariel Sharon of Israel tried to stamp out a political brushfire after an aide said that the planned pullout from Gaza would freeze the peace process. PAGE A11

Turkey Advances In Its Bid to Join European Union

By ELAINE SCIOLINO

BRUSSELS, Oct. 6 — Four decades after Turkey came knocking on Europe's door, the European Union on Wednesday made a crucial overture toward letting it in.

The executive body of the 25-country bloc ruled that Turkey, a poor, large and overwhelmingly Muslim country of 71 million people, had made enough progress in reforming its political and economic systems to merit talks toward membership.

The decision needs the unanimous approval of the 25 heads of member states when they meet in December, although none is expected to challenge it. That does not mean Turkey's membership into the European Union, the world's largest trading bloc, is inevitable. Talks could last up to 15 years. A report on the decision recommending negotiations warned they would be halted if Turkey faltered in its democratic changes.

Even then, Turkey may never become a full member.

"Turkey sufficiently fulfills the political criteria" for talks to start, the report said. But it added, "This is an open-ended process whose outcome cannot be guaranteed beforehand."

Romano Prodi, the departing president of the European Union's executive arm, called the decision "a qualified yes."

Still, the decision was lauded in Turkey as a breakthrough in redrawing the map of Europe and narrow-

Continued on Page A12

NEWS SUMMARY A2

Updated news: nytimes.com
Tomorrow in The Times: Page B8

"All the News That's Fit to Print"

The New York Times

Late Edition

New York: **Today,** mostly sunny, gusty winds, high 30. **Tonight,** clear, cold, low 20. **Tomorrow,** some sun, lighter winds, high 35. **Yesterday,** high 33, low 25. Weather map appears on Page B7.

VOL. CLIV . . No. 53,076 | NEW YORK, MONDAY, DECEMBER 27, 2004 | ONE DOLLAR

Thousands Die as Quake-Spawned Waves Crash Onto Coastlines Across Southern Asia

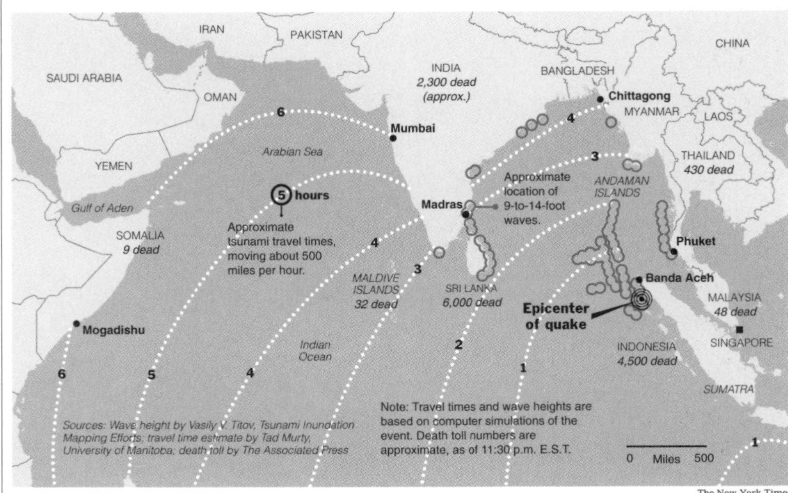

The New York Times

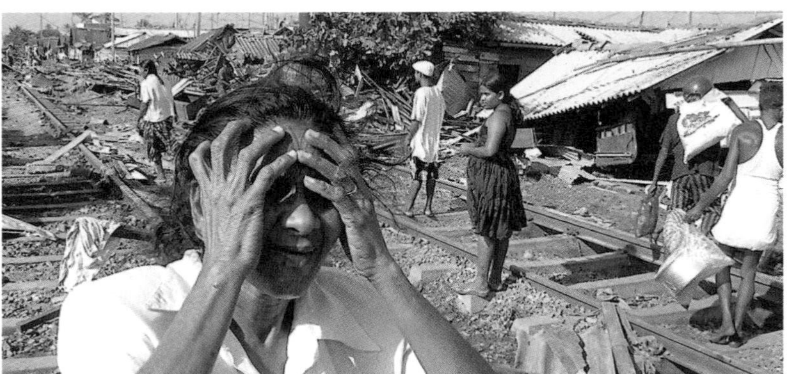

Eranga Jayawardena/Associated Press

SRI LANKA A woman wept after the tsunami destroyed her house in a coastal area in Colombo, the capital.

Agence France-Presse—Getty Images

INDIA The powerful waves battered houses and cars at Marina Beach in Madras, on the eastern coast.

Karim Khamzin/Associated Press

THAILAND A street littered with vehicles and other debris near Patong Beach in Phuket, on the western coast.

Untold Numbers Are Missing in 6 Countries

By AMY WALDMAN

MADRAS, India, Monday, Dec. 27 — The world's most powerful earthquake in 40 years erupted underwater off the Indonesian island of Sumatra on Sunday and sent walls of water barreling thousands of miles, killing more than 13,000 people in half a dozen countries across South and Southeast Asia, with thousands more missing or unreachable.

The earthquake, which measured 9.0 in magnitude, set off tsunamis that built up speeds of as much as 500 miles per hour, then crashed into coastal areas of Sri Lanka, India, Thailand, Indonesia, the Maldives and Malaysia as 40-foot-high walls of water, devouring everything and everyone in their paths.

Its force was felt more than 3,000 miles away in Somalia on the eastern coast of Africa, where nine people were reported killed.

Aid agencies were rushing staff and equipment to the region, warning that rotting bodies were threatening health and water supplies.

It took several hours in some cases on Sunday for the waves to build and reach their targets after the earthquake struck. But none of the most affected countries had warning systems in place to detect the coming onslaught and alert their citizens to move away from the coastline.

"I just couldn't believe what was happening before my eyes," Boree Carlsson, 45, of Sweden, told Reuters from a hotel in the Thai resort of Phuket. "As I was standing there, a car actually floated into the lobby and overturned because the current was so strong."

A tsunami — the term is Japanese — is a series of waves generated by underwater seismic disturbances, in this case the interface of the India and Burma tectonic plates. Seismologists with the United States Geological Survey said the ocean west of Sumatra and the island chains to its north was a hot zone for earthquakes because of a nonstop collision occurring there between the India plate, beneath the Indian Ocean seabed, and the Burma plate under the islands and that part of the continent.

The India plate is moving at about two inches a year to the northeast, creating pressure that releases, sporadically, in seismic activity. But this was an especially devastating earthquake, the fourth most powerful in 100 years.

Television images showed bodies floating in muddied waters. Cars went out to sea; boats came onto land. Snorkelers were dragged onto the beach, and sunbathers out to sea, Simon Clark, a photographer who was vacationing on Ngai Island in Thailand, told The Associated Press.

Indonesia reported nearly 4,500 dead, most in the Banda Aceh area of Sumatra, a region that has been the site of a continuing civil war. In Sri Lanka, at least 6,000 were dead. In India, an estimated 2,300 died, with

Continued on Page A11

More on the Earthquake

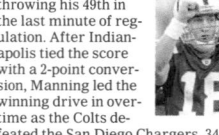

Dimitar Dilkof/Agence France-Presse—Getty Images

Viktor A. Yushchenko flashing a victory sign in Kiev early today.

PRO-WEST LEADER APPEARS TO WIN UKRAINE ELECTION

A THIRD ROUND OF VOTING

Yushchenko, a Survivor of Fraud and Poisoning, Takes the Lead

By C. J. CHIVERS

KIEV, Ukraine, Monday, Dec. 27 — Viktor A. Yushchenko, the opposition leader, appeared headed for a resounding victory early Monday in a riveting presidential race marked by intrigue, charges of poisoning, fervent street demonstrations and widespread abuses of state power.

There were no independent reports of the egregious election violations that had discredited the previous round of voting. Mr. Yushchenko, addressing supporters at this headquarters, predicted an end at last to an extended and bitter election season.

"It has happened," said Mr. Yushchenko, his face still disfigured from dioxin poisoning this fall for which he has blamed his adversaries in the government. "Today we are turning a page of lies, censorship and violence." Ahead, he said, lay a "new epoch of a new great democracy."

With 74 percent of the votes from the Sunday election counted, Mr. Yushchenko was leading Prime Minister Viktor F. Yanukovich by 55 percent to 40 percent, according to the Central Election Commission. The early results placed him within the range predicted by surveys of voters exiting the polls, which gave the opposition a 15- to 20-point lead.

Displays of fireworks lighted up Independence Square, where tens of thousands of Mr. Yushchenko's supporters turned out once more, as they had for more than two weeks in late November and early December to protest the government fraud that discredited the last vote. The Orange Revolution, as Mr. Yushchenko's supporters have taken to calling their peaceful resistance, appeared to be nearing its end.

The election was the second head-to-head contest between Mr. Yushchenko and Mr. Yanukovich, who once had been the handpicked successor to departing President Leonid D. Kuchma, but had publicly broken with Mr. Kuchma and cast himself as an embittered outsider.

A first round of voting in October had narrowed a large field to these two finalists, and the second round of voting, on Nov. 21, which gave the victory to Mr. Yanukovich, was overturned by Ukraine's Supreme Court

Continued on Page A12

Airlines' Woes May Be Worse In Coming Year

By MICHELINE MAYNARD

Passengers who got caught up in the airlines' troubles over Christmas received a glimpse of what may await them in the coming year.

The winter storms and computer malfunctions, which snarled airport traffic from Philadelphia to Atlanta, may have been unavoidable, experts say. But the signs of labor unrest that cropped up over the weekend could be a harbinger of things to come in an industry already buffeted by bankruptcies and structural change.

With the six big airlines expected to lose another $5.5 billion this year, every one of them — American, United, Delta, Continental, Northwest and US Airways — has announced plans for deeper cuts in 2005. All told, they will reach $7.5 billion in spending and at least 20,000 jobs.

"We really have the tough part ahead of us," said Gerald A. Grinstein, the chief executive at Delta Air Lines, which avoided a bankruptcy filing this fall by persuading pilots to cut their pay by a third.

For passengers, the irreversible retrenchment by the airline industry, which has shrunk by a quarter since the start of the decade, has meant the loss of food service, a reduction in routes, flight delays, lost baggage and other headaches.

But if employees' reactions to these kinds of changes are anything like what US Airways experienced over the weekend, consumers are in for more serious disruptions.

Yesterday, US Airways, which is operating in bankruptcy, canceled 29

Continued on Page A14

Autism Therapies Still a Mystery, But Parents Take a Leap of Faith

By BENEDICT CAREY

Desperate parents of autistic children have tried almost everything — hormone injections, exotic diets, faith healing — in the hope of finding a cure.

But more than 60 years after it was first identified, autism remains mystifying and stubbornly difficult to treat. About the only thing parents, doctors and policy makers agree on is that the best chance for autistic children to develop social and language skills is to enroll them in some type of intensive behavioral therapy.

A government-appointed panel has endorsed such therapies, which can cost $40,000 to more than $60,000 per year. Parents fight to get their children placed in behavioral programs, encouraged by the claims of some therapists that they can produce astonishing improvement in up to 50 percent of cases. An estimated 141,000 children with autism receive special education services, in many cases including behavioral therapies, through public schools.

Yet the science behind behavioral treatments is modest at best. Researchers have published very few rigorously controlled studies of the therapies, and the results of those studies have been mixed. While some children thrive, even joining regular classrooms, the studies have found that most show moderate or little improvement. And researchers say most parents now experiment with so many alternative treatments — including vitamins, diets, sensory therapies and computer games — that they muddy the results of behavior treatment, making it very hard to say what is causing a child to gain skills or to decline.

The most recent analysis of treatment research, financed by the National Institutes of Health and scheduled to be published next year, concludes that although behavior treatments benefit many children, there is no evidence that any particular treatment leads to recovery. Doctors do not yet know how to predict which

Continued on Page A15

INSIDE

Disaster Sneaks In and a Village Is Pummeled

By SETH MYDANS

DEHIWALA, Sri Lanka, Monday, Dec. 27 — Disaster crept up on them deceptively, the villagers said, then pounced.

"We were just relaxing here after finishing our morning work," said J. W. Kanti, whose work consists of cooking, washing and caring for her children. "All of a sudden the water from the sea rose up close to our houses. Then it went out again. We all stood and watched."

It withdrew for 1,000 yards, said Christoper Fernando, 30, an electrician, scraping the seabed dry behind it.

"The stones looked like elephants!" said his neighbor Emil Chandradase.

The people who lost everything here in Sri Lanka in Sunday's earthquake were among the country's poorest, mostly subsistence fishermen who lived between the rocky shoreline and the railroad tracks.

Officials say as many as 4,500 people are known to have died in Sri Lanka, one of the most severely hit nations, and that perhaps 500,000 are homeless. The death toll is certain to rise as more people are determined to be missing from seaside villages like this one.

No one died here in Dehiwala, a village south of the capital, Colombo, but hundreds have been left homeless, including 600 people who are taking refuge on the brightly lighted grounds of a Buddhist temple.

Mr. Fernando said the fishermen rushed to secure their boats, in vain. "Then all of a sudden, after a few minutes, the water came back again in a huge wall and we ran, and all our houses were turned into junk."

A huge wind rose for a moment, whipping the four palm trees that stand near his house. "We just grabbed our kids and ran," he said. "That's all we managed to save."

One of those taking refuge at the temple was Aslin Gomus, 58, whose voice was hoarse from shouting.

"The water came, and I started screaming," she said. "I screamed and screamed. I saved a lot of children." But when she was asked, many hours later, she said she had no idea what she had been shouting.

Her niece Kumari Mendis, 29, said she took up the cry, "The water is coming!"

"We were so scared," Ms. Mendis said. "I thought maybe we will die now. We were just running. Thank God nobody is dead. But everything is gone. Everything is nothing."

Before they told their tales, they seemed to be bundles of rags lying

Continued on Page A11

"All the News That's Fit to Print"

The New York Times

Late Edition

New York: **Today:** scattered showers, cool and breezy, high 46. **Tonight,** rain ending, chilly, low 39. **Tomorrow,** breezy, milder, high 57. **Yesterday,** high 57, low 40. Weather map, Page 37.

VOL. CLIV . . No. 53,173 | Copyright © 2005 The New York Times | NEW YORK, SUNDAY, APRIL 3, 2005 | $4.50 beyond the greater New York metropolitan area. | $3.50

POPE JOHN PAUL II DIES AT 84

In 26-Year Reign, Reshaped Church and Papacy

Challenge Posed in Selecting a Successor

By LAURIE GOODSTEIN

When the 117 Roman Catholic cardinals who are eligible to elect a successor to Pope John Paul II gather in the Sistine Chapel to cast their ballots, the worldwide suspense about the outcome will be shared even by the cardinals in the conclave.

There is no clear front-runner, unlike in some past papal elections, many church experts agree. So the cardinals will be weighing a host of factors, including the candidates' country of origin, age, experience and personality.

Among the most critical questions facing the cardinals is, should the papacy be returned to an Italian, or should the cardinals make the bold gesture of choosing a pope from the third world, where Catholicism is both thriving and threatened by competing faiths?

"A third-world pope would clearly indicate that this is no longer a European church, that we are truly catholic in the sense that the word catholic means universal," said the Rev. Thomas Reese, editor of America, a Jesuit weekly.

To qualify as electors, cardinals must be less than 80 years old. In this election, the cardinals come from more than 60 countries, and more than 60 of them were appointed in the past four years. For many of them, the funeral proceedings and the conclave itself, 15 to 20 days after the pope's death, will offer the first opportunity to take the measure of all the potential candidates firsthand.

"Each one of those cardinals is going to walk into that conclave thinking, 'Which of these candidates is going to go over best back in my diocese, in my country,' " Father Reese said.

With all but three of the cardinal electors having been appointed by John Paul, nearly all his potential successors fit his mold of doctrinal conservatism on issues like abortion and euthanasia, birth control, homosexuality and the ordination of women. So the more pivotal factors are likely to be the candidates' nationality and professional experience.

Vatican observers have spent years now honing their ever-changing lists of cardinals who are "papabile," or potential popes. Although the chosen successor may not have made any of these lists, there are certain names that keep cropping up

Continued on Page 44

Derrick Ceyrac/Agence France-Presse

Pope John Paul II listening during a Mass at the Strasbourg cathedral in 1988 on his fourth trip to France.

Krakow and Beyond: Prayers, Tributes and Awe

By RICHARD BERNSTEIN

KRAKOW, Poland, April 2 — They were already there when the end came, perhaps 10,000 or 20,000 people, all gathered under bare trees in the large square under the window of the archbishop's residence where Pope John Paul II used to stand and talk to people on pastoral visits in this city.

There were not very many tears, though some people did weep. It was more a kind of awed and pensive stillness under the dark sky. Candles lined the windows of the residence; in the distance was the sound of a siren. And then, around 10 p.m. on Saturday, the people who had been standing through a chilly evening for hours praying for the pope learned he was dead. They sank collectively to their knees.

The Roman Catholic Church lost one of its most charismatic and influential leaders, but Poland lost one of the great men of this country's turbulent and tragic history. So Krakow was out, lighting candles, saying prayers, pressing knees onto cold pavement or trampled grass, and remembering the man who represented to them nothing less than the savior of the national Polish soul.

"He was like Moses," said Przemyslaw Kalicki, who was standing in the square with his wife, Paulina, and their 13 year-old son Maciej, just minutes after the pope's death became known. "He led us through the Red Sea of Communism."

As Mr. Kalicki spoke, the 16th-century bell of the Wawel Cathedral across town, the biggest bell in Poland, began to ring, and the members of the Kalicki family stopped to listen. The bell, which has a deep and mystical timber, has been rung only on historic occasions.

The sense of history was indeed present. An era began here in 1978, when the city's son, Karol Wojtyla, was elected pope and Poland was a Communist dictatorship. And it ended with Poland democratic and secure, at least in part because of his moral authority.

Continued on Page 46

Succumbs to Illness Suffered at Length and in Public

By IAN FISHER

VATICAN CITY, Sunday, April 3 — Pope John Paul II died Saturday night, succumbing finally to years of illness endured painfully and publicly, ending an extraordinary, if sometimes polarizing, 26-year reign that remade the papacy.

He died at 9:37 p.m. in his apartment three stories above St. Peter's Square, as tens of thousands of the faithful gathered within sight of his lighted window for a second night of vigils, amid millions of prayers for him from Roman Catholics around the world as his health declined rapidly.

People wept and knelt on cobblestones as the news of his death spread across the square, bowing their heads to a man whose long and down-to-earth papacy was the only one that many young and middle-aged Catholics around the world remembered. For more than 10 minutes, not long after his death was announced, the largely Roman crowd simply applauded him.

"I have looked up to this man as a guide, and now it is like a star that has suddenly disappeared," said Caeser Aturi, 38, a priest from Ghana, which the widely traveled pope visited in 1980, on a continent where the Roman Catholic church grew sizably under his reign.

He was born Karol Wojtyla on May 18, 1920 in Wadowice, Poland. He was 84 years old.

Hospitalized twice since Feb. 1 and suffering for a decade from Parkinson's disease, John Paul's health hit its last crisis on Thursday, when the Vatican announced that a urinary tract infection had caused a high fever and unstable blood pressure.

In the next day, his kidneys and cardio-respiratory system began to fail. On Saturday morning, his chief spokesman, Dr. Joaquín Navarro-Valls, announced grimly that the Pope had begun to fade from consciousness.

His last hours were spent, Dr. Navarro-Valls said in a statement early on Sunday, by "the uninterrupted prayer of all those who surrounded him." At 8 p.m. Mass was celebrated in his room, the statement said, and he was administered the final Catholic rite for the sick and dying for the second time, having already received it on Thursday.

He was surrounded at his death by a close circle of aides from Poland: his two personal secretaries, Archbishop Stanislaw Dziwisz and Monsignor Mieczyslaw Mokrzycki; Cardinal Marian Jaworski, Archbishop Stanislaw Rylko; the Rev. Tadeusz Styczen, as well as three Polish nuns who have long worked in his residence. His personal doctor, Renato Buzzonetti, two other doctors and two nurses were also there.

After a doctor certifies his death, tradition calls for the Vatican camerlengo, Cardinal Eduardo Martinez Somalo, who will run the Vatican until a new pope is chosen, to call out his baptismal name three times. He then strikes the pope's forehead with a silver hammer to ensure he is dead. The hammer is then used to destroy the papal ring, the symbol of his authority.

The Vatican said the body of John Paul II would lie in state at St. Peter's Basilica no sooner than Monday. The Italian news agency ANSA reported that his funeral — to be at-

Continued on Page 44

Giuseppe Cacace/Getty Images

The Vatican's doors will not reopen until a new pope is elected.

JOHN PAUL II

A SPECIAL SECTION John Paul II was a politically deft figure who transcended geographical and ideological boundaries. **PAGE 39**

UNEASY FLOCK Under John Paul II, a drifting Catholic Church gained new rigor and a clear direction. But that direction has dismayed many American Catholics. **WEEK IN REVIEW**

AN EDITORIAL Keeper of the flock for a quarter of a century. **PAGE 46**

Janek Skarzynski/Agence France-Presse — Getty Images

In Wadowice, Poland, the hometown of Pope John Paul II, women wept yesterday after hearing of his death.

Aging Warheads Ignite a Debate Among Scientists

By WILLIAM J. BROAD

For over two decades, a compact, powerful warhead called the W-76 has been the centerpiece of the nation's nuclear arsenal, carried aboard the fleet of nuclear submarines that prowl the Atlantic and Pacific Oceans.

But in recent months it has become the subject of a fierce debate among experts inside and outside the government over its reliability and its place in the nuclear arsenal.

The government is readying a plan to spend more than $2 billion on a routine 10-year overhaul to extend the life of the aging warheads. At the same time, some weapons scientists say the warheads have a fundamental design flaw that could cause them to explode with far less force than intended.

Although the government has denied that assertion, officials have disclosed that Washington is nevertheless considering replacing the W-76 altogether.

"This is the one we worry about the most," said Everet H. Beckner, who oversees the arsenal as director of defense programs at the National Nuclear Security Administration.

Some arms-control advocates oppose the 10-year overhaul program, saying it could produce not only refurbishments but also deadly new in-

Continued on Page 27

Drug Makers Race to Cash In on Fight Against Fat

By STEPHANIE SAUL

LOUISVILLE, Ky. — The L-Marc Research clinic stands at the geographic center of an American epidemic, where the meat-and-potatoes Midwest meets the chicken-fried South, and just across the street from a McDonald's.

The clinic is a leading recruitment post in the drug industry's multibillion-dollar war on fat. Desperate to be thin, overweight people eagerly respond to L-Marc's local newspaper ads for volunteers to test experimental weight-loss drugs. For each trial, the clinic is forced to turn away dozens of volunteers.

"I've had people crying on the phone," said Heather Hausberger,

OBESITY INC.

Wanted: A Magic Pill

the dietitian who screens applicants. "They've tried everything. Nothing seems to work. A lot of people are looking for the quick fix, the magic pill."

Many drug makers, too, are seeking that magic pill. From pharmaceutical giants to tiny start-ups, the industry is spending billions of dollars developing obesity drugs. An estimated 200 possibilities are now in the research pipeline or under test among patients at dozens of clinics like L-Marc, according to MedMarket Diligence, a health care research firm.

Some drug makers say they are tackling fat in response to public health warnings of a national obesity epidemic — one that has been linked to diabetes, heart disease and other conditions and now accounts for more than $100 billion of the United States' $1.8 trillion annual medical bill. The obese are defined as those with a so-called body mass index of 30 or more. By that measure, obese people now make up one-third of the adult population.

But many drug industry analysts

Continued on Page 22

INSIDE

Help Wanted in China: Cheap Labor Falls Short

There is a growing shortage of factory workers in two of China's southern provinces at the heart of its export-driven economy, and analysts caution that it could be the start of a long-term trend that could eventually erode China's leadership position for cheap labor. **PAGE 4**

The Filibuster's Defender

With his encyclopedic knowledge of Senate rules and procedure, Senator Robert C. Byrd of West Virginia has emerged as the Democratic leader in fighting to preserve filibusters of judicial nominees. **PAGE 26**

Reaction Shifts on Shootings

The Columbine High School rampage in 1999 inspired gun-control proposals in Congress and the states but recent highly publicized shootings in Chicago, Atlanta, Wisconsin and Minnesota have led to calls to ease gun laws. **PAGE 25**

Apathy Worries AIDS Experts

Despite warnings from New York City health officials about a rare, possibly more virulent strain of H.I.V., many AIDS activists hold out little hope that the news will prompt substantial or lasting changes in the behavior of gay men. **PAGE 29**

Top Teams Advance

Top-ranked Illinois and top-seeded North Carolina advanced to the N.C.A.A. men's basketball title game tomorrow. Illinois defeated Louisville, 72-57, for its first berth in the title game. North Carolina defeated Michigan State, 87-71. **SPORTSSUNDAY**

New Season, Old Faces

Randy Johnson and Roger Clemens are at the head of a class of pitchers who are thriving into their 40's. Stephen King ponders the state of Red Sox fans who enter the season in an unfamiliar position. **BASEBALL PREVIEW**

A Reminder

Daylight saving time resumed at 2 a.m. today. Clocks were set ahead one hour.

Updated news: nytimes.com

FOR HOME DELIVERY CALL 1-800-NYTIMES

"All the News That's Fit to Print"

The New York Times

Late Edition

New York: **Today:** Cloudy, humid, scattered showers, high 82. **Tonight,** a shower, low 73. **Tomorrow,** ample sun, warm, high 89. **Yesterday,** high 85, low 75. Weather map is on Page D9.

VOL. CLIV . . No. 53,323 NEW YORK, WEDNESDAY, AUGUST 31, 2005 ONE DOLLAR

NEW ORLEANS IS INUNDATED AS 2 LEVEES FAIL; MUCH OF GULF COAST IS CRIPPLED; TOLL RISES

Vincent Laforet/The New York Times

Water engulfed much of New Orleans yesterday, and officials feared a steep death toll after breaches in the levees sent the waters of Lake Pontchartrain pouring into the city.

CITY IS OFF LIMITS

Pentagon Joins in the Effort — Bush Cuts Vacation Short

By JOSEPH B. TREASTER and N. R. KLEINFIELD

NEW ORLEANS, Aug. 30 — A day after New Orleans thought it had narrowly escaped the worst of Hurricane Katrina's wrath, water broke through two levees on Tuesday and virtually submerged and isolated the city, causing incalculable destruction and rendering it uninhabitable for weeks to come.

With bridges washed out, highways converted into canals, and power and communications lines inoperable, government officials ordered everyone still remaining out of the city. Officials began planning for the evacuation of the Superdome, where about 10,000 refugees huddled in increasingly grim conditions as water and food were running out and rising water threatened the generators.

The situation was so dire that late in the day the Pentagon ordered five Navy ships and eight Navy maritime rescue teams to the Gulf Coast to bolster relief operations. It also planned to fly in Swift boat rescue teams from California.

As rising water and widespread devastation hobbled rescue and recovery efforts, the authorities could only guess at the death toll in New Orleans and across the Gulf Coast. In Mississippi alone, officials raised the official count of the dead to at least 100.

"It looks like Hiroshima is what it looks like," Gov. Haley Barbour said, describing parts of Harrison County, Miss.

Across the region, rescue workers were not even trying to gather up and count the dead, officials said, but pushed them aside for the time being as they tried to find the living.

As the sweep of the devastation became clear, President Bush cut short his monthlong summer vacation on Tuesday and returned to Washington, where he will meet on Wednesday with a task force established to coordinate the efforts of 14 federal agencies that will be involved in responding to the disaster.

The scope of the catastrophe caught New Orleans by surprise. A certain sense of relief that was felt on Monday afternoon, after the eye of the storm swept east of the city, proved cruelly illusory, as the authorities and residents woke up Tuesday to a more horrifying result than had been anticipated. Mayor Ray

Continued on Page A13

DEMOCRATIC FIELD LAGS IN CITY POLL

Many Choose Bloomberg Over Any of His Rivals

By JIM RUTENBERG and MARJORIE CONNELLY

New York City Democrats are largely unimpressed with their field of mayoral candidates in the coming primary election, and nearly half of them believe that the Republican mayor, Michael R. Bloomberg, deserves re-election, according to the latest New York Times poll.

With two weeks to go before the Sept. 13 primary, more than a quarter of Democratic voters said they remained undecided. And half of Democrats said that if Mr. Bloomberg were in the Democratic primary they would vote for him, giving the mayor more than double the support of the next most popular candidate, Fernando Ferrer, in such a hypothetical matchup.

The poll showed Mr. Bloomberg in an enviable position as he heads to the November general election. It was a startling reversal for a mayor who two years ago had the lowest job approval rating in the history of the New York Times poll, 24 percent. Today, 59 percent of New Yorkers approve of the job he is doing, 9 percentage points higher than his previous high of 50 percent in late June.

But when voters were asked to

Continued on Page B5

Secrecy Veils China's Jailing Of a Journalist

By JIM YARDLEY

BEIJING, Aug. 30 — For the more than 11 months that he has been incarcerated, Zhao Yan has been held in one of the darkest corners of China's legal system because of the accusation against him: that he leaked state secrets to his employer, The New York Times.

The accusation, which Mr. Zhao and The Times deny, deprives a defendant in China of almost all rights. Mr. Zhao still has not had a court hearing. No public explanation has been given for his arrest. He is forbidden to see his family. His lawyer's efforts to post bail were denied not by a judge but by the Ministry of State Security, the agency that arrested him.

Mr. Zhao, 43, who worked as a researcher for the newspaper's bureau in Beijing, was no stranger to State Security when it picked him up last Sept. 17 at a Pizza Hut in Shanghai. His previous work as a muckraking journalist and rural activist earned him regular visits from agents and invited speculation that his past life was the reason for his arrest.

But a confidential State Security report and interviews confirm that Mr. Zhao was the focus of a high-level investigation begun in response to an article in The Times on Sept. 7.

The article, which cited two anony-

Continued on Page A6

Face to Face With Death and Destruction in Biloxi

By SHAILA DEWAN

BILOXI, Miss., Aug. 30 — If an aerial camera flying over this ruined peninsula were to zoom in, past the blocks of flattened houses, past the causeway crumpled like an accordion, past the barges that pulled loose from their moorings and sailed inland, past where the Biloxi Visitors Center and the McDonald's used to be, past the lawnmowers and soup ladles and scissors and tangled Hawaiian shirts and barstools and bathtubs, it might zero in on a pair of bare feet jutting toward the sky, out of a square hole in a concrete slab.

"That's J.D.," said Jimmy Ellzey, who stood studying the wreckage of the Tivoli Hotel on Tuesday with a fixed expression. Then he gestured to a white, waxen knee, barely visible under the slab. "And that's Sue."

He walked along what had been the roof of the two-story building and pointed. "I played poker with him the night before," he said, pointing to an arm, and the top of a head, of a silver-haired man boxed in by the pale green tile of a shower stall. "He actually won 10 bucks from me. I don't know his name. I just know he couldn't swim."

The manager of the Tivoli, a residential hotel, said later that there were eight people under that slab — eight not yet counted in the death toll in Harrison County, one of the hardest hit by Hurricane Katrina.

The authorities said they had no firm tally of the dead, and large parts of the county had yet to be searched. Joe Spraggins, the head of emergency management for the county, said the official count was at 100 but sure to grow.

At a news briefing just east in Gulfport, Gov. Haley Barbour warned that the death toll could soar.

"There is incredible evidence that the casualties are more than 50, maybe 80," Governor Barbour said, "and it seems likely that that's not the end of it. It may be higher, maybe substantially."

Chief Pat Sullivan of the Gulfport

Continued on Page A12

AFTER THE HURRICANE

OIL PRICES As the extent of the damage to offshore platforms became apparent, oil prices soared above $70 a barrel and gasoline futures jumped by 20 percent amid concern that it would take months to restore production. PAGE C1

PUBLIC HEALTH Federal health officials rushed equipment and experts to the Gulf Coast and warned that the consequences of the storm were likely to be enormous. PAGE A14

A CITY'S SOUL People who love what is perhaps America's most distinctive city are wondering what will remain of New Orleans, physically and psychologically. PAGE A11

THE MILITARY RESPONSE Five Navy ships and eight maritime rescue teams were ordered to the Gulf Coast. PAGE A14

Eric Gay/Associated Press

Evelyn Turner's husband, Xavier Bowie, who had cancer, died in New Orleans when his oxygen ran out.

In Search of a Place to Sleep, and News of Home

By KATE ZERNIKE and JODI WILGOREN

SARALAND, Ala., Aug. 30 — Hundreds of thousands of evacuees from the New Orleans area stranded in overcrowded hotels, motels and makeshift shelters and on highways across much of the South underscored a new reality on Tuesday: an extended diaspora of a city's worth of people, one rarely seen in the annals of urban disaster.

As news spread that the devastated, largely emptied and cordoned-off New Orleans area would not be habitable until at least next week, hurricane refugees gathered in hotel lobbies and shelters around television sets beaming images of their waterlogged city and turned to cellphones and laptops, usually in vain, for information about the homes, relatives and neighbors they had left behind.

Hotels as far away as Houston (350 miles from New Orleans), Memphis (395 miles) and Little Rock (445 miles) were booked, and the American Red Cross had opened more than 230 shelters in schools, churches and civic centers spread through six Southern states.

Many found themselves wandering anew after maxing out credit cards or being forced to leave previously booked rooms.

America Williams, 34, evacuated on Sunday, piling into a sport utility vehicle with her boyfriend and 13 of his relatives — seven of them children. "They just told us to drive, to drive east or west to get as far from the storm as possible," Ms. Williams said. "Our intention was to go to Atlanta, but it was raining so hard we stopped in Birmingham."

After two nights in three $50 rooms at a motel, the family ran out of money and moved on Tuesday to the Birmingham Jefferson Civic Center, where the Red Cross had just opened a shelter. "We're down to our very last," Ms. Williams said. "We came

Continued on Page A15

INSIDE

Five Lebanese Detained in Assassination Inquiry

A United Nations investigation into the assassination of former Prime Minister Rafik Hariri of Lebanon has ordered five current or former Lebanese high officials with links to Syria detained for questioning. PAGE A3

Poverty Rate Rose in 2004

Even as the economy grew, incomes stagnated last year and the poverty rate rose, the Census Bureau reported. It was the first time on record that household incomes failed to increase for five straight years. The report reflected lingering weakness in workers' pay. PAGE A9

Hints of Missing Millions

In the first hopeful sign for investors in the Bayou hedge fund, Arizona authorities say that $101 million they seized from a bank account could be from the fund. BUSINESS DAY, PAGE C1

Ebet J. Schechter/European Pressphoto Agency

Roddick Is Ousted at Open

Andy Roddick, seeded fourth in the U.S. Open, was a first-round loser, dropping straight sets to Gilles Muller. SPORTSWEDNESDAY, PAGE D1

Updated news: nytimes.com

Tomorrow in The Times: Page D9

"All the News That's Fit to Print"

The New York Times

Late Edition

New York: **Today,** Clouds with some sun, continued chilly, high 52. **Tonight,** clearing, cool, low 41. **Tomorrow,** warmer, sunny, high 65. **Yesterday,** high 50, low 42. Details, Page B20.

VOL. CLV . . No. 53,382 *NEW YORK, SATURDAY, OCTOBER 29, 2005* *ONE DOLLAR*

Cheney Aide Charged With Lying in Leak Case

Novel Strategy Pits Journalists Against Source

By KATHARINE Q. SEELYE and ADAM LIPTAK

In pressing his indictment of I. Lewis Libby Jr., the special prosecutor is pitting three prominent journalists against their former source, a strategy that experts in law and journalism say has rarely been used or tested.

It is all but unheard of for reporters to turn publicly on their sources or for prosecutors to succeed in conscripting members of a profession that prizes its independence.

Yet Mr. Libby's trial on perjury and obstruction charges will largely turn on whether jurors are more inclined to believe a government official who played a critical role in devising the justifications for the Iraq war or members of a profession whose own credibility has been under assault.

"We don't have much of a track record," said Jeffrey H. Smith, a former general counsel of the Central Intelligence Agency, "because journalists so rarely testify."

The three reporters all initially resisted subpoenas for their testimony, hoping to avoid not only testifying before the grand jury but also having to appear as a prosecution witness at trial. Such challenges have often been successful in the past. But all of them lost, and ultimately relented, saying that Mr. Libby had granted them permission to testify about confidential conversations.

"This is exactly the thing," said Jane Kirtley, a professor of media ethics and law at the University of Minnesota, "that journalists fear most — that they will become an in-

Continued on Page A14

Shift in Focus For Prosecutor

In the Hunt for a Leak, Charging a Cover-Up

By TODD S. PURDUM

News Analysis

WASHINGTON, Oct. 28 — The capital stopped in its tracks on Friday to watch a trim, plain, soft-spoken prosecutor whose voice it had barely heard in two years call the most important aide to the most powerful vice president in American history a liar. Politely, calmly, but firmly — and over and over again.

The prosecutor, Patrick J. Fitzgerald, brought no charges on the issue that prompted his investigation: whether someone in the government committed a crime by leaking the classified C.I.A. identity of the wife of one of the sharpest critics of the administration's rationale for war with Iraq. But he offered renewed evidence of that oldest of Washington axioms: the cover-up is always worse than the crime.

In an hourlong, live television news conference, Mr. Fitzgerald said that Vice President Dick Cheney's chief of staff, I. Lewis Libby Jr., had repeatedly told F.B.I. agents, and later a federal grand jury, that he was "just passing gossip from one reporter to another at the end of a long chain of phone calls" about the identity of the agent, Valerie Wilson. "It would be a compelling story that would lead the F.B.I. to go away," Mr. Fitzgerald said. "If only it were true."

It was as if Mr. Fitzgerald had suddenly morphed from the ominous star of a long-running silent movie into a sympathetic echo of Kevin Costner in "The Untouchables." And Mr. Libby's sworn testimony that he had learned of Ms. Wilson's identity from reporters suddenly seemed to spring from the same confidence that they would never contradict him that led Bill Clinton to assume that Monica S. Lewinsky had not saved evidence of their affair.

"We didn't get the straight story," Mr. Fitzgerald said, explaining his hitherto secret investigation and sometimes inscrutable moves. "And we had to — had to — take action."

As Mr. Fitzgerald spoke from the Justice Department, the cable television networks showed only mute, miniature split-screen images of counterprogrammed live speeches

Continued on Page A15

Photographs by DOUG MILLS/The New York Times

Patrick J. Fitzgerald, the special prosecutor, announcing the indictment yesterday at the Justice Department.

I. Lewis Libby Jr., indicted yesterday, being driven to work at the White House from his home in McLean, Va.

LIBBY QUITS POST

Rove's Fate Unresolved — Political Crisis for the White House

By DAVID JOHNSTON and RICHARD W. STEVENSON

WASHINGTON, Oct. 28 — I. Lewis Libby Jr., Vice President Dick Cheney's chief of staff, was indicted by a federal jury on Friday on five felony charges of lying to investigators and misleading the grand jury in the C.I.A. leak case, deepening the air of political crisis afflicting the White House while leaving many questions unanswered.

The indictment charged Mr. Libby with one count of obstruction of justice, two counts of making false statements to F.B.I. investigators and two counts of lying to the grand jury. It presented Mr. Libby as a deceptive witness who lied repeatedly and provided fictitious accounts to the grand jury about his dealings with reporters. But it did not charge him with the actual leaking of a C.I.A. officer's name.

Mr. Libby, one of the highest-ranking and most influential officials in the administration, immediately resigned and left the White House.

He said in a written statement later that he expected to be exonerated. If convicted of all the charges, he faces up to 30 years in prison and fines up to $1.25 million.

At a news conference at the Justice Department, the special counsel in the case, Patrick J. Fitzgerald, said his investigation "is not over," but he declined to say whether he might seek additional indictments.

The developments left unresolved the fate of Karl Rove, President Bush's senior adviser and deputy chief of staff, who had been warned by the prosecutor that he was in serious legal jeopardy but who was not charged in the indictment against Mr. Libby. With the term of his grand jury at an end, Mr. Fitzgerald said he could present any new evidence to an already impaneled grand jury if needed.

Mr. Rove's lawyer, Robert D. Luskin, said in a statement he was confident Mr. Fitzgerald would conclude Mr. Rove had done nothing wrong.

The charges against Mr. Libby and the prosecutor's decision not to indict Mr. Rove riveted Washington, left the White House scrambling to insulate Mr. Bush from further political damage and emboldened Demo-

Continued on Page A12

MORE ON LEAK INQUIRY

Tim Sloan/Agence France-Presse — Getty Images

RELIEF ABOUT ROVE Republicans were relieved that Karl Rove, above, the president's top adviser, escaped indictment yesterday. PAGE A14

THE INSIDER I. Lewis Libby Jr. counseled others to be discreet, but did not always follow that advice. His exceptions may haunt him. PAGE A13

LOOKING FOR ANSWERS Among the unanswered questions: who told Robert D. Novak that Valerie Wilson was a C.I.A. operative, and was her exposure a crime? PAGE A13

By Pouring It On, Bloomberg Risks Talk of Overkill

By JIM RUTENBERG and PATRICK D. HEALY

Television commercials promoting his candidacy are running not only in English, but are also coming out in Russian, Mandarin, Cantonese, Korean, Hindi and Urdu. New Yorkers are being bombarded with hundreds of thousands of phone calls from Rudolph W. Giuliani, Beverly Sills and Oscar de la Renta promoting his re-election. And thousands of volunteers will be knocking on doors from Staten Island to the Bronx urging people to vote.

The aggressiveness of Mayor Michael R. Bloomberg's re-election drive, even as he surges in the polls, has intensified to the point where it is perplexing to some supporters. They worry his operation will alienate Democrats who are poised to vote for him but may come to see his spending as overkill and his campaign as bullying his Democratic opponent, Fernando Ferrer.

"It's particularly troubling when an incumbent who has so many advantages finds it necessary" to spend so much, said City Councilwoman Eva S. Moskowitz, a Democrat who said she had endorsed Mr. Bloomberg earlier this month in spite of his spending because of his record as mayor. "This is a lot of money."

In the spring of 2001, New York

Continued on Page B4

Youth Power in Liberia: From Bullets to Ballots

By LYDIA POLGREEN

MONROVIA, Liberia — War took James Garmey's childhood. It came at night, in the form of armed men battering down a door and carrying him off, the 8-year-old son of a rural customs collector, to be a soldier for the warlord and future president Charles Taylor.

"I went to training," said Mr. Garmey, now 22, speaking in the smooth patois of the Liberian street, letting consonants and bits of grammar slip away. "I was small, but I learned to hold gun and after a while went to battlefront. I fire gun, I defend my area."

When Mr. Taylor fled in 2003, Mr. Garmey finally put his gun down, saying he had traded it for a different weapon altogether: the ballot.

"I cast my vote and that is my power," he said. "I no need any more gun."

Much of Africa's future belongs to young men and women like Mr. Garmey, members of a generation orphaned by conflict and AIDS, hardened by combat and want, often illiterate and unbound by deep traditions and taboos.

Manipulated by their elders, they helped unleash a cycle of bloodshed that has killed hundreds of thousands of people in West Africa alone. In that way, through their numbers and their physical strength, young people have wielded a kind of indirect and chaotic power in this region for the better part of two decades.

Now, as democracy slowly spreads, the young wield another kind of power. In Liberia people from 18 to 22 make up almost a quarter of registered voters. Add those up to the age of 28, and young people make up a huge bloc of Liberia's voting public, no less than 40 percent.

Across the region, a population explosion has created a similar youth bulge that is only now beginning to make itself manifest at the voting booth.

"They can make anybody win and can make anybody lose," said Sidi M. Diawara, an election expert in Liberia for the National Democratic Institute, a nonpartisan organization that helps develop political parties and monitor elections. "They are now the backbone of political parties, and not just in Liberia. There is a huge number of youth entering the democratic process across the region."

In Liberia, which just held its first election since the end of the 14-year civil war that killed 200,000 and displaced a third of the population, the young helped propel the presidential candidacy of George Weah, 39, a former soccer star in Europe who is

Continued on Page A9

Michael Kamber for The New York Times

Mostly young crowds like this one at a campaign rally in Monrovia earlier this month helped George Weah, a 39-year-old former soccer star, lead the field of candidates in the first round of Liberia's presidential election.

INSIDE

Bush Under Pressure Over Next Court Nominee

As he chooses another Supreme Court nominee, President Bush faces redoubled pressure both from Republicans demanding someone with a clear conservative record on social issues and from Democrats emboldened by the unraveling of the nomination of Harriet E. Miers. PAGE A10

U.S. Broadens Ban on Caviar

The Fish and Wildlife Service extended a ban on the importing of beluga caviar, the most highly prized variety. The new move, intended to help preserve dwindling beluga stocks, will effectively bar all imports to the United States. PAGE A17

New Orleans Loses Its Shade

Hurricane Katrina ravaged not only New Orleans's buildings, but also its trees, leaving shady avenues suddenly sun-dappled. PAGE A11

Syria Shows Border Security

Syria took reporters on a tour of the border to show what it was doing to prevent infiltration of fighters and arms into Iraq, while noting that the border remained porous. PAGE A8

Nobel-Winning Chemist Dies

Richard E. Smalley, a chemistry professor, shared a Nobel prize for discovering a new spherical form of carbon and championed the potential of nanotechnology. PAGE C16

Updated news: nytimes.com
Tomorrow in The Times: Page B20

Health Care: Whose Burden?

As the nation's largest employer, Wal-Mart cannot help being entangled in the increasingly contentious debate over who should be responsible for the health care of working Americans. BUSINESS DAY, PAGE C1

THIS WEEKEND

A Reminder

Standard time resumes at 2 a.m. tomorrow. Clocks are set back one hour.

The Large and Small of It

Television used to be a medium-sized medium; now it either takes up a wall or fits in a pocket. Do these new screens change what it's like to watch? ARTS & LEISURE

Time's Up for Pensions

Corporations were happy to offer generous retirement plans as long as accountants and federal insurance delayed the day of reckoning. But now that day has come. MAGAZINE

Follow the Money

An Upper East Sider who was on his co-op board took millions from the building. He repaid it, but his tactics provide a lesson for others on what to watch out for. REAL ESTATE

"All the News That's Fit to Print"

The New York Times

Late Edition

New York: **Today,** sunshine, clouds, high 64. **Tonight,** a few clouds, low 50. **Tomorrow,** more sun than clouds, warm, high 69. **Yesterday,** high 71, low 51. Weather map is on Page D8.

VOL. CLV . . No. 53,567 NEW YORK, TUESDAY, MAY 2, 2006 — ONE DOLLAR

Republicans Drop a Tax Plan After Business Leaders Protest

Senate Rejects Action to Cushion High Gas Prices

By CARL HULSE

WASHINGTON, May 1 — Senate Republicans on Monday hurriedly abandoned a broad tax proposal opposed by the oil industry and business leaders, another sign of their struggle to come up with an acceptable political and legislative answer to high gasoline prices.

Senator Bill Frist of Tennessee, the majority leader, said he had decided to jettison the provision, which would have generated billions of dollars by changing the way businesses treat inventories for tax purposes. Instead, he said the Senate Finance Committee would hold hearings on the plan "later this year, so the pluses and minuses of the provision can become well known."

The retreat came after a torrent of objections from business leaders and their advocates, who typically view Republicans in Congress as allies. They said they had been blindsided by the inclusion of the proposal as a central element of the Republican leadership's energy package late last week.

The centerpiece of the leadership proposal, a $100 rebate check to compensate taxpayers for higher gasoline prices, continued to receive a rough reception. Members of the public have telephoned and written to ridicule the idea, and even Republican lawmakers are finding fault.

"Political anxiety in an election year is to blame for a lot of the bad bills Congress passes," said Representative Jeff Flake, Republican of Arizona, who on Monday called the rebate a "knee-jerk populist idea" that voters would see through.

Democrats are trying to rally voters against Republicans, pointing to the rising fuel costs as evidence of how consumers were hurt by the opposition's ties to the oil industry.

The Republican energy package was assembled quickly last week after lawmakers returned from a recess punctuated by public complaints about the rapidly rising gas costs. Senate officials acknowledged privately that they were paying a price for rolling out the proposal before having time to vet it fully.

Besides the tax provision and the rebate, the measure includes new protections against price gouging, incentives to expand domestic oil refinery capacity, support for new energy initiatives and tax incentives for buying hybrid vehicles.

Outside Congress, experts have

Continued on Page A21

States Challenge U.S. Over Truck Mileage

Ten states, including California and New York, plan to file suit this week to force the Bush administration to toughen gasoline mileage regulations for sport utility vehicles and other trucks.

The suit contends that the administration did not do a rigorous enough analysis of the environmental benefits of fuel economy regulations before issuing new rules last month.

Article, Page A21.

Immigrants Take to U.S. Streets in Show of Strength

J. Emilio Flores for The New York Times

EFFECT Some businesses in downtown Los Angeles closed in a show of support for immigrant rights.

Charles Rex Arbogast/Associated Press

CAUSE Hundreds of thousands of people marched in Chicago, where demonstrators filled a downtown street.

Planned Boycott Evolves Into Protests

By RANDAL C. ARCHIBOLD

LOS ANGELES, May 1 — Hundreds of thousands of immigrants and their supporters skipped work, school and shopping on Monday and marched in dozens of cities from coast to coast.

The demonstrations did not bring the nation to a halt as planned by some organizers, though they did cause some disruptions and conveyed in peaceful but sometimes boisterous ways the resolve of those who favor loosening the country's laws on immigration.

Originally billed as a nationwide economic boycott under the banner "Day Without an Immigrant," the day evolved into a sweeping round of protests intended to influence the debate in Congress over granting legal status to all or most of the estimated 11 million illegal immigrants in the country.

The protesters, a mix of illegal immigrants and legal residents and citizens, were mostly Latino, but in contrast to similar demonstrations in the past two months, large numbers of people of other ethnicities joined or endorsed many of the events. In some cases, the rallies took on a broader tone of social action, as gay rights advocates, opponents of the war in Iraq and others without a direct stake in the immigration debate took to the streets.

"I think it's only fair that I speak up for those who can't speak for themselves," said Aimee Hernandez, 28, one of an estimated 400,000 people who turned out in Chicago, the site of one of the largest demonstrations. "I think we're just too many that you can't just send them back. How are you going to ignore these people?"

But among those who favor stricter controls on illegal immigration, the protests hardly impressed.

"When the rule of law is dictated by a mob of illegal aliens taking to the streets, especially under a foreign flag, then that means the nation is not governed by a rule of law — it is a mobocracy," Jim Gilchrist, a founder of the Minutemen Project, a volunteer group that patrols the United States-Mexico border, said in an interview.

While the boycott, an idea born several months ago among a small group of grass-roots immigration advocates here, may not have shut down the country, it was strongly felt in a variety of places, particularly those with large Latino populations.

Stores and restaurants in Los Angeles, Chicago and New York closed because workers did not show up or as a display of solidarity with demonstrators. In Los Angeles, the police

Continued on Page A18

Zimbabwe's Prices Rise 900%, Turning Staples Into Luxuries

By MICHAEL WINES

HARARE, Zimbabwe, April 25 — How bad is inflation in Zimbabwe? Well, consider this: at a supermarket near the center of this tatterdemalion capital, toilet paper costs $417.

No, not per roll. Four hundred seventeen Zimbabwean dollars is the value of a single two-ply sheet. A roll costs $145,750 — in American currency, about 69 cents.

The price of toilet paper, like everything else here, soars almost daily, spawning jokes about an impending better use for Zimbabwe's $500 bill, now the smallest in circulation.

But what is happening is no laughing matter. For untold numbers of Zimbabweans, toilet paper — and bread, margarine, meat, even the once ubiquitous morning cup of tea — have become unimaginable luxuries. All are casualties of the hyperinflation that is roaring toward 1,000 percent a year, a rate usually seen only in war zones.

Zimbabwe has been tormented this entire decade by both deep recession and high inflation, but in recent months the economy seems to have abandoned whatever moorings it had left. The national budget for 2006 has already been largely spent. Government services have started to crumble.

The purity of Harare's drinking water, siphoned from a lake downstream of its sewer outfall, has been unreliable for months, and dysentery and cholera swept the city in December and January. The city suffers rolling electrical blackouts. Mounds of uncollected garbage pile up on the streets of the slums.

Zimbabwe's inflation is hardly history's worst — in Weimar Germany in 1923, prices quadrupled each month, compared with doubling about once every three or four months in Zimbabwe. That said, experts agree that Zimbabwe's inflation is currently the world's highest, and has been for some time.

Public-school fees and other ever-rising government surcharges have begun to exceed the monthly incomes of many urban families lucky enough to find work. The jobless — officially 70 percent of Zimbabwe's 4.2 million workers, but widely

Continued on Page A6

Ideals Collide as Vatican Rethinks Condom Ban

By IAN FISHER

ROME, May 1 — Even at the Vatican, not all sacred beliefs are absolute: Thou shalt not kill, but war can be just. Now, behind the quiet walls, a clash is shaping up involving two poles of near certainty: the church's long-held ban on condoms and its advocacy of human life.

The issue is AIDS. Church officials recently confirmed that Pope Benedict XVI had requested a report on whether it might be acceptable for Catholics to use condoms in one narrow circumstance: to protect life inside a marriage when one partner is infected with H.I.V. or is sick with AIDS.

Whatever the pope decides, church officials and other experts broadly agree that it is remarkable that so delicate an issue is being taken up. But they also agree that such an inquiry is logical, and particularly significant from this pope, who was Pope John Paul II's strict enforcer of church doctrine.

"In some ways, maybe he has got the greatest capacity to do it because there is no doubt about his orthodoxy," said the Rev. Jon Fuller, a Jesuit physician who runs an AIDS clinic at the Boston Medical Center.

The issue has surfaced repeatedly as one of the most complicated and delicate facing the church. For years, some influential cardinals and theologians have argued for a change for couples affected by AIDS in the name of protecting life, while others have fiercely attacked the possibility as demoting the church's long advocacy of abstinence and marital fidelity to fight the disease.

The news broke just after Benedict celebrated his first anniversary as pope, a relatively quiet papal year. But he devoted his first encyclical to love, specifically between a man and a woman in marriage.

Indeed, with regard to condoms, the only change apparently being considered is in the specific case of married couples. But any change would be unpopular with conservative Catholics, some of whom have expressed disappointment that Benedict has displayed a softer face now as defender of the faith than he did when he was still Cardinal Joseph Ratzinger, the papal adviser.

"It's just hard to imagine that any pope — and this pope — would change the teaching," said Austin Ruse, president of the Culture of Life Foundation, a Catholic-oriented advocacy group in Washington that opposes abortion and contraception.

It is too soon to know where the pope is heading. Far less contentious issues can take years to inch through the Vatican's nexus of belief and bureaucracy, prayer and politics, and Cardinal Javier Lozano Barragán,

Continued on Page A12

Pensions in Peril Over Exemptions Tied to Churches

By MARY WILLIAMS WALSH

Mary Petti worked for 35 years at a community hospital in Orange, N.J., earning a pension with a government guarantee. But now the hospital has closed, money is leaking out of the plan, and Ms. Petti fears the funds will be exhausted by the time she plans to retire in five years. The government guarantee has vanished as well.

Her plight illustrates a little-known aspect of pension law, which allows churches and organizations affiliated with them to escape the costly and complicated rules that apply to secular employers.

Tens of thousands of people work for organizations that have opted out of the law, as Ms. Petti's did. Most do not know that they are exposed to potential losses with little parallel in the corporate world.

For Ms. Petti and her fellow workers, their retirements were put at risk shortly before the hospital failed, when it exempted itself from federal pension law, citing an agreement it had made with the Roman Catholic Archdiocese of Newark.

"I felt that my pension was safe," said Ms. Petti, 60, who worked her way up from nurse to vice president for patient care services in her years at the Hospital Center at Orange.

Continued on Page C6

INSIDE

Bolivia Nationalizes Oil and Gas Fields

President Evo Morales nationalized Bolivia's plentiful oil and gas fields, further rattling foreign producers already troubled by growing intervention in Latin America's resource-rich energy sector. Indigenous Aymara marched in support of the decision by the president, who is also Aymara. Mr. Morales ordered the military to occupy energy installations to ensure continued production. PAGE A9

Science's Gatekeepers

Disclosures of fraudulent or flawed studies in medical and scientific journals have called into question the peer-review system. Although journals try to weed out bad research, passing peer review is not like a Good Housekeeping seal of approval. SCIENCE TIMES, PAGE F1

Revisiting the 80's Excess

With copious clips and a little poignancy, CBS relives the opulent era of the Carrington in "Dynasty Reunion." But the show, starring Linda Evans, left, John Forsythe and Joan Collins, brings to mind another family of the 80's: the Reagans. A review by Alessandra Stanley. THE ARTS, PAGE E1

Noah Friedman-Rudovsky for The New York Times

Hindus Killed in Kashmir

Thirty-five Hindus were killed in Indian-administered Kashmir. Islamic militants were blamed for the attacks, which came just before talks on the province. PAGE A3

Getting Personal

Marketers are trying to put the consumer first, by using "my" and "your" in advertisements to create a bond. BUSINESS DAY, PAGE C1

A New Old-Fashioned Show

"The Drowsy Chaperone," a lively spoof of a 1920's frolic, is an ingenious exercise in escapism. A review by Ben Brantley. THE ARTS, PAGE E1

In Nebraska Senate Challenge, Pork Is Portrayed as Bad Politics

By MONICA DAVEY

OMAHA, April 26 — In some other year, Pete Ricketts, a wealthy former Ameritrade executive who wants to replace Ben Nelson in the United States Senate, would probably not have considered mentioning all the items Mr. Nelson and his colleagues in Washington have helped bring home to Nebraska: financing for a parking garage at the private Creighton University, for instance, or for a parking lot at the Joslyn Art Museum here.

Those would be left for Senator Nelson, a Democrat, to boast about.

But with days to go before Nebraska's primary election, Mr. Ricketts and at least one other Republican candidate are eagerly discussing such projects in interviews, forums and fund-raisers, portraying them as symbols of corruption and waste in Washington.

And so, in a reversal of tactics, challengers here and in other states like Montana, Ohio and Rhode Island are telling voters what the incumbents have brought home, in the hopes, it seems, that the national controversy over the pet projects known as earmarks has come home, too.

"In a time of war, and with the costs of Katrina, we've got to look at what we want to have and what we've got to have," said Mr. Ricketts, who has never run for office but was ahead of the two other Republican candidates in a recent poll. "We've got to end earmarks — or at least reform them."

For years, with little effect, a small group of Republican senators, including John McCain of Arizona, has fought earmarks, the bits of bill language directing federal dollars to specific projects. But the combination of the Jack Abramoff lobbying scandal and the federal budget deficit has drawn new scrutiny to efforts by lawmakers on both sides of the aisle to secure pet projects for constituents and supporters.

It is uncertain how the issue may

Continued on Page A22

"All the News That's Fit to Print"

The New York Times

Late Edition
New York: **Today,** mild, partly sunny, high 49. **Tonight,** a brief snow shower, colder, low 25. **Tomorrow,** sunshine, chilly winds, high 34. **Yesterday,** high 49, low 31. Weather map, Page D8.

VOL. CLVI . . No. 53,786

NEW YORK, THURSDAY, DECEMBER 7, 2006

ONE DOLLAR

Panel Urges Basic Shift in U.S. Policy in Iraq

Doug Mills/The New York Times

Panel members yesterday, from the front: Alan K. Simpson, William J. Perry, Charles S. Robb, Sandra Day O'Connor, James A. Baker III, Lee H. Hamilton, Edwin Meese III and, to the far left, Vernon E. Jordan Jr.

Rebuke for Bush — Situation Is 'Grave'

By DAVID E. SANGER

WASHINGTON, Dec. 6 — A bipartisan commission warned Wednesday that "the situation in Iraq is grave and deteriorating," and it handed President Bush both a rebuke for his current strategy and a detailed blueprint for a fundamentally different approach, including the pullback of all American combat brigades over the next 15 months.

In unusually sweeping and blunt language, the panel of five Republicans and five Democrats issued 79 specific recommendations.

These included a call for direct engagement with Syria and Iran as part of a "new diplomatic offensive," jump-starting the Israeli-Palestinian peace effort, and a clear declaration that the United States would reduce its support to Iraq unless Baghdad made "substantial progress" on reconciliation and security.

Mr. Bush has refused to deal with Syria and Iran, and as recently as last week, he assured Prime Minister Nuri Kamal al-Maliki that the American commitment to Iraq would be undiminished until victory was achieved.

But the commission, led by James A. Baker III and Lee H. Hamilton, argued that while Americans might be in Iraq for years, the Iraqis must understand that the American military commitment was not "open ended." It is time, the panel said, for the United States to "begin to move its combat forces out of Iraq responsibly."

The detailed prescription called for much more aggressive diplomatic efforts in the Middle East than the Bush administration has been willing to embrace. Its calls for reconciliation and reform in Iraq and an overhaul of the American military role would also mark major departures in the American strategy. [Text of the executive summary, Page A24.]

Members of the commission said they believed that their recommendations would improve prospects for success in Iraq, but they said there was no guarantee against failure.

"The current approach is not working, and the ability of the United States to influence events is diminishing," Mr. Hamilton said at a news conference on Capitol Hill. "Our ship of state has hit rough waters. It must now chart a new way forward."

Administration officials said they expected President Bush to announce his own "way forward" this month. They were careful not to take issue with the report's findings in public, and said Mr. Bush had yet to make firm decisions. But some suggested that the diplomatic strategy in the report better fit the Middle East of 15 years ago, when Mr. Baker served as secretary of state.

What played out on Wednesday morning, from the White House to Capitol Hill, was a remarkable condemnation of American policy drift in the biggest and most divisive military conflict to involve American forces since Vietnam. It was all the more unusual because Mr. Baker was secretary of state to Mr. Bush's father, and because the bipartisan group managed to come up with unanimous recommendations.

The report was delivered in an atmosphere of mounting anxiety about the war, a month after midterm elections that brought the Democrats to power in Congress and prompted Mr. Bush to oust Donald H. Rumsfeld as defense secretary.

On Wednesday the Senate voted overwhelmingly to confirm Robert

Continued on Page A23

NEWS ANALYSIS

Will It Work In the White House?

By SHERYL GAY STOLBERG

WASHINGTON, Dec. 6 — In 142 stark pages, the Iraq Study Group report makes an impassioned plea for bipartisan consensus on the most divisive foreign policy issue of this generation. Without President Bush, that cannot happen.

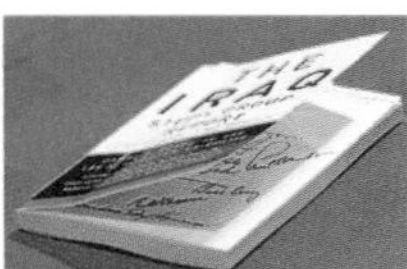

A signed copy of the Iraq Study Group's report.

The commissioners gave a nod to Mr. Bush, adopting his language in accepting the goal of an Iraq that can "govern itself, sustain itself and defend itself." But the administration's talk of Iraq as a beacon of democracy in the Middle East is absent, as is any talk of victory.

Instead, the report confronts the president with a powerful argument that his policy in Iraq is not working and that he must move toward disengagement. For Mr. Bush to embrace the study group's blueprint would mean accepting its implicit criticism of his democracy agenda, reversing course in Iraq and throughout the Middle East and meeting Democrats more than halfway.

Assuming he is not ready to go that far, despite some recent signals of flexibility, he faces the more general question of whether he is ready to embrace the spirit of the report — not to mention the drubbing his party took in the midterm elections a month ago — and produce a new approach of his own that amounts to more than a repackaging of his current worldview.

"In a sense," said Dennis Ross, who worked for both President Clinton and the first President Bush as a Middle East envoy, "what you have here offers the Democrats a ready handle to show, 'We're prepared to be bipartisan on the issue of Iraq, because we'll embrace the bipartisan Iraq Study Group — are you prepared to be bipartisan as well?' "

The study group, for instance, calls for direct engagement with Iran and Syria; so far, Mr. Bush has refused. While Mr. Bush has steadfastly resisted a timetable for

Continued on Page A23

MILITARY ANALYSIS

Will It Work On the Battlefield?

By MICHAEL R. GORDON

The military recommendations issued yesterday by the Iraq Study Group are based more on hope than history and run counter to assessments made by some of its own military advisers.

An attack on a bus killed three in Baghdad yesterday.

Ever since the invasion of Iraq in 2003, the United States has struggled in vain to tamp down the violence in Iraq and to build up the capacity of Iraq's security forces. Now the study group is positing that the United States can accomplish in little more than one year what it has failed to carry out in three.

In essence, the study group is projecting that a rapid infusion of American military trainers will so improve the Iraqi security forces that virtually all of the American combat brigades may be withdrawn by the early part of 2008.

"By the first quarter of 2008, subject to unexpected developments in the security situation on the ground, all combat brigades not necessary for force protection could be out of Iraq," the study group says.

Jack Keane, the retired Army chief of staff who served on the group's panel of military advisers, described that goal as entirely impractical. "Based on where we are now we can't get there," General Keane said in an interview, adding that the report's conclusions say more about "the absence of political will in Washington than the harsh realities in Iraq."

The experience of American commanders shows the difficulties in rapidly handing over security responsibilities to Iraq. In June, Gen. George W. Casey Jr., the senior American commander in Iraq, developed a plan that called for gradually drawing down the number of American brigade combat teams by December 2007, to just 5 or 6 from the 14 combat brigades that were deployed at the time. In keeping with this approach, American troops in Baghdad began to cut back on their patrols

Continued on Page A24

Case of the Dwindling Docket Mystifies the Supreme Court

Legal Scholars Offer Theories on a Drop in Appeals

By LINDA GREENHOUSE

WASHINGTON, Dec. 6 — On the Supreme Court's color-coded master calendar, which was distributed months before the term began on the first Monday in October, Dec. 6 is marked in red to signify a day when the justices are scheduled to be on the bench, hearing arguments.

The courtroom, however, was empty on Wednesday, and for a simple reason: The court was out of cases. The question is, where have all the cases gone?

Last year, during his Senate confirmation hearing, Chief Justice John G. Roberts Jr. said he thought the court had room on its docket and that it "could contribute more to the clarity and uniformity of the law by taking more cases."

But that has not happened. The court has taken about 40 percent fewer cases so far this term than last. It now faces noticeable gaps in its calendar for late winter and early spring. The December shortfall is the result of a pipeline empty of cases granted last term and carried over to this one.

The number of cases the court decided with signed opinions last term, 69, was the lowest since 1953 and fewer than half the number the court was deciding as recently as the mid-1980s. And aside from the school integration and global warming cases the court heard last week, along with the terrorism-related cases it has decided in the last few years, relatively few of the cases it is deciding speak to the core of the country's concerns.

The reasons for the decline all grow out of forces building for decades. The federal government has been losing fewer cases in the lower courts and so has less reason to appeal. As Congress enacts fewer laws, the justices have fewer statutes to interpret. And justices who think they might end up on the losing side of an important case might vote not to take it.

In a divided court, in a divided country, the court's reduced role is perhaps not surprising, nor is it necessarily a bad thing. "In the post-Bush v. Gore era, the court may be concerned about taking the wrong case and making an unpopular decision," said Frederick Schauer, a professor at the John F. Kennedy School of Government at Harvard, in an interview.

Professor Schauer argued in a recent and much-discussed Harvard Law Review article that the court's work "had only minimal direct engagement with the central issues of the nation's public and policy agenda." In an interview, he said, "I think they like being under the radar."

In private conversations, the justices themselves insist that nothing so profound is going on, but rather seem mystified at what they perceive as a paucity of cases that meet the court's standard criteria. The most important of those criteria is whether a case raises a question that has produced conflicting decisions among the lower federal courts.

But there are still plenty of lower-court conflicts that go unresolved, said Thomas C. Goldstein, a Supreme Court practitioner and close student of court statistics who wrote last week on the popular Scotusblog that the justices were "on the cusp of the greatest shortfall in filling the court's docket in recent memory, and likely in its modern history."

"I don't think we're at the end of

Continued on Page A36

Fewer Opinions

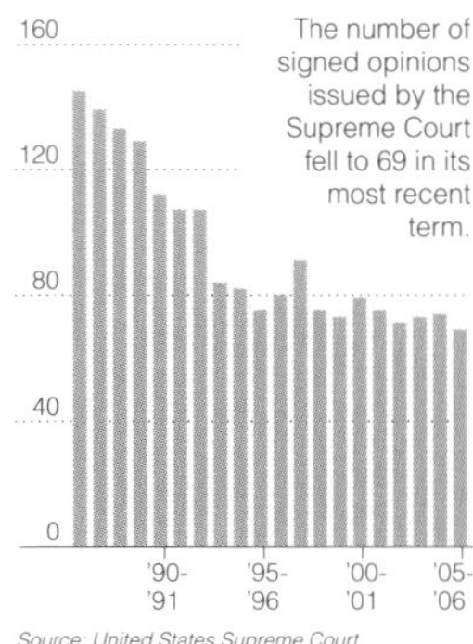

Source: United States Supreme Court

The New York Times

As More Are Stricken by E. Coli, Taco Bell Points to Green Onions

By ANDREW MARTIN and BRUCE LAMBERT

After Taco Bell traced a growing E. coli outbreak to green onions at its restaurants yesterday morning, government investigators began an intensive search to identify the source of the contamination. The total number of cases in three Northeastern states swelled to 99, implicating several additional restaurants and a second food distributor, who said the onions came from a California farm.

Taco Bell officials said early yesterday that their preliminary tests had traced the E. coli to three samples of green onions, which the restaurant chain sprinkles on many of its menu items. In what the company president, Greg Creed, called "an abundance of caution," Taco Bell removed green onions from its 5,800 outlets across the United States.

A Suffolk County laboratory later confirmed E. coli in three of four green onions taken from a previously unopened package at one of the restaurants, "suggesting that it was already contaminated before it arrived," said Suffolk's acting health commissioner, Dr. David G. Graham. County officials retrieved the green onions from a Taco Bell in Deer Park after the franchise identified them as the probable cause of the outbreak.

New cases were reported yesterday in New York, New Jersey and Pennsylvania. In New York, the number of sick people on Long Island nearly doubled to 41, while the outbreak spread to far-flung counties upstate, where several new cases were reported. The Taco Bell franchises in upstate New York get their food from a distribution center in Albany, not the huge warehouse in Burlington, N.J., that serves the Taco Bell outlets first tied to the outbreak.

Three new cases were reported in New Jersey, for a total of 43 under investigation. The new cases included that of a 43-year-old North Plainfield man who ate at a Taco Bell on Dec. 2, far later than most of the other victims, who reported getting sick after

Continued on Page B8

Broadway Baby: Magical Moments, Tantrums or a $250 Lullaby

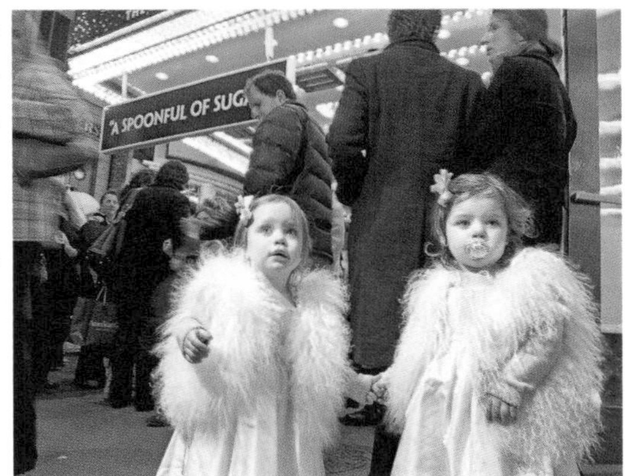

Joe Fornabaio for The New York Times

On the town: Liliana Florencia Falcone, left, and Carolina Alessandra Falcone, 21-month-old twins, seeing the Broadway musical "Mary Poppins."

By CAMPBELL ROBERTSON

Four hundred and fifty bucks. That's what it cost the Agnew family for a Saturday night performance of "The Lion King." Whether that considerable chunk was spent for two hours and 45 minutes of delight or for one flustered and fuss-filled act followed by a hasty escape at intermission came down to one person: Harris Agnew, age 3.

"We're questioning the thought process at this moment," said Jim Agnew of Williamsburg, Va., who was standing in line before the show with his wife, Julie, and their children, Clark, 6, and Harris.

"If it goes well," Ms. Agnew said, "this will be a magical experience." She looked at Harris uncertainly. "We're hoping."

The perception of Broadway as a destination for families with children has been growing for years, keeping pace with the rise of the tourist audience. According to the League of American Theaters and Producers, the proportion of Broadway theatergoers under the age of 18 rose from 4 percent in 1980 to a peak of 11.6 percent in the 2000-01 season. Last season 9.6 percent were under 18, with a third of those — or 384,000 theatergoers — under 12.

The league does not break down age groups more finely than that, though simple observation suggests that most of those under-12's are on the older end of the scale. But the really little ones are also there, and they tend to be a conspicuous minority.

"There are mothers breast-feeding in the audience," said one usher at the Minskoff Theater, where "The Lion King" is playing. "Going to the

Continued on Page B4

INSIDE

New Signs of Water on Mars

Pictures of Martian gullies taken several years apart suggest that water still flows on the surface of the planet, scientists said. PAGE A30

Criticism of Oil Monitoring

A government inquiry found pervasive problems in the monitoring of royalties for oil drilling. PAGE C1

Updated news: nytimes.com
Tomorrow in The Times: Page D7

Stuart Goldenberg

Cameras Under $300

For many consumers, writes David Pogue, buying the right camera is all about looks, as in looking good while taking a picture. PAGE C1

Vote to Ordain Gay Rabbis

Conservative Judaism will allow the ordination of gay rabbis and the celebration of same-sex commitment ceremonies. PAGE A26

"All the News That's Fit to Print"

The New York Times

Late Edition
New York: **Today,** mostly cloudy, light winds, high 48. **Tonight,** clearing, low 36, 20s in suburbs. **Tomorrow,** sunny, clouds late, high 48. **Yesterday,** high 48, low 43. Details, Page B28.

VOL. CLVI . . No. 53,809 + | NEW YORK, SATURDAY, DECEMBER 30, 2006 | ONE DOLLAR

SADDAM HUSSEIN HANGED IN BAGHDAD; SWIFT END TO DRAMA; TROOPS ON ALERT

New Job Title For Druggists: Diabetes Coach

By IAN URBINA

ASHEVILLE, N.C. — In an office behind the Hershey's candy rack at a Kerr Drug here, Stuart Rohrbaugh shifts in his chair as his pharmacist stares at a dangerously high blood sugar reading from last month.

"I think that was the day a buddy of mine brought over his home-brew beer," stammers Mr. Rohrbaugh, whose diabetes was diagnosed six years ago.

Silently, the pharmacist lifts her eyes, sending Mr. Rohrbaugh's gaze to the floor.

"I know, I know," he says.

Mr. Rohrbaugh, 37, learned relatively late in life that he had Type 1 diabetes, a malfunction of the immune system that usually surfaces in childhood. There are hundreds in Asheville with that type, and even more with the more prevalent Type 2, which often hits as a consequence of obesity or age.

And so in this town of 75,000, where people like to use sugar in their coffee and in their iced tea, and as a term of endearment, Mr. Rohrbaugh and the others face the formidable challenge of either managing their diabetes or suffering its potential ravages: blindness, organ failure, stroke.

In trying to meet that challenge, the kind of polite browbeating that Mr. Rohrbaugh faced at his local pharmacy seems to be paying off.

For the past 10 years, the city of Asheville has given free diabetes medicines and supplies to municipal workers who have the disease if they agree to monthly counseling from specially trained pharmacists. The results, city officials say, have been dramatic: Within months of enrolling in the program, almost twice as many have their blood sugar levels under control. In addition, the city's health plan has saved more than $2,000 in medical costs per patient each year.

There are at least 21 million diabetics in the United States, and health officials have begun to despair of combating the disease because it involves getting people to do something much more difficult than taking their medicine or having surgery: altering their daily behavior, like their eating and exercise habits.

But amid this gloom, Asheville's

Continued on Page A15

Pool photo by David Furst

Saddam Hussein yelling at the court as the sentence for crimes against humanity was announced on Nov. 5.

Witness Says He 'Gave Up' — Guilty in 148 Deaths

This article is by ***Marc Santora, James Glanz*** *and* ***Sabrina Tavernise.***

BAGHDAD, Saturday, Dec. 30 — Saddam Hussein, the dictator who led Iraq through three decades of brutality, war and bombast before American forces chased him from his capital city and captured him in a filthy pit near his hometown, was hanged just before dawn Saturday during the morning call to prayer.

The final stages for Mr. Hussein, 69, came with terrible swiftness after he lost the appeal, five days ago, of his death sentence for the killings of 148 men and boys in the northern town of Dujail in 1982. He had received the sentence less than two months before from a special court set up to judge his reign as the almost unchallenged dictator of Iraq.

His execution at 6:10 a.m. was announced on state-run Iraqiya television. Witnesses said 14 Iraqi officials had attended the hanging, at the former military intelligence building in northern Baghdad, now part of an American base. Those in the room said that Mr. Hussein was dressed entirely in black and carrying a Koran and that he was compliant as the noose was draped around his neck.

"He just gave up," said Mowaffak al-Rubaie, Iraq's national security adviser. "We were astonished. It was strange. He just gave up."

He added: "Saddam Hussein is gone. All Iraqis will look to the future after the end of this era."

At President Bush's ranch in Crawford, Tex., a White House spokesman, Scott Stanzel, said Mr. Bush had gone to bed before the execution took place and was not awakened. Mr. Bush had received a briefing from his national security adviser Friday afternoon, when he learned the execution would be carried out within hours, Mr. Stanzel said. Asked why Mr. Bush had gone to sleep before hearing the news, he said Mr. Bush "knew that it was going to happen."

In a statement written in advance, Mr. Bush said Mr. Hussein "was executed after receiving a fair trial — the kind of justice he denied the victims of his brutal regime."

"Saddam Hussein's execution comes at the end of a difficult year for the Iraqi people and for our troops," Mr. Bush said. "Bringing Saddam Hussein to justice will not end the violence in Iraq, but it is an important milestone on Iraq's course to becoming a democracy that can govern, sustain and defend itself, and be an ally in the war on terror."

There were conflicting accounts about whether two of Mr. Hussein's co-defendants were also hanged. The Iraqi state television said the co-defendants, Mr. Hussein's half-brother Barzan Ibrahim, and Awad Hamed al-Bandar, the former chief justice of the Revolutionary Court, were hanged after Mr. Hussein. But Mr. Rubaie could not confirm this.

Concerned that the execution

Continued on Page A8

NEWS ANALYSIS

Joy of Capture Muted at End

Grim Realities in Iraq Alter the Tone for Bush

By JEFF ZELENY

CRAWFORD, Tex., Dec. 29 — The capture of Saddam Hussein three years ago was a jubilant moment for the White House, hailed by President Bush in a televised address from the Cabinet Room. The execution of Mr. Hussein, though, seemed hardly to inspire the same sentiment.

Before the hanging was carried out in Baghdad, Mr. Bush went to sleep here at his ranch and was not roused when the news came. In a statement written in advance, the president said the execution would not end the violence in Iraq.

After Mr. Hussein was arrested Dec. 13, 2003, he gradually faded from view, save for his courtroom outbursts and writings from prison. The growing chaos and violence in Iraq has steadily overshadowed the torturous rule of Mr. Hussein, who for more than two decades held a unique place in the politics and psyche of the United States, a symbol of the manifestation of evil in the Middle East.

Now, what could have been a triumphal bookend to the American invasion of Iraq has instead been dampened by the grim reality of conditions on the ground there. Mr. Hussein's hanging means that the ousted leader has been held accountable for his misdeeds, fulfilling the American

Continued on Page A9

Crowds of Pupils but Little Else in African Schools

By SHARON LaFRANIERE

BAMAKO, Mali — Even before workers hung the last wooden shutter on the new classrooms here, School H was overcrowded.

Makamba Keito, the school's director, was expecting no more than 420 first through sixth graders. But as he opened registration on a sizzling Saturday in September, twice that number were already on the list — and those were only the students who had transferred from other jam-packed schools nearby.

Mr. Keito registered a few dozen more, then halted with a whopping 887 pupils, an average of 126 per teacher. "That's it," he recalled telling parents who had been turned away. "You must go find some other place."

Finding places for millions of new students is one of sub-Saharan Africa's most overwhelming and gratifying missions. After two decades of sluggish growth in enrollment rates, the region's 45 countries find themselves with an embarrassment of eager schoolchildren.

Nearly 22 million more students flooded classrooms between 1999 and 2004, increasing the enrollment rate by 18 percent, more than any other region of the world, according to Unesco. More than 6 out of 10 primary school-age children are now enrolled — and that does not include older students, like 14-year-old second graders, who have also streamed into schools.

Not since the 1970s has sub-Saharan Africa made such strides.

"The whole climate has changed," said Nicholas Burnett, who produces an annual global report on schooling for Unesco. "Resources are becoming available. You can definitely see the attitudes of African parents changing. Africa is starting to move in such a positive direction."

Two trends have converged to produce such change: One is a new willingness by international donors and African governments to spend hundreds of millions of dollars more on basic education. That has fed a rising demand for education by the region's parents, who for perhaps the first time see a chance to give their children a future that they were denied.

The challenges, however, remain staggering. Foremost is a flood tide of school-age children in a region whose birth rate is nearly twice the world's average. Forty-four in 100 sub-Saharan residents are under age 15, the highest proportion on earth. By some estimates, the next decade could raise the school-age population by another 28 million.

AFRICA / MALI / Miles 200 / ALGERIA / MALI / MAURITANIA / Niger R. / Gao / Mopti / Bamako / NIGER / Kinsika / BURKINA FASO / GUINEA / IVORY COAST / GHANA

The New York Times

In Bamako, the newly opened School H is short of textbooks.

The region must absorb those newcomers while trying to lift itself from the subbasement of global education. Sub-Saharan Africa is home to barely one-sixth of the world's children under 15, but fully half the world's uneducated children — the legacy of poverty, colonialism and historically inadequate schools. Those who do make it to primary school are more likely to enroll late, repeat grades and drop out before sixth grade than are students anywhere else, according to Unesco.

The pupil-teacher ratio, averaging 44 to 1, is the world's highest; the percentage of trained teachers is among the lowest.

Mali is a template for those challenges. One of earth's poorest nations, it also has the world's second-highest birth rate, behind only neighboring Niger. It lags even most African nations in the share of children in primary school.

Yet a crusade is under way to get Malian children out of thatched huts and arid fields and into classrooms. Thanks partly to newfound economic growth, Mali more than doubled its spending per child between 1994 and 2004 to educate youngsters aged 6

Continued on Page A6

For 30 Years, a Terror To Iraq and Neighbors

One of the most brutal tyrants of recent history, Saddam Hussein unleashed devastating regional wars and reduced oil-rich Iraq to a claustrophobic police state. His unflinching 30-year hold on Iraq ended in 2003 with the American invasion. **OBITUARY, PAGES A10-11,**

By NEIL MacFARQUHAR

Elder-Care Costs Deplete Savings Of a Generation

By JANE GROSS

To care for her ailing 97-year-old father over the past three years, Elizabeth Rodriguez, a vice president at the Federal Reserve Bank in New York, has borrowed against her 401(k) retirement plan, sold her house on Staten Island and depleted nearly 20 years of savings.

The money has gone to lawyers' fees ($50,000) to win a contested guardianship. It has gone for home-care equipment like the mattress for his hospital bed (about $3,000 in all) and for a food service to deliver meals ($400 a month).

It has gone for a two-bedroom rental apartment big enough for herself, her dad and a home aide ($1,600 a month more than a one-bedroom apartment in the same building), and for a wheelchair-accessible van to get him to doctors' appointments ($330 a trip).

Asked to tally the costs, Ms. Rodriguez, 58, said she had no idea how much she was spending. "A shower chair, body cream with no alcohol, new shoes," she said. "You don't stop and calculate. You just buy what you have to buy."

Ms. Rodriguez is among the legion of adult children — more than 15 million, according to various calculations — who take care of their aging parents, a responsibility that often includes paying for all or part of their housing, medical supplies and incidental expenses. Many costs are out of pocket and largely unnoticed: clothing, home repair, a cellular telephone.

Adult children with the largest out-of-pocket expenses are those supervising care long distance, those who

Continued on Page A16

NEWS SUMMARY A2

Updated news: nytimes.com
Tomorrow in The Times: Page B28

INSIDE

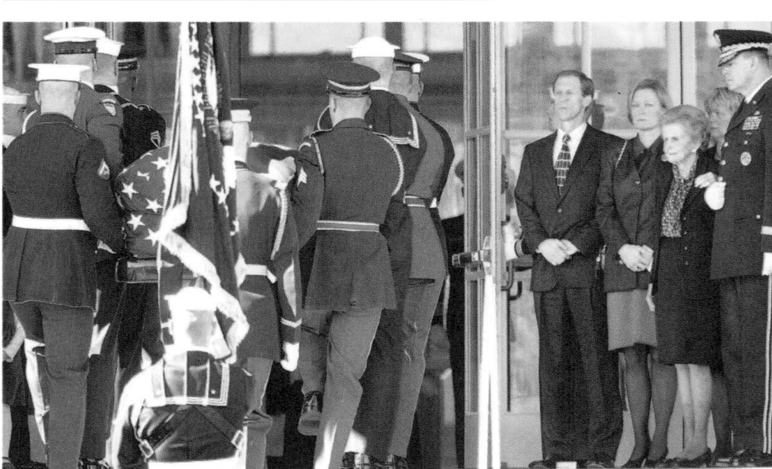

Monica Almeida/The New York Times

For the Fords, a Simple Goodbye

President Gerald R. Ford's coffin arriving at St. Margaret's Episcopal Church in Palm Desert, Calif., as Betty Ford looked on. The repose and prayer service were the first of several events marking the 38th president's life. **PAGE A13**

Somalis Split on Ethiopia Role

Some Somalis protested against Ethiopian troops in the capital, Mogadishu. Others welcomed a former prime minister. **PAGE A4**

Apple Computer Clears Chief

Apple Computer said its chief executive, Steven P. Jobs, was not responsible for the improper dating of stock options. **PAGE C1**

Inquiry in U.S. Oil Program

The Justice Department is investigating Interior Department employees involved in a multibillion-dollar oil-trading program. **PAGE C1**

Coaches' Famous Last Words

In the world of college football, a coach's word is rarely as good as his next job. Often, a coach's vow to stay can be still be heard as he leaves to begin a new job. Notre Dame's Charlie Weis says he has no intention of coaching the Giants. For the fans of the Irish and the Giants, only time will tell. **SPORTSSATURDAY, D1**

THIS WEEKEND

The Neuroscience of Music

Daniel Levitin, a cognitive psychologist, is the rare music scientist to have worked in the music business, as a producer for Blue Öyster Cult. His studies of how humans process music may unlock other mysteries of the brain, like how people with autism think. **ARTS & LEISURE**

Holiday on Ice

Hardy souls who visit St. Petersburg, Russia, during the holiday season discover a city aglow. Winter there may seem cold, dark and forbidding, but it's perfect for a party. *Also:* Elegant dining on both sides of the Rio Grande, in El Paso and Ciudad Juárez, and 36 Hours in London. **TRAVEL**

The Lives They Lived

The 13th annual tribute to notable people who died in the last year. **MAGAZINE**

"All the News That's Fit to Print"

The New York Times

Late Edition
New York: **Today,** Brisk and chilly with ample sunshine, high 33. **Tonight,** colder, low 16. **Tomorrow,** frigid breezes, partly sunny, high 21. **Yesterday,** high 38, low 32. Details, Page A16.

VOL. CLVI . . No. 53,844 | NEW YORK, SATURDAY, FEBRUARY 3, 2007 | ONE DOLLAR

Doug Mills/The New York Times

Deadly Tornadoes Leave a Trail of Devastation in Florida

At least 19 people were killed yesterday after tornadoes spun off from strong thunderstorms that swept through Central Florida before dawn. Rescue workers combed piles of rubble for survivors, and a state of emergency was declared in four counties. Lady Lake, above, was hit hard. Page A9.

SCIENCE PANEL SAYS GLOBAL WARMING IS 'UNEQUIVOCAL'

CITES HUMAN ROLE

3-Year Study Foresees Centuries of Rising Temperatures

By ELISABETH ROSENTHAL and ANDREW C. REVKIN

PARIS, Feb. 2 — In a grim and powerful assessment of the future of the planet, the leading international network of climate scientists has concluded for the first time that global warming is "unequivocal" and that human activity is the main driver, "very likely" causing most of the rise in temperatures since 1950.

They said the world was in for centuries of climbing temperatures, rising seas and shifting weather patterns — unavoidable results of the buildup of heat-trapping gases in the atmosphere.

But their report, released here on Friday by the Intergovernmental Panel on Climate Change, said warming and its harmful consequences could be substantially blunted by prompt action.

While the report provided scant new evidence of a climate apocalypse now, and while it expressly avoided recommending courses of action, officials from the United Nations agencies that created the panel in 1988 said it spoke of the urgent need to limit looming and momentous risks.

"In our daily lives we all respond urgently to dangers that are much less likely than climate change to affect the future of our children," said Achim Steiner, executive director of the United Nations Environment Program, which administers the panel along with the World Meteorological Organization.

"Feb. 2 will be remembered as the date when uncertainty was removed as to whether humans had anything to do with climate change on this planet," he went on. "The evidence is on the table."

The report is the panel's fourth assessment since 1990 on the causes and consequences of climate change, but it is the first in which the group asserts with near certainty — more than 90 percent confidence — that carbon dioxide and other greenhouse gases from human activities have been the main causes of warming in the past half century.

In its last report, in 2001, the panel, consisting of hundreds of scientists and reviewers, said the confidence level for its projections was "likely," or 66 to 90 percent. That level has now been raised to "very likely," better than 90 percent. Both reports are online at www.ipcc.ch.

The Bush administration, which until recently avoided directly accepting that humans were warming the planet in potentially harmful ways, embraced the findings, which had been approved by representatives from the United States and 112 other countries on Thursday night.

Administration officials asserted Friday that the United States had played a leading role in studying and combating climate change, in part by an investment of an average of almost $5 billion a year for the past six

Continued on Page A5

Possible surface temperature increases for the 21st century, based on a midrange scenario for greenhouse gas emissions.

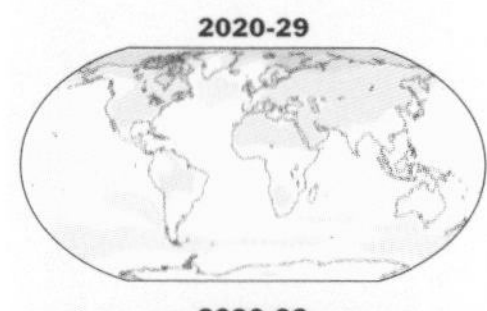

Source: Intergovernmental Panel on Climate Change

The New York Times

Dan Crosbie/Canadian Ice Service

Polar bears adrift on chunks of glacial ice in the Bering Sea in 2004. Much higher temperatures are forecast for the Arctic, scientists say.

ANALYSIS IS BLEAK ON IRAQ'S FUTURE

Both Sides in Debate Cite Intelligence Report

By MARK MAZZETTI

WASHINGTON, Feb. 2 — The release on Friday of portions of a bleak new National Intelligence Estimate about Iraq's future left the White House and its opponents vying over whether its findings buttressed their vastly different views about how to arrest the worsening sectarian chaos there.

The assessment, by American intelligence agencies, expressed deep doubts about the abilities of Iraqi politicians to hold together an increasingly balkanized country, and about whether Iraqi troops might be able to confront powerful militias over the next 18 months and assume more responsibility for security.

The analysis, the first such estimate on Iraq in more than two years, described in sober language a rapidly unraveling country in which security has worsened despite four years of efforts by the administration. [Text, Page A6.]

President Bush acknowledged last month that his strategy had failed so far.

The estimate suggested that the United States now faced an unpalatable decision in which a rapid withdrawal of American troops would only accelerate momentum toward Iraq's collapse, and in which Iraq

Continued on Page A6

Police Report Far More Stops And Searches

By AL BAKER and EMILY VASQUEZ

The New York Police Department released new information yesterday showing that police officers stopped 508,540 individuals on New York City streets last year — an average of 1,393 stops per day — often searching them for illegal weapons. The number was up from 97,296 in 2002, the last time the department divulged 12 months' worth of data.

After inquiries by the City Council and civil rights advocates, the department delivered four bound volumes of statistics to the Council in midafternoon. The raw data showed that more than half of those stopped last year were black: an average of 67,000 per quarter.

At the same time, the average number of people arrested per quarter as a result of such stops almost doubled to 5,317 last year, from 2,819 in 2002, and summonses nearly quintupled, to a quarterly average of 7,292 last year from 1,461 in 2002.

Until yesterday, the most recent information released by the Police Department about how and why it stops people to search them, sometimes looking for illegal guns, was from 2003, according to city officials and city and court records. Some officials have said that lag put the department at odds with a pair of legal requirements that sprang from public outrage at the 1999 fatal police shooting of Amadou Diallo, an un-

Continued on Page B2

Among Hispanics in America, N.F.L. Mania Hits Cultural Wall

By JOHN BRANCH

MIAMI, Feb. 2 — In October 2005, the National Football League played its first regular-season game outside the United States. It drew 103,467 people in Mexico City. The league expects huge audiences this year for a preseason game in Beijing and a regular-season game in London.

But as the N.F.L. has worked to extend its reach globally, it has run headfirst into a language barrier in its own country. Just a few miles from Sunday's Super Bowl XLI, the league's championship game in this largely Hispanic city, is a market of fans that has barely been tapped.

The N.F.L. might be more popular in Mexico than it is among Spanish-speaking people in the United States.

"I think it's very possible," said the former N.F.L. kicker Raul Allegre, who was born in Mexico and is now a well-known Spanish-language football broadcaster. "I think it's a fact."

Recent statistics support Mr. Allegre: In Spanish-speaking households in this country, which account for roughly 10 percent of the population, the N.F.L. is out of sight, out of mind, lagging far behind soccer, boxing, baseball, basketball and other sports in popularity, according to a study commissioned in December by ESPN Deportes, the Spanish-language arm of ESPN in the United States.

That could have long-term consequences for the N.F.L., which has grown accustomed to unbridled growth. Hispanics are the largest ethnic minority in the United States, and they account for one of every two people added to the population through immigration and birth.

The league is midway through a three-year plan to penetrate the Hispanic market both in the United States and Latin America. But it has been handicapped by a disjointed approach to reaching Spanish-speaking fans on television and on its flashy Web sites and by cultural barriers, reflected at least in part by the presence of only about 25 Hispanic players in the 32-team league.

While the Hispanic market was growing, the league spent the past

Continued on Page D2

INSIDE

17 Killed as Factional War Intensifies in Gaza Strip

At least 17 people died in some of the worst internal Palestinian fighting to date as Fatah security force members stormed a Hamas-aligned university, setting fire to several buildings. Some 23 people have been killed in two days, mostly members of security forces, but also civilians, including a 7-year-old boy. PAGE A3

Colleges Queried on Lenders

Colleges and universities nationwide began receiving formal requests for information from the New York attorney general's office as part of an investigation of financial relationships they or individual college officials might have with student loan companies. PAGE A10

YouTube to Remove Videos

YouTube, the video-sharing site, says it will comply with Viacom's request that it remove more than 100,000 clips from the Web. PAGE C1

THIS WEEKEND

Designer-Dog Fights

Puggles (at right), Labradoodles, Maltipoos. Is a hyperdesigned hybrid dog a better dog, an overpriced mutt of a dog or no dog at all? MAGAZINE

Updated news: nytimes.com
Tomorrow in The Times: Page A16

Silicon Valley's High-Tech Hunt for Colleague

By KATIE HAFNER

SAN FRANCISCO, Feb. 2 — When James Gray failed to return home from a sailing trip on Sunday night, Silicon Valley's best and brightest went out to help find him.

After all, Dr. Gray, 63, a Microsoft researcher, is one of their own.

The United States Coast Guard, which started a search Sunday night, suspended it on Thursday, after sending aircraft and boats to scour 132,000 square miles of ocean, stretching from the Channel Islands in Southern California to the Oregon border. Teams turned up nothing, not so much as a shard of aluminum hull or a swatch of sail from Dr. Gray's 40-foot sailboat, Tenacious.

In the meantime, as word swept through the high-technology community, dozens of Dr. Gray's colleagues, friends and former students began banding together on Monday to supplement the Coast Guard's efforts with the tool they know best: computer technology.

James Gray

The flurry of activity, which began in earnest on Tuesday, escalated as the days and nights passed. A veritable Who's Who of computer scientists from Google, Amazon, Microsoft, NASA and universities across the country spent sleepless nights writing ad hoc software, creating a blog and reconfiguring satellite images so that dozens of volunteers could pore over them, searching for a speck of red hull and white deck among a sea of gray pixels.

Coast Guard officials said they had never before seen such a concerted, technically creative effort carried out by friends and family of a missing sailor. "This is the largest strictly civilian, privately sponsored search effort I have ever seen," said Capt. David Swatland, deputy commander of the Coast Guard sector in San Francisco, who has spent most of his 23-year career in search and rescue.

On Tuesday evening, as the Coast Guard's search continued, Joseph M. Hellerstein, a computer science professor at the University of California, Berkeley, sent out an e-mail message with the subject: "Urgent . . . Jim Gray." One recipient, Sergey Brin, co-founder of Google, wrote back within an hour, and offered to enlist Google Earth's satellite imaging expertise.

By Wednesday, Professor Hellerstein had started a blog and earth sciences experts at the Ames Research Center of NASA in Moffett Field, Calif., had sprung into action. They secured the promise of help from a high-altitude aircraft equipped with a high-resolution digital camera that was already scheduled for a flight Friday from Dryden Research Center in Southern California but whose pilot could make sure his path included the search area.

By Thursday morning, in response to calls from Google, NASA and the Coast Guard, DigitalGlobe, an imaging company in Longmont, Colo., had commanded its satellite to capture images of strips of the coastline based on the most likely areas where Dr. Gray's

Continued on Page C5

As Titillating as a Budget Memo, Gossip Blossoms in Washington

By MARK LEIBOVICH

WASHINGTON, Feb. 2 — Some big doings in the nation's capital this week.

Item: Dennis Hastert, the former House speaker, had his gallbladder removed.

Item: Karl Rove was spotted at a performance of "Who's Afraid of Virginia Woolf" at the Kennedy Center.

Item: Representative William Lacy Clay, a Missouri Democrat, got his braces taken off.

Item: A photograph of Paul Wolfowitz, president of the World Bank, revealed holes in his socks.

Item: Senator Norm Coleman, a Minnesota Republican, nearly committed the etiquette-crime of entering the Senate chamber without a tie (he found a loaner at the last minute).

As the globe warms, Iraq burns and a presidential campaign heats up, Washington finds itself red-hot in gossip, or what passes for such here. Never in memory has the political world been so awash in items about every little burp and wart and appendectomy of our nation's leaders.

Ten publications carry a total of 14 columns focusing on political tidbits that appear regularly, up from three columns a decade ago.

They include the Reliable Source and In the Loop columns, The Washington Post's entrenched offerings (the paper's Web site started a new enterprise, the Sleuth, last month); In the Know and Under the Dome, which dish in the tabloid The Hill; and Heard on the Hill, which appears in Roll Call.

The Examiner offers Yeas and Nays, while the latest entry, The Politico, nourishes its politerati with Shenanigans and the Crypt.

So what does this all mean?

"It means I have to spend a lot more of my time fielding calls and e-mails from gossip columnists," said a slightly exasperated Jim Manley, the top communications aide to Senator Harry Reid of Nevada, the Democratic majority leader.

Mr. Manley had just finished responding to an e-mail message from a Roll Call reporter about whether Mr. Reid knew the date of Valentine's Day. (That day's Politico had broken the Watergate-like develop-

Continued on Page A11

"All the News That's Fit to Print"

The New York Times

Late Edition

Today, sun, then clouds late, mild, high 48. **Tonight,** showers, low 42. **Tomorrow,** early clouds, a shower, then clearing, quite mild, high 53. Weather map appears on Page D7.

VOL. CLVII . . No. 54,172

NEW YORK, FRIDAY, DECEMBER 28, 2007

$1.25

BHUTTO IS KILLED, AND PAKISTAN FACES RAGE AND MORE TURMOIL

JOHN MOORE/GETTY IMAGES

A survivor grieved amid the victims Thursday in Rawalpindi, Pakistan, after a bomb blast and gun attack killed Benazir Bhutto.

SLAIN AT A RALLY

Rioting and Disarray Less Than 2 Weeks Before Elections

By SALMAN MASOOD and CARLOTTA GALL

RAWALPINDI, Pakistan — Benazir Bhutto, the Pakistani opposition leader and twice-serving prime minister, was assassinated Thursday evening as she left a political rally here, a scene of fiery carnage that plunged Pakistan deeper into political turmoil and ignited widespread violence by her enraged supporters.

Ms. Bhutto, 54, was shot in the neck or head, according to differing accounts, as she stood in the open sunroof of a car and waved to crowds. Seconds later a suicide attacker detonated his bomb, damaging one of the cars in her motorcade, killing more than 20 people and wounding 50, the Interior Ministry said.

News of her death sent angry protesters swarming the emergency ward of the nearby hospital, where doctors declared Ms. Bhutto dead at 6:16 p.m. Supporters later jostled to carry her bare wooden coffin as it began its journey to her hometown, Larkana, in southern Pakistan, for burial. In Karachi and other cities, frenzied crowds vented their rage, blocking the streets, burning tires and throwing stones.

The death of Ms. Bhutto, leader of Pakistan's largest political party, throws Pakistan's politics into disarray less than two weeks before parliamentary elections scheduled for Jan. 8 and just weeks after a state of emergency was lifted. There was immediate speculation that elections would be postponed and another state of emergency declared.

A deeply polarizing figure, Ms. Bhutto spent 30 years navigating the turbulent and often violent world of Pakistani politics, becoming in 1988 the first woman to lead a modern Muslim country. [Obituary, Page A14.]

She had narrowly escaped an assassination attempt upon her return to Pakistan two months ago. Her death now presents President Pervez Musharraf with one of the most potent crises of his turbulent eight years in power, and Bush administration officials with a new challenge in their efforts to stabilize a frontline state — home to both Al Qae-

Continued on Page A11

NEWS ANALYSIS

A Serious Blow to U.S. Reconciliation Efforts

By HELENE COOPER and STEVEN LEE MYERS

WASHINGTON — The assassination of Benazir Bhutto on Thursday left in ruins the delicate diplomatic effort the Bush administration had pursued in the past year to reconcile Pakistan's deeply divided political factions. Now it is scrambling to sort through ever more limited options, as American influence on Pakistan's internal affairs continues to decline.

On Thursday, officials at the American Embassy in Islamabad reached out to members of the political party of former Prime Minister Nawaz Sharif, according to a senior administration official. The very fact that officials are even talking to backers of Mr. Sharif, who they believe has too many ties to Islamists, suggests how hard it will be to find a partner the United States fully trusts.

The assassination highlighted, in spectacular fashion, the failure of two of President Bush's main objectives in the region: his quest to bring democracy to the Muslim world, and his drive to force out the Islamist militants who have hung on tenaciously in Pakistan, the nuclear-armed state considered ground zero in President Bush's fight against terrorism, despite the administration's long-running effort to root out Al Qaeda from the Pakistan-Afghanistan border.

Administration officials say the United States still wants the Pakistani elections to proceed, either as scheduled on Jan. 8 or soon after. But several senior administration officials acknowledged that President Pervez Mu-

Continued on Page A10

ONLINE: **BHUTTO'S LIFE**

An interactive timeline with photographs and video, plus slide shows and reader reaction:
nytimes.com

CLOCKWISE FROM TOP LEFT, ASIF HASSAN/AFP — GETTY IMAGES, JOHN MOORE/GETTY IMAGES, FAROOQ NAEEMA/AFP — GETTY IMAGES

Buses burned in Karachi, Pakistan's largest city, after the assassination; Ms. Bhutto on a stage minutes before she was killed in Rawalpindi; supporters carrying her coffin from a hospital.

Under Attack, Drug Maker Turned to Giuliani for Help

By BARRY MEIER and ERIC LIPTON

THE LONG RUN
The Lobbyist

In western Virginia, far from the limelight, United States Attorney John L. Brownlee found himself on the telephone last year with a political and legal superstar, Rudolph W. Giuliani.

For years, Mr. Brownlee and his small team had been building a case that the maker of the painkiller OxyContin had misled the public when it claimed the drug was less prone to abuse than competing narcotics. The drug was believed to be a factor in hundreds of deaths involving its abuse.

Mr. Giuliani, celebrated for his stewardship of New York City after 9/11, soon told the prosecutors they were wrong.

In 2002, the drug maker, Purdue Pharma of Stamford, Conn., hired Mr. Giuliani and his consulting firm, Giuliani Partners, to help stem the controversy about OxyContin. Among Mr. Giuliani's missions was the job of convincing public officials that they could trust Purdue because they could trust him.

So it was no small success when, after the call, Mr. Brownlee did what many people might have done when confronted with such celebrity: He went out and bought a copy of Mr. Giuliani's book, "Leadership."

"I wanted to be prepared for my meetings with him," Mr. Brownlee said in a recent interview.

Over the past few weeks, Mr. Giuliani's consulting business has received increasing scrutiny, at times forcing him to defend his business as he campaigns for the Republican presidential nomination.

But his work for Purdue, the company's first and longest-running client, provides a window into how he used his standing as an eminent lawyer, a Republican insider and a national celebrity to aid a controversial client and build a business fortune.

A former top federal prosecutor, Mr. Giuliani participated in two meetings between Purdue officials and the head of the Drug Enforcement Administration, the agency investigating the company. Giuliani Partners took on the job of monitoring security improvements at company facilities making OxyContin, an issue of concern to the D.E.A.

As a celebrity, Mr. Giuliani helped the company win several public relations battles, playing a role in an effort by Purdue to persuade an influential Pennsylvania congressman, Curt Weldon, not to blame it for OxyContin abuse.

Despite these efforts, Purdue suffered a crushing defeat in May at the hands of Mr. Brownlee when the company and three top executives pleaded guilty to criminal charges.

Mr. Giuliani, who declined to discuss his work for Purdue for this article, has refused to talk in detail about his firm's clients. He has said that he is no longer involved in the day-

Continued on Page A20

MIKE WINTROATH/ASSOCIATED PRESS

Rudolph W. Giuliani and Asa Hutchinson, right, former chief of the Drug Enforcement Administration.

Iowa Saturated by Political Ads In 11th-Hour Bid for Undecided

By PATRICK HEALY

DES MOINES — One week before Iowa kicks off the presidential nomination contest, the campaigns are spending three times as much money flooding the airwaves and the Internet as candidates did in 2004, hoping to sway the huge number of undecided voters after months of on-the-ground appeals.

In one of her single biggest television expenditures here, advisers said Thursday, Senator Hillary Rodham Clinton, Democrat of New York, is spending more than $20,000 to broadcast a two-minute taped message during every 6 p.m. newscast in Iowa on the eve of the caucuses, Jan. 2, which will be seen by an estimated 515,510 adults in the state.

Mitt Romney is preparing a new advertising blitz this weekend in hopes of stemming the momentum of his 11th-hour breakaway Republican rival here, Mike Huckabee.

And, signaling the sharpening tone of the advertising wars, Rudolph W. Giuliani's campaign released a commercial Thursday invoking imagery of Sept. 11, a tactic President Bush's campaign was criticized for in 2004.

The campaigns are still unsure whether to use negative advertisements against opponents here. For now, they are calibrating their mainly positive advertisements to reflect the themes playing out here: change vs. status quo politics, new ideas on domestic concerns and Iraq vs. old thinking, the need for fresh leadership, and their respect for the first-in-the-nation Iowa caucuses.

"I believe that on the night of Jan. 3, you're going to say enough is enough," another Democrat, John Edwards, says in one of two television spots that began running Thursday. "There's going to be a rising that begins right here in Iowa," he says, "and it's going to spread across America, and it will be a wave of change that cannot be stopped."

The Democrats are spending by far the most on television advertising here, and smashing records in the process. Senator Barack Obama of Illinois has spent the most, at $8.3 million, Mrs. Clinton has spent $6.5 million, and Mr. Edwards, of North Carolina, has spent $2.7 million, according to an analysis by CMAG, a firm that tracks political advertising spending. Over the last week, Democratic candidates combined have spent at least

Continued on Page A21

After DNA Diagnosis: 'Hello, 16p11.2. Are You Just Like Me?'

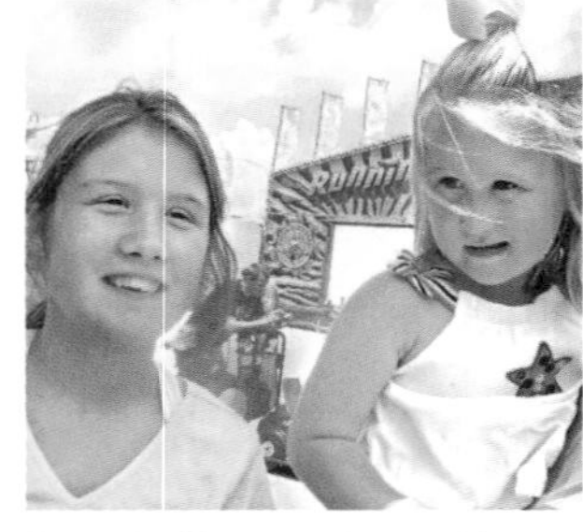

Samantha Napier, 14, left, and Taygen Lane, 4, share a rare genetic mutation.

THE DNA AGE
Chromosome Kinship

By AMY HARMON

The girls had never met, but they looked like sisters.

There was no missing the similarities: the flat bridge of their noses, the thin lips, the fold near the corner of their eyes. And to the families of 14-year-old Samantha Napier and 4-year-old Taygen Lane there was something else, too. In the likeness was lurking an explanation for the learning difficulties, the digestion problems, the head-banging that had troubled each of them, for so long.

Several of the adults wiped tears from their eyes. "It's like meeting family," said Jessica Houk, Samantha's older sister, who accompanied her and their mother to a Kentucky amusement park last July to greet Taygen.

But the two families are not related, and would never have met save for an unusual bond: a few months earlier, a newly available DNA test revealed that Samantha and Taygen share an identical nick in the short arm of their 16th chromosomes.

With technology that can now scan each of an individual's 46 chromosomes for minute aberrations, doctors are providing thousands of children lumped together as "autistic'' or "developmentally delayed" with distinct genetic diagnoses. The symptoms, they are finding, can be traced to one of dozens of deletions or duplications of DNA that were previously hard or impossible to detect.

Some mutations are so rare that they are known only by their chromosomal address: Samantha and Taygen are two of only six children with the diagnosis "16p11.2.''

Few of these mutations were inherited in the traditional sense, and the affected children are typically the only family member with the disorder. So, many parents are searching out strangers struck by the same genetic lightning bolt. They want solace, advice and answers to what the future might hold. From other families of children with the same chromosomal anomaly, they are seeking insight into their own. Sometimes what

Continued on Page A19

INSIDE

Security Help for China

American companies are helping China install high-tech public surveillance systems for the Beijing Olympics, alarming human rights advocates. **PAGE C1**

Credit Crisis? Wait Till '08

The subprime debacle may be just a warm-up to a bigger credit tremor, Floyd Norris writes. **BUSINESS DAY, PAGE C1**

Golden Globes May Go Dark

The writers' strike threatens to push the Golden Globe awards, set for Jan. 13, off the air. **PAGE C1**

NEWS SUMMARY A2

Updated news: nytimes.com
This Weekend: Page D7

"All the News That's Fit to Print"

The New York Times

Late Edition

Today, sunshine yielding to clouds, mild, high 49. **Tonight**, turning colder, clearing, low 24. **Tomorrow**, cold, blustery and mostly sunny, high 32. Weather map appears on Page A16.

VOL. CLVII . . No. 54,221 + ©2008 The New York Times NEW YORK, FRIDAY, FEBRUARY 15, 2008 $1.25

JIM KILLAM/NORTHERN STAR, VIA ASSOCIATED PRESS

One of the injured at Northern Illinois University is taken from the campus building where the shootings occurred.

Gunman Slays Five in Illinois At a University

By SUSAN SAULNY and MONICA DAVEY

DeKALB, Ill. — With minutes left in a class in ocean sciences at Northern Illinois University on Thursday afternoon, a tall skinny man dressed all in black stepped out from behind a curtain on the stage of the lecture hall, said nothing, and opened fire with a shotgun, the authorities and witnesses said.

The man shot again and again, witnesses said, perhaps 20 times or more. Students in the large lecture hall, stunned and screaming, dropped to the floor. They crouched behind anything they could find, even an overhead projector. They scattered, the blood of victims spattering, some said, on those who escaped injury.

Five people, all of them students, were killed, John G. Peters, the president of Northern Illinois University, said at a news conference late Thursday evening. Sixteen others were wounded, two of them critically, Mr. Peters said. Hospital officials said several of the students had been shot in the head.

The gunman, whom the authorities did not identify, also died of a self-inflicted gunshot wound, Mr. Peters said. The gunman, he said, had been a graduate student in sociology at the university in 2007, but was no longer enrolled here. Records suggested that the man, who had more recently attended a different state school, had no previous

Continued on Page A13

Signs in Kenya of a Land Redrawn by Ethnicity

By JEFFREY GETTLEMAN

OTHAYA, Kenya — Sarah Wangoi has spent her entire life — all 70 years of it — in the Rift Valley. But last month, she was chased off her farm by a mob that called her a foreigner. She now sleeps on the cold floor of a stranger's house, seeking refuge in an area of Kenya where her ethnic group, the Kikuyu, is strong. It is, supposedly, her homeland.

"I am safe now," said Ms. Wangoi, though the mob still chases her in her dreams.

Across the country, William Ojiambo sat in a field where the ground was too hard to plow. He, too, sought refuge with his ethnic group, the Luo. He used to live in an ethnically mixed town called Nakuru but was recently evicted by a gang from another ethnic group that burned everything he owned.

"We came here with nothing, like cabbages thrown in the back of a truck," Mr. Ojiambo said.

Kenya used to be considered one of the most promising countries in Africa. Now it is in the throes of ethnically segregating itself. Ever since a deeply flawed election in December kicked off a wave of ethnic and political violence, hundreds of thousands of people have been violently driven from their homes and many are now resettling in ethnically homogenous zones.

Luos have gone back to Luo land, Kikuyus to Kikuyu land, Kambas to Kamba land and Kisiis to Kisii land. Even some of the packed slums in the capital, Nairobi, have split along ethnic lines.

The bloodletting across the country that has killed more than

Waves of Violence Send Refugees on Road to Safety

1,000 people since the election seems to have subsided in the past week. But the trucks piled high with mattresses, furniture, blankets and children keep chugging across the countryside, an endless convoy of frightened people who in their desperation are redrawing the map of Kenya.

The United Nations and Western powers are pushing for a political compromise, and President Bush said he would send Secretary of State Condoleezza Rice to "deliver a message" to Kenya's leaders. [Page A11.]

On Thursday, officials here said that Kenyan government and opposition leaders had agreed in principle to join together in a coalition government but that they remained bitterly divided over the specifics, especially how much power the opposition would have. Two officials close to the negotiations said the government had rejected the opposition's offer to split power between the president, who would remain head of state and the military's commander in chief, and a newly created prime minister position.

Whatever deal is struck will have to address the growing de facto segregation, since a resettlement of the country may further entrench the political and ethnic divisions that have recently erupted. Shattered trust is much harder to rebuild than smashed huts, and many people say they will never go back to where they fled.

"How can we, when it was our friends who did this to us?" said Joseph Ndungu, a shopkeeper in the Rift Valley, who said that men he used to play soccer with burned down his shop.

The government is lending a hand in the country's separation, at least for the moment. Police officers are escorting people back

Continued on Page A10

Black Leader, A Clinton Ally, Tilts to Obama

Shift Comes as Her Bid Takes a Populist Turn

By JEFF ZELENY and PATRICK HEALY

MILWAUKEE — Representative John Lewis, an elder statesman from the civil rights era and one of Senator Hillary Rodham Clinton's most prominent black supporters, said Thursday night that he planned to cast his vote as a superdelegate for Senator Barack Obama in hopes of preventing a fight at the Democratic convention.

"In recent days, there is a sense of movement and a sense of spirit," said Mr. Lewis, a Georgia Democrat who endorsed Mrs. Clinton last fall. "Something is happening in America, and people are prepared and ready to make that great leap."

Mr. Lewis, who carries great influence among other members of Congress, disclosed his decision in an interview in which he said that as a superdelegate he could "never, ever do anything to reverse the action" of the voters of his district, who overwhelmingly supported Mr. Obama.

"I've been very impressed with the campaign of Senator Obama," Mr. Lewis said. "He's getting better and better every single day."

His comments came as fresh signs emerged that Mrs. Clinton's support was beginning to erode from some other African-American lawmakers who also serve as superdelegates. Representative David Scott of Georgia, who was among the first to defect, said he, too, would not go against the will of voters in his district.

The developments came on a day in which Mrs. Clinton set out anew to prove that the fight for the Democratic nomination was far from over. Campaigning in Ohio, she pursued a new strategy of biting attack lines against Mr. Obama, while adopting a newly

Continued on Page A18

Romney Backs McCain

Mitt Romney threw his support — and vowed to try to throw his delegates — behind Senator John McCain. Page A19.

TOP OFFICIALS SEE BLEAKER OUTLOOK FOR THE ECONOMY

NEW RATE CUT POSSIBLE

Bernanke and Paulson Are Criticized as Too Slow in Acting

By EDMUND L. ANDREWS

WASHINGTON — With the credit markets once again deteriorating, the nation's two top economic policy makers acknowledged Thursday that the outlook for the economy had worsened, as both came under criticism for being overtaken by events and failing to act boldly enough.

In testimony to Congress, Ben S. Bernanke, the chairman of the Federal Reserve, signaled that the Fed was ready to reduce interest rates yet again, pointing out that problems in housing and mortgage-related markets had spread more widely and proved more intractable than he predicted three months ago.

His sobering assessment was echoed by Treasury Secretary Henry M. Paulson Jr., who appeared with him. Both continued to avoid predicting a recession but said they were scaling back the more optimistic forecasts they had issued in November.

Ethan S. Harris, chief United States economist for Lehman Brothers, said that both policy makers had "come clean" about the economy's problems but that investors were not impressed.

Stock prices, which normally rally when the Fed hints it will lower borrowing costs, tumbled instead. The Dow Jones industrial average dropped 175 points, or 1.4 percent; broader stock indexes dropped by similar amounts.

Anxiety is escalating among institutional lenders and major borrowers, as the panic over soaring default rates on subprime mortgages that began last summer continues to spread, freezing up credit for municipalities, hospitals, student loans and even investment funds holding the most conservative bonds. [Page C1.]

On Capitol Hill, the economic policy makers found themselves in the line of fire. Senator Robert Menendez, Democrat of New Jersey, accused both Mr. Bernanke and Mr. Paulson of having "hit the snooze button."

Senator Christopher J. Dodd of Connecticut, chairman of the Banking Committee, told reporters after the hearing that "it just seems as if they aren't as concerned about the magnitude of the problem."

Testifying before the committee, Mr. Bernanke said he still ex-

Continued on Page A14

When Strains on Military Families Turn Deadly

By LIZETTE ALVAREZ and DEBORAH SONTAG

A few months after Sgt. William Edwards and his wife, Sgt. Erin Edwards, returned to a Texas Army base from separate missions in Iraq, he assaulted her mercilessly. He struck her, choked her, dragged her over a fence and slammed her into the sidewalk.

As far as Erin Edwards was concerned, that would be the last time he beat her.

Unlike many military wives, she knew how to work the system to protect herself. She was an insider, even more so than her husband, since she served as an aide to a brigadier general at Fort Hood.

With the general's help, she quickly arranged for a future transfer to a base in New York. She pressed charges against her husband and secured an order of protection. She sent her two children to stay with her mother. And she received assurance from her husband's commanders that he would be barred from leaving the base unless accompanied by an officer.

Yet on the morning of July 22, 2004, William Edwards easily slipped off base, skipping his anger-management class, and drove to his wife's house in the Texas town of Killeen. He waited for her to step outside and then, after a struggle, shot her point-blank in the head before turning the gun on himself.

During an investigation, Army officers told the local police that they did not realize Erin Edwards had been afraid of her husband. And they acknowledged that despite his restrictions, William Edwards had not been escorted off base "on every occasion," according to a police report.

That admission troubled the detective handling the case.

"I believe that had he been confined to base and had that confinement been monitored," said Detective Sharon L. Brank of the local police, "she would not be dead at his hands."

The killing of Erin Edwards di-

Sgt. Erin Edwards, shown in Saddam Hussein's hiding hole, was killed by her husband, a fellow soldier. Both served in Iraq.

WAR TORN
Violence at Home

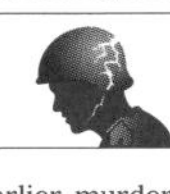

rectly echoed an earlier murder of a military wife that drew far more attention. Almost 10 years ago, at Fort Campbell in Kentucky, a different Army sergeant defied a similar restriction to base, driving out the front gate on his way to a murder almost foretold.

That 1998 homicide, one of several featured in a "60 Minutes" exposé on domestic violence in the military, galvanized a public outcry, Congressional demands for action and the Pentagon's pledge to do everything possible to prevent such violence from claiming more lives.

Yet just as the Defense Department undertook substantial changes, guided by a Congressionally chartered task force on domestic violence that decried a system more adept at protecting offenders than victims, the wars in Afghanistan and then Iraq began.

Pentagon officials say that wartime has not derailed their efforts to make substantive improvements in the way that the military tackles domestic violence.

They say they have, for example, offered more parenting and couples classes, provided additional victims advocates and afforded victims greater confidentiality in reporting abuses.

But interviews with members of the task force, as well as an examination of cases of fatal domestic violence and child abuse, indicate that wartime pressures on military families and on the

Continued on Page A14

INSIDE

House Leaves Surveillance Act to Expire

The House broke for a week's recess without renewing terrorist surveillance authority demanded by President Bush, which expires Saturday, leading him to warn of risky intelligence gaps while Democrats accused him of reckless fear mongering. PAGE A17

House Accuses 2 Bush Aides

The House voted to issue contempt citations against the White House chief of staff and a former White House counsel over the ouster of several federal prosecutors. PAGE A17

U.S. to Produce Iran Data

The Bush administration has agreed to give international inspectors data that it says proves Iran worked on developing a nuclear weapon until a little more than four years ago. PAGE A9

A Solar System Like Ours

Astronomers said that they had found a smaller version of our solar system 5,000 light-years across the galaxy — the first planetary system that really looks like our own. PAGE A20

Housing Dream Comes True

The story could not have had a better ending if he had written it himself: A struggling aspiring novelist lands an East Side studio apartment for $14,000, Susan Dominus writes in Big City. PAGE B1

MONICA ALMEIDA/THE NEW YORK TIMES

A New Home for Art in Los Angeles

Chris Burden's "Urban Light" at the new Broad Contemporary Art Museum, an addition to the Los Angeles County Museum of Art. Reviews by Nicolai Ouroussoff and Roberta Smith. WEEKEND, PAGE E31

U.S. to Attempt To Shoot Down Faulty Satellite

By THOM SHANKER

WASHINGTON — The military will try to shoot down a crippled spy satellite in the next two weeks, senior officials said Thursday. The officials laid out a high-tech plan to intercept the satellite over the Pacific just before it tumbles uncontrollably to Earth carrying toxic fuel.

President Bush ordered the action to prevent any possible contamination from the hazardous rocket fuel on board, and not out of any concern that parts of the spacecraft might survive and reveal its secrets, the officials said.

The challenging mission to demolish the satellite on the fringes of space will rely on an unforeseen use of ship-based weapons developed to defend against ballistic missile attacks.

The effort will be a real-world test of the nation's antiballistic missile systems and its antisatellite abilities, even though the Pentagon said it was not using the effort to test its most exotic weapons or send a message to any adversaries.

The ramifications of the operation are diplomatic, as well as military and scientific, in part because the United States criticized China last year when Beijing tested an antisatellite system with an old weather satellite as a target.

The three-ship convoy assigned to the new task will stalk the satellite's orbital path across the northern Pacific, tracking the satellite as it circles the globe 16

Continued on Page A20

Updated news: nytimes.com
This Weekend: Page A16

"All the News That's Fit to Print"

The New York Times

Late Edition

Today, increasing clouds, snow arriving late, high 37. **Tonight,** light snow will end, low 23. **Tomorrow,** plenty of sunshine, cold, high 35. Weather map appears on Page D8.

VOL. CLVII . . No. 54,226 | NEW YORK, WEDNESDAY, FEBRUARY 20, 2008 | $1.25

WISCONSIN HANDS OBAMA VICTORY, NINTH IN A ROW

McCAIN WINS G.O.P. RACE

Surveys Show Longtime Backers of Clinton Shifting Course

By PATRICK HEALY and JEFF ZELENY

Senator Barack Obama decisively beat Senator Hillary Rodham Clinton in the Wisconsin primary on Tuesday night, accelerating his momentum ahead of crucial primaries in Ohio and Texas and cutting into Mrs. Clinton's support among women and union members.

With the two rivals now battling state by state over margins of victory and allotment of delegates, surveys of voters leaving the Wisconsin polls showed Mr. Obama, of Illinois, making new inroads with those two groups as well as middle-age voters and continuing to win support from white men and younger voters — a performance that yielded grim tidings for Mrs. Clinton, of New York.

On the Republican side, Senator John McCain of Arizona won a commanding victory over Mike Huckabee in the Wisconsin contest and led by a wide margin in Washington State. All but assured of his party's nomination, Mr. McCain immediately went after Mr. Obama during a rally in Ohio, deriding "eloquent but empty" calls for change.

For Mr. Obama, Wisconsin was his ninth consecutive victory, a streak in which he has not only run up big margins in many states but also pulled votes from once-stalwart supporters of Mrs. Clinton, like low- and middle-income people and women. Voters in Hawaii were also holding caucuses, but results were not expected until Wednesday morning.

Mrs. Clinton wasted no time in signaling that she would now take a tougher line against Mr. Obama — a recognition, her advisers said, that she must act to alter the course of the campaign and define Mr. Obama on her terms.

In a speech in Ohio shortly after the polls closed in Wisconsin, she alluded to what her campaign considers Mr. Obama's lack of experience, and his support for a health insurance plan that would not initially seek to cover all Americans.

"This is the choice we face: One of us is ready to be commander in chief in a dangerous world," Mrs. Clinton said in the remarks, which she also planned to expand upon in a speech in

Continued on Page A18

JAVIER GALEANO/ASSOCIATED PRESS

Cubans gathered to talk Tuesday in Havana near a photo of Fidel Castro, who resigned after nearly 50 years as Cuba's president.

Tape Inquiry: Ex-Spymaster In the Middle

By MARK MAZZETTI and SCOTT SHANE

WASHINGTON — It would become known inside the Central Intelligence Agency as "the Italian job," a snide movie reference to the bungling performance of an agency team that snatched a radical Muslim cleric from the streets of Milan in 2003 and flew him to Egypt — a case that led to criminal charges in Italy against 26 Americans.

Porter J. Goss, the C.I.A. director in 2005 when embarrassing news reports about the operation broke, asked the agency's independent inspector general to start a review of amateurish tradecraft in the case, like operatives staying in five-star hotels and using traceable credit cards and cellphones.

But Jose A. Rodriguez Jr., now the central figure in a controversy over destroyed C.I.A. interrogation tapes, fought back. A blunt-spoken Puerto Rico native and former head of the agency's Latin America division, he had been selected by Mr. Goss months earlier to head the agency's troubled clandestine branch. Mr. Rodriguez told his boss that no inspector general review would be necessary — his service would investigate itself.

It was a protective instinct that ran deep inside the C.I.A.'s fabled Directorate of Operations, the

Continued on Page A12

Castro Quits One Role, but May Not Be Done Yet

By ANTHONY DePALMA

HAVANA — Fidel Castro, bedridden for 19 months, on Tuesday gave up the almost unlimited power he has wielded in Cuba for nearly 50 years, but whether the surprise announcement represented a historic change or a symbolic political maneuver remained unclear.

It is expected that his brother Raúl, 76, will be officially named president, and some experts consider him more pragmatic.

Raúl Castro has talked about bringing more accountability to government and possibly working to improve relations with the United States. But since taking over temporarily in the summer of 2006, he has largely operated in his brother's shadow, and, except for facilitating huge investments by Canadian and European resort developers here, he has brought about little change.

MUTED REACTION IN MIAMI

The response in Miami to Fidel Castro's decision was mostly muted, with scattered joy. Page A8.

Under Cuba's Constitution, a newly chosen legislative body, the National Assembly, is scheduled to select a 31-member Council of State on Sunday, including a new president. Fidel Castro said he would not accept the position even if it were offered to him.

In a letter of resignation read over early morning radio and television programs across the country, the 81-year-old Mr. Castro — who has appeared frail in the few videos released by the Cuban government — was said to be too ill to continue as head of state and would not stand in the way of others who were ready to take over, a sentiment he first expressed last December.

Experts on Cuban politics say the decision on a successor remains in the hands of the Castro brothers and their inner circle, many of whom hold cabinet positions. Others said that a younger president could be brought in or that the posts of prime minister and president could be divided between Raúl Castro and one of the ministers.

It was not clear what role, if any, Fidel Castro would play in a new government, or whether he would retain other powerful positions, including head of the Communist Party. But he signaled that he was not yet ready to completely exit the stage.

It is not even certain that Mr. Castro was well enough to actually write the letter of resignation. Doubts have arisen over his

Continued on Page A8

PAKISTAN VICTORS WANT DIALOGUE WITH MILITANTS

LESS MILITARY ACTION

Restrictions on Courts and the Media May Be Reversed

By CARLOTTA GALL and JANE PERLEZ

ISLAMABAD, Pakistan — The winners of Pakistan's parliamentary elections said Tuesday that they would take a new approach to fighting Islamic militants by pursuing more dialogue than military confrontation, and that they would undo the crackdown on the media and restore independence to the judiciary.

With nearly complete returns from Monday's vote giving it the most seats, the party of the assassinated opposition leader Benazir Bhutto, led by her widower, Asif Ali Zardari, made clear that a new political order prevailed in Pakistan.

Mr. Zardari, the leader of the Pakistan Peoples Party, said the new Parliament would reverse many of the unpopular policies that fueled the strong protest vote against President Pervez Musharraf and his party.

Bush administration officials said the United States would still like to see Pakistan's opposition leaders find a way to work with Mr. Musharraf, a staunch ally for more than six years, but conceded that the notion appeared increasingly unlikely. [Page A10.]

Though Mr. Zardari said he wanted a government of national consensus, he ruled out working with anyone from the previous government under Mr. Musharraf.

Instead he said he was talking to the leader of the other main opposition party, Nawaz Sharif, whose party finished second, about forming a coalition.

Although the resounding victory of the two parties was broadly welcomed in Pakistan, there were immediate memories of the failings of civilian governments here in the 1990s. American officials were particularly skeptical of Mr. Zardari, who has faced corruption charges in Pakistan and abroad and has come to his current position of leadership only through his wife's death.

Mr. Sharif was twice prime minister in the 1990s and faced numerous corruption charges himself after being ousted by Mr. Musharraf in a coup.

Mr. Sharif quickly announced several conditions for joining a coalition. They included the impeachment of Mr. Musharraf and the restoration of the chief justice and other Supreme Court judges suspended by the president in November.

Mr. Zardari was less categorical, not calling for Mr. Musharraf's impeachment, for instance. The struggle to end military rule and bring a return to democracy is a long, uphill battle, he said.

"We might have to take soft, small steps," he said at a news briefing at his home in the capital after a meeting of 50 senior members of the party.

Still, the first order of business will be to undo restrictions on the media and restore the independence of the judiciary, he said.

But Mr. Zardari did not specifically call for the reinstatement of the chief justice and his colleagues; there are corruption charges still pending against him.

Though he has little experience

Continued on Page A10

Lacking Cure, a New Tack on a Muscle Disease

By REED ABELSON

For more than four decades, on telethons featuring celebrity performers and children in wheelchairs, Jerry Lewis has been raising money each Labor Day for the Muscular Dystrophy Association and the disease that helped make "poster child" part of the American idiom.

On the most recent telethon, which was staged in Las Vegas and raised $63.8 million, the "Law and Order" actress Mariska Hargitay spoke of patients' "hope that M.D.A. research will lead to treatments and cures." Mr. Lewis, who has never disclosed why he chose this disease as his cause, once again closed the broadcast with an emotional rendition of the song "You'll Never Walk Alone."

But for all the money collected toward a cure, Duchenne muscular dystrophy, the most common form of the disease, still confines thousands of boys in this country to wheelchairs in their early teens. Many do not live past their 20s.

It is a stark reminder of how American medicine — with its focus on breakthrough treatments — can sometimes fail a complex, rare and stubbornly uncurable disease. Single-minded in their pursuit of a cure, doctors and researchers for years all but ignored the necessary and unglamorous work of managing Duchenne (pronounced doo-SHEN) as a chronic condition.

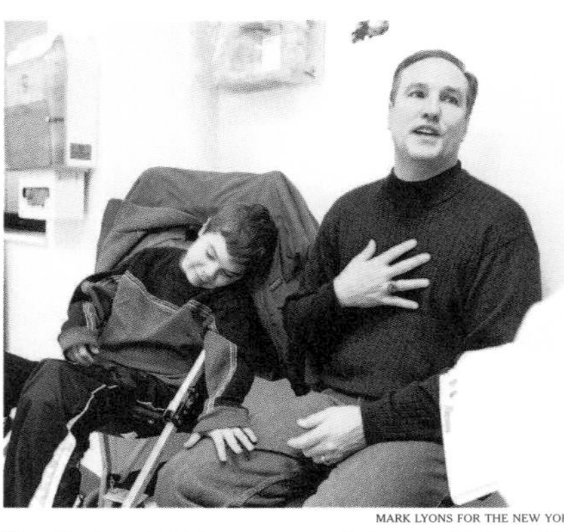

MARK LYONS FOR THE NEW YORK TIMES

Tom Hoel was told two years ago doctors could do nothing for his son Anthony, now 18, who has muscular dystrophy.

HEALTH PLANS

Treating the 'Lost Boys'

The approach is changing at a few medical centers, which are focused on making better use of available therapies to eke out longer lives for their patients. Rather than concentrate only on a cure, some researchers are now intent on developing drugs that may alleviate the effects of the disease.

But, absent a cure, too many doctors around the country still assume there is little or nothing that can be done for the muscle-wasting condition, parents and specialists say.

"We're in a stone age with Duchenne," said Dr. Linda H. Cripe, a pediatric cardiologist at the Cincinnati Children's Hospital Medical Center. She describes Duchenne patients as "a group of

Continued on Page A16

Housing Slowdown Hits Towns At the Outskirts of Texas Boom

ALLISON V. SMITH FOR THE NEW YORK TIMES

Lots abound at the Grand Heritage development in Lavon, Tex.

By LESLIE EATON

LAVON, Tex. — Once little more than a speed trap 25 miles northeast of Dallas, this town started to boom about a year ago, as turreted stone castlettes and modest brick bungalows began springing up in what had been wheat fields.

Big Dallas seemed to be knocking on little Lavon's door. Thousands of lots were laid out and hundreds of houses built, as developers tried to meet what seemed to be an insatiable appetite for inexpensive single-family homes. Land values soared, the population hit 2,500, and by November, the city was finally flush enough to afford a full-time police department.

But that was when the knocking stopped. Banks were no longer giving mortgages to anyone who could fog a mirror. "For sale" signs went up and stayed up. Weeds, not houses, sprouted on the scraped-earth plots.

And now the city government, which had counted on years of growth, is short of money. Plans for a new City Hall have been suspended, street paving jobs have been postponed, and there is even the prospect that programs and personnel will be cut, said J. Michael Jones, the city marshal and chief administrator.

"I say that very quietly," Mr. Jones added, "because I don't want to panic our citizens or our employees."

Unlike many other states with housing troubles, Texas as a whole is booming, continuing to attract new residents and create jobs. But across the state's outermost exurbs, formed by waves of new housing, building has ground almost to a halt.

These were not towns built on the speculation that soaring

Continued on Page A17

INSIDE

Oil Price Passes $100, Dragging Down Stocks

Crude oil closed above $100 a barrel for the first time, feeding fears that energy costs will further weaken consumer spending. The record close helped reverse a 157-point rally in the Dow industrials. BUSINESS DAY, PAGE C1

Judge Shuts Down Web Site

In a move that could test First Amendment rights in the Internet era, a judge ordered the disabling of a Web site that discloses confidential information. PAGE A14

Year-Round Season at NBC

NBC Universal said it would announce in April a full year's schedule of program introductions. The move, meant to appeal to advertisers, is a big step away from one of the industry's oldest traditions, the fall television season. BUSINESS DAY, PAGE C1

A New Band Hits Town

Tokio Hotel, a German band with Bill Kaulitz, right, is charming America's girls. Review by Kelefa Sanneh. THE ARTS, PAGE E1

SPECIAL TODAY

Small Business

With an all-natural energy drink, a young company tries to break into the New York beverage market, where the risks and rewards are high. SECTION H

Reporter Found in Contempt

A federal judge found a former reporter for USA Today in contempt of court for refusing to name confidential sources who had discussed a former Army bioterrorism expert's possible role in the 2001 anthrax attacks. PAGE A15

RAHAV SEGEV FOR THE NEW YORK TIMES

Jason Kidd Sent to Dallas

The off-again, on-again trade of Jason Kidd from the Nets to the Dallas Mavericks was completed. SPORTSWEDNESDAY, PAGE D5

"All the News That's Fit to Print"

The New York Times

Late Edition

Today, a mixture of sun and clouds, high 48. **Tonight,** cloudy, a shower, low 38. **Tomorrow,** mostly cloudy and mild with showers late, high 55. Weather map appears on Page B8.

VOL. CLVII . . No. 54,248 | NEW YORK, THURSDAY, MARCH 13, 2008 | $1.25

SPITZER RESIGNS

Felled by Sex Scandal, He Says His Focus Is on Family

HIROKO MASUIKE FOR THE NEW YORK TIMES

Eliot Spitzer, accompanied by his wife, Silda Wall Spitzer, resigned as governor, two days after news emerged of his involvement with prostitutes.

Lt. Gov. Paterson to Step Up Monday

By DAVID KOCIENIEWSKI and DANNY HAKIM

Gov. Eliot Spitzer, whose rise to political power as a fierce enforcer of ethics in public life was undone by revelations of his own involvement with prostitutes, resigned on Wednesday, becoming the first New York governor to leave office amid scandal in nearly a century.

The resignation will be effective on Monday at noon. Lt. Gov. David A. Paterson, a state legislator for 22 years and the heir to a Harlem political dynasty, will be sworn in as New York's 55th governor, making him the state's first black chief executive.

Mr. Spitzer announced he was stepping down at a grim appearance at his Midtown Manhattan office, less than 48 hours after it emerged that he had been intercepted on a federal wiretap confirming plans to meet a call girl from a high-priced prostitution service in Washington, leaving the public stunned and angered and bringing business in the State Capitol to a halt.

With his wife, Silda Wall Spitzer, at his side, Mr. Spitzer, a Democrat, said he would leave political life to concentrate on healing himself and his family.

"Over the course of my public life, I have insisted — I believe correctly — that people regardless of their position or power take responsibility for their conduct," he said. "I can and will ask no less of myself. For this reason, I am resigning from the office of governor."

Mr. Spitzer, 48, spoke in a somber but steady voice, softening his usual barking tone. He took no questions. His wife, in a dark suit and a brightly colored scarf, looked off to the side, occasionally glancing up to reveal deep circles beneath her eyes.

Though he came into office last January with a sweeping electoral mandate for change, Mr. Spitzer's time as governor was marked by fierce combat and costly stumbles. He faced a scandal last year after members of his staff used the State Police to disseminate damaging information about his chief Republican rival, Joseph L. Bruno, the leader of the State Senate.

Since Monday, Mr. Spitzer has been consumed with crisis, trying to salvage his marriage and his career and avoid federal charges stemming from the case.

A man defined by ambition and relentlessness, Mr. Spitzer appeared to struggle with the decision to relinquish power. On Tuesday af-

Continued on Page A20

Governor Found Himself On a Road With One Exit

The unraveling of Eliot Spitzer's tenure as governor came on Monday morning. He told family and friends the night before that he could not survive the prostitution scandal that had ensnared him. At that point, he decided only to acknowledge the obvious — that his behavior was deeply troubling — and apologized to his family and the public.

He then returned to a blur of passionate talks with advisers and friends, his wife and three criminal defense lawyers, aides said. His wife, Silda, and his mentor and friend, Lloyd Constantine, counseled him to resist resignation.

But others, particularly those from the political realm in Albany who were privately furious with the governor, recognized that he had no good place to go. By Tuesday night, he decided that it was over.

BY MICHAEL POWELL AND NICHOLAS CONFESSORE, PAGE B1

For an Aspiring Singer, A Harsher Spotlight

Ashley A. Dupré

Kristen, the prostitute described as having had a rendezvous with Eliot Spitzer on Feb. 13 in Washington, has spent the last few days in her Manhattan apartment. Born Ashley Youmans, but now known as Ashley Alexandra Dupré, she left a broken home on the Jersey Shore at 17 and came to New York to work the nightclubs as a singer.

In a series of telephone interviews on Tuesday night, she said she had slept very little over the past week. "I just don't want to be thought of as a monster," she said.

BY SERGE F. KOVALESKI AND IAN URBINA, PAGE B1

A Bipartisan Prediction Of Harmony in Albany

Gov. Eliot Spitzer's confrontational, sometimes bellicose manner antagonized his opponents and alienated his allies, and his sweeping electoral mandate dissipated month by month.

Now, as Lt. Gov. David A. Paterson prepares to succeed Mr. Spitzer, Republicans and Democrats alike are predicting an extensive change of atmosphere and a return to comity between the governor and the Legislature. Mr. Paterson's temperament and style, his friends and fellow officials say, are mild and subtle.

In politics, style and tone are crucial, but a major shift in either may be the only sure outcome of Mr. Paterson's ascension to the governor's office on Monday, an event likely to be as transforming as any in New York political history.

BY NICHOLAS CONFESSORE AND JEREMY W. PETERS, PAGE B1

Pentagon Cites Tapes Showing Interrogations

By MARK MAZZETTI and SCOTT SHANE

WASHINGTON — The Defense Department is conducting an extensive review of the videotaping of interrogations at military facilities from Iraq to Guantánamo Bay, and so far it has identified nearly 50 tapes, including one that showed what a military spokesman described as the forcible gagging of a terrorism suspect.

The Pentagon review was begun in late January after the Central Intelligence Agency acknowledged that it had destroyed its own videotapes of harsh interrogations conducted by C.I.A. officers, an action that is now the subject of criminal and Congressional investigations.

Ali al-Marri

The review was intended in part to establish clearer rules for any videotaping of interrogations, Defense officials said. But they acknowledged that it had been complicated by inconsistent taping practices in the past, as well as uncertain policies for when tapes could be destroyed or must be preserved.

The officials said it appeared that only a small fraction of the tens of thousands of interrogations worldwide since 2001 had been recorded.

The officials said the nearly 50 tapes they identified documented interrogations of two terrorism suspects, Jose Padilla and Ali al-Marri, and were made at a Navy detention site in Charleston, S.C., where the two men have been

Continued on Page A8

Racial Issue Bubbles Up Again for Democrats

By PATRICK HEALY and JEFF ZELENY

After the Democratic primary in South Carolina turned racially divisive in January, Senators Hillary Rodham Clinton and Barack Obama essentially declared a truce and put a stop to fighting between their camps. But this week, race has once again begun casting a pall over the battle between the two.

On Wednesday a close ally of Mrs. Clinton, Geraldine A. Ferraro, the Democratic vice-presidential nominee in 1984 who was on the Clinton finance committee, resigned from the campaign after being criticized by Mr. Obama's advisers, among others, for her recent comments that "if Obama was a white man, he would not be in this position" as a leading presidential contender.

Ms. Ferraro did not disavow that remark. Mrs. Clinton, while calling it regrettable, did not break with her.

Mr. Obama, speaking to reporters on Wednesday, said he did not believe that there was "a directive in the Clinton campaign saying, 'Let's heighten the racial elements in the campaign.' I certainly wouldn't want to think that."

He said he was puzzled at how, after more than a year of campaigning, race and sex are at the forefront as never before.

"I don't want to deny the role of race and gender in our society," he said. "They're there, and they're powerful. But I don't think it's productive."

Yet race, as well as sex, have been unavoidable subtexts of the Democratic campaign since the two candidates began seeking to be the first African-American or the first woman to lead a party's presidential ticket. In the primaries and caucuses this winter, too, Mrs. Clinton has enjoyed substantial support from women, while Mr. Obama has increasingly drawn overwhelming votes from blacks.

The Tuesday primary in Mississippi, a state where the electorate has historically been racially polarized, generated one of the most divided votes. Mrs. Clinton received 8 percent of the black vote, and Mr. Obama received 26 percent of the white vote, according to exit polls by Edison/Mitofsky for The Associated Press and television net-

Continued on Page A16

Video Road Hogs Stir Fear of Internet Traffic Jam

By STEVE LOHR

Caution: Heavy Internet traffic ahead. Delays possible.

For months there has been a rising chorus of alarm about the surging growth in the amount of data flying across the Internet. The threat, according to some industry groups, analysts and researchers, stems mainly from the increasing visual richness of online communications and entertainment — video clips and movies, social networks and multiplayer games.

Moving images, far more than words or sounds, are hefty rivers of digital bits as they traverse the Internet's pipes and gateways, requiring, in industry parlance, more bandwidth. Last year, by one estimate, the video site YouTube, owned by Google, consumed as much bandwidth as the entire Internet did in 2000.

In a widely cited report published last November, a research firm projected that user demand for the Internet could outpace network capacity by 2011. The title of a debate scheduled next month at a technology conference in Boston sums up the angst: "The End of the Internet?"

With video and data traffic growing, some analysts warn of slowdowns ahead.

GLOBAL CONSUMER INTERNET TRAFFIC

12 million terabytes

9

6

3

0

PROJECTIONS

'05 '06 '07 '08 '09 '10 '11

Source: Cisco Systems THE NEW YORK TIMES

But the Internet traffic surge represents more a looming challenge than an impending catastrophe. Even those most concerned are not predicting a lights-out Internet crash. An individual user, they say, would experience Internet clogging in the form of sluggish download speeds and frustration with data-heavy services that become much less useful or enjoyable.

"The Internet doesn't collapse, but there would be a growing class of stuff you just can't do online," said Johna Till Johnson, president of Nemertes Research, which predicted the bandwidth squeeze by 2011, anticipating that demand will grow by 100 percent or more a year.

Others are less worried — at least in the short term. Andrew M. Odlyzko, a professor at the University of Minnesota, estimates that digital traffic on the global network is growing about 50 percent a year, in line with a recent analysis by Cisco Systems, the big network equipment maker.

That sounds like a daunting rate of growth. Yet the technology for handling Internet traffic is advancing at an impressive pace as well. The router computers for relaying data get faster, fi-

Continued on Page C5

INSIDE

JOAO SILVA FOR THE NEW YORK TIMES

Iraqi Officials Plan to Reclaim the Nation's Main Port

Senior Iraqi officials have said the government may soon deploy Iraqi Army troops to seize control of Basra's port, which is decrepit and controlled by local militias. The officials also suggested that Western troops might be involved in the operation. PAGE A6

Smog Standard a Bit Tighter

The E.P.A. announced a modest tightening of the smog standard, overruling the advice of its scientific advisory panel for a stronger standard. PAGE A12

Woods, on Par With Palmer

Tiger Woods, the dominant golfer in the sport today, has much in common with Arnold Palmer, one of the game's greats. SPORTSTHURSDAY, PAGE D1

An Idyll for Dollar Seekers

Venezuelans, facing 23 percent inflation, are flocking to the island of Curaçao to get their hands on American dollars. PAGE A4

Israeli Raid Ends 5-Day Lull

Israeli undercover troops killed four Palestinian militants riding in a car in the West Bank city of Bethlehem, shattering a five-day lull in violence and threatening Egyptian efforts to mediate a cease-fire. PAGE A3

Airline Grounds 38 Jets

Southwest Airlines, which was fined $10.2 million last week for an inspection lapse, found another problem and grounded 38 jets for immediate checks, forcing about 125 flight cancellations. BUSINESS DAY, PAGE C1

DONNA McWILLIAM/ASSOCIATED PRESS

News Summary A2

Updated news: nytimes.com

Tomorrow in The Times: Page B6

"All the News That's Fit to Print"

The New York Times

Late Edition

Today, clouds yielding to sun, diminishing winds, high 55. **Tonight,** mostly cloudy, rain, snow late, low 35. **Tomorrow,** clearing, blustery, high 46. Weather map, Page D8.

VOL. CLVII . . No. 54,250 · NEW YORK, SATURDAY, MARCH 15, 2008 · $1.25

REUTERS

Chinese security forces in Lhasa, Tibet, took cover during a fifth day of protests. The banner overhead reads, "Strengthen public safety management, safeguard political stability." Beijing is facing the most serious demonstrations in Tibet since the 1980s.

Run on Big Wall St. Bank Spurs U.S.-Backed Rescue

Bear Stearns Squeezed in Credit Crisis — JPMorgan and the Fed Step In

By LANDON THOMAS Jr.

Just three days ago, the head of Bear Stearns, the beleaguered investment bank, sought to assure Wall Street that his firm was safe.

But those assurances were blown away in what amounted to a bank run at Bear Stearns, prompting JPMorgan Chase and the Federal Reserve Bank of New York to step in on Friday with a financial rescue package intended to keep the firm afloat.

The move underscores the extreme stresses that the credit crisis has imposed on the financial system and raises the once-unthinkable prospect that major Wall Street firms might fail.

The developments may only postpone the eventual sale of all or part of Bear Stearns, which has had crippling losses on mortgage-linked investments. To keep the 85-year-old firm solvent, JPMorgan, backed by the New York Fed, extended a secured line of credit that gives Bear Stearns at least 28 days to shore up its finances or, more likely, to find a buyer.

News of the bailout ignited fears that other big banks remain vulnerable to the continuing credit crisis, and stocks tumbled in another rocky day for the markets. Financial shares led the way, with shares of Bear Stearns plunging 47 percent. Hours after the rescue was announced, another Wall Street firm, Lehman Brothers, said it had secured a three-year credit line from banks. Its stock fell 15 percent.

Policy makers are likely to spend the weekend dealing with the fallout in the financial system, and potential buyers are already circling Bear Stearns.

As the Wall Street drama unfolded, Ben S. Bernanke, the Federal Reserve chairman, added fresh warnings Friday about a gathering wave of home foreclosures bearing down on American communities.

President Bush, meantime, made his most striking acknowledgment yet of the country's economic troubles, even as he defended his administration's re-

Continued on Page A11

Source: Bloomberg · THE NEW YORK TIMES

Violence in Tibet as Monks Clash With the Police

10 Deaths Reported at Demonstrations in the Capital

By JIM YARDLEY

BEIJING — Violence erupted Friday morning in a busy market area of the Tibetan capital, Lhasa, as Buddhist monks and other ethnic Tibetans brawled with Chinese security forces in clashes that brought an official report of 10 deaths. Witnesses say angry Tibetan crowds burned shops, cars, military vehicles and at least one tourist bus.

The chaotic scene was the latest, and most violent, confrontation in a series of protests that began on Monday and now represent a major challenge to the ruling Communist Party as it prepares to play host to the Olympic Games in August. By Saturday morning, Chinese armored vehicles were reportedly patrolling the center of the city.

Beijing is facing the most serious and prolonged demonstrations in Tibet since the late 1980s, when it suppressed a rebellion there with lethal force that left scores, and possibly hundreds, of ethnic Tibetans dead. The leadership is clearly alarmed that a wave of negative publicity could disrupt its elaborate plans for the Olympics and its hopes that the games will showcase its rising influence and prosperity rather than domestic turmoil.

The Dalai Lama, the exiled spiritual leader of Tibet, and his supporters around the world, have embraced the protesters in Lhasa. Thousands of Buddhists in neighboring India and Nepal took to the streets Friday in solidarity. Concerned that the protests might spread elsewhere in China, the authorities appeared to be moving the military police into other regions with large Tibetan populations.

Roughly 1,000 special police officers were deployed in the town of Bamei, in Sichuan Province, the site of a temple sacred to Tibetans, witnesses said by tele-

Continued on Page A8

DELEGATE BATTLES EMBROIL 2 STATES

Clinton's Backers Warn Party on Donations

By MICHAEL LUO and JOHN M. BRODER

Democrats in Michigan and Florida struggled Friday to resolve the impasse over their disputed January primaries, coming up with a plan to hold a June primary in Michigan while remaining deadlocked in Florida.

Reflecting how tense the situation has become, influential fund-raisers for Senator Hillary Rodham Clinton have stepped up their behind-the-scenes pressure on national party leaders to resolve the matter, with some even threatening to withhold their donations to the Democratic National Committee unless it seats the delegates from the two states or holds new primaries there.

The committee penalized Michigan and Florida for holding their primaries early in violation of national party rules, barring their delegates from being seated at the Democratic convention this summer. But with the Democratic contest now a scramble for every remaining delegate, the allocation of delegates from the two states could have a substantial impact on the nomination.

Mrs. Clinton won the primaries in both states, but the contests

Continued on Page A12

NEWS ANALYSIS

A Wall St. Domino Theory

By JENNY ANDERSON and VIKAS BAJAJ

The Federal Reserve's unusual decision to provide emergency assistance to Bear Stearns underscores a long-building concern that one failure could spread across the financial system.

Wall Street firms like Bear Stearns conduct business with many individuals, corporations, financial companies, pension funds and hedge funds. They also do billions of dollars of business with each other every day, borrowing and lending securities at a dizzying pace and fueling the wheels of capitalism.

The sudden collapse of a major player could not only shake client confidence in the entire system, but also make it difficult for sound institutions to conduct business as usual. Hedge funds that rely on Bear to finance their trading and hold their securities would be stranded; investors who wrote financial contracts with Bear would be at risk; markets that depended on Bear to buy and sell securities would screech to a halt, if they were not already halted.

"In a trading firm, trust is everything," said Richard Sylla, a financial historian at New York University. "The person at the other end of the phone or the trading screen has to believe that you will make good on any deal that you make."

Commercial banks, mutual fund companies and other big financial firms with deep pockets would presumably weather such turmoil. Firms that traded extensively with Bear Stearns could be at great risk if the bank failed.

For individual customers, the Federal Deposit Insurance Corporation insures deposits up to

Continued on Page A11

Politics Tests a Town Unity Forged by Gunshots

By MONICA DAVEY

KIRKWOOD, Mo. — After a shared horror, people in tightknit towns often grow still closer. So no one was surprised when signs began sprouting on the wide lawns here: "Kirkwood stands together, grieves together, heals together."

Then came plans for blood drives and for fund-raisers at a V.F.W. hall and in the high school cafeteria to benefit the families of three Kirkwood officials and two police officers who died when a gunman stormed a City Council meeting on Feb. 7 and opened fire.

But now the rush of small-town unity and nurture in this St. Louis suburb is being tested by a political reality that the rampage also left behind. One of the two candidates in an imminent election for mayor, Councilwoman Connie Karr, was among the dead, and the town has been caught up in an awkward — some say disrespectful and unseemly — struggle over leadership even as the mourning continues.

With purple bunting still framing the door to City Hall, some residents have circulated petitions, proposed emergency ordinances and delivered fiery speeches demanding postponement of the election, long planned for April 8.

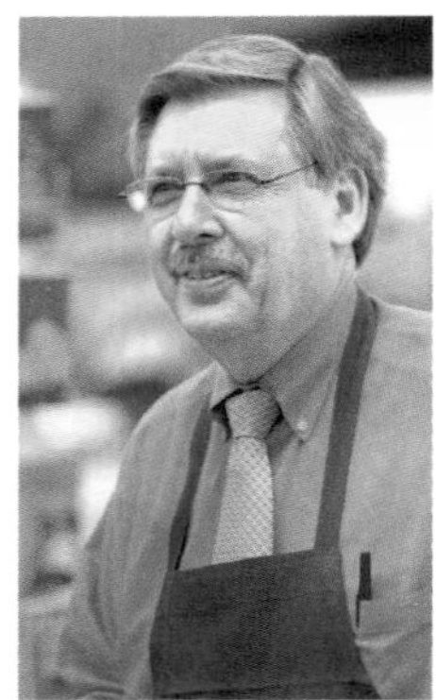

DAN GILL FOR THE NEW YORK TIMES

Arthur J. McDonnell, mayoral hopeful and shooting survivor.

Those calling for a delay insist that voters deserve more choices than the remaining candidate, Councilman Arthur J. McDonnell, a grocer who himself endured the rampage by taking cover behind the dais. (The mayor, Mike Swoboda, who was shot in the head and gravely wounded, was barred from seeking re-election by term limits. He remains in a rehabilitation center.)

Last week's meeting of the Council, its first inside the chamber since the killings, turned into a contentious, sometimes tearful debate over the election, the decision to remove Ms. Karr's name from the ballot and what some have described as distrust of an old guard here, Council members among them, who the dissidents argue have denied newcomers, African-Americans, opponents of development and others a political voice.

"There are many people in this city who feel they don't have any representation," Nancy Seats, 73, told the Council, one of scores of residents who filled the chamber, which smelled of fresh paint and new olive-hued carpeting and

Continued on Page A14

RICHARD PERRY/THE NEW YORK TIMES

The Blood Lines are one of the many bands at the South by Southwest festival in Austin, Tex.

1,700 Bands, Rocking as the CD Industry Reels

By JON PARELES

AUSTIN, Tex. — "I don't want to feel like I don't have a future," sang the Shout Out Louds, one of more than 1,700 bands that have been performing day and night at Austin's clubs, halls, meeting rooms, parking lots and street corners since Wednesday.

The Shout Out Louds, from Stockholm, were singing about a romance, but they could have been speaking for thousands of people attending the 22nd annual South by Southwest Music Festival. It is America's most important music convention, particularly for rising bands, gathering a critical mass of musicians and their supporters and exploiters from the United States and across the world. While major labels have a low profile at this year's gathering, other corporations are highly visible, using sponsorships to latch on to music as a draw and as a symbol of cool.

Southwest is a talent showcase and a schmoozathon, a citywide barbecue party and a brainstorming session for a business that has been radically shaken and stirred by the Internet. For established recording companies, the instantaneous and often unpaid distribution of music online is business hell; CD album sales are on an accelerating slide, and sales of downloads aren't making up for the losses. But for listeners, as well as for musicians who mostly want a chance to be heard, the digital era is fan heaven. As major labels have shrunk in the 21st century, South by Southwest has nearly doubled in

Continued on Page A15

INSIDE

Eli Lilly E-Mail Discussed Unapproved Use for Drug

An Eli Lilly official who is about to become the company's top executive wrote an e-mail message in 2003 that appears to have encouraged the company to promote Zyprexa, its schizophrenia medicine, for a use not approved by federal drug regulators. PAGE C1

A C.I.A. Secret Prisoner

The Central Intelligence Agency secretly detained a Qaeda suspect as part of a program that allows the use of harsh interrogation, officials said. PAGE A6

NATO Expansion in Doubt

President Bush's efforts to cement a trans-Atlantic legacy by adding three nations to NATO appear in disarray as the alliance struggles with internal divisions, tensions with Russia and the combat mission in Afghanistan that have exposed rifts among current members. PAGE A9

Guilty Plea for Trial Lawyer

Richard F. Scruggs, a Mississippi lawyer whose tobacco litigation was portrayed in the film "The Insider," has pleaded guilty to trying to bribe a judge in a case evolving from insurance payments in the wake of Hurricane Katrina. BUSINESS DAY, PAGE C1

Candidates Call Paterson

Lt. Gov. David A. Paterson of New York, who will become governor on Monday, has been called by both Hillary Rodham Clinton and Barack Obama. PAGE B1

THIS WEEKEND

'Lush Life'

Echoes of Raymond Chandler and Saul Bellow course through Richard Price's novel, in which an aspiring writer becomes a murder suspect. BOOK REVIEW

T: Design

The Times Style Magazine looks at the work of a tech-savvy Spanish architect, an artist's open, airy house in Thailand and more. *Also,* the innovative Japanese designer Naoto Fukasawa.

"All the News That's Fit to Print"

The New York Times

Late Edition
Today, milder with periods of rain, high 54. **Tonight,** breezy and mild with showers, low 45. **Tomorrow,** partly cloudy and blustery, high 51. Weather map appears on Page A16.

VOL. CLVII . . No. 54,254 | © 2008 The New York Times | NEW YORK, WEDNESDAY, MARCH 19, 2008 | $1.25

JAMES HILL FOR THE NEW YORK TIMES

Notes From the Field, 5 Years In

Reporters and photographers who covered the Iraq war look back at years of conflict. Page A8.

Stephen Farrell
If the Shiites felt confident enough to loot, it was all over.

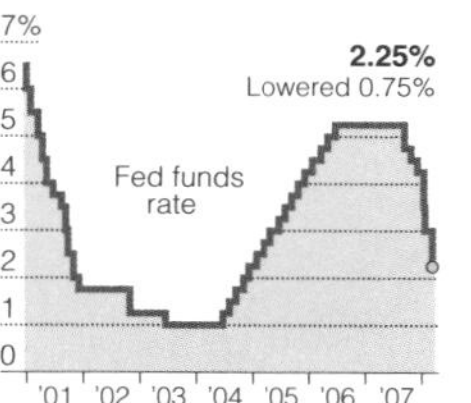

Dexter Filkins
Each of us had his own moment of recognition, when we knew the insurgency was not just a scattering of street gangs but a movement that was blossoming on the support it enjoyed among the country's Sunni Arabs.

Sabrina Tavernise
An American general whose views I shared used to draw the analogy with an abused child: it will grow up to be an abuser. Even a lifetime of tough psychiatric work may not help.

Max Becherer
Today when I look into the abyss of the past five years it is not black. It is populated with faces. And it is not quiet.

In Dollars The Pentagon says the Iraq war's cost is $600 billion; others put it in the trillions. Page A9.

On the road to Baghdad, an American convoy passes an Iraqi killed in a fight with marines in March 2003. More photographs, an interactive timeline, and fuller reminiscences in the Baghdad Bureau blog: **nytimes.com/world**

Fed Trims Rates Sharply, Sending the Markets Up

Cut of 3/4 of a Point Is Less Than Expected — Signs of Split on Policy at Central Bank

By EDMUND L. ANDREWS

WASHINGTON — The Federal Reserve reduced short-term interest rates for the sixth time in six months on Tuesday, capping an extraordinary series of measures it has taken to stabilize financial markets. The cut was smaller than investors had been expecting, though, and exposed some signs of a split among policy makers.

The central bank lowered its federal funds rate — the rate it charges banks for overnight loans — by three-quarters of a percentage point, to 2.25 percent, and left the door open to additional rate cuts in the months ahead.

Though it was one of the biggest one-day rate cuts in decades, investors had been betting heavily that the Fed would cut its benchmark rate a full percentage point in response to strong evidence that a recession has begun and to the deepening crisis on Wall Street.

But two members of the Fed's policy-making committee dissented, saying they favored an even smaller rate cut, and the policy group as a whole expressed new worries about inflation — a possible argument against aggressive rate cuts.

"Inflation has been elevated, and some indicators of inflation expectations have risen," the Fed said in a statement that accompanied the rate decision. "It will be necessary to continue to monitor developments carefully."

Some analysts saw the cut of three-quarters of a point as a compromise to appease those who wanted less. Others surmised that the Fed might have been reluctant to cut rates further immediately in part because as the rates inch closer to zero, the Fed leaves itself less room to maneuver in case of further financial shocks.

Investors reacted ambivalently to the initial news of the rate cut but pushed stock prices sharply higher by the end of the day. A rally began in the morning after two major investment firms, Goldman Sachs and Lehman Brothers, reported profits that were higher than expected and reassured investors that they had adequate capital. Stock prices pulled back within minutes of the Fed's afternoon announcement, before resuming their rise.

By the day's end, the Dow Jones industrial average was up 420 points, or 3.51 percent, to 12,392.66.

The Fed's statement and the

Continued on Page A13

Fed's Benchmark Rate

7%
6
5
4
3
2
1
0
2.25%
Lowered 0.75%
Fed funds rate
'01 '02 '03 '04 '05 '06 '07
Source: Federal Reserve

Can't Grasp Credit Crisis? Join the Club

DAVID LEONHARDT
ECONOMIC SCENE

Raise your hand if you don't quite understand this whole financial crisis.

It has been going on for seven months now, and many people probably feel as if they should understand it. But they don't, not really. The part about the housing crash seems simple enough. With banks whispering sweet encouragement, people bought homes they couldn't afford, and now they are falling behind on their mortgages.

But the overwhelming majority of homeowners are doing just fine. So how is it that a mess concentrated in one part of the mortgage business — subprime loans — has frozen the credit markets, sent stock markets gyrating, caused the collapse of Bear Stearns, left the economy on the brink of the worst recession in a generation and forced the Federal Reserve to take its boldest action since the Depression?

I'm here to urge you not to feel sheepish. This may not be entirely comforting, but your confusion is shared by many people who are in the middle of the crisis.

"We're exposing parts of the capital markets that most of us had never heard of," Ethan Harris, a top Lehman Brothers economist, said last week. Robert Rubin, the former Treasury secretary and current Citigroup executive, has said that he hadn't heard of "liquidity puts," an ob-

Continued on Page A13

New Governor And Wife Talk Of Past Affairs

By DANNY HAKIM and TRYMAINE LEE

ALBANY — In an extraordinary news conference on his first full day on the job, Gov. David A. Paterson acknowledged on Tuesday that he had had several extramarital relationships, including one with a state employee, but said he had done nothing illegal and had been faithful to his wife in recent years.

Mr. Paterson said he made the disclosure because he wanted to clear his conscience and avoid being blackmailed. He said he hoped his openness about his past affairs would help him to gain the trust of New Yorkers and move forward to focus on governing.

"I didn't want to be compromised, I didn't want to be blackmailed, I didn't want to hesitate taking an action because the person on the other end might hurt me or my family," Mr. Paterson, a Democrat, said during the tense and often awkward appearance with his wife, Michelle Paige Paterson, at his side. "I just thought this was the time to come forward and reveal this."

Mr. Paterson said no state funds had been used as he carried out his affairs. He said he may have used his campaign

Continued on Page A17

Court Weighs Right to Guns, And Its Limits

By LINDA GREENHOUSE

WASHINGTON — A majority of the Supreme Court appeared ready on Tuesday to embrace, for the first time in the country's history, an interpretation of the Second Amendment that protects the right to own a gun for personal use.

That may be the easy part.

The harder question in the case challenging the District of Columbia's handgun ban is what kind of restrictions the government could constitutionally place, in the name of public safety, on the newly recognized right. The answer to that question, on which the outcome of the case will turn, was less clear.

The argument was lively and intense, running 22 minutes over its allotted hour and 15 minutes. Despite "starting afresh," as Chief Justice John G. Roberts Jr. put it, on a subject the court had not addressed since 1939, the justices appeared at least as well informed as the lawyers on minute details of English and American legal history. The relevance of that history, on which both sides have their distinguished experts, remains to be seen.

There was also a good deal of linguistic dissection of the Second Amendment's text: "A well regulated Militia, being neces-

Continued on Page A17

Obama Urges U.S. to Grapple With Race Issue

By JEFF ZELENY

PHILADELPHIA — Senator Barack Obama delivered a sweeping assessment of race in America on Tuesday, bluntly confronting the divisions between black and white as he sought to dispel the furor over inflammatory statements by his former pastor.

Mr. Obama again condemned the more incendiary remarks of the pastor, the Rev. Jeremiah A. Wright Jr. But, drawing on his experiences as the son of a white mother and a black father, Mr. Obama went on to try to explain to white voters the anger and frustration behind Mr. Wright's words and to urge blacks to understand the sources of the racial fears and resentments among whites.

While his immediate political goal was to tamp down any doubts that his association with Mr. Wright has caused among voters as he battles for the Democratic presidential nomination, Mr. Obama also sought to link his theme of understanding and reconciliation to more concrete issues at stake in the election as the economy weakens.

"The fact is," he said, "that the comments that have been made and the issues that have surfaced over the last few weeks reflect the complexities of race in this country that we've never really worked through — a part of our Union that we have yet to perfect.

"And if we walk away now," he continued, "if we simply retreat into our respective corners, we will never be able to come together and solve challenges like health care, or education, or the need to find good jobs for every American."

After running a campaign that in many ways tried not to be defined by race, Mr. Obama placed himself squarely in the middle of the debate over how to address it, a living bridge between whites and blacks still divided by the legacy of slavery and all that came after it. [News analysis, Page A14.]

His language reached at times for the inspiration and idealism of

Continued on Page A14

JESSICA KOURKOUNIS FOR THE NEW YORK TIMES

Senator Barack Obama spoke on race Tuesday in Philadelphia.

For Top Medical Students, Appearance Offers an Attractive Field

JOSH HANER/THE NEW YORK TIMES

Meena Singh applied to 90 dermatology programs.

By NATASHA SINGER

BOSTON — March Madness has a different meaning for Thomas Hocker and Meena Singh, a married couple in their final year at the Harvard Medical School, who are waiting to learn Thursday if they have been accepted into their residency programs of choice.

Already saddled with about $330,000 in education loans, they borrowed $20,000 more so they could fly around the country this winter for about two dozen residency interview each. All told, each applied to 90 such training programs.

Ms. Singh, pregnant during interview season, gave birth to their second daughter in early January. Three days later, she flew to Miami for an interview.

The search has been difficult not because they are mediocre students; indeed, each has a brand-name education, academic honors and published research

THE PRICE OF BEAUTY
Specialties in Vogue

on disease. No, it has been hard because they aspire to be dermatologists.

As thousands of medical students await word this week on residency programs, two specialties concerned with physical appearance — dermatology and plastic surgery — are among the most competitive.

Only 61 percent of seniors at American medical schools whose first choice was dermatology received a residency in that field last year, compared with 98 percent for those whose first choice was internal medicine and 99 percent for those seeking family medicine, according to a report by the Association of American Medical Colleges and the National Resident Matching Program, which pairs candidates and programs. Although there are far fewer positions in dermatology (320 residencies in 2007) than in internal medicine (5,517) and family medicine (2,603), the field is attracting some of the best and brightest future doctors.

Seniors accepted in 2007 as residents in dermatology and two other appearance-related fields — plastic surgery and otolaryngology

Continued on Page A12

INSIDE

A Back Channel to Hamas
After ruling out talks with Hamas, the militant Islamist group, the Bush administration is using Egypt to open a channel between Israel and representatives of the group. **PAGE A10**

Easing the 'No Child' Law
The Bush administration, acknowledging that the No Child Left Behind law labels too many schools as failing, is relaxing provisions for some states. **PAGE A11**

Guilty Verdict in Girl's Death
Nixzmary Brown's stepfather was convicted of first-degree manslaughter but acquitted of second-degree murder for his role in her death. **PAGE B1**

Arthur C. Clarke Is Dead
The author of "2001: A Space Odyssey" and numerous other books that blended scientific expertise with poetic imagination and helped usher in the space age was 90. **PAGE C12**

Whitney to Get $131 Million
The art foundation of the cosmetics executive Leonard A. Lauder will give the Whitney Museum the largest donation in its 77-year history. **THE ARTS, PAGE E1**

FRONT PAGE INDEX

Photo Credits

Page 27: National Archives/Matthew Brady (top); National Archives (center right); National Archives (center left); National Archives/Matthew Brady (bottom)

Page 28: National Archives/Timothy Sullivan (top); National Archives (center); National Archives/Alexander Gardner (bottom)

Page 29: National Archives (top); National Archives (center); Library of Congress (bottom)

Page 30: AP Images (top); U.S. Army Signal Corps drawing (bottom)

Page 55: AP Images (top); Landov/Ivy Close photo (center); Stock Montage/Getty Images photo (bottom left); Landov/Ivy Close photos (bottom right)

Page 56: Library of Congress

Page 57: AP Images (top); Library of Congress (bottom)

Page 58: AP Images (top); Library of Congress (bottom)

Page 65: AP Images (top); AP Images (bottom)

Page 66: AP Images

Page 67: Library of Congress (top); AP Images (bottom)

Page 68: AP Images (top); Library of Congress (bottom)

Page 106: Library of Congress (top); Library of Congress (bottom)

Page 107: Library of Congress (top); Library of Congress (center); AP Images (bottom)

Page 108: Library of Congress (top); Library of Congress (bottom)

Page 109: Library of Congress (top); Library of Congress (bottom)

Page 133: AP Images (top); AP Images (center); National Archives (bottom)

Page 134: National Archives (top); AP Images (bottom)

Page 135: Library of Congress (bottom)

Page 136: AP Images

Page 155: AP Images (top); Library of Congress (bottom)

Page 156: Getty Images (top); AP Images (bottom)

Page 157: AP Images (top); Carl van Vechtan/Library of Congress (center); AP Images (bottom)

Page 158: AP Images (top); AP Images (center); AP Images (bottom)

Page 181: AP Images (top); AP Images (bottom)

Page 182: AP Images (top); Library of Congress (center); AP Images (bottom)

Page 183: AP Images (top); AP Images (center); AP Images (bottom)

Page 184: AP Images (top); AP Images (center); AP Images (bottom)

Page 218: Landov/DPA (top); National Archives (bottom)

Page 219: National Archives (top); AP Images (bottom)

Page 220: AP Images (top); National Archives (bottom)

Page 221: National Archives (top); National Archives (center); AP Images (bottom)

Page 236: AP Images (top); AP Images (center); AP Images (bottom)

Page 237: AP Images (top); AP Images (center); AP Images (bottom)

Page 238: AP Images (top); Landov/Reuters (bottom)

Page 239: AP Images (top); AP Images (bottom)

Page 248: AP Images (top); AP Images (bottom)

Page 249: AP Images (top); AP Images (bottom)

Page 250: AP Images (top); AP Images (center); AP Images (bottom)

Page 251: AP Images (top); AP Images (bottom)

Page 291: AP Images (top); AP Images (center); AP Images (bottom)

Page 292: AP Images (top); Library of Congress (center); AP Images (bottom)

Page 293: AP Images (top); AP Images (center); AP Images (bottom)

Page 294: AP Images (top); AP Images (bottom)

Page 325: NASA Photo (top); NASA Photo (bottom)

Page 326: AP Images (top); AP Images (center); AP Images (bottom)

Page 327: NASA Photo (top left); NASA Photo (top right); AP Images (center); NASA Photo (bottom)

Page 328: NASA Photo (top); NASA Photo (bottom)

Page 347: Landov/DPA (top); Landov/DPA (center); Landov/EMPICS (bottom)

Page 348: Landov/Bloomberg News (top); AP Images (bottom)

Page 349: Landov/DPA (top); Landov/DPA (bottom)

Page 350: AP Images (top); AP Images (bottom)

Page 359: AP Images (top); AP Images (center); AP Images (bottom)

Page 360: AP Images (top); AP Images (center); AP Images (bottom left); AP Images (bottom right)

Page 361: AP Images (top); AP Images (center); AP Images (bottom)

Page 362: AP Images (top); AP Images (bottom)

Page 371: AP Images (top); AP Images (center); AP Images (bottom)

Page 372: AP Images (top); AP Images (center); AP Images (bottom)

Page 373: AP Images (top); AP Images (center); AP Images (bottom left); AP Images (bottom right);

Page 374: AP Images (top); AP Images (bottom)

Page 405: AP Images (top); Landov/Bloomberg News (center); Landov/Bloomberg News (bottom)

Page 406: AP Images (top); Landov/Reuters (center); AP Images (bottom)

Page 407: Landov/Bloomberg News (top); Landov/Bloomberg News (center); AP Images (bottom)

Page 408: Landov/Bloomberg News (top); Landov/ Reuters (bottom)

Page 428: AP Images/Charles Krupa (top); George M. Gutierrez for the New York Times (bottom)

Page 429: AP Photo/U.S. Coast Guard, Petty Officer Tom Sperduto (top); AP Photo/Ron Edmonds (bottom)

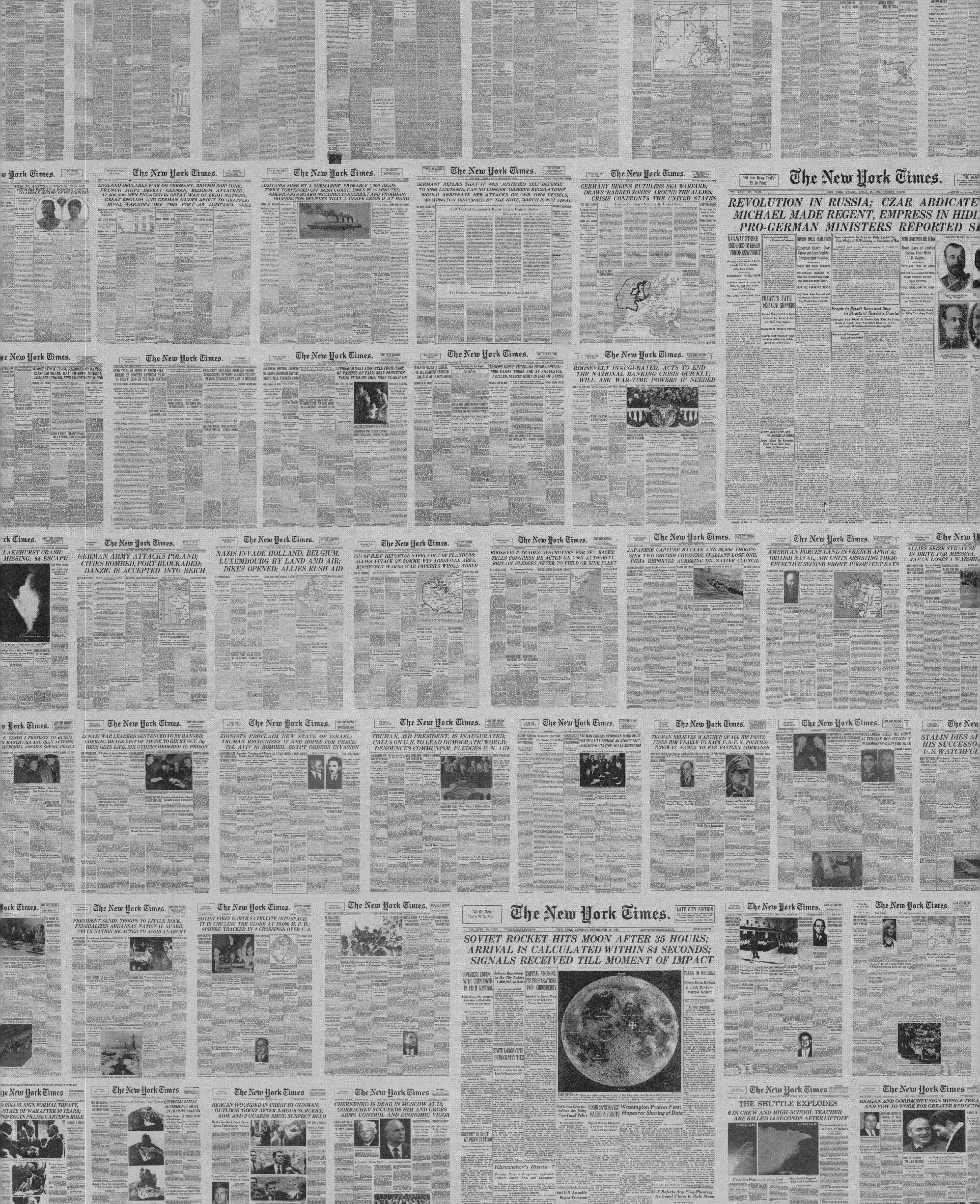

The New York Times.

HEIR TO AUSTRIA'S THRONE IS SLAIN WITH HIS WIFE BY A BOSNIAN YOUTH TO AVENGE SEIZURE OF HIS COUNTRY

ENGLAND DECLARES WAR ON GERMANY; BRITISH SHIP SUNK; FRENCH SHIPS DEFEAT GERMAN, BELGIUM ATTACKED; 17,000,000 MEN ENGAGED IN GREAT WAR OF EIGHT NATIONS; GREAT ENGLISH AND GERMAN NAVIES ABOUT TO GRAPPLE; RIVAL WARSHIPS OFF THIS PORT AS LUSITANIA SAILS

LUSITANIA SUNK BY A SUBMARINE, PROBABLY 1,000 DEAD; TWICE TORPEDOED OFF IRISH COAST; SINKS IN 15 MINUTES; AMERICANS ABOARD INCLUDED VANDERBILT AND FROHMAN; WASHINGTON BELIEVES THAT A GRAVE CRISIS IS AT HAND

GERMANY REPLIES THAT IT WAS 'JUSTIFIED SELF-DEFENSE' TO SINK LUSITANIA; CAN NO LONGER 'OBSERVE REGULATIONS' WOULD ARBITRATE HER ATTACKS ON OUR OWN VESSELS; WASHINGTON DISTURBED BY THE NOTE, WHICH IS NOT FINAL

GERMANY BEGINS RUTHLESS SEA WARFARE; DRAWS 'BARRED ZONES' AROUND THE ALLIES; CRISIS CONFRONTS THE UNITED STATES

REVOLUTION IN RUSSIA; CZAR ABDICATE[S]; MICHAEL MADE REGENT, EMPRESS IN HIDI[NG]; PRO-GERMAN MINISTERS REPORTED S[LAIN]

WORST STOCK CRASH STEMMED BY BANKS; 12,894,650-SHARE DAY SWAMPS MARKET; LEADERS CONFER, FIND CONDITIONS SOUND

LINDBERGH BABY KIDNAPPED FROM HOME OF PARENTS ON FARM NEAR PRINCETON; TAKEN FROM HIS CRIB; WIDE SEARCH ON

TROOPS DRIVE VETERANS FROM CAPITAL; FIRE CAMPS THERE AND AT ANACOSTIA; 1 KILLED, SCORES HURT IN DAY OF STRIFE

ROOSEVELT INAUGURATED, ACTS TO END THE NATIONAL BANKING CRISIS QUICKLY; WILL ASK WAR-TIME POWERS IF NEEDED

LAKEHURST CRASH; ... MISSING; 64 ESCAPE

GERMAN ARMY ATTACKS POLAND; CITIES BOMBED, PORT BLOCKADED; DANZIG IS ACCEPTED INTO REICH

NAZIS INVADE HOLLAND, BELGIUM, LUXEMBOURG BY LAND AND AIR; DIKES OPENED; ALLIES RUSH AID

75% OF B.E.F. REPORTED SAFELY OUT OF FLANDERS; ALLIES ATTACK ON SOMME, WIN ABBEVILLE AREA; ROOSEVELT WARNS WAR IMPERILS WHOLE WORLD

ROOSEVELT TRADES DESTROYERS FOR SEA BASES; TELLS CONGRESS HE ACTED ON OWN AUTHORITY; BRITAIN PLEDGES NEVER TO YIELD OR SINK FLEET

JAPANESE CAPTURE BATAAN AND 36,000 TROOPS; SINK TWO BRITISH CRUISERS; ITALIANS LOSE ONE; INDIA REPORTED AGREEING ON NATIVE COUNCIL

AMERICAN FORCES LAND IN FRENCH AFRICA; BRITISH NAVAL, AIR UNITS ASSISTING THEM; EFFECTIVE SECOND FRONT, ROOSEVELT SAYS

ALLIES SEIZE SYRACUSE IN DRIVE FOR MESSINA; JAPAN LOSES 4 WARSHIPS

U.S. SENDS 2 PROTESTS TO RUSSIA ON MANCHURIA AND IRAN ACTIONS; CHURCHILL ASSAILS SOVIET POLICY

12 NAZI WAR LEADERS SENTENCED TO BE HANGED; GOERING HEADS LIST OF THOSE TO DIE BY OCT. 16; HESS GETS LIFE, SIX OTHERS ORDERED TO PRISON

ZIONISTS PROCLAIM NEW STATE OF ISRAEL; TRUMAN RECOGNIZES IT AND HOPES FOR PEACE; TEL AVIV IS BOMBED, EGYPT ORDERS INVASION

TRUMAN, 32D PRESIDENT, IS INAUGURATED; CALLS ON U.S. TO LEAD DEMOCRATIC WORLD; DENOUNCES COMMUNISM, PLEDGES U.N. AID

TRUMAN ORDERS HYDROGEN BOMB BUILT FOR SECURITY PENDING AN ATOMIC PACT; CONGRESS HAILS STEP; BOARD BEGINS JOB

TRUMAN RELIEVES M'ARTHUR OF ALL HIS POSTS; FINDS HIM UNABLE TO BACK U.S.-U.N. POLICIES; RIDGWAY NAMED TO FAR EASTERN COMMANDS

MOSSADEGH FLEES HIS HOME AS TEHERAN MOB ATTACKS IT IN DEMONSTRATION FOR SHAH

STALIN DIES AFTER 29-YEAR RULE; HIS SUCCESSOR ...; U.S. WATCHFUL

PRESIDENT SENDS TROOPS TO LITTLE ROCK, FEDERALIZES ARKANSAS NATIONAL GUARD; TELLS NATION HE ACTED TO AVOID ANARCHY

SOVIET FIRES EARTH SATELLITE INTO SPACE; IT IS CIRCLING THE GLOBE AT 18,000 M.P.H.; SPHERE TRACKED IN 4 CROSSINGS OVER U.S.

SOVIET ROCKET HITS MOON AFTER 35 HOURS; ARRIVAL IS CALCULATED WITHIN 84 SECONDS; SIGNALS RECEIVED TILL MOMENT OF IMPACT

EGYPT AND ISRAEL SIGN FORMAL TREATY, ENDING A STATE OF WAR AFTER 30 YEARS; SADAT AND BEGIN PRAISE CARTER'S ROLE

REAGAN WOUNDED IN CHEST BY GUNMAN; OUTLOOK 'GOOD' AFTER 2-HOUR SURGERY; AIDE AND 2 GUARDS SHOT; SUSPECT HELD

CHERNENKO IS DEAD IN MOSCOW AT 73; GORBACHEV SUCCEEDS HIM AND URGES ARMS CONTROL AND ECONOMIC VIGOR

THE SHUTTLE EXPLODES
6 IN CREW AND HIGH-SCHOOL TEACHER ARE KILLED 74 SECONDS AFTER LIFTOFF

REAGAN AND GORBACHEV SIGN MISSILE TREATY AND VOW TO WORK FOR GREATER REDUCTIONS